SCOTT®

2021 STANDARD POSTAGE STAMP CATALOGUE

ONE HUNDRED AND SEVENTY-SEVENTH EDITION IN SIX VOLUMES

VOLUME 2B

Cyp-F

Released May 2020
Includes New Stamp Listings through the March 2020 *Linn's Stamp News Monthly* Catalogue Update

AMOS MEDIA

911 S. Vandemark Road, Sidney, OH 45365-4129
Publishers of *Linn's Stamp News, Linn's Stamp News Monthly, Coin World* and *Coin World Monthly.*

Table of Contents

See the following volumes for other country listings:
Volume 1A: United States, United Nations, Abu Dhabi-Australia; Volume 1B: Austria-B
Volume 2A: C-Cur
Volume 3A: G; Volume 3B: H-I
Volume 4A: J-L; Volume 4B: M
Volume 5A: N-Phil; Volume 5B: Pit-Sam
Volume 6A: San-Tete; Volume 6B: Thai-Z

Scott Catalogue Mission Statement

The Scott Catalogue Team exists to serve the recreational, educational and commercial hobby needs of stamp collectors and dealers.

We strive to set the industry standard for philatelic information and products by developing and providing goods that help collectors identify, value, organize and present their collections.

Quality customer service is, and will continue to be, our highest priority. We aspire toward achieving total customer satisfaction.

Copyright Notice

Trademark Notice

ISBN 978-0-89487-584-7

Library of Congress Card No. 2-3301

Acknowledgments

Our appreciation and gratitude go to the following individuals who have assisted us in preparing information included in this year's Scott Catalogues. Some helpers prefer anonymity. These individuals have generously shared their stamp knowledge with others through the medium of the Scott Catalogue.

Those who follow provided information that is in addition to the hundreds of dealer price lists and advertisements and scores of auction catalogues and realizations that were used in producing the catalogue values. It is from those noted here that we have been able to obtain information on items not normally seen in published lists and advertisements. Support from these people goes beyond data leading to catalogue values, for they also are key to editorial changes.

A special acknowledgment to Liane and Sergio Sismondo of The Classic Collector for their assistance and knowledge sharing that have aided in the preparation of this year's Standard and Classic Specialized Catalogues.

Clifford J. Alexander
(Carriers and Locals Society)
Roland Austin
Jim Bardo (Bardo Stamps)
John Birkinbine II
James A. Booth
Les Bootman
Roger S. Brody
Keith & Margie Brown
Tina & John Carlson (JET Stamps)
Carlson Chambliss
Bob Coale
Tony L. Crumbley
(Carolina Coin and Stamp, Inc.)
Christopher Dahle
Markand Dave
Bob and Rita Dumaine
(Sam Houston Duck Co.)
Mark Eastzer
Paul G. Eckman
Steve Farago
Mike Farrell
Robert Finder (Korea Stamp Society)
Jeffrey M. Forster
Ernest E. Fricks
(France & Colonies Philatelic Society)
Bob Genisol (Sultan Stamp Center)
Henning Gmerek
Stan Goldfarb
Marc E. Gonzales
Dan Harding
Sy Harvell
Bruce Hecht (Bruce L. Hecht Co.)
Armen Hovsepian (ArmenStamp)
Robert Jack
Eric Jackson
Peter C. Jeannopoulos
William A. (Bill) Jones
Allan Katz (Ventura Stamp Co.)
Jon Kawaguchi
(Ryukyu Philatelic Specialist Society)
Han Ki Klm
John R. Lewis
(The William Henry Stamp Co.)
Ignacio Llach (Filatelia Llach, S.L.)
William K. McDaniel
Pat McElroy
Gary Morris (Pacific Midwest Co.)
Peter Mosiondz, Jr.
Phillip Moulay
Bruce M. Moyer
(Moyer Stamps & Collectables)
Richard H. Muller (Richard's Stamps)
Scott Murphy
Leonard Nadybal
Dr. Tiong Tak Ngo
Nik & Lisa Oquist
Nicholas Pertwee
Don Peterson (International Philippine
Philatelic Society)
Stanley M. Piller
(Stanley M. Piller & Associates)
Dr. Charles Posner
Peter W. W. Powell
Siddique Mahmudur Rahman
(Bangladesh Institute of Philatelic
Studies)
Ghassan D. Riachi
Omar Rodriguez
Mehrdad Sadri (Persiphila)
Alex Schauss (Schauss Philatelics)
Joyce & Chuck Schmidt
Guy Shaw (Mexico-Elmhurst Philatelic
Society International)
J. Randall Shoemaker (Philatelic Stamp
Authenication and Grading, Inc.)
Jeff Siddiqui
(Pakistan Philatelic Study Circle)
Sergio & Liane Sismondo
(The Classic Collector)
Jay Smith
Telah Smith
Scott R. Trepel
(Siegel Auction Galleries, Inc.)
Steven Unkrich
Herbert R. Volin
Philip T. Wall
Yong S. Yi (Korea Stamp Society)
Ralph Yorio
Dr. Michal Zika (Album)
Alfonso G. Zulueta, Jr.

SCOTT

What's new for 2021 Scott Standard Volume 2?

Another catalog season is upon us as we continue the journey of the 152-year history of the Scott catalogs. The 2021 volumes are the 177th edition of the Scott *Standard Postage Stamp Catalogue*. Vol. 2A includes listings for countries of the world Cambodia through Curacao. Listings for Cyprus through F countries of the world can be found in Vol. 2B.

VOL. 2A

Approximately 200 value changes were made in the listings for Canada. With the Canadian dollar remaining stable during the past year and the cost of a Canadian permanent stamp increasing only slightly, values for many of the modern stamp issues remained unchanged for the 2021 catalogs.

There was a mix of increases and decreases for earlier stamps of Canada. One notable increase was for the watermarked 1868 ½¢ Queen Victoria stamp (Scott 21b), which increased to $25,000 from $22,500 in unused condition.

The market for modern Canadian stamp errors appears to be softening, and a number of values were adjusted accordingly.

Interest in the stamps of specific Canadian provinces remains strong, and few value changes were made. When compared to the major listing of a stamp, it appears varieties of the listing seem to be performing slightly better.

British Columbia and Vancouver Island's first issue, the 1860 2½-penny Queen Victoria stamp (Scott 1), increases from $25,000 to $27,500 in unused condition.

British Columbia and Vancouver Island's 1860 2½-penny Queen Victoria stamp (Scott 1) increased in value from $25,000 to $27,500 in unused condition.

The stamps of Cape Juby were reviewed, with approximately 100 value changes noted. Most of these changes were slight decreases.

Two stamps of the Cape of Good Hope jumped in value. The 1861 1-penny carmine stamp (Scott 7a) increased in used condition from $4,000 to $6,500. The 1863 1p dark carmine stamp increased to $350 from $325 in both unused and used condition.

Interest in Cape Verde is strong, and there were a number of increases and some decreases throughout the listings. The most significant increase was for the 40-reis Crown of Portugal stamp (Scott 5), which went from $85 unused and $50 used to $105 and $55, respectively.

Approximately 400 value changes were made for Chad, most of which were slight decreases.

The stamps of China were reviewed, with approximately 400 values changed. Values appear to be softening, but one exception was the 1897 set of three surcharges (Scott 25-27) that jumped from $472.50 unused to $740 unused.

Almost 4,000 value changes were made for the stamps of the Republic of China (Taiwan). Stamps from 1950 to 1970 are doing very well. There were numerous value increases, some of them fairly large. A mix of increases and decreases were noted for stamps issued after 1970.

The 1958 set of four President's Mansion in Taipei stamps (Scott 1196-1199) increased from $236 unused and $10.35 used to $294.50 and $11.35, respectively.

A line-by-line review of post-1971 Comoro Islands stamps took place. Approximately 175 value changes — a mix of increases and slight decreases — were recorded. A number of souvenir sheets were noted and valued for the first time in footnotes.

The stamps of the People's Republic of Congo were reviewed, with more than 100 value changes made. Most of these changes were decreases.

VOL. 2B

The stamps of Djibouti received a line-by-line review, with more than 130 value changes made. A significant number of footnotes with descriptions and values for souvenir sheets not previously noted were added.

More than 4,000 value changes were made for the stamps of the Republic of China (Taiwan). The 1958 set of four President's Mansion in Taipei stamps (Scott 1196-1199) increased from $236 unused and $10.35 used to $294.50 and $11.35, respectively.

For the Dominican Republic, an editorial note was added about the speculative Universal Postal Union surcharges of 1891. The note includes this explanation:

"Although this issue was authorized by the President the entire supply was given to a single speculative French dealer. A few covers exist most addressed to his wife in New York."

The note also mentions that numerous forgeries of the surcharged UPU set exist.

A complete review of Ethiopia yielded almost 2,000 value changes. Although decreases predominated, earlier issues fared better. The 1903 set of seven overprints (Scott 22-28) increased from $176 in both used and unused condition to $234 both ways in the 2021 catalog.

Three new minors were added to the listings of the surcharged Bird stamps of Fiji.

The stamps of Funchal received a full review, with many slight increases noted for almost all of its stamps.

And lastly, we encourage you to pay special attention to the Number Additions, Deletions & Changes in this volume. We also suggest reading the catalog introduction, which includes an abundance of useful information.

Best wishes in your stamp collecting pursuits!

Jay Bigalke, Scott catalog editor-in-chief

Addresses, Telephone Numbers, Web Sites, E-Mail Addresses of General & Specialized Philatelic Societies

Collectors can contact the following groups for information about the philately of the areas within the scope of these societies, or inquire about membership in these groups. Aside from the general societies, we limit this list to groups that specialize in particular fields of philately, particular areas covered by the Scott Standard Postage Stamp Catalogue, and topical groups. Many more specialized philatelic society exist than those listed below. These addresses are updated yearly, and they are, to the best of our knowledge, correct and current. Groups should inform the editors of address changes whenever they occur. The editors also want to hear from other such specialized groups not listed. Unless otherwise noted all website addresses begin with http://

General Societies

American Philatelic Society
100 Match Factory Place
Bellefonte, PA 16823-1367
(814) 933-3803
https://stamps.org
apsinfo@stamps.org

International Society of Worldwide Stamp Collectors
Joanne Murphy, M.D.
P.O. Box 19006
Sacramento, CA 95819
www.iswsc.org
executivedirector@iswsc.org

Royal Philatelic Society of Canada
P.O. Box 69080
St. Clair Post Office
Toronto, ON M4T 3A1
CANADA
(888) 285-4143
www.rpsc.org
info@rpsc.org

Royal Philatelic Society London
15 Abchurch Lane
London EX4N 7BW
UNITED KINGDOM
+44 (0) 20 7486 1044
www.rpsl.org.uk
secretary@rpsl.org.uk

Libraries, Museums, and Research Groups

American Philatelic Research Library
Scott Tiffney
100 Match Factory Place
Bellefonte, PA 16823
(814) 933-3803
www.stamplibrary.org
library@stamps.org

V. G. Greene Philatelic Research Foundation
P.O. Box 69100
St. Clair Post Office
Toronto, ON M4T 3A1
CANADA
(416) 921-2073
info@greenefoundation.ca

Aero/Astro Philately

American Air Mail Society
Stephen Reinhard
P.O. Box 110
Mineola, NY 11501
www.americanairmailsociety.org
sreinhard1@optonline.net

Postal History

Auxiliary Markings Club
Jerry Johnson
6621 W. Victoria Ave.
Kennewick, WA 99336
www.postal-markings.org
membership-2010@postal-markings.org

Postage Due Mail Study Group
Bob Medland
Camway Cottage
Nanny Hurn's Lane
Cameley, Bristol BS39 5AJ
UNITED KINGDOM
01761 45959
www.postageduemail.org.uk
secretary.pdmsg@gmail.com

Postal History Society
Yamil Kouri
405 Waltham St. #347
Lexington, MA 02421
www.postalhistorysociety.org
yhkouri@massmed.org

Post Mark Collectors Club
Bob Milligan
7014 Woodland Oaks Drive
Magnolia, TX 77354
(281) 259-2735
www.postmarks.org
bob.milligan@gmail.com

U.S. Cancellation Club
Roger Curran
18 Tressler Blvd.
Lewisburg, PA 17837
rdcnrc@ptd.net

Revenues & Cinderellas

American Revenue Association
Lyman Hensley
473 E. Elm St.
Sycamore, IL 60178-1934
www.revenuer.org
ilrno2@netzero.net

Christmas Seal & Charity Stamp Society
John Denune, Jr.
234 E. Broadway
Granville, OH 43023
(740) 814-6031
www.seal-society.org

National Duck Stamp Collectors Society
Anthony J. Monico
P.O. Box 43
Harleysville, PA 19438-0043
www.ndscs.org
ndscs@ndscs.org

State Revenue Society
Kent Gray
P.O. Box 67842
Albuquerque, NM 87193
www.staterevenue.org
srssecretary@comcast.net

Thematic Philately

Americana Unit
Dennis Dengel
17 Peckham Road
Poughkeepsie, NY 12603-2018
www.americanaunit.org
ddengel@americanaunit.org

American Topical Association
Jennifer Miller
P.O. Box 2143
Greer, SC 29652-2143
(618) 985-5100
www.americantopicalassn.org
americantopical@msn.com

Astronomy Study Unit
Leonard Zehr
1009 Treverton Crescent
Windsor, ON N8P 1K2
CANADA
(416) 833-9317
www.astronomystudyunit.net
lenzehr@gmail.com

Bicycle Stamps Club
Corey Hjalseth
1102 Broadway, Suite 200
Tacoma, WA 98402
(253) 318-6222
www.bicyclestampsclub.org
coreyh@evergreenhomeloans.com

Biology Unit
Chris Dahle
1401 Linmar Drive NE
Cedar Rapids, IA 52402-3724
www.biophilately.org
chris-dahle@biophilately.org

Bird Stamp Society
Mr. S. A. H. (Tony) Statham
Ashlyns Lodge
Chesham Road
Berkhamsted, Herts HP4 2ST
UNITED KINGDOM
www.bird-stamps.org/bss
tony.statham@sky.com

Captain Cook Society
Jerry Yucht
8427 Leale Ave.
Stockton, CA 95212
www.captaincooksociety.com
us@captaincooksociety.com

The CartoPhilatelic Society
Marybeth Sulkowski
2885 Sanford Ave., SW, #32361
Grandville, MI 49418-1342
www.mapsonstamps.org
secretary@mapsonstamps.org

Casey Jones Railroad Unit
Jeff Lough
2612 Redbud Land, Apt. C
Lawrence, KS 66046
www.uqp.de/cjr
jeffydplaugh@gmail.com

Cats on Stamps Study Unit
Robert D. Jarvis
2731 Teton Lane
Fairfield, CA 94533
www.catstamps.info
catmews1@yahoo.com

Chemistry & Physics on Stamps Study Unit
Dr. Roland Hirsch
13830 Metcalf Ave., Apt. 15218
Overland Park, KS 66223-8017
(301) 792-6296
www.cpossu.org
rfhirsch@cpossu.org

Chess on Stamps Study Unit
Barry Keith
511 1st St. N., Apt. 106
Charlottesville, VA 22902
www.chessonstamps.org
keithfam@embarqmail.com

Cricket Philatelic Society
A. Melville-Brown
11 Weppons, Ravens Road
Shorham-by-Sea
West Sussex BN43 5AW
UNITED KINGDOM
www.cricketstamp.net
mel.cricket.100@googlemail.com

Earth's Physical Features Study Group
Fred Klein
515 Magdalena Ave.
Los Altos, CA 94024
http://epfsu.jeffhayward.com
epfsu@jeffhayward.com

Ebony Society of Philatelic Events and Reflections (ESPER)
Don Neal
P.O. Box 5245
Somerset, NJ 08875-5245
www.esperstamps.org
esperdon@verizon.net

Europa Study Unit
Tonny E. Van Loij
3002 S. Xanthia St.
Denver, CO 80231-4237
(303) 752-0189
www.europastudyunit.org
tvanloij@gmail.com

Fire Service in Philately
John Zaranek
81 Hillpine Road
Cheektowaga, NY 14227-2259
(716) 668-3352
jczaranek@roadrunner.com

Gastronomy on Stamps Study Unit
David Wolfersburger
5062 NW 35th Lane Road
Ocala, FL 34482
(314) 494-3795
www.gastronomystamps.org

Gay & Lesbian History on Stamps Club
Joe Petronie
P.O. Box 190842
Dallas, TX 75219-0842
www.glhsonline.org
glhsc@aol.com

Gems, Minerals & Jewelry Study Unit
Fred Haynes
10 Country Club Drive
Rochester, NY 14618-3720
fredmhaynes55@gmail.com

Graphics Philately Association
Larry Rosenblum
1030 E. El Camino Real
PMB 107
Sunnyvale, CA 94087-3759
www.graphics-stamps.org
larry@graphics-stamps.org

Journalists, Authors and Poets on Stamps
Christopher D. Cook
7222 Hollywood Rd.
Berrien Springs, MI 49103
cdcook2@gmail.com

Lighthouse Stamp Society
Dalene Thomas
1805 S. Balsam St., #106
Lakewood, CO 80232
(303) 986-6620
www.lighthousestampsociety.org
dalene@lighthousestampsociety.org

Lions International Stamp Club
David McKirdy
s-Gravenwetering 248
3062 SJ Rotterdam
NETHERLANDS
31(0) 10 212 0313
www.lisc.nl
davidmckirdy@aol.com

Masonic Study Unit
Gene Fricks
25 Murray Way
Blackwood, NJ 08012-4400
genefricks@comcast.net

Medical Subjects Unit
Dr. Frederick C. Skvara
P.O. Box 6228
Bridgewater, NJ 08807
fcskvara@optonline.net

Napoleonic Age Philatelists
Ken Berry
4117 NW 146th St.
Oklahoma City, OK 73134-1746
(405) 748-8646
www.nap-stamps.org
krb4117@att.net

Old World Archaeological Study Unit
Caroline Scannell
14 Dawn Drive
Smithtown, NY 11787-1761
www.owasu.org
editor@owasu.org

Petroleum Philatelic Society International
Feitze Papa
922 Meander Drive
Walnut Creek, CA 94598-4239
www.ppsi.org.uk
oildad@astound.net

Rotary on Stamps Fellowship
Gerald L. Fitzsimmons
105 Calle Ricardo
Victoria, TX 77904
www.rotaryonstamps.org
glfitz@suddenlink.net

Scouts on Stamps Society International
Woodrow (Woody) Brooks
498 Baldwin Road
Akron, OH 44312
(330) 612-1294
www.sossi.org
secretary@sossi.org

Ships on Stamps Unit
Erik Th. Matzinger
Voorste Havervelden 30
4822 AL Breda
NETHERLANDS
www.shipsonstamps.org
erikships@gmail.com

Space Topic Study Unit
David Blog
P.O. Box 174
Bergenfield, NJ 07621
www.space-unit.com
davidblognj@gmail.com

Stamps on Stamps Collectors Club
Michael Merritt
73 Mountainside Road
Mendham, NJ 07945
www.stampsonstamps.org
stampsonstamps@yahoo.com

Windmill Study Unit
Walter J. Hallien
607 N. Porter St.
Watkins Glenn, NY 14891-1345
(607) 229-3541
www.windmillworld.com

Wine On Stamps Study Unit
David Wolfersburger
5062 NW 35th Lane Road
Ocala, FL 34482
(314) 494-3795
www.wine-on-stamps.org

United States

American Air Mail Society
Stephen Reinhard
P.O. Box 110
Mineola, NY 11501
www.americanairmailsociety.org
sreinhard1@optonline.net

American First Day Cover Society
Douglas Kelsey
P.O. Box 16277
Tucson, AZ 85732-6277
(520) 321-0880
www.afdcs.org
afdcs@afdcs.org

Auxiliary Markings Club
Jerry Johnson
6621 W. Victoria Ave.
Kennewick, WA 99336
www.postal-markings.org
membership-2010@postal-markings.org

American Plate Number Single Society
Rick Burdsall
APNSS Secretary
P.O. BOX 1023
Palatine, IL 60078-1023
www.apnss.org
apnss.sec@gmail.com

American Revenue Association
Lyman Hensley
473 E. Elm St.
Sycamore, IL 60178-1934
www.revenuer.org
ilrno2@netzero.net

American Society for Philatelic Pages and Panels
Ron Walenciak
P.O. Box 1042
Washington TWP, NJ 07676
www.asppp.org
rwalenciak@aol.com

Canal Zone Study Group
Mike Drabik
P.O. Box 281
Bolton, MA 01740
www.canalzonestudygroup.com
czsgsecretary@gmail.com

Carriers and Locals Society
John Bowman
14409 Pentridge Drive
Corpus Christi, TX 78410
(361) 933-0757
www.pennypost.org
jbowman@stx.rr.com

Christmas Seal & Charity Stamp Society
John Denune, Jr.
234 E. Broadway
Granville, OH 43023
(740) 814-6031
www.seal-society.org
john@christmasseals.net

Confederate Stamp Alliance
Patricia A. Kaufmann
10194 N. Old State Road
Lincoln, DE 19960-3644
(302) 422-2656
www.csalliance.org
trishkauf@comcast.net

Error, Freaks, and Oddities Collectors Club
Scott Shaulis
P.O. Box 549
Murrysville, PA 15668-0549
(724) 733-4134
www.efocc.org
scott@shaulisstamps.com

National Duck Stamp Collectors Society
Anthony J. Monico
P.O. Box 43
Harleysville, PA 19438-0043
www.ndscs.org
ndscs@ndscs.org

Plate Number Coil Collectors Club (PNC3)
Gene Trinks
16415 W. Desert Wren Court
Surprise, AZ 85374
(623) 322-4619
www.pnc3.org
gctrinks@cox.net

Post Mark Collectors Club
Bob Milligan
7014 Woodland Oaks Drive
Magnolia, TX 77354
(281) 259-2735
www.postmarks.org
bob.milligan@gmail.com

Souvenir Card Collectors Society
William V. Kriebel
1923 Manning St.
Philadelphia, PA 19103-5728
www.souvenircards.org
kriebewv@drexel.edu

United Postal Stationery Society
Dave Kandziolka
404 Sundown Drive
Knoxville, TN 37934
www.upss.org
membership@upss.org

U.S. Cancellation Club
Roger Curran
18 Tressler Blvd.
Lewisburg, PA 17837
rdcnrc@ptd.net

U.S. Philatelic Classics Society
Rob Lund
2913 Fulton St.
Everett, WA 98201-3733
www.uspcs.org
membershipchairman@uspcs.org

US Possessions Philatelic Society
Daniel F. Ring
P.O. Box 113
Woodstock, IL 60098
http://uspps.tripod.com
danielfring@hotmail.com

United States Stamp Society
Rod Juell
P.O. Box 3508
Joliet, IL 60434-3508
www.usstamps.org
execsecretary@usstamps.org

Africa

Bechuanalands and Botswana Society
Otto Peetoom
Roos
East Yorkshire HU12 0LD
UNITED KINGDOM
44(0)1964 670239
www.bechuanalandphilately.com
info@bechuanalandphilately.com

Egypt Study Circle
Mike Murphy
11 Waterbank Road
Bellingham
London SE6 3DJ
UNITED KINGDOM
(44) 0203 6737051
www.egyptstudycircle.org.uk
secretary@egyptstudycircle.org.uk

Ethiopian Philatelic Society
Ulf Lindahl
21 Westview Place
Riverside, CT 06878
(203) 722-0769
https://ethiopianphilatelicsociety.weebly.com
ulindahl@optonline.net

Liberian Philatelic Society
P.O. Box 1570
Parker, CO 80134
www.liberiastamps.org
liberiastamps@comcast.net

Orange Free State Study Circle
J. R. Stroud, RDPSA
24 Hooper Close
Burnham-on-sea
Somerset TA8 1JQ
UNITED KINGDOM
44 1278 782235
www.orangefreestatephilately.org.uk
richard@richardstroud.plus.com

Philatelic Society for Greater Southern Africa
Alan Hanks
34 Seaton Drive
Aurora, ON L4G 2K1
CANADA
www.psgsa.org
alan.hanks@sympatico.ca

Rhodesian Study Circle
William R. Wallace
P.O. Box 16381
San Francisco, CA 94116
(415) 564-6069
www.rhodesianstudycircle.org.uk
bwall8rscr@earthlink.net

Society for Moroccan and Tunisian Philately
S.P.L.M.
206, Bld Pereire
75017 PARIS
FRANCE
http://splm-philatelie.org
splm206@aol.com

South Sudan Philatelic Society
William Barclay
1370 Spring Hill Road
South Londonderry, VT 05155
barclayphilatelics@gmail.com

Sudan Study Group
Andy Neal
Bank House, Coedway
Shrewsbury SY5 9AR
UNITED KINGDOM
www.sudanstamps.org
andywneal@gmail.com

Transvaal Study Circle
c/o 9 Meadow Road
Gravesend, Kent DA11 7LR
UNITED KINGDOM
www.transvaalstamps.org.uk
transvaalstudycircle@aol.co.uk

West Africa Study Circle
Martin Bratzel
1233 Virginia Ave.
Windsor, ON N8S 2Z1
CANADA
www.wasc.org.uk
marty_bratzel@yahoo.ca

Asia

Aden & Somaliland Study Group
Gary Brown
P.O. Box 106
Briar Hill, VIC 3088
AUSTRALIA
www.stampdomain.com/aden
garyjohn951@optushome.com.au

Burma (Myanmar) Philatelic Study Circle
Michael Whittaker
1, Ecton Leys, Hillside
Rugby
Warwickshire CV22 5SL
UNITED KINGDOM
https://burmamyanmarphilately.wordpress.com/burma-myanmar-philatelic-study-circle
manningham8@mypostoffice.co.uk

Ceylon Study Circle
Rodney W. P. Frost
42 Lonsdale Road
Cannington
Bridgwater, Somerset TA5 2JS
UNITED KINGDOM
01278 652592
www.ceylonsc.org
rodney.frost@tiscali.co.uk

China Stamp Society
H. James Maxwell
1050 W. Blue Ridge Blvd.
Kansas City, MO 64145-1216
www.chinastampsociety.org
president@chinastampsociety.org

Hong Kong Philatelic Society
John Tang
G.P.O. Box 446
HONG KONG
www.hkpsociety.com
hkpsociety@outlook.com

Hong Kong Study Circle
Robert Newton
www.hongkongstudycircle.com/index.html
newtons100@gmail.com

India Study Circle
John Warren
P.O. Box 7326
Washington, DC 20044
(202) 488-7443
https://indiastudycircle.org
jw-kbw@earthlink.net

International Philippine Philatelic Society
James R. Larot, Jr.
4990 Bayleaf Court
Martinez, CA 94553
(925) 260-5425
www.theipps.info
jlarot@ccwater.com

International Society for Japanese Philately
William Eisenhauer
P.O. Box 230462
Tigard, OR 97281
(503) 496-2634
www.isjp.org
secretary@isjp.org

Iran Philatelic Study Circle
Nigel Gooch
Marchwood, 56, Wickham Ave.
Bexhill-on-Sea
East Sussex TN39 3ER
UNITED KINGDOM
www.iranphilately.org
nigelmgooch@gmail.com

Korea Stamp Society
Peter Corson
1109 Gunnison Place
Raleigh, NC 27609
(919) 787-7611
https://koreastampsociety.org
pbcorson@aol.com

Nepal & Tibet Philatelic Study Circle
Colin Hepper
12 Charnwood Close
Peterborough, Cambs PE2 9BZ
UNITED KINGDOM
http://fuchs-online.com/ntpsc
ntpsc@fuchs-online.com

Pakistan Philatelic Study Circle
Jeff Siddiqui
P.O. Box 7002
Lynnwood, WA 98046
jeffsiddiqui@msn.com

Society of Indo-China Philatelists
Ron Bentley
2600 N. 24th St.
Arlington, VA 22207
(703) 524-1652
www.sicp-online.org
ron.bentley@verizon.net

Society of Israel Philatelists, Inc.
Sarah Berezenko
100 Match Factory Place
Bellefonte, PA 16823-1367
(814) 933-3803 ext. 212
www.israelstamps.com
israelstamps@gmail.com

Australasia and Oceana

Australian States Study Circle of the Royal Sydney Philatelic Club
Ben Palmer
G.P.O. 1751
Sydney, NSW 2001
AUSTRALIA
http://club.philas.org.au/states

Fellowship of Samoa Specialists
Trevor Shimell
18 Aspen Drive, Newton Abbot
Devon TQ12 4TN
UNITED KINGDOM
www.samoaexpress.org
trevor.shimell@gmail.com

Malaya Study Group
Michael Waugh
151 Roker Lane
Pudsey
Leeds LS28 9ND
UNITED KINGDOM
http://malayastudygroup.com
mawpud43@gmail.com

New Zealand Society of Great Britain
Michael Wilkinson
121 London Road
Sevenoaks
Kent TN13 1BH
UNITED KINGDOM
01732 456997
www.nzsgb.org.uk
mwilkin799@aol.com

Pacific Islands Study Circle
John Ray
24 Woodvale Ave.
London SE25 4AE
UNITED KINGDOM
www.pisc.org.uk
secretary@pisc.org.uk

Papuan Philatelic Society
Steven Zirinsky
P.O. Box 49, Ansonia Station
New York, NY 10023
(718) 706-0616
www.papuanphilatelicsociety.com
szirinsky@cs.com

Pitcairn Islands Study Group
Dr. Everett L. Parker
207 Corinth Road
Hudson, ME 04449-3057
(207) 573-1686
www.pisg.net
eparker@hughes.net

Ryukyu Philatelic Specialist Society
Laura Edmonds
P.O. Box 240177
Charlotte, NC 28224-0177
(336) 509-3739
www.ryukyustamps.org
secretary@ryukyustamps.org

Society of Australasian Specialists / Oceania
Steve Zirinsky
P.O. Box 230049
New York, NY 10023-0049
www.sasoceania.org
president@sosoceania.org

Sarawak Specialists' Society
Stephen Schumann
2417 Cabrallo Drive
Hayward, CA 94545
(510) 785-4794
www.britborneostamps.org.uk
vpnam@s-s-s.org.uk

Western Australia Study Group
Brian Pope
P.O. Box 423
Claremont, WA 6910
AUSTRALIA
(61) 419 843 943
www.wastudygroup.com
wastudygroup@hotmail.com

Europe

American Helvetia Philatelic Society
Richard T. Hall
P.O. Box 15053
Asheville, NC 28813-0053
www.swiss-stamps.org
secretary2@swiss-stamps.org

American Society for Netherlands Philately
Hans Kremer
50 Rockport Court
Danville, CA 94526
(925) 820-5841
www.asnp1975.com
hkremer@usa.net

Andorran Philatelic Study Circle
David Hope
17 Hawthorn Drive
Stalybridge
Cheshire SK15 1UE
UNITED KINGDOM
www.andorranpsc.org.uk
andorranpsc@btinternet.com

Austria Philatelic Society
Ralph Schneider
P.O. Box 978
Iowa Park, TX 76376
(940) 213-5004
www.austriaphilatelicsociety.com
rschneiderstamps@gmail.com

Channel Islands Specialists Society
Richard Flemming
Burbage, 64 Falconers Green
Hinckley
Leicestershire LE102SX
UNITED KINGDOM
www.ciss1950.org.uk
secretary@ciss1950.org.uk

Cyprus Study Circle
Rob Wheeler
47 Drayton Ave.
London W13 0LE
UNITED KINGDOM
www.cyprusstudycircle.org
robwheeler47@aol.com

Danish West Indies Study Unit of Scandinavian Collectors Club
Arnold Sorensen
7666 Edgedale Drive
Newburgh, IN 47630
(812) 480-6532
www.scc-online.org
valbydwi@hotmail.com

Eire Philatelic Association
John B. Sharkey
1559 Grouse Lane
Mountainside, NJ 07092-1340
www.eirephilatelicassoc.org
jsharkeyepa@me.com

Faroe Islands Study Circle
Norman Hudson
40 Queen's Road
Vicar's Cross
Chester CH3 5HB
UNITED KINGDOM
www.faroeislandssc.org
jntropics@hotmail.com

France & Colonies Philatelic Society
Edward Grabowski
111 Prospect St., 4C
Westfield, NJ 07090
(908) 233-9318
www.franceandcolsps.org
edjjg@alum.mit.edu

Germany Philatelic Society
P.O. Box 6547
Chesterfield, MO 63006-6547
www.germanyphilatelicusa.org
info@germanyphilatelicsocietyusa.org

Gibraltar Study Circle
Susan Dare
22, Byways Park, Strode Road
Clevedon
North Somerset BS21 6UR
UNITED KINGDOM
www.gibraltarstudycircle.wordpress.com
smldare@yahoo.co.uk

International Society for Portuguese Philately
Clyde Homen
1491 Bonnie View Road
Hollister, CA 95023-5117
www.portugalstamps.com
ispp1962@sbcglobal.net

Italy and Colonies Study Circle
Richard Harlow
7 Duncombe House
8 Manor Road
Teddington, Middlesex TW118BE
UNITED KINGDOM
44 208 977 8737
www.icsc-uk.com
richardharlow@outlook.com

Liechtenstudy USA
Paul Tremaine
410 SW Ninth St.
Dundee, OR 97115-9731
(503) 538-4500
www.liechtenstudy.org
tremaine@liechtenstudy.org

Lithuania Philatelic Society
Audrius Brazdeikis
9915 Murray Landing
Missouri City, TX 77459
(281) 450-6224
www.lithuanianphilately.com/lps
audrius@lithuanianphilately.com

Luxembourg Collectors Club
Gary B. Little
7319 Beau Road
Sechelt, BC V0N 3A8
CANADA
(604) 885-7241
http://lcc.luxcentral.com
gary@luxcentral.com

Plebiscite-Memel-Saar Study Group of the German Philatelic Society
Clayton Wallace
100 Lark Court
Alamo, CA 94507
claytonwallace@comcast.net

Polonus Polish Philatelic Society
Daniel Lubelski
P.O. Box 2212
Benicia, CA 94510
(419) 410-9115
www.polonus.org
info@polonus.org

Rossica Society of Russian Philately
Alexander Kolchinsky
1506 Country Lake Drive
Champaign, IL 61821-6428
www.rossica.org
alexander.kolchinsky@rossica.org

Scandinavian Collectors Club
Steve Lund
P.O. Box 16213
St. Paul, MN 55116
www.scc-online.org
steve88h@aol.com

Society for Czechoslovak Philately
Tom Cossaboom
P.O. Box 4124
Prescott, AZ 86302
(928) 771-9097
www.csphilately.org
klfck1@aol.com

Society for Hungarian Philately
Alan Bauer
P.O. Box 4028
Vineyard Haven, MA 02568
(617) 645-4045
www.hungarianphilately.org

Spanish Study Circle
Edith Knight
www.spaincircle.wixsite.com/spainstudycircle
spaincircle@gmail.com
alan@hungarianstamps.com

Ukrainian Philatelic & Numismatic Society
Martin B. Tatuch
5117 8th Road N.
Arlington, VA 22205-1201
www.upns.org
treasurer@upns.org

Vatican Philatelic Society
Joseph Scholten
1436 Johnston St. SE
Grand Rapids, MI 49507-2829
www.vaticanphilately.org
jscholten@vaticanphilately.org

Yugoslavia Study Group
Michael Chant
1514 N. Third Ave.
Wausau, WI 54401
0208-748-9919
www.yugosg.org
membership@yugosg.org

Interregional Societies

American Society of Polar Philatelists
Alan Warren
P.O. Box 39
Exton, PA 19341-0039
(610) 321-0740
www.polarphilatelists.org
alanwar@att.net

First Issues Collector's Club
Kurt Streepy
3128 E. Mattatha Drive
Bloomington, IN 47401
www.firstissues.org
secretary@firstissues.org

Former French Colonies Specialist Society
Col.fra
BP 628
75367 PARIS Cedex 08
FRANCE
www.colfra.org
postmaster@colfra.org

France & Colonies Philatelic Society
Edward Grabowski
111 Prospect St., 4C
Westfield, NJ 07090
(908) 233-9318
www.franceandcolsps.org
edjjg@alum.mit.edu

Joint Stamp Issues Society
Richard Zimmermann
29A, Rue Des Eviats
67220 LALAYE
FRANCE
www.philarz.net
richard.zimmermann@club-internet.fr

The King George VI Collectors Society
Brian Livingstone
21 York Mansions
Prince of Wales Drive
London SW11 4DL
UNITED KINGDOM
www.kg6.info
livingstone484@btinternet.com

International Society of Reply Coupon Collectors
Peter Robin
P.O. Box 353
Bala Cynwyd, PA 19004
peterrobin@verizon.net

Italy and Colonies Study Circle
Richard Harlow
7 Duncombe House
8 Manor Road
Teddington, Middlesex TW118BE
UNITED KINGDOM
44 208 977 8737
www.icsc-uk.com
richardharlow@outlook.com

St. Helena, Ascension & Tristan Da Cunha Philatelic Society
Dr. Everett L. Parker
207 Corinth Road
Hudson, ME 04449-3057
(207) 573-1686
www.shatps.org
eparker@hughes.net

United Nations Philatelists
Blanton Clement, Jr.
P.O. Box 146
Morrisville, PA 19067-0146
www.unpi.com
bclemjunior@gmail.com

Latin America

Asociación Filatélica de Panamá
Edward D. Vianna B
ASOFILPA
0819-03400
El Dorado, Panama
PANAMA
http://asociacionfilatelicadepanama.blogspot.com
asofilpa@gmail.com

Asociacion Mexicana de Filatelia (AMEXFIL)
Alejandro Grossmann
Jose Maria Rico, 129
Col. Del Valle
3100 Mexico City, DF
MEXICO
www.amexfil.mx
amexfil@gmail.com

Associated Collectors of El Salvador
Joseph D. Hahn
301 Rolling Ridge Drive, Apt. 111
State College, PA 16801-6149
www.elsalvadorphilately.org
joehahn100@hotmail.com

Association Filatelic de Costa Rica
Giana Wayman (McCarty)
#SJO 4935
P.O. Box 025723
Miami, FL 33102-5723
011-506-2-228-1947
scotland@racsa.co.cr

Brazil Philatelic Association
William V. Kriebel
1923 Manning St.
Philadelphia, PA 19103-5728
www.brazilphilatelic.org
info@brazilphilatelic.org

Canal Zone Study Group
Mike Drabik
P.O. Box 281
Bolton, MA 01740
www.canalzonestudygroup.com
czsgsecretary@gmail.com

Colombia-Panama Philatelic Study Group
Thomas P. Myers
P.O. Box 522
Gordonsville, VA 22942
www.copaphil.org
tpmphil@hotmail.com

Falkland Islands Philatelic Study Groups
Morva White
42 Colton Road
Shrivenham
Swindon SN6 8AZ
UNITED KINGDOM
44(0) 1793 783245
www.fipsg.org.uk
morawhite@supanet.com

Federacion Filatelica de la Republica de Honduras
Mauricio Mejia
Apartado Postal 1465
Tegucigalpa, D.C.
HONDURAS
504 3399-7227
www.facebook.com/filateliadehonduras
ffrh@hotmail.com

International Cuban Philatelic Society (ICPS)
Ernesto Cuesta
P.O. Box 34434
Bethesda, MD 20827
(301) 564-3099
www.cubafil.org
ecuesta@philat.com

International Society of Guatemala Collectors
Jaime Marckwordt
449 St. Francis Blvd.
Daly City, CA 94015-2136
(415) 997-0295
www.guatemalastamps.com
president@guatamalastamps.com

Mexico-Elmhurst Philatelic Society International
Eric Stovner
P.O. Box 10097
Santa Ana, CA 92711-0097
www.mepsi.org
treasurer@mepsi.org

Nicaragua Study Group
Erick Rodriguez
11817 S. W. 11th St.
Miami, FL 33184-2501
nsgsec@yahoo.com

North America (excluding United States)

British Caribbean Philatelic Study Group
Bob Stewart
7 West Dune Lane
Long Beach Township, NJ 08008
(941) 379-4108
www.bcpsg.com
bcpsg@comcast.net

British North America Philatelic Society
Andy Ellwood
10 Doris Ave.
Gloucester, ON K1T 3W8
CANADA
www.bnaps.org
secretary@bnaps.org

British West Indies Study Circle
Steve Jarvis
5 Redbridge Drive
Andover
Hants SP10 2LF
UNITED KINGDOM
01264 358065
www.bwisc.org
info@bwisc.org

Bermuda Collectors Society
John Pare
405 Perimeter St.
Mount Horeb, WI 53572
(608) 852-7358
www.bermudacollectorssociety.com
pare16@mhtc.net
john@christmasseals.net

Haiti Philatelic Society
Ubaldo Del Toro
5709 Marble Archway
Alexandria, VA 22315
www.haitiphilately.org
u007ubi@aol.com

Hawaiian Philatelic Society
Gannon Sugimura
P.O. Box 10115
Honolulu, HI 96816-0115
www.stampshows.com/hps.html
hiphilsoc@gmail.com

Stamp Dealer Associations

American Stamp Dealers Association, Inc.
P.O. Box 692
Leesport, PA 19553
(800) 369-8209
www.americanstampdealer.com
asda@americanstampdealer.com

National Stamp Dealers Association
Sheldon Ruckens, President
3643 Private Road 18
Pinckneyville, IL 62274-3426
(618) 357-5497
www.nsdainc.org
nsda@nsdainc.org

Youth Philately

Young Stamp Collectors of America
100 Match Factory Place
Bellefonte, PA 16823
(814) 933-3803
https://stamps.org/stamps.org/Learn/youth-in-philately
ysca@stamps.org

Expertizing Services

The following organizations will, for a fee, provide expert opinions about stamps submitted to them. Collectors should contact these organizations to find out about their fees and requirements before submiting philatelic material to them. The listing of these groups here is not intended as an endorsement by Amos Media Co.

General Expertizing Services

American Philatelic Expertizing Service (a service of the American Philatelic Society)
100 Match Factory Place
Bellefonte PA 16823-1367
(814) 237-3803
www.stamps.org/stamp-authentication
apex@stamps.org
Areas of Expertise: Worldwide

BPA Expertising, Ltd.
P.O. Box 1141
Guildford, Surrey, GU5 0WR
UNITED KINGDOM
www.bpaexpertising.com
sec@bpaexpertising.org
Areas of Expertise: British Commonwealth, Great Britain, Classics of Europe, South America and the Far East

Philatelic Foundation
22 E. 35th St., 4th Floor
New York NY 10016
(212) 221-6555
www.philatelicfoundation.org
philatelicfoundation@verizon.net
Areas of Expertise: U.S. & Worldwide

Philatelic Stamp Authentication and Grading, Inc.
P.O. Box 41-0880
Melbourne FL 32941-0880
(305) 345-9864
www.psaginc.com
info@psaginc.com
Areas of Expertise: U.S., Canal Zone, Hawaii, Philippines, Canada & Provinces

Professional Stamp Experts
P.O. Box 539309
Henderson NV 89053-9309
(702) 776-6522
www.gradingmatters.com
www.psestamp.com
info@gradingmatters.com
Areas of Expertise: Stamps and covers of U.S., U.S. Possessions, British Commonwealth

Royal Philatelic Society London Expert Committee
15 Abchurch Lane
London, EX4N 7BW
UNITED KINGDOM
www.rpsl.limited/experts.aspx
experts@rpsl.limited
Areas of Expertise: Worldwide

Expertizing Services Covering Specific Fields or Countries

China Stamp Society Expertizing Service
1050 W. Blue Ridge Blvd.
Kansas City MO 64145
(816) 942-6300
hjmesq@aol.com
Areas of Expertise: China

Confederate Stamp Alliance Authentication Service
C/O Stefan T. Jaronski
P.O. Box 232
Sidney, MT 59270-0232
www.csalliance.org/CSAAS.shtml
authentication@csalliance.org
Areas of Expertise: Confederate stamps and postal history

Errors, Freaks and Oddities Collectors Club Expertizing Service
138 East Lakemont Drive
Kingsland GA 31548
(912) 729-1573
Areas of Expertise: U.S. errors, freaks and oddities

Hawaiian Philatelic Society Expertizing Service
P.O. Box 10115
Honolulu HI 96816-0115
www.stampshows.com/hps.html
hiphilsoc@gmail.com
Areas of Expertise: Hawaii

Hong Kong Stamp Society Expertizing Service
P.O. Box 206
Glenside PA 19038
Areas of Expertise: Hong Kong

International Association of Philatelic Experts United States Associate members:

Paul Buchsbayew
119 W. 57th St.
New York NY 10019
(212) 977-7734
Areas of Expertise: Russia, Soviet Union

William T. Crowe
P.O. Box 2090
Danbury CT 06813-2090
wtcrowe@aol.com
Areas of Expertise: United States

John Lievsay
(see American Philatelic Expertizing Service and Philatelic Foundation)
Areas of Expertise: France

Robert W. Lyman
P.O. Box 348
Irvington on Hudson NY 10533
(914) 591-6937
Areas of Expertise: British North America, New Zealand

Robert Odenweller
P.O. Box 401
Bernardsville NJ 07924-0401
(908) 766-5460
Areas of Expertise: New Zealand, Samoa to 1900

Sergio Sismondo
The Regency Tower, Suite 1109
770 James St.
Syracuse NY 13203
(315) 422-2331
Areas of Expertise: British East Africa, Camerouns, Cape of Good Hope, Canada, British North America

International Society for Japanese Philately Expertizing Committee
132 North Pine Terrace
Staten Island NY 10312-4052
(718) 227-5229
Areas of Expertise: Japan and related areas, except WWII Japanese Occupation issues

International Society for Portuguese Philately Expertizing Service
P.O. Box 43146
Philadelphia PA 19129-3146
(215) 843-2106
s.s.washburne@worldnet.att.net
Areas of Expertise: Portugal and Colonies

Mexico-Elmhurst Philatelic Society International Expert Committee
Expert Committee Administrator
Marc E. Gonzales
P.O. Box 29040
Denver CO 80229-0040
www.mepsi.org/expert_committeee.htm
expertizations@mepsi.org
Areas of Expertise: Mexico

Ukrainian Philatelic & Numismatic Society Expertizing Service
30552 Dell Lane
Warren MI 48092-1862
Areas of Expertise: Ukraine, Western Ukraine

V. G. Greene Philatelic Research Foundation
P.O. Box 69100
St. Clair Post Office
Toronto, ON M4T 3A1
CANADA
(416) 921-2073
www.greenefoundation.ca
info@greenefoundation.ca
Areas of Expertise: British North America

Information on Catalogue Values, Grade and Condition

Catalogue Value

The Scott Catalogue value is a retail value; that is, an amount you could expect to pay for a stamp in the grade of Very Fine with no faults. Any exceptions to the grade valued will be noted in the text. The general introduction on the following pages and the individual section introductions further explain the type of material that is valued. The value listed for any given stamp is a reference that reflects recent actual dealer selling prices for that item.

Dealer retail price lists, public auction results, published prices in advertising and individual solicitation of retail prices from dealers, collectors and specialty organizations have been used in establishing the values found in this catalogue. Amos Media Co. values stamps, but Amos Media is not a company engaged in the business of buying and selling stamps as a dealer.

Use this catalogue as a guide for buying and selling. The actual price you pay for a stamp may be higher or lower than the catalogue value because of many different factors, including the amount of personal service a dealer offers, or increased or decreased interest in the country or topic represented by a stamp or set. An item may occasionally be offered at a lower price as a "loss leader," or as part of a special sale. You also may obtain an item inexpensively at public auction because of little interest at that time or as part of a large lot.

Stamps that are of a lesser grade than Very Fine, or those with condition problems, generally trade at lower prices than those given in this catalogue. Stamps of exceptional quality in both grade and condition often command higher prices than those listed.

Values for pre-1900 unused issues are for stamps with approximately half or more of their original gum. Stamps with most or all of their original gum may be expected to sell for more, and stamps with less than half of their original gum may be expected to sell for somewhat less than the values listed. On rarer stamps, it may be expected that the original gum will be somewhat more disturbed than it will be on more common issues. Post-1900 unused issues are assumed to have full original gum. From breakpoints in most countries' listings, stamps are valued as never hinged, due to the wide availability of stamps in that condition. These notations are prominently placed in the listings and in the country information preceding the listings. Some countries also feature listings with dual values for hinged and never-hinged stamps.

Grade

A stamp's grade and condition are crucial to its value. The accompanying illustrations show examples of Very Fine stamps from different time periods, along with examples of stamps in Fine to Very Fine and Extremely Fine grades as points of reference. When a stamp seller offers a stamp in any grade from fine to superb without further qualifying statements, that stamp should not only have the centering grade as defined, but it also should be free of faults or other condition problems.

FINE stamps (illustrations not shown) have designs that are quite off center, with the perforations on one or two sides very close to the design but not quite touching it. There is white space between the perforations and the design that is minimal but evident to the unaided eye. Imperforate stamps may have small margins, and earlier issues may show the design just touching one edge of the stamp design. Very early perforated issues normally will have the perforations slightly cutting into the design. Used stamps may have heavier than usual cancellations.

FINE-VERY FINE stamps will be somewhat off center on one side, or slightly off center on two sides. Imperforate stamps will have two margins of at least normal size, and the design will not touch any edge. For perforated stamps, the perfs are well clear of the design, but are still noticeably off center. *However, early issues of a country may be printed in such a way that the design naturally is very close to the edges. In these cases, the perforations may cut into the design very slightly.* Used stamps will not have a cancellation that detracts from the design.

VERY FINE stamps will be just slightly off center on one or two sides, but the design will be well clear of the edge. The stamp will present a nice, balanced appearance. Imperforate stamps will be well centered within normal-sized margins. *However, early issues of many countries may be printed in such a way that the perforations may touch the design on one or more sides. Where this is the case, a boxed note will be found defining the centering and margins of the stamps being valued.* Used stamps will have light or otherwise neat cancellations. This is the grade used to establish Scott Catalogue values.

EXTREMELY FINE stamps are close to being perfectly centered. Imperforate stamps will have even margins that are slightly larger than normal. Even the earliest perforated issues will have perforations clear of the design on all sides.

Amos Media Co. recognizes that there is no formally enforced grading scheme for postage stamps, and that the final price you pay or obtain for a stamp will be determined by individual agreement at the time of transaction.

Condition

Grade addresses only centering and (for used stamps) cancellation. *Condition* refers to factors other than grade that affect a stamp's desirability.

Factors that can increase the value of a stamp include exceptionally wide margins, particularly fresh color, the presence of selvage, and plate or die varieties. Unusual cancels on used stamps (particularly those of the 19th century) can greatly enhance their value as well.

Factors other than faults that decrease the value of a stamp include loss of original gum, regumming, a hinge remnant or foreign object adhering to the gum, natural inclusions, straight edges, and markings or notations applied by collectors or dealers.

Faults include missing pieces, tears, pin or other holes, surface scuffs, thin spots, creases, toning, short or pulled perforations, clipped perforations, oxidation or other forms of color changelings, soiling, stains, and such man-made changes as reperforations or the chemical removal or lightening of a cancellation.

Grading Illustrations

On the following two pages are illustrations of various stamps from countries appearing in this volume. These stamps are arranged by country, and they represent early or important issues that are often found in widely different grades in the marketplace. The editors believe the illustrations will prove useful in showing the margin size and centering that will be seen on the various issues.

In addition to the matters of margin size and centering, collectors are reminded that the very fine stamps valued in the Scott catalogues also will possess fresh color and intact perforations, and they will be free from defects.

Examples shown are computer-manipulated images made from single digitized master illustrations.

Stamp Illustrations Used in the Catalogue

It is important to note that the stamp images used for identification purposes in this catlaogue may not be indicative of the grade of stamp being valued. Refer to the written discussion of grades on this page and to the grading illustrations on the following two pages for grading information.

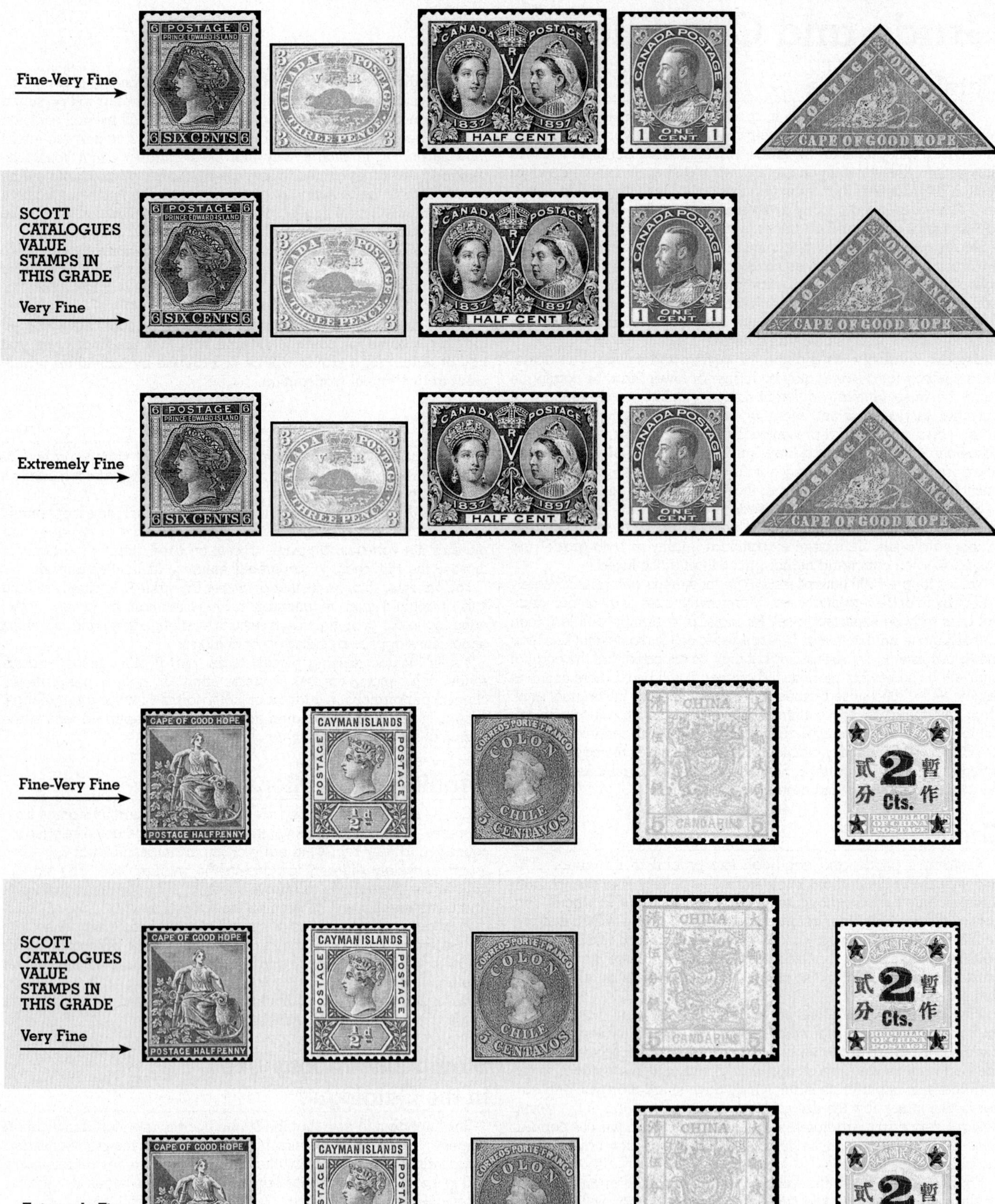
Fine-Very Fine
SCOTT CATALOGUES VALUE STAMPS IN THIS GRADE
Very Fine
Extremely Fine
Fine-Very Fine
SCOTT CATALOGUES VALUE STAMPS IN THIS GRADE
Very Fine
Extremely Fine

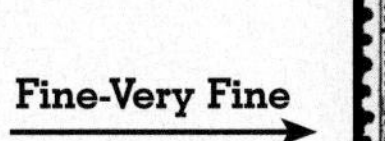

Fine-Very Fine →

SCOTT CATALOGUES VALUE STAMPS IN THIS GRADE

Very Fine →

Extremely Fine →

Fine-Very Fine →

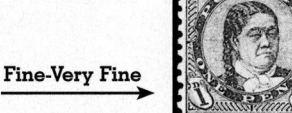

SCOTT CATALOGUES VALUE STAMPS IN THIS GRADE

Very Fine →

Extremely Fine →

For purposes of helping to determine the gum condition and value of an unused stamp, Scott presents the following chart which details different gum conditions and indicates how the conditions correlate with the Scott values for unused stamps. Used together, the Illustrated Grading Chart on the previous pages and this Illustrated Gum Chart should allow catalogue users to better understand the grade and gum condition of stamps valued in the Scott catalogues.

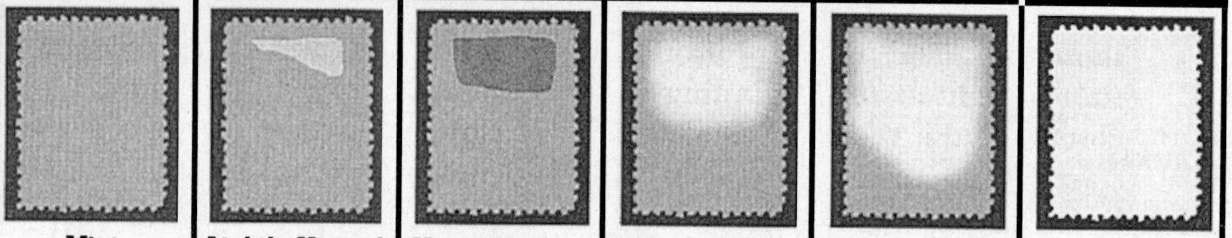

Gum Categories:	MINT N.H.	ORIGINAL GUM (O.G.)				NO GUM
	Mint Never Hinged *Free from any disturbance*	**Lightly Hinged** *Faint impression of a removed hinge over a small area*	**Hinge Mark or Remnant** *Prominent hinged spot with part or all of the hinge remaining*	**Large part o.g.** *Approximately half or more of the gum intact*	**Small part o.g.** *Approximately less than half of the gum intact*	**No gum** *Only if issued with gum*
Commonly Used Symbol:	★★	★	★	★	★	(★)
Pre-1900 Issues (Pre-1881 for U.S.)	*Very fine pre-1900 stamps in these categories trade at a premium over Scott value*			Scott Value for "Unused"		Scott "No Gum" listings for selected unused classic stamps
From 1900 to breakpoints for listings of never-hinged stamps	Scott "Never Hinged" listings for selected unused stamps	Scott Value for "Unused" (Actual value will be affected by the degree of hinging of the full o.g.)				
From breakpoints noted for many countries	Scott Value for "Unused"					

Never Hinged (NH; ★★): A never-hinged stamp will have full original gum that will have no hinge mark or disturbance. The presence of an expertizer's mark does not disqualify a stamp from this designation.

Original Gum (OG; ★): Pre-1900 stamps should have approximately half or more of their original gum. On rarer stamps, it may be expected that the original gum will be somewhat more disturbed than it will be on more common issues. Post-1900 stamps should have full original gum. Original gum will show some disturbance caused by a previous hinge(s) which may be present or entirely removed. The actual value of a post-1900 stamp will be affected by the degree of hinging of the full original gum.

Disturbed Original Gum: Gum showing noticeable effects of humidity, climate or hinging over more than half of the gum. The significance of gum disturbance in valuing a stamp in any of the Original Gum categories depends on the degree of disturbance, the rarity and normal gum condition of the issue and other variables affecting quality.

Regummed (RG; (★)): A regummed stamp is a stamp without gum that has had some type of gum privately applied at a time after it was issued. This normally is done to deceive collectors and/or dealers into thinking that the stamp has original gum and therefore has a higher value. A regummed stamp is considered the same as a stamp with none of its original gum for purposes of grading.

Catalogue Listing Policy

It is the intent of Amos Media Co. to list all postage stamps of the world in the *Scott Standard Postage Stamp Catalogue*. The only strict criteria for listing is that stamps be decreed legal for postage by the issuing country and that the issuing country actually have an operating postal system. Whether the primary intent of issuing a given stamp or set was for sale to postal patrons or to stamp collectors is not part of our listing criteria. Scott's role is to provide basic comprehensive postage stamp information. It is up to each stamp collector to choose which items to include in a collection.

It is Scott's objective to seek reasons why a stamp should be listed, rather than why it should not. Nevertheless, there are certain types of items that will not be listed. These include the following:

1. Unissued items that are not officially distributed or released by the issuing postal authority. If such items are officially issued at a later date by the country, they will be listed. Unissued items consist of those that have been printed and then held from sale for reasons such as change in government, errors found on stamps or something deemed objectionable about a stamp subject or design.
2. Stamps "issued" by non-existent postal entities or fantasy countries, such as Nagaland, Occusi-Ambeno, Staffa, Sedang, Torres Straits and others. Also, stamps "issued" in the names of legitimate, stamp-issuing countries that are not authorized by those countries.
3. Semi-official or unofficial items not required for postage. Examples include items issued by private agencies for their own express services. When such items are required for delivery, or are valid as prepayment of postage, they are listed.
4. Local stamps issued for local use only. Postage stamps issued by governments specifically for "domestic" use, such as Haiti Scott 219-228, or the United States non-denominated stamps, are not considered to be locals, since they are valid for postage throughout the country of origin.
5. Items not valid for postal use. For example, a few countries have issued souvenir sheets that are not valid for postage. This area also includes a number of worldwide charity labels (some denominated) that do not pay postage.
6. Egregiously exploitative issues such as stamps sold for far more than face value, stamps purposefully issued in artificially small quantities or only against advance orders, stamps awarded only to a selected audience such as a philatelic bureau's standing order customers, or stamps sold only in conjunction with other products. All of these kinds of items are usually controlled issues and/or are intended for speculation. These items normally will be included in a footnote.
7. Items distributed by the issuing government only to a limited group, club, philatelic exhibition or a single stamp dealer or other private company. These items normally will be included in a footnote.
8. Stamps not available to collectors. These generally are rare items, all of which are held by public institutions such as museums. The existence of such items often will be cited in footnotes.

The fact that a stamp has been used successfully as postage, even on international mail, is not in itself sufficient proof that it was legitimately issued. Numerous examples of so-called stamps from non-existent countries are known to have been used to post letters that have successfully passed through the international mail system.

There are certain items that are subject to interpretation. When a stamp falls outside our specifications, it may be listed along with a cautionary footnote.

A number of factors are considered in our approach to analyzing how a stamp is listed. The following list of factors is presented to share with you, the catalogue user, the complexity of the listing process.

Additional printings — "Additional printings" of a previously issued stamp may range from an item that is totally different to cases where it is impossible to differentiate from the original. At least a minor number (a small-letter suffix) is assigned if there is a distinct change in stamp shade, noticeably redrawn design, or a significantly different perforation measurement. A major number (numeral or numeral and capital-letter combination) is assigned if the editors feel the "additional printing" is sufficiently different from the original that it constitutes a different issue.

Commemoratives — Where practical, commemoratives with the same theme are placed in a set. For example, the U.S. Civil War Centennial set of 1961-65 and the Constitution Bicentennial series of 1989-90 appear as sets. Countries such as Japan and Korea issue such material on a regular basis, with an announced, or at least predictable, number of stamps known in advance. Occasionally, however, stamp sets that were released over a period of years have been separated. Appropriately placed footnotes will guide you to each set's continuation.

Definitive sets — Blocks of numbers generally have been reserved for definitive sets, based on previous experience with any given country. If a few more stamps were issued in a set than originally expected, they often have been inserted into the original set with a capital-letter suffix, such as U.S. Scott 1059A. If it appears that many more stamps than the originally allotted block will be released before the set is completed, a new block of numbers will be reserved, with the original one being closed off. In some cases, such as the U.S. Transportation and Great Americans series, several blocks of numbers exist. Appropriately placed footnotes will guide you to each set's continuation.

New country — Membership in the Universal Postal Union is not a consideration for listing status or order of placement within the catalogue. The index will tell you in what volume or page number the listings begin.

"No release date" items — The amount of information available for any given stamp issue varies greatly from country to country and even from time to time. Extremely comprehensive information about new stamps is available from some countries well before the stamps are released. By contrast some countries do not provide information about stamps or release dates. Most countries, however, fall between these extremes. A country may provide denominations or subjects of stamps from upcoming issues that are not issued as planned. Sometimes, philatelic agencies, those private firms hired to represent countries, add these later-issued items to sets well after the formal release date. This time period can range from weeks to years. If these items were officially released by the country, they will be added to the appropriate spot in the set. In many cases, the specific release date of a stamp or set of stamps may never be known.

Overprints — The color of an overprint is always noted if it is other than black. Where more than one color of ink has been used on overprints of a single set, the color used is noted. Early overprint and surcharge illustrations were altered to prevent their use by forgers.

Personalized Stamps — Since 1999, the special service of personalizing stamp vignettes, or labels attached to stamps, has been offered to customers by postal administrations of many countries. Sheets of these stamps are sold, singly or in quantity, only through special orders made by mail, in person, or through a sale on a computer website with the postal administrations or their agents for which an extra fee is charged, though some countries offer to collectors at face value personalized stamps having generic images in the vignettes or on the attached labels. It is impossible for any catalogue to know what images have been chosen by customers. Images can be 1) owned or created by the customer, 2) a generic image, or 3) an image pulled from a library of stock images on the stamp creation website. It is also impossible to know the quantity printed for any stamp having a particular image. So from a valuing standpoint, any image is equivalent to any other image for any personalized stamp having the same catalogue number. Illustrations of personalized stamps in the catalogue are not always those of stamps having generic images.

Personalized items are listed with some exceptions. These include:

1. Stamps or sheets that have attached labels that the customer cannot personalize, but which are nonetheless marketed as "personalized," and are sold for far more than the franking value.
2. Stamps or sheets that can be personalized by the customer, but where a portion of the print run must be ceded to the issuing country for sale to other customers.
3. Stamps or sheets that are created exclusively for a particular commercial client, or clients, including stamps that differ from any similar stamp that has been made available to the public.
4. Stamps or sheets that are deliberately conceived by the issuing authority that have been, or are likely to be, created with an excessive number of different face values, sizes, or other features that are changeable.
5. Stamps or sheets that are created by postal administrations using the same system of stamp personalization that has been put in place for use by the public that are printed in limited quantities and sold above face value.
6. Stamps or sheets that are created by licensees not directly affiliated or controlled by a postal administration.

Excluded items may or may not be footnoted.

Se-tenants — Connected stamps of differing features (se-tenants) will be listed in the format most commonly collected. This includes pairs, blocks or larger multiples. Se-tenant units are not always symmetrical. An example is Australia Scott 508, which is a block of seven stamps. If the stamps are primarily collected as a unit, the major number may be assigned to the multiple, with minors going to each component stamp. In cases where continuous-design or other unit se-tenants will receive significant postal use, each stamp is given a major Scott number listing. This includes issues from the United States, Canada, Germany and Great Britain, for example.

Understanding the Listings

On the opposite page is an enlarged "typical" listing from this catalogue. Below are detailed explanations of each of the highlighted parts of the listing.

1 Scott number — Scott catalogue numbers are used to identify specific items when buying, selling or trading stamps. Each listed postage stamp from every country has a unique Scott catalogue number. Therefore, Germany Scott 99, for example, can only refer to a single stamp. Although the Scott catalogue usually lists stamps in chronological order by date of issue, there are exceptions. When a country has issued a set of stamps over a period of time, those stamps within the set are kept together without regard to date of issue. This follows the normal collecting approach of keeping stamps in their natural sets.

When a country issues a set of stamps over a period of time, a group of consecutive catalogue numbers is reserved for the stamps in that set, as issued. If that group of numbers proves to be too few, capital-letter suffixes, such as "A" or "B," may be added to existing numbers to create enough catalogue numbers to cover all items in the set. A capital-letter suffix indicates a major Scott catalogue number listing. Scott generally uses a suffix letter only once. Therefore, a catalogue number listing with a capital-letter suffix will seldom be found with the same letter (lower case) used as a minor-letter listing. If there is a Scott 16A in a set, for example, there will seldom be a Scott 16a. However, a minor-letter "a" listing may be added to a major number containing an "A" suffix (Scott 16Aa, for example).

Suffix letters are cumulative. A minor "b" variety of Scott 16A would be Scott 16Ab, not Scott 16b.

There are times when a reserved block of Scott catalogue numbers is too large for a set, leaving some numbers unused. Such gaps in the numbering sequence also occur when the catalogue editors move an item's listing elsewhere or have removed it entirely from the catalogue. Scott does not attempt to account for every possible number, but rather attempts to assure that each stamp is assigned its own number.

Scott numbers designating regular postage normally are only numerals. Scott numbers for other types of stamps, such as air post, semi-postal, postal tax, postage due, occupation and others have a prefix consisting of one or more capital letters or a combination of numerals and capital letters.

2 Illustration number — Illustration or design-type numbers are used to identify each catalogue illustration. For most sets, the lowest face-value stamp is shown. It then serves as an example of the basic design approach for other stamps not illustrated. Where more than one stamp use the same illustration number, but have differences in design, the design paragraph or the description line clearly indicates the design on each stamp not illustrated. Where there are both vertical and horizontal designs in a set, a single illustration may be used, with the exceptions noted in the design paragraph or description line.

When an illustration is followed by a lower-case letter in parentheses, such as "A2(b)," the trailing letter indicates which overprint or surcharge illustration applies.

Illustrations normally are 70 percent of the original size of the stamp. Oversized stamps, blocks and souvenir sheets are reduced even more. Overprints and surcharges are shown at 100 percent of their original size if shown alone, but are 70 percent of original size if shown on stamps. In some cases, the illustration will be placed above the set, between listings or omitted completely. Overprint and surcharge illustrations are not placed in this catalogue for purposes of expertizing stamps.

3 Paper color — The color of a stamp's paper is noted in italic type when the paper used is not white.

4 Listing styles — There are two principal types of catalogue listings: major and minor.

Major listings are in a larger type style than minor listings. The catalogue number is a numeral that can be found with or without a capital-letter suffix, and with or without a prefix.

Minor listings are in a smaller type style and have a small-letter suffix or (if the listing immediately follows that of the major number) may show only the letter. These listings identify a variety of the major item. Examples include perforation and shade differences, multiples (some souvenir sheets, booklet panes and se-tenant combinations), and singles of multiples.

Examples of major number listings include 16, 28A, B97, C13A, 10N5, and 10N6A. Examples of minor numbers are 16a and C13Ab.

5 Basic information about a stamp or set — Introducing each stamp issue is a small section (usually a line listing) of basic information about a stamp or set. This section normally includes the date of issue, method of printing, perforation, watermark and, sometimes, some additional information of note. *Printing method, perforation and watermark apply to the following sets until a change is noted.* Stamps created by overprinting or surcharging previous issues are assumed to have the same perforation, watermark, printing method and other production characteristics as the original. Dates of issue are as precise as Scott is able to confirm and often reflect the dates on first-day covers, rather than the actual date of release.

6 Denomination — This normally refers to the face value of the stamp; that is, the cost of the unused stamp at the post office at the time of issue. When a denomination is shown in parentheses, it does not appear on the stamp. This includes the non-denominated stamps of the United States, Brazil and Great Britain, for example.

7 Color or other description — This area provides information to solidify identification of a stamp. In many recent cases, a description of the stamp design appears in this space, rather than a listing of colors.

8 Year of issue — In stamp sets that have been released in a period that spans more than a year, the number shown in parentheses is the year that stamp first appeared. Stamps without a date appeared during the first year of the issue. Dates are not always given for minor varieties.

9 Value unused and Value used — The Scott catalogue values are based on stamps that are in a grade of Very Fine unless stated otherwise. Unused values refer to items that have not seen postal, revenue or any other duty for which they were intended. Pre-1900 unused stamps that were issued with gum must have at least most of their original gum. Later issues are assumed to have full original gum. From breakpoints specified in most countries' listings, stamps are valued as never hinged. Stamps issued without gum are noted. Modern issues with PVA or other synthetic adhesives may appear ungummed. Unused self-adhesive stamps are valued as appearing undisturbed on their original backing paper. Values for used self-adhesive stamps are for examples either on piece or off piece. For a more detailed explanation of these values, please see the "Catalogue Value," "Condition" and "Understanding Valuing Notations" sections elsewhere in this introduction.

In some cases, where used stamps are more valuable than unused stamps, the value is for an example with a contemporaneous cancel, rather than a modern cancel or a smudge or other unclear marking. For those stamps that were released for postal and fiscal purposes, the used value represents a postally used stamp. Stamps with revenue cancels generally sell for less.

Stamps separated from a complete se-tenant multiple usually will be worth less than a pro-rated portion of the se-tenant multiple, and stamps lacking the attached labels that are noted in the listings will be worth less than the values shown.

10 Changes in basic set information — Bold type is used to show any changes in the basic data given for a set of stamps. These basic data categories include perforation gauge measurement, paper type, printing method and watermark.

11 Total value of a set — The total value of sets of three or more stamps issued after 1900 are shown. The set line also notes the range of Scott numbers and total number of stamps included in the grouping. The actual value of a set consisting predominantly of stamps having the minimum value of 25 cents may be less than the total value shown. Similarly, the actual value or catalogue value of se-tenant pairs or of blocks consisting of stamps having the minimum value of 25 cents may be less than the catalogue values of the component parts.

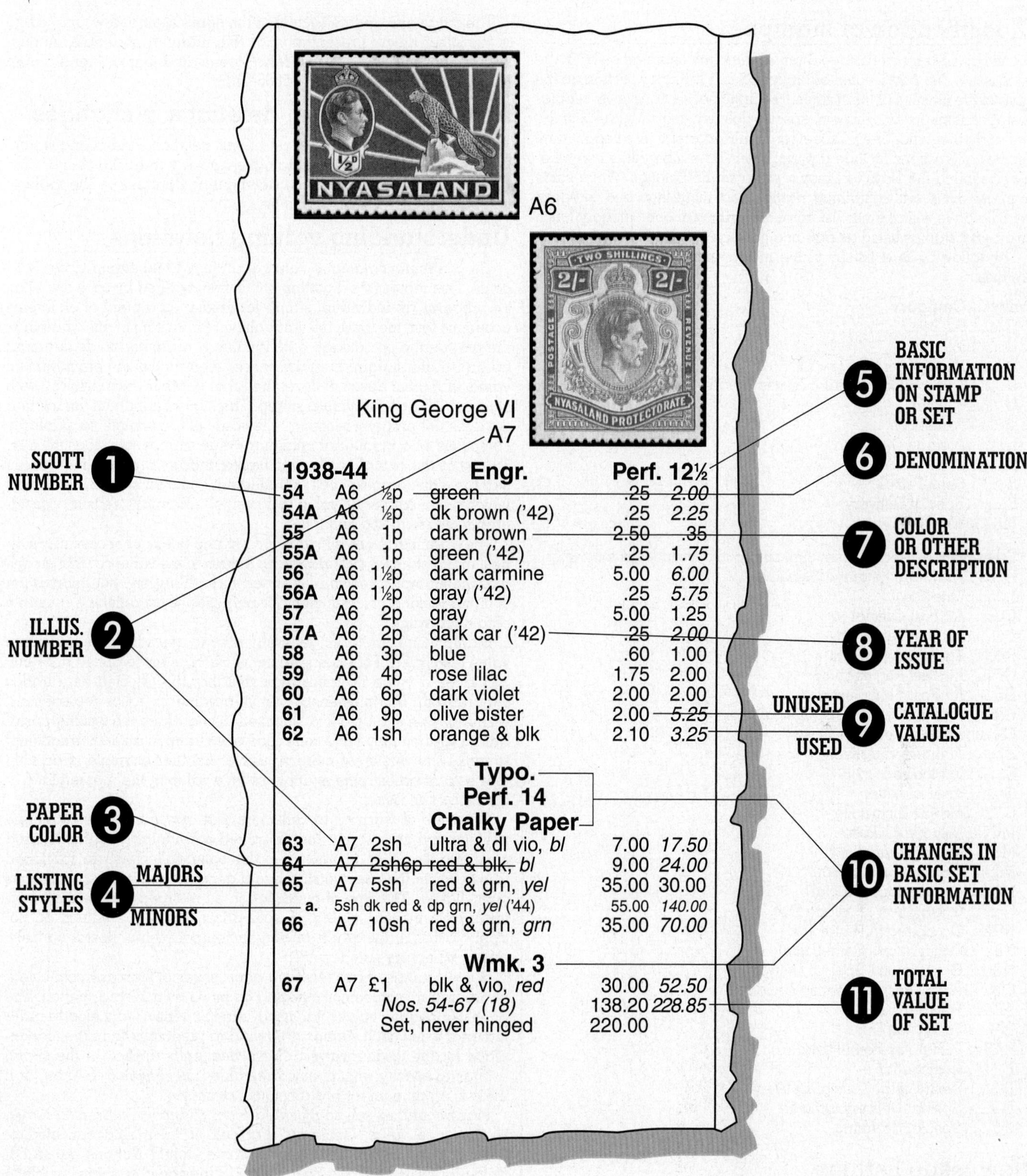

A6

King George VI
A7

1938-44 **Engr.** **Perf. 12½**

54	A6	½p	green	.25	*2.00*
54A	A6	½p	dk brown ('42)	.25	*2.25*
55	A6	1p	dark brown	2.50	.35
55A	A6	1p	green ('42)	.25	*1.75*
56	A6	1½p	dark carmine	5.00	*6.00*
56A	A6	1½p	gray ('42)	.25	*5.75*
57	A6	2p	gray	5.00	1.25
57A	A6	2p	dark car ('42)	.25	*2.00*
58	A6	3p	blue	.60	1.00
59	A6	4p	rose lilac	1.75	2.00
60	A6	6p	dark violet	2.00	2.00
61	A6	9p	olive bister	2.00	*5.25*
62	A6	1sh	orange & blk	2.10	*3.25*

Typo.
Perf. 14
Chalky Paper

63	A7	2sh	ultra & dl vio, *bl*	7.00	*17.50*
64	A7	2sh6p	red & blk, *bl*	9.00	*24.00*
65	A7	5sh	red & grn, *yel*	35.00	30.00
a.		5sh	dk red & dp grn, *yel* ('44)	55.00	*140.00*
66	A7	10sh	red & grn, *grn*	35.00	*70.00*

Wmk. 3

67	A7	£1	blk & vio, *red*	30.00	*52.50*
			Nos. 54-67 (18)	138.20	*228.85*
			Set, never hinged	220.00	

Special Notices

Classification of stamps

The *Scott Standard Postage Stamp Catalogue* lists stamps by country of issue. The next level of organization is a listing by section on the basis of the function of the stamps. The principal sections cover regular postage, semi-postal, air post, special delivery, registration, postage due and other categories. Except for regular postage, catalogue numbers for all sections include a prefix letter (or number-letter combination) denoting the class to which a given stamp belongs. When some countries issue sets containing stamps from more than one category, the catalogue will at times list all of the stamps in one category (such as air post stamps listed as part of a postage set).

The following is a listing of the most commonly used catalogue prefixes.

Prefix .... Category
C......... Air Post
M........ Military
P......... Newspaper
N......... Occupation - Regular Issues
O .... Official
Q .... Parcel Post
J.......... Postage Due
RA ...... Postal Tax
B......... Semi-Postal
E......... Special Delivery
MR...... War Tax

Other prefixes used by more than one country include the following:
H......... Acknowledgment of Receipt
I.......... Late Fee
CO...... Air Post Official
CQ...... Air Post Parcel Post
RAC.... Air Post Postal Tax
CF ...... Air Post Registration
CB ...... Air Post Semi-Postal
CBO ... Air Post Semi-Postal Official
CE ...... Air Post Special Delivery
EY....... Authorized Delivery
S......... Franchise
G .... Insured Letter
GY...... Marine Insurance
MC ..... Military Air Post
MQ..... Military Parcel Post
NC...... Occupation - Air Post
NO...... Occupation - Official
NJ........ Occupation - Postage Due
NRA.... Occupation - Postal Tax
NB ...... Occupation - Semi-Postal
NE ...... Occupation - Special Delivery
QY...... Parcel Post Authorized Delivery
AR ...... Postal-fiscal
RAJ ..... Postal Tax Due
RAB .... Postal Tax Semi-Postal
F......... Registration
EB....... Semi-Postal Special Delivery
EO...... Special Delivery Official
QE...... Special Handling

New issue listings

Updates to this catalogue appear each month in the *Linn's Stamp News* monthly magazine. Included in this update are additions to the listings of countries found in the *Scott Standard Postage Stamp Catalogue* and the *Specialized Catalogue of United States Stamps and Covers*, as well as corrections and updates to current editions of this catalogue.

From time to time there will be changes in the final listings of stamps from the *Linn's Stamp News* magazine to the next edition of the catalogue. This occurs as more information about certain stamps or sets becomes available.

The catalogue update section of the *Linn's Stamp News* magazine is the most timely presentation of this material available. Annual subscriptions to *Linn's Stamp News* are available from Linn's Stamp News, Box 4129, Sidney, OH 45365-4129.

Number additions, deletions & changes

A listing of catalogue number additions, deletions and changes from the previous edition of the catalogue appears in each volume. See Catalogue Number Additions, Deletions & Changes in the table of contents for the location of this list.

Understanding valuing notations

The *minimum catalogue value* of an individual stamp or set is 25 cents. This represents a portion of the cost incurred by a dealer when he prepares an individual stamp for resale. As a point of philatelic-economic fact, the lower the value shown for an item in this catalogue, the greater the percentage of that value is attributed to dealer mark up and profit margin. In many cases, such as the 25-cent minimum value, that price does not cover the labor or other costs involved with stocking it as an individual stamp. The sum of minimum values in a set does not properly represent the value of a complete set primarily composed of a number of minimum-value stamps, nor does the sum represent the actual value of a packet made up of minimum-value stamps. Thus a packet of 1,000 different common stamps — each of which has a catalogue value of 25 cents — normally sells for considerably less than 250 dollars!

The *absence of a retail value* for a stamp does not necessarily suggest that a stamp is scarce or rare. A dash in the value column means that the stamp is known in a stated form or variety, but information is either lacking or insufficient for purposes of establishing a usable catalogue value.

Stamp values in *italics* generally refer to items that are difficult to value accurately. For expensive items, such as those priced at $1,000 or higher, a value in italics indicates that the affected item trades very seldom. For inexpensive items, a value in italics represents a warning. One example is a "blocked" issue where the issuing postal administration may have controlled one stamp in a set in an attempt to make the whole set more valuable. Another example is an item that sold at an extreme multiple of face value in the marketplace at the time of its issue.

One type of warning to collectors that appears in the catalogue is illustrated by a stamp that is valued considerably higher in used condition than it is as unused. In this case, collectors are cautioned to be certain the used version has a genuine and contemporaneous cancellation. The type of cancellation on a stamp can be an important factor in determining its sale price. Catalogue values do not apply to fiscal, telegraph or non-contemporaneous postal cancels, unless otherwise noted.

Some countries have released back issues of stamps in canceled-to-order form, sometimes covering as much as a 10-year period. The Scott Catalogue values for used stamps reflect canceled-to-order material when such stamps are found to predominate in the marketplace for the issue involved. Notes frequently appear in the stamp listings to specify which items are valued as canceled-to-order, or if there is a premium for postally used examples.

Many countries sell canceled-to-order stamps at a marked reduction of face value. Countries that sell or have sold canceled-to-order stamps at *full* face value include United Nations, Australia, Netherlands, France and Switzerland. It may be almost impossible to identify such stamps if the gum has been removed, because official government canceling devices are used. Postally used examples of these items on cover, however, are usually worth more than the canceled-to-order stamps with original gum.

Abbreviations

Scott uses a consistent set of abbreviations throughout this catalogue to conserve space, while still providing necessary information.

COLOR ABBREVIATIONS

amb. amber	crim. crimson	ol ..... olive
anil.. aniline	cr ..... cream	olvn . olivine
ap.... apple	dk .... dark	org... orange
aqua aquamarine	dl ..... dull	pck .. peacock
az .... azure	dp.... deep	pnksh pinkish
bis ... bister	db.... drab	Prus. Prussian
bl ..... blue	emer emerald	pur... purple
bld... blood	gldn. golden	redsh reddish
blk ... black	gryshgrayish	res ... reseda
bril... brilliant	grn... green	ros ... rosine
brn... brown	grnsh greenish	ryl .... royal
brnsh brownish	hel ... heliotrope	sal ... salmon
brnz. bronze	hn .... henna	saph sapphire
brt.... bright	ind .. indigo	scar. scarlet
brnt . burnt	int ..... intense	sep .. sepia
car... carmine	lav ... lavender	sien . sienna
cer ... cerise	lem .. lemon	sil..... silver
chlky chalky	lil ..... lilac	sl..... slate
chamchamois	lt ...... light	stl .... steel
chnt . chestnut	mag. magenta	turq.. turquoise
choc chocolate	man. manila	ultra ultramarine
chr ... chrome	mar.. maroon	Ven.. Venetian
cit .... citron	mv ... mauve	ver ... vermilion
cl...... claret	multi multicolored	vio .. violet
cob .. cobalt	mlky milky	yel ... yellow
cop .. copper	myr.. myrtle	yelsh yellowish

When no color is given for an overprint or surcharge, black is the color used. Abbreviations for colors used for overprints and surcharges include: "(B)" or "(Blk)," black; "(Bl)," blue; "(R)," red; and "(G)," green.

Additional abbreviations in this catalogue are shown below:

Adm. ....Administration
AFL...............American Federation of Labor
Anniv. ....Anniversary
APS ....American Philatelic Society
Assoc. ....Association
ASSR. ....Autonomous Soviet Socialist Republic
b. ....Born
BEP...............Bureau of Engraving and Printing
Bicent. ....Bicentennial
Bklt. ....Booklet
Brit................British
btwn. ....Between
Bur. ....Bureau
c. or ca. ....Circa
Cat. ....Catalogue
Cent. ....Centennial, century, centenary
CIO ....Congress of Industrial Organizations
Conf. ....Conference
Cong. ....Congress
Cpl. ....Corporal
CTO ....Canceled to order
d. ....Died
Dbl. ....Double
EDU..............Earliest documented use
Engr. ....Engraved
Exhib.............Exhibition
Expo..............Exposition
Fed. ....Federation
GB ....Great Britain
Gen. ....General
GPO ....General post office
Horiz. ....Horizontal
Imperf. ....Imperforate
Impt..............Imprint
Intl. ....International
Invtd. ....Inverted
L ....Left
Lieut., lt. ....Lieutenant
Litho. ....Lithographed
LL ....Lower left
LR ....Lower right
mm ....Millimeter
Ms. ....Manuscript
Natl. ....National
No. ....Number
NY ....New York
NYC ....New York City
Ovpt. ....Overprint
Ovptd. ....Overprinted
P ....Plate number
Perf. ....Perforated, perforation
Phil. ....Philatelic
Photo. ....Photogravure
PO ....Post office
Pr. ....Pair
P.R. ....Puerto Rico
Prec. ....Precancel, precanceled
Pres. ....President
PTT ....Post, Telephone and Telegraph
R ....Right
Rio ....Rio de Janeiro
Sgt. ....Sergeant
Soc. ....Society
Souv. ....Souvenir
SSR ....Soviet Socialist Republic, see ASSR
St. ....Saint, street
Surch. ....Surcharge
Typo. ....Typographed
UL ....Upper left
Unwmkd. ....Unwatermarked
UPU ....Universal Postal Union
UR ....Upper Right
US ....United States
USPOD ....United States Post Office Department
USSR ....Union of Soviet Socialist Republics
Vert. ....Vertical
VP ....Vice president
Wmk. ....Watermark
Wmkd. ....Watermarked
WWI ....World War I
WWII ....World War II

Examination

Amos Media Co. will not comment upon the genuineness, grade or condition of stamps, because of the time and responsibility involved. Rather, there are several expertizing groups that undertake this work for both collectors and dealers. Neither will Amos Media Co. appraise or identify philatelic material. The company cannot take responsibility for unsolicited stamps or covers sent by individuals.

All letters, E-mails, etc. are read attentively, but they are not always answered due to time considerations.

How to order from your dealer

When ordering stamps from a dealer, it is not necessary to write the full description of a stamp as listed in this catalogue. All you need is the name of the country, the Scott catalogue number and whether the desired item is unused or used. For example, "Japan Scott 422 unused" is sufficient to identify the unused stamp of Japan listed as "422 A206 5y brown."

Basic Stamp Information

A stamp collector's knowledge of the combined elements that make a given stamp issue unique determines his or her ability to identify stamps. These elements include paper, watermark, method of separation, printing, design and gum. On the following pages each of these important areas is briefly described.

Paper

Paper is an organic material composed of a compacted weave of cellulose fibers and generally formed into sheets. Paper used to print stamps may be manufactured in sheets, or it may have been part of a large roll (called a web) before being cut to size. The fibers most often used to create paper on which stamps are printed include bark, wood, straw and certain grasses. In many cases, linen or cotton rags have been added for greater strength and durability. Grinding, bleaching, cooking and rinsing these raw fibers reduces them to a slushy pulp, referred to by paper makers as "stuff." Sizing and, sometimes, coloring matter is added to the pulp to make different types of finished paper.

After the stuff is prepared, it is poured onto sieve-like frames that allow the water to run off, while retaining the matted pulp. As fibers fall onto the screen and are held by gravity, they form a natural weave that will later hold the paper together. If the screen has metal bits that are formed into letters or images attached, it leaves slightly thinned areas on the paper. These are called watermarks.

When the stuff is almost dry, it is passed under pressure through smooth or engraved rollers - dandy rolls - or placed between cloth in a press to be flattened and dried.

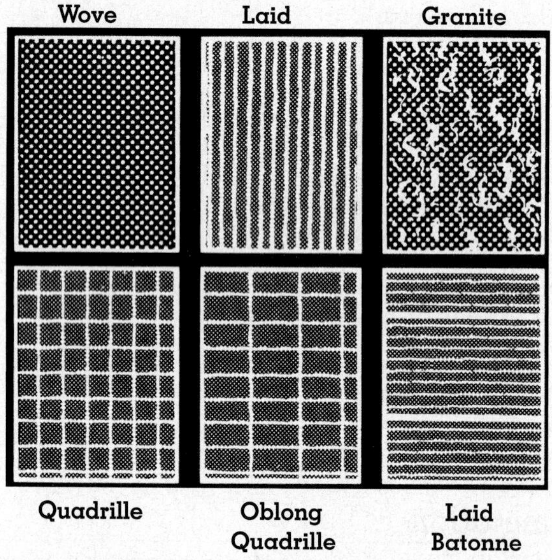

Stamp paper falls broadly into two types: wove and laid. The nature of the surface of the frame onto which the pulp is first deposited causes the differences in appearance between the two. If the surface is smooth and even, the paper will be of fairly uniform texture throughout. This is known as *wove paper*. Early papermaking machines poured the pulp onto a continuously circulating web of felt, but modern machines feed the pulp onto a cloth-like screen made of closely interwoven fine wires. This paper, when held to a light, will show little dots or points very close together. The proper name for this is "wire wove," but the type is still considered wove. Any U.S. or British stamp printed after 1880 will serve as an example of wire wove paper.

Closely spaced parallel wires, with cross wires at wider intervals, make up the frames used for what is known as *laid paper*. A greater thickness of the pulp will settle between the wires. The paper, when held to a light, will show alternate light and dark lines. The spacing and the thickness of the lines may vary, but on any one sheet of paper they are all alike. See Russia Scott 31-38 for examples of laid paper.

Batonne, from the French word meaning "a staff," is a term used if the lines in the paper are spaced quite far apart, like the printed ruling on a writing tablet. Batonne paper may be either wove or laid. If laid, fine laid lines can be seen between the batons.

Quadrille is the term used when the lines in the paper form little squares. *Oblong quadrille* is the term used when rectangles, rather than squares, are formed. Grid patterns vary from distinct to extremely faint. See Mexico-Guadalajara Scott 35-37 for examples of oblong quadrille paper.

Paper also is classified as thick or thin, hard or soft, and by color. Such colors may include yellowish, greenish, bluish and reddish.

Brief explanations of other types of paper used for printing stamps, as well as examples, follow.

Colored — Colored paper is created by the addition of dye in the paper-making process. Such colors may include shades of yellow, green, blue and red. *Surface-colored papers*, most commonly used for British colonial issues in 1913-14, are created when coloring is added only to the surface during the finishing process. Stamps printed on surface-colored paper have white or uncolored backs, while true colored papers are colored through. See Jamaica Scott 71-73.

Pelure — Pelure paper is a very thin, hard and often brittle paper that is sometimes bluish or grayish in appearance. See Serbia Scott 169-170.

Native — This is a term applied to handmade papers used to produce some of the early stamps of the Indian states. Stamps printed on native paper may be expected to display various natural inclusions that are normal and do not negatively affect value. Japanese paper, originally made of mulberry fibers and rice flour, is part of this group. See Japan Scott 1-18.

Manila — This type of paper is often used to make stamped envelopes and wrappers. It is a coarse-textured stock, usually smooth on one side and rough on the other. A variety of colors of manila paper exist, but the most common range is yellowish-brown.

Silk — Introduced by the British in 1847 as a safeguard against counterfeiting, silk paper contains bits of colored silk thread scattered throughout. The density of these fibers varies greatly and can include as few as one fiber per stamp or hundreds. U.S. revenue Scott R152 is a good example of an easy-to-identify silk paper stamp.

Silk-thread paper has uninterrupted threads of colored silk arranged so that one or more threads run through the stamp or postal stationery. See Great Britain Scott 5-6 and Switzerland Scott 14-19.

Granite — Filled with minute cloth or colored paper fibers of various colors and lengths, granite paper should not be confused with either type of silk paper. Austria Scott 172-175 and a number of Swiss stamps are examples of granite paper.

Chalky — A chalk-like substance coats the surface of chalky paper to discourage the cleaning and reuse of canceled stamps, as well as to provide a smoother, more acceptable printing surface. Because the designs of stamps printed on chalky paper are imprinted on what is often a water-soluble coating, any attempt to remove a cancellation will destroy the stamp. *Do not soak these stamps in any fluid.* To remove a stamp printed on chalky paper from an envelope, wet the paper from underneath the stamp until the gum dissolves enough to release the stamp from the paper. See St. Kitts-Nevis Scott 89-90 for examples of stamps printed on this type of chalky paper.

India — Another name for this paper, originally introduced from China about 1750, is "China Paper." It is a thin, opaque paper often used for plate and die proofs by many countries.

Double — In philately, the term double paper has two distinct meanings. The first is a two-ply paper, usually a combination of a thick and a thin sheet, joined during manufacture. This type was used experimentally as a means to discourage the reuse of stamps.

The design is printed on the thin paper. Any attempt to remove a cancellation would destroy the design. U.S. Scott 158 and other Banknote-era stamps exist on this form of double paper.

The second type of double paper occurs on a rotary press, when the end of one paper roll, or web, is affixed to the next roll to save time feeding the paper through the press. Stamp designs are printed over the joined paper and, if overlooked by inspectors, may get into post office stocks.

Goldbeater's Skin — This type of paper was used for the 1866 issue of Prussia, and was a tough, translucent paper. The design was printed in reverse on the back of the stamp, and the gum applied over the printing. It is impossible to remove stamps printed on this type of paper from the paper to which they are affixed without destroying the design.

Ribbed — Ribbed paper has an uneven, corrugated surface made by passing the paper through ridged rollers. This type exists on some copies of U.S. Scott 156-165.

Various other substances, or substrates, have been used for stamp manufacture, including wood, aluminum, copper, silver and gold foil, plastic, and silk and cotton fabrics.

Watermarks

Watermarks are an integral part of some papers. They are formed in the process of paper manufacture. Watermarks consist of small designs, formed of wire or cut from metal and soldered to the surface of the mold or, sometimes, on the dandy roll. The designs may be in the form of crowns, stars, anchors, letters or other characters or symbols. These pieces of metal - known in the paper-making industry as "bits" - impress a design into the paper. The design sometimes may be seen by holding the stamp to the light. Some are more easily seen with a watermark detector. This important tool is a small black tray into which a stamp is placed face down and dampened with a fast-evaporating watermark detection fluid that brings up the watermark image in the form of dark lines against a lighter background. These dark lines are the thinner areas of the paper known as the watermark. Some watermarks are extremely difficult to locate, due to either a faint impression, watermark location or the color of the stamp. There also are electric watermark detectors that come with plastic filter disks of various colors. The disks neutralize the color of the stamp, permitting the watermark to be seen more easily.

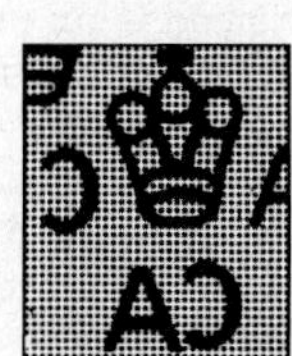

Multiple watermarks of Crown Agents and Burma

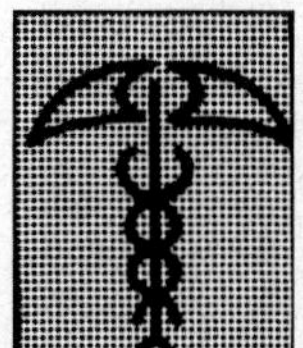

Watermarks of Uruguay, Vatican City and Jamaica

WARNING: Some inks used in the photogravure process dissolve in watermark fluids (Please see the section on Soluble Printing Inks). Also, see "chalky paper."

Watermarks may be found normal, reversed, inverted, reversed and inverted, sideways or diagonal, as seen from the back of the stamp. The relationship of watermark to stamp design depends on the position of the printing plates or how paper is fed through the press. On machine-made paper, watermarks normally are read from right to left. The design is repeated closely throughout the sheet in a "multiple-watermark design." In a "sheet watermark," the design appears only once on the sheet, but extends over many stamps. Individual stamps may carry only a small fraction or none of the watermark.

"Marginal watermarks" occur in the margins of sheets or panes of stamps. They occur on the outside border of paper (ostensibly outside the area where stamps are to be printed). A large row of letters may spell the name of the country or the manufacturer of the paper, or a border of lines may appear. Careless press feeding may cause parts of these letters and/or lines to show on stamps of the outer row of a pane.

Soluble Printing Inks

WARNING: Most stamp colors are permanent; that is, they are not seriously affected by short-term exposure to light or water. Many colors, especially of modern inks, fade from excessive exposure to light. There are stamps printed with inks that dissolve easily in water or in fluids used to detect watermarks. Use of these inks was intentional to prevent the removal of cancellations. Water affects all aniline inks, those on so-called safety paper and some photogravure printings - all such inks are known as fugitive colors. *Removal from paper of such stamps requires care and alternatives to traditional soaking.*

Separation

"Separation" is the general term used to describe methods used to separate stamps. The three standard forms currently in use are perforating, rouletting and die-cutting. These methods are done during the stamp production process, after printing. Sometimes these methods are done on-press or sometimes as a separate step. The earliest issues, such as the 1840 Penny Black of Great Britain (Scott 1), did not have any means provided for separation. It was expected the stamps would be cut apart with scissors or folded and torn. These are examples of imperforate stamps. Many stamps were first issued in imperforate formats and were later issued with perforations. Therefore, care must be observed in buying single imperforate stamps to be certain they were issued imperforate and are not perforated copies that have been altered by having the perforations trimmed away. Stamps issued imperforate usually are valued as singles. However, imperforate varieties of normally perforated stamps should be collected in pairs or larger pieces as indisputable evidence of their imperforate character.

PERFORATION

The chief style of separation of stamps, and the one that is in almost universal use today, is perforating. By this process, paper between the stamps is cut away in a line of holes, usually round, leaving little bridges of paper between the stamps to hold them together. Some types of perforation, such as hyphen-hole perfs, can be confused with roulettes, but a close visual inspection reveals that paper has been removed. The little perforation bridges, which project from the stamp when it is torn from the pane, are called the teeth of the perforation.

As the size of the perforation is sometimes the only way to differentiate between two otherwise identical stamps, it is necessary to be able to accurately measure and describe them. This is done with a perforation gauge, usually a ruler-like device that has dots or graduated lines to show how many perforations may be counted in the space of two centimeters. Two centimeters is the space universally adopted in which to measure perforations.

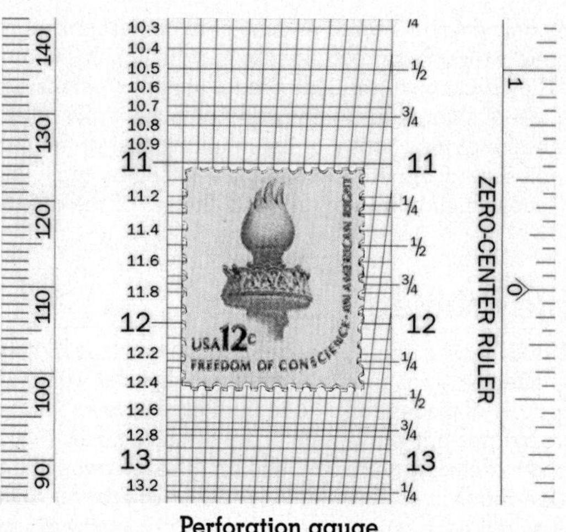

Perforation gauge

To measure a stamp, run it along the gauge until the dots on it fit exactly into the perforations of the stamp. If you are using a graduated-line perforation gauge, simply slide the stamp along the surface until the lines on the gauge perfectly project from the center of the bridges or holes. The number to the side of the line of dots or lines that fit the stamp's perforation is the measurement. For example, an "11" means that 11 perforations fit between two centimeters. The description of the stamp therefore is "perf. 11." If the gauge of the perforations on the top and bottom of a stamp differs from that on the sides, the result is what is known as *compound perforations.* In measuring compound perforations, the gauge at top and bottom is always given first, then the sides. Thus, a stamp that measures 11 at top and bottom and 10½ at the sides is "perf. 11 x 10½." See U.S. Scott 632-642 for examples of compound perforations.

Stamps also are known with perforations different on three or all four sides. Descriptions of such items are clockwise, beginning with the top of the stamp.

A perforation with small holes and teeth close together is a "fine perforation." One with large holes and teeth far apart is a "coarse perforation." Holes that are jagged, rather than clean-cut, are "rough perforations." *Blind perforations* are the slight impressions left by the perforating pins if they fail to puncture the paper. Multiples of stamps showing blind perforations may command a slight premium over normally perforated stamps.

The term *syncopated perfs* describes intentional irregularities in the perforations. The earliest form was used by the Netherlands from 1925-33, where holes were omitted to create distinctive patterns. Beginning in 1992, Great Britain has used an oval perforation to help prevent counterfeiting. Several other countries have started using the oval perfs or other syncopated perf patterns.

A new type of perforation, still primarily used for postal stationery, is known as microperfs. Microperfs are tiny perforations (in some cases hundreds of holes per two centimeters) that allows items to be intentionally separated very easily, while not accidentally breaking apart as easily as standard perforations. These are not currently measured or differentiated by size, as are standard perforations.

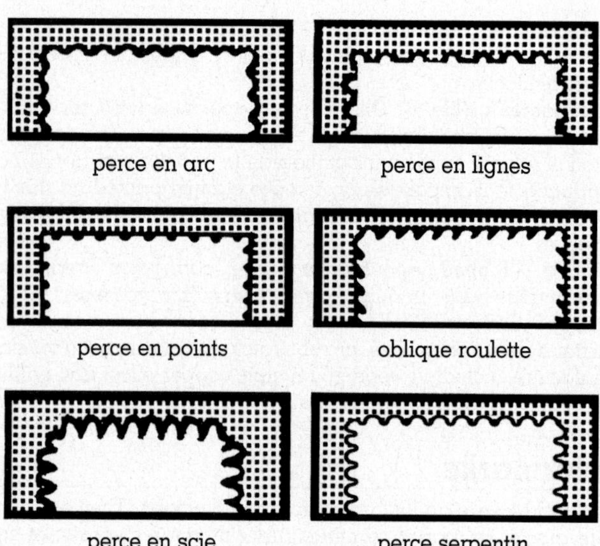

ROULETTING

In rouletting, the stamp paper is cut partly or wholly through, with no paper removed. In perforating, some paper is removed. Rouletting derives its name from the French roulette, a spur-like wheel. As the wheel is rolled over the paper, each point makes a small cut. The number of cuts made in a two-centimeter space determines the gauge of the roulette, just as the number of perforations in two centimeters determines the gauge of the perforation.

The shape and arrangement of the teeth on the wheels varies. Various roulette types generally carry French names:

Perce en lignes - rouletted in lines. The paper receives short, straight cuts in lines. This is the most common type of rouletting. See Mexico Scott 500.

Perce en points - pin-rouletted or pin-perfed. This differs from a small perforation because no paper is removed, although round, equidistant holes are pricked through the paper. See Mexico Scott 242-256.

Perce en arc and *perce en scie* - pierced in an arc or saw-toothed designs, forming half circles or small triangles. See Hanover (German States) Scott 25-29.

Perce en serpentin - serpentine roulettes. The cuts form a serpentine or wavy line. See Brunswick (German States) Scott 13-18.

Once again, no paper is removed by these processes, leaving the stamps easily separated, but closely attached.

DIE-CUTTING

The third major form of stamp separation is die-cutting. This is a method where a die in the pattern of separation is created that later cuts the stamp paper in a stroke motion. Although some standard stamps bear die-cut perforations, this process is primarily used for self-adhesive postage stamps. Die-cutting can appear in straight lines, such as U.S. Scott 2522, shapes, such as U.S. Scott 1551, or imitating the appearance of perforations, such as New Zealand Scott 935A and 935B.

Printing Processes

ENGRAVING (Intaglio, Line-engraving, Etching)

Master die — The initial operation in the process of line engraving is making the master die. The die is a small, flat block of softened steel upon which the stamp design is recess engraved in reverse.

Master die

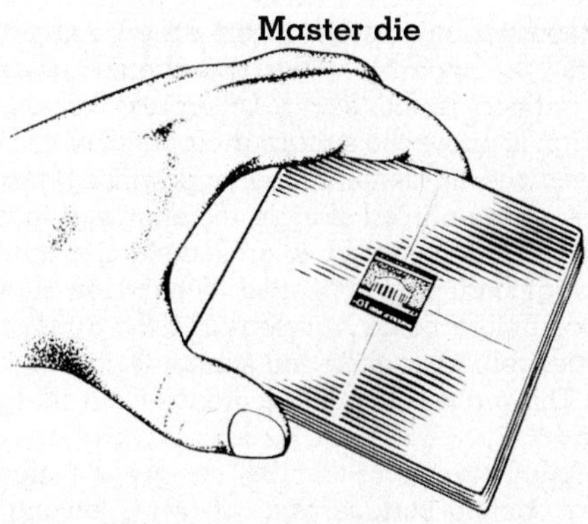

Photographic reduction of the original art is made to the appropriate size. It then serves as a tracing guide for the initial outline of the design. The engraver lightly traces the design on the steel with his graver, then slowly works the design until it is completed. At various points during the engraving process, the engraver hand-inks the die and makes an impression to check his progress. These are known as progressive die proofs. After completion of the engraving, the die is hardened to withstand the stress and pressures of later transfer operations.

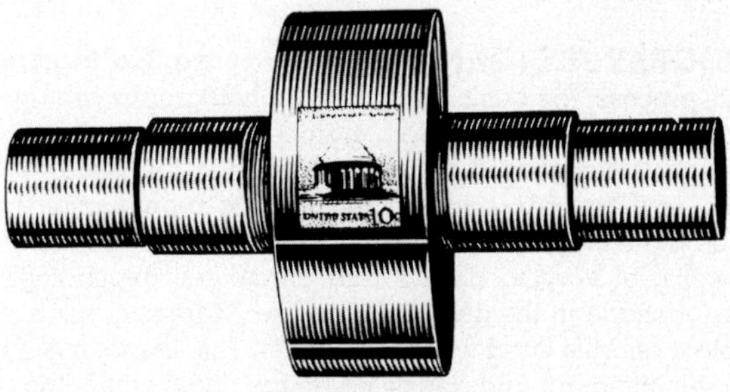

Transfer roll

Transfer roll — Next is production of the transfer roll that, as the name implies, is the medium used to transfer the subject from the master die to the printing plate. A blank roll of soft steel, mounted on a mandrel, is placed under the bearers of the transfer press to allow it to roll freely on its axis. The hardened die is placed on the bed of the press and the face of the transfer roll is applied to the die, under pressure. The bed or the roll is then rocked back and forth under increasing pressure, until the soft steel of the roll is forced into every engraved line of the die. The resulting impression on the roll is known as a "relief" or a "relief transfer." The engraved image is now positive in appearance and stands out from the steel. After the required number of reliefs are "rocked in," the soft steel transfer roll is hardened.

Different flaws may occur during the relief process. A defective relief may occur during the rocking in process because of a minute piece of foreign material lodging on the die, or some other cause. Imperfections in the steel of the transfer roll may result in a breaking away of parts of the design. This is known as a relief break, which will show up on finished stamps as small, unprinted areas. If a damaged relief remains in use, it will transfer a repeating defect to the plate. Deliberate alterations of reliefs sometimes occur. "Altered reliefs" designate these changed conditions.

Plate — The final step in pre-printing production is the making of the printing plate. A flat piece of soft steel replaces the die on the bed of the transfer press. One of the reliefs on the transfer roll is positioned over this soft steel. Position, or layout, dots determine the correct position on the plate. The dots have been lightly marked on the plate in advance. After the correct position of the relief is determined, the design is rocked in by following the same method used in making the transfer roll. The difference is that this time the image is being transferred from the transfer roll, rather than to it. Once the design is entered on the plate, it appears in reverse and is recessed. There are as many transfers entered on the plate as there are subjects printed on the sheet of stamps. It is during this process that double and shifted transfers occur, as well as re-entries. These are the result of improperly entered images that have not been properly burnished out prior to rocking in a new image.

Modern siderography processes, such as those used by the U.S. Bureau of Engraving and Printing, involve an automated form of rocking designs in on preformed cylindrical printing sleeves. The same process also allows for easier removal and re-entry of worn images right on the sleeve.

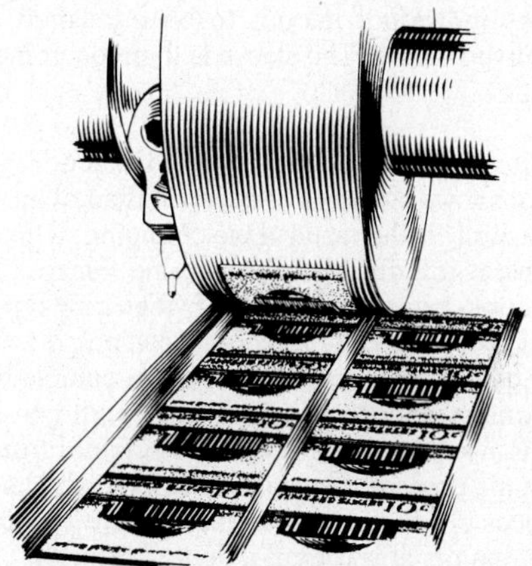

Transferring the design to the plate

Following the entering of the required transfers on the plate, the position dots, layout dots and lines, scratches and other markings generally are burnished out. Added at this time by the siderographer are any required *guide lines, plate numbers* or other *marginal markings.* The plate is then hand-inked and a proof impression is taken. This is known as a plate proof. If the impression is approved, the plate is machined for fitting onto the press, is hardened and sent to the plate vault ready for use.

On press, the plate is inked and the surface is automatically wiped clean, leaving ink only in the recessed lines. Paper is then forced under pressure into the engraved recessed lines, thereby receiving the ink. Thus, the ink lines on engraved stamps are slightly raised, and slight depressions (debossing) occur on the back of the stamp. Prior to the advent of modern high-speed presses and more advanced ink formulations, paper had to be dampened before receiving the ink. This sometimes led to uneven shrinkage by the time the stamps were perforated, resulting in improperly perforated stamps, or misperfs. Newer presses use drier paper, thus both *wet* and *dry printings* exist on some stamps.

Rotary Press — Until 1914, only flat plates were used to print engraved stamps. Rotary press printing was introduced in 1914, and slowly spread. Some countries still use flat-plate printing.

After approval of the plate proof, older *rotary press plates* require additional machining. They are curved to fit the press cylinder. "Gripper slots" are cut into the back of each plate to receive the "grippers," which hold the plate securely on the press. The plate is then hardened. Stamps printed from these bent rotary press plates are longer or wider than the same stamps printed from flat-plate presses. The stretching of the plate during the curving process is what causes this distortion.

Re-entry — To execute a re-entry on a flat plate, the transfer roll is re-applied to the plate, often at some time after its first use on the press. Worn-out designs can be resharpened by carefully burnishing out the original image and re-entering it from the transfer roll. If the original impression has not been sufficiently removed and the transfer roll is not precisely in line with the remaining impression, the resulting double transfer will make the re-entry obvious. If the registration is true, a re-entry may be difficult or impossible to distinguish. Sometimes a stamp printed from a successful re-entry is identified by having a much sharper and clearer impression than its neighbors. With the advent of rotary presses, post-press re-entries were not possible. After a plate was curved for the rotary press, it was impossible to make a re-entry. This is because the plate had already been bent once (with the design distorted).

However, with the introduction of the previously mentioned modern-style siderography machines, entries are made to the preformed cylindrical printing sleeve. Such sleeves are dechromed and softened. This allows individual images to be burnished out and re-entered on the curved sleeve. The sleeve is then rechromed, resulting in longer press life.

Double Transfer — This is a description of the condition of a transfer on a plate that shows evidence of a duplication of all, or a portion of the design. It usually is the result of the changing of the registration between the transfer roll and the plate during the rocking in of the original entry. Double transfers also occur when only a portion of the design has been rocked in and improper positioning is noted. If the worker elected not to burnish out the partial or completed design, a strong double transfer will occur for part or all of the design.

It sometimes is necessary to remove the original transfer from a plate and repeat the process a second time. If the finished re-worked image shows traces of the original impression, attributable to incomplete burnishing, the result is a partial double transfer.

With the modern automatic machines mentioned previously, double transfers are all but impossible to create. Those partially doubled images on stamps printed from such sleeves are more than likely re-entries, rather than true double transfers.

Re-engraved — Alterations to a stamp design are sometimes necessary after some stamps have been printed. In some cases, either the original die or the actual printing plate may have its "temper" drawn (softened), and the design will be re-cut. The resulting impressions from such a re-engraved die or plate may differ slightly from the original issue, and are known as "re-engraved." If the alteration was made to the master die, all future printings will be consistently different from the original. If alterations were made to the printing plate, each altered stamp on the plate will be slightly different from each other, allowing specialists to reconstruct a complete printing plate.

Dropped Transfers — If an impression from the transfer roll has not been properly placed, a dropped transfer may occur. The final stamp image will appear obviously out of line with its neighbors.

Short Transfer — Sometimes a transfer roll is not rocked its entire length when entering a transfer onto a plate. As a result, the finished transfer on the plate fails to show the complete design, and the finished stamp will have an incomplete design printed. This is known as a "short transfer." U.S. Scott No. 8 is a good example of a short transfer.

TYPOGRAPHY (Letterpress, Surface Printing, Flexography, Dry Offset, High Etch)

Although the word "Typography" is obsolete as a term describing a printing method, it was the accepted term throughout the first century of postage stamps. Therefore, appropriate Scott listings in this catalogue refer to typographed stamps. The current term for this form of printing, however, is "letterpress."

As it relates to the production of postage stamps, letterpress printing is the reverse of engraving. Rather than having recessed areas trap the ink and deposit it on paper, only the raised areas of the design are inked. This is comparable to the type of printing seen by inking and using an ordinary rubber stamp. Letterpress includes all printing where the design is above the surface area, whether it is wood, metal or, in some instances, hardened rubber or polymer plastic.

For most letterpress-printed stamps, the engraved master is made in much the same manner as for engraved stamps. In this instance, however, an additional step is needed. The design is transferred to another surface before being transferred to the transfer roll. In this way, the transfer roll has a recessed stamp design, rather than one done in relief. This makes the printing areas on the final plate raised, or relief areas.

For less-detailed stamps of the 19th century, the area on the die not used as a printing surface was cut away, leaving the surface area raised. The original die was then reproduced by stereotyping or electrotyping. The resulting electrotypes were assembled in the required number and format of the desired sheet of stamps. The plate used in printing the stamps was an electroplate of these assembled electrotypes.

Once the final letterpress plates are created, ink is applied to the raised surface and the pressure of the press transfers the ink impression to the paper. In contrast to engraving, the fine lines of letterpress are impressed on the surface of the stamp, leaving a debossed surface. When viewed from the back (as on a typewritten page), the corresponding line work on the stamp will be raised slightly (embossed) above the surface.

PHOTOGRAVURE (Gravure, Rotogravure, Heliogravure)

In this process, the basic principles of photography are applied to a chemically sensitized metal plate, rather than photographic paper. The design is transferred photographically to the plate through a halftone, or dot-matrix screen, breaking the reproduction into tiny dots. The plate is treated chemically and the dots form depressions, called cells, of varying depths and diameters, depending on the degrees of shade in the design. Then, like engraving, ink is applied to the plate and the surface is wiped clean. This leaves ink in the tiny cells that is lifted out and deposited on the paper when it is pressed against the plate.

Gravure is most often used for multicolored stamps, generally using the three primary colors (red, yellow and blue) and black. By varying the dot matrix pattern and density of these colors, virtually any color can be reproduced. A typical full-color gravure stamp will be created from four printing cylinders (one for each color). The original multicolored image will have been photographically separated into its component colors.

Modern gravure printing may use computer-generated dot-matrix screens, and modern plates may be of various types including metal-coated plastic. The catalogue designation of Photogravure (or "Photo") covers any of these older and more modern gravure methods of printing.

For examples of the first photogravure stamps printed (1914), see Bavaria Scott 94-114.

LITHOGRAPHY (Offset Lithography, Stone Lithography, Dilitho, Planography, Collotype)

The principle that oil and water do not mix is the basis for lithography. The stamp design is drawn by hand or transferred from engraving to the surface of a lithographic stone or metal plate in a greasy (oily) substance. This oily substance holds the ink, which will later be transferred to the paper. The stone (or plate) is wet with an acid fluid, causing it to repel the printing ink in all areas not covered by the greasy substance.

Transfer paper is used to transfer the design from the original stone or plate. A series of duplicate transfers are grouped and, in turn, transferred to the final printing plate.

Photolithography — The application of photographic processes to lithography. This process allows greater flexibility of design, related to use of halftone screens combined with line work. Unlike photogravure or engraving, this process can allow large, solid areas to be printed.

Offset — A refinement of the lithographic process. A rubber-covered blanket cylinder takes the impression from the inked lithographic plate. From the "blanket" the impression is *offset* or transferred to the paper. Greater flexibility and speed are the principal reasons offset printing has largely displaced lithography. The term "lithography" covers both processes, and results are almost identical.

EMBOSSED (Relief) Printing

Embossing, not considered one of the four main printing types, is a method in which the design first is sunk into the metal of the die. Printing is done against a yielding platen, such as leather or linoleum. The platen is forced into the depression of the die, thus forming the design on the paper in relief. This process is often used for metallic inks.

Embossing may be done without color (see Sardinia Scott 4-6); with color printed around the embossed area (see Great Britain Scott 5 and most U.S. envelopes); and with color in exact registration with the embossed subject (see Canada Scott 656-657).

HOLOGRAMS

For objects to appear as holograms on stamps, a model exactly the same size as it is to appear on the hologram must be created. Rather than using photographic film to capture the image, holography records an image on a photoresist material. In processing, chemicals eat away at certain exposed areas, leaving a pattern of constructive and destructive interference. When the photoresist is developed, the result is a pattern of uneven ridges that acts as a mold. This mold is then coated with metal, and the resulting form is used to press copies in much the same way phonograph records are produced.

A typical reflective hologram used for stamps consists of a reproduction of the uneven patterns on a plastic film that is applied to a reflective background, usually a silver or gold foil. Light is reflected off the background through the film, making the pattern present on the film visible. Because of the uneven pattern of the film, the viewer will perceive the objects in their proper three-dimensional relationships with appropriate brightness.

The first hologram on a stamp was produced by Austria in 1988 (Scott 1441).

FOIL APPLICATION

A modern technique of applying color to stamps involves the application of metallic foil to the stamp paper. A pattern of foil is applied to the stamp paper by use of a stamping die. The foil usually is flat, but it may be textured. Canada Scott 1735 has three different foil applications in pearl, bronze and gold. The gold foil was textured using a chemical-etch copper embossing die. The printing of this stamp also involved two-color offset lithography plus embossing.

THERMOGRAPHY

In the 1990s stamps began to be enhanced with thermographic printing. In this process, a powdered polymer is applied over a sheet that has just been printed. The powder adheres to ink that lacks drying or hardening agents and does not adhere to areas where the ink has these agents. The excess powder is removed and the sheet is briefly heated to melt the powder. The melted powder solidifies after cooling, producing a raised, shiny effect on the stamps. See Scott New Caledonia C239-C240.

COMBINATION PRINTINGS

Sometimes two or even three printing methods are combined in producing stamps. In these cases, such as Austria Scott 933 or Canada 1735 (described in the preceding paragraph), the multiple-printing technique can be determined by studying the individual characteristics of each printing type. A few stamps, such as Singapore Scott 684-684A, combine as many as three of the four major printing types (lithography, engraving and typography). When this is done it often indicates the incorporation of security devices against counterfeiting.

INK COLORS

Inks or colored papers used in stamp printing often are of mineral origin, although there are numerous examples of organic-based pigments. As a general rule, organic-based pigments are far more subject to varieties and change than those of mineral-based origin.

The appearance of any given color on a stamp may be affected by many aspects, including printing variations, light, color of paper, aging and chemical alterations.

Numerous printing variations may be observed. Heavier pressure or inking will cause a more intense color, while slight interruptions in the ink feed or lighter impressions will cause a lighter appearance. Stamps printed in the same color by water-based and solvent-based inks can differ significantly in appearance. This affects several stamps in the U.S. Prominent Americans series. Hand-mixed ink formulas (primarily from the 19th century) produced under different conditions (humidity and temperature) account for notable color variations in early printings of the same stamp (see U.S. Scott 248-250, 279B, for example). Different sources of pigment can also result in significant differences in color.

Light exposure and aging are closely related in the way they affect stamp color. Both eventually break down the ink and fade colors, so that a carefully kept stamp may differ significantly in color from an identical copy that has been exposed to light. If stamps are exposed to light either intentionally or accidentally, their colors can be faded or completely changed in some cases.

Papers of different quality and consistency used for the same stamp printing may affect color appearance. Most pelure papers, for example, show a richer color when compared with wove or laid papers. See Russia Scott 181a, for an example of this effect.

The very nature of the printing processes can cause a variety of differences in shades or hues of the same stamp. Some of these shades are scarcer than others, and are of particular interest to the advanced collector.

Luminescence

All forms of tagged stamps fall under the general category of luminescence. Within this broad category is fluorescence, dealing with forms of tagging visible under longwave ultraviolet light, and phosphorescence, which deals with tagging visible only under shortwave light. Phosphorescence leaves an afterglow and fluorescence does not. These treated stamps show up in a range of different colors when exposed to UV light. The differing wavelengths of the light activates the tagging material, making it glow in various colors that usually serve different mail processing purposes.

Intentional tagging is a post-World War II phenomenon, brought about by the increased literacy rate and rapidly growing mail volume. It was one of several answers to the problem of the need for more automated mail processes. Early tagged stamps served the purpose of triggering machines to separate different types of mail. A natural outgrowth was to also use the signal to trigger machines that faced all envelopes the same way and canceled them.

Tagged stamps come in many different forms. Some tagged stamps have luminescent shapes or images imprinted on them as a form of security device. Others have blocks (United States), stripes, frames (South Africa and Canada), overall coatings (United States), bars (Great Britain and Canada) and many other types. Some types of tagging are even mixed in with the pigmented printing ink (Australia Scott 366, Netherlands Scott 478 and U.S. Scott 1359 and 2443).

The means of applying taggant to stamps differs as much as the intended purposes for the stamps. The most common form of tagging is a coating applied to the surface of the printed stamp. Since the taggant ink is frequently invisible except under UV light, it does not interfere with the appearance of the stamp. Another common application is the use of phosphored papers. In this case the paper itself either has a coating of taggant applied before the stamp is printed, has taggant applied during the papermaking process (incorporating it into the fibers), or has the taggant mixed into the coating of the paper. The latter method, among others, is currently in use in the United States.

Many countries now use tagging in various forms to either expedite mail handling or to serve as a printing security device against counterfeiting. Following the introduction of tagged stamps for public use in 1959 by Great Britain, other countries have steadily joined the parade. Among those are Germany (1961); Canada and Denmark (1962); United States, Australia, France and Switzerland (1963); Belgium and Japan (1966); Sweden and Norway (1967); Italy (1968); and Russia (1969). Since then, many other countries have begun using forms of tagging, including Brazil, China, Czechoslovakia, Hong Kong, Guatemala, Indonesia, Israel, Lithuania, Luxembourg, Netherlands, Penrhyn Islands, Portugal, St. Vincent, Singapore, South Africa, Spain and Sweden to name a few.

In some cases, including United States, Canada, Great Britain and Switzerland, stamps were released both with and without tagging. Many of these were released during each country's experimental period. Tagged and untagged versions are listed for the aforementioned countries and are noted in some other countries' listings. For at least a few stamps, the experimentally tagged version is worth far more than its untagged counterpart, such as the 1963 experimental tagged version of France Scott 1024.

In some cases, luminescent varieties of stamps were inadvertently created. Several Russian stamps, for example, sport highly fluorescent ink that was not intended as a form of tagging. Older stamps, such as early U.S. postage dues, can be positively identified by the use of UV light, since the organic ink used has become slightly fluorescent over time. Other stamps, such as Austria Scott 70a-82a (varnish bars) and Obock Scott 46-64 (printed quadrille lines), have become fluorescent over time.

Various fluorescent substances have been added to paper to make it appear brighter. These optical brightners, as they are known, greatly affect the appearance of the stamp under UV light. The brightest of these is known as Hi-Brite paper. These paper varieties are beyond the scope of the Scott Catalogue.

Shortwave UV light also is used extensively in expertizing, since each form of paper has its own fluorescent characteristics that are impossible to perfectly match. It is therefore a simple matter to detect filled thins, added perforation teeth and other alterations that involve the addition of paper. UV light also is used to examine stamps that have had cancels chemically removed and for other purposes as well.

Gum

The Illustrated Gum Chart in the first part of this introduction shows and defines various types of gum condition. Because gum condition has an important impact on the value of unused stamps, we recommend studying this chart and the accompanying text carefully.

The gum on the back of a stamp may be shiny, dull, smooth, rough, dark, white, colored or tinted. Most stamp gumming adhesives use gum arabic or dextrine as a base. Certain polymers such as polyvinyl alcohol (PVA) have been used extensively since World War II.

The *Scott Standard Postage Stamp Catalogue* does not list items by types of gum. The *Scott Specialized Catalogue of United States Stamps and Covers* does differentiate among some types of gum for certain issues.

Reprints of stamps may have gum differing from the original issues. In addition, some countries have used different gum formulas for different seasons. These adhesives have different properties that may become more apparent over time.

Many stamps have been issued without gum, and the catalogue will note this fact. See, for example, United States Scott 40-47. Sometimes, gum may have been removed to preserve the stamp. Germany Scott B68, for example, has a highly acidic gum that eventually destroys the stamps. This item is valued in the catalogue with gum removed.

Reprints and Reissues

These are impressions of stamps (usually obsolete) made from the original plates or stones. If they are valid for postage and reproduce obsolete issues (such as U.S. Scott 102-111), the stamps are *reissues.* If they are from current issues, they are designated as *second, third,* etc., *printing.* If designated for a particular purpose, they are called *special printings.*

When special printings are not valid for postage, but are made from original dies and plates by authorized persons, they are *official reprints. Private reprints* are made from the original plates and dies by private hands. An example of a private reprint is that of the 1871-1932 reprints made from the original die of the 1845 New Haven, Conn., postmaster's provisional. *Official reproductions* or imitations are made from new dies and plates by government authorization. Scott will list those reissues that are valid for postage if they differ significantly from the original printing.

The U.S. government made special printings of its first postage stamps in 1875. Produced were official imitations of the first two stamps (listed as Scott 3-4), reprints of the demonetized pre-1861 issues (Scott 40-47) and reissues of the 1861 stamps, the 1869 stamps and the then-current 1875 denominations. Even though the official imitations and the reprints were not valid for postage, Scott lists all of these U.S. special printings.

Most reprints or reissues differ slightly from the original stamp in some characteristic, such as gum, paper, perforation, color or watermark. Sometimes the details are followed so meticulously that only a student of that specific stamp is able to distinguish the reprint or reissue from the original.

Remainders and Canceled to Order

Some countries sell their stock of old stamps when a new issue replaces them. To avoid postal use, the *remainders* usually are canceled with a punch hole, a heavy line or bar, or a more-or-less regular-looking cancellation. The most famous merchant of remainders was Nicholas F. Seebeck. In the 1880s and 1890s, he arranged printing contracts between the Hamilton Bank Note Co., of which he was a director, and several Central and South American countries. The contracts provided that the plates and all remainders of the yearly issues became the property of Hamilton. Seebeck saw to it that ample stock remained. The "Seebecks," both remainders and reprints, were standard packet fillers for decades.

Some countries also issue stamps *canceled-to-order (CTO),* either in sheets with original gum or stuck onto pieces of paper or envelopes and canceled. Such CTO items generally are worth less than postally used stamps. In cases where the CTO material is far more prevalent in the marketplace than postally used examples, the catalogue value relates to the CTO examples, with postally used examples noted as premium items. Most CTOs can be detected by the presence of gum. However, as the CTO practice goes back at least to 1885, the gum inevitably has been soaked off some stamps so they could pass as postally used. The normally applied postmarks usually differ slightly from standard postmarks, and specialists are able to tell the difference. When applied individually to envelopes by philatelically minded persons, CTO material is known as *favor canceled* and generally sells at large discounts.

Cinderellas and Facsimiles

Cinderella is a catch-all term used by stamp collectors to describe phantoms, fantasies, bogus items, municipal issues, exhibition seals, local revenues, transportation stamps, labels, poster stamps and many other types of items. Some cinderella collectors include in their collections local postage issues, telegraph stamps, essays and proofs, forgeries and counterfeits.

A *fantasy* is an adhesive created for a nonexistent stamp-issuing authority. Fantasy items range from imaginary countries (Occusi-Ambeno, Kingdom of Sedang, Principality of Trinidad or Torres Straits), to non-existent locals (Winans City Post), or nonexistent transportation lines (McRobish & Co.'s Acapulco-San Francisco Line).

On the other hand, if the entity exists and could have issued stamps (but did not) or was known to have issued other stamps, the items are considered *bogus* stamps. These would include the Mormon postage stamps of Utah, S. Allan Taylor's Guatemala and Paraguay inventions, the propaganda issues for the South Moluccas and the adhesives of the Page & Keyes local post of Boston.

Phantoms is another term for both fantasy and bogus issues.

Facsimiles are copies or imitations made to represent original stamps, but which do not pretend to be originals. A catalogue illustration is such a facsimile. Illustrations from the Moens catalogue of the last century were occasionally colored and passed off as stamps. Since the beginning of stamp collecting, facsimiles have been made for collectors as space fillers or for reference. They often carry the word "facsimile," "falsch" (German), "sanko" or "mozo" (Japanese), or "faux" (French) overprinted on the face or stamped on the back. Unfortunately, over the years a number of these items have had fake cancels applied over the facsimile notation and have been passed off as genuine.

Forgeries and Counterfeits

Forgeries and counterfeits have been with philately virtually from the beginning of stamp production. Over time, the terminology for the two has been used interchangeably. Although both forgeries and counterfeits are reproductions of stamps, the purposes behind their creation differ considerably.

Among specialists there is an increasing movement to more specifically define such items. Although there is no universally accepted terminology, we feel the following definitions most closely mirror the items and their purposes as they are currently defined.

Forgeries (also often referred to as *Counterfeits*) are reproductions of genuine stamps that have been created to defraud collectors. Such spurious items first appeared on the market around 1860, and most old-time collections contain one or more. Many are crude and easily spotted, but some can deceive experts.

An important supplier of these early philatelic forgeries was the Hamburg printer Gebruder Spiro. Many others with reputations in this craft included S. Allan Taylor, George Hussey, James Chute, George Forune, Benjamin & Sarpy, Julius Goldner, E. Oneglia and L.H. Mercier. Among the noted 20th-century forgers were Francois Fournier, Jean Sperati and the prolific Raoul DeThuin.

Forgeries may be complete replications, or they may be genuine stamps altered to resemble a scarcer (and more valuable) type. Most forgeries, particularly those of rare stamps, are worth only a small fraction of the value of a genuine example, but a few types, created by some of the most notable forgers, such as Sperati, can be worth as much or more than the genuine. Fraudulently produced copies are known of most classic rarities and many medium-priced stamps.

In addition to rare stamps, large numbers of common 19th- and early 20th-century stamps were forged to supply stamps to the early packet trade. Many can still be easily found. Few new philatelic forgeries have appeared in recent decades. Successful imitation of well-engraved work is virtually impossible. It has proven far easier to produce a fake by altering a genuine stamp than to duplicate a stamp completely.

Counterfeit (also often referred to as *Postal Counterfeit* or *Postal Forgery*) is the term generally applied to reproductions of stamps that have been created to defraud the government of revenue. Such items usually are created at the time a stamp is current and, in some cases, are hard to detect. Because most counterfeits are seized when the perpetrator is captured, postal counterfeits, particularly used on cover, are usually worth much more than a genuine example to specialists. The first postal counterfeit was of Spain's 4-cuarto carmine of 1854 (the real one is Scott 25). Apparently, the counterfeiters were not satisfied with their first version, which is now very scarce, and they soon created an engraved counterfeit, which is common. Postal counterfeits quickly followed in Austria, Naples, Sardinia and the Roman States. They have since been created in many other countries as well, including the United States.

An infamous counterfeit to defraud the government is the 1-shilling Great Britain "Stock Exchange" forgery of 1872, used on telegraph forms at the exchange that year. The stamp escaped detection until a stamp dealer noticed it in 1898.

Fakes

Fakes are genuine stamps altered in some way to make them more desirable. One student of this part of stamp collecting has estimated that by the 1950s more than 30,000 varieties of fakes were known. That number has grown greatly since then. The widespread existence of fakes makes it important for stamp collectors to study their philatelic holdings and use relevant literature. Likewise, collectors should buy from reputable dealers who guarantee their stamps and make full and prompt refunds should a purchased item be declared faked or altered by some mutually agreed-upon authority. Because fakes always have some genuine characteristics, it is not always possible to obtain unanimous agreement among experts regarding specific items. These students may change their opinions as philatelic knowledge increases. More than 80 percent of all fakes on the philatelic market today are regummed, reperforated (or perforated for the first time), or bear forged overprints, surcharges or cancellations.

Stamps can be chemically treated to alter or eliminate colors. For example, a pale rose stamp can be re-colored to resemble a blue shade of high market value. In other cases, treated stamps can be made to resemble missing color varieties. Designs may be changed by painting, or a stroke or a dot added or bleached out to turn an ordinary variety into a seemingly scarcer stamp. Part of a stamp can be bleached and reprinted in a different version, achieving an inverted center or frame. Margins can be added or repairs done so deceptively that the stamps move from the "repaired" into the "fake" category.

Fakers have not left the backs of the stamps untouched either. They may create false watermarks, add fake grills or press out genuine grills. A thin India paper proof may be glued onto a thicker backing to create the appearance an issued stamp, or a proof printed on cardboard may be shaved down and perforated to resemble a stamp. Silk threads are impressed into paper and stamps have been split so that a rare paper variety is added to an otherwise inexpensive stamp. The most common treatment to the back of a stamp, however, is regumming.

Some in the business of faking stamps have openly advertised fool-proof application of "original gum" to stamps that lack it, although most publications now ban such ads from their pages. It is believed that very few early stamps have survived without being hinged. The large number of never-hinged examples of such earlier material offered for sale thus suggests the widespread extent of regumming activity. Regumming also may be used to hide repairs or thin spots. Dipping the stamp into watermark fluid, or examining it under longwave ultraviolet light often will reveal these flaws.

Fakers also tamper with separations. Ingenious ways to add margins are known. Perforated wide-margin stamps may be falsely represented as imperforate when trimmed. Reperforating is commonly done to create scarce coil or perforation varieties, and to eliminate the naturally occurring straight-edge stamps found in sheet margin positions of many earlier issues. Custom has made straight-edged stamps less desirable. Fakers have obliged by perforating straight-edged stamps so that many are now uncommon, if not rare.

Another fertile field for the faker is that of overprints, surcharges and cancellations. The forging of rare surcharges or overprints began in the 1880s or 1890s. These forgeries are sometimes difficult to detect, but experts have identified almost all. Occasionally, overprints or cancellations are removed to create non-overprinted stamps or seemingly unused items. This is most commonly done by removing a manuscript cancel to make a stamp resemble an unused example. "SPECIMEN" overprints may be removed by scraping and repainting to create non-overprinted varieties. Fakers use inexpensive revenues or pen-canceled stamps to generate unused stamps for further faking by adding other markings. The quartz lamp or UV lamp and a high-powered magnifying glass help to easily detect removed cancellations.

The bigger problem, however, is the addition of overprints, surcharges or cancellations - many with such precision that they are very difficult to ascertain. Plating of the stamps or the overprint can be an important method of detection.

Fake postmarks may range from many spurious fancy cancellations to a host of markings applied to transatlantic covers, to adding normally appearing postmarks to definitives of some countries with stamps that are valued far higher used than unused. With the increased popularity of cover collecting, and the widespread interest in postal history, a fertile new field for fakers has come about. Some have tried to create entire covers. Others specialize in adding stamps, tied by fake cancellations, to genuine stampless covers, or replacing less expensive or damaged stamps with more valuable ones. Detailed study of postal rates in effect at the time a cover in question was mailed, including the analysis of each handstamp used during the period, ink analysis and similar techniques, usually will unmask the fraud.

Restoration and Repairs

Scott bases its catalogue values on stamps that are free of defects and otherwise meet the standards set forth earlier in this introduction. Most stamp collectors desire to have the finest copy of an item possible. Even within given grading categories there are variances. This leads to a controversial practice that is not defined in any universal manner: stamp *restoration*.

There are broad differences of opinion about what is permissible when it comes to restoration. Carefully applying a soft eraser to a stamp or cover to remove light soiling is one form of restoration, as is washing a stamp in mild soap and water to clean it. These are fairly accepted forms of restoration. More severe forms of restoration include pressing out creases or removing stains caused by tape. To what degree each of these is acceptable is dependent upon the individual situation. Further along the spectrum is the freshening of a stamp's color by removing oxide build-up or the effects of wax paper left next to stamps shipped to the tropics.

At some point in this spectrum the concept of *repair* replaces that of restoration. Repairs include filling thin spots, mending tears by reweaving or adding a missing perforation tooth. Regumming stamps may have been acceptable as a restoration or repair technique many decades ago, but today it is considered a form of fakery.

Restored stamps may or may not sell at a discount, and it is possible that the value of individual restored items may be enhanced over that of their pre-restoration state. Specific situations dictate the resultant value of such an item. Repaired stamps sell at substantial discounts from the value of sound stamps.

Terminology

Booklets — Many countries have issued stamps in small booklets for the convenience of users. This idea continues to become increasingly popular in many countries. Booklets have been issued in many sizes and forms, often with advertising on the covers, the panes of stamps or on the interleaving.

The panes used in booklets may be printed from special plates or made from regular sheets. All panes from booklets issued by the United States and many from those of other countries contain stamps that are straight edged on the sides, but perforated between. Others are distinguished by orientation of watermark or other identifying features. Any stamp-like unit in the pane, either printed or blank, that is not a postage stamp, is considered to be a *label* in the catalogue listings.

Scott lists and values booklet panes. Modern complete booklets also are listed and valued. Individual booklet panes are listed only when they are not fashioned from existing sheet stamps and, therefore, are identifiable from their sheet stamp counterparts.

Panes usually do not have a used value assigned to them because there is little market activity for used booklet panes, even though many exist used and there is some demand for them.

Cancellations — The marks or obliterations put on stamps by postal authorities to show that they have performed service and to prevent their reuse are known as cancellations. If the marking is made with a pen, it is considered a "pen cancel." When the location of the post office appears in the marking, it is a "town cancellation." A "postmark" is technically any postal marking, but in practice the term generally is applied to a town cancellation with a date. When calling attention to a cause or celebration, the marking is known as a "slogan cancellation." Many other types and styles of cancellations exist, such as duplex, numerals, targets, fancy and others. See also "precancels," below.

Coil Stamps — These are stamps that are issued in rolls for use in dispensers, affixing and vending machines. Those coils of the United States, Canada, Sweden and some other countries are perforated horizontally or vertically only, with the outer edges imperforate. Coil stamps of some countries, such as Great Britain and Germany, are perforated on all four sides and may in some cases be distinguished from their sheet stamp counterparts by watermarks, counting numbers on the reverse or other means.

Covers — Entire envelopes, with or without adhesive postage stamps, that have passed through the mail and bear postal or other markings of philatelic interest are known as covers. Before the introduction of envelopes in about 1840, people folded letters and wrote the address on the outside. Some people covered their letters with an extra sheet of paper on the outside for the address, producing the term "cover." Used airletter sheets, stamped envelopes and other items of postal stationery also are considered covers.

Errors — Stamps that have some major, consistent, unintentional deviation from the normal are considered errors. Errors include, but are not limited to, missing or wrong colors, wrong paper, wrong watermarks, inverted centers or frames on multicolor printing, inverted or missing surcharges or overprints, double impressions, missing perforations, unintentionally omitted tagging and others. Factually wrong or misspelled information, if it appears on all examples of a stamp, are not considered errors in the true sense of the word. They are errors of design. Inconsistent or randomly appearing items, such as misperfs or color shifts, are classified as freaks.

Color-Omitted Errors — This term refers to stamps where a missing color is caused by the complete failure of the printing plate to deliver ink to the stamp paper or any other paper. Generally, this is caused by the printing plate not being engaged on the press or the ink station running dry of ink during printing.

Color-Missing Errors — This term refers to stamps where a color or colors were printed somewhere but do not appear on the finished stamp. There are four different classes of color-missing errors, and the catalog indicates with a two-letter code appended to each such listing what caused the color to be missing. These codes are used only for the United States' color-missing error listings.

FO = A *foldover* of the stamp sheet during printing may block ink from appearing on a stamp. Instead, the color will appear on the back of the foldover (where it might fall on the back of the selvage or perhaps on the back of the stamp or another stamp). FO also will be used in the case of foldunders, where the paper may fold underneath the other stamp paper and the color will print on the platen.

EP = A piece of *extraneous paper* falling across the plate or stamp paper will receive the printed ink. When the extraneous paper is removed, an unprinted portion of stamp paper remains and shows partially or totally missing colors.

CM = A misregistration of the printing plates during printing will result in a *color misregistration*, and such a misregistraion may result in a color not appearing on the finished stamp.

PS = A *perforation shift* after printing may remove a color from the finished stamp. Normally, this will occur on a row of stamps at the edge of the stamp pane.

Measurements - When measurements are given in the Scott catalogues for stamp size, grill size or any other reason, the first measurement given is always for the top and bottom dimension, while the second measurement will be for the sides (just as perforation gauges are measured). Thus, a stamp size of 15mm x 21mm will indicate a vertically oriented stamp 15mm wide at top and bottom, and 21mm tall at the sides. The same principle holds for measuring or counting items such as U.S. grills. A grill count of 22x18 points (B grill) indicates that there are 22 grill points across by 18 grill points down.

Overprints and Surcharges — Overprinting involves applying wording or design elements over an already existing stamp. Overprints can be used to alter the place of use (such as "Canal Zone" on U.S. stamps), to adapt them for a special purpose ("Porto" on Denmark's 1913-20 regular issues for use as postage due stamps, Scott J1-J7) or to commemorate a special occasion (United States Scott 647-648).

A *surcharge* is a form of overprint that changes or restates the face value of a stamp or piece of postal stationery.

Surcharges and overprints may be handstamped, typeset or, occasionally, lithographed or engraved. A few hand-written overprints and surcharges are known.

Personalized Stamps — In 1999, Australia issued stamps with se-tenant labels that could be personalized with pictures of the customer's choice. Other countries quickly followed suit, with some offering to print the selected picture on the stamp itself within a frame that was used exclusively for personalized issues. As the picture used on these stamps or labels vary, listings for such stamps are for any picture within the common frame (or any picture on a se-tenant label), be it a "generic" image or one produced especially for a customer, almost invariably at a premium price.

Precancels — Stamps that are canceled before they are placed in the mail are known as precancels. Precanceling usually is done to expedite the handling of large mailings and generally allow the affected mail pieces to skip certain phases of mail handling.

In the United States, precancellations generally identified the point of origin; that is, the city and state. This information appeared across the face of the stamp, usually centered between parallel lines. More recently, bureau precancels retained the parallel lines, but the city and state designations were dropped. Recent coils have a service inscription that is present on the original printing plate. These show the mail service paid for by the stamp. Since these stamps are not intended to receive further cancellations when used as intended, they are considered precancels. Such items often do not have parallel lines as part of the precancellation.

In France, the abbreviation *Affranchts* in a semicircle together with the word *Postes* is the general form of precancel in use. Belgian precancellations usually appear in a box in which the name of the city appears. Netherlands precancels have the name of the city enclosed between concentric circles, sometimes called a "lifesaver." Precancellations of other countries usually follow these patterns, but may be any arrangement of bars, boxes and city names.

Precancels are listed in the Scott catalogues only if the precancel changes the denomination (Belgium Scott 477-478); if the precanceled stamp is different from the non-precanceled version (such as untagged U.S. precancels); or if the stamp exists only precanceled (France Scott 1096-1099, U.S. Scott 2265).

Proofs and Essays — Proofs are impressions taken from an approved die, plate or stone in which the design and color are the same as the stamp issued to the public. Trial color proofs are impressions taken from approved dies, plates or stones in colors that vary from the final version. An essay is the impression of a design that differs in some way from the issued stamp. "Progressive die proofs" generally are considered to be essays.

Provisionals — These are stamps that are issued on short notice and intended for temporary use pending the arrival of regular issues. They usually are issued to meet such contingencies as changes in government or currency, shortage of necessary postage values or military occupation.

During the 1840s, postmasters in certain American cities issued stamps that were valid only at specific post offices. In 1861, postmasters of the Confederate States also issued stamps with limited validity. Both of these examples are known as "postmaster's provisionals."

Se-tenant — This term refers to an unsevered pair, strip or block of stamps that differ in design, denomination or overprint.

Unless the se-tenant item has a continuous design (see U.S. Scott 1451a, 1694a) the stamps do not have to be in the same order as shown in the catalogue (see U.S. Scott 2158a).

Specimens — The Universal Postal Union required member nations to send samples of all stamps they released into service to the International Bureau in Switzerland. Member nations of the UPU received these specimens as samples of what stamps were valid for postage. Many are overprinted, handstamped or initial-perforated "Specimen," "Canceled" or "Muestra." Some are marked with bars across the denominations (China-Taiwan), punched holes (Czechoslovakia) or back inscriptions (Mongolia).

Stamps distributed to government officials or for publicity purposes, and stamps submitted by private security printers for official approval, also may receive such defacements.

The previously described defacement markings prevent postal use, and all such items generally are known as "specimens."

Tete Beche — This term describes a pair of stamps in which one is upside down in relation to the other. Some of these are the result of intentional sheet arrangements, such as Morocco Scott B10-B11. Others occurred when one or more electrotypes accidentally were placed upside down on the plate, such as Colombia Scott 57a. Separation of the tete-beche stamps, of course, destroys the tete beche variety.

Currency Conversion

Country	Dollar	Pound	S Franc	Yen	HK $	Euro	Cdn $	Aus $
Australia	1.4303	1.8803	1.4727	0.0132	0.1836	1.5983	1.1004	—
Canada	1.2998	1.7087	1.3383	0.0120	0.1668	1.4525	—	0.9088
European Union	0.8949	1.1764	0.9214	0.0082	0.1149	—	0.6885	0.6257
Hong Kong	7.7904	10.241	8.0214	0.0717	—	8.7053	5.9935	5.4467
Japan	108.65	142.83	111.87	—	13.947	121.41	83.590	75.963
Switzerland	0.9712	1.2767	—	0.0089	0.1247	1.0853	0.7472	0.6790
United Kingdom	0.7607	—	0.7832	0.0070	0.0976	0.8500	0.5852	0.5318
United States	—	1.3146	1.0297	0.0092	0.1284	1.1174	0.7693	0.6992

Country	Currency	U.S. $ Equiv.
Cyprus	euro	1.1174
Czech Republic	koruna	.0441
Denmark	krone	.1495
Djibouti	franc	.0056
Dominica	East Caribbean dollar	.3704
Dominican Republic	peso	.0189
Ecuador	US dollar	1.0000
Egypt	pound	.0623
Equatorial Guinea	CFA franc	.0017
Eritrea	nakfa	.0667
Estonia	euro	1.1174
Ethiopia	birr	.0312
Falkland Islands	pound	1.3146
Faroe Islands	krone	.1495
Fiji	dollar	.4664
Finland	euro	1.1174
Aland Islands	euro	1.1174
France	euro	1.1174
French Polynesia	Community of French Pacific (CFP) franc	.0094
French So. & Antarctic Terr.	euro	1.1174

Source: **xe.com** *Jan. 2, 2020. Figures reflect values as of Jan. 2, 2020.*

COMMON DESIGN TYPES

Pictured in this section are issues where one illustration has been used for a number of countries in the Catalogue. Not included in this section are overprinted stamps or those issues which are illustrated in each country. Because the location of Never Hinged breakpoints varies from country to country, some of the values in the listings below will be for unused stamps that were previously hinged.

EUROPA

Europa, 1956

The design symbolizing the cooperation among the six countries comprising the Coal and Steel Community is illustrated in each country.

Belgium	*496-497*
France	*805-806*
Germany	*748-749*
Italy	*715-716*
Luxembourg	*318-320*
Netherlands	*368-369*

Nos. 496-497 (2)	9.00	.50
Nos. 805-806 (2)	5.25	1.00
Nos. 748-749 (2)	7.40	1.10
Nos. 715-716 (2)	9.25	1.25
Nos. 318-320 (3)	65.50	42.00
Nos. 368-369 (2)	25.75	1.50
Set total (13) Stamps	122.15	47.35

Europa, 1958

"E" and Dove — CD1

European Postal Union at the service of European integration.

1958, Sept. 13

Belgium	527-528
France	889-890
Germany	790-791
Italy	750-751
Luxembourg	341-343
Netherlands	375-376
Saar	317-318

Nos. 527-528 (2)	3.75	.60
Nos. 889-890 (2)	1.65	.55
Nos. 790-791 (2)	2.95	.60
Nos. 750-751 (2)	1.05	.60
Nos. 341-343 (3)	1.35	.90
Nos. 375-376 (2)	1.25	.75
Nos. 317-318 (2)	1.05	2.30
Set total (15) Stamps	13.05	6.30

Europa, 1959

6-Link Enless Chain — CD2

1959, Sept. 19

Belgium	536-537
France	929-930
Germany	805-806
Italy	791-792
Luxembourg	354-355
Netherlands	379-380

Nos. 536-537 (2)	1.55	.60
Nos. 929-930 (2)	1.40	.80
Nos. 805-806 (2)	1.35	.60
Nos. 791-792 (2)	.80	.50
Nos. 354-355 (2)	2.65	1.00
Nos. 379-380 (2)	2.10	1.85
Set total (12) Stamps	9.85	5.35

Europa, 1960

19-Spoke Wheel CD3

First anniversary of the establishment of C.E.P.T. (Conference Europeenne des Administrations des Postes et des Telecommunications.) The spokes symbolize the 19 founding members of the Conference.

1960, Sept.

Belgium	553-554
Denmark	379
Finland	376-377
France	970-971
Germany	818-820
Great Britain	377-378
Greece	688
Iceland	327-328
Ireland	175-176
Italy	809-810
Luxembourg	374-375
Netherlands	385-386
Norway	387
Portugal	866-867
Spain	941-942
Sweden	562-563
Switzerland	400-401
Turkey	1493-1494

Nos. 553-554 (2)	1.25	.55
No. 379 (1)	.55	.50
Nos. 376-377 (2)	1.70	1.80
Nos. 970-971 (2)	.50	.50
Nos. 818-820 (3)	1.90	1.35
Nos. 377-378 (2)	8.00	5.00
No. 688 (1)	4.25	1.75
Nos. 327-328 (2)	1.30	1.85
Nos. 175-176 (2)	47.50	27.50
Nos. 809-810 (2)	.50	.50
Nos. 374-375 (2)	1.00	.80
Nos. 385-386 (2)	2.00	2.00
No. 387 (1)	1.00	.80
Nos. 866-867 (2)	3.00	1.75
Nos. 941-942 (2)	1.50	.75
Nos. 562-563 (2)	1.05	.55
Nos. 400-401 (2)	1.75	.75
Nos. 1493-1494 (2)	2.10	1.35
Set total (34) Stamps	80.85	50.05

Europa, 1961

19 Doves Flying as One — CD4

The 19 doves represent the 19 members of the Conference of European Postal and Telecommunications Administrations C.E.P.T.

1961-62

Belgium	572-573
Cyprus	201-203
France	1005-1006
Germany	844-845
Great Britain	382-384
Greece	718-719
Iceland	340-341
Italy	845-846
Luxembourg	382-383
Netherlands	387-388
Spain	1010-1011
Switzerland	410-411
Turkey	1518-1520

Nos. 572-573 (2)	.75	.50
Nos. 201-203 (3)	*2.10*	*1.20*
Nos. 1005-1006 (2)	.50	.50
Nos. 844-845 (2)	.60	.75
Nos. 382-384 (3)	.75	.75
Nos. 718-719 (2)	.80	.50
Nos. 340-341 (2)	1.10	1.60
Nos. 845-846 (2)	.50	.50
Nos. 382-383 (2)	.55	.55
Nos. 387-388 (2)	.50	.50
Nos. 1010-1011 (2)	.70	.55
Nos. 410-411 (2)	1.90	.60
Nos. 1518-1520 (3)	1.55	.90
Set total (29) Stamps	12.30	9.40

Europa, 1962

Young Tree with 19 Leaves CD5

The 19 leaves represent the 19 original members of C.E.P.T.

1962-63

Belgium	582-583
Cyprus	219-221
France	1045-1046
Germany	852-853
Greece	739-740
Iceland	348-349
Ireland	184-185
Italy	860-861
Luxembourg	386-387
Netherlands	394-395
Norway	414-415
Switzerland	416-417
Turkey	1553-1555

Nos. 582-583 (2)	.65	.65
Nos. 219-221 (3)	*76.25*	*6.75*
Nos. 1045-1046 (2)	.60	.50
Nos. 852-853 (2)	.65	.75
Nos. 739-740 (2)	2.00	1.15
Nos. 348-349 (2)	.85	.85
Nos. 184-185 (2)	2.00	.50
Nos. 860-861 (2)	1.00	.55
Nos. 386-387 (2)	.75	.55
Nos. 394-395 (2)	1.35	.90
Nos. 414-415 (2)	1.75	1.70
Nos. 416-417 (2)	1.65	1.00
Nos. 1553-1555 (3)	*2.05*	1.10
Set total (28) Stamps	91.55	16.95

Europa, 1963

Stylized Links, Symbolizing Unity — CD6

1963, Sept.

Belgium	598-599
Cyprus	229-231
Finland	419
France	1074-1075
Germany	867-868
Greece	768-769
Iceland	357-358
Ireland	188-189
Italy	880-881
Luxembourg	403-404
Netherlands	416-417
Norway	441-442
Switzerland	429
Turkey	1602-1603

Nos. 598-599 (2)	1.60	.55
Nos. 229-231 (3)	*64.00*	*9.40*
No. 419 (1)	1.25	.55
Nos. 1074-1075 (2)	.60	.50
Nos. 867-868 (2)	.50	.55
Nos. 768-769 (2)	4.65	1.65
Nos. 357-358 (2)	1.20	1.20
Nos. 188-189 (2)	4.75	3.25
Nos. 880-881 (2)	.50	.50
Nos. 403-404 (2)	.75	.55
Nos. 416-417 (2)	1.30	1.00
Nos. 441-442 (2)	2.60	2.40
No. 429 (1)	.90	.60
Nos. 1602-1603 (2)	1.20	.50
Set total (27) Stamps	85.80	23.20

Europa, 1964

Symbolic Daisy — CD7

5th anniversary of the establishment of C.E.P.T. The 22 petals of the flower symbolize the 22 members of the Conference.

1964, Sept.

Austria	738
Belgium	614-615
Cyprus	244-246
France	1109-1110
Germany	897-898
Greece	801-802
Iceland	367-368
Ireland	196-197
Italy	894-895
Luxembourg	411-412
Monaco	590-591
Netherlands	428-429
Norway	458
Portugal	931-933
Spain	1262-1263
Switzerland	438-439
Turkey	1628-1629

No. 738 (1)	1.20	.80
Nos. 614-615 (2)	1.40	.60
Nos. 244-246 (3)	*32.25*	*5.10*
Nos. 1109-1110 (2)	.50	.50
Nos. 897-898 (2)	.50	.50
Nos. 801-802 (2)	4.15	1.55
Nos. 367-368 (2)	1.40	1.15
Nos. 196-197 (2)	17.00	4.25
Nos. 894-895 (2)	.50	.50
Nos. 411-412 (2)	.75	.55
Nos. 590-591 (2)	2.50	.70
Nos. 428-429 (2)	.75	.60
No. 458 (1)	3.50	3.50
Nos. 931-933 (3)	*10.00*	*2.00*
Nos. 1262-1263 (2)	1.30	.80
Nos. 438-439 (2)	1.65	.50
Nos. 1628-1629 (2)	2.00	.80
Set total (34) Stamps	81.35	24.40

Europa, 1965

Leaves and "Fruit" CD8

1965

Belgium	636-637
Cyprus	262-264
Finland	437
France	1131-1132
Germany	934-935
Greece	833-834
Iceland	375-376
Ireland	204-205
Italy	915-916
Luxembourg	432-433
Monaco	616-617
Netherlands	438-439
Norway	475-476
Portugal	958-960
Switzerland	469
Turkey	1665-1666

Nos. 636-637 (2)	.50	.50
Nos. 262-264 (3)	*25.35*	*6.00*
No. 437 (1)	1.25	.55
Nos. 1131-1132 (2)	.70	.55
Nos. 934-935 (2)	.50	.50
Nos. 833-834 (2)	2.25	1.15
Nos. 375-376 (2)	2.50	1.75
Nos. 204-205 (2)	16.00	3.35
Nos. 915-916 (2)	.50	.50
Nos. 432-433 (2)	.75	.55
Nos. 616-617 (2)	3.25	1.65
Nos. 438-439 (2)	.55	.50
Nos. 475-476 (2)	2.40	1.90
Nos. 958-960 (3)	*10.00*	*2.75*
No. 469 (1)	1.15	.50
Nos. 1665-1666 (2)	2.00	1.25
Set total (32) Stamps	69.65	23.95

Europa, 1966

Symbolic Sailboat — CD9

1966, Sept.

Andorra, French	172
Belgium	675-676
Cyprus	275-277
France	1163-1164
Germany	963-964

Greece 862-863
Iceland 384-385
Ireland 216-217
Italy 942-943
Liechtenstein 415
Luxembourg 440-441
Monaco 639-640
Netherlands 441-442
Norway 496-497
Portugal 980-982
Switzerland 477-478
Turkey 1718-1719

No. 172 (1)	3.00	3.00
Nos. 675-676 (2)	.80	.50
Nos. 275-277 (3)	*4.75*	*2.75*
Nos. 1163-1164 (2)	.55	.50
Nos. 963-964 (2)	.50	.55
Nos. 862-863 (2)	2.10	1.05
Nos. 384-385 (2)	4.50	3.50
Nos. 216-217 (2)	6.75	2.00
Nos. 942-943 (2)	.50	.50
No. 415 (1)	.40	.35
Nos. 440-441 (2)	.70	.55
Nos. 639-640 (2)	2.00	.65
Nos. 441-442 (2)	.85	.50
Nos. 496-497 (2)	2.35	2.15
Nos. 980-982 (3)	*9.75*	2.25
Nos. 477-478 (2)	1.40	.60
Nos. 1718-1719 (2)	3.35	1.75
Set total (34) Stamps	44.25	23.15

Europa, 1967

Cogwheels
CD10

1967

Andorra, French 174-175
Belgium 688-689
Cyprus 297-299
France 1178-1179
Germany 969-970
Greece 891-892
Iceland 389-390
Ireland 232-233
Italy 951-952
Liechtenstein 420
Luxembourg 449-450
Monaco 669-670
Netherlands 444-447
Norway 504-505
Portugal 994-996
Spain 1465-1466
Switzerland 482
Turkey B120-B121

Nos. 174-175 (2)	10.75	6.25
Nos. 688-689 (2)	1.05	.55
Nos. 297-299 (3)	*4.25*	*2.50*
Nos. 1178-1179 (2)	.55	.50
Nos. 969-970 (2)	.55	.55
Nos. 891-892 (2)	3.05	.85
Nos. 389-390 (2)	3.00	2.00
Nos. 232-233 (2)	5.90	2.30
Nos. 951-952 (2)	.60	.50
No. 420 (1)	.45	.40
Nos. 449-450 (2)	1.00	.70
Nos. 669-670 (2)	2.75	.70
Nos. 444-447 (4)	2.70	2.05
Nos. 504-505 (2)	2.00	1.80
Nos. 994-996 (3)	*9.50*	1.85
Nos. 1465-1466 (2)	.50	.50
No. 482 (1)	.60	.30
Nos. B120-B121 (2)	2.50	2.00
Set total (38) Stamps	51.70	26.30

Europa, 1968

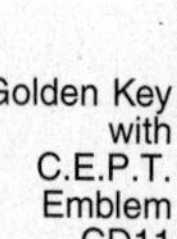

Golden Key with C.E.P.T. Emblem
CD11

1968

Andorra, French 182-183
Belgium 705-706
Cyprus 314-316
France 1209-1210
Germany 983-984
Greece 916-917
Iceland 395-396
Ireland 242-243
Italy 979-980
Liechtenstein 442
Luxembourg 466-467
Monaco 689-691
Netherlands 452-453
Portugal 1019-1021
San Marino 687
Spain 1526
Switzerland 488
Turkey 1775-1776

Nos. 182-183 (2)	16.50	10.00
Nos. 705-706 (2)	1.25	.50
Nos. 314-316 (3)	*2.90*	*2.50*
Nos. 1209-1210 (2)	.85	.55
Nos. 983-984 (2)	.50	.55
Nos. 916-917 (2)	3.10	1.45
Nos. 395-396 (2)	3.00	2.20
Nos. 242-243 (2)	3.30	2.25
Nos. 979-980 (2)	.50	.50
No. 442 (1)	.45	.40
Nos. 466-467 (2)	.80	.70
Nos. 689-691 (3)	*5.40*	.95
Nos. 452-453 (2)	1.05	.70
Nos. 1019-1021 (3)	*9.75*	2.10
No. 687 (1)	.55	.35
No. 1526 (1)	.25	.25
No. 488 (1)	.40	.25
Nos. 1775-1776 (2)	2.50	1.25
Set total (35) Stamps	53.05	27.45

Europa, 1969

"EUROPA" and "CEPT"
CD12

Tenth anniversary of C.E.P.T.

1969

Andorra, French 188-189
Austria 837
Belgium 718-719
Cyprus 326-328
Denmark 458
Finland 483
France 1245-1246
Germany 996-997
Great Britain 585
Greece 947-948
Iceland 406-407
Ireland 270-271
Italy 1000-1001
Liechtenstein 453
Luxembourg 475-476
Monaco 722-724
Netherlands 475-476
Norway 533-534
Portugal 1038-1040
San Marino 701-702
Spain 1567
Sweden 814-816
Switzerland 500-501
Turkey 1799-1800
Vatican 470-472
Yugoslavia 1003-1004

Nos. 188-189 (2)	18.50	12.00
No. 837 (1)	.65	.30
Nos. 718-719 (2)	.75	.50
Nos. 326-328 (3)	*3.00*	*2.25*
No. 458 (1)	.75	.75
No. 483 (1)	3.50	.75
Nos. 1245-1246 (2)	.55	.50
Nos. 996-997 (2)	.70	.50
No. 585 (1)	.25	.25
Nos. 947-948 (2)	4.00	1.25
Nos. 406-407 (2)	4.20	2.40
Nos. 270-271 (2)	3.50	2.00
Nos. 1000-1001 (2)	.50	.50
No. 453 (1)	.45	.45
Nos. 475-476 (2)	.95	.50
Nos. 722-724 (3)	*10.50*	2.00
Nos. 475-476 (2)	1.35	1.00
Nos. 533-534 (2)	2.20	1.95
Nos. 1038-1040 (3)	17.75	2.40
Nos. 701-702 (2)	.90	.90
No. 1567 (1)	.25	.25
Nos. 814-816 (3)	4.00	2.85
Nos. 500-501 (2)	1.85	1.00
Nos. 1799-1800 (2)	2.50	1.65
Nos. 470-472 (3)	.75	.75
Nos. 1003-1004 (2)	4.00	4.00
Set total (51) Stamps	88.30	43.65

Europa, 1970

Interwoven Threads
CD13

1970

Andorra, French 196-197
Belgium 741-742
Cyprus 340-342
France 1271-1272
Germany 1018-1019
Greece 985, 987
Iceland 420-421
Ireland 279-281
Italy 1013-1014
Liechtenstein 470
Luxembourg 489-490
Monaco 768-770
Netherlands 483-484
Portugal 1060-1062
San Marino 729-730
Spain 1607
Switzerland 515-516
Turkey 1848-1849
Yugoslavia 1024-1025

Nos. 196-197 (2)	20.00	8.50
Nos. 741-742 (2)	1.10	.55
Nos. 340-342 (3)	*2.70*	*2.75*
Nos. 1271-1272 (2)	.65	.50
Nos. 1018-1019 (2)	.60	.50
Nos. 985,987 (2)	6.35	1.60
Nos. 420-421 (2)	6.00	4.00
Nos. 279-281 (3)	7.50	2.50
Nos. 1013-1014 (2)	.50	.50
No. 470 (1)	.45	.45
Nos. 489-490 (2)	.80	.55
Nos. 768-770 (3)	*6.35*	2.10
Nos. 483-484 (2)	1.30	1.15
Nos. 1060-1062 (3)	*9.75*	2.35
Nos. 729-730 (2)	.90	.55
No. 1607 (1)	.25	.25
Nos. 515-516 (2)	1.85	.70
Nos. 1848-1849 (2)	2.50	1.50
Nos. 1024-1025 (2)	.80	.80
Set total (40) Stamps	70.35	31.80

Europa, 1971

"Fraternity, Cooperation, Common Effort"
CD14

1971

Andorra, French 205-206
Belgium 803-804
Cyprus 365-367
Finland 504
France 1304
Germany 1064-1065
Greece 1029-1030
Iceland 429-430
Ireland 305-306
Italy 1038-1039
Liechtenstein 485
Luxembourg 500-501
Malta 425-427
Monaco 797-799
Netherlands 488-489
Portugal 1094-1096
San Marino 749-750
Spain 1675-1676
Switzerland 531-532
Turkey 1876-1877
Yugoslavia 1052-1053

Nos. 205-206 (2)	20.00	7.75
Nos. 803-804 (2)	1.30	.55
Nos. 365-367 (3)	*2.60*	*3.25*
No. 504 (1)	5.00	.75
No. 1304 (1)	.45	.40
Nos. 1064-1065 (2)	.60	.50
Nos. 1029-1030 (2)	4.00	1.80
Nos. 429-430 (2)	5.00	3.75
Nos. 305-306 (2)	4.50	1.50
Nos. 1038-1039 (2)	.65	.50
No. 485 (1)	.45	.45
Nos. 500-501 (2)	1.00	.65
Nos. 425-427 (3)	*.80*	*.80*
Nos. 797-799 (3)	*15.00*	2.80
Nos. 488-489 (2)	1.20	.95
Nos. 1094-1096 (3)	*9.75*	1.75
Nos. 749-750 (2)	.65	.55
Nos. 1675-1676 (2)	.75	.55
Nos. 531-532 (2)	1.85	.65
Nos. 1876-1877 (2)	2.50	1.25
Nos. 1052-1053 (2)	.50	.50
Set total (43) Stamps	78.55	31.65

Europa, 1972

Sparkles, Symbolic of Communications
CD15

1972

Andorra, French 210-211
Andorra, Spanish 62
Belgium 825-826
Cyprus 380-382
Finland 512-513
France 1341
Germany 1089-1090
Greece 1049-1050
Iceland 439-440
Ireland 316-317
Italy 1065-1066
Liechtenstein 504
Luxembourg 512-513
Malta 450-453
Monaco 831-832
Netherlands 494-495
Portugal 1141-1143
San Marino 771-772
Spain 1718
Switzerland 544-545
Turkey 1907-1908
Yugoslavia 1100-1101

Nos. 210-211 (2)	21.00	7.00
No. 62 (1)	60.00	60.00
Nos. 825-826 (2)	.95	.55
Nos. 380-382 (3)	*5.95*	*4.25*
Nos. 512-513 (2)	7.00	1.40
No. 1341 (1)	.50	.35
Nos. 1089-1090 (2)	1.10	.50
Nos. 1049-1050 (2)	2.00	1.55
Nos. 439-440 (2)	2.90	2.65
Nos. 316-317 (2)	13.00	4.50
Nos. 1065-1066 (2)	.55	.50
No. 504 (1)	.45	.45
Nos. 512-513 (2)	.95	.65
Nos. 450-453 (4)	1.05	1.40
Nos. 831-832 (2)	5.00	1.40
Nos. 494-495 (2)	1.20	.90
Nos. 1141-1143 (3)	*9.75*	1.50
Nos. 771-772 (2)	.70	.50
No. 1718 (1)	.50	.40
Nos. 544-545 (2)	1.65	.60
Nos. 1907-1908 (2)	4.00	2.00
Nos. 1100-1101 (2)	1.20	1.20
Set total (44) Stamps	141.40	94.25

Europa, 1973

Post Horn and Arrows
CD16

1973

Andorra, French 219-220
Andorra, Spanish 76
Belgium 839-840
Cyprus 396-398
Finland 526
France 1367
Germany 1114-1115
Greece 1090-1092
Iceland 447-448
Ireland 329-330
Italy 1108-1109
Liechtenstein 528-529
Luxembourg 523-524
Malta 469-471
Monaco 866-867
Netherlands 504-505
Norway 604-605
Portugal 1170-1172
San Marino 802-803
Spain 1753
Switzerland 580-581
Turkey 1935-1936
Yugoslavia 1138-1139

Nos. 219-220 (2)	20.00	11.00
No. 76 (1)	1.25	.85
Nos. 839-840 (2)	1.00	.65
Nos. 396-398 (3)	*4.25*	*3.85*
No. 526 (1)	1.25	.55
No. 1367 (1)	1.25	.75
Nos. 1114-1115 (2)	.85	.50
Nos. 1090-1092 (3)	2.10	1.40
Nos. 447-448 (2)	6.65	3.35

Nos. 329-330 (2)	5.25	2.00
Nos. 1108-1109 (2)	.50	.50
Nos. 528-529 (2)	.60	.60
Nos. 523-524 (2)	.90	.75
Nos. 469-471 (3)	.90	1.20
Nos. 866-867 (2)	15.00	2.40
Nos. 504-505 (2)	1.20	.95
Nos. 604-605 (2)	4.00	1.80
Nos. 1170-1172 (3)	*13.00*	2.15
Nos. 802-803 (2)	*1.00*	.60
No. 1753 (1)	.35	.25
Nos. 580-581 (2)	1.55	.60
Nos. 1935-1936 (2)	4.15	2.25
Nos. 1138-1139 (2)	1.15	1.10
Set total (46) Stamps	88.15	40.05

Europa, 2000

CD17

2000

Albania 2621-2622
Andorra, French 522
Andorra, Spanish 262
Armenia 610-611
Austria 1814
Azerbaijan 698-699
Belarus 350
Belgium 1818
Bosnia & Herzegovina (Moslem) 358
Bosnia & Herzegovina (Serb) 111-112
Croatia 428-429
Cyprus 959
Czech Republic 3120
Denmark 1189
Estonia 394
Faroe Islands 376
Finland 1129
Aland Islands 166
France 2771
Georgia 228-229
Germany 2086-2087
Gibraltar 837-840
Great Britain (Jersey) 935-936
Great Britain (Isle of Man) 883
Greece 1959
Greenland 363
Hungary 3699-3700
Iceland 910
Ireland 1230-1231
Italy 2349
Latvia 504
Liechtenstein 1178
Lithuania 668
Luxembourg 1035
Macedonia 187
Malta 1011-1012
Moldova 355
Monaco 2161-2162
Poland 3519
Portugal 2358
Portugal (Azores) 455
Portugal (Madeira) 208
Romania 4370
Russia 6589
San Marino 1480
Slovakia 355
Slovenia 424
Spain 3036
Sweden 2394
Switzerland 1074
Turkey 2762
Turkish Rep. of Northern Cyprus 500
Ukraine 379
Vatican City 1152

Nos. 2621-2622 (2)	11.00	11.00
No. 522 (1)	2.00	1.00
No. 262 (1)	1.75	.80
Nos. 610-611 (2)	4.75	4.75
No. 1814 (1)	1.40	1.40
Nos. 698-699 (2)	6.00	6.00
No. 350 (1)	1.75	1.75
No. 1818 (1)	1.40	.60
No. 358 (1)	4.75	4.75
Nos. 111-112 (2)	110.00	110.00
Nos. 428-429 (2)	6.25	6.25
No. 959 (1)	2.10	1.40
No. 3120 (1)	1.20	.40
No. 1189 (1)	3.50	2.25
No. 394 (1)	1.25	1.25
No. 376 (1)	2.40	2.40
No. 1129 (1)	2.00	.60
No. 166 (1)	2.00	1.10
No. 2771 (1)	1.25	.40
Nos. 228-229 (2)	9.00	9.00
Nos. 2086-2087 (2)	4.35	2.10
Nos. 837-840 (4)	5.50	5.30
Nos. 935-936 (2)	2.40	2.40
No. 883 (1)	1.75	1.75
No. 363 (1)	1.90	1.90
Nos. 3699-3700 (2)	6.50	2.50
No. 910 (1)	1.60	1.60
Nos. 1230-1231 (2)	4.35	4.35
No. 2349 (1)	1.50	.40
No. 504 (1)	5.00	2.40
No. 1178 (1)	2.25	1.75
No. 668 (1)	1.50	1.50
No. 1035 (1)	1.40	.85
No. 187 (1)	3.00	3.00
Nos. 1011-1012 (2)	4.35	4.35
No. 355 (1)	3.50	3.50
Nos. 2161-2162 (2)	2.80	1.40
No. 3519 (1)	1.25	.75
No. 2358 (1)	1.25	.65
No. 455 (1)	1.25	.50
No. 208 (1)	1.25	.50
No. 4370 (1)	2.50	1.25
No. 6589 (1)	2.00	.85
No. 1480 (1)	1.00	1.00
No. 355 (1)	1.60	.80
No. 424 (1)	3.25	3.25
No. 3036 (1)	.75	.40
No. 2394 (1)	3.00	2.25
No. 1074 (1)	2.10	1.05
No. 2762 (1)	2.75	2.00
No. 500 (1)	2.50	2.50
No. 379 (1)	4.50	3.00
No. 1152 (1)	1.25	1.25
Set total (68) Stamps	261.60	230.15

The Gibraltar stamps are similar to the stamp illustrated, but none have the design shown above. All other sets listed above include at least one stamp with the design shown, but some include stamps with entirely different designs. Bulgaria Nos. 4131-4132, Guernsey Nos. 802-803 and Yugoslavia Nos. 2485-2486 are Europa stamps with completely different designs.

PORTUGAL & COLONIES
Vasco da Gama

Fleet Departing CD20

Fleet Arriving at Calicut — CD21

Embarking at Rastello CD22

Muse of History CD23

San Gabriel, da Gama and Camoens CD24

Archangel Gabriel, the Patron Saint CD25

Flagship San Gabriel — CD26

Vasco da Gama — CD27

Fourth centenary of Vasco da Gama's discovery of the route to India.

1898

Azores 93-100
Macao 67-74
Madeira 37-44
Portugal 147-154
Port. Africa 1-8
Port. Congo 75-98
Port. India 189-196
St. Thomas & Prince Islands 170-193
Timor 45-52

Nos. 93-100 (8)	113.50	73.50
Nos. 67-74 (8)	136.00	96.75
Nos. 37-44 (8)	44.55	34.00
Nos. 147-154 (8)	155.00	50.25
Nos. 1-8 (8)	27.00	17.75
Nos. 75-98 (24)	41.50	34.45
Nos. 189-196 (8)	20.25	12.95
Nos. 170-193 (24)	38.75	34.30
Nos. 45-52 (8)	39.75	27.25
Set total (104) Stamps	616.30	381.20

Pombal
POSTAL TAX
POSTAL TAX DUES

Marquis de Pombal — CD28

Planning Reconstruction of Lisbon, 1755 — CD29

Pombal Monument, Lisbon — CD30

Sebastiao Jose de Carvalho e Mello, Marquis de Pombal (1699-1782), statesman, rebuilt Lisbon after earthquake of 1755. Tax was for the erection of Pombal monument. Obligatory on all mail on certain days throughout the year. Postal Tax Dues are inscribed "Multa."

1925

Angola RA1-RA3, RAJ1-RAJ3
Azores RA9-RA11, RAJ2-RAJ4
Cape Verde RA1-RA3, RAJ1-RAJ3
Macao RA1-RA3, RAJ1-RAJ3
Madeira RA1-RA3, RAJ1-RAJ3
Mozambique RA1-RA3, RAJ1-RAJ3
Nyassa RA1-RA3, RAJ1-RAJ3
Portugal RA11-RA13, RAJ2-RAJ4
Port. Guinea RA1-RA3, RAJ1-RAJ3
Port. India RA1-RA3, RAJ1-RAJ3
St. Thomas & Prince Islands RA1-RA3, RAJ1-RAJ3
Timor RA1-RA3, RAJ1-RAJ3

Nos. RA1-RA3,RAJ1-RAJ3 (6)	6.60	6.60
Nos. RA9-RA11,RAJ2-RAJ4 (6)	6.60	6.60
Nos. RA1-RA3,RAJ1-RAJ3 (6)	4.50	3.90
Nos. RA1-RA3,RAJ1-RAJ3 (6)	21.25	10.50
Nos. RA1-RA3,RAJ1-RAJ3 (6)	4.35	12.45
Nos. RA1-RA3,RAJ1-RAJ3 (6)	2.40	2.55
Nos. RA1-RA3,RAJ1-RAJ3 (6)	52.50	38.25
Nos. RA11-RA13,RAJ2-RAJ4 (6)	5.95	5.20
Nos. RA1-RA3,RAJ1-RAJ3 (6)	3.30	2.70
Nos. RA1-RA3,RAJ1-RAJ3 (6)	3.45	3.45
Nos. RA1-RA3,RAJ1-RAJ3 (6)	3.75	3.60
Nos. RA1-RA3,RAJ1-RAJ3 (6)	2.10	3.90
Set total (72) Stamps	116.75	99.70

Vasco da Gama CD34

Mousinho de Albuquerque CD35

Dam CD36

Prince Henry the Navigator CD37

Affonso de Albuquerque CD38

Plane over Globe CD39

1938-39

Angola 274-291, C1-C9
Cape Verde 234-251, C1-C9
Macao 289-305, C7-C15
Mozambique 270-287, C1-C9
Port. Guinea 233-250, C1-C9
Port. India 439-453, C1-C8
St. Thomas & Prince Islands ... 302-319, 323-340, C1-C18
Timor 223-239, C1-C9

Nos. 274-291,C1-C9 (27)	129.40	22.85
Nos. 234-251,C1-C9 (27)	87.00	27.15
Nos. 289-305,C7-C15 (26)	589.45	145.25
Nos. 270-287,C1-C9 (27)	63.45	11.20
Nos. 233-250,C1-C9 (27)	88.05	30.70
Nos. 439-453,C1-C8 (23)	74.75	25.50
Nos. 302-319,323-340,C1-C18 (54)	316.25	191.35
Nos. 223-239,C1-C9 (26)	193.55	94.50
Set total (237) Stamps	1,542.	548.50

Lady of Fatima

Our Lady of the Rosary, Fatima, Portugal — CD40

1948-49

Angola 315-318
Cape Verde 266
Macao 336
Mozambique 325-328
Port. Guinea 271
Port. India 480
St. Thomas & Prince Islands 351
Timor 254

Nos. 315-318 (4)	68.00	17.25
No. 266 (1)	8.50	4.50
No. 336 (1)	42.50	12.00
Nos. 325-328 (4)	73.25	16.85
No. 271 (1)	3.25	3.00
No. 480 (1)	2.50	2.25
No. 351 (1)	7.25	6.50
No. 254 (1)	6.00	6.00
Set total (14) Stamps	211.25	68.35

A souvenir sheet of 9 stamps was issued in 1951 to mark the extension of the 1950 Holy Year. The sheet contains: Angola No. 316, Cape Verde No. 266, Macao No. 336, Mozambique No. 325, Portuguese Guinea No. 271, Portuguese India Nos. 480, 485, St. Thomas & Prince Islands No. 351, Timor No. 254. The sheet also contains a portrait of Pope Pius XII and is inscribed "Encerramento do

"Ano Santo, Fatima 1951." It was sold for 11 escudos.

Holy Year

Church Bells and Dove
CD41

Angel Holding Candelabra
CD42

Holy Year, 1950.

1950-51

Angola 331-332
Cape Verde 268-269
Macao.......................................339-340
Mozambique 330-331
Port. Guinea 273-274
Port. India................. 490-491, 496-503
St. Thomas & Prince Islands...353-354
Timor 258-259

Nos. 331-332 (2) 7.60 1.35
Nos. 268-269 (2) 5.50 3.50
Nos. 339-340 (2) 60.00 14.00
Nos. 330-331 (2) 3.00 1.10
Nos. 273-274 (2) 3.50 2.60
Nos. 490-491,496-503 (10) 12.80 5.40
Nos. 353-354 (2) 7.75 4.90
Nos. 258-259 (2) 8.00 4.00
Set total (24) Stamps 108.15 36.85

A souvenir sheet of 8 stamps was issued in 1951 to mark the extension of the Holy Year. The sheet contains: Angola No. 331, Cape Verde No. 269, Macao No. 340, Mozambique No. 331, Portuguese Guinea No. 275, Portuguese India No. 490, St. Thomas & Prince Islands No. 354, Timor No. 258, some with colors changed. The sheet contains doves and is inscribed 'Encerramento do Ano Santo, Fatima 1951.' It was sold for 17 escudos.

Holy Year Conclusion

Our Lady of Fatima — CD43

Conclusion of Holy Year. Sheets contain alternate vertical rows of stamps and labels bearing quotation from Pope Pius XII, different for each colony.

1951

Angola 357
Cape Verde 270
Macao..352
Mozambique 356
Port. Guinea 275
Port. India 506
St. Thomas & Prince Islands..........355
Timor 270

No. 357 (1) 5.25 1.50
No. 270 (1) 1.50 1.25
No. 352 (1) 45.00 10.00
No. 356 (1) 2.25 1.00
No. 275 (1) 1.00 .65
No. 506 (1) 1.60 1.00
No. 355 (1) 3.00 2.00
No. 270 (1) 5.75 2.40
Set total (8) Stamps 65.35 19.80

Medical Congress

CD44

First National Congress of Tropical Medicine, Lisbon, 1952. Each stamp has a different design.

1952

Angola 358
Cape Verde 287
Macao..364
Mozambique 359
Port. Guinea 276
Port. India 516
St. Thomas & Prince Islands..........356
Timor 271

No. 358 (1) 1.50 .50
No. 287 (1) .75 .60
No. 364 (1) 10.00 6.00
No. 359 (1) 1.25 .55
No. 276 (1) .45 .35
No. 516 (1) 4.75 2.00
No. 356 (1) .35 .30
No. 271 (1) 2.50 1.30
Set total (8) Stamps 21.55 11.60

Postage Due Stamps

CD45

1952

Angola J37-J42
Cape Verde J31-J36
Macao.......................................J53-J58
Mozambique J51-J56
Port. Guinea J40-J45
Port. India J47-J52
St. Thomas & Prince Islands...J52-J57
Timor J31-J36

Nos. J37-J42 (6) 4.30 2.55
Nos. J31-J36 (6) 2.80 2.30
Nos. J53-J58 (6) 17.45 6.85
Nos. J51-J56 (6) 1.80 1.55
Nos. J40-J45 (6) 2.55 2.55
Nos. J47-J52 (6) 6.10 6.10
Nos. J52-J57 (6) 3.85 3.85
Nos. J31-J36 (6) 6.20 3.50
Set total (48) Stamps 45.05 29.25

Sao Paulo

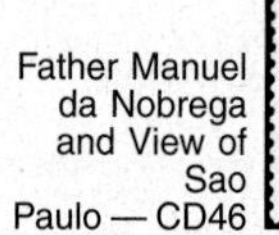

Father Manuel da Nobrega and View of Sao Paulo — CD46

Founding of Sao Paulo, Brazil, 400th anniv.

1954

Angola 385
Cape Verde 297
Macao..382
Mozambique 395
Port. Guinea 291
Port. India 530
St. Thomas & Prince Islands..........369
Timor 279

No. 385 (1) .80 .50
No. 297 (1) .70 .60
No. 382 (1) 15.00 6.00
No. 395 (1) .40 .30
No. 291 (1) .35 .25
No. 530 (1) .80 .40
No. 369 (1) .70 .50
No. 279 (1) 3.00 1.25
Set total (8) Stamps 21.75 9.80

Tropical Medicine Congress

CD47

Sixth International Congress for Tropical Medicine and Malaria, Lisbon, Sept. 1958. Each stamp shows a different plant.

1958

Angola 409
Cape Verde 303
Macao..392
Mozambique 404
Port. Guinea 295
Port. India 569
St. Thomas & Prince Islands..........371
Timor 289

No. 409 (1) 3.50 1.10
No. 303 (1) 5.50 2.10
No. 392 (1) 10.00 5.00
No. 404 (1) 2.50 .85
No. 295 (1) 2.75 1.10
No. 569 (1) 1.75 .75
No. 371 (1) 2.75 2.00
No. 289 (1) 3.50 2.75
Set total (8) Stamps 32.25 15.65

Sports

CD48

Each stamp shows a different sport.

1962

Angola 433-438
Cape Verde 320-325
Macao.......................................394-399
Mozambique 424-429
Port. Guinea 299-304
St. Thomas & Prince Islands...374-379
Timor 313-318

Nos. 433-438 (6) 5.50 3.20
Nos. 320-325 (6) 15.25 5.20
Nos. 394-399 (6) 68.65 14.60
Nos. 424-429 (6) 5.70 2.45
Nos. 299-304 (6) 4.95 2.15
Nos. 374-379 (6) 6.75 3.20
Nos. 313-318 (6) 9.15 5.05
Set total (42) Stamps 115.95 35.85

Anti-Malaria

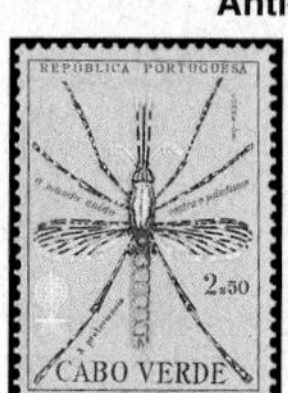

Anopheles Funestus and Malaria Eradication Symbol — CD49

World Health Organization drive to eradicate malaria.

1962

Angola 439
Cape Verde 326
Macao..400
Mozambique 430
Port. Guinea 305
St. Thomas & Prince Islands..........380
Timor 319

No. 439 (1) 1.75 .90
No. 326 (1) 1.40 .90
No. 400 (1) 7.00 2.25
No. 430 (1) 1.40 .40
No. 305 (1) 1.25 .45
No. 380 (1) 2.25 1.25
No. 319 (1) 1.50 1.00
Set total (7) Stamps 16.55 7.15

Airline Anniversary

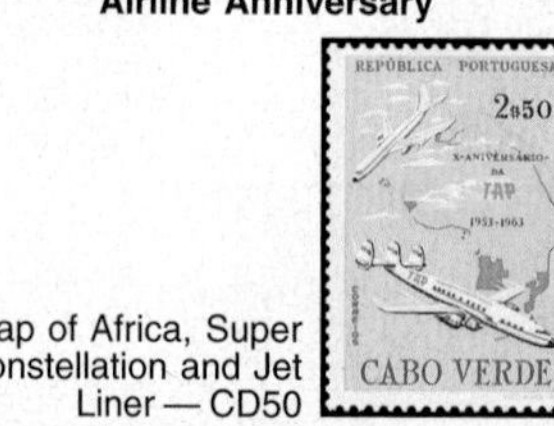

Map of Africa, Super Constellation and Jet Liner — CD50

Tenth anniversary of Transportes Aereos Portugueses (TAP).

1963

Angola 490
Cape Verde 327
Mozambique 434
Port. Guinea 318
St. Thomas & Prince Islands..........381

No. 490 (1) 1.00 .35
No. 327 (1) 1.10 .70
No. 434 (1) .40 .25
No. 318 (1) .65 .35
No. 381 (1) .80 .50
Set total (5) Stamps 3.95 2.15

National Overseas Bank

Antonio Teixeira de Sousa — CD51

Centenary of the National Overseas Bank of Portugal.

1964, May 16

Angola 509
Cape Verde 328
Port. Guinea 319
St. Thomas & Prince Islands..........382
Timor 320

No. 509 (1) .90 .30
No. 328 (1) 1.10 .75
No. 319 (1) .65 .40
No. 382 (1) .70 .50
No. 320 (1) 1.50 .85
Set total (5) Stamps 4.85 2.80

ITU

ITU Emblem and the Archangel Gabriel — CD52

International Communications Union, Cent.

1965, May 17

Angola 511
Cape Verde 329
Macao..402
Mozambique 464
Port. Guinea 320
St. Thomas & Prince Islands..........383
Timor 321

No. 511 (1) 1.25 .65
No. 329 (1) 2.10 1.40
No. 402 (1) 6.00 2.25
No. 464 (1) .45 .25
No. 320 (1) 1.90 .75
No. 383 (1) 2.00 1.00
No. 321 (1) 1.50 .90
Set total (7) Stamps 15.20 7.20

National Revolution

CD53

40th anniv. of the National Revolution. Different buildings on each stamp.

1966, May 28

Angola 525
Cape Verde 338
Macao..403
Mozambique 465
Port. Guinea 329
St. Thomas & Prince Islands..........392
Timor 322

No. 525 (1) .50 .25
No. 338 (1) .60 .45
No. 403 (1) 9.00 2.25
No. 465 (1) .50 .30
No. 329 (1) .55 .35
No. 392 (1) .80 .50
No. 322 (1) 1.75 .95
Set total (7) Stamps 13.70 5.05

Navy Club

CD54

Centenary of Portugal's Navy Club. Each stamp has a different design.

1967, Jan. 31

Angola 527-528
Cape Verde 339-340
Macao 412-413
Mozambique 478-479
Port. Guinea 330-331
St. Thomas & Prince Islands ...393-394
Timor 323-324

Nos. 527-528 (2)	1.75	.75
Nos. 339-340 (2)	2.00	1.40
Nos. 412-413 (2)	11.25	4.00
Nos. 478-479 (2)	1.40	.65
Nos. 330-331 (2)	1.20	.90
Nos. 393-394 (2)	3.30	1.30
Nos. 323-324 (2)	4.65	1.90
Set total (14) Stamps	25.55	10.90

Admiral Coutinho

CD55

Centenary of the birth of Admiral Carlos Viegas Gago Coutinho (1869-1959), explorer and aviation pioneer. Each stamp has a different design.

1969, Feb. 17

Angola 547
Cape Verde 355
Macao 417
Mozambique 484
Port. Guinea 335
St. Thomas & Prince Islands 397
Timor 335

No. 547 (1)	.85	.35
No. 355 (1)	.50	.25
No. 417 (1)	5.00	1.75
No. 484 (1)	.25	.25
No. 335 (1)	.35	.25
No. 397 (1)	.60	.35
No. 335 (1)	2.50	1.05
Set total (7) Stamps	10.05	4.25

Administration Reform

Luiz Augusto Rebello da Silva — CD56

Centenary of the administration reforms of the overseas territories.

1969, Sept. 25

Angola 549
Cape Verde 357
Macao 419
Mozambique 491
Port. Guinea 337
St. Thomas & Prince Islands 399
Timor 338

No. 549 (1)	.35	.25
No. 357 (1)	.50	.25
No. 419 (1)	6.00	1.00
No. 491 (1)	.25	.25
No. 337 (1)	.25	.25
No. 399 (1)	.45	.45
No. 338 (1)	1.25	.50
Set total (7) Stamps	9.05	2.95

Marshal Carmona

CD57

Birth centenary of Marshal Antonio Oscar Carmona de Fragoso (1869-1951), President of Portugal. Each stamp has a different design.

1970, Nov. 15

Angola 563
Cape Verde 359
Macao 422
Mozambique 493
Port. Guinea 340
St. Thomas & Prince Islands 403
Timor 341

No. 563 (1)	.45	.25
No. 359 (1)	.55	.35
No. 422 (1)	2.00	1.00
No. 493 (1)	.40	.25
No. 340 (1)	.35	.25
No. 403 (1)	.75	.40
No. 341 (1)	1.00	.35
Set total (7) Stamps	5.50	2.85

Olympic Games

CD59

20th Olympic Games, Munich, Aug. 26-Sept. 11. Each stamp shows a different sport.

1972, June 20

Angola 569
Cape Verde 361
Macao 426
Mozambique 504
Port. Guinea 342
St. Thomas & Prince Islands 408
Timor 343

No. 569 (1)	.65	.25
No. 361 (1)	.85	.30
No. 426 (1)	4.25	1.00
No. 504 (1)	.30	.25
No. 342 (1)	.45	.25
No. 408 (1)	.45	.25
No. 343 (1)	1.60	.80
Set total (7) Stamps	8.55	3.10

Lisbon-Rio de Janeiro Flight

CD60

50th anniversary of the Lisbon to Rio de Janeiro flight by Arturo de Sacadura and Coutinho, March 30-June 5, 1922. Each stamp shows a different stage of the flight.

1972, Sept. 20

Angola 570
Cape Verde 362
Macao 427
Mozambique 505
Port. Guinea 343
St. Thomas & Prince Islands 409
Timor 344

No. 570 (1)	.35	.25
No. 362 (1)	1.50	.30
No. 427 (1)	22.50	8.50
No. 505 (1)	.25	.25
No. 343 (1)	.25	.25
No. 409 (1)	.50	.25
No. 344 (1)	1.40	.60
Set total (7) Stamps	26.75	10.40

WMO Centenary

WMO Emblem — CD61

Centenary of international meterological cooperation.

1973, Dec. 15

Angola 571
Cape Verde 363
Macao 429
Mozambique 509
Port. Guinea 344
St. Thomas & Prince Islands 410
Timor 345

No. 571 (1)	.45	.25
No. 363 (1)	.65	.30
No. 429 (1)	6.00	1.75
No. 509 (1)	.30	.25
No. 344 (1)	.45	.35
No. 410 (1)	.60	.50
No. 345 (1)	4.25	2.50
Set total (7) Stamps	12.70	5.90

FRENCH COMMUNITY

Upper Volta can be found under Burkina Faso in Vol. 1
Madagascar can be found under Malagasy in Vol. 3

Colonial Exposition

People of French Empire CD70

Women's Heads CD71

France Showing Way to Civilization CD72

"Colonial Commerce" CD73

International Colonial Exposition, Paris.

1931

Cameroun 213-216
Chad 60-63
Dahomey 97-100
Fr. Guiana 152-155
Fr. Guinea 116-119
Fr. India 100-103
Fr. Polynesia 76-79
Fr. Sudan 102-105
Gabon 120-123
Guadeloupe 138-141
Indo-China 140-142
Ivory Coast 92-95
Madagascar 169-172
Martinique 129-132
Mauritania 65-68
Middle Congo 61-64
New Caledonia 176-179
Niger 73-76
Reunion 122-125
St. Pierre & Miquelon 132-135
Senegal 138-141
Somali Coast 135-138
Togo 254-257
Ubangi-Shari 82-85
Upper Volta 66-69
Wallis & Futuna Isls. 85-88

Nos. 213-216 (4)	23.00	18.25
Nos. 60-63 (4)	22.00	22.00
Nos. 97-100 (4)	26.00	26.00
Nos. 152-155 (4)	22.00	22.00
Nos. 116-119 (4)	19.75	19.75
Nos. 100-103 (4)	18.00	*18.00*
Nos. 76-79 (4)	30.00	30.00
Nos. 102-105 (4)	19.00	19.00
Nos. 120-123 (4)	17.50	17.50
Nos. 138-141 (4)	19.00	19.00
Nos. 140-142 (3)	12.00	11.50
Nos. 92-95 (4)	22.50	22.50
Nos. 169-172 (4)	9.25	6.50
Nos. 129-132 (4)	21.00	21.00
Nos. 65-68 (4)	22.00	22.00
Nos. 61-64 (4)	20.00	18.50
Nos. 176-179 (4)	24.00	24.00
Nos. 73-76 (4)	20.50	20.50
Nos. 122-125 (4)	22.00	22.00
Nos. 132-135 (4)	24.00	24.00
Nos. 138-141 (4)	20.00	20.00
Nos. 135-138 (4)	22.00	22.00
Nos. 254-257 (4)	22.00	22.00
Nos. 82-85 (4)	21.00	21.00
Nos. 66-69 (4)	19.00	19.00
Nos. 85-88 (4)	31.00	35.00
Set total (103) Stamps	548.50	543.00

Paris International Exposition
Colonial Arts Exposition

"Colonial Resources"
CD74 CD77

Overseas Commerce CD75

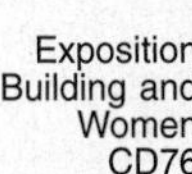

Exposition Building and Women CD76

"France and the Empire" CD78

Cultural Treasures of the Colonies CD79

Souvenir sheets contain one imperf. stamp.

1937

Cameroun 217-222A
Dahomey 101-107
Fr. Equatorial Africa 27-32, 73
Fr. Guiana 162-168
Fr. Guinea 120-126
Fr. India 104-110
Fr. Polynesia 117-123
Fr. Sudan 106-112
Guadeloupe 148-154
Indo-China 193-199
Inini 41
Ivory Coast 152-158
Kwangchowan 132
Madagascar 191-197
Martinique 179-185
Mauritania 69-75
New Caledonia 208-214
Niger 77-83
Reunion 167-173
St. Pierre & Miquelon 165-171
Senegal 172-178
Somali Coast 139-145
Togo 258-264
Wallis & Futuna Isls. 89

Nos. 217-222A (7)	18.80	20.30
Nos. 101-107 (7)	23.60	27.60
Nos. 27-32, 73 (7)	28.10	32.10
Nos. 162-168 (7)	22.50	24.50
Nos. 120-126 (7)	24.00	28.00
Nos. 104-110 (7)	21.15	36.50
Nos. 117-123 (7)	58.50	75.00
Nos. 106-112 (7)	23.60	27.60
Nos. 148-154 (7)	19.55	21.05
Nos. 193-199 (7)	17.70	19.70
No. 41 (1)	21.00	27.50
Nos. 152-158 (7)	22.20	26.20
No. 132 (1)	9.25	11.00
Nos. 191-197 (7)	19.25	21.75
Nos. 179-185 (7)	19.95	21.70
Nos. 69-75 (7)	20.50	24.50
Nos. 208-214 (7)	39.00	50.50
Nos. 73-83 (11)	40.60	45.10
Nos. 167-173 (7)	21.70	23.20
Nos. 165-171 (7)	49.60	64.00
Nos. 172-178 (7)	21.00	23.80
Nos. 139-145 (7)	25.60	32.60
Nos. 258-264 (7)	20.40	20.40
No. 89 (1)	19.00	37.50
Set total (154) Stamps	606.55	742.10

Curie

Pierre and Marie Curie CD80

40th anniversary of the discovery of radium. The surtax was for the benefit of the Intl. Union for the Control of Cancer.

1938

Cameroun	B1
Cuba	B1-B2
Dahomey	B2
France	B76
Fr. Equatorial Africa	B1
Fr. Guiana	B3
Fr. Guinea	B2
Fr. India	B6
Fr. Polynesia	B5
Fr. Sudan	B1
Guadeloupe	B3
Indo-China	B14
Ivory Coast	B2
Madagascar	B2
Martinique	B2
Mauritania	B3
New Caledonia	B4
Niger	B1
Reunion	B4
St. Pierre & Miquelon	B3
Senegal	B3
Somali Coast	B2
Togo	B1

No. B1 (1)	10.00	10.00
Nos. B1-B2 (2)	12.00	3.35
No. B2 (1)	9.50	9.50
No. B76 (1)	21.00	12.50
No. B1 (1)	24.00	24.00
No. B3 (1)	13.50	13.50
No. B2 (1)	8.75	8.75
No. B6 (1)	10.00	10.00
No. B5 (1)	20.00	20.00
No. B1 (1)	12.50	12.50
No. B3 (1)	11.00	10.50
No. B14 (1)	12.00	12.00
No. B2 (1)	11.00	7.50
No. B2 (1)	11.00	11.00
No. B2 (1)	13.00	13.00
No. B3 (1)	7.75	7.75
No. B4 (1)	16.50	17.50
No. B1 (1)	16.50	16.50
No. B4 (1)	14.00	14.00
No. B3 (1)	21.00	22.50
No. B3 (1)	10.50	10.50
No. B2 (1)	7.75	7.75
No. B1 (1)	20.00	20.00
Set total (24) Stamps	313.25	294.60

Caillie

Rene Caillie and Map of Northwestern Africa — CD81

Death centenary of Rene Caillie (1799-1838), French explorer. All three denominations exist with colony name omitted.

1939

Dahomey	108-110
Fr. Guinea	161-163
Fr. Sudan	113-115
Ivory Coast	160-162
Mauritania	109-111
Niger	84-86
Senegal	188-190
Togo	265-267

Nos. 108-110 (3)	1.20	3.60
Nos. 161-163 (3)	1.20	3.20
Nos. 113-115 (3)	1.20	3.20
Nos. 160-162 (3)	1.05	2.55
Nos. 109-111 (3)	1.05	3.80
Nos. 84-86 (3)	2.35	2.35
Nos. 188-190 (3)	1.05	2.90
Nos. 265-267 (3)	1.05	3.30
Set total (24) Stamps	10.15	24.90

New York World's Fair

Natives and New York Skyline CD82

1939

Cameroun	223-224
Dahomey	111-112
Fr. Equatorial Africa	78-79
Fr. Guiana	169-170
Fr. Guinea	164-165
Fr. India	111-112
Fr. Polynesia	124-125
Fr. Sudan	116-117
Guadeloupe	155-156
Indo-China	203-204
Inini	42-43
Ivory Coast	163-164
Kwangchowan	133-134
Madagascar	209-210
Martinique	186-187
Mauritania	112-113
New Caledonia	215-216
Niger	87-88
Reunion	174-175
St. Pierre & Miquelon	205-206
Senegal	191-192
Somali Coast	179-180
Togo	268-269
Wallis & Futuna Isls.	90-91

Nos. 223-224 (2)	2.80	2.40
Nos. 111-112 (2)	1.60	3.20
Nos. 78-79 (2)	1.60	3.20
Nos. 169-170 (2)	2.60	2.60
Nos. 164-165 (2)	1.60	3.20
Nos. 111-112 (2)	3.00	*8.00*
Nos. 124-125 (2)	4.80	4.80
Nos. 116-117 (2)	1.60	3.20
Nos. 155-156 (2)	2.50	2.50
Nos. 203-204 (2)	2.05	2.05
Nos. 42-43 (2)	7.50	9.00
Nos. 163-164 (2)	1.50	3.00
Nos. 133-134 (2)	2.50	2.50
Nos. 209-210 (2)	1.50	2.50
Nos. 186-187 (2)	2.35	2.35
Nos. 112-113 (2)	1.40	2.80
Nos. 215-216 (2)	3.35	3.35
Nos. 87-88 (2)	1.60	2.80
Nos. 174-175 (2)	2.80	2.80
Nos. 205-206 (2)	4.80	6.00
Nos. 191-192 (2)	1.40	2.80
Nos. 179-180 (2)	1.40	2.80
Nos. 268-269 (2)	1.40	2.80
Nos. 90-91 (2)	5.00	6.00
Set total (48) Stamps	62.65	86.65

French Revolution

Storming of the Bastille CD83

French Revolution, 150th anniv. The surtax was for the defense of the colonies.

1939

Cameroun	B2-B6
Dahomey	B3-B7
Fr. Equatorial Africa	B4-B8, CB1
Fr. Guiana	B4-B8, CB1
Fr. Guinea	B3-B7
Fr. India	B7-B11
Fr. Polynesia	B6-B10, CB1
Fr. Sudan	B2-B6
Guadeloupe	B4-B8
Indo-China	B15-B19, CB1
Inini	B1-B5
Ivory Coast	B3-B7
Kwangchowan	B1-B5
Madagascar	B3-B7, CB1
Martinique	B3-B7
Mauritania	B4-B8
New Caledonia	B5-B9, CB1
Niger	B2-B6
Reunion	B5-B9, CB1
St. Pierre & Miquelon	B4-B8
Senegal	B4-B8, CB1
Somali Coast	B3-B7
Togo	B2-B6
Wallis & Futuna Isls.	B1-B5

Nos. B2-B6 (5)	60.00	60.00
Nos. B3-B7 (5)	47.50	47.50
Nos. B4-B8,CB1 (6)	120.00	120.00
Nos. B4-B8,CB1 (6)	79.50	79.50
Nos. B3-B7 (5)	47.50	47.50
Nos. B7-B11 (5)	28.75	*32.50*
Nos. B6-B10,CB1 (6)	122.50	122.50
Nos. B2-B6 (5)	50.00	50.00
Nos. B4-B8 (5)	50.00	50.00
Nos. B15-B19,CB1 (6)	85.00	85.00
Nos. B1-B5 (5)	80.00	100.00
Nos. B3-B7 (5)	43.75	43.75
Nos. B1-B5 (5)	46.25	46.25
Nos. B3-B7,CB1 (6)	65.50	65.50
Nos. B3-B7 (5)	52.50	52.50
Nos. B4-B8 (5)	42.50	42.50
Nos. B5-B9,CB1 (6)	101.50	101.50
Nos. B2-B6 (5)	60.00	60.00
Nos. B5-B9,CB1 (6)	87.50	87.50
Nos. B4-B8 (5)	67.50	72.50
Nos. B4-B8,CB1 (6)	56.50	56.50
Nos. B3-B7 (5)	45.00	45.00
Nos. B2-B6 (5)	42.50	42.50
Nos. B1-B5 (5)	80.00	110.00
Set total (128) Stamps	1,562.	1,621.

Plane over Coastal Area CD85

All five denominations exist with colony name omitted.

1940

Dahomey	C1-C5
Fr. Guinea	C1-C5
Fr. Sudan	C1-C5
Ivory Coast	C1-C5
Mauritania	C1-C5
Niger	C1-C5
Senegal	C12-C16
Togo	C1-C5

Nos. C1-C5 (5)	4.00	4.00
Nos. C1-C5 (5)	4.00	4.00
Nos. C1-C5 (5)	4.00	4.00
Nos. C1-C5 (5)	3.80	3.80
Nos. C1-C5 (5)	3.50	3.50
Nos. C1-C5 (5)	3.50	3.50
Nos. C12-C16 (5)	3.50	3.50
Nos. C1-C5 (5)	3.15	3.15
Set total (40) Stamps	29.45	29.45

Defense of the Empire

Colonial Infantryman — CD86

1941

Cameroun	B13B
Dahomey	B13
Fr. Equatorial Africa	B8B
Fr. Guiana	B10
Fr. Guinea	B13
Fr. India	B13
Fr. Polynesia	B12
Fr. Sudan	B12
Guadeloupe	B10
Indo-China	B19B
Inini	B7
Ivory Coast	B13
Kwangchowan	B7
Madagascar	B9
Martinique	B9
Mauritania	B14
New Caledonia	B11
Niger	B12
Reunion	B11
St. Pierre & Miquelon	B8B
Senegal	B14
Somali Coast	B9
Togo	B10B
Wallis & Futuna Isls.	B7

No. B13B (1)	1.60
No. B13 (1)	1.20
No. B8B (1)	3.50
No. B10 (1)	1.40
No. B13 (1)	1.40
No. B13 (1)	1.25
No. B12 (1)	3.50
No. B12 (1)	1.40
No. B10 (1)	1.00
No. B19B (1)	3.00
No. B7 (1)	1.75
No. B13 (1)	1.25
No. B7 (1)	.85
No. B9 (1)	1.50
No. B9 (1)	1.40
No. B14 (1)	.95
No. B12 (1)	1.40
No. B11 (1)	1.60
No. B8B (1)	4.50
No. B14 (1)	1.25
No. B9 (1)	1.60
No. B10B (1)	1.10
No. B7 (1)	1.75
Set total (23) Stamps	40.15

Each of the CD86 stamps listed above is part of a set of three stamps. The designs of the other two stamps in the set vary from country to country. Only the values of the Common Design stamps are listed here.

Colonial Education Fund

CD86a

1942

Cameroun	CB3
Dahomey	CB4
Fr. Equatorial Africa	CB5
Fr. Guiana	CB4
Fr. Guinea	CB4
Fr. India	CB3
Fr. Polynesia	CB4
Fr. Sudan	CB4
Guadeloupe	CB3
Indo-China	CB5
Inini	CB3
Ivory Coast	CB4
Kwangchowan	CB4
Malagasy	CB5
Martinique	CB3
Mauritania	CB4
New Caledonia	CB4
Niger	CB4
Reunion	CB4
St. Pierre & Miquelon	CB3
Senegal	CB5
Somali Coast	CB3
Togo	CB3
Wallis & Futuna	CB3

No. CB3 (1)	1.10	
No. CB4 (1)	.80	5.50
No. CB5 (1)	.80	
No. CB4 (1)	1.10	
No. CB4 (1)	.40	5.50
No. CB3 (1)	.90	
No. CB4 (1)	2.00	
No. CB4 (1)	.40	5.50
No. CB3 (1)	1.10	
No. CB5 (1)	2.00	
No. CB3 (1)	1.25	
No. CB4 (1)	1.00	5.50
No. CB4 (1)	1.00	
No. CB5 (1)	.65	
No. CB3 (1)	1.00	
No. CB4 (1)	.80	
No. CB4 (1)	2.25	
No. CB4 (1)	.35	
No. CB4 (1)	.90	
No. CB3 (1)	7.00	
No. CB5 (1)	.80	6.50
No. CB3 (1)	.70	
No. CB3 (1)	.35	
No. CB3 (1)	2.00	
Set total (24) Stamps	30.65	28.50

Cross of Lorraine & Four-motor Plane CD87

1941-5

Cameroun	C1-C7
Fr. Equatorial Africa	C17-C23
Fr. Guiana	C9-C10
Fr. India	C1-C6
Fr. Polynesia	C3-C9
Fr. West Africa	C1-C3
Guadeloupe	C1-C2
Madagascar	C37-C43

Martinique	C1-C2
New Caledonia	C7-C13
Reunion	C18-C24
St. Pierre & Miquelon	C1-C7
Somali Coast	C1-C7

Nos. C1-C7 (7)	6.30	6.30
Nos. C17-C23 (7)	10.40	6.35
Nos. C9-C10 (2)	3.80	3.10
Nos. C1-C6 (6)	9.30	*15.00*
Nos. C3-C9 (7)	13.75	10.00
Nos. C1-C3 (3)	9.50	3.90
Nos. C1-C2 (2)	3.75	2.50
Nos. C37-C43 (7)	5.60	3.80
Nos. C1-C2 (2)	3.00	1.60
Nos. C7-C13 (7)	8.85	7.30
Nos. C18-C24 (7)	7.05	5.00
Nos. C1-C7 (7)	11.60	9.40
Nos. C1-C7 (7)	13.95	11.10
Set total (71) Stamps	106.85	85.35

Somali Coast stamps are inscribed "Djibouti".

Transport Plane CD88

Caravan and Plane CD89

1942

Dahomey	C6-C13
Fr. Guinea	C6-C13
Fr. Sudan	C6-C13
Ivory Coast	C6-C13
Mauritania	C6-C13
Niger	C6-C13
Senegal	C17-C25
Togo	C6-C13

Nos. C6-C13 (8)	7.15
Nos. C6-C13 (8)	5.75
Nos. C6-C13 (8)	8.00
Nos. C6-C13 (8)	11.15
Nos. C6-C13 (8)	9.75
Nos. C6-C13 (8)	6.20
Nos. C17-C25 (9)	9.45
Nos. C6-C13 (8)	6.75
Set total (65) Stamps	64.20

Red Cross

Marianne CD90

The surtax was for the French Red Cross and national relief.

1944

Cameroun	B28
Fr. Equatorial Africa	B38
Fr. Guiana	B12
Fr. India	B14
Fr. Polynesia	B13
Fr. West Africa	B1
Guadeloupe	B12
Madagascar	B15
Martinique	B11
New Caledonia	B13
Reunion	B15
St. Pierre & Miquelon	B13
Somali Coast	B13
Wallis & Futuna Isls.	B9

No. B28 (1)	2.00	1.60
No. B38 (1)	1.60	1.20
No. B12 (1)	1.75	1.25
No. B14 (1)	1.50	1.25
No. B13 (1)	2.00	1.60
No. B1 (1)	6.50	4.75
No. B12 (1)	1.40	1.00
No. B15 (1)	.90	.90
No. B11 (1)	1.20	1.20
No. B13 (1)	1.50	1.50
No. B15 (1)	1.60	1.10
No. B13 (1)	2.60	2.60
No. B13 (1)	1.75	2.00
No. B9 (1)	3.00	3.00
Set total (14) Stamps	29.30	24.95

Eboue

CD91

Felix Eboue, first French colonial administrator to proclaim resistance to Germany after French surrender in World War II.

1945

Cameroun	296-297
Fr. Equatorial Africa	156-157
Fr. Guiana	171-172
Fr. India	210-211
Fr. Polynesia	150-151
Fr. West Africa	15-16
Guadeloupe	187-188
Madagascar	259-260
Martinique	196-197
New Caledonia	274-275
Reunion	238-239
St. Pierre & Miquelon	322-323
Somali Coast	238-239

Nos. 296-297 (2)	2.40	1.95
Nos. 156-157 (2)	2.55	2.00
Nos. 171-172 (2)	2.45	2.00
Nos. 210-211 (2)	2.20	1.95
Nos. 150-151 (2)	3.60	2.85
Nos. 15-16 (2)	2.40	2.40
Nos. 187-188 (2)	2.05	1.60
Nos. 259-260 (2)	2.00	1.45
Nos. 196-197 (2)	2.05	1.55
Nos. 274-275 (2)	3.40	3.00
Nos. 238-239 (2)	2.40	2.00
Nos. 322-323 (2)	4.40	3.45
Nos. 238-239 (2)	2.45	2.10
Set total (26) Stamps	34.35	28.30

Victory

Victory — CD92

European victory of the Allied Nations in World War II.

1946, May 8

Cameroun	C8
Fr. Equatorial Africa	C24
Fr. Guiana	C11
Fr. India	C7
Fr. Polynesia	C10
Fr. West Africa	C4
Guadeloupe	C3
Indo-China	C19
Madagascar	C44
Martinique	C3
New Caledonia	C14
Reunion	C25
St. Pierre & Miquelon	C8
Somali Coast	C8
Wallis & Futuna Isls.	C1

No. C8 (1)	1.60	1.20
No. C24 (1)	1.60	1.25
No. C11 (1)	1.75	1.25
No. C7 (1)	1.00	4.00
No. C10 (1)	2.75	2.00
No. C4 (1)	1.60	1.20
No. C3 (1)	1.25	1.00
No. C19 (1)	1.00	.55
No. C44 (1)	1.00	.35
No. C3 (1)	1.30	1.00
No. C14 (1)	1.50	1.25
No. C25 (1)	1.10	.90
No. C8 (1)	2.10	2.10
No. C8 (1)	1.75	1.40
No. C1 (1)	2.25	1.90
Set total (15) Stamps	23.55	21.35

Chad to Rhine

Leclerc's Departure from Chad — CD93

Battle at Cufra Oasis — CD94

Tanks in Action, Mareth — CD95

Normandy Invasion — CD96

Entering Paris — CD97

Liberation of Strasbourg — CD98

"Chad to the Rhine" march, 1942-44, by Gen. Jacques Leclerc's column, later French 2nd Armored Division.

1946, June 6

Cameroun	C9-C14
Fr. Equatorial Africa	C25-C30
Fr. Guiana	C12-C17
Fr. India	C8-C13
Fr. Polynesia	C11-C16
Fr. West Africa	C5-C10
Guadeloupe	C4-C9
Indo-China	C20-C25
Madagascar	C45-C50
Martinique	C4-C9
New Caledonia	C15-C20
Reunion	C26-C31
St. Pierre & Miquelon	C9-C14
Somali Coast	C9-C14
Wallis & Futuna Isls.	C2-C7

Nos. C9-C14 (6)	12.05	9.70
Nos. C25-C30 (6)	14.70	10.80
Nos. C12-C17 (6)	12.65	10.35
Nos. C8-C13 (6)	12.80	*15.00*
Nos. C11-C16 (6)	17.55	13.40
Nos. C5-C10 (6)	16.05	11.95
Nos. C4-C9 (6)	12.00	9.60
Nos. C20-C25 (6)	6.40	6.40
Nos. C45-C50 (6)	10.30	8.40
Nos. C4-C9 (6)	8.85	7.30
Nos. C15-C20 (6)	13.40	11.90
Nos. C26-C31 (6)	10.25	6.55
Nos. C9-C14 (6)	17.30	14.35
Nos. C9-C14 (6)	18.10	12.65
Nos. C2-C7 (6)	13.75	10.45
Set total (90) Stamps	196.15	158.80

UPU

French Colonials, Globe and Plane — CD99

Universal Postal Union, 75th anniv.

1949, July 4

Cameroun	C29
Fr. Equatorial Africa	C34
Fr. India	C17
Fr. Polynesia	C20
Fr. West Africa	C15
Indo-China	C26
Madagascar	C55
New Caledonia	C24
St. Pierre & Miquelon	C18
Somali Coast	C18
Togo	C18
Wallis & Futuna Isls.	C10

No. C29 (1)	8.00	4.75
No. C34 (1)	16.00	12.00
No. C17 (1)	11.50	8.75
No. C20 (1)	20.00	15.00
No. C15 (1)	12.00	8.75
No. C26 (1)	4.75	4.00
No. C55 (1)	4.00	2.75
No. C24 (1)	7.50	5.00
No. C18 (1)	20.00	12.00
No. C18 (1)	14.00	10.50
No. C18 (1)	8.50	7.00
No. C10 (1)	11.00	8.25
Set total (12) Stamps	137.25	98.75

Tropical Medicine

Doctor Treating Infant CD100

The surtax was for charitable work.

1950

Cameroun	B29
Fr. Equatorial Africa	B39
Fr. India	B15
Fr. Polynesia	B14
Fr. West Africa	B3
Madagascar	B17
New Caledonia	B14
St. Pierre & Miquelon	B14
Somali Coast	B14
Togo	B11

No. B29 (1)	7.25	5.50
No. B39 (1)	7.25	5.50
No. B15 (1)	6.00	4.00
No. B14 (1)	10.50	8.00
No. B3 (1)	9.50	7.25
No. B17 (1)	5.50	5.50
No. B14 (1)	6.75	5.25
No. B14 (1)	16.00	15.00
No. B14 (1)	7.75	6.25
No. B11 (1)	5.00	3.50
Set total (10) Stamps	81.50	65.75

Military Medal

Medal, Early Marine and Colonial Soldier — CD101

Centenary of the creation of the French Military Medal.

1952

Cameroun	322
Comoro Isls.	39
Fr. Equatorial Africa	186

Fr. India 233
Fr. Polynesia 179
Fr. West Africa 57
Madagascar 286
New Caledonia 295
St. Pierre & Miquelon 345
Somali Coast 267
Togo 327
Wallis & Futuna Isls. 149

No. 322 (1)	7.25	3.25
No. 39 (1)	45.00	37.50
No. 186 (1)	8.00	5.50
No. 233 (1)	5.50	7.00
No. 179 (1)	13.50	10.00
No. 57 (1)	8.75	6.50
No. 286 (1)	3.75	2.50
No. 295 (1)	6.50	6.00
No. 345 (1)	16.00	15.00
No. 267 (1)	9.00	8.00
No. 327 (1)	5.50	4.75
No. 149 (1)	7.25	7.25
Set total (12) Stamps	136.00	113.25

Liberation

Allied Landing, Victory Sign and Cross of Lorraine — CD102

Liberation of France, 10th anniv.

1954, June 6

Cameroun C32
Comoro Isls. C4
Fr. Equatorial Africa C38
Fr. India C18
Fr. Polynesia C22
Fr. West Africa C17
Madagascar C57
New Caledonia C25
St. Pierre & Miquelon C19
Somali Coast C19
Togo C19
Wallis & Futuna Isls. C11

No. C32 (1)	7.25	4.75
No. C4 (1)	32.50	19.00
No. C38 (1)	12.00	8.00
No. C18 (1)	11.00	8.00
No. C22 (1)	10.00	8.00
No. C17 (1)	12.00	5.50
No. C57 (1)	3.25	2.00
No. C25 (1)	7.50	5.00
No. C19 (1)	19.00	12.00
No. C19 (1)	10.50	8.50
No. C19 (1)	7.00	5.50
No. C11 (1)	11.00	8.25
Set total (12) Stamps	143.00	94.50

FIDES

Plowmen CD103

Efforts of FIDES, the Economic and Social Development Fund for Overseas Possessions (Fonds d' Investissement pour le Developpement Economique et Social). Each stamp has a different design.

1956

Cameroun 326-329
Comoro Isls. 43
Fr. Equatorial Africa 189-192
Fr. Polynesia 181
Fr. West Africa 65-72
Madagascar 292-295
New Caledonia 303
St. Pierre & Miquelon 350
Somali Coast 268-269
Togo 331

Nos. 326-329 (4)	6.90	3.20
No. 43 (1)	2.25	1.60
Nos. 189-192 (4)	3.20	1.65
No. 181 (1)	4.00	2.00
Nos. 65-72 (8)	16.00	6.35
Nos. 292-295 (4)	2.25	1.20
No. 303 (1)	1.90	1.10
No. 350 (1)	6.00	4.00
Nos. 268-269 (2)	5.35	3.15
No. 331 (1)	4.25	2.10
Set total (27) Stamps	52.10	26.35

Flower

CD104

Each stamp shows a different flower.

1958-9

Cameroun 333
Comoro Isls. 45
Fr. Equatorial Africa 200-201
Fr. Polynesia 192
Fr. So. & Antarctic Terr. 11
Fr. West Africa 79-83
Madagascar 301-302
New Caledonia 304-305
St. Pierre & Miquelon 357
Somali Coast 270
Togo 348-349
Wallis & Futuna Isls. 152

No. 333 (1)	1.60	.80
No. 45 (1)	5.25	4.25
Nos. 200-201 (2)	3.60	1.60
No. 192 (1)	6.50	4.00
No. 11 (1)	8.75	7.50
Nos. 79-83 (5)	10.45	5.60
Nos. 301-302 (2)	1.60	.60
Nos. 304-305 (2)	8.00	3.00
No. 357 (1)	4.50	2.25
No. 270 (1)	4.25	1.40
Nos. 348-349 (2)	1.10	.50
No. 152 (1)	3.25	3.25
Set total (20) Stamps	58.85	34.75

Human Rights

Sun, Dove and U.N. Emblem CD105

10th anniversary of the signing of the Universal Declaration of Human Rights.

1958

Comoro Isls. 44
Fr. Equatorial Africa 202
Fr. Polynesia 191
Fr. West Africa 85
Madagascar 300
New Caledonia 306
St. Pierre & Miquelon 356
Somali Coast 274
Wallis & Futuna Isls. 153

No. 44 (1)	9.00	9.00
No. 202 (1)	2.40	1.25
No. 191 (1)	13.00	8.75
No. 85 (1)	2.40	2.00
No. 300 (1)	.80	.40
No. 306 (1)	2.00	1.50
No. 356 (1)	3.50	2.50
No. 274 (1)	3.50	2.10
No. 153 (1)	4.50	4.50
Set total (9) Stamps	41.10	32.00

C.C.T.A.

CD106

Commission for Technical Cooperation in Africa south of the Sahara, 10th anniv.

1960

Cameroun 339
Cent. Africa 3
Chad 66
Congo, P.R. 90
Dahomey 138
Gabon 150
Ivory Coast 180
Madagascar 317
Mali 9
Mauritania 117
Niger 104
Upper Volta 89

No. 339 (1)	1.60	.75
No. 3 (1)	1.60	.75
No. 66 (1)	1.75	.50
No. 90 (1)	1.00	1.00
No. 138 (1)	.50	.25
No. 150 (1)	1.25	1.10
No. 180 (1)	1.10	.50
No. 317 (1)	.60	.30
No. 9 (1)	1.20	.50
No. 117 (1)	.75	.40
No. 104 (1)	.85	.45
No. 89 (1)	.65	.40
Set total (12) Stamps	12.85	6.90

Air Afrique, 1961

Modern and Ancient Africa, Map and Planes — CD107

Founding of Air Afrique (African Airlines).

1961-62

Cameroun C37
Cent. Africa C5
Chad C7
Congo, P.R. C5
Dahomey C17
Gabon C5
Ivory Coast C18
Mauritania C17
Niger C22
Senegal C31
Upper Volta C4

No. C37 (1)	1.00	.50
No. C5 (1)	1.00	.65
No. C7 (1)	1.00	.25
No. C5 (1)	1.75	.90
No. C17 (1)	.80	.40
No. C5 (1)	11.00	6.00
No. C18 (1)	2.00	1.25
No. C17 (1)	2.50	1.25
No. C22 (1)	1.75	.90
No. C31 (1)	.80	.30
No. C4 (1)	3.50	1.75
Set total (11) Stamps	27.10	14.15

Anti-Malaria

CD108

World Health Organization drive to eradicate malaria.

1962, Apr. 7

Cameroun B36
Cent. Africa B1
Chad B1
Comoro Isls. B1
Congo, P.R. B3
Dahomey B15
Gabon B4
Ivory Coast B15
Madagascar B19
Mali B1
Mauritania B16
Niger B14
Senegal B16
Somali Coast B15
Upper Volta B1

No. B36 (1)	1.00	.45
No. B1 (1)	1.40	1.40
No. B1 (1)	1.00	.50
No. B1 (1)	3.50	3.50
No. B3 (1)	1.40	1.00
No. B15 (1)	.75	.75
No. B4 (1)	1.00	1.00
No. B15 (1)	1.25	1.25
No. B19 (1)	.75	.50
No. B1 (1)	1.25	.60
No. B16 (1)	.80	.80
No. B14 (1)	.75	.75
No. B16 (1)	1.10	.65
No. B15 (1)	7.00	7.00
No. B1 (1)	.75	.70
Set total (15) Stamps	23.70	20.85

Abidjan Games

CD109

Abidjan Games, Ivory Coast, Dec. 24-31, 1961. Each stamp shows a different sport.

1962

Cent. Africa 19-20, C6
Chad 83-84, C8
Congo, P.R. 103-104, C7
Gabon 163-164, C6
Niger 109-111
Upper Volta 103-105

Nos. 19-20,C6 (3)	4.15	2.85
Nos. 83-84,C8 (3)	5.80	1.55
Nos. 103-104,C7 (3)	3.85	1.80
Nos. 163-164,C6 (3)	5.00	3.00
Nos. 109-111 (3)	2.60	1.25
Nos. 103-105 (3)	2.80	1.75
Set total (18) Stamps	24.20	12.20

African and Malagasy Union

Flag of Union CD110

First anniversary of the Union.

1962, Sept. 8

Cameroun 373
Cent. Africa 21
Chad 85
Congo, P.R. 105
Dahomey 155
Gabon 165
Ivory Coast 198
Madagascar 332
Mauritania 170
Niger 112
Senegal 211
Upper Volta 106

No. 373 (1)	2.00	.75
No. 21 (1)	1.25	.75
No. 85 (1)	1.25	.25
No. 105 (1)	1.50	.50
No. 155 (1)	1.25	.90
No. 165 (1)	1.60	1.25
No. 198 (1)	2.10	.75
No. 332 (1)	.80	.80
No. 170 (1)	.75	.50
No. 112 (1)	.80	.50
No. 211 (1)	.80	.50
No. 106 (1)	1.10	.75
Set total (12) Stamps	15.20	8.20

Telstar

Telstar and Globe Showing Andover and Pleumeur-Bodou — CD111

First television connection of the United States and Europe through the Telstar satellite, July 11-12, 1962.

1962-63

Andorra, French 154
Comoro Isls. C7
Fr. Polynesia C29
Fr. So. & Antarctic Terr. C5
New Caledonia C33
St. Pierre & Miquelon C26
Somali Coast C31
Wallis & Futuna Isls. C17

No. 154 (1)	2.00	1.60
No. C7 (1)	4.50	2.75
No. C29 (1)	11.50	8.00

No. C5 (1)	29.00	21.00
No. C33 (1)	25.00	18.50
No. C26 (1)	7.25	4.50
No. C31 (1)	1.00	1.00
No. C17 (1)	3.75	3.75
Set total (8) Stamps	84.00	61.10

Freedom From Hunger

World Map and Wheat Emblem CD112

U.N. Food and Agriculture Organization's "Freedom from Hunger" campaign.

1963, Mar. 21

Cameroun....................B37-B38
Cent. Africa....................B2
Chad....................B2
Congo, P.R....................B4
Dahomey....................B16
Gabon....................B5
Ivory Coast....................B16
Madagascar....................B21
Mauritania....................B17
Niger....................B15
Senegal....................B17
Upper Volta....................B2

Nos. B37-B38 (2)	2.25	.75
No. B2 (1)	1.25	1.25
No. B2 (1)	1.10	.50
No. B4 (1)	1.40	1.00
No. B16 (1)	.80	.80
No. B5 (1)	1.00	1.00
No. B16 (1)	1.50	1.50
No. B21 (1)	.60	.45
No. B17 (1)	.80	.80
No. B15 (1)	.75	.75
No. B17 (1)	.80	.50
No. B2 (1)	.75	.70
Set total (13) Stamps	13.00	10.00

Red Cross Centenary

CD113

Centenary of the International Red Cross.

1963, Sept. 2

Comoro Isls....................55
Fr. Polynesia....................205
New Caledonia....................328
St. Pierre & Miquelon....................367
Somali Coast....................297
Wallis & Futuna Isls....................165

No. 55 (1)	7.50	6.00
No. 205 (1)	15.00	12.00
No. 328 (1)	8.00	6.75
No. 367 (1)	12.00	5.50
No. 297 (1)	6.25	6.25
No. 165 (1)	4.00	4.00
Set total (6) Stamps	52.75	40.50

African Postal Union, 1963

UAMPT Emblem, Radio Masts, Plane and Mail CD114

Establishment of the African and Malagasy Posts and Telecommunications Union.

1963, Sept. 8

Cameroun....................C47
Cent. Africa....................C10
Chad....................C9
Congo, P.R....................C13
Dahomey....................C19
Gabon....................C13
Ivory Coast....................C25
Madagascar....................C75
Mauritania....................C22
Niger....................C27
Rwanda....................36
Senegal....................C32
Upper Volta....................C9

No. C47 (1)	2.25	1.00
No. C10 (1)	1.90	.90
No. C9 (1)	1.80	.60
No. C13 (1)	1.40	.75
No. C19 (1)	.75	.25
No. C13 (1)	1.90	.80
No. C25 (1)	2.50	1.50
No. C75 (1)	1.25	.80
No. C22 (1)	1.50	.60
No. C27 (1)	1.25	.60
No. 36 (1)	1.00	.75
No. C32 (1)	1.75	.50
No. C9 (1)	1.50	.75
Set total (13) Stamps	20.75	9.80

Air Afrique, 1963

Symbols of Flight — CD115

First anniversary of Air Afrique and inauguration of DC-8 service.

1963, Nov. 19

Cameroun....................C48
Chad....................C10
Congo, P.R....................C14
Gabon....................C18
Ivory Coast....................C26
Mauritania....................C26
Niger....................C35
Senegal....................C33

No. C48 (1)	1.25	.40
No. C10 (1)	1.80	.60
No. C14 (1)	1.60	.60
No. C18 (1)	1.25	.65
No. C26 (1)	1.00	.50
No. C26 (1)	.70	.25
No. C35 (1)	1.00	.55
No. C33 (1)	2.00	.65
Set total (8) Stamps	10.60	4.20

Europafrica

Europe and Africa Linked — CD116

Signing of an economic agreement between the European Economic Community and the African and Malagasy Union, Yaounde, Cameroun, July 20, 1963.

1963-64

Cameroun....................402
Cent. Africa....................C12
Chad....................C11
Congo, P.R....................C16
Gabon....................C19
Ivory Coast....................217
Niger....................C43
Upper Volta....................C11

No. 402 (1)	2.25	.60
No. C12 (1)	2.50	1.75
No. C11 (1)	1.60	.50
No. C16 (1)	1.60	1.00
No. C19 (1)	1.25	.75
No. 217 (1)	1.10	.35
No. C43 (1)	.85	.50
No. C11 (1)	1.50	.80
Set total (8) Stamps	12.65	6.25

Human Rights

Scales of Justice and Globe CD117

15th anniversary of the Universal Declaration of Human Rights.

1963, Dec. 10

Comoro Isls....................56
Fr. Polynesia....................206
New Caledonia....................329
St. Pierre & Miquelon....................368
Somali Coast....................300
Wallis & Futuna Isls....................166

No. 56 (1)	7.50	6.00
No. 205 (1)	15.00	12.00
No. 329 (1)	7.00	6.00
No. 368 (1)	7.00	3.50
No. 300 (1)	8.50	8.50
No. 166 (1)	7.00	7.00
Set total (6) Stamps	52.00	43.00

PHILATEC

Stamp Album, Champs Elysees Palace and Horses of Marly CD118

Intl. Philatelic and Postal Techniques Exhibition, Paris, June 5-21, 1964.

1963-64

Comoro Isls....................60
France....................1078
Fr. Polynesia....................207
New Caledonia....................341
St. Pierre & Miquelon....................369
Somali Coast....................301
Wallis & Futuna Isls....................167

No. 60 (1)	4.00	3.50
No. 1078 (1)	.25	.25
No. 206 (1)	15.00	10.00
No. 341 (1)	6.50	6.50
No. 369 (1)	11.00	8.00
No. 301 (1)	7.75	7.75
No. 167 (1)	3.00	3.00
Set total (7) Stamps	47.50	39.00

Cooperation

CD119

Cooperation between France and the French-speaking countries of Africa and Madagascar.

1964

Cameroun....................409-410
Cent. Africa....................39
Chad....................103
Congo, P.R....................121
Dahomey....................193
France....................1111
Gabon....................175
Ivory Coast....................221
Madagascar....................360
Mauritania....................181
Niger....................143
Senegal....................236
Togo....................495

Nos. 409-410 (2)	2.50	.50
No. 39 (1)	.90	.50
No. 103 (1)	1.00	.25
No. 121 (1)	.90	.35
No. 193 (1)	.80	.35
No. 1111 (1)	.25	.25
No. 175 (1)	.90	.60
No. 221 (1)	1.10	.35

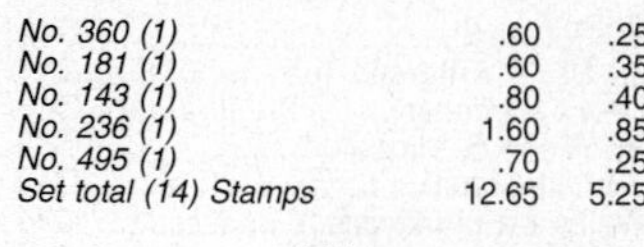

No. 360 (1)	.60	.25
No. 181 (1)	.60	.35
No. 143 (1)	.80	.40
No. 236 (1)	1.60	.85
No. 495 (1)	.70	.25
Set total (14) Stamps	12.65	5.25

ITU

Telegraph, Syncom Satellite and ITU Emblem CD120

Intl. Telecommunication Union, Cent.

1965, May 17

Comoro Isls....................C14
Fr. Polynesia....................C33
Fr. So. & Antarctic Terr....................C8
New Caledonia....................C40
New Hebrides....................124-125
St. Pierre & Miquelon....................C29
Somali Coast....................C36
Wallis & Futuna Isls....................C20

No. C14 (1)	18.00	9.00
No. C33 (1)	80.00	52.50
No. C8 (1)	200.00	160.00
No. C40 (1)	10.00	8.00
Nos. 124-125 (2)	40.50	34.00
No. C29 (1)	24.00	11.50
No. C36 (1)	15.00	9.00
No. C20 (1)	16.00	16.00
Set total (9) Stamps	403.50	300.00

French Satellite A-1

Diamant Rocket and Launching Installation — CD121

Launching of France's first satellite, Nov. 26, 1965.

1965-66

Comoro Isls....................C16a
France....................1138a
Reunion....................359a
Fr. Polynesia....................C41a
Fr. So. & Antarctic Terr....................C10a
New Caledonia....................C45a
St. Pierre & Miquelon....................C31a
Somali Coast....................C40a
Wallis & Futuna Isls....................C23a

No. C16a (1)	9.00	9.00
No. 1138a (1)	.65	.65
No. 359a (1)	3.50	3.00
No. C41a (1)	14.00	14.00
No. C10a (1)	29.00	24.00
No. C45a (1)	7.00	7.00
No. C31a (1)	14.50	14.50
No. C40a (1)	7.00	7.00
No. C23a (1)	8.50	8.50
Set total (9) Stamps	93.15	87.65

French Satellite D-1

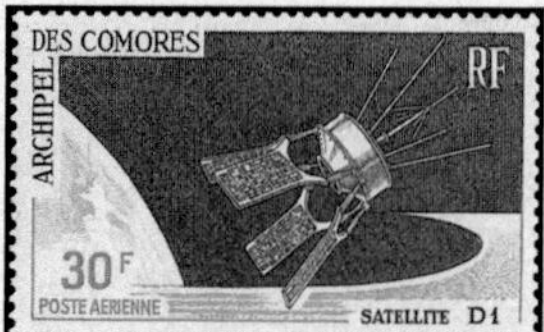

D-1 Satellite in Orbit — CD122

Launching of the D-1 satellite at Hammaguir, Algeria, Feb. 17, 1966.

1966

Comoro Isls....................C17
France....................1148

Fr. Polynesia	C42
Fr. So. & Antarctic Terr.	C11
New Caledonia	C46
St. Pierre & Miquelon	C32
Somali Coast	C49
Wallis & Futuna Isls.	C24

No. C17 (1)	4.00	4.00
No. 1148 (1)	.25	.25
No. C42 (1)	7.00	4.75
No. C11 (1)	57.50	40.00
No. C46 (1)	2.25	2.00
No. C32 (1)	9.00	6.00
No. C49 (1)	4.25	2.75
No. C24 (1)	3.50	3.50
Set total (8) Stamps	87.75	63.25

Air Afrique, 1966

Planes and Air Afrique Emblem — CD123

Introduction of DC-8F planes by Air Afrique.

1966

Cameroun	C79
Cent. Africa	C35
Chad	C26
Congo, P.R.	C42
Dahomey	C42
Gabon	C47
Ivory Coast	C32
Mauritania	C57
Niger	C63
Senegal	C47
Togo	C54
Upper Volta	C31

No. C79 (1)	.80	.25
No. C35 (1)	1.00	.50
No. C26 (1)	.85	.25
No. C42 (1)	1.00	.25
No. C42 (1)	.75	.25
No. C47 (1)	.90	.35
No. C32 (1)	1.00	.60
No. C57 (1)	.80	.30
No. C63 (1)	.70	.35
No. C47 (1)	.80	.30
No. C54 (1)	.80	.25
No. C31 (1)	.75	.50
Set total (12) Stamps	10.15	4.15

African Postal Union, 1967

Telecommunications Symbols and Map of Africa — CD124

Fifth anniversary of the establishment of the African and Malagasy Union of Posts and Telecommunications, UAMPT.

1967

Cameroun	C90
Cent. Africa	C46
Chad	C37
Congo, P.R.	C57
Dahomey	C61
Gabon	C58
Ivory Coast	C34
Madagascar	C85
Mauritania	C65
Niger	C75
Rwanda	C1-C3
Senegal	C60
Togo	C81
Upper Volta	C50

No. C90 (1)	2.40	.65
No. C46 (1)	2.25	.85
No. C37 (1)	2.00	.60
No. C57 (1)	1.60	.60
No. C61 (1)	1.75	.95
No. C58 (1)	2.00	.85
No. C34 (1)	3.50	1.50
No. C85 (1)	1.25	.60
No. C65 (1)	1.25	.60
No. C75 (1)	1.40	.60
Nos. C1-C3 (3)	2.30	1.25
No. C60 (1)	1.75	.50
No. C81 (1)	1.90	.30
No. C50 (1)	1.80	.70
Set total (16) Stamps	27.15	10.55

Monetary Union

Gold Token of the Ashantis, 17-18th Centuries — CD125

West African Monetary Union, 5th anniv.

1967, Nov. 4

Dahomey	244
Ivory Coast	259
Mauritania	238
Niger	204
Senegal	294
Togo	623
Upper Volta	181

No. 244 (1)	.65	.65
No. 259 (1)	.85	.40
No. 238 (1)	.45	.25
No. 204 (1)	.55	.25
No. 294 (1)	.60	.25
No. 623 (1)	.60	.25
No. 181 (1)	.65	.35
Set total (7) Stamps	4.35	2.40

WHO Anniversary

Sun, Flowers and WHO Emblem CD126

World Health Organization, 20th anniv.

1968, May 4

Afars & Issas	317
Comoro Isls.	73
Fr. Polynesia	241-242
Fr. So. & Antarctic Terr.	31
New Caledonia	367
St. Pierre & Miquelon	377
Wallis & Futuna Isls.	169

No. 317 (1)	3.00	3.00
No. 73 (1)	2.40	1.75
Nos. 241-242 (2)	22.00	12.75
No. 31 (1)	62.50	47.50
No. 367 (1)	4.00	2.25
No. 377 (1)	12.00	9.00
No. 169 (1)	5.75	5.75
Set total (8) Stamps	111.65	82.00

Human Rights Year

Human Rights Flame — CD127

1968, Aug. 10

Afars & Issas	322-323
Comoro Isls.	76
Fr. Polynesia	243-244
Fr. So. & Antarctic Terr.	32
New Caledonia	369
St. Pierre & Miquelon	382
Wallis & Futuna Isls.	170

Nos. 322-323 (2)	6.75	4.00
No. 76 (1)	3.25	3.25
Nos. 243-244 (2)	24.00	14.00
No. 32 (1)	55.00	47.50
No. 369 (1)	2.75	1.50
No. 382 (1)	8.00	5.50
No. 170 (1)	3.25	3.25
Set total (9) Stamps	103.00	79.00

2nd PHILEXAFRIQUE

CD128

Opening of PHILEXAFRIQUE, Abidjan, Feb. 14. Each stamp shows a local scene and stamp.

1969, Feb. 14

Cameroun	C118
Cent. Africa	C65
Chad	C48
Congo, P.R.	C77
Dahomey	C94
Gabon	C82
Ivory Coast	C38-C40
Madagascar	C92
Mali	C65
Mauritania	C80
Niger	C104
Senegal	C68
Togo	C104
Upper Volta	C62

No. C118 (1)	3.25	1.25
No. C65 (1)	1.75	1.75
No. C48 (1)	2.40	1.00
No. C77 (1)	2.00	1.75
No. C94 (1)	2.25	2.25
No. C82 (1)	2.00	2.00
Nos. C38-C40 (3)	14.50	14.50
No. C92 (1)	1.75	.85
No. C65 (1)	1.75	1.00
No. C80 (1)	1.90	.75
No. C104 (1)	3.00	1.90
No. C68 (1)	2.00	1.40
No. C104 (1)	2.25	.45
No. C62 (1)	4.00	3.25
Set total (16) Stamps	44.80	34.10

Concorde

Concorde in Flight CD129

First flight of the prototype Concorde supersonic plane at Toulouse, Mar. 1, 1969.

1969

Afars & Issas	C56
Comoro Isls.	C29
France	C42
Fr. Polynesia	C50
Fr. So. & Antarctic Terr.	C18
New Caledonia	C63
St. Pierre & Miquelon	C40
Wallis & Futuna Isls.	C30

No. C56 (1)	26.00	16.00
No. C29 (1)	18.00	12.00
No. C42 (1)	.75	.35
No. C50 (1)	55.00	35.00
No. C18 (1)	55.00	37.50
No. C63 (1)	27.50	20.00
No. C40 (1)	32.50	11.00
No. C30 (1)	15.00	10.00
Set total (8) Stamps	229.75	141.85

Development Bank

Bank Emblem — CD130

African Development Bank, fifth anniv.

1969

Cameroun	499
Chad	217
Congo, P.R.	181-182
Ivory Coast	281
Mali	127-128
Mauritania	267
Niger	220
Senegal	317-318
Upper Volta	201

No. 499 (1)	.80	.25
No. 217 (1)	.90	.25
Nos. 181-182 (2)	1.00	.50
No. 281 (1)	.70	.40
Nos. 127-128 (2)	1.00	.50
No. 267 (1)	.60	.25
No. 220 (1)	.70	.30
Nos. 317-318 (2)	1.55	.50
No. 201 (1)	.65	.30
Set total (12) Stamps	7.90	3.25

ILO

ILO Headquarters, Geneva, and Emblem — CD131

Intl. Labor Organization, 50th anniv.

1969-70

Afars & Issas	337
Comoro Isls.	83
Fr. Polynesia	251-252
Fr. So. & Antarctic Terr.	35
New Caledonia	379
St. Pierre & Miquelon	396
Wallis & Futuna Isls.	172

No. 337 (1)	2.75	2.00
No. 83 (1)	1.25	.75
Nos. 251-252 (2)	24.00	12.50
No. 35 (1)	15.00	10.00
No. 379 (1)	2.25	1.10
No. 396 (1)	10.00	5.50
No. 172 (1)	2.75	2.75
Set total (8) Stamps	58.00	34.60

ASECNA

Map of Africa, Plane and Airport CD132

10th anniversary of the Agency for the Security of Aerial Navigation in Africa and Madagascar (ASECNA, Agence pour la Securite de la Navigation Aerienne en Afrique et a Madagascar).

1969-70

Cameroun	500
Cent. Africa	119
Chad	222
Congo, P.R.	197
Dahomey	269
Gabon	260
Ivory Coast	287
Mali	130
Niger	221
Senegal	321
Upper Volta	204

No. 500 (1)	2.00	.60
No. 119 (1)	2.00	.80
No. 222 (1)	1.00	.25
No. 197 (1)	2.00	.40
No. 269 (1)	.90	.55
No. 260 (1)	1.75	.75
No. 287 (1)	.90	.40
No. 130 (1)	.90	.40
No. 221 (1)	1.40	.70
No. 321 (1)	1.60	.50
No. 204 (1)	1.75	1.00
Set total (11) Stamps	16.20	6.35

U.P.U. Headquarters

CD133

New Universal Postal Union headquarters, Bern, Switzerland.

1970

Afars & Issas ... 342
Algeria ... 443
Cameroun ... 503-504
Cent. Africa ... 125
Chad ... 225
Comoro Isls. ... 84
Congo, P.R. ... 216
Fr. Polynesia ... 261-262
Fr. So. & Antarctic Terr. ... 36
Gabon ... 258
Ivory Coast ... 295
Madagascar ... 444
Mali ... 134-135
Mauritania ... 283
New Caledonia ... 382
Niger ... 231-232
St. Pierre & Miquelon ... 397-398
Senegal ... 328-329
Tunisia ... 535
Wallis & Futuna Isls. ... 173

No. 342 (1)	2.50	1.40
No. 443 (1)	1.10	.40
Nos. 503-504 (2)	2.60	.55
No. 125 (1)	1.75	.70
No. 225 (1)	1.20	.25
No. 84 (1)	5.50	2.00
No. 216 (1)	1.00	.25
Nos. 261-262 (2)	20.00	10.00
No. 36 (1)	40.00	27.50
No. 258 (1)	.90	.55
No. 295 (1)	1.10	.50
No. 444 (1)	.55	.25
Nos. 134-135 (2)	1.05	.50
No. 283 (1)	.60	.30
No. 382 (1)	3.00	1.50
Nos. 231-232 (2)	1.50	.60
Nos. 397-398 (2)	34.00	16.25
Nos. 328-329 (2)	1.55	.55
No. 535 (1)	.60	.25
No. 173 (1)	3.25	3.25
Set total (26) Stamps	123.75	67.55

De Gaulle

CD134

First anniversary of the death of Charles de Gaulle, (1890-1970), President of France.

1971-72

Afars & Issas ... 356-357
Comoro Isls. ... 104-105
France ... 1325a
Fr. Polynesia ... 270-271
Fr. So. & Antarctic Terr. ... 52-53
New Caledonia ... 393-394
Reunion ... 380a
St. Pierre & Miquelon ... 417-418
Wallis & Futuna Isls. ... 177-178

Nos. 356-357 (2)	12.50	7.50
Nos. 104-105 (2)	9.00	5.75
No. 1325a (1)	3.00	2.50
Nos. 270-271 (2)	51.50	29.50
Nos. 52-53 (2)	40.00	29.50
Nos. 393-394 (2)	23.00	11.75
No. 380a (1)	9.25	8.00
Nos. 417-418 (2)	56.50	31.00
Nos. 177-178 (2)	20.00	16.25
Set total (16) Stamps	224.75	141.75

African Postal Union, 1971

UAMPT Building, Brazzaville, Congo — CD135

10th anniversary of the establishment of the African and Malagasy Posts and Telecommunications Union, UAMPT. Each stamp has a different native design.

1971, Nov. 13

Cameroun ... C177
Cent. Africa ... C89
Chad ... C94
Congo, P.R. ... C136
Dahomey ... C146
Gabon ... C120
Ivory Coast ... C47
Mauritania ... C113
Niger ... C164
Rwanda ... C8
Senegal ... C105
Togo ... C166
Upper Volta ... C97

No. C177 (1)	2.00	.50
No. C89 (1)	2.25	.85
No. C94 (1)	1.50	.50
No. C136 (1)	1.60	.75
No. C146 (1)	1.75	.80
No. C120 (1)	1.75	.70
No. C47 (1)	2.00	1.00
No. C113 (1)	1.20	.65
No. C164 (1)	1.25	.60
No. C8 (1)	2.75	2.50
No. C105 (1)	1.60	.50
No. C166 (1)	1.25	.40
No. C97 (1)	1.50	.70
Set total (13) Stamps	22.40	10.45

West African Monetary Union

African Couple, City, Village and Commemorative Coin — CD136

West African Monetary Union, 10th anniv.

1972, Nov. 2

Dahomey ... 300
Ivory Coast ... 331
Mauritania ... 299
Niger ... 258
Senegal ... 374
Togo ... 825
Upper Volta ... 280

No. 300 (1)	.65	.25
No. 331 (1)	1.00	.50
No. 299 (1)	.75	.25
No. 258 (1)	.65	.30
No. 374 (1)	.50	.30
No. 825 (1)	.60	.25
No. 280 (1)	.60	.25
Set total (7) Stamps	4.75	2.10

African Postal Union, 1973

Telecommunications Symbols and Map of Africa — CD137

11th anniversary of the African and Malagasy Posts and Telecommunications Union (UAMPT).

1973, Sept. 12

Cameroun ... 574
Cent. Africa ... 194
Chad ... 294
Congo, P.R. ... 289
Dahomey ... 311
Gabon ... 320
Ivory Coast ... 361
Madagascar ... 500
Mauritania ... 304
Niger ... 287
Rwanda ... 540
Senegal ... 393
Togo ... 849
Upper Volta ... 297

No. 574 (1)	1.75	.40
No. 194 (1)	1.25	.75
No. 294 (1)	1.75	.40
No. 289 (1)	1.60	.50
No. 311 (1)	1.25	.55
No. 320 (1)	1.40	.75
No. 361 (1)	2.50	1.00
No. 500 (1)	1.10	.35
No. 304 (1)	1.10	.40
No. 287 (1)	.90	.60
No. 540 (1)	4.00	2.00
No. 393 (1)	1.60	.50
No. 849 (1)	1.00	.35
No. 297 (1)	1.25	.70
Set total (14) Stamps	22.45	9.25

Philexafrique II — Essen

CD138

CD139

Designs: Indigenous fauna, local and German stamps. Types CD138-CD139 printed horizontally and vertically se-tenant in sheets of 10 (2x5). Label between horizontal pairs alternately commemoratives Philexafrique II, Libreville, Gabon, June 1978, and 2nd International Stamp Fair, Essen, Germany, Nov. 1-5.

1978-1979

Benin ... C286a
Central Africa ... C201a
Chad ... C239a
Congo Republic ... C246a
Djibouti ... C122a
Gabon ... C216a
Ivory Coast ... C65a
Mali ... C357a
Mauritania ... C186a
Niger ... C292a
Rwanda ... C13a
Senegal ... C147a
Togo ... C364a

No. C286a (1)	9.00	8.50
No. C201a (1)	7.50	7.50
No. C239a (1)	7.50	4.00
No. C246a (1)	7.00	7.00
No. C122a (1)	6.50	6.50
No. C216a (1)	6.50	4.00
No. C65a (1)	9.00	9.00
No. C357a (1)	5.00	3.00
No. C186a (1)	4.50	4.00
No. C292a (1)	6.00	6.00
No. C13a (1)	4.00	4.00
No. C147a (1)	10.00	4.00
No. C364a (1)	3.00	1.50
Set total (13) Stamps	85.50	69.00

BRITISH COMMONWEALTH OF NATIONS

The listings follow established trade practices when these issues are offered as units by dealers. The Peace issue, for example, includes only one stamp from the Indian state of Hyderabad. The U.P.U. issue includes the Egypt set. Pairs are included for those varieties issued with bilingual designs se-tenant.

Silver Jubilee

Windsor Castle and King George V CD301

Reign of King George V, 25th anniv.

1935

Antigua ... 77-80
Ascension ... 33-36
Bahamas ... 92-95
Barbados ... 186-189
Basutoland ... 11-14
Bechuanaland Protectorate ... 117-120
Bermuda ... 100-103
British Guiana ... 223-226
British Honduras ... 108-111
Cayman Islands ... 81-84
Ceylon ... 260-263
Cyprus ... 136-139
Dominica ... 90-93
Falkland Islands ... 77-80
Fiji ... 110-113
Gambia ... 125-128
Gibraltar ... 100-103
Gilbert & Ellice Islands ... 33-36
Gold Coast ... 108-111
Grenada ... 124-127
Hong Kong ... 147-150
Jamaica ... 109-112
Kenya, Uganda, Tanzania ... 42-45
Leeward Islands ... 96-99
Malta ... 184-187
Mauritius ... 204-207
Montserrat ... 85-88
Newfoundland ... 226-229
Nigeria ... 34-37
Northern Rhodesia ... 18-21
Nyasaland Protectorate ... 47-50
St. Helena ... 111-114
St. Kitts-Nevis ... 72-75
St. Lucia ... 91-94
St. Vincent ... 134-137
Seychelles ... 118-121
Sierra Leone ... 166-169
Solomon Islands ... 60-63
Somaliland Protectorate ... 77-80
Straits Settlements ... 213-216
Swaziland ... 20-23
Trinidad & Tobago ... 43-46
Turks & Caicos Islands ... 71-74
Virgin Islands ... 69-72

The following have different designs but are included in the omnibus set:

Great Britain ... 226-229
Offices in Morocco (Sp. Curr.) ... 67-70
Offices in Morocco (Br. Curr.) ... 226-229
Offices in Morocco (Fr. Curr.) ... 422-425
Offices in Morocco (Tangier) ... 508-510
Australia ... 152-154
Canada ... 211-216
Cook Islands ... 98-100
India ... 142-148
Nauru ... 31-34
New Guinea ... 46-47
New Zealand ... 199-201
Niue ... 67-69
Papua ... 114-117
Samoa ... 163-165
South Africa ... 68-71
Southern Rhodesia ... 33-36
South-West Africa ... 121-124

Nos. 77-80 (4)	20.25	23.25
Nos. 33-36 (4)	58.50	127.50
Nos. 92-95 (4)	25.00	46.00
Nos. 186-189 (4)	30.00	50.30
Nos. 11-14 (4)	11.60	21.25
Nos. 117-120 (4)	15.75	36.00
Nos. 100-103 (4)	16.80	58.50
Nos. 223-226 (4)	22.35	35.50
Nos. 108-111 (4)	15.25	16.35
Nos. 81-84 (4)	21.60	24.50
Nos. 260-263 (4)	10.40	21.60
Nos. 136-139 (4)	39.75	34.40
Nos. 90-93 (4)	18.85	19.85
Nos. 77-80 (4)	55.00	14.75
Nos. 110-113 (4)	20.25	34.00
Nos. 125-128 (4)	13.05	25.25
Nos. 100-103 (4)	28.75	42.75
Nos. 33-36 (4)	36.80	67.00
Nos. 108-111 (4)	25.75	78.10
Nos. 124-127 (4)	16.70	40.60
Nos. 147-150 (4)	59.00	18.75
Nos. 109-112 (4)	17.00	39.00
Nos. 42-45 (4)	8.75	11.00
Nos. 96-99 (4)	35.75	49.60
Nos. 184-187 (4)	22.00	33.70
Nos. 204-207 (4)	47.60	58.25
Nos. 85-88 (4)	10.25	30.25
Nos. 226-229 (4)	17.50	12.05
Nos. 34-37 (4)	17.50	70.00
Nos. 18-21 (4)	17.00	15.00
Nos. 47-50 (4)	39.75	80.25
Nos. 111-114 (4)	31.15	33.25
Nos. 72-75 (4)	10.80	18.65
Nos. 91-94 (4)	16.00	20.80
Nos. 134-137 (4)	9.45	21.25
Nos. 118-121 (4)	15.75	40.00
Nos. 166-169 (4)	23.60	50.35
Nos. 60-63 (4)	29.00	38.00
Nos. 77-80 (4)	17.00	48.25
Nos. 213-216 (4)	15.00	25.10
Nos. 20-23 (4)	6.80	18.25
Nos. 43-46 (4)	14.05	27.75
Nos. 71-74 (4)	8.40	14.50
Nos. 69-72 (4)	25.00	55.25
Nos. 226-229 (4)	5.15	4.40

Nos. 67-70 (4)	14.35	*26.10*
Nos. 226-229 (4)	8.20	*28.90*
Nos. 422-425 (4)	3.90	2.00
Nos. 508-510 (3)	18.80	*23.85*
Nos. 152-154 (3)	49.50	45.35
Nos. 211-216 (6)	23.85	13.35
Nos. 98-100 (3)	9.65	*12.00*
Nos. 142-148 (7)	28.85	14.00
Nos. 31-34 (4)	9.90	*9.90*
Nos. 46-47 (2)	4.35	1.70
Nos. 199-201 (3)	23.00	*28.50*
Nos. 67-69 (3)	11.80	*26.50*
Nos. 114-117 (4)	9.20	*17.50*
Nos. 163-165 (3)	4.40	6.50
Nos. 68-71 (4)	57.50	*153.00*
Nos. 33-36 (4)	27.75	*45.25*
Nos. 121-124 (4)	13.00	*36.10*
Set total (245) Stamps	1,340.	2,141.

Coronation

Queen Elizabeth and King George VI
CD302

1937

Aden....................13-15
Antigua....................81-83
Ascension....................37-39
Bahamas....................97-99
Barbados....................190-192
Basutoland....................15-17
Bechuanaland Protectorate......121-123
Bermuda....................115-117
British Guiana....................227-229
British Honduras....................112-114
Cayman Islands....................97-99
Ceylon....................275-277
Cyprus....................140-142
Dominica....................94-96
Falkland Islands....................81-83
Fiji....................114-116
Gambia....................129-131
Gibraltar....................104-106
Gilbert & Ellice Islands....................37-39
Gold Coast....................112-114
Grenada....................128-130
Hong Kong....................151-153
Jamaica....................113-115
Kenya, Uganda, Tanzania............60-62
Leeward Islands....................100-102
Malta....................188-190
Mauritius....................208-210
Montserrat....................89-91
Newfoundland....................230-232
Nigeria....................50-52
Northern Rhodesia....................22-24
Nyasaland Protectorate....................51-53
St. Helena....................115-117
St. Kitts-Nevis....................76-78
St. Lucia....................107-109
St. Vincent....................138-140
Seychelles....................122-124
Sierra Leone....................170-172
Solomon Islands....................64-66
Somaliland Protectorate....................81-83
Straits Settlements....................235-237
Swaziland....................24-26
Trinidad & Tobago....................47-49
Turks & Caicos Islands....................75-77
Virgin Islands....................73-75

The following have different designs but are included in the omnibus set:

Great Britain....................234
Offices in Morocco (Sp. Curr.)..........82
Offices in Morocco (Fr. Curr.).........439
Offices in Morocco (Tangier)...........514
Canada....................237
Cook Islands....................109-111
Nauru....................35-38
Newfoundland....................233-243
New Guinea....................48-51
New Zealand....................223-225
Niue....................70-72
Papua....................118-121
South Africa....................74-78
Southern Rhodesia....................38-41
South-West Africa....................125-132

Nos. 13-15 (3)	2.70	*5.65*
Nos. 81-83 (3)	1.85	*8.00*
Nos. 37-39 (3)	2.75	*2.75*
Nos. 97-99 (3)	1.05	*3.05*
Nos. 190-192 (3)	1.10	1.95
Nos. 15-17 (3)	1.15	*3.00*
Nos. 121-123 (3)	.95	3.35
Nos. 115-117 (3)	1.25	5.00
Nos. 227-229 (3)	1.45	3.05
Nos. 112-114 (3)	1.20	2.40
Nos. 97-99 (3)	1.10	2.70
Nos. 275-277 (3)	8.25	10.35
Nos. 140-142 (3)	3.75	6.50
Nos. 94-96 (3)	.85	2.40
Nos. 81-83 (3)	2.90	*2.30*
Nos. 114-116 (3)	1.35	*5.75*
Nos. 129-131 (3)	.85	3.95
Nos. 104-106 (3)	2.25	6.45
Nos. 37-39 (3)	.85	*2.15*
Nos. 112-114 (3)	3.10	*10.00*
Nos. 128-130 (3)	1.00	.85
Nos. 151-153 (3)	23.00	12.50
Nos. 113-115 (3)	1.25	1.25
Nos. 60-62 (3)	1.00	2.35
Nos. 100-102 (3)	1.55	4.00
Nos. 188-190 (3)	1.25	1.60
Nos. 208-210 (3)	2.05	3.75
Nos. 89-91 (3)	1.00	3.35
Nos. 230-232 (3)	7.00	2.80
Nos. 50-52 (3)	3.25	8.50
Nos. 22-24 (3)	.95	2.25
Nos. 51-53 (3)	1.05	1.30
Nos. 115-117 (3)	1.45	2.05
Nos. 76-78 (3)	.95	2.15
Nos. 107-109 (3)	1.05	2.05
Nos. 138-140 (3)	.80	*4.75*
Nos. 122-124 (3)	1.20	*1.90*
Nos. 170-172 (3)	1.95	5.65
Nos. 64-66 (3)	.90	2.00
Nos. 81-83 (3)	1.10	*3.50*
Nos. 235-237 (3)	3.25	1.60
Nos. 24-26 (3)	.75	2.70
Nos. 47-49 (3)	1.00	1.00
Nos. 75-77 (3)	1.30	1.15
Nos. 73-75 (3)	2.20	6.90
No. 234 (1)	.25	.25
No. 82 (1)	.80	.80
No. 439 (1)	.35	.25
No. 514 (1)	.55	.55
No. 237 (1)	.35	.25
Nos. 109-111 (3)	.85	.80
Nos. 35-38 (4)	1.10	*5.50*
Nos. 233-243 (11)	41.90	30.40
Nos. 48-51 (4)	1.40	*7.90*
Nos. 223-225 (3)	1.75	2.25
Nos. 70-72 (3)	.80	*2.05*
Nos. 118-121 (4)	1.60	*5.25*
Nos. 74-78 (5)	7.60	9.35
Nos. 38-41 (4)	3.55	15.50
Nos. 125-132 (8)	5.00	8.40
Set total (189) Stamps	170.80	262.15

Peace

King George VI and Parliament Buildings, London
CD303

Return to peace at the close of World War II.

1945-46

Aden....................28-29
Antigua....................96-97
Ascension....................50-51
Bahamas....................130-131
Barbados....................207-208
Bermuda....................131-132
British Guiana....................242-243
British Honduras....................127-128
Cayman Islands....................112-113
Ceylon....................293-294
Cyprus....................156-157
Dominica....................112-113
Falkland Islands....................97-98
Falkland Islands Dep.............1L9-1L10
Fiji....................137-138
Gambia....................144-145
Gibraltar....................119-120
Gilbert & Ellice Islands....................52-53
Gold Coast....................128-129
Grenada....................143-144
Jamaica....................136-137
Kenya, Uganda, Tanzania............90-91
Leeward Islands....................116-117
Malta....................206-207
Mauritius....................223-224
Montserrat....................104-105
Nigeria....................71-72
Northern Rhodesia....................46-47
Nyasaland Protectorate....................82-83
Pitcairn Islands....................9-10
St. Helena....................128-129
St. Kitts-Nevis....................91-92
St. Lucia....................127-128
St. Vincent....................152-153
Seychelles....................149-150
Sierra Leone....................186-187
Solomon Islands....................80-81
Somaliland Protectorate..........108-109
Trinidad & Tobago....................62-63
Turks & Caicos Islands....................90-91
Virgin Islands....................88-89

The following have different designs but are included in the omnibus set:

Great Britain....................264-265
Offices in Morocco (Tangier)....523-524
Aden
  Kathiri State of Seiyun..............12-13
  Qu'aiti State of Shihr and Mukalla 12-13
Australia....................200-202
Basutoland....................29-31
Bechuanaland Protectorate......137-139
Burma....................66-69
Cook Islands....................127-130
Hong Kong....................174-175
India....................195-198
  Hyderabad....................51-53
New Zealand....................247-257
Niue....................90-93
Pakistan-Bahawalpur....................O16
Samoa....................191-194
South Africa....................100-102
Southern Rhodesia....................67-70
South-West Africa....................153-155
Swaziland....................38-40
Zanzibar....................222-223

Nos. 28-29 (2)	.95	2.50
Nos. 96-97 (2)	.50	*.80*
Nos. 50-51 (2)	.80	*2.00*
Nos. 130-131 (2)	.50	1.40
Nos. 207-208 (2)	.50	1.10
Nos. 131-132 (2)	.55	.55
Nos. 242-243 (2)	1.05	*1.40*
Nos. 127-128 (2)	.50	.50
Nos. 112-113 (2)	.80	.80
Nos. 293-294 (2)	.60	*2.10*
Nos. 156-157 (2)	.90	.70
Nos. 112-113 (2)	.50	.50
Nos. 97-98 (2)	.90	1.35
Nos. 1L9-1L10 (2)	1.30	1.00
Nos. 137-138 (2)	.75	*1.75*
Nos. 144-145 (2)	.50	.95
Nos. 119-120 (2)	.75	*1.00*
Nos. 52-53 (2)	.50	*1.10*
Nos. 128-129 (2)	1.85	*3.75*
Nos. 143-144 (2)	.50	*.95*
Nos. 136-137 (2)	.80	*12.50*
Nos. 90-91 (2)	.65	.65
Nos. 116-117 (2)	.50	1.50
Nos. 206-207 (2)	.65	2.00
Nos. 223-224 (2)	.50	1.05
Nos. 104-105 (2)	.50	.50
Nos. 71-72 (2)	.70	*2.75*
Nos. 46-47 (2)	1.25	*2.00*
Nos. 82-83 (2)	.50	.50
Nos. 9-10 (2)	1.40	1.40
Nos. 128-129 (2)	.65	.70
Nos. 91-92 (2)	.50	.50
Nos. 127-128 (2)	.50	.60
Nos. 152-153 (2)	.50	.50
Nos. 149-150 (2)	.55	.50
Nos. 186-187 (2)	.50	.50
Nos. 80-81 (2)	.50	1.50
Nos. 108-109 (2)	.70	.50
Nos. 62-63 (2)	.50	.50
Nos. 90-91 (2)	.50	.50
Nos. 88-89 (2)	.50	.50
Nos. 264-265 (2)	.50	.50
Nos. 523-524 (2)	1.50	3.00
Nos. 12-13 (2)	.50	.90
Nos. 12-13 (2)	.50	*1.25*
Nos. 200-202 (3)	1.60	*1.25*
Nos. 29-31 (3)	2.10	2.60
Nos. 137-139 (3)	2.05	*4.75*
Nos. 66-69 (4)	1.50	1.25
Nos. 127-130 (4)	2.00	1.85
Nos. 174-175 (2)	6.75	3.15
Nos. 195-198 (4)	5.60	5.50
Nos. 51-53 (3)	1.50	1.70
Nos. 247-257 (11)	3.35	3.65
Nos. 90-93 (4)	1.70	*2.20*
No. O16 (1)	5.50	*7.00*
Nos. 191-194 (4)	2.05	1.00
Nos. 100-102 (3)	1.00	3.25
Nos. 67-70 (4)	1.40	1.75
Nos. 153-155 (3)	1.85	3.25
Nos. 38-40 (3)	2.40	*5.50*
Nos. 222-223 (2)	.65	1.00
Set total (151) Stamps	74.55	114.15

Silver Wedding

King George VI and Queen Elizabeth
CD304 CD305

1948-49

Aden....................30-31
  Kathiri State of Seiyun..............14-15
  Qu'aiti State of Shihr and Mukalla 14-15
Antigua....................98-99
Ascension....................52-53
Bahamas....................148-149
Barbados....................210-211
Basutoland....................39-40
Bechuanaland Protectorate......147-148
Bermuda....................133-134
British Guiana....................244-245
British Honduras....................129-130
Cayman Islands....................116-117
Cyprus....................158-159
Dominica....................114-115
Falkland Islands....................99-100
Falkland Islands Dep............1L11-1L12
Fiji....................139-140
Gambia....................146-147
Gibraltar....................121-122
Gilbert & Ellice Islands....................54-55
Gold Coast....................142-143
Grenada....................145-146
Hong Kong....................178-179
Jamaica....................138-139
Kenya, Uganda, Tanzania............92-93
Leeward Islands....................118-119
Malaya
  Johore....................128-129
  Kedah....................55-56
  Kelantan....................44-45
  Malacca....................1-2
  Negri Sembilan....................36-37
  Pahang....................44-45
  Penang....................1-2
  Perak....................99-100
  Perlis....................1-2
  Selangor....................74-75
  Trengganu....................47-48
Malta....................223-224
Mauritius....................229-230
Montserrat....................106-107
Nigeria....................73-74
North Borneo....................238-239
Northern Rhodesia....................48-49
Nyasaland Protectorate....................85-86
Pitcairn Islands....................11-12
St. Helena....................130-131
St. Kitts-Nevis....................93-94
St. Lucia....................129-130
St. Vincent....................154-155
Sarawak....................174-175
Seychelles....................151-152
Sierra Leone....................188-189
Singapore....................21-22
Solomon Islands....................82-83
Somaliland Protectorate..........110-111
Swaziland....................48-49
Trinidad & Tobago....................64-65
Turks & Caicos Islands....................92-93
Virgin Islands....................90-91
Zanzibar....................224-225

The following have different designs but are included in the omnibus set:

Great Britain....................267-268
  Offices in Morocco (Sp. Curr.) 93-94
  Offices in Morocco (Tangier) 525-526
Bahrain....................62-63
Kuwait....................82-83
Oman....................25-26
South Africa....................106
South-West Africa....................159

Nos. 30-31 (2)	40.40	56.50
Nos. 14-15 (2)	17.85	*16.00*
Nos. 14-15 (2)	18.55	*12.50*
Nos. 98-99 (2)	13.55	*15.75*
Nos. 52-53 (2)	55.55	50.45
Nos. 148-149 (2)	45.25	40.30
Nos. 210-211 (2)	18.35	13.55
Nos. 39-40 (2)	52.80	*55.25*
Nos. 147-148 (2)	42.85	*47.75*
Nos. 133-134 (2)	47.75	*55.25*
Nos. 244-245 (2)	24.25	*28.45*
Nos. 129-130 (2)	25.25	*53.20*
Nos. 116-117 (2)	25.25	*33.50*
Nos. 158-159 (2)	58.50	*78.05*
Nos. 114-115 (2)	25.25	*32.75*
Nos. 99-100 (2)	112.10	76.10
Nos. 1L11-1L12 (2)	4.25	6.00
Nos. 139-140 (2)	18.20	11.50
Nos. 146-147 (2)	21.25	21.25
Nos. 121-122 (2)	61.00	*78.00*
Nos. 54-55 (2)	14.25	*26.25*
Nos. 142-143 (2)	35.25	48.20
Nos. 145-146 (2)	21.75	21.75
Nos. 178-179 (2)	283.50	96.50
Nos. 138-139 (2)	27.85	*60.25*
Nos. 92-93 (2)	50.25	*67.75*
Nos. 118-119 (2)	7.00	8.25
Nos. 128-129 (2)	29.25	*53.25*
Nos. 55-56 (2)	35.25	*50.25*
Nos. 44-45 (2)	35.75	*62.75*
Nos. 1-2 (2)	35.40	*49.75*
Nos. 36-37 (2)	28.10	*38.20*
Nos. 44-45 (2)	28.00	*38.05*
Nos. 1-2 (2)	40.50	37.80

Nos. 99-100 (2)	27.80	*37.75*
Nos. 1-2 (2)	33.50	*58.00*
Nos. 74-75 (2)	30.25	25.30
Nos. 47-48 (2)	32.75	*61.75*
Nos. 223-224 (2)	40.55	45.25
Nos. 229-230 (2)	17.75	*45.25*
Nos. 106-107 (2)	8.75	*17.25*
Nos. 73-74 (2)	17.85	*22.80*
Nos. 238-239 (2)	35.30	*45.75*
Nos. 48-49 (2)	100.30	90.25
Nos. 85-86 (2)	18.25	*30.25*
Nos. 11-12 (2)	44.75	48.50
Nos. 130-131 (2)	32.80	*42.80*
Nos. 93-94 (2)	11.25	10.50
Nos. 129-130 (2)	22.25	*45.25*
Nos. 154-155 (2)	27.75	*30.25*
Nos. 174-175 (2)	50.40	*52.90*
Nos. 151-152 (2)	16.25	*48.25*
Nos. 188-189 (2)	25.25	*29.75*
Nos. 21-22 (2)	116.00	45.40
Nos. 82-83 (2)	13.40	13.40
Nos. 110-111 (2)	8.40	*8.75*
Nos. 48-49 (2)	40.30	*47.75*
Nos. 64-65 (2)	32.75	*38.25*
Nos. 92-93 (2)	11.25	*16.25*
Nos. 90-91 (2)	16.25	22.25
Nos. 224-225 (2)	29.60	38.00
Nos. 267-268 (2)	30.40	25.25
Nos. 93-94 (2)	20.10	25.35
Nos. 525-526 (2)	23.10	29.25
Nos. 62-63 (2)	38.50	*57.75*
Nos. 82-83 (2)	45.50	45.50
Nos. 25-26 (2)	41.00	*42.50*
No. 106 (1)	.80	1.00
No. 159 (1)	1.10	.35
Set total (136) Stamps	2,463.	2,686.

U.P.U.

Mercury and Symbols of Communications — CD306

Plane, Ship and Hemispheres — CD307

Mercury Scattering Letters over Globe CD308

U.P.U. Monument, Bern CD309

Universal Postal Union, 75th anniversary.

1949

Aden 32-35
Kathiri State of Seiyun 16-19
Qu'aiti State of Shihr and Mukalla 16-19
Antigua 100-103
Ascension 57-60
Bahamas 150-153
Barbados 212-215
Basutoland 41-44
Bechuanaland Protectorate 149-152
Bermuda 138-141
British Guiana 246-249
British Honduras 137-140
Brunei 79-82
Cayman Islands 118-121
Cyprus 160-163
Dominica 116-119
Falkland Islands 103-106
Falkland Islands Dep. 1L14-1L17
Fiji 141-144
Gambia 148-151
Gibraltar 123-126
Gilbert & Ellice Islands 56-59
Gold Coast 144-147
Grenada 147-150
Hong Kong 180-183
Jamaica 142-145
Kenya, Uganda, Tanzania 94-97
Leeward Islands 126-129
Malaya
Johore 151-154
Kedah 57-60
Kelantan 46-49
Malacca 18-21
Negri Sembilan 59-62
Pahang 46-49
Penang 23-26
Perak 101-104
Perlis 3-6
Selangor 76-79
Trengganu 49-52
Malta 225-228
Mauritius 231-234
Montserrat 108-111
New Hebrides, British 62-65
New Hebrides, French 79-82
Nigeria 75-78
North Borneo 240-243
Northern Rhodesia 50-53
Nyasaland Protectorate 87-90
Pitcairn Islands 13-16
St. Helena 132-135
St. Kitts-Nevis 95-98
St. Lucia 131-134
St. Vincent 170-173
Sarawak 176-179
Seychelles 153-156
Sierra Leone 190-193
Singapore 23-26
Solomon Islands 84-87
Somaliland Protectorate 112-115
Southern Rhodesia 71-72
Swaziland 50-53
Tonga 87-90
Trinidad & Tobago 66-69
Turks & Caicos Islands 101-104
Virgin Islands 92-95
Zanzibar 226-229

The following have different designs but are included in the omnibus set:

Great Britain 276-279
Offices in Morocco (Tangier) 546-549
Australia 223
Bahrain 68-71
Burma 116-121
Ceylon 304-306
Egypt 281-283
India 223-226
Kuwait 89-92
Oman 31-34
Pakistan-Bahawalpur 26-29, O25-O28
South Africa 109-111
South-West Africa 160-162

Nos. 32-35 (4)	5.85	*8.45*
Nos. 16-19 (4)	2.75	*16.00*
Nos. 16-19 (4)	2.60	8.00
Nos. 100-103 (4)	3.60	*7.70*
Nos. 57-60 (4)	11.10	9.00
Nos. 150-153 (4)	5.35	9.30
Nos. 212-215 (4)	4.40	*14.85*
Nos. 41-44 (4)	4.75	*10.00*
Nos. 149-152 (4)	3.35	*7.25*
Nos. 138-141 (4)	4.75	6.15
Nos. 246-249 (4)	2.75	4.20
Nos. 137-140 (4)	3.30	6.35
Nos. 79-82 (4)	9.50	8.45
Nos. 118-121 (4)	3.60	*7.25*
Nos. 160-163 (4)	4.60	*10.70*
Nos. 116-119 (4)	2.30	5.65
Nos. 103-106 (4)	14.00	17.10
Nos. 1L14-1L17 (4)	14.60	14.50
Nos. 141-144 (4)	3.35	15.75
Nos. 148-151 (4)	2.75	7.10
Nos. 123-126 (4)	5.90	*8.75*
Nos. 56-59 (4)	4.30	*13.00*
Nos. 144-147 (4)	2.55	*10.35*
Nos. 147-150 (4)	2.15	3.55
Nos. 180-183 (4)	57.25	18.25
Nos. 142-145 (4)	2.25	2.45
Nos. 94-97 (4)	2.90	3.40
Nos. 126-129 (4)	3.05	*9.60*
Nos. 151-154 (4)	4.70	8.90
Nos. 57-60 (4)	4.80	12.00
Nos. 46-49 (4)	4.25	12.65
Nos. 18-21 (4)	4.25	*17.30*
Nos. 59-62 (4)	3.50	10.75
Nos. 46-49 (4)	3.00	7.25
Nos. 23-26 (4)	5.10	11.75
Nos. 101-104 (4)	3.65	10.75
Nos. 3-6 (4)	3.95	14.25
Nos. 76-79 (4)	4.90	12.30
Nos. 49-52 (4)	5.55	12.25
Nos. 225-228 (4)	4.50	4.85
Nos. 231-234 (4)	4.35	6.70
Nos. 108-111 (4)	3.30	4.35
Nos. 62-65 (4)	1.60	*4.25*
Nos. 79-82 (4)	24.25	24.25
Nos. 75-78 (4)	2.80	*9.25*
Nos. 240-243 (4)	7.15	6.50
Nos. 50-53 (4)	5.00	*6.50*
Nos. 87-90 (4)	4.05	4.05
Nos. 13-16 (4)	18.50	16.50
Nos. 132-135 (4)	4.85	7.10
Nos. 95-98 (4)	3.35	5.55
Nos. 131-134 (4)	2.55	*3.85*
Nos. 170-173 (4)	2.20	*5.05*
Nos. 176-179 (4)	8.15	10.85
Nos. 153-156 (4)	3.00	5.15
Nos. 190-193 (4)	2.90	*9.15*
Nos. 23-26 (4)	19.00	13.70
Nos. 84-87 (4)	4.05	4.90
Nos. 112-115 (4)	3.95	8.70
Nos. 71-72 (2)	1.95	*2.25*
Nos. 50-53 (4)	2.80	4.65
Nos. 87-90 (4)	3.00	*5.25*
Nos. 66-69 (4)	3.15	3.15
Nos. 101-104 (4)	2.70	4.10
Nos. 92-95 (4)	2.60	5.90
Nos. 226-229 (4)	5.45	13.50
Nos. 276-279 (4)	1.35	1.00
Nos. 546-549 (4)	3.20	*10.15*
No. 223 (1)	.40	.40
Nos. 68-71 (4)	4.75	*16.50*
Nos. 116-121 (6)	7.30	5.35
Nos. 304-306 (3)	3.35	4.25
Nos. 281-283 (3)	5.75	2.70
Nos. 223-226 (4)	27.25	10.50
Nos. 89-92 (4)	6.10	10.25
Nos. 31-34 (4)	8.00	15.75
Nos. 26-29,O25-O28 (8)	2.00	*42.00*
Nos. 109-111 (3)	2.00	2.70
Nos. 160-162 (3)	3.00	5.50
Set total (313) Stamps	462.85	720.30

University

Arms of University College CD310

Alice, Princess of Athlone CD311

1948 opening of University College of the West Indies at Jamaica.

1951

Antigua 104-105
Barbados 228-229
British Guiana 250-251
British Honduras 141-142
Dominica 120-121
Grenada 164-165
Jamaica 146-147
Leeward Islands 130-131
Montserrat 112-113
St. Kitts-Nevis 105-106
St. Lucia 149-150
St. Vincent 174-175
Trinidad & Tobago 70-71
Virgin Islands 96-97

Nos. 104-105 (2)	1.35	*3.75*
Nos. 228-229 (2)	1.75	2.65
Nos. 250-251 (2)	1.10	*1.25*
Nos. 141-142 (2)	1.40	2.20
Nos. 120-121 (2)	1.40	*1.75*
Nos. 164-165 (2)	1.20	*1.60*
Nos. 146-147 (2)	.90	.70
Nos. 130-131 (2)	1.35	4.00
Nos. 112-113 (2)	.85	*2.00*
Nos. 105-106 (2)	.90	2.25
Nos. 149-150 (2)	1.40	1.50
Nos. 174-175 (2)	1.00	*2.15*
Nos. 70-71 (2)	.75	.75
Nos. 96-97 (2)	1.50	*3.75*
Set total (28) Stamps	16.85	30.30

Coronation

Queen Elizabeth II — CD312

1953

Aden 47
Kathiri State of Seiyun 28
Qu'aiti State of Shihr and Mukalla 28
Antigua 106
Ascension 61
Bahamas 157
Barbados 234
Basutoland 45
Bechuanaland Protectorate 153
Bermuda 142
British Guiana 252
British Honduras 143
Cayman Islands 150
Cyprus 167
Dominica 141
Falkland Islands 121
Falkland Islands Dependencies 1L18
Fiji 145
Gambia 152
Gibraltar 131
Gilbert & Ellice Islands 60
Gold Coast 160
Grenada 170
Hong Kong 184
Jamaica 153
Kenya, Uganda, Tanzania 101
Leeward Islands 132
Malaya
Johore 155
Kedah 82
Kelantan 71
Malacca 27
Negri Sembilan 63
Pahang 71
Penang 27
Perak 126
Perlis 28
Selangor 101
Trengganu 74
Malta 241
Mauritius 250
Montserrat 127
New Hebrides, British 77
Nigeria 79
North Borneo 260
Northern Rhodesia 60
Nyasaland Protectorate 96
Pitcairn Islands 19
St. Helena 139
St. Kitts-Nevis 119
St. Lucia 156
St. Vincent 185
Sarawak 196
Seychelles 172
Sierra Leone 194
Singapore 27
Solomon Islands 88
Somaliland Protectorate 127
Swaziland 54
Trinidad & Tobago 84
Tristan da Cunha 13
Turks & Caicos Islands 118
Virgin Islands 114

The following have different designs but are included in the omnibus set:

Great Britain 313-316
Offices in Morocco (Tangier) 579-582
Australia 259-261
Bahrain 92-95
Canada 330
Ceylon 317
Cook Islands 145-146
Kuwait 113-116
New Zealand 280-284
Niue 104-105
Oman 52-55
Samoa 214-215
South Africa 192
Southern Rhodesia 80
South-West Africa 244-248
Tokelau Islands 4

No. 47 (1)	1.25	1.25
No. 28 (1)	.75	*1.50*
No. 28 (1)	1.10	.60
No. 106 (1)	.40	*.75*
No. 61 (1)	1.25	2.75
No. 157 (1)	1.40	.75
No. 234 (1)	1.00	.25
No. 45 (1)	.50	*.60*
No. 153 (1)	.75	.35
No. 142 (1)	.85	.50
No. 252 (1)	.45	.25
No. 143 (1)	.60	.40
No. 150 (1)	.40	*1.75*
No. 167 (1)	1.60	.75
No. 141 (1)	.40	.40
No. 121 (1)	.90	1.50
No. 1L18 (1)	1.80	1.40
No. 145 (1)	1.00	.60
No. 152 (1)	.50	.50
No. 131 (1)	.50	.50
No. 60 (1)	.65	*2.25*
No. 160 (1)	1.00	.25

No. 170 (1)	.30	.25
No. 184 (1)	6.00	.35
No. 153 (1)	.70	.25
No. 101 (1)	.40	.25
No. 132 (1)	1.00	*2.25*
No. 155 (1)	1.40	.30
No. 82 (1)	2.25	.60
No. 71 (1)	1.60	1.60
No. 27 (1)	1.10	*1.50*
No. 63 (1)	1.40	.65
No. 71 (1)	2.25	.25
No. 27 (1)	1.75	.30
No. 126 (1)	1.60	.25
No. 28 (1)	1.75	*4.00*
No. 101 (1)	1.75	.25
No. 74 (1)	1.50	1.00
No. 241 (1)	.50	.25
No. 250 (1)	1.00	.25
No. 127 (1)	.60	.45
No. 77 (1)	.75	.60
No. 79 (1)	.45	.25
No. 260 (1)	1.75	1.00
No. 60 (1)	.70	.25
No. 96 (1)	.75	.75
No. 19 (1)	2.25	2.25
No. 139 (1)	1.25	1.25
No. 119 (1)	.35	.25
No. 156 (1)	.70	.35
No. 185 (1)	.50	.30
No. 196 (1)	2.00	*1.75*
No. 172 (1)	.80	.80
No. 194 (1)	.40	.40
No. 27 (1)	2.50	.40
No. 88 (1)	1.00	1.00
No. 127 (1)	.40	.25
No. 54 (1)	.30	.25
No. 84 (1)	.25	.25
No. 13 (1)	1.00	1.75
No. 118 (1)	.40	*1.10*
No. 114 (1)	.40	*1.00*
Nos. 313-316 (4)	16.35	5.95
Nos. 579-582 (4)	7.40	5.20
Nos. 259-261 (3)	3.60	2.75
Nos. 92-95 (4)	15.25	12.75
No. 330 (1)	.25	.25
No. 317 (1)	1.40	.25
Nos. 145-146 (2)	2.65	2.65
Nos. 113-116 (4)	16.00	8.50
Nos. 280-284 (5)	1.35	*2.00*
Nos. 104-105 (2)	1.60	1.60
Nos. 52-55 (4)	14.25	6.50
Nos. 214-215 (2)	2.50	.80
No. 192 (1)	.45	.30
No. 80 (1)	7.25	7.25
Nos. 244-248 (5)	3.00	2.35
No. 4 (1)	2.75	2.75
Set total (106) Stamps	162.85	112.90

Separate designs for each country for the visit of Queen Elizabeth II and the Duke of Edinburgh.

Royal Visit 1953

1953

Aden 62
Australia 267-269
Bermuda 163
Ceylon 318
Fiji 146
Gibraltar 146
Jamaica 154
Kenya, Uganda, Tanzania 102
Malta 242
New Zealand 286-287

No. 62 (1)	.65	4.00
Nos. 267-269 (3)	2.75	2.05
No. 163 (1)	.50	.25
No. 318 (1)	1.00	.25
No. 146 (1)	.65	.35
No. 146 (1)	.50	.30
No. 154 (1)	.50	.25
No. 102 (1)	.50	.25
No. 242 (1)	.35	.25
Nos. 286-287 (2)	.50	.50
Set total (13) Stamps	7.90	8.45

West Indies Federation

Map of the Caribbean CD313

Federation of the West Indies, April 22, 1958.

1958

Antigua 122-124
Barbados 248-250
Dominica 161-163
Grenada 184-186
Jamaica 175-177
Montserrat 143-145
St. Kitts-Nevis 136-138
St. Lucia 170-172
St. Vincent 198-200
Trinidad & Tobago 86-88

Nos. 122-124 (3)	5.80	3.80
Nos. 248-250 (3)	1.60	*2.90*
Nos. 161-163 (3)	1.95	1.85
Nos. 184-186 (3)	1.50	1.20
Nos. 175-177 (3)	2.65	3.45
Nos. 143-145 (3)	2.35	1.35
Nos. 136-138 (3)	3.00	3.10
Nos. 170-172 (3)	2.05	2.80
Nos. 198-200 (3)	1.50	1.75
Nos. 86-88 (3)	.75	.90
Set total (30) Stamps	23.15	23.10

Freedom from Hunger

Protein Food CD314

U.N. Food and Agricultural Organization's "Freedom from Hunger" campaign.

1963

Aden 65
Antigua 133
Ascension 89
Bahamas 180
Basutoland 83
Bechuanaland Protectorate 194
Bermuda 192
British Guiana 271
British Honduras 179
Brunei 100
Cayman Islands 168
Dominica 181
Falkland Islands 146
Fiji 198
Gambia 172
Gibraltar 161
Gilbert & Ellice Islands 76
Grenada 190
Hong Kong 218
Malta 291
Mauritius 270
Montserrat 150
New Hebrides, British 93
North Borneo 296
Pitcairn Islands 35
St. Helena 173
St. Lucia 179
St. Vincent 201
Sarawak 212
Seychelles 213
Solomon Islands 109
Swaziland 108
Tonga 127
Tristan da Cunha 68
Turks & Caicos Islands 138
Virgin Islands 140
Zanzibar 280

No. 65 (1)	1.50	1.75
No. 133 (1)	.35	.35
No. 89 (1)	1.00	.50
No. 180 (1)	.65	.65
No. 83 (1)	.50	.25
No. 194 (1)	.50	.50
No. 192 (1)	1.00	.50
No. 271 (1)	.45	.25
No. 179 (1)	.60	.25
No. 100 (1)	3.25	2.25
No. 168 (1)	.55	.30
No. 181 (1)	.30	.30
No. 146 (1)	10.50	2.50
No. 198 (1)	3.50	2.25
No. 172 (1)	.50	.25
No. 161 (1)	4.00	2.25
No. 76 (1)	1.40	.40
No. 190 (1)	.30	.25
No. 218 (1)	47.50	7.50
No. 291 (1)	2.00	2.00
No. 270 (1)	.50	.50
No. 150 (1)	.55	.35
No. 93 (1)	.60	.25
No. 296 (1)	1.90	.75
No. 35 (1)	10.00	4.50
No. 173 (1)	2.25	1.10
No. 179 (1)	.40	.40
No. 201 (1)	.90	.50
No. 212 (1)	1.60	*1.75*
No. 213 (1)	.85	.35
No. 109 (1)	3.00	.85
No. 108 (1)	.50	.50
No. 127 (1)	.60	.35
No. 68 (1)	.75	.35
No. 138 (1)	.50	.25
No. 140 (1)	.50	.50
No. 280 (1)	1.50	.80
Set total (37) Stamps	107.25	39.30

Red Cross Centenary

Red Cross and Elizabeth II CD315

1963

Antigua 134-135
Ascension 90-91
Bahamas 183-184
Basutoland 84-85
Bechuanaland Protectorate 195-196
Bermuda 193-194
British Guiana 272-273
British Honduras 180-181
Cayman Islands 169-170
Dominica 182-183
Falkland Islands 147-148
Fiji 203-204
Gambia 173-174
Gibraltar 162-163
Gilbert & Ellice Islands 77-78
Grenada 191-192
Hong Kong 219-220
Jamaica 203-204
Malta 292-293
Mauritius 271-272
Montserrat 151-152
New Hebrides, British 94-95
Pitcairn Islands 36-37
St. Helena 174-175
St. Kitts-Nevis 143-144
St. Lucia 180-181
St. Vincent 202-203
Seychelles 214-215
Solomon Islands 110-111
South Arabia 1-2
Swaziland 109-110
Tonga 134-135
Tristan da Cunha 69-70
Turks & Caicos Islands 139-140
Virgin Islands 141-142

Nos. 134-135 (2)	1.00	*2.00*
Nos. 90-91 (2)	6.75	3.35
Nos. 183-184 (2)	2.30	2.80
Nos. 84-85 (2)	1.20	.90
Nos. 195-196 (2)	.95	.85
Nos. 193-194 (2)	3.00	2.80
Nos. 272-273 (2)	.85	.60
Nos. 180-181 (2)	1.00	2.50
Nos. 169-170 (2)	1.10	*3.00*
Nos. 182-183 (2)	.70	*1.05*
Nos. 147-148 (2)	18.00	5.50
Nos. 203-204 (2)	3.25	2.80
Nos. 173-174 (2)	.75	1.00
Nos. 162-163 (2)	6.25	5.40
Nos. 77-78 (2)	2.00	*3.50*
Nos. 191-192 (2)	.80	.50
Nos. 219-220 (2)	35.00	7.35
Nos. 203-204 (2)	.75	*1.65*
Nos. 292-293 (2)	2.50	4.75
Nos. 271-272 (2)	.90	.90
Nos. 151-152 (2)	1.00	.75
Nos. 94-95 (2)	1.00	.50
Nos. 36-37 (2)	6.50	5.50
Nos. 174-175 (2)	1.70	2.30
Nos. 143-144 (2)	.90	.90
Nos. 180-181 (2)	1.25	1.25
Nos. 202-203 (2)	.90	.90
Nos. 214-215 (2)	1.00	1.50
Nos. 110-111 (2)	1.25	1.15
Nos. 1-2 (2)	1.25	1.25
Nos. 109-110 (2)	1.10	1.10
Nos. 134-135 (2)	1.00	1.25
Nos. 69-70 (2)	1.15	.80
Nos. 139-140 (2)	.85	.75
Nos. 141-142 (2)	.80	1.25
Set total (70) Stamps	110.70	74.35

Shakespeare

Shakespeare Memorial Theatre, Stratford-on-Avon — CD316

400th anniversary of the birth of William Shakespeare.

1964

Antigua 151
Bahamas 201
Bechuanaland Protectorate 197
Cayman Islands 171
Dominica 184
Falkland Islands 149
Gambia 192
Gibraltar 164
Montserrat 153
St. Lucia 196
Turks & Caicos Islands 141
Virgin Islands 143

No. 151 (1)	.35	.25
No. 201 (1)	.60	.35
No. 197 (1)	.35	.35
No. 171 (1)	.35	.30
No. 184 (1)	.35	.35
No. 149 (1)	1.60	.50
No. 192 (1)	.35	.25
No. 164 (1)	.65	.55
No. 153 (1)	.35	.25
No. 196 (1)	.45	.25
No. 141 (1)	.40	.25
No. 143 (1)	.45	.45
Set total (12) Stamps	6.25	4.10

ITU

ITU Emblem CD317

Intl. Telecommunication Union, cent.

1965

Antigua 153-154
Ascension 92-93
Bahamas 219-220
Barbados 265-266
Basutoland 101-102
Bechuanaland Protectorate 202-203
Bermuda 196-197
British Guiana 293-294
British Honduras 187-188
Brunei 116-117
Cayman Islands 172-173
Dominica 185-186
Falkland Islands 154-155
Fiji 211-212
Gibraltar 167-168
Gilbert & Ellice Islands 87-88
Grenada 205-206
Hong Kong 221-222
Mauritius 291-292
Montserrat 157-158
New Hebrides, British 108-109
Pitcairn Islands 52-53
St. Helena 180-181
St. Kitts-Nevis 163-164
St. Lucia 197-198
St. Vincent 224-225
Seychelles 218-219
Solomon Islands 126-127
Swaziland 115-116
Tristan da Cunha 85-86
Turks & Caicos Islands 142-143
Virgin Islands 159-160

Nos. 153-154 (2)	1.45	1.35
Nos. 92-93 (2)	1.90	1.30
Nos. 219-220 (2)	1.35	1.50
Nos. 265-266 (2)	1.50	1.25
Nos. 101-102 (2)	.85	.65
Nos. 202-203 (2)	1.10	.75
Nos. 196-197 (2)	2.15	*2.25*
Nos. 293-294 (2)	.50	.50
Nos. 187-188 (2)	.75	.75
Nos. 116-117 (2)	1.75	1.75
Nos. 172-173 (2)	1.00	.85
Nos. 185-186 (2)	.55	.55
Nos. 154-155 (2)	6.75	3.15
Nos. 211-212 (2)	2.00	1.05
Nos. 167-168 (2)	9.00	5.95
Nos. 87-88 (2)	.85	.60
Nos. 205-206 (2)	.50	.25
Nos. 221-222 (2)	24.50	3.80
Nos. 291-292 (2)	1.20	.65
Nos. 157-158 (2)	1.05	1.15
Nos. 108-109 (2)	.65	.50
Nos. 52-53 (2)	6.25	4.30
Nos. 180-181 (2)	.80	.60
Nos. 163-164 (2)	.60	.60
Nos. 197-198 (2)	1.25	1.25
Nos. 224-225 (2)	.80	.90
Nos. 218-219 (2)	.75	.60
Nos. 126-127 (2)	.70	.55
Nos. 115-116 (2)	.70	.70
Nos. 85-86 (2)	1.00	.65
Nos. 142-143 (2)	.75	.50
Nos. 159-160 (2)	.85	.85
Set total (64) Stamps	75.80	42.30

Intl. Cooperation Year

ICY Emblem CD318

1965

Antigua	155-156
Ascension	94-95
Bahamas	222-223
Basutoland	103-104
Bechuanaland Protectorate	204-205
Bermuda	199-200
British Guiana	295-296
British Honduras	189-190
Brunei	118-119
Cayman Islands	174-175
Dominica	187-188
Falkland Islands	156-157
Fiji	213-214
Gibraltar	169-170
Gilbert & Ellice Islands	104-105
Grenada	207-208
Hong Kong	223-224
Mauritius	293-294
Montserrat	176-177
New Hebrides, British	110-111
New Hebrides, French	126-127
Pitcairn Islands	54-55
St. Helena	182-183
St. Kitts-Nevis	165-166
St. Lucia	199-200
Seychelles	220-221
Solomon Islands	143-144
South Arabia	17-18
Swaziland	117-118
Tristan da Cunha	87-88
Turks & Caicos Islands	144-145
Virgin Islands	161-162

Nos. 155-156 (2)	.55	.50
Nos. 94-95 (2)	1.30	1.40
Nos. 222-223 (2)	.65	1.90
Nos. 103-104 (2)	.75	.85
Nos. 204-205 (2)	.85	1.00
Nos. 199-200 (2)	2.05	1.25
Nos. 295-296 (2)	.55	.50
Nos. 189-190 (2)	.60	.55
Nos. 118-119 (2)	.85	.85
Nos. 174-175 (2)	1.00	.75
Nos. 187-188 (2)	.55	.55
Nos. 156-157 (2)	6.00	1.65
Nos. 213-214 (2)	1.95	1.25
Nos. 169-170 (2)	1.25	*2.75*
Nos. 104-105 (2)	.85	.60
Nos. 207-208 (2)	.50	.50
Nos. 223-224 (2)	22.00	3.10
Nos. 293-294 (2)	.70	.70
Nos. 176-177 (2)	.80	.65
Nos. 110-111 (2)	.50	.50
Nos. 126-127 (2)	12.00	12.00
Nos. 54-55 (2)	6.35	4.50
Nos. 182-183 (2)	.95	.50
Nos. 165-166 (2)	.80	.60
Nos. 199-200 (2)	.55	.55
Nos. 220-221 (2)	.80	.60
Nos. 143-144 (2)	.70	.60
Nos. 17-18 (2)	1.20	.50
Nos. 117-118 (2)	.75	.75
Nos. 87-88 (2)	1.05	.65
Nos. 144-145 (2)	.65	.50
Nos. 161-162 (2)	.65	.50
Set total (64) Stamps	70.70	44.05

Churchill Memorial

Winston Churchill and St. Paul's, London, During Air Attack CD319

1966

Antigua	157-160
Ascension	96-99
Bahamas	224-227
Barbados	281-284
Basutoland	105-108
Bechuanaland Protectorate	206-209
Bermuda	201-204
British Antarctic Territory	16-19
British Honduras	191-194
Brunei	120-123
Cayman Islands	176-179
Dominica	189-192
Falkland Islands	158-161
Fiji	215-218
Gibraltar	171-174
Gilbert & Ellice Islands	106-109
Grenada	209-212
Hong Kong	225-228
Mauritius	295-298
Montserrat	178-181
New Hebrides, British	112-115
New Hebrides, French	128-131
Pitcairn Islands	56-59
St. Helena	184-187
St. Kitts-Nevis	167-170
St. Lucia	201-204
St. Vincent	241-244
Seychelles	222-225
Solomon Islands	145-148
South Arabia	19-22
Swaziland	119-122
Tristan da Cunha	89-92
Turks & Caicos Islands	146-149
Virgin Islands	163-166

Nos. 157-160 (4)	3.05	3.05
Nos. 96-99 (4)	10.00	6.40
Nos. 224-227 (4)	2.30	*3.20*
Nos. 281-284 (4)	3.00	4.95
Nos. 105-108 (4)	2.80	3.25
Nos. 206-209 (4)	2.50	2.50
Nos. 201-204 (4)	4.00	*4.75*
Nos. 16-19 (4)	41.20	18.00
Nos. 191-194 (4)	2.45	1.30
Nos. 120-123 (4)	7.65	6.55
Nos. 176-179 (4)	3.10	3.65
Nos. 189-192 (4)	1.15	1.15
Nos. 158-161 (4)	12.75	9.55
Nos. 215-218 (4)	4.40	3.00
Nos. 171-174 (4)	3.05	5.30
Nos. 106-109 (4)	1.50	1.30
Nos. 209-212 (4)	1.10	1.10
Nos. 225-228 (4)	52.50	11.40
Nos. 295-298 (4)	4.05	4.05
Nos. 178-181 (4)	1.60	1.55
Nos. 112-115 (4)	2.30	1.00
Nos. 128-131 (4)	10.25	10.25
Nos. 56-59 (4)	11.00	6.75
Nos. 184-187 (4)	1.85	1.95
Nos. 167-170 (4)	1.50	1.70
Nos. 201-204 (4)	1.50	1.50
Nos. 241-244 (4)	1.50	1.75
Nos. 222-225 (4)	3.20	4.35
Nos. 145-148 (4)	1.50	1.60
Nos. 19-22 (4)	2.95	2.20
Nos. 119-122 (4)	1.70	2.55
Nos. 89-92 (4)	5.95	2.70
Nos. 146-149 (4)	1.60	1.75
Nos. 163-166 (4)	1.90	1.90
Set total (136) Stamps	212.85	137.95

Royal Visit, 1966

Queen Elizabeth II and Prince Philip CD320

Caribbean visit, Feb. 4 - Mar. 6, 1966.

1966

Antigua	161-162
Bahamas	228-229
Barbados	285-286
British Guiana	299-300
Cayman Islands	180-181
Dominica	193-194
Grenada	213-214
Montserrat	182-183
St. Kitts-Nevis	171-172
St. Lucia	205-206
St. Vincent	245-246
Turks & Caicos Islands	150-151
Virgin Islands	167-168

Nos. 161-162 (2)	3.50	2.60
Nos. 228-229 (2)	3.05	3.05
Nos. 285-286 (2)	3.00	2.00
Nos. 299-300 (2)	2.35	.85
Nos. 180-181 (2)	3.45	1.80
Nos. 193-194 (2)	3.00	.60
Nos. 213-214 (2)	.80	.50
Nos. 182-183 (2)	2.00	1.00
Nos. 171-172 (2)	.90	.75
Nos. 205-206 (2)	1.50	1.35
Nos. 245-246 (2)	2.75	1.35
Nos. 150-151 (2)	1.20	.55
Nos. 167-168 (2)	1.75	1.75
Set total (26) Stamps	29.25	18.15

World Cup Soccer

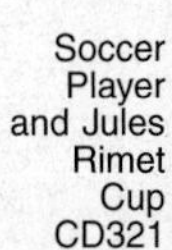

Soccer Player and Jules Rimet Cup CD321

World Cup Soccer Championship, Wembley, England, July 11-30.

1966

Antigua	163-164
Ascension	100-101
Bahamas	245-246
Bermuda	205-206
Brunei	124-125
Cayman Islands	182-183
Dominica	195-196
Fiji	219-220
Gibraltar	175-176
Gilbert & Ellice Islands	125-126
Grenada	230-231
New Hebrides, British	116-117
New Hebrides, French	132-133
Pitcairn Islands	60-61
St. Helena	188-189
St. Kitts-Nevis	173-174
St. Lucia	207-208
Seychelles	226-227
Solomon Islands	167-168
South Arabia	23-24
Tristan da Cunha	93-94

Nos. 163-164 (2)	.80	.85
Nos. 100-101 (2)	2.50	2.00
Nos. 245-246 (2)	.65	.65
Nos. 205-206 (2)	1.75	1.75
Nos. 124-125 (2)	1.30	1.25
Nos. 182-183 (2)	.75	.65
Nos. 195-196 (2)	1.20	.75
Nos. 219-220 (2)	1.70	.60
Nos. 175-176 (2)	1.85	1.75
Nos. 125-126 (2)	.70	.60
Nos. 230-231 (2)	.65	*.95*
Nos. 116-117 (2)	1.00	1.00
Nos. 132-133 (2)	7.00	7.00
Nos. 60-61 (2)	5.50	5.00
Nos. 188-189 (2)	1.25	.60
Nos. 173-174 (2)	.85	.80
Nos. 207-208 (2)	1.15	.90
Nos. 226-227 (2)	.85	.75
Nos. 167-168 (2)	1.10	1.10
Nos. 23-24 (2)	1.90	.55
Nos. 93-94 (2)	1.25	.80
Set total (42) Stamps	35.70	30.30

WHO Headquarters

World Health Organization Headquarters, Geneva — CD322

1966

Antigua	165-166
Ascension	102-103
Bahamas	247-248
Brunei	126-127
Cayman Islands	184-185
Dominica	197-198
Fiji	224-225
Gibraltar	180-181
Gilbert & Ellice Islands	127-128
Grenada	232-233
Hong Kong	229-230
Montserrat	184-185
New Hebrides, British	118-119
New Hebrides, French	134-135
Pitcairn Islands	62-63
St. Helena	190-191
St. Kitts-Nevis	177-178
St. Lucia	209-210
St. Vincent	247-248
Seychelles	228-229
Solomon Islands	169-170
South Arabia	25-26
Tristan da Cunha	99-100

Nos. 165-166 (2)	1.15	.55
Nos. 102-103 (2)	6.60	3.35
Nos. 247-248 (2)	.80	.80
Nos. 126-127 (2)	1.35	1.35
Nos. 184-185 (2)	2.25	1.20
Nos. 197-198 (2)	.75	.75
Nos. 224-225 (2)	4.70	3.30
Nos. 180-181 (2)	6.50	4.50
Nos. 127-128 (2)	.80	.70
Nos. 232-233 (2)	.80	.50
Nos. 229-230 (2)	11.25	2.30
Nos. 184-185 (2)	1.00	1.00
Nos. 118-119 (2)	.75	.50
Nos. 134-135 (2)	8.75	8.75
Nos. 62-63 (2)	7.25	6.50
Nos. 190-191 (2)	3.50	1.50
Nos. 177-178 (2)	.60	.60
Nos. 209-210 (2)	.80	.80
Nos. 247-248 (2)	1.15	1.05
Nos. 228-229 (2)	1.25	.65
Nos. 169-170 (2)	.95	.80
Nos. 25-26 (2)	2.10	.70
Nos. 99-100 (2)	1.90	1.25
Set total (46) Stamps	66.95	43.40

UNESCO Anniversary

"Education" — CD323

"Science" (Wheat ears & flask enclosing globe). "Culture" (lyre & columns). 20th anniversary of the UNESCO.

1966-67

Antigua	183-185
Ascension	108-110
Bahamas	249-251
Barbados	287-289
Bermuda	207-209
Brunei	128-130
Cayman Islands	186-188
Dominica	199-201
Gibraltar	183-185
Gilbert & Ellice Islands	129-131
Grenada	234-236
Hong Kong	231-233
Mauritius	299-301
Montserrat	186-188
New Hebrides, British	120-122
New Hebrides, French	136-138
Pitcairn Islands	64-66
St. Helena	192-194
St. Kitts-Nevis	179-181
St. Lucia	211-213
St. Vincent	249-251
Seychelles	230-232
Solomon Islands	171-173
South Arabia	27-29
Swaziland	123-125
Tristan da Cunha	101-103
Turks & Caicos Islands	155-157
Virgin Islands	176-178

Nos. 183-185 (3)	1.90	*2.50*
Nos. 108-110 (3)	11.00	5.80
Nos. 249-251 (3)	2.35	2.35
Nos. 287-289 (3)	2.35	2.15
Nos. 207-209 (3)	3.80	*3.90*
Nos. 128-130 (3)	4.65	5.40
Nos. 186-188 (3)	2.50	1.50
Nos. 199-201 (3)	1.60	.75
Nos. 183-185 (3)	6.50	3.25
Nos. 129-131 (3)	2.50	*2.45*
Nos. 234-236 (3)	1.10	1.20
Nos. 231-233 (3)	69.50	17.50
Nos. 299-301 (3)	2.10	1.50
Nos. 186-188 (3)	2.40	2.40
Nos. 120-122 (3)	1.90	1.90
Nos. 136-138 (3)	7.75	7.75
Nos. 64-66 (3)	7.10	4.75
Nos. 192-194 (3)	5.25	3.65
Nos. 179-181 (3)	.90	.90
Nos. 211-213 (3)	1.15	1.15
Nos. 249-251 (3)	2.30	1.35
Nos. 230-232 (3)	2.40	2.40
Nos. 171-173 (3)	2.00	1.50
Nos. 27-29 (3)	5.50	5.50
Nos. 123-125 (3)	1.40	1.40
Nos. 101-103 (3)	2.00	1.40
Nos. 155-157 (3)	1.05	.90
Nos. 176-178 (3)	1.40	1.30
Set total (84) Stamps	156.35	88.50

Silver Wedding, 1972

Queen Elizabeth II and Prince Philip — CD324

Designs: borders differ for each country.

1972

Anguilla	161-162
Antigua	295-296
Ascension	164-165
Bahamas	344-345
Bermuda	296-297
British Antarctic Territory	43-44
British Honduras	306-307
British Indian Ocean Territory	48-49

Brunei 186-187
Cayman Islands 304-305
Dominica 352-353
Falkland Islands 223-224
Fiji 328-329
Gibraltar 292-293
Gilbert & Ellice Islands 206-207
Grenada 466-467
Hong Kong 271-272
Montserrat 286-287
New Hebrides, British 169-170
New Hebrides, French 188-189
Pitcairn Islands 127-128
St. Helena 271-272
St. Kitts-Nevis 257-258
St. Lucia 328-329
St.Vincent 344-345
Seychelles 309-310
Solomon Islands 248-249
South Georgia 35-36
Tristan da Cunha 178-179
Turks & Caicos Islands 257-258
Virgin Islands 241-242

Nos. 161-162 (2)	1.10	*1.50*
Nos. 295-296 (2)	.50	.50
Nos. 164-165 (2)	.70	.70
Nos. 344-345 (2)	.60	.60
Nos. 296-297 (2)	.50	*.65*
Nos. 43-44 (2)	6.50	5.65
Nos. 306-307 (2)	.80	.80
Nos. 48-49 (2)	2.00	1.00
Nos. 186-187 (2)	.70	.70
Nos. 304-305 (2)	.75	.75
Nos. 352-353 (2)	.65	.65
Nos. 223-224 (2)	1.00	1.15
Nos. 328-329 (2)	.70	.70
Nos. 292-293 (2)	.50	.50
Nos. 206-207 (2)	.50	.50
Nos. 466-467 (2)	.70	.70
Nos. 271-272 (2)	1.70	1.50
Nos. 286-287 (2)	.50	.50
Nos. 169-170 (2)	.50	.50
Nos. 188-189 (2)	1.05	1.05
Nos. 127-128 (2)	.90	.85
Nos. 271-272 (2)	.70	1.20
Nos. 257-258 (2)	.65	.50
Nos. 328-329 (2)	.75	.75
Nos. 344-345 (2)	.55	.55
Nos. 309-310 (2)	.90	.90
Nos. 248-249 (2)	.50	.50
Nos. 35-36 (2)	1.40	1.40
Nos. 178-179 (2)	.70	.70
Nos. 257-258 (2)	.50	.50
Nos. 241-242 (2)	.50	.50
Set total (62) Stamps	30.00	28.95

Princess Anne's Wedding

Princess Anne and Mark Phillips — CD325

Wedding of Princess Anne and Mark Phillips, Nov. 14, 1973.

1973

Anguilla 179-180
Ascension 177-178
Belize 325-326
Bermuda 302-303
British Antarctic Territory 60-61
Cayman Islands 320-321
Falkland Islands 225-226
Gibraltar 305-306
Gilbert & Ellice Islands 216-217
Hong Kong 289-290
Montserrat 300-301
Pitcairn Islands 135-136
St. Helena 277-278
St. Kitts-Nevis 274-275
St. Lucia 349-350
St. Vincent 358-359
St. Vincent Grenadines 1-2
Seychelles 311-312
Solomon Islands 259-260
South Georgia 37-38
Tristan da Cunha 189-190
Turks & Caicos Islands 286-287
Virgin Islands 260-261

Nos. 179-180 (2)	.55	.55
Nos. 177-178 (2)	.60	.60
Nos. 325-326 (2)	.50	.50
Nos. 302-303 (2)	.50	.50
Nos. 60-61 (2)	1.10	1.10
Nos. 320-321 (2)	.50	.50
Nos. 225-226 (2)	.70	.60
Nos. 305-306 (2)	.55	.55
Nos. 216-217 (2)	.50	.50
Nos. 289-290 (2)	2.65	2.00
Nos. 300-301 (2)	.55	.55
Nos. 135-136 (2)	.70	.60
Nos. 277-278 (2)	.50	.50
Nos. 274-275 (2)	.50	.50
Nos. 349-350 (2)	.50	.50
Nos. 358-359 (2)	.50	.50
Nos. 1-2 (2)	.50	.50
Nos. 311-312 (2)	.65	.65
Nos. 259-260 (2)	.70	.70
Nos. 37-38 (2)	.75	.75
Nos. 189-190 (2)	.50	.50
Nos. 286-287 (2)	.50	.50
Nos. 260-261 (2)	.50	.50
Set total (46) Stamps	15.50	14.65

Elizabeth II Coronation Anniv.

CD326

CD327

CD328

Designs: Royal and local beasts in heraldic form and simulated stonework. Portrait of Elizabeth II by Peter Grugeon. 25th anniversary of coronation of Queen Elizabeth II.

1978

Ascension 229
Barbados 474
Belize 397
British Antarctic Territory 71
Cayman Islands 404
Christmas Island 87
Falkland Islands 275
Fiji 384
Gambia 380
Gilbert Islands 312
Mauritius 464
New Hebrides, British 258
New Hebrides, French 278
St. Helena 317
St. Kitts-Nevis 354
Samoa 472
Solomon Islands 368
South Georgia 51
Swaziland 302
Tristan da Cunha 238
Virgin Islands 337

No. 229 (1)	2.00	2.00
No. 474 (1)	1.35	1.35
No. 397 (1)	1.40	1.75
No. 71 (1)	6.00	6.00
No. 404 (1)	2.00	2.00
No. 87 (1)	3.50	*4.00*
No. 275 (1)	4.00	5.50
No. 384 (1)	1.75	1.75
No. 380 (1)	1.50	1.50
No. 312 (1)	1.25	1.25
No. 464 (1)	2.75	2.75
No. 258 (1)	1.75	1.75
No. 278 (1)	3.50	3.50
No. 317 (1)	1.75	1.75
No. 354 (1)	1.00	1.00
No. 472 (1)	2.10	2.10
No. 368 (1)	2.50	2.50
No. 51 (1)	3.00	3.00
No. 302 (1)	1.60	1.60
No. 238 (1)	1.50	1.50
No. 337 (1)	1.80	1.80
Set total (21) Stamps	48.00	50.35

Queen Mother Elizabeth's 80th Birthday

CD330

Designs: Photographs of Queen Mother Elizabeth. Falkland Islands issued in sheets of 50; others in sheets of 9.

1980

Ascension 261
Bermuda 401
Cayman Islands 443
Falkland Islands 305
Gambia 412
Gibraltar 393
Hong Kong 364
Pitcairn Islands 193
St. Helena 341
Samoa 532
Solomon Islands 426
Tristan da Cunha 277

No. 261 (1)	.40	.40
No. 401 (1)	.45	.75
No. 443 (1)	.40	.40
No. 305 (1)	.40	.40
No. 412 (1)	.40	.50
No. 393 (1)	.35	.35
No. 364 (1)	1.10	1.25
No. 193 (1)	.60	.60
No. 341 (1)	.50	.50
No. 532 (1)	.55	.55
No. 426 (1)	.50	.50
No. 277 (1)	.45	.45
Set total (12) Stamps	6.10	6.65

Royal Wedding, 1981

Prince Charles and Lady Diana — CD331

CD331a

Wedding of Charles, Prince of Wales, and Lady Diana Spencer, St. Paul's Cathedral, London, July 29, 1981.

1981

Antigua 623-627
Ascension 294-296
Barbados 547-549
Barbuda 497-501
Bermuda 412-414
Brunei 268-270
Cayman Islands 471-473
Dominica 701-705
Falkland Islands 324-326
Falkland Islands Dep. 1L59-1L61
Fiji 442-444
Gambia 426-428
Ghana 759-764
Grenada 1051-1055
Grenada Grenadines 440-443
Hong Kong 373-375
Jamaica 500-503
Lesotho 335-337
Maldive Islands 906-909
Mauritius 520-522
Norfolk Island 280-282
Pitcairn Islands 206-208
St. Helena 353-355
St. Lucia 543-549
Samoa 558-560
Sierra Leone 509-518
Solomon Islands 450-452
Swaziland 382-384
Tristan da Cunha 294-296
Turks & Caicos Islands 486-489
Caicos Island 8-11
Uganda 314-317
Vanuatu 308-310
Virgin Islands 406-408

Nos. 623-627 (5)	6.55	2.55
Nos. 294-296 (3)	1.00	1.00
Nos. 547-549 (3)	.90	.90
Nos. 497-501 (5)	10.95	10.95
Nos. 412-414 (3)	2.00	2.00
Nos. 268-270 (3)	2.15	*4.50*
Nos. 471-473 (3)	1.20	1.30
Nos. 701-705 (5)	8.35	2.35
Nos. 324-326 (3)	1.65	1.70
Nos. 1L59-1L61 (3)	1.45	1.45
Nos. 442-444 (3)	1.35	1.35
Nos. 426-428 (3)	.80	.80
Nos. 759-764 (9)	6.20	6.20
Nos. 1051-1055 (5)	9.85	1.85
Nos. 440-443 (4)	2.35	2.35
Nos. 373-375 (3)	3.05	2.85
Nos. 500-503 (4)	1.45	1.35
Nos. 335-337 (3)	.90	.90
Nos. 906-909 (4)	1.55	1.55
Nos. 520-522 (3)	2.75	2.75
Nos. 280-282 (3)	1.35	1.35
Nos. 206-208 (3)	1.10	1.10
Nos. 353-355 (3)	.85	.85
Nos. 543-549 (5)	8.50	8.50
Nos. 558-560 (3)	.85	.85
Nos. 509-518 (10)	15.50	15.50
Nos. 450-452 (3)	1.25	1.25
Nos. 382-384 (3)	1.30	1.25
Nos. 294-296 (3)	.90	.90
Nos. 486-489 (4)	2.20	2.20
Nos. 8-11 (4)	5.00	5.00
Nos. 314-317 (4)	3.30	3.00
Nos. 308-310 (3)	1.15	1.15
Nos. 406-408 (3)	1.10	1.10
Set total (131) Stamps	110.80	94.65

Princess Diana

CD332

CD333

Designs: Photographs and portrait of Princess Diana, wedding or honeymoon photographs, royal residences, arms of issuing country. Portrait photograph by Clive Friend. Souvenir sheet margins show family tree, various people related to the princess. 21st birthday of Princess Diana of Wales, July 1.

1982

Antigua 663-666
Ascension 313-316
Bahamas 510-513
Barbados 585-588
Barbuda 544-547
British Antarctic Territory 92-95
Cayman Islands 486-489
Dominica 773-776
Falkland Islands 348-351
Falkland Islands Dep. 1L72-1L75
Fiji 470-473
Gambia 447-450
Grenada 1101A-1105
Grenada Grenadines 485-491
Lesotho 372-375
Maldive Islands 952-955
Mauritius 548-551
Pitcairn Islands 213-216
St. Helena 372-375
St. Lucia 591-594
Sierra Leone 531-534
Solomon Islands 471-474
Swaziland 406-409
Tristan da Cunha 310-313
Turks and Caicos Islands 531-534
Virgin Islands 430-433

Nos. 663-666 (4)	8.25	7.35
Nos. 313-316 (4)	3.50	3.50
Nos. 510-513 (4)	6.00	3.85
Nos. 585-588 (4)	3.40	3.25
Nos. 544-547 (4)	9.75	7.70
Nos. 92-95 (4)	4.25	3.45
Nos. 486-489 (4)	*4.75*	*2.70*
Nos. 773-776 (4)	7.05	7.05
Nos. 348-351 (4)	2.95	2.95
Nos. 1L72-1L75 (4)	2.50	2.60
Nos. 470-473 (4)	3.25	2.95
Nos. 447-450 (4)	2.85	2.85
Nos. 1101A-1105 (7)	16.05	15.55

Nos. 485-491 (7)	17.65	17.65
Nos. 372-375 (4)	4.00	4.00
Nos. 952-955 (4)	5.50	3.90
Nos. 548-551 (4)	5.50	5.50
Nos. 213-216 (4)	2.15	2.15
Nos. 372-375 (4)	2.95	2.95
Nos. 591-594 (4)	9.90	9.90
Nos. 531-534 (4)	7.20	7.20
Nos. 471-474 (4)	2.90	2.90
Nos. 406-409 (4)	3.85	2.25
Nos. 310-313 (4)	3.65	1.45
Nos. 486-489 (4)	2.20	2.20
Nos. 430-433 (4)	3.00	3.00
Set total (110) Stamps	145.00	130.80

250th anniv. of first edition of Lloyd's List (shipping news publication) & of Lloyd's marine insurance.

CD335

Designs: First page of early edition of the list; historical ships, modern transportation or harbor scenes.

1984

Ascension....................351-354
Bahamas....................555-558
Barbados....................627-630
Cayes of Belize....................10-13
Cayman Islands....................522-526
Falkland Islands....................404-407
Fiji....................509-512
Gambia....................519-522
Mauritius....................587-590
Nauru....................280-283
St. Helena....................412-415
Samoa....................624-627
Seychelles....................538-541
Solomon Islands....................521-524
Vanuatu....................368-371
Virgin Islands....................466-469

Nos. 351-354 (4)	2.90	2.55
Nos. 555-558 (4)	4.15	2.95
Nos. 627-630 (4)	6.10	5.15
Nos. 10-13 (4)	2.65	2.65
Nos. 522-526 (5)	9.30	8.45
Nos. 404-407 (4)	3.50	3.65
Nos. 509-512 (4)	5.30	4.90
Nos. 519-522 (4)	4.20	4.30
Nos. 587-590 (4)	8.95	8.95
Nos. 280-283 (4)	2.40	2.35
Nos. 412-415 (4)	2.40	2.40
Nos. 624-627 (4)	2.55	2.35
Nos. 538-541 (4)	5.00	5.00
Nos. 521-524 (4)	4.65	3.95
Nos. 368-371 (4)	2.40	2.40
Nos. 466-469 (4)	4.25	4.25
Set total (65) Stamps	70.70	66.25

Queen Mother 85th Birthday

CD336

Designs: Photographs tracing the life of the Queen Mother, Elizabeth. The high value in each set pictures the same photograph taken of the Queen Mother holding the infant Prince Henry.

1985

Ascension....................372-376
Bahamas....................580-584
Barbados....................660-664
Bermuda....................469-473
Falkland Islands....................420-424
Falkland Islands Dep....................1L92-1L96
Fiji....................531-535
Hong Kong....................447-450
Jamaica....................599-603
Mauritius....................604-608
Norfolk Island....................364-368
Pitcairn Islands....................253-257
St. Helena....................428-432
Samoa....................649-653
Seychelles....................567-571
Zil Elwannyen Sesel....................101-105
Solomon Islands....................543-547
Swaziland....................476-480
Tristan da Cunha....................372-376
Vanuatu....................392-396

Nos. 372-376 (5)	4.65	4.65
Nos. 580-584 (5)	7.70	6.45
Nos. 660-664 (5)	8.00	6.70
Nos. 469-473 (5)	9.40	9.40
Nos. 420-424 (5)	7.35	6.65
Nos. 1L92-1L96 (5)	8.00	8.00
Nos. 531-535 (5)	6.15	6.15
Nos. 447-450 (4)	9.50	8.50
Nos. 599-603 (5)	6.15	7.00
Nos. 604-608 (5)	11.80	11.80
Nos. 364-368 (5)	5.05	5.05
Nos. 253-257 (5)	5.25	5.95
Nos. 428-432 (5)	5.25	5.25
Nos. 649-653 (5)	8.40	7.55
Nos. 567-571 (5)	8.70	8.70
Nos. 101-105 (5)	6.60	6.60
Nos. 543-547 (5)	3.95	3.95
Nos. 476-480 (5)	7.75	7.25
Nos. 372-376 (5)	5.40	5.40
Nos. 392-396 (5)	5.25	5.25
Set total (99) Stamps	140.30	136.25

Queen Elizabeth II, 60th Birthday

CD337

1986, April 21

Ascension....................389-393
Bahamas....................592-596
Barbados....................675-679
Bermuda....................499-503
Cayman Islands....................555-559
Falkland Islands....................441-445
Fiji....................544-548
Hong Kong....................465-469
Jamaica....................620-624
Kiribati....................470-474
Mauritius....................629-633
Papua New Guinea....................640-644
Pitcairn Islands....................270-274
St. Helena....................451-455
Samoa....................670-674
Seychelles....................592-596
Zil Elwannyen Sesel....................114-118
Solomon Islands....................562-566
South Georgia....................101-105
Swaziland....................490-494
Tristan da Cunha....................388-392
Vanuatu....................414-418
Zambia....................343-347

Nos. 389-393 (5)	2.80	3.30
Nos. 592-596 (5)	2.75	*3.70*
Nos. 675-679 (5)	3.25	3.10
Nos. 499-503 (5)	4.65	*5.15*
Nos. 555-559 (5)	4.55	5.60
Nos. 441-445 (5)	3.95	*4.95*
Nos. 544-548 (5)	3.00	3.00
Nos. 465-469 (5)	8.75	6.75
Nos. 620-624 (5)	2.75	2.70
Nos. 470-474 (5)	2.10	2.10
Nos. 629-633 (5)	3.70	3.70
Nos. 640-644 (5)	4.10	4.10
Nos. 270-274 (5)	2.70	2.70
Nos. 451-455 (5)	3.05	3.05
Nos. 670-674 (5)	2.55	2.55
Nos. 592-596 (5)	2.70	2.70
Nos. 114-118 (5)	2.15	2.15
Nos. 562-566 (5)	2.90	2.90
Nos. 101-105 (5)	3.30	3.65
Nos. 490-494 (5)	2.15	2.15
Nos. 388-392 (5)	3.00	3.00
Nos. 414-418 (5)	3.10	3.10
Nos. 343-347 (5)	1.75	1.75
Set total (115) Stamps	75.70	77.85

Royal Wedding

Marriage of Prince Andrew and Sarah Ferguson CD338

1986, July 23

Ascension....................399-400
Bahamas....................602-603
Barbados....................687-688
Cayman Islands....................560-561
Jamaica....................629-630
Pitcairn Islands....................275-276
St. Helena....................460-461
St. Kitts....................181-182
Seychelles....................602-603
Zil Elwannyen Sesel....................119-120
Solomon Islands....................567-568
Tristan da Cunha....................397-398
Zambia....................348-349

Nos. 399-400 (2)	1.60	1.60
Nos. 602-603 (2)	2.75	2.75
Nos. 687-688 (2)	2.00	1.25
Nos. 560-561 (2)	1.70	*2.35*
Nos. 629-630 (2)	1.35	1.35
Nos. 275-276 (2)	2.40	2.40
Nos. 460-461 (2)	1.05	1.05
Nos. 181-182 (2)	1.50	2.25
Nos. 602-603 (2)	2.50	2.50
Nos. 119-120 (2)	2.30	2.30
Nos. 567-568 (2)	1.00	1.00
Nos. 397-398 (2)	1.40	1.40
Nos. 348-349 (2)	1.10	1.30
Set total (26) Stamps	22.65	23.50

Queen Elizabeth II, 60th Birthday

Queen Elizabeth II & Prince Philip, 1947 Wedding Portrait — CD339

Designs: Photographs tracing the life of Queen Elizabeth II.

1986

Anguilla....................674-677
Antigua....................925-928
Barbuda....................783-786
Dominica....................950-953
Gambia....................611-614
Grenada....................1371-1374
Grenada Grenadines....................749-752
Lesotho....................531-534
Maldive Islands....................1172-1175
Sierra Leone....................760-763
Uganda....................495-498

Nos. 674-677 (4)	8.00	8.00
Nos. 925-928 (4)	5.50	6.20
Nos. 783-786 (4)	23.15	23.15
Nos. 950-953 (4)	7.25	7.25
Nos. 611-614 (4)	8.25	7.90
Nos. 1371-1374 (4)	6.80	6.80
Nos. 749-752 (4)	6.75	6.75
Nos. 531-534 (4)	5.25	5.25
Nos. 1172-1175 (4)	6.25	6.25
Nos. 760-763 (4)	5.25	5.25
Nos. 495-498 (4)	8.50	8.50
Set total (44) Stamps	90.95	91.30

Royal Wedding, 1986

CD340

Designs: Photographs of Prince Andrew and Sarah Ferguson during courtship, engagement and marriage.

1986

Antigua....................939-942
Barbuda....................809-812
Dominica....................970-973
Gambia....................635-638
Grenada....................1385-1388
Grenada Grenadines....................758-761
Lesotho....................545-548
Maldive Islands....................1181-1184
Sierra Leone....................769-772
Uganda....................510-513

Nos. 939-942 (4)	7.00	*8.75*
Nos. 809-812 (4)	14.55	14.55
Nos. 970-973 (4)	7.25	7.25
Nos. 635-638 (4)	7.80	7.80
Nos. 1385-1388 (4)	8.30	8.30
Nos. 758-761 (4)	9.00	9.00
Nos. 545-548 (4)	7.45	7.45
Nos. 1181-1184 (4)	8.45	8.45
Nos. 769-772 (4)	5.35	5.35
Nos. 510-513 (4)	9.25	10.00
Set total (40) Stamps	84.40	86.90

Lloyds of London, 300th Anniv.

CD341

Designs: 17th century aspects of Lloyds, representations of each country's individual connections with Lloyds and publicized disasters insured by the organization.

1986

Ascension....................454-457
Bahamas....................655-658
Barbados....................731-734
Bermuda....................541-544
Falkland Islands....................481-484
Liberia....................1101-1104
Malawi....................534-537
Nevis....................571-574
St. Helena....................501-504
St. Lucia....................923-926
Seychelles....................649-652
Zil Elwannyen Sesel....................146-149
Solomon Islands....................627-630
South Georgia....................131-134
Trinidad & Tobago....................484-487
Tristan da Cunha....................439-442
Vanuatu....................485-488

Nos. 454-457 (4)	5.00	5.00
Nos. 655-658 (4)	8.90	4.95
Nos. 731-734 (4)	12.50	8.35
Nos. 541-544 (4)	8.00	*6.60*
Nos. 481-484 (4)	5.45	3.85
Nos. 1101-1104 (4)	4.25	4.25
Nos. 534-537 (4)	11.00	7.85
Nos. 571-574 (4)	8.35	8.35
Nos. 501-504 (4)	8.70	7.15
Nos. 923-926 (4)	9.40	9.40
Nos. 649-652 (4)	12.85	12.85
Nos. 146-149 (4)	11.25	11.25
Nos. 627-630 (4)	7.00	4.45
Nos. 131-134 (4)	6.30	3.70
Nos. 484-487 (4)	10.25	6.35
Nos. 439-442 (4)	7.60	7.60
Nos. 485-488 (4)	5.90	5.90
Set total (68) Stamps	142.70	117.85

Moon Landing, 20th Anniv.

CD342

Designs: Equipment, crew photographs, spacecraft, official emblems and report profiles created for the Apollo Missions. Two stamps in each set are square in format rather than like the stamp shown; see individual country listings for more information.

1989

Ascension....................468-472
Bahamas....................674-678
Belize....................916-920
Kiribati....................517-521
Liberia....................1125-1129
Nevis....................586-590
St. Kitts....................248-252
Samoa....................760-764
Seychelles....................676-680
Zil Elwannyen Sesel....................154-158
Solomon Islands....................643-647
Vanuatu....................507-511

Nos. 468-472 (5)	9.40	8.60
Nos. 674-678 (5)	23.00	19.70
Nos. 916-920 (5)	22.85	18.10
Nos. 517-521 (5)	12.50	12.50
Nos. 1125-1129 (5)	8.50	8.50
Nos. 586-590 (5)	7.50	7.50

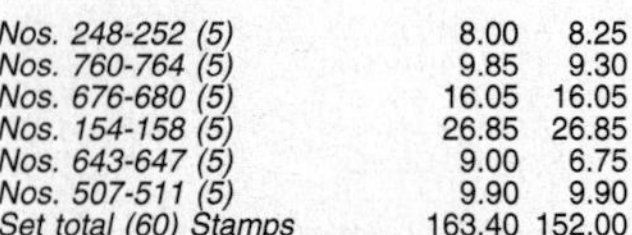

Nos. 248-252 (5)	8.00	8.25
Nos. 760-764 (5)	9.85	9.30
Nos. 676-680 (5)	16.05	16.05
Nos. 154-158 (5)	26.85	26.85
Nos. 643-647 (5)	9.00	6.75
Nos. 507-511 (5)	9.90	9.90
Set total (60) Stamps	163.40	152.00

Queen Mother, 90th Birthday

CD343

CD344

Designs: Portraits of Queen Elizabeth, the Queen Mother. See individual country listings for more information.

1990

Ascension 491-492
Bahamas 698-699
Barbados 782-783
British Antarctic Territory 170-171
British Indian Ocean Territory 106-107
Cayman Islands 622-623
Falkland Islands 524-525
Kenya 527-528
Kiribati 555-556
Liberia 1145-1146
Pitcairn Islands 336-337
St. Helena 532-533
St. Lucia 969-970
Seychelles 710-711
Zil Elwannyen Sesel 171-172
Solomon Islands 671-672
South Georgia 143-144
Swaziland 565-566
Tristan da Cunha 480-481

Nos. 491-492 (2)	4.75	4.75
Nos. 698-699 (2)	5.25	5.25
Nos. 782-783 (2)	4.00	3.70
Nos. 170-171 (2)	6.00	6.00
Nos. 106-107 (2)	18.00	18.50
Nos. 622-623 (2)	4.00	5.50
Nos. 524-525 (2)	4.75	4.75
Nos. 527-528 (2)	7.00	7.00
Nos. 555-556 (2)	4.75	4.75
Nos. 1145-1146 (2)	3.25	3.25
Nos. 336-337 (2)	4.25	4.25
Nos. 532-533 (2)	5.25	5.25
Nos. 969-970 (2)	5.25	5.25
Nos. 710-711 (2)	6.60	6.60
Nos. 171-172 (2)	8.25	8.25
Nos. 671-672 (2)	5.00	5.30
Nos. 143-144 (2)	5.50	6.50
Nos. 565-566 (2)	4.10	4.10
Nos. 480-481 (2)	5.60	5.60
Set total (38) Stamps	111.55	114.55

Queen Elizabeth II, 65th Birthday, and Prince Philip, 70th Birthday

CD345

CD346

Designs: Portraits of Queen Elizabeth II and Prince Philip differ for each country. Printed in sheets of 10 + 5 labels (3 different) between. Stamps alternate, producing 5 different triptychs.

1991

Ascension 506a
Bahamas 731a
Belize 970a
Bermuda 618a
Kiribati 572a
Mauritius 734a
Pitcairn Islands 349a
St. Helena 555a
St. Kitts 319a
Samoa 791a
Seychelles 724a
Zil Elwannyen Sesel 178a
Solomon Islands 689a
South Georgia 150a
Swaziland 587a
Vanuatu 541a

No. 506a (1)	3.50	3.75
No. 731a (1)	4.00	4.00
No. 970a (1)	3.75	3.75
No. 618a (1)	3.50	4.00
No. 572a (1)	4.00	4.00
No. 734a (1)	3.75	3.75
No. 349a (1)	3.25	3.25
No. 555a (1)	2.75	2.75
No. 319a (1)	3.00	3.00
No. 791a (1)	3.75	3.75
No. 724a (1)	5.00	5.00
No. 178a (1)	6.25	6.25
No. 689a (1)	3.75	3.75
No. 150a (1)	4.75	7.00
No. 587a (1)	4.00	4.00
No. 541a (1)	2.50	2.50
Set total (16) Stamps	61.50	64.50

Royal Family Birthday, Anniversary

CD347

Queen Elizabeth II, 65th birthday, Charles and Diana, 10th wedding anniversary: Various photographs of Queen Elizabeth II, Prince Philip, Prince Charles, Princess Diana and their sons William and Henry.

1991

Antigua 1446-1455
Barbuda 1229-1238
Dominica 1328-1337
Gambia 1080-1089
Grenada 2006-2015
Grenada Grenadines 1331-1340
Guyana 2440-2451
Lesotho 871-875
Maldive Islands 1533-1542
Nevis 666-675
St. Vincent 1485-1494
St. Vincent Grenadines 769-778
Sierra Leone 1387-1396
Turks & Caicos Islands 913-922
Uganda 918-927

Nos. 1446-1455 (10)	21.70	20.05
Nos. 1229-1238 (10)	125.00	119.50
Nos. 1328-1337 (10)	30.20	30.20
Nos. 1080-1089 (10)	24.65	24.40
Nos. 2006-2015 (10)	25.45	22.10
Nos. 1331-1340 (10)	23.85	23.35
Nos. 2440-2451 (12)	21.40	21.15
Nos. 871-875 (5)	13.55	13.55
Nos. 1533-1542 (10)	28.10	28.10
Nos. 666-675 (10)	23.65	23.65
Nos. 1485-1494 (10)	26.75	25.90
Nos. 769-778 (10)	25.40	25.40
Nos. 1387-1396 (10)	26.35	26.35
Nos. 913-922 (10)	27.50	25.30
Nos. 918-927 (10)	26.60	26.60
Set total (147) Stamps	470.15	455.60

Queen Elizabeth II's Accession to the Throne, 40th Anniv.

CD348

Various photographs of Queen Elizabeth II with local Scenes.

1992

Antigua 1513-1518
Barbuda 1306-1311
Dominica 1414-1419
Gambia 1172-1177
Grenada 2047-2052
Grenada Grenadines 1368-1373
Lesotho 881-885
Maldive Islands 1637-1642
Nevis 702-707
St. Vincent 1582-1587
St. Vincent Grenadines 829-834
Sierra Leone 1482-1487
Turks and Caicos Islands 978-987
Uganda 990-995
Virgin Islands 742-746

Nos. 1513-1518 (6)	15.00	15.10
Nos. 1306-1311 (6)	125.25	83.65
Nos. 1414-1419 (6)	12.50	12.50
Nos. 1172-1177 (6)	14.95	14.85
Nos. 2047-2052 (6)	15.95	15.95
Nos. 1368-1373 (6)	17.00	15.35
Nos. 881-885 (5)	11.90	11.90
Nos. 1637-1642 (6)	17.55	17.55
Nos. 702-707 (6)	13.55	13.55
Nos. 1582-1587 (6)	14.40	14.40
Nos. 829-834 (6)	19.65	19.65
Nos. 1482-1487 (6)	22.50	22.50
Nos. 913-922 (10)	27.50	25.30
Nos. 990-995 (6)	19.50	19.50
Nos. 742-746 (5)	15.50	15.50
Set total (92) Stamps	362.70	317.25

CD349

1992

Ascension 531-535
Bahamas 744-748
Bermuda 623-627
British Indian Ocean Territory 119-123
Cayman Islands 648-652
Falkland Islands 549-553
Gibraltar 605-609
Hong Kong 619-623
Kenya 563-567
Kiribati 582-586
Pitcairn Islands 362-366
St. Helena 570-574
St. Kitts 332-336
Samoa 805-809
Seychelles 734-738
Zil Elwannyen Sesel 183-187
Solomon Islands 708-712
South Georgia 157-161
Tristan da Cunha 508-512
Vanuatu 555-559
Zambia 561-565

Nos. 531-535 (5)	6.10	6.10
Nos. 744-748 (5)	6.90	4.70
Nos. 623-627 (5)	7.40	7.55
Nos. 119-123 (5)	22.75	19.25
Nos. 648-652 (5)	7.60	6.60
Nos. 549-553 (5)	5.95	5.90
Nos. 605-609 (5)	5.15	5.50
Nos. 619-623 (5)	5.10	5.25
Nos. 563-567 (5)	9.10	9.10
Nos. 582-586 (5)	3.85	3.85
Nos. 362-366 (5)	5.35	5.35
Nos. 570-574 (5)	5.70	5.70
Nos. 332-336 (5)	6.60	5.50
Nos. 805-809 (5)	7.85	5.90
Nos. 734-738 (5)	10.55	10.55
Nos. 183-187 (5)	9.40	9.40
Nos. 708-712 (5)	5.00	5.30
Nos. 157-161 (5)	5.60	5.90
Nos. 508-512 (5)	8.75	8.30
Nos. 555-559 (5)	3.65	3.65
Nos. 561-565 (5)	5.60	5.60
Set total (105) Stamps	153.95	144.95

Royal Air Force, 75th Anniversary

CD350

1993

Ascension 557-561
Bahamas 771-775
Barbados 842-846
Belize 1003-1008
Bermuda 648-651
British Indian Ocean Territory 136-140
Falkland Is. 573-577
Fiji 687-691
Montserrat 830-834
St. Kitts 351-355

Nos. 557-561 (5)	15.60	14.60
Nos. 771-775 (5)	24.65	21.45
Nos. 842-846 (5)	14.15	12.85
Nos. 1003-1008 (6)	16.55	16.50
Nos. 648-651 (4)	9.65	10.45
Nos. 136-140 (5)	16.10	16.10
Nos. 573-577 (5)	10.85	10.85
Nos. 687-691 (5)	17.75	17.40
Nos. 830-834 (5)	14.10	14.10
Nos. 351-355 (5)	22.80	23.55
Set total (50) Stamps	162.20	157.85

Royal Air Force, 80th Anniv.

Design CD350 Re-inscribed

1998

Ascension 697-701
Bahamas 907-911
British Indian Ocean Terr 198-202
Cayman Islands 754-758
Fiji 814-818
Gibraltar 755-759
Samoa 957-961
Turks & Caicos Islands 1258-1265
Tuvalu 763-767
Virgin Islands 879-883

Nos. 697-701 (5)	16.10	16.10
Nos. 907-911 (5)	13.60	12.65
Nos. 136-140 (5)	16.10	16.10
Nos. 754-758 (5)	15.25	15.25
Nos. 814-818 (5)	14.00	12.75
Nos. 755-759 (5)	9.70	9.70
Nos. 957-961 (5)	15.70	14.90
Nos. 1258-1265 (2)	27.50	27.50
Nos. 763-767 (5)	9.75	9.75
Nos. 879-883 (5)	15.00	15.00
Set total (47) Stamps	152.70	149.70

End of World War II, 50th Anniv.

CD351

CD352

1995

Ascension 613-617
Bahamas 824-828
Barbados 891-895
Belize 1047-1050
British Indian Ocean Territory 163-167
Cayman Islands 704-708
Falkland Islands 634-638
Fiji 720-724
Kiribati 662-668
Liberia 1175-1179
Mauritius 803-805
St. Helena 646-654
St. Kitts 389-393
St. Lucia 1018-1022
Samoa 890-894
Solomon Islands 799-803
South Georgia 198-200
Tristan da Cunha 562-566

Nos. 613-617 (5)	21.50	21.50

Nos. 824-828 (5)	22.00	18.70
Nos. 891-895 (5)	14.20	11.90
Nos. 1047-1050 (4)	6.05	5.90
Nos. 163-167 (5)	16.25	16.25
Nos. 704-708 (5)	17.65	13.95
Nos. 634-638 (5)	18.65	17.15
Nos. 720-724 (5)	17.50	14.50
Nos. 662-668 (7)	16.30	16.30
Nos. 1175-1179 (5)	15.25	11.15
Nos. 803-805 (3)	7.50	7.50
Nos. 646-654 (9)	26.10	26.10
Nos. 389-393 (5)	16.40	16.40
Nos. 1018-1022 (5)	14.25	11.15
Nos. 890-894 (5)	15.25	14.50
Nos. 799-803 (5)	14.75	14.75
Nos. 198-200 (3)	14.50	15.50
Nos. 562-566 (5)	20.10	20.10
Set total (91) Stamps	294.20	273.30

UN, 50th Anniv.

CD353

1995

Bahamas 839-842
Barbados 901-904
Belize 1055-1058
Jamaica 847-851
Liberia 1187-1190
Mauritius 813-816
Pitcairn Islands 436-439
St. Kitts 398-401
St. Lucia 1023-1026
Samoa 900-903
Tristan da Cunha 568-571
Virgin Islands 807-810

Nos. 839-842 (4)	7.15	6.40
Nos. 901-904 (4)	7.00	5.75
Nos. 1055-1058 (4)	4.70	4.70
Nos. 847-851 (5)	5.40	5.45
Nos. 1187-1190 (4)	9.65	9.65
Nos. 813-816 (4)	3.90	3.90
Nos. 436-439 (4)	8.15	8.15
Nos. 398-401 (4)	6.15	7.15
Nos. 1023-1026 (4)	7.50	7.25
Nos. 900-903 (4)	9.35	8.20
Nos. 568-571 (4)	13.50	13.50
Nos. 807-810 (4)	7.45	7.45
Set total (49) Stamps	89.90	87.55

Queen Elizabeth, 70th Birthday

CD354

1996

Ascension 632-635
British Antarctic Territory 240-243
British Indian Ocean Territory 176-180
Falkland Islands 653-657
Pitcairn Islands 446-449
St. Helena 672-676
Samoa 912-916
Tokelau 223-227
Tristan da Cunha 576-579
Virgin Islands 824-828

Nos. 632-635 (4)	5.30	5.30
Nos. 240-243 (4)	9.45	8.15
Nos. 176-180 (5)	11.50	11.50
Nos. 653-657 (5)	13.55	11.20
Nos. 446-449 (4)	8.60	8.60
Nos. 672-676 (5)	12.70	12.70
Nos. 912-916 (5)	10.50	10.50
Nos. 223-227 (5)	10.50	10.50
Nos. 576-579 (4)	8.35	8.35
Nos. 824-828 (5)	11.30	11.30
Set total (46) Stamps	101.75	98.10

Diana, Princess of Wales (1961-97)

CD355

1998

Ascension 696
Bahamas 901A-902
Barbados 950
Belize 1091
Bermuda 753
Botswana 659-663
British Antarctic Territory 258
British Indian Ocean Terr. 197
Cayman Islands 752A-753
Falkland Islands 694
Fiji 819-820
Gibraltar 754
Kiribati 719A-720
Namibia 909
Niue 706
Norfolk Island 644-645
Papua New Guinea 937
Pitcairn Islands 487
St. Helena 711
St. Kitts 437A-438
Samoa 955A-956
Seycelles 802
Solomon Islands 866-867
South Georgia 220
Tokelau 252B-253
Tonga 980
Niuafo'ou 201
Tristan da Cunha 618
Tuvalu 762
Vanuatu 718A-719
Virgin Islands 878

No. 696 (1)	5.25	5.25
Nos. 901A-902 (2)	5.30	5.30
No. 950 (1)	6.25	6.25
No. 1091 (1)	5.00	5.00
No. 753 (1)	5.00	5.00
Nos. 659-663 (5)	8.25	8.80
No. 258 (1)	5.50	5.50
No. 197 (1)	5.50	5.50
Nos. 752A-753 (3)	7.40	7.40
No. 694 (1)	5.00	5.00
Nos. 819-820 (2)	5.25	5.25
No. 754 (1)	4.75	4.75
Nos. 719A-720 (2)	4.85	4.85
No. 909 (1)	1.75	1.75
No. 706 (1)	5.50	5.50
Nos. 644-645 (2)	5.25	5.25
No. 937 (1)	6.25	6.25
No. 487 (1)	4.75	4.75
No. 711 (1)	4.25	4.25
Nos. 437A-438 (2)	5.15	5.15
Nos. 955A-956 (2)	7.00	7.00
No. 802 (1)	6.25	6.25
Nos. 866-867 (2)	5.40	5.40
No. 220 (1)	4.50	5.00
Nos. 252B-253 (2)	6.00	6.00
No. 980 (1)	5.75	5.75
No. 201 (1)	6.50	6.50
No. 618 (1)	5.00	5.00
No. 762 (1)	4.00	4.00
Nos. 718A-719 (2)	8.00	8.00
No. 878 (1)	4.50	4.50
Set total (46) Stamps	169.10	170.15

Wedding of Prince Edward and Sophie Rhys-Jones

CD356

1999

Ascension 729-730
Cayman Islands 775-776
Falkland Islands 729-730
Pitcairn Islands 505-506
St. Helena 733-734
Samoa 971-972
Tristan da Cunha 636-637
Virgin Islands 908-909

Nos. 729-730 (2)	4.50	4.50
Nos. 775-776 (2)	4.95	4.95
Nos. 729-730 (2)	14.00	14.00
Nos. 505-506 (2)	7.00	7.00
Nos. 733-734 (2)	5.00	5.00
Nos. 971-972 (2)	5.00	5.00
Nos. 636-637 (2)	7.50	7.50
Nos. 908-909 (2)	7.50	7.50
Set total (16) Stamps	55.45	55.45

1st Manned Moon Landing, 30th Anniv.

CD357

1999

Ascension 731-735
Bahamas 942-946
Barbados 967-971
Bermuda 778
Cayman Islands 777-781
Fiji 853-857
Jamaica 889-893
Kirbati 746-750
Nauru 465-469
St. Kitts 460-464
Samoa 973-977
Solomon Islands 875-879
Tuvalu 800-804
Virgin Islands 910-914

Nos. 731-735 (5)	12.80	12.80
Nos. 942-946 (5)	14.10	14.10
Nos. 967-971 (5)	9.45	8.25
No. 778 (1)	9.00	9.00
Nos. 777-781 (5)	9.25	9.25
Nos. 853-857 (5)	9.25	8.45
Nos. 889-893 (5)	8.30	7.18
Nos. 746-750 (5)	8.85	8.85
Nos. 465-469 (5)	9.25	8.00
Nos. 460-464 (5)	11.35	11.65
Nos. 973-977 (5)	12.60	12.45
Nos. 875-879 (5)	7.50	7.50
Nos. 800-804 (5)	7.45	7.45
Nos. 910-914 (5)	11.75	11.75
Set total (66) Stamps	140.90	136.68

Queen Mother's Century

CD358

1999

Ascension 736-740
Bahamas 951-955
Cayman Islands 782-786
Falkland Islands 734-738
Fiji 858-862
Norfolk Island 688-692
St. Helena 740-744
Samoa 978-982
Solomon Islands 880-884
South Georgia 231-235
Tristan da Cunha 638-642
Tuvalu 805-809

Nos. 736-740 (5)	15.50	15.50
Nos. 951-955 (5)	13.75	12.65
Nos. 782-786 (5)	8.35	8.35
Nos. 734-738 (5)	30.00	28.25
Nos. 858-862 (5)	12.80	13.25
Nos. 688-692 (5)	10.30	10.30
Nos. 740-744 (5)	16.15	16.15
Nos. 978-982 (5)	12.50	12.10
Nos. 880-884 (5)	7.50	7.00
Nos. 231-235 (5)	29.75	30.00
Nos. 638-642 (5)	18.00	18.00
Nos. 805-809 (5)	8.65	8.65
Set total (60) Stamps	183.25	180.20

Prince William, 18th Birthday

CD359

2000

Ascension 755-759
Cayman Islands 797-801
Falkland Islands 762-766
Fiji 889-893
South Georgia 257-261
Tristan da Cunha 664-668
Virgin Islands 925-929

Nos. 755-759 (5)	15.50	15.50
Nos. 797-801 (5)	11.15	10.90
Nos. 762-766 (5)	24.60	22.50
Nos. 889-893 (5)	12.90	12.90
Nos. 257-261 (5)	29.00	28.75
Nos. 664-668 (5)	21.50	21.50
Nos. 925-929 (5)	14.50	14.50
Set total (35) Stamps	129.15	126.55

Reign of Queen Elizabeth II, 50th Anniv.

CD360

2002

Ascension 790-794
Bahamas 1033-1037
Barbados 1019-1023
Belize 1152-1156
Bermuda 822-826
British Antarctic Territory 307-311
British Indian Ocean Territory 239-243
Cayman Islands 844-848
Falkland Islands 804-808
Gibraltar 896-900
Jamaica 952-956
Nauru 491-495
Norfolk Island 758-762
Papua New Guinea 1019-1023
Pitcairn Islands 552
St. Helena 788-792
St. Lucia 1146-1150
Solomon Islands 931-935
South Georgia 274-278
Swaziland 706-710
Tokelau 302-306
Tonga 1059
Niuafo'ou 239
Tristan da Cunha 706-710
Virgin Islands 967-971

Nos. 790-794 (5)	14.10	14.10
Nos. 1033-1037 (5)	15.25	15.25
Nos. 1019-1023 (5)	12.90	12.90
Nos. 1152-1156 (5)	12.65	12.25
Nos. 822-826 (5)	18.00	18.00
Nos. 307-311 (5)	23.00	23.00
Nos. 239-243 (5)	19.40	19.40
Nos. 844-848 (5)	13.25	13.25
Nos. 804-808 (5)	23.00	22.00
Nos. 896-900 (5)	6.65	6.65
Nos. 952-956 (5)	16.65	16.65
Nos. 491-495 (5)	17.75	17.75
Nos. 758-762 (5)	19.50	19.50
Nos. 1019-1023 (5)	14.50	14.50
No. 552 (1)	9.25	9.25
Nos. 788-792 (5)	19.75	19.75
Nos. 1146-1150 (5)	12.25	12.25
Nos. 931-935 (5)	12.40	12.40
Nos. 274-278 (5)	28.00	28.50
Nos. 706-710 (5)	12.50	12.50
Nos. 302-306 (5)	14.50	14.50
No. 1059 (1)	8.50	8.50
No. 239 (1)	8.75	8.75
Nos. 706-710 (5)	18.50	18.50
Nos. 967-971 (5)	16.50	16.50
Set total (113) Stamps	387.50	386.60

Queen Mother Elizabeth (1900-2002)

CD361

2002

Ascension 799-801
Bahamas 1044-1046
Bermuda 834-836
British Antarctic Territory 312-314
British Indian Ocean Territory 245-247
Cayman Islands 857-861
Falkland Islands 812-816
Nauru 499-501
Pitcairn Islands 561-565
St. Helena 808-812
St. Lucia 1155-1159
Seychelles 830
Solomon Islands 945-947
South Georgia 281-285
Tokelau 312-314
Tristan da Cunha 715-717
Virgin Islands 979-983

Nos. 799-801 (3)	8.85	8.85
Nos. 1044-1046 (3)	9.10	9.10
Nos. 834-836 (3)	12.25	12.25
Nos. 312-314 (3)	18.75	18.75
Nos. 245-247 (3)	17.35	17.35
Nos. 857-861 (5)	15.00	15.00
Nos. 812-816 (5)	28.50	28.50
Nos. 499-501 (3)	14.00	14.00
Nos. 561-565 (5)	15.25	15.25
Nos. 808-812 (5)	12.00	12.00
Nos. 1155-1159 (5)	13.00	13.00
No. 830 (1)	6.50	6.50
Nos. 945-947 (3)	9.25	9.25
Nos. 281-285 (5)	19.50	19.50
Nos. 312-314 (3)	11.85	11.85
Nos. 715-717 (3)	16.25	16.25
Nos. 979-983 (5)	23.50	23.50
Set total (63) Stamps	250.90	250.90

Head of Queen Elizabeth II

CD362

2003

Ascension 822
Bermuda 865
British Antarctic Territory 322
British Indian Ocean Territory 261
Cayman Islands 878
Falkland Islands 828
St. Helena 820
South Georgia 294
Tristan da Cunha 731
Virgin Islands 1003

No. 822 (1)	12.50	12.50
No. 865 (1)	50.00	50.00
No. 322 (1)	9.50	9.50
No. 261 (1)	11.00	11.00
No. 878 (1)	14.00	14.00
No. 828 (1)	9.00	9.00
No. 820 (1)	9.00	9.00
No. 294 (1)	8.50	8.50
No. 731 (1)	10.00	10.00
No. 1003 (1)	10.00	10.00
Set total (10) Stamps	143.50	143.50

Coronation of Queen Elizabeth II, 50th Anniv.

CD363

2003

Ascension 823-825
Bahamas 1073-1075
Bermuda 866-868
British Antarctic Territory 323-325
British Indian Ocean Territory 262-264
Cayman Islands 879-881
Jamaica 970-972
Kiribati 825-827
Pitcairn Islands 577-581
St. Helena 821-823
St. Lucia 1171-1173
Tokelau 320-322
Tristan da Cunha 732-734
Virgin Islands 1004-1006

Nos. 823-825 (3)	12.50	12.50
Nos. 1073-1075 (3)	13.00	13.00
Nos. 866-868 (2)	14.25	14.25
Nos. 323-325 (3)	23.00	23.00
Nos. 262-264 (3)	28.00	28.00
Nos. 879-881 (3)	19.25	19.25
Nos. 970-972 (3)	10.00	10.00
Nos. 825-827 (3)	13.50	13.50
Nos. 577-581 (5)	14.40	14.40
Nos. 821-823 (3)	7.25	7.25
Nos. 1171-1173 (3)	8.75	8.75
Nos. 320-322 (3)	17.25	17.25
Nos. 732-734 (3)	16.75	16.75
Nos. 1004-1006 (3)	25.00	25.00
Set total (43) Stamps	222.90	222.90

Prince William, 21st Birthday

CD364

2003

Ascension 826
British Indian Ocean Territory 265
Cayman Islands 882-884
Falkland Islands 829
South Georgia 295
Tokelau 323
Tristan da Cunha 735
Virgin Islands 1007-1009

No. 826 (1)	7.25	7.25
No. 265 (1)	8.00	8.00
Nos. 882-884 (3)	6.95	6.95
No. 829 (1)	13.50	13.50
No. 295 (1)	8.50	8.50
No. 323 (1)	7.25	7.25
No. 735 (1)	6.00	6.00
Nos. 1007-1009 (3)	10.00	10.00
Set total (12) Stamps	67.45	67.45

British Commonwealth of Nations

Dominions, Colonies, Territories, Offices and Independent Members

Comprising stamps of the British Commonwealth and associated nations.

A strict observance of technicalities would bar some or all of the stamps listed under Burma, Ireland, Kuwait, Nepal, New Republic, Orange Free State, Samoa, South Africa, South-West Africa, Stellaland, Sudan, Swaziland, the two Transvaal Republics and others but these are included for the convenience of collectors.

1. Great Britain

Great Britain: Including England, Scotland, Wales and Northern Ireland.

2. The Dominions, Present and Past

AUSTRALIA

The Commonwealth of Australia was proclaimed on January 1, 1901. It consists of six former colonies as follows:

New South Wales
Queensland
South Australia
Victoria
Tasmania
Western Australia

The following islands and territories are, or have been, administered by Australia: Australian Antarctic Territory, Christmas Island, Cocos (Keeling) Islands, Nauru, New Guinea, Norfolk Island, Papua.

CANADA

The Dominion of Canada was created by the British North America Act in 1867. The following provinces were former sepa- rate colonies and issued postage stamps:

British Columbia and Vancouver Island
New Brunswick
Newfoundland
Nova Scotia
Prince Edward Island

FIJI

The colony of Fiji became an independent nation with dominion status on Oct. 10, 1970.

GHANA

This state came into existence Mar. 6, 1957, with dominion status. It consists of the former colony of the Gold Coast and the Trusteeship Territory of Togoland. Ghana became a republic July 1, 1960.

INDIA

The Republic of India was inaugurated on January 26, 1950. It succeeded the Dominion of India which was proclaimed August 15, 1947, when the former Empire of India was divided into Pakistan and the Union of India. The Republic is composed of about 40 predominantly Hindu states of three classes: governor's provinces, chief commissioner's provinces and princely states. India also has various territories, such as the Andaman and Nicobar Islands.

The old Empire of India was a federation of British India and the native states. The more important princely states were autonomous. Of the more than 700 Indian states, these 43 are familiar names to philatelists because of their postage stamps.

CONVENTION STATES

Chamba
Faridkot
Gwalior
Jhind
Nabha
Patiala

FEUDATORY STATES

Alwar
Bahawalpur
Bamra
Barwani
Bhopal
Bhor
Bijawar
Bundi
Bussahir
Charkhari
Cochin
Dhar
Dungarpur
Duttia
Faridkot (1879-85)
Hyderabad
Idar
Indore
Jaipur
Jammu
Jammu and Kashmir
Jasdan
Jhalawar
Jhind (1875-76)
Kashmir
Kishangarh
Kotah
Las Bela
Morvi
Nandgaon
Nowanuggur
Orchha
Poonch
Rajasthan
Rajpeepla
Sirmur
Soruth
Tonk
Travancore
Wadhwan

NEW ZEALAND

Became a dominion on September 26, 1907. The following islands and territories are, or have been, administered by New Zealand:

Aitutaki
Cook Islands (Rarotonga)
Niue
Penrhyn
Ross Dependency
Samoa (Western Samoa)
Tokelau Islands

PAKISTAN

The Republic of Pakistan was proclaimed March 23, 1956. It succeeded the Dominion which was proclaimed August 15, 1947. It is made up of all or part of several Moslem provinces and various districts of the former Empire of India, including Bahawalpur and Las Bela. Pakistan withdrew from the Commonwealth in 1972.

SOUTH AFRICA

Under the terms of the South African Act (1909) the self-governing colonies of Cape of Good Hope, Natal, Orange River Colony and Transvaal united on May 31, 1910, to form the Union of South Africa. It became an independent republic May 3, 1961.

Under the terms of the Treaty of Versailles, South-West Africa, formerly German South-West Africa, was mandated to the Union of South Africa.

SRI LANKA (CEYLON)

The Dominion of Ceylon was proclaimed February 4, 1948. The island had been a Crown Colony from 1802 until then. On May 22, 1972, Ceylon became the Republic of Sri Lanka.

3. Colonies, Past and Present; Controlled Territory and Independent Members of the Commonwealth

Abu Dhabi
Aden
Aitutaki
Alderney
Anguilla
Antigua
Ascension
Australia
Bahamas
Bahrain
Bangladesh
Barbados
Barbuda
Basutoland
Batum
Bechuanaland
Bechuanaland Prot.
Belize
Bermuda
Botswana
British Antarctic Territory
British Central Africa
British Columbia and Vancouver Island
British East Africa
British Guiana

British Honduras
British Indian Ocean Territory
British New Guinea
British Solomon Islands
British Somaliland
Brunei
Burma
Bushire
Cameroons
Canada
Cape of Good Hope
Cayman Islands
Christmas Island
Cocos (Keeling) Islands
Cook Islands
Crete,
British Administration
Cyprus
Dominica
East Africa & Uganda
Protectorates
Egypt
Falkland Islands
Fiji
Gambia
German East Africa
Ghana
Gibraltar
Gilbert Islands
Gilbert & Ellice Islands
Gold Coast
Grenada
Griqualand West
Guernsey
Guyana
Heligoland
Hong Kong
Indian Native States
(see India)
Ionian Islands
Jamaica
Jersey
Jordan
Kenya
Kenya, Uganda & Tanzania
Kiribati
Kuwait
Labuan
Lagos
Leeward Islands
Lesotho
Madagascar
Malawi
Malaya
Federated Malay States
Johore
Kedah
Kelantan
Malacca
Negri Sembilan
Pahang
Penang
Perak
Perlis
Selangor
Singapore
Sungei Ujong
Trengganu
Malaysia
Maldive Islands
Malta
Man, Isle of
Mauritius
Mesopotamia
Montserrat
Mozambique
Muscat
Namibia
Natal
Nauru
Nevis
New Britain
New Brunswick
Newfoundland
New Guinea
New Hebrides
New Republic
New South Wales
New Zealand
Niger Coast Protectorate
Nigeria
Niue
Norfolk Island
North Borneo
Northern Nigeria
Northern Rhodesia
North West Pacific Islands
Nova Scotia
Nyasaland Protectorate
Oman
Orange River Colony
Pakistan
Palestine
Papua New Guinea
Penrhyn Island
Pitcairn Islands
Prince Edward Island
Qatar
Queensland
Rhodesia
Rhodesia & Nyasaland
Ross Dependency
Rwanda
Sabah
St. Christopher
St. Helena
St. Kitts
St. Kitts-Nevis-Anguilla
St. Lucia
St. Vincent
Samoa
Sarawak
Seychelles
Sierra Leone
Singapore
Solomon Islands
Somaliland Protectorate
South Africa
South Arabia
South Australia
South Georgia
Southern Nigeria
Southern Rhodesia
South-West Africa
Sri Lanka
Stellaland
Straits Settlements
Sudan
Swaziland
Tanganyika
Tanzania
Tasmania
Tobago
Togo
Tokelau Islands
Tonga
Transvaal
Trinidad
Trinidad and Tobago
Tristan da Cunha
Trucial States
Turks and Caicos
Turks Islands
Tuvalu
Uganda
United Arab Emirates
Vanuatu
Victoria
Virgin Islands
Western Australia
Zambia
Zanzibar
Zimbabwe
Zululand

POST OFFICES IN FOREIGN COUNTRIES

Africa
East Africa Forces
Middle East Forces
Bangkok
China
Morocco
Turkish Empire

Colonies, Former Colonies, Offices, Territories Controlled by Parent States

Belgium

Belgian Congo
Ruanda-Urundi

Denmark

Danish West Indies
Faroe Islands
Greenland
Iceland

Finland

Aland Islands

France

COLONIES PAST AND PRESENT, CONTROLLED TERRITORIES

Afars & Issas, Territory of
Alaouites
Alexandretta
Algeria
Alsace & Lorraine
Anjouan
Annam & Tonkin
Benin
Cambodia (Khmer)
Cameroun
Castellorizo
Chad
Cilicia
Cochin China
Comoro Islands
Dahomey
Diego Suarez
Djibouti (Somali Coast)
Fezzan
French Congo
French Equatorial Africa
French Guiana
French Guinea
French India
French Morocco
French Polynesia (Oceania)
French Southern & Antarctic Territories
French Sudan
French West Africa
Gabon
Germany
Ghadames
Grand Comoro
Guadeloupe
Indo-China
Inini
Ivory Coast
Laos
Latakia
Lebanon
Madagascar
Martinique
Mauritania
Mayotte
Memel
Middle Congo
Moheli
New Caledonia
New Hebrides
Niger Territory
Nossi-Be
Obock
Reunion
Rouad, Ile
Ste.-Marie de Madagascar
St. Pierre & Miquelon
Senegal
Senegambia & Niger
Somali Coast
Syria
Tahiti
Togo
Tunisia
Ubangi-Shari
Upper Senegal & Niger
Upper Volta
Viet Nam
Wallis & Futuna Islands

POST OFFICES IN FOREIGN COUNTRIES

China
Crete
Egypt
Turkish Empire
Zanzibar

Germany

EARLY STATES

Baden
Bavaria
Bergedorf
Bremen
Brunswick
Hamburg
Hanover
Lubeck
Mecklenburg-Schwerin
Mecklenburg-Strelitz
Oldenburg
Prussia
Saxony
Schleswig-Holstein
Wurttemberg

FORMER COLONIES

Cameroun (Kamerun)
Caroline Islands
German East Africa
German New Guinea
German South-West Africa
Kiauchau
Mariana Islands
Marshall Islands
Samoa
Togo

Italy

EARLY STATES

Modena
Parma
Romagna
Roman States
Sardinia
Tuscany
Two Sicilies
  Naples
  Neapolitan Provinces
  Sicily

FORMER COLONIES, CONTROLLED TERRITORIES, OCCUPATION AREAS

Aegean Islands
  Calimno (Calino)
  Caso
  Cos (Coo)
  Karki (Carchi)
  Leros (Lero)
  Lipso
  Nisiros (Nisiro)
  Patmos (Patmo)
  Piscopi
  Rodi (Rhodes)
  Scarpanto
  Simi
  Stampalia
Castellorizo
Corfu
Cyrenaica
Eritrea
Ethiopia (Abyssinia)
Fiume
Ionian Islands
  Cephalonia
  Ithaca
  Paxos
Italian East Africa
Libya
Oltre Giuba
Saseno
Somalia (Italian Somaliland)
Tripolitania

POST OFFICES IN FOREIGN COUNTRIES

"ESTERO"*
Austria
China
  Peking
  Tientsin
Crete
Tripoli
Turkish Empire
  Constantinople
  Durazzo
  Janina
Jerusalem
Salonika
Scutari
Smyrna
Valona

*Stamps overprinted "ESTERO" were used in various parts of the world.

Netherlands

Aruba
Caribbean Netherlands
Curacao
Netherlands Antilles (Curacao)
Netherlands Indies
Netherlands New Guinea
St. Martin
Surinam (Dutch Guiana)

Portugal

COLONIES PAST AND PRESENT, CONTROLLED TERRITORIES

Angola
Angra
Azores
Cape Verde
Funchal
Horta
Inhambane
Kionga
Lourenco Marques
Macao
Madeira
Mozambique
Mozambique Co.
Nyassa
Ponta Delgada
Portuguese Africa
Portuguese Congo
Portuguese Guinea
Portuguese India
Quelimane
St. Thomas & Prince Islands
Tete
Timor
Zambezia

Russia

ALLIED TERRITORIES AND REPUBLICS, OCCUPATION AREAS

Armenia
Aunus (Olonets)
Azerbaijan
Batum
Estonia
Far Eastern Republic
Georgia
Karelia
Latvia
Lithuania
North Ingermanland
Ostland
Russian Turkestan
Siberia
South Russia
Tannu Tuva
Transcaucasian Fed. Republics
Ukraine
Wenden (Livonia)
Western Ukraine

Spain

COLONIES PAST AND PRESENT, CONTROLLED TERRITORIES

Aguera, La
Cape Juby
Cuba
Elobey, Annobon & Corisco
Fernando Po
Ifni
Mariana Islands
Philippines
Puerto Rico
Rio de Oro
Rio Muni
Spanish Guinea
Spanish Morocco
Spanish Sahara
Spanish West Africa

POST OFFICES IN FOREIGN COUNTRIES

Morocco
Tangier
Tetuan

Dies of British Colonial Stamps

DIE A:

1. The lines in the groundwork vary in thickness and are not uniformly straight.

2. The seventh and eighth lines from the top, in the groundwork, converge where they meet the head.

3. There is a small dash in the upper part of the second jewel in the band of the crown.

4. The vertical color line in front of the throat stops at the sixth line of shading on the neck.

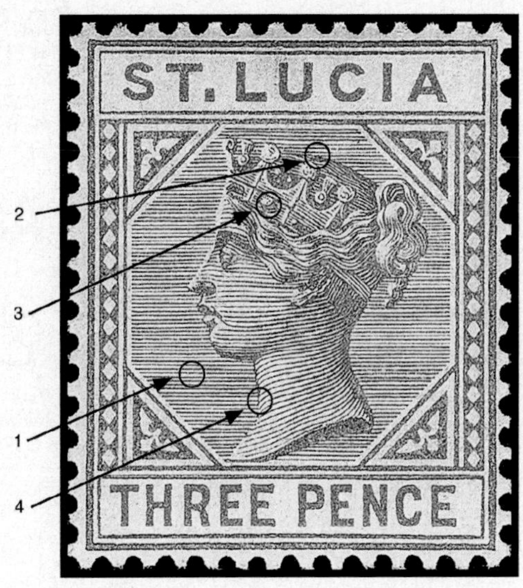

DIE B:

1. The lines in the groundwork are all thin and straight.

2. All the lines of the background are parallel.

3. There is no dash in the upper part of the second jewel in the band of the crown.

4. The vertical color line in front of the throat stops at the eighth line of shading on the neck.

DIE I:

1. The base of the crown is well below the level of the inner white line around the vignette.

2. The labels inscribed "POSTAGE" and "REVENUE" are cut square at the top.

3. There is a white "bud" on the outer side of the main stem of the curved ornaments in each lower corner.

4. The second (thick) line below the country name has the ends next to the crown cut diagonally.

DIE Ia.	DIE Ib.
1 as die II.	1 and 3 as die II.
2 and 3 as die I.	2 as die I.

DIE II:

1. The base of the crown is aligned with the underside of the white line around the vignette.

2. The labels curve inward at the top inner corners.

3. The "bud" has been removed from the outer curve of the ornaments in each corner.

4. The second line below the country name has the ends next to the crown cut vertically.

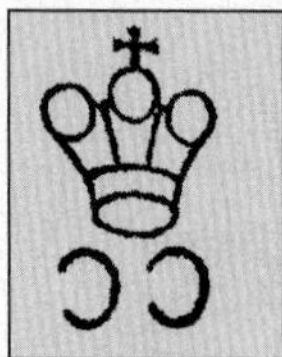
Wmk. 1
Crown and C C

Wmk. 2
Crown and C A

Wmk. 3
Multiple Crown and C A

Wmk. 4
Multiple Crown and Script C A

Wmk. 4a

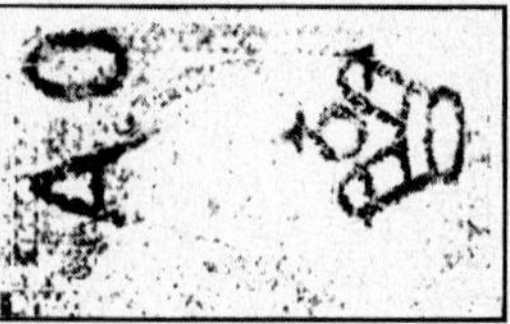
Wmk. 46

Wmk. 314
St. Edward's Crown and C A Multiple

Wmk. 373

Wmk. 384

Wmk. 406

British Colonial and Crown Agents Watermarks

Watermarks 1 to 4, 314, 373, 384 and 406, common to many British territories, are illustrated here to avoid duplication.

The letters "CC" of Wmk. 1 identify the paper as having been made for the use of the Crown Colonies, while the letters "CA" of the others stand for "Crown Agents." Both Wmks. 1 and 2 were used on stamps printed by De La Rue & Co.

Wmk. 3 was adopted in 1904; Wmk. 4 in 1921; Wmk. 46 in 1879; Wmk. 314 in 1957; Wmk. 373 in 1974; Wmk. 384 in 1985; Wmk 406 in 2008.

In Wmk. 4a, a non-matching crown of the general St. Edwards type (bulging on both sides at top) was substituted for one of the Wmk. 4 crowns which fell off the dandy roll. The non-matching crown occurs in 1950-52 printings in a horizontal row of crowns on certain regular stamps of Johore and Seychelles, and on various postage due stamps of Barbados, Basutoland, British Guiana, Gold Coast, Grenada, Northern Rhodesia, St. Lucia, Swaziland and Trinidad and Tobago. A variation of Wmk. 4a, with the non-matching crown in a horizontal row of crown-CA-crown, occurs on regular stamps of Bahamas, St. Kitts-Nevis and Singapore.

Wmk. 314 was intentionally used sideways, starting in 1966. When a stamp was issued with Wmk. 314 both upright and sideways, the sideways varieties usually are listed also – with minor numbers. In many of the later issues, Wmk. 314 is slightly visible.

Wmk. 373 is usually only faintly visible.

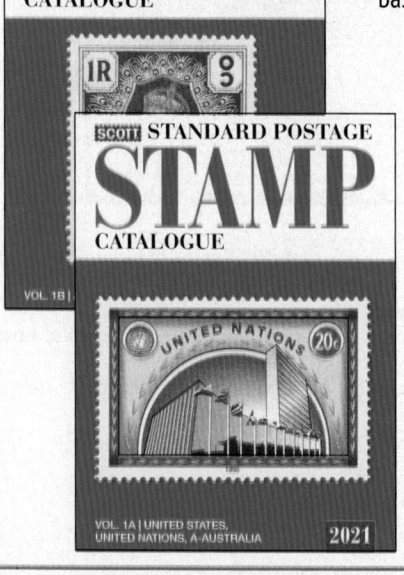

CYPRUS

ˈsī-prəs

LOCATION — An island in the Mediterranean Sea off the coast of Turkey
GOVT. — Republic
AREA — 3,572 sq. mi.
POP. — 754,064 (1999 est.)
CAPITAL — Nicosia

The British Crown Colony of Cyprus became a republic in 1960.

Turkey invaded Cyprus in 1974 resulting in the the northern 40% of the island becoming the Turkish Republic of Northern Cyprus. No other country recognizes this division of the island.

See Turkey in Volume 6.

12 Pence = 1 Shilling
40 Paras = 1 Piaster
9 Piasters = 1 Shilling
20 Shillings = 1 Pound
1000 Milliemes = 1 Pound (1955)
100 Cents = 1 Cyprus Pound (1983)
100 Cents = 1 Euro (2008)

Catalogue values for unused stamps in this country are for Never Hinged items, beginning with Scott 156 in the regular postage section and Scott RA1 in the postal tax section.

Values for unused stamps are for examples with original gum as defined in the catalogue introduction. Very fine examples of Nos. 1, 2 and 7-10 will have perforations touching the design on at least one or more sides due to the narrow spacing of the stamps on the plates and to imperfect perforation methods. Stamps with perfs clear on all four sides are scarce and will command higher prices.

Watermark

Wmk. 344 — Map of Cyprus and KC/K Delta

Queen Victoria — A1

A2 A3

A4 A5

A6 A7

Various Watermarks as in Great Britain (#20, 23, 25, 27 & 29)

1880 Typo. *Perf. 14*

No.	Type	Description	Unused	Used
1	A1	½p rose (P 15)	125.00	115.00
		Plate 12	240.00	*300.00*
		Plate 19	5,750.	950.00
b.		Double overprint (P 15)		*45,000.*
2	A2	1p red (P 216)	24.00	*55.00*
		Plate 217	24.00	*60.00*
		Plate 174	1,500.	1,500.
		Plate 181	525.00	210.00
		Plate 184	22,000.	3,500.
		Plate 193	840.00	
		Plate 196	725.00	
		Plate 201	27.50	*57.50*
		Plate 205	90.00	57.50
		Plate 208	135.00	65.00
		Plate 215	24.00	*57.50*
		Plate 218	32.50	*65.00*
		Plate 220	550.00	475.00
b.		Double overprint (P 218)	5,400.	
		Double overprint (P 208)	*27,500.*	
c.		Pair, one without ovpt. (P 208)	*27,500.*	
3	A3	2½p claret (P 14)	4.50	*19.00*
		Plate 15	8.00	*50.00*
4	A4	4p lt ol grn (P 16)	150.00	*240.00*
5	A5	6p ol gray (P 16)	575.00	*750.00*
6	A6	1sh green (P 13)	900.00	525.00

Black Surcharge

No.	Type	Description	Unused	Used
7	A7	30 paras on 1p red (P 216)	150.00	*95.00*
		Plate 201	180.00	110.00
		Plate 217	210.00	210.00
		Plate 220	175.00	*190.00*
b.		Dbl. surch., one invtd. (P 220)	2,000.	*1,500.*
		Dbl. surch., one invtd. (P 216)	7,750.	

No. 2 Surcharged

18mm Long

1881

No.	Type	Description	Unused	Used
8	A2	½p on 1p (205, 216)	82.50	*100.00*
		Plate 174	250.00	*400.00*
		Plate 181	225.00	*260.00*
		Plate 201	115.00	*140.00*
		Plate 205	85.00	*100.00*
		Plate 208	225.00	*375.00*
		Plate 215	840.00	*1,000.*
		Plate 217	1,000.	900.00
		Plate 218	550.00	*675.00*
		Plate 220	325.00	*450.00*

16mm Long

No.	Type	Description	Unused	Used
9	A2	½p on 1p (P 201)	140.00	*190.00*
		Plate 216	400.00	*460.00*
		Plate 218		*17,500.*
a.		Double surcharge (P 201, 216)	3,750.	3,000.

13mm Long

No.	Type	Description	Unused	Used
10	A2	½p on 1p red (P 215)	52.50	*75.00*
		Plate 205	425.00	
		Plate 217	175.00	110.00
		Plate 218	90.00	*125.00*
c.		Double surcharge (P 215)	550.00	*700.00*
		Double surcharge (P 205)	875.00	
e.		Triple surcharge (P 215)	875.00	
		Triple surcharge (P 205)	*4,750.*	
		Triple surcharge (P 217)	—	
		Triple surcharge (P 218)	*4,750.*	
h.		Quadruple surch. (P 205, 215)	*7,500.*	
j.		"CYPRUS" double (P 218)	*6,000.*	

A8

1881, July Typo. Wmk. 1

No.	Type	Description	Unused	Used
11	A8	½pi emer grn	210.00	52.50
12	A8	1pi rose	425.00	37.50
13	A8	2pi ultramarine	525.00	37.50
14	A8	4pi olive green	1,050.	325.00
15	A8	6pi olive gray	1,900.	500.00

Postage and revenue stamps of Cyprus with "J.A.B." (the initials of Postmaster J.A. Bulmer) in manuscript, or with "POSTAL SURCHARGE" (with or without "J. A. B."), were not Postage Due stamps but were employed for accounting purposes between the chief PO at Larnaca and the sub-offices.

See Nos. 19-25, 28-37. For surcharges see Nos. 16-18, 26-27.

Nos. 1881-1894 Surcharged in Black

1882 Wmk. 1

No.	Type	Description	Unused	Used
16	A8	½pi on ½pi grn	750.00	92.50
17	A8	30pa on 1pi rose	1,750.	140.00
a.		Double surcharge, one inverted	*1,400.*	*850.00*

1884 Wmk. 2

No.	Type	Description	Unused	Used
18	A8	½pi on ½pi grn	190.00	10.00
a.		Double surcharge		*3,200.*

See Nos. 26, 27.

1882-94 Die B

For description of Dies A and B see "Dies of British Colonial Stamps" in Table of Contents.

No.	Type	Description	Unused	Used
19	A8	½pi green	16.00	2.50
20	A8	30pa violet	12.50	*14.00*
21	A8	1pi rose	15.50	11.00
22	A8	2pi blue	15.50	2.10
23	A8	4pi pale ol grn	20.00	*42.50*
24a	A8	6pi	275.00	*800.00*
25a	A8	12pi	190.00	*450.00*
		Nos. 19-25a (7)	544.50	*1,322.*

Die A

No.	Type	Description	Unused	Used
19a	A8	½pi	25.00	3.25
b.		½pi emerald	*6,000.*	525.00
20a	A8	30pa lilac	85.00	30.00
21a	A8	1pi	110.00	4.50
22a	A8	2pi	170.00	4.00
23a	A8	4pi	375.00	40.00
24	A8	6pi olive gray	75.00	21.00
25	A8	12pi brown org	225.00	45.00
		Nos. 19a-25 (7)	1,065.	147.75

Nos. 1881-1894 Surcharged in Black

Type I — Figures "½" 8mm apart.
Type II — Figures "½" 6mm apart.
The space between the fraction bars varies from 5½ to 8½mm but is usually 6 or 8mm.

Black Surcharge Type I

1886 Wmk. 2

No.	Type	Description	Unused	Used
26	A8	½pi on ½pi grn	525.00	17.50
a.		Type II	325.00	100.00
b.		Double surcharge, type II		

Wmk. 1

No.	Type	Description	Unused	Used
27	A8	½pi on ½pi grn	*8,750.*	500.00
a.		Type II	*24,000.*	

No. 27a probably is a proof.

1894-96 Wmk. 2

No.	Type	Description	Unused	Used
28	A8	½pi grn & car rose	5.25	1.75
29	A8	30pa violet & green	5.75	*6.00*
30	A8	1pi rose & ultra	8.50	1.75
31	A8	2pi ultra & mar	19.00	1.75
32	A8	4pi ol green & vio	22.50	17.50
33	A8	6pi ol gray & grn	22.50	*40.00*
34	A8	9pi brown & rose	29.00	*40.00*
35	A8	12pi brn org & blk	25.00	*72.50*
36	A8	18pi slate & brown	60.00	62.50
37	A8	45pi dk vio & ultra	125.00	*165.00*
		Nos. 28-37 (10)	322.50	*408.75*

King Edward VII — A12

1903 Typo.

No.	Type	Description	Unused	Used
38	A12	½pi grn & car rose	16.00	1.40
39	A12	30pa violet & green	26.00	5.50
40	A12	1pi car rose & ultra	42.50	7.50
41	A12	2pi ultra & mar	90.00	18.00
42	A12	4pi ol grn & vio	62.50	27.50
43	A12	6pi ol brn & grn	52.50	*145.00*
44	A12	9pi brn & car rose	125.00	*275.00*
45	A12	12pi org brn & blk	37.50	*87.50*
46	A12	18pi blk & brn	100.00	*175.00*
47	A12	45pi dk vio & ultra	250.00	*600.00*
		Nos. 38-47 (10)	802.00	*1,342.*

1904-07 Wmk. 3

No.	Type	Description	Unused	Used
48	A12	5pa bis & blk ('07)	1.25	2.00
49	A12	10pa org & grn ('07)	6.00	1.90
50	A12	½pi grn & car rose	12.00	1.60
51	A12	30pa redsh vio & grn	21.50	2.75
52	A12	1pi car rose & ultra	17.50	1.10
53	A12	2pi ultra & mar	20.00	2.00
54	A12	4pi ol grn & red vio	32.50	20.00
55	A12	6pi ol brn & grn	32.50	17.00
56	A12	9pi brn & car rose	52.50	9.75
57	A12	12pi org brn & blk	40.00	*67.50*
58	A12	18pi blk & brn	55.00	15.00
59	A12	45pi dk vio & ultra	120.00	*175.00*
		Nos. 48-59 (12)	410.75	*315.60*

King George V — A13

1912

No.	Type	Description	Unused	Used
61a	A13	10pa org yel & br grn ('15)	2.75	1.60
62	A13	½pi grn & car rose	2.90	.35
63	A13	30pa vio & grn	3.25	2.40
64	A13	1pi car & ultra	5.75	1.90
65	A13	2pi ultra & mar	8.50	2.25
66	A13	4pi ol grn & red vio	5.50	*5.25*
67	A13	6pi ol brn & grn	6.00	*11.50*
68	A13	9pi brn & car rose	42.50	28.00
69	A13	12pi org brn & blk	25.00	*57.50*
70	A13	18pi blk & brn	50.00	*50.00*
71	A13	45pi dl vio & ultra	130.00	*170.00*
		Nos. 61a-71 (11)	282.15	330.75

1921-23 Wmk. 4

No.	Type	Description	Unused	Used
72	A13	10pa org & grn	16.00	13.50
73	A13	10pa gray & yel	16.00	9.50
74	A13	30pa violet & grn	3.75	2.00
75	A13	30pa green	9.00	1.75
76	A13	1pi rose & ultra	26.00	*45.00*
77	A13	1pi violet & car	4.00	5.00
78	A13	1½pi org & blk	12.50	7.25
79	A13	2pi ultra & red vio	35.00	25.00
80	A13	2pi rose & ultra	16.00	*27.50*
81	A13	2¾pi ultra & red vio	11.00	*12.00*
82	A13	4pi ol grn & red vio	19.00	*26.00*
83	A13	6pi ol brn & grn	37.50	*80.00*
84	A13	9pi brn & car	47.50	*95.00*
85	A13	18pi black & brn	90.00	*175.00*
86	A13	45pi dl vio & ultra	275.00	*325.00*
		Nos. 72-86 (15)	618.25	*849.50*

Wmk. 3

No.	Type	Description	Unused	Used
87	A13	10sh grn & red, *yel*	425.00	*900.00*
88	A13	£1 vio & blk, *red*	1,400.	*3,250.*

Years of issue: Nos. 73, 75, 77-78, 80-81, 87-88, 1923; others, 1921.

A14

1924-28 Chalky Paper Wmk. 4

No.	Type	Denomination / Color	Unused	Used
89	A14	¼pi gray & brn org	2.10	.55
90	A14	½pi gray blk & blk	6.25	*14.50*
91	A14	½pi grn & dp grn ('25)	2.50	1.10
92	A14	¾pi grn & dp grn	4.25	1.10
93	A14	¾pi gray blk & blk ('25)	4.50	1.10
94	A14	1pi brn vio & org brn	2.40	2.10
95	A14	1½pi org & blk	3.50	*14.50*
96	A14	1½pi car ('25)	5.25	1.60
97	A14	2pi car & grn	4.25	*21.00*
98	A14	2pi org & blk ('25)	15.00	4.25
99	A14	2½pi ultra ('25)	9.00	1.90
100	A14	2¾pi ultra & dl vio	3.75	5.00
101	A14	4pi ap grn & vio	5.25	5.25
102	A14	4½pi blk & yel, *emer*	4.00	5.25
103	A14	6pi grn ol & grn	5.25	*9.00*
104	A14	9pi brn & dk vio	9.00	5.75
105	A14	12pi org brn & blk	14.50	*65.00*
106	A14	18pi blk & org	29.00	5.75
		Revenue cancel		1.00
107	A14	45pi gray vio & ultra	65.00	45.00
		Revenue cancel		1.50
108	A14	90pi grn & red, *yel*	125.00	*270.00*
		Revenue cancel		3.75
109	A14	£5 blk, *yel* ('28)	3,750.	*8,000.*
		On cover (overfranked)		275.00
		Revenue cancel		275.00

Wmk. 3

No.	Type	Denomination / Color	Unused	Used
110	A14	£1 vio & blk, *red*	350.00	*900.00*
		Revenue cancel		12.50
		Nos. 89-108 (20)	319.75	*479.70*

Nos. 96 and 99 are on ordinary paper.

Silver Coin of Amathus — A15

Philosopher Zeno — A16

Map of Cyprus — A17

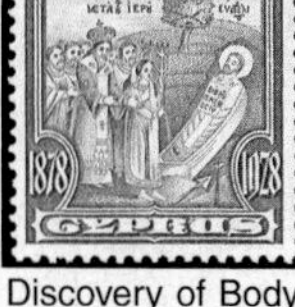
Discovery of Body of St. Barnabas — A18

Cloisters of Bella Paise Monastery — A19

Badge of the Colony — A20

Hospice of Umm Haram at Larnaca — A21

Statue of Richard Coeur de Lion, London — A22

St. Nicholas Cathedral, Famagusta — A23

King George V — A24

Perf. 12

1928, Feb. 1 Engr. Wmk. 4

No.	Type	Denomination / Color	Unused	Used
114	A15	¾pi dark violet	3.75	1.60
115	A16	1pi Prus bl & blk	4.00	2.00
116	A17	1½pi red	7.50	2.25
117	A18	2½pi ultramarine	4.75	2.75
118	A19	4pi dp red brown	9.50	9.50
119	A20	6pi dark blue	14.00	*32.50*
120	A21	9pi violet brown	11.00	*17.50*
121	A22	18pi dk brn & blk	30.00	*35.00*
122	A23	45pi dp blue & vio	52.50	*62.50*
123	A24	£1 ol brn & dp blue	275.00	*400.00*
		Nos. 114-123 (10)	412.00	*565.60*

50th year of Cyprus as a British colony.

Ruins of Vouni Palace — A25

Columns at Salamis — A26

Peristerona Church — A27

Soli Theater — A28

Kyrenia Castle and Harbor — A29

Kolossi Castle — A30

St. Sophia Cathedral — A31

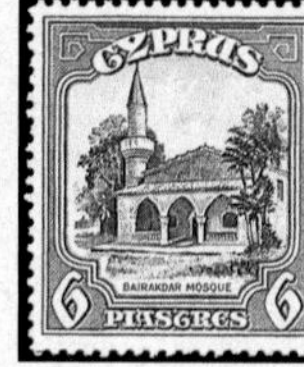
Bairakdar Mosque — A32

Queen's Window, St. Hilarion Castle — A33

Buyuk Khan, Nicosia — A34

Forest Scene — A35

1934, Dec. 1 Engr. *Perf. 12½*

No.	Type	Denomination / Color	Unused	Used
125	A25	¼pi yel brn & ultra	1.40	1.10
		Never hinged	2.10	
	a.	Vert. pair, imperf. between	*52,500.*	*35,000.*
126	A26	½pi green	1.90	1.25
		Never hinged	2.10	
	a.	Vert. pair, imperf. between	*18,000.*	*20,000.*
127	A27	¾pi vio & blk	3.50	.45
		Never hinged	4.50	
	a.	Vert. pair, imperf. between	*52,500.*	
128	A28	1pi brn & blk	3.00	2.50
		Never hinged	4.50	
	a.	Vert. pair, imperf. between	*26,000.*	*26,000.*
	b.	Horiz. pair, imperf. btwn.	*19,000.*	
129	A29	1½pi rose red	4.00	2.10
		Never hinged	6.00	
130	A30	2½pi dk ultra	5.25	2.40
		Never hinged	7.75	
131	A31	4½pi dk car & blk	5.25	5.00
		Never hinged	14.00	
132	A32	6pi blue & blk	12.50	*20.00*
		Never hinged	26.00	
133	A33	9pi dl vio & blk brn	20.00	8.50
		Never hinged	32.50	
134	A34	18pi ol grn & blk	55.00	50.00
		Never hinged	120.00	
135	A35	45pi blk & emer	120.00	85.00
		Never hinged	225.00	
		Nos. 125-135 (11)	231.80	*178.30*
		Set, never hinged	405.00	

Common Design Types pictured following the introduction.

Silver Jubilee Issue

Common Design Type

1935, May 6 *Perf. 11x12*

No.	Type	Denomination / Color	Unused	Used
136	CD301	¾pi gray blk & ultra	4.25	1.50
137	CD301	1½pi car & dk bl	6.25	3.00
138	CD301	2½pi ultra & brn	5.25	1.90
139	CD301	9pi brn vio & ind	24.00	*28.00*
		Nos. 136-139 (4)	39.75	*34.40*
		Set, never hinged	60.00	

Coronation Issue

Common Design Type

1937, May 12 *Perf. 11x11½*

No.	Type	Denomination / Color	Unused	Used
140	CD302	¾pi dark gray	1.00	1.00
141	CD302	1½pi dark car	1.25	*2.50*
142	CD302	2½pi deep ultra	1.50	*3.00*
		Nos. 140-142 (3)	3.75	6.50
		Set, never hinged	7.75	

Ruins of Vouni Palace — A36

Columns at Salamis — A37

Peristerona Church — A38

Soli Theater — A39

Kyrenia Castle and Harbor — A40

Kolossi Castle — A41

Map of Cyprus — A42

Bairakdar Mosque — A43

Citadel, Famagusta — A44

Buyuk Khan — A45

Forest Scene A46

King George VI A47

1938-44 **Wmk. 4** ***Perf. 12½***

143 A36 ¼pi yel brn & ultra .60 .60
144 A37 ½pi green .80 .50
145 A38 ¾pi violet & blk 7.25 1.75
146 A39 1pi orange .90 .40
a. Perf. 13½x12½ ('44) 375.00 30.00
Never hinged 575.00
147 A40 1½pi rose car 3.25 2.00
147A A40 1½pi lt vio ('43) .90 .75
147B A38 2pi car & blk ('42) .90 .45
c. Perf. 12½x13½ ('44) 2.00 *12.50*
Never hinged 3.25
148 A41 2½pi ultramarine 15.00 4.50
148A A41 3pi dp ultra ('42) 1.25 .60
149 A42 4½pi gray .90 .40
150 A43 6pi blue & blk 1.25 *1.10*
151 A44 9pi dk vio & blk 1.00 .80
152 A45 18pi ol grn & blk 5.00 1.75
153 A46 45pi blk & emer 16.00 5.00
154 A47 90pi blk & brt vio 21.00 8.00
155 A47 £1 ind & dl red 45.00 32.50
Nos. 143-155 (16) 121.00 61.10
Set, never hinged 275.00

See Nos. 164-166.

Catalogue values for unused stamps in this section, from this point to the end of the section, are for Never Hinged items.

Peace Issue
Common Design Type

1946, Oct. 21 **Engr.** ***Perf. 13½x14***

156 CD303 1½pi purple .45 .25
157 CD303 3pi deep blue .45 .45

Silver Wedding Issue
Common Design Types

1948, Dec. 20 **Photo.** ***Perf. 14x14½***

158 CD304 1½pi purple 1.00 .55

Engr.; Name Typo.
Perf. 11½x11

159 CD305 £1 dark blue 57.50 *77.50*

UPU Issue
Common Design Types
Perf. 13½, 11x11½

1949, Oct. 10 **Engr.** **Wmk. 4**

160 CD306 1½pi violet .65 *1.60*
161 CD307 2pi deep carmine 1.75 1.60
162 CD308 3pi indigo 1.10 *1.50*
163 CD309 9pi rose violet 1.10 *6.00*
Nos. 160-163 (4) 4.60 *10.70*

Types of 1938-43

1951, July 2 **Engr.** ***Perf. 12½***

164 A37 ½pi purple 3.75 .75
165 A40 1½pi deep green 6.25 1.25
166 A41 4pi deep ultra 6.75 1.40
Nos. 164-166 (3) 16.75 3.40

Coronation Issue
Common Design Type

1953, June 2 ***Perf. 13½x13***

167 CD312 1½pi brt grn & black 1.60 .75

Carobs A48

Copper Pyrites Mine A49

St. Hilarion Castle A50

Queen Elizabeth II and Cyprian Coin Devices — A51

Designs: 3m, Grapes. 5m, Oranges. 15m, Troodos forest. 20m, Aphrodite beach. 25m, Coin of Paphos. 30m, Kyrenia. 35m, Harvest in Mesaoria. 40m, Famagusta harbor. 100m, Hala Sultan Tekke. 250m, Kanakaria church. £1, Queen Elizabeth II and devices of Byzantium, Lusignan, Ottoman Empire and Venice.

Perf. 11½

1955, Aug. 1 **Engr.** **Wmk. 4**

168 A48 2m chocolate .25 *.50*
169 A48 3m violet blue .25 .25
170 A48 5m orange 1.00 .25
171 A49 10m gray grn & chocolate 1.25 .25
172 A49 15m indigo & olive 3.50 .50
173 A49 20m ultra & brown 1.25 .25
174 A49 25m aquamarine 3.25 .70
175 A49 30m carmine & blk 3.00 .25
176 A49 35m aqua & orange 1.25 .50
177 A49 40m choc & dk grn 2.00 .75

Perf. 13½

178 A50 50m red brn & aqua 2.10 .30
179 A50 100m bl green & mag 13.00 .60
180 A50 250m vio brn & dk blue gray 16.00 13.00

Perf. 11x11½

181 A51 500m lilac rose & grnsh gray 37.50 15.00
182 A51 £1 grnsh gray & brn red 30.00 *52.50*
Revenue cancel 1.00
Nos. 168-182 (15) 115.60 85.60

Republic

Nos. 168-182 Overprinted in Dark Blue

1960, Aug. 16 **Ovpt. 10x6½mm**

183 A48 2m chocolate .25 *.75*
184 A48 3m violet blue .25 .25
185 A48 5m orange 2.25 .25

Overprint 12½x11mm

186 A49 10m gray grn & choc 1.00 .25
187 A49 15m indigo & ol 3.25 .30
188 A49 20m ultra & brn 1.75 *1.50*
a. Double overprint *12,000.*
189 A49 25m aquamarine 1.75 1.75
190 A49 30m car & black 1.75 .30
a. Double overprint *45,000.*
191 A49 35m aqua & org 1.75 .70
192 A49 40m choc & dk grn 2.00 *2.50*

2-line overprint 2½mm apart

193 A50 50m red brown & aqua 2.00 .75
194 A50 100m bl grn & mag 9.00 2.50
195 A50 250m vio brn & dk blue gray 30.00 5.50

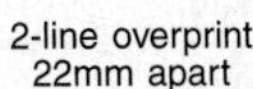

2-line overprint 22mm apart

196 A51 500m lil rose & grnsh gray 45.00 27.00
197 A51 £1 grnsh gray & brn red 50.00 *62.50*
Nos. 183-197 (15) 152.00 106.80

The overprint, in Greek and Turkish, reads "Republic of Cyprus."

Map of Cyprus — A52

Wmk. 314

1960, Aug. 16 **Engr.** ***Perf. 11½***

198 A52 10m brown & green .25 .25
199 A52 30m blue & brown .80 .70
200 A52 100m purple & black 2.40 2.25
Nos. 198-200 (3) 3.45 3.20

Independence of Republic of Cyprus.

Europa Issue

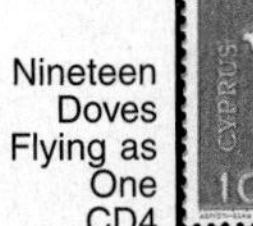

Nineteen Doves Flying as One CD4

Perf. 14x13½

1962, Mar. 19 **Litho.** **Unwmk.**

201 CD4 10m lilac *.30* .25
202 CD4 40m deep ultra *.90* .35
203 CD4 100m emerald *.90* .60
Nos. 201-203 (3) *2.10* 1.20

Admission of Cyprus to Council of Europe.

Malaria Eradication Emblem A54

1962, May 14 ***Perf. 14x13½***

204 A54 10m gray green & black .25 .25
205 A54 30m red brown & black .45 .25

WHO drive to eradicate malaria.

Iron Age Jug — A55

St. Barnabas Church, Salamis A56

Designs: 5m, Grapes. 10m, Head of Apollo. 15m, St. Sophia Church, Nicosia. 30m, Temple of Apollo. 35m, Head of Aphrodite. 40m, Skiing on Mt. Troodos. 50m, Ruins of Gymnasium, Salamis. 100m, Hala Sultan Tekke (sheep, Salt Lake Larnaca and tomb). 250m, Bella Paise Monastery. 500m, Cyprus mouflon. £1, St. Hilarion Castle.

Perf. 13½x14, 14x13½

1962, Sept. 17 **Wmk. 344**

206 A55 3m dk brn & sal .25 .30
207 A55 5m dull green & red lilac .25 .25
208 A55 10m dk slate grn & yel green .25 .25
209 A55 15m dk brn & rose vio .40 .25
210 A56 25m salmon & brn .45 .25
211 A56 30m lt bl & dk bl .25 .25
212 A55 35m dk bl & pale grn .45 .25
213 A56 40m vio bl & dk bl 1.50 *1.75*
214 A56 50m olive bis & dk grn .60 .25
215 A55 100m brn & yel brn 4.25 .30
216 A56 250m tan & black 11.00 2.40
217 A55 500m brown & olive 21.00 9.00
218 A56 £1 gray & green 22.50 *30.00*
Nos. 206-218 (13) 63.15 45.50

Wmk. 344 is found in two positions: normal or inverted on vertical stamps, and reading up or down on horizontal stamps.

For overprints see Nos. 232-236, 265-268. For surcharge see No. 273.

Europa Issue, 1962
Common Design Type
Perf. 14x13½

1963, Jan. 28 **Wmk. 344**

Size: 36x20mm

219 CD5 10m ultra & black *3.75* .25
220 CD5 40m red & black *15.00* *1.50*
221 CD5 150m green & black *57.50* *5.00*
Nos. 219-221 (3) *76.25* *6.75*

Cypriot Farm Girl — A57

75m, Statue of Demeter, goddess of agriculture.

1963, Mar. 21 ***Perf. 13½x14***

222 A57 25m blk, ultra & ocher .50 .45
223 A57 75m dk car, gray & blk 3.25 2.25

FAO "Freedom from Hunger" campaign.

Cub Scout and Tents — A58

20m, Sea Scout. 150m, Boy Scout & mouflon.

1963, Aug. 21 **Wmk. 344**

224 A58 3m multicolored .25 .25
225 A58 20m multicolored .40 .25
226 A58 150m multicolored 2.00 2.50
a. Souvenir sheet of 3 120.00 *175.00*
Nos. 224-226 (3) 2.65 3.00

Boy Scout movement in Cyprus, 50th anniv. No. 226a contains 3 imperf. stamps similar to Nos. 224-226 with simulated perforations. Sold for 250m.

Red Cross Nurse — A59

Children's Home, Kyrenia
A60

Perf. 13½x14, 14x13½

1963, Sept. 9 Litho. Wmk. 344

227 A59 10m multicolored .75 .25
228 A60 100m multicolored 3.50 *4.25*

Intl. Red Cross, cent.

Europa Issue

Stylized Links, Symbolizing Unity — CD6

1963, Nov. 4 Perf. 14x13½

229 CD6 20m multicolored *6.50* *.70*
230 CD6 30m multicolored *7.50* *.70*
231 CD6 150m multicolored *50.00* *8.00*
Nos. 229-231 (3) *64.00* *9.40*

Nos. 208, 211, 213-215 Overprinted in Ultramarine

1964, May 5 Perf. 13½x14, 14x13½

232 A55 10m dk sl grn & yel grn .25 .25
233 A55 30m lt blue & dk blue .25 .25
234 A55 40m vio bl & dull bl .40 .30
235 A55 50m ol bis & dk grn .30 .35
236 A55 100m brn & yel brown .40 *.75*
Nos. 232-236 (5) 1.60 1.90

Decision by the UN and its Security Council to help restore the country to normality and to seek a solution of its problems.

Clay Mask and Soli Theater
A62

Designs: 35m, Curium theater. 50m, Salamis theater. 100m, Performance of "Othello" in front of Othello Tower.

1964, June 15 Perf. 13½x14

237 A62 15m multicolored .45 .25
238 A62 35m multicolored .45 .25
239 A62 50m multicolored .45 .25
240 A62 100m multicolored 1.75 *2.25*
Nos. 237-240 (4) 3.10 3.00

400th anniversary of Shakespeare's birth.

Boxers
A63

14th century B.C. art: 10m, Runners, vert. 75m, Chariot.

1964, July 6 Perf. 13½x14, 14x13½

241 A63 10m brn, bis & blk .25 .25
242 A63 25m gray bl, bl & brn .30 .25
243 A63 75m brick red, blk & brn .65 .80
a. Souvenir sheet of 3 8.00 *15.00*
Nos. 241-243 (3) 1.20 1.30

18th Olympic Games, Tokyo, Oct. 10-25, 1964. No. 243a contains three imperf. stamps similar to Nos. 241-243 with gray marginal inscription. Sheet sold for 250m; the difference between face value and selling price went for the promotion of classical athletics in Cyprus.

Europa Issue

Symbolic Daisy — CD7

Perf. 13½x14

1964, Sept. 14 Litho. Wmk. 344

244 CD7 20m bis brn & red brn *2.25* *.30*
245 CD7 30m lt blue & dk blue *3.00* *.30*
246 CD7 150m grn & ol grn *27.00* *4.50*
Nos. 244-246 (3) *32.25* *5.10*

CEPT, 5th anniv. The 22 petals of the flower symbolize the 22 members of the organization.

Satyr Drinking Wine, 5th Century B.C. Statuette — A65

Modern Winery
A66

Cypriot Wine Industry: 10m, Dionysus and Acme drinking wine, 3rd century mosaic. 50m, Commandaria wine, Knight Templar and Kolossi Castle.

Perf. 14x13½, 13½x14

1964, Oct. 26 Wmk. 344

247 A66 10m multicolored .45 .25
248 A65 40m multicolored .80 *1.00*
249 A65 50m multicolored .80 .30
250 A66 100m multicolored 1.75 *2.00*
Nos. 247-250 (4) 3.80 3.55

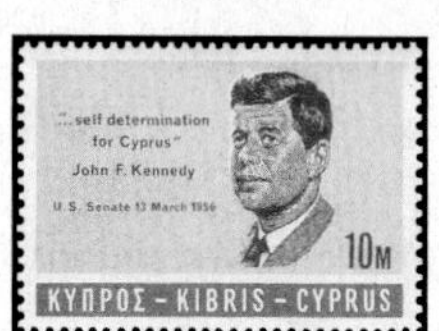

Pres. John F. Kennedy (1917-1963) — A67

Perf. 14x13½

1965, Feb. 15 Litho. Wmk. 344

251 A67 10m violet blue .25 .25
252 A67 40m green .35 .35
253 A67 100m rose claret .45 .35
a. Souvenir sheet of 3 4.00 *7.00*
Nos. 251-253 (3) 1.05 .95

No. 253a contains 3 imperf. stamps similar to Nos. 251-253 with simulated perforations. Sold for 250m, 100m going to charitable organizations in Cyprus.

Old Couple — A68

Mother and Children by A. Diamantis — A69

45m, Man with broken leg (accident insurance).

1965, Apr. 12 Perf. 13½x14

254 A68 30m dull green & tan .25 .25
255 A68 45m dk vio bl, bl & gray .40 .30

Perf. 13½x12½

256 A69 75m buff & red brown 1.25 *1.75*
Nos. 254-256 (3) 1.90 2.30

Introduction of Social Insurance Law.

ITU Emblem, Old and New Communication Equipment — A70

1965, May 17 Litho. Perf. 14x13½

257 A70 15m brn, yel & blk .65 .25
258 A70 60m grn, lt grn & blk 7.00 3.25
259 A70 75m dk & lt bl & blk 8.00 4.75
Nos. 257-259 (3) 15.65 8.25

ITU, cent.

ICY Emblem
A71

1965, May 17 Wmk. 344

260 A71 50m multicolored .90 .25
261 A71 100m multicolored 1.60 .75

International Cooperation Year.

Europa Issue

Leaves and Fruit
CD8

Perf. 14x13½

1965, Sept. 27 Litho. Wmk. 344

262 CD8 5m org, org brn & black 1.10 *.25*
263 CD8 45m lt grn, org brn & black *5.25* *1.75*
264 CD8 150m gray, org brn & black *19.00* *4.00*
Nos. 262-264 (3) *25.35* *6.00*

Nos. 206, 208, 211 and 216 Overprinted in Dark Blue

1966, Jan. 31 Perf. 13½x14, 14x13½

265 A55 3m dk brn & salmon .35 .40
266 A55 10m dk sl grn & yel green .40 .25
267 A56 30m lt bl & dk blue .40 .25
268 A56 250m tan & black 1.35 *2.25*
Nos. 265-268 (4) 2.50 3.15

UN General Assembly's resolution to mediate the dispute between Greeks and Turks on Cyprus, Dec. 18, 1965.

St. Barnabas, Ancient Icon — A73

Chapel over Tomb of St. Barnabas
A74

Bishop Anthemios of Constantine Dreaming of St. Barnabas, Discovering Tomb, etc. — A75

Design: 15m, Discovery of body of St. Barnabas (scene as in type A18).

Perf. 13x14, 14x13

1966, Apr. 25 Litho. Wmk. 344

269 A73 15m multicolored .25 .25
270 A74 25m multicolored .25 .25
271 A73 100m multicolored .65 *2.00*

Size: 110x91mm

Imperf

272 A75 250m multicolored 5.25 *11.00*
Nos. 269-272 (4) 6.40 13.50

1900th anniv. of the death of St. Barnabas.

No. 206 Surcharged with New Value and Three Bars

Perf. 13½x14

1966, May 30 Litho. Wmk. 344

273 A55 5m on 3m dk brn & sal .45 .25

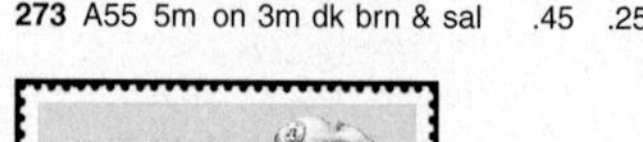

Gen. K. S. Thimayya
A76

1966, June 6 Perf. 14x13½

274 A76 50m tan & black .35 .25

In memory of Gen. Kodendera Subayya Thimayya (1906-1965), commander of the UN Peace-keeping Force on Cyprus.

Europa Issue

Symbolic Sailboat — CD9

Perf. 13½x14

1966, Sept. 26 Litho. Wmk. 344

No.	Type	Description	Unused	Used
275	CD9	20m multicolored	*.50*	*.25*
276	CD9	30m multicolored	*.50*	*.25*
277	CD9	150m multicolored	*3.75*	*2.25*
		Nos. 275-277 (3)	*4.75*	*2.75*

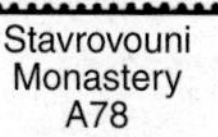

Stavrovouni Monastery A78

St. Nicholas Cathedral, Famagusta A79

Ingot Bearer, Bronze Age — A80

Designs: 5m, St. James' Church, Tricomo, vert. 10m, Zeno of Citium, marble bust, vert. 15m, Ship from 7th cent. BC vase, horiz. 20m, Silver coin, 4th cent. BC (head of Hercules with lion skin). 25m, Sleeping Eros (1st cent. marble statue; horiz.). 35m, Hawks on 11th cent. gold and enamel scepter from Curium. 40m, Marriage of David (7th cent. silver disc). 50m, Silver coin of Alexander the Great showing Hercules and Zeus, horiz. 100m, Bird catching fish on 7th cent. BC jug. 500m, The Rape of Ganymede (3rd cent. mosaic). £1, Aphrodite (1st cent. marble statue).

Perf. 12x12½, 12½x12

1966, Nov. 21 Litho. Wmk. 344

No.	Type	Description	Unused	Used
278	A78	3m bl, dl yel, grn & black	.40	.25
279	A78	5m dk bl, ol & blk	.25	.25
280	A78	10m olive & black	.25	.25
		Perf. 14x13½, 13½x14		
281	A79	15m org brn, blk & red brn	.25	.25
282	A79	20m red brn & blk	1.25	1.25
283	A79	25m red brn, gray & black	.40	.25
284	A79	30m aqua, tan & blk	.60	.30
285	A79	35m dk car, yel & blk	.60	.45
286	A79	40m brt bl, gray & blk	.80	.45
287	A79	50m org brn, gray & blk	1.10	.25
288	A79	100m gray, buff, blk & red	4.00	.25
		Perf. 13x14		
289	A80	250m dull yel, grn & blk	1.10	.50
290	A80	500m multicolored	3.00	.90
291	A80	£1 gray, lt gray & black	2.50	*6.75*
		Nos. 278-291 (14)	16.50	12.35

Electric Power Station, Limassol — A81

Arghaka-Maghounda Dam — A82

Designs: 35m, Troodos Highway. 50m, Cyprus Hilton Hotel. 100m, Ships in Famagusta Harbor.

Perf. 14x13½, 13½x14

1967, Apr. 10 Litho. Wmk. 344

No.	Type	Description	Unused	Used
292	A81	10m lt brn, dark brn & yellow	.25	.25
293	A82	15m lt bl, bl & grn	.25	.25
294	A82	35m dark gray, indigo & dark grn	.30	.25
295	A82	50m gray, olive & blue	.30	.25
296	A82	100m gray, ind & bl	.30	*1.00*
		Nos. 292-296 (5)	1.40	2.00

1st development program, 1962-66, completion.

Europa Issue, 1967

Common Design Type

1967, May 2 ***Perf. 13x14***

Size: 21x37mm

No.	Type	Description	Unused	Used
297	CD10	20m yel grn & olive	*.50*	*.25*
298	CD10	30m rose vio & pur	*.50*	*.25*
299	CD10	150m pale brn & brn	*3.25*	*2.00*
		Nos. 297-299 (3)	*4.25*	*2.50*

Javelin Thrower, Map of Eastern Mediterranean and "Victory" — A83

Map of Eastern Mediterranean, Victory Statue and: 35m, Runner. 100m, High jumper. 250m, Amphora, map of Eastern Mediterranean and Victory statue.

Perf. 13½x13

1967, Sept. 4 Litho. Wmk. 344

No.	Type	Description	Unused	Used
300	A83	15m multicolored	.25	.25
301	A83	35m multicolored	.25	.30
302	A83	100m multicolored	.60	*1.00*
		Size: 97x77mm		
		Imperf		
303	A83	250m multicolored	2.50	*6.50*
		Nos. 300-303 (4)	3.60	8.05

Cyprus-Crete-Salonika Athletic Games.

A84

ITY Emblem and: 10m, Marble Forum at Salamis, Church of St. Barnabas and Bellapais Abbey. 40m, Famagusta Beach. 50m, Plane and Nicosia International Airport. 100m, Youth Hostel and skiing on Mt. Troodos.

Perf. 13½x13

1967, Oct. 16 Litho. Wmk. 344

No.	Type	Description	Unused	Used
304	A84	10m multicolored	.25	.25
305	A84	40m multicolored	.25	*1.00*
306	A84	50m multicolored	.25	.25
307	A84	100m multicolored	.25	*1.00*
		Nos. 304-307 (4)	1.00	2.50

Intl. Tourist Year, 1967.

St. Andrew, 6th Century Mosaic — A85

Crucifixion, 15th Century — A86

The Three Kings, 15th Century Fresco — A87

1967, Nov. 8 ***Perf. 13x13½***

No.	Type	Description	Unused	Used
308	A85	25m multicolored	.25	.25
309	A86	50m multicolored	.25	.25
310	A87	75m multicolored	.25	.25
		Nos. 308-310 (3)	.75	.75

St. Andrew's Monastery, cent. (25m); Exhibition of Art of Cyprus, Paris, Nov. 7, 1967-Jan. 3, 1968 (50m); 20th anniv. of UNESCO (75m).

Human Rights Flame and Stars — A88

Designs: 90m, Human Rights flame and UN emblem. 250m, Scroll showing Article One of the Declaration of Human Rights.

Perf. 13½x14

1968, Mar. 18 Litho. Wmk. 344

No.	Type	Description	Unused	Used
311	A88	50m multicolored	.25	.25
312	A88	90m multicolored	.25	*.70*
		Size: 110x90mm		
		Imperf		
313	A88	250m multicolored	1.25	*4.75*
		Nos. 311-313 (3)	1.75	*5.70*

Intl. Human Rights Year.

Europa Issue, 1968

Common Design Type

1968, Apr. 29 ***Perf. 14x13½***

No.	Type	Description	Unused	Used
314	CD11	20m multicolored	*.40*	*.25*
315	CD11	30m dk car rose, gray brn & blk	*.50*	*.25*
316	CD11	150m multicolored	*2.00*	*2.00*
		Nos. 314-316 (3)	*2.90*	*2.50*

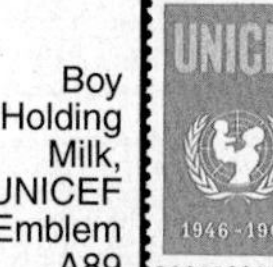

Boy Holding Milk, UNICEF Emblem A89

Aesculapius and WHO Emblem — A90

Perf. 14x13½, 13½x14

1968, Sept. 2 Wmk. 344

No.	Type	Description	Unused	Used
317	A89	35m dk red, lt brn & blk	.25	.25
318	A90	50m gray ol, blk & grn	.25	.25

21st anniv. of UNICEF (No. 317), 20th anniv. of the WHO (No. 318).

Discus Thrower — A91

25m, Runners. 100m, Stadium, Mexico City.

Perf. 13½x14, 14x13½

1968, Oct. 24 Litho.

No.	Type	Description	Unused	Used
319	A91	10m multicolored	.25	.25
320	A91	25m vio blue & multi	.25	.25
321	A91	100m blue & multi, horiz.	.25	*1.25*
		Nos. 319-321 (3)	.75	1.75

19th Olympic Games, Mexico City, 10/12-27.

ILO Emblem — A92

Perf. 12x13½

1969, Mar. 3 Wmk. 344

No.	Type	Description	Unused	Used
322	A92	50m bl, vio bl & org brn	.25	.25
323	A92	90m gray, blk & org brn	.25	*.55*

ILO, 50th anniv.

Ancient Map of Cyprus A93

Design: 50m, Medieval map of Cyprus.

Perf. 13½x13

1969, Apr. 7 Wmk. 344

No.	Type	Description	Unused	Used
324	A93	35m multicolored	.25	.30
325	A93	50m olive & multi	.25	.30

1st Intl. Congress of Cypriot Studies.

Europa Issue

"EUROPA" and "CEPT" CD12

1969, Apr. 28 Litho. ***Perf. 14x13½***

No.	Type	Description	Unused	Used
326	CD12	20m bl, blk & gray	*.55*	*.25*
327	CD12	30m cop red, blk & ocher	*.55*	*.25*
328	CD12	150m grn, blk & yel	*1.90*	*1.75*
		Nos. 326-328 (3)	*3.00*	*2.25*

CEPT, 10th anniv.

European Roller — A95

Birds: 15m, Audouin's gull. 20m, Cyprus warbler. 30m, Eurasian jay, vert. 40m, Hoopoe, vert. 90m, Eleonora's falcon, vert.

Perf. 13½x12, 12x13½

1969, July 7 Wmk. 344

No.	Type	Description	Unused	Used
329	A95	5m multicolored	.45	.25
330	A95	15m multicolored	.60	.25
331	A95	20m multicolored	.60	.25
332	A95	30m multicolored	.65	.25

333 A95 40m multicolored .75 .30
334 A95 90m multicolored 1.90 *4.00*
Nos. 329-334 (6) 4.95 5.30

Nativity, Mural, 1192
A96

Christmas: 45m, Nativity, mural in Church of Ayios Nicolaos tis Steghis, 14th century. 250m, Virgin and Child between Archangels Michael and Gabriel, mosaic in Church of Panayia Angeloktistos, 6th-7th centuries. Design of 20m is a mural in Church of Panayia tou Arakos, Lagoudhera.

1969, Nov. 24 Litho. *Perf. 13½x13*
335 A96 20m multicolored .25 .25
336 A96 45m multicolored .25 .25

Size: 109x89mm

Imperf

337 A96 250m dk blue & multi 5.00 *12.00*
Nos. 335-337 (3) 5.50 12.50

Mahatma Gandhi
A97

1970, Jan. 26 *Perf. 14x13½*
338 A97 25m multicolored .35 .35
339 A97 75m multicolored 1.40 1.50

Birth cent. of Mohandas K. Gandhi (1869-1948), leader in India's struggle for independence.

Europa Issue

Interwoven Threads
CD13

1970, May 4 Litho. Wmk. 344
340 CD13 20m brn, yel & org *.40 .25*
341 CD13 30m brt bl, yel & org *.40 .25*
342 CD13 150m brt rose lil, yel & orange *1.90 2.25*
Nos. 340-342 (3) *2.70 2.75*

Landscape with Flowers — A99

Designs: Various landscapes with flowers.

Perf. 13x14

1970, Aug. 3 Litho. Wmk. 344
343 A99 10m multicolored .25 .25
344 A99 50m multicolored .25 .25
345 A99 90m multicolored .60 *1.25*
Nos. 343-345 (3) 1.10 1.75

European Nature Conservation Year.

Education Year Emblem — A100

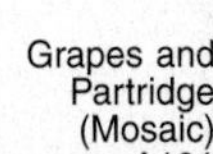

Grapes and Partridge (Mosaic)
A101

UN Emblem, Dove, Globe and Wheat
A102

Perf. 13x14, 14x13

1970, Sept. 7 Litho. Wmk. 344
346 A100 5m tan, blk & brn .25 .25
347 A101 15m multicolored .25 .25
348 A102 75m multicolored .25 *.75*
Nos. 346-348 (3) .75 1.25

Intl. Education Year (No. 346); 50th General Assembly of the Intl. Vine and Wine Office (No. 347); 25th anniv. of the UN (No. 348).

Virgin and Child, Mural from Podhithou Church, 16th Century — A103

Perf. 14x14½

1970, Nov. 23 Photo. Unwmk.
349 A103 Strip of three .45 *.55*
a. 25m Left angel .25 .25
b. 25m Virgin and Child .25 .25
c. 25m Right angel .25 .25
350 A103 75m multicolored .35 .35

Christmas.

Design of No. 349 is same as No. 350, but divided by perforation into 3 stamps with 25m denomination each. Size of No. 349: 71x46mm; size of No. 350: 42x31mm.

Cotton Napkin — A104 Festive Costume — A105

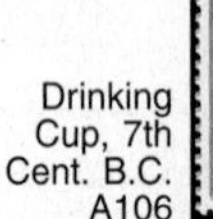

Drinking Cup, 7th Cent. B.C.
A106

Mouflon from Mosaic Pavement, 3rd Century — A107

Cypriot Art: 5m, St. George, bas-relief on pine board, 19th cent. 20m, kneeling donors, painting, Church of St. Mamas, 1465. 25m, Mosaic head, 5th cent. A.D. 30m, Athena mounting horse-drawn chariot, terracotta figurine, 5th cent. B.C. 40m, Shepherd playing pipe, 14th cent. fresco. 50m, Woman's head, limestone, 3rd cent. B.C. 75m, Angel, mosaic, 6th cent. 90m, Mycenaean silver bowl, 14th cent. B.C. 500m, Woman and tree, decoration from amphora, 7th-6th cent. B.C. £1, God statue (horned helmet), from Enkomi, 12th cent. B.C., vert.

Perf. 12½x13½ (A104), 13x14 (A105), 14x13 (A106), 13½x13, 13x13½ (A107)

1971, Feb. 22 Litho. Wmk. 344
351 A104 3m blk, red & brn .35 .50
352 A104 5m citron, red brn & black .25 .25
353 A105 10m multicolored .25 .30
354 A106 15m bister brn, blk & slate .25 .25
355 A105 20m slate, red brn & black .40 .50
356 A105 25m multicolored .30 .25
357 A106 30m multicolored .30 .25
358 A105 40m gray & multi 1.10 1.10
359 A105 50m bl, bis & blk .90 .25
360 A105 75m cit & multi 2.00 1.25
361 A106 90m multicolored 2.25 2.50
362 A107 250m lt red brn, brn & black 1.75 .40
363 A107 500m tan & multi .90 .50
364 A107 £1 multicolored 1.75 .75
Nos. 351-364 (14) 12.75 9.05

For surcharges & overprints see Nos. 403, 424-427, 444, RA1.

Europa Issue

"Fraternity, Co-operation, Common Effort" — CD14

1971, May 3 Litho. *Perf. 14x13½*

Size: 36½x23½mm

365 CD14 20m lt bl, vio bl & blk *.30 .25*
366 CD14 30m brt yel grn, grn & blk *.30 .25*
367 CD14 150m yel, grn & blk *2.00 2.75*
Nos. 365-367 (3) *2.60 3.25*

Archbishop Kyprianos, 1821 — A109

Paintings: 30m, Young Greek Taking Oath, horiz. 100m, Bishop Germanòs of Patras Declaring Greek Independence.

Perf. 13x13½, 13½x13

1971, July 9 Wmk. 344
368 A109 15m multicolored .25 .25
369 A109 30m multicolored .25 .25
370 A109 100m multicolored .25 *.50*
Nos. 368-370 (3) .75 1.00

150th anniversary of Greek independence.

Arch and Castle
A110

Tourist Publicity: 25m, Decorated gourd and sun over shore, vert. 60m, Mountain road, vert. 100m, Village church.

Perf. 13½x13, 13x13½

1971, Sept. 20
371 A110 15m vio bl & multi .25 .25
372 A110 25m ocher & multi .25 .25
373 A110 60m green & multi .25 *.60*
374 A110 100m blue & multi .25 *.65*
Nos. 371-374 (4) 1.00 1.75

Virgin and Child — A111

1971, Nov. 22 *Perf. 13½x14*
375 A111 10m shown .25 .35
376 A111 50m The Three Kings .25 .35
377 A111 100m Shepherds .25 .35
a. Strip of 3, Nos. 375-377 .65 *.95*

Christmas.

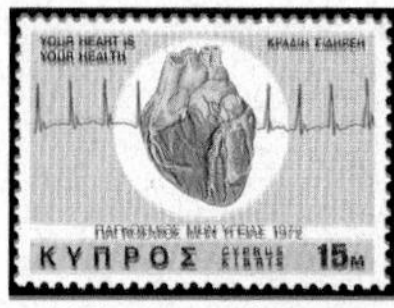

Heart and Electrocardiogram — A112

1972, Apr. 11 *Perf. 13½x12½*
378 A112 15m bister & multi .25 .25
379 A112 50m brown & multi .25 *.45*

"Your heart is your health," World Health Day.

Europa Issue

Sparkles, Symbolic of Communications
CD15

1972, May 22 *Perf. 12½x13½*
380 CD15 20m brn, org & fawn *.60 .30*
381 CD15 30m pur, org & lilac *.60 .45*
382 CD15 150m dk ol, org & brt green *4.75 3.50*
Nos. 380-382 (3) *5.95 4.25*

Archery, Olympic and Motion Emblems
A114

1972, July 24 *Perf. 14x13½*
383 A114 10m shown .25 .25
384 A114 40m Wrestling .35 .25
385 A114 100m Soccer .65 *1.75*
Nos. 383-385 (3) 1.25 2.25

20th Olympic Games, Munich, 8/26-9/11.

Apollo, Silver Stater, Marion, 5th Century B.C.
A115

Silver Staters of Cyprus: 30m, Eagle's head, Paphos, c. 460 B.C. 40m, Pallas Athena, Lapithos, 388-387 B.C. 100m, Sphinx (obverse) and lotus flower (reverse), Idalion, c. 460 B.C.

1972, Sept. 25 Litho. Wmk. 344

Coins in Silver

386 A115 20m lt grnsh bl & blk .25 .25
387 A115 30m pale bl & silver .25 .25
388 A115 40m ol bister & black .25 .30
389 A115 100m pale brn & blk .75 *1.00*
Nos. 386-389 (4) 1.50 1.80

Bathing the Christ Child — A116

Christmas: 20m, The Three Kings. 100m, Nativity. 250m, The Nativity, 1466, mural in Church of the Holy Cross, Platanistasa. The designs of the 10m, 20m, 100m, show details from mural shown entirely on 250m.

1972, Nov. 20 Litho. *Perf. 13½x14*

390	A116	10m multicolored	.25	.25
391	A116	20m multicolored	.25	.25
392	A116	100m multicolored	.25	*.40*

Size: 110x90mm

Imperf

393	A116	250m multicolored	1.75	*4.25*
		Nos. 390-393 (4)	2.50	5.15

Landscape, Troodos Mountains A117

100m, FIS Congress emblem and map of Cyprus.

Perf. 14x13½

1973, Mar. 13 Wmk. 344

394	A117	20m blue & multi	.25	.25
395	A117	100m blue & multi	.25	*.40*

29th Meeting of the Intl. Ski Fed. (FIS), Nicosia, June 1973.

Europa Issue

Post Horn of Arrows CD16

1973, May 7 Size: 37x21mm

396	CD16	20m dl bl & multi	*.50*	*.25*
397	CD16	30m multicolored	*.50*	*.35*
398	CD16	150m multicolored	*3.25*	*3.25*
		Nos. 396-398 (3)	*4.25*	*3.85*

Archbishop's Palace, Nicosia — A119

Traditional Architecture: 30m, Konak, Nicosia, 18th century, vert. 50m, House, Gourri, 1850, vert. 100m, House, Rizokarpaso, 1772.

1973, July 23 *Perf. 14x13, 13x14*

399	A119	20m multicolored	.25	.25
400	A119	30m multicolored	.25	.25
401	A119	50m multicolored	.25	.25
402	A119	100m multicolored	.25	*.85*
		Nos. 399-402 (4)	1.00	1.60

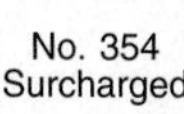

No. 354 Surcharged

1973, Sept. 24 *Perf. 14x13*

403	A106	20m on 15m multi	.35	.35

Cyprus Scout Emblem — A120

EEC Emblem A121

Cyprus Airways Emblem — A122

35m, FAO emblem. 100m, INTERPOL emblem.

1973, Sept. 24 *Perf. 13x14, 14x13*

404	A120	10m brn ol, ol & buff	.30	.30
405	A121	25m pur, bl & plum	.30	.30
406	A121	35m grn, gray grn & citron	.30	.30
407	A122	50m black & blue	.30	.30
408	A120	100m brown & fawn	.40	*.80*
		Nos. 404-408 (5)	1.60	2.00

60th anniv. of Cyprus Boy Scout Organ.; association of Cyprus with EEC; 10th anniv. of FAO; 25th anniv. of Cyprus Airways; 50th anniv. of Intl. Criminal Police Organization.

Archangel Gabriel — A123

Virgin and Child — A124

Christmas: 100m, Panaya tou Araka Church, horiz. Designs of 10m, 20m are from wall paintings in Arakas Church.

1973, Nov. 26 Wmk. 344

409	A123	10m multicolored	.25	.25
410	A124	20m multicolored	.25	.25
411	A124	100m multicolored	.25	*.75*
		Nos. 409-411 (3)	.75	1.25

Grapes — A125

1974, Mar. 18 Litho. *Perf. 13x14*

412	A125	25m shown	.25	.25
413	A125	50m Grapefruit	.25	*.60*
414	A125	50m Oranges	.25	*.60*
415	A125	50m Lemons	.25	*.60*
a.		Strip of 3, #413-415	1.00	*2.00*
		Nos. 412-415 (4)	1.00	*2.05*

Europa Issue

Rape of Europa — A126

Design shows a silver stater of Marion, second half of 5th century B.C.

1974, Apr. 29

416	A126	10m org brn & multi	*.60*	*.30*
417	A126	40m multicolored	*.60*	*.60*
418	A126	150m dk car & multi	*2.75*	*2.75*
		Nos. 416-418 (3)	*3.95*	*3.65*

Solon, 3rd Century Mosaic A127

Designs: 10m, Front page of "History of Cyprus," by Archimandrite Kyprianos, 1788, vert. 100m, St. Neophytos, mural, vert. 250m, Maps of Cyprus and Greek Islands, by Abraham Ortelius, 1584.

Perf. 13x14, 14x13

1974, July 22 Litho. Wmk. 344

419	A127	10m multicolored	.25	.25
420	A127	25m multicolored	.25	.25
421	A127	100m multicolored	.30	.85

Size: 110x90mm

Imperf

422	A127	250m multicolored	2.25	*4.75*
		Nos. 419-422 (4)	3.05	6.10

2nd Intl. Congress of Cypriot Studies, Nicosia, Sept. 15-21. No. 422 has simulated perforations.

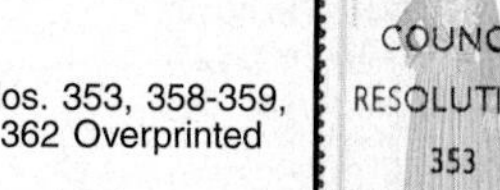

Nos. 353, 358-359, 362 Overprinted

Perf. 13x14, 13½x13

1974, Oct. 14 Litho.

424	A105	10m multicolored	.25	.25
425	A105	40m multicolored	.35	.50
426	A105	50m multicolored	.35	.35
427	A107	250m multicolored	.70	*2.75*
		Nos. 424-427 (4)	1.65	3.85

UN Security Council Resolution No. 353 to end hostilities on Cyprus. Overprint is in 3 lines on No. 427.

Virgin and Child, 1466 A129

Adoration of the Kings, c. 1500 — A130

Christmas: 100m, Flight into Egypt, mural, Monastery Church of Ayios Neophytos, c. 1500. (50m is from same church). Mural on 10m is in Church of Stavros tou Agiasmati.

Perf. 14x13, 13x14

1974, Dec. 2 Wmk. 344

429	A129	10m multicolored	.25	.25
430	A130	50m multicolored	.25	.25
431	A129	100m multicolored	.25	*.45*
		Nos. 429-431 (3)	.75	.95

Disabled Persons, Emblem — A131

Council of Europe Flag — A132

1975, Feb. 17 Unwmk. *Perf. 14½*

432	A131	30m ocher & ultra	.25	.25
433	A132	100m multicolored	.55	*1.25*

8th European Meeting of the Intl. Society for the Rehabilitation of Disabled Persons (30m; design shows society's emblem); 25th anniv. of Council of Europe (100m).

First Mail Coach in Cyprus A133

1975, Feb. 17

434	A133	20m multicolored	.25	.25
435	A133	50m ultra & multi	.80	.40

Centenary (in 1974) of UPU.

The Distaff, by Michael Kashalos — A134

Europa (Paintings): 30m, Still Life, by Christoforos Savva. 150m, Virgin and Child of Liopetri, by Georghios P. Georghiou.

Perf. 13½x14½

1975, Apr. 28 Photo.

436	A134	20m multicolored	*.25*	*.25*
437	A134	30m multicolored	*.30*	*.25*
438	A134	150m multicolored	*.80*	*.60*
a.		Strip of 3, #436-438	*1.40*	*1.60*

Red Cross Flag over Cyprus — A135

Nurse and Nurses Emblem A136

Steatite Female Figure, c. 3000 B.C. — A137

Perf. 12½x13½, 13½x12½

1975, Aug. 4 Litho. Wmk. 344

439 A135 25m blue green & red .25 .25
440 A136 30m dp blue & lt grn .25 .25
441 A137 75m multicolored .25 *.85*
Nos. 439-441 (3) .75 1.35

Cyprus Red Cross, 25th anniv.; Intl. Nurses' Day 1975; IWY.

Submarine Cable — A138

International Telephone A139

Perf. 12½x13½, 13½x12½

1975, Oct. 13 Litho.

442 A138 50m multicolored .30 .25
443 A139 100m purple & org .60 *.85*

Telecommunications achievements.

No. 351 Surcharged

1976, Jan. 5 *Perf. 12½x13½*

444 A104 10m on 3m multi .45 *.90*

Vessel in Shape of Woman, 19th Century — A140

Composite Vessel, 2100-2000 B.C. — A141

Europa: 100m, Byzantine goblet, 15th cent.

Perf. 13x14

1976, May 3 Litho. Wmk. 344

445 A140 20m violet & multi *.35 .25*
446 A141 60m gray & multi *.80 .70*
447 A140 100m brown & multi *1.60 1.60*
Nos. 445-447 (3) *2.75 2.55*

Self-help Housing A142

Cyprus Airways Jet — A143

Designs: 25m, Women sewing in front of tents. 30m, Aforestation.

1976, May 3 *Perf. 14x13*

448 A142 10m multicolored .25 .25
449 A142 25m multicolored .25 .25
450 A142 30m multicolored .25 .25
451 A143 60m multicolored .25 .55
Nos. 448-451 (4) 1.00 1.30

Re-activation of the economy.

Terracotta Statue, 7th-6th Centuries B.C. — A144

Bronze Plate with Inscription, Idalion, 5th Century B.C. A145

Designs: 10m, Limestone head of bearded man, 5th cent. B.C. 20m, Gold necklace, Lamboussa, 6th cent. A.D. 25m, Terracotta warrior on horseback, 7th cent. B.C. 30m, Limestone figure, priest of Aphrodite, 5th cent. B.C. 50m, Mycenaean crater, 13th cent. B.C. 60m, Limestone sarcophagus, Amathus, 550-500 B.C. 100m, Gold bracelet, Lamboussa, 6th cent. A.D. 250m, Silver dish, Lamboussa, 6th cent. A.D. 500m, Bronze stand, 12th cent. B.C. £1, Marble statue of Artemis, Larnaca, 4th cent. B.C.

Perf. 12x13½

1976, June 7 Wmk. 344

Size: 22x33mm

452 A144 5m brn & multi .25 *.75*
453 A144 10m gray & multi .25 *.65*

Size: 24x37mm, 37x24mm

Perf. 13x14, 14x13

454 A144 20m red & multi .25 *.60*
455 A144 25m lt brn & blk .25 .25
456 A144 30m green & multi .25 .25
457 A145 40m bis gray & blk .25 *.60*
458 A145 50m brn & multi .25 .25
459 A145 60m dk brn & multi .25 .25
460 A145 100m crim & multi .40 *.60*

Size: 28x40mm

Perf. 13x12½

461 A144 250m dk bl & multi .50 *1.60*
462 A144 500m yel & multi 1.00 *1.75*
463 A144 £1 slate & multi 2.10 *2.50*
Nos. 452-463 (12) 6.00 *10.05*

George Washington A146

1976, July 5 *Perf. 13x13½*

464 A146 100m multicolored .50 .40

American Bicentennial.

Montreal Olympic Games Emblem — A147

Various Sports A148

100m, like 60m, with different sports.

1976, July 5 Unwmk. *Perf. 14*

465 A147 20m yel, blk & dk car .25 .25
466 A148 60m ultra & multi .25 *.30*
467 A148 100m lilac & multi .35 *.40*
Nos. 465-467 (3) .85 *.95*

21st Olympic Games, Montreal, Canada, July 17-Aug. 1.

Children in Library — A149

Low-cost Housing Development A150

Hands Shielding Eye — A151

Perf. 13½x14, 13x13½

1976, Sept. 27 Litho. Wmk. 344

468 A149 40m black & multi .25 .25
469 A150 50m multicolored .25 .25
470 A151 80m ultra & multi .35 *.55*
Nos. 468-470 (3) .85 1.05

Books for Children (40m); Habitat, UN Conference on Human Settlements, Vancouver, Canada, May 31-June 11 (50m); World Health Day: Foresight prevents blindness (80m).

Archangel Michael — A152

Christmas: 15m, Archangel Gabriel. 150m, Nativity. Icons in Ayios Neophytos Monastery, 16th century.

1976, Nov. 15 Unwmk. *Perf. 12½*

471 A152 10m multicolored .25 .25
472 A152 15m multicolored .25 .25
473 A152 150m multicolored .30 *.80*
Nos. 471-473 (3) .80 1.30

Landscape, by A. Diamantis — A154

Europa (Paintings): 60m, Trees and Meadow, by T. Kanthos. 120m, Harbor, by V. Ioannides.

Perf. 13½x13

1977, May 2 Litho. Unwmk.

475 A154 20m multicolored *.30 .25*
476 A154 60m multicolored *.70 .40*
477 A154 120m multicolored *1.25 2.00*
Nos. 475-477 (3) *2.25 2.65*

Cyprus No. 196 — A155

Perf. 13x13½

1977, June 13 Litho. Wmk. 344

478 A155 120m multicolored .40 .40

25th anniv. of reign of Queen Elizabeth II.

Silver Tetradrachm of Demetrios Poliorcetes — A156

Ancient Coins of Cyprus: 10m, Bronze coin of Emperor Trajan. 60m, Silver Tetradrachm of Ptolemy VIII. 100m, Gold octadrachm of Arsinoe II.

1977, June 13 Unwmk. *Perf. 14*

479 A156 10m multicolored .25 .25
480 A156 40m multicolored .30 .25
481 A156 60m multicolored .35 .30
482 A156 100m multicolored .50 *.85*
Nos. 479-482 (4) 1.40 1.65

Archbishop Makarios (1913-1977), Pres. of Cyprus — A157

20m, Archbishop in full vestments. 250m, Head.

Perf. 13x14

1977, Sept. 10 Litho. Unwmk.

483 A157 20m multicolored .25 .25
484 A157 60m multicolored .25 .25
485 A157 250m multicolored .60 *1.00*
Nos. 483-485 (3) 1.10 1.50

Handicrafts A158

Sputnik over Earth — A159

Designs: 40m, Map of the Mediterranean Sea. 60m, Gold medals and sports emblems.

Perf. 13½x12

1977, Oct. 17		**Wmk. 344**	
486 A158 20m multicolored		.25	.25
487 A158 40m multicolored		.25	.25
488 A158 60m multicolored		.25	.25
489 A159 80m multicolored		.25	*.75*
Nos. 486-489 (4)		1.00	1.50

Revitalization of handicrafts (20m); Man and the biosphere (40m); Gold medals won by secondary school students in France for long jump and 200 meter race (60m); 60th anniv. of Bolshevik Revolution (80m).

Nativity A160

Christmas (Children's Drawings): 10m, Three Kings following the star. 150m, Flight into Egypt.

Perf. 14x13½

1977, Nov. 21	**Litho.**	**Unwmk.**	
490 A160 10m multicolored		.25	.25
491 A160 40m multicolored		.25	.25
492 A160 150m multicolored		.25	*.70*
Nos. 490-492 (3)		.75	1.20

Demetrios Lipertis (1866-1937) — A161

150m, Vasilis Michaelides (1849-1917).

1978, Mar. 6	**Wmk. 344**	***Perf. 14x13***	
493 A161 40m bister & olive		.25	.25
494 A161 150m gray, ver & blk		.35	*.70*

Cypriot poets.

Chrysorrhogiatissa Monastery — A162

Europa: 75m, Kolossi Castle. 125m, Municipal Library, Paphos.

Perf. 14½x13

1978, Apr. 24	**Litho.**	**Unwmk.**	
495 A162 25m multicolored		*.30*	*.25*
496 A162 75m multicolored		*.80*	*.40*
497 A162 125m multicolored		*1.40*	*1.40*
Nos. 495-497 (3)		*2.50*	*2.05*

Makarios as Archbishop 1950-1977 A163

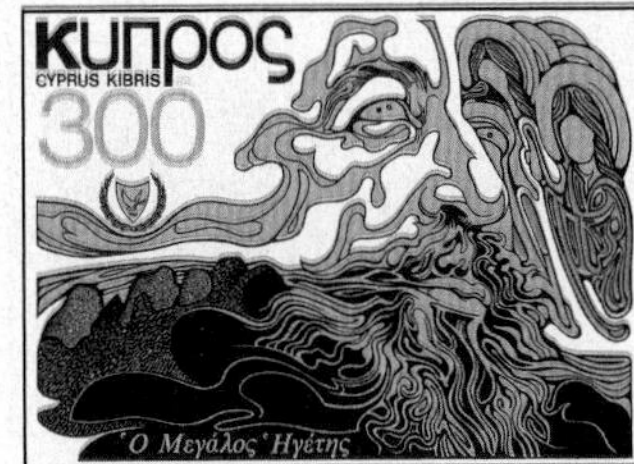

"The Great Leader" — A164

Archbishop Makarios: 25m, Exiled, Seychelles, 1956-1957. 50m, President of Cyprus, 1960-1977. 75m, Soldier of Christ. 100m, Freedom fighter.

Perf. 14x14½

1978, Aug. 3	**Litho.**	**Unwmk.**	
498 A163 15m multicolored		.25	.25
499 A163 25m multicolored		.25	.25
500 A163 50m multicolored		.25	.25
501 A163 75m multicolored		.25	.35
502 A163 100m multicolored		.25	.35
a. Strip of 5, #498-502		1.25	*1.50*

Size: 110x80mm

Imperf

503 A164 300m multicolored		2.00	*2.50*
Nos. 498-503 (6)		3.25	3.95

Archbishop Makarios, President of Cyprus.

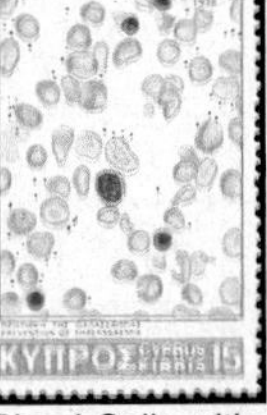

Blood Cells with Low Hemoglobin A165

Bust of Aristotle A166

Heads and Human Rights Emblem A167

Wilbur and Orville Wright, Flyer I A168

Perf. 13x14, 14x13

1978, Oct. 23	**Unwmk.**	**Litho.**	
504 A165 15m multicolored		.25	.25
505 A166 35m multicolored		.25	.25
506 A167 75m black		.25	.35
507 A168 125m multicolored		.35	*.70*
Nos. 504-507 (4)		1.10	1.55

Anemia prevention (15m); 2300th death anniv. of Aristotle (35m); 30th anniv. of Universal Declaration of Human Rights (75m); 75th anniv. of first powered flight (125m).

Kiti Icon Stand — A169

Christmas: 35m, Athienou icon stand. 150m, Omodhos icon stand.

1978, Dec. 4		***Perf. 14x14½***	
508 A169 15m multicolored		.25	.25
509 A169 35m multicolored		.25	.25
510 A169 150m multicolored		.40	*.70*
Nos. 508-510 (3)		.90	1.20

Venus Statue from Soli A170

125m, Birth of Venus, by Botticelli (detail).

1979, Mar. 12	**Litho.**	***Perf. 14x13½***	
511 A170 75m multicolored		.30	.25
512 A170 125m multicolored		.50	.40

Mail Coach, Envelope and Truck A171

Europa: 75m, Old telephone, dish antenna and satellite. 125m, Steamship, jet and envelopes.

1979, Apr. 30	**Litho.**	***Perf. 14x13½***	
513 A171 25m multicolored		*.55*	*.25*
514 A171 75m multicolored		*.95*	*.40*
515 A171 125m multicolored		*2.75*	*1.25*
Nos. 513-515 (3)		*4.25*	*1.90*

Peacock Wrasse A172

Designs: 50m, Black partridge, vert. 75m, Cyprus cedar, vert. 125m, Mule.

Perf. 13½x12½, 12½x13½

1979, June 25		**Litho.**	
516 A172 25m multicolored		.25	.25
517 A172 50m multicolored		.40	*.55*
518 A172 75m multicolored		.40	.35
519 A172 125m multicolored		.60	*1.10*
Nos. 516-519 (4)		1.65	2.25

Children Holding Globe, UNESCO Emblem — A173

Dove, Magnifying Glass, Album A174

Lord Kitchener, Map of Cyprus A175

Smiling Child, IYC Emblem A176

Soccer A177

Rotary Emblem — A178

1979, Oct. 1	**Litho.**	***Perf. 12½***	
520 A173 15m multicolored		.25	.25
521 A174 25m multicolored		.25	.25
522 A175 50m multicolored		.25	.25
523 A176 75m multicolored		.25	.25
524 A177 100m multicolored		.25	*.35*
525 A178 125m multicolored		.25	*.70*
Nos. 520-525 (6)		1.50	2.05

Intl. Bureau of Education, Geneva, 50th anniv.; Cyprus Philatelic Society, 20th anniv.; Horatio Herbert Kitchener's survey of Cyprus, cent.; IYC; European Soccer Assoc., 25th anniv.; Rotary Club of Cyprus, 75th anniv.

Jesus, Icon, 12th Century — A179

Christmas (Icons): 35m, Nativity, 16th cent. 150m, Virgin and Child, 12th cent.

Perf. 13½x14, 13x14

1979, Nov. 5 **Litho.**

Sizes: 24x37mm; 27x40mm (35m)

526 A179 15m multicolored		.25	.25
527 A179 35m multicolored		.25	.25
528 A179 150m multicolored		.25	*.45*
Nos. 526-528 (3)		.75	.95

Cyprus No. 1, Nicosia Cancel A180

Cyprus Stamp Centenary: 125m, #3, Kyrenia cancel. 175m, #6, Larnaca cancel. 500m, #1-6.

1980, Mar. 17	**Litho.**	***Perf. 14x13***	
529 A180 40m multicolored		.25	.25
530 A180 125m multicolored		.25	.25
531 A180 175m multicolored		.50	.50

Size: 105x85mm

Imperf

532 A180 500m multicolored		1.40	1.40
Nos. 529-532 (4)		2.40	2.40

Holy Cross, St. Barnabas Church, Agiasmati — A181

Europa: 125m, Zeno of Citium, Ny Carsberg Glyptothek, Copenhagen.

1980, Apr. 28		***Perf. 12½***	
533 A181 40m multicolored		*.25*	.25
534 A181 125m multicolored		*.45*	*.30*

Sailing, Moscow '80 Emblem A182

1980, June 23 Litho. *Perf. 14x13*

535 A182 40m shown .25 .25
536 A182 125m Swimming .25 .25
537 A182 200m Gymnast .40 .40
Nos. 535-537 (3) .90 .90

22nd Summer Olympic Games, Moscow, July 19-Aug. 3.

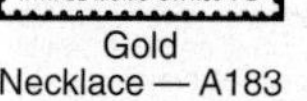

Gold Necklace — A183

Clay Amphora — A184

Archaeological finds on Cyprus, 12th cent. B.C. to 3rd cent. A.D. 15m, 40m, 150m, 500m, horiz.

Perf. 13½x14, 14x13½

1980, Sept. 15 Litho. Wmk. 344

538 A183 10m shown .30 *.90*
539 A184 15m Bronze cow .30 *.90*
540 A184 25m shown .30 .30
541 A184 40m Lion, gold ring .40 *.65*
542 A184 50m Bronze caul-dron .40 .25
543 A184 75m Stele 1.10 *1.40*
544 A184 100m Clay jug .80 .25
545 A184 125m Warrior, terra-cotta bust .80 *.90*
546 A184 150m Lions attack-ing bull 1.25 .25
547 A184 175m Faience and enamel vase .90 *1.25*
548 A184 200m Warrior god, bronze .90 .40
549 A184 500m Stone bowl .90 *1.50*
550 A183 £1 Ivory plaque 1.10 *1.25*
551 A183 £2 Leda and the swan, mosaic 1.90 *2.25*
Nos. 538-551 (14) 11.35 *12.45*

For surcharges see Nos. 584, 600-611.

Cyprus Flag — A185

Archbishop Makarios — A187

Treaty Signing Establishing Republic, 20th Anniversary — A186

1980, Oct. 1 *Perf. 13½x14, 14x13*

552 A185 40m multicolored .25 .25
553 A186 125m multicolored .25 .25
554 A187 175m multicolored .35 .35
Nos. 552-554 (3) .85 .85

Dove and Woman A188

Perf. 14x13

1980, Nov. 29 Litho. Wmk. 344

555 A188 40m shown .25 .25
556 A188 125m Dove and man .40 .40
a. Pair, #555-556 .65 .65

Intl. Palestinian Solidarity Day.

Pulpit, Ayios Lazaros Church, Larnaca — A189

Christmas: 25m, Pulpit, Tripiotis Church, Nicosia. 100m, Iconostatis (Holy Door), Panayia Church, Paralimni.

1980, Nov. 29 *Perf. 13½x14*

557 A189 25m multicolored .25 .25

Size: 24x37mm

558 A189 100m multicolored .25 .25

Size: 21x37mm

559 A189 125m multicolored .25 .25
Nos. 557-559 (3) .75 .75

Europa Issue

Folk Dance — A190

1981, May 4 Photo. *Perf. 14*

560 A190 40m shown *.30* .25
561 A190 175m Dance, diff. *.65* *.50*

Self-portrait, by Leonardo Da Vinci — A191

The Last Supper, by Da Vinci — A192

Perf. 13½x14, 12½x13½

1981, June 15 Wmk. 344 Litho.

562 A191 50m shown .35 .30
563 A192 125m shown .75 .50
564 A191 175m Lace pattern, Milan Cathedral .90 .70
Nos. 562-564 (3) 2.00 1.50

Da Vinci's visit to Cyprus, 500th anniv.

Ophrys Kotschyi — A193

Orchids: 50m, Orchis puntulata. 75m, Ophrys argolica elegantis. 150m, Epipactis veratrifolia.

1981, July 6 *Perf. 13½x14*

565 A193 25m shown .30 .30
566 A193 50m multi .55 .55
567 A193 75m multi .90 .90
568 A193 150m multi 1.50 1.50
a. Block of 4, #565-568 3.25 3.25
Nos. 565-568 (4) 3.25 3.25

Prince Charles and Lady Diana, St. Paul's Cathedral A194

Perf. 14x13

1981, Sept. 28 Wmk. 344

569 A194 200m multicolored .70 *.80*

Royal wedding.

Heinrich von Stephan (1831-1897), UPU Founder — A195

World Food Day (Oct. 16) A196

Intl. Year of the Disabled A197

European Campaign for Urban Renaissance — A198

1981, Sept. 28

570 A195 25m multicolored .25 .25
571 A196 40m multicolored .25 .25
572 A197 125m multicolored .30 .30
573 A198 150m multicolored .35 .35
Nos. 570-573 (4) 1.15 1.15

Our Lady of the Angels, Transfiguration Church, Palekhori A199

Christmas (Frescoes): 100m, Christ, Madonna of Arakas Church, Lagoudera, vert. 125m, Baptism of Christ, Our Lady of Assinou Church, Nikitari.

1981, Nov. 16 *Perf. 12½*

574 A199 25m multicolored .25 .25
575 A199 100m multicolored .60 .35
576 A199 125m multicolored .70 .45
Nos. 574-576 (3) 1.55 1.05

Bathing Aphrodite, Sculpture, Soloi, 250 B.C. — A200

Design: 175m, Aphrodite Emerging from the Water, by Titian, 16th cent.

Perf. 13½x14

1982, Apr. 12 Litho. Wmk. 344

577 A200 125m multicolored .70 .50
578 A200 175m multicolored .90 .70

Europa Issue

Liberation by Emperor Nicephorus II Phocas, 965 A.D. A201

175m, Conversion of Sergius Paulus, 45 A.D.

Perf. 12½

1982, May 3 Photo. Unwmk.

579 A201 40m shown *.45* .25
580 A201 175m multi *.80* *1.75*

Mosaic Chrismon A202

Cultural Heritage: 125m, King of Palaepaphos (High Priest of Aphrodite), sculpture, vert. 225m, Theseus Struggling with the Minotaur, mosaic.

1982, July 5 Litho. Wmk. 344

581 A202 50m multicolored .25 .25
582 A202 125m multicolored .55 .55
583 A202 225m multicolored 1.00 1.00
Nos. 581-583 (3) 1.80 1.80

No. 543 Surcharged

1982, Sept. 6 Litho. *Perf. 13½x14*

584 A184 100m on 75m multi .55 .55

Scouting Year — A203

Perf. 13½x12½, 12½x13½

1982, Nov. 8 Wmk. 344

585 A203 100m Emblem, horiz. .40 .40
586 A203 125m Baden-Powell .50 .50
587 A203 175m Camp site, horiz. .60 *.90*
Nos. 585-587 (3) 1.50 1.80

A203a

Christmas — A204

Designs: 25m, 250m, Christ Giving Holy Communion (bread, 25m: wine, 250m) to the Apostles, St. Neophytos Monastery Church, Paphos. 100m, Chalice, Church of St. Savvas, Nicosia.

Perf. 12½, 13½x14 (100m)

1982, Dec. 6

588 A203a 25m multicolored .25 .25
589 A204 100m multicolored .40 .35
590 A203a 250m multicolored .85 *1.50*
Nos. 588-590 (3) 1.50 2.10

A204a

50m, Cyprus Forest Industries, Ltd. 125m, Mosaic, 3rd cent. 150m, Dancers. 175m, Royal Exhibition Building, Melbourne.

1983, Mar. 14 ***Perf. 14x13½***

591 A204a 50m multi .25 .25
592 A204a 125m multi .25 .25
593 A204a 150m multi .25 .35
594 A204a 175m multi .25 *.45*
Nos. 591-594 (4) 1.00 1.30

Commonwealth Day.

Europa A205

50m, Cyprosyllabic script funerary stele, 6th cent. B.C. 200m, Copper ore, Enkomi ingot, 1400-1250 BC, bronze jug, 2nd cent.

1983, May 3 **Photo.** ***Perf. 14½x14***

595 A205 50m multicolored *.25* .25
596 A205 200m multicolored *.75* *1.75*

Local Butterflies A206

60m, Pararge aegeria. 130m, Aricia medon. 250m, Glaucopsyche paphos.

Wmk. 344

1983, June 28 **Litho.** ***Perf. 12½***

597 A206 60m multi .35 .30
598 A206 130m multi .75 .50
599 A206 250m multi 1.40 *2.00*
Nos. 597-599 (3) 2.50 2.80

Nos. 538-549 Surcharged

Perf. 13½x14, 14x13½

1983, Oct. 3 **Litho.** **Wmk. 344**

600 A183 1c on 10m multi .25 *.90*
601 A184 2c on 15m multi .25 *1.10*
602 A184 3c on 25m multi .25 *.90*
603 A184 4c on 40m multi .25 *.90*
604 A184 5c on 50m multi .40 .40
605 A184 6c on 75m multi .40 *.90*
606 A184 10c on 100m multi .55 .50
607 A184 13c on 125m multi .65 .60
608 A184 15c on 150m multi .65 .70
609 A184 20c on 200m multi .70 *.80*
610 A184 25c on 175m multi 1.10 *1.25*
611 A184 50c on 500m multi 1.90 *2.25*
Nos. 600-611 (12) 7.35 *11.20*

Electricity Authority of Cyprus, 30th Anniv. — A207

World Communications Year — A208

Intl. Maritime Org., 25th Anniv. — A209

Universal Declaration of Human Rights, 35th Anniv. — A210

Nicos Kazantzakis, 100th Birth Anniv. — A211

Archbishop Makarios III, 70th Birth Anniv. — A212

1983, Oct. 27 **Litho.** ***Perf. 13½x14***

612 A207 3c multicolored .25 .25
613 A208 6c multicolored .25 .25
614 A209 13c multicolored .25 .25
615 A210 15c multicolored .25 .25
616 A211 20c multicolored .30 *.75*
617 A212 25c multicolored .30 *.80*
Nos. 612-617 (6) 1.60 2.55

Christmas — A213

Designs: 4c, Belfry, St. Lazaros Church, Larnaca. 13c, Belfry, St. Varvara Church, Kaimakli, Nicosia. 20c, Belfry, St. Ioannis Church, Larnaca.

1983, Dec. 12 ***Perf. 12½x14***

618 A213 4c multicolored .25 .25
619 A213 13c multicolored .60 .60
620 A213 20c multicolored .85 *1.40*
Nos. 618-620 (3) 1.70 2.25

Waterside Cafe at the Marina, Larnaca — A214

19th Century engravings. Size of 6c: 41x27mm; 75c, 110x85mm.

Perf. 14½x14 (6c), 14, Imperf. (75c)

1984, Mar. 6

621 A214 6c shown .25 .25
622 A214 20c Bazaar, Larnaca .40 *.75*
623 A214 30c East Gate, Nicosia .65 *1.40*
624 A214 75c St. Lazarus Church Interior, Larnaca 1.50 *2.10*
Nos. 621-624 (4) 2.80 *4.50*

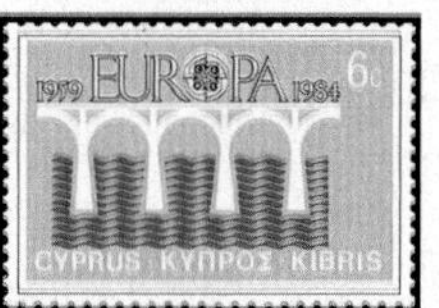

Europa (1959-1984) — A215

1984, Apr. 30 **Wmk. 344** ***Perf. 12½***

625 A215 6c multicolored *.40* .25
626 A215 15c multicolored *.90* *1.75*

1984 Summer Olympics A216

1984, June 18 **Litho.** ***Perf. 14***

627 A216 3c Running .25 .25
628 A216 4c Olympic column .25 .25
629 A216 13c Swimming .50 *.75*
630 A216 20c Gymnastics .70 *1.40*
Nos. 627-630 (4) 1.70 2.65

Turkish Invasion, 10th Anniv. A217

15c, Prisoners, barbed wire. 20c, Map.

1984, July 20 **Litho.** ***Perf. 14x13½***

631 A217 15c multicolored .45 .45
632 A217 20c multicolored .60 .60

Cyprus Philatelic Society, 25th Anniv. — A218

Cyprus Soccer Assoc., 50th Anniv. A219

George Papanicolaou (1883-1962), Cancer Researcher — A220

Medieval Map A221

1984, Oct. 15 **Wmk. 344** ***Perf. 12½***

633 A218 6c multicolored .25 .25
634 A219 10c multicolored .40 .40
635 A220 15c multicolored .70 .70
636 A221 25c multicolored 1.25 *2.00*
Nos. 633-636 (4) 2.60 3.35

Intl. Symposium of Cyprus Cartography and First Intl. Symposium on Medieval Paleography (25c).

Christmas — A222

4c, St. Mark. 13c, Gospel page (St. Mark). 20c, St. Luke.

1984, Nov. 26 **Litho.** ***Perf. 12½***

637 A222 4c multicolored .30 .30
638 A222 13c multicolored .90 .90
639 A222 20c multicolored 1.40 *2.00*
Nos. 637-639 (3) 2.60 3.20

Landscapes — A223

1c, Autumn at Platania. 2c, Ayia Napa Monastery. 3c, Phine Village. 4c, Kykko Monastery. 5c, Beach at Makronissos. 6c, Village Street, Omodhos, vert. 10c, Sea view. 13c, Water sports. 15c, Beach at Protaras. 20c, Forestry, vert. 25c, Sunrise at Protaras, vert. 30c, Village houses, Pera Orinis. 50c, Apollo Hylates Sanctuary. £1, Troodos Mountain, vert. £5, Personification of Autumn, Dionyssos House, vert.

Perf. 15x14, 14x15

1985, Mar. 18 **Litho.**

640 A223 1c multicolored .25 *.65*
641 A223 2c multicolored .25 *.65*
642 A223 3c multicolored .25 *.65*
643 A223 4c multicolored .25 *.35*
644 A223 5c multicolored .25 .25
645 A223 6c multicolored .25 .25
646 A223 10c multicolored .30 .30
647 A223 13c multicolored .40 .30
648 A223 15c multicolored .45 .35
649 A223 20c multicolored .50 .50
650 A223 25c multicolored .80 *.90*
651 A223 30c multicolored 1.10 1.10
652 A223 50c multicolored 2.25 *2.75*
653 A223 £1 multicolored 5.00 3.00
654 A223 £5 multicolored 18.00 16.00
Nos. 640-654 (15) 30.30 28.00

For surcharges see Nos. 684-685, 712.

Europa A224

6c, Ceramic figures playing the double flute, lyre and tambourine, 7th-6th cent. B.C. 15c, Cypriot violin, lute, flute, the Fourth Women's Dance from the Cyprus Suite.

1985, May 6 **Litho.** ***Perf. 12½***

655 A224 6c multicolored *.40* .40
656 A224 15c multicolored *1.10* *2.00*

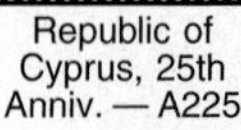

Republic of Cyprus, 25th Anniv. — A225

UN 40th Anniv. — A229

Natl. Liberation Movement, 30th Anniv. — A226

Intl. Youth Year A227

Solon Michaelides (1905-1979), Conductor, European Music Year — A228

Perf. 14½ (#657), 14½x14, 15 (#661)

1985, Sept. 23 **Litho.**

657	A225	4c multicolored	.25	.25
658	A226	6c multicolored	.25	.25
659	A227	13c multicolored	.55	*1.10*
660	A228	15c multicolored	.90	*1.25*
661	A229	20c multicolored	.50	*1.75*
		Nos. 657-661 (5)	2.45	*4.60*

Christmas — A230

Murals of the St. Ioannis Lampadistis Monastery, Kalopanyiotis: 4c, Virgin Mary's Visit to Elizabeth. 13c, The Nativity. 20c, The Candlemas, Church of Our Lady of Assinous, Nikitari.

1985, Nov. 18 **Litho.** ***Perf. 12½***

662	A230	4c multicolored	.25	.25
663	A230	13c multicolored	.50	.50
664	A230	20c multicolored	.85	*7.50*
		Nos. 662-664 (3)	1.60	8.25

Hellenistic Platinum Spoon A231

Designs: 20c, Ionian helmet, foot of a sculpture. 25c, Union of Eros and Intellect personified, abstract. 30c, Statue profile.

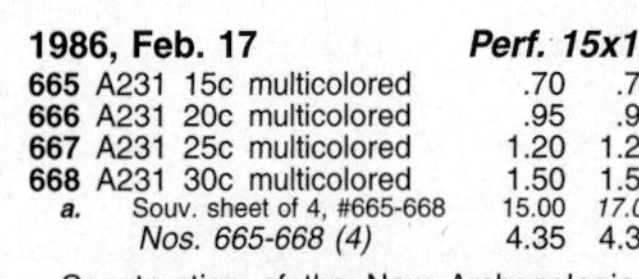

1986, Feb. 17 ***Perf. 15x14***

665	A231	15c multicolored	.70	.70
666	A231	20c multicolored	.95	.95
667	A231	25c multicolored	1.20	1.20
668	A231	30c multicolored	1.50	1.50
a.		Souv. sheet of 4, #665-668	15.00	*17.00*
		Nos. 665-668 (4)	4.35	4.35

Construction of the New Archaeological Museum, Nicosia. Department of Antiquities, 50th anniv. No. 668a sold for £1.

Europa Issue

Mouflon, Cedar Trees A232

17c, Flamingos, Larnaca Salt Lake.

1986, Apr. 28 **Litho.** ***Perf. 14x13***

669	A232	7c shown	*.40*	*.35*
670	A232	17c multicolored	*1.50*	*2.50*

Seashells A233

1986, July 1 ***Perf. 14x13½***

671	A233	5c Chlamys pesfelis	.35	.35
672	A233	7c Charonia variegata	.40	.40
673	A233	18c Murex brandaris	1.00	1.00
674	A233	25c Cypraea spurca	1.30	*2.00*
		Nos. 671-674 (4)	3.05	3.75

Overseas Cypriots Year A234

Halley's Comet A235

Anniversaries and events: No. 677, Comet tail, Edmond Halley.

Perf. 13½x13

1986, Oct. 13 **Litho.** **Wmk. 344**

675	A234	15c multicolored	1.10	.75
676	A235	18c shown	1.60	*2.00*
677	A235	18c multicolored	1.60	*2.00*
a.		Pair, #676-677	3.25	*4.00*
		Nos. 675-677 (3)	4.30	*4.75*

No. 677a has continuous design.

Road Safety A236

5c, Pedestrian crossing. 7c, Helmet, motorcycle controls. 18c, Seatbelt, rearview mirror.

1986, Nov. 10 ***Perf. 14x13***

678	A236	5c multicolored	.60	.50
679	A236	7c multicolored	1.00	.50
680	A236	18c multicolored	2.40	*3.00*
		Nos. 678-680 (3)	4.00	4.00

Intl. Peace Year, Christmas A237

Nativity frescoes (details): 5c, Church of Panayia tou Araka. 15c, Church of Panayia tou Moutoulla. 17c, Church of St. Nicholaos tis Steyis.

1986, Nov. 24 ***Perf. 13½x14***

681	A237	5c multicolored	.40	.30
682	A237	15c multicolored	1.25	.60
683	A237	17c multicolored	1.60	*2.00*
		Nos. 681-683 (3)	3.25	2.90

Nos. 645 and 647 Surcharged

Perf. 14x15, 15x14

1986, Oct. 13 **Litho.** **Wmk. 344**

684	A223	7c on 6c multi	.90	.50
685	A223	18c on 13c multi	1.75	1.00

Miniature Sheet

Troodos Churches on UNESCO World Heritage List — A238

Churches and frescoes: a, Assinou, Nikitari. b, Moutoulla, Moutoullas. c, Podithou, Galata. d, Ayios Ioannis Lampadistis, Kalopanayiotis. e, Timios Stavros, Pelentri. f, Stavros Ayiasmati, Platanistasa. g, Archangelos Pedoula, Pedoulas. h, Ayios Nicolaos tis Steyis, Kakopetria. i, Araka, Lagoudera.

Perf. 12½

1987, Apr. 22 **Photo.** **Unwmk.**

686	A238	Sheet of 9	10.00	10.00
a.-i.		15c any single	1.00	1.00

Europa Issue

Modern Architecture A239

7c, Central Bank of Cyprus. 18c, Cyprus Communications Authority.

Perf. 14x13½

1987, May 11 **Litho.** **Wmk. 344**

687	A239	7c multicolored	*.50*	*.40*
688	A239	18c multicolored	*1.00*	*1.75*

Ships Named Kyrenia A240

2c, The Kyrenia, Kyrenia Castle. 3c, Kyrenia II, Perama Shipyard. 5c, Kyrenia II, Paphos. 17c, Kyrenia II, NY Harbor.

1987, Oct. 3

689	A240	2c multicolored	.45	.30
690	A240	3c multicolored	.60	.75
691	A240	5c multicolored	.80	.50
692	A240	17c multicolored	1.75	1.25
		Nos. 689-692 (4)	3.60	2.80

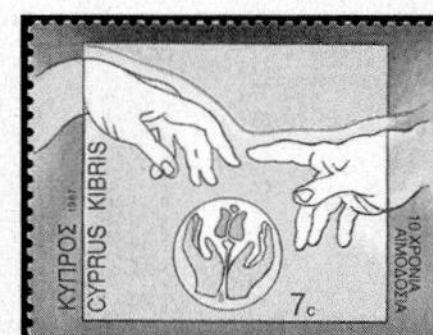

Blood Donation Coordinating Committee, 10th Anniv. — A241

European Campaign for Countryside — A242

TROODOS '87 — A243

Perf. 14x13½

1987, Nov. 2 **Litho.** **Wmk. 344**

693	A241	7c multicolored	.60	.55
694	A242	15c multicolored	1.40	1.25
695	A243	20c multicolored	2.00	*2.75*
		Nos. 693-695 (3)	4.00	4.55

Christmas A244

1987, Nov. 30 ***Perf. 14***

696	A244	5c Babe in a manger	.35	.35
697	A244	15c Ornament	1.25	1.25
698	A244	17c Fruit bowl	1.50	*2.00*
		Nos. 696-698 (3)	3.10	3.60

Cyprus Customs Union in Cooperation with the EEC — A245

15c, Natl. and EEC flags. 18c, Maps.

Perf. 13x13½

1988, Jan. 11 **Wmk. 344**

699	A245	15c multicolored	1.25	*1.60*
700	A245	18c multicolored	1.60	1.60

A246

Europa (Communication and transportation): No. 701, Electronic mail (Intelpost). No. 702, Cellular telephone system. No. 703, Cyprus Airways, technology vs. ecology (jet, 3 flamingos). No. 704, Cyprus Airways (jet, 4 flamingos).

1988, May 9 ***Perf. 14x14½***

701	A246	7c multicolored	*.65*	*1.00*
702	A246	7c multicolored	*.65*	*1.00*
a.		Pair, #701-702	*1.30*	*2.00*

703 A246 18c multicolored 2.25 3.00
704 A246 18c multicolored 2.25 3.00
a. Pair, #703-704 *6.50 6.00*
Nos. 701-704 (4) 5.80 8.00

1988 Summer Olympics, Seoul — A247

Unwmk.

1988, June 27 Photo. *Perf. 12*
Granite Paper

705 A247 5c Sailing .40 .30
706 A247 7c Track .45 .45
707 A247 10c Marksmanship .50 .70
708 A247 20c Judo 1.10 1.50
Nos. 705-708 (4) 2.45 2.95

Non-Aligned Foreign Minister's Conference — A248

Designs: 10c, Natl. coat of arms. 50c, Jawaharlal Nehru, Tito, Gamal Abdel Nasser and Makarios III (1913-77).

Perf. 14x13½

1988, Sept. 5 Litho. Wmk. 344

709 A248 1c shown .25 .25
710 A248 10c multicolored .65 .65
711 A248 50c multicolored 3.00 3.00
Nos. 709-711 (3) 3.90 3.90

No. 643 Srchd.

1988, Oct. 3 Litho. *Perf. 15x14*

712 A223 15c on 4c multi 1.75 1.40

Christmas A249

5c, Candlemas. 15c, Madonna and child. 17c, Adoration of the Magi.

Perf. 13½x14

1988, Nov. 28 Litho. Wmk. 344

713 A249 5c multicolored .40 .25
714 A249 15c multicolored .85 .30
715 A249 17c multicolored 1.30 *1.75*
Nos. 713-715 (3) 2.55 2.30

A250

1988, Dec. 10

716 A250 25c lt ultra & int blue 1.40 1.40

UN Declaration of Human Rights, 40th anniv.

3rd Games of Small European States, Nicosia A251

Perf. 13½

1989, Apr. 10 Litho. Unwmk.

717 A251 1c Discus .40 .30
718 A251 5c Javelin .40 .30
719 A251 15c Wrestling .90 .50
720 A251 18c Running 1.10 1.10

Size: 110x80mm

Imperf

721 A251 £1 Nike, laurel, bird 7.50 7.50
Nos. 717-721 (5) 10.30 9.70

Various Children's Games A252

Perf. 13x13½

1989, May 8 Litho. Unwmk.

722 A252 7c multi (5 boys) *.85 .75*
723 A252 7c multi (6 boys) *.85 .75*
a. Pair, #722-723 *1.90 1.90*
724 A252 18c multi (6 boys) *1.25 1.10*
725 A252 18c multi (5 boys) *1.25 1.10*
a. Pair, #724-725 *2.75 2.75*
Nos. 722-725 (4) 4.20 3.70

Europa.

French Revolution, Bicent. — A253

Perf. 11½

1989, July 7 Litho. Unwmk.
Granite Paper

726 A253 18c multicolored 1.40 1.00

A254

A255

1989, Sept. 4 *Perf. 13½*

727 A254 15c multicolored .65 .65
728 A255 30c multicolored 1.40 1.40

15c for Interparliamentary Union, cent. 30c for 9th Non-Aligned Summit Conf., Belgrade.

Apiculture A256

3c, Honeycomb and bees. 10c, Gathering nectar on pink flower. 15c, Gathering nectar on white flower. 18c, Queen, worker bees.

1989, Oct. 15 *Perf. 13½x14*

729 A256 3c multicolored .50 .30
730 A256 10c multicolored .90 .60
731 A256 15c multicolored 1.10 .60
732 A256 18c multicolored 1.25 *1.75*
Nos. 729-732 (4) 3.75 3.25

Annivs. & Events — A257

Designs: 3c, Armenian earthquake. 5c, Cyprus Philatelic Society. 7c, European Cancer Year. 17c, World Food Day.

1989, Nov. 13

733 A257 3c multicolored .35 *1.10*
734 A257 5c multicolored .50 .30
735 A257 7c multicolored .85 *1.40*
736 A257 17c multicolored 1.25 *1.40*
Nos. 733-736 (4) 2.95 *4.20*

A258

A259

Mosaics, 3rd-5th Cent. A260

Details: 1c, Winter, from *The Four Seasons,* House of Dionysos. 2c, Personification of Crete, from *Theseus Slaying the Minotaur,* Villa of Theseus. 3c, Centaur and Maenad, from *The Dionysiac Procession,* House of Aion, vert. 4c, *Poseidon and Amymone,* House of Dionysos. 5c, Leda, from *Leda and the Swan,* House of Aion. 7c, Apollon, from *Apollo and Marsyas,* House of Aion. 10c, Hermes and Dionysos, from *Hermes Presenting Dionysos to Tropheus,* House of Aion, vert. 15c, Cassiopeia, from *Cassiopeia and the Nereids,* House of Aion. 18c, *Orpheus Playing the Lyre,* House of Orpheus. 20c, Nymphs preparing bath, from *Hermes Presenting Dionysos to Tropheus,* vert. 25c, Amazon holding double ax and reins, House of Orpheus, vert. 40c, Doris, one of 3 Nereids in *Cassiopeia and the Nereids.* 50c, Hercules and the lion, from *The First Labor of Hercules,* House of Orpheus. £1, *Apollon and Daphne,* House of Dionysos. £3, Cupid hunting, Villa of Theseus.

Perf. 13, 13x13½ (2c, 4c, 18c, 40c), 13½x13 (3c, 10c, 20c, 25c)

1989, Dec. 29

737 A258 1c multicolored .50 *1.50*
738 A259 2c multicolored .50 *1.50*
739 A259 3c multicolored .65 *1.50*
740 A259 4c multicolored .85 *1.50*
741 A258 5c multicolored .85 .30
742 A258 7c multicolored 1.10 .35
743 A259 10c multicolored 1.30 .40
744 A258 15c multicolored 2.10 .65
745 A259 18c multicolored 2.10 .70
746 A259 20c multicolored 2.50 .90
747 A259 25c multicolored 2.50 .90
748 A259 40c multicolored 3.75 2.00

Perf. 13½x14

749 A260 50c multicolored 2.75 2.00
750 A260 £1 multicolored 6.25 3.75
751 A260 £3 multicolored 13.00 *14.00*
Nos. 737-751 (15) 40.70 31.95

UNESCO World Literacy Year — A261

83rd Interparliamentary Conference, Nicosia — A262

Lions Europa Forum A263

Anniversaries & events.

1990, Apr. 3 *Perf. 14x13½*

752 A261 15c multicolored .80 .80
753 A262 17c multicolored .95 .95
754 A263 18c multicolored 1.25 1.25
Nos. 752-754 (3) 3.00 3.00

Europa A264

Post Offices: 7c, Paphos. 18c, Limassol City Center.

1990, May 10 Litho. *Perf. 13x13½*

755 A264 7c multicolored *1.00 .45*
756 A264 18c multicolored *1.75 2.50*

European Year of Tourism — A265

Designs: 5c, Hotel and Catering Institute, 25th anniv. 7c, Holy Church of St. Lazarus, 1100th anniv. 15c, Female silhouette, butterflies. 18c, Male silhouette, birds.

1990, July 9 *Perf. 14*

757 A265 5c multicolored .60 .60
758 A265 7c multicolored .75 .75
759 A265 15c multicolored 2.10 1.75
760 A265 18c multicolored 2.40 *3.75*
Nos. 757-760 (4) 5.85 6.85

Republic of Cyprus, 30th Anniv. A266

1990, Sept. 29 Photo. *Perf. 11½*

761 A266 15c Sun .75 .60
762 A266 17c shown .95 .70
763 A266 18c Fish 1.25 .80
764 A266 40c Birds, flowers 3.00 *5.00*

Size: 90x90mm

Imperf

765 A266 £1 Stylized bird 6.50 6.50
Nos. 761-765 (5) 12.45 13.60

Flowers — A267

2c, Chionodoxa lochiae. 3c, Pancrayium maritimum. 5c, Paeonia mascula. 7c, Cyclamen cyprium. 15c, Tulipa cypria. 18c, Crocus cyprius.

1990, Nov. 5 Litho. *Perf. 13½x13*

766 A267 2c multicolored .40 *1.50*
767 A267 3c multicolored .60 *1.50*
768 A267 5c multicolored .85 .65
769 A267 7c multicolored 1.10 1.00
770 A267 15c multicolored 2.25 2.25
771 A267 18c multicolored 2.40 *3.50*
Nos. 766-771 (6) 7.60 10.40

Christmas A268

1990, Dec. 3 *Perf. 13½x14*

772 A268 5c Nativity .90 .30
773 A268 15c Virgin and Child 1.90 .45
774 A268 17c Nativity, diff. 2.25 *3.00*
Nos. 772-774 (3) 5.05 3.75

Mosaics From Kanakaria Church — A269

1991, Mar. 28 Photo. *Perf. 12*

Granite Paper

775 A269 5c Archangel .80 .25
776 A269 15c Christ Child .85 .75
777 A269 17c St. James 1.60 *1.75*
778 A269 18c St. Matthew 1.75 *2.25*
Nos. 775-778 (4) 5.00 5.00

Europa A270

1991, May 6 Litho. *Perf. 13x13½*

779 A270 7c Spacecraft Ulysses *.75 .40*
780 A270 18c Spacecraft Giotto *1.60 2.25*

Oenanthe Cypriaca (Cyprus Wheatear) A271

1991, July 4 Litho. *Perf. 13½*

781 A271 5c Juvenile bird 1.10 .50
782 A271 7c Autumn plumage 1.25 .50
783 A271 15c Male bird 1.50 .75
784 A271 30c Female bird 2.40 *3.75*
Nos. 781-784 (4) 6.25 5.50

UN High Commissioner for Refugees, 40th Anniv. — A272

1991, Oct. 7 Litho. *Perf. 14x13½*

785 A272 5c shown .35 .25
786 A272 15c Legs 1.40 .75
787 A272 18c Faces 1.75 *2.25*
Nos. 785-787 (3) 3.50 3.25

Christmas A273

1991, Nov. 25 Litho. *Perf. 13½*

788 A273 5c Nativity scene .35 .25
789 A273 15c St. Basil .85 .85
790 A273 17c Baptism of Jesus 1.10 1.50
a. Strip of 3, #788-790 2.75 2.75

Strips of 3 are from sheets of 9.

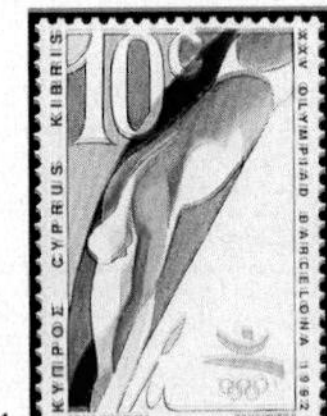

A274

1992, Apr. 3 Litho. *Perf. 12*

Granite Paper

791 A274 10c Swimming 1.10 .60
792 A274 20c Long jump 1.50 1.00
793 A274 30c Running 2.25 2.25
794 A274 35c Discus 2.50 2.50
Nos. 791-794 (4) 7.35 6.35

1992 Summer Olympics, Barcelona.

Expo '92, Seville A275

10th Youth Under 16 European Soccer Tournament — A276

Opening of University of Cyprus A277

1992, Apr. 20 Litho. *Perf. 14*

795 A275 20c multicolored 2.00 .95
796 A276 25c multicolored 2.10 1.25
797 A277 30c multicolored 2.10 *2.75*
Nos. 795-797 (3) 6.20 4.95

Discovery of America, 500th Anniv. A278

No. 798, Map. No. 799, Embarkation at Palos. No. 800, Three ships. No. 801, Columbus.

1992, May 29 Litho. *Perf. 13x13½*

798 A278 10c multicolored *1.00 .90*
799 A278 10c multicolored *1.00 .90*
a. Pair, #798-799 *2.25 2.25*
800 A278 30c multicolored *1.50 1.25*
801 A278 30c multicolored *1.50 1.25*
a. Pair, #800-801 *3.25 3.25*
Nos. 798-801 (4) 5.00 4.30

Europa.

Reptiles A279

Designs: 7c, Chamaeleo chamaeleon. 10c, Lacerta laevis troodica. 15c, Mauremys caspica. 20c, Coluber cypriensis.

1992, Sept. 14 Litho. *Perf. 14x13½*

802 A279 7c multicolored 1.00 .40
803 A279 10c multicolored 1.10 .65
804 A279 15c multicolored 1.60 1.10
805 A279 20c multicolored 2.10 *2.50*
Nos. 802-805 (4) 5.80 4.65

Intl. Maritime and Shipping Conference — A280

Unwmk.

1992, Nov. 9 Litho. *Perf. 14*

806 A280 50c multicolored 4.00 4.00

Christmas A281

Church wall paintings: 7c, "Virgin Mary Greeting Elizabeth," Church of Timios Stavros, Pelendri. 15c, "The Virgin and Child," Church of Panayia tou Araka. 20c, "Holy Mother Odigitria," Church of Ayios Nicolaos tis Steyis.

1992, Nov. 9 *Perf. 13½x14*

807 A281 7c multicolored .65 .35
808 A281 15c multicolored 1.00 .75
809 A281 20c multicolored 1.60 *2.25*
Nos. 807-809 (3) 3.25 3.35

A282

1993, Feb. 15 Litho. *Perf. 14*

810 A282 10c multicolored 1.00 .80

Pancyprian Gymnasium, cent.

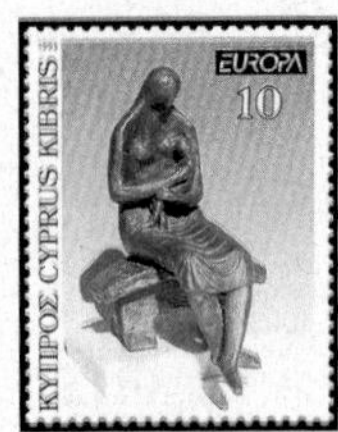

A283

Europa: 10c, Bronze sculpture, Motherhood, by N. Dymiotis (1930-1990). 30c, Applique, Motherhood, by Savva (1924-1968), horiz.

1993, Apr. 3 *Perf. 13½x14, 14x13½*

811 A283 10c multicolored *.90 .65*
812 A283 30c multicolored *1.60 2.00*

13th European Cup for Women Athletes A284

Scouting in Cyprus, 80th Anniv. — A285

Water Skiing Moufflon Encouragement Cup — A286

Archbishop Makarios III, 80th Anniv. of Birth — A287

Perf. 13½x14, 14x13½

1993, May 24 Litho.

813 A284 7c multicolored .50 .40
814 A285 10c multicolored .70 .55
815 A286 20c multicolored 1.25 1.25
a. Inscribed "MUFFLON" *13.00*
816 A287 25c multicolored 1.75 *2.25*
Nos. 813-816 (4) 4.20 4.45

Fish — A288

1993, Sept. 6 Litho. *Perf. 14x13½*

817 A288 7c Holocentrus ruber .60 .35
818 A288 15c Scorpaena scrofa .90 .70
819 A288 20c Serranus scriba 1.00 1.00
820 A288 30c Balistes capriscus 2.00 *2.40*
Nos. 817-820 (4) 4.50 4.45

Maritime Cyprus A289

1993, Oct. 4 *Perf. 14*

821 A289 25c multicolored 2.25 2.25

12th Commonwealth Summit Conference — A290

1993, Oct. 4 *Perf. 14x13½*

822 A290 35c red brown & tan 2.10 2.10
823 A290 40c olive brown & tan 2.75 2.75

Christmas A291

7c, Carved wooden cross, Stavrovouni Monastery. 20c, Crucifixion, cross from Lefkara Church. 25c, Nativity, cross from Pedoulas Church.

1993, Nov. 22 Litho. *Perf. 13½x14*

824 A291 7c multicolored .40 .30
825 A291 20c multicolored .95 .95

Perf. 14x13½

826 A291 25c multi, horiz. 1.40 2.00
Nos. 824-826 (3) 2.75 3.25

Copper Industry A292

Europa: 10c, Early smelting of copper. 30c, Map, boat, copper ingot.

1994, Mar. 1 Litho. *Perf. 13x13½*

827 A292 10c multicolored *.70 .70*
828 A292 30c multicolored *1.25 1.75*

Persons with Special Needs — A293

Intl. Olympic Committee, Cent. — A294

World Gymnasiade, Nicosia — A295

Intl. Year of the Family — A296

1994, May 9 Litho. *Perf. 13*

829 A293 7c multicolored .55 .35
830 A294 15c multicolored 1.00 .65
831 A295 20c multicolored 1.25 1.25
832 A296 25c multicolored 1.50 *2.00*
Nos. 829-832 (4) 4.30 4.25

Turkish Invasion and Occupation of Cyprus, 20th Anniv. — A297

1994, June 27 Litho. *Perf. 14*

833 A297 10c Human rights .80 .40
834 A297 50c Cultural heritage 3.25 3.25

Trees — A298

7c, Pinus nigra. 15c, Cedrus libani. 20c, Quercus alnifolia. 30c, Arbutus andrachne.

1994, Oct. 10 Litho. *Perf. 13½*

835 A298 7c multicolored .70 .40
836 A298 15c multicolored 1.10 .80
837 A298 20c multicolored 1.25 1.25
838 A298 30c multicolored 1.90 *2.50*
Nos. 835-838 (4) 4.95 4.95

ICAO, 50th Anniv. A299

1994, Nov. 21 Litho. *Perf. 14*

839 A299 30c multicolored 3.25 3.25

Christmas A300

Designs: 7c, Virgin Mary (Vlahernitissa). 20c, Nativity. 25c, Archangel Michael.

1994, Nov. 21 *Perf. 13½*

840 A300 7c multicolored .80 .50
841 A300 20c multicolored 1.90 1.00
842 A300 25c multicolored 2.50 *3.00*
Nos. 840-842 (3) 5.20 4.50

Traditional Costumes — A301

Costumes: 1c, Female, Phapos. 2c, Bridal, Karpess. 3c, Female, Phapos, diff. 5c, Female, Messaoria. 7c, Bridegroom's. 10c, Shepherd's, Messaoria. 15c, Festive female, Nicosia. 20c, Festive female, Karpass. 25c, Female, Mountain-Pitsillia. 30c, Festive female, Karpass, diff. 35c, Rural male. 40c, Plain festive male, Messaoria. 50c, Urban male. £1, Urban festive female, Sarka.

1994, Dec. 27 Litho. *Perf. 13½x13*

843 A301 1c multicolored .40 .40
844 A301 2c multicolored .60 .60
845 A301 3c multicolored .65 .65
846 A301 5c multicolored .80 .80
847 A301 7c multicolored .85 .85
848 A301 10c multicolored 1.25 1.25
849 A301 15c multicolored 2.10 2.10
850 A301 20c multicolored 2.10 2.10
851 A301 25c multicolored 2.40 2.40
852 A301 30c multicolored 2.40 2.40
853 A301 35c multicolored 2.40 2.40
854 A301 40c multicolored 2.75 2.75
855 A301 50c multicolored 3.50 3.50
856 A301 £1 multicolored 6.00 6.00
a. Inscribed "1998" 6.00 6.00
Nos. 843-856 (14) 28.20 28.20

Third Intl. Congress of Cypriot Studies — A302

Excavations: 20c, Hearth room, Ashlar building, Paliotaverna. 30c, Hall, Agios Demetrios area, Kalavasos. £1, Old Nicosia Archbishorpic building, 18th cent.

1995, Feb. 27 Litho. *Perf. 14*

859 A302 20c multicolored 1.25 1.25
860 A302 30c multicolored 1.90 1.90

Size: 107x71mm

Imperf

861 A302 £1 multicolored 6.25 6.25
Nos. 859-861 (3) 9.40 9.40

A303

Liberation Monument, Nicosia: a, People walking left. b, Statue of Liberty, prisoners leaving prison. c, People walking right.

1995, Mar. 31 Litho. *Perf. 13x14*

862 Strip of 3 4.25 4.25
a.-c. A303 20c any single 1.35 1.35

No. 862 is a continuous design.

Formation of EOKA (Natl. Organization of Cypriot Struggle), 40th anniv.

Europa — A304

10c, Concentration camp prisoners, dove, rainbow, map of Europe. 30c, Prisoner, dove.

1995, May 8 Litho. *Perf. 13½*

863 A304 10c multicolored *1.00 .75*
864 A304 30c multicolored *2.00 3.00*

Liberation of the concentration camps, 50th anniv.

Health A305

7c, Proper nutrition, exercise. 10c, Fight against AIDS. 15c, Fight against illegal drugs. 20c, Stop smoking campaign.

1995, June 26 Litho. *Perf. 13½*

865 A305 7c multi, vert. .35 .30
866 A305 10c multi .75 .75
867 A305 15c multi .80 .80
868 A305 20c multi, vert. 1.10 *1.50*
Nos. 865-868 (4) 3.00 3.35

European Cultural Month A306

25c, Map of Europe, building.

1995, Sept. 18 Litho. *Perf. 13x13½*

869 A306 20c shown .85 .85
870 A306 25c multicolored 1.10 *1.25*

Souvenir Sheet

Europhilex '95 — A307

Designs: a, Dove carrying letter, stars. b, Stars, exhibition emblem.

1995, Sept. 18 Litho. *Perf. 14*

871 A307 Sheet of 2 8.75 8.75
a.-b. 50c any single 4.00 4.00

A limited number were surcharged £5 on each stamp and sold at "Europhilex '95" on Oct. 27 and 28, 1995.

UN, 50th Anniv. A308

Volleyball, Cent. — A309

European Conservation Year — A310

World Clay Target Shooting Championships — A311

Perf. 13x13½, 13½x13

1995, Oct. 24 **Litho.**

872	A308	10c	multicolored	.65	.65
873	A309	15c	multicolored	1.00	.75
874	A310	20c	multicolored	1.40	1.10
875	A311	25c	multicolored	1.60	*2.25*
			Nos. 872-875 (4)	4.65	4.75

Christmas A312

Various reliquaries, Kykko Monastery.

1995, Nov. 27 **Litho.** ***Perf. 13½x13***

No.					
876	A312	7c	multicolored	.60	.45
877	A312	20c	multicolored	1.40	1.10
878	A312	25c	multicolored	1.75	*2.25*
			Nos. 876-878 (3)	3.75	3.80

A313

A314

A315

Anniversaries and Events — A316

1996, Jan. 4 **Litho.** ***Perf. 13½x13***

879	A313	10c	multicolored	.90	.65
880	A314	20c	multicolored	1.50	1.10
881	A315	35c	multicolored	2.25	2.25
882	A316	40c	multicolored	2.25	*2.75*
			Nos. 879-882 (4)	6.90	6.75

Pancyprian Organization of Large Families, 25th anniv. (No. 879). Motion pictures, cent. (NO. 880). UNICEF, 50th anniv. (No. 881). 13th Conf. of Commonwealth Speakers and Presiding Officers (No. 882).

Portraits of Women

A317 A318

1996, Apr. 8 **Litho.** ***Perf. 14***

883	A317	10c	multicolored	*1.10*	*.50*
884	A318	30c	multicolored	*2.40*	*2.75*

Europa.

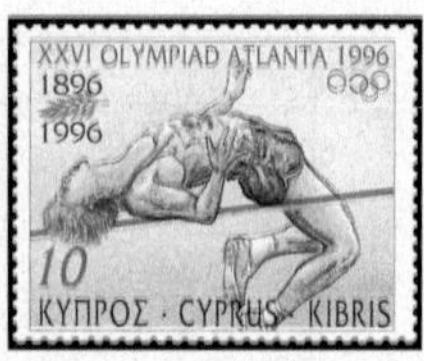

1996 Summer Olympics, Atlanta A319

1996, June 10 **Litho.** ***Perf. 13***

885	A319	10c	High jump	.90	.35
886	A319	20c	Javelin	1.25	.70
887	A319	25c	Wrestling	1.75	1.10
888	A319	30c	Swimming	2.10	*2.50*
			Nos. 885-888 (4)	6.00	4.65

Mills of Cyprus — A320

1996, Sept. 23 **Litho.** ***Perf. 13***

889	A320	10c	Watermill	.95	.70
890	A320	15c	Olivemill	1.40	1.00
891	A320	20c	Windmill	1.50	1.40
892	A320	25c	Handmill	2.00	2.00
			Nos. 889-892 (4)	5.85	5.10

Icons, Religious Landmarks A321

Designs: No. 893, Icon of Our Lady of Iberia, Moscow. No. 894, Holy Monastery of Stavrovouni, Cyprus. No. 895, Icon of St. Nicholas, Cyprus. No. 896, Iveron Mother of God Resurrection Gate, Moscow.

1996, Nov. 13 **Litho.** ***Perf. 11½***

No.					
893	A321	30c	multicolored	2.10	2.10
894	A321	30c	multicolored	2.10	2.10
895	A321	30c	multicolored	2.10	2.10
896	A321	30c	multicolored	2.10	2.10
a.			Block of 4, #893-896	9.00	9.00

See Russia No. 6356.

Christmas A322

Paintings from Church of the Virgin of Asinou: 7c, Detail from Nativity. 20c, Virgin Mary between Archangels Gabriel and Michael. 25c, Christ bestowing blessings, vert.

1996, Dec. 2 ***Perf. 13x13½, 13½x13***

No.					
897	A322	7c	multicolored	.90	.50
898	A322	20c	multicolored	2.00	1.25
899	A322	25c	multicolored	2.40	*2.75*
			Nos. 897-899 (3)	5.30	4.50

Easter A323

1997, Mar. 24 **Litho.** ***Perf. 13x13½***

900	A323	15c	The Last Supper	1.25	.75
901	A323	25c	The Crucifixion	1.75	1.75

A324

1997, Mar. 24 ***Perf. 13½x13***

902	A324	30c	multicolored	4.25	3.75

European Men's Clubs Basketball Cup finals.

A325

Europa (Stories and Legends): 30c, Man in red cape fighting Death, eagle above.

1997, May 5 **Litho.** ***Perf. 13½x13***

903	A325	15c	shown	*1.10*	*.50*
904	A325	30c	multicolored	*2.10*	*2.50*

Insects A326

10c, Oedipoda miniata. 15c, Acherontia atropos. 25c, Daphnis nerii. 35c, Ascalaphus macaronius.

1997, June 30 **Litho.** ***Perf. 13x13½***

905	A326	10c	multicolored	1.00	.40
906	A326	15c	multicolored	1.50	.60
907	A326	25c	multicolored	2.00	1.25
908	A326	35c	multicolored	2.50	2.50
			Nos. 905-908 (4)	7.00	4.75

Archbishop Makarios III (1913-77), 1st Pres. of Cyprus Republic A327

1997, Aug. 1 **Litho.** ***Perf. 13x13½***

909	A327	15c	multicolored	1.50	1.00

Christmas A328

Frescoes from Church of Ayios Ioannis Lambadestis: 10c, Nativity. 25c, Magi on way to Bethlehem. 30c, Flight into Egypt.

1997, Nov. 17 **Litho.** ***Perf. 13½x13***

No.					
910	A328	10c	multicolored	.95	.65
911	A328	25c	multicolored	2.40	1.40
912	A328	30c	multicolored	2.75	2.75
			Nos. 910-912 (3)	6.10	4.80

Minerals A329

1998, Mar. 9 **Litho.** ***Perf. 13x13½***

913	A329	10c	Green jasper	.55	.40
914	A329	15c	Iron pyrite	.80	.65
915	A329	25c	Gypsum	1.30	1.30
916	A329	30c	Chalcedony	1.60	1.60
			Nos. 913-916 (4)	4.25	3.95

1998 World Cup Soccer Championships, France — A330

1998, May 4 **Litho.** ***Perf. 14***

917	A330	35c	multicolored	2.75	1.75

Europa A331

Festivals, holidays: 15c, "Katakklysmos" Larnaca. 30c, People watching proclamation of independence, 1960.

1998, May 4

918	A331	15c multicolored	*1.10*	*.55*
919	A331	30c multicolored	*2.40*	*1.60*

Ovis Gmelini Ophion A332

World Wildlife Fund: No. 920, Male, female, calf. No. 921, Group running. No. 922, Male up close. No. 923, Male with front legs up on rock, one grazing.

1998, June 22 Litho. *Perf. 13x13½*

920	A332	25c multicolored	1.50	1.50
921	A332	25c multicolored	1.50	1.50
922	A332	25c multicolored	1.50	1.50
923	A332	25c multicolored	1.50	1.50
a.		Block of 4, #920-923	6.00	6.00

Issued in sheets of 16.

World Stamp Day A333

1998, Oct. 9 Litho. *Perf. 14*

924	A333	30c multicolored	2.75	2.75
a.		Booklet pane of 8	22.00	
		Complete booklet, #924a	25.00	

A334

1998, Oct. 9

925	A334	50c multicolored	2.00	2.00

Universal Declaration of Human Rights, 50th anniv.

A335

Christmas (Scenes from paintings in the Church of the Virgin of Théosképasti, Kalopanayiotis): 10c, The Annunciation. 25c, The Nativity. 30c, Baptism of Christ.

1998, Nov. 16 Litho. *Perf. 14*

926	A335	10c multicolored	.35	.35
927	A335	25c multicolored	.90	.90
928	A335	30c multicolored	2.75	2.75
a.		Souvenir sheet, #926-928	4.00	4.00
		Nos. 926-928 (3)	4.00	4.00

Mushrooms — A336

10c, Pleurotus eryngii. 15c, Lactarius deliciosus. 25c, Sparassis crispa. 30c, Morchella elata.

1999, Mar. 4 Litho. *Perf. 13½x13*

929	A336	10c multicolored	.50	.50
930	A336	15c multicolored	1.00	.60
931	A336	25c multicolored	1.50	1.50
932	A336	30c multicolored	1.60	*2.50*
		Nos. 929-932 (4)	4.60	5.10

Natl. Parks and Nature Preserves A337

1999, May 6 Litho. *Perf. 14*

933	A337	15c Tripylos Reserve	*.90*	*.50*
934	A337	30c Lara Reserve	*1.60*	*2.10*
a.		Booklet pane, 4 each #933-934	*11.00*	
		Complete booklet, #934a	*12.00*	

Europa.

Council of Europe, 50th Anniv. A338

1999, May 6

935	A338	30c multicolored	2.10	2.10

4000 Years of Hellenism — A339

a, Sanctuary of Apollo Hylates, Kourion. b, Mycenaean "Krater of the Warriors," Athens. c, Mycenaean amphoral krater, Cyprus Museum. d, Sanctuary of Apollo Epikourios, Delphi.

1999, June 28 Litho. *Perf. 13½x13*

936	A339	25c Block of 4, #a.-d.	6.25	6.25

See Greece No. 1938.

UPU, 125th Anniv. A340

1999, Sept. 30 Litho. *Perf. 14*

937	A340	15c shown	1.00	.90
938	A340	35c "125"	2.50	2.00

Souvenir Sheet

Maritime Cyprus Shipping Conference — A341

Cyprus flag and: a, Container ship. b, Binoculars, chart, cap. c, Ship with yellow stripe on tower. d, Tanker.

1999, Sept. 30

939	A341	25c Sheet of 4, #a.-d.	5.00	5.00

Souvenir Sheet

Turkish Invasion of Cyprus, 25th Anniv. — A342

1999, Nov. 11 Litho. *Imperf.*

940	A342	30c multicolored	2.50	2.50

A343

1999, Nov. 11 *Perf. 14*

941	A343	10c Angel	.70	.55
942	A343	25c Magi	1.40	1.25
943	A343	30c Madonna and child	1.60	1.60
		Nos. 941-943 (3)	3.70	3.40

Christmas.

Souvenir Sheet

A344

Miss Universe 2000: a, 15c, Woman, stars. b, 35c, Armless nude statue of woman.

2000, Mar. 30 Litho. *Perf. 13¼x13*

944	A344	Sheet of 2, #a.-b.	3.00	3.00

Jewelry — A345

Various pieces of jewelry. Nos. 945-952 vert.

2000, Mar. 30 Litho. *Perf. 14*

945	A345	10c multi	.45	.45
946	A345	15c multi	.60	.60
947	A345	20c multi	.80	.80
948	A345	25c multi	1.00	1.00
949	A345	30c multi	1.25	1.25
950	A345	35c multi	1.40	1.40
951	A345	40c multi	1.60	1.60
952	A345	50c multi	2.25	2.25
953	A345	75c multi	3.00	3.00
954	A345	£1 multi	4.00	4.00
955	A345	£2 multi	7.50	7.50
956	A345	£3 multi	11.00	11.00
		Nos. 945-956 (12)	34.85	34.85

Cyprus Red Cross, 50th Anniv. A346

2000, May 9 Litho. *Perf. 13x13¼*

957	A346	15c multi	2.25	2.25

Memorial to Heroes of 1955-59 Independence Struggle — A347

2000, May 9 *Perf. 13¼x13*

958	A347	15c multi	2.40	2.40

Europa, 2000

Common Design Type

2000, May 9 *Perf. 14*

959	CD17	30c multi	*2.10*	*1.40*

World Meteorological Org., 50th Anniv. — A348

2000, May 9

960	A348	30c multi	2.25	2.25

European Convention of Human Rights, 50th Anniv. A349

2000, June 29 Litho. *Perf. 13x13¼*

961	A349	30c multi	3.00	3.00

Churches Damaged Under Turkish Occupation A350

Designs: 10c, Monastery of Antifonitis, Kalograia, vert. 15c, Church of St. Themonianos, Lysi, vert. 25c, Church of Panagia Kanakaria, Lytrhagkomi. 30c, Avgasida Monastery Church, Milia.

Perf. 13¼x13, 13x13¼

2000, June 29

962	A350	10c multi	1.10	.60
963	A350	15c multi	1.50	.80
964	A350	25c multi	2.00	1.60
965	A350	30c multi	2.40	2.40
		Nos. 962-965 (4)	7.00	5.40

2000 Summer Olympics, Sydney A351

Designs: 10c, Archery. 15c, Pommel horse. 25c, Diving. 35c, Trampoline.

2000, Sept. 14 Litho. *Perf. 13x13½*

966-969	A351	Set of 4	6.00	6.00

Christmas — A352

Gospel covers: 10c, Annunciation. 25c, Nativity. 30c, Baptism of Jesus.

2000, Nov. 2 ***Perf. 13½x13***
970-972 A352 Set of 3 5.00 5.00

Pavlos Liasides (1901-85), Poet — A353

2001, Mar. 12 Litho. ***Perf. 13¼x13***
973 A353 13c multi 1.25 .65

Commonwealth Day, 25th Anniv. — A354

2001, Mar. 12 ***Perf. 13x13¼***
974 A354 30c multi 2.75 2.75

UN High Commissioner for Refugees, 50th Anniv. — A355

2001, Mar. 12
975 A355 30c multi 2.50 2.50

Europa A356

Designs: 20c, Bridge over Diarizos River. 30c, Akaki River.

2001, May 3
976-977 A356 Set of 2 *4.00 2.00*
977a Booklet pane, 4 each #976-977 *17.00*
Booklet, #977a *19.00*

Crabs A357

Designs: 13c, Parthenope massena. 20c, Calappa granulata. 25c, Ocypode cursor. 30c, Pagurus bernhardus.

2001, June 7
978-981 A357 Set of 4 9.00 9.00

Loukis Akritas (1909-65), Writer — A358

2001, Oct. 25 Litho. ***Perf. 13½x13***
982 A358 20c multi 2.50 1.25

Christmas — A359

Holy Monastery of Macheras, 800th anniv.: 13c, Icon of Madonna. 25c, Monastery building. 30c, Crucifix.

2001, Oct. 25
983-985 A359 Set of 3 5.00 5.00

Cats — A360

No. 986, 20c: a, Red brown panel. b, Green panel.
No. 987, 25c: a, Dark brown panel. b, Orange brown panel.

2002, Mar. 21 Litho. ***Perf. 13x13½***
Horiz. Pairs, #a-b
986-987 A360 Set of 2 7.00 7.00

Europa — A361

Designs: 20c, Equestrian act. 30c, Tightrope walker.

2002, May 9 ***Perf. 13½x13***
988-989 A361 Set of 2 *4.00 2.00*
a. Booklet pane, 4 each #988-989 *17.00* —
Booklet, #989a *19.00*

Medicinal Plants A362

Designs: 13c, Myrtus communis. 20c, Lavandula stoechas. 25c, Capparis spinosa. 30c, Ocimum basilicum.

2002, June 13 ***Perf. 13x13½***
990-993 A362 Set of 4 7.00 7.00

Mother Teresa (1910-97) — A363

2002, Sept. 12 Litho. ***Perf. 13½x13***
994 A363 40c multi 4.00 4.00

Intl. Teachers' Day — A364

No. 995: a, 13c, Blackboard and teachers. b, 30c, Computer and teachers.

2002, Sept. 12 ***Perf. 13x13½***
995 A364 Horiz. pair, #a-b 3.75 3.75

Cyprus-Europhilex 02 Philatelic Exhibition — A365

No. 996: a, Seal, 490-470 B.C. (red brown background). b, Silver coin of Timoharis, 5th-4th cent B.C. (blue background) c, Silver coin of Stasioikos, 449 B.C. (yellow background).
No. 997: a, Clay oil lamp, 2nd cent. A.D. (olive green background). b, Clay statue of Europa on a bull, 7th-6th cent. B.C. (yellow background). c, Clay oil lamp, 1st cent. B.C. (lilac background)
No. 998: a, 15th cent. map of eastern Crete and western Cyprus, and statue of Aphrodite, 1st cent. B.C. b, Map of eastern Cyprus, and Abduction of Europe, by Francesco di Giorgio.

2002, Sept. 22
996 Horiz. strip of 3 4.50 4.50
a.-c. A365 20c Any single 1.50 1.50
997 Horiz. strip of 3 6.75 6.75
a.-c. A365 30c Any single 2.25 2.25

Souvenir Sheet

998 Sheet of 2, #a-b 9.50 9.50
a.-b. A365 50c Any single 3.75 3.75

Christmas A366

Wall painting in Church of Metamorphosis Sotiros, Palechori: 13c, Nativity, detail. 25c, Angels, detail. 30c, Entire painting (37x37mm).

Perf. 13x13½, 13¾ (30c)
2002, Nov. 21
999-1001 A366 Set of 3 5.75 5.75

Antique Automobiles A367

No. 1002: a, 20c, 1946 Triumph Roadster 1800. b, 25c, 1917 Ford Model T. c, 30c, 1932 Baby Ford.

2003, Mar. 20 Litho. ***Perf. 13x13½***
1002 A367 Vert. strip of 3, #a-c 6.50 6.50

Europa — A368

2003, May 8 ***Perf. 13½x13***
Color of Triangles
1003 A368 20c yellow *1.00* .65
a. Perf. 13½x13¾ on 3 sides *1.75 1.10*
1004 A368 30c red *1.60 1.00*
a. Perf. 13½x13¾ on 3 sides *3.00 1.60*
b. Booklet pane, 4 each #1003a-1004a *20.00* —
Complete booklet, #1004b *24.00*

European Ministers of Education, 7th Conference — A369

2003, June 12 Litho. ***Perf. 13½x13***
1005 A369 30c multi 2.25 2.25

Worldwide Fund for Nature (WWF) — A370

Mediterranean horseshoe bat: a, In flight. b, Close-up. c, Hanging from rock. d, With open mouth.

2003, June 12 ***Perf. 13x13½***
1006 A370 25c Block of 4, #a-b 7.00 7.00

Birds of Prey — A371

No. 1007, 20c: a, Eleonora's falcon. b, Eleonora's falcons in flight.
No. 1008, 25c: a, Head of Imperial eagle. b, Imperial eagles in flight.
No. 1009, 30c: a, Owl on branch. b, Owl in flight, eggs.

2003, Sept. 25 Litho. *Perf. 14*
Horiz. pairs, #a-b

1007-1009 A371 Set of 3 9.50 9.50

Famous Men A372

Designs: No. 1010, 5c, Constantinos Spyridakis (1903-76), Education minister. No. 1011, 5c, Tefkros Anthias (1903-68), poet (23x31mm).

Perf. 13x13¼, 13¼x13
2003, Nov. 13

1010-1011 A372 Set of 2 1.25 1.25

Christmas A373

Details of Nativity icon from church in Kourdali: 13c, Angels. 30c, Three Magi on horses. 40c, Entire icon (37x60mm).

Perf. 13¾x13¼, 13¾x14 (40c)
2003, Nov. 13

1012-1014 A373 Set of 3 5.50 5.50

FIFA (Fédération Internationale de Football Association), Cent. — A374

Perf. 13¼x13¾
2004, Mar. 11 Litho.

1015 A374 30c multi 2.25 2.25

UEFA (European Soccer Union), 50th Anniv. — A375

2004, Mar. 11 *Perf. 13¼x13*

1016 A375 30c multi 2.25 2.25

Yiannos Kranidiotis (1947-99), Politician A376

2004, May 1 *Perf. 13¼x13½*

1017 A376 20c multi 1.10 1.10

Admission to European Union — A377

2004, May 1 *Perf. 14¼x14*

1018 A377 30c multi 2.25 2.25

Europa A378

Cliff and: 20c, Amphitheater, ship. 30c, Family at seashore, sculpture

2004, May 1 *Perf. 13¾x13¼*

1019 A378 20c multi *1.25* .60
a. Perf. 13¾ on 3 sides *1.50* .70
1020 A378 30c multi *1.75* .90
a. Perf. 13¾ on 3 sides *2.00* *1.10*
b. Booklet pane, 4 each #1019a, 1020a *16.00* —
Complete booklet, #1020b *18.00*

2004 Summer Olympics, Athens — A379

Designs: 13c, Equestrian. 20c, Runners. 30c, Swimmers. 40c, Athletes, man in robe.

2004, June 10 Litho. *Perf. 13¼x13*

1021-1024 A379 Set of 4 5.75 5.75

Mammals — A380

No. 1025, 20c — Tursiops truncatus: a, Blue background. b, White background.
No. 1026, 30c — Vulpes vulpes indutus: a, Green background. b, White background.
No. 1027, 40c, Lepus europaeus cyprium: a, Orange brown background. b, White background.

2004, Sept. 9 Litho. *Perf. 13¾x13½*
Horiz. Pairs, #a-b

1025-1027 A380 Set of 3 13.00 13.00

Georgios Philippou Pierides (1904-99), Writer — A381

Emilios Chourmouzios (1904-73), Writer — A382

2004, Nov. 11 *Perf. 13¼x13*

1028 A381 5c multi .65 .65
1029 A382 5c multi .65 .65

Christmas A383

Details from icon depicting the birth of Christ, Monastery of Chrysoroyiatissa: 13c, Angels. 30c, Magi on horseback. 40c, Annunciation, vert. (37x60mm).
£1, Adoration of the Shepherds.

Perf. 13¾x13¼, 13¾x14 (40c)
2004, Nov. 11

1030-1032 A383 Set of 3 6.00 6.00

Souvenir Sheet
Perf. 13¾ on 3 Sides

1033 A383 £1 multi 6.75 6.75

No. 1033 contains one 37x38mm stamp.

Carolina Pelendritou, Swimming Gold Medalist at 2004 Paralympics A384

2005, Mar. 3 Litho. *Perf. 13¼x13¾*

1034 A384 20c multi 1.50 1.50

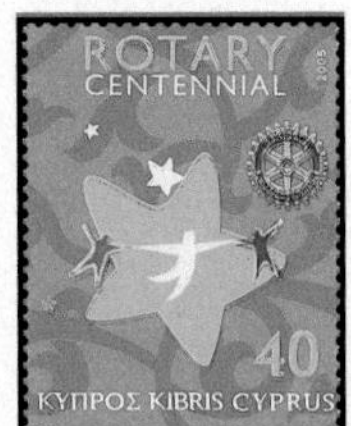

Rotary International, Cent. — A385

2005, Mar. 3

1035 A385 40c multi 2.50 2.50

Natl. Organization of Cypriot Struggle (EOKA), 50th Anniv. — A386

2005, Mar. 3

1036 A386 50c multi 3.00 3.00

Europa — A387

Table with food and: 20c, Purple grapes, sailboat. 30c, Green grapes, steamship.

2005, May 5 *Perf. 13½x13*
White Frame All Around

1037 A387 20c multi .90 .90
1038 A387 30c multi 1.40 1.40

Booklet Stamps
White Frame on 3 Sides
Perf. 13½ on 3 Sides

1039 A387 20c multi *1.25* .75
1040 A387 30c multi *1.75* *1.25*
a. Horiz. pair, #1039-1040 *3.25* *2.25*
b. Booklet pane, 4 #1040a *13.50* —
Complete booklet, #1040b *15.00*
Nos. 1037-1040 (4) 5.30 4.30

Dogs — A388

Designs: 13c, German shepherd. 20c, Hungarian vizsla. 30c, Labrador retriever. 40c, Dalmatian.

2005, June 16 Litho. *Perf. 13¼*

1041-1044 A388 Set of 4 8.00 8.00
1044a Booklet pane, #1041-1044 8.50 —
Complete booklet, #1044a 8.50

Christmas A389

Icons: 13c, Annunciation to the Shepherds. 30c, Adoration of the Magi. 40c, Madonna and Child, vert. (38x60mm).

Perf. 13¼, 13¾x14 (40c)
2005, Nov. 10 Litho.

1045-1047 A389 Set of 3 4.25 4.25

Souvenir Sheet

Europa Stamps, 50th Anniv. — A390

No. 1048: a, Cyprus #246. b, Cyprus #202. c, Cyprus #220. d, Cyprus #231.

2006, Feb. 23 Litho. *Perf. 13¾*

1048 A390 30c Sheet of 4, #a-d 7.00 7.00

Postal Museum, 25th Anniv. A391

2006, Mar. 30 *Perf. 13¾x13¼*

1049 A391 25c multi 1.75 1.75

Rembrandt (1606-69), Painter A392

2006, Mar. 30

1050 A392 40c multi 3.00 3.00

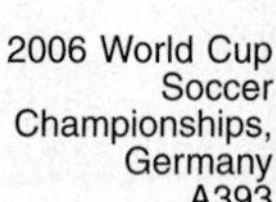

2006 World Cup Soccer Championships, Germany A393

2006, Mar. 30 *Perf. 13¼x13¾*
1051 A393 50c multi 3.25 3.25

Souvenir Sheet

Folk Dances — A394

No. 1052 — Folk dancers from: a, Cyprus. b, India.

2006, Apr. 12 *Perf. 13x13½*
1052 A394 40c Sheet of 2, #a-b 5.50 5.50

See India No. 2151.

Europa — A395

2006, May 4 *Perf. 13½x13*

1053	A395 30c grn & multi	1.60	1.60
a.	Perf. 13½x13¾ on 3 sides	1.60	1.60
1054	A395 40c red & multi	2.10	2.10
a.	Perf. 13½x13¾ on 3 sides	2.10	2.10
b.	Booklet pane, 4 each #1053a-1054a	15.50	—
	Complete booklet, #1054b	15.50	

Organ Transplantation — A396

2006, June 15 **Litho.** *Perf. 13¼*
1055 A396 13c multi .90 .90

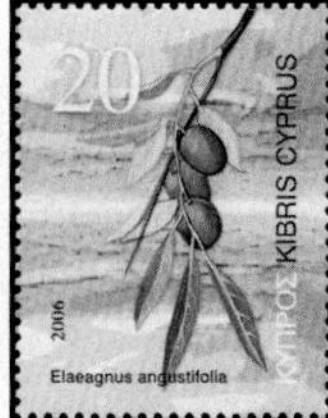

Fruit — A397

Designs: 20c, Elaeagnus angustifolia. 25c, Mespilus germanica, horiz. 60c, Opuntia ficus barbarica.

Perf. 13¼x13½, 13½x13¼

2006, June 15
1056-1058 A397 Set of 3 6.75 6.75

Fire Trucks A398

Designs: 13c, Bedford water carrier. 20c, Hino pump water tender. 50c, Bedford ladder truck.

2006, Sept. 14 *Perf. 13¾x13¼*
1059-1061 A398 Set of 3 6.25 6.25

Nicos Nicolaides (1884-1956), Writer — A399

2006, Nov. 16 Litho. *Perf. 13½x13*
1062 A399 5c multi .60 .60

Christmas — A400

Items from Agiou Eleftheriou Church: 13c, Carved wood iconostasis. 30c, Cross. 40c, Bas-relief of cross, spear and sponge.

2006, Nov. 16 *Perf. 13¼x13¾*
1063-1065 A400 Set of 3 4.75 4.75

St. Xenon, the Postman — A401

Litho. & Embossed

2007, Feb. 8 *Imperf.*
1066 A401 £1 multi 8.00 8.00

Echinoderms — A402

No. 1067: a, Antedon mediterranea. b, Centrostephanus longispinus. c, Astropecten jonstoni. d, Ophioderma longicadum.

2007, Feb. 8 Litho. *Perf. 13¾x13¼*
1067 Horiz. strip of 4 6.50 6.50
a.-d. A402 25c Any single 1.60 1.60

Motorcycles A403

Designs: 13c, 1972 Triumph Daytona. 20c, 1941 Matchless. 40c, 1940 BSA. 60c, 1939 Ariel Red Hunter.

2007, Mar. 15
1068-1071 A403 Set of 4 7.25 7.25

Treaty of Rome, 50th Anniv. — A404

2007, May 3 *Perf. 13¼x13¾*
1072 A404 30c multi 1.60 1.60

Europa — A405

Scouting emblem in gold, knot in: 30c, Light blue. 40c, Buff.

Litho. & Embossed With Foil Application

2007, May 3

1073-1074	A405 Set of 2	3.25	3.25
1074a	Booklet pane, 4 each #1073-1074, perf. on 3 sides	13.00	—
	Complete booklet, #1074a	13.00	

Scouting, cent.

Social Insurance, 50th Anniv. — A406

No. 1075: a, Text in Greek. b, Text in English.

2007, June 14 Litho. *Perf. 13x13¼*
1075 A406 40c Horiz. pair, #a-b 4.00 4.00

Miniature Sheet

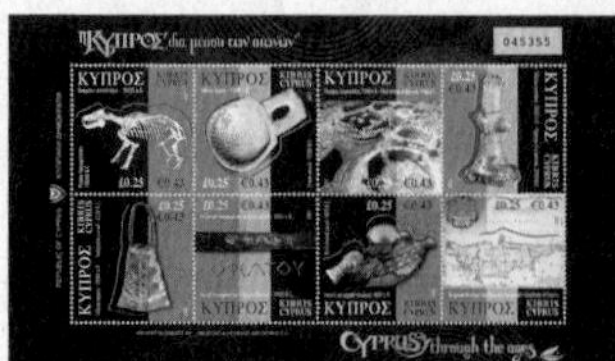

Cyprus Throughout the Ages — A407

No. 1076: a, Skeleton of pygmy hippopotamus, 10,000 B.C. b, Stone vessel, 7000 B.C. c, Choirokoitia Settlement, 7000 B.C. d, Female terracotta figurine, 3000 B.C. e, Terracotta vessel, 2000 B.C. f, Greek inscriptions on bronze skewer, 1000 B.C. g, Bird-shaped vessel, 800 B.C. h, Map of ancient kingdoms of Cyprus.

2007, Oct. 2 *Perf. 13¾*
1076 A407 25c Sheet of 8, #a-h 12.00 12.00

See Nos. 1101, 1116, 1138.

Neoclassical Buildings A408

Designs: 13c, Limassol District Administration Building. 15c, National Bank of Greece Building, Nicosia. 20c, Archaeological Research Unit Building, Nicosia. 30c, National Art Gallery, Nicosia. 40c, Paphos Municipal Library. 50c, A. G. Leventis Foundation Office Building, Nicosia. £1, Limassol Municipal Library. £3, Phaneromeni Gymnasium, Nicosia.

2007, Oct. 2 *Perf. 13¾x13½*

1077	A408 13c multi	.65	.65
1078	A408 15c multi	.75	.75
1079	A408 20c multi	1.00	1.00
1080	A408 30c multi	1.50	1.50
1081	A408 40c multi	2.00	2.00
1082	A408 50c multi	2.40	2.40
1083	A408 £1 multi	5.00	5.00
1084	A408 £3 multi	14.50	14.50
	Nos. 1077-1084 (8)	27.80	27.80

Christmas — A409

Murals from Chapel of St. Themonianus, Lysi: 13c, Virgin Mary. 30c, Archangel Gabriel. 40c, Christ Pantocrator (35x45mm).

Perf. 14x13¾, 13¾ (40c)

2007, Nov. 15
1085-1087 A409 Set of 3 4.75 4.75

100 Cents = 1 Euro

Souvenir Sheet

Introduction of Euro Currency — A410

No. 1088: a, Statue of Aphrodite, map of Cyprus. b, Sleeping Lady statue.

2008, Jan. 1 Litho. *Perf. 13¾*
1088 A410 €1 Sheet of 2, #a-b 5.50 5.50

See Malta No. 1329.

Anemone Flowers — A411

Variously colored Anemone coronaria flowers with background colors of: 26c, Blue. 34c, Red. 51c, Green. 68c, Yellow orange.

2008, Mar. 6 *Perf. 13¼x13¾*
1089-1092 A411 Set of 4 6.25 6.25

Europa — A412

Designs: 51c, Closed and open envelopes. 68c, Envelopes and mail boxes.

2008, May 2 Litho. ***Perf. 13¼x13¾***

1093-1094	A412	Set of 2	3.75	3.75
1094a		Booklet pane, 4 each #1093-1094, perf. 13¼x13¾ on 3 sides	15.00	—
		Complete booklet, #1094a	15.00	

Souvenir Sheet

Fourth Intl. Congress of Cypriot Studies, Nicosia — A413

2008, May 2 ***Perf. 13¾ on 3 Sides***

1095 A413 85c multi 3.50 3.50

12th Francophone Summit, Quebec — A414

2008, June 5 Litho. ***Perf. 13¾***

1096 A414 85c multi 3.25 3.25

2008 Summer Olympics, Beijing A415

Designs: 22c, Sailboarding. 34c, High jump. 43c, Tennis. 51c, Shooting.

2008, June 5 ***Perf. 13x13¼***

1097-1100 A415 Set of 4 4.75 4.75

Cyprus Throughout the Years Type of 2007

Miniature Sheet

No. 1101: a, Coin from Archaic period, 750 B.C.-480 B.C. b, Ship from Archaic period. c, Bust of Kimon the Athenian and ship, Classical period, 480 B.C.-310 B.C. d, Tomb of the Kings, Hellenistic period, 310 B.C.-30 B.C. e, Coin from Hellenistic period. f, Painting of St. Paul from Roman period, 30 B.C.-A.D. 324. g, Bust of Septimus Severus from Roman period. h, Granting of church privileges from Early Byzantine period, 324-841.

2008, Oct. 2 Litho. ***Perf. 13¾***

1101 A407 43c Sheet of 8, #a-h 12.00 12.00

Christmas — A416

Icons from church, Pelendri: 22c, Archangel Gabriel. 51c, Archangel Michael. 68c, Madonna and Child.

2008, Nov. 13 ***Perf. 13¼x13***

1102-1104 A416 Set of 3 4.75 4.75

Cooperative Movement, Cent. A417

2009, Mar. 12 Litho. ***Perf. 13¾***

1105 A417 26c multi 1.00 1.00

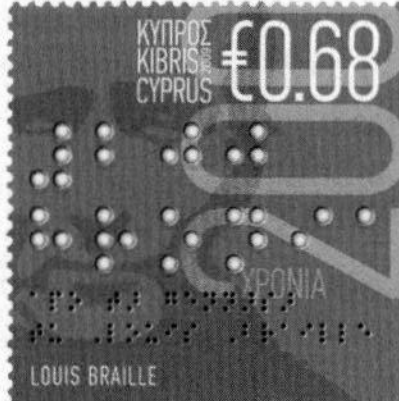

Louis Braille (1809-52), Educator of the Blind A418

2009, Mar. 12 Litho. & Embossed

1106 A418 68c multi 2.50 2.50

Introduction of the Euro, 10th Anniv. A419

Reverse of Cyprus: 51c, Cent coin. 68c, 2-euro coin.

2009, Mar. 12 Litho.

1107-1108 A419 Set of 2 4.75 4.75

Intl. Year of Planet Earth — A420

No. 1109: a, Western Hemisphere. b, Eastern Hemisphere.

2009, May 4 Litho. ***Perf. 13x13¼***

1109 A420 51c Horiz. pair, #a-b 3.75 3.75

Europa — A421

Constellations: 51c, Cassiopeia. 68c, Andromeda.

2009, May 4 ***Perf. 13¼x13¾***

1110-1111	A421	Set of 2	3.75	3.75
1111a		Booklet pane of 8, 4 each #1110-1111, perf. 13¼x13¾ on 3 sides	15.00	—
		Complete booklet, #1111a	15.00	

Intl. Year of Astronomy.

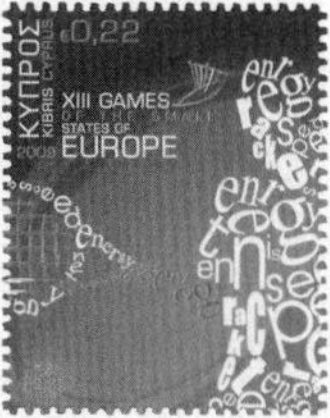

18th Games of the Small States of Europe, Cyprus — A422

Designs: 22c, Tennis. 34c, Sailing. 43c, Cycling.

2009, June 1 Litho. ***Perf. 13¼x13¾***

1112-1114 A422 Set of 3 3.50 3.50

Souvenir Sheet

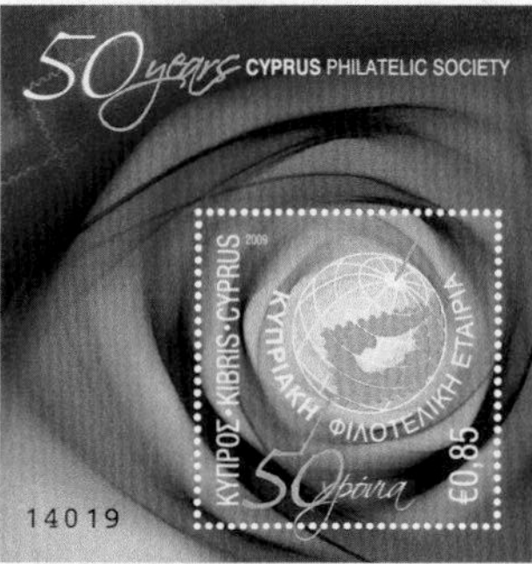

Cyprus Philatelic Society, 50th Anniv. — A423

Litho. & Embossed With Foil Application

2009, June 1 ***Perf. 13¾***

1115 A423 85c multi 3.25 3.25

Cyprus Throughout the Years Type of 2007

Miniature Sheet

No. 1116: a, St. Paraskevi Church, 9th cent. b, Monastery of St. John Chrysostom, 1090-1100. c, Lusignan coat of arms, 1192-1489. d, Chronicle of Leontios Machairas, 15th cent. e, Queen Caterina Cornaro cedes Cyprus to Venice, 1489. f, Venetian Walls, Nicosia, 1567-70. g, Ottoman siege of Nicosia, 1570. h, Larnaca Aqueduct, 18th cent.

2009, Sept. 10 Litho. ***Perf. 13¾***

1116 A407 43c Sheet of 8, #a-h 14.00 14.00

Domesticated Birds — A424

Designs: 22c, Pigeon. 34c, Turkey. 43c, Rooster. 51c, Duck.

2009, Sept. 10 ***Perf. 13¾x13¼***

1117-1120 A424 Set of 4 5.75 5.75

European Court of Human Rights, 50th Anniv. A425

2009, Nov. 12 Litho. ***Perf. 13x13¼***

1121 A425 51c multi 2.00 2.00

A426

Christmas A427

Perf. 13¼x13¾

2009, Nov. 12 Litho.

1122 A426 22c shown .75 .75

Litho. & Embossed With Foil Application

Perf. 13¾

1123	A427	51c shown	1.75	1.75
1124	A427	68c Solid silver star	2.75	2.75
		Nos. 1122-1124 (3)	5.25	5.25

Republic of Cyprus, 50th Anniv. A428

Denomination color: 68c, Bister. 85c, Blue.

Litho. & Embossed With Foil Application

2010, Jan. 27 ***Perf. 13¾x13¼***

1125-1126 A428 Set of 2 5.25 5.25

Expo 2010, Shanghai A429

2010, Mar. 17 Litho. ***Perf. 13x13¼***

1127 A429 51c multi 1.60 1.60

2010 World Cup Soccer Championships, South Africa — A430

2010, Mar. 17 ***Perf. 13¾***

1128 A430 €1.71 multi 5.75 5.75

Barnyard Animals A431

Designs: 22c, Pig. 26c, Sheep. 34c, Goat. 43c, Cow. €1.71, Rabbit.

2010, Mar. 17 ***Perf. 13¾x13¼***

1129-1133 A431 Set of 5 10.00 10.00

Europa — A432

No. 1134 — Stack of books and: a, Sun, flowers, tree, snails, bees. b, Tree, bees.

2010, May 5 ***Perf. 13¼x13¾***

1134 A432 51c Horiz. pair, #a-b 3.25 3.25
c. Booklet pane of 8, 4 each #1134a-1134b, perf. 13¼x13¾ on 3 sides 13.00 —
Complete booklet, #1134c 13.00

Visit of Pope Benedict XVI — A433

2010, June 4 ***Perf. 13¾x14¼***

1135 A433 51c multi 1.60 1.60

Cyprus Railway — A434

No. 1136 — Locomotive with denomination in: a, Black. b, White.

85c, Train, map of stations.

2010, June 4 ***Perf. 13¾x13¼***

1136 A434 43c Pair, #a-b 2.75 2.75

Souvenir Sheet

1137 A434 85c multi 3.00 3.00

Cyprus Through the Ages Type of 2007

Miniature Sheet

No. 1138: a, Treaties of Sevres, 1920, and Lausanne, 1923. b, Burnt Government House, 1931. c, Imprisoned graves, 1955-59. d, Statue of Gregoris Afxentiou (1928-57), anti-colonialist leader. e, Presidential Palace, 1960. f, Black Summer 1974, painting by Telemachos Kanthos. g, Pres. Tassos Papadopoulos signing Treaty of Accession to the European Union, 2004. h, Flag of Cyprus.

2010, Oct. 1 **Litho.** ***Perf. 13¾***

1138 A407 43c Sheet of 8, #a-h 11.00 11.00

Souvenir Sheet

Viticulture — A435

No. 1139: a, Wine barrels, wine glass. b, Grapes, pitcher.

Perf. 14 on 3 Sides

2010, Nov. 10 **Litho.**

1139 A435 51c Sheet of 2, #a-b 3.25 3.25

See Romania Nos. 5216-5217.

Nativity — A436

Christmas Ornament A437

Perf. 13¼x13¾

2010, Nov. 10 **Litho.**

1140 A436 22c shown .65 .65

Litho. & Embossed With Foil Application

Perf. 13¾

1141 A437 51c shown 1.50 1.50
1142 A437 68c Ornament, diff. 2.10 2.10
Nos. 1140-1142 (3) 3.90 3.90

Anorthosis Ammochostos Soccer Team, Cent. — A438

2011, Jan. 28 **Litho.** ***Perf. 13¾***

1143 A438 34c multi .95 .95

Composers — A439

No. 1144: a, Johann Sebastian Bach (1685-1750). b, Wolfgang Amadeus Mozart (1756-91). c, Ludwig van Beethoven (1770-1827).

2011, Jan. 28 ***Perf. 13¾x14¼***

1144 Horiz. strip of 3 4.25 4.25
a.-c. A439 51c Any single 1.40 1.40

Lace A440

Lace with: 26c, Floral pattern. 43c, Diamonds and squares pattern.

2011, Mar. 23 ***Perf. 13¾x14***

1145-1146 A440 Set of 2 2.00 2.00

Rosa Damascena A441

2011, Mar. 23 ***Perf. 13¾***

1147 A441 34c shown 1.00 1.00

Souvenir Sheet

1148 A441 85c Roses, diff. 2.50 2.50

Nos. 1147-1148 are impregnated with a rose scent.

Europa A442

2011, May 4 ***Perf. 14***

1149 A442 51c Blue forest 1.50 1.50
a. Perf. 13x13½ on 3 sides 1.50
1150 A442 68c Green forest 2.00 2.00
a. Perf. 13x13½ on 3 sides 2.00 2.00
b. Booklet pane of 8, 4 each #1149a-1150a 14.00 —
Complete booklet, #1150b 14.00

Intl. Year of Forests.

Lighthouses A443

Map and: 34c, Paphos Lighthouse. 43c, Cape Greco Lighthouse.

€1.71 Cape Kiti Lighthouse.

2011, May 4 ***Perf. 14***

1151-1152 A443 Set of 2 3.00 3.00

Souvenir Sheet

Perf. 13½x13¼

1153 A443 €1.71 multi 6.00 6.00

Booklet Stamp
Self-Adhesive

Die Cut Perf. 13¼x13

1153A A443 43c multi (RA28Ab) 1.50 1.50

No. 1153 contains one 27x35mm stamp.

Christopher A. Pissarides, 2010 Nobel Laureate in Economics — A444

2011, June 8 ***Perf. 14x14¼***

1154 A444 €1.71 multi 5.00 5.00

Tall Ships A445

Designs: 22c, Galleon. 43c, Caravel. 85c, Brig.

2011, June 8 ***Perf. 13¾***

1155-1157 A445 Set of 3 4.25 4.25

The Hare and the Tortoise — A446

No. 1158: a, Hare. b, Tortoise. c, Tortoise passing sleeping hare, horiz. d, Hare running. e, Tortoise crossing finish line.

Die Cut Perf. 11½x12, 12x11½

2011, Oct. 5 **Litho.**

Self-Adhesive

1158 A446 34c Booklet pane of 5, #a-e 4.75 4.75

Nativity — A447

Christmas Ornament A448

Perf. 13¼x13¾

2011, Nov. 11 **Litho.**

1159 A447 22c shown .60 .60

Litho. & Embossed With Foil Application

Perf. 13¾

1160 A448 51c shown 1.40 1.40
1161 A448 68c Ornament, diff. 1.90 1.90
Nos. 1159-1161 (3) 3.90 3.90

Horses A449

Various horses: 26c, 34c, 51c, 85c.

2012, Jan. 31 **Litho.** ***Perf. 13¾x13¼***

1162-1165 A449 Set of 4 6.50 6.50

2012 Summer Olympics, London A450

Designs: 22c, Men's gymnastics. 26c, Men's tennis. 34c, Men's high jump. 43c, Shooting.

Litho. With Foil Application

2012, Mar. 21 ***Perf. 14***

1166-1169 A450 Set of 4 4.00 4.00

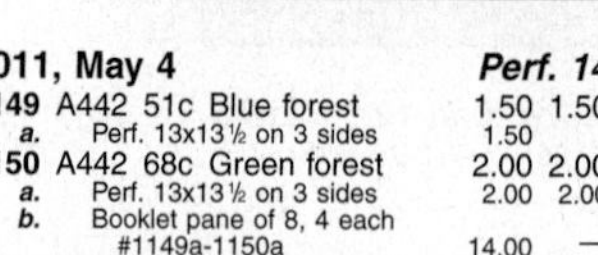

Souvenir Sheet

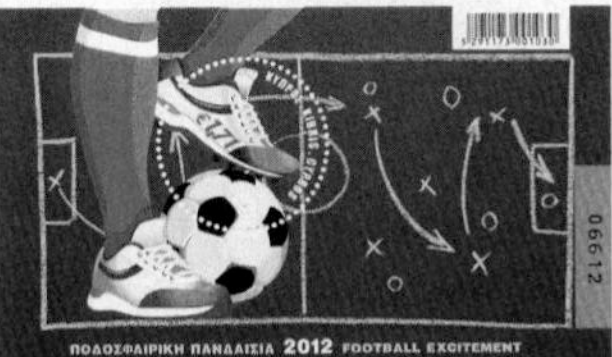

Soccer — A451

2012, Mar. 21 Litho. *Perf.*
1170 A451 €1.71 multi 5.50 5.50

Jasminum Grandiflorum — A452

2012, May 2 *Perf. 13¾*
1171 A452 34c shown 1.10 1.10

Souvenir Sheet

1172 A452 85c Flowers, diff. 2.60 2.60

Nos. 1171-1172 are impregnated with a jaasmine scent.

Europa A453

Various Cyprus tourist attractions and silhouette of: 51c, Family. 68c, Man and woman with bicycles.

2012, May 2 *Perf. 13¾x13½*
1173-1174 A453 Set of 2 3.25 3.25
1174a Booklet pane of 8, 4 each #1173-1174, perf. 13¾x13½ on 3 sides 13.00 —
Complete booklet, #1174a 13.00

Cyprus Presidency of European Union Council A454

Litho. With Foil Application

2012, July 1 *Perf. 13¾*
1175 A454 51c multi 1.75 1.75

Souvenir Sheet

1176 A454 €10 multi 28.00 28.00

The Cricket and the Ant — A455

No. 1177: a, Cricket with fiddle, sun. b, Ant with seeds. c, Ant carrying seeds. d, Cricket fiddling under tree. e, Cricket outside in winter, ant at door.

2012, Oct. 3 *Die Cut Perf. 11¼x12*

Self-Adhesive

1177 A455 34c Booklet pane of 5, #a-e 5.25 5.25

Pavlos Kontides, Silver Medalist in Sailing at 2012 Summer Olympics A456

Litho. With Foil Application

2012, Nov. 14 *Perf. 14*
1178 A456 34c multi .90 .90

Christmas — A457

Icons from: 22c, Madonna and Child, Christ Antiphonitis Church. 51c, Madonna and Child, Panayia Church, Lysi. 68c, Madonna and Child Enthroned Between St. George and St. Nicholas, St. George's Church, Vatyli.

Perf. 13¼x13¾

2012, Nov. 12 Litho.
1179 A457 22c multi .60 .60
1180 A457 51c multi 1.40 1.40

Size: 65x65mm

Imperf

1181 A457 68c multi 1.75 1.75

Admission of Cyprus Red Cross to International Red Cross, 1st Anniv. — A458

2013, Jan. 30 *Perf. 14¼x13¾*
1182 A458 22c multi .80 .80

Cyprus Scouts Association, Cent. A459

2013, Jan. 30 *Perf. 13¾*
1183 A459 43c multi 1.40 1.40

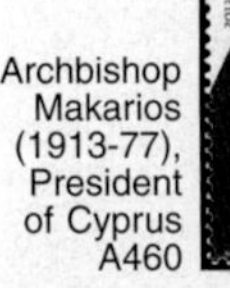

Archbishop Makarios (1913-77), President of Cyprus A460

2013, Jan. 30 *Perf. 14*
1184 A460 85c multi 2.60 2.60

Easter — A461

Icons depicting: 26c, Christ's entry into Jerusalem. 34c, Crucifixion. €1.71, Resurrection (27x40mm).

2013, Apr. 3 *Perf. 14x14¼*
1185-1187 A461 Set of 3 6.50 6.50

Origanum Dubium A462

2013, May 2 *Perf. 13¾*
1188 A462 22c shown .75 .75

Souvenir Sheet

1189 A462 85c Flowers, diff. 2.75 2.75

Nos. 1188-1189 are impregnated with an oregano scent.

Europa A463

Mailbox and postal vehicles: 34c, Automobile, van and airplane. 51c, Automobile.

2013, May 2 *Perf. 14*
1190-1191 A463 Set of 2 2.50 2.50
1191a Booklet pane of 8, 4 each #1190-1191, perf. 14 on 3 sides 10.00 —
Complete booklet, #1191a 10.00

Marine Life — A464

Designs: 34c, Seahorse. 43c, Sea anemone. €1.71, Sea fan coral.

2013, June 5 *Perf. 13¾*
1192-1194 A464 Set of 3 7.50 7.50

For surcharge, see No. 1225.

Cypriot Folk Tale "Spanos and the Forty Dragons" — A465

No. 1195: a, Spanos in cloud near dragon. b, Boar chasing Spanos up a tree, vert. c, Spanos, river, woman holding flowers. d, Spanos sitting near dragon. e, Spanos pouring water on dragon.

Die Cut Perf. 13x13½, 13½x13

2013, Nov. 13 Litho.

Self-Adhesive

1195 A465 34c Booklet pane of 5, #a-e 5.75 5.75

Christmas A466

Winning art in children's stamp design contest: 22c, Santa Claus and Christmas tree. 34c, Snowman, Christmas trees and houses. 85c, Christmas tree and gifts, vert.

Perf. 14¼x14, 14x14¼

2013, Nov. 13 Litho.
1196-1198 A466 Set of 3 4.75 4.75

Olive Production A467

Designs: 34c, Olive tree and grove.
No. 1200: a, Olives. b, Olives, container of olive oil.

2014, Jan. 30 Litho. *Perf. 14*
1199 A467 34c multi 1.00 1.00
1200 A467 51c Horiz. pair, #a-b 3.00 3.00

Four Seasons A468

Designs: 22c, Child under umbrella (winter). 43c, Girl wearing butterfly costume standing in flowers (spring). 85c, Girl with balloons, fish and dolphins (summer). €1.71, Child holding fallen leaf in front of face (autumn).

2014, Mar. 12 Litho. *Perf. 13¾*
1201-1204 A468 Set of 4 9.00 9.00

For surcharges, see Nos. 1212-1214.

Europa A469

Musicians with instruments: 34c, Cyprus flute. 51c, Lute.

2014, May 2 Litho. *Perf. 14*
1205-1206 A469 Set of 2 2.40 2.40
1206a Booklet pane of 8, 4 each #1205-1206, perf. 14 on 3 sides 9.75 —
Complete booklet, #1206a 9.75

Famous Men A470

Designs: 41c, El Greco (1541-1614), painter. 50c, Michelangelo (1475-1564), painter and sculptor. 64c, Galileo Galilei (1564-1642), astronomer. 75c, Henri de Toulouse-Lautrec (1864-1901), painter.

2014, June 30 Litho. *Perf. 14*
1207-1210 A470 Set of 4 6.25 6.25

Euromed Postal Emblem and Mediterranean Sea — A471

2014, July 9 Litho. *Perf. 14*
1211 A471 60c multi 1.60 1.60

Nos. 1201, 1202 and 1204 Surcharged

Methods and Perfs. As Before

2014, Aug. 1

1212 A468 4c on 22c #1201 .25 .25
1213 A468 €1 on 43c #1202 2.75 2.75
1214 A468 €1.88 on €1.71 #1204 5.00 5.00
Nos. 1212-1214 (3) 8.00 8.00

Famous People — A472

No. 1215: a, Theodoulos Kallinikos (1904-2004), cantor and musicologist. b, Stylianos Hourmouzios (1850-1937), cantor and journalist.

No. 1216: a, Sozos Tombolis (1914-2002), cantor and music professor. b, Achilleas Lymbourides (1917-2008), composer.

No. 1217: a, Telemachos Kanthos (1910-93), painter. b, Loukia Nicolaidou (1909-94), painter.

No. 1218: a, George Pol Georgiou (1901-72), painter. b, Michael Kashalos (1885-1974), painter.

No. 1219: a, Kypros Chrysanthis (1915-98), writer. b, Antis Pernaris (1903-80), writer.

No. 1220: a, Glafkos Alithersis (1897-1965), writer. b, Costas Montis (1914-2004), writer.

2014, Oct. 10 Litho. *Perf. 14*

1215 A472 Horiz. pair .25 .25
a.-b. 4c Either single .25 .25
1216 A472 Horiz. pair 1.75 1.75
a.-b. 34c Either single .85 .85
1217 A472 Horiz. pair 2.00 2.00
a.-b. 41c Either single 1.00 1.00
1218 A472 Horiz. pair 2.50 2.50
a.-b. 50c Either single 1.25 1.25
1219 A472 Horiz. pair 3.25 3.25
a.-b. 64c Either single 1.60 1.60
1220 A472 Horiz. pair 4.25 4.25
a.-b. 85c Either single 2.10 2.10
Nos. 1215-1220 (6) 14.00 14.00

See Nos. 1226-1231.

Cypriot Folk Tale "The Prince of Venice" — A473

No. 1221: a, Prince carried by angel. b, Angel carrying sword, vert. c, Woman with veil, vert. d, Angel and woman, vert. e, Ship at sea.

Die Cut Perf. 13½

2014, Nov. 24 Litho.

Self-Adhesive

1221 A473 Booklet pane of 5 5.00
a.-e. 41c Any single 1.00 1.00

Christmas — A474

Icons depicting: 41c, Nativity. 64c, Madonna and Child. 75c, Nativity, diff.

2014, Nov. 24 Litho. *Perf. 14*

1222-1224 A474 Set of 3 4.50 4.50

No. 1193 Surcharged

Method and Perf. As Before

2015, Feb. 4

1225 A464 34c on 43c #1193 .75 .75

Famous People Type of 2014

No. 1226: a, Adamantios Diamantis (1900-94), painter. b, Theodosis Pierides (1908-68), poet.

No. 1227: a, Maria Rousia (1894-1957), writer. b, Melis Nicolaides (1892-1979), writer.

No. 1228: a, Kyriakos Hadjioannou (1909-97), folklorist. b, Polyxeni Loizia (1855-1942), educator.

No. 1229: a, Loizos Philippou (1895-1950), newspaper editor. b, Persefoni Papadopoulou (1888-1948), educator.

No. 1230: a, Georgios Frangoudes (1869-1939), politician. b, Porfyrios Dikaios (1904-71), archaeologist.

No. 1231: a, Nicos Pantelides (1906-84), actor. b, Pavlos Xioutas (1908-91), folklorist.

2015, Feb. 4 Litho. *Perf. 14*

1226 A472 Horiz. pair .25 .25
a.-b. 4c Either single .25 .25
1227 A472 Horiz. pair 2.25 2.25
a.-b. 50c Either single 1.10 1.10
1228 A472 Horiz. pair 2.80 2.80
a.-b. 60c Either single 1.40 1.40
1229 A472 Horiz. pair 3.50 3.50
a.-b. 75c Either single 1.75 1.75
1230 A472 Horiz. pair 4.50 4.50
a.-b. €1 Either single 2.25 2.25
1231 A472 Horiz. pair 7.00 7.00
a.-b. €1.50 Either single 3.50 3.50
Nos. 1226-1231 (6) 20.30 20.30

Melkonian Orphanage — A475

2015, Apr. 2 Litho. *Perf. 13¾x14¼*

1232 A475 64c multi 1.40 1.40

See Armenia No. 1034.

Preserved Fruit — A476

Designs: 34c, Bitter orange. 41c, Bitter orange, diff. €1.88, Cherry.

2015, Apr. 2 Litho. *Perf. 13¾*

1233-1235 A476 Set of 3 5.75 5.75

Souvenir Sheet

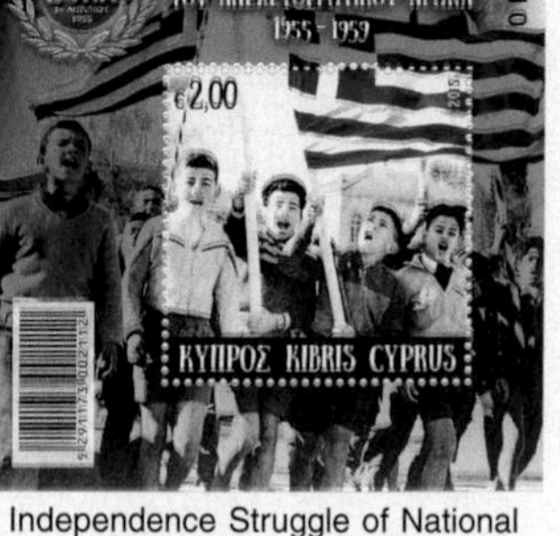

Independence Struggle of National Organization of Cypriot Fighters, 60th Anniv. — A477

Litho., Sheet Margin Litho. With Foil Application

2015, Apr. 2 *Perf. 13¾*

1236 A477 €2 multi 4.50 4.50

Europa — A478

Children and: 34c, Top. 64c, Marbles.

2015, May 5 Litho. *Perf. 14*

1237-1238 A478 Set of 2 2.25 2.25
1238a Booklet pane of 8, 4 each #1237-1238, perf. 14 on 3 sides 9.00 —
Complete booklet, #1238a 9.00

Map of Mediterranean Sea and Cypriot Boats — A479

2015, July 9 Litho. *Perf. 14*

1239 A479 75c multi 1.75 1.75

Akamas Peninsula A480

Avakas Gorge — A481

2015, July 9 Litho. *Perf. 14*

1240 A480 34c multi .75 .75
1241 A481 64c multi 1.40 1.40

International Telecommunication Union, 150th Anniv. — A482

2015, Sept. 14 Litho. *Perf. 14*

1242 A482 64c multi 1.50 1.50

Castles A483

Designs: 4c, Buffavento Castle. 34c, Kantara Castle. 41c, Agios Ilarionas (St. Hilarion) Castle. 75c, Kyrenia Castle.

Perf. 13¾x13½

2015, Sept. 14 Litho.

1243-1246 A483 Set of 4 3.50 3.50

Handicrafts — A484

No. 1247: a, Carved wooden chair. b, Decorated gourds.

No. 1248: a, Silver merrecha. b, Clay vessels.

2015, Sept. 14 Litho. *Perf. 14*

1247 A484 Pair 1.50 1.50
a.-b. 34c Either single .75 .75
1248 A484 Pair 3.00 3.00
a.-b. 64c Either single 1.50 1.50

A485 A486

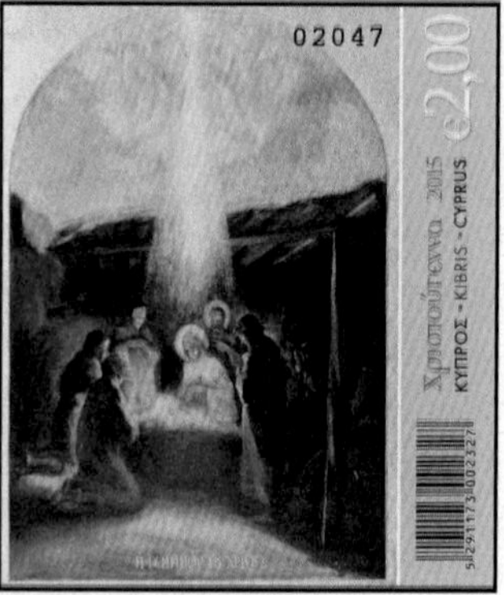

Christmas — A487

Designs: 34c, Girl burning olive leaves. 41c, Madonna and Child icon. 64c, Child mailing letter to Santa Claus. €2, Nativity.

2015, Nov. 19 Litho. *Perf. 14*

1249 A485 34c multi .75 .75
1250 A486 41c multi .90 .90
1251 A485 64c multi 1.40 1.40
Nos. 1249-1251 (3) 3.05 3.05

Imperf

1252 A487 €2 multi 4.25 4.25

Traditional Crafts A488

Designs: 41c, Basket weaving. 64c, Wood carving.

2016, Mar. 10 Litho. *Perf. 14*
1253-1254 A488 Set of 2 2.40 2.40

2016 Summer Olympics, Rio de Janeiro — A489

Designs: 34c, Taekwondo. 41c, Tennis. 64c, High jump. 75c, Sprinter.

2016, Apr. 11 Litho. *Perf. 13¾*
1255-1258 A489 Set of 4 5.00 5.00

No. 1258 is a square stamp.

A490

Europa A491

2016, May 9 Litho. *Perf. 14*
1259 A490 34c multi .80 .80
1260 A491 64c multi 1.50 1.50
a. Booklet pane of 8, 4 each #1259-1260, perf. 14 on 3 sides 9.25 —

Think Green Issue.
No. 1260a was sold with but unattached to a booklet cover.

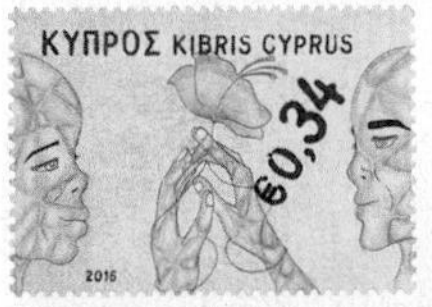
A492

Winning Art in "Principles and Values of the European Union" Children's Stamp Design Contest
A493 A494

2016, May 9 Litho. *Perf. 14*
1261 A492 34c multi .75 .75
1262 A493 41c multi .95 .95
1263 A494 64c multi 1.50 1.50
Nos. 1261-1263 (3) 3.20 3.20

Montage of Fish of the Mediterranean Sea — A495

2016, July 8 Litho. *Perf. 14*
1264 A495 €1.88 multi 4.25 4.25

Fountains A496

Designs: 34c, Children at Panayla Fountain, Paphos. 41c, Woman carrying water jug, Pegeia Fountain, Pegia.

2016, July 8 Litho. *Perf. 14*
1265-1266 A496 Set of 2 1.75 1.75

Stelios Joannou (1915-99), Businessman and Philanthropist A497

Georgios Paraskevaides (1916-2007), Businessman and Philanthropist A498

Anastasios Georgios Leventis (1902-78), Businessman and Philanthropist A499

2016, Oct. 17 Litho. *Perf. 14*
1267 A497 34c multi .75 .75
1268 A498 34c multi .75 .75
1269 A499 34c multi .75 .75
Nos. 1267-1269 (3) 2.25 2.25

Cyprus Chairmanship of the Council of Europe — A500

2016, Nov. 17 Litho. *Perf. 13¾*
1270 A500 €1 multi 2.25 2.25

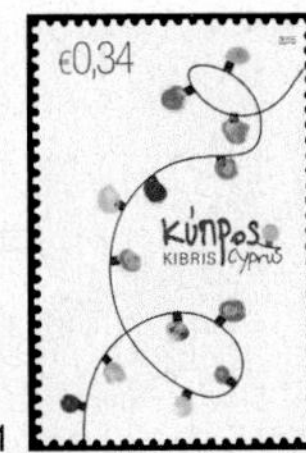
A501

Christmas A502

Designs: 34c, String of Christmas lights. 41c, Christmas tree. 64c, Adoration of the Magi icon.

2016, Nov. 17 Litho. *Perf. 14*
1271 A501 34c multi .75 .75
1272 A501 41c multi .90 .90
1273 A502 64c multi 1.40 1.40
Nos. 1271-1273 (3) 3.05 3.05

Flowers — A503

Designs; 34c, Crocus hartmannianus. 41c, Carlina pygmaea. 64c, Centaurea akamantis. €1, Tulipa cypria.

2017, Feb. 16 Litho. *Perf. 14*
1274-1277 A503 Set of 4 5.00 5.00

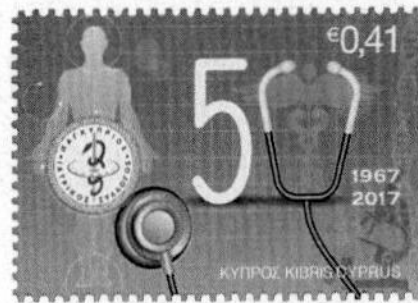
Television Broadcasting in Cyprus, 60th Anniv. — A504

2017, Mar. 24 Litho. *Perf. 14*
1278 A504 34c multi .75 .75

Cyprus Medical Association, 50th Anniv. — A505

2017, Mar. 24 Litho. *Perf. 14*
1279 A505 41c multi .90 .90

Lions Clubs International, Cent. — A506

2017, Mar. 24 Litho. *Perf. 14*
1280 A506 64c multi 1.40 1.40

Paphos, 2017 European Capital of Culture A507

No. 1281: a, Aphrodite's Rock. b, Emblem. c, Pillars of House of Theseus.

2017, Mar. 24 Litho. *Perf. 14*
1281 Horiz. strip of 3 4.25 4.25
a.-c. A507 64c Any single 1.40 1.40

International Year of Sustainable Tourism for Development — A508

2017, May 4 Litho. *Perf. 14*
1282 A508 64c multi 1.50 1.50

Europa A509

Designs: 41c, Larnaka Castle. 64c, Paphos Castle.

2017, May 4 Litho. *Perf. 14*
1283-1284 A509 Set of 2 2.40 2.40
1284a Booklet pane of 8, 4 each #1283-1284, perf. 14 on 3 sides 9.75 —
Complete booklet, #1284a 9.75

Stylized Tree — A510

2017, July 10 Litho. *Perf. 14*
1285 A510 64c multi 1.50 1.50

Triptych From Church of Our Lady Chryseleousa Strovolos — A511

Children Opening Gift — A512

Boy Writing Letter to Santa Claus — A513

No. 1286: a, St. Minas the Egyptian (carmine panel at left). b, Madonna and Child, ship (carmine panel at bottom). c, St. Spyridon (carmine panel at right).
No. 1287: a, Child in red and white striped shirt, Santa Claus and reindeer. b, Child in green shirt.

2017, Nov. 24 Litho. *Perf. 14*

1286	A511	34c Horiz. strip of 3, #a-c	2.50	2.50
1287	A512	41c Horiz. pair, #a-b	2.00	2.00
1288	A513	64c multi	1.60	1.60
		Nos. 1286-1288 (3)	6.10	6.10

Christmas.

Souvenir Sheet

St. Andrew the Apostle Monastery, Rizokarpaso, 150th Anniv. — A514

Litho. With Foil Application

2017, Nov. 30 *Perf. 13¼x13*

1289 A514 €10 sil & multi 24.00 24.00

Flowers — A515

Designs: 34c, Allium sphaerocephalon. 41c, Anthemis tricolor. 64c, Onobrychis venosa. €1.88, Tragopogon porrifolius.

Perf. 13¼x13½

2018, Feb. 12 Litho.

1290-1293 A515 Set of 4 8.00 8.00

Halloumi Cheese A516

2018, Mar. 28 Litho. *Perf. 14*

1294 A516 41c multi 1.00 1.00

2018 World Cup Soccer Championships, Russia — A517

2018, Mar. 28 Litho. *Perf. 14*

1295 A517 64c multi 1.60 1.60

Marios Tokas (1954-2008), Composer — A518

2018, Apr. 27 Litho. *Perf. 13¾x14¼*

1296 A518 64c multi 1.60 1.60

Europa A519

Designs: 34c, Kelefos Bridge. 64c, Akapnou Bridge.

2018, May 2 Litho. *Perf. 14*

1297-1298	A519	Set of 2	2.40	2.40
1298a		Booklet pane of 8, 4 each #1297-1298, perf. 14 on 3 sides	9.75	—
		Complete booklet, #1298a	9.75	

Houses, Lefkosa A520

2018, July 9 Litho. *Perf. 14*

1299 A520 64c multi 1.50 1.50

Interparliamentary Assembly on Orthodoxy, 25th Anniv. — A521

2018, July 9 Litho. *Perf. 13¾x14¼*

1300 A521 64c multi 1.50 1.50

Birds A522

Designs: 34c, Carduelis carduelis. 64c, Chloris chloris. €1, Fringilla coelebs.

2018, Sept. 27 Litho. *Perf. 14*

1301-1303 A522 Set of 3 4.75 4.75

Children and Snowman A523

Nativity Icon, Panagia Odigitria Church, Galata — A524

Children Singing Carols — A525

No. 1306: a, Girl with triangle at left. b, Boy with drum at left.

Perf. 14¼x14, 14 (41c)

2018, Nov. 8 Litho.

1304	A523	34c multi	.80	.80
1305	A524	41c multi	.95	.95
1306	A525	64c Horiz. pair, #a-b	3.00	3.00
		Nos. 1304-1306 (3)	4.75	4.75

Carnival A526

Carnival revelers wearing: 41c, Clown and Native American costumes. 50c, Pirate and witch costumes.

Perf. 13¾x13½

2019, Feb. 20 Litho.

1307-1308 A526 Set of 2 2.10 2.10

Old Trees — A527

Designs: 34c, 800-year old Platanus orientalis. 41c, 700-year old Cupressus sempervirens. 64c, 1500-year old Pistacia atlantica.

2019, Mar. 28 Litho. *Perf. 13¾x14*

1309-1311 A527 Set of 3 3.25 3.25

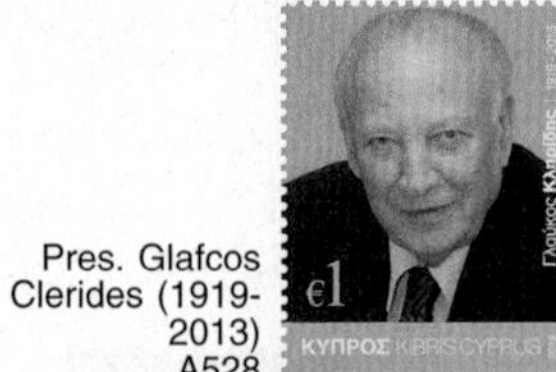

Pres. Glafcos Clerides (1919-2013) A528

2019, Apr. 20 Litho. *Perf. 13¼*

1312 A528 €1 multi 2.25 2.25

Europa A529

Birds: 41c, Gyps fulvus. 64c, Aquila fasciata.

2019, May 2 Litho. *Perf. 13½*

1313-1314	A529	Set of 2	2.40	2.40
1314a		Booklet pane of 8, 4 each #1313-1314, perf. 13½ on 3 sides	9.75	—
		Complete booklet, #1314a	9.75	

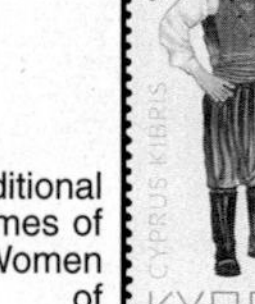

Traditional Costumes of Men and Women of Cyprus — A530

2019, July 9 Litho. *Perf. 13¼x13¾*

1315 A530 €1.88 multi 4.25 4.25

Miniature Sheet

Athletic Associations — A531

No. 1316 — Organization and year of establishment: a, Olympia Athletic Association, 1892. b, Pancypria Athletic Association, 1894. c, Zenon Athletic Association, 1896. d, Korivos Athletic Association, 1898. e, Evagoras Athletic Association of Ammochostos, 1903. f, Praxandros Athletic Association, 1919.

2019, July 9 Litho. *Perf. 13¾x13¼*

1316 A531 34c Sheet of 6, #a-f 4.50 4.50

Council of Europe, 70th Anniv. A532

Perf. 13¾x13¼

2019, Sept. 10 Litho.

1317 A532 34c multi .75 .75

International Civil Aviation Organization, 75th Anniv. — A533

Perf. 13¾x13¼

2019, Sept. 10 Litho.

1318 A533 41c multi .90 .90

Express Mail Service, 20th Anniv. A534

Perf. 13¾x13¼

2019, Sept. 10 Litho.

1319 A534 64c multi 1.40 1.40

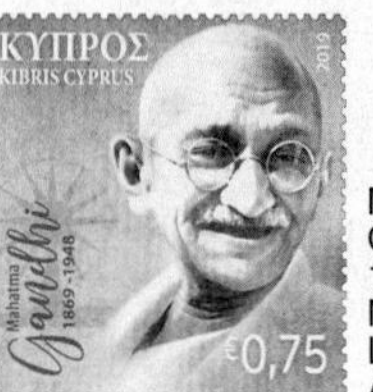

Mohandas K. Gandhi (1869-1948), Indian Nationalist Leader A535

2019, Sept. 10 Litho. *Perf. 13½*

1320 A535 75c multi 1.75 1.75

Angel A536

Snowman A537

Painting of Our Lady of Araka — A538

Perf. 13¾x13¼

2019, Nov. 14 **Litho.**

1321 A536 34c multi .75 .75
1322 A537 41c multi .90 .90

Perf. 13¼x13¾

1323 A538 64c multi 1.40 1.40
Nos. 1321-1323 (3) 3.05 3.05

Christmas.

POSTAL TAX STAMPS

Catalogue values for unused stamps in this section are for Never Hinged items.

Unless otherwise stated, Cyprus postal tax stamps are for the Refugee Fund.

No. 352 Surcharged

Perf. 12x12½

1974, Dec. 2 **Wmk. 344**

RA1 A104 10m on 5m multi .70 .70

Old Woman and Child — PT1

1974, Oct. 1 *Perf. 12½x13½*

RA2 PT1 10m gray & black .60 .60

Child and Barbed Wire — PT2

Perf. 13x12½

1977, Jan. 10 **Litho.** **Wmk. 344**

RA3 PT2 10m black .60 .60

Inscribed 1984

1984, June 18 *Perf. 13x12½*

RA4 PT2 1c black .60 .60

There are two types of No. RA4.

Inscribed 1988 — PT3

1988-2007 *Perf. 13x12½*

Design Size 22x28mm

RA5 PT3 1c black & pale gray .60 .60

Perf. 11½x12

RA6 PT3 1c Inscribed 1989 .60 .60
RA7 PT3 1c Inscribed 1990 .60 .60

Unwmk.

Perf. 13

RA8 PT3 1c Inscribed 1991 .60 .60
RA9 PT3 1c Inscribed 1992 .60 .60
RA10 PT3 1c Inscribed 1993 .60 .60
RA11 PT3 1c Inscribed 1994 .60 .60

Perf. 14½x13¾

Design Size 21x24.5mm

RA12 PT3 1c Inscribed 1995 .60 .60
RA13 PT3 1c Inscribed 1996 .60 .60
RA14 PT3 1c Inscribed 1997 .60 .60
RA15 PT3 1c Inscribed 1998 .60 .60
RA16 PT3 1c Inscribed 1999 .60 .60
RA17 PT3 1c Inscribed 2000 .60 .60
RA18 PT3 1c Inscribed 2001 .60 .60

Size: 22x27mm

Perf. 12¾

RA19 PT3 1c Inscribed 2002 .60 .60
RA20 PT3 1c Inscribed 2003 .60 .60

Perf. 12¾x13

RA21 PT3 1c Inscribed 2004 .60 .60
RA22 PT3 1c Inscribed 2005 .60 .60
RA23 PT3 1c Inscribed 2006 .60 .60

Perf. 13½x14

RA24 PT3 1c Inscribed 2007 .50 .50
Nos. RA5-RA24 (20) 11.90 11.90

Issued: No. RA5, 9/12/88; No. RA6, 9/4/89; No. RA7, 9/29/90; No. RA8, 10/7/91; No. RA9, 11/9/92; No. RA10, 1993; No. RA11, 11/21/94; No. RA12, 10/24/95; No. RA13, 6/10/96; No. RA14, 6/30/97; No. RA15, 1998; No. RA16, 1999; No. RA17, 2000; No. RA18, 2001. No. RA19, 2002. No. RA19, 2003. No. RA20, 2003. No. RA21, 11/11/04. No. RA22, 6/16/05. No. RA23, 5/4/06. No. RA24, 3/15/07.

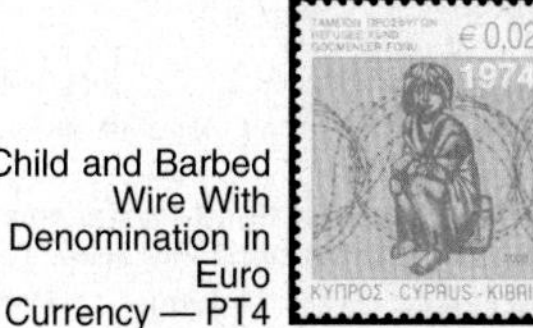

Child and Barbed Wire With Denomination in Euro Currency — PT4

2008-18 **Litho.** *Perf. 13½x14*

RA25 PT4 2c dk gray & gray .50 .50

Inscribed "2009"

RA26 PT4 2c blk & lilac gray .50 .50

Inscribed "2010"

RA27 PT4 2c blk & tan .50 .50

Inscribed "2011"

RA28 PT4 2c blk & lt green .50 .50

Booklet Stamp Self-Adhesive

Die Cut Perf. 13½x14¼

RA28A PT4 2c blk & lt grn .50 .50
b. Booklet pane of 12, 6 each #1153A, RA28A 18.00

Inscribed "2012"

Perf. 13½

RA29 PT4 2c blk & lt blue .50 .50

Inscribed "2013"

RA30 PT4 2c blk & dull org .50 .50

Inscribed "2014"

RA31 PT4 2c blk & gray .50 .50

Inscribed "2015"

RA32 PT4 2c blk & bl gray .50 .50

Inscribed "2016"

RA33 PT4 2c ol gray & lt brnish gray .50 .50

Inscribed "2017"

Perf. 13½x14

RA34 PT4 2c blk & bl gray .50 .50

Inscribed "2018"

Perf. 13½

RA35 PT4 2c blk & grnsh gray .25 .25

Inscribed "2019"

Perf. 13x13¼

RA36 PT4 2c blk & olive grn .25 .25

Issued: Nos. RA28, RA28A, 5/4/11; No. RA29, 1/31/12; No. RA30, 1/30/13; No. RA31, 3/12/14; No. RA32, 4/2/15; No. RA33, 3/10/16; No. RA34, 2/16/17; No. RA35, 2/12/18; No. RA36, 2/20/19.

CYRENAICA

ˌsir-ə-ˈnā-ə-kə

LOCATION — In northern Africa bordering on the Mediterranean Sea
GOVT. — Italian colony
AREA — 75,340 sq. mi.
POP. — 225,000 (approx. 1934)
CAPITAL — Bengasi (Benghazi)

Cyrenaica was an Italian Colony. In 1949 Great Britain granted the Amir of Cyrenaica autonomy in internal affairs. Cyrenaica was incorporated into the kingdom of Libya in 1951.

100 Centesimi = 1 Lira
1000 Milliemes = 1 Pound (1950)

Catalogue values for unused stamps in this country are for Never Hinged items, beginning with Scott 65 in the regular postage section, Scott J1 in the postage due section.

Used values in italics are for postally used stamps. CTO's sell for about the same as unused, hinged stamps.

Watermark

Wmk. 140 — Crown

Propaganda of the Faith Issue
Italy Nos. 143-146 Overprinted

1923, Oct. 24 **Wmk. 140** *Perf. 14*

1 A68 20c ol grn & brn org 8.00 *35.00*
2 A68 30c claret & brn org 8.00 *35.00*
3 A68 50c violet & brn org 5.00 *40.00*
4 A68 1 l blue & brn org 10.00 *60.00*
Nos. 1-4 (4) 31.00 *170.00*
Set, never hinged 65.00

Fascisti Issue

Italy Nos. 159-164 Overprinted in Red or Black

1923, Oct. 29 **Unwmk.** *Perf. 14*

5 A69 10c dk grn (R) 9.00 *13.00*
6 A69 30c dk vio (R) 9.00 *13.00*
7 A69 50c brn car 9.00 *17.50*

Wmk. 140

8 A70 1 l blue 9.00 *32.50*
9 A70 2 l brown 9.00 *37.50*
10 A71 5 l blk & bl (R) 9.00 *60.00*
Nos. 5-10 (6) 54.00 *173.50*
Set, never hinged 112.50

Manzoni Issue

Italy Nos. 165-170 Ovptd. in Red

1924, Apr. 1 *Perf. 14*

11 A72 10c brn red & blk 9.00 *45.00*
12 A72 15c bl grn & blk 9.00 *45.00*
13 A72 30c blk & slate 9.00 *45.00*
14 A72 50c org brn & blk 9.00 *45.00*
15 A72 1 l bl & blk 55.00 *275.00*
a. Double overprint *825.00*
Never hinged *1,250.*
16 A72 5 l vio & blk 350.00 *2,250.*
Nos. 11-16 (6) 441.00 *2,705.*
Set, never hinged 930.00

Vertical overprints on Nos. 11-14 are essays. On Nos. 15-16 the overprint is vertical at the left.

All examples of No. 15a are poorly centered.

Victor Emmanuel Issue

Italy Nos. 175-177 Overprinted

1925-26 **Unwmk.** *Perf. 11*

17 A78 60c brn car 1.35 *7.25*
18 A78 1 l dark blue 1.35 *7.25*
19 A78 1.25 l dk bl ('26) 3.75 *10.00*
a. Perf. 13½ 360.00 *1,000.*
Never hinged 900.00
Nos. 17-19 (3) 6.45 *24.50*
Set, never hinged 16.00

Issue dates: Nov. 1925, July 1926.

Saint Francis of Assisi Issue

Italian Stamps of 1926 Ovptd.

1926, Apr. 12 **Wmk. 140** *Perf. 14*

20 A79 20c gray green 2.00 *8.50*
21 A80 40c dark violet 2.00 *8.50*
22 A81 60c red brown 2.00 *15.00*

Ovptd. in Red

Unwmk.

23 A82 1.25 l dk bl, perf. 11 2.00 *20.00*
24 A83 5 l + 2.50 l ol grn 4.50 *42.50*
Nos. 20-24 (5) 12.50 *94.50*
Set, never hinged 31.50

Volta Issue

Type of Italy 1927, Overprinted

1927, Oct. 10 Wmk. 140 *Perf. 14*

25 A84 20c purple 4.50 *23.00*
26 A84 50c dp org 5.50 *16.00*
27 A84 1.25 l brt bl 9.50 *37.50*
Nos. 25-27 (3) 19.50 *76.50*
Set, never hinged 35.00

Monte Cassino Issue

Types of 1929 Issue of Italy, Ovptd. in Red or Blue

1929, Oct. 14

28 A96 20c dk grn (R) 4.50 *12.75*
29 A96 25c red org (Bl) 4.50 *12.75*
30 A98 50c + 10c crim (Bl) 4.50 *13.50*
31 A98 75c + 15c ol brn (R) 4.50 *13.50*
32 A96 1.25 l + 25c dk vio (R) 9.00 *25.00*
33 A98 5 l + 1 l saph (R) 9.00 *27.50*

Overprinted in Red

Unwmk.

34 A100 10 l + 2 l gray brn 9.00 *40.00*
Nos. 28-34 (7) 45.00 *145.00*
Set, never hinged 114.00

Royal Wedding Issue

Type of Italian Stamps of 1930 Overprinted

1930, Mar. 17 Wmk. 140

35 A101 20c yel grn 2.25 *5.50*
36 A101 50c + 10c dp org 1.60 *7.25*
37 A101 1.25 l + 25c rose red 1.60 *11.00*
Nos. 35-37 (3) 5.45 *23.75*
Set, never hinged 13.75

Ferrucci Issue

Types of Italian Stamps of 1930, Ovptd. in Red or Blue

1930, July 26

38 A102 20c violet (R) 5.50 *4.50*
39 A103 25c dk grn (R) 5.50 *4.50*
40 A103 50c black (R) 5.50 *10.00*
41 A103 1.25 l dp bl (R) 5.50 *16.00*
42 A104 5 l + 2 l dp car 12.00 *35.00*
Nos. 38-42 (5) 34.00 *70.00*
Set, never hinged 84.00

Virgil Issue

Italian Stamps of 1930 Ovptd. in Red or Blue

1930, Dec. 4

43 A106 15c vio blk .75 *7.00*
44 A106 20c org brn (Bl) .75 *2.75*
45 A106 25c dk grn .75 *2.75*
46 A106 30c lt brn (Bl) .75 *2.75*
47 A106 50c dl vio .75 *2.75*
48 A106 75c rose red (Bl) .75 *5.50*
49 A106 1.25 l gray bl .75 *6.75*

Unwmk.

50 A106 5 l + 1.50 l dk vio 2.75 *27.50*
51 A106 10 l + 2.50 l ol brn (Bl) 2.75 *42.50*
Nos. 43-51 (9) 10.75 *100.25*
Set, never hinged 26.00

Saint Anthony of Padua Issue

Italian Stamps of 1931 Ovptd. in Blue or Red

1931, May 7 Wmk. 140

52 A116 20c brown (Bl) 1.10 *13.75*
53 A116 25c green (R) 1.10 *5.50*
54 A118 30c gray brn (Bl) 1.10 *5.50*
55 A118 50c dl vio (Bl) 1.10 *5.50*
56 A120 1.25 l slate bl (R) 1.10 *13.75*

Overprinted like Nos. 23-24 in Red or Black

Unwmk.

57 A121 75c black (R) 1.10 *25.00*
58 A122 5 l + 2.50 l dk brn 8.25 *50.00*
Nos. 52-58 (7) 14.85 *119.00*
Set, never hinged 37.50

Carabineer
A1

1934, Oct. 16 Photo. Wmk. 140

59 A1 5c dk ol grn & brn 4.00 *12.75*
60 A1 10c brn & blk 4.00 *12.75*
61 A1 20c scar & indigo 4.00 *11.50*
62 A1 50c pur & brn 4.00 *11.50*
63 A1 60c org brn & ind 4.00 *16.00*
64 A1 1.25 l dk bl & grn 4.00 *27.50*
Nos. 59-64 (6) 24.00 *92.00*
Set, never hinged 60.00

2nd Colonial Art Exhibition held at Naples. See Nos. C24-C29.

Catalogue values for unused stamps in this section, from this point to the end of the section, are for Never Hinged items.

Autonomous State

Senussi Warrior
A2 A3

Perf. 12½

1950, Jan. 16 Unwmk. Engr.

65 A2 1m dark brown .65 *2.25*
66 A2 2m rose car .85 *2.00*
67 A2 3m orange .85 *2.00*
68 A2 4m dark green 4.25 *3.25*
69 A2 5m gray 1.10 *1.25*
70 A2 8m red orange 1.25 *1.50*
71 A2 10m purple 1.25 *1.50*
72 A2 12m red 1.25 *1.50*
73 A2 20m deep blue 1.25 *1.50*
74 A3 50m choc & ultra 6.75 *8.50*
75 A3 100m bl blk & car rose 21.00 *42.50*
76 A3 200m vio & pur 25.00 *67.50*
77 A3 500m dk grn & org 110.00 *135.00*
Nos. 65-77 (13) 175.45 *270.25*

SEMI-POSTAL STAMPS

Many issues of Italy and Italian Colonies include one or more semipostal denominations. To avoid splitting sets, these issues are generally listed as regular postage unless all values carry a surtax.

Holy Year Issue

Italian Semi-Postal Stamps of 1924 Overprinted in Black or Red

1925, June 1 Wmk. 140 *Perf. 12*

B1 SP4 20c + 10c dk grn & brn 2.25 *14.00*
B2 SP4 30c + 15c dk brn & brn 2.25 *15.00*
B3 SP4 50c + 25c vio & brn 2.25 *14.00*
B4 SP4 60c + 30c dp rose & brn 2.25 *18.00*
B5 SP8 1 l + 50c dp bl & vio (R) 2.25 *22.50*
B6 SP8 5 l + 2.50 l org brn & vio (R) 2.25 *35.00*
Nos. B1-B6 (6) 13.50 *118.50*
Set, never hinged 34.50

Colonial Institute Issue

"Peace" Substituting Spade for Sword — SP1

1926, June 1 Typo. *Perf. 14*

B7 SP1 5c + 5c brown .75 *5.50*
B8 SP1 10c + 5c olive grn .75 *5.50*
B9 SP1 20c + 5c blue grn .75 *5.50*
B10 SP1 40c + 5c brown red .75 *5.50*
B11 SP1 60c + 5c orange .75 *5.50*
B12 SP1 1 l + 5c blue .75 *11.50*
Nos. B7-B12 (6) 4.50 *39.00*
Set, never hinged 10.50

Surtax for Italian Colonial Institute.

Types of Italian Semi-Postal Stamps of 1926 Overprinted like Nos. 17-19

1927, Apr. 21 Unwmk. *Perf. 11*

B13 SP10 40c + 20c dk brn & blk 2.20 *25.00*
B14 SP10 60c + 30c brn red & ol brn 2.20 *25.00*
B15 SP10 1.25 l + 60c dp bl & blk 2.20 *37.50*
a. Double overprint *1,450.*
Never hinged *2,200.*
B16 SP10 5 l + 2.50 l dk grn & blk 3.75 *57.50*
Nos. B13-B16 (4) 10.35 *145.00*
Set, never hinged 21.00

The surtax on these stamps was for the charitable work of the Voluntary Militia for Italian National Defense.

Allegory of Fascism and Victory — SP2

1928, Oct. 15 Wmk. 140 *Perf. 14*

B17 SP2 20c + 5c bl grn 2.25 *8.25*
B18 SP2 30c + 5c red 2.25 *8.25*
B19 SP2 50c + 10c purple 2.25 *14.00*
B20 SP2 1.25 l + 20c dk bl 2.75 *18.00*
Nos. B17-B20 (4) 9.50 *48.50*
Set, never hinged 24.50

46th anniv. of the Societa Africana d'Italia. The surtax aided that society.

Types of Italian Semi-Postal Stamps of 1926 Overprinted in Red or Black like Nos. 52-56

1929, Mar. 4 Unwmk. *Perf. 11*

B21 SP10 30c + 10c red & blk 2.75 *16.00*
B22 SP10 50c + 20c vio & blk 2.75 *17.50*
B23 SP10 1.25 l + 50c brn & bl 4.25 *30.00*
B24 SP10 5 l + 2 l ol grn & blk (Bk) 4.25 *60.00*
Nos. B21-B24 (4) 14.00 *123.50*
Set, never hinged 35.50

Surtax for the charitable work of the Voluntary Militia for Italian Natl. Defense.

Types of Italian Semi-Postal Stamps of 1926 Overprinted in Black or Red like Nos. 52-56

1930, Oct. 20 *Perf. 14*

B25 SP10 30c + 10c dk grn & bl grn (Bk) 25.00 *55.00*
B26 SP10 50c + 10c dk grn & vio 25.00 *80.00*
B27 SP10 1.25 l + 30c ol brn & red brn 25.00 *80.00*
B28 SP10 5 l + 1.50 l ind & grn 100.00 *215.00*
Nos. B25-B28 (4) 175.00 *430.00*
Set, never hinged 438.00

Surtax for the charitable work of the Voluntary Militia for Italian Natl. Defense.

Sower — SP3

1930, Nov. 27 Photo. Wmk. 140

B29 SP3 50c + 20c ol brn 2.75 *16.00*
B30 SP3 1.25 l + 20c dp bl 2.75 *16.00*
B31 SP3 1.75 l + 20c green 2.75 *18.00*
B32 SP3 2.55 l + 50c purple 8.25 *27.50*
B33 SP3 5 l + 1 l dp car 8.25 *42.50*
Nos. B29-B33 (5) 24.75 *120.00*
Set, never hinged 67.00

25th anniv. of the Italian Colonial Agricultural Institute. The surtax was for the aid of that institution.

AIR POST STAMPS

Air Post Stamps of Tripolitania, 1931, Overprinted in Blue like Nos. 38-42

1932, Jan. 7 Wmk. 140 *Perf. 14*

C1 AP1 50c rose car 1.00 *.25*
C2 AP1 60c dp org 4.00 *9.00*
C3 AP1 80c dl vio 4.00 *14.00*
Nos. C1-C3 (3) 9.00 *23.25*
Set, never hinged 22.50

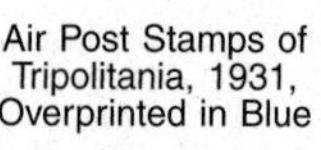

Air Post Stamps of Tripolitania, 1931, Overprinted in Blue

1932, May 12

C4	AP1	50c rose car	1.00	1.20
C5	AP1	80c dull violet	4.50	*17.50*
		Set, never hinged	14.00	

This overprint was also applied to the 60c, Tripolitania No. C9. The overprinted stamp was never used in Cyrenaica, but was sold at Rome in 1943 by the Postmaster General for the Italian Colonies. Value $10.

Arab on Camel — AP2

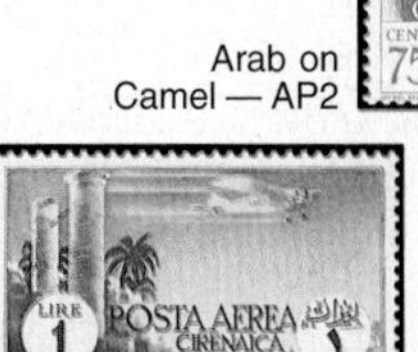

Airplane in Flight AP3

1932, Aug. 8 **Photo.**

C6	AP2	50c purple	11.00	.25
C7	AP2	75c brn rose	11.00	*10.00*
C8	AP2	80c deep blue	11.00	*19.00*
C9	AP3	1 l black	4.50	.25
C10	AP3	2 l green	4.50	*11.50*
C11	AP3	5 l deep car	7.70	*22.50*
		Nos. C6-C11 (6)	49.70	*63.50*
		Set, never hinged	124.50	

For surcharges and overprint see Nos. C20-C23.

Graf Zeppelin Issue

Zeppelin and Clouds forming Pegasus AP4

Zeppelin and Ancient Galley AP5

Zeppelin and Giant Bowman AP6

1933, Apr. 15

C12	AP4	3 l dk brn	10.00	*72.50*
C13	AP5	5 l purple	10.00	*72.50*
C14	AP6	10 l dp grn	10.00	*135.00*
C15	AP5	12 l deep blue	10.00	*150.00*
C16	AP4	15 l carmine	10.00	*150.00*
C17	AP6	20 l black	10.00	*200.00*
		Nos. C12-C17 (6)	60.00	*780.00*
		Set, never hinged	150.00	

North Atlantic Crossing Issue

Airplane Squadron and Constellations — AP7

1933, June 1

C18	AP7	19.75 l grn & dp bl	13.75	*375.00*
C19	AP7	44.75 l red & indigo	14.00	*375.00*
		Set, never hinged	70.00	

Type of 1932 Ovptd. and Srchd.

1934, Jan. 20

C20	AP3	2 l on 5 l org brn	3.25	*55.00*
C21	AP3	3 l on 5 l yel grn	3.25	*55.00*
C22	AP3	5 l ocher	3.25	*65.00*
C23	AP3	10 l on 5 l rose	4.50	*65.00*
		Nos. C20-C23 (4)	14.25	*240.00*
		Set, never hinged	35.50	

For use on mail to be carried on a special flight from Rome to Buenos Aires.

Transport Plane AP8

Venus of Cyrene AP9

1934, Oct. 9

C24	AP8	25c sl bl & org red	4.00	*13.00*
C25	AP8	50c dk grn & ind	4.00	*11.50*
C26	AP8	75c dk brn & org red	4.00	*11.50*
a.		Imperf.	3,000.	
		Never hinged	4,500.	
C27	AP9	80c org brn & ol grn	4.00	*12.50*
C28	AP9	1 l scar & ol grn	4.00	*16.00*
C29	AP9	2 l dk bl & brn	4.00	*27.50*
		Nos. C24-C29 (6)	24.00	*92.00*
		Set, never hinged	24.00	

2nd Colonial Arts Exhib. held at Naples.

AIR POST SEMI-POSTAL STAMPS

King Victor Emmanuel III SPAP1

Wmk. 104

1934, Nov. 5 **Photo.** ***Perf. 14***

CB1	SPAP1	25c + 10c gray grn	9.00	*16.00*
CB2	SPAP1	50c + 10c brn	9.00	*16.00*
CB3	SPAP1	75c + 15c rose red	9.00	*16.00*
CB4	SPAP1	80c + 15c brn blk	9.00	*16.00*
CB5	SPAP1	1 l + 20c red brn	9.00	*16.00*
CB6	SPAP1	2 l + 20c brt bl	9.00	*16.00*
CB7	SPAP1	3 l + 25c pur	22.50	*72.50*
CB8	SPAP1	5 l + 25c org	22.50	*72.50*
CB9	SPAP1	10 l + 30c dp vio	22.50	*72.50*
CB10	SPAP1	25 l + 2 l dp grn	22.50	*72.50*
		Nos. CB1-CB10 (10)	144.00	*386.00*
		Set, never hinged	365.00	

65th birthday of King Victor Emmanuel III and the non-stop flight, Rome-Mogadiscio.

AIR POST SEMI-POSTAL OFFICIAL STAMP

Type of Air Post Semi-Postal Stamps, 1934, Overprinted Crown and "SERVIZIO DI STATO" in Black

1934, Nov. 5 **Wmk. 140** ***Perf. 14***

CBO1	SPAP1	25 l + 2 l cop red	*1,500.*

POSTAGE DUE STAMPS

Catalogue values for unused stamps in this section are for Never Hinged items.

D1

Perf. 12½

1950, July 1 **Unwmk.** **Engr.**

J1	D1	2m dark brown	77.50	*110.00*
J2	D1	4m deep green	77.50	*110.00*
J3	D1	8m scarlet	77.50	*110.00*
J4	D1	10m vermilion	77.50	*120.00*
J5	D1	20m orange yel	77.50	*120.00*
J6	D1	40m deep blue	77.50	*160.00*
J7	D1	100m dark gray	77.50	*250.00*
		Nos. J1-J7 (7)	542.50	*980.00*

CZECHOSLOVAKIA

ˌche-kə-slō-ˈvä-kē-ə

LOCATION — Central Europe
GOVT. — Republic
AREA — 49,355 sq. mi.
POP. — 15,395,970 (1983 est.)
CAPITAL — Prague

The Czechoslovakian Republic consists of Bohemia, Moravia and Silesia, Slovakia and Ruthenia (Carpatho-Ukraine). In March 1939, a German protectorate was established over Bohemia and Moravia, as well as over Slovakia which had meanwhile declared its independence. Ruthenia was incorporated in the territory of Hungary. These territories were returned to the Czechoslovak Republic in 1945, except for Ruthenia, which was ceded to Russia. Czechoslovakia became a federal state on Jan. 2, 1969. On Jan. 1, 1993 Czechoslovakia separated into Slovakia and the Czech Republic. See Volume 5 for the stamps of Slovakia.

100 Haleru = 1 Koruna

Catalogue values for unused stamps in this country are for Never Hinged items, beginning with Scott 142 in the regular postage section, B144 in the semi-postal section, Scott C19 in the air post section, Scott EX1 in the personal delivery section, and Scott J58 in the postage due section, Scott O1 int he officials section, and Scott P14 in the newspaper section.

Watermarks

Wmk. 107 — Linden Leaves (Vertical)

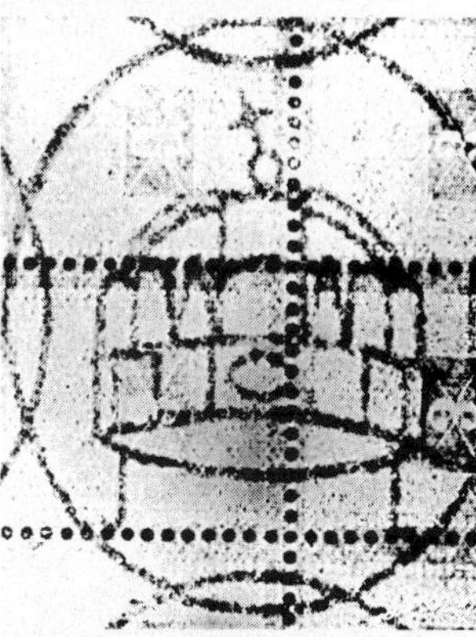
Wmk. 135 — Crown in Oval or Circle, Sideways

Wmk. 136

Wmk. 136a

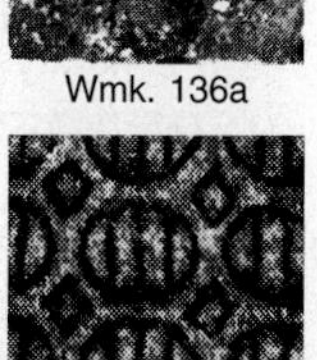
Wmk. 341 — Striped Ovals

Stamps of Austria overprinted "Ceskoslovenska Republika," lion and "Cesko Slovensky Stat," "Provisorni Ceskoslovenska Vlada" and Arms, and "Ceskoslovenska Statni Posta" and Arms were made privately. A few of them were passed through the post but all have been pronounced unofficial and unauthorized by the Postmaster General.

During the occupation of part of Northern Hungary by the Czechoslovak forces, stamps of Hungary were overprinted "Cesko Slovenska Posta," "Ceskoslovenska Statni Posta" and Arms, and "Slovenska Posta" and Arms. These stamps were never officially issued though examples have passed the post.

Hradcany at Prague — A1

1918-19 **Unwmk.** **Typo.** ***Imperf.***

1	A1	3h red violet	.25	.25
2	A1	5h yellow green	.25	.25
3	A1	10h rose	.25	.25
4	A1	20h bluish green	.25	.25
5	A1	25h deep blue	.25	.25
6	A1	30h bister	.35	.25
7	A1	40h red orange	.35	.25

8 A1 100h brown .75 .25
9 A1 200h ultra 1.50 .25
10 A1 400h purple 3.00 .25

On the 3h-40h "Posta Ceskoslovenska" is in white on a colored background; on the higher values the words are in color on a white background.

No. 5c was not valid for postage.

Nos. 1-6 exist as tete-beche gutter pairs.

See Nos. 368, 1554, 1600. For surcharges see Nos. B130, C1, C4, J15, J19-J20, J22-J23, J30.

Perf. 11½, 13½

13 A1 5h yellow green .60 .25
a. Perf. 11½x10¾ 3.00 .45
14 A1 10h rose .35 .25
15 A1 20h bluish green .35 .25
a. Perf. 11½ .35 .25
16 A1 25h deep blue .75 .35
a. Perf. 11½ 1.50 .35
20 A1 200h ultra 6.00 .25
Nos. 1-10,13-16,20 (15) 15.25 3.85

All values of this issue exist with various private perforations and examples have been used on letters.

The 3h, 30h, 40h, 100h and 400h formerly listed are now known to have been privately perforated.

For overprints see Eastern Silesia Nos. 2, 5, 7-8, 14, 16, 18, 30.

A2

Type II

Type III

Type IV

Type II — Sun behind cathedral. Colorless foliage in foreground.

Type III — Without sun. Shaded foliage in foreground.

Type IV — No foliage in foreground. Positions of buildings changed. Letters redrawn.

1919 ***Imperf.***

23 A2 1h dark brown (II) .25 .25
25 A2 5h blue green (IV) .35 .25
27 A2 15h red (IV) .35 .25
29 A2 25h dull violet (IV) .65 .25
30 A2 50h dull violet (II) .40 .25
31 A2 50h dark blue (IV) .35 .25
32 A2 60h orange (III) 1.50 .25
33 A2 75h slate (IV) 1.10 .25
34 A2 80h olive grn (III) .75 .25
36 A2 120h gray black (IV) 2.25 .25
38 A2 300h dark green (III) 7.00 .35
39 A2 500h red brown (IV) 7.00 .25
40 A2 1000h violet (III) 15.00 1.10
a. 1000h bluish violet 35.00 2.25
Nos. 23-40 (13) 36.95 4.20

For overprints see Eastern Silesia Nos. 1, 3-4, 6, 9-13, 15, 17, 20-21.

1919-20 ***Perf. 11½, 13¾, 13¾x11½***

41 A2 1h dk brown (II) .25 .25
42 A2 5h blue grn (IV), perf. 13½ .60 .25
a. Perf. 11½ 25.00 5.00
43 A2 10h yellow grn (IV) .35 .25
a. Imperf. 17.50 14.00
b. Perf. 11¾ 10.00 1.00
44 A2 15h brick red (IV) .35 .25
a. Perf. 11½x10¾ 27.50 5.00
b. Perf. 11½x13¾ 75.00 22.50
c. Perf. 13¾x10¾ 100.00 22.50
45 A2 20h rose (IV) .60 .25
a. Imperf. 90.00 85.00
46 A2 25h dull vio (IV), perf. 11½ .65 .25
a. Perf. 11½x10¾ 4.50 1.10
b. Perf. 13¾x10¾ 150.00 37.50
47 A2 30h red violet (IV) .35 .25
a. Imperf. 150.00 175.00
b. Perf. 13¾x13½ 450.00 175.00
c. 30h deep violet .60 .25
d. As "c," perf. 13¾x13½ 525.00 190.00
e. As "c," imperf. 150.00 160.00
50 A2 60h orange (III) .40 .25
a. Perf. 13¾x13½ 15.00 4.50
53 A2 120h gray black (IV) 4.00 1.00
Nos. 41-53 (9) 7.55 3.00

Nos. 43a, 45a, 47a and 47e were imperforate by accident and not issued in quantities as were Nos. 23 to 40.

Rouletted stamps of the preceding issues are said to have been made by a postmaster in a branch post office at Prague, or by private firms, but without authority from the Post Office Department.

The 50, 75, 80, 300, 500 and 1000h have been privately perforated.

Unlisted color varieties of types A1 and A2 were not officially released, and some are printer's waste.

For surcharges and overprints see Nos. B131, C2-C3, C5-C6, J16-J18, J21, J24-J29, J31, J42-J43, Eastern Silesia 22-29.

Pres. Thomas Garrigue Masaryk — A4

1920 ***Perf. 13½***

61 A4 125h gray blue 1.50 .25
a. 125h ultramarine 20.00 19.00
62 A4 500h slate, *grysh* 2.50 1.50
63 A4 1000h blk brn, *brnsh* 6.50 3.00
Nos. 61-63 (3) 10.50 4.75

Nos. 61, 61a, 63 imperf. were not regularly issued. Values: unused singles, No. 61 $30; No. 61a $150; No. 63 $40.

For surcharge and overprints, see Nos. B131, Eastern Silesia 31-32.

Carrier Pigeon with Letter — A5

Czechoslovakia Breaking Chains to Freedom — A6

Hussite Priest — A7

Agriculture and Science — A8

Type I

Type II

Two types of 40h:
Type I: 9 leaves by woman's hip.
Type II: 10 leaves by woman's hip.

1920 ***Perf. 14***

65 A5 5h dark blue .25 .25
a. Perf. 13¾ *275.00* *150.00*
66 A5 10h blue green .25 .25
a. Perf. 13¾ *125.00* 110.00
67 A5 15h red brown .25 .25
68 A6 20h rose .25 .25
69 A6 25h lilac brown .25 .25
70 A6 30h red violet .25 .25
71 A6 40h red brown (I) .50 .25
a. As "b," tête bêche pair 2.50 1.50
b. Perf. 13½ .60 .25
c. Type II .25 .25
72 A6 50h carmine .35 .25
73 A6 60h dark blue .35 .25
a. As "b," tête bêche pair 3.50 3.50
b. Perf. 13½ .35 1.50

Photo.

74 A7 80h purple .25 .25
75 A7 90h black brown .30 .25

Typo.

Perf. 13¾

76 A8 100h dark green .50 .25
77 A8 200h violet .75 .25
78 A8 300h vermilion 1.50 .25
a. Perf. 13¾x13½ 4.50 .35
79 A8 400h brown 3.50 .45
80 A8 500h deep green 3.50 .45
a. Perf. 13¾x13½ 40.00 5.50
81 A8 600h deep violet 4.50 .45
a. Perf. 13¾x13½ 125.00 7.00
Nos. 65-81 (17) 17.50 4.85

No. 69 has background of horizontal lines.

Imperfs. were not regularly issued.

Nos. 71 and 73 exist as tete-beche gutter pairs.

For surcharges and overprint see Nos. C7-C9, J44-J56.

Type I

Type II

Two types of 20h:
Type I: Base of 2 is long, interior of 0 is angular.
Type II: Base of 2 is short, interior of 0 is an oval.

Type I

Type II

Two types of 25h:
Type I: Top of 2 curves up.
Type II: Top of 2 curves down.

1920-25 ***Perf. 14***

82 A5 5h violet .25 .25
a. As "b," tête bêche pair 2.00 1.00
b. Perf. 13½ 1.00 .35
83 A5 10h olive bister .25 .25
a. As "b," tête bêche pair 2.00 1.50
b. Perf. 13½ .60 .35
84 A5 20h deep orange (II) .25 .25
a. As "b," tête bêche pair 14.00 15.00
b. Perf. 13½ 3.50 .60
c. Type I — —
85 A5 25h blue green (I) .25 .25
a. Type II .25 .25
86 A5 30h deep violet ('25) 3.00 .25
87 A6 50h yellow green .60 .25
a. As "b," tête bêche pair 27.50 27.50
b. Perf. 13½ 7.50 2.00
88 A6 100h dark brown 1.00 .25
a. Perf. 13½ 15.00 .30
89 A6 150h rose 2.00 .50
a. Perf. 13½ 35.00 2.00
90 A6 185h orange 1.50 .30
91 A6 250h dark green 2.25 .50
Nos. 82-91 (10) 11.35 3.05

Imperfs. were not regularly issued.

Nos. 82-84, 87 exist as tete-beche gutter pairs.

Type of 1920 Issue Redrawn

Type I

Type II

Type III

Type I — Rib of leaf below "O" of POSTA is straight and extends to tip. White triangle above book is entirely at left of twig. "P" has a stubby, abnormal appendage.

Type II — Rib is extremely bent; does not reach tip. Triangle extends at right of twig. "P" like Type I.

Type III — Rib of top left leaf is broken in two. Triangle like Type II. "P" has no appendage.

1923 ***Perf. 13¾, 13¾x13½***

92 A8 100h red, *yellow,* III, perf. 14x13½ .75 .50
a. Type I, perf. 13¾ 1.00 .25
b. Type I, perf. 13¾x13½ .75 .25
c. Type II, perf. 13¾ 1.25 .25
d. Type II, perf. 13¾x13½ 1.10 .25
e. Type III, perf. 13¾ 7.50 .25
93 A8 200h blue, *yellow,* II, perf. 14 10.00 .30
a. Type II, perf. 13¾x13½ 10.00 .30
b. Type III, perf. 13¾ 6.50 .30
c. Type III, perf. 13¾x13½ 45.00 .50
94 A8 300h violet, *yellow,* I, perf. 13¾ 4.50 .25
a. Type II, perf. 13¾ 35.00 .35
b. Type II, perf. 13¾x13½ 50.00 .50
c. Type III, perf. 13¾x13½ 6.00 .25
d. Type III, perf. 13¾ 27.50 .35
Nos. 92-94 (3) 15.25 1.05

President Masaryk
A9 A10

Perf. 13¾x13½, 13¾

1925 **Photo.** **Wmk. 107**

Size: 19½x23mm

95 A9 40h brown orange .75 .25
96 A9 50h olive green 1.50 .25
97 A9 60h red violet 1.75 .25
Nos. 95-97 (3) 4.00 .75

Distinctive Marks of the Engravings.

I, II, III — Background of horizontal lines in top and bottom tablets. Inscriptions in Roman letters with serifs.

IV — Crossed horizontal and vertical lines in the tablets. Inscriptions in Antique letters without serifs.

I, II, IV — Shading of crossed diagonal lines on the shoulder at the right.

III — Shading of single lines only.

I — "T" of "Posta" over middle of "V" of "Ceskoslovenska." Three short horizontal lines in lower part of "A" of "Ceskoslovenska."

II — "T" over right arm of "V." One short line in "A."

III — "T" as in II. Blank space in lower part of "A."

IV — "T" over left arm of "V."

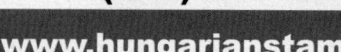

Wmk. Horizontally (107)
Engr.
I. First Engraving
Size: 19¾x22½mm

98 A10 1k carmine .85 .25
99 A10 2k deep blue 1.75 .35
100 A10 3k brown 3.75 .65
101 A10 5k blue green 1.25 .35
Nos. 98-101 (4) 7.60 1.60

Wmk. Vertically (107)
Size: 19¼x23mm

101A A10 1k carmine 60.00 3.50
101B A10 2k deep blue 60.00 12.50
101C A10 3k brown 150.00 12.50
101D A10 5k blue green 3.50 .60
Nos. 101A-101D (4) 273.50 29.10

II. Second Engraving
Wmk. Horizontally (107)
Size: 19x21½mm

102 A10 1k carmine 35.00 .60
103 A10 2k deep blue 3.50 .30
104 A10 3k brown 4.50 .35
Nos. 102-104 (3) 43.00 1.25

III. Third Engraving
Size: 19-19½x21½-22mm
Perf. 10

105 A10 1k carmine rose .75 .25
a. Perf. 14 6.00 .25

IV. Fourth Engraving
Size: 19x22mm

1926 ***Perf. 10***
106 A10 1k carmine rose 1.00 .25

Perf. 14
108 A10 3k brown 4.50 .25

There is a 2nd type of No. 106: with long mustache. Same values. See No. 130, design SP3.

Karlstein Castle — A11

1926, June 1 **Engr.** ***Perf. 10***
109 A11 1.20k red violet .50 .30
110 A11 1.50k car rose .35 .25
111 A11 2.50k dark blue 3.25 .35
Nos. 109-111 (3) 4.10 .90

See Nos. 133, 135.

Karlstein Castle — A12

Pernstein Castle — A13

Orava Castle A14

Masaryk A15

Strahov Monastery — A16

Hradcany at Prague A17

Great Tatra — A18

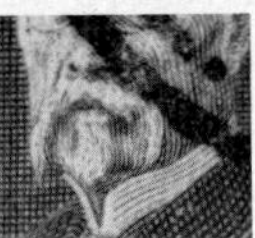
Short Mustache

Long, Wavy Mustache

1926-27 **Engr.** **Wmk. 107**
114 A13 30h gray green 1.25 .25
115 A14 40h red brown .50 .25
116 A15 50h deep green .50 .25
117 A15 60h red vio, *lil* .85 .25
118 A16 1.20k red violet 4.00 1.50

Perf. 13½
119 A17 2k blue 1.00 .25
a. 2k ultramarine 6.00 .75
120 A17 3k deep red 1.25 .25
121 A18 4k brn vio ('27) 4.50 .60
122 A18 5k dk grn ('27) 14.00 3.00
Nos. 114-122 (9) 27.85 6.60

No. 116 exists in two types. The one with short, straight mustache at left sells for several times as much as that with longer wavy mustache.

See Nos. 137-140.

Coil Stamps
Perf. 10 Vertically

123 A12 20h brick red .50 .40
a. Vert. pair, imperf. horiz. 100.00
124 A13 30h gray green .35 .25
a. Vert. pair, imperf. horiz. 100.00
125 A15 50h deep green .25 .25
Nos. 123-125 (3) 1.10 .90

See No. 141.

Short Mustache

Long, Wavy Mustache

1927-31 **Unwmk.** ***Perf. 10***
126 A13 30h gray green .25 .25
127 A14 40h deep brown .70 .25
128 A15 50h deep green .25 .25
129 A15 60h red violet .70 .25
130 A10 1k carmine rose 1.10 .25
131 A15 1k deep red .75 .25
132 A16 1.20k red violet .40 .25
133 A11 1.50k carmine ('29) .55 .25
134 A13 2k dp grn ('29) .50 .25
135 A11 2.50k dark blue 5.50 .30
136 A14 3k red brown ('31) .60 .25
Nos. 126-136 (11) 11.30 2.80

No. 130 exists in two types. The one with longer mustache at right sells for several times as much as that with the short mustache.

1927-28 ***Perf. 13½***
137 A17 2k ultra .85 .25
138 A17 3k deep red ('28) 1.90 .65
139 A18 4k brown violet ('28) 6.00 1.00
140 A18 5k dark green ('28) 6.25 .50
Nos. 137-140 (4) 15.00 2.40

Coil Stamp
1927 ***Perf. 10 Vertically***
141 A12 20h brick red .50 .25

Catalogue values for unused stamps in this section, from this point to the end of the section, are for Never Hinged items.

Hradec Castle A19

Brno Cathedral A25

Masaryk — A27

10th anniv. of Czech. independence: 40h, Town Hall, Levoca. 50h, Telephone exchange, Prague. 60h, Town of Jasina. 1k, Hluboka Castle. 1.20k, Pilgrims' House, Velehrad. 2.50k, Great Tatra. 5k, Old City Square, Prague.

1928, Oct. 22 ***Perf. 13½***
142 A19 30h black .25 .25
143 A19 40h red brown .25 .25
144 A19 50h dark green .25 .25
145 A19 60h orange red .25 .25
146 A19 1k carmine .30 .25
147 A19 1.20k brown vio 1.00 .45
148 A25 2k ultra 1.00 .75
149 A19 2.50k dark blue 3.00 2.50
150 A27 3k dark brown 1.50 1.25
151 A25 5k deep violet 3.00 3.00
Nos. 142-151 (10) 10.80 9.20

From one to three sheets each of Nos. 142-148, perf 12½, appeared on the market in the early 1950's.

Coat of Arms — A29

1929-37 ***Perf. 10***
152 A29 5h dark ultra ('31) .25 .25
153 A29 10h bister brn ('31) .25 .25
154 A29 20h red .25 .25
155 A29 25h green .25 .25
156 A29 30h red violet .25 .25
157 A29 40h dk brown ('37) 1.60 .25
a. 40h red brown ('29) .25 .25
Nos. 152-157 (6) 2.85 1.50

Coil Stamp
Perf. 10 Vertically
158 A29 20h red .25 .25

For overprints, see Bohemia and Moravia Nos. 1-5, Slovakia Nos. 2-6.

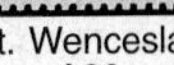
St. Wenceslas A30

Founding St. Vitus' Cathedral A31

Design: 3k, 5k, St. Wenceslas martyred.

1929, May 14 ***Perf. 13½***
159 A30 50h gray green .30 .25
160 A30 60h slate violet .45 .25
161 A31 2k dull blue 1.10 .30
162 A30 3k brown 1.50 .35
163 A30 5k brown violet 5.50 3.50
Nos. 159-163 (5) 8.85 4.65

Millenary of the death of St. Wenceslas.

Statue of St. Wenceslas and National Museum, Prague — A33

1929 ***Perf. 10***
164 A33 2.50k deep blue 1.00 .25

Brno Cathedral A34

Tatra Mountain Scene A35

Design: 5k, Old City Square, Prague.

1929, Oct. 15 ***Perf. 13½***
165 A34 3k red brown 3.00 .25
166 A35 4k indigo 6.75 .25
167 A35 5k gray green 11.00 .30
Nos. 165-167 (3) 20.75 .80

See No. 183.

A37

Type I

Type II

Two types of 50h:

I — A white space exists across the bottom of the vignette between the coat, shirt and tie and the "HALERU" frame panel.

II — An extra frame line has been added just above the "HALERU" panel which finishes off the coat and tie shading evenly.

1930, Jan. 2 ***Perf. 10***
168 A37 50h myrtle green (II) .25 .25
a. Type I 1.10 .25
169 A37 60h brown violet 1.00 .25
170 A37 1k brown red .40 .25
Nos. 168-170 (3) 1.65 .75

See No. 234.

Coil Stamp
1931 ***Perf. 10 Vertically***
171 A37 1k brown red 1.50 .60

President Masaryk — A38

1930, Mar. 1 ***Perf. 13½***
175 A38 2k gray green 1.50 .35
176 A38 3k red brown 2.25 .35
177 A38 5k slate blue 6.00 1.50
178 A38 10k gray black 16.00 3.50
Nos. 175-178 (4) 25.75 5.70

Eightieth birthday of President Masaryk.

Nos. 175-178 were each issued in sheets with ornamental tabs at the bottom. Value, set with tabs $65.50.

St. Nicholas' Church, Prague — A39

1931, May 15
183 A39 10k black violet 11.00 1.10

Krivoklat Castle — A40

Krumlov Castle — A42

Design: 4k, Orlik Castle.

1932, Jan. 2 *Perf. 10*

184 A40 3.50k violet 2.40 1.10
185 A40 4k deep blue 3.25 .60
186 A42 5k gray green 4.75 .60
Nos. 184-186 (3) 10.40 2.30

A43

A44

1932, Mar. 16

187 A43 50h yellow green .35 .25
188 A43 1k brown carmine 1.10 .25
189 A44 2k dark blue 9.00 .35
190 A44 3k red brown 19.00 .35
Nos. 187-190 (4) 29.45 1.20

Miroslav Tyrs — A45

1933, Feb. 1

191 A45 60h dull violet .40 .25

Miroslav Tyrs (1832-84), founder of the Sokol movement; and the 9th Sokol Congress (Nos. 187-190).

First Christian Church at Nitra
A46 A47

1933, June 20

192 A46 50h yellow green .75 .25
193 A47 1k carmine rose 7.00 .25

Prince Pribina who introduced Christianity into Slovakia and founded there the 1st Christian church in A.D. 833.

All gutter pairs are vertical. Values unused: No. 192 $300; No. 193 $15,000.

Bedrich Smetana, Czech Composer and Pianist, 50th Death Anniv. — A48

1934, Mar. 26 **Engr.** *Perf. 10*

194 A48 50h yellow green .40 .25

Consecration of Legion Colors at Kiev, Sept. 21, 1914 — A49

Ensign Heyduk with Colors A51

Legionnaires A52

1k, Legion receiving battle flag at Bayonne.

1934, Aug. 15 *Perf. 10*

195 A49 50h green .35 .25
196 A49 1k rose lake .50 .25
197 A51 2k deep blue 2.75 .25
198 A52 3k red brown 4.50 .45
Nos. 195-198 (4) 8.10 1.20

20th anniv. of the Czechoslovakian Legion which fought in WWI.

Antonin Dvorák, (1841-1904), Composer — A53

1934, Nov. 22

199 A53 50h green .40 .25

Pastoral Scene — A54

1934, Dec. 17 *Perf. 10*

200 A54 1k claret .60 .25
a. Souv. sheet of 15, perf. 13½ 160.00 *250.00*
b. As "a," single stamp 10.00 *12.50*
201 A54 2k blue 1.75 .45
a. Souv. sheet of 15, perf. 13½ 600.00 *900.00*
b. As "a," single stamp 35.00 27.50

Centenary of the National Anthem.

Nos. 200-201 were each issued in sheets of 100 stamps and 12 blank labels. Value, set with attached labels: mint $21; used $7.

Nos. 200a & 201a have thick paper, darker shades, no gum. Forgeries exist.

A55

President Masaryk — A56

1935, Mar. 1

202 A55 50h green, *buff* .35 .25
203 A55 1k claret, *buff* .35 .25
204 A56 2k gray blue, *buff* .50 .60
205 A56 3k brown, *buff* 3.00 .50
Nos. 202-205 (4) 4.20 1.60

85th birthday of President Masaryk.

Nos. 204-205 were each issued in sheets of 100 stamps and 12 blank labels. Value with attached labels: mint $30; used $30.

See No. 235.

Monument to Czech Heroes at Arras, France — A57

1935, May 4

206 A57 1k rose .35 .25
207 A57 2k dull blue 1.50 .45

20th anniversary of the Battle of Arras.

Nos. 206-207 were each issued in sheets of 100 stamps and 12 blank labels. Value, set with attached labels: mint $8; used $8.

Gen. Milan Stefánik — A58

1935, May 18

208 A58 50h green .25 .25

Sts. Cyril and Methodius — A59

1935, June 22

209 A59 50h green .25 .25
210 A59 1k claret .45 .25
211 A59 2k deep blue 1.50 .25
Nos. 209-211 (3) 2.20 .75

Millenary of the arrival in Moravia of the Apostles Cyril and Methodius.

Masaryk — A60

1935, Oct. 20 *Perf. 12½*

212 A60 1k rose lake .25 .25

No. 212 exists imperforate. See Bohemia and Moravia No. 1A. For overprints see Bohemia and Moravia Nos. 9-10, Slovakia 12.

Statue of Macha, Prague — A61

1936, Apr. 30

213 A61 50h deep green .25 .25
214 A61 1k rose lake .40 .25

Karel Hynek Macha (1810-1836), Bohemian poet.

Nos. 213-214 were each issued in sheets of 100 stamps and 12 blank labels. Value, set with attached labels: mint $1; used 75c.

Jan Amos Komensky (Comenius) — A61a

Pres. Eduard Benes A62

Gen. Milan Stefánik A63

1936

215 A61a 40h dark blue .25 .25
216 A62 50h dull green .25 .25
217 A63 60h dull violet .25 .25
Nos. 215-217 (3) .75 .75

See no. 252, Slovakia 23A. For overprints see Bohemia and Moravia Nos. 6, 8, Slovakia 7, 9-11.

Castle Palanok near Mukacevo A64

Town of Banska Bystrica A65

Castle at Zvikov — A66

Ruins of Castle at Strecno — A67

Castle at Cesky Raj A68

Palace at Slavkov (Austerlitz) A69

Statue of King George of Podebrad A70

Town Square at Olomouc — A71

Castle Ruins at Bratislava A72

1936, Aug. 1

218 A64 1.20k rose lilac .25 .25
219 A65 1.50k carmine .25 .25
220 A66 2k dark blue green .25 .25
221 A67 2.50k dark blue .25 .25
222 A68 3k brown .25 .25
223 A69 3.50k dark violet 1.50 .25
224 A70 4k dark violet .60 .25
225 A71 5k green .60 .25
226 A72 10k blue 1.00 .25
Nos. 218-226 (9) 4.95 2.25

Nos. 224-226 were each issued in sheets of 100 stamps and 12 blank labels. Value, with attached labels: mint $6; used $6.

For overprints and surcharge see Nos. 237-238, 254A, Bohemia and Moravia 11-12, 14-19, Slovakia 13-14, 16-23.

President Benes — A73

1937, Apr. 26 Unwmk. *Perf. 12½*

227	A73 50h deep green	.25	.25

For overprints see Nos. 236, Slovakia 8.

Soldiers of the Czech Legion — A74

1937, June 15

228	A74 50h deep green	.25	.25
229	A74 1k rose lake	.30	.25

20th anniv. of the Battle of Zborov.

Nos. 228-229 were each issued in sheets of 100 stamps and 12 blank labels. Value, set with attached labels: mint $2; used $1.50.

Cathedral at Prague — A75

1937, July 1

230	A75 2k green	.90	.25
231	A75 2.50k blue	1.40	.30

Founding of the "Little Entente," 16th anniv.

Nos. 230-231 were each issued in sheets with blank labels. Value, set with attached labels: mint $17.50; used $9.

Jan Evangelista Purkyne — A76

1937, Sept. 2

232	A76 50h slate green	.25	.25
233	A76 1k dull rose	.30	.25

150th anniv. of the birth of Purkyne, Czech physiologist.

Nos. 232-233 were printed in sheets of 100 with 12 decorated labels. Value, set with labels, $2.50.

Masaryk Types of 1930-35

1937, Sept. *Perf. 12½*

234	A37 50h black	.25	.25

With date "14.IX. 1937" in design

235	A56 2k black	.30	.25

Death of former President Thomas G. Masaryk on Sept. 14, 1937.

No. 235 was issued in sheets of 100 stamps and 12 inscribed labels. Value, with attached label: mint $3.50; used $3.50.

International Labor Bureau Issue

Stamps of 1936-37 Overprinted in Violet or Black

1937, Oct. 6 *Perf. 12½*

236	A73 50h dp green (Bk)	.35	.35
237	A65 1.50k carmine (V)	.35	.35
238	A66 2k dp green (V)	.70	.35
	Nos. 236-238 (3)	1.40	1.05

Bratislava Philatelic Exhibition Issue

Souvenir Sheet

A77

1937, Oct. 24 *Perf. 12½*

239	A77 Sheet of 2	2.50	*2.75*
a.	50h dark blue	.80	1.20
b.	1k brown carmine	.80	1.20

The stamps show a view of Poprad Lake (50h) and the tomb of General Milan Stefanik (1k).

No. 239 overprinted with the Czechoslovak arms and "Czecho-Slovak Participation New York World's Fair 1939 and 1940, Czecho-Slovak Pavilion" were privately produced to finance Czechoslovak participation in the exhibition. The overprint exists in black, green, red, blue, gold and silver.

No. 239 overprinted "Liberation de la Tchechoslovaquie, 28-X-1945" etc., was sold at a philatelic exhibition in Brussels, Belgium.

St. Barbara's Church, Kutna Hora — A79

1937, Dec. 4

240	A79 1.60k olive green	.25	.25

For overprints see Bohemia and Moravia Nos. 13, Slovakia 15.

Peregrine Falcon, Sokol Emblem — A80

1938, Jan. 21

241	A80 50h deep green	.25	.25
242	A80 1k rose lake	.25	.25

10th Intl. Sokol Games.

Nos. 241-242 were each issued in sheets of 100 stamps and 12 inscribed labels. Value, set with attached labels: mint $1.50; used $2.50.

Imperf. examples of No. 242 are essays.

Legionnaires

A81 A82

Legionnaire — A83

1938

243	A81 50h deep green	.25	.25
244	A82 50h deep green	.25	.25
245	A83 50h deep green	.25	.25
	Nos. 243-245 (3)	.75	.75

20th anniv. of the Battle of Bachmac, Vouziers and Doss Alto.

Nos. 243-245 were each issued in sheets of 100 stamps and 12 inscribed labels. Value, set with attached labels $2, mint or used.

Jindrich Fügner, Co-Founder of Sokol Movement — A84

1938, June 18 *Perf. 12½*

246	A84 50h deep green	.25	.25
247	A84 1k rose lake	.25	.25
248	A84 2k slate blue	.40	.25
	Nos. 246-248 (3)	.90	.75

10th Sokol Summer Games.

Nos. 246-248 were each issued in sheets of 100 stamps and 12 inscribed labels. Value, set with attached labels: mint $2.50; used $2.

View of Pilsen — A85

1938, June 24

249	A85 50h deep green	.25	.25

Provincial Economic Council meeting, Pilsen.

No. 249 was issued in sheets of 150 stamps and 10 labels depicting a flower within a cog-wheel. Value, with attached label $1, mint or used.

For overprint see Bohemia & Moravia No. 7.

Cathedral of Kosice — A86

1938, July 15 *Perf. 12½*

250	A86 50h deep green	.25	.25

Kosice Cultural Exhibition.

No. 250 was issued in sheets of 150 stamps and 10 labels depicting grapes. Value, with attached label $1, $7.50 mint, $4.50 used.

Prague Philatelic Exhibition Issue

Souvenir Sheet

Vysehrad Castle — Hradcany — A87

1938, June 26 *Perf. 12½*

251	A87 Sheet of 2	5.00	5.00
a.	50h dark blue	1.50	1.50
b.	1k deep carmine	1.50	1.50

See No. 3036.

Stefánik Type of 1936

1938, Nov. 21

252	A63 50h deep green	.25	.25

Allegory of the Republic — A89

1938, Dec. 19 Unwmk.

253	A89 2k lt ultra	.30	.25
254	A89 3k pale brown	.50	.40

20th anniv. of Independence.

Nos. 253-254 were each issued in sheets of 100 stamps and 12 blank labels. Value, set with attached labels $2, mint or used.

See No. B153.

"Wir sind frei!"

Stamps of Czechoslovakia, 1918-37, overprinted with a swastika in black or red and "Wir sind frei!" were issued locally and unofficially in 1938 as Czech authorities were evacuating and German authorities arriving. They appeared in the towns of Asch, Karlsbad, Reichenberg-Maffersdorf, Rumburg, etc.

The overprint, sometimes including a surcharge or the town name (as in Karlsbad), exists on many values of postage, air post, semi-postal, postage due and newspaper stamps.

No. 226 Surcharged in Orange Red

1939, Jan. 18 Unwmk. *Perf. 12½*

254A	A72 300h on 10k blue	1.25	*1.75*

Opening of the Slovakian Parliament.

No. 254A was issued in sheets of 100 stamps with 12 blank labels. Value with attached labels, mint $4.

View of Jasina — A89a

Perf. 12½

1939, Mar. 15 Engr. Unwmk.

254B	A89a 3k ultra	*4.00*	*40.00*

Inauguration of the Carpatho-Ukraine Diet, Mar. 2, 1939.

Printed for use in the province of Carpatho-Ukraine but issued in Prague at the same time.

No. 254B was issued in sheets of 100 stamps with 12 blank labels. Values with attached labels: mint $12, used $80. Used value is for red commemorative cancel.

The stamps formerly listed as Czechoslovakia Nos. 255, 256 and C18 are now listed with Bohemia and Moravia and Slovakia. No. 255 is now Slovakia No. 23A. No. 256 and C18 are now listed as Bohemia and Moravia 1A and C1, respectively.

Linden Leaves and Buds — A90

1945 Photo. *Perf. 14*

256A	A90 10h black	.25	.25
257	A90 30h yellow brown	.25	.25
258	A90 50h dark green	.25	.25
258A	A90 60h dark blue	.25	.25

Engr.

(Buds Open)

Perf. 12½

259	A90 60h blue	.25	.25
259A	A90 80h orange ver	.25	.25
260	A90 1.20k rose	.25	.25
261	A90 3k violet brown	.25	.25
262	A90 5k green	.25	.25
	Nos. 256A-262 (9)	2.25	2.25

Compare with Bohemia-Moravia type A1.

Thomas G. Masaryk — A91

1945-46 Photo. *Perf. 12*

262A	A91	5h dull violet ('46)	.25	.25
262B	A91	10h orange yel ('46)	.25	.25
262C	A91	20h dk brown ('46)	.25	.25
263	A91	50h brt green	.25	.25
264	A91	1k orange red	.25	.25
265	A91	2k chalky blue	.25	.25
		Nos. 262A-265 (6)	1.50	1.50

Coat of Arms — A92

1945 *Imperf.*

266	A92	50h olive gray	.25	.25
267	A92	1k brt red vio	.25	.25
268	A92	1.50k dk carmine	.25	.25
269	A92	2k deep blue	.25	.25
269A	A92	2.40k henna brn	.25	.25
270	A92	3k brown	.25	.25
270A	A92	4k dk slate grn	.25	.25
271	A92	6k violet blue	.25	.25
271A	A92	10k sepia	.25	.25
		Nos. 266-271A (9)	2.25	2.25

Nos. 266, 268, 269, 270 and 271 exist in 2 printings. Stamps of the 1st printing have a coarse impression and are on thin, hard paper in sheets of 100; all values exist in the 2nd printing, with fine impressions on thick, soft wove paper in sheets of 200. Values are the same.

Staff Capt. Ridky (British Army) — A93

Dr. Miroslav Novak (French Army) — A94

Capt. Otakar Jaros (Russian Army) — A95

Staff Capt. Stanislav Zimprich (Foreign Legion) — A96

2nd Lt. Jiri Kral (French Air Force) A97

Josef Gabcik (Parachutist) A98

Staff Capt. Alois Vasatko (Royal Air Force) A99

Private Frantisek Adamek (British Colonial Service) A100

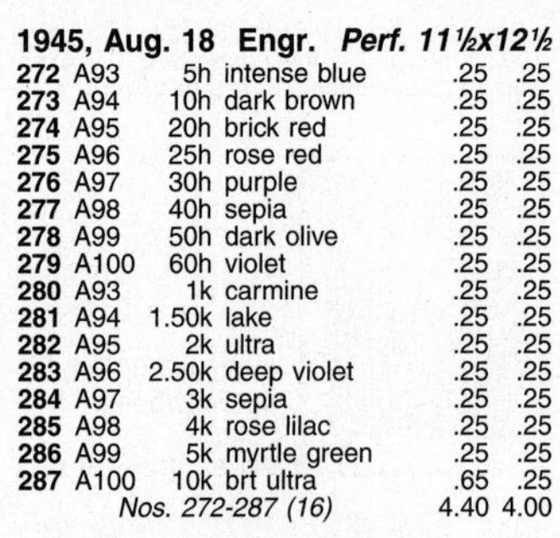

1945, Aug. 18 Engr. *Perf. 11½x12½*

272	A93	5h intense blue	.25	.25
273	A94	10h dark brown	.25	.25
274	A95	20h brick red	.25	.25
275	A96	25h rose red	.25	.25
276	A97	30h purple	.25	.25
277	A98	40h sepia	.25	.25
278	A99	50h dark olive	.25	.25
279	A100	60h violet	.25	.25
280	A93	1k carmine	.25	.25
281	A94	1.50k lake	.25	.25
282	A95	2k ultra	.25	.25
283	A96	2.50k deep violet	.25	.25
284	A97	3k sepia	.25	.25
285	A98	4k rose lilac	.25	.25
286	A99	5k myrtle green	.25	.25
287	A100	10k brt ultra	.65	.25
		Nos. 272-287 (16)	4.40	4.00

Flags of Russia, Great Britain, US and Czechoslovakia — A101

View of Banská Bystrica A102

Patriot Welcoming Russian Soldier, Turciansky A103

Ruins of Castle at Sklabina A104

Czech Patriot, Strecno A105

1945, Aug. 29 Photo. *Perf. 10*

288	A101	1.50k brt carmine	.25	.25
289	A102	2k brt blue	.25	.25
290	A103	4k dark brown	.25	.25
291	A104	4.50k purple	.25	.30
292	A105	5k deep green	.50	.50
		Nos. 288-292 (5)	1.50	1.55

National uprising against the Germans.

A card contains one each of Nos. 288-292 on thin cardboard, ungummed. Size: 148x210mm. Sold for 50k. Value, $20 unused, $120 used. Forged cancellations exist.

Stefánik A106

Benes A107

Masaryk — A108

1945-47 Engr. *Perf. 12, 12½*

293	A106	30h rose violet	.25	.25
294	A107	60h blue	.25	.25
294A	A106	1k red org ('47)	.25	.25
295	A108	1.20k car rose	.25	.25
295A	A108	1.20(k) rose lil ('46)	.25	.25
296	A106	2.40(k) rose	.25	.25
297	A107	3k red violet	.25	.25
297A	A108	4k dark blue ('46)	.25	.25
298	A108	5k Prus green	.25	.25
299	A107	7k gray	.25	.25
300	A106	10k gray blue	.30	.25
300A	A106	20k sepia ('46)	.30	.25
		Nos. 293-300A (12)	3.10	3.00

1945 Photo. *Perf. 14*

301	A108	50h brown	.25	.25
302	A106	80h dark green	.25	.25
303	A107	1.60(k) olive green	.25	.25
304	A108	15k red violet	.30	.25
		Nos. 301-304 (4)	1.05	1.00

Statue of Kozina and Chod Castle, Domazlice — A109

1945, Nov. 28 Engr. *Perf. 12½*

305	A109	2.40k rose carmine	.25	.25
306	A109	4k blue	.25	.25

250th anniv. of the death of Jan Sladky Kozina, peasant leader.

Nos. 305-306 were issued in sheets of 100 stamps with 12 blank labels. Value, set with attached labels, mint $6.

Red Army Soldier — A110

1945, Mar. 26 Litho. *Imperf.*

307	A110	2k crimson rose	.40	.40
308	A110	5k slate black	1.10	1.10
309	A110	6k ultramarine	1.10	1.10
		Nos. 307-309 (3)	2.60	2.60

Souvenir Sheet

1945, July 16 Gray Burelage

310	Sheet of 3	4.00	4.00
a.	A110 2k crimson rose	.75	.75
b.	A110 5k slate black	.75	.75
c.	A110 6k ultramarine	.75	.75

Return of Pres. Benes, Apr., 1945.

Clasped Hands — A112

1945 *Rouletted 12½*

311	A112	1.50k brown red	1.50	1.50
312	A112	9k red orange	.35	.35
313	A112	13k orange brown	.65	.65
314	A112	20k blue	1.50	1.50
		Nos. 311-314 (4)	4.00	4.00

Karel Havlícek Borovsky — A113

1946, July 5 Engr. *Perf. 12½*

315	A113	1.20k gray black	.25	.25

Borovsky (1821-56), editor and writer.

Issued in sheets of 100 stamps and 12 inscribed labels. Value with attached label: $1.25.

Old Town Hall, Brno — A114

Hodonin Square — A115

Perf. 12½x12, 12x12½

1946, Aug. 3 Engr. Unwmk.

316	A114	2.40k deep rose	.25	.25
317	A115	7.40k dull violet	.25	.25

See No. B159.

President Eduard Benes — A116

1946, Oct. 28

318	A116	60h indigo	.25	.25
319	A116	1.60k dull green	.25	.25
320	A116	3k red lilac	.25	.25
321	A116	8k sepia	.25	.25
		Nos. 318-321 (4)	1.00	1.00

Flag, Symbols — A117

1947, Jan. 1 *Perf. 12½*

322	A117	1.20k Prus green	.25	.25
323	A117	2.40k deep rose	.25	.25
324	A117	4k deep blue	.45	.25
		Nos. 322-324 (3)	.95	.75

Czechoslovakia's two-year reconstruction and rehabilitation program.

Nos. 322-324 each issued in sheets of 100 stamps and 12 inscribed labels. Value, set with attached labels, $3.

Saint Adalbert — A118

1947, Apr. 23

326	A118	1.60k gray	.75	.60
327	A118	2.40k rose carmine	.90	.60
328	A118	5k blue green	1.10	.45
		Nos. 326-328 (3)	2.75	1.65

950th anniv. of the death of Saint Adalbert, Bishop of Prague.

Nos. 326-328 each issued in sheets of 100 stamps and 12 monogrammed labels. Value, set with attached labels, $35.

Grief — A119

Allegorical Figure — A120

1947, June 10 **Engr.**

329 A119 1.20k black .40 .25
330 A119 1.60k slate black .45 .45
331 A120 2.40k brown violet .45 .45
Nos. 329-331 (3) 1.30 1.15

Destruction of Lidice, 5th anniversary.
Nos. 329-331 each issued in sheets of 100 stamps and 12 inscribed labels. Value, set with attached labels, $15.

World Federation of Youth Symbol — A121

1947, July 20

332 A121 1.20k violet brown .50 .35
333 A121 4k slate .50 .35

World Youth Festival held in Prague, July 20-Aug. 17.

Thomas G. Masaryk — A122

1947, Sept. 14

334 A122 1.20k gray blk, *buff* .25 .25
335 A122 4k blue blk, *cream* .30 .25

Death of Masaryk, 10th anniv.
Nos. 334-335 each issued in sheets of 100 stamps and 12 inscribed labels. Value, set with attached labels, $5.

Msgr. Stefan Moyses A123

1947, Oct. 19

336 A123 1.20k rose violet .25 .25
337 A123 4k deep blue .25 .25

150th anniversary of the birth of Stefan Moyses, first Slovakian chairman of the Slavic movement.
Each issued in sheets of 100 stamps and 12 labels with "MOYSES" and floral decoration. Value, set with attached labels, $7.50.

"Freedom from Social Oppression" A124

1947, Oct. 26 **Photo.** ***Perf. 14***

338 A124 2.40k brt carmine .40 .30
339 A124 4k brt ultra .50 .25

Russian revolution of Oct., 1917, 30th anniv.

Benes — A125

1948, Feb. 15 **Photo.**

Size: 17½x21½mm

340 A125 1.50k brown .25 .25

Size: 19x23mm

341 A125 2k deep plum .25 .25
342 A125 5k brt ultra .25 .25
Nos. 340-342 (3) .75 .75

"Czechoslovakia" Greeting Sokol Marchers — A126

1948, Mar. 7 **Engr.** ***Perf. 12½***

343 A126 1.50k brown .25 .25
344 A126 3k rose carmine .25 .25
345 A126 5k blue .50 .25
Nos. 343-345 (3) 1.00 .75

The 11th Sokol Congress.
Nos. 343-345 each issued in sheets of 100 stamps and 12 labels depicting dates and bouquet. Values, set with attached labels: mint $4.50; used $3.75.

King Charles IV — A127

St. Wenceslas, King Charles IV — A128

1948, Apr. 7

346 A127 1.50k black brown .25 .25
347 A128 2k dark brown .25 .25
348 A128 3k brown red .25 .25
349 A127 5k dark blue .25 .25
Nos. 346-349 (4) 1.00 1.00

600th anniv. of the foundation of Charles University, Prague.
Nos. 346-349 each issued in sheets of 100 stamps and 12 inscribed labels. Value, set with attached labels, $4.50.

Czech Peasants in Revolt — A129

Unwmk.

1948, May 14 **Photo.** ***Perf. 14***

350 A129 1.50k dk olive brown .25 .25

Centenary of abolition of serfdom.

Jindrich Vanicek — A130

Designs: 1.50k, 2k, Josef Scheiner.

1948, June 10 **Engr.** ***Perf. 12½***

351 A130 1k dark green .25 .25
352 A130 1.50k sepia .25 .25
353 A130 2k gray blue .25 .25
354 A130 3k claret .25 .25
Nos. 351-354 (4) 1.00 1.00

11th Sokol Congress, Prague, 1948.
Nos. 351-354 each issued in sheets of 100 stamps and 12 labels depicting a sunflower. Values, set with attached labels: $3.75 mint; $3 used.

Frantisek Palacky & F. L. Rieger — A131

1948, June 20 **Unwmk.**

355 A131 1.50k gray .25 .25
356 A131 3k brown carmine .25 .25

Constituent Assembly at Kromeriz, cent.
Nos. 355-356 each issued in sheets of 100 stamps and 12 labels depicting a wreath. Value, set with attached labels, $1.50.

Miloslav Josef Hurban — A132

3k, Ludovit Stur. 5k, Michael M. Hodza.

1948, Aug. 27 ***Perf. 12½***

357 A132 1.50k dark brown .25 .25
358 A132 3k carmine lake .25 .25
359 A132 5k indigo .25 .25
Nos. 357-359 (3) .75 .75

Cent. of 1848 insurrection against Hungary.
Nos. 357-359 each issued in sheets of 100 stamps and 12 labels depicting signatures. Values, set with attached labels: mint $5; used $3.50.

Eduard Benes — A133

1948, Sept. 28

360 A133 8k black .25 .25

President Eduard Benes, 1884-1948.

Czechoslovak Family — A134

1948, Oct. 28 ***Perf. 12½x12***

361 A134 1.50k deep blue .25 .25
362 A134 3k rose carmine .25 .25

Czechoslovakia's Independence, 30th anniv.
Nos. 361-362 each issued in sheets of 100 stamps and 12 labels depicting dates, leaves. Value, set with attached labels, $2.

Pres. Klement Gottwald — A135

1948-49 ***Perf. 12½***

Size: 18½x23½mm

363 A135 1.50k dk brown .25 .25
364 A135 3k car rose .30 .25
a. 3k rose brown 1.00 .25
365 A135 5k gray blue .25 .25

Size: 23½x29mm

366 A135 20k purple .90 .25
Nos. 363-366 (4) 1.70 1.00

No. 366 was issued in sheets of 100 stamps and 12 monogrammed labels. Value, with attached label, $3.50.
See Nos. 373, 564, 600-604.

Souvenir Sheet

1948, Nov. 23 **Unwmk.** ***Imperf.***

367 A135 30k rose brown 4.25 3.00

52nd birthday of Pres. Klement Gottwald (1896-1953).

Hradcany Castle Type of 1918

Souvenir Sheet

1948, Dec. 18

368 A1 10k dk blue violet 3.00 2.40

1st Czech postage stamp, 30th anniv.

Czechoslovak and Russian Workmen Shaking Hands — A138

1948, Dec. 12 ***Perf. 12½***

369 A138 3k rose carmine .25 .25

5th anniv. of the treaty of alliance between Czechoslovakia and Russia.
No. 369 issued in sheets of 100 stamps and 12 labels depicting Czech and Soviet flags. Value with attached label 60c.

Lenin — A139

1949, Jan. 21 **Engr.** ***Perf. 12½***

370 A139 1.50k violet brown .30 .25
371 A139 5k deep blue .30 .30

25th anniversary of the death of Lenin.
Nos. 370-371 each issued in sheets of 100 stamps and 12 labels depicting torch. Value, set with attached labels: mint $1.75; used $1.50.

Gottwald Type of 1948 Inscribed: "UNOR 1948" and

Gottwald Addressing Meeting A140

1949, Feb. 25 **Photo.** ***Perf. 14***

372 A140 3k red brown .25 .25

Perf. 12½

Engr.

Size: 23½x29mm

373 A135 10k deep green .40 .25

1st anniv. of Gottwald's speech announcing the appointment of a new government. No. 372 exists in a souvenir sheet of 1. It was not sold to the public.
No. 373 issued in sheets of 100 stamps and 12 inscribed labels. Values with attached label: mint $2.50; used $1.50.

A141

Writers: 50h, P. O. Hviezdoslav. 80h, V. Vancura. 1k, J. Sverma. 2k, Julius Fucik. 4k, Jiri Wolker. 8k, Alois Jirasek.

1949 **Photo.** ***Perf. 14***

374 A141 50h violet brown .25 .25
375 A141 80h scarlet .25 .25
376 A141 1k dk olive green .25 .25
377 A141 2k brt blue .40 .25

Perf. 12½

Engr.

378 A141 4k violet brown .40 .25
379 A141 8k brown black .50 .25
Nos. 374-379 (6) 2.05 1.50

A142

3k, Stagecoach and Train. 5k, Postrider and post bus. 13k, Sailing ship and plane.

1949, May 20

380 A142	3k brown carmine	1.50	1.50
381 A142	5k deep blue	1.00	.45
382 A142	13k deep green	1.50	1.00
	Nos. 380-382 (3)	4.00	2.95

75th anniv. of the UPU.

Reaping A143

Communist Emblem and Workers A144

Workman, Symbol of Industry — A145

Perf. 12½x12, 12x12½

1949, May 24 **Unwmk.**

383 A143	1.50k deep green	.50	.45
384 A144	3k brown carmine	.50	.45
385 A145	5k deep blue	.50	.45
	Nos. 383-385 (3)	1.50	1.35

No. 384 for the 9th meeting of the Communist Party of Czechoslovakia, 5/25/49.

Nos. 383-385 each issued in sheets of 100 stamps and 12 inscribed labels. Value, set with attached labels, $12.

Bedrich Smetana and Natl. Theater, Prague — A146

1949, June 4 ***Perf. 12½x12***

386 A146	1.50k dull green	.25	.25
387 A146	5k deep blue	.75	.25

Birth of Bedrich Smetana, composer, 125th anniv.

Aleksander Pushkin — A147

1949, June 6 ***Perf. 12x12½***

388 A147 2k olive gray .25 .25

Birth of Aleksander S. Pushkin, 150th anniv.

Frederic Chopin and Conservatory, Warsaw A148

1949, June 24 ***Perf. 12½x12***

389 A148	3k dark red	.40	.25
390 A148	8k violet brown	.75	.50

Cent. of the death of Frederic F. Chopin.

Globe and Ribbon — A149

1949, Aug. 20 ***Perf. 12½x12***

391 A149	1.50k violet brown	.35	.35
392 A149	5k ultra	.90	.90

50th Prague Sample Fair, Sept. 11-18, 1949.

Starting in October, 1949, some commemorative sets included one "blocked" value, which could be obtained only by purchasing the complete set. These restricted values were printed in smaller quantities than other stamps in the set and were typically sold for more than face value.

Zvolen Castle — A150

1949, Aug. 28 ***Perf. 12½***

393 A150 10k rose lake .75 .25

Early Miners — A151

Miner of Today — A152

Design: 5k, Mining Machine.

1949, Sept. 11 ***Perf. 12½***

394 A151	1.50k sepia	.70	.50
395 A152	3k carmine rose	5.50	2.00
396 A151	5k deep blue	4.00	1.50
	Nos. 394-396 (3)	10.20	4.00

700th anniv. of the Czechoslovak mining industry; 150th anniv. of the miner's laws.

Construction Workers — A153

1949, Dec. 11 ***Perf. 12½***

397 A153	1k shown	3.00	1.40
398 A153	2k Machinist	2.00	.70

2nd Trade Union Congress, Prague, 1949.

Joseph V. Stalin — A154

Design: 3k, Stalin facing left.

Cream Paper

1949, Dec. 21 **Unwmk.**

399 A154	1.50k greenish gray	.75	.35
400 A154	3k claret	4.50	1.75

70th birthday of Joseph V. Stalin.

Skier — A155

Efficiency Badge — A156

Engr., Photo. (3k)

1950, Feb. 15 ***Perf. 12½, 13½***

401 A155	1.50k gray blue	2.75	1.50
402 A156	3k vio brn, *cr*	2.75	1.50
403 A155	5k ultramarine	2.00	1.10
	Nos. 401-403 (3)	7.50	4.10

51st Ski Championship for the Tatra cup, Feb. 15-26, 1950.

Vladimir V. Mayakovsky, Poet, 20th Death Anniv. — A157

1950, Apr. 14 **Engr.** ***Perf. 12½***

404 A157	1.50k dark brown	2.25	1.10
405 A157	3k brown red	2.25	1.10

See Nos. 414-417, 422-423, 432-433, 464-465, 477-478.

Soviet Tank Soldier and Hradcany A158

2k, Hero of Labor medal. 3k, Two workers (militiamen) and Town Hall, Prague. 5k, Text of government program and heraldic lion.

1950, May 5

406 A158	1.50k gray green	.35	.25
407 A158	2k dark brown	1.00	1.00
408 A158	3k brown red	.25	.25
409 A158	5k dark blue	.50	.25
	Nos. 406-409 (4)	2.10	1.75

5th anniv. of the Czechoslovak People's Democratic Republic.

Factory and Young Couple with Tools A159

Designs: 2k, Steam shovel. 3k, Farmer and farm scene. 5k, Three workers leaving factory.

1950, May 9 **Engr.**

410 A159	1.50k dark green	1.75	.85
411 A159	2k dark brown	1.75	.85
412 A159	3k rose red	1.00	.35
413 A159	5k deep blue	1.00	.35
	Nos. 410-413 (4)	5.50	2.40

Canceled to Order

The government philatelic department started about 1950 to sell canceled sets of new issues. Values in the second ("used") column are for these canceled-to-order stamps. Postally used stamps are worth more.

Portrait Type of 1950

Design: S. K. Neumann.

1950, June 5 **Unwmk.** ***Perf. 12½***

414 A157	1.50k deep blue	.35	.25
415 A157	3k violet brown	1.10	1.00

Stanislav Kostka Neumann (1875-1947), journalist and poet.

1950, June 21

Design: Bozena Nemcova.

416 A157	1.50k deep blue	1.25	.75
417 A157	7k dark brown	.30	.25

Bozena Nemcova (1820-1862), writer.

Liberation of Colonies A160

Designs: 2k, Allegory, Fight for Peace. 3k, Group of Students. 5k, Marching Students with flags.

1950, Aug. 14

418 A160	1.50k dark green	.25	.25
419 A160	2k sepia	.25	.25
420 A160	3k rose carmine	.25	.25
421 A160	5k ultra	.60	.45
	Nos. 418-421 (4)	1.35	1.20

2nd International Students World Congress, Prague, Aug. 12-24, 1950.

Portrait Type of 1950

Design: Zdenek Fibich.

1950, Oct. 15

422 A157	3k rose brown	.90	.55
423 A157	8k gray green	.35	.25

Zdenek Fibich, musician, birth centenary.

Miner, Soldier and Farmer A161

Czech and Soviet Soldiers A162

1950, Oct. 6

424 A161	1.50k slate	.35	.35
425 A162	3k carmine rose	.35	.35

Issued to publicize Czech Army Day.

Prague Castle, 16th Century A163

Prague, 1493 A164

3k, Prague, 1606. 5k, Prague, 1794.

1950, Oct. 21 ***Perf. 14***

426 A163	1.50k black	4.50	2.25
427 A164	2k chocolate	4.50	2.25
428 A164	3k brown car	4.50	2.25
429 A164	5k gray	4.50	2.25
a.	Block of 4, #426-429	25.00	15.00

See Nos. 434-435.

Communications Symbols — A165

1950, Oct. 25 *Perf. 12½*

430 A165	1.50k chocolate	.35	.25
431 A165	3k brown carmine	.75	.60

1st anniv. of the foundation of the Intl. League of P.T.T. Employees.

Portrait Type of 1950

Design: J. Gregor Tajovsky.

1950, Oct. 26

432 A157	1.50k brown	1.00	.75
433 A157	5k deep blue	1.00	.75

10th anniversary of the death of J. Gregor Tajovsky (1874-1940), Slovakian writer.

Scenic Type of 1950

Design: Prague, 1950.

1950, Oct. 28

434 A164	1.50k indigo	.35	.25
a.	Souvenir sheet of 4, imperf.	30.00	11.00
435 A164	3k brown car	.90	.50

Czech and Soviet Steel Workers A166

1950, Nov. 4 **Unwmk.**

436 A166	1.50k chocolate	.45	.30
437 A166	5k deep blue	.90	.60

Issued to publicize the 2nd meeting of the Union of Czechoslovak-Soviet Friendship.

Dove by Picasso A167

1951, Jan. 20 **Photo.** *Perf. 14*

438 A167	2k deep blue	6.00	4.50
439 A167	3k rose brown	4.00	1.50

1st Czechoslovak Congress of Fighters for Peace, held in Prague.

Julius Fucik — A168

1951, Feb. 17 **Engr.** *Perf. 12½*

440 A168	1.50k gray	.75	.75
441 A168	5k gray blue	1.50	1.50

No. 441 exists in a sheet of 12. Value, $500.

Drop Hammer — A169

Installing Gear — A170

1951, Feb. 24

442 A169	1.50k gray blk	.25	.25
443 A170	3k violet brn	.25	.25
444 A169	4k gray blue	.60	.50
	Nos. 442-444 (3)	1.10	1.00

Women Machinists — A171

Designs: 3k, Woman tractor operator. 5k, Women of different races.

1951, Mar. 8 **Photo.** *Perf. 14*

445 A171	1.50k olive brown	.40	.30
446 A171	3k brown car	1.40	1.00
447 A171	5k blue	.70	.40
	Nos. 445-447 (3)	2.50	1.70

International Women's Day, Mar. 8.

Apprentice Miners — A172

1951, Apr. 12 **Engr.** *Perf. 12½*

448 A172	1.50k gray	.55	.50
449 A172	3k red brown	.25	.25

Plowing A173

Collective Cattle Breeding A174

1951, Apr. 28 **Photo.** *Perf. 14*

450 A173	1.50k brown	.70	.70
451 A174	2k dk green	1.40	1.40

Tatra Mountain Recreation Center — A175

Mountain Recreation Centers: 2k, Beskydy (Beskids). 3k, Krkonose (Carpathians).

1951, May 5 **Engr.** *Perf. 12½*

452 A175	1.50k deep green	.25	.25
453 A175	2k dark brown	1.00	.75
454 A175	3k rose brown	.25	.25
	Nos. 452-454 (3)	1.50	1.25

Issued to publicize the summer opening of trade union recreation centers.

Klement Gottwald and Joseph Stalin A176

Factory Militiaman A177

Red Army Soldier and Partisan A178

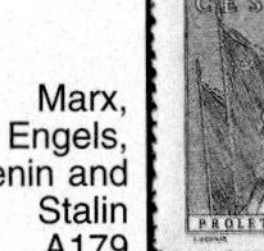

Marx, Engels, Lenin and Stalin A179

1951 **Unwmk.** *Perf. 12½*

455 A176	1.50k olive gray	.75	.25
456 A177	2k red brown	.35	.25
457 A178	3k rose brown	.35	.25
458 A176	5k deep blue	1.40	1.00
459 A179	8k gray	.70	.25
	Nos. 455-459 (5)	3.55	2.00

30th anniv. of the founding of the Czechoslovak Communist Party.

A180

Design: 1k, 2k, Antonin Dvorák. 1.50k, 3k, Bedrich Smetana.

1951, May 30

460 A180	1k redsh brown	.35	.25
461 A180	1.50k olive gray	1.40	.70
462 A180	2k dk redsh brn	1.40	.70
463 A180	3k rose brown	.35	.25
	Nos. 460-463 (4)	3.50	1.90

International Music Festival, Prague.

Nos. 461 and 462 were each issued in sheets of 10 stamps. Value, $700 for 461, $600 for 462.

Portrait Type of 1950

Portrait: Bohumir Smeral (facing right).

1951, June 21

464 A157	1.50k dark gray	.75	.50
465 A157	3k rose brown	.35	.25

10th anniv. of the death of Bohumir Smeral, political leader.

A181

1951, June 21

466 A181	1k shown	.75	.35
467 A181	1.50k Discus	.75	.35
468 A181	3k Soccer	1.50	.35
469 A181	5k Skier	3.50	1.50
	Nos. 466-469 (4)	6.50	2.55

Issued to honor the 9th Congress of the Czechoslovak Sokol Federation.

Scene from "Fall of Berlin" A182

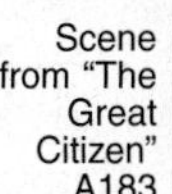

Scene from "The Great Citizen" A183

1951, July 14

470 A182	80h rose brown	.35	.35
471 A183	1.50k dark gray	.35	.35
472 A182	4k gray blue	1.40	1.10
	Nos. 470-472 (3)	2.10	1.80

Intl. Film Festival, Karlovy Vary, July 14-29.

Alois Jirásek — A184

"Fables and Fate" A185

Design: 4k, Scene from "Reign of Tabor."

1951, Aug. 23 **Engr.** *Perf. 12½*

473 A184	1.50k gray	.35	.25
474 A184	5k dark blue	2.10	.80

Photo.

Perf. 14

475 A185	3k dark red	.50	.25
476 A185	4k dark brown	.50	.25
	Nos. 473-476 (4)	3.45	1.55

Cent. of the birth of Alois Jirásek, author.

No. 474 was issued in a sheet of 10 stamps. Value: mint *$1,000.*

Portrait Type of 1950

Design: Josef Hybes (1850-1921), co-founder of Czech Communist Party.

1951, July 21 **Engr.**

477 A157	1.50k chocolate	.35	.25
478 A157	2k rose brown	.75	.40

"Ostrava Region" — A186

Mining Iron Ore — A187

1951, Sept. 9

479 A186	1.50k dk brown	.25	.25
480 A187	3k rose brown	.25	.25
481 A186	5k deep blue	1.00	.65
	Nos. 479-481 (3)	1.50	1.15

Miner's Day, Sept. 9, 1951.

Soldiers on Parade — A188

1k, Gunner and field gun. 1.50k, Klement Gottwald. 3k, Tankman and tank. 5k, Aviators.

Photo. (80h, 5k), Engr.

1951, Oct. 6 *Perf. 14 (80h, 5k), 12½*

Inscribed: "Den CS Armady 1951"

482	A188	80h olive brown	.35	.30
483	A188	1k dk olive grn	.35	.30
484	A188	1.50k sepia	.35	.30
485	A188	3k claret	.75	.35
486	A188	5k blue	1.75	.75
		Nos. 482-486 (5)	3.55	2.00

Issued to publicize Army Day, Oct. 6, 1951.

Stalin and Gottwald — A189

Lenin, Stalin and Soldiers — A190

1951, Nov. 3 **Engr.** *Perf. 12½*

487	A189	1.50k sepia	.25	.25
488	A190	3k red brown	.25	.25
489	A189	4k deep blue	1.00	.45
		Nos. 487-489 (3)	1.50	.95

Issued to publicize the month of Czechoslovak-Soviet friendship, 1951.

Peter Jilemnicky — A191

1951, Dec. 5 **Unwmk.**

491	A191	1.50k redsh brown	.25	.25
492	A191	2k dull blue	.80	.30

Peter Jilemnicky (1901-1949), writer.

Ladislav Zapotocky — A192

1952, Jan. 12 *Perf. 11½*

493	A192	1.50k brown red	.25	.25
494	A192	4k gray	1.00	.45

Centenary of the birth of Ladislav Zapotocky, Bohemian socialist pioneer.

Jan Kollar — A193

1952, Jan. 30 **Unwmk.** *Perf. 11½*

495	A193	3k dark carmine	.25	.25
496	A193	5k violet blue	1.10	.60

Jan Kollar (1793-1852), poet.

Lenin and Lenin Hall — A194

1952, Jan. 30 *Perf. 12½*

497	A194	1.50k rose carmine	.30	.25
498	A194	5k deep blue	1.10	.75

6th All-Russian Party Conf., 40th anniv.

Emil Holub and African — A195

1952, Feb. 21 *Perf. 11½*

499	A195	3k red brown	.35	.25
500	A195	5k gray	1.50	.90

Death of Emil Holub, explorer, 50th anniv.

Gottwald Metallurgical Plant — A196

Designs: 2k, Foundry. 3k, Chemical plant.

1952, Feb. 25 **Photo.** *Perf. 14*

501	A196	1.50k sepia	.25	.25
502	A196	2k red brown	1.50	.60
503	A196	3k scarlet	.25	.25
		Nos. 501-503 (3)	2.00	1.10

Student, Soldier and Miner — A197

Youths of Three Races — A198

1952, Mar. 21 **Unwmk.** *Perf. 14*

504	A197	1.50k blue	.25	.25
505	A198	2k olive black	.25	.25
506	A197	3k lake	1.00	.50
		Nos. 504-506 (3)	1.50	1.00

International Youth Day, Mar. 25, 1952.

Similar to Type of 1951

Portrait: Otakar Sevcik.

1952, Mar. 22 **Engr.** *Perf. 12½*

507	A184	2k choc, *cr*	.80	.35
508	A184	3k rose brn, *cr*	.25	.25

Otakar Sevcik, violinist, birth cent.

Jan A. Komensky — A199

1952, Mar. 28

509	A199	1.50k dk brown, *cr*	1.50	.65
510	A199	11k dk blue, *cr*	.35	.25

360th anniv. of the birth of Jan Amos Komensky (Comenius), teacher and philosopher.

Industrial and Farm Women — A200

1952, Mar. 8

511	A200	1.50k dp blue, *cr*	1.20	.50

International Women's Day Mar. 8, 1952.

Woman and Children — A201

1952, Apr. 12

512	A201	2k chocolate, *cr*	1.60	1.00
513	A201	3k dp claret, *cr*	.25	.25

Intl. Conf. for the Protection of Children, Vienna, Apr. 12-16, 1952.

Antifascist — A202

1952, Apr. 11 **Photo.** *Perf. 14*

514	A202	1.50k red brown	.25	.25
515	A202	2k ultra	1.10	.60

Day of International Solidarity of Fighters against Fascism, Apr. 11, 1952.

Harvester A203

Design: 3k, Tractor and Seeders.

1952, Apr. 30

516	A203	1.50k deep blue	2.10	1.20
517	A203	2k brown	.30	.30
518	A203	3k brown red	.30	.30
		Nos. 516-518 (3)	2.70	1.80

Youths Carrying Flags — A204

1952, May 1

519	A204	3k brown red	.35	.25
520	A204	4k dk red brown	1.40	1.25

Issued to publicize Labor Day, May 1, 1952.

Crowd Cheering Soviet Soldiers — A205

1952, May 9

521	A205	1.50k dark red	.55	.45
522	A205	5k deep blue	2.25	1.25

Liberation of Czechoslovakia from German occupation, 7th anniversary.

Children A206

Design: 3k, "Pioneer" teaching children.

1952, May 31 **Engr.** *Perf. 12½*

523	A206	1.50k dk brn, *cr*	.25	.25
524	A206	2k Prus grn, *cr*	1.50	.60
525	A206	3k rose brn, *cr*	.25	.25
		Nos. 523-525 (3)	2.00	1.10

International Children's Day May 31, 1952.

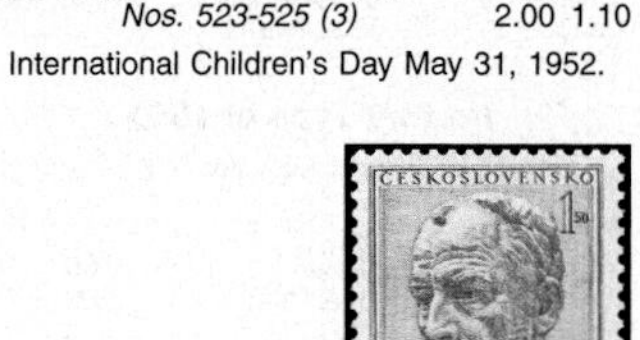

J. V. Myslbek — A207

Design: 8k, Allegory, "Music."

1952, June 2

526	A207	1.50k red brown	.30	.25
527	A207	2k dark brown	1.25	.90
528	A207	8k gray green	.25	.25
		Nos. 526-528 (3)	1.80	1.40

Joseph V. Myslbek (1848-1922), sculptor.

Beethoven — A208

House of Artists — A209

1952, June 7 **Unwmk.** *Perf. 11½*

529	A208	1.50k sepia	.35	.25
530	A209	3k red brown	.35	.25
531	A208	5k indigo	1.40	1.10
		Nos. 529-531 (3)	2.10	1.60

International Music Festival, Prague, 1952.

Lidice, Symbol of a New Life — A210

1952, June 10 *Perf. 12½*

532	A210	1.50k dk violet brn	.25	.25
533	A210	5k dark blue	1.00	.60

Destruction of Lidice, 10th anniversary.

Jan Hus — A211

Bethlehem Chapel — A212

1952, July 5

534	A211	1.50k brown	.25	.25
535	A212	3k red brown	.25	.25
536	A211	5k black	1.10	.65
		Nos. 534-536 (3)	1.60	1.15

550th anniv. of the installation of Jan Hus as pastor of Bethlehem Chapel, Prague.

Doctor Examining Patient — A213

2k, Doctor, Nurse, Mother and child.

1952, July 31

537 A213 1.50k dark brown 1.40 .80
538 A213 2k blue violet .35 .25
539 A213 3k rose brown .35 .25
Nos. 537-539 (3) 2.10 1.30

Czechoslovakia's Unified Health Service.

A214

United Physical Education Program — A214a

1952, Aug. 2 ***Perf. 11½***

540 A214 1.50k Relay race .95 .60
541 A214a 2k Canoeing 2.50 1.10
542 A214a 3k Cycling .60 .55
543 A214a 4k Hockey *3.25* *3.00*
Nos. 540-543 (4) 7.30 5.25

Issued to publicize Czechoslovakia's Unified Physical Education program.

F. L. Celakovski — A215

1952, Aug. 5 ***Perf. 12½***

544 A215 1.50k dark brown .25 .25
545 A215 2k dark green 1.40 .90

Centenary of the death of Frantisek L. Celakovski, poet and writer.

Mikulas Ales — A216

Perf. 11x11½

1952, Aug. 30 **Engr.** **Unwmk.**

546 A216 1.50k dk gray grn .45 .35
547 A216 6k red brown 3.00 2.25

Birth centenary of Mikulas Ales, painter.

17th Century Mining Towers — A217

Designs: 1.50k, Coal Excavator. 2k, Peter Bezruc mine. 3k, Automatic coaling crane.

1952, Sept. 14 ***Perf. 12½***

548 A217 1k sepia 1.25 .45
549 A217 1.50k dark blue .25 .25
550 A217 2k olive gray .25 .25
551 A217 3k violet brown .25 .25
Nos. 548-551 (4) 2.00 1.20

Miners' Day, Sept. 14, 1952. No. 550 also for the 85th anniv. of the birth of Peter Bezruc (Vladimir Vasek), poet.

Jan Zizka — A218

Designs: 2k, Fraternization with Russians. 3k, Marching with flag.

Inscribed: ". . . . Armady 1952,"

1952, Oct. 5 **Engr.** ***Perf. 11½***

552 A218 1.50k rose lake .25 .25
553 A218 2k olive bister .25 .25
554 A218 3k dk car rose .25 .25
555 A218 4k gray 1.50 .45
Nos. 552-555 (4) 2.25 1.20

Issued to publicize Army Day, Oct. 5, 1952.

Souvenir Sheet

Statues to Bulgarian Partisans and to Soviet Army — A219

1952, Oct. 18 **Unwmk.** ***Perf. 12½***

556 A219 Sheet of 2 85.00 16.00
a. 2k deep carmine 35.00 7.50
b. 3k ultramarine 35.00 7.50

National Philatelic Exhibition, Bratislava, Oct. 18-Nov. 2, 1952.

Danube River, Bratislava A220

1952, Oct. 18

557 A220 1.50k dark brown .25 .25

National Philatelic Exhibition, Bratislava.

Conference with Lenin and Stalin — A221

1952, Nov. 7

558 A221 2k brown black 1.40 .95
559 A221 3k carmine .25 .25

35th anniv. of the Russian Revolution and to publicize Czechoslovak-Soviet friendship.

Worker and Nurse Holding Dove and Olive Branch — A222

1952, Nov. 15 **Photo.** ***Perf. 14***

560 A222 2k brown 1.40 .80
561 A222 3k red .25 .25

Issued to publicize the first State Congress of the Czechoslovak Red Cross.

Matej Louda, Hussite Leader, Painted by Mikulas Ales A223

3k, Dragon-killer Trutnov, painted by Ales.

1952, Nov. 18 **Engr.** ***Perf. 11½***

562 A223 2k red brown .35 .25
563 A223 3k grnsh gray .75 .25

Mikulas Ales, painter, birth cent.

Gottwald Type of 1948-49

1952, June 2 **Unwmk.** ***Perf. 12½***

Size: 19x24mm

564 A135 1k dark green .60 .25

"Peace" Flags — A224

1952, Dec. 12 **Photo.** ***Perf. 14***

565 A224 3k red brown .35 .25
566 A224 4k deep blue .75 1.00

Issued to publicize the Congress of Nations for Peace, Vienna, Dec. 12-19, 1952.

Dove by Picasso — A225

Design: 4k, Czech Family.

1953, Jan. 17

567 A225 1.50k dark brown .25 .25
568 A225 4k slate blue .65 .30

2nd Czechoslovak Peace Congress.

Smetana Museum — A226

Design: 4k, Jirásek Museum.

1953, Feb. 10 **Engr.** ***Perf. 11½***

569 A226 1.50k dk violet brn .25 .25
570 A226 4k dark gray 1.50 .75

Prof. Zdenek Nejedly, 75th birth anniv.

Martin Kukucin — A227

Jaroslav Vrchlicky — A228

Designs: 2k, Karel Jaromir Erben. 3k, Vaclav Matej Kramerius. 5k, Josef Dobrovsky.

1953, Feb. 28

571 A227 1k gray .25 .25
572 A228 1.50k olive .25 .25
573 A228 2k rose lake .25 .25
574 A228 3k lt brown .50 .25
575 A228 5k slate blue 1.50 .75
Nos. 571-575 (5) 2.75 1.75

Issued to honor Czech writers and poets: 1k, 25th anniv. of death of Kukucin. 1.50k, birth cent. of Vrchlicky. 2k, cent. of completion of "Kytice" by Erben. 3k, birth bicent. of Kramerius. 5k, birth bicent. of Dobrovsky.

Militia — A229

Gottwald — A230

Design: 8k, Portraits of Stalin and Gottwald and Peoples Assembly.

Perf. 13½x14

1953, Feb. 25 **Photo.** **Unwmk.**

576 A229 1.50k deep blue .25 .25
577 A230 3k red .25 .25
578 A229 8k dark brown 2.10 .75
Nos. 576-578 (3) 2.60 1.25

5th anniv. of the defeat of the attempt to reinstate capitalism.

Book and Torch — A231

Design: 3k, Bedrich Vaclavek.

1953, Mar. 5 **Engr.** ***Perf. 11½***

579 A231 1k sepia 1.50 .60
580 A231 3k orange brown .25 .25

Bedrich Vaclavek (1897-1943), socialist writer.

Stalin Type of 1949

Inscribed "21 XII 1879-5 III 1953"

1953, Mar. 12

581 A154 1.50k black .35 .25

Death of Joseph Stalin, Mar. 5, 1953.

Mother and Child — A232

Girl Revolutionist A233

1953, Mar. 8

582 A232 1.50k ultra .25 .25
583 A233 2k brown red 1.25 .60

International Women's Day.

Klement Gottwald — A234

1953, Mar. 19

584 A234 1.50k black .25 .25
585 A234 3k black .25 .25

Souvenir Sheet

Imperf

586 A234 5k black 5.00 4.00

Death of Pres. Klement Gottwald, 3/14/53.

Josef Pecka, Ladislav Zapotocky and Josef Hybes — A236

1953, Apr. 7 Unwmk. *Perf. 11½*

587 A236 2k lt violet brn .25 .25

75th anniversary of the first congress of the Czech Social Democratic Party.

Cyclists — A237

1953, Apr. 29

588 A237 3k deep blue .75 .35

6th International Peace Bicycle Race, Prague-Berlin-Warsaw.

Medal of "May 1, 1890" A238

Designs: 1.50k, Lenin and Stalin. 3k, May Day Parade. 8k, Marx and Engels.

Engraved and Photogravure

1953, Apr. 30 *Perf. 11½x11, 14*

589 A238 1k chocolate 1.40 .35
590 A238 1.50k dark gray .25 .25
591 A238 3k carmine lake .25 .25
592 A238 8k dk gray green .30 .25
Nos. 589-592 (4) 2.20 1.10

Issued to publicize Labor Day, May 1, 1953.

Sowing Grain — A239

1953, May 8 Photo. *Perf. 14*

593 A239 1.50k shown .35 .25
594 A239 7k Reaper 1.60 1.40

Socialization of the village.

Dam — A240

Welder — A241

Design: 3k, Iron works.

1953, May 8 *Perf. 11½*

595 A240 1.50k gray 1.10 .30
596 A241 2k blue gray .25 .25
597 A240 3k red brown .25 .25
Nos. 595-597 (3) 1.60 .80

Josef Slavik — A242

Leos Janacek — A243

1953, June 19 Photo.

598 A242 75h dp gray blue .75 .25
599 A243 1.60k dark brown 1.00 .25

Issued on the occasion of the International Music Festival, Prague, 1953.

Gottwald Type of 1948-49

Perf. 12½ (15h, 1k), 11½ (20h, 3k)

1953

600 A135 15h yellow green .35 .25
601 A135 20h dk violet brn .45 .25
602 A135 1k purple 1.10 .25
603 A135 3k brown car .25 .25
604 A135 3k gray .75 .25
Nos. 600-604 (5) 2.90 1.25

Nos. 600-604 vary slightly in size.

Pres. Antonin Zapotocky — A244

1953, June 19 *Perf. 14*

605 A244 30h violet blue .75 .25
606 A244 60h cerise 1.00 .25

Julius Fucik A245

Book and Carnation A246

1953, Sept. 8 Engr. *Perf. 12½*

607 A245 40h dk violet brn .30 .25
608 A246 60h pink .50 .30

10th anniv. of the death of Julius Fucik, Communist leader executed by the Nazis.

Miner and Flag — A247

Design: 60h, Oil field and workers.

1953, Sept. 10 *Perf. 11½*

609 A247 30h gray .30 .25
610 A247 60h brown vio 1.25 .50

Miner's Day, Sept. 10, 1953.

Volleyball Game — A248

Motorcyclist A249

Design: 60h, Woman throwing javelin.

1953, Sept. 15

611 A248 30h brown red 4.50 1.50
612 A249 40h dk violet brn 2.75 .85
613 A248 60h rose violet 2.50 .85
Nos. 611-613 (3) 9.75 3.20

Hussite Warrior — A250

Designs: 60h, Soldier presenting arms. 1k, Red army soldiers.

1953, Oct. 8

614 A250 30h brown .30 .25
615 A250 60h rose lake .35 .25
616 A250 1k brown red 1.50 1.25
Nos. 614-616 (3) 2.15 1.75

Issued to publicize Army Day, Oct. 3, 1953.

Pres. Antonin Zapotocky — A251

1953 Unwmk. *Perf. 11½, 12½*

617 A251 30h violet blue .50 .25
618 A251 60h carmine rose .80 .25

No. 617 is perf. 11½ & measures 19x23mm, No. 618 perf. 12½ & 18½x23½mm.

See No. 780.

Charles Bridge and Prague Castle — A252

1953, Aug. 15 Engr. *Perf. 11½*

619 A252 5k gray 4.00 .25

Korean and Czech Girls — A253

1953, Oct. 11 *Perf. 11x11½*

620 A253 30h dark brown 2.40 1.50

Czechoslovakia's friendship with Korea.

Flags, Hradcany Castle and Kremlin — A254

Designs: 60h, Lomonosov University, Moscow. 1.20k, Lenin Ship Canal.

1953, Nov. 7

621 A254 30h dark gray .75 .50
622 A254 60h dark brown 1.10 .85
623 A254 1.20k ultra 3.00 1.90
Nos. 621-623 (3) 4.85 3.25

Czechoslovak-Soviet friendship month.

Emmy Destinn, Opera Singer — A255

National Theater, Prague — A256

Portrait: 2k, Eduard Vojan, actor.

1953, Nov. 18 *Perf. 14*

624 A255 30h blue black 1.10 .75
625 A256 60h brown .35 .35
626 A255 2k sepia 2.75 1.10
Nos. 624-626 (3) 4.20 2.20

Natl. Theater founding, 70th anniv.

Nos. 624 and 626 each were issued in sheets of 10. Values: No. 624, $100; No. 626, $75.

Josef Manes — A257

1953, Nov. 28 *Perf. 11x11½*

627 A257 60h brown carmine .35 .25
628 A257 1.20k deep blue 1.50 .90

Issued to honor Josef Manes, painter.

Vaclav Hollar — A258

Portrait: 1.20k, Head framed, facing right.

1953, Dec. 5

629 A258 30h brown black .35 .25
630 A258 1.20k dark brown 1.50 .65

Vaclav Hollar, artist and etcher.

Leo N. Tolstoy — A259

1953, Dec. 29 Unwmk.

631 A259 60h dark green .35 .25
632 A259 1k chocolate 1.50 .50

Leo N. Tolstoi, 125th birth anniv.

Locomotive — A260

Design: 1k, Plane loading mail.

Engraved, Center Photogravure

1953, Dec. 29 ***Perf. 11½x11***

633 A260 60h brn org & gray vio 1.50 .45
634 A260 1k org brn & brt bl 3.50 1.10

Lenin — A261

Lenin Museum, Prague — A262

1954, Jan. 21 **Engr.** ***Perf. 11½***

635 A261 30h dark brown .45 .25
636 A262 1.40k chocolate 1.50 .65

30th anniversary of the death of Lenin.

Klement Gottwald — A263

Design: 2.40k, Revolutionist with flag.

1954, Feb. 18 ***Perf. 11x11½, 14x13½***

637 A263 60h dark brown .30 .25
638 A263 2.40k rose lake 3.50 1.50

25th anniversary of the fifth congress of the Communist Party in Czechoslovakia.

No. 638 was issued in a sheet of 10 stamps. Value, $90.

Gottwald Mausoleum, Prague — A264

Gottwald and Stalin A265

1.20k, Lenin & Stalin mausoleum, Moscow.

1954, Mar. 5 ***Perf. 11½, 14x13½***

639 A264 30h olive brown .35 .25
640 A265 60h deep ultra .35 .25
641 A264 1.20k rose brown 2.25 1.00
Nos. 639-641 (3) 2.95 1.50

1st anniv. of the deaths of Stalin and Gottwald.

No. 641 was issued in a sheet of 10 stamps. Value, $120.

Two Runners — A266

Group of Hikers — A267

Design: 1k, Woman swimmer.

1954, Apr. 24 ***Perf. 11¼, 13¾ (#643)***

642 A266 30h dark brown 2.10 1.10
643 A267 80h dark green 7.00 3.50
644 A266 1k dk violet blue 1.75 .75
Nos. 642-644 (3) 10.85 5.35

No. 643 was issued in a sheet of 10 stamps. Value, $350.

Nurse — A268

Designs: 15h, Construction worker. 40h, Postwoman. 45h, Ironworker. 50h, Soldier. 75h, Lathe operator. 80h, Textile worker. 1k, Farm woman. 1.20k, Scientist and microscope. 1.60k, Miner. 2k, Physician and baby. 2.40k, Engineer. 3k, Chemist.

1954 ***Perf. 12½x12, 11½x11***

645 A268 15h dark green .35 .25
646 A268 20h lt violet .40 .25
647 A268 40h dark brown .50 .25
648 A268 45h dk gray blue .40 .25
649 A268 50h dk gray green .50 .25
650 A268 75h deep blue .50 .25
651 A268 80h violet brown .50 .25
652 A268 1k green .80 .25
653 A268 1.20k dk violet blue .50 .25
654 A268 1.60k brown blk 1.20 .25
655 A268 2k orange brown 1.60 .25
656 A268 2.40k violet blue 1.60 .25
657 A268 3k carmine 1.60 .25
Nos. 645-657 (13) 10.45 3.25

Antonin Dvorák — A269

40h, Leos Janacek. 60h, Bedrich Smetana.

1954, May 22 ***Perf. 11x11½***

658 A269 30h violet brown 2.25 .25
659 A269 40h brick red 3.00 .35
660 A269 60h dark blue .90 .25
Nos. 658-660 (3) 6.15 .85

"Year of Czech Music," 1954.

Prokop Divis — A270

1954, June 15

661 A270 30h gray .35 .25
662 A270 75h violet brown 1.40 .50

200th anniv. of the invention of a lightning conductor by Prokop Divis.

Slovak Insurrectionist A271

Design: 1.20k, Partisan woman.

1954, Aug. 28 ***Perf. 11½***

663 A271 30h brown orange .25 .25
664 A271 1.20k dark blue .85 .50

Slovak national uprising, 10th anniv.

Anton P. Chekhov — A272

1954, Sept. 24

665 A272 30h dull gray grn .30 .25
666 A272 45h dull gray brn 1.10 .50

50th anniv. of the death of Chekhov, writer.

Soviet Representative Giving Agricultural Instruction — A273

Designs: 60h, Soviet industrial instruction. 2k, Dancers (cultural collaboration).

1954, Nov. 6 ***Perf. 11½x11***

667 A273 30h yellow brown .25 .25
668 A273 60h dark blue .25 .25
669 A273 2k vermilion 1.40 .90
Nos. 667-669 (3) 1.90 1.40

Czechoslovak-Soviet friendship month.

Jan Neruda — A274

60h, Janko Jesensky. 1.60k, Jiri Wolker.

1954, Nov. 25 ***Perf. 11x11½***

670 A274 30h dark blue .85 .25
671 A274 60h dull red 1.40 .50
672 A274 1.60k sepia .35 .25
Nos. 670-672 (3) 2.60 1.00

Issued to honor Czechoslovak poets.

View of Telc A275

Views: 60h, Levoca. 3k, Ceske Budejovice.

1954, Dec. 10 **Engr. & Photo.**

673 A275 30h black & bis .70 .25
674 A275 60h brown & bis .80 .25
675 A275 3k black & bis 2.50 1.25
Nos. 673-675 (3) 4.00 1.75

Pres. Antonin Zapotocky — A276

1954, Dec. 18 **Engr.** ***Perf. 11½***

676 A276 30h black brown .50 .25
677 A276 60h dark blue .55 .25

Souvenir Sheet

Imperf

678 A276 2k deep claret 15.00 6.00

70th birthday of Pres. Antonin Zapotocky. See Nos. 829-831.

Attacking Soldiers — A278

Design: 2k, Soldier holding child.

1954, Oct. 3 ***Perf. 11½***

679 A278 60h dark green .30 .25
680 A278 2k dark brown 1.40 1.25

Army Day, Oct. 6, 1954.

Woman Holding Torch — A279

Design: 45h, Ski jumper.

1955, Jan. 20 **Engr.**

681 A279 30h red 2.10 .50

Engraved and Photogravure

682 A279 45h black & blue 3.50 .50

First National Spartacist Games, 1955.

Comenius University Building A280

Design: 75h, Jan A. Komensky medal.

1955, Jan. 28 **Engr.** ***Perf. 11½***

683 A280 60h deep green .30 .25
684 A280 75h chocolate 1.40 .65

35th anniversary of the founding of Comenius University, Bratislava.

Czechoslovak Automobile A281

60h, Textile worker. 75h, Lathe operator.

1955, Mar. 15 **Unwmk.**

685 A281 45h dull green 1.40 .30
686 A281 60h dk violet blue .60 .25
687 A281 75h sepia .90 .25
Nos. 685-687 (3) 2.90 .80

Woman Decorating Soviet Soldier — A282

Stalin Memorial, Prague — A283

Designs: 35h, Tankman with flowers. 60h, Children greeting soldier.

1955, May 5 Engr. *Perf. 11½*

688 A282 30h blue .35 .25
689 A282 35h dark brown 1.50 .30
690 A282 60h cerise .35 .25

Photo.

691 A283 60h sepia .35 .25
Nos. 688-691 (4) 2.55 1.05

10th anniv. of Czechoslovakia's liberation.

Music and Spring — A284

Design: 1k, Woman with lyre.

1955, May 12 Engr. & Photo.

692 A284 30h black & pale blue .35 .25
693 A284 1k black & pale rose 1.40 1.20

International Music Festival, Prague, 1955.

Foundry Worker — A285

Design: 45h, Farm workers.

1955, May 12 Engr.

694 A285 30h violet .25 .25
695 A285 45h green 1.20 .60

Issued to publicize the third congress of the Trade Union Revolutionary Movement.

Woman Athlete — A286

60h, Dancing couple. 1.60k, Athlete.

1955, June 21

696 A286 20h violet blue 1.00 .40
697 A286 60h green .35 .25
698 A286 1.60k red .75 .25
Nos. 696-698 (3) 2.10 .90

Issued to publicize the first National Spartacist Games, Prague, June-July, 1955.

Jakub Arbes — A287

Portraits: 30h, Jan Stursa. 40h, Elena Marothy-Soltesova. 60h, Josef Vaclav Sladek. 75h, Alexander Stepanovic Popov. 1.40k, Jan Holly. 1.60k, Pavel Josef Safarik.

1955

699 A287 20h brown .25 .25
700 A287 30h black .25 .25
701 A287 40h gray green .60 .25
702 A287 60h black .50 .25
703 A287 75h claret 1.75 .25
704 A287 1.40k black, *cr* .50 .25
705 A287 1.60k dark blue .50 .25
Nos. 699-705 (7) 4.35 1.75

Various anniversaries of prominent Slavs.

Girl and Boy of Two Races — A288

1955, July 20

706 A288 60h violet blue .75 .25

5th World Festival of Youth in Warsaw, July 31-Aug. 14.

Costume of Ocova, Slovakia — A289

Regional Costumes: 75h, Detva man, Slovakia. 1.60k, Chodsko man, Bohemia. 2k, Hana woman, Moravia.

1955, July 25

Frame and Outlines in Brown

707 A289 60h orange & rose 10.00 7.00
708 A289 75h orange & lilac 4.00 4.00
709 A289 1.60k blue & orange 11.50 7.00
710 A289 2k yellow & rose 11.50 7.00
Nos. 707-710 (4) 37.00 25.00

Nos. 707-710 were each issued in sheets of 10 stamps. Value, $450.

Carp A290

Designs: 30h, Beetle. 35h, Gray Partridge. 1.40k, Butterfly. 1.50k, Hare.

1955, Aug. 8 Engr. & Photo.

711 A290 20h sepia & lt bl 2.25 .35
712 A290 30h sepia & pink 1.50 .30
713 A290 35h sepia & buff 1.50 .75
714 A290 1.40k sepia & cream 7.50 4.50
715 A290 1.50k sepia & lt grn 2.75 1.10
Nos. 711-715 (5) 15.50 7.00

Tabor A291

45h, Prachatice. 60h, Jindrichuv Hradec.

1955, Aug. 26 Engr.

716 A291 30h violet brown .50 .25
717 A291 45h rose carmine 2.00 .45
718 A291 60h sage green 1.00 .25
Nos. 716-718 (3) 3.50 .95

Issued to publicize the architectural beauty of the towns of Southern Bohemia.

Souvenir Sheet

Various Views of Prague — A292

1955, Sept. 10 Engr. *Perf. 14x13½*

719 A292 Sheet of 5 27.50 27.50
a. 30h gray black 4.75 5.25
b. 45h gray black 4.75 5.25
c. 60h rose lake 4.75 5.25
d. 75h rose lake 4.75 5.25
e. 1.60k gray black 4.75 5.25

International Philatelic Exhibition, Prague, Sept. 10-25, 1955. Size: 145x110mm. Exists imperf., value $47.50.

Motorcyclists A293

1955, Aug. 28

720 A293 60h violet brown 3.00 .75

30th International Motorcycle Races at Gottwaldov, Sept. 13-18, 1955.

Workers, Soldier and Pioneer — A294

Army Day: 60h, Tanks and planes.

1955, Oct. 6 Unwmk. *Perf. 11½*

721 A294 30h violet brown .35 .25
722 A294 60h slate 1.75 .75

Hans Christian Andersen — A295

Portraits: 40h, Friedrich von Schiller. 60h, Adam Mickiewicz. 75h, Walt Whitman.

1955, Oct. 27

723 A295 30h brown red .35 .25
724 A295 40h dark blue 2.25 1.00
725 A295 60h deep claret .35 .25
726 A295 75h greenish black .75 .35
Nos. 723-726 (4) 3.70 1.85

Issued in honor of these four poets and to mark the 100th anniversary of the publication of Walt Whitman's "Leaves of Grass."

Railroad Bridge A296

30h, Train crossing bridge. 60h, Train approaching tunnel. 1.60k, Miners' housing project.

Inscribed: "Stavba Socialismu"

1955, Dec. 15

727 A296 20h dull green .75 .25
728 A296 30h violet brown .75 .25
729 A296 60h slate .75 .25
730 A296 1.60k carmine rose .75 .25
Nos. 727-730 (4) 3.00 1.00

Issued to publicize socialist public works.

Hydroelectric Plant — A297

2nd Five Year Plan: 10h, Miner with drill. 25h, Building construction. 30h, Harvester. 60h, Metallurgical plant.

Inscribed: "Druhy Petilety Plan 1956-1960."

1956, Feb. 20 *Perf. 11½x11*

731 A297 5h violet brown .30 .25
732 A297 10h gray black .30 .25
733 A297 25h dk car rose .45 .25
734 A297 30h green .30 .25
735 A297 60h violet blue .30 .25
Nos. 731-735 (5) 1.65 1.25

Jewelry — A298

1956, Mar. 17 *Perf. 11x11½*

736 A298 30h shown .45 .25
737 A298 45h Glassware 3.50 1.60
738 A298 60h Ceramics .45 .25
739 A298 75h Textiles .45 .30
Nos. 736-739 (4) 4.85 2.40

Products of Czechoslovakian industries.

Karlovy Vary (Karlsbad) — A299

Various Spas: 45h, Marianske Lazne (Marienbad). 75h, Piestany. 1.20k, Tatry Vysne Ruzbachy (Tatra Mountains).

1956, Mar. 17

740 A299 30h olive green 1.50 .30
741 A299 45h brown 1.10 .30
742 A299 75h claret 6.00 3.00
743 A299 1.20k ultra .75 .30
Nos. 740-743 (4) 9.35 3.90

Issued to publicize Czechoslovakian spas.

"We Serve our People" — A300

Designs: 60h, Russian War Memorial, Berlin. 1k, Tank crewman with standard.

1956, Apr. 9 Photo. *Perf. 11x11½*

744	A300	30h olive brown	.75	.25
745	A300	60h carmine rose	.75	.25
746	A300	1k ultra	4.50	2.75
		Nos. 744-746 (3)	6.00	3.25

Exhibition: "The Construction and Defense of our Country," Prague, Apr., 1956.

Cyclists — A301

Girl Basketball Players — A302

Athletes and Olympic Rings — A303

Engraved and Photogravure

1956, Apr. 25 Unwmk. *Perf. 11½*

747	A301	30h green & lt blue	3.50	.35
748	A302	45h dk blue & car	1.40	.35
749	A303	75h brown & lemon	1.10	.70
		Nos. 747-749 (3)	6.00	1.40

9th Intl. Peace Cycling Race, Warsaw-Berlin-Prague, May 1-15, 1956 (No. 747). 5th European Womens' Basketball Championship (No. 748). Summer Olympics, Melbourne, Nov. 22-Dec. 8, 1956 (No. 749).

See No. 765.

Mozart — A304

45h, Josef Myslivecek. 60h, Jiri Benda. 1k, Bertramka House, Prague. 1.40k, Xaver Dusek (1731-99) and wife Josepha. 1.60k, Nostic Theater, Prague.

1956, May 12 Engr.

Design in Gray Black

750	A304	30h bister	1.50	.35
751	A304	45h gray green	8.50	6.00
752	A304	60h pale rose lilac	1.50	.35
753	A304	1k salmon	1.50	.35
754	A304	1.40k lt blue	4.50	.75
755	A304	1.60k lemon	3.00	.35
		Nos. 750-755 (6)	20.50	8.15

200th anniv. of the birth of Wolfgang Amadeus Mozart and to publicize the International Music Festival in Prague.

Home Guard — A305

1956, May 25

756	A305	60h violet blue	.75	.25

Issued to commemorate the first meeting of the Home Guard, Prague, May 25-27, 1956.

Josef Kajetan Tyl — A306

Portraits: 20h, Ludovit Stur. 30h, Frana Sramek. 1.40k, Karel Havlicek Borovsky.

1956, June 23

757	A306	20h dull purple	.75	.25
758	A306	30h blue	.45	.25
759	A306	60h black	.45	.25
760	A306	1.40k claret	3.00	1.75
		Nos. 757-760 (4)	4.65	2.50

Issued to honor various Czechoslovakian writers. See Nos. 781-784, 873-876.

River Patrol — A307

Design: 60h, Guard and dog.

1956, July 8 *Perf. 11x11½*

761	A307	30h ultra	.75	.25
762	A307	60h green	.60	.25

Issued to honor men of Frontier Guard.

Type of 1956 and

Steeplechase — A308

1956, Sept. 8 Unwmk. *Perf. 11½*

763	A308	60h indigo & bister	3.00	.75
764	A308	80h brown vio & vio	1.50	.35
765	A303	1.20k slate & orange	3.00	1.50
		Nos. 763-765 (3)	7.50	2.60

Steeplechase, Pardubice, 1956 (No. 763). Marathon race, Kosice, 1956 (No. 764). Olympic Games, Melbourne, Nov. 22-Dec. 8 (No. 765).

Woman Gathering Grapes — A309

Fishermen — A310

35h, Women gathering hops. 95h, Logging.

1956, Sept. 20 Engr.

766	A309	30h brown lake	.35	.25
767	A309	35h gray green	.35	.25
768	A310	80h dark blue	.75	.25
769	A310	95h chocolate	2.25	1.00
		Nos. 766-769 (4)	3.70	1.75

Issued to publicize natural resources.

European Timetable Conf., Prague, Nov. 9-13 — A311

A312

Locomotives: 10h, 1846. 30h, 1855. 40h, 1945. 45h, 1952. 60h, 1955. 1k, 1954.

1956, Nov. 9 Unwmk. *Perf. 11½*

770	A311	10h brown	2.50	.35
771	A312	30h gray	2.50	.35
772	A312	40h green	5.00	.35
773	A312	45h brown car	8.50	5.00
774	A312	60h indigo	2.50	.35
775	A312	1k ultra	6.00	.35
		Nos. 770-775 (6)	27.00	6.75

Costume of Moravia — A313

Regional Costumes (women): 1.20k, Blata, Bohemia. 1.40k, Cicmany, Slovakia. 1.60k, Novohradsko, Slovakia.

1956, Dec. 15 *Perf. 13½*

776	A313	30h brn, ultra & car	1.75	1.75
777	A313	1.20k brn, car & ultra	2.75	.40
778	A313	1.40k brn, ocher & ver	10.00	3.25
779	A313	1.60k brn, car & grn	3.50	.80
		Nos. 776-779 (4)	18.00	6.20

See Nos. 832-835.

Nos. 776-779 each were issued in sheets of 10 stamps. Value, $160.

Zapotocky Type of 1953

1956, Oct. 7 Unwmk. *Perf. 12½*

780	A251	30h blue	.75	.25

Portrait Type of 1956

15h, Ivan Olbracht. 20h, Karel Toman. 30h, F. X. Salda. 1.60k, Terezia Vansova.

1957, Jan. 18 Engr. *Perf. 11½*

781	A306	15h dk red brn, *cr*	.30	.25
782	A306	20h dk green, *cr*	.30	.25
783	A306	30h dk brown, *cr*	.30	.25
784	A306	1.60k dk blue, *cr*	.60	.25
		Nos. 781-784 (4)	1.50	1.00

Issued in honor of Czechoslovakian writers.

Kolin Cathedral — A315

Views: No. 786, Banska Stiavnica. No. 787, Uherske Hradiste. No. 788, Karlstein. No. 789, Charles Bridge, Prague. 1.25k, Moravska Trebova.

1957, Feb. 23

785	A315	30h dk blue gray	.40	.25
786	A315	30h rose violet	.50	.25
787	A315	60h deep rose	.50	.25
788	A315	60h gray green	.50	.25
789	A315	60h brown	.75	.25
790	A315	1.25k gray	3.00	1.25
		Nos. 785-790 (6)	5.65	2.50

Anniversaries of various towns and landmarks.

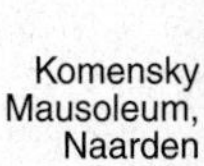

Komensky Mausoleum, Naarden A316

Jan A. Komensky A317

Old Prints: 40h, Komensky teaching. 1k, Sun, moon, stars and earth.

Perf. 11½x11, 14 (A317)

1957, Mar. 28 Engr. Unwmk.

791	A316	30h pale brown	.45	.25
792	A316	40h dark green	.45	.25
793	A317	60h chocolate	3.00	.75
794	A316	1k carmine rose	.60	.25
		Nos. 791-794 (4)	4.50	1.50

300th anniv. of the publication of "Didactica Opera Omnia" by J. A. Komensky (Comenius). No. 793 issued in sheets of four. Value, $24.

Farm Woman — A318

1957, Mar. 22 *Perf. 11½*

795	A318	30h lt blue green	.75	.25

3rd Cong. of Agricultural Cooperatives.

Cyclists A319

Woman Archer A320

Boxers — A321

Rescue Team A322

1957, Apr. 30 ***Perf. 11½x11, 11x11½***

796 A319 30h sepia & ultra .60 .25
797 A319 60h dull grn & bis *2.25 1.25*
798 A320 60h gray & emer .45 .25
799 A321 60h sepia & org .45 .25
800 A322 60h violet & choc .75 .25
Nos. 796-800 (5) 4.50 2.25

10th Intl. Peace Cycling Race, Prague-Berlin-Warsaw (Nos. 796-797). Intl. Archery Championships (No. 798). European Boxing Championships, Prague (No. 799). Mountain Climbing Rescue Service (No. 800).

Jan V. Stamic — A323

Musicians: No. 802, Ferdinand Laub. No. 803, Frantisek Ondricek. No. 804, Josef B. Foerster. No. 805, Vitezslav Novak. No. 806, Josef Suk.

1957, May 12 ***Perf. 11½***

801 A323 60h purple .35 .25
802 A323 60h black .35 .25
803 A323 60h slate blue .35 .25
804 A323 60h brown .35 .25
805 A323 60h dull red brn .90 .25
806 A323 60h blue green .35 .25
Nos. 801-806 (6) 2.65 1.50

Spring Music Festival, Prague.

Josef Bozek — A324

School of Engineering A325

60h, F. J. Gerstner. 1k, R. Skuhersky.

1957, May 25

807 A324 30h bluish black .25 .25
808 A324 60h gray brown .30 .25
809 A324 1k rose lake .30 .25
810 A325 1.40k blue violet .65 .25
Nos. 807-810 (4) 1.50 1.00

School of Engineering in Prague, 250th anniv.

Pioneer and Philatelic Symbols A326

Design: 60h, Girl and carrier pigeon.

Engraved and Photogravure

1957, June 8 ***Perf. 11½***

811 A326 30h olive grn & org .45 .25

Engr. ***Perf. 13½***

812 A326 60h brn & vio bl 3.00 2.25

Youth Philatelic Exhibition, Pardubice.
No. 812 was printed in miniature sheets of 4. Value $12.

"Grief" — A327

Design: 60h, Rose, symbol of new life.

1957, June 10

813 A327 30h black .35 .25
814 A327 60h blk & rose red 1.25 .35

Destruction of Lidice, 15th anniversary.
No. 814 was issued in a sheet of 10 stamps. Value, $28.

Motorcyclists A328

1957, July 5 ***Perf. 11½***

815 A328 60h dk gray & blue 1.50 .30

32nd International Motorcycle Race.

Karel Klic — A329

Josef Ressel — A330

1957, July 5

816 A329 30h gray black .60 .25
817 A330 60h violet blue .60 .25

Klic, inventor of photogravure, and Ressel, inventor of the ship screw.

Chamois — A331

Gentian A332

Designs: 30h, Brown bear. 60h, Edelweiss. 1.25k, Tatra Mountains.

1957, Aug. 28 **Engr.** ***Perf. 11½***

818 A331 20h emer & brnsh gray 1.00 .25
819 A331 30h lt blue & brn 1.00 .25
820 A332 40h gldn brn & vio bl 1.60 .30
821 A332 60h yellow & grn 1.00 .25

Size: 48x28½mm

822 A332 1.25k ol grn & bis 1.60 .80
Nos. 818-822 (5) 6.20 1.85

Tatra Mountains National Park.

"Marycka Magdonova" A333

Engraved and Photogravure

1957, Sept. 15 **Unwmk.** ***Perf. 11½***

823 A333 60h black & dull red .45 .25

90th birthday of Petr Bezruc, poet and author of "Marycka Magdonova."

Man Holding Banner of Trade Union Cong. — A334

1957, Sept. 28 **Engr.**

824 A334 75h rose red .45 .25

4th Intl. Trade Union Cong., Leipzig, 10/4-15.

Television Transmitter and Antennas — A335

Design: 60h, Family watching television.

1957, Oct. 19 **Engr.** ***Perf. 11½***

825 A335 40h dk blue & car .30 .25
826 A335 60h redsh brown & emer .45 .25

Issued to publicize the television industry.

Worker, Globe and Lenin A336

60h, Worker, factory, hammer and sickle.

1957, Nov. 7 ***Perf. 12x11½***

827 A336 30h claret .25 .25
828 A336 60h gray blue .25 .25

Russian Revolution, 40th anniversary.

Zapotocky Type of 1954 dated: 19 XII 1884-13 XI 1957

1957, Nov. 18 **Unwmk.** ***Perf. 11½***

829 A276 30h black .25 .25
830 A276 60h black .25 .25

Souvenir Sheet

Imperf

831 A276 2k black 5.00 1.25

Death of Pres. Antonin Zapotocky.

Costume Type of 1956

Regional Costumes: 45h, Pilsen woman, Bohemia. 75h, Slovacko man, Moravia. 1.25k, Hana woman, Moravia. 1.95k, Teshinsko woman, Silesia.

1957, Dec. 18 **Engr.** ***Perf. 13½***

832 A313 45h brn, bl & dk red 4.25 1.50
833 A313 75h dk brn, red & grn 3.00 .80
834 A313 1.25k dk brn, scar & ocher 5.25 1.50
835 A313 1.95k sepia, bl & ver 6.00 3.75
Nos. 832-835 (4) 18.50 7.55

Nos. 832-835 each was issued in sheets of 10 stamps. Value, set $200.

A337

A338

Designs: 30h, Radio telescope and observatory. 45h, Meteorological station in High Tatra. 75h, Sputnik 2 over Earth.

1957, Dec. 20 ***Perf. 11½***

836 A337 30h violet brn & yel 1.60 .50
837 A338 45h sepia & lt bl .65 .30
838 A337 75h claret & blue 2.00 .85
Nos. 836-838 (3) 4.25 1.65

IGY, 1957-58. No. 838 also for the launching of Sputnik 2, Nov. 3, 1957.

Girl Skater — A339

Designs: 40h, Canoeing. 60h, Volleyball. 80h, Parachutist. 1.60k, Soccer.

1958, Jan. 25 **Engr.** ***Perf. 11½x12***

839 A339 30h rose violet 1.75 .25
840 A339 40h blue .35 .25
841 A339 60h redsh brown .35 .25
842 A339 80h violet blue 1.50 .45
843 A339 1.60k brt green .65 .25
Nos. 839-843 (5) 4.60 1.45

Issued to publicize various sports championship events in 1958.

Litomysl Castle — A340

Design: 60h, Bethlehem Chapel.

1958, Feb. 10 ***Perf. 11½***

844 A340 30h green .30 .25
845 A340 60h redsh brown .30 .25

80th anniversary of the birth of Zdenek Nejedly, restorer of Bethlehem Chapel.

Giant Excavator A341

Peace Dove and: 60h, Soldiers, flame and banner, horiz. 1.60k, Harvester and rainbow, horiz.

1958, Feb. 25

846 A341 30h gray violet & yel .25 .25
847 A341 60h gray brown & car .25 .25
848 A341 1.60k green & dull yel .45 .25
Nos. 846-848 (3) .95 .75

10th anniv. of the "Victorious February."

Jewelry — A342

Designs: 45h, Dolls. 60h, Textiles. 75h, Kaplan turbine. 1.20k, Glass.

Engraved and Photogravure

1958 Unwmk. *Perf. 11½*

849	A342	30h rose car & blue	.40	.25
850	A342	45h rose red & pale lil	.40	.25
851	A342	60h violet & aqua	.60	.25
852	A342	75h ultra & salmon	1.50	.75
853	A342	1.20k blue grn & pink	.60	.25
		Nos. 849-853 (5)	3.50	1.75

Issued for the Universal and International Exposition at Brussels.

King George of Podebrad — A343

Design: 60h, View of Prague, 1628.

1958, May 19 Engr.

854	A343	30h carmine rose	.50	.25
855	A343	60h violet blue	.30	.25

Issued to publicize the National Archives Exhibition, Prague, May 15-Aug. 15.

"Towards the Stars" — A344

Women of Three Races — A345

Boy, Girl and Globes A346

1958, May 26

856	A344	30h carmine rose	.45	.25
857	A345	45h rose violet	.45	.25
858	A346	60h blue	.45	.25
		Nos. 856-858 (3)	1.35	.75

The Soc. for Dissemination of Political and Cultural Knowledge (No. 856). 4th Cong. of the Intl. Democratic Women's Fed. (No. 857). 1st World Trade Union Conf. of Working Youths, Prague, July 14-20 (No. 858).

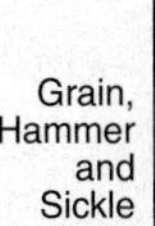

Grain, Hammer and Sickle A347

Atomic Reactor A348

45h, Map of Czechoslovakia, hammer & sickle.

1958, May 26

859	A347	30h dull red	.25	.25
860	A347	45h green	.30	.25
861	A348	60h dark blue	.30	.25
		Nos. 859-861 (3)	.85	.75

11th Congress of the Czech Communist Party and the 15th anniv. of the Russo-Czechoslovakian Treaty.

Karlovy Vary A349

Various Spas: 40h, Podebrady. 60h, Marianske Lazne. 80h, Luhacovice. 1.20k, Strbske Pleso. 1.60k, Trencianske Teplice.

1958, June 25

862	A349	30h rose claret	.45	.25
863	A349	40h redsh brown	.45	.25
864	A349	60h gray green	.30	.25
865	A349	80h sepia	.45	.25
866	A349	1.20k violet blue	.60	.25
867	A349	1.60k lt violet	1.20	.75
		Nos. 862-867 (6)	3.45	2.00

Telephone Operator — A350

Design: 45h, Radio transmitter.

1958, June 20

868	A350	30h black & brn org	.40	.25
869	A350	45h black & lt grn	.40	.25

Conference of Postal Ministers of Communist Countries, Prague, June 30-July 9.

Pres. Novotny — A351

1958-59 *Perf. 12½*

870	A351	30h brt violet blue	.65	.25
b.		Perf. 11½	.50	.25
870A	A351	30h violet ('59)	4.00	1.75
871	A351	60h carmine rose	.45	.25

Perf. 11½

Redrawn

871A	A351	60h rose red	.50	.25
		Nos. 870-871A (4)	5.60	2.50

On No. 871 the top of the "6" turns down; on No. 871A it is open.

Czechoslovak Pavilion, Brussels — A352

1958, July 15 Engr. & Photo.

872	A352	1.95k lt blue & bis brn	.90	.25

Czechoslovakia Week at the Universal and International Exhibition at Brussels.

Portrait Type of 1956

30h, Julius Fucik. 45h, G. K. Zechenter 60h, Karel Capek. 1.40k, Svatopluk Cech.

1958, Aug. 20 Engr. *Perf. 11½*

873	A306	30h rose red	.30	.25
874	A306	45h violet	1.50	.25
875	A306	60h dk blue gray	.60	.25
876	A306	1.40k gray	.60	.25
		Nos. 873-876 (4)	3.00	1.00

Death anniversaries of four famous Czechs.

The Artist and the Muse — A353

1958, Aug. 20 *Perf. 14*

877	A353	1.60k black	3.50	1.10

85th birthday of Max Svabinsky, artist and engraver.

No. 877 was printed in miniature sheets of 4. Value $24.

Children's Hospital, Brno — A354

Designs: 60h, New Town Hall, Brno. 1k, St. Thomas Church. 1.60k, View of Brno.

1958, Sept. 6 Unwmk. *Perf. 11½*

Size: 40x23mm

878	A354	30h violet	.25	.25
879	A354	60h rose red	.25	.25
880	A354	1k brown	.35	.25

Perf. 14

Size: 50x28mm

881	A354	1.60k dk slate grn	1.75	1.25
		Nos. 878-881 (4)	2.60	2.00

Natl. Phil. Exhib., Brno, Sept. 9.

No. 881 sold for 3.10k, including entrance ticket to exhibition. Issued in sheets of four. Value, $10.

Lepiota Procera — A355

Mushrooms: 40h, Boletus edulis. 60h, Krombholzia rufescens. 1.40k, Amanita muscaria L. 1.60k, Armillariella mellea.

1958, Oct. 6 *Perf. 14*

882	A355	30h dk brn, grn & buff	1.60	.35
883	A355	40h vio brn & brn org	1.60	.35
884	A355	60h black, red & buff	2.40	.35
885	A355	1.40k brown, scar & grn	4.00	1.60
886	A355	1.60k blk, red brn & ol	8.00	4.50
		Nos. 882-886 (5)	17.60	7.15

Nos. 882-886 were each issued in a miniature sheet of 10 stamps. Value, set $275.

Children on Beach — A356

45h, Mother, child and bird. 60h, Skier.

1958, Oct. 24 Unwmk. *Perf. 14*

887	A356	30h blue, yel & red	.35	.25
888	A356	45h ultra & carmine	1.40	.60
889	A356	60h brown, blue & yel	.35	.25
		Nos. 887-889 (3)	2.10	1.10

UNESCO Headquarters in Paris opening, Nov. 3. Nos. 887-889 each were issued in sheets of 10. Value, set $75.

Bozek's Steam Car of 1815 A357

Designs: 45h, "Präsident" car of 1897. 60h, "Skoda" sports car. 80h, "Tatra" sedan. 1k, "Autocar Skoda" bus. 1.25k, Trucks.

Engraved and Photogravure

1958, Dec. 1 *Perf. 11½x11*

890	A357	30h vio blk & buff	.70	.25
891	A357	45h ol & lt ol grn	.70	.25
892	A357	60h ol gray & sal	1.75	.25
893	A357	80h claret & bl grn	1.10	.25
894	A357	1k brn & lt yel grn	1.40	.30
895	A357	1.25k green & buff	2.10	.45
		Nos. 890-895 (6)	7.75	1.75

Issued to honor the automobile industry.

Stamp of 1918 and Allegory — A358

1958, Dec. 18 Engr. *Perf. 11x11½*

896	A358	60h dark blue gray	.85	.30

1st Czechoslovakian postage stamp, 40th anniv.

Ice Hockey A359

30h, Girl throwing javelin. 60h, Ice hockey. 1k, Hurdling. 1.60k, Rowing. 2k, High jump.

1959, Feb. 14 *Perf. 11½x11*

897	A359	20h dk brown & gray	.50	.25
898	A359	30h red brn & org brn	.40	.25
899	A359	60h dk bl & pale grn	.65	.25
900	A359	1k maroon & citron	.50	.25
901	A359	1.60k dull vio & lt bl	.80	.25
902	A359	2k red brn & lt bl	1.75	.25
		Nos. 897-902 (6)	4.60	1.50

Congress Emblem — A360

60h, Industrial & agricultural workers, emblem.

1959, Feb. 27 *Perf. 11½*

903	A360	30h maroon & lt blue	.45	.25
904	A360	60h dk blue & yellow	.45	.25

4th Agricultural Cooperative Cong. in Prague.

"Equality of All Races" — A361

Designs: 1k, "Peace." 2k, Mother and Child: "Freedom for Colonial People."

1959, Mar. 23

905	A361	60h gray green	.30	.25
906	A361	1k gray	.45	.25
907	A361	2k dk gray blue	1.50	.50
		Nos. 905-907 (3)	2.25	1.00

10th anniversary of the signing of the Universal Declaration of Human Rights.

Girl Holding Puppet — A362

40h, Pioneer studying map. 60h, Pioneer with radio. 80h, Girl pioneer planting tree.

1959, Mar. 28 Engr. & Photo.

908	A362	30h violet bl & yel	.35	.25
909	A362	40h indigo & ultra	.45	.25
910	A362	60h black & lilac	.35	.25
911	A362	80h brown & lt green	.65	.25
		Nos. 908-911 (4)	1.80	1.00

10th anniv. of the Pioneer organization.

Frederic Joliot Curie — A363

1959, Apr. 17 Engr.

912	A363	60h sepia	1.40	.30

Frederic Joliot Curie and the 10th anniversary of the World Peace Movement.

"Reaching for the Moon" — A364

1959, Apr. 17

913	A364	30h violet blue	1.10	.30

2nd Cong. of the Czechoslovak Assoc. for the Propagation of Political and Cultural knowledge.

Town Hall Pilsen — A365

Designs: 60h, Part of steam condenser turbine. 1k, St. Bartholomew's Church, Pilsen. 1.60k, Part of lathe.

1959, May 2

914	A365	30h lt brown	.30	.25
915	A365	60h violet & lt grn	.30	.25
916	A365	1k violet blue	.40	.25
917	A365	1.60k black & yellow	1.10	.50
		Nos. 914-917 (4)	2.10	1.25

2nd Pilsen Stamp Exhib. in connection with the centenary of the Skoda (Lenin) armament works.

Factory and Emblem A366

Inscribed: "IV Vseodborovy sjezd, 1959"

1959, May 13

918	A366	30h shown	.45	.25
919	A366	60h Dam	.30	.25

4th Trade Union Congress.

Zvolen Castle A367

1959, June 13

920	A367	60h gray olive & yel	.60	.25

Regional Stamp Exhibition, Zvolen, 1959.

Frantisek Benda — A368

Aurel Stodola — A369

30h, Vaclav Kliment Klicpera. 60h, Karel V. Rais. 80h, Antonin Slavicek. 1k, Peter Bezruc.

1959, June 22 ***Perf. 11½x11***

921	A368	15h violet blue	.25	.25
922	A368	30h orange brown	.25	.25
923	A369	40h dull green	.25	.25
924	A369	60h dull red brn	.35	.25
925	A369	80h dull violet	.55	.25
926	A368	1k dark brown	.55	.25
		Nos. 921-926 (6)	2.20	1.50

View of the Fair Grounds A370

Designs: 60h, Fair emblem and world map. 1.60k, Pavilion "Z."

Inscribed: "Mezinarodni Veletrh Brne 6.-20.IX. 1959"

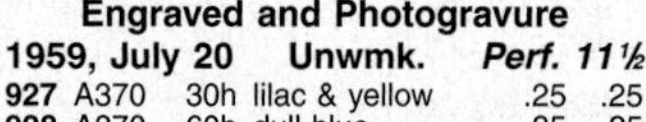

Engraved and Photogravure

1959, July 20 Unwmk. ***Perf. 11½***

927	A370	30h lilac & yellow	.25	.25
928	A370	60h dull blue	.25	.25
929	A370	1.60k dk blue & bister	.75	.25
		Nos. 927-929 (3)	1.25	.75

International Fair at Brno, Sept. 6-20.

Revolutionist and Flag — A371

Slovakian Fighter — A372

1.60k, Linden leaves, sun and factory.

Perf. 11½

1959, Aug. 29 Unwmk. Engr.

930	A371	30h black & rose	.25	.25
931	A372	60h carmine rose	.25	.25
932	A371	1.60k dk blue & yel	.45	.25
		Nos. 930-932 (3)	.95	.75

Natl. Slovakian revolution, 15th anniv. and Slovakian Soviet Republic, 40th anniv.

Alpine Marmots A373

1959, Sept. 25 Engr. & Photo.

933	A373	30h shown	1.25	.25
934	A373	40h Bison	1.00	.40
935	A373	60h Lynx, vert.	2.60	.30
936	A373	1k Wolf	2.60	1.00
937	A373	1.60k Red deer	2.25	.55
		Nos. 933-937 (5)	9.70	2.50

Tatra National Park, 10th anniv.

Lunik 2 Hitting Moon and Russian Flag A374

1959, Sept. 23 ***Perf. 11½***

938	A374	60h dk red & lt ultra	1.50	.30

Issued to commemorate the landing of the Soviet rocket on the moon, Sept. 13, 1959.

Stamp Printing Works, Peking A375

1959, Oct. 1

939	A375	30h pale green & red	.40	.25

10 years of Czechoslovakian-Chinese friendship.

Haydn — A376

Design: 3k, Charles Darwin.

1959, Oct. 16 Engr. ***Perf. 11½***

940	A376	60h violet black	.50	.25
941	A376	3k dark red brown	1.25	.65

150th death anniv. of Franz Joseph Haydn, Austrian composer, and 150th birth anniv. of Charles Darwin, English naturalist.

Great Spotted Woodpecker A377

Birds: 30h, Blue tits. 40h, Nuthatch. 60th, Golden oriole. 80h, Goldfinch. 1k, Bullfinch. 1.20k, European kingfisher.

1959, Nov. 16 ***Perf. 14***

942	A377	20h multicolored	1.50	.60
943	A377	30h multicolored	1.50	.60
944	A377	40h multicolored	4.50	1.50
945	A377	60h multicolored	1.50	.60
946	A377	80h multicolored	2.25	.75
947	A377	1k multicolored	2.25	.75
948	A377	1.20k multicolored	3.00	.75
		Nos. 942-948 (7)	16.50	5.55

Nos. 942-948 were each issued in miniature sheets of 10. Value, set $275.

Nikola Tesla A378

Designs: 30h, Alexander S. Popov. 35h, Edouard Branly. 60h, Guglielmo Marconi. 1k, Heinrich Hertz. 2k, Edwin Howard Armstrong and research tower, Alpine, N. J.

Engraved and Photogravure

1959, Dec. 7 ***Perf. 11½***

949	A378	25h black & pink	1.00	.25
950	A378	30h black & orange	.25	.25
951	A378	35h black & lt vio	.25	.25
952	A378	60h black & blue	.25	.25
953	A378	1k black & lt grn	.25	.25
954	A378	2k black & bister	1.25	.25
		Nos. 949-954 (6)	3.25	1.50

Issued to honor inventors in the fields of telegraphy and radio.

Gymnast — A379

2nd Winter Spartacist Games: 60h, Skier. 1.60k, Basketball players.

1960, Jan. 20 ***Perf. 11½***

955	A379	30h salmon pink & brn	1.00	.25
956	A379	60h lt blue & blk	1.00	.25
957	A379	1.60k bister & brn	.85	.25
		Nos. 955-957 (3)	2.85	.75

1960, June 15 **Unwmk.**

Designs: 30h, Two girls in "Red Ball" drill. 60h, Gymnast with stick. 1k, Three girls with hoops.

958 A379 30h lt grn & rose claret .65 .25
959 A379 60h pink & black .50 .25
960 A379 1k ocher & vio bl .85 .25
Nos. 958-960 (3) 2.00 .75

2nd Summer Spartacist Games, Prague, June 23-July 3.

River Dredge Boat A380

Ships: 60h, River tug. 1k, Tourist steamer. 1.20k, Cargo ship "Lidice."

1960, Feb. 22 ***Perf. 11½***

961 A380 30h slate grn & sal 2.75 .30
962 A380 60h maroon & pale bl 1.40 .30
963 A380 1k dk violet & yel 2.50 .30
964 A380 1.20k lilac & pale grn 3.50 .90
Nos. 961-964 (4) 10.15 1.80

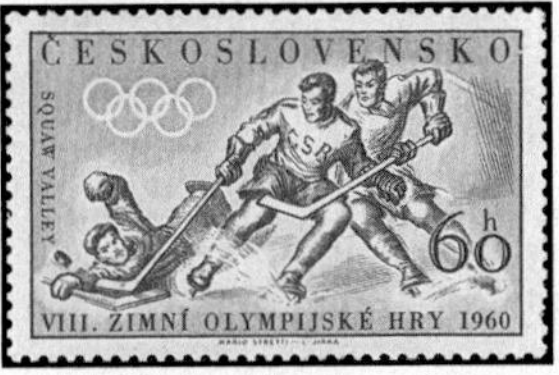

Ice Hockey Players — A381

Design: 1.80k, Figure skaters.

1960, Feb. 27

965 A381 60h sepia & lt blue 2.00 .40
966 A381 1.80k black & lt green 6.00 1.75

8th Olympic Winter Games, Squaw Valley, Calif., Feb. 18-29, 1960.

1960, June 15 **Unwmk.**

Designs: 1k, Running. 1.80k, Women's gymnastics. 2k, Rowing.

967 A381 1k black & orange .85 .30
968 A381 1.80k black & sal pink 1.40 .40
969 A381 2k black & blue 2.50 .75
Nos. 967-969 (3) 4.75 1.45

17th Olympic Games, Rome, 8/25-9/11.

Trencin Castle — A382

Castles: 10h, Bezdez. 20h, Kost. 30h, Pernstein. 40h, Kremnica. 50h, Krivoklát castle. 60h, Karlstein. 1k, Smolenice. 1.60k, Kokorin.

1960-63 **Engr.** ***Perf. 11½***

970 A382 5h gray violet .30 .25
971 A382 10h black .30 .25
972 A382 20h brown org .35 .25
973 A382 30h green .30 .25
974 A382 40h brown .35 .25
974A A382 50h black ('63) 3.50 .25
975 A382 60h rose red .45 .25
976 A382 1k lilac .45 .25
977 A382 1.60k dark blue .75 .25
Nos. 970-977 (9) 6.75 2.25

1961, Oct. **Wmk. 341**

977A A382 30h green 3.00 .40

Lenin — A383

1960, Apr. 22 **Unwmk.**

978 A383 60h gray olive 1.40 .25

90th anniversary of the birth of Lenin.

Soldier Holding Child — A384

Designs: No. 980, Child eating pie. No. 981, Soldier helping concentration camp victim. No. 982, Welder and factory, horiz. No. 983, Tractor driver and farm, horiz.

1960, May 5 **Engr. & Photo.**

979 A384 30h maroon & lt blue .35 .25
980 A384 30h dull red .35 .25
981 A384 30h green & dull blue .40 .25
982 A384 60h dk blue & buff .35 .25
983 A384 60h redsh brn & yel grn .40 .25
Nos. 979-983 (5) 1.85 1.25

15th anniversary of liberation.

Steelworker — A385

Design: 60h, Farm woman and child.

1960, May 24

984 A385 30h maroon & gray .30 .25
985 A385 60h green & pale blue .30 .25

1960 parliamentary elections.

Red Cross Nurse Holding Dove A386

Fire Fighters A387

1960, May 26 **Unwmk.**

986 A386 30h brown car & bl .30 .25
987 A387 60h dk blue & pink .45 .25

3rd Congress of the Czechoslovakian Red Cross (No. 986), and the 2nd Fire Fighters' Congress (No. 987).

Hand of Philatelist with Tongs and Two Stamps — A388

Design: 1k, Globe and 1937 Bratislava stamp (shown in miniature on 60h).

1960, July 11 ***Perf. 11½***

988 A388 60h black & dull yel .75 .25
989 A388 1k black & blue .90 .25

Issued to publicize the National Stamp Exhibition, Bratislava, Sept. 24-Oct. 9.
See Nos. C49-C50.

Stalin Mine, Ostrava-Hermanovice — A390

Designs: 20h, Power station, Hodonin. 30h, Gottwald iron works, Kuncice. 40h, Harvester. 60h, Oil refinery.

1960, July 25

992 A390 10h black & pale grn .30 .25
993 A390 20h maroon & lt bl .30 .25
994 A390 30h indigo & pink .30 .25
995 A390 40h green & pale lilac .30 .25
996 A390 60h dk blue & yel .30 .25
Nos. 992-996 (5) 1.50 1.25

Issued to publicize the new five-year plan.

Viktorin Cornelius, Lawyer — A391

Portraits: 20h, Karel Matej Capek-Chod, writer. 30h, Hana Kvapilova, actress. 40h, Oskar Nedbal, composer. 60h, Otakar Ostrcil, composer.

1960, Aug. 23 **Engr.**

997 A391 10h black .30 .25
998 A391 20h red brown .45 .25
999 A391 30h rose red .55 .25
1000 A391 40h dull green 1.40 .60
1001 A391 60h gray violet .45 .25
Nos. 997-1001 (5) 3.15 1.60

See Nos. 1037-1041.

Skoda Sports Plane Flying Upside Down A392

1960, Aug. 28 **Engr. & Photo.**

1002 A392 60h violet blue & blue 1.40 .30

1st aerobatic world championships, Bratislava.

Constitution and "Czechoslovakia" — A393

1960, Sept. 18

1003 A393 30h violet bl & pink .40 .25

Proclamation of the new socialist constitution.

Workers Reading Newspaper — A394

Man Holding Newspaper — A395

1960, Sept. 18

1004 A394 30h slate & ver .25 .25
1005 A395 60h black & rose .25 .25

Day of the Czechoslovak Press, Sept. 21, 1960, and 40th anniv. of the Rudé Právo paper.

Globes and Laurel A396

1960, Sept. 18 **Engr.**

1006 A396 30h dk blue & bister .40 .25

World Federation of Trade Unions, 15th anniv.

Black-crowned Night Heron — A397

Birds: 30h, Great crested grebe. 40h, Lapwing. 60h, Gray heron. 1k, Graylag goose, horiz. 1.60k, Mallard, horiz.

Engraved and Photogravure

1960, Oct. 24 **Unwmk.** ***Perf. 11½***

Designs in Black

1007 A397 25h pale vio blue .90 .25
1008 A397 30h pale citron .80 .25
1009 A397 40h pale blue .90 .30
1010 A397 60h pink .60 .25
1011 A397 1k pale yellow 1.75 .25
1012 A397 1.60k lt violet 4.50 1.25
Nos. 1007-1012 (6) 9.45 2.55

Doronicum Clusii (Thistle) — A398

Flowers: 30h, Cyclamen. 40h, Primrose. 60h, Hen-and-chickens. 1k, Gentian. 2k, Pasqueflower.

1960, Nov. 21 **Engr.** ***Perf. 14***

1013 A398 20h black, yel & grn .80 .40
1014 A398 30h black, car rose & grn .80 .40
1015 A398 40h black, yel & grn .80 .40
1016 A398 60h black, pink & grn .80 .40
1017 A398 1k black, bl, vio & grn 2.00 .40
1018 A398 2k black, lil, yel & grn 2.75 1.60
Nos. 1013-1018 (6) 7.95 3.60

Nos. 1013-1018 were each issued in sheets of 10. Value, set $100.

Alfons Mucha — A399

1960, Dec. 18 Engr. *Perf. 11½x12*

1019 A399 60h dk blue gray 3.00 .25

Day of the Czechoslovak Postage Stamp and birth cent. of Alfons Mucha, designer of the 1st Czechoslovakian stamp (Type A1).

Rolling-mill Control Bridge — A400

Designs: 30h, Turbo generator. 60h, Ditch-digging machine.

1961, Jan. 20 Unwmk. *Perf. 11½*

1020 A400 20h blue .30 .25
1021 A400 30h rose .30 .25
1022 A400 60h brt green .30 .25
Nos. 1020-1022 (3) .90 .75

Third Five-Year Plan.

Athletes with Flags — A401

Designs: No. 1024, Motorcycle race, horiz. 40h, Sculling, horiz. 60h, Ice skater. 1k, Rugby. 1.20k, Soccer. 1.60k, Long-distance runners.

Perf. 11x11½, 11½x11

1961, Feb. 20 Engr. & Photo.

1023 A401 30h rose red & bl .30 .25
1024 A401 30h dk blue & car .30 .25
1025 A401 40h dk gray & car .45 .25
1026 A401 60h lilac & blue .45 .25
1027 A401 1k ultra & yel .45 .25
1028 A401 1.20k green & buff 1.10 .25
1029 A401 1.60k sepia & salmon 1.50 .30
Nos. 1023-1029 (7) 4.55 1.80

Various sports events.

Exhibition Emblem — A402

1961, Mar. 6 Engr. *Perf. 11½*

1030 A402 2k dk blue & red 2.25 .25

"Praga 1962" International Stamp Exhibition, Prague, Sept. 1962.

Rocket Launching — A403

30h, Sputnik III, horiz. 40h, As 20h, but inscribed "Start Kosmicke Rakety k Venusi — 12.II.1961". 60h, Luna I, horiz. 1.60k, Interplanetary station, horiz. 2k, Similar to type A404, without commemorative inscription.

1961, Mar. 6 Engr. & Photo.

1031 A403 20h violet & pink .30 .25
1032 A403 30h dk green & buff .65 .25
1033 A403 40h dk red & yel grn .65 .30
1034 A403 60h violet & buff .80 .25
1035 A403 1.60k dk bl & pale grn .55 .25
1036 A403 2k mar & pale bl 1.25 .75
Nos. 1031-1036 (6) 4.20 2.05

Issued to publicize Soviet space research.

Portrait Type of 1960

No. 1037, Jindrich Mosna. No. 1038, Pavol Orszagh Hviezdoslav. No. 1039, Alois Mrstik. No. 1040, Joza Uprka. No. 1041, Josef Hora.

1961, Mar. 27 *Perf. 11½*

1037 A391 60h green .30 .25
1038 A391 60h dark blue .60 .25
a. "ORSZACH" instead of "ORSZAGH" 175.00 25.00
1039 A391 60h dull claret .75 .25
1040 A391 60h gray .55 .25
1041 A391 60h sepia .30 .25
Nos. 1037-1041 (5) 2.50 1.25

Man Flying into Space A404

1961, Apr. 13

1042 A404 60h car & pale bl .65 .25
1043 A404 3k ultra & yel 2.00 .60

1st man in space, Yuri A. Gagarin, Apr. 12, 1961. See No. 1036.

Flute Player — A405

1961, Apr. 24 Engr.

1044 A405 30h shown .45 .25
1045 A405 30h Dancer .45 .25
1046 A405 60h Lyre player .65 .25
Nos. 1044-1046 (3) 1.55 .75

Prague Conservatory of Music, 150th anniv.

Blast Furnace and Mine, Kladno — A406

1961, Apr. 24

1047 A406 3k dull red .65 .25

City of Kladno, 400th anniv.

Marching Workers — A407

Woman with Hammer and Sickle — A408

Klement Gottwald Museum A409

Designs: No. 1050, Lenin Museum. No. 1051, Crowd with flags. No. 1053, Man saluting Red Star.

1961, May 10

1048 A407 30h dull violet .30 .25
1049 A409 30h dark blue .30 .25
1050 A409 30h redsh brown .30 .25
1051 A407 60h vermilion .30 .25
1052 A408 60h dark green .30 .25
1053 A408 60h carmine .30 .25
Nos. 1048-1053 (6) 1.80 1.50

Czech Communist Party, 40th anniversary.

Puppet — A410

Designs: Various Puppets.

Engraved and Photogravure

1961, June 20 Unwmk. *Perf. 11½*

1054 A410 30h ver & yel .30 .25
1055 A410 40h sepia & bluish grn .30 .25
1056 A410 60h vio bl & sal .30 .25
1057 A410 1k green & lt blue .30 .25
1058 A410 1.60k mar & pale vio .95 .25
Nos. 1054-1058 (5) 2.15 1.25

Woman, Map of Africa and Flag of Czechoslovakia — A411

1961, June 26

1059 A411 60h red & blue .35 .25

Issued to publicize the friendship between the people of Africa and Czechoslovakia.

Map of Europe and Fair Emblem A412

Fair emblem and: 60h Horizontal boring machine, vert. 1k, Scientists' meeting and nuclear physics emblem.

1961, Aug. 14 *Perf. 11½*

1060 A412 30h dk bl & pale grn .30 .25
1061 A412 60h green & pink .30 .25
1062 A412 1k vio brn & lt bl .60 .25
Nos. 1060-1062 (3) 1.20 .75

International Trade Fair, Brno, Sept. 10-24.

Sugar Beet, Cup of Coffee and Bags of Sugar — A413

1961, Sept. 18 Unwmk. *Perf. 11½*

1063 A413 20h shown .25 .25
1064 A413 30h Clover .25 .25
1065 A413 40h Wheat .25 .25
1066 A413 60h Hops .25 .25
1067 A413 1.40k Corn .30 .25
1068 A413 2k Potatoes 2.00 .35
Nos. 1063-1068 (6) 3.30 1.60

Charles Bridge, St. Nicholas Church and Hradcany — A414

1961, Sept. 25

1069 A414 60h violet bl & car 1.20 .25

26th session of the Governor's Council of the Red Cross Societies League, Prague.

Orlik Dam and Kaplan Turbine A415

Designs: 30h, View of Prague, flags and stamps. 40h, Hluboká Castle, river and fish. 60h, Karlovy Vary and cup. 1k, Pilsen and beer bottle. 1.20k, North Bohemia landscape and vase. 1.60k, Tatra mountains, boots, ice pick and rope. 2k, Ironworks, Ostrava Kuncice and pulley. 3k, Brno and ball bearing. 4k, Bratislava and grapes. 5k, Prague and flags.

1961 Unwmk. *Perf. 11½*

Size: 41x23mm

1070 A415 20h gray & blue *1.50* .45
1071 A415 30h vio blue & red 1.50 .75
1072 A415 40h dk blue & lt grn 1.60 .75
1073 A415 60h dk blue & yel 1.10 .75
1074 A415 1k mar & grn 1.60 .75
1075 A415 1.20k green & pink 1.60 1.10
1076 A415 1.60k brn & vio bl 1.90 1.10
1077 A415 2k blk & ocher 1.90 .45
1078 A415 3k ultra & yel 2.00 .55
1079 A415 4k purple & sal 2.40 1.10

Perf. 13½

Engr.

Size: 50x29mm

1080 A415 5k multicolored 20.00 20.00
Nos. 1070-1080 (11) 37.10 27.75

"PRAGA 1962 World Exhib. of Postage Stamps," Aug. 18-Sept. 2, 1962.

No. 1080 was printed in sheet of 4. Value $120.

Globe A416

Engraved and Photogravure

1961, Nov. 27 *Perf. 11½*

1081 A416 60h red & ultra .50 .25

Issued to publicize the Fifth World Congress of Trade Unions, Moscow, Dec. 4-16.

Orange Tip Butterfly — A417

Designs (butterflies): 20h, Zerynthia hypsipyle Sch. 30h, Apollo. 40h, Swallowtail. 60h, Peacock. 80h, Mourning cloak (Camberwell beauty). 1k, Underwing (moth). 1.60k, Red admiral. 2k, Brimstone (sulphur).

1961, Nov. 27 **Engr.**

1082	A417	15h	multicolored	.80	.30
1083	A417	20h	multicolored	.80	.30
1084	A417	30h	multicolored	.80	.30
1085	A417	40h	multicolored	.80	.30
1086	A417	60h	multicolored	.80	.30
1087	A417	80h	multicolored	2.40	.90
1088	A417	1k	multicolored	2.40	.90
1089	A417	1.60k	multicolored	2.40	.90
1090	A417	2k	multicolored	6.50	3.00
			Nos. 1082-1090 (9)	17.70	7.20

Nos.1082-1090 were each issued in sheets of 10. Value, set $400.

Bicyclists — A418

Sports: 40h, Woman gymnast. 60h, Figure skaters. 1k, Woman bowler. 1.20k, Goalkeeper, soccer. 1.60k, Discus thrower.

Engraved and Photogravure

1962, Feb. 5 **Unwmk.** ***Perf. 11½***

1091	A418	30h	black & vio bl	.25	.25
1092	A418	40h	black & yel	.25	.25
1093	A418	60h	slate & grnsh bl	.35	.25
1094	A418	1k	black & pink	.35	.25
1095	A418	1.20k	black & green	.35	.25
1096	A418	1.60k	blk & dull grn	1.50	.45
			Nos. 1091-1096 (6)	3.05	1.70

Various 1962 sports events.

No. 1095 does not have the commemorative inscription.

Karel Kovarovic — A419

Frantisek Zaviska and Karel Petr A420

20h, Frantisek Skroup. 30h, Bozena Nemcova. 60h, View of Prague & staff of Aesculapius. 1.60k, Ladislav Celakovsky. 1.80k, Miloslav Valouch & Juraj Hronec.

1962, Feb. 26 **Engr.**

1097	A419	10h	red brown	.25	.25
1098	A419	20h	violet blue	.25	.25
1099	A419	30h	brown	.25	.25
1100	A420	40h	claret	.50	.25
1101	A419	60h	black	.25	.25
1102	A419	1.60k	slate green	.25	.25
1103	A420	1.80k	dark blue	.60	.25
			Nos. 1097-1103 (7)	2.35	1.75

Various cultural personalities and events.

Miner and Flag A421

1962, Mar. 19 **Engr. & Photo.**

1104	A421	60h	indigo & rose	.25	.25

30th anniv. of the miners' strike at Most.

"Man Conquering Space" — A422

Soviet Spaceship Vostok 2 — A423

40h, Launching of Soviet space rocket. 80h, Multi-stage automatic rocket. 1k, Automatic station on moon. 1.60k, Television satellite.

1962, Mar. 26

1105	A422	30h	dk red & lt blue	.35	.25
1106	A422	40h	dk blue & sal	.35	.25
1107	A423	60h	dk blue & pink	.35	.25
1108	A423	80h	rose vio & lt grn	.35	.25
1109	A422	1k	indigo & citron	.35	.25
1110	A423	1.60k	green & buff	1.90	.25
			Nos. 1105-1110 (6)	3.65	1.50

Issued to publicize space research.

Polar Bear — A424

Zoo Animals: 30h, Chimpanzee. 60h, Camel. 1k, African and Indian elephants, horiz. 1.40k, Leopard, horiz. 1.60k, Przewalski horse, horiz.

1962, Apr. 24 **Unwmk.** ***Perf. 11½***

Design and Inscriptions in Black

1111	A424	20h	grnsh blue	.75	.25
1112	A424	30h	violet	.75	.25
1113	A424	60h	orange	.75	.25
1114	A424	1k	green	.75	.25
1115	A424	1.40k	carmine rose	.75	.25
1116	A424	1.60k	lt brown	1.90	1.25
			Nos. 1111-1116 (6)	5.65	2.50

Child and Grieving Mother — A425

60h, Flowers growing from ruins of Lezáky.

1962, June 9 **Engr. & Photo.**

1118	A425	30h	black & red	.45	.25
1119	A425	60h	black & dull bl	.75	.25

20th anniversary of the destruction of Lidice and Lezáky by the Nazis.

Klary's Fountain, Teplice — A426

1962, June 9

1120	A426	60h	dull grn & yel	.40	.25

1,200th anniversary of the discovery of the medicinal springs of Teplice.

Malaria Eradication Emblem, Cross and Dove — A427

3k, Dove and malaria eradication emblem.

1962, June 18

1121	A427	60h	black & crimson	.45	.25
1122	A427	3k	dk blue & yel	1.10	.35

WHO drive to eradicate malaria.

Soccer Goalkeeper — A428

1962, June 20 **Unwmk.** ***Perf. 11½***

1123	A428	1.60k	green & yellow	1.50	.25

Czechoslovakia's participation in the World Cup Soccer Championship, Chile, May 30-June 17. See No. 1095.

Soldier in Swimming Relay Race — A429

Designs: 40h, Soldier hurdling. 60h, Soccer player. 1k, Soldier with rifle in relay race.

1962, July 20

1124	A429	30h	green & lt ultra	.25	.25
1125	A429	40h	dk purple & yel	.25	.25
1126	A429	60h	brown & green	.25	.25
1127	A429	1k	dk blue & sal pink	.25	.25
			Nos. 1124-1127 (4)	1.00	1.00

2nd Summer Spartacist Games of Friendly Armies, Prague, Sept., 1962.

"Agriculture" A430

Designs: 60h, Astronaut in capsule. 80h, Boy with flute, horiz. 1k, Workers of three races, horiz. 1.40k, Children dancing around tree. 1.60k, Flying bird, horiz. 5k, View of Prague, horiz.

1962 **Engr.** ***Perf. 13½***

1128	A430	30h	multicolored	1.20	.60
1129	A430	60h	multicolored	.60	.30
a.			Miniature sheet of 8	*20.00*	*20.00*
1130	A430	80h	multicolored	1.75	1.25
1131	A430	1k	multicolored	1.75	1.25
1132	A430	1.40k	multicolored	1.75	1.25
1133	A430	1.60k	multicolored	3.00	2.10
			Nos. 1128-1133 (6)	10.05	6.75

Souvenir Sheet

1134	A430	5k	multicolored	13.00	10.00
a.			Imperf.	40.00	35.00

"PRAGA 1962 World Exhib. of Postage Stamps," 8/18-9/2/62. No. 1133 also for FIP Day, Sept. 1. Printed in sheets of 10. Value: Nos. 1128-1133 $150; No. 1134 $80.

No. 1129a contains 4 each of Nos. 1128-1129 and 2 labels arranged in 2 rows of 2 se-tenant pairs of Nos. 1128-1129 with label between. Sold for 5k, only with ticket.

No. 1134 contains one 51x30mm stamp. Sold only with ticket.

Children in Day Nursery and Factory A431

Sailboat and Trade Union Rest Home, Zinkovy — A432

Engraved and Photogravure

1962, Oct. 29 **Unwmk.** ***Perf. 11½***

1135	A431	30h	black & lt blue	.25	.25
1136	A432	60h	brown & yellow	.25	.25

Cruiser "Aurora" A433

1962, Nov. 7

1137	A433	30h	black & gray bl	.25	.25
1138	A433	60h	black & pink	.25	.25

Russian October revolution, 45th anniv.

Cosmonaut and Worker — A434

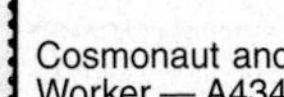

Lenin — A435

1962, Nov. 7

1139	A434	30h	dark red & blue	.25	.25
1140	A435	60h	black & dp rose	.25	.25

40th anniversary of the USSR.

Symbolic Crane — A436

40h, Agricultural products, vert. 60h, Factories.

1962, Dec. 4

1141 A436 30h dk red & yel .25 .25
1142 A436 40h gray blue & yel .25 .25
1143 A436 60h black & dp rose .30 .25
Nos. 1141-1143 (3) .80 .75

Communist Party of Czechoslovakia, 12th cong.

Ground Beetle — A437

Beetles: 30h, Cardinal beetle. 60h, Stag beetle, vert. 1k, Great water beetle. 1.60k, Alpine longicorn, vert. 2k, Ground beetle, vert.

1962, Dec. 15 Engr. *Perf. 14*

1144 A437 20h multicolored .80 .40
1145 A437 30h multicolored .80 .40
1146 A437 60h multicolored .80 .40
1147 A437 1k multicolored 1.60 .60
1148 A437 1.60k multicolored 3.25 .60
1149 A437 2k multicolored 4.50 2.00
Nos. 1144-1149 (6) 11.75 4.40

Nos. 1144-1149 were each printed in sheets of 10. Value, set $225.

Table Tennis — A438

Sports: 60h, Bicyclist. 80h, Skier. 1k, Motorcyclist. 1.20k, Weight lifter. 1.60k, Hurdler.

Engraved and Photogravure

1963, Jan. *Perf. 11½*

1150 A438 30h black & dp grn .25 .25
1151 A438 60h black & orange .25 .25
1152 A438 80h black & ultra .25 .25
1153 A438 1k black & violet .40 .25
1154 A438 1.20k blk & pale brn .40 .25
1155 A438 1.60k blk & car .85 .25
Nos. 1150-1155 (6) 2.40 1.50

Various 1963 sports events.

Industrial Plant, Laurel and Star — A439

Symbol of Pioneer Summer Camp — A440

Industrial Plant and Symbol of Growth — A441

1963, Feb. 25 Unwmk. *Perf. 11½*

1156 A439 30h carmine & lt bl .25 .25
1157 A440 60h black & car .25 .25
1158 A441 60h black & red .25 .25
Nos. 1156-1158 (3) .75 .75

15th anniv. of the "Victorious February" and 5th Trade Union Cong.

Artists' Guild Emblem — A442

Juraj Jánosik — A443

Eduard Urx — A444

National Theater, Prague — A445

No. 1163, Woman reading to children. No. 1164, Juraj Pálkovic. 1.60k, Max Svabinsky.

Engr. & Photo.; Engr. (A444)

1963, Mar. 25 Unwmk. *Perf. 11½*

1159 A442 20h black & Prus bl .25 .25
1160 A443 30h car & lt bl .25 .25
1161 A444 30h carmine .25 .25
1162 A445 60h dl red brn & lt bl .25 .25
1163 A444 60h green .25 .25
1164 A444 60h black .25 .25
1165 A444 1.60k brown .50 .25
Nos. 1159-1165 (7) 2.00 1.75

Various cultural personalities and events.

Boy and Girl with Flag — A446

Engraved and Photogravure

1963, Apr. 18 *Perf. 11½*

1166 A446 30h slate & rose red .35 .25

The 4th Congress of Czechoslovak Youth.

Television Transmitter — A447

40h, Television camera, mast and set, horiz.

1963, Apr. 25

1167 A447 40h buff & slate .40 .25
1168 A447 60h dk red & lt blue .40 .25

Czechoslovak television, 10th anniversary.

Rocket to the Sun A448

50h, Rockets & Sputniks leaving Earth. 60h, Spacecraft to & from Moon. 1k, 3k, Interplanetary station & Mars 1. 1.60k, Atomic rocket & Jupiter. 2k, Rocket returning from Saturn.

1963, Apr. 25

1169 A448 30h red brn & buff .45 .25
1170 A448 50h slate & bluish grn .45 .25
1171 A448 60h dk green & yel .40 .25
1172 A448 1k dk gray & sal .65 .25
1173 A448 1.60k gray brn & lt grn .65 .25
1174 A448 2k dk purple & yel *1.25* .75
Nos. 1169-1174 (6) *3.85 2.00*

Souvenir Sheet

Imperf

1175 A448 3k Prus grn & org red *10.00 5.00*

No. 1175 issued for 1st Space Research Exhib., Prague, Apr. 1963.

Studio and Radio A449

1k, Globe inscribed "Peace" & aerial mast, vert.

1963, May 18 Unwmk. *Perf. 11½*

1176 A449 30h choc & pale grn .40 .25
1177 A449 1k bluish grn & lilac .40 .25

40th anniversary of Czechoslovak radio.

Tupolev Tu-104B Turbojet A450

Design: 1.80k, Ilyushin Il-18 Moskva.

1963, May 25

1178 A450 80h violet & lt bl 1.00 .35
1179 A450 1.80k dk blue & lt grn 1.50 .35

40th anniversary of Czechoslovak airlines.

9th Cent. Ring, Map of Moravian Settlements — A451

1.60k, Falconer, 9th cent. silver disk.

1963, May 25

1180 A451 30h lt green & blk .25 .25
1181 A451 1.60k dull yel & blk .75 .25

1100th anniversary of Moravian empire.

Woman Singing — A452

1963, May 25 Engr.

1182 A452 30h bright red .55 .25

60th anniversary of the founding of the Moravian Teachers' Singing Club.

Kromeriz Castle and Barley — A453

Engraved and Photogravure

1963, June 20 Unwmk. *Perf. 11½*

1183 A453 30h slate grn & yel .55 .25

Natl. Agricultural Exhib. and 700th anniv. of Kromeriz.

Centenary Emblem, Nurse and Playing Child — A454

1963, June 20

1184 A454 30h dk gray & car .50 .25

Centenary of the International Red Cross.

Bee, Honeycomb and Emblem A455

1963, June 20

1185 A455 1k brown & yellow .75 .25

19th Intl. Beekeepers Cong., Apimondia, 1963.

Liberec Fair Emblem — A456

1963, July 13

1186 A456 30h black & dp rose .40 .25

Liberec Consumer Goods Fair.

Town Hall, Brno — A457

Design: 60h, Town Hall tower, Brno.

1963, July 29

1187 A457 30h lt blue & maroon .35 .25
1188 A457 60h pink & dk blue .35 .25

International Trade Fair, Brno.

Cave, Moravian Karst — A458

No. 1190, Trout, Hornad Valley. 60h, Great Hawk Gorge. 80h, Macocha mountains.

1963, July 29

1189 A458 30h brown & lt bl .80 .25
1190 A458 30h dk bl & dull grn .95 .25
1191 A458 60h green & blue .80 .25
1192 A458 80h sepia & pink .80 .25
Nos. 1189-1192 (4) 3.35 1.00

Blast Furnace A459

1963, Aug. 15 Unwmk. *Perf. 11½*
1193 A459 60h blk & bluish grn .40 .25

30th Intl. Cong. of Iron Founders, Prague.

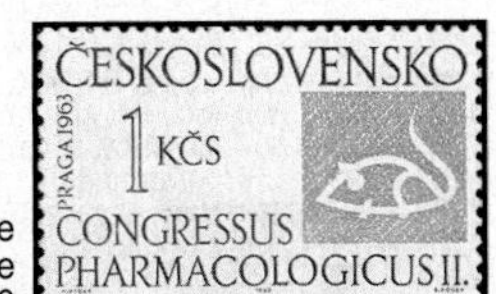

White Mouse A460

1963, Aug. 15
1194 A460 1k black & carmine .60 .25

2nd Intl. Pharmacological Cong., Prague.

Farm Machinery for Underfed Nations — A461

1963, Aug. 15 Engr.
1195 A461 1.60k black .50 .25

FAO "Freedom from Hunger" campaign.

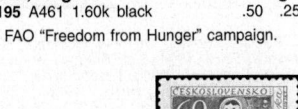

Wooden Toys — A462

Folk Art (Inscribed "UNESCO"): 80h, Cock and flowers. 1k, Flowers in vase. 1.20k, Janosik, Slovak hero. 1.60k, Stag. 2k, Postilion.

1963, Sept. 2 Engr. *Perf. 13½*
1196 A462 60h red & vio bl .65 .30
1197 A462 80h multi .65 .30
1198 A462 1k multi .65 .30
1199 A462 1.20k multi .65 .30
1200 A462 1.60k multi .65 .30
1201 A462 2k multi 2.75 1.75
Nos. 1196-1201 (6) 6.00 3.25

Nos. 1196-1201 were printed in sheets of 10. Value, set $100.

Canoeing A463

Sports: 40h, Volleyball. 60h, Wrestling. 80h, Basketball. 1k, Boxing. 1.60k, Gymnastics.

Engraved and Photogravure
1963, Oct. 26 *Perf. 11½*
1202 A463 30h indigo & grn .30 .25
1203 A463 40h red brn & lt bl .30 .25
1204 A463 60h brn red & yel .35 .25
1205 A463 80h dk pur & dp org .45 .25
1206 A463 1k ultra & dp rose .60 .35
1207 A463 1.60k vio bl & ultra 2.00 1.00
Nos. 1202-1207 (6) 4.00 2.35

1964 Olympic Games, Tokyo.

Tree and Star — A464

Design: 60h, Star, hammer and sickle.

1963, Dec. 11 Unwmk. *Perf. 11½*
1208 A464 30h bis brn & lt bl .30 .25
1209 A464 60h carmine & gray .30 .25

Russo-Czechoslovakian Treaty, 20th anniv.

Atom Diagrams Surrounding Head — A465

1963, Dec. 12 Engr.
1210 A465 60h dark purple .40 .25

3rd Congress of the Association for the Propagation of Scientific Knowledge.

Chamois — A466

40h, Alpine ibex. 60h, Mouflon. 1.20k, Roe deer. 1.60k, Fallow deer. 2k, Red deer.

1963, Dec. 14 *Perf. 14*
1211 A466 30h multi 1.25 .35
1212 A466 40h multi 1.25 .35
1213 A466 60h brn, yel & grn 1.25 .35
1214 A466 1.20k multi 2.00 1.00
1215 A466 1.60k multi 2.50 1.25
1216 A466 2k multi 5.00 2.50
Nos. 1211-1216 (6) 13.25 5.80

Nos. 1211-1216 were each issued in sheets of 10 stamps. Value, set $400.

Figure Skating — A467

80h, Skiing, horiz. 1k, Field ball player.

Engraved and Photogravure
1964, Jan. 20 Unwmk. *Perf. 11½*
1217 A467 30h violet bl & yel .30 .25
1218 A467 80h dk blue & org .45 .25
1219 A467 1k brown & lilac .75 .25
Nos. 1217-1219 (3) 1.50 .75

Intl. University Games (30h, 80h) and the World Field Ball Championships (1k).

Ice Hockey — A468

1964, Jan. 20
1220 A468 1k shown 1.10 .45
1221 A468 1.80k Toboggan 1.20 .60
1222 A468 2k Ski jump 2.25 1.00
Nos. 1220-1222 (3) 4.55 2.05

9th Winter Olympic Games, Innsbruck, Jan. 29-Feb. 9, 1964.

Magura Rest Home, High Tatra — A469

Design: 80h, Slovak National Insurrection Rest Home, Low Tatra.

1964, Feb. 19 Unwmk. *Perf. 11½*
1223 A469 60h green & yellow .30 .25
1224 A469 80h violet bl & pink .30 .25

Skiers and Ski Lift A470

60h, Automobile camp, Telc. 1k, Fishing, Spis Castle. 1.80k, Lake & boats, Cesky Krumlov.

1964, Feb. 19 Engr. & Photo.
1225 A470 30h dk vio brn & bl .40 .25
1226 A470 60h slate & car .45 .25
1227 A470 1k brown & olive .80 .25
1228 A470 1.80k slate grn & org 1.10 .35
Nos. 1225-1228 (4) 2.75 1.10

Moses, Day and Night by Michelangelo — A471

Designs: 60h, "A Midsummer Night's Dream," by Shakespeare. 1k, Man, telescope and heaven, vert. 1.60k, King George of Podebrad (1420-71).

1964, Mar. 20
1229 A471 40h black & yel grn .35 .25
1230 A471 60h slate & car .35 .25
1231 A471 1k black & lt blue 1.25 .25
1232 A471 1.60k black & yellow 1.25 .25
a. Souvenir sheet of 4, imperf. ('88) 9.50 6.50
Nos. 1229-1232 (4) 3.20 1.00

400th anniv. of the death of Michelangelo (40h); 400th anniv. of the birth of Shakespeare (60h); 400th anniv. of the birth of Galileo (1k); 500th anniv. of the pacifist efforts of King George of Podebrad (1.60k).

No. 1232a for PRAGA '88.

Yuri A. Gagarin — A472

Astronauts: 60h, Gherman Titov. 80h, John H. Glenn, Jr. 1k, Scott M. Carpenter, vert. 1.20k, Pavel R. Popovich and Andrian G. Nikolayev. 1.40k, Walter M. Schirra, vert. 1.60k, Gordon L. Cooper, vert. 2k, Valentina Tereshkova and Valeri Bykovski, vert.

1964, Apr. 27 Unwmk. *Perf. 11½*
Yellow Paper
1233 A472 30h black & vio bl .50 .25
1234 A472 60h dk grn & dk car .50 .25
1235 A472 80h dk car & vio .55 .25
1236 A472 1k ultra & rose vio .75 .25
1237 A472 1.20k ver & ol gray .60 .30
1238 A472 1.40k black & dl grn 1.00 .45
1239 A472 1.60k pale pur & Prus grn 2.25 1.50
1240 A472 2k dk blue & red .75 .40
Nos. 1233-1240 (8) 6.90 3.65

World's first 10 astronauts.

Creeping Bellflower — A473

Flowers: 80h, Musk thistle. 1k, Chicory. 1.20k, Yellow iris. 1.60k, Gentian. 2k, Corn poppy.

1964, June 15 Engr. *Perf. 14*
1241 A473 60h dk grn, lil & org .75 .25
1242 A473 80h blk, grn & red lil 1.10 .25
1243 A473 1k vio bl, grn & pink 1.10 .45
1244 A473 1.20k black, yel & grn 1.10 .30
1245 A473 1.60k violet & grn 1.10 .40
1246 A473 2k vio, red & grn 4.50 1.50
Nos. 1241-1246 (6) 9.65 3.15

Nos. 1241-1246 were each issued in sheets of 10. Value, set $250.

Film "Flower" and Karlovy Vary Colonnade — A474

Engraved and Photogravure
1964, June 20 Unwmk. *Perf. 13½*
1247 A474 60h black, blue & car 2.00 .50

14th Intl. Film Festival at Karlovy Vary, July 4-19.

Issued in sheets of 10. Value, $80.

Silesian Coat of Arms — A475

1964, June 20 *Perf. 11½*
1248 A475 30h black & yel .30 .25

150th anniv. of the Silesian Museum, Opava.

Young Miner of 1764 — A476

1964, June 20
1249 A476 60h sepia & lt grn .30 .25

Mining School at Banska Stiavnica, bicent.

Skoda Fire Engine A477

1964, June 20
1250 A477 60h car rose & lt bl 1.00 .25

Voluntary fire brigades in Bohemia, cent.

Gulls, Hradcany Castle, Red Cross — A478

1964, July 10
1251 A478 60h car & bluish gray .55 .25

4th Czechoslovak Red Cross Congress at Prague.

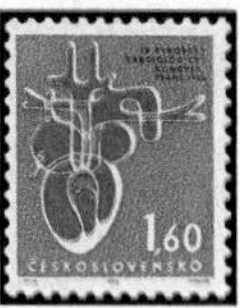

Human Heart — A479

1964, July 10
1252 A479 1.60k ultra & car 1.10 .25

4th European Cardiological Cong. at Prague.

Partisans, Girl and Factories A480

Battle Scene, 1944 — A481

Design: No. 1254, Partisans and flame.

Engraved and Photogravure
1964, Aug. 17 Unwmk. *Perf. 11½*
1253 A480 30h brown & red .25 .25
1254 A480 60h dk blue & red .25 .25
1255 A481 60h black & red .25 .25
Nos. 1253-1255 (3) .75 .75

20th anniv. of the Slovak Natl. Uprising; No. 1255, 20th anniv. of the Battles of Dukla Pass.

Hradcany at Prague — A482

Design: 5k, Charles Bridge and Hradcany.

1964, Aug. 30 *Perf. 11½x12*
1256 A482 60h black & red .65 .25

Souvenir Sheet
Engr. *Imperf.*
1257 A482 5k deep claret 3.50 2.50

Millenium of the Hradcany, Prague. No. 1257 stamp size: 30x50mm.

Discus Thrower and Pole Vaulter — A483

Designs: 60h, Bicycling, horiz. 1k, Soccer. 1.20k, Rowing. 1.60k, Swimming, horiz. 2.80k, Weight lifting, horiz.

Engraved and Photogravure
1964, Sept. 2 *Perf. 13½*
1258 A483 60h multi .80 .30
1259 A483 80h multi .80 .30
1260 A483 1k multi .80 .30
1261 A483 1.20k multi .80 .30
1262 A483 1.60k multi .80 .30
1263 A483 2.80k multi 4.00 2.00
Nos. 1258-1263 (6) 8.00 3.50

Issued to commemorate the 18th Olympic Games, Tokyo, Oct. 10-25.

Nos. 1258-1263 were issued in sheets of 10. Value, set $125.

Miniature Sheet

Space Ship Voskhod I, Astronauts and Globe — A484

1964, Nov. 12 Unwmk. *Perf. 11½*
1264 A484 3k dk bl & dl lil, *buff* 5.00 3.50

Russian 3-man space flight of Vladimir M. Komarov, Boris B. Yegorov and Konstantin Feoktistov, Oct. 12-13.

Steam Engine and Atomic Power Plant — A485

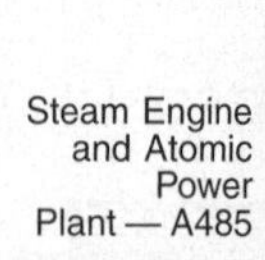

Diesel Engine "CKD Praha" — A486

1964, Nov. 16 Engr.
1265 A485 30h dull red brown .25 .25

Engraved and Photogravure
1266 A486 60h green & salmon 1.00 .25

Traditions and development of engineering; No. 1265 for 150th anniv. of the First Brno Engineering Works, No. 1266 for the engineering concern CKD Praha.

European Redstart — A487

Birds: 60h, Green woodpecker. 80h, Hawfinch. 1k, Black woodpecker. 1.20k, European robin. 1.60k, European roller.

1964, Nov. 16 Litho. *Perf. 10½*
1267 A487 30h multicolored 1.10 .30
1268 A487 60h black & multi 1.10 .30
1269 A487 80h multicolored 1.40 .35
1270 A487 1k multicolored 1.75 .40
1271 A487 1.20k lt vio bl & blk 1.75 .40
1272 A487 1.60k yellow & blk 3.50 1.00
Nos. 1267-1272 (6) 10.60 2.75

Dancer A488

"In the Sun" Preschool Children A489

Designs: 60h, "Over the Obstacles," teenagers. 1k, "Movement and Beauty," woman flag twirler. 1.60k, Runners at start.

Engraved and Photogravure
1965 Unwmk. *Perf. 11½*
1273 A488 30h red & lt blue .25 .25

Perf. 11½x12
1274 A489 30h vio bl & car .25 .25
1275 A489 60h brown & ultra .25 .25
1276 A489 1k black & yellow .25 .25
1277 A489 1.60k maroon & gray .60 .25
Nos. 1273-1277 (5) 1.60 1.25

3rd Natl. Spartacist Games. Issue dates: No. 1273, Jan. 3; Nos. 1274-1277, May 24.

Mountain Rescue Service — A490

Designs: No. 1279, Woman gymnast. No. 1280, Bicyclists. No. 1281, Women hurdlers.

1965, Jan. 15 Unwmk. *Perf. 11½*
1278 A490 60h violet & blue .30 .25
1279 A490 60h maroon & ocher .30 .25
1280 A490 60h black & carmine .30 .25
1281 A490 60h green & yellow .30 .25
Nos. 1278-1281 (4) 1.20 1.00

Mountain Rescue Service (No. 1278); 1st World Championship in Artistic Gymnastics, Prague, Dec. 1965 (No. 1279); World Championship in Indoor Bicycling, Prague, Oct. 1965 (No. 1280); "Universiada 1965," Brno (No. 1281).

Arms and View, Beroun — A491

Designs: No. 1283, Town Square, Domazlice. No. 1284, Old and new buildings, Frydek-Mystek. No. 1285, Arms and view, Lipnik. No. 1286, Fortified wall, City Hall and Arms, Policka. No. 1287, View and hops, Zatek. No. 1288, Small fortress and rose, Terezin.

1965, Feb. 15
1282 A491 30h vio bl & lt bl .30 .25
1283 A491 30h dull pur & yel .30 .25
1284 A491 30h slate & gray .30 .25
1285 A491 30h green & bis .30 .25
1286 A491 30h brown & tan .30 .25
1287 A491 30h dk blue & cit .30 .25
1288 A491 30h black & rose .30 .25
Nos. 1282-1288 (7) 2.10 1.75

Nos. 1282-1287 for 700th anniv. of the founding of various Bohemian towns; No. 1288 the 20th anniv. of the liberation of the Theresienstadt (Terezin) concentration camp.

Sun's Corona A492

Space Research: 30h, Sun. 60h, Exploration of the Moon. 1k, Twin space craft, vert. 1.40k, Space station. 1.60k, Exploration of Mars, vert. 2k, USSR and US Meteorological collaboration.

1965, Mar. 15 *Perf. 12x11½, 11½x12*
1289 A492 20h rose & red lilac .25 .25
1290 A492 30h rose red & yel .25 .25
1291 A492 60h bluish blk & yel .25 .25
1292 A492 1k pur & pale bl .25 .25
1293 A492 1.40k black & salmon .35 .25
1294 A492 1.60k black & pink .50 .25
1295 A492 2k bluish blk & lt bl *1.50 1.00*
Nos. 1289-1295 (7) *3.35 2.50*

Space research; Nos. 1289-1290 also for the Intl. Quiet Sun Year, 1964-65.

Frantisek Ventura, Equestrian; Amsterdam, 1928 — A493

Czechoslovakian Olympic Victories: 30h, Discus, Paris, 1900. 60h, Running, Helsinki, 1952. 1k, Weight lifting, Los Angeles, 1932. 1.40k, Gymnastics, Berlin, 1936. 1.60k, Double sculling, Rome, 1960. 2k, Women's gymnastics, Tokyo, 1964.

1965, Apr. 16 *Perf. 11½x12*
1296 A493 20h choc & gold .25 .25
1297 A493 30h indigo & emer .25 .25
1298 A493 60h ultra & gold .25 .25
1299 A493 1k red brn & gold .25 .25
1300 A493 1.40k dk sl grn & gold 1.10 .45
1301 A493 1.60k black & gold 1.10 .45
1302 A493 2k maroon & gold .55 .30
Nos. 1296-1302 (7) 3.75 2.20

Astronauts Virgil Grissom and John Young — A494

Designs: No. 1304, Alexei Leonov floating in space. No. 1305, Launching pad at Cape Kennedy. No. 1306, Leonov leaving space ship.

1965, Apr. 17 *Perf. 11x11½*
1303 A494 60h slate bl & lil rose .45 .25
1304 A494 60h vio blk & blue .45 .25
1305 A494 3k slate bl & lil rose 1.60 1.00
a. Pair, #1303, 1305 3.50 1.50
1306 A494 3k vio blk & blue 1.60 1.00
a. Pair, #1304, 1306 3.50 1.50
Nos. 1303-1306 (4) 4.10 2.50

Issued to honor American and Soviet astronauts. Printed in sheets of 25; one sheet contains 20 No. 1303 and 5 No. 1305, the other sheet contains 20 No. 1304 and 5 No. 1306. Value, $125 each.

Russian Soldier, View of Prague and Guerrilla Fighters A495

Designs: No. 1308, Blast furnace, workers and tank. 60h, Worker and factory. 1k, Worker and new constructions. 1.60k, Woman farmer, new farm buildings and machinery.

1965, May 5 Engr. *Perf. 13½*
1307 A495 30h dk red, blk & ol .35 .25
1308 A495 30h multicolored .35 .25
1309 A495 60h vio bl, red & blk .35 .25

No.	Type	Description	Unused	Used
1310	A495	1k dp org, blk & brn	.50	.25
1311	A495	1.60k yel, red & blk	.55	.25
		Nos. 1307-1311 (5)	2.10	1.25

20th anniv. of liberation from the Nazis.

Nos. 1307-1311 were each printed in sheets of 10. Value, set $120.

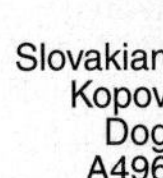

Slovakian Kopov Dog A496

Dogs: 40h, German shepherd. 60h, Czech hunting dog with pheasant. 1k, Poodle. 1.60k, Czech terrier. 2k, Afghan hound.

1965, June 10 ***Perf. 12x11½***

No.	Type	Description	Unused	Used
1312	A496	30h black & red org	.45	.25
1313	A496	40h black & yellow	.45	.25
1314	A496	60h black & ver	.70	.25
1315	A496	1k black & dk car rose	1.00	.25
1316	A496	1.60k black & orange	1.25	.25
1317	A496	2k black & orange	2.00	1.25
		Nos. 1312-1317 (6)	5.85	2.50

World Dog Show at Brno and the International Dog Breeders Congress, Prague.

UN Headquarters Building, NY — A497

Emblems: 60h, UN & inscription. 1.60k, ICY.

1965, June 24 ***Perf. 12x11½***

No.	Type	Description	Unused	Used
1318	A497	60h dk red brn & yel	.25	.25
1319	A497	1k ultra & lt blue	.65	.25
1320	A497	1.60k gold & dk red	.55	.25
		Nos. 1318-1320 (3)	1.45	.75

20th anniv. of the UN and the ICY, 1965.

Trade Union Emblem A498

1965, June 24 **Engr.**

No.	Type	Description	Unused	Used
1321	A498	60h dk red & ultra	.40	.25

Intl. Trade Union Federation, 20th anniv.

Women and Globe — A499

1965, June 24 ***Perf. 11½x12***

No.	Type	Description	Unused	Used
1322	A499	60h violet blue	.40	.25

20th anniv. of the Intl. Women's Federation.

Children's House (Burgraves' Palace), Hradcany A500

Matthias Tower — A501

1965, June 25 ***Perf. 11½***

No.	Type	Description	Unused	Used
1323	A500	30h slate green	.30	.25
1324	A501	60h dark brown	.30	.25

Issued to publicize the Hradcany, Prague.

Marx and Lenin — A502

1965, July 1 **Engr. & Photo.**

No.	Type	Description	Unused	Used
1325	A502	60h car rose & gold	.40	.25

6th conf. of Postal Ministers of Communist Countries, Peking, June 21-July 15.

Joseph Navratil — A503

Jan Hus — A504

Gregor Johann Mendel A505

Costume Jewelry A506

Bohuslav Martinu A507

Seated Woman and University of Bratislava A508

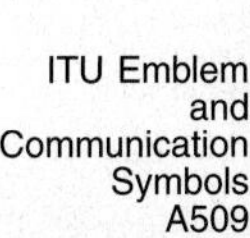

ITU Emblem and Communication Symbols A509

Macromolecular Symposium Emblem A510

Design: No. 1327, Ludovit Stur (diff. frame).

1965 **Unwmk.** ***Perf. 11½***

No.	Type	Description	Unused	Used
1326	A503	30h black & fawn	.25	.25
1327	A503	30h black & dull grn	.25	.25
1328	A504	60h black & crimson	.25	.25
1329	A505	60h vio bl & red	.25	.25
1330	A506	60h purple & gold	.25	.25
1331	A507	60h black & orange	.25	.25
1332	A508	60h brn, *yel*	.25	.25
1333	A509	1k orange & blue	.35	.25
1334	A510	1k black & dp org	.35	.25
		Nos. 1326-1334 (9)	2.45	2.25

No. 1326, Navratil (1798-1865), painter; No. 1327, Stur (1815-56), Slovak author and historian; No. 1328, the 550th anniv. of the death of Hus, religious reformer;

No. 1329, cent. of publication of Mendel's laws of inheritance; No. 1330 publicizes the "Jablonec 1965" costume jewelry exhib.; No. 1331, Martinu (1890-1959), composer; No. 1332, 500th anniv. of the founding of the University of Bratislava as Academia Istropolitana; No. 1333, cent. of the ITU; No. 1334, Intl. Symposium on Macromolecular Chemistry, Prague, Sept. 1-8.

Issued: No. 1333, 7/10.

Miniature Sheet

"Young Woman at her Toilette," by Titian — A512

1965, Aug. 12

No.	Type	Description	Unused	Used
1336	A512	5k multicolored	6.00	4.00

Hradcany Art Gallery. No. 1336 contains one stamp.

Help for Flood Victims — A513

Rescue of Flood Victims A514

1965, Sept. 6 **Engr.**

No.	Type	Description	Unused	Used
1337	A513	30h violet blue	.25	.25

Engraved and Photogravure

No.	Type	Description	Unused	Used
1338	A514	2k dk ol grn & ol	.65	.45

Help for Danube flood victims in Slovakia.

Dotterel A515

Mountain Birds: 60h, Wall creeper, vert. 1.20k, Lesser redpoll. 1.40k, Golden eagle, vert. 1.60k, Ring ouzel. 2k, Eurasian nutcracker, vert.

1965, Sept. 20 **Litho.** ***Perf. 11***

No.	Type	Description	Unused	Used
1339	A515	30h multi	.80	.25
1340	A515	60h multi	.80	.25
1341	A515	1.20k multi	.80	.25
1342	A515	1.40k multi	1.50	.25
1343	A515	1.60k multi	1.00	.45
1344	A515	2k multi	4.00	1.75
		Nos. 1339-1344 (6)	8.90	3.20

Levoca — A516

Views of Towns: 10h, Jindrichuv Hradec. 20h, Nitra. 30h, Kosice. 40h, Hradec Králové. 50h, Telc. 60h, Ostrava. 1k, Olomouc. 1.20k, Ceske Budejovice. 1.60k, Cheb. 2k, Brno. 3k, Bratislava. 5k, Prague.

Engraved and Photogravure

1965-66 ***Perf. 11½x12***

Size: 23x19mm

No.	Type	Description	Unused	Used
1345	A516	5h black & yel	.25	.25
1346	A516	10h ultra & ol bis	.80	.25
1347	A516	20h black & lt bl	.25	.25
1348	A516	30h vio bl & lt grn	.25	.25
1348A	A516	40h dk brn & lt bl ('66)	.25	.25
1348B	A516	50h black & ocher ('66)	.50	.25
1348C	A516	60h red & gray ('66)	1.00	.25
1348D	A516	1k pur & pale grn ('66)	1.00	.25

Perf. 11½x11

Size: 30x23mm

No.	Type	Description	Unused	Used
1349	A516	1.20k slate & lt bl	.75	.25
1350	A516	1.60k indigo & yel	.75	.25
1351	A516	2k sl grn & pale yel	.75	.25
1352	A516	3k brn & yel	1.25	.25
1353	A516	5k black & pink	1.75	.25
		Nos. 1345-1353 (13)	9.55	3.25

Medicinal Plants — A517

1965, Dec. 3 **Engr.** ***Perf. 14***

No.	Type	Description	Unused	Used
1354	A517	30h Coltsfoot	.35	.25
1355	A517	60h Meadow saffron	.35	.25
1356	A517	80h Corn poppy	1.00	.25
1357	A517	1k Foxglove	1.00	.40
1358	A517	1.20k Arnica	1.40	.60
1359	A517	1.60k Cornflower	1.40	.45
1360	A517	2k Dog rose	3.50	1.50
		Nos. 1354-1360 (7)	9.00	3.70

Nos. 1354-1360 were each printed in sheets of 10. Value, set $225.

Strip of "Stamps" — A518

Engraved and Photogravure

1965, Dec. 18 ***Perf. 11½***

No.	Type	Description	Unused	Used
1361	A518	1k dark red & gold	3.50	2.00

Issued for Stamp Day, 1965.

Romain Rolland (1866-1944), French Writer — A519

Portraits: No. 1362, Stanislav Sucharda (1866-1916), sculptor. No. 1363, Ignac Josef Pesina (1766-1808), veterinarian. No. 1365, Donatello (1386-1466), Italian sculptor.

1966, Feb. 14 **Engr.** ***Perf. 11½***

No.	Type	Description	Unused	Used
1362	A519	30h deep green	.25	.25
1363	A519	30h violet blue	.25	.25
1364	A519	60h rose lake	.25	.25
1365	A519	60h brown	.25	.25
		Nos. 1362-1365 (4)	1.00	1.00

Symbolic Musical Instruments & Names of Composers — A520

1966, Jan. 15 Engr. & Photo.

1366 A520 30h black & gold .55 .25

Czech Philharmonic Orchestra, 70th anniv.

Figure Skating Pair A521

No. 1368, Man skater. No. 1369, Volleyball player, spiking, vert. 1k, Volleyball player, saving, vert. 1.60k, Woman skater. 2k, Figure skating pair.

1966, Feb. 17

1367 A521 30h dk car rose .30 .25
1368 A521 60h green .30 .25
1369 A521 60h carmine & buff .30 .25
1370 A521 1k vio & lt bl .40 .25
1371 A521 1.60k brown & yellow .50 .25
1372 A521 2k blue & grnsh bl 2.40 .40
Nos. 1367-1372 (6) 4.20 1.65

Nos. 1367-1368, 1371-1372 for the European Figure Skating Championships, Bratislava; Nos. 1369-1370 for the World Volleyball Championships.

Souvenir Sheet

Girl Dancing — A522

1966, Mar. 21 Engr. *Imperf.*

1373 A522 3k slate bl, red & bl 3.50 1.50

Cent. of the opera "The Bartered Bride" by Bedrich Smetana.

"Ajax" 1841 A523

Locomotives: 30h, "Karlstejn" 1865. 60h, Steam engine, 1946. 1k, Steam engine with tender, 1946. 1.60k, Electric locomotive, 1964. 2k, Diesel locomotive, 1964.

1966, Mar. 21 *Perf. 11½x11*

Buff Paper

1374 A523 20h sepia 1.10 .25
1375 A523 30h dull violet 1.60 .25
1376 A523 60h dull purple 1.10 .25
1377 A523 1k dark blue 1.25 .50
1378 A523 1.60k dk blue grn 1.75 .40
1379 A523 2k dark red 3.25 2.10
Nos. 1374-1379 (6) 10.05 3.75

European Perch A524

30h, Brown trout, vert. 1k, Carp. 1.20k, Northern pike. 1.40k, Grayling. 1.60k, Eel.

Perf. 13x13½, 13½x13

1966, Apr. 22 Litho. Unwmk.

1380 A524 30h multi .60 .25
1381 A524 60h multi .60 .25
1382 A524 1k multi 1.25 .25
1383 A524 1.20k multi .60 .25
1384 A524 1.40k multi 1.10 .50
1385 A524 1.60k multi 2.50 1.00
Nos. 1380-1385 (6) 6.65 2.50

Intl. Fishing Championships, Svit, Sept. 3-5.

WHO Headquarters, Geneva — A525

Engraved and Photogravure

1966, Apr. 25 *Perf. 12x11½*

1386 A525 1k dk blue & lt blue .35 .25

Opening of the WHO Headquarters, Geneva.

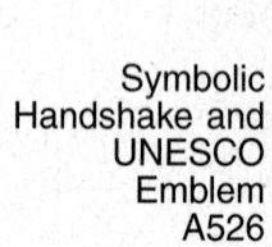

Symbolic Handshake and UNESCO Emblem A526

1966, Apr. 25 *Perf. 11½*

1387 A526 60h bister & olive gray .45 .25

20th anniv. of UNESCO.

Prague Castle Issue

Belvedere Palace and St. Vitus' Cathedral A527

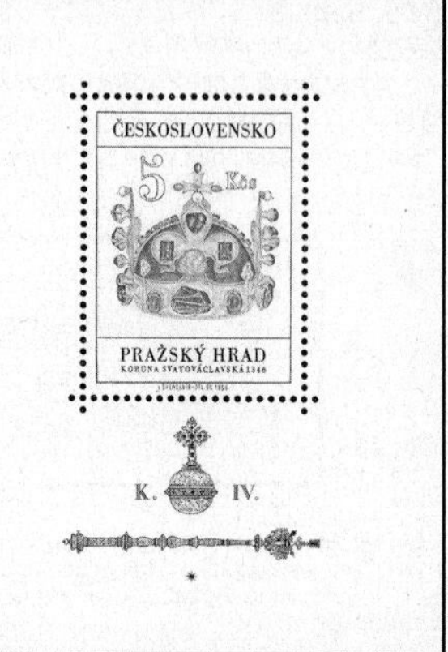

Crown of St. Wenceslas, 1346 — A528

Design: 60h, Madonna, altarpiece from St. George's Church.

1966, May 9 Engr. *Perf. 11½*

1388 A527 30h dark blue .50 .25

Engraved and Photogravure

1389 A527 60h blk & yel bis .75 .25

Souvenir Sheet

Engr.

1390 A528 5k multi 5.00 2.50

See Nos. 1537-1539.

Tiger Swallowtail A529

Butterflies and Moths: 60h, Clouded sulphur. 80h, European purple emperor. 1k, Apollo. 1.20k, Burnet moth. 2k, Tiger moth.

1966, May 23 Engr. *Perf. 14*

1391 A529 30h multi .90 .25
1392 A529 60h multi .90 .25
1393 A529 80h multi 1.25 .40
1394 A529 1k multi 1.90 .60
1395 A529 1.20k multi 1.90 .50
1396 A529 2k multi 5.50 2.00
Nos. 1391-1396 (6) 12.35 4.00

Nos. 1391-1396 were issued in sheets of 10. Value, set $250.

Flags of Russia and Czechoslovakia — A530

Designs: 60h, Rays surrounding hammer and sickle "sun." 1.60k, Girl's head and stars.

Engraved and Photogravure

1966, May 31 *Perf. 11½*

1397 A530 30h dk bl & crim .25 .25
1398 A530 60h dk bl & red .25 .25
1399 A530 1.60k red & dk bl .30 .25
Nos. 1397-1399 (3) .80 .75

13th Congress of the Communist Party of Czechoslovakia.

Dakota Chief — A531

Designs: 20h, Indians, canoe and tepee, horiz. 30h, Tomahawk. 40h, Haida totem poles. 60h, Kachina, good spirit of the Hopis. 1k, Indian on horseback hunting buffalo, horiz. 1.20k, Calumet, Dakota peace pipe.

1966, June 20 Size: 23x40mm

1400 A531 20h vio bl & dp org .25 .25
1401 A531 30h blk & dl org .25 .25
1402 A531 40h blk & lt bl .25 .25
1403 A531 60h grn & yel .25 .25
1404 A531 1k pur & emer .40 .25
1405 A531 1.20k vio bl & rose lil .65 .30

Perf. 14

Engr.

Size: 23x37mm

1406 A531 1.40k multi 1.60 .90
Nos. 1400-1406 (7) 3.65 2.45

Cent. of the Náprstek Ethnographic Museum, Prague, and "The Indians of North America" exhibition.

No. 1406 was issued in sheets of 10. Value, $500.

Model of Molecule — A532

Engraved and Photogravure

1966, July 4 Unwmk. *Perf. 11½*

1407 A532 60h blk & lt bl .50 .25

Czechoslovak Chemical Society, cent.

"Guernica" by Pablo Picasso — A533

1966, July 5 Size: 75x30mm

1408 A533 60h blk & pale bl 2.75 1.40

30th anniversary of International Brigade in Spanish Civil War.

Sheets of 15 stamps and 5 labels inscribed "Picasso-Guernica 1937." Values: with tab attached, $6; sheet $75.

Pantheon, Bratislava — A534

Designs: No. 1410, Devin Castle and Ludovit Stur. No. 1411, View of Nachod. No. 1412, State Science Library, Olomouc.

1966, July 25 Engr.

1409 A534 30h dl pur .30 .25
1410 A534 60h dk bl .35 .25
1411 A534 60h green .35 .25
1412 A534 60h sepia .30 .25
Nos. 1409-1412 (4) 1.30 1.00

No. 1409, Russian War Memorial, Bratislava; No. 1410, the 9th cent. Devin Castle as symbol of Slovak nationalism; No. 1411, 700th anniv. of the founding of Nachod; No. 1412, the 400th anniv. of the State Science Library, Olomouc.

Atom Symbol and Sun — A535

Engraved and Photogravure

1966, Aug. 29 *Perf. 11½*

1413 A535 60h blk & red .40 .25

Issued to publicize Jachymov (Joachimsthal), where pitchblende was first discovered, "cradle of the atomic age."

Brno Fair Emblem — A536

1966, Aug. 29

1414 A536 60h blk & red .40 .25

8th International Trade Fair, Brno.

Olympia Coin and Olympic Rings — A537

Design: 1k, Olympic flame, Czechoslovak flag and Olympic rings.

1966, Aug. 29

1415	A537	60h blk & gold	.30	.25
1416	A537	1k dk bl & red	1.10	.30

70th anniv. of the Olympic Committee.

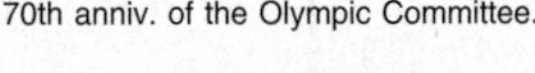

Missile Carrier, Tank and Jet Plane A538

1966, Aug. 31

1417	A538	60h blk & apple grn	.40	.25

Issued to commemorate the maneuvers of the armies of the Warsaw Pact countries.

Mercury A539

30h, Moravian silver thaler, 1620, reverse & obverse, vert. 1.60k, Old & new buildings of Brno State Theater. 5k, Intl. Trade Fair Administration Tower & postmark, vert.

1966, Sept. 10

1418	A539	30h dk red & blk	.45	.25
1419	A539	60h org & blk	.45	.25
1420	A539	1.60k blk & brt grn	.75	.25
		Nos. 1418-1420 (3)	1.65	.75

Souvenir Sheet

1421	A539	5k multi	3.00	3.00

Brno Philatelic Exhibition, Sept. 11-25. No. 1421 contains one 30x40mm stamp.

First Meeting in Orbit — A540

30h, Photograph of far side of Moon & Russian satellite. 60h, Photograph of Mars & Mariner 4. 80th, Soft landing on Moon. 1k, Satellite, laser beam & binary code. 1.20k, Telstar over Earth & receiving station.

1966, Sept. 26 *Perf. 11½*

1422	A540	20h vio & lt grn	.25	.25
1423	A540	30h blk & sal pink	.25	.25
1424	A540	60h slate & lilac	.35	.25
1425	A540	80h dk pur & lt bl	.35	.25
1426	A540	1k blk & vio	.40	.25
1427	A540	1.20k red & bl	1.75	.25
		Nos. 1422-1427 (6)	3.35	1.50

Issued to publicize American and Russian achievements in space research.

Badger A541

Game Animals: 40h, Red deer, vert. 60h, Lynx. 80h, Hare. 1k, Red fox. 1.20k, Brown bear, vert. 2k, Wild boar.

1966, Nov. 28 **Litho.** *Perf. 13½*

1428	A541	30h multi	.60	.25
1429	A541	40h multi	.60	.25
1430	A541	60h multi	.50	.25
1431	A541	80h multi *(europaens)*	1.25	.25
a.		80h multi *(europaeus)*	6.00	3.50
1432	A541	1k multi	.90	.30
1433	A541	1.20k multi	1.25	.50
1434	A541	2k multi	3.00	1.25
		Nos. 1428-1434 (7)	8.10	3.05

The sheet of 50 of the 80h contains 40 with misspelling "europaens" and 10 with "europaeus."

"Spring" by Vaclav Hollar, 1607-77 A542

Paintings: No. 1436, Portrait of Mrs. F. Wussin, by Jan Kupecky (1667-1740). No. 1437, Snow Owl by Karel Purkyne (1834-1868). No. 1438, Tulips by Vaclav Spála (1885-1964). No. 1439, Recruit by Ludovít Fulla (1902-1980).

1966, Dec. 8 **Engr.** *Perf. 14*

1435	A542	1k black	3.75	3.50
1436	A542	1k multicolored	5.25	1.90
1437	A542	1k multicolored	2.40	1.90
1438	A542	1k multicolored	2.40	1.90
1439	A542	1k multicolored	19.00	16.00
		Nos. 1435-1439 (5)	32.80	25.20

Printed in sheets of 4 stamps and 2 labels. The labels in sheet of No. 1435 are inscribed "Vaclav Hollar 1607-1677" in fancy frame. Other labels are blank. Value, set $135.

See No. 1484.

Symbolic Bird — A543

Engraved and Photogravure

1966, Dec. 17 *Perf. 11½*

1440	A543	1k dp blue & yel	1.25	.80

Issued for Stamp Day.

Youth — A544

1967, Jan. 16 *Perf. 11½*

1441	A544	30h ver & lt bl	.30	.25

5th Cong. of the Czechoslovak Youth Org.

Symbolic Flower and Machinery A545

1967, Jan. 16

1442	A545	30h carmine & yel	.30	.25

6th Trade Union Congress, Prague.

Parents with Dead Child — A545a

1967, Jan. 16 *Perf. 11½*

1442A	A545a	60h blk & sal	.30	.25

"Peace and Freedom in Viet Nam."

View of Jihlava and Tourist Year Emblem A546

Views and Tourist Year Emblem: 40h, Spielberg Castle and churches, Brno. 1.20k, Danube, castle and churches, Bratislava. 1.60k, Vlatava River bridges, Hradcany and churches, Prague.

1967, Feb. 13 **Engr.** *Perf. 11½*

Size: 40x23mm

1443	A546	30h brown violet	.25	.25
1444	A546	40h maroon	.25	.25

Size: 75x30mm

1445	A546	1.20k violet blue	.60	.25
1446	A546	1.60k black	2.00	.80
		Nos. 1443-1446 (4)	3.10	1.55

International Tourist Year, 1967.

Black-tailed Godwit — A547

Birds: 40h, Shoveler, horiz. 60h, Purple heron. 80h, Penduline tit. 1k, Avocet. 1.40k, Black stork. 1.60k, Tufted duck, horiz.

1967, Feb. 20 **Litho.** *Perf. 13½*

1447	A547	30h multi	.75	.30
1448	A547	40h multi	.75	.30
1449	A547	60h multi	.75	.30
1450	A547	80h multi	.75	.30
1451	A547	1k multi	.75	.30
1452	A547	1.40k multi	1.40	.60
1453	A547	1.60k multi	2.75	1.20
		Nos. 1447-1453 (7)	7.90	3.30

Solar Research and Satellite — A548

Space Research: 40h, Space craft, rocket and construction of station. 60h, Man on moon and orientation system. 1k, Exploration of solar system and rocket. 1.20k, Lunar satellites and moon photograph. 1.60k, Planned lunar architecture and moon landing.

Engraved and Photogravure

1967, Mar. 24 *Perf. 11½*

1454	A548	30h yel & dk red	.30	.25
1455	A548	40h vio bl & blk	.45	.25
1456	A548	60h lilac & grn	.45	.25
1457	A548	1k brt pink & sl	.45	.25
1458	A548	1.20k lt violet & blk	.70	.25
1459	A548	1.60k brn lake & blk	2.10	.60
		Nos. 1454-1459 (6)	4.45	1.85

Gothic Painting, by Master Theodoric A549

Designs: 40h, "Burning of Master Hus," from Litomerice Hymnal. 60h, Modern glass sculpture. 80h, "The Shepherdess and the Chimney Sweep," Andersen fairy tale, painting by J. Trnka. 1k, Section of pressure vessel from atomic power station. 1.20k, Three ceramic figurines, by P. Rada. 3k, Montreal skyline and EXPO '67 emblem.

1967, Apr. 10 **Engr.** *Perf. 14*

Size: 37x23mm

1460	A549	30h multi	.25	.25
1461	A549	40h multi	.25	.25
1462	A549	60h multi	.25	.25
1463	A549	80h multi	.25	.25
1464	A549	1k multi	1.00	.25
1465	A549	1.20k multi	1.25	.60
		Nos. 1460-1465 (6)	3.25	1.85

Souvenir Sheet

Perf. 11½

Size: 40x30mm

1466	A549	3k multi	3.00	2.50

EXPO '67, International Exhibition, Montreal, Apr. 28-Oct. 27, 1967.

Nos. 1460-1465 were each issued in a miniature sheet of 10 stamps. Value, set $50.

Examples of No. 1466 imperf. were not issued.

Canoe Race A550

Women Playing Basketball — A551

No. 1468, Wheels, dove & emblems of Warsaw, Berlin, Prague. 1.60k, Canoe slalom.

Perf. 12x11½, 11½x12

1967, Apr. 17 **Engr. & Photo.**

1467	A550	60h black & brt bl	.25	.25
1468	A550	60h black & salmon	.25	.25
1469	A551	60h blk & grnsh bl	.25	.25
1470	A551	1.60k black & brt vio	1.10	.55
		Nos. 1467-1470 (4)	1.85	1.30

No. 1467, 5th Intl. Wild-Water Canoeing Championships; No. 1468, 20th Warsaw-Berlin-Prague Bicycle Race; No. 1469, Women's Basketball Championships; No. 1470, 10th Intl. Water Slalom Championships.

"Golden Street" — A552

Designs: 60h, Interior of Hall of King Wenceslas. 5k, St. Matthew, from illuminated manuscript, 11th century.

1967, May 9 *Perf. 11½x11*

1471	A552	30h rose claret	.25	.25
1472	A552	60h bluish black	.50	.25

Souvenir Sheet

Perf. 11½

1473 A552 5k multicolored 2.60 2.40

Issued to publicize the Castle of Prague.

Stylized Lyre with Flowers — A553

1967, May 10 *Perf. 11½*

1474 A553 60h dull pur & brt grn .30 .25

Prague Music Festival.

Old-New Synagogue, Prague — A554

30h, Detail from Torah curtain, 1593. 60h, Prague Printer's emblem, 1530. 1k, Mikulov jug, 1804. 1.40k, Memorial for Concentration Camp Victims 1939-45, Pincas Synagogue (menorah & tablet). 1.60k, Tombstone of David Gans, 1613.

1967, May 22 *Perf. 11½*

1475 A554 30h dull red & lt bl .30 .25
1476 A554 60h blk & lt grn .25 .25
1477 A554 1k dk bl & rose lil .35 .25
1478 A554 1.20k dk brn & mar .65 .25
1479 A554 1.40k black & yellow .55 .25
1480 A554 1.60k green & yel 4.50 2.75
Nos. 1475-1480 (6) 6.60 4.00

Issued to show Jewish relics. The items shown on the 30h, 60h and 1k are from the State Jewish Museum, Prague.

"Lidice" — A555

1967, June 9 Unwmk. *Perf. 11½*

1481 A555 30h black & brt rose .30 .25

Destruction of Lidice by the Nazis, 25th anniv.

Prague Architecture — A556

1967, June 10 Engr. & Photo.

1482 A556 1k black & gold .35 .25

Issued to publicize the 9th Congress of the International Union of Architects, Prague.

Peter Bezruc A557

1967, June 21

1483 A557 60h dull rose & blk .30 .25

Peter Bezruc, poet & writer, birth cent.

Painting Type of 1966

2k, Henri Rousseau (1844-1910), self-portrait.

1967, June 22 Engr. *Perf. 11½*

1484 A542 2k multicolored 2.00 1.60

Praga 68, World Stamp Exhibition, Prague, June 22-July 7, 1968.

Printed in sheets of 4 stamps (2x2), separated by horizontal gutter with inscription and picture of Natl. Gallery, site of Praga 68. Value, $10.

View of Skalitz — A558

No. 1486, Mining tower & church steeple, Pribram. No. 1487, Hands holding book & view of Presov.

1967, Aug. 21 Engr. *Perf. 11½*

1485 A558 30h violet blue .25 .25
1486 A558 30h slate green .25 .25
1487 A558 30h claret .25 .25
Nos. 1485-1487 (3) .75 .75

Towns of Skalitz, Pribram, Presov, annivs.

Colonnade and Spring, Karlovy Vary and Communications Emblem — A559

1967, Aug. 21 Engr. & Photo.

1488 A559 30h violet bl & gold .30 .25

5th Sports & Cultural Festival of the Employees of the Ministry of Communications, Karlovy Vary.

Ondrejov Observatory and Galaxy — A560

1967, Aug. 22 Engr.

1489 A560 60h vio bl, rose lil & sil 1.50 .25

13th Cong. of the Intl. Astronomical Union.

No. 1489 was issued in a sheet of 10 stamps. Value, set $60.

Orchid — A561

Flowers from the Botanical Gardens: 30h, Cobaea scandens. 40h, Lycaste deppei. 60h, Glottiphyllum davisii. 1k, Anthurium. 1.20k, Rhodocactus. 1.40k, Moth orchid.

1967, Aug. 30 Litho. *Perf. 12½*

1490 A561 20h multicolored .30 .25
1491 A561 30h pink & multi .30 .25
1492 A561 40h multicolored .45 .25
1493 A561 60h lt blue & multi .45 .25
1494 A561 1k multicolored .60 .25
1495 A561 1.20k lt yellow & multi .65 .30
1496 A561 1.40k multicolored 1.75 .70
Nos. 1490-1496 (7) 4.50 2.25

Red Squirrel A562

Animals from the Tatra National Park: 60h, Wild cat. 1k, Ermine. 1.20k, Dormouse. 1.40k, Hedgehog. 1.60k, Pine marten.

Engraved and Photogravure

1967, Sept. 25 *Perf. 11½*

1497 A562 30h black, yel & org .35 .25
1498 A562 60h black & buff .35 .25
1499 A562 1k black & lt blue .40 .25
1500 A562 1.20k brn, pale grn & yel .50 .25
1501 A562 1.40k blk, pink & yel .55 .25
1502 A562 1.60k black, org & yel 2.75 1.25
Nos. 1497-1502 (6) 4.90 2.50

Rockets and Weapons — A563

1967, Oct. 6 Engr. *Perf. 11½*

1503 A563 30h slate green .30 .25

Day of the Czechoslovak People's Army.

Cruiser "Aurora" Firing at Winter Palace A564

Designs: 60h, Hammer and sickle emblems and Red Star, vert. 1k, Hands reaching for hammer and sickle, vert.

1967, Nov. 7 Engr. & Photo.

1504 A564 30h black & dk car .25 .25
1505 A564 60h black & dk car .25 .25
1506 A564 1k black & dk car .25 .25
Nos. 1504-1506 (3) .75 .75

Russian October Revolution, 50th anniv.

The Conjurer, by Frantisek Tichy A565

Paintings: 80h, Don Quixote, by Cyprian Majernik. 1k, Promenade in the Park, by Norbert Grund. 1.20k, Self-portrait, by Peter J. Brandl. 1.60k, Saints from Jan of Jeren Epitaph, by Czech Master of 1395.

1967, Nov. 13 Engr. *Perf. 11½*

1507 A565 60h multi .35 .25
1508 A565 80h multi .50 .30
1509 A565 1k multi .75 .50
1510 A565 1.20k multi .75 .50
1511 A565 1.60k multi 3.25 2.75
Nos. 1507-1511 (5) 5.60 4.30

Nos. 1507-1511 were issued in sheets of 4. Value, set $24.

See Nos. 1589-1593, 1658-1662, 1711-1715, 1779-1783, 1847-1851, 1908-1913, 2043-2047, 2090-2093, 2147-2151, 2265-2269, 2335-2339, 2386-2390, 2437-2441, 2534-2538, 2586-2590, 2634-2638, 2810-2813, 2843-2847, 2872-2874, 2908-2910, 2936-2938, 2973-2975, 2995, 3001-3002, 3028-3030, 3054-3055, 3075-3076, 3105-3107, 3133-3135, 3160-3162, 3188-3190, 3224-3226, 3233, 3255-3257, 3287-3289, 3323-3325, 3359-3361, 3401-3402, 3435-3436, 3478-3480, 3518-3520, 3552-3553, 3591-3593, 3616, 3618, 3656-3658, 3680, 3690-3692, 3726-3727, 3729, 3774-3776, 3794-3795, 3810-3811.

Pres. Antonin Novotny — A566

1967, Dec. 9 Engr. *Perf. 11½*

1512 A566 2k blue gray 1.40 .25
1513 A566 3k brown 1.40 .25

Czechoslovakia Nos. 65, 71 and 81 of 1920 — A567

1967, Dec. 18

1514 A567 1k maroon & silver 1.60 1.10

Issued for Stamp Day.

Symbolic Flag and Dates — A568

1968, Jan. 15 Engr. *Perf. 11½*

1515 A568 30h red, dk bl & ultra .75 .25

50th anniversary of Czechoslovakia.

No. 1515 was issued in a sheet of 10. Value, $30.

Figure Skating and Olympic Rings — A569

Olympic Rings and: 1k, Ski course. 1.60k, Toboggan chute. 2k, Ice hockey.

1968, Jan. 29 Engr. & Photo.

1516 A569 60h blk, yel & ocher .30 .25
1517 A569 1k ol grn, lt bl & lem .55 .25
1518 A569 1.60k blk, lil & bl grn .70 .25
1519 A569 2k blk, ap grn & lt bl 1.10 .25
Nos. 1516-1519 (4) 2.65 1.00

10th Winter Olympic Games, Grenoble, France, Feb. 6-18.

Factories and Rising Sun — A570

Design: 60h, Workers and banner.

1968, Feb. 25 *Perf. 11½x12*

1520 A570 30h car & dk bl .25 .25
1521 A570 60h car & dk bl .25 .25

20th anniversary of February Revolution.

Map of Battle of Sokolovo A571

Human Rights Flame — A572

1968, Mar. 8 *Perf. 11½*

1522 A571 30h blk, brt bl & car .40 .25

Engr.

1523 A572 1k rose carmine 1.10 .40

25th anniv. of the Battle of Sokolovo, Mar. 8, 1943, against the German Army, No. 1522; Intl. Human Rights Year, No. 1523.

Janko Kral and Liptovsky Mikulas — A573

Karl Marx — A574

Girl's Head — A575

Arms and Allegory — A576

Head — A577

1968, Mar. 25 **Engr.**

1524 A573 30h green .30 .25
1525 A574 30h claret .25 .25

Engraved and Photogravure

1526 A575 30h dk red & gold .25 .25
1527 A576 30h dk blue & dp org .25 .25
1528 A577 1k multicolored .50 .25
Nos. 1524-1528 (5) 1.55 1.25

The writer Janko Kral and the Slovak town Liptovsky Mikulas (No. 1524); 150th anniv. of the birth of Karl Marx (No. 1525); cent. of the cornerstone laying of the Prague Natl. Theater (No. 1526); 150th anniv. of the Prague Natl. Museum (No. 1527); 20th anniv. of WHO (1k).

Symbolic Radio Waves A578

No. 1530, Symbolic television screens.

1968, Apr. 29 *Perf. 11½*

1529 A578 30h blk, car & vio bl .25 .25
1530 A578 30h blk, car & vio bl .25 .25

45th anniv. of Czechoslovak broadcasting (No. 1529), 15th anniv. of television (No. 1530).

Olympic Rings, Mexican Sculpture and Diver — A579

Olympic Rings and: 40h, Runner and "The Sanctification of Quetzalcoatl." 60h, Volleyball and Mexican ornaments. 1k, Czechoslovak and Mexican Olympic emblems and carved altar. 1.60k, Soccer and ornaments. 2k, View of Hradcany, weather vane and key.

1968, Apr. 30

1531 A579 30h black, bl & car .25 .25
1532 A579 40h multi .25 .25
1533 A579 60h multi .25 .25
1534 A579 1k multi .35 .25
1535 A579 1.60k multi .35 .25
1536 A579 2k black & multi 1.75 .40
Nos. 1531-1536 (6) 3.20 1.65

19th Olympic Games, Mexico City, 10/12-27.

Prague Castle Types of 1966

Designs: 30h, Tombstone of Bretislav I. 60h, Romanesque door knocker, St. Wenceslas Chapel. 5k, Head of St. Peter, mosaic from Golden Gate of St. Vitus Cathedral.

1968, May 9 *Perf. 11½*

1537 A527 30h multicolored .40 .25
1538 A527 60h black, red & cit .40 .25

Souvenir Sheet

Engr.

1539 A528 5k multicolored 2.75 2.75

Pres. Ludvik Svoboda — A580

1968-70 **Engr.** *Perf. 11½*

1540 A580 30h ultramarine .25 .25
1540A A580 50h green ('70) .25 .25
1541 A580 60h maroon .25 .25
1541A A580 1k rose car ('70) .30 .25
Nos. 1540-1541A (4) 1.05 1.00

Shades exist of No. 1541A.

"Business," Sculpture by Otto Gutfreund A581

Cabaret Performer, by Frantisek Kupka — A582

Designs (The New Prague): 40h, Broadcasting Corporation Building. 60h, New Parliament. 1.40k, Tapestry by Jan Bauch "Prague 1787." 3k, Presidential standard.

Engr. & Photo.; Engr. (2k)

1968, June 5

1542 A581 30h black & multi .25 .25
1543 A581 40h black & multi .25 .25
1544 A581 60h dk brn & multi .25 .25
1545 A581 1.40k dk brn & multi .40 .25
1546 A582 2k indigo & multi .85 .70
1547 A581 3k black & multi .85 .30
Nos. 1542-1547 (6) 2.85 2.00

Designs (The Old Prague): 30h, St. George's Basilica. 60h, Renaissance fountain. 1k, Villa America-Dvorak Museum, 18th cent. building. 1.60k, Emblem from the House of Three Violins, 18th cent. 2k, Josefina, by Josef Manes. 3k, Emblem of Prague, 1475.

1968, June 21 *Perf. 11½*

1548 A581 30h green, gray & yel .25 .25
1549 A581 60h dk vio, ap grn & gold .25 .25
1550 A581 1k black, lt bl & pink .30 .25
1551 A581 1.60k slate grn & multi .55 .25
1552 A582 2k brown & multi 1.25 .60
1553 A581 3k blk, yel, bl & pink 1.25 .60
Nos. 1548-1553 (6) 3.85 2.20

Nos. 1542-1553 publicized the Praga 68 Philatelic Exhibition. Nos. 1542-1545, 1547-1551, 1553 issued in sheets of 15 + 15 labels with Praga 68 emblem and inscription.

Nos. 1546, 1552 issued in sheets of 4 (2x2) with one horizontal label between top and bottom rows showing Praga 68 emblem. Values for sheets of 4, each $8.

Souvenir Sheet

View of Prague and Emblems — A583

Engraved and Photogravure

1968, June 22 *Imperf.*

1554 A583 10k multicolored 3.25 2.50

Praga 68 and 50th anniv. of Czechoslovak postage stamps. Sold only together with a 5k admission ticket to the Praga 68 philatelic Exhibition. Value $20.

Madonna with the Rose Garlands, by Dürer — A584

1968, July 6 *Perf. 11½*

1555 A584 5k multicolored 3.75 2.75

FIP Day, July 6. Issued in sheets of 4 (2x2) with one horizontal label between, showing Praga 68 emblem. Value, $20.

Stagecoach on Rails — A585

Design: 1k, Steam and electric locomotives.

1968, Aug. 6

1556 A585 60h multicolored .45 .25
1557 A585 1k multicolored 1.60 .60

No. 1556: 140th anniv. of the horse-drawn railroad Ceské Budejovice to Linz; No. 1557: cent. of the Ceské Budejovice to Plzen railroad.

6th Intl. Slavonic Cong. in Prague — A586

1968, Aug. 7 *Perf. 11½*

1558 A586 30h vio blue & car .40 .25

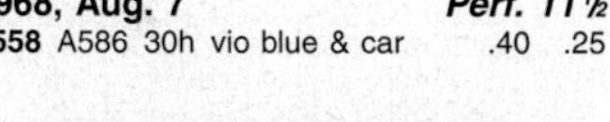

Ardspach Rocks and Ammonite — A587

60h, Basalt formation & frog skeleton fossil. 80h, Rocks, basalt veins & polished agate. 1k, Pelecypoda (fossil shell) & Belanske Tatra mountains. 1.60k, Trilobite & Barrande rock formation.

1968, Aug. 8

1559 A587 30h black & citron .25 .25
1560 A587 60h black & rose cl .25 .25
1561 A587 80h black, lt vio & pink .30 .25
1562 A587 1k black & lt blue .40 .25
1563 A587 1.60k black & bister 1.40 .65
Nos. 1559-1563 (5) 2.60 1.65

Issued to publicize the 23rd International Geological Congress, Prague, Aug. 8-Sept. 3.

Raising Slovak Flag A588

60h, Slovak partisans, and mountain.

1968, Sept. 9 Engr. *Perf. 11½*

1564 A588 30h ultra .25 .25
1565 A588 60h red .25 .25

No. 1564 for the Slovak Natl. Council, No. 1565 the 120th anniv. of the Slovak national uprising.

Flowerpot, by Jiri Schlessinger (age 10) — A589

Drawings by Children in Terezin Concentration Camp: 30h, Jew and Guard, by Jiri Beutler (age 10). 60h, Butterflies, by Kitty Brunnerova (age 11).

Engraved and Photogravure

1968, Sept. 30 *Perf. 11½*

Size: 30x23mm

1566 A589 30h blk, buff & rose lil .30 .25
1567 A589 60h black & multi .30 .25

Perf. 12x11½

Size: 41x23mm

1568 A589 1k black & multi .80 .25
Nos. 1566-1568 (3) 1.40 .75

30th anniversary of Munich Pact.

Arms of Regional Capitals A590

Arms of Prague — A591

1968, Oct. 21 *Perf. 11½*

1569 A590 60h Banská Bystrica .25 .25
1570 A590 60h Bratislava .25 .25
1571 A590 60h Brno .25 .25
1572 A590 60h Ceské Budejovice .25 .25
1573 A590 60h Hradec Králové .25 .25
1574 A590 60h Kosice .25 .25
1575 A590 60h Ostrava (horse) .25 .25
1576 A590 60h Plzen .25 .25
1577 A590 60h Ustí nad Labem .25 .25

Perf. 11½x16

1578 A591 1k shown .25 .25
Nos. 1569-1578 (10) 2.50 2.50

No. 1578 issued in sheets of 10. Value, $40.
See Nos. 1652-1657, 1742-1747, 1886-1888, 2000-2001.

Flag and Linden Leaves A592

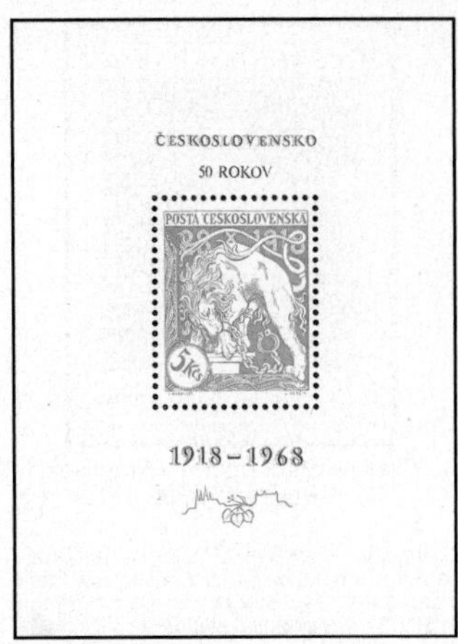

Bohemian Lion Breaking Chains (Type SP1 of 1919) — A593

Design: 60h, Map of Czechoslovakia, linden leaves, Hradcany in Prague and Castle in Bratislava.

1968, Oct. 28 *Perf. 12x11½*

1579 A592 30h dp blue & mag .30 .25
1580 A592 60h blk, gold, red & ultra .30 .25

Souvenir Sheet

Engr.

Perf. 11½x12

1581 A593 5k red 3.50 2.75

Founding of Czechoslovakia, 50th anniv.

Ernest Hemingway — A594

Caricatures: 30h, Karel Capek (1890-1938), writer. 40h, George Bernard Shaw. 60h, Maxim Gorki. 1k, Pablo Picasso. 1.20k, Taikan Yokoyama (1868-1958), painter. 1.40k, Charlie Chaplin.

Engraved and Photogravure

1968, Nov. 18 *Perf. 11½x12*

1582 A594 20h black, org & red .25 .25
1583 A594 30h black & multi .30 .25
1584 A594 40h blk, lic & car .30 .25
1585 A594 60h black, sky bl & grn .25 .25
1586 A594 1k black, brn & yel .45 .25
1587 A594 1.20k black, dp car & vio .45 .25
1588 A594 1.40k black, brn & dp org 1.75 .40
Nos. 1582-1588 (7) 3.75 1.90

Cultural personalities of the 20th cent. and UNESCO. See Nos. 1628-1633.

Painting Type of 1967

Czechoslovakian Art: 60h, Cleopatra II, by Jan Zrzavy (1890-1977). 80h, Black Lake (man and horse), by Jan Preisler (1872-1918). 1.20k, Giovanni Francisci as a Volunteer, by Peter Michal Bohun (1822-1879). 1.60k, Princess Hyacinth, by Alfons Mucha (1860-1939). 3k, Madonna and Child, woodcarving, 1518, by Master Paul of Levoca.

1968, Nov. 29 Engr. *Perf. 11½*

1589 A565 60h multi .75 .35
1590 A565 80h multi .75 .35
1591 A565 1.20k multi .75 .35
1592 A565 1.60k multi .75 .35
1593 A565 3k multi 2.50 2.50
Nos. 1589-1593 (5) 5.50 3.90

Nos. 1589-1593 were issued in sheets of 4. Value, set $25.

Cinderlad — A595

Slovak Fairy Tales: 60h, The Proud Lady. 80h, The Ruling Knight. 1k, Good Day, Little Bench. 1.20k, The Spellbound Castle. 1.80k, The Miraculous Hunter. The designs are from illustrations by Ludovit Fulla for "Slovak Stories."

1968, Dec. 18 Engr. & Photo.

1594 A595 30h multi .25 .25
1595 A595 60h multi .25 .25
1596 A595 80h multi .40 .25
1597 A595 1k multi .55 .25
1598 A595 1.20k multi .55 .25
1599 A595 1.80k multi 1.50 .65
Nos. 1594-1599 (6) 3.50 1.90

Czechoslovakia Nos. 2 and 3 — A596

1968, Dec. 18

1600 A596 1k violet bl & gold .95 .65

50th anniv. of Czechoslovakian postage stamps.

Crescent, Cross and Lion and Sun Emblems — A597

60h, 12 crosses in circles forming large cross.

1969, Jan. 31 *Perf. 11½*

1601 A597 60h black, red & gold .25 .25
1602 A597 1k black, ultra & red .35 .25

No. 1601: 50th anniv. of the Czechoslovak Red Cross. No. 1602: 50th anniv. of the League of Red Cross Societies.

ILO Emblem — A598

1969, Jan. 31

1603 A598 1k black & gray .30 .25

50th anniv. of the ILO.

Cheb Pistol A599

Historical Firearms: 40h, Italian pistol with Dutch decorations, c. 1600. 60h, Wheellock rifle from Matej Kubik workshop c. 1720. 1k, Flintlock pistol, Devieuxe workshop, Liege, c. 1760. 1.40k, Duelling pistols, from Lebeda workshop, Prague, c. 1835. 1.60k, Derringer pistols, US, c. 1865.

1969, Feb. 18

1604 A599 30h black & multi .25 .25
1605 A599 40h black & multi .25 .25
1606 A599 60h black & multi .25 .25
1607 A599 1k black & multi .25 .25
1608 A599 1.40k black & multi .35 .25
1609 A599 1.60k black & multi 1.40 .25
Nos. 1604-1609 (6) 2.75 1.50

Bratislava Castle, Muse and Book — A600

No. 1611, Science symbols & emblem (Brno University). No. 1612, Harp, laurel & musicians' names. No. 1613, Theatrical scene. No. 1614, Arms of Slovakia, banner & blossoms. No. 1615, School, outstretched hands & woman with linden leaves.

1969, Mar. 24 Engr. *Perf. 11½*

1610 A600 60h violet blue .25 .25

Engraved and Photogravure

1611 A600 60h blk, gold & slate .25 .25
1612 A600 60h gold, blue, blk & red .25 .25
1613 A600 60h black & rose red .25 .25
1614 A600 60h rose red, sil & bl .25 .25
1615 A600 60h black & gold .25 .25
Nos. 1610-1615 (6) 1.50 1.50

50th anniv. of: Komensky University in Bratislava (No. 1610); Brno University (No. 1611); Brno Conservatory of Music (No. 1612); Slovak Natl. Theater (No. 1613); Slovak Soviet Republic (No. 1614); cent. of the Zniev Gymnasium (academic high school) (No. 1615).

Baldachin-top Car and Four-seat Coupé of 1900-1905 — A601

Designs: 1.60k, Laurin & Klement Voiturette, 1907, and L & K touring car with American top, 1907. 1.80k, First Prague bus, 1907, and sectionalized Skoda bus, 1967.

1969, Mar. 25 Engr. & Photo.

1616 A601 30h blk, lil & lt grn .60 .25
1617 A601 1.60k blk, org brn & lt bl .75 .25
1618 A601 1.80k multi 1.40 .60
Nos. 1616-1618 (3) 2.75 1.10

Peace, by Ladislav Guderna — A602

1969, Apr. 21 *Perf. 11*

1619 A602 1.60k multi .50 .35

20th anniv. of the Peace Movement. Issued in sheets of 15 stamps and 5 tabs. Stamp with tab $2.50.

Horse and Rider, by Vaclav Hollar — A603

Old Engravings of Horses: 30h, Prancing Stallion, by Hendrik Goltzius, horiz. 80h, Groom Leading Horse, by Matthäus Merian, horiz. 1.80k, Horse and Soldier, by Albrecht Dürer. 2.40k, Groom and Horse, by Johann E. Ridinger.

1969, Apr. 24 ***Perf. 11x11½, 11½x11***

Yellowish Paper

1620 A603 30h dark brown .25 .25
1621 A603 80h violet brown .25 .25
1622 A603 1.60k slate .45 .25
1623 A603 1.80k sepia .50 .25
1624 A603 2.40k multi 2.40 .60
Nos. 1620-1624 (5) 3.85 1.60

M. R. Stefánik as Astronomy Professor and French General — A604

1969, May 4 **Engr.** ***Perf. 11½***

1625 A604 60h rose claret .40 .25

Gen. Milan R. Stefánik, 50th death anniv.

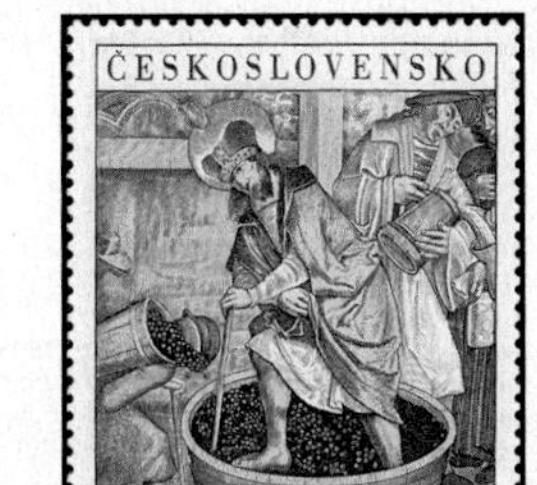

St. Wenceslas Pressing Wine, Mural by the Master of Litomerice — A605

Design: No. 1627, Coronation banner of the Estates, 1723, with St. Wenceslas and coats of arms of Bohemia and Czech Crown lands.

1969, May 9 **Engr.** ***Perf. 11½***

1626 A605 3k multicolored 2.00 1.40
1627 A605 3k multicolored 2.00 1.40

Issued to publicize the art treasures of the Castle of Prague.

Issued in sheets of 4. Value, set $20.

See Nos. 1689-1690.

Caricature Type of 1968

Caricatures: 30h, Pavol Orszagh Hviezdoslav (1849-1921), Slovak writer. 40h, Gilbert K. Chesterton (1874-1936), English writer. 60h, Vladimir Mayakovski (1893-1930), Russian poet. 1k, Henri Matisse (1869-1954), French painter. 1.80k, Ales Hrdlicka (1869-1943), Czech-born American anthropologist. 2k, Franz Kafka (1883-1924), Austrian writer.

Engraved and Photogravure

1969, June 17 ***Perf. 11½x12***

1628 A594 30h blk, red & bl .25 .25
1629 A594 40h blk, bl & lt vio .25 .25
1630 A594 60h blk, rose & yel .25 .25
1631 A594 1k black & multi .25 .25
1632 A594 1.80k blk, ultra & ocher .25 .25
1633 A594 2k blk, yel & brt grn 1.50 .50
Nos. 1628-1633 (6) 2.75 1.75

Issued to honor cultural personalities of the 20th century and UNESCO.

"Music," by Alfons Mucha — A606

Paintings by Mucha: 60h, "Painting." 1k, "Dance." 2.40k, "Ruby" and "Amethyst."

1969, July 14 ***Perf. 11½x11***

Size: 30x49mm

1634 A606 30h black & multi .80 .25
1635 A606 60h black & multi .80 .25
1636 A606 1k black & multi 1.00 .25

Size: 39x51mm

1637 A606 2.40k black & multi 2.00 1.25
Nos. 1634-1637 (4) 4.60 2.00

Alfons Mucha (1860-1930), painter and stamp designer (Type A1).

No. 1637 was issued in sheets of 4. Value $12.50.

Pres. Svoboda and Partisans A607

No. 1639, Slovak fighters and mourners.

1969, Aug. 29 ***Perf. 11***

1638 A607 30h ol grn & red, *yel* .25 .25
1639 A607 30h vio bl & red, *yel* .25 .25

25th anniversary of the Slovak uprising and of the Battle of Dukla.

Tatra Mountain Stream and Gentians — A608

Designs: 60h, Various views in Tatra Mountains. No. 1644, Mountain pass and gentians. No. 1645, Houses, Krivan Mountain and autumn crocuses.

1969, Sept. 8 **Engr.** ***Perf. 11***

Size: 71x33mm

1640 A608 60h gray .25 .25
1641 A608 60h dark blue .25 .25
1642 A608 60h dull gray vio .25 .25

Perf. 11½

Size: 40x23mm

1643 A608 1.60k multi .55 .25
1644 A608 1.60k multi 1.25 .50
1645 A608 1.60k multi .55 .25
Nos. 1640-1645 (6) 3.10 1.75

20th anniv. of the creation of the Tatra Mountains Natl. Park.

Nos. 1640-1642 are printed in sheets of 15 (3x5) with 5 labels showing mountain plants. Value, set with tabs $2.50.

Nos. 1643-1645 were issued in sheets of 10. Value, $70.

Bronze Belt Ornaments A609

Archaeological Treasures from Bohemia and Moravia: 30h, Gilt ornament with 6 masks. 1k, Jeweled earrings. 1.80k, Front and back of lead cross with Greek inscription. 2k, Gilt strap ornament with human figure.

Engraved and Photogravure

1969, Sept. 30 ***Perf. 11½x11***

1646 A609 20h gold & multi .25 .25
1647 A609 30h gold & multi .25 .25
1648 A609 1k red & multi .25 .25
1649 A609 1.80k dull org & multi .45 .25
1650 A609 2k gold & multi 1.75 .25
Nos. 1646-1650 (5) 2.95 1.25

"Mail Circling the World" A610

1969, Oct. 1 **Engr.** ***Perf. 12***

1651 A610 3.20k multi .95 .60

16th UPU Cong., Tokyo, Oct. 1-Nov. 14.

Issued in sheets of 4. Value $9.

Coat of Arms Type of 1968

Engraved and Photogravure

1969, Oct. 25 ***Perf. 11½***

1652 A590 50h Bardejov .25 .25
1653 A590 50h Hranice .25 .25
1654 A590 50h Kezmarok .25 .25
1655 A590 50h Krnov .25 .25
1656 A590 50h Litomerice .25 .25
1657 A590 50h Manetin .25 .25
Nos. 1652-1657 (6) 1.50 1.50

Painting Type of 1967

Designs: 60h, Requiem, 1944, by Frantisek Muzika. 1k, Resurrection, 1380, by the Master of the Trebon Altar. 1.60k, Crucifixion, 1950, by Vincent Hloznik. 1.80k, Girl with Doll, 1863, by Julius Bencur. 2.20k, St. Jerome, 1357-67, by Master Theodorik.

1969, Nov. 25 ***Perf. 11½***

1658 A565 60h multi .75 .25
1659 A565 1k multi .75 .25
1660 A565 1.60k multi .75 .40
1661 A565 1.80k multi .75 .40
1662 A565 2.20k multi 3.00 2.00
Nos. 1658-1662 (5) 6.00 3.30

Nos. 1658-1662 were each issued in sheets of 4. Value, set $30.

Symbolic Sheet of Stamps — A611

1969, Dec. 18 ***Perf. 11½x12***

1663 A611 1k dk brn, ultra & gold .30 .30

Issued for Stamp Day 1969.

Ski Jump — A612

Designs: 60h, Long distance skier. 1k, Ski jump and slope. 1.60k, Woman skier.

1970, Jan. 6 ***Perf. 11½***

1664 A612 50h multi .25 .25
1665 A612 60h multi .25 .25
1666 A612 1k multi .25 .25
1667 A612 1.60k multi .60 .30
Nos. 1664-1667 (4) 1.35 1.05

Intl. Ski Championships "Tatra 1970."

Ludwig van Beethoven — A613

Portraits: No. 1669, Friedrich Engels (1820-95), German socialist. No. 1670, Maximilian Hell (1720-92), Slovakian Jesuit and astronomer. No. 1671, Lenin, Russian Communist leader. No. 1672, Josef Manes (1820-71), Czech painter. No. 1673, Comenius (1592-1670), theologian and educator.

1970, Feb. 17 **Engr.** ***Perf. 11x11½***

1668 A613 40h black .25 .25
1669 A613 40h dull red .25 .25
1670 A613 40h yellow brn .25 .25
1671 A613 40h dull red .25 .25
1672 A613 40h brown .25 .25
1673 A613 40h black .25 .25
Nos. 1668-1673 (6) 1.50 1.50

Anniversaries of birth of Beethoven, Engels, Hell, Lenin and Manes, 300th anniv. of the death of Comenius, and to honor UNESCO.

Bells A614

80h, Machine tools & lathe. 1k, Folklore masks. 1.60k, Angel & Three Wise Men, 17th cent. icon from Koniec. 2k, View of Orlik Castle, 1787, by F. K. Wolf. 3k, "Passing through Koshu down to Mishima" from Hokusai's 36 Views of Fuji.

Engraved and Photogravure

1970, Mar. 13 ***Perf. 11½x11***

Size: 40x23mm

1674 A614 50h multi .25 .25
1675 A614 80h multi .25 .25
1676 A614 1k multi .25 .25

Size: 50x40mm

Perf. 11½

1677 A614 1.60k multi .35 .30
1678 A614 2k multi .45 .25
1679 A614 3k multi 2.10 .70
Nos. 1674-1679 (6) 3.65 2.00

EXPO '70 Intl. Exhib., Osaka, Japan, Mar. 15-Sept. 13, 1970.

Nos. 1674-1676 issued in sheets of 50, Nos. 1677-1679 in sheets of 4. Value, set of 3 sheets, $18.

Kosice Townhall, Laurel and Czechoslovak Arms — A615

1970, Apr. 5 ***Perf. 11***

1680 A615 60h slate, ver & gold .40 .25

Government's Kosice Program, 25th anniv.

"The Remarkable Horse" by Josef Lada — A616

Paintings by Josef Lada: 60h, Autumn, 1955, horiz. 1.80k, "The Water Sprite." 2.40k, Children in Winter, 1943, horiz.

1970, Apr. 21 ***Perf. 11½***

1681 A616 60h black & multi .30 .25
1682 A616 1k black & multi .45 .25
1683 A616 1.80k black & multi .75 .25
1684 A616 2.40k black & multi 1.50 .25
Nos. 1681-1684 (4) 3.00 1.00

Lenin — A617

Design: 60h, Lenin without cap, facing left.

1970, Apr. 22

1685	A617	30h dk red & gold	.25	.25
1686	A617	60h black & gold	.25	.25

Lenin (1870-1924), Russian communist leader.

Fighters on the Barricades — A618

No. 1688, Lilac, Russian tank and castle.

1970, May 5 ***Perf. 11x11½***

1687	A618	30h dull pur, gold & bl	.25	.25
1688	A618	30h dull grn, gold & red	.25	.25

No. 1687: 25th anniv. of the Prague uprising. No. 1688: 25th anniv. of the liberation of Czechoslovakia from the Germans.

Prague Castle Art Type of 1969

No. 1689, Bust of St. Vitus, 1486. No. 1690, Hermes and Athena, by Bartholomy Spranger (1546-1611), mural from White Tower.

1970, May 7 **Engr.** ***Perf. 11½***

1689	A605	3k maroon & multi	1.90	1.25
1690	A605	3k lt blue & multi	1.75	1.00

Nos. 1689-1690 were issued in sheets of 4. Value, set of 2 sheets, $18.

Compass Rose, UN Headquarters and Famous Buildings of the World — A619

Engraved and Photogravure

1970, June 26 ***Perf. 11***

1691	A619	1k black & multi	.40	.25

25th anniv. of the UN. Issued in sheets of 15 (3x5) and 5 labels showing UN emblem. Value of single with tab attached: unused $1; used 75c.

Cannon from 30 Years' War and Baron Munchhausen — A620

Historical Cannons: 60h, Cannon from Hussite war and St. Barbara. 1.20k, Cannon from Prussian-Austrian war, and legendary cannoneer Javurek. 1.80k, Early 20th century cannon and spaceship "La Colombiad" (Jules Verne). 2.40k, World War I cannon and "Good Soldier Schweik."

1970, Aug. 31 ***Perf. 11½***

1692	A620	30h black & multi	.25	.25
1693	A620	60h black & multi	.25	.25
1694	A620	1.20k black & multi	.25	.25
1695	A620	1.80k black & multi	.25	.25
1696	A620	2.40k black & multi	1.25	.25
		Nos. 1692-1696 (5)	2.25	1.25

"Rude Pravo" (Red Truth) A621

1970, Sept. 21 ***Perf. 11½x11***

1697	A621	60h car, gold & blk	.25	.25

50th anniv. of the Rude Pravo newspaper.

"Great Sun" House Sign and Old Town Tower Bridge, Prague — A622

60h, "Blue Lion" & Town Hall Tower, Brno. 1k, Gothic corner stone & Town Hall Tower, Bratislava. 1.40k, Coat of Arms & Gothic Tower, Bratislava, & medallion. 1.60k, Moravian Eagle & Gothic Town Hall Tower, Brno. 1.80k, "Black Sun" & "Green Frog" house signs & New Town Hall, Prague.

1970, Sept. 23 ***Perf. 11x11½***

1698	A622	40h black & multi	.25	.25
1699	A622	60h black & multi	.25	.25
1700	A622	1k black & multi	.25	.25
1701	A622	1.40k black & multi	1.40	.25
1702	A622	1.60k black & multi	.30	.25
1703	A622	1.80k black & multi	.80	.25
		Nos. 1698-1703 (6)	3.25	1.50

Germany-Uruguay Semifinal Soccer Match — A623

Designs: 20h, Sundisk Games' emblem and flags of participating nations. 60h, England-Czechoslovakia match and coats of arms. 1k, Romania-Czechoslovakia match and coats of arms. 1.20k, Brazil-Italy, final match and emblems. 1.80k, Brazil-Czechoslovakia match and emblems.

1970, Oct. 29 ***Perf. 11½***

1704	A623	20h blk & multi	.25	.25
1705	A623	40h blk & multi	.25	.25
1706	A623	60h blk & multi	.30	.25
1707	A623	1k blk & multi	.45	.25
1708	A623	1.20k blk & multi	.45	.25
1709	A623	1.80k blk & multi	1.50	.25
		Nos. 1704-1709 (6)	3.20	1.50

9th World Soccer Championships for the Jules Rimet Cup, Mexico City, 5/30-6/21.

Congress Emblem — A624

1970, Nov. 9 **Engr. & Photo.**

1710	A624	30h blk, gold, ultra & red	.25	.25

Congress of the Czechoslovak Socialist Youth Federation.

Painting Type of 1967

Paintings: 1k, Seated Mother, by Mikulas Galanda. 1.20k, Bridesmaid, by Karel Svolinsky. 1.40k, Walk by Night, 1944, by Frantisek Hudecek. 1.80k, Banska Bystrica Market, by Dominik Skutecky. 2.40k, Adoration of the Kings, from the Vysehrad Codex, 1085.

1970, Nov. 27 **Engr.** ***Perf. 11½***

1711	A565	1k multi	.35	.25
1712	A565	1.20k multi	.70	.30
1713	A565	1.40k multi	.35	.30
1714	A565	1.80k multi	.70	.30
1715	A565	2.40k multi	3.00	2.00
		Nos. 1711-1715 (5)	5.10	3.15

Nos. 1711-1715 were each issued in sheets of 4. Value, set $20.

Radar A625

Designs: 40h, Interkosmos 3, geophysical satellite. 60h, Kosmos meteorological satellite. 1k, Astronaut and Vostok satellite. No. 1720, Interkosmos 4, solar research satellite. No. 1720A, Space satellite (Sputnik) over city. 1.60k, Two-stage rocket on launching pad.

1970-71 **Engr. & Photo.** ***Perf. 11***

1716	A625	20h black & multi	.25	.25
1717	A625	40h black & multi	.25	.25
1718	A625	60h black & multi	.25	.25
1719	A625	1k black & multi	.25	.25
1720	A625	1.20k black & multi	.25	.25
1720A	A625	1.20k black & multi ('71)	.25	.25
1721	A625	1.60k black & multi	.90	.25
		Nos. 1716-1721 (7)	2.40	1.75

"Interkosmos," the collaboration of communist countries in various phases of space research.

Issued: No. 1720A, 11/15/71; others, 11/30/70.

Face of Christ on Veronica's Veil — A626

Slovak Ikons, 16th-18th Centuries: 60h, Adam and Eve in the Garden, vert. 2k, St. George and the Dragon. 2.80k, St. Michael, vert.

1970, Dec. 17 **Engr.** ***Perf. 11½***

Cream Paper

1722	A626	60h multi	.70	.35
1723	A626	1k multi	1.00	.35
1724	A626	2k multi	1.00	.70
1725	A626	2.80k multi	2.10	1.40
		Nos. 1722-1725 (4)	4.80	2.80

Nos. 1722-1725 were each issued in sheets of 4. Value, set $22.50.

Carrier Pigeon Type of 1920 — A627

Engraved and Photogravure

1970, Dec. 18 ***Perf. 11x11½***

1726	A627	1k red, blk & yel grn	.40	.30

Stamp Day.

Song of the Barricades, 1938, by Karel Stika — A628

Czech and Slovak Graphic Art: 50h, Fruit Grower's Barge, 1941, by Cyril Bouda. 60h, Moon (woman) Searching for Lilies of the Valley, 1913, by Jan Zrzavy. 1k, At the Edge of Town (working man and woman), 1931, by Koloman Sokol. 1.60k, Summer, 1641, by Vaclav Hollar. 2k, Gamekeeper and Shepherd of Orava Castle, 1847, by Peter M. Bohun.

Engr. & Photo.; Engr. (40h, 60h, 1k)

1971, Jan. 28 ***Perf. 11½***

1727	A628	40h brown	.25	.25
1728	A628	50h black & multi	.25	.25
1729	A628	60h slate	.25	.25
1730	A628	1k black	.30	.25
1731	A628	1.60k black & buff	.30	.25
1732	A628	2k black & multi	1.25	.25
		Nos. 1727-1732 (6)	2.60	1.50

Church of St. Bartholomew, Chrudim A629

Bell Tower, Hronsek A630

Designs: 1k, Roofs and folk art, Horácko. 1.60k, Saris Church. 2.40k, House, Jicin. 3k, House and folk art, Melnik. 5k, Watch Tower, Nachod. 5.40k, Baroque house, Posumavi. 6k, Cottage, Orava. 9k, Cottage, Turnov. 10k, Old houses, Liptov. 14k, House and wayside bell stand. 20k, Houses, Cicmany.

Engraved and Photogravure

1971-72 ***Perf. 11½x11, 11x11½***

1733	A630	1k multi	.25	.25
1734	A629	1.60k multi	1.50	.25
1735	A630	2k multi	2.10	.25
1736	A629	2.40k multi	1.10	.25
1736A	A630	3k multi ('72)	2.10	.25
1737	A629	3.60k multi	1.40	.25
1737A	A630	5k multi ('72)	2.10	.25
1738	A629	5.40k multi	.75	.25
1739	A630	6k multi	3.50	.25
1740	A630	9k multi	1.40	.25
1740A	A629	10k multi ('72)	2.10	.25
1741	A629	14k multi	2.25	.25
1741A	A629	20k multi ('72)	2.10	.30
		Nos. 1733-1741A (13)	22.65	3.30

Nos. 1736A, 1738, 1740 are horizontal.

See No. 2870.

Coat of Arms Type of 1968

1971, Mar. 26 ***Perf. 11½***

1742	A590	60h Zilina	.25	.25
1743	A590	60h Levoca	.25	.25
1744	A590	60h Ceska Trebova	.25	.25
1745	A590	60h Uhersky Brod	.25	.25
1746	A590	60h Trutnov	.25	.25
1747	A590	60h Karlovy Vary	.25	.25
		Nos. 1742-1747 (6)	1.50	1.50

"Fight of the Communards and Rise of the International" — A631

Design: No. 1749, World fight against racial discrimination, and "UNESCO."

1971, Mar. 18 ***Perf. 11***

1748	A631	1k multicolored	.30	.25

1749 A631 1k multicolored .30 .25

No. 1748 for cent. of the Paris Commune. No. 1749 for the Year against Racial Discrimination. Issued in sheets of 15 stamps and 5 labels. Value for single with attached tab, each $1.

A632

Edelweiss, mountaineering map & equipment.

1971, Apr. 27 *Perf. 11½x11*
1750 A632 30h multicolored .25 .25

50th anniversary of Slovak Alpine Club.

A633

1971, Apr. 27 *Perf. 11½*
1751 A633 30h Singer .25 .25

50th anniversary of Slovak Teachers' Choir.

Abbess' Crosier, 16th Century
A634

No. 1753, Allegory of Music, 16th cent. mural.

1971, May 9
1752 A634 3k gold & multi 1.90 1.40
1753 A634 3k blk, dk brn & buff 1.90 1.40

Nos. 1752-1753 were each issued in sheets of 4. Value, set $15.

See Nos. 1817-1818, 1884-1885, 1937-1938, 2040-2041, 2081-2082, 2114-2115, 2176-2177, 2238-2239, 2329-2330, 2384-2385, 2420-2421.

Lenin
A635

40h, Hammer & sickle allegory. 60h, Raised fists. 1k, Star, hammer & sickle.

1971, May 14 *Perf. 11*
1754 A635 30h blk, red & gold .25 .25
1755 A635 40h blk, ultra, red & gold .25 .25
1756 A635 60h blk, ultra, red & gold .25 .25
1757 A635 1k blk, ultra, red & gold .30 .25
Nos. 1754-1757 (4) 1.05 1.00

Czechoslovak Communist Party, 50th anniv.

Star, Hammer-Sickle Emblems — A636

60h, Hammer-sickle emblem, fist & people, vert.

Perf. 11½x11, 11x11½
1971, May 24 **Engr. & Photo.**
1758 A636 30h blk, red, gold & yel .25 .25
1759 A636 60h blk, red, gold & bl .25 .25

14th Congress of Communist Party of Czechoslovakia.

Ring-necked Pheasant — A637

Designs: 60h, Rainbow trout. 80h, Mouflon. 1k, Chamois. 2k, Stag. 2.60k, Wild boar.

1971, Aug. 17 *Perf. 11½x11*
1760 A637 20h orange & multi .25 .25
1761 A637 60h lt blue & multi .25 .25
1762 A637 80h yellow & multi .25 .25
1763 A637 1k lt green & multi .30 .25
1764 A637 2k lilac & multi .40 .25
1765 A637 2.60k bister & multi 2.25 .65
Nos. 1760-1765 (6) 3.70 1.90

World Hunting Exhib., Budapest, Aug. 27-30.

Diesel Locomotive — A638

1971, Sept. 2 *Perf. 11x11½*
1766 A638 30h lt bl, blk & red .40 .25

Cent. of CKD, Prague Machine Foundry.

Gymnasts and Banners — A639

1971, Sept. 2 *Perf. 11½x11*
1767 A639 30h red brn, gold & ultra .25 .25

50th anniversary of Workers' Physical Exercise Federation.

Road Intersections and Bridge — A640

1971, Sept. 2 **Engr. & Photo.**
1768 A640 1k blk, gold, red & bl .30 .25

14th World Highways and Bridges Congress. Sheets of 25 stamps and 25 labels printed se-tenant with continuous design. Value, single with attached tab, unused 60c; used 30c.

Chinese Fairytale, by Eva Bednarova
A641

Designs: 1k, Tiger and other animals, by Mirko Hanak. 1.60k, The Miraculous Bamboo Shoot, by Yasuo Segawa, horiz.

Perf. 11½x11, 11x11½
1971, Sept. 10
1769 A641 60h multi .25 .25
1770 A641 1k multi .30 .25
1771 A641 1.60k multi .45 .25
Nos. 1769-1771 (3) 1.00 .75

Bratislava BIB 71 biennial exhibition of illustrations for children's books.

Apothecary Jars and Coltsfoot — A642

Intl. Pharmaceutical Cong.: 60h, Jars and dog rose. 1k, Scales and adonis vernalis. 1.20k, Mortars and valerian. 1.80k, Retorts and chicory. 2.40k, Mill, mortar and henbane.

1971, Sept. 20 *Perf. 11½x11*
Yellow Paper
1772 A642 30h multi .25 .25
1773 A642 60h multi .25 .25
1774 A642 1k multi .25 .25
1775 A642 1.20k multi .25 .25
1776 A642 1.80k multi .25 .25
1777 A642 2.40k multi 1.25 .25
Nos. 1772-1777 (6) 2.50 1.50

Painting Type of 1967

Paintings: 1k, "Waiting" (woman's head), 1967, by Imro Weiner-Král. 1.20k, Resurrection, by Master of Vyssi Brod, 14th century. 1.40k, Woman with Pitcher, by Milos Bazovsky. 1.80k, Veruna Cudova (in folk costume), by Josef Mánes. 2.40k, Detail from "Feast of the Rose Garlands," by Albrecht Dürer.

1971, Nov. 27 *Perf. 11½*
1779 A565 1k multi .30 .30
1780 A565 1.20k multi .75 .45
1781 A565 1.40k multi .60 .30
1782 A565 1.80k multi 1.10 .50
1783 A565 2.40k multi 1.75 .75
Nos. 1779-1783 (5) 4.50 2.30

Nos. 1779-1783 were each issued in sheets of 4. Value, set $25.

Workers Revolt in Krompachy, by Julius Nemcik — A643

1971, Nov. 28 *Perf. 11x11½*
1784 A643 60h multi .30 .25

History of the Czechoslovak Communist Party.

Wooden Dolls and Birds — A644

Folk Art and UNICEF Emblem: 80h, Jug handles, carved. 1k, Horseback rider. 1.60k, Shepherd carrying lamb. 2k, Easter eggs and rattle. 3k, "Zbojnik," folk hero.

1971, Dec. 11 *Perf. 11½*
1785 A644 60h multi .40 .25
1786 A644 80h multi .80 .25
1787 A644 1k multi .40 .25
1788 A644 1.60k multi .40 .25
1789 A644 2k multi .40 .30
1790 A644 3k multi 2.00 .60
Nos. 1785-1790 (6) 4.40 1.90

25th anniv. of UNICEF.

Nos. 1785-1790 were each issued in sheets of 10. Value, set $45.

Runners, Parthenon, Czechoslovak Olympic Emblem — A645

Designs: 40h, Women's high jump, Olympic emblem and plan for Prague Stadium. 1.60k, Cross-country skiers, Sapporo '72 emblem and ski jump in High Tatras. 2.60k, Discus thrower, Discobolus and St. Vitus Cathedral.

1971, Dec. 16 **Engr. & Photo.**
1791 A645 30h multi .25 .25
1792 A645 40h multi .25 .25
1793 A645 1.60k multi .25 .25
1794 A645 2.60k multi 1.50 .75
Nos. 1791-1794 (4) 2.25 1.50

75th anniversary of Czechoslovak Olympic Committee (30h, 2.60k); 20th Summer Olympic Games, Munich, Aug. 26-Sept. 10, 1972 (40h); 11th Winter Olympic Games, Sapporo, Japan, Feb. 3-13, 1972 (1.60k).

Post Horns and Lion — A646

1971, Dec. 17 *Perf. 11x11½*
1795 A646 1k blk, gold, car & bl .30 .25

Stamp Day.

Figure Skating — A647

Olympic Emblems and: 50h, Ski jump. 1k, Ice hockey. 1.60k, Sledding, women's.

1972, Jan. 13 *Perf. 11½*
1796 A647 40h pur, org & red .25 .25
1797 A647 50h dk bl, org & red .25 .25
1798 A647 1k mag, org & red .30 .25
1799 A647 1.60k bl grn, org & red 1.25 .25
Nos. 1796-1799 (4) 2.05 1.00

11th Winter Olympic Games, Sapporo, Japan, Feb. 3-13.

"Ležáky" — A648

No. 1801, Boy's head behind barbed wire, horiz. No. 1802, Hand rising from ruins. No. 1803, Soldier and banner, horiz.

1972, Feb. 16

1800 A648 30h blk, dl org & red .25 .25
1801 A648 30h blk & brn org .25 .25
1802 A648 60h blk, yel & red .25 .25
1803 A648 60h sl grn & multi .25 .25
Nos. 1800-1803 (4) 1.00 1.00

30th anniv. of: destruction of Lezáky (No. 1800) and Lidice (No. 1802); Terezin concentration camp (No. 1801); Czechoslovak Army unit in Russia (No. 1803).

Book Year Emblem — A649

1972, Mar. 17 ***Perf. 11½x11***
1804 A649 1k blk & org brn .30 .25

International Book Year 1972.

Steam and Diesel Locomotives A650

1972, Mar. 17 ***Perf. 11½x11***
1805 A650 30h multi .75 .25

Centenary of the Kosice-Bohumin railroad.

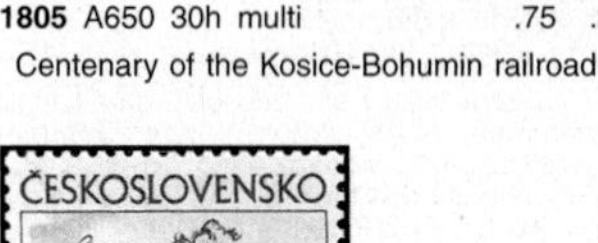

"Pasture," by Vojtech Sedlacek A651

Designs: 50h, Dressage, by Frantisek Tichy. 60th, Otakar Kubin, by Vaclav Fiala. 1k, The Three Kings, by Ernest Zmetak. 1.60k, Woman Dressing, by Ludovit Fulla.

1972, Mar. 27 ***Perf. 11½x11***
1806 A651 40h multi .25 .25
1807 A651 50h multi .25 .25
1808 A651 60h multi .25 .25
1809 A651 1k multi .25 .25
1810 A651 1.60k multi 1.25 .90
Nos. 1806-1810 (5) 2.25 1.90

Czech and Slovak graphic art.
1.60k issued in sheets of 4. Value $9.
See Nos. 1859-1862, 1921-1924.

Ice Hockey A652

Design: 1k, Two players.

1972, Apr. 7 ***Perf. 11***
1811 A652 60h blk & multi .25 .25
1812 A652 1k blk & multi .40 .25

World and European Ice Hockey Championships, Prague.
For overprint see Nos. 1845-1846.

Bicycling, Olympic Rings and Emblem A653

1972, Apr. 7
1813 A653 50h shown .25 .25
1814 A653 1.60k Diving .35 .25
1815 A653 1.80k Canoeing .55 .25
1816 A653 2k Gymnast 1.10 .25
Nos. 1813-1816 (4) 2.25 1.00

20th Olympic Games, Munich, 8/26-9/11.

Prague Castle Art Type of 1971

Designs: No. 1817, Adam and Eve, column capital, St. Vitus Cathedral. No. 1818, Czech coat of arms (lion), c. 1500.

1972, May 9 ***Perf. 11½***
1817 A634 3k blk & multi 2.10 1.40
1818 A634 3k blk, red, sil & gold 1.40 .85

Nos. 1817-1818 were each issued in sheets of 4. Value, set $15.

Andrej Sladkovic (1820-1872), Poet — A654

No. 1820, Janko Kral (1822-1876), poet. No. 1821, Ludmilla Podjavorinska (1872-1951), writer. No. 1822, Antonin Hudecek (1872-1941), painter. No. 1823, Frantisek Bilek (1872-1941), sculptor. No. 1824, Jan Preisler (1872-1918), painter.

1972, June 14 ***Perf. 11***
1819 A654 40h pur, ol & bl .25 .25
1820 A654 40h dk grn, bl & yel .25 .25
1821 A654 40h blk & multi .25 .25
1822 A654 40h brn, grn & bl .25 .25
1823 A654 40h choc, grn & org .25 .25
1824 A654 40h grn, sl & dp org .25 .25
Nos. 1819-1824 (6) 1.50 1.50

Men with Banners — A655

1972, June 14 ***Perf. 11x11½***
1825 A655 30h dk vio bl, red & yel .25 .25

8th Trade Union Congress, Prague.

Art Forms of Wire A656

Ornamental Wirework: 60h, Plane and rosette. 80h, Four-headed dragon and ornament. 1k, Locomotive and loops. 2.60k, Tray and owl.

1972, Aug. 28 ***Perf. 11½x11***
1826 A656 20h sal & multi .25 .25
1827 A656 60h multi .25 .25
1828 A656 80h pink & multi .25 .25
1829 A656 1k multi .25 .25
1830 A656 2.60k rose & multi 1.40 .25
Nos. 1826-1830 (5) 2.40 1.25

"Jiskra" A657

Engr. & Photo.

1972, Sept. 27 ***Perf. 11½x11***

Size: 40x22mm

Multicolored Design on Blue Paper

1831 A657 50h shown .25 .25
1832 A657 60h "Mir" .25 .25
1833 A657 80h "Republika" .25 .25

Size: 48x29mm

Perf. 11x11½

1834 A657 1k "Kosice" .30 .25
1835 A657 1.60k "Dukla" .45 .25
1836 A657 2k "Kladno" 1.40 .55
Nos. 1831-1836 (6) 2.90 1.80

Czechoslovak sea-going vessels.

Hussar, 18th Century Tile — A658

60h, Janissary. 80h, St. Martin. 1.60k, St. George. 1.80k, Nobleman's guard. 2.20k, Slovakian horseman.

1972, Oct. 24 ***Perf. 11½x11***
1837 A658 30h shown .25 .25
1838 A658 60h multicolored .25 .25
1839 A658 80h multicolored .25 .25
1840 A658 1.60k multicolored .45 .25
1841 A658 1.80k multicolored .70 .25
1842 A658 2.20k multicolored 1.25 .25
Nos. 1837-1842 (6) 3.15 1.50

Horsemen from 18th-19th century tiles or enamel paintings on glass.

Worker, Flag Hoisted on Bayonet A659

Star, Hammer and Sickle A660

1972, Nov. 7 ***Perf. 11x11½***
1843 A659 30h gold & multi .25 .25
1844 A660 60h rose car & gold .25 .25

55th anniv. of the Russian October Revolution (30h); 50th anniv. of the Soviet Union (60h).

Nos. 1811-1812 Overprinted in Violet Blue or Black

1972 ***Perf. 11***
1845 A652 60h multi (VBl) 7.00 6.50
1846 A652 1k multi (Bk) 7.00 6.50

Czechoslovakia's victorious ice hockey team. The overprint on the 60h (shown) is in Czech and reads CSSR/MISTREM/SVETA; the overprint on the 1k is in Slovak.

Painting Type of 1967

Designs: 1k, "Nosegay" (nudes and flowers), by Max Svabinsky. 1.20k, Struggle of St. Ladislas with Kuman nomad, anonymous, 14th century. 1.40k, Lady with Fur Hat, by Vaclav Hollar. 1.80k, Midsummer Night's Dream, 1962, by Josef Liesler. 2.40k, Pablo Picasso, self-portrait.

1972, Nov. 27 **Engr. & Photo.**
1847 A565 1k multi .85 .40
1848 A565 1.20k multi .85 .40
1849 A565 1.40k blk & cream 1.10 .40
1850 A565 1.80k multi .85 .50
1851 A565 2.40k multi 2.10 1.40
Nos. 1847-1851 (5) 5.75 3.10

Nos. 1847-1851 were each issued in sheets of 4. Value, set $24.

Goldfinch A661

Songbirds: 60h, Warbler feeding young cuckoo. 80h, Cuckoo. 1k, Black-billed magpie. 1.60k, Bullfinch. 3k, Song thrush.

1972, Dec. 15 **Size: 30x48½mm**
1852 A661 60h yel & multi .25 .25
1853 A661 80h multi .25 .25
1854 A661 1k lt bl & multi .25 .25

Engr.

Size: 30x23mm

1855 A661 1.60k multi 1.50 .70
1856 A661 2k multi 1.50 .70
1857 A661 3k multi 1.50 .70
Nos. 1852-1857 (6) 5.25 2.85

Nos. 1855-1857 were each issued in a sheet of 10. Value, set $55.

Post Horn and Allegory — A662

1972, Dec. 18 **Engr. & Photo.**
1858 A662 1k blk, red lil & gold .30 .30

Stamp Day.

Art Type of 1972

Designs: 30h, Flowers in Window, by Jaroslav Grus. 60h, Quest for Happiness, by Josef Balaz. 1.60k, Balloon, by Kamil Lhotak. 1.80k, Woman with Viola, by Richard Wiesner.

1973, Jan. 25 ***Perf. 11½x11***
1859 A651 30h multi .25 .25
1860 A651 60h multi .25 .25
1861 A651 1.60k multi .30 .25
1862 A651 1.80k multi .25 .35
Nos. 1859-1862 (4) 1.05 1.10

Czech and Slovak graphic art.

Tennis Player — A663

Figure Skater — A664

Torch and Star — A665

1973, Feb. 22 ***Perf. 11***

1863	A663	30h vio & multi	.25	.25
1864	A664	60h blk & multi	.25	.25
1865	A665	1k multi	.30	.25
		Nos. 1863-1865 (3)	.80	.75

80th anniversary of the tennis organization in Czechoslovakia (30h); World figure skating championships, Bratislava (60h); 3rd summer army Spartakiad of socialist countries (1k).

Star and Factories A666

Workers' Militia, Emblem and Flag — A667

1973, Feb. 23

1866	A666	30h multi	.25	.25
1867	A667	60h multi	.25	.25

25th anniversary of the Communist revolution in Czechoslovakia and of the Militia.

A668

Torch &: 30h, Capt. Jan Nalepka, Major Antonin Sochor and Laurel. 40h, Evzen Rosicky, Mirko Nespor & ivy leaves. 60h, Vlado Clementis, Karol Smidke & linden leaves. 80h, Jan Osoha, Josef Molak & oak leaves. 1k, Marie Kuderikova, Jozka Jaburkova & rose. 1.60k, Vaclav Sinkule, Eduard Urx & palm leaf.

1973, Mar. 20 ***Perf. 11½x11***

Yellow Paper

1868	A668	30h blk, ver & gold	.30	.25
1869	A668	40h blk, ver & grn	.30	.25
1870	A668	60h blk, ver & gold	.30	.25
1871	A668	80h blk, ver & gold	.30	.25
1872	A668	1k blk, ver & grn	.30	.25
1873	A668	1.60k blk, ver & sil	.75	.25
		Nos. 1868-1873 (6)	2.25	1.50

Fighters against and victims of Fascism and Nazism during German Occupation.

Virgil I. Grissom, Edward H. White, Roger B. Chaffee — A669

Designs: 20h, Soviet planetary station "Venera." 30h, "Intercosmos" station. 40h, Lunokhod on moon. 3.60k, Vladimir M. Komarov, Georgi T. Dobrovolsky, Vladislav N. Volkov, Victor I. Patsayev. 5k, Yuri A. Gagarin.

Two types of 3.60k: type I, Cosmonaut on background of cross-hatched lines; type 2, Cosmonaut on background of parallel diagonal lines.

1973, Apr. 12 ***Perf. 11½x11***

Size: 40x22mm

1874	A669	20h multi	.25	.25
1875	A669	30h multi	.25	.25
1876	A669	40h multi	.25	.25

Engr.

Perf. 11½

Size: 49x30mm

1877	A669	3k multi	1.00	.50
1878	A669	3.60k multi, type 1	1.00	.75
a.		Type 2	20.00	7.50
1879	A669	5k multi	2.50	2.00
		Nos. 1874-1879 (6)	5.25	4.00

In memory of American and Russian astronauts.

Nos. 1877-1879 were each issued in sheets of 4. Values: set (with No. 1878) $30; mset (with No. 1878a) $90.

Radio — A670

Telephone and Map of Czechoslovakia A671

Television A672

1973, May 1 ***Perf. 11½x11***

1880	A670	30h blk & multi	.25	.25
1881	A671	30h lt bl, pink & blk	.25	.25
1882	A672	30h dp bl & multi	.25	.25
		Nos. 1880-1882 (3)	.75	.75

Czechoslovak anniversaries: 50 years of broadcasting (No. 1880); 20 years of telephone service to all communities (No. 1881); 20 years of television (No. 1882).

Coat of Arms and Linden Branch — A673

1973, May 9 ***Perf. 11x11½***

1883	A673	60h red & multi	.25	.25

25th anniv. of the Constitution of May 9.

Prague Castle Art Type of 1971

No. 1884, Royal Legate, 14th century. No. 1885, Seal of King Charles IV, 1351.

1973, May 9 ***Perf. 11½***

1884	A634	3k blue & multi	1.25	.75
1885	A634	3k gold, grn & dk brn	1.75	1.50

Nos. 1884-1885 were each issued in sheets of 4. Value, set $13.

Coat of Arms Type of 1968

1973, June 20

1886	A590	60h Mikulov	.25	.25
1887	A590	60h Zlutice	.30	.25
1888	A590	60h Smolenice	.35	.25
		Nos. 1886-1888 (3)	.90	.75

Coats of arms of Czechoslovakian cities.

Heraldic Colors of Olomouc and Moravia — A674

1973, Aug. 23 **Engr. & Photo.**

1889	A674	30h multi	.25	.25

University of Olomouc, 400th anniv.

Flower Show — A675

60h, Tulips (30x50mm). 1k, Rose (30x50mm). 1.60k, Anthurium (23x39mm). 1.80k, Iris (23x39mm). 2k, Chrysanthemum (30x50mm). 3.60k, Cymbidium (23x39mm).

1973, Aug. 23 ***Perf. 11½***

1890	A675	60h multi	.75	.35
1891	A675	1k multi	.75	.35
1892	A675	1.60k shown	.40	.35
1893	A675	1.80k multi	.40	.35
1894	A675	2k multi	1.90	1.00
1895	A675	3.60k multi	.75	.35
		Nos. 1890-1895 (6)	4.95	2.75

Olomouc, Aug. 18-Sept. 2. 60h, 1k, 2k issued in sheets of 4, others in sheets of 10. Value, set $50.

Hunting Dogs A676

1973, Sept. 5

1896	A676	20h Irish setter	.45	.25
1897	A676	30h Czech terrier	.45	.25
1898	A676	40h Bavarian hunting dog	.55	.25
1899	A676	60h German pointer	.55	.25
1900	A676	1k Cocker spaniel	.85	.25
1901	A676	1.60k Dachshund	2.10	.50
		Nos. 1896-1901 (6)	4.95	1.75

Czechoslovak United Hunting Org., 50th anniv.

St. John, the Baptist, by Svabinsky A677

Works by Max Svabinsky: 60h, "August Noon" (woman). 80h, "Marriage of True Minds" (artist and muse). 1k, "Paradise Sonata I" (Adam dreaming of Eve). 2.60k, Last Judgment, stained glass window, St. Vitus Cathedral.

1973, Sept. 17 **Litho. & Engr.**

1902	A677	20h blk & pale grn	.25	.25
1903	A677	60h black & buff	.25	.25

Engr.

1904	A677	80h black	.75	.25
1905	A677	1k slate green	.75	.25
1906	A677	2.60k multi	1.90	1.25
		Nos. 1902-1906 (5)	3.90	2.25

Centenary of the birth of Max Svabinsky (1873-1962), artist and stamp designer. 20h and 60h issued in sheets of 25; 80h and 1k se-tenant in sheets of 4 checkerwise (value $4); 2.60k in sheets of 4 (value $10).

Trade Union Emblem A678

1973, Oct. 15 **Engr. & Photo.**

1907	A678	1k red, bl & yel	.25	.25

8t (valueh Congress of the World Federation of Trade Unions, Varna, Bulgaria.

Painting Type of 1967

1k, Boy from Martinique, by Antonin Pelc. 1.20k, "Fortitude" (mountaineer), by Martin Benka. 1.80k, Rembrandt, self-portrait. 2k, Pierrot, by Bohumil Kubista. 2.40k, Ilona Kubinyiova, by Peter M. Bohun. 3.60k, Virgin and Child (Veveri Madonna), c. 1350.

1973, Nov. 27 ***Perf. 11½***

1908	A565	1k multi, vio bl inscriptions	2.50	1.25
a.		1k multi, black inscriptions	9.00	9.00
1909	A565	1.20k multi	*2.50*	*1.25*
1910	A565	1.80k multi	.80	.80
1911	A565	2k multi	.80	.80
1912	A565	2.40k multi	.80	.80
1913	A565	3.60k multi	.80	.80
		Nos. 1908-1913 (6)	8.20	5.70

Nos. 1908-1909 were each issued in sheets of 4. Nos. 1910-1913 were printed se-tenant with gold and black inscription on gutter. Value, sheet $35. No. 1908a in sheet of 4, value $45.

The central backgroundis light bluish green on No. 1908; grayish blue on No. 1908a.

Postilion — A679

1973, Dec. 18

1914	A679	1k gold & multi	.30	.25

Stamp Day 1974 and 55th anniversary of Czechoslovak postage stamps. Printed with 2 labels showing telephone and telegraph. Value of single with two labels, $1.75.

"CSSR" — A680

1974, Jan. 1

1915	A680	30h red, gold & ultra	.25	.25

5th anniversary of Federal Government in the Czechoslovak Socialist Republic.

Bedrich Smetana — A681

Pablo Neruda, Chilean Flag — A682

1974, Jan. 4 ***Perf. 11x11½***

1916	A681	60h shown	.25	.25
1917	A681	60h Josef Suk	.25	.25
1918	A682	60h shown	.25	.25
		Nos. 1916-1918 (3)	.75	.75

Smetana (1824-84), composer; Suk (1874-1935), composer, and Pablo Neruda (Neftali Ricardo Reyes, 1904-73), Chilean poet.

Comecon Building, Moscow — A683

1974, Jan. 23

1919	A683	1k gold, red & vio bl	.25	.25

25th anniversary of the Council of Mutual Economic Assistance (COMECON).

Symbols of Postal Service — A684

1974, Feb. 20 *Perf. 11½*
1920 A684 3.60k multi .85 .45

BRNO '74 National Stamp Exhibition, Brno, June 8-23.

No. 1920 was issue both in normal sheets of 25 stamps and in sheets containing 16 stamps se-tenant with 9 labels depicting Brno. Values: single stamp with attached tab unused $2.50; used $2.50; full sheet of 16 stamps and 9 labels $35.

Art Type of 1972

Designs: 60h, Tulips 1973, by Josef Broz. 1k, Structures 1961 (poppy and building), by Orest Dubay. 1.60k, Bird and flowers (Golden Sun-Glowing Day), by Adolf Zabransky. 1.80k, Artificial flowers, by Frantisek Gross.

1974, Feb. 21 *Perf. 11½x11*

1921	A651	60h multi	.25	.25
1922	A651	1k multi	.30	.25
1923	A651	1.60k multi	.40	.25
1924	A651	1.80k multi	1.10	.30
		Nos. 1921-1924 (4)	2.05	1.05

Czech and Slovak graphic art.

Oskar Benes and Vaclav Prochazka — A685

40h, Milos Uher, Anton Sedlacek. 60h, Jan Hajecek, Marie Sedlackova. 80h, Jan Sverma, Albin Grznar. 1k, Jaroslav Neliba, Alois Hovorka. 1.60k, Ladislav Exnar, Ludovit Kukorelli.

1974, Mar. 21 *Perf. 11½x11*

1925	A685	30h indigo & multi	.25	.25
1926	A685	40h indigo & multi	.25	.25
1927	A685	60h indigo & multi	.25	.25
1928	A685	80h indigo & multi	.25	.25
1929	A685	1k indigo & multi	.30	.25
1930	A685	1.60k indigo & multi	.85	.25
		Nos. 1925-1930 (6)	2.15	1.50

Partisan commanders and fighters.

"Water, the Source of Energy" A686

Symbolic Designs: 1k, Importance of water for agriculture. 1.20k, Study of the oceans. 1.60k, "Hydrological Decade." 2k, Struggle for unpolluted water.

1974, Apr. 25 **Engr.** *Perf. 11½*

1931	A686	60h multi	.55	.25
1932	A686	1k multi	.55	.25
1933	A686	1.20k multi	1.10	.45
1934	A686	1.60k multi	1.10	.45
1935	A686	2k multi	2.10	1.40
		Nos. 1931-1935 (5)	5.40	2.80

Hydrological Decade (UNESCO), 1965-1974.

Nos. 1931-1935 were each issued in sheets of 4. Value $25.

Allegory Holding "Molniya," and Ground Station — A687

1974, Apr. 30 **Engr. & Photo.**
1936 A687 30h vio bl & multi .25 .25

"Intersputnik," first satellite communications ground station in Czechoslovakia.

Prague Castle Art Type of 1971

No. 1937, Golden Cock, 17th century locket. No. 1938, Glass monstrance, 1840.

1974, May 9 **Engr.** *Perf. 11½*

1937	A634	3k gold & multi	1.50	1.10
1938	A634	3k blk & multi	2.25	1.50

Nos. 1937-1938 werre each issued in sheets of 4. Value, set $15.

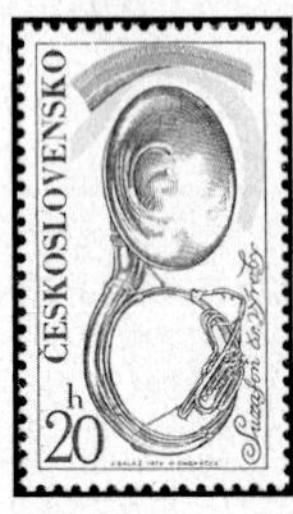
Sousaphone A688

30h, Bagpipe. 40h, Violin, by Martin Benka. 1k, Pyramid piano. 1.60k, Tenor quinton, 1754.

Engraved and Photogravure

1974, May 12 *Perf. 11x11½*

1939	A688	20h shown	.25	.25
1940	A688	30h multi	.25	.25
1941	A688	40h multi	.25	.25
1942	A688	1k multi	.25	.25
1943	A688	1.60k multi	.80	.25
		Nos. 1939-1943 (5)	1.80	1.25

Prague and Bratislava Music Festivals. The 1.60k also commemorates 25th anniversary of Slovak Philharmonic Orchestra.

Child — A689

1974, June 1 *Perf. 11½*
1944 A689 60h multi .25 .25

Children's Day. Design is from illustration for children's book by Adolf Zabransky.

Globe, People and Exhibition Emblems — A690

Design: 6k, Rays and emblems symbolizing "Oneness and Mutuality."

1974, June 1

1945	A690	30h multi	.25	.25
1946	A690	6k multi	1.50	.75

BRNO 74 Natl. Stamp Exhib., Brno, June 8-23.

Nos. 2171-2172 were each issued both in sheet of 50 stamps and in sheets of 16 stamps and 14 labels. Values: stamps with attached labels, $1.75; 2 sheets of 16 stamps and 14 labels $35.

Resistance Fighter — A691

1974, Aug. 29 *Perf. 11½*
1947 A691 30h multi .25 .25

Slovak National Uprising, 30th anniversary.

Actress Holding Tragedy and Comedy Masks — A692

1974, Aug. 29
1948 A692 30h red, sil & blk .25 .25

Bratislava Academy of Music and Drama, 25th anniversary.

Slovak Girl with Flower — A693

1974, Aug. 29
1949 A693 30h multi .25 .25

SLUK, Slovak folksong and dance ensemble, 25th anniversary.

Hero and Leander A694

Design: 2.40k, Hero watching Leander swim the Hellespont. No. 1952, Leander reaching shore. No. 1953, Hero mourning over Leander's body. No. 1954, Hermione, Leander's sister. No. 1955, Mourning Cupid. Designs are from 17th century English tapestries in Bratislava Council Palace.

1974-76

1950	A694	2k multi	1.25	1.10
1951	A694	2.40k multi	1.50	1.25
1952	A694	3k multi	1.00	.45
1953	A694	3k multi	1.75	1.75
1954	A694	3.60k multi	2.50	1.10
1955	A694	3.60k multi	.85	.60
		Nos. 1950-1955 (6)	8.85	6.25

Issued: Nos. 1950-1951, 9/25/74; Nos. 1952, 1954, 8/29/75; Nos. 1953, 1955, 5/9/76.

Nos. 1950-1951 were each issued in sheets of 4, with 2 blank labels; Nos. 1952-1955 were issued in sheets of 4. Value, set $50.

Soldier Standing Guard, Target, 1840 — A695

Painted Folk-art Targets: 60h, Landscape with Pierrot and flags, 1828. 1k, Diana crowning champion marksman, 1832. 1.60k, Still life with guitar, 1839. 2.40k, Salvo and stag in flight, 1834. 3k, Turk and giraffe, 1831.

1974, Sept. 26 *Perf. 11½*

Size: 30x50mm

1956	A695	30h black & multi	.25	.25
1957	A695	60h black & multi	.25	.25
1958	A695	1k black & multi	.30	.25

Engr.

Perf. 12

Size: 40x50mm

1959	A695	1.60k green & multi	.50	.45
1960	A695	2.40k sepia & multi	.90	.75
1961	A695	3k multi	*3.00*	*3.00*
		Nos. 1956-1961 (6)	*5.20*	*4.95*

Nos. 1959-1961 were each issued in sheets of 4. Value, set $17.50.

UPU Emblem and Postilion — A696

UPU Cent. (UPU Emblem and): 40h, Mail coach. 60h, Railroad mail coach, 1851. 80h, Early mail truck. 1k, Czechoslovak Airlines mail plane. 1.60k, Radar.

Engraved and Photogravure

1974, Oct. 9 *Perf. 11½*

1962	A696	30h multi	.25	.25
1963	A696	40h multi	.25	.25
1964	A696	60h multi	.25	.25
1965	A696	80h multi	.25	.25
1966	A696	1k multi	.40	.25
1967	A696	1.60k multi	1.25	.25
		Nos. 1962-1967 (6)	2.65	1.50

Sealed Letter — A697

Post Rider — A698

20h, Post Horn, Old Town Bridge Tower. No. 1971, Carrier pigeon.

1974, Oct. 31 *Perf. 11½x11*

1968	A698	20h multi	.25	.25
1969	A697	30h brn, bl & red	.25	.25
1970	A698	40h multi	.25	.25
1971	A697	60h bl, yel & red	.25	.25
		Nos. 1968-1971 (4)	1.00	1.00

Nos. 1968-1971 were reissued in 1979, printed on fluorescent paper. Value, set $15.

See No. 2675.

Stylized Bird — A699

No. 1977, Same design as No. 1976. No. 1979, Map of Czechoslovakia with postal code numbers.

Coil Stamps

1975 **Photo.** *Perf. 14*

1976	A699	30h brt bl	.25	.25
1977	A699	60h carmine	.25	.25

Postal Code Symbol — A699a

1976			*Perf. 11½*	
1978	A699a	30h emer	.25	.25
1979	A699a	60h scar	.25	.25

Nos. 1976-1979 have black control number on back of every fifth stamp.

Ludvik Kuba, Self-portrait, 1941 — A700

Paintings: 1.20k, Violinist Frantisek Ondricek, by Vaclav Brozik. 1.60k, Vase with Flowers, by Otakar Kubin. 1.80k, Woman with Pitcher, by Janko Alexy. 2.40k, Bacchanalia, c. 1635, by Karel Skreta.

1974, Nov. 27		**Engr.**	*Perf. 11½*	
1980	A700	1k multi	.50	.30
1981	A700	1.20k multi	.80	.40
1982	A700	1.60k multi	.80	.60
1983	A700	1.80k multi	1.00	.40
1984	A700	2.40k multi	2.50	1.75
		Nos. 1980-1984 (5)	5.60	3.45

Czech and Slovak art.

Nos. 1980-1984 were each issued in sheets of 4. Value, set $25.

See Nos. 2209-2211, 2678-2682, 2721-2723, 2743, 2766-2768.

Post Horn — A701

Engraved and Photogravure

1974, Dec. 18			*Perf. 11x11½*	
1985	A701	1k multicolored	.30	.25

Stamp Day.

Still-life with Hare, by Hollar — A702

Designs: 1k, The Lion and the Mouse, by Vaclav Hollar. 1.60k, Deer Hunt, by Philip Galle. 1.80k, Grand Hunt, by Jacques Callot.

1975, Feb. 26			*Perf. 11½x11*	
1988	A702	60h blk & buff	.25	.25
1989	A702	1k blk & buff	.25	.25
1990	A702	1.60k blk & yel	.25	.25
1991	A702	1.80k blk & buff	1.25	.65
		Nos. 1988-1991 (4)	2.00	1.40

Hunting scenes from old engravings.

Guns Pointing at Family A703

Designs: 1k, Women and building on fire. 1.20k, People and roses. All designs include names of destroyed villages.

1975, Feb. 26			*Perf. 11*	
1992	A703	60h multi	.25	.25
1993	A703	1k multi	.25	.25
1994	A703	1.20k multi	.30	.25
		Nos. 1992-1994 (3)	.80	.75

Destruction of 14 villages by the Nazis, 30th anniversary.

Young Woman and Globe — A704

1975, Mar. 7			*Perf. 11½x11*	
1995	A704	30h red & multi	.25	.25

International Women's Year 1975.

Little Queens, Moravian Folk Custom A705

Folk Customs: 1k, Straw masks (animal heads and blackened faces), Slovak. 1.40k, The Tale of Maid Dorothea (executioner, girl, king and devil). 2k, Drowning of Morena, symbol of death and winter.

1975, Mar. 26		**Engr.**	*Perf. 11½*	
1996	A705	60h blk & multi	.45	.25
1997	A705	1k blk & multi	.70	.45
1998	A705	1.40k blk & multi	.85	.60
1999	A705	2k blk & multi	1.00	.75
		Nos. 1996-1999 (4)	3.00	2.05

Nos. 1996-1999 were each issued in sheets of four. Value $12.50.

Coat of Arms Type of 1968

Engraved and Photogravure

1975, Apr. 17			*Perf. 11½*	
2000	A590	60h Nymburk	.25	.25
2001	A590	60h Znojmo	.25	.25

Coats of arms of Czechoslovakian cities.

Czech May Uprising — A706

Liberation by Soviet Army — A707

Czechoslovak-Russian Friendship — A708

Engr. & Photo.; Engr. (A707)

1975, May 9				
2002	A706	1k multi	.25	.25
2003	A707	1k multi	.25	.25
2004	A708	1k multi	.25	.25
		Nos. 2002-2004 (3)	.75	.75

30th anniv. of the May uprising of the Czech people and of liberation by the Soviet Army; 5th anniv. of the Czechoslovak-Soviet Treaty of Friendship, Cooperation and Mutual Aid.

Adolescents' Exercises — A709

Designs: 60th, Children's exercises. 1k, Men's and women's exercises.

Engraved and Photogravure

1975, June 15			*Perf. 12x11½*	
2005	A709	30h lil & multi	.25	.25
2006	A709	60h multi	.25	.25
2007	A709	1k vio & multi	.25	.25
		Nos. 2005-2007 (3)	.75	.75

Spartakiad 1975, Prague, June 26-29. Nos. 2005-2007 each issued in sheets of 30 stamps and 40 labels, showing different Spartakiad emblems. Value, set with tabs, $1.

Datrioides Microlepis and Sea Horse — A710

Tropical Fish (Aquarium): 1k, Beta splendens regan and Pterophyllum scalare. 1.20k, Carassius auratus. 1.60k, Amphiprion percula and Chaetodon sp. 2k, Pomacanthodes semicirculatus, Pomocanthus maculosus and Paracanthorus hepatus.

1975, June 27			*Perf. 11½*	
2008	A710	60h multi	.25	.25
2009	A710	1k multi	.35	.25
2010	A710	1.20k multi	.40	.25
2011	A710	1.60k multi	.55	.25
2012	A710	2k multi	1.75	.50
		Nos. 2008-2012 (5)	3.30	1.50

Pelicans, by Nikita Charushin — A711

Book Illustrations: 30h, The Dreamer, by Lieselotte Schwarz. 40h, Hero on horseback, by Val Munteanau. 60h, Peacock, by Klaus Ensikat. 80h, Woman on horseback, by Robert Dubravec.

1975, Sept. 5				
2013	A711	20h multi	.25	.25
2014	A711	30h multi	.25	.25
2015	A711	40h multi	.30	.25
2016	A711	60h multi	.30	.25
2017	A711	80h multi	.60	.25
		Nos. 2013-2017 (5)	1.70	1.25

Bratislava BIB 75 biennial exhibition of illustrations for children's books.

Nos. 2013-2017 issued in sheets of 25 stamps and 15 labels with designs and inscriptions in various languages. Value, set with attached labels, $2.

Strakonice, 1951 — A712

Designs: Motorcycles.

1975, Sept. 29			*Perf. 11½*	
2018	A712	20h shown	.25	.25
2019	A712	40h Jawa 250, 1945	.25	.25
2020	A712	60h Jawa 175, 1935	.25	.25
2021	A712	1k ITAR, 1921	.25	.25
2022	A712	1.20k ORION, 1903	.25	.25
2023	A712	1.80k Laurin & Klement, 1898	1.40	.40
		Nos. 2018-2023 (6)	2.65	1.65

Study of Shortwave Solar Radiation — A713

Soyuz-Apollo Link-up in Space — A714

60h, Study of aurora borealis & Oréol satellite. 1k, Study of ionosphere & cosmic radiation. 2k, Copernicus, radio map of the sun & satellite.

1975, Sept. 30				
2024	A713	30h multi	.25	.25
2025	A713	60h yel, rose red & vio	.25	.25
2026	A713	1k bl, yel & vio	.25	.25
2027	A713	2k red, vio & yel	.35	.25
		Engr.		
2028	A714	5k vio & multi	2.00	1.50
		Nos. 2024-2028 (5)	3.10	2.50

International cooperation in space research.

No. 2028 issued in sheets of 4. Value $15.

The design of No. 2026 appears to be inverted.

Slovnaft, Petrochemical Plant — A715

Designs: 60h, Atomic power station. 1k, Construction of Prague subway. 1.20k, Construction of Friendship pipeline. 1.40k, Combine harvesters. 1.60k, Apartment house construction.

Engraved and Photogravure

1975, Oct. 28				
2029	A715	30h multi	.25	.25
2030	A715	60h multi	.25	.25
2031	A715	1k multi	.25	.25
2032	A715	1.20k multi	.25	.25
2033	A715	1.40k multi	.25	.25
2034	A715	1.60k multi	.75	.30
		Nos. 2029-2034 (6)	2.00	1.55

Socialist construction, 30th anniversary. Nos. 2029-2034 printed se-tenant with labels. Value, set with attached labels, $2.50.

Pres. Gustav Husak — A716

1975, Oct. 28 **Engr.**

2035 A716 30h ultra .25 .25
2036 A716 60h rose red .25 .25

Prague Castle Art Type of 1971

3k, Gold earring, 9th cent. 3.60k, Arms of Premysl Dynasty & Bohemia from lid of leather case containing Bohemian crown, 14th cent.

1975, Oct. 29

2040 A634 3k blk, grn, pur & gold .95 .50
2041 A634 3.60k red & multi 2.00 1.60

Nos. 2040-2041 each issued in sheets of 4. Value, set $12.50.

Miniature Sheet

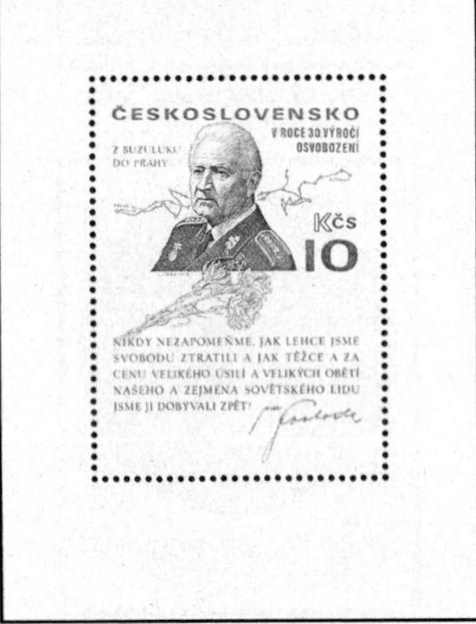

Ludvik Svoboda, Map of Journey from Buzuluk to Prague, Carnations — A717

1975, Nov. 25

2042 A717 10k multi 9.00 7.00

Pres. Ludvik Svoboda, 80th birthday.
Exists imperf. Value, $40 unused, $25 used.

Painting Type of 1967

Paintings: 1k, "May 1975" (Woman and doves for 30th anniv. of peace), by Zdenek Sklenar. 1.40k, Woman in national costume, by Eugen Nevan. 1.80k, "Liberation of Prague," by Alena Cermakova, horiz. 2.40k, "Fire 1938" (woman raising fist), by Josef Capek. 3.40k, Old Prague, 1828, by Vincenc Morstadt.

1975, Nov. 27 **Engr.** ***Perf. 11½***

2043 A565 1k blk, buff & brn .30 .25
2044 A565 1.40k multi .55 .25
2045 A565 1.80k multi .55 .30
2046 A565 2.40k multi 1.50 .75
2047 A565 3.40k multi 1.50 1.25
Nos. 2043-2047 (5) 4.40 2.80

Nos. 2043-2047 were each issued in sheets of 4. Value, set $20.

Carrier Pigeon — A718

Engraved and Photogravure

1975, Dec. 18 ***Perf. 11½***

2048 A718 1k red & multi .30 .25

Stamp Day 1975.

Frantisek Halas — A719

Wilhelm Pieck — A720

Frantisek Lexa — A721

Jindrich Jindrich — A722

Ivan Krasko — A723

1976, Feb. 25 ***Perf. 11½***

2049 A719 60h multi .25 .25
2050 A720 60h multi .25 .25
2051 A721 60h multi .25 .25
2052 A722 60h multi .25 .25
2053 A723 60h multi .25 .25
Nos. 2049-2053 (5) 1.25 1.25

Halas (1901-49), poet; Pieck (1876-1960), pres. of German Democratic Republic; Lexa (1876-1960), professor of Egyptology; Jindrich (1876-1967), composer and writer; Krasko (1876-1958), Slovak poet.

No. 2051 printed in sheets of 10, others in sheets of 50. Value, No. 2051 sheet, $4.

Ski Jump, Olympic Emblem A724

Winter Olympic Games Emblem and: 1.40k, Figure skating, women's. 1.60k, Ice hockey.

1976, Mar. 22 ***Perf. 12x11½***

2054 A724 1k gold & multi .25 .25
2055 A724 1.40k gold & multi .25 .25
2056 A724 1.60k gold & multi 1.00 .30
Nos. 2054-2056 (3) 1.50 .80

12th Winter Olympic Games, Innsbruck, Austria, Feb. 4-15.

Javelin and Olympic Rings — A725

1976, Mar. 22 ***Perf. 11½***

2057 A725 2k shown .30 .25
2058 A725 3k Relay race .45 .25
2059 A725 3.60k Shot put 1.40 .90
Nos. 2057-2059 (3) 2.15 1.40

21st Olympic Games, Montreal, Canada, July 17-Aug. 1.

Table Tennis — A726

1976, Mar. 22 ***Perf. 11x12***

2060 A726 1k multi .30 .25

European Table Tennis Championship, Prague, Mar. 26-Apr. 4.

Symbolic of Communist Party — A727

Worker, Derrick, Emblem — A728

1976, Apr. 12 ***Perf. 11x12***

2061 A727 30h gold & multi .25 .25
2062 A728 60h gold & multi .25 .25

15th Congress of the Communist Party of Czechoslovakia.

Radio Prague Orchestra A729

Dancer, Violin, Tragic Mask — A730

Actors — A731

Folk Dancers A732

Film Festival — A733

1976, Apr. 26 ***Perf. 11½***

2063 A729 20h gold & multi .25 .25
2064 A730 20h pink & multi .25 .25
2065 A731 20h lt bl & multi .25 .25
2066 A732 30h blk & multi .25 .25
2067 A733 30h vio bl, rose & grn .25 .25
Nos. 2063-2067 (5) 1.25 1.25

Czechoslovak Radio Symphony Orchestra, Prague, 50th anniv. (No. 2063); Academy of Music and Dramatic Art, Prague, 50th anniv. (No. 2064); Nova Scena Theater Co., Bratislava, 30th anniv. (No. 2065); Intl. Folk Song and Dance Festival, Straznice, 30th anniv. (No. 2066); 20th Intl. Film Festival, Karlovy Vary (No. 2067).

Hammer and Sickle
A734 A735

Design: 6k, Hammer and sickle, horiz.

1976, May 14

2068 A734 30h gold, red & dk bl .25 .25
2069 A735 60h gold, red & dp car .25 .25

Souvenir Sheet

2070 A735 6k red & multi 2.00 2.00

Czechoslovak Communist Party, 55th anniv. No. 2070 contains a 50x30mm stamp.

Ships in Storm, by Frans Huys (1522-1562) A736

Old Engravings of Ships: 60h, by Václav Hollar (1607-77). 1k, by Regnier Nooms Zeeman (1623-68). 2k, by Francois Chereau (1680-1729).

Engraved and Photogravure

1976, July 21 ***Perf. 11x11½***

2071 A736 40h buff & blk .25 .25
2072 A736 60h gray, buff & blk .25 .25
2073 A736 1k lt grn, buff & blk .25 .25
2074 A736 2k lt bl, buff & blk 1.40 .25
Nos. 2071-2074 (4) 2.15 1.00

"UNESCO" A737

1976, July 30 ***Perf. 11½***

2075 A737 2k gray & multi .35 .30

30th anniversary of UNESCO. Issued in sheets of 10. Value $5.

Souvenir Sheet

Hands Holding Infant, Globe and Dove — A738

1976, July 30

2076 A738 Sheet of 2 4.00 3.50
a. 6k multi 2.50 2.00

European Security and Cooperation Conference, Helsinki, Finland, 2nd anniv.

Merino Ram — A739

Designs: 40h, Bern-Hana milk cow. 1.60k, Kladruby stallion Generalissimus XXVII.

1976, Aug. 28 ***Perf. 11½x12***

2077 A739 30h multi .25 .25
2078 A739 40h multi .25 .25
2079 A739 1.60k multi .35 .25
Nos. 2077-2079 (3) .85 .75

Bountiful Earth Exhibition, Ceske Budejovice, Aug. 28-Sept. 12.

Couple Smoking, WHO Emblem and Skull — A740

1976, Sept. 7 ***Perf. 12x11½***

2080 A740 2k multi .60 .30

Fight against smoking, WHO drive against drug addiction.
Printed in sheets of 10 (2x5) with WHO emblems and inscription in margin. Value $10.

Prague Castle Art Type of 1971

Designs: 3k, View of Prague Castle, by F. Hoogenberghe, 1572. 3.60k, Faun and Satyr, sculptured panel, 16th century.

1976, Oct. 22 **Engr.** ***Perf. 11½***

2081 A634 3k multi 2.50 2.10
2082 A634 3.60k multi .90 .60

Nos. 2081-2082 were each issued in sheets of 4. Value $15.

Guernica 1937, by Imro Weiner-Kral A741

1976, Oct. 22

2083 A741 5k multi .80 .40

40th anniv. of the Intl. Brigade in Spain.

Zebras A742

20h, Elephants. 30h, Cheetah. 40h, Giraffes. 60h, Rhinoceros. 3k, Bongos.

Engraved and Photogravure

1976, Nov. 3 ***Perf. 11½x11, 11x11½***

2084 A742 10h multi .25 .25
2085 A742 20h multi, vert. .25 .25
2086 A742 30h multi .30 .25
2087 A742 40h multi, vert. .45 .25
2088 A742 60h multi .45 .25
2089 A742 3k multi, vert. 2.00 .25
Nos. 2084-2089 (6) 3.70 1.50

African animals in Dvur Kralove Zoo.

Painting Type of 1967

Paintings of Flowers: 1k, by Peter Matejka. 1.40k, by Cyril Bouda. 2k, by Jan Brueghel. 3.60k, J. Rudolf Bys.

1976, Nov. 27 **Engr.** ***Perf. 11½***

2090 A565 1k multi .75 .50
2091 A565 1.40k multi 1.50 .90
2092 A565 2k multi 1.20 .90
2093 A565 3.60k multi .80 .40
Nos. 2090-2093 (4) 4.25 2.70

Nos. 2090-2093 were each issued in sheets of 4, with emblem and name of Praga 1978 on horizontal gutter. Value, set $17.50.

Postrider, 17th Century, and Satellites — A743

1976, Dec. 18 **Engr. & Photo.**

2094 A743 1k multi .25 .25

Stamp Day 1976.

Ice Hockey — A744

1977, Feb. 11 ***Perf. 11½***

2095 A744 60h shown .25 .25
2096 A744 1k Biathlon .25 .25
2097 A744 1.60k Ski jump .85 .25
2098 A744 2k Downhill skiing .25 .25
Nos. 2095-2098 (4) 1.60 1.00

6th Winter Spartakiad of Socialist Countries' Armies.

Arms of Vranov — A745

Coats of Arms of Czechoslovak towns.

1977, Feb. 20

2099 A745 60h shown .25 .25
2100 A745 60h Kralupy nad Vltavou .25 .25
2101 A745 60h Jicin .25 .25
2102 A745 60h Valasske Mezirici .25 .25
Nos. 2099-2102 (4) 1.00 1.00

See Nos. 2297-2300.

Window, Michna Palace — A746

Prague Renaissance Windows: 30h, Michna Palace. 40h, Thun Palace. 60h, Archbishop's Palace, Hradcany. 5k, St. Nicholas Church.

1977, Mar. 10

2103 A746 20h multi .25 .25
2104 A746 30h multi .25 .25
2105 A746 40h multi .25 .25
2106 A746 60h multi .25 .25
2107 A746 5k multi 1.50 .25
Nos. 2103-2107 (5) 2.50 1.25

PRAGA 1978 International Philatelic Exhibition, Prague, Sept. 8-17, 1978.

Children, Auxiliary Police A747

1977, Apr. 21 ***Perf. 11½***

2108 A747 60h multi .25 .25

Auxiliary Police, 25th anniversary.

Warsaw, Polish Flag, Bicyclists A748

Designs: 60h, Berlin, DDR flag, bicyclists. 1k, Prague, Czechoslovakian flag, victorious bicyclist. 1.40k, Bicyclists on highways, modern views of Berlin, Prague and Warsaw.

1977, May 7

2109 A748 30h multi .25 .25
2110 A748 60h multi .25 .25
2111 A748 1k multi .60 .25
2112 A748 1.40k multi .40 .25
Nos. 2109-2112 (4) 1.50 1.00

30th International Bicycle Peace Race Warsaw-Prague-Berlin.

Congress Emblem — A749

1977, May 25 ***Perf. 11½***

2113 A749 30h car, red & gold .25 .25

9th Trade Union Congress, Prague 1977.

Prague Castle Art Type of 1971

Designs: 3k, Onyx footed bowl, 1350. 3.60k, Bronze horse, 1619.

1977, June 7 **Engr.**

2114 A634 3k multi 1.25 1.10
2115 A634 3.60k multi 1.10 1.10

Nos. 2114-2115 were each issued in sheets of 4. Value, set $11.

French Postrider, 19th Century, PRAGA '78 Emblem — A750

Postal Uniforms: 1k, Austrian, 1838. 2k, Austrian, late 18th century. 3.60k, Germany, early 18th century.

1977, June 8 **Engr. & Photo.**

2116 A750 60h multi .25 .25
2117 A750 1k multi .25 .25
2118 A750 2k multi .40 .25
2119 A750 3.60k multi 1.50 .35
Nos. 2116-2119 (4) 2.40 1.10

PRAGA 1978 International Philatelic Exhibition, Prague, Sept. 8-17, 1978.
Nos. 2116-2119 were each issued both in sheets of 50 and in sheets of 4 stamps with 4 inscribed labels and 2 blank labels. Value, set of sheets of 4, $10.

Coffeepots, Porcelain Mark — A751

Czechoslovak Porcelain and Porcelain Marks: 30h, Urn. 40h, Vase. 60h, Cup and saucer, jugs. 1k, Candlestick and plate. 3k, Cup and saucer, coffeepot.

1977, June 15

2120 A751 20h multi .25 .25
2121 A751 30h multi .25 .25
2122 A751 40h multi .25 .35
2123 A751 60h multi .25 .25
2124 A751 1k multi .25 .25
2125 A751 3k multi 1.10 .35
Nos. 2120-2125 (6) 2.35 1.60

Mlada Boleslav Costume — A752

PRAGA Emblem and Folk Costumes from: 1.60k, Vazek. 3.60k, Zavadka. 5k, Belkovice.

1977, Aug. 31 Engr. *Perf. 11½*

2126	A752	1k multi	1.25	.95
2127	A752	1.60k multi	1.25	.95
2128	A752	3.60k multi	1.25	.95
2129	A752	5k multi	1.25	.95
		Nos. 2126-2129 (4)	5.00	3.80

Issued in sheets of 10 and in sheets of 8 plus 2 labels showing PRAGA '78 emblem. Value, set: sheets of 10 $50; sheets of 8 $40.

Old Woman, Devil and Spinner, by Viera Bombova A753

Book Illustrations: 60h, Bear and tiger, by Genadij Pavlisin. 1k, Coach drawn by 4 horses (Hans Christian Andersen), by Ulf Lovgren. 2k, Bear and flamingos (Lewis Carroll), by Nicole Claveloux. 3k, King with keys, and toys, by Jiri Trnka.

1977, Sept. 9 Engr. & Photo.

2130	A753	40h multi	.25	.25
2131	A753	60h multi	.25	.25
2132	A753	1k multi	.25	.25
2133	A753	2k multi	.25	.25
2134	A753	3k multi	1.00	.35
		Nos. 2130-2134 (5)	2.00	1.35

Prize-winning designs, 6th biennial exhibition of illustrations for children's books, Bratislava.

Globe, Violin, Doves, View of Prague — A754

1977, Sept. 28 *Perf. 11½*

2135	A754	60h multi	.25	.25

Congress of International Music Council of UNESCO, Prague and Bratislava.

Souvenir Sheets

"For a Europe of Peace" — A755

1.60k, "For a Europe of Cooperation." 2.40k, "For a Europe of Social Progress."

1977, Oct. 3

2136	A755	Sheet of 2	.50	.50
a.		60h multi	.25	.25
2137	A755	Sheet of 2	1.00	1.00
a.		1.60k multi	.25	.25
2138	A755	Sheet of 2	2.00	1.75
a.		2.40k multi	.50	.50

2nd European Security and Cooperation Conference, Belgrade. Nos. 2136-2138 each contain 2 stamps and 2 blue on buff inscriptions and ornaments.

Nos. 2136-2138 were issued imperforate in sheets of 2. Value, $30.

For overprint of No. 2137, see No. 2334.

S. P. Korolev, Sputnik I Emblem — A756

30h, Yuri A. Gagarin & Vostok I. 40h, Alexei Leonov. 1k, Neil A. Armstrong & footprint on moon. 1.60k, Construction of orbital space station.

1977, Oct. 4

2139	A756	20h multi	.25	.25
2140	A756	30h multi	.25	.25
2141	A756	40h multi	.25	.25
2142	A756	1k multi	.25	.25
2143	A756	1.60k multi	.60	.25
		Nos. 2139-2143 (5)	1.60	1.25

Space research, 20th anniv. of 1st earth satellite.

Sailors, Cruiser Aurora — A757

1977, Nov. 7

2144	A757	30h multi	.25	.25

60th anniv. of Russian October Revolution.

"Russia," Arms of USSR, Kremlin — A758

1977, Nov. 7

2145	A758	30h multi	.25	.25

55th anniversary of the USSR.

"Science" — A759

1977, Nov. 17

2146	A759	3k multi	.50	.25

Czechoslovak Academy of Science, 25th anniversary.

Painting Type of 1967

Paintings: 2k, "Fear" (woman), by Jan Mudroch. 2.40k, Jan Francisci, portrait by Peter M. Bohun. 2.60k, Vaclav Hollar, self-portrait, 1647. 3k, Young Woman, 1528, by Lucas Cranach. 5k, Cleopatra, by Rubens.

1977, Nov. 27 Engr. *Perf. 11½*

2147	A565	2k multi	.75	.45
2148	A565	2.40k multi	1.20	.90
2149	A565	2.60k multi	1.20	.90
2150	A565	3k multi	.75	.60
2151	A565	5k multi	1.50	1.50
		Nos. 2147-2151 (5)	5.40	4.35

Nos. 2147-2151 were each issued in sheets of 4. Value, set $25.

View of Bratislava, by Georg Hoefnagel — A760

Design: 3.60k, Arms of Bratislava, 1436.

1977, Dec. 6

2152	A760	3k multi	1.90	1.60
2153	A760	3.60k multi	.80	.50

Nos. 2152-21531 were each issued in sheets of 4. Value, set $12.50.

See Nos. 2174-2175, 2270-2271, 2331-2332, 2364-2365, 2422-2423, 2478-2479, 2514-2515, 2570-2571, 2618-2619.

Stamp Pattern and Post Horn — A761

1977, Dec. 18 Engr. & Photo.

2154	A761	1k multi	.25	.25

Stamp Day.

Zdenek Nejedly — A762

Karl Marx — A763

1978, Feb. 10 *Perf. 11½*

2155	A762	30h multi	.25	.25
2156	A763	40h multi	.25	.25

Zdenek Nejedly (1878-1962), musicologist and historian; Karl Marx (1818-1883), political philosopher.

Civilians Greeting Guardsmen — A764

Intellectual, Farm Woman and Steel Worker, Flag — A765

1978, Feb. 25

2157	A764	1k gold & multi	.25	.25
2158	A765	1k gold & multi	.25	.25

30th anniv. of "Victorious February" (No. 2157), and Natl. Front (No. 2158).

An imperforate sheet of four of No. 2157 was sold with an admission ticket to PRAGA 78 international philatelic exhibition. Value, $4.

See note after 2190.

Yuri A. Gagarin, Vostok I — A766

Design: 30h, 3.60k, like No. 2140.

Engraved; Overprint Photogravure (Blue and carmine on 30h, green and lilac rose on 3.60k)

1978, Mar. 2 *Perf. 11½x12*

2159	A766	30h dk red	.25	.25
2160	A766	3.60k vio bl	2.40	2.40

Capt. V. Remek, 1st Czechoslovakian cosmonaut on Russian spaceship Soyuz 28, Mar. 2-9.

10k Coin, 1964, and 25k Coin, 1965 — A767

40h, Medal for Culture, 1972. 1.40k, Charles University medal, 1948. 3k, Ferdinand I medal, 1568. 5k, Gold florin, 1335.

1978, Mar. 14 Engr. & Photo.

2161	A767	20h sil & multi	.25	.25
2162	A767	40h sil & multi	.25	.25
2163	A767	1.40k gold & multi	1.00	.25
2164	A767	3k gold & multi	.35	.25
2165	A767	5k gold & multi	.35	.25
		Nos. 2161-2165 (5)	2.20	1.25

650th anniversary of Kremnica Mint.

Tire Tracks and Ball — A768

1978, Mar. 15

2166	A768	60h multi	.25	.25

Road safety.

Congress Emblem — A769

1978, Apr. 16 *Perf. 11½*

2167	A769	1k multi	.25	.25

9th World Trade Union Cong., Prague 1978.

Shot Put and Praha '78 Emblem A770

1k, Pole vault. 3.60k, Women runners.

1978, Apr. 26

2168	A770	40h multi	.30	.30
2169	A770	1k multi	.40	.30
2170	A770	3.60k multi	.90	.50
		Nos. 2168-2170 (3)	1.60	1.10

5th European Athletic Championships, Prague 1978.

Ice Hockey — A771

Designs: 30h, Hockey. 2k, Ice hockey play.

1978, Apr. 26

2171	A771	30h multi	.25	.25
2172	A771	60h multi	.35	.25
2173	A771	2k multi	.35	.25
		Nos. 2171-2173 (3)	.95	.75

5th European Ice Hockey Championships and 70th anniversary of Bandy hockey.

Bratislava Type of 1977

Designs: 3k, Bratislava, 1955, by Orest Dubay. 3.60k, Fishpound Square, Bratislava, 1955, by Imro Weiner-Kral.

1978, May 9 Engr. *Perf. 11½*

2174	A760	3k multi	.95	.80
2175	A760	3.60k multi	1.25	.80

Nos. 2174-2175 were each issued in sheets of 4. Value, set $10.

Prague Castle Art Type of 1971

3k, King Ottokar II, detail from tomb. 3.60k, Charles IV, detail from votive panel by Jan Ocka.

1978, May 9

2176	A634	3k multi	.75	.60
2177	A634	3.60k multi	3.50	2.40

Nos. 2176-2177 were each issued in sheets of 4. Value, set $18.

Ministry of Post, Prague A772

Engraved and Photogravure

1978, May 29 *Perf. 12x11½*

2178	A772	60h multi	.25	.25

14th session of permanent COMECOM Commission (Ministers of Post and Telecommunications of Socialist Countries).

Palacky Bridge A773

Prague Bridges and PRAGA '78 Emblem: 40h, Railroad bridge. 1k, Bridge of May 1. 2k, Manes Bridge. 3k, Svatopluk Cech Bridge. 5.40k, Charles Bridge.

1978, May 30

2179	A773	20h blk & multi	.25	.25
2180	A773	40h blk & multi	.25	.25
2181	A773	1k blk & multi	.25	.25
2182	A773	2k blk & multi	.25	.25
2183	A773	3k blk & multi	.30	.25
2184	A773	5.40k blk & multi	1.40	.25
		Nos. 2179-2184 (6)	2.70	1.50

PRAGA 1978 International Philatelic Exhibition, Prague, Sept. 8-17.

St. Peter and Apostles, Clock Tower, and Emblem A774

Town Hall Clock, Prague, by Josef Manes, and PRAGA '78 Emblem: 1k, Astronomical clock. 2k, Prague's coat of arms. 3k, Grape harvest (September). 3.60k, Libra. 10k, Arms surrounded by zodiac signs and scenes symbolic of 12 months, horiz. 2k, 3k, 3.60k show details from design of 10k.

1978, June 20 *Perf. 11½x11*

2185	A774	40h multi	.25	.25
2186	A774	1k multi	.25	.25
2187	A774	2k multi	.25	.25
2188	A774	3k multi	1.50	.35
2189	A774	3.60k multi	.55	.25
		Nos. 2185-2189 (5)	2.80	1.35

Souvenir Sheet

Perf. 12x12

2190	A774	10k multi	10.00	7.50

PRAGA '78 Intl. Philatelic Exhibition, Prague, Sept. 8-17. No. 2190 contains one 50x40mm stamp. Sheet exists imperf. Value $27.50.

A non-valid souvenir sheet contains 4 imperf. examples of No. 2157. Sold only with PRAGA ticket.

Folk Dancers — A775

1978, July 7 *Perf. 11½x12*

2191	A775	30h multi	.25	.25

25th Folklore Festival, Vychodna.

Overpass and PRAGA Emblem — A776

1k, 2k, Modern office buildings, diff. 6k, Old & new Prague. 20k, Charles Bridge & Old Town, by Vincent Morstadt, 1828.

1978 *Perf. 12x11½*

2192	A776	60h blk & multi	.25	.25
2193	A776	1k blk & multi	.25	.25
2194	A776	2k blk & multi	.25	.25
2195	A776	6k blk & multi	1.50	.75
		Nos. 2192-2195 (4)	2.25	1.50

Souvenir Sheet

Engr.

2196	A776	20k multi	9.50	7.50

PRAGA 1978 Intl. Phil. Exhib., Prague, Sept. 8-17. No. 2196 also for 60th anniv. of Czechoslovak postage stamps. No. 2196 contains one 61x45mm stamp.

Issued: Nos. 2192-2195, 9/8; No. 2196, 9/10.

Souvenir Sheet

Titian (1488-1576), Venetian painter — A777

No. 2197a, Apollo's Companion, by Titian. No. 2197b, King Midas. Stamps show details from "Apollo Flaying Marsya" by Titian.

1978, Sept. 12 *Perf. 11½*

2197	A777	Sheet of 2	11.00	8.75
a.		10k multi	5.00	4.25
b.		10k multi	5.00	4.25

No. 2197 with dark blue marginal inscription "FIP" was sold only with entrance ticket to PRAGA Philatelic Exhibition. Value $25.

Exhibition Hall — A778

Engraved and Photogravure

1978, Sept. 13 *Perf. 11½x11*

2198	A778	30h multi	.25	.25

22nd International Engineering Fair, Brno.

Postal Newspaper Service — A779

TV Screen, Headquarters and Logo — A780

Newspaper, Microphone A781

1978, Sept. 21 *Perf. 11½*

2199	A779	30h multi	.25	.25
2200	A780	30h multi	.25	.25
2201	A781	30h multi	.25	.25
		Nos. 2199-2201 (3)	.75	.75

Postal News Service, 25th anniv.; Czechoslovakian television, 25th anniv.; Press, Broadcasting and Television Day.

Sulky Race A782

Pardubice Steeplechase: 10h, Falling horses and jockeys at fence. 30h, Race. 40h, Horses passing post. 1.60k, Hurdling. 4.40k, Winner.

1978, Oct. 6 *Perf. 12x11½*

2202	A782	10h multi	.25	.25
2203	A782	20h multi	.25	.25
2204	A782	30h multi	.25	.25
2205	A782	40h multi	.25	.25
2206	A782	1.60k multi	.25	.25
2207	A782	4.40k multi	1.25	.25
		Nos. 2202-2207 (6)	2.50	1.50

Woman Holding Arms of Czechoslovakia A783

1978, Oct. 28 *Perf. 11½*

2208	A783	60h multi	.25	.25

60th anniversary of independence.

Art Type of 1974

2.40k, Flowers, by Jakub Bohdan (1660-1724). 3k, The Dream of Salas, by Ludovit Fulla, horiz. 3.60k, Apostle with Censer, Master of the Spissko Capitals (c. 1480-90).

1978, Nov. 27 Engr.

2209	A700	2.40k multi	.90	.45
2210	A700	3k multi	1.00	.75
2211	A700	3.60k multi	2.75	2.25
		Nos. 2209-2211 (3)	4.65	3.45

Slovak National Gallery, 30th anniversary.

Nos. 2209-2211 were each issued in sheets of 4. Value, set $20.

Musicians, by Jan Könyves — A784

Slovak Ceramics: 30h, Janosik on Horseback, by Jozef Franko. 40h, Woman in Folk Costume by Michal Polasko. 1k, Three Girls Singing, by Ignac Bizmayer. 1.60k, Janosik Dancing, by Ferdis Kostka.

Engraved and Photogravure

1978, Dec. 5 *Perf. 11½x12*

2212	A784	20h multi	.25	.25
2213	A784	30h multi	.25	.25
2214	A784	40h multi	.25	.25
2215	A784	1k multi	.25	.25
2216	A784	1.60k multi	.60	.25
		Nos. 2212-2216 (5)	1.60	1.25

Alfons Mucha and his Design for 1918 Issue — A785

1978, Dec. 18 *Perf. 11½*

2217	A785	1k multi	.25	.25

60th Stamp Day.

COMECON Building, Moscow — A786

1979, Jan. 1 *Perf. 11½*

2218	A786	1k multi	.25	.25

Council for Mutual Economic Aid (COMECON), 30th anniversary.

Woman's Head and Grain — A787

Woman, Workers, Child, Doves — A788

1979, Jan. 1

2219	A787	30h multi	.25	.25
2220	A788	60h multi	.25	.25

United Agricultural Production Assoc., 30th anniv. (30h); Czechoslovakian Federation, 10th anniv. (60h).

Soyuz 28, Rockets and Capsule — A789

60h, Astronauts Aleksei Gubarev and Vladimir Remek on launching pad, vert. 1.60k, Soviet astronauts J. Romanenko and G. Grecko, Salyut 6 and recovery ship. 2k, Salyut-Soyuz orbital complex, post office in space and Czechoslovakia No. 2153. 4k, Soyuz 28, crew after landing and trajectory map, vert. 10k, Gubarev and Remek, Intercosmos emblem, arms of Czechoslovakia and USSR.

1979, Mar. 2

2221	A789	30h multi	.25	.25
2222	A789	60h multi	.25	.25
2223	A789	1.60k multi	.25	.25
2224	A789	2k multi	1.40	.25
2225	A789	4k multi	.60	.25
		Nos. 2221-2225 (5)	2.75	1.25

Souvenir Sheet

2226	A789	10k multi	4.50	2.75

1st anniv. of joint Czechoslovak-Soviet space flight. Size of No. 2226: 76x93mm (stamp 39x55mm). No. 2226 has Cyrillic inscription, No. 2455a does not.

No. 2226 exists imperf. Value, $30.

Alpine Bellflowers — A790

Mountain Flowers: 20h, Crocus. 30h, Pinks. 40h, Alpine hawkweed. 3k, Larkspur.

1979, Mar. 23 ***Perf. 11½***

2227	A790	10h multi	.25	.25
2228	A790	20h multi	.25	.25
2229	A790	30h multi	.25	.25
2230	A790	40h multi	.25	.25

Perf. 14

2231	A790	3k multi	1.10	.25
		Nos. 2227-2231 (5)	2.10	1.25

Mountain Rescue Service, 25th anniversary.

The 3k exists perf. 11½. Value, $20 unused, $10 used.

The 3k was issued in sheets of 10. Values: perf 14 (No. 2231), $25; perf 11½, $180.

Stylized Satellite, Dial, Tape — A791

1979, Apr. 2

2232	A791	10h multi	.25	.25

Telecommunications research, 30th anniv.

Artist and Model, Dove, Bratislava Castle — A792

Cog Wheels, Transformer and Student — A793

Musical Instruments, Bratislava Castle — A794

Pioneer Scarf, IYC Emblem — A795

Red Star, Man, Child and Doves — A796

1979, Apr. 2

2233	A792	20h multi	.25	.25
2234	A793	20h multi	.25	.25
2235	A794	30h multi	.25	.25
2236	A795	30h multi	.25	.25
2237	A796	60h multi	.25	.25
		Nos. 2233-2237 (5)	1.25	1.25

Fine Arts Academy, Bratislava, 30th anniv.; Slovak Technical University, 40th anniv.; Radio Symphony Orchestra, Bratislava, 30th anniv.; Young Pioneers, 30th anniv. and IYC; Peace Movement, 30th anniversary.

Prague Castle Art Type of 1971

3k, Burial crown of King Ottokar II. 3.60k, Portrait of Mrs. Reitmayer, by Karel Purkyne.

1979, May 9 ***Perf. 11½***

2238	A634	3k multi	1.75	1.10
2239	A634	3.60k multi	1.75	.80

Nos. 2238-2239 were each issued in sheets of 4. Value, set $13.50.

Arms of Vlachovo Brezi, 1538 — A797

Animals in Heraldry: 60h, Jesenik, 1509 (bear and eagle). 1.20k, Vysoke Myto, 1471 (St. George slaying dragon). 1.80k,Martin, 1854 (St. Martin giving coat to beggar). 2k, Zebrak, 1674 (mythological beast).

1979, May 25 ***Perf. 11½x12***

2240	A797	30h multi	.25	.25
2241	A797	60h multi	.25	.25
2242	A797	1.20k multi	.25	.25
2243	A797	1.80k multi	*1.00*	*.25*
2244	A797	2k multi	.60	.25
		Nos. 2240-2244 (5)	*2.35*	*1.25*

Forest, Thriving and Destroyed A798

Designs: 1.80k, Water. 3.60k, City. 4k, Cattle. All designs show good and bad environment, separated by exclamation point; Man and Biosphere emblem.

1979, June 22 **Engr.** ***Perf. 11½***

2245	A798	60h multi	.25	.25
2246	A798	1.80k multi	.25	.25
2247	A798	3.60k multi	*1.60*	*.60*
2248	A798	4k multi	1.10	.25
		Nos. 2245-2248 (4)	*3.20*	*1.35*

Man and Biosphere Program of UNESCO.

Nos. 2245-2248 were each issued in sheets of 10. Value, set $32.50.

Refinery, Smokestacks A799

Engraved and Photogravure

1979, Aug. 29 ***Perf. 11x11½***

2249	A799	30h multi	.25	.25

Slovak National Uprising, 35th anniversary.

Frog and Goat A800

Book Illustrations (IYC Emblem and): 40h, Knight on horseback. 60h, Maidens. 1k, Boy with sled following rooster. 3k, King riding flying beast.

1979, Apr. 2 ***Perf. 11½x11***

2250	A800	20h multi	.25	.25
2251	A800	40h multi	.25	.25
2252	A800	60h multi	.25	.25
2253	A800	1k multi	.25	.25
2254	A800	3k multi	*1.10*	*.25*
		Nos. 2250-2254 (5)	*2.10*	*1.25*

Prize-winning designs, 7th biennial exhibition of illustrations for children's books, Bratislava; International Year of the Child.

Printed with labels showing story characters. Value, set with attached labels, $2.75.

"Bone Shaker" Bicycles, 1870 A801

Bicycles from: 20h, 1978. 40h, 1910. 60h, 1886. 3.60k, 1820.

1979, Sept. 14 ***Perf. 12x11½***

2255	A801	20h multi	.25	.25
2256	A801	40h multi	.25	.25
2257	A801	60h multi	.25	.25
2258	A801	2k multi	.25	.25
2259	A801	3.60k multi	1.50	.30
		Nos. 2255-2259 (5)	2.50	1.30

Bracket Clock, 18th Century A802

Designs: 18th century clocks.

1979, Oct. 1 ***Perf. 11½***

2260	A802	40h multi	.25	.25
2261	A802	60h multi	.25	.25
2262	A802	80h multi	1.25	.25
2263	A802	1k multi	.25	.25
2264	A802	2k multi	.35	.25
		Nos. 2260-2264 (5)	2.35	1.25

Painting Type of 1967

Paintings: 1.60k, Sunday by the River, by Alois Moravec. 2k, Self-portrait, by Gustav Mally. 3k, Self-portrait, by Ilia Yefimovic Repin. 3.60k, Horseback Rider, by Jan Bauch. 5k, Dancing Peasants, by Albrecht Dürer.

1979, Nov. 27 **Engr.** ***Perf. 12***

2265	A565	1.60k multi	.40	.35
2266	A565	2k multi	.60	.50
2267	A565	3k multi	.60	.50
2268	A565	3.60k multi	2.00	1.75
2269	A565	5k multi	1.60	1.25
		Nos. 2265-2269 (5)	5.20	4.35

Nos. 2265-2269 were each issued in sheets of 4. Value, set $20.

Bratislava Type of 1977

Designs: 3k, Bratislava Castle on the Danube, by L. Janscha, 1787. 3.60k, Bratislava Castle, stone engraving by Wolf, 1815.

1979, Dec. 5

2270	A760	3k multi	1.00	.80
2271	A760	3.60k multi	1.75	1.50

Nos. 2270-2272 were each issued in sheets of 4. Value, set $12.50.

Stamp Day — A803

Engraved and Photogravure

1979, Dec. 18 ***Perf. 11½x12***

2272	A803	1k multi	.25	.25

Electronic Circuits — A804

Designs: 50h, Satellite dish. 2k, Airplane. 3k, Computer punch tape.

1979-80 **Photo.** ***Perf. 11½x12***

Coil Stamps

2273	A804	50h red	.25	.25
2274	A804	1k brown	.25	.25
2275	A804	2k green ('80)	.30	.25
2276	A804	3k lake ('80)	.45	.25
		Nos. 2273-2276 (4)	1.25	1.00

The 1k comes in two shades.

Runners and Dove A805

Engraved and Photogravure

1980, Jan. 29 ***Perf. 12x11½***

2289	A805	50h multi	.25	.25

50th Intl. Peace Marathon, Kosice, Oct. 4.

Downhill Skiing — A806

1980, Jan. 29 ***Perf. 11½x12***

2290	A806	1k shown	.30	.25
2291	A806	2k Speed skating	.95	.35
2292	A806	3k Four-man bobsled	.80	.35
		Nos. 2290-2292 (3)	2.05	.95

13th Winter Olympic Games, Lake Placid, NY, Feb. 12-24.

Basketball — A807

1980, Jan. 29 *Perf. 11½*

2293 A807 40h shown .25 .25
2294 A807 1k Swimming .25 .25
2295 A807 2k Hurdles 1.50 .35
2296 A807 3.60k Fencing 1.10 .30
Nos. 2293-2296 (4) 3.10 1.15

22nd Olympic Games, Moscow, 7/19-8/3.

Arms Type of 1977

No. 2297, Bystrice Nad Pernstejnem. No. 2298, Kunstat. No. 2299, Rozmital Pod Tremsinem. No. 2300, Zlata Idka.

1980, Feb. 20 *Perf. 11½*

2297 A745 50h multi .25 .25
2298 A745 50h multi .25 .25
2299 A745 50h multi .25 .25
2300 A745 50h multi .25 .25
Nos. 2297-2300 (4) 1.00 1.00

Theatrical Mask — A808

Slovak National Theater, Actors — A809

1980, Mar. 1

2301 A808 50h multi .25 .25
2302 A809 1k multi .25 .25

50th Jiraskuv Hronov Theatrical Ensemble Review; Slovak National Theater, Bratislava, 60th anniversary.

Mouse in Space, Satellite — A810

Intercosmos: 1k, Weather map, satellite. 1.60k, Intersputnik television transmission. 4k, Camera, satellite. 5k, Czech satellite station, 1978, horiz. 10k, Intercosmos emblem, horiz.

1980, Apr. 12 *Perf. 11½x12, 12x11½*

2303 A810 50h multi .25 .25
2304 A810 1k multi .25 .25
2305 A810 1.60k multi 1.40 .25
2306 A810 4k multi 1.00 .25
2307 A810 5k multi 1.40 .25
Nos. 2303-2307 (5) 4.30 1.25

Souvenir Sheet

2308 A810 10k multi 3.50 2.50

Intercosmos cooperative space program.
No. 2305 was issued in a sheet of 10. Value, $25.
No. 2308 exists imperf. Value, $30.

Police Corps Banner, Emblem — A811

1980, Apr. 17 *Perf. 11½*

2309 A811 50h multi .25 .25

National Police Corps, 35th anniversary.

Lenin's 110th Birth Anniversary — A812

Design: No. 2311, Engels's 160th birth anniv.

1980, Apr. 22

2310 A812 1k tan & brn .25 .25
2311 A812 1k lt grn & brn .25 .25

Old and Modern Prague, Czech Flag, Bouquet A813

Boy Writing "Peace" A814

Pact Members' Flags, Dove — A815

Czech and Soviet Arms, Prague and Moscow Views A816

1980, May 6 *Perf. 12x11½*

2312 A813 50h multi .25 .25
2313 A814 1k multi .25 .25
2314 A815 1k multi .25 .25
2315 A816 1k multi .25 .25
Nos. 2312-2315 (4) 1.00 1.00

Liberation by Soviet army, 35th anniv.; Soviet victory in WWII, 35th anniv.; Signing of Warsaw Pact (Bulgaria, Czechoslovakia, German Democratic Rep., Hungary, Poland, Romania, USSR), 25th anniv.; Czechoslovak-Soviet Treaty of Friendship, Cooperation and Mutual Aid, 10th anniv.

Souvenir Sheet

UN, 35th Anniv. — A817

1980, June 3 **Engr.** *Perf. 12*

2316 A817 Sheet of 2 3.25 2.50
a. 4k multicolored 1.25 1.25

Athletes Parading Banners in Strahov Stadium, Prague, Spartakiad Emblem — A818

Engraved and Photogravure

1980, June 3 *Perf. 12x11½*

2317 A818 50h shown .25 .25
2318 A818 1k Gymnast, vert. .25 .25

Spartakiad 1980, Prague, June 26-29.

Aechmea Fasciata — A819

Flowers: 50ch, Gerbera Jamesonii. 1k, Aechmea fasciata. 2k, Strelitzia reginae. 4k, Paphiopedilum.

1980, Aug. 13 *Perf. 12*

2319 A819 50h multicolored .45 .25
2320 A819 1k multicolored 2.10 .65
2321 A819 2k multicolored .55 .25
2322 A819 4k multicolored 2.25 .25
Nos. 2319-2322 (4) 5.35 1.40

Olomouc and Bratislava Flower Shows.
Nos. 2319-2322 were each issued in sheets of 10. Values, set: unused, $65; used, $30.

A820

Designs: Folktale character embroideries.

1980, Sept. 24 *Perf. 11½x12*

2323 A820 50h Chad girl .25 .25
2324 A820 1k Punch and dog .25 .25
2325 A820 2k Dandy and Posy .35 .25
2326 A820 4k Lion and moon 1.30 .75
2327 A820 5k Wallachian dance .65 .25
Nos. 2323-2327 (5) 2.80 1.75

National Census A821

1980, Sept. 24 *Perf. 12x11½*

2328 A821 1k multi .25 .25

Prague Castle Type of 1971

Designs: 3k, Old Palace gateway. 4k, Armorial lion, 16th century.

1980, Oct. 28 *Perf. 12*

2329 A634 3k multi 1.60 1.25
2330 A634 4k multi 1.10 .65

Nos. 2329-2330 were each issued in sheets of 4. Value, set: unused, $12; used, $9.

Bratislava Type of 1977

3k, View across the Danube, by J. Eder, 1810. 4k, The Old Royal Bridge, by J.A. Lantz, 1820.

1980, Oct. 28

2331 A760 3k multi 1.60 1.40
2332 A760 4k multi 1.25 .80

Nos. 2331-2332 were each issued in sheets of 4. Value, set $16.

10th Anniversary of Socialist Youth Federation — A822

1980, Nov. 9 *Perf. 12x11½*

2333 A822 50h multi .25 .25

No. 2137 Overprinted 3. / MEZINARODNI VELETRH ZNAMEK / ESSEN '80 in Red

1980, Nov. 18

2334 A755 1.60k multi 18.00 10.00

Czechoslovak Day/ ESSEN '80, 3rd International Stamp Exhibition, No. 2334 has overprinted red marginal inscription.

Painting Type of 1967

Designs: 1k, Pavel Jozef Safarik, by Jozef B. Klemens. 2k, Peasant Revolt mosaic, Anna Podzemna. 3k, St. Lucia, 14th century statue. 4k, Waste Heaps, by Jan Zrzavy, horiz. 5k, Labor, sculpture by Jan Stursa.

1980, Nov. 27 **Engr.** *Perf. 12*

2335 A565 1k multi 1.25 1.10
2336 A565 2k multi 1.25 1.10
2337 A565 3k multi .65 .45
2338 A565 4k multi .75 .55
2339 A565 5k multi .75 .55
Nos. 2335-2339 (5) 4.65 3.75

Nos. 2335-2339 were each issued in sheets of 4. Value, set $27.

Stamp Day — A823

Engraved and Photogravure

1980, Dec. 18 *Perf. 11½x12*

2340 A823 1k multi .25 .25

7th Five-year Plan, 1981-1985 A824

1981, Jan. 1 *Perf. 11½*

2341 A824 50h multi .25 .25

International Year of the Disabled A825

1981, Feb. 24

2342 A825 1k multi .25 .25

Landau, 1800 A826

1k, Mail coach, 1830. 3.60k, Mail sled, 1840. 5k, 4-horse mail coach, 1860. 7k, Open carriage, 1840.

1981, Feb. 25 *Perf. 12x11½*

2343 A826 50h shown .25 .25
2344 A826 1k multi .25 .25
2345 A826 3.60k multi 1.00 .35
2346 A826 5k multi .75 .25

2347 A826 7k multi 1.10 .75
a. Sheet of 4 15.00 10.00
Nos. 2343-2347 (5) 3.35 1.85

WIPA '81 Intl. Philatelic Exhibition, Vienna, Austria, May 22-31. No. 2347a issued May 10.

Wolfgang Amadeus Mozart — A827

Famous Men: No. 2348, Josef Hlavka (1831-1908). No. 2349, Juraj Hronec (1881-1959). No. 2350, Jan Sverma (1901-44). No. 2351, Mikulas Schneider-Trnavsky (1881-1958). No. 2352, B. Bolzano (1781-1848). No. 2353, Dimitri Shostakovich, composer. No. 2354, George Bernard Shaw, playwright.

1981, Mar. 10 ***Perf. 11½***

2348 A827 50h multi .25 .25
2349 A827 50h multi .25 .25
2350 A827 50h multi .25 .25
2351 A827 50h multi .25 .25
2352 A827 1k multi .45 .25
2353 A827 1k multi .25 .25
2354 A827 1k multi .25 .25
2355 A827 1k multi .25 .25
Nos. 2348-2355 (8) 2.20 2.00

Souvenir Sheet

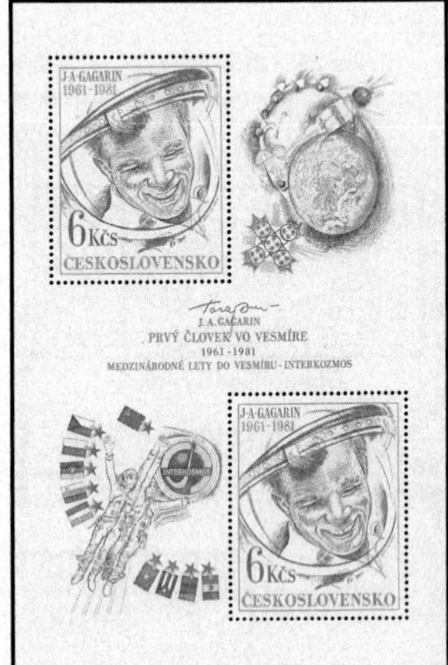

Yuri Gagarin — A828

1981, Apr. 5 ***Perf. 12***

2356 A828 Sheet of 2 4.50 4.00
a. 6k multicolored 2.00 1.60

20th anniv. of 1st manned space flight.

Workers and Banner A829

1k, Hands holding banner. 4k, Worker holding banner, vert.

1981, Apr. 6 ***Perf. 12x11½***

2357 A829 50h shown .25 .25
2358 A829 1k multi .25 .25
2359 A829 4k multi .35 .25
Nos. 2357-2359 (3) .85 .75

Czechoslovakian Communist Party, 60th anniv.

Congress Emblem, View of Prague — A830

1981, Apr. 6

2360 A830 50h shown .25 .25
2361 A830 1k Bratislava .25 .25

16th Communist Party Congress.

Agriculture Museum, 90th Anniv. — A831

1981, May 14 ***Perf. 11½x12***

2362 A831 1k multi .25 .25

Natl. Assembly Elections — A832

1981, June 1

2363 A832 50h multi .25 .25

Bratislava Type of 1977

Designs: 3k, Bratislava Castle, by G.B. Probst, 1760. 4k, Grassalkovic Palace, by C. Bschor, 1815.

1981, June 10 ***Perf. 12***

2364 A760 3k multi 1.40 1.25
2365 A760 4k multi 1.00 .75

Nos. 2364-2365 were each issued in sheets of 4. Value, set: unused, $12; used, $9.

Uran and Red October (Health) Resorts A833

Successes of Socialist Achievements Exhibition: 1k, Brno-Bratislava Highway, Jihlava. 2k, Nuclear power station, Jaslovske Bohunice.

1981, June 10 ***Perf. 12x11½***

2366 A833 80h multi .25 .25
2367 A833 1k multi .25 .25
2368 A833 2k multi .25 .25
Nos. 2366-2368 (3) .75 .75

Border Defense Units, 30th Anniv. A834

Civil Defense, 30th Anniv. A835

Union for Cooperation with the Army (SVAZARM), 30th Anniv. — A836

Intl.Youth Character Building Contest, Rysy Mtn., 25th Anniv. — A837

Engraved and Photogravure

1981, July 11 ***Perf. 11½***

2369 A834 40h multi .25 .25
2370 A835 50h multi .25 .25
2371 A836 1k multi .25 .25
2372 A837 3.60k multi .75 .30
Nos. 2369-2372 (4) 1.50 1.05

30th Natl. Festival of Amateur Puppet Ensembles — A838

1981, July 2 ***Perf. 11½***

2373 A838 2k Punch and Devil .50 .25

Souvenir Sheet

Guernica, by Pablo Picasso — A839

1981, July 2 **Engr.** ***Perf. 11½x12***

2374 A839 10k multi 3.50 2.50

Picasso's birth centenary; 45th anniv. of Intl. Brigades in Spain.

Cat Holding Flower, by Etienne Delessert A840

8th Biennial Exhibition of Children's Book Illustrations (Designs by): 50h, Albin Brunovsky, vert. 1k, Adolf Born. 2k, Vive Tolli. 10k, Suekichi Akaba.

Engraved and Photogravure

1981, Sept. 5 ***Perf. 11½***

2375 A840 50h multi .25 .25
2376 A840 1k multi .25 .25
2377 A840 2k multi .25 .25
2378 A840 4k multi .55 .25
2379 A840 10k multi 1.50 .25
Nos. 2375-2379 (5) 2.80 1.25

Prague Zoo, 50th Anniv. — A841

1981, Sept. 28 ***Perf. 11½x12***

2380 A841 50h Gorillas .45 .25
2381 A841 1k Lions .80 .25
2382 A841 7k Przewalski's horses 2.25 .80
Nos. 2380-2382 (3) 3.50 1.30

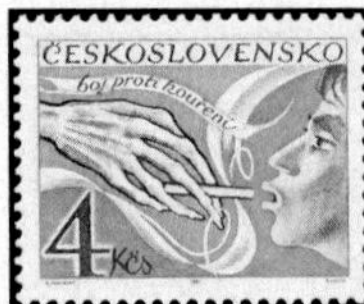

Anti-smoking Campaign A842

1981, Oct. 27 ***Perf. 12***

2383 A842 4k multi .85 .45

No. 2383 was issued in sheets of 10, containing 8 stamps and 2 labels. Values: single with label attached, $1.25; sheet, $9.

Prague Castle Art Type of 1971

Designs: 3k, Carved dragon, Palais Lobkovitz, 16th cent. 4k, St. Vitus Cathedral, by J. Sember and G. Dobler, 19th cent.

1981, Oct. 28

2384 A634 3k multi .75 .45
2385 A634 4k multi 1.75 1.40

Nos. 2384-2385 were each issued in sheets of 4. Value, set $12.

Painting Type of 1967

Designs: 1k, View of Prague, by Vaclav Hollar (1607-1677). 2k, Czechoslovak Academy medallion, engraved by Otakar Spaniel (1881-1955). 3k, Jihoceska Vysivka, by Zdenek Sklenar (b. 1910). 4k, Still Life, by A.M. Gerasimov (1881-1963). 5k, Standing Woman, by Pablo Picasso (1881-1973).

1981, Nov. 27 **Engr.** ***Perf. 12***

2386 A565 1k multi 2.10 1.40
2387 A565 2k multi .55 .30
2388 A565 3k multi .70 .45
2389 A565 4k multi .85 .45
2390 A565 5k multi 1.40 1.10
Nos. 2386-2390 (5) 5.60 3.70

Nos. 2386-2390 were each issued in sheets of 4. Value, set $27.50.

Sheets of No. 2390 exist with center gutter inscribed with Philexfrance 82 and FIP emblems. Value, $10.

Stamp Day — A843

Engraved and Photogravure

1981, Dec. 18 ***Perf. 11½x12***

2391 A843 1k Engraver Edward Karel .25 .25

Russian Workers' Party, Prague Congress, 70th Anniv. — A844

1982, Jan. 18 ***Perf. 12***

2392 A844 2k Lenin .50 .25
a. Sheet of 4 *4.50 4.00*

No. 2392 issued in sheet of 8. Value $10.

1982 World Cup Soccer A845

Designs: Various soccer players.

1982, Jan. 29 ***Perf. 12x11½***

2393 A845 1k multi .25 .25
2394 A845 3.60k multi .70 .30
2395 A845 4k multi 1.40 .50
Nos. 2393-2395 (3) 2.35 1.05

10th World Trade Union Congress, Havana — A846

1982, Feb. 10 ***Perf. 11½***

2396 A846 1k multi .25 .25

Arms of Hrob — A847

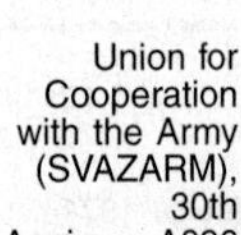

Arms of various cities: No. 2398, Nove Mesto Nad Metuji. No. 2399, Trencin. No. 2400, Mlada Boleslav.

1982, Feb. 10 ***Perf. 12x11½***

2397 A847 50h shown .25 .25
2398 A847 50h multicolored .25 .25
2399 A847 50h multicolored .25 .25
2400 A847 50h multicolored .25 .25
Nos. 2397-2400 (4) 1.00 1.00

See Nos. 2499-2502, 2542-2544, 2595-2597, 2783-2786.

50th Anniv. of the Great Strike at Most — A848

1982, Mar. 23 ***Perf. 11½***

2401 A848 1k multi .25 .25

60th Intl. Railway Union Congress — A849

6k, Steam locomotive, 1922, electric, 1982.

1982, Mar. 23 ***Perf. 12x11½***

2402 A849 6k multicolored 3.25 .95

10th Workers' Congress, Prague — A850

1982, Apr. 15

2403 A850 1k multi .25 .25

George Dimitrov — A851

1982, May 1

2404 A851 50h multi .25 .25

A852

Engravings: 40h, The Muse Euterpe Playing a Flute, by Crispin de Passe (1565-1637). 50h, The Lute Player, by Jacob de Gheyn (1565-1629). 1k, Woman Flautist, by Adriaen Collaert (1560-1618). 2k, Musicians in a Hostel, by Rembrandt (1606-1669). 3k, Hurdy-gurdy Player, by Jacques Callot (1594-1635).

1982, May 18 ***Perf. 11½x12***

2405 A852 40h multi .25 .25
2406 A852 50h multi .25 .25
2407 A852 1k multi .25 .25
2408 A852 2k multi .30 .25
2409 A852 3k multi 1.10 .60
Nos. 2405-2409 (5) 2.15 1.60

10th Lidice Intl. Children's Drawing Contest — A853

1982, May 18

2410 A853 2k multi 1.25 .90

Issued in sheets of 6 with 3 labels. Value $9.

40th Anniv. of Destruction of Lidice and Lezaky — A854

1982, June 4 ***Perf. 11½***

2411 A854 1k Girl, rose .45 .25
2412 A854 1k Hands, barbed wire .45 .25

Souvenir Sheet

UN Disarmament Conference — A855

1982, June 4 ***Perf. 12***

2413 A855 Sheet of 2 9.00 7.00
a. 6k Woman holding doves 4.00 3.00

Souvenir Sheet

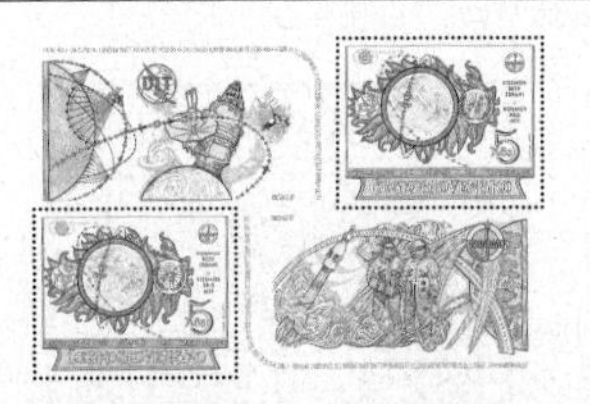

2nd UN Conference on Peaceful Uses of Outer Space, Vienna, Aug. 9-21 — A856

1982, Aug. 9 **Engr. & Photo.**

2414 A856 Sheet of 2 12.50 9.00
a. 5k multi 4.50 3.50

Krivoklat Castle A857

1k, Statues (Krivoklat). 2k, Nitra Castle. 3k, Pottery, lock (Nitra).

1982, Aug. 31 ***Perf. 12x11½***

2415 A857 50h shown .25 .25
2416 A857 1k multi .25 .25
2417 A857 2k multi .30 .25
2418 A857 3k multi .40 .35
a. Souv. sheet of 4, #2415-2418 2.00 1.60
Nos. 2415-2418 (4) 1.20 1.10

50th Anniv. of Zizkov Hill Natl. Monument — A858

1982, Sept. 16

2419 A858 1k multi .25 .25

Prague Castle Art Type of 1971

Designs: 3k, St. George and the Dragon, 1373. 4k, Tomb of King Vratislav I, 10th cent.

1982, Sept. 28 ***Perf. 12***

2420 A634 3k multi 1.60 1.25
2421 A634 4k multi .85 .85

Nos. 2420-2421 were each issued in sheets of 4. Value, set: unused, $11; used, $10.

Bratislava Type of 1977

Designs: 3k, Paddle steamer, Parnik, 1818. 4k, View from Bridge, 19th cent.

1982, Sept. 29

2422 A760 3k multi 1.40 1.00
2423 A760 4k multi 1.40 1.00

Nos. 2422-2423 were each issued in sheets of 4. Value, set $15.

European Danube Commission — A859

3k, Steamer, Bratislava Bridge. 3.60k, Ferry, Budapest.

1982, Sept. 29 ***Perf. 11½x12***

2424 A859 3k multi .65 .25
a. Souvenir sheet of 4 4.00 3.00
2425 A859 3.60k multi .85 .25
a. Souvenir sheet of 4 6.00 5.00

16th Communist Party Congress — A860

1982, Oct. 28 ***Perf. 12x11½***

2426 A860 20h Agriculture .25 .25
2427 A860 1k Industry .25 .25
2428 A860 3k Engineering .25 .25
Nos. 2426-2428 (3) .75 .75

30th Anniv. of Academy of Sciences — A861

1982, Oct. 29 ***Perf. 11½***

2429 A861 6k Emblem .90 .35

65th Anniv. of October Revolution — A862

Design: 1k, 60th anniv. of USSR.

1982, Nov. 7 ***Perf. 12x11½***

2430 A862 50h multi .25 .25
2431 A862 1k multi .25 .25

Jaroslav Hasek, Writer, Sculpture by Josef Malejovsky — A863

Sculptures: 2k, Jan Zrzavy, painter and graphic artist, by Jan Simota. 4.40k, Leos Janacek, composer, by Milos Axman. 6k, Martin Kukucin, freedom fighter, by Jan Kulich. 7k, Peaceful Work, by Rudolf Pribis.

Engraved and Photogravure

1982, Nov. 26 ***Perf. 11½x12***

2432 A863 1k multi .25 .25
2433 A863 2k multi .25 .25
2434 A863 4.40k multi .75 .25
2435 A863 6k multi .80 .25
2436 A863 7k multi 1.20 .50
Nos. 2432-2436 (5) 3.25 1.50

Nos. 2432-2436 were each issued in sheets of 4. Value, set $20.

Painting Type of 1967

1k, Revolution in Spain, by Josef Sima (1891-1971). 2k, Woman Dressing, by Rudolf Kremlicka (1886-1932). 3k, The Girl Bride, by Dezider Milly (1906-1971). 4k, Performers, by Jan Zelibsky (b. 1907). 5k, The Complaint of the Birds, by Emil Filla (1882-1953).

1982, Nov. 27 ***Perf. 12***

2437 A565 1k multi .70 .45
2438 A565 2k multi 1.40 1.00
2439 A565 3k multi .70 .45
2440 A565 4k multi .70 .45
2441 A565 5k multi 1.40 1.00
Nos. 2437-2441 (5) 4.90 3.35

Nos. 2437-2441 were each issued in sheets of 4. Value, set $20.

Stamp Day — A864

1k, Engraver Jaroslav Goldschmied (1890-1977).

1982, Dec. 8 ***Perf. 11½***

2442 A864 1k multicolored .25 .25

A865

1983, Jan. 10 **Engr.** ***Perf. 12x11½***

2443 A865 50h dark blue .25 .25

Pres. Gustav Husak, 70th birthday. See No. 2686.

A866

Designs: 50h, Jaroslav Hasek (1882-1923), writer. 1k, Julius Fucik (1903-1943), antifascist martyr. 2k, Martin Luther (1483-1546). 5k, Johannes Brahms (1833-1897), composer.

1983, Feb. 24 **Engr. & Photo.**

2444 A866 50h multi .25 .25
2445 A866 1k multi .25 .25
2446 A866 2k multi .25 .25
a. Souvenir sheet of 4 24.00 12.50
2447 A866 5k multi .65 .25
Nos. 2444-2447 (4) 1.40 1.00

Nordposta '83 Intl. Stamp Exhibition, Hamburg.
No. 2446a issued Nov. 1.

Workers Marching A867

Family — A868

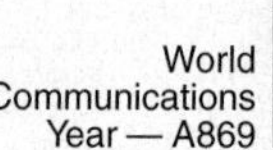

1983, Feb. 25 *Perf. 11½*

2448	A867 50h multi		.25	.25
2449	A868 1k multi		.25	.25

35th anniv. of "Victorious February" (50h), and Natl. Front (1k).

World Communications Year — A869

Perf. 11½, 12x11½ (2k)

1983, Mar. 16

2450	A869 40h multi	.25	.25
2451	A869 1k multi	.25	.25
2452	A869 2k multi	.25	.25
2453	A869 3.60k multi	.40	.25
	Nos. 2450-2453 (4)	1.15	1.00

Various wave patterns. 2k, 40x23mm; 3.60k, 49x19mm.

7th World Ski-jumping Championships A870

1983, Mar. 16 *Perf. 11½*

2454	A870 1k multi	.25	.25

Souvenir Sheet

5th Anniv. of Czechoslovak-USSR Intercosmos Cooperative Space Program — A871

1983, Apr. 12 *Perf. 12*

2455	A871 Sheet of 2	11.00	7.50
a.	10k multi	3.50	3.50

See No. 2226.

Protected Species — A872

50h, Butterfly, violets. 1k, Water lilies, frog. 2k, Pine cones, crossbill. 3.60k, Herons. 5k, Gentians, lynx. 7k, Stag.

1983, Apr. 28 *Perf. 12x11½*

2456	A872 50h multi	.30	.25
2457	A872 1k multi	.65	.25
2458	A872 2k multi	.65	.30
2459	A872 3.60k multi	.80	.35
2460	A872 5k multi	1.10	.45
2461	A872 7k multi	2.50	1.00
	Nos. 2456-2461 (6)	6.00	2.60

Soviet Marshals — A873

50h, Ivan S. Konev. 1k, Andrei I. Yeremenko. 2k, Rodion J. Malinovsky.

1983, May 5 *Perf. 11½*

2462	A873 50h multi	.25	.25
2463	A873 1k multi	.25	.25
2464	A873 2k multi	.25	.25
	Nos. 2462-2464 (3)	.75	.75

30th anniv. of Czechoslovak-Soviet defense treaty.

A874

1983, July 13 *Perf. 12*

2465	A874 2k multi	.35	.25
a.	Souvenir sheet of 4	6.50	5.50

World Peace and Life Congress, Prague. No. 2465 issued in sheets of 8. Value $4.50.

Emperor Rudolf II by Adrian De Vries (1560-1626) A875

Art treasures of the Prague Castle: 5k, Kinetic relief, Timepiece, Rudolf Svoboda.

1983, Aug. 25 *Perf. 11½*

2466	A875 4k multi	.80	.60
2467	A875 5k multi	.80	.60

Nos. 2466-2467 were each issued in sheets of 6. Value, set $12.

See Nos. 2518-2519, 2610-2611, 2654-2655, 2717-2718, 2744-2745, 2792-2793.

9th Biennial of Illustrations for Children and Youth — A876

Illustrators: 50h, Oleg K. Zotov, USSR. 1k, Zbigniew Rychlicki, Poland. 4k, Lisbeth Zwerger, Austria. 7k, Antonio Dominques, Angola.

1983, Sept. 9 **Engr. & Photo.**

2468	A876 50h multi	.25	.25
2469	A876 1k multi	.25	.25
2470	A876 4k multi	.25	.25
2471	A876 7k multi	.50	.25
a.	Souv. sheet of 4, #2468-2471	5.00	3.00
	Nos. 2468-2471 (4)	1.25	1.00

World Communications Year — A877

Emblems and aircraft.

1983, Sept. 30 *Perf. 11½*

2472	A877 50h red & black	.25	.25
2473	A877 1k red & black, vert.	.25	.25
2474	A877 4k red & black	.75	.25
	Nos. 2472-2474 (3)	1.25	.75

60th anniv. of the Czechoslovak Airlines.

16th Party Congress Achievements — A878

1983, Oct. 20 *Perf. 12x11½*

2475	A878 50h Civil engineering construction	.25	.25
2476	A878 1k Chemical industry	.25	.25
2477	A878 3k Health services	.40	.25
	Nos. 2475-2477 (3)	.90	.75

Bratislava Type of 1977

Designs: 3k, Two sculptures, Viktor Tilgner (1844-96). 4k, Mirbachov Palace, 1939, by Julius Schubert (1888-1947).

1983, Oct. 28 *Perf. 12*

2478	A760 3k multi	1.50	1.25
2479	A760 4k multi	1.25	1.00

Nos. 2478-2479 were each issued in sheets of 4 stamps. Value, set $12.

Natl. Theater, Prague, Centenary — A879

50h, Natl. Theater building. 2k, State Theater, Natl. Theater.

1983, Nov. 8 **Engr.** *Perf. 11½*

2480	A879 50h brown	.25	.25
2481	A879 2k green	.30	.25

Messenger of Mourning, by Mikolas Ales — A880

Designs: 2k, Genius, theater curtain by Vojtech Hynais (1854-1925). 3k, Music, Lyric drawings by Frantisek Zenisek (1849-1916). 4k, Symbolic figure of Prague, by Vaclav Brozik (1851-1901). 5k, Hradcany Castle, by Julius Marak (1832-1899).

1983, Nov. 18 **Engr.**

2482	A880 1k multi	1.20	.75
2483	A880 2k multi	1.50	1.10
2484	A880 3k multi	.90	.45
2485	A880 4k multi	1.40	.45
2486	A880 5k multi	1.10	.60
	Nos. 2482-2486 (5)	6.10	3.35

Nos. 2482-2486 were each issued in sheets of 4 stamps. Value, set $30.

Warrior with Sword and Shield, Engraving, 17th Cent. — A881

Engravings of Costumes: 50h, Bodyguard of Rudolf II, by Jacob de Gheyn (1565-1629). 1k, Lady with Lace Collar, by Jacques Callot (1592-1635). 4k, Lady, by Vaclav Hollar (1607-77). 5k, Man, by Antoine Watteau (1684-1721).

Engraved and Photogravure

1983, Dec. 2 *Perf. 11½x12*

2487	A881 40h multi	.25	.25
2488	A881 50h multi	.25	.25
2489	A881 1k multi	.25	.25
2490	A881 4k multi	.55	.25
2491	A881 5k multi	1.25	.75
	Nos. 2487-2491 (5)	2.55	1.75

Stamp Day — A882

1k, Karl Seizinger (1889-1978), #114.

1983, Dec. 18

2492	A882 1k multicolored	.25	.25

Czechoslovak Federation, 15th Anniv. — A883

50h, Bratislava, Prague Castles.

1984, Jan. 1 *Perf. 11½*

2493	A883 50h multicolored	.25	.25

35th Anniv. of COMECON A884

1k, Headquarters, Moscow.

1984, Jan. 23

2494	A884 1k dark blue & red brown	.25	.25

1984 Winter Olympics A885

1984, Feb. 7 *Perf. 12x11½*

2495	A885 2k Cross-country skiing	.40	.25
2496	A885 3k Hockey	.50	.25
a.	Souvenir sheet of 4	5.00	4.00
2497	A885 5k Biathlon	1.25	.35
	Nos. 2495-2497 (3)	2.15	.85

Intl. Olympic Committee, 90th Anniv. — A886

1984, Feb. 7 *Perf. 11½x12*

2498	A886 7k Rings, runners, torch	1.25	.35

City Arms Type of 1982

1984, Mar. 1 *Perf. 12x11½*

2499 A847 50h Kutna Hora .25 .25
2500 A847 50h Turnov .25 .25
2501 A847 1k Martin .25 .25
2502 A847 1k Milevsko .25 .25
Nos. 2499-2502 (4) 1.00 1.00

Intercosmos Space Program — A887

Various satellites. Nos. 2503-2507 se-tenant with labels showing flags.

1984, Apr. 12 *Perf. 11½x12*

2503 A887 50h multi .30 .25
2504 A887 1k multi .45 .25
2505 A887 2k multi .45 .25
2506 A887 4k multi .75 .25
2507 A887 5k multi .75 .25
Nos. 2503-2507 (5) 2.70 1.25

Resistance Heroes — A888

Designs: 50h, Vendelin Opatrny (1908-44). 1k, Ladislav Novomesky (1904-76). 2k, Rudolf Jasiok (1919-44). 4k, Jan Nalepka (1912-43).

1984, May 9 *Perf. 11x11½*

2508 A888 50h multi .25 .25
2509 A888 1k multi .25 .25
2510 A888 2k multi .25 .25
2511 A888 4k multi .25 .25
Nos. 2508-2511 (4) 1.00 1.00

Music Year — A889

1984, May 11 *Perf. 11½*

2512 A889 50h Instruments .25 .25
2513 A889 1k Organ pipes, vert. .25 .25

Bratislava Type of 1977

Designs: 3k, Vintners' Guild arms, 19th cent. 4k, View of Bratislava (painting commemorating shooting competition, 1827).

1984, June 1 *Perf. 12*

2514 A760 3k multi 1.10 .85
2515 A760 4k multi 1.60 1.10

Nos. 2514-2515 were each issued in sheets of 4 stamps. Value, set $12.

Central Telecommunications Building, Bratislava — A890

1984, June 1 *Perf. 11½*

2516 A890 2k multi .25 .25

A891

1984, June 12 *Perf. 12*

2517 A891 5k UPU emblem, dove, globe 2.50 2.50

1984 UPU Congress. Issued in sheet of 4 with and without Philatelic Salon text. Values, $30 with text, $12 without text.

Prague Castle Type of 1983

Designs: 3k, Crowing rooster, St. Vitus Cathedral, 19th cent. 4k, King David from the Roundnice, Book of Psalms illuminated manuscript, Bohemia, 15th cent.

1984, Aug. 9 **Engr. & Photo.**

2518 A875 3k multi .75 .60
2519 A875 4k multi 1.00 .75

Nos. 2518-2519 were each issued in sheets of 6 stamps. Value, set $10.

Playing Cards — A893

50h, Jack of Spades, 16th cent. 1k, Queen of spades, 17th cent. 2k, 9 of hearts, 18th cent. 3k, Jack of clubs, 18th cent. 5k, King of hearts, 19th cent.

1984, Aug. 28 *Perf. 11½x12*

2520 A893 50h multi .25 .25
2521 A893 1k multi .25 .25
2522 A893 2k multi .25 .25
2523 A893 3k multi .35 .25
2524 A893 5k multi 1.00 .25
Nos. 2520-2524 (5) 2.10 1.25

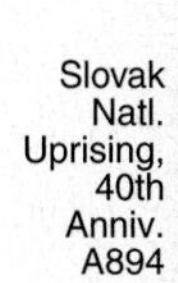

Slovak Natl. Uprising, 40th Anniv. A894

1984, Aug. 29 *Perf. 12x11½*

2525 A894 50h Family, factories, flowers .25 .25

Battle of Dukla Pass (Carpathians), 40th Anniv. — A895

1984, Sept. 8 *Perf. 11½x12*

2526 A895 2k Soldiers, flag .40 .25

1984 Summer Olympics A896

1984, Sept. 9 *Perf. 12x11½*

2527 A896 1k Pole vault .25 .25
2528 A896 2k Bicycling .40 .25
2529 A896 3k Rowing .60 .35
2530 A896 5k Weight lifting 1.00 .45
a. Souv. sheet of 4, #2527-2530 4.00 3.25
Nos. 2527-2530 (4) 2.25 1.30

16th Party Congress Goals and Projects — A897

1984, Oct. 28 *Perf. 12x11½*

2531 A897 1k Communications .25 .25
2532 A897 2k Transportation .25 .25
2533 A897 3k Transgas pipeline .35 .25
a. Souvenir sheet of 3 2.00 1.60
Nos. 2531-2533 (3) .85 .75

Painting Type of 1967

1k, The Milevsky River, by Karel Stehlik (b. 1912). 2k, Under the Trees, by Viktor Barvitius (1834-1902). 3k, Landscape with Flowers, by Zolo Palugyay (1898-1935). 4k, King in Palace, Visehrad Codex miniature, 1085. 5k, View of Kokorin Castles, by Antonin Manes. Nos. 2534-2537 horiz.; issued in sheets of 4.

1984, Nov. 16 *Perf. 11½*

2534 A565 1k multi 1.75 .90
2535 A565 2k multi 1.75 .90
2536 A565 3k multi 1.75 .90
2537 A565 4k multi 2.75 .90
2538 A565 5k multi 3.25 .90
Nos. 2534-2538 (5) 11.25 4.50

Nos. 2534-2538 were each issued in sheets of 4 stamps. Value, set $45.

Students' Intl., 45th Anniv. — A898

1984, Nov. 17

2539 A898 1k Head, dove .25 .25

Birth Cent., Antonin Zapotocky — A899

Engr. & Photo.

1984, Dec. 18 *Perf. 11½*

2540 A899 50h multi .25 .25

Stamp Day — A900

1k, Engraver Bohumil Heinz (1894-1940).

1984, Dec. 18 *Perf. 11½x12*

2541 A900 1k multi .25 .25

City Arms Type of 1982

1985, Feb. 5 *Perf. 12x11½*

2542 A847 50h Kamyk nad Vltavou .25 .25
2543 A847 50h Havirov .25 .25
2544 A847 50h Trnava .25 .25
Nos. 2542-2544 (3) .75 .75

University of Applied Arts, Prague, Centenary — A901

1985, Feb. 6 *Perf. 11½x12*

2545 A901 3k Art and Pleasure, sculpture .40 .25

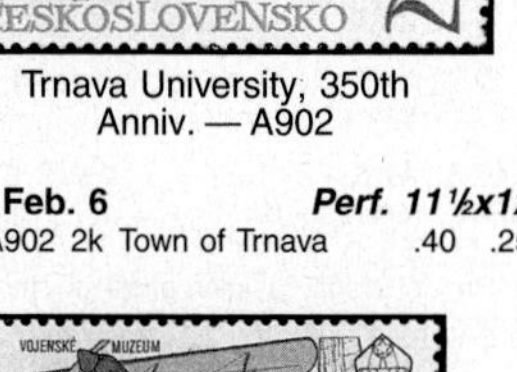

Trnava University, 350th Anniv. — A902

1985, Feb. 6 *Perf. 11½x12*

2546 A902 2k Town of Trnava .40 .25

Military Museum Exposition — A903

50h, Armor, crossbow, vert. 1k, Medals, vert. 2k, Biplane, spacecraft.

1985, Feb. 7 *Perf. 11½x12, 12x11½*

2547 A903 50h multi .25 .25
2548 A903 1k multi .25 .25
2549 A903 2k multi .40 .25
Nos. 2547-2549 (3) .90 .75

Vladimir I. Lenin (1870-1924), 1st Chairman of Russia — A904

1985, Mar. 15 **Engr.** *Perf. 12*

2550 A904 2k multi .80 .40

No. 2550 printed in sheets of 6 stamps. Value $5.

UN 40th Anniv., Peace Year 1986 A905

1985, Mar. 15

2551 A905 6k UN, Peace Year emblems 2.75 2.40

Issued in sheets of 4 stamps. Value $12.

Natl. Arms, Twig, Crowd — A906

Engraved and Photogravure

1985, Apr. 5 *Perf. 11½*

2552 A906 4k multicolored .60 .25

Kosice govt. plan, Apr. 5, 1945.

Natl. Arms, Flag, Soldiers — A907

1985, Apr. 5

2553 A907 50h multicolored .25 .25

Natl. Security Forces, 40th anniv.

Halley's Comet, INTERCOSMOS Project Vega — A908

Design: Emblem, space platform, interstellar map, intercept data.

1985, Apr. 12 — *Perf. 12x11½*

2554 Sheet of 2 — 9.00 9.00
a. A908 5k multicolored — 4.00 3.25

Project Vega, a joint effort of the USSR, France, German Democratic Republic, Austria, Poland, Bulgaria and CSSR, was for the geophysical study of Halley's Comet, Dec. 1984-Mar. 1986.

European Ice Hockey Championships, Prague, Apr. 17-May 3 — A909

1985, Apr. 13

2555 A909 1k Hockey players, emblem — .25 .25

No. 2555 Ovptd. "CSSR MISTREM SVETA" in Violet Blue

1985, May 31 — *Perf. 12x11½*

2556 A909 1k multi — 2.00 2.00

Natl. Chess Org., 80th Anniv. — A910

1985, Apr. 13 — *Perf. 11½*

2557 A910 6k Emblem, game board, chessmen — 1.25 .50

Anniversaries — A911

No. 2558, May Uprising, 1945. No. 2559, Soviet Army in CSSR, 1945. No. 2560, Warsaw Treaty, 1950. No. 2561, Czech-Soviet Treaty, 1970.

1985, May 5 — *Perf. 11½x12*

2558 A911 1k multicolored — .25 .25
2559 A911 1k multicolored — .25 .25
2560 A911 1k multicolored — .25 .25
2561 A911 1k multicolored — .25 .25
Nos. 2558-2561 (4) — 1.00 1.00

Spartakiad '85, Strahov Stadium, Prague, June 27 — A912

Designs: 50h, Gymnasts warming up with rackets and balls. 1k, Rhythmic gymnastics floor exercise, Prague Castle.

1985, June 3 — *Perf. 11½, 11½x12*

2562 A912 50h multi — .25 .25

Size: 53x22mm

2563 A912 1k multi — .25 .25

WWII Anti-Fascist Political Art — A913

Drawings and caricatures: 50h, Fire, and From the Concentration Camp, by Joseph Capek (1887-1945). 2k, The Conference on Disarmament in Geneva, 1927 and The Prophecy of Three Parrots, 1933, by Frantisek Bidlo (1895-1945). 4k, The Unknown Warrior to Order, 1936, and The Almost Peaceful Dove, 1937, by Antonin Pelc (1895-1967).

1985, June 4 — *Perf. 12x11½*

2564 A913 50h multi — .25 .25
2565 A913 2k multi — .25 .25
2566 A913 4k multi — .90 .25
Nos. 2564-2566 (3) — 1.40 .75

Helsinki Conference on European Security and Cooperation, 10th Anniv. — A914

1985, July 1 — **Engr. & Photo.**

2567 A914 7k multi — 2.25 1.50
a. Souvenir sheet of 4 — 9.00 7.00

An imperf. souv. sheet similar to No. 2567a was issued June 1, 1988 for FINLANDIA '88 and PRAGA '88. Value $35.

12th World Youth Festival, Moscow A915

1985, July 2

2568 A915 1k Kremlin, youths — .25 .25

A916

1985, Sept. 3 — *Perf. 11½*

2569 A916 50h multi — .25 .25

Federation of World Trade Unions, 40th anniv.

Bratislava Type of 1977

Designs: 3k, Castle and river, lace embroidery by Elena Holeczyova (1906-1983). 4k, Pottery cups and mugs, 1600-1500 B.C.

1985, Sept. 4 — **Engr.** — *Perf. 12*

2570 A760 3k multi — 1.60 .45
2571 A760 4k multi — 2.10 .60

Nos. 2570-2571 were each issued in sheets of 4 stamps. Value, set $14.

A918

Children's book illustrations: 1k, Rocking Horse, by Kveta Pacovska, USSR. 2k, Fairies, by Gennadij Spirin, USSR. 3k, Butterfly and Girl, by Kaarina Kaila, Finland. 4k, Boy and Animals, by Erick Ingraham, US.

Engraved and Photogravure

1985, Sept. 5 — *Perf. 11½*

2572 A918 1k multi — .25 .25
2573 A918 2k multi — .25 .25
2574 A918 3k multi — .70 .25
2575 A918 4k multi — .70 .30
a. Souv. sheet of 4, #2572-2575 — 4.50 3.00
Nos. 2572-2575 (4) — 1.90 1.05

10th biennial of illustrations.

5-Year Development Plan — A919

50h, Construction machinery. 1k, Prague subway, map. 2k, Modern textile spinning.

1985, Oct. 28 — *Perf. 12x11½*

2576 A919 50h multicolored — .25 .25
2577 A919 1k multicolored — .25 .25
2578 A919 2k multicolored — .25 .25
Nos. 2576-2578 (3) — .75 .75

16th Communist Party Congress goals.

Prague Castle — A920

2k, Presidential Palace Gate, 1768. 3k, St. Vitus' Cathedral.

Engr., Engr. & Photo. (3k)

1985, Oct. 28 — *Perf. 12*

2579 A920 2k multicolored — .40 .40
2580 A920 3k multicolored — .50 .50

Nos. 2579-2580 were each issued in sheets of 6 stamps. Value, set $9.

A921

Glassware: 50h, Pitcher, Near East, 4th cent. 1k, Venetian pitcher, 16th cent. 2k, Bohemian goblet, c. 1720. 4k, Harrachov Bohemian vase, 18th cent. 6k, Jablonec Bohemian vase, c. 1900.

Engraved and Photogravure

1985, Nov. 23 — *Perf. 11½x12*

2581 A921 50h multi — .25 .25
2582 A921 1k multi — .25 .25
2583 A921 2k multi — .30 .25
2584 A921 4k multi — .50 .25
2585 A921 6k multi — 1.00 .35
Nos. 2581-2585 (5) — 2.30 1.35

Arts and Crafts Museum, Prague, cent.

Painting Type of 1967

Designs: 1k, Young Woman in a Blue Gown, by Jozef Ginovsky (1800-1857). 2k, Lenin on the Charles Bridge, Prague, 1952, by Martin Sladky (b. 1920). 3k, Avenue of Poplars, 1935, by Vaclav Rabas (1885-1954). 4k, The Martyrom of St. Dorothea, 1516, by Hans Baldung Grien (c. 1484-1545). 5k, Portrait of Jasper Schade van Westrum, 1645, by Frans Hals (c. 1581-1666).

1985, Nov. 27 — **Engr.** — *Perf. 12*

2586 A565 1k multi — 1.60 .80
2587 A565 2k multi — 1.10 .35
2588 A565 3k multi — 1.50 .35
2589 A565 4k multi — .90 .50
2590 A565 5k multi — .90 .50
Nos. 2586-2590 (5) — 6.00 2.50

Nos. 2586-2590 were each issued in sheets of 4 stamps. Value, set $30.

Bohdan Roule (1921-1960), Engraver — A922

Engraved and Photogravure

1985, Dec. 18 — *Perf. 11½x12*

2591 A922 1k multicolored — .25 .25

Stamp Day 1985.

Intl. Peace Year — A923

1986, Jan. 2

2592 A923 1k multi — .25 .25

Philharmonic Orchestra, 90th Anniv. — A924

1986, Jan. 2 — *Perf. 11½*

2593 A924 1k Victory Statue, Prague — .25 .25

EXPO '86, Vancouver A925

Design: Z 50 LS monoplane, Cenyerth Prague-Kladno locomotive, Sahara Desert rock drawing, 5th-6th cent. B.C.

1986, Jan. 23 — *Perf. 11½*

2594 A925 4k multicolored — .85 .25

City Arms Type of 1982

1986, Feb. 10 — *Perf. 12x11½*

Size: 42x54mm

2595 A847 50h Myjava — .25 .25
2596 A847 50h Vodnany — .25 .25
2597 A847 50h Zamberk — .25 .25
Nos. 2595-2597 (3) — .75 .75

17th Natl. Communist Party Congress, Prague, Mar. 24 — A926

1986, Mar. 20 — *Perf. 11½*

2598 A926 50h shown — .25 .25
2599 A926 1k Industry — .25 .25

Natl. Communist Party, 65th Anniv. — A927

50h, Star, man, woman. 1k, Hammer, sickle, laborers.

1986, Mar. 20 *Perf. 12x11½*

2600 A927 50h multi .25 .25
2601 A927 1k multi .25 .25

Natl. Front Election Program A928

1986, Mar. 28

2602 A928 50h multi .25 .25

Karlovy Vary Intl. Film Festival, 25th Anniv. — A929

1986, Apr. 3 *Perf. 11½*

2603 A929 1k multi .25 .25

A930

1986, Apr. 8 **Engr. & Photo.**

2604 A930 1k multi .25 .25

Spring of Prague Music Festival.

A931

1986, Apr. 25

2605 A931 50h multi .40 .25

Prague-Moscow air service, 50th anniv.

Intl. Olympic Committee, 90th Anniv. — A932

1986, May 12 *Perf. 11½x12*

2606 A932 2k multi .30 .25

1986 World Cup Soccer Championships, Mexico — A933

1986, May 15 *Perf. 12x11½*

2607 A933 4k multi .80 .40

Women's World Volleyball Championships, Prague — A934

1986, May 19

2608 A934 1k multi .25 .25

Souvenir Sheet

Intl. Philatelic Federation, FIP, 60th Anniv. — A935

1986, June 3 **Engr.** *Perf. 12*

2609 A935 20k multi 6.50 5.00

Exists imperf and with perforations between stamps omitted. Values, $15 and $27.50, respectively.

Prague Castle Type of 1983

Designs: 2k, Jewelled funerary pendant, 9th cent. 3k, Allegory of Blossoms, sculpture by Jaroslav Horejc (1886-1983), St. Vitus' Cathedral.

1986, June 6 **Engr.** *Perf. 12*

2610 A875 2k multi .40 .30
2611 A875 3k multi .70 .45

Nos. 2610-2611 were each issued in sheets of 6 stamps. Value, set $8.

UN Child Survival Campaign — A937

Toys.

Engraved and Photogravure

1986, Sept. 1 *Perf. 11½*

2612 A937 10h Rooster .25 .25
2613 A937 20h Horse and rider .25 .25
2614 A937 1k Doll .25 .25
2615 A937 2k Doll, diff. .50 .25
2616 A937 3k Tin omnibus, c. 1910 .65 .30
Nos. 2612-2616 (5) 1.90 1.30

UNICEF, 40th anniv.

Registration, Cent. — A938

1986, Sept. 2 *Perf. 11½x12*

2617 A938 4k Label, mail coach .45 .25

Bratislava Type of 1977

1986, Sept. 11 **Engr.** *Perf. 12*

2618 A760 3k Sigismund Gate 1.25 .80
2619 A760 4k St. Margaret, bas-relief 1.25 .65

Nos. 2618-2619 were each issued in sheets of 4 stamps. Value, set $12.

Owls — A939

Engraved and Photogravure

1986, Sept. 18 *Perf. 11½*

2620 A939 50h Bubo bubo .70 .25
2621 A939 2k Asio otus .85 .25
2622 A939 3k Strix aluco 1.40 .30
2623 A939 4k Tyto alba 1.40 .45
2624 A939 5k Asio flammeus 2.10 .60
Nos. 2620-2624 (5) 6.45 1.85

Souvenir Sheet

Intl. Brigades in Spain — A940

Theater curtain: Woman Savaged by Horses, 1936, by Vladimir Sychra (1903-1963), Natl Gallery, Prague.

1986, Oct. 1 **Engr.** *Perf. 12*

2625 A940 Sheet of 2 4.50 3.50
a. 5k multi 2.00 1.25

Locomotives and Streetcars — A941

Engraved and Photogravure

1986, Oct. 6 *Perf. 12x11½*

2626 A941 50h KT-8 .25 .25
2627 A941 1k E458.1 .25 .25
2628 A941 3k T466.2 .75 .30
2629 A941 5k M152.0 .80 .25
Nos. 2626-2629 (4) 2.05 1.05

Paintings in the Prague and Bratislava Natl. Galleries — A942

Designs: 1k, The Circus Rider, 1980, by Jan Bauch (b. 1898). 2k, The Ventriloquist, 1954, by Frantisek Tichy (1896-1961). 3k, In the Circus, 1946, by Vincent Hloznik (b. 1919). 6k, Clown, 1985, by Karel Svolinsky (1896-1986).

1986, Oct. 13 **Engr.** *Perf. 12*

2630 A942 1k multi 1.25 .65
2631 A942 2k multi 1.60 .85
2632 A942 3k multi 1.60 .85
2633 A942 6k multi 1.10 .95
Nos. 2630-2633 (4) 5.55 3.30

Nos. 2630-2633 were each issued in sheets of 4 stamps. Value, set $25.

Painting Type of 1967

1k, The Czech Lion, May 1918, by Vratislav H. Brunner (1886-1928). 2k, Boy with Mandolin, 1945, by Jozef Sturdik (b. 1920). 3k, Metra Building, 1984, by Frantisek Gross (1909-1985). 4k, Portrait of Maria Maximiliana at Sternberk, 1665, by Karel Skreta (1610-1674). 5k, Adam & Eve, 1538, by Lucas Cranach (1472-1553).

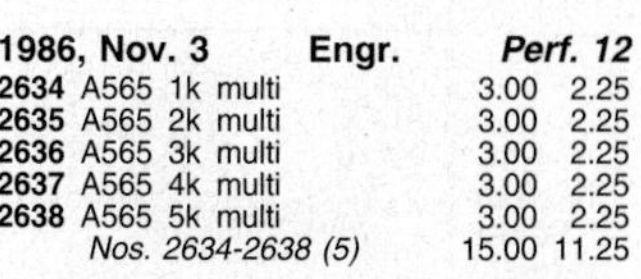

1986, Nov. 3 **Engr.** *Perf. 12*

2634 A565 1k multi 3.00 2.25
2635 A565 2k multi 3.00 2.25
2636 A565 3k multi 3.00 2.25
2637 A565 4k multi 3.00 2.25
2638 A565 5k multi 3.00 2.25
Nos. 2634-2638 (5) 15.00 11.25

Nos. 2634-2638 were each issued in sheets of 4 stamps. Value, set $75.

Stamp Day — A943

Design: V.H. Brunner (1886-1928), stamp designer, and No. 88.

Photo. & Engr.

1986, Dec. 18 *Perf. 11½x12*

2639 A943 1k multicolored .25 .25

World Cyclocross Championships, Jan. 24-25, Central Bohemia — A944

1987, Jan. 22 *Perf. 11½*

2640 A944 6k multi .80 .25

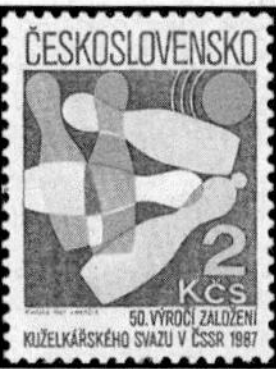

Czechoslovakian Bowling Union, 50th Anniv. — A945

1987, Jan. 22 *Perf. 11½*

2641 A945 2k multi .35 .25

State Decorations — A946

Designs: 50h, Gold Stars of Socialist Labor and Czechoslovakia. 2k, Order of Klement Gottwald. 3k, Order of the Republic. 4k, Order of Victorious February. 5k, Order of Labor.

1987, Feb. 4 *Perf. 12x11½*

2642 A946 50h multi .25 .25
2643 A946 2k multi .25 .25
2644 A946 3k multi .30 .25
2645 A946 4k multi .45 .25
2646 A946 5k multi .60 .40
Nos. 2642-2646 (5) 1.85 1.40

Butterflies — A947

1k, Limenitis populi. 2k, Smerinthus ocellatus. 3k, Pericallia matronula. 4k, Saturnia pyri.

1987, Mar. 4

2647 A947 1k multi .65 .25
2648 A947 2k multi 1.00 .25
2649 A947 3k multi 1.25 .35
2650 A947 4k multi 1.60 .35
Nos. 2647-2650 (4) 4.50 1.20

Natl. Nuclear Power Industry A948

1987, Apr. 6
2651 A948 5k multi .60 .25

11th Revolutionary Trade Union Movement Congress, Apr. 14-17, Prague — A949

1987, Apr. 7 ***Perf. 11½***
2652 A949 1k multi .25 .25

Souvenir Sheet

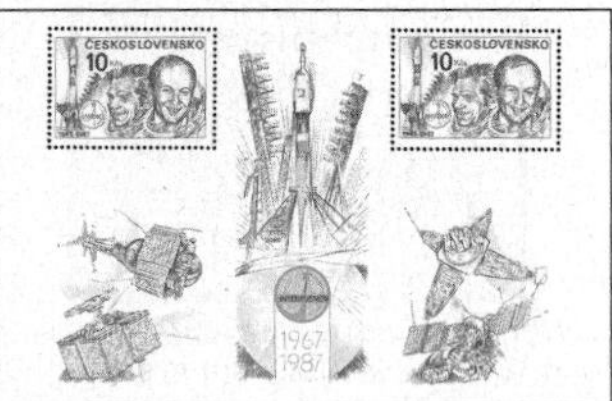

INTERCOSMOS, 20th Anniv. — A950

Cosmonauts Alexei Gubarev of the USSR & Vladimir Remek of Czechoslovakia, rocket & emblem.

1987, Apr. 12 Engr. ***Perf. 12***
2653 A950 Sheet of 2 6.00 5.00
a. 10k multi 2.75 1.75
b. Souv. sheet of 4, litho. & engr., imperf. 9.00 7.00

No. 2653b issued Nov. 15, 1987, and exists in two formats with either exhibition embelm or "Dni Nametove Filatelie" at top.

Prague Castle Type of 1983

Designs: 2k, Three Saints, stained-glass window detail, c. 1870, St. Vitus Cathedral, by Frantisek Sequens (1830-1896). 3k, Coat of Arms, New Land Rolls Hall, 1605.

1987, May 9 ***Perf. 11½***
2654 A875 2k multi .40 .30
2655 A875 3k dk red, slate gray & yel org .60 .45

Nos. 2634-2638 were each issued in sheets of 6 stamps. Value, set $6.

PRAGA '88 A951

Photo. & Engr.

1987, May 12 ***Perf. 12x11½***
2656 A951 3k Telephone, 1894 .75 .25
2657 A951 3k Postal van, 1924 .75 .30
2658 A951 4k Locomotive tender, 1907 .75 .30
2659 A951 4k Tram, 1900 .75 .30
2660 A951 5k Steam roller, 1936 .75 .30
Nos. 2656-2660 (5) 3.75 1.45

Printed in sheets of 8 + 2 labels picturing telephone or vehicles. Value $25.
Nos. 2657-2658 were also printed in sheets of 4 + label picturing vehicles. Value, $30 for both sheets.

Destruction of Lidice and Lezaky, 45th Anniv. — A952

Drawings: No. 2661, When the Fighting Ended, 1945, by Pavel Simon. No. 2662, The End of the game, 1945, by Ludmila Jirincova.

1987, June ***Perf. 11½***
2661 A952 1k blk, cerise & vio .25 .25
2662 A952 1k blk, gold, pale lil & cerise .25 .25

Union of Czechoslovakian Mathematicians and Physicists, 125th Anniv. — A953

Designs: No. 2663, Prague Town Hall mathematical clock, Theory of Functions diagram. No. 2664, J.M. Petzval (1807-1891), C. Strouhal (1850-1922) and V. Jarnik (1897-1970). No. 2665, Geographical measurement from A.M. Malletta's book, 1672, earth fold and Brownian motion diagrams.

1987, July 6 ***Perf. 11½x12***
2663 A953 50h multi .25 .25
2664 A953 50h multi .25 .25
2665 A953 50h multi .25 .25
Nos. 2663-2665 (3) .75 .75

11th Biennial of Children's Book Illustration — A954

Award-winning illustrations: 50h, Asun Balzola, Spain. 1k, Frederic Clement, France. 2k, Elzbieta Gaudasinska, Poland. 4k, Marija Lucija Stupica, Yugoslavia.

1987, Sept. 3 ***Perf. 11½***
2666 A954 50h multi .25 .25
2667 A954 1k multi .25 .25
2668 A954 2k multi .25 .25
a. Souv. sheet of 2 + label 2.00 1.50
2669 A954 4k multi .55 .35
Nos. 2666-2669 (4) 1.30 1.10

Sept. 11-Oct. 30, Bratislava.

Eternal Flame, Flower — A955

1987, Sept. 23
2670 A955 50h multicolored .25 .25

Theresienstadt Memorial for the victims from 23 European countries who died in the Small Fortress, Terezin, a Nazi concentration camp.

Socialist Communications Organization, 30th Anniv. — A956

1987, Sept. 23
2671 A956 4k Emblem, satellite, dish receiver .40 .25

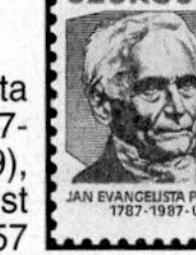

Jan Evangelista Purkyne (1787-1869), Physiologist A957

1987, Sept. 30
2672 A957 7k multicolored .80 .25

Views of Bratislava — A958

Designs: 3k, Male and female figures supporting an oriel, Arkier Palace, c. 1552. 4k, View of Bratislava from Ware Conterfactur de Stadt Presburg, from an engraving by Hans Mayer, 1563.

1987, Oct. 1 Engr. ***Perf. 12***
2673 A958 3k multicolored .50 .35
2674 A958 4k multicolored .70 .45

Each printed in sheets of 4 with Bratislava Castle (from Mayer's engraving) between. Value, set $5.
See Nos. 2719-2720, 2763-2764, 2800-2801.

Type of 1974

Photo. & Engr.

1987, Nov. 1 ***Perf. 12x11½***
2675 A699 1k Post rider .25 .25

PRAGA '88, Aug. 26-Sept. 4, 1988. No. 2675 printed se-tenant with label picturing exhibition emblem. Value for single with attached label 40c.

October Revolution, Russia, 70th Anniv. — A959

Establishment of the Union of Soviet Socialist Republics, 65th Anniv. — A960

1987, Nov. 6 ***Perf. 12x11½***
2676 A959 50h multicolored .25 .25
2677 A960 50h multicolored .25 .25

Art Type of 1974

Paintings in national galleries: 1k, Enclosure of Dreams, by Kamil Lhotak (b. 1912). 2k, Tulips, by Ester Simerova-Martincekova (b. 1909). 3k, Triptych with Bohemian Landscape, by Josef Lada (1887-1957). 4k, Accordion Player, by Josef Capek (1887-1945). 5k, Self-portrait, by Jiri Trnka (1912-1969).

1987, Nov. 18 Engr. ***Perf. 12***
2678 A700 1k multi 3.00 .75
2679 A700 2k multi 3.00 1.60
2680 A700 3k multi 3.00 1.10
2681 A700 4k multi 3.00 .80
2682 A700 5k multi 3.00 1.25
Nos. 2678-2682 (5) 15.00 5.50

Czech and Slovak art.
Nos. 2678-2682 were each issued in sheets of 4. Value, set $65.

69th Stamp Day — A961

Portrait of Jacob Obrovsky (1882-1949), stamp designer, Bohemian Lion (Type SP1), sketch of a lion and PRAGA '88 emblem.

Photo. & Engr.

1987, Dec. 18 ***Perf. 11½x12***
2683 A961 1k multicolored .25 .25

No. 2683 printed in sheet of four with eight labels se-tenant with stamps, inscribed "100 Years of the National Philatelic Movement in Czechoslovakia" in Czech. The four labels between the "blocks of six" are blank. Value, sheet $3.

Czechoslovak Republic, 70th Anniv. — A962

1k, Woman, natl. arms, linden branch.

1988, Jan. 1 ***Perf. 12x11½***
2684 A962 1k multicolored .25 .25

Natl. Front, 40th Anniv. — A963

1988, Feb. 25 ***Perf. 11½***
2685 A963 50h multicolored .25 .25

Husak Type of 1983

Photo. & Engr.

1988, Jan. 10 ***Perf. 12x11½***
2686 A865 1k brt rose & dk carmine .25 .25

Olympics — A965

50h, Ski jumping, ice hockey. 1k, Basketball, soccer. 6k, Discus, weight lifting.

1988, Feb. 1 ***Perf. 11½x12***
2687 A965 50h multicolored .25 .25
2688 A965 1k multicolored .25 .25
2689 A965 6k multicolored .70 .25
Nos. 2687-2689 (3) 1.20 .75

Exist in souv. sheets of 2, imperf. between and in souv. sheets of 2, imperf. Value, each set, $16.

Victorious February, 40th Anniv. — A966

Statue of Klement Gottwald by Rudolf Svoboda.

1988, Feb. 25 ***Perf. 11½***
2690 A966 50h multicolored .25 .25

No. 2690 exists in a souvenir sheet of two No. 2690 and two postally invalid imperf impressions of No. 637. Value $5.
Sheet exists imperf. Value $9.

Classic Automobiles — A967

50h, 1914 Laurin & Klement. 1k, 1902 Tatra NW Type B. 2k, 1905 Tatra NW Type E. 3k, 1929 Tatra 12 Normandie. 4k, 1899 Meteor.

1988, Mar. 1 ***Perf. 12x11½***
2691 A967 50h multi .25 .25
2692 A967 1k multi .25 .25
2693 A967 2k multi .25 .25
2694 A967 3k multi .45 .25
2695 A967 4k multi .75 .25
a. Bklt. pane, 2 3k, 3 4k + label 4.00
Complete booklet, #2695a 5.00
Nos. 2691-2695 (5) 1.95 1.25

Postal Museum, 70th Anniv. A968

Praga '88 emblem and: 50h, Postman, Malostranske Namesti Square p.o., Prague, c. 1742, and Velka Javorina television transmitter, 1979. 1k, Telecommunications Center, Mlada Boleslav, 1986, and Carmelite Street p.o., Prague, c. 1792. 2k, Prague 1 (1873) and Bratislava 56 (1984) post offices. 4k, Communications Center, Prachatice (1982), postman and Maltetske Nameski Square p.o., Prague, c. 1622.

1988, Mar. 10

2696 A968 50h multi .25 .25
2697 A968 1k multi .25 .25
2698 A968 2k multi .25 .25
2699 A968 4k multi .30 .25
a. Souv. sheet, 2 ea #2698-2699 2.25 1.25
Nos. 2696-2699 (4) 1.05 1.00

In No. 2699a the top pair of Nos. 2698-2699 is imperf. at top and sides.

A969

1988, Mar. 29 ***Perf. 11½***

2700 A969 50h multicolored .25 .25

Matice Slovenska Cultural Assoc., 125th anniv.

A970

PRAGA '88. (Exhibition emblem and aspects of the Museum of Natl. Literature, Prague): 1k, Gate and distant view of museum. 2k, Celestial globe, illuminated manuscript, bookshelves and ornately decorated ceiling. 5k, Illuminated "B" and decorated binder of a medieval Bible. 7k, Celestial globe, illuminated manuscript, Zodiacal signs (Aries and Leo), view of museum.

1988, May 12 **Photo. & Engr.**

2701 A970 1k multicolored .30 .25
a. Souvenir sheet of 4 1.50 1.25
2702 A970 2k multicolored .55 .25
a. Souvenir sheet of 4 3.25 2.00
2703 A970 5k multicolored .80 .30
a. Souvenir sheet of 4 5.75 4.75
2704 A970 7k multicolored 1.75 .65
a. Souvenir sheet of 4 11.00 9.00
b. Souv. sheet of 4, imperf., #2701-2704 3.75 3.00
Nos. 2701-2704 (4) 3.40 1.45

PRAGA '88 — A971

Exhibition emblem and fountains, Prague.

1988, June 1 ***Perf. 11½x12***

2705 A971 1k Waldstein Palace .30 .25
2706 A971 2k Old town square .30 .25
2707 A971 3k Charles University .45 .25
2708 A971 4k Prague Castle .75 .30
a. Souv. sheet of 4, #2705-2708 4.00 2.00
Nos. 2705-2708 (4) 1.80 1.05

Souvenir Sheet

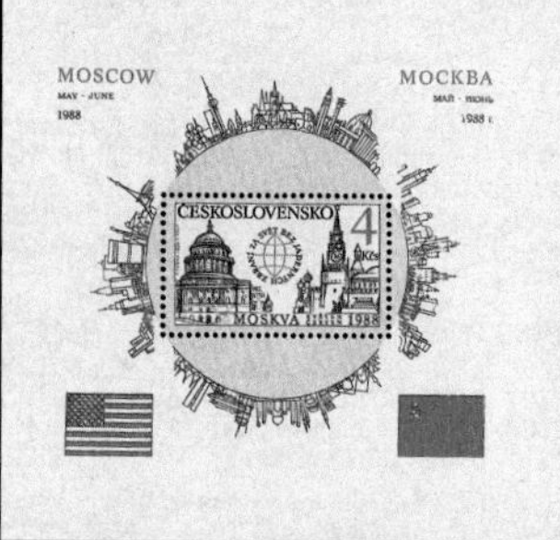

Soviet-US Summit Conference on Arms Reduction, Moscow — A972

Design: The Capitol, Washington, and the Kremlin, Moscow.

1988, June 1 ***Perf. 12x11½***

2709 A972 4k blue blk, dark red & gold 2.50 1.50

Exists imperf. Value $7.

PRAGA '88 A973

Exhibition emblem and modern architecture, Prague: 50h, Trade Unions Central Recreation Center. 1k, Koospol foreign trade company. 2k, Motol Teaching Hospital. 4k, Culture Palace.

1988, July 1 ***Perf. 12x11½***

2710 A973 50h multicolored .25 .25
2711 A973 1k blk, lt blue & bister .25 .25
2712 A973 2k multicolored .25 .25
a. Souv. sheet, 2 1k, 2 2k + 4 labels, imperf. 2.00 1.50
2713 A973 4k multicolored .25 .25
a. Souv. sheet, 2 50h, 2 4k + 4 labels, imperf. 2.00 1.50
Nos. 2710-2713 (4) 1.00 1.00

Souvenir Sheet

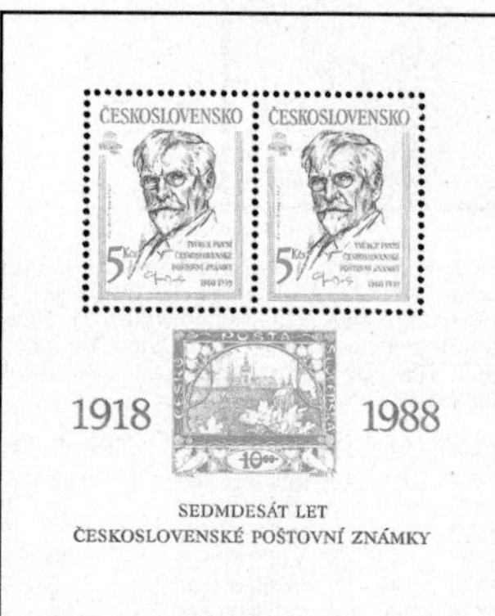

PRAGA '88 — A974

Design: Exhibition emblem and Alfons Mucha (1860-1939), designer of first Czech postage stamp.

1988, Aug. 18 **Engr.** ***Perf. 12***

2714 A974 Sheet of 2 5.50 3.25
a. 5k multicolored 2.40 1.25

Czech postage stamps, 70th anniv.

Souvenir Sheets

PRAGA '88 — A975

5k, *Turin, Monte Superga,* by Josef Navratil (1798-1865), Postal Museum, Prague.

Details of *Bacchus and Ariadne,* by Sebastiano Ricci (1659-1734), Natl. Gallery, Prague: No. 2716a, Ariadne. No. 2716b, Bacchus and creatures.

1988

2715 A975 Sheet of 2 5.00 4.00
a. 5k multi 2.50 1.60
2716 A975 Sheet of 2 9.00 6.00
a.-b. 10k any single 4.00 2.40

No. 2716 exists with emblem and inscription "DEN F.I.P. JOURNEE DE LA FEDERATION INTERNATIONALE DE PHILATELIE." Value $12.

Issue dates: 5k, Aug. 19; 10k, Aug. 26.

Prague Castle Type of 1983

2k, Pottery jug, 17th cent. 3k, *St. Catherine with Angel,* 1580, by Paolo Veronese.

1988, Sept. 28 **Engr.** ***Perf. 12***

2717 A875 2k shown .40 .40
2718 A875 3k multi .45 .45

Nos. 2717-2718 were each issued in sheets of 6. Value, set $6.

Bratislava Views Type of 1987

3k, *Hlavne Square, circa 1840* an etching by R. Alt-Sandman, 1840. 4k, *Ferdinand House, circa 1850,* a pen-and-ink drawing by V. Reim.

1988, Oct. 19

2719 A958 3k multicolored .50 .50
2720 A958 4k multicolored .65 .65

Nos. 2719-2720 were each issued in sheets of 4. Value, set $4.50.

Art Type of 1974

Paintings in natl. galleries: 2k, *With Bundles,* 1931, by Martin Benka (1888-1971). 6k, *Blue Bird,* 1903, by Vojtech Preissig (1873-1944). 7k, *A Jaguar Attacking a Rider,* c. 1850, by Eugene Delacroix (1798-1863).

1988, Nov. 17 **Engr.** ***Perf. 12***

2721 A700 2k multicolored 2.00 1.00
2722 A700 6k multicolored 3.50 1.50
2723 A700 7k multicolored 3.50 1.50
Nos. 2721-2723 (3) 9.00 4.00

Czech and Slovak art.

Nos. 2721-2723 were each issued in sheets of 4. Value, set $40.

Stamp Day — A978

Design: 1k, Jaroslav Benda (1882-1970), illustrator and stamp designer.

Photo. & Engr.

1988, Dec. 18 ***Perf. 11½x12***

2724 A978 1k multicolored .25 .25

Paris-Dakar Rally — A979

Trucks: 50h, Earth, Motokov Liaz. 1k, Liaz, globe. 2k, Earth, Motokov Tatra. No. 607. 4k, Map of racecourse, turban, Tatra.

1989, Jan. 2 ***Perf. 12x11½***

2725 A979 50h multicolored .35 .25
2726 A979 1k multicolored .35 .25
2727 A979 2k multicolored .45 .25
2728 A979 4k multicolored .75 .25
Nos. 2725-2728 (4) 1.90 1.00

Czechoslovakian Federation, 20th Anniv. — A980

1989, Jan. 1

2729 A980 50h multicolored .25 .25

Jan Botto (1829-1881) A981

Taras Grigorievich Shevchenko (1814-1861) A982

Jean Cocteau (1889-1963) A983

Charlie Chaplin (1889-1977) A984

Jawaharlal Nehru (1889-1964) and "UNESCO" — A985

Famous men: No. 2732, Modest Petrovich Musorgsky (1839-1881).

Photo. & Engr.

1989, Mar. 9 ***Perf. 12x11½***

2730 A981 50h brn blk & lt blue green .25 .25
2731 A982 50h shown .25 .25
2732 A982 50h multicolored .25 .25
2733 A983 50h red brn, grnh blk & org brn .25 .25
2734 A984 50h blk, int blue & dark red .25 .25
2735 A985 50h brn blk & lt yel green .25 .25
Nos. 2730-2735 (6) 1.50 1.50

Shipping Industry A986

1989, Mar. 27

2736 A986 50h Republika .25 .25
2737 A986 1k Pionyr, flags .25 .25
2738 A986 2k Brno, flags .25 .25
2739 A986 3k Trinec .35 .25
2740 A986 4k Flags, mast, Orlik .75 .25
2741 A986 5k Vltava, communication hardware 1.00 .30
Nos. 2736-2741 (6) 2.85 1.55

Pioneer Organization, 40th Anniv. — A987

Photo. & Engr.

1989, Apr. 20 ***Perf. 11½***

2742 A987 50h multi .25 .25

Art Type of 1974

Details of *Feast of Rose Garlands*, 1506, by Albrecht Durer, Natl. Gallery, Prague: a, Virgin and Child. b, Angel playing mandolin.

1989, Apr. 21 **Engr.** ***Perf. 12***

Miniature Sheet

2743 Sheet of 2 7.50 4.00
a.-b. A700 10k any single 3.50 2.00

Prague Castle Art Type of 1983

2k, Bas-relief picturing Kaiser Karl IV, from Kralovske tomb by Alexander Colin (c. 1527-1612). 3k, Self-portrait, by V.V. Reiner (1689-1743).

1989, May 9 **Photo. & Engr.**

2744 A875 2k dark red, sepia & buff .35 .30
2745 A875 3k multi .50 .40

Nos. 2744-2745 were each issued in sheets of 6. Value, set $6.

Souvenir Sheet

PHILEXFRANCE '89, French Revolution Bicent. — A988

1989, July 14 **Engr.** ***Perf. 12***

2746 A988 5k brt blue, blk & dk red 2.00 1.50

Haliaeetus albicilla — A989

Photo. & Engr.

1989, July 17 ***Perf. 12x11½***

2747 A989 1k multicolored .50 .25

World Wildlife Fund — A990

Toads and newts.

1989, July 18 ***Perf. 11½x12***

2748 A990 2k Bombina bombina .65 .30
2749 A990 3k Bombina variegata 1.00 .45
2750 A990 4k Triturus alpestris 1.40 .60
2751 A990 5k Triturus montandoni 1.60 .70
Nos. 2748-2751 (4) 4.65 2.05

Slovak Folk Art Collective, 40th Anniv. — A991

1989, Aug. 29 ***Perf. 12x11½***

2752 A991 50h multicolored .25 .25

Slovak Uprising, 45th Anniv. — A992

Photo. & Engr.

1989, Aug. 29 ***Perf. 11½x12***

2753 A992 1k multicolored .25 .25

A993

Award-winning illustrations: 50h, Hannu Taina, Finland. 1k, Aleksander Aleksov, Bulgaria. 2k, Jurgen Spohn, West Berlin. 4k, Robert Brun, Czechoslovakia.

1989, Sept. 4 ***Perf. 11½***

2754 A993 50h multicolored .25 .25
2755 A993 1k multicolored .25 .25
2756 A993 2k multicolored .25 .25
2757 A993 4k multicolored .60 .25
a. Souvenir sheet of 2 2.00 .80
Nos. 2754-2757 (4) 1.35 1.00

12th Biennial of Children's Book Illustration, Bratislava.

A994

Poisonous mushrooms: 50h, Nolanea verna. 1k, Amanita phalloides. 2k, Amanita virosa. 3k, Cortinarius orellanus. 5k, Galerina marginata.

1989, Sept. 5 **Engr.** ***Perf. 11½x12***

2758 A994 50h multicolored .30 .25
2759 A994 1k multicolored .40 .25
2760 A994 2k multicolored .55 .25
2761 A994 3k multicolored .90 .25
2762 A994 5k multicolored 1.00 .25
Nos. 2758-2762 (5) 3.15 1.25

Nos. 2758-2762 were each issued in sheets of 10. Value, set $40.

Bratislava Views Type of 1987

Views of Devin, a Slavic castle above the Danube, Bratislava.

1989, Oct. 16 **Engr.** ***Perf. 12***

2763 A958 3k Castle, flower .60 .60
2764 A958 4k Castle, urn .80 .80

Nos. 2763-2764 were each issued in sheets of 4. Value, set $6.

Jan Opletal (1915-39) — A996

Photo. & Engr.

1989, Nov. 17 ***Perf. 12x11½***

2765 A996 1k multicolored .25 .25

Intl. Student's Day. Funeral of Opletal, a Nazi victim, on Nov. 15, 1939, sparked student demonstrations that resulted in the closing of all universities in occupied Bohemia and Moravia.

Art Type of 1974

Paintings in Natl. Galleries: 2k, *Nirvana*, c. 1920, by Anton Jasusch (1882-1965). 4k, *Winter Evening in Town*, c. 1907, by Jakub Schikaneder (1855-1924), horiz. 5k, *The Bakers*, 1926, by Pravoslav Kotik (1889-1970), horiz.

1989, Nov. 27 **Engr.** ***Perf. 12***

2766 A700 2k multicolored .80 .60
2767 A700 4k multicolored 1.40 1.10
2768 A700 5k multicolored 1.40 1.10
Nos. 2766-2768 (3) 3.60 2.80

Nos. 2766-2768 were each issued in sheets of 4. Value, set $15.

Stamp Day — A997

Design: Portrait of Cyril Bouda, stamp designer, art tools and falcon.

Photo. & Engr.

1989, Dec. 18 ***Perf. 11½x12***

2769 A997 1k multicolored .25 .25

A998

Photo. & Engr.

1990, Jan. 8 ***Perf. 11½x12***

2770 A998 1k multicolored .60 .25

UNESCO World Literacy Year. Printed se-tenant with inscribed label picturing UN and UNESCO emblems. Value, single with label attached 75c.

A999

Famous men: No. 2771, Karel Capek, writer. No. 2772, Thomas G. Masaryk. 1k, Lenin. 2k, Emile Zola, French writer. 3k, Jaroslav Heyrovsky (1890-1987), chemical physicist. 10k, Bohuslav Martinu (1890-1959), composer.

1990, Jan. 9 ***Perf. 11½***

2771 A999 50h multicolored .25 .25
2772 A999 50h multicolored .25 .25
2773 A999 1k multicolored .25 .25
2774 A999 2k multicolored .30 .25
2775 A999 3k multicolored .50 .30
2776 A999 10k multicolored 1.60 .90
Nos. 2771-2776 (6) 3.15 2.20

Nos. 2771, 2775-2776 inscribed "UNESCO."

Pres. Vaclav Havel — A1000

1990, Jan. 9 ***Perf. 12x11½***

2777 A1000 50h red, brt vio & bl .30 .25

See Nos. 2879, 2948.

Handball Players — A1001

1990, Feb. 1 ***Perf. 11½***

2778 A1001 50h multicolored .25 .25

1990 Men's World Handball Championships, Czechoslovakia.

Flora — A1002

Flowers: 50h, Antirrhinum majus. 1k, Zinnia elegans. 3k, Tigridia pavonia. 5k, Lilium candidum.

Photo. & Engr.

1990, Mar. 1 ***Perf. 11½***

2779 A1002 50h multicolored .55 .25
2780 A1002 1k multicolored .80 .25
2781 A1002 3k multicolored 1.00 .25

Perf. 12x12½

2782 A1002 5k multicolored 1.40 .60
Nos. 2779-2782 (4) 3.75 1.35

No. 2782 was issued in a sheet of 10. Value, $12.50.

City Arms Type of 1982

Photo. & Engr.

1990, Mar. 28 ***Perf. 12x11½***

2783 A847 50h Prostejov .25 .25
2784 A847 50h Bytca .25 .25
2785 A847 50h Sobeslav .25 .25
2786 A847 50h Podebrady .25 .25
Nos. 2783-2786 (4) 1.00 1.00

A1003

1990, Apr. 16 ***Perf. 11½x12***

2787 A1003 1k brn vio, rose & buff .60 .25

Visit of Pope John Paul II.

World War II Liberation A1004

Photo. & Engr.

1990, May 5 ***Perf. 11½***

2788 A1004 1k multicolored .25 .25

Souvenir Sheet

150th Anniv. of the Postage Stamp — A1005

1990, May 6 **Engr.** ***Perf. 12***
2789 A1005 7k multicolored 4.00 1.50

Stamp World London 90.

A1006

Photo. & Engr.

1990, May 8 ***Perf. 11½***
2790 A1006 1k multicolored .60 .25

World Cup Soccer Championships, Italy.

Free Elections A1007

1990, June 1
2791 A1007 1k multicolored .60 .25

Prague Castle Type of 1983

2k, Gold and jeweled hand. 3k, King Otakar II's Seal.

1990, June 6, 1990 **Engr.**
2792 A875 2k multicolored .55 .30
2793 A875 3k multicolored .80 .40

Art treasures of Prague Castle.

Nos. 2792-2793 were each issued in sheets of 6. Value, set $9.

Helsinki Conference, 15th Anniv. — A1008

Photo & Engr.

1990, June 21 ***Perf. 12x11½***
2794 A1008 7k multicolored .90 .40

Dr. Milada Horakova A1009

1990, June 25 ***Perf. 12x11½***
2795 A1009 1k multicolored .30 .25

Intercanis Dog Show, Brno — A1010

Designs: 50h, Poodles, 1k, Afghan hound, Irish wolfhound, greyhound. 4k, Czech terrier, bloodhound, Hannoverian hound. 7k, Cavalier King Charles Spaniel, cocker spaniel, American cocker spaniel.

1990, July 2
2796 A1010 50h multicolored .50 .25
2797 A1010 1k multicolored .75 .25
2798 A1010 4k multicolored 1.25 .30
2799 A1010 7k multicolored 1.75 .65
Nos. 2796-2799 (4) 4.25 1.45

Bratislava Art Type of 1987

1990 **Engr.** ***Perf. 12***
2800 A958 3k Ancient Celtic coin .65 .40
2801 A958 4k Gen. Milan Stefanik .65 .45

Issue dates: 3k, Sept. 29. 4k, July 21.
Nos. 2800-2801 were each issued in sheets of 4. Value, set $6.

Grand Pardubice Steeplechase, Cent. — A1011

Photo. & Engr.

1990, Sept. 7 ***Perf. 12x11½***
2802 A1011 50h multicolored .25 .25
2803 A1011 4k multi, diff. .50 .25

Protected Animals — A1012

Litho. & Engr.

1990, Oct. 1 ***Perf. 12x11***
2804 A1012 50h Marmota marmota 1.00 .25
2805 A1012 1k Felis silvestris 1.00 .25
2806 A1012 4k Castor fiber 1.75 .30
2807 A1012 5k Plecotus auritus 1.75 .75
Nos. 2804-2807 (4) 5.50 1.55

Conf. of Civic Associations, Helsinki — A1013

Litho. & Engr.

1990, Oct. 15 ***Perf. 12x11½***
2808 A1013 3k blue, gold & yel .50 .30

Christmas — A1014

Photo. & Engr.

1990, Nov. 15 ***Perf. 11½x12***
2809 A1014 50h multicolored .25 .25

Painting Type of 1967

Works of art: 2k, Krucemburk by Jan Zrzavy (1890-1977), horiz. 3k, St. Agnes of Bohemia from the St. Wenceslas Monument, Prague by Josef V. Myslbek (1848-1922). 4k, The Slavs in their Homeland by Alfons Mucha (1860-1939). 5k, St. John the Baptist by Auguste Rodin (1840-1917).

1990, Nov. 27 **Engr.** ***Perf. 11½***
2810 A565 2k multicolored 1.25 .50
2811 A565 3k multicolored 1.25 .60
2812 A565 4k multicolored 2.10 .60
2813 A565 5k multicolored 2.10 .60
Nos. 2810-2813 (4) 6.70 2.30

Nos. 2810-2813 were each issued in sheets of 4. Value, set $30.

Karel Svolinsky (1896-1986), Vignette from No. 1182 — A1016

1990, Dec. 18 **Photo. & Engr.**
2814 A1016 1k multicolored .25 .25

Stamp Day.

A1017

1991, Jan. 10 ***Perf. 11½***
2815 A1017 1k multicolored .30 .25

European Judo Championships, Prague.

A1018

Design: A. B. Svojsik (1876-1938), Czech Scouting Founder.

1991, Jan. 10
2816 A1018 3k multicolored .75 .30

Scouting in Czechoslovakia, 80th Anniv.

Bethlehem Chapel, Prague, 600th Anniv. — A1019

1991, Feb. 4 ***Perf. 12x11½***
2817 A1019 50h multicolored .25 .25

Wolfgang Amadeus Mozart (1756-1791), Old Theatre — A1020

1991, Feb. 4
2818 A1020 1k multicolored .25 .25

Steamship Bohemia, 150th Anniv. — A1021

1991, Feb. 4 ***Perf. 11½x12***
2819 A1021 5k multicolored .85 .30

Famous Men A1022

Designs: No. 2820, Antonin Dvorak (1841-1904), composer. No. 2821, Andrej Kmet (1841-1908), botanist. No. 2822, Jaroslav Seifert (1901-1986), poet, Nobel laureate for Literature. No. 2823, Jan Masaryk (1886-1948), diplomat. No. 2824, Alois Senefelder (1771-1834), lithographer.

1991, Feb. 18 ***Perf. 12x11½***
2820 A1022 1k multicolored .25 .25
2821 A1022 1k multicolored .25 .25
2822 A1022 1k multicolored .25 .25
2823 A1022 1k multicolored .25 .25
2824 A1022 1k multicolored .25 .25
Nos. 2820-2824 (5) 1.25 1.25

Nos. 2820-2824 printed with se-tenant labels. See No. 2831.

Europa — A1023

Photo. & Engr.

1991, May 6 ***Perf. 11½x12***
2825 A1023 6k blk, bl & red 2.00 .60

A1024

Photo. & Engr.

1991, May 10 ***Perf. 11½x12***
2826 A1024 1k multicolored .25 .25

General Exhibition in Prague, cent.

Antarctic Treaty, 30th Anniv. A1025

1991, May 20 ***Perf. 12x11½***
2827 A1025 8k multicolored 1.75 .60

Castles — A1026

1991, June 3 ***Perf. 11½***
2828 A1026 50h Blatna .25 .25
2829 A1026 1k Bouzov .40 .25
2830 A1026 3k Kezmarok .60 .25
Nos. 2828-2830 (3) 1.25 .75

Famous Men Type

Design: Jan Palach (1948-1969), Student.

Photo. & Engr.

1991, Aug. 9 ***Perf. 12x11½***
2831 A1022 4k black 2.00 .30

Printed se-tenant with label.

Scenic Views — A1027

Photo. & Engr.

1991, Aug. 28 ***Perf. 11½***
2832 A1027 4k Krivan mountains 1.00 .60
2833 A1027 4k Rip mountain 1.00 .60

A1028

Illustrations by: 1k, Binette Schroeder, Germany. 2k, Stasys Eidrigevicius, Poland.

Photo. & Engr.

1991, Sept. 2 ***Perf. 11½***
2834 A1028 1k multicolored .25 .25
2835 A1028 2k multicolored .35 .25

13th Biennial Exhibition of Children's Book Illustrators, Bratislava.

A1029

Design: Father Andrej Hlinka (1864-1938), Slovak nationalist.

1991, Sept. 27 **Engr.** ***Perf. 11½***
2836 A1029 10k blue black 1.40 .30

Art of Prague and Bratislava A1030

Designs: No. 2837, Holy Infant of Prague. No. 2838, Blue Church of Bratislava.

1991, Sept. 30
2837 A1030 3k multicolored 1.25 .50
2838 A1030 3k multicolored 1.25 .50

Nos. 2837-2838 were each issued in sheets of 8. Value, set $15.

Flowers — A1031

1k, Gagea bohemica. 2k, Aster alpinus. 5k, Fritillaria meleagris. 11k, Daphne cneorum.

Photo. & Engr.

1991, Nov. 3 ***Perf. 12x11½***
2839 A1031 1k multicolored .60 .25
2840 A1031 2k multicolored .85 .25
2841 A1031 5k multicolored 1.25 .30
2842 A1031 11k multicolored 2.50 .45
Nos. 2839-2842 (4) 5.20 1.25

Painting Type of 1967

Paintings: 2k, Everyday Homelife by Max Ernst. 3k, Lovers by Auguste Renoir. 4k, Head of Christ by El Greco. 5k, Coincidence by Ladislav Guderna. 7k, Two Maidens by Utamaro.

1991, Nov. 3 **Engr.** ***Perf. 11½***
2843 A565 2k multicolored 1.25 .60
2844 A565 3k multicolored 1.25 .60
2845 A565 4k multicolored 1.25 .75
2846 A565 5k multicolored 1.75 1.25
2847 A565 7k multicolored 1.75 1.25
Nos. 2843-2847 (5) 7.25 4.45

Nos. 2843-2847 were each issued in sheets of 4. Value, set $30.

Christmas — A1033

1991, Nov. 19
2848 A1033 50h multicolored .30 .25

Stamp Day — A1034

Martin Benka (1888-1971), stamp engraver.

Photo. & Engr.

1991, Dec. 18 ***Perf. 11½x12***
2849 A1034 2k multicolored .45 .25

1992 Winter Olympics, Albertville — A1035

1992, Jan. 6 ***Perf. 11½***
2850 A1035 1k Biathlon .25 .25

Photo. & Engr.

1992, May 21 ***Perf. 11½***
2851 A1035 2k Tennis .30 .25

1992 Summer Olympics, Barcelona.

Souvenir Sheet

Jan Amos Komensky (Comenius), Educator — A1036

1992, Mar. 5 **Engr.**
2852 A1036 10k multicolored 4.00 3.50

World Ice Hockey Championships, Prague and Bratislava — A1037

1992, Mar. 31 **Photo. & Engr.**
2853 A1037 3k multicolored .75 .25

Traffic Safety A1038

1992, Apr. 2
2854 A1038 2k multicolored .50 .25

Expo '92, Seville — A1039

1992, Apr. 2
2855 A1039 4k multicolored .75 .25

Discovery of America, 500th Anniv. — A1040

1992, May 5 **Engr.**
2856 A1040 22k multicolored 2.00 2.00

Europa. Printed in sheets of 8. Value $18.

Czechoslovak Military Actions in WWII — A1041

Designs: 1k, J. Kubis and J. Gabcik, assassins of Reinhard Heydrich, 1942. 2k, Pilots flying for France and Great Britain. 3k, Defense of Tobruk. 6k, Capture of Dunkirk, 1944-45.

1992, May 21 **Engr.** ***Perf. 12x11½***
2857 A1041 1k multicolored .50 .25
2858 A1041 2k multicolored .60 .25
2859 A1041 3k multicolored .75 .25
2860 A1041 6k multicolored 1.60 .35
Nos. 2857-2860 (4) 3.45 1.10

A1042

Photo. & Engr.

1992, June 10 ***Perf. 11½***
2861 A1042 2k multicolored .30 .25

Czechoslovakian Red Cross.

A1043

1992, June 30
2862 A1043 1k multicolored .30 .25

Junior European Table Tennis Championships, Topolcany.

Beetles A1044

1992, July 15
2863 A1044 1k Polyphylla fullo .65 .25
2864 A1044 2k Ergates faber .90 .25
2865 A1044 3k Meloe violaceus 1.90 .45
2866 A1044 4k Dytiscus latissimus 1.90 .45
Nos. 2863-2866 (4) 5.35 1.40

The 1k exists with denomination omitted.

Troja Castle A1045

1992, Aug. 28 **Engr.** ***Perf. 11½***
2867 A1045 6k shown 2.60 1.00
2868 A1045 7k Statue of St. Martin, vert. 3.00 1.10
2869 A1045 8k Lednice Castle 3.50 1.25
Nos. 2867-2869 (3) 9.10 3.35

Nos. 2867-2869 were each issued in sheets of 8. Value, set $75.

Chrudim Church Type of 1971

Photo. & Engr.

1992, Aug. 28 ***Perf. 11½x11***
2870 A629 50h multicolored .75 .25

Postal Bank — A1045a

Photo. & Engr.

1992, Aug. 28 ***Perf. 11½x12***
2870A A1045a 20k multicolored 2.00 .75

Antonius Bernolak, Georgius Fandly — A1046

Photo. & Engr.

1992, Oct. 6 ***Perf. 12x11½***
2871 A1046 5k multicolored .75 .30

Slovakian Educational Society, bicent.

Cesky Krumlov — A1046a

Photo. & Engr.

1992, Oct. 19 ***Perf. 11½x12***
2871A A1046a 3k brick red & brn .75 .25

See No. 2890.

Painting Type of 1967

6k Old Man on a Raft, by Koloman Sokol. 7k, Still Life of Grapes and Raisins, by Georges Braque, horiz. 8k, Abandoned Corset, by Toyen.

Perf. 11½x12, 12x11½

1992, Nov. 2 **Engr.**
2872 A565 6k multicolored 2.00 .95

2873 A565 7k multicolored 3.25 1.10
2874 A565 8k multicolored 3.25 1.25
Nos. 2872-2874 (3) 8.50 3.30

Nos. 2872-2874 were each issued in sheets of 4. Value, set $37.50.

Christmas — A1047

Photo. & Engr.

1992, Nov. 9 ***Perf. 12x11½***
2875 A1047 2k multicolored .75 .25

Jindra Schmidt (1897-1984), Graphic Artist and Engraver — A1048

Photo. & Engr.

1992, Dec. 18 ***Perf. 11½x12***
2876 A1048 2k multicolored .75 .25

Stamp Day.

On January 1, 1993, Czechoslovakia split into Czech Republic and Slovakia. Czech Republic listings continue here. Slovakia can be found in Volume 5.

CZECH REPUBLIC

AREA — 30,449 sq. mi.
POP. — 10,280,513 (1999 est.)

Natl. Arms A1049

Photo. & Engr.

1993, Jan. 20 ***Perf. 11***
2877 A1049 3k multicolored .40 .25

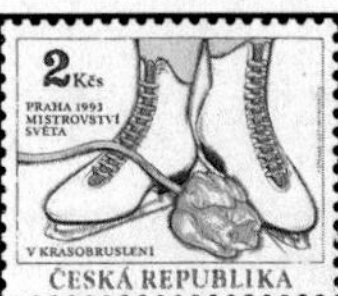

1993 World Figure Skating Championships, Prague A1050

1993, Feb. 25 ***Perf. 11½x11***
2878 A1050 2k multicolored .30 .25

Havel Type of 1990 Inscribed "Ceska Republika"

Photo. & Engr.

1993, Mar. 2 ***Perf. 12x11½***
2879 A1000 2k vio, vio brn & blue .30 .25

St. John Nepomuk, Patron Saint of Czechs, 600th Death Anniv. — A1051

1993, Mar. 11
2880 A1051 8k multicolored 1.00 .35

See Germany No. 1776; Slovakia No. 158.

Holy Hunger, by Mikulas Medek — A1052

1993, Mar. 11 ***Perf. 11½***
2881 A1052 14k multicolored *3.75 2.00*

Europa.
Issued in sheets of 4. Value, $16.

Sacred Heart Church, Prague A1053

1993, Mar. 30 **Engr.** ***Perf. 11½***
2882 A1053 5k multicolored 1.00 .50

Issued in sheets of 8. Value, $10.

Brevnov Monastery, 1000th Anniv. — A1054

Litho. & Engr.

1993, Apr. 12 ***Perf. 12x11½***
2883 A1054 4k multicolored .55 .25

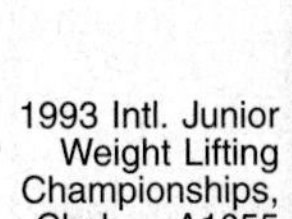
1993 Intl. Junior Weight Lifting Championships, Cheb — A1055

Photo. & Engr.

1993, May 12 ***Perf. 11½***
2884 A1055 6k multicolored 1.00 .35

Clock Tower and Church, Brno — A1056

1993, June 16 **Engr.** ***Perf. 12x11½***
2885 A1056 8k multicolored 1.50 1.50

Brno, 750th anniv.
Issued in sheets of 8. Value, $12.

Arrival of St. Cyril and St. Methodius, 1130th Anniv. — A1057

1993, June 22 **Photo. & Engr.**
2886 A1057 8k multicolored 1.00 .50

See Slovakia No. 167.

Souvenir Sheet

State Arms — A1058

1993, June 22 ***Perf. 11½***
2887 A1058 8k Sheet of 2 2.60 2.60

Architecture Type of 1992 Inscribed "Ceska Republika" and

A1059

Cities: 1k, Ceske Budejovice. 2k, Usti Nad Labem. No. 2890, like #2871A. No. 2891, Brno. 5k, Plzen. 6k, Slany. 7k, Ostrava. 8k, Olomouc. 10k, Hradec Kralove. 20k, Prague. 50k, Opava.

Perf. 12x11½, 11½x12

1993-94 **Photo. & Engr.**

2888	A1059	1k dp cl & org	.25	.25
2889	A1059	2k red vio & bl	.25	.25
2890	A1046a	3k gray bl & red	.25	.25
		Complete booklet, 5 #2890	4.50	
2891	A1059	3k dk bl & red	.25	.25
		Complete booklet, 5 #2891	3.75	
2892	A1059	5k bluish green & brn	.25	.25
2893	A1059	6k grn & org yel	1.00	.30
2894	A1059	7k blk brn & grn	1.00	.30
2895	A1059	8k dp vio & yel	.80	.30
2896	A1059	10k olive gray & red	.90	.40
2897	A1059	20k red & blue	2.50	.75
2898	A1059	50k brn & grn	4.75	1.75
		Nos. 2888-2898 (11)	12.20	5.05

Issued: No. 2891, 3/30/94; 6k, 10/1/94; 7k, 11/23/94; others, 7/1/93.

World Rowing Championships, Racice A1060

Photo. & Engr.

1993, Aug. 18 ***Perf. 11½***
2901 A1060 3k multicolored .40 .25

A1061

Famous men: 2k, August Sedlacek (1843-1926), historian. 3k, Eduard Cech (1893-1960), mathematician.

1993, Aug. 26 ***Perf. 12x11½***
2902 A1061 2k multicolored .40 .25
2903 A1061 3k multicolored .55 .25

Trees — A1062

1993, Oct. 26 ***Perf. 11½***
2904 A1062 5k Quercus robur .60 .30
2905 A1062 7k Carpinus betulus .80 .40
2906 A1062 9k Pinus silvestris 1.25 .50
Nos. 2904-2906 (3) 2.65 1.20

See Slovakia Nos. 160-162.

Christmas — A1063

Photo. & Engr.

1993, Nov. 8 ***Perf. 11½***
2907 A1063 2k multicolored .30 .25

Painting Type of 1967 Inscribed "ČESKA REPUBLIKA"

Paintings: 9k, Strahovska Madonna, by "Bohemian Master" in the year 1350. 11k, Composition, by Miro, horiz. 14k, Field of Green, by Van Gogh, horiz.

1993 **Engr.** ***Perf. 11½x12***
2908 A565 9k multicolored 2.00 2.00

Perf. 12x11½

2909 A565 11k multicolored 2.25 2.25
2910 A565 14k multicolored 3.25 3.25
Nos. 2908-2910 (3) 7.50 7.50

Issued: 11k, 14k, Nov. 8; 9k, Dec. 15.
Nos. 2908-2910 were each issued in sheets of 4. Value, set $30.

Intl. Year of the Family — A1064

Photo. & Engr.

1994, Jan. 19 ***Perf. 11½***
2911 A1064 2k multicolored .30 .25

Jan Kubelik (1880-1940), Composer A1065

Photo. & Engr.

1994, Jan. 19 ***Perf. 11½***
2912 A1065 3k multicolored .40 .25

UNESCO — A1065a

Designs: 2k, Voltaire (1694-1778), philosopher. 6k, Georgius Agricola (1494-1555), mineralogist, humanist.

1994, Feb. 2 ***Perf. 12x11½***
2913 A1065a 2k multicolored .25 .25
2914 A1065a 6k multicolored .80 .35

1994 Winter Olympics, Lillehammer A1066

Photo. & Engr.

1994, Feb. 2 ***Perf. 11½***
2915 A1066 5k multicolored .70 .35

A1067

Europa (Marco Polo &): No. 2916, Stylized animals, Chinese woman. No. 2917, Stylized animals.

Photo. & Engr.

1994, May 4 *Perf. 11½*

2916 A1067 14k multicolored 1.75 1.75
2917 A1067 14k multicolored 1.75 1.75
a. Pair, #2916-2917 3.50 3.50

Nos. 2916-2917 were issued in sheets of 2 + 2 labels. Value, $8.

Eduard Benes — A1068

1994, May 18

2918 A1068 5k violet & brt purple .60 .25

Architectural Sights — A1069

UNESCO: 8k, Houses at the square, Telc. 9k, Cubist house designed by Chochol, Prague.

1994, May 18

2919 A1069 8k multicolored 1.25 .75
2920 A1069 9k multicolored 1.25 .75

Issued in sheets of 8. Value, pair of sheets $20.

Children's Day — A1070

Photo. & Engr.

1994, June 1 *Perf. 11½*

2921 A1070 2k multicolored .40 .25

Dinosaurs — A1071

Perf. 11½x11, 11x11½

1994, June 1 **Litho.**

2922 A1071 2k Stegosaurus .30 .25
2923 A1071 3k Apatosaurus .50 .25
2924 A1071 5k Tarbosaurus, vert. .70 .35
Nos. 2922-2924 (3) 1.50 .85

A1072

Photo. & Engr.

1994, June 1 *Perf. 11½x11*

2925 A1072 8k multicolored 1.00 .50

1994 World Cup Soccer Championships, US.

A1073

1994, June 15 *Perf. 11x11½*

2926 A1073 2k multicolored .35 .25

12th Pan-Sokol Rally, Prague.

Intl. Olympic Committee, Cent. — A1074

1994, June 15

2927 A1074 7k multicolored 1.00 .50

UPU, 120th Anniv. A1075

1994, Aug. 3 **Engr.** *Perf. 11½*

2928 A1075 11k multicolored 1.40 1.00

No. 2928 was issued in sheets of 4 + 4 labels. Value, $11.50.

Songbirds — A1076

Designs: 3k, Saxicola torquata. 5k, Carpodacus erythrinus. 14k, Luscinia svecica.

Photo. & Engr.

1994, Aug. 24 *Perf. 11x11½*

2929 A1076 3k multicolored .40 .25
2930 A1076 5k multicolored .60 .30
2931 A1076 14k multicolored 1.50 .80
Nos. 2929-2931 (3) 2.50 1.35

Historic Race Cars — A1077

Photo. & Engr.

1994, Oct. 5 *Perf. 11½*

2932 A1077 2k 1900 NW .25 .25
Complete booklet, 10 #2932 3.00
2933 A1077 3k 1908 L&K .45 .25
Complete booklet, 5 #2933 2.75
2934 A1077 9k 1912 Praga 1.10 .50
Nos. 2932-2934 (3) 1.80 1.00

Christmas — A1078

Photo. & Engr.

1994, Nov. 9 *Perf. 11½*

2935 A1078 2k multicolored .45 .25

Painting Type of 1967 Inscribed "CESKA REPUBLIKA"

Engraving or paintings: 7k, Stary Posetilec A Zena, by Lucas Van Leyden. 10k, Moulin Rouge, by Henri de Toulouse-Lautrec. 14k, St. Vitus Madonna, St. Vitus Cathedral, Prague.

1994, Nov. 9 **Engr.** *Perf. 12*

2936 A565 7k multicolored .95 .95
2937 A565 10k multicolored 1.40 1.40
2938 A565 14k multicolored 2.00 2.00
Nos. 2936-2938 (3) 4.35 4.35

Nos. 2936-2938 were each printed in sheets of 4. Value, set $17.

World Tourism Organization, 20th Anniv. — A1079

Photo. & Engr.

1995, Jan. 2 *Perf. 11x12*

2939 A1079 8k green blue & red .95 .50

Czech Stamp Production — A1080

1995, Jan. 20

2940 A1080 3k Design N1 .60 .25

Czech Republic & European Union Association Agreement A1081

1995, Jan. 20 **Litho.** *Perf. 13½x12½*

2941 A1081 8k multicolored 1.20 .65

Famous Men A1082

Designs: 2k, Johannes Marcus Marci (1595-1667). 5k, Ferdinand Peroutka (1895-1978). 7k, Premysl Pitter (1895-1976).

Photo. & Engr.

1995, Feb. 1 *Perf. 12x11*

2942 A1082 2k multicolored .30 .25
2943 A1082 5k multicolored .30 .25
2944 A1082 7k multicolored .90 .35
Nos. 2942-2944 (3) 1.50 .85

Theater Personalities — A1083

Designs: No. 2945, Jiri Voskovec (1905-81). No. 2946, Jan Werich (1905-80). No. 2947, Jaroslav Jezek (1906-42). 22k, Caricatures of Voskovec, Werich, and Jezek with piano.

1995 **Photo. & Engr.** *Perf. 12x11*

2945 A1083 3k multicolored .35 .25
Complete booklet, 3 #2945 6.00
2946 A1083 3k multicolored .35 .25
Complete booklet, 3 #2946 6.00
2947 A1083 3k multicolored .35 .25
Complete booklet, 3 #2947 6.00
a. Strip of 3, #2945-2947 1.10 1.10
Complete booklet, 2 #2947a 9.00
Nos. 2945-2947 (3) 1.05 .75

Souvenir Sheet

Photo.

Perf. 12

2947B A1083 22k yellow & black 2.50 2.50

Issued: 3k, 3/15; 22k, 9/20.

Havel Type of 1990 Inscribed "Ceska Republika"

Photo. & Engr.

1995, Mar. 22 *Perf. 12x11½*

2948 A1000 3.60k bl, vio & mag .45 .25
Complete booklet, 5 #2948 4.00

Rural Architecture A1084

1995, Mar. 22 *Perf. 11½*

2949 A1084 40h shown .25 .25
2950 A1084 60h Homes, diff. .25 .25

European Nature Conservation Year — A1085

1995, Apr. 12

2951 A1085 3k Bombus terrestris .55 .30
Complete booklet, 5 #2951 4.00
2952 A1085 5k Mantis religiosa .70 .30
Complete booklet, 5 #2952 4.50
2953 A1085 6k Calopteryx splendens .80 .30
Complete booklet, 5 #2953 5.00
Nos. 2951-2953 (3) 2.05 .90

Peace & Freedom A1086

Photo. & Engr.

1995, May 3 *Perf. 11½*

2954 A1086 9k Rose, profiles 1.00 .35
2955 A1086 14k Butterfly, profiles 1.50 .75

Europa.

Natural Beauties in Czech Republic A1087

Designs: 8k, "Stone Organ" scenic mountain. 9k, Largest sandstone bridge in Europe.

Photo. & Engr.

1995, May 3 *Perf. 11½*

2956 A1087 8k multicolored .95 .95
2957 A1087 9k multicolored 1.00 1.00

Nos. 2956-2957 were each issued in sheets of 8. Value, set $16.

Children's Day — A1088

Photo. & Engr.

1995, June 1 *Perf. 11½*

2958 A1088 3.60k multicolored .60 .25

First Train from Vienna to Prague, 150th Anniv. A1089

3k, Chocen Tunnel. 9.60k, Entering Prague.

1995, June 21

2959 A1089 3k multicolored .35 .25
Complete booklet, 5 #2959 4.00
2960 A1089 9.60k multicolored 1.15 .50

World Wrestling Championships, Prague A1090

Photo. & Engr.

1995, Sept. 6 *Perf. 11½*

2961 A1090 3k multicolored .75 .25

Cartoon Characters A1091

Designs: 3k, Man playing violin, woman washing, by Vladimir Rencin. 3.60k, Angel, naked man, by Vladimir Jiranek. 5k, Circus trainer holding ring for champagne cork to pop through, by Jiri Sliva.

1995, Sept. 6

2962 A1091 3k multicolored .35 .25
Complete booklet, 5 #2962 3.50
2963 A1091 3.60k multicolored .35 .25
Complete booklet, 5 #2963 3.50
2964 A1091 5k multicolored .35 .30
Complete booklet, 5 #2964 3.50
Nos. 2962-2964 (3) 1.05 .80

A1092

1995, Sept. 20 Litho. *Perf. 13½x13*

2965 A1092 3k multicolored .35 .25

SOS Children's Villages, 25th anniv.

A1093

Designs: 2.40k, Gothic. 3k, Secession. 3.60k, Romance. 4k, Classic portal; 4.60k, Rococo. 9.60k, Renaissance Portal. 12.60k, Cubist. 14k, Baroque.

Photo. & Engr.

1995-97 *Perf. 12x11½*

2966 A1093 2.40k red & green .30 .25
2967 A1093 3k grn & bl .35 .25
2967A A1093 3.60k pur & grn .45 .25
2968 A1093 4k blue & red .50 .25
Complete booklet, 5 #2967A 3.00
2968A A1093 4.60k multicolored .55 .25
2969 A1093 9.60k blue & red 1.10 .45
2969A A1093 12.60k red brn & bl 1.50 .45
2970 A1093 14k grn & pur 1.60 .60
Nos. 2966-2970 (8) 6.35 2.75

Issued: 9.60k, 9/27; 2.40k, 14k, 10/11; 3k, 3.60k, 10/25; 4k, 6/12/96; 4.60k, 3/26/97; 12.60k, 6/25/97.

UN, 50th Anniv. A1094

1995, Oct. 11 Litho. *Perf. 12x11½*

2971 A1094 14k multicolored 1.60 .80

Wilhelm Röntgen (1845-1923), Discovery of the X-Ray, Cent. — A1095

1995, Oct. 11 Photo. & Engr.

2972 A1095 6k blk, buff & bl vio .75 .35

Painting Type of 1967 Inscribed "CESKA REPUBLIKA"

Designs: 6k, Parisiene, by Ludek Marold. 9k, Vase of Flowers, by J.K. Hirschely. 14k, Portrait of J. Malinsky, by Antoinín Machek.

1995, Nov. 8 *Perf. 12*

2973 A565 6k multicolored .95 .45
2974 A565 9k multicolored 1.25 .65
2975 A565 14k multicolored 2.00 1.00
Nos. 2973-2975 (3) 4.20 2.10

Nos. 2973-2975 were each printed in sheets of 4. Value, set $13.50.

Christmas — A1096

1995, Nov. 8 *Perf. 11½*

2976 A1096 3k multicolored .50 .25
Complete booklet, 5 #2976 3.00

Czech Philharmonic Orchestra, Cent. — A1097

Photo. & Engr.

1996, Jan. 2 *Perf. 12x11½*

2977 A1097 3.60k multicolored .55 .25

Tradition of Czech Stamp Production — A1098

Photo. & Engr.

1996, Jan. 20 *Perf. 11½x12*

2978 A1098 3.60k Design A5 of 1920 .55 .25

Vera Mencikova (1906-44), Chess Player — A1099

Photo. & Engr.

1996, Feb. 14 *Perf. 12x11½*

2979 A1099 6k multicolored .75 .35

Easter — A1100

1996, Mar. 13 *Perf. 11½x12*

2980 A1100 3k multicolored .45 .25
Complete booklet, 5 #2980 2.00

Josef Sudek (1896-1976), Photographer A1101

Photo. & Engr.

1996, Mar. 13 *Perf. 11*

2981 A1101 9.60k multicolored 1.10 .60

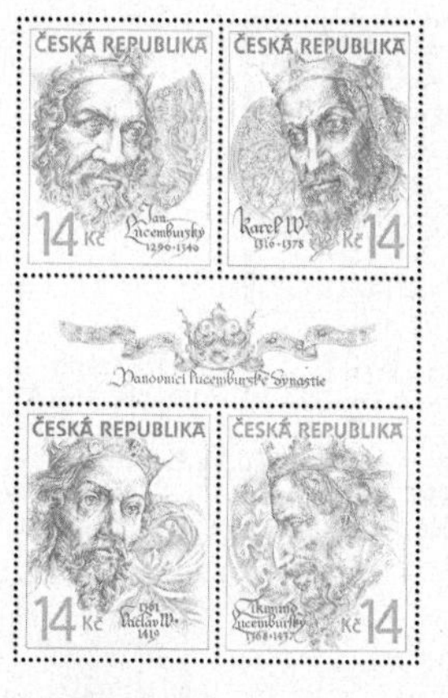
Rulers from House of Luxembourg — A1102

Designs: a, John of Luxembourg (1296-1346). b, Charles IV (1316-78). c, Wenceslas IV. (1361-1419). d, Sigismund (1368-1437).

1996, Mar. 27 Engr. *Perf. 11½*

2982 A1102 14k Sheet of 4, #a.-d. + label 6.00 6.00

Jiri Guth-Jarkovsky, Participant in First Modern Olympic Games, Athens A1103

Photo. & Engr.

1996, Mar. 27 *Perf. 11½*

2983 A1103 9.60k multicolored 1.25 .60

Modern Olympic Games, cent.

World Wildlife Fund — A1104

Designs: a, 3.60k, Eliomys quercinus. b, 5k, Dryomys nitedula. c, 6k, Spermophilus citellus. d, 8k, Sicista betulina.

Photo. & Engr.

1996, Apr. 24 *Perf. 11½x12*

2984 A1104 Block of 4, #a.-d. 2.50 2.50

Issued in sheets of 8 stamps. Value $5.

Ema Destinnova (1878-1930), Singer — A1105

1996, May 2 *Perf. 11½*

2985 A1105 8k multicolored .85 .35

Europa.

No. 2985 was issued in sheets of 10. Value $8.50.

A1106

Photo. & Engr.

1996, May 15 *Perf. 11x11½*

2986 A1106 12k multicolored 1.20 .65

Jean Gaspart Deburau (1796-1846), mime.

A1107

1996, May 29

2987 A1107 3k multicolored .35 .25

1996 Summmer Olympic Games, Atlanta.

Intl. Children's Day — A1108

Photo. & Engr.

1996, May 29 *Perf. 11½*

2988 A1108 3k multicolored .35 .25

Architectural Sites — A1109

UNESCO: 8k, St. Nepomuk Church, Zelena Hora. 9k, Loreta Tower, Prague.

1996, June 26 **Engr.** *Perf. 11½*

2989 A1109 8k multicolored 1.00 1.00
2990 A1109 9k multicolored 1.10 1.10

Nos. 2989-2990 were each issued in sheets of 8. Value, set $16.

See Nos. 3056-3057.

UNICEF, 50th Anniv. A1110

Photo. & Engr.

1996, Sept. 11 *Perf. 12x11*

2991 A1110 3k multicolored .35 .25

Horses

A1111 A1112

Photo. & Engr.

1996, Sept. 25 *Perf. 11x11½*

2992 A1111 3k multicolored .50 .25
2993 A1112 3k multicolored .50 .25
a. Pair, #2992-2993 1.00 .75
Complete booklet, 3 #2992, 2 #2993 3.00
Complete booklet, 2 #2992, 3 #2993 3.00

Souvenir Sheet

Vaclav Havel, 60th Birthday — A1113

1996, Oct. 5

2994 A1113 Sheet of 2 1.25 1.25
a. 6k red & blue .60 .50

Painting Type of 1967 Inscribed "CESKA REPUBLIKA"

The Baroque Chair, by Endre Nemes (1909-85).

1996, Oct. 5 **Engr.** *Perf. 11½*

2995 A565 20k multicolored 2.00 2.00

No. 2995 was issued in sheets of 4. Value $8.

See Slovakia No. 255; Sweden No. 2199.

Tycho Brahe (1546-1601), Astronomer — A1114

Photo. & Engr.

1996, Oct. 9 *Perf. 11½x11*

2996 A1114 5k multicolored .85 .30

Biplanes A1115

1996, Oct. 9

2997 A1115 7k Letov S1 .70 .40
2998 A1115 8k Aero A11 .90 .40
2999 A1115 10k Avia BH21 1.00 .50
Nos. 2997-2999 (3) 2.60 1.30

Christmas A1116

Photo. & Engr.

1996, Nov. 13 *Perf. 11½*

3000 A1116 3k multicolored .45 .25
Complete booklet, 5 #3000 3.50

Painting Type of 1967 Inscribed "CESKA REPUBLIKA"

Designs: 9k, Garden of Eden, by Josef Váchal (1884-1969), horiz. 11k, Breakfast, by Georg Flegel (1566-1638).

1996, Nov. 13 **Engr.** *Perf. 11½*

3001 A565 9k multicolored 1.00 1.00
3002 A565 11k multicolored 1.25 1.25

Nos. 3001-3002 were each issued in sheets of 4. Value, set $10.

Czech Stamp Production — A1117

Photo. & Engr.

1997, Jan. 20 *Perf. 11½x12*

3003 A1117 3.60k #68, bl & red .75 .25

Easter — A1118

Photo. & Engr.

1997, Mar. 12 *Perf. 11½*

3004 A1118 3k multicolored .75 .25
Complete booklet, 5 #3004 4.00

Flowers — A1119

3.60k, Erythronium dens-canis. 4k, Calla palustris. 5k, Cypripedium calceolus. 8k, Iris pumila.

1997, Mar. 12 *Perf. 11x11½*

3005 A1119 3.60k multicolored .30 .25
Complete booklet, 5 #3005 2.50
3006 A1119 4k multicolored .30 .25
Complete booklet, 5 #3006 2.50
3007 A1119 5k multicolored .50 .30
Complete booklet, 5 #3007 3.50
3008 A1119 8k multicolored .60 .45
Complete booklet, 5 #3008 5.00
Nos. 3005-3008 (4) 1.70 1.25

A1120

Jewish Monuments in Prague: 8k, Altneuschul Synagogue. 10k, Tombstone of Rabbi Judah Loew MaHaRal.

1997, Apr. 30 *Perf. 11½*

3009 A1120 8k multicolored .75 .45
3010 A1120 10k multicolored .90 .55
a. Sheet, 4 each #3009-3010 7.00 4.00

See Israel Nos. 1302-1303.

Greetings Stamp — A1121

1997, Mar. 26 **Litho.** *Perf. 13x13½*

3011 A1121 4k Girl with cats .50 .25

A1122

1997, Apr. 23 **Engr.** *Perf. 11½*

3012 A1122 7k deep violet .95 .40

St. Adalbert (956-97). See Germany No. 1964, Hungary No. 3569, Poland No. 3337, Vatican City No. 1040.

No. 3012 was issued in sheets of 4 + 4 labels. Value, $7.

A1123

Europa (Stories and Legends): No. 3013, Queen, knight with sword, lion, snakes. No. 3014, Man riding in chariot drawn by chickens, King looking through window.

Photo. & Engr.

1997, Apr. 30 *Perf. 11½x12*

3013 A1123 8k multicolored 1.00 .60
3014 A1123 8k multicolored 1.00 .60

Nos. 3013-3014 were each issued in sheets of 8. Value, set $16.

Souvenir Sheet

Collections of Rudolf II (1522-1612), Prague Exhibition — A1124

Designs: a, 6k, Musical instruments, flowers, face of bearded man. b, 8k, Rudolf II wearing laurel wreath, holding rose, Muses. c, 10k, Rudolf II, skull, moth's wings, tree, flowers, leaves, fruit.

1997, May 14 **Engr.** *Perf. 12*

3015 A1124 Sheet of 3, #a.-c. 2.25 2.25

Intl. Children's Day — A1125

Photo. & Engr.

1997, May 28 *Perf. 11½*

3016 A1125 4.60k multicolored .75 .25

Frantisek Krizik (1847-1941), Electrical Engineer, Inventor of Arc Lamp — A1126

Photo. & Engr.

1997, June 25 *Perf. 12x11½*

3017 A1126 6k multicolored .85 .25

European Swimming & Diving Championships, Prague — A1127

Photo. & Engr.

1997, Aug. 27 *Perf. 11½*

3018 A1127 11k multicolored 1.00 .40

"The Good Soldier Schweik," by Jaroslav Hasek, 110th Anniv. — A1128

4k, Mrs. Müller, Schweik in wheelchair. 4.60k, Lt. Lukás, Col. Kraus von Zillergut, dog. 6k, Schweik smoking pipe, winter scene.

Photo. & Engr.

1997, Sept. 10 *Perf. 12x11½*
3019 A1128 4k multicolored .50 .25
a. Booklet pane of 8 + 4 labels 4.50
Complete booklet, #3019a 4.50
3020 A1128 4.60k multicolored .50 .25
a. Booklet pane of 8 + 4 labels 5.00
Complete booklet, #3020a 5.00
3021 A1128 6k multicolored .50 .30
a. Booklet pane of 8 + 4 labels 6.00
Complete booklet, #3021a 6.00
Nos. 3019-3021 (3) 1.50 .80

Praga 1998, Intl. Stamp Exhibition — A1129

No. 3022, Lesser Town, Prague Castle. No. 3023, Old Town, bridges over Vltava River.

Photo. & Engr.

1997, Sept. 24 *Perf. 11½*
3022 A1129 15k multicolored 1.40 .60
3023 A1129 15k multicolored 1.40 .60
a. Souvenir sheet, #3022-3023 + 2 labels 3.75 3.00

Historic Service Vehicles A1130

Designs: 4k, Postal bus, Prague. 4.60k, Sentinel truck, Skoda. 8k, Fire truck, Tatra.

1997, Oct. 8 *Perf. 12x11½*
3024 A1130 4k multicolored .30 .25
Complete booklet, 5 #3024 2.50
3025 A1130 4.60k multicolored .30 .25
Complete booklet, 5 #3025 3.50
3026 A1130 8k multicolored .60 .40
Complete booklet, 5 #3026 5.00
Nos. 3024-3026 (3) 1.20 .90

A1131

Photo. & Engr.

1997, Nov. 12 *Perf. 11½*
3027 A1131 4k multicolored .50 .25
Complete booklet, 5 #3027 2.75

Christmas.

Painting Type of 1967 Inscribed "CESKA REPUBLIKA"

7k, Landscape with Chateau in Chantilly, by Antonín Chittussi (1847-91). 12k, The Prophets Came Out of the Desert, by Frantisek Bílek (1872-1941). 1 6k, Parisian Antiquarians, by T. F. Simon (1877-1942).

1997, Nov. 12 **Engr.** *Perf. 12*
3028 A565 7k multi, horiz. .50 .50
3029 A565 12k multi 1.00 1.00
3030 A565 16k multi 1.50 1.50
Nos. 3028-3030 (3) 3.00 3.00

Nos. 3028-3030 were each issued in sheets of 4. Value, set $12.

A1132

1998, Jan. 20 **Litho.** *Perf. 11½x12*
3031 A1132 7k multicolored .85 .30

1998 Winter Olympic Games, Nagano.

Tradition of Czech Stamp Production — A1133

Photo. & Engr.

1998, Jan. 20 *Perf. 12x11½*
3032 A1133 12.60k Type A8 1.25 .55
a. Booklet pane of 8 + 4 labels 12.50
Complete booklet, #3032a 12.50

Pres. Václav Havel — A1134

1998, Jan. 22
3033 A1134 4.60k dark grn & red .85 .25

See No. 3114.

Love — A1135

1998, Feb. 4 *Perf. 11½*
3034 A1135 4k multicolored .50 .25
Complete booklet, 5 #3034 2.50

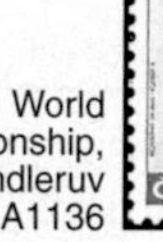

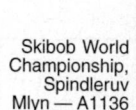

Skibob World Championship, Spindleruv Mlyn — A1136

1998, Feb. 25
3035 A1136 8k multicolored .85 .35

Prague Philatelic Exhibition Type of 1938

Souvenir Sheet

1998, Feb. 25 **Engr.** *Perf. 12x11½*
3036 A87 Sheet of 2 5.00 5.00
a. 30k like #251a 2.50 2.00

Prague '98, Intl. Philatelic Exhibition.

Easter — A1137

Photo. & Engr.

1998, Mar. 25 *Perf. 11x11½*
3037 A1137 4k multicolored .55 .25
Complete booklet, 5 #3037 2.75

Ondrejov Observatory, Cent. — A1138

1998, Mar. 25 *Perf. 12x11½*
3038 A1138 4.60k multicolored .85 .25

Czech Ice Hockey Team, Gold Medalists at Nagano Winter Olympic Games — A1139

1998, Apr. 1 **Litho.** *Perf. 11½x12*
3039 A1139 23k Dominik Hasek 1.50 1.50

No. 3039 was issued in a sheet with two labels. Value, $2.

Charles University and New Town, Prague, 650th Anniv. — A1140

Designs: a, 15k, Hands forming arch, University seal. b, 22k, Charles IV (1316-78), Holy Roman Emperor, King of Bohemia. c, 23k, Groin vault, St. Vitus Cathedral, Prague.

1998, Apr. 1 **Engr.** *Perf. 12*
3040 A1140 Sheet of 3, #a.-c. 5.50 5.50

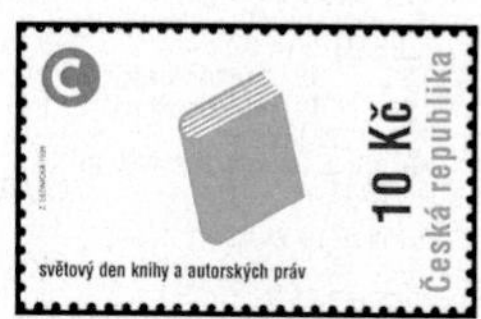

World Book and Copyright Day — A1141

1998, Apr. 23 **Litho.** *Perf. 12x11½*
3041 A1141 10k multicolored 1.00 .45

Nature Conservation A1142

1998, Apr. 23 *Perf. 13x13½*
3042 A1142 4.60k Perdix perdix .45 .25
3043 A1142 4.60k Lyrurus tetrix .45 .25
a. Pair, #3042-3043 1.10 .60
3044 A1142 8k Cervus elaphus .65 .30
3045 A1142 8k Alces alces .65 .30
a. Pair, #3044-3045 1.50 1.10
Nos. 3042-3045 (4) 2.20 1.10

Natl. Festivals and Holidays A1143

Europa: 11k, King's Ride. 15k, Wearing masks for Carnival.

Litho. & Engr.

1998, May 5 *Perf. 11½*
3046 A1143 11k multicolored .90 .55
3047 A1143 15k multicolored 1.40 .75

Intl. Children's Day — A1144

Designs: 4k, Two satyr musicians. 4.60k, Character riding on fish.

Photo. & Engr.

1998, May 27 *Perf. 11½*
3048 A1144 4k multicolored .60 .25
a. Booklet of 6 +4 labels 4.00
Complete booklet, #3048a 4.00
3049 A1144 4.60k multicolored .60 .25
a. Booklet of 6 + 4 labels 4.50
Complete booklet, #3049a 4.50

Famous Men — A1145

Designs: 4k, Frantisek Kmoch (1848-1912), bandleader, composer. 4.60k, Frantisek Palacky (1798-1876), historian, politician. 6k, Rafael Kubelík (1914-96), composer, conductor.

1998, May 27 *Perf. 11½x12*
3050 A1145 4k multicolored .35 .25
3051 A1145 4.60k multicolored .45 .25
3052 A1145 6k multicolored .55 .25
Nos. 3050-3052 (3) 1.35 .75

Revolt of 1848, 150th Anniv. A1146

1998, May 27 *Perf. 12x11½*
3053 A1146 15k multicolored 1.60 .75

Painting Type of 1967 Inscribed "CESKA REPUBLIKA"

Praga 1998 Intl. Stamp Exhibition, works of art: 22k, Amorfa Dvoubarevna Fuga, by Frantisek Kupka (1871-1957), horiz. 23k, Escape, by Paul Gauguin (1848-1903), horiz.

1998, June 17 **Engr.** *Perf. 12*
3054 A565 22k multicolored 1.75 1.75
3055 A565 23k multicolored 2.25 1.75

Nos. 3054-3055 were each issued in sheets of 4. Value, set $16.

UNESCO World Heritage Sites Type of 1996

8k, St. Barbara Cathedral, Kutná Hora, horiz. 11k, The Chateau of Valtice, horiz.

1998, Oct. 7 **Engr.** *Perf. 11½x12*
3056 A1109 8k multicolored .70 .40
3057 A1109 11k multicolored 1.00 .60

Nos. 3056-3057 were each issued in sheets of 8. Value, set $15.

Czechoslovak Republic, 80th Anniv. — A1147

Designs based on World War I recruitment posters by Vojtech Preissig (1873-1944): 4.60k, Soldiers holding flags, guns. 5k, Three soldiers marching. 12.60k, Flags waving from city buildings.

Perf. 11½x11¾

1998, Oct. 28 **Litho. & Engr.**

3058 A1147 4.60k multicolored .50 .30

3059 A1147 5k multicolored .70 .30

3060 A1147 12.60k multicolored 1.25 .90

Nos. 3058-3060 (3) 2.45 1.50

No. 3060 was issued in sheets of 6+2 labels. Value $25.

Christmas A1148

Designs: 4k, People following star. 6k, Angel blowing trumpet over town, vert.

Photo. & Engr.

1998, Nov. 18 ***Perf. 11½***

3061 A1148 4k multicolored .45 .25
Complete booklet, 5 #3061 2.50

3062 A1148 6k multicolored .70 .25
Complete booklet, 5 #3062 4.00

Signs of the Zodiac — A1149

3063 A1149 1k

1998-2003 ***Perf. 11¾x11½***

3064 A1149 10k Aquarius .75 .25

3065 A1149 9k Libra .75 .25

3066 A1149 8k Cancer .65 .25

3067 A1149 20k Sagittarius 1.60 .45

3068 A1149 5k Taurus .55 .25
Booklet, 5 #3068 2.75

3069 A1149 5.40k Scorpio .60 .25
Booklet, 5 #3069 3.00

3070 A1149 2k Virgo .25 .25

3071 A1149 40h Pisces .65 .25

3072 A1149 12k Leo 1.00 .30

3073 A1149 17k Gemini 1.60 .65

3074 A1149 26k Aries 2.40 .95

Nos. 3063-3074 (12) 11.05 4.35

Issued: 1k, 10k, 11/18; 9k, 5/5/99; 8k, 20k, 9/8/99; 5k, 5.40k, 12/8/99; 2k, 5/9/00. 40h, 1/20/01. 12k, 2/21/01. 17k, 9/1/02. 26k, 2/12/03.

Painting Type of 1967 Inscribed "CESKA REPUBLIKA"

15k, Painting from the Greater Cycle, 1902, by Jan Preisler (1872-1918), horiz. 16k, Spinner, by Josef Navrátil (1798-1865).

1998, Dec. 9 ***Perf. 12***

3075 A565 15k multicolored 1.40 1.00

3076 A565 16k multicolored 1.40 1.00

Nos. 3075-3076 were each issued in sheets of 4. Value, set $11.

A1150

Photo. & Engr.

1999, Jan. 20 ***Perf. 11½x11¾***

3077 A1150 4.60k #164 .85 .25

a. Booklet pane of 8 + 4 labels 5.00
Complete booklet, #3077a 5.50

Tradition of Czech stamp production.

Domestic Cats — A1151

Photo. & Engr.

1999, Feb. 17 ***Perf. 11½***

3078 A1151 4.60k shown .55 .25
Complete booklet, 5 #3078 3.50

3079 A1151 5k Adult, kitten .55 .25
Complete booklet, 5 #3079 3.50

3080 A1151 7k Two cats .80 .30
Complete booklet, 5 #3080 3.50

Nos. 3078-3080 (3) 1.90 .80

Easter — A1152

Photo. & Engr.

1999, Mar. 10 ***Perf. 11¼x11½***

3081 A1152 3k multicolored .35 .25

Protected Birds — A1153

No. 3082, Merops apiaster. No. 3083, Upupa epops.

Protected butterflies: No. 3084, Catocala electa. No. 3085, Euphydryas maturna.

Perf. 12¾x13¼

1999, Mar. 10 **Litho.**

3082 A1153 4.60k multicolored .45 .25

3083 A1153 4.60k multicolored .45 .25

a. Pair, #3082-3083 .95 .60
Complete booklet, 3 #3082, 2 #3083 5.00

3084 A1153 5k multicolored .45 .25

3085 A1153 5k multicolored .45 .25

a. Pair, #3084-3085 .95 .60
Complete booklet, 3 #3084, 2 #3085 5.00

Nature conservation.

Czech Republic's Entry Into NATO — A1154

Photo. & Engr.

1999, Mar. 12 ***Perf. 12x11½***

3086 A1154 4.60k multicolored .45 .25

Council of Europe, 50th Anniv. A1155

Photo. & Engr.

1999, Apr. 14 ***Perf. 11¾x11¼***

3087 A1155 7k multicolored 1.20 .40

Natl. Olympic Committee, Cent. — A1156

Design: Josef Rössler-Orovsky (1869-1933), founder of Czech Olympic Committee.

1999, Apr. 14 ***Perf. 11¼x11¾***

3088 A1156 9k multicolored 1.20 .35

Europa A1157

Natl. Parks: 11k, Sumava. 17k, Podyji.

1999, May 5 ***Perf. 11¾x11¼***

3089 A1157 11k multicolored .90 .40

3090 A1157 17k multicolored 1.40 .65

Nos. 3089-3090 were each issued in sheets of 8. Value, set $27.

Ferda the Ant, Pytlik the Beetle and Ladybird A1158

Photo. & Engr.

1999, May 26 ***Perf. 11½x11¼***

3091 A1158 4.60k multicolored .75 .25
Complete booklet, 8 #3091 6.00

Bridges A1159

1999, May 26 **Engr.** ***Perf. 11¾***

3092 A1159 8k Stádlec, vert. .60 .40

3093 A1159 11k Cernvír 1.00 .60

Nos. 3092-3094 were each issued in sheets of 8. Value, set $13.

Souvenir Sheet

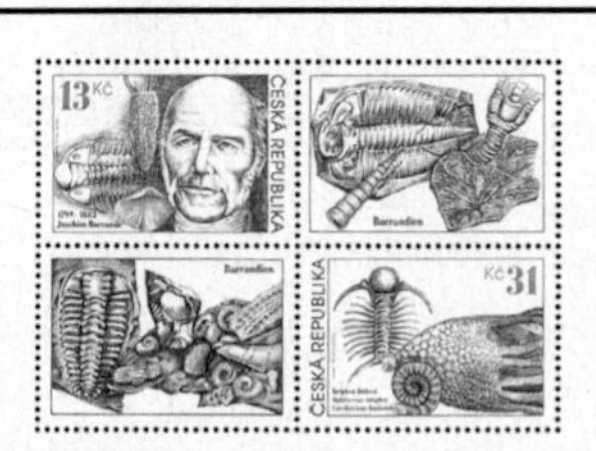

Paleontologist Joachim Barrande (1799-1883) and Trilobite Fossils — A1160

a, 13k, Barrande, fossils. b, 31k, Delphon forbesi, Ophioceras simplex, Carolicrinus barrandei.

1999, June 23 **Engr.** ***Perf. 11¾***

3094 A1160 Sheet of 2, #a.-b. + 2 labels 4.00 4.00

Jihlava Mining Rights, 750th Anniv. A1161

Photo. & Engr.

1999, June 23 ***Perf. 11¾x11¼***

3095 A1161 8k multicolored .95 .35

a. Bklt. pane of 8 + 4 labels 8.00
Complete booklet, #3095a 8.00

UPU, 125th Anniv. — A1162

Litho. & Engr.

1999, June 23 ***Perf. 11¾***

3096 A1162 9k multicolored 1.00 .40

No. 3096 was issued in sheets of 5 + 10 labels. Value, $6.

Vincenc Preissnitz (1799-1851), Hydrotherapy Advocate A1163

Photo. & Engr.

1999, Sept. 8 ***Perf. 11¼***

3097 A1163 4.60k multicolored .50 .25

UNESCO.

Carved Beehives — A1164

Designs: 4.60k, Woman. 5k, St. Joseph and Infant Jesus. 7k, Chimney sweep.

Photo. & Engr.

1999, Sept. 29 ***Perf. 11¼x11½***

3098 A1164 4.60k multi .55 .25
Complete booklet, 5 #3098 2.75

3099 A1164 5k multi .60 .25
Complete booklet, 5 #3099 3.00

3100 A1164 7k multi .80 .30
Complete booklet, 5 #3100 4.00

Nos. 3098-3100 (3) 1.95 .80

Cartoons by Miroslav Bartak — A1165

Designs: 4.60k, Doctor in clown mask, infant. 5k, Dog with pipe. 7k, Night seeping through window sill.

1999, Oct. 20

3101	A1165	4.60k multi	.45	.25
3102	A1165	5k multi	.55	.25
3103	A1165	7k multi	.70	.30
		Nos. 3101-3103 (3)	1.70	.80

Souvenir Sheet

Beuron Art School — A1166

Designs: a, 11k, Mater Dei, 1898. b, 13k, Pantocrator, 1911.

Litho. & Engr.

1999, Oct. 20 ***Perf. 11¾***

3104 A1166 Sheet of 2, #a.-b. 2.25 2.25

Painting Type of 1967 Inscribed "CESKA REPUBLIKA"

Designs: 13k, Red Orchid, by Jindrich Styrsky (1899-1942). 17k, Landscape with Marsh, by Julius Marák (1832-99). 26k, Monument, by Frantisek Hudecek (1909-90).

1999, Nov. 10 **Engr.** ***Perf. 11¾***

3105	A565	13k multi	1.00	1.00
3106	A565	17k multi	1.50	1.50
3107	A565	26k multi	2.50	2.00
		Nos. 3105-3107 (3)	5.00	4.50

Nos. 3105-3107 were each issued in sheets of 4. Value, set $20.

Christmas — A1167

Photo. & Engr.

1999, Nov. 10 ***Perf. 11¼x11½***

3108 A1167 3k multi .35 .25

A1168

Photo. & Engr.

2000, Jan. 20 ***Perf. 11¼x11¾***

3109 A1168 5.40k #B151 .75 .25
a. Bklt. pane of 8 + 4 labels 6.00
Booklet, #3109a 6.00

Tradition of Czech stamp production.

Brno 2000 Philatelic Exhibition — A1169

Designs: 5k, 1593 view of Brno. 50k, St. James's Church, vert.

2000, Jan. 20 ***Perf. 11¾x11¼***

3110 A1169 5k multi .60 .25

Souvenir Sheet

Perf. 11¼x11¾

3111 A1169 50k multi 5.00 4.25

No. 3110 printed in sheets of 35 stamps and 30 labels.

Kutna Hora Royal Mining Law, 700th Anniv. — A1170

2000, Mar. 1 ***Perf. 11¼x11¾***

3112 A1170 5k multi .60 .25
a. Booklet pane of 8 + 4 labels 5.00
Booklet, #3112a 5.00

Souvenir Sheet

Pres. Thomas Garrigue Masaryk (1850-1937) — A1171

2000, Mar. 1 **Engr.** ***Perf. 11¾***

3113 A1171 17k multi 1.75 1.50

Pres. Havel Type of 1998

Photo. & Engr.

2000, Mar. 1 ***Perf. 11¾x11¼***

3114 A1134 5.40k Prus bl & org brn .60 .25

Easter — A1172

Photo. & Engr.

2000, Apr. 5 ***Perf. 11¼x11½***

3115 A1172 5k multi .60 .25

Souvenir Sheet

Prague, 2000 European City of Culture — A1173

No. 3116: a, 9k, Statue of man. b, 11k, Statue of harpist. c, 17k, Statue of King Charles IV.

Litho. & Engr.

2000, Apr. 5 ***Perf. 11¾***

3116 A1173 Sheet of 3, #a-c + 3 labels 4.00 4.00

Souvenir Sheet

Trains — A1174

No. 3117: a, 8k, Train from 1900. b, 15k, Train from 2000.

Litho. & Engr.

2000, May 5 ***Perf. 11¾***

3117 A1174 Sheet of 2, #a-b, +3 labels 3.00 3.00

Czech Personalities A1175

5k, Vítezslav Nezval (1900-58), writer. 8k, Gustav Mahler (1860-1911), composer.

Photo. & Engr.

2000, May 5 ***Perf. 11¼x11¾***

3118-3119 A1175 Set of 2 1.40 .50

Europa, 2000

Common Design Type

2000, May 5 **Litho.** ***Perf. 12¾x13¼***

3120 CD17 9k multi 1.20 .40

Intl. Children's Year — A1176

Photo. & Engr.

2000, May 31 ***Perf. 11½x11¼***

3121 A1176 5.40k multi .75 .25
a. Booklet pane of 8 + 2 labels 6.00
Booklet, #3121a 6.00

1995 Proof of Fermat's Last Theorem by Andrew Wiles A1177

2000, May 31 ***Perf. 11¾x11¼***

3122 A1177 7k multi .80 .25

Intl. Mathematics Year.

Prague Landmarks — A1178

Designs: 9k, Charles Bridge tower. 11k, St. Nicholas's Church. 13k, Town Hall.

2000, June 28 **Engr.** ***Perf. 11¾***

3123-3125 A1178 Set of 3 3.00 1.10

Issued in sheets of 8. Value, set $24.

Mushrooms — A1179

No. 3126, 5k: a, Geastrum pouzarii. b, Boletus satanoides.
No. 3127, 5.40k: a, Morchella pragensis. b, Verpa bohemica.

Photo. & Engr.

2000, June 28 ***Perf. 11¼x11½***

Pairs, #a-b

3126-3127 A1179 Set of 2 2.40 .70
Booklet, 3 #3126a, 2 #3126b 3.50
Booklet, 3 #3127b, 2 #3127a 3.50

Meeting of Intl. Monetary Fund and World Bank Group, Prague — A1180

2000, Aug. 30 ***Perf. 11¾x11¼***

3128 A1180 7k multi .95 .25

Ancient Olympics A1181

2000, Aug. 30

3129 A1181 9k multi 1.00 .35

2000 Summer Olympics, Sydney — A1182

2000, Aug. 30
3130 A1182 13k multi 1.25 .45

No. 3130 was issued in sheets of 35 + 25 labels. Values: stamp + 1 label, $1.50; stamp + 2 labels, $1.75.

Hunting — A1183

No. 3131: a, 5k, Falconry. b, 5k, Deer at feed trough.
No. 3132: a, 5.40k, Ducks and blind. b, 5.40k, Deer and blind.

Photo. & Engr.
2000, Oct. 4 ***Perf. 11¼x11¾***
Horiz. Pairs, #a-b
3131-3132 A1183 Set of 2 2.40 .55
Booklet, 3 #3131a, 2 #3131b 3.50
Booklet, 3 #3132a, 2 #3132b 3.50

Painting Type of 1967 Inscribed "CESKA REPUBLIKA"

Designs: 13k, St. Luke the Evangelist, by Master Theodoricus. 17k, Simeon With Infant Jesus, by Petr Jan Brandl. 26k, Brunette, by Alfons Mucha.

2000, Nov. 15 Engr. *Perf. 11¾*
3133-3135 A565 Set of 3 5.00 4.50

Nos. 3133-3135 were each issued in sheets of 4. Value, set $20.

Christmas — A1184

Photo. & Engr.
2000, Nov. 15 ***Perf. 11¼x11½***
3136 A1184 5k multi .60 .25

End of Millennium A1185

2000, Nov. 22
3137 A1185 9k multi 1.20 .35

Advent of New Millennium A1186

2001, Jan. 2
3138 A1186 9k multi 1.20 .35

Tradition of Czech Stamp Production A1187

2001, Jan. 20 ***Perf. 11¼x11¾***
3139 A1187 5.40k #474 .75 .25
a. Booklet pane of 8 + 4 labels 6.00
Booklet, #3139a 6.00

Jan Amos Komensky (Comenius, 1592-1670), Theologian — A1188

Photo. & Engr.
2001, Mar. 14 ***Perf. 11¼x11½***
3140 A1188 9k red & black 1.10 .35

Souvenir Sheet

Architecture — A1189

No. 3141: a, 13k, Church and decorations, Jakub. b, 17k, Arcade decorations, Bucovice Castle. c, 31k, Dance Hall, Prague.

2001, Mar. 28 Engr. *Perf. 11¾x11½*
3141 A1189 Sheet of 3, #a-c 6.00 4.50

Easter — A1190

Photo. & Engr.
2001, Mar. 28 ***Perf. 11¼x11½***
3142 A1190 5.40k multi .75 .25

Souvenir Sheet

Allegory of Art, by Vaclav Vavrinec Reiner — A1191

Litho. & Engr.
2001, Apr. 18 ***Perf. 11¾***
3143 A1191 50k multi 5.00 4.25

Europa A1192

Photo. & Engr.
2001, May 9 ***Perf. 11¾x11¼***
3144 A1192 9k pur & lilac 1.20 .35

European Men's Volleyball Championships, Ostrova — A1193

Photo. & Engr.
2001, May 9 ***Perf. 11¼x11½***
3145 A1193 12k multi 1.25 .50

Intl. Children's Day — A1194

Photo. & Engr.
2001, May 30 ***Perf. 11¼x11½***
3146 A1194 5.40k multi .60 .25
a. Booklet pane of 8 + 2 labels 5.00 —
Booklet, #3146a 5.00

Famous Men — A1195

Designs: 5.40k, Frantisek Skroup (1801-62), composer. 16k, Frantisek Halas (1901-49), writer.

2001, May 30
3147-3148 A1195 Set of 2 2.50 .80

Congratulations A1196

2001, June 20
3149 A1196 5.40k multi .75 .25
Booklet, 5 #3149 4.00

Dogs — A1197

No. 3150: a, West Highland terrier. b, Beagle.
No. 3151: a, German shepherd. b, Golden retriever.

Photo. & Engr.
2001, June 20 ***Perf. 11½x11¼***
3150 Pair 1.25 1.00
a.-b. A1197 5.40k Any single .60 .25
Booklet, 3 #3150a, 2 #3150b 3.25
Booklet, 3 #3150b, 2 #3150a 3.25
3151 Pair 1.25 1.00
a.-b. A1197 5.40k Any single .60 .25
Booklet, 3 #3151a, 2 #3151b 3.25

Zoo Animals A1198

No. 3152: a, Pongo pygmaeus. b, Panthera tigris altaica.
No. 3153: a, Ailurus fulgens. b, Fennecus zerda.

Photo. & Engr.
2001, Sept. 5 ***Perf. 11¾x11¼***
3152 Pair 1.00 1.00
a.-b. A1198 5.40k Any single .50 .25
Booklet, 3 #3152b, 2 #3152a 3.25
3153 Pair 1.00 1.00
a.-b. A1198 5.40k Any single .50 .25
Booklet, 3 #3153b, 2 #3153a 3.25

UNESCO World Heritage Sites A1199

Designs: 12k, Kormeríz Castle and Gardens. 14k, Holasovice Historical Village Restoration.

2001, Oct. 9 Engr. *Perf. 11½x11¾*
3154-3155 A1199 Set of 2 2.00 1.25

See Nos. 3177-3178, 3267-3268.

Year of Dialogue Among Civilizations A1200

Photo. & Engr.
2001, Oct. 9 ***Perf. 11¼x11½***
3156 A1200 9k multi .85 .35

Mills — A1201

Designs: 9k, Windmill. 14.40k, Water mill.

2001, Oct. 9
3157-3158 A1201 Set of 2 2.25 1.00

Christmas — A1202

Photo. & Engr.
2001, Nov. 14 ***Perf. 11¼x11½***
3159 A1202 5.40k multi .60 .30

Painting Type of 1967 Inscribed "CESKA REPUBLIKA"

Designs: 12k, The Annunciation of the Virgin Mary, by Michael J. Rentz. 17k, The Sans Souci Bar in Nimes, by Cyril Bouda. 26k, The Goose Keeper, by Vaclav Brozík.

2001, Nov. 14 Engr. *Perf. 11¾*
3160-3162 A565 Set of 3 4.50 4.25

Nos. 3160-3162 were each issued in sheets of 4. Value, set $18.

Tradition of Czech Stamp Production — A1203

Photo. & Engr.

2002, Jan. 20 ***Perf. 11¼x11¾***

3163 A1203 5.40k Type A89		.75	.25
a.	Booklet pane of 8 + 4 labels	5.00	—
	Booklet, #3163a	5.00	

2002 Winter Olympics, Salt Lake City — A1204

2002, Jan. 30 ***Perf. 11¼***

3164 A1204 12k multi 1.25 .45

For overprint, see No. 3168.

2002 Winter Paralympics, Salt Lake City — A1205

2002, Jan. 30 ***Perf. 11¼x11½***

3165 A1205 5.40k multi .85 .25

Composers Jaromír Vejvoda (1902-88), Josef Poncar (1902-86) and Karel Vacek (1902-82) — A1206

2002, Mar. 6 ***Perf. 11¾x11¼***

3166 A1206 9k multi 1.10 .35

Easter — A1207

2002, Mar. 6 ***Perf. 11¼x11½***

3167 A1207 5.40k multi .85 .25

No. 3164 Overprinted in Blue

Photo. & Engr.

2002, Mar. 8 ***Perf. 11¼***

3168 A1204 12k multi 1.25 .65

Divan, by Vlaho Bukovac (1855-1922) — A1208

Litho. & Engr.

2002, Apr. 23 ***Perf. 11¾***

3169 A1208 17k multi 2.00 1.40

Printed in sheets of 4 + 2 labels. Value $8. See Croatia No. 487.

Europa A1209

Photo. & Engr.

2002, May 7 ***Perf. 11¾x11¼***

3170 A1209 9k multi 1.20 .35

Souvenir Sheet

Czech Culture and France — A1210

No. 3171: a, 23k, Klávesy Piana-Jezero, by Frantisek Kupka. b, 31k, Man with Broken Nose, sculpture by Auguste Rodin.

Perf. 11¾x11½

2002, May 7 **Litho. & Engr.**

3171 A1210 Sheet of 2, #a-b 5.25 4.00

Intl. Children's Day — A1211

Photo. & Engr.

2002, May 29 ***Perf. 11¼x11½***

3172 A1211 5.40k multi		.60	.25
a.	Booklet pane of 8 + 2 labels	5.00	—
	Complete booklet, #3172a	5.00	

Margaritifera Margaritifera A1212

2002, June 6

3173 A1212 9k multi 1.00 .35

Jan Hus (1372-1415), Religious Leader — A1213

2002, June 19

3174 A1213 9k multi + label 1.00 .35

Souvenir Sheet

Worldwide Fund for Nature (WWF) — A1214

Butterflies: a, 5.40k, Maculinea nausithous. b, 5.40k, Maculinea alcon. c, 9k, Maculinea teleius. d, 9k, Maculinea arion.

Litho. & Engr.

2002, June 19 ***Perf. 11¾***

3175 A1214 Sheet of 4, #a-d + 4 labels 3.50 2.75

Pansy — A1215

Photo. & Engr.

2002, Sept. 1 ***Perf. 11¾x11¼***

3176 A1215 6.40k multi .85 .25

See Nos. 3220-3221, 3262-3263, 3293-3294, 3340, 3345-3347, 3363-3366, 3467-3469, 3500, 3756, 3789.

World Heritage Sites Type of 2001

Designs: 12k, Litomysl Castle. 14k, Holy Trinity Column, Olomouc, vert.

Perf. 11½x11¾, 11¾x11½

2002, Sept. 11 **Engr.**

3177-3178 A1199 Set of 2 2.75 2.00

Nos. 3177-3178 were each issued in sheets of 8. Value, set $25.

Emil Zátopek (1922-2000), Olympic Long Distance Runner — A1216

Photo. & Engr.

2002, Sept. 11 ***Perf. 11¼x11¾***

3179 A1216 9k multi 1.10 .35

Pres. Havel Type of 1998

Photo. & Engr.

2002, Nov. 6 ***Perf. 11¾x11¼***

3180 A1134 6.40k pur & blue .85 .25

St. Nicholas' Day — A1217

2002, Nov. 6 ***Perf. 11¼x11½***

3181 A1217 6.40k multi		.85	.25
a.	Booklet pane of 8 + 2 labels	6.00	—
	Complete booklet, #3181a	6.00	

Christmas — A1218

2002, Nov. 13

3182 A1218 6.40k multi .85 .25

NATO Summit, Prague — A1219

2002, Nov. 14 ***Perf. 11¼x11¾***

3183 A1219 9k multi 1.00 .30

Furniture — A1220

Designs: 6.40k, Armchair, 17th cent. 9k, Sewing table with hemispheric cover, 1820. 12k, Dressing table with mirror, 1860. 17k, Art deco amchair, 1923.

2002, Dec. 11

3184-3187 A1220 Set of 4 4.50 2.25

Painting Type of 1967 Inscribed "CESKA REPUBLIKA"

Designs: 12k, The Abandoned, by Jaroslav Panuska, horiz. 20k, St. Wenceslas, by Mikolás Ales. 26k, Portrait of a Young Man with a Lute, by Jan Petr Molitor.

2002, Dec. 11 **Engr.** ***Perf. 11¾***

3188-3190 A565 Set of 3 5.75 3.75

Nos. 3188-3190 were each issued in sheets of 4. Value, set $23.

Souvenir Sheet

Czech Republic, 10th Anniv. — A1221

Litho. & Engr.

2003, Jan. 1 ***Perf. 11¾***
3191 A1221 25k multi 2.75 1.60

Tradition of Czech Stamp Production — A1222

Photo. & Engr.

2003, Jan. 20 ***Perf. 11¼x11¾***
3192 A1222 6.40k Type A75 .95 .25
a. Booklet pane of 8 + 2 labels 7.50 —
Complete booklet, #3192a 7.50

Famous Men — A1223

Designs: 6.40k, Jaroslav Vrchlicky (1853-1912), poet. 8k, Josef Thomayer (1853-1927), physician and writer.

2003, Feb. 12 ***Perf. 11½x11¼***
3193-3194 A1223 Set of 2 1.75 .50

Easter — A1224

2003, Mar. 26 ***Perf. 11¼x11½***
3195 A1224 6.40k multi .95 .25

Roses Above Prague — A1225

Perf. 12¾x13¼

2003, Mar. 26 **Litho.**
3196 A1225 6.40k multi + label .75 .35

Labels could be personalized.
Issued in sheets of 9 stamps and 12 labels. Value $9.
See No. 3517.

Lace A1226

Designs: 6.40k, Netted lace. 9k, Bobbin lace.

Photo. & Engr.

2003, Mar. 26 ***Perf. 11¼***
3197 A1226 6.40k bl, dk bl & red .75 .25
a. Booklet pane of 6 + 4 labels 4.50 —
Complete booklet, #3197a 4.50
3198 A1226 9k dk bl, bl & red 1.00 .35
a. Booklet pane of 6 + 4 labels 6.00 —
Complete booklet, #3197a 6.00

Europa — A1227

Litho. & Engr.

2003, May 7 ***Perf. 11¾***
3199 A1227 9k multi 1.20 .65

Geologic Attractions — A1228

Designs: 12k, Sandstone towers, Hrubá Skála Region. 14k, Punkva Caves, Moravian karst area.

2003, May 7 **Engr.** ***Perf. 11½x11¾***
3200-3201 A1228 Set of 2 3.00 2.00

Nos. 3200-3201 were each issued in sheets of 8. Value, set $25.

Mach and Sebestova, Children's Television Show Characters — A1229

Photo. & Engr.

2003, May 28 ***Perf. 11¼x11½***
3202 A1229 6.40k multi .95 .35
a. Booklet pane of 8 + 2 labels 7.50 —
Complete booklet, #3202a 7.50

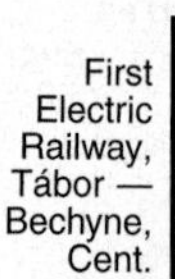

First Electric Railway, Tábor — Bechyne, Cent. A1230

2003, May 28 ***Perf. 11¾x11¼***
3203 A1230 10k multi 1.25 .50

A1231

Observation towers: No. 3204, 6.40k, Klet. No. 3205, 6.40k, Slovanka.

2003, May 28 ***Perf. 11¼x11½***
3204-3205 A1231 Set of 2 1.50 .50

A1232

2003, June 25 ***Perf. 11¾x11¼***
3206 A1232 9k multi 1.25 .35

European Shooting Championships, Plzen and Brno.

A1233

2003, June 25 ***Perf. 11¼x11½***
3207 A1233 9k multi 1.20 .35

Josef Dobrovsky (1753-1829), linguist.

Pres. Vaclav Klaus — A1234

Photo. & Engr.

2003 ***Perf. 11¾x11¼***
3208 A1234 6.40k buff, red & vio bl .95 .35
3209 A1234 6.50k Prus bl & pur .95 .35

Issued: 6.40k, 7/30; 6.50k, 11/5.
See No. 3264.

Souvenir Sheet

Tropical Fish — A1235

No. 3210: a, 12k, Betta splendens (27x44mm). b, 14k, Pterophyllum scalare (27x44mm). c, 16k, Carassius auratus (54x44mm). d, 20k, Symphysodon aequifasciatus (54x44mm).

Litho. & Engr.

2003, Sept. 10 ***Perf. 11¾***
3210 A1235 Sheet of 4, #a-d 6.00 5.00

No. 3210 exists in six different varieties, which may be distinguished by the number of horizontal lines in the stone in the bottom sheet margin below the 14k stamp. Values given are for sheets with 1, 2 or 5 lines in the stone; value for sheet with no lines or 3 lines in the stone, $21; value for sheet with 4 lines in the stone, $72.50.

Oriental Carpets A1236

Designs: 9k, Turkish prayer carpet, 19th cent. 12k, Turkish carpet, 18th cent.

2003, Oct. 1 **Engr.** ***Perf. 11¾***
3211-3212 A1236 Set of 2 2.50 1.75

Nos. 3211-3212 were each issued in sheets of 4. Value, set $10.

Tympanum, Porta Coeli Monastery, Predklásterí — A1237

Photo. & Engr.

2003, Oct. 15 ***Perf. 11¾x11¼***
3213 A1237 6.50k multi .95 .45
a. Booklet pane of 8 + 4 labels 7.50 —
Complete booklet, #3213a 7.50

Birds of Prey — A1238

Designs: 6.50k, Milvus milvus. 8k, Falco peregrinus. 9k, Hieraaetus pennatus.

2003, Oct. 15 ***Perf. 11¼x11½***
3214 A1238 6.50k multi .75 .25
Booklet, 5 #3214 3.75
3215 A1238 8k multi .90 .30
Booklet, 5 #3215 4.50
3216 A1238 9k multi 1.00 .30
Booklet, 5 #3216 5.00
Nos. 3214-3216 (3) 2.65 .85

Czech Fire Fighters, 140th Anniv. A1239

Fire engines: 6.50k, Wooden fire engine, 1822. 9k, Motorized fire engine, 1933. 12k, CAS 8/Avia Daewoo fire truck, 2002.

2003, Oct. 15 ***Perf. 11¾x11¼***
3217-3219 A1239 Set of 3 3.00 1.50

Flower Type of 2002

Designs: 50h, Cornflower (chrpa). 6.50k, Dahlia (jirina).

2003, Oct. 22
3220 A1215 50h multi .25 .25
3221 A1215 6.50k multi .75 .25

Roses Over Prague Type of 2003 and

Prague Castle Lantern — A1240

2003, Oct. 22 Litho. ***Perf. 12¾x13¼***
3222 A1225 6.50k multi + label .75 .25
3223 A1240 9k multi + label 1.00 .30

Labels could be personalized.
Nos. 3222-3223 were each issued in sheets of 9 stamps and 12 labels. Value, set $17.50.

Painting Type of 1967 Inscribed "CESKA REPUBLIKA"

Designs: 17k, Poor Countryside, by Max Svabinsky, horiz. 20k, Autumn in Veltrusy, by Antonín Slavícek. 26k, Eleanora de Toledo, by Agnolo Bronzino.

2003, Nov. 5 Engr. ***Perf. 11¾***
3224-3226 A565 Set of 3 6.50 4.00

Nos. 3224-3226 were each issued in sheets of 4. Value, set $26.

Christmas A1241

Photo. & Engr.
2003, Nov. 5 ***Perf. 11¼x11½***
3227 A1241 6.50k multi .75 .35

Tradition of Czech Stamp Production A1242

Photo. & Engr.
2004, Jan. 20 ***Perf. 11¼x11¾***
3228 A1242 6.50k Vignette of #1703 .95 .35
a. Booklet pane of 8 + 4 labels 7.50 —
Complete booklet, #3228a 7.50

Church of the Assumption of the Virgin Mary, Brno — A1243

2004, Feb. 18 Engr. ***Perf. 11¾***
3229 A1243 17k multi 1.90 1.00

Brno 2005 Philatelic Exhibition.
No. 3229 was issued in sheets of 4. Value $8.

Industrial Building Historical Preservation A1244

Designs: 6.50k, Busek's Water Forging Hammer, Lniste. 17k, Iron Furnace, Stará Hut u Adamova.

Photo. & Engr.
2004, Feb. 18 ***Perf. 11½x11¼***
3230-3231 A1244 Set of 2 2.40 .90

Easter A1245

2004, Mar. 17
3232 A1245 6.50k multi .95 .25

Painting Type of 1967 Inscribed "CESKA REPUBLIKA"

Design: Prometheus, by Antonín Procházka.

2004, Mar. 17 Engr. ***Perf. 11¾***
3233 A565 26k multi 2.60 1.60

Brno 2005 Philatelic Exhibition. No. 3233 was issued in sheets of 4. Value $11.

World Ice Hockey Championships, Prague and Ostrava — A1246

Photo. & Engr.
2004, Apr. 14 ***Perf. 11¼x11¾***
3234 A1246 12k multi 1.50 .50

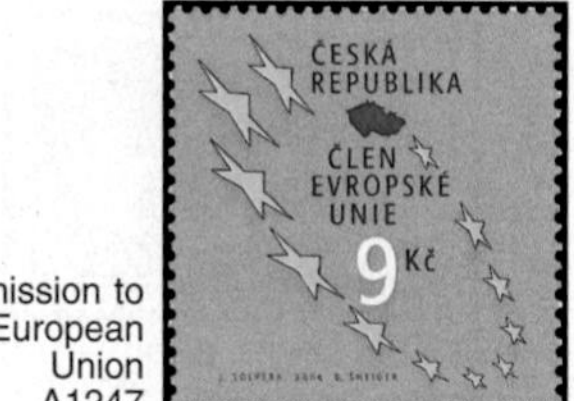
Admission to European Union A1247

Photo. & Engr.
2004, May 1 ***Perf. 11¼***
3235 A1247 9k multi 1.20 .35

Admission to the European Union — A1248

2004, May 1 Litho. ***Perf. 11¾x11¼***
3236 A1248 9k multi 1.10 .35

No. 3236 was issued in sheets of 10. Value $11.

Europa A1249

2004, May 5 ***Perf. 11¼***
3237 A1249 9k multi 1.10 .35

Composers of Czech Operas — A1250

Designs: 6.50k, Dalibor, by Bedrich Smetana (1824-84). 8k, Jakobín, by Antonín Dvorák (1841-1904). 10k, Její Pastorkyna, by Leos Janácek (1854-1928).

Photo. & Engr.
2004, May 5 ***Perf. 11¼x11¾***
3238-3240 A1250 Set of 3 2.60 1.10

For Children A1251

Photo. & Engr.
2004, May 26 ***Perf. 11½x11¼***
3241 A1251 6.50k multi .85 .25
a. Booklet pane of 8 + 2 labels 7.00 —
Complete booklet, #3241a 7.00

Statue of Radegast, by Albín Polásek — A1252

2004, May 26 ***Perf. 11¼x11½***
3242 A1252 6.50k multi .85 .25

Brno 2005 Philatelic Exhibition.

Tourist Attractions — A1253

Designs: 12k, Holy Mountain, Príbram. 14k, Holy Shrine, Bystrice pod Hostynem.

2004, May 26 Engr. ***Perf. 11½x11¾***
3243-3244 A1253 Set of 2 2.60 1.50

Nos. 3243-3244 were each issued in sheets of 8. Value, set $24.

A1254

Photo. & Engr.
2004, June 23 ***Perf. 11¼x11¾***
3245 A1254 6.50k multi 1.20 .25

2004 Paralympics, Athens.

A1255

2004, June 23
3246 A1255 9k multi 1.00 .35

2004 Summer Olympics, Athens.

Petrarch (1304-74), Poet — A1256

2004, June 23 ***Perf. 11¾x11¼***
3247 A1256 14k multi 1.40 .60

Famous Trees — A1257

Designs: 6.50k, Singing lime tree, Telecí. 8k, Jan Zizka oak tree, Podhradí.

Photo. & Engr.
2004, Sept. 8 ***Perf. 11¼x11½***
3248 A1257 6.50k multi .75 .25
Complete booklet, 5 #3248 3.75
3249 A1257 8k multi .90 .30
Complete booklet, 5 #3249 4.50

Miniature Sheet

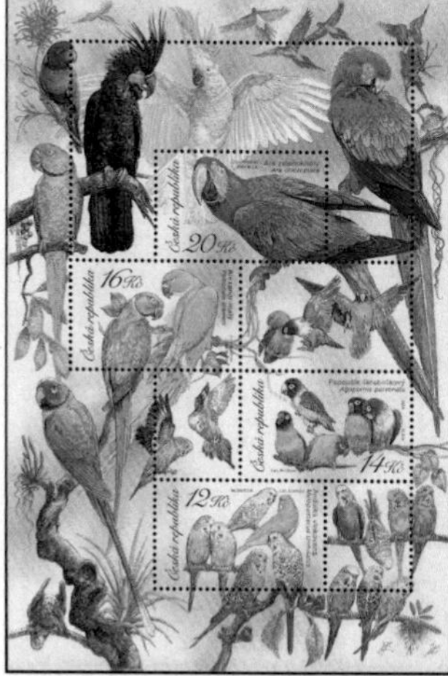
Parrots — A1258

No. 3250: a, 12k, Melopsittacus undulatus. b, 14k, Agapornis personata. c, 16k, Psittacula krameri. d, 20k, Ara chloroptera.

Litho. & Engr.
2004, Sept. 8 ***Perf. 11¾***
3250 A1258 Sheet of 4, #a-d, + 4 labels 6.00 4.50

Compulsory School Attendance, 230th Anniv. — A1259

Photo. & Engr.

2004, Sept. 29 *Perf. 11¼x11½*

3251 A1259 6.50k multi .85 .25

Baby Carriages — A1260

Carriages made about: 12k, 1880. 14k, 1890. 16k, 1900.

2004, Oct. 20

3252-3254 A1260 Set of 3 4.00 2.00

Painting Type of 1967 Inscribed "CESKA REPUBLIKA"

Designs: 20k, On the Outskirts of the Cesky Ráj Region, by Alois Bubák, horiz. 22k, The Long, the Broad and the Sharpsight, by Hanus Schwaiger. 26k, The Spring, by Vojtěch Hynais.

2004, Nov. 10 **Engr.** *Perf. 11¾*

3255-3257 A565 Set of 3 6.50 4.25

Nos. 3255-3257 were each issued in sheets of 4. Value, set $32.

Christmas — A1261

Photo. & Engr.

2004, Nov. 10 *Perf. 11¼x11½*

3258 A1261 6.50k multi .75 .25

Tradition of Czech Stamp Production A1262

2005, Jan. 18 *Perf. 11¼x11¾*

3259 A1262 6.50k Design of #975 .95 .30

a. Booklet pane of 8 + 4 labels 7.50 —

Complete booklet, #3259a 7.50

Peacock and Bugler Portal Decoration — A1263

2005, Jan. 18 **Litho.** *Perf. 12¾x13¼*

3260 A1263 7.50k multi + label .95 .30

Labels could be personalized for an additional fee.

Issued in sheets of 9 stamps and 12 labels. Value $9.

See Nos. 3372, 3516.

Souvenir Sheet

Moonscape, by Petr Ginz — A1264

Perf. 11¾x11½

2005, Jan. 18 **Litho. & Engr.**

3261 A1264 31k multi 3.00 2.00

Flower Type of 2002

Designs: 7.50k, Lily (lilie). 19k, Fuchsia (fuchsie).

Photo. & Engr.

2005 *Perf. 11¾x11¼*

3262 A1215 7.50k multi .85 .30

3263 A1215 19k multi 2.25 .85

Issued: 7.50k, 1/20; 19k, 3/2.

Pres. Vaclav Klaus Type of 2003

2005, Feb. 9

3264 A1234 7.50k claret & red .85 .30

Granny, by Bozena Nemcová, 150th Anniv. of Publication A1265

2005, Feb. 9 *Perf. 11¼x11¾*

3265 A1265 7.50k multi .85 .30

Easter — A1266

Photo. & Engr.

2005, Mar. 2 *Perf. 11¼x11½*

3266 A1266 7.50k multi .85 .30

UNESCO World Heritage Sites Type of 2001

Designs: 14k, St. Prokop's Basilica, Trebíc, vert. 16k, Villa Tugendhat, Brno.

Perf. 11¾x11½, 11½x11¾

2005, Mar. 23 **Engr.**

3267-3268 A1199 Set of 2 3.25 1.90

Nos. 3267-32682 were each issued in sheets of 8. Value, set $26.

Famous Men — A1267

Designs: 7.50k, Bohuslav Brauner (1855-1935), chemist. 12k, Adalbert Stifter (1805-68), writer, painter. 19k, Mikulás Dacicky of Heslov (1555-1626), poet.

Photo. & Engr.

2005, Apr. 13 *Perf. 11¼x11¾*

3269-3271 A1267 Set of 3 3.75 1.60

Europa A1268

2005, May 4 **Litho.** *Perf. 11¼*

3272 A1268 9k multi 1.20 .35

Issued in sheets of 6. Value, $7.50.

Battle of Austerlitz, Bicent. — A1269

Napoleon Before the Battle of Austerlitz, by Louis-François Lejeune — A1270

Photo. & Engr.

2005, May 4 *Perf. 11¾x11¼*

3273 A1269 19k multi 2.25 .90

Souvenir Sheet

Litho. & Engr.

Perf. 11¾

3274 A1270 30k multi 3.50 2.25

Brno 2005 Stamp Exhibition (No. 3274).

No. 3273 was issued in sheets of 40 + 20 labels. Value, one stamp + label $3.25.

See France No. 3115.

Kremílek and Vochomurka, by Václav Ctvrtek — A1271

Photo. & Engr.

2005, May 25 *Perf. 11¼x11½*

3275 A1271 7.50k multi .85 .30

a. Booklet pane of 8 + 2 labels 7.00 —

Complete booklet, #3275a 7.00

Intl. Year of Physics A1272

2005, May 25 *Perf. 11¼x11¾*

3276 A1272 12k multi 1.40 .75

2005 European Baseball Championships A1273

2005, June 22

3277 A1273 9k multi 1.10 .50

Souvenir Sheet

Protected Flora and Fauna of the Krkonose Mountains — A1274

No. 3278: a, 12k, Viola lutea sudetica, Hedysarum hedysaroides (44x28mm). b, 14k, Cinclus cinclus, Leucojum vernum (44x28mm). c, 15k, Sorex alpinus, Salamandra salamandra, Primula minima (44x54mm). d, 22k, Mt. Snezka, Luscinia svecica svecica, Aeschna coerulea, Pneumonanthe asclepiadea (44x54mm).

Litho. & Engr.

2005, June 22 *Perf. 11¾*

3278 A1274 Sheet of 4, #a-d, + 4 labels 7.00 4.25

Church Bells — A1275

Bells from: 7.50k, Benesov, 1322, Havlíckuv Brod, 1335. 9k, Dobrs, 1561, 1596. 12k, Olomouc, 1827.

Photo. & Engr.

2005, Sept. 7 *Perf. 11½x11¾*

3279 A1275 7.50k multi .80 .30

Complete booklet, 5 #3279 4.00

3280 A1275 9k multi .90 .40

Complete booklet, 5 #3280 4.50

3281 A1275 12k multi 1.20 .50

Complete booklet, 5 #3281 6.00

Nos. 3279-3281 (3) 2.90 1.20

Tractors A1276

Designs: 7.50k, 1923 John Deere 15/27. 9k, 1921 Lanz Bulldog HL-12, 1596. 18k, 1937 Skoda HT 40.

2005, Sept. 21 ***Perf. 11½x11¼***

3282 A1276 7.50k multi		.60	.30
Complete booklet, 5 #3282		3.50	
3283 A1276 9k multi		.90	.35
Complete booklet, 5 #3283		5.00	
3284 A1276 18k multi		1.90	.75
Complete booklet, 5 #3284		9.50	
Nos. 3282-3284 (3)		3.40	1.40

World Summit on the Information Society, Tunis A1277

2005, Sept. 21 ***Perf. 11¼***

3285 A1277 9k org & violet 1.10 .35

Curling A1278

Photo. & Engr.

2005, Oct. 12 ***Perf. 11¾x11¼***

3286 A1278 17k multi 2.00 .70

Painting Type of 1967 Inscribed "ČESKÁ REPUBLIKA"

Designs: 22k, Summer Landscape, by Adolf Kosárek. 25k, Deinotherium, by Zdeněk Burian. 26k, Osiky Near Velké Nemcice, by Alois Kalvoda.

2005, Nov. 9 **Engr.** ***Perf. 11¾***

3287-3289 A565 Set of 3 8.00 5.25

Nos. 3287-3289 were each issued in sheets of 4. Value, set $32.50.

A1279

Christmas A1280

Photo. & Engr.

2005, Nov. 9 ***Perf. 11¼x11½***

3290 A1279 7.50k multi .85 .30

Perf. 11½x11¼

3291 A1280 9k multi 1.00 .35

Tradition of Czech Stamp Production A1281

Photo. & Engr.

2006, Jan. 20 ***Perf. 11¼x11¾***

3292 A1281 7.50k Portion of #C59		.95	.30
a. Booklet pane of 8 + 2 labels		7.50	—
Complete booklet, #3292a		7.50	

Flower Type of 2002

Designs: 11k, Marshmallow (ibisek). 24k, Daffodil (narcis).

2006 ***Perf. 11¾x11¼***

3293 A1215 11k multi		1.25	.45
3294 A1215 24k multi		2.75	1.00

Issued: 11k, 2/1; 24k, 2/22.

Flowers — A1282

Flowers, Grapes, Glass of Wine — A1283

2006 **Litho.** ***Perf. 12¾x13¼***

3295 A1282 10k multi + label		1.10	.60
3296 A1283 12k multi + label		1.40	.75

Issued: 10k, 2/1; 12k, 2/22. Labels could be personalized for an additional fee.

Nos. 3295-3296 were issued in sheets of 9 stamps and 12 labels. Value, set $22.50.

See No. 3373.

Madonna of Zbraslav — A1284

2006, Feb. 8 **Engr.** ***Perf. 11¾***

3297 A1284 25k multi 2.50 1.75

Printed in sheets of 4. Value $10.

2006 Winter Paralympics, Turin — A1285

Photo. & Engr.

2006, Feb. 8 ***Perf. 11¾x11¼***

3298 A1285 7.50k multi .85 .30

2006 Winter Olympics, Turin — A1286

2006 ***Perf. 11¼x11¾***

3299 A1286 9k multi 1.00 .40

With "K. NEUMANNOVA / ZLATA MEDAILE" Overprinted in Red Reading Up

3300 A1286 9k multi 1.10 .40

Issued: No. 3299, 2/8; No. 3300, 3/15.

Famous Men — A1287

Designs: 11k, Frantisek Josef Gerstner (1756-1832), mathematician and educator. 12k, Jaroslav Jezek (1906-42), composer. 19k, Sigmund Freud (1856-1939), psychoanalyst.

2006, Feb. 22 ***Perf. 11½x11¼***

3301-3303 A1287 Set of 3 4.00 1.75

Easter — A1288

2006, Mar. 22 ***Perf. 11¼x11½***

3304 A1288 7.50k multi 1.20 .30

Osek Monastery — A1289

Kokorinsko Capstones — A1290

2006, Mar. 22 **Engr.** ***Perf. 11½x11¾***

3305 A1289 12k multi		1.20	.65
3306 A1290 15k multi		1.40	.85

Nos. 3305-3306 were each issued in sheets of 8. Value, set $22.

Love — A1291

Photo. & Engr.

2006, Apr. 26 ***Perf. 11¼x11½***

3307 A1291 7.50k multi		.95	.35
Complete booklet, 5 #3307		4.75	

Europa A1292

Silhouette of person and: 10k, Horse. 20k, Dog.

2006, May 3 ***Perf. 11¾x11¼***

3308-3309 A1292 Set of 2 3.00 1.40

Issued in sheets of 8. Value, set $24.

Rumcajs, Manka and Cipísek, by V. Ctvrtek — A1293

Photo. & Engr.

2006, May 31 ***Perf. 11¼x11½***

3310 A1293 7.50k multi		.95	.35
a. Booklet pane of 8 + 2 labels		7.50	—
Complete booklet, #3310a		7.50	

A1294

2006, June 14 ***Perf. 11¼x11¾***

3311 A1294 19k multi 2.00 .90

Kamenice Pass, Czech Switzerland National Park.

A1295

Jewelry with garnets: 15k, Silver brooch with pearl, 1904. 18k, Gold pendant, 1930.

2006, June 14

3312-3313 A1295 Set of 2 3.00 1.75

Miniature Sheet

Bohemian Kings of Premyslid Dynasty — A1296

No. 3314: a, 12k, Otakar I Premysl (c. 1155-1230). b, 14k, Václav (Wenceslas) I (1205-53). c, 15k, Otakar II Premysl (1230-78). d, 22k, Václav (Wenceslas) II (1271-1305). e, 28k, Václav (Wenceslas) III (1289-1306).

2006, June 14 Engr. ***Perf. 11¾***
3314 A1296 Sheet of 5, #a-e, + label 8.25 6.00

Souvenir Sheet

Mosaic of Prague Castle, by Giovanni Castrucci — A1297

Litho. & Engr.

2006, Sept. 13 ***Perf. 11¾***
3315 A1297 35k multi 3.50 2.25

Cacti — A1298

No. 3316: a, Gymnocalycium denudatum. b, Obregonia denegrii.

No. 3317: a, Astrophytum asterias. b, Cintia knizei.

Perf. 11¼x11¾

2006, Sept. 13 **Litho.**
3316 A1298 7.50k Pair, #a-b 1.50 .90
Complete booklet, 2 #3316a, 3 #3316b 3.50
3317 A1298 10k Pair, #a-b 2.00 1.25
Complete booklet, 2 #3317a, 3 #3317b 5.00

Ecology A1299

2006, Sept. 27 ***Perf. 11¾x11¼***
3318 A1299 7.50k multi .95 .35

Christmas — A1300

2006, Oct. 11 ***Perf. 12¾x13¼***
3319 A1300 7.50k multi + label 1.10 .35

Printed in sheets of 9 stamps + 12 labels. Labels could be personalized. Value, $11.

Vrtbovská Garden, Prague — A1301

Photo. & Engr.

2006, Oct. 11 ***Perf. 11½x11¾***
3320 A1301 7.50k multi .95 .35
a. Booklet pane of 8 + 4 labels 7.50 —
Complete booklet, #3320a 7.50

Praga 2008 Intl. Philatelic Exhibition, Prague.

Wooden Churches — A1302

Designs: 7.50k, Church of the Virgin Mary, Broumov. 19k, Church of St. Andrew, Hodslavice.

Photo. & Engr.

2006, Oct. 11 ***Perf. 11¾x11¼***
3321-3322 A1302 Set of 2 2.60 1.60

Painting Type of 1967 Inscribed "CESKA REPUBLIKA"

Designs: 22k, Still Life with Fruit, by Jan Davidsz de Heem. 25k, Montenegrin Madonna, by Jaroslav Cermák. 28k, Pod Suchym Skalim, by Frantisek Kaván, horiz.

2006, Nov. 8 Engr. ***Perf. 11¾***
3323-3325 A565 Set of 3 7.00 4.50

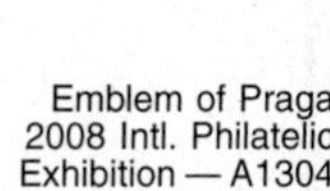

Emblem of Praga 2008 Intl. Philatelic Exhibition — A1304

2006, Dec. 1 **Litho.**
3327 A1304 7.50k multi .95 .35

See Nos. 3341, 3368.

Czech Technical University, Prague, 300th Anniv. — A1305

Photo. & Engr.

2007, Jan. 10 ***Perf. 11¾x11½***
3328 A1305 9k multi 1.10 .50

Famous Men — A1306

Designs: 7.50k, Frána Srámek (1877-1952), writer. 19k, Karel Slavoj Amerling (1807-84), educator.

2007, Jan. 10 ***Perf. 11½x11¼***
3329-3330 A1306 Set of 2 2.50 1.40

Tradition of Czech Stamp Production A1307

2007, Jan. 20 ***Perf. 11½x11¾***
3331 A1307 7.50k Type A242 .85 .35
a. Booklet pane of 8 + 4 labels 6.75 —
Complete booklet, #3331a 6.75

Cancer Prevention A1308

Photo. & Engr.

2007, Feb. 21 ***Perf. 11¼x11½***
3332 A1308 7.50k multi .85 .35

Snake — A1309

Perf. 11¼x11¾

2007, Feb. 21 **Litho.**
3333 A1309 12k multi 1.20 .70

Oriental Art A1310

Designs: 12k, Girl with a Puppet, by Kunisawa Utagawa. 24k, Siva, Parvati and Ganesa, 19th cent. Indian glass painting.

Litho. & Engr.

2007, Feb. 21 ***Perf. 11¾***
3334-3335 A1310 Set of 2 3.50 2.10

Easter — A1311

Photo. & Engr.

2007, Mar. 14 ***Perf. 11¼x11½***
3336 A1311 7.50k multi .85 .35

Model of Mala Strana Area of Prague, by Antonín Langweil — A1312

2007, Mar. 14 ***Perf. 11¾x11¼***
3337 A1312 7.50k multi .85 .35
a. Booklet pane of 8 + 4 labels 7.00 —
Complete booklet, #3337a 7.00

Praga 2008 Intl. Philatelic Exhibition, Prague.

No. 3337 was issued in sheets of 8 + 4 labels. Value, $10.

Stoclet House, Brussels, Designed by Josef Hoffmann — A1313

Designs: 20k, Building interior. 35k, Building exterior.

2007, Mar. 26 ***Perf. 11¼x11¾***
3338-3339 A1313 Set of 2 5.00 3.25

See Belgium Nos. 2228-2229.

Flowers Type of 2002

Perf. 12¾x13¼

2007, Mar. 26 **Litho.**
3340 A1282 11k multi + label 1.25 .60

Label could be personalized for an additional fee.

Praga 2008 Emblem Type of 2006

2007, Apr. 4 ***Perf. 11¾x11½***
3341 A1304 11k blue & multi 1.25 .60

Spas
A1314

Designs: 12k, Jurkovic House, Luhacovice. 15k, Gocár Pavillion, Lázne Bohdanec.

2007, Apr. 4 Engr. *Perf. 11½x11¾*
3342-3343 A1314 Set of 2 2.50 1.75

Issued in sheets of 8. Value, $20.

Europa
A1315

Photo. & Engr.

2007, May 9 *Perf. 11¼*
3344 A1315 11k multi 1.25 .60

Scouting, cent.

Flowers Type of 2002

Designs: 1k, Cyclamen (bramborik). 15k, Tropaeolum (lichorerisnice). 23k, Geranium (pelargonie).

Photo. & Engr.

2007 *Perf. 11¾x11¼*
3345 A1215 1k multi .25 .25
3346 A1215 15k multi 1.60 .90
3347 A1215 23k multi 2.00 1.25
Nos. 3345-3347 (3) 3.85 2.40

Issued: 1k, 23k, 5/9. 15k, 9/5.

Fast Arrows, Comic Strip by Jaroslav Foglar
A1316

Photo. & Engr.

2007, May 30 *Perf. 11¾x11¼*
3348 A1316 7.50k multi .85 .35
a. Booklet pane of 8 + 4 labels 7.00 —
Complete booklet, #3348a 7.00

Historic Stoves — A1317

Designs: 7.50k, Gothic era stove, Olomouc, and tile. 12k, Renaissance era stove, Rícany u Prahy and tile.

Photo. & Engr.

2007, June 20 *Perf. 11½x11¾*
3349 A1317 7.50k multi .70 .35
Complete booklet, 5 #3349 3.50
3350 A1317 12k multi 1.25 .60
Complete booklet, 5 #3350 6.25

Souvenir Sheet

Vaclav Hollar (1607-77), Engraver — A1318

Litho. & Engr.

2007, June 20 *Perf. 11¾*
3351 A1318 35k multi + 2 labels 3.00 2.10

Souvenir Sheet

Charles Bridge, Prague, 650th Anniv. — A1319

2007, June 20
3352 A1319 45k multi 4.50 3.00

Praga 2008 World Philatelic Exhibition.

First Movie Theater in Prague, Cent.
A1320

Photo. & Engr.

2007, Sept. 5 *Perf. 11¾x11¼*
3353 A1320 7.50k multi .75 .35

Didactica Opera Omnia, by Comenius, 350th Anniv. — A1321

2007, Sept. 5
3354 A1321 12k multi 1.25 .75

Miniature Sheet

Flora and Fauna of the White Carpathians — A1322

No. 3355: a, 9k, Ophrys holosericea (27x44mm). b, 10k, Colias myrmidone, Anacamptis pyramidalis (27x44mm). c, 11k, Ophrys apifera (27x44mm). d, 12k, Coracias garrulus, Gymnadenia densiflora (54x44mm).

Litho. & Engr.

2007, Sept. 5 *Perf. 11¾*
3355 A1322 Sheet of 4, #a-d, + 4 labels 4.25 2.75

Emil Holub (1847-1902), Naturalist — A1323

Photo. & Engr.

2007, Oct. 3 *Perf. 11¾x11¼*
3356 A1323 11k multi 1.25 .65

Water Towers — A1324

Towers in: 7.50k, Karviná. 18k, Plzen.

2007, Oct. 3 *Perf. 11¼x11¾*
3357-3358 A1324 Set of 2 2.75 1.50

Painting Type of 1967 Inscribed "CESKÁ REPUBLIKA"

Designs: 22k, Vrbicany Castle, by Amálie Mánesova, horiz. 25k, Way to Bechnye Castle, by Otakar Lebeda. 28k, Montmartre, by Sobeslav Hippolyt Pinkas, horiz.

2007, Nov. 7 Engr. *Perf. 11¾*
3359-3361 A565 Set of 3 7.25 4.50

Christmas — A1325

Photo. & Engr.

2007, Nov. 7 *Perf. 11¼x11½*
3362 A1325 7.50k multi .85 .40

Flower Type of 2002

Design: 2.50k, Gaillardia (kokarda); 3k, Azalea (azalka); 10k, Rose (ruze); 21k, Gerbera daisy (gerbera).

Photo. & Engr.

2007-08 *Perf. 11¾x11¼*
3363 A1215 2.50k multi .30 .25
3364 A1215 3k multi .30 .25
3365 A1215 10k multi 1.10 .60
3366 A1215 21k multi 2.00 1.40
Nos. 3363-3366 (4) 3.70 2.50

Issued: 2.50k, 12/12/07; 3k, 3/19/08; 10k, 1/30/08; 21k, 3/5/08.

Czech Republic's Entry Into Schengen Border-Free Zone
A1326

2007, Dec. 19 Litho. *Perf. 11¼*
3367 A1326 10k multi 1.10 .55

Praga 2008 Emblem Type of 2006

2007, Dec. 19 *Perf. 11¾x11¼*
3368 A1304 18k bl grn & blue 2.00 1.00

Tradition of Czech Stamp Production
A1327

Photo. & Engr.

2008, Jan. 20 *Perf. 11¼x11¾*
3369 A1327 10k Type A311 .95 .60
a. Booklet pane of 8 + 4 labels 8.00 —
Complete booklet, #3369a 8.00

Famous Men — A1328

Designs: 11k, Karel Klostermann (1848-1923), writer. 14k, Josef Kajetán Tyl (1808-56), playwright.

2008, Jan. 20 *Perf. 11¼x11½*
3370-3371 A1328 Set of 2 2.50 1.50

Peacock and Bugler Type of 2005 and Flowers, Grapes and Glass of Wine Type of 2006 Redrawn

2008, Jan. 30 Litho. *Perf. 12¾x13¼*
3372 A1263 10k multi + label 1.00 .60
3373 A1283 17k multi + label 1.75 1.00

Nos. 3372-3373 were issued in sheets of 9 stamps and 12 labels. Labels could be personalized for an additional fee.

George of Podebrady (1420-71), King of Bohemia — A1329

Photo. & Engr.

2008, Feb. 20 *Perf. 11¼x11¾*
3374 A1329 12k multi 1.25 .75

No. 3374 was issued in sheets of 8 + 1 label. Values: single stamp + label, $4; complete sheet, $10.

Intl. Year of Planet Earth
A1330

2008, Feb. 20 Litho. *Perf. 11¼*
3375 A1330 18k multi 1.75 1.10

Easter
A1331

Photo. & Engr.

2008, Mar. 5 *Perf. 11½x11¼*
3376 A1331 10k multi 1.25 .60

Bath Servant Zuzana Carrying King Wenceslas IV Over the Vltava River, by J. Navrátil — A1332

2008, Mar. 5 *Perf. 11¾x11¼*

3377 A1332 10k multi 1.10 .60
a. Booklet pane of 8 + 4 labels 9.00 —
Complete booklet, #3377a 9.00

Praga 2008 Intl. Philatelic Exhibition, Prague.

Publication of Orbis Pictus, Children's Picture Book, by Comenius, 350th Anniv. — A1333

2008, Mar. 19 *Perf. 11¼x11¾*

3378 A1333 10k multi 1.25 .60

Mountaintop Hotel With Broadcast Tower, Jested — A1334

Hradec Kralové Buildings and Monuments A1335

2008, Mar. 19 Engr. *Perf. 11½*

3379 A1334 12k multi 1.10 .75
3380 A1335 15k multi 1.50 .95

Pres. Klaus Type of 2003

Photo. & Engr.

2008, Apr. 2 *Perf. 11¾x11¼*

3381 A1234 10k multi 1.10 .60

A1336

Items in National Technical Museum: 10k, Reichenbach-Ertel astronomical theodolite, c. 1830. 14k, 1935 Jawa 750 sports car, horiz. 18k, Märky, Bromovsky-Schulz gasoline combustion engine, c. 1889.

Perf. 11¼x11¾, 11¾x11¼

2008, Apr. 16 Photo. & Engr.

3382-3384 A1336 Set of 3 4.25 2.60

National Technical Museum, Prague, cent.

A1337

2008, Apr. 16 *Perf. 11¼x11¾*

3385 A1337 17k multi 1.75 1.10

Czech Hockey Association, cent.

Europa A1338

2008, May 7 Litho. *Perf. 11¾x11¼*

3386 A1338 17k multi 1.75 1.10

The Doggy's and Pussy's Tales, Children's Book by Josef Capek A1339

Photo. & Engr.

2008, May 28 *Perf. 11½x11¼*

3387 A1339 10k multi 1.00 .70
a. Booklet pane of 8 + 2 labels 9.00 —
Complete booklet, #3387a 9.00

Souvenir Sheet

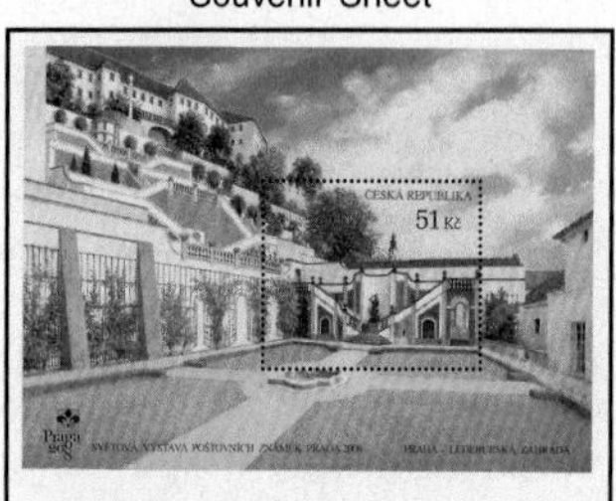

Ledeburk Gardens, Prague — A1340

Litho. & Engr.

2008, May 28 *Perf. 11¾*

3388 A1340 51k multi 5.50 3.25

Praga 2008 World Philatelic Exhibition.

Miniature Sheet

Flora and Fauna of Trebon Basin UNESCO Biosphere Reservation — A1341

No. 3389: a, 10k, Alcedo atthis (28x44mm). b, 12k, Lutra lutra and Spiraea salicifolia (54x44mm). c, 14k, Haliaeetus albicilla (54x44mm). d, 18k, Netta rufina and Nymphaea alba (54x44mm).

2008, May 28

3389 A1341 Sheet of 4, #a-d, + 3 labels 6.25 3.50

2008 Paralympics, Beijing — A1342

Perf. 11¾x11¼

2008, June 18 Litho.

3390 A1342 10k multi 1.10 .70

2008 Summer Olympics, Beijing — A1343

2008, June 18

3391 A1343 18k multi 1.75 1.25

Explorers — A1344

Designs: 12k, Ferdinand Stolicka (1838-74), explorer of Himalayas. 21k, Alois Musil (1868-1944), explorer of Jordanian desert.

2008, June 18 Photo. & Engr.

3392-3393 A1344 Set of 2 3.25 2.25

Children's Book Illustration by Josef Palacek — A1345

2008, Sept. 3 Litho. *Perf. 12¾x13¼*

3394 A1345 10k multi + label 1.10 .60

Printed in sheets of 9 stamps + 12 labels. Labels could be personalized. Value, $10.

Emmaus Monastery, Prague — A1346

Photo. & Engr.

2008, Sept. 3 *Perf. 11¼x11¾*

3395 A1346 10k multi 1.00 .60
Tete-beche pair 2.00 *2.00*

Praga 2008 World Philatelic Exhibition.

Applied Art Designers' Association, Cent. — A1347

2008, Sept. 3 *Perf. 11¾x11¼*

3396 A1347 26k multi 2.75 1.60

Karel Plicka (1894-1987), Photographer — A1348

Litho. & Engr.

2008, Sept. 12 *Perf. 11¾*

3397 A1348 35k multi + 2 labels 4.00 2.10

See Slovakia No. 548.

Souvenir Sheet

Mail Coach — A1349

2008, Sept. 12

3398 A1349 35k multi 4.00 2.10

Praga 2008 Intl. Stamp Exhibition, Prague, and 2008 Vienna Intl. Stamp Exhibition. See Austria No. 2172.

Stoves — A1350

Stove from: 10k, Sternberk Castle. 17k, Archbishop's Palace, Prague.

Photo. & Engr.

2008, Oct. 15 *Perf. 11¼x11¾*

3399 A1350 10k multi 1.00 .55
Complete booklet, 5 #3399 5.50
3400 A1350 17k multi 1.75 .95
Complete booklet, 5 #3400 9.50

Painting Type of 1967 Inscribed "CESKA REPUBLIKA"

Designs: 23k, Vltava River at Klecany, by Zdenka Braunerová, horiz. 26k, Autumn Road, by Otakar Nejedly.

2008, Nov. 5 Engr. *Perf. 11¾*

3401-3402 A565 Set of 2 5.25 3.00

Issued in sheets of 4. Value, set $21.

Souvenir Sheet

Allegory of Water, by Jan Jakub Hartman — A1351

2008, Nov. 5 Litho. & Engr.

3403 A1351 30k multi 3.25 1.75

Basket With Apples — A1352

Winter Scene — A1353

Mechanical Christmas Display — A1354

Photo. & Engr.

2008, Nov. 5 ***Perf. 11¼x11½***

3404 A1352 10k multi .95 .55

Litho.

Perf. 12¾x13¼

3405 A1353 10k multi + label .95 .55

Souvenir Sheet

Litho. & Engr.

Perf. 11¾

3406 A1354 30k multi 3.25 1.75

Christmas.

No. 3405 was printed in sheets of 9 stamps + 12 labels. Value $10. Labels could be personalized.

Czech Republic Presidency of European Union, January to June 2009 — A1355

Perf. 11¾x11¼

2008, Nov. 25 **Litho.**

3407 A1355 17k multi + label 1.75 .90

No. 3407 was issued in sheets of 30 stamps + 30 labels.

Louis Braille (1809-52), Educator of the Blind — A1356

Charles Darwin (1809-82), Naturalist — A1357

2009, Jan. 2 **Photo. & Engr.**

3408 A1356 10k multi .95 .55

3409 A1357 12k multi 1.10 .60

Tradition of Czech Stamp Production A1358

2009, Jan. 20 ***Perf. 11¼x11¾***

3410 A1358 10k Design of #980 1.00 .50

a. Booklet pane of 8 + 4 labels 8.25 —

Complete booklet, #3410a 8.25

Nordic World Skiing Championships, Liberec — A1359

Perf. 11¾x11¼

2009, Feb. 11 **Litho.**

3411 A1359 18k multi 1.25 1.25

Souvenir Sheet

Preservation of Polar Regions and Glaciers — A1360

Litho. & Engr.

2009, Feb. 11 ***Perf. 11¾***

3412 A1360 35k multi 3.50 1.90

Easter A1361

Photo. & Engr.

2009, Mar. 18 ***Perf. 11½x11¼***

3413 A1361 10k multi .95 .55

Lu Tung-pin, by Unknown Chinese Artist — A1362

Mythical Beings, by Unknown Balinese Artist — A1363

Litho. & Engr.

2009, Mar. 18 ***Perf. 11¾***

3414 A1362 18k multi 1.75 1.00

3415 A1363 24k multi 2.25 1.40

Souvenir Sheet

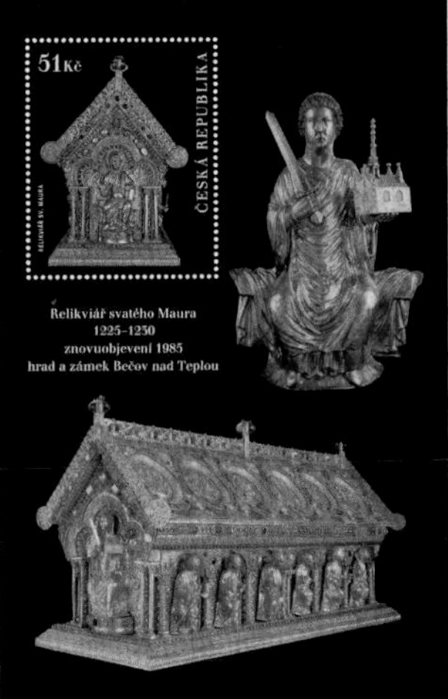

Reliquary of St. Maurus, Becov nad Teplou Castle — A1364

2009, Apr. 8

3416 A1364 51k multi 5.00 3.00

Pardubice to Liberec Rail Line, 150th Anniv. — A1365

Photo. & Engr.

2009, Apr. 22 ***Perf. 11¾x11¼***

3417 A1365 10k multi 1.00 .60

Industry and Trade Ministry Building, 75th Anniv. A1366

Photo. & Engr.

2009, Apr. 22 ***Perf. 11¾x11½***

3418 A1366 10k multi 1.00 .60

Europa A1367

2009, May 6 **Litho.** ***Perf. 11¼***

3419 A1367 17k multi 1.75 1.00

Intl. Year of Astronomy.

Buildings A1368

Designs: 12k, Cistercian Monastery, Vyssí Brod. 14k, Horsovsky Castle, Tyn.

2009, May 6 **Engr.** ***Perf. 11¾x11½***

3420-3421 A1368 Set of 2 2.50 1.50

Nos. 3420-3421 also were issued in souvenir sheets of 1. Value, set of two sheets $27.

Marionettes Spejbl and Hurvínek — A1369

Photo. & Engr.

2009, May 27 ***Perf. 11¼x11½***

3422 A1369 10k multi 1.10 .60

a. Booklet pane of 8 + 2 labels 9.00 —

Complete booklet, #3422a 9.00

Rabbi Jehuda Löw (c. 1525-1609) A1370

2009, May 27 **Litho.** ***Perf. 11¼x11¾***

3423 A1370 21k multi 2.00 1.25

Printed in sheets of 5 + 4 labels. Value, $10.

Granting of Religious Freedom by Rudolf II, 400th Anniv. A1371

Photo. & Engr.

2009, June 17 ***Perf. 11¼***

3424 A1371 26k multi 2.50 1.50

Intl. Firefighters' Games, Ostrava — A1372

Perf. 11¾x11¼

2009, June 17 **Litho.**
3425 A1372 17k multi 1.75 1.00

Miniature Sheet

Krivoklát UNESCO Biosphere Reservation — A1373

No. 3426: a, 10k, Eudia pavonia (44x27mm). b, 12k, Aglia tau, Cervus elaphus (44x54mm). c, 14k, Bubo bubo, Lunaria rediviva, Ciconia nigra (44x54mm). d, 17k, Tyto alba, Krivoklát Castle (44x54mm).

Litho. & Engr.

2009, Sept. 2 *Perf. 11¾*
3426 A1373 Sheet of 4, #a-d, + 4 labels 5.50 4.50

Souvenir Sheet

Bohemian-Moravian Highlands — A1374

2009, Sept. 2
3427 A1374 43k multi 4.00 2.50

Windmill, Ruprechtov A1375

Water Mill, Hoslovice A1376

Photo. & Engr.

2009, Sept. 23 *Perf. 11¼x11½*
3428 A1375 10k multi 1.00 .60
Complete booklet, 5 #3428 5.50

Perf. 11½x11¼

3429 A1376 12k multi 1.25 .70
Complete booklet, 5 #3429 7.00

Czech National Anthem, 175th Anniv. — A1377

2009, Oct. 14 *Perf. 11¼x11¾*
3430 A1377 10k multi 1.00 .60

Barbora Markéta Eliásová (1874-1957), Travel Writer — A1378

2009, Oct. 14 *Perf. 11¾x11¼*
3431 A1378 18k multi 1.75 1.10

Stoves — A1379

Designs: 10k, Empire stove, Litomysl Castle. 14k, Biedermeier stove, Vyskov Castle.

2009, Oct. 14 *Perf. 11¼x11¾*
3432 A1379 10k multi 1.00 .60
Complete booklet, 5 #3432 5.50
3433 A1379 14k multi 1.25 .80
Complete booklet, 5 #3433 7.50

Protest Rallies of Nov. 17, 1939, and Nov. 17, 1989 — A1380

2009, Nov. 4 **Litho.**
3434 A1380 14k multi 1.25 .80

Painting Type of 1967 Inscribed "CESKA REPUBLIKA"

Designs: 24k, Canal Lock in Moret, by Alfred Sisley, horiz. 26k, Alley, by Alfred Justitz, horiz.

2009, Nov. 4 **Engr.** *Perf. 11¾*
3435-3436 A565 Set of 2 5.25 3.00

Souvenir Sheet

Oldrich and Bozena, by Frantisek Zenísek — A1381

Litho. & Engr.

2009, Nov. 4 *Perf. 11¾*
3437 A1381 34k multi 3.50 2.00

Christmas — A1382

Photo. & Engr.

2009, Nov. 4 *Perf. 11¼x11½*
3438 A1382 10k multi 1.10 .60

Tradition of Czech Stamp Production A1383

2010, Jan. 20 *Perf. 11¼x11¾*
3439 A1383 10k Vignette of #2121 1.10 .55
a. Booklet pane of 8 + 4 labels 9.00 —
Complete booklet, #3439a 9.00

Magdalena Dobromila Rettigová (1785-1845), Writer — A1384

2010, Jan. 20 *Perf. 11¾x11¼*
3440 A1384 12k multi 1.25 .65

2010 Winter Olympics, Vancouver — A1385

2010, Feb. 10 *Perf. 11¼x11¾*
3441 A1385 18k multi 1.25 .95

2010 Winter Paralympics, Vancouver — A1386

2010, Feb. 10
3442 A1386 18k multi 1.25 .95

Souvenir Sheet

Expo 2010, Shanghai — A1387

2010, Feb. 10 **Litho.**
3443 A1387 35k multi + 3 labels 3.00 1.90

Easter A1388

Photo. & Engr.

2010, Mar. 10 *Perf. 11½x11¼*
3444 A1388 10k multi 1.10 .55

Martina Sáblíková, Gold Medalist at 2010 Winter Olympic Games — A1389

Perf. 11¼x11¾

2010, Mar. 24 **Litho.**
3445 A1389 10k multi 1.10 .55

Souvenir Sheet

Karel Hynek Macha (1810-36), Writer — A1390

Perf. 11½x11¾

2010, Mar. 10 **Litho. & Engr.**
3446 A1390 43k multi 4.00 2.40

Enrique Stanko Vráz (1860-1932), Travel Writer — A1391

Photo. & Engr.

2010, Apr. 14 ***Perf. 11¾x11¼***
3447 A1391 24k multi 2.25 1.25

19th Century Transcaucasian Carpets — A1392

Designs: 21k, Kasim Usak carpet. 24k, Celaberd carpet.

Litho. & Engr.

2010, Apr. 14 ***Perf. 11¾***
3448-3449 A1392 Set of 2 4.00 2.40

Ctyrlístek Comic Strip Character Fifinka — A1393

Serpentine Die Cut 15x16½

2010, Apr. 28 **Litho.**

Booklet Stamp
Self-Adhesive

3450 A1393 A multi 1.10 .55
a. Booklet pane of 10 11.00

No. 3450 sold for 10k on day of issue.

Prague Castle — A1394

2010, May 5 **Engr.** ***Perf. 11¾***
3451 A1394 17k brown 1.50 .85

Prague Castle in the Art of the Postage Stamp Exhibition, Prague. Printed in sheets of 4 + label. Value, $6.

Dásenka, Children's Book by Karel Capek A1395

2010, May 5 **Litho.** ***Perf. 11¼***
3452 A1395 17k multi 1.50 .85

Europa.

Children's Book Illustration by Helena Zmatlíková (1923-2005) A1396

Photo. & Engr.

2010, May 26 ***Perf. 11¼x11½***
3453 A1396 10k multi 1.10 .50
a. Booklet pane of 8 + 2 labels 9.00 —
Complete booklet, #3453a 9.00

Alphonse Mucha (1860-1939), Illustrator — A1397

Designs: E, Gismonda. Z, Zodiac.

Serpentine Die Cut 14¼x14½

2010, May 26 **Litho.**

Booklet Stamps
Self-Adhesive

3454 A1397 E multi 1.60 .80
a. Booklet pane of 6 9.75

Size: 43x54mm

Serpentine Die Cut 14½

3455 A1397 Z multi 1.75 .85
a. Booklet pane of 6 10.50

No. 3454 sold for 17k and No. 3455 sold for 18k on day of issue.

Zd'árské Hills Protected Landscape — A1398

Photo. & Engr.

2010, June 16 ***Perf. 11¾x11½***
3456 A1398 10k multi 1.10 .50

Marriage of John of Luxembourg and Elizabeth of Bohemia, 700th Anniv. — A1399

Photo. & Engr.

2010, June 16 ***Perf. 11¾x11¼***
3457 A1399 17k multi 1.50 .85

Accession to the throne of Bohemia by the House of Luxembourg. See Luxembourg No. 1292.

No. 3457 was issued in sheets 5 stamps + 4 labels. Values: single stamp + label, $1.75; complete sheet, $9.

Astronomical Clock, Prague, 600th Anniv. — A1400

2010, June 16 **Litho.**
3458 A1400 21k multi 2.25 1.10

Towns — A1401

Designs: 12k, Klatovy. 14k, Stramberk.

2010, June 16 **Engr.**
3459-3460 A1401 Set of 2 2.40 1.25

Czech Republic, Winners of 2010 World Ice Hockey Championships A1402

Perf. 11¼x11¾

2010, June 23 **Litho.**
3461 A1402 10k multi 1.10 .50

Ctyrlístek Comic Strip Characters Fifinka, Pind'a, Bobík and Myspulín — A1403

2010, Sept. 1 **Litho.** ***Perf. 12¾x13¼***
3462 A1403 A multi + label 1.10 .55

No. 3462 was printed in sheets of 9 + 12 labels that could be personalized and had a franking value of 10k on day of issue.

Children With Magnifying Glass and Stamp Album — A1404

Boy Examining Stamp — A1405

2010, Sept. 1
3463 A1404 A multi + label 1.10 .55
3464 A1405 E multi + label 2.10 1.10

Nos. 3463-3464 each were printed in sheets of 9 + 12 labels that could be personalized. On day of issue, No. 3463 had a franking value of 10k and No. 3464 had a franking value of 20k.

2010 Women's World Basketball Championships, Czech Republic — A1406

2010, Sept. 1 ***Perf. 11¼x11¾***
3465 A1406 17k multi 1.75 .90

Miniature Sheet

Flora and Fauna of Lower Morava UNESCO Biosphere Reserve — A1407

No. 3466: a, 10k, Tichodroma muraria, Papilio machaon, Aster amellus (45x55mm). b, 12k, Saga pedo, Iris variegata (45x27mm). c, 14k, Lacerta viridis, Pulsatilla grandis (45x27mm). d, 18k, Upupa epops, Arenaria grandiflora (45x55mm).

Litho. & Engr.

2010, Sept. 1 ***Perf. 11¾***
3466 A1407 Sheet of 4, #a-d, + 3 labels 6.00 3.00

Flowers Type of 2002

Designs: 4k, Anemone (sasanka). 25k, Iris (kosatec). 30k, Tulip (tulipán).

Photo. & Engr.

2010 ***Perf. 11¾x11¼***
3467 A1215 4k multi .45 .25
3468 A1215 25k multi 2.00 1.50
3469 A1215 30k multi 2.25 1.75
Nos. 3467-3469 (3) 4.70 3.50

Issued: 4k, 9/29; 25k, 30k, 9/15.

Austrian Empire Post Office Sign, Postal Map, Dwarves with Letters, Handstamp and Posthorn A1408

2010, Sept. 29 **Litho.** ***Perf. 11¼***
3470 A1408 A multi 1.10 .55

Postal Musuem, Prague. No. 3470 sold for 10k on day of issue.

Famous Men — A1409

Designs: 10k, Adolf Branald (1910-2008), writer. 12k, Karel Zeman (1910-89), film director and animator.

Photo. & Engr.

2010, Sept. 29 ***Perf. 11¼x11½***
3471-3472 A1409 Set of 2 2.25 1.25

Ctyrlístek Comic Strip Character Myspulín — A1410

Serpentine Die Cut 15x16½
2010, Oct. 20 **Litho.**
Booklet Stamp
Self-Adhesive

3473 A1410 A multi 1.25 .60
a. Booklet pane of 10 12.50

No. 3473 sold for 10k on day of issue.

Bridges A1411

Designs: 10k, Mariánsky Bridge, Ustí nad Labem. 12k, Stone Bridge, Písek.

Photo. & Engr.

2010, Oct. 20 ***Perf. 11¾x11¼***
3474 A1411 10k multi 1.00 .60
Complete booklet, 5 #3474 5.50
3475 A1411 12k multi 1.25 .70
Complete booklet, 5 #3475 7.00

Stoves — A1412

Designs: 10k, Art Nouveau stove. 20k, Art Deco stove.

2010, Oct. 20 ***Perf. 11¼x11¾***
3476 A1412 10k multi 1.00 .60
Complete booklet, 5 #3476 6.25
3477 A1412 20k multi 1.75 1.25
Complete booklet, 5 #3477 12.00

Art Type of 1967 Inscribed "CESKA REPUBLIKA"

Designs: 24k, Paris and Helen, by Karel Skréta. 26k, Sand Bargemen, by Milos Jiránek. 30k, Spring, by Karel Spillar, horiz.

Litho. & Engr. (24k), Engr.

2010, Nov. 10 ***Perf. 11¾***
3478-3480 A565 Set of 3 7.50 4.50

Illumination From 1558 Zlutice Hymn Book — A1413

Perf. 11¼x11¾
2010, Nov. 10 **Litho.**
3481 A1413 10k multi 1.10 .55

Christmas.

2011 Census — A1414

2011, Jan. 5
3482 A1414 10k black & green 1.10 .55

Souvenir Sheet

Kaspar Maria von Sternberg (1761-1838), Paleobotanist — A1415

Perf. 11¾x11½
2011, Jan. 5 **Litho. & Engr.**
3483 A1415 43k multi 5.00 2.40

Mail Coach on Charles Bridge, 1966 Envelope Indicia by Josef Hercík — A1416

Photo. & Engr.

2011, Jan. 20 ***Perf. 11¾x11¼***
3484 A1416 10k multi 1.10 .55
a. Booklet pane of 8 + 4 labels 9.00 —
Complete booklet, #3484a 9.50

Tradition of Czech stamp production.

St. Agnes of Bohemia (1211-82) — A1417

2011, Jan. 20 ***Perf. 11¼x11¾***
3485 A1417 12k multi 1.25 .70

Ctyrlístek Comic Strip Character Pind'a — A1418

Booklet Stamp
Serpentine Die Cut 15x16½
2011, Feb. 9 **Litho.** **Self-Adhesive**
3486 A1418 A multi 1.10 .55
a. Booklet pane of 10 11.00

No. 3486 sold for 10k on day of issue.

Jirí Melantrich of Aventinum (c. 1511-80), Printer — A1419

Photo. & Engr.

2011, Feb. 9 ***Perf. 11¼x11¾***
3487 A1419 30k multi 3.00 1.75

Cheb, 950th Anniv. — A1420

Black Madonna House, Prague, Cent. — A1421

2011, Feb. 9 **Engr.** ***Perf. 11¾x11½***
3488 A1420 12k multi 1.10 .70
Perf. 11½x11¾
3489 A1421 14k multi 1.40 .80

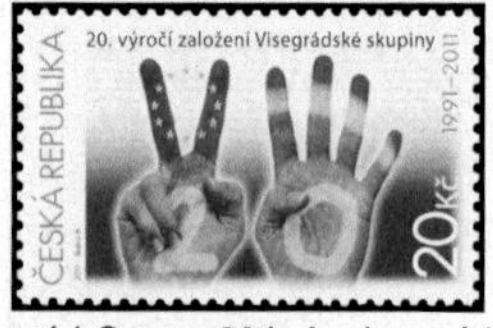
Visegrád Group, 20th Anniv. — A1422

Perf. 11¾x11¼
2011, Feb. 11 **Litho.**
3490 A1422 20k multi 2.00 1.10

See Hungary No. 4183, Poland No. 4001, and Slovakia No. 611.

No. 3490 was issued in sheets of 8 + 8 labels. Values: single stamp + label, $2.25; complete sheet, $18.

Architecture A1423

Designs: A, House gables from Blatensko region, North Moravia and West Bohemia, gable shutter from North Bohemia. E, House gables from North Bohemia and South Bohemia, Wallachian cottage, Central Bohemian gate. Z, Houses from North Bohemia, West Bohemia and Wallachia, vert.

Photo. & Engr.

2011 ***Perf. 11¼x11¾***
3491 A1423 A blk, lt bl & bl 1.00 .60
3492 A1423 E blk, beige & brn 2.25 1.25

Perf. 11¾x11¼
3493 A1423 Z blk, gray grn & bl grn 2.25 1.25
Nos. 3491-3493 (3) 5.50 3.10

Issued: Nos. 3491-3492, 2/23; No. 3493, 5/27. On day of issue Nos. 3491-3493 sold for 10k, 20k and 21k, respectively.

See No. 3559.

Souvenir Sheet

Petr Vok (1539-1611) and Vilém (1535-92) von Rosenberg, Aristocrats — A1424

2011, Mar. 9 **Engr.** ***Perf. 11¾***
3494 A1424 49k multi 4.50 3.00

Easter — A1425

Perf. 11¼x11¾
2011, Mar. 23 **Litho.**
3495 A1425 A multi 1.10 .60

No. 3495 sold for 10k on day of issue.

Vlasta Burian (1891-1962), Actor — A1426

Photo. & Engr.

2011, Apr. 6 ***Perf. 11¾x11¼***
3496 A1426 10k multi 1.10 .60

Teaching at Prague Conservatory, Bicent. — A1427

2011, Apr. 6 ***Perf. 11¼x11¾***
3497 A1427 10k multi 1.10 .60

Ctyrlistek Comic Strip Character Bobík — A1428

Booklet Stamp

Serpentine Die Cut 15x16½

2011, May 4 Litho. Self-Adhesive

3498 A1428 A multi 1.25 .60
a. Booklet pane of 10 12.50

No. 3498 sold for 10k on day of issue.

Europa A1429

2011, May 4 Litho. *Perf. 11¼*

3499 A1429 20k multi 2.00 1.25

Intl. Year of Forests.

Flower Type of 2002

Design: 2k, Chrysanthemum (chryzantéma).

Photo. & Engr.

2011, May 27 *Perf. 11¾x11¼*

3500 A1215 2k multi .25 .25

Souvenir Sheet

Johann Gerstner (1851-1939), Violinist — A1430

Litho. & Engr.

2011, May 27 *Perf. 11¾*

3501 A1430 34k multi 3.50 2.10

See Slovenia No. 891.

The Little Witch and Abraxas, the Raven, Animated Characters by Zdenek Smetana A1431

Photo. & Engr.

2011, June 1 *Perf. 11½x11¼*

3502 A1431 10k multi 1.25 .60
a. Booklet pane of 8 + 2 labels 10.00 —
Complete booklet, #3502a 10.00

First Public Long-Distance Flight of Jan Kaspar (1883-1927), Cent. — A1432

2011, June 1 *Perf. 11¼x11¾*

3503 A1432 21k multi 2.25 1.25

Execution of 27 Protestant Leaders in Prague, 390th Anniv. — A1433

Litho. & Engr.

2011, June 1 *Perf. 11¾*

3504 A1433 26k rose pink & blk 2.50 1.60

Cricetus Cricetus — A1434

Perf. 11¼x11¾

2011, June 15 Litho.

3505 A1434 10k multi 1.10 .60
Complete booklet, 5 #3505 6.00

Floral Arrangement A1435

2011, June 15

3506 A1435 25k multi 2.50 1.50

Europa Cup, Championships of European Federation of Professional Florist Associations, Havirov.

Men's European Volleyball Championships, Prague and Karlovy Vary — A1436

Perf. 11¼x11¾

2011, Aug. 31 Litho.

3507 A1436 20k multi 2.25 1.10

Wolfgang Amadeus Mozart (1756-91), Composer — A1437

Booklet Stamp

Serpentine Die Cut 11½

2011, Aug. 31 Self-Adhesive

3508 A1437 E multi 2.25 1.10
a. Booklet pane of 6 13.50

No. 3508 sold for 20k on day of issue.

Miniature Sheet

Flora and Fauna of Sumava UNESCO Biosphere Reserve — A1438

No. 3509: a, 10k,Turdus torquatus, Erebia euryale, Tetrao urogallus (54x44mm). b, 14k, Dactylorhiza traunsteineri, Colias palaeno (27x44mm). c, 18k, Aeshna juncea, Alces alces, Tetrao tetrix (54x44mm). d, 20k, Lynx lynx, Picoides tridactylus (54x44mm).

Litho. & Engr.

2011, Aug. 31 *Perf. 11¾*

3509 A1438 Sheet of 4, #a-d, + 4 labels 6.00 3.50

Organ, Church of the Assumption of Our Lady, Plasy — A1439

Perf. 11¼x11¾

2011, Sept. 14 Litho.

3510 A1439 10k multi 1.10 .55

Frantisek Alexander Elstner (1902-74), Travel Writer — A1440

Photo. & Engr.

2011, Sept. 14 *Perf. 11¾x11¼*

3511 A1440 14k multi 1.40 .80

Pat and Mat, Characters From Children's Television Show — A1441

Booklet Stamp

Serpentine Die Cut 15x16½

2011, Oct. 5 Litho. Self-Adhesive

3512 A1441 A multi 1.10 .55
a. Booklet pane of 10 11.00

No. 3512 sold for 10k on day of issue.

World Post Day A1442

2011, Oct. 5 *Perf. 11¼*

3513 A1442 21k multi 2.25 1.25

Film Posters A1443

Poster for: No. 3514, 10k, Une Femme Douce, 1970. No. 3515, 10k, Markéta Lazarová, 1966.

2011, Oct. 5 Litho. *Perf. 11¾x11¼*

3514-3515 A1443 Set of 2 2.25 1.10

Peacock & Bugler Type of 2005 and Roses Above Prague Type of 2003

2011, Oct. 27 *Perf. 11¼x11¾*

3516 A1263 A multi + label 1.10 .55
3517 A1225 E multi + label 2.25 1.10

On day of issue, No. 3516 sold for 10k and No. 3517 sold for 20k. Nos. 3516-3517 each were issued in sheets of 9 stamps and 12 labels that could be personalized. Value, $30.

Art Type of 1967 Inscribed "CESKA REPUBLIKA"

Designs: 24k, Lovers, by Jaroslav Vozniak, horiz. 26k, Woman in Corn Field, by Joza Uprka. 30k, Winter Landscape, by August Bedrich Piepenhagen, horiz.

2011, Nov. 9 Engr. *Perf. 11¾*

3518-3520 A565 Set of 3 8.00 4.50

Christmas A1444

2011, Nov. 9 Litho. *Perf. 11¾x11¼*

3521 A1444 A multi 1.10 .55

No. 3521 sold for 10k on day of issue.

House, Vidim — A1445

Photo. & Engr.

2012, Jan. 20 *Perf. 11¼x11¾*

3522 A1445 6k multi .65 .30

Josef Liesler (1912-2005), Stamp Designer — A1446

2012, Jan. 20 *Perf. 11¾x11¼*

3523 A1446 10k multi 1.10 .55
a. Booklet pane of 8 + 4 labels 9.00 —
Complete booklet, #3523a 9.00

Tradition of Czech stamp production.

Jirí Trnka (1912-69), Film Animator and Director — A1447

2012, Feb. 15

3524 A1447 10k multi 1.10 .55

Sokol Movement, 150th Anniv. — A1448

Perf. 11¼x11¾

2012, Feb. 15 **Litho.**

3525 A1448 14k multi 1.50 .75

Union of Czech Mathematicians and Physicists, 150th Anniv. — A1449

2012, Mar. 7 ***Perf. 11¾x11¼***

3526 A1449 10k multi 1.10 .55

Kuks A1450

Designs: 14k, Buildings in Kuks. 18k, Statue by Matthias B. Braun, vert.

Perf. 11½x11¾, 11¾x11½

2012, Mar. 7 **Engr.**

3527-3528 A1450 Set of 2 3.00 1.75

Hiker at Signpost — A1451

Perf. 11¼x11¾

2012, Mar. 21 **Litho.**

3529 A1451 A multi + label 1.10 .55

No. 3529 was printed in sheets of 9 + 12 labels that could be personalized and had a franking value of 10k on day of issue.

Gregor Mendel (1822-84), Genetics Pioneer — A1452

Photo. & Engr.

2012, Apr. 4 ***Perf. 11¾x11¼***

3530 A1452 20k multi 1.90 1.10

First Hebrew Book Printed in Prague, 500th Anniv. A1453

2012, Apr. 18 **Litho.** ***Perf. 11¼***

3531 A1453 25k multi 2.40 1.40

Prague Tourist Attractions A1454

Photo. & Engr.

2012, May 2 ***Perf. 11¼x11¾***

3532 A1454 20k multi 2.00 1.10

Europa.

Scouting in Czechoslovakia, Cent. — A1455

2012, May 2 **Litho.** ***Perf. 11¼***

3533 A1455 21k multi 2.00 1.10

Boats on Bat'a Canal A1456

2012, May 16 **Engr.** ***Perf. 11¾x11¼***

Booklet Stamp

3534 A1456 10k dark blue 1.20 .50

a. Booklet pane of 8 + 4 labels 9.50 —

Complete booklet, #3534a 9.50

The Whipping of Christ, by Tintoretto — A1457

2012, May 16 ***Perf. 11¾***

3535 A1457 30k multi 3.50 1.50

Art in Prague Castle. See Nos. 3569, 3605, 3642, 3674, 3705, 3755, 3790.

St. Wenceslas (c. 907-35) A1458

Serpentine Die Cut 11 Syncopated

2012, June 6 **Litho.**

Self-Adhesive

3536 A1458 A multi 1.00 .50

No. 3536 sold for 10k on day of issue. See No. 3576.

Lezáky Massacre, 70th Anniv. — A1459

2012, June 6 ***Perf. 11¾x11¼***

3537 A1459 10k multi 1.00 .50

Lidice Massacre, 70th Anniv. — A1460

2012, June 6 **Photo. & Engr.**

3538 A1460 20k multi 2.00 1.00

Coronation of Statue of Our Lady of Hostyn, Cent. — A1461

Litho. & Engr.

2012, June 20 ***Perf. 11¾***

3539 A1461 21k multi 1.90 1.00

No. 3539 was issued in sheets of 8 stamps + 1 label. Values: single stamp + label, $2.50; complete sheet, $16.

A1462

A1463

Personalized Stamps A1464

Serpentine Die Cut 11 Syncopated

2012, June 20 **Litho.**

Self-Adhesive

3540 A1462 A multi .95 .50

3541 A1463 A multi .95 .50

3542 A1464 E multi 1.90 .95

Nos. 3540-3542 (3) 3.80 1.95

Nos. 3540-3542 each were printed in sheets of 25. Vignette portions of each stamp could be personalized. The generic vignettes of these stamps are shown. On day of issue, the franking value of Nos. 3540-3541 each were 10k, and of No. 3542, 20k.

2012 Summer Olympics, London — A1465

Litho. & Engr.

2012, June 20 ***Perf. 11¾***

3543 A1465 20k multi 1.90 .95

No. 3543 was issued in sheets of 3 stamps + 2 labels. Values: single stamp + label, $2.25; complete sheet, $6.

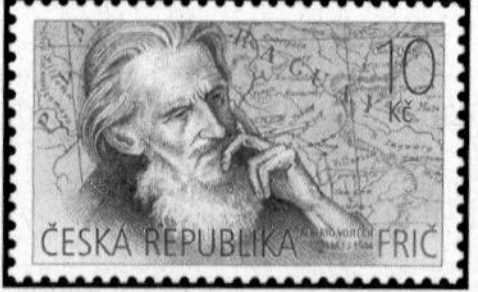

Alberto Vojtech Fric (1882-1944), Cactus Collector, Botanist and Ethnographer — A1466

2012, Sept. 5 **Litho.** ***Perf. 11¾x11¼***

3544 A1466 10k multi 1.10 .55

Illustrations of Antique Automobiles by Václav Zapadlík — A1467

No. 3545: a, 1933 Duesenberg SJ. b, 1931, Wikov 70. c, 1936 Mercedes-Benz 540. d, 1938 Rolls Royce Phantom III. e, 1934 Bugatti Royale 41. f, 1929 Isotta Fraschini Tipo 8A.

Serpentine Die Cut 11½

2012, Sept. 5

Self-Adhesive

3545 Booklet pane of 6 13.00

a.-f. A1467 E Any single 2.10 1.10

On day of issue, Nos. 3545a-3545f each sold for 20k. See Nos. 3580-3581, 3610-3611, 3645-3646.

Miniature Sheet

Orchids — A1468

No. 3546: a, 10k, Dendrobium peguanum (44x27mm). b, 14k, Stanhopea tigrina and Coryanthes feildingii (44x54mm). c, 18k, Cattleya aclandiae and Cattleya maxima (44x54mm). d, 20k, Paphiopedilum charlesworthii, Paphiopedilum insigne, and Paphiopedilum hirsutissimum (44x54mm).

Litho. & Engr.

2012, Sept. 5 ***Perf. 11¾***

3546 A1468 Sheet of 4, #a-d, + 4 labels 6.00 3.25

Souvenir Sheet

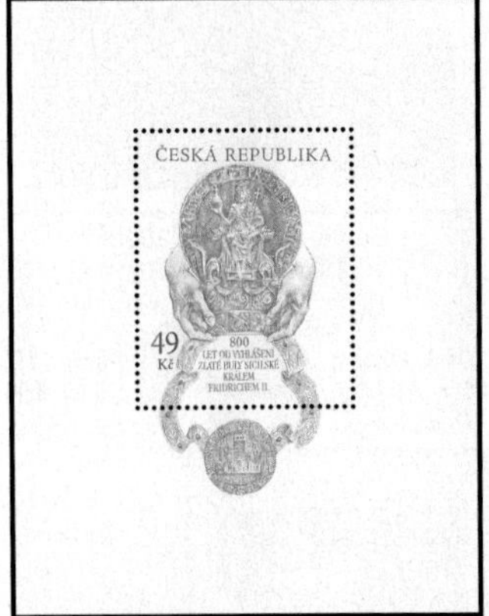

Golden Bull of Sicily, 800th Anniv. — A1469

2012, Sept. 19 Engr. ***Perf. 11¾***

3547 A1469 49k multi 4.75 2.60

Paphiopedilum Venustum — A1470

2012, Oct. 3 Litho. ***Perf. 11¼x11¾***

3548 A1470 A multi + label 1.10 .55

No. 3548 was printed in sheets of 9 + 12 labels that could be personalized. On day of issue, No. 3548 had a franking value of 10k.

Masaryk Circuit Racers — A1471

Designs: 18k, Frantisek St'astny (1927-2000), motorcycle racer. 25k, Louis Chiron (1899-1979), automobile racer.

2012, Oct. 3 **Photo. & Engr.**

3549-3550 A1471 Set of 2 4.50 2.25

1891 Ericsson Desk Telephone A1472

2012, Oct. 3 Litho. ***Perf. 11¼***

3551 A1472 26k multi 2.75 1.40

World Post Day.

Art Type of 1967 Inscribed "CESKA REPUBLIKA" and

Life's Pleasures, by Frantisek Kupka — A1473

Designs: 26k, A Long-haired Girl, by Kamil Lhoták. 32k, Self-portrait with Family, by Jan Kupecky. No. 3554: a, Blonde nude on horse. b, Brunette nude on pony, vert.

2012, Nov. 7 Engr. ***Perf. 11¾***

3552-3553 A565 Set of 2 5.50 3.00

Litho. & Engr.

Souvenir Sheet

3554 A1473 30k Sheet of 2, #a-b 6.00 3.00

Christmas — A1474

2012, Nov. 7 Litho. ***Perf. 11¼x11¾***

3555 A1474 A multi + label 1.00 .50

No. 3555 sold for 10k on day of issue and was printed in sheets of 9 + 12 labels that could be personalized.

Pinda, Bobik, Myspulin and Fifinka Riding Griffin A1475

Myspulin Taking Picture of Bobik, Fifinka, King Rudolf II, Aurix the Lion and Pinda — A1476

Serpentine Die Cut 16½x15

2012, Nov. 7 **Self-Adhesive**

Booklet Stamps

3556 A1475 A multi 1.00 .50
3557 A1476 A multi 1.00 .50
a. Booklet pane of 10, 5 each #3556-3557 10.00

On day of issue, Nos. 3556-3557 each sold for 10k.

Architecture Type of 2011 and

Building, Busanovice, 1847 — A1477

Photo. & Engr.

2012 ***Perf. 11¼x11¾***

3558 A1477 5k multi .75 .25
3559 A1423 A black & blue 1.25 .50

Issued: No. 3558, 12/19; No. 3559, 11/8. No. 3559 sold for 10k on day of issue. Compare No. 3559 with No. 3491.

Ivan Strnad (1926-2005), Stamp Designer — A1478

2013, Jan. 20 ***Perf. 11¾x11¼***

3560 A1478 10k multi 1.10 .55
a. Booklet pane of 8 + 4 labels 9.00 —
Complete booklet, #3560a 9.00

Tradition of Czech stamp production.

Bertha von Suttner (1843-1914), 1905 Nobel Peace Laureate — A1479

Perf. 11¼x11¾

2013, Feb. 13 **Litho.**

3561 A1479 18k multi 1.90 .95

Cottage, Novy Hrozenkov — A1480

Photo. & Engr.

2013, Mar. 6 ***Perf. 11¾x11¼***

3562 A1480 14k brn & dk brn 1.50 .75

Transportation — A1481

No. 3563: a, Aero HC2 Heli Baby helicopter. b, Pécko-18 tugboat.

2013, Mar. 6 **Litho.**

3563 A1481 25k Vert. pair, #a-b 4.50 2.60

Zlatá Koruna Monastery, 750th Anniv. — A1482

2013, Apr. 3 Engr. ***Perf. 11¾x11½***

3564 A1482 14k multi 1.40 .70

George Orwell (1903-50), Writer — A1483

Photo. & Engr.

2013, Apr. 3 ***Perf. 11¼x11¾***

3565 A1483 26k multi 2.60 1.40

Pres. Milos Zeman — A1484

2013, Apr. 24 ***Perf. 11¾x11¼***

3566 A1484 A red & purple 1.00 .50

No. 3566 sold for 10k on day of issue. See No. 3752.

Europa A1485

2013, May 2 Litho. ***Perf. 11¼***

3567 A1485 25k multi 2.25 1.40

Fláje Dam A1486

2013, May 15 Engr. ***Perf. 11¾x11¼***
3568 A1486 14k green 1.25 .75
a. Booklet pane of 8 + 4 labels 10.50 —
Complete booklet, #3568a 10.50

Art in Prague Castle Type of 2012

Design: 25k, Portrait of Jacob König, Goldsmith and Bookseller, by Paolo Veronese.

2013, May 15 Engr. ***Perf. 11¾***
3569 A1457 25k multi 2.25 1.40

Cross of Závis of Falkenstejn A1487

2013, May 29 ***Perf. 11¾***
3570 A1487 26k multi 2.40 1.40

Krtek the Mole — A1488

Serpentine Die Cut 16½x15
2013, May 29 Litho.
Booklet Stamp Self-Adhesive
3571 A1488 A multi 1.25 .55
a. Booklet pane of 10 12.50
b. As No. 3571, serpentine die cut 11x11¼ syncopated ('15) 1.50 .55
c. Booklet pane of 10 #3571b 15.00

No. 3571 sold for 10k on day of issue. No. 3571b sold for 13k when issued.

Historic Methods of Transportation — A1489

No. 3572: a, Tatra 15/30 automobile. b, Cechie 33 Böhmerland motorcycle.

Perf. 11¾x11¼
2013, June 12 Litho.
3572 A1489 10k Horiz. pair, #a-b 2.40 1.10

Souvenir Sheet

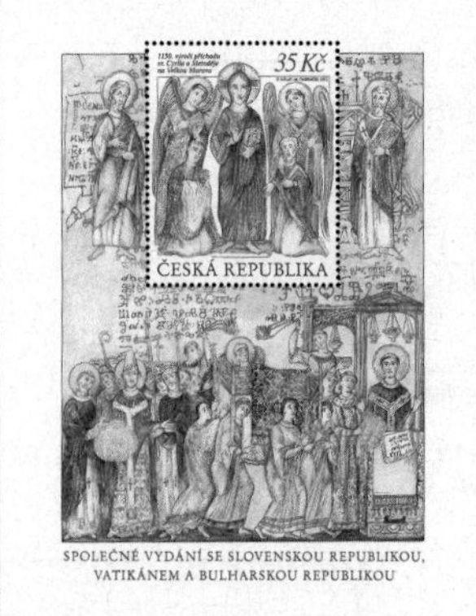

Mission of Sts. Cyril and Methodius to Slavic Lands, 1150th Anniv. — A1490

Litho. & Engr.
2013, June 12 ***Perf. 11¾***
3573 A1490 35k multi 3.75 1.90

See Bulgaria No. 4647, Slovakia No. 666 and Vatican City No. 1536.

Postal Banking Services, 130th Anniv. A1491

Perf. 11¾x11¼
2013, June 26 Litho.
3574 A1491 20k multi 1.75 1.00

Franz Kafka (1883-1924), Writer — A1492

Serpentine Die Cut 11½
2013, June 26 Litho.
Booklet Stamp Self-Adhesive
3575 A1492 E multi 2.00 1.00
a. Booklet pane of 6 12.00

No. 3575 sold for 20k on day of issue.

St. Wenceslas Type of 2012

2013, July 31 Litho. ***Perf. 11¼x11¾***
3576 A1458 13k multi 1.40 .70

2013 Canoe Slalom World Championships, Prague — A1493

Photo. & Engr.
2013, Sept. 4 ***Perf. 11¾x11¼***
3577 A1493 10k multi 1.10 .55

Novy Jicín, 700th Anniv. — A1494

2013, Sept. 4 Engr. ***Perf. 11¾***
3578 A1494 20k multi 1.75 1.75

Miniature Sheet

Flora and Fauna of the Karlstejn Region — A1495

No. 3579: a, 10k, Dracocephalum austriacum, Chorthippus vagans (27x44mm). b, 14k, Oenanthe oenanthe, Velká Amerika Limestone Quarry (27x44mm). c, 18k, Polyommatus coridon, Pulsatilla pratensis, Colias crocea (54x44mm). d, 20k, Rosa gallica, Karlstejn Castle (54x44mm).

Litho. & Engr.
2013, Sept. 4 ***Perf. 11¾***
3579 A1495 Sheet of 4, #a-d, + 4 labels 6.00 3.25

Antique Automobiles Type of 2012

Illustrations by Václav Zapadlík: No. 3580, 1930 Skoda 860. No. 3581, 1932 Skoda 645.

Serpentine Die Cut 11¼ Syncopated
2013, Sept. 4 Litho.
Booklet Stamps Self-Adhesive
3580 A1467 A multi 1.25 .70
3581 A1467 A multi 1.25 .70
a. Booklet pane of 8, 4 each #3580-3581 10.00

Nos. 3580-3581 each sold for 13k on day of issue.

A1496

Personalized Stamps — A1497

Serpentine Die Cut 11¼ Syncopated
2013, Sept. 4 Litho.
Booklet Stamps Self-Adhesive
3582 A1496 A black 1.50 .70
a. Booklet pane of 8 12.00
3583 A1497 E black 3.00 1.25
a. Booklet pane of 8 24.00

On day of issue, No. 3582 sold for 13k, and No. 3583 sold for 25k. Nos. 3582 and 3583 could have the image portions of the stamp personalized for an additional fee. The horizontal generic vignettes of these stamps are shown. Nos. 3582a and 3583a contain four stamps with these horizontal generic vignettes and four stamps with similar generic vignettes but with a vertical orientation. Values for Nos. 3582 and Nos. 3583 are for stamps with images with either a horizontal or vertical orientation.

Josef Bican (1913-2001), Soccer Player — A1498

Photo. & Engr.
2013, Sept. 18 ***Perf. 11¼x11¾***
3584 A1498 13k multi 1.25 .70

Horses From Chlumetz Stud Farm — A1499

Design: 13k, Kinsky horse. 17k, Palomino horse.

Perf. 11¼x11¾
2013, Sept. 18 Litho.
3585-3586 A1499 Set of 2 2.75 1.60

Cottage, Salajna — A1500

2013, Oct. 2 Engr. ***Perf. 11¼x11¾***
3587 A1500 29k green 2.60 1.60

Souvenir Sheet

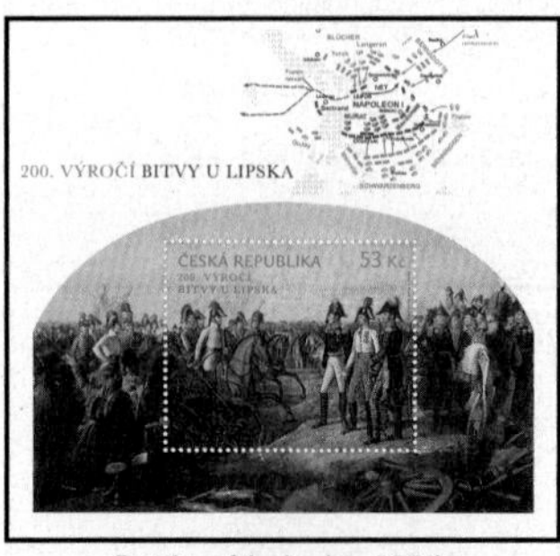

Battle of Leipzig, 200th Anniv. — A1501

Litho. & Engr.
2013, Oct. 2 ***Perf. 11¾***
3588 A1501 53k multi 5.50 3.00

Bible of Kralice, 400th Anniv. A1502

2013, Oct. 16 Litho. ***Perf. 11¼***
3589 A1502 17k multi 1.75 .85

Otto Wichterle (1912-98), Inventor of Soft Contact Lenses — A1503

Photo. & Engr.
2013, Oct. 16 ***Perf. 11¼x11¾***
3590 A1503 21k multi 1.90 1.10

Art Type of 1967 Inscribed "CESKA REPUBLIKA"

Designs: 25k, A View of Roman Churches, by Giovanni Battista Piranesi, horiz. 30k, Still Life with the Author, by Bohuslav Reynek. 35k, Round Portrait, by Max Svabinsky.

Engr., Litho & Engr. (30k)
2013, Nov. 27 ***Perf. 11¾***
3591-3593 A565 Set of 3 7.50 4.50

Ladislav Jirka (1914-86), Stamp Engraver — A1504

2014, Jan. 20 Litho. ***Perf. 11¾x11¼***
3594 A1504 13k multi 1.25 .65
a. Booklet pane of 8 + 4 labels 10.00 —
Complete booklet, #3594a 10.00

Tradition of Czech stamp production.

Dog and Four-Leaf Clover — A1505

2014, Jan. 20 Litho. ***Perf. 11¼x11¾***
3595 A1505 A multi + label 1.25 .65

No. 3595 was printed in sheets of 9 + 12 labels that could be personalized. On day of issue, No. 3595 had a franking value of 13k.

2014 Winter Olympics, Sochi, Russia — A1506

2014, Feb. 5 Litho. ***Perf. 11¾x11¼***
3596 A1506 25k multi 2.50 1.25

2014 Winter Paralympics, Sochi, Russia A1507

2014, Feb. 5 Litho. ***Perf. 11¾x11¼***
3597 A1507 13k multi 1.25 .70
a. Tête-bêche pair 2.50 1.40

Czech Firefighters, 150th Anniv. — A1508

2014, Mar. 5 Litho. ***Perf. 11¾x11¼***
3598 A1508 13k multi 1.25 .70

Transportation — A1509

No. 3599: a, Rapid, 1912 airplane of Eugen Cihák. b, Type R1 Prague Metro train.

2014, Mar. 5 Litho. ***Perf. 11¾x11¼***
3599 A1509 13k Pair, #a-b 2.25 1.40

Bohumil Hrabal (1914-97), Writer — A1510

Photo. & Engr.
2014, Mar. 26 ***Perf. 11¼x11¾***
3600 A1510 17k blk & brn 1.75 .85

Cervená Lhota Castle — A1511

2014, Mar. 26 Engr. ***Perf. 11¾***
3601 A1511 17k multi 1.50 .85

Zdenek Kopal (1914-93), Astronomer — A1512

Perf. 11¾x11¼
2014, Mar. 26 Litho.
3602 A1512 21k multi 2.10 1.10

Silesian Museum, Opava, 200th Anniv. — A1513

Photo. & Engr.
2014, Apr. 30 ***Perf. 11¼x11¾***
3603 A1513 13k multi 1.25 .70

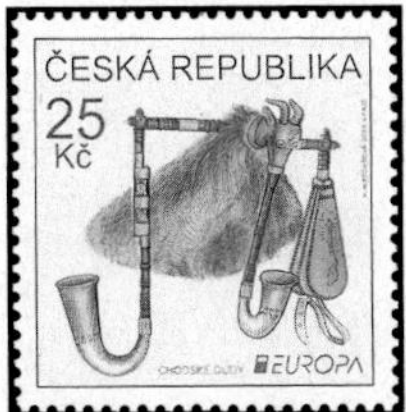
Bagpipes A1514

Photo. & Engr.
2014, Apr. 30 ***Perf. 11¼***
3604 A1514 25k multi 2.10 1.25

Europa.

Art in Prague Castle Type of 2012

Design: 37k, Assembly of Olympian Gods, by Peter Paul Rubens.

Litho. & Engr.
2014, May 28 ***Perf. 11¾***
3605 A1457 37k multi 3.75 1.90

No. 3605 was printed in sheets of 2. Value, $7.50.

Paper Mill, Velké Losiny A1515

Photo. & Engr.
2014, May 28 ***Perf. 11¾x11¼***
3606 A1515 13k multi 1.25 .70

Animated Characters Ju and Hele — A1516

Serpentine Die Cut 11 Syncopated
2014, May 28 Litho.
Booklet Stamp Self-Adhesive
3607 A1516 A multi 1.25 .70
a. Booklet pane of 10 12.50

No. 3607 sold for 13k on day of issue.

Historic Methods of Transportation — A1517

No. 3608: a, Paddle steamer Franz Joseph I. b, 1936 Zbrojovka Brno Z4 automobile.

Perf. 11¾x11¼
2014, June 11 Litho.
3608 A1517 25k Horiz. pair, #a-b 4.50 2.50

Souvenir Sheet

World War I, Cent. — A1518

No. 3609: a, Soldier carrying rifle, mother holding child. b, Soldiers, people falling into pit.

2014, June 11 Litho. ***Perf. 11¾***
3609 A1518 29k Sheet of 2, #a-b, + 3 labels 5.00 3.00

Antique Automobiles Type of 2012

Designs: No. 3610, 1938 Skoda Popular Monte Carlo. No. 3611, 1941 Skoda Superb 3000.

Serpentine Die Cut 11¼ Syncopated
2014, Sept. 3 Litho.
Booklet Stamps Self-Adhesive
3610 A1467 A multi 1.10 .60
3611 A1467 A multi 1.10 .60
a. Booklet pane of 8, 4 each #3610-3611 9.00

Nos. 3610-3611 each sold for 13k on day of issue.

Karel, Elder of Zierotín (1564-1636), Governor of Moravia — A1519

Photo. & Engr.
2014, Sept. 3 ***Perf. 11¾x11¼***
3612 A1519 29k multi 2.50 1.40

Miniature Sheet

Flora and Fauna of the Beskid Mountains — A1520

No. 3613: a, 13k, Meles meles (44x27mm). b, 17k, Felis silvestris (44x27mm). c, 21k, Ursus arctos, Carabus variolosus (44x54mm). d, 25k, Nucifraga caryocatactes, Canis lupus (44x54mm).

Litho. & Engr.
2014, Sept. 3 ***Perf. 11¾***
3613 A1520 Sheet of 4, #a-d, + 3 labels 7.00 3.50

Flower Bouquet in Wine Bottle — A1521

2014, Oct. 15 Litho. ***Perf. 11¼x11¾***
3614 A1521 A multi + label 1.25 .60

No. 3614 was printed in sheets of 9 + 12 labels that could be personalized. On day of issue No. 3614 had a franking value of 13k.

Souvenir Sheet

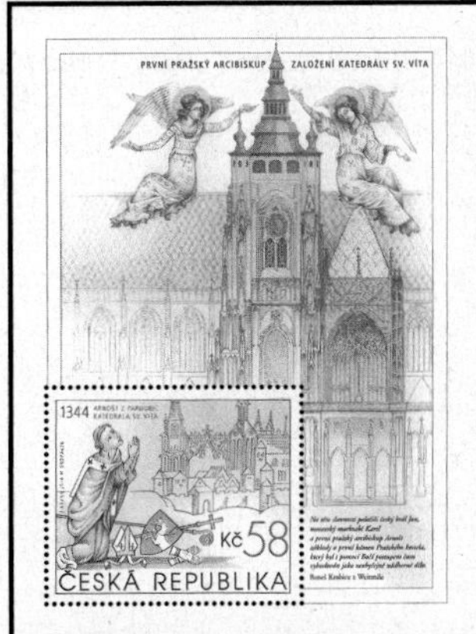
St. Vitus Cathedral, Prague, 670th Anniv. — A1522

Litho. & Engr.

2014, Oct. 15 *Perf. 11¾*
3615 A1522 58k multi 5.25 2.60

Art Type of 1967 Inscribed "CESKA REPUBLIKA" and

Solitude and Spectacles, Photograph by Jaromír Funke — A1523

Designs: 25k, Street in Winter, by Jakub Schikaneder. 37k, Leda Atomica, by Salvador Dalí.

Engr., Litho. (29k)

2014, Nov. 5 *Perf. 11¾*
3616 A565 25k multi 2.25 1.10
3617 A1523 29k multi 2.60 1.40
3618 A565 37k multi 3.50 1.75
Nos. 3616-3618 (3) 8.35 4.25

Historical Events of November 17 — A1524

2014, Nov. 5 Litho. *Perf. 11¼x11¾*
3619 A1524 13k multi 1.25 .60

Nazi attack on Czech university students, 75th anniv.; start of Velvet Revolution, 25th anniv.

Andreas Vesalius (1514-64), Anatomist — A1525

Photo. & Engr.

2014, Nov. 5 *Perf. 11¼x11¾*
3620 A1525 25k multi 2.25 1.10

Bethlehem in Winter, by Josef Lada — A1526

2014, Nov. 5 Litho. *Perf. 11¾x11¼*
3621 A1526 A multi 1.25 .60

Christmas. No. 3621 sold for 13k on day of issue.

A1527

Personalized Stamps A1528

Serpentine Die Cut Syncopated

2014, Nov. 26 **Litho.**

Self-Adhesive

3622 A1527 A multi 1.25 .60
3623 A1528 Z multi 2.75 1.40

Nos. 3622-3623 were each printed in sheets of 25. Vignette portions of each stamp could be personalized. The generic vignettes of these stamps are shown. On day of issue, the franking value of No. 3622 was 13k; No. 3623, 30k.

Oldrich Kulhánek (1940-2013), Stamp Designer — A1529

Photo. & Engr.

2015, Jan. 20 *Perf. 11¾x11¼*
3624 A1529 13k multi 1.20 .55
a. Booklet pane of 8 + 4 labels 9.50 —
Complete booklet, #3624a 9.50

Vitezslava Kaprálová (1915-40), Composer — A1530

2015, Jan. 20 Litho. *Perf. 11¾x11¼*
3625 A1530 17k multi 1.40 .70

Military Aircraft and Vehicles — A1531

Designs: No. 3626, Supermarine Spitfire LF Mk IXE. No. 3627, T-34/76.2 tank. No. 3628, Harley-Davidson motorcycle. No. 3629, Jeep-Ford GPW.

Serpentine Die Cut 11¼ Syncopated

2015, Jan. 20 **Litho.**

Booklet Stamps

Self-Adhesive

3626 A1531 A multi 1.10 .55
3627 A1531 A multi 1.10 .55
3628 A1531 A multi 1.10 .55
3629 A1531 A multi 1.10 .55
a. Bookklet pane of 8, 2 each #3626-3629 9.00
Nos. 3626-3629 (4) 4.40 2.20

On day of issue, Nos. 3626-3629 each sold for 13k.

Cartoon Character Vecerníček, 50th Anniv. A1532

Serpentine Die Cut 11 Syncopated

2015, Feb. 18 **Litho.**

Self-Adhesive

3630 A1532 A multi 1.10 .55

No. 3630 sold for 13k on day of issue.

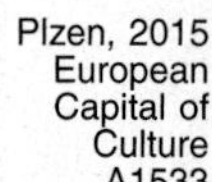

Plzen, 2015 European Capital of Culture A1533

Photo. & Engr.

2015, Feb. 18 *Perf. 11¼*
3631 A1533 25k multi 2.00 1.00

Printed in sheets of 3, with 3 labels. Value, $9.50.

Historic Methods of Transportation — A1534

No. 3632: a, Walter 6B automobile. b, Monoplane of Metodej Vlach.

Perf. 11¾x11¼

2015, Feb. 18 **Litho.**
3632 A1534 13k Horiz. pair, #a-b 2.10 1.10

Easter — A1535

2015, Mar. 4 Litho. *Perf. 11¼x11¾*
3633 A1535 A multi 1.10 .55

No. 3633 sold for 13k on day of issue.

Postmen on Geese Above Charles Bridge — A1536

2015, Mar. 4 Litho. *Perf. 11¼x11¾*
3634 A1536 A multi + label 1.10 .55

No. 3633 has a franking value of 13k on day of issue and was printed in sheets of 9 + 12 labels that could be personalized.

Souvenir Sheet

The Last Supper, by Leonardo da Vinci — A1537

Perf. 11¼x11¾

2015, Mar. 18 **Litho.**
3635 A1537 25k multi 2.25 1.00

Expo 2015, Milan.

Church of St. Ignatius and Spejchar Gallery, Chomutov — A1538

Photo. & Engr.

2015, Apr. 15 *Perf. 11¼x11¾*
3636 A1538 25k multi 2.10 2.10
a. Booklet pane of 8 + 4 labels 17.00 —
Complete booklet, #3636a 17.00

Sixth Czech and German Philatelic Exhibition, Chomutov.

2015 Men's Ice Hockey World Championships, Czech Republic — A1539

2015, Apr. 15 Litho. *Perf. 11¾x11¼*
3637 A1539 30k multi 2.50 1.25

Animated Film Characters Bob and Bobek A1540

Bob and Bobek: No. 3638, Playing ice hockey. No. 3639, Rowing raft.

Serpentine Die Cut 11 Syncopated

2015, Apr. 29 **Litho.**

Booklet Stamps

Self-Adhesive

3638 A1540 A multi 1.10 .55
3639 A1540 A multi 1.10 .55
a. Booklet pane of 10, 5 each #3638-3639 11.00

Nos. 3638-3639 each sold for 13k on day of issue.

Moldava Railway, 130th Anniv. A1541

2015, May 6 Engr. *Perf. 11¾x11¼*
3640 A1541 13k black 1.10 .55
a. Booklet pane of 8 + 4 labels 9.00 —
Complete booklet, #3640a 9.00

Europa A1542

2015, May 6 Litho. *Perf. 11¼*
3641 A1542 25k multi 2.10 2.10

Art in Prague Castle Type of 2012

Design: 34k, Head of a Woman, by Hans von Aachen.

2015, May 27 Engr. *Perf. 11¾*
3642 A1457 34k multi 3.00 1.40

Rabí Castle Ruins A1543

2015, May 27 Engr. *Perf. 11¾*
3643 A1543 17k multi 1.50 .70

Jan Hus (c. 1370-1415), Church Reformer — A1544

Perf. 11¼x11¾
2015, June 17 Litho.
3644 A1544 13k multi 1.25 .55

Antique Automobiles Type of 2012

Illustrations by Václav Zapadlik: No. 3645, 1955 Skoda 1201. No. 3646, 1947 Skoda Rapid 1500.

Serpentine Die Cut 11¼ Syncopated
2015, Sept. 2 Litho.
Booklet Stamps
Self-Adhesive

3645 A1467 A multi 1.10 .55
3646 A1467 A multi 1.10 .55
a. Booklet pane of 8, 4 each #3645-3646 9.00

Nos. 3645-3646 each sold for 13k on day of issue.

Sir Nicholas Winton (1909-2015), Rescuer of Jewish Children During World War II — A1545

2015, Sept. 2 Litho. *Perf. 11¾x11¼*
3647 A1545 13k multi 1.25 .55

Postcrossing A1546

Serpentine Die Cut 11¼ Syncopated
2015, Sept. 2 Litho.
Self-Adhesive

3648 A1546 E multi 2.50 1.10

No. 3648 sold for 25k on day of issue.

Miniature Sheet

Owls — A1547

No. 3649: a, 13k, Athene noctua (27x44mm). b, 17k, Aegolius funereus (27x44mm). c, 21k, Nyctea scandiaca (27x44mm). d, 25k, Bubo bubo (44x54mm).

Litho. & Engr.
2015, Sept. 2 *Perf. 11¾*
3649 A1547 Sheet of 4, #a-d, + 4 labels 6.50 3.25

Historic Methods of Transportation — A1548

No. 3650: a, Tatra T3 tram, 1960s. b, Primátor Dittrich paddle steamer.

Perf. 11¾x11¼
2015, Sept. 23 Litho.
3650 A1548 25k Vert. pair, #a-b 4.25 2.10

Flag of Czech Republic A1549

Serpentine Die Cut 11¼ on 1 Side Syncopated
2015, Oct. 14 Litho.
Self-Adhesive

3651 A1549 A multi 1.25 .55

No. 3651 sold for 13k on day of issue.

Organ and Jakub Jan Ryba (1765-1815), Composer — A1550

Photo. & Engr.
2015, Oct. 14 *Perf. 11¼x11¾*
3652 A1550 13k multi 1.25 .55

Wedding of Oldrich and Bozena, Painting From Dalimil's Chronicle — A1551

2015, Oct. 14 Litho. *Perf. 11¾x11¼*
3653 A1551 21k multi 2.00 .85

Souvenir Sheet

World War I, Cent. — A1552

No. 3654: a, Unveiling of statue of Jan Hus burning at the stake. b, Soldier carrying dying comrade.

2015, Oct. 14 Litho. *Perf. 11¾*
3654 A1552 27k Sheet of 2, #a-b, + 3 labels 4.50 2.25

Jan Opletal (1915-39), Medical Student Killed in Anti-Nazi Protests — A1553

Photo. & Engr.
2015, Nov. 11 *Perf. 11¼x11¾*
3655 A1553 13k blue & red 1.25 .55

Art Type of 1967 Inscribed "CESKA REPUBLIKA"

Designs: 27k, The Bride, book illustration by Antonín Strnadel. 30k, Sitting, by Bohumír Matal. 34k, Great Dialogue, sculpture by Karel Nepras, horiz.

Engr., Litho. & Engr. (34k)
2015, Dec. 16 *Perf. 11¾*
3656-3658 A565 Set of 3 8.00 3.75

Postman With Posthorn — A1554

Perf. 11¼x11¾
2015, Dec. 16 Litho.
3659 A1554 Z multi + label 2.60 1.25

No. 3659 was printed in sheets of 9 + 12 labels that could be personalized. On day of issue, No. 3659 had a franking value of 30k.

Karel Svolinsky (1896-1986), Stamp Designer — A1555

2016, Jan. 20 Litho. *Perf. 11¾x11¼*
3660 A1555 13k multi 1.25 .55
a. Booklet pane of 8 + 4 labels 10.00 —
Complete booklet, #3660a 10.00

Tradition of Czech stamp production.

Jerome of Prague (c. 1378-1416), Church Reformer — A1556

2016, Jan. 20 Litho. *Perf. 11¾x11¼*
3661 A1556 17k multi 1.60 .70

Czech Spotted Dogs — A1557

2016, Feb. 3 Litho. *Perf. 12*
3662 A1557 13k multi 1.25 .55

Transportation — A1558

No. 3663: a, Tatra rail coach M290.0. b, Paddle steamer Vysehrad.

Perf. 11¾x11¼
2016, Feb. 17 Litho.
3663 A1558 27k Pair, #a-b 5.00 2.25

Tomás Bat'a (1876-1932), Shoe Manufacturer A1559

Photo. & Engr.
2016, Mar. 16 *Perf. 11¼x11¾*
3664 A1559 13k black & red 1.25 .55

Petrín Observation Tower and Funicular, 125th Anniv. — A1560

Photo. & Engr.

2016, Mar. 16 ***Perf. 11¼x11¾***
3665 A1560 13k redsh brn & cream 1.25 .55
a. Booklet pane of 8 + 4 labels 10.00 —
Complete booklet, #3665a 10.00

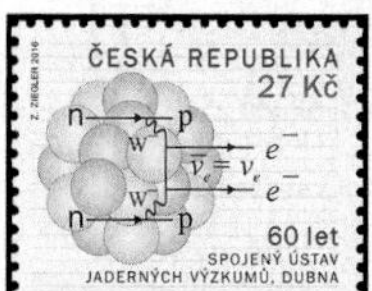
Joint Institute for Nuclear Research, Dubna, Russia, 60th Anniv. A1561

Perf. 11¾x11¼

2016, Mar. 16 **Litho.**
3666 A1561 27k multi 2.50 1.10

Buchlov Castle A1562

2016, Apr. 6 **Engr.** ***Perf. 11½x11¾***
3667 A1562 17k multi 1.50 .75

Czech and Slovak Philatelic Exhibition, Zd'ár nad Sázavou — A1563

2016, Apr. 27 **Litho.** ***Perf. 11¼x11¾***
3668 A1563 13k multi 1.25 .55
a. Booklet pane of 8 + 4 labels 10.00 —
Complete booklet, #3668a 10.00

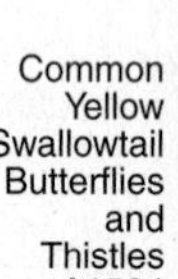

Common Yellow Swallowtail Butterflies and Thistles A1564

2016, Apr. 27 **Litho.** ***Perf. 12***
3669 A1564 16k multi 1.50 .70

Europa A1565

2016, May 4 **Litho.** ***Perf. 11¾x11¼***
3670 A1565 27k multi 2.50 1.10

Think Green Issue.
Printed in sheets of 8. Value, $20.

Souvenir Sheet

Holy Roman Emperor Charles IV (1316-78) — A1566

Litho. & Engr.

2016, May 4 ***Perf. 11¾***
3671 A1566 54k multi + 2 labels *8.00 5.00*

No. 3671 was issued on May 4 with the incorrectly-spelled Latin inscription "Karolus Quatrus" in the sheet margin. Value, $100. The sheet was withdrawn from sale on May 5, and replaced soon thereafter with sheets bearing the correct inscription "Karolus Quartus."

Animated Cartoon Character Amálka the Fairy — A1567

Serpentine Die Cut 11¼ Syncopated

2016, May 18 **Litho.**

Booklet Stamp Self-Adhesive

3672 A1567 A multi 1.50 .70
a. Booklet pane of 10 15.00

No. 3672 sold for 16k on day of issue.

Premiere of *The Bartered Bride*, by Bedrich Smetana, 150th Anniv. — A1567a

2016, May 18 **Litho.** ***Perf. 11¼x11¾***
3673 A1567a 16k multi 1.50 .70

Art in Prague Castle Type of 2012

Design: 38k, Prague Altarpiece detail depicting St. Barbara, by Lucas Cranach the Elder.

2016, May 18 **Engr.** ***Perf. 11¾***
3674 A1457 38k multi 3.25 1.60

Flower Arrangement A1568

2016, June 8 **Litho.** ***Perf. 11¾x11¼***
3675 A1568 A multi + label 1.40 .70

No. 3675 was printed in sheets of 9 + 12 labels that could be personalized. On day of issue, No. 3675 had a franking value of 16k.

International Folklore Festival, Stráznice — A1569

Photo. & Engr.

2016, June 22 ***Perf. 11¼x11¾***
3676 A1569 20k multi 1.75 .85

Jan Jessenius (1566-1621), Physician and Professor of Anatomy — A1570

Photo. & Engr.

2016, June 22 ***Perf. 11¼x11¾***
3677 A1570 27k multi + label 2.50 1.10

See Hungary No. 4393, Poland No. 4232, Slovakia No. 743.

2016 Summer Olympics, Rio de Janeiro — A1571

Perf. 11¾x11¼

2016, June 22 **Litho.**
3678 A1571 32k multi 3.00 1.40

2016 Summer Paralympics, Rio de Janeiro — A1572

Perf. 11¾x11¼

2016, June 22 **Litho.**
3679 A1572 16k multi 1.50 .70

Art Type of 1967 Inscribed "CESKA REPUBLIKA"

Design: Young Woman on a Balcony, by Gerrit Dou.

2016, Sept. 7 **Engr.** ***Perf. 11¾***
3680 A565 27k multi 2.50 1.10

See Liechtenstein No. 1691.

Tree Frog — A1573

2016, Sept. 7 **Litho.** ***Perf. 11¾x11¼***
3681 A1573 A multi 1.50 .70

No. 3681 sold for 16k on day of issue.

Dr. Antonín Holy (1936-2012), Developer of Antiretroviral Drugs — A1574

2016, Sept. 7 **Litho.** ***Perf. 11¼x11¾***
3682 A1574 20k multi 2.00 .85

UNESCO World Heritage Sites in Czech Republic — A1575

Designs: 16k, Lednice-Valtice Cultural Landscape. 27k, Historic Center of Prague.

2016, Sept. 7 **Litho.** ***Perf. 11¼x11¾***
3683-3684 A1575 Set of 2 4.00 1.90

See United Nations Nos. 1142, 1144a, 1144e; Offices in Geneva Nos. 626, 627a, 627e; Offices in Vienna Nos. 594a, 594e.

Miniature Sheet

Animals in Czech Republic Zoos — A1576

No. 3685: a, 16k, Panthera uncia, Jihlava Zoo. b, 20k, Oryx gazella gazella, Panthera leo leo, Olomouc Zoo. c, 24k, Diceros bicornis, Lycaon pictus, Dvur Králové Zoo. d, 27k, Equus przewalskii, Prague Zoo.

Litho. & Engr.

2016, Sept. 7 *Perf. 11¾*

3685 A1576 Sheet of 4, #a-d, + 3 labels 8.00 3.75

Historic Methods of Transportation — A1577

No. 3686: a, Tatra 87 automobile. b, Aero Ab-11 biplane.

Perf. 11¾x11¼

2016, Sept. 21 **Litho.**

3686 A1577 16k Horiz. pair, #a-b 3.00 1.40

Zelezné Hory Protected Landscape Area, 25th Anniv. — A1578

2016, Oct. 12 Litho. *Perf. 11¾x11¼*

3687 A1578 16k multi 1.50 .70

Bee-eaters — A1579

2016, Oct. 12 Litho. *Perf. 11¾x11¼*

3688 A1579 20k multi 2,00 .85

Souvenir Sheet

Fight for Czech Statehood — A1580

No. 3689: a, St. Wenceslas, King Ottokar II of Bohemia, Holy Roman Emperor Charles IV, flags, soldiers. b, Grieving widow and children, Austrian imperial eagle.

2016, Oct. 12 Litho. *Perf. 11¾*

3689 A1580 27k Sheet of 2, #a-b, + 3 labels 5.00 2.25

Art Type of 1967 Inscribed "CESKA REPUBLIKA"

Designs: 27k, Two Women, by Jaroslav Král, horiz. 30k, Girl with Absinthe, sculpture by Bedrich Stefan. 38k, Clown with Monkey, by Frantisek Tichy.

2016, Nov. 9 Litho. *Perf. 11¾*

3690-3692 A565 Set of 3 8.50 3.75

United Nations Educational, Scientific and Cultural Organization, 70th Anniv. — A1581

2016, Nov. 9 Litho. *Perf. 12*

3693 A1581 32k multi 2.90 1.40

Oldrich Posmurny (1942-2010), Stamp Designer — A1582

Photo. & Engr.

2017, Jan. 20 *Perf. 11¼x11¾*

3694 A1582 16k multi 1.50 .70

a. Booklet pane of 8 + 4 labels 12.00 —

Complete booklet, #3694a 12.00

Tradition of Czech stamp production.

Czech Crown Jewels — A1583

Serpentine Die Cut 11½ Syncopated

2017, Jan. 20 **Litho.**

Booklet Stamp Self-Adhesive

3695 A1583 E multi 2.90 1.40

a. Booklet pane of 8 24.00

No. 3695 sold for 32k on day of issue.

Historic Methods of Transportation — A1584

Designs: No. 3696a, Skoda 606DNd postal bus. No. 3696b, Fk-5-1401 railroad mail car. No. 3697, Paddle steamer "Prague." 32k, Aero A-14 biplane.

2017 Litho. *Perf. 11¾x11¼*

3696 A1584 16k Horiz. pair, #a-b 3.00 1.25

3697 A1584 16k multi 1.50 .65

3698 A1584 32k multi 3.00 1.40

Nos. 3696-3698 (3) 7.50 3.30

Issued: No. 3696, 2/15; No. 3697, 3/8; No. 3698, 1/20.

Straka Academy, 120th Anniv. — A1585

2017, Mar. 8 Litho. *Perf. 11¾x11¼*

3699 A1585 24k multi 2.25 .95

Porta Bohemica River Valley — A1586

2017, Apr. 5 Engr. *Perf. 11¾*

3700 A1586 20k multi 1.75 .85

Prague Airport, 80th Anniv. A1587

Photo. & Engr.

2017, Apr. 5 *Perf. 11¾x11¼*

3701 A1587 32k multi 2.60 1.40

Vera Cáslavská (1942-2016), Gymnast and President of Czech Olympic Committee A1588

2017, May 3 Litho. *Perf. 11¼x11¾*

3702 A1588 16k multi 1.40 .70

Frydlant Castle A1589

Photo. & Engr.

2017, May 3 *Perf. 11¼*

3703 A1589 32k multi 2.75 1.40

Europa.

Holy Roman Empress Maria Theresa (1717-80) — A1590

Photo. & Engr.

2017, May 3 *Perf. 11¾*

3704 A1590 32k multi 2.75 1.40

Art in Prague Castle Type of 2012

No. 3705 — St. Catherine with Angel, by Paolo Veronese: a, Black image. b, Multicolored image.

2017, May 17 Engr. *Perf. 11¾*

3705 A1457 32k Horiz. pair, #a-b 5.50 2.75

Printed in sheets containing two each of Nos. 3705a-3705b + central label.

Souvenir Sheet

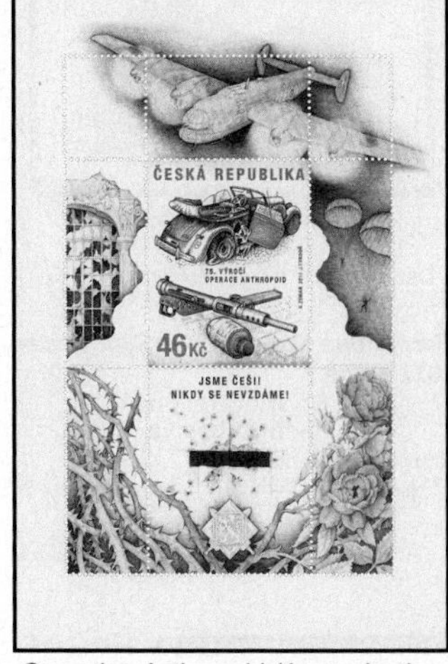

Operation Anthropoid (Assassination of Reinhard Heydrich), 75th Anniv. — A1591

Litho. & Engr.

2017, May 17 *Perf. 11¾*

3706 A1591 46k multi + 7 labels 4.00 2.00

Josef Kainar (1917-71), Writer — A1592

Photo. & Engr.

2017, June 7 *Perf. 11¼x11¾*

3707 A1592 16k multi 1.40 .70

Heliodor Píka (1897-1949), General Executed by Communists A1593

Photo. & Engr.

2017, June 7 *Perf. 11¼x11¾*

3708 A1593 37k multi 3.25 1.60

Joze Plecnik (1872-1957), Architect — A1594

Perf. 11½x11¾

2017, June 7 **Litho. & Engr.**

3709 A1594 32k multi 2.75 1.40

No. 3709 was printed in sheets of 2 + central label.

Locomotives — A1595

Designs: No. 3710, Steam locomotive No. 7. No. 3711, Cog locomotive "The Austrian."

Serpentine Die Cut 11½ Syncopated

2017, June 7 Litho.

Booklet Stamps Self-Adhesive

3710 A1595 A multi		1.40	.70
3711 A1595 A multi		1.40	.70
a. Booklet pane of 8, 4 each #3710-3711		11.50	

On day of issue, Nos. 3710-3711 each sold for 16k.

Prague Pneumatic Mail System A1596

2017, June 21 Litho. *Perf. 11¼*

3712 A1596 A multi	1.40	.70

No. 3712 sold for 16k on day of issue.

Church of the Assumption of Our Lady, Most, 500th Anniv. — A1597

Photo. & Engr.

2017, June 21 *Perf. 11¼x11¾*

3713 A1597 16k multi	1.40	.70

Moravian Museum, Brno, 200th Anniv. A1598

Photo. & Engr.

2017, June 21 *Perf. 11¾x11¼*

3714 A1598 20k multi	1.75	.85

Gas Street Lighting in Prague, 170th Anniv. — A1599

Photo. & Engr.

2017, Sept. 6 *Perf. 11¼x11¾*

3715 A1599 16k multi	1.50	.75
a. Booklet pane of 8 + 4 labels	12.00	—
Complete booklet, #3715a	12.00	

Josef Balabán (1894-1941), Václav Morávek (1904-42), and Josef Masín (1896-1942), Members of "Three Kings" Anti-Nazi Resistance Group — A1600

2017, Sept. 6 Litho. *Perf. 11¾x11¼*

3716 A1600 16k multi	1.50	.75

Mauritius No. 2 — A1601

2017, Sept. 6 Litho. *Perf. 12*

3717 A1601 A multi	1.50	.75

No. 3717 sold for 16k on day of issue.

Worker for Partner Post Office — A1602

2017, Sept. 6 Litho. *Perf. 11¾x11¼*

3718 A1602 A multi	1.50	.75
Complete booklet, 5 #3718	7.50	

No. 3718 sold for 16k on day of issue.

Miniature Sheet

Animals in Czech Republic Zoos — A1603

No. 3719: a, 16k, Bison bonasus, Chomutov Zoo. b, 20k, Pan troglodytes, Panthera leo krugeri, Hodonín Zoo. c, 24k, Ursus maritimus, Brno Zoo. d, 30k, Rhinoceros unicornis, Varanus macraei, Plzen Zoo.

Litho. & Engr.

2017, Sept. 6 *Perf. 11¾*

3719 A1603 Sheet of 4, #a-d, + 4 labels	8.25	4.25

Nature Protection.

Václav Hollar Association of Czech Graphic Artists, Cent. — A1604

Photo. & Engr.

2017, Sept. 20 *Perf. 11¼x11¾*

3720 A1604 20k multi	1.90	.95

Imperial Austrian Letter Boxes, 200th Anniv. — A1605

Photo. & Engr.

2017, Oct. 4 *Perf. 11¼x11¾*

3721 A1605 16k multi	1.50	.75
a. Booklet pane of 8 + 4 labels	12.00	—
Complete booklet, #3721a	12.00	

Family on Bicycle A1606

Photo. & Engr.

2017, Oct. 4 *Perf. 11½x11¼*

3722 A1606 16k blk & red	1.50	.75

Self-Sculpture of Fictional Character Jára Cimrman, 50th Anniv. — A1607

Serpentine Die Cut 11¼ Syncopated

2017, Oct. 4 Litho.

Booklet Stamp Self-Adhesive

3723 A1607 A multi	1.50	.75
a. Booklet pane of 8	12.00	

Jára Cimrman, fictional character created for 1967 Czech radio program, selected as "Greatest Czech" in 2005. No. 3723 sold for 16k on day of issue.

Souvenir Sheet

Fight for Czech Statehood — A1608

No. 3724: a, Soldiers, flag, independence leaders Milan R. Stefánik (1880-1919), Tomás G. Masaryk (1850-1937), and Jan Syrovy (1880-1970). b, Writers Alois Jirásek (1851-1930), and Jaroslav Kvapil (1868-1950) and Manifesto of Czech Writers.

Litho., Sheet Margin Litho. With Foil Application

2017, Oct. 4 *Perf. 11¾*

3724 A1608 30k Sheet of 2, #a-b, + 3 labels	5.50	2.75

Tatra Automobile at Railroad Crossing A1609

2017, Oct. 18 Litho. *Perf. 11¾x11½*

3725 A1609 A multi + label	1.50	.75

No. 3725 was printed in sheets of 9 + 12 labels that could be personalized. On day of issue No. 3725 had a franking value of 16k.

Art Type of 1967 Inscribed "CESKA REPUBLIKA"

Designs: 32k, Cuddled, photograph by Taras Kuscynskyj. 38k, Tempter, painting by Norbert Grund.

Litho. (32k), Engr. (38k)

2017, Nov. 8 *Perf. 11¾*

3726-3727 A565 Set of 2	6.50	3.25

Czech Astronomical Society, Cent. — A1610

2017, Nov. 8 Litho. *Perf. 11¼x11¾*

3728 A1610 16k multi	1.50	.75

Art Type of 1967 Inscribed "CESKA REPUBLIKA"

Design: Winner, by Jaroslava Pesicová.

2017, Dec. 13 Engr. *Perf. 11¾*

3729 A565 30k multi	3.00	1.50

Souvenir Sheet

Postal Officials — A1611

No. 3730: a, 32k, Jirí Stríbny (1880-1955), first Czechoslovakian minister of Posts and Telegraphs. b, 37k, Maxmilián Fatka (1868-1962), first director general of Czechoslovak Post.

Litho. & Engr.

2017, Dec. 13 *Perf. 11¾*

3730 A1611 Sheet of 2, #a-b	6.50	3.25

Czech Republic, 25th Anniv. — A1612

2018, Jan. 3 Litho. *Perf. 12*

3731 A1612 24k multi 2.40 1.25

No. 3731 was printed in sheets of 2 + central label.

2018 Winter Paralympics, PyeongChang, South Korea — A1613

2018 Winter Olympics, PyeongChang, South Korea — A1614

2018, Jan. 20 Litho. *Perf. 11¾x11¼*

3732 A1613 16k multi 1.60 .80

Perf. 11¼x11¾

3733 A1614 37k multi 3.75 1.90

Jirí Bouda (1934-2015), Stamp Designer — A1615

Perf. 11¾x11¼

2018, Jan. 20 Litho. & Engr.

3734 A1615 A multi 1.90 .95

a. Booklet pane of 8 + 4 labels 15.50 —

Complete booklet, #3734a 15.50

Tradition of Czech stamp production. No. 3734 sold for 19k on day of issue.

Prague Castle A1616

Perf. 11¾x11¼

2018, Feb. 21 Litho.

3735 A1616 A red & indigo + label 1.90 .95

No. 3735 was printed in sheets of 9 + 12 labels that could be personalized. On day of issue, No. 3735 had a franking value of 19k.

Person Making Willow Whip — A1617

Perf. 11¾x11¼

2018, Feb. 21 Litho.

3736 A1617 A multi 1.90 .95

Easter. On day of issue, No. 3736 sold for 19k.

Prague Municipal Library — A1618

Perf. 11¼x11¾

2018, Feb. 21 Litho.

3737 A1618 A multi 1.90 .95

On day of issue, No. 3737 sold for 19k.

Silesian Eagle in National Coat of Arms — A1619

Moravian Eagle in National Coat of Arms — A1620

Presidential Standard — A1621

National Seal — A1622

Bohemian Lion in National Coat of Arms — A1623

National Flag — A1624

National Colors — A1625

National Anthem — A1626

Serpentine Die Cut 11½ Syncopated

2018, Feb. 21 Litho.

Booklet Stamps
Self-Adhesive

3738 A1619 A multi 1.90 .95
3739 A1620 A multi 1.90 .95
3740 A1621 A multi 1.90 .95
3741 A1622 A multi 1.90 .95
3742 A1623 A multi 1.90 .95
3743 A1624 A multi 1.90 .95
3744 A1625 A multi 1.90 .95
3745 A1626 A multi 1.90 .95
a. Booklet pane of 8, #3738-3745 15.50
Nos. 3738-3745 (8) 15.20 7.60

On day of issue, Nos. 3738-3745 each sold for 19k.

Dr. Frantisek Hamza (1868-1930), and Hamza Hospital — A1627

Photo. & Engr.

2018, Feb. 21 *Perf. 11¼x11¾*

3746 A1627 20k blue & claret 1.90 .95

Paddle Steamer Vltava A1628

Perf. 11¾x11¼

2018, Mar. 14 Litho.

3747 A1628 A multi 1.90 .95

On day of issue, No. 3747 sold for 19k.

Dlouhé Stráne Hydroelectric Power Plant — A1629

Perf. 11¾x11¼

2018, Mar. 14 Litho.

3748 A1629 23k multi 2.25 1.10

Carriage of Emperor Ferdinand I of Austria A1630

Carriage of Princess Pauline Clémentine von Metternich-Sándor — A1631

Postal Coach, Zamberk A1632

Carriage of Johann Adolf II, Prince of Schwarzenberg — A1633

Passenger Coach A1634

Serpentine Die Cut Syncopated

2018, Mar. 14 Litho.

Self-Adhesive

3749 Strip of 5 17.50 8.75
a. A1630 E multi 3.50 1.75
b. A1631 E multi 3.50 1.75
c. A1632 E multi 3.50 1.75
d. A1633 E multi 3.50 1.75
e. A1634 E multi 3.50 1.75

Coaches and carriages from Postal Museum. Praga 2018 International Philatelic Exhibition. Nos. 3749a-3749e each sold for 35k on day of issue.

Eduard Storch (1878-1959), Archaeologist and Writer — A1635

2018, Apr. 4 Litho. *Perf. 11¾x11¼*

3750 A1635 19k multi 1.75 .90

Czech National Library Architectural Design of Jan Kaplicky (1937-2009) — A1636

Photo. & Engr.

2018, Apr. 4 *Perf. 11¼x11¾*
3751 A1636 E multi 3.25 1.60

No. 3751 sold for 35k on day of issue.

Pres. Zeman Type of 2013

Photo. & Engr.

2018, Apr. 18 *Perf. 11¾x11¼*
3752 A1484 A red & dk blue 1.75 .90

No. 3752 sold for 19k on day of issue.

Stadlec Bridge and Podolsko Bridge A1637

2018, May 2 Litho. *Perf. 11*
3753 A1637 E gold & multi 3.25 1.60

Europa. No. 3751 sold for 35k on day of issue.

Czech Jazz Music — A1638

2018, May 2 Litho. *Perf. 11¼x11¾*
3754 A1638 Z multi 3.75 1.90

No. 3754 sold for 41k on day of issue.

Art in Prague Castle Type of 2012

Design: 32k, Sacrifice at the Temple, by Francesco da Ponte, the Younger.

2018, May 23 Engr. *Perf. 11¾*
3755 A1457 32k multi 3.00 1.50

Flowers Type of 2002

Design: 1k, Lily of the valley (konvalinka).

Perf. 11¾x11¼

2018, June 20 Litho.
3756 A1215 1k multi .25 .25

Bentwood Chairs by Factory Established by Michael Thonet (1796-1871) A1639

Perf. 11¼x11¾

2018, June 20 Litho.
3757 A1639 19k multi 1.75 .85
a. Booklet pane of 8 + 4 labels 14.00 —
Complete booklet, #3757a 14.00

Mushrooms A1640

Designs: No. 3758, Leccinum rufescens. No. 3759, Amanita rubescens.

Serpentine Die Cut 11¼ Syncopated

2018, June 20 Litho.

Booklet Stamps
Self-Adhesive

3758 A1640 A multi 1.75 .85
3759 A1640 A multi 1.75 .85
a. Booklet pane of 10, 5 each #3758-3759 17.50

Souvenir Sheet

Czechoslovakian Postage Stamps, Cent. — A1641

No. 3760: a, 27k, Czechoslovakia Nos. B125, P3, 244, P27, 575, 152, 329, 1133. b, 44k, Czech Republic Nos. 3040b, 3210b, 3467, 3567, 3615, 3692.

2018, June 20 Litho. *Perf. 11¾*
3760 A1641 Sheet of 2, #a-b, + 3 labels 6.50 3.25

Souvenir Sheet

Czech Postal Museum, Cent. — A1642

Directors: a, 19k, Václav Dragoun (1865-1950). b, 23k, Jirí Karásek (1871-1951). c, 27k, Pavel Ctvrtnik (1947-2008).

Litho. & Engr., Litho. Sheet Margin

2018, Aug. 8 *Perf. 11¾x11½*
3761 A1642 Sheet of 3, #a-c 6.25 3.25

Praga 2018 International Philatelic Exhibition, Prague.

Souvenir Sheet

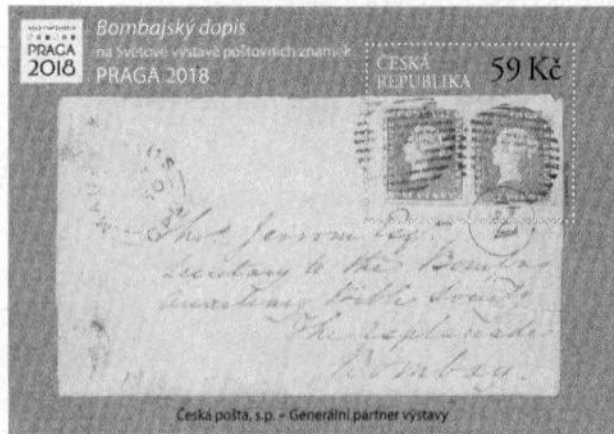

1850 Cover to Bombay, India From Port Louis, Mauritius — A1643

2018, Aug. 8 Litho. *Perf. 11¾*
3762 A1643 59k multi 5.50 2.75

Sale of Bombay Cover to Czech collector. Praga 2018 International Philatelic Exhibition, Prague.

Locomotives — A1644

Designs: No. 3763, 1939 M260001 locomotive. No. 3764, Steam locomotive 365024, 1923.

Serpentine Die Cut 11½ Syncopated

2018, Sept. 5 Litho.

Booklet Stamps
Self-Adhesive

3763 A1644 A multi 1.75 .85
3764 A1644 A multi 1.75 .85
a. Booklet pane of 8, 4 each #3763-3764 14.00

On day of issue, Nos. 3763-3764 each sold for 19k.

Miniature Sheet

Animals in Czech Republic Zoos — A1645

No. 3765: a, 19k, Ursus arctos horribilis, Decín Zoo. b, 23k, Pongo pygmaeus, Ustí nad Labem Zoo. c, 27k, Loxodonta africana, Zlín Zoo. d, 33k, Cercopithecus diana, Hippopotamus amphibius, Ostrava Zoo.

Litho. & Engr.

2018, Sept. 5 *Perf. 11¾*
3765 A1645 Sheet of 4, #a-d, + 4 labels 9.25 4.75

National Agricultural Museum, Prague, Cent. — A1646

Photo. & Engr.

2018, Sept. 19 *Perf. 11¾x11¼*
3766 A1646 27k multi 2.50 1.25

Souvenir Sheet

Fight for Czech Statehood — A1647

No. 3767 — Flags and: a, Monument to St. Wenceslas, Prague. b, Tomás G. Masaryk (1850-1937), first president of Czechoslovakia.

Litho., Sheet Margin Litho. With Foil Application

2018, Oct. 10 *Perf. 11¾*
3767 A1647 33k Sheet of 2, #a-b, + 3 labels 6.00 3.00

National Museum, Prague, 200th Anniv. — A1648

2018, Oct. 10 Litho. *Perf. 11¼x11¾*
3768 A1648 19k multi 1.75 .85

Goose and Wine Bottle — A1649

2018, Oct. 24 Litho. *Perf. 11¼x11¾*
3769 A1649 A multi 1.75 .85
a. Booklet pane of 8 + 4 labels 14.00 —
Complete booklet, #3769a 14.00
b. Tete-beche pair 3.50 3.50

St. Martin's Day. No. 3769 sold for 19k on day of issue. No. 3769b is found in No. 3769a.

Miroslav Hornícek (1918-2003), Actor — A1650

Photo. & Engr.

2018, Oct. 24 *Perf. 11¼x11¾*
3770 A1650 19k multi 1.75 .85

Frantisek Ladislav Rieger (1818-1903), Politician — A1651

Photo. & Engr.

2018, Oct. 24 ***Perf. 11¼x11¾***
3771 A1651 27k multi 2.40 1.25

Miniature Sheet

Czech Orders and Medals, Cent. — A1652

No. 3772: a, 19k, Medal of Merit. b, 23k, Order of Thomas Garrigue Masaryk. c, 27k, Order of the White Lion. d, 33k, Medal for Heroism.

2018, Oct. 24 **Litho.** ***Perf. 12***
3772 A1652 Sheet of 4, #a-d 9.00 4.50

Christmas A1653

No. 3773: a, Christmas ornament and apple. b, Christmas ornament and cookie.

2018, Oct. 24 **Litho.** ***Perf. 11¾x11¼***
3773 A1653 A Pair, #a-b 3.50 1.75

On day of issue, Nos. 3773a-3773b each sold for 19k.

Art Type of 1967 Inscribed "CESKA REPUBLIKA"

Designs: 27k, The Great Angel's Others I, II, sculpture by Stanislav Libensky. 33k, Birds of Jevis, painting by Vladimir Komárek. 41k, Diego de Guzmán, engraving by Paulus Pontius.

Litho. (27k), Litho. & Engr. (33k), Engr. (41k)

2018, Nov. 14 ***Perf. 11¾***
3774-3776 A565 Set of 3 9.00 4.50

Thomas Garrigue Masaryk (1850-1937), First President of Czechoslovakia A1654

Photo. & Engr.

2018, Nov. 14 ***Perf. 11¼x11¾***
3777 A1654 A multi 1.75 .85
a. Souvenir sheet of 1 1.75 .85

No. 3777 sold for 19k on day of issue.

Prague Castle Guard, Cent. — A1655

2018, Dec. 5 **Litho.** ***Perf. 11¼x11¾***
3778 A1655 A multi 1.75 .85
a. Booklet pane of 8 + 4 labels 14.00 —
Complete booklet, #3778a 14.00

No. 3778 sold for 19k on day of issue.

Petr Eben (1929-2007), Composer — A1656

2019, Jan. 20 **Litho.** ***Perf. 11¼x11¾***
3779 A1656 19k multi 1.75 .85

Masaryk University, Brno, Cent. — A1657

2019, Jan. 20 **Litho.** ***Perf. 11¼x11¾***
3780 A1657 A multi 1.75 .85

No. 3780 sold for 19k on day of issue.

Adolf Born (1930-2016), Illustrator — A1658

2019, Jan. 20 **Litho.** ***Perf. 11¾x11¼***
3781 A1658 A multi 1.75 .85
a. Booklet pane of 8 + 4 labels 14.00 —
Complete booklet, #3781a 14.00

Tradition of Czech stamp production. No. 3781 sold for 19k on day of issue.

Rudolf Tomás Jedlicka (1869-1926), Surgeon and Radiologist — A1659

Perf. 11¾x11¼

2019, Feb. 14 **Litho.**
3782 A1659 19k multi 1.75 .85

Souvenir Sheet

Jirí Hanzelka (1920-2003) and Miroslav Zikmund, Travel Writers and Film Makers — A1660

No. 3783: a, Zikmund holding camera. b, Hanzelka.

Perf. 11¾x11½

2019, Feb. 14 **Litho. & Engr.**
3783 A1660 45k Sheet of 2, #a-b + 2 labels 8.00 4.00

100th birthday of Zikmund.

Process of Making Sugar Cubes by Jakub Krystof Rad, 175th Anniv. — A1661

2019, Mar. 6 **Litho.** ***Perf. 11¼x11¾***
3784 A1661 19k multi 1.75 .85

Les Království Dam, Cent. — A1662

2019, Mar. 6 **Litho.** ***Perf. 11¾x11¼***
3785 A1662 A multi 1.75 .85
a. Booklet pane of 8 + 4 labels 14.00 —
Complete booklet, #3785a 14.00

No. 3785 sold for 19k on day of issue.

Maltese Cross and Church of Our Lady Under the Chain, Prague, Headquarters of Grand Priory of Bohemia of the Sovereign Military Order of Malta — A1663

2019, Mar. 6 **Litho.** ***Perf. 11¼x11¾***
3786 A1663 45k multi 4.00 2.00

Alois Rasin (1867-1923), Minister of Finance — A1664

2019, Apr. 3 **Litho.** ***Perf. 11¾x11¼***
3787 A1664 23k multi 2.00 1.00

Czechoslovakian currency, cent.

Alcedo Atthis A1665

2019, Apr. 24 **Litho.** ***Perf. 11***
3788 A1665 E multi 3.50 1.75

Europa. No. 3788 sold for 39k on day of issue.

Flowers Type of 2002

Design: E, Dandelion (pampeliska).

2019, May 22 **Litho.** ***Perf. 11¾x11¼***
3789 A1215 E multi 3.50 1.75

No. 3789 sold for 39k on day of issue.

Art in Prague Castle Type of 2012

No. 3790 — Paintings by Adolf Absolon: a, Prague Castle in Summer. b, Prague Castle in Winter.

Litho. & Engr.

2019, May 22 ***Perf. 11¾***
3790 A1457 Horiz. pair 7.00 3.50
a.-b. E Either single 3.50 1.75

Nos. 3790a-3790b each sold for 39k on day of issue.

Gelasius Dobner (1719-90), Historian — A1666

2019, May 22 **Litho.** ***Perf. 11¾x11¼***
3791 A1666 27k multi 2.40 1.25

A1667

Ctylistek Comic Strip, 50th Anniv. A1668

Serpentine Die Cut 11 Syncopated

2019, May 22 **Litho.**

Booklet Stamps Self-Adhesive

3792 A1667 A blue & multi 1.75 .85
3793 A1668 A red & multi 1.75 .85
a. Booklet pane of 10, 5 each #3792-3793 17.50

Nos. 3792-3793 each sold for 19k on day of issue.

Art Type of 1967 Inscribed "CESKA REPUBLIKA"

Designs: 27k, Line No. 56, by Zdenek Sykora (1920-2011). 45k, Poplars, by Václav Radimsky (1867-1946).

Litho. (27k), Engr. (45k)

2019, June 12 ***Perf. 11¾***
3794-3795 A565 Set of 2 6.50 3.25

First Horse-drawn Tram in Brno, 150th Anniv. — A1669

Perf. 11¾x11¼

2019, June 26 **Litho.**
3796 A1669 A multi 1.75 .85

No. 3796 sold for 19k on day of issue.

Jan Palach (1948-1969) and Jan Zajic (1950-69), Student Protestors Who Set Themselves Afire — A1670

Perf. 11¾x11¼

2019, June 26 **Litho.**
3797 A1670 A multi 1.75 .85

No. 3797 sold for 19k on day of issue.

Mohandas K. Gandhi (1869-1948), Indian Nationalist Leader — A1671

Perf. 11¼x11¾

2019, June 26 **Litho.**
3798 A1671 Z multi 4.00 2.00

No. 3798 sold for 45k on day of issue.

Electra 10A in Flight — A1672

Electra 10A at Airport — A1673

Serpentine Die Cut 11½ Syncopated

2019, Sept. 4 **Litho.**

Booklet Stamps
Self-Adhesive

3799 A1672 E multi 3.50 1.75
3800 A1673 E multi 3.50 1.75
a. Booklet pane of 8, 4 each #3799-3800 28.00

Nos. 3799 and 3800 each sold for 39k on day of issue.

Clock and Horseman Lancing Dragon — A1674

2019, Sept. 4 **Litho.** ***Perf. 11¼x11¾***
3801 A1674 A multi + label 1.60 .80

No. 3801 was printed in sheets of 9 + 12 labels that could be personalized. On day of issue, No. 3801 had a franking value of 19k.

Miniature Sheet

Animals in Czech Republic Zoos — A1675

No. 3802: a, 19k, Crocodylus mindorensis, Protivín Zoo (45x27mm). b, 23k, Ovis aries strepsiceros, Vyskov Zoopark (45x27mm). c, 27k, Platalea leucordia, Lutra lutra, Hluboká Zoo (45x54mm). e, 33k, Budorcas taxicolor bedfordi, Liberec Zoo (45x54mm).

Litho. & Engr.

2019, Sept. 4 ***Perf. 11¾***
3802 A1675 Sheet of 4, #a-d, + 4 labels 8.75 4.50

Automobile Designed by Václav Král (1936-2005) — A1676

2019, Oct. 2 **Litho.** ***Perf. 11¾x11¼***
3803 A1676 A multi 1.75 .85
a. Booklet pane of 8 + 4 labels 14.00 —
Complete booklet, #3803a 14.00

No. 3803 sold for 19k on day of issue.

Souvenir Sheet

Service of Czechoslovakians in Royal Air Force in World War II — A1677

No. 3804: a, Flag of Czechoslovakia, Royal Air Force emblem and emblems of four Czechoslovak squadrons. b, Frantisek Perina (1911-2006), pilot.

2019, Oct. 2 **Litho.** ***Perf. 11¾***
3804 A1677 E Sheet of 2, #a-b 7.00 3.50

Nos. 3804a-3804b each sold for 39k on day of issue.

Ivan Blatny (1919-90), Poet — A1680

Perf. 11¼x11¾

2019, Nov. 13 **Litho.**
3807 A1680 A multi 1.75 .85

No. 3807 sold for 19k on day of issue.

Czechoslovakian Red Cross, Cent. — A1681

Perf. 11¾x11¼

2019, Nov. 13 **Litho.**
3808 A1681 19k multi 1.75 .85

Souvenir Sheet

Velvet Revolution, 30th Anniv. — A1682

Litho. & Engr.

2019, Nov. 13 ***Perf. 11¾***
3809 A1682 44k multi 4.00 2.00

Art Type of 1967 Inscribed "CESKA REPUBLIKA"

Designs: 39k, Touch of Fate II, sculpture by Ladislav Saloun. 45k, Flora, painting by Ota Janecek, horiz.

Litho. (39k), Litho. & Engr. (45k)

2019 ***Perf. 11¾***
3810-3811 A565 Set of 2 7.25 7.25

Issued: 39k, 11/27; 45k, 11/13.

SEMI-POSTAL STAMPS

Nos. B1-B123 were sold at 1½ times face value at the Philatelists' Window of the Prague P.O. for charity benefit. They were available for ordinary postage.

Almost all stamps between Nos. B1-B123 are known with misplaced or inverted overprints and/or in pairs with one stamp missing the overprint.

The overprints of Nos. B1-B123 have been well forged.

Austrian Stamps of 1916-18 Overprinted in Black or Blue — a

Two sizes of type A40:
Type I: 25x30mm.
Type II: 26x29mm.

1919 ***Perf. 12½***

B1	A37	3h brt violet	.25	*.25*
B2	A37	5h lt green	.25	*.25*
B3	A37	6h dp orange (Bl)	.50	*.70*
B4	A37	6h dp orange (Bk)	*3,250.*	*2,500.*
B5	A37	10h magenta	1.00	*.85*
B6	A37	12h lt blue	.70	.70
B7	A42	15h dull red	.35	*.35*
B8	A42	20h dark green	.35	*.35*
a.		20h green	55.00	40.00
B9	A42	25h blue	.30	.25
B10	A42	30h dull violet	.30	.25
B11	A39	40h olive grn	.35	.35
B12	A39	50h dk green	.35	.35
B13	A39	60h dp blue	.35	.35
B14	A39	80h orange brn	.35	.35
B15	A39	90h red violet	.70	.70
B16	A39	1k car, *yel* (Bl)	.50	.50
B17	A39	1k car, *yel* (Bk)	52.50	52.50
B18	A40	2k light blue (I)	3.00	3.00
a.		2k dark blue (II)	*5,000.*	*3,500.*
B19	A40	3k car rose (I)	32.50	32.50
a.		3k claret (I)	3,750.	1,500.
B20	A40	4k yellow grn (I)	27.50	21.00
a.		4k deep green (I)	55.00	45.00
B21	A40	10k violet	300.00	160.00
a.		10k deep violet	375.00	275.00
b.		10k black violet	450.00	300.00

The used value of No. B18a is for a stamp that has only a Czechoslovakian cancellation. Some examples of Austria No. 160, which were officially overprinted with type "a" and sold by the post office, had previously been used and lightly canceled with Austrian cancellations. These canceled-before-overprinting stamps, which were postally valid, sell for about one-fourth as much.

Granite Paper

B22 A40 2k light blue 3.50 2.50
B23 A40 3k carmine rose 9.00 7.00

The 4k and 10k on granite paper with this overprint were not regularly issued.

Excellent counterfeits of Nos. B1-B23 exist.

Austrian Newspaper Stamps Overprinted — b

Imperf

On Stamp of 1908

B26 N8 10h carmine *3,500.* 2,000.

On Stamps of 1916

B27 N9 2h brown .25 .25
B28 N9 4h green .35 .35
B29 N9 6h deep blue .35 .35
B30 N9 10h orange 4.25 4.25
B31 N9 30h claret 1.40 1.40
Nos. B27-B31 (5) 6.60 6.60

Austrian Special Handling Stamps Overprinted in Blue or Black — c

Perf. 12½
Stamps of 1916 Overprinted

B32 SH1 2h claret, *yel* (Bl) 25.00 25.00
B33 SH1 5h dp grn, *yel* (Bk) *800.00 700.00*

Stamps of 1917 Overprinted — d

B34 SH2 2h cl, *yel* (Bl) .25 *.35*
a. Vert. pair, imperf. btwn. *250.00*
B35 SH2 2h cl, *yel* (Bk) 35.00 32.50
B36 SH2 5h grn, *yel* (Bk) .25 .25

Austrian Air Post Stamps, #C1-C3, Overprinted Type "c" Diagonally

B37 A40 1.50k on 2k lil 90.00 70.00
B38 A40 2.50k on 3k ocher 110.00 90.00
B39 A40 4k gray *800.00 650.00*

1919

Austrian Postage Due Stamps of 1908-13 Overprinted Type "b"

B40 D3 2h carmine *4,500. 2,750.*
B41 D3 4h carmine 17.50 17.50
B42 D3 6h carmine 10.50 9.00
B43 D3 14h carmine 35.00 32.50
B44 D3 25h carmine 30.00 30.00
B45 D3 30h carmine 325.00 250.00
B46 D3 50h carmine *650.00 650.00*

Austria Nos. J49-J56 Overprinted Type "b"

B47 D4 5h rose red .25 *.30*
B48 D4 10h rose red .25 *.30*
B49 D4 15h rose red .25 *.30*
B50 D4 20h rose red 1.75 1.75
B51 D4 25h rose red 1.75 1.75
B52 D4 30h rose red .60 .60
B53 D4 40h rose red 1.75 1.75
B54 D4 50h rose red *300.00* 250.00

Austria Nos. J57-J59 Overprinted Type "a"

B55 D5 1k ultra 10.50 9.00
B56 D5 5k ultra 21.00 21.00
B57 D5 10k ultra 225.00 200.00

Austria Nos. J47-J48, J60-J63 Overprinted Type "c" Diagonally

B58 A22 1h gray 20.00 16.00
B59 A23 15h on 2h vio 95.00 90.00
B60 A38 10h on 24h blue 80.00 70.00
B61 A38 15h on 36h vio .35 .35
B62 A38 20h on 54h org 70.00 65.00
B63 A38 50h on 42h choc .75 .75

Hungarian Stamps Ovptd. Type "b"

1919 **Wmk. 137** ***Perf. 15***

On Stamps of 1913-16

B64 A4 1f slate *2,200. 1,800.*
B65 A4 2f yellow 5.25 4.50
B66 A4 3f orange 32.50 25.00
B67 A4 6f olive green 5.00 5.00
B68 A4 50f lake, *bl* .90 .75
B69 A4 60f grn, *sal* 45.00 35.00
B70 A4 70f red brn, *grn* *2,250. 1,750.*

On Stamps of 1916

B71 A8 10f rose 300.00 225.00
B72 A8 15f violet 150.00 100.00

On Stamps of 1916-18

B73 A9 2f brown orange .25 .25
B74 A9 3f red lilac .25 .25
B75 A9 5f green .25 .25
B76 A9 6f grnsh blue .50 .50
B77 A9 10f rose red 1.40 1.00
B78 A9 15f violet .25 .25
B79 A9 20f gray brown 12.00 11.00
B80 A9 25f dull blue .90 .70
B81 A9 35f brown 9.00 9.00
B82 A9 40f olive green 3.00 2.25

Overprinted Type "d"

B83 A10 50f red vio & lil 1.10 *1.40*
B84 A10 75f brt bl & pale bl 1.10 *1.40*
B85 A10 80f yel grn & pale grn 1.10 *1.40*
B86 A10 1k red brn & cl 2.10 2.00
B87 A10 2k ol brn & bis 9.00 9.00
B88 A10 3k dk vio & ind 37.50 35.00
B89 A10 5k dk brn & lt brn 90.00 60.00
B90 A10 10k vio brn & vio *1,300.* 800.00

Overprinted Type "b"
On Stamps of 1918

B91 A11 10f scarlet .25 .25
B92 A11 20f dark brown .30 .30
B93 A11 25f deep blue 1.10 .75
B94 A12 40f olive grn 3.50 2.75
B95 A12 50f lilac 30.00 22.50

On Stamps of 1919

B96 A13 10f red 9.00 7.00
B97 A13 20f dk brn *6,500. 4,500.*

Same Overprint On Hungarian Newspaper Stamp of 1914
Imperf

B98 N5 (2f) orange .25 *.25*

Same Overprint On Hungarian Special Delivery Stamp
Perf. 15

B99 SD1 2f gray grn & red .25 *.25*

Same Ovpt. On Hungarian Semi-Postal Stamps

B100 SP3 10f + 2f rose red .70 .70
B101 SP4 15f + 2f violet 1.10 1.10
B102 SP5 40f + 2f brn car 3.50 3.50
Nos. B98-B102 (5) 5.80 5.80

Hungarian Postage Due Stamps of 1903-18 Overprinted Type "b"

1919 **Wmk. 135** ***Perf. 11½, 12***

B103 D1 50f green & black *350.00 300.00*

Wmk. Crown (136, 136a)
Perf. 11½x12, 15

B104 D1 1f green & black *1,200. 1,000.*
B105 D1 2f green & black *750.00 650.00*
B106 D1 12f green & black *4,250. 3,500.*
B107 D1 50f green & black 275. 150.

Wmk. Double Cross (137)
Perf. 15
On Stamps of 1914

B110 D1 1f green & black 1,250. 600.
B111 D1 2f green & black 700. 550.
B112 D1 5f green & black 1,325. 900.
B113 D1 12f green & black *5,250. 4,000.*
B114 D1 50f green & black 275. 150.

On Stamps of 1915-18

B115 D1 1f green & red 125.00 100.00
B116 D1 2f green & red .75 .75
B117 D1 5f green & red 12.50 10.00
B118 D1 6f green & red 2.00 2.00
B119 D1 10f green & red .50 .50
a. Pair, one without overprint
B120 D1 12f green & red 2.00 2.00
B121 D1 15f green & red 5.00 4.50
B122 D1 20f green & red 1.25 1.25
B123 D1 30f green & red 40.00 35.00
Nos. B115-B123 (9) 189.00 156.00

Excellent counterfeits of Nos. B1-B123 exist.

Bohemian Lion Breaking its Chains — SP1

Mother and Child — SP2

Perf. 11½, 13¾ and Compound

1919 **Typo.** **Unwmk.**

Pinkish Paper

B124 SP1 15h gray green .25 .25
a. 15h light green 32.50 25.00
B125 SP1 25h dark brown .25 .25
a. 25h light brown *5.00* 4.00
B126 SP1 50h dark blue .25 .25

Photo.
Yellowish Paper

B127 SP2 75h slate .25 .25
B128 SP2 100h brn vio .25 .25
B129 SP2 120h vio, *yel* .25 .25
Nos. B124-B129 (6) 1.50 1.50

Values are for perf 13¾. Other perfs are valued higher.

Nos. B124-B126 commemorate the 1st anniv. of Czechoslovak independence. Nos. B127-B129 were sold for the benefit of Legionnaires' orphans. Imperforates exist.

See No. 1581.

Regular Issues of Czechoslovakia Surcharged in Red

a

b

1920 ***Perf. 13¾***

B130 A1(a) 40h + 20h bister .75 *1.00*
B131 A2(a) 60h + 20h green .75 *1.00*
B132 A4(b) 125h + 25h gray bl 3.25 *2.75*
Nos. B130-B132 (3) 4.75 *4.75*
Set, never hinged 12.00

President Masaryk — SP3

Wmk. Linden Leaves (107)

1923 **Engr.** ***Perf. 13¾x14¾***

B133 SP3 50h gray green .60 .40
B134 SP3 100h carmine 1.10 .75
B135 SP3 200h blue 3.25 2.50
B136 SP3 300h dark brown 3.25 3.50
Nos. B133-B136 (4) 8.20 7.15
Set, never hinged 15.00

5th anniv. of the Republic.

The gum was applied through a screen and shows the monogram "CSP" (Ceskoslovenska Posta). These stamps were sold at double their face values, the excess being given to the Red Cross and other charitable organizations.

International Olympic Congress Issue

Semi-Postal Stamps of 1923 Overprinted in Blue or Red

1925

B137 SP3 50h gray green 5.50 7.50
B138 SP3 100h carmine 7.00 12.00
B139 SP3 200h blue (R) 35.00 45.00
Nos. B137-B139 (3) 47.50 64.50
Set, never hinged 120.00

These stamps were sold at double their face values, the excess being divided between a fund for post office clerks and the Olympic Games Committee.

Sokol Issue

Semi-Postal Stamps of 1923 Overprinted in Blue or Red

1926

B140 SP3 50h gray green 1.60 *4.00*
B141 SP3 100h carmine 3.25 *4.00*
B142 SP3 200h blue (R) 10.00 11.00
a. Double overprint
B143 SP3 300h dk brn (R) 20.00 15.00
Nos. B140-B143 (4) 34.85 34.00
Set, never hinged 100.00

These stamps were sold at double their face values, the excess being given to the Congress of Sokols, June, 1926.

Catalogue values for unused stamps in this section, from this point to the end of the section, are for Never Hinged items.

Midwife Presenting Newborn Child to its Father; after a Painting by Josef Manes

SP4 SP5

1936 **Unwmk.** **Engr.** ***Perf. 12½***

B144 SP4 50h + 50h green .50 .35
B145 SP5 1k + 50h claret 1.00 .60
B146 SP4 2k + 50h blue 2.50 1.25
Nos. B144-B146 (3) 4.00 2.20

Nos. B144-B146 were each issued in sheets of 100 with 12 labels. Value, set $40.

SP6

"Lullaby" by Stanislav Sucharda SP7

1937 ***Perf. 12½***

B147 SP6 50h + 50h dull green .50 .25
B148 SP6 1k + 50h rose lake 1.00 .60
B149 SP7 2k + 1k dull blue 2.50 1.25
Nos. B147-B149 (3) 4.00 2.10

Nos. B147-B149 were each issued in sheets of 100 with 12 labels. Value, set of singles with attached labels hinged mint $5; used $5.

President Masaryk and Little Girl in Native Costume — SP8

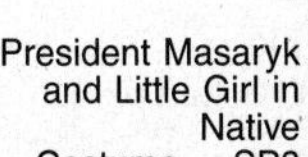

1938 ***Perf. 12½***

B150 SP8 50h + 50h deep green .75 .50
B151 SP8 1k + 50h rose lake .70 .55

Souvenir Sheet
Imperf

B152 SP8 2k + 3k black 4.25 5.00

88th anniv. of the birth of Masaryk (1850-1937).

Nos. B150-B151 were each issued in sheets of 100 stamps and 12 blank labels. Value, set of singles with attached labels: mint $4; used $3.

Allegory of the Republic Type
Souvenir Sheet

1938 ***Perf. 12½***

B153 A89 2k (+ 8k) dark blue 3.00 3.50

The surtax was devoted to national relief for refugees.

"Republic" and Congress Emblem — SP10

1945 **Engr.**
B154 SP10 1.50k + 1.50k car rose .25 .25
B155 SP10 2.50k + 2.50k blue .25 .25

Students' World Cong., Prague, 11/17/45.

St. George Slaying the Dragon — SP11

1946
B156 SP11 2.40k + 2.60k car rose .25 .25
B157 SP11 4k + 6k blue .25 .25

Souvenir Sheet

Imperf

B158 SP11 4k + 6k blue 1.50 1.50

1st anniv. of Czechoslovakia's liberation. The surtax aided WW II orphans.

Nos. B156-B157 were each issued in sheets of 100 stamps and 12 inscribed labels. Value for set of singles with attached labels, mint or used $3.50.

Old Town Hall Type of 1946

Souvenir Sheet

1946, Aug. 3 ***Imperf.***
B159 A114 2.40k rose brown 1.10 .75

Brno Natl. Stamp Exhib., Aug., 1946. The sheet was sold for 10k.

"You Went Away" — SP14

"You Remained Ours" — SP15

"You Came Back" — SP16

1946, Oct. 28 **Photo.** ***Perf. 14***
B160 SP14 1.60k + 1.40k red brn .35 .35
B161 SP15 2.40k + 2.60k scarlet .35 .35
B162 SP16 4k + 4k deep blue .70 .70
Nos. B160-B162 (3) 1.40 1.40

The surtax was for repatriated Slovaks.

Barefoot Boy — SP17

2k+1k, Mother and child. 3k+1k, Little girl.

Perf. 12½

1948, Dec. 18 **Unwmk.** **Engr.**
B163 SP17 1.50k + 1k rose lilac .45 .25
B164 SP17 2k + 1k dp blue .25 .25
B165 SP17 3k + 1k rose car .35 .25
Nos. B163-B165 (3) 1.05 .75

The surtax was for child welfare.

Nos. B163-B165 were each issued in sheets of 100 stamps and 12 inscribed labels. Value for set of singles with attached labels: mint $3; used $2.

Woman and Child — SP18

Design: 3k+1k, Man lifting child.

1949, Dec. 18 ***Perf. 12½***
B166 SP18 1.50k + 50h gray 4.75 1.90
B167 SP18 3k + 1k claret 7.00 2.75

The surtax was for child welfare.

SP19

Dove Carrying Olive Branch — SP20

1949, Dec. 18
B168 SP19 1.50k + 50h claret 4.50 1.50
B169 SP20 3k + 1k rose red 4.50 1.50

The surtax was for the Red Cross.

AIR POST STAMPS

Nos. 9, 39-40, 20, and Types of 1919 Srchd. in Red, Blue or Green

1920 **Unwmk.** ***Imperf.***
C1 A1 14k on 200h (R) 15.00 12.00
a. Inverted surcharge 125.00
C2 A2 24k on 500h (Bl) 40.00 25.00
a. Inverted surcharge 225.00
C3 A2 28k on 1000h (G) 25.00 20.00
a. Inverted surcharge 150.00
b. Double surcharge 200.00
Nos. C1-C3 (3) 80.00 57.00

Perf. 13¾

C4 A1 14k on 200h (R) 22.50 *22.50*
a. Perf. 13¾x13½ 150.00 95.00
C5 A2 24k on 500h (Bl) 45.00 *70.00*
a. Perf. 13¾x13½ 150.00 75.00

Perf. 13¾x13½

C6 A2 28k on 1000h (G) 20.00 17.50
a. Inverted surcharge 400.00 —
b. Perf. 13¾ 475.00 475.00
c. As "b," invtd. surcharge 350.00 —
Nos. C4-C6 (3) 87.50 110.00
Nos. C1-C6 (6) 167.50 167.00

Excellent counterfeits of the overprint are known.

Stamps of 1920 Srchd. in Black or Violet

1922, June 15 ***Perf. 13¾***
C7 A8 50h on 100h dl grn 1.75 1.50
a. Inverted surcharge 150.00
b. Double surcharge 160.00
C8 A8 100h on 200h vio 3.50 2.25
a. Inverted surcharge 150.00
C9 A8 250h on 400h brn (V) 5.00 3.50
a. Inverted surcharge 275.00
Nos. C7-C9 (3) 10.25 7.25
Set, never hinged 20.00

Fokker Monoplane AP3

Smolik S 19 AP4

Smolik S 19 — AP5

Fokker over Prague AP6

1930, Dec. 16 **Engr.** ***Perf. 13½***
C10 AP3 50h deep green .25 .25
C11 AP3 1k deep red .25 *.45*
C12 AP4 2k dark green .40 *.90*
C13 AP4 3k red violet .85 1.10
C14 AP5 4k indigo .75 1.10
C15 AP5 5k red brown 1.75 *3.50*
C16 AP6 10k vio blue 3.00 3.50
a. 10k ultra 8.50 10.00
C17 AP6 20k gray violet 3.00 4.50
Nos. C10-C17 (8) 10.25 15.30
Set, never hinged 17.50

Two types exist of the 50h, 1k and 2k, and three types of the 3k, differing chiefly in the size of the printed area. A "no hill at left" variety of the 3k exists.

Imperf. examples of Nos. C10-C17 are proofs.

See Bohemia and Moravia No. C1.

Perf. 12

C10a AP3 50h deep green 2.50 *4.50*
C11a AP3 1k deep red 13.00 *22.50*
C12a AP4 2k dark green 13.00 *22.50*
C14a AP5 4k indigo 2.00 *3.50*
C17a AP6 20k gray violet 3.00 *7.00*

Perf. 12x13½, 13½x12

C11b AP3 1k deep red 3.50 *6.50*
C12b AP4 2k dark green 10.00 *15.00*

Perf. 13¾x12¼

C17b AP6 20k gray violet *1,750.*

Perf. 12½

C15a AP5 5k red brown *2,000.*

Catalogue values for unused stamps in this section, from this point to the end of the section, are for Never Hinged items.

Capt. Frantisek Novak — AP7

Plane over Bratislava Castle — AP8

Plane over Charles Bridge, Prague — AP9

1946-47 ***Perf. 12½***
C19 AP7 1.50k rose red .25 .25
C20 AP7 5.50k dk gray bl .50 .25
C21 AP7 9k sepia ('47) .85 .25
C22 AP8 10k dl grn .85 .35
C23 AP7 16k violet 1.50 .60
C24 AP8 20k light blue 1.60 1.10
C25 AP9 24k dk bl, *cr* 1.00 .65
C26 AP9 24k rose lake 1.75 1.00
C27 AP9 50k dk gray bl 3.25 2.60
Nos. C19-C27 (9) 11.55 7.05

No. C25 was issued June 12, 1946, for use on the first Prague-New York flight.

Nos. C22, C24-C27 were each issued in sheets of 100 stamps and 12 labels depicting airplane over globe. Values for singles with attached labels (mint/used): C22, $2/$1.50; C24, $4/$3; C25, $7.50/$4; C26, $5.50/$4.50; C27, $9/$7.50.

Nos. C19-C24, C26-C27 Surcharged with New Value and Bars in Various Colors

1949, Sept. 1 ***Perf. 12½***
C28 AP7 1k on 1.50k (Bl) .25 .25
C29 AP7 3k on 5.50k (C) .35 .25
C30 AP7 6k on 9k (Br) .55 .25
C31 AP7 7.50k on 16k (C) .75 .25
C32 AP8 8k on 10k (G) .75 .75
C33 AP8 12.50k on 20k (Bl) 1.10 .55
C34 AP9 15k on 24k rose lake (Bl) 2.75 1.00
C35 AP9 30k on 50k (Bl) 2.00 .90
Nos. C28-C35 (8) 8.50 4.20

Karlovy Vary (Karlsbad) — AP10

1951, Apr. 2 **Engr.** ***Perf. 13½***
C36 AP10 6k shown 3.50 1.75
C37 AP10 10k Piestany 3.50 1.75
C38 AP10 15k Marienbad 6.00 1.75
C39 AP10 20k Silac 9.50 4.50
Nos. C36-C39 (4) 22.50 9.75

Nos. C36-C39 were each issued in a sheet of 10 stamps. Value, set *$950.*

View of Cesky Krumlov — AP11

Views: 1.55k, Olomouc. 2.35k, Banska Bystrica. 2.75k, Bratislava. 10k, Prague.

1955 **Cream Paper** ***Perf. 11½***
C40 AP11 80h olive green 1.00 .25
C41 AP11 1.55k violet brn 1.40 .45
C42 AP11 2.35k violet blue 1.90 .25
C43 AP11 2.75k rose brown 2.75 .45
C44 AP11 10k indigo 5.50 2.75
Nos. C40-C44 (5) 12.55 4.15

Issue dates: 10k, Feb. 20. Others, Mar. 28.

Airline: Moscow-Prague-Paris — AP12

2.35k, Airline: Prague-Cairo-Beirut-Damascus.

Engraved and Photogravure

1957, Oct. 15 **Unwmk.** ***Perf. 11½***
C45 AP12 75h ultra & rose 1.00 .25
C46 AP12 2.35k ultra & org yel 1.00 .30

Planes at First Czech Aviation School, Pardubice — AP13

Design: 1.80k, Jan Kaspar and flight of first Czech plane, 1909.

1959, Oct. 15

C47	AP13	1k gray & yel	.25	.25
C48	AP13	1.80k blk & pale bl	.75	.25

50th anniv. of Jan Kaspar's 1st flight Aug. 25, 1909, at Pardubice.

Mail Coach, Plane and Arms of Bratislava — AP14

Design: 2.80k, Helicopter over Bratislava.

1960, Sept. 24 Unwmk. *Perf. 11½*

C49	AP14	1.60k dk bl & gray	1.50	.75
C50	AP14	2.80k grn & buff	1.75	1.10

Issued to publicize the National Stamp Exhibition, Bratislava, Sept. 24-Oct. 9.

AP15

Designs: 60h, Prague hails Gagarin. 1.80k, Gagarin, rocket and dove.

1961, June 22

C51	AP15	60h gray & car	.30	.25
C52	AP15	1.80k gray & blue	.45	.25

No. C51 commemorates Maj. Gagarin's visit to Prague, Apr. 28-29; No. C52 commemorates the first man in space, Yuri A. Gagarin, Apr. 12, 1961.

AP16

"PRAGA" emblem and: 80h, Dove & Nest of Eggs. 1.40k, Dove. 2.80k, Symbolic flower with five petals. 4.20k, Five leaves.

1962, May 14 Engr. *Perf. 14*

C53	AP16	80h multicolored	.75	.35
C54	AP16	1.40k blk, dk red & bl	1.50	1.50
C55	AP16	2.80k multicolored	1.50	1.50
C56	AP16	4.20k multicolored	1.50	1.50
		Nos. C53-C56 (4)	5.25	4.85

PRAGA 1962 World Exhibition of Postage Stamps, Aug. 18-Sept. 2, 1962.

Nos. C53-C56 were each issued in sheets of 10. Value, set $85.

Vostok 5 and Lt. Col. Valeri Bykovski AP17

2.80k, Vostok VI & Lt. Valentina Tereshkova.

1963, June 26

C57	AP17	80h slate bl & pink	1.00	.35
C58	AP17	2.80k dl red brn & lt bl	1.75	.35

Space flights of Valeri Bykovski, June 14-19, and Valentina Tereshkova, first woman astronaut, June 16-19, 1963.

PRAGA 1962 Emblem, View of Prague and Plane — AP18

Designs: 60h, Istanbul '63 (Hagia Sophia). 1k, Philatec Paris 1964 (Ile de la Cité). 1.40k, WIPA 1965 (Belvedere Palace, Vienna). 1.60k, SIPEX 1966 (Capitol, Washington). 2k, Amphilex '67 (harbor and old town, Amsterdam). 5k, PRAGA 1968 (View of Prague).

Engraved and Photogravure

1967, Oct. 30 *Perf. 11½*

Size: 30x50mm

C59	AP18	30h choc, yel & rose	.25	.25
C60	AP18	60h dk grn, yel & lil	.25	.25
C61	AP18	1k blk, brick red & lt bl	.35	.25
C62	AP18	1.40k vio, yel & dp org	.45	.25
C63	AP18	1.60k ind, tan & lil	.45	.25
C64	AP18	2k dk grn, org & red	.45	.25

Size: 40x50mm

C65	AP18	5k multi	2.50	1.60
		Nos. C59-C65 (7)	4.70	3.10

PRAGA 1968 World Stamp Exhibition, Prague, June 22-July 7, 1968. No. C59-C64 issued in sheets of 15 stamps and 15 bilingual labels. Values, set of singles with attached labels: mint $6.50; used $4.50. No. C65 issued in sheets of 4 stamps and one center label. Value $15.

Glider L-13 — AP19

Airplanes: 60h, Sports plane L-40. 80h, Aero taxi L-200. 1k, Crop-spraying plane Z-37. 1.60k, Aerobatics trainer Z-526. 2k, Jet trainer L-29.

1967, Dec. 11

C66	AP19	30h multi	.25	.25
C67	AP19	60h multi	.25	.25
C68	AP19	80h multi	.25	.25
C69	AP19	1k multi	.30	.25
C70	AP19	1.60k multi	.50	.25
C71	AP19	2k multi	1.60	.90
		Nos. C66-C71 (6)	3.15	2.15

Charles Bridge, Prague, and Balloon — AP20

Designs: 1k, Belvedere, fountain and early plane. 2k, Hradcany, Prague, and airship.

1968, Feb. 5 Unwmk. *Perf. 11½*

C72	AP20	60h multicolored	.30	.25
C73	AP20	1k multicolored	.45	.30
C74	AP20	2k multicolored	.75	.30
		Nos. C72-C74 (3)	1.50	.85

PRAGA 1968 World Stamp Exhibition, Prague, June 22-July 7, 1968.

Nos. C72-C74 were each issued in a sheet of 10 stamps, Value, set $24.

Astronaut, Moon and Manhattan AP21

Design: 3k, Lunar landing module and J. F. Kennedy Airport, New York.

1969, July 21

C75	AP21	60h blk, vio, yel & sil	.40	.25
C76	AP21	3k blk, bl, ocher & sil	1.60	.25

Man's 1st landing on the moon, July 20, 1969, US astronauts Neil A. Armstrong and Col. Edwin E. Aldrin, Jr., with Lieut. Col. Michael Collins piloting Apollo 11.

Nos. C75-C76 printed with label inscribed with names of astronauts and European date of moon landing. Values for pair of singles with attached labels: mint $3; used $1.

TU-104A over Bitov Castle AP22

Designs: 60h, IL-62 over Bezdez Castle. 1.40k, TU-13A over Orava Castle. 1.90k, IL-18 over Veveri Castle. 2.40k, IL-14 over Pernstejn Castle. 3.60k, TU-154 over Trencin Castle.

1973, Oct. 24 Engr. *Perf. 11½*

C77	AP22	30h multi	.25	.25
C78	AP22	60h multi	.25	.25
C79	AP22	1.40k multi	.25	.25
C80	AP22	1.90k multi	.40	.25
C81	AP22	2.40k multi	1.50	.75
C82	AP22	3.60k multi	.70	.25
		Nos. C77-C82 (6)	3.35	2.00

50 years of Czechoslovakian aviation.

Nos. C77-C82 were each printed in sheets of 10. Values, set: mint $50; used $25.

Old Water Tower and Manes Hall — AP23

Designs (Praga 1978 Emblem, Plane Silhouette and): 1.60k, Congress Hall. 2k, Powder Tower, vert. 2.40k, Charles Bridge and Old Bridge Tower. 4k, Old Town Hall on Old Town Square, vert. 6k, Prague Castle and St. Vitus' Cathedral, vert.

Engraved and Photogravure

1976, June 23 *Perf. 11½*

C83	AP23	60h ind & multi	.25	.25
C84	AP23	1.60k ind & multi	.25	.25
C85	AP23	2k ind & multi	.35	.25
C86	AP23	2.40k ind & multi	.40	.25
C87	AP23	4k ind & multi	.80	.30
C88	AP23	6k ind & multi	2.00	.80
		Nos. C83-C88 (6)	4.05	2.10

PRAGA 1978 International Philatelic Exhibition, Prague, Sept. 8-17, 1978.

Zeppelin, 1909 and 1928 — AP24

PRAGA '78 Emblem and: 1k, Ader, 1890, L'Eole & Dunn, 1914. 1.60k, Jeffries-Blanchard balloon, 1785. 2k, Otto Lilienthal's glider, 1896. 4.40k, Jan Kaspar's plane, Pardubice, 1911.

1977, Sept. 15 *Perf. 11½*

C89	AP24	60h multi	.25	.25
C90	AP24	1k multi	.30	.25
C91	AP24	1.60k multi	.35	.25
C92	AP24	2k multi	.45	.25
C93	AP24	4.40k multi	2.25	.50
		Nos. C89-C93 (5)	3.60	1.50

History of aviation.

Nos. C89-C93 were each issued in sheets of 30 stamps, 15 labels depicting the exhibition emblem, and 5 blank labels. Values for set of singles with attached inscribed labels: mint $5; used $2.50.

SPECIAL DELIVERY STAMPS

Doves — SD1

1919-20 Unwmk. Typo. *Imperf.*

E1	SD1	2h red vio, *yel*	.25	.25
E2	SD1	5h yel grn, *yel*	.25	.25
E3	SD1	10h red brn, *yel* ('20)	.75	.75
		Nos. E1-E3 (3)	1.25	1.25

For overprints and surcharge see Nos. P11-P13, Eastern Silesia E1-E2.

1921 White Paper

E1a	SD1	2h red violet	9.00
E2a	SD1	5h yellow green	6.00
E3a	SD1	10h red brown	140.00
		Nos. E1a-E3a (3)	155.00

It is doubted that Nos. E1a-E3a were regularly issued.

PERSONAL DELIVERY STAMPS

Catalogue values for unused stamps in this section are for Never Hinged items.

PD1

Design: No. EX2, "D" in each corner.

1937 Unwmk. Photo. *Perf. 13½*

No.	Type	Description	Unused	Used
EX1	PD1	50h blue	.25	*.25*
EX2	PD1	50h carmine	.25	*.25*

PD3

1946 *Perf. 13½*

No.	Type	Description	Unused	Used
EX3	PD3	2k deep blue	.50	*.75*

POSTAGE DUE STAMPS

D1

1918-20 Unwmk. Typo. *Imperf.*

No.	Type	Description	Unused	Used
J1	D1	5h deep bister	.25	.25
J2	D1	10h deep bister	.25	.25
J3	D1	15h deep bister	.25	.25
J4	D1	20h deep bister	.30	.25
J5	D1	25h deep bister	.45	.25
J6	D1	30h deep bister	.45	.25
J7	D1	40h deep bister	.60	.25
J8	D1	50h deep bister	.75	.25
J9	D1	100h blk brn	1.50	.25
J10	D1	250h orange	11.00	1.40
J11	D1	400h scarlet	15.00	1.40
J12	D1	500h gray grn	7.50	.25
J13	D1	1000h purple	7.50	.25
J14	D1	2000h dark blue	22.50	.60
		Nos. J1-J14 (14)	68.30	6.15

For surcharges and overprints see Nos. J32-J41, J57, Eastern Silesia J1-J11.

Nos. 1, 33-34, 10 Surcharged in Blue

1922

No.	Type	Description	Unused	Used
J15	A1	20h on 3h red vio	.30	.25
J16	A2	50h on 75h slate	1.50	.25
J17	A2	60h on 80h olive grn	.80	.25
J18	A2	100h on 80h olive grn	3.00	.25
J19	A1	200h on 400h purple	4.00	.25
		Nos. J15-J19 (5)	9.60	1.25

Same Surcharge on Nos. 1, 10, 30-31, 33-34, 36, 40 in Violet

1923-26

No.	Type	Description	Unused	Used
J20	A1	10h on 3h red vio	.25	.25
J21	A1	20h on 3h red vio	.30	.25
J22	A1	30h on 3h red vio	.25	.25
J23	A1	40h on 3h red vio	.25	.25
J24	A2	50h on 75h slate	1.25	.25
J25	A2	60h on 50h dk vio ('26)	4.00	1.25
J26	A2	60h on 50h dk bl ('26)	4.00	1.50
J27	A2	60h on 75h slate	.50	.25
J28	A2	100h on 80h ol grn	27.50	.25
J29	A2	100h on 120h gray blk	1.00	.25
J30	A1	100h on 400h pur ('26)	1.00	.25
J31	A2	100h on 1000h dp vio ('26)	1.60	.25
		Nos. J20-J31 (12)	41.90	5.25

Postage Due Stamp of 1918-20 Surcharged in Violet

1924

No.	Type	Description	Unused	Used
J32	D1	50h on 400h scar	.90	.25
J33	D1	60h on 400h scar	3.25	.60
J34	D1	100h on 400h scar	2.00	.25
		Nos. J32-J34 (3)	6.15	1.10

Postage Due Stamps of 1918-20 Surcharged with New Values in Violet as in 1924

1925

No.	Type	Description	Unused	Used
J35	D1	10h on 5h bister	.25	.25
J36	D1	20h on 5h bister	.25	.25
J37	D1	30h on 15h bister	.25	.25
J38	D1	40h on 15h bister	.25	.25
J39	D1	50h on 250h org	1.10	.25
J40	D1	60h on 250h org	1.50	.60
J41	D1	100h on 250h org	2.25	.25
		Nos. J35-J41 (7)	5.85	2.10

Stamps of 1918-19 Surcharged with New Values in Violet as in 1922

1926 *Perf. 14, 11½*

No.	Type	Description	Unused	Used
J42	A2	30h on 15h red	.50	.30
J43	A2	40h on 15h red	.50	.30

Surcharged in Violet

1926 *Perf. 14*

No.	Type	Description	Unused	Used
J44	A8	30h on 100h dk grn	.25	.25
J45	A8	40h on 200h violet	.25	.25
J46	A8	40h on 300h ver	.95	.25
a.		Perf. 14x13½		60.00
J47	A8	50h on 500h dp grn	.50	.25
a.		Perf. 14x13½	2.75	
J48	A8	60h on 400h brown	1.00	.25
J49	A8	100h on 600h dp vio	2.50	.35
a.		Perf. 14x13½	30.00	1.25
		Nos. J44-J49 (6)	5.45	1.60

Surcharged in Violet

1927

No.	Type	Description	Unused	Used
J50	A6	100h dark brown	.55	.25
a.		Perf. 13½	*200.00*	10.00

Surcharged in Violet

No.	Type	Description	Unused	Used
J51	A6	40h on 185h org	.25	.25
J52	A6	50h on 20h car	.25	.25
a.		50h on 50h carmine (error)		*55,000.*
J53	A6	50h on 150h rose	.25	.25
a.		Perf. 13½	12.50	2.00
J54	A6	60h on 25h brown	.25	.25
J55	A6	60h on 185h orange	.55	.25
J56	A6	100h on 25h brown	.55	.25
		Nos. J50-J56 (7)	2.65	1.75

No. J52a is known only used.

No. J12 Surcharged in Deep Violet

1927 *Imperf.*

No.	Type	Description	Unused	Used
J57	D1	200h on 500h gray grn	8.00	2.50

Catalogue values for unused stamps in this section, from this point to the end of the section, are for Never Hinged items.

D5

1928 *Perf. 14x13½*

No.	Type	Description	Unused	Used
J58	D5	5h dark red	.25	.25
J59	D5	10h dark red	.25	.25
J60	D5	20h dark red	.25	.25
J61	D5	30h dark red	.25	.25
J62	D5	40h dark red	.25	.25
J63	D5	50h dark red	.25	.25
J64	D5	60h dark red	.25	.25
J65	D5	1k ultra	.25	.25
J66	D5	2k ultra	.50	.25
J67	D5	5k ultra	.75	.25
J68	D5	10k ultra	1.90	.25
J69	D5	20k ultra	3.75	.30
		Nos. J58-J69 (12)	8.90	3.05

D6

1946-48 Photo. *Perf. 14*

No.	Type	Description	Unused	Used
J70	D6	10h dark blue	.25	.25
J71	D6	20h dark blue	.25	.25
J72	D6	50h dark blue	.25	.25
J73	D6	1k carmine rose	.25	.25
J74	D6	1.20k carmine rose	.25	.25
J75	D6	1.50k carmine rose ('48)	.25	.25
J76	D6	1.60k carmine rose	.25	.25
J77	D6	2k carmine rose ('48)	.25	.25
J78	D6	2.40k carmine rose	.25	.25
J79	D6	3k carmine rose	.25	.25
J80	D6	5k carmine rose	.25	.25
J81	D6	6k carmine rose ('48)	.25	.25
		Nos. J70-J81 (12)	3.00	3.00

D7

D8

1954-55 Engr. *Perf. 12½, 11½*

No.	Type	Description	Unused	Used
J82	D7	5h gray green ('55)	.25	.25
J83	D7	10h gray green ('55)	.25	.25
J84	D7	30h gray green	.25	.25
J85	D7	50h gray green ('55)	.25	.25
J86	D7	60h gray green ('55)	.25	.25
J87	D7	95h gray green	.35	.25
J88	D8	1k violet	.35	.25
J89	D8	1.20k violet ('55)	.35	.25
J90	D8	1.50k violet	.70	.25
J91	D8	1.60k violet ('55)	.45	.25
J92	D8	2k violet	.85	.25
J93	D8	3k violet	1.10	.25
J94	D8	5k violet ('55)	1.40	.25
		Nos. J82-J94 (13)	6.80	3.25

Perf. 11½ stamps are from a 1963 printing which lacks the 95h, 1.60k, and 2k.

Stylized Flower — D9

Designs: Various stylized flowers.

Engraved and Photogravure

1971-72 *Perf. 11½*

No.	Type	Description	Unused	Used
J95	D9	10h vio bl & pink	.25	.25
J96	D9	20h vio & lt bl	.25	.25
J97	D9	30h emer & lil rose	.25	.25
J98	D9	60h pur & emer	.25	.25
J99	D9	80h org & vio bl	.25	.25
J100	D9	1k dk red & emer	.25	.25
J101	D9	1.20k grn & org	.25	.25
J102	D9	2k blue & red	.25	.25
J103	D9	3k blk & yel	.30	.25
J104	D9	4k brn & ultra	.45	.25
J105	D9	5.40k red & lilac	.60	.25
J106	D9	6k brick red & org	.75	.25
		Nos. J95-J106 (12)	4.10	3.00

All except 5.40k issued in 1972.

OFFICIAL STAMPS

Catalogue values for unused stamps in this section are for Never Hinged items.

Coat of Arms — O1

1945 Unwmk. Litho. *Perf. 10½x10*

No.	Type	Description	Unused	Used
O1	O1	50h dp slate grn	.25	.25
O2	O1	1k dp bl vio	.25	.25
O3	O1	1.20k plum	.25	.25
O4	O1	1.50k crimson rose	.25	.25
O5	O1	2.50k bright ultra	.25	.25
O6	O1	5k dk vio brn	.30	.25
O7	O1	8k rose pink	.30	.30
		Nos. O1-O7 (7)	1.85	1.80

Redrawn

1947 Photo. *Perf. 14*

No.	Type	Description	Unused	Used
O8	O1	60h red	.25	.25
O9	O1	80h dk olive grn	.25	.25
O10	O1	1k dk lilac gray	.25	.25
O11	O1	1.20k dp plum	.25	.25
O12	O1	2.40k dk car rose	.25	.25
O13	O1	4k brt ultra	.25	.25
O14	O1	5k dk vio brn	.25	.25
O15	O1	7.40k purple	.25	.25
		Nos. O8-O15 (8)	2.00	2.00

There are many minor changes in design, size of numerals, etc., of the redrawn stamps.

NEWSPAPER STAMPS

Windhover — N1

1918-20 Unwmk. Typo. *Imperf.*

No.	Type	Description	Unused	Used
P1	N1	2h gray green	.25	.25
P2	N1	5h green ('20)	.25	.25
a.		5h dark green	.40	.25
P3	N1	6h red	.30	.25
P4	N1	10h dull violet	.25	.25
P5	N1	20h blue	.25	.25
P6	N1	30h gray brown	.25	.25
P7	N1	50h orange ('20)	.30	.25
P8	N1	100h red brown ('20)	.40	.25
		Nos. P1-P8 (8)	2.25	2.00

Nos. P1-P8 exist privately perforated.

For surcharges and overprints see Nos. P9-P10, P14-P16, Eastern Silesia P1-P5.

Stamps of 1918-20 Surcharged in Violet

1925-26

No.	Type	Description	Unused	Used
P9	N1	5h on 2h gray green	.50	.40
P10	N1	5h on 6h red ('26)	.25	*.40*

Special Delivery Stamps of 1918-20 Overprinted in Violet

1926

No.	Type	Description	Unused	Used
P11	SD1	5h apple grn, *yel*	.25	.25
a.		5h dull green, *yellow*	.50	.40
P12	SD1	10h red brn, *yel*	.25	.25

With Additional Surcharge of New Value

P13	SD1	5h on 2h red vio, *yel*	.35	.35
		Nos. P11-P13 (3)	.85	.85

Catalogue values for unused stamps in this section, from this point to the end of the section, are for Never Hinged items.

Newspaper Stamps of 1918-20 Overprinted in Violet

1934

P14	N1	10h dull violet	.25	.25
P15	N1	20h blue	.25	.25
P16	N1	30h gray brown	.25	.25
		Nos. P14-P16 (3)	.75	.75

Overprinted for use by commercial firms only.

Carrier Pigeon — N2

1937 *Imperf.*

P17	N2	2h bister brown	.25	.25
P18	N2	5h dull blue	.25	.25
P19	N2	7h red orange	.25	.25
P20	N2	9h emerald	.25	.25
P21	N2	10h henna brown	.25	.25
P22	N2	12h ultra	.25	.25
P23	N2	20h dark green	.25	.25
P24	N2	50h dark brown	.25	.25
P25	N2	1k olive gray	.25	.25
		Nos. P17-P25 (9)	2.25	2.25

For overprint see Slovakia Nos. P1-P9.

Bratislava Philatelic Exhibition Issue
Souvenir Sheet

1937 *Imperf.*

P26	N2	10h henna brn, sheet of 25	4.00	4.00

Newspaper Delivery Boy — N4

1945 Unwmk. Typo. *Imperf.*

P27	N4	5h dull blue	.25	.25
P28	N4	10h red	.25	.25
P29	N4	15h emerald	.25	.25
P30	N4	20h dark slate green	.25	.25
P31	N4	25h bright red vio	.25	.25
P32	N4	30h ocher	.25	.25
P33	N4	40h red orange	.25	.25
P34	N4	50h brown red	.25	.25
P35	N4	1k slate gray	.25	.25
P36	N4	5k deep vio blue	.25	.25
		Nos. P27-P36 (10)	2.50	2.50

CZECHOSLOVAK LEGION POST

The Czechoslovak Legion in Siberia issued these stamps for use on its mail and that of local residents. Forgeries exist.

For more detailed listings of Czechoslovak Legion Post issues, see the *Classic Specialized Catalogue of Stamps and Covers.*

Russia No. 79 Overprinted

1918 Typo. *Perf. 14x14½*

A1	A15	10k dark blue	2,500.	—

No. A1 was sold for a few days in Chelyabinsk. It was withdrawn because of a spelling error ("CZESZKJA," instead of "CZESZKAJA").

This overprint was also applied to Russia Nos. 73-78, 80-81, 83-85, 119-121, 123 and 130-131. These were trial printings, never sold to the public, although favor-cancelled covers exist.

Urn and Cathedral at Irkutsk — A1

Armored Railroad Car — A2

Sentinel — A3

1919-20 Litho. *Imperf.*

1	A1	25k carmine	10.50	—
a.		Perf 11½ ('20)	15.00	—
2	A2	50k yellow green	10.50	—
a.		Perf 11½ ('20)	15.00	—
3	A3	1r red brown	19.00	—
a.		Perf 11½ ('20)	22.50	—

Originals of Nos. 1-3 and 1a-3a have a crackled yellow gum. Ungummed remainders, which were given a white gum, exist imperforate and perforated 11½ and 13¼. Value per set, $3.

Lion of Bohemia — A4

Two types: 1 — 6 points on star-like mace head at right of goblet; large saber handle; measures 20x25¼mm. 2 — 5 points on mace head; small saber handle; measures 19½x25mm.

Perce en Arc in Blue

1920 Embossed

4	A4	(25k) blue & rose	3.00	—

No. 4 Overprinted

1920

5	A4	(25k) bl & rose	10.00	—

Both types of No. 4 received overprint.

No. 5 Surcharged with New Values in Green

6	A4	2k bl & rose	35.00
7	A4	3k bl & rose	35.00
8	A4	5k bl & rose	35.00
9	A4	10k bl & rose	35.00
10	A4	15k bl & rose	35.00
11	A4	25k bl & rose	35.00
12	A4	35k bl & rose	35.00
13	A4	50k bl & rose	35.00
14	A4	1r bl & rose	35.00
		Nos. 6-14 (9)	315.00

BOHEMIA AND MORAVIA

Catalogue values for unused stamps in this country are for never hinged items, beginning with Scott 20 in the regular postage section, Scott B1 in the semi-postal section, Scott J1 in the postage due section, and Scott P1 in the newspaper section.

Masaryk Type of Czechoslovakia with hyphen in "Cesko-Slovensko" A60

1939, Apr. 23

1A	A60	1k rose lake	.25	.25

Prepared by Czechoslovakia prior to the German occupation March 15, 1939. Subsequently issued for use in Bohemia and Moravia.

See No. C1.

German Protectorate

Stamps of Czechoslovakia, 1928-39, Overprinted in Black

Perf. 10, 12½, 12x12½

1939, July 15 Unwmk.

1	A29	5h dk ultra	.25	*1.25*
2	A29	10h brown	.25	*1.25*
3	A29	20h red	.25	*1.25*
4	A29	25h green	.25	*1.25*
5	A29	30h red vio	.25	*1.25*
6	A61a	40h dk bl	2.50	*5.00*
7	A85	50h dp grn	.25	*1.25*
8	A63	60h dl vio	2.50	*5.00*
9	A60	1k rose lake (#212)	.75	*1.75*
10	A60	1k rose lake	.30	*1.25*
11	A64	1.20k rose lilac	3.00	*5.00*
12	A65	1.50k carmine	3.00	*5.75*
13	A79	1.60k olive grn	5.00	*5.75*
a.		"Mähnen"	32.50	*75.00*
14	A66	2k dk bl grn	1.10	*4.00*
15	A67	2.50k dk bl	3.00	*5.00*
16	A68	3k brown	3.00	*5.75*
17	A70	4k dk vio	9.50	*6.50*
18	A71	5k green	5.50	*10.00*
19	A72	10k blue	5.50	*15.00*
		Nos. 1-19 (19)	46.15	*83.25*
		Set, never hinged	60.00	

The size of the overprint varies, Nos. 1-10 measure 17½x15½mm, Nos. 11-16 19x18mm, Nos. 17 and 19 28x17½mm and No. 18 23½x23mm.

Catalogue values for unused stamps in this section, from this point to the end of the section, are for never hinged items.

Linden Leaves and Closed Buds — A1

1939-41 Photo. *Perf. 14*

20	A1	5h dark blue	.25	*.30*
21	A1	10h blk brn	.25	*.40*
22	A1	20h crimson	.25	*.30*
23	A1	25h dk bl grn	.25	*.30*
24	A1	30h dp plum	.25	*.30*
24A	A1	30h golden brn ('41)	.25	*.30*
25	A1	40h orange ('40)	.25	.25
26	A1	50h slate grn ('40)	.25	.25
		Nos. 20-26 (8)	2.00	2.40

See Nos. 49-51.

Castle at Zvikov — A2

Karlstein Castle — A3

St. Barbara's Church, Kutna Hora — A4

Cathedral at Prague — A5

Brno Cathedral — A6

Town Square, Olomouc — A7

1939 Engr. *Perf. 12½*

27	A2	40h dark blue	.25	*.30*
28	A3	50h dk bl grn	.25	*.30*
29	A4	60h dl vio	.25	*.30*
30	A5	1k dp rose	.25	*.30*
31	A6	1.20k rose lilac	.25	*.50*
32	A6	1.50k rose car	.25	*.30*
33	A7	2k dk bl grn	.25	*.45*
34	A7	2.50k dark blue	.25	*.30*
		Nos. 27-34 (8)	2.00	*2.75*

No. 31 measures 23½x29½mm, No. 42 measures 18½x23mm.

See #52-53, 53B. For overprints see #60-61.

Zlin — A8

Iron Works at Moravská Ostrava — A9

Prague — A10

1939-40

35	A8	3k dl rose vio	.25	*.30*
36	A9	4k slate ('40)	.25	*.40*
37	A10	5k green	.45	*.65*
38	A10	10k lt ultra	.35	*.75*
39	A10	20k yel brn	1.00	*1.50*
		Nos. 35-39 (5)	2.30	*3.60*

Types of 1939 and

Neuhaus A11

Pernstein Castle A12

Pardubice Castle — A13

Lainsitz Bridge near Bechyne A14

Samson Fountain, Budweis — A15

Kromeriz A16

Wallenstein Palace, Prague — A17

1940 Engr. *Perf. 12½*

40	A11	50h dk bl grn	.25	.25
41	A12	80h dp bl	.25	*.30*
42	A6	1.20k vio brn	.30	.25
43	A13	2k gray grn	.25	.25
44	A14	5k dk bl grn	.25	.25
45	A15	6k brn vio	.25	*.50*
46	A16	8k slate grn	.25	*.30*
47	A17	10k blue	.45	.30
48	A10	20k sepia	.75	*2.00*
		Nos. 40-48 (9)	3.00	*4.40*

No. 42 measures 18½x23mm; No. 31, 23½x29½mm.

Types of 1939-40

1941

49	A1	60h violet	.25	.25
50	A1	80h red org	.25	.25
51	A1	1k brown	.25	.25
52	A5	1.20k rose red	.25	.25
53	A4	1.50k lil rose	.25	.25
53A	A13	2k light blue	.25	.25
53B	A6	2.50k ultra	.25	.25
53C	A12	3k olive	.25	.25
		Nos. 49-53C (8)	2.00	2.00

Nos. 49-51 show buds open. Nos. 52 and 53B measure 18¾x23½mm and have no inscriptions below design.

For overprints see Nos. 60-61.

Antonin Dvorák — A18

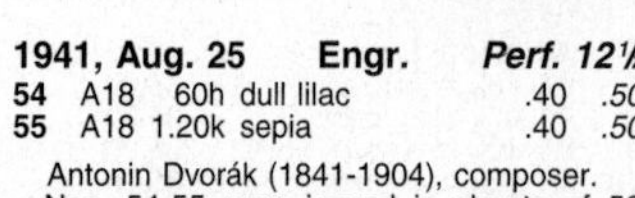

1941, Aug. 25 Engr. *Perf. 12½*

54	A18	60h dull lilac	.40	*.50*
55	A18	1.20k sepia	.40	*.50*

Antonin Dvorák (1841-1904), composer.

Nos. 54-55 were issued in sheets of 50 stamps and 50 alternating inscribed labels. Value for set of singles with attached labels, unused or used, $1.25.

Farming Scene — A19

Factories — A20

1941, Sept. 7 Photo. *Perf. 13½*

56	A19	30h dk red brn	.25	*.30*
57	A19	60h dark green	.25	*.30*
58	A20	1.20k dk plum	.25	*.30*
59	A20	2.50k sapphire	.25	*1.50*
		Nos. 56-59 (4)	1.00	*2.40*

Issued to publicize the Prague Fair.

Nos. 52 and 53B Overprinted in Blue or Red

1942, Mar. 15 *Perf. 12½*

60	A5	1.20k rose red (Bl)	.70	*1.00*
61	A6	2.50k ultra (R)	.70	*1.00*

3rd anniv. of the Protectorate of Bohemia and Moravia.

Adolf Hitler — A21

1942 Photo. *Perf. 14*

Size: 17½x21½mm

62	A21	10(h) gray blk	.25	*.25*
63	A21	30(h) bister brn	.25	*.25*
64	A21	40(h) slate blue	.25	*.25*
65	A21	50(h) slate grn	.25	*.25*
66	A21	60(h) purple	.25	*.25*
67	A21	80(h) org ver	.25	*.25*

Perf. 12½

Engr.

Size: 18x21mm

68	A21	1k dl brn	.25	*.25*
69	A21	1.20(k) carmine	.25	*.30*
70	A21	1.50(k) claret	.25	*.30*
71	A21	1.60(k) Prus grn	.25	*.30*
72	A21	2k light blue	.25	*.30*
73	A21	2.40(k) fawn	.25	*.30*

Size: 18½x24mm

74	A21	2.50(k) ultra	.25	*.30*
75	A21	3k olive grn	.25	*.30*
76	A21	4k brt red vio	.25	*.30*
77	A21	5k myrtle grn	.25	*.30*
78	A21	6k claret brn	.25	*.40*
79	A21	8k indigo	.25	*.40*

Size: 23½x29¾mm

80	A21	10k dk gray grn	.25	*.75*
81	A21	20k gray vio	.50	*.90*
82	A21	30k red	.75	*1.50*
83	A21	50k deep blue	1.50	*2.50*
		Nos. 62-83 (22)	7.50	*10.90*

17th Century Messenger — A22

1943, Jan. 10 Photo. *Perf. 13½*

84	A22	60h dark rose violet	.40	.40

Stamp Day.

Scene from "Die Meistersinger" A23

Richard Wagner A24

Scene from "Siegfried" — A25

1943, May 22

85	A23	60h violet	.25	.25
86	A24	1.20k carmine rose	.25	.25
87	A25	2.50k deep ultra	.25	.25
		Nos. 85-87 (3)	.75	.75

Richard Wagner (1813-83).

St. Vitus' Cathedral, Prague — A26

1944, Nov. 21 Engr. *Perf. 12½*

88	A26	1.50k dull rose brn	.25	.25
89	A26	2.50k dull lilac blue	.25	*.35*

Adolf Hitler — A27

1944

90	A27	4.20k green	.50	.50

SEMI-POSTAL STAMPS

Catalogue values for unused stamps in this section are for never hinged items.

Nurse and Wounded Soldier — SP1

Perf. 13½

1940, June 29 Photo. Unwmk.

B1	SP1	60h + 40h indigo	.35	*.75*
B2	SP1	1.20k + 80h deep plum	.35	*.75*

Surtax for German Red Cross.

Nos. B1-B2 were issued in sheets of 50 stamps and 50 alternating inscribed labels. Value for set of singles with attached labels: unused $4.50; used $4.

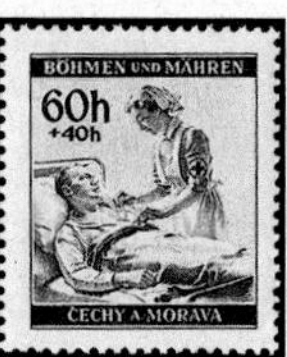

Red Cross Nurse and Patient — SP2

1941, Apr. 20

B3	SP2	60h + 40h indigo	.40	*.75*
B4	SP2	1.20k + 80h dp plum	.40	*.75*

Surtax for German Red Cross.

Nos. B3-B4 were issued in sheets of 50 stamps and 50 alternating inscribed labels. Value for set of singles with attached labels: unused $3.50; used $4.50.

Old Theater, Prague — SP3

Mozart — SP4

1941, Oct. 26

B5	SP3	30h + 30h brown	.25	.25
B6	SP3	60h + 60h Prus grn	.25	.25
B7	SP4	1.20k + 1.20k scar	.25	*.25*
B8	SP4	2.50k + 2.50k dk bl	.45	*.45*
		Nos. B5-B8 (4)	1.20	*1.20*

150th anniversary of Mozart's death.

Labels alternate with stamps in sheets of Nos. B5-B8. The labels with Nos. B5-B6 show two bars of Mozart's opera "Don Giovanni." Those with Nos. B7-B8 show Mozart's piano. Value for set of singles with attached labels: unused $2.50; used $3.50.

Adolf Hitler — SP5

1942, Apr. 20 Engr. *Perf. 12½*

B9	SP5	30h + 20h dl brn vio	.25	.25
B10	SP5	60h + 40h dl grn	.25	.25
B11	SP5	1.20k + 80h dp claret	.25	.35
B12	SP5	2.50k + 1.50k dl bl	.40	*.75*
		Nos. B9-B12 (4)	1.15	*1.60*

Hitler's 53rd birthday.

Nos. B9-B12 were issued in sheets of 100 stamps and 12 blank labels. Value for set of singles with attached labels: unused $3; used $2.25.

Nurse and Soldier — SP6

1942, Sept. 4 *Perf. 13½*

B13	SP6	60h + 40h deep blue	.25	.25
B14	SP6	1.20(k) + 80(h) dp plum	.25	.25

The surtax aided the German Red Cross.

Emperor Charles IV SP7

Peter Parler SP8

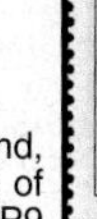

John the Blind, King of Bohemia — SP9

1943, Jan. 29

B15	SP7	60h + 40h violet	.25	.25
B16	SP8	1.20k + 80h carmine	.25	.25
B17	SP9	2.50k + 1.50k vio bl	.25	.25
		Nos. B15-B17 (3)	.75	*.75*

The surtax was for the benefit of the German wartime winter relief.

Adolf Hitler — SP10

1943, Apr. 20 Engr. *Perf. 12½*

B18	SP10	60h + 1.40k dl vio	.25	*.45*
B19	SP10	1.20k + 3.80k carmine	.25	*.45*

Hitler's 54th birthday.

Nos. B18-B19 were issued in sheets of 100 stamps and 12 blank labels. Value for set of singles with attached labels: unused $1.10; used $1.

Deathmask of Reinhard Heydrich — SP11

1943, May 28 Photo. *Perf. 13½*

B20	SP11	60h + 4.40k black	.75	*1.50*

No. B20 exists in a souvenir sheet containing a single stamp. It was given to high Nazi officials attending a ceremony one year after Heydrich's assassination. Value $15,000.

Eagle and Red Cross — SP12

1943, Sept. 16 *Perf. 13*

B21	SP12	1.20k + 8.80k blk & car	.60	.35

The surtax aided the German Red Cross.

Native Costumes SP13

Nazi Emblem, Arms of Bohemia, Moravia SP14

1944, Mar. 15 *Perf. 13½*

B22	SP13	1.20(k) + 3.80(k) rose lake	.25	.25
B23	SP14	4.20(k) + 10.80(k) golden brn	.25	.25
B24	SP13	10k + 20k saph	.25	*.25*
		Nos. B22-B24 (3)	.75	*.75*

Fifth anniversary of protectorate.

Adolf Hitler — SP15

1944, Apr. 20

B25	SP15	60h + 1.40k olive blk	.30	.25
B26	SP15	1.20k + 3.80k slate grn	.30	.25

Bedrich Smetana — SP16

1944, May 12 Engr. *Perf. 12½*

B27	SP16	60h + 1.40k dk gray grn	.25	.25
B28	SP16	1.20k + 3.80k brn car	.25	.25

Bedrich Smetana (1824-84), Czech composer and pianist.

AIR POST STAMP

Catalogue values for unused stamps in this section are for never hinged items.

Type of Czechoslovakia 1930 with hyphen in "Cesko-Slovensko"

Fokker Monoplane — AP3

1939, Apr. 22 *Perf. 13½*

C1	AP3	30h rose lilac	1.60	.25

Prepared by Czechoslovakia prior to the German occupation March 15, 1939. Subsequently issued for use in Bohemia and Moravia. See No. 1A.

PERSONAL DELIVERY STAMPS

PD1

1939-40 Unwmk. Photo. *Perf. 13½*

EX1	PD1	50h indigo & blue ('40)	1.00	*2.50*
		Never hinged	2.25	
EX2	PD1	50h carmine & rose	.60	*3.00*
		Never hinged	1.60	

POSTAGE DUE STAMPS

Catalogue values for unused stamps in this section are for never hinged items.

D1

1939-40 Unwmk. Typo. *Perf. 14*

J1	D1	5h dark carmine	.25	*.30*
J2	D1	10h dark carmine	.25	*.30*
J3	D1	20h dark carmine	.25	*.30*
J4	D1	30h dark carmine	.25	*.30*
J5	D1	40h dark carmine	.25	*.30*
J6	D1	50h dark carmine	.25	*.30*
J7	D1	60h dark carmine	.25	*.30*
J8	D1	80h dark carmine	.25	*.30*
J9	D1	1k bright ultra	.25	*.35*
J10	D1	1.20k brt ultra ('40)	.30	*.35*
J11	D1	2k bright ultra	.80	*1.00*
J12	D1	5k bright ultra	1.00	*1.40*
J13	D1	10k bright ultra	1.75	*1.75*
J14	D1	20k bright ultra	3.50	*3.50*
		Nos. J1-J14 (14)	9.60	*10.75*

OFFICIAL STAMPS

Catalogue values for unused stamps in this section are for never hinged items.

Numeral — O1

Unwmk.

1941, Jan. 1 Typo. *Perf. 14*

O1	O1	30h ocher	.25	.25
O2	O1	40h indigo	.25	.25
O3	O1	50h emerald	.25	.25
O4	O1	60h slate grn	.25	.25
O5	O1	80h org red	.65	.25
O6	O1	1k red brn	.35	.25
O7	O1	1.20k carmine	.35	.25
O8	O1	1.50k dp plum	.50	.25
O9	O1	2k brt bl	.50	.25
O10	O1	3k olive	.50	.25
O11	O1	4k red vio	.70	.40
O12	O1	5k org yel	1.60	.90
		Nos. O1-O12 (12)	6.15	3.80

Eagle — O2

1943, Feb. 15

O13	O2	30(h) bister	.25	*.30*
O14	O2	40(h) indigo	.25	*.30*
O15	O2	50(h) yel grn	.25	*.30*
O16	O2	60(h) dp vio	.25	*.30*
O17	O2	80(h) org red	.25	*.30*
O18	O2	1k chocolate	.25	*.30*
O19	O2	1.20(k) carmine	.25	*.30*
O20	O2	1.50(k) brn red	.25	*.30*
O21	O2	2k lt bl	.25	*.30*
O22	O2	3k olive	.25	*.30*
O23	O2	4k red vio	.25	*.40*
O24	O2	5k dk grn	.25	*.40*
		Nos. O13-O24 (12)	3.00	3.80

NEWSPAPER STAMPS

Catalogue values for unused stamps in this section are for never hinged items.

Carrier Pigeon — N1

1939 Unwmk. Typo. *Imperf.*

P1	N1	2h ocher	.25	*.30*
P2	N1	5h ultra	.25	*.30*
P3	N1	7h red orange	.25	*.30*
P4	N1	9h emerald	.25	*.30*
P5	N1	10h henna brown	.25	*.30*
P6	N1	12h dark ultra	.25	*.30*
P7	N1	20h dark green	.25	*.30*
P8	N1	50h red brown	.25	*.35*
P9	N1	1k greenish gray	.25	*.80*
		Nos. P1-P9 (9)	2.25	3.25

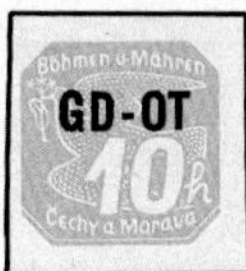

No. P5 Overprinted in Black

1940

P10	N1	10h henna brown	.45	*.65*

Overprinted for use by commercial firms.

N2

1943, Feb. 15

P11	N2	2(h) ocher	.25	.25
P12	N2	5(h) light blue	.25	.25
P13	N2	7(h) red orange	.25	.25
P14	N2	9(h) emerald	.25	.25
P15	N2	10(h) henna brown	.25	.25
P16	N2	12(h) dark ultra	.25	.25
P17	N2	20(h) dark green	.25	.25
P18	N2	50(h) red brown	.25	.25
P19	N2	1k slate green	.25	.25
		Nos. P11-P19 (9)	2.25	2.25

DAHOMEY

də-'hō-mē

LOCATION — West coast of Africa
AREA — 43,483 sq. mi.
POP. — 3,030,000 (est. 1974)
CAPITAL — Porto-Novo

Formerly a native kingdom including Benin, Dahomey was annexed by France in 1894. It became part of the colonial administrative unit of French West Africa in 1895. Stamps of French West Africa superseded those of Dahomey in 1945. The Republic of Dahomey was proclaimed Dec. 4, 1958.

The republic changed its name to the People's Republic of Benin on Nov. 30, 1975. See Benin for stamps issued after that date.

100 Centimes = 1 Franc

Catalog values for unused stamps in this country are for Never Hinged items, beginning with Scott 137 in the regular postage section, Scott B15 in the semi-postal section, Scott C14 in the airpost section, Scott CQ1 in the airpost parcel post section, Scott J29 in the postage due section, and Scott Q1 in the parcel post section.

See French West Africa No. 71 for stamp inscribed "Dahomey" and "Afrique Occidentale Francaise."

Navigation and Commerce — A1

Perf. 14x13½

1899-1905 Typo. Unwmk.

Name of Colony in Blue or Carmine

1	A1	1c black, *lil bl* ('01)	1.60	.80
2	A1	2c brown, *buff* ('04)	1.60	.80
3	A1	4c claret, *lav* ('04)	2.40	2.40
4	A1	5c yellow grn ('04)	6.50	4.00
5	A1	10c red ('01)	8.00	4.00
6	A1	15c gray ('01)	4.00	4.00
7	A1	20c red, *grn* ('04)	20.00	16.00
8	A1	25c black, *rose* ('99)	24.00	24.00
9	A1	25c blue ('01)	20.00	16.00
10	A1	30c brown, *bis* ('04)	24.00	12.00
11	A1	40c red, *straw* ('04)	24.00	16.00
12	A1	50c brn, *az* (name in red) ('01)	40.00	24.00
12A	A1	50c brn, *az* (name in bl) ('05)	32.50	24.00
13	A1	75c dp vio, *org* ('04)	85.00	55.00
14	A1	1fr brnz grn, *straw* ('04)	40.00	32.50
15	A1	2fr violet, *rose* ('04)	110.00	72.50
16	A1	5fr red lilac, *lav* ('04)	135.00	105.00
		Nos. 1-16 (17)	578.60	413.00

Perf. 13½x14 stamps are counterfeits.
For surcharges see Nos. 32-41.

Gen. Louis Faidherbe A2

Oil Palm — A3

Dr. Noel Eugène Ballay A4

1906-07 ***Perf. 13½x14***

Name of Colony in Red or Blue

17	A2	1c slate	1.60	.80
18	A2	2c chocolate	2.40	.80
19	A2	4c choc, *gray bl*	4.00	3.25
20	A2	5c green	8.00	3.25
21	A2	10c carmine (B)	24.00	4.00
22	A3	20c black & red, *azure*	16.00	12.00
23	A3	25c blue, *pnksh*	16.00	12.00
24	A3	30c choc, *pnksh*	16.00	16.00
25	A3	35c black, *yellow*	87.50	12.00
26	A3	45c choc, *grnsh* ('07)	24.00	16.00
27	A3	50c deep violet	20.00	20.00
28	A3	75c blue, *orange*	24.00	24.00
29	A4	1fr black, *azure*	32.00	24.00
30	A4	2fr blue, *pink*	110.00	110.00
31	A4	5fr car, *straw* (B)	95.00	110.00
		Nos. 17-31 (15)	480.50	368.10

Nos. 2-3, 6-7, 9-13 Surcharged in Black or Carmine

Spacing between figures of surcharge 1.5mm (5c), 2mm (10c)

1912 ***Perf. 14x13½***

32	5c on 2c brn, *buff*	2.00	*2.40*
33	5c on 4c claret, *lav* (C)	1.60	*2.00*
a.	Double surcharge	275.00	
34	5c on 15c gray (C)	2.00	*2.40*
35	5c on 20c red, *grn*	2.00	*2.40*
36	5c on 25c blue (C)	2.00	*2.40*
a.	Inverted surcharge	240.00	
37	5c on 30c brown, *bis* (C)	2.00	*2.40*
38	10c on 40c red, *straw*	2.00	*2.40*
a.	Inverted surcharge	325.00	
39	10c on 50c brn, *az*, name in bl (C)	2.40	2.75
40	10c on 50c brn, *az*, name in red (C)	1,125.	1,300.
41	10c on 75c violet, *org*	8.00	8.00
a.	Double surcharge	*5,500.*	
	Nos. 32-39,41 (9)	24.00	27.15

Two spacings between the surcharged numerals are found on Nos. 32 to 41. For detailed listings, see the *Scott Classic Specialized Catalogue of Stamps and Covers.*

Man Climbing Oil Palm — A5

1913-39 ***Perf. 13½x14***

42	A5	1c violet & blk	.40	.30
43	A5	2c choc & rose	.40	.40
44	A5	4c black & brn	.40	.40
45	A5	5c yel grn & bl grn	1.20	.55
46	A5	5c vio brn & vio ('22)	.40	.80
47	A5	10c org red & rose	1.60	.80
a.		Half used as 5c on wrapper or printed matter		—
48	A5	10c yel grn & bl grn ('22)	.80	.80
49	A5	10c red & ol ('25)	.40	.40
50	A5	15c brn org & dk vio ('17)	.80	.80
51	A5	20c gray & red brown	.80	.75
52	A5	20c bluish grn & grn ('26)	.40	.40
53	A5	20c mag & blk ('27)	.40	.40
54	A5	25c ultra & dp blue	2.00	1.60
55	A5	25c vio brn & org ('22)	1.20	.80
56	A5	30c choc & vio	2.75	2.40
57	A5	30c red org & rose ('22)	3.25	3.25
58	A5	30c yellow & vio ('25)	.40	.40
59	A5	30c dl grn & grn ('27)	.40	.40
60	A5	35c brown & blk	.80	.80
61	A5	35c bl grn & grn ('38)	.40	.30
62	A5	40c black & red org	.80	.80
63	A5	45c gray & ultra	.80	.80
64	A5	50c chocolate & brn	6.50	6.00
a.		Half used as 25c on cover		*500.00*
65	A5	50c ultra & bl ('22)	1.60	1.60
66	A5	50c brn red & bl ('26)	1.20	1.20
67	A5	55c gray grn & choc ('38)	.80	.55
68	A5	60c vio, *pnksh* ('25)	.40	.40
69	A5	65c yel brn & ol grn ('26)	1.20	1.20
70	A5	75c blue & violet	1.20	1.20
71	A5	80c henna brn & ultra ('38)	.40	.40
72	A5	85c dk bl & ver ('26)	1.60	1.60
73	A5	90c rose & brn red ('30)	.80	.80
74	A5	90c yel bis & red org ('39)	1.20	.80
75	A5	1fr blue grn & blk	1.20	1.20
76	A5	1fr dk bl & ultra ('26)	1.60	1.60
77	A5	1fr yel brn & lt red ('28)	1.60	1.20
78	A5	1fr dk red & red org ('38)	1.05	.95
79	A5	1.10fr vio & bis ('28)	5.50	*6.00*
80	A5	1.25fr dp bl & dk brn ('33)	17.50	7.25
81	A5	1.50fr dk bl & lt bl ('30)	1.60	.80
82	A5	1.75fr dk brn & dp buff ('33)	4.00	2.00
83	A5	1.75fr ind & ultra ('38)	1.60	.95
84	A5	2fr yel org & choc	1.20	*1.60*
85	A5	3fr red violet ('30)	2.40	1.75
86	A5	5fr violet & dp bl	2.40	2.75
		Nos. 42-86 (45)	79.35	62.15

The 1c gray and yellow green and 5c dull red and black are Togo Nos. 193a, 196a.

Nos. 47a and 64a were authorized for use in Paouignan during the last part of November 1921. Other values exist as bisects but were not authorized.

For surcharges see Nos. 87-96, B1, B8-B11.

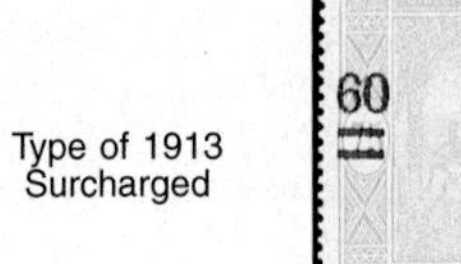

Type of 1913 Surcharged

1922-25

87	A5	60c on 75c vio, *pnksh*	1.20	1.20
a.		Double surcharge	200.00	
88	A5	65c on 15c brn org & dk vio ('25)	2.00	2.00
89	A5	85c on 15c brn org & dk vio ('25)	2.00	2.00
		Nos. 87-89 (3)	5.20	5.20

Stamps and Type of 1913-39 Surcharged with New Value and Bars

1924-27

90	A5	25c on 2fr org & choc	1.20	1.20
91	A5	90c on 75c cer & brn red ('27)	2.00	2.00
92	A5	1.25fr on 1fr dk bl & ultra (R) ('26)	1.60	1.60
93	A5	1.50fr on 1fr dk bl & grnsh bl ('27)	2.75	2.75
94	A5	3fr on 5fr olvn & dp org ('27)	10.50	10.50
95	A5	10fr on 5fr bl vio & red brn ('27)	8.00	8.00
96	A5	20fr on 5fr ver & dl grn ('27)	8.75	8.75
		Nos. 90-96 (7)	34.80	34.80

Common Design Types pictured following the introduction.

Colonial Exposition Issue

Common Design Types

1931 Engr. ***Perf. 12½***

Name of Country in Black

97	CD70	40c deep green	6.50	6.50
98	CD71	50c violet	6.50	6.50
99	CD72	90c red orange	6.50	6.50
100	CD73	1.50fr dull blue	6.50	6.50
		Nos. 97-100 (4)	26.00	26.00

Paris International Exposition Issue

Common Design Types

1937 Engr. ***Perf. 13***

101	CD74	20c deep violet	2.00	2.00
102	CD75	30c dark green	2.00	2.00
103	CD76	40c car rose	2.00	2.00
104	CD77	50c dark brown	1.60	1.60
105	CD78	90c red	1.60	1.60
106	CD79	1.50fr ultra	2.40	2.40
		Nos. 101-106 (6)	11.60	11.60

Souvenir Sheet

Imperf

107	CD77	3fr dp blue & blk	12.00	*16.00*
a.		Inscription inverted	1,600.	1,600.

Caillié Issue

Common Design Type

1939, Apr. 5 Engr. ***Perf. 12½x12***

108	CD81	90c org brn & org	.40	1.20
109	CD81	2fr brt violet	.40	1.20
110	CD81	2.25fr ultra & dk blue	.40	1.20
		Nos. 108-110 (3)	1.20	3.60

New York World's Fair Issue

Common Design Type

1939 **Engr.**

111	CD82	1.25fr car lake	.80	1.60
112	CD82	2.25fr ultra	.80	1.60

Man Poling a Canoe — A7

Pile House A8

Sailboat on Lake Nokoué — A9

Dahomey Warrior — A10

1941 ***Perf. 13***

113	A7	2c scarlet	.25	.25
114	A7	3c deep blue	.25	.25
115	A7	5c brown violet	.70	.70
116	A7	10c green	.30	.30
117	A7	15c black	.25	.25
118	A8	20c violet brown	.30	.30
119	A8	30c dk violet	.30	.30
120	A8	40c scarlet	.70	.70
121	A8	50c slate green	.95	.95
122	A8	60c black	.30	.30
123	A8	70c brt red violet	1.20	1.20
124	A9	80c brown black	1.20	1.20
125	A9	1fr violet	1.20	1.20
126	A9	1.30fr brown violet	1.20	1.20
127	A9	1.40fr green	1.20	1.20
128	A9	1.50fr brt rose	1.20	1.20
129	A9	2fr brown orange	1.20	1.20
130	A10	2.50fr dark blue	1.20	1.20
131	A10	3fr scarlet	1.20	1.20
132	A10	5fr slate green	1.20	1.20
133	A10	10fr violet brown	2.00	2.00
134	A10	20fr black	2.40	2.40
		Nos. 113-134 (22)	20.70	20.70

Nos. 121, 122 without "RF," see Nos. 136A-136B.

Pile House and Marshal Pétain
A11

1941 ***Perf. 12½x12***
135 A11 1fr green .80 —
136 A11 2.50fr blue .80 —

For surcharges see Nos. B14A-B14B.

Type of 1941 without "RF"

1944 ***Perf. 13***
136A A8 50c slate green 1.20
136B A8 60c black 1.20

Nos. 136A-136B were issued by the Vichy government in France, but were not placed on sale in Dahomey.

Catalogue values for unused stamps in this section, from this point to the end of the section, are for Never Hinged items.

Republic

Village Ganvié — A12

Unwmk.
1960, Mar. 1 Engr. ***Perf. 12***
137 A12 25fr dk blue, brn & red .65 .25

For overprint see No. 152.

Imperforates
Most Dahomey stamps from 1960 onward exist imperforate in issued and trial colors, and also in small presentation sheets in issued colors.

C.C.T.A. Issue
Common Design Type

1960, May 16
138 CD106 5fr rose lilac & ultra .50 .25

Emblem of the Entente — A13

Council of the Entente Issue

1960, May 29 Photo. ***Perf. 13x13½***
139 A13 25fr multicolored .65 .40

1st anniv. of the Council of the Entente (Dahomey, Ivory Coast, Niger and Upper Volta).

Prime Minister Hubert Maga — A14

1960, Aug. Engr. ***Perf. 13***
140 A14 85fr deep claret & blk 1.60 .90

Issued on the occasion of Dahomey's proclamation of independence, Aug. 1, 1960.
For surcharge see No. 149.

Weaver — A15

2fr, 10fr, Wood sculptor. 3fr, 15fr, Fisherman and net, horiz. 4fr, 20fr, Potter, horiz.

1961, Feb. 17 Engr. ***Perf. 13***
141 A15 1fr rose, org & red lilac .25 .25
142 A15 2fr bister brn & choc .25 .25
143 A15 3fr green & orange .25 .25
144 A15 4fr olive bis & claret .25 .25
145 A15 6fr rose, lt vio & ver .40 .25
146 A15 10fr blue & green .55 .40
147 A15 15fr red lilac & violet .75 .40
148 A15 20fr bluish vio & Prus bl .90 .55
Nos. 141-148 (8) 3.60 2.60

For surcharges see Nos. 1374, Q1-Q7.

No. 140 Surcharged in Black

1961, Aug. 1
149 A14 100fr on 85fr dp cl & blk 3.25 3.25

First anniversary of Independence.

Doves, UN Building and Emblem — A16

1961, Sept. 20 Unwmk. ***Perf. 13***
150 A16 5fr multicolored .35 .25
151 A16 60fr multicolored 1.20 .90

1st anniv. of Dahomey's admission to the UN. See No. C16 and souvenir sheet No. C16a.

No. 137 Overprinted in Black

1961, Dec. 24
152 A12 25fr dk blue, brn & red .65 .40

Abidjan Games, Dec 24-31.

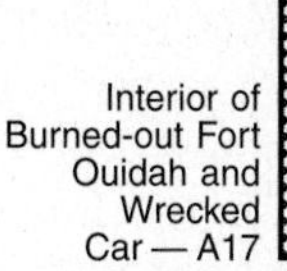
Interior of Burned-out Fort Ouidah and Wrecked Car — A17

1962, July 31 Photo. ***Perf. 12½***
153 A17 30fr multicolored .45 .45
154 A17 60fr multicolored .75 .60

Evacuation of Fort Ouidah by the Portuguese, and its occupation by Dahomey. 1st anniv.

African and Malgache Union Issue
Common Design Type

1962, Sept. 8 ***Perf. 12½x12***
155 CD110 30fr red lil, bluish grn, red & gold 1.25 .90

Red Cross Nurses and Map — A18

1962, Oct. 5 Engr. ***Perf. 13***
156 A18 5fr blue, choc & red .30 .25
157 A18 20fr blue, dk grn & red .60 .45
158 A18 25fr blue, brown & red .65 .45
159 A18 30fr blue, black & red .85 .70
Nos. 156-159 (4) 2.40 1.85

Ganvié Woman in Canoe — A19

Peuhl Herdsman and Cattle A20

Designs: 3fr, 65fr, Bariba chief of Nikki. 15fr, 50fr, Ouidah witch doctor, rock python. 20fr, 30fr, Nessoukoué women carrying vases on heads, Abomey. 25fr, 40fr, Dahomey girl. 60fr, Peuhl herdsman and cattle. 85fr, Ganvié woman in canoe.

1963, Feb. 18 Unwmk. ***Perf. 13***
160 A19 2fr grnsh blue & vio .25 .25
161 A19 3fr blue & black .25 .25
162 A20 5fr brown, blk & grn .35 .25
163 A19 15fr brn, bl grn & red brn .35 .25
164 A19 20fr green, blk & car .30 .25
165 A20 25fr dk brn, bl & bl grn .40 .25
166 A19 30fr brn org, choc & mag .60 .40
167 A20 40fr choc, grn & brt bl 1.00 .40
168 A19 50fr blk, grn, brn & red brn 1.60 .55
169 A20 60fr choc, org red & ol 3.50 1.00
170 A19 65fr orange brn & choc 1.75 .65
171 A19 85fr brt blue & choc 2.50 1.00
Nos. 160-171 (12) 12.85 5.50

For surcharges see Nos. 211, 232, Benin 655A, 690F, 700, 722, 1375, 1417.

Boxers — A21

Designs: 1fr, 20fr, Soccer goalkeeper, horiz. 2fr, 5fr, Runners.

1963, Apr. 11 **Engr.**
172 A21 50c green & black .25 .25
173 A21 1fr olive, blk & brn .25 .25
174 A21 2fr olive, blue & brn .25 .25
175 A21 5fr brown, crim & blk .25 .25
176 A21 15fr dk violet & brn .35 .25
177 A21 20fr multicolored .55 .55
Nos. 172-177 (6) 1.90 1.80

Friendship Games, Dakar, Apr. 11-21.
For surcharges & overprint see Benin Nos. 697, 704, 716, 1372, 1382, 1384.

President's Palace, Cotonou — A22

1963, Aug. 1 Photo. ***Perf. 12½x12***
178 A22 25fr multicolored .45 .25

Third anniversary of independence.

Gen. Toussaint L'Ouverture
A23

1963, Nov. 18 Unwmk. ***Perf. 12x13***
179 A23 25fr multicolored .55 .25
180 A23 30fr multicolored .70 .25
181 A23 100fr ultra, brn & red 1.60 .80
Nos. 179-181 (3) 2.85 1.30

Pierre Dominique Toussaint L'Ouverture (1743-1803), Haitian gen., statesman and descendant of the kings of Allada (Dahomey). For overprint, see Benin No. 1367. For surcharge, see Benin No. 1466.

UN Emblem, Flame, "15" — A24

1963, Dec. 10 ***Perf. 12***
182 A24 4fr multicolored .25 .25
183 A24 6fr multicolored .25 .25
184 A24 25fr multicolored .45 .25
Nos. 182-184 (3) .95 .75

15th anniversary of the Universal Declaration of Human Rights. For surcharge, see Benin No. 1377.

Somba Dance — A25

Regional Dances: 3fr, Nago dance, Pobe-Ketou, horiz. 10fr, Dance of the baton. 15fr, Nago dance, Ouidah, horiz. 25fr, Dance of the Sakpatassi. 30fr, Dance of the Nessouhouessi, horiz.

1964, Aug. 8 Engr. ***Perf. 13***
185 A25 2fr red, emerald & blk .25 .25
186 A25 3fr dull red, blue & grn .25 .25
187 A25 10fr purple, blk & red .45 .25
188 A25 15fr magenta, blk & grn .45 .25
189 A25 25fr Prus blue, brn & org .90 .30
190 A25 30fr dk red, choc & org 1.15 .40
Nos. 185-190 (6) 3.45 1.70

Runner — A26

1964, Oct. 20 Photo. *Perf. 11*

191	A26 60fr shown		1.60	1.00
192	A26 85fr Bicyclist		2.75	1.40

18th Olympic Games, Tokyo, Oct. 10-25.

Cooperation Issue

Common Design Type

1964, Nov. 7 Engr. *Perf. 13*

193	CD119 25fr org, vio & dk brn	.80	.35

UNICEF Emblem, Mother and Child — A27

25fr, Mother holding child in her arms.

1964, Dec. 11 Unwmk. *Perf. 13*

194	A27 20fr yel grn, dk red & blk	.40	.25
195	A27 25fr blue, dk red & blk	.60	.45

18th anniv. of UNICEF. For overprints, see Benin Nos. 691A, and 1368.

IQSY Emblem and Apollo — A28

100fr, IQSY emblem, Nimbus weather satellite.

1964, Dec. 22 Photo. *Perf. 13x12½*

196	A28 25fr green & lt yellow	.55	.25
197	A28 100fr deep plum & yellow	2.00	.95

International Quiet Sun Year, 1964-65.

Abomey Tapestry — A29

Designs (Abomey tapestries): 25fr, Warrior and fight scenes. 50fr, Birds and warriors, horiz. 85fr, Animals, ship and plants, horiz.

1965, Apr. 12 Photo. *Perf. 12½*

198	A29 20fr multicolored	.80	.25
199	A29 25fr multicolored	.95	.40
200	A29 50fr multicolored	1.50	.80
201	A29 85fr multicolored	3.25	1.10
a.	Min. sheet of 4, #198-201	8.00	8.00
	Nos. 198-201 (4)	6.50	2.55

Issued to publicize the local rug weaving industry.

Baudot Telegraph Distributor and Ader Telephone A30

1965, May 17 Engr. *Perf. 13*

202	A30 100fr lilac, org & blk	1.75	1.60

Cent. of the ITU.

Cotonou Harbor — A31

100fr, Cotonou Harbor, denomination at left.

1965, Aug. 1 Photo. *Perf. 12½*

203	25fr multicolored	1.10	.25
204	100fr multicolored	2.50	1.10
a.	A31 Pair, #203-204	4.50	2.10

The opening of Cotonou Harbor. No. 204a has a continuous design.

For surcharges see Nos. 219-220.

Cybium Tritor A32

Fish: 25fr, Dentex filosus. 30fr, Atlantic sailfish. 50fr, Blackish tripletail.

1965, Sept. 20 Engr. *Perf. 13*

205	A32 10fr black & brt blue	.75	.25
206	A32 25fr brt blue, org & blk	1.00	.55
207	A32 30fr violet bl & grnsh bl	1.75	.80
208	A32 50fr black, gray bl & org	2.75	1.00
	Nos. 205-208 (4)	6.25	2.60

For surcharge see Benin No. 911.

Independence Monument — A33

1965, Oct. 28 Photo. *Perf. 12x12½*

209	A33 25fr gray, black & red	.40	.25
210	A33 30fr lt ultra, black & red	.65	.25

October 28 Revolution, 2nd anniv. For surcharge, see Benin No. 1385.

No. 165 Surcharged

1965, Nov. Engr. *Perf. 13*

211	A20 1fr on 25fr	.30	.25

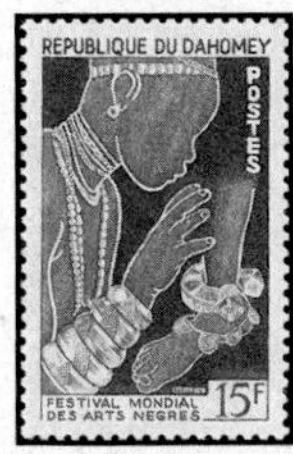
Porto Novo Cathedral A34

Designs: 50fr, Ouidah Pro-Cathedral, vert. 70fr, Cotonou Cathedral.

1966, Mar. 21 Engr. *Perf. 13*

212	A34 30fr Prus bl, vio brn & grn	.55	.25
213	A34 50fr vio brn, Prus bl & brn	.70	.50
214	A34 70fr grn, Prus bl & vio brn	1.25	.75
	Nos. 212-214 (3)	2.50	1.50

Jewelry — A35

Designs: 30fr, Architecture. 50fr, Musician. 70fr, Crucifixion, sculpture.

1966, Apr. 4 Engr. *Perf. 13*

215	A35 15fr dull red brn & blk	.45	.25
216	A35 30fr dk brn, ultra & brn red	.70	.45
217	A35 50fr brt blue & dk brn	1.20	.55
218	A35 70fr red brown & blk	2.50	.85
	Nos. 215-218 (4)	4.85	2.10

International Negro Arts Festival, Dakar, Senegal, Apr. 1-24.

Nos. 203-204 Surcharged

1966, Apr. 24 Photo. *Perf. 12½*

219	A31 15fr on 25fr multi	.55	.35
220	A31 15fr on 100fr multi	.55	.35
a.	Pair, #219-220	1.50	1.10

Fifth anniversary of the Cooperation Agreement between France and Dahomey.

WHO Headquarters from the East — A36

1966, May 3 *Perf. 12½x13*

Size: 35x22½mm

221	A36 30fr multicolored	.75	.25

Inauguration of the WHO Headquarters, Geneva. See No. C32.

For surcharge see Benin No. 717.

Boy Scout Signaling A37

Designs: 10fr, Patrol standard with pennant, vert. 30fr, Campfire and map of Dahomey, vert. 50fr, Scouts building foot bridge.

1966, Oct. 17 Engr. *Perf. 13*

222	A37 5fr dk brn, ocher & red	.30	.25
223	A37 10fr black, grn & rose cl	.30	.25
224	A37 30fr org, red brn & pur	.70	.35
225	A37 50fr vio bl, grn & dk brn	1.20	.45
a.	Min. sheet of 4, #222-225	3.00	3.00
	Nos. 222-225 (4)	2.50	1.30

Clappertonia Ficifolia — A38

Flowers: 3fr, Hewittia sublobata. 5fr, Butterfly pea. 10fr, Water lily. 15fr, Commelina forskalaei. 30fr, Eremomastax speciosa.

1967, Feb. 20 Photo. *Perf. 12x12½*

226	A38 1fr multicolored	.25	.25
227	A38 3fr multicolored	.35	.25
228	A38 5fr multicolored	.55	.25
229	A38 10fr multicolored	.90	.35
230	A38 15fr multicolored	1.10	.55
231	A38 30fr multicolored	2.10	.90
	Nos. 226-231 (6)	5.25	2.55

For surcharges see Benin Nos. 707, 715, 1376, 1390, 1402.

Nos. 170-171 Surcharged

1967, Mar. 1 Engr. *Perf. 13*

232	A19 30fr on 65fr	.85	.60
a.	Double surcharge	36.00	
233	A19 30fr on 85fr	.85	.60
a.	Double surcharge	60.00	
b.	Inverted surcharge	60.00	

Lions Emblem, Dancing Children, Bird — A39

1967, Mar. 20

234	A39 100fr dl vio, dp bl & grn	1.50	1.10

50th anniversary of Lions International.

"Man in the City" Pavilion A40

"The New Africa" Exhibit — A40a

1967, June 12 Engr. *Perf. 13*

235	A40 30fr green & choc	.70	.25
236	A40a 70fr green & brn red	1.50	.65

EXPO '67, International Exhibition, Montreal, Apr. 28-Oct. 27, 1967. See No. C57 and miniature sheet No. C57a.

For surcharges see Benin No. 897.

Europafrica Issue

Trade (Blood) Circulation, Map of Europe and Africa — A41

1967, July 20 Photo. *Perf. 12x12½*

237	A41 30fr multicolored	.70	.25
238	A41 45fr multicolored	1.10	.45

For surcharge, see Benin No. 1386.

Scouts Climbing Mountain, Jamboree Emblem A42

70fr, Jamboree emblem, Scouts launching canoe.

1967, Aug. 7 Engr. *Perf. 13*
239 A42 30fr brt bl, red brn & sl .80 .25
240 A42 70fr brt bl, sl grn & dk brn 1.60 .65

12th Boy Scout World Jamboree, Farragut State Park, Idaho, Aug. 1-9. For souvenir sheet see No. C59a.
For surcharges see Benin Nos. 902, 912, 1391.

Rhone River and Olympic Emblems A43

Designs (Olympic Emblems and): 45fr, View of Grenoble, vert. 100fr, Rhone Bridge, Grenoble, and Pierre de Coubertin.

1967, Sept. 2 Engr. *Perf. 13*
241 A43 30fr bis, dp bl & grn .70 .40
242 A43 45fr ultra, grn & brn .90 .55
243 A43 100fr choc, grn & brt bl 2.25 1.00
a. Min. sheet of 3, #241-243 4.50 4.50
Nos. 241-243 (3) 3.85 1.95

10th Winter Olympic Games, Grenoble, Feb. 6-18, 1968.
For surcharges, see Benin Nos. 903, 1054E, 1054F, 1392.

Monetary Union Issue
Common Design Type

1967, Nov. 4 Engr. *Perf. 13*
244 CD125 30fr grn, dk car & dk brn .65 .65

Animals from the Pendjari Reservation A45

Designs: 15fr, Cape Buffalo. 30fr, Lion. 45fr, Buffon's kob. 70fr, African slender-snouted crocodile. 100fr, Hippopotamus.

1968, Mar. 18 Photo. *Perf. 12½x13*
245 A45 15fr multicolored .55 .25
246 A45 30fr purple & multi .65 .50
247 A45 45fr blue & multi 1.25 .60
248 A45 70fr multicolored 2.25 .75
249 A45 100fr multicolored 4.00 2.25
Nos. 245-249 (5) 8.70 4.35

See Nos. 252-256.
For surcharges see No. 310, Benin Nos. 655E, 725, 1415, 1420, 1421.

WHO Emblem A46

1968, Apr. 22 Engr. *Perf. 13*
250 A46 30fr multicolored .60 .25
251 A46 70fr multicolored 1.40 .70

20th anniv. of WHO. For surcharges, see Benin Nos. 1012, 1387, 1465.

Animals from the Pendjari Reservation A47

Animals: 5fr, Warthog. 30fr, Leopard. 60fr, Spotted hyena. 75fr, Anubius baboon. 90fr, Hartebeest.

1969, Feb. 10 Photo. *Perf. 12½x12*
252 A47 5fr dark brown & multi .25 .25
253 A47 30fr deep ultra & multi .70 .50
254 A47 60fr dark green & multi 1.25 .70
255 A47 75fr dark blue & multi 3.00 1.00
256 A47 90fr dark green & multi 4.00 2.25
Nos. 252-256 (5) 9.20 4.70

For surcharges, see Benin Nos. 708, 1438.

Heads, Symbols of Agriculture and Science, and Globe A48

1969, Mar. 10 Engr. *Perf. 13*
257 A48 30fr orange & multi .50 .25
258 A48 70fr maroon & multi 1.50 .70

50th anniv. of the ILO.
For surcharges see Benin Nos. 904, 913.

Arms of Dahomey — A49

1969, June 30 Litho. *Perf. 13½x13*
259 A49 5fr yellow & multi .35 .30
260 A49 30fr orange red & multi 1.50 .45

See No. C101.

Development Bank Issue

Cornucopia and Bank Emblem — A50

1969, Sept. 10 Photo. *Perf. 13*
261 A50 30fr black, grn & ocher .75 .55

African Development Bank, 5th anniv.
For surcharge see Benin No. 905.

Europafrica Issue

Ambary (Kenaf) Industry, Cotonou A51

Design: 45fr, Cotton industry, Parakou.

1969, Sept. 22 Litho. *Perf. 14*
262 A51 30fr multicolored 1.00 .50
263 A51 45fr multicolored 1.25 .75

See Nos. C105-C105a.
For overprints and surcharges see Benin No. 1054A.

Sakpata Dance and Tourist Year Emblem — A52

Dances and Tourist Year Emblem: 30fr, Guelede dance. 45fr, Sato dance.

1969, Dec. 15 Litho. *Perf. 14*
264 A52 10fr multicolored .75 .30
265 A52 30fr multicolored 1.45 .45
266 A52 45fr multicolored 2.00 .55
Nos. 264-266 (3) 4.20 1.30

See No. C108. For surcharges see Benin Nos. 690J, 1054B, 1388, 1433.

UN Emblem, Garden and Wall — A53

1970, Apr. 6 Engr. *Perf. 13*
267 A53 30fr ultra, red org & slate .70 .25
268 A53 40fr ultra, brn & sl grn 1.25 .50

25th anniversary of the United Nations.
For surcharge see No. 294. For overprint see Benin 647B.

ASECNA Issue
Common Design Type

1970, June 1 Engr. *Perf. 13*
269 CD132 40fr red & purple .90 .55

For surcharges, see Benin Nos. 906, 1396.

Mt. Fuji, EXPO '70 Emblem, Monorail Train — A54

1970, June 15 Litho. *Perf. 13½x14*
270 A54 5fr green, red & vio bl .40 .25

EXPO '70 International Exhibition, Osaka, Japan, 3/15-9/13/70. See Nos. C124-C125.

Alkemy, King of Ardres — A55

40fr, Sailing ships "La Justice" & "La Concorde," Ardres, 1670. 50fr, Matheo Lopes, ambassador of the King of Ardres & his coat of arms. 200fr, Louis XIV & fleur-de-lis.

1970, July 6 Engr. *Perf. 13*
271 A55 40fr brt grn, ultra & brn .75 .25
272 A55 50fr dk car, choc & emer 1.05 .40
273 A55 70fr gray, lemon & choc 1.60 .65
274 A55 200fr Prus bl, dk car & choc 4.00 1.25
Nos. 271-274 (4) 7.40 2.55

300th anniv. of the mission from the King of Ardres to the King of France, and of the audience with Louis XIV on Dec. 19, 1670.
For surcharges see Benin Nos. 721, 724, 914.

Star of the Order of Independence — A56

1970, Aug. 1 Photo. *Perf. 12*
275 A56 30fr multicolored .40 .25
276 A56 40fr multicolored .60 .25

10th anniversary of independence.
For surcharge see Benin Nos. 720, 1464.

Bariba Warrior — A57

Designs: 2fr, 50fr, Two horsemen. 10fr, 70fr, Horseman facing left.

1970, Aug. 24 *Perf. 12½x13*
277 A57 1fr yellow & multi .30 .25
278 A57 2fr gray grn & multi .45 .25
279 A57 10fr blue & multi .60 .25
280 A57 40fr yellow grn & multi 1.90 .35
281 A57 50fr gold & multi 2.40 .50
282 A57 70fr lilac rose & multi 3.00 .80
Nos. 277-282 (6) 8.65 2.40

For surcharges see Benin Nos. 350-351, 613, 703, 1373, 1401.

Globe and Heart A58

Design: 40fr, Hands holding heart, vert.

1971, June 7 Engr. *Perf. 13*
283 A58 40fr red, green & dk brn 2.00 .50
284 A58 100fr green, red & blue 4.00 1.25

For surcharges see Benin Nos. 617, 647A, 712, 907, 1429.

Intl. year against racial discrimination.

Ancestral Figures and Lottery Ticket — A59

1971, June 24 Litho. *Perf. 14*
285 A59 35fr multicolored .80 .25
286 A59 40fr multicolored 1.25 .35

4th anniv. of the National Lottery.
For overprint and surcharge, see Benin Nos. 710, 1430.

King Behanzin's Emblem (1889-1894) A60

Emblems of the Kings of Abomey: 25fr, Agoliagbo (1894-1900). 35fr, Ganyehoussou (1620-45), bird and cup, horiz. 100fr, Guezo (1818-58), bull, tree and birds. 135fr, Ouegbadja (1645-85), horiz. 140fr, Glèle (1858-89), lion and sword, horiz.

Photo.; Litho. (25fr, 135fr)

1971-72 *Perf. 12½*
287 A60 25fr multicolored .55 .25
288 A60 35fr green & multi .90 .25
289 A60 40fr green & multi 1.25 .55
290 A60 100fr red & multi 2.25 .90
291 A60 135fr multicolored 3.25 1.40
292 A60 140fr brown & multi 3.75 1.90
Nos. 287-292 (6) 11.95 5.25

Issued: 25fr, 135fr, 7/17/72; others, 8/3/71.

For surcharges and overprint, see Benin Nos. 614, 634B, 708A, 726, 791, 1054D, 1369, 1422, 1431, 1467, 1470.

Kabuki Actor, Long-distance Skiing — A61

1972, Feb. Engr. *Perf. 13*

293 A61 35fr dk car, brn & bl grn 2.50 .75

11th Winter Olympic Games, Sapporo, Japan, Feb. 3-13. See No. C153.

No. 268 Surcharged

1972

294 A53 35fr on 40fr multi .90 .35

Brahms and "Soir d'été" — A62

Design: 65fr, Brahms, woman at piano & music, horiz.

1972, June 29 Engr. *Perf. 13*

295 A62 30fr red brn, blk & lilac 4.00 .80
296 A62 65fr red brn, blk & lilac 6.75 1.50

75th anniversary of the death of Johannes Brahms (1833-1897), German composer.
For surcharges see Benin Nos. 654B, 718, 1389.

The Hare and The Tortoise, by La Fontaine — A63

Fables: 35fr, The Fox and The Stork, vert. 40fr, The Cat, The Weasel and Rabbit.

1972, Aug. 28 Engr. *Perf. 13*

297 A63 10fr multicolored 2.25 .75
298 A63 35fr dark red & multi 4.25 1.25
299 A63 40fr ultra & multi 5.50 1.75
Nos. 297-299 (3) 12.00 3.75

Jean de La Fontaine (1621-1695), French fabulist. For surcharges, see Benin Nos. 1380, 1393, 1397.

West African Monetary Union Issue
Common Design Type

1972, Nov. 2 Engr. *Perf. 13*

300 CD136 40fr choc, ocher & gray .65 .25

Dr. Armauer Hansen, Microscope, Bacilli — A65

Design: 85fr, Portrait of Dr. Hansen.

1973, May 14 Engr. *Perf. 13*

301 A65 35fr ultra, vio brn & brn .50 .35
302 A65 85fr yel grn, bis & ver 1.25 .75

Centenary of the discovery by Dr. Armauer G. Hansen of the Hansen bacillus, the cause of leprosy.
For surcharges see Benin Nos. 655G, 1084, 1437.

Arms of Dahomey — A66

1973, June 25 Photo. *Perf. 13*

303 A66 5fr ultra & multi .25 .25
304 A66 35fr ocher & multi .40 .25
305 A66 40fr red orange & multi .60 .25
Nos. 303-305 (3) 1.25 .75

For overprint and surcharge see Benin Nos. 690A, 1403.

INTERPOL Emblem and Spiderweb A67

Design: 50fr, INTERPOL emblem and communications symbols, vert.

1973, July Engr.

306 A67 35fr ver, grn & brn .60 .30
307 A67 50fr green, brn & red .85 .45

50th anniversary of International Criminal Police Organization (INTERPOL).
For overprints and surcharges, see Benin Nos. 634A, 810, 1434, 1471.

Education in Hygiene and Nutrition A68

WHO, 25th Anniv.: 100fr, Prenatal examination and care, WHO emblem.

1973, Aug. 2 Photo. *Perf. 12½x13*

308 A68 35fr multicolored .50 .30
309 A68 100fr multicolored 1.50 .65

For surcharges, see Benin Nos. 655B, 1439.

No. 248 Srchd. and Ovptd. in Red

1973, Aug. 16

310 A45 100fr on 70fr multi 2.50 1.00

African solidarity in drought emergency.

African Postal Union Issue
Common Design Type

1973, Sept. 12 Engr. *Perf. 13*

311 CD137 100fr red, purple & blk 1.25 .55

For surcharges, see Benin Nos. 690I, 1440.

Epinephelus Aeneus — A69

Fish: 15fr, Drepane africana. 35fr, Pragus ehrenbergi.

1973, Sept. 18

312 A69 5fr slate blue & indigo 1.00 .30
313 A69 15fr black & brt blue 1.50 .35
314 A69 35fr emerald, ocher & sep 4.00 .60
Nos. 312-314 (3) 6.50 1.25

For surcharges, see Benin No. 698, 1378, 1383, 1394.

Chameleon A70

40fr, Emblem over map of Dahomey, vert.

1973, Nov. 30 Photo. *Perf. 13*

315 A70 35fr olive & multi .55 .30
316 A70 40fr multicolored 1.25 .35

1st anniv. of the Oct. 26 revolution.

The Chameleon in the Tree — A71

Designs: 5fr, The elephant, the hen and the dog, vert. 10fr, The sparrowhawk and the dog, vert. 25fr, The chameleon in the tree. 40fr, The eagle, the viper and the hen.

1974, Feb. 14 Photo. *Perf. 13*

317 A71 5fr emerald & multi .75 .25
318 A71 10fr slate blue & multi .90 .25
319 A71 25fr slate blue & multi 1.75 .30
320 A71 40fr light blue & multi 2.50 .45
Nos. 317-320 (4) 5.90 1.25

Folktales of Dahomey.
For surcharges and overprint see Benin Nos. 699, 709, 908, 1363, 1370, 1379, 1381, 1432.

German Shepherd — A72

1974, Apr. 25 Photo. *Perf. 13*

321 A72 40fr shown 1.50 .35
322 A72 50fr Boxer 1.75 .35
323 A72 100fr Saluki 3.50 .80
Nos. 321-323 (3) 6.75 1.50

For surcharges, see Benin No. 1398, 1435, 1441.

Council Issue

Map and Flags of Members A73

1974, May 29 Photo. *Perf. 13x12½*

324 A73 40fr blue & multi .80 .25

15th anniversary of the Council of Accord.

Locomotive 232, 1911 — A74

Designs: Locomotives.

1974, Sept. 2 Photo. *Perf. 13x12½*

325 A74 35fr shown 1.00 .30
326 A74 40fr Freight, 1877 2.00 .30
327 A74 100fr Crampton, 1849 3.00 1.00
328 A74 200fr Stephenson, 1846 6.00 1.60
Nos. 325-328 (4) 12.00 3.20

For surcharges see Benin Nos. 654E, 690D, 690K, 727, 909, 1395, 1399, 1442, 1444.

Globe, Money, People in Bank A75

1974, Oct. 31 Engr. *Perf. 13*

329 A75 35fr multicolored .50 .35

World Savings Day. For surcharge, see Benin No. 1468.

Dompago Dance, Hissi Tribe — A76

Folk Dances: 25fr, Fetish Dance, Vaudou-Tchinan. 40fr, Bamboo Dance, Agbehoun. 100fr, Somba Dance, Sandoua, horiz.

1975, Aug. 4 Litho. *Perf. 12*

330 A76 10fr yellow & multi .65 .25
331 A76 25fr dk green & multi 1.25 .25
332 A76 40fr red & multi 1.60 .50
333 A76 100fr multicolored 3.00 .60
Nos. 330-333 (4) 6.50 1.60

For surcharges and overprints see Benin Nos. 655D, 690C, 713, 1371,1404, 1414, 1443.

Flags of Dahomey and Nigeria over Africa — A77

Design: 100fr, Arrows connecting maps of Dahomey and Nigeria, horiz.

1975, Aug. 11 Photo. *Perf. 12½x13*

334 A77 65fr multicolored .75 .25
335 A77 100fr green & multi 1.00 .45

Year of intensified cooperation between Dahomey and Nigeria.
For surcharges & overprint see Benin Nos. 690H, 701, 899, 901, 1419, 1423.

Map, Pylons, Emblem — A78

Benin Electric Community Emblem and Pylon — A79

1975, Aug. 18
336 A78 40fr multicolored .75 .35
337 A79 150fr multicolored 2.00 1.00

Benin Electric Community and Ghana-Togo-Dahomey cooperation.
For surcharges see Benin Nos. 601, 900, 910, 1400, 1405, Q12A, Q12B.

Map of Dahomey, Rising Sun — A80

1975, Aug. 25 Photo. *Perf. 12½x13*
338 A80 35fr multicolored .50 .25

Cooperation Year for the creation of a new Dahoman society.
For overprint see Benin No. 690E. For surcharge, see Benin No. 1362.

Albert Schweitzer, Nurse, Patient — A81

1975, Sept. 22 Engr. *Perf. 13*
339 A81 200fr olive, grn & red brn 6.25 1.50

Birth centenary of Albert Schweitzer (1875-1965), medical missionary and musician.
For surcharges, see Benin Nos. 655F, 1445.

Woman Speaking on Telephone, IWY Emblem — A82

150fr, IWY emblem and linked rings.

1975, Oct. 20 Engr. *Perf. 12½x13*
340 A82 50fr Prus blue & lilac .75 .35
341 A82 150fr emerald, brn & org 2.00 .80

International Women's Year 1975.
For surcharges, see Benin Nos. 655C, 1054C, 1436, 1469.

SEMI-POSTAL STAMPS

Regular Issue of 1913 Surcharged in Red

1915 Unwmk. *Perf. 14x13½*
B1 A5 10c + 5c orange red & rose 1.60 1.60

Curie Issue
Common Design Type

1938 *Perf. 13*
B2 CD80 1.75fr + 50c brt ultra 9.50 9.50

French Revolution Issue
Common Design Type

1939 Photo.
Name and Value Typo. in Black
B3 CD83 45c + 25c green 9.50 9.50
B4 CD83 70c + 30c brown 9.50 9.50
B5 CD83 90c + 35c red org 9.50 9.50
B6 CD83 1.25fr + 1fr rose pink 9.50 9.50
B7 CD83 2.25fr + 2fr blue 9.50 9.50
Nos. B3-B7 (5) 47.50 47.50

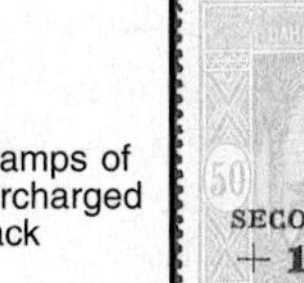

Postage Stamps of 1913-38 Surcharged in Black

1941 *Perf. 13½x14*
B8 A5 50c + 1fr brn red & bl 3.25 3.25
B9 A5 80c + 2fr hn brn & ultra 7.25 7.25
B10 A5 1.50fr + 2fr dk bl & lt bl 7.25 7.25
B11 A5 2fr + 3fr yel org & choc 7.25 7.25
Nos. B8-B11 (4) 25.00 25.00

Common Design Type and

Radio Operator — SP1

Senegalese Artillerymen SP2

1941 Photo. *Perf. 13½*
B12 SP1 1fr + 1fr red 1.20
B13 CD86 1.50fr + 3fr claret 1.20
B14 SP2 2.50fr + 1fr blue 1.20
Nos. B12-B14 (3) 3.60

Surtax for the defense of the colonies.
Nos. B12-B14 were issued by the Vichy government in France, but were not placed on sale in Dahomey.

Nos. 135-136 Srchd. in Black or Red

1944 Engr. *Perf. 12½x12*
B14A 50c + 1.50fr on 2.50fr deep blue (R) .80
B14B + 2.50fr on 1fr green .80

Colonial Development Fund.
Nos. B14A-B14B were issued by the Vichy government in France, but were not placed on sale in Dahomey.

Catalogue values for unused stamps in this section, from this point to the end of the section, are for Never Hinged items.

Republic
Anti-Malaria Issue
Common Design Type

1962, Apr. 7 Engr. *Perf. 12½x12*
B15 CD108 25fr + 5fr orange brn .75 .75

Freedom from Hunger Issue
Common Design Type

1963, Mar. 21 Unwmk. *Perf. 13*
B16 CD112 25fr + 5fr ol, brn red & brn .80 .80

AIR POST STAMPS

Common Design Type

1940 Unwmk. Engr. *Perf. 12½*
C1 CD85 1.90fr ultra .40 .40
C2 CD85 2.90fr dk red .40 .40
C3 CD85 4.50fr dk gray grn .80 .80
C4 CD85 4.90fr yel bister .80 .80
C5 CD85 6.90fr deep org 1.60 1.60
Nos. C1-C5 (5) 4.00 4.00

Common Design Types

1942
C6 CD88 50c car & bl .30
C7 CD88 1fr brn & blk .30
C8 CD88 2fr dk grn & red brn .50
C9 CD88 3fr dk bl & scar .95
C10 CD88 5fr vio & brn red 1.05

Frame Engr., Center Typo.
C11 CD89 10fr ultra, ind & org 1.05
C12 CD89 20fr rose car, mag & gray blk 1.10
C13 CD89 50fr yel grn, dl grn & dp bl 1.90 *3.25*
a. 50fr yellow green, dull green & pale blue 2.75 *3.75*
Nos. C6-C13 (8) 7.15

Nos. C6-C12 were issued by the Vichy government in France, but were not placed on sale in Dahomey.

Catalogue values for unused stamps in this section, from this point to the end of the section, are for Never Hinged items.

Republic

Somba House — AP4

Design: 500fr, Royal Court of Abomey.

Unwmk.
1960, Apr. 1 Engr. *Perf. 13*
C14 AP4 100fr multi 3.25 .80
C15 AP4 500fr multi 13.50 4.00

For overprint see Benin No. C419. For surcharges, see No. CQ5, Benin Nos. C541, C609.

Type of Regular Issue, 1961

1961, Sept. 20
C16 A16 200fr multi 3.50 2.25
a. Souv. sheet of 3, #150-151, C16 7.00 7.00

Air Afrique Issue
Common Design Type

1962, Feb. 17 *Perf. 13*
C17 CD107 25fr ultra, blk & org brn .80 .40

Palace of the African and Malgache Union, Cotonou — AP5

1963, July 27 Photo. *Perf. 13x12*
C18 AP5 250fr multi 5.00 2.75

Assembly of chiefs of state of the African and Malgache Union held at Cotonou in July.

African Postal Union Issue
Common Design Type

1963, Sept. 8 Unwmk. *Perf. 12½*
C19 CD114 25fr brt bl, ocher & red .75 .25

See note after Cameroun No. C47.

Boeing 707 — AP6

Boeing 707: 200fr, On the ground. 300fr, Over Cotonou airport. 500fr, In the air.

1963, Oct. 25 Engr. *Perf. 13*
C20 AP6 100fr multi 2.00 .60
C21 AP6 200fr multi 3.00 2.00
C22 AP6 300fr multi 5.00 2.00
C23 AP6 500fr multi 10.00 2.50
Nos. C20-C23 (4) 20.00 7.10

For surcharges see Nos. CQ1-CQ5, Benin No. C610.

Priests Carrying Funerary Boat, Isis Temple, Philae — AP7

1964, Mar. 9 Unwmk. *Perf. 13*
C24 AP7 25fr vio bl & brn 2.00 .95

UNESCO world campaign to save historic monuments in Nubia.

Weather Map and Symbols — AP8

1965, Mar. 23 Photo. *Perf. 12½*
C25 AP8 50fr multi .80 .55

Fifth World Meteorological Day.

ICY Emblem and Men of Various Races — AP9

1965, June 26 Engr. *Perf. 13*
C26 AP9 25fr dl pur, mar & grn .65 .25
C27 AP9 85fr dp bl, mar & sl grn 1.25 .80

International Cooperation Year, 1965

Winston Churchill — AP10

1965, June 15 Photo. *Perf. 12½*

C28 AP10 100fr multi 2.25 1.75

For surcharges, see Benin Nos. C519, C611.

Abraham Lincoln — AP11

1965, July 15 *Perf. 13*

C29 AP11 100fr multi 2.00 1.00

Centenary of death of Lincoln

For surcharge see No. C55.

John F. Kennedy and Arms of Dahomey — AP12

1965, Nov. 22 Photo. *Perf. 12½*

C30 AP12 100fr dp grn & blk 2.75 1.10

President John F. Kennedy (1917-63).

For surcharge see No. C56.

Dr. Albert Schweitzer and Patients — AP13

1966, Jan. 17 Photo. *Perf. 12½*

C31 AP13 100fr multi 3.00 1.25

Dr. Albert Schweitzer (1875-1965), medical missionary, theologian and musician.

For surcharge see Benin No. C435.

WHO Type of Regular Issue

Design: WHO Headquarters from the West.

1966, May 3 Unwmk. *Perf. 13*
Size: 47x28mm

C32 A36 100fr ultra, yel & blk 1.75 1.50

Pygmy Goose — AP14

Broad-billed Rollers — AP15

Birds: 100fr, Fiery-breasted bush-shrike. 250fr, Emerald cuckoos. 500fr, Emerald starling.

1966-67 *Perf. 12½*

C33 AP14 50fr multi 2.00 .55
C34 AP14 100fr multi 3.00 .85
C35 AP15 200fr multi 10.00 2.25
C36 AP15 250fr multi 10.00 3.00
C37 AP14 500fr multi 15.00 6.00
Nos. C33-C37 (5) 40.00 12.65

Issued: 50fr, 100fr, 500fr, 6/13/66; others, 1/20/67.

For surcharges see No. C107, Benin Nos. 1472, C353-C355, C357, C368, C426, C436, C511, C550, C590.

Industrial Symbols — AP16

1966, July 21 Photo. *Perf. 12x13*

C38 AP16 100fr multi 1.75 .80

Agreement between European Economic Community & the African & Malagache Union, 3rd anniv.

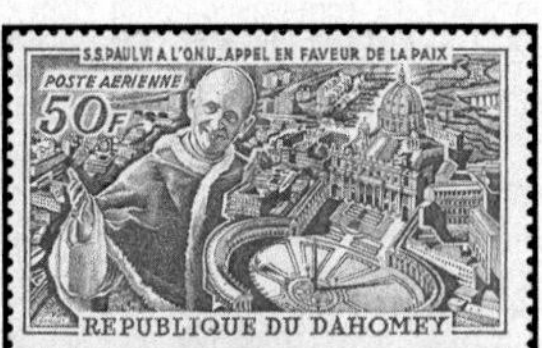

Pope Paul VI and St. Peter's, Rome — AP17

Pope Paul VI and UN General Assembly AP18

70fr, Pope Paul VI and view of NYC.

1966, Aug. 22 Engr. *Perf. 13*

C39 AP17 50fr multi .75 .45
C40 AP17 70fr multi .95 .55
C41 AP18 100fr multi 1.75 1.00
a. Min. sheet of 3, #C39-C41 4.50 4.50
Nos. C39-C41 (3) 3.45 2.00

Pope Paul's appeal for peace before the UN General Assembly, Oct. 4, 1965.

Air Afrique Issue, 1966

Common Design Type

1966, Aug. 31 Photo. *Perf. 12½*

C42 CD123 30fr dk vio, blk & gray .75 .25

"Science" — AP20

Designs: 45fr, "Art" (carved female statue), vert. 100fr, "Education" (book and letters).

1966, Nov. 4 Engr. *Perf. 13*

C43 AP20 30fr mag, ultra & vio brn .45 .25
C44 AP20 45fr mar & grn .80 .55
C45 AP20 100fr blk, mar & brt bl 1.90 1.00
a. Min. sheet of 3, #C43-C45 3.25 3.25
Nos. C43-C45 (3) 3.15 1.80

20th anniversary of UNESCO.

Madonna by Alessio Baldovinetti AP21

Christmas: 50fr, Nativity after 15th century Beaune tapestry. 100fr, Adoration of the Shepherds, by José Ribera.

1966, Dec. 25 Photo. *Perf. 12½x12*

C46 AP21 50fr multi 3.25 2.25
C47 AP21 100fr multi 4.50 3.25
C48 AP21 200fr multi 9.00 5.00
Nos. C46-C48 (3) 16.75 10.50

See Nos. C95-C96, C109-C115. For surcharges, see No. C60, Benin Nos. C427, C520. For overprint, see Benin No. C544

1967, Apr. 10 *Perf. 12½x12*

Paintings by Ingres: No. C49, Self-portrait, 1804. No. C50, Oedipus and the Sphinx.

C49 AP21 100fr multi 3.25 1.75
C50 AP21 100fr multi 3.25 1.75

Jean Auguste Dominique Ingres (1780-1867), French painter.

Three-master Suzanne — AP22

Windjammers: 45fr, Three-master Esmeralda, vert. 80fr, Schooner Marie Alice, vert. 100fr, Four-master Antonin.

1967, May 8 *Perf. 13*

C51 AP22 30fr multi 1.00 .50
C52 AP22 45fr multi 1.25 .75
C53 AP22 80fr multi 2.50 1.25
C54 AP22 100fr multi 3.25 1.50
Nos. C51-C54 (4) 8.00 4.00

For overprint and surcharges see Benin Nos. C369, C420, C606, C612.

Nos. C29-C30 Surcharged

1967, May 29 Photo. *Perf. 13, 12½*

C55 AP11 125fr on 100fr 2.75 1.25
C56 AP12 125fr on 100fr 2.75 1.25

50th anniv. of the birth of Pres. John F. Kennedy.

EXPO '67 "Man In Space" Pavilion — AP23

1967, June 12 Engr. *Perf. 13*

C57 AP23 100fr dl red & Prus bl 2.00 .75
a. Min. sheet of 3, #235-236, C57 4.00 4.00

EXPO '67, International Exhibition, Montreal, Apr. 28-Oct. 27, 1967.

Europafrica Issue

Konrad Adenauer, by Oscar Kokoschká AP24

1967, July 19 Photo. *Perf. 12½x12*

C58 AP24 70fr multi 2.00 1.25
a. Souv. sheet of 4 8.50 8.50

Konrad Adenauer (1876-1967), chancellor of West Germany (1949-1963). For surcharges, see Benin Nos. C428, C572, C602.

Jamboree Emblem, Ropes and World Map — AP25

1967, Aug. 7 Engr. *Perf. 13*

C59 AP25 100fr lil, sl grn & dp bl 1.60 .75
a. Souv. sheet of 3, #239-240, C59 3.50 3.50

12th Boy Scout World Jamboree, Farragut State Park, Idaho, Aug. 1-9.

No. C48 Srchd. in Red

1967, Aug. 12 Photo. *Perf. 12½x12*

C60 AP21 150fr on 200fr 3.50 2.75
a. "150F" omitted 300.00 300.00

Riccione, Italy Stamp Exhibition.

African Postal Union Issue, 1967
Common Design Type

1967, Sept. 9 Engr. *Perf. 13*
C61 CD124 100fr red, brt lil & emer 1.75 .95

For surcharge see Benin No. C471.

Charles de Gaulle AP26

1967, Nov. 21 Photo. *Perf. 12½x13*
C62 AP26 100fr multi 3.75 2.50
a. Souv. sheet of 4 16.00 16.00

Pres. Charles de Gaulle of France on the occasion of Pres. Christophe Soglo's state visit to Paris, Nov. 1967.

Madonna, by Matthias Grunewald AP27

Paintings: 50fr, Holy Family by the Master of St. Sebastian, horiz. 100fr, Adoration of the Magi by Ulrich Apt the Elder. 200fr, Annunciation, by Matthias Grunewald.

1967, Dec. 11 Photo. *Perf. 12½*
C63 AP27 30fr multi .55 .45
C64 AP27 50fr multi 1.10 .60
C65 AP27 100fr multi 2.00 1.25
C66 AP27 200fr multi 5.00 2.00
Nos. C63-C66 (4) 8.65 4.30

Christmas 1967.

Venus de Milo and Mariner 5 — AP28

#C68, Venus de Milo and Venera 4 rocket.

1968, Feb. 17 Photo. *Perf. 13*
C67 AP28 70fr grnsh bl & multi 1.75 .75
C68 AP28 70fr dp bl & multi 1.75 .75
a. Souv. sheet of 2, #C67-C68 4.00 4.00

Explorations of the planet Venus, Oct. 18-19, 1967.
For surcharges see Nos. C103-C104, Benin Nos. C573, C587.

Gutenberg Monument, Strasbourg Cathedral AP29

Design: 100fr, Gutenberg Monument, Mainz, and Gutenberg press.

1968, May 20 Litho. *Perf. 14x13½*
C69 AP29 45fr grn & org 1.00 .40
C70 AP29 100fr dk & lt bl 2.00 1.00
a. Souv. sheet of 2, #C69-C70 3.75 3.75

500th anniv. of the death of Johann Gutenberg, inventor of printing from movable type.
For surcharges see Benin Nos. C512, C516.

Martin Luther King, Jr. — AP30

Designs: 30fr, "We must meet hate with creative love" in French, English and German. 100fr, Full-face portrait.

Perf. 12½, 13½x13
1968, June 17 Photo.
Size: 26x46mm
C71 AP30 30fr red brn, yel & blk .60 .35
Size: 26x37mm
C72 AP30 55fr multi 1.00 .45
C73 AP30 100fr multi 1.50 .90
a. Min. sheet of 3, #C71-C73 4.00 4.00
Nos. C71-C73 (3) 3.10 1.70

Martin Luther King, Jr. (1929-68), American civil rights leader.
For surcharges, see Benin Nos. C517, C561, C613.

Robert Schuman — AP31

45fr, Alcide de Gasperi. 70fr, Konrad Adenauer.

1968, July 20 Photo. *Perf. 13*
C74 AP31 30fr dp yel, blk & grn .40 .40
C75 AP31 45fr org, dk brn & ol .85 .50
C76 AP31 70fr multi 1.40 .50
Nos. C74-C76 (3) 2.65 1.40

5th anniversary of the economic agreement between the European Economic Community and the African and Malgache Union.
For surcharges, see Benin Nos. C462, C562, C603.

Battle of Montebello, by Henri Philippoteaux — AP32

Paintings: 45fr, 2nd Zouave Regiment at Magenta, by Riballier. 70fr, Battle of Magenta, by Louis Eugène Charpentier. 100fr, Battle of Solferino, by Charpentier.

1968, Aug. 12 *Perf. 12½x12*
C77 AP32 30fr multi 1.15 .50
C78 AP32 45fr multi 1.60 .65
C79 AP32 70fr multi 3.25 1.25
C80 AP32 100fr multi 4.00 1.00
Nos. C77-C80 (4) 10.00 3.40

Issued for the Red Cross. For surcharges, see Benin Nos. C574, C594, C614.

Mail Truck in Village — AP33

Designs: 45fr, Mail truck stopping at rural post office. 55fr, Mail truck at river bank. 70fr, Mail truck and train.

1968, Oct. 7 Photo. *Perf. 13x12½*
C81 AP33 30fr multi .90 .50
C82 AP33 45fr multi 1.10 .55
C83 AP33 55fr multi 1.75 .55
C84 AP33 70fr multi 4.25 1.00
Nos. C81-C84 (4) 8.00 2.60

For surcharges see Benin Nos. C352, C357A, C584.

Aztec Stadium, Mexico City — AP34

45fr, Ball player, Mayan sculpture, vert. 70fr, Wrestler, sculpture from Uxpanapan, vert. 150fr, Olympic Stadium, Mexico City.

1968, Nov. 20 Engr. *Perf. 13*
C85 AP34 30fr dp cl & sl grn .80 .30
C86 AP34 45fr ultra & dk rose brn 1.50 .60
C87 AP34 70fr sl grn & dk brn 2.10 .65
C88 AP34 150fr dk car & dk brn 3.00 1.25
a. Min. sheet of 4, #C85-C88 7.50 7.50
Nos. C85-C88 (4) 7.40 2.80

19th Olympic Games, Mexico City, Oct. 12-27. No. C88a is folded down the vertical gutter separating Nos. C85-C86 se-tenant at left and Nos. C87-C88 se-tenant at right.
For overprint and surcharges see Benin Nos. C457, C461, C513.

The Annunciation, by Foujita — AP35

Paintings by Foujita: 30fr, Nativity, horiz. 100fr, The Virgin and Child. 200fr, The Baptism of Christ.

Perf. 12x12½, 12½x12
1968, Nov. 25 Photo.
C89 AP35 30fr multi .80 .55
C90 AP35 70fr multi 1.60 .80
C91 AP35 100fr multi 1.75 1.25
C92 AP35 200fr multi 4.00 2.75
Nos. C89-C92 (4) 8.15 5.35

Christmas 1968. For surcharges, see Benin Nos. C531, C563, C575, C615, C648.

PHILEXAFRIQUE Issue

Painting: Diderot, by Louis Michel Vanloo.

1968, Dec. 16 *Perf. 12½x12*
C93 AP35 100fr multi 3.75 3.75

PHILEXAFRIQUE, Philatelic Exhibition in Abidjan, Feb. 14-23. Printed with alternating label.
For surcharges, see Benin Nos. C522, C629.

2nd PHILEXAFRIQUE Issue
Common Design Type

50fr, Dahomey #119 and aerial view of Cotonou.

1969, Feb. 14 Engr. *Perf. 13*
C94 CD128 50fr bl, brn & pur 2.25 2.25

For surcharge see Benin Nos. C467, C651.

Christmas Painting Type

Paintings: No. C95, Virgin of the Rocks, by Leonardo da Vinci. No. C96, Virgin with the Scales, by Cesare da Sesto.

1969, Mar. 17 Photo. *Perf. 12½x12*
C95 AP21 100fr vio & multi 2.00 1.00
C96 AP21 100fr grn & multi 2.00 1.00

Leonardo da Vinci (1452-1519).
For surcharge see Benin No. C651B.

General Bonaparte, by Jacques Louis David AP36

Paintings: 60fr, Napoleon I in 1809, by Robert J. Lefevre. 75fr, Napoleon on the Battlefield of Eylau, by Antoine Jean Gros, horiz. 200fr, Gen. Bonaparte at Arcole, by Gros.

1969, Apr. 14 Photo. *Perf. 12½x12*
C97 AP36 30fr multi 1.50 1.25
C98 AP36 60fr multi 2.75 1.75
C99 AP36 75fr multi 3.25 2.50
C100 AP36 200fr multi 7.50 5.50
Nos. C97-C100 (4) 15.00 11.00

Bicentenary of the birth of Napoleon I. For surcharges, see Benin Nos. C599, C605.

Arms Type of Regular Issue, 1969

1969, June 30 Litho. *Perf. 13½x13*
C101 A49 50fr multi .75 .30

For overprint and surcharge see Benin Nos. C417, C596.

Apollo 8 Trip Around the Moon — AP37

Embossed on Gold Foil
1969, July *Die-cut Perf. 10½*
C102 AP37 1000fr gold 20.00 20.00

US Apollo 8 mission, which put the 1st men into orbit around the moon, Dec. 21-27, 1968.

Nos. C67-C68 Surcharged

1969, Aug. 1 Photo. *Perf. 13*
C103 AP28 125fr on 70fr, #C67 2.50 1.75
C104 AP28 125fr on 70fr, #C68 2.50 1.75

Man's 1st landing on the moon, July 20, 1969; US astronauts Neil A. Armstrong, Col.

Edwin E. Aldrin, Jr., with Lieut. Col. Michael Collins piloting Apollo 11.

Europafrica Issue

Type of Regular Issue, 1969

Design: 100fr, Oil palm industry, Cotonou.

1969, Sept. 22 Litho. *Perf. 14*

C105 A51 100fr multi 2.25 .35
a. Souv. sheet of 3, #262-263, C105 4.25 4.25

For surcharge see Benin No. C523.

Dahomey Rotary Emblem — AP38

1969, Sept. 25 *Perf. 14x13½*

C106 AP38 50fr multi 1.00 .75

For surcharge see Benin No. C468.

No. C33 Surcharged

1969, Nov. 15 Photo. *Perf. 12½*

C107 AP14 10fr on 50fr multi .45 .25

Dance Type of Regular Issue

Design: Teke dance and Tourist Year emblem.

1969, Dec. 15 Litho. *Perf. 14*

C108 A52 70fr multi 2.50 1.50

For surcharge see Benin No. C398.

Painting Type of 1966

Christmas: 30fr, Annunciation, by Vrancke van der Stockt. 45fr, Nativity, Swabian School, horiz. 110fr, Madonna and Child, by the Master of the Gold Brocade. 200fr, Adoration of the Kings, Antwerp School.

1969, Dec. 20 *Perf. 12½x12, 12x12½*

C109 AP21 30fr multi .50 .40
C110 AP21 45fr red & multi .85 .65
C111 AP21 110fr multi 2.10 1.25
C112 AP21 200fr multi 3.75 2.25
Nos. C109-C112 (4) 7.20 4.55

For surcharges see Benin #C425, C463, C475, C532, C595.

1969, Dec. 27 *Perf. 12½x12*

Paintings: No. C113, The Artist's Studio (detail), by Gustave Courbet. No. C114, Self-portrait with Gold Chain, by Rembrandt. 150fr, Hendrickje Stoffels, by Rembrandt.

C113 AP21 100fr red & multi 2.25 1.25
C114 AP21 100fr grn & multi 2.25 1.25
C115 AP21 150fr multi 3.75 1.75
Nos. C113-C115 (3) 8.25 4.25

For overprints and surcharges see Benin Nos. C458, C472, C524.

Franklin D. Roosevelt AP39

1970, Feb. Photo. *Perf. 12½*

C116 AP39 100fr ultra, yel grn & blk 1.75 .80

25th anniversary of the death of Pres. Franklin Delano Roosevelt (1882-1945). For surcharges see Benin Nos. C525, C637.

Astronauts, Rocket, US Flag — AP40

Astronauts: 50fr, Riding rocket through space. 70fr, In landing module approaching moon. 110fr, Planting US flag on moon.

1970, Mar. 9 Photo. *Perf. 12½*

C117 AP40 30fr multi .65 .25

Souvenir Sheet

C118 Sheet of 4 8.00 8.00
a. AP40 50fr violet blue & multi .75 .75
b. AP40 70fr violet blue & multi 1.00 1.00
c. AP40 110fr violet blue & multi 1.25 1.25

See note after No. C104. No. C118 contains Nos. C117, C118a, C118b and C118c.
For surcharge see No. C120.

Walt Whitman and Dahoman Huts — AP41

1970, Apr. 30 Engr. *Perf. 13*

C119 AP41 100fr Prus bl, brn & emer 1.40 .80

Walt Whitman (1818-92), American poet. For surcharge, see Benin No. C510.

No. C117 Surcharged in Silver

1970, May 15 Photo. *Perf. 12½*

C120 AP40 40fr on 30fr multi 1.20 .75

The flight of Apollo 13.
For surcharge see Benin No. C464.

Soccer Players and Globe — AP42

Designs: 50fr, Goalkeeper catching ball. 200fr, Players kicking ball.

1970, May 19

C121 AP42 40fr multi .75 .40
C122 AP42 50fr multi .95 .50
C123 AP42 200fr multi 3.50 1.25
Nos. C121-C123 (3) 5.20 2.15

9th World Soccer Championships for the Jules Rimet Cup, Mexico City, May 30-June 21, 1970.
For surcharges, see No. C126, Benin Nos. C502, C504.

EXPO '70 Type of Regular Issue

EXPO '70 Emblems and: 70fr, Dahomey pavilion. 120fr, Mt. Fuji, temple and torii.

1970, June 15 Litho. *Perf. 13½x14*

C124 A54 70fr yel, red & dk vio 1.25 .60
C125 A54 120fr yel, red & grn 2.25 1.00

For surcharges see Benin Nos. C470, C477.

No. C123 Surcharged and Overprinted

1970, July 13 Photo. *Perf. 12½*

C126 AP42 100fr on 200fr multi 2.10 1.00

Brazil's victory in the 9th World Soccer Championships, Mexico City.
For surcharge see Benin No. C515.

Mercury, Map of Africa and Europe — AP43

Europafrica Issue, 1970

1970, July 20 Photo. *Perf. 12x13*

C127 AP43 40fr multi .90 .40
C128 AP43 70fr multi 1.50 .60

For surcharges see Benin Nos. C429, C488, C566.

Ludwig van Beethoven AP44

1970, Sept. 21 Litho. *Perf. 14x13½*

C129 AP44 90fr brt bl & vio blk 1.40 .45
C130 AP44 110fr yel grn & dk brn 1.75 .65

Bicentenary of the birth of Ludwig van Beethoven (1770-1827), composer.
For surcharges, see Benin Nos. C476, C608.

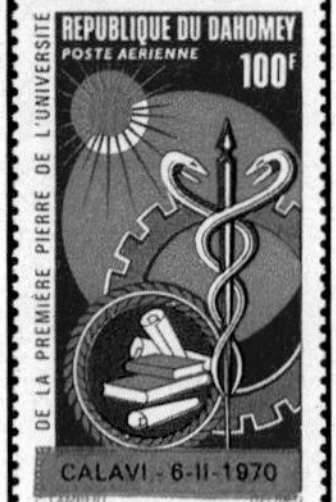

Symbols of Learning — AP45

1970, Nov. 6 Photo. *Perf. 12½*

C131 AP45 100fr multi 1.40 .75

Laying of the foundation stone for the University at Calavi.
For overprint and surcharges see Benin Nos. C356, C399, C616.

Annunciation, Rhenish School, c.1340 — AP46

Paintings of Rhenish School, circa 1340: 70fr, Nativity. 110fr, Adoration of the Kings. 200fr, Presentation at the Temple.

1970, Nov. 9 *Perf. 12½x12*

C132 AP46 40fr gold & multi .55 .40
C133 AP46 70fr gold & multi 1.00 .55
C134 AP46 110fr gold & multi 2.40 1.25
C135 AP46 200fr gold & multi 4.00 2.00
Nos. C132-C135 (4) 7.95 4.20

Christmas 1970.
For surcharges see Benin Nos. C479, C518, C527.

Charles de Gaulle, Arc de Triomphe and Flag — AP47

Design: 500fr, de Gaulle as old man and Notre Dame Cathedral, Paris.

1971, Mar. 15 Photo. *Perf. 12½*

C136 AP47 40fr multi .80 .45
C137 AP47 500fr multi 6.50 3.25

Gen. Charles de Gaulle (1890-1970), President of France.
For surcharges see Benin Nos. C465, C567.

L'Indifférent, by Watteau — AP48

Painting: No. C139, Woman playing stringed instrument, by Watteau.

1971, May 3 Photo. *Perf. 13*

C138 AP48 100fr red brn & multi 3.25 1.75
C139 AP48 100fr red brn & multi 3.25 1.75

For overprints and surcharge see Nos. C151-C152, Benin Nos. C357D, C372, C456, C526, C617, C638.

1971, May 29 Photo. *Perf. 13*

Dürer Paintings: 100fr, Self-portrait, 1498. 200fr, Self-portrait, 1500.

C140 AP48 100fr bl grn & multi 2.25 1.25
C141 AP48 200fr dk grn & multi 4.50 2.25

Albrecht Dürer (1471-1528), German painter and engraver. See Nos. C151-C152, C174-C175. For surcharges and overprints see Benin Nos. C357B, C381, C533, C545, C618.

Johannes Kepler and Diagram — AP49

200fr, Kepler, trajectories, satellite and rocket.

1971, July 12 Engr. *Perf. 13*
C142 AP49 40fr brt rose lil, blk & vio bl .90 .55
C143 AP49 200fr red, blk & dk bl 3.25 1.75

Kepler (1571-1630), German astronomer.
For overprint and surcharges see Benin Nos. C342, C348, C466, C480, C568.

Europafrica Issue

Jet Plane, Maps of Europe and Africa — AP50

100fr, Ocean liner, maps of Europe and Africa.

1971, July 19 Photo. *Perf. 12½x12*
C144 AP50 50fr blk, lt bl & org 1.60 .60
C145 AP50 100fr multi 2.50 1.00

For surcharges see Benin Nos. C374, C404, C421, C585, C630.

African Postal Union Issue, 1971
Common Design Type

Design: 100fr, Dahomey coat of arms and UAMPT building, Brazzaville, Congo.

1971, Nov. 13 *Perf. 13x13½*
C146 CD135 100fr bl & multi 1.75 .80

For overprint and surcharge see Benin Nos. C357E, C619.

Flight into Egypt, by Van Dyck — AP51

Paintings: 40fr, Adoration of the Shepherds, by the Master of the Hausbuch, c. 1500, vert. 70fr, Adoration of the Kings, by Holbein the Elder, vert. 200fr, The Birth of Christ, by Dürer.

1971, Nov. 22 *Perf. 13*
C147 AP51 40fr gold & multi .85 .45
C148 AP51 70fr gold & multi 1.40 .55
C149 AP51 100fr gold & multi 2.10 .80
C150 AP51 200fr gold & multi 5.00 1.75
Nos. C147-C150 (4) 9.35 3.55

Christmas 1971
For overprint and surcharges see Benin Nos. C394, C394A, C397, C403, C403A, C405, C481, C503, C546, C581, C604, C631.

Painting Type of 1971 Inscribed: "25e ANNIVERSAIRE DE L'UNICEF"

Paintings: 40fr, Prince Balthazar, by Velasquez. 100fr, Infanta Margarita Maria, by Velázquez.

1971, Dec. 11
C151 AP48 40fr gold & multi 1.75 .55
C152 AP48 100fr gold & multi 3.00 .85

25th anniv. of UNICEF.
For surcharges see Benin Nos. C366, C418, C437, C592, C639.

Olympic Games Type

Design: 150fr, Sapporo '72 emblem, ski jump and stork flying.

1972, Feb. Engr. *Perf. 13*
C153 A61 150fr brn, dp rose lil & bl 3.50 1.25

11th Winter Olympic Games, Sapporo, Japan, Feb. 3-13.
For overprint and surcharge see Benin Nos. C347, C433, C645.

Boy Scout and Scout Flag — AP52

Designs: 40fr, Scout playing marimba. 100fr, Scouts doing farm work.

1972, Mar. 19 Photo. *Perf. 13*
Size: 26x35mm
C154 AP52 35fr multi .50 .25
C155 AP52 40fr multi .85 .40
Size: 26x46mm
C156 AP52 100fr yel & multi 1.75 .85
a. Souvenir sheet of 3, #C154-C156, perf. 12½ 4.25 4.25
Nos. C154-C156 (3) 3.10 1.50

World Boy Scout Seminar, Cotonou, Mar. 1972.
For overprint and surcharges see Benin Nos. C373, C414, C569.

Workers Training Institute and Friedrich Naumann — AP53

Design: 250fr, Workers Training Institute and Pres. Theodor Heuss of Germany.

1972, Mar. 29 Photo. *Perf. 13x12*
C157 AP53 100fr brt rose, blk & vio 1.50 .65
C158 AP53 250fr bl, blk & vio 3.50 1.40

Laying of foundation stone for National Workers Training Institute.
For surcharges see Benin Nos. C380, C473, C640, C649, Q25A.

Mosaic Floor, St. Mark's, Venice — AP54

12th Century Mosaics from St. Mark's Basilica: 40fr, Roosters carrying fox on a pole. 65fr, Noah sending out dove.

1972, Apr. 10 *Perf. 13*
C159 AP54 35fr gold & multi 1.35 .75
C160 AP54 40fr gold & multi 1.50 .90
C161 AP54 65fr gold & multi 3.00 1.50
Nos. C159-C161 (3) 5.85 3.15

UNESCO campaign to save Venice.
For surcharges see Benin Nos. 690G, C600.

Neapolitan and Dahoman Dancers — AP55

1972, May 3 *Perf. 13½x13*
C162 AP55 100fr multi 1.50 .65

12th Philatelic Exhibition, Naples.
For surcharges, see Benin Nos. C395, C620.

Running, German Eagle, Olympic Rings — AP56

85fr, High jump and Glyptothek, Munich. 150fr, Shot put and Propylaeum, Munich.

1972, June 12 Engr. *Perf. 13*
C163 AP56 20fr ultra, grn & brn .40 .25
C164 AP56 85fr brn, grn & ultra .95 .60
C165 AP56 150fr grn, brn & ultra 2.00 1.00
a. Min. sheet of 3, #C163-C165 4.00 4.00
Nos. C163-C165 (3) 3.35 1.85

20th Olympic Games, Munich, 8/26-9/10.
For overprints and surcharges see Nos. C170-C172, Benin C343, C346, C370, C404A, C559, C577, C651A.

Louis Blériot and his Plane — AP57

1972, June 26
C166 AP57 100fr vio, cl & brt bl 4.00 1.75

Birth centenary of Louis Blériot (1872-1936), French aviation pioneer.
For surcharges see Benin Nos. C386, C621.

Adam, by Lucas Cranach — AP58

Design: 200fr, Eve, by Lucas Cranach.

1972, Oct. 24 Photo.
C167 AP58 150fr multi 2.75 1.25
C168 AP58 200fr multi 4.50 1.75

Cranach (1472-1553), German painter.
For surcharges see Benin Nos. C402, C434A, C537, C643.

Pauline Borghese, by Canova — AP59

1972, Nov. 8
C169 AP59 250fr multi 7.00 1.75

Antonio Canova (1757-1822), Italian sculptor.
For surcharge, see Benin No. 1366.

Nos. C163-C165 Overprinted

a

b

c

1972, Nov. 13 Engr. *Perf. 13*
C170 AP56(a) 20fr multi .45 .25
C171 AP56(b) 85fr multi 1.25 .60
C172 AP56(c) 150fr multi 2.25 1.25
a. Miniature sheet of 3 5.25 5.25
Nos. C170-C172 (3) 3.95 2.10

Gold medal winners in 20th Olympic Games: Lasse Viren, Finland, 5,000m. and 10,000m. races (20fr); Ulrike Meyfarth, Germany, women's high jump (85fr); Wladyslaw Komar, Poland, shot put (150fr).
For surcharges, see Benin Nos. C343A, C371, C538, C607.

Louis Pasteur — AP60

1972, Nov. 30
C173 AP60 100fr brt grn, lil & brn 2.50 1.00

Pasteur (1822-95), chemist and bacteriologist.
For surcharges see Benin Nos. C344, C622.

Painting Type of 1971

Paintings by Georges de La Tour (1593-1652), French painter: 35fr, Vielle player. 150fr, The Newborn, horiz.

1972, Dec. 11 **Photo.**
C174 AP48 35fr multi .80 .40
C175 AP48 150fr multi 2.25 1.25

For surcharges see Benin Nos. C364, C490, C578.

Annunciation, School of Agnolo Gaddi — AP61

Paintings: 125fr, Nativity, by Simone dei Crocifissi. 140fr, Adoration of the Shepherds, by Giovanni di Pietro. 250fr, Adoration of the Kings, by Giotto.

1972, Dec. 15
C176 AP61 35fr gold & multi .75 .25
C177 AP61 125fr gold & multi 2.00 .65
C178 AP61 140fr gold & multi 2.75 1.00
C179 AP61 250fr gold & multi 4.50 1.50
Nos. C176-C179 (4) 10.00 3.40

Christmas 1972. See Nos. C195-C198, C234, C251, C253-C254. For overprint and surcharges see Benin Nos. C383A, C384, C392, C401, C444, C528, C628, C652.

Statue of St. Teresa, Basilica of Lisieux — AP62

100fr, St. Teresa, roses, and globe, vert.

1973, May 14 **Photo.** ***Perf. 13***
C180 AP62 40fr blk, gold & lt ultra .75 .45
C181 AP62 100fr gold & multi 2.50 1.00

St. Teresa of Lisieux (Therese Martin, 1873-97), Carmelite nun.
For surcharges see Benin Nos. C390, C570, C623.

Scouts, African Scout Emblem — AP63

Designs (African Scout Emblem and): 20fr, Lord Baden-Powell, vert. 40fr, Scouts building bridge.

1973, July 2 **Engr.** ***Perf. 13***
C182 AP63 15fr bl, grn & choc .45 .25
C183 AP63 20fr ol & Prus bl .75 .25
C184 AP63 40fr grn, Prus bl & brn .90 .35
a. Souvenir sheet of 3 3.00 3.00
Nos. C182-C184 (3) 2.10 .85

24th Boy Scout World Conference, Nairobi, Kenya, July 16-21. No. C184a contains 3 stamps similar to Nos. C182-C184 in changed colors (15fr in ultramarine, slate green and chocolate; 20fr in chocolate, ultramarine and indigo; 40fr in slate green, indigo and chocolate).
For surcharges see Nos. C217-C218, Benin C365, C409, C558, C560, C571.

Copernicus, Venera and Mariner Satellites — AP64

125fr, Copernicus, sun, earth & moon, vert.

1973, Aug. 20 **Engr.** ***Perf. 13***
C185 AP64 65fr blk, dk brn & org 1.50 .55
C186 AP64 125fr bl, slate grn & pur 2.75 1.00

For surcharges and overprints see Benin Nos. C345, C349A, C375, C601, C642.

Head and City Hall, Brussels AP64a

1973, Sept. 17 **Engr.** ***Perf. 13***
C187 AP64a 100fr blk, Prus bl & dk grn 1.10 .60

African Weeks, Brussels, Sept. 15-30, 1973.
For surcharge see Benin No. C400.

WMO Emblem, World Weather Map — AP65

1973, Sept. 25
C188 AP65 100fr ol grn & lt brn 1.40 .75

Cent. of intl. meteorological cooperation.
For surcharges and overprint see Nos. C199, Benin Nos. C382, C624.

Europafrica Issue

AP66

Design: 40fr, similar to 35fr.

1973, Oct. 1 **Engr.** ***Perf. 13***
C189 AP66 35fr multi .55 .35
C190 AP66 40fr bl, sepia & ultra .70 .40

For overprint and surcharges, see Benin Nos. C411, C564, C593.

John F. Kennedy — AP67

1973, Oct. 18
C191 AP67 200fr bl grn, vio & sl grn 2.75 2.75

Souvenir Sheet

C191A AP67 200fr bl, rd brn, brn 5.00 5.00

For surcharge and overprint, see Benin Nos. C377, C441, C547.

Soccer — AP68

40fr, 2 soccer players. 100fr, 3 soccer players.

1973, Nov. 19 **Engr.** ***Perf. 13***
C192 AP68 35fr multi .55 .25
C193 AP68 40fr multi .65 .25
C194 AP68 100fr multi 1.25 .65
Nos. C192-C194 (3) 2.45 1.15

World Soccer Cup, Munich 1974.
For surcharges and overprint see Nos. C219-C220, Benin Nos. C396, C591, C644.

Painting Type of 1972

Christmas: 35fr, Annunciation, by Dirk Bouts. 100fr, Nativity, by Giotto. 150fr, Adoration of the Kings, by Botticelli. 200fr, Adoration of the Shepherds, by Jacopo Bassano, horiz.

1973, Dec. 20 **Photo.** ***Perf. 13***
C195 AP61 35fr gold & multi .80 .40
C196 AP61 100fr gold & multi 1.50 .65
C197 AP61 150fr gold & multi 3.00 1.10
C198 AP61 200fr gold & multi 3.25 1.75
Nos. C195-C198 (4) 8.55 3.90

For surcharges see Benin Nos. C378, C388, C410, C434, C438, C442, C487, C565, C646.

No C188 Surcharged in Violet

1974, Feb. 4 **Engr.** ***Perf. 13***
C199 AP65 200fr on 100fr multi 2.25 1.25

Skylab US space missions, 1973-74.

Skiers, Snowflake, Olympic Rings — AP69

1974, Feb. 25 **Engr.** ***Perf. 13***
C200 AP69 100fr vio bl, brn & brt bl 1.75 1.10

50th anniversary of first Winter Olympic Games, Chamonix, France. For surcharges, see Benin Nos. C625, C389.

Marie Curie AP70

1974, June 7 **Engr.** ***Perf. 13***
C201 AP70 50fr Lenin 1.75 .65
C202 AP70 125fr shown 2.25 .90
C203 AP70 150fr Churchill 2.50 1.40
Nos. C201-C203 (3) 6.50 2.95

50th anniv. of the death of Lenin; 40th anniv. of the death of Marie Sklodowska Curie; cent. of the birth of Winston Churchill.
For surcharges see Benin Nos. C387A, C391A, C489, C529, C597, C632, C634.

Bishop, Persian, 18th Century — AP71

200fr, Queen, Siamese chess piece, 19th cent.

1974, June 14 **Photo.** ***Perf. 12½x13***
C204 AP71 50fr org & multi 2.50 1.00
C205 AP71 200fr brt grn & multi 6.00 2.50

21st Chess Olympiad, Nice, 6/6-30/74.
For surcharges and overprint see Benin Nos. C469, C482, C598, C627, Q11.

Frederic Chopin — AP72

Design: No. C207, Ludwig van Beethoven.

1974, June 24 **Engr.** ***Perf. 13***
C206 AP72 150fr blk & copper red 4.50 1.40
C207 AP72 150fr blk & copper red 4.50 1.40

Famous musicians: Frederic Chopin and Ludwig van Beethoven.
For surcharges see Benin Nos. C376, C452, C459, C539, C579, C647, C655.

Astronaut on Moon, and Earth AP73

1974, July 10 **Engr.** ***Perf. 13***
C208 AP73 150fr multi 2.75 1.50

5th anniversary of the first moon walk.
For surcharges and overprint see Benin Nos. C391, C460, C635.

Litho. & Embossed 'Gold Foil' Stamps

These stamps generally are of a different design format than the rest of the issue. Since there is a commemorative inscription tying them to the issue a separate illustration is not being shown.

World Cup Soccer Championships, Munich — AP74

World Cup trophy and players and flags of: 35fr, West Germany, Chile, Australia, DDR. 40fr, Zaire, Scotland, Brazil, Yugoslavia. 100fr, Sweden, Bulgaria, Uruguay, Netherlands. 200fr, Italy, Haiti, Poland, Argentina. 300fr, Stadium. 500fr, Trophy and flags.

Perf. 14x13, 13x14

1974, July 16 — Litho.

C209 AP74 35fr multicolored .40 .25
C210 AP74 40fr multicolored .55 .25
C211 AP74 100fr multicolored 1.10 .70
C212 AP74 200fr multicolored 2.50 1.25
C213 AP74 300fr multi, horiz. 2.50 1.50

Souvenir Sheet

C215 AP74 500fr multi, horiz. 7.25 7.25

It is uncertain if this issue was valid for postage or recognized by the Dahomey government.

Nos. C182-C183 Srchd. and Ovptd. in Black or Red

1974, July 19

C217 AP63 100fr on 15fr multi 1.25 .60
C218 AP63 140fr on 20fr multi (R) 1.75 .90

11th Pan-Arab Jamboree, Batrun, Lebanon, Aug. 1974. Overprint includes 2 bars over old denomination; 2-line overprint on No. C217, 3 lines on No. C218.

Nos. C193-C194 Overprinted and Surcharged

1974, July 26 — Engr. — *Perf. 13*

C219 AP68 100fr on 40fr 1.10 .65
C220 AP68 150fr on 100fr 1.60 1.00

World Cup Soccer Championship, 1974, victory of German Federal Republic.

Earth and UPU Emblem — AP75

Designs (UPU Emblem and): 65fr, Concorde in flight. 125fr, French railroad car, c. 1860. 200fr, African drummer and Renault mail truck, pre-1939.

1974, Aug. 5 — Engr. — *Perf. 13*

C221 AP75 35fr rose cl & vio .75 .40
C222 AP75 65fr Prus grn & cl 1.50 .95
C223 AP75 125fr multi 3.50 1.50
C224 AP75 200fr multi 3.50 2.00
Nos. C221-C224 (4) 9.25 4.85

Centenary of Universal Postal Union.
For surcharges, see Benin Nos. C422, C530, C540, C586, C653, C657, Q13B, Q17B.

UPU, Cent. — AP76

Communications and transportation: 50fr, Rocket, Indian shooting arrow. 100fr, Airplane, dog sled, vert. 125fr, Rocket launch, balloon. 150fr, Rocket re-entry into Earth's atmosphere, drum. 200fr, Locomotive, Pony Express rider. 500fr, UPU headquarters. No. C230, Train, 1829. No. C232, Astronaut canceling envelope on moon.

1974 — Litho. — *Perf. 13x14, 14x13*

C225 AP76 50fr multicolored .50 .30
C226 AP76 100fr multicolored .75 .60
C227 AP76 125fr multicolored 1.00 .85
C228 AP76 150fr multicolored 1.75 1.00
C229 AP76 200fr multicolored 2.50 1.25

Litho. & Embossed

Perf. 13½

Size: 48x60mm

C230 AP76 1000fr gold & multi 12.00 12.00

Souvenir Sheets

Litho.

Perf. 13x14

C231 AP76 500fr multicolored 4.50 4.50

Litho. & Embossed

Perf. 13½

C232 AP76 1000fr gold & multi 7.25 7.25

Issued: #C230, C232, Oct. 9; others, Aug. 5.
It is uncertain if this issue was valid for postage or recognized by the Dahomey government.

Lion of Belfort by Frederic A. Bartholdi — AP77

1974, Aug. 20 — Engr. — *Perf. 13*

C233 AP77 100fr rose brn 2.50 1.00

For surcharges see Benin Nos. C387, C551, C626.

Paintins Type of 1972

1974, Aug. 20 — Engr. — *Perf. 13*

Painting: 250fr, Girl with Falcon, by Philippe de Champaigne.

C234 AP61 250fr multi 4.00 2.40

For surcharges see Benin Nos. C363, C445.

Prehistoric Animals — AP78

1974, Sept. 23 — Photo.

C235 AP78 35fr Rhamphorhynchus 1.50 .80
C236 AP78 150fr Stegosaurus 5.00 2.25
C237 AP78 200fr Tyrannosaurus 7.00 2.75
Nos. C235-C237 (3) 13.50 5.80

For surcharges and overprint, see Benin Nos. C349, C350, C440, C443, C548, C636.

Conquest of Space — AP79

Various spacecraft and: 50fr, Mercury. 100fr, Venus. 150fr, Mars. 200fr, Jupiter. 400fr, Sun.

1974, Oct. 31 — Litho. — *Perf. 13x14*

C238 AP79 50fr multicolored .40 .30
C239 AP79 100fr multicolored 1.00 .50
C240 AP79 150fr multicolored 1.75 .90
C241 AP79 200fr multicolored 2.25 1.25
Nos. C238-C241 (4) 5.40 2.95

Souvenir Sheet

C242 AP79 400fr multicolored 5.25 5.25

It is uncertain if this issue was valid for postage or recognized by the Dahomey government.

West Germany, World Cup Soccer Champions — AP80

Designs: 100fr, Team. 125fr, Paul Breitner. 150fr, Gerd Muller. 300fr, Presentation of trophy. 500fr, German team positioned on field.

1974, Nov. — Litho. — *Perf. 13x14*

C243 AP80 100fr multicolored .75 .50
C244 AP80 125fr multicolored 1.00 .75
C245 AP80 150fr multicolored 1.50 1.00
C246 AP80 300fr multicolored 3.25 2.00
Nos. C243-C246 (4) 6.50 4.25

Souvenir Sheet

C248 AP80 500fr multicolored 5.25 5.25

It is uncertain if this issue was valid for postage or recognized by the Dahomey government.

Europafrica Issue

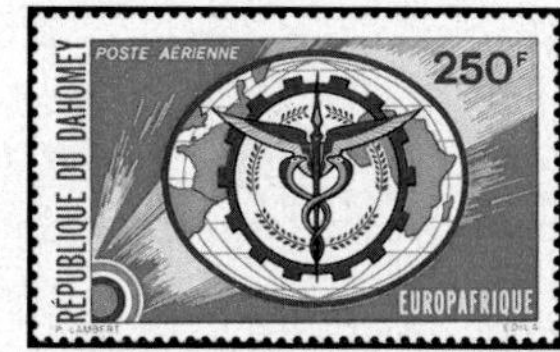

Globe, Cogwheel, Emblem — AP81

1974, Dec. 20 — Typo. — *Perf. 13*

C250 AP81 250fr red & multi 3.25 2.75

Printed tête bêche in sheets of 10.
For surcharges see Benin Nos. C430, C509, C650.

Christmas Type of 1972 and

Nativity, by Martin Schongauer — AP82

Paintings: 35fr, Annunciation, by Schongauer. 100fr, Virgin in Rose Arbor, by Schongauer. 250fr, Virgin and Child, with St. John the Baptist, by Botticelli.

1974, Dec. 23 — Photo. — *Perf. 13*

C251 AP61 35fr gold & multi .60 .30
C252 AP82 40fr gold & multi .60 .40
C253 AP61 100fr gold & multi 1.60 .55
C254 AP61 250fr gold & multi 4.25 1.75
Nos. C251-C254 (4) 7.05 3.00

For surcharges, see Benin Nos. C413, C431, C439, C446, C552, C641.

Apollo and Soyuz Spacecraft AP83

200fr, American and Russian flags, rocket take-off. 500fr, Apollo-Soyuz link-up.

1975, July 16 — Litho. — *Perf. 12½*

C255 AP83 35fr multi .50 .30
C256 AP83 200fr vio bl, red & bl 2.40 1.25
C257 AP83 500fr vio bl, ind & red 5.50 3.00
Nos. C255-C257 (3) 8.40 4.55

Apollo Soyuz space test project (Russo-American cooperation); launching July 15; link-up, July 17.
For surcharges and overprints, see Benin Nos. C406, C415-C416, C451, C542-C543, C549, C580.

Nos. C255-C256 Surcharged

No. C258

No. C259

1975, July 17 — Litho. — *Perf. 12½*

C258 AP83 100fr on 35fr (S) 1.25 .60
C259 AP83 300fr on 200fr 3.25 1.40

Apollo-Soyuz link-up in space, July 17, 1975.

ARPHILA Emblem, "Stamps" and Head of Ceres — AP84

1975, Aug. 22 Engr. *Perf. 13*

C260	AP84	100fr blk, bl & lilac	1.50	.75

ARPHILA 75, International Philatelic Exhibition, Paris, June 6-16.

For surcharges see Benin Nos. C383, C474.

Europafrica Issue

Holy Family, by Michelangelo AP85

1975, Sept. 29 Litho. *Perf. 12*

C261	AP85	300fr gold & multi	4.50	1.50

For surcharge and overprint, see Benin Nos. C447, C554.

Infantry and Stars — AP86

American bicentennial (Stars and): 135fr, Drummers and fifer. 300fr, Artillery with cannon. 500fr, Cavalry.

1975, Nov. 18 Engr. *Perf. 13*

C262	AP86	75fr grn car & pur	1.00	.45
C263	AP86	135fr bl, mag & sep	1.75	.90
C264	AP86	300fr vio bl, ver & choc	3.25	1.75
C265	AP86	500fr ver, dk grn & brn	5.75	2.50
		Nos. C262-C265 (4)	11.75	5.60

For overprints and surcharges see Benin Nos. C247-C249, C385, C412, C429A, C453, C478, C534, C555, C557, C576, C588.

Diving and Olympic Rings AP87

Design: 250fr, Soccer and Olympic rings.

1975, Nov. 24

C266	AP87	40fr vio, grnsh bl & ol brn	.55	.25
C267	AP87	250fr red, emer & brn	2.40	1.25

Pre-Olympic Year 1975.

For surcharges see Benin Nos. C341, C393, C553, C582.

AIR POST SEMI-POSTAL STAMPS

Maternity Hospital, Dakar — SPAP1

Dispensary, Mopti — SPAP2

Nurse Weighing Baby — SPAP3

Perf. 13½x12½, 13 (#CB3)

Photo, Engr. (#CB3)

1942, June 22

CB1	SPAP1	1.50fr + 3.50fr green	.80	*5.50*
CB2	SPAP2	2fr + 6fr brown	.80	*5.50*
CB3	SPAP3	3fr + 9fr car red	.80	*5.50*
		Nos. CB1-CB3 (3)	2.40	*16.50*

Native children's welfare fund.

Colonial Education Fund

Common Design Type

Perf. 12½x13½

1942, June 22 Engr.

CB4	CD86a	1.20fr + 1.80fr blue & red	.80	*5.50*

AIR POST PARCEL POST STAMPS

Catalogue values for unused stamps in this section are for Never Hinged items.

Nos. C20-C23, C14 Surcharged in Black or Red

No. CQ2

No. CQ5

1967-69 Engr. *Perf. 13*

CQ1	AP6	200fr on 200fr	2.10	2.10
CQ2	AP6	300fr on 100fr	2.40	2.40
CQ3	AP6	500fr on 300fr	4.50	4.50
CQ4	AP6	1000fr on 500fr	9.50	9.50
CQ5	AP4	5000fr on 100fr (R) ('69)	35.00	35.00
		Nos. CQ1-CQ5 (5)	53.50	53.50

On No. CQ5, "Colis Postaux" is at top, bar at right.

POSTAGE DUE STAMPS

Dahomey Natives — D1

1906 Unwmk. Typo. *Perf. 14x13½*

J1	D1	5c grn, *grnsh*	4.00	4.00
J2	D1	10c red brn	4.00	4.00
J3	D1	15c dark blue	8.00	8.00
J4	D1	20c blk, *yellow*	8.00	8.00
J5	D1	30c red, *straw*	12.00	12.00
J6	D1	50c violet	24.00	24.00
J7	D1	60c blk, *buff*	16.00	16.00
J8	D1	1fr blk, *pinkish*	52.50	40.00
		Nos. J1-J8 (8)	128.50	116.00

D2

1914

J9	D2	5c green	.25	.25
J10	D2	10c rose	.55	.55
J11	D2	15c gray	.55	.55
J12	D2	20c brown	1.10	1.10
J13	D2	30c blue	1.40	1.40
J14	D2	50c black	1.60	1.60
J15	D2	60c orange	2.00	2.00
J16	D2	1fr violet	2.10	2.10
		Nos. J9-J16 (8)	9.55	9.55

Type of 1914 Issue Surcharged

1927

J17	D2	2fr on 1fr lilac rose	5.50	5.50
J18	D2	3fr on 1fr org brn	5.50	5.50

Carved Mask — D3

1941 Engr. *Perf. 14x13*

J19	D3	5c black	.25	.25
J20	D3	10c lilac rose	.25	.25
J21	D3	15c dark blue	.25	.25
J22	D3	20c bright yel green	.30	.30
J23	D3	30c orange	.50	.50
J24	D3	50c violet brown	.70	.70
J25	D3	60c slate green	1.10	1.10
J26	D3	1fr rose red	1.40	1.40
J27	D3	2fr yellow	1.50	1.50
J28	D3	3fr dark purple	1.90	1.90
		Nos. J19-J28 (10)	8.15	8.15

Type D3 without "RF"

1944

J28A	D3	10c lilac rose	.50
J28B	D3	15c dark blue	.55
J28C	D3	20c bright yel green	.55
		Nos. J28A-J28C (3)	1.60

Nos. J28A-J28C were issued by the Vichy government in France, but were not placed on sale in Dahomey.

Catalogue values for unused stamps in this section, from this point to the end of the section, are for Never Hinged items.

Republic

Panther and Man — D4

Perf. 14x13½

1963, July 22 Typo. Unwmk.

J29	D4	1fr green & rose	.25	.25
J30	D4	2fr brn & emerald	.30	.30
J31	D4	5fr org & vio bl	.30	.30
J32	D4	10fr magenta & blk	.65	.65
J33	D4	20fr vio bl & org	1.10	1.10
		Nos. J29-J33 (5)	2.60	2.60

Heliograph — D5

No. J35, Mail boat. No. J36, Morse receiver. No. J37, Mailman on bicycle. No. J38, Early telephone. No. J39, Autorail. No. J40, Mail truck. No. J41, Radio tower. No. J42, DC-8F jet plane. No. J43, Early Bird communications satellite.

1967, Oct. 24 Engr. *Perf. 11*

J34	D5	1fr brn, dl pur & bl	.25	.25
J35	D5	1fr dl pur, brn & bl	.25	.25
a.		Pair, #J34-J35	.25	
J36	D5	3fr dk brn, dk grn & org	.25	.25
J37	D5	3fr dk grn, dk brn & org	.25	.25
a.		Pair, #J36-J37	.25	
J38	D5	5fr ol bis, lil & bl	.35	.35
J39	D5	5fr lil, ol bis & bl	.35	.35
a.		Pair, #J38-J39	.75	
J40	D5	10fr brn org, vio & grn	.50	.50
J41	D5	10fr vio, brn org & grn	.50	.50
a.		Pair, #J40-J41	1.10	
J42	D5	30fr Prus bl, mar & vio	1.00	1.00
J43	D5	30fr vio, Prus bl & mar	1.00	1.00
a.		Pair, #J42-J43	2.25	
		Nos. J34-J43 (10)	4.70	4.70

Pairs printed tete beche, se-tenant at the base.

PARCEL POST STAMPS

Catalogue values for unused stamps in this section are for Never Hinged items.

Nos. 141-146 and 148 Surcharged

1967, Jan. Unwmk. Engr. *Perf. 13*

Q1	A15	5fr on 1fr multi	.25	.25
Q2	A15	10fr on 2fr multi	.35	.35
Q3	A15	20fr on 6fr multi	.60	.60
Q4	A15	25fr on 3fr multi	.90	.90
Q5	A15	30fr on 4fr multi	1.00	1.00
Q6	A15	50fr on 10fr multi	1.40	1.40
a.		"20" instead of "50"	100.00	
Q7	A15	100fr on 20fr multi	2.50	2.50
		Nos. Q1-Q7 (7)	7.00	7.00

The surcharge is arranged to fit the shape of the stamp.

No. Q6a occurred once on the sheet.

DALMATIA

dal-ˈmā-sh͵ē-͵ə

LOCATION — A promontory in the northwestern part of the Balkan Peninsula, together with several small islands in the Adriatic Sea.
GOVT. — Part of the former Austro-Hungarian crownland of the same name.
AREA — 113 sq. mi.
POP. — 18,719 (1921)
CAPITAL — Zara.

Stamps were issued during Italian occupation. This territory was subsequently annexed by Italy.

100 Centesimi = 1 Corona = 1 Lira

Used values are for postally used stamps.

Issued under Italian Occupation

Italy No. 87 Surcharged

1919, May 1 Wmk. 140 *Perf. 14*

1	A46 1cor on 1 l brn & grn	3.00	*12.00*
a.	Pair, one without surcharge	*1,050.*	*1,050.*

Italian Stamps of 1906-08 Surcharged — a

1921-22

2	A48 5c on 5c green	4.00	*8.00*
3	A48 10c on 10c claret	4.00	*8.00*
a.	Pair, one without surcharge	775.00	
4	A49 25c on 25c blue ('22)	6.00	*11.25*
5	A49 50c on 50c vio ('22)	6.00	*11.00*
a.	Double surcharge		*300.00*
b.	Pair, one without surcharge	*1,000.*	

Italian Stamps of 1901-10 Surcharged — b

6	A46 1cor on 1 l brn & grn ('22)	10.00	*24.00*
7	A46 5cor on 5 l bl & rose ('22)	40.00	*110.00*
8	A51 10cor on 10 l gray grn & red ('22)	40.00	*110.00*
	Nos. 2-8 (7)	110.00	*282.25*

Surcharges similar to these but differing in style or arrangement of type were used in Austria under Italian occupation.

SPECIAL DELIVERY STAMPS

Italian Special Delivery No. E1 Srchd. Type "a"

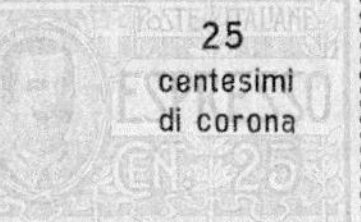

1921 Wmk. 140 *Perf. 14*

E1	SD1 25c on 25c rose red	3.00	*12.00*
a.	Double surcharge	290.00	*500.00*

Italian Special Delivery Stamp Surcharged

1922

E2	SD2 1.20 l on 1.20 l	195.00

No. E2 was not placed in use.

POSTAGE DUE STAMPS

Italian Postage Due Stamps and Type Surcharged types "a" or "b"

1922 Wmk. 140 *Perf. 14*

J1	D3 (a) 50c on 50c buff & mag	4.00	*9.00*
J2	D3 (b) 1cor on 1 l bl & red	9.00	*32.50*
J3	D3 (b) 2cor on 2 l bl & red	55.00	*135.00*
J4	D3 (b) 5cor on 5 l bl & red	55.00	*135.00*
	Nos. J1-J4 (4)	123.00	*311.50*

DANISH WEST INDIES

ˈdā-nish ˈwest ˈin-dēs

LOCATION — Group of islands in the West Indies, lying east of Puerto Rico
GOVT. — Danish colony
AREA — 132 sq. mi.
POP. — 27,086 (1911)
CAPITAL — Charlotte Amalie

The US bought these islands in 1917 and they became the US Virgin Islands, using US stamps and currency.

100 Cents = 1 Dollar
100 Bit = 1 Franc (1905)

Wmk. 111 — Small Crown

Wmk. 112 — Crown

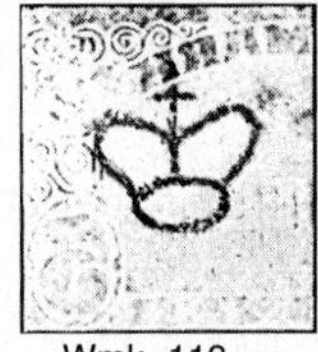

Wmk. 113 — Crown

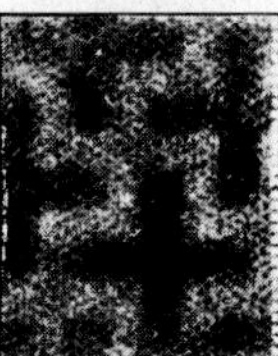

Wmk. 114 — Multiple Crosses

Coat of Arms — A1

Yellowish Paper
Yellow Wavy-line Burelage, UL to LR

1856 Typo. Wmk. 111 *Imperf.*

1	A1 3c dark carmine, brown gum	200.	*275.*
a.	3c dark carmine, yellow gum	225.	*275.*
b.	3c carmine, white gum	*4,250.*	—

The brown and yellow gums were applied locally.

Reprint: 1981, carmine, back-printed across two stamps ("Reprint by Dansk Post og Telegrafmuseum 1978"), value, pair, $10.

White Paper

1866

Yellow Wavy-line Burelage UR to LL

2	A1 3c rose	40.	*65.*

No. 2 reprints, unwatermarked: 1930, carmine, value $100. 1942, rose carmine, back-printed across each row ("Nytryk 1942 G. A. Hagemann Danmark og Dansk Vestindiens Frimaerker Bind 2"), value $50.

1872 *Perf. 12½*

3	A1 3c rose	100.	*275.*

1873 Without Burelage

4	A1 4c dull blue	250.	*475.*
a.	Imperf., pair	775.	
b.	Horiz. pair, imperf. vert.	575.	

The 1930 reprint of No. 4 is ultramarine, unwatermarked and imperf., value $100.

The 1942 4c reprint is blue, unwatermarked, imperf. and has printing on back (see note below No. 2), value $60.

A2

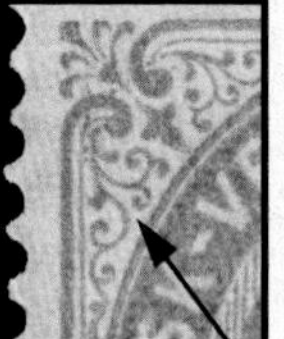

Normal Frame

Inverted Frame

The arabesques in the corners have a main stem and a branch. When the frame is in normal position, in the upper left corner the branch leaves the main stem half way between two little leaflets. In the lower right corner the branch starts at the foot of the second leaflet. When the frame is inverted the corner designs are, of course, transposed.

Values for inverted frames, covers and blocks are for the cheapest variety.

White Wove Paper
Varying from Thin to Thick

1874-79 Wmk. 112 *Perf. 14x13½*

5	A2 1c green & brown red	22.50	*30.00*
a.	1c green & rose lilac, thin paper	80.00	*125.00*
b.	1c green & red violet, medium paper	45.00	*65.00*
c.	1c green & claret, thick paper	20.00	*30.00*
e.	As "c," inverted frame	25.00	*32.50*
f.	As "a," inverted frame	*475.00*	
6	A2 3c blue & carmine	27.50	20.00
a.	3c light blue & rose carmine, thin paper	65.00	50.00
b.	3c deep blue & dark carmine, medium paper	40.00	17.00
c.	3c greenish blue & lake, thick paper	32.50	17.00
d.	Imperf., pair	375.00	—
e.	Inverted frame, thick paper	30.00	20.00
f.	As "a," inverted frame	*350.00*	
7	A2 4c brown & dull blue	16.00	*19.00*
b.	4c brown & ultramarine, thin paper	225.00	*225.00*
c.	Diagonal half used as 2c on cover		140.00
d.	As "b," inverted frame	*900.00*	*1,400.*
8	A2 5c grn & gray ('76)	30.00	20.00
a.	5c yellow green & dark gray, thin paper	55.00	32.50
b.	Inverted frame, thick paper	30.00	20.00
9	A2 7c lilac & orange	35.00	*95.00*
a.	7c lilac & yellow	90.00	*100.00*
b.	Inverted frame	65.00	*150.00*
10	A2 10c blue & brn ('76)	30.00	25.00
a.	10c dark blue & black brown, thin paper	70.00	40.00
b.	Period between "t" & "s" of "cents"	35.00	25.00
c.	Inverted frame	27.50	*32.50*
11	A2 12c red lil & yel grn ('77)	42.50	*175.00*
a.	12c lilac & deep green	160.00	*200.00*
12	A2 14c lilac & green	650.00	*1,250.*
a.	Inverted frame	*2,500.*	*3,500.*
13	A2 50c vio, thin paper ('79)	190.00	*300.00*
a.	50c gray violet, thick paper	250.00	*375.00*
	Nos. 5-13 (9)	1,044.	1,934.

No. 5 exists with a surcharge similar to the surcharge on No. 15, with 10 CENTS value and 1895 date. This stamp is an essay.

The central element in the fan-shaped scrollwork at the outside of the lower left corner of Nos. 5a and 7b looks like an elongated diamond.

See Nos. 16-20. For surcharges see Nos. 14-15, 23-28, 40.

No. 9 Surcharged in Black

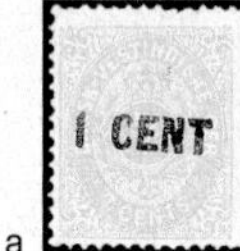

a

1887

14	A2 (a) 1c on 7c lilac & orange	100.00	*200.00*
a.	1c on 7c lilac & yellow	120.00	*225.00*
b.	Double surcharge	250.00	*500.00*
c.	Inverted frame	110.00	*350.00*

No. 13 Surcharged in Black

b

1895

15 A2 (b) 10c on 50c violet, thin paper 42.50 *67.50*

The "b" surcharge also exists on No. 5, with "10" found in two sizes. These are essays.

Type of 1874-79

1896-1901 ***Perf. 13***

16 A2 1c grn & red vio, inverted frame ('98) 15.00 *22.50*
- a. Normal frame 300.00 *450.00*

17 A2 3c blue & lake, inverted frame ('98) 12.00 *17.50*
- a. Normal frame 250.00 *425.00*

18 A2 4c bister & dull blue ('01) 17.50 11.00
- a. Diagonal half used as 2c on cover 100.00
- b. Inverted frame 60.00 *80.00*
- c. As "b," diagonal half used as 2c on cover 350.00

19 A2 5c green & gray, inverted frame 35.00 35.00
- a. Normal frame 800.00 *1,200.*

20 A2 10c blue & brn ('01) 80.00 *150.00*
- a. Inverted frame 1,000. *2,000.*
- b. Period between "t" and "s" of "cents" 170.00 160.00

Nos. 16-20 (5) 159.50 *236.00*

Arms — A5

1900

21 A5 1c light green 3.00 3.00
22 A5 5c light blue 17.50 *25.00*

See Nos. 29-30. For surcharges see Nos. 41-42.

Nos. 6, 17, 20 Surcharged

c

Surcharge "c" in Black

1902 ***Perf. 14x13½***

23 A2 2c on 3c blue & carmine, inverted frame 700.00 *900.00*
- a. "2" in date with straight tail 750.00 *950.00*
- b. Normal frame —

Perf. 13

24 A2 2c on 3c blue & lake, inverted frame 10.00 *27.50*
- a. "2" in date with straight tail 12.00 *32.50*
- b. Dated "1901" 750.00 750.00
- c. Normal frame 175.00 *300.00*
- d. Dark green surcharge 2,750.
- e. As "d" & "a" — —
- f. As "d" & "c" —

The overprint on No. 24b exists in two types: with "1901" measuring 2.5 mm or 2.2 mm high.

Only one example of No. 24f can exist.

25 A2 8c on 10c blue & brown 25.00 *42.50*
- a. "2" with straight tail 30.00 *45.00*
- b. On No. 20b 32.50 *45.00*
- c. Inverted frame 250.00 *425.00*

d

Surcharge "d" in Black

1902 ***Perf. 13***

27 A2 2c on 3c blue & lake, inverted frame 12.00 *32.50*
- a. Normal frame 240.00 *425.00*

28 A2 8c on 10c blue & brown 12.00 12.00
- a. On No. 20b 18.50 *25.00*
- b. Inverted frame 225.00 *400.00*

Nos. 23-28 (5) 759.00 1,015.

1903 **Wmk. 113**

29 A5 2c carmine 8.00 *22.50*
30 A5 8c brown 27.50 *35.00*

King Christian IX — A8

St. Thomas Harbor — A9

1905 **Typo.** ***Perf. 13***

31 A8 5b green 3.75 3.25
32 A8 10b red 3.75 3.25
33 A8 20b green & blue 8.75 8.75
34 A8 25b ultramarine 8.75 *10.50*
35 A8 40b red & gray 8.25 *9.50*
36 A8 50b yellow & gray 10.00 10.00

Perf. 12

Wmk. Two Crowns (113)

Frame Typographed, Center Engraved

37 A9 1fr green & blue 17.50 *40.00*
38 A9 2fr orange red & brown 30.00 *55.00*
39 A9 5fr yellow & brown 77.50 *275.00*

Nos. 31-39 (9) 168.25 *415.25*

Favor cancels exist on Nos. 37-39. Value 25% less.

Nos. 18, 22 and 30 Surcharged in Black

1905 **Wmk. 112**

40 A2 5b on 4c bister & dull blue 16.00 *50.00*
- a. Inverted frame 45.00 *90.00*

41 A5 5b on 5c light blue 10.00 *47.50*

Wmk. 113

42 A5 5b on 8c brown 12.50 *50.00*

Nos. 40-42 (3) 38.50 147.50

Favor cancels exist on Nos. 40-42. Value 25% less.

Frederik VIII — A10

Frame Typographed, Center Engraved

1908

43 A10 5b green 1.90 1.90
44 A10 10b red 1.90 1.90
45 A10 15b violet & brown 3.75 *4.50*
46 A10 20b green & blue 30.00 27.50
47 A10 25b blue & dark blue 1.90 *2.50*
48 A10 30b claret & slate 50.00 *52.50*
49 A10 40b vermilion & gray 5.75 *9.50*
50 A10 50b yellow & brown 5.75 *14.00*

Nos. 43-50 (8) 100.95 114.30

Christian X — A11

1915 **Wmk. 114** ***Perf. 14x14½***

51 A11 5b yellow green 4.00 *5.50*
52 A11 10b red 4.00 *55.00*
53 A11 15b lilac & red brown 4.00 *55.00*
54 A11 20b green & blue 4.00 *55.00*
55 A11 25b blue & dark blue 4.00 *17.50*
56 A11 30b claret & black 4.00 *100.00*
57 A11 40b orange & black 4.00 *100.00*
58 A11 50b yellow & brown 3.75 *100.00*

Nos. 51-58 (8) 31.75 *488.00*

Forged and favor cancellations exist.

POSTAGE DUE STAMPS

Royal Cipher, "Christian 9 Rex" D1

1902 **Litho.** **Unwmk.** ***Perf. 11½***

J1 D1 1c dark blue 5.00 *17.50*
J2 D1 4c dark blue 12.50 *22.50*
J3 D1 6c dark blue 22.50 *60.00*
J4 D1 10c dark blue 20.00 *65.00*

Nos. J1-J4 (4) 60.00 *165.00*

There are five types of each value. On the 4c they may be distinguished by differences in the figure "4"; on the other values differences are minute.

Used values of Nos. J1-J8 are for canceled stamps. Uncanceled stamps without gum have probably been used. Value 60% of unused.

Excellent counterfeits of Nos. J1-J4 exist.

Numeral of value — D2

1905-13 ***Perf. 13***

J5 D2 5b red & gray 4.50 *6.75*
J6 D2 20b red & gray 7.50 *14.00*
J7 D2 30b red & gray 6.75 *14.00*
J8 D2 50b red & gray 6.00 *30.00*
- a. Perf. 14x14½ ('13) 90.00 *375.00*
- b. Perf. 11½ 375.00

Nos. J5-J8 (4) 24.75 *64.75*

All values of this issue are known imperforate, but were not regularly issued.

Used values of Nos. J5-J8 are for canceled stamps. Uncanceled examples without gum have probably been used. Value 60% of unused.

No. J8b is valued in the grade of fine.

Counterfeits of Nos. J5-J8 exist.

Danish West Indies stamps were replaced by those of the U.S. in 1917, after the U.S. bought the islands.

DANZIG

'dan,t,-sig

LOCATION — In northern Europe bordering on the Baltic Sea
AREA — 754 sq. mi.
POP. — 407,000 (approx. 1939)
CAPITAL — Danzig

Established as a "Free City and State" under the protection of the League of Nations in 1920, Danzig was seized by Germany in 1939. It became a Polish province in 1945.

100 Pfennig = 1 Gulden (1923)
100 Pfennig = 1 Mark

Watermarks

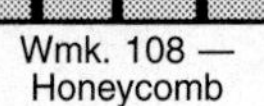

Wmk. 108 — Honeycomb

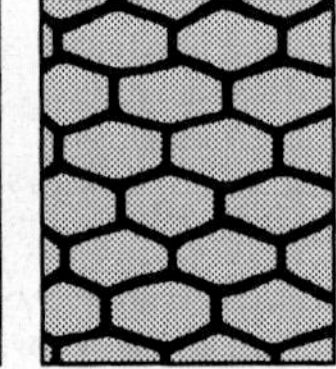

Wmk. 109 — Webbing

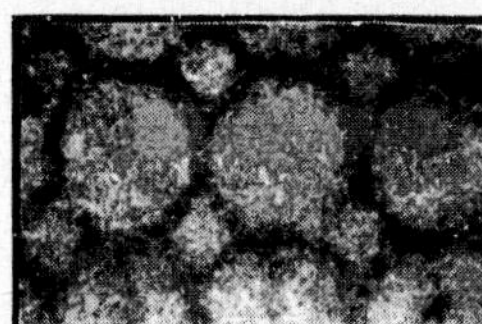

Wmk. 110 — Octagons

Wmk. 125 — Lozenges

Wmk. 237 — Swastikas

Used Values of 1920-23 are for favor-canceled stamps unless otherwise noted. Postally used examples bring much higher prices.

For additional varieties, see the *Scott Classic Catalogue.*

German Stamps of 1906-20 Overprinted in Black

Perf. 14, 14½, 15x14½

1920 **Wmk. 125**

1 A16 5pf green .30 *.50*
- a. Pair, one without overprint 100.00
- b. Double overprint —

2 A16 10pf car rose .30 .30
3 A22 15pf violet brown .30 .30
4 A16 20pf blue violet .30 *1.10*
5 A16 30pf org & blk, *buff* .30 .30
- a. Pair, one without overprint — —

6 A16 40pf car rose .30 .30
7 A16 50pf pur & blk, *buff* .50 .30
- a. Pair, one without overprint 175.00

8 A17 1m red .50 .60
- a. Pair, one without overprint 100.00

9 A17 1.25m green .50 .60
10 A17 1.50m yellow brn .90 *1.60*
11 A21 2m blue 3.25 *7.25*
- a. Double overprint *375.00*

12 A21 2.50m lilac rose 3.00 *4.50*
- c. Double overprint 1,000.

13 A19 3m black violet 7.50 *10.50*
- a. 3m blackish slate-violet 67.50 *135.00*
- b. Double overprint

14 A16 4m black & rose 4.75 *6.00*
15 A20 5m slate & car (25x17 holes) 2.50 *3.75*
- a. Center & "Danzig" invtd. *15,000.*
- b. Inverted overprint *20,000.*

Nos. 1-15 (15) 25.20 37.90
Set, never hinged 122.50

The 5pf brown, 10pf orange and 40pf lake and black with this overprint were not regularly issued. Value for trio, $450.

For surcharges see Nos. 19-23, C1-C3.

Issued: 40pf, 9/13; 1.50m, 3m 7/20; 4m, 12/21; others 6/14.

Nos. 5, 4 Surcharged in Various Sizes

1920

19 A16 5pf on 30pf (V) .25 .25
20 A16 10pf on 20pf (R) .25 .25
a. Double surcharge 110.00 —
21 A16 25pf on 30pf (G) .25 .25
a. Inverted surcharge 85.00 *275.00*
22 A16 60pf on 30pf (Br) .70 *1.00*
a. Double surcharge 85.00 *290.00*
b. Pair, one without surcharge *75.00* —
23 A16 80pf on 30pf (V) .70 *1.00*

Issued: No. 21, 8/10. No. 20, 8/17. Nos. 19, 22-23, 11/1.

German Stamps Surcharged in Various Styles

No. 25

No. 27

No. 30

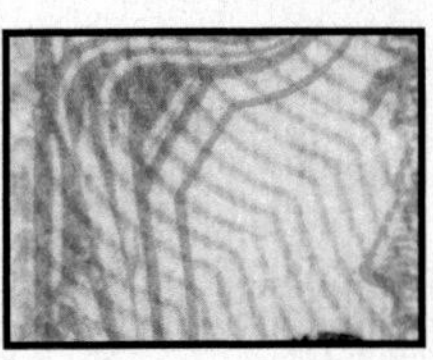
Burelage With Points Up

Gray Burelage with Points Up

25 A16 1m on 30pf org & blk, *buff* (Bk) .85 *1.50*
a. Pair, one without surcharge
26 A16 1¼m on 3pf brn (R) 1.00 *1.50*
27 A22 2m on 35pf red brn (Bl) 1.50 1.50
d. Surcharge omitted 70.00 —
28 A22 3m on 7½pf org (G) 1.00 *1.50*
29 A22 5m on 2pf gray (R) 1.00 *2.00*
30 A22 10m on 7½pf org (Bk) 3.00 *7.00*
Nos. 19-30 (11) 10.50 *17.75*
Set, never hinged 64.00

Gray Burelage with Points Down

26a A16 1¼m on 3pf brown 36.00 *42.50*
27a A22 2m on 35pf red brn 400.00 325.00
28a A22 3m on 7½pf orange 25.00 17.00
29a A22 5m on 2pf gray 25.00 *30.00*
30a A22 10m on 7½pf orange 5.75 *11.00*
Nos. 26a-30a (5) 491.75 *425.50*
Set, never hinged 2,100.

Violet Burelage with Points Up

25b A16 1m on 30pf org & blk, *buff* 85.00 30.00
26b A16 1¼m on 3pf brown 4.50 *6.50*
27b A22 2m on 35pf red brn 11.50 *37.50*
28b A22 3m on 7½pf orange 2.50 *2.50*
29b A22 5m on 2pf gray 1.25 *2.50*
30b A22 10m on 7½pf orange 1.25 *2.50*
h. Double overprint 70.00
Nos. 25b-30b (6) 106.00 *81.50*
Set, never hinged 430.00

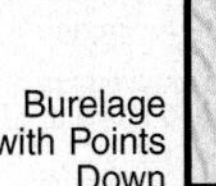

Burelage with Points Down

Violet Burelage with Points Down

25c A16 1m on 30pf org & blk, *buff* 1.25 2.50
26c A16 1¼m on 3pf brown 6.50 *11.00*
e. Double overprint 450.00
27c A22 2m on 35pf red brn 30.00 *50.00*
28c A22 3m on 7½pf orange 40.00 *85.00*
29c A22 5m on 2pf gray 6.50 *8.50*
30c A22 10m on 7½pf orange 13.50 *29.00*
Nos. 25c-30c (6) 97.75 *186.00*
Set, never hinged 380.00

Excellent counterfeits of the surcharges are known.

German Stamps of 1906-20 Overprinted in Blue

1920

31 A22 2pf gray 110.00 *200.00*
32 A22 2½pf gray 150.00 *300.00*
33 A16 3pf brown 11.00 *17.00*
a. Double overprint 75.00 —
34 A16 5pf green .60 *.70*
a. Double overprint 85.00
35 A22 7½pf orange 40.00 *57.50*
36 A16 10pf carmine 3.75 *7.00*
b. Double overprint 75.00
37 A22 15pf dk violet .60 *.70*
b. Double overprint 85.00
38 A16 20pf blue violet .60 *.70*

Overprinted in Carmine or Blue

39 A16 25pf org & blk, *yel* .60 *.70*
40 A16 30pf org & blk, *buff* 50.00 *92.50*
42 A16 40pf lake & blk 2.25 *2.50*
a. Inverted overprint 210.00
b. Double overprint 425.00
43 A16 50pf pur & blk, *buff* 175.00 *300.00*
44 A16 60pf mag (Bl) 1,250. *2,100.*
45 A16 75pf green & blk .60 *.70*
a. Double overprint *450.00*
46 A16 80pf lake & blk, *rose* 2.40 *4.25*
47 A17 1m carmine 1,200. *2,100.*
a. Double overprint *4,250.*

Overprinted in Carmine

48 A21 2m gray blue 1,200. *2,100.*

Counterfeit overprints of Nos. 31-48 exist.

Nos. 44, 47 and 48 were issued in small quantities and usually affixed directly to the mail by the postal clerk.

For surcharge see No. 62.

A8

Hanseatic Trading Ship — A9

Serrate Roulette 13½

1921, Jan. 31 Typo. Wmk. 108

49 A8 5pf brown & violet .25 .25
50 A8 10pf orange & dk vio .25 .25
51 A8 25pf green & car rose .50 .65
52 A8 40pf carmine rose 3.75 3.25
53 A8 80pf ultra .50 .50
54 A9 1m car rose & blk 1.60 *2.00*
55 A9 2m dk blue & dk grn 5.00 5.00
56 A9 3m blk & grnsh bl 2.00 *2.00*
57 A9 5m indigo & rose red 2.00 *2.00*
58 A9 10m dk grn & brn org 2.50 *4.50*
Nos. 49-58 (10) 18.35 *20.40*
Set, never hinged 82.50

Issued in honor of the Constitution.

Nos. 49 and 50 with center in red instead of violet and Nos. 49-51, 54-58 with center inverted are probably proofs. All values of this issue exist imperforate but are not known to have been regularly issued in that condition.

1921, Mar. 11 ***Perf. 14***

59 A8 25pf green & car rose .50 *.85*
60 A8 40pf carmine rose .50 .85
61 A8 80pf ultra 5.50 *10.00*
Nos. 59-61 (3) 6.50 *11.70*
Set, never hinged 34.00

No. 45 Surcharged in Black

1921, May 6 Wmk. 125

62 A16 60pf on 75pf .95 .90
Never hinged 5.50
a. Double surcharge 100.00 *110.00*

Surcharge on No. 62 normally appears at top of design.

Arms — A11

Coat of Arms — A12

Wmk. 108 (Upright or Sideways)

1921-22 ***Perf. 14***

63 A11 5(pf) orange .25 .25
64 A11 10(pf) dark brown .25 .25
65 A11 15(pf) green .25 .25
66 A11 20(pf) slate .25 .25
67 A11 25(pf) dark green .25 .25
68 A11 30(pf) blue & car .25 .25
a. Center inverted 75.00 *150.00*
69 A11 40pf green & car .25 .25
a. Center inverted 75.00 *150.00*
70 A11 50pf dk grn & car .25 .25
71 A11 60pf carmine .45 .45
72 A11 80pf black & car .35 *.45*

Paper With Faint Gray Network

73 A11 1m org & car .50 .40
a. Center inverted 75.00 150.00
74 A11 1.20m blue violet 1.25 1.25
75 A11 2m gray & car 3.25 *4.25*
76 A11 3m violet & car 9.00 10.00

Serrate Roulette 13½
Wmk. 108 Upright

77 A12 5m grn, red & blk 1.25 *3.00*
78 A12 9m rose, red & org ('22) 3.00 *8.50*
79 A12 10m ultra, red & blk 1.25 *3.00*
80 A12 20m red & black 1.25 *3.00*
Nos. 63-80 (18) 23.55 *36.30*
Set, never hinged 85.00

In this and succeeding issues the mark values usually have the face of the paper covered with a gray network. This network is often very faint and occasionally is omitted.

Nos. 64-76 exist imperf. Value, each $16-$50 unused, $50-$150 never hinged.

See Nos. 81-93, 99-105. For surcharges and overprints see Nos. 96-98, O1-O33.

Type of 1921 and

A13

Coat of Arms — A13a

1922 Wmk. 108 Upright ***Perf. 14***

81 A11 75(pf) deep vio .25 *.25*
82 A11 80(pf) green .25 *.25*
83 A11 1.25m vio & car .25 *.25*
84 A11 1.50m slate gray .25 *.40*
85 A11 2m car rose .25 *.25*
86 A11 2.40m dk brn & car 1.15 *2.00*
87 A11 3m car lake .25 *.40*
88 A11 4m dark blue 1.15 *2.00*
89 A11 5m deep grn .25 *.35*
90 A11 6m car lake .25 *.35*
a. 6m car rose, wmk. 109 sideways *1,800.*
91 A11 8m light blue .45 *1.60*
92 A11 10m orange .25 *.35*
93 A11 20m org brn .25 *.35*
94 A13 50m gold & car 2.00 *6.50*
95 A13a 100m metallic grn & red 3.25 *6.00*
Nos. 81-95 (15) 10.50 *21.30*
Set, never hinged 42.50

No. 95 has buff instead of gray network.

Nos. 81-83, 85-86, 88 exist imperf. Value, each $12.50.

Nos. 94-95 exist imperf. Value, each $50

Nos. 87, 88 and 91 Surcharged in Black or Carmine

1922

96 A11 6m on 3m car lake .35 *.60*
a. Double surcharge
97 A11 8m on 4m dk blue .35 *.85*
a. Double surcharge 70.00 *145.00*
b. Pair, one without surcharge 150.00
98 A11 20m on 8m lt bl (C) .35 *.60*
Nos. 96-98 (3) 1.05 *2.05*
Set, never hinged 4.00

Wmk. 109 Sideways

1922-23 ***Perf. 14***

99 A11 4m dark blue .25 *.40*
100 A11 5m dark green .25 *.40*
102 A11 10m orange .25 *.40*
103 A11 20m orange brn .25 *.40*

Paper Without Network
Wmk. 109 Upright

104 A11 40m pale blue .25 *.60*
105 A11 80m red .25 *.60*
Nos. 99-105 (6) 1.50 *2.80*
Set, never hinged 5.40

Nos. 100, 102 and 103 also exist with watermark vertical. Values slightly higher.

Nos. 104-105 exist imperf. Value, each $12.50 unused, $32.50 never hinged.

A15

A15a

Coat of Arms A16

1922-23 Wmk. 109 Upright ***Perf. 14***

Paper With Gray Network

106 A15 50m pale bl & red .25 *.40*
107 A15a 100m dk grn & red .25 *.40*
108 A15a 150m violet & red .25 *.40*
109 A16 250m violet & red .40 *.40*
110 A16 500m gray blk & red .40 *.40*
111 A16 1000m brn & red .40 *.40*
112 A16 5000m silver & red 1.50 *6.00*

Paper Without Network

113 A15 50m pale blue .40 *.60*
114 A15a 100m deep green .40 *.60*
115 A15 200m orange .40 *.60*
Nos. 106-115 (10) 4.65 *10.20*
Set, never hinged 19.00

Nos. 108-112 exist imperf. Value, each $50 unused, $125 never hinged.

Nos. 113-115 exist imperf. Value, each $35 unused, $92.50 never hinged.

See Nos. 123-125. For surcharges and overprints see Nos. 126, 137-140, 143, 156-167, O35-O38.

A17

1923 *Perf. 14*

Paper With Gray Network

117 A17 250m violet & red .25 *.55*
118 A17 300m bl grn & red .25 *.55*
119 A17 500m gray & red .25 *.55*
120 A17 1000m brown & red .25 *.55*
121 A17 3000m violet & red .25 *.55*
123 A16 10,000m orange & red .60 .60
124 A16 20,000m pale bl & red .60 *1.00*
125 A16 50,000m green & red .60 *1.00*
Nos. 117-125 (8) 3.05 *5.35*
Set, never hinged 12.50

Nos. 117, 119-121 exist imperf. Value, each $19 unused, $45 never hinged; Nos. 123-125 also exist imperf. Values each, $25 unused, $85 never hinged.

See Nos. 127-135. For surcharges & overprints see Nos. 141-142, 144-155, O39-O41.

No. 124 Surcharged in Red

1923, Aug. 14

126 A16 100,000m on #124 1.00 *6.00*
Never hinged 4.50

No. 126 exists imperf. Value $50 unused, $125 never hinged.

1923 *Perf. 14*

Paper Without Network

127 A17 1000m brown .25 *.40*
129 A17 5000m rose .25 *.40*
131 A17 20,000m pale blue .25 *.40*
132 A17 50,000m green .25 *.40*

Paper With Gray Network

133 A17 100,000m deep blue .25 *.40*
b. Double impression 80.00
134 A17 250,000m violet .25 *.40*
135 A17 500,000m slate .25 *.40*
Nos. 127-135 (7) 1.75 2.80
Set, never hinged 5.00

Abbreviations:
th=(tausend) thousand
mil=million

Nos. 115, 114, 132, and Type of 1923 Surcharged

No. 137-139

No. 140

No. 141

No. 142

1923 *Perf. 14*

Paper Without Network

137 A15 40th m on 200m .85 *2.00*
a. Double surcharge 85.00
138 A15 100th m on 200m .85 *2.00*
139 A15 250th m on 200m 6.25 *13.00*
140 A15a 400th m on 100m .60 .60
141 A17 500th m on #132 .40 *.60*

On 10,000m

142 A17 1mil m org 3.75 *6.25*

The surcharges on Nos. 140-142 differ in details from those on Nos. 137-139.

Type of 1923 Surcharged

Paper With Gray Network
On 1,000,000m

143 A16 10mil m org .40 *1.25*
Nos. 137-143 (7) 13.10 *25.70*
Set, never hinged 60.00

Nos. 142-143 exist imperf. Values: No. 142 unused $50, never hinged $125; No. 143 unused $25, never hinged $85.

Type of 1923 Surcharged

Wmk. 109 Upright
Perf. 14

10,000m rose on paper without Network

144 A17 1mil m on 10,000m .25 *.60*
145 A17 2mil m on 10,000m .25 *.60*
146 A17 3mil m on 10,000m .25 *.60*
147 A17 5mil m on 10,000m .35 *.60*
b. Double surcharge 85.00

10,000m gray lilac on paper without Network

148 A17 10mil m on 10,000m .40 *.75*
149 A17 20mil m on 10,000m .40 *.75*
150 A17 25mil m on 10,000m .25 *.75*
151 A17 40mil m on 10,000m .25 *.75*
a. Double surcharge 52.50
152 A17 50mil m on 10,000m .25 *.75*

Type of 1923 Surcharged in Red

10,000m gray lilac on paper without Network

153 A17 100mil m on 10,000m .25 *.75*
154 A17 300mil m on 10,000m .25 *.75*
155 A17 500mil m on 10,000m .25 *.75*
Nos. 144-155 (12) 3.40 *8.40*
Set, never hinged 15.00

Nos. 144-147 exist imperf. Value, each $25 unused, $85 never hinged. Nos. 148-155 exist imperf. Value, each $32.50 unused, $85 never hinged.

Types of 1923 Surcharged

1923, Oct. 31 **Wmk. 110** *Perf. 14*

156 A15 5pf on 50m .45 .40
157 A15 10pf on 50m .45 .40
158 A15a 20pf on 100m .45 .40
159 A15 25pf on 50m 3.50 *9.00*
160 A15 30pf on 50m 3.50 2.00
161 A15a 40pf on 100m 2.25 2.00
162 A15a 50pf on 100m 2.25 *3.00*
163 A15a 75pf on 100m 8.00 *16.00*

Type of 1923 Surcharged

1923, Nov. 5

164 A16 1g on 1mil m rose 4.50 *6.25*
165 A16 2g on 1mil m rose 12.00 *17.50*
166 A16 3g on 1mil m rose 22.00 *62.50*
167 A16 5g on 1mil m rose 25.00 *67.50*
Nos. 156-167 (12) 84.35 *186.95*
Set, never hinged 400.00

Coat of Arms — A19

1924-37 **Wmk. 109** ***Perf. 14***

168 A19 3pf brn, *yelsh* ('35) 1.25 *1.50*
a. 3pf dp brn, *white* ('27) 2.10 1.90
170 A19 5pf org, *yelsh* 3.25 .55
a. White paper 8.50 2.00
c. Tête bêche pair 375.00
d. Syncopated perf., #170 10.50 9.25
e. Syncopated perf., #170a 25.00 22.50
171 A19 7pf yel grn ('33) 1.60 *3.00*
172 A19 8pf yel grn ('37) 1.60 *6.00*
173 A19 10pf grn, *yelsh* 5.50 .50
a. White paper 11.50 2.50
c. 10pf blue grn, *yellowish* 7.75 1.10
d. Tête bêche pair 325.00
e. Syncopated perf., #173 18.00 11.00
f. Syncopated perf., #173a 27.50 13.00
g. Syncopated perf., #173c 11.00 *14.50*
175 A19 15pf gray 3.75 .65
176 A19 15pf red, *yelsh* ('35) 2.10 1.10
a. White paper ('25) 4.50 1.10
177 A19 20pf carmine & red 15.00 .65
178 A19 20pf gray ('35) 2.25 *2.50*
179 A19 25pf slate & red 27.00 3.75
180 A19 25pf carmine ('35) 16.00 1.60
181 A19 30pf green & red 14.00 .85
182 A19 30pf dk violet ('35) 2.25 *4.25*
183 A19 35pf ultra 4.50 1.50
184 A19 40pf dk blue & blue 12.00 1.00
185 A19 40pf yel brn & red 6.50 *12.50*
186 A19 40pf dk blue ('35) 2.25 *3.75*
a. Imperf. 60.00
187 A19 50pf blue & red 16.00 7.50
a. Yellowish paper 17.50 *32.50*
188 A19 55pf plum & scar 5.00 *14.50*
189 A19 60pf dk grn & red 6.25 *17.50*
190 A19 70pf yel grn & red ('35) 2.25 *7.50*
191 A19 75pf violet & red, *yellowish* 7.50 *29.00*
a. White paper 10.00 8.50
192 A19 80pf dk org brn & red ('35) 2.25 *7.50*
Nos. 168-192 (23) 160.05 *129.15*
Set, never hinged 675.00

The 5pf and 10pf with syncopated perforations (Netherlands type C) are coils.

See Nos. 225-232. For overprints and surcharges see Nos. 200-209, 211-215, 241-252, B9-B11, O42-O52.

Oliva Castle and Cathedral A20

St. Mary's Church A23

Council Chamber on the Langenmarkt A24

2g, Mottlau River & Krantor. 3g, View of Zoppot.

1924-32 **Engr.** **Wmk. 125**

193 A20 1g yel grn & blk 21.00 *45.00*
Parcel post cancel 20.00
194 A20 1g org & gray blk ('32) 17.00 3.75
Parcel post cancel 1.00
a. 1g red orange & blk 17.00 11.00
Parcel post cancel 1.00
195 A20 2g red vio & blk 45.00 *110.00*
Parcel post cancel 40.00
196 A20 2g rose & blk 3.75 *8.00*
Parcel post cancel 1.75
197 A20 3g dk blue & blk 4.75 *5.00*
Parcel post cancel 2.25
198 A23 5g brn red & blk 4.75 *8.50*
Parcel post cancel 1.90
199 A24 10g dk brn & blk 21.00 *110.00*
Parcel post cancel 18.00
Nos. 193-199 (7) 117.25 *290.25*
Set, never hinged 600.00

See No. 233. For overprints and surcharges see Nos. 210, 253-254, C31-C35.

Stamps of 1924-25 Overprinted in Black, Violet or Red

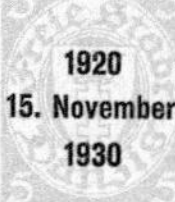

1930, Nov. 15 **Typo.** **Wmk. 109**

200 A19 5pf orange 2.50 *3.50*
201 A19 10pf yellow grn (V) 3.50 4.25
202 A19 15pf red 6.00 *10.00*
203 A19 20pf carmine & red 3.00 *5.50*
204 A19 25pf slate & red 4.25 *10.00*
205 A19 30pf green & red 8.50 *22.50*
206 A19 35pf ultra (R) 32.50 *90.00*
207 A19 40pf dk bl & bl (R) 11.50 *35.00*
208 A19 50pf dp blue & red 32.50 *75.00*
209 A19 75pf violet & red 32.50 *82.50*

Engr. **Wmk. (125)**

210 A20 1g orange & blk (R) 32.50 *75.00*
Nos. 200-210 (11) 169.25 *413.25*
Set, never hinged 675.00

10th anniv. of the Free State. Counterfeits exist.

Nos. 171 and 183 Surcharged in Red, Blue or Green

Nos. 211-214

No. 215

1934-36

211 A19 6pf on 7pf (R) 1.00 *1.50*
212 A19 8pf on 7pf (Bl) 2.00 *2.25*
213 A19 8pf on 7pf (R) 1.15 *2.40*
214 A19 8pf on 7pf (G) .75 *2.40*
215 A19 30pf on 35pf (Bl) 11.00 *24.50*
Nos. 211-215 (5) 15.90 *33.05*
Set, never hinged 60.00

Bathing Beach, Brösen A25

View of Brösen Beach A26

War Memorial at Brösen — A27

1936, June 23 **Typo.** **Wmk. 109**

216 A25 10pf deep green .70 *.70*
217 A26 25pf rose red 1.25 *2.40*
218 A27 40pf bright blue 2.25 *4.50*
Nos. 216-218 (3) 4.20 *7.60*
Set, never hinged 15.00

Village of Brösen, 125th anniversary.
Exist imperf. Value each, $40 unused, $110 never hinged.

Skyline of Danzig — A28

1937, Mar. 27

219 A28 10pf dark blue .50 *1.40*
220 A28 15pf violet brown 1.60 *2.00*
Set, never hinged 11.25
Set of 2, #219-220 on one 1st day cover 20.00

Air Defense League.

Danzig Philatelic Exhibition Issue
Souvenir Sheet

St. Mary's Church — A29

1937, June 6 Wmk. 109 *Perf. 14*

221 A29 50pf dark opal green 4.00 *20.00*
Never hinged 11.00

Danzig Philatelic Exhib., June 6-8, 1937.

Arthur Schopenhauer
A30 A31

Design: 40pf, Full-face portrait, white hair.

Unwmk.

1938, Feb. 22 Photo. *Perf. 14*

222 A30 15pf dull blue 1.35 *2.40*
223 A31 25pf sepia 3.25 *8.00*
224 A31 40pf orange ver 1.35 *3.25*
Nos. 222-224 (3) 5.95 *13.65*
Set, never hinged 20.00
Set of 3, #222-224 on one 1st day cover 37.50

150th anniv. of the birth of Schopenhauer.

Type of 1924-35

1938-39 Typo. Wmk. 237 *Perf. 14*

225 A19 3pf brown .90 *7.25*
226 A19 5pf orange .90 *2.00*
b. Syncopated perf. 1.40 *7.50*
227 A19 8pf yellow grn 4.00 *32.50*
228 A19 10pf blue green .90 *2.00*
b. Syncopated perf. 3.00 *10.00*
229 A19 15pf scarlet 1.60 *10.00*
230 A19 25pf carmine 2.10 *7.50*
231 A19 40pf dark blue 2.10 *27.50*
232 A19 50pf brt bl & red 2.10 *130.00*

Engr.

233 A20 1g red org & blk 6.75 *110.00*
Nos. 225-233 (9) 21.35 *328.75*
Set, never hinged 90.00

Sizes: No. 233, 32½x21¼mm; No. 194, 31x21mm.

Nos. 226b and 228b are coils with Netherlands type C perforation.

Knights in Tournament, 1500 — A33
French Leaving Danzig, 1814 — A35

Stamp Day: 10pf, Signing of Danzig-Sweden neutrality treaty, 1630. 25pf, Battle of Weichselmünde, 1577.

Unwmk.

1939, Jan. 7 Photo. *Perf. 14*

234 A33 5pf dark green .40 *2.00*
235 A33 10pf copper brown .85 *2.25*
236 A35 15pf slate black 1.25 *2.75*
237 A35 25pf brown violet 1.60 *3.75*
Nos. 234-237 (4) 4.10 *10.75*
Set, never hinged 14.00
Set of 4, #234-237 on one 1st day cover 30.00

Gregor Mendel — A37

15pf, Dr. Robert Koch. 25pf, Wilhelm Roentgen.

1939, Apr. 29 Photo. *Perf. 13x14*

238 A37 10pf copper brown .65 *.85*
239 A37 15pf indigo .65 *2.00*
240 A37 25pf dark olive green 1.25 *2.75*
Nos. 238-240 (3) 2.55 *5.60*
Set, never hinged 7.25

Issued in honor of the achievements of Mendel, Koch and Roentgen.

Issued under German Administration

Stamps of Danzig, 1925-39, Surcharged in Black

a

b

c

1939 Wmk. 109 *Perf. 14*

241 A19(b) 4rpf on 35pf ultra .75 *2.25*
242 A19(b) 12rpf on 7pf yel grn 1.50 *2.25*
243 A19(a) 20rpf gray 3.00 *8.50*

Wmk. 237

244 A19(a) 3rpf brown .75 *2.40*
245 A19(a) 5rpf orange .65 *3.00*
246 A19(a) 8rpf yellow grn 1.10 *4.25*
247 A19(a) 10rpf blue grn 2.25 *4.25*
248 A19(a) 15rpf scarlet 6.00 *11.00*
249 A19(a) 25rpf carmine 4.50 *10.00*
250 A19(a) 30rpf dk violet 2.00 *4.50*
251 A19(a) 40rpf dk blue 2.75 *6.00*
252 A19(a) 50rpf brt bl & red 4.00 *7.00*

Thick Paper

253 A20(c) 1rm on 1g red org & blk 14.00 *57.50*

Wmk. 125

Thin White Paper

254 A20(c) 2rm on 2g rose & blk 20.00 *62.50*
Nos. 241-254 (14) 63.25 *185.40*
Set, never hinged 190.00

Nos. 241-254 were valid throughout Germany.

SEMI-POSTAL STAMPS

St. George and Dragon — SP1

Wmk. 108

1921, Oct. 16 Typo. *Perf. 14*

Size: 19x22mm

B1 SP1 30pf + 30pf grn & org .45 .95
B2 SP1 60pf + 60pf rose & org 1.25 *1.60*

Size: 25x30mm

Serrate Roulette 13½

B3 SP1 1.20m + 1.20m dk bl & org 2.00 *2.25*
Nos. B1-B3 (3) 3.70 4.80
Set, never hinged 16.00

Nos. B1-B3 exist imperf. Value each, $45 unused, $125 never hinged.

Aged Pensioner SP2

1923, Mar. Wmk. 109 *Perf. 14*

Paper With Gray Network

B4 SP2 50m + 20m lake .25 *.60*
B5 SP2 100m + 30m red vio .25 *.60*
Set, never hinged 2.50

Nos. B4-B5 exist imperf. Value each, $50 unused, $30 used, $210 never hinged.

Philatelic Exhibition Issue

Neptune Fountain — SP3

Various Frames.

1929, July 7 Engr. Unwmk.

B6 SP3 10pf yel grn & gray 2.40 1.60
B7 SP3 15pf car & gray 2.40 1.60
B8 SP3 25pf ultra & gray 8.50 *13.00*
a. 25pf violet blue & black 25.00 *80.00*
Nos. B6-B8 (3) 13.30 16.20
Set, never hinged 45.00
Set of 3, #B6-B8 on one 1st day cover 200.00

These stamps were sold exclusively at the Danzig Philatelic Exhibition, June 7-14, 1929, at double their face values, the excess being for the aid of the exhibition.

Regular Issue of 1924-25 Surcharged in Black

1934, Jan. 15 Wmk. 109

B9 A19 5pf + 5pf orange 9.50 *19.00*
B10 A19 10pf + 5pf yel grn 22.50 *45.00*
B11 A19 15pf + 5pf carmine 13.50 *35.00*
Nos. B9-B11 (3) 45.50 *99.00*
Set, never hinged 220.00

Surtax for winter welfare. Counterfeits exist.

Stock Tower — SP4
George Hall — SP6

City Gate, 16th Century SP5

1935, Dec. 16 Typo. *Perf. 14*

B12 SP4 5pf + 5pf orange .65 *1.50*
B13 SP5 10pf + 5pf green 1.10 *2.25*
B14 SP6 15pf + 10pf scarlet 2.75 *3.50*
Nos. B12-B14 (3) 4.50 *7.25*
Set, never hinged 16.00
Set of 3, #B12-B14 on one 1st day cover 40.00

Surtax for winter welfare.

Milk Can Tower SP7
Frauentor SP8

Krantor — SP9

Langgarter Gate — SP10

High Gate SP11

1936, Nov. 25

B15 SP7 10pf + 5pf dk bl 1.60 *4.50*
a. Imperf. 75.00
B16 SP8 15pf + 5pf dull grn 1.60 *5.75*
B17 SP9 25pf + 10pf red brn 2.25 *9.00*
B18 SP10 40pf + 20pf brn & red brn 3.00 *10.00*
B19 SP11 50pf + 20pf bl & dk bl 5.25 *15.00*
Nos. B15-B19 (5) 13.70 *44.25*
Set, never hinged 80.00

Surtax for winter welfare.

SP12 SP13

1937, Oct. 30 Wmk. 109 Sideways

B20 SP12 25pf + 25pf dk car 2.75 *5.25*

Wmk. 109 Upright

B21 SP13 40pf + 40pf blue & red 2.75 *5.25*
a. Souvenir sheet of 2, #B20a-B21 60.00 *110.00*
Set, never hinged 27.50

Founding of Danzig community at Magdeburg. No. B21a exists imperf. Value, $1,600 unused, $3,250 never hinged.

Madonna SP14

Mercury SP15

Weather Vane, Town Hall SP16

Neptune Fountain SP17

St. George and Dragon — SP18

1937, Dec. 13

B23	SP14	5pf + 5pf brt violet	2.50	*7.50*
B24	SP15	10pf + 10pf dk brn	2.50	*5.75*
B25	SP16	15pf + 5pf bl & yel brn	2.50	*8.25*
B26	SP17	25pf + 10pf bl grn & grn	3.25	*11.00*
B27	SP18	40pf + 25pf brt car & bl	5.75	*15.00*
		Nos. B23-B27 (5)	16.50	*47.50*
		Set, never hinged	65.00	
		Set of 5, #B23-B27 on one 1st day cover		100.00

Surtax for winter welfare. Designs are from frieze of the Artushof.

"Peter von Danzig" Yacht Race — SP19

Ships: 10pf+5pf, Dredger Fu Shing. 15pf+10pf, S. S. Columbus. 25pf+10pf, S. S. City of Danzig. 40pf+15pf, Peter von Danzig, 1472.

1938, Nov. 28 Photo. Unwmk.

B28	SP19	5pf + 5pf dk bl grn	1.40	*1.50*
B29	SP19	10pf + 5pf gldn brn	1.40	*3.00*
B30	SP19	15pf + 10pf ol grn	1.60	*3.00*
B31	SP19	25pf + 10pf indigo	2.50	*4.00*
B32	SP19	40pf + 15pf vio brn	3.00	*6.75*
		Nos. B28-B32 (5)	9.90	*18.25*
		Set, never hinged	50.00	
		Set of 5, #B28-B32 on one 1st day cover		60.00

Surtax for winter welfare.

AIR POST STAMPS

No. 6 Surcharged in Blue or Carmine

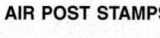

1920, Sept. 29 Wmk. 125 *Perf. 14*

C1	A16	40pf on 40pf	1.25	*2.60*
a.		Double surcharge	160.00	*250.00*
C2	A16	60pf on 40pf (C)	1.25	*2.60*
a.		Double surcharge	125.00	*250.00*
C3	A16	1m on 40pf	1.25	*2.60*
a.		Double surcharge	125.00	250.00
		Nos. C1-C3 (3)	3.75	*7.80*
		Set, never hinged	13.50	

Plane faces left on No. C2.

AP3

Plane over Danzig AP4

Wmk. (108) Upright

1921-22 Typo. *Perf. 14*

C4	AP3	40(pf) blue green	.25	*.45*
C5	AP3	60(pf) dk violet	.25	*.45*
C6	AP3	1m carmine	.25	*.45*
C7	AP3	2m org brn	.25	*.45*

Serrate Roulette 13½

Size: 34½x23mm

C8	AP4	5m violet blue	1.25	*2.25*
C9	AP4	10m dp grn	2.00	*4.25*
		Nos. C4-C9 (6)	4.25	*8.30*
		Set, never hinged	18.00	

Nos. C4-C9 exist imperf. Value, each $32.50 unused, $125 never hinged.

1923 Wmk. (109) Upright *Perf. 14*

C10	AP3	40(pf) blue green	.55	*1.90*
C11	AP3	60(pf) dk violet	.55	*1.90*
a.		Double impression		
C12	AP3	1m carmine	.55	*1.90*
C13	AP3	2m org brown	.55	*1.90*
C14	AP3	25m pale blue	.40	*.70*

Serrate Roulette 13½

Size: 34½x23mm

C15	AP4	5m violet blue	.55	*1.00*
C16	AP4	10m deep green	.55	*1.00*

Paper With Gray Network

C17	AP4	20m org brn	.55	*1.00*

Size: 40x23mm

C18	AP4	50m orange	.40	*.70*
C19	AP4	100m red	.40	*.70*
C20	AP4	250m dark brown	.60	*.70*
C21	AP4	500m car rose	.60	*.70*
		Nos. C10-C21 (12)	6.25	*14.10*
		Set, never hinged	30.00	

Nos. C11, C12, C14-C21 exist imperf. Value, Nos. C11, C12, C15-C17, each $8.50 unused, $32.50 never hinged. Value, No. C14, C18-C21, each $40 unused, $125 never hinged.

Nos. C18, C19 and C21 exist with wmk. sideways, both perf and imperf. Value each, $60 unused, $160 never hinged.

Post Horn and Airplanes — AP5

1923, Oct. 18 *Perf. 14*

Paper Without Network

C22	AP5	250,000m scarlet	.35	*1.25*
C23	AP5	500,000m scarlet	.35	*1.25*
		Set, never hinged	2.50	

Exist imperf. Value, each: $50 unused; $125 never hinged.

Surcharged

On 100,000m

C24	AP5	2mil m scarlet	.35	*1.25*

On 50,000m

C25	AP5	5mil m scarlet	.35	*1.25*
b.		Cliché of 10,000m in sheet of 50,000m	32.50	*160.00*

Exist imperf. Value, each $125 unused, $290 never hinged.

Nos. C24 and C25 were not regularly issued without surcharge, although examples have been passed through the post. Values: C24 unused $8.50, never hinged $32.50; C25 unused $12, never hinged $21.

AP6

Plane over Danzig — AP7

1924

C26	AP6	10(pf) vermilion	21.00	3.50
C27	AP6	20(pf) carmine rose	2.10	1.50
C28	AP6	40(pf) olive brown	3.00	1.75
C29	AP6	1g deep green	3.00	3.00
C30	AP7	2½g violet brown	17.50	*32.50*
		Nos. C26-C30 (5)	46.60	*42.25*
		Set, never hinged	175.00	

Exist imperf. Value Nos. C26, C30, $85 unused, $200 never hinged; others, each $40 unused, $110 never hinged.

Nos. 193, 195, 197-199 Srchd. in Various Colors

1932 Wmk. 125

C31	A20	10pf on 1g (G)	9.00	*21.00*
C32	A20	15pf on 2g (V)	9.00	*21.00*
C33	A20	20pf on 3g (Bl)	9.00	*21.00*
C34	A23	25pf on 5g (R)	9.00	*21.00*
C35	A24	30pf on 10g (Br)	9.00	*21.00*
		Nos. C31-C35 (5)	45.00	*105.00*
		Set, never hinged	200.00	

Intl. Air Post Exhib. of 1932. The surcharges were variously arranged to suit the shapes and designs of the stamps. The stamps were sold at double their surcharged values, the excess being donated to the exhibition funds.

No. C31 exists with inverted surcharge and with double surcharge. Value each, $85 unused, $210 never hinged.

Airplane

AP8 AP9

1935, Oct. 24 Wmk. 109

C36	AP8	10pf scarlet	1.75	.85
C37	AP8	15pf yellow	1.75	1.25
C38	AP8	25pf dark green	1.75	1.50
C39	AP8	50pf gray blue	9.00	*9.25*
C40	AP9	1g magenta	3.50	*13.00*
		Nos. C36-C40 (5)	17.75	*25.85*
		Set, never hinged	65.00	

Nos. C36 and C40 exist imperf. Values: C36 unused $20, never hinged $62.50; C40 unused $29, never hinged $85.

See Nos. C42-C45.

Souvenir Sheet

St. Mary's Church — AP10

1937, June 6 *Perf. 14*

C41	AP10	50pf dark grayish blue	3.75	*16.00*

Danzig Phil. Exhib., June 6-8, 1937.

Type of 1935

1938-39 Wmk. 237

C42	AP8	10pf scarlet	1.25	*3.75*
C43	AP8	15pf yellow ('39)	2.00	*12.00*
C44	AP8	25pf dark green	1.60	*6.50*
C45	AP8	50pf gray blue ('39)	4.00	*57.50*
		Nos. C42-C45 (4)	8.85	*79.75*
		Set, never hinged	42.50	

POSTAGE DUE STAMPS

Danzig Coat of Arms — D1

1921-22 Typo. Wmk. (108) *Perf. 14*

Paper Without Network

J1	D1	10(pf) deep violet	.35	*.45*
J2	D1	20(pf) deep violet	.35	*.45*
J3	D1	40(pf) deep violet	.35	*.45*
J4	D1	60(pf) deep violet	.35	*.45*
J5	D1	75(pf) dp violet ('22)	.35	*.45*
J6	D1	80(pf) deep violet	.35	*.45*
J7	D1	120(pf) deep violet	.35	*.45*
J8	D1	200(pf) dp violet ('22)	.95	*1.00*
J9	D1	240(pf) deep violet	.35	*1.00*
J10	D1	300(pf) dp violet ('22)	.95	*1.00*
J11	D1	400(pf) deep violet	.95	*1.00*
J12	D1	500(pf) deep violet	.95	*1.00*
J13	D1	800(pf) deep violet ('22)	.95	*1.00*
J14	D1	20m dp violet ('22)	.95	*1.00*
		Nos. J1-J14 (14)	8.50	*10.15*
		Set, never hinged	27.50	

Nos. J1-J14 exist imperf. Value, each $30 unused, $75 never hinged.

1923 Wmk. 109 Sideways

J15	D1	100(pf) deep violet	.60	*.75*
J16	D1	200(pf) deep violet	2.50	*3.75*
J17	D1	300(pf) deep violet	.60	*.75*
J18	D1	400(pf) deep violet	.60	*.75*
J19	D1	500(pf) deep violet	.60	*.75*
J20	D1	800(pf) deep violet	1.25	*3.75*
J21	D1	10m deep violet	.60	*1.00*
J22	D1	20m deep violet	.60	*.75*
J23	D1	50m deep violet	.60	*.75*

Paper With Gray Network

J24	D1	100m deep violet	.60	*1.00*
J25	D1	500m deep violet	.60	*1.00*
		Nos. J15-J25 (11)	9.15	15.00
		Set, never hinged	25.00	

Nos. J15, J17, J22-J25 exist imperf. Value each, $12.50 unused, $40 never hinged.

Nos. J22-J23 and Type of 1923 Surcharged

1923, Oct. 1

Paper without Network

No.	Type	Denomination	Unused	Used
J26	D1	5000m on 50m	.40	*.75*
J27	D1	10,000m on 20m	.40	*.75*
J28	D1	50,000m on 500m	.40	*.75*
J29	D1	100,000m on 20m	.85	*1.25*
		Nos. J26-J29 (4)	2.05	*3.50*
		Set, never hinged	8.00	

On No. J26 the numerals of the surcharge are all of the larger size.

A 1000(m) on 100m deep violet was prepared but not issued. Value, $145, never hinged $350.

Nos. J26-J28 exist imperf. Value each, $18 unused, $45 never hinged.

Danzig Coat of Arms — D2

1923-28 **Wmk. 110**

No.	Type	Denomination	Unused	Used
J30	D2	5(pf) blue & blk	.85	.75
J31	D2	10(pf) blue & blk	.40	*.75*
J32	D2	15(pf) blue & blk	1.25	1.10
J33	D2	20(pf) blue & blk	1.25	*2.00*
J34	D2	30(pf) blue & blk	9.00	2.00
J35	D2	40(pf) blue & blk	2.10	*3.00*
J36	D2	50(pf) blue & blk	2.10	*2.25*
J37	D2	60(pf) blue & blk	13.00	*18.00*
J38	D2	100(pf) blue & blk	17.50	9.75
J39	D2	3g blue & car	10.00	*40.00*
a.		"Guldeu" instead of "Gulden"	325.00	*1,050.*
		Nos. J30-J39 (10)	57.45	*79.60*
		Set, never hinged	225.00	

Used values of Nos. J30-J39 are for postally used stamps.

See Nos. J43-J47.

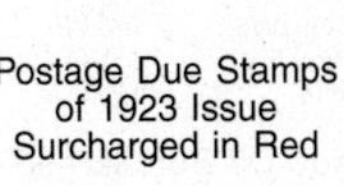

Postage Due Stamps of 1923 Issue Surcharged in Red

1932, Dec. 20

No.	Type	Denomination	Unused	Used
J40	D2	5pf on 40(pf)	4.25	*7.50*
J41	D2	10pf on 60(pf)	32.50	9.00
J42	D2	20pf on 100(pf)	2.75	*7.50*
		Nos. J40-J42 (3)	39.50	*24.00*
		Set, never hinged	160.00	

Type of 1923

1938-39 **Wmk. 237** ***Perf. 14***

No.	Type	Denomination	Unused	Used
J43	D2	10(pf) bl & blk ('39)	1.25	*62.50*
J44	D2	30(pf) bl & blk	2.25	*50.00*
J45	D2	40(pf) bl & blk ('39)	6.75	*100.00*
J46	D2	60(pf) bl & blk ('39)	6.75	*100.00*
J47	D2	100(pf) bl & blk	11.00	*72.50*
		Nos. J43-J47 (5)	28.00	*385.00*
		Set, never hinged	125.00	

OFFICIAL STAMPS

Regular Issues of 1921-22 Overprinted — a

1921-22 **Wmk. 108** ***Perf. 14x14½***

No.	Type	Denomination	Unused	Used
O1	A11	5(pf) orange	.25	.25
O2	A11	10(pf) dark brown	.25	.25
a.		Inverted overprint	60.00	
O3	A11	15(pf) green	.25	.25
O4	A11	20(pf) slate	.25	.25
O5	A11	25(pf) dark green	.25	.25
a.		Pair, one without overprint	170.00	
O6	A11	30(pf) blue & car	.60	.60
O7	A11	40(pf) grn & car	.25	.25
O8	A11	50(pf) dk grn & car	.25	.25
O9	A11	60(pf) carmine	.25	.25
O10	A11	75(pf) dp vio	.25	*.40*
O11	A11	80(pf) black & car	.85	.85
O12	A11	80(pf) green	.25	*2.40*

Paper With Faint Gray Network

No.	Type	Denomination	Unused	Used
O14	A11	1m org & car	.25	.25
O15	A11	1.20m blue violet	1.25	1.25
O16	A11	1.25m vio & car	.25	*.40*
O17	A11	1.50m slate gray	.25	*.40*
O18	A11	2m gray & car	16.00	12.00
a.		Inverted overprint	110.00	
O19	A11	2m car rose	.25	*.40*
O20	A11	2.40m dk brn & car	1.25	*2.40*
O21	A11	3m violet & car	8.50	*10.00*
O22	A11	3m car lake	.25	*.40*
O23	A11	4m dk blue	1.25	.85
O24	A11	5m dp grn	.25	*.40*
O25	A11	6m car lake	.25	*.40*
O26	A11	10m orange	.25	*.40*
O27	A11	20m org brn	.25	*.40*
		Nos. O1-O27 (26)	34.45	*36.20*
		Set, never hinged	175.00	

Double overprints exist on Nos. O1-O2, O5-O7, O10 and O12.

Same Overprint on No. 96

No.	Type	Denomination	Unused	Used
O28	A11	6m on 3m	.35	*.75*
		Never hinged	1.00	
a.		Inverted overprint	30.00	
		Never hinged	85.00	

No. 77 Overprinted

Serrate Roulette 13½

1922 **Wmk. 108 Sideways**

No.	Type	Denomination	Unused	Used
O29	A12	5m grn, red & blk	3.75	*6.00*
		Never hinged	18.00	

Nos. 99-103, 106-107 Overprinted Type "a"

1922-23 **Wmk. 109** ***Perf. 14***

No.	Type	Denomination	Unused	Used
O30	A11	4m dark blue	.25	*.60*
O31	A11	5m dark green	.25	*.60*
O32	A11	10m orange	.25	*.60*
O33	A11	20m orange brn	.25	*.60*
O34	A15	50m pale blue & red	.25	*.60*
O35	A15a	100m dk grn & red	.25	*.60*

Nos. 113-115, 118-120 Overprinted Type "a"

No.	Type	Denomination	Unused	Used
O36	A15	50m pale blue	.25	*.75*
a.		Inverted overprint	25.00	
O37	A15a	100m dark green	.25	*.75*
O38	A15	200m orange	.25	*.75*
a.		Inverted overprint	25.00	

Paper With Gray Network

No.	Type	Denomination	Unused	Used
O39	A17	300m bl grn & red	.25	*.60*
O40	A17	500m gray & red	.25	*.75*
O41	A17	1000m brn & red	.25	*.75*
		Nos. O30-O41 (12)	3.00	*7.95*
		Set, never hinged	16.80	

Regular Issue of 1924-25 Overprinted

1924-25 ***Perf. 14x14½***

No.	Type	Denomination	Unused	Used
O42	A19	5pf red orange	2.10	*3.25*
O43	A19	10pf green	2.10	*9.00*
O44	A19	15pf gray	2.10	3.25
O45	A19	15pf red	19.00	10.00
O46	A19	20pf car & red	2.10	2.10
O47	A19	25pf slate & red	19.00	27.50
O48	A19	30pf green & red	3.00	*3.75*
O49	A19	35pf ultra	60.00	50.00
O50	A19	40pf dk bl & dull bl	7.00	*8.50*
O51	A19	50pf dp blue & red	21.00	*42.50*
O52	A19	75pf violet & red	42.50	*120.00*
		Nos. O42-O52 (11)	179.90	*279.85*
		Set, never hinged	640.00	

Double overprints exist on Nos. O42-O44, O47, O50-O52.

DENMARK

ˈden-ˌmärk

LOCATION — Northern part of a peninsula which separates the North and Baltic Seas, and includes the surrounding islands
GOVT. — Kingdom
AREA — 16,631 sq. mi.
POP. — 5,294,860 (1/1/1999)
CAPITAL — Copenhagen

96 Skilling = 1 Rigsbank Daler
100 Ore = 1 Krone (1875)

Catalogue values for unused stamps in this country are for Never Hinged items, beginning with Scott 297 in the regular postage section, Scott B15 in the semipostal section, and Scott Q28 in the parcel post section.

Values for unused stamps are for examples with original gum as defined in the catalogue introduction. Very fine examples of Nos. 9-37 and O1-O9 will have perforations clear of the framelines but with the design noticeably off center. Well centered stamps are quite scarce and will command substantial premiums.

Watermarks

Wmk. 111 — Small Crown

Wmk. 112 — Crown

Wmk. 113 — Crown

Wmk. 114 — Multiple Crosses

A1

Royal Emblems — A2

1851 **Typo.** **Wmk. 111** ***Imperf.***

With Yellow Brown Burelage

No.	Type	Denomination	Unused	Used
1	A1	2rs blue	*3,500.*	1,000.
a.		First printing	*8,250.*	*2,400.*
2	A2	4rs brown	600.00	40.00
a.		First printing	600.00	40.00
b.		4rs yellow brown	875.00	55.00

The first printing of Nos. 1 and 2 had the burelage printed from a copper plate, giving a clear impression with the lines in slight relief. The subsequent impressions had the burelage typographed, with the lines fainter and not rising above the surface of the paper.

Nos. 1-2 were reprinted in 1885 and 1901 on heavy yellowish paper, unwatermarked and imperforate, with a brown burelage. No. 1 was also reprinted without burelage, on both yellowish and white paper. Value for least costly reprint of No. 1, $50.

No. 2 was reprinted in 1951 in 10 shades with "Colour Specimen 1951" printed on the back. It was also reprinted in 1961 in 2 shades without burelage and with "Farve Nytryk 1961" printed on the back. Value for least costly reprint of No. 2, $8.50.

Dotting in Spandrels — A3

1854-57

No.	Type	Denomination	Unused	Used
3	A3	2s blue ('55)	75.00	60.00
4	A3	4s brown	325.00	15.00
a.		4s yellow brown	350.00	15.00
5	A3	8s green ('57)	300.00	67.50
a.		8s yellow green	300.00	80.00
6	A3	16s gray lilac ('57)	525.00	190.00
		Nos. 3-6 (4)	1,225.	332.50

See No. 10. For denominations in cents see Danish West Indies Nos. 1-4.

Wavy Lines in Spandrels — A4

1858-62

7 A4 4s yellow brown 65.00 8.50
a. 4s brown 67.50 8.00
b. Wmk. 112 ('62) 62.50 9.00
8 A4 8s green 800.00 82.50

Nos. 2 to 8 inclusive are known with unofficial perforation 12 or 13, and Nos. 4, 5, 7 and 8 with unofficial roulette 9½.

Nos. 3, 6-8 were reprinted in 1885 on heavy yellowish paper, unwatermarked, imperforate and without burelage. Nos. 4-5 were reprinted in 1924 on white paper, unwatermarked, imperforate, gummed and without burelage. Value for No. 3, $15; Nos. 4-5, each $110; No. 6, $20; Nos. 7-8, each $15.

1863 Wmk. 112 *Rouletted 11*

9 A4 4s brown 100.00 15.00
a. 4s deep brown 100.00 15.00
10 A3 16s violet 1,400. 650.00

Royal Emblems — A5

1864-68 *Perf. 13*

11 A5 2s blue ('65) 65.00 35.00
12 A5 3s red vio ('65) 80.00 75.00
13 A5 4s red 40.00 8.00
14 A5 8s bister ('68) 275.00 95.00
15 A5 16s olive green 475.00 175.00
Nos. 11-15 (5) 935.00 388.00

Nos. 11-15 were reprinted in 1886 on heavy yellowish paper, unwatermarked, imperforate and without gum. The reprints of all values except the 4s were printed in two vertical rows of six, inverted with respect to each other, so that horizontal pairs are always tête bêche. Value $12 each.

Nos. 13 and 15 were reprinted in 1942 with printing on the back across each horizontal row: "Nytryk 1942. G. A. Hagemann: Danmarks og Vestindiens Frimaerker, Bind 2." Value, $70 each.

Imperf, single

11a A5 2s blue 95.00 95.00
12a A5 3s red violet 140.00
13a A5 4s red 77.50 90.00
14a A5 8s bister 375.00
15a A5 16s olive green 450.00

1870 *Perf. 12½*

11b A5 2s blue 275.00 350.00
12b A5 3s red violet 475.00 650.00
14b A5 8s bister 475.00 475.00
15b A5 16s olive green 725.00 *1,450.*
Nos. 11b-15b (4) 1,950. 2,925.

A6

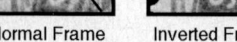

Normal Frame

Inverted Frame

The arabesques in the corners have a main stem and a branch. When the frame is in normal position, in the upper left corner the branch leaves the main stem half way between two little leaflets. In the lower right corner the branch starts at the foot of the second leaflet. When the frame is inverted the corner designs are, of course, transposed.

1870-71 Wmk. 112 *Perf. 14x13½*
Paper Varying from Thin to Thick

16 A6 2s gray & ultra ('71) 70.00 27.50
a. 2s gray & blue 70.00 27.50
17 A6 3s gray & brt lil ('71) 100.00 110.00
18 A6 4s gray & car 40.00 10.00
19 A6 8s gray & brn ('71) 200.00 75.00
20 A6 16s gray & grn ('71) 275.00 175.00

Perf. 12½

21 A6 2s gray & bl ('71) 2,000. *3,250.*
22 A6 4s gray & car 150.00 125.00
24 A6 48s brn & lilac 450.00 275.00

Nos. 16-20, 24 were reprinted in 1886 on thin white paper, unwatermarked, imperforate and without gum. These were printed in sheets of 10 in which 1 stamp has the normal frame (value $32.50 each) and 9 the inverted (value $11 each).

Imperf, single

16b A6 2s *250.*
17a A6 3s *240.*
18a A6 4s *200.*
19a A6 8s *250.*
20a A6 16s *400.*
24a A6 48s *425.* —

Inverted Frame

16c A6 2s 1,000. 775.
17b A6 3s 2,500. 2,000.
18b A6 4s 775. 87.50
19b A6 8s 1,750. 900.
20b A6 16s 2,000. 1,750.
24b A6 48s 2,750. 1,900.

1875-79 *Perf. 14x13½*

25 A6 3o gray blue & gray 18.00 15.00
a. 1st "A" of "DANMARK" missing 60.00 150.00
b. Imperf *750.00*
c. Inverted frame 18.00 16.00
26 A6 4o slate & blue 25.00 .50
a. 4o gray & blue 25.00 1.10
b. 4o slate & ultra 90.00 17.00
c. 4o gray & ultra 75.00 16.00
d. Imperf 75.00 —
e. As #26, inverted frame 25.00 .50
27 A6 5o rose & blue ('79) 30.00 72.50
a. Ball of lower curve of large "5" missing 125.00 300.00
b. Inverted frame 1,000. *2,250.*
28 A6 8o slate & car 22.50 .50
a. 8o gray & carmine 75.00 5.00
b. Imperf 150.00 —
c. Inverted frame 22.50 .50
29 A6 12o sl & dull lake 10.00 4.00
a. 12o gray & bright lilac 65.00 8.00
b. 12o gray & dull magenta 72.50 10.00
c. Inverted frame 14.00 4.00
30 A6 16o slate & brn 77.50 6.50
a. 16o light gray & brown 77.50 17.00
b. Inverted frame 52.50 4.50
31 A6 20o rose & gray 90.00 32.50
a. 20o carmine & gray 90.00 32.50
b. Inverted frame 90.00 32.50
32 A6 25o gray & green 65.00 40.00
a. Inverted frame 77.50 62.50
33 A6 50o brown & vio 70.00 37.50
a. 50o brown & blue violet 400.00 175.00
b. Inverted frame 70.00 32.50
34 A6 100o gray & org ('77) 110.00 60.00
a. Imperf, single 375.00
b. Inverted frame 150.00 60.00
Nos. 25-34 (10) 518.00 269.00
Set, never hinged 1,625.

The stamps of this issue on thin semi-transparent paper are far scarcer than those on thicker paper.

See Nos. 41-42, 44, 46-47, 50-52. For surcharges see Nos. 55, 79-80, 136.

Arms — A7

Two types of numerals in corners

Small Numerals

Large Numerals

1882
Small Corner Numerals

35 A7 5o green 240.00 100.00
Never hinged 725.00
37 A7 20o blue 190.00 70.00
Never hinged 650.00

1884-88
Larger Corner Numerals

38 A7 5o green 15.00 3.50
a. Imperf —
39 A7 10o carmine ('85) 16.00 2.50
a. Small numerals in corners ('88) 550.00 *725.00*
b. Imperf, single 175.00
c. Pair, Nos. 39, 39a 600.00 *875.00*
40 A7 20o blue 30.00 5.00
a. Pair, Nos. 37, 40 400.00 *875.00*
b. Imperf —
Nos. 38-40 (3) 61.00 11.00
Set, never hinged 285.00

Stamps with large corner numerals have white line around crown and lower oval touches frame.

The plate for No. 39, was damaged and 3 clichés in the bottom row were replaced by clichés for post cards, which had small numerals in the corners.

Two clichés with small numerals were inserted in the plate of No. 40.

See Nos. 43, 45, 48-49, 53-54. For surcharge see No. 56.

1895-1901 Wmk. 112 *Perf. 13*

41 A6 3o blue & gray 10.00 7.25
42 A6 4o slate & bl ('96) 4.50 .40
43 A7 5o green 12.00 .75
44 A6 8o slate & car 4.50 .45
45 A7 10o rose car 24.00 .65
46 A6 12o sl & dull lake 7.00 4.00
47 A6 16o slate & brown 19.00 4.50
48 A7 20o blue 30.00 2.40
49 A7 24o brown ('01) 7.00 6.00
50 A6 25o gray & grn ('98) 110.00 19.50
51 A6 50o brown & vio ('97) 60.00 24.00
52 A6 100o slate & org 90.00 35.00
Nos. 41-52 (12) 378.00 104.90
Set, never hinged 875.00

Inverted Frame

41b A6 3o 12.00 7.00
42a A6 4o 4.50 .45
44a A6 8o 4.50 .50
46a A6 12o 14.00 4.50
47a A6 16o 30.00 5.00
50a A6 25o 60.00 27.50
51a A6 50o 95.00 32.50
52a A6 100o 90.00 57.50
Nos. 41b-52a (8) 310.00 134.95
Set, never hinged 635.00

1902-04 Wmk. 113

41c A6 3o blue & gray 2.75 3.00
42b A6 4o slate & blue 17.00 20.00
43a A7 5o green 2.00 .25
44d A6 8o slate & carmine 525.00 425.00
45a A7 10o rose carmine 3.00 .25
48a A7 20o blue 20.00 4.75
50b A6 25o gray & green 10.50 4.50
51b A6 50o brown & violet 27.50 20.00
52b A6 100o slate & orange 30.00 15.00
Nos. 41c-52b (9) 637.75 492.75
Set, never hinged 1,325.

Inverted Frame

41d A6 3o 75.00 130.00
42c A6 4o 140.00 130.00
50c A6 25o 210.00 60.00
51c A6 50o 260.00 240.00
52c A6 100o 225.00 240.00
Nos. 41d-52c (5) 910.00 800.00
Set, never hinged 2,500.

1902 Wmk. 113

53 A7 1o orange .75 .65
a. Imperf — —
54 A7 15o lilac 11.00 .75
a. Imperf, single *4,250.*

Nos. 44d, 44, 49 Surcharged

a

b

1904-12 Wmk. 113

55 A6(a) 4o on 8o sl & car 3.50 4.00
a. Wmk. 112 ('12) 21.00 *60.00*
Never hinged 42.50
b. As "a," inverted frame — *6,000.*

Wmk. 112

56 A7(b) 15o on 24o brown 5.75 17.50
a. Short "15" at right 27.50 *105.00*
Never hinged 60.00
Set, never hinged 16.00

A10

1905-17 Wmk. 113 *Perf. 13*

57 A10 1o orange ('06) 2.25 .75
58 A10 2o carmine 4.75 .40
a. Perf. 14x14½ ('17) 3.75 *19.00*
59 A10 3o gray 9.75 .65
60 A10 4o dull blue 7.00 .60
a. Perf. 14x14½ ('17) 11.00 *37.50*
61 A10 5o dp green ('12) 5.25 .35
62 A10 10o dp rose ('12) 6.75 .35
63 A10 15o lilac 25.00 2.25
64 A10 20o dk blue ('12) 35.00 .90
Nos. 57-64 (8) 95.75 6.25
Set, never hinged 310.00

The three wavy lines in design A10 are symbolical of the three waters which separate the principal Danish islands.

See Nos. 85-96, 1338-1342A, 1468-1473. For surcharges and overprints see Nos. 163, 181, J1, J38, Q1-Q2.

King Christian IX — A11

1904-05 Engr.

65 A11 10o scarlet 4.00 .65
66 A11 20o blue 22.50 3.00
67 A11 25o brown ('05) 27.50 8.00
68 A11 50o dull vio ('05) 110.00 *120.00*
69 A11 100o ocher ('05) 13.00 *60.00*
Nos. 65-69 (5) 177.00 *191.65*
Set, never hinged 565.00

1905-06 Re-engraved

70 A11 5o green 4.50 .35
71 A11 10o scarlet ('06) 21.00 .60
Set, never hinged 56.00

The re-engraved stamps are much clearer than the originals, and the decoration on the king's left breast has been removed.

King Frederik VIII — A12

1907-12

72 A12 5o green 1.75 .40
a. Imperf. —
73 A12 10o red 4.25 .40
a. Imperf. —
74 A12 20o indigo 19.00 .65
a. 20o bright blue ('11) 40.00 2.75
75 A12 25o olive brn 35.00 1.25
76 A12 35o dp org ('12) 6.00 *10.00*
77 A12 50o claret 35.00 7.00
78 A12 100o bister brn 100.00 5.00
Nos. 72-78 (7) 201.00 24.70
Set, never hinged 525.00

Nos. 47, 31 and O9 Surcharged

c

d

Dark Blue Surcharge

1912 Wmk. 112 *Perf. 13*

79 A6(c) 35o on 16o 17.00 *50.00*
a. Inverted frame 325.00 *625.00*

Perf. 14x13½

80 A6(c) 35o on 20o 30.00 *85.00*
a. Inverted frame 130.00 *325.00*

Black Surcharge

81 O1(d) 35o on 32o 42.50 *120.00*
Nos. 79-81 (3) 89.50 *255.00*
Set, never hinged 185.00

General Post Office, Copenhagen — A15

1912 Engr. Wmk. 113 *Perf. 13*

82 A15 5k dark red 500.00 200.00
Never hinged 1,500.

See Nos. 135, 843.

Perf. 14x14½

1913-30 Typo. Wmk. 114

85 A10 1o dp orange ('14) .40 .45
a. Bklt. pane, 2 ea #85, 91 + 2 labels 20.00

86 A10 2o car ('13) 3.75 .35
a. Imperf 150.00 300.00
b. Booklet pane, 4 + 2 labels 27.50
87 A10 3o gray ('13) 6.75 .40
88 A10 4o blue ('13) 8.00 .45
a. Half used as 2o on cover 1,250.
89 A10 5o dk brown ('21) .75 .35
a. Imperf 190.00
b. Booklet pane, 4 + 2 labels 14.00
90 A10 5o lt green ('30) 1.50 .40
a. Booklet pane, 4 + 2 labels 16.00
b. Booklet pane of 50
91 A10 7o apple grn ('26) 5.75 *7.25*
a. Booklet pane, 4 + 2 labels 20.00
92 A10 7o dk violet ('30) 16.00 6.50
93 A10 8o gray ('21) 7.00 3.25
94 A10 10o green ('21) .85 .35
a. Imperf 225.00
b. Booklet pane, 4 + 2 labels 37.50
95 A10 10o bister brn ('30) 2.25 .35
a. Booklet pane, 4 + 2 labels 16.00
b. Booklet pane of 50
96 A10 12o violet ('26) 25.00 9.75
Nos. 85-96 (12) 78.00 29.85
Set, never hinged 200.00

No. 88a was used with No. 97 in Faroe Islands, Jan. 3-23, 1919.

See surcharge and overprint note following No. 64.

King Christian X — A16

1913-28 Typo. *Perf. 14x14½*

97 A16 5o green 1.40 .35
a. Bklt. pane of 4, with P# 400.00
98 A16 7o orange ('18) 2.25 *2.75*
99 A16 8o dk gray ('20) 14.00 6.50
100 A16 10o red 2.40 .40
a. Imperf 300.00
b. Bklt. pane of 4, with P# 500.00
101 A16 12o gray grn ('18) 7.50 *10.00*
102 A16 15o violet 3.25 .40
103 A16 20o dp blue 13.00 .35
104 A16 20o brown ('21) 1.25 .40
105 A16 20o red ('26) 1.50 .40
106 A16 25o dk brown 13.50 .50
107 A16 25o brn & blk ('20) 85.00 8.75
108 A16 25o red ('22) 4.25 .95
109 A16 25o yel grn ('25) 3.00 .50
110 A16 27o ver & blk ('18) 30.00 *50.00*
111 A16 30o green & blk ('18) 35.00 3.25
112 A16 30o orange ('21) 3.00 2.00
113 A16 30o dk blue ('25) 1.75 1.00
114 A16 35o orange 29.00 7.50
115 A16 35o yel & blk ('19) 9.00 6.50
116 A16 40o vio & blk ('18) 18.00 4.00
117 A16 40o gray bl & blk ('20) 37.50 7.50
118 A16 40o dk blue ('22) 6.00 1.60
119 A16 40o orange ('25) 1.50 *1.50*
120 A16 50o claret 37.50 5.75
121 A16 50o claret & blk ('19) 75.00 2.50
122 A16 50o lt gray ('22) 9.25 .40
a. 50o olive gray ('21) 75.00 8.00
Never hinged 210.00
123 A16 60o brn & bl ('19) 60.00 3.75
a. 60o brown & ultra ('19) 225.00 12.50
Never hinged 750.00
124 A16 60o grn bl ('21) 9.00 .75
125 A16 70o brn & grn ('20) 26.00 2.25
126 A16 80o bl grn ('15) 50.00 22.50
127 A16 90o brn & red ('20) 18.00 3.25
128 A16 1k brn & bl ('22) 75.00 3.00
129 A16 2k gray & cl ('25) 67.50 15.00
130 A16 5k vio & brn ('27) 7.00 *5.75*
131 A16 10k ver & yel grn ('28) 325.00 65.00
Nos. 97-131 (35) 1,082. 247.00
Set, never hinged 3,085.

No. 97 surcharged "2 ORE" is Faroe Islands No. 1. Two of the 14 printings of No. 97a have no P# in the selvage. These sell for more.

Nos. 87 and 98, 89 and 94, 89 and 104, 90 and 95, 97 and 103, 100 and 102 exist se-tenant in coils for use in vending machines.

For surcharges and overprints see Nos. 161-162, 176-177, 182-184, J2-J8, M1-M2, Q3-Q10.

King Christian X — A17

1913-20 Engr.

132 A17 1k yellow brown 95.00 1.25
133 A17 2k gray 150.00 7.00
134 A17 5k purple ('20) 15.00 10.00
Nos. 132-134 (3) 260.00 18.25
Set, never hinged 940.00

For overprint see No. Q11.

G.P.O. Type of 1912

Perf. 14x14½

1915 Wmk. 114 Engr.

135 A15 5k dark red ('15) 500.00 175.00
Never hinged 1,500.

Nos. 46 and O10 Surcharged in Black type "c" and

e

1915 Wmk. 112 Typo. *Perf. 13*

136 A6 (c) 80o on 12o 40.00 *100.00*
a. Inverted frame 600.00 *1,100.*
Never hinged 825.00
137 O1 (e) 80o on 8o 47.50 *140.00*
a. "POSTERIM" 95.00 *325.00*
Never hinged 140.00
Set, never hinged 155.00

Newspaper Stamps Surcharged

On Issue of 1907

1918 Wmk. 113 *Perf. 13*

138 N1 27o on 1o olive 105.00 *325.00*
139 N1 27o on 5o blue 105.00 *325.00*
140 N1 27o on 7o car 105.00 *325.00*
141 N1 27o on 10o dp lil 105.00 *325.00*
142 N1 27o on 68o yel brn 7.50 *37.50*
143 N1 27o on 5k rose & yel grn 6.75 *26.00*
144 N1 27o on 10k bis & bl 7.50 *35.00*
Nos. 138-144 (7) 441.75 *1,399.*
Set, never hinged 940.00

On Issue of 1914-15

Wmk. Multiple Crosses (114)

Perf. 14x14½

145 N1 27o on 1o ol gray 5.00 *15.50*
146 N1 27o on 5o blue 7.50 *30.00*
147 N1 27o on 7o rose 5.00 *12.50*
148 N1 27o on 8o green 7.50 *16.00*
149 N1 27o on 10o dp lil 3.25 *17.00*
150 N1 27o on 20o green 8.00 *16.50*
151 N1 27o on 29o org yel 3.25 *14.50*
152 N1 27o on 38o orange 32.50 *110.00*
153 N1 27o on 41o yel brn 7.50 *45.00*
154 N1 27o on 1k bl grn & mar 5.00 *14.50*
Nos. 145-154 (10) 84.50 *291.50*
Set, never hinged 150.00

Kronborg Castle — A20

Sonderborg Castle — A21

Roskilde Cathedral — A22

Perf. 14½x14, 14x14½

1920, Oct. 5 Typo.

156 A20 10o red 7.00 .50
157 A21 20o slate 5.00 .50
158 A22 40o dark brown 17.00 4.50
Nos. 156-158 (3) 29.00 5.50
Set, never hinged 52.00

Reunion of Northern Schleswig with Denmark.

See Nos. 159-160. For surcharges see Nos. B1-B2.

1921

159 A20 10o green 9.00 .55
160 A22 40o dark blue 67.50 11.50
Set, never hinged 174.00

Stamps of 1918 Surcharged in Blue

1921-22

161 A16 8o on 7o org ('22) 2.25 *5.00*
162 A16 8o on 12o gray grn 2.25 *15.00*
Set, never hinged 15.75

No. 87 Surcharged

1921

163 A10 8o on 3o gray 3.75 *5.25*
Never hinged 8.25

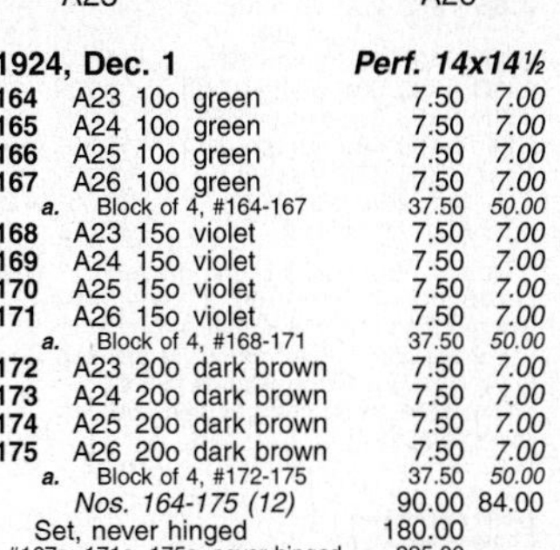

Christian X A23 — Christian IV A24 — A25 — A26

1924, Dec. 1 *Perf. 14x14½*

164 A23 10o green 7.50 *7.00*
165 A24 10o green 7.50 *7.00*
166 A25 10o green 7.50 *7.00*
167 A26 10o green 7.50 *7.00*
a. Block of 4, #164-167 37.50 *50.00*
168 A23 15o violet 7.50 *7.00*
169 A24 15o violet 7.50 *7.00*
170 A25 15o violet 7.50 *7.00*
171 A26 15o violet 7.50 *7.00*
a. Block of 4, #168-171 37.50 *50.00*
172 A23 20o dark brown 7.50 *7.00*
173 A24 20o dark brown 7.50 *7.00*
174 A25 20o dark brown 7.50 *7.00*
175 A26 20o dark brown 7.50 *7.00*
a. Block of 4, #172-175 37.50 *50.00*
Nos. 164-175 (12) 90.00 84.00
Set, never hinged 180.00
#167a, 171a, 175a, never hinged 225.00

300th anniv. of the Danish postal service.

Stamps of 1921-22 Surcharged

k

l

1926

176 A16 (k) 20o on 30o org 6.75 *15.00*
177 A16 (l) 20o on 40o dk bl 9.00 *18.00*
Set, never hinged 31.00

A27

A28

1926, Mar. 11 *Perf. 14x14½*

178 A27 10o dull green 1.50 .45
179 A28 20o dark red 2.00 .45
180 A28 30o dark blue 8.50 1.50
Nos. 178-180 (3) 12.00 2.40
Set, never hinged 24.50

75th anniv. of the introduction of postage stamps in Denmark.

Stamps of 1913-26 Surcharged in Blue or Black

No. 181

Nos. 182-184

1926-27 *Perf. 14x14½*

181 A10 7o on 8o gray (Bl) 1.50 *4.75*
182 A16 7o on 27o ver & blk 4.50 *17.00*
183 A16 7o on 20o red ('27) .75 *2.50*
184 A16 12o on 15o violet 2.25 *6.00*

Surcharged on Official Stamps of 1914-23

185 O1 (e) 7o on 1o org 4.00 *16.00*
186 O1 (e) 7o on 3o gray 7.50 *32.50*
187 O1 (e) 7o on 4o blue 3.75 *7.75*
188 O1 (e) 7o on 5o grn 52.50 *150.00*
189 O1 (e) 7o on 10o grn 4.50 *15.50*
190 O1 (e) 7o on 15o vio 4.50 *15.50*
191 O1 (e) 7o on 20o ind 19.00 *77.50*
a. Double surcharge 750.00 *975.00*
Nos. 181-191 (11) 104.75 *345.00*
Set, never hinged 155.00

Caravel — A30

1927 Typo. *Perf. 14x14½*

192 A30 15o red 6.00 .40
193 A30 20o gray 11.00 2.40
194 A30 25o light blue 1.25 .40
195 A30 30o ocher 1.25 .40
196 A30 35o red brown 25.00 1.50
197 A30 40o yel green 25.00 .40
Nos. 192-197 (6) 69.50 5.50
Set, never hinged 200.00

See Nos. 232-238J. For surcharges & overprints see Nos. 244-245, 269-272, Q12-Q14, Q19-Q25.

Christian X — A31

1930, Sept. 26

210 A31 5o apple grn 2.50 .35
a. Booklet pane, 4 + 2 labels 18.00
211 A31 7o violet 6.75 3.00
212 A31 8o dk gray 22.50 32.50
213 A31 10o yel brn 5.00 .35
a. Booklet pane, 4 + 2 labels 29.00
214 A31 15o red 10.00 .35
215 A31 20o lt gray 25.00 9.75
216 A31 25o lt blue 8.50 1.25
217 A31 30o yel buff 9.00 1.75
218 A31 35o red brown 12.00 4.50
219 A31 40o dp green 10.00 1.25
Nos. 210-219 (10) 111.25 55.05
Set, never hinged 295.00

60th birthday of King Christian X.

Wavy Lines and Numeral of Value — A32

Type A10 Redrawn

1933-40 Unwmk. Engr. *Perf. 13*

220 A32 1o gray blk .45 .30
221 A32 2o scarlet .35 .30
222 A32 4o blue .40 .35
223 A32 5o yel grn 1.00 .35
a. 5o gray green 37.50 *60.00*
b. Tête bêche gutter pair 8.00 *15.50*
c. Booklet pane of 4 11.00
d. Bklt. pane, 1 #223a, 3 #B6 37.50 70.00
Never hinged 60.00
e. As "b," without gutter 17.50 *27.50*
224 A32 5o rose lake ('38) .30 .30
a. Booklet pane of 4 1.20
b. Booklet pane of 10 12.00
224C A32 6o orange ('40) .30 .30
225 A32 7o violet 2.00 .35
226 A32 7o yel grn ('38) 1.10 .45
226A A32 7o lt brown ('40) .35 .35
227 A32 8o gray .45 .50
227A A32 8o yellow grn ('40) .30 .35
228 A32 10o yellow org 12.50 .35
a. Tête bêche gutter pair 50.00 55.00
b. Booklet pane of 4 110.00
c. As "a," without gutter 60.00 *70.00*
Never hinged 100.00
229 A32 10o lt brown ('37) 9.50 .35
a. Booklet pane of 4 100.00
b. Booklet pane of 4, 1 #229, 3 #B7 32.50 45.00
230 A32 10o violet ('38) .75 .35
a. Booklet pane of 4 2.75
b. Bklt. pane, 2 #230, 2 #B10 2.50 7.00
Never hinged 6.00
Nos. 220-230 (14) 29.75 4.95
Set, never hinged 75.00

Design A10 was typographed. They had a solid background with groups of small hearts below the heraldic lions in the upper corners and below "DA" and "RK" of "DANMARK." The numerals of value were enclosed in single-lined ovals.

Design A32 is line-engraved and has a background of crossed lines. The hearts have been removed and the numerals of value are now in double-lined ovals. Two types exist of some values.

The 1ö, No. 220, was issued on fluorescent paper in 1969.

No. 230 with wide margins is from booklet pane No. 230b.

Surcharges of 20, 50 & 60öre on #220, 224 and 224C are listed as Faroe Islands #2-3, 5-6.

See Nos. 318, 333, 382, 416, 437-437A, 493-498, 629, 631, 688-695, 793-795, 883-886, 1111-1113, 1116. For overprints and surcharges see Nos. 257, 263, 267-268, 355-356, Q15-Q17, Q31, Q43.

Certain tête-bêche pairs of 1938-55 issues which reached the market in 1971, and were not regularly issued, are not listed. This group comprises 24 different major-number vertical pairs of types A32, A47, A61 and SP3 (13 with gutters, 11 without), and pairs of some minor numbers and shades. They were removed from booklet pane sheets.

Type of 1927 Issue
Type I

Type I — Two columns of squares between sail and left frame line.

1933-34 Engr. *Perf. 13*

232 A30 20o gray 15.00 .35
233 A30 25o blue 85.00 30.00
234 A30 25o brown ('34) 30.00 .35
235 A30 30o orange yel 1.50 1.40
236 A30 30o blue ('34) 1.50 .40
237 A30 35o violet .60 .35
238 A30 40o yellow grn 6.25 .35
Nos. 232-238 (7) 139.85 33.20
Set, never hinged 325.00

Type II

Type II — One column of squares between sail and left frame line.

1933-40

238A A30 15o deep red 3.00 .35
k. Booklet pane of 4 26.00
l. Bklt. pane, 1 #238A, 3 #B8 45.00
Never hinged 115.00
238B A30 15o yel grn ('40) 9.00 .40
238C A30 20o gray blk ('39) 4.50 .70
238D A30 20o red ('40) .90 .35
238E A30 25o dp brown ('39) .90 .35
238F A30 30o blue ('39) 2.25 .70
238G A30 30o orange ('40) .75 .35
238H A30 35o violet ('40) 1.00 .35
238I A30 40o yel grn ('39) 15.00 .35
238J A30 40o blue ('40) 1.40 .35
Nos. 238A-238J (10) 38.70 4.25
Set, never hinged 95.00

Nos. 232-238J, engraved, have crosshatched background. Nos. 192-197, typographed, have solid background.

For No. 238A surcharged 20 ore see Denmark No. 271, Faroe Islands No. 4.

See note on surcharges and overprints following No. 197.

King Christian X — A33

1934-41 *Perf. 13*

239 A33 50o gray 1.20 .30
240 A33 60o blue grn 2.40 .35
240A A33 75o dk blue ('41) .45 .35
241 A33 1k lt brown 3.75 .35
242 A33 2k dull red 6.00 1.00
243 A33 5k violet 9.00 3.50
Nos. 239-243 (6) 22.80 5.85
Set, never hinged 75.00

For overprints see Nos. Q26-Q27.

Nos. 233, 235 Surcharged in Black

1934, June 9

244 A30 4o on 25o blue .50 .50
245 A30 10o on 30o org yel 2.40 *3.25*
Set, never hinged 7.50

"The Ugly Duckling" A34

Andersen A35

"The Little Mermaid" — A36

1935, Oct. 1 *Perf. 13*

246 A34 5o lt green 3.00 .30
a. Tête bêche gutter pair 15.00 *22.50*
b. Booklet pane of 4 40.00
c. As "a," without gutter 17.00 *21.00*
Never hinged 45.00
247 A35 7o dull vio 2.50 *2.50*
248 A36 10o orange 4.50 .30
a. Tête bêche gutter pair 18.00 *32.50*
b. Booklet pane of 4 65.00
c. As "a," without gutter 20.00 *40.00*
Never hinged 65.00
249 A35 15o red 11.00 .30
a. Tête bêche gutter pair 45.00 *52.50*
b. Booklet pane of 4 160.00
c. As "a," without gutter 42.50 *75.00*
Never hinged 110.00
250 A35 20o gray 9.50 1.25
251 A35 30o dl bl 3.00 .35
Nos. 246-251 (6) 33.50 *5.00*
Set, never hinged 87.50

Centenary of the publication of the earliest installment of Hans Christian Andersen's "Fairy Tales."

Nikolai Church A37

Hans Tausen A38

Ribe Cathedral — A39

1936 *Perf. 13*

252 A37 5o green 1.40 .40
a. Booklet pane of 4 21.00
253 A37 7o violet 2.00 *4.50*
254 A38 10o lt brown 2.00 .40
a. Booklet pane of 4 25.00
255 A38 15o dull rose 3.00 .30
256 A39 30o blue 16.00 1.40
Nos. 252-256 (5) 24.40 7.00
Set, never hinged 62.50

Church Reformation in Denmark, 400th anniv.

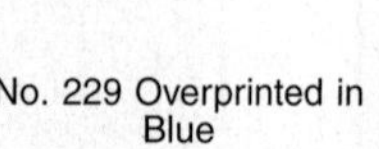
No. 229 Overprinted in Blue

1937, Sept. 17

257 A32 10o lt brown 1.50 *1.60*
Never hinged 2.00

Jubilee Exhib. held by the Copenhagen Phil. Club on their 50th anniv. The stamps were on sale at the Exhib. only, each holder of a ticket of admission (1k) being entitled to purchase 20 stamps at face value; of a season ticket (5k), 100 stamps.

Yacht and Summer Palace, Marselisborg A40

Christian X in Streets of Copenhagen A41

Equestrian Statue of Frederik V and Amalienborg Palace — A42

1937, May 15 *Perf. 13*

258 A40 5o green 1.40 .30
a. Booklet pane of 4 15.00
259 A41 10o brown 1.40 .30
a. Booklet pane of 4 15.00
260 A42 15o scarlet 1.40 .30
a. Booklet pane of 4 17.00
261 A41 30o blue 15.00 2.40
Nos. 258-261 (4) 19.20 3.30
Set, never hinged 42.50

25th anniv. of the accession to the throne of King Christian X.

Emancipation Column, Copenhagen — A43

1938, June 20 *Perf. 13*

262 A43 15o scarlet .60 .30
Never hinged 1.40

Abolition of serfdom in Denmark, 150th anniv.

No. 223 Overprinted in Red on Alternate Stamps

1938, Sept. 2

263 A32 5o yellow grn, pair 3.25 *7.00*
Never hinged 4.50

10th Danish Philatelic Exhibition.

Bertel Thorvaldsen A44

Statue of Jason A45

1938, Nov. 17 Engr. *Perf. 13*

264 A44 5o rose lake .45 .30
265 A45 10o purple .45 .30
266 A44 30o dark blue 1.50 .60
Nos. 264-266 (3) 2.40 1.20
Set, never hinged 5.25

The return to Denmark in 1838 of Bertel Thorvaldsen, Danish sculptor.

Stamps of 1933-39 Surcharged with New Values in Black

a

b

20
c

1940

267 A32 (a) 6o on 7o yel grn .30 *.35*
268 A32 (a) 6o on 8o gray .45 *.35*
269 A30 (b) 15o on 40o #238 .90 *6.00*
270 A30 (b) 15o on 40o #238I .75 *.95*
271 A30 (c) 20o on 15o dp red 1.10 .30
272 A30 (b) 40o on 30o #238F 1.00 .35
Nos. 267-272 (6) 4.50 *8.30*
Set, never hinged 9.25

Stamps previously listed as Denmark No. 273-276 are listed as Faroe Islands Nos. 2-6 .

Bering's Ship — A46

1941, Nov. 27 **Engr.** ***Perf. 13***

277	A46	10o dk violet	.35	.30
278	A46	20o red brown	.60	.30
279	A46	40o dk blue	.40	.35
		Nos. 277-279 (3)	1.35	.95
		Set, never hinged	3.00	

Death of Vitus Bering, explorer, 200th anniv.

King Christian X — A47

1942-46 **Unwmk.** ***Perf. 13***

280	A47	10o violet	.30	.35
281	A47	15o yel grn	.35	.35
282	A47	20o red	.40	.35
283	A47	25o brown ('43)	.50	.45
284	A47	30o orange ('43)	.45	.35
285	A47	35o brt red vio ('44)	.40	.35
286	A47	40o blue ('43)	.40	.35
286A	A47	45o ol brn ('46)	.35	.35
286B	A47	50o gray ('45)	.60	.35
287	A47	60o bluish grn ('44)	.55	.35
287A	A47	75o dk blue ('46)	.55	.35
		Nos. 280-287A (11)	4.85	3.95
		Set, never hinged	8.00	

For overprints see Nos. Q28-Q30.

Round Tower — A48

1942, Nov. 27

288	A48	10o violet	.35	.30
		Never hinged	.75	

300th anniv. of the Round Tower, Copenhagen.

For surcharge see No. B14.

Condor Plane — A49

1943, Oct. 29

289	A49	20o red	.25	.25
		Never hinged	.35	

25th anniv. of the Danish Aviation Company (Det Danske Luftfartsselskab).

Ejby Church — A50

15ö, Oesterlars Church. 20ö, Hvidbjerg Church.

1944 **Engr.** ***Perf. 13***

290	A50	10o violet	.30	.25
291	A50	15o yellow grn	.30	.25
292	A50	20o red	.30	.25
		Nos. 290-292 (3)	.90	.75
		Set, never hinged	1.75	

Ole Roemer — A53

1944, Sept. 25

293	A53	20o henna brown	.35	.30
		Never hinged	.65	

Birth of Ole Roemer, astronomer, 300th anniv.

Christian X — A54

1945, Sept. 26

294	A54	10o lilac	.25	.25
295	A54	20o red	.25	.25
296	A54	40o deep blue	.25	.25
		Nos. 294-296 (3)	.75	.75
		Set, never hinged	1.75	

75th birthday of King Christian X.

Catalogue values for unused stamps in this section, from this point to the end of the section, are for Never Hinged items.

Small State Seal — A55

1946-47 **Unwmk.** ***Perf. 13***

297	A55	1k brown	1.00	.25
298	A55	2k red ('47)	2.40	.25
299	A55	5k dull blue	6.00	.25
		Nos. 297-299 (3)	9.40	.75

Nos. 297-299 issued on ordinary and fluorescent paper. Values for ordinary paper are much higher.

See Nos. 395-400, 441A-444D, 499-506, 643-650, 716-720A, 804-815, 909, 1134-1138, 1304-1313, 1474-1478, 1508. For overprints see Nos. Q35, Q40, Q46-Q48.

Tycho Brahe — A56

1946, Dec. 14 **Engr.**

300	A56	20o dark red	.30	.25

Birth of Tycho Brahe, astronomer, 400th anniv.

First Danish Locomotive A57

Modern Steam Locomotive A58

Diesel Locomotive A59

1947, June 27

301	A57	15o steel blue	.60	.35
302	A58	20o red	1.10	.35
303	A59	40o deep blue	3.50	2.25
		Nos. 301-303 (3)	5.20	2.95

Inauguration of the Danish State Railways, cent.

Jacobsen — A60

1947, Nov. 10 ***Perf. 13***

304	A60	20o dark red	.30	.25

60th anniv. of the death of Jacob Christian Jacobsen, founder of the Glyptothek Art Museum, Copenhagen.

Frederik IX — A61

Three types among 15ö, 20ö, 30ö:

I — Background of horizontal lines. No outline at left for cheek and ear. King's uniform textured in strong lines.

II — Background of vertical and horizontal lines. Contour of cheek and ear at left. Uniform same.

III — Background and facial contour lines as in II. Uniform lines double and thinner.

1948-50 **Unwmk.** ***Perf. 13***

306	A61	15(o) green (II)	2.50	.30
a.		Type III ('49)	1.60	.50
307	A61	20(o) dk red (I)	1.10	.25
a.		Type III ('49)	1.40	.30
308	A61	25(o) lt brown	1.40	.25
309	A61	30(o) org (II)	13.00	.50
a.		Type III ('50)	21.00	.50
310	A61	40(o) dl blue ('49)	4.75	1.00
311	A61	45(o) olive ('50)	2.10	.35
312	A61	50(o) gray ('49)	1.75	.30
313	A61	60(o) grnsh bl ('50)	2.50	.30
314	A61	75(o) lil rose ('50)	2.00	.30
		Nos. 306-314 (9)	31.10	3.55

See Nos. 319-326, 334-341, 354. For surcharges see Nos. 357-358, 370, B20, B24-B25, Q32-Q34, Q36-Q39.

Legislative Assembly, 1849 — A62

1949, June 5

315	A62	20o red brown	.35	.25

Adoption of the Danish constitution, cent.

Symbol of UPU — A63

1949, Oct. 9

316	A63	40o dull blue	.65	.35

75th anniv. of the UPU.

Kalundborg Radio Station and Masts — A64

1950, Apr. 1 **Engr.** ***Perf. 13***

317	A64	20o brown red	.50	.25

Radio broadcasting in Denmark, 25th anniv.

Types of 1933-50

1950-51 **Unwmk.** ***Perf. 13***

318	A32	10o green	.30	.25
319	A61	15(o) lilac	1.00	.30
b.		15(o) gray lilac	4.00	.25
320	A61	20(o) lt brown	1.10	.30
321	A61	25(o) dark red	3.50	.25
322	A61	35(o) gray grn ('51)	.95	.25
323	A61	40(o) gray	.95	.25
324	A61	50(o) dark blue	3.25	.25
325	A61	55(o) brown ('51)	32.50	2.75
326	A61	70(o) deep green	3.00	.30
		Nos. 318-326 (9)	46.55	4.90

Warship of 1701 — A65

1951, Feb. 26 **Engr.** ***Perf. 13***

327	A65	25o dark red	.50	.30
328	A65	50o deep blue	4.00	.80

250th anniv. of the foundation of the Naval Officers' College.

Oersted — A66

1951, Mar. 9 **Unwmk.**

329 A66 50o blue 1.40 .60

Cent. of the death of Hans Christian Oersted, physicist.

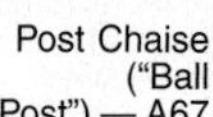

Post Chaise ("Ball Post") — A67

1951, Apr. 1 ***Perf. 13***

330 A67 15o purple .65 .25
331 A67 25o henna brown .65 .25

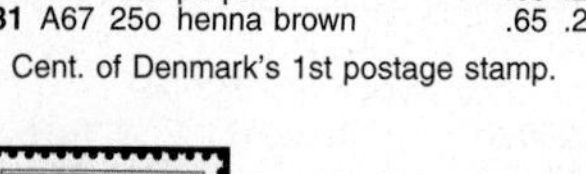

Cent. of Denmark's 1st postage stamp.

Marine Rescue — A68

1952, Mar. 26

332 A68 25o red brown .45 .35

Cent. of the foundation of the Danish Lifesaving Service.

Types of 1933-50

1952-53 ***Perf. 13***

333	A32	12o lt yel grn	.30	.25
334	A61	25(o) lt blue	1.10	.30
335	A61	30(o) brown red	1.00	.35
336	A61	50(o) aqua ('53)	1.00	.30
337	A61	60(o) dp blue ('53)	1.10	.35
338	A61	65(o) gray ('53)	1.10	.35
339	A61	80(o) orange ('53)	1.10	.35
340	A61	90(o) olive ('53)	3.00	.30
341	A61	95(o) red org ('53)	1.10	.25
		Nos. 333-341 (9)	10.80	2.80

Jelling Runic Stone — A69

Designs: 15o, Vikings' camp, Trelleborg. 20o, Church of Kalundborg. 30o, Nyborg castle. 60o, Goose tower, Vordinborg.

1953-56 ***Perf. 13***

342	A69	10o dp green	.30	.25
343	A69	15o lt rose vio	.30	.25
344	A69	20o brown	.30	.25
345	A69	30o red ('54)	.30	.25
346	A69	60o dp blue ('54)	.35	.25

Designs: 10o, Manor house, Spottrup. 15o, Hammershus castle ruins. 20o, Copenhagen stock exchange. 30o, Statue of Frederik V, Amalienborg. 60o, Soldier statue at Fredericia.

347	A69	10o green ('54)	.30	.25
348	A69	15o lilac ('55)	.30	.25
349	A69	20o brown ('55)	.30	.25
350	A69	30o red ('55)	.30	.25
351	A69	60o deep blue ('56)	.60	.25
		Nos. 342-351 (10)	3.35	2.50

1000th anniv. of the Kingdom of Denmark. Each stamp represents a different century.

Telegraph Equipment of 1854 — A70

1954, Feb. 2 ***Perf. 13***

352 A70 30o red brown .40 .25

Cent. of the telegraph in Denmark.

Frederik V — A71

1954, Mar. 31

353 A71 30o dark red .55 .35

200th anniv. of the founding of the Royal Academy of Fine Arts.

Type of 1948-50

1955, Apr. 27

354 A61 25o lilac 1.00 .30

Nos. 224C and 226A Surcharged with New Value in Black. Nos. 307 and 321 Surcharged with New Value and 4 Bars

1955-56

355	A32	5o on 6o org	.30	.25
356	A32	5o on 7o lt brn	.30	.25
357	A61	30(o) on 20(o) dk red (I)	.80	.30
a.		Type III	1.40	.35
b.		Double surcharge	*1,150.*	*1,150.*
c.		Inverted surcharge	*650.00*	
358	A61	30(o) on 25(o) dk red ('56)	.60	.25
a.		Double surcharge		—
		Nos. 355-358 (4)	2.00	1.05

A72

1955, Nov. 11 **Unwmk.**

359 A72 30o dark red .50 .25

100th anniv. of the death of Sören Kierkegaard, philosopher and theologian.

A73

1956, Sept. 12 **Engr.**

360 A73 30o Ellehammer's plane .50 .25

50th anniv. of the 1st flight made by Jacob Christian Hansen Ellehammer in a heavier-than-air craft.

Northern Countries Issue

Whooper Swans — A74

1956, Oct. 30 ***Perf. 13***

361 A74 30o rose red 1.75 .25
362 A74 60o ultramarine 1.60 .80

Issued to emphasize the close bonds among the northern countries: Denmark, Finland, Iceland, Norway and Sweden.

Prince's Palace — A75

Design: 60ö, Sun God's Chariot.

1957, May 15 **Unwmk.**

363 A75 30o dull red .90 .25
364 A75 60o dark blue .90 .75

150th anniv. of the National Museum.

Harvester — A76

1958, Sept. 4 **Engr.** ***Perf. 13***

365 A76 30o fawn .30 .25

Centenary of the Royal Veterinary and Agricultural College.

Frederik IX — A77

1959, Mar. 11

366	A77	30o rose red	.40	.25
367	A77	35o rose lilac	.50	.25
368	A77	60o ultra	.50	.25
		Nos. 366-368 (3)	1.40	.75

King Frederik's 60th birthday.

Ballet Dancer — A78

1959, May 16

369 A78 35o rose lilac .30 .25

Danish Ballet and Music Festival, May 17-31. See Nos. 401, 422.

No. 319 Surcharged

1960, Apr. 7

370 A61 30o on 15o lilac .30 .25

World Refugee Year, 7/1/59-6/30/60.

Seeder and Farm A79

30ö, Harvester combine. 60ö, Plow.

1960, Apr. 28 **Engr.** ***Perf. 13***

371	A79	12o green	.25	.25
372	A79	30o dull red	.30	.25
373	A79	60o dk blue	.65	.50
		Nos. 371-373 (3)	1.20	1.00

King Frederik IX and Queen Ingrid — A80

1960, May 24 **Unwmk.**

374 A80 30o dull red .45 .25
375 A80 60o blue .65 .60

25th anniversary of the marriage of King Frederik IX and Queen Ingrid.

Bascule Light — A81

1960, June 8 **Engr.**

376 A81 30o dull red .30 .25

400th anniv. of the Lighthouse Service.

Finsen — A82

1960, Aug. 1 ***Perf. 13***

377 A82 30o dark red .30 .25

Centenary of the birth of Dr. Niels R. Finsen, physician and scientist.

Nursing Mother — A83

1960, Aug. 16 **Unwmk.**

378 A83 60o ultra .55 .50

10th meeting of the regional committee for Europe of WHO, Copenhagen, Aug. 16-20.

Europa Issue, 1960

Common Design Type

1960, Sept. 19 ***Perf. 13***

Size: 28x21mm

379 CD3 60o ultra .55 .50

DC-8 Airliner — A84

1961, Feb. 24

380 A84 60o ultra .75 .50

10th anniv. of the Scandinavian Airlines System, SAS.

Landscape A85

1961, Apr. 21 ***Perf. 13***

381 A85 30o copper brown .30 .25

Denmark's Soc. of Nature Lovers, 50th anniv.

Fluorescent Paper
as well as ordinary paper, was used in printing many definitive and commemorative stamps, starting in 1962. These include No. 220, 224; the 15, 20, 25, 30, 35 (Nos. 386 and 387), 50 and 60ö, 1.50k and 25k definitives of following set, and Nos. 297-299, 318, 333, 380, 401-427, 429-435, 438-439, 493, 543, 548, B30.
Only fluorescent paper was used for Nos. 436-437, 437A and 440 onward; in semipostals from B31 onward.

Frederik IX — A86

1961-63 Engr. *Perf. 13*

382	A32	15o green ('63)	.50	.35
383	A86	20o brown	.45	.35
384	A86	25o brown ('63)	.30	.35
385	A86	30o rose red	.65	.35
386	A86	35o olive grn	.85	.75
387	A86	35o rose red ('63)	.30	.35
388	A86	40o gray	1.20	.35
389	A86	50o aqua	.55	.30
390	A86	60o ultra	1.10	.35
391	A86	70o green	1.60	.35
392	A86	80o red orange	1.60	.35
393	A86	90o olive bister	4.25	.35
394	A86	95o claret ('63)	1.00	.90
		Nos. 382-394 (13)	14.35	5.45

See Nos. 417-419, 438-441. For overprints see Nos. Q41-Q42, Q44-Q45.

State Seal Type of 1946-47

1962-65

395	A55	1.10k lilac ('65)	5.25	2.00
396	A55	1.20k gray	3.00	.35
397	A55	1.25k orange	3.00	.35
398	A55	1.30k green ('65)	5.50	1.75
399	A55	1.50k red lilac	2.75	.35
400	A55	25k yellow grn	8.00	.35
		Nos. 395-400 (6)	27.50	5.15

Dancer Type of 1959 Inscribed "15-31 MAJ"

1962, Apr. 26
401 A78 60o ultra .30 .25

Issued to publicize the Danish Ballet and Music Festival, May 15-31.

Old Mill — A87

1962, May 10 Unwmk. *Perf. 13*
402 A87 10o red brown .30 .25

Cent. of the abolition of mill monopolies.

M.S. Selandia — A88

1962, June 14 Engr.
403 A88 60o dark blue 1.60 1.50

M.S. Selandia, the 1st Diesel ship, 50th anniv.

Violin Scroll, Leaves, Lights and Balloon A89

1962, Aug. 31
404 A89 35o rose violet .35 .25

150th anniv. of the birth of Georg Carstensen, founder of Tivoli amusement park, Copenhagen.

Cliffs on Moen Island — A90

1962, Nov. 22
405 A90 20o pale brown .30 .25

Issued to publicize preservation of natural treasures and landmarks.

Germinating Wheat — A91

1963, Mar. 21 Engr.
406 A91 35o fawn .35 .25

FAO "Freedom from Hunger" campaign.

Railroad Wheel, Tire Tracks, Waves and Swallow — A92

1963, May 14 Unwmk. *Perf. 13*
407 A92 15o green .60 .40

Inauguration of the "Bird Flight Line" railroad link between Denmark and Germany.

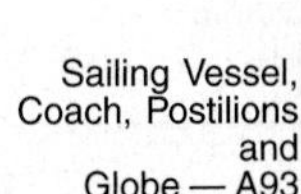

Sailing Vessel, Coach, Postilions and Globe — A93

1963, May 27
408 A93 60o dark blue .40 .40

Cent. of the 1st Intl. Postal Conf., Paris, 1863.

Niels Bohr and Atom Diagram — A94

1963, Nov. 21 Engr.
409 A94 35o red brown .40 .35
410 A94 60o dark blue .65 .25

50th anniv. of Prof. Niels Bohr's (1885-1962) atom theory.
See Greeland Nos. 66-67.

Early Public School Drawn on Slate — A95

1964, June 19 Unwmk. *Perf. 13*
411 A95 35o red brown .60 .25

150th anniversary of the royal decrees for the public school system.

Fish and Chart — A96

1964, Sept. 7 Engr.
412 A96 60o violet blue .35 .40

Conference of the International Council for the Exploration of the Sea, Copenhagen.

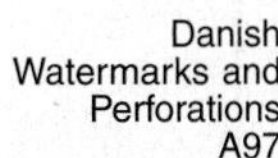

Danish Watermarks and Perforations A97

1964, Oct. 10 *Perf. 13*
413 A97 35o pink .30 .25

25th anniv. of Stamp Day and to publicize the Odense Stamp Exhibition, Oct. 10-11.

Landscape A98

1964, Nov. 12 Engr.
414 A98 25o brown .30 .25

Issued to publicize preservation of natural treasures and landmarks.

Calculator, Ledger and Inkwell — A99

1965, Mar. 8 Unwmk.
415 A99 15o light olive green .30 .25

First Business School in Denmark, cent.

Types of 1933 and 1961

1965, May 15 Engr. *Perf. 13*

416	A32	25o apple green	.55	.50
417	A86	40o brown	.45	.35
418	A86	50o rose red	.75	.35
419	A86	80o ultra	.75	.65
		Nos. 416-419 (4)	2.50	1.85

For overprints see Nos. Q41-Q42.

ITU Emblem, Telegraph Key, Teletype Paper — A100

1965, May 17
420 A100 80o dark blue .35 .25

Cent. of the ITU.

Carl Nielsen (1865-1931), Composer — A101

1965, June 9 Engr.
421 A101 50o brown red .40 .25

Dancer Type of 1959 Inscribed "15-31 MAJ"

1965, Sept. 23
422 A78 50o rose red .30 .25

Issued to publicize the Danish Ballet and Music Festival, May 15-31.

Bogo Windmill — A102

1965, Nov. 10 Engr. *Perf. 13*
423 A102 40o brown .30 .25

Issued to publicize the preservation of natural treasures and landmarks.

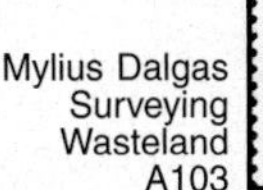

Mylius Dalgas Surveying Wasteland A103

1966, Feb. 24
424 A103 25o olive green .50 .30

Cent. of the Danish Heath Soc. (reclamation of wastelands), founded by Enrico Mylius Dalgas.

Christen Kold (1816-70), Educator — A104

1966, Mar. 29 *Perf. 13*
425 A104 50o dull red .50 .50

Poorhouse, Copenhagen A105

Holte Allée, Bregentved A106

Dolmen (Grave) in Jutland — A107

1966 Unwmk.

426	A105	50o dull red	.55	.50
427	A106	80o dk blue	1.00	.40
428	A107	1.50k dk slate grn	1.40	.25
		Nos. 426-428 (3)	2.95	1.15

Publicizing preservation of national treasures and ancient monuments. Issued: 50o, May 12; 80o, June 16; 1.50k, Nov. 24.

George Jensen by Ejnar Nielsen — A108

1966, Aug. 31 Engr. *Perf. 13*
429 A108 80o dark blue 1.00 .40

George Jensen, silversmith, birth cent.

Music Bar and Instruments A109

1967, Jan. 9

430 A109 50o dark red .70 .25

Royal Danish Academy of Music, cent.

Cogwheels, and Broken Customs Duty Ribbon — A110

1967, Mar. 2

431 A110 80o dark blue .70 .25

European Free Trade Association. Industrial tariffs were abolished Dec. 31, 1966, among EFTA members: Austria, Denmark, Finland, Great Britain, Norway, Portugal, Sweden and Switzerland.

Windmill and Medieval Fortress — A111

Designs: 40ö, Ship's rigging and baroque house front. 50ö, Old Town Hall. 80ö, New building construction.

1967 Engr. *Perf. 13*

432 A111 25o green .60 .25
433 A111 40o sepia .35 .25
434 A111 50o red brown .35 .40
435 A111 80o dk blue .85 .80
Nos. 432-435 (4) 2.15 1.70

The 800th anniversary of Copenhagen.
Issued: Nos. 432-433, 4/6; Nos. 434-435, 5/11.

Princess Margrethe and Prince Henri — A112

1967, June 10

436 A112 50o red .30 .25

Marriage of Crown Princess Margrethe and Prince Henri de Monpezat.

Types of 1933-1961

1967-71 Engr. *Perf. 13*

437 A32 30o dk green .70 .35
437A A32 40o orange ('71) .80 .35
438 A86 50o brown 1.25 .35
Complete booklet, 4 #318, 2 each #437, 438 20.00
439 A86 60o rose red 1.25 .35
440 A86 80o green .85 .35
441 A86 90o ultra .90 .35
441A A55 1.20k Prus grn ('71) 2.00 .45
442 A55 2.20k orange 3.50 .35
443 A55 2.80k gray 3.00 .35
444 A55 2.90k rose vio 5.25 .35
444A A55 3k dk sl grn ('69) 1.00 .35
444B A55 3.10k plum ('70) 8.50 .35
444C A55 4k gray ('69) 1.40 .35
444D A55 4.10k olive ('70) 8.50 .35
Nos. 437-444D (14) 38.90 5.00

Issued: Nos. 437-441, 6/30/67; Nos. 442-443, 7/8/67; No. 444, 4/29/68; Nos. 444A, 444C, 8/28/69; Nos. 444B, 444D, 8/27/70; Nos. 437A, 441A, 6/24/71.

For overprints see Nos. Q44-Q45.

Sonne — A113

1967, Sept. 21

445 A113 60o red .30 .25

150th anniv. of the birth of Hans Christian Sonne, pioneer of the cooperative movement in Denmark.

Cross-anchor and Porpoise — A114

1967, Nov. 9 Engr. *Perf. 13*

446 A114 90o dk blue .35 .25

Centenary of the Danish Seamen's Church in Foreign Ports.

Esbjerg Harbor — A115

1968, Apr. 24

447 A115 30o dk yellow grn .30 .25

Centenary of Esbjerg Harbor.

Koldinghus A116

1968, June 13

448 A116 60o copper red .65 .25

700th anniversary of Koldinghus Castle.

Shipbuilding Industry — A117

Designs: 50o, Chemical industry. 60o, Electric power. 90o, Engineering.

1968, Oct. 24 Engr. *Perf. 13*

449 A117 30o green .25 .25
450 A117 50o brown .25 .25
451 A117 60o red brown .25 .25
452 A117 90o dark blue 1.00 1.00
Nos. 449-452 (4) 1.75 1.75

Issued to publicize Danish industries.

Sower — A118

1969, Jan. 29

453 A118 30o gray green .30 .25

Royal Agricultural Soc. of Denmark, 200th anniv.

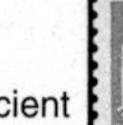

Five Ancient Ships — A119

Nordic Cooperation Issue

1969, Feb. 28 Engr. *Perf. 13*

454 A119 60o brown red .80 .25
455 A119 90o blue 1.60 1.60

50th anniv. of the Nordic Soc. and cent. of postal cooperation among the northern countries. The design is taken from a coin found at the site of Birka, an ancient Swedish town. See also Finland No. 481, Iceland Nos. 404-405, Norway Nos. 523-524 and Sweden Nos. 808-810.

Frederik IX — A120

1969, Mar. 11

456 A120 50o sepia .30 .25
457 A120 60o dull red .30 .25

70th birthday of King Frederik IX.

Common Design Types pictured following the introduction.

Europa Issue, 1969
Common Design Type

1969, Apr. 28

Size: 28x20mm

458 CD12 90o chalky blue .75 .75

Kronborg Castle — A121

1969, May 22 Engr. *Perf. 13*

459 A121 50o brown .30 .25

Association of Danes living abroad, 50th anniv.

Danish Flag — A122

1969, June 12

460 A122 60o bluish blk, red & gray .30 .25

750th anniversary of the fall of the Dannebrog (Danish flag) from heaven.

Nexo — A123

1969, Aug. 28

461 A123 80o deep green .30 .25

Centenary of the birth of Martin Andersen Nexo (1869-1954), novelist.

Stensen — A124

1969, Sept. 25

462 A124 1k deep brown .35 .25

300th anniv. of the publication of Niels Stensen's geological work "On Solid Bodies."

Abstract Design — A125

1969, Nov. 10 Engr. *Perf. 13*

463 A125 60o rose, red & ultra .30 .25

Symbolic Design — A126

1969, Nov. 20

464 A126 30o olive green .30 .25

Valdemar Poulsen (1869-1942), electrical engineer and inventor.

Post Office Bank — A127

1970, Jan. 15 Engr. *Perf. 13*

465 A127 60o dk red & org .30 .25

50th anniv. of post office banking service.

School Safety Patrol — A128

1970, Feb. 19

466 A128 50o brown .30 .25

Issued to publicize road safety.

Candle in Window — A129

1970, May 4 Engr. *Perf. 13*

467 A129 50o slate, dull bl & yel .30 .25

25th anniv. of liberation from the Germans.

Deer — A130

1970, May 28

468 A130 60o yel grn, red & brn .30 .25

Tercentenary of Jaegersborg Deer Park.

Elephant Figurehead, 1741 — A131

1970, June 15 ***Perf. 11½***
469 A131 30o multicolored .30 .25

Royal Naval Museum, tercentenary.

"The Homecoming" by Povl Christensen — A132

1970, June 15 ***Perf. 13***
470 A132 60o org, dl vio & ol grn .30 .25

Union of North Schleswig and Denmark, 50th anniv.

Electromagnet A133

1970, Aug. 13 **Engr.**
471 A133 80o gray green .30 .25

150th anniversary of Hans Christian Oersted's discovery of electromagnetism.

Bronze Age Ship A134

Ships: 50o, Viking shipbuilding, from Bayeux tapestry. 60o, Thuroe schooner with topgallant. 90o, Tanker.

1970, Sept. 24
472 A134 30o ocher & brown .25 .25
473 A134 50o brn red & rose brn .25 .25
474 A134 60o gray ol & red brn .35 .25
475 A134 90o blue grn & ultra 1.25 1.25
Nos. 472-475 (4) 2.10 2.00

UN Emblem A135

1970, Oct. 22 **Engr.** ***Perf. 13***
476 A135 90o blue, grn & red 1.00 1.00

25th anniversary of the United Nations.

Bertel Thorvaldsen — A136

1970, Nov. 19
477 A136 2k slate blue .60 .50

Bicentenary of the birth of Bertel Thorvaldsen (1768-1844), sculptor.

Mathide Fibiger — A137

1971, Feb. 25
478 A137 80o olive green .30 .25

Danish Women's Association centenary.

Refugees — A138

1971, Mar. 26 **Engr.** ***Perf. 13***
479 A138 50o brown .25 .25
480 A138 60o brown red .35 .25

Joint northern campaign for the benefit of refugees.

Hans Egede — A139

1971, May 27
481 A139 1k brown .35 .25

250th anniversary of arrival of Hans Egede in Greenland and beginning of its colonization.

A140

1971, Oct. 14
482 A140 30o Swimming .25 .25
483 A140 50o Gymnastics .50 .25
484 A140 60o Soccer .75 .25
485 A140 90o Sailing .75 .75
Nos. 482-485 (4) 2.25 1.50

A141

1971, Nov. 11 **Engr.** ***Perf. 13***
486 A141 90o dark blue .35 .35

Centenary of first lectures given by Georg Brandes (1842-1927), writer and literary critic.

A142

1972, Jan. 27
487 A142 80o slate green .35 .25

Centenary of Danish sugar production.

A143

1972, Mar. 11 **Engr.** ***Perf. 13***
488 A143 60o red brown .30 .25

Frederik IX (1899-1972).

Abstract Design A144

1972, Mar. 11
489 A144 1.20k brt rose lil, bl gray & brn .65 .65

Danish Meteorological Institute, cent.

Nikolai F. S. Grundtvig — A145

1972, May 4 **Engr.** ***Perf. 13***
490 A145 1k sepia .50 .50

Nikolai Frederik Severin Grundtvig (1783-1872), theologian and poet.

Locomotive, 1847, Ferry, Travelers A146

1972, June 26
491 A146 70o rose red .30 .25

125th anniversary of Danish State Railways.

Rebild Hills — A147

1972, June 26
492 A147 1k bl, sl grn & mar .35 .25

Types of 1933-46

1972-78 **Engr.** ***Perf. 13***
493 A32 20o slate bl ('74) .35 .35
494 A32 50o sepia ('74) .30 .30
a. Bklt. pane of 12 (4 #318, 4 #493, 4 #494) ('85) 15.00
495 A32 60o apple grn ('76) 1.75 .90
496 A32 60o gray ('78) .70 .70
497 A32 70o red 1.00 .35
498 A32 70o apple grn ('77) 1.10 .35
499 A55 2.50k orange 1.75 .35
500 A55 2.80k olive ('75) 1.25 .65
501 A55 3.50k lilac 2.00 .35
502 A55 4.5k olive 5.50 .35
503 A55 6k vio blk ('76) 2.00 .35
504 A55 7k red lilac ('78) 2.10 .35
505 A55 9k brown ol ('77) 3.00 .35

With Vertical and Horizontal Engraving Lines

506 A55 10k lemon ('76) 3.00 .35
Nos. 493-506 (14) 25.80 6.05

See footnote after No. 1313.

"Tinker Turned Politician" — A148

1972, Sept. 14
507 A148 70o dark red .30 .25

250th anniv. of the comedies of Ludvig Holberg (1684-1754) on the Danish stage.

WHO Building, Copenhagen — A149

1972, Sept. 14
508 A149 2k bl, blk & lt red brn .60 .60

Opening of WHO Building, Copenhagen.

Bridge Across Little Belt — A150

Highway engineering (Diagrams): 60o, Hanstholm Harbor. 70o, Lim Fjord Tunnel. 90o, Knudshoved Harbor.

1972, Oct. 19 **Engr.** ***Perf. 13***
509 A150 40o dk green .25 .25
510 A150 60o dk brown .35 .25
511 A150 70o dk red .35 .25
512 A150 90o dk blue grn 1.40 .50
Nos. 509-512 (4) 2.35 1.25

Aeroskobing House c. 1740 — A151

Danish Architecture: 60o, East Bornholm farmhouse, 17th century, horiz. 70o, House, Christianshavn, c. 1710. 1.20k, Hvide Sande Farmhouse, c. 1810, horiz.

1972, Nov. 23

Size: 20x28mm, 27x20mm

513 A151 40o red, brn & blk .35 .25
514 A151 60o blk, vio bl & grn .35 .25

Size: 18x37mm, 36x20mm

515 A151 70o red, dk red & blk .45 .30
516 A151 1.20k dk brn, red & grn 1.40 1.00
Nos. 513-516 (4) 2.55 1.80

Jensen — A152

1973, Feb. 22 **Engr.** ***Perf. 13***
517 A152 90o green .35 .25

Centenary of the birth of Johannes Vilhelm Jensen (1873-1950), lyric poet and novelist.

Guard Rails, Cogwheels — A153

1973, Mar. 22

518 A153 50o sepia .55 .25

Centenary of first Danish Factory Act for labor protection.

Abildgaard — A154

1973, Mar. 22

519 A154 1k dull blue .70 .35

Bicentenary of Royal Veterinary College, Christianshaven, founded by Prof. P. C. Abildgaard.

Rhododendron A155

Design: 70o, Dronningen of Denmark rose.

1973, Apr. 26

520 A155 60o brn, grn & vio .50 .25
521 A155 70o dk red, rose & grn .50 .25

Centenary of the founding of the Horticultural Society of Denmark.

Nordic Cooperation Issue

Nordic House, Reykjavik A156

1973, June 26 Engr. *Perf. 13*

522 A156 70o multicolored .50 .25
523 A156 1k multicolored 1.50 1.25

A century of postal cooperation among Denmark, Finland, Iceland, Norway and Sweden, and in connection with the Nordic Postal Conference, Reykjavik.

Sextant, Stella Nova, Cassiopeia — A157

1973, Oct. 18 Engr. *Perf. 13*

524 A157 2k dark blue 1.75 .30

400th anniversary of the publication of "De Nova Stella," by Tycho Brahe.

St. Mark, from 11th Cent. Book of Dalby — A158

1973, Oct. 18 Photo. *Perf. 14x14½*

525 A158 120o buff & multi 1.10 .65

300th anniversary of Royal Library.

Devil and Gossips, Fanefjord Church, 1480 — A159

Frescoes: No. 527, Queen Esther and King Ahasuerus, Tirsted Church, c.1400. No. 528, Miraculous Harvest, Jetsmark Church, c.1474. No. 529, Jesus carrying cross, and wearing crown of thorns, Biersted Church, c.1400. No. 530, Creation of Eve, Fanefjord Church, c.1480.

1973, Nov. 28 Engr. *Perf. 13*

Cream Paper

526 A159 70o dk red, yel & grn 1.40 .30
527 A159 70o dk red, yel & grn 1.40 .30
528 A159 70o dk red, yel & grn 1.40 .30
529 A159 70o dk red, yel & grn 1.40 .30
530 A159 70o dk red, yel & grn 1.40 .30
a. Bklt. pane, 2 each #526-530 35.00
b. Strip of 5, #526-530 6.75

Blood Donors — A160

1974, Jan. 24

531 A160 90o purple & red 1.10 .25

"Blood Saves Lives."

Queen Margrethe — A161

1974-81 Engr. *Perf. 13*

532 A161 60o brown 1.00 .50
533 A161 60o orange .60 .45
534 A161 70o red 1.00 .25
535 A161 70o dk brown .80 .25
536 A161 80o green .80 .25
537 A161 80o dp brn ('76) 1.10 .25
538 A161 90o red lilac 1.10 .25
539 A161 90o dull red 1.40 .30
540 A161 90o slate grn ('76) 1.10 .30
541 A161 100o dp ultra 1.10 .25
542 A161 100o gray ('75) 1.10 .25
543 A161 100o red ('76) 1.10 .35
544 A161 100o brown ('77) 1.00 .25
a. Bklt. pane of 5 (#544, #494, 2 #493, #318) 2.50
Complete booklet, #544a 2.50
545 A161 110o orange ('78) 1.20 .25
546 A161 120o slate 1.00 .50
547 A161 120o red ('77) 1.40 .25
Complete booklet, 4 each #318, 493, 544, 547 13.50
548 A161 130o ultra ('75) 1.60 1.40
549 A161 150o vio bl ('78) 1.40 .85
550 A161 180o slate grn ('77) 1.40 .40
551 A161 200o blue ('81) 1.40 1.00
Nos. 532-551 (20) 22.60 8.55

See Nos. 630, 632-642. For overprint see No. Q49.

Pantomime Theater — A162

1974, May 16

552 A162 100o indigo .40 .30

Cent. of the Pantomime Theater, Tivoli.

Hverringe A163

Views: 60o, Norre Lyndelse, Carl Nielsen's childhood home. 70o, Odense, Hans Chr. Andersen's childhood home. 90o, Hesselagergaard, vert. 120o, Hindsholm.

1974, June 20 Engr. *Perf. 13*

553 A163 50o brown & multi .50 .50
554 A163 60o sl grn & multi .65 .65
555 A163 70o red brn & multi .50 .50
556 A163 90o dk green & mar .55 .25
557 A163 120o red org & dk grn .70 .50
Nos. 553-557 (5) 2.90 2.40

Emblem, Runner with Map — A164

1974, Aug. 22 Engr. *Perf. 13*

558 A164 70o shown .70 .70
559 A164 80o Compass .25 .25

World Orienteering Championships 1974.

Iris — A165

1974, Sept. 19

560 A165 90o shown .50 .25
561 A165 120o Purple orchid .75 .75

Copenhagen Botanical Garden centenary.

Mailman, 1624, and Postilion, 1780 — A166

Carrier Pigeon — A167

Design: 90o, Balloon and sailing ships.

1974, Oct. 9 Engr. *Perf. 13*

562 A166 70o lemon & dk brn .40 .25
563 A166 90o dull grn & sepia .40 .25
564 A167 120o dark blue .65 .65
Nos. 562-564 (3) 1.45 1.15

350th anniv. of Danish PO (70o, 90o) and cent. of UPU (120o).

Souvenir Sheet

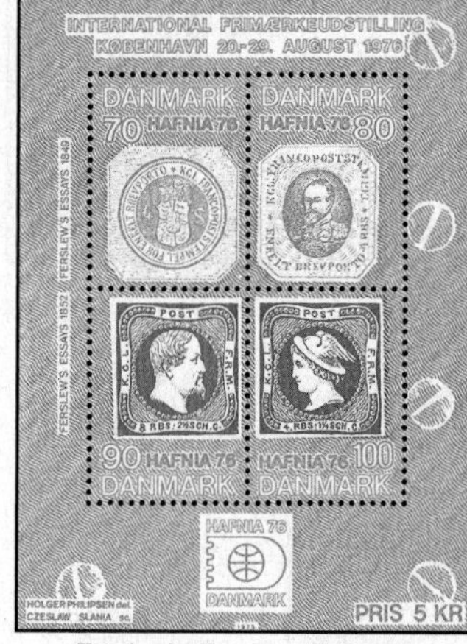

Ferslew's Essays, 1849 and 1852 — A168

Engraved and Photogravure

1975, Feb. 27 *Perf. 13*

565 A168 Sheet of 4 7.50 *8.50*
a. 70o Coat of arms 1.75 *2.00*
b. 80o King Frederik VII 1.75 *2.00*
c. 90o King Frederik VII 1.75 *2.00*
d. 100o Mercury 1.75 *2.00*

HAFNIA 76 Intl. Stamp Exhib., Copenhagen, Aug. 20-29, 1976. Sold for 5k.

See No. 585.

Early Radio Equipment — A169

1975, Mar. 20 Engr. *Perf. 13*

566 A169 90o dull red .35 .30

Danish broadcasting, 50th anniversary.

Flora Danica Plate — A170

Danish China: 90o, Flora Danica tureen. 130o, Vase and tea caddy, blue fluted china.

1975, May 22

567 A170 50o slate grn .30 .25
568 A170 90o brown red .65 .65
569 A170 130o violet bl 1.10 1.10
Nos. 567-569 (3) 2.05 2.00

Church of Moravian Brethren, Christiansfeld A171

120o, Kongsgaard farmhouse, Lejre. 150o, Anna Queenstraede, Helsingor, vert.

1975, June 19

570 A171 70o sepia .65 .65
571 A171 120o olive green .80 .80
572 A171 150o violet black .65 .25
Nos. 570-572 (3) 2.10 1.70

European Architectural Heritage Year 1975.

Andersen — A172

Designs: 70o, Numbskull Jack, drawing by Vilh. Pedersen. 130o, The Marshking's Daughter, drawing by L. Frohlich.

1975, Aug. 28 Engr. *Perf. 13*

573 A172 70o brown & blk .60 .60
574 A172 90o brn red & dk brn .75 .30
575 A172 130o blue blk & sepia 1.75 1.75
Nos. 573-575 (3) 3.10 2.65

Hans Christian Andersen (1805-75), writer.

Watchman's Square, Abenra — A173

Designs: 90o, Haderslev Cathedral, vert. 100o, Mögeltönder Polder. 120o, Mouth of Vidaaen at Höjer Floodgates.

1975, Sept. 25

576 A173 70o multicolored .45 .45
577 A173 90o multicolored .40 .25
578 A173 100o multicolored .50 .25
579 A173 120o multicolored .55 .50
Nos. 576-579 (4) 1.90 1.45

European Kingfisher A174

1975, Oct. 23 Engr. *Perf. 13*

580 A174 50o shown .45 .45
581 A174 70o Hedgehog .45 .45
582 A174 90o Cats .45 .45
583 A174 130o Avocets 1.25 1.25
584 A174 200o Otter .65 .25
Nos. 580-584 (5) 3.25 2.85

Protected animals, and for the centenary of the Danish Society for the Prevention of Cruelty to Animals (90o).

HAFNIA Type of 1974
Souvenir Sheet

1975, Nov. 20 Engr. & Photo.

585 A168 Sheet of 4 4.50 *6.75*
a. 50o buff & brown, No. 2 1.10 *1.60*
b. 70o buff, brown & blue, No. 1 1.10 *1.60*
c. 90o buff, blue & brown, No. 11 1.10 *1.60*
d. 130o olive, brown & buff, No. 19 1.10 *1.60*

HAFNIA 76 Intl. Stamp Exhib., Copenhagen, Aug. 20-29, 1976. Sold for 5k.

Copenhagen, Center — A175

View from Round Tower — A176

Copenhagen, Views: 100o, Central Station, interior. 130o, Harbor.

1976, Mar. 25 Engr. *Perf. 12½*

586 A175 60o multicolored .45 .45
587 A176 80o multicolored .45 .45
588 A176 100o multicolored .45 .25
589 A175 130o multicolored 1.50 1.50
Nos. 586-589 (4) 2.85 2.65

Postilion, by Otto Bache — A177

1976, June 17 Engr. *Perf. 12½*

590 A177 130o multicolored 1.00 1.25

Souvenir Sheet

591 A177 130o multicolored 10.00 *16.00*

HAFNIA 76 Intl. Stamp Exhib., Copenhagen, Aug. 20-29. No. 591 contains one stamp similar to No. 590 with design continuous into sheet margin. Sheet shows painting "A String of Horses Outside an Inn" of which No. 590 shows a detail. Sheet sold for 15k including exhibition ticket.

Emil Chr. Hansen, Physiologist, in Laboratory — A178

1976, Sept. 23 Engr. *Perf. 13*

592 A178 100o orange red .40 .30

Carlsberg Foundation (art and science), centenary.

Glass Blower Molding Glass — A179

Danish Glass Production: 80o, Finished glass removed from pipe. 130o, Glass cut off from foot. 150o, Glass blown up in mold.

1976, Nov. 18 Engr. *Perf. 13*

593 A179 60o slate .50 .50
594 A179 80o dk brown .50 .25
595 A179 130o dk blue 1.00 1.00
596 A179 150o red brown .60 .25
Nos. 593-596 (4) 2.60 2.00

Five Water Lilies — A180

Photogravure and Engraved

1977, Feb. 2 *Perf. 12½*

597 A180 100o brt green & multi .50 .35
598 A180 130o ultra & multi 2.00 2.00

Nordic countries cooperation for protection of the environment and 25th Session of Nordic Council, Helsinki, Feb. 19.

Road Accident — A181

1977, Mar. 24 Engr. *Perf. 12½*

599 A181 100o brown red .40 .30

Road Safety Traffic Act, May 1, 1977.

Europa — A182

1977, May 2 Engr. *Perf. 12½*

600 A182 1k Allinge *.60 .30*
601 A182 1.30k View, Ringsted *3.00 3.00*

Kongeaen A183

Landscapes, Southern Jutland: 90o, Skallingen. 150o, Torskind. 200o, Jelling.

1977, June 30 Engr. *Perf. 12½*

602 A183 60o multicolored 1.25 1.25
603 A183 90o multicolored .65 .65
604 A183 150o multicolored .60 .50
605 A183 200o multicolored .75 .50
Nos. 602-605 (4) 3.25 2.90

See Nos. 616-619, 655-658, 666-669.

Hammers and Horseshoes A184

Designs: 1k, Chisel, square and plane. 1.30k, Trowel, ceiling brush and folding ruler.

1977, Sept. 22 Engr. *Perf. 12½*

606 A184 80o dk brown .30 .25
607 A184 1k red .40 .25
608 A184 1.30k violet bl .75 .60
Nos. 606-608 (3) 1.45 1.10

Danish crafts.

Globe Flower — A185

Endangered Flora: 1.50k, Cnidium dubium.

1977, Nov. 17 Engr. *Perf. 12½*

609 A185 1k multicolored .40 .25
610 A185 1.50k multicolored 1.25 1.25

Handball — A186

1978, Jan. 19 *Perf. 12½*

611 A186 1.20k red .40 .30

Men's World Handball Championships.

Christian IV, Frederiksborg Castle A187

Frederiksborg Museum A188

1978, Mar. 16

612 A187 1.20k brown red .50 .50
613 A188 1.80k black .60 .30

Frederiksborg Museum, centenary.

Europa Issue

Jens Bang's House, Aalborg A189

Frederiksborg Castle, Ground Plan and Elevation A190

1978, May 11 Engr. *Perf. 12½*

614 A189 1.20k red *.30* .25
615 A190 1.50k dk bl & vio bl *1.25 1.25*

Landscape Type of 1977

Landscapes, Central Jutland: 70o, Kongenshus Memorial Park. 120o, Post Office, Old Town in Aarhus. 150o, Lignite fields, Soby. 180o, Church wall, Stadil Church.

1978, June 15 Engr. *Perf. 12½*

616 A183 70o multicolored .50 .50
617 A183 120o multicolored .55 .25
Complete booklet, 10 #617 9.00
618 A183 150o multicolored .80 .80
619 A183 180o multicolored .60 .60
Nos. 616-619 (4) 2.45 2.15

Boats in Harbor — A191

Danish fishing industry: 1k, Eel traps. 1.80k, Boats in berth. 2.50k, Drying nets.

1978, Sept. 7 Engr. *Perf. 12½*

620 A191 70o olive gray .50 .50
621 A191 1k redsh brown .50 .25
622 A191 1.80k slate .60 .50
623 A191 2.50k sepia .85 .60
Nos. 620-623 (4) 2.45 1.85

Edible Morel — A192

Design: 1.20k, Satan's mushroom.

1978, Nov. 16 Engr. *Perf. 12½*

624 A192 1k sepia .65 .55
625 A192 1.20k dull red .65 .55

Telephones — A193

1979, Jan. 25 Engr. *Perf. 12½*

626 A193 1.20k dull red .40 .30

Centenary of Danish telephone.

University Seal A194

Pentagram: University Faculties A195

1979, Apr. 5 Engr. *Perf. 12½*

627 A194 1.30k vermilion .40 .25
628 A195 1.60k dk vio blue .55 .55

University of Copenhagen, 500th anniv.

Types of 1933-1974

1979-82 Engr. *Perf. 13*

629 A32 80o green .35 .40
630 A161 90o slate 3.00 3.25
631 A32 100o dp green ('81) .50 .40
632 A161 110o brown .65 .40
a. Bklt. pane, #493-494, 632, 2 #318 ('79) 1.50
complete booklet, #632a 1.50
633 A161 130o red .65 .40
a. Bklt. pane, 2 ea #494, 629, 632, 4 #633 ('79) 7.50
Complete booklet, #633a 8.00
634 A161 130o brown ('81) .65 .60
635 A161 140o red org ('80) 2.00 2.50
636 A161 150o red org ('81) .65 .80
637 A161 160o ultra 1.25 1.25
638 A161 160o red ('81) .65 .40
a. Bklt. pane, 2 ea #318, 634, 638, 8 #494) 12.00
Complete booklet, #638a 12.00

639 A161 180o ultra ('80) 1.40 1.40
640 A161 210o gray ('80) 2.00 2.50
641 A161 230o ol grn ('81) 1.00 .65
642 A161 250o blue grn ('81) 1.40 1.00
643 A55 2.80k dull grn 1.40 1.10
644 A55 3.30k brn red ('81) 1.40 .80
645 A55 3.50k grnsh bl ('82) 2.50 3.00
646 A55 4.30k brn red ('80) 4.00 5.25
647 A55 4.70k rose lil ('81) 3.50 5.25
648 A55 8k orange 2.75 .40
649 A55 12k red brn ('81) 5.00 .65
650 A55 14k dk red brn ('82) 5.75 .80
Nos. 629-650 (22) 42.45 33.20

A196

Europa: 1.30k, Mail cart, 1785. 1.60k, Morse key and amplifier.

1979, May 10 ***Perf. 12½***
651 A196 1.30k red *1.00* .25
652 A196 1.60k dark blue *3.00* 1.10

A197

Viking Art: 1.10k, Gripping beast pendant. 2k, Key with gripping beast design.

1979, June 14 Engr. ***Perf. 13***
653 A197 1.10k sepia .40 .40
654 A197 2k grnsh gray .50 .40

Landscape Type of 1977

Landscapes, Northern Jutland: 80o, Mols Bjerge. 90o, Orslev Kloster. 200o, Trans. 280o, Bovbjerg.

1979, Sept. 6 Engr. ***Perf. 12½***
655 A183 80o multicolored .50 .50
656 A183 90o multicolored 1.60 1.60
657 A183 200o multicolored .90 .35
658 A183 280o multicolored 1.10 1.10
Nos. 655-658 (4) 4.10 3.55

Adam Oehlenschläger (1799-1850), Poet and Dramatist A198

1979, Oct, 4 Engr. ***Perf. 13***
659 A198 1.30k dk carmine .40 .30

Score, Violin, Dancing Couple — A199

Ballerina — A200

1979, Nov. 8 Engr. ***Perf. 13x12½***
660 A199 1.10k brown .40 .30
661 A200 1.60k ultra .60 .65

Jacob Gade (1879-63), composer; August Bournonville (1805-79), ballet master.

Royal Mail Guards' Office, Copenhagen, 1779 — A201

1980, Feb. 14 Engr. ***Perf. 13***
662 A201 1.30k brown red .50 .35

National Postal Service, 200th anniversary.

Symbols of Occupation, Health and Education A202

1980, May 5 Engr. ***Perf. 13***
663 A202 1.60k dark blue .65 .50

World Conference of the UN Decade for Women, Copenhagen, July 14-30.

Karen Blixen (1885-1962), Writer (Pen Name Isak Dinesen) — A203

Europa: 1.60k, August Krogh (1874-1949), physiologist.

1980, May 5
664 A203 1.30k red *.65* .25
665 A203 1.60k blue *1.40* *1.40*

Landscape Type of 1977

Northern Jutland: 80o, Viking ship burial grounds, Lindholm Hoje. 110o, Lighthouse, Skagen, vert. 200o, Boreglum Monastery. 280o, Fishing boats, Vorupor Beach.

1980, June 19 Engr. ***Perf. 13***
666 A183 80o multicolored .50 .50
667 A183 110o multicolored .50 .50
668 A183 200o multicolored .70 .30
669 A183 280o multicolored 2.00 2.00
Nos. 666-669 (4) 3.70 3.30

Nordic Cooperation Issue

Silver Tankard, by Borchardt Rollufse, 1641 — A204

1.80K, Bishop's bowl, Copenhagen faience, 18th cent.

1980, Sept. 9 Engr. ***Perf. 13***
670 A204 1.30k shown .50 .35
671 A204 1.80k multicolored 1.40 1.40

Frisian Sceat Facsimile, Obverse and Reverse, 9th Century A205

Coins: 1.40k Silver coin of Valdemar the Great and Absalom, 1157-1182, 1.80k, Gold 12-mark coin of Christian VII, 1781.

1980, Oct. 9 Engr. ***Perf. 13***
672 A205 1.30k red & redsh brn .50 .45
673 A205 1.40k ol gray & sl grn 1.60 1.40
674 A205 1.80k dk bl & sl bl 1.25 1.25
Nos. 672-674 (3) 3.35 3.10

Tonder Lace Pattern, North Schleswig — A206

Designs: Tonder lace patterns.

1980, Nov. 13 Engr. ***Perf. 13***
675 A206 1.10k brown .65 .65
676 A206 1.30k brown red .50 .30
677 A206 2k olive gray .70 .30
Nos. 675-677 (3) 1.85 1.25

Nyboder Development, Copenhagen, 350th Anniversary A207

Design: 1.30k, View of Nyboder, diff.

1981, Mar. 19
678 A207 1.30k dp org & ocher .90 .90
679 A207 1.60k dp org & ocher .55 .30

Tilting at a Barrel on Shrovetide A208

Design: 2k, Midsummer's Eve bonfire.

1981, May 4 Engr. ***Perf. 13***
680 A208 1.60k brown red *.40* .25
Complete booklet, 10 #680 *4.00*
681 A208 2k dk blue *1.25* *.75*

Soro Lake and Academy, Zealand — A209

Designs: Views of Zealand: 150o, Poet N.F.S. Grundtvig's home, Udby. 160o, Kaj Munk's home, Opager. 200o, Gronsund. 230o, Bornholm Island.

1981, June 18 Engr. ***Perf. 13***
682 A209 100o shown .50 .50
683 A209 150o multicolored .65 .65
684 A209 160o multicolored .65 .30
685 A209 200o multicolored .80 .80
686 A209 230o multicolored 1.10 .85
Nos. 682-686 (5) 3.70 3.10

European Urban Renaissance Year — A210

1981, Sept. 10 Engr. ***Perf. 12½x13***
687 A210 1.60k dull red .65 .35

Type of 1933

1981-85 Engr. ***Perf. 13***
688 A32 30o orange .60 .40
a. Bklt. pane 10 (2 #318, 2 #688, 6 #494)('84) 30.00
Complete booklet, #688a, 6 #708 30.00
689 A32 40o purple .50 .40
a. Bklt. pane of 10 (4 #318, 2 #689, 4 #494) ('89) 4.50
690 A32 80o ol bis ('85) 1.00 .80
691 A32 100o blue ('83) .85 .40
b. Bklt. pane of 8 (2 #494, 4 #691, 2 #706) ('83) 21.00
Complete booklet, #691b 21.00
692 A32 150o dk green ('82) .85 .40
693 A32 200o green ('83) 1.00 .90
694 A32 230o brt yel grn ('84) 1.50 .60
695 A32 250o brt yel grn ('85) 1.50 .60
Nos. 688-695 (8) 7.80 4.50

Ellehammer's 18-horsepower Biplane, 1906 — A211

1.30k, R-1 Fokker CV reconnaissance plane, 1926. 1.60k, Bellanca J-300, 1931. 2.30k, DC-7C, 1957.

1981, Oct. 8 Engr. ***Perf. 13***
696 A211 1k black & bluish green .65 .65
697 A211 1.30k brown & lt brown 1.10 1.10
698 A211 1.60k red & orange .65 .30
699 A211 2.30k dark blue & pale blue .90 .70
Nos. 696-699 (4) 3.30 2.75

Arms Type of 1946 and

Queen Margrethe II, 10th Anniv. of Accession — A212

1982-85 Engr. ***Perf. 13***
700 A212 1.60k dull red .65 .40
701 A212 1.60k dk ol grn 2.50 3.00
702 A212 1.80k sepia .85 .70
703 A212 2k dull red .90 .30
b. Bklt. pane, 4 #494, 2 ea #493, 702, 703 20.00
704 A212 2.20k ol grn ('83) 1.50 2.75
705 A212 2.30k violet 1.00 1.20
706 A212 2.50k org red ('83) .85 .30
707 A212 2.70k dk blue 1.20 .80
708 A212 2.70k cop red ('84) 1.25 .40
c. Booklet pane, 3 #688, 2 #494, 3 #708 ('84) 13.00
709 A212 2.80k cop red ('85) 1.00 .50
Complete booklet, #494a, 6 #709 13.50
b. Booklet pane, 3 #493, 2 #494, 3 #709 ('85) 6.75
Complete booklet, #709b 7.00
710 A212 3k violet ('83) 1.20 .50
711 A212 3.30k bluish blk ('84) 1.75 1.00
712 A212 3.50k blue ('83) 1.50 .65
713 A212 3.50k dk vio ('85) 1.50 .80
714 A212 3.70k dp blue ('84) 1.75 .80
715 A212 3.80k dk blue ('85) 1.40 .60
716 A55 4.30k dk ol grn ('84) 4.50 4.75
717 A55 5.50k dk bl grn ('84) 2.75 1.25
718 A55 16k cop red ('83) 6.00 .90
719 A55 17k cop red ('84) 7.75 1.25
720 A55 18k brn vio ('85) 8.50 1.25
720A A55 50k dk red ('85) 17.00 3.25
Nos. 700-720A (22) 67.30 27.35

See Nos. 796-803, 887, 889, 896, 899.

World Figure Skating Championships A213

1982, Feb. 25
721 A213 2k dark blue .80 .50

Revenue Schooner Argus — A214

1982, Feb. 25 Engr. ***Perf. 12½***
722 A214 1.60k carmine red .65 .35

Customs Service centenary

Europa — A215

2k, Abolition of adscription, 1788. 2.70k, Women's voting right, 1915.

1982, May 3 Engr. ***Perf. 12½***
723 A215 2k brown lake *.75* .25
Complete booklet, 10 #723 7.50
724 A215 2.70k deep blue *1.75* *1.00*

Butter Churn, Barn, Hjedding — A216

1982, June 10 Engr. ***Perf. 13***
725 A216 1.80k brown .80 .65

Cooperative dairy farming centenary.

Records Office, 400th Anniv. — A217

1982, June 10
726 A217 2.70k green 1.20 .50

Steen Steensen Blicher (1782-1848), Poet, by J.V. Gertner — A218

1982, Aug. 26 **Engr.** ***Perf. 13***
727 A218 2k brown red .35 .30

Robert Storm Petersen (1882-1949), Cartoonist — A219

Characters: 1.50k, Three little men and the number man. 2k, Peter and Ping the penguin, horiz.

1982, Sept. 23 **Engr.** ***Perf. 12½***
728 A219 1.50k dk bl & red .70 .50
729 A219 2k red & ol grn 1.10 .40

Printing in Denmark, 500th Anniv. — A220

1982, Sept. 23
730 A220 1.80k Press, text, ink balls .80 .85

A221

1982, Nov. 4
731 A221 2.70k Library seal 1.20 .50

500th anniv. of University Library.

World Communications Year — A222

1983, Jan. 27 **Engr.** ***Perf. 13***
732 A222 2k multicolored .80 .35

Amusement Park, 400th Anniv. — A223

1983, Feb. 24
733 A223 2k multicolored .80 .35

Badminton Championship A224

1983, Feb. 24
734 A224 2.70k multicolored 1.20 .50

Nordic Cooperation Issue — A225

1983, Mar. 24
735 A225 2.50k Egeskov Castle .90 .40
736 A225 3.50k Troll Church, North Jutland 1.40 .75

50th Anniv. of Steel Plate Printed Stamps — A226

1983, Mar. 24 **Engr.** ***Perf. 13***
737 A226 2.50k car rose 1.00 .35

Europa 1983 — A227

2.50k, Kildekovshallen Recreation Center, Copenhagen. 3.50k, Salling Sound Bridge.

1983, May 5 **Engr.** ***Perf. 13***
738 A227 2.50k multicolored *1.10* .25
739 A227 3.50k multicolored *2.00 1.00*

Weights and Measures Ordinance, 300th Anniv. — A228

1983, June 16
740 A228 2.50k red 1.00 .35

Christian V Danish Law, 300th Anniv. — A229

1983, Sept. 8 **Engr.**
741 A229 5k Codex titlepage 2.00 1.00

A230

1k, Car crash, police. 2.50k, Fire, ambulance service. 3.50k, Sea rescue.

1983, Oct. 6 **Engr.** ***Perf. 13***
742 A230 1k brown .50 .50
743 A230 2.50k red 1.00 .35
744 A230 3.50k blue 1.25 .85
Nos. 742-744 (3) 2.75 1.70

Life saving and salvage services.

Elderly in Society — A231

1983, Oct. 6
745 A231 2k Stages of life .80 .80
746 A231 2.50k Train passengers 1.00 .30

N.F.S. Grundtvig (1783-1872), Poet — A232

Street Scene, by C.W. Eckersberg (1783-1853) A233

1983, Nov. 3 **Engr.**
747 A232 2.50k brown red 1.20 .50
748 A233 2.50k brown red 1.00 .35

Tree Planting Campaign — A234

1984, Jan. 26 **Litho. & Engr.**
749 A234 2.70k Shovel, sapling 1.20 .35

A235

1984, Jan. 26 **Engr.**
750 A235 3.70k Game 1.75 .50

1984 Billiards World Championships, Copenhagen, May 10-13.

Hydrographic Dept. Bicentenary A236

Pilotage Service, 300th Anniv. — A237

1984, Mar. 22 **Engr.** ***Perf. 13***
751 A236 2.30k Compass 1.25 .90
752 A237 2.70k Boat 1.25 .50

2nd European Parliament Elections A238

Scouts Around Campfire, Emblems A239

Litho. & Engr.

1984, Apr. 12 ***Perf. 13***
753 A238 2.70k org & dk bl 1.75 .35
754 A239 2.70k multi 1.20 .35

Europa (1959-84) A240

1984, May 3 **Engr.** ***Perf. 12½***
755 A240 2.70k red *1.75* .25
756 A240 3.70k blue *2.25 1.60*

Prince Henrik, 50th Birthday A241

D Day, 40th Anniv. A242

1984, June 6 **Engr.**
757 A241 2.70k brown red 1.20 .35
758 A242 2.70k War Memorial, Copenhagen 1.20 .35

See Greenland No. 160.

17th Cent. Inn — A243

1984, June 6
759 A243 3k multicolored 1.50 1.40

Fishing and Shipping A244

1984, Sept. 6 **Engr.**
760 A244 2.30k Research (Herring) 1.60 1.75
761 A244 2.70k Sea transport 1.10 .60
762 A244 3.30k Deep-sea fishing 1.60 1.75
763 A244 3.70k Deep-sea, diff. 1.60 1.75
Nos. 760-763 (4) 5.90 5.85

A245

1984, Oct. 5 **Litho. & Engr.**
764 A245 1k Post bird .35 .35

A246

Holberg Meets with an Officer, by Wilhelm Marstrand (1810-73).

1984, Oct. 5
765 A246 2.70k multicolored 1.20 .35

Ludvig Holberg (1684-1754), writer.

Jewish Community in Copenhagen, 300th Anniv. — A247

3.70k, Woman blessing Sabbath candles.

1984, Oct. 5
766 A247 3.70k multicolored 1.75 1.40

Carnival in Rome, by Christoffer W. Eckersberg (1783-1853) — A248

Paintings: 10k, Ymer and Odhumble (Nordic mythology figures), by Nicolai A. Abildgaard (1743-1809), vert.

Perf. 12½x13, 13x12½

1984, Nov. 22 **Litho. & Engr.**

767 A248 5k multicolored 3.25 3.25
768 A248 10k multicolored 5.75 5.75

German and French Reform Church, 300th Anniv. — A249

1985, Jan. 24 **Engr.** ***Perf. 13***

769 A249 2.80k magenta 1.75 .35

Bonn-Copenhagen Declaration, 30th Anniv. — A250

1985, Feb. 21 **Litho.** ***Perf. 14***

770 A250 2.80k Map, flags 1.90 .65

Intl. Youth Year — A251

1985, Mar. 14 ***Perf. 13***

771 A251 3.80k multicolored 1.75 .90

Souvenir Sheet

HAFNIA '87 Philatelic Exhibition — A252

Early Postal Ordinances — 1k, Christian IV's Ordinance on Postmen, 1624. 2.50k, Plague Mandate, 1711. 2.80k, Ordinance on Prohibition of Mail by Means other than the Post, 1775. 3.80k, Act on Postal Articles, 1831.

1985, Mar. 14 **Litho. & Engr.**

772 Sheet of 4 5.50 *6.50*
a. A252 1k multi 1.25 *1.60*
b. A252 2.50k multi 1.25 *1.60*
c. A252 2.80k multi 1.25 *1.60*
d. A252 3.80k multi 1.25 *1.60*

Sold for 15k.

Europa 1985 — A253

1985, May 2

773 A253 2.80k Musical staff *1.50* *.50*
774 A253 3.80k Musical staff, diff. *1.90* *1.25*

Arrival of Queen Ingrid in Denmark, 50th Anniv. — A254

2.80k, Queen Mother, chrysanthemums.

1985, May 21

775 A254 2.80k multicolored 1.20 .35

See Greenland No. 163.

Opening of the Faro Bridges — A255

1985, May 21 **Litho.** ***Perf. 13***

776 A255 2.80k Faro-Falster Bridge 1.20 .35

St. Cnut's Land Grant to Lund Cathedral, 900th Anniv. — A256

Seal of King Cnut and: 2.80k, Lund Cathedral. 3k, City of Helsingdorg, Sweden.

1985, May 21 **Engr.**

777 A256 2.80k multi 1.10 .45
778 A256 3k multi 2.00 2.00

See Sweden Nos. 1538-1539.

UN Decade for Women — A257

1985, June 27 **Litho. & Engr.**

779 A257 3.80k Cyclist 1.75 1.00

Sports — A258

1985, June 27

780 A258 2.80k Women's floor exercise 1.25 .30
781 A258 3.80k Canoe & kayak 1.75 .95
782 A258 6k Cycling 2.90 1.75
Nos. 780-782 (3) 5.90 3.00

Kronborg Castle, Elsinore, 400th Anniv. — A259

1985, Sept. 5

783 A259 2.80k multi 1.75 .35

UN 40th Anniv. — A260

1985, Sept. 5

784 A260 3.80k Dove, emblem 1.75 1.20

Niels Bohr (1885-1962), Physicist — A261

1985, Oct. 3 ***Perf. 13x12½***

785 A261 2.80k With wife Margrethe 1.75 1.40

Winner of 1922 Nobel Prize in Physics for theory of atomic structure.

Hand Signing "D" — A262

1985, Nov. 7 **Engr.** ***Perf. 13***

786 A262 2.80k multicolored 1.40 .35

Danish Assoc. for the Deaf, 50th anniv.

Boat, by Helge Refn — A263

1985, Nov. 7 **Litho.**

787 A263 2.80k multicolored 1.40 .35

Abstract Iron Sculpture by Robert Jacobsen A264

Lithographed and Engraved

1985, Nov. 7 ***Perf. 13x12½***

788 A264 3.80k multicolored 3.50 3.75

Painting by Bjorn Wiinblad A265

1986, Jan. 23 **Litho.** ***Perf. 13x12½***

789 A265 2.80k multicolored 1.75 1.40

Amnesty Intl., 25th Anniv. A266

Lithographed and Engraved

1986, Jan. 23 ***Perf. 13***

790 A266 2.80k multicolored 1.20 .35

Miniature Sheet

HAFNIA '87 — A267

1986, Feb. 20

791 A267 Sheet of 4 7.50 11.00
a. 100o Holstein carriage, c. 1840 1.75 2.50
b. 250o Iceboat, c. 1880 1.75 2.50
c. 280o 1st mail van, 1908 1.75 2.50
d. 380o Airmail service 1919 1.75 2.50

Sold for 15k.

Changing of the Guard — A268

1986, Mar. 20 ***Perf. 13***

792 A268 2.80k multicolored 1.20 .35

Royal Danish Life Guards barracks and Rosenborg Drilling Ground, bicent.

Types of 1933-85

1986-90 **Engr.** ***Perf. 13***

793 A32 5o brn org ('89) .35 .40
794 A32 270o brt yel grn 1.90 1.75
b. Bklt. pane, 6 #318, 2 #691, 2 #794 18.00
795 A32 300o brt yel grn 1.75 .40
Complete booklet, #794b, 4 #795 22.50
796 A212 3k cop red 1.20 .60
Complete booklet, #691, #794, 3 #318, 2 #796 6.00
797 A212 3.20k deep vio 1.00 .80
798 A212 3.20k carmine 1.25 .40
c. Bklt. pane, 2 #693, 4 #798 9.00
Complete booklet, #689a, #798c 15.00
Complete booklet, #693, 2 #798, 2 #318, #689, 2 #494 15.50
799 A212 3.40k dk grn 2.25 3.00
800 A212 3.80k dark vio 1.20 2.90
801 A212 4.10k dark blue 1.40 .60
802 A212 4.20k dk pur 3.50 3.00
803 A212 4.40k dp bl 2.50 .60
804 A55 4.60k gray 5.00 5.50
805 A55 6.50k dp grn 2.50 1.00

806	A55	6.60k	green	5.00	5.50
807	A55	7.10k	brn vio	3.50	3.50
808	A55	7.30k	green	4.75	5.50
809	A55	7.70k	dk brn vio	4.50	2.10
810	A55	11k	brown	5.50	5.25
811	A55	20k	dp ultra	6.75	.80
812	A55	22k	henna brn	7.25	2.25
813	A55	23k	dark olive grn	10.50	2.25
814	A55	24k	dark olive grn	10.50	2.00
815	A55	26k	dark olive grn	12.50	2.25
		Nos. 793-815 (23)		96.55	52.35

Issued: 6.50k, 20k, 1/9/86; 22k, 1/3/87; 270o, 3k, No. 797, 3.80k, 4.10k, 4.60k, 6.60k, 7.10k, 24k, 1/7/88; No. 794b, 1/28/88; 300o, No. 798, 3.40k, 4.20k, 4.40k, 7.30k, 7.70k, 11k, 26k, 1/26/89; 5o, 1989; 23k, 1/11/90.

No. 793 issued for use in lieu of currency of the same face value.

Soro Academy, 400th Anniv. — A269

1986, Apr. 28 **Litho. & Engr.**
816 A269 2.80k multi 1.40 .50

Intl. Peace Year — A270

1986, Apr. 28
817 A270 3.80k multi 1.60 1.10

A271

1986, May 26 **Litho.**
818 A271 2.80k multi 1.75 .50

Crown Prince Frederik, 18th birthday.

Nordic Cooperation Issue 1986 — A272

Sister towns.

1986, May 27 **Engr.**
819 A272 2.80k Aalborg Harbor 1.40 .35
820 A272 3.80k Thisted Church and Town Hall 1.60 1.25

Hoje Tastrup Train Station Opening, May 31 — A273

1986, May 27 **Litho.**
821 A273 2.80k multi 1.20 .35

Mailbox, Telegraph Lines, Telephone — A274

1986, June 19 **Litho.** ***Perf. 13***
822 A274 2.80k multi 1.00 .35

19th European Intl. PTT Congress, Copenhagen, Aug. 12-16.

Natl. Bird Candidates — A275

Finalists: a, Corvus corax. b, Sturnus vulgaris. c, Cygnus olor (winner). d, Vanellus vanellus. e, Alauda arvensis.

1986, June 19 **Litho. & Engr.**
823 Strip of 5 10.50 24.00
a.-e. A275 2.80k any single 2.00 1.00
Complete booklet, 2 #823 21.00

A276

1986, June 19
824 A276 2.80k multi 1.20 .35

Danish Rifle, Gymnastics and Sports Club, 125th anniv.

Souvenir Sheet

HAFNIA '87 — A277

1986, Sept. 4
825 Sheet of 4 10.00 12.50
a. A277 100o Mailcoach, c. 1841 2.25 3.00
b. A277 250o Postmaster, c. 1840 2.25 3.00
c. A277 280o Postman, c. 1851 2.25 3.00
d. A277 380o Rural postman, c. 1893 2.25 3.00

Sold for 15k.

Europa 1986 — A278

1986, Sept. 4 **Engr.**
826 A278 2.80k Street sweeper *2.50* .25
827 A278 3.80k Garbage truck *3.50* *1.50*

Cupid — A279

1986, Oct. 9 **Litho.**
828 A279 3.80k multi 1.50 1.00

Premiere of The Whims of Cupid and the Ballet Master, by Vincenzo Galeotti, bicent.

Refugee — A280

1986, Oct. 9 **Litho. & Engr.**
829 A280 2.80k multi 1.20 .35

Danish Refugee Council Relief Campaign.

A281

Protestant Reformation in Denmark, 450th Anniv.: Sermon, altarpiece detail, 1561, Thorslunde Church, Copenhagen.

1986, Oct. 9 **Litho.** ***Perf. 13***
830 A281 6.50k multi 2.50 1.75

A282

1986, Nov. 6 **Litho. & Engr.**
831 A282 3.80k multi 3.00 3.00

Organization for Economic Cooperation and Development, 25th anniv.

Abstract by Lin Utzon — A283

1987, Jan. 22 **Litho.** ***Perf. 13***
832 A283 2.80k multi 1.00 .35
Complete booklet, 10 #832 11.00

Art appreciation.

A284

1987, Feb. 26 **Engr.** ***Perf. 13***
833 A284 2.80k lake & black 1.00 .35

Danish Consumer Council, 40th anniv.

A285

Religious art (details) from Ribe Cathedral.

1987, Apr. 9 **Litho.** ***Perf. 13***
834 A285 3k Fresco 1.40 .60
835 A285 3.80k Stained-glass window 2.10 2.10
Complete booklet, 10 #835 21.00
836 A285 6.50k Mosaic 3.50 3.50
Nos. 834-836 (3) 7.00 6.20

Ribe Cathedral redecoration, 1982-1987, by Carl-Henning Pedersen.

A286

Europa (Modern architecture): 2.80k, Central Library, Gentofte, 1985. 3.80k, Hoje Tastrup High School, 1985, horiz.

1987, May 4 **Engr.** ***Perf. 13***
837 A286 2.80k rose claret *2.50* *.35*
838 A286 3.80k bright ultra *3.50* *2.25*

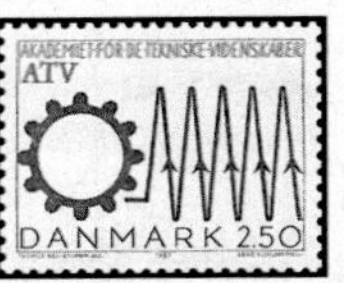

A287

1987, May 4
839 A287 2.50k dk red & bl blk 2.00 2.00

Danish Academy of Technical Sciences (ATV), 50th anniv.

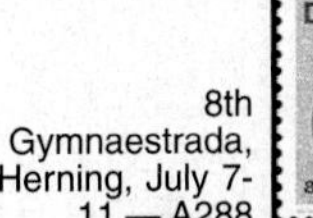

8th Gymnaestrada, Herning, July 7-11 — A288

1987, June 18 **Litho. & Engr.**
840 A288 2.80k multi 1.00 .35
Complete booklet, 10 #840 10.00

A289

1987, June 18
841 A289 3.80k multi 1.60 1.40

Danish Cooperative Bacon Factories, cent.

A290

1987, Aug. 27 **Litho.**
842 A290 3.80k Single-sculler 1.60 1.20

World Rowing Championships, Aug. 23-30.

HAFNIA '87, Bella Center, Copenhagen, Oct. 16-25 — A291

No. 843, Type A15, mail train c. 1912.

Litho. & Engr.

1987, Aug. 27 ***Perf. 13x12½***
843 A291 280o multi 1.90 1.50

Souvenir Sheet

843A A291 280o like No. 843 20.00 26.00

Purchase of No. 843A included admission to the exhibition. Sold for 45k.

Due to a color shift, some examples of No. 843A have a green lawn and locomotive.

Abstact by Ejler Bille — A292

1987, Sept. 24 **Litho.** ***Perf. 13***

844 A292 2.80k multi 1.00 .35
Complete booklet, 10 #844 10.00

Rasmus Rask (1787-1832), Linguist — A293

1987, Oct. 15 **Engr.** ***Perf. 13x12½***

845 A293 2.80k dk hen brn 1.00 .45

A294

Emblem: Miraculous Catch (Luke 5:4-7), New Testament.

1987, Oct. 15 ***Perf. 13***

846 A294 3k carmine lake 1.25 .50

Clerical Assoc. for the Home Mission in Denmark, 125th anniv.

A295

Designs: 3k, Two lions from the gate of Rosenburg Castle around the monogram of Christian IV. 4.10k, Portrait of the monarch painted by P. Isaacsz, vert.

Photo. & Engr., Litho. (4.10k)

1988, Feb. 18 ***Perf. 13***

847 A295 3k blue gray & gold 1.25 .30
Complete booklet, 10 #847 12.50
848 A295 4.10k multi 1.60 .75

Accession of Christian IV (1577-1648), King of Denmark and Norway (1588-1648), 400th anniv.

Ole Worm (1588-1654), Archaeologist, and Runic Artifacts — A296

1988, Feb. 18 **Engr.**

849 A296 7.10k chocolate 2.75 2.75

Odense, 1000th Anniv. — A297

Design: St. Cnut's Church and statue of Hans Christian Andersen, Odense.

1988, Mar. 10 **Engr.**

850 A297 3k multi 1.00 .35
Complete booklet, 10 #850 10.00

A298

1988, Apr. 7 **Litho.**

851 A298 2.70k multi 1.25 1.25

Danish Civil Defense and Emergency Planning Agency, 50th Anniv.

WHO, 40th Anniv. — A299

1988, Apr. 7 **Litho. & Engr.**

852 A299 4.10k multi 1.75 1.00

Abolition of *Stavnsbaand,* 200th Anniv. — A300

Painting: King Christian VII riding past the Liberty Memorial, Copenhagen, by C.W. Eckersberg (1783-1853).

1988, May 5 **Litho.**

853 A300 3.20k multi 1.40 1.00

Stavnsbaand (adscription) provided that all Danish farmers' sons from age 4 to 40 would be bound as villeins to the estates on which they were born, thus providing landowners with free labor.

A301

Europa: Transport and communication — 3k, Postwoman on bicycle. 4.10k, Mobile telephone.

1988, May 5

854 A301 3k multicolored *1.75* .25
855 A301 4.10k multicolored *2.50* *1.00*

A302

1988, June 16 **Litho.**

856 A302 4.10k multi 1.60 .75

1988 Individual Speedway World Motorcycle Championships, Denmark, Sept. 3.

Federation of Danish Industries, 150th Anniv. — A303

Painting (detail): *The Industrialists,* by P.S. Kroyer.

1988, June 16 ***Perf. 13½x13***

857 A303 3k multi 1.00 .50

Danish Metalworkers' Union, Cent. — A304

3k, Glass mosaic by Niels Winkel.

1988, Aug. 18 **Litho.** ***Perf. 13***

858 A304 3k multicolored 1.00 .50

Tonder Teachers' Training College, 200th Anniv. — A305

1988, Aug. 18 **Engr.** ***Perf. 13x12½***

859 A305 3k lake 1.00 .50

Homage to Leon Degand, Sculpture by Robert Jacobsen A306

1988, Sept. 22 ***Perf. 11½x13***

860 A306 4.10k blk, lake & gray 3.75 *5.00*

Danish-French cultural exchange program, 10th anniv. See France No. 2130.

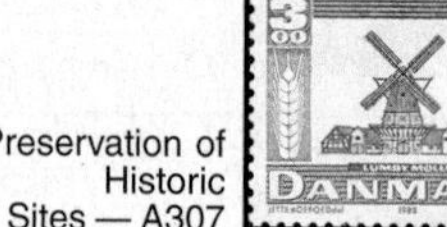

Preservation of Historic Sites — A307

3k, Lumby Windmill, 1818. 7.10k, Vejstrup Water Mill, 1837.

1988, Oct. 13 **Engr.** ***Perf. 13x12½***

861 A307 3k red & org 1.60 .50
Complete booklet, 10 #861 16.00
862 A307 7.10k dp blue & bluish grn 4.00 2.75

Paintings in the State Museum of Art, Copenhagen — A308

4.10k, *Bathing Boys,* 1902, by Peter Hansen (1868-1928). 10k, *The Hill at Overkaerby,* 1917, by Fritz Syberg (1862-1939).

Litho. & Engr.

1988, Nov. 3 ***Perf. 13***

863 A308 4.10k multi 3.25 *4.50*
864 A308 10k multi 6.50 *8.00*

See Nos. 881-882, 951-952, 972-973, 1018-1019.

The Little Mermaid, Sculpture by Edvard Eriksen — A309

1989, Feb. 16 **Engr.**

865 A309 3.20k dark green 1.75 .50
Complete booklet, 10 #865 17.50

Tourism industry, cent.

Danish Soccer Assoc., Cent. — A310

1989, Mar. 16 **Litho.**

866 A310 3.20k multi 1.60 .50
Complete booklet, 10 #866 16.00

NATO Membership, 40th Anniv. — A311

1989, Mar. 16

867 A311 4.40k dk blue, gold & lt blue 2.00 1.25

Nordic Cooperation Issue — A312

Folk costumes.

1989, Apr. 20 **Litho. & Engr.**

868 A312 3.20k Woman from Valby 1.40 .40
869 A312 4.40k Pork butcher 2.10 1.60

European Parliament 3rd Elections A313

1989, May 11 **Litho.**

870 A313 3k blue & yellow 1.60 1.50

Europa 1989 — A314

Children's toys.

1989, May 11 **Litho. & Engr.**

871 A314 3.20k Lego blocks *1.90* .25
872 A314 4.40k Wooden soldiers, by Kay Bojesen *3.00* *.90*

Agricultural Museum, Cent. A315

1989, June 15 **Engr.** ***Perf. 13***

873 A315 3.20k Tractor, 1889 1.25 .50

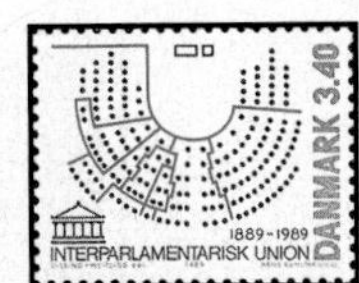

Interparliamentary Union, Cent. — A316

1989, June 15 **Litho. & Engr.**
874 A316 3.40k Folketing Chamber layout 3.50 4.00

Danish Fishery and Marine Research Institute, Cent. A317

1989, Aug. 24 **Litho. & Engr.**
875 A317 3.20k multi 1.25 .50

Bernhard Severin Ingemann (1789-1862), Poet and Novelist — A318

1989, Aug. 24 **Engr.**
876 A318 7.70k dark green 3.00 1.90

A319

Danish Film Office, 50th Anniv.: 3k, Scene from the short feature film *They Reached the Ferry*, 1948. 3.20k, Bodil Ipsen (d. 1964), actress. 4.40k, Carl Th. Dreyer (1889-1968), screenwriter and director.

1989, Sept. 28 **Litho.**
877 A319 3k multi 1.40 1.40
878 A319 3.20k multi 1.25 .50
879 A319 4.40k multi 1.75 1.00
Nos. 877-879 (3) 4.40 2.90

Stamp Day, 50th Anniv. — A320

1989, Nov. 10 **Litho. & Engr.**
880 A320 3.20k multi 1.25 .50

Art Type of 1988

Paintings: 4.40k, *Part of the Northern Gate of the Citadel Bridge*, c. 1837, by Christen Kobke (1810-1848). 10k, *A Little Girl, Elise Kobke, With a Cup in Front of Her*, c. 1850, by Constantin Hansen (1804-1880).

1989, Nov. 10 ***Perf. 12½x13***
881 A308 4.40k multi 3.00 4.00
882 A308 10k multi 6.25 8.50

Types of 1933-82 and

A321

A321a

Queen Margrethe II

1990-98 **Engr.** ***Perf. 12¾***
883 A32 25o bluish black .55 .40
a. Bklt. pane, 4 #691, 2 #883 4.75
884 A32 125o carmine lake .95 .40
885 A32 325o lt yel grn 2.10 1.75
886 A32 350o yellow green 2.00 .95
887 A212 3.50k dark red 1.25 .40
a. Bklt. pane, 2 each #691, 885, 887 8.00
Complete booklet, #883, #885, #887, 3 #691 16.00
Complete booklet, #883a, #887a 13.50
888 A321 3.50k henna brown 1.40 .40
b. Bklt. pane, 4 each #883, #884, #888 ('91) 20.00
Complete booklet, #888b 20.00
Complete booklet, 2 each #883, #884, #888 16.00
889 A212 3.75k dark green 2.25 2.40
890 A321 3.75k green 4.00 3.75
891 A321 3.75k red 3.00 .40
a. Bklt. pane, 4 each #884, #891 17.50
Complete booklet, #891a 17.50
b. Booklet pane, 2 each #691, 883, 891 8.75
Complete booklet, #891b 8.75
892 A321a 3.75k red 2.25 .50
a. Booklet pane, 2 each #691, 883, 892 14.50
Complete booklet, #892a 14.50
b. Booklet pane, 2 #883, 4 #494, 2 #892 12.00
Complete booklet, #892b 12.00
893 A321 4k brown 2.50 1.20
894 A321a 4k deep bl grn 2.25 .80
895 A321a 4.25k olive brown 2.90 1.90
896 A212 4.50k brown violet 2.75 3.25
897 A321 4.50k violet 2.50 2.40
898 A321a 4.50k deep bl blk 2.60 2.40
899 A212 4.75k dark blue 1.90 .40
900 A321 4.75k blue 2.50 .40
901 A321 4.75k violet 3.50 2.00
902 A321a 4.75k brown *3.50* 2.10
903 A321a 5k violet 2.50 1.75
904 A321 5k blue 3.50 .40
905 A321 5.25k black 3.50 1.75
906 A321a 5.25k deep blue 3.25 .80
907 A321 5.50k green 3.25 3.75
908 A321a 5.50k henna brown 3.50 2.75
909 A55 7.50k dark bl grn 3.00 2.75
Nos. 883-909 (27) 69.15 42.15

Queen Margrethe II's 50th birthday (No. 888).

Issued: No. 888, 4/5; Nos. 890, 897, 900, 1990; No. 888a, 2/14/91; Nos. 886, 891, 891a, 901, 904, 6/10/92; 5.50k, 1/13/94; 4k, 5.25k, 6/27/96; Nos. 892, 892a, 1/14/97; Nos. 894, 902, 903, 906, 8/28/97; Nos. 895, 898, 908, 909, 3/26/98; others, 1/11/90.

See Nos. 1114, 1125, 1130.

Museum of Decorative Art, Cent. — A322

Design: Silver coffee pot designed by Axel Johannes Kroyer, Copenhagen, 1726.

1990, Feb. 15 **Engr.** ***Perf. 13***
911 A322 3.50k dark blue & blk 1.20 .80
Complete booklet, 10 #911 12.00

A323

Steam engine, 200th anniv.: Steam engine built by Andrew Mitchell, 1790.

1990, Feb. 15
912 A323 8.25k dull red brown 2.75 1.75

Nyholm, 300th Anniv. A324

1990, Apr. 5 **Engr.**
913 A324 4.75k black 1.75 .90

Europa 1990 — A325

3.50k, Royal Monogram, Haderslev P.O. 4.75k, Odense P.O.

1990, Apr. 5 **Litho.**
914 A325 3.50k multi *1.10* .25
915 A325 4.75k multi *1.75* .60

A326

Pieces from the Flora Danica Banquet Service produced for King Christian VII: No. 916, Bell-shaped lid, dish. No. 917, Gravy boat, dish. No. 918, Ice pot, casserole, lid. No. 919, Serving dish.

1990, May 3 **Litho.**
916 A326 3.50k multicolored 1.25 1.90
917 A326 3.50k multicolored 1.25 1.90
918 A326 3.50k multicolored 1.25 1.90
919 A326 3.50k multicolored 1.25 1.90
a. Strip of 4, #916-919 5.00 8.50

Flora Danica porcelain, 200th anniv.

A327

Endangered plant species.

1990, June 14
920 A327 3.25k Marshmallow 1.25 1.25
921 A327 3.50k Red helleborine 2.25 .35
Complete booklet, 10 #921 30.00
922 A327 3.75k Purple orchis 1.50 1.50
923 A327 4.75k Lady's slipper 1.90 .65
Nos. 920-923 (4) 6.90 3.75

Village Churches, Jutland — A328

Perf. 13x12½, 12½x13
1990, Aug. 30 **Engr.**
924 A328 3.50k Gjellerup 1.20 .35
Complete booklet, 10 #924 12.00
925 A328 4.75k Veng 1.60 .75
926 A328 8.25k Bredsten, vert. 3.00 2.00
Nos. 924-926 (3) 5.80 3.10

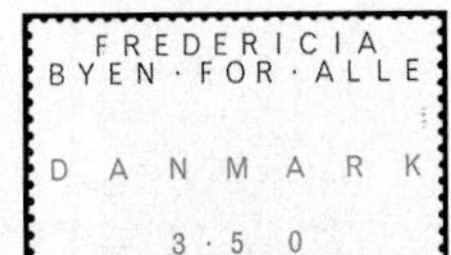

Fredericia, "The Town for Everybody" A329

Engr. & Embossed
1990, Oct. 5 ***Perf. 13***
927 A329 3.50k black & red 1.20 .90

Tordenskiold (Peter Wessel, 1690-1720), Admiral — A330

1990, Oct. 5 **Litho.** ***Perf. 13½x13***
928 A330 3.50k multicolored 1.20 .60
Complete booklet, 10 #928 12.00

Prevent Bicycle Thefts — A331

Design: 3.50k, Stop drunk driving.

1990, Nov. 8 **Litho.** ***Perf. 13x12½***
930 A331 3.25k shown 1.10 1.10
931 A331 3.50k Automobile, wine glass 1.10 .30

Locomotives — A332

1991, Mar. 14 **Engr.** ***Perf. 13***
932 A332 3.25k IC3 1990 1.40 1.50
933 A332 3.50k Class A 1882 1.10 .35
Complete booklet, 10 #933 11.00
934 A332 3.75k Class MY 1954 1.25 1.75
935 A332 4.75k Class P 1907 1.50 1.50
Nos. 932-935 (4) 5.25 5.10

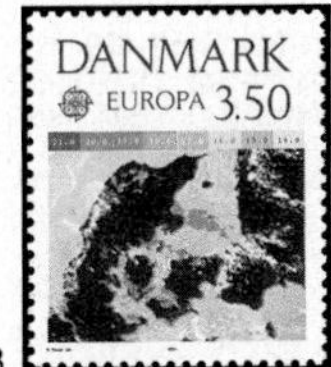

Europa — A333

Satellite photographs showing temperatures of Danish: 3.50k, Waters. 4.75k, Land.

1991, May 2 **Litho.** ***Perf. 13***
936 A333 3.50k multicolored *1.75* .25
937 A333 4.75k multicolored *2.10* 1.00

Jutland Law, 750th Anniv. — A334

1991, May 2
938 A334 8.25k multicolored 3.00 2.75

Danish Islands — A335

1991, June 6
939 A335 3.50k Fano 1.40 .30
Complete booklet, 10 #939 18.00
940 A335 4.75k Christianso 1.60 .90

Decorative Art — A336

Designs: 3.25k, Earthenware bowl and jars by Christian Poulsen. 3.50k, Chair by Hans Wegner, vert. 4.75k, Silver cutlery by Kay Bojesen, vert. 8k, Lamp by Poul Henningsen.

1991, Aug. 22 **Litho.** ***Perf. 13***
941 A336 3.25k multicolored 1.10 1.50
942 A336 3.50k multicolored 1.00 .35
Complete booklet, 10 #942 10.00
943 A336 4.75k multicolored 1.25 1.75
944 A336 8.25k multicolored 3.00 4.50
Nos. 941-944 (4) 6.35 8.10

Keep Denmark Clean — A337

Designs: 3.50k, Cleaning up after dog. 4.75k, Picking up litter.

1991, Sept. 19 **Engr.** ***Perf. 13***

945 A337 3.50k red 2.00 .30
Complete booklet, 10 #945 20.00
946 A337 4.75k blue 2.00 1.00

Posters from Danish Museum of Decorative Arts — A338

Posters for: 3.50k, Nordic Advertising Congress, by Arne Ungermann (1902-1981). 4.50k, Poster Exhibition at Copenhagen Zoo (baboon), by Valdemar Andersen (1875-1928). 4.75k, Danish Air Lines, by Ib Andersen (1907-1969). 12k, The Sinner, by Sven Brasch (1886-1970).

1991, Sept. 19 **Litho.**

947 A338 3.50k multicolored 1.00 .30
948 A338 4.50k multicolored 1.75 2.50
949 A338 4.75k multicolored 1.25 1.50
950 A338 12k multicolored 4.00 3.50
Nos. 947-950 (4) 8.00 7.80

Art Type of 1988

Designs: 4.75k, Lady at her Toilet by Harald Giersing (1881-1927), vert. 14k, Road through a Wood by Edvard Weie (1879-1943), vert.

Litho. & Engr.

1991, Nov. 7 ***Perf. 13x12½***

951 A308 4.75k multicolored 1.75 1.75
952 A308 14k multicolored 4.50 4.00

A339

Treasures of Natl. Museum: 3.50k, Earthenware bowl, Skarpsalling. 4.50k, Bronze dancer, Grevensvaenge. 4.75k, Bottom plate of silver cauldron, Gundestrup. 8.25k, Flint knife, Hindsgavl.

1992, Feb. 13 **Engr.** ***Perf. 13***

953 A339 3.50k dk vio & brown 1.10 .30
Complete booklet, 10 #953 11.00
954 A339 4.50k dk bl & dk ol green 2.40 2.40
955 A339 4.75k brown & black 1.25 1.10
956 A339 8.25k dk ol grn & vio brown 2.75 2.75
Nos. 953-956 (4) 7.50 6.55

A340

1992, Mar. 12 ***Perf. 13½x13***

957 A340 3.50k rose carmine 1.25 .65

Danish Society of Chemical, Civil, Electrical, and Mechanical Engineers, cent.

Souvenir Sheet

Queen Margaret I (1353-1412) — A341

Litho. & Engr.

1992, Mar. 12 ***Perf. 12½***

958 A341 Sheet of 2 6.25 7.25
a. 3.50k Fresco 3.00 3.50
b. 4.75k Alabaster bust 3.00 3.50

Nordia '94, Scandinavian Philatelic Exhibition. No. 958 sold for 12k to benefit the exhibition.

Discovery of America, 500th Anniv. — A342

1992, May 7 **Engr.** ***Perf. 12½***

959 A342 3.50k Potato plant *2.25 .40*
Complete booklet, 10 #959 *22.50*
960 A342 4.75k Ear of corn *4.25 1.75*

Europa.

Protect the Environment — A343

3.75k, Hare beside road. 5k, Fish, water pollution. 8.75k, Cut trees, vert.

Litho. & Engr.

1992, June 10 ***Perf. 13***

961 A343 3.75k multi 1.25 .30
Complete booklet, 10 #961 12.50
962 A343 5k multi 1.75 .70
963 A343 8.75k multi 3.50 2.00
Nos. 961-963 (3) 6.50 3.00

Queen Margrethe II and Prince Henrik, 25th Wedding Anniv. — A344

1992, June 10 **Litho.** ***Perf. 12½x13***

964 A344 3.75k multicolored .90 1.60

See Greenland No. 253.

A345

1992, July 16 ***Perf. 13***

965 A345 3.75k multicolored 1.75 .75

Denmark, European soccer champions.

Danish Pavilion, Expo '92, Seville — A346

1992, Aug. 27 **Engr.** ***Perf. 13***

966 A346 3.75k blue 1.50 .75

Single European Market — A347

1992, Oct. 8 **Litho. & Engr.** ***Perf. 13***

967 A347 3.75k blue & org 1.50 .75

A348

Cartoon characters: 3.50k, A Hug, by Ivar Gjorup. 3.75k, Love Letter, by Phillip Stein Jonsson. 4.75k, Domestic Triangle, by Nikoline Werdelin. 5k, Poet and His Little Wife, by Jorgen Mogensen.

Litho. & Engr.

1992, Oct. 8 ***Perf. 12½***

968 A348 3.50k multicolored 1.75 1.00

Engr.

969 A348 3.75k red & purple 1.40 .30
970 A348 4.75k blk & red brn 2.50 2.50
971 A348 5k blue & red brn 1.75 .70
Nos. 968-971 (4) 7.40 4.50

Art Type of 1988

5k, Landscape from Vejby, 1843, by John Thomas Lundbye. 10k, Motif from Halleby Brook, 1847, by Peter Christian Skovgaard.

Litho. & Engr.

1992, Nov. 12 ***Perf. 12½x13***

972 A308 5k multicolored 2.10 2.00
973 A308 10k multicolored 4.00 3.25

Publication of New Danish Bible — A349

3.75k, Jacob's fight with angel.

1992, Nov. 12 ***Perf. 13***

974 A349 3.75k multi 1.75 1.20

A350

Archaeological Treasures. Anthropomorphic gold foil figures found in: 3.75k, Lundeborg, horiz. 5k, Bornholm.

Litho. & Engr.

1993, Feb. 4 ***Perf. 13***

975 A350 3.75k multicolored 1.40 .30
976 A350 5k multicolored 1.90 .70

Butterflies — A351

3.75k, Small tortoiseshell. 5k, Large blue. 8.75k, Marsh fritillary. 12k, Red admiral.

1993, Mar. 11 **Litho.**

977 A351 3.75k multi 1.75 .40
Complete booklet, 10 #977 17.50
978 A351 5k multi 2.50 .80
979 A351 8.75k multi 5.25 3.50
980 A351 12k multi 5.25 3.50
Nos. 977-980 (4) 14.75 8.20

Tivoli Gardens, 150th Anniv. — A352

Posters: 3.75k, Pierrot, by Thor Bogelund, 1947, horiz. 5k, Balloons, by Wilhelm Freddie, 1987.

1993, May 6 **Litho.** ***Perf. 12½***

981 A352 3.75k multicolored 1.75 1.00
Complete booklet, 10 #981 17.50
982 A352 5k multicolored 1.75 .90

A353

Europa (Contemporary paintings by): 3.75k, Troels Worsel, horiz. 5k, Stig Brogger.

1993, May 6 ***Perf. 13***

983 A353 3.75k multicolored *1.40 1.10*
984 A353 5k multicolored *1.90 .90*

A354

1993, June 17 **Engr.** ***Perf. 13***

985 A354 5k dark blue green 4.00 1.00

Danish-Russian relations, 500th anniv. See Russia No. 6154.

Training Ships
A355 A356

Perf. 13, 13½x13 (#987)

1993, June 17 Litho. & Engr.

986 A355 3.75k Danmark 2.00 .30

987 A356 4.75k Jens Krogh 4.00 4.50

988 A355 5k Georg Stage, horiz. 3.00 1.75

Size: 39x28mm

Perf. 13x13½

989 A356 9.50k Marilyn Anne, horiz. 5.50 5.25

Nos. 986-989 (4) 14.50 11.80

Child's Drawing of Viking Ships — A357

Letter Writing Campaign — A358

1993, Aug. 19 Litho. *Perf. 13*

990 A357 3.75k multicolored 2.25 .65

991 A358 5k lt & dk bl & blk 2.50 1.40

Ethnic Jewelry — A359

1993, Sept. 16 Litho. *Perf. 13*

992 A359 3.50k Falster 1.75 1.25

993 A359 3.75k Amager 1.75 .30

Complete booklet, 10 #993 17.50

994 A359 5k Laeso 2.00 .90

995 A359 8.75k Romo 4.50 3.00

Nos. 992-995 (4) 10.00 5.45

Cubist Paintings A360

5k, Assemblage, by Vilhelm Lundstrom, 1929. 15k, Composition, by Franciska Clausen, 1929.

Litho. & Engr.

1993, Nov. 11 *Perf. 12½*

996 A360 5k multicolored 2.75 2.25

997 A360 15k multicolored 6.75 5.00

See Nos. 1033-1034, 1080-1081.

Conservation — A361

1994, Jan. 27 Litho. *Perf. 13*

998 A361 3.75k Save water *3.50 .30*

999 A361 5k CO2 *4.50 1.10*

Castles A362

Castles: 3.50k, Marselisborg, Aarhus. 3.75k, Amalienborg, Copenhagen. 5k, Fredensborg, North Zealand. 8.75k, Graasten, South Jutland.

Litho. & Engr.

1994, Mar. 17 *Perf. 13x12½*

1000 A362 3.50k multicolored 1.50 .70

1001 A362 3.75k multicolored 1.75 .30

Complete booklet, 10 #1001 17.50

1002 A362 5k multicolored 2.25 .30

1003 A362 8.75k multicolored 3.75 3.50

a. Bklt. pane, #1000-1003 30.00 30.00

No. 1003a printed with 2 different labels. One shows a marching band, the other shows a ship.

Danmark Expedition, 1906-08 — A363

Europa: 3.75k, Expedition ship, Danmark, Alfred Wegener's weather balloon. 5k, Theodolite, Johan Peter Koch, cartographer.

1994, May 5 Engr. *Perf. 13*

1004 A363 3.75k deep brn vio *1.90 .25*

1005 A363 5k dp slate grn *2.60 1.25*

Complete booklet, 10 #1005 *35.00*

Trams — A364

Designs: 3.75k, Copenhagen tram (Engelhardt). 4.75k, Aarhus car. 5k, Odense tram, vert. 12k, Horse-drawn tram.

Litho. & Engr.

1994, June 9 *Perf. 13*

1006 A364 3.75k multicolored 1.25 .30

1007 A364 4.75k multicolored 2.25 2.75

1008 A364 5k multicolored 1.75 1.40

Size: 38x21mm

1009 A364 12k multicolored 5.25 5.25

Nos. 1006-1009 (4) 10.50 9.70

Children's Stamp Competition — A365

1994, Aug. 25 Litho. *Perf. 12½*

1010 A365 3.75k multicolored 1.50 .70

ILO, 75th Anniv. — A366

1994, Aug. 25 *Perf. 13*

1011 A366 5k multicolored 2.00 1.00

Wild Animals — A367

Litho. & Engr.

1994, Oct. 20 *Perf. 12½*

1012 A367 3.75k House sparrows 2.00 .35

1013 A367 4.75k Badger 3.00 2.25

1014 A367 5k Squirrel, vert. 2.60 1.00

1015 A367 9.50k Black grouse 5.00 4.50

Size: 36x26mm

Perf. 13

1016 A367 12k Grass snake 6.00 5.25

Nos. 1012-1016 (5) 18.60 13.35

A368

1994, Nov. 10 Litho. *Perf. 13*

1017 A368 3.75k multicolored 1.75 .70

Folk High Schools, 150th anniv.

Painting Type of 1988

Designs: 5k, Study of Italian Woman and Sleeping Child, by Wilhelm Marstrand. 15k, Interior from Amaliegade with the Artist's Brothers, by Wilhelm Bendz.

Litho. & Engr.

1994, Nov. 10 *Perf. 12½x13*

1018 A308 5k multicolored 2.00 1.40

1019 A308 15k multicolored 6.00 3.25

Aarhus Cathedral School, 800th Anniv. — A369

Litho. & Engr.

1995, Jan. 26 *Perf. 13*

1020 A369 3.75k multicolored 1.75 .70

UN, 50th Anniv. — A370

Litho. & Engr.

1995, Jan. 26 *Perf. 13*

1021 A370 5k multicolored 2.50 1.20

Complete booklet, 10 #1021 35.00

Danish Islands A371

1995, Mar. 16 Engr. *Perf. 13*

1022 A371 3.75k Avernako 2.25 .30

Complete booklet, 10 #1022 22.50

1023 A371 4.75k Fejo 2.75 2.50

1024 A371 5k Fur 3.50 .90

1025 A371 9.50k Endelave 4.50 4.50

a. Booklet pane, #1022-1025 + 2 labels 15.00

Complete booklet, 2 #1025a 32.50

Nos. 1022-1025 (4) 13.00 8.20

No. 1025a printed with four different large labels. Labels with one pane are MF Faaborg II and MF Endelave. The other pane has MF Bukken-bruse and MF Fursund.

Liberation of Denmark, 50th Anniv. A372

Designs: 3.75k, Gen. Montgomery, Town Hall Square, vert. 5k, White busses returning from concentration camps. 8.75k, Airplane dropping supplies to resistance. 12k, Jews escape across the Sound to Sweden.

1995, May 4 Litho. *Perf. 13*

1026 A372 3.75k multicolored 2.10 .30

Complete booklet, 10 #1026 21.00

1027 A372 5k multicolored 2.75 1.00

1028 A372 8.75k multicolored 4.25 4.00

1029 A372 12k multicolored 6.00 6.00

Nos. 1026-1029 (4) 15.10 11.30

Europa (Nos. 1026-1027).

A373

1995, June 8 Litho. *Perf. 13*

1030 A373 3.50k multicolored 1.50 .70

Danish Rhymed Chronicle, 500th anniv.

A374

3.75k, Roskilde Festival. 5k, Tonder Festival.

1995, June 8

1031 A374 3.75k multi, horiz. 1.60 .30

Complete booklet, 10 #1031 16.00

1032 A374 5k multi 2.25 1.00

No. 1031 is 28x21mm.

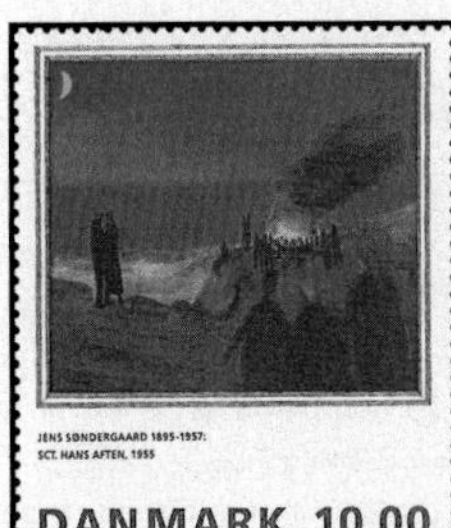

Paintings A375

Designs: 10k, "Sct. Hans Aften, 1955," by Jens Sondergaard. 15k, "Landskab-Gudhjem, 1939," by Niels Lergaard.

Litho. & Engr.

1995, Aug. 24 *Perf. 13x12½*

1033 A375 10k multicolored 5.00 5.75

1034 A375 15k multicolored 7.50 7.50

Tycho Brahe (1546-1601), Astronomer A376

3.75k, Uranienborg Observatory. 5.50k, Sextant.

Litho. & Engr.

1995, Oct. 27 *Perf. 13*

1035 A376 3.75k multicolored 2.00 .65

1036 A376 5.50k multicolored 2.75 2.75

See Sweden Nos. 2149-2150.

Toys A377

Designs: 3.75k, Tekno cars. 5k, Dolls, teddy bear. 8.75k, Model trains. 12k, Glud & Marstrand tin horse-drawn carriage & fire pumper.

1995, Nov. 9 *Perf. 13x12½*

1037	A377 3.75k multicolored		1.60	.30
	Complete booklet, 10 #1037		16.00	
1038	A377 5k multicolored		2.10	1.00
1039	A377 8.75k multicolored		3.25	3.25
1040	A377 12k multicolored		4.25	4.25
	Nos. 1037-1040 (4)		11.20	8.80

A378

Cartoonlike views of Copenhagen: 3.75k, Round Tower as music box. 5k, Christiansborg Castle. 8.75k, Marble Church as top of balloon. 12k, The Little Mermaid statue on stage.

1996, Jan. 25 **Litho.** *Perf. 13*

1041	A378 3.75k multicolored	1.25	.30
	Complete booklet, 10 #1041	13.00	
1042	A378 5k multicolored	1.75	.70
1043	A378 8.75k multicolored	3.00	3.00
1044	A378 12k multicolored	4.00	4.50
	Nos. 1041-1044 (4)	10.00	8.50

Copenhagen, 1996 cultural capital of Europe.

A379

1996, Mar. 21 **Litho.** *Perf. 13*

1045	A379 3.75k Sports for disabled	1.25	.30
	Complete booklet, 10 #1045	13.00	
1046	A379 4.75k Swimming	1.60	1.60
1047	A379 5k Sailing	1.75	.50
1048	A379 9.50k Cycling	3.25	3.25
a.	Bklt. pane of 4, #1045-1048 + 2 labels	14.00	
	Complete booklet, 2 #1048a	28.00	

No. 1048a printed with two different large labels. One shows hands and soccer ball, second shows tennis racket and tennis balls.

Danish Federation for Sports for the Disabled (No. 1045). Modern Olympic Games, cent., Sports Confederation of Denmark, cent., 1996 Summer Olympics, Atlanta (Nos. 1046-1048).

A380

1996, May 9 **Litho.** *Perf. 13*

1049	A380 3.75k multicolored	1.50	1.00

Danish Employers' Confederation, cent.

A381

Famous Danish Women (Europa): 3.75k, Karen Blixen (1885-1962), writer. 5k, Asta Nielsen (1881-1972), silent screen actress.

1996, May 9

1050	A381 3.75k lt brn & dk brn	*1.50*	*.50*
1051	A381 5k gray & dk blue	*2.00*	*.75*
	Complete booklet, 10 #1051	*20.00*	

A382

Wooden Dinghies: 3.50k, Roskilde Fjord sail boat. 3.75k, Limfjorden skiff. 12.25k, Two-masted smack, South Funen Archipelago.

Perf. 13, 12½ (#1053)

1996, June 13 **Engr.**

1052	A382 3.50k multicolored	1.25	1.00
1053	A382 3.75k multicolored	1.50	.50
	Complete booklet, 10 #1053	16.00	
1054	A382 12.25k multicolored	4.50	5.25
	Nos. 1052-1054 (3)	7.25	6.75

No. 1053 is 20x39mm.

Lighthouses — A383

Litho. & Engr.

1996, Sept. 12 *Perf. 13x12½*

1055	A383 3.75k Fornaes	1.50	.30
	Complete booklet, 10 #1055	16.00	
1056	A383 5k Blavandshuk	1.75	.50
a.	Bklt. pane, 8 #1055, 2 #1056	22.00	
	Complete booklet, #1056a	22.00	
1057	A383 5.25k Bovbjerg	2.00	2.00
1058	A383 8.75k Mon	3.00	3.00
	Nos. 1055-1058 (4)	8.25	5.80

Art Works of Thorvald Bindesboll (1846-1908) — A384

Litho. & Engr.

1996, Oct. 10 *Perf. 13*

1059	A384 3.75k Pitcher	1.50	.30
	Complete booklet, 10 #1059	16.00	

Litho.

1060	A384 4k Portfolio cover	1.60	1.10

Paintings A385

Designs: 10k, "At Lunch," by P.S. Kroyer, 1893. 15k, "The Girl with Sunflowers," by Michael Ancher, 1889.

Litho. & Engr.

1996, Nov. 7 *Perf. 13x12½*

1061	A385 10k multicolored	4.00	4.00
1062	A385 15k multicolored	5.25	5.25

A386

Queen Margrethe II: 3.50k, With Prince Henrik. 3.75k, With Crown Prince Frederik. 4k, Delivering New Year speech. 5.25k, Waving to crowd.

1997, Jan. 14 **Litho.** *Perf. 13*

1063	A386 3.50k multicolored	1.25	1.25
1064	A386 3.75k multicolored	1.50	.30
	Complete booklet, 10 #1064	16.00	
1065	A386 4k multicolored	1.40	.70
1066	A386 5.25k multicolored	2.00	1.50
a.	Sheet of 4, #1063-1066 + 2 labels	6.50	6.50
	Nos. 1063-1066 (4)	6.15	3.75

Queen Margrethe II, 25th anniv. of coronation.

A387

Open Air Museum, Copenhagen, Cent.: 3.50k, Kalstrup post mill. 3.75k, Ellested water mill. 5k, Fjellerup manor barn. 8.75k, Romo farm.

1997, Mar. 13 **Engr.** *Perf. 13*

1067	A387 3.50k multicolored	1.25	1.00
1068	A387 3.75k multicolored	1.25	.30
	Complete booklet, 10 #1068	12.50	
1069	A387 5k multicolored	1.75	.75
	Complete booklet, 10 #1069	17.50	
1070	A387 8.75k multicolored	3.00	2.50
a.	Booklet pane, #1067-1070 + label	14.00	
	Complete booklet, 2 #1070a	28.00	
	Nos. 1067-1070 (4)	7.25	4.55

No. 1070a printed with two different large labels. One shows a view of Ellested water mill, the other shows a farm in Ejersted.

Great Belt Railway Link — A388

1997, May 15 **Litho.** *Perf. 13*

1071	A388 3.75k East Tunnel	1.50	.50
	Complete booklet, 10 #1071	15.00	
1072	A388 4.75k West Bridge	1.75	1.75

A389

Kalmar Union, 600th Anniv.: No. 1073, Margrete I and Eric of Pomerania. No. 1074, The Three Graces symbolizing Denmark, Norway and Sweden.

1997, June 12 **Litho.** *Perf. 13*

1073	4k multicolored	2.60	2.75
1074	4k multicolored	2.60	2.75
a.	A389 Pair, #1073-1074	5.25	6.50

No. 1074a is a continuous design.

Copenhagen-Roskilde Railway, 150th Anniv. — A390

Designs: 3.75k, Two modern trains under Carlsberg Bridge. 8.75k, Early steam train going under Carlsberg Bridge.

Litho. & Engr.

1997, June 12 *Perf. 13*

1075	A390 3.75k multicolored	2.75	.30
	Complete booklet, 10 #1075	27.50	
1076	A390 8.75k multicolored	5.00	2.50

End of Railway Mail Service A391

1997, June 12 **Litho.**

1077	A391 5k multicolored	1.75	.70

Stories and Legends A392

Europa: 3.75k, Large cat on top of treasure chest, from "The Tinder Box." 5.25k, Butterfly, pond, frog, from "Thumbelina."

1997, Aug. 28 **Engr.** *Perf. 13*

1078	A392 3.75k multicolored	*1.40*	*.40*
1079	A392 5.25k multicolored	*1.75*	*1.50*

Painting Type of 1993

Designs: 9.75k, "Dust Dancing in the Sun," by Vilhelm Hammershoi (1864-1916). 13k, "Woman Mountaineer," by J.F. Willumsen (1863-1958).

Litho. & Engr.

1997, Sept. 18 *Perf. 13x12½*

1080	A360 9.75k multicolored	4.75	5.50
1081	A360 13k multicolored	6.25	7.00

A393

Danish Design: 3.75k, Faaborg chair, vert. 4k, Margrethe bowl, vert. 5k, The Ant (chair). 12.25k, Georg Jensen silver bowl, vert.

1997, Nov. 6 **Litho.** *Perf. 13*

1082	A393 3.75k multicolored	1.25	.30
	Complete booklet, 10 #1082	12.50	
1083	A393 4k multicolored	1.25	.75
1084	A393 5k multicolored	2.00	.45
1085	A393 12.25k multicolored	4.50	5.25
	Nos. 1082-1085 (4)	9.00	6.75

Danish Confederation of Trade Unions, Cent. — A394

3.50k, General Workers Union in Denmark (SiD). 3.75k, Danish Confederation of Trade Unions (LO). 4.75k, Danish Nurse's Organization. 5k, Union of Commercial and Clerical Employees in Denmark (HK).

1998, Jan. 22 **Litho.** *Perf. 13*

1086	A394 3.50k multicolored	1.10	.90
1087	A394 3.75k multicolored	1.25	.30
	Complete booklet, 10 #1087	12.50	

1088 A394 4.75k multicolored 1.90 2.50
1089 A394 5k multicolored 2.00 .65
Complete booklet, 10 #1089 20.00
Nos. 1086-1089 (4) 6.25 4.35

City of Roskilde, 1000th Anniv. — A395

Litho. & Engr.

1998, Mar. 26 ***Perf. 13***
1090 A395 3.75k multicolored 1.50 .90
Complete booklet, 10 #1090 15.00

A396

1998, Mar. 26 **Litho.** ***Perf. 13***
1091 A396 5k Ladybug 1.75 .50

Reduce poison.

A397

New Post & Tele Museum, Copenhagen: 3.75k, Postman, 1922. 4.50k, Morse code operator, c. 1910. 5.50k, Telephone operator, 1910. 8.75k, Modern postman.

1998, May 28 **Litho.** ***Perf. 13***
1092 A397 3.75k multicolored 1.25 .30
Complete booklet, 10 #1092 12.50
a. Booklet pane, 2 each #1087, 1089, 3 ea. 1090, 1092 30.00
Complete booklet, #1092a 30.00
1093 A397 4.50k multicolored 1.50 1.50
1094 A397 5.50k multicolored 2.00 2.00
1095 A397 8.75k multicolored 2.75 2.75
a. Booklet pane, #1092-1095 14.00
Complete booklet, 2 #1095a 28.00
Nos. 1092-1095 (4) 7.50 6.55

No. 1095a is printed with two backgrounds. One shows part of King Christian IV's "Order Concerning Postmen," 1624. The other shows part of Copenhagen c. 1923. Complete booklets contain panes with each background.

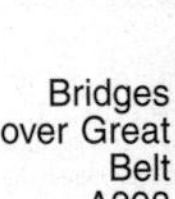

Bridges over Great Belt A398

No. 1096, West Bridge. No. 1097, East Bridge (suspension).

1998, May 28 **Engr.** ***Perf. 13***
1096 A398 5k shown 2.75 .75
1097 A398 5k multi 2.75 .75
a. Pair, #1096-1097 + label 6.00 1.50

Nordic Stamps — A399

Shipping: No. 1098, Signal flags, harbor master with binoculars. No. 1099, Radar image of entrance to Copenhagen harbor, sextant.

1998, May 28 **Litho.** ***Perf. 13***
1098 A399 6.50k multicolored 3.50 3.50
1099 A399 6.50k multicolored 3.50 3.50
a. Pair, #1098-1099 7.25 7.25
b. Souvenir sheet, #1099a 8.00 10.00

National Festivals — A400

Europa: 3.75k, Horse at Danish agricultural show. 4.50k, Theater, tents at Arhus Festival Week, Arhus.

Litho. & Engr.

1998, Sept. 3 ***Perf. 13***
1100 A400 3.75k multicolored *1.50 .60*
Complete booklet, 10 #1100 *15.00*
1101 A400 4.50k multicolored *1.75 1.00*

Contemporary Art — A401

Paintings: 3.75k, Danish Autumn, by Per Kirkeby. 5k, Alpha, by Mogens Andersen, vert. 8.75k, Imagery, by Ejler Bille, vert. 19k, Celestial Horse, by Carl-Henning Pedersen.

Perf. 12½x13, 13x12½

1998, Oct. 15 **Litho. & Engr.**
1102 A401 3.75k multicolored 1.25 1.25

Litho.

1103 A401 5k multicolored 2.00 1.50
1104 A401 8.75k multicolored 3.25 3.25
1105 A401 19k multicolored 6.50 7.75
Nos. 1102-1105 (4) 13.00 13.75

See Nos. 1160-1161, 1190-1191, 1204-1205, 1235-1236, 1255-1256, 1282-1283, 1333-1336.

A402

Fossil, name of Danish geologist: 3.75k, Ammonite, Ole Worm (1588-1654). 4.50k, Shark's teeth, Niels Stensen (1638-86). 5.50k, Sea Urchin, Soren Abildgaard (1718-91). 15k, Slit-shell snail, Erich Pontoppidan (1698-1764).

1998, Nov. 5 **Engr.** ***Perf. 13***
1106 A402 3.75k multicolored 1.25 .30
Complete booklet, 10 #1106 12.50
1107 A402 4.50k multicolored 1.75 1.75
1108 A402 5.50k multicolored 1.75 1.75
1109 A402 15k multicolored 5.00 4.50
a. Souvenir sheet, #1106-1109 12.00 12.50

Wavy Lines and Queen Types of 1933, 1997 and

Queen Margrethe II — A402a

1999-2004 **Engr.** ***Perf. 12¾***
1111 A32 150o purple .60 .25
1112 A32 375o green 2.60 .70
1113 A32 400o green 1.75 .65
1114 A321a 4k red 2.60 .50
a. Booklet pane, 4 #883, 2 #494, 2 #1114 6.75
Complete booklet, #1114a 7.00
1115 A402a 4k red 1.75 .50
b. Booklet pane, 4 #883, 2 #494, 2 #1115 5.00
Booklet, #1115b 5.00
c. Sheet of 8 + label 16.00
1116 A32 425o green 2.75 .65
1117 A402a 4.25k blue 2.60 1.00
1118 A402a 4.25k red 1.75 .70
b. Booklet pane, 6 #883, 2 #1118 5.00
c. Sheet of 8 + central label 36.00 —
1119 A402a 4.50k orange 2.00 1.50
a. Vert. strip of 10 + 10 etiquettes 24.00
1120 A402a 4.50k red 2.90 1.10
a. Booklet pane, 2 #494, 2 #1120 6.00 —
Complete booklet, #1120a 6.00
b. Sheet of 8 + central label 26.00 —
1121 A402a 4.75k sepia 3.25 1.75
1122 A402a 5k dk green 2.00 1.00
a. Sheet of 8 + 8 etiquettes *65.00* —
1123 A402a 5.25k ultra 2.10 1.00
1124 A402a 5.50k violet 2.50 .90
a. Sheet of 8 + label 24.00
b. Sheet of 8 + 8 etiquettes 30.00
1125 A321a 5.75k blue 2.25 1.25
1126 A402a 5.75k emerald 2.50 1.25
1127 A402a 6k bister 2.50 .75
a. Sheet of 10 + 10 etiquettes 45.00 —
1128 A402a 6.25k green 4.00 2.00
1129 A402a 6.50k slate grn *2.50* .90
a. Sheet of 8 + 8 etiquettes 32.00
b. Sheet of 8 + central label 42.00 —
1130 A321a 6.75k slate green 4.25 2.75
1131 A402a 6.75k henna brn 3.25 2.50
1132 A402a 7k rose lilac 3.00 2.50
1133 A402a 8.50k bright blue *3.00* 3.00
1134 A55 10.50k dk bl gray *4.00* 2.50
1135 A55 11.50k dk bl gray 5.75 4.00
1136 A55 12.50k gray 6.00 4.50
1137 A55 13k orange 5.50 4.50
1138 A55 15k blue 6.50 5.25
Nos. 1111-1138 (28) 86.15 49.85

Issued: 375o, Nos. 1114, 1118, 1130, 1/13/99; No. 1125, 1/3/00; Nos. 1115, 1119, 1119a, 4.25k, 4.50k, 5k, 5.25k, 5.50k, Nos. 1126, 1131, 4/12/00; No. 1119b, 6k, 7k, 5/9/01; Nos. 1119c, 1121a, 1124a, 4/17/01; 150o, 4.75k, 6.50k, 10.50k, 1/2/02. 400o, No. 1120, 6.25k, 8.50k, 11.50k, 1/2/03. No. 1120b, 3/12. Nos. 1124b, 1129a, 3/12/03. Nos. 1128b, 1/2/03; No. 1122a, 4/2/02; 425o, No. 1120, 12.50k, 13k, 15k, 1/2/04. Nos. 1120b, 1127a, 1/2/04.

See Nos. 1295, 1296-1303.

A403

1999, Jan. 13 **Litho.** ***Perf. 13***
1143 A403 4k Oersted Satellite 1.40 .90

Deciduous Trees A404

4k, Fagus sylvatica. 5k, Fraxinus excelsior, vert. 5.25k, Tilia cordata, vert. 9.25k, Quercus robur.

1999, Jan. 13 **Litho. & Engr.**
1144 A404 4k multicolored 1.25 .30
Complete booklet, 10 #1144 12.50
1145 A404 5k multicolored 1.75 1.00
1146 A404 5.25k multicolored 1.75 .65
1147 A404 9.25k multicolored 3.00 3.00
Nos. 1144-1147 (4) 7.75 4.95

50th Anniversaries — A405

Litho. & Engr.

1999, Feb. 24 ***Perf. 13***
1148 A405 3.75k Home Guard 1.40 .90
1149 A405 4.25k NATO 2.00 1.00

Harbingers of Spring — A406

1999, Feb. 24 **Litho.**
1150 A406 4k Lapwing in flight 1.60 .30
Complete booklet, 10 #1150 16.00
1151 A406 5.25k Geese 1.75 .90
a. Souvenir sheet, #1150-1151 6.50 5.00

Nature Reserves — A407

Litho. & Engr.

1999, Apr. 28 ***Perf. 13***
1152 A407 4.50k Vejlerne *1.75 1.00*
1153 A407 5.50k Langli *2.00 1.25*

Europa.

Council of Europe, 50th Anniv. A408

1999, Apr. 28 **Engr.**
1154 A408 9.75k blue 3.00 3.00

Danish Constitution, 150th Anniv. — A409

1999, June 2 **Litho.** ***Perf. 13***
1155 A409 4k red & black 1.40 .70

Danish Revue, 150th Anniv. A410

Performers: 4k, Kjeld Petersen and Dirch Passer, comedians. 4.50k, Osvald Helmuth, singer. 5.25k, Preben Kaas and Jorgen Ryg, comedians, singers. 6.75k, Liva Weel, singer.

1999, June 2 **Engr.** ***Perf. 13***
1156 A410 4k deep red 1.60 .50
Complete booklet, 10 #1156 16.00
1157 A410 4.50k slate 1.75 1.40
1158 A410 5.25k deep blue 1.75 .85
Complete booklet, 10 #1158 17.50
1159 A410 6.75k deep claret 2.25 1.60
a. Bklt. pane, #1156-1159 + 2 labels 14.00 15.00
Complete booklet, 2 #1159a 28.00
Nos. 1156-1159 (4) 7.35 4.35

No. 1159a printed with two different pairs of labels. One version has showgirl label at left, the second version has showgirl label at right. Complete booklets contain one of each pane.

Contemporary Paintings Type

9.25k, Fire Farver, by Thomas Kluge. 16k, Dreng, by Lise Malinovsky.

1999, Aug. 25 Litho. *Perf. 12¾*

1160 A401 9.25k multi, vert. 3.25 4.00
1161 A401 16k multi, vert. 5.25 5.25

Opening of New Extension of the Royal Library, "The Black Diamond" A411

1999, Aug. 25 Engr. *Perf. 13¾*

1162 A411 8.75k black 4.00 3.00

Migratory Birds — A412

Litho. & Engr.

1999, Sept. 29 *Perf. 12¾*

1163 A412 4k Swallows 1.60 .30
Complete booklet, 10 #1163 16.00
1164 A412 5.25k Gray-lag geese 1.75 1.00
a. Souvenir sheet, #1163-1164 5.25 6.50
1165 A412 5.50k Common eider 1.75 .90
1166 A412 12.25k Arctic tern 4.50 5.25
a. Souvenir sheet, #1165-1166 9.00 10.00
Nos. 1163-1166 (4) 9.60 7.45

Stamps from Nos. 1164a and 1166a lack white border found on Nos. 1163-1166.

New Year 2000 — A413

1999, Nov. 10 Litho. *Perf. 13¼*

1167 A413 4k Hearts 1.40 .50
1168 A413 4k Wavy lines 1.40 .50
a. Bklt. pane, 5 ea #1167-1168 35.00
Complete booklet, #1168a 35.00

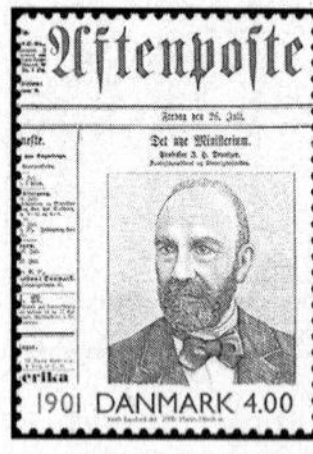

The 20th Century — A414

4k, Prof. J.H. Deuntzer on front page of newspaper, 1901. 4.50k, Newspaper illustration, 1903. 5.25k, Asta Nielsen and Poul Reumert in the film "The Abyss," 1910. 5.75k, Advertising sticker showing woman on telephone, 1914.

See sheet of 16, #1184a.

2000, Jan. 12 Litho. & Engr.

1169 A414 4k buff & blk 1.40 .50
Complete booklet, 10 #1169 14.00
1170 A414 4.50k multicolored 1.75 1.00
1171 A414 5.25k multicolored 1.75 1.00
Complete booklet, 10 #1171 17.50
1172 A414 5.75k multicolored 1.75 1.25
Nos. 1169-1172 (4) 6.65 3.75

2000, May 9

4k, Allegory of women suffrage on front page of newspaper, 1915. 5k, Newspaper caricature of the Kanslergade Agreement, 1933. 5.50k, Film "Long and Short," 1927. 6.75k, Front page of Radio Weekly Review, 1925.

1173 A414 4k multi 1.40 .55
Booklet, 10 #1173 14.00
1174 A414 5k multi 1.75 1.00
1175 A414 5.50k multi 2.00 1.60
1176 A414 6.75k multi 2.25 2.50
Nos. 1173-1176 (4) 7.40 5.65

2000, Aug. 23

4k, Liberation of Denmark on front page of newspaper, 1945. 5.75k, Newspaper caricature of new constitution, 1953. 6.75k, Poster for film "Café Paradise," 1950. 12.25k, Advertisement for Arena television, 1957.

1177 A414 4k multi 1.40 .90
Booklet, 10 #1177 14.00
1178 A414 5.75k multi 2.00 1.60
1179 A414 6.75k multi 2.25 2.50
1180 A414 12.25k multi 4.00 4.25
Nos. 1177-1180 (4) 9.65 9.25

2000, Nov. 8

4k, Entry of Denmark into European Community on front page of newspaper, 1972. 4.50k, Newspaper caricature of youth revolt, 1969. 5.25k, Poster for film "The Olsen Gang," 1968. 5.50k, Denmark Post website on Internet, 1999.

1181 A414 4k multi 1.40 .90
Booklet, 10 #1181 14.00
1182 A414 4.50k multi 1.60 1.60
1183 A414 5.25k multi 1.75 1.00
Booklet, 10 #1183 17.50
a. Booklet pane, #1171, 1175, 1179, 1183 + label 8.00
Booklet, 2 #1183a 16.00
1184 A414 5.50k multi 2.00 1.25
a. Sheet of 16, #1169-1184 47.50 42.50
Nos. 1181-1184 (4) 6.75 4.75

No. 1183a comes with two different labels. Booklet contains one of each.

60th Birthday of Queen Margrethe II — A415

2000, Apr. 12 Litho. *Perf. 12¾*

1185 A415 4k gray & car 1.60 .60
Complete booklet, 10 #1185 16.00
1186 A415 5.25k gray & blue 1.75 .90
a. Souvenir sheet, #1185-1186 4.00 4.25

Oresund Bridge, Sweden-Denmark — A416

Litho. & Engr.

2000, May 9 *Perf. 12¾*

1187 A416 4.50k shown 2.00 1.90

Litho.

1188 A416 4.50k Map 2.00 1.90
a. Pair, #1187-1188 4.25 3.75

See Sweden Nos. 2391-2393.

Europa, 2000

Common Design Type

2000, May 9 Litho. *Perf. 13*

1189 CD17 9.75k multi *3.50 2.25*

Contemporary Art Type of 1998

Designs: 4k, Pegasus, by Kurt Trampedach. 5.25k, Landscape, by Nina Sten-Knudsen.

2000, Sept. 27 *Perf. 12¾*

1190 A401 4k multi 1.50 1.50
1191 A401 5.25k multi 1.50 1.50

Royal Danish Air Force, 50th Anniv. A417

2000, Sept. 27 Engr.

1192 A417 9.75k black & red 3.00 2.50
a. Souvenir sheet of 1 3.00 3.50

Botanical Gardens, Copenhagen — A418

Litho. & Engr.

2001, Jan. 24 *Perf. 12¾*

1193 A418 4k Palm House 1.40 .60
Booklet, 10 #1193 14.00

Size: 28x21mm

1194 A418 6k Lake 2.00 .85
1195 A418 12.25k Water lilies 4.00 4.50
Nos. 1193-1195 (3) 7.40 5.95

"Use the Language" A419

2001, Mar. 28 Litho. *Perf. 13*

1196 A419 4k "A," text 1.40 .55
Booklet, 10 #1196 14.00
1197 A419 7k "Z," text 2.75 .90

Danish Postage Stamps, 150th Anniv. — A420

Portion of #2 and: 4k, Engraver Martinus William Ferslew. 5.50k, Printer Andreas Thiele. 6k, Head Copenhagen postmaster Frantz Christopher von Jessen. 10.25k, Postmaster General Magrius Otto Spohus Count Danneskjold-Samsoe.

Litho. & Engr.

2001, Apr. 1 *Perf. 13¼x13*

1198 A420 4k multi 1.50 1.00
1199 A420 5.50k multi 1.90 1.25
Booklet, 10 #1199 19.00
1200 A420 6k multi 2.00 1.25
1201 A420 10.25k multi 4.00 2.50
a. Booklet pane, #1198-1201 + label 20.00 21.00
Booklet, 2 #1201a 40.00
Nos. 1198-1201 (4) 9.40 6.00

No. 1201a printed with two different labels. One version has proof of stamp design, sketch of proposed design and Ferslew's letter to Danneskjold-Samsoe, and other shows two essays and letter from M. T. C. Bartholdy.

Europa — A421

Designs: 4.50k, Hands in water. 9.75k, Woman's head, water.

2001, May 9 Litho. *Perf. 13¼x13*

1202 A421 4.50k multi 1.25 .90
a. Booklet pane of 5 + 5 etiquettes 7.50
Booklet, 2 #1202a 15.00
1203 A421 9.75k multi 3.00 3.50

Contemporary Paintings Type of 1998

Designs: 18k, Missus, by Jorn Larsen, horiz. 22k, Postbillede, by Henning Damgaard-Sorensen.

Perf. 13x12½, 12½x13

2001, Aug. 22 Litho.

1204 A401 18k multi 6.00 6.50
1205 A401 22k multi 7.25 7.75

Youth Culture A422

Designs: 4k, Skateboarding. 5.50k, Kissing. 6k, Creating music. 10.25k, Tongue piercing.

2001, Aug. 22 *Perf. 13*

1206 A422 4k multi 1.60 .60
Booklet, 10 #1206 16.00
1207 A422 5.50k multi 1.75 1.10
Booklet, 10 #1207 17.50
1208 A422 6k multi 1.90 1.90
1209 A422 10.25k multi 4.00 4.00
a. Souvenir sheet, #1206-1209 9.00 9.75
Nos. 1206-1209 (4) 9.25 7.60

Hafnia 01 Philatelic Exhibition, Copenhagen A423

Monarch and stamps: 4k, Queen Margrethe II, #757, 1000. 4.50k, King Frederik IX, #775, 1003. 5.50k, King Christian X, #1001, B10. 7k, King Christian IX, #1002, 66.

Litho. & Engr.

2001, Oct. 16 *Perf. 13x13¼*

1210 A423 4k multi 1.60 .75
1211 A423 4.50k multi 1.75 1.75
1212 A423 5.50k multi 1.75 1.75
1213 A423 7k multi 2.50 2.75
a. Souvenir sheet, #1210-1213 6.50 7.50
b. Strip, #1210-1213 + central label 10.00 11.50
Nos. 1210-1213 (4) 7.60 7.00

Island Ferries A424

Designs: 3.75k, Bukken-Bruse. 4k, Ouro. 4.25k, Hjarno. 6k, Barsofaergen.

2001, Nov. 7 *Perf. 12¾*

1214 A424 3.75k multi 1.25 1.60
1215 A424 4k multi 1.60 .60
Booklet, 10 #1215 16.00
1216 A424 4.25k multi 1.60 1.60
1217 A424 6k multi 2.00 2.25
Nos. 1214-1217 (4) 6.45 6.05

Comics and Cartoons — A425

Designs: 4k, Rasmus Klump, by Vilhelm Hansen. 5.50k, Valhalla, by Peter Madsen. 6.50k, Jungledyret Hugo, by Flemming Quist Moller. 10.50k, Cirkeline, by Hanne Hastrup.

2002, Jan. 16 Litho. *Perf. 13¼x13*

1218 A425 4k multi 1.50 .55
Booklet, 10 #1218 15.00
a. Sheet of 8 + label 50.00
1219 A425 5.50k multi 1.75 1.00
Booklet, 10 #1219 17.50
a. Sheet of 8 + label 27.50
1220 A425 6.50k multi 2.10 1.75
1221 A425 10.50k multi 4.00 4.50
a. Souvenir sheet, #1218-1221 8.00 9.00
Nos. 1218-1221 (4) 9.35 7.80

The Girls in the Airport, Sculpture by Hanne Varming — A426

Designs: 4k, Rear view. 5k, Front view.

Photo. & Engr.

2002, Mar. 13 *Perf. 12¾*

1222 A426 4k multi, *cream* 1.60 .55
Booklet, 10 #1222 16.00
1223 A426 5k multi, *cream* 1.75 1.60

Europa — A427

Winning drawings in children's stamp design contest: 4k, Clown, by Luna Ostergard. 5k, Clown, by Camille Wagner Larsen.

2002, May 15 **Litho.** *Perf. 13*

1224 A427 4k multi *1.50 .90*
Booklet, 10 #1224 *15.00*
1225 A427 5k multi *1.75 1.75*
a. Booklet pane of 5 + 5 etiquettes *8.75* —
Booklet, 2 #1225a *17.50*

Landscapes A428

2002, May 15 **Engr.**

1226 A428 4k Bornholm 1.60 .90
1227 A428 6k West Jutland 1.90 1.90
1228 A428 6.50k Langeland 1.75 2.25
1229 A428 12.50k Thy 4.50 4.50
Nos. 1226-1229 (4) 9.75 9.55

Historic Postal Vehicles A429

Designs: 4k, 1953 Nimbus motorcycle. 5.50k, 1962 Bedford van. 10k, 1984 Renault 4 van. 19k, 1998 Volvo FH12 tractor trailer.

Litho. & Engr.

2002, Aug. 21 *Perf. 13x13¼*

1230 A429 4k multi 1.60 .65
Booklet, 10 #1230 16.00
a. Sheet of 8 + central label 36.00 —
1231 A429 5.50k multi 1.90 1.50
Booklet, 10 #1231 19.00
1232 A429 10k multi 4.00 4.00
1233 A429 19k multi 7.00 7.00
a. Booklet pane of 4, #1230-1233 20.00
Booklet, 2 #1233a 40.00
Nos. 1230-1233 (4) 14.50 13.15

No. 1233a is printed with two different labels. One shows a 1908 Berliet van and the other a 2002 Peugeot Partner. Both are included in the booklet.

Opening of Copenhagen Metro — A430

2002, Sept. 25 **Engr.** *Perf. 12¾*

1234 A430 5.50k multi, *tan* 1.50 1.40

Contemporary Paintngs Type of 1998

Designs: 5k, Children's Corner, by Jens Birkemose, vert. 6.50k, Maleren og Modellen, by Frans Kannik, vert.

2002, Sept. 25 *Perf. 13x12½*

1235 A401 5k red & blue 1.75 1.75
1236 A401 6.50k multi 2.25 2.25

Intl. Council for the Exploration of the Sea, Cent. — A431

Atlantic cod and: 4k, Exploration ship Dana. 10.50k, Hirtshals lighthouse.

Litho. & Engr.

2002, Sept. 25 *Perf. 13¼x13*

1237 A431 4k multi 1.60 .65
1238 A431 10.50k multi 4.00 4.00
a. Souvenir sheet, #1237-1238 4.50 5.00

See Faroe Islands No. 426, Greenland Nos. 401-402.

Danish House Architecture A432

Designs: 4k, Dianas Have, Horsholm, by Vandkusten Design Studio, 1992. 4.25k, Blangstedgard, Odense, by Poul Ingemann, 1988. 5.50k, Dansk Folkeferie, Karrebaeksminde, by Stephan Kappel, 1979. 6.50k, Fredensborg Terraces, Fredensborg, by Jorn Utzon, 1963. 9k, Soholm, Klampenborg, by Arne Jacobsen, 1950.

Litho. & Engr.

2002, Nov. 8 *Perf. 12¾*

1239 A432 4k multi 1.60 1.00
Booklet, 10 #1239 16.00
1240 A432 4.25k multi 1.60 .70
1241 A432 5.50k multi 1.90 1.50
1242 A432 6.50k multi 2.25 1.75
1243 A432 9k multi 3.00 3.00
Nos. 1239-1243 (5) 10.35 7.95

See Nos. 1257-1261, 1267-1271, 1317-1321.

Youth Sports — A433

2003, Jan. 15 **Litho.** *Perf. 12¾*

1244 A433 4.25k Soccer 1.50 .70
Booklet, 10 #1244 16.00
a. Sheet of 8 + central label *13.00 13.00*
1245 A433 5.50k Swimming 1.75 1.50
Booklet, 10 #1245 17.50
1246 A433 8.50k Gymnastics 3.25 3.25
1247 A433 11.50k Handball 4.00 4.25
Nos. 1244-1247 (4) 10.50 9.70

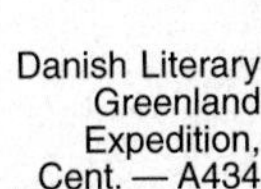

Danish Literary Greenland Expedition, Cent. — A434

Designs: 4.25k, Expedition members Harald Moltke, Knud Rasmussen, Jorgen Bronlund, Ludvig Mylius-Erichsen and Gabriel Olsen. 7k, Campsite.

2003, Mar. 12 **Engr.** *Perf. 12¾*

1248 A434 4.25k blue gray 1.25 .70

Size: 61x22mm

1249 A434 7k multi 2.25 2.25
a. Souvenir sheet, #1248-1249 + label *5.00 5.00*

See Greenland Nos. 407-408.

Europa — A435

Poster art: 4.25k, Poster for Copenhagen International Theater Festival, by Ole Fick, 1985. 5.50k, Poster for Bertel Thorvaldsen Museum, by Ole Woldbye, 1970.

2003, May 14 **Litho.** *Perf. 12¾*

1250 A435 4.25k multi *1.50 .60*
Booklet, 10 #1250 *15.00*

Engr.

1251 A435 5.50k black *1.75 1.40*
Booklet, 10 #1251 *17.50*
a. Sheet of 8 + central label *40.00*

Insects — A436

Designs: 4.25k, Ephemera danica. 6.50k, Dytiscus latissimus. 12k, Cordulegaster boltoni, vert.

2003, May 14 **Litho. & Engr.**

1252 A436 4.25k multi 1.50 .50
a. Sheet of 8 + central label 25.00 —
1253 A436 6.50k multi 2.00 2.00
a. Sheet of 8 + central label 50.00 —

Size: 21x39mm

1254 A436 12k multi 3.75 3.75
a. Souvenir sheet, #1252-1254 7.00 7.50
Nos. 1252-1254 (3) 7.25 6.25

Contemporary Art Type of 1998

Designs: 5.50k, Baering, by Sys Hindsbo. 19k, Det Forjaettede Land, by Poul Anker Bech.

Litho. & Engr.

2003, Aug. 27 *Perf. 12½x13*

1255 A401 5.50k multi 1.75 1.75

Litho.

1256 A401 19k multi 6.50 6.50

Danish House Architecture Type of 2002

Designs: 4k, Bellahoj Apartment Complex, Copenhagen, by Tage Nielsen and Mogens Irming, 1944-58. 4.25k, Anchersvej, Klampenborg, by Mogens Lassen, 1935. 5.25k, Gerthasminde, Odense, by Anton Rosen, 1912-35. 9k, Solvang, Vallekilde College, by Andreas Bentsen and Martin Nyrop, 1889. 15k, Stenbrogard, Brorup, by Peter Holdensen, 1868.

Litho. & Engr.

2003, Aug. 27 *Perf. 12¾*

1257 A432 4k multi 1.60 1.60
1258 A432 4.25k multi 1.60 .90
Complete booklet, 10 #1258 16.00
1259 A432 5.25k multi 1.75 1.75
1260 A432 9k multi 3.25 3.25
1261 A432 15k multi 4.50 4.50
Nos. 1257-1261 (5) 12.70 12.00

A437

2003, Nov. 7 **Engr.** *Perf. 12¾*

1262 A437 6.50k gray blue 2.00 1.75

Awarding of first Nobel Prize to a Dane (Niels Finsen for Physiology and Medicine), cent.

A438

Artifacts from Royal Jelling World Heritage Site: 4.25k, Queen Thyra's stone. 5.50k, King Gorm's cup. 8.50k, King Harald's stone. 11.50k, Wall paintings, Jelling Church.

2003, Nov. 7 **Litho. & Engr.**

1263 A438 4.25k multi 1.50 1.25
Booklet, 10 #1263 17.50
1264 A438 5.50k multi 1.75 1.50
Booklet, 10 #1264 22.50
1265 A438 8.50k multi 2.75 2.75
1266 A438 11.50k multi 3.75 3.75
Nos. 1263-1266 (4) 9.75 9.25

A spiral-bound booklet, enclosed in a slipcase, with four booklet panes containing single stamps of Nos. 1263-1266, and a booklet pane containing a strip of Nos. 1263-1266, sold for 99k. Value, $35.

Danish House Architecture Type of 2002

Designs: 4.50k, Spurveskjul, Virum, by Nicolai Abildgaard, 1805. 6k, Liselund, Mon, by Andreas Kirkerup, 1792. 7k, Kampmann's Yard, Varde, by Hans Wolff Ollgaard, Hack Kampmann and Mikkel Stobberup, 1781. 12.50k, Harsdorff's House, Copenhagen, by Caspar Frederik Harsdorff, 1780. 15k, Nyso Manor, Praesto, by Jens Lauridsen.

Litho. & Engr.

2004, Jan.14 *Perf. 12¾*

1267 A432 4.50k multi 1.60 1.00
Booklet, 10 #1267 16.00
1268 A432 6k multi 2.40 1.60
1269 A432 7k multi 2.50 2.50
1270 A432 12.50k multi 4.00 4.00
1271 A432 15k multi 5.25 5.25
Nos. 1267-1271 (5) 15.75 14.35

Academy of Fine Arts, Copenhagen, 250th Anniv. — A439

Litho. & Engr.

2004, Mar. 26 *Perf. 13¼x13*

1272 A439 5.50k multi 2.10 1.25
Booklet, 10 #1272 21.00

Norse Gods — A440

Designs: 4.50k, Heimdal guarding Bifrost bridge. 6k, Gefion plowing Sjaelland out of Sweden.

2004, Mar. 26

1273 A440 4.50k multi 1.75 .85
a. Sheet of 8 + central label 35.00 35.00
1274 A440 6k multi 2.40 1.10
a. Souvenir sheet, #1273-1274 8.00 8.00
b. Sheet of 8 + central label 55.00 55.00

Wedding of Crown Prince Frederik and Mary Donaldson — A441

No. 1275: a, Couple facing right. b, Couple facing left.

Litho. & Photo.

2004, May 14 *Perf. 13x13¼*

1275 A441 Horiz. pair 3.50 3.50
Booklet, 5 #1275 20.00
a.-b. 4.50k Either single, denomination 8½ mm wide 1.75 1.25
c.-d. 4.50k Either single, denomination 7½ mm wide 1.75 1.25
e. Souvenir sheet, #1275c-1275d + central label 4.00 4.00

See Faroe Islands No. 444 and Greenland Nos. 429-430.

Frederiksberg Palace, 300th Anniv. — A442

Designs: 4.25k, Doorway overlooking Sondermarken Park. 4.50k, Gatehouse archway, castle yard. 6.50k, Aerial view.

Litho. & Engr.

2004, May 14 *Perf. 13*

1276 A442 4.25k multi 1.60 1.60
1277 A442 4.50k multi 1.75 1.00

Size: 55x32mm

1278 A442 6.50k multi 2.50 2.00
a. Souvenir sheet, #1276-1278 6.00 7.00
Nos. 1276-1278 (3) 5.85 4.60

Prince Henrik, 70th Birthday — A443

2004, June 9 **Litho.** *Perf. 12¾*

1279 A443 4.50k multi 1.60 1.00

Europa A444

2004, June 9 *Perf. 13*

1280 A444 6k Cyclists 2.50 1.60
1281 A444 9k Sailboats 3.50 3.00

Contemporary Paintings Type of 1998

Designs: 13k, Senses the Body Landscape, by Lars Ravn, vert. 21k, The Dog Bites, by Lars Norgard, vert.

Litho. & Engr.

2004, Aug. 25 *Perf. 13x12½*

1282 A401 13k multi 5.00 5.00

Litho.

1283 A401 21k multi 7.50 7.50

Viking Ship Museum, Roskilde A445

Designs: 4.50k, Skuldelev 1 on Roskilde Fjord. 5.50k, Reconstruction of Skuldelev 2. 6.50k, Cross-section of ship. 12.50k, Excavation of archaelogical site where ships were found.

Litho. & Engr.

2004, Aug. 25 *Perf. 13x13¼*

1284 A445 4.50k multi 1.60 1.00
Complete booklet, 10 #1284 16.00
1285 A445 5.50k multi 2.00 1.60
Complete booklet, 10 #1285 20.00
1286 A445 6.50k multi 2.40 2.00
1287 A445 12.50k multi 4.50 4.50
Nos. 1284-1287 (4) 10.50 9.10

A spiral-bound booklet, enclosed in a slipcase, with four booklet panes containing single stamps of Nos. 1284-1287 and a booklet pane containing a strip of Nos. 1284-1287, sold for 99k. Value, $40.

Birds of Prey A446

Designs: 4.50k, Falco tinnunculus. 5.50k, Accipiter nisus. 6k, Buteo buteo. 7k, Circus aeruginosus.

Litho. & Engr.

2004, Nov. 5 *Perf. 13*

1288 A446 4.50k multi 1.75 .90
Complete booklet, 10 #1288 17.50
a. Sheet of 8 + central label 17.50 17.50
1289 A446 5.50k multi 2.10 1.00
a. Sheet of 8 + central label 22.50 22.50
1290 A446 6k multi 2.40 2.00
1291 A446 7k multi 2.75 2.25
Nos. 1288-1291 (4) 9.00 6.15

Queen and Small State Seal Types of 1946-2000

2005-09 **Engr.** *Perf. 12¾*

1295 A402a 4.75k red 1.90 1.00
a. Sheet of 8 + central label 17.00 —
1296 A402a 5.50k red 2.25 .50
b. Sheet of 8 #1296 + central label 20.00 —
1296A A402a 6.50k blue 2.75 .50
1297 A402a 7.25k blk vio 3.00 2.50
1298 A402a 7.50k blue 3.25 2.50
1299 A402a 7.75k vio blk 3.50 .90
1300 A402a 8k indigo 4.00 2.50
1301 A402a 8.25k Prus blue *2.50* 2.50
1302 A402a 8.75k Prus blue 3.75 1.00
1303 A402a 9k blue 3.25 3.25

With Diagonal Engraving Lines

1304 A55 10k olive yellow 3.50 1.25
1304A A55 10.50k car rose 4.00 3.25
1305 A55 13.50k green 5.00 4.25
1308 A55 16k Prus grn 7.25 1.25
1309 A55 16.50k red brn 6.00 5.25
1310 A55 17k sl grn 6.25 5.25
1311 A55 17.50k purple 6.25 5.25
1312 A55 20k blue 8.25 1.75
1312A A55 20.50k purple 9.25 1.75
1313 A55 22k brn vio 8.25 6.00
Nos. 1295-1313 (20) 94.15 52.40

Issued: 7.50k, 16.50k, 22k, 1/3. 4.75k, 8k, 11/11. 4.75k, 10k, 17k, 1/2/06. 7.25k, 8.25k, 11/10/06. 13.50k, 17.50k, 1/2/07. 20k, 11/8/07. 5.50k, 6.50k, 7.75k, 8.75k, 1/2/08. Nos. 1296b, 1308, 1312, 3/27/08. Nos. 1303, 1304A, 1/2/09. Type A55 stamps with diagonal engraving lines have engraver's name of Mörck at lower right. Earlier stamps of type A55 have vertical and horizontal engraving lines. The lettering was also changed slightly in the Mörck engraving.

Danish House Architecture Type of 2002

Designs: 4.25k, Hjarup Manse, Vamdrup, c. 1665. 4.50k, Ejdersted Farm, Southwest Schleswig, 1653. 7.50k, Provstegade, Randers, c. 1650. 9.50k, Smith's Yard, Koge, c. 1550. 16.50k, Carmelite Monastery, Elsinore, c. 1500.

Litho. & Engr.

2005, Jan. 12 *Perf. 12¾*

1317 A432 4.25k multi 1.75 1.75
1318 A432 4.50k multi 1.75 .65
Complete booklet, 10 #1318 17.50
a. Booklet pane, 4 #691, 8 #1318 17.00 —
Complete booklet, #1318a 17.00
1319 A432 7.50k multi 2.90 2.90
1320 A432 9.50k multi 3.50 3.50
1321 A432 16.50k multi 7.25 7.25
Nos. 1317-1321 (5) 17.15 16.05

Bonn-Copenhagen Declaration, 50th Anniv. — A447

2005, Mar. 2 **Litho.**

1322 A447 6.50k multi 2.50 2.00

See Germany No. 2330.

Hans Christian Andersen (1805-75), Author — A448

Paper Cutting by Andersen, Scissors — A449

Designs: 6.50k, Pen, inkwell, illustration of duckling, manuscript handwritten by Andersen. 7.50k, Andersen's drawing of Casino dell'Orlogio, Rome, and boots.

2005, Mar. 2 **Engr.**

1323 A448 4.50k black 1.60 1.60
a. Sheet of 8 + central label 20.00 20.00

Litho. & Engr.

1324 A449 5.50k multi 2.00 2.00
Complete booklet, 10 #1324 20.00
a. Sheet of 8 + central label 25.00 25.00
1325 A449 6.50k multi 2.25 2.00
1326 A449 7.50k multi 3.00 2.50
Nos. 1323-1326 (4) 8.85 8.10

A spiral-bound booklet, enclosed in a slipcase, with four booklet panes containing single stamps of Nos. 1323-1326, and a booklet pane containing a strip of Nos. 1323-1326, sold fof 99k. Value, $40.

See Malta Nos. 1196-1199.

August Bournonville (1805-79), Choreographer A450

Bournonville and: 4.50k, Dancer. 5.50k, Dancers.

Litho. & Engr.

2005, May 4 *Perf. 13¼x13*

1327 A450 4.50k multi 1.75 1.75
Complete booklet, 10 #1327 17.50
a. Sheet of 8 + central label 19.00 —
1328 A450 5.50k multi 2.00 2.00
a. Sheet of 8 + central label 17.50 —
b. Souvenir sheet, #1327-1328 4.00 4.00

Sailors in World War II — A451

Designs: 4.50k, Ship convoy. 7.50k, Unloading of ship's cargo.

2005, May 4 **Litho.** *Perf. 13*

1329 A451 4.50k multi 1.60 1.60
1330 A451 7.50k multi 2.75 2.75

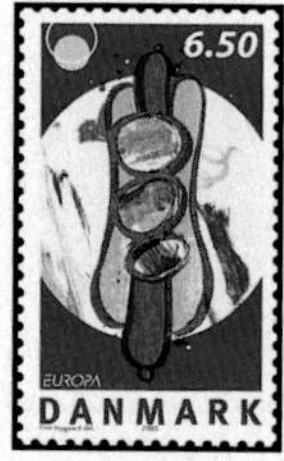

Europa — A452

2005, May 4 *Perf. 12¾*

1331 A452 6.50k Hot dog *3.00 1.90*
1332 A452 9.50k Fish *4.50 3.75*

Contemporary Art Type of 1998

Designs: 5.50k, Telepathy, by Anna Fro Vodder, vert. 6.50k, Home Again, by Kaspar Bonnén, vert. 7.50k, Unrest, by John Korner, vert. 12.50k, Palace in the Morning, by Tal Rosenzweig.

Perf. 13x12½, 12½x13

2005, Aug. 24 **Litho.**

1333 A401 5.50k multi 2.40 2.40
1334 A401 6.50k multi 2.75 2.75
1335 A401 7.50k multi 3.00 3.00
1336 A401 12.50k multi 6.00 6.00
Nos. 1333-1336 (4) 14.15 14.15

INDEX:2005 Intl. Design Exhibition, Copenhagen A453

2005, Aug. 24 **Engr.** *Perf. 13¼*

1337 A453 4.50k black 1.75 1.25
Complete booklet, 10 #1337 17.50

Wavy Lines Type of 1905-17

2005-08 **Engr.** *Perf. 12¾*

1338 A10 25o indigo .25 .25
a. Booklet pane, 2 each #1295, 1338 ('06) 4.00 —
Complete booklet, #1338a 4.00
1339 A10 50o brown .25 .25
1340 A10 100o bright blue .35 .25
1341 A10 200o dark green .70 .25
1342 A10 450o green 1.60 .65
1342A A10 500o brt yel grn 2.25 .65
Nos. 1338-1342A (6) 5.40 2.30

Wavy Line stamps, cent.

Issued: Nos. 1338-1342, 10/28/05. No. 1338a, 1/2/06. No. 1342A, 3/27/08.

Seals A454

Designs: 4.50k, Phoca vitulina. 5.50k, Halichoerus grypus.

2005, Nov. 11 **Engr.** *Perf. 13x13¼*

1343 A454 4.50k multi 1.75 1.25
Complete booklet, 10 #1343 17.50
1344 A454 5.50k indigo 2.00 1.50
a. Souvenir sheet, #1343-1344 4.00 4.00

Flowers — A455

Designs: 4.75k, Calanthus nivalis. 5.50k, Eranthis hyemalis. 7k, Crocus vernus hybrid. 8k, Anemone nemorosa.

2006, Jan. 11 Engr. *Perf. 12¾*

1345 A455 4.75k multi 1.60 .90
Complete booklet, 10 #1345 16.00
a. Sheet of 8 + central label 15.00 —
1346 A455 5.50k multi 1.75 1.75
Complete booklet, 10 #1346 17.50
a. Sheet of 8 + central label 17.00 —
1347 A455 7k multi 2.25 2.25
1348 A455 8k multi 2.50 2.50
Nos. 1345-1348 (4) 8.10 7.40

Creatures in Norse Mythology — A456

Designs: 4.75k, Elf king and elf girls. 7k, Incubi, werewolves, hel-horse, gnome and troll.

Litho. & Engr.

2006, Mar. 29 *Perf. 13¼x13*

1349 A456 4.75k multi 1.60 1.60
1350 A456 7k multi 2.40 2.40
a. Souvenir sheet, #1349-1350 4.50 7.00

Rosenborg Castle, 400th Anniv. — A457

Designs: 4.75k, Castle exterior. 5.50k, Silver lion, thrones of king and queen. 13k, Royal coat of arms ceiling decoration.

2006, Mar. 29

1351 A457 4.75k multi 1.60 1.60
Complete booklet, 10 #1351 16.00
1352 A457 5.50k multi 2.00 2.00
1353 A457 13k multi 4.50 4.50
Nos. 1351-1353 (3) 8.10 8.10

A spiral-bound booklet, enclosed in a slip-case, with four booklet panes containing single stamps of Nos. 1351-1353 and a booklet pane containing a strip of Nos. 1351-1353, sold for 99k. Value, $35.

New Carlsberg Glyptotek, Cent. — A458

Designs: 4.75k, Marble relief from Athenian graveyard. 5.50k, Conservatory dome. 8k, Dancer Looking at the Sole of Her Right Foot, sculpture by Edgar Degas.

2006, June 7

1354 A458 4.75k multi 1.60 1.60
Complete booklet, 10 #1354 16.00
1355 A458 5.50k multi 2.00 2.00
1356 A458 8k multi 2.75 2.75
a. Souvenir sheet, #1354-1356 6.50 6.50
Nos. 1354-1356 (3) 6.35 6.35

Race Cars A459

Designs: 4.75k, 1958 Alfa Dana Midget, Swebe Jap. 5.50k, 1965 Austin Mini Cooper S, 1965 Ford Cortina GT, 1965 Alfa Romeo 1600 GTA. 10k, 1963 Jaguar E Type, 1967 Volvo P 1800. 17k, 1965 Lotus Elan, Renault Alpine A 110.

2006, June 7 *Perf. 13x13¼*

1357 A459 4.75k multi 1.75 1.75
Complete booklet, 10 #1357 17.50
1358 A459 5.50k multi 2.00 2.00
Complete booklet, 10 #1358 20.00
1359 A459 10k multi 3.75 3.75
1360 A459 17k multi 6.00 6.00
Nos. 1357-1360 (4) 13.50 13.50

Europa — A460

Winning designs in children's stamp design contest: 4.75k, Smiling children, by Rikke Veber Rasmussen. 7k, Two smiling children, by Anette Bertram Nielsen.

2006, Aug. 23 Litho. *Perf. 13¼x13*

1361 A460 4.75k multi 1.90 .90
Booklet, 10 #1361 19.00
1362 A460 7k blk & dull grn 2.75 1.25

Airplanes A461

Designs: 4.50k, J. C. H. Ellehammer's 1906 biplane. 4.75k, KZ II, 1946. 5.50k, KZ IV, 1944. 13k, KZ VII, 1947.

Litho. & Engr.

2006, Aug. 23 *Perf. 12¾*

1363 A461 4.50k multi 1.75 1.75
1364 A461 4.75k multi 1.75 1.75
a. Miniature sheet of 8 + central label 14.00 14.00
1365 A461 5.50k multi 2.00 2.00
a. Miniature sheet of 8 + central label 16.00 16.00
1366 A461 13k multi 4.50 4.50
Nos. 1363-1366 (4) 10.00 10.00

Paintings by COBRA Group Artists A462

Designs: 4.75k, Untitled, by Asger Jorn. 5.50k, Landscape of the Night, by Else Alfelt, vert. 7k, New Skin, by Pierre Alechinsky. 8k, The Olive Eater, by Egill Jacobsen, vert.

Perf. 13x13¼, 13¼x13

2006, Nov. 10 Litho.

1367 A462 4.75k multi 1.75 1.75
Booklet, 10 #1367 17.50
1368 A462 5.50k multi 2.00 2.00
1369 A462 7k multi 2.75 2.75
1370 A462 8k multi 3.00 3.00
Nos. 1367-1370 (4) 9.50 9.50

See Belgium Nos. 2168-2169.

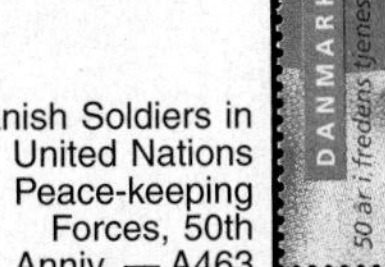

Danish Soldiers in United Nations Peace-keeping Forces, 50th Anniv. — A463

Litho. & Engr.

2007, Jan. 10 *Perf. 13*

1371 A463 4.75k multi 1.75 1.75

Intl. Polar Year A464

Designs: 7.25k, Wooden and walrus tusk carvings of Norse, Late Dorset and Thule cultures of Greenland. 13.50k, Research airplane used for measuring thickness of polar ice.

2007, Jan. 10 *Perf. 13¼*

1372 A464 7.25k multi 2.50 2.50
1373 A464 13.50k multi 4.75 4.75
a. Souvenir sheet, #1372-1373 5.00 5.00

Windmills — A465

Designs: 4.50k, Askov Mill, 1891. 4.75k, Gedser Mil, 1957. 6k, Bogo Mill, 1989. 8.25k, Middelgrunden, 2000.

2007, Jan. 10 Engr.

1374 A465 4.50k brown 1.75 1.75
1375 A465 4.75k red 1.75 1.75
Complete booklet, 10 #1375 17.50
a. Sheet of 8 + central label 15.00 15.00
1376 A465 6k green 2.00 2.00
Complete booklet, 10 #1376 20.00
a. Sheet of 8 + central label 19.00 19.00
1377 A465 8.25k blue 3.00 3.00
Nos. 1374-1377 (4) 8.50 8.50

Galathea 3 Scientific Expedition — A466

Satellite, ship and: 4.75k, Marine life. 7.25k, Globe showing route of expedition.

Litho. & Engr.

2007, Mar. 28 *Perf. 12¾*

1378 A466 4.75k multi 1.75 1.75
1379 A466 7.25k multi 2.50 2.50
a. Souvenir sheet, #1378-1379 4.50 4.50

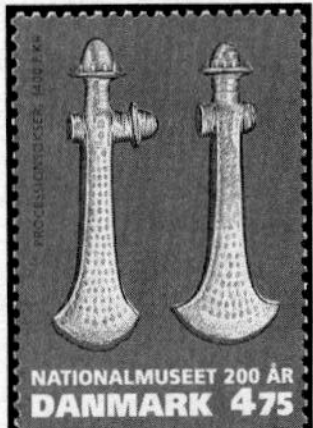

National Museum, Bicent. — A467

Designs: 4.75k, Ceremonial axes. 6k, Funen aquaemanale. 8.25k, Armillary sphere. 10.25k, Wooden mask, Borneo.

2007, Mar. 28 *Perf. 13¼*

1380 A467 4.75k Prus bl & blk 1.75 1.75
Complete booklet, 10 #1380 17.50
1381 A467 6k brn lake & blk 2.00 2.00
1382 A467 8.25k orange & blk 3.00 3.00
1383 A467 10.25k bl gray, blk & org 3.75 3.75
Nos. 1380-1383 (4) 10.50 10.50

A spiral-bound booklet, enclosed in a slip-case, with four booklet panes containing single stamps of Nos. 1380-1383 and a booklet pane containing a strip of Nos. 1380-1383, sold for 109k. Value, $40.

Europa A468

Scouts: 4.75k, On hike. 7.25k, Around campfire.

2007, June 6 *Perf. 13x13¼*

1384 A468 4.75k multi 1.75 1.75
Complete booklet, 10 #1384 17.50
1385 A468 7.25k multi 2.75 2.75

Scouting, cent.

Modern Art A469

Designs: 4.75k, The Traveler, by Arne Haugen Sorensen. 8.25k, Trionfale, by Seppo Mattinen.

2007, June 6 Litho. *Perf. 13x12½*

1386 A469 4.75k multi 1.75 1.60
a. Miniature sheet of 8 + central label 15.00 15.00
1387 A469 8.25k multi 3.00 2.50

Mandatory Use of Metric System in Denmark, Cent. A470

Litho. & Engr.

2007, Aug. 22 *Perf. 12¾*

1388 A470 4.75k black & red 1.90 .85

Nature of Denmark A471

Flora and fauna of Rabjerg Dune: 4.75k, Niobe fritillary butterfly (klitperlemorsommerfugl). 6k, Northern dune tiger beetle (sandspringer). 7.25k, Sand lizard (markfirben). 13.50k, Seaside pansy (klitstedmoderblomst).

2007, Aug. 22

1389 A471 4.75k multi 1.75 .70
Complete booklet, 10 #1389 17.50
1390 A471 6k multi 2.25 .90
Complete booklet, 10 #1390 22.50
1391 A471 7.25k multi 2.75 1.00
1392 A471 13.50k multi 5.00 1.75
a. Souvenir sheet, #1389-1392 12.50 12.50
Nos. 1389-1392 (4) 11.75 4.35

Famous Men — A472

Designs: 4.75k, Poul Henningsen (1894-1967), designer, and Artichoke lamp. 6k, Victor Borge (1909-2000), comedian, and piano keys. 7.25k, Arne Jacobsen (1902-71), architect, and Egg chair. 8.25k, Piet Hein (1905-96), inventor, and superellipse.

2007, Nov. 8 Engr. *Perf. 12¾*

1393 A472 4.75k multi 1.75 .85
Complete booklet, 10 #1393 17.50
1394 A472 6k blk & blue 2.00 1.00
1395 A472 7.25k multi 2.75 1.25
1396 A472 8.25k blk & purple 3.00 1.60
Nos. 1393-1396 (4) 9.50 4.70

See Nos. 1412-1415, 1502-1505.

Danish National Theater A473

Designs: 5.50k, Old Stage. 6.50k, Playhouse. 7.75k, Copenhagen Opera House.

Litho. & Engr.

2008, Jan. 9 ***Perf. 13x13¼***

1397 A473 5.50k multi 2.25 1.10
Complete booklet, 10 #1397 22.50
a. Sheet of 8 + central label 19.00 —
1398 A473 6.50k multi 2.60 1.25
Complete booklet, 10 #1398 26.00
1399 A473 7.75k multi 3.25 1.60
Nos. 1397-1399 (3) 8.10 3.95

Royal Life Guards, 350th Anniv. — A474

Guards in: 5.50k, Red dress uniforms. 10k, Camouflage uniforms.

Litho. & Engr.

2008, Mar. 27 ***Perf. 13¼x13***

1400 A474 5.50k multi 2.50 1.25
Complete booklet, 10 #1400 25.00
1401 A474 10k multi 4.50 2.10
a. Souvenir sheet, #1400-1401 7.00 7.00

Nordic Mythology A475

Places associated with mythology: 5.50k, Lindholm Hoje burial grounds. 7.75k, Feggeklit.

2008, Mar. 27 **Litho.**

1402 A475 5.50k black 2.40 1.25
1403 A475 7.75k black 3.25 1.60
a. Souvenir sheet, #1402-1403 6.00 6.00

Europa — A476

Designs: 5.50k, Boy writing letter. 7.75k, Girl reading letter.

2008, June 4 **Litho.** ***Perf. 13***

1404 A476 5.50k multi 2.40 1.25
Complete booklet, 10 #1404 24.00
1405 A476 7.75k multi 3.25 1.60

Allotment Gardens A477

Designs: 5.50k, Man tending Hjelm Allotment Association garden. 6.50k, Men sitting in Vennelyst Allotment Association garden.

Litho. & Engr.

2008, June 4 ***Perf. 13x13¼***

1406 A477 5.50k multi 2.40 1.25
Complete booklet, 10 #1406 24.00
a. Miniature sheet of 8 + central label 20.00
1407 A477 6.50k multi 2.75 1.40
a. Miniature sheet of 8 + central label 23.00

Louisiana Museum of Art, Humlebaek, 50th Anniv. — A478

Designs: 5.50k, Original Museum building, Figures in Landscape, by Roy Lichtenstein, I Am in You, by Doug Aitken. 7.75k, I Am in You, glass corridor, A Closer Grand Canyon, by David Hockney. 8.75k, Reclining Figure No. 5, by Henry Moore, Walking Man, by Albert Giacometti, Big Head, by Giacometti, Slender Ribs, by Alexander Calder. 16k, Slender Ribs, people in concert hall, Untitled, by Sam Francis, seat designed by Poul Kjaerholm.

2008, June 4

1408 A478 5.50k multi 2.40 1.25
1409 A478 7.75k multi 3.25 1.60
a. Booklet pane, #1408-1409 8.00 —
1410 A478 8.75k multi 3.75 1.90
1411 A478 16k multi 6.75 3.50
a. Booklet pane, #1410-1411 14.50 —
b. Booklet pane, #1408-1411 22.00 —
c. Horiz. strip of 4, #1408-1411 19.00 19.00
Complete booklet, #1409a, 1411a, 1411b 50.00
Nos. 1408-1411 (4) 16.15 8.25

Complete booklet sold for 102.40k.

Famous Men Type of 2007

Designs: 5k, Halfdan Rasmussen (1915-2002), poet, and line from poem. 5.50k, Erik Balling (1924-2005), film and television director, and actors in movie. 6.50k, Bodil Kjer (1917-2003), actress. 10k, Niels-Henning Orsted Pedersen (1946-2005), jazz musician, and bass.

2008, Aug. 27 **Engr.** ***Perf. 12¾***

1412 A472 5k blk & claret 2.40 .90
1413 A472 5.50k multi 2.75 1.10
Complete booklet, 10 #1413 27.50
1414 A472 6.50k multi 3.25 1.10
Complete booklet, 10 #1414 32.50
1415 A472 10k multi 4.50 1.75
Nos. 1412-1415 (4) 12.90 4.85

Art Photography — A479

Designs: 5.50k, Trappe, by Viggo Rivad. 7.75k, Berlin, by Krass Clement, horiz.

2008, Aug. 27 **Litho.** ***Perf. 13x12¾***

1416 A479 5.50k black 2.50 2.00

Perf. 12¾x13

1417 A479 7.75k black 3.25 2.50

Winter Berries and Flowers — A480

Designs: 5.50k, Ilex aquifolium berries. 6.50k, Helleborus niger flower. 7.75k, Taxus baccata berries. 8.75k, Symphoricarpos rivularis berries.

Litho. & Engr.

2008, Nov. 7 ***Perf. 13***

1418 A480 5.50k multi 1.90 .95
Complete booklet, 10 #1418 19.00
a. Booklet pane of 4 7.75 —
1419 A480 6.50k multi 2.25 1.10
1420 A480 7.75k multi 2.75 1.40
1421 A480 8.75k multi 3.00 1.50
a. Souvenir sheet, #1418-1421 10.00 5.00
b. Booklet pane of 4, #1418-1421 10.00 —
Complete booklet, #1418a, 1421b 18.00
Nos. 1418-1421 (4) 9.90 4.95

No. 1421b is No. 1421a sewn into the booklet.

COP15 Climate Change Conference, Copenhagen — A481

Designs: 5.50k, Bioenergy. 9k, Low-energy building.

2009, Jan. 7 **Engr.** ***Perf. 13x13¼***

1422 A481 5.50k dark blue 2.00 1.00
1423 A481 9k dark blue 3.25 1.75

Old Town Open-Air Museum, Aarhus, Cent. A482

Designs: 5.50k, Mintmaster's Mansion, drummer. 6.50k, Mayor's House, woman in period costume. 8k, Museum of Clocks and Watches and Danish Poster Museum, painter. 10.50k, Steps to Kerteminde School, farm hand.

Litho. & Engr.

2009, Jan. 7 ***Perf. 13x13¼***

1424 A482 5.50k multi 2.00 1.00
Complete booklet, 10 #1424 20.00
1425 A482 6.50k multi 2.40 1.25
Complete booklet, 10 #1425 24.00
1426 A482 8k multi 3.00 1.50
1427 A482 10.50k multi 3.75 1.90
a. Souvenir sheet, #1424-1427 11.00 11.00
Nos. 1424-1427 (4) 11.15 5.65

Europa — A483

Designs: 5.50k, Round Tower, Copenhagen. 8k, Tycho Brahe Planetarium.

2009, Mar. 25 **Litho.** ***Perf. 13¼***

1428 A483 5.50k multi 2.00 .95
Complete booklet, 10 #1428 20.00
1429 A483 8k multi 3.25 1.40

Flora and Fauna — A484

Designs: 5k, Anacamptus pyramidalis. 5.50k, Falco peregrinus. 8k, Zygaena purpuralis. 17k, Tooth of Mosasaurus lemonnieri.

2009, Mar. 25 **Litho.** ***Perf. 12¾***

1430 A484 5k multi 1.90 .85
1431 A484 5.50k multi 2.40 .95
Complete booklet, 10 #1431 24.00
a. Miniature sheet of 8 + central label 17.00 17.00
1432 A484 8k multi 3.00 1.40
1433 A484 17k multi 6.75 3.00
a. Souvenir sheet, #1430-1433 13.50 13.50
Nos. 1430-1433 (4) 14.05 6.20

Copenhagen Zoo, 150th Anniv. — A485

Designs: 5.50k, Zoo Tower, rhinoceros. 6.50k, Elephants. 8k, Red-eyed tree frog, flamingos. 9k, Tiger python, golden lion tamarin.

2009, June 10 **Litho.** ***Perf. 13¼x13***

1434 A485 5.50k multi 2.10 1.10
Complete booklet, 10 #1434 21.00
a. Miniature sheet of 8 + central label 17.00 17.00
1435 A485 6.50k multi 2.50 1.25
a. Miniature sheet of 8 + central label 20.00 20.00
b. Booklet pane of 2, #1434-1435 8.00 —
1436 A485 8k multi 3.00 1.50
1437 A485 9k multi 3.50 1.75
a. Booklet pane of 2, #1436-1437 12.00 —
b. Booklet pane of 4, #1434-1437 20.00 —
Complete booklet, #1435b, 1437a, 1437b 40.00
Nos. 1434-1437 (4) 11.10 5.60

Complete booklet containing Nos. 1435b, 1437a, 1437b sold for 109k.

Historic Maps A486

Maps of Denmark by: 5.50k, Royal Danish Academy of Sciences and Letters, 1841. 6.50k, Johannes Mejer, 1650. 12k, Marcus Jordan, 1585. 18k, Abraham Ortelius, 1570.

2009, July 15 **Litho.** ***Perf. 12½***

1438 A486 5.50k multi 2.10 1.10

Size: 41x24mm

Perf. 12¾

1439 A486 6.50k multi 2.50 1.25
1440 A486 12k multi 4.75 2.40
1441 A486 18k multi 7.00 3.50
Nos. 1438-1441 (4) 16.35 8.25

Intl. Conference on the History of Cartography, Copenhagen.

Metropolitanskolen, 800th Anniv. — A487

Designs: 5.50k, Author Hans Scherfig as boy and Metropolitanskolen building, Copenhagen. 6.50k, Two students and current school building, Norrebro.

2009, Sept. 9 **Engr.** ***Perf. 13x13¼***

1442 A487 5.50k red & black 2.25 1.10
1443 A487 6.50k black & grn 2.60 1.40

COP15, United Nations Climate Conference, Copenhagen — A488

Designs: 5.50k, Fuel cell technology. 8k, Wind turbine.

2009, Sept. 9

1444 A488 5.50k dark blue 2.25 1.10
Complete booklet, 10 #1444 22.50
1445 A488 8k dark blue 3.25 1.60

Modern Art — A489

Designs: 5.50k, Houses in Motion, by Jes Fomsgaard. 12k, Garlic, by Karin Birgitte Lund, vert.

2009 Litho. *Perf. 12¾x13*

1446 A489 5.50k multi 2.25 1.10
a. Sheet of 8 + central label 18.00 18.00

Perf. 12½x12¾

1447 A489 12k multi 5.00 2.40

Issued: 5.50k, 9/9; 12k, 10/27.

Children Playing in Snow — A490

Designs: 5.50k, Child rolling snow into large ball, snowman. 6.50k, Child in snow, child sledding. 8k, Child throwing snowball at two children. 9k, Two children making snow angels.

2009, Oct. 27 Litho. *Perf. 12½x12¾*

1448 A490 Sheet of 4 12.50 12.50
a. 5.50k multi 2.25 1.10
b. 6.50k multi 2.60 1.40
c. 8k multi 3.25 1.60
d. 9k multi 3.75 1.90

Self-Adhesive

Die Cut Perf. 13x13½

1449 A490 5.50k multi 2.40 1.10
a. Booklet pane of 12 29.00
1450 A490 6.50k multi 2.75 1.40
a. Booklet pane of 12 33.00
1451 A490 8k multi 3.25 1.60
1452 A490 9k multi 3.75 1.90
a. Sheet of 8, 2 each #1449-1452 25.00
Nos. 1449-1452 (4) 12.15 6.00

Nos. 1449a and 1450a each exist with six different booklet covers.

Flora and Fauna — A491

Designs: 8.50k, Bufo calamita. 9.50k, Lycaena phlaeas. 12.50k, Alauda arvensis. 18.50k, Astragalus danicus.

2010, Jan. 2 Litho. *Perf. 12¼*

1453 Souvenir sheet of 4 19.00 19.00
a. A491 8.50k multi 3.25 1.60
b. A491 9.50k multi 3.50 1.75
c. A491 12.50k multi 4.75 2.40
d. A491 18.50k multi 7.00 3.50

Self-Adhesive

Die Cut Perf. 13x13½

1454 A491 8.50k multi 3.25 1.60
1455 A491 9.50k multi 3.50 1.75
1456 A491 12.50k multi 5.00 2.40
1457 A491 18.50k multi 7.00 3.50
Nos. 1454-1457 (4) 18.75 9.25

Queen Margrethe II — A492

Die Cut Perf. 13

2010, Feb. 10 Litho. & Engr.

Self-Adhesive

Panel Color

1458 A492 5.50k red 2.25 1.00
1459 A492 6.50k Prus blue 2.60 1.25
a. Booklet pane of 10 26.00
1460 A492 8.50k yel green 3.25 1.60
1461 A492 9.50k dark blue 3.75 1.75
a. Miniature sheet of 8, 2 each #1458-1461 25.00
Nos. 1458-1461 (4) 11.85 5.60

No. 1458 was issued in coils as well as sheets. Every fifth coil stamp has a control number printed on the backing paper.

No. 1461a sold for 99k. See Nos. 1516-1519, 1574-1575, 1619-1620, 1635, 1665-1666, 1697-1700.

Issued: No. 1459a, 1/2/14.

Queen Margrethe II and Family A493

Die Cut Perf. 13¼

2010, Mar. 24 Litho. & Engr.

Self-Adhesive

1462 A493 5.50k multi 2.25 2.00
a. Booklet pane of 12 27.00

Queen Margrethe II, 70th birthday.

Ribe, 1300th Anniv. — A494

Designs: 5.50k, Ribe Cathedral. 6.50k, Statue of Queen Dagmar.

2010, Mar. 24 Engr.

Self-Adhesive

1463 A494 5.50k black 2.25 1.00
1464 A494 6.50k black 2.40 1.25
a. Booklet pane of 12 29.00
b. Miniature sheet of 6, 3 each #1463-1464 16.00

Nordic Coastlines A495

Designs: 5.50k, Ship at Lindo Shipyard. 8.50k, Crane, Port of Aarhus.

Perf. 12¼x12½

2010, Mar. 24 Litho.

1465 Sheet of 2 5.50 6.00
a. A495 5.50k multi 2.00 1.00
b. A495 8.50k multi 3.25 1.60

Self-Adhesive

Die Cut Perf. 13¼

1466 A495 5.50k multi 2.00 1.00
1467 A495 8.50k multi 3.25 1.60

Wavy Lines Type of 1905 and Small State Seal Type of 1946

2010 Engr. *Die Cut Perf. 13*

Self-Adhesive

1468 A10 50o brown .25 .25
1469 A10 100o blue .40 .25
1470 A10 200o dark green .75 .25
1471 A10 300o orange 1.20 .25
1472 A10 400o purple 1.60 .35
1473 A10 500o green 1.90 .45
1474 A55 10k lemon 3.75 .80
1475 A55 15k blue 5.50 1.25
1476 A55 20k dark blue 7.50 1.60
1477 A55 30k red brown 11.50 2.75
1478 A55 50k red 18.00 4.00
Nos. 1468-1478 (11) 52.35 12.20

Issued: 50o, 100o, 200o, 500o, 4/28; 300o, 400o, 30k, 3/24; 10k, 15k, 20k, 50k, 6/1.

Nos. 1474, 1476, 1478 were reissued in slightly different shades Mar. 10, 2014. No. 1476 was reissued Dec. 17, 2015. No. 1478 was reissued Oct. 1, 2016 in a pinker shade.

Album Cover for Gasolin' 3, by Gasolin' A496

Die Cut Perf. 13½x13¼

2010, Apr. 28 Litho.

Self-Adhesive

1479 A496 5.50k multi 2.25 1.50
a. Booklet pane of 12 27.00
b. Sheet of 4 19.00 15.00

Klampenborg Racetrack, Cent. — A497

Designs: 5.50k, Horses at finish line. 24k, Spectators watching race.

2010, June 1 Self-Adhesive

1480 A497 5.50k multi 2.25 1.10
1481 A497 24k multi 9.25 4.50

Europa — A498

Children's book characters: 5.50k, Sporge-Jorgen. 8.50k, Orla Fro-Snapper, horiz.

Die Cut Perf. 13¼x13½

2010, June 1

Self-Adhesive

1482 A498 5.50k multi 2.10 1.00
a. Sheet of 8 18.00

Die Cut Perf. 13½x13¼

1483 A498 8.50k multi 3.25 2.00

Booklet Stamp

Serpentine Die Cut 13½

1484 A498 5.50k multi 8.00 3.50
a. Booklet pane of 12 96.00
b. Serpentine Die Cut 10 8.00 3.50
c. Booklet pane of 12 #1484b 96.00

Royal Danish Navy, 500th Anniv. A499

Designs: 5.50k, Frigate Iver Huitfeldt. 6.50k, Artillery ship Niels Iuel. 8.50k, Ironclad warship Todenskjold. 9.50k, Screw frigate Jylland. 16k, Caravel Maria.

Die Cut Perf. 13¼x13

2010, June 1 Litho. & Engr.

Self-Adhesive (#1485-1489, 1491-1495)

1485 A499 5.50k red & black 2.00 .90
1486 A499 6.50k red & black 2.50 1.10
a. Booklet pane of 12 25.00
1487 A499 8.50k red & black 3.25 1.40
1488 A499 9.50k red & black 4.00 1.60
1489 A499 16k red & black 6.25 2.60
Nos. 1485-1489 (5) 18.00 7.60

Booklet Stamps

Perf. 12¼x12½

1490 Booklet pane of 5 30.00 —
a. A499 5.50k red & black 3.00 2.60
b. A499 6.50k red & black 3.75 3.00
c. A499 8.50k red & black 5.25 4.25
d. A499 9.50k red & black 5.75 4.75
e. A499 16k red & black 9.50 7.75

Booklet Panes of 1

Serpentine Die Cut 13¼x13½

1491 A499 5.50k red & black 3.25 2.75
1492 A499 6.50k red & black 4.00 3.50
1493 A499 8.50k red & black 5.50 4.50
1494 A499 9.50k red & black 6.25 5.00
1495 A499 16k red & black 10.00 8.00
Complete booklet, #1490-1495 60.00
Nos. 1491-1495 (5) 29.00 23.75

Complete booklet sold for 139k.

Greetings — A500

Die Cut Perf. 13x13¼

2010, June 1 Litho.

Self-Adhesive

1496 A500 5.50k Heart 2.25 .90
1497 A500 5.50k Danish Flag 2.25 .90
1498 A500 5.50k "Tillykke" 2.25 .90
1499 A500 5.50k Gift 2.25 .90
1500 A500 5.50k Flower 2.25 .90
a. Sheet of 10, 2 each #1496-1500 22.50
Nos. 1496-1500 (5) 11.25 4.50

The right third of Nos. 1496-1500 has straight-edged die cutting. See Nos. 1552-1556.

A501

A502

A503

A504

A505

A506

A507

A508

A509

Post Danmark Rundt Bicycle Race — A510

2010, Aug. 4 ***Die Cut Perf. 13x13¼***
1501 Sheet of 10 *65.00*
a. A501 5.50k multi *6.50 3.25*
b. A502 5.50k multi *6.50 3.25*
c. A503 5.50k multi *6.50 3.25*
d. A504 5.50k multi *6.50 3.25*
e. A505 5.50k multi *6.50 3.25*
f. A506 5.50k multi *6.50 3.25*
g. A507 5.50k multi *6.50 3.25*
h. A508 5.50k multi *6.50 3.25*
i. A509 5.50k multi *6.50 3.25*
j. A510 5.50k multi *6.50 3.25*

The right third of Nos. 1501a-1501j has straight-edged die cutting.

Famous Men Type of 2007

Designs: 5.50k, Dan Turèll (1946-93), writer, and lines from poem. 6.50k, Tove Ditlevsen (1917-76), poet, and her childhood home. 9.50k, Henry Heerup (1907-93), and "Love in the Coffee Pot." 12.50k, Dea Trier Morch (1941-2001), writer and artist, and illustation from her novel, *Winter's Child.*

Die Cut Perf. 13½x12¾
2010, Aug. 25 **Litho. & Engr.**
Self-Adhesive
1502 A472 5.50k multi 2.25 .80
a. Souvenir sheet of 8 17.50
b. Booklet pane of 12 27.50
1503 A472 6.50k multi 2.50 1.10
1504 A472 9.50k multi 3.50 1.60
1505 A472 12.50k multi 5.00 3.25
Nos. 1502-1505 (4) 13.25 6.75

Art — A511

Designs: 5.50k, Two Roses, by Inge Ellegaard. 18.50k, Night Flower, by Kirstine Roepstorff, vert.

Die Cut Perf. 13¼x13½
2010, Aug. 25 **Litho.**
Self-Adhesive
1506 A511 5.50k multi 2.25 1.50
Die Cut Perf. 13½x13¼
1507 A511 18.50k multi 7.25 5.00

Small State Seal Type of 1946
Die Cut Perf. 13
2010, Oct. 26 **Engr.**
1508 A55 25k green 9.50 4.75

"Winter Tales" — A512

Designs: 5.50k, Woman on park bench, ducks. 6.50k, Woman on park bench hugging snowman. 8.50k, Woman kissing snowman. 12.50k, Snowman coming to life, dog.

2010, Oct. 26 **Litho.** ***Perf. 12¼x13***
1509 Sheet of 4 13.00 6.50
a. A512 5.50k multi 2.10 1.10
b. A512 6.50k multi 2.50 1.25
c. A512 8.50k multi 3.25 1.60
d. A512 12.50k multi 4.75 2.40

Self-Adhesive
Die Cut Perf. 13¼
1510 A512 5.50k multi 2.10 1.10
1511 A512 6.50k multi 2.50 1.25
1512 A512 8.50k multi 3.25 1.60
1513 A512 12.50k multi 4.75 2.40
a, Sheet of 8, #1511-1513, 5 #1510 21.00
Nos. 1510-1513 (4) 12.60 6.35

Booklet Stamps
Serpentine Die Cut 13½
1514 A512 5.50k multi 5.00 5.00
a. Booklet pane of 12 60.00
1515 A512 6.50k multi 5.00 5.00
a. Booklet pane of 12 60.00

Queen Margrethe II Type of 2010
Die Cut Perf. 13
2011, Mar. 9 **Litho. & Engr.**
Self-Adhesive
Panel Color
1516 A492 6k Prus blue 2.50 1.10
1517 A492 8k red 3.25 1.50
1518 A492 9k yel green 3.75 1.75
1519 A492 11k dark blue 4.50 2.10
Nos. 1516-1519 (4) 14.00 6.45

Nos. 1516 and 1517 were issued in coils as well as sheets. Every fifth coil stamp has a control number printed on the backing paper.

Art A513

Designs: 8k, Untitled (for Karl Pichert), by Claus Carstensen. 13k, Det Her Sted (This Place), by Lise Harlev.

Die Cut Perf. 13½x13¼
2011, Mar. 23 **Litho. & Engr.**
Self-Adhesive
1520 A513 8k sil & black 3.25 1.60
Litho.
1521 A513 13k multi 5.00 2.50

Supreme Court, 350th Anniv. — A514

Designs: 6k, Supreme Court decree of King Frederik III, 1661. 8k, Court and judges.

Litho. & Engr.
2011, Mar. 23 ***Perf. 13x12½***
1522 Sheet of 2 5.75 6.25
a. A514 6k multi 2.40 2.40
b. A514 8k multi 3.25 1.60

Self-Adhesive
Die Cut Perf. 13x13½
1523 A514 6k multi 2.40 1.25
1524 A514 8k multi 3.25 1.60

Camping — A515

Designs: 6k, Man wearing t-shirt and shorts in front of trailer. 8k, Garden gnome in front of trailer.

Die Cut Perf. 13x13¼
2011, Mar. 23 **Litho.**
Self-Adhesive
1525 A515 6k multi 2.50 1.25
1526 A515 8k multi 3.25 1.60
Serpentine Die Cut 13½
1527 A515 6k multi 2.50 1.25
a. Booklet pane of 12 30.00
1528 A515 8k multi 3.25 1.60
a. Booklet pane of 12 39.00
b. Pair, #1527-1528 5.75
Nos. 1525-1528 (4) 11.50 5.70

Nos. 1527-1528 were printed in sheets of 8 containing four of each stamp. Sheet sold for 56k.

Europa — A516

Designs: 8k, Caterpillar on branch in spring. 11k, Squirrel, tree in autumn.

2011, May 4 ***Die Cut Perf. 13x13¼***
Self-Adhesive
1529 A516 8k multi 3.25 1.60
1530 A516 11k multi 4.25 2.10
Booklet Stamp
Serpentine Die Cut 13½
1531 A516 8k multi 3.25 3.00
a. Booklet pane of 12 39.00

Intl. Year of Forests.

Manor Houses A517

Designs: No. 1532, Norre Vosborg, near Holstebro. No. 1533, Voergaard Castle, Vendsyssel. No. 1534, Englesholm Castle, near Vejle. No. 1535, Gammel Estrup, near Randers.

Die Cut Perf. 13¼x13
2011, May 4 **Litho. & Engr.**
Self-Adhesive
1532 A517 6k multi 2.40 1.25
1533 A517 6k multi 2.40 1.25
1534 A517 8k multi 3.25 1.60
1535 A517 8k multi 3.25 1.60
Nos. 1532-1535 (4) 11.30 5.70

Arabian Expedition of Carsten Niebuhr, 250th Anniv. — A518

Compass rose and: 8k, Niebuhr (1733-1815), explorer. 13k, Horse-drawn grain mill from Egypt.

2011, May 4 ***Die Cut Perf. 13x13¼***
Self-Adhesive
1536 A518 8k multi 3.50 1.60
1537 A518 13k multi 5.25 2.50
a. Souvenir sheet of 2, #1536-1537, + label 8.75
Booklet Stamp
Serpentine Die Cut 13½
1538 A518 8k multi 3.25 1.60
a. Booklet pane of 12 39.00

Paddle Steamer SS Hjejlen, 150th Anniv. A519

2011, June 8 ***Die Cut Perf. 13***
Self-Adhesive
1539 A519 8k multi 3.50 1.60
a. Miniature sheet of 6 21.00

Children's Television Characters A520

Designs: 6k, Bruno the Bear and French fries. 8k, Bamse the Bear and balloons.

Die Cut Perf. 13¼x13
2011, June 8 **Litho.**
Self-Adhesive
1540 A520 6k multi 2.50 1.25
a. Miniature sheet of 6 15.00
1541 A520 8k multi 3.50 1.60
a. Miniature sheet of 6 21.00
Booklet Stamps
Serpentine Die Cut 13½
1542 A520 6k multi 2.50 2.00
a. Booklet pane of 10 + 10 etiquettes 25.00
1543 A520 8k multi 3.50 3.00
a. Booklet pane of 12 35.00

Summer Flowers — A521

Designs: 2k, Papaver rhoeas. 6k, Geranium. 8k, Astrantia major. 10k, Papaver nudicaule.

2011, June 8 ***Perf. 12x12¾***
1544 Miniature sheet of 4 11.00 11.00
a. A521 2k multi .80 .40
b. A521 6k multi 2.40 1.25
c. A521 8k multi 3.25 1.60
d. A521 10k multi 4.00 2.00
Self-Adhesive
Die Cut Perf. 13x13¼
1545 A521 2k multi .80 .40
1546 A521 6k multi 2.40 1.25
1547 A521 8k multi 3.25 1.60
1548 A521 10k multi 4.00 2.00
Nos. 1545-1548 (4) 10.45 5.25
Booklet Stamp
Serpentine Die Cut 13½
1549 A521 6k multi 2.50 2.25
a. Booklet pane of 10 + 10 etiquettes 25.00

Sketch of Woman's Clothing Designed by Malene Birger — A522

Fashion Accessories Designed by Silas Adler — A523

Die Cut Perf. 13x13¼

2011, Aug. 4 Litho. & Engr.

Self-Adhesive

1550 A522 6k black 2.40 1.25
1551 A523 8k multi 3.25 1.60
a. Souvenir sheet of 2, #1550-1551 5.75

Greetings Type of 2010

Die Cut Perf. 13x13¼

2011, Aug. 4 Litho.

Self-Adhesive

1552 A500 8k Heart 3.25 1.60
1553 A500 8k Danish Flag 3.25 1.60
1554 A500 8k "Tillykke" 3.25 1.60
1555 A500 8k Open envelope 3.25 1.60
1556 A500 8k Flower 3.25 1.60
a. Sheet of 10, 2 each #1552-1556 32.50
Nos. 1552-1556 (5) 16.25 8.00

The right third of Nos. 1552-1556 has straight-edged die cutting.

International Cycling Union Road World Championships, Denmark — A524

2011, Aug. 4 *Die Cut Perf. 13x13¼*

Self-Adhesive

1557 A524 8k multi 3.25 1.60
a. Souvenir sheet of 6 19.50

Copenhagen Central Railway Station, Cent. — A525

People and: 6k, Station's front. 8k, Clock. 9k, Arches. 16k, Train at platform.

Litho. & Engr.

2011, Sept. 10 *Perf. 13x12¼*

Booklet Stamps (#1558-1561, 1566)

1558 A525 6k multi 6.00 6.00
1559 A525 8k multi 6.00 6.00
a. Booklet pane of 2, #1558-1559 12.00 —
1560 A525 9k multi 9.00 9.00
1561 A525 16k multi 9.00 9.00
a. Booklet pane of 4, #1558-1561 30.00 —
b. Booklet pane of 2, #1560-1561 18.00 —
Complete booklet, #1559a, 1561a, 1561b 60.00
Nos. 1558-1561 (4) 30.00 30.00

Self-Adhesive

Die Cut Perf. 13¼x13

1562 A525 6k multi 2.25 1.25
1563 A525 8k multi 3.00 1.75
1564 A525 9k multi 3.50 2.00
1565 A525 16k multi 6.00 3.00
Nos. 1562-1565 (4) 14.75 8.00

Serpentine Die Cut 13½

1566 A525 8k multi 3.25 3.00
a. Booklet pane of 12 39.00

The complete booklet sold for 139k.

People in Winter — A526

Designs: 6k, Bathing Viking. 8k, Woman feeding duck. 11k, Man walking dog. 13k, Ice fisherman.

2011, Oct. 25 Litho. *Perf. 12¼*

1567 Sheet of 4 15.00 7.50
a. A526 6k multi 2.40 1.25
b. A526 8k multi 3.00 1.75
c. A526 11k multi 4.25 2.90
d. A526 13k multi 5.00 3.25

Self-Adhesive

Die Cut Perf. 13x13¼

1568 A526 6k multi 2.40 1.25
1569 A526 8k multi 3.00 1.75
1570 A526 11k multi 4.25 2.90
1571 A526 13k multi 5.00 3.25
Nos. 1568-1571 (4) 14.65 9.15

Booklet Stamps

Serpentine Die Cut 13½

1572 A526 6k multi 2.50 2.25
a. Booklet pane of 10 + 10 etiquettes 25.00
1573 A526 8k multi 3.50 3.25
a. Booklet pane of 12 42.50

Queen Margrethe II Type of 2010

Die Cut Perf. 13

2012, Jan. 2 Litho. & Engr.

Self-Adhesive

Panel Color

1574 A492 12k purple 4.50 3.75
1575 A492 14k black 5.25 2.90

Armillary Spheres A527

Designs: No. 1576, Equatorial armillary sphere built by Tycho Brahe, 1595. No. 1577, Simplified armillary sphere built by Guo Shouj-ing, 1276.

Die Cut Perf. 13¾

2012, Jan. 4 Litho. & Engr.

Self-Adhesive

1576 A527 6k multi 2.50 1.50
1577 A527 6k multi 2.50 1.50

See People's Republic of China Nos. 3980-3981.

Reign of Queen Margrethe II, 40th Anniv. — A528

2012, Jan. 4 *Perf. 13½*

Souvenir Sheet

1578 A528 8k multi 3.00 3.00

Self-Adhesive

Die Cut Perf. 13¼x13½

1579 A528 8k multi 3.00 3.00

Bridges A529

Designs: 6k, Queen Alexandrine Bridge. 8k, Faro Bridge.

2012, Jan. 4 Litho. *Perf. 13¼*

Souvenir Sheet

1580 Sheet of 2 8.25 8.25
a. A529 6k multi 3.00 2.00
b. A529 8k multi 5.00 3.00

Self-Adhesive

Die Cut Perf. 13¼

1581 A529 6k multi 2.10 1.40
1582 A529 8k multi 3.25 2.00

Booklet Stamps

Serpentine Die Cut 13½

1583 A529 6k multi 2.10 1.40
a. Booklet pane of 10 + 10 etiquettes 21.00
1584 A529 8k multi 3.25 2.00
a. Booklet pane of 10 + 10 etiquettes 32.50

Nordia 2012 Stamp Exhibition, Roskilde.

Europa — A530

2012, Mar. 21 *Perf. 14*

Souvenir Sheet

1585 A530 12k multi 4.50 4.50

Self-Adhesive

Die Cut Perf. 14

1586 A530 12k multi 4.50 2.75

No. 1586 was printed in sheets of 30.

Sea Rescue — A531

Designs: 6k, Helicopter and rescue boat. 11k, Helicopter over Copenhagen University Hospital helipad.

2012, Mar. 21 *Perf. 13½x13¼*

Souvenir Sheet

1587 A531 Sheet of 2 6.50 6.50
a. 6k multi 2.40 1.60
b. 11k multi 4.00 2.40

Self-Adhesive

Die Cut Perf. 13½x13¼

1588 A531 6k multi 2.40 1.60
1589 A531 11k multi 4.00 2.40

Scenes From Tales by Hans Christian Andersen A532

Designs: 2k, The Shepherdess and the Chimney Sweep. 3k, The Nightingale. 6k, The Wild Swans. 8k, What the Old Man Does Is Always Right.

Die Cut Perf. 13½x13¼

2012, June 1 Litho. & Engr.

Self-Adhesive

1590 A532 2k multi 1.10 .70
1591 A532 3k multi 1.00 1.00
1592 A532 6k multi 2.10 1.40
1593 A532 8k multi 2.75 1.75
Nos. 1590-1593 (4) 6.95 4.85

Booklet Stamps

Serpentine Die Cut 13½x13¼

1594 A532 6k multi 2.25 1.50
a. Booklet pane of 10 + 10 etiquettes 22.50
1595 A532 8k multi 3.00 1.75
a. Booklet pane of 10 + sticker 30.00

Sandwiches
A533 A534

Designs: Nos. 1596, 1600, 1604, Egg and shrimp sandwich. Nos. 1597, 1601, 1605, Rolled sausage sandwich. 8k, Potato sandwich. 16k, Roast beef sandwich.

2012, June 1 Litho. *Perf. 13x13¼*

Booklet Stamps

1596 A533 6k multi 4.00 4.00
a. Booklet pane of 1 4.00 —
1597 A534 6k multi 4.00 4.00
a. Booklet pane of 1 4.00 —
1598 A534 8k multi 5.25 5.25
a. Booklet pane of 1 5.25 —
1599 A534 16k multi 10.50 10.50
a. Booklet pane of 1 10.50 —
b. Booklet pane of 4, #1596-1599 24.00 —
Complete booklet, #1596a, 1597a, 1598a, 1599a, 1599b 48.00
Nos. 1596-1599 (4) 23.75 23.75

Self-Adhesive

Die Cut Perf. 13x13¼

1600 A533 6k multi 2.00 1.00
1601 A534 6k multi 2.00 1.00
1602 A534 8k multi 2.75 1.40
1603 A534 16k multi 5.50 2.75
Nos. 1600-1603 (4) 12.25 6.15

Serpentine Die Cut 13½

1604 A533 6k multi 2.10 1.10
1605 A534 6k multi 2.10 1.10
a. Booklet pane of 10, 5 each #1604-1605 + 10 etiquettes 20.00
1606 A534 8k multi 2.90 1.75
a. Booklet pane of 10 27.50
Nos. 1604-1606 (3) 7.10 3.95

Complete booklet sold for 139k. Nos. 1604-1606 weree printed in a sheet of 8 containing 3 each nos. 1604-1605 and 2 No. 1606.

Portrait of Johanne Luise Heiberg, by Emilius Baerentzen — A535

Die Cut Perf. 14x13¾

2012, Sept. 5 Litho. & Engr.

Self-Adhesive

1607 A535 8k multi 3.00 1.75

Heiberg (1812-90), theater actress and director.

Flowers — A536

Designs: 8k, Saponaria officinalis. 12k, Centaurea scabiosa. 14k, Leontodon autumnalis.

Die Cut Perf. 13x13½

2012, Sept. 5 **Litho.**

Self-Adhesive

1608 A536 8k multi 3.00 1.75
1609 A536 12k multi 4.50 2.40
1610 A536 14k multi 5.25 3.75
Nos. 1608-1610 (3) 12.75 7.90

Booklet Stamp

Serpentine Die Cut 13½

1611 A536 8k multi 3.00 2.50
a. Booklet pane of 10 30.00

Copenhagen Central Post Office, Cent. — A537

2012, Sept. 12 **Engr.** ***Perf. 13x13¼***

1612 A537 8k dark red 3.00 3.00

Post Scriptum, by Christian Vind — A538

Die Cut Perf. 14x13¾

2012, Nov. 2 **Litho. & Engr.**

Self-Adhesive

1613 A538 16k blk & yel org 5.75 4.00

Tree in Winter — A539

Tree and: 6k, Bird and musical notes. 8k, Birdhouse, bird. 12k, Moon, bird on branch of bush.

Die Cut Perf. 13x13¼

2012, Nov. 2 **Litho.** **Self-Adhesive**

1614 A539 6k blue 2.10 1.10
1615 A539 8k dull blue 2.90 1.75
1616 A539 12k blue 4.25 3.50
Nos. 1614-1616 (3) 9.25 6.35

Booklet Stamps

Serpentine Die Cut 13½

1617 A539 6k blue 2.10 1.10
a. Booklet pane of 10 + 10 etiquettes 21.00
1618 A539 8k dull blue 2.90 1.75
a. Booklet pane of 10 29.00

Queen Margrethe II Type of 2010

Self-Adhesive

Die Cut Perf. 13

Litho. & Engr.

2013, Jan. 2 **Panel Color**

1619 A492 12.50k purple 4.75 2.75
1620 A492 14.50k dark gray 5.25 2.75

Kaj and Andrea A540

Mr. Beard — A541

Die Cut Perf. 13½x13¼

2013, Jan. 7 **Self-Adhesive** **Litho.**

1621 A540 8k multi 3.00 2.50
a. Sheet of 6 18.00 15.00

Die Cut Perf. 13¼x13½

1622 A541 8k multi 3.00 2.50

Booklet Stamps

Serpentine Die Cut 13½

1623 A540 8k multi 3.00 2.50
1624 A541 8k multi 3.00 2.50
a. Booklet pane of 10, 5 each #1623-1624 30.00

Characters on children's television programs.

Fish — A542

Designs: 6k, Clupea harengus. 8k, Gadus morhua. 12.50k, Platichthys flesus. 14.50k, Anguilla anguilla.

Booklet Stamps (#1625-1628, 1633-1634)

2013, Jan. 7 **Litho.** ***Perf. 13***

1625 A542 6k multi 3.50 3.50
a. Booklet pane of 1 3.50 —
1626 A542 8k multi 5.00 5.00
a. Booklet pane of 1 5.00 —
1627 A542 12.50k multi 7.50 7.50
a. Booklet pane of 1 7.50 —
1628 A542 14.50k multi 9.00 9.00
a. Booklet pane of 1 9.00 —
b. Booklet pane of 4, #1625-1628 25.00 —
Complete booklet, #1625a, 1626a, 1627a, 1628a, 1628b 50.00
Nos. 1625-1628 (4) 25.00 25.00

Self-Adhesive

Die Cut Perf. 13

1629 A542 6k multi 2.25 1.20
1630 A542 8k multi 3.00 1.75
1631 A542 12.50k multi 4.50 3.75
1632 A542 14.50k multi 5.25 3.75
Nos. 1629-1632 (4) 15.00 10.45

Serpentine Die Cut 13½

1633 A542 6k multi 2.25 1.20
a. Booklet pane of 10 + 10 etiquettes 22.50
1634 A542 8k multi 3.00 1.75
a. Booklet pane of 10 30.00

Complete booklet sold for 139k.

Queen Margrethe II Type of 2010

Die Cut Perf. 13

2013, Mar. 4 **Litho. & Engr.**

Self-Adhesive

Panel Color

1635 A492 16k orange 6.00 5.00

Soren Kierkegaard (1813-55), Philosopher A543

2013, Mar. 4 ***Die Cut Perf. 13¼x13***

1636 A543 8k multi 3.00 2.50

Electric Postal Bicycle, Europa A544

2013, Mar. 4 ***Perf. 13½x13***

Souvenir Sheet

1637 A544 12.50k multi 4.75 3.00

Self-Adhesive

Die Cut Perf. 13¼x13

1638 A544 12.50k multi 4.75 2.25

Manor Houses A545

Designs: Nos. 1639, 1641, Egeskov Castle. Nos. 1640, 1642, Valdemar's Castle.

2013, Mar. 4 ***Die Cut Perf. 13¼x13***

Self-Adhesive

1639 A545 8k multi 3.00 2.50
1640 A545 8k multi 3.00 2.50

Booklet Stamps

Serpentine Die Cut 13½

1641 A545 8k multi 3.00 2.50
1642 A545 8k multi 3.00 2.50
a. Booklet pane of 10, 5 each #1641-1642 30.00

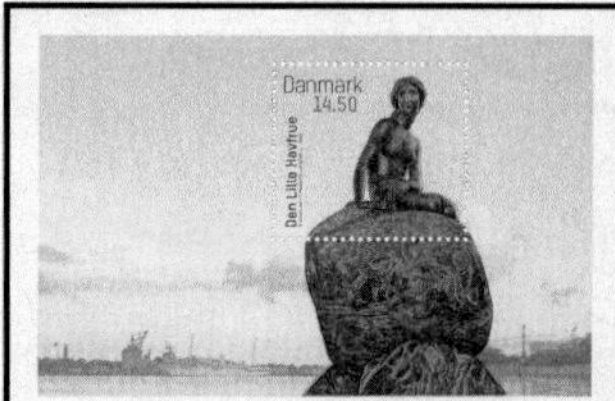

The Little Mermaid Statue, Copenhagen, Cent. — A546

Litho. & Engr.

2013, May 27 ***Perf. 13½x13***

Souvenir Sheet

1643 A546 14.50k multi *5.25* 5.25

Self-Adhesive

Die Cut Perf. 13¼x13

1644 A546 14.50k multi 5.25 4.50

Danish Rock Music A547

Designs: Nos. 1645, 1647, Crowd at rock concert. Nos. 1646, 1648, Electric guitar of Kasper Eistrup.

Die Cut Perf. 13¼x13

2013, May 27 **Litho.**

Self-Adhesive

1645 A547 8k multi 3.00 1.75
1646 A547 8k multi 3.00 1.75

Serpentine Die Cut 13½

1647 A547 8k multi 3.00 1.75
1648 A547 8k multi 3.00 1.75
a. Booklet pane of 10, 5 each #1647-1648 30.00
Nos. 1645-1648 (4) 12.00 7.00

Nos. 1647-1648 were printed in sheets containing 3 of each stamp.

Culture Yard, Elsinore — A548

Designs: 8k, Wing of building and reflecting pond. 12.50k, Building entrance and reflecting pond.

2013, Aug. 29 **Litho.** ***Perf. 13x13¼***

Souvenir Sheet

1649 A548 Sheet of 2 7.50 4.50
a. 8k multi 3.00 1.75
b. 12.50k multi 4.50 2.75

Self-Adhesive

Die Cut Perf. 13x13¼

1650 A548 8k multi 3.00 1.75
1651 A548 12.50k multi 4.50 2.75

Fifth INDEX: Intl. Design award ceremonies, Elsinore.

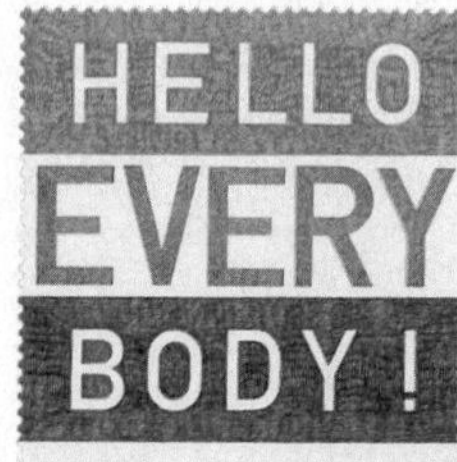

Best Wishes, by Jytte Hoy A549

Die Cut Perf. 13¼x13½

2013, Sept. 2 **Litho. & Engr.**

Self-Adhesive

1652 A549 8k multi 3.00 1.75

Scenes from Stories by Hans Christian Andersen A550

Scenes from: 6k, The Tinderbox. 8k, The Flying Trunk. 12.50k, The Sweethearts (The Top and the Ball). 14.50k, The Little Match Girl.

Die Cut Perf. 13¼x13

2013, Sept. 2 **Litho. & Engr.**

Self-Adhesive

1653 A550 6k multi 2.25 1.50
a. Booklet pane of 10 + 10 etiquettes 22.50
1654 A550 8k multi 3.00 1.75
a. Booklet pane of 10 30.00
1655 A550 12.50k multi 4.50 3.00
1656 A550 14.50k multi 5.25 3.75
Nos. 1653-1656 (4) 15.00 10.00

Christmas — A551

Designs: 6k, Christmas rose. 8k, Skating girl. 12.50k, Robins.

2013, Oct. 29 Litho. *Perf. 13x12¾*

Souvenir Sheet

1657 Sheet of 3 9.75 9.75
a. A551 6k multi 2.25 1.20
b. A551 8k multi 3.00 1.75
c. A551 12.50k multi 4.50 3.75

Self-Adhesive

Die Cut Perf. 13x13¼

1658 A551 6k multi 2.25 1.20
1659 A551 8k multi 3.00 1.75
1660 A551 12.50k multi 4.50 3.00
Nos. 1658-1660 (3) 9.75 5.95

Booklet Stamps

Serpentine Die Cut 13½

1661 A551 6k multi 2.25 1.20
a. Booklet pane of 10 + 10 etiquettes 22.50
1662 A551 8k multi 3.00 1.75
a. Booklet pane of 10 30.00

Trade Treaty Between Denmark and France, 350th Anniv. A552

Map and compass rose with ship at: 8k, Right. 12.50k, Left.

Die Cut Perf. 13½x13¼

2013, Nov. 7 Litho. & Engr.

Self-Adhesive

1663 A552 8k rose & blue 3.00 1.75
1664 A552 12.50k blue & rose 4.50 2.75

See France Nos. 4526-4527.

Queen Margrethe II Type of 2010

Die Cut Perf. 13

2014, Jan. 2 Litho. & Engr.

Self-Adhesive

Panel Color

1665 A492 9k red 3.75 2.50
a. Booklet pane of 10 37.50
1666 A492 18k blue 7.50 4.50
a. Booklet pane of 10 75.00

Nordic Cuisine — A553

Aebleflaesk: 6.50k, Raw ingredients (Pig and apples). 14k, Finished dish.

Die Cut Perf. 13½x13

2014, Jan. 2 Litho.

Self-Adhesive

1667 A553 6.50k multi 2.50 1.50
a. Booklet pane of 10 25.00
1668 A553 14k multi 5.25 2.60

Flowers — A554

Designs: No. 1669, Fritillaria meleagris. No. 1670, Muscari botryoides.

Die Cut Perf. 13¾

2014, Jan. 2 Litho.

Self-Adhesive

1669 A554 9k multi 3.50 1.75
1670 A554 9k multi 3.50 1.75
a. Horiz. pair, #1669-1670 on backing paper without printing 7.00
b. Booklet pane of 10, 5 each #1669-1670 35.00

Nos. 1669 and 1670 were printed in sheets of 6 containing 3 of each stamp.

PH Grand Piano — A555

Die Cut Perf. 13½x13

2014, Mar. 15 Litho. & Engr.

Self-Adhesive

1671 A555 14k multi 5.25 3.75

Europa.

General Peter du Plat (1809-64) — A556

Prussian Soldiers at Battle of Dybbol — A557

Litho. & Engr.

2014, Mar. 15 *Perf. 13x12¾*

Souvenir Sheet

1672 Sheet of 2 + label 10.50 10.50
a. A556 9k multi 3.50 1.75
b. A557 18k multi 6.75 3.50

Self-Adhesive

Die Cut Perf. 13½

1673 A556 9k multi 3.50 1.75
a. Booklet pane of 10 35.00

Die Cut Perf. 13x13½

1674 A557 18k multi 6.75 3.50

Battle of Dybbol, 150th anniv,

Chairs — A558

Designs: 6.50k, Three-legged shell chair, designed by Hans J. Wegner (1914-2007). 16k, Spanish chair, designed by Borge Mogensen (1914-72).

Die Cut Perf. 13½x13

2014, Mar. 15 Litho. & Engr.

Self-Adhesive

1675 A558 6.50k org & gray 2.40 1.50
a. Booklet pane of 10 24.00
1676 A558 16k brn & lt brn 6.00 3.00
a. Booklet pane of 5 30.00

A booklet containing perf. 13½x13 stamps with water-activated gum having designs identical to Nos. 1675 and 1676 sold for 139k. The booklet contained a pane containing one example of the 6.50k, another containing one example of the 16k, and another containing one example each of the 6.50k and 16k.

Sailboats A559

Designs: 6.50k, Laser Radial dinghy. 14k, Hanse 430e yacht.

Perf. 12½x12¾

2014, Mar. 17 Litho.

Souvenir Sheet

1677 Sheet of 2 7.75 7.75
a. A559 6.50k multi 2.40 1.50
b. A559 14k multi 5.25 2.75

Self-Adhesive

Die Cut Perf. 13x13½

1678 A559 6.50k multi 2.40 1.50
a. Booklet pane of 10 24.00
1679 A559 14k multi 5.25 2.60

Princess Benedikte and Scouts A560

Die Cut Perf. 13x13½

2014, Apr. 29 Litho.

Self-Adhesive

1680 A560 9k multi + label 3.50 3.50
a. Booklet pane of 5 + 5 labels 17.50

Princess Benedikte, 70th birthday.

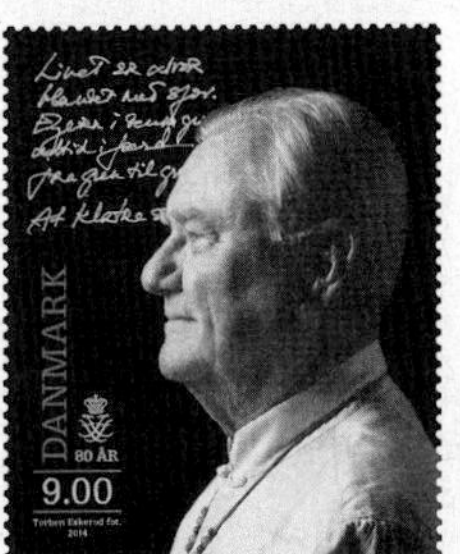

Danish School System, 200th Anniv. — A561

Die Cut Perf. 13½

2014, June 11 Litho.

Self-Adhesive

1681 A561 6.50k multi 2.40 1.50
a. Booklet pane of 10 24.00

Prince Henrik, 80th Birthday A562

Die Cut Perf. 13½

2014, June 11 Litho.

Self-Adhesive

1682 A562 9k multi 3.50 1.75
a. Booklet pane of 4 14.00

Den Frie Center of Contemporary Art, Cent. — A563

Die Cut Perf. 13½

2014, June 11 Litho. & Engr.

Self-Adhesive

1683 A563 9k multi 3.50 1.75
a. Booklet pane of 2 7.00

Manor Houses A564

Designs: 6.50k, Knuthenborg. 9k, Ledreborg Palace.

Die Cut Perf. 13x13½

2014, June 11 Litho. & Engr.

Self-Adhesive

1684 A564 6.50k multi 2.40 1.25
a. Booklet pane of 10 24.00
1685 A564 9k multi 3.50 1.75
a. Booklet pane of 10 35.00

Guard Hussar Regiment, 400th Anniv. — A565

Die Cut Perf. 13½

2014, Aug. 30 Litho. & Engr.

Self-Adhesive

1686 A565 6.50k multi 2.40 1.25
a. Booklet pane of 10 24.00

Blank Space for Greetings, by Olafur Eliasson — A566

Serpentine Die Cut 10¼

2014, Aug. 30 Litho. & Engr.

Self-Adhesive

1687 A566 9k blk & olive 3.25 1.60
a. Booklet pane of 4 13.00

The central portion of the stamp is die cut.

Characters from Stories by Hans Christian Andersen — A567

Designs: 6.50k, Klods-Hans (Clumsy Hans) and dead crow. 9k, Tommelise (Thumbelina) and toad.

Perf. 12¾x13¼

2014, Aug. 30 Litho. & Engr.

Souvenir Sheet

1688 Sheet of 2 5.75 3.00
a. A567 6.50k multi 2.40 1.25
b. A567 9k multi 3.25 1.60

Self-Adhesive

Die Cut Perf. 13½x13

1689 A567 6.50k multi 2.40 1.25
a. Booklet pane of 10 24.00
1690 A567 9k multi 3.25 1.60
a. Booklet pane of 10 32.50

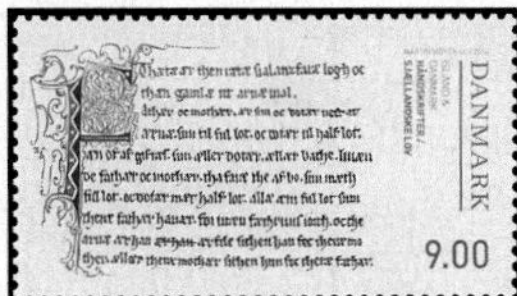

Manuscripts — A568

Designs: 9k, Valdemar's Law of Zealand, 13th cent. 14k, Njáls Saga, c. 1350.

Litho. & Engr.

2014, Aug. 30 ***Perf. 13x12¾***

Souvenir Sheet

1691 Sheet of 2 8.25 4.25
a. A568 9k multi 3.25 1.60
b. A568 14k multi 5.00 2.50

Self-Adhesive

Die Cut Perf. 13½

1692 A568 9k multi 3.25 1.60
a. Booklet pane of 10 32.50
1693 A568 14k multi 5.00 2.50
a. Booklet pane of 5 25.00

See Iceland Nos. 1350-1352.

Berries — A569

Designs: 6.50k, Snowberries. 9k, Lingonberries. 14k, Firethorn.

Die Cut Perf. 13½x13¼

2014, Oct. 18 **Litho.**

Self-Adhesive

1694 A569 6.50k multi 2.25 1.10
a. Booklet pane of 10 22.50
1695 A569 9k multi 3.00 1.50
a. Booklet pane of 10 30.00
1696 A569 14k multi 4.75 2.40
a. Booklet pane of 5 24.00
Nos. 1694-1696 (3) 10.00 5.00

Queen Margrethe II Type of 2010

Die Cut Perf. 13

2014, Nov. 17 **Litho. & Engr.**

Self-Adhesive

Panel Color

1697 A492 7k Prus blue 2.40 1.25
a. Booklet pane of 10 24.00
1698 A492 10k red 3.50 1.75
a. Booklet pane of 10 35.00
1699 A492 16.50k orange 5.50 2.75
a. Booklet pane of 10 55.00
1700 A492 19k blue 6.50 3.25
a. Booklet pane of 10 65.00
Nos. 1697-1700 (4) 17.90 9.00

Children's Poems by Halfdan Rasmussen (1915-2002) — A570

Poems from *Halfdans ABC*: No. 1701, Bennys Bukser Braendte (Benn's Trouser's Burned). No. 1702, Kanonkongen Knold (Cannon King Knold).

Die Cut Perf. 13¾x13½

2015, Jan. 2 **Litho. & Engr.**

Self-Adhesive

1701 A570 7k blue & multi 2.25 1.10
1702 A570 7k dl grn & multi 2.25 1.10
a. Booklet pane of 10, 6 #1701, 4 #1702 22.50

Lego Blocks — A571

Blocks of various colors and: 10k, Boy. 14.50k, Girl.

Die Cut Perf. 13½x13

2015, Jan. 2 **Self-Adhesive** **Litho.**

1703 A571 10k multi 3.25 1.60
a. Booklet pane of 10 32.50
b. Sheet of 6 + 20 stickers 22.50
1704 A571 14.50k multi 4.75 2.40
a. Booklet pane of 10 4.75 2.40

No. 1703b sold for 70k.

Animals in Wadden Sea National Park — A572

Designs: Nos. 1705a, 1706, Texel sheep. Nos. 1705b, 1707, Black-tailed godwit, vert. Nos. 1705c, 1708, Harbor seals.

Litho. & Engr.

2015, Jan. 2 ***Perf. 13***

1705 Souvenir sheet of 3 9.75 5.00
a.-c. A572 10k Any single 3.25 1.60

Self-Adhesive

Die Cut Perf. 13¼x13½, 13½x13¼

1706 A572 10k multi 3.25 1.60
1707 A572 10k multi 3.25 1.60
1708 A572 10k multi 3.25 1.60
a. Booklet pane of 10, 4 #1706, 6 #1708 32.50
Nos. 1706-1708 (3) 9.75 4.80

Herlufsholm, 450th Anniv. — A573

Die Cut Perf. 13½x13

2015, Mar. 14 **Litho.**

Self-Adhesive

1709 A573 10k multi 3.00 1.50
a. Booklet pane of 10 30.00 —

Inventions — A574

Inventions: Nos. 1710a, 1711, Dry cell battery, by Wilhelm Hellesen, 1887. Nos. 1710b, 1712, Ready-mix concrete truck, by Kristian Hindhede, 1929, horiz. Nos. 1710c, 1713, Long John delivery bicycle, by Morten Rasmussen Mortensen, 1929, horiz. Nos. 1710d, 1714, Writing ball, by Rasmus Mallin-Hansen, 1867.

2015, Mar. 14 **Litho.** ***Perf. 13***

Souvenir Sheet

1710 Sheet of 4 12.00 6.00
a.-d. A574 10k Any single 3.00 1.50

Booklet Stamps

Self-Adhesive

Litho. & Engr.

Die Cut Perf. 13½x13, 13x13½

1711 A574 10k multi 3.00 1.50
1712 A574 10k multi 3.00 1.50
1713 A574 10k multi 3.00 1.50
a. Booklet pane of 10, 6 #1713, 4 #1712 30.00
1714 A574 10k multi 3.00 1.50
a. Booklet pane of 10, 6 #1711, 4 #1714 30.00
Nos. 1711-1714 (4) 12.00 6.00

Medal of Merit — A575

Order of the Elephant — A576

Order of Dannebrog — A577

Die Cut Perf. 13½x13

2015, Mar. 14 **Litho. & Engr.**

Self-Adhesive

1715 A575 7k multi 2.10 1.10

Booklet Stamps

1716 A576 7k multi 2.10 1.10
1717 A577 7k multi 2.10 1.10
a. Booklet pane of 10, 6 #1716, 4 #1717 21.00
Nos. 1715-1717 (3) 6.30 3.30

A booklet containing perforated examples of Nos. 1715-1717 (three booklet panes containing one of each stamp and one booklet pane containing all three stamps) sold for 199k.

Woman Suffrage, Cent. A578

Die Cut Perf. 13¼

2015, June 13 **Litho.**

Self-Adhesive

1718 A578 10k multi 3.00 1.50

Samosvej 8, 2300 Kobenhaven S, Danmark, by Jesper Christiansen — A579

Die Cut Perf. 13¼

2015, June 13 **Litho. & Engr.**

Self-Adhesive

1719 A579 10k multi 3.00 1.50

Copenhagen Carpenters' Guild, 500th Anniv. — A580

Die Cut Perf. 13½x13

2015, June 13 **Litho. & Engr.**

Self-Adhesive

1720 A580 10k multi 3.00 1.50
a. Booklet pane of 10 30.00

Ships — A581

Designs: Nos. 1721a, 1723, Georg Stage. Nos. 1721b, 1722, Danmark. Nos. 1721c, 1724, Kobenhavn. Nos. 1721d, 1725, Fulton.

2015, June 13 **Litho.** ***Perf. 13x12¾***

1721 A581 Sheet of 4 8.50 8.50
a.-d. 7k Any single 2.10 1.10

Self-Adhesive

Die Cut Perf. 13x13½

1722 A581 7k multi 2.10 1.10
1723 A581 7k multi 2.10 1.10
a. Vert. pair, #1722-1723, on backing paper without printing 4.25
1724 A581 7k multi 2.10 1.10
1725 A581 7k multi 2.10 1.10
a. Vert. pair, #1724-1725, on backing paper without printing 4.25
b. Booklet pane of 10, 2 each #1723-1725, 4 #1722 21.00
Nos. 1722-1725 (4) 8.40 4.40

Miniature Sheet

25th Post Danmark Rundt Bicycle Race — A582

No. 1726: a, Moreno Argentin. b, Jakob Fuglsang. c, Cyclists in Randers. d, Matti Breschel. e, Cyclists on Kiddesvej climb, Velje. f, Fabian Cancellara. g, Cyclists on Storebaelts Bridge. h, Cyclist on Frederiksberg Allé, Copenhagen. i, Mark Cavendish. j, Michael Valgren.

Die Cut Perf. 13x13¼ on 3 Sides

2015, June 27 **Litho.**

Self-Adhesive

1726 A582 Sheet of 10 25.50
a.-e. 7k Any single 2.10 1.10
f.-j. 10k Any single 3.00 1.50

Christmas — A583

Honey cakes shaped as: Nos. 1727a, 1728, Man. Nos. 1727b, 1729, Woman. Nos. 1727c, 1730, Heart.

2015, Oct. 17 **Litho.** ***Perf. 12¾x13¼***

Souvenir Sheet

1727 Sheet of 3 7.25 3.75
a.-b. A583 7k Either single 2.10 1.10
c. A583 10k multi 3.00 1.50

Self-Adhesive

Die Cut Perf. 13½x13

1728 A583 7k multi 2.10 1.10
1729 A583 7k multi 2.10 1.10
a. Booklet pane of 10, 6 #1728, 4 #1729 21.00

Size:22x32mm

Die Cut Perf. 12¼x13 Syncopated

1730 A583 10k multi 3.00 1.50
Nos. 1728-1730 (3) 7.20 3.70

Maribo Cathedral, 600th Anniv. — A584

Litho. & Engr.
2016, Jan. 4 *Perf. 13½x13*
Self-Adhesive

1731 A584 19k multi 5.50 2.75
a. Booklet pane of 10 55.00

Nordic Food Culture
A585 A586

2016, Jan. 4 Litho. *Perf. 13*
Souvenir Sheet

1732 Sheet of 2 4.80 2.50
a. A585 8k multi 2.40 1.25
b. A586 8k multi 2.40 1.25

Self-Adhesive
Die Cut Perf. 13 Syncopated

1733 A585 8k multi 2.40 1.25
a. Booklet pane of 5 12.00
1734 A586 8k multi 2.40 1.25
a. Booklet pane of 5 12.00

Souvenir Sheet

Europa — A587

No. 1735: a, Hands holding Earth wrapped in leaves. b, Bicylcist, wind generators, paint roller.

2016, Mar. 31 Litho. *Perf. 13*
1735 A587 Sheet of 2 15.50 15.50
a.-b. 25k Either single 7.75 3.75

Think Green Issue.

Sports — A588

Designs: No. 1736, Runner in Lillebaelt Half Marathon. No. 1737, Cyclists in Fyen Rundt Bicycle Race. No. 1738, Cyclist in Haervejslobet Mountain Bike Race. No. 1739, Swimmer in Christiansborg Rundt Swimming Race. No. 1740, Bicycle helmet, running shoes, swimming goggles.

Die Cut Perf. 13¼ Syncopated
2016, Mar. 31 Litho.
Booklet Stamps
Self-Adhesive

1736 A588 8k multi 2.50 1.25
1737 A588 8k multi 2.50 1.25
1738 A588 8k multi 2.50 1.25
1739 A588 8k multi 2.50 1.25
1740 A588 8k multi 2.50 1.25
a. Booklet pane of 10, 2 each #1736-1740 25.00
Nos. 1736-1740 (5) 12.50 6.25

Prize-Winning Animals at Agricultural Shows — A589

Designs: No. 1741, Wyandotte cockerel. No. 1742, Danish Red Holstein cow. No. 1743, Oldenburg stallion. No. 1744, Shropshire ram. No. 1745, Satin rabbit.

Die Cut Perf. 13¼ Syncopated
2016, Mar. 31 Litho.
Booklet Stamps
Self-Adhesive

1741 A589 8k multi 2.50 1.25
1742 A589 8k multi 2.50 1.25
1743 A589 8k multi 2.50 1.25
1744 A589 8k multi 2.50 1.25
1745 A589 8k multi 2.50 1.25
a. Booklet pane of 10, 2 each #1741-1745 25.00
Nos. 1741-1745 (5) 12.50 6.25

Famous Men — A590

Designs: No. 1746, Maersk Mc-Kinney Moller (1913-2012), shipping magnate, and M/S Emma Maersk. No. 1747, Jorn Utzon (1918-2008), architect, and Sydney Opera House.

Die Cut Perf. 13¼ Syncopated
2016, Mar. 31 Litho. & Engr.
Booklet Stamps
Self-Adhesive

1746 A590 19k multi 6.00 3.00
1747 A590 19k multi 6.00 3.00
a. Booklet pane of 10, 6 #1746, 4 #1747 60.00

Souvenir Sheet

Art by Trine Sondergaard — A591

No. 1748: a, Interior #12. b, Guldnakke #16.

2016, June 23 Litho. *Perf. 12½*
1748 A591 Sheet of 2 15.00 15.00
a.-b. 25k Either single 7.50 3.75

Children's Songs — A592

Illustrations by Bitte Böcher from children's songbook *De Sma Synger.* Nos. 1749a, 1751, Den Lille Ole Med Paraplyen. Nos. 1749b, 1750, Der Sad to Katte pa et Bord. Nos. 1749c, 1753, Bro, Bro, Brille. Nos. 1749d, 1752, Mors Lille Ole.

2016, June 23 Litho. *Perf. 12¾x13*
1749 Sheet of 4 9.75 9.75
a.-d. A592 8k Any single 2.40 1.25

Booklet Stamps
Self-Adhesive
Litho. & Engr.
Die Cut Perf. 13¼ Syncopated

1750 A592 8k blk & brt grn 2.40 1.25
1751 A592 8k blk & brt org 2.40 1.25
1752 A592 8k blk & brt grn 2.40 1.25
1753 A592 8k blk & brt org 2.40 1.25
a. Booklet pane of 10, 2 each #1751-1753, 4 #1750 24.00
Nos. 1750-1753 (4) 9.60 5.00

Danish Porcelain Designs — A593

Designs: No. 1754, Magestellet (Seagull), 1892. No. 1755, Flora Danica, 1790. No. 1756, Bla Blomst Svejfet (Blue Flower Curved), 1779. No. 1757, Sort Mega Riflet (Black Fluted Mega), 2006. No. 1758, Musselmalet Halvblonde (Blue Fluted Half Lace), 1888.

Die Cut Perf. 13¼ Syncopated
2016, June 23 Litho.
Booklet Stamps
Self-Adhesive

1754 A593 8k multi 2.40 1.25
1755 A593 8k multi 2.40 1.25
1756 A593 8k multi 2.40 1.25
1757 A593 8k multi 2.40 1.25
1758 A593 8k multi 2.40 1.25
a. Booklet pane of 10, 2 each #1754-1758 24.00
Nos. 1754-1758 (5) 12.00 6.25

A booklet containing 11 perf. 12¾x13¼ stamps with the designs of Nos. 1754-1758 and four perforated progressive proofs of the Flora Danica design sold for 199k.

Illustrations of Pixies by Peter Moller (1838-1910) A594

Designs: No. 1759, Pixie carrying baskets of toys and balloon. No. 1760, Pixie dancing with cat. No. 1761, Dog biting pixie's cap. No. 1762, Pixies dancing and playing concertina. No. 1763, Five pixie musicians.

Die Cut Perf. 13¼ Syncopated
2016, Sept. 29 Litho.
Booklet Stamps
Self-Adhesive

1759 A594 8k multi 2.40 1.25
1760 A594 8k multi 2.40 1.25
1761 A594 8k multi 2.40 1.25
1762 A594 8k multi 2.40 1.25
1763 A594 8k multi 2.40 1.25
a. Booklet pane of 5, #1759-1763 12.00
Nos. 1759-1763 (5) 12.00 6.25

Christmas.

Souvenir Sheet

Frederksborg Castle, Hillerod — A595

No. 1764 — Aerial views of: a, Baroque Gardens. b, Castle.

2017, Jan. 2 Litho. *Perf. 13*
1764 A595 Sheet of 2 14.00 7.00
a.-b. 25k Either single 7.00 3.50

Shellfish — A596

Designs: No. 1765, Taskekrabbe (crab). No. 1766, Jomfruhummer (lobster). No. 1767, Nordsoreje (shrimp). No. 1768, Blamusling (mussel). No. 1769, Limfjordsosters (oyster).

Die Cut Perf. 13¾ Syncopated
2017, Jan. 2 Litho.
Booklet Stamps
Self-Adhesive

1765 A596 8k multi 2.25 1.10
1766 A596 8k multi 2.25 1.10
1767 A596 8k multi 2.25 1.10
1768 A596 8k multi 2.25 1.10
1769 A596 8k multi 2.25 1.10
a. Booklet pane of 10, 2 each #1765-1769 22.50
Nos. 1765-1769 (5) 11.25 5.50

Heart With Gay Pride Flag Stripes — A597

Heart at: No. 1770, Top. No. 1771, Bottom.

Die Cut Perf. 13¼ Syncopated
2017, Mar. 30 Litho.
Booklet Stamps
Self-Adhesive

1770 A597 8k multi 2.40 2.40
1771 A597 8k multi 2.40 2.40
a. Booklet pane of 10, 6 #1770, 4 #1771 24.00

Aarhus, 2017 European Capital of Culture A598

Buildings in Aarhus: No. 1772, ARoS Art Museum. No. 1773, Moesgaard Museum. No. 1774, DOKK1 Culture Center. No. 1775, The Iceberg Apartment Complex. No. 1776, City Hall.

Die Cut Perf. 13¼ Syncopated
2017, Mar. 30 Litho.
Booklet Stamps
Self-Adhesive

1772 A598 25k multi 7.25 7.25
1773 A598 25k multi 7.25 7.25
1774 A598 25k multi 7.25 7.25
1775 A598 25k multi 7.25 7.25
1776 A598 25k multi 7.25 7.25
a. Booklet pane of 10, 2 each #1772-1776 72.50
Nos. 1772-1776 (5) 36.25 36.25

Souvenir Sheet

Queen Margrethe II and Prince Henrik, 50th Wedding Anniversary — A599

2017, May 15 Litho. *Perf. 13½*
1777 A599 50k gold & multi 15.00 15.00

See Faroe Islands No. 686, Greenland No. 754.

A600

A601

A602

A603

Summer Houses A604

Die Cut Perf. 13¼ Syncopated

2017, June 15 **Litho.**

Booklet Stamps
Self-Adhesive

1778 A600 8k multi 2.50 2.50
1779 A601 8k multi 2.50 2.50
1780 A602 8k multi 2.50 2.50
1781 A603 8k multi 2.50 2.50
1782 A604 8k multi 2.50 2.50
a. Booklet pane of 10, 2 each #1778-1782 25.00
Nos. 1778-1782 (5) 12.50 12.50

Automobiles — A605

No. 1783: a, 1960 BMW Isetta 300. b, 1959 Volkswagen 1200 De Luxe. c, 1973 Citroen DS21 Pallas.

2017, June 15 **Litho.** ***Perf. 13x13¼***

1783 A605 Sheet of 3 23.50 23.50
a.-c. 25k Any single 7.75 7.75
d. Booklet pane of 1 #1783a 15.00 —
e. Booklet pane of 1 #1783b 15.00 —
f. Booklet pane of 1 #1783c 15.00 —
g. Booklet pane of 1 #1783c + 4 invalid for postage progressive proofs of #1783 15.00 —
Complete booklet, #1783d, 1783e, 1783f, 1783g 60.00
h. As #1783, with Nordia 2017 emblem and text in sheet margin 23.50 23.50

Complete booklet sold for 199k.
Issued: No. 1783h, 10/27.

A606

A607

A608

A609

Flowers — A610

Die Cut Perf. 13¼ Syncopated

2017, Sept. 28 **Litho.**

Booklet Stamps
Self-Adhesive

1784 A606 8k multi 2.60 2.60
1785 A607 8k multi 2.60 2.60
1786 A608 8k multi 2.60 2.60
1787 A609 8k multi 2.60 2.60
1788 A610 8k multi 2.60 2.60
a. Booklet pane of 10, 2 each #1784-1788 26.00
Nos. 1784-1788 (5) 13.00 13.00

A611

A612

A613

A614

Art by Bjorn Wiinblad (1918-2006) A615

Die Cut Perf. 13¼ Syncopated

2018, Jan. 2 **Litho.**

Booklet Stamps
Self-Adhesive

1789 A611 9k multi 3.00 3.00
1790 A612 9k multi 3.00 3.00
1791 A613 9k multi 3.00 3.00
1792 A614 9k multi 3.00 3.00
1793 A615 9k multi 3.00 3.00
a. Booklet pane of 10, 2 each #1789-1793 30.00
Nos. 1789-1793 (5) 15.00 15.00

A booklet, issued on Sept. 6, 2018, containing 11 perf. 14¼ water-activated gum examples of Nos. 1789-1793 and four progressive proofs of No. 1790, sold for 199k.

Rose Varieties — A616

Designs: No. 1794, Jubilee Celebration. No. 1795, Rhapsody in Blue. No. 1796, Sekel. No. 1797, Ingrid Bergman. No. 1798, Crocus Rose.

Die Cut Perf. 13¾ Syncopated

2018, Jan. 2 **Litho.**

Booklet Stamps
Self-Adhesive

1794 A616 27k multi 8.75 8.75
1795 A616 27k multi 8.75 8.75
1796 A616 27k multi 8.75 8.75
1797 A616 27k multi 8.75 8.75
1798 A616 27k multi 8.75 8.75
a. Booklet pane of 10, 2 each #1794-1798 87.50
Nos. 1794-1798 (5) 43.75 43.75

Souvenir Sheet

A617

No. 1799 — Stamps designed by Yoko Ono: a, Moon and "Dream." b, Sun and "Smile."

2018, Jan. 2 **Litho.** ***Perf. 13¼x13¾***

1799 A617 Sheet of 2 17.50 17.50
a.-b. 27k Either single 8.75 8.75

Souvenir Sheet

Great Belt Bridge — A618

No. 1800: a, Bridge towers. b, Bridge approach.

2018, May 17 **Litho.** ***Perf. 13¼***

1800 A618 Sheet of 2 17.00 17.00
a.-b. 27k Either single 8.50 4.25

Europa.

Souvenir Sheet

Fish — A619

No. 1801: a, Esox lucius (75x36mm). b, Perca fluviatilis (25x36mm).

2018, May 17 **Litho.** ***Perf. 13½x13¼***

1801 A619 Sheet of 2 17.00 17.00
a.-b. 27k Either single 8.50 4.25

Europa.

Wild Food — A620

Designs: No. 1802, Braende naelde (stinging nettles). No. 1803, Karljohan svamp (Karl Johan mushroom). No. 1804, Japansk pileurt (Japanese knotweed). No. 1805, Skvalder kal (ground elder). No. 1806, Hyben rose (rosehips).

Die Cut Perf. 13¼ Syncopated

2018, Sept. 6 **Litho.**

Booklet Stamps
Self-Adhesive

1802 A620 9k multi 3.00 3.00
1803 A620 9k multi 3.00 3.00
1804 A620 9k multi 3.00 3.00
1805 A620 9k multi 3.00 3.00
1806 A620 9k multi 3.00 3.00
a. Booklet pane of 10, 2 each #1802-1806 30.00

Lines and Hearts — A621

2019, Jan. 2 **Litho.** ***Die Cut Perf. 13***

Booklet Stamp
Self-Adhesive

1807 A621 1k dark blue .30 .30
a. Booklet pane of 10 3.00

Thor's Hammer with Runic Inscriptions A622

Necklace of Glass Beads A623

Buckle in Shape of Ship — A624

Valkyrie Figurine — A625

Decorative Clip — A626

Die Cut Perf. 13¼x13½ Syncopated

2019, Jan. 2 **Litho.**

Booklet Stamps
Self-Adhesive

1808 A622 10k multi 3.00 3.00
1809 A623 10k multi 3.00 3.00
1810 A624 10k multi 3.00 3.00
1811 A625 10k multi 3.00 3.00
1812 A626 10k multi 3.00 3.00
a. Booklet pane of 10, 2 each #1808-1812 30.00
Nos. 1808-1812 (5) 15.00 15.00

Viking era artifacts.

Danish Flag, 800th Anniv. — A627

Flags and: Nos. 1813, 1818, Christianborg Palace Tower. Nos. 1814, 1819, Birthday cake, horiz. Nos. 1815, 1820, Soccer ball and net. Nos. 1816, 1821, Royal Yacht Dannebrog, horiz. Nos. 1817, 1822, Houses.

2019 **Litho.** ***Perf. 13¼***

Booklet Stamps

1813 A627 10k multi 5.50 5.50
1814 A627 10k multi 5.50 5.50
a. Booklet pane of 1 + 4 perforated progressive proofs 5.50 —
1815 A627 10k multi 5.50 5.50
1816 A627 10k multi 5.50 5.50
a. Booklet pane of 2, #1814, 1816 11.00 —
1817 A627 10k multi 5.50 5.50
a. Booklet pane of 5, #1813-1817 27.50 —
b. Booklet pane of 3, #1813, 1815, 1817 16.50 —
Complete booklet, #1814a, 1816a, 1817a, 1817b 61.00
Nos. 1813-1817 (5) 27.50 27.50

Self-Adhesive

Die Cut Perf. 13¼ Syncopated

1818 A627 10k multi 3.00 3.00
a. Coil single on translucent paper 3.00
1819 A627 10k multi 3.00 3.00
1820 A627 10k multi 3.00 3.00
1821 A627 10k multi 3.00 3.00

1822 A627 10k multi 3.00 3.00
a. Booklet pane of 10, 2 each #1818-1822 30.00
Nos. 1818-1822 (5) 15.00 15.00

Issued: Nos. 1813-1817, 5/16; Nos. 1818-1822, 1/2. Complete booklet sold for 199k.

Lighthouses A628

Designs: No. 1823, Hammeren Lighthouse. No. 1824, Lyngvig Lighthouse. No. 1825, Hirtshals Lighthouse. No. 1826, Taksensand Lighthouse. No. 1827, Omo Lighthouse.

Die Cut Perf. 13¼x13 Syncopated

2019, May 16 **Litho.**

Booklet Stamps
Self-Adhesive

1823 A628 10k multi 3.00 3.00
1824 A628 10k multi 3.00 3.00
1825 A628 10k multi 3.00 3.00
1826 A628 10k multi 3.00 3.00
1827 A628 10k multi 3.00 3.00
a. Booklet pane of 10, 2 each #1823-1827 30.00
Nos. 1823-1827 (5) 15.00 15.00

Souvenir Sheet

Europa — A629

No. 1828: a, Mute swans and chicks (60x40mm). b, Mute swan and chick (30x40mm).

2019, May 16 **Litho.** ***Perf. 13¼x13***

1828 A629 Sheet of 2 18.00 18.00
a.-b. 30k Either single 9.00 9.00

Dogs — A630

Designs: No. 1829, Labrador retriever named Audi. No. 1830, Golden retriever named Chivas. No. 1831, Smooth fox terrier named Mille. No. 1832, Icelandic sheepdogs named Píla, Gaia and Blidha. No. 1833, German shepherd named Theo.

Die Cut Perf. 13x13½ Syncopated

2019, Sept. 19 **Litho.**

Booklet Stamps
Self-Adhesive

1829 A630 10k multi 3.00 3.00
1830 A630 10k multi 3.00 3.00
1831 A630 10k multi 3.00 3.00
1832 A630 10k multi 3.00 3.00
1833 A630 10k multi 3.00 3.00
a. Booklet pane of 10, 2 each #1829-1833 30.00
Nos. 1829-1833 (5) 15.00 15.00

Miniature Sheet

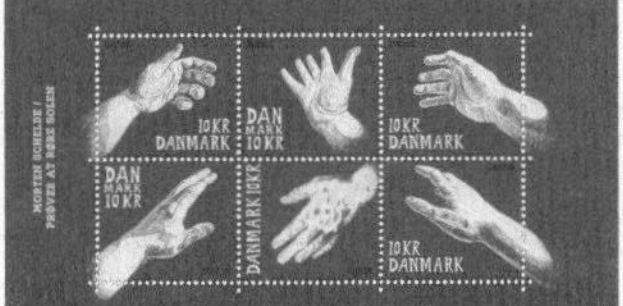
Trying to Touch the Sun, by Morten Schelde — A631

No. 1834 — Hand with country name and denomination at: a, LR. b, LL, country name on two lines. c, LL, country name on one line, palm visible. d, UL, country name on two lines. e, Left. f, LL, country name on one line, palm not visible.

2019, Sept. 19 **Litho.** ***Perf. 13½***

1834 A631 Sheet of 6 18.00 18.00
a.-f. 10k Any single 3.00 3.00

SEMI-POSTAL STAMPS

Nos. 159, 157 Surcharged in Red

Wmk. Multiple Crosses (114)

1921, June 17 ***Perf. 14½x14***

B1 A20 10o + 5o green 27.50 *60.00*
B2 A21 20o + 10o slate 30.00 *77.50*
Set, never hinged 167.50

Crown and Staff of Aesculapius — SP1

1929, Aug. 1 **Engr.**

B3 SP1 10o yellow green 4.50 *7.00*
a. Booklet pane of 2 27.50
B4 SP1 15o brick red 9.00 *12.00*
a. Booklet pane of 2 32.50
B5 SP1 25o deep blue 25.00 *40.00*
a. Booklet pane of 2 135.00
Nos. B3-B5 (3) 38.50 *59.00*
Set, never hinged 100.00

These stamps were sold at a premium of 5 öre each for benefit of the Danish Cancer Committee.

Dybbol Mill — SP2

1937, Jan. 20 **Unwmk.** ***Perf. 13***

B6 SP2 5o + 5o green .60 *1.40*
B7 SP2 10o + 5o lt brown 2.25 *9.00*
B8 SP2 15o + 5o carmine 3.25 *9.00*
Nos. B6-B8 (3) 6.10 *19.40*
Set, never hinged 13.00

The surtax was for a fund in memory of H. P. Hanssen, statesman.

Nos. 223a and B6, Nos. 229 and B7, Nos. 238A and B8 are found se-tenant in booklets. For booklet panes, see Nos. 223d, 229b and 238Al.

Queen Alexandrine — SP3

1939-40 ***Perf. 13***

B9 SP3 5o + 3o rose lake & red ('40) .25 .35
a. Booklet pane of 4 2.00 2.00
B10 SP3 10o + 5o dk violet & red .35 .25
B11 SP3 15o + 5o scarlet & red .30 *.50*
Nos. B9-B11 (3) .90 1.10
Set, never hinged 1.35

The surtax was for the Danish Red Cross.

Nos. 230 and B10 have been issued se-tenant in booklets. See No. 230b. In this pane No. 230 measures 23½x31mm from perf. to perf.

Crown Princess Ingrid and Princess Margrethe — SP4

1941-43

B12 SP4 10o + 5o dk violet .25 .25
a. Booklet pane of 10 32.50
B13 SP4 20o + 5o red ('43) .25 .25
Set, never hinged .60

Surtax for the Children's Charity Fund.

No. 288 Surcharged in Red

1944, May 11

B14 A48 10o + 5o violet .25 .25
Never hinged .30
a. Booklet pane of 10 27.50

The surtax was for the Danish Red Cross.

Catalogue values for unused stamps in this section, from this point to the end of the section, are for Never Hinged items.

Symbols of Freedom SP5

Explosions at Rail Junction SP6

Danish Flag — SP7

1947, May 4 **Engr.** ***Perf. 13***

B15 SP5 15o + 5o green .35 .35
B16 SP6 20o + 5o dark red .35 .35
B17 SP7 40o + 5o deep blue .85 .85
Nos. B15-B17 (3) 1.55 1.55

Issued in memory of the Danish struggle for liberty and the liberation of Denmark. The surtax was for the Liberty Fund.

For surcharges see Nos. B22-B23.

Princess Anne-Marie — SP8

1950, Oct. 19 **Unwmk.**

B18 SP8 25o + 5o rose brown .55 .50

The surtax was for the National Children's Welfare Association.

S. S. Jutlandia — SP9

1951, Sept. 13 ***Perf. 13***

B19 SP9 25o + 5o red .65 .60

The surtax was for the Red Cross.

No. 335 Surcharged in Black

1953, Feb. 13

B20 A61 30o + 10o brown red 1.50 1.50

The surtax was for flood relief in the Netherlands.

Stone Memorial — SP10

1953, Mar. 26 ***Perf. 13***

B21 SP10 30o + 5o dark red 1.40 1.25

The surtax was for cultural work of the Danish Border Union.

Nos. B15 and B16 Surcharged in Black

1955, Feb. 17

B22 SP5 20o + 5o on No. B15 1.00 .85
B23 SP6 30o + 5o on No. B16 1.00 .85

The surtax was for the Liberty Fund.

No. 341 Surcharged

1957, Mar. 25

B24 A61 30o + 5o on 95o red org .65 .65

The surtax went to the Danish Red Cross for aid to Hungary.

No. 335 Surcharged in Black

1959, Feb. 23

B25 A61 30o + 10o brown red .80 .90

The surtax was for the Greenland Fund.

Globe Encircled by Red Cross Flags — SP11

1959, June 24 Engr. *Perf. 13*
B26 SP11 30o + 5o rose red .50 .50
B27 SP11 60o + 5o lt ultra & car .75 .75

Centenary of the Intl. Red Cross idea. The surtax was for the Red Cross. Crosses photogravure on No. B27.

Queen Ingrid — SP12

1960, Oct. 25 Unwmk.
B28 SP12 30o + 10o dark red 1.00 1.00

Queen Ingrid's 25th anniv. as a Girl Scout. The surtax was for the Scouts' fund for needy and sick children.

African Mother, Child — SP13

1962, May 24
B29 SP13 30o + 10o dark red .75 1.00

Issued to aid underdeveloped countries.

Healthy and Crippled Hands — SP14

1963, June 24 *Perf. 13*
B30 SP14 35o + 10o dark red 1.10 1.10

The surtax was for the benefit of the Cripples' Foundation.

Old Bridge at Danish-German Border — SP15

1964, May 28 Engr.
B31 SP15 35o + 10o henna brn .85 .90

Surtax for the Danish Border Union.

Princesses Margrethe, Benedikte, Anne-Marie SP16

1964, Aug. 24
B32 SP16 35o + 10o dull red .85 .75
B33 SP16 60o + 10o dk bl & red 1.10 .95

The surtax was for the Red Cross.

Happy Child — SP17

1965, Oct. 21 Engr. *Perf. 13*
B34 SP17 50o + 10o brick red .65 .65

The surtax was for the National Children's Welfare Association.

"Red Cross" in 32 Languages and Red Cross, Red Lion and Sun, and Red Crescent Emblems SP18

1966, Jan. 20 Engr. *Perf. 13*
B35 SP18 50o + 10o red .65 .65

Engraved and Photogravure

B36 SP18 80o + 10o dk bl & red .80 .80

The surtax was for the Red Cross.

"Refugees 66" — SP19

1966, Oct. 24 Engr. *Perf. 13*
B37 SP19 40o + 10o sepia .80 .80
B38 SP19 50o + 10o rose red .80 .80
B39 SP19 80o + 10o blue 1.60 1.60
Nos. B37-B39 (3) 3.20 3.20

The surtax was for aid to refugees.

Symbolic Rose — SP20

1967, Oct. 12
B40 SP20 60o + 10o brown red .50 .55

The surcharge was for the Salvation Army.

Two Greenland Boys in Round Tower — SP21

1968, Sept. 12 Engr. *Perf. 13*
B41 SP21 60o + 10o dark red .65 .65

The surtax was for child welfare work in Greenland.

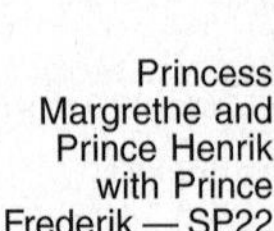

Princess Margrethe and Prince Henrik with Prince Frederik — SP22

1969, Dec. 11
B42 SP22 50o + 10o brn & red .65 .65
B43 SP22 60o + 10o brn red & red .65 .65

The surtax was for the Danish Red Cross.

Child Seeking Help — SP23

1970, Mar. 13
B44 SP23 60o + 10o brown red .65 .65

Surtax for "Save the Children Fund."

Child — SP24

1971, Apr. 29 Engr. *Perf. 13*
B45 SP24 60o + 10o copper red .65 .65

Surtax was for the National Children's Welfare Association.

Marsh Marigold — SP25

1972, Aug. 17
B46 SP25 70o + 10o green & yel .50 .55

Soc. and Home for the Disabled, cent.

Heimaey Town and Volcano — SP26

1973, Oct. 17 Engr. *Perf. 13*
B47 SP26 70o + 20o vio blue & red 1.00 1.00

The surtax was for the victims of the eruption of Heimaey Volcano, Jan. 23, 1973.

Queen Margrethe, IWY Emblem — SP27

1975, Mar. 20 Engr. *Perf. 13*
B48 SP27 90o + 20o red & cream .95 .80

International Women's Year 1975. Surtax was for a foundation to benefit women primarily in Greenland and Faroe Islands.

Skuldelev I SP28

Ships: 90o+20o, Thingvalla, emigrant steamer. 100o+20o, Liner Frederick VIII, c. 1930. 130o+20o, Three-master Danmark.

1976, Jan. 22 Engr. *Perf. 13*
B49 SP28 70 + 20o olive brown .75 .85
B50 SP28 90 + 20o brick red .75 .85
B51 SP28 100 + 20o olive green .85 1.10
B52 SP28 130 + 20o violet blue .90 1.60
Nos. B49-B52 (4) 3.25 4.40

American Declaration of Independence, 200th anniv.

People and Red Cross — SP29

1976, Feb. 26 Engr. *Perf. 13*
B53 SP29 100o + 20o red & black .65 .65
B54 SP29 130o + 20o bl, red & blk .80 .80

Centenary of Danish Red Cross.

Invalid in Wheelchair — SP30

1976, May 6 Engr. *Perf. 13*
B55 SP30 100o + 20o ver & blk .65 .65

The surtax was for the Foundation to Aid the Disabled.

Mother and Child — SP31

1977, Mar. 24 Engr. *Perf. 12½*
B56 SP31 1k + 20o multicolored .80 .80

Danish Society for the Mentally Handicapped, 25th anniv. Surtax was for the Society.

Anti-Cancer Campaign SP32

1978, Oct. 12 Engr. *Perf. 13*
B57 SP32 120o + 20o red .65 .65

Danish Anti-Cancer Campaign, 50th anniversary. Surtax was for campaign.

Child and IYC Emblem — SP33

1979, Jan. 25 Engr. *Perf. 12½*
B58 SP33 1.20k + 20o red & brown .65 .65

International Year of the Child.

Foundation for the Disabled, 25th Anniversary SP34

1980, Apr. 10 Engr. *Perf. 13*
B59 SP34 130o + 20o brown red .65 .70

Children Playing Ball — SP35

1981, Feb. 5 Engr. *Perf. 12½x13*
B60 SP35 1.60k + 20o brown red .70 .90

Surtax was for child welfare.

Intl. Year of the Disabled — SP36

1981, Sept. 10 Engr. *Perf. 12½x13*
B61 SP36 2k + 20o dark blue 1.00 1.10

Stem and Broken Line — SP37

1982, May 3 **Engr.** ***Perf. 13***
B62 SP37 2k + 40o dull red 1.10 1.20

Surtax was for Danish Multiple Sclerosis Society.

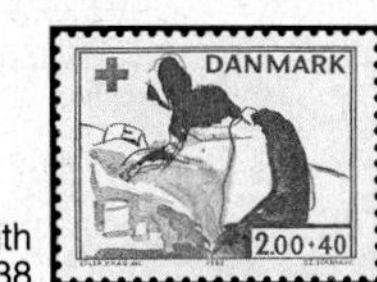

Nurse with Patient — SP38

1983, Jan. 27 **Engr.**
B63 SP38 2k + 40o multicolored 1.40 1.40

1984 Olympic Games — SP39

1984, Feb. 23 **Litho. & Engr.**
B64 SP39 2.70k + 40o multi 1.75 1.40

Electrocardiogram Reading, Heart — SP40

1984, Sept. 6 **Engr.** ***Perf. 12½***
B65 SP40 2.70k + 40o red 1.75 2.00

Surtax was for Heart Foundation.

SP41

1985, May 2 **Litho.** ***Perf. 13***
B66 SP41 2.80k + 50o multi 1.40 2.25

Liberation from German Occupation, 40th Anniv. Surtax for benefit of World War II veterans.

SP42

Design: Tapestry detail, by Caroline Ebbeson (1852-1936), former patient, St. Hans Hospital, Roskilade.

1985, Oct. 3 **Litho. & Engr.**
B67 SP42 2.80k + 40o multi 1.40 1.90

Natl. Soc. for the Welfare of the Mentally Ill, 25th Anniv. Surtax benefited the mentally ill.

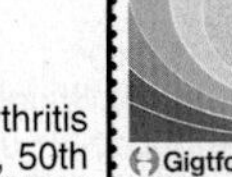

Danish Arthritis Assoc., 50th Anniv. — SP43

1986, Mar. 20 **Litho.** ***Perf. 13***
B68 SP43 2.80k + 50o multi 2.25 2.25

Surtax for the Arthritis Assoc.

Poul Reichhart (1913-1985), as Papageno in The Magic Flute — SP44

1986, Feb. 6 **Litho.** ***Perf. 13***
B69 SP44 2.80k + 50o multi 2.25 2.25

Surtax for the physically handicapped.

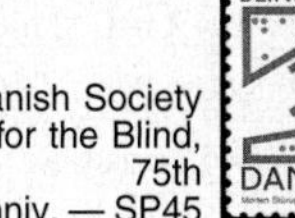

Danish Society for the Blind, 75th Anniv. — SP45

Litho. & Engr.
1986, Feb. 20 ***Perf. 13***
B70 SP45 2.80k +50o blk, vio brn & dk red 2.25 2.75

Danish Assoc. of Epileptics, 25th Anniv. SP46

1987, Sept. 24 **Engr.** ***Perf. 13***
B71 SP46 2.80k +50o dk red, brt ultra & dk grn 2.40 3.00

Folkekirkens Nodhjaelp Relief Organization — SP47

1988, Mar. 10 **Engr.**
B72 SP47 3k +50o multicolored 2.25 2.75

Surtax for the relief organization.

Natl. Council for Unwed Mothers, 5th Anniv. — SP48

1988, Sept. 22 **Photo.**
B73 SP48 3k +50o dk rose brn 2.50 3.25

Salvation Army — SP49

1989, Feb. 16 **Litho.**
B74 SP49 3.20k +50o multi 2.50 3.00

Insulin Crystal — SP50

1990, Aug. 30 **Litho.** ***Perf. 13***
B75 SP50 3.50k +50o multi 3.25 4.50

Danish Diabetes Assoc., 50th anniv.

Children's Telephone SP51

1991, June 6 **Engr.** ***Perf. 13***
B76 SP51 3.50k +50o dark blue 2.40 2.75

Surtax benefits Borns Vilkar, children's welfare organization.

Danish Dyslexia Assoc., 50th Anniv. SP52

Litho. & Engr.
1992, Aug. 27 ***Perf. 13***
B77 SP52 3.75k +50o multi 3.75 5.00

YMCA Social Work, 75th Anniv. — SP53

1993, Aug. 19 **Litho.** ***Perf. 13***
B78 SP53 3.75k +50o multi 2.75 3.25

Prince Henrik, 60th Birthday — SP54

Litho. & Engr.
1994, June 9 ***Perf. 13***
B79 SP54 3.75k +50o multi 2.10 3.00

Surtax for Danish Red Cross.

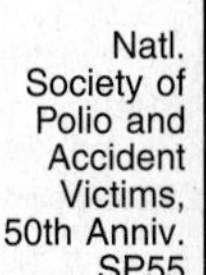

Natl. Society of Polio and Accident Victims, 50th Anniv. SP55

1995, June 8 **Litho.** ***Perf. 13***
B80 SP55 3.75k +50o red 1.90 2.75

The AIDS Foundation — SP56

1996, Oct. 10 **Litho.** ***Perf. 13***
B81 SP56 3.75k +50o red & black 3.50 2.25

Asthma-Allergy Assoc. — SP57

1997, May 15 **Litho.** ***Perf. 13***
B82 SP57 3.75k +50o multi 2.50 2.75

Danish Cancer Society SP58

1998, Sept. 3 **Litho.** ***Perf. 13***
B83 SP58 3.75k +50o multi 2.25 2.50

SP59

1999, Aug. 25 **Litho.** ***Perf. 13***
B84 SP59 4k +50o blue & red 2.00 2.25

For the Alzheimer's Association.

SP60

2000, Sept. 27 **Engr.** ***Perf. 13***
B85 SP60 4k +50o red & blue 1.60 2.00

For the Cerebral Palsy Association.

Amnesty International — SP61

2001, Jan. 24 **Engr.** ***Perf. 12¾***
B86 SP61 4k +50o blk & red 2.25 2.25

LEV National Association SP62

2002, Mar. 13 **Engr.** ***Perf. 12¾***
B87 SP62 4k + 50o multi, *greenish* 2.25 2.25

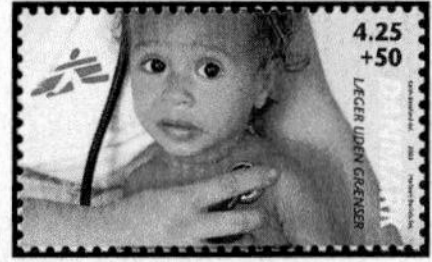

Doctors Without Borders SP63

2003, Mar. 12 **Litho.** ***Perf. 12¾***
B88 SP63 4.25k +50o multi 1.60 1.25
Booklet, 10 #B88 16.00

Children's Aid Day — SP64

2004, Jan. 14 Litho. *Perf. 12¾*

B89 SP64 4.50k +50o multi 1.75 2.10
Booklet, 10 #B89 17.50

SOS Children's Villages SP65

2005, Jan. 12 Litho. *Perf. 12¾*

B90 SP65 4.50k +50o multi 2.40 2.75
Complete booklet, 10 #B90 24.00

Surtax was originally intended for an SOS Children's Village in Burundi, but surtax went to the relief fund for Dec. 26, 2004 tsunami victims. A sticker noting this change was to be applied to the front covers of the booklets.

Danish Refugee Council, 50th Anniv. SP66

2006, Jan. 11 Engr. *Perf. 12¾*

B91 SP66 4.75k +50o blk & red, *tan* 2.75 2.75
Complete booklet, 10 #B91 27.50

Crown Prince Frederik, Crown Princess Mary, and Prince Christian SP67

2007, Jan. 10 Engr. *Perf. 13x13¼*

B92 SP67 4.75k +50o multi 2.75 2.40
Complete booklet, 10 #B92 27.50

Surtax for Crown Prince Frederik and Crown Princess Mary's Fund for Charitable and Humanitarian Purposes.

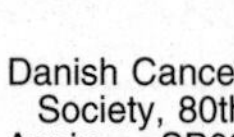

Danish Cancer Society, 80th Anniv. — SP68

2008, Jan. 9 Engr. *Perf. 12¾*

B93 SP68 5.50k +50o blk & red 2.50 2.40
Complete booklet, 10 #B93 25.00

SP69

Design: Prince Henrik, Farm Field, Viet Nam, Emblem of Worldwide Fund for Nature (WWF).

2009, Jan. 7 Litho. *Perf. 13x13¼*

B94 SP69 5.50k + 50o multi 2.75 3.25
Complete booklet, 10 #B94 27.50

Surtax for Worldwide Fund for Nature.

Danish Children's Cancer Foundation SP70

Die Cut Perf. 13¼x13½

2010, Jan. 6 Litho.

Self-Adhesive

B95 SP70 5.50k +50o multi 2.40 2.50
a. Souvenir sheet of 4 9.75

Booklet Stamp

Serpentine Die Cut 10

B96 SP70 5.50k +50o multi 2.40 2.50
a. Booklet pane of 12 29.00

Issued: No. B95a, 8/4.

Eight People SP71

2011 Litho. *Die Cut Perf. 13½x13*

Self-Adhesive

B97 SP71 5.50k+50o blk & red 2.50 2.50
B98 SP71 8k+50o blk & red 3.50 3.50

Booklet Stamps

Serpentine Die Cut 13½

B99 SP71 5.50k+50o blk & red 2.50 2.50
a. Booklet pane of 10 25.00
B100 SP71 8k+50o blk & red 3.50 3.50
a. Booklet pane of 10 35.00
b. Sheet of 6 + 7 labels 21.00 21.00

Surtax for Danish Rheumatism Association. Issued: Nos. B97, B99, 1/6; Nos. B98, B100, 3/9. No. B100b, 8/4.

Crown Princess Mary — SP72

2012, June 10 *Die Cut Perf. 13x13½*

Self-Adhesive

B101 SP72 8k+50o multi 3.00 3.00

Booklet Stamp

Serpentine Die Cut 13½

B102 SP72 8k+50o multi 3.00 3.00
a. Booklet pane of 10 + sticker 30.00

Surtax for Danish Heart Foundation.

Crown Princess Mary Type of 2012

Serpentine Die Cut 13½

2012, June 10

Self-Adhesive

Stochastic Litho. Printing

B103 SP72 8k+50o multi 3.50 3.50

The black dots that make up the design on No. B102 are arranged in lines, but are randomly placed on No. B103. No. B103 was printed in sheets of 6.

Girl's Head — SP73

Die Cut Perf. 13x13¼

2013-14 Litho.

B104 SP73 8k+1k multi 3.25 3.25

Booklet Stamp

Serpentine Die Cut 13½

B105 SP73 8k+1k multi 3.25 3.25
a. Booklet pane of 10 32.50

Self-Adhesive

Die Cut Perf. 13½x13

B106 SP73 9k+1k multi 3.75 3.75
a. Booklet pane of 10 37.50

Surtax for Save the Children charity.
Issued: Nos. B104-B105, 5/27; No. B106, 1/2/14.
No. B106 was printed in sheets of 6. Surtax was for Save the Children charity.

Red Cross, 150th Anniv. — SP74

2014-15 Litho. *Die Cut Perf. 13½*

Self-Adhesive

B107 SP74 9k+1k gray & red 3.75 3.75
a. Booklet pane of 10 37.50
B108 SP74 10k+1k gray & red 3.50 3.50
a. Booklet pane of 10 35.00

Surtax for Red Cross. Issued: No. B107, 6/3; No. B108, 1/2/15.

Worldwide Fund for Nature (WWF) — SP75

Sun, bird and: No. B109, Deer. No. B110, Farmhouse and wind generator.

Die Cut Perf. 13¼ Syncopated

2015, May 7 Litho.

Self-Adhesive

B109 SP75 10k+1k multi 3.25 3.25
B110 SP75 10k+1k multi 3.25 3.25
a. Booklet pane of 10, 6 #B109, 4 #B110 32.50

Surtax for Worldwide Fund for Nature. See Sweden No. B63.

WWF Type of 2015

Designs: No. B111, Like #B109. No. B112, Like #B110.

Die Cut Perf. 13½ Syncopated

2016, Jan. 4 Litho.

Self-Adhesive

B111 SP75 8k+1k multi 2.60 2.60
B112 SP75 8k+1k multi 2.60 2.60
a. Booklet pane of 5, 3 #B111, 2 #B112 13.00

AIR POST STAMPS

Airplane and Plowman — AP1

Wmk. Multiple Crosses (114)

1925-29 Typo. *Perf. 12x12½*

C1 AP1 10o yellow green 27.50 *50.00*
C2 AP1 15o violet ('26) 70.00 *110.00*
C3 AP1 25o scarlet 45.00 *72.50*
C4 AP1 50o lt gray ('29) 130.00 *315.00*
C5 AP1 1k choc ('29) 105.00 *300.00*
Nos. C1-C5 (5) 377.50 *847.50*
Set, never hinged 975.00

Towers of Copenhagen — AP2

Unwmk.

1934, June 9 Engr. *Perf. 13*

C6 AP2 10o orange .75 *1.10*
C7 AP2 15o red 2.60 *5.50*
C8 AP2 20o Prus blue 2.60 *5.50*
C9 AP2 50o olive black 2.60 *5.50*
C10 AP2 1k brown 10.50 *19.00*
Nos. C6-C10 (5) 19.05 *36.60*
Set, never hinged 40.00

LATE FEE STAMPS

LF1

Perf. 14x14½

1923 Typo. Wmk. 114

I1 LF1 10o green 17.00 5.25
Never hinged 50.00
a. Double overprint *3,000.*

No. I1 was, at first, not a postage stamp but represented a tax for the services of the post office clerks in filling out postal forms and writing addresses. In 1923 it was put into use as a Late Fee stamp.

Coat of Arms — LF2

1926-31

I2 LF2 10o green 13.50 1.00
I3 LF2 10o brown ('31) 9.00 .70
Set, never hinged 60.00

1934 Unwmk. Engr. *Perf. 13*

I4 LF2 5o green .35 .30
I5 LF2 10o orange .35 .30
Set, never hinged 1.30

POSTAGE DUE STAMPS

Regular Issues of 1913-20 Overprinted

Perf. 14x14½

1921, May 1 Wmk. 114

J1 A10 1o deep orange 2.50 7.00
J2 A16 5o green 7.00 7.00
J3 A16 7o orange 4.50 8.50
J4 A16 10o red 30.00 17.00
J5 A16 20o deep blue 22.50 14.00
J6 A16 25o brown & blk 30.00 10.00
J7 A16 50o claret & blk 13.50 8.50
Nos. J1-J7 (7) 110.00 72.00
Set, never hinged 300.00

Same Overprint in Dark Blue On Military Stamp of 1917

1921, Nov. 23

J8 A16 10o red 15.00 20.00
Never hinged 37.50
a. "S" inverted 175.00 240.00
Never hinged 350.00

Numeral of Value — D1

Typographed (Solid Panel)

1921-30 *Perf. 14x14½*

J9 D1 1o orange ('22) 2.00 2.50
J10 D1 4o blue ('25) 3.75 3.25
J11 D1 5o brown ('22) 3.25 2.50
J12 D1 5o lt green ('30) 3.75 2.50
J13 D1 7o apple grn ('27) 18.00 24.00
J14 D1 7o dk violet ('30) 50.00 40.00
J15 D1 10o yellow grn ('22) 4.50 2.25
J16 D1 10o lt brown ('30) 4.50 2.25
J17 D1 20o grnsh blue ('21) 3.50 3.25
a. Double impression 2,700.
J18 D1 20o gray ('30) 4.75 5.00
J19 D1 25o scarlet ('23) 4.50 6.00
J20 D1 25o violet ('26) 3.75 7.75
J21 D1 25o lt blue ('30) 7.25 10.75
J22 D1 1k dk blue ('21) 90.00 20.00
J23 D1 1k brn & dk bl ('25) 10.00 18.00
J24 D1 5k purple ('25) 22.50 18.00
Nos. J9-J24 (16) 236.00 168.00
Set, never hinged 615.00

Engraved (Lined Panel)

1934-55 Unwmk. *Perf. 13*

J25 D1 1o slate .30 .30
J26 D1 2o carmine .35 .30
J27 D1 5o yellow green .45 .30
J28 D1 6o dk olive ('41) .45 .30
J29 D1 8o magenta ('50) 2.00 *4.00*
J30 D1 10o orange .35 .30
J31 D1 12o dp ultra ('55) .55 1.50
J32 D1 15o lt violet ('54) .85 .30
J33 D1 20o gray .65 .30
J34 D1 25o blue .75 .30
J35 D1 30o green ('53) .50 .30
J36 D1 40o claret ('49) .60 .25
J37 D1 1k brown .80 .30
Nos. J25-J37 (13) 8.60 *8.75*
Set, never hinged 14.50

No. 96 Surcharged in Black

1934 Wmk. 114 *Perf. 14x14½*

J38 A10 15o on 12o violet 6.00 4.50
Never hinged 18.00

MILITARY STAMPS

Nos. 97 and 100 Overprinted in Blue

1917 Wmk. 114 *Perf. 14x14½*

M1 A16 5o green 19.00 *40.00*
a. "S" inverted 300.00 *375.00*
M2 A16 10o red 16.00 *27.00*
a. "S" inverted 225.00 *375.00*
Set, never hinged 70.00
#M1a, M2a, never hinged 975.00

The letters "S F" are the initials of "Soldater Frimaerke" (Soldier's Stamp).

For overprint see No. J8.

OFFICIAL STAMPS

Small State Seal — O1

Wmk. Crown (112)

1871 Typo. *Perf. 14x13½*

O1 O1 2s blue 275.00 200.00
a. 2s ultra 275.00 200.00
b. Imperf *450.00*
O2 O1 4s carmine 77.50 40.00
a. Imperf *450.00*
O3 O1 16s green 450.00 350.00
a. Imperf *450.00*

Perf. 12½

O4 O1 4s carmine 6,500. 650.00
O5 O1 16s green 450.00 600.00
#O1-O3, O5, never hinged 3,575.

Nos. O4-O5 values are for stamps with defective perfs.

Nos. O1-O3 were reprinted in 1886 upon white wove paper, unwatermarked and imperforate. Value $10 each.

1875 *Perf. 14x13½*

O6 O1 3o violet 15.00 *55.00*
O7 O1 4o grnsh blue 18.00 6.25
O8 O1 8o carmine 15.00 2.00
a. Imperf —
O9 O1 32o green 32.50 *30.00*
Nos. O6-O9 (4) 80.50 *93.25*
Set, never hinged 245.00

For surcharge see No. 81.

1899-02 *Perf. 13*

O9A O1 3o red lilac ('02) 4.50 *15.00*
c. Imperf *400.00*
As "c," pair *1,100.*
O9B O1 4o blue 3.75 *4.50*
O10 O1 8o carmine 20.00 *26.00*
Nos. O9A-O10 (3) 28.25 45.50
Set, never hinged 85.00

For surcharge see No. 137.

1902-06 Wmk. 113

O11 O1 1o orange 2.25 *3.25*
O12 O1 3o red lilac ('06) 1.50 *1.90*
O13 O1 4o blue ('03) 3.00 *4.50*
O14 O1 5o green 3.00 .85
O15 O1 10o carmine 4.50 3.50
Nos. O11-O15 (5) 14.25 14.00
Set, never hinged 36.00

1914-23 Wmk. 114 *Perf. 14x14½*

O16 O1 1o orange 1.25 *2.75*
O17 O1 3o gray ('18) 4.50 *17.00*
O18 O1 4o blue ('16) 30.00 *60.00*
O19 O1 5o green ('15) 3.00 2.25
O20 O1 5o choc ('23) 7.50 *30.00*
O21 O1 10o red ('17) 15.00 8.00
O22 O1 10o green ('21) 5.25 *6.00*
O23 O1 15o violet ('19) 20.00 *37.50*
O24 O1 20o indigo ('20) 22.50 20.00
Nos. O16-O24 (9) 109.00 *183.50*
Set, never hinged 250.00

For surcharges see Nos. 185-191.

No. O20 is valued CTO.

Official stamps were discontinued Apr. 1, 1924.

NEWSPAPER STAMPS

Numeral of Value — N1

1907 Typo. Wmk. 113 *Perf. 13*

P1 N1 1o olive 20.00 3.00
P2 N1 5o blue 30.00 15.00
P3 N1 7o carmine 18.00 1.25
P4 N1 10o deep lilac 57.50 5.00
P5 N1 20o green 45.00 1.50
P6 N1 38o orange 62.50 2.50
P7 N1 68o yellow brown 150.00 27.50
P8 N1 1k bl grn & claret 37.50 6.00
P9 N1 5k rose & yel grn 225.00 45.00
P10 N1 10k bister & blue 225.00 45.00
Nos. P1-P10 (10) 870.50 151.75
Set, never hinged 3,050.

For surcharges see Nos. 138-144.

1914-15 Wmk. 114 *Perf. 14x14½*

P11 N1 1o olive gray 18.00 2.00
P12 N1 5o blue 45.00 12.50
P13 N1 7o rose 45.00 3.00
P14 N1 8o green ('15) 45.00 7.00
P15 N1 10o deep lilac 75.00 3.00
P16 N1 20o green 300.00 3.25
a. Imperf., pair *1,200.*
P17 N1 29o orange yel ('15) 75.00 8.00
P18 N1 38o orange 2,000. 190.00
P19 N1 41o yellow brn ('15) 95.00 5.75
P20 N1 1k blue grn & mar 125.00 3.25
Nos. P11-P17,P19-P20 (9) 823.00 47.75
Set, never hinged 3,200.

For surcharges see Nos. 145-154.

PARCEL POST STAMPS

These stamps were for use on postal packets sent by the Esbjerg-Fano Ferry Service.

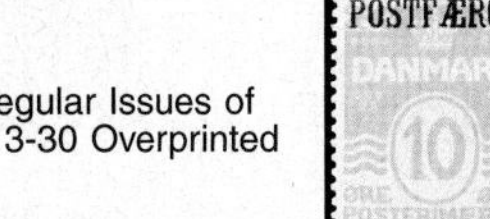

Regular Issues of 1913-30 Overprinted

1919-41 Wmk. 114 *Perf. 14x14½*

Q1 A10 10o green ('22) 20.00 20.00
Q2 A10 10o bister brn ('30) 15.00 8.50
Q3 A16 10o red 45.00 *90.00*
a. "POSFFAERGE" 200.00 *500.00*
Q4 A16 15o violet 20.00 *35.00*
a. "POSFFAERGE" 250.00 *525.00*
Q5 A16 30o orange ('22) 22.50 *47.50*
Q6 A16 30o dk blue ('26) 4.50 8.00
Q7 A16 50o cl & blk ('20) 300.00 *350.00*
Q8 A16 50o lt gray ('22) 30.00 30.00
a. 50o olive gray ('22) 225.00 *450.00*
Q9 A16 1k brn & bl ('24) 60.00 30.00
Q9A A16 5k vio & brn ('41) 3.75 *3.25*
Q10 A16 10k ver & grn ('30) 80.00 *150.00*

Engr.

Q11 A17 1k yellow brn 120.00 *225.00*
a. "POSFFAERGE" 1,500. *2,600.*
Nos. Q1-Q11 (12) 720.75 *997.25*
Set, never hinged 1,750.

1927-30

Q12 A30 15o red ('27) 27.00 15.00
Q13 A30 30o ocher ('27) 18.00 *20.00*
Q14 A30 40o yel grn ('30) 27.00 17.00
Nos. Q12-Q14 (3) 72.00 52.00
Set, never hinged 180.00

Overprinted on Regular Issues of 1933-40

1936-42 Unwmk. *Perf. 13*

Q15 A32 5o rose lake ('42) .35 .35
Q16 A32 10o yellow org 35.00 *35.00*
Q17 A32 10o lt brown ('38) 1.50 *2.75*
Q18 A32 10o purple ('39) .35 .35
Q19 A30 15o deep red 1.50 *2.00*
Q20 A30 30o blue, I 4.50 *7.50*
Q21 A30 30o blue, II ('40) 15.00 *32.50*
Q22 A30 30o org, II ('42) .60 *1.25*
Q23 A30 40o yel grn, I 4.50 *7.00*
Q24 A30 40o yel grn, II ('40) 15.00 *32.50*
Q25 A30 40o blue, II ('42) .60 *1.10*
Q26 A33 50o gray 1.20 *2.40*
Q27 A33 1k lt brown 1.40 *1.40*
Nos. Q15-Q27 (13) 81.50 *126.10*
Set, never hinged 160.00

Catalogue values for unused stamps in this section, from this point to the end of the section, are for Never Hinged items.

Overprinted on Nos. 284, 286, 286B

1945

Q28 A47 30o orange 4.00 2.40
Q29 A47 40o blue 1.90 1.90
Q30 A47 50o gray 2.00 2.00
Nos. Q28-Q30 (3) 7.90 6.30

Ovptd. on #318, 309, 310, 312, 297

1949-53

Q31 A32 10o green ('53) .65 .50
Q32 A61 30o orange 5.50 2.25
Q33 A61 40o dull blue 4.50 2.25
Q34 A61 50o gray ('50) 24.00 1.25
Q35 A55 1k brown ('50) 2.40 1.50
Nos. Q31-Q35 (5) 37.05 7.75

Ovptd. on #335, 323, 336, 326, 397

1955-65

Q36 A61 30o brown red 2.25 2.25
Q37 A61 40o gray 2.25 2.25
Q38 A61 50o aqua 2.25 2.25
Q39 A61 70o deep green 2.25 2.25
Q40 A55 1.25k orange ('65) 10.00 12.00
Nos. Q36-Q40 (5) 19.00 21.00

Overprinted on Nos. 417 and 419

1967 Engr. *Perf. 13*

Q41 A86 40o brown .65 1.25
Q42 A86 80o ultra .65 1.25

Nos. 224, 438, 441, 297-299 Overprinted

1967-74 Engr. *Perf. 13*

Q43 A32 5o rose lake .60 .50
Q44 A86 50o brown ('74) .65 .90
Q45 A86 90o ultra ('70) 1.10 1.60
Q46 A55 1k brown 2.50 2.75
Q47 A55 2k red ('72) 2.90 4.25
Q48 A55 5k dull bl ('72) 3.50 4.50
Nos. Q43-Q48 (6) 11.25 14.50

Nos. Q44-Q45, Q47-Q48 are on fluorescent paper.

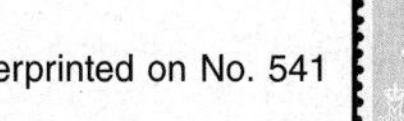

Overprinted on No. 541

1975, Feb. 27

Q49 A161 100o deep ultra 1.60 2.40

DIEGO-SUAREZ

dē-ˌā-gō 'swär-əs

LOCATION — A town at the northern end of Madagascar
GOVT. — French colony
POP. — 12,237

From 1885 to 1896 Diego-Suarez, (Antsirane), a French naval base, was a separate colony and issued its own stamps. These were succeeded by stamps of Madagascar.

100 Centimes = 1 Franc

Values for unused stamps are for examples with original gum as defined in the catalogue introduction except for Nos. 6-10 and J1-J2 which are valued without gum.

Stamps of French Colonies Handstamp Surcharged in Violet

1890 **Unwmk.** ***Perf. 14x13½***

1 A9 15c on 1c blk, *bl* 300.00 100.00
2 A9 15c on 5c grn, *grnsh* 650.00 100.00
3 A9 15c on 10c blk, *lav* 300.00 92.50
4 A9 15c on 20c red, *grn* 650.00 80.00
5 A9 15c on 25c blk, *rose* 130.00 52.50

This surcharge is found inverted, double, etc. See the *Scott Classic Catalogue.* Counterfeits exist.

Ship Flying French Flag — A2

France — A5

Symbolical of Union of France and Madagascar
A3 A4

1890 **Litho.** ***Imperf.***

6 A2 1c black 1,150. 240.00
7 A3 5c black 1,100. 200.00
8 A4 15c black 210.00 95.00
9 A5 25c black 225.00 110.00

Counterfeits exist of Nos. 6-9.

A6

1891

10 A6 5c black 350.00 100.00

Excellent counterfeits exist of No. 10.

Stamps of French Colonies Surcharged in Red or Black

No. 11

No. 12

1892 ***Perf. 14x13½***

11 A9 5c on 10c blk, *lav* (R) 210.00 105.00
a. Inverted surcharge 475.00 400.00
12 A9 5c on 20c red, *grn* 190.00 72.50
a. Inverted surcharge 450.00 400.00

Stamps of French Colonies Overprinted in Black or Red

1892

13 A9 1c blk, *lilac blue* (R) 32.50 20.00
14 A9 2c brown, *buff* 32.50 20.00
15 A9 4c claret, *lav* 55.00 45.00
16 A9 5c green, *grnsh* 120.00 80.00
17 A9 10c black, *lavender* 40.00 32.50
b. Double overprint 240.00 180.00
18 A9 15c blue, *pale blue* 32.50 20.00
19 A9 20c red, *grn* 40.00 32.50
20 A9 25c black, *rose* 36.00 20.00
21 A9 30c brown, *bis* (R) 1,300. 925.00
22 A9 35c black, *yellow* 1,300. 925.00
23 A9 75c carmine, *rose* 72.50 52.50
a. Double overprint 400.00
24 A9 1fr brnz grn, *straw* (R) 80.00 52.50
a. Double overprint 240.00 210.00

Inverted Overprint

13a A9 1c 225.00 190.00
14a A9 2c 225.00 190.00
15a A9 4c 325.00
16a A9 5c 240.00 200.00
17a A9 10c 240.00 200.00
20a A9 25c 240.00 200.00
21a A9 30c 1,700.
22a A9 35c 1,700.

Navigation and Commerce
A10 A11

1892 **Typo.** ***Perf. 14x13½***

Name of Colony in Blue or Carmine

25 A10 1c black, *blue* 2.00 2.00
26 A10 2c brown, *buff* 2.75 2.75
27 A10 4c claret, *lav* 3.25 3.25
28 A10 5c green, *grnsh* 6.50 6.50
29 A10 10c black, *lavender* 8.75 7.25
30 A10 15c bl, quadrille paper 16.50 11.00
31 A10 20c red, *green* 22.50 16.00
32 A10 25c black, *rose* 17.50 14.50
33 A10 30c brown, *bister* 22.50 16.00
34 A10 40c red, *straw* 27.50 21.00
35 A10 50c carmine, *rose* 45.00 35.00
36 A10 75c violet, *org* 52.50 45.00
37 A10 1fr brnz grn, *straw* 75.00 60.00
Nos. 25-37 (13) 302.25 240.25

Perf. 13½x14 stamps are counterfeits.

1894 ***Perf. 14x13½***

38 A11 1c black, *blue* 2.00 2.00
39 A11 2c brown, *buff* 2.75 2.40
40 A11 4c claret, *lav* 3.25 2.75
41 A11 5c green, *grnsh* 5.50 4.75
42 A11 10c black, *lavender* 7.25 7.25
43 A11 15c blue, quadrille paper 12.00 6.50
44 A11 20c red, *grn* 20.00 13.50
45 A11 25c black, *rose* 12.00 9.50
46 A11 30c brown, *bister* 13.50 6.50
47 A11 40c red, *straw* 13.50 6.50
48 A11 50c carmine, *rose* 20.00 13.50
49 A11 75c violet, *org* 12.00 8.75
50 A11 1fr brnz grn, *straw* 27.50 24.00
Nos. 38-50 (13) 151.25 107.90

Bisected stamps of type A11 are mentioned in note after Madagascar No. 62.

For surcharges see Madagascar Nos. 56-57, 61-62.

Perf. 13½x14 stamps are counterfeits.

POSTAGE DUE STAMPS

D1

D2

1891 **Unwmk.** **Litho.** ***Imperf.***

J1 D1 5c violet 240.00 120.00
J2 D2 50c black 260.00 140.00

Excellent counterfeits exist of Nos. J1-J2.

Postage Due Stamps of French Colonies Ovptd. Like Nos. 13-24

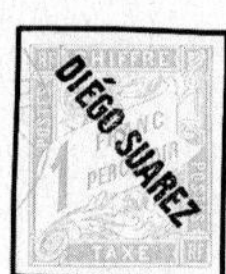

1892

J3 D1 1c black 130.00 72.50
J4 D1 2c black 130.00 65.00
a. Inverted overprint 450.00 300.00
J5 D1 3c black 130.00 65.00
J6 D1 4c black 130.00 60.00
J7 D1 5c black 130.00 72.50
J8 D1 10c black 40.00 32.50
a. Inverted overprint 460.00 450.00
J9 D1 15c black 36.00 32.50
a. Double overprint 575.00 500.00
J10 D1 20c black 200.00 135.00
a. Double overprint 600.00 500.00
J11 D1 30c black 120.00 60.00
a. Inverted overprint 450.00 300.00
J12 D1 60c black 1,200. 775.00
J13 D1 1fr brown 2,800. 1,500.

DJIBOUTI

jə-'bü-tē

LOCATION — East Africa
GOVT. — Republic
AREA — 8,958 sq. mi.
POP. — 447,439 (1999 est.)
CAPITAL — Djibouti

The French territory of Afars and Issas became the Republic of Djibouti June 27, 1977. For 1894-1902 issues with "Djibouti" or "DJ," see Somali Coast.

Catalogue values for all unused stamps in this country are for Never Hinged items.

Afars and Issas Issues of 1972-1977 Ovptd. and Srchd. in Black, Dark Green, Blue or Brown

No. 439

No. 440

No. 441

Nos. 442, 447

Nos. 443, 445

Nos. 444, 451

No. 446

Nos. 448, 453

No. 449

No. 450

No. 452

No. 454

No. 455

No. 456

Printing and Perforations as Before

1977

439	A63	1fr on 4fr (#358;B)	2.50	.25
440	A81	2fr on 5fr (#433;B)	2.50	.25
441	A75	5fr on 20fr (#421;B)	.40	.25
442	A70	8fr (#380;B)	.40	.25
443	A71	20fr (#387;DG)	3.75	1.00
444	A81	30fr (#434;B)	4.00	.80
445	A71	40fr (#388;DG)	5.50	1.25
446	A71	45fr (#389;Bl)	5.50	5.50
447	A78	45fr (#428;B)	8.00	5.00
448	A72	50fr (#394;B)	9.00	2.50
449	A71	60fr (#391;Br)	7.50	2.50
450	A79	70fr (#430;B)	8.50	2.50
451	A81	70fr (#435;B)	6.50	3.00
452	A74	100fr (#418;B)	12.00	4.00
453	A72	150fr (#399;B)	12.00	5.00
454	A76	200fr (#422;B)	6.00	4.50
455	A80	200fr (#432;B)	10.00	10.00
456	A74	300fr (#419;B)	10.00	10.00
		Nos. 439-456,C106-C108 (21)	140.05	77.80

Map and Flag of Djibouti — A83

Design: 65fr, Map and flag of Djibouti, map of Africa, horiz.

1977, June 27 Litho. *Perf. 12½*

457	A83	45fr multicolored	1.50	.85
458	A83	65fr multicolored	2.25	.85

Independence, June 27.

A84

1977, July 4

459	A84	10fr Headrest, horiz.	.35	.25
460	A84	20fr Water cask	.70	.25
461	A84	25fr Pitcher	1.00	.45
		Nos. 459-461 (3)	2.05	.95

Ostrich — A85

1977, Aug. 11 Litho. *Perf. 12½*

462	A85	90fr shown	3.00	.80
463	A85	100fr Weaver	4.50	1.25

Snail A86

Designs: 15fr, Fiddler crab. 50fr, Klipspringers. 70fr, Green turtle. 80fr, Priacanthus hamrur (fish). 150fr, Dolphinfish.

1977 Litho. *Perf. 12½*

464	A86	15fr multicolored	.65	.25
465	A86	45fr multicolored	1.25	.60
466	A86	50fr multicolored	1.75	.50
467	A86	70fr multicolored	1.75	.60
468	A86	80fr multicolored	2.25	.85
469	A86	150fr multicolored	4.50	1.75
		Nos. 464-469 (6)	12.15	4.55

Issued: 45fr, 70fr, 80fr, 9/14; others, 12/5.

Pres. Hassan Gouled Aptidon and Djibouti Flag — A87

1978, Feb. 12 Litho. *Perf. 13*

470	A87	65fr multicolored	1.50	.50

Charaxes Hansali — A88

Butterflies: 20fr, Colias electo. 25fr, Acraea chilo. 150fr, Junonia hierta.

1978, Mar. 13 Litho. *Perf. 12½x13*

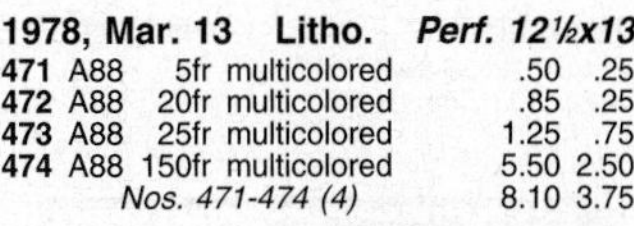

471	A88	5fr multicolored	.50	.25
472	A88	20fr multicolored	.85	.25
473	A88	25fr multicolored	1.25	.75
474	A88	150fr multicolored	5.50	2.50
		Nos. 471-474 (4)	8.10	3.75

Necklace — A89

Design: 55fr, Necklace, diff.

1978, May 29 Litho. *Perf. 12½x13*

475	A89	45fr pink & multi	1.25	.35
476	A89	55fr blue & multi	1.25	.45

Bougainvillea A90

Flowers: 35fr, Hibiscus schizopetalus. 250fr, Caesalpinia pulcherrima.

1978, July 10 Photo. *Perf. 12½x13*

477	A90	15fr multicolored	.50	.25
478	A90	35fr multicolored	.85	.25
479	A90	250fr multicolored	6.00	.90
		Nos. 477-479 (3)	7.35	1.40

Charonia Nodifera — A91

Sea Shell: 80fr, Charonia variegata.

1978, Oct. 9 Litho. *Perf. 13*

480	A91	10fr multicolored	1.10	.25
481	A91	80fr multicolored	4.25	.95

Chaetodon A92

30fr, Yellow surgeonfish. 40fr, Harlequinfish.

1978, Nov. 20 Litho. *Perf. 13x12½*

482	A92	8fr multicolored	.55	.25
483	A92	30fr multicolored	1.10	.25
484	A92	40fr multicolored	2.75	.75
		Nos. 482-484 (3)	4.40	1.25

Alsthom BB 1201 at Dock — A93

55fr, Steam locomotive 231. 60fr, Steam locomotive 130 and map of route. 75fr, Diesel.

1979, Jan. 29 Litho. *Perf. 13*

485	A93	40fr multicolored	1.25	.25
486	A93	55fr multicolored	1.40	.30
487	A93	60fr multicolored	1.75	.30
488	A93	75fr multicolored	2.25	.40
		Nos. 485-488 (4)	6.65	1.25

Djibouti-Addis Ababa railroad.

Children and IYC Emblem — A94

Design: 200fr, Mother, child, IYC emblem.

1979, Feb. 26 Litho. *Perf. 13*

489	A94	20fr multicolored	.50	.25
490	A94	200fr multicolored	4.00	1.10

International Year of the Child.

Nos. 489-490 exist in souvenir sheets of one. Value, set, $20.

Plane over Ardoukoba Volcano — A95

30fr, Helicopter over Ardoukoba Volcano.

1979, Mar. 19

491	A95	30fr multi, vert.	1.00	.35
492	A95	90fr multi	3.00	.65

Rowland Hill, Postal Clerks, No. C109 — A96

100fr, Somali Coast #22, Djibouti #457, letters, Rowland Hill. 150fr, Letters hoisted onto ship, smoke signals, Rowland Hill.

1979, Apr. 17 Litho. *Perf. 13x12½*

493	A96	25fr multicolored	.40	.25
494	A96	100fr multicolored	2.00	.45
495	A96	150fr multicolored	3.00	.70
		Nos. 493-495 (3)	5.40	1.40

Sir Rowland Hill (1795-1879), originator of penny postage.

Nos. 493-495 exist in souvenir sheets of one. Value, set, $50.

View of Djibouti, Bird and Local Woman — A97

Design: 80fr, Map and flag of Djibouti, UPU emblem, Boeing 747, train and mail runner.

1979, June 8 Litho. *Perf. 13x12½*

496	A97	55fr multicolored	4.00	.85
497	A97	80fr multicolored	4.75	1.10

Philexafrique II, Libreville, Gabon, June 8-17. Nos. 496, 497 each printed in sheets of 10 with 5 labels showing exhibition emblem.

Solanacea A98

Flowers: 2fr, Opuntia, vert. 15fr, Trichodesma. 45fr, Acacia etbaica. 50fr, Thunbergia alata, vert.

Perf. 13x13½, 13½x13

1979, June 18

498 A98 2fr multicolored .25 .25
499 A98 8fr multicolored .25 .25
500 A98 15fr multicolored .50 .25
501 A98 45fr multicolored 1.00 .25
502 A98 50fr multicolored 1.25 .25
Nos. 498-502 (5) 3.25 1.25

Running — A99

Olympic Emblem and: 70fr, Basketball, vert. 200fr, Soccer.

Perf. 12½x13, 13x12½

1979, Oct. 22 **Litho.**

503 A99 70fr multicolored 1.50 .25
504 A99 120fr multicolored 2.25 .50
505 A99 200fr multicolored 3.75 .75
Nos. 503-505 (3) 7.50 1.50

Pre-Olympic Year.

Cypraecassis Rufa — A100

Shells: 40fr, Lambis chiragra arthritica. 300fr, Harpa connaidalis.

1979, Dec. 22 **Litho.** ***Perf. 13***

506 A100 10fr multicolored .25 .25
507 A100 40fr multicolored 1.00 .25
508 A100 300fr multicolored 6.50 1.50
Nos. 506-508 (3) 7.75 2.00

Rotary International, 75th Anniversary — A101

1980, Feb. 19 **Litho.** ***Perf. 13x12½***

509 A101 90fr multicolored 2.25 .75
a. Souvenir sheet of 1 #509 15.00 15.00

Lions Club of Djibouti — A102

1980, Feb. 19

510 A102 100fr multicolored 2.25 .75

Colotis Danae — A103

1980, Mar. 17 ***Perf. 13x13½***

511 A103 5fr shown .90 .50
512 A103 55fr Danaus chrysippus 3.75 1.50

Chess Players, Knight — A104

Chess Federation Creation: 75fr, Chess Game, Florence, 1493.

1980, June 9 **Litho.** ***Perf. 13***

513 A104 20fr multicolored 1.25 .25
514 A104 75fr multicolored 3.25 .35

Cribraria A105

1980, Aug. 12 **Litho.** ***Perf. 13***

515 A105 15fr shown .75 .25
516 A105 85fr Nautilius pompilius 2.75 .50

Alexander Fleming, Discoverer of Penicillin — A106

Design: 130fr, Jules Verne, French science fiction writer; earth, moon and spacecraft.

1980, Sept. 1

517 A106 20fr multicolored 1.00 .35
518 A106 130fr multicolored 3.00 .60

Capt. Cook and Endeavor — A107

Capt. James Cook Death Bicentenary: 90fr, Ships and Maps of voyages.

1980, Nov. 20 **Litho.** ***Perf. 13***

519 A107 55fr multicolored 1.40 .65
520 A107 90fr multicolored 2.25 .90

Souvenir sheets of 1 exist, perf. 12½x12. Value, each $10.

Angel Fish A108

1981, Apr. 13 **Litho.** ***Perf. 12½***

521 A108 25fr shown 1.75 .25
522 A108 55fr Moorish idol 3.25 .50
523 A108 70fr Scad 3.75 1.50
Nos. 521-523 (3) 8.75 2.25

13th World Telecommunications Day — A109

1981, May 17 **Litho.** ***Perf. 13***

524 A109 140fr multicolored 2.75 .70

Type 231 Steam Locomotive, Germany, 1958 and Amtrak, US, 1980 — A110

Locomotives: 55fr, Stephenson and his Rocket, Djibouti Railways 230 engine. 65fr, Type TGV, France, Type 962, Japan.

1981, June 9 **Litho.** ***Perf. 13***

525 A110 40fr multicolored 1.50 .30
526 A110 55fr multicolored 2.00 .35
527 A110 65fr multicolored 2.50 .40
Nos. 525-527 (3) 6.00 1.05

Radio Amateurs Club — A111

1981, June 25

528 A111 250fr multicolored 5.00 1.00

Prince Charles and Lady Diana — A112

1981, June 29

529 A112 180fr shown 2.50 .75
530 A112 200fr Couple, diff. 3.00 1.00

Royal Wedding.

Nos. 529-530 exist in souvenir sheets of one. Value, set, $30.

Lord Nelson and Victory — A113

1981, July 6 **Litho.** ***Perf. 13x12½***

531 A113 100fr multicolored 1.90 .45
532 A113 175fr multicolored 3.25 .90

Lord Horatio Nelson (1758-1805).

Scout Tending Campfire — A114

Design: 105fr, Scout giving sign.

1981, July 16 **Litho.** ***Perf. 13***

533 A114 60fr shown 3.00 .70
534 A114 105fr multicolored 3.75 .80

28th World Scouting Conference, Dakar, Aug. (60fr); 4th Pan-African Scouting Conference, Abidjan, Aug. (105fr).

Pawn and Queen, Swedish Bone Chess Pieces, 13th Cent. — A115

130fr, Pawn, knight, Chinese, 19th cent., vert.

1981, Oct. 15 **Litho.** ***Perf. 13***

535 A115 50fr shown 1.50 .35
536 A115 130fr multicolored 3.00 .85

For overprints see Nos. 542-543.

Sheraton Hotel Opening — A116

1981, Nov. 15 **Litho.** ***Perf. 13x12½***

537 A116 75fr multicolored 1.50 .45

For surcharge see No. 623.

Acacia Mellifera A117

Designs: 10fr, Clitoria ternatea, vert. 35fr, Punica granatum. 45fr, Malvaceous plant, vert.

1981, Dec. 21 ***Perf. 13***

538 A117 10fr multicolored .40 .25
539 A117 30fr shown .80 .25
540 A117 35fr multicolored 1.15 .25
541 A117 45fr multicolored 1.40 .30
Nos. 538-541 (4) 3.75 1.05

See Nos. 558-560.

Nos. 535-536 Overprinted

1981, Dec. **Litho.** ***Perf. 13***

542 A115 50fr multicolored 2.00 .50
543 A115 130fr multicolored 4.00 1.00

World Chess Championship.

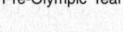

TB Bacillus Centenary A117a

Design: Koch, slide, microscope.

1982, Mar. 24 Litho. *Perf. 13*
544 A117a 305fr multicolored 7.00 1.50

A117b

Designs: 125fr, Ivory bishop. 175fr, Queen, pawn, 19th cent.

1982, Apr. 8 Litho. *Perf. 13*
545 A117b 125fr multi 3.50 .75
546 A117b 175fr multi 4.25 1.25

1982 World Chess Championship.

A118

1982, May 17
547 A118 150fr multicolored 3.00 .85

14th World Telecommunications Day.
For surcharge see No. 647.

Bus and Jeep — A119

1982, July 27 Litho. *Perf. 13*
548 A119 20fr shown .55 .25
549 A119 25fr Dhow, ferry .70 .25
550 A119 55fr Train, jet 1.50 .45
Nos. 548-550 (3) 2.75 .95

Nos. 548-550 exist in souvenir sheets of one. Value, set, $25.

Shells from the Red Sea A120

10fr, Cypraea erythraeensis. 15fr, Conus sumatrensis. 25fr, Cypraea pulchra. 30fr, Conus inscriptus. 70fr, Casmaria ponderosa. 150fr, Cypraea exusta.

1982, Nov. 20 Litho. *Perf. 12½*
551 A120 10fr multicolored .45 .25
552 A120 15fr multicolored .75 .30
553 A120 25fr multicolored .90 .35
554 A120 30fr multicolored 1.10 .40
555 A120 70fr multicolored 2.25 .50
556 A120 150fr multicolored 4.50 1.50
a. Strip of 6, #551-556 9.95 3.30
Nos. 551-556 (6) 9.95 3.30

See Nos. 563-567.

Intl. Palestinian Solidarity Day — A121

1982, Nov. 29 Litho. *Perf. 13*
557 A121 40fr multicolored 1.00 .25

Local Flowers type of 1981

Various flowers. 5fr, 55fr, vert.

1983, Apr. 14 Litho. *Perf. 13*
558 A117 5fr multicolored .25 .25
559 A117 50fr multicolored 1.25 .40
560 A117 55fr multicolored 1.40 .40
Nos. 558-560 (3) 2.90 1.05

World Communications Year — A123

1983, June 20 Litho. *Perf. 13*
561 A123 500fr multicolored 9.00 2.25

Conference of Donors, Nov. 21-23 — A124

1983, Nov. 21 Litho. *Perf. 13x12½*
562 A124 75fr multicolored 1.50 .40

Shell Type of 1982

15fr, Marginella obtusa. 30fr, Conus jickelli. 55fr, Cypraea macandrewi. 80fr, Conus cuvieri. 100fr, Turbo petholatus.

1983, Dec. 20 Litho. *Perf. 12½*
563 A120 15fr multicolored .50 .25
564 A120 30fr multicolored 1.00 .25
565 A120 55fr multicolored 1.60 .40
566 A120 80fr multicolored 2.25 .50
567 A120 100fr multicolored 2.50 .65
Nos. 563-567 (5) 7.85 2.05

Local Butterflies A125

5fr, Colotis chrysonome. 20fr, Colias erate. 30fr, Junonia orithyia. 75fr, Acraea doubledayi. 110fr, Byblia ilithya.

1984, Jan. 24 Litho. *Perf. 13½x13*
568 A125 5fr multicolored .50 .25
569 A125 20fr multicolored 1.00 .25
570 A125 30fr multicolored 1.50 .35
571 A125 75fr multicolored 4.25 1.00
572 A125 110fr multicolored 5.50 1.50
Nos. 568-572 (5) 12.75 3.35

Landscapes and Animals — A126

2fr, Randa Klipspringer. 8fr, Ali Sabieh, gazelles. 10fr, Lake Assal, oryx. 15fr, Tadjoura, gazelle. 40fr, Alaila Dada, jackal, vert. 45fr, Lake Abbe, warthog. 55fr, Obock, seagull. 125fr, Presidential Palace, bird.

1984, Apr. 29 Litho. *Perf. 13*
573 A126 2fr multicolored .25 .25
574 A126 8fr multicolored .25 .25
575 A126 10fr multicolored .25 .25
576 A126 15fr multicolored .25 .25
577 A126 40fr multicolored .75 .25
578 A126 45fr multicolored .75 .30
579 A126 55fr multicolored 1.90 .75
580 A126 125fr multicolored 3.75 1.25
Nos. 573-580 (8) 8.15 3.55

For surcharges see Nos. 646, 657-658, 660.

Fire Prevention — A127

1984, Sept. 9 Litho. *Perf. 13*
581 A127 25fr Fire truck 1.00 .25
582 A127 95fr Hook & ladder 3.25 .50
583 A127 100fr Fire plane 3.25 1.00
Nos. 581-583 (3) 7.50 1.75

International Olympic Committee Membership A128

1984, July 22 Litho. *Perf. 13*
584 A128 45fr Runners .90 .35

Motor Carriage, 1886 A128a

1984, Nov. 11 Litho. *Perf. 12½*
585 A128a 35fr shown .80 .30
586 A128a 65fr Cabriolet, 1896 1.60 .65
587 A128a 90fr Phoenix, 1900 2.25 .95
Nos. 585-587 (3) 4.65 1.90

Gottlieb Daimler (1834-1900), pioneer automobile manufacturer.

Marie and Pierre Curie — A129

1984, Dec. 3 Litho. *Perf. 12½*
588 A129 150fr Pierre Curie 3.25 1.10
589 A129 150fr Marie Curie 3.25 1.10

Nos. 588-589 exist in souvenir sheet of two. Value, set, $30.

A130

Audubon Bicentenary — A130a

5fr, Merops albicollis. 15fr, Pterocles exustus. 20fr, Trachyphonus margaritatus somalicus. 25fr, Coracias garrulus.
200fr, Pandion haliaetus, vert.

1985, Jan. 27 Litho. *Perf. 13*
590 A130 5fr multi .75 .35
591 A130 15fr multi 3.25 .85
592 A130 20fr multi 3.75 1.00
593 A130 25fr multi 4.50 1.10
Nos. 590-593 (4) 12.25 3.30

Souvenir Sheet
Self-Adhesive
Perf. 12½

593A A130a 200fr multi 27.50 27.50

No. 593A is airmail and printed on wood.

Intl. Youth Year — A131

1985, Mar. 26 Litho. *Perf. 13*
594 A131 10fr multicolored .30 .25
595 A131 30fr multicolored .65 .30
596 A131 40fr multicolored .90 .40
Nos. 594-596 (3) 1.85 .95

German Railways, 150th Anniv. — A132

Designs: 55fr, Engine No. 29, Addis Ababa-Djibouti Railways. 75fr, Adler, museum facsimile of the first German locomotive.

1985, Apr. 22 Litho. *Perf. 13*
597 A132 55fr multicolored 2.25 .65
598 A132 75fr multicolored 3.25 .90

Scouting — A133

35fr, Planting saplings. 65fr, Hygiene, family health care.

1985, May 23

599 A133 35fr multicolored 1.00 .45
600 A133 65fr multicolored 1.75 .75

A134

80fr, Victor Hugo (1802-1885), Novelist. 100fr, Arthur Rimbaud (1854-1891), poet.

1985, June 24 **Litho.**

601 A134 80fr brt blue & slate 1.60 .80
602 A134 100fr multicolored 2.00 1.00

Sea Shells A135

Designs: 10fr, Cypraea nebrites. 15fr, Cypraea turdus. 30fr, Conus acuminatus. 40fr, Cypraea camelopardalis. 55fr, Conus terebra.

1985, July 15 **Litho.** ***Perf. 12½***

603 A135 10fr multicolored .40 .25
604 A135 15fr multicolored .60 .25
605 A135 30fr multicolored 1.50 .30
606 A135 40fr multicolored 1.75 .55
607 A135 55fr multicolored 2.75 .70
Nos. 603-607 (5) 7.00 2.05

1st World Cup Marathon '85, Hiroshima A136

Designs: 75fr, Winners. 100fr, Approaching finish.

1985, Sept. 2 ***Perf. 12½x13***

608 A136 75fr multicolored 1.25 .75
609 A136 100fr multicolored 2.00 1.00

Halley's Comet — A137

Designs: 85fr, Bayeux Tapestry, Comet and Halley. 90fr, Vega I, Giotto space probes, map of planets, comet trajectory.

1986, Jan. 27 **Litho.** ***Perf. 13***

610 A137 85fr multicolored 1.50 .50
611 A137 90fr multicolored 1.75 .85

ISERST Solar Energy Installation — A138

Designs: 50fr, Runners on beach. 150fr, Windmill, headquarters, power control station.

1986, Mar. 20

612 A138 50fr multicolored .95 .40
613 A138 150fr multicolored 2.75 1.25

Ships from Columbus's Fleet, 1492 — A139

1986, Apr. 14

614 A139 60fr Santa Maria 1.90 .55
615 A139 90fr Nina, Pinta 3.25 .95

Fish, Red Sea — A140

Designs: 20fr, Elagatis bipinnulatus. 25fr, Valamugil seheli. 55fr, Lutjanus rivulatus.

1986, June 16 **Litho.** ***Perf. 13½x13***

616 A140 20fr multicolored .65 .30
617 A140 25fr multicolored .75 .45
618 A140 55fr multicolored 2.00 .75
Nos. 616-618 (3) 3.40 1.50

Public Buildings — A141

105fr, People's Palace. 115fr, Ministry of the Interior, Posts & Telecommunications.

1986, July 21 **Litho.** ***Perf. 13***

619 A141 105fr multicolored 1.75 .90
620 A141 115fr multicolored 2.10 1.00

Sea-Me-We Building, Keyboard — A142

1986, Sept. 8 **Litho.** ***Perf. 13***

621 A142 100fr multicolored 2.00 .70

Souvenir Sheet

Perf. 12½

622 A142 250fr multicolored 13.50 13.50

Southeast Asia, Middle East, Western Europe Submarine Cable System inauguration.

No. 537 Surcharged

1986, Nov. 15 ***Perf. 13x12½***

623 A116 55fr on 75fr multi 1.40 .50

Pasteur Institute, Cent. — A143

1987, Feb. 19 **Litho.** ***Perf. 13***

624 A143 220fr multicolored 5.00 1.60

Natl. Vaccination Campaign.

Edible Mushrooms A144

35fr, Macrolepiota imbricata. 50fr, Lentinus squarrosulus. 95fr, Terfezia boudieri.

1987, Apr. 16 **Litho.** ***Perf. 13x12½***

625 A144 35fr multicolored 1.50 .65
626 A144 50fr multicolored 2.25 .85
627 A144 95fr multicolored 3.00 1.50
Nos. 625-627 (3) 6.75 3.00

Wildlife A145

1987, May 14 ***Perf. 12½x13***

628 A145 5fr Hare .50 .25
629 A145 30fr Dromedary 1.25 .30
630 A145 140fr Cheetah 5.00 1.00
Nos. 628-630 (3) 6.75 1.55

1988 Olympics, Seoul and Calgary — A146

85fr, Pierre de Coubertin (1863-1937), founder of the modern Olympics, & lighting of the flame. 135fr, Ski jumping. 140fr, Running.

1987, July 16 ***Perf. 13***

631 A146 85fr multicolored 1.60 .55
632 A146 135fr multicolored 2.75 .95
633 A146 140fr multicolored 3.00 1.00
Nos. 631-633 (3) 7.35 2.50

Traditional Art — A147

1988, Jan. 20 **Litho.** ***Perf. 13***

634 A147 30fr Nomad's comb .60 .30
635 A147 70fr Wash jug 1.25 .60

UN Universal Immunization by 1990 Campaign A148

1988, Apr. 10 ***Perf. 12½***

636 A148 125fr multicolored 2.50 1.00

16th Africa Cup Soccer Championships, Morocco — A149

Design: Athletes, view of Rabat.

1988, Mar. 13 ***Perf. 13***

637 A149 55fr multicolored 1.20 .50

1988 Winter Olympics, Calgary — A150

1988, May 7 **Litho.** ***Perf. 13***

638 A150 45fr Ski jump 1.00 .40

Campaign Against Thirst A151

1988, Sept. 10 Litho. *Perf. 12½x13*

639 A151 50fr multicolored 1.25 .45

Intl. Fund for Agricultural Development, 10th Anniv. — A152

1988, Nov. 14 *Perf. 13*

640 A152 135fr multicolored 2.50 1.00

Michel Lafoux Air Club, 40th Anniv. — A153

Design: 145fr, 1948 Tiger Moth, 1988 Tobago-10.

1988, Dec. 6

641 A153 145fr multi 2.75 1.00

Marine Life A154

Designs: 90fr, Lobophyllia costata. 160fr, Lambis truncata.

1989, Jan. 20 Litho. *Perf. 12½*

642 A154 90fr multicolored 2.25 .30
643 A154 160fr multicolored 4.25 1.40

Colotis protomedia A155

1989, Feb. 15

644 A155 70fr multicolored 5.00 2.10

Nos. 573 and 547 Surcharged

1989 *Perf. 13*

646 A126 70fr on 2fr No. 573 2.25 .50
647 A118 70fr on 150fr No. 547 2.25 .50

Issued: 646, 12/20; 647, 12/29.

Folk Dances — A157

1989, Mar. 20

648 A157 30fr shown .50 .25
649 A157 70fr multicolored, diff. 1.40 .50

Francolin of Djibouti — A159

1989, Apr. 10 Litho. *Perf. 12½*

651 A159 35fr multicolored 2.50 .75

Rare Flora A160

1989, June 12

652 A160 25fr Calotropis procera .90 .25

A161

1989, Aug. 10 Litho. *Perf. 13*

653 A161 70fr multicolored 1.60 .75

Interparliamentary Union, cent.

Intl. Literacy Year — A162

1989, Oct. 1

654 A162 145fr multicolored 2.75 1.10

Petroglyph — A163

1989, Nov. 18 Litho. *Perf. 13*

655 A163 5fr multicolored 1.00 .40

Girl — A164

1989, Dec. 6

656 A164 55fr multicolored 1.60 .65

Nos. 574, 576-577 Surcharged

1989-1990 Litho. *Perf. 13*

657 A126 30fr on 8fr multi .50 .30
658 A126 50fr on 40fr multi 2.00 .55
660 A126 120fr on 15fr multi 2.25 1.00
Nos. 657-660 (3) 4.75 1.85

Issue dates: 30fr, 12/20/89; 50fr, 7/3/90; 120fr, 3/17/90.

Water Conservation — A165

1990, May 5 Litho. *Perf. 11½*

665 A165 120fr multicolored 2.25 .90

Traditional Jewelry A166

1990, Mar. 10

666 A166 70fr multicolored 1.75 .45

Commiphora — A167

1990, Feb. 20 *Perf. 12*

667 A167 30fr multicolored 1.50 .35

Baskets — A168

1990, July 3

668 A168 30fr multicolored .70 .40

A169

1990, June 12 *Perf. 11½*

669 A169 100fr multicolored 2.00 .80

World Cup Soccer Championships, Italy.

A170

1990, Apr. 16 *Perf. 11½*

670 A170 55fr shown 1.50 .45

20 kilometer race of Djibouti.

Vaccination Campaign A171

1990, Aug. 22 Litho. *Perf. 11½*
Granite Paper

671 A171 300fr multicolored 4.75 2.00

Charles de Gaulle — A172

1990, Sept. 16 Granite Paper

672 A172 200fr multicolored 4.00 1.25

African Tourism Year — A173

1991, Jan. 23 Litho. *Perf. 13*
673 A173 115fr multicolored 2.25 .80

Corals — A174

1991, Jan. 28 *Perf. 12½*
674 A174 40fr Acropora .90 .50
675 A174 45fr Seriatopora hytrise 1.25 .50

Aquatic Birds — A175

10fr, Pelecanus rufescens. 15fr, Egretta gularis. 20fr, Ardea goliath, horiz. 25fr, Platalea leucorodia, horiz.

1991, Feb. 12
676 A175 10fr multicolored .70 .25
677 A175 15fr multicolored 1.50 .25
678 A175 20fr multicolored 1.75 .30
679 A175 25fr multicolored 1.90 .35
Nos. 676-679 (4) 5.85 1.15

UNO Development Conference — A176

1990, Oct. 9 Litho. *Perf. 11½x12*
Granite Paper
680 A176 45fr multicolored 1.10 .45

Fossils — A177

1990, Nov. 1 Granite Paper
681 A177 90fr pur, org & blk 5.25 1.75

Papio Hamadryas — A178

1990, Dec. 6 Granite Paper
682 A178 50fr multicolored 1.75 .55

Pandion Haliaetus A179

1991, Mar. 20 Litho. *Perf. 12x11½*
683 A179 200fr multicolored 5.00 1.60

Traditional Game A180

1991, Apr. 4
684 A180 250fr multicolored 5.25 3.25

See No. 696.

Djibouti-Ethiopia Railroad — A181

1991, May 25 Litho. *Perf. 11½*
685 A181 85fr multicolored 4.00 2.25

World Environment Day — A182

1991, June 10
686 A182 110fr multicolored 2.75 .65

Philexafrique — A183

1991, Jul. 16 Litho. *Perf. 11½*
687 A183 120fr Islands 3.25 1.75

Pre-Olympic Year — A184

1991, Sept. 25
688 A184 175fr Handball 4.50 3.00

World Food Day — A185

1991, Oct. 16 Litho. *Perf. 11½x12*
689 A185 105fr multicolored 2.50 1.10

Underwater Cable Network — A186

1991, Nov. 28 *Perf. 12x11½*
690 A186 130fr multicolored 3.00 1.00

Discovery of America, 500th Anniv. A187

1991, Dec. 19 Litho. *Perf. 11½*
691 A187 145fr multicolored 3.25 1.60

Arthur Rimbaud (1854-1891) Poet and Merchant — A188

1991-92 *Perf. 11½*
692 A188 90fr Young man, ship 2.75 .90
693 A188 150fr Old man, camels 3.00 .90

Issued: 90fr, 2/5/92; 150fr, 12/23/91.

Djibouti-Ethiopia Railroad — A189

Design: 250fr, Locomotive, map.

1992 Litho. *Perf. 12x11½*
694 A189 70fr multicolored 2.75 1.10

Souvenir Sheet
Perf. 13x12½
695 A189 250fr multicolored 5.25 5.25

Issue dates: 70fr, Feb. 2; 250fr, Jan. 30.

Traditional Game Type of 1991

1992, Feb. 10 *Perf. 11½*
696 A180 100fr Boys playing Go 2.10 .85

A190

1992, June 9 Litho. *Perf. 14*
697 A190 80fr multicolored 2.10 1.25

1992 Summer Olympics, Barcelona.

A191

Traditional food preparation — 30fr, Pounding grain. 45fr, Preparing mofo. 70fr, Winnowing grain. 75fr, Cooking mofo.

1992 Litho. *Perf. 14x13½*
698 A191 30fr multi 1.25 .50
698A A191 45fr multi 90.00 —
699 A191 70fr multi 1.25 .65
699A A191 75fr multi 90.00 —

Issued: Nos. 698, 699, 4/20; No. 698A, 12/6.

Discovery of America, 500th Anniv. A192

1992, May 16 Litho. *Perf. 11½*
700 A192 125fr multicolored 3.25 .95

African Soccer Championships A193

1992, July 22 *Perf. 14*
701 A193 15fr multicolored .75 .25

Intl. Space Year — A194

Designs: 120fr, Rocket, satellite. 135fr, Astronaut, satellite, horiz.

Perf. 14x13½, 13½x14

1992, Sept. 28

702	A194	120fr multi	2.75	.85
703	A194	135fr multi	2.75	.95

Wildlife—A195

1992, Nov. 11 *Perf. 14*

704	A195	5fr Dik-dik	1.25	.25
705	A195	200fr Caretta caretta	5.00	1.60

Taeniura Lymma — A195a

Perf. 11½x11¾

1990, Mar. 24 **Litho.**

Panel Color

705A	A195a	30fr pink	—	—
705B	A195a	70fr yellow	—	—
705C	A195a	100fr green	—	—
705D	A195a	120fr lilac	—	—

Nomad Girls in Traditional Costumes A196

1993, Jan. 26 **Litho.** *Perf. 13*

706	A196	70fr Girl beside hut	1.75	.45
707	A196	120fr shown	2.75	.75

White-eyed Seagull A197

1993, Feb. 28 **Litho.** *Perf. 12½*

708	A197	300fr multicolored	5.75	1.75

Amin Salman Mosque — A198

1993, Feb. 17 **Litho.** *Perf. 13¾x14*

709	A198	500fr multicolored	*52.50*	*5.50*

Handcrafts — A199

1993, Apr. 23 **Litho.** *Perf. 13¾x14*

710	A199	100fr Neck rest	100.00	15.00
711	A199	125fr Sword	100.00	15.00

Cercopithecus Aethiops — A200

1993, May 29 **Litho.** *Perf. 14¼x13½*

712	A200	150fr multi	80.00	5.00

Organization of African Unity, 30th Anniv. — A201

Perf. 14¼x13½

1993, June 20 **Litho.**

713	A201	200fr multi	100.00	2.25

Water Carriers — A202

1993, July 6 **Litho.** *Perf. 14x13¾*

714	A202	30fr Woman	100.00	—
715	A202	50fr Man	100.00	—

Conquest of Space — A203

1993, Sept. 30 **Litho.** *Perf. 14x13¾*

716	A203	90fr multicolored	—	—

A204

Traditional utensils.

1993, Sept. 30 **Litho.** *Perf. 13½*

717	A204	15fr Weyso	.45	.25
718	A204	20fr Hangol	.90	.25
719	A204	25fr Saqaf	1.00	.25
720	A204	30fr Subrar	1.40	.45
		Nos. 717-720 (4)	3.75	1.20

A205

Traditional musical instruments.

1993, Nov. 10 **Litho.** *Perf. 14*

721	A205	5fr Flute	1.00	1.00
722	A205	10fr Drum	1.00	1.00

Souvenir Sheet

Wedding of Japan's Crown Prince Naruhito and Masako Owada — A206

1994, Jan. 10 **Litho.** *Perf. 13x12½*

Self-Adhesive

723	A206	500fr multicolored	22.50	22.50

No. 723 printed on wood.

20 Kilometer Race of Djibouti — A207

1994 **Litho.** *Perf. 11½*

724	A207	50fr multicolored	2.50	1.00

Promotion of Breastfeeding A208

1994

725	A208	40fr shown	1.90	.40
726	A208	45fr Mother, infant	2.10	.40

Hassan Gouled Aptidon Stadium A209

1994

727	A209	70fr multicolored	2.50	1.10

Stenella Longirostris — A210

1994, May 1 **Litho.** *Perf. 11¾x11½*

728	A210	120fr multicolored	—	—

World Housing Day — A211

1994, May 9 **Litho.** *Perf. 11½x11¾*

729	A211	30fr multi	*100.00*	—

Eupodotis Senegalensis — A212

Perf. 11¾x11½

1994, June 16 **Litho.**

730	A212	10fr multicolored	180.00	—

1994 World Cup Soccer Tournament — A213

1994, Sept. 7

731	A213	200fr multicolored	*150.00*	—

Dress of a Village Leader — A214

Design: 100fr, Traditional nomad costume.

Perf. 11½x11¾

1994, Sept. 18 **Litho.**

732	A214	100fr multicolored	*100.00*	—

Perf. 11¾

733	A214	150fr multicolored	*10.00*	—

Canis Aureus A215

Perf. 11¾x11½

1994, Sept. 28 **Litho.**

734	A215	400fr multi	*135.00*	—

World Walking Day A216

1994, Oct. 19 Litho. *Perf. 11¾x11½*
735 A216 75fr multicolored *150.00* —

A217

1994, Nov. 26 Litho. *Perf. 11¾*
736 A217 55fr Book stand 75.00 —

A218

1994, Dec. 6 Litho. *Perf. 11½x11¾*
737 A218 35fr Traditional dance 60.00 12.00

Souvenir Sheet

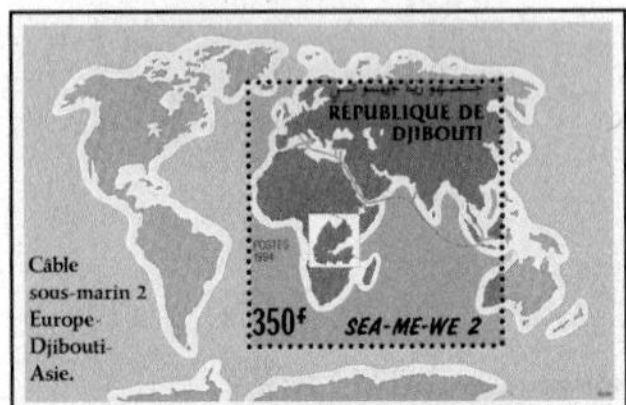

Sea-Me-We 2 Submarine Cable — A218a

1994 *Perf. 12½*
737A A218a 350fr multi *175.00* —

Volleyball, Cent. — A219

1995, Feb. 25 Litho. *Perf. 11¾*
738 A219 70fr multicolored — —

United Nations, 50th Anniv. — A220

1995, Feb. 25
739 A220 120fr multicolored — —

Fight Against Thirst A221

Perf. 11¾x11½
1995, Mar. 29 Litho.
740 A221 100fr multicolored — —

Threskiornis Aethiopica — A222

Design: 30fr, Phoenicopterus ruber

1995, Apr. 5 Litho. *Perf. 11¾*
741 A222 30fr multicolored — —
742 A222 50fr multicolored — —

World Telecommunications Day — A223

Perf. 11¾x11½
1995, June 10 Litho.
743 A223 125fr multicolored *70.00* 1.25

Crocuta Crocuta A224

1995, June 12 Litho. *Perf. 11¾*
744 A224 200fr multi *105.00* —

People Meeting Under Tree A225

1995, July 3 Litho. *Perf. 11¾x11½*
745 A225 150fr multi *65.00* —

Nomads Around Fire — A226

1995, Aug. 9 *Perf. 11¾*
746 A226 45fr multi *60.00* 12.00

FAO, 50th Anniv. — A227

1995, Sept. 27 *Perf. 11½x11¾*
747 A227 250fr multi *70.00* 12.00

Traditional Costume — A228

1995, Dec. 6 *Perf. 11¾*
748 A228 90fr multicolored — 12.00

African Development Bank, 30th Anniv. — A229

1995. Dec. 18 *Perf. 11¾x11½*
749 A229 300fr multi *60.00* 12.00

African Soccer Cup — A230

1996, Feb. 28
750 A230 70fr multicolored *180.00* —

Ostrich — A231

1996, Apr. 23
751 A231 120fr multi *100.00* —

Leopard A232

1996, May 6
752 A232 70fr multi 105.00 —

Amber Necklace — A233

1996, June 13 Litho.
753 A233 30fr multi 100.00 —

1996 Summer Olympic Games, Atlanta — A234

Perf. 11½x11¾
1996, Sept. 21 Litho.
754 A234 105fr multicolored *125.00* 12.00

Commicarpus Grandiflorus A236

1996, Oct. 6 Litho. *Perf. 11½x11¾*
756 A236 350fr multi *60.00* 12.00

Djibouti Folklore — A237

1996, Nov. 28 Litho. *Perf. 11¾*
757 A237 95fr multi *60.00* —

Legend of the Lion and Three Bulls A238

1996, Nov. 28 Litho. *Perf. 11¾*
758 A238 95fr multi *80.00* 12.00

Children's Day A239

1996, Dec. 17 *Perf. 11¾x11½*
759 A239 130fr multi *60.00* 12.00

A240

Legend of the Tortoise and the Fox: No. 760, Tortoise and fox at starting line. No. 761, Fox leaves tortoise behind. No. 762, Tortoise passes sleeping fox.

1997, Jan. 17 ***Perf. 11¾***

760 A240 60fr multi — —
761 A240 60fr multi — —
762 A240 60fr multi — —
a. Horiz. strip, #760-762 *135.00*

UNICEF, 50th Anniv. — A241

1997, Feb. 9 **Litho.** ***Perf. 11¾***

763 A241 80fr Mother, child *50.00* 10.00
764 A241 90fr Hands around globe *100.00* 12.00

Dancers — A242

1997, May 14 **Litho.** ***Perf. 11¾***

765 A242 70fr multi *70.00* 12.00

Fortune Teller A243

Designs: 200fr, Fortune teller and woman. 300fr, Fortune teller, camel.

1997, May 29 **Litho.** ***Perf. 11¾***

766 A243 200fr multi 60.00 12.00
767 A243 300fr multi 60.00 12.00

Woman's Day — A244

1997, May 30 **Litho.** ***Perf. 11¾***

768 A244 250fr multi *160.00 12.00*

Traditional Objects A245

Design: 30fr, Writing board, horiz. 400fr, Bowl and spoon.

1997, June 5 **Litho.** ***Perf. 11¾***

769 A245 30fr multi 45.00 10.00
770 A245 400fr multi 45.00 10.00

Telecommunications A246

Designs: 30fr, Arta post office. 100fr, Map, building with antenna and satellite dishes. 120fr, Ships, map showing submarine cable route, horiz.

1997, June 27 **Litho.** ***Perf. 11¾***

771 A246 30fr multi — 12.00
772 A246 100fr multi — 12.00
773 A246 120fr multi — 12.00

Goats in Tree A247

1997, July 26 **Litho.** ***Perf. 11¾***

774 A247 120fr multi 50.00 15.00

A248

Portrait of Diana: a, 125fr. b, 130fr. c, 150fr.

1998, Mar. 25 **Litho.** ***Perf. 13½***

775 A248 Strip of 3, #a.-c. 5.00 5.00

Diana, Princess of Wales (1961-97).
No. 775 was isssued in sheets of 6 stamps.

Mother Teresa (1910-97) — A249

1998 **Litho.** ***Perf. 13½***

776 A249 130fr multicolored 2.75 1.40

No. 776 was issued in sheets of 4.

Intl. Year of the Ocean A250

a, Tangara chilensis. b, Agalychnis callidryas. c, Delphinus delphis, megaptera novaeangliae. d, Cercopithecus aethiops (h). e, Laticaudia colubrina (i), sphyrna mokarran. f, Lactoria cornuta, delphinus delphis (g). g, Delphinus delphis (k). h, Aspidontus taeniatus, lo vulpinus. i, Sepioteuthis lessoniana. j, Prionace glauca (i), chaetodon ornatissimus. k, Eupagurus bernherdus. l, Octopus vulgaris (k).

1998, Apr. 20 **Litho.** ***Perf. 13½***

777 A250 75fr Sheet of 12, #a.-l. 16.00 16.00

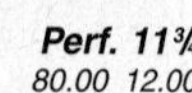

Mahatma Gandhi (1869-1948) A251

1998, Apr. 20 **Litho.** ***Perf. 11¾***

778 A251 250fr multi *80.00 12.00*

Traditional Art — A252

1998, Apr. 25 **Litho.** ***Perf. 11½x11¾***

779 A252 30fr multicolored *120.00* 12.00

Women's Rights and International Peace — A253

1998, May 3 ***Perf. 11¾x11½***

780 A253 70fr multicolored *60.00* 12.00

World Water Day A254

1998, May 10 **Litho.** ***Perf. 11¾***

781 A254 45fr multi *60.00* 12.00

1998 World Cup Soccer Championships, France — A255

1998, June 10 **Litho.** ***Perf. 11¾***

782 A255 200fr multi 145.00 —

Marine Life — A256

Perf. 11½x11¾, 11¾x11½

1998, July 2 **Litho.**

783 A256 20fr Octopus *135.00* —
784 A256 25fr Shark, horiz. *135.00* —

Cats and Bush — A257

1998, Aug. 30 ***Perf. 11½x11¾***

785 A257 120fr multi *135.00* —

World Telecommunications Day — A258

1996, Sept. 27 **Litho.** ***Perf. 11¾***

786 A258 150fr multi 100.00 —

National Bank — A259

1998, Sept. 30 **Litho.** ***Perf. 11¾***

787 A259 100fr multi 135.00 12.00

Flags and IGAD Emblem — A260

Perf. 11½x11¾

1998, Sept. 30 **Litho.**

788 A260 85fr multi *75.00* —

Traditional Game Goos A261

1998, Oct. 1 ***Perf. 11¾x11½***

789 A261 110fr multi *60.00* —

Fishing Port A262

1998

790 A262 100fr multi *115.00* —

Maskali Island A263

1998
791 A263 500fr multi 140.00 —

Fish A264

1999 Litho. *Perf. 13¼x13½*
792 A264 70fr multi 100.00 —

Antelope — A264a

Perf. 13¼x13½
1999, Mar. 16 Litho.
792A A264a 120fr multi 90.00 —

Djibouti Franc, 50th Anniv. A265

1999
793 A265 100fr multi 60.00 —

World Telecommunications Day — A266

1999
794 A266 125fr multi 55.00 —

Worldwide Fund for Nature (WWF) — A267

Phacochoerus africanus aeliani: a, Adult and young. b, Adult standing. c, Head. d, Adult walking.

2000, Apr. 13 Litho. *Perf. 14*
795 A267 100fr Block of 4, #a-d 9.00 9.00

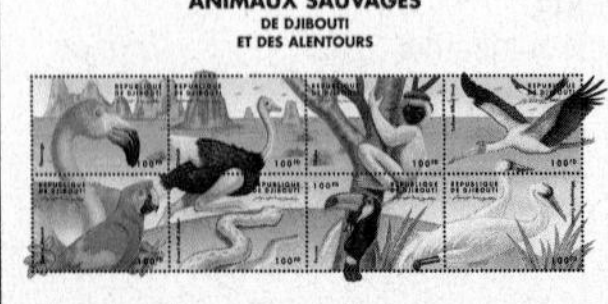
Wild Animals — A268

No. 796: a, Flamingo. b, Ostrich. c, Sifaka. d, Yellow-billed stork. e, Scarlet macaw. f, Dwarf puff adder. g, Toucan. h, Whooping crane.

2000, Apr. 13
796 A268 100fr Sheet of 8, #a-h 22.50 22.50

Butterflies — A269

No. 797: a, Doxocopa cherubina. b, Heliconius charitonius. c, Cantonephele numili. d, Danaus gilippus. e, Morpho peleides. f, Heliconius doris.
No. 798, 250fr, Agraulis vanillae. No. 799, 250fr, Strymon melinus.

2000, Apr. 13
797 A269 100fr Sheet of 6, #a-f 12.00 12.00
Souvenir Sheets
798-799 A269 Set of 2 11.00 11.00

No. 797 contains six 28x42mm stamps.

Water Resources — A270

2000, Apr. 13
800 A270 500fr multi 8.00 8.00

Trains and Landmarks — A271

No. 801: a, 5fr, Class OJ 2-10-2, China. b, 25fr, Eurostar, France-England. c, 15fr, Glacier Express, Switzerland. d, 40fr, Unidentified train. e, 35fr, Class WP 4-6-2, India.
No. 802, 110fr: a, Nord Chapelon Pacific, France. b, Class 23 2-6-2, Germany. c, Class GS-4 4-8-4, US. d, Class A4 4-6-2, Great Britain. e, Pacific 4-6-2, South Africa. f, Class HP, India.
No. 803, 120fr: a, VT601, Germany. b, ICIII Bo-Bo EMU, Netherlands. c, TGV, France. d, ETR 450, Italy. e, AVE, Spain. f, Bullet Train, Japan.
No. 804, 250fr, GM War Bonnet, US. No. 805, 250fr, Class 8 Pacific, Great Britain.

2000, Apr. 28
801 A271 Horiz. strip of 5, #a-e 3.00 3.00
Sheets of 6, #a-f
802-803 A271 Set of 2 15.00 15.00
Souvenir Sheets
804-805 A271 Set of 2 6.00 6.00

Dancers A272

2000, Apr. 28
806 A272 75fr multi 4.00 1.50

Blacksmith — A273

2000, May 14
807 A273 100fr multi 6.00 2.50

Marine Life — A274

No. 808, vert.: a, Dendrochirus biocellatus. b, Hippocampus. c, Amphiprion ocellaris, Amphiprion percula. d, Periclimenes imperator. e, Pomacnetridae. f, Octopus vulgaris.
No. 809, 50fr: a, Cephalopholis miniata. b, Ptereleotris hanae. c, Sphyraena genie. d, Tripterygion segmentatum. e, Odontaspididae. f, Cirrhitidae. g, Amphiprion. h, Capros aper. i, Balistidae. j, Trygonorhina fasciata. k, Cephalopholis. l, Corythoichthys ocellatus.
No. 810, 60fr: a, Lutjanus kasmira. b, Chaetodon fasciatus. c, Epinephelinae. d, Hypoplectrus gutavarius. e, Loligo opalescens. f, Diodontinae. g, Coelenterata. h, Sargocentron xantherythrum. i, Thalassoma lunare. j, Hemichromis bimaculatus. k, Dasyatis. l, Fromia monilis.
No. 811, 250fr, Eschrichtis robustus. No. 812, 250fr, Cheloniidae.

2000, May 14
808 A274 55fr Sheet of 6, #a-f 8.00 8.00
Sheets of 12, #a-l
809-810 A274 Set of 2 30.00 30.00
Souvenir Sheets
811-812 A274 Set of 2 8.00 8.00

Camels and Tender A275

2000, June 26
813 A275 35fr multi 4.75 .90

Ships A276

Designs: 10fr, Thomas W. Lawson, 1902. 15fr, BT Global Challenge, 2000. 20fr, Reliance and Shamrock III, 1903. 25fr, Archibald Russell, 1905. 50fr, Greek merchantman, 8th cent. B.C.
No. 819, 130fr: a, Norman warship, 1066. b, Hanseatic cog, c. 1300. c, Santa Maria, 1492. d, Mary Rose, 1510. e, Golden Hind, 1577. f, Sovereign of the Seas, 1637.
No. 820:, 135fr: a, HMS Endeavour, 1768. b, USS Constitution, 1797. c, Chasse-Maree, 1800. d, Baltimore clipper, 1812. e, Lightning, 1853. f, Bluenose, 1921.
No. 821, 250fr, HM Yacht Britannia, 1893. No. 822, 250fr, Herzogin Cecilie, 1902.

2000, June 26
814-818 A276 Set of 5 2.00 2.00
Sheets of 6, #a-f
819-820 A276 Set of 2 25.00 25.00
Souvenir Sheets
821-822 A276 Set of 2 8.00 8.00

Millennium A277

2000, July 18
823 A277 125fr multi 2.75 2.75

Birds A278

2000, Aug. 23
824 Horiz. strip of 5 2.75 2.75
a. A278 5fr Lanius excubitor .35 .35
b. A278 10fr Phoenicopterus minor .35 .35
c. A278 15fr Eupodatis senegalensis .35 .35
d. A278 40fr Noephron perchopterus .60 .60
e. A278 50fr Pterocles lichtensteinii .75 .75

Space Exploration — A279

No. 825, 100fr, vert.: a, John Glenn and Mercury capsule, 1962. b, Soyuz capsule, Apollo-Soyuz mission, 1975. c, Hubble Telescope, 1990. d, Apollo capsule, Apollo-Soyuz mission. e, Glenn at speaker's stand, 1974. f, Space Shuttle Columbia, 1981.
No. 826, 100fr, vert.: a, Apollo 11 service module, 1969. b, Telstar, 1962. c, Ariane 4, 1988. d, Apollo 11 lunar module. e, Neil Armstrong, 1969. f, Splashdown of Apollo 11, 1969.
No. 827, 200fr, Astronaut on moon saluting. No. 828, 250fr, Astronauts conducting experiments on moon. No. 829, 250fr, Space Shuttle Challenger.

2000, Aug. 23 Sheets of 6, #a-f
825-826 A279 Set of 2 20.00 20.00
Souvenir Sheets
827-829 A279 Set of 3 12.00 12.00

2000 Summer Olympics, Sydney
A280

Olympic flame, flag and: 80fr, Runner. 90fr, Tennis player.

2000 ***Perf. 14***
830-831 A280 Set of 2 4.00 4.00

Unknown Soldier Monument—A280a

2004, Apr. 18 Litho. ***Perf. 13x12¾***
832 A280a 175fr multi 50.00 20.00

Independence, 27th Anniv. — A281

2004, June 27 Litho. ***Perf. 13***
833 A281 45fr multi — —

Dragon Tree
A282

Pregnant Woman at Hospital — A283

Camel Caravan
A284

Natl. Union of Djibouti Women — A285

National Arms
A286

Perf. 12¾x13, 13x12¾

2004, Dec. 18 **Litho.**
834 A282 15fr multi 37.50 20.00
835 A283 25fr multi 37.50 20.00
836 A284 45fr multi 37.50 20.00
837 A285 70fr multi 37.50 20.00
838 A286 100fr multi 25.00 20.00
Nos. 834-838 (5) 175.00 100.00

Friendship Between Djibouti and People's Republic of China, 25th Anniv.

Designs: 5fr, Djibouti Electricity Building. 10fr, Hassan Gouled Stadium. 15fr, Djibouti Central Bank. 30fr, People's Palace. 45fr, Ministry of Foreign Affairs Building.

2004, Dec. 27 ***Perf. 12***
839-843 A286a Set of 5 115.00 115.00

Items commemorating the death of Pope John Paul II were declared as "fraudulent" by Djibouti Post.

2006 World Cup Soccer Championships, Germany — A287

2005, June 8 Litho. ***Perf. 13***
844 A287 100fr multi *95.00* —

Tanker in Port of Doraleh — A288

2006, Nov. 6 Litho. ***Perf. 13***
845 A288 120fr multi *50.00* —

Printed in sheets of 4.

Common Market for Eastern and Southern Africa Summit, Djibouti — A289

2006, Nov. 6 Litho. ***Perf. 13¼x13***
846 A289 150fr multi *50.00* —

Djibouti Chamber of Commerce, Cent. — A290

2007 Litho. ***Perf. 12¾***
847 A290 50fr multi *12.00* —
a. Souvenir sheet of 2 *52.50* —

Independence, 30th Anniv. — A291

2007, June 27 Litho. ***Perf. 13***
848 A291 75fr multi 25.00 —
a. Souvenir sheet of 2 50.00 —

Mahamoud Harbi (1921-60), Politician — A292

2007, Aug. 17 Litho. ***Perf. 13x12¾***
849 A292 165fr multi 30.00 5.00

Indo-Suez Red Sea Bank — A293

2008, Oct. 19 Litho. ***Perf. 13x13½***
850 A293 220fr multi *25.00 6.00*
a. Souvenir sheet of 2 50.00 —

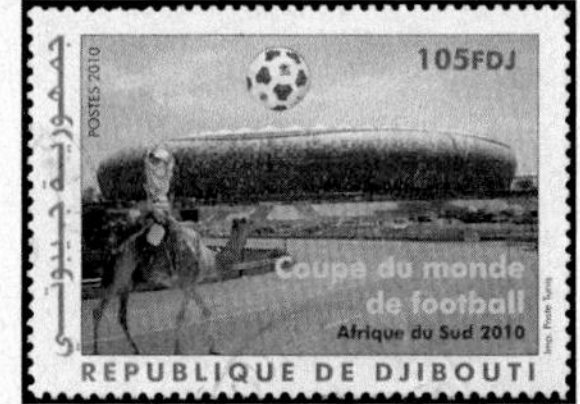

2010 World Cup Soccer Championships, South Africa — A295

2010, May Litho. ***Perf. 13***
852 A295 105fr multi 25.00 —
a. Souvenir sheet of 1 27.50 —

Djibouti postal authorities have declared "illegal" the following items:

Sheets of 8 stamps of various values: Mushrooms

Sheets of 6 stamps of various values: Fire trucks and Scouts (3 different)

Sheets of 6 700f stamps: Butterflies and Orchids, Butterflies and Scouts, Trains

Sheets of 6 300f stamps: Birds

Sheets of 4 800f stamps: Bonsai

Sheets of 4 700f stamps: Dogs (4 different), Cats (4 different), Babe Ruth and Tiger Woods, Dinosaurs

Sheets of 2 stamps of various values: Fire trucks (2 different).

2014 Africa Internet Summit, Djibouti — A296

2014 Litho. ***Perf. 13***
853 A296 170fr multi *15.00* —
a. Souvenir sheet of 1 50.00 —

A297

A298

A299

Personalized Stamps — A300

2016, Jan. 25 Litho. ***Perf. 13¼x13***
854 A297 250fr multi 3.00 3.00
855 A298 250fr multi 3.00 3.00
856 A299 250fr multi 3.00 3.00
857 A300 250fr multi 3.00 3.00
Nos. 854-857 (4) 12.00 12.00

Nos. 854-857 were each printed in sheets of 16 that could be personalized. A generic image showing Santa Claus with the inscription "Bonne Année 2016!" was made available. Values are for stamps with or without any printed vignette.

Fauna — A301

No. 858, 260fr — Primates: a, Lemur catta. b, Leontopithecus rosalia. c, Macaca fuscata. d, Mandrillus sphinx.

No. 859, 260fr — Bats: a, Plecotus auritus. b, Erophylla sezekorni. c, Sturnira lilium. d, Desmodus rotundus.

No. 860, 260fr — Wild cats: a, Panthera tigris. b, Panthera pardus melas. c, Panthera onca. d, Panthera leo.

No. 861, 260fr — Lions: a, Panthera leo nubica. b, Panthera leo bleyenberghi. c, Panthera leo leo. d, Panthera leo azandica.

No. 862, 260fr — Dugong dugon: a, One dugong surfacing, fish at LR. b, Two dugongs, and calf. c, Dugong swimming, surrounded by fish. d, One dugong on sea floor, two fish at UL.

No. 863, 260fr — Dolphins: a, Delphinus capensis. b, Lagenorhynchus obscurus. c, Stenella frontalis. d, Delphinus delphis.

No. 864, 260fr — Whales: a, Delphinapterus leucas. b, Megaptera novaeangliae. c, Eubalaena australis. d, Physeter macrocephalus.

No. 865, 260fr — Eagles: a, Lophaetus occipitalis. b, Geranoaetus melanoleucus. c, Haliaeetus leucogaster. d, Aquila heliaca.

No. 866, 260fr — Parrots: a, Eclectus roratus. b, Anodorhynchus hyacinthinus. c, Conuropsis carolinensis. d, Trichoglossus moluccanus.

No. 867, 260fr — Owls: a, Megascops asio. b, Pulsatrix perspicillata. c, Bubo sumatranus. d, Ptilopsis leucotis.

No. 868, 260fr — Starlings: a, Sturnus vulgaris. b, Spreo fischeri. c, Sturnia sinensis. d, Mino dumontii.

No. 869, 260fr — Sunbirds: a, Leptocoma minima. b, Nectarinia famosa. c, Leptocoma sperata and Aetopyga siparaja. d, Anthreptes malacensis and Nectarinia tacazze.

No. 870, 260fr — Warblers: a, Lioparus chrysotis. b, Psittiparus gularis. c, Sylvia rueppelli. d, Parophasma galinieri.

No. 871, 260fr — Butterflies: a, Limenitis archippus. b, Apatura iris. c, Teinopalpus imperialis. d, Iphiclides podalirius.

No. 872, 260fr — Turtles: a, Terrapene carolina bauri. b, Chelonoidis nigra. c, Testudo graeca. d, Stigmochelys pardalis.

No. 873, 260fr — Snakes: a, Bitis arietans. b, Dispholidus typus. c, Echis pyramidum. d, Atractaspis fallax.

No. 874, 260fr — Crocodiles: a, Crocodylus siamensis. b, Crocodylus porosus. c, Crocodylus rhombifer. d, Crocodylus acutus.

No. 875, 260fr — Chameleons: a, Chamaeleo calyptratus. b, Chameleon hoehnelii. c, Chamaeleo chamaeleon. d, Furcifer pardalis.

No. 876, 260fr — Scorpions: a, Centruroides margaritatus. b, Parabuthus liosoma. c, Androctonus crassicauda, Blaptica dubia. d, Babycurus jacksoni.

No. 877, 960fr, Cebus capucinus. No. 878, 960fr, Acerodon jubatus. No. 879, 960fr, Puma concolor. No. 880, 960fr, Panthera leo senegalensis. No. 881, 960fr, Two dugong dugon. No. 882, 960fr, Stenella coeruleoalba. No. 883, 960fr, Physeter macrocephalus, diff. No. 884, 960fr, Aquila rapax. No. 885, 960fr, Psittacus erithacus. No. 886, 960fr, Strix nebulosa. No. 887, 960fr, Lamprotornis hildebrandti. No. 888, 960fr, Cinnyris chalybeus. No. 889, 960fr, Myzornis pyrrhoura. No. 890, 960fr, Lasiommata megera. No. 891, 960fr, Aldabrachelys gigantea. No. 892, 960fr, Naja pallida. No. 893, 960fr, Crocodylus acutus, diff. No. 894, 960fr, Kinyongia fischeri. No. 895, 960fr, Hottentotta tamulus.

2016, Jan. 25 Litho. *Perf. 13¼*

Sheets of 4, #a-d

858-876 A301 Set of 19 225.00 225.00

Souvenir Sheets

877-895 A301 Set of 19 205.00 205.00

A302

No. 896, 260fr — Nelson Mandela (1918-2013), President of South Africa, and: a, Three doves. b, Prison cell. c, Amethyst crystal. d, Dove and flag of South Africa.

No. 897, 270fr — Mahatma Gandhi (1869-1948), Indian nationalist leader: a, Sitting at small table. b, With spinning wheel, automobile. c, Seated, pulling thread. d, Seated in chair.

No. 898, 270fr — St. John Paul II (1920-2005): a, With two doves. b, With Nelson Mandela. c, With Mother Teresa. d, Holding crucifix.

No. 899, 270fr — Queen Elizabeth II, longest-reigning British monarch, wearing: a, Crown and blue sash. b, Pink hat. c, Green hat. d, Tiara and orange sash.

No. 900, 270fr — Princess Diana (1961-97), with: a, Princes William and Harry. b, Mother Teresa. c, Child and Red Cross flag. d, Princes Charles and William.

No. 901, 270fr — Lord Robert Baden-Powell (1857-1941), founder of Scouting movement, Scouting emblem: a, Wearing military uniform. b, Wearing Indian headdress. c, Holding animal horn, British flag in background. d, With Scout bugler.

No. 902, 270fr — Nobel laureates: a, Ei-ichi Negishi, 2010 Chemistry laureate. b, Malala Yousafzai, 2014 Peace laureate. c, James D. Watson, 1962 Physiology or Medicine laureate. d, Doris Lessing, 2007 Literature laureate.

No. 903, 270fr — Soccer players and stadiums for 2016 European Soccer Championships, France: a, Stade Pierre Mauroy, Lille. b, Stade Vélodrome, Marseille. c, Stade de Lyon, Lyon. d, Stade de Bordeaux, Bordeaux.

No. 904, 270fr — Sports of the 2016 Summer Olympics, Rio de Janeiro: a, Artistic gymnastics. b, Kayak slalom. c, Women's beach volleyball. d, Rugby.

No. 905, 270fr — Attack on Pearl Harbor, 75th anniv.: a, USS Arizona. b, U.S. P-40B airplane. c, Japanese Mitsubishi A6M Zero airplane. d, USS Missouri.

No. 906, 270fr — Walt Disney (1901-66), animated filmmaker, and: a, Bavarian Castle. b, Awards. c, Film camera. d, Drawing board and sketches.

No. 907, 270fr — Marilyn Monroe (1926-62), actress, wearing: a, Necklace. b, Black bathing suit. c, Blue bathing suit. d, White dress and gloves.

No. 908, 270fr — Elvis Presley (1935-77): a, Playing guitar. b, Holding microphone. c, Wearing striped shirt. d, With Hollywood Walk of Fame star.

No. 909, 270fr — Wolfgang Amadeus Mozart (1756-91), composer, and: a, His father, Johann Georg Leopold Mozart (1719-87). b, His mother, Anna Maria Pertl Mozart (1720-78). c, His wife, Maria Constanze Mozart (1762-1842). d, Young Mozart blindfolded behind piano.

No. 910, 270fr — Georg Alfred Schumann (1866-1952), composer: a, Violin, score, hands of conductor. b, Wearing black suit. c, At piano. d, Conducting musicians.

No. 911, 270fr — Paintings by Vincent van Gogh (1853-90): a, Self-portrait, 1889. b, Vase with Twelve Sunflowers, 1889. c, Portrait of Doctor Gachet, 1890. d, Starry Night Over the Rhône, 1888.

No. 912, 270fr — Paintings by Claude Monet (1840-1926): a, Flowering Garden in Saint-Adresse, 1866. b, Les Meules à Giverny, 1884. c, The Bridge at Argenteuil, 1874. d, The Bridge Over the Water Lily Pond, 1905.

No. 913, 270fr — Paintings by Pablo Picasso (1881-1973): a, Self-portrait, 1907. b, Boy with a Pipe, 1905. c, The Old Guitarist, 1903. d, Portrait of Daniel-Henry Kahnweiler, 1910.

No. 914, 270fr — Christmas: a, Ded Moroz and Snegurochka. b, Santa Claus and reindeer. c, Saint Nicholas on horse. d, Joulupukki.

No. 915, 270fr — New Year 2016 (Year of the Monkey): a, Monkey on branch. b, Monkey with open mouth. c, Head of monkey. d, Adult and juvenile monkey.

No. 916, 960fr, Mandela, diff. No. 917, 960fr, Gandhi and tiger. No. 918, 960fr, St. John Paul II and 14th Dalai Lama. No. 919, 960fr, Queen Elizabeth II and Prince Philip. No. 920, 960fr, Princess Diana and Queen Elizabeth II. No. 921, 960fr, Baden-Powell, Boy Scout and Scouting emblem. No. 922, 960fr, 14th Dalai Lama receiving 1989 Nobel Peace Prize. No. 923, 960fr, Soccer player, Stade de France, Saint-Denis. No. 924, 960fr, Women's 100-meter sprint, boxers. No. 925, 960fr, Explosion on USS Shaw, Herbert C. Jones, Medal of Honor. No. 926, 960fr, Disney, diff. No. 927, 960fr, Monroe, diff. No. 928, 960fr, Presley playing guitar, diff. No. 929, 960fr, Mozart, Masonic compass and square. No. 930, 960fr, Schumann conducting musicians, diff. No. 931, 960fr, Self-portrait with Bandaged Ear and Pipe, by van Gogh, 1889. No. 932, 960fr, Woman with a Parasol, by Monet, 1875. No. 933, 960fr, Seated Woman, by Picasso, 1937. No. 934, 960fr, Saint Nicholas waving. No. 935, 960fr, Adult and juvenile monkeys, diff.

2016, Mar. 15 Litho. *Perf. 13¼*

Sheets of 4, #a-d

896-915 A302 Set of 20 245.00 245.00

Souvenir Sheets

916-935 A302 Set of 20 220.00 220.00

Inscriptions on Nos. 911b and 932 are incorrect.

A303

No. 936, 280fr — Campaign against malaria: a, Two adults watching sleeping child. b, Mosquito, person tending to patient. c, Mother watching sleeping child. d, Child behind mosquito netting.

No. 937, 280fr — Rugby players: a, Player kicking ball. b, Two players with red shirts attempting tackle. c, Player running with ball and opponent. d, Player with black shirt tackling ball carrier.

No. 938, 280fr — Table tennis players: a, Fan Zhendong. b, Liu Shiwen. c, Kasumi Ishikawa. d, Xu Xin.

No. 939, 280fr — Chess players: a, Magnus Carlsen. b, Sergey Karjakin. c, Viswanathan Anand. d, Judit Polgár.

No. 940, 280fr — Pilgrimage to Mecca: a, Pilgrims circling Ka'aba. b, Stoning of the devil. c, Great Mosque of Mecca, Koran. d, Shaving of heads.

No. 941, 280fr — Lighthouses: a, Les Eclaireurs Lighthouse, Argentina. b, Jeddah Lighthouse, Saudi Arabia. c, Lindau Lighthouse, Germany. d, New London Ledge Lighthouse, U.S.

No. 942, 280fr — Ships: a, Kruzenshtern. b, Flying Dutchman and Phocéa. c, Götheborg. d, Europa.

No. 943, 280fr — Steam locomotives: a, Class C38, Australia. b, Class 19D, South Africa. c, DRB Class 52, Germany. d, Class P36, Russia.

No. 944, 280fr — High-speed trains: a, CRH380A, People's Republic of China. b, Shinkansen Series E6, E621-1, Japan. c, Shinkansen Series N700A, Japan. d, Shinkansen Series H5, H523-1, Japan.

No. 945, 280fr — Race cars: a, Aston Martin DBRS 9. b, Ferrari F150 Italia. c, Ford Fiesta RS WRC. d, Maserati MC12 GT1.

No. 946, 280fr — Fire trucks: a, 1964 Bedford. b, 1962 Chevrolet Apache. c, 1959 Ford Galaxie. d, 1937 Chevrolet.

No. 947, 280fr — First commercial flight of the Concorde, 40th anniv.: a, Concorde in flight, passenger cabin. b, Concorde in flight, nose of Concorde. c, Concorde taking off. d, Under wing view of Concorde.

No. 948, 280fr — Scenes from Apollo space missions: a, Apollo 11. b, Apollo 16. c, Apollo 15. d, Apollo 17.

No. 949, 280fr — Sled dogs: a, Samoyeds. b, Siberian huskies and Alaskan malamutes. c, Alaskan malamutes. d, Man carrying Siberian husky.

No. 950, 280fr — Raptors: a, Melierax poliopterus. b, Torgos tracheliotus. c, Glaucidium passerinum. d, Terathopius ecaudatus.

No. 951, 280fr — Butterflies: a, Boloria aquilonaris. b, Pontia protodice. c, Strymon melinus. d, Aricia agestis.

No. 952, 280fr — Dinosaurs: a, Tyrannosaurus rex. b, Microraptor zhaoianus. c, Dakotaraptor steini. d, Chasmosaurus.

No. 953, 280fr — Orchids: a, Caucaea mimetica. b, Diuris magnifica. c, Thelymitra pulcherrima. d, Thelymitra campanulata.

No. 954, 280fr — Mushrooms: a, Craterellus tubaeformis. b, Tricholoma matsutake. c, Cantharellus cibarius. d, Stropharia rugoso.

No. 955, 280fr — Minerals: a, Sulfur. b, Chalcanthite. c, Colemanite. d, Legrandite.

No. 956, 960fr, Malaria-carrying mosquito, horiz. No. 957, 960fr, Rugby players, horiz. No. 958, 960fr, Ma Long playing table tennis, horiz. No. 959, 960fr, Chess players Anatoly Karpov and Garry Kasparov, horiz. No. 960, 960fr, Pilgrims on Mount Arafat, horiz. No. 961, 960fr, Cape Hatteras Lighthouse, U.S., Onychoprion fuscatus, horiz. No. 962, 960fr, El Galeón, horiz. No. 963, 960fr, Erie Berkshire locomotive, horiz. No. 964, 960fr, Frecciarossa 1000 train, Italy, horiz. No. 965, 960fr, Aston Martin DBR9, horiz. No. 966, 960fr, 1927 Ahrens-Fox fire truck, horiz. No. 967, 960fr, Concorde in flight and cockpit, horiz. No. 968, 960fr, Apollo 16 astronaut John Young on Moon, horiz. No. 969, 960fr, Dogs pulling sled, horiz. No. 970, 960fr, Aquila pomarina, horiz. No. 971, 960fr, Colotis danae, horiz. No. 972, 960fr, Deinocheirus mirificus, horiz. No. 973, 960fr, Cattleya schroederae, horiz. No. 974, 960fr, Boletus edulis, horiz. No. 975, 960fr, Galèna and fluorite, horiz.

2016, May 5 Litho. *Perf. 13¼*

Sheets of 4, #a-d

936-955 A303 Set of 20 255.00 255.00

Souvenir Sheets

956-975 A303 Set of 20 220.00 220.00

No. 940a inscription is missing "c" of circumambulation. Nos. 956-975 each contain one 66x42mm stamp.

Investiture of Pres. Ismail Omar Guelleh — A304

2016, May 8 Litho. *Perf. 13¼*

976 A304 1000fr bister & multi 11.50 11.50

Litho. With Foil Application

Souvenir Sheet

977 A304 5000fr gold & multi 57.50 57.50

No. 976 was printed in sheets of 4. No. 977 contains one 51x51mm stamp.

A305

Independence, 39th Anniv. — A306

2016, June 27 Litho. *Perf. 13½x13*

978 A305 250fr multi 3.00 3.00

Souvenir Sheet

Perf. 13¼

979 A306 500fr multi 5.75 5.75

Souvenir Sheet

Hassan Gouled Aptidon (1916-2006), First President of Djibouti — A307

2016, June 27 Litho. *Perf. 13¼*

980 A307 500fr multi 5.75 5.75

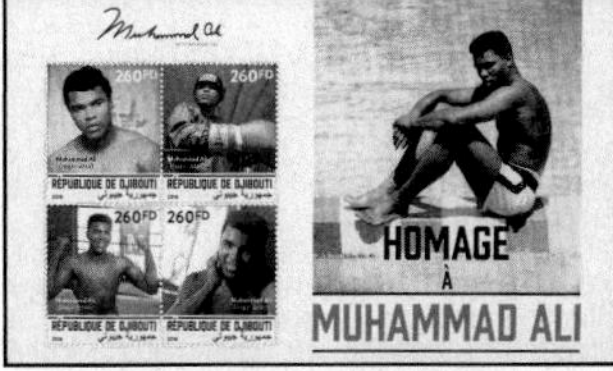

Muhammad Ali (1942-2016), Boxer — A308

No. 981 — Ali: a, With sign taped to wall. b, Wearing boxing gloves and headgear. c, In boxing ring. d, With hand touching face.

960fr, Ali running.

2016, July 28 Litho. *Perf. 13¼*

981 A308 260fr Sheet of 4, #a-d 12.00 12.00

Souvenir Sheet

982 A308 960fr multi 11.00 11.00

No. 982 contains one 38x54mm stamp.

A309

No. 983, 260fr — Steve Jobs (1955-2011), co-founder and chief executive officer of Apple Inc., and: a, Steve Wozniak, co-founder of Apple. b, Three computers. c, Apple 1 computer. d, Computer and apple.

No. 984, 260fr — Pope Francis: a, With Patriarch Cyril of Moscow. b, With child and dove. c, With statue and rosary beads. d, Washing feet of refugees.

No. 985, 260fr — Paintings by Pierre-Auguste Renoir (1841-1919): a, Young Woman Sewing, 1879. b, Luncheon of the Boating Party, 1880-81. c, Two Girls at the Piano, 1892. d, The Bridge at Chatou, 1875.

No. 986, 260fr — Paintings by Francisco de Goya (1746-1828): a, The Umbrella, 1777. b, Clothed Maja, 1800. c, Saturn Devouring His Son, 1819-23. d, Charles IV of Spain and His Family, 1800.

No. 987, 260fr — Paintings by Berthe Morisot (1841-95): a, The Garden at Bougival, 1884. b, Hide-and-Seek, 1873. c, Lucie Leon at the Piano, 1892. d, Dahlias, 1876.

No. 988, 260fr — Paintings by Paul Cézanne (1839-1906): a, Kitchen Table, 1888-90. b, The Bridge at Maincy, 1879. c, Still Life with Apples and Oranges, 1895. d, Mont Sainte-Victoire with Large Pine, 1887.

No. 989, 260fr — Museum visitors looking at paintings in the Musée d'Orsay: a, Yellow Haystacks, by Paul Gauguin, 1889. b, Luncheon on the Grass, by Edouard Manet, 1862-63. c, The Floor Scrapers, by Gustave Caillebotte, 1875. d, Self-portrait, by Vincent van Gogh, 1889.

No. 990, 260fr — Items from ancient Egypt: a, Bust of Nefertiti. b, Gayer-Anderson Cat. c, Horus and Temple of Amun, Luxor. d, Funerary mask of Tutankhamun and Giza Pyramids.

No. 991, 260fr — Royal Mail, 500th anniv.: a, Postman emptying pillar box, Morris J Type mail van. b, Horse-drawn mail wagon. c, Postal worker rowing to SS Mona's Queen. d, Postmen on bicycles.

No. 992, 260fr — Battle of Moscow, 75th anniv.: a, German soldier and battlefield map. b, T-34 tank. c, Telegrapher and telegraph key. d, German General Erich Hoepner (1886-1944) and Sturmgeschütz III.

No. 993, 260fr — First flight of LZ-129 (Hindenburg), 80th anniv.: a, Pianist and singer on Hindenburg. b, Workers under docked Hindenburg. c, Hindenburg and hangar. d, Hindenburg, tables and chairs.

No. 994, 260fr — Yuri Gagarin (1934-68), 55th anniv. of first spaceflight, and: a, Launch of rocket. b, Vostok 1 in space. c, Gagarin seated in spacesuit. d, Monument to Gagarin, Moscow.

No. 995, 260fr — Intl. Year of Pulses: a, Woman, child and legumes. b, Hands holding seedling. c, Farm machinery, sprout. d, Poicephalus senegalus, legume.

No. 996, 260fr — Gold medalists at 2014 Winter Olympics, Sochi, Russia: a, Alexander Tretyakov, skeleton. b, Matthias Mayer, downhill skiing. c, Darya Domracheva, mass start, pursuit and individual biathlon. d, Michel Mulder, speed skating.

No. 997, 260fr — Host cities for 2018 World Cup soccer championships, Russia: a, Yekaterinburg. b, St. Petersburg. c, Kazan. d, Volgograd.

No. 998, 260fr — Cat breeds: a, Ragdoll, standing. b, Siamese. c, Ragdoll, prone. d, Australian Mist.

No. 999, 260fr — Dolphins: a, Stenella longirostris. b, Tursiops truncatus with open mouth, beak of Stenella longirostris. c, Stenella coeruleoalba. d, Two Tursiops truncatus.

No. 1000, 260fr — Owls: a, Asio stygius. b, Strix leptogrammica. c, Surnia ulula. d, Tyto alba.

No. 1001, 260fr — Turtles: a, Cuora flavomarginata, Terrapene carolina carolina. b, Terrapene carolina carolina, Geochelone elegans. c, Trachemys scripta elegans. d, Terrapene ornata ornata, Stigmochelys pardalis.

No. 1002, 960fr, Jobs, computer and iPhone. No. 1003, 960fr, Pope Francis and dove. No. 1004, 960fr, Portrait of Marie-Thérèse Durand Ruel, by Renoir, 1882. No. 1005, 960fr, Witches' Sabbath, by Goya, 1789. No. 1006, 960fr, On the Balcony of Eugene Manet's room at Bougival, by Morisot, 1881. No. 1007, 960fr, A Modern Olympia, by Cézanne, 1870. No. 1008, 960fr, Visitor looking at Portrait of Doctor Paul Gachet , 1890 at Musée d'Orsay. No. 1009, 960fr, Painting from Tomb of Userhat. No. 1010, 960fr, British postman, pillar box, Titan Airways Boeing 737. No. 1011, 960fr, Soviet General Georgy Zhukov (1896-1974), anti-aircraft fire of Battle of Moscow. No. 1012, 960fr, Mooring of the Hindenburg at Lakehurst, New Jersey. No. 1013, 960fr, Gagarin, Vostok 1, flag of Soviet Union. No. 1014, 960fr, Hands holding legumes. No. 1015, 960fr, Sage Kotsenburg, 2014 Winter Olympics snowboarding gold medalist. No. 1016, 960fr, Moscow, host city for 2018 World Cup. No. 1017, 960fr, Burmese cat. No. 1018, 960fr, Inia geoffrensis. No. 1019, 960fr, Bubo scandiacus. No. 1020, 960fr, Centrochelys sulcata.

2016, July 28 Litho. *Perf. 13¼*

Sheets of 4, #a-d

983-1001 A309 Set of 19 225.00 225.00

Souvenir Sheets

1002-1020 A309 Set of 19 205.00 205.00

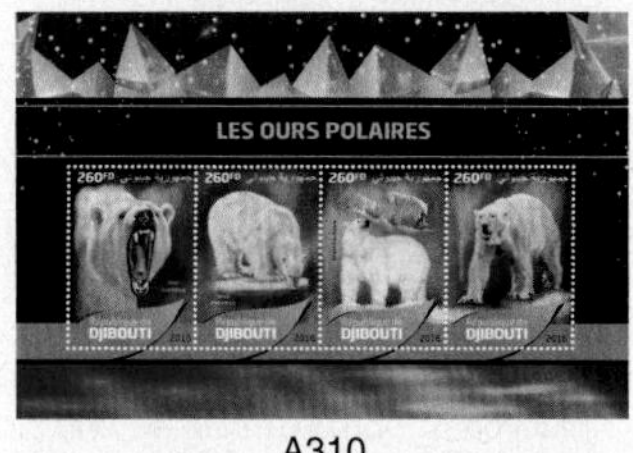

A310

No. 1021, 260fr — Ursus maritimus: a, Head of bear with open mouth. b, Looking at water. c, Two adults and cub. d, Bear walking.

No. 1022, 260fr — Hippopotamus amphibius: a, One animal with head near ground. b, One animal with open mouth, Latin name on two lines. c, Adult and juvenile. d, One adult with open mouth, Latin name on one line.

No. 1023, 260fr — Pandas: a, Ailuropoda melanoleuca eating. b, Ailurus fulgens, feet on mound. c, Ailurus fulgens, prone. d, Adult and juvenile Ailuropoda melanoleuca.

No. 1024, 260fr — Tigers: a, Head of Panthera tigris altaica. b, Panthera tigris tigris with open mouth. c, Panthera tigris tigris with closed mouth. d, Panthera tigris altaica walking.

No. 1025, 260fr — Dog breeds: a, Brussels griffon. b, Neapolitan mastiff. c, Canary Island hound. d, Kerry Blue terrier.

No. 1026, 260fr — Elephants: a, Loxodonta africana and tree. b, Two Loxodonta africana. c, Loxodonta africana and man. d, Loxodonta cyclotis.

No. 1027, 260fr — Water birds: a, Morus bassanus. b, Tadorna ferruginea. c, Dendrocygna bicolor. d, Cygnus atratus.

No. 1028, 260fr — Kingfishers: a, Corythornis cristatus, Halcyon smyrnensis. b, Alcedo atthis. c, Corythornis cristatus. d, Ceyx erithaca, Halcyon smyrnensis.

No. 1029, 260fr — Pigeons: a, Columba palumbus. b, Gymnophaps albertisii. c, Columba livia. d, Patagioenas leucocephala.

No. 1030, 260fr — Falcons: a, Falco vespertinus. b, Falco fasciinucha. c, Falco amurensis. d, Falco sparverius.

No. 1031, 260fr — Bees: a, Xylocopa micans. b, Euglossa dilemma. c, Anthidium manicatum. d, Augochlorella aurata.

No. 1032, 260fr — Butterflies: a, Cupidopsis cissus. b, Graphium porthaon. c, Myrina silenus. d, Tarucus sybaris.

No. 1033, 260fr — Fish: a, Acanthurus leucosternon, Acanthurus triostegus. b, Pterois volitans. c, Pygoplites diacanthus. d, Manta alfredi.

No. 1034, 260fr — Shells: a, Cypraecassis rufa. b, Charonia tritonis. c, Trochus nodulosus. d, Conus mustelinus.

No. 1035, 260fr — Extinct animals: a, Mammuthus columbi. b, Moropus elatus. c, Elasmotherium sibiricum. d, Smilodon populator.

No. 1036, 260fr — Prehistoric aquatic animals: a, Enchodus. b, Mosasaurus hoffmannii. c, Ammonoidea. d, Helicoprion bessonovi.

No. 1037, 260fr — Mushrooms: a, Rhodotus palmatus. b, Phallus indusiatus. c, Lactarius deliciosus. d, Leccinum scabrum.

No. 1038, 260fr — Minerals: a, Chalcanthite. b, Legrandite. c, Gadolinite. d, Fluorite.

No. 1039, 260fr — Cartoon characters on stamps: a, U.S. Nos. 4399-4402 (Characters from *The Simpsons*). b, U.S. No. 4470, Switzerland Nos. 1536-1537 (Characters from *Garfield*). c, U.S. Zazzle personalized stamps depicting *SpongeBob SquarePants*. d, Switzerland No. 1497, Belgium Nos. 2320-2321 (Characters from *The Smurfs*).

No. 1040, 960fr, Ursus maritimus adult and cub. No. 1041, 960fr, Hippopotamus amphibius adult and juvenile, diff. No. 1042, 960fr, Two Ailuropoda melanoleuca. No. 1043, 960fr, Two Panthera tigris altaica. No. 1044, 960fr, Akita. No. 1045, 960fr, Elephas maximus. No. 1046, 960fr, Gavia immer. No. 1047, 960fr, Alcedo atthis, diff. No. 1048, 960fr, Goura scheepmakeri. No. 1049, 960fr, Falco peregrinus. No. 1050, 960fr, Andrena cineraria. No. 1051, 960fr, Myrina silenus ficedula. No. 1052, 960fr, Plectorhinchus vittatus, Heniochus pleurotaenia. No. 1053, 960fr, Lambis lambis. No. 1054, 960fr, Glyptodon clavipes. No. 1055, 960fr, Dinichthys terrelli. No. 1056, 960fr, Morchella esculenta. No. 1057, 960fr, Cassiterite. No. 1058, 960fr, Netherlands No.1080a, U.S. Zazzle srtamps depicting *Tom and Jerry*.

2016, Sept. 26 Litho. *Perf. 13¼*

Sheets of 4, #a-d

1021-1039 A310 Set of 19 225.00 225.00

Souvenir Sheets

1040-1058 A310 Set of 19 210.00 210.00

Worldwide Fund for Nature (WWF) — A311

No. 1059 — Torgos tracheliotos: a, Bird on branch. b, Two birds. c, Two birds and carrion. d, Bird and animal bones.

960fr, Torgos tracheliotos in flight.

2016, Sept. 26 Litho. *Perf. 13¼*

1059 A311 260fr Sheet of 4, #a-d 12.00 12.00

Souvenir Sheet

1060 A311 960fr multi 11.00 11.00

No. 1060 lacks the WWF emblem on the stamp and sheet margin. For surcharges, see Nos. 1814-1821.

Miniature Sheet

First Batallion of Somali Snipers, Cent. — A312

No. 1061: a, Medal, Battle of Douaumont. b, Tank and Malmaison, 1917. c, Monument. d, Airplane over Pointe de Grave and Cordouan Lighthouse, France, 1945.

2016, Oct. 24 Litho. *Perf. 13¼*

1061 A312 500fr Sheet of 4, #a-d 22.50 22.50

A313

No. 1062, 280fr — Rotary International in Djibouti: a, Boy holding stick and water bottle. b, Woman and children at well. c, Woman holding child to receive vaccination. d, Children.

No. 1063, 280fr — Red Cross-Red Crescent in Djibouti: a, Red Crescent, map of Africa,

Red Crescent workers carrying litter. b, Red Crescent worker assisting woman. c, Red Crescent worker looking at notebook. d, Red Crescent worker holding water bucket.

No. 1064, 280fr — Canonization of Mother Teresa (1910-97): a, Mother Teresa and building. b, Mother Teresa, dove, Pres. Ronald Reagan and wife, Nancy. c, Mother Teresa holding child. d, Mother Teresa and flag of India.

No. 1065, 280fr — Extraordinary Jubilee of Mercy: a, Pope Francis in Kenya. b, Pope Francis opening holy doors. c, Pope Benedict XVI. d, Dove and Popes Francis, Benedict XVI.

No. 1066, 280fr — British royal family: a, Queen Elizabeth II. b, Duke and Duchess of Cambridge. c, Prince George and Princess Charlotte. d, Duke and Duchess of Cambridge, Prince George and Princess Charlotte.

No. 1067, 280fr — Publication of Albert Einstein's Theory of General Relativity, cent.: a, Einstein, globes, equation, model of atom. b, Einstein and equation. c, Hand holding orb depicting Einstein. d, Einstein and light bulb.

No. 1068, 280fr — Battle of the Somme, cent.: a, Mark I tank. b, British Gen. Ivor Maxse (1862-1958) and soldiers. c, French soldiers at munitions wagon. d, German soldier on horse.

No. 1069, 280fr — Navy ships: a, San Marco, Italy. b, Zubr Class hovercraft, Russia, and tank. c, USS Coronado, United States. d, BSF Azov 151, BF Minsk 127, Russia.

No. 1070, 280fr — Submarines.: a, Type 035, People's Republic of China. b, Typhoon Class Project 941, Russia. c, A26 submarine. d, HMS Triumph, Great Britain.

No. 1071, 280fr — High-speed trains.: a, ETR 500 Frecciarossa, Italy. b, SNCF TGV Duplex, France. c, AVE Class 103, Spain. d, Eurostar e320, Great Britain.

No. 1072, 280fr — Motorcycles: a, BMW K1600GTL. b, Suzuki TU250X. c, MV Agusta F3 800. d, Yamaha Star VMAX.

No. 1073, 280fr — Russian military aircraft: a, Sukhoi Su-35. b, Mil Mi-28 helicopter. c, Kamov KA-50 helicopter. d, Mikoyan MiG-41.

No. 1074, 280fr — Space exploration: a, Mars Rover Spirit, 2004. b, Neil Armstrong (1930-2012) on ladder of Lunar Module, 1969. c, Yuri Gagarin (1934-68), and Vostok 1, 1961. d, Final mission of Space Shuttle Atlantis, 2011.

No. 1075, 280fr — 2016 Ice Hockey World Championships, Russia: a, Players fighting for puck near goaltender. b, U.S. player and Russian goaltender. c, Canadian and Russian players. d, Finnish player and Canadian goaltender.

No. 1076, 280fr — Chess players: a, Magnus Carlsen. b, Anatoly Karpov. c, Bobby Fischer. d, Mariya Muzychuk.

No. 1077, 280fr — Islamic art: a, Battle scene from the Shahnameh. b, Interior of Cathedral-Mosque of Córdoba, Spain. c, Jameh Mosque, Isfahan, Iran. d, Pyxis of al-Mughira.

No. 1078, 280fr — Lighthouses: a, Petit Minou Lighthouse, France. b, Hornby Lighthouse, Australia. c, Store Faerder Lighthouse, Norway. d, Point Betsie Lighthouse, Michigan.

No. 1079, 280fr — Orchids: a, Cattleya labiata. b, Cypripedium kentuckiense. c, Vanda denisoniana. d, Orchis purpurea.

No. 1080, 280fr — New Year 2017 (Year of the Rooster): a, Rooster with leg raised and wings extended. b, Rooster facing right, pagoda in background. c, Rooster facing right, torii in background. d, Rooster in air, flapping wings.

No. 1081, 960fr, Child and containers, Rotary International emblem. No. 1082, 960fr, Red Crescent worker with water bottle tending to injured person. No. 1083, 960fr, Mother Teresa and child, diff. No. 1084, 960fr, Pope Francis kissing creche figure of infant Jesus. No. 1085, 960fr, Queen Elizabeth II, diff. No. 1086, 960fr, Einstein at blackboard. No. 1087, 960fr, German soldier at Battle of the Somme. No. 1088, 960fr, USS Essex and CH-53E helicopters. No. 1089, 960fr, USS Scorpion. No. 1090, 960fr, IC3 3 train, Germany. No. 1091, 960fr, Beta 450 RR motorcycle. No. 1092, 960fr, Mikoyan MiG-35. No. 1093, 960fr, Sputnik 1, 1957. No. 1094, 960fr, Russian ice hockey player sprawled on ice. No. 1095, 960fr, Sergey Karjakin, chess pieces. No. 1096, 960fr, Qutub Minar and Alai Darwaza, India. No. 1097, 960fr, La Vieille Lighthouse, France. No. 1098, 960fr, Vanda coerulea. No. 1099, 960fr, Rooster and Great Wall of China.

2016, Nov. 25 Litho. *Perf. 13¼*

Sheets of 4, #a-d

1062-1080 A313 Set of 19 240.00 240.00

Souvenir Sheets

1081-1099 A313 Set of 19 205.00 205.00

Election of Donald Trump as U.S. President — A314

No. 1100: a, Trump and stars. b, Trump and Republican Party emblem. c, Trump with wife, Melania, and son, Barron. d, Trump and running mate, Mike Pence.

960fr, Trump, diff.

2016, Nov. 25 Litho. *Perf. 13¼*

1100 A314 280fr Sheet of 4, #a-d 12.50 12.50

Souvenir Sheet

1101 A314 960fr multi 11.00 11.00

No. 1101 contains one 51x90mm stamp.

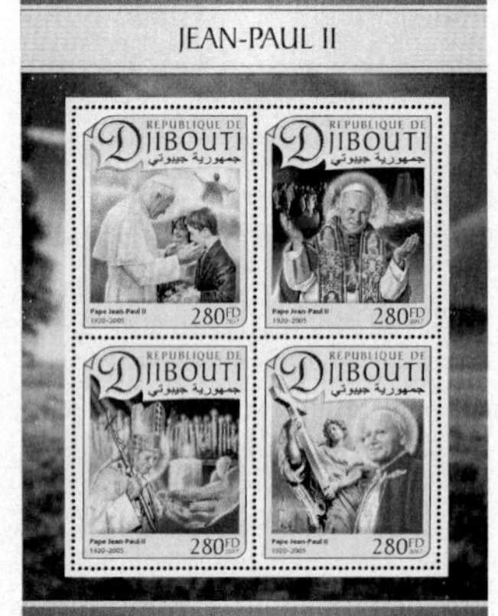

A315

No. 1102, 280fr — St. John Paul II (1920-2005), with: a, Boy and girl. b, Crowd worshiping. c, Candles. d, Religious sculpture.

No. 1103, 280fr — Michèle Morgan (1920-2016), actress, with: a, Unidentified actor. b, Hand on head. c, Clapboard and film reel. d, Gérard Philipe (1922-59), actor.

No. 1104, 280fr — John Glenn, Jr. (1921-2016), astronaut: a, U.S. flag, Mercury capsule, launch of Atlas 8 rocket. b, Glenn and Space Shuttle Discovery. c, Glenn, military airplane and Pres. John F. Kennedy (1917-63). d, Glenn, U.S. flag and rocket launch.

No. 1105, 280fr — Rotary International emblem and: a, Paul P. Harris (1868-1947), founder of Rotary International, holding book. b, Rotary volunteer giving vaccine to child. c, Children reading. d, Harris with reversed Paul Harris Fellow pin.

No. 1106, 280fr — Scouting, 110th anniv.: a, Scouts in canoe, Nettapus auritus. b, Scout with binoculars, Circaetus cinereus. c, Scouts with Scouting flag. d, Scout and Lentinus squarrosolus.

No. 1107, 280fr — Paintings by Ivan Aivazovsky (1817-1900): a, Portrait of Loris-Melikov, 1888. b, Battle of Cesme at Night, 1848. c, Boat Ride by Kumpaki in Constantinople, 1846. d, Odessa, 1840.

No. 1108, 280fr — Paintings by Edgar Degas (1834-1917): a, In a Café, 1875-76. b, Emma Dobigny, 1869. c, A Cotton Office in New Orleans, 1873. d, Ballet Rehearsal on Stage, 1874.

No. 1109, 280fr — Paintings by Frida Kahlo (1907-54): a, Tree of Hope, Keep Firm, 1946. b, Still Life with Parrot, 1951. c, The Wounded Deer, 1946. d, Portrait of Lucha Maria, a Girl from Tehuacan, 1942.

No. 1110, 280fr — Sculptures by Auguste Rodin (1840-1917): a, The Thinker, 1903. b, Lady Sackville-West, 1913. c, Young Woman with Flowered Hat, 1870-75. d, The Clenched Hand, 1885, The Gates of Hell, 1880-90.

No. 1111, 280fr — Primates: a, Pongo pygmaeus. b, Indri indri. c, Loris tardigradus. d, Papio hamadryas.

No. 1112, 280fr — Wild cats: a, Panthera tigris altaica. b, Panthera neofelis nebulosa. c, Puma concolor. d, Panthera pardus kotiya.

No. 1113, 280fr — Dolphins: a, Stenella longirostris. b, Grampus griseus. c, Lagenorhynchus obscurus. d, Tursiops truncatus.

No. 1114, 280fr — Whales: a, Balaena mysticetus. b, Delphinapterus leucas. c, Physeter macrocephalus. d, Balaenoptera musculus.

No. 1115, 280fr — Owls: a, Aegolius harrisii, Aegolius acadicus. b, Athene noctua. c, Bubo virginianus. d, Glaucidium passerinum.

No. 1116, 280fr — Birds of prey: a, Caracara plancus. b, Aegolicus acadicus. c, Coragyps atratus. d, Gymnogyps californianus.

No. 1117, 280fr — Water birds: a, Rynchops niger. b, Eudocimus ruber. c, Gavia immer. d, Mycteria leucocephala.

No. 1118, 280fr — Butterflies: a, Perrhybris pamela. b, Junonia lemonias lemonias. c, Ixias pyrene. d, Colotis euippe.

No. 1119, 280fr — Fish: a, Acanthurus leucosternon. b, Ostracion cubicus. c, Antennarius coccineus. d, Scarus coelestinus.

No. 1120, 280fr — Turtles: a, Batagur trivittata. b, Chelus fimbriatus. c, Lepidochelys kempii. d, Lepidochelys olivacea.

No. 1121, 280fr — Snakes: a, Pituophis catenifer. b, Diadophis punctatus. c, Oxyrhopus trigeminus. d, Natrix natrix.

No. 1122, 280fr — Dinosaurs: a, Iguanodon. b, Spinops sternbergorum. c, Cryolophosaurus. d, Spinosaurus.

No. 1123, 280fr — Endangered animals: a, Campephilus principalis. b, Panthera pardus orientalis. c, Helarctos malayanus. d, Lepilemur septentrionalis.

No. 1124, 280fr — Mushrooms: a, Cantharellus cibarius. b, Gyromitra esculenta. c, Ramaria formosa. d, Tylopilus felleus.

No. 1125, 280fr — Orchids: a, Vanda coerulea. b, Cattleya. c, White Phalaenopsis. d, Zygopetalum.

No. 1126, 280fr — Minerals: a, Amazonite. b, Wulfenite. c, Rhodochrosite. d, Aquamarine.

No. 1127, 960fr, St. John Paul II and crosses. No. 1128, 960fr, Morgan with strings of pearls. No. 1129, 960fr, Glenn receiving Presidential Medal of Freedom from Pres. Barack Obama. No. 1130, 960fr, Rotary International emblem and bust of Harris. No. 1131, 960fr, Scout blowing horn, Colotis danae. No. 1132, 960fr, The Roads at Kronstadt, by Aivazovsky, 1840. No. 1133, 960fr, The Dance Class, by Degas, 1874. No. 1134, 960fr, Portrait of My Father, by Kahlo, 1951. No. 1135, 960fr, The Burghers of Calais, by Rodin, 1884-89. No. 1136, 960fr, Leontopithecus rosalia. No. 1137, 960fr, Lynx pardinus. No. 1138, 960fr, Cephalorhynchus heavisidii. No. 1139, 960fr, Megaptera novaeangliae. No. 1140, 960fr, Asio capensis. No. 1141, 960fr, Buteo lagopus. No. 1142, 960fr, Anas rhynchotis. No. 1143, 960fr, Delias eucharis. No. 1144, 960fr, Sparisoma cretense. No. 1145, 960fr, Geochelone elephantopus. No. 1146, 960fr, Naja sumatrana. No. 1147, 960fr, Parasaurolophus. No. 1148, 960fr, Gyps indicus. No. 1149, 960fr, Clitocybe phyllophila. No. 1150, 960fr, Black Phalaenopsis orchid. No. 1151, 960fr, Pyromorphite.

2017, Jan. 20 Litho. *Perf. 13¼*

Sheets of 4, #a-d

1102-1126 A315 Set of 25 310.00 310.00

Souvenir Sheets

1127-1151 A315 Set of 25 265.00 265.00

Varanus Komodoensis — A316

No. 1152 — Komodo dragon: a, With head down, tongue out. b, With head raised, tongue not visible. c, Climbing rock. d, With head raised, tongue out.

950fr, Komodo dragon, tongue touching ground.

2017, Mar. 15 Litho. *Perf. 13¼*

1152 A316 240fr Sheet of 4, #a-d 11.00 11.00

Souvenir Sheet

1153 A316 950fr multi 10.50 10.50

Bandung 2017 World Stamp Exhibition. No. 1153 contains one 48x48mm stamp.

A317

No. 1154, 240fr — Wilbur Wright (1867-1912), aviation pioneer: a, Wright, with brother, Orville (1871-1948) and Wright Flyer. b, Wind testing of Wright Flyer, 1901. c, Wilbur and Wright Flyer in flight. d, Wilbur at controls of airplane.

No. 1155, 240fr — Concorde: a, British Airways Concorde over Paris. b, British Airways Concorde over Nice, France. c, Air France Concorde over London. d, British Airways Concorde over Mecca, Saudi Arabia.

No. 1156, 240fr — Military aircraft: a, Mikoyan-Gurevich MiG-29. b, A-10 Thunderbolt II. c, Junkers Ju 52. d, Boeing-Bell V-22 Osprey.

No. 1157, 240fr — Disappearance of Amelia Earhart (1897-1937), pilot: a, Earhart and her airplane. b, Earhart, airplane and hangar. c, Earhart and husband, George P. Putnam (1887-1950). d, Electra 10E in flight.

No. 1158, 240fr — Ferdinand von Zeppelin (1838-1917), airship manufacturer: a, Zeppelin, passengers boarding Graf Zeppelin. b, Zeppelin LZ-1. c, Zeppelin LZ-4. d, Zeppelin and schematic drawings of airship.

No. 1159, 240fr — 80th birthday of Valentina Tereshkova, first woman in space: a, In car with Russia Premier Nikita Khrushchev (1894-1971). b, With Yuri Gagarin (1934-68), first man in space. c, With obverse and reverse of 1983 1-ruble Russian coin depicting her. d, With Vostok 6.

No. 1160, 240fr — Steam trains: a, Pennsylvania Railroad 1223. b, London and North Eastern Railway Class A4 Mallard 4468. c, Great Western Railway 4-4-0 City of Truro 3717. d, Deutsche Reichsbahn 18 201.

No. 1161, 240fr — High-speed trains: a, Talgo 350. b, NTV Alstom AGV 575. c, Shinkansen Series 500. d, Renfe Series S-103.

No. 1162, 240fr — Sinking of the Titanic, 105th anniv.: a, Titanic and map of voyage. b, Titanic sinking and overturned lifeboat. c, Titanic and iceberg. d, Titanic and Thomas Andrews (1873-1912), designer of Titanic.

No. 1163, 240fr — Submarines: a, HMAS Collins, Australia. b, SSK Kilo Class Type 636 and Icebreaker Ivan Kruzenshtern, Russia. c, HMS Ambush, Great Britain. d, Terrible, France.

No. 1164, 240fr — Donald Campbell (1921-67), land and water speed record holder: a, Wearing helmet. b, In Bluebird K7, waving. c, Sitting. d, With wife, Tonia Bern-Campbell.

No. 1165, 240fr — Special transportation: a, Telescope transporter. b, Victoria, Australia police vehicle. c, Euclid dump truck. d, Snowcat.

No. 1166, 240fr — Fire-fighting vehicles: a, Caterpillar CT660 fire truck, United States. b, Foremost Nodwell 240, Canada. c, Delta 2 wheeled carrier, Canada. d, Hopedale, Massachusets Tanker 1, United States.

No. 1167, 240fr — 1947 Ferrari 125 S, 70th anniv., with background design of: a, Trees. b, Ferrari emblem. c, Steering wheel and dashboard. d, Clouds.

No. 1168, 240fr — Motorcycles: a, 1912 Henderson 4-cylinder. b, 1923 BMW R32. c, 1962-63 BSA Rocket Gold Star A10. d, 1974 Hercules-Wankel 2000.

No. 1169, 240fr — Transportation for Pres. Donald Trump: a, Sikorsky S-76 helicopter. b, 2015 Mercedes-Benz Class S600. c, 1997 Lamborghini Diablo. d, Boeing 757.

No. 1170, 240fr — Sled dogs: a, Five sled dogs and two drivers. b, Two Seppala Siberian sled dogs. c, Husky and Malamutes. d, Sled dogs resting with driver.

No. 1171, 240fr — Jacques Cousteau (1910-97), conservationist and filmmaker: a, Calypso and hot air balloon in Antarctica. b, Cousteau and SP-350 Denise. c, Cousteau holding cup. d, Cousteau and Calypso.

No. 1172, 240fr — Charles Darwin (1809-82), naturalist: a, Portrait of Darwin and his wife, Emma, by George Richmond. b, HMS Beagle and map of its voyage, Conolophus subcristatus. c, Darwin, primate and skulls of Homo neanderthalensis and Homo sapiens. d, Darwin and specimens of Pseudoscarus lepidus, Eleginops maclovinus, and Ceroglossus darwinii.

No. 1173, 240fr — Russian October Revolution, cent.: a, Barricades at St. Isaac Cathedral, St. Petersburg. b, Soldiers at Hermitage and Winter Palace, St. Petersburg. c, Deomonstrators in St. Petersburg. d, Lenin (1870-1924), and Cruiser Aurora.

No. 1174, 240fr — Battle of Stalingrad, 75th anniv.: a, Aug. 23, 1942 air raid. b, Soviet Gen. Georgi Zhukov (1896-1974). c, German Gen. Friedrich Paulus (1890-1957). d, Soviet troops, Feb. 1943.

No. 1175, 240fr — Lighthouses: a, Punta Palascia Lighthouse, Italy. b, Lindesnes Lighthouse, Norway. c, Pointe aux Barques Lighthouse, Michigan. d, North Head Lighthouse, Washington.

No. 1176, 240fr — Windmills and tulips: a, Kinderdijk, Netherlands windmills, red and white tulips. b, Kuremaa, Estonia windmill, yellow tulips. c, Sonderho, Denmark windmill, orange tulips. d, Halanker, Great Britain windmill, red tulips.

No. 1177, 240fr — Endangered animals: a, Anolis gorgonae. b, Anolis proboscis. c, Neurergus kaiseri. d, Tokay gecko.

No. 1178, 950fr, Orville Wright on bicycle, Wright Flyer in flight. No. 1179, 950fr, British Airways Concorde over New York City. No. 1180, 950fr, F-16 Fighting Falcon. No. 1181, 950fr, Earhart holding propeller. No. 1182, 950fr, Zeppelin and his signature. No. 1183, 950fr, Tereshkova and stylized rocket. No. 1184, 950fr, St. Louis-San Francisco train. No. 1185, 950fr, Shinkansen Series E6. No. 1186, 950fr, Titanic and its captain, Edward Smith (1850-1912). No. 1187, 950fr, Victoria Class submarine, Canada. No. 1188, 950fr, Campbell in Bluebird K7. No. 1189, 950fr, Lockheed Martin hybrid dirigibles. No. 1190, 950fr, San José, California fire truck. No. 1191, 950fr, Enzo Ferrari (1898-1988), automobile manufacturer in 1947 Ferrari 125 S. No. 1192, 950fr, 2006 Royal Enfield Bullet motorcycle. No. 1193, 950fr, Gold Trump motorcyle. No. 1194, 950fr, Siberian husky sled dogs. No. 1195, 950fr, Cousteau holding walkie-talkie. No. 1196, 950fr, Darwin, Geospiza fortis, heads of Galapagos finches. No. 1197, 950fr, Lenin and Cruiser Aurora, diff. No. 1198, 950fr, Vasily Zaytsev (1915-91), Soviet sniper at Battle of Stalingrad. No. 1199, 950fr, Petit Minou Lighthouse, France. No. 1200, 950fr, Mostert, South Africa windmill, red and yellow tulips. No. 1201, 950fr, Neurergus kaiseri, diff.

2017, Mar. 15 Litho. *Perf. 13¼*

Sheet of 4, #a-d

1154-1177 A317 Set of 24 260.00 260.00

Souvenir Sheets

1178-1201 A317 Set of 24 255.00 255.00

Miniature Sheets

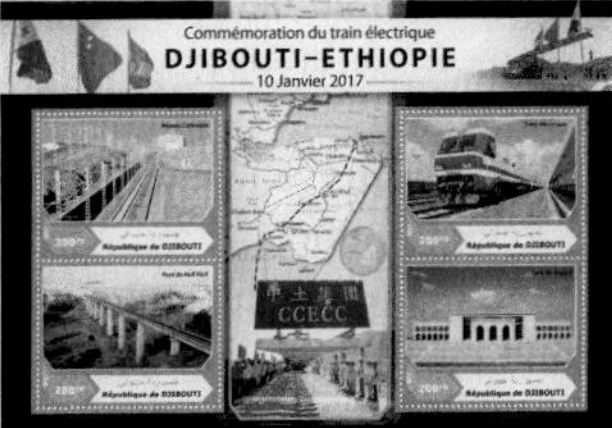

Opening of Djibouti-Ethiopia Electric Rail Line — A318

Nos. 1202 and 1203: a, Tracks and catenary network. b, Electric train. c, Holl Holl Bridge. d, Nagad Station.

2017, Apr. 25 Litho. *Perf. 12¾x13¼*

1202 A318 200fr Sheet of 4, #a-d 9.00 9.00

1203 A318 250fr Sheet of 4, #a-d 11.00 11.00

A319

No. 1204, 240fr — Ailuropoda melanoleuca (Giant panda): a, On branch. b, Adult and cub. c, On back. d, Facing left.

No. 1205, 240fr — Dogs: a, Papillons. b, French bulldog. c, English cocker spaniel. d, Basset hounds.

No. 1206, 240fr — Dolphins: a, Lagenorhynchus obscurus. b, Tursiops truncatus. c, Cephalorhynchus commersonii. d, Stenella frontalis.

No. 1207, 240fr — Owls: a, Tyto alba. b, Bubo cinerascens. c, Bubo lacteus. d, Glaucidium perlatum.

No. 1208, 240fr — Bees and orchids: a, Euglossa imperialis, Cattleya aclandiae. b, Exaerete frontalis, Cymbidium madidum. c, Euglossa tridentata, Maxillaria tenufolia. d, Euglossa dilemma, Cattleya lueddemanniana.

No. 1209, 240fr — Butterflies: a, Batesia hypochlora. b, Papilio demoleus. c, Melitaea didyma. d, Phengaris arion.

No. 1210, 240fr — Turtles: a, Graptemys pseudogeographica kohni. b, Rhinoclemmys pulcherrima. c, Trachemys scripta scripta. d, Trachemys scripta elegans.

No. 1211, 240fr — Extinct animals: a, Mammuthus meridionalis. b, Raphus cucullatus. c, Megacerops coloradensis. d, Thalassocnus antiquus.

No. 1212, 240fr — Mahatma Gandhi (1869-1948), Indian nationalist: a, With spinning wheel. b, Walking, holding walking stick. c, With building. d, With decorated cow.

No. 1213, 240fr — Princess Diana (1961-97): a, With Prince Charles and coat of arms. b, Wearing white blouse. c, Wearing white blouse, with sunglasses in hair. d, Holding Prince Harry.

No. 1214, 950fr, Ailuropoda melanoleuca adult and cub, diff. No. 1215, 950fr, Rottweilers. No. 1216, 950fr, Sotalia fluviatilis. No. 1217, 950fr, Otus senegalensis. No. 1218, 950fr, Euglossa imperialis, Laelia anceps. No. 1219, 950fr, Colotis ione. No. 1220, 950fr, Apalone mutica. No. 1221, 950fr, Glyptodon clavipes. No. 1222, 950fr, Gandhi and Taj Mahal. No. 1223, 950fr, Princess Diana, Duke and Duchess of Cambrige, Prince Harry.

2017, July 5 Litho. *Perf. 13¼*

Sheets of 4, #a-d

1204-1213 A319 Set of 10 110.00 110.00

Souvenir Sheets

1214-1223 A319 Set of 10 105.00 105.00

International Day of Girls in Information and Communications Technology — A319a

2017, July 13 Litho. *Perf. 13¼*

1223A A319a 100fr multi 1.10 1.10

Souvenir Sheet

1223B A319a 200fr multi 2.25 2.25

"Eid Mubarak" — A319b

Designs: 150fr, Lantern at right, Arabic text at left.

300fr, Lantern and star at left, Arabic text at right.

2017, July 20 Litho. *Perf. 13x13¼*

1223C A319b 150fr multi 1.75 1.75

Souvenir Sheet

Perf. 13½x13¼

1223D A319b 300fr multi 3.50 3.50

A319c

Independence, 40th Anniv. — A319d

No. 1223E — Flag of Djibouti and: g, "Unité" at LL. h, Arabic inscription at LL. i, "Inkitino" at LL. j, "Midnimo" at LL.

2017, July 20 Litho. *Perf. 13¼*

1223E A319c 150fr Sheet of 4, #g-j 6.75 6.75

Souvenir Sheet

Litho. With Foil Application

1223F A319d 500fr sil & multi 5.75 5.75

A320

No. 1224, 240fr — Formula I race cars: a, Blue and yellow cars. b, Orange car. c, Bright red car. d, Red and orange cars.

No. 1225, 240fr — Ice hockey: a, Norwegian player in dark blue jersey, player in white and blue jersey. b, Henrik Lundqvist, goaltender for New York Rangers. c, Referee and Washington Capitals player with stick raised. d, Boston Bruins player in black and yellow jersey, player in red and white jersey.

No. 1226, 240fr — Cricket players: a, Batsman swinging and falling fielder. b, Shikhar Dhawan. c, Josh Hazlewood. d, Batsman holding bat behind back, celebrating player.

No. 1227, 240fr — Tennis players: a, Rafael Nadal. b, Stan Wawrinka. c, Angelique Kerber. d, Serena Williams.

No. 1228, 240fr — Table tennis players: a, Zhang Jike. b, Liu Shiwen. c, Ding Ning. d, Liu Guoliang.

No. 1229, 240fr — Golfers: a, Dustin Johnson. b, So-yeon Ryu. c, Lydia Ko. d, Rory McIlroy.

No. 1230, 240fr — Pierre de Coubertin (1863-1937), President of International Olympic Committee: a, Coubertin, wrestlers in background. b, Statue of Coubertin, Beijing. c, Coubertin facing right. d, Coubertin, ancient Greek soldiers in background.

No. 1231, 240fr — Chess pieces: a, Black knight, queen in silhouette. b, White queen, hand moving black piece. c, White queen and king, black king. d, Carved piece depicting elephant carrying howdah, queen in background.

No. 1232, 240fr — Metropolitan Museum of Art, 145th anniv.: a, Fragment of bust of Roman Emperor Caracalla. b, Charles Engelhard Court. c, Bust of Young Girl Identified as Anne Audéoud of Geneva, by Jean Antoine Houdon. d, Silver Buffalo Figure from Benin, 19th cent.

No. 1233, 240fr — Red Cross-Red Crescent Campaign Against Malaria: a, Man spraying insecticide in village. b, Woman and mosquito netting. c, Medical worker examining child. d, Medical worker taking blood sample from child.

No. 1234, 240fr — Pres. John F. Kennedy (1917-63), and: a, U.S. flag. b, Wife, Jacqueline. c, Daughter, Caroline. d, Wife, daughter, and son, John, Jr.

No. 1235, 240fr — 35th birthday of Prince William of Cambridge: a, In helicopter. b, With wife and children. c, As child, with parents and brother. d, Playing polo with brother, Prince Harry.

No. 1236, 240fr — Tall ships: a, Royal Clipper, Sweden. b, Belem, France. c, Palinuro, Italy. d, Juan Sebastián de Elcano, Spain.

No. 1237, 240fr — Naval vessels: a, Gloire, France, 1859. b, USS Texas, 1912. c, Yamato, Japan, 1940. d, La Fayette, France, 1996.

No. 1238, 240fr — European high-speed trains: a, TGV Thalys PBKA, France. b, TGV Lyria, France and Switzerland. c, ICE 3, Germany. d, TCDD HT80000, Turkey.

No. 1239, 240fr — Fire trucks: a, Citroen 46 CDU. b, Rosenbauer Panther. c, MAZ7310 Airfield Crash Tender. d, Ladder truck with tank treads.

No. 1240, 240fr — Opel automobiles: a, Opel Ascona A. b, Opel Kapitän. c, Opel Mokka. d, Opel Tigra.

No. 1241, 240fr — Supersonic aircraft: a, Aerion SBJ. b, North American XB-70 Valkyrie. c, Tupolev Tu-22M. d, Lockheed SR-71 Blackbird.

No. 1242, 240fr — Sergei Korolev (1907-66), spacecraft designer: a, Luna 3, Sputnik 1. b, Korolev and Luna 8K72. c, Korolev and R-7 Semyorka missile. d, Yuri Gagarin (1934-68), cosmonaut, and Vostok 1.

No. 1243, 240fr — Birds of Djibouti: a, Dendropicos namaquus. b, Phoeniculus somaliensis. c, Caprimulgus stellatus. d, Trachyphonus darnaudii.

No. 1244, 950fr, Nico Rosberg, 2016 Formula 1 racing champion and car. No. 1245, 950fr, Ice hockey player taking shot. No. 1246, 950fr, Cricket batsman and wicket-keeper. No. 1247, 950fr, Tennis player Andy Murray. No. 1248, 950fr, Table tennis player Ma Long. No. 1249, 950fr, Golfer Jason Day. No. 1250, 950fr, Coubertin and hurdlers. No. 1251, 950fr, King and queen chess pieces. No. 1252, 950fr, Statue of William Shakespeare, by John Quincy Adams Ward. No. 1253, 950fr, Woman carrying child, Anopheles maculipennis. No. 1254, 950fr, Pres. Kennedy and U.S. flag, diff. No. 1255, 950fr, Wedding of Prince William of Cambridge and Catherine Middleton. No. 1256, 950fr, Tovarishch, Russia. No. 1257, 950fr, Gloire, France, 1935. No. 1258, Renfe Series S-114, Spain. No. 1259, 950fr, Bulldog 4x4 fire truck. No. 1260, 950fr, Opel Astra J. No. 1261, 950fr, Panavia Tornado IDS. No. 1262, 950fr, Korolev and Vostok 1. No. 1263, 950fr, Tricholaema melanocephala.

2017, July 28 Litho. *Perf. 13¼*

Sheets of 4, #a-d

1224-1243 A320 Set of 20 215.00 215.00

Souvenir Sheets

1244-1263 A320 Set of 20 215.00 215.00

Birdpex 8 Philatlelic Exhibition, Mondorf-les-Bains, Luxembourg (Nos. 1243, 1263).

A321

No. 1264, 240fr — Marilyn Monroe (1926-62), actress: a, Wearing white fur coat. b, With signature. c, With star from Hollywood Walk of Fame. d, Wearing black sweater.

No. 1265, 240fr — Paul McCartney, rock musician, and: a, Emblem of the Beatles. b, Wife, Linda. c, Beatle bandmates, John Lennon, Ringo Starr and George Harrison. d, Musical score and curved piano keyboard.

No. 1266, 240fr — Charlie Chaplin (1889-1977), film actor, and: a, Actor Ben Turpin. b, Signature. c, Woman holding flower. d, Child actor.

No. 1267, 240fr — Marie Curie (1867-1934), chemist and physicist, and: a, Pitchblende, husband, Pierre (1859-1906). b, Nobel medals and Daughter, Irène Joliot-Curie (1897-1956). c, Curie Pavilion of Institut du Radium. d, World War I mobile radiological unit.

No. 1268, 240fr — Nelson Mandela (1918-2013), President of South Africa: a, With F. W. de Klerk, Pres. of South Africa, and Nobel medals and diplomas. b, With fist raised. c, Holding dove. d, With trophy and South African rugby player.

No. 1269, 240fr — Pres. Franklin D. Roosevelt (1882-1945): a, Signing declaration of war against Germany. b, Wearing top hat. c, With wife, Eleanor (1884-1962). d, Signing Social Security legislation.

No. 1270, 240fr — Battle of Dunkirk: a, British Admiral Bertram Home Ramsay (1883-1945). b, Airplane flying over battle. c, Battle aftermath. d, Troops in water.

No. 1271, 240fr — Pompidou Center, Paris, 40th anniv.: a, La Roue Rouge, by Fernand Léger. b, Quatre Passagers Roses de Face, by Jean Dubuffet. c, Blue in Violet, by Wassily Kandinsky. d, Vieilles Maisons, Saint-Ilpize en Haute Loire.

No. 1272, 240fr — Alexander Pushkin (1799-1837), poet: a, Portrait. b, Dueling pistols. c, Pushkin sitting on railing, signature. d, Sculpture and drawing of Pushkin.

No. 1273, 240fr — Tigers: a, Panthera tigris altaica. b, Panthera tigris tigris cub. c, Two Panthera tigris tigris. d, Panthera tigris tigris with white fur.

No. 1274, 240fr — Shells: a, Lunella smaragdus. b, Nautilus macromphalus. c, Cymbiola innexa. d, Bolinus brandaris.

No. 1275, 240fr — Mushrooms: a, Suillus luteus. b, Macrolepiota rhacodes. c, Boletus edulis. d, Tricholoma portentosum.

No. 1276, 240fr — Windmills and birds: a, Oud-Zuilen, Netherlands windmill and Alopochen aegyptiaca. b, East Hampton, New York windmill and Tyrannus tyrannus. c, Ramsey, United Kingdom windmill and Carduelis carduelis. d, Lautrec, France windmill and Cyanistes caeruleus.

No. 1277, 240fr — Lighthouses: a, Lorain Lighthouse, Ohio. b, Big Sable Point Lighthouse, Michigan. c, Cape Lookout Lighthouse, North Carolina. d, Block Island Southeast Lighthouse, Rhode Island.

No. 1278, 240fr — Japanese high-speed trains: a, Shinkansen Series E3. b, Shinkansen Series E4. c, Shinkansen Series 800. d, Shinkansen Series E5.

No. 1279, 240fr — Louis Renault (1877-1944), automobile manufacturer, and: a, Renault Dauphinoise Juvaquatre fire vehicle. b, Renault FT-17 tank. c, Renault Type B. d, Renault Reinastella, Arc de Triomphe.

No. 1280, 240fr — Louis Blériot (1872-1936), aviation pioneer: a, Blériot XI airplane on ground. b, Blériot and Eiffel Tower. c, Blériot and mountains. d, Blériot XI in flight.

No. 1281, 240fr — Outer Space Treaty, 50th anniv.: a, World Map. b, Moon, planets, balance. c, Earth, satellites in orbit, gavel. d, Satellite and nuclear missile.

No. 1282, 240fr — Christmas: a, Children placing ornaments on Christmas tree. b, Carolers and violinist near Christmas tree. c, Santa Claus and child. d, Child pulling sled carrying Christmas tree.

No. 1283, 240fr — New Year 2018 (Year of the Dog): a, Pekingese dog facing right. b, Pekingese dog facing forward, Chinese characters at top left. c, Pekingese dog facing forward, Chinese characters at top right. d, Pekingese dog facing left.

No. 1284, 950fr, Monroe in automobile. No. 1285, 950fr, McCartney playing guitar. No. 1286, 950fr, Chaplin dancing. No. 1287, 950fr, Marie Curie and model of atom. No. 1288, 950fr, Mandela with fist raised, diff. No. 1289, 950fr, Roosevelt at desk. No. 1290, 950fr, Map of Battle of Dunkirk, troops boarding ship. No. 1291, 950fr, Rythmes, by Robert Delaunay. No. 1292, 950fr, Pushkin holding quill pen. No. 1293, 950fr, Two Panthera tigris altaica. No. 1294, 950fr, Ceratosoma amoenum, Cypraea aurantia. No. 1295, 950fr, Lycoperdon perlatum. No. 1296, 950fr, Kuremaa, Estonia windmill and Ciconia ciconia. No. 1297, 950fr, Greens Ledge Lighthouse, Connecticut. No. 1298, 950fr, Shinkansen Series 500 Type EVA. No. 1299, 950fr, Renault and Renault 4CV. No. 1300, 950fr, Blériot and Eiffel Tower, diff. No. 1301, 950fr, Sputnik 1. No. 1302, 950fr, Santa Claus and reindeer. No. 1303, 950fr, Pekingese dog, diff.

2017, Sept. 29 Litho. *Perf. 13¼*

Sheets of 4, #a-d

1264-1283 A321 Set of 20 215.00 215.00

Souvenir Sheets

1284-1303 A321 Set of 20 215.00 215.00

Television Broadcasting in Djibouti, 50th Anniv. — A321a

2017, Nov. 9 Litho. *Perf. 13¼x13*

1303A A321a 50fr multi .60 .60

Miniature Sheet

Landscapes — A321b

No. 1303B: c, Grand Bara. d, Port of Obock (land at top). e, Sable Blanc. f, Ras Bir. g, Port of Obock (no land at top). h, Dikhil Region. i, Village of Assamo ("humilité, jaillir, slalomer" inscription). j, Tewo Daba. k, Village of Assamo ("apurer, adepte, décuivrer" inscription). l, Djibouti City.

2017, Nov. 9 Litho. *Perf. 13¼*

1303B A321b 300fr Sheet of 10, #c-l 34.00 34.00

A322

A323

A324

Polar Bear — A325

Design: 950fr, Polar bear, diff.

Perf. 12¾x13¼

2017, Dec. 11 Litho.

1304	A322 240fr multi		2.75	2.75
1305	A323 240fr multi		2.75	2.75
1306	A324 240fr multi		2.75	2.75
1307	A325 240fr multi		2.75	2.75
	Nos. 1304-1307 (4)		11.00	11.00

Souvenir Sheet

Perf. 13¼

1308 A325 950fr multi 11.00 11.00

Nos. 1304-1307 were each printed in sheets of 16 + 4 labels. No. 1308 contains one 45x38mm stamp.

A326

No. 1309, 240fr — Ursus maritimus: a, One polar bear, tree at left. b, Polar bear with head at right. c, Adult and two cubs. d, Polar bear with head at left, mouth open.

No. 1310, 240fr — Cat breeds: a, Korat. b, Toyger. c, Selkirk Rex. d, Chantilly.

No. 1311, 240fr — Wild dogs: a, Cuon alpinus. b, One Canis lupus dingo. c, Lycaon pictus. d, Two Canis lupus dingo.

No. 1312, 240fr — Loxodonta africana: a, One elephant facing right. b, One elephant facing left. c, Two elephants with trunks touching. d, Two elephants walking.

No. 1313, 240fr — Dolphins: a, Inia geoffrensis. b, Stenella coeruleoalba. c, Cephalorhynchus commersonii. d, Grampus griseus.

No. 1314, 240fr — Parrots: a, One Ara ararauna in flight. b, Psittacula krameri. c, Two Ara ararauna. d, Eolophus roseicapilla.

No. 1315, 240fr — Pigeon breeds: a, African Owl. b, Bouclier de Saxe (Saxon Shield). c, American Domestic Show Flight. d, Barbe Anglais (English Barb).

No. 1316, 240fr — Bee-eaters: a, Merops apiaster. b, Merops variegatus. c, Merops malimbicus. d, Merops breweri.

No. 1317, 240fr — Owls: a, Bubo scandiacus. b, Bubo lacteus. c, Bubo bubo. d, Strix seloputo.

No. 1318, 240fr — Butterflies: a, Apatura iris. b, Papilio glaucus. c, Battus philenor. d, Callophrys rubi.

No. 1319, 240fr — Turtles: a, Aldabrachelys gigantea. b, Malaclemys terrapin. c, Trachemys scripta elegans. d, Chelonia mydas.

No. 1320, 240fr — Dinosaurs: a, Lambeosaurus lambei. b, Oviraptor philoceratops. c, Archaeopteryx siemensii. d, Stegosaurus ungulatus.

No. 1321, 240fr — Prehistoric marine animals: a, Pteraspis stensioei, Prognathodon solvayi. b, Dearcmhara shawcrossi. c, Parapuzosia seppenradensis. d, Shastasaurus pacificus.

No. 1322, 240fr — Global warming: a, Giraffa camelopardalis tippelskirchi and text. b, Ursus maritimus and text. c, Cervus elaphus and text. d, Turbinaria reniformis and text.

No. 1323, 240fr — Orchids: a, Odontoglossum crispum. b, Cattleya "Blc. Greenwich." c, Vanda coerulea. d, Miltonia regnellii.

No. 1324, 240fr — Minerals: a, Brookite, quartz. b, Uvarovite. c, Andradite. d, Willemite.

No. 1325, 240fr — Fire trucks: a, 2010 Oshkosh Striker 3000. b, 2012 Iveco Trakker. c, 2011 DAF LF. d, 2011 Scania P.

No. 1326, 240fr — Protestant Reformation, 500th anniv.: a, Martin Luther (1483-1546). b, Martin Bucer (1491-1551). c, Ulrich Zwingli (1484-1531). d, John Calvin (1509-64).

No. 1327, 240fr — 2017 Nobel Laureates: a, Michael Rosbach (Physiology or Medicine). b, Joachim Frank (Chemistry). c, Beatrice Fihn, director of International Campaign to Abolish Nuclear Weapons (Peace). d, Kazuo Ishiguro (Literature).

No. 1328, 950fr, Ursus maritiumus, diff. No. 1329, 950fr, Abyssinian cat. No. 1330, 950fr, Cuon alpinus, diff. No. 1331, 950fr, Loxodonta africana, diff. No. 1332, 950fr, Lagenorhynchus acutus. No. 1333, 950fr, Guaruba guarouba. No. 1334, 950fr, Belgian Ringbeater pigeon. No. 1335, 950fr, Merops nubicoides. No. 1336, 950fr, Megascops kennicottii. No. 1337, 950fr, Papilio troilus. No. 1338, 950fr, Graptemys geographica. No. 1339, 950fr, Pterodactylus antiquus. No. 1340, 950fr, Dunkleosteus terrelli. No. 1341, 950fr, Aptenodytes forsteri. No. 1342, 950fr, Beallara marfitch "Howard's Dream." No. 1343, 950fr, Brazilianite. No. 1344, 950fr, 1984 Oshkosh P19 fire truck. No. 1345, 950fr, Luther, diff. No. 1346, 950fr, Richard H. Thaler, 2017 Nobel Laureate in Economics, Nobel medal, Robert Fludd (1574-1637), mathematician.

2017, Dec. 11 Litho. *Perf. 13¼*

Sheets of 4, #a-d

1309-1327 A326 Set of 19 200.00 200.00

Souvenir Sheets

1328-1346 A326 Set of 19 200.00 200.00

Souvenir Sheet

Djibouti Chamber of Commerce, 110th Anniv. — A326a

Perf. 13¼x13½

2017, Dec. 21 Litho.

1346A A326a 110fr multi 1.25 1.25

Souvenir Sheet

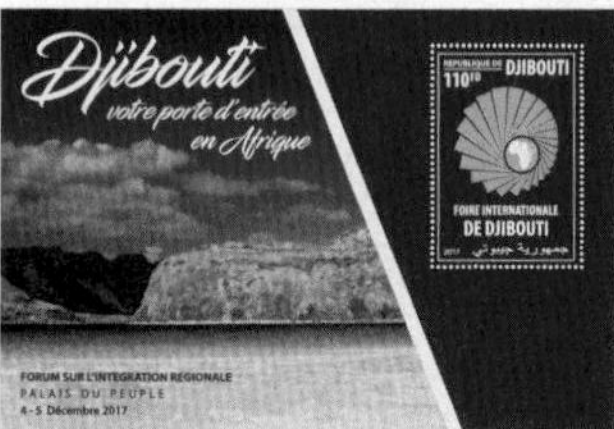

Emblem of Djibouti International Fair — A326b

Perf. 13¼x13½

2017, Dec. 21 Litho.

1346B A326b 110fr multi 1.25 1.25

A327

No. 1347, 240fr — Bobby Fischer (1943-2008), World Chess Champion: a, Scratching face and holding clock. b, Playing against Mikhail Tal (1936-92). c, Without hands visible. d, With hand on forehead.

No. 1348, 240fr — Garry Kasparov, World Chess Champion: a, With hands covering ears. b, Holding chess piece. c, Scratching head. d, Looking down at chess board, two chess pieces.

No. 1349, 240fr — Golf: a, Player wearing green shirt addressing ball, player in red shirt carrying golf bag and club. b, Golf bag and player in red shirt swinging. c, Golf ball and player finishing swing. d, Player carrying golf bag.

No. 1350, 240fr — Ice hockey players: a, Nikita Gusev. b, Nathan MacKinnon. c, Nikita Kucherov. d, Bogdan Kiselevich.

No. 1351, 240fr — Formula I race cars of team: a, Mercedes-AMG Petronas. b, Renault Sport. c, Sauber. d, McLaren.

No. 1352, 240fr — Ferrari automobiles: a, Ferrari Enzo. b, Ferrari F12 Berlinetta. c, Ferrari Pininfarina Sergio Concept, Ferrari F40. d, Ferrari 125 S.

No. 1353, 240fr — Special transportation: a, B-377-SG/SGT Super Guppy ariplane. b, GAZ 47 all-terrain vehicle. c, ZIL-4906 Blue Bird all-terrain vehicle. d, Mil V-12 Homer helicopter.

No. 1354, 240fr — Wright Flyer and Orville Wright (1871-1948): a, Wright Flyer. b, Wright and Wright Flyer. c, Wright Flyer, Orville and Wilbur Wright. d, Wright Flyer, Orville and Wilbur Wright, American flag.

No. 1355, 240fr — Concorde: a, British Airways airplane, nose at UL. b, British Airways airplane, nose at LL. c, Air France airplane, nose at UR. d, Air France airplane, nose at UL.

No. 1356, 240fr — Sailing ships: a, Palinuro, Italy. b, ARC Gloria, Colombia. c, Coast Guard Cutter Eagle, United States. d, STS Sedov, Russia.

No. 1357, 240fr — Submarines: a, Victoria Class submarine. b, HMAS Collins. c, K-535 Yury Dolgorukiy. d, USS Virginia.

No. 1358, 240fr — Steam trains: a, Jacobite, flag of Great Britain. b, Class 520 Sir Malcolm Barclay Harvey, flag of Australia. c, North and Western Class J611, flag of Great Britain. d, Class 26 4-8-4 Red Devil, flag of South Africa.

No. 1359, 240fr — High-speed trains: a, 0 series Shinkansen, flag of Japan. b, NTV ETR575, flag of Italy. c, TGV Lyria, flag of Switzerland. d, CRH, flag of People's Republic of China.

No. 1360, 240fr — Launch of Vostok 6, 55th anniv.: a, Earth, arrow and rocket. b, Statue of Valentina Tereshkova, Moscow, and medal. c, Tereshkova and Vostok 6. d, Vostok 6 and red star.

No. 1361, 240fr — End of World War I, cent.: a, 155-mm cannon of Saint Chamond tank. b, Signing of armistice, 1918. c, Marshal Ferdinand Foch (1851-1929). d, Two soldiers.

No. 1362, 240fr — 50th birthday of King Felipe VI of Spain: a, With Prince William. b, With Queen Elizabeth II. c, With Pope Francis. d, With father, King Juan Carlos I.

No. 1363, 240fr — Dogs: a, Bedlington terrier. b, Chihuahua. c, Lancashire heeler. d, Pomeranian.

No. 1364, 240fr — Butterflies: a, Euphaedra themis. b, Bebearia tentyris. c, Cymothoe egesta. d, Junonia sophia.

No. 1365, 240fr — Marine life: a, Eretmochelys imbricata. b, Octopus vulgaris. c, Amphiprion ocellaris. d, Paguristes cadenati.

No. 1366, 950fr, Fischer, diff. No. 1367, 950fr, Kasparov, diff. No. 1368, 950fr, Golfer placing ball on ground. No. 1369, 950fr, Artemi Panarin. No. 1370, 950fr, Red Bull Racing Team Formula I car. No. 1371, 950fr, Ferrari 250. No. 1372, 950fr, Mil Mi-6 Hook helicopter. No. 1373, 950fr, Orville Wright, wearing hat and aviation headgear. No. 1374, 950fr, British Airways Concorde, diff. No. 1375, 950fr, Royal Clipper, Sweden. No. 1376, 950fr, Seawolf Class submarine. No. 1377, 950fr, Japan Railways C11-171 SL Hakodate Onuma Go, flag of Japan. No. 1378, 950fr, N700 Series Shinkansen, flag of Japan. No. 1379, 950fr, Launch of Vostok 6, red star and dove. No. 1380, 950fr, Foch and soldiers, diff. No. 1381, 950fr, King Felipe VI of Spain. No. 1382, 950fr, Swedish vallhund. No. 1383, 950fr, Rhetus periander. No. 1384, 950fr, Synchiropus splendidus.

2018, Feb. 19 Litho. *Perf. 13¼*

Sheets of 4, #a-d

1347-1365 A327 Set of 19 205.00 205.00

Souvenir Sheets

1366-1384 A327 Set of 19 205.00 205.00

See Nos. 1387-1388.

2018 Winter Olympics, PyeongChang, South Korea — A328

No. 1385 — Venues of 2014 and 2018 Winter Olympics: a, Fisht Olympic Stadium, Sochi, Russia. b, PyeongChang Olympic Stadium. c, Sochi Olympic Complex. d, Speed skating venue, PyeongChang.

950fr, Yin yang with Russian and South Korean flags.

2018, Feb. 19 Litho. *Perf. 13¼*

1385 A328 240fr Sheet of 4, #a-d, + central label 11.00 11.00

Souvenir Sheet

1386 A328 950fr multi 11.00 11.00

No. 1386 contains one 72x72mm diamond-shaped stamp.

Type of 2018

No. 1387 — Fire trucks: a, Robur LO 2002A. b, Barkas B 1000 KLF. c, Ural-43206. d, 1960 Ford Thames 800.

950fr, American-La France Type 0-11A.

2018, Mar. 15 Litho. *Perf. 13¼*

1387 A327 240fr Sheet of 4, #a-d 11.00 11.00

Souvenir Sheet

1388 A327 950fr multi 11.00 11.00

February 6, 2018 SpaceX Flight — A329

No. 1389: a, Launch of Falcon Heavy rocket. b, Tesla Roadster in opened rocket hatch. c, Recovery of two launched rockets. d, Tesla Roadster in space.

950fr, View from front seat of Tesla Roadster in space.

2018, Mar. 15 Litho. *Perf. 13¼*

1389 A329 240fr Sheet of 4, #a-d 11.00 11.00

Souvenir Sheet

1390 A329 950fr multi 11.00 11.00

A330

No. 1391, 240fr — Ursus maritimus: a, Leaping. b, Two adult bears on ice. c, Two cubs in ice den. d, Swimming underwater.

No. 1392, 240fr — Ailuropoda melanoleuca: a, Eating in bamboo forest. b, Walking. c, Rolling on back. d, Eating on hillside.

No. 1393, 240fr — Wild cats: a, Felis chaus. b, Puma concolor. c, Catopuma temminckii. d, Caracal caracal.

No. 1394, 240fr — Whales: a, Kogia breviceps. b, Mesoplodon mirus. c, Eubalaena glacialis. d, Balaenoptera brydei.

No. 1395, 240fr — Owls: a, Tyto alba. b, Bubo bubo sibiricus. c, Glaucidium passerinum. d, Bubo scandiacus.

No. 1396, 240fr — Birds of prey: a, Terathopius ecaudatus. b, Pandion haliaetus. c, Aquila nipalensis. d, Lophaetus occipitalis.

No. 1397, 240fr — Turtles: a, Malaclemys terrapin. b, Emydoidea blandingii. c, Graptemys pseudogeographica. d, Stigmochelys pardalis.

No. 1398, 240fr — Extinct animals a, Diprotodon optatum. b, Coelodonta antiquitatis. c, Megatherium americanum. d, Incilius periglenes (incorrect Latin name).

No. 1399, 240fr — Mushrooms: a, Cantharellus cibarius, Parnassius mnemosyne. b, Entoloma hochstetteri, Vespa mandarinia. c, Laccaria amethystina, Chrysodeixis chalcites. d, Boletus edulis.

No. 1400, 240fr — Bird illustrations of Alexander Wilson (1766-1813), ornithologist: a, Portrait of Wilson and Bonasa umbellus. b, Anas strepera, Somateria mollissima, Mergellus albellus, Oxyura jamaicensis. c, Charadrius wilsonia, Fulica atra, Porphyrio martinicus, Phalaropus fulicarius. d, Tympanuchus cupido.

No. 1401, 240fr — Paintings by Edouard Manet (1832-83): a, The Railway, 1873. b, The Execution of Emperor Maximilian, 1867. c, Music in the Tuileries Gardens, 1862. d, At Father Lathuille, 1879.

No. 1402, 240fr — Paintings by Paul Gauguin (1848-1903): a, Winter at Pont-Aven, and Small Breton Shepherd, 1888. b, The Siesta, c. 1892-94. c, Pastorales Tahitiennes, 1892. d, Sacred Spring, Sweet Dreams (Nave Nave Moe), 1894.

No. 1403, 240fr — Paintings by Vincent van Gogh (1853-90) and various self-portraits: a, A Pair of Shoes, 1887. b, The Old Mill, 1888. c, Prisoners Exercising, 1890. d, Old Man in Sorrow, 1890.

No. 1404, 240fr — Paintings by Pablo Picasso (1881-1973): a, Cat Devouring a Bird, 1939. b, Au Lapin Agile, 1905. c, Mother and Child, 1921. d, Portrait of Dora Maar, 1937.

No. 1405, 240fr — Paintings in the Louvre Museum, Paris: a, Mona Lisa, by Leonardo da Vinci (1452-1519). b, An Old Man and His Grandson, by Domenico Ghirlandaio (1448-94). c, The Veiled Woman, by Raphael (1483-1520). d, Portrait of Daniele Barbaro, by Paolo Veronese (1528-88).

No. 1406, 240fr — Famous people associated with the International Red Cross: a, Agatha Christie (1890-1976), writer. b, Jackie Chan, actor. c, LL Cool J, actor. d, Marie Curie (1867-1934), physicist and chemist.

No. 1407, 240fr — Paul P. Harris (1868-1947), founder of Rotary International: a, Three people near modern bookmobile sponsored by Rotary International. b, Harris, his wife, Jean (1881-1963), Sarcochilus falcatus. c, Harris, Rotary International emblem, Cymbidium sanderae. d, Two children near old bookmobile sponsored by Rotary International.

No. 1408, 240fr — Princess Diana (1961-97): a, Skiing with young sons, Princes William and Harry. b, With small boy. c, With small girl. d, With sons, as adults.

No. 1409, 950fr, Ursus maritimus, diff. No. 1410, 950fr, Ailuropoda melanoleuca, diff., No. 1411, 950fr, Felis margarita. No. 1412, 950fr, Delphinapterus leucas. No. 1413, 950fr, Aegolius funereus. No. 1414, 950fr, Falco hypoleucos. No. 1415, 950fr, Chelonia mydas. No. 1416, 950fr, Incilius periglenes (frog). No. 1417, 950fr, Russula emetica and Rana sylvatica. No. 1418, 950fr, Haliaeetus leucocephala illustration by Wilson. No. 1419, 950fr, A Studio at Batignolles, by Henri Fantin-Latour (1836-1904). No. 1420, 950fr, Self-portrait with Portrait of Emile Bernard (Les Misérables), by Gauguin. No. 1421, 950fr, Self-portraits by van Gogh. No. 1422, 950fr, Acrobat's Family with a Monkey, by Picasso. No. 1423, 950fr, Portrait of a Man, by Antonello da Messina (c. 1430-79). No. 1424, 950fr, Walt Disney (1901-66), movie producer, Ford Model T Red Cross vehicle. No. 1425, 950fr, Harris and Rotary International emblem. No. 1426, 950fr, Princess Diana and Queen Elizabeth II.

2018, Mar. 15 Litho. *Perf. 13¼*

Sheets of 4, #a-d

1391-1408 A330 Set of 18 195.00 195.00

Souvenir Sheets

1409-1426 A330 Set of 18 195.00 195.00

A331

No. 1427, 240fr — Marilyn Monroe (1926-62), actress: a, Brushing hair. b, Sitting on staircase. c, Sitting near plants. d, Near movie camera.

No. 1428, 240fr — Pres. John F. Kennedy (1917-63): a, And Frank Sinatra (1915-98), singer. b, Wearing naval uniform, sitting behind desk. c, And wife, Jacqueline (1929-94). d, With U.S. flag.

No. 1429, 240fr — Nelson Mandela (1918-2013), President of South Africa, and minerals: a, Phosphophyllite. b, Spessartine. c, Anglesite. d, Red beryl.

No. 1430, 240fr — Fifth birthday of Prince George of Cambridge: a, With mother, Catherine, Duchess of Cambridge. b, With sister, Princess Charlotte. c, Sitting alone. d, With father, Prince William.

No. 1431, 240fr — Wedding of Prince Harry and Meghan Markle: a, Couple, flags of Great Britain and United States. b, Couple and foliage. c, Couple kissing in background. d, Couple and castle in background.

No. 1432, 240fr — Ferdinand von Zeppelin (1838-1917), airship builder: a, Zeppelin wearing helmet and Hindenburg (LZ129). b, Zeppelin LZ4. c, Medal depicting Zeppelin and Graf Zeppelin (LZ127). d, Zeppelin wearing red tie.

No. 1433, 240fr — Motorcycle racers in Isle of Man TT races: a, Morgan Govignon, 2016. b, Bruce Anstey, 2007. c, Gary Johnson, 2016. d, James Hillier, 2011.

No. 1434, 240fr — Lamborghini automobiles, 55th anniv.: a, Lamborghini Centenario. b, Lamborghini Gallardo. c, Lamborghini Aventador. d, Lamborghini Diablo.

No. 1435, 240fr — Fire trucks: a, GPM-54. b, CCFM. c, Mercedes-Benz Zetros. d, OES Type III.

No. 1436, 240fr — European high-speed trains: a, Eurostar, France. b, ICE 3, Germany. c, Bombardier Zefiro V300, Italy. d, RENFE Series S-130, Spain.

No. 1437, 240fr — 1958 Munich airplane crash, 60th anniv.: a, Airplane and Manchester United soccer team. b, Refueling of Airspeed Ambassador airplane. c, Rescuers at crash site. d, Nose of crashed airplane.

No. 1438, 240fr — Yuri Gagarin (1934-68), first man in space: a, Gagarin waving. b, Vostok-K rocket, statue of Gagarin, Moscow. c, Gagarin and dove. d, Gagarin in spacesuit.

No. 1439, 240fr — Lighthouses: a, Vlaming Head Lighthouse, Australia. b, Esopus Meadows Lighthouse, New York. c, Cabo de la Huerta Lighthouse, Spain. d, Eckmühl Lighthouse, France.

No. 1440, 240fr — Scouts: a, Two Boy Scouts and campfire. b, Four Girl Scouts and leader. c, Two Boy Scouts saluting. d, Boy Scout and Scoutmaster.

No. 1441, 240fr — Organization of African Unity (African Union), 55th anniv.: a, Pan-African Parliament. b, Roger Nkodo Dang, Parliamentary President. c, African Union building, Addis Ababa, Ethiopia. d, Amara Essy, 2001-02 Secretary-General of OAU.

No. 1442, 240fr — Dolphins: a, Two Tursiops truncatus, one facing right. b, Stenella longirostris. c, Two Tursiops truncatus facing left. d, Orcinus orca.

No. 1443, 240fr — Butterflies: a, Papilio machaon. b, Melanargia galathea. c, Parnassius apollo. d, Morpho helenor.

No. 1444, 240fr — Dinosaurs: a, Velociraptor mongoliensis. b, Triceratops horridus. c, Tyrannosaurus rex. d, Parasaurolophus walkeri.

No. 1445, 240fr — Orchids: a, Laeliocattleya. b, Ophrys apifera. c, Vanda coerulea. d, Anacamptis papilionacea.

No. 1446, 240fr — Minerals: a, Kunzite, California. b, Red beryl, New Mexico. c, Anglesite, Morocco. d, Celestine, Madagascar.

No. 1447, 950fr, Monroe, diff. No. 1448, 950fr, Pres. Kennedy, diff. No. 1449, 950fr, Mandela and Brookite. No. 1450, 950fr, Prince George of Cambridge. No. 1451, 950fr, Prince Harry and Meghan Markle, diff. No. 1452, 950fr, Graf Zeppelin (LZ127) and LZ4. No. 1453, 950fr, Motorcycle racer Ryan Farquhar, 2015. No. 1454, 950fr, Ferruccio Lamborghini (1916-93), industrialist, and Lamborghini Urraco. No. 1455, 950fr, Russian fire truck. No. 1456, 950fr, RABDe 500, Switzerland. No. 1457, 950fr, Harry Gregg, goaltender for Manchester United soccer team who survived plane crash. No. 1458, 950fr, Gagarin in spacesuit, diff. No. 1459, 950fr, St. Nicholas Church Lighthouse, Ukraine. No. 1460, 950fr, Two Boy Scouts following map. No. 1461, 950fr, Gamal Abdel Nasser (1918-70), 1964-65 Chairman of Organization of African Unity. No. 1462, 950fr, One Tursiops truncatus. No. 1463, 950fr, Ypthima baldus. No. 1464, 950fr, Compsognathus longipes. No. 1465, 950fr, Phalaenopsis lueddemanniana. No. 1466, 950fr, Brookite, Pakistan.

2018, June 12 Litho. *Perf. 13¼*

Sheets of 4, #a-d

1427-1446 A331 Set of 20 215.00 215.00

Souvenir Sheets

1447-1466 A331 Set of 20 215.00 215.00

Medals — A332

DesignsL Nos. 1467, 1470a, 200fr, Star of Devotion Military Order. Nos. 1468, 1470b, 300fr, Order of June 27. Nos. 1469, 1470c, 400fr, Order of the Grand Star of Djibouti.

2018, June 27 Litho. *Perf. 13¼x13*

1467-1469 A332 Set of 3 10.00 10.00

Souvenir Sheet

Perf. 13¼

1470 A332 Sheet of 3, #a-c 10.00 10.00

No. 1470 contains three 30x51mm stamps.

Armed Forces Emblem — A333

Police Emblem — A334

Republican Guard Emblem — A335

Gendarmerie Emblem — A336

Coast Guard Emblem — A337

2018, June 27 Litho. *Perf. 13¼x13*

1471	A333 400fr multi		4.50	4.50
1472	A334 400fr multi		4.50	4.50
1473	A335 400fr multi		4.50	4.50
1474	A336 400fr multi		4.50	4.50
1475	A337 400fr multi		4.50	4.50
	Nos. 1471-1475 (5)		22.50	22.50

Souvenir Sheets
Stamps With Colored Frames

Perf. 13¼

1476	A333 500fr multi		5.75	5.75
1477	A334 500fr multi		5.75	5.75
1478	A335 500fr multi		5.75	5.75
1479	A336 500fr multi		5.75	5.75
1480	A337 500fr multi		5.75	5.75
	Nos. 1476-1480 (5)		28.75	28.75

Nos. 1476-1480 each contain one 39x51mm stamp.

Homage to Army Martyrs A338

2018, June 27 Litho. *Perf. 13x13¼*

1481 A338 400fr multi 4.50 4.50

Souvenir Sheet
Stamp With Colored Frame

Perf. 13¼

1482 A338 500fr multi 5.75 5.75

No. 1482 contains one 51x39mm stamp.

Soldiers of African Union Mission in Somalia — A339

2018, June 27 Litho. *Perf. 13¼x13*

1483 A339 400fr multi 4.50 4.50

Souvenir Sheet
Stamp With Colored Frame

Perf. 13¼

1484 A339 500fr multi 5.75 5.75

No. 1484 contains one 39x51mm stamp.

Firefighters A340

2018, June 27 Litho. *Perf. 13¼x13*

1485 A340 400fr multi 4.50 4.50

Souvenir Sheet
Stamp With Colored Frame

Perf. 13¼

1486 A340 500fr multi 5.75 5.75

No. 1486 contains one 33x51mm stamp.

Souvenir Sheets

Flags — A341

Flag of: No. 1487, 500fr, United States. No. 1488, 500fr, People's Republic of China. No. 1489, 500fr, France. No. 1490, 500fr, Germany. No. 1491, 500fr, Italy. No. 1492, 500fr, Japan. No. 1493, 500fr, Spain.

2018, June 27 Litho. *Perf. 13¼*

1487-1493 A341 Set of 7 40.00 40.00

Souvenir Sheet

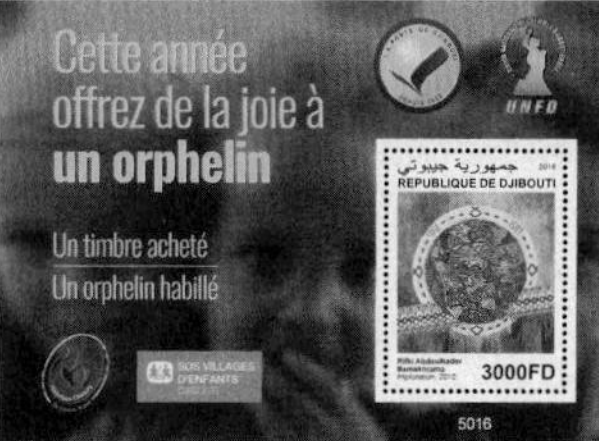

Imploration, by Rifki Abdoulkader Bamakhrama — A342

2018, June 27 Litho. *Perf. 13¼*

1494 A342 3000fr multi 34.00 34.00

Aid for orphans.

Flag of Djibouti and Barkat Gourad Hamadou (1930-2001), Prime Minister — A343

2018, June 27 Litho. *Perf. 13¼x13*

1495 A343 500fr multi 5.75 5.75
a. Souvenir sheet of 1 5.75 5.75

Isao Takahata (1935-2018), Film Director — A344

No. 1496 — Takahata and: a, Hayao Miyazaki, film director. b, Firefly. c, Japanese raccoon dog. d, Princess Kaguya.
950fr, Takahata and Miyazaki, diff.

2018, July 27 Litho. *Perf. 13¼*

1496 A344 240fr Sheet of 4, #a-d 11.00 11.00

Souvenir Sheet

1497 A344 950fr multi 11.00 11.00

A345

No. 1498, 240fr — Milos Forman (1932-2018), film director, and: a, Scene from *Amadeus.* b, Clapboard and signature. c, Poster for *One Flew Over the Cuckoo's Nest.* d, Poster for *Loves of a Blonde.*

No. 1499, 240fr — Frank Sinatra (1915-98), singer and actor, and: a, Microphone. b, Luciano Pavarotti (1935-2007), opera singer. c, Kim Novak, actress. d, Academy Award.

No. 1500, 240fr — Film actors who have portrayed James Bond: a, Daniel Craig. b, Timothy Dalton. c, Roger Moore (1927-2017). d, Pierce Brosnan.

No. 1501, 240fr — Composers: a, Ludwig van Beethoven (1770-1827). b, Johann Sebastian Bach (1685-1750). c, Franz Schubert (1797-1828). d, Joseph Haydn (1732-1809).

No. 1502, 240fr — David Livingstone (1813-73), African explorer and missionary, and: a, David Livingstone Memorial Church, Blantyre, Scotland. b, Henry Morton Stanley (1841-1904), journalist and explorer. c, Livingstone Monument, Zambia. d, African people.

No. 1503, 240fr — Mahatma Gandhi (1869-1948), Indian nationalist: a, Gandhi Assassination Memorial, Delhi. b, Gandhi and *Mountain Landscape with Indians,* by John Mix Stanley. c, Gandhi, dove, flag of India. d, Birthplace of Gandhi, Porbandar, India.

No. 1504, 240fr — Queen Elizabeth II, 65th anniv. of coronation: a, With coat of arms. b, With husband, Prince Philip. c, Riding in coach. d, At coronation.

No. 1505, 240fr — Dr. Martin Luther King, Jr. (1929-68), civil rights activist, and: a, Malcolm X (1925-65), civil rights activist. b, Iwo Jima Memorial. c, Pres. John F. Kennedy (1917-63). d, Bald eagle.

No. 1506, 240fr — Ships and airplanes used by Roald Amundsen (1872-1928), polar explorer: a, Gjoa. b, Dornier Wal N25. c, Maud. d, Latham 47.

No. 1507, 240fr — André Citroen (1878-1935), automobile manufacturer: a, Citroen GT. b, Citroen ZX Rallye-Raid. c, Citroen and Citroen Traction Avant. d, Citroen and Citroen Mehari.

No. 1508, 240fr — Motorcycles from Isle of Man Tourist Trophy Races: a, Suzuki GSX-R1000. b, BMW S1000RR. c, Yamaha YZF R1. d, Honda CBR1000RR.

No. 1509, 240fr — Japanese high-speed trains: a, Shinkansen Series E5. b, Shinkansen Series E3. c, SC Maglev L0. d, Shinkansen Series E6.

No. 1510, 240fr — Naval vessels: a, USS Coronado. b, HMS Gloucester. c, HMAS Anzac. d, USS San Antonio.

No. 1511, 240fr — World War II watercraft and tanks: a, Type VII U-boat. b, Tiger II tank. c, Churchill tank. d, USS Missouri.

No. 1512, 240fr — Sled dogs: a, Greenland dogs. b, Siberian huskies. c, Chinooks. d, Samoyeds.

No. 1513, 240fr — Henry Dunant (1828-1910), founder of Red Cross: a, On horse carrying flag, nurse caring for patient. b, With Nobel medal, 1864 Geneva Convention. c, With Red Cross flag, medic treating injured soldier. d, With nurses and Red Crescent flags.

No. 1514, 240fr — Launch of Apollo 8, 50th anniv.: a, Frank Borman, mission commander and rocket launch. b, Apollo 8 crew members, Jim Lovell, William Anders and Borman. c, Lovell and Apollo 8 capsule in ocean. d, Anders and Apollo 8 in space.

No. 1515, 240fr — Rugby players: a, Player wearing No. 6 at left. b, Player with green shirt at left. c, Player with white and red shirt at left. d, Female rugby players.

No. 1516, 240fr — Chess: a, Chess Players, by Ernest Meissonier. b, 12th century chess pieces. c, Chess clock, pieces on chess board. d, Game of Chess, by Benjamin Eugène Fichel.

No. 1517, 950fr, Forman and Jim Carrey, actor. No. 1518, 950fr, Sinatra shooting revolver. No. 1519, 950fr, Sean Connery, actor, and diamonds. No. 1520, 950fr, Wolfgang Amadeus Mozart (1756-91), composer. No. 1521, 950fr, Livingstone and Victoria Falls. No. 1522, 950fr, Gandhi, dove and flag of India, diff. No. 1523, 950fr, Queen Elizabeth II at coronation, diff. No. 1524, 950fr, Dr. King, White House. No. 1525, 950fr, Amundsen and airship Norge. No. 1526, 950fr, Citroen and Citroen DS21. No. 1527, 950fr, Yamaha YZR-M1, Tower of Refuge. No. 1528, 950fr, Shinkansen Series E7. No. 1529, 950fr, USS Oakland. No. 1530, 950fr, Lockheed P-38 Lightning. No. 1531, 950fr, Alaskan malamutes. No. 1532, 950fr, Dunant, Red Cross flag, Red Cross workers carrying corpse. No. 1533, 950fr, Moon and Apollo 8 crew members. No. 1534, 950fr, American football players. No. 1535, 950fr, Magnus Carlsen, chess player, chess board and pieces.

2018, July 27 Litho. *Perf. 13¼*

Sheets of 4, #a-d

1498-1516 A345 Set of 19 205.00 205.00

Souvenir Sheets

1517-1535 A345 Set of 19 205.00 205.00

Beagle — A346

2018, Aug. 27 Litho. *Perf. 13¼*

1536 A346 240fr multi 2.75 2.75

Souvenir Sheet

1537 A346 950fr multi 11.00 11.00

No. 1536 was printed in sheets of 4.

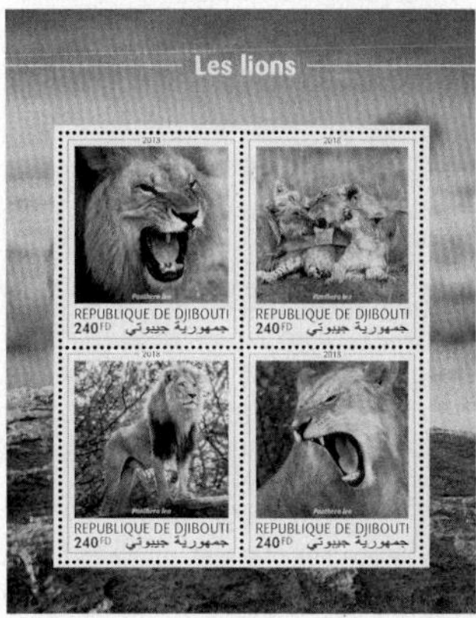

A347

No. 1538, 240fr — Panthera leo: a, Male lion roaring. b, Female lion and cubs. c, Male lion standing on rock. d, Female lion roaring.

No. 1539, 240fr — Panthera tigris: a, Tiger with mouth open. b, Tiger and trees. c, Streak of tigers. d, Tiger in snow.

No. 1540, 240fr — Cats: a, American bobtail. b, Canadian Sphynx. c, Mekong bobtail. d, Abyssinian.

No. 1541, 240fr — Elephants: a, Two Elephas maximus. b, Loxodonta africana and zebras. c, Loxodonta africana with trunk raised. d, One Elephas maximus calf.

No. 1542, 240fr — Primates: a, Rhinopithecus roxellana. b, Hylobates lar. c, Nasalis larvatus. d, Colobus guereza.

No. 1543, 240fr — Water birds: a, Anas platyrhynchos. b, Chauna torquata. c, Bucephala albeola. d, Cygnus olor.

No. 1544, 240fr — Owls: a, Tyto alba. b, Bubo bubo. c, Strix nebulosa. d, Strix aluco.

No. 1545, 240fr — Pigeons: a, Phaps chalcoptera. b, Columbina inca. c, Zenaida graysoni. d, Columba guinea.

No. 1546, 240fr — Kingfishers: a, Tanysiptera sylvia. b, Megaceryle maxima. c, Ceryle rudis. d, Syma torotoro.

No. 1547, 240fr — Apis mellifera: a, Bee on flower, facing right. b, Swarm of bees. c, Line of bees. d, Bee on flower facing left.

No. 1548, 240fr — Butterflies: a, Papilio glaucus. b, Vanessa virginiensis. c, Pochliopta aristolochiae. d, Aglais io.

No. 1549, 240fr — Turtles: a, Aldebrachelys gigantea. b, Chelodina longicollis. c, Chelydra serpentina. d, Eretmochelys imbricata.

No. 1550, 240fr — Snakes: a, Lampropeltis getula. b, Lampropeltis zonata. c, Morelia viridis. d, Trimeresurus albolabris.

No. 1551, 240fr — Prehistoric marine creatures: a, Drepanaspis gemuendenensis. b, Eurhinosaurus longirostris. c, Plesiosaurus dolichodeirus. d, Dinichthys terrelli.

No. 1552, 240fr — Orchids: a, Paphiopedilum hennisianum. b, Paphiopedilum callosum. c, Oncidium incurvum. d, Anguloa superba.

No. 1553, 240fr — Mushrooms: a, Mycena polygramma. b, Cantharellus cibarius. c, Lactarius deliciosus. d, Macrolepiota procera.

No. 1554, 240fr — High-speed Japanese trains: a, Train with two blue stripes on side and orange lights. b, Train with hot pink stripe on front in foreground. c, Train with one blue and two brown stripes. d, Train with two blue stripes, no lights.

No. 1555, 950fr, Panthera leo, diff. No. 1556, 950fr, Panthera tigris, diff. No. 1557, 950fr, American curl cat. No. 1558, 950fr, Loxodonta africana, diff. No. 1559, 950fr, Mandrillus sphinx. No. 1560, 950fr, Chen caerulescens. No. 1561, 950fr, Bubo scandiacus. No. 1562, 950fr, Spilopelia chinensis. No. 1563, 950fr, Ceyx erithaca. No. 1564, 950fr, Apis mellifera on flower, diff. No. 1565, 950fr, Troides helena. No. 1566, 950fr, Chelonia mydas. No. 1567, 950fr, Elaphe obsoleta lindheimeri. No. 1568, 950fr, Carcharocles megalodon. No. 1569, 950fr, Miltonia vexillaria. No. 1570, 950fr, Handkea utriformis. No. 1571, 950fr, JR700 Japanese bullet train on bridge.

2018, Aug. 27 Litho. *Perf. 13¼*

Sheets of 4, #a-d

1538-1554 A347 Set of 17 185.00 185.00

Souvenir Sheets

1555-1571 A347 Set of 17 185.00 185.00

New Year 2019 (Year of the Pig) — A348

No. 1572 — Pig: a, Facing right. b, Facing forward. c, Sleeping. d, Facing left.

950fr, Pig wearing santa hat.

2018, Aug. 27 Litho. *Perf. 13¼*

1572 A348 240fr Sheet of 4, #a-d 11.00 11.00

Souvenir Sheet

1573 A348 950fr multi 11.00 11.00

Miniature Sheets

Chinese Zodiac Animals — A349

Nos. 1574 and 1575: a, Rat. b, Ox (buffle). c, Tiger (tigre). d, Rabbit (lapin). e, Dragon. f, Snake (serpent). g, Horse (cheval). h, Goat (chèvre). i, Monkey (singe), j, Rooster (coq). k, Dog (chien). l, Pig (cochon).

2018, Aug. 27 Litho. *Perf. 13¼x13*

1574 A349 300fr Sheet of 12, #a-l 40.00 40.00

m.	Souvenir sheet of 1, #1574a	3.25	3.25
n.	Souvenir sheet of 1, #1574b	3.25	3.25
o.	Souvenir sheet of 1, #1574c	3.25	3.25
p.	Souvenir sheet of 1, #1574d	3.25	3.25
q.	Souvenir sheet of 1, #1574e	3.25	3.25
r.	Souvenir sheet of 1, #1574f	3.25	3.25
s.	Souvenir sheet of 1, #1574g	3.25	3.25
t.	Souvenir sheet of 1, #1574h	3.25	3.25
u.	Souvenir sheet of 1, #1574i	3.25	3.25
v.	Souvenir sheet of 1, #1574j	3.25	3.25
w.	Souvenir sheet of 1, #1574k	3.25	3.25
x.	Souvenir sheet of 1, #1574l	3.25	3.25

Printed on Wood Veneer Self-Adhesive

1575 A349 300fr Sheet of 12, #a-l 40.00 40.00

See Central Africa No. , Guinea No. , Sierra Leone No.

Diplomatic Relations Between Djibouti and Japan, 40th Anniv. — A349a

2018, Dec. 1 Litho. *Perf. 13¼x13*

1575M A349a 400fr multi 4.50 4.50

Labor Inspection Laws — A349b

2018, Dec. 1 Litho. *Perf. 13¼*

1575N A349b 5000fr multi 57.50 57.50

Nelson Mandela (1918-2013), President of South Africa — A350

2018, Dec. 13 Litho. *Perf. 13¼*

1576 A350 210fr multi 2.40 2.40

Souvenir Sheet

1577 A350 500fr multi 5.75 5.75

A351

No. 1578, 240fr — Michael Jackson (1958-2009), singer: a, With hand over groin at right. b, With heart in background at right. c, As child at right. d, With both arms extended to side at right.

No. 1579, 240fr — 2018 Chess Olympics gold medalists: a, Ju Wenjun, flag of People's Republic of China. b, Ding Liren, flag of People's Republic of China. c, Nguyen Ngoc Truong Son, flag of Viet Nam. d, Mariya Muzychuk, flag of Ukraine.

No. 1580, 240fr — 2018 Nobel laureates: a, Nadia Murad, Peace. b, George P. Smith, Chemistry. c, Gregory P. Winter, Chemistry. d, Denis Mukwege, Peace.

No. 1581, 240fr — Scouts: a, Three Scouts lighting campfire. b, Queen Elizabeth II greeting Scout leaders. c, Girl Scouts raising U.S. flag. d, Scouts and Lord Robert Baden-Powell (1857-1941), founder of Scouting movement.

No. 1582, 240fr — Russian trains: a, Sinara GT1s at Balashikha Station. b, ER-200 at Riga Station, Moscow. c, L-3653 locomotive at Kazan Station. d, Novocherkassk VL85 at Velsk Station.

No. 1583, 240fr — Japanese Shinkansen high-speed trains: a, Series 500. b, Series N700. c, Series E2. d, Series 700.

No. 1584, 240fr — Voyage of USS Nautilus under North Pole, 60th anniv.: a, USS Nautilus under water, emblem. b, USS Nautilus, Commander William R. Anderson (1921-2007), Legion of Merit medal. c, USS Nautilus, Admiral Hyman G. Rickover (1900-86). d, USS Nautilus, map of Arctic, Presidential Unit Citation and National Defense Service Medal.

No. 1585, 240fr — Streamliner motorcycles that broke motorcycle speed records: a, Harley-Davidson, 1970. b, BUB Seven, 2009. c, Yamaha Silver Bird, 1975. d, Ack Attack, 2010.

No. 1586, 240fr — Fire engines: a, FAUN TLF 20 Crashtender. b, Oshkosh MB1. c, Oshkosh P-23 ARFF. d, MAZ-543.

No. 1587, 240fr — Airplanes: a, Antonov An-225 Mriya carrying Buran space shuttle. b, Airbus A300-600ST Beluga. c, Lockheed C-5 Galaxy and F-15s. d, N911NA shuttle carrier with Space Shuttle Endeavour.

No. 1588, 240fr — Space exploration: a, TESS. b, InSight on Mars. c, OSIRIS-REx. d, Falcon Heavy.

No. 1589, 240fr — Minerals: a, Disthene (kyanite). b, Anatase. c, Andradite. d, Cassiterite.

No. 1590, 240fr — Dolphins: a, Lagenorhynchus obscurus. b, Delphinus delphis. c, Stenella frontalis. d, Tursiops truncatus.

No. 1591, 240fr — Fish: a, Acanthurus xanthopterus. b, Zebrasoma xanthurum. c, Carangoides bajad. d, Acanthurus leucopareius.

No. 1592, 240fr — Shells and lighthouses: a, Cypraea mappa and La Vieille Lighthouse, France. b, Cypraecassis rufa and Ile Verte Lighthouse, Canada. c, Cassis cornuta and Cape Meares Lighthouse, Oregon. d, Cymbiola imperialis and Point Loma Lighthouse, California.

No. 1593, 240fr — Dinosaurs: a, Dilophosaurus wetherilli. b, Brontosaurus excelsus. c, Stegosaurus stenops. d, Therizinosaurus cheloniformis.

No. 1594, 240fr — Endangered species: a, Elephas maximus. b, Panthera tigris. c, Aloeides nubilus. d, Equus grevyi.

No. 1595, 240fr — Animals threatened by climate change: a, Pygoscelis antarcticus. b, Ursus maritimus. c, Bombus pascuorum. d, Phascolarctos cinereus.

No. 1596, 240fr — Animals on stamps: a, Panthera tigris on Russia #6181. b, Coracias garrulus on Lithuania #877. c, Lutra lutra on German Democratic Republic #2620. d, Vulpes corsac on Kyrgyzstan #384a.

No. 1597, 950fr, Jackson, diff. No. 1598, 950fr, Jorge Cori, chess gold medalist, flag of Peru. No. 1599, 950fr, Arthur Ashkin 2018 Nobel Physics laureate. No. 1600, 950fr, Two scouts practicing first aid. No. 1601, 950fr, ER-9 train at Yalutorovsk Station, Russia. No. 1602, 950fr, Shinkansen Series 200. No. 1603, 950fr, USS Nautilus under water. No. 1604, 950fr, Gyronaut X-1, 1966. No. 1605, 950fr, Dennis Mk9 fire truck. No. 1606, 950fr, Antonov An-124 and MiG-29. No. 1607, 950fr, Hayabusa 2. No. 1608, 950fr, Red beryl. No. 1609, 950fr, Platanista gangetica. No. 1610, 950fr, Balistapus undulatus. No. 1611, 950fr, Pinctada margaritifera and Point Reyes Lighthouse, California. No. 1612, 950fr, Giganotosaurus carolinii. No. 1613, 950fr, Ailurus fulgens. No. 1614, 950fr, Two Ursus maritimus. No. 1615, 950fr, Castor fiber on Belarus #119.

2018, Dec. 13 Litho. *Perf. 13¼*

Sheets of 4, #a-d

1578-1596 A351 Set of 19 205.00 205.00

Souvenir Sheets

1597-1615 A351 Set of 19 205.00 205.00

Mohandas K. Gandhi (1869-1948), Indian Nationalist Leader A352

2019, Feb. 27 Litho. *Perf. 13¼x13*

1616 A352 100fr multi 1.10 1.10

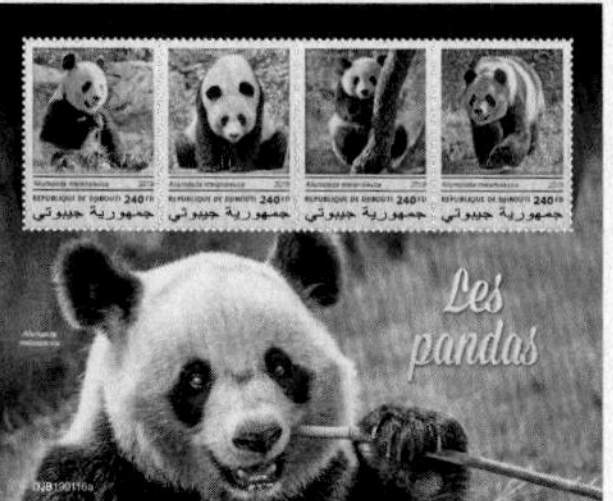

Fauna and Mushrooms — A353

No. 1617, 240fr — Ailuropoda melanoleuca: a, Eating. b, Sitting. c, Climbing on tree. d, Walking.

No. 1618, 240fr — Bats: a, Rhinolophus hipposideros. b, Pteropus lylei. c, Micropteropus pussilus. d, Pteropus poliocephalus.

No. 1619, 240fr — Dogs: a, Airedale terrier. b, Akitai. c, American pit bull terrier. d, Boston terrier.

No. 1620, 240fr — Orcinus orca: a, Head above water, fins at right. b, Pair leaping out of water to right. c, Head above water, fins at left. d, Pair leaping out of water to left.

No. 1621, 240fr — Owls: a, Athene brama. b, Aegolius acadicus. c, Bubo virginianus. d, Bubo scandiacus.

No. 1622, 240fr — Bee-eaters: a, Nyctiornis amictus. b, Merops viridis. c, Merops orientalis. d, Merops nubicoides.

No. 1623, 240fr — Butterflies: a, Papilio glaucus. b, Limenitis arthemis. c, Pachliopta hector. d, Papilio dardanus.

No. 1624, 240fr — Turtles: a, Caretta caretta. b, Emys orbicularis. c, Carettochelys insculpta. d, Pangshura smithii.

No. 1625, 240fr — Spiders: a, Latrodectus mactans. b, Hogna radians. c, Verrucosa arenata. d, Aranea pilipes.

No. 1626, 240fr — Mushrooms: a, Macrolepiota procera. b, Leccinum aurantiacum. c, Boletus edulis. d, Lactaris deterrimus.

No. 1627, 950fr, Ailuropoda melanoleuca, diff. No. 1628, 950fr, Eptesicus fuscus. No. 1629, 950fr, Dalmatian. No. 1630, 950fr, Orcinus orca, diff. No. 1631, 950fr, Athene noctua. No. 1632, 950fr, Merops leschenaulti. No. 1633, 950fr, Battus philenor. No. 1634, 950fr, Geoclemys hamiltonii. No. 1635, 950fr, Araneus diadematus. No. 1636, 950fr, Leccinum versipelle.

2019, Feb. 27 Litho. *Perf. 13¼*

Sheets of 4, #a-d

1617-1626 A353 Set of 10 110.00 110.00

Souvenir Sheets

1627-1636 A353 Set of 10 110.00 110.00

Nos. 1627-1636 each contain one 45x60mm stamp.

A354

No. 1637, 240fr — Princess Diana (1961-97): a, With British flags in background. b, Holding infant. c, Touching face of young boy. d, With building and statue in background.

No. 1638, 240fr — Princess Grace of Monaco (1929-82): a, In automobile with Frank Sinatra (1915-98). b, With two children. c, With royal monogram. d, With her coat of arms.

No. 1639, 240fr — Yuri Gagarin (1934-68), first man in space: a, Standing beside automobile. b, Wearing spacesuit, with Vostok 1. c, Wearing military uniform. d, With wife, Valentina and infant daughter.

No. 1640, 240fr — Niki Lauda (1949-2019), race car driver: a, Lauda and McLaren MP4/1. b, Ferrari 312 T2. c, March 721 G. d, Brabham BT48 and Brabham BT46.

No. 1641, 240fr — European high-speed trains: a, Frecciarossa 1000, flag of Italy. b, TGV Réseau, flag of France. c, ICE 4, flag of Germany. d, Eurostar e320, flag of Great Britain.

No. 1642, 240fr — Submarines: a, USS Los Angeles. b, Akula II class SSN Project 971U, Russia. c, USS Skate. d, Alfa class Project 705 Lyra, Russia.

No. 1643, 240fr — Red Cross campaign against malaria: a, Insect exterminator and Anopheles gambiae. b, Medical staffer, Plasmodium malariae and chemical structure of Primaquine. c, Doctor inoculating child. d, Malaria patient and hand holding hypodermic needle.

No. 1644, 240fr — Ice hockey players: a, Sidney Crosby, Canada. b, Alexander Ovechkin, Russia. c, Patrick Kane, U.S. d, Erik Karlsson, Sweden.

No. 1645, 950fr, Princess Diana and Prince Charles on wedding day. No. 1646, 950fr, Princess Grace and Academy Award. No. 1647, 950fr, Gagarin and technician. No. 1648, 950fr, Lauda and Ferrari 312 B3 cars. No. 1649, 950fr, Eurostar e300, flag of Great Britain. No. 1650, 950fr, USS Triton. No. 1651, 950fr, Hands of malaria patient and medical staffer, mosquito and giraffe. No. 1652, 950fr, Evgeni Malkin, Russia.

2019, Feb. 27 Litho. *Perf. 13¼*

Sheets of 4, #a-d

1637-1644 A354 Set of 8 87.50 87.50

Souvenir Sheets

1645-1652 A354 Set of 8 87.50 87.50

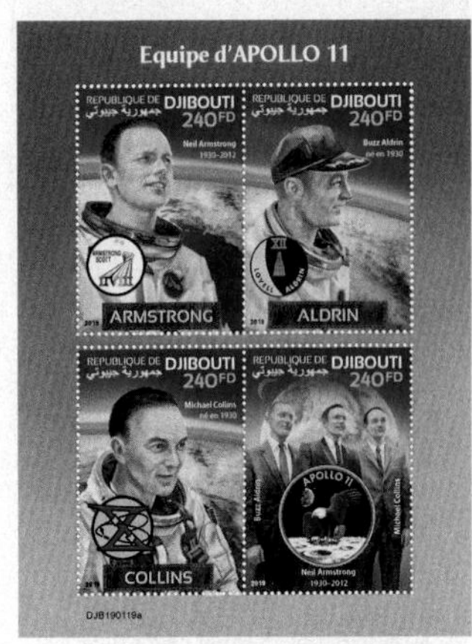

First Man on the Moon, 50th Anniv. — A355

No. 1653: a, Apollo 11 astronaut Neil Armstrong (1930-2012), patch of Gemini 8. b, Apollo 11 astronaut Edwin E. "Buzz" Aldrin, Jr. patch of Gemini 12. c, Apollo 11 astronaut Michael Collins, patch of Gemini 10. c, Aldrin, Armstrong, Collins and patch of Apollo 11.

950fr, Aldrin on moon, Pres. John F. Kennedy (1917-63).

2019, Feb. 27 Litho. *Perf. 13¼*

1653 A355 240fr Sheet of 4, #a-d 11.00 11.00

Souvenir Sheet

1654 A355 950fr multi 11.00 11.00

No. 1654 contains one 45x51mm stamp.

Paintings by Pablo Picasso (1881-1973) — A356

No. 1655: a, Mother and Child, 1902. b, Le Pigeon aux Petits Pois, 1911. c, Vase of Flowers on a Table, 1969. d, The Card Player, 1913-14.

1000fr, Portrait of Woman with an Ermine Collar (Olga), 1923.

2019, Mar. 14 Litho. *Perf. 13¼x13*

1655 A356 250fr Sheet of 4, #a-d 11.50 11.50

Souvenir Sheet

1656 A356 1000fr multi 11.50 11.50

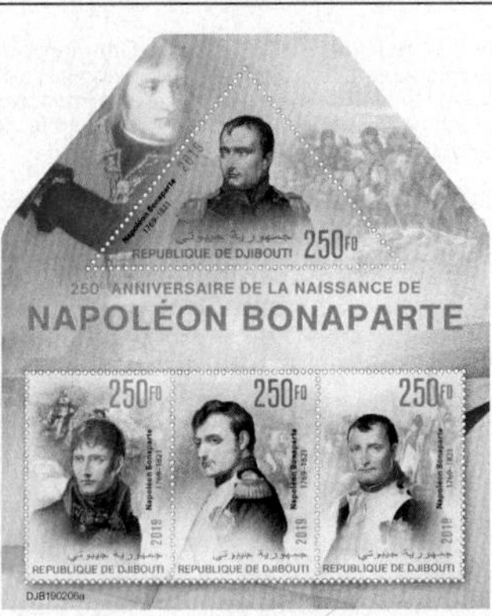

A357

No. 1657, 250fr — Napoleon Bonaparte (1769-1821), Emperor of France, with denomination in: a, Gray lilac (66x40mm triangular stamp). b, Rose (30x42mm). c, Dull violet blue (30x42mm). d, Bright green (30x42mm).

No. 1658, 250fr — Composers: a, Ludwig van Beethoven (1770-1827) (66x40mm triangular stamp). b, Franz Schubert (1797-1828) (30x42mm). c, Johann Sebastian Bach (1685-1750) (30x42mm). d, Joseph Haydn (1732-1809) (30x42mm).

No. 1659, 250fr — Tennis players: a, Novak Djokovic (66x40mm triangular stamp). b, Rafael Nadal (30x42mm). c, Petra Kvitova (30x42mm). d, Alexander Zverev (30x42mm).

No. 1660, 250fr — Chess players: a, Bobby Fischer (1943-2008) (66x40mm triangular stamp). b, Ding Liren (30x42mm). c, Judit Polgár (30x42mm). d, Magnus Carlsen (30x42mm).

No. 1661, 250fr — Scouts: a, Scout examining rocks (66x40mm triangular stamp). b, Scout cooking (30x42mm). c, Scout holding laptop computer (30x42mm). d, Scout writing in notebook (30x42mm).

No. 1662, 250fr — Trains of India: a, Jabalpur Express (66x40mm triangular stamp). b, WAG 9 electric locomotive (30x42mm). c, Maharajas' Express car interior (30x42mm). d, DEMU (30x42mm).

No. 1663, 250fr — Fire engines: a, Ford C series (66x40mm triangular stamp). b, ZIL-157 (30x42mm). c, GAZ-51 (30x42mm). d, IFA W 50 (30x42mm).

No. 1664, 250fr — Concorde, 50th anniv., with denomination in: a, Gray violet (66x40mm triangular stamp). b, Rose (30x42mm). c, Dull violet blue (30x42mm). d, Bright green (30x42mm).

No. 1665, 250fr — Prehistoric aquatic animals: a, Nothosaurus mirabilis (66x40mm triangular stamp). b, Carcharocles megalodon (30x42mm). c, Mosasaurus hoffmanni (30x42mm). d, Plesiosaurus dolichodeirus (30x42mm).

No. 1666, 1000fr, Bonaparte, diff. No. 1667, 1000fr, Wolfgang Amadeus Mozart (1756-91), composer. No. 1668, 1000fr, Tennis player Naomi Osaka. No. 1669, 1000fr, Chess player Garry Kasparov. No. 1670, Lord Robert Baden-Powell (1857-1941), founder of Scouting movement. No. 1671, 1000fr, WCP1 Diesel locomotive. No. 1672, 1000fr, Dennis F2 fire engine. No. 1673, 1000fr, Concorde, diff. No. 1674, 1000fr, Geosaurus giganteus.

2019, Mar. 14 Litho. *Perf. 13¼*

Sheets of 4, #a-d

1657-1665 A357 Set of 9 100.00 100.00

Souvenir Sheets

1666-1674 A357 Set of 9 100.00 100.00

Nos. 1666-1674 each contain one 66x40mm triangular stamp.

A358

No. 1675, 250fr — Primates: a, Leontopithecus rosalia (40mm diameter). b, Pan paniscus (40mm diameter). c, Saimiri sciureus (50x30mm). d, Macaca sinica (50x30mm).

No. 1676, 250fr — Cats: a, Korat (40mm diameter). b, Selkirk Rex (40mm diameter). c, Turkish Angora (50x30mm). d, American Shorthair (50x30mm).

No. 1677, 250fr — Sharks: a, Sphyrna lewini (40mm diameter). b, Triaenodon obesus (40mm diameter). c, Prionace glauca (50x30mm). d, Rhincodon typus (50x30mm).

No. 1678, 250fr — Kingfishers: a, Alcedo azurea (40mm diameter). b, Alcedo atthis (40mm diameter). c, Ceyx erithaca (50x30mm). d, Pelargopsis capensis (50x30mm).

No. 1679, 250fr — Bees: a, Bombus sylvarum (40mm diameter). b, Megachile lagopoda (40mm diameter). c, Apis mellifera facing right (50x30mm). d, Apis mellifera facing left (50x30mm).

No. 1680, 250fr — Orchids: a, Paphiopedilum hirsutissimum (40mm diameter). b, Brassovola nodosa (40mm diameter). c, Phalaenopsis hybrid (50x30mm). d, Dendrobium kingianum (50x30mm).

No. 1681, 250fr — Minerals: a, Apophyllite (40mm diameter). b, Amethyst (40mm diameter). c, Grossular (50x30mm). d, Apatite (50x30mm).

No. 1682, 250fr — Lighthouses and various unnamed shells: a, Marblehead Light, Ohio (40mm diameter). b, Tawas Point Light, Michigan (40mm diameter). c, Castle Hill Lighthouse, Rhode Island (50x30mm). d, West Point Light, Washington (50x30mm).

No. 1683, 1000fr, Pongo abelii. No. 1684, 1000fr, Ocicat. No. 1685, 1000fr, Carcharodon carcharias. No. 1686, 1000fr, Dacelo leachii. No. 1687, 1000fr, Bombus ruderarius. No. 1688, 1000fr, Phalaenopsis Sogo Yukidian. No. 1689, 1000fr, Emerald. No. 1690, 1000fr, Fastnet Lighthouse, Ireland, shell and starfish.

2019, Mar. 14 Litho. *Perf. 13¼*

Sheets of 4, #a-d

1675-1682 A358 Set of 8 90.00 90.00

Souvenir Sheets

Perf.

1683-1690 A358 Set of 8 90.00 90.00

Nos. 1683-1690 each conatin one 40mm diameter stamp.

Souvenir Sheets

Nobel Laureates — A359

Designs: No. 1691, 1000fr, Dr. Martin Luther King, Jr. (1929-68), 1964 Peace laureate. No. 1692, 1000fr, Pablo Neruda (1904-73), 1971 Literature laureate. No. 1693, 1000fr, Mikhail Gorbachev, 1990 Peace laureate. No. 1694, 1000fr, Tu Youyou, 2015 Physiology or Medicine laureate.

2019, Mar. 14 Litho. *Perf.*

1691-1694 A359 Set of 4 45.00 45.00

New Year 2019 (Year of the Pig) — A360

No. 1695: a, Pig and bowl. b, Pig facing left. c, Pig sitting. d, Pig in mud.

1000fr, Pig snout.

Litho. With Foil Application

2019, Mar. 14 *Perf.*

1695 A360 250fr Sheet of 4, #a-d 11.50 11.50

Souvenir Sheet

1696 A360 1000fr multi 11.50 11.50

Naval Vessels of the People's Republic of China A361

Flag of the Navy of People's Republic of China and: No. 1697, 200fr, Type 001A aircraft carrier. No. 1698, 200fr, Type 075 amphibious assault ship.

No. 1699, 500fr, Like #1697. No. 1700, 500fr, Like #1698.

2019, May 27 Litho. *Perf. 13*

1697-1698 A361 Set of 2 4.50 4.50

Souvenir Sheets

1699-1700 A361 Set of 2 11.50 11.50

Eid ul-Fitr Activities — A362

Emblem and: 1000fr, People making art for disabled children. 3000fr, People in march for equality, horiz.

Litho. & Embossed

2019, May 27 *Perf. 13*

1701-1702 A362 Set of 2 45.00 45.00

A363

No. 1703, 250fr — 50th birthday of Vassily Ivanchuk, chess player: a, Touching chess piece at bottom. b, With chin resting on hands at bottom. c, Writing. d, With hands on forehead at left.

No. 1704, 250fr — Richard F. Gordon, Jr. (1929-2017), astronaut: a, Apollo 12 service and command modules, mission patch. b, Wearing spacesuit without helmet. c, Wearing spacesuit and helmet. d, With astronaut Pete Conrad (1930-99).

No. 1705, 250fr — Ernest H. Shackleton (1874-1922), Antarctic explorer: a, Standing with penguins. b, Marine chronometer. c, Sled dog. d, His ship, Endurance.

No. 1706, 250fr — Birth of Archie Harrison Mountbatten-Windsor, son of the Duke and Duchess of Sussex: a, With parents. b, With mother. c, Duke of Sussex. d, Duke of Sussex as child, with his mother, Princess Diana.

No. 1707, 250fr — Paintings by Pierre-Auguste Renoir (1841-1919): a, Children at the Seashore, Guernsey, 1883. b, The Swing, 1876. c, Riding in the Bois du Boulogne, 1873. d, Woman Sitting by the sea, 1883.

No. 1708, 250fr — Japanese high-speed trains: a, Shinkansen Series E6. b, Shinkansen Series 500, blue black trim. c, Shinkansen Series E7. d, Shinkansen Series 500, blue trim.

No. 1709, 250fr — Fire trucks: a, Isuzu Elf. b, Opel Blitz 1.75t. c, Opel Blitz LF8 TS. d, Ford Transit MK1.

No. 1710, 250fr — Motorcycles: a, Moto Guzzi V85TT. b, 2019 BMW R 1250 GS. c, Suzuki GSX1100S Katana. d, Kawasaki Z125.

No. 1711, 250fr — Dinosaurs: a, Beipiaosaurus inexpectus. b, Caudipteryx dongi. c, Archaeoceratops oshimai. d, Rubeosaurus ovatus.

No. 1712, 1000fr, Ivanchuk and Magnus Carlsen playing chess, horiz. No. 1713, 1000fr, Gordon and Apollo 12 mission patch, horiz. No. 1714, 1000fr, Shackleton and foundering ship, horiz. No. 1715, 1000fr, Feet of Mountbatten-Windsor, horiz. No. 1716, 1000fr, Odalisque, by Renoir, horiz. No. 1717, 1000fr, Shinkansen Series E5, horiz. No. 1718, 1000fr, IFA W50 La fire truck, horiz. No. 1719, 1000fr, Yamaha YZF-R125 motorcycle, horiz. No. 1720, 1000fr, Brachylophosaurus canadensis, horiz.

Perf. 13¼x12¾

2019, June 12 Litho.

Sheets of 4, #a-d

1703-1711 A363 Set of 9 100.00 100.00

Souvenir Sheets

Perf. 12¾x13¼

1712-1720 A363 Set of 9 100.00 100.00

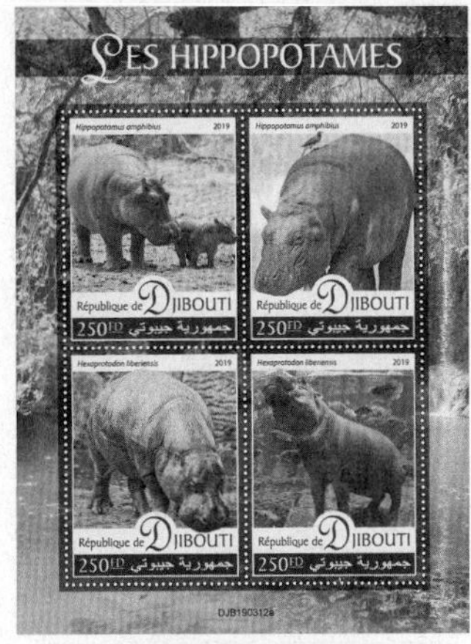

Animals — A364

No. 1721, 250fr — Hippopotamus amphibius: a, Adult and calf. b, Bird sitting on adult. c, Adult. d, Adult underwater.

No. 1722, 250fr — Wild cats: a, Panthera tigris tigris. b, Panthera uncia. c, Puma concolor. d, Panthera pardus orientalis.

No. 1723, 250fr — Sled dogs: a, Siberian huskies. b, Sakhalin husky. c, Alaskan malamute. d, Greenland dogs.

No. 1724, 250fr — Dolphins: a, Lagenorhynchus obscurus. b, Delphinus capensis. c, Tursiops truncatus. d, Stenella frontalis.

No. 1725, 250fr — Birds of prey: a, Aquila rapax. b, Pandion haliaetus. c, Milvus migrans. d, Aquila clanga.

No. 1726, 250fr — Hummingbirds: a, Chlorostilbon lucidus. b, Mellisuga helenae. c, Calypte anna. d, Archilochus colubris.

No. 1727, 250fr — Hornbills: a, Rhyticeros cassidix. b, Buceros bicornis. c, Tockus erythrorhynchus. d, Anthracoceros albirostris.

No. 1728, 250fr — Fish and coral: a, Paracanthurus hepatus, Acabaria splendens. b, Pomacanthus xanthometopon, Zoanthus gigantus. c, Pomacanthus imperator, Discosoma nummiforme. d, Balistoides conspicillum, Ricordea florida.

No. 1729, 250fr — Snakes: a, Trimeresurus insularis. b, Natrix natrix. c, Morelia viridis. d, Atheris ceratophora.

No. 1730, 250fr — Extinct animals: a, Ara gossei. b, Numenius borealis. c, Macropus greyi. d, Pyrenean ibex.

No. 1731, 1000fr, Choeropsis liberiensis. No. 1732, 1000fr, Panthera onca. No. 1733, 1000fr, Alaskan malamute, diff. No. 1734, 1000fr, Stenella coeruleoalba. No. 1735, 1000fr, Aquila heliaca. No. 1736, 1000fr, Calypte anna, diff. No. 1737, 1000fr, Tockus leucomelas. No. 1738, 1000fr, Zebrasoma desjardinii, Annella mollis. No. 1739, 1000fr, Drepanoides anomalus and Heliconia rostrata. No. 1740, 1000fr, Ectopistes migratorius.

Perf. 13¼x12¾

2019, June 12 Litho.

Sheets of 4, #a-d

1721-1730 A364 Set of 10 115.00 115.00

Souvenir Sheets

1731-1740 A364 Set of 10 115.00 115.00

Chinese Bridges A365

Various unnamed Chinese bridges numbered: 100fr, (15-01). 125fr, (15-02). 150fr, (15-03). 175fr, (15-04). 200fr, (15-05). 225fr, (15-06). 250fr, (15-07). 275fr, (15-08). 300fr, (15-09). 325fr, (15-10). 350fr, (15-11). 375fr, (15-12). 400fr (15-13). 425fr (15-14). 450fr, (15-15).

2019, June 12 Litho. *Perf. 13x13¼*

1741-1755 A365 Set of 15 46.50 46.50

Diplomatic relations between Djibouti and People's Republic of China, 40th anniv. Nos. 1741-1755 were each printed in sheets of 15 + label.

Chinese Buildings A366

Various unnamed Chinese buildings numbered: 100fr, (15-01). 125fr, (15-02). 150fr, (15-03). 175fr, (15-04). 200fr, (15-05). 225fr, (15-06). 250fr, (15-07). 275fr, (15-08). 300fr, (15-09). 325fr, (15-10). 350fr, (15-11). 375fr, (15-12). 400fr (15-13). 425fr (15-14). 450fr, (15-15).

2019, June 12 Litho. *Perf. 13x13¼*

1756-1770 A366 Set of 15 46.50 46.50

Diplomatic relations between Djibouti and People's Republic of China, 40th anniv. Nos. 1756-1770 were each printed in sheets of 15 + label.

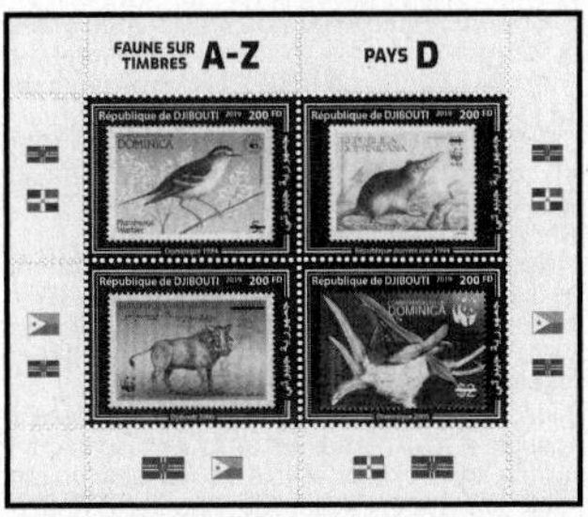

Stamps With Emblem of Worldwide Fund for Nature (WWF) — A367

No. 1771: a, Dominica #827. b, Domincan Republic #1158c. c, Djibouti #795b. d, Dominica #2520b.

No. 1772, 300fr, Dominica #829. No. 1773, 300fr, Dominican Republic #1158b. No. 1774, 300fr, Djibouti #795a. No. 1775, 300fr, Dominica #2520a.

2019, July 27 Litho. *Perf. 13x13¼*

1771 A367 200fr Sheet of 4, #a-d 9.00 9.00

Souvenir Sheets

1772-1775 A367 Set of 4 13.50 13.50

Nos. 1772-1775 each contain one 50x39mm stamp.

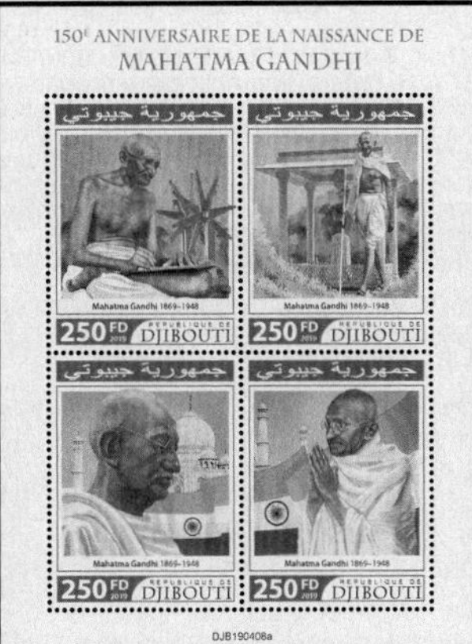

A368

No. 1776, 250fr — Mohandas K. Gandhi (1869-1948), Indian nationalist leader: a, With spinning wheel. b, Holding walking stick. c, Facing right, flag of India and Taj Mahal in background. d, Facing left with hands together, flags of India and Taj Mahal in background.

No. 1777, 250fr — 50th birthday of Michael Schumacher, race car driver: a, With race car in background. b, With Eddie Irvine and Jean Todt. c, In race car. d, With arms raised.

No. 1778, 250fr — Golfers: a, Phil Mickelson. b, Tiger Woods. c, Rory McIlroy. d, Brooks Koepka.

No. 1779, 250fr — 2018 Nobel laureates: a, Peace laureates Nadia Murad and Denis Mukwege. b, Physiology or Medicine laureates Tasuku Honjo and James P. Allison. c, Economics laureates Paul Romer and William Nordhaus. d, Chemistry laureates George Smith, Gregory Winter and Frances Arnold.

No. 1780, 250fr — Paintings by Vincent van Gogh (1853-90): a, The Drinkers, 1890. b, The Langlois Bridge at Arles with Women Washing, 1888. c, Boats on the Banks of the Oise at Auvers, 1890. d, Two Peasants Digging (After Millet), 1889.

No. 1781, 250fr — World War II tanks: a, TKS, Poland. b, 7TP, Poland. c, Panzer IV, Germany. d, Panzer I, Germany.

No. 1782, 250fr — Spaceflight of Apollo 11, 50th anniv.: a, Launch. b, Lunar Module landing on Moon. c, Command and Service Modules above Moon. d, Capsule returning to Earth.

No. 1783, 1000fr, Gandhi and crowd holding flags of India. No. 1784, 1000fr, Schumacher and race car, diff. No. 1785, 1000fr, Woods, diff. No. 1786, 1000fr, 2018 Nobel laureates in Physics, Donna Strickland, Arthur Ashkin, and Gérard Mourou. No. 1787, 1000fr, Self-portrait with Straw Hat, by van Gogh. No. 1788, 1000fr, Panzer III tank, Germany. No. 1789, 1000fr, Astronaut Neil Armstrong on Moon, holding U.S. flag, Apollo 11 mission patch.

2019, July 27 Litho. *Perf. 13¼x12¾*

Sheets of 4, #a-d

1776-1782 A368 Set of 7 80.00 80.00

Souvenir Sheets

1783-1789 A368 Set of 7 80.00 80.00

A369

No. 1790, 250fr — Panthera tigris tigris: a, Two tigers. b, One tiger facing forward with front legs apart. c, One tiger, standing in water. d, Tiger, reclining, with cub.

No. 1791, 250fr — Elephants: a, Three Loxodonta africana. b, Loxodonta cyclotis looking forward. c, Loxodonta cyclotis walking to right. d, Two Loxodonta africana.

No. 1792, 250fr — Whales: a, Megaptera novaeangliae, head at right. b, Megaptera novaeangliae, head at left. c, Two Megaptera novaeangliae. d, Physeter macrocephalus.

No. 1793, 250fr — Pigeons: a, Streptopelia turtur. b, Streptopelia decaocto. c, Ocyphaps lophotes. d, Goura victoria.

No. 1794, 250fr — Owls: a, Glaucidium californicum. b, Bubo africanus. c, Megascops asio. d, Bubo sumatranus.

No. 1795, 250fr — Parrots: a, Ara ararauna. b, Anodorhynchus hyacinthinus. c, Psittacus erithacus. d, Nymphicus hollandicus.

No. 1796, 250fr — Butterflies: a, Danaus eresimus. b, Gonepteryx cleopatra. c, Graphium sarpedon. d, Caligo eurilochus.

No. 1797, 250fr — Turtles: a, Clemmys guttata. b, Apalone spinifera. c, Trachemys scripta. d, Chelydra serpentina.

No. 1798, 250fr — Endangered animals: a, Canis lupus baileyi. b, Grus americana. c, Lynx pardinus. d, Gorilla beringei.

No. 1799, 250fr — Mushrooms: a, Tricholoma equestre. b, Gyroporus cyanescens. c, Boletus betulicola. d, Boletus aereus.

No. 1800, 250fr — Volcanoes: a, Volcán de Fuego, Guatemala. b, Piton de la Fournaise, Reunion Island. c, Parinacota, Bolivia, and Vicugna pacos. d, Sakurajima, Japan.

No. 1801, 250fr — Ships: a, HMS Diadem. b, Lai Fong. c, HMS Prince Royal. d, HMS Bounty.

No. 1802, 1000fr, Panthera tigris tigris, diff. No. 1803, 1000fr, Loxodonta cyclotis adult and calf. No. 1804, 1000fr, Megaptera novaeangliae, diff. No. 1805, 1000fr, Columba livia domestica. No. 1806, 1000fr, Aegolius funereus. No. 1807, 1000fr, Psittacula krameri. No. 1808, 1000fr, Agalis io. No. 1809, 1000fr, Pseudemys nelsoni. No. 1810, 1000fr, Crocodylus siamensis. No. 1811, 1000fr, Hydnum repandum. No. 1812, 1000fr, Popocatepetl, Mexico. No. 1813, 1000fr, USS Providence.

2019, July 27 Litho. *Perf. 13¼x12¾*

Sheets of 4, #a-d

1790-1801 A369 Set of 12 135.00 135.00

Souvenir Sheets

1802-1813 A369 Set of 12 135.00 135.00

Nos. 1059a-1059d Surcharged in Gold or Metallic Red

Methods and Perfs. As Before

2019, Aug. 27

1814 A311 590fr on 260fr #1059a (G) 6.75 6.75
1815 A311 590fr on 260fr #1059a (MR) 6.75 6.75
1816 A311 590fr on 260fr #1059b (G) 6.75 6.75
1817 A311 590fr on 260fr #1059b (MR) 6.75 6.75
1818 A311 590fr on 260fr #1059c (G) 6.75 6.75
1819 A311 590fr on 260fr #1059c (MR) 6.75 6.75
1820 A311 590fr on 260fr #1059d (G) 6.75 6.75
1821 A311 590fr on 260fr #1059d (MR) 6.75 6.75
Nos. 1814-1821 (8) 54.00 54.00

A370

No. 1822, 250fr — Cats: a, Balinese. b, American Shorthair. c, Russian Blue. d, Japanese bobtail.

No. 1823, 250fr — Horses: a, Paint horse. b, Lusitano. c, Knabstruper. d, Holsteiner.

No. 1824, 250fr, vert. — Bee-eaters: a, Merops albicollis. b, Merops apiaster. c, Merops leschenaulti. d, Merops bulocki.

No. 1825, 250fr, vert. — Sunbirds: a, Hedydipna collaris. b, Aethopyga gouldiae. c, Aethopyga siparaja. d, Aethopyga nipalensis.

No. 1826, 250fr, vert. — Ducks: a, Netta rufina. b, Aythya fuligula. c, Bucephala clangula. d, Tadorna tadorna.

No. 1827, 250fr, vert. — Bees: a, Bombus pascuorum. b, Xylocopa virginica. c, Apis cerana. d, Bombus terrestris.

No. 1828, 250fr, vert. — Orchids: a, Prosthechea brassavolae. b, Phalaenopsis mariae. c, Zygopetalum crinitum. d, Ondidium flexuosum.

No. 1829, 250fr, vert. — Minerals: a, Azurite. b, Pyrite. c, Celestine. d, Demantoid.

No. 1830, 1000fr, Abyssinian cats. No. 1831, 1000fr, Shire horses. No. 1832, 1000fr, Merops nubicus, vert. No. 1833, 1000fr, Arachnothera magna, vert. No. 1834, 1000fr, Marmaronetta angustirostris, vert. No. 1835, 1000fr, Apis mellifera, vert. No. 1836, 1000fr, Catasetum fimbriatum, vert. No. 1837, 1000fr, Heliodor.

Perf. 13x13¼, 13¼x13

2019, Aug. 27 Litho.

Sheets of 4, #a-d

1822-1829 A370 Set of 8 90.00 90.00

Souvenir Sheets

1830-1837 A370 Set of 8 90.00 90.00

A371

No. 1838, 250fr — Marilyn Monroe (1926-62), actress: a, Holding dogs. b, Wearing blue dress at right. c, Wearing red dress at right. d, Seated in chair.

No. 1839, 250fr — Charlie Chaplin (1889-1977), actor, in scene from 1914 film: a, *Charlot garde-malade* (His New Profession). b, *Charlot est content de lui* (Kid Auto Races at Venice). c, *Charlot et le Mannequin* (Mabel's Married Life). d, *Charlot artiste peintre* (The Face on the Bar Room Floor).

No. 1840, 250fr — Tigran Petrosian (1929-84), chess player, wearing: a, Gray pinstripe suit. b, Brown suit. c, White shirt and tie. d, White and green plaid shirt.

No. 1841, 250fr — Rotary International emblem and: a, Paul P. Harris (1868-1947), founder, world map and doves. b, Child at water spigot. c, Doctor examining child. d, Children carrying blackboard.

No. 1842, 250fr — Duke and Duchess of Sussex: a, Duke and Duchess with son Archie carried by Duke. b, Duke of Sussex holding baby clothes. c, Archie Mountbatten-Windsor. d, Duke and Duchess with son carried by Duchess.

No. 1843, 250fr — Robert Stephenson (1803-59), civil engineer: a, With flag of Great Britain. b, Signature of Stephenson and Rocket locomotive. c, Standing on Planet locomotive. d, With his yacht, Titania.

No. 1844, 250fr — Scout: a, Fishing. b, At campfire. c, Birdwatching. d, Playing guitar.

No. 1845, 250fr — Japanese Shinkansen high-speed trains: a, Series 400. b, Series N700. c, Series 700. d, Series E3-1000.

No. 1846, 250fr — Operation Market Garden, 75th anniv.: a, DeHavilland DH.98 Mosquitos. b, Douglas C-47 Skytrains. c, Airspeed AS.51 Horsa gliders and Short Stirling Mark IV airplanes. d, Spitfire F Mk II and Messerschmitt Bf 109 airplanes.

No. 1847, 250fr — Flying dinosaurs: a, Eudimorphodon ranzii. b, Caviramus schesaplanensis. c, Caulkicephalus trimicrodon. d, Pterosaur.

No. 1848, 1000fr, Monroe, diff. No. 1849, 1000fr, Chaplin in *Making a Living.* No. 1850, 1000fr, Petrosian, diff. No. 1851, 1000fr, Harris and Rotary International emblem. No. 1852, 1000fr, Archie Mountabtten-Windsor, diff. No. 1853, 1000fr, Britannia Bridge, built by Stephenson. No. 1854, 1000fr, Scout, badge and canoe. No. 1855, 1000fr, Shinkansen Series 500. No. 1856, 1000fr, Hawker Tempest and Junkers Ju88 airplanes. No. 1857, 1000fr, Harpactognathus gentryii.

2019, Aug. 27 Litho. *Perf. 13¼x13*

1838-1847 A371 Set of 10 115.00 115.00

Souvenir Sheets

1848-1857 A371 Set of 10 115.00 115.00

New Year 2020 (Year of the Rat) — A372

No. 1858 — Rat and: a, "2020." b, Fireworks. c, Lantern. d, Fireworks and "2020."

1000fr, Rat with gift.

Litho. With Foil Application

2019, Aug. 27 *Perf. 13¼x13*

1858 A372 250fr Sheet of 4, #a-d 11.50 11.50

Souvenir Sheet

1859 A372 1000fr multi 11.50 11.50

AIR POST STAMPS

Afars and Issas Nos. C104-C105, C103 Overprinted in Brown or Black

Nos. C106, C107

No. C108

1977 Engr. *Perf. 13*

C106 AP37 55fr multi (Br) 2.00 1.75
C107 AP37 75fr multi 9.00 4.00

Litho. *Perf. 12*

C108 AP36 500fr multi 15.00 13.50
Nos. C106-C108 (3) 26.00 19.25

Map of Djibouti, Dove, UN Emblem — AP38

1977, Oct. 19 Photo. *Perf. 13*

C109 AP38 300fr multi 6.50 4.25

Djibouti's admission to the United Nations.

Marcel Brochet MB 101, 1955 — AP39

Djibouti Aero Club: 85fr, Tiger Moth, 1960. 200fr, Rallye-Commodore, 1973.

1978, Feb. 27 Litho. *Perf. 13*

C110 AP39 60fr multi 1.10 .40
C111 AP39 85fr multi 1.60 .65
C112 AP39 200fr multi 4.00 1.10
Nos. C110-C112 (3) 6.70 2.15

Old Man, by Rubens AP40

500fr, Hippopotamus Hunt, by Rubens.

1978, Apr. 24 Photo. *Perf. 13*

C113 AP40 50fr multi 1.50 .50
C114 AP40 500fr multi, horiz. 11.00 5.00

Peter Paul Rubens (1577-1640).

Player Holding Soccer Cup — AP41

Design: 300fr, Soccer player, map of South America with Argentina, Cup and emblem.

1978, June 20 Litho. *Perf. 13*

C115 AP41 100fr multi 1.75 .50
C116 AP41 300fr multi 5.50 1.25

11th World Cup Soccer Championship, Argentina, June 1-25.

For overprints see Nos. C117-C118.

Nos. C115-C116 Overprinted

a

b

1978, Aug. 20 Litho. *Perf. 13*

C117 AP41 (a) 100fr multi 1.60 .75
C118 AP41 (b) 300fr multi 5.50 2.00

Argentina's victory in 1978 Soccer Championship.

Tahitian Women, by Gauguin — AP42

Young Hare, by Dürer AP43

Perf. 13x12½, 12½x13

1978, Sept. 25 **Litho.**
C119 AP42 100fr multi 2.75 .40
C120 AP43 250fr multi 5.50 2.50

Paul Gauguin (1848-1903) and Albrecht Dürer (1471-1528), painters.

Common Design Types pictured following the introduction.

Philexafrique II-Essen Issue
Common Design Types

Designs: No. C121, Lynx and Djibouti No. 456. No. C122, Jay and Brunswick No. 3.

1978, Dec. 13 **Litho.** ***Perf. 13x12½***
C121 CD138 90fr multi 3.00 1.50
C122 CD139 90fr multi 3.00 1.50
a. Pair, Nos. C121-C122 + label 6.50 6.50

UPU Emblem, Map of Djibouti, Dove — AP44

1978, Dec. 18 **Engr.** ***Perf. 13***
C123 AP44 200fr multi 3.25 1.10

Centenary of Congress of Paris.

Junkers JU-52 and Dewoitine D-338 — AP45

Powered Flight, 75th Anniversary: 250fr, Potez P63-11, 1941 and Supermarine Spitfire HF-VII, 1942. 500fr, Concorde, 1969 and Sikorsky S-40 "American Clipper," 1931.

1979, May 21 **Litho.** ***Perf. 13x12½***
C124 AP45 140fr multi 3.00 .60
C125 AP45 250fr multi 4.50 1.00
C126 AP45 500fr multi 9.00 1.75
Nos. C124-C126 (3) 16.50 3.35

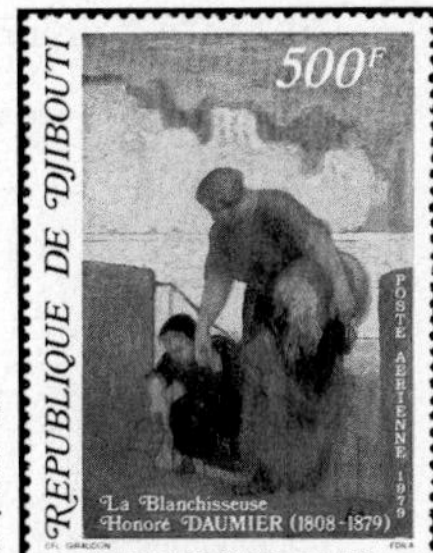

The Laundress, by Honore Daumier AP46

1979, July 10 **Litho.** ***Perf. 12½x13***
C127 AP46 500fr multi 12.00 3.00

Olympic Emblem, Skis, Sleds — AP47

1980, Jan. 21 **Litho.** ***Perf. 13***
C128 AP47 150fr multi 3.00 .60

13th Winter Olympic Games, Lake Placid, N.Y., Feb. 12-24.
For surcharges see Nos. C133-C134.

Cathedral of the Archangel, Basketball, Moscow '80 Emblem — AP48

120fr, Lomonossov Univ., Moscow, soccer. 250fr, Cathedral of the Annunciation, running.

1980, Apr. 10 **Litho.** ***Perf. 13***
C129 AP48 60fr multi 1.05 .25
C130 AP48 120fr multi 2.10 .40
C131 AP48 250fr multi 4.25 1.00
Nos. C129-C131 (3) 7.40 1.65

22nd Summer Olympic Games, Moscow, July 18-Aug. 3.

Air Djibouti, 1st Anniversary — AP49

1980, Mar. 29 **Litho.** ***Perf. 13x12½***
C132 AP49 400fr multi 9.00 2.50

No. C128 Surcharged in Black and Blue or Purple

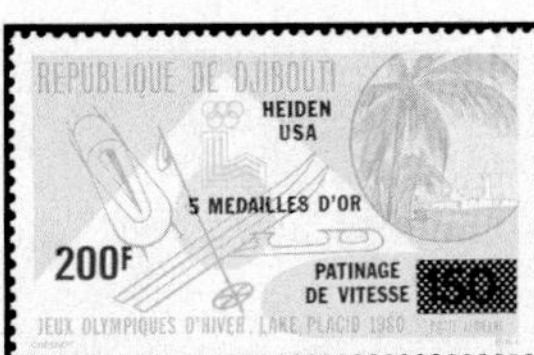

1980, Apr. 5 **Litho.** ***Perf. 13***
C133 AP47 80fr on 150fr 1.75 .50
C134 AP47 200fr on 150fr (P) 4.00 1.50

Apollo 11 Moon Landing, 10th Anniversary — AP50

Space Conquests: 300fr, Apollo-Soyuz space project, 5th anniversary.

1980, May 8
C135 AP50 200fr multi 4.00 .75
C136 AP50 300fr multi 6.50 1.25

Nos. C135-C136 exist in souvenir sheets of one. Value, set, $22.50.

Satellite Earth Station Inauguration — AP51

1980, July 3 **Litho.** ***Perf. 13***
C137 AP51 500fr multi 9.50 1.75

Graf Zeppelin — AP52

1980, Oct. 2 **Litho.** ***Perf. 13***
C138 AP52 100fr shown 2.25 .40
C139 AP52 150fr Ferdinand von Zeppelin, blimp 3.25 .60

Zeppelin flight, 80th anniversary.

Voyager Passing Saturn — AP53

1980, Dec. 21 **Litho.** ***Perf. 13***
C140 AP53 250fr multi 5.50 1.00

AP54

World Cup Soccer Preliminary Games: 200fr, Players, diff.

1981, Jan. 14
C141 AP54 80fr multi 1.75 .30
C142 AP54 200fr multi 4.25 .65

AP55

1981, Feb. 10 **Litho.** ***Perf. 13***
C143 AP55 100fr multi 3.50 .50

European-African Economic Convention.

5th Anniversary of Viking I Take-off to Mars — AP56

20th Anniversary of Various Space Flights: 75fr, Vostok I, Yuri Gagarin, vert. 150fr, Freedom 7, Alan B. Shepard, vert.

1981, Mar. 9 **Litho.** ***Perf. 13***
C144 AP56 75fr multi 1.75 .35
C145 AP56 120fr multi 2.25 .45
C146 AP56 150fr multi 3.00 .65
Nos. C144-C146 (3) 7.00 1.45

Football Players, by Picasso (1881-1973) — AP57

Design: 400fr Man Wearing a Turban, by Rembrandt (1606-1669), vert.

Perf. 13x12½, 12½x13

1981, Aug. 3 **Litho.**
C147 AP57 300fr multi 7.00 1.40
C148 AP57 400fr multi 7.50 1.75

Columbia Space Shuttle — AP58

90fr, Shuttle launching.

1981, Sept. 24 **Litho.** ***Perf. 13***
C149 AP58 90fr multicolored 1.75 .40
C150 AP58 120fr shown 2.50 .60

Nos. C149-C150 exist in souvenir sheets of one. Value, set, $22.50.

Nos. C149-C150 Overprinted in Brown

No. C151

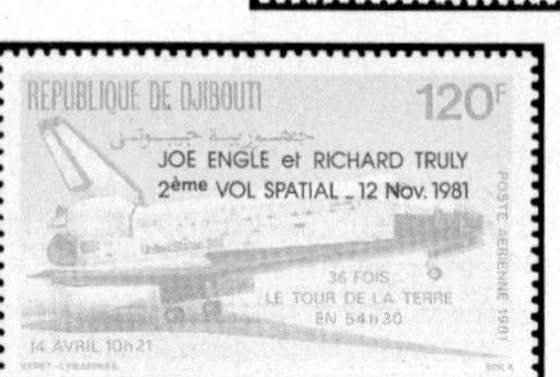

No. C152

1981, Nov. 12 Litho. *Perf. 13*

C151 AP58 90fr multi 1.75 .50
C152 AP58 120fr multi 2.50 .75

1982 World Cup Soccer — AP59

Designs: Various soccer players.

1982, Jan. 20

C153 AP59 110fr multi 2.10 .60
C154 AP59 220fr multi 4.75 1.25

For overprints see Nos. C166-C167.

Space Anniversaries — AP60

Designs: 40fr, Luna 9 moon landing, 15th, vert. 60fr, John Glenn's flight, 20th, vert. 180fr, Viking I Mars landing, 5th.

1982, Feb. 15

C155 AP60 40fr multi .70 .25
C156 AP60 60fr multi 1.10 .30
C157 AP60 180fr multi 3.00 1.00
Nos. C155-C157 (3) 4.80 1.55

21st Birthday of Princess Diana of Wales AP61

1982, Apr. 29 Litho. *Perf. 12½x13*

C158 AP61 120fr Portrait 2.25 .75
C159 AP61 180fr Portrait, diff. 3.50 1.00

For overprints see Nos. C168-C169.

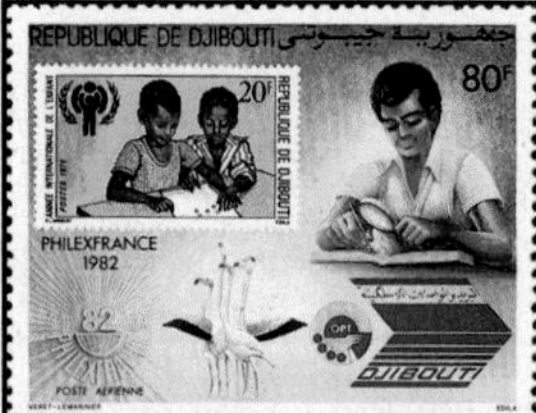

No. 489, Boy Examining Collection — AP62

1982, May 10 *Perf. 13x12½*

C160 AP62 80fr shown 2.50 .75
C161 AP62 140fr No. 495 3.75 1.00
a. Pair, Nos. C160-C161 + label 6.50 6.50

PHILEXFRANCE '82 Stamp Exhibition, Paris, June 11-21.

1350th Anniv. of Mohammed's Death at Medina — AP63

1982, June 8 Litho. *Perf. 13*

C162 AP63 500fr Medina Mosque 9.00 2.00

Scouting Year — AP64

1982, June 28

C163 AP64 95fr Baden-Powell 1.75 .50
C164 AP64 200fr Camp, scouts 4.00 1.25

2nd UN Conference on Peaceful Uses of Outer Space, Vienna, Aug. 9-21 — AP65

1982, Aug. 19

C165 AP65 350fr multi 6.75 3.00

Nos. C153-C154 Overprinted

1982, July 21 Litho. *Perf. 13*

C166 AP59 110fr multi 2.00 .60
C167 AP59 220fr multi 4.00 1.10

Italy's victory in 1982 World Cup.

Nos. C158-C159 Overprinted in Blue or Red

No. C168

No. C169

1982, Aug. 9 *Perf. 12½x13*

C168 AP61 120fr multi 2.50 .75
C169 AP61 180fr multi (R) 3.50 1.00

Birth of Prince William of Wales, June 21.

Franklin D. Roosevelt (1882-1945) AP66

1982, Oct. 7 Litho. *Perf. 13*

C170 AP66 115fr shown 2.00 .50
C171 AP66 250fr George Washington 5.25 1.00

Manned Flight Bicentenary AP67

35fr, Montgolfiere, 1783. 45fr, Giffard, Paris Exposition, 1878. 120fr, Double Eagle II, 1978.

1983, Jan. 20 Litho.

C172 AP67 35fr multi .80 .25
C173 AP67 45fr multi 1.35 .30
C174 AP67 120fr multi 3.50 .80
Nos. C172-C174 (3) 5.65 1.35

Pre-olympic Year — AP68

1983, Feb. 15

C175 AP68 75fr Volleyball 1.50 .55
C176 AP68 125fr Wind surfing 2.75 .85

Nos. C175-C176 exist in souvenir sheets of one. Value, set, $25.

50th Anniv. of Air France — AP69

1983, Mar. 20 Litho. *Perf. 13*

C177 AP69 25fr Bloch 220 .50 .25
C178 AP69 100fr DC-4 1.75 .70
C179 AP69 175fr Boeing 747 3.50 1.10
Nos. C177-C179 (3) 5.75 2.05

AP70

180fr, Martin Luther King, Jr. (1929-68), civil rights leader. 250fr, Alfred Nobel (1833-96)

1983, May 18 Litho. *Perf. 13*

C180 AP70 180fr multi 3.50 1.25
C181 AP70 250fr multi 4.50 2.00

AP71

Service Clubs: 90fr, Rotary Club Intl., Sailing Show, Toronto, June 5-9. 150fr, Lions Club Intl., Honolulu Meeting, June 22-24, Djibouti lighthouse.

1983, July 18 Litho. *Perf. 13*

C182 AP71 90fr multi 3.00 1.50
C183 AP71 150fr multi 3.00 1.00
a. Pair, Nos. C182-C183 + label 5.50 5.50

Vintage Motor Cars — AP72

Designs: 60fr, Renault, 1904. 80fr, Mercedes, 1910, vert. 110fr, Lorraine-Dietrich, 1912.

1983, Sep. 20 Litho. *Perf. 13x12½*

C184 AP72 60fr multi 1.90 .50
C185 AP72 80fr multi 2.50 .65
C186 AP72 110fr multi 3.00 .85
Nos. C184-C186 (3) 7.40 2.00

Souvenir Sheet

Air France, 50th Anniv. — AP73

1983, Oct. 7 **Litho.** ***Perf. 12½***

Self-Adhesive

C187 AP73 250fr multicolored 25.00 25.00

Printed on wood.

Vostok VI AP74

1983, Oct. 20 **Litho.** ***Perf. 12***

C188 AP74 120fr shown 2.25 .80
C189 AP74 200fr Explorer I 3.75 1.10

1984 Winter Olympics — AP75

1984, Feb. 14 **Litho.** ***Perf. 13***

C190 AP75 70fr Speed skating 1.50 .55
C191 AP75 130fr Figure skating 2.50 1.10

For overprints see Nos. C196-C197.

Souvenir Sheet

Ship — AP76

1984, Feb. 14 **Litho.** ***Perf. 12½***

C192 AP76 250fr multi 11.00 11.00

Sea-Me-We (South-east Asia-Middle East-Western Europe) submarine cable construction agreement.

No. C192 exists in a souvenir sheet of one. Value, $12.50.

Motorized Hang Gliders — AP77

Various hang gliders.

1984, Mar. 12 ***Perf. 13x12½***

C193 AP77 65fr multi 1.25 .50
C194 AP77 85fr multi 1.60 .60
C195 AP77 100fr multi 2.10 .75
Nos. C193-C195 (3) 4.95 1.85

Nos. C190-C191 Overprinted with Winners' Names and Country

1984, Mar. 28 ***Perf. 13***

C196 AP75 70fr multi 1.50 .50
C197 AP75 130fr multi 2.75 1.00

Portrait of Marguerite Matisse, 1910, by Henri Matisse AP78

Design: 200fr, Portrait of Mario Varvogli, by Amedeo Modigliani.

1984, Apr. 15 **Litho.** ***Perf. 12½x13***

C198 AP78 150fr multi 3.75 1.00
C199 AP78 200fr multi 4.75 1.40

1984 Summer Olympics — AP79

1984, May 24 ***Perf. 13***

C200 AP79 50fr Running 1.00 .40
C201 AP79 60fr High jump 1.25 .40
C202 AP79 80fr Swimming 1.50 .60
Nos. C200-C202 (3) 3.75 1.40

Nos. C200-C202 exist in a souvenir sheet of 3. Value, $32.50.

Battle Scene — AP80

1984, June 16 **Litho.** ***Perf. 13x12½***

C203 AP80 300fr multi 6.00 2.75

125th anniv. of Battle of Solferino and 120th anniv. of Red Cross.

Bleriot's Flight over English Channel, 75th Anniv. — AP81

Designs: 40fr, 14-Bis plans. 75fr, Britten-Norman Islander. 90fr, Air Djibouti jet.

1984, July 8

C204 AP81 40fr multi .90 .40
C205 AP81 75fr multi 1.40 .75
C206 AP81 90fr multi 1.50 1.00
Nos. C204-C206 (3) 3.80 2.15

375th Anniv., Galileo's Telescope AP82

120fr, Telescopes, spacecraft. 180fr, Galileo, telescopes.

1984, Oct. 7 **Litho.** ***Perf. 13***

C207 AP82 120fr multicolored 2.50 .80
C208 AP82 180fr multicolored 3.50 1.10

1984 Soccer Events — AP83

Designs: No. C209, Euro Cup. No. C210, Los Angeles Olympics.

1984, Oct. 20 **Litho.** ***Perf. 13***

C209 AP83 80fr multi 2.50 .60
C210 AP83 80fr multi 2.50 .60
a. Pair, Nos. C209-C210 + label 4.50 4.00

Service Clubs — AP84

50fr, Lions, World Leprosy Day. 60fr, Rotary, chess board, pieces.

1985, Feb. 23 **Litho.** ***Perf. 13***

C211 AP84 50fr multicolored 1.40 .50
C212 AP84 60fr multicolored 1.60 .55

Nos. C211-C212 exist in souvenir sheets of 1.

Telecommunications Technology — AP85

No. C213, Technician, researchist, operator. No. C214, Offshore oil rig, transmission tower, government building.

1985, July 2 ***Perf. 13x12½***

C213 AP85 80fr multi 2.50 .55
C214 AP85 80fr multi 2.50 .55
a. Pair, Nos. C213-C214 + label 6.25 1.25

PHILEXAFRICA '85, Lome.

Telecommunications Development — AP86

50fr, Intl. transmission center. 90fr, Ariane rocket, vert. 120fr, ARABSAT satellite.

1985, Oct. 2 ***Perf. 13***

C215 AP86 50fr multi .90 .35
C216 AP86 90fr multi 1.60 .65
C217 AP86 120fr multi 2.00 .90
Nos. C215-C217 (3) 4.50 1.90

Youths Windsurfing, Playing Tennis — AP87

No. C219, Tadjoura Highway construction.

1985, Nov. 13 ***Perf. 13x12½***

C218 AP87 100fr multi 2.50 1.00
C219 AP87 100fr multi 2.50 1.00
a. Pair, Nos. C218-C219 + label 6.00 5.00

PHILEXAFRICA '85, Lome, Togo, 11/16-24.

1986 World Cup Soccer Championships, Mexico — AP88

Design: 100fr, Players, stadium.

1986, Feb. 24 **Litho.** ***Perf. 13***

C220 AP88 75fr shown 1.50 .50
C221 AP88 100fr multi 2.00 .70

For overprints see Nos. C223-C224.

Statue of Liberty, Cent. — AP89

1986, May 21

C222 AP89 250fr multi 4.50 1.75

Nos. C220-C221 Ovptd. with Winners

1986, Sept. 15 **Litho.** ***Perf. 13***

C223 AP88 75fr "FRANCE - BELGIQUE / 4-2" 1.25 .65
C224 AP88 100fr "3-2 ARGEN-TINE-RFA" 1.75 .80

1986 World Chess Championships, May 1-19 — AP89a

Malayan animal chess pieces: 80fr, Knight, bishops. 120fr, Rook, king, pawn.

1986, Oct. 13 Litho. *Perf. 13*

C225	AP89a	80fr multi	2.00	.60
C226	AP89a	120fr multi	3.25	.90

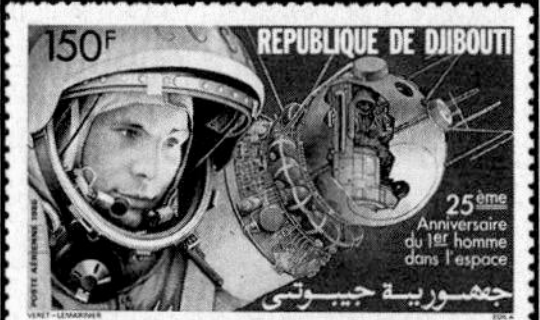

Yuri Gagarin, Sputnik Spacecraft — AP90

Design: 200fr, Space rendezvous, 1966.

1986, Nov. 27 Litho. *Perf. 13*

C227	AP90	150fr shown	3.00	1.10
C228	AP90	200fr multi	4.25	1.25

First man in space, 25th anniv.; Gemini 8-Agena link-up, 20th anniv.

Historic Flights — AP91

Designs: 55fr, Amiot 370. 80fr, Spirit of St. Louis. 120fr, Voyager.

1987, Jan. 22 Litho. *Perf. 13*

C229	AP91	55fr multi	1.25	.40
C230	AP91	80fr multi	1.75	.55
C231	AP91	120fr multi	2.50	.90
		Nos. C229-C231 (3)	5.50	1.85

First flight from Istria to Djibouti, 1942; Lindbergh's Transatlantic flight, 1927; nonstop world circumnavigation without refueling.

For surcharge see No. C240.

Souvenir Sheet

Fight Against Leprosy — AP91a

Design: Raoul Follereau (b. 1903), care giver to lepers, Gerhard Hansen (1841-1912), discoverer of bacillus of leprosy.

1987, Mar. 23 Litho. *Perf. 13x12½*

Self-Adhesive

C231A	AP91a	500fr multi	20.00	15.00

No. C231A printed on wood.

Pres. Aptidon, Natl. Crest and Flag AP92

1987, June 27 Litho. *Perf. 12½x13*

C232	AP92	250fr multi	4.50	1.50

Natl. independence, 10th anniv.

Telstar, 25th Anniv. — AP93

Design: 250fr, Samuel Morse, telegraph key.

1987, Oct. 1 *Perf. 13*

C233	AP93	190fr shown	3.50	1.25
a.		Souvenir sheet, 1 #C233	14.00	—
C234	AP93	250fr multi	4.50	1.50
a.		Souvenir sheet, 1 #C234	14.00	—

Invention of the telegraph, 150th anniv. (250fr).

Nos. C233a and C234a also exist imperf. Value, set of 2, $40.

City of Djibouti, Cent. — AP94

100fr, Djibouti Creek & quay, 1887. 150fr, Aerial view of city, 1987. 250fr, Somali Coast #6, 20, postmarks of 1898 & 1903.

1987, Nov. 15 Litho. *Perf. 13x12½*

C235	AP94	100fr blk & buff	2.00	1.10
C236	AP94	150fr multi	3.00	1.60
a.		Pair, Nos. C235-C236 + label	6.00	2.75

Souvenir Sheet

C237	AP94	250fr multi	6.00	5.50

No. C237 has decorative margin like design of 100fr.

Intl. Red Cross and Red Crescent Organizations, 125th Anniv. — AP95

1988, Feb. 17 Litho. *Perf. 13*

C238	AP95	300fr multi	6.00	3.25

1988 Summer Olympics, Seoul — AP96

1988, June 15 Litho. *Perf. 13*

C239	AP96	105fr multi	3.00	1.00

For overprint see No. C242.

No. C239 exists in a souvenir sheet of one. Value, $25.

No. C229 Surcharged in Black

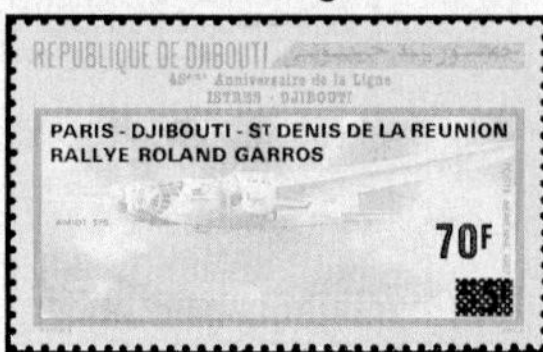

1988, June 28

C240	AP91	70fr on 55fr multi	3.00	1.50

Air race in memory of the Paris-Djibouti-St. Denis flight of French aviator Roland Garros (1888-1913).

World Post Day — AP97

1988, Oct. 9 Litho. *Perf. 13*

C241	AP97	1000fr multi	18.00	10.00

No. C239 Overprinted

1988, Dec. 15 Litho. *Perf. 13*

C242	AP96	105fr multi	2.25	1.50

World Telecommunications Day — AP98

1989, May 17 Litho. *Perf. 12½*

C243	AP98	150fr multi	2.75	1.50

PHILEXFRANCE '89, Declaration of Human Rights and Citizenship Bicent. — AP99

1989, July 14 Litho. *Perf. 12½x13*

C244	AP99	120fr multi	2.75	1.25

Salt, Lake Assal — AP100

1989, Sept. 15 Litho. *Perf. 13*

C245	AP100	300fr multicolored	6.75	3.50

POSTAGE DUE STAMP

Urn for Milking Camel — D1

1988, Jan. 20 Litho. *Perf. 13*

J1	D1	60fr multicolored	1.20	.65

DOMINICA

ˌdä-mə-ˈnē-kə

LOCATION — The largest island of the Windward group in the West Indies. Southeast of Puerto Rico.
GOVT. — Republic in British Commonwealth
AREA — 290 sq. mi.
POP. — 64,881 (1999 est.)
CAPITAL — Roseau

Formerly a Presidency of the Leeward Islands, Dominica became a separate colony under the governor of the Windward Islands on January 1, 1940. Dominica joined the West Indies federation April 22, 1958. In 1968, Dominica became an associate state of Britain; in 1978, an independent nation.

12 Pence = 1 Shilling
20 Shillings = 1 Pound
100 Cents = 1 Dollar (1949)

Catalogue values for unused stamps in this country are for Never Hinged items, beginning with Scott 112.

Watermark

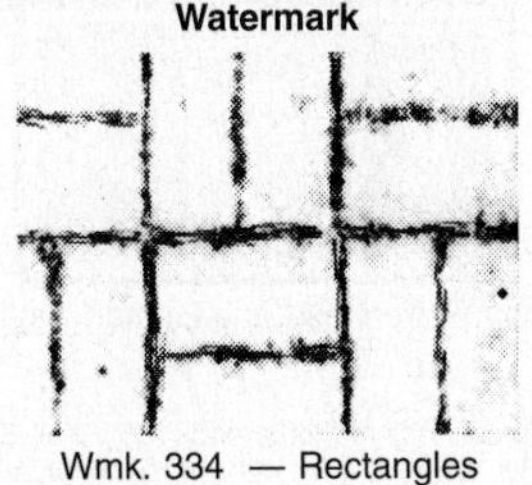

Wmk. 334 — Rectangles

Queen Victoria — A1

Perf. 12½

1874, May 4 Typo. Wmk. 1

1	A1	1p violet	170.00	55.00
a.		Vertical half used as ½p on cover		*9,000.*
2	A1	6p green	625.00	115.00
3	A1	1sh deep lilac rose	375.00	80.00
		Nos. 1-3 (3)	1,170.	250.00

During 1875-87 some issues were manuscript dated with village names. These are considered postally used. Stamps with entire village names sell for much more, starting at $100.

1877-79 *Perf. 14*

4	A1	½p bister ('79)	20.00	*62.50*
5	A1	1p violet	24.00	3.75
a.		Diagonal or vertical half used as ½p on cover		2,600.
6	A1	2½p red brown ('79)	275.00	45.00
7	A1	4p blue ('79)	130.00	3.75
8	A1	6p green	170.00	22.50
9	A1	1sh dp lilac rose	140.00	57.50
		Nos. 4-9 (6)	759.00	195.00

For surcharges see Nos. 10-15.

No. 5 Bisected and Surcharged in Black or Red

a b c

1882

10	A1(a)	½p on half of 1p	240.00	57.50
a.		Inverted surcharge	1,150.	900.00
b.		Surcharge tete beche pair	*2,600.*	*2,000.*
11	A1(b)	½p on half of 1p	72.50	42.50
a.		Surch. reading downward	72.50	42.50
b.		Double surcharge	900.00	
12	A1(c)	½p on half of 1p (R)	40.00	20.00
a.		Inverted surcharge	1,150.	550.00
b.		Double surcharge	1,850.	750.00
		Nos. 10-12 (3)	352.50	120.00

The existence of genuine examples of No. 10b has been questioned.

Nos. 8 and 9 Surcharged in Black

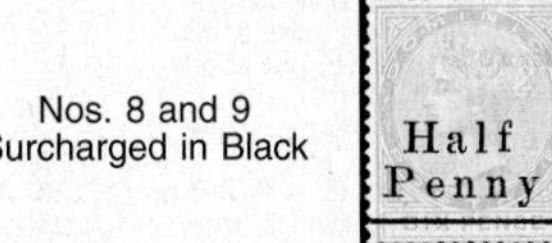

1886

13	A1	½p on 6p green	13.00	15.00
14	A1	1p on 6p green	*45,000.*	*12,500.*
15	A1	1p on 1sh	24.00	*22.00*
a.		Double surcharge	11,500.	4,250.

All examples of No. 14 may have small pin marks which may have been part of the surcharging process.

1883-89 Wmk. 2

16	A1	½p bister ('83)	7.50	*11.50*
17	A1	½p green ('86)	6.00	*5.75*
18	A1	1p violet ('86)	60.00	16.00
a.		Half used as ½p on cover		2,350.
19	A1	1p dp carmine ('89)	5.75	*15.00*
a.		1p rose ('87)	19.00	*28.00*
b.		Vert. half used as ½p on cover		2,100.
20	A1	2½p red brn ('84)	160.00	5.00
21	A1	2½p ultra ('88)	4.25	*9.00*
22	A1	4p gray ('86)	9.00	*7.75*
23	A1	6p orange ('88)	23.00	*92.50*
24	A1	1sh dp lil rose ('88)	200.00	*500.00*
		Nos. 16-24 (9)	475.50	*662.50*

Roseau, Capital of Dominica — A6

King Edward VII — A7

1903 Wmk. 1 *Perf. 14*
Ordinary Paper

25	A6	½p gray green	5.25	4.75
26	A6	1p car & black	17.50	.80
27	A6	2p brn & gray grn	6.00	*8.00*
28	A6	2½p ultra & blk	13.00	5.25
29	A6	3p black & vio	11.50	4.50
30	A6	6p org brn & blk	15.00	*22.50*
31	A6	1sh gray grn & red vio	42.50	*52.50*
32	A6	2sh red vio & blk	40.00	*35.00*
33	A6	2sh6p ocher & gray grn	23.00	*92.50*
34	A7	5sh brown & blk	125.00	*175.00*
		Nos. 25-34 (10)	298.75	*400.80*

Nos. 25 to 29 and 31 are on both ordinary and chalky paper. For detailed listings, see the *Scott Classic Specialized Catalogue of Stamps & Covers.*

1907-20 Chalky Paper Wmk. 3

35	A6	½p gray green	15.00	11.00
36	A6	1p car & black	2.50	.55
37	A6	2p brn & gray grn	16.00	*24.00*
38	A6	2½p ultra & black	5.50	27.50
39	A6	3p black & vio	5.00	*20.00*
40	A6	3p vio, *yel,* chalky paper ('09)	3.75	*5.25*
41	A6	6p org brn & blk ('08)	65.00	*100.00*
42	A6	6p vio & dl vio, chalky paper ('09)	12.50	*19.00*
43	A6	1sh gray grn & red vio	4.75	*67.50*
44	A6	1sh blk, *green,* chalky paper ('10)	3.75	5.00
45	A6	2sh red vio & blk ('08)	30.00	*40.00*
46	A6	2sh ultra & vio, *bl* ('19)	32.50	*110.00*
47	A6	2sh6p ocher & gray grn ('08)	27.50	*75.00*
48	A6	2sh6p red & blk, *bl* ('20)	32.50	*125.00*
49	A7	5sh brn & blk ('08)	75.00	75.00
		Nos. 35-49 (15)	331.25	*704.80*

Nos. 40, 42 and 44 are on both ordinary and chalky paper. For detailed listings, see the *Scott Classic Specialized Catalogue of Stamps & Covers.*

For type surcharged see No. 55.

1908-09 Ordinary Paper

50	A6	½p green	9.50	6.25
51	A6	1p scarlet	2.00	.75
a.		1p carmine	4.50	.45
52	A6	2p gray ('09)	5.00	*17.50*
53	A6	2½p ultramarine	9.50	*9.75*
a.		2½p bright blue ('18)	5.75	*10.50*
		Nos. 50-53 (4)	26.00	*34.25*

King George V — A8

1914 Chalky Paper *Perf. 14*

54	A8	5sh grn & scar, *yel*	70.00	*100.00*

Type of 1903 Surcharged

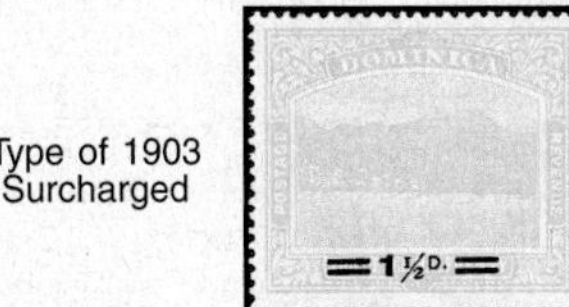

1920

55	A6	1½p on 2½p orange	8.25	4.75

1921 Ordinary Paper Wmk. 4

56	A6	½p green	3.50	*25.00*
57	A6	1p rose red	3.00	*4.00*
58	A6	1½p orange	4.75	*21.00*
59	A6	2p gray	4.25	*4.00*
60	A6	2½p ultra	3.25	*17.50*
61	A6	6p vio & dl vio	5.00	*50.00*
62	A6	2sh ultra & vio, *bl*	50.00	*145.00*
63	A6	2sh6p red & blk, *bl*	45.00	*165.00*
		Nos. 56-63 (8)	118.75	*431.50*

No. 61 is on chalky paper.

Seal of Colony and George V — A9

1923-33 Chalky Paper Wmk. 4

65	A9	½p green & blk	2.50	.85
66	A9	1p violet & blk	7.50	2.25
67	A9	1p scar & black	18.00	1.40
68	A9	1½p car & black	6.75	.90
69	A9	1½p dp brn & blk	15.50	.95
70	A9	2p gray & black	4.50	.65
71	A9	2½p org & black	4.50	*10.00*
72	A9	2½p ultra & black	7.75	2.25
73	A9	3p ultra & black	4.50	*19.00*
74	A9	3p red & blk, *yel*	4.75	1.40
75	A9	4p brown & blk	5.25	*7.25*
76	A9	6p red vio & blk	5.50	*9.00*
77	A9	1sh blk, *emerald*	3.50	*4.25*
78	A9	2sh ultra & blk, *bl*	26.00	*40.00*
79	A9	2sh6p red & blk, *bl*	27.50	*40.00*
80	A9	3sh vio & blk, *yel*	4.50	*15.00*
81	A9	4sh red & blk, *emer*	23.00	*40.00*
82	A9	5sh grn & blk, *yel*	42.50	*62.50*
		Nos. 65-82 (18)	214.00	*257.65*

Issue years: Nos. 80, 82, 1927; Nos. 72, 74, 1928; Nos. 67, 69, 1933; others, 1923.

Many values of this set are known with a forged G.P.O. cancellation dated "MY 19 27".

1923 Wmk. 3

83	A9	3sh vio & blk, *yel*	5.75	*72.50*
84	A9	5sh grn & blk, *yel*	10.00	*65.00*
85	A9	£1 vio & blk, *red*	240.00	*375.00*
		Nos. 83-85 (3)	255.75	*512.50*

Common Design Types pictured following the introduction.

Silver Jubilee Issue
Common Design Type
Perf. 13½x14

1935, May 6 Wmk. 4 Engr.

90	CD301	1p car & blue	1.60	.35
91	CD301	1½p gray blk & ultra	5.75	3.25
92	CD301	2½p blue & brn	5.75	*4.75*
93	CD301	1sh brt vio & ind	5.75	*11.50*
		Nos. 90-93 (4)	18.85	19.85
		Set, never hinged	27.50	

Coronation Issue
Common Design Type

1937, May 12 *Perf. 11x11½*

94	CD302	1p dark carmine	.25	.25
95	CD302	1½p brown	.25	.25
96	CD302	2½p deep ultra	.35	*1.90*
		Nos. 94-96 (3)	.85	2.40
		Set, never hinged	1.50	

Fresh-Water Lake — A10

Layou River — A11

Picking Limes — A12

Boiling Lake — A13

1938-47 Wmk. 4 *Perf. 12½*

97	A10	½p grn & red brn	.25	.25
98	A11	1p car & gray	.25	.25
99	A12	1½p rose vio & grn	.25	*.75*
100	A13	2p brn blk & dp rose	.35	*2.25*
101	A12	2½p ultra & rose vio	.25	*2.25*
a.		2½p bl & rose vio	2.75	1.90
102	A11	3p red brn & ol	.25	*.60*
103	A12	3½p red vio & brt ultra	1.00	*2.10*
104	A10	6p vio & yel grn	.50	*1.60*
105	A10	7p org brn & grn	1.00	*1.60*
106	A13	1sh olive & vio	2.50	1.60
107	A11	2sh red vio & blk	4.50	*12.50*
108	A10	2sh6p scar ver & blk	10.00	5.75
109	A11	5sh dk brn & bl	8.00	*12.00*
110	A13	10sh dl org & blk	10.00	*22.50*
		Nos. 97-110 (14)	39.10	*66.00*
		Set, never hinged	80.00	

Issued: No. 101, 8/42; 3½p, 7p, 2sh, 10sh, 10/15/47; others, 8/15/38.

King George VI — A14

1940, Apr. 15 Photo. ***Perf. 14½x14***
111 A14 ¼p brown violet 1.00 *.25*
a. Ordinary paper ('42) .25 *1.50*

No. 111 is on chalky paper.

Catalogue values for unused stamps in this section, from this point to the end of the section, are for Never Hinged items.

Peace Issue
Common Design Type

1946, Oct. 14 Engr. ***Perf. 13½x14***
112 CD303 1p carmine .25 .25
113 CD303 3½p deep blue .25 .25

Silver Wedding Issue
Common Design Types

1948, Dec. 1 Photo. ***Perf. 14x14½***
114 CD304 1p scarlet .25 .25

Engraved; Name Typographed
Perf. 11½x11
115 CD305 10sh orange brn 25.00 *32.50*

UPU Issue
Common Design Types

Engr.: Name Typo. on 6c and 12c
1949, Oct. 10 ***Perf. 13½, 11x11½***
116 CD306 5c blue .25 .25
117 CD307 6c chocolate 1.25 *3.00*
118 CD308 12c rose violet .50 *2.10*
119 CD309 24c olive .30 .30
Nos. 116-119 (4) 2.30 5.65

University Issue
Common Design Types

1951, Feb. 16 Engr. ***Perf. 14x14½***
120 CD310 3c purple & green .60 *1.25*
121 CD311 12c dp car & dk bl grn .80 .50

George VI
A15

Drying Cocoa
A16

Picking Oranges — A17

Designs: 2c and 60c, Carib Baskets. 3c and 48c, Lime Plantation. 4c, Picking Oranges. 5c, Bananas. 6c, Botanical Gardens. 8c, Drying Vanilla Beans. 12c and $1.20, Fresh Water Lake. 14c, Layou River. 24c, Boiling Lake.

Perf. 14½x14
1951, July 1 Photo. Wmk. 4
122 A15 ½c brown .25 .25

Perf. 13x13½
Engr.
123 A16 1c red org & blk .25 .30
124 A16 2c dp grn & red brn .25 .25
125 A16 3c red vio & bl grn .25 *3.50*
126 A16 4c dk brn & brn org .75 *3.75*
127 A16 5c rose red & blk .85 .30
128 A16 6c org brn & ol grn 1.00 .30
129 A16 8c dp bl & dp grn 3.00 1.75
130 A16 12c emer & gray .75 *1.25*
131 A16 14c pur & blue 1.25 *3.50*
132 A16 24c rose car & red vio 1.00 .40
133 A16 48c red org & bl grn 5.00 *13.50*
134 A16 60c gray & car 4.00 *9.25*
135 A16 $1.20 gray & emer 8.25 *7.25*

Perf. 13½x13
136 A17 $2.40 gray & org 30.00 *52.50*
Nos. 122-136 (15) 56.85 *98.05*

Nos. 125, 127, 129 and 131 Overprinted in Black or Carmine

1951, Oct. 15 ***Perf. 13x13½***
137 A16 3c red vio & bl green .25 *.60*
138 A16 5c rose red & black .25 *1.75*
139 A16 8c dp blue & dp grn (C) .30 .25
140 A16 14c purple & blue (C) 1.75 .30
Nos. 137-140 (4) 2.55 2.90

Adoption of a new constitution for the Windward Islands, 1951.

Coronation Issue
Common Design Type

1953, June 2 Engr. ***Perf. 13½x13***
141 CD312 2c dk green & black .40 .40

Types of 1951 with Portrait of Queen Elizabeth II

1954, Oct. 1 Photo. ***Perf. 14½x14***
142 A15 ½c brown .25 1.25

Perf. 13x13½
Engr.
143 A16 1c red org & blk .25 .30
144 A16 2c dp grn & red brn 1.10 *2.00*
145 A16 3c red vio & bl grn 1.50 .40
146 A16 4c dk brn & brn org .25 .30
147 A16 5c rose red & blk 2.75 1.00
148 A16 6c org brn & ol grn .55 .30
149 A16 8c dp bl & dp grn 1.50 .30
150 A16 12c emer & gray .60 .25
151 A16 14c pur & bl .45 .25
152 A16 24c rose car & red vio .55 .30
153 A16 48c red org & bl grn 2.75 *11.00*
154 A16 60c gray & car 3.50 1.50
155 A16 $1.20 gray & emer 22.50 7.00

Perf. 13½x13
156 A17 $2.40 gray & org 22.50 14.00
Nos. 142-156 (15) 61.00 40.15

Mat Making — A18

5c, Canoe making. 10c, Bananas.

1957, Oct. 15 Wmk. 4 ***Perf. 13x13½***
157 A18 3c car rose & black 4.00 2.50
158 A18 5c brown & blue 12.00 1.10
159 A18 10c redsh brn & brt grn 6.00 3.25
160 A18 48c violet & brown 3.25 2.75
Nos. 157-160 (4) 25.25 9.60

West Indies Federation
Common Design Type
Perf. 11½x11

1958, Apr. 22 Wmk. 314
161 CD313 3c green .50 .35
162 CD313 6c blue .60 *1.10*
163 CD313 12c car rose .85 .40
Nos. 161-163 (3) 1.95 1.85

Sailing Canoe — A19

Traditional Costume — A20

Designs: 1c, Seashore, Rosalie. 2c, 5c, Queen Elizabeth II by Annigoni. 4c, Sulphur Springs. 6c, Road making. 8c, Dugout canoe. 10c, Frog (mountain chicken). 12c, Boats and Scotts Head. 15c, Bananas. 24c, Imperial parrot. 48c, View of Goodwill. 60c, Cacao tree. $1.20, Coat of Arms. $2.40, Trafalgar Falls. $4.80, Coconut palm.

Two types of 14c:
I — Mountain light violet. Girl's eyes look straight out.
II — Mountain blue. Eyes look sideways.

Perf. 14½x14, 14x14½
1963, May 16 Photo. Wmk. 314
164 A19 1c bl, brn & grn .25 *.90*
165 A20 2c ultramarine .30 .25
166 A19 3c lt ultra & blk 1.50 1.10
167 A19 4c sl, grn & brn .25 .25
168 A20 5c magenta .30 .25
169 A19 6c lt grn, vio & buff .25 .50
170 A19 8c tan, blk & lt grn .30 .25
171 A19 10c pink & brn .25 .25
172 A19 12c bl, blk, grn & brn .90 .25
173 A20 14c multi (II) 2.50 2.50
a. Type I .90 .30
174 A19 15c grn, yel & brn 1.25 .25
175 A20 24c multicolored 8.50 .25
176 A19 48c bl, blk & grn .90 .90
177 A19 60c blk, grn, org & brn 1.00 .75
178 A19 $1.20 multicolored 6.25 1.60
179 A20 $2.40 grn, bl, brn & blk 4.75 4.00
180 A20 $4.80 bl, brn & grn 20.00 *30.00*
Nos. 164-180 (17) 49.45 44.25

For overprints see Nos. 211-232.

1966-67 Wmk. 314 Sideways
167a A19 4c ('67) 1.25 .90
169a A19 6c .25 .80
170a A19 8c .45 .90
171a A19 10c ('67) .70 .95
174a A19 15c ('67) .85 1.50
Nos. 167a-174a (5) 3.50 5.05

Freedom from Hunger Issue
Common Design Type

1963, June 4 ***Perf. 14x14½***
181 CD314 15c lilac .30 .30

Red Cross Centenary Issue
Common Design Type
Wmk. 314

1963, Sept. 2 Litho. ***Perf. 13***
182 CD315 5c black & red .25 .25
183 CD315 15c ultra & red .45 *.80*

Shakespeare Issue
Common Design Type

1964, Apr. 23 Photo. ***Perf. 14x14½***
184 CD316 15c lilac rose .35 .35

ITU Issue
Common Design Type

1965, May 17 Litho. ***Perf. 11x11½***
185 CD317 2c emerald & blue .25 .25
186 CD317 48c grnsh blue & slate .30 .30

Intl. Cooperation Year Issue
Common Design Type

1965, Oct. 25 ***Perf. 14½***
187 CD318 1c blue grn & claret .25 .25
188 CD318 15c lt violet & grn .30 .30

Churchill Memorial Issue
Common Design Type

1966, Jan. 24 Photo. ***Perf. 14***
Design in Black, Gold and Carmine Rose
189 CD319 1c bright blue .25 .25
a. Gold omitted *2,000.*
190 CD319 5c green .25 .25
191 CD319 15c brown .30 .30
192 CD319 24c violet .35 .35
Nos. 189-192 (4) 1.15 1.15

Royal Visit Issue
Common Design Type

1966, Feb. 4 Litho. ***Perf. 11x12***
193 CD320 5c violet blue .75 .25
194 CD320 15c dk car rose 2.25 .35

World Cup Soccer Issue
Common Design Type

1966, July 1 Litho. ***Perf. 14***
195 CD321 5c multicolored .35 .25
196 CD321 24c multicolored .85 .50

WHO Headquarters Issue
Common Design Type

1966, Sept. 20 Litho. ***Perf. 14***
197 CD322 5c multicolored .25 .25
198 CD322 24c multicolored .50 .50

UNESCO Anniversary Issue
Common Design Type

1966, Dec. 1 Litho. ***Perf. 14***
199 CD323 5c "Education" .35 .25
200 CD323 15c "Science" .45 .25
201 CD323 24c "Culture" .80 .25
Nos. 199-201 (3) 1.60 .75

Carib, Negro and Caucasian Children — A21

10c, Columbus' ship Santa Maria & banderol. 15c, Hands with banderol. 24c, Belaire dancers.

Perf. 14½x14
1967, Nov. 3 Photo. Wmk. 314
202 A21 5c multicolored .25 .25
203 A21 10c multicolored .25 .25
204 A21 15c multicolored .25 .25
205 A21 24c multicolored .25 .25
Nos. 202-205 (4) 1.00 1.00

Issued for National Day, Nov. 3.

John F. Kennedy and Human Rights Flame — A22

Human Rights Flame and: 10c, Cecil E. A. Rawle (1891-1938), Dominican crusader for human rights. 12c, Pope John XXIII. 48c, Florence Nightingale. 60c, Dr. Albert Schweitzer.

Wmk. 314 Sideways
1968, Apr. 20 Litho. ***Perf. 14***
206 A22 1c multicolored .25 .25
207 A22 10c multicolored .25 .25
208 A22 12c multicolored .25 .25
209 A22 48c multicolored .25 .25
210 A22 60c multicolored .25 .25
Nos. 206-210 (5) 1.25 1.25

International Human Rights Year.

Stamps and Types of 1963-67 Overprinted in Silver or Black: "ASSOCIATED / STATEHOOD"

Perf. 14½x14, 14x14½
1968, July 8 Photo. Wmk. 314
211 A19 1c multi .25 .25
212 A20 2c ultra .25 .25
213 A19 3c lt ultra & blk .25 .25
214 A19 4c multi .25 .25
215 A20 5c magenta .25 .25
216 A19 6c multi (B) .25 .25
217 A19 8c multi (B) .25 .25
218 A19 10c pink & brn .55 .25
219 A19 12c multi .25 *.50*
a. Watermark upright .25 .25
220 A20 14c multi (II) .25 .25
221 A19 15c multi .25 .25
222 A20 24c multi 4.00 .25
223 A19 48c multi .55 *2.25*
a. Watermark upright .50 *1.00*
224 A19 60c multi (B) .90 .75
225 A19 $1.20 multi (B) 1.00 *3.00*
226 A20 $2.40 multi 1.00 *2.25*
227 A20 $4.80 multi 1.25 8.00
Nos. 211-227 (17) 11.75 19.50

In this set, overprint was applied to 2c, 3c, 12c, 14c, 24c, 48c, 60c, $1.20, $2.40 and $4.80 with watermark upright. A reprinting of the 1c, 4c, 6c, 8c, 10c, 12c, No. 219, 15c and 48c, No. 223 on paper with watermark sideways was made. Same value.

Nos. 164-166, 173 and 178 Overprinted: "NATIONAL DAY / 3 NOVEMBER 1968"

Perf. 14½x14, 14x14½
1968, Nov. 3 Photo. Wmk. 314
228 A19 1c blue, brn & grn .25 .25
229 A20 2c ultra .25 .25
230 A19 3c lt ultra & blk .25 .25
231 A20 14c multi (I) .25 .25
232 A19 $1.20 multicolored .55 .55
Nos. 228-232 (5) 1.55 1.55

A23

No. 233: a, 3 soccer players; b, Soccer player, goalie. No. 234: a, Swimmers at start; b, Divers. No. 235: a, Javelin thrower, hurdlers; b, Hurdlers. No. 236: a, Basketball; b, 3 basketball players.

Perf. 11½

1968, Nov. 23 Unwmk. Litho.

233 A23 1c Pair, #a-b .25 .25
234 A23 5c Pair, #a-b .25 .25
235 A23 48c Pair, #a-b .50 .50
236 A23 60c Pair, #a-b 1.40 1.40
Nos. 233-236 (4) 2.40 2.40

19th Olympic Games, Mexico City, 10/12-27.

The Small Cowper Madonna, by Raphael A24

Perf. 12½x12

1968, Dec. 23 Photo. Unwmk.

241 A24 5c multicolored .30 .30

Christmas. No. 241 printed in sheets of 20. Sheets of 6 (3x2) exist containing two each of 12c, 24c, and $1.20 stamps, each picturing a different madonna painting. Value $6.

Venus and Adonis, by Rubens — A25

Paintings: 15c, The Death of Socrates, by Louis Jacques David. 24c, Christ at Emmaus, by Velazquez. 50c, Pilate Washing his Hands, by Rembrandt.

Perf. 14½x15

1969, Jan. 30 Litho. Wmk. 314

242 A25 5c lilac & multi .25 .25
243 A25 15c emerald & multi .25 .25
244 A25 24c lt blue & multi .25 .25
245 A25 50c crimson & multi .45 .45
Nos. 242-245 (4) 1.20 1.20

20th anniv. (in 1968) of the WHO.

Citrus Fruit Picker — A26

No. 247, Woman and child. No. 248, Hotel. No. 249, Red-necked parrots. No. 250, Calypso band. No. 251, Women dancers. No. 252, Tropical fish and coelenterates. No. 253, Diver and turtle.

1969, Mar. 10 *Perf. 14½*

246 A26 10c multicolored .25 .25
247 A26 10c multicolored .25 .25
a. Pair, #246-247 .25 .25
248 A26 12c multicolored .25 .25
249 A26 12c multicolored .25 .25
a. Pair, #248-249 .25 .25
250 A26 24c multicolored .25 .25
251 A26 24c multicolored .25 .25
a. Pair, #250-251 .50 .50
252 A26 48c multicolored .65 .65
253 A26 48c multicolored .65 .65
a. Pair, #252-253 1.30 1.30
Nos. 246-253 (8) 2.80 2.80

Tourist publicity.

Spinning, by Millet, Flags and ILO Emblem — A27

50th anniv. of the ILO (Etchings by Jean F. Millet, Flags and ILO Emblem): 30c, Threshing. 30c, Flax pulling.

1969, July Unwmk. *Perf. 13½*

254 A27 15c multicolored .25 .25
255 A27 30c multicolored .30 .30
256 A27 38c multicolored .30 .30
Nos. 254-256 (3) .85 .85

"Strength in Unity," Bananas and Cacao A28

"Strength in Unity" Emblem and: 8c, Map of Dominica and Hawker Siddeley 748. 12c, Map of Caribbean. 24c, Ships in harbor.

1969, July Litho.

257 A28 5c orange & multi .30 .30
258 A28 8c gray & multi .30 .30
259 A28 12c lilac & multi .30 .30
260 A28 24c lt blue & multi .30 .30
Nos. 257-260 (4) 1.20 1.20

Caribbean Free Trade Area (CARIFTA).

Gandhi at Spinning Wheel and Big Ben, London A29

38c, Gandhi, Nehru and Fatehpur Sikri Mausoleum. $1.20, Gandhi & Taj Mahal.

1969, Oct. Litho. *Perf. 14½*

261 A29 6c multicolored .55 .25
262 A29 38c multicolored .75 .25
263 A29 $1.20 multicolored .85 .85
Nos. 261-263 (3) 2.15 1.35

Mohandas K. Gandhi (1869-1948), leader in India's fight for independence. "Gandhi" is misspelled "Ghandi" on Nos. 261-263.

St. Joseph — A30

Stained Glass Windows, from 17th Century French Churches: 8c, St. John. 12c, St. Peter. 60c, St. Paul.

1969, Nov. 10 Litho. *Perf. 14*

264 A30 6c black & multi .25 .25
265 A30 8c black & multi .25 .25
266 A30 12c black & multi .25 .25
267 A30 60c black & multi .40 .40
Nos. 264-267 (4) 1.15 1.15

National Day, Nov. 3. Issued in sheets of 16 (4x4) with control numbers and 4 tabs with a patriotic poem by W. O. M. Pond.

Queen Elizabeth II — A31

Purplethroated Carib (Hummingbird) — A32

2c, Poinsettia. 3c, Red-necked pigeon. 4c, Imperial parrot. 5c, Swallowtail butterfly. 6c, Brown Julia butterfly. 8c, Banana shipment. 10c, Portsmouth Harbor. 12c, Copra processing plant. 15c, Women with straw work. 25c, Timber plant. 30c, Mining pumice. 38c, Cricket, Grammar School. 50c, Roman Catholic Cathedral. 60c, Government headquarters. $1.20, Melville Hall Airport. $2.40, Coat of Arms. $4.80, Queen Elizabeth II.

Perf. 13½

1969, Nov. 26 Unwmk. Photo.

Chalky Paper

268 A31 ½c silver & multi .25 *1.50*
269 A32 1c yellow & multi .75 *2.00*
270 A32 2c yellow & multi .25 .25
271 A32 3c yellow & multi 2.50 2.50
272 A32 4c yellow & multi 2.50 2.50
273 A32 5c yellow & multi 2.50 2.50
274 A32 6c brown & multi 2.00 *3.50*
275 A32 8c brown & multi .25 .25
276 A32 10c yellow & multi .25 .25
277 A32 12c citron & multi .25 .25
278 A32 15c blue & multi .25 .25
279 A32 25c pink & multi .40 .25
280 A32 30c olive & multi 1.50 .25
281 A32 38c multicolored 8.50 1.75
282 A32 50c brown & multi .65 .65

Wmk. Rectangles (334)

Perf. 14

Size: 38x26mm, 26x38mm

283 A32 60c yel & multi 1.00 *1.50*
284 A32 $1.20 yel & multi 2.00 2.00
285 A32 $2.40 gold & multi 1.50 *4.00*
286 A31 $4.80 gold & multi 3.00 *7.50*
Nos. 268-286 (19) 30.30 *33.65*

1972 On glazed Paper

268a A31 ½c silver & multi .30 *2.00*
269a A32 1c yellow & multi 1.40 *1.50*
270a A32 2c yellow & multi .50 .50
271a A32 3c yellow & multi 3.00 1.50
272a A32 4c yellow & multi 3.00 1.50
273a A32 5c yellow & multi 2.75 1.25
274a A32 6c brown & multi 2.75 2.75
275a A32 8c brown & multi .45 *.60*
276a A32 10c yellow & multi .35 .25
277a A32 12c citron & multi .35 .25
278a A32 15c blue & multi .35 .30
279a A32 25c pink & multi .30 .25
280a A32 30c olive & multi 1.50 .65
281a A32 38c multicolored 8.00 *14.00*
282a A32 50c brown & multi .85 *1.25*
Nos. 268a-282a (15) 25.85 *28.55*

Madonna and Child, by Filippino Lippi — A33

Paintings: 10c, Holy Family with Lamb, by Raphael. 15c, Virgin and Child, by Perugino. $1.20, Madonna of the Rose Hedge, by Botticelli.

Perf. 14½

1969, Dec. Unwmk. Litho.

287 A33 6c lt blue & multi .25 .25
288 A33 10c multicolored .25 .25
289 A33 15c lilac & multi .25 .25
290 A33 $1.20 lt grn & multi .25 .25
a. Souvenir sheet of 2 1.25 1.25
Nos. 287-290 (4) 1.00 1.00

Christmas. No. 290a contains 2 imperf. stamps with simulated perforations similar to Nos. 289-290.

Neil A. Armstrong, First Man on the Moon — A34

Designs: 5c, American flag and astronauts on moon. 8c, Astronauts collecting moon rocks. 30c, Landing module, moon and earth. 50c, Memorial tablet left on moon. 60c, Astronauts Armstrong, Aldrin and Collins.

1970, Feb. 2 Litho. *Perf. 12½*

291 A34 ½c lilac & multi .25 .25
292 A34 5c lt blue & multi .25 .25
293 A34 8c orange & multi .25 .25
294 A34 30c blue & multi .25 .25
295 A34 50c red brn & multi .40 .30
296 A34 60c rose & multi .50 .45
a. Souvenir sheet of 4 2.60 2.60
Nos. 291-296 (6) 1.90 1.75

See note after US No. C76. No. 296a contains 4 stamps similar to Nos. 293-296, but imperf. with simulated perforations.

Giant Green Turtle — A35

Designs: 24c, Flying fish. 38c, Anthurium lily. 60c, Imperial and red-necked parrots.

1970, Sept. 6 Litho. *Perf. 13½x13*

297 A35 6c lt green & multi .50 .50
298 A35 24c multicolored .65 .65
299 A35 38c green & multi .75 .75
300 A35 60c yellow & multi 3.50 3.50
a. Souvenir sheet of 4, #297-300 8.50 8.50
Nos. 297-300 (4) 5.40 5.40

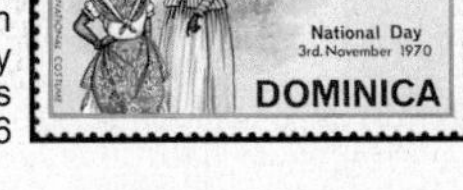

Women in 18th Century Dress A36

Natl. Day: 8c, Carib mace & wife leader, 18th cent. $1, Map & flag of Dominica.

1970, Nov. 3 Litho. *Perf. 14*

301 A36 5c yellow & multi .25 .25
302 A36 8c green & multi .25 .25
303 A36 $1 lt blue & multi .40 .40
a. Souv. sheet of 3, #301-303 + 3 labels 1.25 *1.50*
Nos. 301-303 (3) .90 .90

Marley's Ghost — A37

Designs (from A Christmas Carol, by Dickens): 15c, Fezziwig's Ball. 24c, Scrooge and his Nephew's Christmas Party. $1.20, The Ghost of Christmas Present.

1970, Nov. 23 Litho. *Perf. 14x14½*

304 A37 2c blue & multi .25 .25
305 A37 15c multicolored .25 .25
306 A37 24c red & multi .25 .25
307 A37 $1.20 multicolored .75 .75
a. Souvenir sheet of 4, #304-307 2.75 2.75
Nos. 304-307 (4) 1.50 1.50

Christmas; Charles Dickens (1812-1870).

Hands and Red Cross A38

Designs: 8c, The Doctor, by Sir Luke Fildes. 15c, Dominica flag and Red Cross. 50c, The Sick Child, by Edvard Munch.

1970, Dec. 28 ***Perf. 14½x14***

308 A38 8c multicolored .25 .25
309 A38 10c multicolored .25 .25
310 A38 15c multicolored .25 .25
311 A38 50c multicolored .50 .50
a. Souvenir sheet of 4, #308-311 2.00 2.00
Nos. 308-311 (4) 1.25 1.25

Centenary of the British Red Cross Society.

Marigot Primary School — A39

Education Year Emblem and: 8c, Goodwill Junior High School. 14c, University of the West Indies. $1, Trinity College, Cambridge, England.

1971, Mar. 1 **Litho.** ***Perf. 13½***

312 A39 5c multicolored .25 .25
313 A39 8c multicolored .25 .25
314 A39 14c multicolored .25 .25
315 A39 $1 multicolored .45 .45
a. Souvenir sheet of 2, #314-315 1.50 1.50
Nos. 312-315 (4) 1.20 1.20

International Education Year.

Waterfall and Bird-of-Paradise Flower — A40

Tourist Publicity: 10c, Boat building. 30c, Sailboat along North Coast. 50c, Speed boat and steamer.

1971, Mar. 22 ***Perf. 13½x14***

316 A40 5c multicolored .25 .25
317 A40 10c multicolored .25 .25
318 A40 30c multicolored .25 .25
319 A40 50c multicolored .35 .35
a. Souvenir sheet of 4, #316-319 1.10 1.10
Nos. 316-319 (4) 1.10 1.10

UNICEF Emblem, Letter "D" A41

1971, June 14 **Litho.** ***Perf. 14***

320 A41 5c multicolored .25 .25
321 A41 10c multicolored .25 .25
322 A41 38c multicolored .25 .25
323 A41 $1.20 multicolored .25 .25
a. Souvenir sheet of 2, #321, 323 .85 .85
Nos. 320-323 (4) 1.00 1.00

25th anniv. of UNICEF.

Boy Scout, Jamboree Emblem, Torii, Camp and Mt. Fuji — A42

24c, British Scout, flag. 30c, Japanese Scout, flag. $1, Dominican Scout, flag.

1971, Oct. 18 **Unwmk.** ***Perf. 11***

324 A42 20c bister & multi .25 .25
325 A42 24c green & multi .30 .30
326 A42 30c red lilac & multi .40 .40
327 A42 $1 blue & multi .80 .80
a. Souvenir sheet of 2, #326-327 1.75 1.75
Nos. 324-327 (4) 1.75 1.75

13th Boy Scout World Jamboree, Asagiri Plain, Japan, Aug. 2-10.

Boats at Portsmouth — A43

15c, Carnival street scene. 20c, $1.20, Anthea Mondesire, Carifta Queen. 50c, Rock of Atkinson.

Perf. 13½x14, 14x13½

1971, Nov. 15 **Litho.**

328 A43 8c multi .25 .25
329 A43 15c multi .25 .25
330 A43 20c multi, vert. .25 .25
331 A43 50c multi, vert. .25 .25
Nos. 328-331 (4) 1.00 1.00

Souvenir Sheet

Perf. 15

332 A43 $1.20 multi, vert. .85 .85

National Day.

First Dominica Coin, 8 Reals, 1761 — A44

Early Dominica Coins: 30c, Eleven and 3-bit pieces, 1798. 35c, Two-real coin, 1770, vert. 50c, Three "mocos" and piece of 8, 1798.

1972, Feb. 7 **Litho.** ***Perf. 14***

333 A44 10c violet, silver & blk .25 .25
334 A44 30c green, silver & blk .25 .25
335 A44 35c ultra, silver & blk .25 .25
336 A44 50c red, silver & blk .25 .25
a. Souvenir sheet of 2, #335-336 1.00 1.00
Nos. 333-336 (4) 1.00 1.00

Margin of No. 336a inscribed "Christmas 1971."

Common Opossum, Environment Emblem — A45

Environment Emblem and: 35c, Agouti. 60c, Oncidium papillo (orchid). $1.20, Hibiscus.

1972, June 5

337 A45 ½c yel grn & multi .25 .25
338 A45 35c org brn & multi .30 .30
339 A45 60c lt blue & multi 2.25 2.25
340 A45 $1.20 yellow & multi 1.75 1.75
a. Souvenir sheet of 4, #337-340 6.75 6.75
Nos. 337-340 (4) 4.55 4.55

UN Conf. on Human Environment, Stockholm, June 5-16.

100-meter Sprint, Olympic Rings — A46

Olympic Rings and: 35m, 400-meter hurdles. 58c, Hammer throw, vert. 72c, Broad jump, vert.

1972, Oct. 9 **Litho.** ***Perf. 14***

341 A46 30c dp org & multi .25 .25
342 A46 35c blue & multi .25 .25
343 A46 58c lilac rose & multi .30 .30
344 A46 72c yel green & multi .40 .40
a. Souv. sheet, #343-344, perf. 15 1.25 1.25
Nos. 341-344 (4) 1.20 1.20

20th Olympic Games, Munich, Aug. 26-Sept. 11.

General Post Office — A47

1972, Nov. 1 ***Perf. 13½***

345 A47 10c shown .25 .25
346 A47 20c Morne Diablotin Mountain .25 .25
347 A47 30c Rodney's Rock .25 .25
a. Souv. sheet, #346-347, perf. 15 .60 .60
Nos. 345-347 (3) .75 .75

National Day.

Adoration of the Shepherds, by Caravaggio A48

Paintings: 14c, Madonna and Child, by Rubens. 30c, Madonna and Child, with St. Anne by Orazio Gentileschi. $1, Adoration of the Kings, by Jan Mostaert. (On 8c, painting is mistakenly attributed to Boccaccino, according to Fine Arts Philatelist.)

1972, Dec. 4.

348 A48 8c gold & multi .25 .25
349 A48 14c gold & multi .25 .25
350 A48 30c gold & multi .25 .25
351 A48 $1 gold & multi .35 .35
a. Souvenir sheet of 2 1.10 1.10
Nos. 348-351 (4) 1.10 1.10

Christmas. No. 351a contains one each of Nos. 350-351 with simulated perforations.

Silver Wedding Issue, 1972

Common Design Type

Design: Queen Elizabeth II, Prince Philip, bananas, sisseron parrot.

Perf. 14x14½

1972, Nov. 13 **Photo.** **Wmk. 314**

352 CD324 5c olive & multi .25 .25
353 CD324 $1 multicolored .40 .40

See note after Antigua No. 296.

Launching of Tiros Weather Satellite — A49

1c, Nimbus satellite. 2c, Radiosonde balloon & equipment. 30c, Radarscope. 35c, General circulation of atmosphere. 50c, Picture of hurricane transmitted by satellite. $1, Computer weather map. 30c, 35c, 50c, $1, horiz.

Perf. 14½

1973, July 16 **Unwmk.** **Litho.**

354 A49 ½c black & multi .25 .25
355 A49 1c black & multi .25 .25
356 A49 2c black & multi .25 .25
357 A49 30c black & multi .25 .25
358 A49 35c black & multi .25 .25
359 A49 50c black & multi .30 .30
360 A49 $1 black & multi .55 .55
a. Souvenir sheet of 2, #359-360 1.40 1.40
Nos. 354-360 (7) 2.10 2.10

Intl. meteorological cooperation, cent.

Going to the Hospital A50

WHO Emblem and: 1c, Maternity and infant care. 2c, Inoculation against smallpox. 30c, Emergency service. 35c, Waiting patients. 50c, Examination. $1, Traveling physician.

1973, Aug. 20 **Unwmk.** ***Perf. 14½***

361 A50 ½c lt blue & multi .25 .25
362 A50 1c gray grn & multi .25 .25
363 A50 2c yellow & multi .25 .25
364 A50 30c lt vio & multi .25 .25
365 A50 35c yel grn & multi .30 .30
366 A50 50c multicolored .30 .30
367 A50 $1 bister & multi .45 .45
a. Souvenir sheet of 2, #366-367, perf. 14x14½ 1.25 1.25
Nos. 361-367 (7) 2.05 2.05

WHO, 25th anniv. No. 367a exists perf. 14½.

Cyrique Crab — A51

1973, Oct.

368 A51 ½c shown .25 .25
369 A51 22c Blue land crab .35 .35
370 A51 25c Breadfruit .45 .45
371 A51 $1.20 Sunflower 1.00 1.00
a. Souvenir sheet of 4, #368-371 2.75 2.75
Nos. 368-371 (4) 2.05 2.05

Princess Anne and Mark Phillips — A52

1973, Nov. 14 ***Perf. 13½***

372 A52 25c salmon & multi .25 .25
373 A52 $2 blue & multi .60 .60
a. Souv. sheet of 2 (75c, $1.20) .60 .60

Wedding of Princess Anne and Capt. Mark Phillips.

Nos. 372-373 were issued in sheets of 5 + label. No. 373a contains 2 stamps of type A52: 75c in colors of the 25c, and $1.20 in colors of the $2.

Nativity, by Brueghel A53

Paintings of the Nativity by: 1c, Botticelli. 2c, Dürer. 12c, Botticelli. 22c, Rubens. 35c, Dürer. $1, Giorgione (inscribed "Giorgeone").

1973 Unwmk. Perf. 14½x15

374 A53 ½c gray & multi .25 .25
375 A53 1c gray & multi .25 .25
376 A53 2c gray & multi .25 .25
377 A53 12c gray & multi .25 .25
378 A53 22c gray & multi .25 .25
379 A53 35c gray & multi .25 .25
380 A53 $1 gray & multi .60 .60
a. Souvenir sheet of 2 1.30 1.30
Nos. 374-380 (7) 2.10 2.10

Christmas. No. 380a contains one each of Nos. 379-380 in changed colors.

Carib Basket Weaving — A54

Designs: 10c, Staircase of the Snake. 50c, Miss Caribbean Queen, Kathleen Telemacque, vert. 60c, Miss Carifta Queen, Esther Fadelle, vert. $1, La Jeune Etoille Dancers.

1973, Dec. 17 Perf. 13½x14, 14x13½

381 A54 5c buff & multi .25 .25
382 A54 10c multicolored .25 .25
383 A54 50c multicolored .25 .25
384 A54 60c multicolored .25 .25
385 A54 $1 multicolored .25 .25
a. Souv. sheet of 3, #381-382, 385 .75 .75
Nos. 381-385 (5) 1.25 1.25

National Day.

U.W.I. Center, Dominica — A55

30c, Graduation. $1, University coat of arms.

1974, Jan. 21 Litho. Perf. 13½x14

386 A55 12c dp orange & multi .25 .25
387 A55 30c violet & multi .25 .25
388 A55 $1 multicolored .35 .35
a. Souvenir sheet of 3, #386-388 .50 .50
Nos. 386-388 (3) .85 .85

University of the West Indies, 25th anniv.

Dominica No. 1 and Map of Island A56

Designs: 1c, 50c, No. 8 and post horn. 2c, $1.20, No. 9 and coat of arms. 10c, Like ½c.

1974, May 4 Litho. Perf. 14½

389 A56 ½c brt pur & multi .25 .25
390 A56 1c salmon & multi .25 .25
391 A56 2c ultra & multi .25 .25
392 A56 10c violet & multi .25 .25
393 A56 50c yel grn & multi .40 .40
394 A56 $1.20 rose & multi .65 .65
a. Souv. sheet, #392-394, perf. 15 1.60 1.60
Nos. 389-394 (6) 2.05 2.05

Centenary of Dominican postage stamps.

Soccer Player and Cup, Brazilian Flag — A57

Soccer cup, various players and flags: 1c, Germany, Fed. Rep. 2c, Italy. 30c, Scotland. 40c, Sweden. 50c, Netherlands. $1, Yugoslavia.

1974, July Litho. Perf. 14½

395 A57 ½c shown .25 .25
396 A57 1c multicolored .25 .25
397 A57 2c multicolored .25 .25
398 A57 30c multicolored .25 .25
399 A57 40c multicolored .30 .30
400 A57 50c multicolored .75 .75
401 A57 $1 multicolored 1.10 1.10
a. Souvenir sheet of 2, #400-401, perf. 13½ 1.25 1.25
Nos. 395-401 (7) 3.15 3.15

World Cup Soccer Championship, Munich, June 13-July 7.

Indian Hole A58

40c, Teachers' Training College. $1, Petite Savane Co-operative Bay Oil Distillery.

1974, Nov. 1 Litho. Perf. 13½x14

402 A58 10c multicolored .25 .25
403 A58 40c multicolored .25 .25
404 A58 $1 multicolored .50 .50
a. Souvenir sheet of 3, #402-404 .80 .80
Nos. 402-404 (3) 1.00 1.00

Churchill at Race Track A59

Sir Winston Churchill (1874-1965): 1c, with Gen. Eisenhower. 2c, with Franklin D. Roosevelt. 20c, as First Lord of the Admiralty. 45c, painting outdoors. $2, giving "V" sign.

1974, Nov. 25 Litho. Perf. 14½

405 A59 ½c multicolored .25 .25
406 A59 1c multicolored .25 .25
407 A59 2c multicolored .25 .25
408 A59 20c multicolored .25 .25
409 A59 45c multicolored .25 .25
410 A59 $2 multicolored .50 .50
a. Souvenir sheet of 2, #409-410, perf. 13½ 1.25 1.25
Nos. 405-410 (6) 1.75 1.75

Virgin and Child, by Oronzo Tiso — A60

Paintings (Virgin and Child): 1c, by Lorenzo Costa. 2c, by unknown Master. 10c, by G. F. Romanelli. 25c, Holy Family, by G. S. da Sermoneta. 45c, Adoration of the Shepherds, by Guido Reni. $1, Adoration of the Kings, by Cristoforo Caselli.

1974, Dec. 16 Litho. Perf. 14

411 A60 ½c multicolored .25 .25
412 A60 1c multicolored .25 .25
413 A60 2c multicolored .25 .25
414 A60 10c multicolored .25 .25
415 A60 25c multicolored .25 .25
416 A60 45c multicolored .35 .25
417 A60 $1 multicolored .65 .50
a. Souvenir sheet of 2, #416-417 1.10 1.10
Nos. 411-417 (7) 2.25 2.00

Christmas.

Seamail, "Orinoco," 1851, and "Geesthaven," 1966 — A61

Cent. of UPU: $2, $2.40, Airmail, De Havilland 4, 1918, and Boeing 747, 1974.

1974, Dec. 4 Litho. Perf. 13½

418 A61 10c multicolored .25 .25
419 A61 $2 multicolored 1.25 1.25

Souvenir Sheet

419A Sheet of 2 1.50 1.50
b. A61 $1.20 multicolored .45 .45
c. A61 $2.40 multicolored .90 .90

Nos. 418-419 were each printed in sheets of 50 and 5 + label.

Oldwife A62

1c, Ocyurus chrysurus. 2c, Blue marlin. 3c, Swordfish. 20c, Great barracuda. $2, Grouper.

1975, June 2 Litho. Perf. 14½

421 A62 ½c shown .25 .25
422 A62 1c multicolored .25 .25
423 A62 2c multicolored .25 .25
424 A62 3c multicolored .25 .25
425 A62 20c multicolored .90 .90
426 A62 $2 multicolored 2.75 2.75
a. Souvenir sheet, perf. 13½ 4.00 4.00
Nos. 421-426 (6) 4.65 4.65

Myscelia Antholia A63

Butterflies: 1c, Lycorea ceres. 2c, Siderone nemesis. 6c, Battus polydamas. 30c, Anartia lytrea. 40c, Morpho peleides. $2, Dryas Julia.

1975, July 28 Litho. Perf. 14½

427 A63 ½c shown .25 .25
428 A63 1c multicolored .25 .25
429 A63 2c multicolored .25 .25
430 A63 6c multicolored .75 .75
431 A63 30c multicolored 1.50 1.00
432 A63 40c multicolored 1.50 1.00
433 A63 $2 multicolored 2.25 *6.75*
a. Souvenir sheet, perf. 13½ 4.00 4.00
Nos. 427-433 (7) 6.75 10.25

Royal Mail Ship Yare A64

Ships Tied in with Dominican History: 1c, Royal mail ship Thames. 2c, Canadian National S.S. Lady Nelson. 20c, C.N. S.S. Lady Rodney. 45c, Harrison Line M.V. Statesman. 50c, Geest Line M.V. Geestcape. $2, Geest Line M.V. Geeststar.

1975, Sept. 1 Perf. 14

434 A64 ½c black & multi .40 .35
435 A64 1c black & multi .40 .35
436 A64 2c black & multi .45 .40
437 A64 20c black & multi 1.25 .60
438 A64 45c black & multi 1.50 .80
439 A64 50c black & multi 1.50 1.00
440 A64 $2 black & multi 2.50 *4.50*
a. Souvenir sheet of 2, #439-440 4.00 4.00
Nos. 434-440 (7) 8.00 8.00

IWY Emblem, Farm Women A65

$2, IWY emblem, dressmaker & saleswoman.

1975, Oct. 30 Litho. Perf. 14

441 A65 10c pink & multi .25 .25
442 A65 $2 yellow & multi .65 .65

International Women's Year.

Public Library — A66

5c, Miss Caribbean Queen 1975. 30c, Citrus factory. $1, National Day Cup.

1975, Nov. 6

443 A66 5c multi, vert. .25 .25
444 A66 10c multi .25 .25
445 A66 30c multi .25 .25
446 A66 $1 multi, vert. .40 .40
a. Souvenir sheet of 3 .90 .90
Nos. 443-446 (4) 1.15 1.15

National Day. No. 446a contains 3 stamps similar to Nos. 444-446 with simulated perforations.

Virgin and Child, by Mantegna — A67

Christmas: Paintings of the Virgin and Child.

1975, Nov. 24

447 A67 ½c shown .25 .25
448 A67 1c Fra Filippo Lippi .25 .25
449 A67 2c Bellini .25 .25
450 A67 10c Botticelli .25 .25
451 A67 25c Bellini .25 .25
452 A67 45c Correggio .25 .25
453 A67 $1 Durer .50 .50
a. Souvenir sheet of 2, #452-453 1.25 1.25
Nos. 447-453 (7) 2.00 2.00

Hibiscus A68

Queen Elizabeth II — A69

Designs: 1c, African tulip. 2c, Castor oil tree. 3c, White cedar flower. 4c, Eggplant. 5c, Garfish. 6c, Okra. 8c, Zenaida doves. 10c, Screw pine. 20c, Mangoes. 25c, Crayfish. 30c, Manicou. 40c, Bay leaf groves. 50c, Tomatoes. $1, Lime factory. $2, Rum distillery. $5, Bay oil distillery.

1975, Dec. 8 Litho. *Perf. 14½*

454	A68	½c ultra & multi	.25	*.80*
455	A68	1c lilac & multi	.25	*.80*
456	A68	2c orange & multi	.25	*.80*
457	A68	3c multicolored	.25	*.80*
458	A68	4c pink & multi	.25	*.80*
459	A68	5c multicolored	.25	*.80*
460	A68	6c gray & multi	.25	*1.00*
461	A68	8c multicolored	3.25	1.10
462	A68	10c violet & multi	.25	.25
a.		Perf. 13½	30.00	—
463	A68	20c yellow & multi	.35	.25
464	A68	25c lemon & multi	.40	.25
465	A68	30c salmon & multi	.85	.80
466	A68	40c multicolored	.85	.80
467	A68	50c red & multi	.50	.50
468	A68	$1 citron & multi	.75	.65
469	A68	$2 multicolored	1.30	*3.25*
470	A68	$5 multicolored	1.60	*5.00*

Perf. 14

471	A69	$10 blue & multi	2.25	*14.50*
		Nos. 454-471 (18)	14.10	*33.15*

Nos. 454-465 measure 38½mm x 25mm; nos. 466-470 measure 44½mm x 28mm.

For overprints see Nos. 584-601, 640-643.

All except 3c and 25c exist imperf.

American Infantry — A70

Designs: 1c, English three-decker, 1782. 2c, George Washington. 45c, English sailors. 75c, English ensign with regimental flag. $2, Admiral Hood. All designs have old maps in background.

1976, Apr. 12 Litho. *Perf. 14½*

472	A70	½c green & multi	.25	.25
473	A70	1c purple & multi	.25	.25
474	A70	2c orange & multi	.25	.25
475	A70	45c brown & multi	.45	.25
476	A70	75c ultra & multi	.75	.75
477	A70	$2 red & multi	.90	*1.50*
a.		Souvenir sheet of 2	2.75	*2.75*
		Nos. 472-477 (6)	2.85	3.25

American Bicentennial. No. 477a contains 2 stamps similar to Nos. 476-477, perf. 13.

Rowing — A71

1c, Shot put. 2c, Swimming. 40c, Relay race. 45c, Gymnastics. 60c, Sailing. $2, Archery.

1976, May 24 Litho. *Perf. 14½*

478	A71	½c ocher & multi	.25	.25
479	A71	1c ocher & multi	.25	.25
480	A71	2c ocher & multi	.25	.25
481	A71	40c ocher & multi	.25	.25
482	A71	45c ocher & multi	.25	.25
483	A71	60c ocher & multi	.25	.25
484	A71	$2 ocher & multi	.65	.65
a.		Souv. sheet, #483-484, perf 13	1.75	1.75
		Nos. 478-484 (7)	2.15	2.15

21st Olympic Games, Montreal, Canada, July 17-Aug. 1.

Ringed Kingfisher A72

Birds: 1c, Mourning dove. 2c, Green heron. 15c, Broad-winged hawk. 30c, Blue-headed hummingbird. 45c, Banana-quit. $2, Imperial parrot. 15c, 30c, 45c, $2, vert.

1976, June 28

485	A72	½c multicolored	.25	.25
486	A72	1c multicolored	.25	.25
487	A72	2c multicolored	.25	.25
488	A72	15c multicolored	.90	.90
489	A72	30c multicolored	1.25	1.25
490	A72	45c multicolored	1.50	1.50
491	A72	$2 multicolored	3.00	3.00
a.		Souv. sheet of 3, #489-491, perf. 13	7.00	7.00
		Nos. 485-491 (7)	7.40	7.40

Map of West Indies, Bats, Wicket and Ball A72a

Prudential Cup — A72b

1976, July 26 Litho. *Perf. 14*

492	A72a	15c lt blue & multi	.45	.45
493	A72b	25c lilac rose & black	.85	.85

World Cricket Cup, won by West Indies Team, 1975.

Viking Spacecraft — A73

1c, Titan launch center, horiz. 2c, Titan 3-D & Centaur D-IT. 3c, Orbiter & landing capsule. 45c, Capsule with closed parachute. 75c, Capsule with open parachute. $1, Landing capsule descending on Mars, horiz. $2, Viking on Mars, horiz.

1976, Sept. 20 Litho. *Perf. 15*

494	A73	½c multicolored	.25	.25
495	A73	1c multicolored	.25	.25
496	A73	2c multicolored	.25	.25
497	A73	3c multicolored	.25	.25
498	A73	45c multicolored	.25	.25
499	A73	75c multicolored	.30	.30
500	A73	$1 multicolored	.35	.35
501	A73	$2 multicolored	.60	.60
a.		Souvenir sheet of 2, #500, 501, perf. 13½	1.75	1.75
		Nos. 494-501 (8)	2.50	2.50

Viking mission to Mars.

Virgin and Child, by Giorgione — A74

Virgin and Child by: 1c, Bellini. 2c, Mantegna. 6c, Mantegna. 25c, Memling. 45c, 50c, Correggio. $1, $3, Raphael.

1976, Nov. 1 Litho. *Perf. 14*

502	A74	½c multicolored	.25	.25
503	A74	1c multicolored	.25	.25
504	A74	2c multicolored	.25	.25
505	A74	6c multicolored	.25	.25
506	A74	25c multicolored	.25	.25
507	A74	45c multicolored	.25	.25
508	A74	$3 multicolored	.60	.60
		Nos. 502-508 (7)	2.10	2.10

Souvenir Sheet

509		Sheet of 2	1.10	1.10
a.	A74	50c multicolored	.35	.35
b.	A74	$1 multicolored	.75	.75

Christmas.

Island Craft Co-operative — A75

National Day: 50c, Banana harvest, Castle Bruce Co-operative. $1, Banana shipping plant, Bourne Farmers' Co-operative.

1976, Nov. 22 Litho. *Perf. 13½x14*

510	A75	10c multicolored	.25	.25
511	A75	50c multicolored	.25	.25
512	A75	$1 multicolored	.30	.30
a.		Souvenir sheet of 3, #510-512	.75	.75
		Nos. 510-512 (3)	.80	.80

Common Sundial — A76

Sea Shells: 1c, Flame helmet. 2c, Mouse cone. 20c, Caribbean vase. 40c, West Indian fighting conch. 50c, Short coral shell. $2, Long-spined star shell. $3, Apple murex.

1976, Dec. 20 Litho. *Perf. 14*

513	A76	½c black & multi	.25	.25
514	A76	1c black & multi	.25	.25
515	A76	2c black & multi	.25	.25
516	A76	20c black & multi	.30	.25
517	A76	40c black & multi	.55	.45
518	A76	50c black & multi	.60	.50
519	A76	$3 black & multi	2.25	2.25
		Nos. 513-519 (7)	4.45	4.20

Souvenir Sheet

520	A76	$2 black & multi	2.00	2.00

Queen Enthroned — A77

Designs: 1c, Imperial crown. 45c, Elizabeth II and Princess Anne. $2, Coronation ring. $2.50, Ampulla and spoon. $5, Royal visit to Dominica.

1977, Feb. 7 *Perf. 14*

521	A77	½c multicolored	.25	.25
522	A77	1c multicolored	.25	.25
523	A77	45c multicolored	.25	.25
524	A77	$2 multicolored	.35	.35
525	A77	$2.50 multicolored	.50	.50
		Nos. 521-525 (5)	1.60	1.60

Souvenir Sheet

526	A77	$5 multicolored	1.40	1.40

25th anniv. of the reign of Elizabeth II.

Nos. 521-525 were printed in sheets of 40 (4x10), perf. 14, and sheets of 5 plus label, perf. 12, in changed colors.

For overprints see Nos. 549-554.

Joseph Haydn — A78

Designs: 1c, Fidelio, act I, scene IV. 2c, Dancer Maria Casentini. 15c, Beethoven working on Pastoral Symphony. 30c, "Wellington's Victory." 40c, Soprano Henriette Sontag. $2, Young Beethoven.

1977, Apr. 25 Litho. *Perf. 14*

527	A78	½c multicolored	.25	.25
528	A78	1c multicolored	.25	.25
529	A78	2c multicolored	.25	.25
530	A78	15c multicolored	.50	.50
531	A78	30c multicolored	.50	.50
532	A78	40c multicolored	.50	.50
533	A78	$2 multicolored	1.60	1.60
a.		Souvenir sheet of 3, #531-533	2.60	2.60
		Nos. 527-533 (7)	3.85	3.85

Ludwig van Beethoven (1770-1827), composer.

Boy Scouts on Hike A79

Saluting Boy Scout and: 1c, First aid. 2c, Scouts setting up camp. 45c, Rock climbing. 50c, Kayaking. 75c, Map reading. $2, Campfire. $3, Sailing.

1977, Aug. 8 Litho. *Perf. 14*

534	A79	½c multicolored	.25	.25
535	A79	1c multicolored	.25	.25
536	A79	2c multicolored	.25	.25
537	A79	45c multicolored	.35	.35
538	A79	50c multicolored	.50	.50
539	A79	$3 multicolored	2.00	2.00
		Nos. 534-539 (6)	3.60	3.60

Souvenir Sheet

540		Sheet of 2	1.90	1.90
a.	A79	75c multicolored	.55	.55
b.	A79	$2 multicolored	1.35	1.35

6th Caribbean Jamboree, Kingston, Jamaica, Aug. 5-14.

Nativity A80

Christmas: 1c, Annunciation to the Shepherds. 2c, 45c, Presentation at the Temple (different). 6c, $2, $3, Flight into Egypt (different). 15c, Adoration of the Kings. 50c, Virgin and Child with Angels. ½c to 45c are illustrations from De Lisle Psalter, 14th century. 50c, $2, $3 are from other Psalters.

1977, Nov. 14 Litho. *Perf. 14*

541	A80	½c multicolored	.25	.25
542	A80	1c multicolored	.25	.25
543	A80	2c multicolored	.25	.25
544	A80	6c multicolored	.25	.25
545	A80	15c multicolored	.25	.25
546	A80	45c multicolored	.35	.35
547	A80	$3 multicolored	.85	.85
		Nos. 541-547 (7)	2.45	2.45

Souvenir Sheet

548		Sheet of 2	1.35	1.35
a.	A80	50c multicolored	.25	.25
b.	A80	$2 multicolored	1.10	1.10

Nos. 521-526 Overprinted

1977, Nov. 24 Litho. *Perf. 12, 14*

549	A77	½c multicolored	.25	.25
550	A77	1c multicolored	.25	.25
551	A77	45c multicolored	.25	.25
552	A77	$2 multicolored	.40	.40
553	A77	$2.50 multicolored	.45	.45
		Nos. 549-553 (5)	1.60	1.60

Souvenir Sheet

Perf. 14

554	A77	$5 multicolored	1.10	1.10

Caribbean visit of Queen Elizabeth II. Nos. 549-550 are perf. 12, others perf. 12 and 14.

Two types of No. 554: I. Overprinted only on stamp. II. Overprinted "W.I. 1977" on stamp and "Royal Visit W.I. 1977" on margin.

Masqueraders — A81

Designs: 1c, Sensay costume. 2c, Street musicians. 45c, Douiette band. 50c, Pappy Show wedding. $2, $2.50, Masquerade band.

1978, Jan. 9 *Perf. 14*

No.	Type	Description		
555	A81	½c multicolored	.25	.25
556	A81	1c multicolored	.25	.25
557	A81	2c multicolored	.25	.25
558	A81	45c multicolored	.25	.25
559	A81	50c multicolored	.30	.30
560	A81	$2 multicolored	.50	.50
		Nos. 555-560 (6)	1.80	1.80

Souvenir Sheet

No.	Type	Description		
561	A81	$2.50 multicolored	1.50	1.50

History of Carnival.

Lindbergh and Spirit of St. Louis A82

Designs: 10c, Spirit of St. Louis take-off, Long Island, May 20, 1927. 15c, Lindbergh and map of route New York to Paris. 20c, Lindbergh and plane in Paris. 40c, 1st Zeppelin, trial over Lake Constance. 50c, Spirit of St. Louis. 60c, Count Zeppelin and Zeppelin LZ-2, 1906. $2, Graf Zeppelin, 1928. $3, LZ-127, 1928.

1978, Mar. 13 **Litho.** *Perf. 14½*

No.	Type	Description		
562	A82	6c multicolored	.25	.25
563	A82	10c multicolored	.25	.25
564	A82	15c multicolored	.30	.30
565	A82	20c multicolored	.40	.40
566	A82	40c multicolored	.60	.60
567	A82	60c multicolored	.85	.85
568	A82	$3 multicolored	2.25	2.25
		Nos. 562-568 (7)	4.90	4.90

Souvenir Sheet

No.	Type	Description		
569		Sheet of 2	2.00	2.00
a.	A82	50c multicolored	.40	.40
b.	A82	$2 multicolored	1.60	1.60

Charles A. Lindbergh's solo transatlantic flight from New York to Paris, 50th anniv., and flights of Graf Zeppelin.

Royal Family on Balcony — A83

Designs: 45c, Coronation. $2.50, Elizabeth II and Prince Philip. $5, Elizabeth II.

1978, June 2 **Litho.** *Perf. 14*

No.	Type	Description		
570	A83	45c multicolored	.25	.25
571	A83	$2 multicolored	.45	.45
572	A83	$2.50 multicolored	.55	.55
		Nos. 570-572 (3)	1.25	1.25

Souvenir Sheet

No.	Type	Description		
573	A83	$5 multicolored	1.00	1.00

Coronation of Queen Elizabeth II, 25th anniv. Nos. 570-572 were issued in sheets of 50, and in sheets of 3 stamps and label, in changed colors, perf. 12.

Wright Plane Coming out of Hangar A84

Designs: 40c, 1908 plane. 60c, Flyer I gliding. $2, Flyer I taking off. $3, Wilbur and Orville Wright and Flyer I.

1978, July 10 **Litho.** *Perf. 14½*

No.	Type	Description		
574	A84	30c multicolored	.25	.25
575	A84	40c multicolored	.25	.25
576	A84	60c multicolored	.30	.30
577	A84	$2 multicolored	1.25	1.25
		Nos. 574-577 (4)	2.05	2.05

Souvenir Sheet

No.	Type	Description		
578	A84	$3 multicolored	1.75	1.75

75th anniv. of first powered flight.

A set of 30 stamps embossed on gold foil exists. Value, $400.

Two Apostles, by Rubens — A85

Rubens Paintings: 45c, Descent from the Cross. 50c, St. Ildefonso Receiving Chasuble. $2, Holy Family. $3, Assumption of the Virgin.

1978, Oct. 16 **Litho.** *Perf. 14*

No.	Type	Description		
579	A85	20c multicolored	.25	.25
580	A85	45c multicolored	.25	.25
581	A85	50c multicolored	.25	.25
582	A85	$3 multicolored	.90	.90
		Nos. 579-582 (4)	1.65	1.65

Souvenir Sheet

No.	Type	Description		
583	A85	$2 multicolored	1.00	1.00

Christmas.

Nos. 454-471 Overprinted

1978 Nov. 1 **Litho.** *Perf. 14½*

No.	Type	Description		
584	A68	½c ultra & multi	.25	.25
585	A68	1c lilac & multi	.25	.25
586	A68	2c orange & multi	.30	.25
587	A68	3c multicolored	.30	.25
588	A68	4c pink & multi	.30	.25
589	A68	5c multicolored	.30	.25
590	A68	6c gray & multi	.35	.25
591	A68	8c multicolored	3.00	.25
592	A68	10c violet & multi	1.00	.25
a.		Perf. 13½ ('79)	.50	.25
593	A68	20c yellow & multi	.60	.25
594	A68	25c lemon & multi	.65	.25
595	A68	30c salmon & multi	.70	.30
596	A68	40c multicolored	.70	.55
597	A68	50c red & multi	.75	.75
598	A68	$1 citron & multi	.80	1.40
599	A68	$2 multicolored	1.50	2.75
600	A68	$5 multicolored	2.00	5.50

Perf. 14

No.	Type	Description		
601	A69	$10 blue & multi	3.00	12.50
		Nos. 584-601 (18)	16.75	26.50

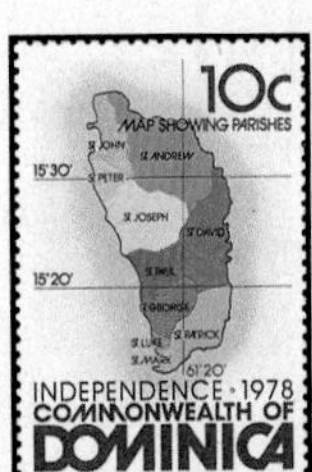

Map of Dominica with Parishes — A86

25c, Sabinea carinalis, natl. flower, & map. 45c, New flag & map. 50c, Coat of arms & map. $2, Prime Minister Patrick John.

1978, Nov. 1 *Perf. 14*

No.	Type	Description		
602	A86	10c multicolored	.75	.40
603	A86	25c multicolored	.55	.25
604	A86	45c multicolored	1.50	.35
605	A86	50c multicolored	.65	.35
606	A86	$2 multicolored	1.50	*2.75*
		Nos. 602-606 (5)	4.95	4.10

Souvenir Sheet

No.	Type	Description		
607	A86	$2.50 multicolored	2.60	2.60

Dominican independence.

Rowland Hill — A87

45c, Great Britain #2. 50c, Dominica #1. $2, Maltese Cross handstamps. $5, Penny Black.

1979, Mar. 19

No.	Type	Description		
608	A87	25c multicolored	.25	.25
609	A87	45c multicolored	.25	.25
610	A87	50c multicolored	.25	.25
611	A87	$2 multicolored	.35	.35
		Nos. 608-611 (4)	1.10	1.10

Souvenir Sheet

No.	Type	Description		
612	A87	$5 multicolored	1.40	1.40

Sir Rowland Hill (1795-1879), originator of penny postage.

Nos. 608-611 printed in sheets of 5 plus label, perf. 12x12½, in changed colors.

For overprints see Nos. 663A-663D.

Boys and Dugout Canoe A88

IYC Emblem and: 40c, Children carrying bananas. 50c, Boys playing cricket. $3, Child feeding rabbits. $5, Boy showing catch of fish.

1979, Apr. 23 **Litho.** *Perf. 14*

No.	Type	Description		
613	A88	30c multicolored	.30	.30
614	A88	40c multicolored	.45	.45
615	A88	50c multicolored	.50	.50
616	A88	$3 multicolored	2.00	2.00
		Nos. 613-616 (4)	3.25	3.25

Souvenir Sheet

No.	Type	Description		
617	A88	$5 multicolored	2.00	2.00

Grouper A89

30c, Striped dolphin. 50c, White-tailed tropic birds. 60c, Brown pelicans. $1, Pilot whale. $2, Brown booby. $3, Elkhorn coral.

1979, May 21 **Litho.** *Perf. 14*

No.	Type	Description		
618	A89	10c multicolored	.50	.25
619	A89	30c multicolored	1.00	.50
620	A89	50c multicolored	1.75	.75
621	A89	60c multicolored	2.00	2.00
622	A89	$1 multicolored	2.50	2.50
623	A89	$2 multicolored	4.25	4.25
		Nos. 618-623 (6)	12.00	10.25

Souvenir Sheet

No.	Type	Description		
624	A89	$3 multicolored	2.75	2.75

Wildlife protection.

Capt. Cook, Bark Endeavour — A90

Capt. Cook and: 50c, Resolution, map of 2nd voyage. 60c, Discovery, map of 3rd voyage. $2, Cook's map of New Zealand, 1770. $5, Portrait.

1979, July 16 **Litho.** *Perf. 14*

No.	Type	Description		
625	A90	10c multicolored	.60	.40
626	A90	50c multicolored	1.00	1.00
627	A90	60c multicolored	1.25	1.25
628	A90	$2 multicolored	1.50	*2.50*
		Nos. 625-628 (4)	4.35	5.15

Souvenir Sheet

No.	Type	Description		
629	A90	$5 multicolored	2.00	2.00

200th death anniv. of Capt. James Cook (1728-1779).

Girl Guides Cooking A91

Girl Guides: 20c, Setting up emergency rain tent. 50c, Raising flag of independent Dominica. $2.50, Playing accordion and singing. $3, Leader and Guides of different ages.

1979, July 30

No.	Type	Description		
630	A91	10c multicolored	.25	.25
631	A91	20c multicolored	.25	.25
632	A91	50c multicolored	.30	.30
633	A91	$2.50 multicolored	1.25	1.25
		Nos. 630-633 (4)	2.05	2.05

Souvenir Sheet

No.	Type	Description		
634	A91	$3 multicolored	1.50	1.50

50th anniv. of Dominican Girl Guides.

Colvillea — A92

Flowering Trees: 40c, Lignum vitae. 60c, Dwarf poinciana. $2, Fern tree. $3, Perfume tree.

1979, Sept. 3 **Litho.** *Perf. 14*

No.	Type	Description		
635	A92	20c multicolored	.25	.25
636	A92	40c multicolored	.25	.25
637	A92	60c multicolored	.35	.35
638	A92	$2 multicolored	.90	.90
		Nos. 635-638 (4)	1.75	1.75

Souvenir Sheet

No.	Type	Description		
639	A92	$3 multicolored	1.75	1.75

Nos. 459, 466, 470-471 Overprinted

No. 640

No. 643

Perf. 14½, 13½, 13½x14, 14

1979, Oct. 29 **Litho.**

640 A68 5c multicolored .25 .25
641 A68 40c multicolored .30 .30
642 A68 $5 multicolored 2.00 2.00
643 A69 $10 multicolored 3.50 3.50
Nos. 640-643 (4) 6.05 6.05

Hurricane devastation, Aug. 29. Vertical overprint on No. 643, others horizontal.

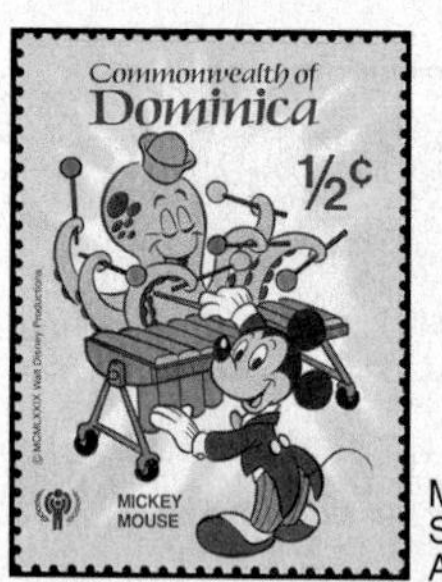

Music Scenes A92a

½c, Mickey Mouse. 1c, Goofy playing guitar. 2c, Mickey Mouse and Goofy. 3c, Donald Duck. 4c, Minnie Mouse. 5c, Goofy playing accordion. 10c, Horace Horsecollar and Dale. $2, Huey, Dewey, Louie. $2.50, Donald and Huey.
$3, Mickey Mouse playing piano.

1979, Nov. 2 **Litho.** ***Perf. 11***

644 A92a ½c multicolored .25 .25
645 A92a 1c multicolored .25 .25
646 A92a 2c multicolored .25 .25
647 A92a 3c multicolored .25 .25
648 A92a 4c multicolored .25 .25
649 A92a 5c multicolored .25 .25
650 A92a 10c multicolored .25 .25
651 A92a $2 multicolored 1.50 1.50
652 A92a $2.50 multicolored 1.50 1.50
Nos. 644-652 (9) 4.75 4.75

Souvenir Sheet

Perf. 13

653 A92a $3 multicolored 3.25 3.25

Cathedral of the Assumption — A93

Cathedrals: 40c, St. Patrick's, New York. 45c, St. Paul's, London, vert. 60c, St. Peter's, Rome. $2, Cologne Cathedral. $3, Notre Dame, Paris, vert.

1979, Nov. 26 **Litho.** ***Perf. 14***

654 A93 6c multicolored .25 .25
655 A93 45c multicolored .25 .25
656 A93 60c multicolored .25 .25
657 A93 $3 multicolored .90 .90
Nos. 654-657 (4) 1.65 1.65

Souvenir Sheet

658 Sheet of 2 .80 .80
a. A93 40c multicolored .25 .25
b. A93 $2 multicolored .55 .55

Christmas.

Nurse and Patients, Rotary Emblem A94

20c, Electrocardiogram machine. 40c, Mental hospital. $2.50, Paul Harris, founder. $3, Map of Africa and Europe.

1980, Mar. 31 **Litho.** ***Perf. 14***

659 A94 10c shown .25 .25
660 A94 20c multicolored .25 .25
661 A94 40c multicolored .25 .25
662 A94 $2.50 multicolored .75 .75
Nos. 659-662 (4) 1.50 1.50

Souvenir Sheet

663 A94 $3 multicolored 1.25 1.25

Rotary International, 75th anniv. Nos. 659-662 each contain quadrant of Rotary emblem.

Nos. 608-611 Overprinted in Black

1980, May 6 **Litho.** ***Perf. 12***

663A A87 25c multicolored .35 .35
663B A87 45c multicolored .55 .55
663C A87 50c multicolored .60 .60
663D A87 $2 multicolored 1.50 1.50
Nos. 663A-663D (4) 3.00 3.00

London 80 Intl. Stamp Exhib., May 6-14.

Shot Put, Moscow '80 Emblem A95

1980, May 27 **Litho.** ***Perf. 14***

664 A95 30c shown .25 .25
665 A95 40c Basketball .60 .30
666 A95 60c Swimming .40 .40
667 A95 $2 Gymnast .70 .70
Nos. 664-667 (4) 1.95 1.65

Souvenir Sheet

668 A95 $3 Running 1.25 1.25

22nd Summer Olympic Games, Moscow, July 19-Aug. 3.

Embarkation for Cythera, by Watteau — A96

Paintings: 20c, Supper at Emmaus, by Caravaggio. 25c, Charles I Hunting, by Van Dyck, vert. 30c, The Maids of Honor, by Velazquez, vert. 45c, Rape of the Sabine Women, by Poussin. $1, Embarkation for Cythera, by Watteau. $3, Holy Family, by Rembrandt. $5, Girl before a Mirror, by Picasso, vert.

Perf. 14x13½, 13½x14

1980, July 22 **Litho.**

669 A96 20c multicolored .25 .25
670 A96 25c multicolored .25 .25
671 A96 30c multicolored .25 .25
672 A96 45c multicolored .25 .25
673 A96 $1 multicolored .40 .40
674 A96 $5 multicolored 1.50 1.50
Nos. 669-674 (6) 2.90 2.90

Souvenir Sheet

675 A96 $3 multicolored 1.10 1.10

Queen Mother Elizabeth, 80th Birthday A97

1980, Aug. 4 ***Perf. 12, 14***

676 A97 40c multicolored .25 .25
677 A97 $2.50 multicolored .50 .50

Souvenir Sheet

678 A97 $3 multicolored .75 .75

Tinkerbell — A98

Designs: Scenes from Disney's Peter Pan.

1980, Oct. 1 **Litho.** ***Perf. 11***

679 A98 ½c multicolored .25 .25
680 A98 1c multicolored .25 .25
681 A98 2c multicolored .25 .25
682 A98 3c multicolored .25 .25
683 A98 4c multicolored .25 .25
684 A98 5c multicolored .25 .25
685 A98 10c multicolored .25 .25
686 A98 $2 multicolored 2.25 1.60
687 A98 $2.50 multicolored 2.25 1.75
Nos. 679-687 (9) 6.25 5.10

Souvenir Sheet

688 A98 $4 multicolored 5.00 5.00

Christmas.

Douglas Bay A99

30c, Valley of Desolation. 40c, Emerald Pool, vert. $3, Indian River, vert.
$4, Trafalgar Falls.

1981, Feb. 12 **Litho.** ***Perf. 14***

689 A99 20c shown .25 .25
690 A99 30c multicolored .25 .25
691 A99 40c multicolored .25 .25
692 A99 $3 multicolored .70 .70
Nos. 689-692 (4) 1.45 1.45

Souvenir Sheet

693 A99 $4 multicolored 1.40 1.40

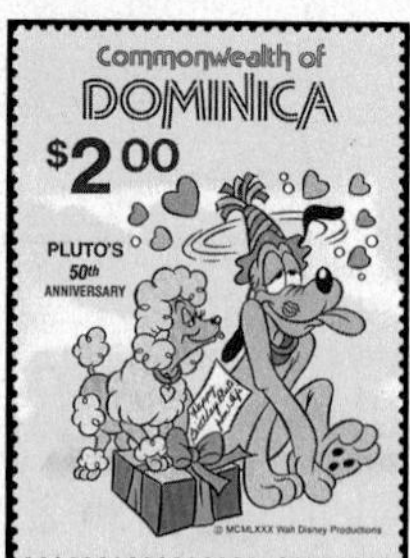

Pluto and Fifi — A100

$4, Pluto in Blue Note (1947 cartoon).

1981, Apr. 30 **Litho.** ***Perf. 13½x14***

694 A100 $2 multicolored 1.75 1.75

Souvenir Sheet

695 A100 $4 multicolored 2.75 2.75

50th anniversary of Walt Disney's Pluto.

Forest Thrush A101

30c, Stolid flycatcher. 40c, Blue-hooded euphonia. $5, Lesser antillean peewee.
$3, Sisserou parrot.

1981, Apr. 30 ***Perf. 14***

696 A101 20c shown .60 .25
697 A101 30c multicolored .70 .35
698 A101 40c multicolored .80 .45
699 A101 $5 multicolored 4.75 4.75
Nos. 696-699 (4) 6.85 5.80

Souvenir Sheet

700 A101 $3 multicolored 3.75 3.75

Royal Wedding Issue
Common Design Type

45c, Couple. 60c, Windsor Castle. $4, Charles.
$5, Helicopter.

1981, June 16 **Litho.** ***Perf. 14***

701 CD331a 45c multi .25 .25
702 CD331a 60c multi .25 .25
703 CD331a $4 multi .60 .60
Nos. 701-703 (3) 1.10 1.10

Souvenir Sheet

704 CD331 $5 multi 1.25 1.25

Booklet

705 CD331 multi 6.00
a. Pane of 6 (3x25c, Lady Diana, 3x$2, Charles) 2.25 *4.50*
b. Pane of 1, $5, Couple 3.00 *3.50*

No. 705 contains imperf., self-adhesive stamps.

Nos. 701-703 also printed in sheets of 5 plus label, perf. 12, in changed colors. Value, set of three sheets $10.

Elves Repairing Santa's Sleigh — A102

Christmas: Scenes from Walt Disney's Santa's Workshop.

1981, Nov. 2 **Litho.** ***Perf. 14***

706 A102 ½c multicolored .25 .25
707 A102 1c multicolored .25 .25
708 A102 2c multicolored .25 .25
709 A102 3c multicolored .25 .25
710 A102 4c multicolored .25 .25
711 A102 5c multicolored .25 .25
712 A102 10c multicolored .25 .25
713 A102 45c multicolored 2.00 .40
714 A102 $5 multicolored 4.00 *5.50*
Nos. 706-714 (9) 7.75 7.65

Souvenir Sheet

715 A102 $4 multicolored 5.75 5.75

Ixora A103

2c, Flamboyant. 4c, Poinsettia. 5c, Sabinea carinalis. 8c, Annatto roucou. 10c, Passion fruit. 15c, Breadfruit. 20c, Allamanda buttercup. 25c, Cashew. 35c, Soursop. 40c, Bougainvillea. 45c, Anthurium. 60c, Cacao. 90c, Pawpaw tree. $1, Coconut palm. $2, Coffee tree. $5, Lobster claw. $10, Banana fig.

1981, Dec. 1 **Litho.** ***Perf. 14***

716 A103 1c shown .25 .90
717 A103 2c multicolored .25 .90
718 A103 4c multicolored .25 .90
719 A103 5c multicolored .25 .60
720 A103 8c multicolored .25 .90
721 A103 10c multicolored .30 .25
722 A103 15c multicolored .50 .50
723 A103 20c multicolored .35 .25
724 A103 25c multicolored .40 .25
725 A103 35c multicolored .45 .40
726 A103 40c multicolored .45 .65
727 A103 45c multicolored .50 .70
728 A103 60c multicolored 1.00 .95
729 A103 90c multicolored .75 1.40
730 A103 $1 multicolored 2.00 1.50
731 A103 $2 multicolored 1.50 3.00
732 A103 $5 multicolored 2.00 *7.00*
c. Perf. 12½x12 ('85) 3.25 *5.00*
733 A103 $10 multicolored 3.50 *13.00*
Nos. 716-733 (18) 14.95 34.05

For overprints see Nos. 852-853.

1984 Inscribed "1984" *Perf. 12*

721a	A103	10c	1.75	.40
730a	A103	$1	2.50	*3.00*
732a	A103	$5	3.25	*5.00*
733a	A103	$10	5.25	*10.00*
		Nos. 721a-733a (4)	12.75	*18.40*

1985 Inscribed "1985" *Perf. 14*

721b	A103	10c	1.00	.65
722b	A103	15c Breadfruit	4.00	2.00
728b	A103	60c Cacao	5.00	3.50
732b	A103	$5 Lobster claw	3.25	*5.00*
		Nos. 721b-732b (4)	13.25	11.15

Intl. Year of the Disabled — A104

45c, Ramp curb. 60c, Bus steps. 75c, Hand-operated car. $4, Bus lift.
$5, Elevator buttons.

1981, Dec. 22 Litho. *Perf. 14*

734	A104	45c multicolored	.45	.30
735	A104	60c multicolored	.55	.40
736	A104	75c multicolored	.65	.50
737	A104	$4 multicolored	2.00	*2.40*
		Nos. 734-737 (4)	3.65	3.60

Souvenir Sheet

738	A104	$5 multicolored	5.00	5.00

Bathers, by Picasso — A105

45c, Olga in Armchair. 75c, Woman in Spanish Costume. $4, Dog and Cock.
$5, Sleeping Peasants.

1981, Dec. 30 *Perf. 14½*

739	A105	45c multicolored	.30	.30
740	A105	60c shown	.40	.40
741	A105	75c multicolored	.50	.50
742	A105	$4 multicolored	2.25	2.25
		Nos. 739-742 (4)	3.45	3.45

Souvenir Sheet

743	A105	$5 multicolored	4.00	4.00

1982 World Cup Soccer — A106

Various Disney characters playing soccer.

1982, Jan. 29 *Perf. 14*

744	A106	½c multicolored	.25	.25
745	A106	1c multicolored	.25	.25
746	A106	2c multicolored	.25	.25
747	A106	3c multicolored	.25	.25
748	A106	4c multicolored	.25	.25
749	A106	5c multicolored	.25	.25
750	A106	10c multicolored	.25	.25
751	A106	60c multicolored	1.25	1.25
752	A106	$5 multicolored	6.25	6.25
		Nos. 744-752 (9)	9.25	9.25

Souvenir Sheet

753	A106	$4 multicolored	5.75	5.75

Golden Days, by Norman Rockwell A107

25c, The Morning News. 45c, The Marbles Champ. $1, Speeding Along.

1982, Mar. 10 Litho. *Perf. 14x13½*

754	A107	10c shown	.25	.25
755	A107	25c multicolored	.25	.25
756	A107	45c multicolored	.30	.30
757	A107	$1 multicolored	.55	.55
		Nos. 754-757 (4)	1.35	1.35

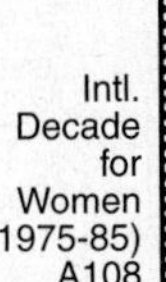

Intl. Decade for Women (1975-85) A108

Famous Women: 10c, Elma Napier (1890-1973), first woman elected to Legislative Council in British West Indies, 1940. 45c, Margaret Mead (1901-1978), anthropologist. $1, Mabel Caudiron (1909-1968), musician and folk historian. $3, Florence Nightingale, founder of modern nursing. $4, Eleanor Roosevelt.

1982, Apr. 15 Litho. *Perf. 14*

758	A108	10c multicolored	.25	.25
759	A108	45c multicolored	.35	.35
760	A108	$1 multicolored	.60	.60
761	A108	$4 multicolored	2.50	2.50
		Nos. 758-761 (4)	3.70	3.70

Souvenir Sheet

762	A108	$3 multicolored	3.00	3.00

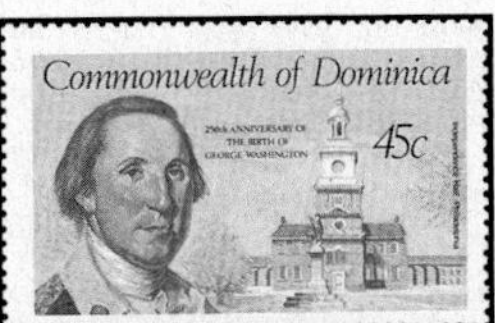

George Washington and Independence Hall, Philadelphia — A109

Washington or Roosevelt and: 60c, Capitol Building. 90c, The Surrender of Cornwallis, by John Trumbull. $2, Dam construction during New Deal (mural by William Gropper). $5, Washington, Roosevelt.

1982, May 1 *Perf. 14½*

763	A109	45c multicolored	.35	.35
764	A109	60c multicolored	.40	.40
765	A109	90c multicolored	.55	.55
766	A109	$2 multicolored	1.00	1.00
		Nos. 763-766 (4)	2.30	2.30

Souvenir Sheet

767	A109	$5 multicolored	3.00	3.00

George Washington's 250th birth anniv. and Franklin D. Roosevelt's birth cent.

Godman's Leaf Butterfly — A110

45c, Zebra. 60c, Mimic. $3, Red rim.
$5, Southern dagger tail.

1982, June 1 Litho. *Perf. 14*

768	A110	15c shown	1.75	1.75
769	A110	45c multicolored	2.75	2.75
770	A110	60c multicolored	3.00	3.00
771	A110	$3 multicolored	6.25	6.25
		Nos. 768-771 (4)	13.75	13.75

Souvenir Sheet

772	A110	$5 multicolored	7.00	7.00

Princess Diana Issue
Common Design Type

45c, Buckingham Palace. $2, Engagement portrait. $4, Diana in wedding dress.
$5, Diana sitting in chair in white dress.

1982, July 1 Litho. *Perf. 14½x14*

773	CD332	45c multicolored	.30	.30
774	CD332	$2 multicolored	1.00	1.00
775	CD332	$4 multicolored	2.25	2.25
		Nos. 773-775 (3)	3.55	3.55

Souvenir Sheet

776	CD332	$5 multicolored	3.50	3.50

Also issued in sheet of 5 plus label.
For overprints see Nos. 782-785.

Scouting Year A111

45c, Cooking. 60c, Meteorological study. 75c, Sisserou parrot, cub scouts. $3, Canoeing, Indian River.
$5, Flagbearer.

1982, July 1 Litho. *Perf. 14*

777	A111	45c multicolored	1.25	1.25
778	A111	60c multicolored	1.75	1.75
779	A111	75c multicolored	2.25	2.25
780	A111	$3 multicolored	5.25	5.25
		Nos. 777-780 (4)	10.50	10.50

Souvenir Sheet

781	A111	$5 multicolored	3.50	3.50

Nos. 773-776 Overprinted

1982, Sept. 1 Litho. *Perf. 14½x14*

782	CD332	45c multicolored	.30	.30
783	CD332	$2 multicolored	1.00	1.00
784	CD332	$4 multicolored	2.25	2.25
		Nos. 782-784 (3)	3.55	3.55

Souvenir Sheet

785	CD332	$5 multicolored	3.50	3.50

Birth of Prince William of Wales, June 21.
Also issued in sheet of 5 plus label.

Christmas — A112

Holy Family Paintings by Raphael.

1982, Oct. 18 Litho. *Perf. 14*

786	A112	25c multicolored	.25	.25
787	A112	30c multicolored	.25	.25
788	A112	90c multicolored	.40	.40
789	A112	$4 multicolored	1.75	1.75
		Nos. 786-789 (4)	2.65	2.65

Souvenir Sheet

790	A112	$5 multicolored	3.50	3.50

Goosebeak Whale Eating Squid — A113

60c, Humpback whale. 75c, Great right whale. $3, Melonhead whale.
$5, Pygmy sperm whale.

1983, Feb. 15 Litho. *Perf. 14*

791	A113	45c shown	1.75	1.75
792	A113	60c multicolored	2.00	2.00
793	A113	75c multicolored	2.25	2.25
794	A113	$3 multicolored	7.50	7.50
		Nos. 791-794 (4)	13.50	13.50

Souvenir Sheet

795	A113	$5 multicolored	6.25	6.25

Commonwealth Day — A113a

25c, Banana industry. 30c, Road construction. 90c, Community nursing. $3, Basket weavers.

1983, Mar. 14

796	A113a	25c multicolored	.25	.25
797	A113a	30c multicolored	.25	.25
798	A113a	90c multicolored	.40	.40
799	A113a	$3 multicolored	1.25	1.25
		Nos. 796-799 (4)	2.15	2.15

World Communications Year — A114

45c, Hurricane pattern, map. 60c, Air-to-ship communication. 90c, Columbia shuttle, dish antenna. $2, Walkie-talkie.
$5, Satellite.

1983, Apr. 18 Litho. *Perf. 14*

800	A114	45c multicolored	.30	.30
801	A114	60c multicolored	.35	.35
802	A114	90c multicolored	.50	.50
803	A114	$2 multicolored	1.00	1.00
		Nos. 800-803 (4)	2.15	2.15

Souvenir Sheet

804	A114	$5 multicolored	2.50	2.50

Manned Flight Bicentenary — A115

45c, Mayo Composite. 60c, Macchi M-39. 90c, Fairey Swordfish. $4, Zeppelin LZ-3.
$5, Double Eagle II, vert.

1983, July 19 Litho. *Perf. 15*

805	A115	45c multicolored	.50	.50
806	A115	60c multicolored	.60	.60
807	A115	90c multicolored	.85	.85
808	A115	$4 multicolored	3.00	3.00
		Nos. 805-808 (4)	4.95	4.95

Souvenir Sheet

809	A115	$5 multicolored	3.00	3.00

Duesenberg SJ, 1935 — A116

45c, Studebaker Avanti, 1962. 60c, Cord 812, 1936. 75c, MG-TC, 1945. 90c, Camaro 350-SS, 1967. $3, Porsche 356, 1948.
$5, Ferrari 312-T, 1975.

1983, Sept. 1 Litho. *Perf. 14*

810	A116	10c shown	.35	.35
811	A116	45c multicolored	.45	.45
812	A116	60c multicolored	.50	.50
813	A116	75c multicolored	.55	.55
814	A116	90c multicolored	.60	.60
815	A116	$3 multicolored	1.75	1.75
		Nos. 810-815 (6)	4.20	4.20

Souvenir Sheet

816	A116	$5 multicolored	3.00	3.00

Christmas — A117

Raphael Paintings.

1983, Oct. 4 Litho. *Perf. 13½*

817	A117	45c multicolored	.30	.30
818	A117	60c multicolored	.35	.35
819	A117	90c multicolored	.50	.50
820	A117	$4 multicolored	2.00	2.00
		Nos. 817-820 (4)	3.15	3.15

Souvenir Sheet

821	A117	$5 multicolored	3.00	3.00

23rd Olympic Games, Los Angeles, July 28-Aug. 12 — A118

30c, Gymnastics. 45c, Javelin. 60c, Diving. $4, Fencing.
$5, Equestrian.

1984, Mar. Litho. *Perf. 14*

822	A118	30c multicolored	.25	.25
823	A118	45c multicolored	.35	.35
824	A118	60c multicolored	.45	.45
825	A118	$4 multicolored	2.50	2.50
		Nos. 822-825 (4)	3.55	3.55

Souvenir Sheet

826	A118	$5 multicolored	3.75	3.75

Local Birds A119

5c, Plumbeous warbler. 45c, Imperial parrot. 60c, Blue-headed hummingbird. 90c, Red-necked parrot.
$5, Roseate flamingoes.

1984, May Litho.

827	A119	5c multicolored	3.00	3.00
828	A119	45c multicolored	7.00	7.00
829	A119	60c multicolored	8.50	8.50
830	A119	90c multicolored	11.00	11.00
		Nos. 827-830 (4)	29.50	29.50

Souvenir Sheet

831	A119	$5 multicolored	9.00	9.00

Easter A120

Various Disney characters and Easter bunnies.

1984, Apr. 15 Litho. *Perf. 11*

832	A120	½c multicolored	.25	.25
833	A120	1c multicolored	.25	.25
834	A120	2c multicolored	.25	.25
835	A120	3c multicolored	.25	.25
836	A120	4c multicolored	.25	.25
837	A120	5c multicolored	.25	.25
838	A120	10c multicolored	.25	.25
839	A120	$2 multicolored	3.00	3.00
840	A120	$4 multicolored	6.25	6.25
		Nos. 832-840 (9)	11.00	11.00

Souvenir Sheet

Perf. 14

841	A120	$5 multicolored	5.75	5.75

Ships A121

45c, Atlantic Star. 60c, Atlantic. 90c, Carib fishing pirogue. $4, Norway.
$5, Santa Maria.

1984, June 14 Litho. *Perf. 14*

842	A121	45c multicolored	1.75	1.75
843	A121	60c multicolored	2.00	2.00
844	A121	90c multicolored	2.50	2.50
845	A121	$4 multicolored	6.75	6.75
		Nos. 842-845 (4)	13.00	13.00

Souvenir Sheet

846	A121	$5 multicolored	5.00	5.00

Local Plants — A122

45c, Guzmania lingulata. 60c, Pitcairnia angustifolia. 75c, Tillandsia fasciculata. $3, Aechmea smithiorum.
$5, Tillandsia utriculata.

1984, Aug. 13

847	A122	45c multicolored	.40	.40
848	A122	60c multicolored	.50	.50
849	A122	75c multicolored	.60	.60
850	A122	$3 multicolored	2.40	2.40
		Nos. 847-850 (4)	3.90	3.90

Souvenir Sheet

851	A122	$5 multicolored	3.75	3.75

Ausipex Intl. Stamp Exhibition.

Nos. 721, 732 Overprinted

1984 Litho. *Perf. 14*

852	A103	10c multicolored	.25	.25
853	A103	$5 multicolored	4.00	4.00

Correggio & Degas — A122a

Correggio: 25c, Virgin and Child with Young St. John. 60c, Christ Bids Farewell to the Virgin Mary. 90c, Do Not Touch Me. $4, The Mystical Marriage of St. Catherine. No. 862, Adoration of the Magi,
Degas, horiz.: 30c, Before the Start. 45c, On the Racecourse. $1, Jockeys at the Flagpole. $3, Racehorses at Longchamp. No. 863, Self-portrait.

1984, Nov. Litho. *Perf. 15*

854	A122a	25c multicolored	.35	.35
855	A122a	30c multicolored	.40	.40
856	A122a	45c multicolored	.45	.45
857	A122a	60c multicolored	.50	.50
858	A122a	90c multicolored	.65	.65
859	A122a	$1 multicolored	.75	.75
860	A122a	$3 multicolored	1.75	1.75
861	A122a	$4 multicolored	1.90	1.90
		Nos. 854-861 (8)	6.75	6.75

Souvenir Sheets

862	A122a	$5 multicolored	3.00	3.00
863	A122a	$5 multicolored	3.00	3.00

A123

1984, Dec. *Perf. 14*

864	A123	30c Avro 748	1.25	1.25
865	A123	60c Twin Otter	2.25	2.25
866	A123	$1 Islander	2.50	2.50
867	A123	$3 Casa	4.75	4.75
		Nos. 864-867 (4)	10.75	10.75

Souvenir Sheet

868	A123	$5 Boeing 747	5.50	5.50

Intl. Civil Aviation Org., 40th anniv.

A124

Scenes from various Donald Duck movies.

1984, Nov. Litho.

869	A124	45c multicolored	1.25	1.25
870	A124	60c multicolored	1.50	1.50
871	A124	90c multicolored	2.00	2.00
872	A124	$2 multicolored, perf. 12x12½	3.50	3.50
873	A124	$4 multicolored	5.75	5.75
		Nos. 869-873 (5)	14.00	14.00

Souvenir Sheet

Perf. 13½x14

874	A124	$5 multicolored	5.50	5.50

Christmas and 50th anniv. of Donald Duck.

Cats A125

10c, Tabby. 15c, Calico shorthair. 20c, Siamese. 25c, Manx. 45c, Abyssinian. 60c, Tortoise shell longhair. $1, Rex. $2, Persian. $3, Himalayan. No. 884, $5, Burmese.
No. 885, $5, Gray Burmese, Persian, American shorthair.

1984, Nov. 12 Litho. *Perf. 15*

875	A125	10c multicolored	.25	.25
876	A125	15c multicolored	.25	.25
877	A125	20c multicolored	.25	.25
878	A125	25c multicolored	.25	.25
879	A125	45c multicolored	.40	.40
880	A125	60c multicolored	.50	.50
881	A125	$1 multicolored	.75	.75
882	A125	$2 multicolored	1.00	1.00
883	A125	$3 multicolored	2.00	2.00
884	A125	$5 multicolored	3.50	3.50
		Nos. 875-884 (10)	9.15	9.15

Souvenir Sheet

885	A125	$5 multicolored	5.50	5.50

Girl Guides, 75th Anniv. A126

35c, Lady Baden-Powell. 45c, Inspecting Dominican troop. 60c, With Dominican troop leaders. $3, Lord and Lady Baden-Powell, vert.
$5, Flag ceremony.

1985, Feb. 18 *Perf. 14*

886	A126	35c multicolored	.60	.60
887	A126	45c multicolored	.70	.70
888	A126	60c multicolored	.90	.90
889	A126	$3 multicolored	3.50	3.50
		Nos. 886-889 (4)	5.70	5.70

Souvenir Sheet

890	A126	$5 multicolored	5.50	5.50

John James Audubon A127

45c, King rails. $1, Black & white warbler, vert. $2, Broad-winged hawks, vert. $3, Ring-necked ducks.
$5, Reddish egrets, vert.

1985, Apr. 4

891	A127	45c multicolored	1.25	1.25
892	A127	$1 multicolored	2.00	2.00
893	A127	$2 multicolored	3.25	3.25
894	A127	$3 multicolored	4.25	4.25
		Nos. 891-894 (4)	10.75	10.75

Souvenir Sheet

895	A127	$5 multicolored	5.50	5.50

Nos. 891-894 exist vertically se-tenant with labels showing additional bird species.
See Nos. 965-969.

Duke of Edinburgh Awards, 1984 — A128

45c, Woman at computer terminal. 60c, Medical staff, patient. 90c, Runners. $4, Family jogging.
$5, Duke of Edinburgh.

1985, Apr. 30

896	A128	45c multicolored	.50	.50
897	A128	60c multicolored	1.60	1.60
898	A128	90c multicolored	2.00	2.00
899	A128	$4 multicolored	3.25	3.25
		Nos. 896-899 (4)	7.35	7.35

Souvenir Sheet

900	A128	$5 multicolored	4.00	4.00

Intl. Youth Year A129

45c, Cricket match. 60c, Environmental study, parrot. $1, Stamp collecting. $3, Boating, leisure.
$5, Youths join hands.

1985, July 8 Litho. *Perf. 14*

No.	Type	Value	Description	Unused	Used
901	A129	45c	multicolored	3.00	2.00
902	A129	60c	multicolored	3.75	2.50
903	A129	$1	multicolored	4.00	3.50
904	A129	$3	multicolored	5.25	*7.50*
			Nos. 901-904 (4)	16.00	15.50

Souvenir Sheet

No.	Type	Value	Description	Unused	Used
905	A129	$5	multicolored	4.00	4.00

Queen Mother, 85th Birthday — A130

60c, Visiting Sadlers Wells. $1, Fishing. $3, At Clarence House, 1984.
$5, Attending Windsor Castle Garter Ceremony.

1985, July 15

No.	Type	Value	Description	Unused	Used
906	A130	60c	multicolored	1.00	.75
907	A130	$1	multicolored	1.50	.75
908	A130	$3	multicolored	2.00	2.00
			Nos. 906-908 (3)	4.50	3.50

Souvenir Sheet

No.	Type	Value	Description	Unused	Used
909	A130	$5	multicolored	3.75	3.75

Johann Sebastian Bach — A131

Portrait, signature, music from Explication and: 45c, Cornett 60c, Coiled trumpet. $1, Piccolo. $3, Violoncello piccolo.

1985, Sept. 2

No.	Type	Value	Description	Unused	Used
910	A131	45c	multicolored	1.00	1.00
911	A131	60c	multicolored	1.50	1.50
912	A131	$1	multicolored	2.00	2.00
913	A131	$3	multicolored	4.25	4.25
			Nos. 910-913 (4)	8.75	8.75

Souvenir Sheet

No.	Type	Value	Description	Unused	Used
914	A131	$5	Portrait	4.00	4.00

State Visit of Elizabeth II, Oct. 25 — A132

60c, Flags of UK, Dominica. $1, Elizabeth II, vert. $4, HMS Britannia.
$5, Map.

1985, Oct. 25 *Perf. 14½*

No.	Type	Value	Description	Unused	Used
915	A132	60c	multicolored	.75	.75
916	A132	$1	multicolored	.75	.75
917	A132	$4	multicolored	3.50	3.50
			Nos. 915-917 (3)	5.00	5.00

Souvenir Sheet

No.	Type	Value	Description	Unused	Used
918	A132	$5	multicolored	3.75	3.75

Mark Twain — A133

Disney characters in Tom Sawyer.

1985, Nov. 11 Litho. *Perf. 14*

No.	Type	Value	Description	Unused	Used
919	A133	20c	multicolored	.75	.35
920	A133	60c	multicolored	1.50	.35
921	A133	$1	multicolored	2.00	2.00
922	A133	$1.50	multicolored	2.50	2.50
923	A133	$2	multicolored	3.00	3.00
			Nos. 919-923 (5)	9.75	8.20

Souvenir Sheet

No.	Type	Value	Description	Unused	Used
924	A133	$5	multicolored	6.50	6.50

Christmas.

The Brothers Grimm — A134

Disney characters in Little Red Cap (Little Red Riding Hood).

1985, Nov. 11

No.	Type	Value	Description	Unused	Used
925	A134	10c	multicolored	.40	.40
926	A134	45c	multicolored	1.00	.50
927	A134	90c	multicolored	2.00	2.00
928	A134	$1	multicolored	2.25	2.25
929	A134	$3	multicolored	4.25	4.25
			Nos. 925-929 (5)	9.90	9.40

Souvenir Sheet

No.	Type	Value	Description	Unused	Used
930	A134	$5	multicolored	7.75	7.75

Christmas.

UN, 40th Anniv. A135

Stamps of UN, famous men and events: 45c, No. 442 and Lord Baden-Powell. $2, No. 157 and Maimonides (1135-1204) Judaic scholar. $3, No. 278 and Sir Rowland Hill. $5, Apollo-Soyuz Mission, 10th anniv.

1985, Nov. 22 *Perf. 14½*

No.	Type	Value	Description	Unused	Used
931	A135	45c	multicolored	.90	.90
932	A135	$2	multicolored	2.00	2.00
933	A135	$3	multicolored	2.00	2.00
			Nos. 931-933 (3)	4.90	4.90

Souvenir Sheet

No.	Type	Value	Description	Unused	Used
934	A135	$5	multicolored	3.75	3.75

1986 World Cup Soccer Championships, Mexico — A136

Various soccer plays.

1986, Mar. 26 *Perf. 14*

No.	Type	Value	Description	Unused	Used
935	A136	45c	multicolored	1.25	1.25
936	A136	60c	multicolored	1.75	1.75
937	A136	$1	multicolored	2.25	2.25
938	A136	$3	multicolored	5.50	5.50
			Nos. 935-938 (4)	10.75	10.75

Souvenir Sheet

No.	Type	Value	Description	Unused	Used
939	A136	$5	multicolored	8.50	8.50

For overprints see Nos. 974-978.

Statue of Liberty, Cent. A137

Statue and: 15c, New York police pursuing river pirates, c. 1890. 25c, Police patrol boat. 45c, Hoboken Ferry Terminal, c. 1890. $4, Holland Tunnel.
$5, Statue, vert.

1986, Mar. 26

No.	Type	Value	Description	Unused	Used
940	A137	15c	multicolored	1.50	.75
941	A137	25c	multicolored	1.50	1.00
942	A137	45c	multicolored	2.50	1.00
943	A137	$4	multicolored	5.00	5.00
			Nos. 940-943 (4)	10.50	7.75

Souvenir Sheet

No.	Type	Value	Description	Unused	Used
944	A137	$5	multicolored	5.50	5.50

Halley's Comet A138

5c, Jantal Mantar Observatory, Delhi, India, Nasir al Din al Tusi (1201-1274), astronomer. 10c, US Bell X-1 rocket plane breaking sound barrier. 45c, Astronomicum Caesareum, 1540, manuscript diagram of comet's trajectory, 1531. $4, Mark Twain, comet appeared at birth and death. $5, Comet.

1986, Apr. 17

No.	Type	Value	Description	Unused	Used
945	A138	5c	multicolored	.60	.60
946	A138	10c	multicolored	.60	.60
947	A138	45c	multicolored	1.25	1.25
948	A138	$4	multicolored	3.25	3.25
			Nos. 945-948 (4)	5.70	5.70

Souvenir Sheet

No.	Type	Value	Description	Unused	Used
949	A138	$5	multicolored	3.75	3.75

For overprints see Nos. 984-988.

Queen Elizabeth II, 60th Birthday
Common Design Type

2c, Wedding, 1947. $1, With Pope John Paul II, 1982. $4, Royal visit, 1971.
$5, Age 10.

1986, Apr. 21 Litho. *Perf. 14*

No.	Type	Value	Description	Unused	Used
950	CD339	2c	multicolored	.25	.25
951	CD339	$1	multicolored	.75	.75
952	CD339	$4	multicolored	2.50	2.50
			Nos. 950-952 (3)	3.50	3.50

Souvenir Sheet

No.	Type	Value	Description	Unused	Used
953	CD339	$5	multicolored	3.75	3.75

AMERIPEX '86 — A139

Walt Disney characters involved in stamp collecting: 25c, Mickey Mouse and Pluto. 45c, Donald Duck. 60c, Chip-n-Dale. $4, Donald, nephews.
$5, Uncle Scrooge.

1986, May 22 *Perf. 11*

No.	Type	Value	Description	Unused	Used
954	A139	25c	multicolored	.75	.75
955	A139	45c	multicolored	.95	.95
956	A139	60c	multicolored	1.25	1.25
957	A139	$4	multicolored	4.00	4.00
			Nos. 954-957 (4)	6.95	6.95

Souvenir Sheet
Perf. 14

No.	Type	Value	Description	Unused	Used
958	A139	$5	multicolored	6.00	6.00

British Monarchs — A140

1986, June 9 *Perf. 14*

No.	Type	Value	Description	Unused	Used
959	A140	10c	William I	.40	.40
960	A140	40c	Richard II	.75	.75
961	A140	50c	Henry VIII	.90	.90
962	A140	$1	Charles II	1.00	1.00
963	A140	$2	Queen Anne	1.50	1.50
964	A140	$4	Queen Victoria	3.00	3.00
			Nos. 959-964 (6)	7.55	7.55

Audubon Type of 1985

25c, Black-throated diver. 60c, Great blue heron. 90c, Yellow-crowned night heron. $4, Shoveler duck.
$5, Goose.

Perf. 12½x12, 12x12½

1986, June 18

No.	Type	Value	Description	Unused	Used
965	A127	25c	multicolored	1.25	.50
966	A127	60c	multicolored	1.75	1.75
967	A127	90c	multicolored	2.25	2.25
968	A127	$4	multicolored	4.50	4.50
			Nos. 965-968 (4)	9.75	9.00

Souvenir Sheet
Perf. 14

No.	Type	Value	Description	Unused	Used
969	A127	$5	multicolored	10.00	10.00

Nos. 966-967 vert.

Royal Wedding Issue, 1986
Common Design Type

1986, July 23 *Perf. 14*

No.	Type	Value	Description	Unused	Used
970	CD340	45c	Couple	.40	.40
971	CD340	60c	Prince Andrew	.60	.60
972	CD340	$4	Prince, aircraft	2.50	2.50
			Nos. 970-972 (3)	3.50	3.50

Souvenir Sheet

No.	Type	Value	Description	Unused	Used
973	CD340	$5	Couple, diff.	3.75	3.75
			Nos. 970-973 (4)	7.25	7.25

Nos. 935-939 Overprinted in Gold

1986, Sept. 15 Litho. *Perf. 14*

No.	Type	Value	Description	Unused	Used
974	A136	45c	multicolored	1.25	.50
975	A136	60c	multicolored	1.50	1.50
976	A136	$1	multicolored	2.00	2.00
977	A136	$3	multicolored	4.75	4.75
			Nos. 974-977 (4)	9.50	8.75

Souvenir Sheet

No.	Type	Value	Description	Unused	Used
978	A136	$5	multicolored	8.75	8.75

Paintings by Albrecht Durer — A141

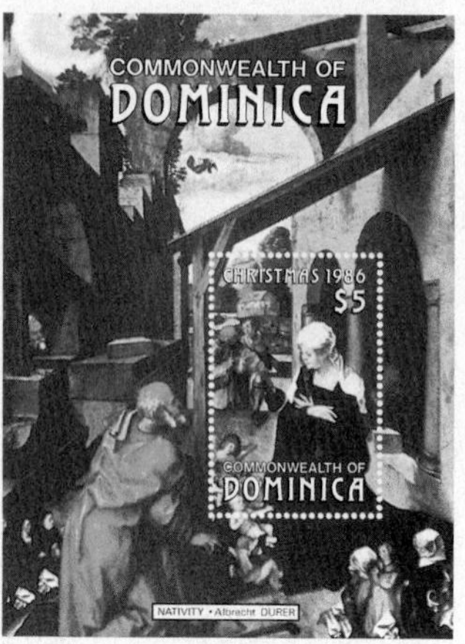

A142

45c, Virgin in Prayer. 60c, Madonna and Child. $1, Madonna and Child, diff. $3, Madonna and Child with St. Anne.
$5, Nativity.

1986, Dec. 2	Litho.		*Perf. 14*	
979	A141	45c multicolored	.85	.35
980	A141	60c multicolored	1.40	1.40
981	A141	$1 multicolored	2.00	2.00
982	A141	$3 multicolored	5.50	5.50
		Nos. 979-982 (4)	9.75	9.25

Souvenir Sheet

983	A142	$5 multicolored	8.75	8.75

Nos. 945-949 Printed with Halley's Comet Logo in Black or Silver

1986, Dec. 16				
984	A138	5c multicolored	.25	.25
985	A138	10c multicolored	.25	.25
986	A138	45c multicolored	.50	.50
987	A138	$4 multicolored	3.75	3.75
		Nos. 984-987 (4)	4.75	4.75

Souvenir Sheet

988	A138	$5 multi (S)	4.50	4.50

Birds — A143

1c, Broad-winged hawk. 2c, Ruddy quail dove. 5c, Red-necked pigeon. 10c, Green heron. 15c, Common gallinule. 20c, Ringed kingfisher. 25c, Brown pelican. 35c, White-tailed tropicbird. 45c, Red-legged thrush. 60c, Purple throated carib. 90c, Magnificent frigatebird. $1, Trembler. $2, Black-capped petrel. $5, Barn owl. $10, Imperial parrot.

1987, Jan. 20	Litho.		*Perf. 15*	
989	A143	1c multicolored	.25	*.75*
990	A143	2c multicolored	.25	*.75*
991	A143	5c multicolored	.30	*.75*
992	A143	10c multicolored	.30	.25
993	A143	15c multicolored	.40	.30
994	A143	20c multicolored	.40	.30
995	A143	25c multicolored	.40	.25
996	A143	35c multicolored	.40	.30
997	A143	45c multicolored	.50	.40
998	A143	60c multicolored	.60	.55
999	A143	90c multicolored	.70	.70
1000	A143	$1 multicolored	.80	.80
1001	A143	$2 multicolored	1.50	1.50
1002	A143	$5 multicolored	3.75	3.75
1003	A143	$10 multicolored	6.25	6.25
		Nos. 989-1003 (15)	16.80	17.60

Inscribed "1989" and "Questa"

1989, Aug. 31	Litho.		*Perf. 14*	
990a	A143	2c	.35	*.90*
991a	A143	5c	.35	*.80*
992a	A143	10c	.40	.25
993a	A143	15c	.55	.30
994a	A143	20c	.65	.35
995a	A143	25c	.65	.35
996a	A143	35c	.85	.30
997a	A143	45c	1.00	.30
998a	A143	60c	1.50	.50
1000a	A143	$1	1.75	1.00
1001a	A143	$2	3.00	3.00
1002a	A143	$5	6.00	6.00
1003a	A143	$10	8.00	8.00
		Nos. 990a-1003a (13)	25.05	22.05

Inscribed "1990" and "Questa"

1990	Litho.		*Perf. 12*	
990b	A143	2c	.40	*.95*
991b	A143	5c	.40	*.85*
992b	A143	10c	.45	.35
993b	A143	15c	.45	.35
994b	A143	20c	.70	.40
995b	A143	25c	.70	.40
996b	A143	35c	.85	.35
997b	A143	45c	1.00	.35
998b	A143	60c	1.50	1.60
1000b	A143	$1	1.75	1.00
1001b	A143	$2	3.00	3.00
1002b	A143	$5	6.25	6.25
1003b	A143	$10	8.25	8.25
		Nos. 990b-1003b (13)	25.70	24.10

Inscribed "1991" and "Questa"

1991	Litho.		*Perf. 13x11½*	
990c	A143	2c	.50	*1.10*
991c	A143	5c	.50	*.95*
992c	A143	10c	.55	.40
993c	A143	15c	.55	.35
994c	A143	20c	.75	.35
995c	A143	25c	.75	.40
996c	A143	35c	.85	.40
997c	A143	45c	1.40	1.25
998c	A143	60c	2.00	1.40
1000c	A143	$1	2.00	1.50
1001c	A143	$2	3.50	3.50
1002c	A143	$5	7.00	7.00
1003c	A143	$10	10.00	10.00
		Nos. 990c-1003c (13)	30.35	28.60

Paintings by Marc Chagall (1887-1985) A144

Designs: 25c, Artist and His Model. 35c, Midsummer Night's Dream. 45c, Joseph the Shepherd. 60c, the Cellist. 90c, Woman with Pigs. $1, the Blue Circus. $3, For Vava. $4, the Rider. No. 1012, Purim. No. 1013, Firebird design for the curtain of the Stravinsky Ballet production.

1987, Mar. 2			*Perf. 14*	
1004	A144	25c multicolored	.50	.25
1005	A144	35c multicolored	.65	.30
1006	A144	45c multicolored	.85	.35
1007	A144	60c multicolored	1.00	.50
1008	A144	90c multicolored	1.10	.70
1009	A144	$1 multicolored	1.25	1.25
1010	A144	$3 multicolored	2.50	2.50
1011	A144	$4 multicolored	3.50	3.50

Size: 110x95mm

Imperf

1012	A144	$5 multicolored	4.00	4.00
1013	A144	$5 multicolored	4.00	4.00
		Nos. 1004-1013 (10)	19.35	17.35

A145

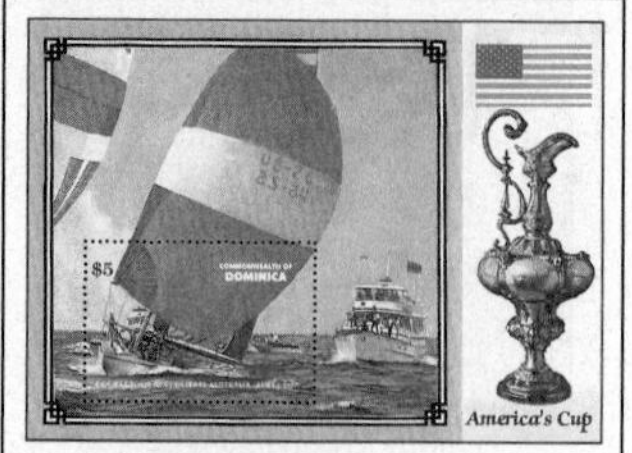

America's Cup — A146

45c, Reliance, 1903. 60c, Freedom, 1980. $1, Mischief, 1881. $3, Australia, 1977.
$5, Courageous, Australia, 1977.

1987, Feb. 5			*Perf. 15*	
1014	A145	45c multicolored	.60	.45
1015	A145	60c multicolored	.70	.50
1016	A145	$1 multicolored	.90	1.00
1017	A145	$3 multicolored	2.75	2.00
		Nos. 1014-1017 (4)	4.95	3.95

Souvenir Sheet

1018	A146	$5 multicolored	3.75	3.75

Conch Shells — A147

Designs: 35c, Morch Poulsen's triton. 45c, Swainson globe purple sea snail. 60c, Banded tulip. No. 1022, Lamarck deltoid rock shell. No. 1023, Junoia volute.

1987, Apr. 13			Litho.	
1019	A147	35c multicolored	.35	.35
1020	A147	45c multicolored	.45	.45
1021	A147	60c multicolored	.55	.55
1022	A147	$5 multicolored	3.50	3.50
		Nos. 1019-1022 (4)	4.85	4.85

Souvenir Sheet

1023	A147	$5 multicolored	4.50	4.50

CAPEX '87 A148

Mushrooms: 45c, Cantharellus cinnabarinus. 60c, Boletellus cubenis. $2, Eccilia cystiophorus. $3, Xerocomus guadelupae.
$5, Gymnopilus chrysopellus.

1987, June 15	Litho.		*Perf. 14*	
1024	A148	45c multicolored	1.50	.75
1025	A148	60c multicolored	2.00	2.00
1026	A148	$2 multicolored	3.75	3.75
1027	A148	$3 multicolored	4.50	4.50
		Nos. 1024-1027 (4)	11.75	11.00

Souvenir Sheet

1028	A148	$5 multicolored	10.00	10.00

A149

Discovery of America, 500th Anniv. (in 1992) — A150

Explorations of Christopher Columbus: 10c, Discovery of Dominica. 15c, Ships greeted by Carib Indians. 45c, Claiming New World for Spain. 60c, Wrecking of the Santa Maria. 90c, Fleet setting sail. $1, Sighting land. $3, Trading with the Indians. No. 1036, First settlement. No. 1037, Arrival of Second Fleet at Dominica, Nov. 3, 1493. No. 1038, Map of exploration of the Leeward Islands.

1987, July 27			*Perf. 15*	
1029	A149	10c multicolored	.40	.40
1030	A149	15c multicolored	.50	.50
1031	A149	45c multicolored	.75	.75
1032	A149	60c multicolored	.95	.95
1033	A149	90c multicolored	1.20	1.20
1034	A149	$1 multicolored	1.25	1.25
1035	A149	$3 multicolored	2.50	2.50
1036	A149	$5 multicolored	3.25	3.25
		Nos. 1029-1036 (8)	10.80	10.80

Souvenir Sheets

1037	A150	$5 multicolored	4.75	4.75
1038	A150	$5 multicolored	4.75	4.75

For overprints see Nos. 1083-1084.

Transportation — A151

10c, Warrior, 1st iron-clad warship. 15c, Maglev-MLU 001, fastest passenger train. 25c, Clipper Flying Cloud, fastest NYC-San Francisco voyage, 1852. 35c, 1st elevated railway, NYC. 45c, Tom Thumb, 1st US passenger train locomotive. 60c, Joshua Slocum, 1st solo circumnavigation of the world in a sloop. 90c, Se-Land Commerce, fastest Pacific crossing. $1, 1st cable car, San Francisco. $3, Orient Express. $4, The North River Steamboat of Clermont, invented by Robert Fulton, 1st successful commercial steamboat.

1987	Litho.		*Perf. 14*	
1039	A151	10c multicolored	.50	.50
1040	A151	15c multicolored	.75	.75
1041	A151	25c multi, vert.	.80	.80
1042	A151	35c multi, vert.	1.00	1.00
1043	A151	45c multicolored	1.10	1.10
1044	A151	60c multi, vert.	1.25	1.25
1045	A151	90c multi, vert.	1.40	1.40
1046	A151	$1 multicolored	1.50	1.50
1047	A151	$3 multicolored	3.75	3.75
1048	A151	$4 multicolored	4.00	4.00
		Nos. 1039-1048 (10)	16.05	16.05

Issued: 10c, 15c, 45c, 60c, $4, 9/28; others 8/1.

For overprints see Nos. 1081-1082.

Christmas — A152

Paintings (details): 20c, Virgin and Child with St. Anne, by Durer. 25c, The Virgin and Child, by Murillo. $2, Madonna and Child, by Vincenzo Foppa (c. 1427-1516). $4, Madonna and Child, by Paolo Veronese (1528-1588). $5, Angel of the Annunciation, anonymous.

1987, Nov. 16				
1049	A152	20c multicolored	.30	.30
1050	A152	25c multicolored	.30	.30
1051	A152	$2 multicolored	2.00	2.00
1052	A152	$4 multicolored	4.25	4.25
		Nos. 1049-1052 (4)	6.85	6.85

Souvenir Sheet

1053	A152	$5 multicolored	3.75	3.75

Mickey Mouse, 60th Anniv. A153

Disney theme parks and trains: 20c, People Mover, Disney World. 25c, Horse-drawn Trolley, Disneyland. 45c, Roger E. Broggie, Disney World. 60c, Big Thunder Mountain, Disneyland. 90c, Walter E. Disney, Disneyland. $1, Monorail, Disney World. $3, Casey Jr. from Dumbo. $4, Lilly Belle, Disney World. No. 1062, Rainbow Caverns Mine Train, Disneyland, horiz. No. 1063, Toy train from movie Out of Scale, horiz.

1987, Dec. 7 Litho. *Perf. 14*

1054 A153 20c multicolored .55 .55
1055 A153 25c multicolored .55 .55
1056 A153 45c multicolored .90 .90
1057 A153 60c multicolored 1.00 1.00
1058 A153 90c multicolored 1.60 1.60
1059 A153 $1 multicolored 1.75 1.75
1060 A153 $3 multicolored 4.00 4.00
1061 A153 $4 multicolored 5.25 5.25
Nos. 1054-1061 (8) 15.60 15.60

Souvenir Sheets

1062 A153 $5 multicolored 4.00 4.00
1063 A153 $5 multicolored 4.00 4.00

40th Wedding Anniv. of Queen Elizabeth II and Prince Philip — A154

45c, Couple, wedding party, 1947. 60c, Elizabeth, Charles, c. 1952. $1, Royal Family, c. 1952. $3, Queen with tiara, c. 1960.
$5, Elizabeth, 1947.

1988, Feb. 15 Litho. *Perf. 14*

1064 A154 45c multicolored .75 .75
1065 A154 60c multicolored .80 .80
1066 A154 $1 multicolored 1.00 1.00
1067 A154 $3 multicolored 2.40 2.40
Nos. 1064-1067 (4) 4.95 4.95

Souvenir Sheet

1068 A154 $5 multicolored 3.50 3.50

1988 Summer Olympics, Seoul — A155

1988, Mar. 15

1069 A155 45c Kayaking .85 .85
1070 A155 60c Tae kwon-do 1.25 1.25
1071 A155 $1 Diving 1.40 1.40
1072 A155 $3 Parallel bars 2.50 2.50
Nos. 1069-1072 (4) 6.00 6.00

Souvenir Sheet

1073 A155 $5 Soccer 3.25 3.25

For overprints see Nos. 1151-1155.

Reunion '88 Tourism Campaign A156

10c, Carib Indian, vert. 25c, Mountainous interior. 35c, Indian River, vert. 60c, Belaire dancer, vert. 90c, The Boiling Lake, vert. $3, Coral reef.
$5, Belaire dancer, diff., vert.

1988, Apr. 13 Litho. *Perf. 15*

1074 A156 10c multicolored .25 .25
1075 A156 25c multicolored .25 .25
1076 A156 35c multicolored .25 .25
1077 A156 60c multicolored .25 .25
1078 A156 90c multicolored .30 .30
1079 A156 $3 multicolored .90 .90
Nos. 1074-1079 (6) 2.20 2.20

Souvenir Sheet

1080 A156 $5 multicolored 3.00 3.00

Independence, 10th anniv.

Nos. 1046-1047, 1037-1038 Ovptd. for Philatelic Exhibitions in Black

a

b

c

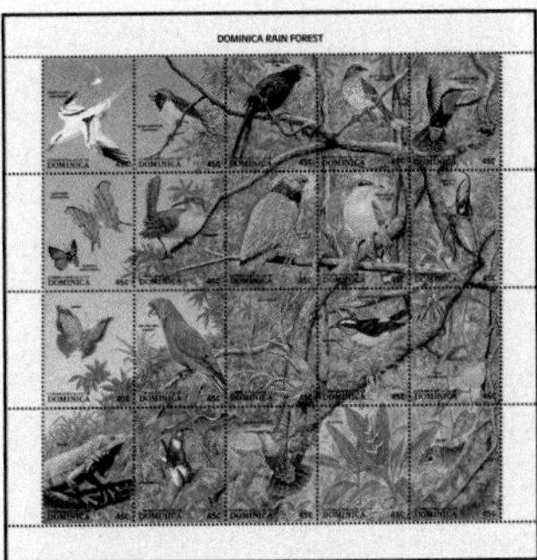

d

1988, June 1 Litho. *Perf. 14*

1081 A151(a) $1 multi 1.00 1.00
1082 A151(b) $3 multi 3.75 3.75

Souvenir Sheets

Perf. 15

1083 A150(c) $5 multi 4.00 4.00
1084 A150(d) $5 multi 4.00 4.00

Miniature Sheet

Rain Forest Flora and Fauna — A157

Designs: a, White-tailed tropicbirds. b, Blue-throated euphonia. c, Smooth-billed ani. d, Scaly-breasted thrasher. e, Purple-throated carib. f, Southern daggertail and Clench's hairstreak. g, Trembler. h, Imperial parrot. i, Mangrove cuckoo. j, Hercules beetle. k, Orion. l, Red-necked parrot. m, Tillandsia. n, Polystacha luteola and bananaquit. o, False chameleon. p, Iguana. q, Hypolimnas. r, Green-throated carib. s, Heliconia. t, Agouti.

1988, July 25 *Perf. 14½*

1085 A157 Sheet of 20 14.00 14.00
a.-t. 45c any single .60 .60

Intl. Fund for Agricultural Development (IFAD), 10th Anniv. — A158

1988, Sept. 5 Litho. *Perf. 14*

1086 A158 45c Hen house .65 .65
1087 A158 60c Pig farm .90 .90
1088 A158 90c Cattle 1.25 1.25
1089 A158 $3 Black-belly sheep 3.50 3.50
Nos. 1086-1089 (4) 6.30 6.30

Souvenir Sheet

1090 A158 $5 Mixed crops, vert. 3.75 3.75

Entertainers A159

10c, Gary Cooper. 35c, Josephine Baker. 45c, Maurice Chevalier. 60c, James Cagney. $1, Clark Gable. $2, Louis Armstrong. $3, Liberace. $4, Spencer Tracy.
No. 1099, Elvis Presley. No. 1100, Humphrey Bogart.

1988, Sept. 8

1091 A159 10c multicolored .40 .25
1092 A159 35c multicolored .50 .25
1093 A159 45c multicolored .55 .30
1094 A159 60c multicolored .75 .30
1095 A159 $1 multicolored 1.00 .30
1096 A159 $2 multicolored 1.75 1.75
1097 A159 $3 multicolored 2.00 2.00
1098 A159 $4 multicolored 2.50 2.50
Nos. 1091-1098 (8) 9.45 7.65

Souvenir Sheets

1099 A159 $5 multicolored 4.25 4.25
1100 A159 $5 multicolored 4.25 4.25

Flowering Trees and Shrubs A160

1988, Sept. 29 Litho. *Perf. 14*

1101 A160 15c Sapodilla .25 .25
1102 A160 20c Tangerine .25 .25
1103 A160 25c Avocado pear .25 .25
1104 A160 45c Amherstia .30 .30
1105 A160 90c Lipstick tree .55 .55
1106 A160 $1 Cannonball tree .60 .60
1107 A160 $3 Saman 1.50 1.50
1108 A160 $4 Pineapple 2.00 2.00
Nos. 1101-1108 (8) 5.70 5.70

Souvenir Sheets

1109 A160 $5 Lignum vitae 3.75 3.75
1110 A160 $5 Sea grape 3.75 3.75

Paintings by Titian A161

Designs: 25c, Jacopo Strada, c. 1567. 35c, Titian's Daughter Lavinia, c. 1565. 45c, Andrea Navagero, c. 1515. 60c, Judith with Head of Holoferenes, c. 1570. $1, Emilia di Spilimbergo, c. 1560. $2, Martyrdom of St. Lawrence, c. 1548. $3, Salome With the Head of St. John the Baptist, c. 1560. $4, St. John the Baptist, c. 1540. No. 1119, Self-portrait, c. 1555. No. 1120, Sisyphus, 1549.

1988, Oct. 10 Litho. *Perf. 13½x14*

1111 A161 25c multicolored .25 .25
1112 A161 35c multicolored .25 .25
1113 A161 45c multicolored .35 .35
1114 A161 60c multicolored .45 .45
1115 A161 $1 multicolored .90 .90
1116 A161 $2 multicolored 1.25 1.25
1117 A161 $3 multicolored 2.00 2.00
1118 A161 $4 multicolored 2.50 2.50
Nos. 1111-1118 (8) 7.95 7.95

Souvenir Sheets

1119 A161 $5 multicolored 3.50 3.50
1120 A161 $5 multicolored 3.50 3.50

Independence, 10th Anniv. — A162

20c, Imperial parrot. 45c, No. 1, landscape. $2, No. 602, waterfall. $3, Carib wood.
$5, Natl. band performing.

1988, Oct. 31 Litho. *Perf. 14*

1121 A162 20c multicolored 1.75 .50
1122 A162 45c multicolored 1.00 .40
1123 A162 $2 multicolored 1.75 1.75
1124 A162 $3 multicolored 2.00 *3.00*
Nos. 1121-1124 (4) 6.50 5.65

Souvenir Sheet

1125 A162 $5 multicolored 3.75 3.75

Nos. 1122-1123 horiz.

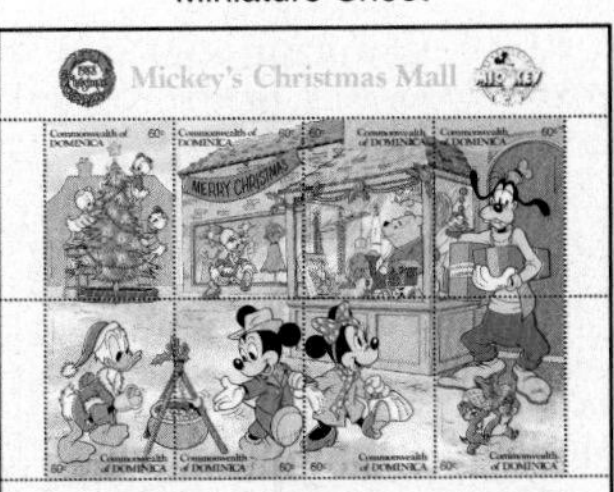

John F. Kennedy — A163

20c, With Jackie. 25c, Sailing Vicuna. $2, Walking in Hyannis Port. $4, Berlin Wall speech.
$5, Portrait.

1988, Nov. 22

1126 A163 20c multicolored .25 .25
1127 A163 25c multicolored .25 .25
1128 A163 $2 multicolored .95 .95
1129 A163 $4 multicolored 2.25 2.25
Nos. 1126-1129 (4) 3.70 3.70

Souvenir Sheet

1130 A163 $5 multicolored 3.50 3.50

Nos. 1126-1128 horiz.

Miniature Sheet

Christmas, Mickey Mouse 60th Anniv. — A164

No. 1131: a, Huey, Dewey, Louie. b, Daisy Duck. c, Winnie-the-Pooh. d, Goofy. e, Donald Duck. f, Mickey Mouse. g, Minnie Mouse. h, Chip-n-Dale.
No. 1132, Mickey, Morty and Ferdy. No. 1133, Characters visiting shopping mall Santa.

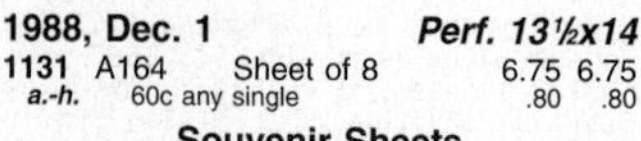

1988, Dec. 1 *Perf. 13½x14*

1131 A164 Sheet of 8 6.75 6.75
a.-h. 60c any single .80 .80

Souvenir Sheets

1132 A164 $6 multi 5.00 5.00
1133 A164 $6 multi, horiz. 5.00 5.00

UN Declaration of Human Rights, 40th Anniv. — A165

Designs: $3, Flag of Sweden and Raoul Wallenberg, who helped save 100,000 Jews in Budapest from deportation to Nazi concentration camps.
$5, Human Rights Flame.

1988, Dec. 12 *Perf. 14*

1134 A165 $3 multicolored 3.00 3.00

Souvenir Sheet

1135 A165 $5 multi, vert. 4.00 4.00

Coastal Game Fish A166

10c, Greater amberjack. 15c, Blue marlin. 35c, Cobia. 45c, Dolphin. 60c, Cero. 90c, Mahogany snapper. $3, Yellowfin tuna. $4, Rainbow parrotfish.
No. 1144, Manta ray. No. 1145, Tarpon.

1988, Dec. 22 **Litho.** *Perf. 14*

1136 A166 10c multicolored .25 .25
1137 A166 15c multicolored .25 .25
1138 A166 35c multicolored .40 .40
1139 A166 45c multicolored .50 .50
1140 A166 60c multicolored .75 .75
1141 A166 90c multicolored 1.00 1.00
1142 A166 $3 multicolored 2.50 2.50
1143 A166 $4 multicolored 3.50 3.50
Nos. 1136-1143 (8) 9.15 9.15

Souvenir Sheets

1144 A166 $5 multicolored 5.00 5.00
1145 A166 $5 multicolored 5.00 5.00

Caribbean Insects and Reptiles A167

10c, Leatherback turtle. 25c, Monarch butterfly. 60c, Green anole. $3, Praying mantis.
$5, Hercules beetle.

1988, Dec. 29

1146 A167 10c multicolored .60 .60
1147 A167 25c multicolored 1.75 1.75
1148 A167 60c multicolored 2.00 2.00
1149 A167 $3 multicolored 5.50 5.50
Nos. 1146-1149 (4) 9.85 9.85

Souvenir Sheet

1150 A167 $5 multicolored 5.00 5.00

Nos. 1069-1073 Overprinted

a

b

c

d

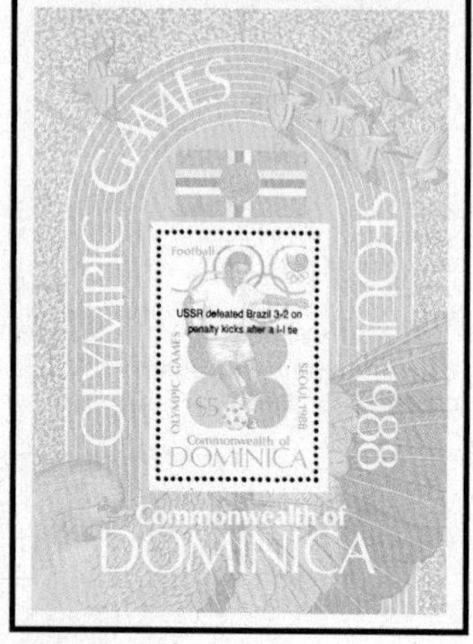

e

1989, Mar. 20 **Litho.** *Perf. 14*

1151 A155(a) 45c multi .30 .30
1152 A155(b) 60c multi .40 .40
1153 A155(c) $1 multi .75 .75
1154 A155(d) $3 multi 1.90 1.90
Nos. 1151-1154 (4) 3.35 3.35

Souvenir Sheet

1155 A155(e) $5 multi 3.75 3.75

Pre-Columbian Societies and Their Customs — A168

UPAE and discovery of America anniv. emblems and: 20c, Carib Indians canoeing. 35c, Bow hunting. $1, Canoe making. $3, Shield wrestling. $6, Dancing.

1989, May 8 **Litho.** *Perf. 14*

1156 A168 20c multicolored .25 .25
1157 A168 35c multicolored .35 .35
1158 A168 $1 multicolored 1.00 1.00
1159 A168 $3 multicolored 2.75 2.75
Nos. 1156-1159 (4) 4.35 4.35

Souvenir Sheet

1160 A168 $6 multicolored 4.25 4.25

Discovery of America 500th anniv. (in 1992).

Paintings by Yokoyama Taikan (1868-1958) A169

Designs: 10c, Lao-tzu. 20c, Red Maple Leaves (panels 1-2). 45c, King Wen Learns a Lesson from His Cook. 60c, Red Maple Leaves (panels 3-4). $1, Wild Flowers. $2, Red Maple Leaves (panels 5-6). $3, Red Maple Leaves (panels 7-8). $4, The Indian Ceremony of Floating Lamps on the River. No. 1169, Innocence. No. 1170, Red Maple Leaves (4 panels).

1989, Aug. 8 **Litho.** *Perf. 13½x14*

1161 A169 10c multicolored .25 .25
1162 A169 20c multicolored .25 .25
1163 A169 45c multicolored .30 .30
1164 A169 60c multicolored .40 .40
1165 A169 $1 multicolored .65 .65
1166 A169 $2 multicolored 1.25 1.25
1167 A169 $3 multicolored 1.75 1.75
1168 A169 $4 multicolored 2.25 2.25
Nos. 1161-1168 (8) 7.10 7.10

Souvenir Sheets

1169 A169 $5 multicolored 3.75 3.75
1170 A169 $5 multicolored 3.75 3.75

Hirohito (1901-89) and enthronement of Akihito as emperor of Japan.

PHILEXFRANCE '89, July 7-17, Paris — A170

Designs: 10c, Map of Dominica with French place names, 1766. 35c, French coin, 1688. $1, French ship, 1720. $4, Introduction of coffee to Dominica by the French, 1772. $5, Text.

1989, July 17 **Litho.** *Perf. 14*

1171 A170 10c multi, vert. 1.00 1.00
1172 A170 35c shown 1.00 1.00
1173 A170 $1 multicolored 1.50 1.50
1174 A170 $4 multicolored 3.00 3.00
Nos. 1171-1174 (4) 6.50 6.50

Souvenir Sheet

1175 A170 $5 multicolored 5.25 5.25

Butterflies A171

Designs: 10c, Homerus swallowtail. 15c, *Morpho peleides*. 25c, Julia. 35c, Gundlach's swallowtail. 60c, Monarch. $1, Gulf fritillary. $3, Red-splashed sulphur. $5, *Papilio andraemon*. No. 1184, *Heliconius doris, Adelpha cytherea, Calliona argenissa, Eurema proterpia*. No. 1185, *Adelpha iphicla, Dismorphia spio, Lucinia sida*.

1989, Sept. 11 **Litho.** *Perf. 14*

1176 A171 10c multicolored .40 .40
1177 A171 15c multicolored .40 .40
1178 A171 25c multicolored .70 .70
1179 A171 35c multicolored .80 .80
1180 A171 60c multicolored 1.10 1.10
1181 A171 $1 multicolored 1.50 1.50
1182 A171 $3 multicolored 3.50 3.50
1183 A171 $5 multicolored 6.00 6.00
Nos. 1176-1183 (8) 14.40 14.40

Souvenir Sheets

1184 A171 $6 multicolored 6.50 6.50
1185 A171 $6 multicolored 6.50 6.50

Misspellings: No. 1181, "Frittillary"; No. 1182, "Sulper."

Orchids — A172

10c, Oncidium pusillum. 35c, Epidendrum cochleata. 45c, Epidendrum ciliare. 60c, Cyrtopodium andersonii. $1, Habenaria pauciflora. $2, Maxillaria alba. $3, Selenipedium palmifolium. $4, Brassavola cucullata.
No. 1194, Oncidium lanceanum. No. 1195, Comparettia falcata.

1989, Sept. 28

1186 A172 10c multicolored .40 .40
1187 A172 35c multicolored .75 .75
1188 A172 45c multicolored .85 .85
1189 A172 60c multicolored 1.10 1.10
1190 A172 $1 multicolored 1.50 1.50
1191 A172 $2 multicolored 2.50 2.50
1192 A172 $3 multicolored 3.00 3.00
1193 A172 $4 multicolored 4.75 4.75
Nos. 1186-1193 (8) 14.85 14.85

Souvenir Sheets

1194 A172 $5 multicolored 6.50 6.50
1195 A172 $5 multicolored 6.50 6.50

1st Moon Landing, 20th Anniv. A173

10c, Columbia in lunar orbit. 60c, Aldrin descending ladder. $2, Aldrin, Sea of Tranquility. $3, Flag raising.
$6, Liftoff.

1989, Oct. 31 **Litho.** *Perf. 14*

1196 A173 10c multicolored .35 .35
1197 A173 60c multicolored .80 .80
1198 A173 $2 multicolored 2.25 2.25
1199 A173 $3 multicolored 3.25 3.25
Nos. 1196-1199 (4) 6.65 6.65

Souvenir Sheet

1200 A173 $6 multicolored 7.00 7.00

Souvenir Sheets

A174

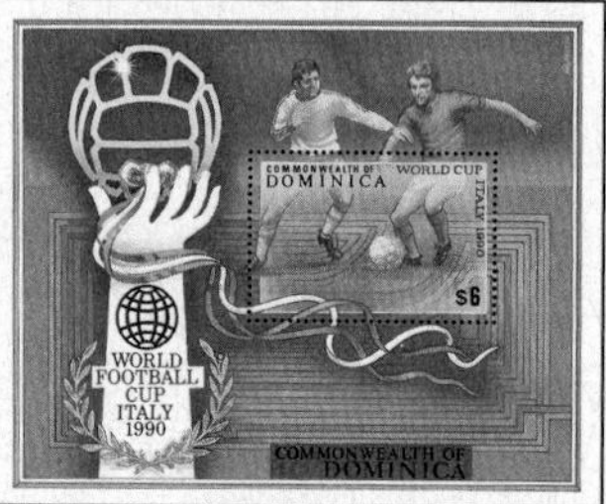

1990 World Cup Soccer Championships, Italy — A175

Past championship match scenes, flags and soccer ball: a, Brazil vs. Italy, Mexico, 1970. b, England vs. West Germany, England, 1966. c, West Germany vs. Netherlands, West Germany, 1974. d, Italy vs. West Germany, Spain, 1982.

1989, Nov. 7 *Perf. 14*

1201 A174 Sheet of 4 8.75 8.75
a.-d. $1 any single 2.00 2.00

Perf. 14

1202 A175 $6 shown 6.00 6.00

Souvenir Sheet

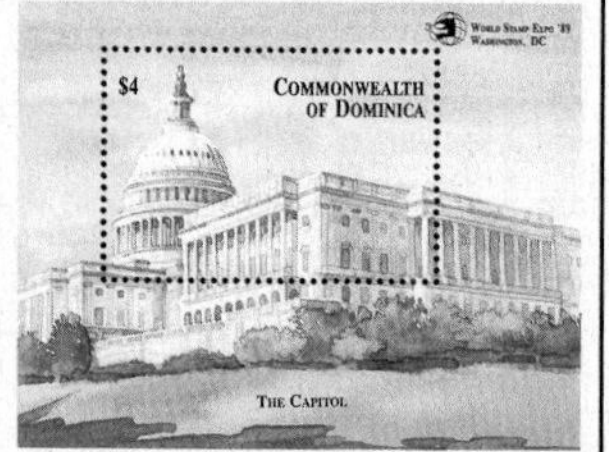

The Capitol, Washington, DC — A176

1989, Nov. 17 **Litho.** *Perf. 14*

1203 A176 $4 multicolored 3.75 3.75

World Stamp Expo '89.

Miniature Sheets

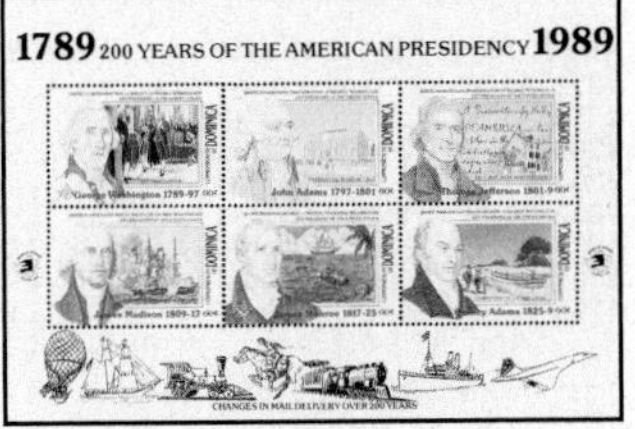

American Presidency, 200th Anniv. — A177

US presidents, historic events and monuments.

No. 1204: a, Washington, 1st inauguration. b, John Adams, presidential mansion, 1800. c, Jefferson, Graff House in Philadelphia, excerpt from the 1st draft of the Declaration of Independence. d, Madison, USS *Constitution* at the defeat of HMS *Guerriere,* 1812. e, Monroe, freed slaves settle Liberia, 1822. f, John Quincy Adams, opening of the Erie Canal, 1825.

No. 1205: a, Fillmore, Commodore Perry laying groundwork for US trade agreement with Japan. b, Pierce, Jefferson Davis and San Xavier del Bac mission, Tucson, AZ, Gadsden Purchase, 1853. c, Buchanan, Pony Express stamp, Buffalo Bill Cody as express rider. d, Lincoln, UPU emblem, Intl. Postal Congress, Paris, 1863. e, Andrew Johnson, polar bear, purchase of Alaska from Russia, 1867. f, Grant, 1st transcontinental railway link, Promontory Point, Utah, 1869.

No. 1206: a, Theodore Roosevelt, construction of the Panama Canal, 1904. b, Taft, Adm. Peary becomes 1st man to reach the North Pole, 1909. c, Wilson, US #C3, cancel commemorating 1st scheduled airmail service, 1918. d, Harding, airship USS *Shenandoah* at Lakehurst, NJ. e, Coolidge, Lindbergh's solo transatlantic flight, 1927. f, Mt. Rushmore, by Gutzon Borglum, 1927.

No. 1207: a, Lyndon B. Johnson, space exploration. b, Nixon visiting PRChina, 1971. c, Ford, tall ship in NY Harbor for Operation Sail, 1976, US bicentennial celebrations. d, Carter, Sadat of Egypt and Begin of Israel during the Camp David Accords, 1979. e, Reagan, European Space Agency emblem, flags and *Columbia* space shuttle. f, Bush, Grumman Avenger bomber he piloted during WWII.

1989, Nov. 17 *Perf. 14*

1204 A177 Sheet of 6 6.50 6.50
a.-f. 60c any single 1.00 1.00
1205 A177 Sheet of 6 6.50 6.50
a.-f. 60c any single 1.00 1.00
1206 A177 Sheet of 6 6.50 6.50
a.-f. 60c any single 1.00 1.00
1207 A177 Sheet of 6 6.50 6.50
a.-f. 60c any single 1.00 1.00

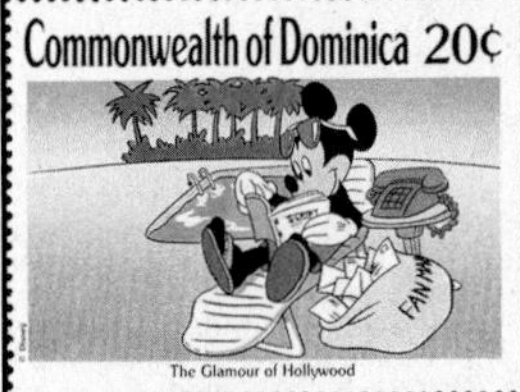

Mickey Mouse as a Hollywood Star — A178

Walt Disney characters: 20c, Reading script. 35c, Television interview. 45c, Named a star in tabloid headline. 60c, Signing autographs. $1, In dressing room, holding fans at bay. $2, Riding in limousine. $3, With Minnie in the limelight. $4, Accepting award. No. 1216, Giving interview during celebrity tennis tournament. No. 1217, Footprint impression in cement outside theater.

1989, Nov. 30 Litho. *Perf. 14x13½*

1208 A178 20c multicolored .50 .50
1209 A178 35c multicolored .70 .70
1210 A178 45c multicolored .80 .80
1211 A178 60c multicolored .90 .90
1212 A178 $1 multicolored 1.25 1.25
1213 A178 $2 multicolored 2.25 2.25
1214 A178 $3 multicolored 3.00 3.00
1215 A178 $4 multicolored 4.00 4.00
Nos. 1208-1215 (8) 13.40 13.40

Souvenir Sheets

1216 A178 $5 multicolored 5.50 5.50
1217 A178 $5 multicolored 5.50 5.50

Christmas — A179

Religious paintings by Botticelli: 20c, *Madonna in Glory with Seraphim.* 25c, *The Annunciation.* 35c, *Madonna of the Pomegranate.* 45c, *Madonna of the Rose Garden.* 60c, *Madonna of the Book.* $1, *Madonna and Child Under a Baldachin with Three Angels.* $4, *Madonna and Child with Angels.* No. 1225, *Bardi Madonna.* No. 1226, *The Mystic Nativity.* No. 1227, *The Adoration of the Magi.*

1989, Dec. 4 *Perf. 14*

1218 A179 20c multicolored .45 .45
1219 A179 25c multicolored .45 .45
1220 A179 35c multicolored .60 .60
1221 A179 45c multicolored .75 .75
1222 A179 60c multicolored .90 .90
1223 A179 $1 multicolored 1.10 1.10
1224 A179 $4 multicolored 3.00 3.00
1225 A179 $5 multicolored 4.75 4.75
Nos. 1218-1225 (8) 12.00 12.00

Souvenir Sheets

1226 A179 $5 multicolored 5.00 5.00
1227 A179 $5 multicolored 5.00 5.00

Nehru — A180

$5, Parliament House, New Delhi, horiz.

1989, Dec. 27 Litho. *Perf. 14*

1228 A180 60c shown 2.00 2.00

Souvenir Sheet

1229 A180 $5 multicolored 6.00 6.00

Jawaharlal Nehru (1889-1964), 1st prime minister of independent India.

Girl Guides — A181

Guide movement in Dominica, 60th anniv.: 60c, Lady Baden-Powell and Agatha Robinson, former Guide leader on Dominica. $5, Dorris Stockmann, chairman of the world committee of the World Assoc. of Girl Guides and Girl Scouts, and Judith Pestaina, chief commissioner of the Dominica Girl Guides Assoc., horiz.

1989, Dec. 29

1230 A181 60c multicolored 1.25 1.25

Souvenir Sheet

1231 A181 $5 multi, horiz. 5.25 5.25

Miniature Sheet

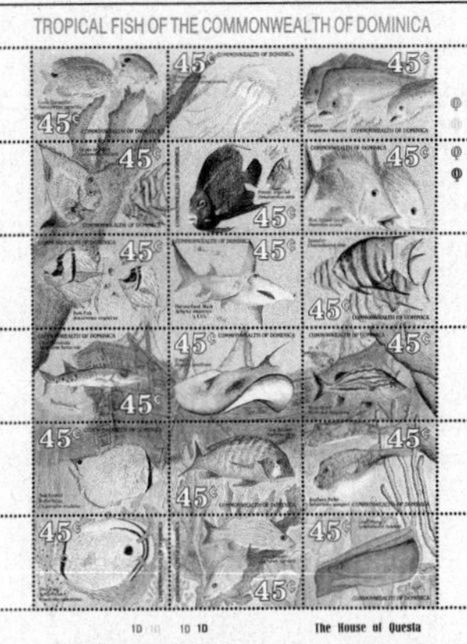

Marine Life — A182

Designs: a, Cocoa damselfish. b, Stinging jellyfish. c, Dolphin. d, Queen angelfish. e, French angelfish. f, Blue striped grunt. g, Pork fish. h, Hammerhead shark. i, Spadefish. j, Great barracuda. k, Stingray. l, Black grunt. m, Two-spotted butterflyfish. n, Dog snapper. o, Southern puffer. p, Four-eyed butterflyfish. q, Lane snapper. r, Green moray.

1990 Litho. *Perf. 14*

1232 A182 Sheet of 18 11.00 11.00
a.-r. 45c any single .55 .55

Penny Black, 150th Anniv. A183

Stamp World London '90: 50c, Post Office accelerator, 1830. 60c, $4, No. 1239, London skyline, St. Paul's Cathedral. 90c, Railway post car, 1838. $3, Center cycle, 1883. No. 1240, Mail truck, 1899.

1990, May 3 Litho. *Perf. 13½*

1233 A183 45c green & black .60 .60
1234 A183 50c blk & slate blue .80 .80
1235 A183 60c dk blue & blk .85 .85
1236 A183 90c black & green 1.50 1.50
1237 A183 $3 blk & dk bl vio 2.75 2.75
1238 A183 $4 dk bl vio & blk 3.75 3.75
Nos. 1233-1238 (6) 10.25 10.25

Souvenir Sheet

1239 A183 $5 beige & black 4.50 4.50
1240 A183 $5 gray & red brn 4.50 4.50

A184

Birds: 10c, Blue-headed hummingbird. 20c, Black-capped petrel. 45c, Red-necked parrot. 60c, Black swift. $1, Troupial. $2, Brown noddy. $4, Lesser Antillean pewee. $5. Little blue heron. No. 1249, House wren. No. 1250, Imperial parrot.

1990, July 16 Litho. *Perf. 14*

1241 A184 10c multicolored .40 .40
1242 A184 20c multicolored .55 .55
1243 A184 45c multicolored .75 .75
1244 A184 60c multicolored .95 .95
1245 A184 $1 multicolored 1.60 1.60
1246 A184 $2 multicolored 2.25 2.25
1247 A184 $4 multicolored 3.75 3.75
1248 A184 $5 multicolored 4.25 4.25
Nos. 1241-1248 (8) 14.50 14.50

Souvenir Sheets

1249 A184 $6 multicolored 5.00 5.00
1250 A184 $6 multicolored 5.00 5.00

A185

Shells: 10c, Reticulated cowrie-helmet. 20c, West Indian chank. 35c, West Indian fighting conch. 60c, True tulip. $1, Sunrise tellin. $2, Crown cone. $3, Common dove shell. $4, Atlantic fig shell. No. 1259, Giant tun. No. 1260, King helmet.

1990, July 19

1251 A185 10c multicolored .40 .40
1252 A185 20c multicolored .55 .55
1253 A185 35c multicolored .70 .70
1254 A185 60c multicolored 1.00 1.00
1255 A185 $1 multicolored 1.40 1.40
1256 A185 $2 multicolored 2.25 2.25
1257 A185 $3 multicolored 3.00 3.00
1258 A185 $4 multicolored 3.75 3.75
Nos. 1251-1258 (8) 13.05 13.05

Souvenir Sheets

1259 A185 $5 multicolored 5.00 5.00
1260 A185 $5 multicolored 5.00 5.00

A186

Queen Mother, 90th Birthday: various photos.

1990, Sept. 10

1261 A186 20c multicolored .25 .25
1262 A186 45c multicolored .40 .40
1263 A186 60c multicolored .60 .60
1264 A186 $3 multicolored 2.50 2.50
Nos. 1261-1264 (4) 3.75 3.75

Souvenir Sheet

1265 A186 $5 multicolored 3.50 3.50

A187

45c, Men's singles, tennis. 60c, Men's foil fencing. $2, 100m freestyle swimming. $3, Star class yachting.

$5, Coxless pairs, rowing.

1990, Nov. 5 Litho. *Perf. 14*

1266 A187 45c multicolored 1.25 1.25
1267 A187 60c multicolored 1.40 1.40
1268 A187 $2 multicolored 2.25 2.25
1269 A187 $3 multicolored 3.25 3.25
Nos. 1266-1269 (4) 8.15 8.15

Souvenir Sheet

1270 A187 $5 multicolored 6.75 6.75

1992 Summer Olympics, Barcelona.

Christmas A188

Walt Disney characters on carousel animals: 10c, Mickey, frog. 15c, Huey, Dewey & Louie, white elephant. 25c, Donald, polar bear. 45c, Goofy, goat. $1, Donald, giraffe. $2, Daisy, stork. $4, Goofy, lion. $5, Daisy, horse. No. 1279, Mickey, swan chariot, horiz. No. 1280, Mickey, Minnie & Goofy, griffin chariot.

1990, Dec. 13 *Perf. 13½x14*

1271	A188	10c multicolored	.40	.40
1272	A188	15c multicolored	.50	.50
1273	A188	25c multicolored	.60	.60
1274	A188	45c multicolored	.90	.90
1275	A188	$1 multicolored	1.25	1.25
1276	A188	$2 multicolored	2.00	2.00
1277	A188	$4 multicolored	4.00	4.00
1278	A188	$5 multicolored	5.00	5.00
		Nos. 1271-1278 (8)	14.65	14.65

Souvenir Sheets

Perf. 14x13½

1279	A188	$6 multicolored	7.00	7.00
1280	A188	$6 multicolored	7.00	7.00

World Cup Soccer Championships, Italy — A189

Players and coaches from participating countries.

1990, Dec. 28 Litho. *Perf. 14*

1281	A189	15c England	.45	.45
1282	A189	45c Brazil	.75	.75
1283	A189	60c West Germany	1.00	1.00
1284	A189	$4 Austria	4.25	4.25
		Nos. 1281-1284 (4)	6.45	6.45

Souvenir Sheets

1285	A189	$6 Ireland, vert.	5.00	5.00
1286	A189	$6 USSR, vert.	5.00	5.00

Cog Trains of Switzerland — A190

Designs: 10c, Glion-Roches de Naye, 1890. 35c, Electric cog rail car ascending Mt. Pilatus. 45c, Cog railway to Schynige Platte, view of Eiger, Monch and Jungfrau Mountains. 60c, Furka-Oberalp train on Bugnli Viaduct, vert. $1, 1910 Jungfraubahn Cog Railway, Jungfrau Mountain, 1910. $2, Testing Swiss rail cars built for Pike's Peak on Arth-Rigibahn, 1963. $4, Brienz-Rothorn Bahn, 1991. $5, Private 1870 Rigi-Scheideck Hotel post stamp, 1890 Arth-Rigi Railway Engine. No. 1295, Sherlock Holmes watching Brunigline train descending from Brunig Pass. No. 1296, Switzerland #738 and first passenger train to ascend Mt. Rigi, 1871.

1991, Mar. 26 Litho. *Perf. 14*

1287	A190	10c multicolored	.60	.60
1288	A190	35c multicolored	1.00	1.00
1289	A190	45c multicolored	1.10	1.10
1290	A190	60c multicolored	1.25	1.25
1291	A190	$1 multicolored	1.40	1.40
1292	A190	$2 multicolored	2.00	2.00
1293	A190	$4 multicolored	3.00	3.00
1294	A190	$5 multicolored	3.50	3.50
		Nos. 1287-1294 (8)	13.85	13.85

Souvenir Sheets

Perf. 13½

1295	A190	$6 multicolored	6.00	6.00
1296	A190	$6 multicolored	6.00	6.00

Nos. 1295-1296 each contain one 50x37mm stamp.

Voyages of Discovery A191

Explorer's ships: 10c, Gil Eannes, 1433-1434. 25c, Alfonso Gonclaves Baldaya, 1436. 45c, Bartolomeu Dias, 1487. 60c, Vasco da Gama, 1497-1499. $1, Vallarte the Dane. $2, Aloisio Cadamosto, 1456-1458. $4, Diogo Gomes, 1457. $5, Diogo Cao, 1482-1485.

No. 1305, Blue and yellow macaw. No. 1306, Red and yellow macaw.

1991, Apr. 8 Litho. *Perf. 14*

1297	A191	10c multicolored	.45	.45
1298	A191	25c multicolored	.55	.55
1299	A191	45c multicolored	.65	.65
1300	A191	60c multicolored	.75	.75
1301	A191	$1 multicolored	1.10	1.10
1302	A191	$2 multicolored	1.60	1.60
1303	A191	$4 multicolored	2.75	2.75
1304	A191	$5 multicolored	3.25	3.25
		Nos. 1297-1304 (8)	11.10	11.10

Souvenir Sheets

1305	A191	$6 multicolored	4.75	4.75
1306	A191	$6 multicolored	4.75	4.75

Discovery of America, 500th anniv. (in 1992).

Japanese Costumes — A192

Walt Disney characters wearing Japanese costumes: 10c, Donald as soldier. 15c, Mickey as Kabuki actor. 25c, Mickey, Minnie in traditional wedding clothes. 45c, Daisy as Geisha girl, vert. $1, Mickey in sokutai dress of high government official, vert. $2, Goofy as mino farmer, vert. $4, Pete as shogun, vert. $5, Donald as warlord. No. 1315, Mickey, as Noh player, vert. No. 1316, Goofy as Kabubei-Jishi street performer, vert.

1991, May 22 Litho. *Perf. 14*

1307	A192	10c multicolored	.65	.65
1308	A192	15c multicolored	.75	.75
1309	A192	25c multicolored	.90	.90
1310	A192	45c multicolored	1.10	1.10
1311	A192	$1 multicolored	2.00	2.00
1312	A192	$2 multicolored	2.75	2.75
1313	A192	$4 multicolored	3.50	3.50
1314	A192	$5 multicolored	4.25	4.25
		Nos. 1307-1314 (8)	15.90	15.90

Souvenir Sheets

1315	A192	$6 multicolored	7.50	7.50
1316	A192	$6 multicolored	7.50	7.50

Phila Nippon '91.

Mushrooms A193

10c, Horn of plenty. 15c, Shaggy mane. 45c, Yellow morel. 60c, Chanterelle. $1, Blewit. $2, Slippery jack. $4, Emetic russula. $5, Honey mushroom.

No. 1326, Beefsteak polypore. No. 1327, Voluminous-latex milky.

1991, June 3 Litho. *Perf. 14*

1318	A193	10c multicolored	.25	.25
1319	A193	15c multicolored	.45	.45
1320	A193	45c multicolored	.55	.55
1321	A193	60c multicolored	.65	.65
1322	A193	$1 multicolored	1.00	1.00
1323	A193	$2 multicolored	1.75	1.75
1324	A193	$4 multicolored	3.00	3.00
1325	A193	$5 multicolored	4.00	4.00
		Nos. 1318-1325 (8)	11.65	11.65

Souvenir Sheets

1326	A193	$6 multicolored	5.00	5.00
1327	A193	$6 multicolored	5.00	5.00

Royal Family Birthday, Anniversary

Common Design Type

1991, June 17 Litho. *Perf. 14*

1328	CD347	10c multicolored	.45	.45
1329	CD347	15c multicolored	.90	.90
1330	CD347	40c multicolored	1.00	1.00
1331	CD347	60c multicolored	1.10	1.10
1332	CD347	$1 multicolored	2.00	2.00
1333	CD347	$2 multicolored	2.75	2.75
1334	CD347	$4 multicolored	4.00	4.00
1335	CD347	$5 multicolored	4.50	4.50
		Nos. 1328-1335 (8)	16.70	16.70

Souvenir Sheets

1336	CD347	$5 Elizabeth, Philip	5.00	5.00
1337	CD347	$5 Charles, Diana, sons	8.50	8.50

10c, 60c, $2, $4, No. 1336, Queen Elizabeth II, 65th birthday. Others, Charles and Diana, 10th wedding anniversary.

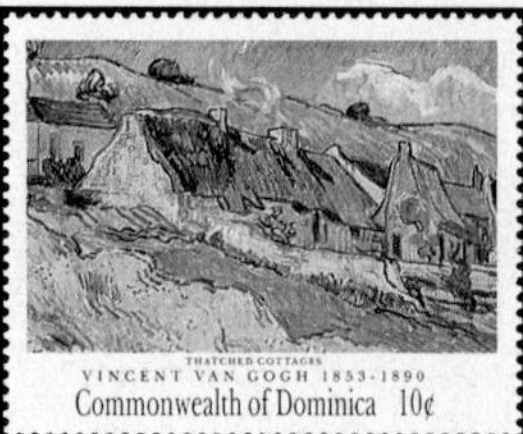

Vincent Van Gogh (1853-1890), Painter — A194

Paintings: 10c, Thatched Cottages. 25c, The House of Pere Eloi. 45c, The Midday Siesta. 60c, Portrait of a Young Peasant, vert. $1, Still Life: Vase with Irises Against a Yellow Background, vert. $2, Still Life Vase with Irises. $4, Blossoming Almond Tree. $5, Irises. No. 1346, A Meadow in the Mountains: Le Mas De Saint-Paul. No. 1347, Doctor Gachet's Garden in Auvers, vert.

1991, July 8 Litho. *Perf. 13½*

1338	A194	10c multicolored	.65	.65
1339	A194	25c multicolored	.90	.90
1340	A194	45c multicolored	1.10	1.10
1341	A194	60c multicolored	1.40	1.40
1342	A194	$1 multicolored	2.00	2.00
1343	A194	$2 multicolored	2.50	2.50
1344	A194	$4 multicolored	3.75	3.75
1345	A194	$5 multicolored	4.00	4.00
		Nos. 1338-1345 (8)	16.30	16.30

Size: 101x75mm

Imperf

1346	A194	$6 multicolored	6.50	6.50
1347	A194	$6 multicolored	6.50	6.50

Intl. Literacy Year — A195

Scenes from Walt Disney's "The Little Mermaid": 10c, Ariel with Flounder and Sebastian. 25c, King Triton. 45c, Sebastian drums in "Kiss De Girl" concert. 60c, Flotsam and Jetsam taunt Ariel. $1, Scuttle, Flounder and Ariel. $2, Ariel and Flounder discover a book. $4, Prince Eric, dog Max, manservant Grimsby, and crew. $5, Ursula the sea witch. No. 1356, Ariel transformed into human being. No. 1357, Ariel and Prince Eric dancing in town, vert.

1991, Aug. 6 *Perf. 14*

1348	A195	10c multicolored	.35	.35
1349	A195	25c multicolored	.45	.45
1350	A195	45c multicolored	.65	.65
1351	A195	60c multicolored	.90	.90
1352	A195	$1 multicolored	1.50	1.50
1353	A195	$2 multicolored	2.75	2.75
1354	A195	$4 multicolored	4.50	4.50
1355	A195	$5 multicolored	5.50	5.50
		Nos. 1348-1355 (8)	16.60	16.60

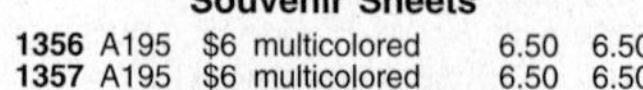

Souvenir Sheets

1356	A195	$6 multicolored	6.50	6.50
1357	A195	$6 multicolored	6.50	6.50

World Landmarks — A196

Designs: 10c, Empire State Building, US, vert. 25c, Kremlin, USSR. 45c, Buckingham Palace, United Kingdom. 60c, Eiffel Tower, France, vert. $1, Taj Mahal, India. $2, Sydney Opera House, Australia. $4, Colosseum, Italy. $5, Pyramids, Egypt. No. 1366, Galileo demonstrating laws of physics from Tower of Pisa, Italy. No. 1367, Great Wall of China and Emperor Shi Huang Ti.

1991, Aug. 12 Litho. *Perf. 14*

1358	A196	10c multicolored	.45	.45
1359	A196	25c multicolored	.55	.55
1360	A196	45c multicolored	.90	.90
1361	A196	60c multicolored	1.10	1.10
1362	A196	$1 multicolored	2.00	2.00
1363	A196	$2 multicolored	3.00	3.00
1364	A196	$4 multicolored	4.75	4.75
1365	A196	$5 multicolored	5.50	5.50
		Nos. 1358-1365 (8)	18.25	18.25

Souvenir Sheets

1366	A196	$6 multicolored	8.00	8.00
1367	A196	$6 multicolored	8.00	8.00

Japanese Attack on Pearl Harbor, 50th Anniv. A197

Designs: 10c, 6:00am, First wave of Japanese planes leave carrier Akagi. 15c, 6:40am, Destroyer Ward and PBY attack midget submarine. 45c, 7:00am, Second wave of Japanese planes leave carriers. 60c, 7:48am, Japanese Zeros attack on Kaneohe Air Station. $1, 8:30am, Destroyers Breeze, Medusa and Curtiss sink midget submarine. $2, 8:45am, Damaged battleship Nevada sorties. $4, 8:10am, Battleship Arizona explodes, killing 1,177 men. $5, 9:45am, Japanese attack ends. No. 1376, 8:00am, Japanese fighters and bombers attack Hickam Air Base. No. 1377, 7:55am, Pearl Harbor attack begins.

1991, Sept. 2

1368	A197	10c multicolored	.60	.60
1369	A197	15c multicolored	.70	.70
1370	A197	45c multicolored	1.10	1.10
1371	A197	60c multicolored	1.25	1.25
1372	A197	$1 multicolored	1.50	1.50
1373	A197	$2 multicolored	2.00	2.00
1374	A197	$4 multicolored	2.75	2.75
1375	A197	$5 multicolored	3.00	3.00
		Nos. 1368-1375 (8)	12.90	12.90

Souvenir Sheets

1376	A197	$6 multicolored	5.25	5.25
1377	A197	$6 multicolored	5.25	5.25

Butterflies — A198

1c, Little yellow. 2c, Gulf fritillary. 5c, Monarch. 10c, Red rim. 15c, Flambeau. 20c, Large orange sulphur. 25c, Caribbean buckeye. 35c, Polydamas swallowtail. 45c, Cassius blue. 55c, Great southern white. 60c, Godman's leaf. 65c, Hanno blue. 90c, Mimic. $1, Long-tailed skipper. $1.20, Orion. $2, Cloudless sulphur. $5, Painted lady. $10, Southern daggertail. $20, White peacock.

Perf. 13½x13, 13½x14 (2c, 10c, 15c, 25c, 45c, 90c, $1, $20)

1991-93

1378	A198	1c multi	.35	*.90*
1379	A198	2c multi	.35	*.90*
1380	A198	5c multi	.65	*.90*
1381	A198	10c multi	.65	.25
1382	A198	15c multi	.75	.25
1383	A198	20c multi	.75	.25
1384	A198	25c multi	.75	.25
1385	A198	35c multi	.85	.35
1386	A198	45c multi	.85	.35
1386A	A198	55c multi	1.25	.60
1387	A198	60c multi	1.00	.40
1387A	A198	65c multi	1.25	.60
1388	A198	90c multi	1.40	.60
1389	A198	$1 multi	1.40	.75
1389A	A198	$1.20 multi	1.50	1.50
1390	A198	$2 multi	2.25	2.25
1391	A198	$5 multi	3.75	*5.50*
1391A	A198	$10 multi	9.00	*11.00*
1391B	A198	$20 multi	14.00	*16.00*
		Nos. 1378-1391B (19)	42.75	43.60

Issued: 55c, 65c, $1.20, 1/11/93; others, 10/14/91.

Charles de Gaulle, Birth Cent. — A199

1991, Nov. 1

1392 A199 45c shown 2.25 2.25

Souvenir Sheet

1393 A199 $5 blk & bl, horiz. 6.00 6.00

Creole Week — A200

45c, Man in 18th cent. costume. 60c, Accordion player. $1, Dancers. $5, Stick fight c. 1785.

1991, Nov. 1 ***Perf. 14***

1394 A200 45c multicolored .60 .60
1395 A200 60c multicolored .90 .90
1396 A200 $1 multicolored 1.50 1.50
Nos. 1394-1396 (3) 3.00 3.00

Souvenir Sheet

1397 A200 $5 multicolored 6.50 6.50

Credit Union, 40th Anniv. — A201

60c, Emblem, founder, horiz.

1991, Nov. 1

1398 A201 10c black .55 .55
1399 A201 60c blk, red, org, yel 1.50 1.50

Year of the Environment and Shelter — A202

15c, Keep the beaches clean. 60c, No. 1402, Amazona imperalis. No. 1403, Lagoon outlet.

1991, Nov. 18

1400 A202 15c multicolored .50 .50
1401 A202 60c multicolored 2.75 2.75

Souvenir Sheets

1402 A202 $5 multicolored 7.75 7.75
1403 A202 $5 multicolored 7.75 7.75

Christmas A203

Paintings by Jan van Eyck: 10c, The Virgin Enthroned with Child (detail). 20c, The Madonna at the Fountain. 35c, The Virgin in a Church. 45c, The Madonna with Canon van der Paele. 60c, The Madonna with Canon van der Paele (detail). $1, The Madonna in an Interior. $3, The Annunciation. $5, The Annunciation, diff. No. 1412, The Madonna with Chancellor Rolin. No. 1413, Virgin and Child with Saints and Donor.

1991, Dec. 2 ***Perf. 12***

1404 A203 10c multicolored .55 .55
1405 A203 20c multicolored .75 .75
1406 A203 35c multicolored .90 .90
1407 A203 45c multicolored 1.00 1.00
1408 A203 60c multicolored 1.50 1.50
1409 A203 $1 multicolored 1.75 1.75
1410 A203 $3 multicolored 2.75 2.75
1411 A203 $5 multicolored 4.00 4.00
Nos. 1404-1411 (8) 13.20 13.20

Souvenir Sheets

Perf. 14x14½

1412 A203 $6 multicolored 6.50 6.50
1413 A203 $6 multicolored 6.50 6.50

Queen Elizabeth II's Accession to the Throne, 40th Anniv.

Common Design Type

1992, Feb. 6 **Litho.** ***Perf. 14***

1414 CD348 10c multicolored .25 .25
1415 CD348 15c multicolored .25 .25
1416 CD348 $1 multicolored .75 .75
1417 CD348 $5 multicolored 3.75 3.75
Nos. 1414-1417 (4) 5.00 5.00

Souvenir Sheets

1418 CD348 $6 River scene 3.75 3.75
1419 CD348 $6 Seaside village 3.75 3.75

Botanical Gardens, Cent. — A204

Designs: 10c, Cricket match. 15c, Scenic entrance. 45c, Traveller's tree. 60c, Bamboo house. $1, Old pavilion. $2, Ficus benjamina. $4, Cricket ground. $5, Thirty-five steps. No. 1428, Fountain. No. 1429, Cricket masters.

1992, Mar. 30 **Litho.** ***Perf. 14***

1420 A204 10c multicolored .40 .40
1421 A204 15c multicolored .40 .40
1422 A204 45c multicolored .40 .40
1423 A204 60c multicolored .60 .60
1424 A204 $1 multicolored 1.00 1.00
1425 A204 $2 multicolored 1.75 1.75
1426 A204 $4 multicolored 4.25 4.25
1427 A204 $5 multicolored 4.50 4.50
Nos. 1420-1427 (8) 13.30 13.30

Souvenir Sheets

1428 A204 $6 multicolored 5.00 5.00
1429 A204 $6 multicolored 5.00 5.00

Spanish Art — A205

Paintings or details from paintings by Velazquez: 10c, Pope Innocent X. 15c, 45c The Forge of Vulcan (different details). 60c, Queen Mariana of Austria. $1, Pablo de Valladolid. $2, Sebastian de Morra. $3, Felipe IV (detail). $4, Felipe IV. No. 1438, Surrender of Breda. No. 1439, The Drunkards.

1992, May 4 ***Perf. 13***

1430 A205 10c multicolored .25 .25
1431 A205 15c multicolored .25 .25
1432 A205 45c multicolored .45 .45
1433 A205 60c multicolored .55 .55
1434 A205 $1 multicolored .80 .80
1435 A205 $2 multicolored 1.50 1.50
1436 A205 $3 multicolored 2.25 2.25
1437 A205 $4 multicolored 2.75 2.75

Size: 120x95mm

Imperf

1438 A205 $6 multicolored 4.75 4.75
1439 A205 $6 multicolored 4.75 4.75
Nos. 1430-1439 (10) 18.30 18.30

Granada '92.

Easter — A206

Paintings: 10c, The Supper at Emmaus, studio of Gerrit Van Honthorst. 15c, Christ before Caiaphas, by Van Honthorst, vert. 45c, The Taking of Christ, by Valentin de Boulogne. 60c, Pilate Washing his Hands, by Mattia Preti, vert. $1, The Last Supper (detail), by Master of the Reredos of The Chapel of the Church of S. Francisco D'Evora. $2, The Three Marys at the Tomb (detail), by Adolphe William Bouguereau, vert. $3, Denial of St. Peter, by Hendrik Terbrugghen. $5, Doubting Thomas, by Bernardo Strozzi, vert. No. 1448, The Crucifixion (detail), by Mathias Grunewald, vert. No. 1449, The Resurrection (detail), by Caravaggio, vert.

1992 ***Perf. 14***

1440 A206 10c multicolored .25 .25
1441 A206 15c multicolored .25 .25
1442 A206 45c multicolored .50 .50
1443 A206 60c multicolored .75 .75
1444 A206 $1 multicolored .90 .90
1445 A206 $2 multicolored 1.50 1.50
1446 A206 $3 multicolored 2.25 2.25
1447 A206 $5 multicolored 3.75 3.75
Nos. 1440-1447 (8) 10.15 10.15

Souvenir Sheets

1448 A206 $6 multicolored 5.00 5.00
1449 A206 $6 multicolored 5.00 5.00

Columbus and New World Flora and Fauna — A207

10c, Hercules beetle. 25c, Crapaud frog. 75c, Parrot. $2, Anole. $4, Royal gramma. $5, Hibiscus.

No. 1456, Giant katydid. No. 1457, Columbus' fleet.

1992, May 18

1450 A207 10c multi .50 .50
1451 A207 25c multi 1.00 1.00
1452 A207 75c multi 1.75 1.75
1453 A207 $2 multi 2.00 2.00
1454 A207 $4 multi 2.75 2.75
1455 A207 $5 multi 3.50 3.50
Nos. 1450-1455 (6) 11.50 11.50

Souvenir Sheets

1456 A207 $6 multi 5.00 5.00
1457 A207 $6 multi 5.00 5.00

Nos. 1456-1457 are horiz.

Hummingbirds — A208

10c, Purple throated carib. 15c, Rufous breasted hermit. 45c, Puerto Rican emerald. 60c, Antillean mango. $1, Green throated carib. $2, Blue headed. $4, Eastern streamertail. $5, Antillean crested. No. 1466, Green mango. No. 1467, Vervain hummingbird.

1992, May 28

1458 A208 10c multicolored .50 .50
1459 A208 15c multicolored .50 .50
1460 A208 45c multicolored .75 .75
1461 A208 60c multicolored .90 .90
1462 A208 $1 multicolored 1.25 1.25
1463 A208 $2 multicolored 2.25 2.25
1464 A208 $4 multicolored 3.75 3.75
1465 A208 $5 multicolored 4.50 4.50
Nos. 1458-1465 (8) 14.40 14.40

Souvenir Sheets

1466 A208 $6 multicolored 6.75 6.75
1467 A208 $6 multicolored 6.75 6.75

Genoa '92.

Dinosaurs A209

10c, Camptosaurus. 15c, Edmontosaurus. 25c, Corythosaurus. 60c, Stegosaurus. $1, Torosaurus. $3, Euoplocephalus. $4, Tyrannosaurus. $5, Parasaurolophus.

1992, June 23 **Litho.** ***Perf. 14***

1468 A209 10c multi .50 .50
1469 A209 15c multi .60 .60
1470 A209 25c multi .75 .75
1471 A209 60c multi .85 .85
1472 A209 $1 multi 1.00 1.00
1473 A209 $3 multi 1.90 1.90
1474 A209 $4 multi 3.00 3.00
1475 A209 $5 multi 3.50 3.50
Nos. 1468-1475 (8) 12.10 12.10

Souvenir Sheets

1476 A209 $6 like #1472 4.75 4.75
1477 A209 $6 like #1470 4.75 4.75

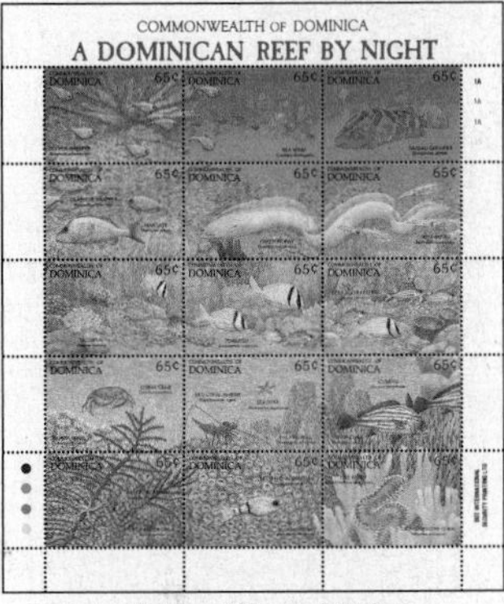

Marine Life — A210

No. 1478: a, Copper sweeper (b). b, Sea wasp (c). c, Nassau grouper. d, Glasseye snapper, margate. e, Green moray (f). f, Reef squid. g, Octopus. h, Porkfish (g, i). i, Reef squirrelfish (h). j, Coral crab, flower coral. k, Red coral shrimp, sea star, pillar coral (l, n). l, Cubbyu, brain coral (o). m, Basket starfish, thick finger coral. n, Belted cardinal fish, boulder coral (k, m). o, Fire worm, crenelated fire coral.

No. 1479: a, Trumpetfish, blue chromis. b, Queen triggerfish. c, Hawksbill turtle. d, Sergeant major, rock beauty. e, Sharksucker. f, Lemon shark. g, Spotted trunkfish, bluehead. h, Blue tang, yellowtail damselfish. i, Queen angelfish, banded butterflyfish. j, Spotted seahorse, flower coral. k, Stoplight parrotfish, pillar coral. l, Smallmouth grunt, brain coral. m, Flamingo tongue, thick finger coral. n, Arrow crab, boulder coral. o, Sharknose goby, crenelated fire coral.

No. 1480, Harlequin bass. No. 1481, Flamefish.

1992, July 20 **Litho.** ***Perf. 14***

1478 A210 65c Sheet of 15, #a.-o. 7.75 7.75
1479 A210 65c Sheet of 15, #a.-o. 7.75 7.75

Souvenir Sheets

1480 A210 $6 multicolored 6.50 6.50
1481 A210 $6 multicolored 6.50 6.50

A211

10c, Archery. 15c, Two-man canoeing. 25c, 110-meter hurdles. 60c, Men's high jump. $1, Greco-Roman wrestling. $2, Men's rings. $4, Men's parallel bars. $5, Equestrian.

No. 1490, Field hockey. No. 1491, Women's platform diving.

1992, Aug. 10 Litho. *Perf. 14*

1482	A211	10c multi	.30	.30
1483	A211	15c multi	.35	.35
1484	A211	25c multi	.40	.40
1485	A211	60c multi	.65	.65
1486	A211	$1 multi	.90	.90
1487	A211	$2 multi	1.50	1.50
1488	A211	$4 multi	2.75	2.75
1489	A211	$5 multi	3.25	3.25
		Nos. 1482-1489 (8)	10.10	10.10

Souvenir Sheets

1490	A211	$6 multi	5.50	5.50
1491	A211	$6 multi	5.50	5.50

1992 Summer Olympics, Barcelona.

A212

1992 Litho. *Perf. 14½*

1492	A212	$1 Coming ashore	1.00	1.00
1493	A212	$2 Natives, ships	1.75	2.00

Discovery of America, 500th anniv. Organization of East Caribbean States.

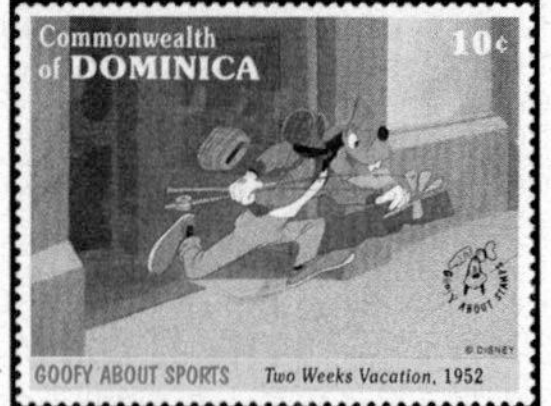

Walt Disney's Goofy, 60th Anniv. — A213

Scenes from Disney cartoon films: 10c, Two Weeks Vacation, 1952. 15c, Aquamania, 1961. 25c, Goofy Gymnastics, 1949. 45c, How to Ride a Horse, 1941. $1, Foul Hunting, 1947. $2, For Whom the Bulls Toil, 1953. $4, Tennis Racquet, 1949. $5, Double Dribble, 1946. No. 1502, Aquamania, 1961, vert. No. 1503, The Goofy Sports Story, 1956, vert.

1992, Nov. 11 Litho. *Perf. 14x13½*

1494	A213	10c multicolored	.45	.45
1495	A213	15c multicolored	.55	.55
1496	A213	25c multicolored	.80	.80
1497	A213	45c multicolored	.90	.90
1498	A213	$1 multicolored	1.50	1.50
1499	A213	$2 multicolored	2.75	2.75
1500	A213	$4 multicolored	4.75	4.75
1501	A213	$5 multicolored	5.25	5.25
		Nos. 1494-1501 (8)	16.95	16.95

Souvenir Sheets

Perf. 13½x14

1502	A213	$6 multicolored	7.75	7.75
1503	A213	$6 multicolored	7.75	7.75

Model Trains A214

15c, Brass Reno 4-4-0, HO scale, c. 1963. 25c, Union Pacific Golden Classic, G gauge, 1992. 55c, LMS 3rd class brake coach, OO scale, 1970s. 65c, Brass Wabash 2-6-0, HO scale, c. 1958. 75c, Pennsylvania RR T-1 duplex, O gauge, 1991. $1, Streamline engine 2-6-0, O gauge, post World War II. $3, Japanese Natl. Railways class C62, HO scale, c. 1960. $5, Tinplate friction-drive floor trains, 1960s. No. 1512, 1st "toy" train in Japan, 1854. No. 1513, Stephenson's Rocket, 1:26 scale, c. 1972, vert.

1992, Nov. 11 *Perf. 14*

1504	A214	15c multicolored	.45	.45
1505	A214	25c multicolored	.50	.55
1506	A214	55c multicolored	.75	.75
1507	A214	65c multicolored	.90	.90
1508	A214	75c multicolored	1.00	1.00
1509	A214	$1 multicolored	1.25	1.25
1510	A214	$3 multicolored	2.75	2.75
1511	A214	$5 multicolored	4.50	4.50
		Nos. 1504-1511 (8)	12.10	12.15

Souvenir Sheets

Perf. 13

1512	A214	$6 multicolored	5.50	5.50
1513	A214	$6 multicolored	5.50	5.50

No. 1512 contains one 52x40mm stamp, No. 1513 one 39x51mm stamp.

Hummel Figurines — A215

Angel: 20c, Playing violin. 25c, Playing horn. 55c, Playing mandolin. 65c, Seated, playing trumpet. 90c, On cloud with lantern. $1, Holding candle. $1.20, Flying. $6, On cloud with candle.

1992, Nov. 2 *Perf. 14*

1514	A215	20c multicolored	.35	.35
1515	A215	25c multicolored	.35	.35
1516	A215	55c multicolored	.55	.55
1517	A215	65c multicolored	.70	.70
a.		Sheet of 4, #1514-1517	2.25	2.25
1518	A215	90c multicolored	1.00	1.00
1519	A215	$1 multicolored	1.25	1.25
1520	A215	$1.20 multicolored	1.50	1.50
1521	A215	$6 multicolored	3.25	3.25
a.		Sheet of 4, #1518-1521	8.00	8.00
		Nos. 1514-1521 (8)	8.95	8.95

Anniversaries and Events
A216 A217

Designs: 25c, Graf Zeppelin, 1929. No. 1523, Elderly man, plant. No. 1524, Elderly man on bicycle. No. 1525, Elderly man helping boy bait hook. No. 1526, Konrad Adenauer. No. 1527, Space shuttle. No. 1528, Wolfgang Amadeus Mozart. No. 1529, Snowy egret. No. 1530, Sir Thomas Lipton, Shamrock V, 1930. $2, Men pulling fishing net toward beach. $3, Helen Keller. No. 1533, Earth Resources Satellite. No. 1534, Map of Germany, 1949. No. 1535, Eland. $5, Count Ferdinand von Zeppelin. No. 1537, Cologne Cathedral, Germany. No. 1538, Scene from the Magic Flute. No. 1539, Mir Space Station. No. 1540, Engine of Graf Zeppelin. No. 1541, Rhinoceros hornbill.

1992 Litho. *Perf. 14*

1522	A216	25c multicolored	.60	.60
1523	A216	45c multicolored	.80	.80
1524	A216	45c multicolored	.80	.80
1525	A216	45c multicolored	.80	.80
1526	A216	90c multicolored	.90	.90
1527	A216	90c multicolored	.90	.90
1528	A217	$1.20 multicolored	2.00	2.00
1529	A216	$1.20 multicolored	1.50	1.50
1530	A216	$1.20 multicolored	1.75	1.75
1531	A216	$2 multicolored	1.75	1.75
1532	A216	$3 multicolored	3.00	3.00
1533	A216	$4 multicolored	3.00	3.00
1534	A216	$4 multicolored	4.25	4.25
1535	A216	$4 multicolored	4.25	4.25
1536	A216	$5 multicolored	5.00	5.00
		Nos. 1522-1536 (15)	31.30	31.30

Souvenir Sheets

1537	A216	$6 multicolored	6.25	6.25
1538	A217	$6 multicolored	6.75	6.75
1539	A216	$6 multicolored	6.25	6.25
1540	A216	$6 multicolored	6.25	6.25
1541	A216	$6 multicolored	5.75	5.75

Konrad Adenauer, 25th anniv. of death (Nos. 1526, 1534, 1537). Intl. Space Year (Nos. 1527, 1533, 1539). Mozart, 200th anniv. of death (in 1991) (Nos. 1528, 1538). Count Zeppelin, 75th anniv. of death (Nos. 1522, 1536, 1540). Intl. Day of the Elderly (Nos. 1523-1525). UN Earth Summit, Rio (Nos. 1529, 1535, 1541). America's Cup yacht race (No. 1530). WHO Intl. Conference on Nutrition, Rome (No. 1531). Lions Intl., 75th anniv. (No. 1532).

Issued: Nos. 1528, 1539, Oct.; Nos. 1523-1527, 1533-1534, 1537-1538, Nov.; Nos. 1522, 1529, 1535-1536, 1540-1541, Dec.

Miniature Sheet

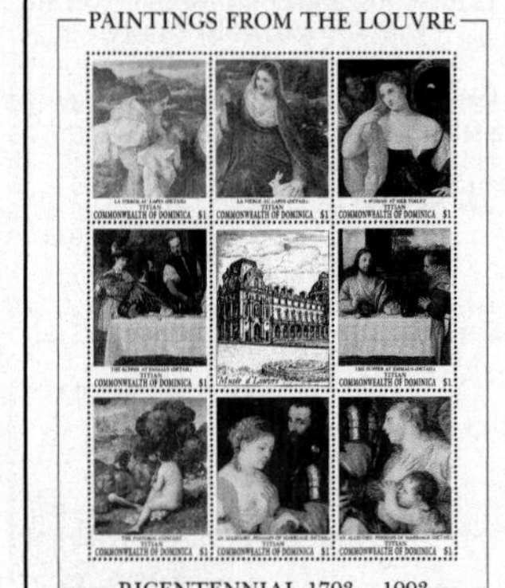

Louvre Museum, Bicent. — A218

Details or entire paintings by Titian: a-b, Madonna and Child with St. Catherine and a Rabbit (diff. details). c, A Woman at Her Toilet. d-e, The Supper at Emmaus (diff. details). f, The Pastoral Concert. g-h, An Allegory, Perhaps of Marriage (diff. details).

Painting by Hieronymus Bosch: $6, The Ship of Fools.

1993, Mar. 24 Litho. *Perf. 12*

1542	A218	$1 Sheet of 8, #a.-h. + label	9.50	9.50

Souvenir Sheet

Perf. 14½

1543	A218	$6 multicolored	5.75	5.75

No. 1543 contains one 55x88mm stamp.

Elvis Presley, 15th Anniv. of Death (in 1992) A219

a, Portrait. b, With guitar. c, Holding microphone.

1993, Feb. *Perf. 14*

1544	A219	$1 Strip of 3, #a.-c.	3.75	3.75

Miniature Sheet

Birds of Dominica — A220

a, Plumbeous warbler. b, Black swift. c, Blue-hooded euphonia. d, Rufous-throated solitaire. e, Ringed kingfisher. f, Blue-headed hummingbird. g, Bananaquit. h, Trembler. i, Forest thrush. j, Purple-throated carib. k, Ruddy quail dove. l, Least bittern.

No. 1546, Imperial parrot. No. 1547, Red-necked parrot (Amazona arausiaca).

1993, Apr. 30

1545	A220	90c Sheet of 12, #a.-l.	18.00	18.00

Souvenir Sheets

1546	A220	$6 multicolored	6.50	6.50
1547	A220	$6 multicolored	6.50	6.50

Turtles A221

25c, Leatherback laying eggs. 55c, Hawksbill. 65c, Atlantic Ridley. 90c, Green turtle laying eggs. $1, Green turtle at sea. $2, Hawksbill, diff. $4, Loggerhead. $5, Leatherback at sea. No. 1556, Green turtle hatchling. No. 1557, Head of hawksbill.

1993, May 26 Litho. *Perf. 14*

1548	A221	25c multicolored	.45	.45
1549	A221	55c multicolored	.55	.55
1550	A221	65c multicolored	.75	.75
1551	A221	90c multicolored	.95	.95
1552	A221	$1 multicolored	1.10	1.10
1553	A221	$2 multicolored	1.75	1.75
1554	A221	$4 multicolored	3.25	3.25
1555	A221	$5 multicolored	4.25	4.25
		Nos. 1548-1555 (8)	13.05	13.05

Souvenir Sheets

1556	A221	$6 multicolored	5.75	5.75
1557	A221	$6 multicolored	5.75	5.75

For overprints see Nos. 2103-2107.

Automobiles — A222

Designs: 90c, 1928 Model A Ford. $1.20, Mercedes-Benz winning Swiss Grand Prix, 1936. $4, Mercedes-Benz winning German Grand Prix, 1935. $5, 1915 Model T Ford.

No. 1562: a, 1993 Mercedes-Benz coupe/roadster. b, 1893 Benz Viktoria.

No. 1563, Ford GT-40.

1993, May Litho. *Perf. 14*

1558	A222	90c multicolored	.80	.80
1559	A222	$1.20 multicolored	1.10	1.10
1560	A222	$4 multicolored	2.75	2.75
1561	A222	$5 multicolored	3.75	3.75
		Nos. 1558-1561 (4)	8.40	8.40

Souvenir Sheets

1562	A222	$3 Sheet of 2, #a.-b.	5.00	5.00
1563	A222	$6 multicolored	5.00	5.00

No. 1563 contains one 57x42mm stamp.

First Ford gasoline engine, cent. (Nos. 1558, 1561, 1563). Benz's first four-wheeled vehicle, cent. (Nos. 1559-1560, 1562).

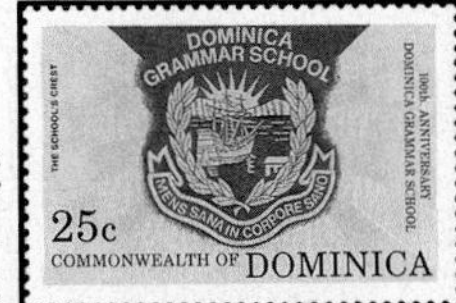

Dominica Grammar School, Cent. A223

Designs: 25c, School crest. 30c, V. A. A. Archer, first West Indian headmaster. 65c, Hubert A. Charles, first Dominican headmaster. 90c, Present school building.

1993, May

1564 A223 25c multicolored .25 .25
1565 A223 30c multicolored .30 .30
1566 A223 65c multicolored .60 .60
1567 A223 90c multicolored .85 .85
Nos. 1564-1567 (4) 2.00 2.00

Aviation Anniversaries — A224

Designs: 25c, New York ticker tape parade, 1928. 55c, BAC Lightning F2. 65c, Graf Zeppelin over Sphinx, pyramids, 1929. $1, Boeing 314 flying boat. $2, Astronaut stepping onto moon. $4, Viktoria Louise over Kiel harbor, 1912. $5, Supermarine Spitfire, vert. No. 1575, Royal Air Force Crest, vert. No. 1576, Hugo Eckener in airship cockpit, vert. No. 1577, Jean-Pierre Blanchard's hot air balloon, 1793, vert.

1993, May 28 Litho. *Perf. 14*

1568 A224 25c multicolored .90 .90
1569 A224 55c multicolored 1.10 1.10
1570 A224 65c multicolored 1.50 1.50
1571 A224 $1 multicolored 1.75 1.75
1572 A224 $2 multicolored 3.00 3.00
1573 A224 $4 multicolored 4.00 4.00
1574 A224 $5 multicolored 4.25 4.25
Nos. 1568-1574 (7) 16.50 16.50

Souvenir Sheets

1575 A224 $6 multicolored 6.25 6.25
1576 A224 $6 multicolored 6.25 6.25
1577 A224 $6 multicolored 5.75 5.75

Zeppelin Capt. Hugo Eckener, 125th anniv. of birth (Nos. 1568, 1570, 1573, 1576). Royal Air Force, 75th anniv. (Nos. 1569, 1574-1575). Nos. 1575-1576 each contain one 42x57mm stamp.

Miniature Sheet

Coronation of Queen Elizabeth II, 40th Anniv. — A225

Designs: No. 1578a, 20c, Official coronation photograph. b, 25c, Ceremony. c, 65c, Gold State Coach. d, $5, Queen Elizabeth II, Queen Mother.

$6, Portrait, by Norman Hutchinson, 1969.

1993, June 2 Litho. *Perf. 13½x14*

1578 A225 Sheet, 2 each #a.-d. 13.00 13.00

Souvenir Sheet

Perf. 14

1579 A225 $6 multicolored 6.75 6.75

No. 1579 contains one 28x42mm stamp.
For overprints see Nos. 1688-1689.

A226

Cameo photos of couple and: 90c, Crown Prince holding flowers. $5, Princess wearing full-length coat.

$6, Princess riding in limousine.

1993, June 14 Litho. *Perf. 14*

1580 A226 90c multicolored .75 .75
1581 A226 $5 multicolored 5.00 5.00

Souvenir Sheet

1582 A226 $6 multicolored 6.00 6.00

Wedding of Japan's Crown Prince Naruhito and Masako Owada.

Inauguration of Pres. William J. Clinton — A227

$5, Bill, Hillary Clinton. $6, Bill Clinton, vert.

1993, July 30 Litho. *Perf. 14*

1583 A227 $5 multicolored 4.25 4.25

Souvenir Sheet

1584 A227 $6 multicolored 6.00 6.00

Willy Brandt (1913-92), German Chancellor — A228

Brandt and: 65c, Pres. Eisenhower, 1959. $5, N.K. Winston, 1964. $6, Portrait.

1993, July 30

1585 A228 65c black & brown .90 .90
1586 A228 $5 black & brown 4.75 4.75

Souvenir Sheet

1587 A228 $6 black & brown 6.00 6.00

Picasso (1881-1973) A229

Paintings: 25c, Bather with Beach Ball, 1929. 90c, Portrait of Leo Stein, 1906. $5, Portrait of Wilhelm Unde, 1910. $6, Man with a Pipe, 1915.

1993, July 30

1588 A229 25c multicolored .40 .40
1589 A229 90c multicolored .85 .85
1590 A229 $5 multicolored 4.75 4.75
Nos. 1588-1590 (3) 6.00 6.00

Souvenir Sheet

1591 A229 $6 multicolored 6.00 6.00

Polska '93 — A230

Paintings: 90c, Self-portrait, by Marian Szczyrbula, 1921. $3, Portrait of Bruno Jasienski, by Tytus Czyzewski, 1921. $6, Miser, by Tadeusz Makowski, 1973.

1993, July 30

1592 A230 90c multicolored 1.50 1.50
1593 A230 $3 multicolored 3.50 3.50

Souvenir Sheet

1594 A230 $6 multicolored 6.00 6.00

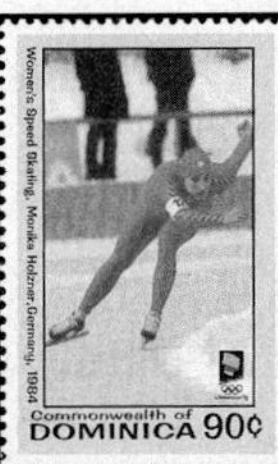

A231

90c, Monika Holzner, speedskating, 1984. $4, US hockey players, Ray Leblanc, Tim Sweeney, 1992. $6, Men's ski jump.

1993, July 30

1595 A231 90c multicolored 1.50 1.50
1596 A231 $4 multicolored 4.00 4.00

Souvenir Sheet

1597 A231 $6 multicolored 5.75 5.75

1994 Winter Olympics, Lillehammer, Norway.

Copernicus (1473-1543) A232

Designs: $1.20, Astronomer using quadrant. $3, Observatory. $5, Copernicus.

1993, July 30

1598 A232 $1.20 multicolored 1.50 1.50
1599 A232 $3 multicolored 3.75 3.75

Souvenir Sheet

1600 A232 $5 multicolored 6.00 6.00

Opening of New General Post Office A233

New General Post Office and: 25c, Prince Philip. 90c, Queen Elizabeth II.

1993, July 30

1601 A233 25c multicolored .25 .25
1602 A233 90c multicolored 1.00 1.00

1994 World Cup Soccer Championships, US — A234

25c, Maradona, Buchwald. 55c, Gullit. 65c, Chavarria, Bliss. No. 1606, 90c, Maradona. No. 1607, 90c, Alvares. $1, Altobelli, Yonghwang. $2, Referee, Stopyra. $5, Renquin, Yaremtchuk.

No. 1611, Brehme. No. 1612, Fabbri.

1993, Sept. 8 Litho. *Perf. 14*

1603 A234 25c multicolored .65 .65
1604 A234 55c multicolored .75 .75
1605 A234 65c multicolored .85 .85
1606 A234 90c multicolored 1.00 1.00
1607 A234 90c multicolored 1.00 1.00
1608 A234 $1 multicolored 1.25 1.25
1609 A234 $2 multicolored 2.00 2.00
1610 A234 $5 multicolored 3.00 3.00
Nos. 1603-1610 (8) 10.50 10.50

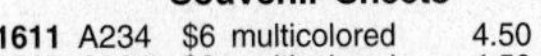

Souvenir Sheets

1611 A234 $6 multicolored 4.50 4.50
1612 A234 $6 multicolored 4.50 4.50

Taipei '93 — A235

25c, Tiger Balm Gardens. 65c, Building, Kenting Park. 90c, Tzu-en Tower. $5, Villa, Lan Tao Island.

No. 1617 — Chinese kites: a, Chang E Rising up to the Moon. b, Red Phoenix and Rising Sun. c, Heavenly Judge. d, Monkey King. e, Goddess of the Luo River. f, Heavenly Maiden Scatters Flowers.

$6, Jade Girl, Liao Dynasty.

1993, Oct. 4 Litho. *Perf. 13½x14*

1613 A235 25c multi .30 .30
1614 A235 65c multi .55 .55
1615 A235 90c multi 1.00 1.00
1616 A235 $5 multi 4.25 4.25
Nos. 1613-1616 (4) 6.10 6.10

Miniature Sheet

1617 A235 $1.65 Sheet of 6, #a.-f. 10.00 10.00

Souvenir Sheet

1618 A235 $6 multi 5.25 5.25

With Bangkok '93 Emblem

25c, Tugu Monument, Java. 55c, Candi Cangkuang, West Java. 90c, Pura Taman Ayun, Mengwi. $5, Stone mosaics, Ceto.

No. 1623 — Puppets: a, Thai, Rama and Sita. b, Burmese, Tha Khi Lek. c, Burmese, diff. d, Thai, Demons, Wat Phra Kaew. e, Thai, Hun Lek performing Khun Chang, Khun Phaen. f, Thai, Hun Lek performing Ramakien.

$6, Stone carving, Thailand.

1993

1619 A235 25c multi .30 .30
1620 A235 55c multi .55 .55
1621 A235 90c multi 1.00 1.00
1622 A235 $5 multi 4.00 4.00
Nos. 1619-1622 (4) 5.85 5.85

Miniature Sheet

1623 A235 $1.65 Sheet of 6, #a.-f. 10.00 10.00

Souvenir Sheet

1624 A235 $6 multi 5.25 5.25

With Indopex '93 Emblem

Designs: 25c, Ornate Chedi, Wat Phra Boromathat Chaiya. 55c, Preserved temple ruins, Sukhothai Historical Park. 90c, Prasat Hin Phimai, Thailand. $5, Main sanctuary, Prasat Phanom Rung, Thailand.

Indonesian puppets — No. 1629: a, Arjuna & Prabu Gilling Wesi. b, Loro Blonyo. c, Yogyanese puppets, Menak cycle. d, Wayang gedog, Ng Setro. e, Wayang golek, Kencana Wungu. f, Wayang gedog, Raden Damar Wulan.

$6, Sculpture of Majapahit noble, Pura Sada, Kapel.

1993, Oct. 4 Litho. *Perf. 13½x14*

1625 A235 25c multicolored .40 .40
1626 A235 55c multicolored .60 .60
1627 A235 90c multicolored 1.25 1.25
1628 A235 $5 multicolored 4.00 4.00
Nos. 1625-1628 (4) 6.25 6.25

Miniature Sheet

1629 A235 $1.65 Sheet of 6, #a.-f. 10.00 10.00

Souvenir Sheet

1630 A235 $6 multicolored 5.25 5.25

Miniature Sheet

Willie the Operatic Whale — A236

Nos. 1631-1633, Characters and scenes from Disney's animated film Willie the Operatic Whale.

1993, Nov. 1 Litho. *Perf. 14x13½*

1631 A236 $1 Sheet of 9, #a.-i. 14.00 14.00

Souvenir Sheets

1632 A236 $6 multicolored 5.00 5.00

Perf. 13½x14

1633 A236 $6 multi, vert. 5.00 5.00

Christmas A237

25c, 55c, 65c, 90c (No. 1637), Details or entire woodcut, The Adoration of the Magi, by Durer.

90c (No. 1638), $1, $3, $5, Details or entire painting, The Foligni Madonna, by Raphael.

Souvenir Sheets: No. 1642, $6, The Adoration of the Magi, by Durer. No. 1643, $6, The Foligni Madonna, by Raphael.

1993, Nov. 8 Litho. *Perf. 13*

1634-1643 A237 Set of 10 20.00 20.00

A238

Hong Kong '94 — A239

Stamps, scene from Peak Tram: No. 1644, Hong Kong #527, city buildings, trees. No. 1645, Trees, tram, #1292.

Chinese jade: No. 1646a, Horse. b, Cup with handle. c, Vase with birthday peaches. d, Vase. e, Fu dog and puppy. f, Drinking vessel.

1994, Feb. 18 Litho. *Perf. 14*

1644 A238 65c multicolored .50 .50
1645 A238 65c multicolored .50 .50
a. Pair, #1644-1645 1.10 1.10

Miniature Sheet

1646 A239 65c Sheet of 6, #a.-f. 5.75 5.75

Nos. 1644-1645 issued in sheets of 5 pairs. No. 1645a is a continuous design.

New Year 1994 (Year of the Dog) (No. 1646e).

Insects, Butterflies, & Birds — A240

Various Hercules beetles: 20c, 25c, 65c, Male. 90c, Female.

$1, Imperial parrot. $2, Southern dagger tail. $3, The mimic. $5, Purple-throated carib.

Each $6: No. 1655, Snout butterfly. No. 1656, Blue-headed hummingbird.

1994, Mar. 15 Litho. *Perf. 14*

1647-1654 A240 Set of 8 11.00 11.00
1650a Min. sheet, 3 each #1647-1650 10.00 10.00

Souvenir Sheets

1655-1656 A240 Set of 2 12.00 12.00

World Wildlife Fund (Nos. 1647-1650).

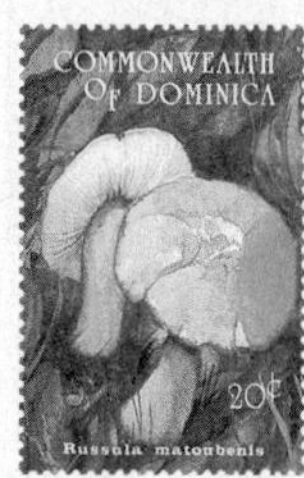

Mushrooms A241

Designs: 20c, Russula matoubenis. 25c, Leptonia caeruleocapita. 65c, Inocybe littoralis. 90c, Russula hygrophytica. $1, Pyrrhoglossum lilaceipes. $2, Hygrocybe konradii. $3, Inopilus magnificus. $5, Boletellus cubensis.

No. 1665, Gerronema citrinum. No. 1666, Lentinus strigosus.

1994, Apr. 18

1657 A241 20c multicolored .45 .45
1658 A241 25c multicolored .50 .50
1659 A241 65c multicolored .65 .65
1660 A241 90c multicolored .80 .80
1661 A241 $1 multicolored .95 .95
1662 A241 $2 multicolored 1.50 1.50
1663 A241 $3 multicolored 2.00 2.00
1664 A241 $5 multicolored 3.00 3.00
Nos. 1657-1664 (8) 9.85 9.85

Souvenir Sheets

1665 A241 $6 multicolored 4.75 4.75
1666 A241 $6 multicolored 4.75 4.75

Orchids — A242

Designs: 20c, Laeliocattleya. 25c, Sophrolaeliocattleya. 65c, Odontocidium. 90c, Laeliocattleya, diff. $1, Cattleya. $2, Odontocidium, diff. $3, Epiphronitis. $4, Oncidium.

Each $6: No. 1675, Schombocattleya. No. 1676, Cattleya, diff.

1994, May 3

1667-1674 A242 Set of 8 10.00 10.00

Souvenir Sheets

1675-1676 A242 Set of 2 10.00 10.00

New Year 1994 (Year of the Dog) — A243

Designs: 20c, Dachshund. 25c, Beagle. 55c, Greyhound. 90c, Jack Russell terrier. $1, Pekingese. $2, White fox terrier. $4, English toy spaniel. $5, Irish setter.

No. 1686, Welsh corgi. No. 1687, Labrador retriever.

1994, May 17

1678 A243 20c multicolored .30 .30
1679 A243 25c multicolored .35 .35
1680 A243 55c multicolored .50 .50
1681 A243 90c multicolored .80 .80
1682 A243 $1 multicolored 1.00 1.00
1683 A243 $2 multicolored 1.50 1.50
1684 A243 $4 multicolored 2.50 2.50
1685 A243 $5 multicolored 3.00 3.00
Nos. 1678-1685 (8) 9.95 9.95

Souvenir Sheets

1686 A243 $6 multicolored 5.00 5.00
1687 A243 $6 multicolored 5.00 5.00

Nos. 1578-1579 Ovptd. in Black or Silver

1994, June 27 Litho. *Perf. 13½x14*

1688 A225 Sheet, 2 ea #a-d 15.00 15.00

Souvenir Sheet

1689 A225 $6 multicolored (S) 7.25 7.25

Overprint on No. 1689 appears in sheet margin.

Miniature Sheet

1994 World Cup Soccer Championships, US — A244

No. 1690: a, Dos Armstrong, US. b, Dennis Bergkamp, Netherlands. c, Roberto Baggio, Italy. d, Rai, Brazil. e, Cafu, Brazil. f, Marco Van Baston, Netherlands.

Each $6: No. 1691, Roberto Mancini, Italy. No. 1692, Stanford Stadium, Palo Alto.

1994, July 5 *Perf. 14*

1690 A244 $1 Sheet of 6, #a.-f. 6.00 6.00

Souvenir Sheets

1691-1692 A244 Set of 2 10.00 10.00

Butterflies A245

20c, Florida white. 25c, Red rim. 55c, Barred sulphur. 65c, Mimic. $1, Large orange sulphur. $2, Southern dagger tail. $3, Dominican snout butterfly. $5, Caribbean buckeye.

No. 1700, Clench's hairstreak. No. 1701, Painted lady.

1994, May 3 Litho. *Perf. 14*

1693 A245 20c multi .40 .40
1694 A245 25c multi .40 .40
1695 A245 55c multi .75 .75
1696 A245 65c multi .80 .80
1697 A245 $1 multi 1.00 1.00
1698 A245 $2 multi 1.50 1.50
1698A A245 $3 multi 2.00 2.00
1699 A245 $5 multi 3.50 3.50
Nos. 1693-1699 (8) 10.35 10.35

Souvenir Sheets

1700 A245 $6 multi 5.50 5.50
1701 A245 $6 multi 5.50 5.50

10th Caribbean Scout Jamboree A246

Designs: 20c, Backpacking. 25c, Cooking over campfire. 55c, Making camp. 65c, Camping. $1, Scout drum unit. $2, Planting trees. $4, Sailing. $5, Scout salute.

Each $6: No. 1710, Early Scout troop. No. 1711, Pres. C.A. Sorhaindo, vert.

1994, July 18 Litho. *Perf. 14*

1702-1709 A246 Set of 8 11.50 11.50

Souvenir Sheets

1710-1711 A246 Set of 2 11.50 11.50

For overprints see Nos. 1762-1766.

D-Day, 50th Anniv. A247

Designs: 65c, US Waco glider brings reinforcements. $2, British Horsa gliders land more troops. $3, Glider troops take Pegasus Bridge.

$6, Hadrian glider.

1994, July 26

1712-1714 A247 Set of 3 5.00 5.00

Souvenir Sheet

1715 A247 $6 multicolored 4.75 4.75

A248

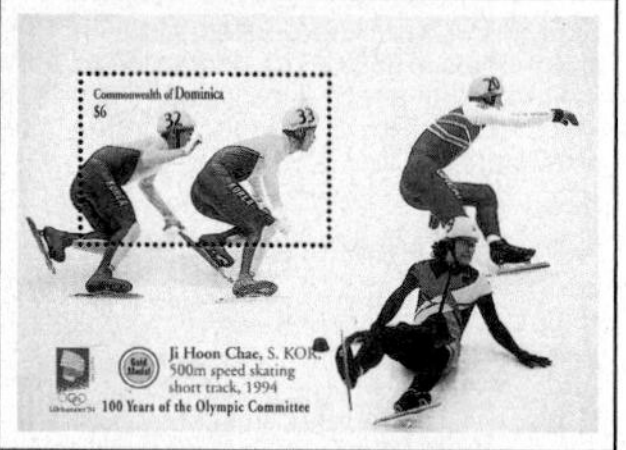

Intl. Olympic Committee, Cent. — A249

Designs: 55c, Ulrike Meyfarth, Germany, high jump, 1984. $1.45, Dieter Baumann, Germany, 5000-meter run, 1992.

$6, Ji Hoon Chae, South Korea, 500-meter short track speed skating, 1994.

1994, July 26

1716 A248 55c multicolored .90 .90
1717 A248 $1.45 multicolored 2.00 2.00

Souvenir Sheet

1718 A249 $6 multicolored 5.75 5.75

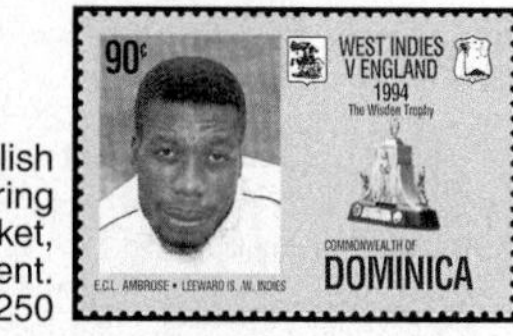

English Touring Cricket, Cent. A250

Designs: 55c, D.I. Goweer Leics, England, vert. 90c, E.C.L. Ambrose, Leeward Islands. $1, G.A. Gooch, England, vert.

$3, First English team, 1895.

1994, July 26

1719-1721 A250 Set of 3 4.00 4.00

Souvenir Sheet

1722 A250 $3 multicolored 5.75 5.75

Miniature Sheet of 6

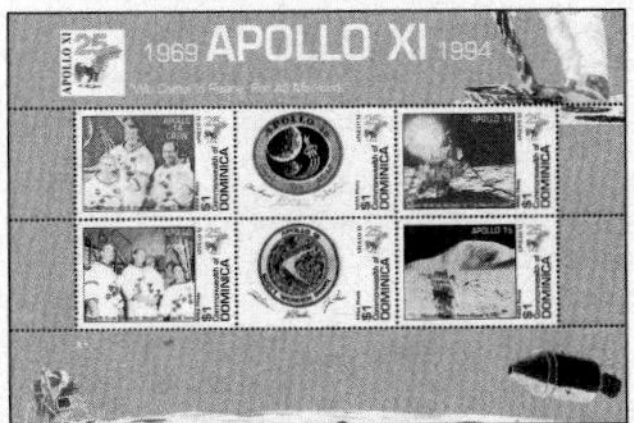

First Manned Moon Landing, 25th Anniv. — A251

No. 1723: a, Apollo 14 crew. b, Apollo 14 patch. c, Apollo 14 lunar module Antares at Fra Mauro Crater. d, Apollo 15 crew. e, Apollo 15 patch. f, Apollo 15 mission, Mount Hadley from rover.
$6, 25th anniv. emblem, lunar surface.

1994, July 26
1723 A251 $1 #a.-f. 7.75 7.75

Souvenir Sheet

1724 A251 $6 multicolored 6.50 6.50

A252

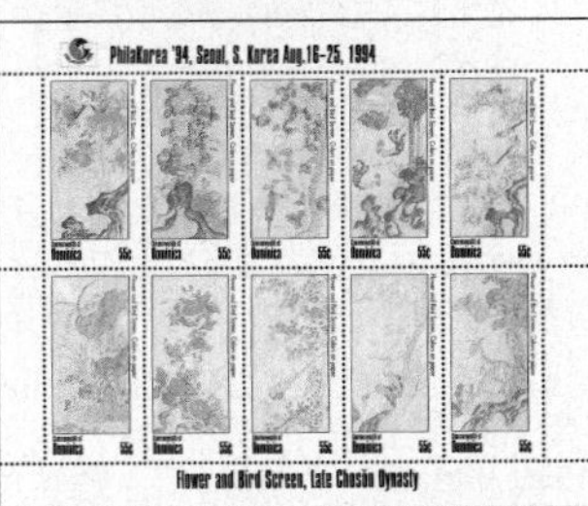

PHILAKOREA '94 — A253

Designs: 65c, P'alsang-jon Hall, Korea. 90c, Popchu-sa Temple. $2, Uhwajong Pavillion, Korea.
Screen, Late Choson Dynasty showing flowers and: No. 1728a, c, e, Birds. b, g, Butterfly. d, Roosters. f, Duck. h, Pheasant. i, Cranes. j, Deer.
$4, Stylized "spirit post" guardian.

1994, July 26 ***Perf. 14, 13 (#1728)***
1725-1727 A252 Set of 3 3.50 3.50

Miniature Sheet of 10

1728 A253 55c #a.-j. 6.00 6.00

Souvenir Sheet

1729 A252 $4 multicolored 3.00 3.00

Mickey Mouse, 65th Birthday A254

Disney characters: 20c, Dippy dawg. 25c, Clarabelle Cow. 55c, Horace Horsecollar. 65c, Mortimer Mouse. $1, Joe Piper. $3, Mr. Casey. $4, Chief O'Hara. $5, Mickey and the Blot.
Each $6: No. 1738, Minnie, Tanglefoot. No. 1739, Pluto, Minnie, horiz.

Perf. 13½x14, 14x13½ (#1739)

1994, Oct. 3
1730-1737 A254 Set of 8 14.00 14.00

Souvenir Sheets

1738-1739 A254 Set of 2 13.00 13.00

A255

Local Entertainers: 20c, Sonia Llyod, folk singer. 25c, Ophelia Marie, singer. 55c, Edney Francis, accordionist. 65c, Norman Letang, saxophonist. 90c, Edie Andre, steel drummer.

1994, Dec. 1 **Litho.** ***Perf. 14***
1740-1744 A255 Set of 5 3.25 3.25

Miniature Sheet

A256

Marilyn Monroe (1926-62), Actress: Nos. 1745a-1745i, Various portraits. No. 1746, $6, Hands above head. No. 1747, $6, Holding hat.

1994, Dec. 1
1745 A256 90c #a.-i. 11.50 11.50

Souvenir Sheets

1746-1747 A256 Set of 2 10.00 10.00

Christmas A257

Details or entire Spanish paintings: 20c, Madonna and child, by Luis de Morales. 25c, Madonna and Child with Yarn Winder, by Morales. 55c, Our Lady of the Rosary, by Zurbaran. 65c, Dream of the Patrician, by Bartolome Murillo. 90c, Madonna of Charity, by El Greco. $1, The Annunciation, by Zurbaran. $2, Mystical Marriage of St. Catherine, by Jusepe de Ribera. $3, The Holy Family with St. Bruno and Other Saints, by Ribera.
Each $6: No. 1756, Vision of the Virgin to St. Bernard, by Murillo. No. 1757, Adoration of the Shepherds, by Murillo.

1994, Dec. 2 ***Perf. 13½x14***
1748-1755 A257 Set of 8 7.00 7.00

Souvenir Sheets

1756-1757 A257 Set of 2 10.00 10.00

Order of the Caribbean Community — A258

First award recipients: 25c, Sir Shridath Ramphal, statesman, Guyana. 65c, William Gilbert Demas, economist, Trinidad & Tobago. 90c, Derek Walcott, writer, St. Lucia.

1994, Dec. 16 ***Perf. 14***
1758-1760 A258 Set of 3 2.00 2.00

Jeffrey Edmund, 1994 World Cup Soccer Player A259

1994, Dec. 28
1761 A259 25c multicolored .35 .35

Nos. 1705, 1708-1711 Ovptd.

1995, Mar. 21 **Litho.** ***Perf. 14***
1762-1764 A246 Set of 3 7.00 7.00

Souvenir Sheets

1765-1766 A246 Set of 2 10.00 10.00

Location of overprint varies.

New Year 1995 (Year of the Boar) — A260

Stylized boars: a, 25c, Facing right. b, 65c, Facing forward. c, $1, Facing left.
$2, Two facing each other, horiz.

1995, Apr. 15 **Litho.** ***Perf. 14½***
1767 A260 Strip of 3, #a.-c. 1.60 1.60
d. Souv. sheet of 3, #1767a-1767c 1.60 1.60

Souvenir Sheet

1768 A260 $2 multicolored 1.50 1.50

No. 1767 was issued in sheets of 4 strips.

Birds A261

Designs: 25c, Wood duck. 55c, Mallard. 65c, Blue-winged teal. $5, Blood eared parakeet.
No. 1773, vert.: a, Cattle egret. b, Snow goose (a, c). c, Peregrine falcon. d, Barn owl. e, Black-crowned night heron. f, Common grackle. g, Brown pelican. h, Great egret. i, Ruby-throated hummingbird. j, Laughing gull. k, Greater flamingo. l, Common moorhen.
No. 1774, Trumpeter swan, vert. No. 1775, White-eyed vireo.

1995, Apr. 15 **Litho.** ***Perf. 14***
1769-1772 A261 Set of 4 5.00 5.00

Miniature Sheet of 12

1773 A261 65c #a.-l. 16.00 16.00

Souvenir Sheets

1774 A261 $5 multicolored 5.00 5.00
1775 A261 $6 multicolored 6.00 6.00

Miniature Sheets

End of World War II, 50th Anniv. — A262

No. 1776: a, Mitsubishi A6M2 Zero. b, Aichi D3A1 Type 99 "Val." c, Nakajima 97-B5N "Kate." d, Zuikaku. e, Akagi. f, Ryuho.
No. 1777: a, German Panther tank, Ardennes. b, Allied fighter bomber. c, Patton's army crosses the Rhine. d, Rocket-powered ME 163. e, V-2 rocket on launcher. f, German U-boat surrenders in North Atlantic. g, Round the clock bombardment of Berlin. h, Soviet soldiers reach center of Berlin.
Each $6: No. 1778, Statue atop Dresden's town hall after Allied bombing. No. 1779, Japanese attack plane.

1995 **Litho.** ***Perf. 14***
1776 A262 $2 #a.-f. + label 9.00 9.00
1777 A262 $2 #a.-h. + label 13.00 13.00

Souvenir Sheets

1778-1779 A262 Set of 2 14.00 14.00

Issued: Nos. 1777-1778, 5/18; others, 7/21.

1996 Summer Olympics, Atlanta A263

Designs: 15c, Mark Breland, boxing. 20c, Lou Banach, Joseph Atiyeh, freestyle wrestling. 25c, Judo. 55c, Fencing. 65c, Matt Biondi, swimming. $1, Gushiken on rings, vert. $2, Cycling, vert. $5, Volleyball.
Each $6: No. 1788, Joe Fargis on Touch of Class, equestrian. No. 1789, Soccer, vert.

1995, July 21
1780-1787 A263 Set of 8 9.50 9.50

Souvenir Sheets

1788-1789 A263 Set of 2 10.50 10.50

UN, 50th Anniv. — A264

No. 1790: a, 65c, Signatures on UN charter, attendee. b, $1, Attendee. $2, Attendees.
$6, Winston Churchill.

1995, Aug. 16 **Litho.** ***Perf. 14***
1790 A264 Strip of 3, #a.-c. 2.75 2.75

Souvenir Sheet

1791 A264 $6 multicolored 5.00 5.00

No. 1790 is a continuous design.

Souvenir Sheets

FAO, 50th Anniv. — A265

Street market scene: a, 90c, Woman in red dress. b, $1, Woman seated. c, $2, Vendors, women.
$6, Woman in field, woman holding water cans, vert.

1995, Aug. 16

1792 A265 Sheet of 3, #a.-c. 2.50 2.50
1793 A265 $6 multicolored 4.50 4.50

No. 1792 is a continuous design.

Queen Mother, 95th Birthday A266

No. 1794: a, Drawing. b, Wearing crown, green dress. c, Formal portrait. d, Blue dress.
$6, Portrait as younger woman.

1995, Aug. 16 ***Perf. 13½x14***

1794 A266 $1.65 Strip or block of 4, #a.-d. 5.50 5.50

Souvenir Sheet

1795 A266 $6 multicolored 5.50 5.50

No. 1794 was issued in sheets of 8 stamps.
Sheet margins of Nos. 1794-1795 exist with black frame and text "In Memoriam — 1900-2002" overprinted in sheet margins.

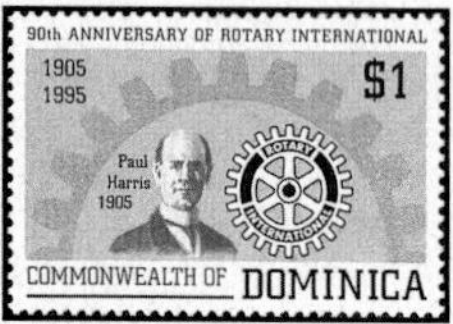

Rotary, 90th Anniv. A267

1995 ***Perf. 14***

1796 A267 $1 Paul Harris, emblem 1.00 1.00

Souvenir Sheet

1797 A267 $6 Rotary emblems 4.75 4.75

Dinosaurs A268

20c, Monoclonius. 25c, Euoplocephalus. 55c, Coelophysis. 65c, Compsognathus.
No. 1802: a, Dimorphodon. b, Ramphorynchus. c, Giant alligator. d, Pentaceratops.
No. 1803, vert: a, Ceratosaurus. b, Comptosaurus (a). c, Stegosaur. d, Camarasaurs. e, Baronyx. f, Dilophosaurus. g, Dromaeosaurids (f). h, Deinonychus. i, Dinicthys. j, Carcharodon (k). k, Nautiloid. l, Trilobite.
$5, Sauropelta. $6, Triceratops, vert.

1995, Sept. 8

1798-1801 A268 Set of 4 1.75 1.75
1802 A268 90c Strip of 4, #a.-d. 3.00 3.00

Miniature Sheet of 12

1803 A268 $1 #a.-l. 10.00 10.00

Souvenir Sheets

1804 A268 $5 multicolored 5.00 5.00
1805 A268 $6 multicolored 5.00 5.00

Singapore '95 (Nos. 1798-1801, 1803-1805).

Miniature Sheets of 6

Nobel Prize Fund Established, Cent. — A269

Recipients, each $2: No. 1806a, Oscar A. Sanchez, peace, 1987. b, Ernst B. Chain, medicine, 1945. c, Aage Bohr, physics, 1975. d, Jaroslav Seifert, literature, 1984. e, Joseph E. Murray, medicine, 1990. f, Jaroslav Heyrovsky, chemistry, 1959.
No. 1807, each $2: a, Adolf von Baeyer, chemistry, 1905. b, Edward Buchner, chemistry, 1907. c, Carl Bosch, chemistry, 1931. d, Otto Hahn, chemistry, 1944. e, Otto Paul Herman Diels, chemistry, 1950. f, Kurt Alder, chemistry, 1950.
No. 1808, Emil A. von Behring, medicine, 1901.

1995, Oct. 24 **Litho.** ***Perf. 14***

1806-1807 A269 Set of 2 19.00 19.00

Souvenir Sheet

1808 A269 $2 multicolored 1.75 1.75

Christmas A270

Details or entire paintings: 20c, Madonna and Child, by Pontormo. 25c, The Immaculate Conception, by Murillo. 55c, The Adoration of the Magi, by Filippino Lippi. 65c, Rest on the Flight into Egypt, by Van Dyck. 90c, Sacred Family, by Van Dyck. $5, The Annunciation, by Van Eyck.
No. 1815, The Virgin and the Infant, by Van Eyck. No. 1816, The Holy Family, by Ribera.

1995, Nov. 30 **Litho.** ***Perf. 13½x14***

1809-1814 A270 Set of 6 6.00 6.00

Souvenir Sheets

1815 A270 $5 multicolored 3.75 3.75
1816 A270 $6 multicolored 4.75 4.75

Miniature Sheets

Sierra Club, Cent. — A271

Designs: No. 1817, each $1: a, Florida panther with mouth open. b, Florida panther looking right. c, Manatee. d, Two manatees. e, Three sockeye salmon. f, Group of sockeye salmon. g, Two southern sea otters. h, Southern sea otter. i, Southern sea otter showing both front paws.
No. 1818, vert, each $1: a, Florida panther. b, Manatee. c, Sockeye salmon. d, Key deer facing left. e, Key deer. f, Key deer with antlers, up close. g, Wallaby with young in pouch. h, Wallaby. i, Wallaby with young.

1995, Dec. 10 ***Perf. 14***

1817-1818 A271 Set of 2 13.00 13.00

Chinese Paintings, A City of Cathay A272

No. 1819, brown lettering, each 90c: a, Boats docked, people on shore. b, River, bridge. c, Two boats on river. d, River, pavilion along shore. e, Open sea, people in courtyard.
No. 1820, black lettering, each 90c: a, City scene. b, City scene, wall. c, Outside wall, river. d, Large boat on river. e, People crossing over bridge.
No. 1821, $2: a, Boat on river, city above. b, People walking across bridge.
No. 1822, $2: a, Lifting ramp to another boat, vert. b, Holding lines in water, tree, vert.

1995, Dec. 27 **Litho.** ***Perf. 14½***

Strips of 5

1819-1820 A272 Set of 2 7.50 7.50

Souvenir Sheets of 2

1821-1822 A272 Set of 2 6.00 6.00

Nos. 1819-1822 are each continuous designs.

Classic Western Art — A273

Paintings by Raphael: No. 1823, Agony in the Garden. No. 1824, Pope Leo X with Two Cardinals. No. 1825, Bindo Altoviti.
$6, Triumphant entry of Constantine into Rome, by Rubens.

1995, Dec. 27 ***Perf. 14***

1823-1825 A273 $2 Set of 3 5.25 5.25

Souvenir Sheet

1826 A273 $6 multicolored 5.25 5.25

New Year 1996 (Year of the Rat) — A274

Stylized rats, Chinese inscriptions: No. 1827a, 25c, purple & brown. b, 65c, orange & green. c. $1, red lilac & blue.
$2, Two rats, horiz.

1996, Jan. 16 ***Perf. 14½***

1827 A274 Strip of 3, #a.-c. 1.90 1.90

Miniature Sheet

1828 A274 Sheet of 1 #1827 1.60 1.60

Souvenir Sheet

1829 A274 $2 multicolored 1.75 1.75

No. 1827 was issued in sheets of 12 stamps.

Miniature Sheet

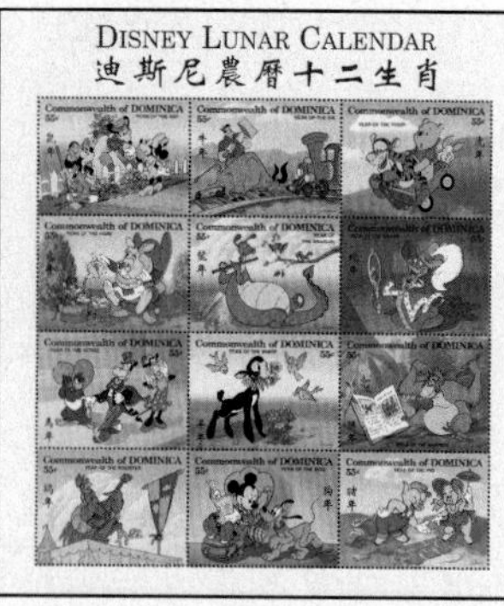

Disney Lunar New Year — A275

Disney characters representing year of the: No. 1830a, Rat. b, Ox. c, Tiger. d, Hare. e, Dragon. f, Snake. g, Horse. h, Sheep. i, Monkey. j, Rooster. k, Dog. l, Pig.
$3, Rat character. $6, Pig, rat, ox characters on lunar calendar wheel.

1996, Jan. 16 ***Perf. 14x13½***

1830 A275 55c Sheet of 12, #a.-l. 11.00 11.00

Souvenir Sheets

1831 A275 $3 multicolored 4.00 4.00
1832 A275 $6 multicolored 8.00 8.00

Methods of Transportation — A276

Designs: 65c, Donkey cart, 1965. 90c, 1910 Car. $2, 1950 Taxi. $3, 1955 Bus.

1996, Jan. 29 **Litho.** ***Perf. 14***

1833-1836 A276 Set of 4 8.00 8.00

Miniature Sheets

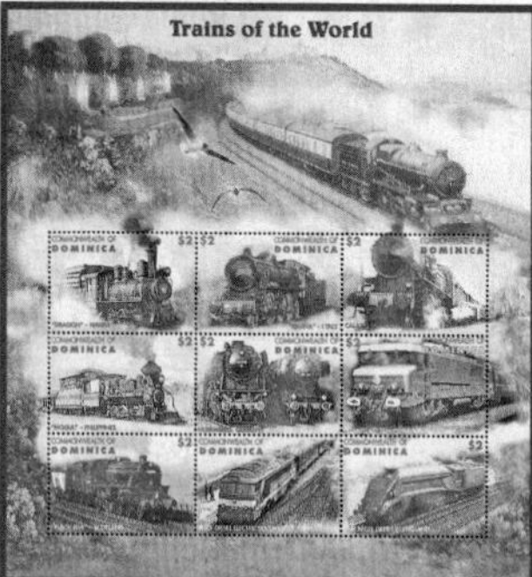

Locomotives — A277

No. 1837, each $2: a, "Dragon," Hawaii. b, "Regina," Italy. c, Calazo to Padua, Italy. d, "Mogul," Philippines. e, Nuremberg, Germany. f, "Stanislas," French Natl. Railway. g, "Black Five," Scotland. h, SNCF diesel electric, France. i, "Sir Nigel Gresley," England.
No. 1838, each $2: a, Hohi Line 9600 class, Japan. b, Peloponnese Express, Greece. c, Porter 2-4-0S, Hawaii. d, Norway-Swedish Jodemans Railway. e, 220 Diesel, Federal German Railway. f, 2-8-4T Indian Railways. g, East African Railways. h, Electrical trains, USSR. i, 0-8-0, Austria.
$5, "Duchess of Hamilton," England. $6, Diesel engine, China.

1996, Jan. 29

1837-1838 A277 Set of 2 28.00 28.00

Souvenir Sheets

1839 A277 $5 multicolored 4.75 4.75
1840 A277 $6 multicolored 5.25 5.25

No. 1837h has a face value of $1.

Giant Panda A278

Designs: a, With right leg up on rock. b, Front legs up on rock. c, Seated. d, Holding head down.

1996, May 15 Litho. *Perf. 13½x14*
1841 A278 55c Block of 4, #a.-d. 4.50 4.50

Souvenir Sheet
Perf. 14x13½
1842 A278 $3 Panda, horiz. 3.75 3.75

CHINA '96, 9th Asian Intl. Philatelic Exhibition. No. 1841 was issued in sheets of 8 stamps.
See No. 1911.

Queen Elizabeth II, 70th Birthday A279

No. 1843: a, Portrait. b, Wearing regalia of Order of the Garter. c, Wearing bright blue dress, pearls.
$6, In uniform.

1996, May 16 Litho. *Perf. 13½x14*
1843 A279 $2 Strip of 3, #a.-c. 4.25 4.25

Souvenir Sheet
1844 A279 $6 multicolored 4.25 4.25

No. 1843 was issued in sheets of 9 stamps.

Legendary Film Detectives A280

Designs: a, Humphrey Bogart as Sam Spade. b, Sean Connery as James Bond. c, Warren Beatty as Dick Tracy. d, Basil Rathbone as Sherlock Holmes. e, William Powell as the Thin Man. f, Sidney Toler as Charlie Chan, g, Peter Sellers as Inspector Clouseau. h, Robert Mitchum as Philip Marlowe. i, Peter Ustinov as Inspector Poirot.
$6, Margaret Rutherford as Miss Marple.

1996, July
1845 A280 $1 Sheet of 9, #a.-i. 13.00 13.00

Souvenir Sheet
1846 A280 $6 multicolored 6.00 6.00

1996 Summer Olympics, Atlanta A281

Designs: 20c, Olympic Stadium, Moscow, 1980. 25c, Hermine Joseph, vert. 55c, Women's field hockey, Zimbabwe, 1980. 90c, Jerome Romain, vert. $1, Polo, discontinued sport, vert. $2, Greg Louganis, diving.

1996 *Perf. 14*
1847-1852 A281 Set of 6 4.25 4.25

See Nos. 1897-1900.

Local Entertainers A282

Designs: 25c, Irene Peltier, national dress of Dominica. 55c, Rupert Bartley, street band player. 65c, Rosemary Cools-Lartigue, pianist. 90c, Celestine "Orion" Theophile, belle queen, Grand Bay. $1, Cecil Bellot, former government band master.

1996, July 31 Litho. *Perf. 14*
1853-1857 A282 Set of 5 2.75 2.75

Jerusalem, 3000th Anniv. — A283

Designs: a, 90c, Shrine of the Book, Israel Museum. b, $1, Church of All Nations. c, $2, The Great Synagogue.
$5, Hebrew University, Mount Scopus.

1996, July 31
1858 A283 Sheet of 3, #a.-c. 3.00 3.00

Souvenir Sheet
1859 A283 $5 multicolored 4.50 4.50

Radio, Cent. A284

Entertainers: 90c, Artie Shaw. $1, Benny Goodman. $2, Duke Ellington. $4, Harry James.
$6, Tommy Dorsey, Jimmy Dorsey, horiz.

1996, July 31
1860-1863 A284 Set of 4 6.25 6.25

Souvenir Sheet
1864 A284 $6 multicolored 5.00 5.00

UNICEF, 50th Anniv. A285

20c, Girl looking at globe. 55c, Boy with stethoscope, syringe. $5, Doctor examining child.
No. 1868, Girl, vert.

1996, July 31
1865-1867 A285 Set of 3 4.25 4.25

Souvenir Sheet
1868 A285 $5 multicolored 4.50 4.50

World Post Day — A286

Scenes of 18th cent. life in Dominica: 10c, Captain of ship taking letters by hand. 25c, Anthony Trollope vists Dominica to organize postal service. 55c, Steam vessel "Yare" carries mail around island. 65c, Post offices and agencies. 90c, Country postman carrying mail around mountain tracks. $1, West Indies Federation stamp, first airmail sent on German "goose" seaplane. $2, #602, General Post Office, old and new.
$5, Captain of ship.

1996, Oct. 1 Litho. *Perf. 14*
1869-1875 A286 Set of 7 6.25 6.25

Souvenir Sheet
1876 A286 $5 multicolored 5.50 5.50

Fish — A287

Designs: 1c, Scrawled filefish. 2c, Lion fish. 5c, Porcupine fish. 10c, Powder blue surgeonfish. 15c, Red hind. 20c, Golden butterfly fish. 25c, Long-nosed butterfly fish. 35c, Pennant butterfly fish. 45c, Spotted drum. 55c, Blue-girdled angelfish. 60c, Scorpion fish. 65c, Harlequin sweetlips. 90c, Flame angelfish. $1, Queen trigger. $1.20, Stoplight parrot. $1.45, Black durgon. $2, Glasseye snapper. $5, Balloon fish. $10, Creole wrasse. $20, Seabass.

1996, Oct. 1 Litho. *Perf. 14*

1877	A287	1c	multicolored	.30	.50
1878	A287	2c	multicolored	.30	.50
1879	A287	5c	multicolored	.35	.50
1880	A287	10c	multicolored	.45	.45
1881	A287	15c	multicolored	.50	.50
1882	A287	20c	multicolored	.55	.55
1883	A287	25c	multicolored	.55	.55
1884	A287	35c	multicolored	.70	.70
1885	A287	45c	multicolored	.90	.90
1886	A287	55c	multicolored	1.00	1.00
1887	A287	60c	multicolored	1.00	1.00
1888	A287	65c	multicolored	1.00	1.00
1889	A287	90c	multicolored	1.25	1.00
1890	A287	$1	multicolored	1.50	1.00
1891	A287	$1.20	multicolored	1.60	1.00
1892	A287	$1.45	multicolored	1.75	1.25
1893	A287	$2	multicolored	2.00	2.00
1894	A287	$5	multicolored	5.00	5.00
1895	A287	$10	multicolored	10.00	10.00
1896	A287	$20	multicolored	19.00	19.00
	Nos. 1877-1896 (20)			49.70	48.40

See Nos. 2024-2039B for size 20x18mm stamps.

1996 Summer Olympic Games Type

Past Olympic medalists, vert, each 90c: No. 1897a, Ulrike Meyfarth, high jump. b, Pat McCormick, diving. c, Takeichi Nishi, equestrian. d, Peter Farkas, Greco-Roman wrestling. e, Carl Lewis, track & field. f, Agnes Keleti, gymnastics. g, Yasuhiro Yamashita, judo. h, John Kelly, single sculls. i, Naim Suleymanoglu, weight lifting.
No. 1898, vert, each 90c: a, Sammy Lee, diving. b, Bruce Jenner, decathlon. c, Olga Korbut, gymnastics. d, Steffi Graf, tennis. e, Florence Griffith-Joyner, track and field. f, Mark Spitz, swimming. g, Li Ning, gymnastics. h, Erika Salumae, cycling. i, Abebe Bikila, marathon.
#1899, $5, Joan Benoit, 1st women's marathon, vert.
#1900, $5, Milt Campbell, discus.

1996, June 7 Litho. *Perf. 14*
Sheets of 9
1897-1898 A281 Set of 2 15.00 15.00

Souvenir Sheets
1899-1900 A281 Set of 2 8.25 8.25

A288

Christmas (Details or entire paintings): 25c, Enthroned Madonna and Child, by Stefano Veneziano. 55c, Noli Me Tangere, by Beato Angelico. 65c, Madonna and Child, by Angelico. 90c, Madonna of Corneta Tarquinia, by Filippo Lippi. $2, Annunciation, by Angelico. $5, Madonna with Child, by Angelico, diff.
Each $6: No. 1907, Coronation of the Virgin, by Beato Angelico. No. 1908, Holy Family with St. Barbara, by Veronese, horiz.

1996, Nov. 25
1901-1906 A288 Set of 6 8.50 8.50

Souvenir Sheets
1907-1908 A288 Set of 2 10.00 10.00

A289

Paintings of "Herdboy and Buffalo," by Li Keran (1907-89): No. 1909: a, f, Herdboy Plays the Flute. b, g, Playing Cricket in the Autumn. c, h, Listen to the Summer Cicada. d, i, Grazing in the Spring.
$2, Return in Wind and Rain.

1997 Litho. *Perf. 14*
1909 A289 90c Strip of 4, #a.-d. 3.25 3.25

Souvenir Sheets
1909E A289 55c Sheet of 4, #f.-i. 2.00 2.00
Perf. 15x14½
1910 A289 $2 multicolored 2.00 2.00

New Year 1997 (Year of the Ox).
No. 1909 was printed in sheets of 8 stamps.
No. 1910 contains one 34x52mm stamp.

Souvenir Sheet

Huangshan Mountain, China — A290

1996, May 15 Litho. *Perf. 12*
1911 A290 $2 multicolored 2.25 2.25

China '96. No. 1911 was not available until March 1997.

A291

Lee Lai-Shan, 1996 Olympic Gold Medalist in Wind Surfing — A291a

1997 Litho. *Perf. 15x14*

1912 A291 $2 multicolored 1.75 1.75

Souvenir Sheet

Perf. 14

1913 A291 $5 multicolored 4.25 4.25

No. 1912 was issued in sheets of 3.
No. 1913 contains one 38x51mm stamp.

Litho. & Embossed

Perf. 9

Without Gum

1913A A291a $35 gold & multi, like #1913

Butterflies A292

No. 1914: a, Meticalla metis. b, Coeliades forestan. c, Papilio dardanus. d, Mylothris chloris. e, Poecilmitis thyshe. f, Myrina silenus. g, Bematistes aganice. h, Euphaedra neophron. i, Precis hierta.

No. 1915, vert: a, Striped policeman. b, Mountain sandman. c, Brown-veined white. d, Bowker's widow. e, Foxy charaxes. f, Pirate. g, African clouded yellow. h, Garden inspector.

Each $6: No. 1916, Acraea natalica. No. 1917, Eurytela dryope.

1997, Apr. 1 Litho. *Perf. 14*

1914 A292 55c Sheet of 9, #a.-i. 4.75 4.75

1915 A292 90c Sheet of 8, #a.-h. 6.75 6.75

Souvenir Sheets

1916-1917 A292 Set of 2 12.00 12.00

UNESCO, 50th Anniv. A293

55c, View from temple, China. 65c, Palace of Diocletian, Croatia. 90c, St. Mary's Cathedral, Hildesheim, Germany. $1, Monastery of Rossanou, Mount Athos, Greece. $2, Scandola Nature Reserve, France. $4, Church of San Antao, Portugal.

No. 1924: a, Ruins of Copan, Honduras. b, Cuzco Cathedral, Peru. c, Olinda, Brazil, d, Canaima Natl. Park, Venezuela. e, Galapagos Islands Natl. Park, Ecuador. f, Ruins of Church, Jesuit missions of Santisima, Paraguay. g, Fortress, San Lorenzo, Panama. h, Natl. Park, Fortress, Haiti.

Each $6: No. 1925, Chengde Lakes, China. No. 1926, Kyoto, Japan.

1997, Apr. 7 *Perf. 13½x14*

1918-1923 A293 Set of 6 8.75 8.75

1924 A293 $1 Sheet of 8, #a.-h. + label 7.75 7.75

Souvenir Sheets

1925-1926 A293 Set of 2 10.50 10.50

Disney Scenes "Sealed with a Kiss" A294

Cartoon film, year released: 25c, Mickey's Horse, Tanglefoot, 1933. 35c, Shanghaied, 1935. 55c, Pluto's Judgment Day, 1935. 65c, Race for Riches, 1935. 90c, Elmer Elephant, 1936. $1, Brave Little Tailor, 1938. $2, Donald's Crime, 1945. $4, In Dutch, 1946.

Each $6: No. 1935, Nifty Nineties, 1941. No. 1936, Mickey's Surprise Party, 1939.

1997, Apr. 15 *Perf. 13½x14*

1927-1934 A294 Set of 8 11.00 11.00

Souvenir Sheets

1935-1936 A294 Set of 2 10.00 10.00

Cats — A295

25c, Cream Burmese. $1, Snowshoe. $2, Sorrell Abyssinian. $5, Torbie Persian.

No. 1941: a, British bicolor shorthair (d, e). b, Maine coon kitten, Somali kitten (c). c, Maine coon kitten, diff. d, Lynx point Siamese (e). e, Blue Burmese kitten, white Persian (odd-eyed) (f). f, Persian kitten.

No. 1942, Silver tabby.

1997, Apr. 24 *Perf. 14*

1937-1940 A295 Set of 4 7.00 7.00

1941 A295 $2 Sheet of 6, #a.-f. 10.50 10.50

Souvenir Sheet

1942 A295 $6 multicolored 5.50 5.50

Dogs — A296

Designs: 20c, Afghan hound. 55c, Cocker spaniel. 65c, Smooth fox terrier. 90c, West Highland white terrier.

No. 1947a, St. Bernard. b, Boy with grand basset. c, Rough collie. d, Golden retriever. e, Golden retriever, Tibetan spaniel, smooth fox terrier. f, Smooth fox terrier, diff.

$6, Shetland sheepdog.

1997, Apr. 24

1943-1946 A296 Set of 4 2.00 2.00

1947 A296 90c Sheet of 6, #a.-f. 5.25 5.25

Souvenir Sheet

1948 A296 $6 multicolored 5.50 5.50

A297

No. 1949: a, Queen Elizabeth II. b, Royal Arms. c, Prince, Queen walking among crowd. d, Queen, Prince in military attire. e, Buckingham Palace. f, Prince Philip.

$6, Portrait of Queen and Prince on balcony.

1997, May 29 Litho. *Perf. 14*

1949 A297 $1 Sheet of 6, #a.-f. 5.50 5.50

Souvenir Sheet

1950 A297 $6 multicolored 5.00 5.00

Queen Elizabeth II and Prince Philip, 50th wedding anniv.

Paintings by Hiroshige (1797-1858) A298

No. 1951: a, Ichigaya Hachiman Shrine. b, Blossoms on the Tama River Embankment. c, Kumano Junisha Shrine, Tsunohazu ("Juniso"). d, Benkei Moat from Soto-Sakurada to Kojimachi. e, Kinokuni Hill & View of Akasak Tameike. f, Naito Shinjuku, Yotsuya.

Each $6: No. 1952, Kasumigaseki. No. 1952A, Sanno Festival Procession at Kojimachi I-chome.

1997, May 29

1951 A298 $1.55 Sheet of 6, #a.-f. 10.50 10.50

Souvenir Sheets

1952-1952A A298 Set of 2 12.50 12.50

Orchids A299

Designs, vert: 20c, Oncidium altissimum. 25c, Oncidium papilio. 55c, Epidendrum fragrans. 65c, Oncidium lanceanum. 90c, Campylocentrum micranthum. $4, Pogonia rosea.

No. 1959: a, Brassavola cucculata. b, Epidendrum ibaguense. c, Ionopsis utricularioides. d, Rodriguezia lanceolata. e, Oncidium cebolleta. f, Epidendrum ciliare.

Each $5: No. 1960, Stanhopea grandiflora. No. 1961, Oncidium ampliatum.

1997, May 10 Litho. *Perf. 14*

1953-1958 A299 Set of 6 8.00 8.00

1959 A299 $1 Sheet of 6, #a.-f. 7.00 7.00

Souvenir Sheets

1960-1961 A299 Set of 2 11.00 11.00

Paul P. Harris (1868-1947), Founder of Rotary, Intl. — A300

Portrait of Harris and: $2, Rotary Village Corps, irrigation project, Honduras. $6, Emblems, world community service.

1997, May 29

1962 A300 $2 multicolored 1.60 1.60

Souvenir Sheet

1963 A300 $6 multicolored 6.00 6.00

Heinrich von Stephan (1831-97) A301

Portraits of Von Stephan and: No. 1964 a, Kaiser Wilhelm II. b, UPU emblem. c, Postal messenger, ancient Japan.

$6, Von Stephan, Russian dog team carrying post, 1859.

1997, May 29

1964 A301 $2 Sheet of 3, #a.-c. 4.25 4.25

Souvenir Sheet

1965 A301 $6 multicolored 4.50 4.50

PACIFIC 97.

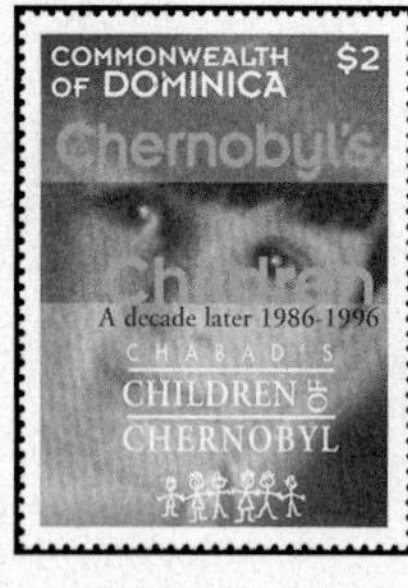

Chernobyl Disaster, 10th Anniv. A302

Designs: No. 1966, Chabad's Children of Chernobyl. No. 1967, UNESCO.

1997, May 29 *Perf. 13½x14*

1966 A302 $2 multicolored 2.25 2.25

1967 A302 $2 multicolored 2.25 2.25

Grimm's Fairy Tales A303

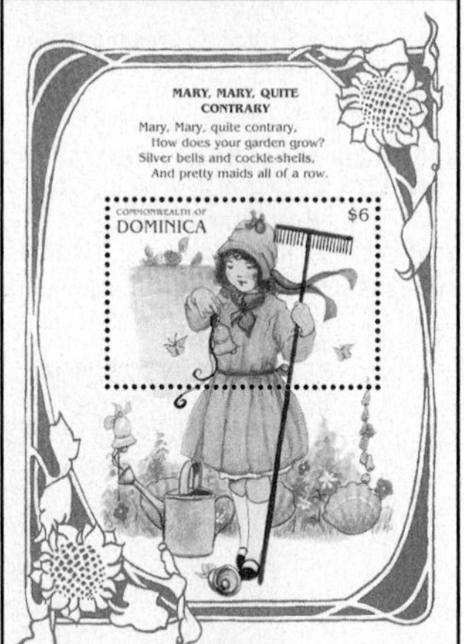

Mother Goose Rhymes — A304

The Goose Girl: No. 1968: a, Girl with horse. b, Geese, pond, castle. c, Girl. No. 1969, Girl, horiz.

No. 1970: Mary, Mary, Quite Contrary.

1997, May 29 *Perf. 13½x14*

1968 A303 $2 Sheet of 3, #a.-c. 6.00 6.00

Souvenir Sheets

Perf. 14x13½

1969 A303 $6 multicolored 6.00 6.00

Perf. 14

1970 A304 $6 multicolored 5.00 5.00

Return of Hong Kong to China — A305

Designs: $1, View of Hong Kong at night. $1.45, View of Hong Kong in daytime. $2, View of Hong Kong at night, diff.

Hong Kong skyline at dusk: No. 1974: a, 65c. b, 90c. c, $1. d, $3.

1997, July 1 ***Perf. 14***

1971-1973 A305 Set of 3 3.75 3.75
1974 A305 Sheet of 4, #a.-d. 5.00 5.00

Nos. 1971-1973 were issued in sheets of 4.

1998 Winter Olympics, Nagano — A306

Medal winners: 20c, Yukio Kasaya, 1972 ski jump. 25c, Jens Weissflog, 1994 ski jump. No. 1977, 55c, Anton Maier, 1968 men's speed skating. No. 1978, 55c, Ljubov Egorova, 1994 women's cross-country skiing. 65c, 1994 Ice hockey, Sweden. 90c, Bernhard Glass, 1980 men's luge. $4, Frank-Peter Roetsch, 1988 men's biathlon.

No. 1982: a, like #1975. b, like #1976. c, like #1977. d, Christa Rothenburger, 1988 women's speed skating.

Each $5: No. 1983, Jacob Tullin Thams, 1924 ski jumping. No. 1984, Charles Jewtraw, 1924 men's speed skating.

1997, July 15

1975-1981 A306 Set of 7 8.75 8.75
1982 A306 $1 Strip or block of 4, #a.-d. 5.00 5.00

Souvenir Sheets

1983-1984 A306 Set of 2 9.00 9.00

No. 1982 issued in sheets of 8 stamps.

1998 World Cup Soccer Championships, France — A307

Players, vert: 20c, Klinsmann, Germany. 55c, Bergkamp, Holland. 65c, Ravanelli, Italy. 90c, Kinkladze, Georgia. $2, Shearer, England. $4, Dani, Portugal.

Stadiums: No. 1991, each 65c: a, Wembley, England. b, Bernabeu, Spain. c, Maracana, Brazil. d, Torino, Italy. e, Centenary, Uruguay. f, Olympic, Germany. g, Rose Bowl, US. h, Azteca, Mexico.

Team Captains: No. 1992, each 65c: a, Meazza, Italy, 1934. b, Matthaus, Germany, 1990. c, Walter, W. Germany, 1954. d, Maradona, Argentina, 1986. e, Beckenbauer, Germany, 1974. f, Moore, England, 1966. g, Dunga, Brazil, 1994. h, Zoff, Italy, 1982.

$5, Mario Kempes, Argentina, vert. $6, Ally McCoist, Scotland, vert.

1997, July 21 **Litho.** ***Perf. 14***

1985-1990 A307 Set of 6 8.00 8.00

Sheets of 8 + Label

1991-1992 A307 Set of 2 9.00 9.00

Souvenir Sheets

1993 A307 $5 multicolored 4.50 4.50
1994 A307 $6 multicolored 5.50 5.50

Dominica Credit Union — A308

25c, Joffre Robinson, former Credit Union president. 55c, Sister Alicia, founder credit union movement in Dominica. 65c, Lorrel Bruce, 1st Cooperative Credit Union president. 90c, Roseau Credit Union Building.

$5, Bruce, Robinson, Sister Alicia.

1997, Aug. 15 **Litho.** ***Perf. 14x13½***

1995-1998 A308 Set of 4 2.25 2.25

Souvenir Sheet

Perf. 14

1999 A308 $5 multicolored 4.50 4.50

No. 1999 contains one 28x60mm stamp.

A309

Medical Pioneers: 20c, Louis Pasteur, father of bacteriology. 25c, Christiaan Barnard, performed first heart transplant. 55c, Sir Alexander Fleming, developer of penicillin. 65c, Camillo Golgi, neurologist. 90c, Jonas Salk, developer of polio vaccine. $1, Har Ghobind Khorana, geneticist. $2, Elizabeth Blackwell, first woman physician. $3, Sir Frank Macfarlane Burnet, immunologist.

$5, Fleming, diff. $6, Pasteur, diff.

1997, Sept. 1 **Litho.** ***Perf. 14***

2000-2007 A309 Set of 8 10.00 10.00

Souvenir Sheets

2008 A309 $5 multicolored 5.25 5.25
2009 A309 $6 multicolored 6.25 6.25

A310

Diana, Princess of Wales (1961-97): Various portraits.

1997, Oct. 20 **Litho.** ***Perf. 14***

2010 A310 $2 Sheet of 4, #a.-d. 6.50 6.50

Souvenir Sheet

2011 A310 $5 multicolored 4.75 4.75

Christmas — A311

Entire paintings or details: 20c, Echo and Narcissus, by Poussin. 55c, Angel Departing from the Family of Tobias, by Rembrandt. 65c, Seated Nymphs with Flute, by Francois Boucher. 90c, Angel, by Rembrandt. $2, Dispute of the Holy Sacrament, by Raphael. $4, Garden of Love, by Rubens.

Each $6: No. 2018, Annunciation, by Botticelli. No. 2019, Christ on the Mount of Olives, by El Greco.

1997, Nov. 10 **Litho.** ***Perf. 14***

2012-2017 A311 Set of 6 7.00 7.00

Souvenir Sheets

2018-2019 A311 Set of 2 11.00 11.00

The $4 is incorrectly inscribed Holy Trinity, by Raphael. No. 2018 is incorrectly inscribed Study of a Muse, by Raphael.

A312

Paintings of tigers, by Ling-Nan School: No. 2020: a, 55c, Gao Qifeng. b, 65c, Zhao Shao'ang. c, 90c, Gao Jianfu. d, $1.20, Gao Jianfu, diff.

$3, Tiger running down mountain, by Gao Jianfu.

1998, Jan. 5 **Litho.** ***Perf. 14½***

2020 A312 Sheet of 4, #a.-d. 3.00 3.00

Souvenir Sheet

Perf. 14x14½

2021 A312 $3 multicolored 2.25 2.25

New Year 1998 (Year of the Tiger). No. 2021 contains one 44x36mm stamp.

Fish Type of 1996

5c, Porcupine fish. 10c, Powder-blue surgeonfish. 15c, Red hind. 20c, Golden butterflyfish. 25c, Long-nosed butterflyfish. 35c, Pennant butterflyfish. 45c, Spotted drum. 55c, Blue-girdled angelfish. 60c, Scorpion fish. 65c, Harlequin sweetlips. 90c, Flame angelfish. $1, Queen trigger. $1.20, Stoplight parrot. $1.45, Black durgon. $2, Glasseye snapper. $5, Balloon fish. $10, Creole wrasse. $20, Seabass.

1998 ***Perf. 13x13½***

Size: 20x18mm

2024	A287	5c multi	.30	.50
2025	A287	10c multi	.30	.50
2026	A287	15c multi	.40	.50
2027	A287	20c multi	.40	.40
2028	A287	25c multi	.45	.45
2029	A287	35c multi	.50	.50
2030	A287	45c multi	.70	.70
2031	A287	55c multi	.80	.80
2032	A287	60c multi	.90	.90
2033	A287	65c multi	.90	.90
2034	A287	90c multi	1.00	.90
2035	A287	$1 multi	1.25	1.25
2036	A287	$1.20 multi	1.50	1.40
2037	A287	$1.45 multi	1.75	1.75
2038	A287	$2 multi	2.25	2.25
2039	A287	$5 multi	5.00	5.00
2039A	A287	$10 multi	9.50	9.50
2039B	A287	$20 multi	20.00	20.00
	Nos. 2024-2039B (18)		47.90	48.20

A313

Famous 20th cent. athletes — No. 2040: a, Jesse Owens. b, Owens jumping in 1936 Summer Olympic Games, Berlin. c, Isaac Berger lifting weights. d, Berger. e, Boris Becker. f, Becker playing tennis. g, Arthur Ashe playing tennis, holding Wimbledon trophy. h, Ashe.

No. 2041, Franz Beckenbauer, soccer player, horiz.

1998, Feb. 9 **Litho.** ***Perf. 14***

Sheet of 8

2040 A313 $1 #a.-h. 7.50 7.50

Souvenir Sheet

2041 A313 $6 multi 6.25 6.25

Nos. 2040b-2040c, 2040f-2040g are each 53x38mm.

A314

Japanese Cinema Stars — No. 2042: a, Akira Kurosawa. b, Kurosawa's 1950 film, "Rashomon." c, Toshiro Mifune in 1954 film, "Seven Samurai." d, Mifune. e, Yasujiro Ozu. f, Ozu's 1949 film, "Late Spring." g, Sessue Hayakawa in 1957 film, "Bridge on the River Kwai." h, Hayakawa.

No. 2043, Akira Kurosawa, director.

1998, Feb. 9 **Litho.** ***Perf. 14***

Sheet of 8

2042 A314 $1 #a.-h. 7.50 7.50

Souvenir Sheet

2043 A314 $6 multi 6.25 6.25

Nos. 2042b-2042c, 2042f-2042g are each 53x38mm.

A315

Mushrooms: 10c, Omphalotus illudens. 15c, Inocybe fastigiata. 20c, Marasmius plicatulus. 50c, Mycena lilacifolia. 55c, Armillaria straminea. 90c, Tricholomopsis rutilans.

No. 2050, each $1: a, Lepiota naucina. b, Cortinarius violaceus. c, Boletus aereus. d, Tricholoma aurantium. e, Lepiota procera. f, Clitocybe geotropa. g, Lepiota acutesquamosa. h, Tricholoma saponaceum. i, Lycoperdon gemmatum.

No. 2051, each $1: a, Boletus ornatipes. b, Russula xerampelina. c, Cortinarius collinitus. d, Agaricus meleagris. e, Coprinus comatus. f, Amanita caesarea. g, Amanita brunnescens. h, Amanita muscaria. i, Morchella esculenta.

$6, Cortinarius violaceus.

1998, Mar. 2 **Litho.** ***Perf. 14***

2044-2049 A315 Set of 6 3.00 3.00

Sheets of 9

2050-2051 A315 Set of 2 17.50 17.50

Souvenir Sheet

2052 A315 $6 multicolored 5.25 5.25

Sailing Ships A316

Designs: 65c, Greek bireme. 90c, Egyptian felucca. $1, Viking longboat. $2, Chinese junk.

No. 2057: a, Two-masted topsail schooner. b, The Golden Hinde. c, Roman merchant ship. d, Gazela Primeiro. e, Moshulu. f, Bluenose.

Each $5: No. 2058, Pinta. No. 2059, Chesapeake Bay skipjack.

1998, Mar. 16 **Litho.** ***Perf. 14***

2053-2056 A316 Set of 4 4.50 4.50
2057 A316 55c Block of 6, #a.-f. 3.25 3.25

Souvenir Sheets

2058-2059 A316 Set of 2 10.00 10.00

No. 2053 incorrectly inscribed "Egyptian felucca."

No. 2057 was issued in sheets of 12 stamps.

Mickey & Minnie Mouse's 70th Anniv. — A317

25c, Steamboat Willie, 1928. 55c, The Brave Little Tailor, 1938. 65c, Nifty Nineties, 1941. 90c, Mickey Mouse Club, 1955. $1, Mickey, Minnie at the opening of Walt Disney World, 1971. $1.45, Mousercise Mickey & Minnie, 1980.

Each $5: No. 2061, Walt Disney, Mickey, Minnie. No. 2062, Surprise Party for Mickey & Minnie.

1998, June 16 Litho. *Perf. 14x13½*

2060A	A317	25c black	.30	.30
2060B	A317	55c multi	.60	.60
2060C	A317	65c multi	.75	.75
2060D	A317	90c multi	1.00	1.00
2060E	A317	$1 multi	1.10	1.10
2060F	A317	$1.45 multi	1.60	1.60
	Nos. 2060A-2060F (6)		5.35	5.35

Souvenir Sheet of 7

2060G	#2060A-2060F, 2060h	11.50	11.50
h.	$5 Runaway brain, perf 13½ at left	3.50	3.50

Size: 130x104mm

Imperf

2061-2062	A317	Set of 2	10.00	10.00

Souvenir Sheet

Disney's The Lion King — A318

1998, June 16 Litho. *Perf. 13½x14*

2063	A318	$5 multicolored	7.00	7.00

Sea Birds A319

25c, Erect crested penguin. 65c, Humboldt penguin. 90c, Red knot. $1, Audubon's shearwater.

No. 2068: a, Crested tern. b, Franklin's gull. c, Australian pelican. d, Fairy prion. e, Andean gull. f, Imperial shag. g, Red phalarope. h, Hooded grebe. i, Least auklet. j, Little grebe. k, Cape petrel. l, Horned grebe.

Each $5: No. 2069, Sula nebouxii. No. 2070, Fulmarus glacialis.

1998, Aug. 4 *Perf. 14*

2064-2067	A319	Set of 4	2.50	2.50
2068	A319	90c Sheet of 12, #a.-l.	10.00	10.00

Souvenir Sheets

2069-2070	A319	Set of 2	10.50	10.50

Airplanes A320

20c, Jetstar II. 25c, AN 225. 55c, Dash-8. 65c, Beech-99. 90c, American Eagle. $2, HFB 320 Itansa Jet.

No. 2077, each $1: a, SR 71 "Blackbird." b, Stealth bomber. c, Northrop YF23. d, F-14 A "Tomcat." e, F-15 "Eagle S." f, MiG 29 "Fulcrum." g, Europa X5. h, Camion.

No. 2078, each $1: a, E400. b, CL-215 C-GKDN Amphibian. c, Piper jet. d, Beech Hawker. e, Lockheed YF22. f, Piper Seneca V. g, CL-215 Amphibian. h, Vantase.

Each $6: No. 2079, F-1 Fighter. No. 2080, Sea Hopper.

1998, Aug. 17

2071-2076	A320	Set of 6	4.50	4.50

Sheets of 8

2077-2078	A320	Set of 2	17.00	17.00

Souvenir Sheets

2079-2080	A320	Set of 2	11.00	11.00

Intl. Year of the Ocean A321

Marine life: 25c, Fridman fish. 55c, Hydrocoral. 65c, Feather star. 90c, Royal angelfish.

No. 2085, each $1: a, Monk seal. b, Galapagos penguin. c, Manta ray. d, Hawksbill turtle. e, Moorish idol. f, Nautilus. g, Giant clam. h, Tubeworms. i, Nudibranch.

No. 2086, each $1: a, Spotted dolphin. b, Atlantic sailfish. c, Sailfin flying fish. d, Fairy basslet. e, Atlantic spadefish. f, Leatherback turtle. g, Blue tang. h, Coral banded shrimp. i, Rock beauty.

No. 2087, Humpback whale. No. 2088, Leafy sea dragon.

1998, Sept. 7 Litho. *Perf. 14*

2081-2084	A321	Set of 4	2.50	2.50

Sheets of 9

2085-2086	A321	Set of 2	19.00	19.00

Souvenir Sheets

2087	A321	$5 multicolored	4.75	4.75
2088	A321	$6 multicolored	5.50	5.50

Organization of American States, 50th Anniv. A322

1998, Sept. 1 Litho. *Perf. 14*

2089	A322	$1 multicolored	1.25	1.25

Ferrari Sports Cars A323

55c, 365 GT 2+2. 90c, Boano/Ellena 250 GT. $1, 375 MM coupe. $5, 212.

1998, Sept. 1

2090-2092	A323	Set of 3	3.75	3.75

Souvenir Sheet

2093	A323	$5 multicolored	5.50	5.50

No. 2093 contains one 91x35mm stamp.

Gandhi — A324

1998, Sept. 1

2094	A324	90c shown	1.50	1.50

Souvenir Sheet

2095	A324	$6 Seated	5.25	5.25

No. 2094 was issued in sheets of 4.

Pablo Picasso A325

Paintings: 90c, The Painter and His Model, 1926. $1, The Crucifixion, 1930. $2, Nude with Raised Arms, 1908, vert.

$6, Cafe at Royan, 1940.

1998, Sept. 1 *Perf. 14½*

2096-2098	A325	Set of 3	4.50	4.50

Souvenir Sheet

2099	A325	$6 multicolored	5.75	5.75

Royal Air Force, 80th Anniv. A326

No. 2100: a, Nimrod MR2P. b, C-130 Hercules Mk3. c, Panavia Tornado GR1. d, C-130 Hercules landing.

$5, Biplane, hawk. $6, Hawker Hart, jet.

1998, Sept. 1 *Perf. 14*

2100	A326	$2 Sheet of 4, #a.-d.	7.00	7.00

Souvenir Sheets

2101	A326	$5 multicolored	4.75	4.75
2102	A326	$6 multicolored	5.25	5.25

No. 2100d incorrectly inscribed Panavia Tornado GR1.

Nos. 1548-1549, 1551-1552, 1554 Ovptd.

1998, Sept. 14

2103-2107	A221	Set of 5	6.00	6.00

A327

1998 World Scouting Jamboree, Chile: 65c, Scout sign. $1, Scout handshake. $2, World Scout flag.

$5, Lord Baden-Powell.

1998

2108-2110	A327	Set of 3	3.25	3.25

Souvenir Sheet

2111	A327	$5 multicolored	5.25	5.25

A328

Birds: 25c, Northern cardinal. 55c, Eastern bluebird. 65c, Carolina wren. 90c, Blue jay. $1, Evening grosbeak. $2, Bohemian waxwing.

$5, Northern parula. $6, Painted bunting.

1998, Dec. 1 Litho. *Perf. 14*

2112-2117	A328	Set of 6	5.50	5.50

Souvenir Sheets

2118	A328	$5 multicolored	5.25	5.25
2119	A328	$6 multicolored	6.25	6.25

Christmas.

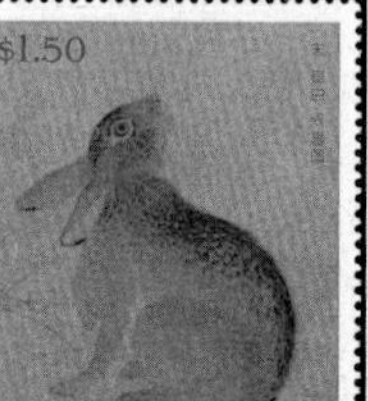

New Year 1999 (Year of the Rabbit) A329

1999, Jan. 4 Litho. *Perf. 14*

2120	A329	$1.50 multicolored	2.00	2.00

No. 2120 was issued in sheets of 4.

Orchids — A330

55c, Broughtonia sanguinea. 65c, Cattleyonia Keith Roth "Roma." 90c, Comparettia falcata. $2, Cochleanthes discolor.

No. 2125, each $1: a, Dracula erythiochaete. b, Lycaste aromatica. c, Masdevallia marguerile. d, Encyclia marfae. e, Laelia gouldiana. f, Huntleya meleagris. g, Galeandria baueri. h, Lycale deppei.

No. 2126, each $1: a, Anguloa clowesii. b, Lemboglossum cervantesii. c, Oncidium cebolleta. d, Millonia. e, Pescatorea lehmannll. f, Sophronitis coccinea. g, Pescatorea cerina. h, Encyclia vitellina.

Each $5: No. 2127, Lepanthes ovalis. No. 2128, Encyclia cochleata.

1999, Apr. 26 Litho. *Perf. 14*

2121-2124	A330	Set of 4	4.50	4.50

Sheets of 8

2125-2126	A330	Set of 2	17.50	17.50

Souvenir Sheets

2127-2128	A330	Set of 2	10.00	10.00

Trains A331

No. 2129, each $1: a, Class 103.1 Co-Co, Germany. b, Class .24, "Trans Pennine," UK. c, GG1 2-Co-Co-2, US. d, LRC Bo-Bo, Canada. e, Class EW, New Zealand. f, Class SS1 "Shao-Shani," China. g, Gulf, Mobile Ohio, US. h, Class 9100 2-Do-2, France.

No. 2130, each $1: a, County Donegal Petrol Rail Car No. 10, Ireland. b, RDC Single Rail Car, US. c, WDM Class Co-Co, India. d, Bi-

Polar No. E-2, US. e, Class X Co-Co, Australia. f, Beijing Bo-Bo, China. g, Class E428 2-Bo-Bo-2, Italy. h, Class 581 Twelve-Car Train, Japan.
$5, X-2000 Tilting Express Train, Sweden, vert. $6, Class 87 Bo-Bo, Great Britain, vert.

1999, May 10 Litho. *Perf. 14*

Sheets of 8

2129-2130 A331 Set of 2 13.00 13.00

Souvenir Sheets

2131 A331 $5 multicolored 4.00 4.00
2132 A331 $6 multicolored 5.00 5.00

Australia '99, World Stamp Expo.

Prehistoric Animals — A332

25c, Tyrannosaurus, vert. 65c, Hypacrosaurus. 90c, Sauropelta. $2, Zalambdalestes.
No. 2137, each $1: a, Barosaurus. b, Rhamphorhynchus. c, Apatosaurus. d, Archaeopteryx. e, Diplodocus. f, Ceratosaurus. g, Stegosaurus. h, Elaphrosaurus. i, Vulcanodon.
No. 2138, each $1: a, Psittacosaurus. b, Pteranodon. c, Ichthyornis. d, Spinosaurus. e, Parasaurolophus. f, Ornithomimus. g, Anatosaurus. h, Triceratops. i, Baronyx.
$5, Yangchuanosaurus. $6, Brachiosaurus.

1999, June 1 Litho. *Perf. 14*

2133-2136 A332 Set of 4 3.50 3.50

Sheets of 9

2137-2138 A332 Set of 2 18.00 18.00

Souvenir Sheets

2139 A332 $5 multicolored 4.50 4.50
2140 A332 $6 multicolored 5.50 5.50

Wedding of Prince Edward and Sophie Rhys-Jones A333

No. 2141: a, Sophie. b, Sophie, Edward. c, Edward.
$6, like No. 2141b.

1999, June 19 Litho. *Perf. 13½*

2141 A333 $3 Sheet of 3, #a.-c. 7.25 7.25

Souvenir Sheet

2142 A333 $6 multicolored 5.00 5.00

IBRA '99, World Philatelic Exhibition, Nuremberg — A334

Exhibition emblem, sailing ship Eendraght and: 65c, Cameroun #58, #56. 90c, Cameroun #11, #9.
Emblem, early German train and: $1, Cameroun #19. $2, Cameroun #6.
$6, Cover with Cameroun #19.

1999, June 22 *Perf. 14*

2143-2146 A334 Set of 4 4.00 4.00

Souvenir Sheet

2147 A334 $6 multicolored 6.25 6.25

Souvenir Sheets

PhilexFrance '99 — A335

Trains: $5, L'Aigle, 1855. $6, Mainline diesel locomotive, 1963.

1999, June 22 *Perf. 13¾*

2148 A335 $5 multicolored 4.50 4.50
2149 A335 $6 multicolored 5.50 5.50

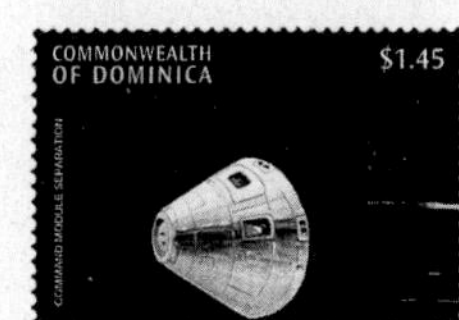

Apollo 11 Moon Landing, 30th Anniv. A336

No. 2150: a, Command Module separation b, Service Module separation. c, 3rd Stage Booster separation. d, Landing, Command Modules go to the moon. e, Apollo Ground Tracker. f, Goldstone Radio Telescope.
$6, Apollo 11 after splashdown.

1999, June 22 *Perf. 14*

2150 A336 $1.45 Sheet of 6, #a.-f. 9.00 9.00

Souvenir Sheet

2151 A336 $6 multicolored 6.00 6.00

Paintings by Hokusai (1760-1849) A337

Details or entire paintings — No. 2152:, each $2 a, Pilgrims at Kirifuri Waterfall. b, Kakura-Sato (rats looking at book, pulling on rope). c, Travelers on the Bridge by Ono Waterfall. d, Fast Cargo Boat Battling the Waves. e, Kakura-Sato (rats working with bales). f, Buufinfinh and Weeping cherry.
No. 2153, each $2: a, Cuckoo and Azalea. b, Soldiers (spear in left hand). c, Lover in the snow. d, Ghost of Koheiji. e, Soldiers (spear in right hand). f, Chinese Poet in Snow.
$5, Empress Jitó. $6, One Hundred Poems by One Hundred Poets.

Perf. 13½x13¾

1999, June 22 Litho.

Sheets of 6

2152-2153 A337 Set of 2 19.00 19.00

Souvenir Sheets

2154 A337 $5 multicolored 4.50 4.50
2155 A337 $6 multicolored 5.50 5.50

Johann Wolfgang von Goethe (1749-1832), Poet — A338

No. 2156: a, Faust perceives an astrological sign. b, Portrait of Goethe and Friedrich von Schiller (1759-1805). c, Faust tempted by Mephistopheles.
$6, Profile portrait of Goethe.

1999, June 22 *Perf. 14*

2156 A338 $2 Sheet of 3, #a.-c. 5.00 5.00

Souvenir Sheet

2157 A338 $6 multicolored 5.00 5.00

Rights of the Child — A339

No. 2158: a, Woman, child. b, Child in blue sweater. c, Two children.
$6, Dove, horiz.

1999, June 22 Litho. *Perf. 14*

2158 A339 $3 Sheet of 3, #a.-c. 7.50 7.50

Souvenir Sheet

2159 A339 $6 multicolored 5.00 5.00

Queen Mother (b. 1900) — A340

A340a

Gold Frames

No. 2160: a, In 1939. b, In Australia, 1958. c, At Badminton, 1982. d, Hatless, in 1982.
$6, In 1953.

1999, Aug. 4 *Perf. 14*

2160 A340 $2 Sheet of 4, #a.-d. + label 7.50 7.50

Souvenir Sheet

Perf. 13¾

2161 A340 $6 multicolored 5.00 5.00

No. 2161 contains one 38x51mm stamp.
Compare with Nos. 2345-2346. Backdrop of photo is more pink on No. 2161 than on No. 2346. No. 2161 has embossed arms in margin, while No. 2346 does not.

Litho. & Embossed

Die Cut Perf. 8¾

Without Gum

2161A A340a $20 gold & multi 20.00 20.00

See Nos. 2345-2346.

Flora & Fauna A341

Designs: 25c, Heliconia lobster claw. 65c, Broad winged hawk. $1, Anthurium. $1.55, Blue-headed hummingbird. $2, Bananaquit. $4 Agouti.
No. 2168: a, White-throated sparrow. b, Blue-winged teal. c, Raccoon. d, Alfalf butterfly. e, Bridge. f, Whitetail deer. g, Gray squirrel. h, Banded purple butterfly. i, Snowdrop. j, Bullfrog. k, Mushrooms. l, Large-blotched ensatina.
$5, Eastern chipmunk. $6, Black-footed ferret.

1999

2162-2167 A341 Set of 6 9.00 9.00

Sheet of 12

2168 A341 90c #a.-l. 10.00 10.00

Souvenir Sheets

2169 A341 $5 multicolored 5.00 5.00
2170 A341 $6 multicolored 6.00 6.00

A342

Dominica Festival Commission: 25c, Domfesta. 55c, $5, Dominica's 21st anniv. as a republic. 65c, Carnival development committee. 90c, World Creole Music Festival.

1999 *Perf. 12½*

2171-2174 A342 Set of 4 2.00 2.00

Souvenir Sheet

Perf. 13¼

2175 A342 $5 multicolored 4.50 4.50

No. 2175 contains one 38x51mm stamp.

A343

Intl. Year of the Elderly: 25c, Family. 65c, Four people. 90c, Four people, one in chair.

1999, Aug. 4 *Perf. 14*

2176 A343 Sheet of 3, #a.-c. 1.50 1.50

A345

Christmas: 25c, Yellow-crowned parrot. 55c, Red bishop. 65c, Troupial. 90c, Puerto Rican woodpecker. $2, Mangrove cuckoo. $3, American robin.
$6, Mary with Child Beside the Wall, by Albrecht Dürer.

1999, Dec. 7 Litho. *Perf. 14*

2178-2183 A345 Set of 6 6.75 6.75

Souvenir Sheet

2184 A345 $6 multi 5.25 5.25

Inscription on No. 2181 is misspelled.

A346

Millennium (Highlights of the early 13th Cent.) — No. 2185: a, Leonardo Fibonacci publishes "Liber Abaci," 1202. b, St. Francis of Assisi. c, Mongols conquer China. d, Children's Crusade begins, 1212. e, Magna Carta signed, 1215. f, Founding of Salamanca University, 1218. g, Snorri Sturluson writes "Prose Edda". h, Chinese painter Ma Yuan dies, 1225. i, Genghis Khan dies, 1227. j, Zen Buddhism in Japan. k, Sixth Crusade. l, Lubeck-Hamburg League. m, Inquisitions begin, 1231. n, Cordoba conquered by Castilians, 1236. o, Democracy in San Marino. p, Maimonides (60x40mm). q, Notre Dame Cathedral, Paris.

Highlights of the 1940s — No. 2186: a, Japan bombs Pearl Harbor. b, Churchill becomes Prime Minister of Great Britain. c, Regular television broadcasting begins in the US. d, Anne Frank hid in Amsterdam. e, D-Day Invasion. f, Yalta Conference. g, Establishment of the UN. h, Germany surrenders, concentration camps exposed. i, Russians hoist flag over gutted Reichstag building. j, Eniac computer. k, Independence for India. l, Bell Laboratories produce 1st transistor. m, Gandhi assassinated. n, Israel achieves statehood. o, Blockade of West Berlin, Berlin Airlift. p, Atomic bomb tested in New Mexico (60x40mm). q, Establishment of People's Republic of China.

Perf. 12¾x12½

1999, Dec. 31 Sheets of 17 Litho.

2185 A346 55c #a.-q. + label 8.50 8.50
2186 A346 55c #a.-q. + label 8.50 8.50

See Nos. 2249-2252.

New Year 2000 (Year of the Dragon) A347

2000, Feb. 5 ***Perf. 13¾***

2187 A347 $1.50 shown 1.25 1.25

Souvenir Sheet

2188 A347 $4 Dragon, horiz. 3.75 3.75

No. 2187 printed in sheets of 4.

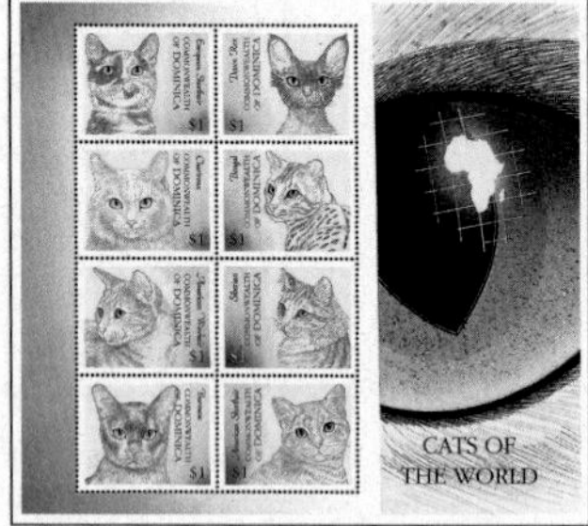

Cats — A348

No. 2189, each $1: a, European Shorthair. b, Devon Rex. c, Chartreux. d, Bengal. e, American Wirehair. f, Siberian. g, Burmese. h, American Shorthair.

No. 2190, each $1: a, Asian Longhair. b, Burmilla. c, Snowshoe. d, Pekeface Persian. e, Himalayan Persian. f, Japanese Bobtail. g, Seychelles Longhair. h, Exotic Shorthair.

Each $6: No. 2191, Awake cat. No. 2192, Sleeping cat.

2000, Feb. 21 ***Perf. 14¼***

Sheets of 8, #a.-h.

2189-2190 A348 Set of 2 16.00 16.00

Souvenir Sheets

2191-2192 A348 Set of 2 12.00 12.00

Puppies — A349

No. 2193: a, Jack Russell Terrier. b, Shar Peis. c, Basset Hound. d, Boxers. e, Wire-haired Terrier. f, Golden Retrievers.

No. 2194, Beagle.

2000, Feb. 21 ***Perf. 14½x14¼***

2193 A349 $1 Sheet of 6, #a.-f. 6.00 6.00

Souvenir Sheet

2194 A349 $6 multi 6.00 6.00

Flowers A350

Various flowers making up a photomosaic of Princess Diana.

2000, Apr. 3 ***Perf. 13¾***

2195 A350 $1 Sheet of 8, #a.-h. 7.50 7.50

See No. 2225.

Butterflies A351

No. 2196, each $1.50: a, Giant swallowtail. b, Tiger pierid. c, Orange theope. d, White peacock. e, Blue tharops. f, Mosaic.

No. 2197, each $1.50: a, Banded king shoemaker. b, Figure-of-eight. c, Grecian shoemaker. d, Blue night. e, Monarch. f, Common morpho.

No. 2198, each $1.50: a, Orange-barred sulphur. b, Clorinde. c, Small flambeau. d, Small lace-wing. e, Polydamas swallowtail. f, Atala.

Each $6: No. 2199, Polydamas swallowtail, vert. No. 2200, Sloane's urania, vert. No. 2201, Blue-green reflector, vert.

2000, Apr. 10 ***Perf. 14***

Sheets of 6, #a.-f.

2196-2198 A351 Set of 3 24.00 24.00

Souvenir Sheets

2199-2201 A351 Set of 3 17.50 17.50

Flowers — A352

Designs: 65c, Passion flower. 90c, Spray orchid. $1, Peach angel's trumpet. $4, Allamanda.

No. 2206, each $1.65: a, Bird of paradise. b, Lobster claw heliconia. c, Candle bush. d, Flor de San Miguel. e, Hibiscus. f, Oleander.

No. 2207, each $1.65: a, Anthurium. b, Fire ginger. c, Shrimp plant. d, Sky vine thunbergia. e, Ceriman. f, Morning glory.

Each $6: No. 2208, Bird of paradise, diff. No. 2109, Hibiscus, diff.

2000, Apr. 25 Litho. ***Perf. 14***

2202-2205 A352 Set of 4 6.00 6.00

Sheets of 6, #a-f

Perf. 13¾

2206-2207 A352 Set of 2 17.00 17.00

Souvenir Sheets

Perf. 13½x 13¾

2208-2209 A352 Set of 2 12.00 12.00

Size of stamps: Nos. 2106-2107, 32x48mm; Nos. 2108-2109, 38x51mm.

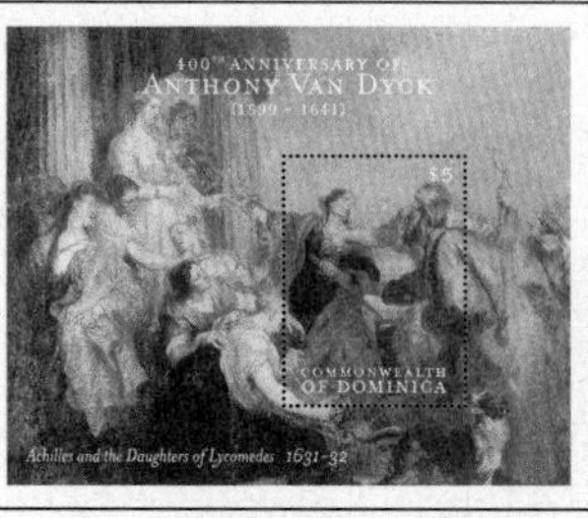

Paintings of Anthony Van Dyck — A353

No. 2210, each $1.65: a, Lady Jane Goodwin. b, Philip Herbert, 4th Earl of Pembroke. c, Philip, Lord Wharton. d, Sir Thomas Hammer. e, Olivia Porter, Wife of Enymion Porter. f, Sir Thomas Chaloner.

No. 2211, horiz, each $1.65: a, Ladies in Waiting. b, Thomas Wentworth, Earl of Strafford, with Sir Philip Mainwaring. c, Dorothy Rivers Savage, Viscountess Andover and Her Sister Lady Elizabeth Thimbleby. d, Mountjoy Blount, Earl of Newport, and Lord George Goring with a Page. e, Thomas Killigrew and an Unidentified Man. f, Elizabeth Villiers, Lady Dalkeith, and Cecilia Killigrew.

No. 2212, horiz, each $1.65: a, The Ages of Man. b, Portrait of a Girl as Erminia Accompanied by Cupid. c, Cupid and Psyche. d, Vertumnus and Pomona. e, The Continence of Scipio. f, Diana and Endymion Surprised by a Satyr.

No. 2213, $5, Achilles and the Daughters of Lycomedes. No. 2214, $5, Amaryllis and Mirtillo. No. 2215, $6, Thomas Howard, 2nd Earl of Arundel, with Alathea, Countess of Arundel.

2000, May 29 ***Perf. 13¾***

Sheets of 6, #a-f

2210-2212 A353 Set of 3 27.00 27.00

Souvenir Sheets

2213-2214 A353 Set of 2 9.00 9.00
2215 A353 $6 multi 5.50 5.50

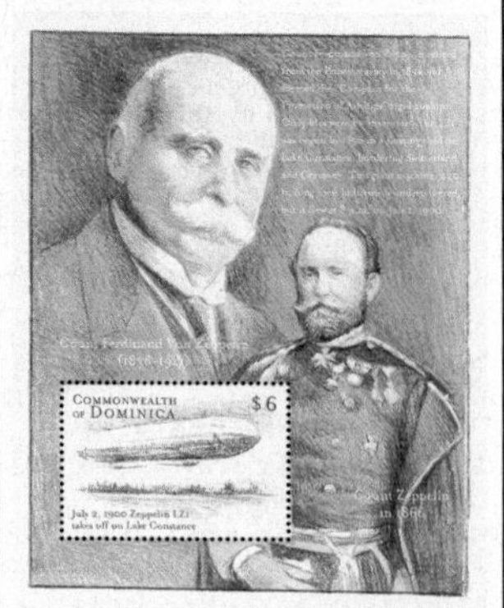

First Zeppelin Flight, Cent. — A354

No. 2216: a, Count Ferdinand von Zeppelin (1838-1917). b, First takeoff of LZ-1. c, LZ-10 over field. d, LZ-6 and Deutschland in hangar. e, Arrival of Z-4 at Luneville. f, Victoria Luise.

No. 2217, LZ-1, diff.

2000, June 21 Litho. ***Perf. 14***

2216 A354 $1.65 Sheet of 6, #a-f 9.00 9.00

Souvenir Sheet

2217 A354 $6 multi 5.50 5.50

Berlin Film Festival, 50th Anniv. — A355

No. 2218: a, Director Satyajit Ray. b, Mahangar. c, Fanfan La Tulipe. d, Le Salaire de la Peur. e, Les Cousins. f, Hon Dansade en Sommar.

No. 2219, Buffalo Bill and the Indians.

2000, June 21

2218 A355 $1.65 Sheet of 6, #a-f 9.00 9.00

Souvenir Sheet

2219 A355 $6 multi 5.50 5.50

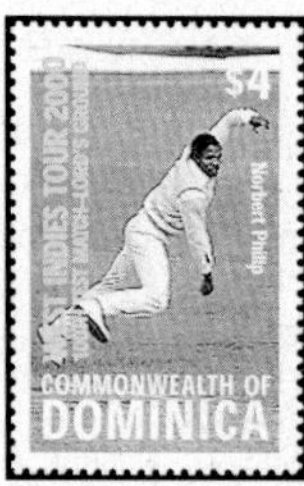

100th Test Match at Lord's Ground — A356

2000, June 21

2220 A356 $4 Norbert Phillip 3.50 3.50

Souvenir Sheet

2221 A356 $6 Lord's Ground 5.50 5.50

Souvenir Sheets

2000 Summer Olympics, Sydney — A357

a, Jesse Owens. b, Pole vault. c, Lenin Stadium Moscow, Soviet Union flag. d, Ancient Greek discus thrower.

2000, June 21

2222 A357 $2 Sheet of 4, #a-d 8.00 8.00

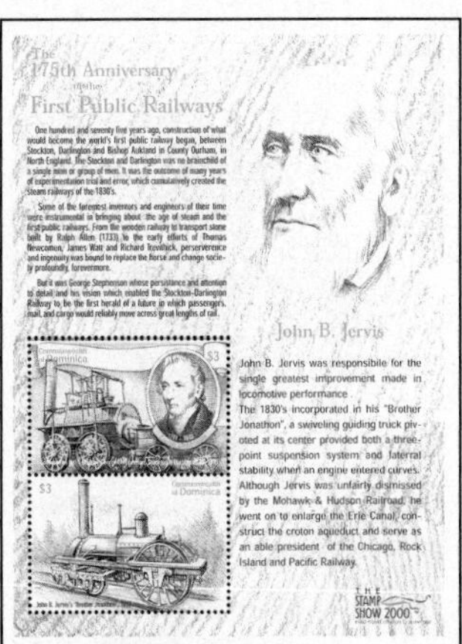

Public Railways, 175th Anniv. — A358

No. 2223: a, Locomotion No. 1, George Stephenson. b, Brother Jonathon.

2000, June 21

2223 A358 $3 Sheet of 2, #a-b 6.25 6.25

The Stamp Show 2000, London.

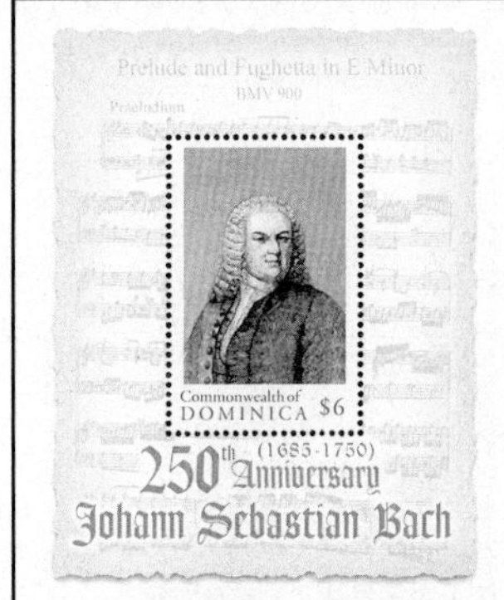

Johann Sebastian Bach — A359

2000, June 21

2224 A359 $6 multi 5.50 5.50

Flower Type of 2000

Various pictures of religious sites making up a photomosaic of Pope John Paul II.

2000, June 21 Litho. *Perf. 13¾*

2225 A350 $1 Sheet of 8, #a-h 8.00 8.00

Apollo-Soyuz Mission, 25th Anniv. — A360

No. 2226, vert.: a, Saturn IB launch vehicle. b, Apollo 18. c, Donald K. Slayton.
$6, Apollo and Soyuz docking.

2000, June 21 ***Perf. 14***

2226 A360 $3 Sheet of 3, #a-c 9.50 9.50

Souvenir Sheet

2227 A360 $6 multi 6.00 6.00

Souvenir Sheet

Albert Einstein (1879-1955) — A361

2000, June 21 ***Perf. 14¼***

2228 A361 $6 multi 5.50 5.50

Prince William, 18th Birthday — A362

No. 2229: a, In ski gear. b, In jacket and red sweater. c, In suit and tie. d, In plaid shirt.
$6, With Prince Harry.

2000, June 22 ***Perf. 14***

2229 A362 $1.65 Sheet of 4, #a-d 6.25 6.25

Souvenir Sheet

Perf. 13¾

2230 A362 $6 multi 5.50 5.50

No. 2229 contains four 28x42mm stamps.

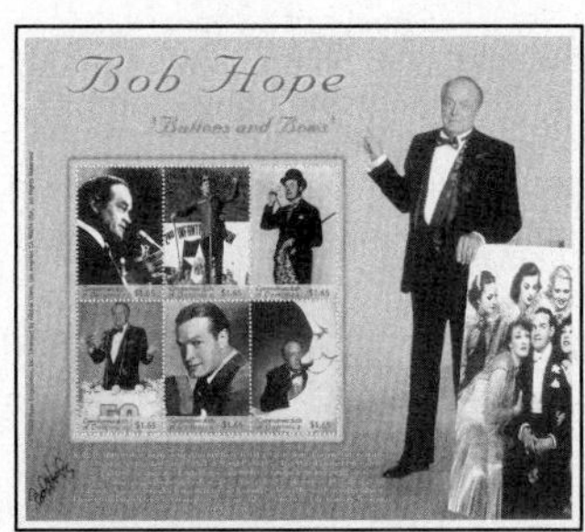

Bob Hope — A363

No. 2231: a, Microphone at right. b, Entertaining troops. c, Wearing bowler. d, Standing in cake. e, Microphone at left. f, With moon.

2000, Aug. 7 ***Perf. 14***

2231 A363 $1.65 Sheet of 6, #a-f 10.00 10.00

Monty Python and the Holy Grail, 25th Anniv. — A364

No. 2232: a, Close-up of Eric Idle. b, Terry Jones, Graham Chapman and John Cleese as three-headed giant, horiz. c, Knights facing castle wall. d, Chapman as King Arthur, with helmeted knight. e, Beheaded knight. f, Armless and legless Black Knight and King Arthur.

2000, Aug. 7 ***Perf. 13¾***

2232 A364 90c Sheet of 6, #a-f 5.25 5.25

Popes — A365

No. 2233: a, Clement X, 1670-76. b, Innocent X, 1644-55. c, Nicholas V, 1447-55. d, Martin V, 1417-31. e, Julius III, 1550-55. f, Innocent XII, 1691-1700.
$6, Clement XIV, 1769-74.

2000, Sept. 5

2233 A365 $1.65 Sheet of 6, #a-f 10.00 10.00

Souvenir Sheet

2234 A365 $6 multi 5.50 5.50

Monarchs — A366

No. 2235: a, Edward IV of England, 1461-83. b, Peter the Great of Russia, 1682-1725. c, Henry VI of England, 1422-61. d, Henry III of England, 1216-72. e, Richard III of England, 1483-85. f, Edward I of England, 1272-1307.
$6, Henry VIII of England, 1509-47.

2000, Sept. 5

2235 A366 $1.65 Sheet of 6, #a-f 10.00 10.00

Souvenir Sheet

2236 A366 $6 multi 5.50 5.50

World Stamp Expo 2000, Anaheim — A367

Spacecraft — No. 2237, $1.65: a, Explorer 14. b, Luna 16. c, Copernicus. d, Explorer 16. e, Luna 10. f, Arybhattan.
No. 2238, $1.65: a, ESSA 8. b, Echo 1. c, Topex Poseidon. d, Diademe. e, Early Bird. f, Molniya.
No. 2239, $6, Hipparcos. No. 2240, $6, Eole.

2000, June 21 Litho. *Perf. 14¼x14*

Sheets of 6, #a-f

2237-2238 A367 Set of 2 20.00 20.00

Souvenir Sheets

2239-2240 A367 Set of 2 11.00 11.00

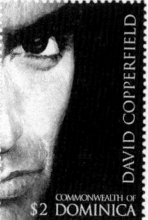

David Copperfield, Magician — A368

2000, Aug. 8 ***Perf. 14***

2241 A368 $2 multi 1.75 1.75

Printed in sheets of 4.

Souvenir Sheet

Female Recording Groups of the 1960s — A369

No. 2242 — The Crystals, yellow spotlight covering: a, UR, LL and LR corners. b, UL and LL corners. c, UR and LR corners. d, UL, LL and LR corners.

2000, Aug. 8

2242 A369 90c Sheet of 4, #a-d 3.50 3.50

Christmas — A370

Angel: 25c, No. 2247a, Looking right, purple and yellow green background. 65c, No. 2247b, At left, looking left, purple background. 90c, No. 2247c, At right, purple and orange background. $5, No. 2247d, At center, blue and purple background.

2000, Dec. 4

2243-2246 A370 Set of 4 6.25 6.25

Sheet of 4

2247 A370 $1.90 #a-d 7.00 7.00

Souvenir Sheet

2248 A370 $6 Angel 5.50 5.50

Millennium Type of 1999

Chinese Art — No. 2249, 55c: a, Eight Prize Steeds, by Giuseppe Castiglione. b, Oleanders, by Wu Hsi Tsai. c, Mynah and Autumn Flowers, by Chang Hsiung. d, Hen and Chicks Beneath Chrysanthemums, by Chu Ch'ao. e, Long Living Pine and Crane, by Xugu. f, Flowers and Fruits, by Chu Lien. g, Lotus and Willow, by Pu Hua. h, Kuan-Yin, by Ch'ien Hui-An. i, Human Figures, by Jen hsun. j, Han-Shan and Shih-Te, by Ren Yi. k, Landscape and Human Figure, by Jen Yu. l, Poetic Thoughts While Walking With a Staff, by Wangchen. m, Peony, by Chen Heng-Ko. n, Plum and Orchids, by Wu Chang-Shih. o, Monkey, by Kao Chi-Feng. p, Grapes and Locust, by Ch'i Pai-Shih and Galloping Horse, by Xu Beihong (60x40mm). q, The Beauty, by Lin Fengmian.

History of Change — No. 2250, 55c: a, Star charts. b, Precision tools. c, Science of the stars. d, Investigation into healing a human being. e, Sharing of medical information. f, Church. g, Water alarm clock. h, Weighted clock. i, Spring-loaded miniature clock. j, New technology of glass blowing. k, First screws. l, Wood lathe. m, New systems for assembly blocks for ships. n, Interchangeable parts for rifles. o, Study of movement. p, Efficiency and the Industrial Revolution (60x40mm). q, Concept of efficiency.

Highlights of the 1960s — No. 2251, 55c: a, First birth control pill developed. b, Yuri Gagarin becomes first man in space. c, The first hit for the Beatles in Britain. d, Assassination of John F. Kennedy. e, Dr. Martin Luther King's "I Have a Dream" speech. f, Betty Friedan writes "The Feminine Mystique." g, Kenya gains independence. h, U.S. Surgeon General warns about smoking-related health hazards. i, U.S. Congress passes Civil Rights Act. j, U.S. increases military presence in South Viet Nam. k, Ernesto "Che" Guevara. l,

First heart transplant. m, Israel wins Six-day War. n, Ho Chi Minh dies. o, First man on the Moon. p, Communists build wall to divide East and West Berlin (60x40mm). q, Woodstock rock concert.

Highlights of the late 14th Century — No. 2252: a, Minnesingers. b, Acampitzin, King of the Aztecs. c, Black Death eases. d, Giotto's campanile built. e, First French franc. f, Ming Dynasty in China. g, Tamerlane begins conquest of Asia. h, Triumph of Death painted by Francesco Traini. i, Robin Hood. j, Geoffrey Chaucer writes "The Canterbury Tales." k, Succession dispute in Japan. l, Jewish exodus from France. m, Temple of the Golden Pavilion built . n, Strasbourg Cathedral built. o, Alhambra Palace (60x40mm). p, Ife bronzes in Nigeria.

2000, Dec. 31 ***Perf. 12¾x12½***

Sheets of 17, #a-q

2249-2251 A346 Set of 3 26.00 26.00
2252 A347 65c Sheet of 17, #a-h, j-p, 2 #i 10.00 10.00

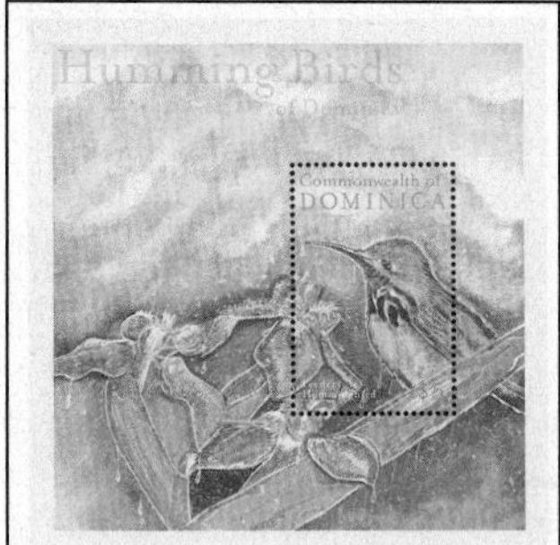

Hummingbirds — A371

No. 2253, $1.25: a, Green-throated carib. b, Bee, on branch. c, Bee, in flight. d, Bahama woodstar. e, Antillean mango. f, Blue-headed.

No. 2254, $1.65: a, Eastern streamertail. b, Purple-throated carib. c, Vervain. d, Bahama woodstar. e, Puerto Rican emerald. f, Antillean crested.

No. 2255, $5, Feeders. No. 2256, $6, Hispaniolan.

2000, Dec. 18 Litho. ***Perf. 14***

Sheets of 6, #a-f

2253-2254 A371 Set of 2 16.00 16.00

Souvenir Sheets

2255-2256 A371 Set of 2 10.00 10.00

Misspellings abound on Nos. 2253-2254.

New Year 2001 (Year of the Snake) A372

2001, Jan. 2 ***Perf. 12x12¼***

2257 A372 $1.20 multi 1.00 1.00

Printed in sheets of 4.

Fauna A373

Designs: 15c, Puerto Rican crested toad. 20c, Axolotl. $1.90, Panamanian golden frog. $2.20, Manatee.

No. 2262, $1.45: a, St. Vincent parrot. b, Indigo macaw. c, Cock of the rock. d, Cuban solenodon. e, Cuban hutia. f, Chinchilla.

No. 2263, $1.45: a, South American flamingo. b, Golden conure. c, Ocelot. d, Giant armadillo. e, Margay. f, Maned wolf.

No. 2264, $6, Anteater. No. 2265, $6, Hawksbill turtle.

2000, Dec. 18 Litho. ***Perf. 14***

2258-2261 A373 Set of 4 4.75 4.75

Sheets of 6, #a-f

2262-2263 A373 Set of 2 17.00 17.00

Souvenir Sheets

2264-2265 A373 Set of 2 12.00 12.00

Pokémon — A374

No. 2266, horiz.: a, Butterfree. b, Bulbasaur. c, Caterpie. d, Charmander. e, Squirtle. f, Pidgeotto.

2001, Feb. ***Perf. 13¾***

2266 A374 $1.65 Sheet of 6, #a-f 7.00 7.00

Souvenir Sheet

2267 A374 $6 Nidoking 4.25 4.25

A375

Marine Life A376

Designs: No. 2268, 15c, Banded sea snake. 25c, Soldier fish. 55c, Banner fish. No. 2271, 90c, Crown of thorns starfish.

No. 2272, 15c, Fish. 65c, Ray. No. 2274, 90c, Octopus. $3, Fish, diff.

No. 2276, $1.65: a, White-tip reef shark, lionfish, sergeant major. b, Blue-striped snappers. c, Great hammerhead shark, stovepipe sponge, pink vase sponge. d, Hawaiian monk seal, blue tube coral. e, Seahorse, common clownfish, red feather star coral. f, Bat starfish, brown octopus.

No. 2277, $1.65: a, Red sponge, shoal of Anthias. b, Orange-striped triggerfish. c, Coral grouper, soft tree coral. d, Peacock fan worms, gorgonian sea fan. e, Sweetlips, sea fan. f, Giant clam, golden cup coral.

No. 2278: a, Shark. b, Starfish. c, Seahorse. d, Fish. e, Crab. f, Eel.

No. 2279, $5, Royal angelfish. No. 2280, $5, Pink anemone fish. No. 2281, Turtle.

2001, Feb. 27 ***Perf. 14***

2268-2271 A375 Set of 4 2.00 2.00
2272-2275 A376 Set of 4 5.00 5.00

Sheets of 6, #a-f

2276-2277 A375 Set of 2 19.00 19.00
2278 A376 $2 Sheet of 6, #a-f 11.00 11.00

Souvenir Sheets

2279-2280 A375 Set of 2 10.00 10.00
2281 A376 $5 multi 5.00 5.00

Phila Nippon '01, Japan — A377

Art: 25c, Gathering of Chinese Women, by Tsuji Kako. 55c, Village by Bamboo Grove, by Takeuchi Seiho. 65c, Mountain Village in Spring, by Suzuki Hyakunen. 90c, Gentleman Amusing Himself, by Domoto Insho. $1, Calmness of Spring Light, by Seiho. $2, Su's Embankment on a Spring Morning, by Tomioka Tessai.

No. 2288, $1.65: a, Thatched Cottages in the Willows, by Kako. b, Joy in the Garden, by Kako. c, Azalea and butterfly, by Kikuchi Hobun. d, Pine Grove, by Kako. e, Woodcutters Talking in Autumn Valley, by Kubota Beisen.

No. 2289, $1.65: a, Waterfowl in Snow, by Kako. b, Heron and Willow, by Kako. c, Crow and Cherry Blossoms, by Hobun. d, Chrysanthemum Immortal, by Yamamoto Shunkyo. e, Cranes of Immortality, by Kako.

No. 2290, $6, Kamo Riverbank in the Misty Rain, by Kako. No. 2291, $6, Diamond Gate, by Kako. No. 2292, $6, Woman, by Suzuki Harunobu.

2001, May 15 Litho. ***Perf. 14***

2282-2287 A377 Set of 6 5.25 5.25

Sheets of 5, #a-e

2288-2289 A377 Set of 2 15.00 15.00

Souvenir Sheets

Perf. 13¾

2290-2292 A377 Set of 3 12.00 12.00

Nos. 2290-2292 each contain one 38x51mm stamp.

Queen Victoria (1819-1901) — A378

No. 2293: a, Prince Albert in uniform. b, Victoria with silver crown. c, Victoria with gold crown. d, Albert in suit.

$6, Victoria as old woman.

2001, May 15 ***Perf. 14***

2293 A378 $2 Sheet of 4, #a-d 7.25 7.25

Souvenir Sheet

Perf. 13¾

2294 A378 $6 multi 5.50 5.50

No. 2294 contains one 38x51mm stamp.

Queen Elizabeth II, 75th Birthday — A379

No. 2295: a, With crown. b, With white dress. c, Formal portrait by Pietro Annigoni. d, With orange coat. e, With child. f, With green dress.

$6, In uniform.

2001, May 15 ***Perf. 14***

2295 A379 $1.20 Sheet of 6, #a-f 6.25 6.25

Souvenir Sheet

2296 A379 $6 multi 5.50 5.50

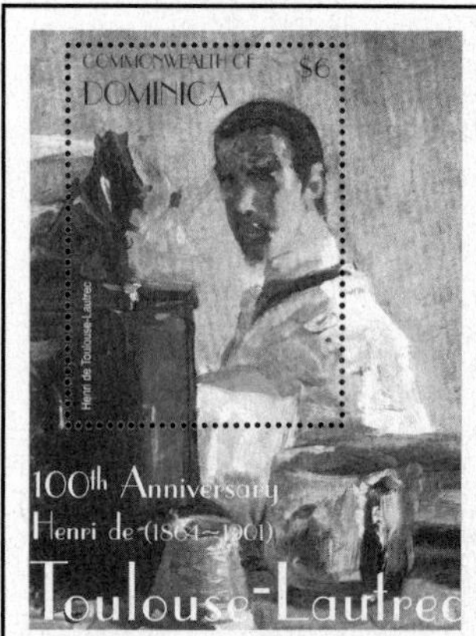

Toulouse-Lautrec Paintings — A380

No. 2297: a, Two Women Waltzing. b, The Medical Inspection. c, The Two Girlfriends. d, Woman Pulling Up Her Stocking.

2001, May 15 Litho. ***Perf. 13¾***

2297 A380 $2 Sheet of 4, #a-d 7.25 7.25

Souvenir Sheet

2298 A380 $6 Self-portrait 5.50 5.50

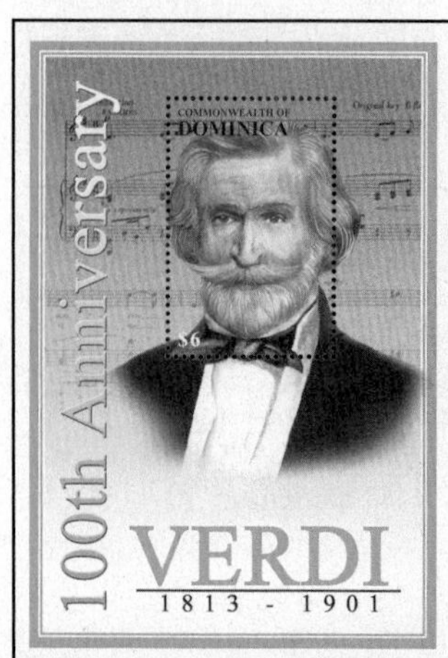

Giuseppe Verdi (1813-1901), Opera Composer — A381

No. 2299: a, Verdi. b, Lady Macbeth. c, Orchestra. d, Score.

2001, May 15 ***Perf. 14***
2299 A381 $2 Sheet of 4, #a-d 7.25 7.25

Souvenir Sheet

2300 A381 $6 Verdi, score 5.50 5.50

Mushrooms A382

Designs: 15c, Cantharellus cibarius. 25c, Hygrocybe pratensis. 55c, Leccinum aurantiacum. $3, Mycena haematopus.
No. 2305, 90c, horiz.: a, Caesar's amanita. b, Agaricus augustus. c, Clitocybe nuda. d, Hygrocybe plavescens. e, Stropharia kaufmanii. f, Hygrophorus speciosus.
No. 2306, $2: a, Marasmiellus candidus. b, Calostoma cinnabarina. c, Cantharellus infundibuliformis. d, Hygrocybe punicea. e, Basket stinkhorn. f, Agrocybe praecox.
No. 2307, $5, Fly agaric, horiz. No. 2308, $5, Gymnopilus spectabilis, horiz.

2001, June 18
2301-2304 A382 Set of 4 4.50 4.50

Sheets of 6, #a-f

2305-2306 A382 Set of 2 18.00 18.00

Souvenir Sheets

2307-2308 A382 Set of 2 10.00 10.00

Mao Zedong (1893-1976) — A383

No. 2309 — Picture from: a, 1945. b, 1926. c, 1949.
$3, 1930.

2001, May 15 **Litho.** ***Perf. 14***
2309 A383 $2 Sheet of 3, #a-c 5.25 5.25

Souvenir Sheet

2310 A383 $3 multi 2.75 2.75

Monet Paintings — A384

No. 2311, horiz.: a, The Basin of Argenteuil. b, The Bridge at Argenteuil. c, The Railway Bridge, Argenteuil. d, The Seine Bridge at Argenteuil.
$6, Woman with a Parasol — Madame Monet and Her Son.

2001, May 15 ***Perf. 13¾***
2311 A384 $2 Sheet of 4, #a-d 7.25 7.25

Souvenir Sheet

2312 A384 $6 multi 5.25 5.25

Fauna — A385

No. 2313: a, St. Vincent parrot. b, Painted bunting. c, Jamaican giant anole. d, White-fronted capuchin. e, Strand racerunner. f, Agouti.
No. 2314: a, Cook's tree boa. b, Tamandua. c, Common iguana. d, Solenodon.
No. 2315, $5, Purple gallinule. No. 2316, $5, Rufous-tailed jacamar. No. 2317, $5, Ruby-throated hummingbird, horiz. No. 2318, $5, Bottlenose dolphins, horiz.

2001, Sept. 3 ***Perf. 14***
2313 A385 $1.45 Sheet of 6, #a-f 8.75 8.75
2314 A385 $2 Sheet of 4, #a-d 8.25 8.25

Souvenir Sheets

2315-2318 A385 Set of 4 19.00 19.00

Birds — A386

Designs: 5c, Yellow warbler. 10c, Palmchat. 15c, Snowy cotinga. 20c, Blue-gray gnatcatcher. 25c, Belted kingfisher. 55c, Red-legged thrush. 65c, Bananaquit. 90c, Yellow-bellied sapsucker. $1, White-tailed tropicbird. $1.45, Ruby-throated hummingbird. $1.90, Painted bunting. $2, Great frigatebird. $5, Brown trembler. $10, Red-footed booby. $20, Sooty tern.

2001, Sept. 3 **Litho.** ***Perf. 14¾x14***

2319	A386	5c	multi	.30	.80
2320	A386	10c	multi	.30	.80
2321	A386	15c	multi	.35	.35
2322	A386	20c	multi	.35	.35
2323	A386	25c	multi	.35	.35
2324	A386	55c	multi	.65	.65
2325	A386	65c	multi	.75	.75
2326	A386	90c	multi	1.00	.80
2327	A386	$1	multi	1.25	1.25
2328	A386	$1.45	multi	1.60	1.60
2329	A386	$1.90	multi	2.00	2.00
2330	A386	$2	multi	2.50	2.50
2331	A386	$5	multi	5.00	5.00
2332	A386	$10	multi	8.50	8.50
2333	A386	$20	multi	17.50	17.50
	Nos. 2319-2333 (15)			42.40	43.20

No. 2323 exists dated "2005."
See No. 2513.

Photomosaic of Queen Elizabeth II — A387

2001, Nov. 15 ***Perf. 14***
2334 A387 $1 multi 1.00 1.00

Issued in sheets of 8.

Christmas — A388

Paintings by Giovanni Bellini: 25c, Madonna and Child. 65c, Madonna and Child, diff. 90c, Baptism of Christ. $1.20, Madonna and Child, diff. $4, Madonna and Child, diff.
$6, Madonna and Child with Sts. Catherine and Mary Magdalene.

2001, Dec. 3
2335-2339 A388 Set of 5 6.75 6.75

Souvenir Sheet

2340 A388 $6 multi 5.50 5.50

2002 World Cup Soccer Championships, Japan and Korea — A389

No. 2341, $2: a, US team, 1950. b, Poster, 1954. c, Poster, 1958. d, Zozimo, 1962. e, Gordon Banks, 1966. f, Pelé, 1970.
No. 2342, $2: a, Daniel Passarella, 1978. b, Paolo Rossi, 1982. c, Diego Maradona, 1986. d, Poster, 1990. e, Seo Jungulon, 1994. f, Jürgen Klinsmann, 1998.
No. 2343, $5, Face on World Cup, 1930. No. 2344, $5, Face and globe on Jules Rimet Trophy, 2002.

2001, Dec. 13 ***Perf. 13¾x14¼***

Sheets of 6, #a-f

2341-2342 A389 Set of 2 21.00 21.00

Souvenir Sheets

Perf. 14¼

2343-2344 A389 Set of 2 10.00 10.00

Queen Mother Type of 1999 Redrawn

No. 2345: a, In 1939. b, In Australia, 1958. c, At Badminton, 1982. d, Hatless, in 1982.
$6, In 1953.

2001, Dec. ***Perf. 14***

Yellow Orange Frames

2345 A340 $2 Sheet of 4, #a-d, + label 7.00 7.00

Souvenir Sheet

Perf. 13¾

2346 A340 $6 multi 5.25 5.25

Queen Mother's 101st birthday. No. 2346 contains one 38x51mm stamp with a bluer backdrop than that found on No. 2161. Sheet margins of Nos. 2345-2346 lack embossing and gold arms and frames found on Nos. 2160-2161.

Souvenir Sheets

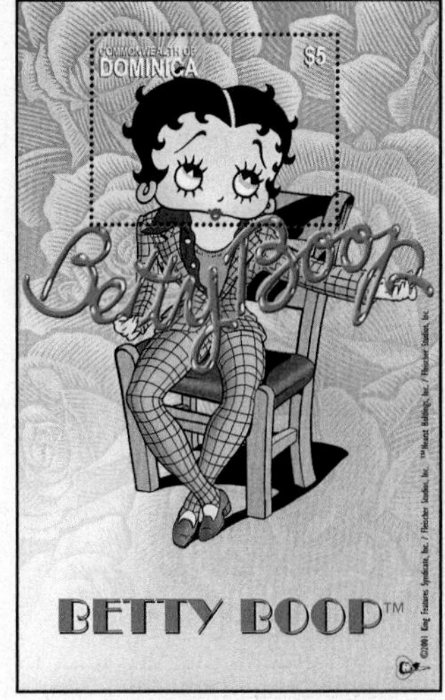

Betty Boop — A390

Betty Boop: No. 2347, $5, In chair, pink rose background. No. 2348, $5, Wearing blue blouse, in jungle. No. 2349, $5, With heart and stars, cat with film reel. No. 2350, $5, Wearing nurse's cap.

2001, Oct. 1 **Litho.** ***Perf. 13¾***
2347-2350 A390 Set of 4 18.00 18.00

The Three Stooges — A391

No. 2351: a, Man, Larry, Moe with sledgehammer, Joe Besser. b, Larry, woman, Joe Besser, Moe. c, Joe Besser, Larry and Moe on hands and knees. d, Larry grabbing throat of woman holding Joe Besser and Moe. e, Joe Besser drinking from baby bottle, pony, Moe and Larry. f, Military policeman, Joe Besser, Larry, woman. g, Larry. h, Joe Besser. i, Moe.
No. 2352, $5, Moe and Larry, "On the air" sign. No. 2353, $5, Larry and pony.

2001, Oct. 1 **Litho.** ***Perf. 13¾***
2351 A391 $1 Sheet of 9, #a-i 8.00 8.00

Souvenir Sheets

2352-2353 A391 Set of 2 9.00 9.00

Souvenir Sheet

New Year 2002 (Year of the Horse) — A392

No. 2354: a, Man with pole, horse. b, Horses grazing. c, Man currying horse. d, Horses with heads up.

2001, Dec. 17 ***Perf. 14***
2354 A392 $1.65 Sheet of 4, #a-d 6.00 6.00

Reign of Queen Elizabeth II, 50th Anniv. — A393

No. 2355: a, Wearing blue coat. b, With Prince Philip. c, Wearing tiara. d, Wearing flowered hat.
$6, With Prince Philip, diff.

2002, Feb. 6 ***Perf. 14¼***
2355 A393 $2 Sheet of 4, #a-d 7.00 7.00

Souvenir Sheet

2356 A393 $6 multi 5.00 5.00

United We Stand — A394

2002, Feb. ***Perf. 13½x13¼***
2357 A394 $2 multi 1.50 1.50

Printed in sheets of 4.

Shirley Temple in "Just Around the Corner" — A395

No. 2358, horiz.: a, Temple, woman with dogs. b, Temple, man and woman. c, Temple and man. d, Boy eating turkey leg, Temple carving turkey. e, Temple with old man. f, Temple with group of boys.
No. 2359: a, Boy, Temple with purse. b, Man and Temple using fingers as guns. c, Temple and man. d, Temple cutting boy's hair.
$6, Temple with black man on toadstool.

2002, Apr. 8 ***Perf. 12¼***
2358 A395 $1.90 Sheet of 6, #a-f 10.00 10.00
2359 A395 $2 Sheet of 4, #a-d 7.25 7.25

Souvenir Sheet

2360 A395 $6 multi 5.25 5.25

Japanese Art — A396

No. 2361, $1.20: a, The Courtesan Tsukioka of the Teahouse Hyogo-Ya, by Eisui Ichirakutei. b, Woman and Servant in the Snow, by Choki Eishosai. c, The Courtesan Shiratsuyu of the Teahouse Wakana-Ya, by Eisho Chokosai. d, Ohisa of the Takashima-Ya, by Toyokuni Utagawa. e, Woman and a Cat, by Kunimasa Utagawa. f, One of "Genre Scenes of Beauties," by Eisen Keisai.
No. 2362, $1.65: a, Women Inside and Outside a Mosquito Net, by Harushige Suzuki. b, Komachi at Shimizu, by Harushige Suzuki. c, Women Viewing Plum Blossoms, by Harunobu Suzuki. d, Women Cooling Themselves at Shijogawara in Kyoto, by Toyohiro Utagawa. e, Woman Reading a Letter, by Utamaro Kitagawa. f, Women Dressed for the Kashima Dance at the Niwaka Festival, by Utamaro Kitagawa.
No. 2363, $1.90: a, Actor Kiyotaro Iwai, by Kunimasa Utagawa. b, Actors Hiriji Otani III and Ryuzo Arashi, by Sharaku Toshusai. c, Actor Komazo Ichikawa II, by Shunko Katsukawa. d, Actors Yaozo Ichikawa and Hangoro Sakata III, by Sharaku Toshusai. e, Actor Torazo Tanimura, by Sharaku Toshusai. f, Actor Kiyotaro Iwai as Oishi, by Toyokuni Utagawa.
No. 2464, $5, Actor Riko Nakamura, by Shunsho Katsukawa. No. 2365, $5, Actors Hanshiro Iwai IV and Sojuro Sawamura III, by Kiyonaga Torii, horiz. No. 2366, $6, Ofuji, Daughter of the Motoyanagi-Ya, by Harunobu Suzuki.

2002, June 17 ***Perf. 14¼***

Sheets of 6, #a-f

2361-2363 A396 Set of 3 24.00 24.00

Souvenir Sheets

2364-2366 A396 Set of 3 12.00 12.00

Souvenir Sheet

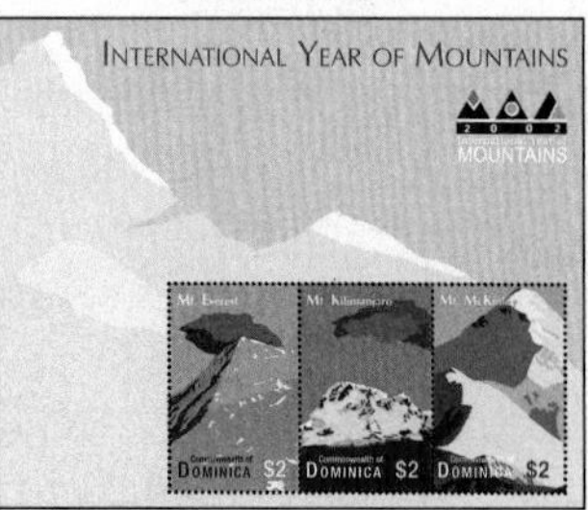

Intl. Year of Mountains — A397

No. 2367: a, Mt. Everest. b, Mt. Kilimanjaro. c, Mt. McKinley.

2002, July 15 ***Perf. 14***
2367 A397 $2 Sheet of 3, #a-c 5.00 5.00

2002 Winter Olympics, Salt Lake City A398

Designs: No. 2368, $2, Skiing. No. 2369, $2, Bobsled.

2002, July 15 ***Perf. 13½***
2368-2369 A398 Set of 2 3.50 3.50
a. Souvenir sheet, #2368-2369 3.50 3.50

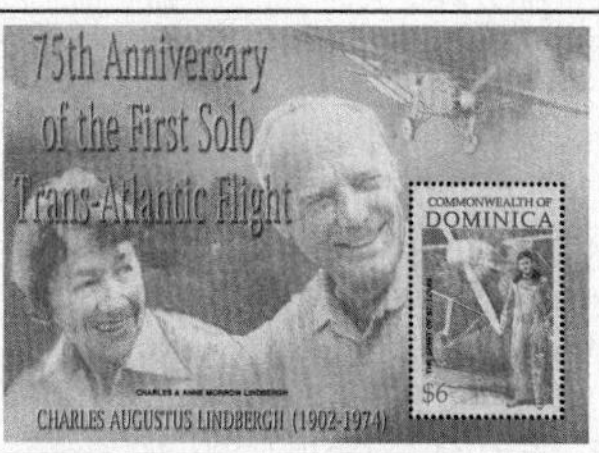

First Solo Trans-Atlantic Flight, 75th Anniv. — A399

No. 2370: a, Charles Lindbergh and Spirit of St. Louis. b, Charles and Anne Morrow Lindbergh.
$6, Charles Lindbergh and Spirit of St. Louis, diff.

2002, July 15 ***Perf. 14***
2370 A399 $3 Sheet of 2, #a-b 5.00 5.00

Souvenir Sheet

2371 A399 $6 multi 5.00 5.00

Popeye in New York — A400

No. 2372, $1: a, Olive Oyl. b, Brutus. c, Sweet Pea. d, Wimpy. e, Jeep. f, Popeye.
No. 2373, $1.90: a, Popeye and Olive Oyl, giraffe at Bronx Zoo. b, Popeye and Olive Oyl, Statue of Liberty. c, Popeye, Olive Oyl, Empire State Building. d, Popeye skating at Rockefeller Center. e, Popeye at Yankee Stadium. f, Popeye helping firefighters.
No. 2374, $6, Popeye, Atlas Statue, Rockefeller Center. No. 2375, $6, Popeye, Olive Oyl and Radio City Music Hall Rockettes, horiz.

2002, July 22

Sheets of 6, #a-f

2372-2373 A400 Set of 2 15.00 15.00

Souvenir Sheets

2374-2375 A400 Set of 2 10.50 10.50

20th World Scout Jamboree, Thailand — A401

No. 2376: a, Lord Robert Baden-Powell (facing forward). b, Lady Olave Baden-Powell. c, Maceo Johnson.
$6, Lord Baden-Powell (profile).

2002, July 15 Litho. ***Perf. 14¼x14***
2376 A401 $3 Sheet of 3, #a-c 8.00 8.00

Souvenir Sheet

2377 A401 $6 multi 5.25 5.25

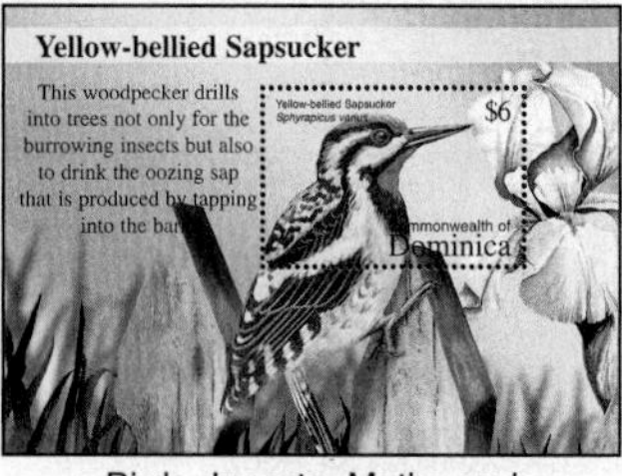

Birds, Insects, Moths and Whales — A402

No. 2378, $1.50, vert. — Birds: a, Brown trembler. b, Snowy ctinga. c, Bananaquit. d, Painted bunting. e, Belted kingfisher. f, Ruby-throated hummingbird.
No. 2379, $1.50, vert. — Insects: a, Field cricket. b, Migratory grasshopper. c, Honey bee. d, Hercules beetle. e, Black ant. f, Cicada.
No. 2380, $1.50, vert. — Moths: a, Carolina sphinx. b, White-lined sphinx. c, Orizaba silkmoth. d, Hieroglyphic moth. e, Hickory tussock moth. f, Diva moth.
No. 2381, $1.50, vert. — Whales: a, Sei. b, Killer. c, Blue. d, White. e, Pygmy. f, Sperm.
No. 2382, $6, Yellow-bellied sapsucker. No. 2383, $6, Bumble bee. No. 2384, $6, Ornate moth. No. 2385, $6, Gray whale.

2002, July 29 ***Perf. 14***

Sheets of 6, #a-f

2378-2381 A402 Set of 4 28.00 28.00

Souvenir Sheets

2382-2385 A402 Set of 4 22.00 22.00

A403

A404

Amphilex 2002 Intl. Stamp Exhibition, Amsterdam — A405

No. 2386 — Dutch Nobel Prize winners: a, Willem Einthoven, Medicine, 1924. b, Nobel Economics medal. c, Peter J. W. Debye, Chemistry, 1936. d, Frits Zernike, Physics, 1953. e, Jan Tinbergen, Economics, 1969. f, Simon van der Meer, Physics, 1984.

No. 2387 — Dutch lighthouses: a, Marken. b, Harlingen. c, Den Oever. d, De Ven. e, Urk. f, Oosterleek.

No. 2388 — Traditional women's costumes: a, South Holland woman with small white head covering (facing forward). b, Zeeland woman with large white head covering (facing backwards). c, Limburg woman with black scarf.

2002, Aug. 30 ***Perf. 13½x13¼***

2386 A403 $1.50 Sheet of 6, #a-f 8.00 8.00

2387 A404 $1.50 Sheet of 6, #a-f 8.00 8.00

Perf. 13½

2388 A405 $3 Sheet of 3, #a-c 8.00 8.00

Intl. Year of Ecotourism A406

Island scenes and cartoon characters: 45c, Detective H2O. 50c, Factman. 55c, B.B. 60c, Stanley the Starfish. 90c, Toxi. $1.20, Adopt. $6, Litterbit.

2002, Oct. 16 ***Perf. 14¼***

2389-2394 A406 Set of 6 3.25 3.25

Souvenir Sheet

2395 A406 $6 multi 5.00 5.00

Elvis Presley (1935-77) A407

2002, Oct. 28 ***Perf. 13¾***

2396 A407 $1.50 multi 1.10 1.10

Printed in sheets of 6 stamps with slightly differing frames.

Amerigo Vespucci (1454-1512), Explorer — A408

No. 2397: a, Compass rose. b, Vespucci with map. c, Map scroll.
$5, Two men.

2002, Nov. 28 ***Perf. 13¾***

2397 A408 $3 Sheet of 3, #a-c 8.00 8.00

Souvenir Sheet

Perf. 14

2398 A408 $5 multi 4.50 4.50

No. 2397 contains three 50x38mm stamps.

Pres. John F. Kennedy (1917-63) — A409

No. 2399, $1.90: a, Wearing military uniform. b, With red denomination at UL. c, With blue denomination at UR. d, Wearing tan suit.

No. 2400, $1.90 (denominations at UL in blue): a, Wearing red tie. b, Wearing blue tie (profile). c, Wearing black tie. d, With hand on chin.

2002, Dec. 16 ***Perf. 14***

Sheets of 4, #a-d

2399-2400 A409 Set of 2 13.50 13.50

Pres. Ronald Reagan — A410

No. 2401, $1.90: a, Wearing cowboy hat. b, Wearing blue green sweater. c, Wearing red sweater. d, Wearing blue sweater.

No. 2402, $1.90, horiz.: a, Wearing blue shirt, and with wife, Nancy. b, Nancy and US flag. c, Ronald. d, Wearing pink shirt, and with wife.

2002, Dec. 16 **Litho.** ***Perf. 14***

Sheets of 4, #a-d

2401-2402 A410 Set of 2 13.50 13.50

Princess Diana (1961-97) — A411

No. 2403 — Various depictions of Princess Diana with background colors of: a, Tan. b, Pink. c, Light blue. d, Light green.

2002, Dec. 16

2403 A411 $1.90 Sheet of 4, #a-d 7.00 7.00

Souvenir Sheet

2404 A411 $5 multi 4.50 4.50

Elizabeth "Ma Pampo" Israel, 128th Birthday — A412

2003, Jan. 27 ***Perf. 13½x13¼***

2405 A412 90c multi .70 .70

New Year 2003 (Year of the Ram) — A413

2003, Feb. 10 ***Perf. 13¾***

2406 A413 $1.65 multi 1.25 1.25

Printed in sheets of 4.

Souvenir Sheets

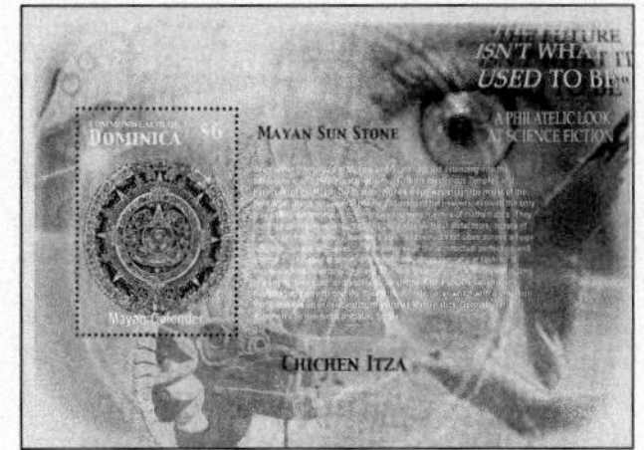

Science Fiction — A414

Designs: No. 2407, $6, Mayan calendar. No. 2408, $6, Atlas. No. 2409, $6, Confucius. No. 2410, $6, Nazca Lines. No. 2411, $6, Pres. Franklin D. Roosevelt and Pres. John F. Kennedy. No. 2412, $6, Zoroaster.

2003, Feb. 10 ***Perf. 13¼***

2407-2412 A414 Set of 6 27.50 27.50

A415

Coronation of Queen Elizabeth II, 50th Anniv. — A416

No. 2413: a, Wearing white dress, no crown. b, Wearing black robe. c, Wearing crown.
$6, Wearing crown, diff. $20, Wearing red robe.

2003 **Litho.** ***Perf. 14***

2413 A415 $3 Sheet of 3, #a-c 6.25 6.25

Souvenir Sheet

2414 A415 $6 multi 4.25 4.25

Miniature Sheet

Litho. & Embossed

Perf. 13¼x13

2415 A416 $20 gold & multi 14.00 14.00

Issued: Nos. 2413-2414, 5/13; No. 2415, 2/24.

Prince William, 21st Birthday — A417

No. 2416: a, Wearing dark blue shirt. b, Wearing blue suit, holding flowers. c, In polo uniform.
$6, Wearing black suit.

2003, June 21 **Litho.** ***Perf. 14***

2416 A417 $3 Sheet of 3, #a-c 6.50 6.50

Souvenir Sheet

2417 A417 $6 multi 4.50 4.50

Intl. Year of Fresh Water — A418

No. 2418: a, Trafalgar Falls. b, YS Falls. c, Dunn's River.
$6, Annandale Falls.

2003, June 21 ***Perf. 13½***

2418 A418 $3 Sheet of 3, #a-c 6.75 6.75

Souvenir Sheet

2419 A418 $6 multi 4.50 4.50

Teddy Bears, Cent. — A419

No. 2420 — Bear with: a, Purple shirt. b, Pink shirt and party favor. c, Green shirt and party favor. d, Black hat. e, Purple hat. f, Pink shirt and birthday cake.

No. 2421 — Bear with: a, Reindeer sweater, text at top. b, Santa Claus costume, text at top. c, Santa Claus costume, text at bottom. d, Reindeer sweater, text at bottom.

2003, June 21 ***Perf. 13½***

2420 A419 $1.65 Sheet of 6, #a-f 7.50 7.50
2421 A419 $2 Sheet of 4, #a-d 6.00 6.00

No. 2421 contains four 37x51mm stamps.

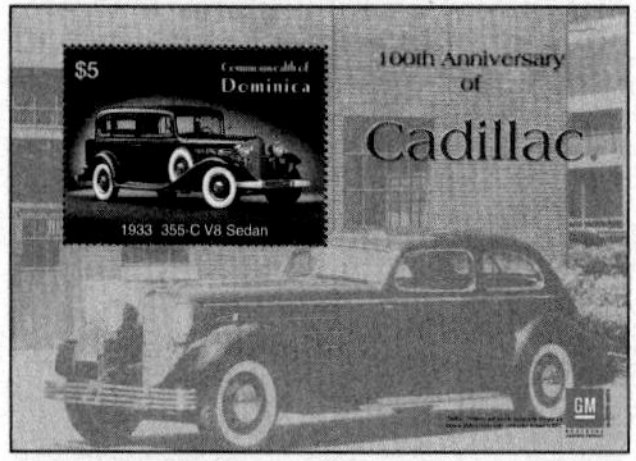

General Motors Automobiles — A420

No. 2422, $2 — Cadillacs: a, 1903 Model A Runabout. b, 1912 Model 30. c, 1918 Type 57 Victoria Coupe. d, 1927 Lasalle Convertible Coupe.

No. 2423, $2 — Corvettes: a, 1953. b, 1956. c, 1957. d, 1962.

No. 2424, $5, 1933 Cadillac 355-C V8 sedan. No. 2425, $5, 1959 Corvette.

2003, June 21 ***Perf. 13¼***

Sheets of 4, #a-d

2422-2423 A420 Set of 2 12.00 12.00

Souvenir Sheets

2424-2425 A420 Set of 2 7.50 7.50

Tour de France Bicycle Race, Cent. — A421

No. 2426 — Champions: a, Firmin Lambot, 1919. b, Phillippe Thys, 1920. c, Léon Scieur, 1921. d, Lambot, 1922.
$5, François Faber.

2003, June 21

2426 A421 $2 Sheet of 4, #a-d 6.00 6.00

Souvenir Sheet

2427 A421 $5 multi 3.75 3.75

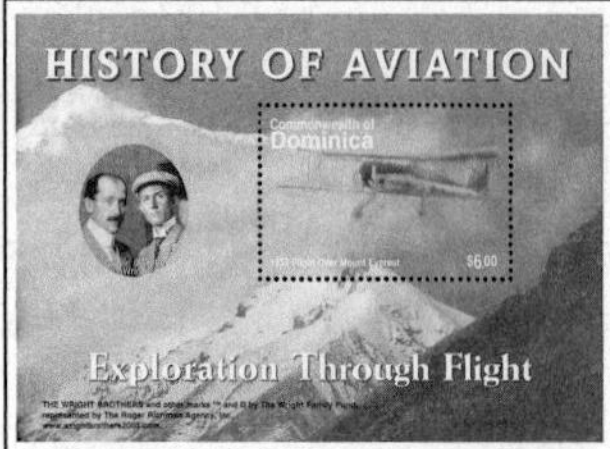

History of Aviation — A422

No. 2428: a, Sputnik, first orbiting satellite, 1957. b, Yuri Gagarin, first man in space, 1961. c, Neil Armstrong, first man on the Moon, 1969. d, Skylab 1, 1973.

$6, Flight over Mt. Everest, 1933.

2003, June 21 ***Perf. 14***

2428 A422 $2 Sheet of 4, #a-d 6.50 6.50

Souvenir Sheet

2429 A422 $6 multi 5.00 5.00

Lewis & Clark Expedition A423

Designs: 20c, Dealing with the Chinook Indians. 50c, Compass used in expedition. 55c, Rocky Mountains. 65c, Medals presented to the Indians, vert. 90c, First encounter with grizzly bear. $1, Befriending Shoshone Indians. $2, Lewis after the expedition, vert. $4, Lewis & Clark, vert.

No. 2438, $5, Meriwether Lewis, vert. No. 2439, $5, William Clark, vert.

2003, June 21

2430-2437 A423 Set of 8 7.50 7.50

Souvenir Sheets

2438-2439 A423 Set of 2 7.00 7.00

2002 World Cup Soccer Championships, Japan and Korea — A424

No. 2440, $1.45: a, Danny Mills. b, Paul Scholes. c, Darius Vassell. d, Michael Owen. e, Emile Heskey. f, Rio Ferdinand.

No. 2441, $1.45: a, Bobby Moore. b, Roger Hunt. c, Gordon Banks. d, Bobby Charlton. e, Alan Ball. f, Geoff Hurst.

No. 2442, $3: a, Ashley Cole. b, David Seaman.

No. 2443, $3: a, Sven-Goran Eriksson. b, Nikki Butt.

No. 2444, $3: a, Robbie Fowler. b, Sol Campbell.

No. 2445, $3: a, Charlton, Ball and Hunt. b, Nobby Stiles.

No. 2446, $3: a, Franz Beckenbauer. b, Oliver Kahn.

2003, June 21 ***Perf. 13¼***

Sheets of 6, #a-f

2440-2441 A424 Set of 2 11.00 11.00

Souvenir Sheets of 2, #a-b

2442-2446 A424 Set of 5 20.00 20.00

CARICOM, 30th Anniv. — A425

2003, July 25 ***Perf. 13½***

2447 A425 $1 multi .75 .75

Christmas A426

Painting details: 50c, Madonna and Child with the Young St. John, by Correggio. 90c, Madonna in Glory with the Christ Child and Sts. Frances and Alvise with the Donor, by Titian. $1.45, Madonna and Child with Angels Playing Musical Instruments, by Correggio. $3, Madonna of the Cherries, by Titian.

$6, Holy Family with John the Baptist, by Andrea del Sarto.

2003, Nov. 17 **Litho.** ***Perf. 14¼***

2448-2451 A426 Set of 4 4.50 4.50

Souvenir Sheet

2452 A426 $6 multi 4.50 4.50

New Year 2004 (Year of the Monkey) — A427

No. 2453: a, Orange monkey, hindquarters of brown monkey. b, Monkey with brown face. c, Brown monkey drinking water. d, Monkey with blue face.

2004, Jan. 5 **Litho.** ***Perf. 14***

2453 A427 $1.50 Sheet of 4, #a.-d. 4.50 4.50

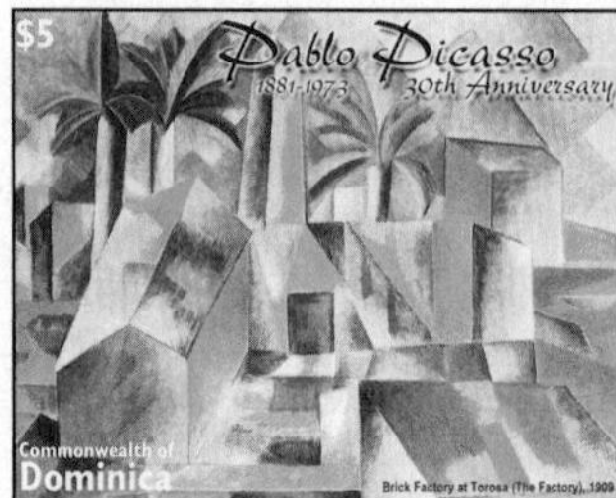

Paintings of Pablo Picasso — A428

No. 2454, vert.: a, Portrait of Manuel Pallarés. b, Woman with Vase of Flowers. c, Woman with a Fan (Fernande). d, Portrait of Clovis Sagot.

$5, Brick Factory at Torosa (The Factory).

2004, Mar. 8 ***Perf. 14¼***

2454 A428 $1 Sheet of 4, #a.-d. 3.00 3.00

Imperf

2455 A428 $5 multi 3.75 3.75

No. 2454 contains four 38x50mm stamps.

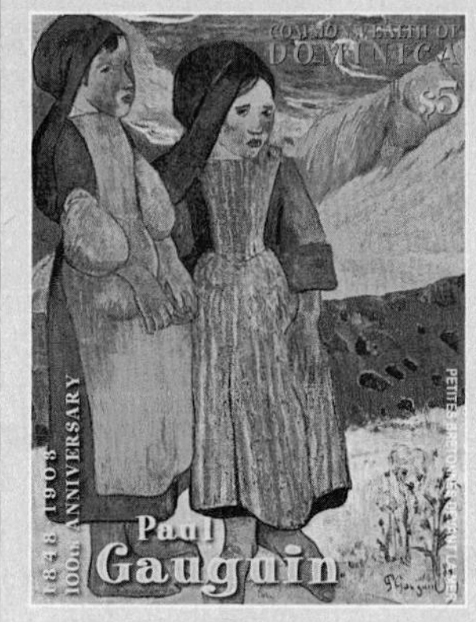

Paintings of Paul Gauguin — A429

No. 2456: a, Village Tahitien avec la Femme en Marche. b, La Barriere. c, Bonjour, Monsieur Gauguin. d, Vegetation Tropicale.

$5, Petites Bretonnes Devant la Mer.

2004, Mar. 8 ***Perf. 14¼***

2456 A429 $2 Sheet of 4, #a.-d. 6.00 6.00

Imperf

2457 A429 $5 multi 3.75 3.75

No. 2456 contains four 38x50mm stamps.

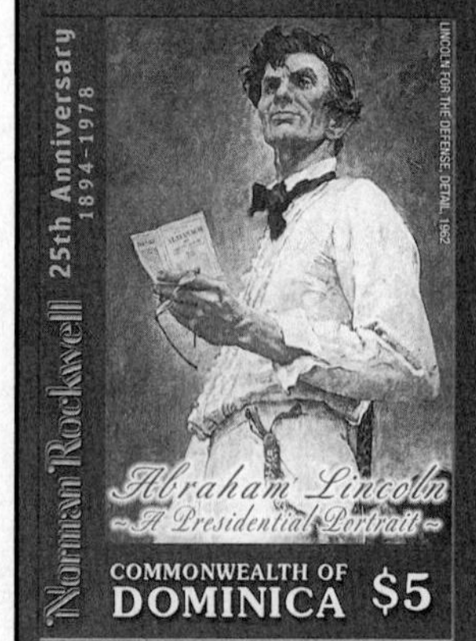

Paintings of Presidents by Norman Rockwell — A430

No. 2458: a, Dwight D. Eisenhower. b, John F. Kennedy. c, Lyndon B. Johnson. d, Richard M. Nixon.

$5, Abraham Lincoln.

2004, Mar. 8 ***Perf. 14¼***

2458 A430 $2 Sheet of 4, #a.-d. 6.00 6.00

Imperf

2459 A430 $5 multi 3.75 3.75

No. 2458 contains four 38x50mm stamps.

Paintings of James McNeill Whistler — A431

Designs: 50c, Symphony in White No. 3. $1, The Artist's Studio, vert. $1.65, The Thames in Ice, vert. No. 2463, $2, Arrangement in Black: Portrait of F. R. Leyland, vert.

No. 2464, $2, vert.: a, Arrangement in Brown & Black: Portrait of Miss Rosa Corder. b, Harmony in Red: Lamplight. c, Symphony in Flesh Color & Pink: Portrait of Mrs. Frances Leyland. d, Arrangement in Yellow & Gray: Effie Deans.

$5, Harmony in Gray and Green: Miss Cicely Alexander, vert.

2004, Mar. 8 *Perf. 14¼*
2460-2463 A431 Set of 4 4.00 4.00
Perf. 13½
2464 A431 $2 Sheet of 4, #a-d 6.00 6.00
Imperf
Size: 71x103mm
2465 A431 $5 multi 3.75 3.75

No. 2464 contains four 35x70mm stamps.

Fish A432

Designs: 20c, Banded butterflyfish. 25c, Queen angelfish. 55c, Porkfish. No. 2469, $5, Redband parrotfish.

No. 2470: a, Beaugregory. b, Porkfish, diff. c, Bicolor cherubfish. d, Rock beauty. e, Blackfin snapper. f, Blue tang.

No. 2471, $5, Indigo hamlet.

2004, Mar. 8 *Perf. 14¼x14¾*
2466-2469 A432 Set of 4 4.50 4.50
Perf. 14
2470 A432 $2 Sheet of 6, #a-f 9.00 9.00
Souvenir Sheet
2471 A432 $5 multi 3.75 3.75

Nos. 2470-2471 each contain 42x28mm stamps.

Shells A433

Designs: 20c, Siratus perelegans. 90c, Polystira albida. $1.45, Cypraea cervus. $2, Strombus gallus.

No. 2476: a, Strombus pugilis. b, Cittarium pica. c, Distorsio clathrata. d, Melongena morio. e, Prunum labiata. f, Chione paphia.

$5, Strombus alatus, vert.

2004, Mar. 8 *Perf. 14¼x14¾*
2472-2475 A433 Set of 4 3.50 3.50
Perf. 14
2476 A433 $1.90 Sheet of 6, #a-f 8.50 8.50
Souvenir Sheet
2477 A433 $5 multi 3.75 3.75

No. 2476 contain six 42x28mm stamps; No. 2477 contains one 28x42mm stamp.

Orchids — A434

Designs: 25c, Epidendrum pseudepidendrum. 55c, Aspasia epidendroides. $1.50, Cochleanthes discolor. $4, Brassavola nodosa.

No. 2482: a, Laelia anceps. b, Caularthron bicornutum. c, Cattleya velutina. d, Cattleya warneri. e, Oncidium splendidum. f, Psychlis atropurpurea.

$5, Maxillaria cuculata, vert.

2004, Mar. 8 *Perf. 14¼x14¾*
2478-2481 A434 Set of 4 4.75 4.75
Perf. 14
2482 A434 $1.90 Sheet of 6, #a-f 8.50 8.50
Souvenir Sheet
2483 A434 $5 multi 3.75 3.75

No. 2482 contains six 42x28mm stamps; No. 2483 contains one 28x42mm stamp.

Butterflies — A435

Designs: 50c, Small flambeau. 90c, Tiger pierid. $1, White peacock. No. 2469, $2, Cramer's mesene.

No. 2488, $2: a, Figure-of-eight. b, Orange theope. c, Clorinde. d, Grecian shoemaker. e, Orange-barred sulphur. f, Common morpho.

$5, Giant swallowtail, vert.

2004, Mar. 8 *Perf. 14¼x14¾*
2484-2487 A435 Set of 4 3.00 3.00
Perf. 14
2488 A435 $2 Sheet of 6, #a-f 8.00 8.00
Souvenir Sheets
2489 A435 $5 multi 3.75 3.75

No. 2488 contains six 42x28mm stamps; No. 2489 contains one 28x42mm stamp.

Olympic Gold Medalists A436

Designs: 20c, Elizabeth Robinson, Amsterdam, 1928. 25c, Károly Takács, London, 1948. 55c, Bob Beamon, Mexico City, 1968. 65c, Mildred Didrikson, Los Angeles, 1932. $1, Ville Ritola, Paris, 1924. $1.65, Alfred Hajós (Guttman), Athens, 1896. $2, Paavo Nurmi, Antwerp, 1920. $4, Nedo Nadi, Antwerp, 1920.

2004, Apr. 12 *Perf. 13¼*
2490-2497 A436 Set of 8 7.75 7.75

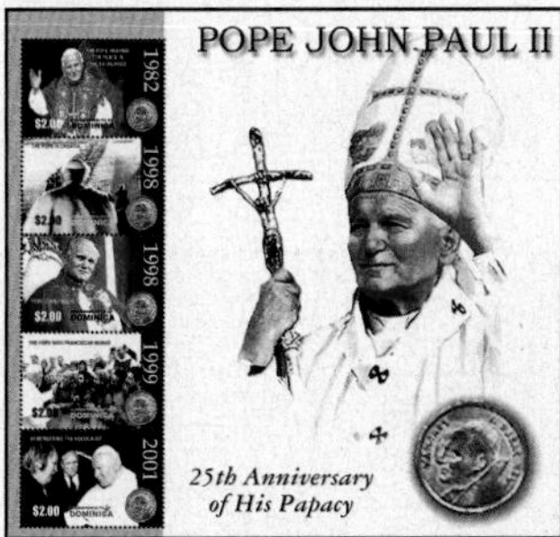

Election of Pope John Paul II, 25th Anniv. (in 2003) — A437

No. 2498: a, Praying for peace in Falkland Islands, 1982. b, In Croatia, 1998. c, Seated, 1998. d, With Franciscan monks, 1999. e, Remembering the Holocaust, 2001.

2004, June 21 **Litho.** *Perf. 14*
2498 A437 $2 Sheet of 5, #a-e 7.50 7.50

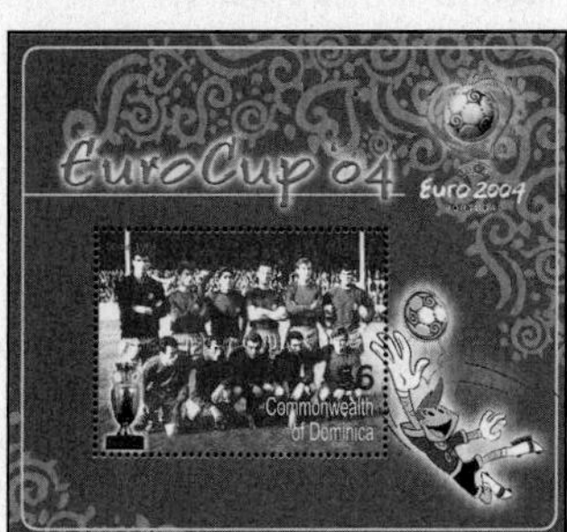

European Soccer Championships, Portugal — A438

No. 2499, vert.: a, Jose Luis Villalonga. b, Lev Yashin. c, Marcelino Martinez. d, Santiago Bernabeu Stadium.

$6, 1964 Spain team.

2004, June 21 *Perf. 14*
2499 A438 $2 Sheet of 4, #a-d 6.00 6.00
Souvenir Sheet
Perf. 14¼
2500 A438 $6 multi 4.50 4.50

No. 2499 contains four 28x42mm stamps.

Trains — A439

No. 2501, $1: a, Engine #22, V7 T4-4-0, V7T4-6-0. b, Don J12. c, Baldwin 2-D-D. d, Southern Engine #20. e, 143-890 2DB class electric locomotive. f, Engine #1.

No. 2502, $1: a, Canadian Pacific freight train. b, Queensland Rail IM U railroad. c, Green and white Shinkansen locomotive. d, Amtrak locomotive. e, Shinkansen locomotive in station. f, YPDMU rail cars.

No. 2503, $1: a, Santa Fe Railroad locomotive. b, Via Rail train, Canada. c, Two Conrail road switchers. d, Strasburg Railroad #90. e, Deltic diesel-electric engine. f, Brighton Belle.

No. 2504, $6, Golsdorf two cylinder compound locomotive 4-4-0. No. 2505, $6, Southern Pacific 4449 4-8-4. No. 2506, $6, White, yellow and blue Shinkansen.

2004, July 12 *Perf. 13¼x13½*
Sheets of 6, #a-f
2501-2503 A439 Set of 3 13.50 13.50
Souvenir Sheets
2504-2506 A439 Set of 3 13.50 13.50

D-Day, 60th Anniv. A440

Designs: $1, Eddie Hannath. $4, Pres. Franklin D. Roosevelt.

No. 2509: a, Rangers make their way towards the cliffs of Pointe du Hoc. b, Rangers begin scaling the cliffs of Pointe du Hoc. c, British troops advance on Sword Beach. d, An AVRE Petard heads inland off Sword Beach.

$6, British troops landing on Sword Beach.

2004, July 22 *Perf. 14*
Stamp + Label (#2507-2508)
2507-2508 A440 Set of 2 3.75 3.75
2509 A440 $2 Sheet of 4, #a-d 6.00 6.00
Souvenir Sheet
2510 A440 $6 multi 4.50 4.50

George Herman "Babe" Ruth (1895-1948), Baseball Player — A441

No. 2511: a, Swinging bat. b, Swinging bat, looking up. c, Holding three bats. d, Hand on knee.

2004, Aug. 18 *Perf. 13½x13¼*
2511 A441 $2 Sheet of 4, #a-d 6.00 6.00

Marilyn Monroe (1926-62), Actress — A442

No. 2512: a, Wearing earrings and necklace. b, Wearing earrings. c, Wearing no earrings or necklace. d, Wearing necklace.

2004, Aug. 18
2512 A442 $2 Sheet of 4, #a-d 6.00 6.00

Bird Type of 2001

2004, Sept. 3 *Perf. 14¾x14*
2513 A386 50c Baltimore oriole .45 .45

Exists dated "2005."

Queen Juliana of the Netherlands (1909-2004) A443

2004, Sept. 21 *Perf. 13¼*
2514 A443 $2 multi 1.50 1.50

Printed in sheets of 6.

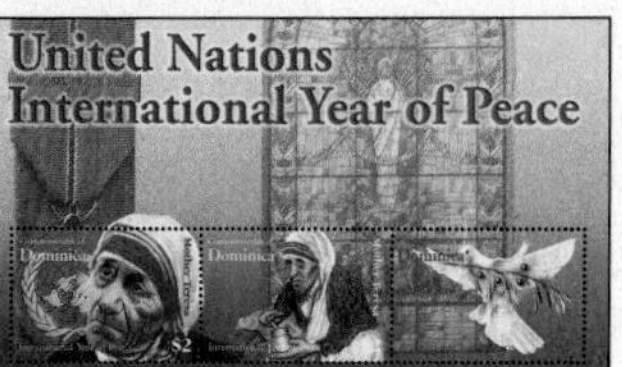

Intl. Year of Peace — A444

No. 2515: a, Mother Teresa, UN emblem. b, Mother Teresa feeding poor. c, Dove.

2004, Sept. 21 *Perf. 14*
2515 A444 $2 Sheet of 3, #a-c 4.50 4.50

Souvenir Sheet

Deng Xiaoping (1904-97) and Mao Zedong (1893-1976), Chinese Leaders — A445

2004, Sept. 21 *Perf. 14*
2516 A445 $6 multi 4.50 4.50

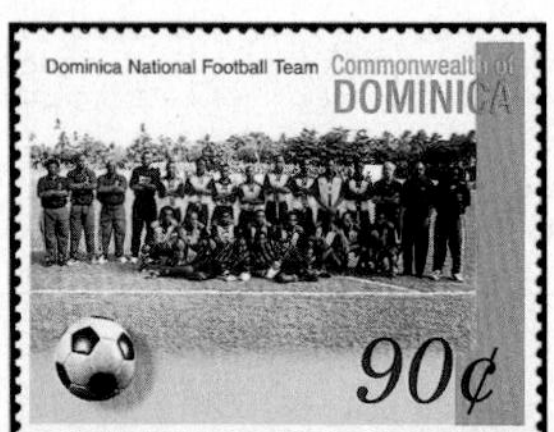

National Soccer Team — A446

2004, Nov. 8 Litho. *Perf. 12*
2517 A446 90c multi .70 .70

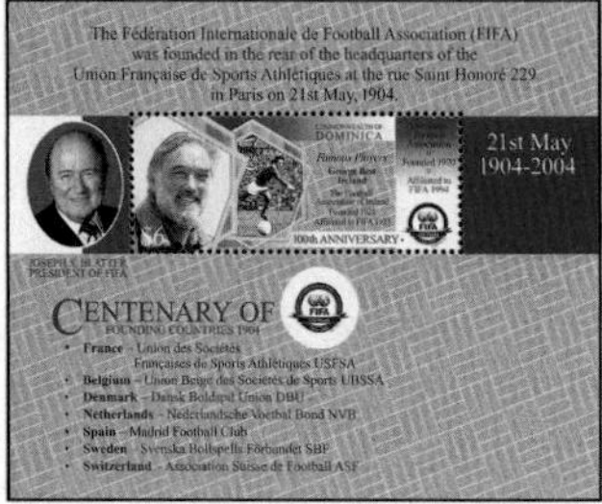

FIFA (Fédération Internationale de Football Association), Cent. — A447

No. 2518: a, Ferenc Puskas. b, Rivaldo. c, Carsten Jancker. d, Johan Cruyff.
$6, George Best.

2004, Nov. 8 *Perf. 12¾x12½*
2518 A447 $2 Sheet of 4, #a-d 6.00 6.00
Souvenir Sheet
2519 A447 $6 multi 4.50 4.50

Worldwide Fund for Nature (WWF) — A448

No. 2520: a, Green-throated Carib (denomination in blue). b, Purple-throated Carib (denomination in white). c, Green-throated Carib (denomination in white). d, Purple-throated Carib (denomination in red).

2005, Jan. 10 *Perf. 14*
2520 A448 $2 Block of 4, #a-d 5.50 5.50
e. Miniature sheet, 2 each #2520a-2520d 11.00 11.00

Prehistoric Animals — A449

No. 2521, $2: a, Tyrannosaurus rex. b, Velociraptor. c, Stegosaurus. d, Psittacosaurus.
No. 2522, $2: a, Mammuthus columbi. b, Spinosaurus. c, Ankylosaurus. d, Mammuthus primigenius.
No. 2523, $2: a, Pterodactylus. b, Pteranodon. c, Sordes. d, Caudiptheryx zoui.
$3, Compsognathus. $5, Archaeopteryx. $6, Mammuthus primigenius, diff.

2005, Jan. 10 *Perf. 12¾*
Sheets of 4, #a-d
2521-2523 A449 Set of 3 18.00 18.00
Souvenir Sheets
2524-2526 A449 Set of 3 10.50 10.50

Birds A450

Designs: 25c, Brown booby. 90c, Brown pelican. $1, Red-billed tropicbird. $4, Northern gannet.
No. 2531: a, Great egret. b, Black-necked grebe. c, Turkey vulture. d, Snail kite.
$6, Red knot.

2005, Jan. 10 *Perf. 14*
2527-2530 A450 Set of 4 4.50 4.50
2531 A450 $2 Sheet of 4, #a-d 5.75 5.75
Souvenir Sheet
2532 A450 $6 multi 4.00 4.00

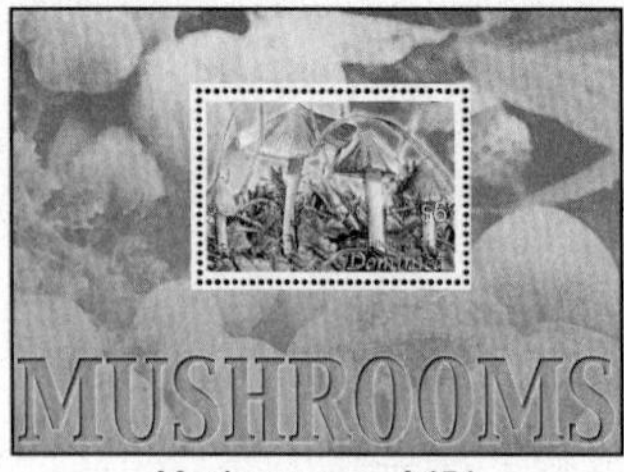

Mushrooms — A451

No. 2533: a, Cortinarius mucosus. b, Cortinarius splendens. c, Cortinarius rufo-olivaceus. d, Inocybe erubescens.
$6, Split fibercap.

2005, Jan. 10
2533 A451 $2 Sheet of 4, #a-d 6.00 6.00
Souvenir Sheet
2534 A451 $6 multi 4.50 4.50

Miniature Sheet

Flowers — A452

No. 2535: a, Sweetshrub. b, Pink turtleheads. c, Flowering quince. d, Water lily.
$6, Glory of the snow, vert.

2005, Jan. 10 Litho. *Perf. 14*
2535 A452 $2 Sheet of 4, #a-d 6.00 6.00
Souvenir Sheet
2535E A452 $6 multi 4.50 4.50

New Year 2005 (Year of the Rooster) — A453

2005, Jan. 24 *Perf. 12¾x12½*
2536 A453 $1 shown .75 .75
Souvenir Sheet
Perf. 12
2537 A453 $4 Roosters 3.00 3.00

No. 2537 contains one 56x36mm stamp.

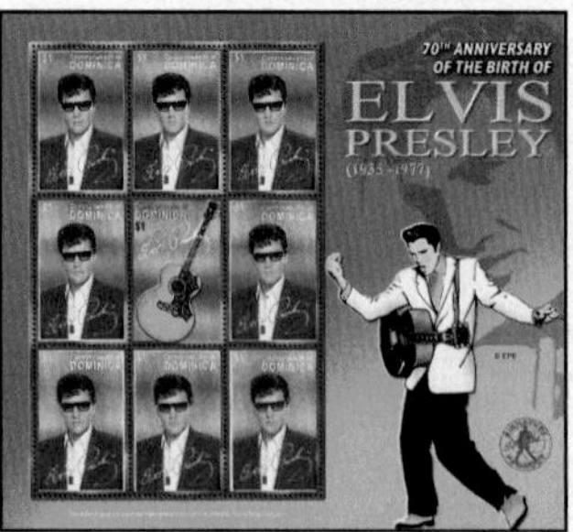

A454

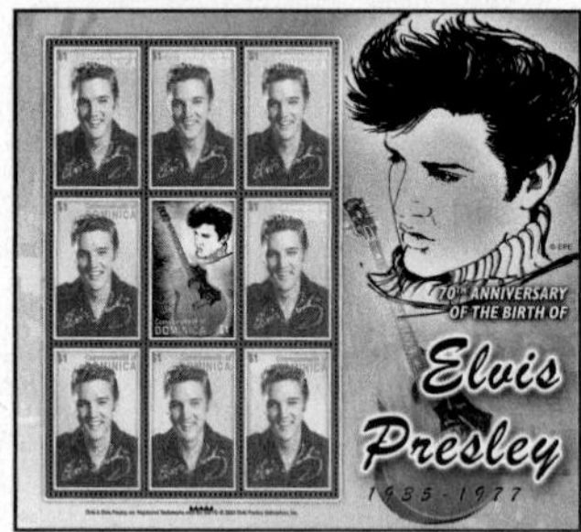

Elvis Presley (1935-77) — A455

Elvis Presley (1935-77) — A455a

No. 2538: a, Green background under country name and near shirt collar. b, Guitar. c, Large red violet areas at side of head. d, Dark green background under country name, blue background near shirt collar. e, Purple background near shirt collar. f, Small red violet areas at side of head.
No. 2539: a, Country name in white, blue background at UR. b, Country name in white, pink background at UR. c, Country name in white, orange background at UR. d, Country name in blue, green background at UR. e, Presley and guitar. f, Country name in blue, yellow background at UR. g, Country name in blue, blue background at UR.
No. 2539H illustration reduced.

2005, Apr. 5 *Perf. 13½*
2538 A454 $1 Sheet of 9, #a-c, 2 each #d-f 6.75 6.75
2539 A455 $1 Sheet of 9, #a, c, e-g, 2 each #b, d 6.75 6.75

Litho. & Embossed
Variable Serpentine Die Cut
Without Gum
2539H A455a $20 gold & multi 14.00 14.00

No. 2539H was not available in the marketplace until 2006.

Miniature Sheet

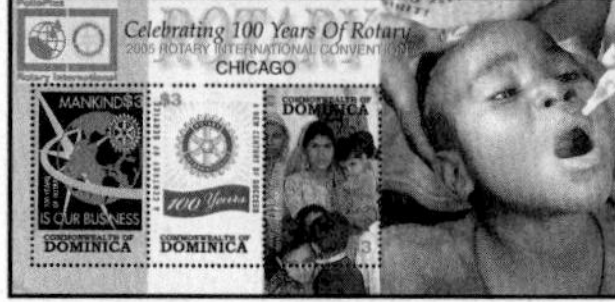

Rotary International, Cent. — A456

No. 2540: a, Globe and Rotary emblem. b, Rotary emblem. c, Women and children.

2005, Sept. 7 *Perf. 12½x12¾*
2540 A456 $3 Sheet of 3, #a-c 6.75 6.75

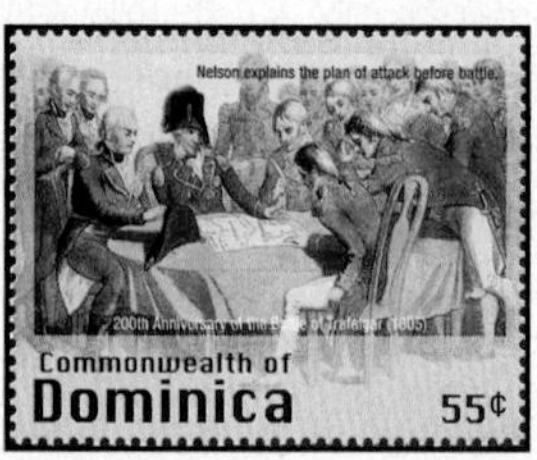

Battle of Trafalgar, Bicent. — A457

Designs: 55c, Admiral Horatio Nelson explaining plan of attack before battle. 65c, Orient explodes during the Battle of the Nile, vert. $1, Nelson and his men board San Nicolas during the Battle of Cape St. Vincent, vert. $2, Ships Agamemnon and Ca Ira in battle.
$6, HMS Victory.

2005, Sept. 7 *Perf. 13¼*
2541-2544 A457 Set of 4 3.25 3.25
Souvenir Sheet
Perf. 12
2545 A457 $6 multi 4.50 4.50

Hans Christian Andersen (1805-75), Author — A458

No. 2546: a, The Swineherd. b, The Nightingale. c, The Fir Tree.
$6, The Ugly Duckling.

2005, Sept. 7 *Perf. 12¾*
2546 A458 $2 Sheet of 3, #a-c 4.50 4.50
Souvenir Sheet
Perf. 12
2547 A458 $6 multi 4.50 4.50

No. 2546 contains three 42x28mm stamps.

Friedrich von Schiller (1759-1805), Writer — A459

No. 2548, vert. — Schiller and German Democratic Republic stamps: a, #241. b, #242. c, #243.
$6, Statue of Schiller.

2005, Sept. 7 ***Perf. 12¾***
2548 A459 $3 Sheet of 3, #a-c 6.75 6.75

Souvenir Sheet

2549 A459 $6 multi 4.50 4.50

Jules Verne (1828-1905), Writer — A460

No. 2550: a, Men, dog and rooster in space. b, Astronauts. c, Men looking at undersea creature. d, Submarine.
$6, Portrait of Verne.

2005, Sept. 7
2550 A460 $2 Sheet of 4, #a-d 6.00 6.00

Souvenir Sheet

2551 A460 $6 multi 4.50 4.50

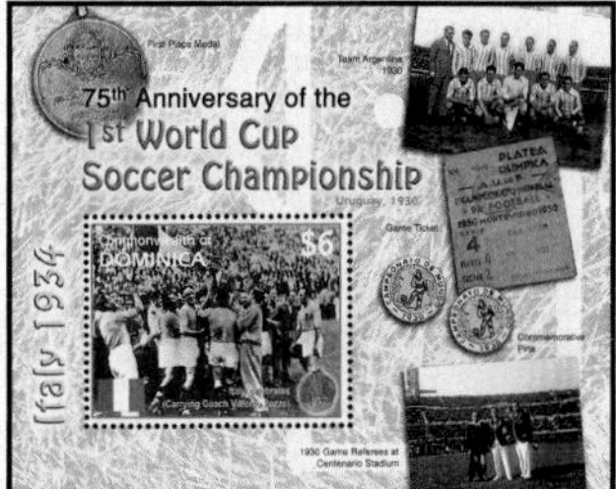

World Cup Soccer Championships, 75th Anniv. — A461

No. 2552: a, 1934 Italy team. b, Scene from 1934 Italy victory over Czechoslovakia. c, Flaminio Stadium. d, Angelos Schiavo.
$6, Italian team celebrating.

2005, Sept. 7 ***Perf. 12***
2552 A461 $2 Sheet of 4, #a-d 6.00 6.00

Souvenir Sheet

2553 A461 $6 multi 4.50 4.50

Christmas — A462

Painting details: 25c, Madonna and Child with Two Angels, by Sandro Botticelli. 50c, Madonna and Child with Angels, by Botticelli. 65c, Madonna and Child, by Pietro Lorenzetti. 90c, Madonna del Roseto, by Botticelli. $1.20, Adoration of the Magi, by Lorenzetti. $3, Madonna in Glory with the Seraphim, by Botticelli.
$5, Madonna of Frari, by Titian, horiz.

2005, Nov. 15 ***Perf. 12¾***
2554-2559 A462 Set of 6 5.00 5.00

Souvenir Sheet

2560 A462 $5 multi 3.75 3.75

Pope John Paul II (1920-2005) and Princess Diana (1961-97) — A463

2005 ***Perf. 13½x13¼***
2561 A463 $3 multi 2.25 2.25

Pope Benedict XVI — A464

2005 **Litho.** ***Perf. 13½x13¼***
2562 A464 $2 multi 1.50 1.50

Printed in sheets of 4.

Souvenir Sheet

New Year 2006 (Year of the Dog) — A465

No. 2563 — Dog figurines with background colors of: a, Pale green and green. b, Orange and pink. c, Rose pink and yellow.

2006, Jan. 3 ***Perf. 13¼x13½***
2563 A465 $1 Sheet of 3, #a-c 2.25 2.25

Miniature Sheets

National Basketball Association Players and Team Emblems — A466

No. 2564, 90c: a, Orlando Magic emblem. b, Hedo Turkoglu.
No. 2565, 90c: a, Denver Nuggets emblem. b, Kenyon Martin.
No. 2566, 90c: a, Miami Heat emblem. b, Antoine Walker.
No. 2567, 90c: a, Golden State Warriors emblem. b, Jason Richardson.
No. 2568, 90c: a, Phoenix Suns emblem. b, Amaré Stoudemire.
No. 2569, 90c: a, Los Angeles Clippers emblem. b, Elton Brand.

2006, Feb. 14 ***Perf. 14***

Sheets of 12, 2 each #a, 10 each #b

2564-2569 A466 Set of 6 47.50 47.50

Léopold Sédar Senghor (1906-2001), First President of Senegal — A467

2006, Mar. 20 ***Perf. 13¼***
2570 A467 $2 multi 1.50 1.50

2006 Winter Olympics, Turin — A468

Designs: 75c, Yugoslavia #1670. 90c, 1984 Sarajevo Winter Olympics poster, vert. $2, Japan #2607g, vert. $3, 1998 Nagano Winter Olympics poster, vert.

2006, Mar. 29
2571-2574 A468 Set of 4 5.00 5.00

Each stamp printed in sheets of 4.

Queen Elizabeth II, 80th Birthday — A469

No. 2575: a, As infant, with mother. b, As young child. c, As baby, wearing bonnet. d, As young girl, wearing jacket.
$5, Wearing tiara and sash.

2006, Mar. 29
2575 A469 $2 Sheet of 4, #a-d 6.00 6.00

Souvenir Sheet

2576 A469 $5 multi 3.75 3.75

Marilyn Monroe (1926-62), Actress — A470

2006, Apr. 7
2577 A470 $3 multi 2.25 2.25

Printed in sheets of 4.

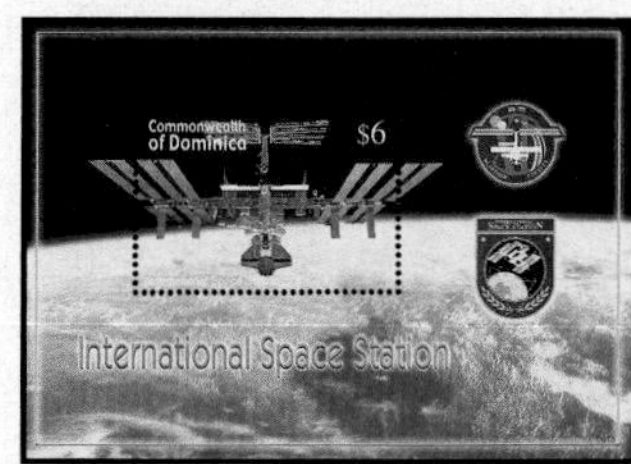

Space Achievements — A471

No. 2578 — Viking I: a, Trenches dug by Viking I. b, Sunset at Viking I landing site. c, Chryse Planitia looking northwest over Viking I. d, First panoramic image of Chryse Planitia, country name and denomination in white. e, As "d," country name in black, denomination in white. f, As "d", country name and denomination in black.
No. 2579, $3, vert. — Luna 9: a, Flight apparatus. b, Modified SS-6 Sapwood rocket. c, Luna 9 Soft Lander. d, Tyuratam.
No. 2580, $3, vert. — Giotto Comet Probe: a, Launch of Giotto. b, Giotto during solar simulation test. c, Halley's Comet develops seven tails. d, Giotto and Comet Grigg-Skjellerup approach trajectories.
No. 2581, $6, Intl. Space Station. No. 2582, $6, Mars Reconnaissance Orbiter. No. 2583, $6, Venus Express Orbiter.

2006, June 6 **Litho.** ***Perf. 14***
2578 A471 $2 Sheet of 6, #a-f 9.00 9.00

Sheets of 4, #a-d

2579-2580 A471 Set of 2 18.00 18.00

Souvenir Sheets

2581-2583 A471 Set of 3 13.50 13.50

Miniature Sheet

Wolfgang Amadeus Mozart (1756-91), Composer — A472

No. 2584: a, Oval portrait. b, Playing harpsichord. c, Wearing red coat. d, Head of Mozart.

2006, Sept. 1 *Perf. 13¼*

2584 A472 $3 Sheet of 4, #a-d 9.00 9.00

Miniature Sheet

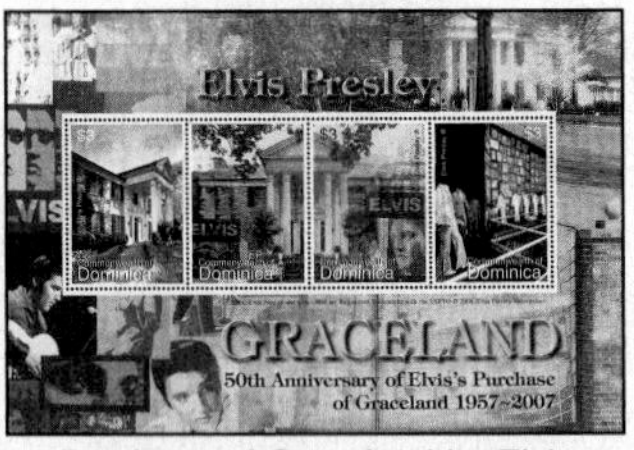

Purchase of Graceland by Elvis Presley, 50th Anniv. — A473

No. 2585: a, View of path leading to front door. b, Graceland, columns at right. c, Graceland, columns at left. d, Room with Presley's costumes.

2006, Sept. 1 *Perf. 13¼*

2585 A473 $3 Sheet of 4, #a-d 9.00 9.00

Miniature Sheets

Pres. John F. Kennedy (1917-63) — A474

No. 2586, $3: a, Supporters holding campaign sign. b, Kennedy campaigning. c, Kennedy waiting for concession. d, Kennedy addressing the nation.

No. 2587, $3: a, Kennedy on crutches from war injuries. b, Kennedy on stretcher. c, Dust jacket of *Profiles in Courage*. d, Kennedy as senator.

2006, Oct. 1 *Perf. 13¼*

Sheets of 4, #a-d

2586-2587 A474 Set of 2 18.00 18.00

Shells — A475

Designs: 5c, Turbinella angulata. 10c, Vasum muricatum. 15c, Fusinus closter. 20c, Crasispira gibbosa. 25c, Terebra strigata. 50c, Prunum carneum. 65c, Purpura patula. 90c, C. chrysostoma. $1, M. nodulosa. $2, Conus regius. $3.50, Conus hieroglyphus. $5, Anodontia alba, vert. $10, C. cassidiformis. $20, Strigilla carnaria, vert.

2006, Oct. 1 *Perf. 14x15, 15x14*

2588	A475	5c multi	.30	*.50*
2589	A475	10c multi	.30	*.50*
2590	A475	15c multi	.40	*.80*
2591	A475	20c multi	.40	.30
2592	A475	25c multi	.40	.30
2593	A475	50c multi	.55	.35
2594	A475	65c multi	.75	.50
2595	A475	90c multi	1.00	.75
2596	A475	$1 multi	1.25	1.25
2597	A475	$2 multi	2.00	2.00
2598	A475	$3.50 multi	3.25	3.25
2599	A475	$5 multi	4.00	4.00
2600	A475	$10 multi	7.00	7.00
2601	A475	$20 multi	14.00	14.00
		Nos. 2588-2601 (14)	35.60	35.50

Souvenir Sheet

Ludwig Durr (1878-1956), Engineer — A476

2006, Nov. 15 **Litho.** *Perf. 12¾*

2602 A476 $5 multi 3.75 3.75

Betty Boop — A477

No. 2603, vert.: a, Betty Boop with black background and leg raised. b, Lips. c, Betty Boop with black background. d, Dog on leash, star. e, Betty Boop, white background. f, Dog, two stars.

No. 2604 — Betty Boop with: a, Light blue panel at top. b, Light yellow panel at top.

2006, Nov. 15

2603 A477 $2 Sheet of 6, #a-f 9.00 9.00

Souvenir Sheet

2604 A477 $3.50 Sheet of 2, #a-b 5.25 5.25

Christmas A478

Christmas stocking showing: No. 2605, 25c, No. 2609a, $2, Christmas tree. No. 2606, 50c, No. 2609b, $2, Bell. No. 2607, 90c, No. 2609c, $2, Candy canes. No. 2608, $1, No. 2609d, $2, Stars.

2006, Dec. 1 *Perf. 14¼*

2605-2608 A478 Set of 4 2.00 2.00

Souvenir Sheet

2609 A478 $2 Sheet of 4, #a-d 5.00 3.00

Souvenir Sheet

Christopher Columbus (1451-1506), Explorer — A479

2007, Jan. 10 *Perf. 12*

2610 A479 $5 brn & black 3.75 3.75

Scouting, Cent. — A480

2007, Jan. 10

2611 A480 $3.50 blue & multi 2.60 2.60

Souvenir Sheet

2612 A480 $5 org & multi 3.75 3.75

No. 2611 was printed in sheets of 3.

Concorde Prototype 001 F-WTSS — A481

No. 2613: a, $1, Airplane in hangar. b, $2, Airplane out of hangar.

2007, Jan. 23 *Perf. 13¼*

2613 A481 Pair, #a-b 2.25 2.25

Printed in sheets containing 3 of each stamp.

Rembrandt (1606-69), Painter — A482

No. 2614, vert. — Details from Christ Driving the Money Changers from the Temple: a, Christ. b, Man with moustache looking up. c, Man with striped headdress. d, Man protecting face with hands.

$5, Jesus and His Disciples.

2007, Jan. 23 *Perf. 13¼*

2614 A482 $2 Sheet of 4, #a-d 6.00 6.00

Imperf

2615 A482 $5 shown 3.75 3.75

No. 2614 contains four 38x50mm stamps.

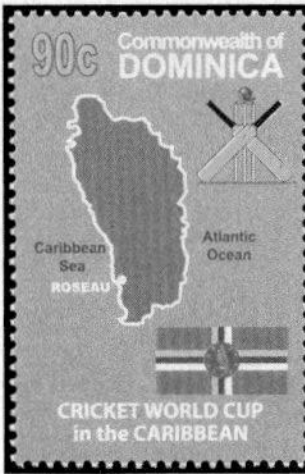

Cricket World Cup — A483

Designs: 90c, Cricket bats, ball and wicket, map and flag of Dominica. $1, Umpire Billy Doctrove.

$5, Cricket bats, ball and wicket.

2007, Apr. 11 *Perf. 14*

2616-2617 A483 Set of 2 2.50 2.50

Souvenir Sheet

2618 A483 $5 multi 4.00 4.00

Birds A484

Designs: 10c, Great frigatebird. 25c, Peruvian booby. 90c, Black stork, vert. No. 2622, $5, Lipkin, vert.

No. 2623: a, Antillean crested hummingbird. b, Rufous-breasted hermit. c, Cuban hummingbird. d, Blue-headed hummingbird.

No. 2624, $5, Red-capped manakin, vert.

2007, Apr. 11 *Perf. 12¾*

2619-2622 A484 Set of 4 5.25 5.25

2623 A484 $2 Sheet of 4, #a-d 7.50 7.50

Souvenir Sheet

2624 A484 $5 multi 5.25 5.25

Flowers — A485

Designs: 10c, Red jasmine. 25c, Bougainvillea. 90c, Portia tree. No. 2628, $5, Rose bay.

No. 2629 — Orchids: a, $1, Tolumnia urophylla. b, $1, Brassavola cucullata. c, $2, Isochilus linearis. d, Spathoglottis plicata.

No. 2630, horiz.: a, Red ginger. b, Baobab. c, Purple wreath. d, Thunbergia.

No. 2631, $5, Flamboyant. No. 2632, $5, Oncidium altissimum.

2007, Apr. 11 **Litho.** *Perf. 12¾*

2625-2628 A485 Set of 4 4.75 4.75

2629 A485 $1 Sheet of 4, #a-d 4.50 4.50

2630 A485 $2 Sheet of 4, #a-d 6.00 6.00

Souvenir Sheets

2631-2632 A485 Set of 2 7.50 7.50

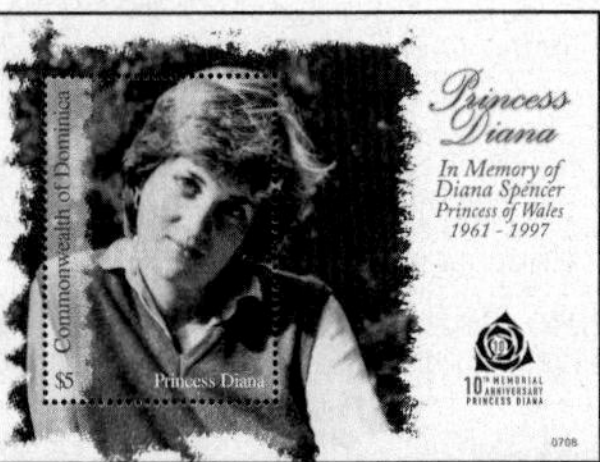

Princess Diana (1961-97) — A486

No. 2633: a, Holding flowers, wearing purple hat. b, Without hat. c, Not holding flowers, wearing purple hat. d, Close-up of #2633a, lines on face. e, Close-up of #2633b, lines on face. f, Close-up of #2633c, lines on face.

$5, Wearing purple sweater.

2007, June 11 *Perf. 13½*
2633 A486 $1 Sheet of 6, #a-f 4.50 4.50

Souvenir Sheet

2634 A486 $5 multi 3.75 3.75

No. 2633 contains six 28x42mm stamps.

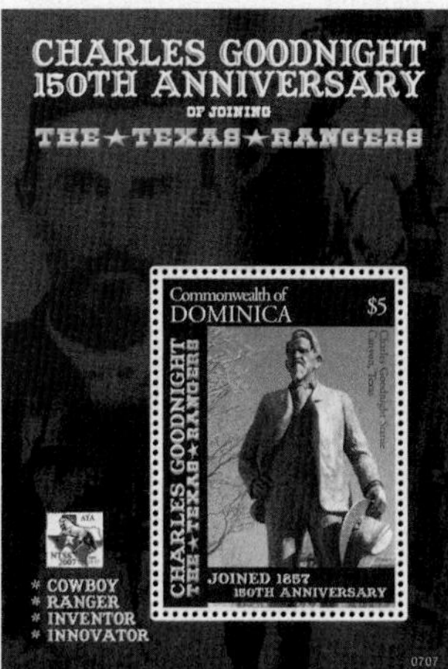

Texas Rangers — A487

No. 2635, horiz.: a, Two Rangers on horses. b, Seven Rangers in front of building with pillars. c, Ten rangers showing rifles. d, Rangers on horses. e, Rangers around still. f, Three Rangers at Justice of the Peace office. g, Rangers and tents. h, Rangers and locomotive. i, Five Rangers on horses near house.
$5, Statue of Charles Goodnight.

2007, June 15 *Perf. 13½*
2635 A487 $1 Sheet of 9, #a-i 6.75 6.75

Souvenir Sheet

2636 A487 $5 multi 3.75 3.75

American Topical Association National Topical Stamp Show, Irving, TX.

Miniature Sheet

New Year 2007 (Year of the Pig) — A488

No. 2637 — Text in: a, Red. b, Green. c, Blue green. d, Purple.

2007, July 2
2637 A488 $2 Sheet of 4, #a-d 6.00 6.00

A489

A490

A491

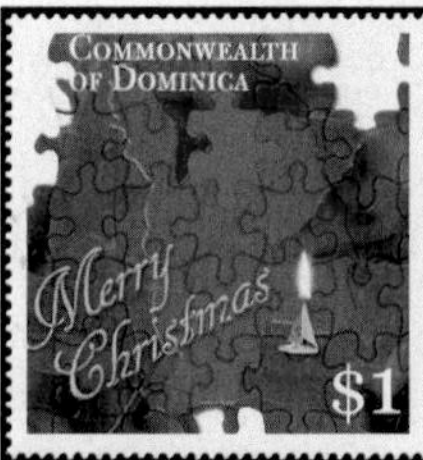

Christmas A492

2007, Nov. 19 **Litho.** *Perf. 14¾x14*

2638	A489	25c multi	.25	.25
2639	A490	50c multi	.40	.40
2640	A491	90c multi	.70	.70
2641	A492	$1 multi	.75	.75
		Nos. 2638-2641 (4)	2.10	2.10

New Year 2008 (Year of the Rat) — A493

2008, Feb. 28 *Perf. 12*
2642 A493 $1 multi .75 .75

Printed in sheets of 4.

University of the West Indies, 60th Anniv. A494

University crest, Dr. Bernard A. Sorhaindo and denomination in: 50c, Red brown. 65c, Green. 90c, Brown.
No. 2646, $5, Crest, Sorhaindo, denomination in black. No. 2647, $5, Crest, Sorhaindo, denomination in blue. No. 2648, $5, Crest, diploma, 60th anniversary emblem.

2008, Apr. 8 *Perf. 13¼*
2643-2645 A494 Set of 3 1.60 1.60

Souvenir Sheets

2646-2648 A494 Set of 3 11.50 11.50

Miniature Sheet

2008 Summer Olympics, Beijing — A495

No. 2649: a, Archery. b, Men's gymnastics. c, Badminton. d, Boxing.

2008, Apr. 8 *Perf. 13¼x13*
2649 A495 $1.40 Sheet of 4, #a-d 4.25 4.25

Miniature Sheet

Visit of Pope Benedict XVI to New York — A496

No. 2650 — Pope and part of St. Patrick's Cathedral in background: a, Small circular window under spire. b, Large central circular window. c, Archway below spire. d, Archway above main door.

2008, June 16 **Litho.** *Perf. 13½*
2650 A496 $1.40 Sheet of 4, #a-d 4.25 4.25

Miniature Sheet

Wedding of Queen Elizabeth II and Prince Philip, 60th Anniv. — A497

No. 2651: a, Couple, denomination in white. b, Queen, denomination in red violet. c, Couple, denomination in black. d, Queen, denomination in white. e, Couple, denomination in red violet. f, Queen, denomination in black.

2008, June 16
2651 A497 $1 Sheet of 6, #a-f 4.50 4.50

Miniature Sheet

Elvis Presley (1935-77) — A498

No. 2652 — Presley and: a, Black and red background, Prussian blue denomination. b, Gray and black background, purple denomination. c, Blue and black background, Prussian blue denomination. d, Purple and black background, purple denomination. e, Gray and black background, Prussian blue denomination. f, Brown and black background, purple denomination.

2008, June 16
2652 A498 $1.50 Sheet of 6 #a-f 6.75 6.75

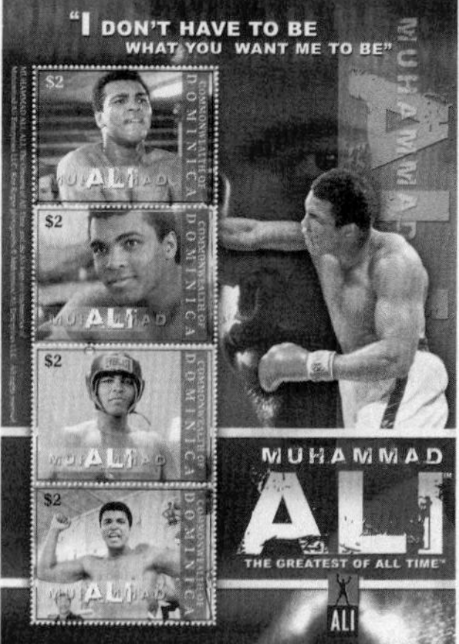

A499

Muhammad Ali, Boxer — A500

No. 2653 — Ali: a, Sweating, denomination in white. b, Smiling, denomination in black. c, Wearing headgear. d, With arms raised.
No. 2654 — Ali: a, Seated in corner of boxing ring. b, Speaking to the press. c, Punching bag. d, Wearing headgear and mouth guard.

2008, July 7
2653 A499 $2 Sheet of 4, #a-d 6.25 6.25
2654 A500 $2 Sheet of 4, #a-d 6.25 6.25

Convent High School, 150th Anniv. A501

Panel color: 50c, Red violet. 65c, Yellow orange. 90c, Blue. $1, Red.
$5, Denomination in LR corner.

2008, Oct. 1 *Perf. 12½*
2655-2658 A501 Set of 4 2.40 2.40

Souvenir Sheet

2659 A501 $5 multi 4.00 4.00

Dogs — A502

Designs: 25c, Dandie Dinmont terrier. 50c, Alaskan malamute. 90c, Welsh Springer spaniel. $1, Pug. $2, Norfolk terrier. $5, Vizsla.
No. 2666: a, Akita. b, Australian cattle dog. c, Border collie. d, Staffordshire bull terrier cross.

Perf. 14¼x14¾

2008, Dec. 11 **Litho.**
2660-2665 A502 Set of 6 8.50 8.50
2666 A502 $2.50 Sheet of 4, #a-d 9.00 9.00

Miniature Sheet

Marilyn Monroe (1926-62), Actress — A503

No. 2667 — Monroe wearing: a, Purple sweater, hand on arm. b, Orange sweater, looking in mirror. c, Purple sweater, holding post. d, Orange sweater, holding wine glass.

2008, Dec. 11 ***Perf. 14***
2667 A503 $2 Sheet of 4, #a-d 6.00 6.00

Christmas A504

Designs: 25c, Santa Claus. 50c, Palm tree with Christmas ornaments. 90c, Christmas stocking. $1, Poinsettias.

2008, Dec. 15 ***Perf. 12***
2668-2671 A504 Set of 4 2.00 2.00

New Year 2009 (Year of the Ox) A505

2009, Jan. 5 ***Perf. 14¾x14¼***
2672 A505 $2 multi 1.50 1.50

Printed in sheets of 4.

Inauguration of Barack Obama as US President A506

Pres. Obama: 65c, With raised hand. 90c, Hand not showing.

No. 2675: a, $2.25, Like 65c. b, $2.25, Looking over shoulder. c, $2.25, Like 90c. d, $2.50, Like 90c. e, $2.50, Looking over shoulder. f, $2.50, Like 65c.

2009, Jan. 20 ***Perf. 11½***
2673-2674 A506 Set of 2 1.25 1.25
2675 A506 Sheet of 6, #a-f 11.00 11.00

A507

Denominations: 50c, 65c, 90c, $1.

2009, Mar. 23 ***Perf. 14¾x14¼***
2676-2679 A507 Set of 4 2.40 2.40

Souvenir Sheet

2680 A507 $5 multi 3.75 3.75

Diplomatic relations between Dominica and People's Republic of China, 5th anniv.

Peony A508

2009, Apr. 10 ***Perf. 13¼***
2681 A508 75c shown .55 .55

Souvenir Sheet

2682 A508 $5 Peonies 3.75 3.75

No. 2682 contains one 44x44mm stamp.

Miniature Sheet

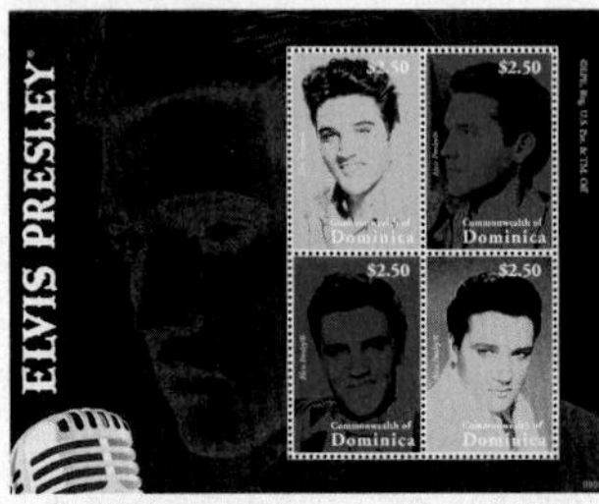

Elvis Presley (1935-77) — A509

No. 2683 — Various photos of Presley with background colors of: a, Yellow orange. b, Gray and blue. c, Blue. d, Gray.

2009, May 23 ***Perf. 13¼***
2683 A509 $2.50 Sheet of 4, #a-d 7.75 7.75

Miniature Sheet

Joseph Haydn (1732-1809), Composer — A510

No. 2684: a, Haydn. b, Haydn's birthplace, Rohrau, Austria. c, Wolfgang Amadeus Mozart. d, St. Stephen's Cathedral, Vienna. e, Nikolaus Esterházy, sponsor of Haydn. f, Esterházy Palace, Fertod, Hungary.

2009, June 10 ***Perf. 11½***
2684 A510 $2.25 Sheet of 6, #a-f 10.00 10.00

Mushrooms A511

Designs: 50c, Leucopaxillus gracillimus. 65c, Calvatia cyathiformis. 90c, Hygrocybe viridiphylla. $1, Boletellus coccineus.

No. 2689, $2: a, Hygrocybe acutoconica. b, Lepiota sulphureocyanescens. c, Lactarius rubrilacteus. d, Lactarius ferrugineus. e, Asterophera lycoperdoides. f, Amanita polypyramis.

2009, Sept. 8 Litho. ***Perf. 14x14¾***
2685-2688 A511 Set of 4 2.25 2.25
2689 A511 $2 Sheet of 6, #a-f 9.00 9.00

A512

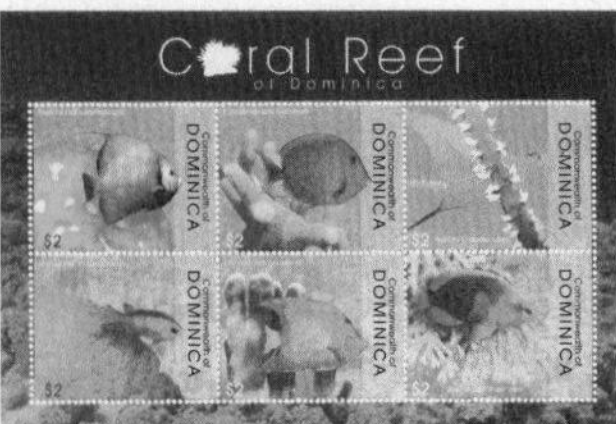

Corals and Marine Life — A513

Designs: 50c, Lobed star coral and shark. 65c, Orange cup coral and fish. 90c, Grooved brain coral and turtle. $1, Elkhorn coral and fish.

No. 2694, $2: a, Rough star coral and fish. b, Branched finger coral and fish. c, Wire coral and ray. d, Great star coral and fish. e, Pillar coral and fish. f, Rose lace coral and fish.

2009, Sept. 8 ***Perf. 14¾x14***
2690-2693 A512 Set of 4 2.25 2.25
2694 A513 $2 Sheet of 6, #a-f 9.00 9.00

Butterflies A514

Designs: 90c, Banded orange heliconian. $1, Gulf fritillary. $2, Julia longwing. $5, Zebra longwing.

No. 2699: a, Cuban cattleheart. b, White peacock. c, Bahamian swallowtail. d, Tropical buckeye.

No. 2700, $6, Purple emperor. No. 2701, $6, Atala black.

2009, Sept. 8 ***Perf. 14¾x14***
2695-2698 A514 Set of 4 6.75 6.75
2699 A514 $2.50 Sheet of 4, #a-d 7.50 7.50

Souvenir Sheets

Perf. 14¼

2700-2701 A514 Set of 2 9.00 9.00

Nos. 2700-2701 each contain one 50x38mm stamp.

Dolphins and Whales A515

Designs: 50c, Irawaddy dolphin. 65c, Pantropical spotted dolphin. 90c, Atlantic humpback dolphin. $1, Indian humpback dolphin.

No. 2706: a, Melon-headed whale. b, Striped dolphin. c, Atlantic spotted dolphin. d, Clymene dolphin. e, Pantropical spotted dolphin (Stenella attenuata graffmani). f, Pantropical spotted dolphin (Stenella attenuata).

2009, Sept. 8 Litho. ***Perf. 14¾x14***
2702-2705 A515 Set of 4 2.25 2.25
2706 A515 $2 Sheet of 6, #a-f 9.00 9.00

See No. 2732.

Shells A516

Designs: 50c, Oliva reticularis. 65c, Vasum muricatum. 90c, Olivella nivea. $1, Olivella mutica.

No. 2711: a, Hyalina avena. b, Persicula fluctuata. c, Agatrix agassizi. d, Trigonostoma rugosum. e, Olivella floralia. f, Marginella eburneola.

2009, Sept. 8
2707-2710 A516 Set of 4 2.25 2.25
2711 A516 $2 Sheet of 6, #a-f 9.00 9.00

Miniature Sheet

Expo 2010, Shanghai — A517

No. 2712: a, Bund. b, Shanghai Museum. c, Yangpu Bridge. d, Shanghai Theater.

2009, Oct. 16 ***Perf. 13x12¾***
2712 A517 $1.50 Sheet of 4, #a-d 4.50 4.50

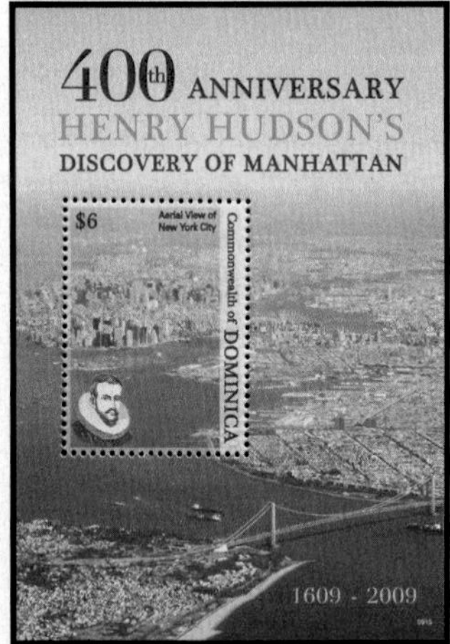

Discovery of Manhattan Island by Henry Hudson, 400th Anniv. — A518

No. 2713, horiz.: a, Panoramic view of New York City, 1913. b, Hudson, the Dreamer, by Jean L.G. Ferris. c, Henry Hudson. d, Hudson's ship, Half Moon. e, Map of Hudson River, c. 1600. f, Henry Hudson Memorial Column, Bronx, NY.

$6, Hudson, aerial view of New York City.

2009, Oct. 16 ***Perf. 13x12¾***
2713 A518 $2.25 Sheet of 6, #a-f 10.00 10.00

Souvenir Sheet

Perf. 12¾x13

2714 A518 $6 multi 4.50 4.50

Miniature Sheet

Pres. John F. Kennedy (1917-63) — A519

No. 2715 — Pres. Kennedy: a, On telephone. b, With family. c, With Vice-president Lyndon B. Johnson. d, Pointing.

2009, Oct. 30 ***Perf. 11½x12***
2715 A519 $2.50 Sheet of 4, #a-d 7.50 7.50

Miniature Sheet

First Man on the Moon, 40th Anniv. — A520

No. 2716: a, Apollo 11 crew. b, Moon landing on television. c, Apollo 11 capsule with parachutes. d, Earth, Apollo 11 modules and patch. e, Command Module in Moon orbit. f, Project Orion.

2009, Nov. 2 ***Perf. 11½***
2716 A520 $2 Sheet of 6, #a-f 9.00 9.00

Chinese Aviation, Cent. — A521

No. 2717: a, H-5. b, H-6. c, H-6H. d, H-6L. $6, H-6U.

2009, Nov. 12 ***Perf. 14***
2717 A521 $2 Sheet of 4, #a-d 6.50 6.50

Souvenir Sheet

Perf. 14¼

2718 A521 $6 multi 4.75 4.75

Aeropex 2009 Intl. Philatelic Exhibition, Beijing. No. 2717 contains four 42x28mm stamps.

Christmas A522

Designs: 50c, Bell-shaped Christmas tree ornament. 65c, Candles and poinsettia. 90c, Gingerbread man. $1.10, Decorated palm tree. $2.25, Christmas tree ornaments. $2.75, Women dancers.

2009, Nov. 16 ***Perf. 11½***
2719-2724 A522 Set of 6 6.25 6.25

Personalized Stamp — A523

2009, Dec. 18 ***Perf. 14x14¾***
2725 A523 $3 gray 2.25 2.25

The vignette on the stamp shown is a generic image. Stamps without a vignette were also made available. Printed in sheets of 12.

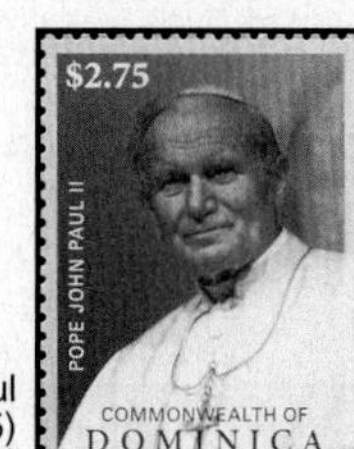

Pope John Paul II (1920-2005) A524

2010, Jan. 4 ***Perf. 12x11½***
2726 A524 $2.75 multi 2.10 2.10

Printed in sheets of 4.

Miniature Sheet

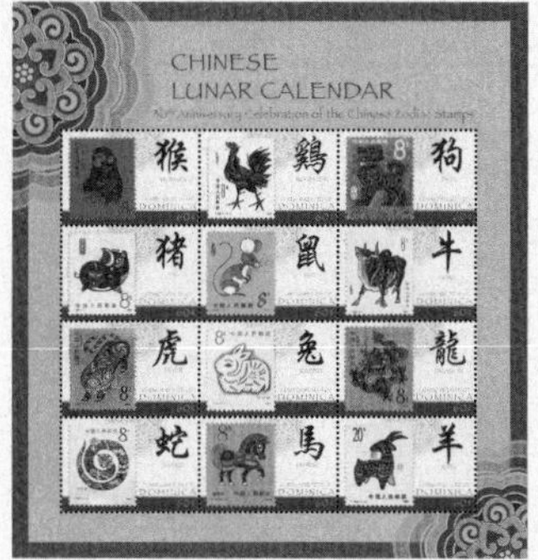

Chinese Zodiac Animals — A524a

No. 2726A — Various stamps of People's Republic of China depicting Zodiac animals: b, Monkey. c, Rooster. d, Dog. e, Pig. f, Rat. g, Ox. h, Tiger. i, Rabbit. j, Dragon. k, Snake. l, Horse. m, Ram.

2010, Jan. 4 **Litho.** ***Perf. 12¾***
2726A A524a 60c Sheet of 12, #b-m 6.00 6.00

Souvenir Sheet

New Year 2010 (Year of the Tiger) — A525

2010, Jan. 4 ***Perf. 12¾***
2727 A525 $5 multi 4.00 4.00

Miniature Sheet

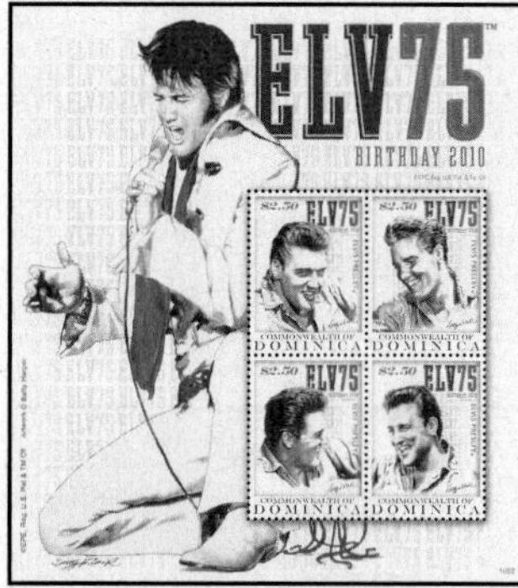

Elvis Presley (1935-77) — A526

Various drawings of Presley.

2010, Jan. 8 ***Perf. 11½***
2728 A526 $2.50 Sheet of 4, #a-d 7.75 7.75

Miniature Sheet

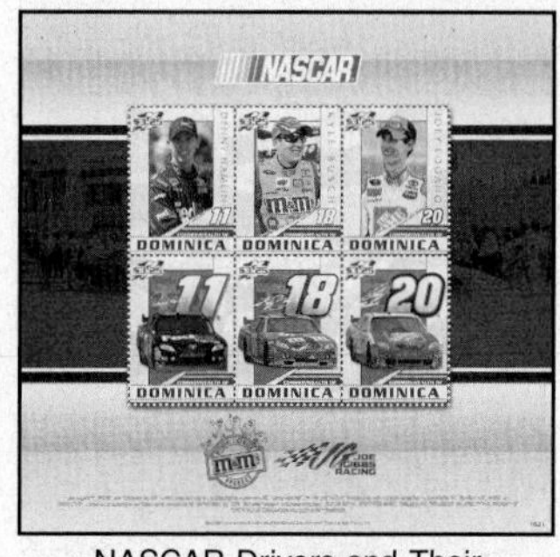

NASCAR Drivers and Their Cars — A527

No. 2729: a, Denny Hamlin. b, Kyle Busch. c, Joey Logano. d, Hamlin's car (#11). e, Busch's car (#18). f, Logano's car (#20).

2010, Jan. 19 **Litho.**
2729 A527 $3.25 Sheet of 6, #a-f 15.00 15.00

Miniature Sheets

Dogs — A528

No. 2730, $2.50 — Dalmatian and: a, Books. b, Stone wall. c, Swimming pool. d, Stack of logs.
No. 2731, $2.50 — Boxer and: a, Brick wall. b, Bush. c, Window. d, Fence.

2010, Jan. 19 ***Perf. 11½x11¾***

Sheets of 4, #a-d

2730-2731 A528 Set of 2 15.50 15.50

No. 2706 With "Haiti Earthquake Relief Fund" and Map of Haiti Added to Stamps and Sheet Margin

Miniature Sheet

Designs as before.

2010, Feb. 4 ***Perf. 14¾x14***
2732 A515 $2 Sheet of 6, #a-f 9.25 9.25

Position of added text varies on each stamp.

Ferraris and Their Parts A529

No. 2733, $1.25: a, Engine of 1982 208 GTB Turbo. b, 1982 208 GTB Turbo.
No. 2734, $1.25: a, Engine of 1983 126 C3. b, 1983 126 C3.
No. 2735, $1.25: a, Side panel and rear wheel of 1984 Testarossa. b, 1984 Testarossa.
No. 2736, $1.25: a, Suspension of 1987 408 4RM. b, 1987 408 4RM.

2010, Feb. 17 ***Perf. 12***

Vert. Pairs, #a-b

2733-2736 A529 Set of 4 8.00 8.00

Nos. 2733-2736 each were printed in sheets containing four pairs.

Miniature Sheet

Mother Teresa (1910-97), Humanitarian — A530

No. 2737 — Mother Teresa: a, Denomination in black. b, Holding rosary. c, Wearing white habit. d, Kissing hand of Pope John Paul II.

2010, Feb. 24 ***Perf. 11¼x11½***
2737 A530 $2.50 Sheet of 4, #a-d 8.00 8.00

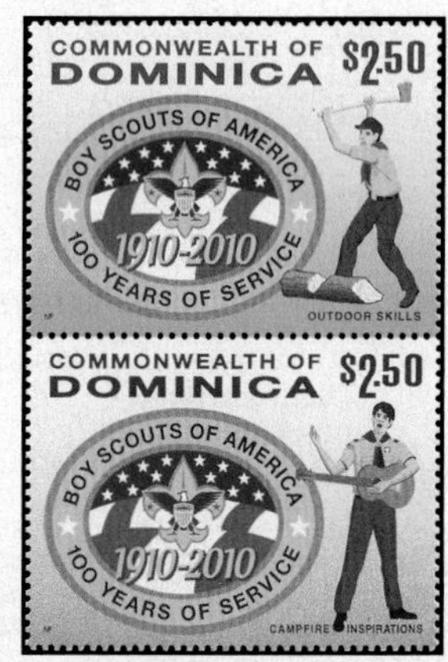

Boy Scouts of America, Cent. — A531

No. 2738, $2.50: a, Outdoor skills. b, Campfire inspirations.
No. 2739, $2.50: a, Emergency one-man carry. b, Swimming fun with safety.

2010, Feb. 24 ***Perf. 13¼***

Pairs, #a-b

2738-2739 A531 Set of 2 8.00 8.00

Nos. 2738-2739 each were printed in sheets containing two pairs.

Miniature Sheet

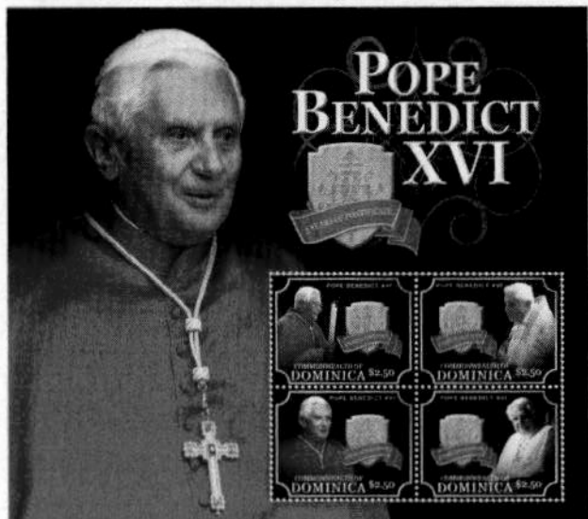

Pope Benedict XVI — A532

No. 2740 — Pope Benedict XVI: a, Wearing red, holding candle. b, Wearing white, hands clasped. c, Wearing red, not holding candle. d, Wearing white, hands not clasped.

2010, Mar. 23 ***Perf. 11½x12***

2740 A532 $2.50 Sheet of 4, #a-d 7.50 7.50

Caravaggio Paintings — A533

No. 2741, vert.: a, Mary Magdalene. b, Sick Bacchus. c, Bacchus. d, The Inspiration of Saint Matthew.
$6, Saint Gerolamo.

2010, Mar. 23 ***Perf. 12x11½***

2741 A533 $2.50 Sheet of 4, #a-d 7.50 7.50

Souvenir Sheet

Perf. 11½

2742 A533 $6 multi 4.50 4.50

Miniature Sheet

Girl Guides, Cent. — A534

No. 2743: a, Rainbows. b, Brownies. c, Guides. d, Senior Section. $6, Girl Guide, vert.

2010, Apr. 19 ***Perf. 11½x12***

2743 A534 $2.75 Sheet of 4, #a-d 8.25 8.25

Souvenir Sheet

Perf. 11¼x11½

2743E A534 $6 multi 4.50 4.50

Souvenir Sheets

A535

A536

A537

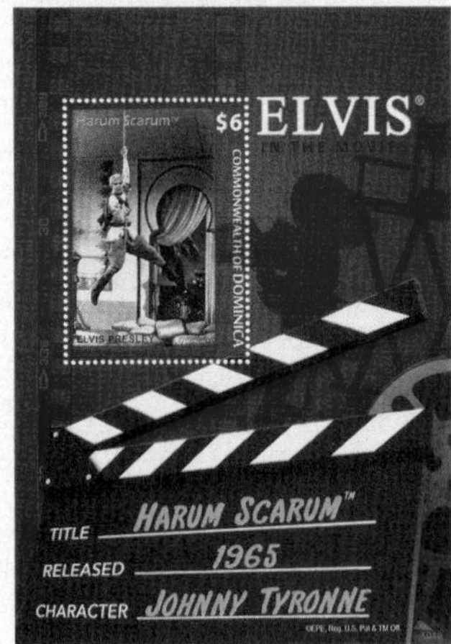

Elvis Presley (1935-77) — A538

2010, May 12 ***Perf. 13½***

2744 A535 $6 multi 4.50 4.50
2745 A536 $6 multi 4.50 4.50
2746 A537 $6 multi 4.50 4.50
2747 A538 $6 multi 4.50 4.50
Nos. 2744-2747 (4) 18.00 18.00

Miniature Sheets

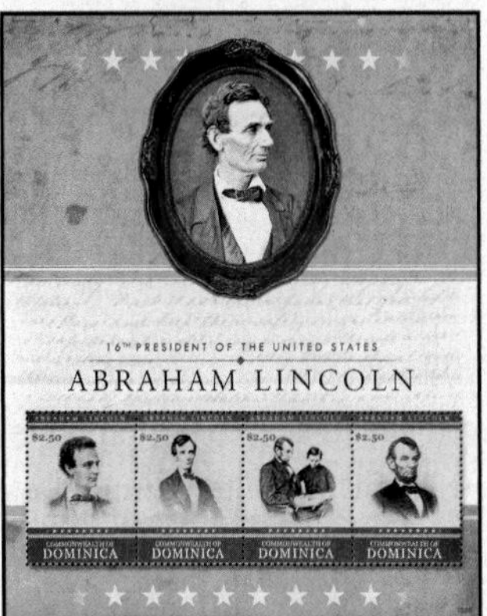

Pres. Abraham Lincoln (1809-65) — A539

No. 2748, $2.50 — Photographs of Lincoln: a, Without beard. b, Without beard, arms crossed. c, Reading to son, Tad. d, With beard.

No. 2749, $2.50: a, Statue of Lincoln, Bascom Hill, University of Wisconsin. b, Aerial view of Lincoln Memorial. c, Statue of Lincoln in Lincoln Memorial. d, Sculpture of Lincoln, Mount Rushmore.

2010, June 22 Litho. ***Perf. 11½***

Sheets of 4, #a-d

2748-2749 A539 Set of 2 15.00 15.00

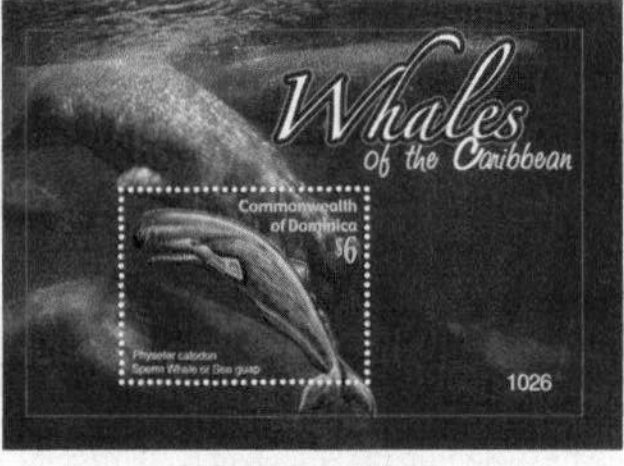

Whales — A540

No. 2750: a, Sowerby's beaked whale. b, Blainville's beaked whale. c, Short-finned pilot whale. d, True's beaked whale. e, False killer whale. f, Dwarf sperm whale.
$6, Sperm whale.

2010, June 22 Litho. ***Perf. 13x13½***

2750 A540 $2 Sheet of 6, #a-f 9.00 9.00

Souvenir Sheet

2751 A540 $6 multi 4.50 4.50

Miniature Sheets

A541

Princess Diana (1961-97) — A542

No. 2752 — Princess Diana wearing: a, Plaid jacket. b, Wedding gown. c, Black jacket. d, Red and white dress.

No. 2753 — Princess Diana with: a, Prince Charles. b, Princes Charles, William and Harry. c, Crowd, holding flowers. d, Small child.

2010, May 12 Litho. ***Perf. 13x13¼***

2752 A541 $2.75 Sheet of 4, #a-d 8.25 8.25
2753 A542 $2.75 Sheet of 4, #a-d 8.25 8.25

Christmas — A543

Painting details: 90c, Geburt Christi (Birth of Christ), by Hans Baldung. $1.45, Thomas Altar, by Meister Francke. $2, Nativity, by Baldung.

2010, Dec. 1 ***Perf. 13x13½***

2754-2756 A543 Set of 3 3.25 3.25

Nos. 2754-2756 each were printed in sheets of 6.

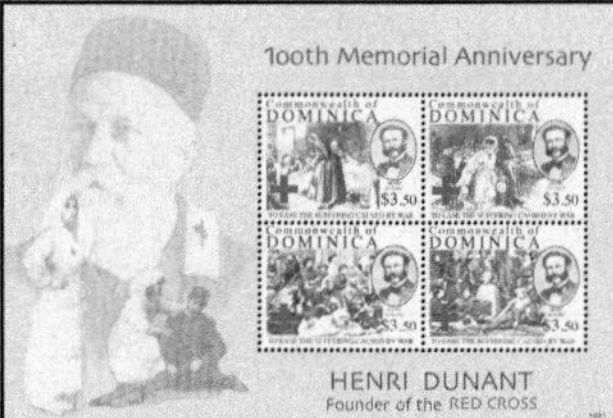

Henri Dunant (1828-1910), Founder of Red Cross — A544

No. 2757 — Red Cross, nurses aiding wounded and portrait of Dunant in: a, Green. b, Brown. c, Purple. d, Blue.
$5, Red Cross, nurses, Dunant in purplish gray.

2010, Dec. 15 ***Perf. 12½x12***

2757 A544 $3.50 Sheet of 4, #a-d 10.50 10.50

Souvenir Sheet

2758 A544 $5 multi 3.75 3.75

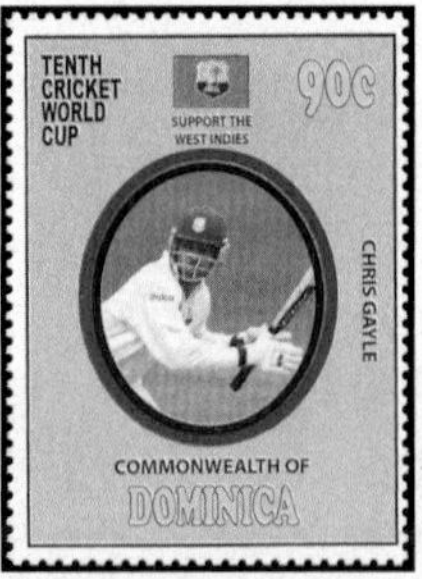

Tenth Cricket World Cup, India, Sri Lanka and Bangladesh A545

Designs: 90c, Chris Gayle. $2, Windsor Park Sports Stadium, Roseau, horiz.
$5, Cricket World Cup.

2011, June 1 Litho. ***Perf. 12½***

2759-2760 A545 Set of 2 2.25 2.25

Souvenir Sheet

Perf. 12

2761 A545 $5 multi 3.75 3.75

No. 2761 contains one 30x40mm stamp.

National HIV and AIDS Response Program — A545a

2011, June 1 Litho. ***Perf. 13½***

2761A A545a 90c multi — —

Lizards — A546

Designs: 5c, Golden skink. 10c, Dominican ground lizard. 15c, Crested anole. 20c, Dominican tree lizard. 25c, Pygmy skink. 50c, House gecko. 65c, Fantastic gecko. 90c, Iguana. $1, Vincent's least gecko. $2, Turnip-tailed gecko. $5, House gecko, diff. $10, Fantastic gecko, diff. $20, Vincent's least gecko, diff.

2011, Oct. 1 ***Perf. 14***

2762 A546 5c multi .25 .25
2763 A546 10c multi .25 .25
2764 A546 15c multi .25 .25
2765 A546 20c multi .25 .25
2766 A546 25c multi .25 .25
2767 A546 50c multi .40 .40
2768 A546 65c multi .50 .50
2769 A546 90c multi .70 .70
2770 A546 $1 multi .75 .75

2771 A546 $2 multi 1.50 1.50
2772 A546 $5 multi 3.75 3.75
2773 A546 $10 multi 7.50 7.50
2774 A546 $20 multi 15.00 15.00
Nos. 2762-2774 (13) 31.35 31.35

Christmas A547

Paintings: 90c, The Annunciation, by Andrea del Sarto. $1.45, Madonna with Child, by Jacopo Bellini. $2, The Virgin, by Carlo Dolci.

2011, Nov. 1
2775-2777 A547 Set of 3 3.25 3.25

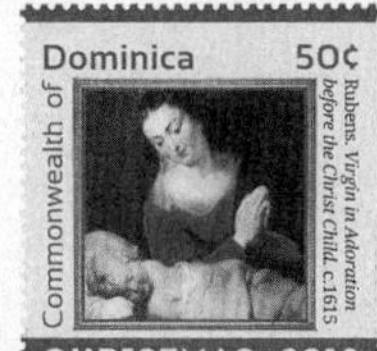

Christmas A548

Paintings: 50c, Virgin in Adoration Before the Christ Child, by Peter Paul Rubens. 90c, Altarpiece of the Rose Garlands, by Albrecht Dürer. $3.50, Crowning of St. Catherine, by Rubens. $5, Adoration of the Magi, by Dürer.

2012, Nov. 19 ***Perf. 13¾***
2778-2781 A548 Set of 4 7.50 7.50

New Year 2011 (Year of the Rabbit) A549

2013, Aug. 29 **Litho.** ***Perf. 12***
2782 A549 $4 multi 3.00 3.00

No. 2782 was printed in sheets of 2.

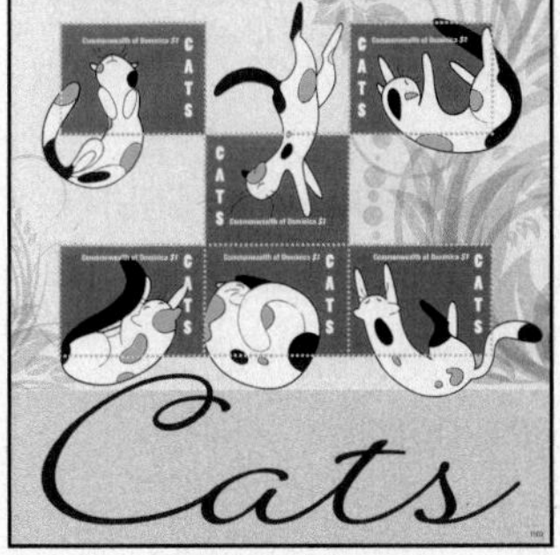

Cats — A550

No. 2783: a, Cat with brown-tipped tail, eyes not visible. b, Cat with black tail and four white paws. c, Head of cat and two front paws. d, Cat with black tail, paw touching "A" in "Cats." e, Cat with white tail, with one black paw visible. f, Cat with one black and three white paws.
$5, Cat, diff.

2013, Sept. 2 **Litho.** ***Perf. 14***
2783 A550 $1 Sheet of 6, #a-f 4.50 4.50

Souvenir Sheet

Perf. 12

2784 A550 $5 multi 3.75 3.75

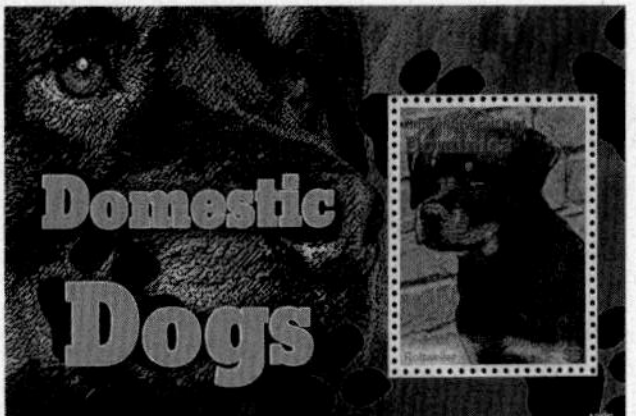

Dogs — A551

No. 2785, $1.45: a, Airedale terrier. b, Bernese mountain dog. c, Pekingese. d, Samoyed.
No. 2786, $1.45, horiz.: a, Labrador retriever. b, Border collie. c, Cocker spaniel. d, Dalmatian.
No. 2787, $5, Rottweiler. No. 2788, $5, Great Dane.

2013, Sept. 2 **Litho.** ***Perf. 12***

Sheets of 4, #a-d

2785-2786 A551 Set of 2 8.75 8.75

Souvenir Sheets

2787-2788 A551 Set of 2 7.50 7.50

Bees and Wasps — A552

No. 2789: a, Carpenter bee. b, Golden digger wasp. c, Bumblebee. d, Yellowjacket.
$5, Golden paper wasp.

2013, Sept. 2 **Litho.** ***Perf. 13¾***
2789 A552 $2 Sheet of 4, #a-d 6.00 6.00

Souvenir Sheet

2790 A552 $5 multi 3.75 3.75

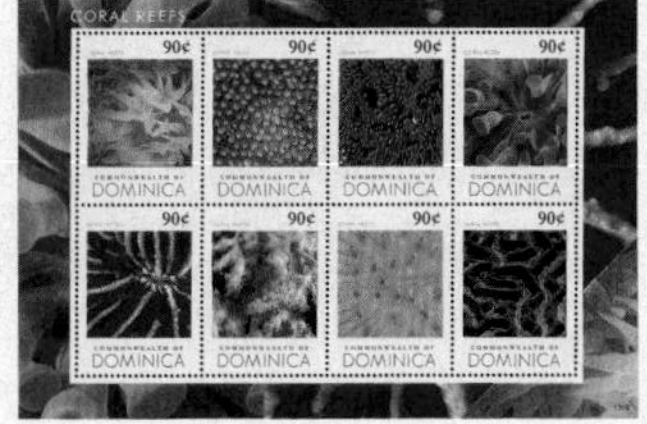

Corals — A553

No. 2791 — Various unnamed corals with colors of; a, Pink (with anemone-like tips). b, Purple and pink (small bead-like appearance). c, Dark red. d, Blue (tubes). e, Purple and pink (with lines). f, Pink (with branches). g, Yellow green. h, Blue (with black curved lines).
$5, Nephthyigorgia sp.

2013, Sept. 2 **Litho.** ***Perf. 14***
2791 A553 90c Sheet of 8, #a-h 5.50 5.50

Souvenir Sheet

Perf. 12¾x12½

2792 A553 $5 multi 3.75 3.75

No. 2792 contains one 38x51mm stamp.

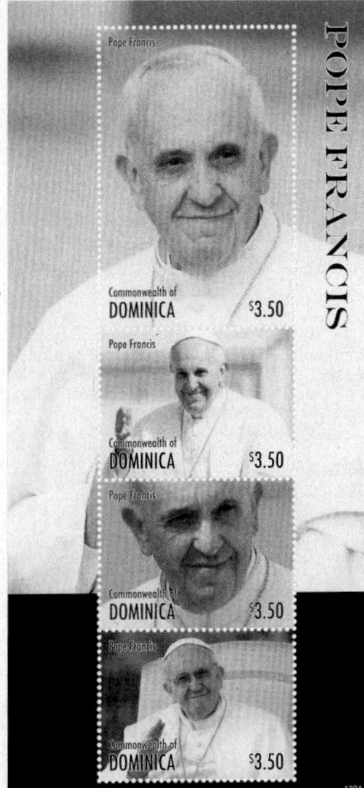

Election of Pope Francis — A554

No. 2793 — Pope Francis: a, With top of head visible (40x60mm). b, Waving, without eyeglasses, horiz. (40x30mm). c, With top of head not visible, horiz. (40x30mm). d, Waving, wearing eyeglasses, horiz. (40x30mm).
$5, Pope Francis, horiz.

2013, Sept. 2 **Litho.** ***Perf. 14***
2793 A554 $3.50 Sheet of 4, #a-d 10.50 10.50

Souvenir Sheet

Perf. 12¾x12½

2794 A554 $5 multi 3.75 3.75

No. 2794 contains one 51x38mm stamp.

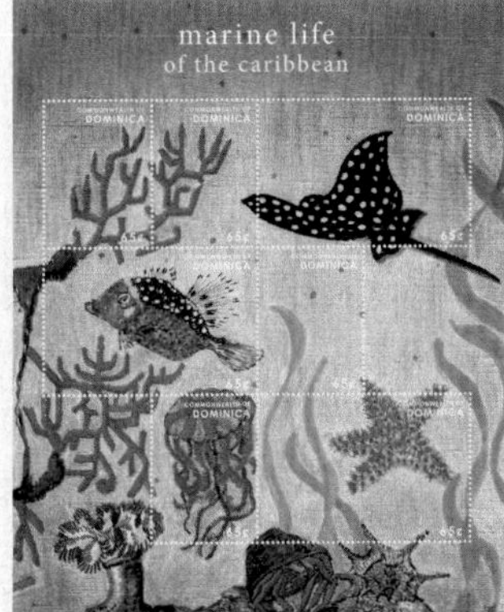

Painting of Marine Life — A555

Painting of Parrot — A556

No. 2795: a, Coral, denomination on coral (30x40mm). b, Coral, denomination on blue background (30x40mm). c, Ray (60x40mm). d, Fish and coral (60x40mm). e, Sea grass (30x40mm). f, Jellyfish (30x40mm). g, Sea grass and starfish (60x40mm).

2013, Sept. 2 **Litho.** ***Perf. 14***
2795 A555 65c Sheet of 7, #a-g 3.50 3.50

Souvenir Sheet

Perf. 12

2796 A556 $5 multi 3.75 3.75

Butterflies A557

No. 2797, $2: a, Malachite. b, Silver-banded hairstreak.
No. 2798, $2: a, Gold rim swallowtail. b, Mangrove buckeye.

2013, Sept. 2 **Litho.** ***Perf. 13¾***

Pairs, #a-b

2797-2798 A557 Set of 2 6.00 6.00

Nos. 2797 and 2798 each were printed in sheets containing two pairs.

Birth of Prince George of Cambridge — A558

No. 2799: a, Duke and Duchess of Cambridge, Prince George. b, Duke of Cambridge holding Prince George. c, Duchess of Cambridge holding Prince George. d, Close-up of Prince George.
$6, Duke and Duchess of Cambridge, Prince George, diff.

2013 **Litho.** ***Perf. 14***
2799 A558 $2 Sheet of 4, #a-d 6.00 6.00

Souvenir Sheet

2800 A558 $6 multi 4.50 4.50

A559

Nelson Mandela (1918-2013), President of South Africa — A560

No. 2801 — Mandela: a, Holding loud-speaker. b, Wearing green and black shirt and jacket. c, With arms raised, color photograph. d, With arms raised, black-and-white photograph. e, Wearing black and gray shirt. f, Wearing black shirt.
$5, Mandela wearing gray shirt. $20, Mandela wearing shirt with leaf design.

2014, Jan. 6 Litho. *Perf. 13¾*

2801 A559 $2.50 Sheet of 6, #a-f 11.00 11.00

Souvenir Sheets

2802 A559 $5 multi 3.75 3.75

Litho., Margin Embossed With Foil Application

Imperf

2803 A560 $20 multi 15.00 15.00

New Year 2014 (Year of the Horse) — A561

No. 2804 — Various Chinese characters for "horse" and: a, Horse in red at left, red chop at right, orange background. b, Horse in yellow at left, yellow chop at left, red orange background. c, Horse in red at left, red chop at left, yellow orange background. d, Horse in yellow at right, red chop at left, brown background. e, Horse in red at right, red chop at left, yellow orange background. f, Horse in yellow at right, red chop at left, dull orange background.
No. 2805 — Chinese characters for "horse" and: a, Horse in red at right. b, Horse in yellow brown at right.

2014, Jan. 8 Litho. *Perf. 14*

2804 A561 $2.50 Sheet of 6, #a-f 11.00 11.00

Souvenir Sheet

2805 A561 $5 Sheet of 2, #a-b 7.50 7.50

Sea Turtles — A562

No. 2806: a, Leatherback turtle. b, Green sea turtle. c, Hawksbill turtle.
$5, Green sea turtle, diff.

2014, May 1 Litho. *Perf. 11½x12*

2806 A562 $3.50 Sheet of 3, #a-c 7.75 7.75

Souvenir Sheet

2807 A562 $5 multi 3.75 3.75

Morne Trois Pitons National Park UNESCO World Heritage Site, 70th Anniv. — A563

No. 2808: a, Fumarole, mountain in background. b, Fumarole, rocks in foreground. c, Lesser Antillean iguana. d, Smoke-enshrouded landscape. e, Smoke above waterfall. g. Waterfall.
$10, Waterfall, diff.

2015, Dec. 1 Litho. *Perf. 12*

2808 A563 $3.50 Sheet of 6, #a-f 15.50 15.50

Souvenir Sheet

2809 A563 $10 multi 7.50 7.50

WAR TAX STAMPS

No. 50 Surcharged in Red

1916 Wmk. 3 *Perf. 14*

MR1 A6 ½p on ½p green 3.50 .85

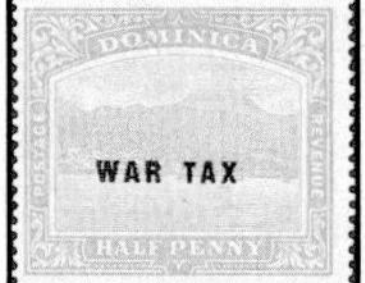

No. 50 Overprinted in Black

1918

MR2 A6 ½p green 7.50 *6.25*

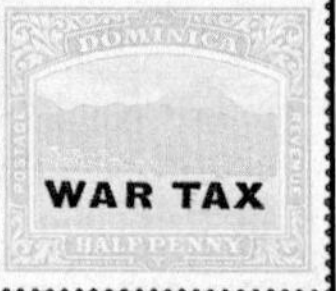

Nos. 50, 40 in Black or Red

1918

MR3 A6 ½p green .25 *.30*

MR4 A6 3p violet, *yel* (R) 5.50 *4.50*

Type of 1908-09 Surcharged in Red

1919

MR5 A6 1½p on 2½p orange .25 *.60*

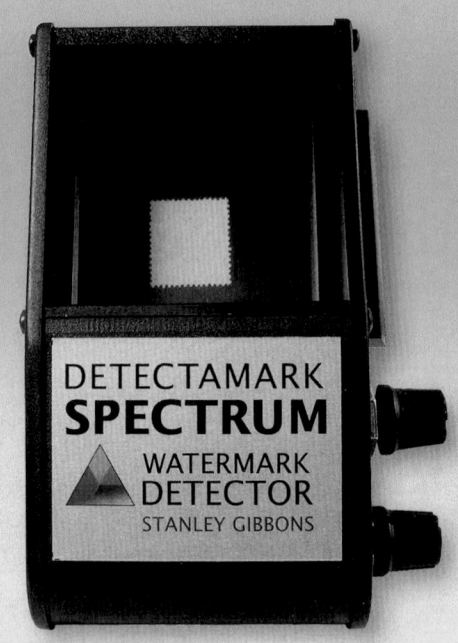

DOMINICAN REPUBLIC

də-'mi-ni-kən ri-'pə-blik

LOCATION — Comprises about two-thirds of the island of Hispaniola in the West Indies
GOVT. — Republic
AREA — 18,700 sq. mi.
POP. — 8,129,734 (1999 est.)
CAPITAL — Santo Domingo

8 Reales = 1 Peso
100 Centavos = 1 Peso (1880)
100 Centimos = 1 Franco (1883)
100 Centavos = 1 Peso (1885)

Catalogue values for unused stamps in this country are for Never Hinged items, beginning with Scott 437 in the regular postage section, Scott B1 in the semi-postal section, Scott C75 in the airpost section, Scott CB1 in the airpost semi-postal section, Scott E7 in the special delivery section, Scott G13 in the insured letter section, Scott J14 in the postage due section, Scott O26 in the officials section, and Scott RA20 in the postal tax section.

Watermarks

Wmk. 115 Diamonds

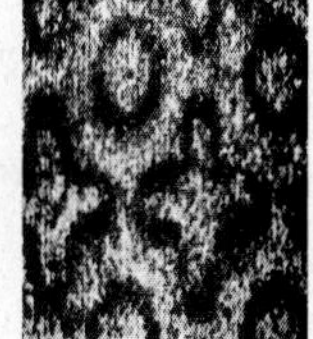
Wmk. 116 Crosses and Circles

Coat of Arms
A1 A2

1865 Unwmk. Typo. *Imperf.*
Wove Paper

No.	Type	Description	Unused	Used
1	A1	½r black, *rose*	700.	650.
2	A1	1r black, *dp green*	1,100.	1,000.

Twelve varieties of each.

Laid Paper

No.	Type	Description	Unused	Used
3	A2	½r black, *pale green*	550.	475.
4	A2	1r black, *straw*	1,800.	1,200.

Twelve varieties of the ½r, ten of the 1r.

A3

A4

1866 Laid Paper Unwmk.

No.	Type	Description	Unused	Used
5	A3	½r black, *straw*	200.00	160.00
6	A3	1r black, *pale green*	2,500.	2,000.
7	A4	1r black, *pale green*	175.00	125.00

Nos. 5-8 have 21 varieties (sheets of 21).

Wmk. 115

No.	Type	Description	Unused	Used
8	A3	1r blk, *pale grn*	13,000.	13,000.
a.		"CORREOS" and "Un Real" doubled	21,000.	

The unique example of No. 8a is centered in the grade of fine, has a shallow thin spot and pinhole.

1866-67 Wove Paper Unwmk.

No.	Type	Description	Unused	Used
9	A3	½r blk, *rose* ('67)	60.00	60.00
10	A3	1r blk, *pale green*	85.00	75.00
a.		Inscription dbl., top & bottom	*400.00*	*400.00*
11	A3	1r black, *blue* ('67)	60.00	37.50
a.		1r black, *light blue* ('67)	50.00	30.00
b.		No space btwn. "Un" and "real"	*600.00*	500.00
c.		Without inscription at top & bottom	*1,500.*	1,000.
d.		Inscription invtd., top & bottom		—
		Nos. 9-11 (3)	205.00	172.50

1867-71 Pelure Paper

No.	Type	Description	Unused	Used
13	A3	½r black, *rose*	150.00	75.00
15	A3	½r black, *lav* ('68)	250.00	210.00
a.		Without inscription at top and bottom		525.00
b.		Dbl. inscriptions, one invtd.		*425.00*
16	A3	½r black, *grnsh gray* ('68)	260.00	225.00
17	A3	½r black, *yel* ('68)	12,000.	
18	A3	½r blk, *ol* ('69)	3,000.	5,500.
22	A3	1r black, *blue*	4,000.	
23	A3	1r black, *lav*	225.00	200.00
24	A4	1r blk, *rose* ('68)	225.00	225.00
25	A4	1r blk, *mag* ('69)	2,250.	1,300.
26	A4	1r blk, *sal* ('71)	300.00	225.00

Value for No. 17 is for an example with very fine centering and small faults. Value for No. 22 is for a faulty example with very fine centering and appearance.

1870-73 Ordinary Paper

No.	Type	Description	Unused	Used
27	A3	½r blk, *mag*	2,500.	4,750.
28	A3	½r blue, *rose* (blk inscription) ('71)	50.00	42.50
a.		Blue inscription	500.00	500.00
b.		Without inscription at top and bottom		
29	A3	½r blk, *yel* ('73)	30.00	21.00
a.		Without inscription at top and bottom	700.00	700.00
30	A4	1r blk, *vio* ('73)	30.00	21.00
a.		Without inscription at top and bottom	700.00	700.00
31	A4	1r black, *dk grn*	60.00	50.00

Nos. 9-31 have 21 varieties (sheets of 21). Nos. 29 and 30 are known pin-perforated, unofficially.

Bisects are known of several of the early 1r stamps.

A5

1879 *Perf. 12½x13*

No.	Type	Description	Unused	Used
32	A5	½r violet	3.00	2.10
a.		Imperf., pair	9.00	9.00
b.		Horiz. pair, imperf. vert.	17.00	
33	A5	½r violet, *bluish*	2.50	1.80
a.		Imperf., pair	9.00	7.50
34	A5	1r carmine	4.50	2.10
a.		Imperf., pair	11.50	9.00
b.		Perf. 13	11.50	7.50
c.		Perf. 13x12½	11.50	7.50
35	A5	1r carmine, *sal*	2.50	1.50
a.		Imperf., pair	8.25	8.25
		Nos. 32-35 (4)	12.50	7.50

In 1891 15 stamps of 1879-83 were surcharged "U P U," new values and crossed diagonal lines.

A6

1880 Typo. *Rouletted in Color*

No.	Type	Description	Unused	Used
36	A6	1c green	1.40	.90
b.		Laid paper	50.00	50.00
37	A6	2c red	1.00	.75
a.		Pelure paper	40.00	40.00
b.		Laid paper	40.00	40.00
38	A6	5c blue	1.50	.70
39	A6	10c rose	3.25	.90
40	A6	20c brown	2.00	.75
41	A6	25c violet	2.25	1.25
42	A6	50c orange	3.00	1.75
43	A6	75c ultra	5.75	3.00
a.		Laid paper	40.00	40.00
44	A6	1p gold	7.50	4.50
a.		Laid paper	50.00	50.00
b.		Double impression	42.50	42.50
		Nos. 36-44 (9)	27.65	14.50

1881 Network Covering Stamp

No.	Type	Description	Unused	Used
45	A6	1c green	.90	.50
46	A6	2c red	.90	.50
47	A6	5c blue	1.25	.50
48	A6	10c rose	1.50	.65
49	A6	20c brown	1.50	.90
50	A6	25c violet	1.75	1.00
51	A6	50c orange	2.00	1.40
52	A6	75c ultra	6.00	4.50
53	A6	1p gold	8.00	7.00
		Nos. 45-53 (9)	23.80	16.95

Preceding Issues (Type A6) Srch. with Value in New Currency

5 céntimos.
a

5 céntimos
b

50 céntimos.
c

1 franco.
d

1 Franco.
e

1 franco
f

1 franco, 25 céntimos.
g

5 francos.
h

5 francos
i

1883 Without Network

No.	Type	Description	Unused	Used
54	(a)	5c on 1c green	1.50	1.60
b.		Inverted surcharge	21.00	21.00
c.		Surcharged "25 céntimos"	50.00	50.00
d.		Surcharged "10 céntimos"	27.50	27.50
55	(b)	5c on 1c green	25.00	9.00
b.		Double surcharge	100.00	
c.		Inverted surcharge	65.00	65.00
56	(c)	5c on 1c green	17.00	9.50
b.		Surcharged "10 céntimos"	35.00	35.00
c.		Surcharged "25 céntimos"	37.50	37.50
57	(a)	10c on 2c red	5.00	3.00
a.		Inverted surcharge	27.50	27.50
d.		Surcharged "5 céntimos"	52.50	52.50
e.		Surcharged "25 céntimos"	75.00	75.00
58	(c)	10c on 2c red	4.50	3.50
a.		"Céntimso"		
b.		Inverted surcharge	37.50	37.50
c.		Surcharged "25 céntimos"	60.00	60.00
d.		"10" omitted	60.00	
59	(a)	25c on 5c blue	7.00	4.50
a.		Surcharged "5 céntimos"	52.50	
b.		Surcharged "10 céntimos"	52.50	52.50
c.		Surcharged "50 céntimos"	75.00	75.00
d.		Inverted surcharge	50.00	50.00
60	(c)	25c on 5c blue	7.50	3.50
a.		Inverted surcharge	45.00	37.50
b.		Surcharged "10 céntimos"	45.00	37.50
e.		"25" omitted	75.00	
f.		Surcharged on back		75.00
61	(a)	50c on 10c rose	27.50	12.50
a.		Inverted surcharge	70.00	60.00
62	(c)	50c on 10c rose	35.00	17.50
a.		Inverted surcharge	52.50	52.50
63	(d)	1fr on 20c brn	15.00	10.00
64	(e)	1fr on 20c brn	17.50	10.00
a.		Comma after "Franco,"	27.50	27.50
65	(f)	1fr on 20c brn	25.00	20.00
a.		Inverted surcharge		75.00
66	(g)	1fr25c on 25c violet	21.00	15.00
a.		Inverted surcharge	65.00	65.00
67	(g)	2fr50c on 50c org	16.00	12.00
a.		Inverted surcharge	35.00	27.50
68	(g)	3fr75c on 75c ultra	30.00	25.00
b.		Inverted surcharge	60.00	60.00
c.		Laid paper	75.00	75.00
70	(i)	5fr on 1p gold	550.00	500.00
a.		"s" of "francos" inverted	700.00	700.00

With Network

No.	Type	Description	Unused	Used
71	(a)	5c on 1c green	3.00	2.50
b.		Inverted surcharge	22.50	22.50
c.		Double surcharge	22.50	22.50
d.		Surcharged "25 céntimos"	42.50	42.50
e.		"5" omitted	75.00	75.00
72	(b)	5c on 1c green	21.00	9.00
b.		Inverted surcharge	60.00	60.00
73	(c)	5c on 1c green	27.50	11.50
b.		Surcharged "10 céntimos"	50.00	42.50
c.		Surcharged "25 céntimos"	60.00	
74	(a)	10c on 2c red	3.75	2.25
a.		Surcharged "5 céntimos"	52.50	45.00
b.		Surcharged "25 céntimos"	67.50	67.50
c.		"10" omitted	57.50	
75	(c)	10c on 2c red	3.00	2.00
a.		Inverted surcharge	30.00	20.00
76	(a)	25c on 5c blue	7.50	3.50
a.		Surcharged "10 céntimos"	75.00	
b.		Surcharged "5 céntimos"	60.00	
c.		Surcharged "50 céntimos"	67.50	
77	(c)	25c on 5c blue	60.00	30.00
a.		Inverted surcharge		
b.		Surcharged on back		
78	(a)	50c on 10c rose	25.00	7.50
a.		Inverted surcharge	50.00	30.00
b.		Surcharged "25 céntimos"	60.00	
79	(c)	50c on 10c rose	30.00	9.50
a.		Inverted surcharge	60.00	
80	(d)	1fr on 20c brn	12.00	10.00
81	(e)	1fr on 20c brn	14.50	12.50
a.		Comma after "Franco"	35.00	35.00
b.		Inverted surcharge	75.00	
82	(f)	1fr on 20c brown	25.00	20.00
83	(g)	1fr25c on 25c violet	45.00	30.00
a.		Inverted surcharge	75.00	
84	(g)	2fr50c on 50c org	19.00	12.50
a.		Inverted surcharge	35.00	27.50
85	(g)	3fr75c on 75c ultra	45.00	42.50
86	(h)	5fr on 1p gold	140.00	140.00
a.		Inverted surcharge		
87	(i)	5fr on 1p gold	190.00	190.00

Many minor varieties exist in Nos. 54-87: accent on "i" of "centimos"; "5" with straight top; "1" with straight serif.

A7

A7a

1885-91 Engr. *Perf. 12*

No.	Type	Description	Unused	Used
88	A7	1c green	1.00	.50
89	A7	2c vermilion	1.00	.50
90	A7	5c blue	1.40	.50
91	A7a	10c orange	2.25	.65
92	A7a	20c dark brown	2.25	.80
93	A7a	50c violet ('91)	7.50	7.50
94	A7	1p carmine ('91)	20.00	20.00
95	A7	2p red brown ('91)	25.00	25.00
		Nos. 88-95 (8)	60.40	55.45

Nos. 93, 94, 95 were issued without gum.
Imperf. varieties are proofs.
For surcharges see Nos. 166-168.

In 1891 certain denominations of the 1879-83 issues were overprinted with a large "X" separating the stamp into four triangles. The top triangle has the letter "U," and the left and right triangles have the letter "P". The bottom triangle is surcharged with a new value. Although this issue was authorized by the president, the entire supply was given to a single French dealer. A few covers exist, most addressed to the dealer's wife in New York. Numerous forgeries exist.

Coat of Arms — A8

1895 *Perf. 12½x14*

No.	Type	Description	Unused	Used
96	A8	1c green	1.25	.50
97	A8	2c orange red	1.25	.50
98	A8	5c blue	1.40	.50
99	A8	10c orange	3.25	1.60
		Nos. 96-99 (4)	7.15	3.10

Exist imperforate but were not issued.

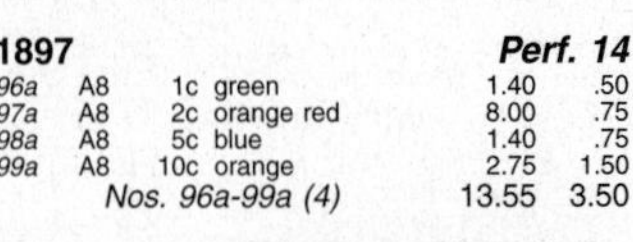

1897 ***Perf. 14***

96a	A8	1c green	1.40	.50
97a	A8	2c orange red	8.00	.75
98a	A8	5c blue	1.40	.75
99a	A8	10c orange	2.75	1.50
		Nos. 96a-99a (4)	13.55	3.50

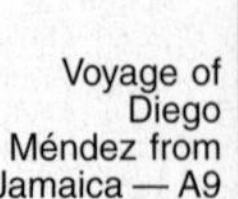

Voyage of Diego Méndez from Jamaica — A9

Enriquillo's Revolt — A10

Sarcophagus of Columbus A11

"Española" Guarding Remains of Columbus A12

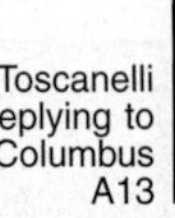

Toscanelli Replying to Columbus A13

Bartolomé de las Casas Defending Indians — A14

Columbus at Salamanca A15

Columbus' Mausoleum A16

1899, Feb. 27 **Litho.** ***Perf. 11½***

100	A9	1c brown violet	7.25	5.25
102	A10	2c rose red	1.75	.70
103	A11	5c blue	2.00	.70
104	A12	10c orange	5.00	1.60
a.		Tête bêche pair	42.50	42.50
105	A13	20c brown	10.00	8.25
106	A14	50c yellow green	11.50	9.75
a.		Tête bêche pair	60.00	60.00
107	A15	1p black, *gray bl*	27.00	22.00
108	A16	2p bister brown	45.00	47.50

1900, Jan.

109	A11	¼c black	.75	*1.60*
110	A15	½c black	.75	*1.60*
110A	A9	1c gray green	.75	.65
		Nos. 100-110A (11)	111.75	99.60

Nos. 100-110A were issued to raise funds for a Columbus mausoleum.

Imperf., Pairs

100a	A9	1c brown violet	16.50	16.50
102a	A10	2c rose red	5.00	
103a	A11	5c blue	5.75	
104b	A12	10c orange	8.75	
105a	A13	20c brown	15.00	
106b	A14	50c yellow green	17.50	
c.		As "b," tête bêche pair	125.00	
107a	A15	1p black, *gray blue*	42.50	
108a	A16	2p bister brown	70.00	
109a	A11	¼c black	3.75	*4.25*
110b	A15	½c black	3.75	*4.25*
110c	A9	1c gray green	3.50	

Map of Hispaniola A17

1900, Oct. 21 **Unwmk.** ***Perf. 14***

111	A17	¼c dark blue	.75	.40
112	A17	½c rose	.75	.40
113	A17	1c olive green	.75	.40
114	A17	2c deep green	.75	.40
115	A17	5c red brown	.75	.40
a.		Vertical pair, imperf. between	17.50	

Perf. 12

116	A17	10c orange	.75	.40
117	A17	20c lilac	3.00	2.50
a.		20c rose (error)	25.00	25.00
118	A17	50c black	2.75	2.50
119	A17	1p brown	3.00	2.50
		Nos. 111-119 (9)	13.25	9.90

Several varieties in design are known in this issue. They were deliberately made. Counterfeits of Nos. 111-119 abound.

A18

1901-06 **Typo.** ***Perf. 14***

120	A18	½c carmine & vio	.70	.40
121	A18	½c blk & org ('05)	1.80	.95
122	A18	½c grn & blk ('06)	.85	.30
123	A18	1c ol grn & vio	.70	.30
124	A18	1c blk & ultra ('05)	1.80	.85
125	A18	1c car & blk ('06)	1.00	.45
126	A18	2c dp grn & vio	.80	.30
127	A18	2c blk & vio ('05)	2.25	.70
128	A18	2c org brn & blk ('06)	1.40	.30
129	A18	5c org brn & vio	.80	.30
130	A18	5c blk & cl ('05)	2.50	1.25
131	A18	5c blue & blk ('06)	1.25	.30
132	A18	10c orange & vio	1.40	.45
133	A18	10c blk & grn ('05)	4.25	2.25
134	A18	10c red vio & blk ('06)	1.40	.40
135	A18	20c brn vio & vio	2.50	.95
136	A18	20c blk & ol ('05)	13.50	8.75
137	A18	20c ol grn & blk ('06)	7.25	3.25
138	A18	50c gray blk & vio	8.00	5.50
139	A18	50c blk & red brn ('05)	47.50	34.00
140	A18	50c brn & blk ('06)	8.75	7.75
141	A18	1p brn & vio	18.00	10.00
142	A18	1p blk & gray ('05)	200.00	*225.00*
143	A18	1p vio & blk ('06)	21.00	13.50
		Nos. 120-143 (24)	349.40	318.20

Issued: 11/15/01; 5/11/05; 8/17/06.

See Nos. 172-176. For surcharges see Nos.151-156.

Francisco Sánchez — A19

Juan Pablo Duarte — A20

Ramón Mella — A21

Ft. Santo Domingo — A22

1902, Feb. 25 **Engr.** ***Perf. 12***

144	A19	1c dk grn & blk	.35	.35
145	A20	2c scarlet & blk	.35	.35
146	A20	5c blue & blk	.35	.35
147	A19	10c orange & blk	.35	.35
148	A21	12c purple & blk	.35	.35
149	A21	20c rose & blk	.60	.60
150	A22	50c brown & blk	.90	.90
		Nos. 144-150 (7)	3.25	3.25

Center Inverted

144a	A19	1c	17.50	*17.50*
145a	A20	2c	17.50	*17.50*
146a	A20	5c	17.50	*17.50*
148a	A21	12c	17.50	*17.50*
149a	A21	20c	17.50	*17.50*
150a	A22	50c	17.50	*17.50*
		Nos. 144a-150a (6)	105.00	*105.00*

400th anniversary of Santo Domingo.

Imperforate varieties of Nos. 144 to 150 were never sold to the public.

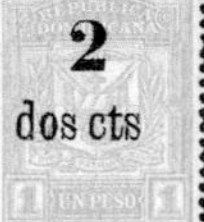

Nos. 138, 141 Surcharged in Black

1904, Aug.

151	A18	2c on 50c	9.25	7.25
152	A18	2c on 1p	13.50	9.25
b.		"2" omitted	50.00	50.00
153	A18	5c on 50c	4.25	2.25
154	A18	5c on 1p	5.25	4.00
155	A18	10c on 50c	8.25	6.75
156	A18	10c on 1p	8.75	6.75
		Nos. 151-156 (6)	49.25	36.25

Inverted Surcharge

151a	A18	2c on 50c	15.00	15.00
152a	A18	2c on 1p	15.00	15.00
c.		As "a," "2" omitted	85.00	85.00
153a	A18	5c on 50c	5.50	5.50
154a	A18	5c on 1p	7.00	6.50
155a	A18	10c on 50c	14.00	14.00
156a	A18	10c on 1p	10.00	10.00
		Nos. 151a-156a (6)	66.50	66.00

Official Stamps of 1902 Overprinted

1904, Aug. 16 **Red Overprint**

157	O1	5c dk blue & blk	5.75	3.00
a.		Inverted overprint	7.25	5.75

Black Overprint

158	O1	2c scarlet & blk	17.00	5.25
a.		Inverted overprint	20.00	6.50
159	O1	5c dk blue & blk	3,500.	3,500.
160	O1	10c yellow grn & blk	10.50	10.50
a.		Inverted overprint	15.00	15.00

Official Stamps of 1902 Surcharged

161	O1	1c on 20c yellow & blk	4.75	3.00
a.		Inverted surcharge	7.25	7.25

Nos. J1-J2 Surcharged or Overprinted in Black

1904-05 **Surcharged "CENTAVOS"**

162	D1	1c on 2c olive gray	250.00	200.00
a.		"entavos"		—
b.		"Dominican"	350.00	300.00
c.		"Centavo"	350.00	300.00

Carmine Surcharge or Overprint

163	D1	1c on 2c olive gray	3.50	1.10
a.		Inverted surcharge	4.75	4.75
b.		"Domihicana"	15.00	15.00
c.		As "b," inverted	40.00	40.00
d.		"Dominican"	10.50	10.50
e.		"Centavos" omitted	30.00	30.00
g.		"entavos"	30.00	
163F	D1	1c on 4c olive gray	35.00	7.00
164	D1	2c olive gray	.95	.60
a.		"Domihicana"	11.00	11.00
b.		Inverted overprint	2.00	2.00
c.		As "a," inverted	25.00	25.00
d.		"Dominican"	25.00	25.00
e.		"Centavo" omitted	12.50	10.00
f.		"entavos"	12.50	12.50
g.		As "f," inverted	40.00	40.00
h.		As "d," inverted	40.00	40.00

Surcharged "CENTAVO"

165	D1	1c on 4c olive gray	.95	.70
a.		"Domihicana"	10.00	10.00
c.		Inverted surcharge	1.75	1.75
d.		"1" omitted	3.50	3.50
e.		As "a," inverted	32.50	32.50
f.		As "d," inverted	40.00	40.00
g.		Double surcharge	30.00	30.00

No. 92 Surcharged in Red

1905, Apr. 4

166	A7a	2c on 20c dk brown	8.75	7.25
a.		Inverted surcharge	15.00	15.00
167	A7a	5c on 20c dk brown	4.75	2.50
a.		Inverted surcharge	16.00	16.00
b.		Double surcharge	25.00	25.00
168	A7a	10c on 20c dk brown	8.75	7.25
		Nos. 166-168 (3)	22.25	17.00

Nos. 166-168 exist with inverted "A" for "V" in "CENTAVOS" in surcharge.

No. J2 Surcharged in Red

1906, Jan. 16 ***Perf. 14***

169	D1	1c on 4c olive gray	.95	.50
a.		Inverted surcharge	10.50	10.50
b.		Double surcharge	25.00	

Nos. J4, J3 Surcharged in Black

1906, May 1

170	D1	1c on 10c olive gray	1.10	.40
a.		Inverted surcharge	10.50	10.50
b.		Double surcharge	14.00	14.00
c.		"OMINICANA"	20.00	20.00
d.		As "c," inverted	150.00	
171	D1	2c on 5c olive gray	1.10	.40
a.		Inverted surcharge	10.50	10.50
b.		Double surcharge	35.00	

The varieties small "C" or small "A" in "REPUBLICA" are found on Nos.169, 170, 171.

Arms Type of 1901-06

1907-10 **Wmk. 116**

172	A18	½c grn & blk ('08)	.85	.25
173	A18	1c carmine & blk	.85	.25
174	A18	2c orange brn & blk	.85	.25
175	A18	5c blue & blk	.85	.25
176	A18	10c red vio & blk ('10)	8.00	1.00
		Nos. 172-176 (5)	11.40	2.00

No. O6 Overprinted in Red

1911, July 11 ***Perf. 13½x14, 13½x13***

177	O2	2c scarlet & black	1.60	.60
a.		"HABILITAOO"	8.75	6.00
b.		Inverted overprint	21.00	
c.		Double overprint	21.00	

A23

1911-13 **Center in Black** ***Perf. 14***

178	A23	½c orange ('13)	.25	.25
179	A23	1c green	.25	.25
180	A23	2c carmine	.25	.25
181	A23	5c gray blue ('13)	.80	.25
182	A23	10c red violet	1.60	.45
183	A23	20c olive green	11.50	11.50

184 A23 50c yellow brn ('12) 3.75 3.75
185 A23 1p violet ('12) 5.75 4.25
Nos. 178-185 (8) 24.15 20.95

See Nos. 230-232.

Juan Pablo Duarte — A24

1914, Apr. 13 ***Perf. 13x14***

Background Red, White and Blue

186 A24 ½c orange & blk .60 .30
187 A24 1c green & blk .60 .30
188 A24 2c rose & blk .60 .30
189 A24 5c slate & blk .60 .40
190 A24 10c magenta & blk 1.40 .70
191 A24 20c olive grn & blk 2.50 1.90
192 A24 50c brown & blk 3.50 2.75
193 A24 1p dull lilac & blk 5.50 4.00
Nos. 186-193 (8) 15.30 10.65

Cent. of the birth of Juan Pablo Duarte (1813-1876), patriot and revolutionary.

Official Stamps of 1909-12 Surcharged in Violet or Overprinted in Red

a

b

1915, Feb. ***Perf. 13½x13, 13½x14***

194 O2 (a) ½c on 20c org & blk .50 .35
a. Inverted surcharge 6.00 6.00
b. Double surcharge 8.75 8.75
c. "Habilitado" omitted 5.25 5.25
195 O2 (b) 1c blue grn & blk .80 .25
a. Inverted overprint 6.00 6.00
b. Double overprint 7.00
c. Overprinted "1915" only 12.50
196 O2 (b) 2c scarlet & blk 1.25 .25
a. Inverted overprint 5.25 5.25
b. Double overprint 7.75 7.75
c. Overprinted "1915" only 8.75
d. "1915" double
197 O2 (b) 5c dk blue & blk 1.00 .25
a. Inverted overprint 7.00 7.00
b. Double overprint 8.75 8.75
c. Double ovpt., one invtd. 27.50
d. Overprinted "1915" only 8.50
198 O2 (b) 10c yel grn & blk 2.75 2.50
a. Inverted overprint 15.00
199 O2 (b) 20c orange & blk 9.25 7.25
a. "Habilitado" omitted
Nos. 194-199 (6) 15.55 10.85

Nos. 194, 196-198 are known with both perforations. Nos. 195, 199 are only perf. 13½x13.

The variety capital "I" for "1" in "Habilitado" occurs once in each sheet in all denominations.

Type of 1911-13 Redrawn

A25

SMALL LETTERS

LARGE LETTERS

TWO CENTAVOS:
Type I — "DOS" in small letters.
Type II — "DOS" in larger letters with white dot at each end of the word.

Overprinted "1915" in Red

1915 Unwmk. Litho. ***Perf. 11½***

200 A25 ½c violet & blk .85 .25
a. Imperf., pair 5.75
201 A25 1c yel brn & blk .85 .25
a. Imperf., pair 6.50
b. Vert. pair, imperf. horiz. 10.50
c. Horiz. pair, imperf. vert. 10.50
202 A25 2c ol grn & blk (I) 3.75 .25
a. Imperf., pair 10.00
203 A25 2c ol grn & blk (II) 6.00 .25
a. Center omitted 87.50
b. Frame omitted 87.50
c. Imperf., pair 15.00
d. Horiz. pair, imperf. vert. 15.00
204 A25 5c magenta & blk 3.75 .25
a. Pair, one without overprint 65.00
b. Imperf., pair 6.50
205 A25 10c gray blue & blk 3.75 .50
a. Imperf., pair 10.00
b. Horiz. pair, imperf. vert. 35.00
206 A25 20c rose red & blk 8.25 1.40
a. Imperf., pair 12.50
207 A25 50c green & blk 10.50 4.00
a. Imperf., pair 25.00
208 A25 1p orange & blk 21.00 7.00
a. Imperf., pair 52.50
Nos. 200-208 (9) 58.70 14.15

Type of 1915 Overprinted "1916" in Red

1916

209 A25 ½c violet & blk 2.25 .25
a. Imperf., pair 21.00
210 A25 1c green & blk 3.25 .25
a. Imperf., pair 21.00

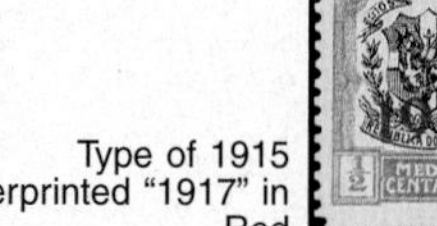
Type of 1915 Overprinted "1917" in Red

1917-19

213 A25 ½c red lilac & blk 3.50 .30
a. Horiz. pair, imperf. btwn. 47.50 47.50
214 A25 1c yellow grn & blk 1.60 .25
a. Vert. pair, imperf. btwn. 50.00
215 A25 2c olive grn & blk 2.25 .25
a. Imperf., pair 35.00
216 A25 5c magenta & blk 23.00 .85
Nos. 213-216 (4) 30.35 1.65

Type of 1915 Overprinted "1919" in Red

1919

219 A25 2c olive grn & blk 17.00 .25

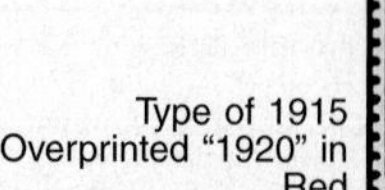

Type of 1915 Overprinted "1920" in Red

1920-27

220 A25 ½c lilac rose & blk .60 .25
a. Horiz. pair, imperf. btwn. 25.00 25.00
b. Inverted overprint
c. Double overprint
d. Double overprint, one invtd.
221 A25 1c yellow grn & blk .75 .25
a. Overprint omitted 70.00
b. Horiz. pair, imperf. btwn. 40.00
222 A25 2c olive grn & blk .75 .25
a. Vertical pair, imperf. between 27.50
223 A25 5c dp rose & blk 9.00 .50
224 A25 10c blue & black 5.75 .25
225 A25 20c rose red & blk ('27) 7.75 .50
226 A25 50c green & blk ('27) 65.00 21.00
Nos. 220-226 (7) 89.60 23.00

Type of 1915 Overprinted "1921" in Red

1921

227 A25 1c yellow grn & blk 5.25 .30
a. Horiz. pair, imperf. btwn. 45.00 45.00
b. Imperf., pair 45.00 45.00
228 A25 2c olive grn & blk 5.75 .40
a. Vert. pair, imperf. btwn. 45.00

Redrawn Design of 1915 without Overprint

1922

230 A25 1c green 3.75 .30
231 A25 2c carmine (II) 3.75 .30
232 A25 5c blue 5.75 .30
Nos. 230-232 (3) 13.25 .90

Nos. 230-232 exist imperf.

A26

Type I

Type II

TEN CENTAVOS:
Type I — Numerals 2mm high. "DIEZ" in thick letters with large white dot at each end.
Type II — Numerals 3mm high. "DIEZ" in thin letters with white dot with colored center at each end.

1924-27 **Second Redrawing**

233 A26 1c green 1.60 .25
a. Vert. pair, imperf. btwn. 35.00 35.00
234 A26 2c red .85 .25
235 A26 5c blue 2.25 .25
236 A26 10c pale bl & blk (I) ('26) 12.00 3.00
236A A26 10c pale bl & blk (II) 22.50 1.10
236B A26 50c gray grn & blk ('26) 60.00 33.00
237 A26 1p org & blk ('27) 19.00 12.50
Nos. 233-237 (7) 118.20 50.35

In the second redrawing the shield has a flat top and the design differs in many details from the stamps of 1911-13 and 1915-22.

A27

1927

238 A27 ½c lilac rose & blk .30 .25

Exhibition Pavilion — A28

1927 **Unwmk.** ***Perf. 12***

239 A28 2c carmine 1.10 .50
240 A28 5c ultra 2.10 .50

Natl. and West Indian Exhib. at Santiago de los Caballeros.

Ruins of Columbus' Fortress A29

1928

241 A29 ½c lilac rose .95 .35
242 A29 1c deep green .70 .25
a. Horiz. pair, imperf. btwn. 25.00
243 A29 2c red .95 .25
244 A29 5c dark blue 2.75 .35
245 A29 10c light blue 2.75 .30
246 A29 20c rose 4.75 .40
247 A29 50c yellow green 13.50 8.25
248 A29 1p orange yellow 35.00 27.00
Nos. 241-248 (8) 61.35 37.15

Reprints exist of 1c, 2c and 10c.
Issued: 1c, 2c, 10c, Oct. 1; others, Dec.

Horacio Vasquez — A30

1929, May-June

249 A30 ½c dull rose .60 .30
250 A30 1c gray green .60 .25
251 A30 2c red .70 .25
252 A30 5c dark ultra 1.40 .35
253 A30 10c pale blue 2.10 .50
Nos. 249-253 (5) 5.40 1.65

Signing of the "Frontier" treaty with Haiti.
Issue dates: 2c, May; others, June.

Imperf., Pairs

249a A30 ½c 12.50
250a A30 1c 12.50
251a A30 2c 12.50
252a A30 5c 14.00

Convent of San Ignacio de Loyola — A31

1930, May 1 ***Perf. 11½***

254 A31 ½c red brown .70 .45
a. Imperf., pair 55.00 55.00
255 A31 1c deep green .65 .25
256 A31 2c vermilion .65 .25
a. Imperf., pair 60.00
257 A31 5c deep blue 2.10 .35
258 A31 10c light blue 4.25 1.25
Nos. 254-258 (5) 8.35 2.55

Cathedral of Santo Domingo, First Church in America
A32

1931 ***Perf. 12***

260 A32 1c deep green	.85	.25
a. Imperf., pair	50.00	
261 A32 2c scarlet	.60	.25
a. Imperf., pair	50.00	
262 A32 3c violet	.85	.25
263 A32 7c dark blue	2.50	.25
264 A32 8c bister	3.00	.85
265 A32 10c light blue	5.75	1.25
a. Imperf., pair	35.00	
Nos. 260-265 (6)	13.55	3.10

Issued: 3c-7c, Aug. 1; others, July 11.
For overprint see No. RAC8.

A33

Overprinted or Surcharged in Black

1932, Dec. 20 ***Perf. 12***

Cross in Red

265B A33 1c yellow green	.55	.50
265C A33 3c on 2c violet	.80	.60
265D A33 5c blue	4.50	4.75
265E A33 7c on 10c turq bl	6.00	6.25
Nos. 265B-265E (4)	11.85	12.10

Proceeds of sale given to Red Cross. Valid Dec. 20 to Jan. 5, 1933.

Inverted and pairs, one without surcharge or overprint, exist on Nos. 265B-265D, as well as missing letters.

Fernando Arturo de Merino (1833-1906) as President — A35

Cathedral of Santo Domingo
A36

Designs: ½c, 5c, 8c, Tomb of Merino. 1c, 3c, 10c, as Archbishop.

1933, Feb. 27 **Engr.** ***Perf. 14***

266 A35 ½c lt violet	.45	.35
267 A35 1c yellow green	.60	.25
268 A35 2c lt red	1.00	.75
269 A35 3c deep violet	.70	.30
270 A35 5c dark blue	.80	.35
271 A35 7c ultra	1.40	.50
272 A35 8c dark green	1.75	1.00
273 A35 10c orange yel	1.50	.60
274 A35 20c carmine rose	3.00	1.75
275 A36 50c lemon	11.25	7.75
276 A36 1p dark brown	26.00	19.00
Nos. 266-276 (11)	48.45	32.60

For surcharges see Nos. G1-G7.

Tower of Homage, Ozama Fortress — A37

1932 **Litho.** ***Perf. 12***

278 A37 1c green	1.75	.25
279 A37 3c violet	1.10	.25

Issue dates: 1c, July 2; 3c, June 22.

"CORREOS" added at left

1933, May 28

283 A37 1c dark green	.50	.25

President Rafael L. Trujillo
A38 A39

1933, Aug. 16 **Engr.** ***Perf. 14***

286 A38 1c yellow grn & blk	1.75	.35
287 A39 3c dp violet & blk	2.50	.35
288 A38 7c ultra & blk	5.75	.75
Nos. 286-288 (3)	10.00	1.45

42nd birthday of President Rafael Leonidas Trujillo Molina.

San Rafael Bridge — A40

1934 **Litho.** ***Perf. 12***

289 A40 ½c dull violet	.70	.40
290 A40 1c dark green	1.00	.25
291 A40 3c violet	1.75	.25
Nos. 289-291 (3)	3.45	.90

Opening of San Rafael Bridge.
Issue dates: ½c, 3c, Mar. 3; 1c, Feb. 17.

Trujillo Bridge
A41

1934

292 A41 ½c red brown	.70	.25
293 A41 1c green	1.00	.25
294 A41 3c purple	1.40	.25
Nos. 292-294 (3)	3.10	.75

Opening of the General Trujillo Bridge near Ciudad Trujillo.
Issue dates: 1c, Aug. 24. Others, Sept. 7.

Ramfis Bridge
A42

1935, Apr. 6

295 A42 1c green	.70	.25
296 A42 3c yellow brown	.70	.25
297 A42 5c brown violet	2.10	1.00
298 A42 10c rose	4.25	1.40
Nos. 295-298 (4)	7.75	2.90

Opening of the Ramfis Bridge over the Higuamo River.

President Trujillo — A43

A44

A45

1935 ***Perf. 11***

299 A43 3c yellow & brown	.30	.25
300 A44 5c org red, bl, red & bis	.40	.25
301 A45 7c ultra, bl, red & brn	.60	.25
302 A44 10c red vio, bl, red & bis	1.00	.25
Nos. 299-302 (4)	2.30	1.00

Ratification of a treaty setting the frontier between Dominican Republic and Haiti.
Issued: 3c, 10/29; 5c, 10c, 11/25; 7c, 11/8.

National Palace
A46

1935, Apr. 1 ***Perf. 11½***

303 A46 25c yellow orange	3.75	.30

Obligatory for all mail addressed to the president and cabinet ministers.

Post Office, Santiago
A47

1936

304 A47 ½c bright violet	.30	.35
305 A47 1c green	.30	.25

Issue dates: ½c, Jan. 14; 1c, Jan. 4.

George Washington Ave., Ciudad Trujillo — A48

1936, Feb. 22

306 A48 ½c brn & vio brn	.40	.45
a. Imperf., pair	52.50	
307 A48 2c carmine & brn	.40	.30
308 A48 3c yel org & red brn	.70	.25
309 A48 7c ultra, blue & brn	1.60	1.25
a. Imperf., pair	52.50	
Nos. 306-309 (4)	3.10	2.25

Dedication of George Washington Avenue, Ciudad Trujillo.

José Nuñez de Cáceres — A49 Felix M. del Monte — A55

Proposed National Library — A56

1c, Gen. Gregorio Luperon. 2c, Emiliano Tejera. 3c, Pres. Trujillo. 5c, Jose Reyes. 7c, Gen. Antonio Duverge. 25c, Francisco J. Peynado. 30c, Salome Urena. 50c, Gen. Jose M. Cabral. 1p, Manuel de Jesus Galvan. 2p, Gaston F. Deligne.

1936 **Unwmk.** **Engr.** ***Perf. 13½, 14***

310 A49 ½c dull violet	.40	.25
311 A49 1c dark green	.30	.25
312 A49 2c carmine	.30	.25
313 A49 3c violet	.40	.25
314 A49 5c deep ultra	.70	.30
315 A49 7c slate blue	1.25	.60
316 A55 10c orange	1.25	.30
317 A56 20c olive green	5.75	3.00
318 A55 25c gray violet	6.75	8.75
319 A55 30c scarlet	8.25	11.50
320 A55 50c black brown	9.75	6.25
321 A55 1p black	27.50	35.00
322 A55 2p yellow brown	80.00	90.00
Nos. 310-322 (13)	142.60	156.70

The funds derived from the sale of these stamps were returned to the National Treasury Fund for the erection of a building for the National Library and Archives.
Issued: 3c, 7c, Mar. 18; others, May 22.

President Trujillo and Obelisk — A62

1937, Jan. 11 **Litho.** ***Perf. 11½***

323 A62 1c green	.30	.25
324 A62 3c violet	.40	.25
325 A62 7c blue & turq blue	1.10	1.10
Nos. 323-325 (3)	1.80	1.60

1st anniv. of naming Ciudad Trujillo.

Discus Thrower and Flag — A63

Flag in Red and Blue

1937, Aug. 14

326 A63 1c dark green	6.00	.75
327 A63 3c violet	9.00	.75
328 A63 7c dark blue	15.00	3.50
Nos. 326-328 (3)	30.00	5.00

1st Natl. Olympic Games, Aug. 16, 1937.

Symbolical of Peace, Labor and Progress — A64

1937, Sept. 18 ***Perf. 12***

329 A64 3c purple	.50	.25

"8th Year of the Benefactor."

Monument to Father Francisco Xavier Billini (1837-90) — A65

1937, Dec. 29

330 A65 ½c deep orange	.25	.25
331 A65 5c purple	.60	.25

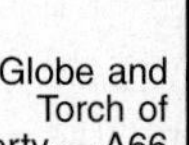

Globe and Torch of Liberty — A66

1938, Feb. 22 ***Perf. 11½***

332 A66 1c green .50 .25
333 A66 3c purple .70 .25
334 A66 10c orange 1.40 .25
Nos. 332-334 (3) 2.60 .75

150th anniv. of the Constitution of the US.

Pledge of Trinitarians, City Gate and National Flag — A67

1938, July 16 ***Perf. 12***

335 A67 1c green, red & dk bl .50 .25
336 A67 3c purple, red & bl .60 .25
337 A67 10c orange, red & bl 1.25 .40
Nos. 335-337 (3) 2.35 .90

Trinitarians and patriots, Francisco Del Rosario Sanchez, Matías Ramón Mella and Juan Pablo Duarte, who helped free their country from foreign domination.

Seal of the University of Santo Domingo — A68

1938, Oct. 28

338 A68 ½c orange .40 .25
339 A68 1c dp green & lt green .40 .25
340 A68 3c purple & pale vio .50 .25
341 A68 7c dp blue & lt blue 1.00 .50
Nos. 338-341 (4) 2.30 1.25

Founding of the University of Santo Domingo, on Oct. 28, 1538.

Trylon and Perisphere, Flag and Proposed Columbus Lighthouse — A69

Flag in Blue and Red

1939, Apr. 30 **Litho.** ***Perf. 12***

342 A69 ½c red org & org .35 .25
343 A69 1c green & lt green .40 .25
344 A69 3c purple & pale vio .40 .25
345 A69 10c orange & yellow 1.40 .65
Nos. 342-345,C33 (5) 4.55 2.25

New York World's Fair.

A70

1939, Sept. **Typo.**

346 A70 ½c black & pale gray .40 .25
347 A70 1c black & yel grn .50 .25
348 A70 3c black & yel brn .50 .25
349 A70 7c black & dp ultra 1.10 .90
350 A70 10c black & brt red vio 2.10 .40
Nos. 346-350 (5) 4.60 2.05

José Trujillo Valdez (1863-1935), father of President Trujillo Molina.

A71

Map of the Americas and flags of 21 American republics.

Flags in National Colors

1940, Apr. 14 **Litho.** ***Perf. 11½***

351 A71 1c deep green .35 .25
352 A71 2c carmine .45 .25
353 A71 3c red violet .60 .25
354 A71 10c orange 1.25 .25
355 A71 1p chestnut 18.00 13.50
Nos. 351-355 (5) 20.65 14.50

Pan American Union, 50th anniv.

Sir Rowland Hill — A72

1940, May 6 ***Perf. 12***

356 A72 3c brt red vio & rose lil 3.25 .40
357 A72 7c dk blue & lt blue 6.75 1.75

Centenary of first postage stamp.

Julia Molina Trujillo A73

1940, May 26

358 A73 1c grn, lt grn & dk grn .40 .25
359 A73 2c brt red, buff & dp rose .40 .25
360 A73 3c org, dl org & brn org .55 .25
361 A73 7c bl, pale bl & dk bl 1.10 .35
Nos. 358-361 (4) 2.45 1.10

Issued in commemoration of Mother's Day.

Map of Caribbean A74

1940, June 6 ***Perf. 11½***

362 A74 3c brt car & pale rose .50 .25
363 A74 7c dk blue & lt blue 1.00 .25
364 A74 1p yel grn & pale grn 10.00 9.00
Nos. 362-364 (3) 11.50 9.50

2nd Inter-American Caribbean Conf. held at Ciudad Trujillo, May 31 to June 6.

Marion Military Hospital — A75

1940, Dec. 24

365 A75 ½c chestnut & fawn .25 .25

Fortress, Ciudad Trujillo A76

Statue of Columbus, Ciudad Trujillo — A77

1941

366 A76 1c dk green & lt green .25 .25
367 A77 2c brt red & rose .25 .25
368 A77 10c orange brn & buff .70 .25
Nos. 366-368 (3) 1.20 .75

Issue dates: 1c, Mar. 27; others, Apr. 7.

Sánchez, Duarte, Mella and Trujillo — A78

1941, May 16

369 A78 3c brt red lil & red vio .30 .25
370 A78 4c brt red, crim & pale rose .40 .25
371 A78 13c dk blue & lt blue .85 .35
372 A78 15c orange brn & buff 2.75 2.10
373 A78 17c lt bl, bl & pale bl 2.75 2.10
374 A78 1p org, yel brn & pale org 11.50 10.50
375 A78 2p lt gray & pale gray 25.00 10.50
Nos. 369-375 (7) 43.55 26.05

Trujillo-Hull Treaty signed Sept. 24, 1940 and effective Apr. 1, 1941.

Bastion of February 27 — A79

1941, Oct. 20

376 A79 5c brt blue & lt blue .50 .25

School, Torch of Knowledge, Pres. Trujillo — A80

1941

377 A80 ½c chestnut & fawn .25 .25
378 A80 1c dk green & lt green .25 .25

Education campaign.
Issue dates: ½c, Dec. 12, 1c, Dec. 2.

Reserve Bank of Dominican Republic A81

1942 **Unwmk.**

379 A81 5c lt brown & buff .50 .25
380 A81 17c dp blue & lt blue 1.00 .45

Founding of the Reserve Bank, 10/24/41.

Representation of Transportation A82

1942, Aug. 15

381 A82 3c dk brn, grn yel & lt bl 4.25 .50
382 A82 15c pur, grn, yel & lt bl 11.00 5.50

Day of Posts and Telegraph, 8th anniv.

Virgin of Altagracia — A83

1942, Aug. 15

383 A83 ½c gray & pale gray 1.00 .25
384 A83 1c dp grn & lt grn 2.10 .25
385 A83 3c brt red lil & lil 13.50 .25
386 A83 5c dk vio brn & vio brn 2.75 .25
387 A83 10c rose pink & pink 4.75 .25
388 A83 15c dp blue & lt blue 10.50 .30
Nos. 383-388 (6) 34.60 1.55

20th anniv. of the coronation of Our Lady of Altagracia.

Bananas — A84

Cows — A85

1942-43

389 A84 3c dk brn & grn ('43) .60 .25
390 A84 4c vermilion & blk ('43) .60 .40
391 A85 5c dp blue & cop brn .60 .25
392 A85 15c dk pur & blue grn 1.00 .50
Nos. 389-392 (4) 2.80 1.40

Issue date: 5c, 15c, Aug. 18.

Emblems of Dominican and Trujillista Parties A86

1943, Jan. 15

393 A86 3c orange .50 .25
394 A86 4c dark red .60 .25
395 A86 13c brt red lilac 1.40 .25
396 A86 1p lt blue 6.75 1.60
Nos. 393-396 (4) 9.25 2.35

Re-election of President Rafael Trujillo Molina, May 16, 1942.

Model Market, Ciudad Trujillo A87

1944

397 A87 2c dk brown & buff .25 .25

Bastion of Feb. 27 and National Flag — A88

1944, Feb. 27 **Unwmk.**

Flag in Dark Blue and Carmine

No.	Type	Description	Unused	Used
398	A88	½c ocher	.25	.25
399	A88	1c yellow green	.25	.25
400	A88	2c scarlet	.25	.25
401	A88	3c brt red vio	.25	.25
402	A88	5c yellow orange	.25	.25
403	A88	7c brt blue	.25	.25
404	A88	10c orange brown	.40	.30
405	A88	20c olive green	.65	.60
406	A88	50c lt blue	1.90	1.75
		Nos. 398-406,C46-C48 (12)	7.25	6.15

Souvenir Sheet

Imperf

No.	Type	Description	Unused	Used
407	A88	Sheet of 12	110.00	110.00
a.-l.		Single stamp	3.00	3.00

Centenary of Independence.

No. 407 contains 1 each of Nos. 398-406 and C46-C48 with simulated perforations. Size: 141x205mm.

Battlefield and Nurse with Child A90

1944, Aug. 1

No.	Type	Description	Unused	Used
408	A90	1c dk bl grn, buff & car	.25	.25
a.		Vertical pair, imperf. btwn.	15.00	
b.		Horiz. pair, imperf. vert.	15.00	
409	A90	2c dk brn, buff & car	.40	.25
410	A90	3c brt bl, buff & car	.40	.25
411	A90	10c rose car, buff & car	.80	.25
		Nos. 408-411 (4)	1.85	1.00

80th anniv. of the Intl. Red Cross.

Municipal Building, San Cristóbal — A91

Unwmk.

1945, Jan. 10 **Litho.** ***Perf. 12***

No.	Type	Description	Unused	Used
412	A91	½c blue & lt blue	.25	.25
413	A91	1c dk green & green	.25	.25
414	A91	2c red org & org	.25	.25
415	A91	3c dk brown & brown	.25	.25
416	A91	10c ultra & gray blue	1.25	.25
		Nos. 412-416 (5)	2.25	1.25

Centenary of the constitution.

Emblem of Communications A92

1945, Sept. 1

Center in Dark Blue and Carmine

No.	Type	Description	Unused	Used
417	A92	3c orange	.25	.25
418	A92	20c yellow green	.85	.25
419	A92	50c light blue	1.75	.70
		Nos. 417-419,C53-C56 (7)	5.00	2.20

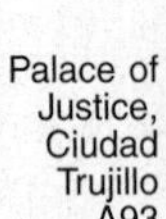

Palace of Justice, Ciudad Trujillo A93

1946 ***Perf. 11½***

No.	Type	Description	Unused	Used
420	A93	3c dk red brown & buff	.25	.25

Map of Hispaniola — A94

1946, Aug. 4 ***Perf. 12***

No.	Type	Description	Unused	Used
421	A94	10c multicolored	.75	.25
		Nos. 421,C62-C63 (3)	2.85	.75

450th anniv. of the founding of Santo Domingo.

Waterfall of Jimenoa — A95

1946-47 **Center Multicolored**

No.	Type	Description	Unused	Used
422	A95	1c yellow grn ('47)	.25	.25
423	A95	2c carmine ('47)	.25	.25
424	A95	3c deep blue	.25	.25
425	A95	13c red violet ('47)	.45	.35
426	A95	20c chocolate ('47)	.80	.35
427	A95	50c orange ('47)	1.75	1.25
		Nos. 422-427,C64-C67 (10)	11.45	5.50

Nos. 422-423, 425-427 issued Mar. 18.

For surcharge see No. 540.

Executive Palace A96

1948, Feb. 27

No.	Type	Description	Unused	Used
428	A96	1c yellow green	.25	.25
429	A96	3c deep blue	.25	.25
		Nos. 428-429,C68-C69 (4)	8.35	3.60

Church of San Francisco Ruins — A97

1949, Apr. 13 ***Perf. 11½***

No.	Type	Description	Unused	Used
430	A97	1c dk grn & pale grn	.25	.25
431	A97	3c dp bl & pale bl	.25	.25
		Nos. 430-431,C70-C73 (6)	4.30	1.90

Gen. Pedro Santana — A98

1949, Aug. 10

No.	Type	Description	Unused	Used
432	A98	3c deep blue & blue	.25	.25

Battle of Las Carreras, cent. See No. C74.

Pigeon and Globe — A99

Center and Inscriptions in Brown

1950, Mar. 23

No.	Type	Description	Unused	Used
433	A99	1c green & pale green	.25	.25
434	A99	2c yel grn & yel	.25	.25
435	A99	5c blue & pale blue	.25	.25
436	A99	7c dk vio bl & pale bl	.40	.25
		Nos. 433-436 (4)	1.15	1.00

75th anniv. of the UPU.

Catalogue values for unused stamps in this section, from this point to the end of the section, are for Never Hinged items.

Hotel Jimani A100

Hotels: 1c, 2c, Hamaca. 5c, Montana. 15c, San Cristobal. 20c, Maguana.

1950-52

No.	Type	Description	Unused	Used
437	A100	½c org brn & buff	.25	.25
438	A100	1c dp grn & grn ('51)	.25	.25
439	A100	2c red org & sal ('52)	.25	.25
440	A100	5c blue & lt blue	.50	.25
441	A100	15c dp orange & yel	.75	.25
442	A100	20c lilac & rose lilac	1.40	.25
443	A100	1p chocolate & yel	5.75	1.90
		Nos. 437-443,C75-C76 (9)	12.90	6.15

Issue dates: 1c, Dec. 1, 1951; 2c, Jan. 11, 1952; others, Sept. 8, 1950.

The ½c, 15c and 20c exist imperf.

Ruins of Church and Hospital of San Nicolas de Bari A101

School of Medicine — A102

1950, Oct. 2

No.	Type	Description	Unused	Used
444	A101	2c dk green & rose brn	.55	.25
445	A102	5c vio blue & org brn	.70	.25
		Nos. 444-445,C77 (3)	2.25	.75

13th Pan-American Health Conference. Nos. 444-445 and C77 exist imperf.

Queen Isabella I — A103

1951, Oct. 12

No.	Type	Description	Unused	Used
446	A103	5c dk blue & red brn	.95	.25

500th anniversary of the birth of Queen Isabella I of Spain. Exists imperf.

Dr. Salvador B. Gautier Hospital A104

1952, Aug.

No.	Type	Description	Unused	Used
447	A104	1c dark green	.35	.25
448	A104	2c red	.35	.25
449	A104	5c violet blue	.55	.25
		Nos. 447-449,C78-C79 (5)	5.70	4.20

Columbus Lighthouse and Flags of 21 Republics A105

1953, Jan. 6 **Engr.** ***Perf. 13***

No.	Type	Description	Unused	Used
450	A105	2c dark green	.30	.25
451	A105	5c deep blue	.40	.25
452	A105	10c deep carmine	.70	.25
		Nos. 450-452,C80-C86 (10)	6.75	4.80

Treasury Building, Ciudad Trujillo A106

Sugar Industry, "Central Rio Haina" A107

1953 **Litho.** ***Perf. 11½***

No.	Type	Description	Unused	Used
453	A106	½c brown	.45	.25
454	A106	2c dark blue	.45	.25
455	A107	5c blue & vio brn	.45	.25
456	A106	15c orange	1.40	.25
		Nos. 453-456 (4)	2.75	1.00

For surcharge see No. 539.

José Marti — A108

1954 ***Perf. 12½***

No.	Type	Description	Unused	Used
457	A108	10c dp blue & dk brown	.85	.25

Centenary of the birth of Jose Marti (1853-1895), Cuban patriot.

Monument to the Peace of Trujillo — A109

1954, May 25

458 A109 2c green .50 .25
459 A109 7c blue .50 .25
460 A109 20c orange 1.75 .25
Nos. 458-460 (3) 2.75 .75

See No. 493.

Rotary Emblem A110

1955, Feb. 23 *Perf. 12*

461 A110 7c deep blue 1.00 .25

50th anniv., Rotary Intl. See No. C90.

Gen. Rafael L. Trujillo — A111

4c, Trujillo in civilian clothes. 7c, Trujillo statue. 10c, Symbols of culture & prosperity.

1955, May 16 **Engr.** *Perf. 13½x13*

462 A111 2c red .50 .25
463 A111 4c lt olive green .50 .25
464 A111 7c indigo .65 .25
465 A111 10c brown 1.25 .25
Nos. 462-465,C91-C93 (7) 7.10 2.05

25th anniversary of the Trujillo era.

General Rafael L. Trujillo — A112

1955, Dec. 20 **Unwmk.** *Perf. 13*

466 A112 7c deep claret .60 .25
467 A112 10c dark blue .80 .25
Nos. 466-467,C94 (3) 2.00 .75

Angelita Trujillo — A113

1955, Dec. 20 **Litho.** *Perf. 12½*

468 A113 10c blue & ultra .75 .25

Nos. 466-468 were issued to publicize the International Fair of Peace and Brotherhood in Ciudad Trujillo, Dec. 1955.

Airport A114

1956, Apr. 6 *Perf. 12½*

469 A114 1c brown .25 .25
470 A114 2c red orange .25 .25
Nos. 469-470,C95 (3) 1.75 .75

3rd Caribbean conf. of the ICAO.

Cedar — A115

1956, Dec. 8 *Perf. 11½x12*

471 A115 5c car rose & grn *1.75* .25
472 A115 6c red vio & grn *2.00* .25
Nos. 471-472,C96 (3) 6.00 .75

Reforestation program.

Fair Emblem — A116

1957, Jan. 10 *Perf. 12½*

473 A116 7c blue, lt brn & ver .40 .25

2nd International Livestock Show, Ciudad Trujillo, Jan. 10-20, 1957. Exists imperf.

Fanny Blankers-Koen, Netherlands A117

Olympic Winners and Flags: 2c, Jesse Owens, US. 3c, Kee Chung Sohn, Japan. 5c, Lord Burghley, England. 7c, Bob Mathias, US.

Flags in National Colors

Engraved & Lithographed

1957, Jan. 24 *Perf. 11½, Imperf.*

474 A117 1c brn, lt bl, vio & mar .30 .25
475 A117 2c dk brn, lt bl & vio .30 .25
476 A117 3c red lilac & red .30 .25
477 A117 5c red org & vio .40 .25
478 A117 7c green & violet .50 .25
Nos. 474-478,C97-C99 (8) 2.75 2.00

16th Olympic Games, Melbourne, Nov. 22-Dec. 8, 1956.

Miniature sheets of 5 exist, perf. and imperf., containing Nos. 474-478. Value, 2 sheets, perf. and imperf., $16.

For surcharges see Nos. B1-B5, B26-B30, CB1-CB3, CB16-CB18.

Lars Hall, Sweden, Pentathlon — A118

Olympic Winners and Flags: 2c, Betty Cuthbert, Australia, 100 & 200 meter dash. 3c, Egil Danielsen, Norway, javelin. 5c, Alain Mimoun, France, marathon. 7c, Norman Read, New Zealand, 50 km. walk.

Perf. 13½, Imperf.

1957, July 18 **Photo.** **Unwmk.**

Flags in National Colors

479 A118 1c brn & brt bl .50 .25
480 A118 2c org ver & dk bl .50 .25
481 A118 3c dark blue .50 .25
482 A118 5c ol & dk bl .50 .25
483 A118 7c rose brn & dk bl .50 .30
Nos. 479-483,C100-C102 (8) 3.45 2.05

1956 Olympic winners.

Miniature sheets of 8 exist, perf. and imperf., containing Nos. 479-483 and C100-C102. The center label in these sheets is printed in two forms: Olympic gold medal or Olympic flag. Sheets measure 140x140mm. Value, 4 sheets, perf. and imperf., medal and flag, $20.

A third set of similar miniature sheets (perf. and imperf.) with center label showing an incorrect version of the Dominican Republic flag (colors transposed) was printed. These sheets are said to have been briefly sold on the first day, then withdrawn as the misprint was discovered. Value, 2 sheets, perf. & imperf., $150.

For surcharges see Nos. B6-B10, CB4-CB6.

Gerald Ouellette, Canada, Small Bore Rifle, Prone — A119

Ron Delaney, Ireland, 1,500 Meter Run — A120

Olympic Winners and Flags: 3c, Tenley Albright, US, figure skating. 5c, Joaquin Capilla, Mexico, platform diving. 7c, Ercole Baldini, Italy, individual road race (cycling).

Engraved and Lithographed

1957, Nov. 12 *Perf. 13½, Imperf.*

Flags in National Colors

484 A119 1c red brown .30 .25
485 A120 2c gray brown .30 .25
486 A119 3c violet .30 .25
487 A120 5c red orange .30 .25
488 A119 7c Prus green .30 .25
Nos. 484-488,C103-C105 (8) 2.55 2.00

1956 Olympic winners.

Miniature sheets of 5 exist, perf. and imperf., containing Nos. 484-488. Value, 2 sheets, perf. and imperf., $5.50.

For surcharges see Nos. B11-B20, CB7-CB12.

Mahogany Flower — A121

1957-58 **Litho.** *Perf. 12½*

489 A121 2c green & maroon .30 .25

Perf. 12

490 A121 4c lilac & rose ('58) .30 .25
491 A121 7c ultra & gray grn .40 .25
492 A121 25c brown & org ('58) 1.20 .35
Nos. 489-492 (4) 2.20 1.10

Sizes: No. 489, 25x29¼mm; Nos. 490-492, 24x28¾mm. In 1959, the 2c was reissued in size 24¼x28½mm with slightly different tones of green and maroon.

Issued: 2c, 10/24; 7c, 11/6; 4c, 25c, 4/7/58.

For surcharges see Nos. 537-538.

Type of 1954, Redrawn

Perf. 12x11½

1957, June 12 **Unwmk.**

493 A109 7c bright blue .75 .25

On No. 493 the cent symbol is smaller, the shading of the sky and steps stronger and the letters in "Correos" shorter and bolder.

Cervantes, Globe, Book — A122

1958, Apr. 23 **Litho.** *Perf. 12½*

494 A122 4c yellow green .45 .25
495 A122 7c red lilac .45 .25
496 A122 10c lt olive brown .75 .25
Nos. 494-496 (3) 1.65 .75

4th Book Fair, Apr. 23-28. Exist imperf.

Gen. Rafael L. Trujillo — A123

1958, Aug. 16 *Perf. 12*

497 A123 2c red lilac & yel .35 .25
498 A123 4c green & yel .35 .25
499 A123 7c brown & yel .35 .25
a. Souv. sheet of 3, #497-499, imperf. 1.25 .80
Nos. 497-499 (3) 1.05 .75

25th anniv. of Gen. Trujillo's designation as "Benefactor of his country."

S. S. Rhadames A124

1958, Oct. 27 *Perf. 12½*

500 A124 7c bright blue 1.50 .30

Day of the Dominican Merchant Marine. Exists imperf.

Shozo Sasahara, Japan, Featherweight Wrestling — A125

Olympic Winners and Flags: 1c, Gillian Sheen, England, fencing, vert. 2c, Milton Campbell, US, decathlon, vert. 5c, Madeleine Berthod, Switzerland, downhill skiing. 7c, Murray Rose, Australia, 400 & 1,500 meter freestyle.

Perf. 13½, Imperf.

1958, Oct. 30 Photo.

Flags in National Colors

501 A125 1c rose, ind & ultra .40 .25
502 A125 2c brown & blue .40 .25
503 A125 3c gray, vio, blk & buff .40 .25
504 A125 5c rose, dk bl, brn & red .40 .25
505 A125 7c lt brn, dk bl & red .40 .25
Nos. 501-505,C106-C108 (8) 3.10 2.00

1956 Olympic winners.
Miniature sheets of 5 exist, perf. and imperf. containing Nos. 501-505. Value, 2 sheets, perf. and imperf., $5.
For surcharges see Nos. B21-B25, CB13-CB15.

Globe and Symbolic Fire — A126

1958, Nov. 3 Litho. *Perf. 11½*

506 A126 7c blue & dp carmine .50 .25

UNESCO Headquarters in Paris opening, Nov. 3.

Dominican Republic Pavilion, Brussels Fair — A127

1958, Dec. 9 Unwmk. *Perf. 12½*

507 A127 7c blue green .30 .25
Nos. 507,C109-C110 (3) 1.45 .90

Universal & Intl. Exposition at Brussels.

Gen. Trujillo Placing Wreath on Altar of the Nation — A128

1959, July 10 *Perf. 12*

508 A128 9c brn, grn, red & gold .45 .25
a. Souv. sheet of 1, imperf. 1.25 .75

29th anniversary of the Trujillo regime.

Lt. Leonidas Rhadames Trujillo, Team Captain — A129

Jamaican Polo Team A130

Design: 10c, Lt. Trujillo on polo pony.

1959, May 15

509 A129 2c violet .25 .25
510 A130 7c yellow brown .50 .25
511 A130 10c green .60 .25
Nos. 509-511,C111 (4) 1.75 1.05

Jamaica-Dominican Republic polo match at Ciudad Trujillo.

Symbolical of Census A131

1959, Aug. 15 Litho. *Perf. 12½*

Flag in Ultramarine and Red

512 A131 1c blue & black .30 .25
513 A131 9c green & black .50 .25
514 A131 13c orange & black .60 .30
Nos. 512-514 (3) 1.40 .80

Issued to publicize the 1960 census.

Trujillo Stadium — A132

1959, Aug. 27

515 A132 9c green & gray .60 .25

Issued to publicize the 3rd Pan American Games, Chicago, Aug. 27-Sept. 7.

Charles V A133

1959, Oct. 12 Unwmk. *Perf. 12*

516 A133 5c bright pink .40 .25
517 A133 9c violet blue .60 .25

400th anniv. of the death of Charles V (1500-1558), Holy Roman Emperor.

Rhadames Bridge — A134

1c and No. 520, Different view of bridge.

1959-60 Litho. *Perf. 12*

518 A134 1c green & gray ('60) .40 .25
519 A134 2c ultra & gray .40 .25
520 A134 2c red & gray ('60) .40 .25
521 A134 5c brn & dull red brn .40 .25
Nos. 518-521 (4) 1.60 1.00

Issued: No. 519, 10/22; 5c, 11/30; 1c, No. 520, 2/6.
For surcharge see No. 536.

Sosua Refugee Settlement and WRY Emblem — A135

1960, Apr. 7 *Perf. 12½*

Center in Gray

522 A135 5c red brn & yel grn .25 .25
523 A135 9c carmine & lt blue .25 .25
524 A135 13c orange & green .50 .25
Nos. 522-524,C113-C114 (5) 2.55 1.35

World Refugee Year, 7/1/59-6/30/60.
For surcharges see Nos. B31-B33.

Sholam Takhti, Iran, Lightweight Wrestling — A136

Olympic Winners: 2c, Masaru Furukawa, Japan, 200 meter breast stroke. 3c, Mildred McDaniel, US, high jump. 5c, Terence Spinks, England, featherweight boxing. 7c, Carlo Pavesi, Italy, fencing.

Perf. 13½, Imperf.

1960, Sept. 14 Photo.

Flags in National Colors

525 A136 1c red, yel grn & blk .35 .25
526 A136 2c org, grnsh bl & brn .35 .25
527 A136 3c henna brn & bl .35 .25
528 A136 5c brown & ultra .35 .25
529 A136 7c grn, bl & rose brn .35 .25
Nos. 525-529,C115-C117 (8) 2.80 2.20

17th Olympic Games, Rome, 8/25-9/11.
Miniature sheets of 5 exist, perf. and imperf., containing Nos. 525-529. Value, 2 sheets, perf. & imperf., $5.
For surcharges see Nos. B34-B38, CB21-CB23.

Post Office, Ciudad Trujillo A137

1960, Aug. 26 Litho. *Perf. 11½x12*

530 A137 2c ultra & gray .30 .25

Exists imperf.

Cattle A138

1960, Aug. 30

531 A138 9c carmine & gray .30 .25

Issued to publicize the Agricultural and Industrial Fair, San Juan de la Maguana.

Nos. 518, 490-491, 453, 427 Surcharged in Red, Black or Blue

1960-61 *Perf. 12*

536 A134 2c on 1c grn & gray (R) .30 .25
537 A121 9c on 4c lilac & rose .60 .25
a. Inverted surcharge 21.00
538 A121 9c on 7c ultra & gray grn (R) .60 .25
539 A106 36c on ½c brown 1.90 1.75
a. Inverted surcharge 18.00
540 A95 1p on 50c multi (Bl) 4.25 3.25
Nos. 536-540 (5) 7.65 5.75

Issue dates: No. 536, Dec. 30, 1960; No. 537, Dec. 20, 1960; others, Feb. 4, 1961.

Trujillo Memorial — A139

1961 Unwmk. *Perf. 11½*

548 A139 1c brown .30 .25
549 A139 2c green .30 .25
550 A139 4c rose lilac .50 .30
551 A139 5c light blue .60 .25
552 A139 9c red orange .50 .25
Nos. 548-552 (5) 2.20 1.30

Gen. Rafael L. Trujillo (1891-1961).
Issued: 2c, 8/7; 4c, 10/24; others 8/30.

Coffee, Cacao — A140

1961, Dec. 30 Litho. *Perf. 12½*

553 A140 1c blue green .35 .25
554 A140 2c orange brown .35 .25
555 A140 4c violet .35 .25
556 A140 5c blue .35 .25
557 A140 9c gray .45 .25
Nos. 553-557,C118-C119 (7) 3.00 2.25

Nos. 553-557 exist imperf.

Dagger Pointing at Mosquito — A141

1962, Apr. 29 Photo. *Perf. 12*

558 A141 10c brt pink & red lilac .30 .25
559 A141 20c pale brn & brn .60 .30
560 A141 25c pale grn & yel grn .85 .40
Nos. 558-560,B39-B40,C120-C121 (9) 6.05 3.75

WHO drive to eradicate malaria.

Broken Fetters and Laurel A142

"Justice," Map of Dominican Republic — A143

Design: 20c, Flag, torch and inscription.

1962, May 30 Litho. *Perf. 12½*

561 A142 1c grn, yel, ultra & red .25 .25
562 A143 9c bister ultra & red .40 .25
563 A142 20c lt blue, ultra & red .85 .25
a. Souvenir sheet of 3, #561-563 1.90 1.90
564 A143 1p lilac, ultra & red 4.50 2.50
Nos. 561-564,C122-C123 (6) 7.80 4.55

1st anniv. of end of Trujillo era. Nos. 561-564 exist imperf.

Farm, Factory and Flag — A144

1962, May 22

565 A144 1c ultra, red & green .30 .25
566 A144 2c ultra & red .30 .25
567 A144 3c ultra, red & brown .30 .25
568 A144 5c ultra, red & blue .30 .25
569 A144 15c ultra, red & orange .40 .30
Nos. 565-569 (5) 1.60 1.30

Map and Laurel A145

1962, June 14 **Litho.**

570 A145 1c black .45 .25

Honoring the martyrs of June 1959 revolution.

Western Hemisphere and Carrier Pigeon — A146

1962, Oct. 23 **Unwmk.** ***Perf. 12½***

571 A146 2c rose red .30 .25
572 A146 9c orange .30 .25
573 A146 14c blue green .60 .25
Nos. 571-573,C124-C125 (5) 2.25 1.50

50th anniv. of the founding of the Postal Union of the Americas and Spain, UPAE.

Archbishop Adolfo Alejandro Nouel — A147

1962, Dec. 18

574 A147 2c bl grn & dull bl .30 .25
575 A147 9c orange & red brn .35 .25
576 A147 13c maroon & vio brn .45 .25
Nos. 574-576,C126-C127 (5) 2.30 1.50

Cent. of the birth of Archbishop Adolfo Alejandro Nouel, President of Dominican Republic in 1911.

Globe, Banner and Emblems A148

1963, Apr. 15 **Unwmk.** ***Perf. 11½***

Banner in Dark Blue & Red

577 A148 2c green .30 .25
578 A148 5c brt rose lilac .30 .25
579 A148 9c orange .60 .25
Nos. 577-579,B41-B43 (6) 2.25 1.50

FAO "Freedom from Hunger" campaign.

Juan Pablo Duarte — A149

1963, July 7 **Litho.** ***Perf. 12x11½***

580 A149 2c shown .30 .25
581 A149 7c Francisco Sanchez .35 .25
582 A149 9c Ramon Mella .45 .25
Nos. 580-582 (3) 1.10 .75

120th anniv. of separation from Haiti. See No. C128.

Ulises F. Espaillat, Benigno F. de Rojas and Pedro F. Bono — A150

Designs: 4c, Generals Santiago Rodriguez, Jose Cabrera and Benito Moncion. 5c, Capotillo monument. 9c, Generals Gaspar Polanco, Gregorio Luperon and Jose A. Salcedo.

1963, Aug. 16 **Unwmk.** ***Perf. 11½***

583 A150 2c green .30 .25
584 A150 4c red orange .30 .25
585 A150 5c brown .75 .25
586 A150 9c bright blue .35 .25
a. Souvenir sheet of 4 1.20 1.00
Nos. 583-586 (4) 1.70 1.00

Cent. of the Restoration. No. 586a contains 4 imperf. stamps similar to Nos. 583-586.

Patient and Nurse — A151

1963, Oct. 25 **Unwmk.** ***Perf. 12½***

587 A151 3c gray & carmine .35 .25
588 A151 6c emerald & red .35 .25
Nos. 587-588,C129 (3) 1.15 .75

Centenary of International Red Cross. Nos. 587-588 exist imperf. Value, set of pairs $18. See No. C129.

Scales, Globe, UNESCO Emblem A152

1963, Dec. 10 **Litho.**

589 A152 6c pink & deep pink .30 .25
590 A152 50c lt green & green .85 .85
Nos. 589-590,C130-C131 (4) 1.75 1.60

Universal Declaration of Human Rights, 15th anniv. Nos. 589-590 exist imperf.

Ramses II Battling the Hittites (from Abu Simbel) — A153

Design: 6c, Two heads of Ramses II.

1964, Mar. 8 **Unwmk.** ***Perf. 12½***

591 A153 3c pale pink & ver .30 .25
592 A153 6c pale blue & ultra .30 .25
593 A153 9c pale rose & red brn .30 .25
Nos. 591-593,C132-C133 (5) 1.50 1.25

UNESCO world campaign to save historic monuments in Nubia.

For surcharges see Nos. B44-B46.

Maximo Gomez — A154

1964, Apr. 30 **Litho.**

594 A154 2c lt blue & blue .30 .25
595 A154 6c dull pink & dull claret .30 .25

Bicent. of the founding of the town of Bani.

Palm Chat — A155

Design: 6c, Hispaniolan parrot.

Size: 27x37½mm

1964, June 8 **Unwmk.** ***Perf. 12½***

596 A155 3c ultra, brn & yel 2.50 .25
597 A155 6c gray & multi 3.25 .25
Nos. 596-597,C134 (3) 11.50 .75

See Nos. 602-604.

Rocket Leaving Earth A156

Designs: 1c, Launching of rocket, vert. 3c, Space capsule orbiting earth. 6c, As 2c.

1964, July 28 **Litho.**

598 A156 1c sky blue .30 .25
599 A156 2c emerald .30 .25
600 A156 3c blue .30 .25
601 A156 6c sky blue .40 .25
Nos. 598-601,C135-C136 (6) 2.00 1.55

Conquest of space.

Bird Type of 1964

Designs: 1c, Narrow-billed tody. 2c, Hispaniolan emerald hummingbird. 6c, Hispaniolan trogon.

1964, Nov. 7 ***Perf. 11½***

Size: 26x37mm

Birds in Natural Colors

602 A155 1c bright pink 2.50 .25
603 A155 2c dark brown 2.50 .25
604 A155 6c blue 4.25 .25
Nos. 602-604 (3) 9.25 .75

Universal Postal Union and United Nations Emblems A157

1964, Dec. 5 **Litho.** ***Perf. 12½***

605 A157 1c red .35 .25
606 A157 4c green .35 .25
607 A157 5c orange .35 .25
Nos. 605-607,C138 (4) 1.40 1.00

15th UPU Cong., Vienna, May-June 1964.

International Cooperation Year Emblem A158

1965, Feb. 16 **Unwmk.** ***Perf. 12½***

608 A158 2c lt blue & ultra .35 .25
609 A158 3c emerald & dk grn .35 .25
610 A158 6c salmon pink & red .35 .25
Nos. 608-610,C139 (4) 1.50 1.05

UN Intl. Cooperation Year.

Virgin of Altagracia A159

Design: 2c, Hands holding lily.

1965, Mar. 18 **Unwmk.** ***Perf. 12½***

611 A159 2c grn, emer & dp rose .35 .25
612 A159 6c multicolored .45 .25
Nos. 611-612,C140 (3) 1.30 .75

4th Mariological Cong. and 11th Intl. Marian Cong. No. 612 exists imperf.

Flags of 21 American Nations — A160

1965, Apr. 14 **Litho.** ***Perf. 11½***

613 A160 2c brown, yel & multi .30 .25
614 A160 6c red lilac & multi .50 .25

Organization of American States.

Stamp of 1865 (No. 1) — A161

1965, Dec. 28 **Litho.** ***Perf. 12½***

615 A161 1c pink, buff & blk .35 .25
616 A161 2c blue, buff & blk .35 .25
617 A161 6c emerald, buff & blk .35 .25
a. Souvenir sheet of 2 1.20 1.10
Nos. 615-617,C142-C143 (5) 1.85 1.30

Cent. of 1st Dominican postage stamps. No. 617a shows replicas of Nos. 1-2. Sold for 50c.

WHO Headquarters, Geneva — A162

1966, May 21 **Litho.** ***Perf. 12½***

618 A162 6c blue .30 .25
619 A162 10c red lilac .50 .25

New WHO Headquarters, Geneva.

Man Holding Map of Republic — A163

1966, May 23

620 A163 2c black & brt green .30 .25
621 A163 6c black & dp orange .50 .25

General elections, June 1, 1966.

Ascia Monuste A164

1966 Litho. *Perf. 12½*

Various Butterflies in Natural Colors

Size: 31x21mm

622 A164 1c blue & vio bl 1.50 .25
623 A164 2c lt grn & brt grn 1.50 .25
624 A164 3c lt gray & gray 2.00 .25
625 A164 6c pink & magenta 2.25 1.00
626 A164 8c buff & brown 4.00 1.40
Nos. 622-626,C146-C148 (8) 41.50 7.90

Issued: 1c, 9/7; 3c, 9/11; others, 11/8.

For surcharges see Nos. B47-B51, CB28-CB30.

Natl. Altar — A165

1967, Jan. 18 Litho. *Perf. 11½*

627 A165 1c bright blue .30 .25
628 A165 2c carmine rose .30 .25
629 A165 3c emerald .30 .25
630 A165 4c gray .30 .25
631 A165 5c orange yellow .30 .25
632 A165 6c orange .30 .25
Nos. 627-632,C149-C151 (9) 2.95 2.30

Map of Republic and Emblem A166

1967, Mar. 30 Litho. *Perf. 12½*

633 A166 2c yellow, blue & blk .30 .25
634 A166 6c orange, blue & blk .30 .25
635 A166 10c emerald, blue & blk .85 .45
Nos. 633-635 (3) 1.45 .95

Development Year, 1967.

Rook and Knight A167

1967, June 23 Litho. *Perf. 12½*

636 A167 25c multicolored 3.00 .50

5th Central American Chess Championships, Santo Domingo. See Nos. C152-C152a.

Alliance for Progress — A168

1967, Sept. 16 Litho. *Perf. 12½*

637 A168 1c bright green .35 .25
Nos. 637,C153-C154 (3) 1.45 .85

6th anniv. of the Alliance for Progress.

Institute Emblem — A169

1967, Oct. 7

638 A169 3c bright green .35 .25
639 A169 6c salmon pink .35 .25
Nos. 638-639,C155 (3) 1.45 .80

25th anniversary of the Inter-American Agriculture Institute.

Globe and Satellite A170

1968, June 15 Typo. *Perf. 12*

640 A170 6c black & multi .35 .25
Nos. 640,C156-C157 (3) 1.20 .80

World Meteorological Day, Mar. 23.

Boxers A171

1968, June 29

641 A171 6c rose red & dp claret .35 .25
Nos. 641,C158-C159 (3) 1.70 .75

Fight between Carlos Ortiz, Puerto Rico, and Teo Cruz, Dominican Republic, for the World Lightweight Boxing Championship.

Lions Emblem — A172

1968, Aug. 9 Litho. *Perf. 11½*

642 A172 6c brown & multi .30 .25

Lions Intl., 50th anniv. (in 1967). See No. C160.

Wrestling and Olympic Emblem A173

1968, Nov. 12 Litho. *Perf. 11½*

643 A173 1c shown .30 .25
644 A173 6c Running .35 .25
645 A173 25c Boxing 1.25 .40
Nos. 643-645,C161-C162 (5) 3.50 1.90

19th Olympic Games, Mexico City, 10/12-27.

Map of Americas and House — A174

1969, Jan. 25 Litho. *Perf. 12½*

646 A174 6c brt bl, lt bl & grn .35 .25

7th Inter-American Conference for Savings and Loans, Santo Domingo, Jan. 25-31. See No. C163.

Stool in Human Form A175

Taino Art: 2c, Wood carved mother figure, vert. 3c, Face carved on 3-cornered stone. 4c, Stone hatchet, vert. 5c, Clay pot.

1969, Jan. 31 Litho. *Perf. 12½*

647 A175 1c yellow, org & blk .40 .25
648 A175 2c lt grn, grn & blk .40 .25
649 A175 3c citron, ol & brt grn .40 .25
650 A175 4c lt lil, lil & brt grn .40 .25
651 A175 5c yellow, org & brn .40 .25
Nos. 647-651,C164-C166 (8) 3.50 2.05

Taino art flourished in the West Indies at the time of Columbus.

Community Day Emblem — A176

1969, Mar. 25 Litho. *Perf. 12½*

652 A176 6c dull green & gold .30 .25

Community Development Day, Mar. 22.

COTAL Emblem — A177

Headquarters Building and COTAL Emblem — A178

Design: 2c, Boy and COTAL emblem.

1969, May 25 Litho. *Perf. 12½*

653 A177 1c lt & dk blue & red .40 .25
654 A177 2c emerald & dk grn .40 .25
655 A178 6c vermilion & pink .40 .25
Nos. 653-655,C167 (4) 1.60 1.00

12th Congress of the Confederation of Latin American Tourist Organizations (COTAL), Santo Domingo, May 25-29.

ILO Emblem — A179

1969, June 27 Litho. *Perf. 12½*

656 A179 6c lt grnsh bl, grnsh bl & blk .40 .25

50th anniv. of the ILO. See No. C168.

Sliding into Base — A180

Designs: 1c, Catching a fly ball. 2c, View of Cibao Stadium, horiz.

Size: 21x31mm (1c, 3c); 43x30mm (2c)

1969, Aug. 15 Litho. *Perf. 12½*

657 A180 1c green & gray .35 .25
658 A180 2c green & lt green .35 .25
659 A180 3c purple & red brown .35 .25
Nos. 657-659,C169-C171 (6) 7.30 4.85

17th World Amateur Baseball Championships, Santo Domingo.

Las Damas Dam A181

Tavera Dam — A182

Designs: 2c, Las Damas hydroelectric station, vert. 6c, Arroyo Hondo substation.

1969 Litho. *Perf. 12*

660 A181 2c green & multi .35 .25
661 A181 3c dk blue & multi .35 .25
662 A181 6c brt rose lilac .35 .25
663 A182 6c multicolored .60 .25
Nos. 660-663,C172-C173 (6) 2.70 1.50

National electrification plan.

Issued: Nos. 660-662, Sept. 15; No. 663, Oct. 15.

Juan Pablo Duarte — A183

1970, Jan. 26 Litho. *Perf. 12*

664 A183 1c emerald & dk grn .35 .25
665 A183 2c sal pink & dp car .35 .25
666 A183 3c brt pink & plum .35 .25
667 A183 6c blue & violet blue .35 .25
Nos. 664-667,C174 (5) 2.15 1.25

Issued for Duarte Day in memory of Juan Pablo Duarte (1813-1876), liberator.

Map of Republic, People, Census Emblem A184

Design: 6c, Census emblem and inscription.

1970, Feb. 6 *Perf. 11*

668 A184 5c emerald & blk .35 .25
669 A184 6c ultra & blue .35 .25
Nos. 668-669,C175 (3) 1.45 .75

Census of 1970.

Abelardo Rodriguez Urdaneta — A185

"One of Many" A186

1970, Feb. 20 Litho. *Perf. 12½*

670 A185 3c ultramarine .35 .25
671 A186 6c green & yel grn .35 .25
Nos. 670-671,C176 (3) 1.25 .75

Issued to honor Abelardo Rodriguez Urdaneta, sculptor.

Masonic Symbols — A187

1970, Mar. 2

672 A187 6c green .30 .25

8th Inter-American Masonic Conference, Santo Domingo, Mar. 1-7. See No. C177.

Communications Satellite — A188

1970, May 25 Litho. *Perf. 12½*

673 A188 20c olive & gray .80 .30

World Telecommunications Day. See No. C178.

UPU Headquarters, Bern — A189

1970, June 5 *Perf. 11*

674 A189 6c gray & brown .40 .25

Inauguration of the new UPU headquarters in Bern. See No. C179.

Education Year Emblem — A190

1970, June 26 Litho. *Perf. 12½*

675 A190 4c rose lilac .40 .25

Issued for International Education Year, 1970. See No. C180.

Pedro Alejandrino Pina — A191

1970, Aug. 24 Litho. *Perf. 12½*

676 A191 6c lt red brn & blk .40 .25

Pedro Alejandrino Pina (1820-70), author.

Children Reading A192

1970, Oct. 12 Litho. *Perf. 12½*

677 A192 5c dull green .40 .25
Nos. 677,C181-C182 (3) 1.25 .75

1st World Exhibition of Books and Culture Festival, Santo Domingo, Oct. 11-Dec. 11.

Virgin of Altagracia A193

1971, Jan. 20 Litho. *Perf. 12½*

678 A193 3c multicolored .45 .25

Inauguration of the Basilica of Our Lady of Altagracia. See No. C184.

Rodriguez Objio — A194

1971, June 18 Litho. *Perf. 11*

679 A194 6c light blue .45 .25

Manuel Rodriguez Objio (1838-1871), poet.

Boxing and Canoeing — A195

1971, Sept. 10

680 A195 2c shown .30 .25
681 A195 5c Basketball .30 .25
Nos. 680-681,C186 (3) 1.00 .75

2nd National Games.

Goat and Fruit A196

Designs: 2c, Cow and goose. 3c, Cacao and horse. 6c, Bananas, coffee and pig.

1971, Sept. 29 *Perf. 12½*

682 A196 1c brown & multi .40 .25
683 A196 2c plum & multi .40 .25
684 A196 3c green & multi .40 .25
685 A196 6c blue & multi .40 .25
Nos. 682-685,C187 (5) 3.60 1.35

6th Natl. agriculture and livestock census.

José Nuñez de Cáceres — A197

1971, Dec. 1 *Perf. 11*

686 A197 6c lt bl, lil & dk bl .45 .25

Sesquicentennial of first national independence. See No. C188.

Shepherds and Star — A198

1971, Dec. 10 *Perf. 12½*

687 A198 6c blue, brown & yel .45 .25

Christmas 1971. See No. C189.

UNICEF Emblem, Child on Beach — A199

1971, Dec. 14 Litho. *Perf. 11*

688 A199 6c gray blue & multi .30 .25

UNICEF, 25th anniv. See No. C190.

Book Year Emblem A200

1972, Jan. 25 *Perf. 12½*

689 A200 1c green, ultra & red .30 .25
690 A200 2c brown, ultra & red .30 .25
Nos. 689-690,C191 (3) 1.35 .80

Intl. Book Year 1972.

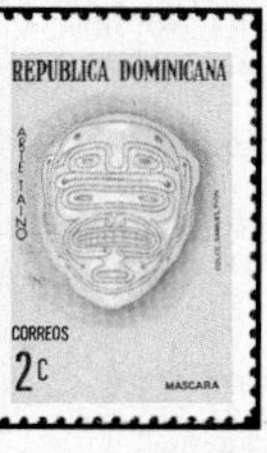

Taino Mask — A201

4c, Ladle and amulet. 6c, Human figure.

1972, May 10 Litho. *Perf. 11*

691 A201 2c pink & multi .50 .25
692 A201 4c black, bl & ocher .50 .25
693 A201 6c gray & multi .50 .25
Nos. 691-693,C194-C196 (6) 4.20 1.70

Taino art. See note after No. 651.

Globe A202

1972, May 17 *Perf. 12½*

694 A202 6c blue & multi .35 .25

4th World Telecommunications Day. See No. C197.

"1972," Stamps and Map of Dominican Republic A203

1972, June 3

695 A203 2c green & multi .30 .25

First National Philatelic Exhibition, Santo Domingo, June 3-17. See No. C198.

Basketball — A204

1972, Aug. 25 Litho. *Perf. 12½*

696 A204 2c blue & multi .30 .25

20th Olympic Games, Munich, Aug. 26-Sept. 11. See No. C199.

Club Emblem A205

1972, Sept. 29 Litho. *Perf. 10½*

697 A205 1c lt green & multi .30 .25

50th anniversary of the Club Activo 20-30 International. See No. C200.

Emilio A. Morel A206

1972, Oct. 20 *Perf. 12½*

698 A206 6c brt pink & multi .30 .25

Emilio A. Morel (1884-1958), poet and journalist. See No. C201.

Central Bank Building A207

1972, Oct. 23

699 A207 1c shown .30 .25

700 A207 5c 1-peso note .30 .25

Nos. 699-700,C202 (3) 1.85 1.05

25th anniv. of Central Bank.

Holy Family — A208

Poinsettia A209

1972, Nov. 21

701 A208 2c rose lil, pur & gold .30 .25

702 A209 6c red & multi .30 .25

Nos. 701-702,C203 (3) 1.55 .75

Christmas 1972.

Mail Box and Student A210

1972, Dec. 15

703 A210 2c rose red .30 .25

704 A210 6c blue .30 .25

705 A210 10c emerald .50 .25

Nos. 703-705 (3) 1.10 .75

Publicity for correspondence schools.

Tavera Dam A211

1973, Feb. 26 Litho. *Perf. 12½*

706 A211 10c multicolored .45 .25

Inauguration of the Tavera Dam.

Various Sports — A212

Designs: a, UL. b, UR. c, LL. d, LR.

1973, Mar. 30 *Perf. 13½x13*

707 A212 Block of 4 1.00 1.00

a.-d. 2c, any single .30 .25

708 A212 Block of 4 5.50 5.50

a.-d. 25c, any single 1.00 .35

Nos. 707-708,C204-C205 (4) 11.00 11.00

12th Central American and Caribbean Games, Santo Domingo, Summer 1974.

Christ Carrying the Cross A213

6c, Belfry of Church of Our Lady of Carmen.

1973, Apr. 18 Litho. *Perf. 10½*

709 A213 2c multicolored .30 .25

710 A213 6c multicolored, vert. .30 .25

Nos. 709-710,C206 (3) 1.35 .75

Holy Week, 1973.

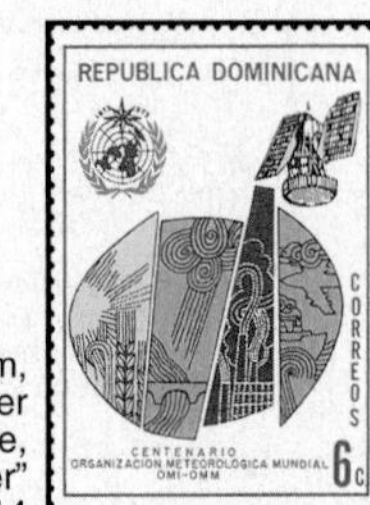

WMO Emblem, Weather Satellite, "Weather" A214

1973, Aug. 10 Litho. *Perf. 13½x13*

711 A214 6c magenta & multi .35 .25

Centenary of international meteorological cooperation. See No. C208.

Mask, Cibao — A215

1973, Oct. 12 Litho. *Perf. 10½*

712 A215 1c Maguey drum, horiz .40 .25

713 A215 2c Carved amber, horiz .40 .25

714 A215 4c shown .40 .25

715 A215 6c Pottery .40 .25

Nos. 712-715,C210-C211 (6) 3.35 1.50

Opening of Museum of Mankind in Santo Domingo.

Nativity A216

Christmas: 6c, Stained glass window, vert.

Perf. 13½x13, 13x13½

1973, Nov. 26

716 A216 2c black, bl & yel .35 .25

717 A216 6c rose & multi .35 .25

Nos. 716-717,C212 (3) 1.20 .75

No. 717 exists imperf.

Dominican Scout Emblem A217

Design: 5c, Scouts and flag.

1973, Dec. 7 Litho. *Perf. 12*

Size: 35x35mm

718 A217 1c ultra & multi .35 .25

Size: 26x36mm

719 A217 5c black & multi .35 .25

Nos. 718-719,C213 (3) 1.95 1.25

Dominican Republic Boy Scouts, 50th anniv.

Sports Palace, Basketball Players A218

Design: 6c, Bicyclist and race track.

1974, Feb. 25 Litho. *Perf. 13½*

720 A218 2c red brown & multi .30 .25

721 A218 6c yellow & multi .30 .25

Nos. 720-721,C214-C215 (4) 2.00 1.00

12th Central American and Caribbean Games, Santo Domingo, 1974.

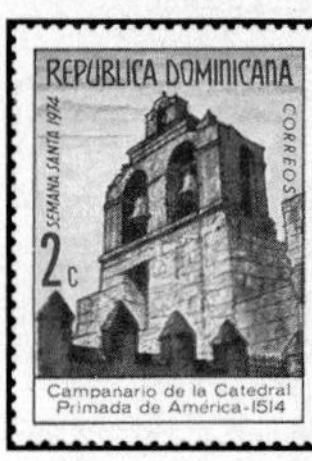

Bell Tower, Cathedral of Santo Domingo — A219

Mater Dolorosa — A220

1974, June 27 Litho. *Perf. 13½*

722 A219 2c multicolored .30 .25

723 A220 6c multicolored .40 .25

Nos. 722-723,C216 (3) 1.35 .75

Holy Week 1974.

Francisco del Rosario Sanchez Bridge — A221

1974, July 12 *Perf. 12*

724 A221 6c multicolored .45 .25

See No. C217.

Map, Emblem and Patient — A222

Design: 5c, Map of Dominican Republic, diabetics' emblem and pancreas.

1974, Aug. 22 Litho. *Perf. 13*

725 A222 4c blue & multi .30 .25

726 A222 5c yellow grn & multi .30 .25

Nos. 725-726,C218-C219 (4) 3.05 1.50

Fight against diabetes.

Train and UPU Emblem A223

Design: 6c, Mail coach and UPU emblem.

1974, Oct. 9 Litho. *Perf. 13½*

727 A223 2c blue & multi .60 .60

728 A223 6c brown & multi .45 .25

Nos. 727-728,C220-C221 (4) 5.55 1.95

Cent. of UPU.

Golfers — A224

Design: 2c, Championship emblem and badge of Dominican Golf Association, horiz.

1974, Oct. 24 ***Perf. 13x13½, 13½x13***

729 A224 2c yellow & blk *1.00* .25
730 A224 6c blue & multi *1.25* .25
Nos. 729-730,C222-C223 (4) 3.55 1.15

World Amateur Golf Championships.

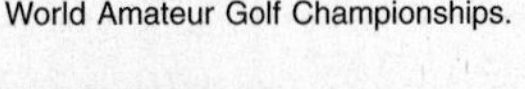

Christmas Decorations A225

Virgin and Child — A226

1974, Dec. 3 **Litho.** ***Perf. 12***

731 A225 2c multicolored .30 .25
732 A226 6c multicolored .40 .25
Nos. 731-732,C224 (3) 1.20 .75

Christmas 1974.

Tomatoes, FAO Emblem — A227

1974, Dec. 5

733 A227 2c shown 1.00 .25
734 A227 3c Avocados 1.00 .25
735 A227 5c Coconuts 1.00 .25
Nos. 733-735,C225 (4) 4.75 1.00

World Food Program, 10th anniv.

Dr. Fernando A. Defillo (1874-1949), Physician — A228

1975, Feb. 14 **Litho.** ***Perf. 13½x13***

736 A228 1c dull brown .40 .25
737 A228 6c dull green .40 .25

Tower, Our Lady of the Rosary Convent — A229

Design: 2c, Jesus saying "I am the Resurrection and the Life."

1975, Mar. 26 **Litho.** ***Perf. 13½***

738 A229 2c brown & multi .30 .25
739 A229 6c multicolored .30 .25
Nos. 738-739,C226 (3) 1.25 .75

Holy Week 1975.

Hands (Steel Beams) with Symbols of Agriculture, Industry A230

1975, May 19 **Litho.** ***Perf. 10½x10***

740 A230 6c dull blue & multi .35 .25

16th Assembly of the Governors of the International Development Bank, Santo Domingo, May 1975. See No. C228.

Satellite Tracking Station — A231

1975, June 21 **Litho.** ***Perf. 13½***

741 A231 5c multicolored .30 .25

Opening of first earth satellite tracking station in Dominican Republic. See No. C229.

Apollo A232

1975, July 24 **Size: 35x25mm**

742 A232 1c shown .30 .25
743 A232 4c Soyuz .30 .25
Nos. 742-743,C230 (3) 6.60 4.50

Apollo Soyuz space test project (Russo-American cooperation), launching July 15; link-up, July 17.

Father Rafael C. Castellanos A233

1975, Aug. 6 **Litho.** ***Perf. 12***

744 A233 6c brown & buff .45 .25

Castellanos (1875-1934), 1st Apostolic Administrator in Dominican Republic.

Women and Men Around IWY Emblem — A234

1975, Aug. 6 ***Perf. 13***

745 A234 3c orange & multi .45 .25

International Women's Year 1975.

Guacanagarix A235

Indian Chiefs: 2c, Guarionex. 3c, Caonabo. 4c, Bohechio. 5c, Cayacoa. 6c, Anacona (woman). 9c, Hatuey.

1975, Sept. 27 **Litho.** ***Perf. 12***

746 A235 1c yellow & multi .60 .25
747 A235 2c salmon & multi .60 .25
748 A235 3c violet bl & multi .60 .25
749 A235 4c green & multi .60 .25
750 A235 5c blue & multi .60 .25
751 A235 6c violet & multi .60 .25
752 A235 9c rose & multi 1.00 .25
Nos. 746-752,C231-C233 (10) 7.10 2.60

Basketball A236

Design: 6c, Baseball and Games' emblem.

1975, Oct. 24 **Litho.** ***Perf. 12***

753 A236 2c pink & multi .50 .25
754 A236 6c orange & multi .50 .25
Nos. 753-754,C234-C235 (4) 3.00 1.05

7th Pan-American Games, Mexico City, Oct. 13-26.

Carolers — A237

6c, Dominican nativity with farmers & shepherds.

1975, Dec. 12 **Litho.** ***Perf. 13x13½***

755 A237 2c yellow & multi .40 .25
756 A237 6c blue & multi .40 .25
Nos. 755-756,C236 (3) 1.40 .75

Christmas 1975.

Abudefdul Marginatus — A238

1976, Jan. 23 **Litho.** ***Perf. 13***

757 A238 10c shown .75 .25
758 A238 10c Doncella .75 .25
759 A238 10c Carajuelo .75 .25
760 A238 10c Reina de los Angeles .75 .25
761 A238 10c Pargo Colorado .75 .25
a. Strip of 5, #757-761 7.00 7.00

Ascension, by J. Priego — A239

2c, Mary Magdalene, by Enrique Godoy.

1976, Apr. 14 **Litho.** ***Perf. 13½***

762 A239 2c blue & multi .40 .25
763 A239 6c yellow & multi .40 .25
Nos. 762-763,C238 (3) 1.55 .80

Holy Week 1976.

"Separacion Dominicana" and Adm. Cambiaso A240

1976, Apr. 15 ***Perf. 13½x13***

764 A240 20c multicolored 1.25 .45

Naval Battle off Tortuga, Apr. 15, 1844.

Maps of US and Dominican Republic — A241

Design: 9c, Maps within cogwheels.

1976, May 29 **Litho.** ***Perf. 13½***

765 A241 6c violet bl & multi .40 .25
766 A241 9c violet bl & multi .40 .25
Nos. 765-766,C239-C240 (4) 3.15 2.00

American Bicentennial.

Flags of Dominican Republic and Spain A242

1976, May 31

767 A242 6c multicolored .65 .25

Visit of King Juan Carlos I and Queen Sofia of Spain. See No. C241.

Various Telephones A243

1976, July 15 ***Perf. 12x12½***

768 A243 6c multicolored .40 .25

Cent. of 1st telephone call by Alexander Graham Bell, Mar. 10, 1876. See No. C242.

Vision of Duarte, by Luis Desangles — A244

Juan Pablo Duarte, by Rhadames Mejia — A245

1976, July 20 Litho. ***Perf. 13x13½***

769 A244 2c multicolored .30 .25

Perf. 13½

770 A245 6c multicolored .30 .25
Nos. 769-770,C243-C244 (4) 3.25 1.85

Juan Pablo Duarte, liberation hero, death centenary.

Fire Hydrant — A246

Design: 6c, Firemen's emblem.

1976, Sept. 13 Litho. ***Perf. 12***

771 A246 4c multicolored .50 .25
772 A246 6c multicolored .50 .25
Nos. 771-772,C245 (3) 4.50 .80

Honoring firemen. Nos. 771-772 inscribed "Corrreos."

Radio and Atom Symbols A247

1976, Oct. 8 Litho. ***Perf. 13½***

773 A247 6c red & black .40 .25

Dominican Radio Club, 50th anniv. See No. C246.

Spain, Central and South America, Galleon A248

1976, Oct. 22 Litho. ***Perf. 13½***

774 A248 6c multicolored .40 .25

Spanish heritage. See No. C247.

Boxing and Montreal Emblem A249

Design: 3c, Weight lifting.

1976, Oct. 22 ***Perf. 12***

775 A249 2c blue & multi .40 .25
776 A249 3c multicolored .40 .25
Nos. 775-776,C248-C249 (4) 2.90 1.50

21st Olympic Games, Montreal, Canada, July 17-Aug. 1.

Virgin and Child — A250

Three Kings — A251

1976, Dec. 8 Litho. ***Perf. 13½***

777 A250 2c multicolored .40 .25
778 A251 6c multicolored .40 .25
Nos. 777-778,C250 (3) 1.55 .80

Christmas 1976.

Cable Car and Beach Scenes A252

1977, Jan. 7

779 A252 6c multicolored .40 .25
Nos. 779,C251-C253 (4) 2.35 1.20

Tourist publicity.

Championship Emblem — A253

1977, Mar. 4 Litho. ***Perf. 13½***

780 A253 3c rose & multi .40 .25
781 A253 5c yellow & multi .40 .25
Nos. 780-781,C254-C255 (4) 2.90 1.50

10th Central American and Caribbean Children's and Young People's Swimming Championships, Santo Domingo.

Christ Carrying Cross — A254

Design: 6c, Head with crown of thorns.

1977, Apr. 18 Litho. ***Perf. 13½x13***

782 A254 2c multicolored .40 .25
783 A254 6c black & rose .40 .25
Nos. 782-783,C256 (3) 1.55 .75

Holy Week 1977.

Doves, Lions Emblem A255

1977, May 6 ***Perf. 13½x13***

784 A255 2c lt blue & multi .40 .25
785 A255 6c salmon & multi .40 .25
Nos. 784-785,C257 (3) 1.40 .75

12th annual Dominican Republic Lions Convention.

Battle Scene A256

1977, June 15 Litho. ***Perf. 13x13½***

786 A256 20c multicolored 1.20 .35

Dominican Navy.

Water Lily — A257

National Botanical Garden: 4c, "Flor de Mayo" (orchid). 6c, Sebesten.

1977, Aug. 19 Litho. ***Perf. 12***

787 A257 2c multicolored .50 .25
788 A257 4c multicolored .50 .25
789 A257 6c multicolored .60 .25
Nos. 787-789,C259-C260 (5) 5.10 2.10

Chart and Computers — A258

1977, Nov. 30 Litho. ***Perf. 13***

790 A258 6c multicolored .40 .25

7th Interamerican Statistics Conf. See No. C261.

Solenodon Paradoxus — A259

Design: 20c, Iguana and Congress emblem.

1977, Dec. 29 Litho. ***Perf. 13***

791 A259 6c multicolored 2.50 .25
792 A259 20c multicolored 4.25 .30
Nos. 791-792,C262-C263 (4) 14.75 1.35

8th Pan-American Veterinary and Zoo-technical Congress.

Main Gate, Casa del Cordon, 1503 — A260

1978, Jan. 19 ***Perf. 13x13½***

Size: 26x36mm

793 A260 6c multicolored .40 .25

Spanish heritage. See No. C264.

Crown of Thorns, Tools at the Cross — A261

6c, Head of Jesus with crown of thorns.

Size: 22x33mm

1978, Mar. 21 Litho. ***Perf. 12***

794 A261 2c multicolored .40 .25
795 A261 6c slate .40 .25
Nos. 794-795,C265-C266 (4) 2.30 1.05

Holy Week 1978.

Cardinal Octavio A. Beras Rojas — A262

1978, May 5 Litho. ***Perf. 13***

796 A262 6c multicolored .40 .25

First Cardinal from Dominican Republic, consecrated May 24, 1976. See No. C268.

Pres. Manuel de Troncoso — A263

1978, June 12 Litho. ***Perf. 13½***

797 A263 2c black, rose & brn .40 .25
798 A263 6c black, gray & brn .60 .25

Manuel de Jesus Troncoso de la Concha (1878-1955), pres. of Dominican Republic, 1940-42.

Father Juan N. Zegri y Moreno — A264

1978, July 11 Litho. ***Perf. 13x13½***
799 A264 6c multicolored .40 .25

Congregation of the Merciful Sisters of Charity, centenary. See No. C273.

Boxing and Games' Emblem A265

1978, July 21 ***Perf. 12***
800 A265 2c shown .50 .25
801 A265 6c Weight lifting .75 .25
Nos. 800-801,C274-C275 (4) 3.75 1.00

13th Central American & Caribbean Games, Medellin, Colombia.

Sun over Landscape A266

Design: 6c, Sun over beach and boat.

1978, Sept. 12 Litho. ***Perf. 12***
802 A266 2c multicolored .40 .25
803 A266 6c multicolored .40 .25
Nos. 802-803,C280-C281 (4) 2.35 1.00

Tourist publicity.

Ships of Columbus, Map of Dominican Republic — A267

1978, Oct. 12 Litho. ***Perf. 13½***
804 A267 2c multicolored .40 .25

Spanish heritage. See No. C282.

Dove, Lamp, Poinsettia A268

Design: 6c, Dominican family and star, vert.

1978, Dec. 5 Litho. ***Perf. 12***
805 A268 2c multicolored .40 .25
806 A268 6c multicolored .50 .25
Nos. 805-806,C284 (3) 1.65 .80

Christmas 1978.

Starving Child, IYC Emblem — A269

1979, Feb. 26 Litho. ***Perf. 12***
807 A269 2c orange & black .40 .25
Nos. 807,C287-C289 (4) 3.15 1.85

Intl. Year of the Child.

Crucifixion A270

Design: 3c, Jesus carrying cross, horiz.

1979, Apr. 9 Litho. ***Perf. 13½***
808 A270 2c multicolored .40 .25
809 A270 3c multicolored .60 .25
Nos. 808-809,C290 (3) 5.00 1.75

Holy Week.

Stigmaphyllon Periplocifolium — A271

1979, May 17 Litho. ***Perf. 12***
810 A271 50c multicolored 2.00 .50
Nos. 810,C293-C295 (4) 7.00 1.80

Dr. Rafael M. Moscoso National Botanical Garden.

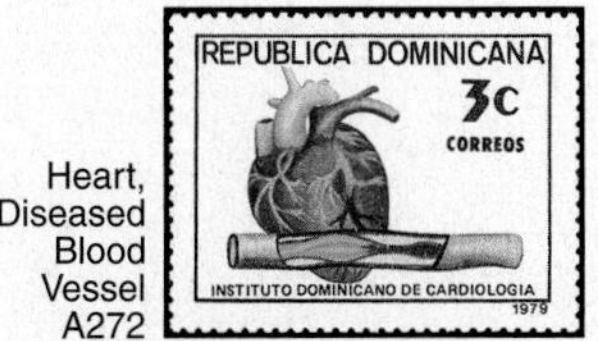

Heart, Diseased Blood Vessel A272

Design: 1p, Cardiology Institute and heart.

1979, June 2 Litho. ***Perf. 13½***
811 A272 3c multicolored .40 .25
812 A272 1p multicolored 2.75 .75
Nos. 811-812,C296 (3) 3.90 1.40

Dominican Cardiology Institute.

Baseball, Games' Emblem A273

3c, Bicycling and Games' emblem, vert.

1979, June 20
813 A273 2c multicolored .40 .25
814 A273 3c multicolored .40 .25
Nos. 813-814,C297 (3) 2.30 .80

8th Pan American Games, Puerto Rico, June 30-July 15.

Soccer — A274

Design: 25c, Swimming, horiz.

1979, Aug. 9 Litho. ***Perf. 12***
815 A274 2c multicolored .40 .25
816 A274 25c multicolored .50 .25
Nos. 815-816,C298 (3) 1.55 .80

Third National Games.

Thomas A. Edison — A275

1979, Aug. 27 ***Perf. 13½***
817 A275 25c multicolored 1.00 .45

Cent. of invention of electric light. See No. C300.

Hand Holding Electric Plug A276

Design: 6c, Filling automobile gas tank.

1979, Aug. 30
818 A276 2c multicolored .40 .25
819 A276 6c multicolored .50 .25

Energy conservation.

Parrot A277

Birds: 6c, Temnotrogon roseigaster.

1979, Sept. 12 Litho. ***Perf. 12***
820 A277 2c multicolored 2.10 .25
821 A277 6c multicolored 2.10 .25
Nos. 820-821,C301-C303 (5) 20.20 2.10

A278

Lions Emblem, Map of Dominican Republic.

1979, Nov. 13 Litho. ***Perf. 12***
822 A278 20c multicolored .75 .40

Lions International Club of Dominican Republic, 15th anniversary. See No. C304.

Christmas A279

1979, Dec. 18 Litho. ***Perf. 12***
823 A279 2c Holy Family .40 .25

See No. C305.

Holy Week — A280

Design: Jesus Carrying Cross.

1980, Mar. 27 Litho. ***Perf. 12***
824 A280 3c multicolored .40 .25
Nos. 824,C306-C307 (3) 1.55 .80

A281

1980, May 15 Litho. ***Perf. 13½***
825 A281 1c shown .60 .25
826 A281 2c Coffee .60 .25
827 A281 3c Plantain .60 .25
828 A281 4c Sugar cane .60 .25
829 A281 5c Corn .60 .25
Nos. 825-829 (5) 3.00 1.25

Cacao Harvest (Agriculture Year)

Cotuf Gold Mine, Pueblo Viejo, Flag of Dominican Republic A282

1980, July 8 Litho. ***Perf. 13½***
830 A282 6c multicolored .40 .25
Nos. 830,C310-C311 (3) 2.40 1.15

Nationalization of gold mining.

Blind Man's Buff A283

1980, July 21 ***Perf. 12***
831 A283 3c shown .40 .25
832 A283 4c Marbles .40 .25
833 A283 5c Drawing in sand .50 .25
834 A283 6c Hopscotch .50 .25
Nos. 831-834 (4) 1.80 1.00

Iguana A284

1980, Aug. 30 **Litho.** ***Perf. 12***
835 A284 20c multicolored 2.75 .45
Nos. 835,C314-C317 (5) 16.15 2.80

Dance, by Jaime Colson
A285

50c, *Woman, by Gilberto Hernandez Ortega*, vert.

Perf. 13x13½, 13½x13
1980, Sept. 23 **Litho.**
836 A285 3c shown .40 .25
837 A285 50c multicolored 1.50 .90
Nos. 836-837,C318-C319 (4) 3.40 2.00

Three Kings — A286

1980, Dec. 5 **Litho.** ***Perf. 13½***
838 A286 3c shown .40 .25
839 A286 6c Carolers .40 .25
Nos. 838-839,C327 (3) 1.45 .80

Christmas 1980.

Salcedo Province Cent. — A287

1981, Jan. 14 **Litho.** ***Perf. 13½***
840 A287 6c multicolored .40 .25

See No. C328.

Juan Pablo Duarte, Liberation Hero, 105th Anniv. of Death — A288

1981, Feb. 6 **Litho.** ***Perf. 12***
841 A288 2c sepia & deep bister .60 .25

Gymnast — A289

1981, Mar. 31 **Litho.** ***Perf. 13½***
842 A289 1c shown .50 .25
843 A289 2c Running .50 .25
844 A289 3c Pole vault .50 .25
845 A289 6c Boxing 1.00 .25
Nos. 842-845,C331 (5) 5.00 1.35

5th National Games.

Mother Mazzarello
A290

1981, Apr. 14 ***Perf. 12***
846 A290 6c multicolored .45 .25

Mother Maria Mazzarello (1837-1881), founder of Daughters of Mary.

A291

1981, May 18 **Litho.** ***Perf. 13½***
847 A291 6c gray vio & lt gray .45 .25

Pedro Henriquez Urena, Historian (1884-1946)

Forest Conservation
A292

1981, June 30 **Litho.** ***Perf. 12***
848 A292 2c shown .45 .25
849 A292 6c River, forest .45 .25

Family in House, Census Emblem
A293

1981, Aug. 14 **Litho.** ***Perf. 12***
850 A293 3c shown .45 .25
851 A293 6c Farmer .45 .25

1981 natl. population and housing census.

Christmas
A294

1981, Dec. 23 **Litho.** ***Perf. 13½***
852 A294 2c Bells .45 .25
853 A294 3c Poinsettia .45 .25
Nos. 852-853,C353 (3) 1.80 .95

A295

1982, Jan. 29 **Litho.** ***Perf. 13½***
854 A295 2c Juan Pablo Duarte .80 .25

National Elections
A296

Designs: Voters casting votes. 3c, 6c vert.

1982, Mar. 30 **Litho.** ***Perf. 13½***
855 A296 2c multicolored .40 .25
856 A296 3c multicolored .40 .25
857 A296 6c multicolored .50 .25
Nos. 855-857 (3) 1.30 .75

A297

Energy Conservation: Various forms of energy.

1982, May 10 **Litho.** ***Perf. 12***
858 A297 1c multicolored .40 .25
859 A297 2c multicolored .40 .25
860 A297 3c multicolored .40 .25
861 A297 4c multicolored .50 .25
862 A297 5c multicolored .50 .25
863 A297 6c multicolored .50 .25
Nos. 858-863 (6) 2.70 1.50

A298

1982, Aug. 2 ***Perf. 12x12½***
864 A298 6c multicolored .40 .25

Emilio Prud'Homme (1856-1932), composer.

Pres. Antonio Guzman Fernandez (1911-1982)
A299

1982, Aug. 4 ***Perf. 13x13½***
865 A299 6c multicolored .40 .25

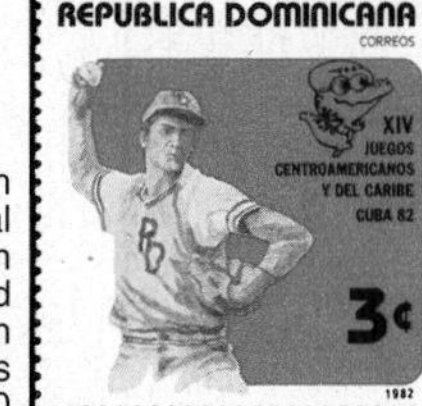

14th Central American and Caribbean Games
A300

1982, Aug. 13 ***Perf. 12, Imperf.***
866 A300 3c Baseball 1.00 .25

See Nos. C368-C370.

San Pedro de Macoris Province Centenary — A301

Designs: 1c, Wagon. 2c, Stained-glass window. 5c, Views.

1982, Aug. 26 ***Perf. 13***
867 A301 1c multicolored .40 .25
868 A301 2c multicolored .40 .25
869 A301 5c multicolored .50 .25
Nos. 867-869,C375 (4) 2.05 1.05

Size of 2c, 25x35mm.

St. Teresa of Jesus of Avila (1515-1582)
A302

1982, Nov. 17 **Litho.** ***Perf. 13½***
870 A302 6c multicolored .60 .25

Christmas 1982 — A303

Various Christmas balls.

1982, Dec. 8
871 A303 6c multicolored 1.10 .25

See No. C380.

Environmental Protection
A304

1982, Dec. 15 ***Perf. 12***
872 A304 2c Bird .40 .25
873 A304 3c Water .40 .25
874 A304 6c Forest .40 .25
875 A304 20c Fish 1.25 .35
Nos. 872-875 (4) 2.45 1.10

Natl. Literacy Campaign A305

Designs: 2c, Vowels on blackboard. 3c, Writing, reading. 6c, Children, pencil.

1983, Mar. 9 Litho. *Perf. 13½*

876 A305 2c multicolored .40 .25
877 A305 3c multicolored .40 .25
878 A305 6c multicolored .50 .25
Nos. 876-878 (3) 1.30 .75

A306

5c, similar arms, incorporating stylized centenary monument.

1983, Apr. 4 *Perf. 12*

879 A306 1c multicolored .40 .25
880 A306 5c multicolored .50 .25

Mao City centenary.

A307

Dominican Historians: 2c, Antonio del Monte y Tejada (1780-1861). 3c, Manuel Ubaldo Gomez (1857-1941). 5c, Emiliano Tejera (1841-1923). 6c, Bernardo Pichardo (1877-1924). 7c, Americo Lugo (1870-1952). 10c, José Gabriel Garcia (1834-1910). 7c, 10c airmail.

1983, Apr. 25 Litho. *Perf. 12*

881 A307 2c multicolored .40 .25
882 A307 3c multicolored .40 .25
883 A307 5c multicolored .40 .25
884 A307 6c multicolored .40 .25
885 A307 7c multicolored .50 .25
886 A307 10c multicolored .75 .30
Nos. 881-886 (6) 2.85 1.55

National Anthem, 100th Anniv. A308

Emilio Prud'Homme, & Jose Reyes, composer.

1983, Sept. 13 Litho. *Perf. 13½*

887 A308 6c copper red & blk .45 .25

Free Masons, 125th Anniv. — A309

1983, Oct. 24 Litho. *Perf. 12*

888 A309 4c Emblem .45 .25

Church of Our Lady of Regla, 300th Anniv. — A310

1983, Nov. 5 *Perf. 13½*

889 A310 3c Church .40 .25
890 A310 6c Statue .50 .25

450th Anniv. of Monte Cristi Province — A311

Designs: 1c, Tower. 2c, Arms. 5c, Cuban independence site, horiz. 7c, Workers, horiz.

1983, Nov. 25 *Perf. 12*

891 A311 1c dark grn & blk .45 .25
892 A311 2c multicolored .45 .25
893 A311 5c gray .45 .25
894 A311 7c gray & blue .45 .25
Nos. 891-894 (4) 1.80 1.00

6th Natl. Games — A312

6c, Bicycling, boxing, baseball. 10c, Runner, weight lifting, swimming.

1983, Dec. 9

895 A312 6c multicolored .40 .25
896 A312 10c multicolored .65 .25

10c airmail.

Restoration of the Republic, 120th Anniv. — A313

Design: 1c, Capotillo Heroes Monument.

1983, Dec. 30 Litho. *Perf. 13½*

897 A313 1c multicolored .45 .25

140th Anniv. of Independence — A314

Designs: 6c, Matia Ramon Mella (Patriot), flag. 25c, Mella's Blunderbuss rifle, Gate of Deliverance (independence declaration site).

1984, Feb. 24 Litho. *Perf. 13½*

898 A314 6c multicolored .40 .25
899 A314 25c multicolored 1.00 .35

Heriberto Pieter (1884-1972), Physician, First Negro Graduate — A315

1984, Mar. 16

900 A315 3c multicolored .45 .25

Battle of Barranquita, 67th Anniv. — A316

1983, Dec. 30 *Perf. 12*

901 A316 5c multicolored .45 .25

Battle of Santiago, 140th Anniv. A317

1984, Mar. 29 *Perf. 13½*

902 A317 7c multicolored .45 .25

Coast Guard Ship DC-1, 1934 A318

1984, Apr. 13 Litho.

903 A318 10c multicolored .65 .25

Navy Day and 140th anniv. of Battle of Tortuguero.

Birth Centenary of Pedro Henriquez Urena — A319

Designs: 7c, Salome Urena. 10, Poem "Mi Pedro." 22c, Pedro Henriquez Urena.

1984, June 29 Litho. *Perf. 12*

904 A319 7c pink & brown .45 .25
905 A319 10c cream & chestnut .65 .25
906 A319 22c cream & brown .60 .25
Nos. 904-906 (3) 1.70 .75

Monument to Heroes of June 1959 A320

1984, June 20 *Perf. 13½*

907 A320 6c silver & blue .60 .25

Costal towns of Constanza, Maimon and Estero Hondo - sites of attempted overthrow of Rafael Trujillo, 25th anniv.

1984 Summer Olympics A321

1984, Aug. 1

908 A321 1p Hurdles 2.50 1.90
909 A321 1p Weightlifting 2.50 1.90
910 A321 1p Boxing 2.50 1.90
911 A321 1p Baseball 2.50 1.90
a. Block of 4, #908-911 18.00 18.00
Nos. 908-911 (4) 10.00 7.60

Protection of Fauna — A322

1984, Oct. 3 Litho. *Perf. 12*

912 A322 10c Owl 3.50 .25
913 A322 15c Flamingo 4.00 .35
914 A322 25c Wild Pig 6.00 .50
915 A322 35c Solenodon 7.00 .70
Nos. 912-915 (4) 20.50 1.80

500th Anniv. of Discovery of America A323

10c, Landing on Hispaniola. 35c, Destruction of Ft. Navidad. 65c, First Mass in America. 1p, Battle of Santo Cerro.

1984, Oct. 10 Litho. *Perf. 13½x13*

916 A323 10c multicolored .45 .25
917 A323 35c multicolored .80 .35
918 A323 65c multicolored 1.50 .80
919 A323 1p multicolored 2.50 1.10
Nos. 916-919 (4) 5.25 2.50

Visit of Pope John Paul II — A324

1984, Oct. 11 Litho. *Perf. 13x13½*

920 Block of 4 9.00 9.00
a. A324 75c shown 1.90 1.90
b. A324 75c Pope, map of Caribbean 1.90 1.90
c. A324 75c Pope, globe 1.90 1.90
d. A324 75c Bishop's crozier 1.90 1.90

150th Anniv. of Birth of Maximo Gomez (1986) A325

10c, Gomez on horseback. 20c, Maximo Gomez.

1984, Dec. 6 Litho. *Perf. 13½*

No.	Type	Description	Unused	Used
921	A325	10c multicolored	.45	.25
922	A325	20c multicolored	.55	.25

Christmas 1984 A326

Perf. 13½x13, 13x13½

1984, Dec. 14 Litho.

No.	Type	Description	Unused	Used
923	A326	5c multicolored	.40	.25
924	A326	10c multicolored, vert.	.50	.25

Sacrifice of the Goat, by Eligio Pichardo A327

Paintings and sculpture: 10c, The Pumpkin Sellers, by Gaspar Mario Cruz; 25c, The Market, by Celeste Woss y Gil; 50c, Horses in the Rain, by Dario Suro.

1984, Dec. 19 Litho. *Perf. 13½*

No.	Type	Description	Unused	Used
925	A327	5c multi	.50	.25
926	A327	10c multi, vert.	.50	.25
927	A327	25c multi	.85	.45
928	A327	50c multi	1.50	.65
		Nos. 925-928 (4)	3.35	1.60

Day of Our Lady of Altagracia A328

5c, Old church at Higuey, 1572. 10c, Our Lady of Altagracia 1514, vert. 25c, Basilica of the Protector, Higuey 1971, vert.

1985, Jan. 21

No.	Type	Description	Unused	Used
929	A328	5c multicolored	.40	.25
930	A328	10c multicolored	.50	.25
931	A328	25c multicolored	.75	.35
		Nos. 929-931 (3)	1.65	.85

Independence, 141st Anniv. — A329

Painting: The Fathers of Our Country (Duarte, Sanchez and Mella).

1985, Mar. 8 *Perf. 12½*

No.	Type	Description	Unused	Used
932	A329	5c multicolored	.40	.25
933	A329	10c multicolored	.45	.25
934	A329	25c multicolored	.70	.25
		Nos. 932-934 (3)	1.55	.75

Battle of Azua, 141st Anniv. A330

10c, Gen. Antonio Duverge, Statue.

1985, Apr. 8 Litho. *Perf. 13½*

No.	Type	Description	Unused	Used
935	A330	10c multicolored	.55	.25

Santo Domingo Lighthouse, 1853 — A331

1985, Apr. 15 Litho.

No.	Type	Description	Unused	Used
936	A331	25c multicolored	.85	.25

Battle of Tortuguero, 141st anniv.

A332

1985, Apr. 15 Litho. *Perf. 12*

No.	Type	Description	Unused	Used
937	A332	35c multicolored	1.10	.45

American Airforces Cooperation System, 25th anniv.

Espaillat Province Cent. — A333

10c, Don Carlos M. Rojas, 1st governor.

1985, May 24 Litho. *Perf. 13½*

No.	Type	Description	Unused	Used
938	A333	10c multicolored	.55	.30

A334

1985, July 5 Litho. *Perf. 12*

No.	Type	Description	Unused	Used
939	A334	5c Table tennis	.40	.25
940	A334	10c Walking race	.50	.30

MOCA '85, 7th Natl. Games.

Intl. Youth Year A335

1985, July 29 *Perf. 13½*

No.	Type	Description	Unused	Used
941	A335	5c Youth	.35	.25
942	A335	25c The Haitises	1.10	.45
943	A335	35c Mt. Duarte summit	1.25	.50
944	A335	2p Mt. Duarte	7.25	2.75
		Nos. 941-944 (4)	9.95	3.95

Interamerican Development Bank, 25th Anniv. — A336

10c, Haina Harbor. 25c, Map of development sites. 1p, Tavera-Bao-Lopez Hydroelectric Complex.

1985, Aug. 23

No.	Type	Description	Unused	Used
945	A336	10c multicolored	.40	.25
946	A336	25c multicolored	.85	.40
947	A336	1p multicolored	2.75	1.75
		Nos. 945-947 (3)	4.00	2.40

Intl. Decade for Women — A337

Design: Evangelina Rodriguez (1879-1947), first Dominican woman doctor.

1985, Sept. 26

No.	Type	Description	Unused	Used
948	A337	10c multicolored	.55	.25

15th Central American and Caribbean Games, Santiago — A338

1985, Oct. 9 *Perf. 12*

No.	Type	Description	Unused	Used
949	A338	5c multicolored	.50	.25
950	A338	25c multicolored	1.40	.45

4th Adm. Christopher Columbus Regatta, Casa de Espana A339

Designs: 50c, Founding of Santo Domingo, 1496. 65c, Chapel of Our Lady of the Rosary, 1496, Santo Domingo. 1p, Columbus, American Indian and old Spanish coat of arms.

1985, Oct. 10 *Perf. 13½*

No.	Type	Description	Unused	Used
951	A339	35c multicolored	1.40	.85
952	A339	50c multicolored	1.80	1.20
953	A339	65c multicolored	2.50	1.50
954	A339	1p multicolored	4.50	2.40
		Nos. 951-954 (4)	10.20	5.95

Discovery of America, 500th anniv. (in 1992).

Cacique Enriquillo — A340

Designs: 5c, Enriquillo in the Bahuroco Mountains, mural detail.

1985, Oct. 31

No.	Type	Description	Unused	Used
955	A340	5c multicolored	.50	.25
956	A340	10c multicolored	.75	.25

Enriquillo (d. 1536), leader of revolution against Spain. Size of No. 955: 47x33mm.

Archbishop Fernando Arturo de Merino — A341

1985, Dec. 3 *Perf. 12*

No.	Type	Description	Unused	Used
957	A341	25c multicolored	.75	.40

Cent. of holy orders granted to Merino (1833-1906), pres. of the republic 1880-82.

Mirabal Sisters, Political Martyrs 1960 A342

1985, Dec. 18 *Perf. 13½*

No.	Type	Description	Unused	Used
958	A342	10c multicolored	.50	.25

Christmas A343

1985, Dec. 18

No.	Type	Description	Unused	Used
959	A343	10c multicolored	.40	.25
960	A343	25c multicolored	.90	.35

Day of Independence, Feb. 27 — A344

Design: Mausoleum of founding fathers Duarte, Sanchez and Mella.

1986, Feb. 26 Litho. *Perf. 13½*

No.	Type	Description	Unused	Used
961	A344	5c multicolored	.40	.25
962	A344	10c multicolored	.50	.25

Holy Week A345

Colonial churches.

1986, Apr. 10

No.	Type	Description	Unused	Used
963	A345	5c San Miguel	.60	.25
964	A345	5c San Andres	.60	.25
965	A345	10c Santa Barbara	.65	.25
966	A345	10c San Lazaro	.65	.25
967	A345	10c San Carlos	.65	.25
		Nos. 963-967 (5)	3.15	1.25

Navy Day A346

Design: Juan Bautista Cambiaso, Juan Bautista Maggiolo and Juan Alejandro Acosta, 1844 independence battle heroes.

1986, Apr. 15

968	A346	10c multicolored	.60	.25

Natl. Elections — A347

1986, Apr. 29

969	A347	5c Voters, map	.45	.25
970	A347	10c Ballot box	.55	.25

Natl. Postal Institute Inauguration A348

1986, June 10

971	A348	10c gold, blue & red	.40	.25
972	A348	25c silver, blue & red	1.00	.30
973	A348	50c black, blue & red	1.75	.65
		Nos. 971-973 (3)	3.15	1.20

Central America and Caribbean Games, Santiago — A349

1986, July 17 Litho. *Perf. 13½*

974	A349	10c Weight lifting	.40	.25
975	A349	25c Gymnastics	.85	.30
976	A349	35c Diving	1.25	.45
977	A349	50c Equestrian	1.50	.70
		Nos. 974-977 (4)	4.00	1.70

Historians A350

Designs: 5c, Ercilia Pepin (b. 1886), vert. 10c, Ramon Emilio Jimenez (b. 1886) and Victor Garrido (1886-1972).

1986, Aug. 1 Litho. *Perf. 13½*

978	A350	5c silver & dull brn	.40	.25
979	A350	10c silver & dull brn	.55	.25

A351

A352

Discovery of America, 500th Anniv. (in 1992) — A353

Designs: 25c, Yachts racing, 5th Adm. Christopher Columbus Regatta, Casa de Espana. 50c, Columbus founding La Isabela City. 65c, Exploration of the hidalgos. 1p, Columbus returning to the Court of Ferdinand and Isabella. 1.50p, Emblems.

1986, Oct. 10 Litho. *Perf. 13½*

980	A351	25c multicolored	.75	.35
981	A352	50c multicolored	1.50	.55
982	A352	65c multicolored	2.00	.95
983	A352	1p multicolored	3.50	1.30

Textured Paper

Size: 86x58mm

Imperf

984	A353	1.50p multicolored	6.25	6.00
		Nos. 980-984 (5)	14.00	9.15

1986 World Cup Soccer Championships, Mexico — A354

Various soccer plays.

1986, Oct. 21 *Perf. 13½*

985	A354	50c multicolored	1.40	.65
986	A354	75c multicolored	3.00	1.10

Medicinal Plants — A355

5c, Zea mays. 10c, Bixa orellana. 25c, Momordica charantia. 50c, Annona muricata.

1986, Dec. 5

987	A355	5c multicolored	.40	.25
988	A355	10c multicolored	.45	.25
989	A355	25c multicolored	.75	.25
990	A355	50c multicolored	1.60	.55
		Nos. 987-990 (4)	3.20	1.30

Second Caribbean Pharmacopeia Seminar.

Christmas A356

1986, Dec. 19

991	A356	5c Urban scene	.50	.25
992	A356	25c Rural scene	1.50	.35

A357

1986, Dec. 31 Litho. *Perf. 13½*

993	A357	10c shown	.40	.25
994	A357	25c Portrait, c. 1900	1.00	.40

Maximo Gomez (1836-1905), revolutionary, statesman.

A358

1987, Mar. 30 Litho. *Perf. 13½*

995	A358	50c brt blue, blk & red	1.40	.65

16th Pan American Ophthalmological Conf., Apr. 5-10.

A359

Stained-glass window, San Juan Bosco church, Santo Domingo: Ascension of Christ to Heaven.

1987, May 28

996	A359	35c multicolored	1.50	.50

Edible Plants — A360

5c, Sorghum bicolor. 25c, Martanta arundinacea. 65c, Calathaea allouia. 1p, Voandzeia subterranea.

1987, Aug. 21

997	A360	5c multicolored	.25	.25
998	A360	25c multicolored	.60	.30
999	A360	65c multicolored	1.90	.95
1000	A360	1p multicolored	3.00	1.40
		Nos. 997-1000 (4)	5.75	2.90

Activo 20-30 Intl., 25th Anniv. A361

1987, Aug. 26

1001	A361	35c multicolored	1.75	.50

Adm. Christopher Columbus Regatta A362

A363

Columbus Memorial, Santo Domingo — A364

1p, Building Ft. Santiago. 1.50p, Columbus imprisoned by Bombadilla.

1987, Oct. 14

1002	A362	50c shown	1.50	.70
1003	A363	75c shown	2.25	1.00
1004	A363	1p multicolored	3.00	1.30
1005	A363	1.50p multicolored	4.50	2.00

Size: 82x70mm

Imperf

1006	A364	2.50p shown	10.00	6.50
		Nos. 1002-1006 (5)	21.25	11.50

Discovery of America, 500th anniv. in 1992.

A365

1987, Sept. 28

1007	A365	40c multicolored	1.20	.50

Junior Olympics, La Vega, 50th anniv.

A366

Historians and authors: 10c, Jose Antonio Hungria. 25c, Joaquin Sergio Inchaustegui.

1987, Nov. 10 Litho. *Perf. 13½*

1008	A366	10c buff & brown	.35	.25
1009	A366	25c pale grn & grn	.90	.25

SAN CRISTOBAL '87, 8th Natl. Games — A367

1987, Nov. 19

1010	A367	5c Baseball	.90	.25
1011	A367	10c Boxing	1.00	.25
1012	A367	50c Judo	3.00	.70
		Nos. 1010-1012 (3)	4.90	1.20

Christmas 1987 A368

1987, Dec. 9 Litho. *Perf. 13½*

1013	A368	10c Roasting pig	.55	.25
1014	A368	50c Arriving at airport	1.75	.60

Fr. Xavier Billini (b. 1837) — A369

10c, Statue. 25c, Portrait. 75c, Ana Hernandez de Billini, his mother.

1987, Dec. 18 Litho. *Perf. 13½*

1015	A369	10c blue gray & dark blue	.35	.25
1016	A369	25c cream & dark grn	.75	.35
1017	A369	75c pink & blkish pur	2.25	1.10
		Nos. 1015-1017 (3)	3.35	1.70

Frank Feliz, Sr., and Aircraft A370

1987, Dec. 22

1018	A370	25c shown	.80	.25

Size: 86x106mm

Imperf

1019	A370	2p No. C30, map	12.50	6.50

Pan-American goodwill flight to South American countries by the planes Colon, Pinta, Nina and Santa Maria, 50th anniv.

Flora A371

No. 1020, Bromelia pinguin. No. 1021, Tillandsia fasciculata. No. 1022, Tillandsia hotteana, vert. No. 1023, Tillandsia compacta, vert.

1988, Feb. 3 Litho. *Perf. 13½*

1020	A371	50c multi	2.10	.70
1021	A371	50c multi	2.10	.70
1022	A371	50c multi	2.10	.70
1023	A371	50c multi	2.10	.70
		Nos. 1020-1023 (4)	8.40	2.80

St. John Bosco (1815-1888) A372

1988, Feb. 23 Litho. *Perf. 13½*

1024	A372	10c shown	.45	.25
1025	A372	70c Stained-glass window	2.70	.95

Dominican Rehabilitation Assoc., 25th Anniv. — A373

1988, Mar. 1

1026	A373	20c multicolored	.75	.30

A374

1988, Apr. 6 Litho. *Perf. 13½*

1027	A374	20c dk red brn & lt fawn	.75	.30

Dr. Manuel Emilio Perdomo (b.1886).

A375

1988, Apr. 29 Litho. *Perf. 13½*

1028	A375	20c multicolored	.75	.30

Dominican College of Engineers, Architects and Surveyors (CODIA), 25th Anniv.

Independence Day, Mexico — A376

Flags and: No. 1029, Fr. Miguel Hidalgo y Costilla (1753-1811), Mexican revolutionary. No. 1030, Juan Pablo Duarte (1813-1876), father of Dominican independence.

1988, Sept. 12 Litho. *Perf. 13½*

1029	A376	50c multicolored	1.40	.65
1030	A376	50c multicolored	1.40	.65

1988 Summer Olympics, Seoul A377

50c, Running, vert. 70c, Table tennis, vert. 1p, Judo, vert. 1.50p, Mural by Tete Marella.

1988, Sept. 21 Litho. *Perf. 13½*

1031	A377	50c multicolored	1.10	.50
1032	A377	70c multicolored	1.60	.75
1033	A377	1p multicolored	2.50	.95
1034	A377	1.50p multicolored	3.75	1.50
		Nos. 1031-1034 (4)	8.95	3.70

A378

Discovery of America, 500th Anniv. (in 1992) — A379

Designs: 50c, 7th Adm. Christopher Columbus Regatta, Casa de Espana, 1988. 70c, La Concepcion Fortress, La Vega Real, 1494. 1.50p, Ft. Bonao. 2p, Nicolas de Ovando (c. 1451-1511), governor of Spanish possessions in America from 1502 to 1509. 3p, Mausoleum of Christopher Columbus, Santo Domingo Cathedral.

1988, Oct. 14 *Perf. 13½*

1035	A378	50c multicolored	1.10	.65
1036	A378	70c multicolored	1.75	.95
1037	A378	1.50p multicolored	3.50	1.90
1038	A378	2p multicolored	5.00	2.40

Size: 78x109mm

Imperf

1039	A379	3p multicolored	6.25	5.50
		Nos. 1035-1039 (5)	17.60	11.40

Discovery of America, 500th anniv. (in 1992). No. 1038 inscribed "1501-1509."

Duverge Parish, Cent. — A380

1988, July 13 Litho. *Perf. 13½*

1040	A380	50c multicolored	1.25	.40

A381

Trinitarians, 150th Anniv. — A382

Designs: 10c, Freedom fighters. 1p, Trinitarian Plaza. 5p, Independence Plaza.

1988, Nov. 11

1041	A381	10c red, blue, gray	.45	.25
1042	A382	1p multicolored	2.00	.45
1043	A382	5p multicolored	13.00	4.75
		Nos. 1041-1043 (3)	15.45	5.45

See footnote after No. 337.

Pharmacology and Biochemistry A383

1988, Nov. 28 Litho. *Perf. 13½*

1044	A383	1p multicolored	2.00	1.40

13th Pan American and 16th Central American Congresses.

The Holy Family, 1504, by Miguel Angel — A384

Design: 20c, Stained-glass window.

1988, Dec. 12

1045	A384	10c shown	.45	.25
1046	A384	20c multicolored	.75	.30

Christmas.

Municipal Technical Advisory Organization (LIGA), 50th Anniv. — A385

1988, Dec. 23

1047	A385	20c multicolored	.75	.35

Ana Teresa Paradas (1890-1960), 1st Female Lawyer of the Republic, 1913 — A386

1988, Dec. 26

1048	A386	20c deep claret	.75	.35

French Revolution Bicent. A387

1989, Mar. 10 Litho. *Perf. 13½*

1049	A387	3p red & violet blue	3.25	2.75

Battle of Tortuga, Apr. 15, 1844
A388

1989, Apr. 14 Litho. *Perf. 13½*

1050 A388 40c multicolored 1.10 .50

Natl. Anti-drug Campaign
A389

1989, May 15

1051	A389	10c multicolored	.30	.25
1052	A389	20c multicolored	.35	.25
1053	A389	50c multicolored	.65	.25
1054	A389	70c multicolored	.90	.30
1055	A389	1p multicolored	1.40	.45
1056	A389	1.50p multicolored	1.90	.50
1057	A389	2p multicolored	2.60	.70
1058	A389	5p multicolored	6.50	1.50
1059	A389	10p multicolored	12.50	3.75
		Nos. 1051-1059 (9)	27.10	7.95

Mother's Day
A390

1989, May 30 Litho. *Perf. 13½*

1060 A390 20c multicolored .70 .25

Eugenio Maria de Hostos (b. 1839) — A391

1989, Aug. 22 Litho. *Perf. 13½*

1061 A391 20c multicolored .70 .25

Gen. Gregorio Luperon (b. 1839) — A392

1989, Aug. 28

1062 A392 20c multicolored .70 .25

Little League Baseball, 50th Anniv.
A393

1989, Sept. 29

1063 A393 1p multicolored 1.75 1.00

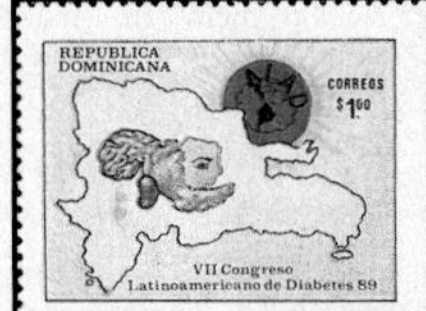

Diabetes '89, 7th Latin American Congress
A394

1989, Oct. 9 Litho. *Perf. 13½*

1064 A394 1p multicolored 1.75 .60

America Issue
A395

UPAE emblem, pre-Columbian artifacts and customs: 20c, Cohoba silver statue and ritual dance. 1p, Taina mortar, pestle and family preparing cazabe.

1989, Oct. 12

1065	A395	20c multicolored	.75	.25
1066	A395	1p multicolored	3.75	2.10

8th Adm. Christopher Columbus Regatta, Casa de Espana — A396

European Colonization of the Americas — A397

Designs: 70c, Fr. Pedro de Cordoba converting the Indians to Catholicism. 1p, Christopher Columbus trading with the Indians. 3p, Sermon of Pedro de Cordoba.

1989, Oct. 13

1067	A396	50c shown	.65	.30
1068	A397	70c shown	.85	.55
1069	A397	1p multicolored	1.75	.75
1070	A397	3p multicolored	3.25	2.10
		Nos. 1067-1070 (4)	6.50	3.70

Discovery of America, 500th anniv. (in 1992).

Natl. Afforestation
A398

Designs: 20c, Tree. 50c, Forest. 1p, Sapling, mature trees.

1989, Oct. 30 Litho. *Perf. 13½*

1071	A398	10c shown	.30	.25
1072	A398	20c multicolored	.35	.25
1073	A398	50c multicolored	1.10	.55
1074	A398	1p multicolored	2.25	1.20
		Nos. 1071-1074 (4)	4.00	2.25

9th Natl. Games, La Vega — A399

1990, Mar. 20 Litho. *Perf. 13½*

1075	A399	10c Cycling	.30	.25
1076	A399	20c Running	.45	.30
1077	A399	50c Basketball	1.40	.75
		Nos. 1075-1077 (3)	2.15	1.30

Holy Week (Easter) — A400

Design: 50c, Jesus carrying cross.

1990, Apr. 5

1078	A400	20c shown	.50	.30
1079	A400	50c multicolored	1.25	.75

Labor Day, Cent.
A401

1990, Apr. 30 Litho. *Perf. 13½*

1080 A401 1p multicolored 1.60 .65

Urban Renewal
A402

Designs: 20c, Highway underpass. 50c, Library. 1p, City street.

1990, May 10

1081	A402	10c shown	.30	.25
1082	A402	20c multi	.40	.25
1083	A402	50c multi	.85	.25
1084	A402	1p multi	2.00	.80
		Nos. 1081-1084 (4)	3.55	1.55

No. 1084 inscribed $100 instead of $1.00.

Penny Black, 150th Anniv. — A403

Design: 3p, Sir Rowland Hill, Penny Black.

1990, May 29

1085 A403 1p multicolored 2.25 1.60

Size: 62x80mm

Imperf

1086 A403 3p multi 6.25 6.25

A404

1990, Oct. 5 Litho. *Perf. 13½*

1087 A404 2p Flags 4.00 2.40

Organization of American States, Cent.

Children's Drawings
A405

No. 1088, House of Tostado. No. 1089, Ruins of St. Nicolas of Bari.

1990, Aug. 7

1088	A405	50c multicolored	1.25	.75
1089	A405	50c multicolored	1.25	.75

Discovery of America, 500th Anniv. (in 1992)
A406

Designs: 1p, Fight at the Gulf of Arrows. 2p, Columbus talking with Guacanagari Indians. 5p, Columbus and Caonabo Indian prisoner.

1990, Oct. 12

1090	A406	1p multicolored	2.25	1.40
1091	A406	2p multicolored	4.50	3.00
1092	A406	5p multicolored	11.00	7.50
		Nos. 1090-1092 (3)	17.75	11.90

9th Adm. Christopher Columbus Regatta — A407

1990, Oct. 12

1093 A407 50c multicolored 1.50 .70

America Issue
A408

UPAE emblem and: 50c, Men in canoe. 3p, Man on hammock.

1990, Nov. 7 Litho. *Perf. 13½*

1094	A408	50c multicolored	1.90	.70
1095	A408	3p multicolored	8.00	4.75

A409

Discovery of Hispaniola: 50c, 1st official mass in Americas. 1p, Arms of 1st religious order in Americas. 3p, Map of island, horiz. 4p, Christopher Columbus, 1st viceroy and governor in Americas.

1991, July 17 Litho. *Perf. 13½*

1096 A409 50c multicolored .90 .55
1097 A409 1p multicolored 1.75 1.20
1098 A409 3p multicolored 4.75 2.75
1099 A409 4p multicolored 8.25 5.00
Nos. 1096-1099 (4) 15.65 9.50

A410

1991

1100 A410 30c Boxing .40 .25
1101 A410 50c Cycling 1.25 .50
1102 A410 1p Bowling 2.50 1.00
Nos. 1100-1102 (3) 4.15 1.75

11th Pan American Games, Havana.

Dr. Tomas Eudoro Perez Rancier, Birth Cent. — A411

1991, July 3

1103 A411 2p yellow & black 7.50 1.90

10th Columbus Regatta, Casa de Espana — A412

Discovery of America, 500th Anniv. (in 1992) A413

Designs: 50c, Encounter of three cultures. 3p, Columbus and Dr. Alvarez Chanca caring for sick. 4p, Rebellion of Enriquillo.

1991, Oct. 15 Litho. *Perf. 13½*

1104 A412 30c multicolored .65 .25
1105 A413 50c multicolored .90 .50
1106 A413 3p multicolored 5.50 3.00
1107 A413 4p multicolored 7.50 4.00
Nos. 1104-1107 (4) 14.55 7.75

See No. 1116.

A414

1991, Nov. 18

1108 A414 3p black & red 4.75 2.10

Cornea Bank.

America Issue — A415

Designs: 1p, Santa Maria. 3p, Christopher Columbus.

1991 Litho. *Perf. 13½*

1109 A415 1p multi 3.00 .85
1110 A415 3p multi 7.00 3.50

33rd Meeting of Inter-American Development Bank Governors, Santo Domingo — A416

1992 Litho. *Perf. 13½*

1111 A416 1p multicolored 1.75 .85

A417

1992 Litho. *Perf. 13½*

1112 A417 3p multicolored 5.25 2.75

Espanola '92 Philatelic Exposition.

A418

Valentin Salinero, Order of the Apostles founder.

1992 Litho. *Perf. 13½*

1113 A418 1p blue & brown 1.75 .90

Order of the Apostles, cent.

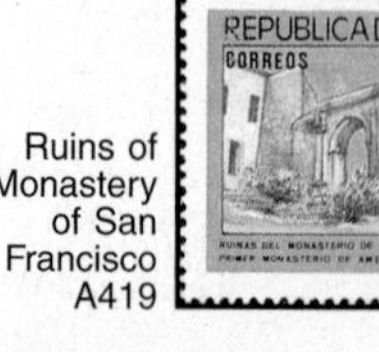

Ruins of Monastery of San Francisco A419

Designs: 3p, Ruins of San Nicolas hospital, first in the Americas.

1992, July 28

1114 A419 50c multicolored .75 .50
1115 A419 3p multicolored 5.50 3.25

Type of 1991 and

A420

Designs: 50c, Racing yacht. 1p, Native women, Columbus. 2p, Natives offering Columbus tobacco. 3p, Native woman, Columbus, corn.

1992, Oct. 6 Litho. *Perf. 13½*

1116 A412 50c multicolored .70 .35
1117 A420 1p multicolored 1.60 .75
1118 A420 2p multicolored 4.50 2.75
1119 A420 3p multicolored 6.50 3.25
Nos. 1116-1119 (4) 13.30 7.10

11th Columbus Regatta (No. 1116), Discovery of America, 500th anniv. (Nos. 1117-1119).

23rd Convention of the Alliance of Panamerican Round Tables, Santo Domingo — A421

1992, Oct. 14

1120 A421 1p multicolored 1.75 .85

Visit by Pope John Paul II A422

Cathedrals: 50c, Vega. 3p, Santo Domingo.

1992, Oct. 1 Photo.

1121 A422 50c multicolored 1.40 .60
1122 A422 3p multicolored 4.75 2.25

Columbus Lighthouse A423

Design: 3p, Lighthouse at night.

1992, Oct. 12 Litho.

1123 A423 30c multicolored 1.00 .45
1124 A423 1p multicolored 2.00 .70

Size: 70x133mm

Imperf

1125 A423 3p multicolored 10.00 10.00

America Issue A424

Designs: 50c, First royal residence in America, Santo Domingo. 3p, First viceregal residence in America, Royal Palace, Colon.

1992, Nov. 13 Litho. *Perf. 13½*

1126 A424 50c multicolored .75 .40
1127 A424 3p multicolored 4.00 2.50

A425

1992, Dec. 2 Litho. *Perf. 13½*

1128 A425 30c Torch bearer .45 .25
1129 A425 1p Emblems 1.50 .80
1130 A425 4p Judo 7.00 3.50
Nos. 1128-1130 (3) 8.95 4.55

1992 Natl. Sports Games, San Juan. Secretary of Sports, Education, Exercise and Recreation (No. 1129).

Natl. Census — A426

1992-93 Litho. *Perf. 13½*

1131 A426 50c black, buff & blue .70 .25
1132 A426 1p blk, brn & blue 1.40 .75
1133 A426 3p blk, gray & bl 4.75 2.50
1134 A426 4p blk, yel grn & bl 6.00 3.00
Nos. 1131-1134 (4) 12.85 6.50

Issued: 50c, 1p, 5/12/92; 3p, 4p, 9/9/93.

A427

1993, May 30

1135 A427 30c multicolored .50 .25
1136 A427 50c multicolored .90 .30
1137 A427 1p multicolored 1.90 .80
Nos. 1135-1137 (3) 3.30 1.35

Ema Balaguer, humanitarian.

A428

1993, Oct. 7 Litho. *Perf. 13½*

1138 A428 30c shown 1.00 .45
1139 A428 1p Emblem, flags 2.75 1.00

Rotary Club of Santo Domingo, 50th anniv.

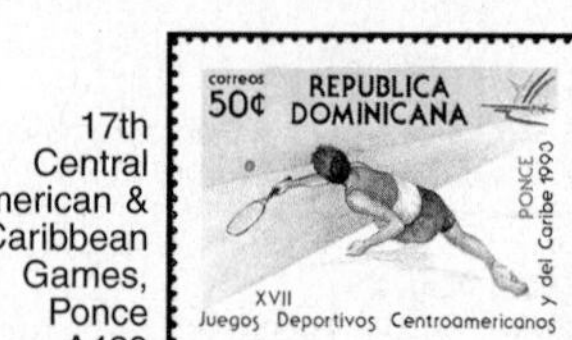

17th Central American & Caribbean Games, Ponce A429

1993, Dec. 21 Litho. *Perf. 13½*

1140 A429 50c Tennis .65 .25
1141 A429 4p Swimming 7.00 2.00

Natl. Education Plan — A430

1993, Dec. 8

1142 A430 1.50p multicolored 2.40 .90

Spanish America — A431

Designs: 50c, First university lecturn. 3p, First city coat of arms.

1993, Dec. 28

1143 A431 50c multi .75 .25
1144 A431 3p multi 5.25 1.50

America Issue A432

Designs: 1p, Aratinga chloroptera. 3p, Cyclura cornuta.

1993, Dec. 30

1145 A432 1p multi 1.25 .50
1146 A432 3p multi 5.25 2.75

Opening of New Natl. Post Office A433

1993, Nov. 12

Color of Inscription

1147 A433 1p olive 1.00 .55
1148 A433 3p red 3.00 1.60
1149 A433 4p blue 3.75 1.90
1150 A433 5p green 4.75 2.25
1151 A433 10p black 9.50 4.50

Size: 105x96mm

Imperf

1152 A433 5p black 12.50 12.50
Nos. 1147-1152 (6) 34.50 23.30

First Mass in America, 500th Anniv. — A434

1994, Feb. 3 Litho. *Perf. 13½*

1153 A434 2p multicolored 3.00 1.25

5th Natl. Philatelic Exhibition A435

1994, Feb. 25

1154 A435 3p multicolored 4.50 1.60

Natl. Independence, 150th Anniv. — A436

No. 1155: a, Men with document, left side of table. b, Document on right side of table, men. c, Flag. d, Couple at window. e, Child holding material, mother making flag.

No. 1156: a, Men looking upward, shooting muskets. b, Men with guns, swords looking backwards. c, Natl. coat of arms. d, Men with guns, swords, one pointing upward. e, Men with weapons, one with flag.

10p, Three men, angel carrying musket, flag.

1994, Feb. 26 Strips of 5

1155 A436 2p #a.-e. 8.25 4.00
1156 A436 3p #a.-e. 12.50 6.00

Size: 161x104mm

Imperf

1157 A436 10p multicolored 11.50 11.50
Nos. 1155-1157 (3) 32.25 21.50

Nos. 1155a-1155b, 1155d-1155e, 1156a-1156b, 1156d-1156e have a continuous design.

Solenodon Paradoxus — A437

Designs: a, Crawling on rock. b, Walking in leaves. c, Looking up. d, With food in mouth.

1994, Mar. 15 Litho. *Perf. 13½*

1158 A437 1p Block of 4, #a.-d. 9.00 5.25

World Wildlife Fund.

Battle of March 19, 150th Anniv. A438

No. 1160, Soldiers advancing uphill toward fort.

1994

1159 A438 2p multicolored 3.00 1.50
1160 A438 2p multicolored 3.00 1.50

Issued: No. 1159, Mar. 18; No. 1160, Mar. 29.

Virgin of Amparo — A439

1994, Apr. 15 Litho. *Perf. 13½*

1161 A439 3p multicolored 4.50 1.75

Battle of Puerto Tortuguero, 150th anniv.

Natl. Elections, May 16 — A440

1994, Apr. 4

1162 A440 2p multicolored 3.00 1.50

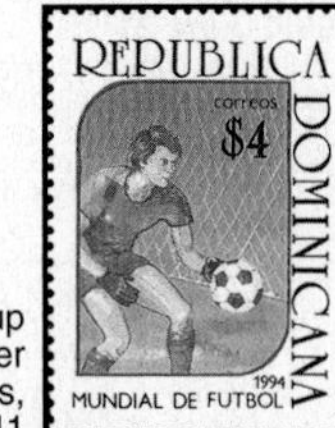

1994 World Cup Soccer Championships, US — A441

1994, June 24 Litho. *Perf. 13½*

1163 A441 4p multicolored 5.00 2.25
1164 A441 6p multicolored 7.00 3.25

Ema Balaguer City of Children A442

1994, July 20 Litho. *Perf. 13½*

1165 A442 1p magenta & brown 2.75 .60

Stamp Day A443

1994, Oct. 18 Litho. *Perf. 13½*

1166 A443 5p Type A3 7.75 3.00

America Issue — A444

1994, Oct. 28

1167 A444 2p Pony Express 3.00 1.50
1168 A444 6p Sailing ship 10.00 4.00

Province of LaVega, 500th Anniv. A445

3p, Ruins of San Francisco Monastery.

1994, Nov. 24 Litho. *Perf. 13½*

1169 A445 3p multicolored 7.25 1.60

First Church the New World, 500th Anniv. — A446

a, "La Isabela," cradle of evangelization. b, "Temple of the Americas," first mission.

1994, Dec. 5 *Perf. 11½*

1170 A446 3p Pair, #a.-b. 10.00 3.00

Constitution, 150th Anniv. — A447

1994, Nov. 6 *Perf. 13½*

1171 A447 3p multicolored 5.00 1.60

Christmas A448

2p, Holy family's flight into Egypt. 3p, Modern family of three standing at river's edge.

1994, Nov. 18

1172 A448 2p multicolored 3.50 1.25
1173 A448 3p multicolored 4.75 1.60

Intl. Year of the Family.

Firsts in America — A449

1994, Dec. 21 Litho. *Perf. 13½*

1174 A449 2p Circulating coins 3.50 .75
1175 A449 5p Sermon for Justice 7.75 2.00

Snakes A450

No. 1176, Hypsirhynchus ferox. No. 1177, Antillophis parvifrons. No. 1178, Uromacer catesbyi. No. 1179, Epicrates striatus.

1994, Dec. 26

1176 2p multicolored 3.00 1.00
1177 2p multicolored 3.00 1.00
a. A450 Pair, #1176-1177 6.00 5.50
1178 2p multicolored 3.00 1.00
1179 2p multicolored 3.00 1.00
a. A450 Pair, #1178-1179 6.00 5.50

Nos. 1177a, 1179a are continuous designs.

Pan American Games, Mar Del Plata, Argentina A451

1995, Apr. 20 *Perf. 13½*

1180 A451 4p Tae kwon do 4.75 1.75
1181 A451 13p Tennis 14.50 5.00

FAO, 50th Anniv. — A452

1995, Apr. 21 **Litho.** *Perf. 11½*

1182 A452 4p multicolored 4.50 2.25

A453

Designs: 2p, Jose Marti, Maximo Gomez. 3p, Marti. 4p, Marti seated at desk, Gomez.

1995, May 19 **Litho.** *Perf. 13½*

1183 A453 2p multicolored 1.90 .75
1184 A453 3p multicolored 2.50 1.40
1185 A453 4p multicolored 3.75 2.00
Nos. 1183-1185 (3) 8.15 4.15

Jose Marti (1853-95), Montecristi Manifesto, cent.

Basketball, Cent. — A454

1995, May 22

1186 A454 3p multicolored 3.00 .45

Medicinal Plants — A455

Designs: No. 1187, Pimenta ozua. No. 1188, Melocactus communis. No. 1189, Smilax. No. 1190, Zamia.

1995, May 26

1187 A455 2p multicolored 2.00 1.00
1188 A455 2p multicolored 2.00 1.00
1189 A455 3p multicolored 3.00 1.50
1190 A455 3p multicolored 3.00 1.50
Nos. 1187-1190 (4) 10.00 5.00

Tourism A456

4p, San Souci Port. 5p, Barahona Airport. 6p, G. Luperon Airport. 13p, Airport of the Americas.

1995, June 21

1191 A456 4p multicolored 3.00 .50
1192 A456 5p multicolored 3.75 .75
1193 A456 6p multicolored 4.75 .85
1194 A456 13p multicolored 10.00 1.75
Nos. 1191-1194 (4) 21.50 3.85

Santiago de Los Caballeros, 500th Anniv. A457

1995, July 29 **Litho.** *Perf. 13½*

1195 A457 3p Jacagua ruins 4.75 .90

Whales A458

Designs: No. 1196, Physeter macrocephalus. No. 1197, Balaenoptera borealis. No. 1198, Ziphius cavirostris. No. 1199, Megaptera novaeangliae.

1995, Aug. 14

1196 A458 3p multicolored 3.00 .50
1197 A458 3p multicolored 3.00 .50
1198 A458 3p multicolored 3.00 .50
1199 A458 3p multicolored 3.00 .50
Nos. 1196-1199 (4) 12.00 2.00

Stamp Day A459

1995, Oct. 18 **Litho.** *Perf. 13½*

1200 A459 4p No. 37 3.25 .50

Popular Singers — A460

1995, Oct. 8

1201 A460 2p Rafael Colon 1.75 .75
1202 A460 3p Casandra Damiron 2.25 1.10

Cathedral of Santiago, Cent. A461

1995, Dec. 28 **Litho.** *Perf. 13½*

1203 A461 3p multicolored 2.50 1.10

4th World Conference of Women, Beijing — A462

1995, Nov. 23

1204 A462 2p multicolored 5.25 1.10

Volleyball, Cent. — A463

Norceca '95 — A464

1995, Oct. 19 ***Imperf.***

1205 A463 5p multicolored 4.75 1.90

Perf. 13½

1206 A464 6p multicolored 5.00 4.25

Singers — A465

1995, Dec. 27 *Perf. 13½*

1207 A465 2p Antonio Mesa 1.75 .80
1208 A465 2p Julieta Otero 1.75 .80
1209 A465 2p Susano Polanco 1.75 .80
Nos. 1207-1209 (3) 5.25 2.40

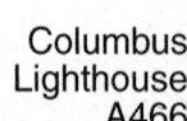

Columbus Lighthouse A466

1995, Dec. 5

1210 A466 10p dk bl, bl & gray 11.00 3.50

See Nos. 1241, 1265, 1299, 1337, 1371, 1375, 1382.

A467

UN, 50th Anniv. A468

1995, Oct. 24

1211 A467 2p multicolored 1.75 .75

Perf. 11½

1212 A468 6p multicolored 5.00 1.00

Environmental Protection — A469

America issue: 2p, Flamingos, sea gull. 6p, Manglar.

1995, Dec. 19 **Litho.** *Perf. 13½*

1213 A469 2p multicolored 1.75 .65
1214 A469 6p multicolored 5.00 1.00

Dominican Republic Air Force, 50th Anniv. — A470

Aircraft: a, O2U-35D Corsair. b, PT-17 Stearman. c, AT-6 Texan. d, PBY-5A Catalina. e, TF-10 Beaufighter. f, FB-6 Mosquito. g, P-38 Lightning. h, P-51D Mustang. i, B-17G Flying Fortress. j, P-47D Thunderbolt. k, FB-5 Vampire. l, C-46 Commander. m, B-26 Invader. n, C-47 Skytrain. o, T-28D Trojan. p, T-33A Silverstar. q, Cessna T-41D. r, T-34 Mentor. s, Cessna O-2A. t, A-37B Dragonfly.

1995, Dec. 30

1215 A470 2p Sheet of 20, #a-t 30.00 17.00

See No. 1228.

UNICEF, 50th Anniv. — A471

1996, Feb. 23

1216 A471 2p shown 1.50 .45
1217 A471 4p Mirror image of #1216 3.00 1.40

Intl. Sailing Competition A472

1996, Mar. 8
1218 A472 5p multicolored 3.25 1.60

Eduardo Brito, Singer, 50th Death Anniv. — A473

1996, Jan. 15
1219 A473 1p shown .65 .30
1220 A473 2p With maracas 1.40 .75
1221 A473 3p Portrait 2.10 1.10
Nos. 1219-1221 (3) 4.15 2.15

No. 1220 is 54x35mm.

Natl. Journalist Day — A474

Design: Arturo J. Pellerano Alfau, Dr. Freddy Gaton Arce, Rafael Herrera Cabral.

1996, Apr. 17 Litho. *Perf. 13½*
1222 A474 5p multicolored 3.75 1.75

ESPAMER '96, Seville — A475

1996, June 7 Litho. *Perf. 13½*
1223 A475 15p multicolored 9.50 4.75

1996 Summer Olympic Games, Atlanta — A476

1996, July 5
1224 A476 5p Judo 3.75 1.40
1225 A476 15p Torch 9.75 4.25

Modern Olympic Games, Cent. — A477

1996, July 5
1226 A477 6p Greece No. 118 3.75 1.90
1227 A477 15p No. 328 9.00 4.25

Dominican Republic Air Force, 50th Anniv. Type of 1995

Helicoptors: a, Sikorsky S-55. b, Alouette II. c, Alouette III. d, OH-6A Cayuse. e, Bell 205 A-1. f, Dauphin II SA.365C.

1996, July 31 Litho. *Perf. 13½*
1228 A470 3p Sheet of 6, #a.-f. 8.00 8.00

World Day Against Illegal Drugs — A478

1996, Sept. 23 Litho. *Perf. 13½*
1229 A478 15p multicolored 9.75 4.25

Mail Delivery A479

No. 1230, World delivery, putting mail in letter box, mailman receiving mail on motorcycle. No. 1231, Woman giving mail to man on horseback, vert. No. 1232, Child holding letter beside mailbox.

1996, July 17 Litho. *Perf. 13½*
1230 A479 3p multicolored 2.50 1.25
1231 A479 3p multicolored 2.50 1.25
1232 A479 3p multicolored 2.50 1.25
Nos. 1230-1232 (3) 7.50 3.75

America Issue — A480

1996, Oct. 15 Litho. *Perf. 13½*
1233 A480 2p Men's costume 1.40 .65
1234 A480 6p Women's costume 3.75 1.75

Stamp Day A481

1996, Oct. 18
1235 A481 5p No. 142 3.25 1.40

26th Intl. Sunfish Championships — A482

6p, Sun, natl. flag, sailboat, vert. 10p, Man sailing boat.

1996, Oct. 16
1236 A482 6p multicolored 3.75 1.75
1237 A482 10p multicolored 6.25 3.25

A483

1996, Nov. 25 Litho. *Perf. 13½*
1238 A483 5p green & multi 3.25 1.60
1239 A483 10p pink & multi 6.25 3.25

Intl. Day to End Violence Against Women.

Birds — A484

a, Buteo ridgwayi. b, Aratinga chloroptera. c, Amazona ventralis. d, Hyetornis rufigularis. e, Saurothera longirostris. f, Siphonorhis brewsteri. g, Chlorostilbon swainsonii. h, Todus angustirostris. i, Todus subulatus. j, Temnotrogon roseigaster. k, Nesoctites micromegas. l, Melanerpes striatus. m, Turdus swalesi. n, Carduelis dominicensis. o, Dulus dominicus. p, Microligea palustris. q, Vireo nanus. r, Xenoligea montanta. s, Turdus swalesi dodae. t, Calyptophilus frugivorus tertius. u, Corvus leucognaphalus. v, Calyptophilus frugivorus neibae.

1996, Nov. 11
1240 A484 2p Sheet of 22, #a-v 45.00 30.00

Lighthouse Type of 1995

1996, Dec. 27 Litho. *Perf. 13½*
1241 A466 10p grn, sil & gray 7.00 3.50

Turtles — A485

a, Dermochelys coriacea. b, Caretta caretta. c, Chelonia mydas. d, Eretmochelys imbricata.

1996, Dec. 30
1242 A485 5p Block of 4, #a.-d. 12.00 10.00

Natl. Youth Day — A486

1997, Jan. 31
1243 A486 3p multicolored 2.00 1.00

National Anthem — A487

Designs: 2p, Lyrics, by Emilio Prudhome. 3p, Music, by Jose Reyes.

1997, Feb. 26
1244 A487 2p multicolored 1.50 .65
1245 A487 3p multicolored 2.00 .95

Salomé Urena (1850-97), Poet — A488

1997, Mar. 6 *Perf. 13½*
1246 A488 3p multicolored 1.90 .95

Comet Hale-Bopp A489

1997, Apr. 1
1247 A489 5p multicolored 4.25 1.60

Size: 72x47mm

Imperf

1248 A489 10p multicolored 11.00 11.00

A490

11th Natl. Sports Games, Mao '97 — A491

2p, Mascot running with torch. 3p, Mascot in batting stance, vert. 5p, Runner breaking finish line.

1997, Apr. 3
1249 A490 2p multicolored 1.75 .65
1250 A491 3p multicolored 2.75 1.00
1251 A491 5p multicolored 4.25 1.60
Nos. 1249-1251 (3) 8.75 3.25

A492

Design: 10p, 5p, Heinrich von Stephan (1831-97), founder of UPU.

1997, Apr. 8 Litho. *Perf. 13½*
1252 A492 10p multicolored 6.25 3.25

Souvenir Sheet

Imperf

1253 A492 5p like #1252 3.25 2.75

No. 1253 has simulated perforations.

A493

1997, Apr. 29 *Perf. 13½*
1254 A493 10p multicolored 9.50 3.25

25th Intl. Congress of CLAHT (Caracas and Latin American Group of Hemostasis and Thrombosis).

Gregorio Luperón (1839-1897), Politician — A494

1997, May 21
1255 A494 3p multicolored 2.00 1.00

House of Spain, 80th Anniv. — A495

1997, July 4
1256 A495 5p multicolored 3.25 1.60

First Peso Coin, Cent. A496

1997, Aug. 6 Litho. *Perf. 13½*
1257 A496 2p multicolored 1.50 .65

A497

Coronation of the Image of Our Lady of Alta Gracia, 75th Anniv. — A498

1997, Aug. 12
1258 A497 3p multicolored 1.90 .85
1259 A498 5p multicolored 3.25 1.60

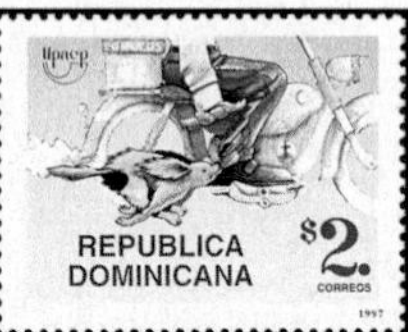

America Issue A499

Life of a postman: 2p, Dog grabbing pants leg of postman on motorcycle. 6p, Dog tearing pants leg of postman with letter.

1997, Oct. 9 Litho. *Perf. 13½*
1260 A499 2p multicolored 1.25 .65

Size: 35½x35½mm

1261 A499 6p multicolored 3.25 1.60

Mother Teresa (1910-97) A500

1997, Oct. 17
1262 A500 5p multicolored 3.00 1.60

Stamp Day — A501

1997, Oct. 18
1263 A501 5p Nos. 108, 322 2.75 1.60

Central Bank of the Dominican Republic, 50th Anniv. — A502

1997, Oct. 30 *Perf. 11½*
1264 A502 10p multicolored 5.50 3.25

Lighthouse Type of 1995

1997, Dec. 15 Litho. *Perf. 13½*
1265 A466 10p bright rose & gray 7.50 3.25

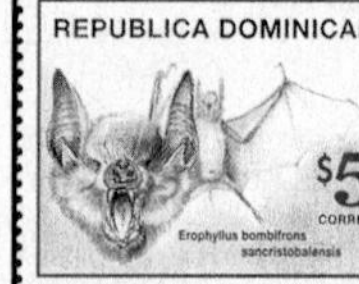

Bats A503

a, Erophylius bombifrons. b, Brachyphylla nana. c, Molossus molossus. d, Lasiurus borealis.

1997, Nov. 11
1266 A503 5p Block of 4, #a.-d. 11.00 11.00

Dominican Air Force, 50th Anniv. A504

Insignias: a, Air Force, red, white, and blue target. b, Northern Air Command, "shark plane." c, Air Command, eagle's wings over target. d, Rescue Force, eagle. e, Maintenance Command. f, Combat Force, dragon, target.

1997, Dec. 19
1267 A504 3p Sheet of 6, #a.-f. 11.00 11.00

Construction of the National Palace, 50th Anniv. — A505

1997, Dec. 30 Litho. *Perf. 13½*
1268 A505 10p multicolored 6.25 3.50

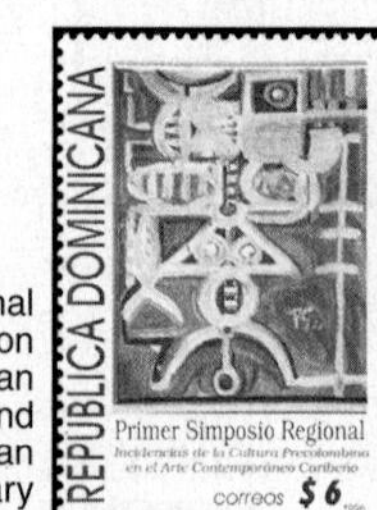

First Regional Symposium on Pre-Columbian Culture and Caribbean Contemporary Art — A506

1998, Jan. 28
1269 A506 6p multicolored 3.75 1.60

A507

1998, Apr. 2 Litho. *Perf. 13½*
1270 A507 10p multicolored 6.25 3.25

American Chamber of Commerce of the Dominican Republic, 75th anniv.

A508

Book Fair: 3p, Natl. Book Fair, 25th anniv. 5p, Intl. Book Fair, Santo Domingo '98.

1998, Apr. 26
1271 A508 3p black, blue & red 1.90 .85

Size: 35x33mm

1272 A508 5p black, blue & red 3.25 1.60

Organization of American States, 50th Anniv. — A509

1998, Apr. 30
1273 A509 5p blue & multi 3.25 1.60
1274 A509 5p pink & multi 3.25 1.60

Establishment of the State of Israel, 50th Anniv. — A510

1998, Apr. 30
1275 A510 10p multicolored 9.00 4.50

Dominican Air Force, 50th Anniv. — A511

a, Gen. Frank Felix Miranda, portrait at left. b, Early aircraft. c, Col. Ernesto Tejeda, portrait at right. d, As "c," portrait at left. e, As "a," portrait at right.

1998, June 26 Sheet of 6
1276 A511 3p Sheet of 6, #a, c-e, 2 #b 11.00 11.00

City of Santo Domingo, 500th Anniv. A512

2p, Sun clock. 3p, St. Lazaro Church & Hospital. 4p, First Cathedral in America. 5p, Royal Palace. 6p, Tower of Honor. 10p, St. Nicolas of Bari Church & Hospital.

1998, Aug. 6 Litho. *Perf. 13½*
1277 A512 2p multi, vert. 1.25 .65
1278 A512 3p multi 1.90 .90
1279 A512 4p multi 2.50 1.25
1280 A512 5p multi 3.25 1.60
1281 A512 6p multi 3.75 1.90
1282 A512 10p multi, vert. 6.25 3.25
Nos. 1277-1282 (6) 18.90 9.55

National Theater, 25th Anniv. — A513

1998, Aug. 14 *Perf. 13x13½*
1283 A513 10p multicolored 6.25 3.00

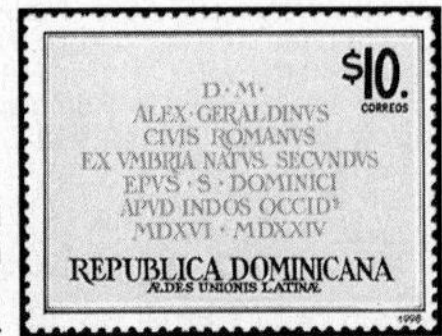

Latin Union, 44th Anniv. A514

1998, Aug. 26 *Perf. 13½*
1284 A514 10p multicolored 6.25 3.00

ICCO (Intl. Cocoa Organization of America & Europe), 25th Anniv. — A515

1998, Sept. 3
1285 A515 10p multicolored 7.75 3.50

Nino Ferrua (1909-79), Stamp Designer A516

1998, Oct. 18 **Litho.** *Perf. 13½x13*
1286 A516 5p multicolored 3.25 1.50

Stamp Day.

Pontificate of John Paul II, 20th Anniv. A517

1998, Oct. 22 *Perf. 13½*
1287 A517 5p shown 3.25 1.50
1288 A517 10p Portrait, diff. 6.75 2.10

Medicinal Plants — A518

a, Pimenta racemosa. b, Pimenta haitiensis. c, Cymbopogon citratus. d, Citrus aurantium.

1998, Nov. 2
1289 A518 3p Block of 4, #a.-d. 7.00 3.25

Famous Women A519

America Issue: 2p, Juana Saltitopa standing with cannon. 6p, Anacaona, Indian maiden, group of Indians.

1998, Nov. 5
1290 A519 2p multicolored 2.00 .65
1291 A519 6p multicolored 4.50 2.00

Intl. Year of the Ocean — A520

1998, Nov. 20
1292 A520 5p multicolored 4.00 1.50

A521

1998, Nov. 23
1293 A521 5p multicolored 2.75 1.50

Expofila '98, Santo Domingo. Santo Domingo, 500th anniv.

National Military Heroes — A522

Designs: a, Fernando Valerio. b, Benito Moncion. c, Jose Maria Cabral. d, Antonio Duverge. e, Gregorio Luperon. f, Jose A. Salcedo. g, Fco. A. Salcedo. h, Gaspar Polanco. i, Santiago Rodriguez. j, Juan Bta. Cambiaso. k, Jose J. Puello. l, Jose Ma. Imbert. m, Juan A. Acosta. n, Marcos Adon. o, Matias R. Mella. p, Francisco R. Sanchez. q, Juan Pablo Duarte. r, Olegario Tenares. s, Pedro Santana. t, Juan Sanchez Ramirez.

1998, Nov. 29
1294 A522 3p Sheet of 20, #a.-t. 27.50 24.50

1st Natl. Paper Money, 150th Anniv. — A523

1998, Nov. 30 *Perf. 11½*
1295 A523 10p multicolored 4.75 2.10

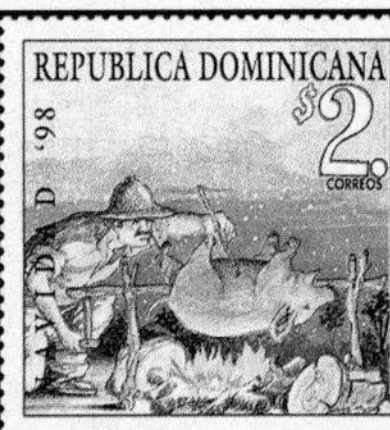

Christmas A524

1998, Dec. 7 *Perf. 13½*
1296 A524 2p Roasting hog .90 .45
1297 A524 5p Magi 2.25 1.10

Universal Declaration of Human Rights, 50th Anniv. A525

1998, Dec. 10
1298 A525 10p multicolored 4.50 2.10

Columbus Lighthouse Type of 1995

1998, Dec. 11
1299 A466 10p orange & black 6.00 3.00

Shells A526

Designs: a, Lyria vegai. b, Strombus gigas. c, Cittarium pica. d, Nerita peloronta.

1998, Dec. 16
1300 A526 5p Block of 4, #a.-d. 11.00 5.25

Gaspar Hernández (1798-1858), Priest — A527

1998, Dec. 18
1301 A527 3p multicolored 1.40 .70

Dominican Society of Endocrinology and Nutrition, 25th Anniv. — A528

1999, Feb. 24 **Litho.** *Perf. 13¼*
1302 A528 10p multicolored 4.00 2.00

Office of Comptroller General — A529

1999, May 4 **Litho.** *Perf. 13¼*
1303 A529 2p multicolored 1.00 .45

Export Industries A530

Perf. 13½x13¼, 13¼x13½

1999, Apr. 30 **Litho.**
1304 A530 6p Tobacco 2.25 1.10
1305 A530 10p Textiles, vert. 3.75 1.60

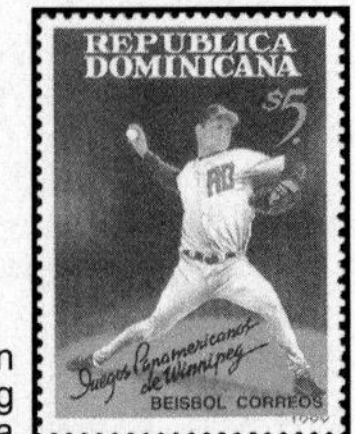

Pan American Games, Winnipeg A530a

1999, July 29 **Litho.** *Perf. 13¼x13½*
1306 A530a 5p Baseball 2.75 1.25
1307 A530a 6p Weight lifting 3.25 1.50

Native Plants — A531

Designs: a, Pseudophoenix ekmanii. b, Murtigia calabura. c, Pouteria dominguensis. d, Rubus dominguensis focke.

1999, July 13
1308 A531 5p Block of 4, #a.-d. 9.50 9.50

Presidents of the Dominican Republic A532

Designs: a, Tomas Bobadilla y Briones. b, Pedro Santana. c, Manuel Jimenez. d, Buenaventura Baez. e, Manuel de Regla Mota. f, José Desiderio Valverde. g, José A. Salcedo. h, Gaspar Polanco.

1999, Aug. 31 *Perf. 13½x13¼*
1309 A532 3p Sheet of 8, #a.-h. + label 10.00 10.00

A533

Sovereign Military Order of Malta A534

Perf. 13¼x13½

1999, Sept. 20 **Litho.**

1310 A533 2p multicolored .85 .45

Perf. 13½

1311 A534 10p multicolored 4.50 2.75

Paintings by José Vela Zanetti (1913-99) — A535

Various paintings.

Perf. 13½x13¼, 13¼x 13½

1999, Sept. 8

1312 A535 2p multi, vert. .70 .45
1313 A535 3p multi, vert. 1.25 .80
1314 A535 5p multi 1.90 1.10
1315 A535 6p multi, vert. 2.40 1.40
1316 A535 10p multi, vert. 3.75 2.10
Nos. 1312-1316 (5) 10.00 5.85

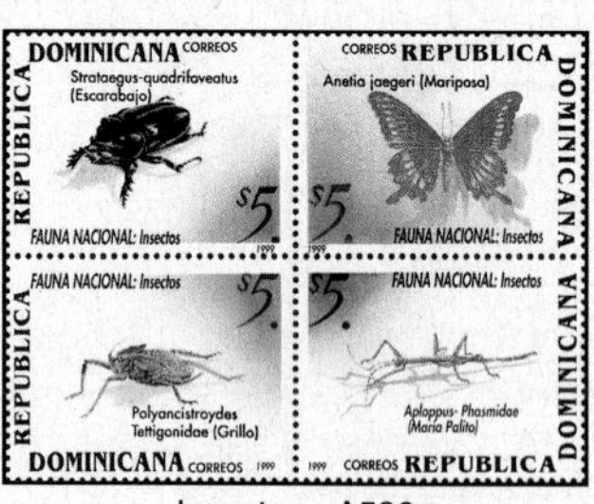

Insects — A536

Designs: a, Strataegus quadrifoveatus. b, Anetia jaegeri. c, Polyancistroydes tettigonidae. d, Aploppus phasmidae.

1999, Sept. 10 *Perf. 13½x13¼*

1317 A536 5p Block of 4, #a.-d. 8.00 8.00

SOS Children's Villages, 50th Anniv. — A537

1999, Sept. 29 *Perf. 13¼x13½*

1318 A537 10p multicolored 4.00 2.10

Intl. Year of the Elderly — A538

1999, Oct. 1

1319 A538 2p Man .75 .25
1320 A538 5p Woman 2.00 1.00

World Education Day — A539

1999, Oct. 5

1321 A539 5p multicolored 2.00 .90

A540

Designs: 2p, Skull and crossbones, land mines, shattered gun. 6p, Mushroom cloud.

1999, Oct. 18

1322 A540 2p multicolored .80 .50
1323 A540 6p multicolored 2.60 1.25

America Issue, a new millennium without arms.

Stamp Day — A541

1999, Oct. 22

1324 A541 5p Luis F. Thomen 2.00 .90

Account of Gen. Juan Pablo Duarte A542

1999, July 16 *Perf. 13½*

1325 A542 3p multicolored 1.25 .25

A543

Contemporary Writers — A544

Perf. 13¼x13½, 13½x13¼

1999, June 23

1326 A543 2p multicolored .75 .25
1327 A544 10p multicolored 4.75 2.25

Dermatological Society, 50th Anniv. — A545

1999, Sept. 15 **Litho.** *Perf. 13¼*

1328 A545 3p multi 1.75 .80

Millennium — A546

3p, Earth, trees. 5p, Scientific achievements.

Perf. 13¼x13½

1999, Nov. 10 **Litho.**

1329 A546 3p multi 1.25 .75
1330 A546 5p multi 2.25 1.10

2nd Summit of African, Caribbean and Pacific Heads of State — A547

Emblem and: 5p, Map of Caribbean area, whale. 6p, Map of Pacific area, Easter Island statues. 10p, Map of Africa, lion.

1999, Nov. 23

1331 A547 5p multi 2.00 1.00
1332 A547 6p multi 2.50 1.10
1333 A547 10p multi 4.00 2.00
Nos. 1331-1333 (3) 8.50 4.10

UPU, 125th Anniv. A548

6p, Globe, envelope, computer, electronic circuits. 10p, Envelope, electronic circuits.

1999, Nov. 29

1334 A548 6p multi 2.25 1.00

Size: 50x75mm

Imperf

1335 A548 10p multi 4.50 2.10

Union of Latin American Universities, 50th Anniv. — A549

1999, Dec. 3 *Perf. 13½x13¼*

1336 A549 6p multi 2.25 1.00

Lighthouse Type of 1995

1999, Dec. 14 *Perf. 13¼x13½*

1337 A466 10p brown & silver 4.50 2.10

Municipal Notes, Cent. — A551

Classical Musicians A550

No. 1338, José de Jésus Ravelo (1876-1951), clarinet. No. 1339, Juan Francisco Garcia (1892-1974), cornet. No. 1340, Manuel Simo (1916-88), saxophone.

1999, Dec. 17

1338 A550 5p multi 2.00 1.00
1339 A550 5p multi 2.00 1.00
1340 A550 5p multi 2.00 1.00
Nos. 1338-1340 (3) 6.00 3.00

Notes and background colors — No. 1341: a, Santo Domingo, San Pedro de Macorís, deep purple. b, Puerto Plata, Moca, purple.

No. 1342, vert.: a, Santiago, Cotui, blue green. b, San Francisco de Macorís, La Vega, golden brown. c, San Cristobal, Samana, peacock blue.

No. 1343: a, As No. 1342a, green background. b, As No. 1342b, brown background. c, As No. 1342c, Prussian blue background.

1999, Dec. 30 *Perf. 13¼*

1341 A551 2p Pair, #a.-b. 2.00 1.00
1342 A551 2p Strip of 3, #a.-c. 2.50 1.10

Souvenir Sheet

Imperf

1343 A551 2p Sheet of 5, Nos. 1341a-1341b, 1343a-1343c 4.50 2.25

Chamber of Spanish Commerce and Industry, 75th Anniv. — A552

1999, Dec. 30 *Perf. 13¼x13½*

1344 A552 10p multi 4.50 2.40

Fight Against Drugs A553

2000, Feb. 17 **Litho.** *Perf. 13½*

1345 A553 5p multi 2.25 1.10

Hogar Crea Dominicana Inc., 25th anniv.

Duarte Institute — A554

2000, Feb. 25 *Perf. 13¼*

1346 A554 2p multi 1.00 .50

Prevention of Child Abuse — A555

2000, Mar. 31

1347 A555 2p multi 1.00 .45

National Police A556

2000, Apr. 6 ***Perf. 13½***
1348 A556 2p shown 1.50 .45

Size: 37x28mm
Perf. 13½x13¼

1349 A556 5p Crest 3.00 1.10

Dominican Institute of Industrial Technology, 25th Anniv. A557

2000, Apr. 11 ***Perf. 13½***
1350 A557 2p multi 1.00 .45

Independencia Province, 50th Anniv. — A558

2000, Apr. 15
1351 A558 3p multi 1.25 .65

A559

12th Natl. Games, La Romana A560

2000, Apr. 27 ***Perf. 13½x13¼***
1352 A559 2p Baseball 1.00 .45
1353 A559 3p Boxing 2.00 .80

Perf. 13½

1354 A560 5p Emblem 3.00 1.00
Nos. 1352-1354 (3) 6.00 2.25

Paintings A561

Designs: 5p, The Violinist, by Darío Suro. 10p, Self-portrait, by Théodore Chassériau.

2000, May 5 ***Perf. 13¼***
1355 A561 5p multi 3.25 1.10
1356 A561 10p multi 5.50 2.50

Presidential Elections A562

2000, May 12
1357 A562 2p multi 1.40 .45

Classical Musicians A563

No. 1358, Julio Alberto Hernandez Camejo (1900-99), pianist. No. 1359, Ramon Diaz (1901-76), bassoonist. No. 1360, Enrique de Marchena Dujarric (1908-88), pianist.

2000, May 31 ***Perf. 13½***
1358 A563 5p multi 3.25 1.10
1359 A563 5p multi 3.25 1.10
1360 A563 5p multi 3.25 1.10
Nos. 1358-1360 (3) 9.75 3.30

Expo 2000, Hanover A564

2000, June 1
1361 A564 5p shown 2.25 1.10
1362 A564 10p Emblem, diff. 4.50 2.10

Art by Jaime Colson — A565

Designs: 2p, Woman on horseback. 3p, Abstract. 5p, Musicians and dancers, horiz. 6p, Nudes. 10p, Colson.

2000 **Litho.** ***Perf. 13¼***
1363-1367 A565 Set of 5 19.00 6.75

Holy Year 2000 A566

Churches: 2p, Santo Cristo de los Milagros de Bayaguana Sanctuary. 5p, Santa Maria la Menor Cathedral, first in the Americas, vert. 10p, Nuestra Señora de la Altagracia Basilica, vert.

2000 ***Perf. 13½x13¼, 13¼x13½***
1368-1370 A566 Set of 3 10.00 4.00

Lighthouse Type of 1995

2000 ***Perf. 13¼x13½***
1371 A466 10p buff, brn & sil 7.25 3.50

Dominican Republic — Republic of China Diplomatic Relations A566a

Flags of Dominican Republic and Republic of China and: 5p, Illustration of dragon. 10p, Carved dragon.

Serpentine Die Cut 11¼

2000, Dec. 15 **Litho.**

Self-Adhesive

1371A-1371B A566a Set of 2 12.00 3.50

America Issue — Campaign Against AIDS — A566b

Designs: 2p, Child. 6p, AIDS patient (38x38mm).

2000, Dec. 21 **Self-Adhesive**
1371C-1371D A566b Set of 2 4.00 2.00

UN High Commissioner for Refugees, 50th Anniv. — A566c

2000, Dec. 29 **Self-Adhesive**
1371E A566c 10p multi 4.50 2.25

Environmental Protection — A567

Designs: 2p, Lizard on leaf, vert. $3, House. $5, River rapids, vert.

Serpentine Die Cut 11¼

2000 **Litho.**

Self-Adhesive

1372-1374 A567 Set of 3 6.50 2.50

Lighthouse Type of 1995

2001 **Litho.** ***Perf. 13¼x13½***
1375 A466 15p lt bl, dk bl & sil 9.00 3.50

Concepcion Bona, Seamstress of First Dominican Republic Flag, Cent. of Death — A568

2001 ***Perf. 13½x13¼***
1376 A568 10p multi 5.50 2.75

Stamp Day — A569

2001
1377 A569 5p multi 3.00 1.10

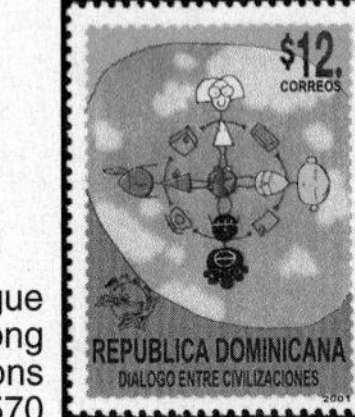

Year of Dialogue Among Civilizations A570

2001 ***Perf. 13¼x13½***
1378 A570 12p multi 5.50 2.50

America Issue — UNESCO World Heritage A571

Designs: 4p, San Felipe Fort. 15p, Ruins of San Nicolas de Bari Hospital (27x37mm).

2001 ***Perf. 13½, 13¼x13½ (15p)***
1379-1380 A571 Set of 2 10.00 4.25

Lighthouse Type of 1995

2002, Oct. 17 **Litho.** ***Perf. 13½x13¾***
1382 A466 15p yel & multi 5.00 2.00

Mushrooms — A572

No. 1383: a, Pycnoporus sanguineus. b, Morchella elata. c, Mycena epipterygia. d, Coriolopsis polyzona.

Perf. 13¼x13½

2001, Sept. 13 **Litho.**
1383 A572 6p Block of 4, #a-d 13.00 6.50

National Botanical Gardens, 25th Anniv. — A573

No. 1384: a, Isidorea pungens. b, Pereskia quisqueyana. c, Goetzea ekmanii. d, Cubanola domingensis.

Perf. 13¼x13½

2001, Sept. 20 **Litho.**

1384 A573 4p Block of 4, #a-d *9.50 9.50*

Presidents of the Dominican Republic — A574

No. 1385: a, Gen. José María Cabral. b, Gen. Gregório Luperón. c, Gen. Ignacio María González. d, Ulises Espaillat. e, Pedro A. Pimentel. f, Federico de Jesús García. g, Fernando Arturo de Mariño. h, Gen. Ulises Heureaux.

2001, Sept. 27 **Litho.** ***Perf. 13¼***

1385 A574 6p Sheet of 8, #a-h, + label 27.50 15.00

Blessed Josemaría Escrivá de Balaguer (1902-75), Founder of Opus Dei — A575

2002, Aug. 29 ***Perf. 13½x13¼***

1386 A575 10p multi 6.50 1.90

Loyola Polytechnic Institute, 50th Anniv. — A576

2002, Oct. 24 ***Perf. 13¼x13½***

1387 A576 6p multi 2.25 1.40

12th Iberoamerican Heads of State Summit — A577

Designs: 12p, Flags below map. 15p, Flags above map.

Perf. 13¾x13½

2002, Nov. 14 **Litho.**

1388-1389 A577 Set of 2 12.00 4.75

Compare with Type A637a.

America Issue — Youth Education and Literacy — A578

Designs: 4p, Teacher helping child write. 15p, Child writing on blackboard.

2002, Dec. 20 ***Perf. 13¼x13½***

1390-1391 A578 Set of 2 8.50 3.00

Coccothrinax Spissa — A579

Perf. 13¼x13½

2002, Dec. 20 **Litho.**

1392 A579 10p multi 4.00 1.50

2003 Pan American Games, Santo Domingo — A580

Color of "2003" in design: 4p, Light green blue. 6p, Blue. 12p, Red.

2003, Feb. 25

1393-1395 A580 Set of 3 6.50 3.00

Medicinal Plants — A581

No. 1396: a, Hymenaea courbaril. b, Spondias mombin. c, Genipa americana. d, Guazuma ulmifonia.

2003, June 17

1396 A581 5p Block of 4, #a-d 6.00 2.75

Dr. José Francisco Peña Gomez (1937-98), Politician A582

Litho. & Engr.

2003, Dec. 17 ***Perf. 11½***

1397 A582 10p multi 4.00 1.40

José Marti (1853-95), Cuban Patriot — A583

2003, Nov. 5 **Litho.** ***Perf. 13x13¼***

1398 A583 15p multi 4.50 2.25

Pan American Health Organization, Cent. (in 2002) — A583a

Perf. 13½x13¼

2006, July. 12 **Litho.**

1398A A583a 20p multi 5.00 2.00

America Issue — Flora and Fauna — A584

Designs: 5p, Aristelliger lar. 15p, Corpernicia berteroana, vert.

Perf. 13½x13¼, 13¼x13½

2004, Jan. 19

1399-1400 A584 Set of 2 8.50 3.00

Nos. 1399-1400 are dated "2003."

Election of Pope John Paul II, 25th Anniv. — A585

Pope John Paul II: 10p, With hand touching face. 15p, Blessing crowd, horiz. 25p, Vignettes of 10p and 15p stamps.

Perf. 13¼x13½, 13½x13¼

2005, Nov. 26

1401-1402 A585 Set of 2 11.00 3.25

Size: 57x85mm

Imperf

1403 A585 25p multi 12.00 3.50

National Council for Children A586

2004, Mar. 10 ***Perf. 13½x13¼***

1404 A586 7p multi 2.75 1.10

Exfilna National Philatelic Exhibition A587

2004, Dec. 8 **Litho.** ***Perf. 13½x13¼***

1405 A587 7p multi 3.00 1.10

America Issue — Fight Against Poverty A588

Design: 10p, Shack. 20p, Poor woman.

2004, Dec. 23

1406-1407 A588 Set of 2 12.00 5.75

Dominican Republic - Canada Diplomatic Relations, 50th Anniv. A589

2004, Dec. 31

1408 A589 20p multi 8.50 3.75

Interexpo '05 Intl. Philatelic Exhibition A590

Designs: 7p, Dove and stamp. 20p, Map highlighting Dominican Republic, vert. 10p, Similar to 7p.

Perf. 13½x13¼, 13¼x13½

2005 **Litho.**
1409-1410 A590 Set of 2 11.00 4.75

Souvenir Sheet

1410A A590 10p multi *15.00* 2.00

Dominican Republic Philatelic Society, 50th anniv.
Issued: 20p, 10/16; 7p, 10/17; 10p, 2005.

America Issue — Environmental Protection A591

Prevention of: 10p, Water pollution. 20p, Air pollution.

2005 *Perf. 13¼x13½*
1411-1412 A591 Set of 2 11.00 4.75

Monte Plata Maternity Clinic A592

Perf. 13½x13¼

2005, Nov. 14 **Litho.**
1413 A592 15p multi 6.25 2.50

Proclamation of Sister City Status of Santo Domingo and La Guardia, Spain — A593

2005, Nov. 11
1414 A593 10p multi 3.50 1.50

Stamp Day A594

2005 **Litho.** *Perf. 13½x13¼*
1415 A594 10p multi 3.50 1.50

Palace of Fine Arts, 50th Anniv. A595

2006, Oct. 10 **Litho.** *Perf. 13¾x13¼*
1416 A595 7p multi 3.00 1.10

Dominican History Academy, 75th Anniv. — A596

2006, Oct. 30 *Perf. 13¼*
1417 A596 10p multi 3.75 1.50

16th Intl. Boxing Congress, Santo Domingo — A597

2006, Nov. 2 *Perf. 13¼x13½*
1418 A597 20p multi 6.50 2.50

Pope John Paul II (1920-2005) A598

Pope and: 10p, Crucifix. 20p, Dove, horiz.

2006, Nov. 4 *Perf. 13½*
1419-1420 A598 Set of 2 11.50 4.50

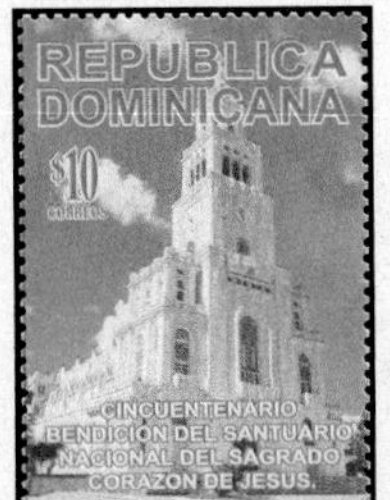

Blessing of Natl. Sacred Heart of Jesus Sanctuary, 50th Anniv. — A599

2006, Nov. 24 *Perf. 13½x13¼*
1421 A599 10p multi 4.50 1.50

Ninth Latin American Botanical Congress A600

2007, Feb/ 26 *Perf. 13¼x13½*
1422 A600 20p multi 7.00 3.00

America Issue, Energy Conservation — A601

Designs: 10p, Light bulb in hands. 20p, Transmission lines and tower.

2007, June 11 *Perf. 13x13¼*
1423-1424 A601 Set of 2 8.50 4.25

Pres. Joaquin Balaguer (1906-2002) A602

Balaguer: 7p, Wearing bow tie. 10p, Holding book.

2006, Sept. 1 *Perf. 13¼x13½*
1425-1426 A602 Set of 2 7.00 2.75

Office of the First Lady A603

Emblem and: 10p, Tree. 25p, Computer and keyboard.

2007, Mar. 1 *Perf. 13½x13¼*
1427-1428 A603 Set of 2 11.00 4.75

Selection of Nicolás de Jesus Cardinal López Rodríguez as Archbishop of Santo Domingo, 25th Anniv. — A604

López Rodríguez: 10p, Standing next to chair. 15p, With Pope John Paul II. 25p, Holding crucifix.

2007, May 25 *Perf. 13¼x13½*
1429-1431 A604 Set of 3 15.00 6.00

2007 Pan American Games, Rio de Janeiro — A605

Designs: 15p, High jump. 20p, Weight lifting.

2007, July 6 **Litho.**
1432-1433 A605 Set of 2 11.00 4.50

Podilymbus Podiceps A606

2007, Sept. 7 **Litho.** *Perf. 13½x13¼*
1434 A606 20p multi 7.00 3.00

Dated 2006.

Stamp Day — A607

2007, Oct. 4 *Perf. 13¼x13½*
1435 A607 15p multi 5.00 2.00

America Issue, Education For All — A608

Top panel in: 10p, Red. 20p, Blue.

2007, Dec. 26
1436-1437 A608 Set of 2 11.00 4.50

Treaty of Friendship With the Netherlands, 150th Anniv. — A609

2007, Nov. 9 *Perf. 13½x13¼*
1438 A609 25p multi 7.00 3.00

Palace of Columbus A610

2008, Apr. 18
1439 A610 10p multi 3.50 1.50

Barahona Province, Cent. — A611

2007, Nov. 23 *Perf. 13¼x13*
1440 A611 10p multi 2.50 1.00

Salvaléon de Higuey, 500th Anniv. A612

2008, Jan. 17 *Perf. 13½*
1441 A612 15p multi 4.00 1.50

Friendship and Cooperation Between Dominican Republic and Republic of China — A613

Designs: 10p, Prunus mume, Swietenia mahagonni. 15p, Urocissa caeruela, Dulus dominicus. 35p, Buildings from China and Dominican Republic.

2008, Feb. 6
1442-1444 A613 Set of 3 13.00 5.50

Children's Book Illustrations by Dr. Sophie Jakowska A614

Initials of Dr. Jakowska and: No. 1445, 7p, Trichechus manatus manatus. No. 1446, 7p, Eretmochelys imbricata, horiz. No. 1447, 10p, Photograph of Jakowska. No. 1448, 10p, Amazona ventralis. 15p, Crocodylus acutus, horiz.

2007, Dec. 7 ***Perf. 13¼x13, 13x13¼***
1445-1449 A614 Set of 5 12.50 5.00

Scouting, Cent. — A615

Designs: 10p, Dominican Republic Scouting emblem. 15p, Scouts, knotted rope.

2008, Jun. 5 **Litho.** ***Perf. 13½***
1450-1451 A615 Set of 2 6.50 2.50

Dominican Diaspora — A616

2008, Apr. 5 ***Perf. 13¼x13***
1452 A616 15p multi 3.50 1.50

Freemasonry in Dominican Republic, 150th Anniv. — A617

2008, Oct. 25 ***Perf. 13¼x13½***
1453 A617 25p multi 6.50 2.50

Stamp Day A618

2008, Oct. 2 ***Perf. 13¼***
1454 A618 20p brown 5.25 2.00

2008 Summer Olympics, Beijing — A619

No. 1455: a, Taekwondo. b, Boxing. c, Table tennis. d, Judo.

2008, Aug. 15 ***Perf. 13x13¼***
1455 A619 10p Block of 4, #a-d 10.00 4.00

Women Involved in Fight for Independence — A620

No. 1456: a, Juana de la Merced Trinidad (d. 1860). b, Joaquina Filomena Gomez de la Cova (1800-93). c, Maria Baltasara de los Reyes (1789-1867). d, Rosa Protomartir Duarte y Diaz (1820-88). e, Manuela Diaz y Jimenez (1786-1858). f, Petronila Abreu y Delgado (1815-1904). g, Micaela de Rivera de Santana (1785-1854). h, Froilana Febles de Santana (1814-88). i, Rosa Montas de Duvergé (1813-95). j, Josefa Antonia Perez de la Paz (1788-1855). k, Ana Valverde (1798-1864). l, Maria de la Concepción Bona y Hernandez (1824-1901). m, Maria de Jesus Pina y Benitez (1825-58). n, Maria Trinidad Sanchez y Ramona (1794-1845).

2008, Mar. 10 ***Perf. 13¼x13½***
1456 A620 Sheet of 14 + 31 labels 32.50 16.00
a.-n. 10p Any single 1.75 .90

Arms of Santiago, 500th Anniv. A621

2008, Dec. 7 **Litho.** ***Perf. 13x13¼***
1457 A621 10p multi 1.50 .50

Discovery of Quisqueya (Hispaniola) by Christopher Columbus, 1492 — A622

2008, Dec. 17
1458 A622 10p multi 1.50 .50

General Timoteo Ogando Encarnación (1818-1908) A623

2008 ***Perf. 13¼x13***
1459 A623 10p multi 1.50 .50

Campaign Against Commercial Sexual Exploitation A624

2008, Nov. 14
1460 A624 10p multi 1.50 .50

Intl. Swimming Federation, Cent. — A625

2009, Feb. 23 ***Perf. 13½***
1461 A625 15p multi 1.50 .50

America Issue, National Festivals — A626

No. 1462: a, 15p, Shot of Independence. b, 25p, Sword of the Restoration.

2008 ***Perf. 13¼x13***
1462 A626 Horiz. pair, #a-b 6.50 2.50

Duarte y Díez Family Tree — A627

No. 1463: a, Juan J. Duarte (1768-1843) and wife, Manuela Díez (1786-1858). b, Juan J. Duarte's sons, Juan Pablo (1813-76), Dominican independence leader, and Vicente (1802-65). c, Juan J. Duarte's son, Manuel (1826-90), and daughter, Rosa (1820-88). d, Juan J. Duarte's daughters, Francisca (1831-99), and Filomena (1818-65).

2009, Feb. 26 ***Perf. 13½x13¼***
1463 A627 10p Block of 4, #a-d 6.50 2.50

Chinatown, Santo Domingo A628

Designs: 15p, Confucius Plaza. 20p, Gateway.

2009, Apr. 17
1464-1465 A628 Set of 2 7.50 3.00

De La Salle Schools in Dominican Republic, 75th Anniv. A629

St. Jean Baptiste de la Salle (1651-1719) A630

2009, May 14 ***Perf. 13½x13¼***
1466 A629 7p multi 1.50 .60
Perf. 13¼x13½
1467 A630 10p multi 2.50 1.10

Invasion of Constanza, Maimón and Estero Hondo by Dominican Exiles, 50th Anniv. A631

2009, June 17 ***Perf. 13½***
1468 A631 10p multi 2.75 1.10

Pres. Juan Bosch (1909-2001) A632

2009, Jun. 19 ***Perf. 13¼x13***
1469 A632 20p multi 4.25 1.90

Crabs — A633

No. 1470: a, Epilobocera haytensis. b, Gecarcinus ruricola. c, Coenobita clypeatus. d, Callinectes sapidus.

Perf. 13½x13¼

2009, Sept. 17 **Litho.**
1470 A633 10p Block of 4, #a-d 4.50 2.25

Winning Designs in Children's Christmas Stamp Design Contest — A634

No. 1471: a, Dancers and musicians in front of house. b, Parade. c, Family and livestock. d, Villagers, manger and Christmas tree.

2009, Oct. 5 **Litho.** *Perf. 13x13¼*
1471 A634 10p Block of 4, #a-d 6.00 2.25

Plazas A635

Designs: 15p, Galicia Plaza, Santo Domingo. 25p, Santo Domingo Plaza, La Guardia, Spain.

2009, Oct. 15 *Perf. 13¼*
1472-1473 A635 Set of 2 5.00 2.25

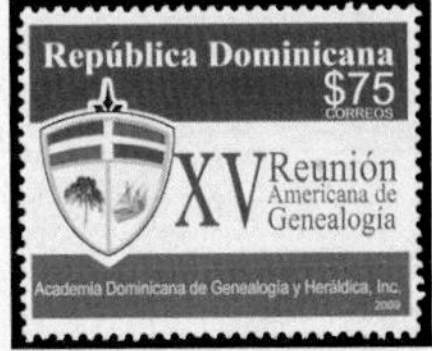

15th American Genealogical Reunion — A636

2009, Nov. 3 *Perf. 13x13¼*
1474 A636 75p multi 10.00 4.25

Natl. School of Judicature A637

2009, Nov. 4 *Perf. 13½*
1475 A637 7p multi .85 .40

12th Iberoamerican Heads of State Summit — A637a

Designs: 12p, Ribbon of flags below map. 15p, Flags above and to sides of map.

2009 **Litho.** *Perf. 13¾x13½*
1475A-1475B A637a Set of 2 7.00 —

Dated 2002. Compare with type A577.

America Issue, Toys and Games — A638

Designs: 10p, Fu-fu. 15p, Hopscotch, horiz. 20p, Pañuelo, horiz.

2009, Dec. 15 *Perf. 13x13, 13x13¼*
1476-1477 A638 Set of 2 5.00 1.75

Imperf

Size: 76x50mm

1478 A638 20p multi 4.50 1.75

Miniature Sheet

Dominican Republic Presidents — A639

No. 1479: a, Benigno Filomeno De Rojas. b, Jacinto B. De Castro. c, Maetos Cabral. d, Gen. Cesáreo Guillermo. e, Francisco G. Billini. f, Alejandro Woss y Gil. g, Carlos Felipe Morales Languasco. h, Ramón Cáceres.

2009 *Perf. 13¼*
1479 A639 7p Sheet of 8, #a-h, + central label 7.50 3.25

See Nos. 1531, 1585.

National Coat of Arms — A640

2010, Feb. 10 *Perf. 13¼x13½*
1480 A640 50p multi 5.00 2.75

14th Ibero-American Notaries Meeting — A641

2010, June 3 **Litho.** *Perf. 13¼x13*
1481 A641 26p multi 3.25 1.40

Preservation of Polar Regions — A642

2010, July 7 *Perf. 13½x13¼*
1482 A642 20p multi 2.25 1.10

Solenodon Paradoxus A643

2010, July 28
1483 A643 25p multi 3.00 1.40

Biodiversity protection.

National Philatelic and Numismatic Museum, 25th Anniv. — A644

2010, Aug. 10 *Perf. 13¼x13*
1484 A644 33p ocher & black 4.00 1.90

Juan Pablo Duarte (1813-76), Independence Leader, and Birthplace, Santo Domingo — A645

2010, Aug. 30 *Perf. 11½x13¼*
1485 A645 25p multi 3.25 1.40

Delivery of the Flag A646

National Pantheon A647

2010, Oct. 12 **Litho.** *Perf. 13½*
1486 A646 26p multi 3.25 1.40

Perf. 13¼x13

1487 A647 33p multi 4.25 1.75

America Issue.

Stamp Day A648

2010, Oct. 18 *Perf. 13x13¼*
1488 A648 15p multi 1.75 .80

Miniature Sheet

Tourism — A649

No. 1489 — Tourist attractions: a, Los Tres Ojos. b, Juan Dolio Beach. c, Altos de Chavón. d, Bayahibe Beach. e, Bávaro Beach. f, Cayo Levantado. g, Las Terrenas Beach. h, Cabarete Beach. i, River rafters, Jarabacoa. j, Lake Enriquillo.

2010, Nov. 4
1489 A649 10p Sheet of 10, #a-j, + 2 labels 10.00 10.00

Veritas Odd Fellows Lodge, Santo Domingo A650

2010, Nov. 26 *Perf. 13½x13¼*
1490 A650 60p multi 6.50 3.25

World AIDS Day — A651

Designs: 15p, Hands with AIDS ribbons on thumbs. 46p, Flower with AIDS ribbon petals.

2010, Dec. 1 *Perf. 13¼x13*
1491-1492 A651 Set of 2 6.50 3.25

Dominican Order in the Americas, 500th Anniv. A652

Designs: 15p, Monastery. 26p, Dominican monk and native boy, vert.

2010, Dec. 7 *Perf. 13x13¼, 13¼x13*
1493-1494 A652 Set of 2 4.50 2.25

National Archives, 75th Anniv. A653

2010, Dec. 14 *Perf. 13½x13¼*
1495 A653 20p multi 2.50 1.10

Santo Domingo, 2010 American Capital of Culture — A654

2010, Dec. 16 *Imperf.*
1496 A654 26p multi 3.00 3.00

Santo Domingo Gates — A655

No. 1497: a, Puerta de la Misericordia, "Republica" at bottom. b, Puerta del Conde, "Republica" at left. c, Puerta del Conde, "Republica" at top. d, Puerta de la Misericordia, "Republica" at left.

20p, Puerta de la Misericordia, Puerta del Conde, arms of Dominican Republic.

2011, Feb. 21 *Perf. 13x13¼*
1497 A655 10p Block of 4, #a-d 4.50 4.50

Size: 90x70mm
Imperf

1498 A655 20p multi 2.25 2.25

Sur Futuro Foundation A656

Designs: 15p, Tree and rainbow. 20p, Lake.

2011, Mar. 3 *Perf. 13¼x13½*
1499-1500 A656 Set of 2 4.00 1.90

Caves — A657

No. 1501: a, Pomier Caves, San Cristobal. b, Fun Fun Cave, Hato Mayor del Rey. c, Guácara de Hernando Alonzo, La Mata, Sánchez Ramírez. d, Golondrinas Cave, Río San Juan.

2011, Mar. 15 *Perf. 13½x13¼*
1501 A657 10p Block of 4, #a-d 4.50 4.50

Dated 2010.

Postal Union of the Americas, Spain and Portugal (UPAEP), Cent. A658

Designs: 20p, "100" with map of Americas and Iberian peninsula in zeroes. 26p, Map of Americas and Iberian peninsula, doves with letters.

2011, Mar. 18 **Litho.**
1502-1503 A658 Set of 2 4.50 2.50

Flowers — A659

No. 1504: a, Pereskia quisqueyana. b, Cereus hexagonus. c, Catalpa longissima. d, Tolumnia variegata.

2011, Mar. 31 *Perf. 13¼x13*
1504 A659 10p Block of 4, #a-d 4.50 4.50

Dated 2010.

Colonel Rafael T. Fernandez Dominguez (1934-65) A660

2011, May 19 **Litho.** *Perf. 13¼x13*
1505 A660 15p multi 1.75 .80

Liberty Day, 50th Anniv. — A661

2011, June 2 *Imperf.*
1506 A661 33p multi 4.00 4.00

Assassination of Pres. Rafael Trujillo, 50th anniv.

Aviation A662

No. 1507: a, 20p, Airplane of Zoilo H. Garcia. b, 25p, Garcia (1849-1922), first Dominican pilot.

2011, June 16 *Perf. 13x13¼*
1507 A662 Vert. pair, #a-b 5.00 5.00

Places Associated With Independence Leader Juan Pablo Duarte — A663

Designs: 15p, Santa Barbara Church, Santo Domingo. 20p, Baptismal font.

2011, Aug. 30
1508-1509 A663 Set of 2 4.25 1.90

Worldwide Fund for Nature (WWF) — A664

No. 1510 — Hypsiboas heilprini: a, Blue denomination at LR. b, Red denomination at LL. c, Red denomination at LR. d, Blue denomination at LL.

2011, Sept. 7
1510 A664 10p Block of 4, #a-d 5.00 5.00

Father of the Fatherland, by Martin de San Juan — A665

2011, Nov. 9 **Litho.** *Imperf.*
1511 A665 20p multi 2.50 2.50

Execution of Francisco del Rosario Sánchez, 150th anniv.

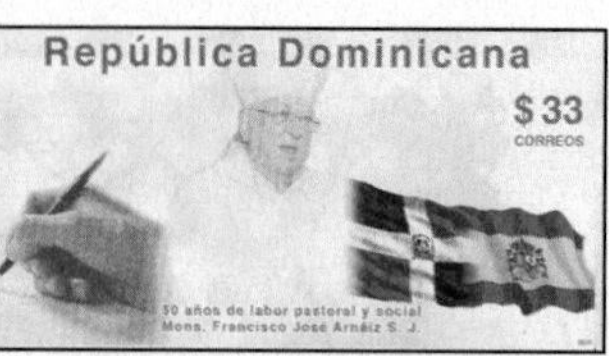

Pastoral and Social Work in Dominican Republic of Bishop Francisco José Arnáiz, 50th Anniv. — A666

2011, Dec. 21
1512 A666 33p multi 3.00 1.75

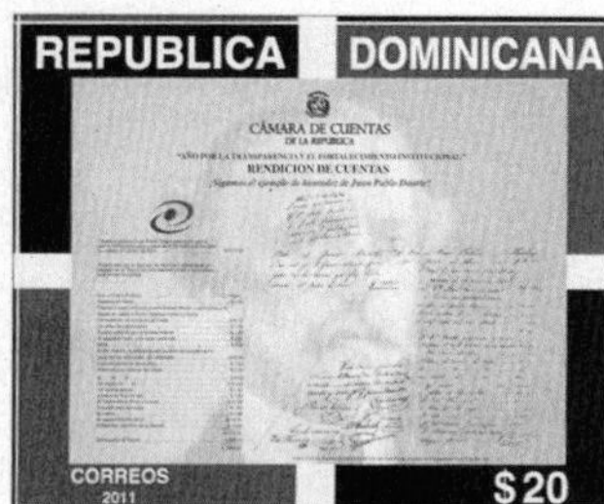

Juan Pablo Duarte and Camara de Cuentas (Governmental Accounting Office) Document — A667

2011
1513 A667 20p multi 2.50 1.10

Sermon Denouncing Mistreatment of Indians of Friar Antonio de Montesinos, 500th Anniv. (in 2011) — A668

2012, Jan. 5 *Perf. 11½*
1514 A668 60p multi 7.50 3.25

Dated 2011.

National Police, 75th Anniv. (in 2011) A669

2012, Jan. 12 ***Perf. 13x13¼***

1515 A669 20p multi 2.50 1.10

Dated 2011.

Order of the Pilgrims of the Way of St. James — A670

2012, Feb. 8 ***Perf. 13¼x13½***

1516 A670 33p multi 3.50 1.75

Miniature Sheets

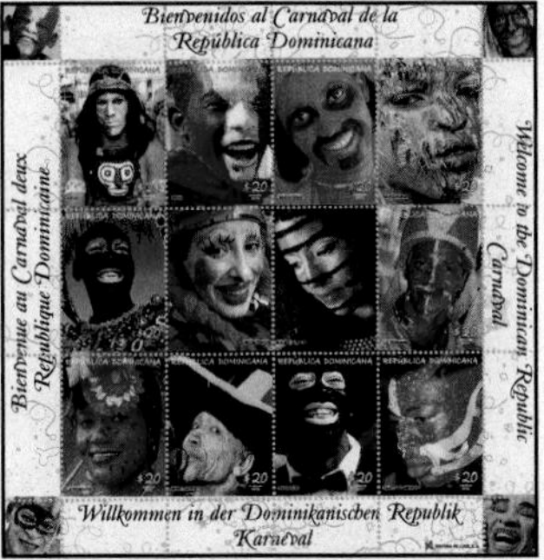

A671

A672

A673

A674

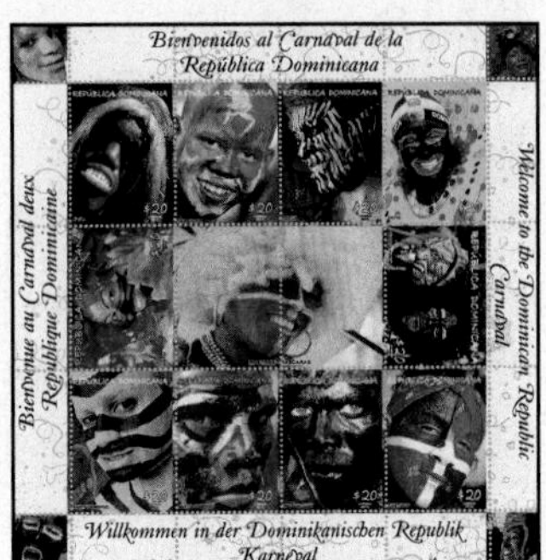

Carnival Masks and Painted Faces — A675

No. 1517: a, Azua (white face with headband). b, Bani. c, Barahona (red and black face). d, Barahona (green, yellow and red face). e, Cotuí (black and red face). f, La Romana (red, white and blue face with hat). g, La Romana (red and blue face with flower). h, Montecristi (yellow face with black and yellow hat). i, San Luis. j, Santo Domingo (red and yellow face with blue spots).

No. 1518: a, Cotuí (pink and red woman's face mask with blue eye lashes), horiz. b, Navarrette. c, Puerto Plata (white and brown mask). d, La Vega (mask with large pointed teeth), horiz. e, Rio San Juan (fish-head mask with large teeth), horiz. f, Samaná. g, San Juan de la Maguana. h, San Pedro de Macoris. i, Santo Domingo (green mask with horns). j, Villa Rivas.

No. 1519: a, Bonao (blue, green and red dragon's head mask). b, Cotuí (hat in flag colors with slits for eyes and mouth). c, La Vega (green and red dragon's head mask). d, Montecristi (red, gold, white, black and green mask). e, La Joya, Guerra, horiz. f, La Romana (yellow and blue bull's head mask with open mouth), horiz. g, Rio San Juan (blue, yellow, green and red demon-head mask with projections). h, Salcedo. i, Santiago (red, white and blue mask with spiked horns). j, Santo Domingo (mask with yellow beard).

No. 1520: a, Barahona (red, white and blue bull's head mask with horns), horiz. b, Bonao (mask with beard, moustache and gold hat). c, Constanza. d, Cabral, horiz. e, Elias Piña. f, La Vega (black, green and red cat's head mask). g, Valverde-Mao, horiz. h, Santiago (white, red and orange mask with spiked horns). i, Santo Domingo (red and yellow mask with horns). j, Puerto Plata (green, white and black pottery head mask), horiz.

No. 1521: a, Azua (red face with green hair). b, Barahona (blue, red, white and black face). c, Cotuí (black and white striped face with green hat). d, Cotuí (black face with flag hat). e, Cotuí (yellow, green, red and black face), horiz. f, Puerto Plata (brown and red mask, black, red and white face), horiz. g, Santo Domingo (yellow and black striped face). h, Santo Domingo (red, blue, white, green and black face). i, Rio San Juan (black face). j, Santiago (red, white and blue face).

Perf. 13¼x13 (vert. stamps), 13x13¼ (horiz. stamps)

2012, Feb. 27

1517 A671 20p Sheet of 10, #a-j, + 2 central labels 20.00 20.00

1518 A672 20p Sheet of 10, #a-j, + 2 central labels 20.00 20.00

1519 A673 20p Sheet of 10, #a-j, + 2 central labels 20.00 20.00

1520 A674 20p Sheet of 10, #a-j, + 2 central labels 20.00 20.00

1521 A675 20p Sheet of 10, #a-j, + 2 central labels 20.00 20.00

Nos. 1517-1521 (5) 100.00 100.00

A676

2012, Mar. 1 ***Perf. 13½x13¼***

1522 A676 20p multi 2.50 1.10

Dated 2011.
Diplomatic Relations Between Dominican Republic and Ecuador, 125th Anniv.

Pontifical Catholic University, Santo Domingo, 50th Anniv. — A677

2012, Apr. 17 ***Perf. 13¼x13***

1523 A677 25p multi 4.50 1.40

Mailboxes A678

Designs: 20p, Mailbox with legs. 25p, Mailbox without legs.

2012, May 8 ***Perf. 13¼x13½***

1524-1525 A678 Set of 2 5.00 2.40

America Issue. Dated 2011.

Maria Montez (1912-51), Actress — A679

2012, June 2 ***Perf. 13¼x13***

1526 A679 100p multi 10.00 5.25

Juan Pablo Duarte (1813-76), Patriot — A680

No. 1527: a, 15p, Photograph of Duarte in Hamburg. b, 25p, Oath of the Trinitaria.

2012, July 24 ***Perf. 13½x13¼***

1527 A680 Pair, #a-b 4.50 2.10

Expo Cibao, 25th Anniv. — A681

2012, Sept. 5 ***Perf. 13¼x13***

1528 A681 20p multi 2.00 1.10

a. Tete-beche pair 4.50 4.50

Miniature Sheet

Birds — A682

No. 1529: a, Caprimulgus eckmani. b, Contopus hispaniolensis. c, Phaenicophilus palmarum. d, Icterus dominicensis. e, Loxia megaplaga. f, Calyptophilus frugivorus. g, Geotrygon leucometopia. h, Spindalis dominicensis. i, Corvus palmarum. j, Tyto glaucops.

2012, Sept. 19

1529 A682 20p Sheet of 10, #a-j, + 2 central labels 25.00 25.00

No. 1529d in the sheet of 10 was inscribed "CIGUA AMARILLA" in the first part of the print run. The error was discovered and corrected to "CIGUA CANARIA" on the remainder of the printing.

Orchids — A683

No. 1530: a, Sudamerylcaste peguerol. b, Tolumnia calochila. c, Quisqueya ekmanii. d, Tolumnia henekenii.

2012, Oct. 18

1530 A683 15p Block of 4, #a-d 6.50 6.50

Presidents Type of 2009

Miniature Sheet

No. 1531: a, Pedro Guillermo. b, Wenceslao Figuereo. c, Horacio Vásquez. d, Juan Isidro Jiménez. e, Eladio Victoria. f, Adolfo Alejandro Nouel. g, José Bordas Valdéz. h, Ramón Báez Machado.

2012 ***Perf. 13¼***

1531 A639 15p Sheet of 8, #a-h, + central label 12.00 12.00

America Issue — A684

No. 1532 — Legend of: a, El Caracaracol. b, La Ciguapa.

2012, Dec. 18 ***Perf. 13¼x13***
1532 A684 20p Horiz. pair, #a-b 15.00 15.00

Miniature Sheet

Tourism — A685

No. 1533: a, Beach, Saona Island. b, Beach, Bahia de las Aguilas. c, San Rafael Beach. d, Gri-Gri Lagoon. e, Dominican Republic flag. f, Playa Dorada. g, El Morro Beach. h, Puerto Plata. i, Monument to the Heroes of the Restoration, Santiago. j, Historic center of Santiago. k, Jordobadas Whale Sanctuary. l, Beach, Punta Cana.

2013, May 23 ***Perf. 13½x13¼***
1533 A685 10p Sheet of 12, #a-l 15.00 15.00

Arachnids — A686

No. 1534: a, Phrynus longipes. b, Mastigoproctus proscorpio. c, Phormictopus cancerides. d, Rhopalurus princeps.

2013, May 28
1534 A686 20p Block of 4, #a-d 10.00 10.00

Pedro Mir (1913-2000), Poet — A687

2013, June 24 ***Perf. 13¼x13***
1535 A687 50p multi 3.00 2.40

La Trinitaria Secret Society, 175th Anniv. — A688

2013, July 15 ***Imperf.***
1536 A688 60p multi 3.75 3.75

María Ugarte (1914-2011), Investigative Reporter — A689

2013, July 31 Litho. ***Perf. 13¼x13***
1537 A689 33p multi 2.25 1.60

A690

General Gregoio Luperón (1839-97) — A691

Perf. 13½x13¼
2013, Aug. 12 Litho.
1538 A690 15p multi 1.10 .70

Imperf
1539 A691 33p multi 2.10 2.10

Dominican War of the Restoration, 150th anniv.

Dominican Rehabilitation Association, Inc., 50th Anniv. — A692

2013, Oct. 23 Litho. ***Perf. 13½x13***
1540 A692 15p red & blue 1.10 .70

Dominican Postal Institute (Inposdom), 50th Anniv. — A693

Designs: 15p, Emblem for InposPak service. 20p, Inposdom emblem, vert. 25p, Exhibit frames at stamp exhibition. 80p, Inposdom Headquarters.

2013, Nov. 28 Litho. ***Perf. 13¼***
1541 A693 15p multi .70 .70

Size: 30x40mm
Perf. 13¼x13½
1542 A693 20p multi .95 .95

Size: 40x30mm
Perf. 13½x13¼
1543 A693 25p multi 1.25 1.25
Nos. 1541-1543 (3) 2.90 2.90

Size: 80x50mm
Imperf
1544 A693 80p multi 5.50 5.50

A694

Juan Pablo Duarte (1813-76), Leader of Independence Movement — A695

No. 1545: a, Atarazana School where Duarte taught fencing. b, House of Josefa Pérez de la Paz, birthplace of La Trinitaria Secret Society. c, Duarte directing "La Dramatica." d, 1844 return of Duarte from exile. e, Duarte and Dominican Republic Constitution and flag.

2013, Dec. 9 Litho. ***Perf. 13***
1545 Horiz. strip of 5 5.00 5.00
a.-e. A694 15p Any single 1.00 1.00

Imperf
1546 A695 25p multi *1.90 1.90*

Campaign Against Discrimination — A696

Designs: 15p, Five children. 20p, Map of Dominican Republic, hands.

2014, Jan. 30 Litho. ***Perf. 13x13¼***
1547-1548 A696 Set of 2 2.75 1.75

America issue. Dated 2013.

A697

Designs: 20p, Building. 25p, Buildings and university crest.

2014, Feb. 14 Litho. ***Perf. 13x13¼***
1549 A697 20p multi 1.40 .95

Size: 89x60mm
Imperf
1550 A697 25p multi 1.75 1.75

Dated 2013.
Founding of St. Thomas Aquinas University, Santo Domingo, 475th Anniv. (in 2013). Reopening of university as Autonomous University of Santo Domingo, cent.

Julia de Burgos (1914-53), Poet — A698

2014, Mar. 28 Litho. ***Perf. 13¼x13***
1551 A698 100p multi 6.75 4.75

Souvenir Sheets

Centro León Museum — A699

National Botanical Gardens — A700

Bellapart Museum — A701

Numismatic and Philatelic Museum — A702

National Museum of Natural History — A703

Museum of Modern Art — A704

No. 1552: a, Entrance to Jimenes Cultural Center. b, Caribeño Patio of Eduardo León Jimenes Cultural Center.

No. 1553: a, Bridge in Japanese Garden. b, Path in Japanese Garden.

No. 1554: a, Permanent Gallery. b, Merengue, painting by Jaime Colson.

No. 1555: a, Exhibit of money with metal ingot. b, Display case in Numismatics Gallery.

No. 1556: a, Museum entrance. b, Skeleton of humpback whale.

No. 1557: a, Sculptures. b, Sculptures and paintings in Permanent Gallery.

2014, May 21 Litho. *Perf. 13½*

1552 A699 50p Sheet of 2, #a-b, + 2 labels 6.50 6.50
1553 A700 50p Sheet of 2, #a-b, + 2 labels 6.50 6.50
1554 A701 50p Sheet of 2, #a-b, + 2 labels 6.50 6.50
1555 A702 50p Sheet of 2, #a-b, + 2 labels 6.50 6.50
1556 A703 50p Sheet of 2, #a-b, + 2 labels 6.50 6.50
1557 A704 50p Sheet of 2, #a-b, + 2 labels 6.50 6.50
Nos. 1552-1557 (6) 39.00 39.00

World Museum Day.

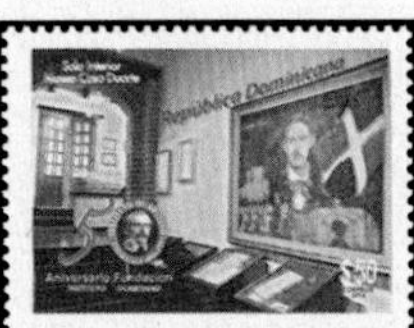

Duarte Institute, 50th Anniv. A705

2014, June 24 Litho. *Perf. 13½*

1558 A705 50p multi 3.50 2.40

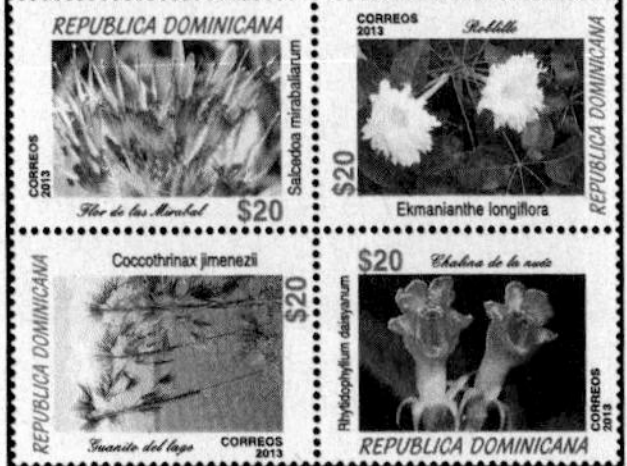

Flowers — A706

No. 1559: a, Salcedoa mirabaliarum. b, Ekmanianthe longiflora, vert. c, Coccothrinax jienezii, vert. d, Rhytidophyllum daisyanum.

2014, Aug. 27 Litho. *Perf. 13x13¼*

1559 A706 20p Block of 4, #a-d 5.75 5.75

Dated 2013.

National Literacy Plan A707

2014, Sept. 8 Litho. *Perf. 13½*

1560 A707 15p multi 1.10 .70

Dated 2013.

Miniature Sheets

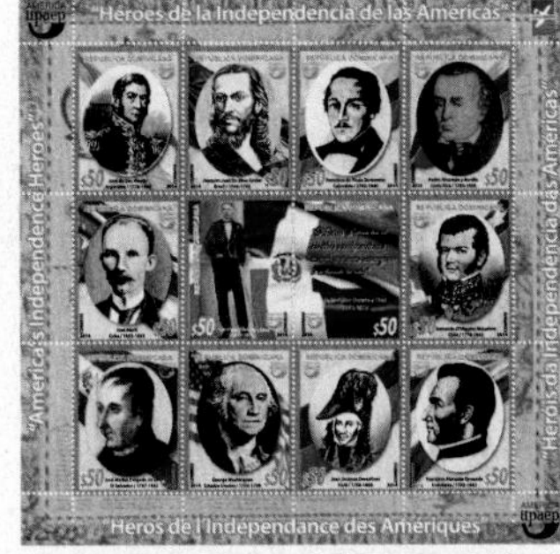

Heroes and Flags of Nations of North and South America — A708

No. 1561, 50p: a, José de San Martín, flag of Argentina. b, Joaquim José Da Silva Xavier (Tiradentes), flag of Brazil. c, Francisco de Paula Santander, flag of Colombia. d, Pedro Alvarado y Bonilla, flag of Costa Rica. e, José Martí, flag of Cuba. f, Juan Pablo Duarte (standing), flag of Dominican Republic. g, Quote by Duarte, flag of Dominican Republic. h, Bernardo O'Higgins Riquelme, flag of Chile. i, José Matías Delgado de León, flag of El Salvador. j, George Washington, flag of United States. k, Jean Jacques Dessalines, flag of Haiti. l, Francisco Morazán Quezada, flag of Honduras.

No. 1562, 50p: a, Simón Bolívar, flag of Bolivia. b, Georges-Etienne Cartier, flag of Canada. c, Máximo Gómez y Báez, flag of Cuba. d, Manuela Sáenz y Aizpuru, flag of Ecuador. e, Pedro Molina Mazariegos, flag of Guatemala. f, Miguel Hidalgo y Costilla, flag of Mexico. g, Head of Duarte, flag of Dominican Republic. h, Augusto César Sandino, flag of Nicaragua. i, Gaspar Rodríguez de Francia, flag of Paraguay. j, José Gabriel Condorcanqui (Túpac Amaru II), flag of Peru. k, José Gervado Artigas Arnal, flag of Uruguay. l, Bolívar, flag of Venezuela.

2014, Sept. 30 Litho. *Perf. 13¼x13*
Sheets of 12, #a-l

1561-1562 A708 Set of 2 70.00 70.00

America issue.

World Food Day — A709

No. 1563: a, Boy holding apple. b, Boy eating broccoli, vert. c, Fruit picker on ladder. d, Girl eating cob of corn, vert.

2014, Oct. 15 Litho. *Perf. 13½*

1563 A709 25p Block of 4, #a-d 7.00 7.00

Miniature Sheet

Wildlife — A710

No. 1564, 25p — Fish: a, Pomacanthus paru. b, Holacanthus ciliaris. c, Serranus tigrinus. d, Nandopsis haitensis. e, Haemulon flavolineatum. f, Anisotremus virginicus. g, Cantherhines macrocerus. h, Agonostomus monticola. i, Epinephelus striatus. j, Gymnothorax funebris. k, Aulostomus maculatus. l, Dasyatis americana.

No. 1565, 25p — Butterflies: a, Anaea troglodyta. b, Anartia lytrea. c, Burca stillmani. d, Burca hispaniolae. e, Myscelia aracynthia. f, Archimestra teleboas. g, Atlante cryptadia. h, Greta diaphanus quisqueya. i, Heraclides machaonides. j, Choranthus haitensis. k, Memphis verticordia. l, Pyrisitia pyro.

Perf. 13½x13¼

2014, Nov. 20 Litho.
Sheets of 12, #a-l

1564-1565 A710 Set of 2 35.00 35.00

Miniature Sheet

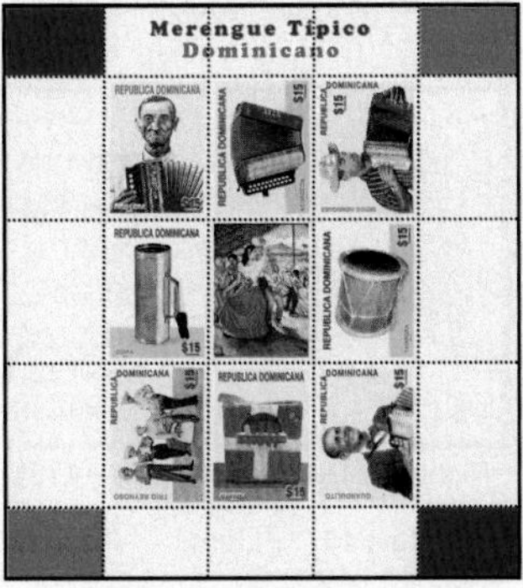

Merengue Musicians and Instruments — A711

No. 1566: a, Nico Lora playing accordion. b, Accordion, horiz. c, Tatico Henriquez playing accordion, horiz. d, Güira. e, Tambora. f, Trio Reynosa performing, horiz. g, Marimba. g, Guandulito playing accordion, horiz.

Perf. 13¼x13½, 13½x13¼

2014, Nov. 26 Litho.

1566 A711 15p Sheet of 8, #a-h, + central label 7.50 7.50

Scouting in the Dominican Republic, Cent. A712

2014, Dec. 3 Litho. *Perf. 13½x13¼*

1567 A712 20p multi 1.25 .90

ISA University, 50th Anniv. (in 2014) A713

2015, Mar. 5 Litho. *Perf. 13½*

1568 A713 200p multi 10.00 9.00

Bani, 250th Anniv. (in 2014) A714

2015, Mar. 6 Litho. *Perf. 13¼*

1569 A714 100p multi 5.50 4.50

Dated 2014.

Gustavo A. Moré González (1925-2002), President of Dominican Philatelic Society — A715

2015, Apr. 9 Litho. *Perf. 13½*

1570 A715 75p multi 4.00 3.50

Stamp Day. Dated 2014.

Programs Run Through Office of the First Lady — A716

No. 1571: a, Newborn Screening Program. b, Comprehensive Care Center for Disability.

2015, Apr. 28 Litho. *Perf. 13¼x13*

1571 A716 250p Horiz. pair, #a-b 25.00 25.00

Miniature Sheets

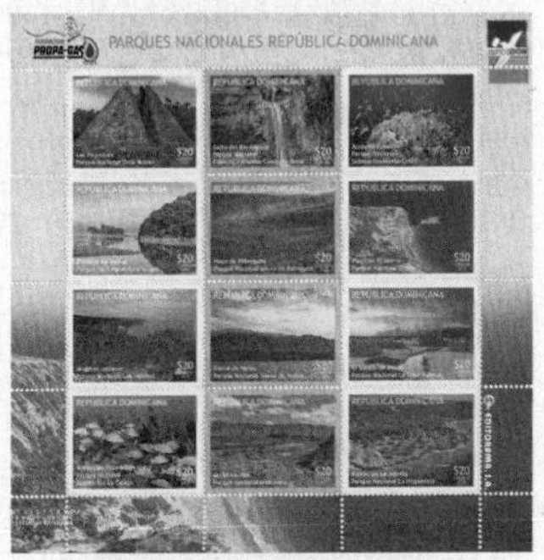

National Parks — A717

No. 1572, 20p: a, Pyramids, Valle Nuevo National Park. b, Rio Grande Waterfall, Francisco Alberto Caamaño Deñó National Park. c, Coral reef and fish, Monte Cristi Underwater National Park. d, Hatillo Dam Reservoir with small islands at left, Aniana Vargas National Park. e, Hoyo de Pelempito, Sierra de Bahoruco National Park. f, Aerial view of El Morro Beach, El Morro National Park. g, Coastal hills, Los Haitises National Park. h, Sierra de Neiba, Sierra de Neiba National Park. i, Salado de Neiba, La Gran Sabana National Park. j, Haemulon spp., La Caleta Underwater National Park. k, Quita Coraza, Anacona National Park. l, La Isabela ruins, La Hispaniola National Park.

No. 1573, 20p: a, Baiguate Waterfall, Baiguate National Park. b, Punta Aguila Cliffs, Jaragua National Park. c, Waterfall, Saltos de la Jalda National Park, vert. d, Cliffs, Sierra Martin García National Park. e, Cyclura ricordii, Lago Enriquillo e Isla Cabritos National Park. f, Offshore rocks, Los Haitises National Park. g, Rock art, Aniana Vargas National Park, vert. h, Whales, Cabo Cabrón National Park. i, Plagiodontia aedium, Sierra de Bahoruco National Park. j, Mountains, Nalga de Maco National Park. k, Sea level view of cliffs and El Morro Beach, El Morro National Park. l, Palm trees, Sierra Martin García National Park.

No. 1574, 20p: a, Tetero Valley, José del Carmen Ramírez National Park. b, Isla Saona, Este National Park. c, Fregata magnificens, Este National Park. d, Mountains, Armando Bermúdez National Park. e, Sun over water, Lago Enriquillo e Isla Cabritos National Park. f, Cabo Cabrón, Cabo Cabrón National Park. g, Epilobocera wetherbeei, Valle Nuevo National Park. h, Punta Espada, Punta Espada National Park. i, Río Amina, Manolo Tavárez Justo National Park. j, La Humeadora, La Humeadora National Park. k, Rivers, Humedales del Ozama National Park. l, Río Mana, Máximo Gómez National Park, vert.

No. 1575, 20p: a, Balsa Estuary, Mangiares de Estero Balsa National Park. b, Río Mao, Piky Lora National Park. c, Lakes, Humedales del Ozama National Park. d, Shoreline, Mangiares del Bajo Yuna National Park. e, Foggy landscape, Valle Nuevo National Park. f, Bahia de las Aguilas, Jaragua National Park. g, Siproeta stelenes, Máximo Gómez National Park, vert. h, Hatillo Dam Reservoir with rocks at LR, Aniana Vargas National Park. i, Phaenicophilus palmarum, Luis Quin National Park. j, Loma La Tachuela, Luis Quin National Park. k, Shoreline, Este National Park. l, Mountains, Manolo Tavárez Justo National Park.

2015, May 22 Litho. *Perf. 13½*
Sheets of 12, #a-l

1572-1575 A717 Set of 4 55.00 55.00

Dominican Chapter of Lions International, 50th Anniv. — A718

2015, May 24 Litho. *Perf. 13¼*
1576 A718 50p multi 2.75 2.25

Matías Ramón Mella Castillo (1816-64), Vice-President — A719

2015, June 10 Litho. *Imperf.*
1577 A719 300p multi 16.00 16.00

Dated 2014.

Cooperation Between Brazilian and Dominican Republic Universities, 50th Anniv. — A720

2015, June 22 Litho. *Perf. 13½*
1578 A720 50p multi 2.50 2.25

Santiago Chamber of Commerce, Cent. — A721

2015, July 9 Litho. *Perf. 13¼*
1579 A721 50p multi 2.50 2.25

Oscar de la Renta (1932-2014), Fashion Designer — A722

2015, Oct. 13 Litho. *Perf. 13¼x13*
1580 A722 250p multi 12.50 11.00

St. Teresa of Avila (1515-82) — A723

2015, Oct. 16 Litho. *Perf. 13¼x13½*
1581 A723 45p multi 2.25 2.00

Rights for Disabled People — A724

2015, Nov. 16 Litho. *Perf. 13¼*
1582 A724 100p multi 5.00 4.50

Campaign to End Violence Against Women — A725

Perf. 13¼x13½
2015, Nov. 25 Litho.
1583 A725 35p multi 1.75 1.60

See Ecuador No. 2173, Guatemala No. 717, El Salvador No. 1747, and Venezuela No. 1731.

Religious Objects — A726

No. 1584: a, Pax, 17th cent. (portapaz). b, Processional cross, 18th cent. (cruz procesional). c, Monstrance, 19th cent. (custodia). d, Eucharistic ark, 16th cent. (arca eucaristica). e, Chalice, 16th cent. (cáliz).

2015, Dec. 1 Litho. *Perf. 13¼x13½*
1584 Strip of 5 12.00 12.00
a.-e. A726 45p Any single 2.00 2.00

Presidents Type of 2009
Miniature Sheet

No. 1585: a, Francisco Henríquez y Carvajal. b, Juan Bautista Vicini Burgos. c, Rafael Estrella Ureña. d, Inscriptions "1930-1938" and "1942-1952" (rule of Rafael Trujillo). e, Inscription "1952-1960" (rule of Hector Trujillo). f, Jacinto Bienvenido Peynado. g, Manuel de Jesús Troncoso de la Concha. h, Joaquín Balaguer Ricardo.

2015, Dec. 18 Litho. *Perf. 13¼*
1585 A639 20p Sheet of 8, #a-h, + central label 9.00 9.00

Dated 2014.

Campaign Against Human Trafficking A727

No. 1586: a, People in suitcase. b, Chained hands holding Earth.

2015, Dec. 18 Litho. *Perf. 13x13½*
1586 A727 50p Pair, #a-b 5.25 5.25

America Issue.

Dominican Republic Postage Stamps, 150th Anniv. A728

Designs: 30p, Dominican Republic #1. 35p, Dominican Republic #2. 45p, Dominican Republic #3. 50p, Dominican Republic #4.

150p, Dominican Republic #1-4, cover bearing #1, printing press.

2015, Dec. 18 Litho. *Perf. 13x13½*
1587-1590 A728 Set of 4 8.50 7.00

Size: 140x100mm
Imperf

1591 A728 150p multi 7.50 7.50

Luis María "Billo" Frómeta (1915-88), Orchestra Conductor A729

2016, Mar. 30 Litho. *Perf. 13½*
1592 A729 150p multi 8.50 6.75

Pedro Henriquez Ureña National University, 50th Anniv. A730

2016, Apr. 20 Litho. *Perf. 13½*
1593 A730 50p multi 2.50 2.25

Marine Mammals — A731

No. 1594: a, Tursiops truncatus. b, Trichechus manatus manatus. c, Megaptera novaeangliae. d, Globicephala.

Perf. 13½x13¼
2016, June 15 Litho.
1594 A731 50p Block of 4, #a-d 11.00 11.00

Anoles — A732

No. 1595: a, Anolis divius. b, Anolis prasinorius. c, Anolis viridius. d, Anolis eladioi.

Perf. 13½x13¼
2016, June 15 Litho.
1595 A732 50p Block of 4, #a-d 11.00 11.00

Miniature Sheet

Dominican Scientists — A733

No. 1596: a, Dr. Pedro Troncoso Sánchez (1904-89), ambassador and historian. b, Dr. Henri Alain Liogier (1916-2009), botanist. c, Dr. Pablo Rafael Iñiguez Pérez (1925-2007), gastroenterologist. d, Dr. José Luís Alemán Dupuy (1928-2007), economist. e, Dr. Juan Manuel Taveras Rodríguez (1919-2002), neuroradiologist. f, Dr. José Altagracia Silié Gatón (1919-2014), judge. g, Dr. Hugo R. Mendoza Tapia (1930-2009), pediatrician. h, Dr. Francisco R. Guarocuya Batista del Villar (1934-2013), cardiologist.

2016, Aug. 10 Litho. *Perf. 13½*
1596 A733 20p Sheet of 8, #a-h 11.00 11.00

Matías Ramón Mella Castillo (1816-64), National Hero — A734

2016, Sept. 29 Litho. *Imperf.*
1597 A734 150p multi 9.50 9.50

A735

Designs: 35p, Florence Terry Griswold (1875-1941), Founder of Pan America Round Tables, and Hotel Menger, San Antonio, Texas.

2016, Oct. 12 Litho. *Perf. 13x13¼*
1598 A735 35p multi 2.75 1.50

First Pan American Round Table, cent.

2016 Summer Olympics, Rio de Janeiro — A736

No. 1599: a, Track and field. b, Boxing. c, Weight lifting. d, Taekwondo.

2016, Oct. 18 Litho. *Perf. 13½x13¼*
1599 A736 15p Block of 4, #a-d 4.75 4.75

America Issue.

Miniature Sheet

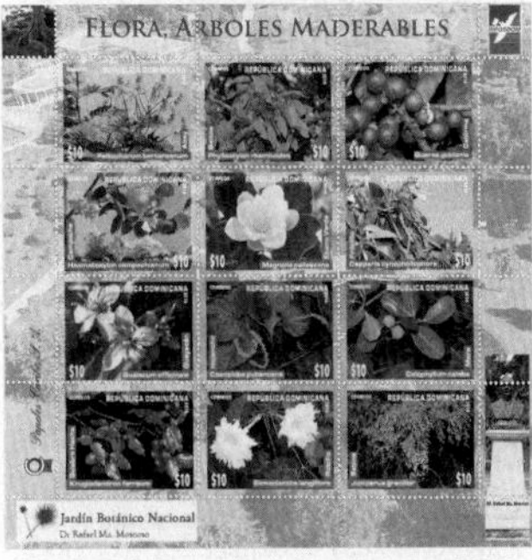
National Botanical Garden — A737

No. 1600: a, Peltophorum berteroanum. b, Phyllostylon rhamnoides. c, Guarea guidonia. d, Haematoxylon campechianum. e, Magnolia pallescens. f, Capparis cynophollophora. g, Guaiacum officinale. h, Coccoloba pubescens. i, Calophyllum calaba. j, Krugiodendron ferreum. k, Ekmanianthe longiflora. l, Juniperus gracilior.

2016, Oct. 27 Litho. *Perf. 13x13¼*
1600 A737 10p Sheet of 12, #a-l 9.50 9.50

No. 1600h "pubescens" is spelled wrong on stamp.

Dr. Román Bautista Brache (1905-65), Physician and Politician — A738

2016, Nov. 4 Litho. *Perf. 13¼x13½*
1601 A738 20p multi 1.25 .90

Mountains — A739

No. 1602: a, Matterhorn, Switzerland. b, Loma Isabel de Torres, Dominican Republic.

Perf. 13½x13¼
2016, Nov. 17 Litho.
1602 A739 60p Pair, #a-b 8.00 8.00

80th anniv. of relations between Dominican Republic and Switzerland.
See Switzerland Nos. 1617.

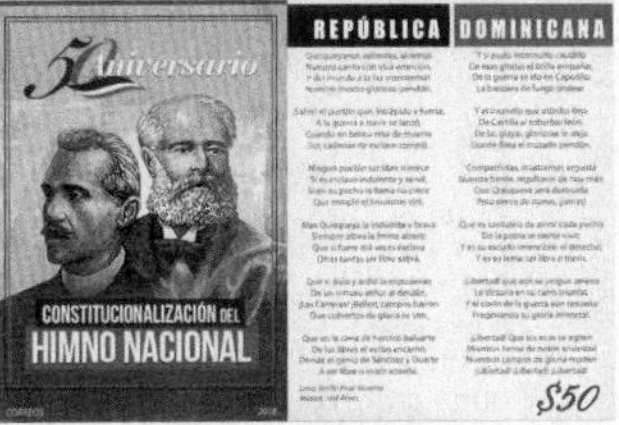
Specification of Dominican Republic National Anthem in National Constitution, 50th Anniv, — A740

2016, Nov. 28 Litho. *Imperf.*
1603 A740 50p multi 3.50 3.50

Miguel de Cervantes (1547-1616), Writer — A741

2017, Jan. 31 Litho. *Perf. 13¼x13½*
1604 A741 100p multi + label 4.50 4.50

BanReservas (Reserve Bank), 75th Anniv. — A742

2017, Mar. 2 Litho. *Perf. 13¼x13½*
1605 A742 75p multi 3.25 3.25

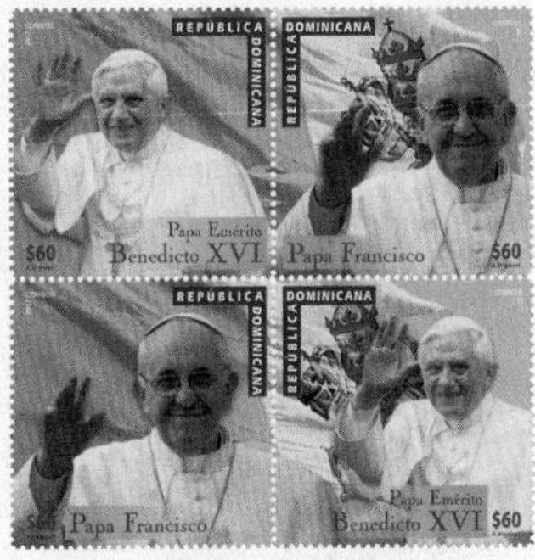
Popes — A743

No. 1606: a, Pope Emeritus Benedict XVI, denomination at LL. b, Pope Francis, denomination at LR. c, Pope Francis, denomination at LL. d, Pope Emeritus Benedict XVI, denomination at LR.

2017, Mar. 14 Litho. *Perf. 13½*
1606 A743 60p Block of 4, #a-d 10.50 10.50

Francisco del Rosario Sánchez (1817-61), Leader in Dominican War of Independence — A744

2017, Mar. 29 Litho. *Imperf.*
1607 A744 150p multi 6.50 6.50

Bridges — A745

No. 1608: a, Mauricio Báez Bridge. b, Matías Ramón Mella Bridge. c, Rio Chavón Bridge. d, Hermanos Patiño Bridge.

2017, Apr. 24 Litho. *Perf. 13½x13¼*
1608 A745 50p Block of 4, #a-d 8.50 8.50

Painters and Their Paintings — A746

No. 1609: a, Silvano Lora (1931-2003). b, Domingo Líz (1931-2013), horiz. c, Gordas en Bicicletas, by Líz, horiz. d, Serie Concieno Ecologico, by Lora.

Perf. 13¼x13½, 13½x13¼ (horiz. stamps)
2017, Apr. 24 Litho.
1609 A746 25p Block of 4, #a-d 4.25 4.25

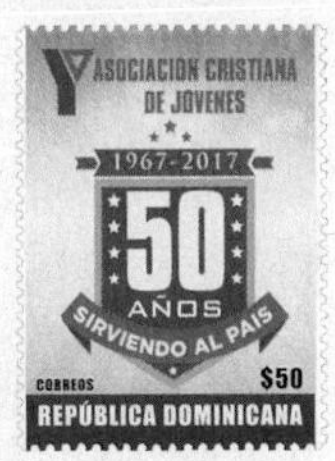
YMCA in Dominican Republic, 50th Anniv. — A747

2017, Apr. 28 Litho. *Perf. 13¼x13½*
1610 A747 50p multi 2.10 2.10

Miniature Sheet

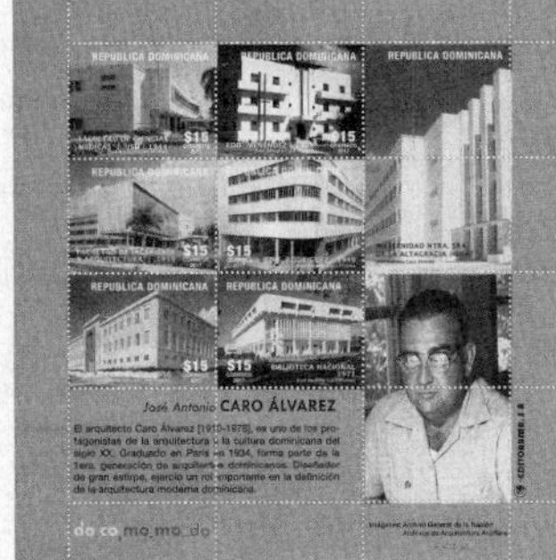
Buildings Designed by José Antonio Caro Alvarez (1910-78) — A748

No. 1611: a, University of Santo Domingo Faculty of Medical Science Building, 1944. b, Menendez Building, 1941. c, Faculty of Engineering and Architecture Building, 1959. d, Rodriguez Building, 1949. e, Central Bank Building, 1956. f, National Library, 1971.

2017, May 9 Litho. *Perf. 13½x13¼*
1611 A748 15p Sheet of 6, #a-f, + 6 labels 4.00 4.00

Fe y Alegría Organization in Dominican Republic, 25th Anniv. — A749

2017, May 17 Litho. *Perf. 13¼x13½*
1612 A749 25p multi 1.10 1.10

Lions Clubs International, Cent. (in 2016) — A750

2017, May 21 Litho. *Perf. 13½x13¼*
1613 A750 100p multi 4.25 4.25

Casa de España Organization, Cent. — A751

2017, June 14 Litho. *Perf. 13½*
1614 A751 12p multi .50 .50

Miniature Sheet

Fruit — A752

No. 1615: a, Annona squamosa. b, Chrysophyllum cainito. c, Malpighia punicifolia. d, Eugenia domingensis. e, Chrisobalanus icaco. f, Genipa americana. g, Spondias mombin. h, Mammea americana. i, Annona reticulata. j, Byrsonima spicata. k, Ziziphus rhodoxylon. l, Coccoloba uvifera.

Perf. 13½x13¼
2017, Sept. 12 Litho.
1615 A752 20p Sheet of 12, #a-l 10.50 10.50

Miniature Sheets

Historic Maps of Hispaniola — A753

No. 1616, 10p — Map by: a, Christopher Columbus, 1493. b, Bologna, 1516. c, Benedetto Bordone, 1528. d, Giovanni B. Ramusio, 1534. e, Giacomo Gastaldi, 1548. f, Giacomo Ruscelli, 1561. g, Paolo Forlani, 1564. h, Ramusio, 1565. i, Bertelli Lafreri, 1566. j, Tomasso Porcacchi, 1572. k, Girolamo Ruscelli, 1580. l, Cornelius Wytfliet, 1597.

No. 1617, 10p — Map by: a, Laugenes, 1598. b, Metellus, 1598. c, Petrus Bertius, 1616. d, Arent Roggeveen, 1675. e, P. Coronelli, 1696. f, Guillaume de l'Isle, 1722-23. g, Emanuel Bowen, 1747. h, M. Bellin, 1754. i, M. Bonne, 1788. j, William Foden, 1795. k, I. Sonis, 1796. l, Tardieu, 1802.

2017, Sept. 26 Litho. *Perf. 13x13¼*
Sheets of 12, #a-l

1616-1617 A753 Set of 2 10.50 10.50

Martin Luther (1483-1546), Religious Reformer — A754

2017, Oct. 9 Litho. *Perf. 13½x13¼*

1618 A754 100p multi 4.25 4.25

Protestant Reformation, 500th anniv.

Women's Citizenship and Suffrage, 75th Anniv. A755

2017, Nov. 7 Litho. *Perf. 13½x13¼*

1619 A755 75p multi 3.25 3.25

Manuel Corripio García (1908-2004), Businessman, and His House — A756

2017, Nov. 29 Litho. *Perf. 13½*

1620 A756 20p multi .85 .85

A vertical column of perforations runs through the center of No. 1620.

Miniature Sheet

Santo Domingo Colonial Era Buildings — A757

No. 1621: a, Santa Maria de la Encarnacion Basilica Cathedral. b, Ruins of San Nicolás di Bari Hospital. c, Imperial Convent. d, Church of the Convent of Our Lady of Mercy. e, Ozama Fortress. f, Museum of the Royal Houses. g, Rosario Chapel. h, Ruins of Monastery of San Francisco.

2017, Dec. 11 Litho. *Perf. 13½*

1621 A757 12p Sheet of 8, #a-h, + 4 central labels 4.00 4.00

Jarabacoa — A758

2017, Dec. 20 Litho. *Perf. 13¼*

1622 A758 25p multi 1.10 1.10

International Year of Sustainable Tourism for Development.

Miniature Sheet

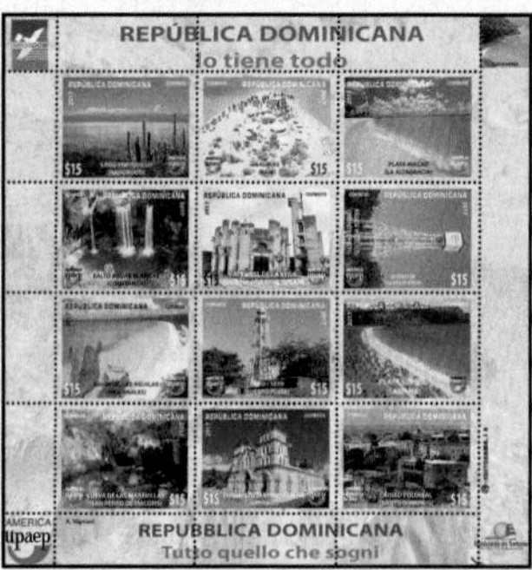

Tourist Attractions — A759

No. 1623: a, Lago Enriquillo, Bahoruco Province. b, Salinas Sand Dunes, Baní. c, Playo Macao, La Altagracia Province. d, Waterfall, Constanza. e, Cathedral of the Immaculate Conception, La Vega. f, Clock tower designed by Gustave Eiffel, Montecristi, vert. g, Bahia de las Aguilas, Pedernales Province. h, Lighthouse, Puerto Plata Province. i, Playa Rincón, Samaná Province. j, Cueva de las Maravillas, San Pedro de Macoris Province. k, St. James the Apostle Cathedral, Santiago de los Caballeros. l, Colonial City, Santo Domingo.

2017, Dec. 20 Litho. *Perf. 13½*

1623 A759 15p Sheet of 12, #a-l 7.50 7.50

America Issue.

Introduction of Basketball in the Dominican Republic, Cent. (in 2017) — A760

2018, Jan. 23 Litho. *Perf. 13x13¼*

1624 A760 25p multi 1.10 1.10

Dated 2017.

Vincentian Charism, 400th Anniv. (in 2017) A761

2018, Jan. 25 Litho. *Perf. 13x13¼*

1625 A761 100p multi 4.25 4.25

Dated 2017.

Souvenir Sheet

Friendship Between Dominican Republic and Peru — A762

No. 1626: a, Ramón Castilla y Marquesado (1797-1867), 20th President of Peru, and flag of Peru. b, Gregorio Luperón (1839-97), 20th President of Dominican Republic, flag of Dominican Republic.

2018, Feb. 7 Litho. *Perf. 13½*

1626 A762 50p Sheet of 2, #a-b 4.25 4.25

Dated 2017. See Peru No. 1957.

Miniature Sheet

Buildings Designed by Guillermo González Sánchez (1900-70) — A763

No. 1627: a, Ramfis Park, 1936. b, Feria de la Paz (Peace Fair), 1955. c, Copello Building, 1938. d, Hotel Jaragua. e, Centro Social Obrero (Social Worker Center), 1945. f, Hotel Hamaca, 1949.

Perf. 13½x13¼

2018, Feb. 15 Litho.

1627 A763 15p Sheet of 6, #a-f, + 6 labels 3.75 3.75

Dated 2017.

Rotary International in Dominican Repulbic, 75th Anniv. — A764

2018, May 15 Litho. *Perf. 13½*

1628 A764 75p multi 3.00 3.00

Miniature Sheet

Buildings Designed by Humberto Ruiz Castillo (1897-1966) — A765

No. 1629: a, St. John Cosco Church, 1938. b, Santo Domingo College, 1939. c, San Rafael Chapel, 1942. d, Anatomy Faculty Building, University of Santo Domingo, 1945. e, Gonzalez Ramos Building, 1946. f, Alma Mater, University of Santo Domingo, 1955.

2018, May 29 Litho. *Perf. 13½x13¼*

1629 A765 15p Sheet of 6, #a-f, + 6 labels 3.75 3.75

Inter-American Institute for Cooperation on Agriculture, 50th Anniv. — A766

Perf. 13½x13¼

2018, June 27 Litho.

1630 A766 50p multi 2.00 2.00

Miniature Sheet

23rd Central American and Caribbean Games, Barranquilla, Colombia — A767

No. 1631: a, Basketball. b, Baseball. c, Artistic gymnastics. d, Volleyball.

2018, July 4 Litho. *Perf. 13½x13¼*

1631 A767 25p Sheet of 4, #a-d 4.00 4.00

Miniature Sheets

Artists and Their Works — A768

No. 1632, 50p: a, Celeste Woss y Gil (1891-1985). b, Nude, by Woss y Gil. c, Mother Selling Dolls, by Cándido Bidó (1936-2011). d, Bidó.

No. 1633, 50p: a, Rooster, by Guillo Perez (1923-2014). b, Perez. c, Marianela Jiménez (1925-2008). d, Carnaval, by Jiménez.

No. 1634, 50p: a, Soucy de Pellerano (1928-2014). b, Maqui-barca del Progresso, sculpture by de Pellerano. c, Untitled work by Fernando Ureña Rib (1951-2014). d, Ureña Rib.

2018, July 18 Litho. *Perf. 13¼x13½*
Sheets of 4, #a-d

1632-1634 A768 Set of 3 24.00 24.00

National Symphony Orchestra — A769

2018, Aug. 22 Litho. *Imperf.*

1635 A769 100p multi 4.00 4.00

Miniature Sheets

Aviators and Flags of Their Countries — A770

No. 1636, 20p: a, Ramón Franco (1896-1938), Spain. b, Frank Andrés Féliz Miranda (1901-54), Dominican Republic. c, Charles Lindbergh (1902-74), United States. d, Juan Guillermo Villasana López (1891-1959), Mexico. e, Silvio Pettirossi (1887-1916), Paraguay. f, Jorge Antonio Chávez Dartnell (1887-1910), Peru. g, Cesáreo L. Berisso (1887-1971), Uruguay. h, Artur de Sacadura Cabral (1881-1924) and Carlos Viegas Gago Cutinho (1869-1959), Portugal, horiz.

No. 1637, 20p: a, Jorge Alejandro Newbery (1875-1914), Argentina, horiz. b, Rafael Pabón Cuevas (1903-34), Bolivia. c, Alberto Santos-Dumont (1873-1932), Brazil. d, Arturo Meriño Benítez (1888-1970), Chile. e, Camilo Daza Alvarez Mutiscua (1898-1975), Colombia. f, Domingo Rosillo del Toro (1878-1957), Cuba, g, Zoilo Hermógenes García (1881-1916), Dominican Republic. h, Cosme Rennella Barbatto (1890-1937), Ecuador.

Perf. 13¼x13½, 13½x13¼ (#1636h, 1637a)

2018, Oct. 3 Litho.
Sheets of 8, #a-h

1636-1637 A770 Set of 2 13.00 13.00

Spanish International Cooperation Agency in the Dominican Republic — A771

2018, Oct. 17 Litho. *Perf. 13½*

1638 A771 60p multi 2.40 2.40

17th Congress of Aeronautical and Space History, Santo Domingo — A772

2018, Nov. 19 Litho. *Perf. 13½*

1639 A772 25p multi 1.00 1.00

Dr. Salvador B. Gautier (1868-1938), First President of Dominican Republic Red Cross — A773

Perf. 13¼x13½

2018, Nov. 27 Litho.

1640 A773 100p multi 4.00 4.00

Miniature Sheet

Winning Art In Zero Hunger Generation Children's Stamp Design Contest — A774

No. 1641: a, Child licking bowl, by Anabelys Estévez. b, Child and plate of food, by Angela María Ramírez Ciriaco. c, Children watering seedling and dreaming of giving apples to other children, by Victor Manuel Pérez. d, Children on globe, by Anderson Alvarez Carpio.

2018, Dec. 12 Litho. *Perf. 13x13¼*

1641 A774 25p Sheet of 4, #a-d 4.00 4.00

Miniature Sheet

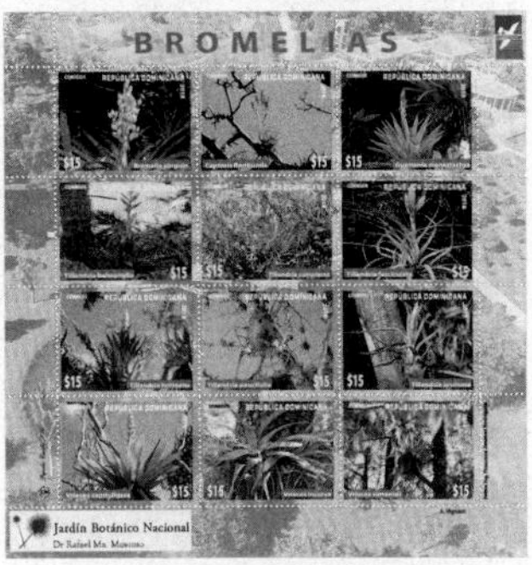

Bromeliads — A775

No. 1642: a, Bromelia pinguin. b, Captosis floribunda. c, Guzmania monestachya. d, Tillandsia baliophylla. e, Tillandsia compressa. f, Tillandsia fasciculata. g, Tillandsia hotteana. h, Tillandsia paucifolia. i, Tillandsia pruinosa. j, Vriesea capituligera. k, Vriesea incurva. l, Vriesea sintenisii.

2019, Feb. 26 Litho. *Perf. 13x13¼*

1642 A775 15p Sheet of 12, #a-l 7.25 7.25

Expo-Independencia 2019 Numismatic and Philatelic Exhibition, Santo Domingo — A776

2019, Apr. 21 Litho. *Imperf.*

1643 A776 25p multi 1.00 1.00

Cooperation Between the Dominican Republic and the European Union — A777

2019, May 8 Litho. *Perf. 13¼*

1644 A777 60p multi 2.40 2.40

A778

A779

A780

A781

Santo Domingo Rotary Club, 50th Anniv. A782

2019, May 24 Litho. *Perf. 13½x13¼*

1645	Horiz. strip of 5	4.00	4.00
a.	A778 20p multi	.80	.80
b.	A779 20p multi	.80	.80
c.	A780 20p multi	.80	.80
d.	A781 20p multi	.80	.80
e.	A782 20p multi	.80	.80

Miniature Sheets

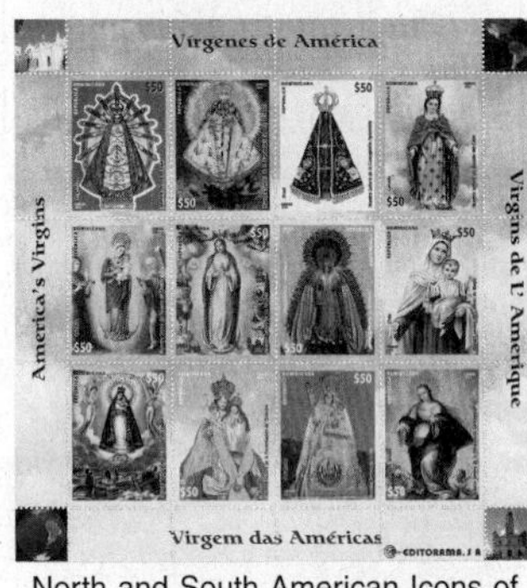

North and South American Icons of the Virgin Mary — A783

No. 1646, 50p — Icon from: a, Argentina. b, Bolivia. c, Brazil. d, Canada. e, Colombia. f, Costa Rica. g, Dominican Republic (Nuestra Señora de las Mercedes). h, Chile. i, Cuba. j, Ecuador. k, El Salvador. l, United States.

No. 1647, 50p — Icon from: a, Guatemala. b, Haiti. c, Honduras. d, Mexico. e, Nicaragua. f, Dominican Republic (Nuestra Señora de la Altagracia). g, Panama. h, Paraguay. i, Peru. j, Puerto Rico. k, Uruguay. l, Venezuela.

Perf. 13¼x13½

2019, June 13 Litho.
Sheets of 12, #a-l

1646-1647 A783 Set of 2 47.50 47.50

A784

Dominican Numismatic Society, 50th Anniv. — A785

Designs: 60p, Dominican Numismatic Society 50th anniversary emblem.

No. 1649 — Obverse and reverse of: a, King Ferdinand II era real coin (denomination at UR). b, Two reales silver coin minted in Santo Domingo (denomination at LR). c, 1844 quarter real coin (denomination at UL). d, 1937 half peso coin (denomination at LL).

2019, June 21 Litho. *Perf. 13½*
1648 A784 60p multi 2.40 2.40

Perf. 13x13¼
1649 A785 20p Sheet of 4, #a-d 3.25 3.25

Dr. Zoraida Heredia Suncar (1917-2011), Educator — A786

2019, July 17 Litho. *Perf. 13¼x13*
1650 A786 60p multi 2.40 2.40

Establishment of Diplomatic Relations Between the Dominican Republic and People's Republic of China — A787

2019, Aug. 2 Litho. *Imperf.*
1651 A787 75p multi 3.00 3.00

Miniature Sheet

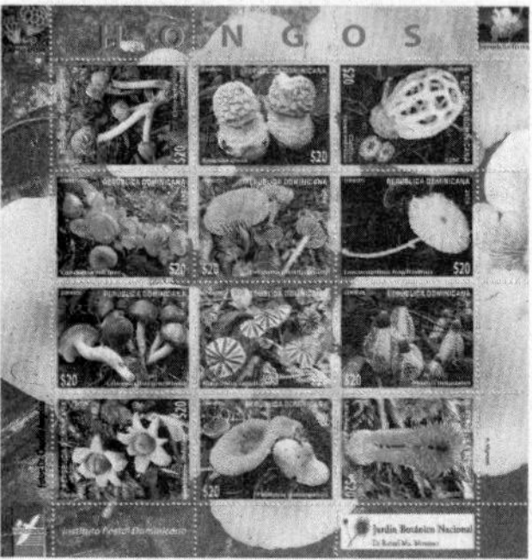
Mushrooms — A788

No. 1652: a, Chlorophyllum molybdites, vert. b, Amanita cruzii. c, Clathrus rose-ovolvatus, vert. d, Coockeina sulcipes. e, Entoloma aff. altissimum. f, Leucocoprinus fragilissimus. g, Leucopaxillus gracillimus. h, Marasmius tageticolor. i, Phallus indusiatus. j, Geastrum violaceum, vert. k, Phillipsia domingensis. l, Laternea pusilla, vert.

Perf. 13½x13¼, 13¼x13½ (vert. stamps)
2019, Aug. 21 Litho.
1652 A788 20p Sheet of 12, #a-l 9.50 9.50

Mohandas K. Gandhi (1869-1948), Indian Nationalist Leader — A789

Perf. 13¼x13½
2019, Aug. 27 Litho.
1653 A789 100p multi 4.00 4.00

Alexander von Humboldt (1769-1859), Naturalist, and Andira Inermis — A790

Perf. 13¼x13½
2019, Sept. 18 Litho.
1654 A790 250p multi 9.75 9.75

A vertical column of perforations runs through the center of the stamp, with the denomination on the left side, and the country name on the right side.

Miniature Sheets

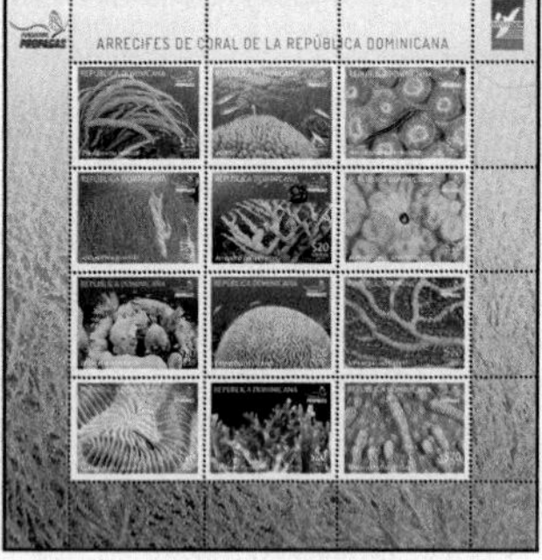
Corals — A791

No. 1655, 20p: a, Plexaurella nutans. b, Madracis auretenra. c, Black fish over blue and red Montastraea cavernosa. d, Antipathes gracilis. e, Acropora palmata. f, Yellow Montastraea cavernosa. g, Orbicella annularis. h, Two fish over Colpophyllia natans. i, Iciligorgia schrammi. j, Fish and close-up view of Colpophyllia natans. k, Stylaster roseus. l, Mycetophyllia aliciae.

No. 1656, 20p: a, Acropora cervicornis. b, Neospongodes portoricensis. c, Mycetophyllia ferox. d, Dendrogyra cylindrus. e, Pseudopterogorgia sp. f, Tubastraea coccinea. g, Antipathes caribbeana. h, Orbicella faveolata. i, Millepora complenata. j, Agaricia tenuifolia. k, Gorgonia ventalina. l, Helioseris cucullata.

2019, Oct. 9 Litho. *Perf. 13½x13¼*
Sheets of 12, #a-l
1655-1656 A791 Set of 2 18.50 18.50

Color Television Broadcasting in Dominican Republic, 50th Anniv. — A792

2019, Nov. 7 Litho. *Perf. 13½x13¼*
1657 A792 50p multi 1.90 1.90

Miniature Sheet

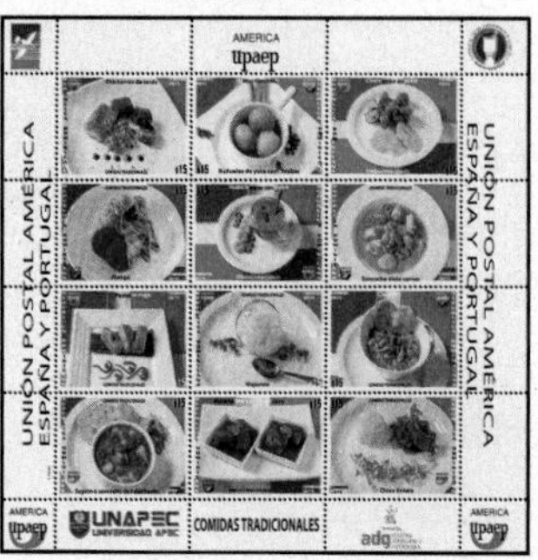
America Issue — A793

No. 1658 — Native cuisine: a, Chicharrón de cerdo (pork rinds). b, Buñuelos de yuca con almíbar (yucca fritters with syrup). c, Chicharrón de pollo (fried chicken). d, Mangú (pureed plantains). e, Habichuelas con dulce (sweet beans). f, Sancocho siete carnes (stew with seven meats). g, Pastel en hoja (Dominican tamales). h, Majarete (corn pudding). i, Chambre (meat and vegetable soup). j, Sopión o sancocho de habichuelas (bean soup). k, Plátano maduro al caldero (plantains in sweet syrup). l, Chivo liniero (goat stew).

Perf. 13½x13¼
2019, Nov. 14 Litho.
1658 A793 15p Sheet of 12, #a-l 7.00 7.00

SEMI-POSTAL STAMPS

Catalogue values for unused stamps in this section are for Never Hinged items.

Nos. 474-478 Surcharged in Red

Engraved and Lithographed
1957, Feb. 8 Unwmk. *Perf. 11½*
Flags in National Colors

B1	A117	1c + 2c brn, lt bl, vio & mar	.40	.40
B2	A117	2c + 2c dk brn, lt bl & vio	.40	.40
B3	A117	3c + 2c red lilac & red	.40	.40
B4	A117	5c + 2c red orange & vio	.40	.40
B5	A117	7c + 2c green & violet	.50	.50
		Nos. B1-B5,CB1-CB3 (8)	3.90	3.90

The surtax was to aid Hungarian refugees. A similar 25c surcharge was applied to the miniature sheets described in the footnote following No. 478. Value, 2 sheets, perf. and imperf., $45

Nos. 479-483 Surcharged in Red Orange

1957, Sept. 9 Photo. *Perf. 13½*
Flags in National Colors

B6	A118	1c + 2c brown & brt bl	.30	.30
B7	A118	2c + 2c org ver & dk bl	.35	.35
B8	A118	3c + 2c dark blue	.40	.40
B9	A118	5c + 2c olive & dk bl	.55	.55
B10	A118	7c + 2c rose brn & dk bl	.60	.60
		Nos. B6-B10,CB4-CB6 (8)	4.75	4.15

Cent. of the birth of Lord Baden Powell and the 50th anniv. of the Scout Movement. The surtax was for the Dominican Republic Boy Scouts.

A similar 5c surcharge was applied to the miniature sheets described in the footnote following No. 483. Value 4 sheets, perf. and imperf., medal and flag, $62.50

Types of Olympic Regular Issue, 1957, Surcharged in Carmine

a

b

1958, May 26 Engr. & Litho.
Flags in National Colors
Pink Paper

B11	A119(a)	1c + 2c red brown	.30	.30
B12	A119(b)	1c + 2c red brown	.30	.30
B13	A120(a)	2c + 2c gray brown	.40	.40
B14	A120(b)	2c + 2c gray brown	.40	.40
B15	A119(a)	3c + 2c violet	.40	.40
B16	A119(b)	3c + 2c violet	.40	.40
B17	A120(a)	5c + 2c red orange	.55	.55
B18	A120(b)	5c + 2c red orange	.55	.55
B19	A119(a)	7c + 2c Prus green	.65	.65
B20	A119(b)	7c + 2c Prus green	.65	.65
		Nos. B11-B20,CB7-CB12 (16)	7.80	7.80

Surtax for the UN Relief and Works Agency for Palestine Refugees.

A similar 5c surcharge, plus marginal United Nations emblem and "UNRWA," was applied to the miniature sheets described in the footnote following No. 488. Value, 4 sheets, perf. and imperf., $20.

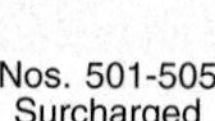
Nos. 501-505 Surcharged

Perf. 13½
1959, Apr. 13 Photo. Unwmk.
Flags in National Colors

B21	A125	1c + 2c rose, indigo & ultra	.45	.45
B22	A125	1c + 2c brown & blue	.45	.45
B23	A125	3c + 2c gray, vio, blk & buff	.55	.55
B24	A125	5c + 2c rose, dk bl, brn & red	.70	.70
B25	A125	7c + 2c lt brn, dk bl & red	.80	.80
		Nos. B21-B25,CB13-CB15 (8)	6.45	6.45

International Geophysical Year, 1957-58.

A similar 5c surcharge was applied to the miniature sheets described in the footnote following No. 505. Value, 2 sheets, perf. and imperf., $40.

Type of 1957 Surcharged in Red

Engraved and Lithographed
1959, Sept. 10 Unwmk. *Imperf.*
Flags in National Colors

B26 A117 1c + 2c brn, lt bl, vio & mar .40 .40
B27 A117 2c + 2c dk brn, lt bl & vio .40 .40
B28 A117 3c + 2c red lilac & red .45 .45
B29 A117 5c + 2c red org & vio .45 .45
B30 A117 7c + 2c green & violet .55 .55
Nos. B26-B30,CB16-CB18 (8) 4.85 4.85

3rd Pan American Games, Chicago, Aug. 27-Sept. 7, 1959.

Nos. 522-524 Surcharged in Red

1960, Apr. 7 Litho. *Perf. 12½*
Center in Gray

B31 A135 5c + 5c red brn & yel grn .35 .35
B32 A135 9c + 5c car & lt bl .35 .35
B33 A135 13c + 5c org & grn .80 .80
Nos. B31-B33,CB19-CB20 (5) 2.40 2.40

World Refugee Year, July 1, 1959-June 30, 1960. The surtax was for aid to refugees.

Souvenir sheets exist perf. and imperf., containing one each of Nos. B31-B33 and CB19-CB20. Value, 2 sheets, perf. and imperf., $12.50

Nos. 525-529 Surcharged

1962, Jan. 8 Photo. *Perf. 13½*
Flags in National Colors

B34 A136 1c + 2c red, yel grn & blk .35 .35
B35 A136 2c + 2c org, grnsh bl & brn .35 .35
B36 A136 3c + 2c henna brn & bl .35 .35
B37 A136 5c + 2c brown & ultra .35 .35
B38 A136 7c + 2c grn, bl & rose brn .35 .35
Nos. B34-B38,CB21-CB23 (8) 3.10 3.10

15th anniv. (in 1961) of UNESCO.

A similar 5c surcharge was applied to the miniature sheets described in the footnote following No. 529. Value, 2 sheets, perf. and imperf., $20.

Anti-Malaria Type of 1962
1962, Apr. 29 Litho. *Perf. 12*

B39 A141 10c + 2c brt pink & red lil .50 .40
B40 A141 20c + 2c pale brn & brn .75 .55

Freedom from Hunger Type of 1963
1963, Apr. 15 Unwmk. *Perf. 11½*
Banner in Dark Blue & Red

B41 A148 2c + 1c green .35 .25
B42 A148 5c + 2c brt rose lil .35 .25
B43 A148 9c + 2c orange .35 .25
Nos. B41-B43 (3) 1.05 .75

A souvenir sheet contains three imperf. stamps similar to Nos. B41-B43. Value, $1.50.

Nos. 591-593 Surcharged

1964, Mar. 8 *Perf. 12½*

B44 A153 3c + 2c pale pink & ver .35 .35
B45 A153 6c + 2c pale bl & ultra .35 .35
B46 A153 9c + 2c pale rose & red brn .35 .35
Nos. B44-B46,CB26-CB27 (5) 1.80 1.80

UNESCO world campaign to save historic monuments in Nubia.

Nos. 622-626 Surcharged

1966, Dec. 9 Litho. *Perf. 12½*
Size: 31x21mm

B47 A164 1c + 2c multi *8.50 1.25*
B48 A164 2c + 2c multi *8.50 1.25*
B49 A164 3c + 2c multi *8.50 1.25*
B50 A164 6c + 4c multi *8.50 1.25*
B51 A164 8c + 4c multi *8.50 1.25*
Nos. B47-B51,CB28-CB30 (8) 56.00 14.00

Surtax for victims of Hurricane Inez.

AIR POST STAMPS

Map of Hispaniola — AP1

Perf. 11½
1928, May 31 Litho. Unwmk.

C1 AP1 10c deep ultra 5.25 2.50

1930

C2 AP1 10c ocher 3.50 3.00
a. Vert. pair, imperf. btwn. *600.00*
C3 AP1 15c scarlet 6.75 4.00
C4 AP1 20c dull green 3.25 .85
C5 AP1 30c violet 6.75 4.50
Nos. C2-C5 (4) 20.25 12.35

Nos. C2-C5 have only "CENTAVOS" in lower panel. Issued: 10c, 20c, 1/24; 15c, 30c, 2/14.

1930

C6 AP1 10c light blue 1.75 .60
C7 AP1 15c blue green 3.25 1.00
C8 AP1 20c yellow brown 3.50 .85
a. Horiz. pair, imperf. vert. 450.00 450.00
C9 AP1 30c chocolate 6.25 1.75
Nos. C6-C9 (4) 14.75 4.20

Issue dates: 10c, 15c, 20c, Sept.; 30c, Oct.

Batwing Sundial Erected in 1753 — AP2

1931-33 *Perf. 12*

C10 AP2 10c carmine 3.50 .50
C11 AP2 10c light blue 1.75 .50
C12 AP2 10c dark green 6.25 2.75
C13 AP2 15c rose lilac 2.75 .50
C14 AP2 20c dark blue 6.25 2.25
a. Numerals reading up at left and down at right 5.75 2.75
b. Imperf., pair 250.00
C15 AP2 30c green 2.50 .25
C16 AP2 50c red brown 6.25 .50
C17 AP2 1p deep orange 10.00 2.75
Nos. C10-C17 (8) 39.25 10.00

Issued: No. C11, 7/2/32; No. C12, 5/28/33; others 8/16.

Airplane and Ozama Fortress AP3

1933, Nov. 20

C18 AP3 10c dark blue 3.50 .60

Airplane and Trujillo Bridge AP4

1934, Sept. 20

C19 AP4 10c dark blue 3.00 .50

Symbolic of Flight AP5

1935, Apr. 29

C20 AP5 10c lt blue & dk blue 1.60 .50

AP6

1936, Feb. 11 *Perf. 11½*

C21 AP6 10c dk bl & turq bl 2.50 .50

Allegory of Flight AP7

1936, Oct. 17

C22 AP7 10c dk bl, bl & turq bl 2.25 .40

Macoris Airport AP8

1937, Oct. 22

C23 AP8 10c green 1.00 .25

Fleet of Columbus AP9

Air Fleet AP10

Proposed Columbus Lighthouse — AP11

1937, Nov. 9 *Perf. 12*

C24 AP9 10c rose red 1.75 1.40
C25 AP10 15c purple 1.40 .95
C26 AP11 20c dk bl & lt bl 1.40 1.25
C27 AP10 25c red violet 2.00 1.25
C28 AP11 30c yellow green 1.75 1.25
C29 AP10 50c brown 3.50 1.75
C30 AP11 75c dk olive grn 10.50 10.50
C31 AP9 1p orange 6.25 2.50
Nos. C24-C31 (8) 28.55 20.85

Goodwill flight to all American countries by the planes "Colon," "Pinta," "Nina" and "Santa Maria."

No. C30 was reproduced imperf. on No. 1019.

Pan American Clipper AP12

1938, July 30

C32 AP12 10c green 1.25 .25

Trylon and Perisphere, Plane and Proposed Columbus Lighthouse — AP13

1939, Apr. 30

C33 AP13 10c green & lt green 2.00 .85

New York World's Fair.

Airplane AP14

1939, Oct. 18

C34 AP14 10c green & dp green 1.60 .25
a. Pair, imperf. btwn. *450.00*

Proposed Columbus Lighthouse, Plane and Caravels — AP15

Christopher Columbus and Proposed Lighthouse — AP16

Proposed Lighthouse — AP17

Christopher Columbus — AP18

Caravel — AP19

1940, Oct. 12

C35	AP15	10c sapphire & lt bl	1.10	.60
C36	AP16	15c org brn & brn	1.60	1.00
C37	AP17	20c rose red & red	1.60	1.00
C38	AP18	25c brt red lil & red vio	1.60	.50
C39	AP19	50c green & lt green	3.00	1.75
		Nos. C35-C39 (5)	8.90	4.85

Discovery of America by Columbus and proposed Columbus memorial lighthouse in Dominican Republic.

Posts and Telegraph Building, San Cristobal
AP20

1941, Feb. 21

C40	AP20	10c brt red lil & pale lil rose	.50	.25

Globe, Wing and Letter
AP21

1942, Feb. 13

C41	AP21	10c dark violet brn	.60	.30
C42	AP21	75c deep orange	3.25	2.00

Plane
AP22

1943, Sept. 1

C43	AP22	10c brt red lilac	.40	.25
C44	AP22	20c dp blue & blue	.40	.25
C45	AP22	25c yellow olive	5.75	3.25
		Nos. C43-C45 (3)	6.55	3.75

Plane, Flag, Coat of Arms and Torch of Liberty — AP23

1944, Feb. 27 ***Perf. 11½***
Flag in Gray, Dark Blue, Carmine

C46	AP23	10c multicolored	.35	.25
C47	AP23	20c multicolored	.45	.25
C48	AP23	1p multicolored	2.00	1.50
		Nos. C46-C48 (3)	2.80	2.00

Centenary of Independence. See No. 407 for souvenir sheet listing.

Communications Building, Ciudad Trujillo — AP24

1944, Nov. 12 **Litho.** ***Perf. 12***

C49	AP24	9c yel grn & blue	.25	.25
C50	AP24	13c dull brn & rose car	.25	.25
C51	AP24	25c org & dull red	.35	.25
b.		Vert. pair, imperf. btwn.	45.00	
C52	AP24	30c black & ultra	.75	.65
		Nos. C49-C52 (4)	1.60	1.40

Twenty booklets of 100 (25 panes of 4) of the 25c were issued. All booklets are still intact.

Communications Type

1945, Sept. 1
Center in Dark Blue and Carmine

C53	A92	7c deep yellow green	.35	.25
C54	A92	12c red orange	.40	.25
C55	A92	13c deep blue	.50	.25
C56	A92	25c orange brown	.90	.25
		Nos. C53-C56 (4)	2.15	1.00

AP26

Flags and National Anthem
AP27

Unwmk.
1946, Feb. 27 **Litho.** ***Perf. 12***
Center in Dark Blue, Deep Carmine and Black

C57	AP26	10c carmine	.95	.40
C58	AP26	15c blue	2.10	.85
C59	AP26	20c chocolate	2.50	.85
C60	AP26	35c orange	3.00	.95
C61	AP27	1p grn, yel grn & cit	25.00	10.00
		Nos. C57-C61 (5)	33.55	13.05

Nos. C57-C61 exist imperf.

Map Type of Regular Issue

1946, Aug. 4

C62	A94	10c multicolored	.75	.25
C63	A94	13c multicolored	1.35	.25

Waterfall Type of Regular Issue

1947, Mar. 18 **Litho.**
Center Multicolored

C64	A95	18c light blue	1.00	.50
C65	A95	23c carmine	1.60	.60
C66	A95	50c red violet	2.10	.60
C67	A95	75c chocolate	3.00	1.10
		Nos. C64-C67 (4)	7.70	2.80

Palace Type of Regular Issue

1948, Feb. 27

C68	A96	37c orange brown	2.10	1.00
C69	A96	1p orange yellow	5.75	2.10

Ruins Type of Regular Issue

1949 **Unwmk.** ***Perf. 11½***

C70	A97	7c ol grn & pale ol grn	.40	.25
C71	A97	10c orange brn & buff	.40	.25
C72	A97	15c brt rose & pale pink	1.25	.30
C73	A97	20c green & pale green	1.75	.60
		Nos. C70-C73 (4)	3.80	1.40

Issue dates: 10c, Apr. 4; others, Apr. 13.

Las Carreras Monument — AP32

1949, Aug. 10

C74	AP32	10c red & pink	.75	.25

Cent. of the Battle of Las Carreras.

Catalogue values for unused stamps in this section, from this point to the end of the section, are for Never Hinged items.

Hotel Type of Regular Issue

Hotels: 12c, Montana. 37c, San Cristobal.

1950, Sept. 8

C75	A100	12c dk blue & blue	.50	.25
C76	A100	37c carmine & pink	3.25	2.50

Map, Plane and Caduceus
AP34

1950, Oct. 2

C77	AP34	12c orange brn & yel	1.00	.25

13th Pan-American Health Conf. Exists imperf.

Hospital Type of Regular Issue

1952, Aug.

C78	A104	23c deep blue	1.20	1.20
C79	A104	29c carmine	3.25	2.25

Columbus Lighthouse and Plane — AP36

1953, Jan. 6 **Engr.** ***Perf. 13***

C80	AP36	12c ocher	.30	.25
C81	AP36	14c dark blue	.30	.25
C82	AP36	20c black brown	.70	.60
C83	AP36	23c deep plum	.40	.40
C84	AP36	25c dark blue	.95	.70
C85	AP36	29c deep green	.70	.60
C86	AP36	1p red brown	2.00	1.25
a.		Miniature sheet of 10	21.00	21.00
		Nos. C80-C86 (7)	5.35	4.05

No. C86a is lithographed and contains Nos. 450-452 and C80-C86, in slightly different shades. Sheet measures 190x130mm and is imperf. with simulated perforations.

A miniature sheet similar to No. C86a, but measuring 200x163mm and in folder, exists. Value $100.

Ano Mariano Initials in Monogram — AP37

1954, Aug. 5 **Litho.** ***Perf. 11½***

C87	AP37	8c claret	.30	.25
C88	AP37	11c blue	.35	.25
C89	AP37	33c brown orange	1.20	.60
		Nos. C87-C89 (3)	1.85	1.10

Marian Year. Nos. C87-C89 exist imperf.

Rotary Type of Regular Issue

1955, Feb. 23 ***Perf. 12***

C90	A110	11c rose red	.50	.25

Flags — AP39

Portraits of General Hector B. Trujillo: 25c, In civilian clothes. 33c, In uniform.

1955, May 16 **Engr.** ***Perf. 13½x13***

C91	AP39	11c blue, yel & car	.80	.25
C92	AP39	25c rose violet	1.40	.30
C93	AP39	33c orange brown	2.00	.50
		Nos. C91-C93 (3)	4.20	1.05

The center of No. C91 is litho. 25th anniv. of the inauguration of the Trujillo era.

Fair Type of Regular Issue

1955, Dec. 20 **Unwmk.** ***Perf. 13***

C94	A112	11c vermilion	.60	.25

ICAO Type of Regular Issue

1956, Apr. 6 **Litho.** ***Perf. 12½***

C95	A114	11c ultra	1.25	.25

Tree Type of Regular Issue

Design: 13c, Mahogany tree.

1956, Dec. 8 **Litho.** ***Perf. 11½x12***

C96	A115	13c orange & green	*2.25*	.25

Type of Regular Issue, 1957

Olympic Winners and Flags: 11c, Paavo Nurmi, Finland. 16c, Ugo Frigerio, Italy. 17c, Mildred Didrikson ("Didrickson" on stamp), US.

Engraved and Lithographed
Perf. 11½, Imperf.
1957, Jan. 24 **Unwmk.**
Flags in National Colors

C97	A117	11c ultra & red org	.25	.25
C98	A117	16c carmine & lt grn	.30	.25
C99	A117	17c black, vio & red	.40	.25
		Nos. C97-C99 (3)	.95	.75

16th Olympic Games, Melbourne, Nov. 22-Dec. 8, 1956.

Souvenir sheets of 3 exist, perf. and imperf., containing Nos. C97-C99. Value, 2 sheets, perf. & imperf., $15.

For surcharges see Nos. CB1-CB3, CB16-CB18.

Type of Regular Issue

Olympic Winners and Flags: 11c, Robert Morrow, US, 100 & 200 meter dash. 16c, Chris Brasher, England, steeplechase. 17c, A. Ferreira Da Silva, Brazil, hop, step and jump.

Perf. 13½, Imperf.
1957, July 18 **Photo.**
Flags in National Colors

C100	A118	11c yellow grn & dk bl	.25	.25
C101	A118	16c lilac & dk blue	.30	.25
C102	A118	17c brown & blue grn	.40	.25
		Nos. C100-C102 (3)	.95	.75

1956 Olympic winners.

See note on miniature sheets following No. 483.

For surcharges see Nos. CB4-CB6.

Types of Regular Issue

Olympic Winners and Flags: 11c, Hans Winkler, Germany, individual jumping. 16c, Alfred Oerter, US, discus throw. 17c, Shirley Strickland, Australia, 800 meter hurdles.

Engraved and Lithographed
Perf. 13½, Imperf.
1957, Nov. 12 **Unwmk.**
Flags in National Colors

C103	A119	11c ultra	.25	.25
C104	A120	16c rose carmine	.40	.25
C105	A119	17c claret	.40	.25
		Nos. C103-C105 (3)	1.05	.75

1956 Olympic winners.

Miniature sheets of 3 exist, perf. and imperf., containing Nos. C103-C105. Value, 2 sheets, perf. and imperf., $5.50.

For surcharges see Nos. CB7-CB12.

Type of Regular Issue

Olympic Winners and Flags: 11c, Charles Jenkins, 400 & 800 meter run, and Thomas Courtney, 1,600 meter relay, US. 16c, Field hockey team, India. 17c, Yachting team, Sweden.

Perf. 13½, Imperf.

1958, Oct. 30 Unwmk. Photo.

Flags in National Colors

C106 A125 11c blue, olive & brn .30 .25
C107 A125 16c lt grn, org & dk bl .40 .25
C108 A125 17c ver, blue & yel .40 .25
Nos. C106-C108 (3) 1.10 .75

1956 Olympic winners.

Miniature sheets of 3 exist, perf. and imperf., containing Nos. C106-C108. Value, 2 sheets, perf. and imperf., $3.

For surcharges see Nos. CB13-CB15.

Fair Type of Regular Issue

1958, Dec. 9 Litho. *Perf. 12½*

C109 A127 9c gray .30 .25
C110 A127 25c lt violet .85 .40
a. Souv. sheet of 3, #C109-C110, 507, imperf. 2.25 2.25

Polo Type of Regular Issue

1959, May 15 *Perf. 12*

C111 A130 11c Dominican polo team .40 .30

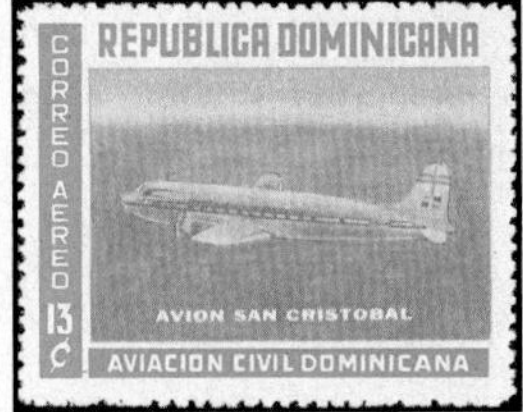

"San Cristobal" Plane — AP42

Perf. 11½

1960, Feb. 25 Unwmk. Litho.

C112 AP42 13c org, bl, grn & gray .50 .25

Dominican Civil Aviation.

Children and WRY Emblem AP43

1960, Apr. 7 *Perf. 12½*

C113 AP43 10c plum, gray & grn .65 .30
C114 AP43 13c gray & green .90 .30

World Refugee Year, 7/1/59-6/30/60.

For surcharges see Nos. CB19-CB20.

Olympic Type of Regular Issue

Olympic Winners: 11c, Pat McCormick, US, diving. 16c, Mithat Bayrack, Turkey, welterweight wrestling. 17c, Ursula Happe, Germany, 200 meter breast stroke.

Perf. 13½, Imperf.

1960, Sept. 14 Photo.

Flags in National Colors

C115 A136 11c blue, gray & brn .35 .25
C116 A136 16c red, brown & ol .35 .30
C117 A136 17c black, blue & ocher .35 .40
Nos. C115-C117 (3) 1.05 .95

17th Olympic Games, Rome, 8/25-9/11.

Miniature sheets of 3 exist, perf. and imperf., containing Nos. C115-C117. Value, 2 sheets, perf. and imperf., $3.75.

For surcharges see Nos. CB21-CB23.

Coffee-Cacao Type of Regular Issue

1961, Dec. 30 Litho. *Perf. 12½*

C118 A140 13c orange ver .35 .30
C119 A140 33c brt yellow .80 .70

Nos. C118-C119 exist imperf.

Anti-Malaria Type of Regular Issue

1962, Apr. 29 Unwmk. *Perf. 12*

C120 A141 13c pink & red .50 .25
C121 A141 33c org & dp org .95 .50

See Nos. CB24-CB25.

Type of Regular Issue

Designs: 13c, Broken fetters and laurel. 50c, Flag, torch and inscription.

1962, May 30 *Perf. 12½*

C122 A142 13c brn, yel, ol, ultra & red .40 .30
C123 A142 50c rose lilac, ultra & red 1.40 1.00

No. C122 exists imperf.

UPAE Type of Regular Issue

1962, Oct. 23 *Perf. 12½*

C124 A146 13c bright blue .45 .25
C125 A146 22c dull red brown .60 .50

Nos. C124-C125 exist imperf.

Nouel Type of Regular Issue

Design: Frame altered with rosary and cross surrounding portrait.

1962, Dec. 18

C126 A147 13c blue & pale blue .45 .25
C127 A147 25c vio & pale vio .75 .50
a. Souv. sheet, #C126-C127, imperf 1.25 1.25

Nos. C126-C127 exist imperf.

Sanchez, Duarte, Mella AP44

1963, July 7 Litho. *Perf. 11½x12*

C128 AP44 15c orange .50 .25

120th anniv. of separation from Haiti.

World Map AP45

1963, Oct. 25 Unwmk. *Perf. 12½*

C129 AP45 10c gray & carmine .45 .25

Cent. of Intl. Red Cross. Exists imperf.

Human Rights Type

1963, Dec. 10 Litho.

C130 A152 7c fawn & red brn .30 .25
C131 A152 10c lt blue & blue .30 .25

Nos. C130-C131 exist imperf.

Ramses II Battling the Hittites (from Abu Simbel) — AP46

1964, Mar. 8 *Perf. 12½*

C132 AP46 10c brt violet .30 .25
C133 AP46 13c yellow .30 .25

UNESCO world campaign to save historic monuments in Nubia.

Nos. C132-C133 exist imperf.

For surcharges see Nos. CB26-CB27.

Striated Woodpecker — AP47

1964, June 8 Litho.

C134 AP47 10c multicolored 5.75 .25

Type of Space Issue

Designs: 7c, Rocket leaving earth. 10c, Space capsule orbiting earth.

1964, July 28 Unwmk. *Perf. 12½*

C135 A156 7c brt green .30 .25
C136 A156 10c violet blue .40 .30
a. Souvenir sheet 4.25 3.50

No. C136a contains 7c and 10c stamps similar to Nos. C135-C136 with simulated perforations.

Pres. John F. Kennedy — AP48

1964, Nov. 22 *Perf. 11½*

C137 AP48 10c buff & dk brown .60 .25

President John F. Kennedy (1917-63). Sheets of 10 (5x2) and sheets of 50.

UPU Type of Regular Issue

1964, Dec. 5 Litho. *Perf. 12½*

C138 A157 7c blue .35 .25

ICY Type of Regular Issue

1965, Feb. 16 Unwmk. *Perf. 12½*

C139 A158 10c lilac & violet .45 .30

Basilica of Our Lady of Altagracia — AP49

1965, Mar. 18 Unwmk. *Perf. 12½*

C140 AP49 10c multicolored .50 .25

Fourth Mariological Congress and the Eleventh International Marian Congress.

Abraham Lincoln — AP50

1965, Apr. 15 Litho. *Perf. 12½*

C141 AP50 17c bright blue .65 .40

Cent. of the death of Abraham Lincoln.

Stamp Centenary Type of 1965

Design: Stamp of 1865, (No. 2).

1965, Dec. 28 Litho. *Perf. 12½*

C142 A161 7c violet, lt grn & blk .40 .25
C143 A161 10c yellow, lt grn & blk .40 .30

ITU Emblem, Old and New Communication Equipment — AP51

1966, Apr. 6 Litho. *Perf. 12½*

C144 AP51 28c pink & carmine .85 .85
C145 AP51 45c brt grn & grn 1.50 1.50

Cent. (in 1965) of the ITU.

Butterfly Type of Regular Issue

1966, Nov. 8 Litho. *Perf. 12½*

Various Butterflies in Natural Colors

Size: 35x24mm

C146 A164 10c lt violet & violet 7.75 .75
C147 A164 50c org & dp org 10.00 1.50
C148 A164 75c pink & rose red 12.50 2.50
Nos. C146-C148 (3) 30.25 4.75

For surcharges see Nos. CB28-CB30.

Altar Type of Regular Issue

1967, Jan. 18 Litho. *Perf. 11½*

C149 A165 7c lt olive green .35 .25
C150 A165 10c lilac .35 .25
C151 A165 20c yellow brown .45 .30
Nos. C149-C151 (3) 1.15 .80

Chess Type of Regular Issue

Design: 10c, Pawn and Bishop.

1967, June 23 Litho. *Perf. 12½*

C152 A167 10c ol, lt ol & blk 1.25 .30
a. Souvenir sheet 10.00 1.90

No. C152a contains 2 imperf. stamps similar to Nos. 636 and C152.

Alliance for Progress Type

1967, Sept. 16 Litho. *Perf. 12½*

C153 A168 8c gray .50 .30
C154 A168 10c blue .60 .30

Cornucopia and Emblem — AP52

1967, Oct. 7

C155 AP52 12c multicolored .75 .30

25th anniversary of the Inter-American Agriculture Institute.

Satellite Type of Regular Issue

1968, June 15 Typo. *Perf. 12*

C156 A170 10c dp blue & multi .35 .25
C157 A170 15c purple & multi .50 .30

Boxing Type of Regular Issue

Designs: Two views of boxing match.

1968, June 29

C158 A171 7c orange yel & grn .60 .25
C159 A171 10c gray & blue .75 .25

See note after No. 641.

Lions Type of Regular Issue

1968, Aug. 9 Litho. *Perf. 11½*

C160 A172 10c ultra & multi .30 .25

Olympic Type of Regular Issue

Designs (Olympic Emblem and): 10c, Weight lifting. 33c, Pistol shooting.

1968, Nov. 12 Litho. *Perf. 11½*

C161 A173 10c buff & multi .35 .25
C162 A173 33c pink & multi 1.25 .75

Latin American Flags — AP53

1969, Jan. 25 Litho. *Perf. 12½*
C163 AP53 10c pink & multi .45 .25

7th Inter-American Savings and Loan Conference, Santo Domingo, Jan. 25-31.

Taino Art Type of Regular Issue

7c, Various vomiting spoons with human heads, vert. 10c, Female torso forming drinking vessel. 20c, Vase with human head, vert.

1969, Jan. 31 Litho. *Perf. 12½*
C164 A175 7c lt bl, bl & lem .40 .25
C165 A175 10c pink, ver & brn .50 .25
C166 A175 20c yellow, org & brn .60 .30
Nos. C164-C166 (3) 1.50 .80

COTAL Type of Regular Issue

10c, Airport of the Americas and COTAL emblem.

1969, May 25 Litho. *Perf. 12½*
C167 A178 10c brown & pale fawn .40 .25

ILO Type of Regular Issue

1969, June 27 Litho. *Perf. 12½*
C168 A179 10c rose, red & black .40 .25

Baseball Type of Regular Issue

Designs: 7c, Bleachers, Tetelo Vargas Stadium, horiz. 10c, Batter, catcher and umpire. 1p, Quisqueya Stadium, horiz.

1969, Aug. 15 Litho. *Perf. 12½*
Size: 43x30mm (7c, 1p); 21x31mm (10c)
C169 A180 7c magenta & org .55 .30
C170 A180 10c mar & rose red .70 .30
C171 A180 1p violet blue & brn 5.00 3.50
Nos. C169-C171 (3) 6.25 4.10

Electrification Types of Regular Issue

Design: No. C172, Rio Haina steam plant. No. C173, Valdesa Dam.

1969 Litho. *Perf. 12*
C172 A181 10c orange ver .50 .25
C173 A182 10c multicolored .55 .25

Issued: No. C172, Sept. 15; No. C173, Oct. 15.

Duarte Type of Regular Issue

1970, Jan. 26 Litho. *Perf. 12*
C174 A183 10c brown & dk brown .75 .25

Census Type of Regular Issue

Design: 10c, Buildings and census emblem.

1970, Feb. 6 *Perf. 11*
C175 A184 10c lt blue & multi .75 .25

Sculpture Type of Regular Issue

Design: 10c, The Prisoner, by Abelardo Rodriguez Urdaneta, vert.

1970, Feb. 20 Litho. *Perf. 12½*
C176 A186 10c bluish gray .55 .25

Masonic Type of Regular Issue

1970, Mar. 2
C177 A187 10c brown .30 .25

Satellite Type of Regular Issue

1970, May 25 Litho. *Perf. 12½*
C178 A188 7c blue & gray .40 .25

UPU Type of Regular Issue

1970, June 5 *Perf. 11*
C179 A189 10c yellow & brown .40 .25

Education Year Type of Regular Issue

1970, June 26 Litho. *Perf. 12½*
C180 A190 15c bright pink .60 .25

Dancers AP54

Design: 10c, UN emblem and wheel.

1970, Oct. 12 Litho. *Perf. 12½*
C181 AP54 7c blue & multi .35 .25
C182 AP54 10c pink & multi .50 .25

1st World Exhib. of Books and Culture Festival, Santo Domingo, Oct. 11-Dec. 11.

Album, Globe and Emblem — AP55

1970, Oct. 26 Litho. *Perf. 11*
C183 AP55 10c multicolored .65 .25

EXFILCA 70, 2nd Interamerican Philatelic Exhibition, Caracas, Venezuela, 11/27-12/6.

Basilica of Our Lady of Altagracia — AP56

1971, Jan. 20 Litho. *Perf. 12½*
C184 AP56 17c multicolored 1.00 .45

Inauguration of the Basilica of Our Lady of Altagracia.

Map of Dominican Republic, CARE Package AP57

1971, May 28 Litho. *Perf. 12½*
C185 AP57 10c blue & green .45 .25

25th anniversary of CARE, a US-Canadian Cooperative for American Relief Everywhere.

Sports Type of Regular Issue

1971, Sept. 10 *Perf. 11*
C186 A195 7c Volleyball .40 .25

Animal Type of Regular Issue

Design: 25c, Cock and grain.

1971, Sept. 29 *Perf. 12½*
C187 A196 25c black & multi 2.00 .35

Independence Type

10c, Dominican-Colombian flag of 1821.

1971, Dec. 1 *Perf. 11*
C188 A197 10c vio bl, yel & red .75 .30

Christmas Type of Regular Issue

1971, Dec. 10 *Perf. 12½*
C189 A198 10c Bell, 1493 .45 .25

UNICEF Type of Regular Issue

Design: UNICEF emblem & child on beach.

1971, Dec. 14 *Perf. 11*
C190 A199 15c multicolored .80 .45

Book Year Type of Regular Issue

1972, Jan. 25 Litho. *Perf. 12½*
C191 A200 12c lilac, dk bl & red .75 .30

Magnifying Glass over Peru on Map of Americas — AP58

1972, Mar. 7 Litho. *Perf. 12*
C192 AP58 10c blue & multi .60 .30

EXFILIMA '71, 3rd Inter-American Philatelic Exposition, Lima, Peru, Nov. 6-14, 1971.

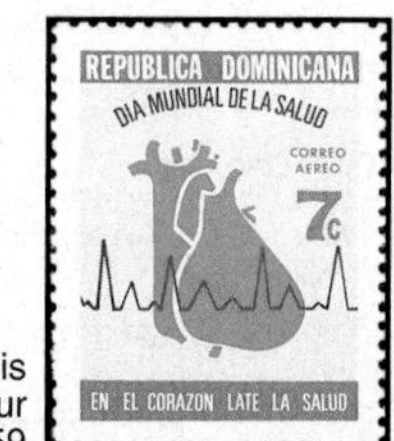
"Your Heart is your Health" — AP59

1972, Apr. 27 Litho. *Perf. 11*
C193 AP59 7c red & multi .50 .25

World Health Day.

Taino Art Type of 1972

Taino Art: 8c, Ritual vessel showing human figures. 10c, Trumpet (shell). 25c, Carved vomiting spoons. All horiz.

1972, May 10 Litho. *Perf. 11*
C194 A201 8c multicolored .50 .25
C195 A201 10c lt blue & multi .70 .25
C196 A201 25c multicolored 1.50 .45
Nos. C194-C196 (3) 2.70 .95

Telecommunications Type of Regular Issue

1972, May 17 *Perf. 12½*
C197 A202 21c yellow & multi 1.00 .45

Exhibition Type of Regular Issue

1972, June 3
C198 A203 33c orange & multi 1.00 .55

Olympic Type of Regular Issue

1972, Aug. 25 Litho. *Perf. 12½*
C199 A204 33c Running 1.25 .75

Club Type of Regular Issue

1972, Sept. 29 Litho. *Perf. 10½*
C200 A205 20c blue & multi .75 .25

Morel Type of Regular Issue

1972, Oct. 20 Litho. *Perf. 12½*
C201 A206 10c multicolored .50 .25

Bank Type of Regular Issue

25c, 1947 silver coin, entrance to the Mint.

1972, Oct. 23
C202 A207 25c ocher & multi 1.25 .55

"La Navidad" Fortress, 1492 AP60

1972, Nov. 21 Litho. *Perf. 12½*
C203 AP60 10c multicolored .95 .25

Christmas 1972.

Sports Type of Regular Issue

Various sports; a, UL. b, UR. c, LL. d, LR.

1973, Mar. 30 Litho. *Perf. 13½x13*
C204 A212 Block of 4 1.75 1.75
a.-d. 8c, any single .30 .25
C205 A212 Block of 4 2.75 2.75
a.-d. 10c, any single .50 .30

Easter Type 1973

10c, Belfry of Church of Our Lady of Help.

1973, Apr. 18 Litho. *Perf. 10½*
C206 A213 10c multi, vert. .75 .25

North and South America on Globe — AP61

1973, May 29 Litho. *Perf. 12*
C207 AP61 7c multicolored .45 .25

Pan-American Health Organization, 70th anniversary (in 1972).

WMO Type of Regular Issue

1973, Aug. 10 Litho. *Perf. 13½x13*
C208 A214 7c green & multi .50 .25

INTERPOL Emblem Police Scientist AP62

1973, Sept. 28 Litho. *Perf. 10½*
C209 AP62 10c vio bl, bl & emer .60 .25

50th anniversary of International Criminal Police Organization.

Handicraft Type of Regular Issue

1973, Oct. 12
C210 A215 7c Sailing ship, mosaic .75 .25
C211 A215 10c Maracas rattles, horiz. 1.00 .25

Christmas Type of Regular Issue

Design: 10c, Angels adoring Christ Child.

1973, Nov. 26 Litho. *Perf. 13½x13*
C212 A216 10c multicolored .50 .25

Scout Type of Regular Issue

21c, Scouts cooking, Lord Baden-Powell.

1973, Dec. 7 Litho. *Perf. 12*
C213 A217 21c red & multi 1.25 .75

Sport Type of Regular Issue

10c, Olympic swimming pool and diver. 25c, Olympic Stadium, soccer and discus.

1974, Feb. 25 Litho. *Perf. 13½*
C214 A218 10c blue & multi .40 .25
C215 A218 25c multicolored 1.00 .25

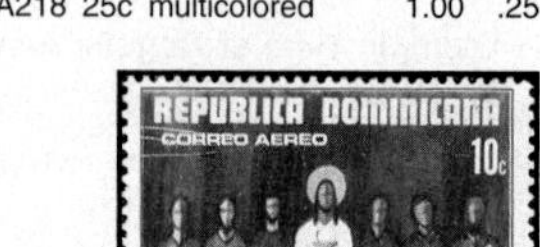
The Last Supper AP63

1974, June 27 Litho. *Perf. 13½*
C216 AP63 10c multicolored .65 .25

Holy Week 1974.

Bridge Type

Design: 10c, Higuamo Bridge.

1974, July 12 *Perf. 12*
C217 A221 10c multicolored .65 .25

Diabetes Type

Map of Dominican Republic, Diabetics' Emblem and: 7c, Kidney. 33c, Eye & heart.

1974, Aug. 22 Litho. *Perf. 13*
C218 A222 7c yellow & multi .45 .25
C219 A222 33c lt blue & multi 2.00 .75

UPU Type

1974, Oct. 9 Litho. *Perf. 13½*

C220 A223 7c Ships 1.75 .35
C221 A223 33c Jet 2.75 .75
a. Souvenir sheet of 4 7.50 7.50

No. C221a contains Nos. 727-728, C220-C221 forming continuous design.

Golfers and Championship Emblem — AP64

20c, Golfer and Golf Association emblem.

1974, Oct. 24 Litho. *Perf. 13x13½*

C222 AP64 10c green & multi *.50* .25
C223 AP64 20c green & multi *.80* .40

World Amateur Golf Championships.

Hand Holding Dove AP65

1974, Dec. 3 Litho. *Perf. 12*

C224 AP65 10c multicolored .50 .25

Christmas 1974.

FAO Type

10c, Bee, beehive and barrel of honey.

1974, Dec. 5

C225 A227 10c multicolored 1.75 .25

Chrismon, Lamb, Candle and Palm — AP66

1975, Mar. 26 Litho. *Perf. 13½*

C226 AP66 10c gold & multi .65 .25

Holy Week 1975.

Spain No. 1, España 75 Emblem — AP67

1975, Apr. 10

C227 AP67 12c red, yel & blk .65 .30

Espana 75, International Philatelic Exhibition, Madrid, Apr. 4-13.

Development Bank Type

1975, May 19 Litho. *Perf. 10½x10*

C228 A230 10c rose car & multi .60 .25

Three Satellites and Globe AP68

1975, June 21 Litho. *Perf. 13½*

C229 AP68 15c multicolored .60 .35

Opening of first earth satellite tracking station in Dominican Republic.

Apollo Type

Design: 2p, Apollo-Soyuz link-up over earth.

1975, July 24 *Perf. 13*
Size: 42x28mm

C230 A232 2p multicolored 6.00 4.00

Indian Chief Type

7c, Mayobanex. 8c, Cotubanama & Juan de Esquivel. 10c, Enriquillo & Mencia.

1975, Sept. 27 Litho. *Perf. 12*

C231 A235 7c lt green & multi .60 .25
C232 A235 8c orange & multi .90 .30
C233 A235 10c gray & multi 1.00 .30
Nos. C231-C233 (3) 2.50 .85

Volleyball AP69

10c, Weight lifting and Games' emblem.

1975, Oct. 24 Litho. *Perf. 12*

C234 AP69 7c blue & multi .75 .25
C235 AP69 10c multicolored 1.25 .30

7th Pan-American Games, Mexico City, Oct. 13-26.

Christmas Type

Design: 10c, Dove and peace message.

1975, Dec. 12 Litho. *Perf. 13x13½*

C236 A237 10c yellow & multi .60 .25

Valdesia Dam — AP70

1976, Jan. 26 Litho. *Perf. 13*

C237 AP70 10c multicolored .50 .25

Holy Week Type 1976

Design: 10c, Crucifixion, by Eliezer Castillo.

1976, Apr. 14 Litho. *Perf. 13½*

C238 A239 10c multicolored .75 .30

Bicentennial Type and

George Washington, Independence Hall — AP71

Design: 10c, Hands holding maps of US and Dominican Republic.

1976, May 29 Litho. *Perf. 13½*

C239 A241 10c vio bl, grn & blk .60 .25
C240 AP71 75c black & orange 1.75 1.25

American Bicentennial; No. C240 also for Interphil 76 International Philatelic Exhibition, Philadelphia, Pa., May 29-June 6.

King Juan Carlos I and Queen Sofia — AP72

1976, May 31

C241 AP72 21c multicolored 1.25 .85

Visit of King Juan Carlos I and Queen Sofia of Spain.

Telephone Type

Design: 10c, Alexander Graham Bell and telephones, 1876 and 1976.

1976, July 15

C242 A243 10c multicolored .65 .25

Duarte Types

10c, Scroll with Duarte letter and Dominican flag. 33c, Duarte return from Exile, by E. Godoy.

1976, July 20 Litho. *Perf. 13½*

C243 A245 10c blue & multi .65 .25

Perf. 13x13½

C244 A244 33c brown & multi 2.00 1.10

Fire Engine AP73

1976, Sept. 13 Litho. *Perf. 12*

C245 AP73 10c multicolored 3.50 .30

Honoring firemen.

Radio Club Type

1976, Oct. 8 Litho. *Perf. 13½*

C246 A247 10c blue & black .60 .25

Various People — AP74

1976, Oct. 22 Litho. *Perf. 13½*

C247 AP74 21c multicolored .90 .55

Spanish heritage.

Olympic Games Type

1976, Oct. 22 *Perf. 12*

C248 A249 10c Running .60 .25
C249 A249 25c Basketball 1.50 .75

Christmas Type

Design: 10c, Angel with bells.

1976, Dec. 8 Litho. *Perf. 13½*

C250 A251 10c multicolored .75 .30

Tourist Activities AP75

Tourist publicity: 12c, Angling and hotel. 25c, Horseback riding and waterfall, vert.

1977, Jan. 7 Size: 36x36mm

C251 AP75 10c multicolored .45 .25

Size: 34x25½mm, 25½x34mm

C252 AP75 12c multicolored .50 .25
C253 AP75 25c multicolored 1.00 .45
Nos. C251-C253 (3) 1.95 .95

Championship Type

1977, Mar. 4 Litho. *Perf. 13½*

C254 A253 10c yel grn & multi .60 .25
C255 A253 25c lt brown & multi 1.50 .75

Holy Week Type 1977

Design: 10c, Belfry and open book.

1977, Apr. 18 Litho. *Perf. 13½x13*

C256 A254 10c multicolored .75 .25

Lions Type

1977, May 6 *Perf. 13½x13*

C257 A255 7c lt green & multi .60 .25

Caravel under Sail — AP76

1977, July 16 Litho. *Perf. 13*

C258 AP76 10c multicolored .60 .30

Miss Universe Contest, held in Dominican Republic.

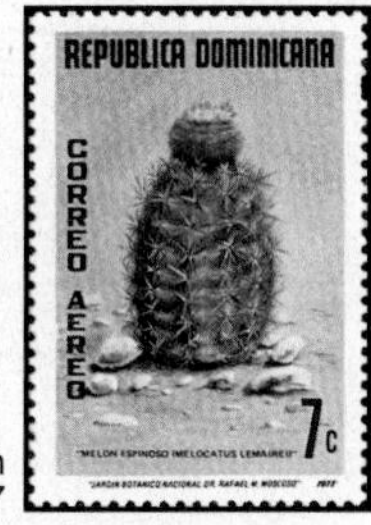

Melon Cactus — AP77

Design: 33c, Coccothrinax (tree).

1977, Aug. 19 Litho. *Perf. 12*

C259 AP77 7c multicolored 1.00 .25
C260 AP77 33c multicolored 2.50 1.10

National Botanical Garden.

Chart and Factories — AP78

1977, Nov. 30 Litho. *Perf. 13x13½*

C261 AP78 28c multicolored 1.00 .65

7th Interamerican Statistics Conference.

Animal Type

Congress Emblem and: 10c, "Dorado," red Roman stud bull. 25c, Flamingo, vert.

1977, Dec. 29 Litho. *Perf. 13*

C262 A259 10c multicolored 3.00 .30
C263 A259 25c multicolored 5.00 .50

Spanish Heritage Type

21c, Window, Casa del Tostado, 16th cent.

1978, Jan. 19 *Perf. 13x13½*
Size: 28x41mm

C264 A260 21c multicolored .85 .55

Holy Week Type, 1978

7c, Facade, Santo Domingo Cathedral. 10c, Facade of Dominican Convent.

1978, Mar. 21 Litho. *Perf. 12*
Size: 27x36mm

C265 A261 7c multicolored .50 .25
C266 A261 10c multicolored 1.00 .30

Schooner Duarte AP79

1978, Apr. 15 Litho. *Perf. 13½*

C267 AP79 7c multicolored .70 .25

Dominican naval forces training ship.

Cardinal Type

1978, May 5 Litho. *Perf. 13*

C268 A262 10c multicolored .60 .25

Antenna AP80

1978, May 17 Litho. *Perf. 13½*

C269 AP80 25c silver & multi 1.00 .55

10th World Telecommunications Day.

No. C1 and Map AP81

1978, June 6

C270 AP81 10c multicolored .60 .25

1st Dominican Rep. airmail stamp, 50th anniv.

Globe, Soccer Ball, Emblem — AP82

33c, Soccer field, Argentina '78 emblem, globe.

1978, June 29

C271 AP82 12c multicolored .65 .35
C272 AP82 33c multicolored 1.40 1.00

11th World Cup Soccer Championship, Argentina, June 1-25.

Crown, Cross and Rosary Emblem — AP83

1978, July 11 *Perf. 13x13½*

C273 AP83 21c multicolored .85 .65

Congregation of the Merciful Sisters of Charity, centenary.

Sports Type

1978, July 21 Litho. *Perf. 13½*

C274 A265 7c Baseball, vert. 1.00 .25
C275 A265 10c Basketball, vert. 1.50 .25

Wright Brothers and Glider, 1902 AP84

Designs: 7c, Diagrams of Flyer I and jet, vert. 13c, Diagram of air flow over wing. 45c, Flyer I over world map.

1978, Aug. 8 *Perf. 12*

C276 AP84 7c multicolored .25 .25
C277 AP84 10c multicolored .60 .25
C278 AP84 13c multicolored .85 .30
C279 AP84 45c multicolored 2.25 1.40
Nos. C276-C279 (4) 3.95 2.20

75th anniversary of first powered flight.

Tourist Type

Designs: 7c, Sun and musical instruments. 10c, Sun and plane over Santo Domingo.

1978, Sept. 12 Litho. *Perf. 12*

C280 A266 7c multicolored .65 .25
C281 A266 10c multicolored .90 .25

People and Globe AP85

1978, Oct. 12 Litho. *Perf. 13½*

C282 AP85 21c multicolored .90 .70

Spanish heritage.

Dominican Republic and UN Flags AP86

1978, Oct. 23 *Perf. 12*

C283 AP86 33c multicolored 1.25 .75

33rd anniversary of the United Nations.

Statue of the Virgin — AP87

1978, Dec. 5 Litho. *Perf. 12*

C284 AP87 10c multicolored .75 .30

Christmas 1978.

Pope John Paul II — AP88

1979, Jan. 25 Litho. *Perf. 13½*

C285 AP88 10c multicolored 3.75 3.25

Visit of Pope John Paul II to the Dominican Republic, Jan. 25-26.

Map of Beata Island AP89

1979, Jan. 25 *Perf. 12*

C286 AP89 10c multicolored 1.50 .30

1st expedition of radio amateurs to Beata Is.

Year of the Child Type, 1979

Designs (ICY Emblem and): 7c, Children reading book. 10c, Symbolic head and protective hands. 33c, Hands and jars.

1979, Feb. 26

C287 A269 7c multicolored .40 .25
C288 A269 10c multicolored .60 .25
C289 A269 33c multicolored 1.75 1.10
Nos. C287-C289 (3) 2.75 1.60

Pope John Paul II Giving Benediction AP90

1979, Apr. 9 Litho. *Perf. 13½*

C290 AP90 10c multicolored 4.00 1.25

Holy Week.

Adm. Juan Bautista Cambiaso AP91

1979, Apr. 14 *Perf. 12*

C291 AP91 10c multicolored .60 .25

135th anniv. of the Battle of Tortuguero.

Map of Dominican Rep., Album, Magnifier AP92

1979, Apr. 18

C292 AP92 33c multicolored 1.10 .75

EXFILNA, 3rd National Philatelic Exhibition, Apr. 18-22.

Flower Type

Designs: 7c, Passionflower. 10c, Isidorea pungens. 13c, Calotropis procera.

1979, May 17 Litho. *Perf. 12*

C293 A271 7c multicolored 1.00 .30
C294 A271 10c multicolored 1.50 .35
C295 A271 13c multicolored 2.50 .65
Nos. C293-C295 (3) 5.00 1.30

Cardiology Type, 1979

10c, Figure of man showing blood circulation.

1979, June 2 Litho. *Perf. 13½*

C296 A272 10c multi, vert. .75 .40

Sports Type

7c, Runner and Games' emblem, vert.

1979, June 20

C297 A273 7c multicolored 1.50 .30

Soccer Type

1979, Aug. 9 Litho. *Perf. 12*

C298 A273 10c Tennis, vert. .65 .30

Rowland Hill, Dominican Republic No. 1 — AP93

1979, Aug. 21 *Perf. 13½*

C299 AP93 2p multicolored 4.75 3.25

Sir Rowland Hill (1795-1879), originator of penny postage.

Electric Light Type

Design: 10c, "100" and light bulb, horiz.

1979, Aug. 27 *Perf. 13½*

C300 A275 10c multicolored .50 .30

Bird Type

Birds: 7c, Phaenicophilus palmarum. 10c, Calyptophilus frugivorus tertius. 45c, Icterus dominicensis.

1979, Sept. 12 Litho. *Perf. 12*

C301 A277 7c multicolored 2.75 .30
C302 A277 10c multicolored 3.75 .30
C303 A277 45c multicolored 9.50 1.00
Nos. C301-C303 (3) 16.00 1.60

Lions Type

10c, Melvin Jones, organization founder.

1979, Nov. 13 Litho. *Perf. 12*

C304 A278 10c multicolored .60 .30

Christmas Type

Christmas: 10c, Three Kings riding camels.

1979, Dec. 18 Litho. *Perf. 12*

C305 A279 10c multicolored .50 .25

Holy Week Type

1980, Mar. 27 Litho. *Perf. 12*

C306 A280 7c Crucifixion .40 .25
C307 A280 10c Resurrection .75 .30

Navy Day — AP94

1980, Apr. 15 Litho. *Perf. 13½*

C308 AP94 21c multicolored .75 .55

Dominican Philatelic Society, 25th Anniversary
AP95

1980, Apr. 18

C309 AP95 10c multicolored .55 .30

Gold Type

1980, July 8 Litho. *Perf. 13½*

C310 A282 10c Drag line mining .75 .35
C311 A282 33c Mine 1.25 .55

Tourism Secretariat Emblem — AP96

1980, Aug. 26 Litho. *Perf. 13½*

C312 AP96 10c shown .45 .30
C313 AP96 33c Conf. emblem 1.60 1.10

World Tourism Conf., Manila, Sept. 27.

Iguana Type

Designs: 7c, American crocodile. 10c, Cuban rat. 25c, Manatee. 45c, Turtle.

1980, Aug. 30 *Perf. 12*

C314 A284 7c multi 2.00 .35
C315 A284 10c multi 2.40 .40
C316 A284 25c multi 3.75 .65
C317 A284 45c multi 5.25 .95
Nos. C314-C317 (4) 13.40 2.35

Painting Type

Designs: 10c, Abstract, by Paul Guidicelli, vert. 17c, Farmer, by Yoryi Morel, vert.

1980, Sept. 23 Litho. *Perf. 13½x13*

C318 A285 10c multi .60 .30
C319 A285 17c multi .90 .55

Visit of Radio Amateurs to Catalina Island
AP97

1980, Oct. 3

C320 AP97 7c multicolored .60 .50

Rotary International, 75th Anniversary — AP98

Design: 10c, Globe, emblem, vert.

1980, Oct. 23 Litho. *Perf. 12*

C321 AP98 10c multi .60 .45
C322 AP98 33c shown 1.25 .85

Carrier Pigeons, UPU Emblem
AP99

1980, Oct. 31 *Perf. 13½*

C323 AP99 33c shown .75 .50
C324 AP99 45c Pigeons, diff. 1.00 .65
C325 AP99 50c Pigeon, stamp 1.40 .75
Nos. C323-C325 (3) 3.15 1.90

Souvenir Sheet

Imperf

C326 AP99 1.10p UPU emblem 2.00 2.00

UPU cent. No. C326 contains one 48½x31mm stamp.

Christmas Type

1980, Dec. 5 Litho. *Perf. 13½*

C327 A286 10c Holy Family .65 .30

Christmas 1980.

Salcedo Type

Design: Map and arms of Salcedo.

1981, Jan. 14 Litho. *Perf. 13½*

C328 A287 10c multicolored .50 .25

AP100

Industrial Symbols, Seminar Emblem.

1981, Feb. 18 Litho. *Perf. 13½*

C329 AP100 10c shown .55 .30
C330 AP100 33c Seminar emblem .90 .55

CODIA Chemical Engineering Seminar.

National Games Type

1981, Mar. 31 Litho. *Perf. 13½*

C331 A289 10c Baseball 2.50 .35

AP101

Design: Admiral Juan Alejandro Acosta.

1981, Apr. 15

C332 AP101 10c multicolored .40 .25

Battle of Tortuguero anniversary.

13th World Telecommunications Day — AP102

1981, May 16 Litho. *Perf. 12*

C333 AP102 10c multicolored .65 .25

Heinrich von Stephan
AP103

1981, July 15 Litho. *Perf. 13½*

C334 AP103 33c tan & lt red brn 1.10 .75

Birth sesquicentennial of UPU founder.

Worker in Wheelchair
AP104

1981, July 24

C335 AP104 7c Stylized people .50 .30
C336 AP104 33c shown 1.25 .75

Intl. Year of the Disabled.

EXPURIDOM '81 Intl. Stamp Show, Santo Domingo, July 31-Aug. 2 — AP105

1981, July 31

C337 AP105 7c multicolored .75 .35

Bullet Holes in Target, Competition Emblem
AP106

1981, Aug. 12

C338 AP106 10c shown .35 .25
C339 AP106 15c Riflemen .55 .30
C340 AP106 25c Pistol shooting 1.00 .65
Nos. C338-C340 (3) 1.90 1.20

2nd World Sharpshooting Championship.

Exports — AP107

1981, Oct. 16 Litho. *Perf. 12*

C341 AP107 7c Jewelry .55 .25
C342 AP107 10c Handicrafts .65 .30
C343 AP107 11c Fruit .80 .30
C344 AP107 17c Vegetables 1.00 .35
Nos. C341-C344 (4) 3.00 1.20

World Food Day — AP108

1981, Oct. 16 Litho. *Perf. 13½*

C345 AP108 10c Fruits .75 .30
C346 AP108 50c Vegetables 1.75 1.40

5th Natl. Games
AP109

1981, Dec. 5 Litho. *Perf. 13½*

C347 AP109 10c Javelin, vert. .45 .35
C348 AP109 50c Cycling 2.10 1.75

Orchids
AP110

7c, Encyclia cochleata. 10c, Broughtonia domingensis. 25c, Encyclia truncata. 75c, Elleanthus capitatus.

1981, Dec. 14

C349 AP110 7c multicolored .85 .25
C350 AP110 10c multicolored 1.00 .30
C351 AP110 25c multicolored 1.60 .75
C352 AP110 75c multicolored 4.00 2.25
Nos. C349-C352 (4) 7.45 3.55

Christmas Type

1981, Dec. 23

C353 A294 10c Dove, sun .90 .45

Battle of Tortuguero Anniv.
AP111

Design: Naval Academy, cadets.

1982, Apr. 15 Litho. *Perf. 13½*

C354 AP111 10c multi .60 .30

1982 World Cup Soccer — AP112

Designs: Various soccer players.

1982, Apr. 19

C355 AP112 10c multicolored .60 .35
C356 AP112 21c multicolored .75 .45
C357 AP112 33c multicolored 1.40 .90
Nos. C355-C357 (3) 2.75 1.70

American Air Forces Cooperation System — AP113

1982, Apr. 12 *Perf. 12*

C358 AP113 10c multicolored .70 .30

Scouting Year
AP114

10c, Baden-Powell, vert. 15c, Globe. 25c, Baden-Powell, scout, vert.

1982, Apr. 30 Litho. *Perf. 13½*

C359 AP114 10c multi .45 .25
C360 AP114 15c multi .65 .30
C361 AP114 25c multi .95 .45
Nos. C359-C361 (3) 2.05 1.00

Dancers — AP115

7c, Emblem. 10c, Cathedral, Casa del Tostado, Santo Domingo.

1982, June 1 Litho. *Perf. 13½*

C362	AP115 7c multi	.30	.25
C363	AP115 10c multi	.35	.25
C364	AP115 33c shown	1.75	.85
	Nos. C362-C364 (3)	2.40	1.35

Tourist Org. of the Americas, 25th Congress (COTAL '82), Santo Domingo.

Espamer '82 Emblem — AP116

Espamer '82 Intl. Stamp Exhibition, San Juan, Oct. 12-17: Symbolic stamps.

1982, July 5

C365	AP116 7c multi	.30	.25
C366	AP116 13c multi, horiz.	.50	.30
C367	AP116 50c multi	2.10	1.60
	Nos. C365-C367 (3)	2.90	2.15

Sports Type

1982, Aug. 13 *Perf. 12, Imperf.*

C368	A300 10c Basketball	1.00	.25
C369	A300 13c Boxing	1.50	.30
C370	A300 25c Gymnast	2.00	.45
	Nos. C368-C370 (3)	4.50	1.00

Harbor, by Alejandro Bonilla — AP117

Paintings: 10c, Portrait of a Woman, by Leopoldo Navarro. 45c, Amelia Francasci, by Luis Desangles. 2p, Portrait, by Abelardo Rodriguez Urdaneta. 10c, 45c, 2p vert.

1982, Aug. 20 *Perf. 13, Imperf.*

C371	AP117 7c multicolored	.30	.25
C372	AP117 10c multicolored	.45	.30
C373	AP117 45c multicolored	2.10	1.40
C374	AP117 2p multicolored	9.00	6.00
	Nos. C371-C374 (4)	11.85	7.95

San Pedro de Macoris Type

1982, Aug. 26

Size: 42x29mm

C375	A301 7c Lake	.75	.30

35th Anniv. of Central Bank AP118

1982, Oct. 22 Litho. *Perf. 13½x13*

C376	AP118 10c multicolored	.60	.35

490th Anniv. of Discovery of America AP119

Designs: 7c, Map. 10c, Santa Maria, vert. 21c, Columbus, vert.

1982, Oct. 7 Litho. *Perf. 13½*

C377	AP119 7c multi	1.25	.95
C378	AP119 10c multi	1.60	1.10
C379	AP119 21c multi	2.10	1.10
	Nos. C377-C379 (3)	4.95	3.15

Christmas Type

1982, Dec. 8

C380	A303 10c multicolored	.55	.35

French Alliance Centenary AP120

1983, Mar. 31 Litho. *Perf. 13½*

C381	AP120 33c multicolored	.85	.55

Battle of Tortuguero Anniv. AP121

Design: 15c, Frigate Mella-451.

1983, Apr. 15 Litho. *Perf. 13½*

C382	AP121 15c multi	.95	.35

World Communications Year — AP122

1983, May 6 Litho. *Perf. 13½*

C383	AP122 10c dk blue & blue	.60	.30

AP123

1983, July 5 Litho. *Perf. 13½*

C384	AP123 9c multicolored	.60	.35

Simon Bolivar (1783-1830).

AP124

7c, Gymnast, basketball. 10c, Highjump, boxing. 15c, Baseball, weight lifting, bicycling.

1983, Aug. 22 Litho. *Perf. 12*

C385	AP124 7c multi	.70	.25
C386	AP124 10c multi	.80	.25
C387	AP124 15c multi	1.00	.30
	Nos. C385-C387 (3)	2.50	.80

9th Pan American Games, Caracas, Aug. 13-28.

491st Anniv. of Discovery of America AP125

10c, Columbus' ships, map. 21c, Santa Maria (trophy). 33c, Yacht Sotavento, vert. 50c, Ship models.

1983, Oct. 11 Litho. *Perf. 13½*

C388	AP125 10c multi	1.25	.45
C389	AP125 21c multi	1.90	.75
C390	AP125 33c multi	2.10	.85
	Nos. C388-C390 (3)	5.25	2.05

Size: 103x103mm

Imperf

C391	AP125 50c multi	15.00	15.00

10th Anniv. of Latin American Civil Aviation Commission AP126

1983, Dec. 7

C392	AP126 10c dark blue	.60	.35

Funeral Procession, by Juan Bautista Gomez — AP127

Designs: 15c, Meeting of Maximo Gomez and Jose Marti in Guayubin, by Enrique Garcia Godoy. 21c, St. Francis, by Angel Perdomo, vert. 33c, Portrait of a Girl, by Adriana Billini, vert.

1983, Dec. 26 *Perf. 13½*

C393	AP127 10c multicolored	.40	.25
C394	AP127 15c multicolored	.40	.25
C395	AP127 21c multicolored	.50	.25
C396	AP127 33c multicolored	.75	.25
	Nos. C393-C396 (4)	2.05	1.00

Christmas 1983 — AP128

1983, Dec. 13 Litho. *Perf. 13½*

C397	AP128 10c Bells, ornaments	.60	.25

AIR POST SEMI-POSTAL STAMPS

Catalogue values for unused stamps in this section are for Never Hinged items.

Nos. C97-C99 Surcharged in Red like Nos. B1-B5

Engraved and Lithographed

1957, Feb. 8 Unwmk. *Perf. 11½*

Flags in National Colors

CB1	A117 11c + 2c ultra & red org	.40	.40
CB2	A117 16c + 2c car & lt grn	.70	.70
CB3	A117 17c + 2c blk, vio & red	.70	.70
	Nos. CB1-CB3 (3)	1.80	1.80

The surtax was to aid Hungarian refugees. A similar 25c surcharge was applied to the souvenir sheets described in the footnote following No. C99. Value, 2 sheets, perf. and imperf., $17.50.

Nos. C100-C102 Surcharged in Red Orange like Nos. B6-B10

1957, Sept. 9 Photo. *Perf. 13½*

Flags in National Colors

CB4	A118 11c + 2c yel grn & dk bl	.70	.50
CB5	A118 16c + 2c lilac & dk bl	.85	.70
CB6	A118 17c + 2c brn & bl grn	1.00	.75
	Nos. CB4-CB6 (3)	2.55	1.95

See note after No. B10.

A similar 5c surcharge was applied to the miniature sheets described in the footnote following No. 483. Value, 4 sheets, perf. & imperf., medal and flag, $40.

Types of Olympic Air Post Stamps, 1957, Surcharged in Carmine like Nos. B11-B20

1958, May 26 Engr. & Litho.

Flags in National Colors

Pink Paper

CB7	A119(a) 11c + 2c ultra	.40	.40
CB8	A119(b) 11c + 2c ultra	.40	.40
CB9	A120(a) 16c + 2c rose car	.55	.55
CB10	A120(b) 16c + 2c rose car	.55	.55
CB11	A119(a) 17c + 2c claret	.65	.65
CB12	A119(b) 17c + 2c claret	.65	.65
	Nos. CB7-CB12 (6)	3.20	3.20

A similar 5c surcharge, plus marginal UN emblem and "UNRWA," was applied to the miniature sheets described in the footnote following No. C105. Value, 4 sheets, perf. and imperf., $20.

Nos. C106-C108 Surcharged like Nos. B21-B25

1959, Apr. 13 Photo. *Perf. 13½*

Flags in National Colors

CB13	A125 11c + 2c blue, ol & brn	.80	.80
CB14	A125 16c + 2c lt grn, org & dk bl	1.10	1.10
CB15	A125 17c + 2c ver bl & yel	1.60	1.60
	Nos. CB13-CB15 (3)	3.50	3.50

A similar 5c surcharge was applied to the miniature sheets described in the footnote following No. C108. Value, 2 sheets, perf. and imperf., $25.

Type of Regular Issue 1957 Surcharged in Red like Nos. B26-B30

Engraved and Lithographed

1959, Sept. 10 *Imperf.*

Flags in National Colors

CB16	A117 11c + 2c ultra & red org	.80	.80
CB17	A117 16c + 2c carmine & lt grn	.90	.90
CB18	A117 17c + 2c black, vio & red	.90	.90
	Nos. CB16-CB18 (3)	2.60	2.60

Nos. C113-C114 Surcharged in Red like Nos. B31-B33

1960, Apr. 7 Litho. *Perf. 12½*

CB19	AP43 10c + 5c plum, gray & grn	.35	.35
CB20	AP43 13c + 5c gray & green	.55	.55

World Refugee Year.

For souvenir sheets see note after No. B33.

Nos. C115-C117 Surcharged

Perf. 13½

1962, Jan. 8 Unwmk. Photo.

Flags in National Colors

CB21	A136 11c + 2c blue, gray & brn	.35	.35
CB22	A136 16c + 2c red, brn & ol	.50	.50
CB23	A136 17c + 2c blk, bl & ocher	.50	.50
	Nos. CB21-CB23 (3)	1.35	1.35

See note after No. B38.

A similar 5c surcharge was applied to the miniature sheets described in the footnote following No. C117. Value, 2 sheets, perf. and imperf., $9.

Anti-Malaria Type of 1962

1962, Apr. 29 Litho. *Perf. 12*

CB24	A141 13c + 2c pink & red	.50	.35
CB25	A141 33c + 2c org & dp org	1.10	.75

Souvenir sheets exist, perf. and imperf. containing one each of Nos. B39-B40, CB24-CB25 and a 25c+2c pale grn and yel grn. Value, 2 sheets, perf. and imperf., $7.50.

Nos. C132-C133 Surcharged like Nos. B44-B46

1964, Mar. 8

CB26	AP46 10c + 2c brt violet	.35	.35
CB27	AP46 13c + 2c yellow	.40	.40

Nos. C146-C148 Surcharged like Nos. B47-B51

1966, Dec. 9 Litho. *Perf. 12½*

Size: 35x24mm

CB28	A164 10c + 5c multi	*3.00*	*1.00*
CB29	A164 50c + 10c multi	*4.50*	*3.00*
CB30	A164 75c + 10c multi	*6.00*	*3.75*
	Nos. CB28-CB30 (3)	*13.50*	*7.75*

AIR POST OFFICIAL STAMPS

Nos. O13-O14 Overprinted in Blue

Unwmk.

1930, Dec. 3 Typo. *Perf. 12*

CO1	O3 10c light blue	17.50	*17.50*
a.	Pair, one without ovpt.	*1,100.*	
CO2	O3 20c orange	17.50	*17.50*

SPECIAL DELIVERY STAMPS

Biplane SD1

Perf. 11½

1920, Apr. Unwmk. Litho.

E1	SD1 10c deep ultra	6.75	1.40
a.	Imperf., pair		

Special Delivery Messenger — SD2

1925

E2	SD2 10c dark blue	21.00	5.75

SD3

1927

E3	SD3 10c red brown	6.75	1.40
a.	"E EXPRESO" at top	55.00	55.00

Type of 1927

1941 Redrawn

E4	SD3 10c yellow green	3.00	3.25
E5	SD3 10c dark blue green	2.75	.60

The redrawn design differs slightly from SD3.

Issue dates: No. E4, Mar. 27; No. E5, Aug. 7.

Emblem of Communications — SD4

1945, Sept. 1 *Perf. 12*

E6	SD4 10c rose car, car & dk bl	1.25	.25

Catalogue values for unused stamps in this section, from this point to the end of the section, are for Never Hinged items.

SD5

1950 Litho. Unwmk.

E7	SD5 10c multicolored	.70	.25

Exists imperf.

Modern Communications System — SD6

1956, Aug. 18 *Perf. 11½*

E8	SD6 25c green	1.25	.30

Carrier Pigeon SD7

1967 Litho. *Perf. 11½*

E9	SD7 25c light blue	.80	.30

Carrier Pigeon, Globe — SD8

1978, Aug. 2 Litho. *Perf. 13½*

E10	SD8 25c multicolored	1.10	.45

Messenger, Plane — SD9

1979, Nov. 30 *Perf. 13½*

E11	SD9 25c multicolored	.75	.45

Motorcycling — SD10

1989, May Litho. *Perf. 13½*

E12	SD10 1p multicolored	2.50	1.10

Postman SD11

1999 Litho. *Perf. 13½x13¼*

E13	SD11 8p multicolored	3.25	2.75

INSURED LETTER STAMPS

Merino Issue of 1933 Surcharged in Red or Black

1935, Feb. 1 Unwmk. *Perf. 14*

G1	A35 8c on 7c ultra	.60	.25
a.	Inverted surcharge	18.00	
G2	A35 15c on 10c org yel	.65	.25
a.	Inverted surcharge	18.00	
G3	A35 30c on 8c dk green	2.25	.90
G4	A35 45c on 20c car rose (Bk)	3.25	1.10
G5	A36 70c on 50c lemon	7.75	1.75
	Nos. G1-G5 (5)	14.50	4.25

Merino Issue of 1933 Surcharged in Red

1940

G6	A35 8c on ½c lt vio	2.75	2.75
G7	A35 8c on 7c ultra	3.25	3.25

Coat of Arms — IL1

1940-45 Litho. *Perf. 11½*

Arms in Black

G8	IL1 8c brown red	.85	.25
a.	8c dk red, no shading on inner frame	1.10	.25
G9	IL1 15c dp orange ('45)	1.75	.25
G10	IL1 30c dk green ('41)	2.00	.25
a.	30c yellow green	2.00	.25
G11	IL1 45c ultra ('44)	2.25	.30
G12	IL1 70c olive brn ('44)	2.10	.30
	Nos. G8-G12 (5)	8.95	1.35

See Nos. G13-G16, G24-G27.

Catalogue values for unused stamps in this section, from this point to the end of the section, are for Never Hinged items.

Redrawn Type of 1940-45

1952-53 Arms in Black

G13	IL1 8c car lake ('53)	4.00	.50
G14	IL1 15c red orange ('53)	2.50	.75
G15	IL1 70c dp brown car	9.50	1.75
	Nos. G13-G15 (3)	16.00	3.00

Larger and bolder numerals on 8c and 15c. Smaller and bolder "70." There are many other minor differences in the design.

Type of 1940-45

1954 Arms in Black, 15x16mm

G16	IL1 10c carmine	.85	.25

Coat of Arms — IL2

1955-69 Unwmk. Litho. *Perf. 11½*

Arms in Black, 13½x11½mm

G17	IL2 10c carmine rose	.40	.25
G18	IL2 15c red orange ('56)	5.25	2.25
G19	IL2 20c red orange ('58)	1.25	.30
a.	20c orange ('69)	1.25	.30
b.	20c orange, retouched ('69)	3.50	1.25
G20	IL2 30c dark green ('55)	2.00	.40
G21	IL2 40c dark green ('58)	2.10	.90
a.	40c lt yellow grn ('62)	2.10	.45
G22	IL2 45c ultra ('56)	4.00	3.75
G23	IL2 70c dp brn car ('56)	6.75	2.25
	Nos. G17-G23 (7)	21.75	10.10

On No. G19b the horizontal shading lines of shield are omitted.

See Nos. G28-G37.

Type of 1940-45

Second Redrawing

1963 *Perf. 12½*

Arms in Black, 17x16mm

G24	IL1 10c red orange	1.25	.30
G25	IL1 20c orange	1.90	1.25

Third Redrawing

1966 Litho. *Perf. 12½*

Arms in Black, 14x14mm

G26	IL1 10c violet	.40	.25
G27	IL1 40c orange	1.50	1.00

Type of 1955-62

1968 Litho. *Perf. 11½*

Arms in Black, 13½x11½mm

G28	IL2 20c red	2.50	1.00
G29	IL2 60c yellow	2.10	2.10

1973-76 Litho. *Perf. 12½*

Arms in Black, 11x11mm

G30	IL2 10c car rose ('76)	.50	.35
G31	IL2 20c yellow	1.40	.90
G32	IL2 20c orange ('76)	1.75	.50
G33	IL2 40c yel grn	1.60	1.00
a.	40c green ('76)	3.00	3.00
G34	IL2 70c blue	1.90	1.90
	Nos. G30-G34 (5)	7.15	4.65

1973 *Perf. 11½*

Arms in Black, 13½x11½mm

G35	IL2 10c dark violet	.90	.30

1978, Aug. 9 *Perf. 10½*

Arms in Black, 11x11mm

G36 IL2 10c rose magenta .45 .25
G37 IL2 40c bright green 1.75 1.50

IL3

1982-83 **Litho.** *Perf. 10½*

Arms in Black

G38 IL3 10c deep magenta .30 .25
G39 IL3 20c deep orange .45 .30
G40 IL3 40c bluish green 1.00 .50
Nos. G38-G40 (3) 1.75 1.05

IL4

1986 **Litho.** *Perf. 10½*

Arms in Black

G41 IL4 20c brt rose lilac .35 .25
G42 IL4 60c orange 1.20 .85
G43 IL4 1p light blue 2.10 1.40
G44 IL4 1.25p pink 2.75 1.75
G45 IL4 1.50p vermilion 3.25 2.50
G46 IL4 3p light green 6.25 4.25
G47 IL4 3.50p olive bister 7.00 4.50
G48 IL4 4p yellow 8.75 5.50
G49 IL4 4.50p lt blue grn 9.75 6.25
G50 IL4 5p brown olive 10.50 7.00
G51 IL4 6p gray 12.50 8.50
G52 IL4 6.50p lt ultra 14.50 9.50
Nos. G41-G52 (12) 78.90 52.25

Issue dates: Nos. G42-G43, G45, July 16. Nos. G46-G52, Sept. 2. Nos. G41, G44, Nov. 6.

Coat of Arms — IL5

1989-90 **Litho.** *Perf. 13½*

Arms in Black

G53 IL5 20c brt lilac rose .35 .25
G54 IL5 60c orange ('90) 1.00 .45
G55 IL5 1p sky blue 1.60 .75
G56 IL5 1.25p lt salmon pink 1.90 .90
G57 IL5 1.50p dark red 2.40 1.40
Nos. G53-G57 (5) 7.25 3.75

"RD$" in lower left square on Nos. G55-G57.

IL6

1994, Oct. **Litho.** *Perf. 13½*

Arms in Black

G58 IL6 50c lilac rose .35 .25
G59 IL6 1p sky blue .50 .25
G60 IL6 1.50p red .65 .30
G61 IL6 2p pink .85 .50
G62 IL6 3p violet blue 1.40 .60
G63 IL6 5p yellow 1.90 .90
G64 IL6 6p apple green 2.50 1.25
G65 IL6 8p green 3.00 1.50
G66 IL6 10p silver gray 4.25 2.00
Nos. G58-G66 (9) 15.40 7.55

POSTAGE DUE STAMPS

D1

1901 **Unwmk.** **Typo.** *Perf. 14*

J1 D1 2c olive gray .90 .25
J2 D1 4c olive gray 1.10 .25
J3 D1 5c olive gray 1.90 .30
J4 D1 10c olive gray 3.25 .95
Nos. J1-J4 (4) 7.15 1.75

For surcharges and overprint see Nos. 162-165, 169-171.

1909 **Wmk. 116**

J5 D1 2c olive gray 1.50 .50
J6 D1 4c olive gray 1.50 .50
J7 D1 6c olive gray 2.00 .75
J8 D1 10c olive gray 4.00 2.50
Nos. J5-J8 (4) 9.00 4.25

1913

J9 D1 2c olive green .60 .30
J10 D1 4c olive green .70 .40
J11 D1 6c olive green 1.10 .50
J12 D1 10c olive green 1.25 .60
Nos. J9-J12 (4) 3.65 1.80

1922 **Unwmk.** **Litho.** *Perf. 11½*

J13 D1 1c olive green .70 .70

Catalogue values for unused stamps in this section, from this point to the end of the section, are for Never Hinged items.

D2

1942

J14 D2 1c dk red & pale pink .40 .25
J15 D2 2c dk bl & pale bl .40 .25
J16 D2 4c dk grn & pale grn .40 .25
J17 D2 6c green & buff .50 .25
J18 D2 8c yel org & pale yel .50 .30
J19 D2 10c mag & pale pink .75 .50
Nos. J14-J19 (6) 2.95 1.80

1955 **Size: 20½x25mm**

J20 D2 2c dark blue 1.40 1.00

D3

1959 **Litho.** *Perf. 11½*

Size: 21x25½mm

J21 D3 1c dark car rose 1.25 1.25
J22 D3 2c dark blue 1.25 1.25
J23 D3 4c green 3.00 3.00
Nos. J21-J23 (3) 5.50 5.50

OFFICIAL STAMPS

Bastion of February 27 O1

Unwmk.

1902, Feb. 25 **Litho.** *Perf. 12*

O1 O1 2c scarlet & blk .65 .30
O2 O1 5c dk blue & blk .85 .25
O3 O1 10c yel grn & blk 1.00 .55
O4 O1 20c yellow & blk 1.25 .55
a. Imperf., pair 11.00
Nos. O1-O4 (4) 3.75 1.65

For overprints and surcharge see Nos. 157-161.

Bastion of Feb. 27 — O2

Perf. 13½x13, 13½x14

1909-12 **Wmk. 116** **Typo.**

O5 O2 1c blue grn & blk .40 .25
O6 O2 2c scarlet & blk .50 .30
O7 O2 5c dk blue & blk 1.00 .40
O8 O2 10c yel grn & blk ('12) 1.60 .95
O9 O2 20c orange & blk ('12) 2.75 2.25
Nos. O5-O9 (5) 6.25 4.15

The 2c, 5c are found in both perforations; 1c, 20c perf. 13½x13; 10c perf. 13½x14.

For overprints and surcharge see Nos. 177, 194-199.

Columbus Lighthouse — O3

1928 **Unwmk.** *Perf. 12*

O10 O3 1c green .30 .30
O11 O3 2c red .30 .30
O12 O3 5c ultramarine .35 .35
O13 O3 10c light blue .40 .40
O14 O3 20c orange .60 .60
Nos. O10-O14 (5) 1.95 1.95

For overprints see Nos. CO1-CO2.

Proposed Columbus Lighthouse O4

1937 **Litho.** *Perf. 11½*

O15 O4 3c dark purple 1.60 .50
O16 O4 7c indigo & blue 1.90 .60
O17 O4 10c orange yellow 2.25 .85
Nos. O15-O17 (3) 5.75 1.95

Proposed Columbus Lighthouse O5

1939-41

O18 O5 1c dp grn & lt grn .90 .40
O19 O5 2c crim & pale pink .90 .40
O20 O5 3c purple & lt vio .90 .40
O21 O5 5c dk bl & lt bl ('40) 1.20 .60
O21A O5 5c lt blue ('41) 2.40 1.25
O22 O5 7c brt bl & lt bl ('41) 2.10 .40
O23 O5 10c yel org & pale org ('41) 2.10 .60
O24 O5 20c brn org & buff ('41) 7.00 1.00
O25 O5 50c brt red lil & pale lil ('41) 8.50 3.00
Nos. O18-O25 (9) 26.00 8.05

Catalogue values for unused stamps in this section, from this point to the end of the section, are for Never Hinged items.

Type of 1939

1950 **Redrawn**

O26 O5 50c dp car & rose 10.00 2.00

The numerals "50" measure 3mm, and are close to left and right frames; numerals measure 4mm on No. O25. There are other minor differences.

Denominations in "Centavos Oro"

1950

O27 O5 5c light blue 1.00 .40
O28 O5 10c yel & pale yel 1.25 .60
O29 O5 20c dl org brn & buff 2.50 2.25
Nos. O27-O29 (3) 4.75 3.25

Letters of top inscription are 1½mm high.

Second Redrawing

Type of 1939-41 Denominations in "Centavos Oro"

1956 **Unwmk.** *Perf. 11½*

O30 O5 7c blue & lt blue 1.00 1.00
O31 O5 20c yellow brn & buff 2.50 2.50
O32 O5 50c red lil & brt pink 6.00 6.00
Nos. O30-O32 (3) 9.50 9.50

The letters of top inscription are 2mm high, the trees at base of monument have been redrawn, etc. On No. O32 the numerals are similar to No. O26.

POSTAL TAX STAMPS

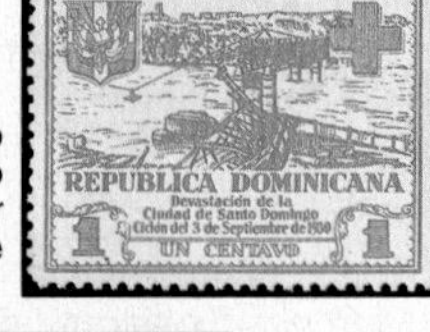

Santo Domingo after Hurricane PT1

Hurricane's Effect on Capital PT2

1930, Dec. **Unwmk.** **Litho.** *Perf. 12*

RA1 PT1 1c green & rose .25 .25
RA2 PT1 2c red rose .25 .25
RA3 PT2 5c ultra & rose .30 .25
RA4 PT2 10c yellow & rose .40 .30

Imperf

RA5 PT1 1c green & rose .40 .30
RA6 PT1 2c red & rose .50 .30
RA7 PT2 5c ultra & rose .60 .50
RA8 PT2 10c yellow & rose .90 .75
Nos. RA1-RA8 (8) 3.60 2.90

For surcharges see Nos. RAC1-RAC7.

Tête bêche Pairs

RA1a PT1 1c green & rose 1.75 1.75
RA2a PT1 2c red rose 1.75 1.50
RA3a PT1 5c ultra & rose 1.75 2.10
RA4a PT1 10c yellow & rose 2.10 2.10
RA5a PT1 1c green & rose 1.75 1.75
RA6a PT1 2c red & rose 1.75 1.75
RA7a PT1 5c ultra & rose 2.10 2.10
RA8a PT1 10c yellow & rose 2.10 2.10
Nos. RA1a-RA8a (8) 15.05 15.15

Dr. Martos Sanatorium PT3

1944, Apr. 1 **Litho.** *Perf. 11½*

RA9 PT3 1c dp bl, sl bl & red .40 .30

Nurse and Child — PT4

1947, Apr. 1 **Unwmk.**
RA10 PT4 1c dp bl, pale bl & car .50 .30

Sanatorium of the Holy Help — PT5

1949, Apr. 1
RA11 PT5 1c dp bl, pale bl & car .35 .25

Youth Holding Banner — PT6

1950, Apr. 1 ***Perf. 11½***
RA12 PT6 1c dp bl, pale bl & car .30 .25

"Suffer Little Children to Come Unto Me" — PT7

1950, Dec. 1 ***Perf. 12***
Size: 22½x32mm
RA13 PT7 1c lt bl & pale bl 1.25 .30
b. Perf. 12½ ('52) 4.50 .25

Vertical line centering side borders merges into dots toward the bottom. See Nos. RA13A, RA17, RA19, RA26, RA32, RA35.
The tax was for child welfare.

1951, Dec. 1 **Redrawn**
RA13A PT7 1c lt blue & pale blue 6.25 .30

In the redrawn stamp, the standing child, a blonde in No. RA13, is changed to a brunette; more foliage has been added above child's head and to branches showing in upper right corner. Vertical dashes in side borders.

Tuberculosis Sanatorium, Santiago — PT8

1952, Apr. 1 **Litho.** ***Perf. 11½***
RA14 PT8 1c lt blue & car .30 .25

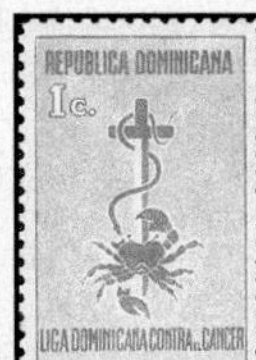
Sword, Serpent and Crab — PT9

1953, Feb. 1 **Unwmk.** ***Perf. 12.***
RA15 PT9 1c carmine .50 .30

The tax was for the Dominican League Against Cancer. See Nos. RA18, RA21, RA43, RA46, RA51, RA56, RA61, RA67, RA72, RA76, RA82, RA88, RA93, RA96.

Tuberculosis Dispensary for Children — PT10

1953, Apr. 1 **Litho.** ***Perf. 12½***
RA16 PT10 1c dp bl, pale bl & red .40 .30

See No. RA22.

Jesus Type of 1950
Second Redrawing

1953, Dec. 1 ***Perf. 11½***
Size: 22x31mm
RA17 PT7 1c blue .35 .25

Solid shading in sky reduced to a few scattered dots. Girl's left arm indicated. Rough white dots in side borders.

Cancer Type of 1952

1954, Oct. 1 **Redrawn** ***Perf. 12½***
RA18 PT9 1c rose carmine .30 .25
a. 1c red orange ('58) .40 .25
b. 1c carmine ('70) 1.25 .25

Upper right serif of numeral "1" eliminated; diagonal line added through "C" and period removed; sword extended, placing top on a line with top of "1." Dots of background screen arranged diagonally. Many other differences.
The tax was for the Dominican League Against Cancer. No. RA18a exists imperf.
On No. RA18b background screen eliminates white outline of crab.

Jesus Type of 1950

1954, Dec. 1 **Third Redrawing**
Size: 23x32¾mm
RA19 PT7 1c bright blue .40 .30
a. 1c pale blue ('59) .40 .30

Center completely screened. Tiny white horizontal rectangles in side borders.

Catalogue values for unused stamps in this section, from this point to the end of the section, are for Never Hinged items.

Lorraine Cross as Bell Clapper — PT11

1955, Apr. 1 **Litho.** ***Perf. 11½x12***
RA20 PT11 1c black, yel & red .50 .30

Cancer Type of 1952
Second Redrawing

1956, Oct. 1 ***Perf. 12½***
RA21 PT9 1c carmine .70 .30
a. 1c red orange ('64) 1.25 .50

Similar to No. RA18, but dots of background screen arranged in vertical and horizontal rows. Outlines of central device, lettering and frame clearly delineated. "C" of cent-sign smaller. Upper claw in solid color.

TB Dispensary Type of 1953
Redrawn

1954, Apr. 1
RA22 PT10 1c blue & red .90 .25
a. Red (cross) omitted 55.00

No. RA22 has third color omitted; clouds added; bolder letters and numerals.

Angelita Trujillo — PT12

1955, Dec. 1 **Unwmk.** ***Perf. 12½***
RA23 PT12 1c violet .95 .30

The tax was for child welfare.

Lorraine Cross — PT13

1956, Apr. 1 **Litho.** ***Perf. 11½***
RA24 PT13 1c blk, grn, lem & red .50 .30

The tax was for the Anti-Tuberculosis League. Inscribed: B.C.G. (Bacillus Calmette-Guerin).

PT14

1957, Apr. 1
RA25 PT14 1c red, blk, yel, grn & bl .50 .30

Jesus Type of 1950
Fourth Redrawing

1956, Dec. 1 **Unwmk.** ***Perf. 12***
Size: 21¾x31¼mm
RA26 PT7 1c blue .40 .25

Thin white lines around numeral boxes. Girl's bouquet touches Jesus' sleeve. Tiny white squares or rectangles in side borders. Foliage at either side of "Era de Trujillo" panel.

PT15

1958, Apr. 1 **Litho.** ***Perf. 12½***
RA27 PT15 1c brown car & red .45 .25

1959, Apr. 1 **Inscribed "1959"**
RA28 PT15 1c brown car & red .45 .25

PT16

1960, Apr. 1 **Litho.** ***Perf. 12***
RA29 PT16 1c bl, pale yel & red .55 .30

PT17

1961, Apr. 1 **Unwmk.** ***Perf. 11½***
RA30 PT17 1c blue & red .40 .25

Nos. RA29-RA30: tax was for the Anti-Tuberculosis League.
See No. RA33.

PT18

Design: 1c, Maria de los Angeles M. de Trujillo and Housing Project.

1961, Aug. 1 **Litho.** ***Perf. 12***
RA31 PT18 1c carmine rose .40 .25

The tax was for aid to the needy.
Nos. RA31-RA33 exist imperf.

Jesus Type of 1950
Fifth Redrawing

1961, Dec. 1 **Unwmk.** ***Perf. 12½***
RA32 PT7 1c blue .40 .25

No. RA32 is similar to No. RA19, but "Era de Trujillo" has been replaced by a solid color panel.

Type of 1961 Dated "1962"

1962, Apr. 2 ***Perf. 12½***
RA33 PT17 1c blue & red .95 .30

Tax for the Anti-Tuberculosis League.

Man's Chest — PT19

1963, Apr. 1 ***Perf. 12x11½***
RA34 PT19 1c ultra & red .50 .30

Jesus Type of 1950
Sixth Redrawing

1963, Dec. 1 ***Perf. 11½***
Size: 21¾x32mm
RA35 PT7 1c blue .40 .25
a. 1c deep blue ('64) .40 .25

No. RA35 is similar to No. RA26, but "Era de Trujillo" panel has been omitted.

Hibiscus — PT20

1966, Apr. 1 **Litho.** ***Perf. 11½***
RA36 PT20 1c emerald & car .40 .25

Tax for the Anti-Tuberculosis League.

Domingoa Nodosa — PT21

1967, Apr. 1 **Litho.** ***Perf. 12½***
RA37 PT21 1c lilac & red 1.00 .30

Tax for the Anti-Tuberculosis League.

Civil Defense Emblem — PT22

1967, July 1 Litho. *Rouletted 13*
RA38 PT22 1c multicolored .40 .25

Tax for the Civil Defense Organization.

Boy, School and Yule Bells — PT23

1967, Dec. 1 Litho. *Perf. 12½*
RA39 PT23 1c rose red & pink .50 .30

1968 *Perf. 11*
RA40 PT23 1c vermilion .45 .25

No. RA40 has screened background; No. RA39, smooth background.
The tax was for child welfare.
See Nos. RA49A, RA52, RA57, RA62, RA68, RA73, RA77, RA81.

Hand Holding Invalid — PT24

1968, Mar. 19 Litho. *Perf. 12½*
RA41 PT24 1c green & yellow .40 .25
a. 1c olive green & deep yellow, perf. 11½x12 ('69) .40 .25

The tax was for the rehabilitation of the handicapped. See Nos. RA47, RA50, RA54.

Dogbane — PT25

1968, Apr. 25 Litho. *Perf. 12½*
RA42 PT25 1c emerald, yel & red .40 .25

The tax was for the Anti-Tuberculosis League. See Nos. RA45, RA49.

Redrawn Cancer Type of 1955

1968, Oct. 1 Litho. *Perf. 12*
RA43 PT9 1c emerald .40 .25

The tax was for the Dominican League against Cancer.

Schoolyard, Torch — PT26

1969, Feb. 1 Litho. *Perf. 12½*
RA44 PT26 1c light blue .40 .25

Issued for Education Year 1969.

Flower Type of 1968

Design: No. RA45, Violets.

1969, Apr. 25 Litho. *Perf. 12½*
RA45 PT25 1c emerald, lil & red .70 .30

Tax for the Anti-Tuberculosis League.

Redrawn Cancer Type of 1955

1969, Oct. 1 Litho. *Perf. 11*
RA46 PT9 1c brt rose lilac .40 .25

Tax for Dominican League against Cancer.

Invalid Type of 1968

1970, Mar. 2 *Perf. 12½*
RA47 PT24 1c blue .40 .25

The tax was for the rehabilitation of the handicapped.

Book, Sun and Education Year Emblem — PT27

1970, Feb. 6 *Perf. 11*
RA48 PT27 1c bright pink .40 .25

International Education Year.

Flower Type of 1968

Design: 1c, Elleanthus capitatus; cross in upper left corner, denomination in lower right.

1970, Apr. 30 *Perf. 11*
RA49 PT25 1c emerald, red & yel 1.10 .30

Tax for Anti-Tuberculosis League.

Boy Type of 1967

1970, Dec. 1 *Perf. 12½*
RA49A PT23 1c orange .45 .30

Communications Emblem — PT28

1971, Jan. 2 Litho. *Perf. 11*
Size: 17½x20½mm
RA49B PT28 1c vio bl & red (white frame) .55 .30

Tax was for Postal and Telegraph Communications School.
See Nos. RA53, RA58, RA63, RA69, RA78, RA91.

Invalid Type of 1968

1971, Mar. 1 Litho. *Perf. 11*
RA50 PT24 1c brt rose lilac .40 .25

Tax for rehabilitation of the handicapped.

Cancer Type of 1952
Third Redrawing

1971, Oct. 1 *Perf. 11½*
RA51 PT9 1c dp yellow green .40 .25

Background of No. RA51 appears white and design stands out. No. RA43 has greenish background and design appears faint. Numeral "1" on No. RA51 is 3½mm high, on No. RA43 it is 3mm.

Boy Type of 1967

1971, Dec. 1 Litho. *Perf. 11*
RA52 PT23 1c green .45 .25

Communications Type of 1971

1972, Jan. 3 Litho. *Perf. 12½*
Size: 19x22mm
RA53 PT28 1c dk bl & red (bl frame) .40 .25

Tax was for the Postal and Telegraph Communications School.

Invalid Type of 1968

1972, Mar. 1 Litho. *Perf. 11½*
RA54 PT24 1c brown .75 .25

Orchid — PT29

1972, Apr. 2 *Perf. 11*
RA55 PT29 1c lt grn, red & yel 1.60 .45

Tax was for the Anti-Tuberculosis League.

Redrawn Cancer Type of 1954-58

1972, Oct. 2 *Perf. 12½*
RA56 PT9 1c orange .45 .25

Tax for Dominican League against Cancer.

Boy Type of 1967

1972, Dec. 1 *Perf. 12*
RA57 PT23 1c violet .40 .25

Tax was for child welfare.

Communications Type of 1971

1973, Jan. 2 *Perf. 10½*
Size: 19x22mm
RA58 PT28 1c dk bl & red (red frame) .40 .25

Tax was for Postal and Telegraph Communications School.

Invalid — PT30

1973, Mar. 1 Litho. *Perf. 12½*
Size: 21x25mm
RA59 PT30 1c olive .40 .25

Tax was for the Dominican Rehabilitation Association. See Nos. RA66, RA70, RA74, RA79, RA86.

Hibiscus — PT31

1973, Apr. 17 Litho. *Perf. 10½*
RA60 PT31 1c multicolored 1.20 .30

Tax was for Anti-Tuberculosis League. Exists imperf.

Cancer Type of 1952 Redrawn and "1973" Added

1973, Oct. 1 *Perf. 13½*
RA61 PT9 1c olive green .55 .30

Tax was for Dominican League Against Cancer.

Boy Type of 1967

1973, Dec. 1 Litho. *Perf. 13x13½*
RA62 PT23 1c blue .70 .25

Communications Type of 1971

1973, Nov. 3 *Perf. 10½*
Size: 19x22mm
RA63 PT28 1c bl & red (lt grn frame) .40 .25

Tax was for Postal and Telegraph Communications School. Exists imperf.

Invalid Type of 1973

1974, Mar. 1 Litho. *Perf. 10½*
Size: 22x27½mm
RA66 PT30 1c light ultra .55 .30

See note after No. RA59.

Cancer Type of 1952 Redrawn and "1974" Added

1974, Oct. 1 *Perf. 12*
RA67 PT9 1c orange .55 .30

Tax for Dominican League Against Cancer.

Boy Type of 1967

1974, Dec. 2 Litho. *Perf. 11½*
RA68 PT23 1c dk brown & buff .40 .25

Communications Type of 1971

1974, Nov. 13 *Perf. 10½*
RA69 PT28 1c blue & red (yel frame) .40 .25

Invalid Type of 1973 Dated "1975"

1975, Mar. 1 *Perf. 13½x13*
Size: 21x32mm
RA70 PT30 1c olive brown .55 .30

See note after No. RA59.

Catteeyopsis Rosea — PT32

1975, Apr. 1 *Perf. 12*
RA71 PT32 1c blue & multi 1.40 .95

Tax was for Anti-Tuberculosis League.

Cancer Type of 1952 Redrawn and "1975" Added

1975, Oct. 1 Litho. *Perf. 12*
RA72 PT9 1c violet blue .55 .30

Tax was for Dominican League Against Cancer. Exists imperf.

Boy Type of 1967

1975, Dec. 1 Litho. *Perf. 12*
RA73 PT23 1c red orange .40 .25

Tax was for child welfare.

Invalid Type of 1973 Dated "1976"

1976, Mar. 1 Litho. *Perf. 12*
Size: 21x31mm
RA74 PT30 1c ultra .55 .30

See note after No. RA59.

Oncidium Colochilum — PT33

1976, Apr. 6 *Perf. 13x13½*
RA75 PT33 1c green & multi 1.00 .30

Tax was for Anti-Tuberculosis League.
See Nos. RA80, RA84.

Cancer Type of 1952 Redrawn and "1976" Added

1976, Oct. 1 Litho. *Perf. 13½*
RA76 PT9 1c green .55 .30

Tax was for Dominican League Against Cancer.

Boy Type of 1967

1976, Dec. 1 Litho. *Perf. 13½*
RA77 PT23 1c purple .55 .30

Tax was for child welfare.

Communications Type of 1971

1977, Jan. 7 Litho. *Perf. 10½*
Size: 19x22mm

RA78 PT28 1c blue & red (lil frame) .40 .25
a. Perf. 12½x10½ — —

Tax was for Postal and Telegraph Communications School.

Invalid Type of 1973 Dated "1977"

1977, Mar. 11 *Perf. 12*
Size: 21x31mm

RA79 PT30 1c ultra .55 .30

See note after No. RA59.

Orchid Type of 1976 Dated "1977"

Orchid: Oncidium variegatum.

1977, Apr. 22 Litho. *Perf. 13½*
RA80 PT33 1c multicolored 1.25 .30

Tax was for Anti-Tuberculosis League.

Boy Type of 1967

1977, Dec. 27 Litho. *Perf. 12*
RA81 PT23 1c emerald .40 .25

Tax was for child welfare.

Cancer Type of 1952 Redrawn and "1977" Added

1978, Oct. 2 Litho. *Perf. 13½*
RA82 PT9 1c lilac rose .55 .30

Tax for Dominican League Against Cancer.

Mother, Child, Holly — PT34

1978, Dec. 1 Litho. *Perf. 13½*
RA83 PT34 1c green .40 .25

Tax was for child welfare.
See Nos. RA89, RA92, RA97.

Orchid Type of 1973 Dated "1978"

Flower: Yellow alder.

1979, Apr. Litho. *Perf. 13½*
RA84 PT33 1c lt blue & multi 1.10 .30

Tax was for Anti-Tuberculosis League.

University Seal — PT35

1979, Feb. 10 Litho. *Perf. 13½*
RA85 PT35 2c ultra & gray .40 .25

450th anniv. of University of Santo Domingo.

Invalid Type of 1973 Dated "1978"

1979, Mar. 1 Litho. *Perf. 12*
RA86 PT30 1c emerald .95 .30

See note after No. RA59.

Invalid — PT36

1980, Mar. 28 Litho. *Perf. 13½*
RA87 PT36 1c olive & citron .95 .30

Cancer Type of 1952 Redrawn and "1980" Added

1980, Oct. 1
RA88 PT9 1c violet & dk pur .40 .25

Mother and Child Type of 1978

1980, Dec. 1 Litho. *Perf. 13½*
RA89 PT34 1c bright blue .40 .25

Turnera Ulmifolia (Marilope) — PT37

1981, Apr. 27 Litho. *Perf. 12*
RA90 PT37 1c multicolored .60 .25

Tax was for Anti-Tuberculosis League.
See Nos. RA98-RA99.

Communications Type of 1971

1981, Feb. Litho. *Perf. 10½*
RA91 PT28 1c blue & red (lt bl frame) .75 .25

Mother and Child Type of 1978

1982, Dec. 1 Litho. *Perf. 12x12½*
RA92 PT34 1c lt bluish green .40 .25

Inscribed 1981.

Cancer Type of 1952 Redrawn and "1981" Added

1982 Litho. *Perf. 13½*
RA93 PT9 1c blue & dp blue .95 .30

PT38

1983, Apr. 29 Litho. *Perf. 12*
RA94 PT38 1c multicolored .40 .25

Tax was for Red Cross.

Disabled — PT39

1984 Litho. *Perf. 13½*
RA95 PT39 1c sky blue .60 .25

Cancer Type of 1952 Redrawn and "1983" Added

1983, Oct. 1 Litho. *Perf. 13½*
RA96 PT9 1c lt bluish grn & dk grn 1.00 .25

Mother and Child Type of 1978

1983, Dec. 1 Litho. *Perf. 12*
RA97 PT34 1c light green 1.00 .25

Inscribed 1983.

Flower Type of 1981 Dated "1983" or "1984"

1983-85 Litho. *Perf. 12x12½*
RA98 PT37 1c 1983 2.25 .25
RA99 PT37 1c 1984 2.25 .25

Issued: #RA98, 4/19/83; #RA99, 4/1/85.

POSTAL TAX AIR POST STAMPS

Postal Tax Stamps Surcharged in Red or Gold

1930, Dec. 3 Unwmk. *Perf. 12*
RAC1 PT2 5c + 5c blk & rose (R) *27.00 31.00*
a. Tête bêche pair *125.00*
b. "Habilitado Para" missing *52.50*
RAC2 PT2 10c + 10c blk & rose (R) *27.00 31.00*
a. Tête bêche pair *125.00*
b. "Habilitado Para" missing *52.50*
c. Gold surcharge *95.00 95.00*
d. As "c," tête bêche pair *450.00*
e. As "c" and "b" *250.00*

Nos. RAC1-RAC2 were on sale one day.

RAC4 PT2 5c + 5c ultra & rose (R) *6.75 6.75*
a. Tête bêche pair *45.00*
b. Inverted surcharge *42.50*
c. Tête bêche pair, inverted surcharge *600.00*
d. Pair, one without surcharge *190.00*
e. "Habilitado Para" missing *15.00*
RAC5 PT2 10c + 10c yel & rose (G) *5.25 5.25*
a. Tête bêche pair *42.50*
b. "Habilitado Para" missing *18.00*

Imperf

RAC6 PT2 5c + 5c ultra & rose (R) *6.75 6.75*
a. Tête bêche pair *52.50*
b. "Habilitado Para" missing *18.00*
RAC7 PT2 10c + 10c yel & rose (G) *6.75 6.75*
a. Tête bêche pair *52.50*
b. "Habilitado Para" missing *18.00*
Nos. RAC1-RAC7 (6) *79.50 87.50*

It was obligatory to use Nos. RA1-RA8 and RAC1-RAC7 on all postal matter, in amounts equal to the ordinary postage.

This surtax was for the aid of sufferers from the hurricane of Sept. 3, 1930.

No. 261 Overprinted in Green

1933, Oct. 11
RAC8 A32 2c scarlet .50 .40
a. Double overprint 9.00
b. Pair, one without overprint 375.00

By official decree this stamp, in addition to the regular postage, had to be used on every letter, etc., sent by the internal air post service.

DUBAI

ˌdü-ˈbī

LOCATION — Oman Peninsula, Arabia, on Persian Gulf
GOVT. — Sheikdom under British protection
AREA — 1,500 sq. mi.
POP. — 60,000
CAPITAL — Dubai

Dubai is one of six Persian Gulf sheikdoms to join the United Arab Emirates which proclaimed its independence Dec. 2, 1971. See United Arab Emirates.

100 Naye Paise = 1 Rupee
100 Dirhams = 1 Riyal (1966)

Imperforate

Many issues were accompanied by smaller quantities of imperforate stamps.

Catalogue values for all unused stamps in this country are for Never Hinged items.

Hermit Crab — A1

Sheik Rashid bin Said al Maktum — A2

2np, 20np, Cuttlefish. 3np, 25np, Snail. 4np, 30np, Crab. 5np, 35np, Sea urchin. 10np, 50np, Sea shell. 1r, Fortress wall. 2r, View of Dubai. 3r, Fortress wall. 5r, View of Dubai.

Perf. 12x11½

1963, June 15 Litho. Unwmk.

1	A1	1np dl bl & car rose	.30	.25
2	A1	2np lt bl & bis brn	.35	.25
3	A1	3np green & sepia	.35	.25
4	A1	4np pink & orange	.35	.25
5	A1	5np violet & blk	.35	.25
6	A1	10np brn org & blk	.35	.25
7	A1	15np gray ol & dp car	.70	.25
8	A1	20np rose red & org brn	.75	.40
9	A1	25np ap grn & red brn	.90	.40
10	A1	30np gray & red	1.50	.40
11	A1	35np dl lil & dl vio	1.50	.40
12	A1	50np org & sepia	2.25	.75
13	A1	1r brt bl & red org	6.00	1.50
14	A1	2r dull yel & brn	9.50	3.50
15	A1	3r rose car & blk	16.00	5.50
16	A1	5r grn & dl red brn	27.50	9.50

Perf. 12

17	A2	10r rose lake, grnsh bl & blk	60.00	19.00
		Nos. 1-17 (17)	128.65	43.10

Nos. 13-17 exist perf 10½. Values are much higher.

Dhows A3

Designs: 2np, First-aid tent. 3np, Camel caravan. 4np, Butterfly.

1963, Sept. 1 Unwmk. *Perf. 12*

18	A3	1np ultra, yel & red	.80	.35
19	A3	2np brn, yel & red	.80	.35
20	A3	3np red brn, org & red	.80	.35
21	A3	4np brn, brt grn & red	.80	.35
		Nos. 18-21,C9-C12 (8)	11.00	4.10

Intl. Red Cross, cent. Exist perf. 10½. Values, each $1.75.

Four imperf. souvenir sheets exist in the denominations and designs of Nos. C9-C12, with "Air-Mail" omitted and colors changed. Size: 119x99mm. Value $50.

For overprints see Nos. C52-C54.

A4

Anopheles Mosquito: 2np, Mosquito and entwined snakes. 3np, Mosquitoes over swamp.

1963, Dec. 20 Unwmk. *Perf. 12*

22	A4	1np emer & red brn	.35	.25
23	A4	1np red & dark brn	.35	.25
24	A4	1np blue & carmine	.35	.25
25	A4	2np brn & orange	.35	.25

26	A4	2np carmine & blue	.35	.25
27	A4	3np org brn & blue	.35	.25
		Nos. 22-27,C13-C15 (9)	4.55	2.35

WHO drive to eradicate malaria.

A5

Designs: 1np, Scouts forming pyramid. 2np, Bugler. 3np, Cub Scouts. 4np, Scouts and bugler. 5np, Scouts presenting flag.

1964 **Unwmk.**

28	A5	1np dk brn & ocher	.25	.25
29	A5	2np car rose & sep	.25	.25
30	A5	3np blue & red org	.25	.25
31	A5	4np carmine & blue	.25	.25
32	A5	5np ind & bluish grn	.35	.25
		Nos. 28-32,C20-C24 (10)	6.35	3.20

11th Boy Scout Jamboree, Marathon, Greece, Aug., 1963.

For overprints see Nos. C47-C51.

Unisphere, New York Skyline and Dubai Harbor — A6

2np, 4np, 10np, Views of NYC and Dubai.

1964, Apr. 22 **Litho.** ***Perf. 12***

33	A6	1np dk bl & rose red	.25	.25
34	A6	2np dl red, lil rose & bl	.25	.25
35	A6	3np brown & green	.25	.25
36	A6	4np emer, brt grn & red	.25	.25
37	A6	5np ol, sl grn & lil	.25	.25
38	A6	10np brn org, red org & blk	.70	.50
		Nos. 33-38,C36-C38 (9)	6.15	4.05

New York World's Fair, 1964-65.

Gymnast — A8

Designs: 2np, 5np, 20np, 40np, Various exercises on bar. 3np, 30np, Various exercises on vaulting horse. 4np, 10np, 1r, Various exercises on rings.

1964 **Photo.** ***Perf. 14***

43	A8	1np org brn & yel grn	.25	.25
44	A8	2np dk brn & grnsh bl	.25	.25
45	A8	3np ultra & org brn	.25	.25
46	A8	4np dk pur & yel	.25	.25
47	A8	5np ocher & dk bl	.25	.25
48	A8	10np brt bl & ocher	.40	.25
49	A8	20np ol & lil rose	.50	.25
50	A8	30np dk bl & yel	1.00	.25
51	A8	40np Prus grn & dl org	1.75	.50
52	A8	1r rose vio & grnsh bl	3.75	1.25
		Nos. 43-52 (10)	8.65	3.75

18th Olympic Games, Tokyo, Oct. 10-25, 1964. An imperf. miniature sheet contains a 67x67mm stamp similar to No. 52. Value $11.

Palace — A9

Sheik Rashid bin Said — A10

Designs: 20np, 25np, View of new Dubai. 35np, 40np, Bridge and dhow. 60np, 1r, Bridge. 1.25r, Minaret. 1.50r, 3r, Old Dubai.

1966, May 30 **Photo.** ***Perf. 14x14½***

Size: 23x18mm

53	A9	5np brown & indigo	.25	.25
54	A9	10np black & orange	.30	.25
55	A9	15np ultra & brown	.40	.25

Perf. 13

Size: 27½x20½mm

56	A9	20np blue & red brn	.50	.30
57	A9	25np org ver & ultra	.55	.40
58	A9	35np violet & emer	.75	.50
59	A9	40np grnsh bl & bl	1.10	.50

Perf. 14½

Size: 31½x24mm

60	A9	60np yel grn & org ver	1.75	1.00
61	A9	1r ultra & blue	2.75	1.50
62	A9	1.25r brn org & blk	3.00	2.00
63	A9	1.50r rose lil & yel grn	5.50	2.10
64	A9	3r dk ol bis & vio	10.00	4.00

Engr.

Perf. 14

65	A10	5r rose carmine	18.00	7.50
66	A10	10r dark blue	37.50	16.00
		Nos. 53-66 (14)	82.35	36.55

Nos. 53-62, 64-66 Overprinted with New Currency Names and Bars

1967

67	A9	5d on 5np	.30	.25
68	A9	10d on 10np	.35	.25
69	A9	15d on 15np	.50	.25
70	A9	20d on 20np	1.00	.25
71	A9	25d on 25np	1.25	.25
72	A9	35d on 35np	1.50	.25
73	A9	40d on 40np	1.75	.30
74	A9	60d on 60np	3.00	.40
75	A9	1r on 1r	4.00	.95
76	A9	1.25r on 1.25r	7.25	1.30
77	A9	3r on 3r	15.00	3.75
78	A10	5r on 5r	27.50	7.50
79	A10	10r on 10r	40.00	14.00
		Nos. 67-79 (13)	103.40	29.70

Sheik and Falcon — A11

Dhow — A12

Litho. & Engr.

1967, Aug. 21 ***Perf. 13½***

80	A11	5d dp car & org	1.10	.30
81	A11	10d sepia & green	1.25	.25
82	A11	20d dp cl & bl gray	1.40	.30
83	A11	35d slate & car	1.75	.30
84	A11	60d vio bl & emer	3.25	.50
85	A11	1r green & lilac	4.50	.50
86	A12	1.25r lt bl & claret	5.50	.65
87	A12	3r dull vio & claret	11.00	1.75
88	A12	5r brt grn & vio	22.50	3.75
89	A12	10r lil rose & grn	30.00	6.75
		Nos. 80-89 (10)	82.25	15.05

S. S. Bamora, 1914 — A13

35d, De Havilland 66 plane, 1930. 60d, S. S. Sirdhana, 1947. 1r, Armstrong Whitworth 15 "Atlanta," 1938. 1.25r, S. S. Chandpara, 1949. 3r, BOAC Sunderland amphibian plane, 1943. No. 96, Freighter Bombala, 1961, and BOAC Super VC10, 1967.

1969, Feb. 12 **Litho.** ***Perf. 14x13½***

90	A13	25d lt grn, bl & blk	.25	*.25*
91	A13	35d multicolored	.25	*.25*
92	A13	60d multicolored	.70	*.25*
93	A13	1r lil, blk & dl yel	1.15	*.25*
94	A13	1.25r gray, blk & dp org	1.60	*.25*
95	A13	3r pink, blk & bl grn	2.50	*.35*
		Nos. 90-95 (6)	6.45	*1.60*

Miniature Sheet

Imperf

96	A13	1.25r pink, blk & bl grn	16.00	16.00

60 years of postal service.

Mother and Children, by Rubens A14

Arab Mother's Day: 60d, Madonna and Child, by Murillo. 1r, Mother and Child, by Francesco Mazzuoli. 3r, Madonna and Child, by Correggio.

1969, Mar. 21 **Litho.** ***Perf. 13½***

97	A14	60d silver & multi	.75	*.25*
98	A14	1r silver & multi	1.50	*.25*
99	A14	1.25r silver & multi	1.75	*.25*
100	A14	3r silver & multi	3.50	*.45*
		Nos. 97-100 (4)	7.50	*1.20*

Porkfish — A15

1969, May 26 **Litho.** ***Perf. 11***

101	A15	60d shown	2.00	*.35*
102	A15	60d Spotted grouper	2.00	*.35*
103	A15	60d Moonfish	2.00	*.35*
104	A15	60d Sweetlips	2.00	*.35*
105	A15	60d Blue angel	2.00	*.35*
106	A15	60d Texas skate	2.00	*.35*
107	A15	60d Striped butterflyfish	2.00	*.35*
108	A15	60d Imperial angelfish	2.00	*.35*
a.		Block of 8, #101-108	35.00	
		Nos. 101-108 (8)	16.00	*2.80*

Nos. 101-108 printed in se-tenant blocks of 8, each sheet containing two such blocks.

Explorers and Map of Arabia — A16

1969, July 21 **Litho.** ***Perf. 13½x13***

109	A16	35d brown & green	1.50	*.35*
110	A16	60d vio & sepia	2.00	*.45*
111	A16	1r green & dl bl	5.50	*.55*
112	A16	1.25r gray & rose car	7.00	*.65*
		Nos. 109-112 (4)	16.00	*2.00*

European explorers of Arabia: Sir Richard Francis Burton (1821-1890), Charles Montagu Doughty (1843-1926), Johann Ludwig Burckhardt (1784-1817) and Wilfred Patrick Thesiger (1910-).

Construction of World's First Underwater Oil Storage Tank — A17

Designs: 20d, Launching of oil storage tank. 35d, Oil storage tank in place on ocean ground. 60d, Sheik Rashid bin Said, offshore drilling platform and monument commemorating first oil export. 1r, Offshore production platform and helicopter port.

1969, Oct. 13 **Litho.** ***Perf. 11***

113	A17	5d blue & multi	.30	*.25*
114	A17	20d blue & multi	1.00	*.25*
115	A17	35d blue & multi	1.90	*.25*
116	A17	60d blue & multi	2.75	*.25*
117	A17	1r blue & multi	4.00	*.25*
		Nos. 113-117 (5)	9.95	*1.25*

Astronauts Collecting Moon Rocks — A18

Designs: 1r, Astronaut at foot of ladder. 1.25r, Astronauts planting American flag.

1969, Dec. 15 **Litho.** ***Perf. 14½***

118		Strip of 3	3.75	*1.00*
a.	A18	60d multicolored	.40	*.25*
b.	A18	1r multicolored	.80	*.25*
c.	A18	1.25r multicolored (airmail)	1.50	*.25*

The 1.25r is inscribed "AIRMAIL."

Sizes: 60d and 1r, 28½x41mm; 1.25r, 60½x41mm.

See note after US No. C76.

Ocean Weather Ship Launching Radio Sonde, and Hastings Plane — A19

WMO Emblem and: 1r, Kew-type radio sonde, weather balloon and radar antenna. 1.25r, Tiros satellite and weather sounding rocket. 3r, Ariel satellite and rocket launching.

1970, Mar. 23 **Litho.** ***Perf. 11***

121	A19	60d dl grn, brn & blk	.40	*.25*
122	A19	1r brown & multi	.75	*.25*
123	A19	1.25r dk blue & multi	.90	*.25*
124	A19	3r multicolored	2.00	*.30*
		Nos. 121-124 (4)	4.05	*1.05*

10th World Meteorological Day.

UPU Headquarters and Monument, Bern — A20

60d, UPU monument, Bern, telecommunications satellite and London PO tower.

1970, May 20 Litho. *Perf. 13½x14*
125 A20 5d lt green & multi .75 *.25*
126 A20 60d dp blue & multi 1.90 *.25*

UPU Headquarters opening, May 20.

Charles Dickens, London Skyline — A21

60d, Dickens' portrait, vert. 1.25r, Dickens & "Old Curiosity Shop." 3r, Bound volumes.

1970, July 23 Litho. *Perf. 13½*
127 A21 60d olive & multi .85 *.25*
128 A21 1r multicolored 1.00 *.25*
129 A21 1.25r buff & multi 1.20 *.25*
130 A21 3r multicolored 4.00 *.50*
Nos. 127-130 (4) 7.05 *1.25*

Dickens (1812-70), English novelist.

The Graham Children, by William Hogarth — A22

Paintings: 60d, Caroline Murat and her Children, by François Pascal Gerard, vert. 1r, Napoleon with the Children on the Terrace in St. Cloud, by Louis Ducis.

1970, Oct. 1 Litho. *Perf. 13½*
131 A22 35d multicolored .75 .25
132 A22 60d multicolored 1.25 .25
133 A22 1r multicolored 2.00 .25
Nos. 131-133 (3) 4.00 .75

Issued for Children's Day.

Sheik Rashid bin Said — A23 Television Station — A25

National Bank of Dubai A24

Designs: 10d, Boat building. 20d, Al Maktum Bascule Bridge. 35d, Great Mosque, Dubai, vert. 1r, Dubai International Airport, horiz. 1.25r, Port Rashid harbor project, horiz. 3r, Rashid Hospital, horiz. 5r, Dubai Trade School, horiz.

Perf. 14x14½, 14½x14
1970-71 Litho.
134 A23 5d multi ('71) .30 .25
135 A24 10d multi ('71) .30 .25
136 A24 20d multi ('71) .40 .25
137 A24 35d multi ('71) .55 .25
138 A24 60d multicolored .80 .25

Perf. 14
139 A25 1r multicolored 1.20 .25
140 A25 1.25r multicolored 1.20 .25
141 A25 3r multicolored 3.75 .25
142 A25 5r multicolored 6.00 .40
143 A25 10r multi ('71) 14.00 .85
Nos. 134-143 (10) 28.50 3.25

Dubai Airport A26

Designs: 1.25r, Airport entrance.

1971, May 15 Litho. *Perf. 13½x14*
144 A26 1r multicolored 3.25 .25
145 A26 1.25r multicolored 4.00 .25

Opening of Dubai International Airport.

Map With Tracking Stations, Satellites A27

1971, June 21 Litho. *Perf. 14½*
146 A27 60d multicolored .60 .30

Outer Space Telecommunications Cong., Paris, Mar. 29-Apr. 2. See Nos. C55-C56.

Fan, Scout Emblem, Map of Japan — A28

Designs: 1r, Boy Scouts in kayaks. 1.25r, Mountaineering. 3r, Campfire, horiz.

Perf. 14x13½, 13½x14
1971, Aug. 30 Litho.
147 A28 60d multicolored .45 *.25*
148 A28 1r multicolored .90 *.25*
149 A28 1.25r multicolored 1.15 *.25*
150 A28 3r multicolored 2.50 *.30*
Nos. 147-150 (4) 5.00 *1.05*

13th Boy Scout World Jamboree, Asagiri Plain, Japan, Aug. 2-10.

Albrecht Dürer, Self-portrait A29

1971, Oct. 18 *Perf. 14x13½*
151 A29 60d gold & multi .80 *.25*

See Nos. C57-C59.

Boy in Meadow A30

5r, Boys playing and UNICEF emblem.

1971, Dec. 11 *Perf. 13½*
152 A30 60d multi .45 *.25*
153 A30 5r multi, horiz. 3.50 *.50*

25th anniv. of UNICEF. See No. C60.

Ludwig van Beethoven A31

Portrait: 10d, Leonardo da Vinci.

1972, Feb. 7
154 A31 10d lt tan & multi .30 *.25*
155 A31 35d lt tan & multi .45 *.25*

See Nos. C61-C62.

Olympic Emblems, Gymnast on Rings — A32

1972, July 31 Litho. *Perf. 13½*
156 A32 35d shown .55 *.25*
157 A32 40d Fencing .65 *.25*
158 A32 65d Hockey .80 *.25*
Nos. 156-158,C65-C67 (6) 7.50 1.50

20th Olympic Games, Munich, 8/26-9/11.

Stamps of Dubai were replaced in 1972 by those of United Arab Emirates.

AIR POST STAMPS

Type of Regular Issue and

Peregrine Falcon — AP1

Design: A1, Falcon over bridge.

Perf. 12x11½, 11½x12
1963, June 15 Litho. Unwmk.
C1 A1 20np dk red brn & lt blue 2.50 .35
C2 AP1 25np ol & blk brn 2.75 .45
C3 A1 30np red org & blk 3.25 .55
C4 AP1 40np grayish brn & dk violet 3.50 .65
C5 A1 50np emer & rose cl 4.25 .75
C6 AP1 60np brn org & blk 5.25 .85
C7 A1 75np vio & dp grn 6.50 1.00
C8 AP1 1r org & red brn 9.00 1.25
Nos. C1-C8 (8) 37.00 5.85

Red Cross Type

Designs: 20np, Dhows. 30np, First-aid tent. 40np, Camel caravan. 50np, Butterfly.

1963, Sept. 1 Unwmk. *Perf. 12*
C9 A3 20np brown, yel & red 1.40 .50
C10 A3 30np dk bl, buff & red 1.40 .50
C11 A3 40np black, yel & red 1.75 .60
C12 A3 50np vio, lt bl & red 3.25 1.10
Nos. C9-C12 (4) 7.80 2.70

Malaria Type

Designs: 30np, Anopheles mosquito. 40np, Mosquito and coiled arrows. 70np, Mosquitoes over swamp.

1963, Dec. 20 Unwmk. *Perf. 12*
C13 A4 30np purple & emer .65 .25
C14 A4 40np red & dull grn .75 .25
C15 A4 70np slate & citron 1.05 .35
Nos. C13-C15 (3) 2.45 .85

Three imperf. souv. sheets exist containing 4 stamps each in changed colors similar to Nos. C13-C15. Value $30.

Wheat — AP2

40np, Wheat and palm tree. 70np, Hands holding wheat. 1r, Woman carrying basket.

1963, Dec. 30 Litho.
C16 AP2 30np vio bl & ocher .50 .30
C17 AP2 40np red & olive .75 .45
C18 AP2 70np green & orange 1.15 .65
C19 AP2 1r org brn & Prus bl 1.75 1.00
Nos. C16-C19 (4) 4.15 2.40

Boy Scout Type

Designs: 20np, Human pyramid. 30np, Bugler. 40np, Cub Scouts. 70np, Scouts and bugler. 1r, Scouts presenting flag.

1964, Jan. 20
C20 A5 20np green & dk brn .30 .25
C21 A5 30np lilac & ocher .60 .25
C22 A5 40np vio bl & yel grn .80 .30
C23 A5 70np dk grn & gray 1.40 .45
C24 A5 1r vio bl & red org 1.90 .70
Nos. C20-C24 (5) 5.00 1.95

Five imperf. souv. sheets exist containing 4 stamps each in changed colors similar to Nos. C20-C24. Value $60.

For overprints see Nos. C47-C51.

John F. Kennedy and US Seal AP3

1964, Jan. 15 Litho.
C25 AP3 75np grn & blk, *lt grn* .90 .55
C26 AP3 1r ocher & blk, *tan* 1.25 .60
C27 AP3 1.25r mag & blk, *gray* 1.60 .85
Nos. C25-C27 (3) 3.75 2.00

Pres. John F. Kennedy (1917-1963).

Nos. C25-C27 exist imperf. Value, set $9.50.

A souvenir sheet contains one imperf. 1.25r in buff and black with simulated perforations. Value $5.

For overprints see Nos. C52-C54.

Spacecraft — AP4

Designs: 1np, 5np, Ascending rocket, vert. 2np, 1r, Mercury capsule, vert. 4np, 2r, Twin spacecraft.

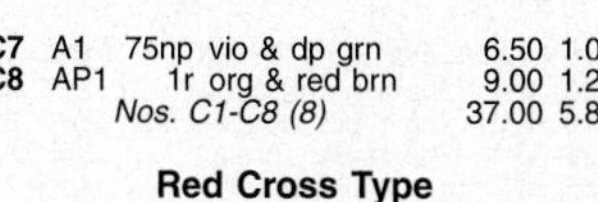

1964, Jan. 25 Unwmk. *Perf. 12*
C28 AP4 1np emerald & org .25 .25
C29 AP4 2np multicolored .30 .25
C30 AP4 3np multicolored .35 .25
C31 AP4 4np multicolored .40 .25
C32 AP4 5np blue & orange .45 .25
C33 AP4 1r vio bl, dp car & buff 1.25 .70
C34 AP4 1.50r vio bl, dp car & buff 2.00 1.25
C35 AP4 2r blue, yel & red 2.75 1.50
Nos. C28-C35 (8) 7.75 4.70

Issued to honor the astronauts.
Nos. C28-C35 exist imperf. Value, set $10.
An imperf. souvenir sheet contains one stamp similar to No. C35. Value $7.

New York World's Fair Type

Statue of Liberty and ships in Dubai harbor.

1964, Apr. 22 Litho.
C36 A6 75np gray bl, ultra & blk .80 .40
C37 A6 2r gray grn, dk brn & bis 1.40 .80
C38 A6 3r dl grn, gray ol & dp org 2.00 1.10
Nos. C36-C38 (3) 4.20 2.30

An imperf. souvenir sheet contains 2 stamps in Statue of Liberty design: 2r dark brown and rose carmine, and 3r ultramarine and gold. Value $10.

Scales and Flame
AP5

1964, Apr. 30 Litho. *Perf. 12*
C39 AP5 35np bl, brn & scar .60 .30
C40 AP5 50np lt bl, dk grn & scar .75 .35
C41 AP5 1r grnsh bl, blk & scar 1.40 .60
C42 AP5 3r lt ultra, ultra, & scar 4.00 2.00
Nos. C39-C42 (4) 6.75 3.25

15th anniv. of the Universal Declaration of Human Rights. An imperf. souvenir sheet contains one 3r light green, ultramarine and scarlet stamp. Value $7.50.

Nos. C20-C24 Overprinted in Red and Black (Shield in Red)

1964, June 20
C47 A5 20np green & dk brn 1.15 .40
C48 A5 30np lilac & ocher 1.35 .50
C49 A5 40np vio bl & yel grn 2.00 .75
C50 A5 70np dk grn & gray 3.25 1.50
C51 A5 1r vio bl & red org 4.50 2.00
Nos. C47-C51 (5) 12.25 5.15

9th Winter Olympic Games, Innsbruck, Austria, Jan. 29-Feb. 9, 1964.
A similar but unauthorized overprint, with shield in black, exists on Nos. 28-32, C20-C24, and the five souvenir sheets mentioned below No. C24. The Dubai G.P.O. calls this black-shield overprint "bogus."

Nos. C25-C27 Overprinted in Brown or Green

1964, Sept. 15
C52 AP3 75np (Br) 2.00 2.00
C53 AP3 1r (G) 2.40 2.40
C54 AP3 1.25r (G) 3.00 3.00
Nos. C52-C54 (3) 7.40 7.40

Pres. John F. Kennedy 48th birth anniv. The same overprint in black was applied to the souv. sheet noted after No. C27.

Communications Type

Designs: 1r, Intelsat 4, tracking station on globe and rocket. 5r, Eiffel Tower, Syncom 3 and Goonhilly radar station.

1971, June 21 Litho. *Perf. 14½*
C55 A27 1r lt brown & multi .60 *.25*
C56 A27 5r multicolored 3.00 *.45*

Portrait Type

1r, Newton. 1.25r, Avicenna. 3r, Voltaire.

1971, Oct. 18 Litho. *Perf. 14x13½*
C57 A29 1r gold & multi 1.10 *.25*
C58 A29 1.25r gold & multi 1.40 *.25*
C59 A29 3r gold & multi 4.00 *.50*
Nos. C57-C59 (3) 6.50 *1.00*

UNICEF Type

1r, Mother, children, UNICEF emblem.

1971, Dec. 11 *Perf. 13½*
C60 A30 1r gold & multi 1.00 *.25*

Portrait Type

75d, Khalil Gibran. 5r, Charles de Gaulle.

1972, Feb. 7 Litho. *Perf. 13½*
C61 A31 75d lt tan & multi .75 *.25*
C62 A31 5r lt tan & multi 5.25 *.35*

Infant Health Care
AP6

Design: 75d, Nurse supervising children at meal, and WHO emblem, vert.

1972, Apr. 7 Litho. *Perf. 14x13½*
C63 AP6 75d multicolored 1.60 *.25*
C64 AP6 1.25r multicolored 2.40 *.25*

World Health Day.

Olympic Type

1972, July 31 Litho. *Perf. 13½*
C65 A32 75d Water polo 1.50 *.25*
C66 A32 1r Steeplechase 1.75 *.25*
C67 A32 1.25r Running 2.25 *.25*
Nos. C65-C67 (3) 5.50 *.60*

POSTAGE DUE STAMPS

Type of Regular Issue

Designs: 1np, 4np, 15np, Clam. 2np, 5np, 25np, Mussel. 3np, 10np, 35np, Oyster.

Perf. 12x11½
1963, June 15 Litho. Unwmk.
J1 A1 1np gray grn & ver 1.00 .35
J2 A1 2np lemon & brt bl 1.50 .45
J3 A1 3np dl rose & green 1.75 .75
J4 A1 4np light grn & mag 2.50 1.00
J5 A1 5np vermilion & blk 3.00 1.25
J6 A1 10np citron & violet 3.50 1.50
J7 A1 15np brt ultra & ver 4.50 1.90
J8 A1 25np buff & olive grn 6.00 2.00
J9 A1 35np turq bl & dp org 6.50 2.75
Nos. J1-J9 (9) 30.25 11.95

Sheik Rashid bin Said — D1

1972, May 22 Litho. *Perf. 14x14½*
J10 D1 5d blk & gray grn 2.00 .75
J11 D1 10d vio bl, blk & bis 2.50 .85
J12 D1 20d sl grn, blk & brick red 4.25 1.50
J13 D1 30d grnsh gray, blk & lil 7.00 2.25
J14 D1 50d lilac, brn & bis 11.00 4.50
Nos. J10-J14 (5) 26.75 9.85

EAST AFRICA & UGANDA PROTECTORATES

ˈest ˈa-fri-kə and ü-ˈgan-də
prə-ˈtek-tˌə-ˌrəts

LOCATION — Central East Africa, bordering on the Indian Ocean
GOVT. — British Protectorate
AREA — 350,000 sq. mi. (approx.)
POP. — 6,503,507 (approx.)
CAPITAL — Mombasa

This territory, formerly administered by the British East Africa Colony, was divided between Kenya Colony and the Uganda Protectorate. See Kenya, Uganda and Tanzania.

16 Annas = 1 Rupee
100 Cents = 1 Rupee (1907)

Altered high value stamps of East Africa and Uganda are plentiful. Expertization by competent authorities is recommended.

A1

A2

King Edward VII

1903 Typo. Wmk. 2 *Perf. 14*
1 A1 ½a gray green 7.00 *23.00*
2 A1 1a car & black 3.00 2.00
3 A1 2a vio & dull vio 10.50 3.00
4 A1 2½a ultramarine 14.50 *60.00*
5 A1 3a gray grn & brn 30.00 *75.00*
6 A1 4a blk & gray grn 13.50 *27.50*
7 A1 5a org brn & blk 22.50 *60.00*
8 A1 8a pale blue & blk 28.00 *50.00*

Wmk. 1
9 A2 1r gray green 27.50 *65.00*
10 A2 2r vio & dull vio 95.00 *100.00*
11 A2 3r blk & gray grn 175.00 *325.00*
12 A2 4r lt green & blk 175.00 *350.00*
13 A2 5r car & black 175.00 *350.00*
14 A2 10r ultra & black 475.00 *675.00*
15 A2 20r ol gray & blk 850.00 *1,950.*
16 A2 50r org brn & blk 2,600. *4,750.*
Nos. 1-14 (14) 1,252. *2,166.*

Nos. 9 and 14 are on both ordinary and chalky paper. Values are for examples on ordinary paper. Values are for the least expensive varieties. See *Scott Classic Specialized Catalogue of Stamps & Covers* for detailed listings.

1904-07 Wmk. 3 Chalky Paper
17 A1 ½a gray green 16.00 3.75
18a A1 1a car & black 11.00 1.00
19 A1 2a vio & dull vio 3.50 3.25
20 A1 2½a blue 10.00 37.50
a. 2½a blue & ultramarine 9.50 *35.00*
21 A1 3a gray grn & brn 4.75 *45.00*
22 A1 4a blk & gray grn 9.25 *22.50*
23 A1 5a org brn & blk 8.00 *32.50*
24a A1 8a pale blue & blk 8.75 10.50
25 A2 1r gray green 35.00 *75.00*
26 A2 2r vio & dl vio 50.00 *77.50*
27 A2 3r blk & gray grn 100.00 *160.00*
28 A2 4r lt green & blk 140.00 *200.00*
29 A2 5r car & black 175.00 *700.00*
29A A2 10r ultra & black 400.00 *450.00*
30 A2 20r ol gray & blk 875.00 *1,600.*
30A A2 50r org brn & blk 2,750. *4,500.*
Nos. 17-29 (10) 541.50 *1,320.*

Nos. 17-19, 21-24 are on both ordinary and chalky paper. No. 20 is on ordinary paper. Values are for the least expensive varieties. See *Scott Classic Specialized Catalogue of Stamps & Covers* for detailed listings.

1907-08
31 A1 1c brown ('08) 3.00 .25
32 A1 3c gray green 22.50 .80
33 A1 6c carmine 3.25 .25
34 A1 10c citron & violet 13.00 10.00
35 A1 12c red vio & dl vio 12.00 3.50
36 A1 15c ultramarine 34.00 11.00
37 A1 25c blk & blue green 22.50 *8.50*
38 A1 50c org brn & green 20.00 17.50
39 A1 75c pale bl & gray blk ('08) 5.50 *40.00*
Nos. 31-39 (9) 135.75 *91.80*

Nos. 31-33, 36 are on ordinary paper.
There are two dies of the 6c differing very slightly in many details.

King George V
A3 A4

1912-18 Ordinary Paper Wmk. 3
40 A3 1c black .40 *2.10*
41 A3 3c green 2.50 .75
a. Booklet pane of 6
42 A3 6c carmine 1.50 .70
a. Booklet pane of 6
43 A3 10c yel orange 2.50 .65
44 A3 12c gray 3.25 .65
45 A3 15c ultramarine 3.25 1.00

Chalky Paper
46 A3 25c scar & blk, *yel* .65 *1.60*
47 A3 50c violet & black 1.90 1.60
48 A3 75c black, *green* 1.90 *21.00*
a. 75c black, *emerald* 13.50 *65.00*
b. 75c blk, *bl grn, olive back* 12.00 9.25
c. 75c blk, *emer, olive back* 50.00 *175.00*
49 A4 1r black, *green* 3.00 *5.25*
a. 1r black, *emerald* 6.00 *60.00*
50 A4 2r blk & red, *bl* 26.00 *45.00*
51 A4 3r gray grn & vio 32.50 *130.00*
52 A4 4r grn & red, *yel* 65.00 *130.00*
53 A4 5r dl vio & ultra 65.00 *160.00*
54 A4 10r grn & red, *grn* 260.00 *375.00*
55 A4 20r vio & blk, *red* 500.00 475.00
56 A4 20r bl & violet, *blue* ('18) 575.00 *875.00*
57 A4 50r gray grn & rose red 925.00 *975.00*
58 A4 100r blk & vio, *red* *9,750.* *4,000.*
59 A4 500r red & grn, *grn* *40,000.*
Nos. 40-54 (15) 469.35 *875.30*

1914 Surface-colored Paper
60 A3 25c scarlet & blk, *yel* .65 *5.50*
61 A3 75c black, *green* 1.25 *19.50*

Stamps of types A3 and A4 with watermark 4 are listed under Kenya, Uganda and Tanzania.
The 1r through 50r with revenue cancellations sell for minimal prices. The 100r and 500r were available for postage but were nearly always used fiscally.
For surcharge see No. 62.

No. 42 Surcharged

1919
62 A3 4c on 6c carmine 1.50 .25
a. Double surcharge 160.00 *250.00*
b. Without squares over old value 50.00 *85.00*
c. Pair, one without surcharge 2,000. *2,250.*
d. Inverted surcharge 350.00 *475.00*

For later issues see Kenya, Uganda and Tanzania.
For stamps of East Africa and Uganda overprinted "G. E. A." see German East Africa.

EASTERN RUMELIA

'ē-stərn rü-'mēl-yə

(South Bulgaria)

LOCATION — In southern Bulgaria
GOVT. — An autonomous unit of the Turkish Empire.
CAPITAL — Philippopolis (Plovdiv)

In 1885 the province of Eastern Rumelia revolted against Turkish rule and united with Bulgaria, adopting the new name of South Bulgaria. This union was assured by the Treaty of Bucharest in 1886, following the war between Serbia and Bulgaria.

40 Paras = 1 Piaster

Counterfeits of all overprints are plentiful.

Stamps of Turkey, 1876-84, Overprinted in Blue

No. 1

A2

A3

1880		Unwmk.		Perf. 13½
1	A5	½pi on 20pa yel grn	67.50	57.50
a.		Horiz. pair, one without overprint		*400.00*
3	A2	10pa blk & rose	*55.00*	
4	A2	20pa vio & grn	87.50	67.50
6	A2	2pi blk & buff	115.00	100.00
7	A2	5pi red & bl	450.00	*500.00*
8	A3	10pa blk & red lil	57.50	

Nos. 3 & 8 were not placed in use.
Inverted and double overprints of all values exist.

Same, with Extra Overprint "R. O."

9	A3	10pa blk & red lil	97.50	95.00

Crescent and Turkish Inscriptions of Value — A4

1881		Typo.		Perf. 13½
10	A4	5pa blk & olive	17.00	1.35
11	A4	10pa blk & green	65.00	1.35
12	A4	20pa blk & rose	1.75	1.25
13	A4	1pi blk & blue	5.75	4.50
14	A4	5pi rose & blue	57.50	*82.50*

Tête bêche pairs, imperforates and all perf. 11½ examples of Nos. 10-14 were not placed in use, and were found only in the remainder stock. This is true also of a 10pa cliché in the 20pa plate, and of a cliché of Turkey No. 63 in the 1pi plate. See the *Scott Classic Catalogue.*

1884				Perf. 11½
15	A4	5pa lil & pale lil	.75	.45
16	A4	10pa grn & pale grn	.25	.45
17	A4	20pa car & pale rose	.55	
18	A4	1pi bl & pale bl	1.15	
19	A4	5pi brn & pale brn	*400.00*	

Nos. 17-19 were not placed in use, and were found only in the remainder stock.
Nos. 15-19 imperf. are from remainders.
See the *Scott Classic Catalogue for perf 13½ listings.*
For overprints see Turkey Nos. 542-545.

South Bulgaria

Counterfeits of all overprints are plentiful.

Nos. 10-14 Overprinted in Two Types

a

b

Type a — Four toes on each foot.
Type b — Three toes on each foot.

Blue Overprint

1885		Unwmk.		Perf. 13½
20	A4 (a)	5pa blk & olive	*325.00*	*375.00*
21	A4 (a)	10pa blk & grn	*875.00*	*825.00*
22	A4 (a)	20pa blk & rose	325.00	—
23	A4 (a)	1pi blk & blue	37.50	*72.50*
24	A4 (b)	5pi rose & blue	*1,100.*	—

See the *Scott Classic Catalogue* for Nos. 22-23, type b, No. 24, type a, and No. 22, perf 11½, types a and b.

Black Overprint

24B	A4 (a)	20pa blk & rose	275.00	—
25	A4 (a)	1pi blk & bl	55.00	*115.00*
26	A4 (b)	5pi rose & bl	*675.00*	—

See the *Scott Classic Catalogue* for No. 25 type b.

Same Overprint on Nos. 15-17

Blue Overprint

Perf. 11½

27	A4 (b)	5pa lil & pale lil, type "b"	22.50	*57.50*
28	A4 (b)	10pa grn & pale grn	40.00	*75.00*
29	A4 (b)	20pa car & pale rose	275.00	*375.00*

Black Overprint

Perf. 13½

30	A4 (b)	5pa lil & pale lil	40.00	*67.50*

Perf. 11½

31	A4 (a)	10pa grn & pale grn	42.50	*85.00*
32	A4 (b)	20pa car & pale rose	55.00	*65.00*

See the *Scott Classic Catalogue* for detailed listings of Nos. 27-32.

Nos. 10-17 Handstamped in Black in Two Types

a

b

Type a — First letter at top circular.
Type b — First letter at top oval.

1885				Perf. 13½
33	A4 (b)	5pa blk & olive	*300.00*	250.00
34	A4 (b)	10pa blk & grn	*225.00*	250.00
35	A4 (b)	20pa blk & rose	72.50	*85.00*
36	A4 (a)	1pi blk & bl	87.50	*115.00*
37	A4 (a)	5pi rose & blue, type "a"	*2,500.*	—

Perf. 13½

38	A4 (a)	5pa lil & pale lil	26.00	*44.00*

Perf. 11½

39	A4 (a)	10pa grn & pale grn	29.00	*35.00*
40	A4 (a)	20pa car & pale rose	29.00	*50.00*

See the *Scott Classic Catalogue* for Nos. 38-40, type b, and No. 38, perf 11½, types a and b.
Nos. 20-40 exist with inverted and double handstamps. Overprints in unlisted colors are proofs.
The stamps of South Bulgaria were superseded in 1886 by those of Bulgaria.

EASTERN SILESIA

'ē-stərn sī-'lē-zh,ē-,ə

LOCATION — In central Europe
GOVT. — Austrian crownland
AREA — 1,987 sq. mi.
POP. — 680,422 (estimated 1920)
CAPITAL — Troppau

After World War I, this territory was occupied by Czechoslovakia and eventually was divided between Poland and Czechoslovakia, the dividing line running through Teschen.

100 Heller = 1 Krone
100 Fennigi = 1 Marka

Plebiscite Issues

Stamps of Czechoslovakia 1918-20, Overprinted in Black, Blue, Violet or Red

1920		Unwmk.		Imperf.
1	A2	1h dark brown	.25	.30
2	A1	3h red violet	.25	.25
3	A2	5h blue green	23.50	22.50
4	A2	15h red	11.50	11.00
5	A1	20h blue green	.25	.25
6	A2	25h dull violet	.75	.75
7	A1	30h bister (R)	.25	.25
8	A1	40h red orange	.30	.30
9	A2	50h dull violet	.60	.45
10	A2	50h dark blue	2.60	1.50
11	A2	60h orange (Bl)	.75	.75
12	A2	75h slate (R)	.50	.75
13	A2	80h olive grn (R)	.50	.75
14	A1	100h brown	1.10	1.10
15	A2	120h gray blk (R)	1.60	*2.25*
16	A1	200h ultra (R)	1.60	*2.00*
17	A2	300h green (R)	6.25	*7.50*
18	A1	400h purple (R)	2.60	*3.00*
20	A2	500h red brn (Bl)	5.25	*6.00*
a.		Black overprint	6.25	*9.00*
21	A2	1000h violet (Bl)	13.00	*13.50*
a.		Black overprint	62.50	*75.00*
		Nos. 1-21 (20)	73.40	75.15

Perf. 11½, 13¾

22	A2	1h dark brown	.25	.25
23	A2	5h blue green	.30	.25
24	A2	10h yellow green	.30	.25
a.		Imperf.	*260.00*	*210.00*
25	A2	15h red	.50	.25
26	A2	20h rose	.50	.35
a.		Imperf.	*300.00*	*250.00*
27	A2	25h dull violet	.50	.35
28	A2	30h red violet (Bl)	.35	.35
29	A2	60h orange (Bl)	.50	.50
30	A1	200h ultra (R)	3.00	3.00
		Nos. 22-30 (9)	6.20	5.55

The letters "S. O." are the initials of "Silésie Orientale."
Forged cancellations are found on Nos. 1-30.

Overprinted in Carmine or Violet

31	A4	500h sl, *grysh* (C)	40.00	
32	A4	1000h blk brn, *brnsh*	40.00	

Excellent counterfeits of this overprint exist.

Stamps of Poland, 1919, Overprinted

1920				Perf. 11½
41	A10	5f green	.25	.25
42	A10	10f red brown	.25	.25
43	A10	15f light red	.25	.25
44	A11	25f olive green	.25	.25
45	A11	50f blue green	.25	.25

Overprinted

46	A12	1k deep green	.25	.25
47	A12	1.50k brown	.25	.25
48	A12	2k dark blue	.25	.25
49	A13	2.50k dull violet	.30	.25
50	A14	5k slate blue	.50	.25
		Nos. 41-50 (10)	2.80	2.50

SPECIAL DELIVERY STAMPS

Czechoslovakia Special Delivery Stamps Ovptd. in Blue

1920		Unwmk.		Imperf.
E1	SD1	2h red violet, *yel*	.25	.25
a.		Black overprint	4.75	.80
E2	SD1	5h yellow green, *yel*	.25	.25
a.		Black overprint	8.00	5.00

Nos. E1-E2a exist on white paper.

POSTAGE DUE STAMPS

Czechoslovakia Postage Due Stamps Overprinted In Blue or Red

1920		Unwmk.		Imperf.
J1	D1	5h deep bis (Bl)	.25	.25
a.		Black overprint	72.50	62.50
J2	D1	10h deep bister	.25	.25
J3	D1	15h deep bister	.25	.25
J4	D1	20h deep bister	.25	.25
J5	D1	25h deep bister	.25	.25
J6	D1	30h deep bister	.25	.25
J7	D1	40h deep bister	.50	.25
J8	D1	50h deep bister	2.60	3.00
J9	D1	100h blk brn (R)	2.60	3.00
J10	D1	500h gray grn (R)	5.75	4.50
J11	D1	1000h purple (R)	8.50	11.50
		Nos. J1-J11 (11)	21.45	23.75

Forged cancellations exist.

NEWSPAPER STAMPS

Czechoslovakia Newspaper Stamps Overprinted in Black like Nos. 1-30

1920		Unwmk.		Imperf.
P1	N1	2h gray green	.30	.30
P2	N1	6h red	.25	.25
P3	N1	10h dull violet	.40	.25
P4	N1	20h blue	.65	.25
P5	N1	30h gray brown	.65	.25
		Nos. P1-P5 (5)	2.25	1.30

ECUADOR

'e-kwə-,dor

LOCATION — Northwest coast of South America, bordering on the Pacific Ocean
GOVT. — Republic
AREA — 116,270 (?) sq. mi.
POP. — 12,562,496 (1999 est.)
CAPITAL — Quito

The Republic of Ecuador was so constituted on May 11, 1830, after the Civil War that separated the original members of the Republic of Colombia, founded by Simon Bolivar by uniting the Presidency of Quito with the Viceroyalty of New Grenada and the Captaincy of Venezuela. The Presidency of Quito became the Republic of Ecuador.

8 Reales = 1 Peso
100 Centavos = 1 Sucre (1881)
100 Cents = 1 Dollar (2000)

Catalogue values for unused stamps in this country are for Never Hinged items, beginning with Scott 453 in the regular postage section, Scott C147 in the airpost section, Scott CO19 in the airpost officials section, Scott O201 in the officials section, Scott RA60 in the postal tax section, and all entries in the Galapagos section.

Watermarks

Wmk. 117 — Liberty Cap

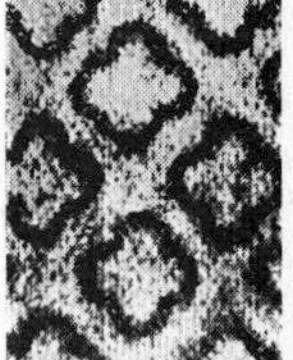

Wmk. 127 Quatrefoils

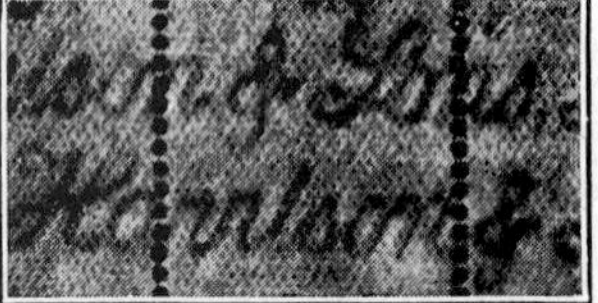

Wmk. 233 — "Harrison & Sons, London" in Script Letters

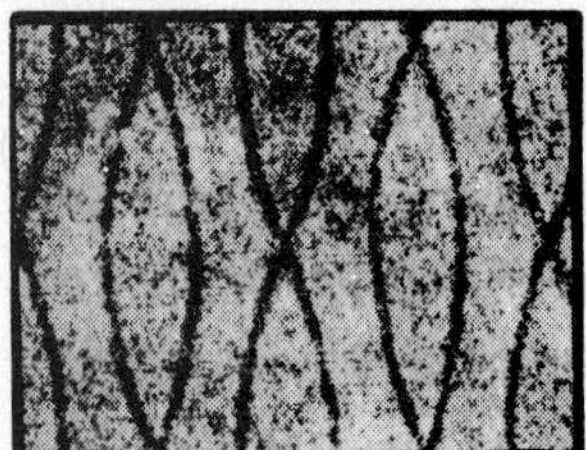

Wmk. 340 — Alternating Interlaced Wavy Lines

Wmk. 367 — Liberty Cap, Emblem, Inscription

Wmk. 377 — Interlocking Circles

Wmk. 395 — Emblem, Inscription

Coat of Arms
A1 A2

1865-72 Unwmk. Typo. *Imperf.*

Quadrille Paper

1	A1	1r yellow ('72)	60.00	55.00

Wove Paper

2	A1	½r ultra	40.00	20.00
a.		½r gray blue ('67)	40.00	15.00
b.		Batonne paper ('70)	50.00	25.00
c.		Blue paper ('72)	250.00	100.00
3	A1	1r buff	25.00	18.00
a.		1r orange buff	30.00	20.00
4	A1	1r yellow	25.00	15.00
a.		1r olive yellow ('66)	32.50	22.50
b.		Laid paper	175.00	110.00
c.		Half used as ½r on cover		900.00
d.		Batonne paper	40.00	30.00
5	A1	1r green	300.00	55.00
a.		Half used as ½r on cover		*900.00*
6	A2	4r red ('66)	500.00	200.00
a.		4r red brown ('66)	700.00	200.00
b.		Arms in circle	500.00	250.00
c.		Printed on both sides	550.00	—
d.		Half used as 2r on cover		1,600.
		Nos. 1-6 (6)	950.00	363.00

Letter paper embossed with arms of Ecuador was used in printing a number of sheets of Nos. 2, 4-6.

On the 4r the oval holding the coat of arms is usually 13½-14mm wide, but on about one-fifth of the stamps in the sheet it is 15-15½mm wide, almost a circle.

The 2r, 8r and 12r, type A1, are bogus.

Proofs of the ½r, type A1, are known in black and green.

An essay of type A2 shows the condor's head facing right.

1871-72 Blue-surface Paper

7	A1	½r ultra	50.00	25.00
8	A1	1r yellow	300.00	100.00

Unofficial reprints of types A1-A2 differ in color, have a different sheet makeup and lack gum. Type A1 reprints usually have a double frameline at left. All stamps on blue paper with horiz. blue lines are reprints.

A3 A4

1872 White Paper Litho. *Perf. 11*

9	A3	½r blue	30.00	5.00
10	A4	1r orange	40.00	7.00
11	A3	1p rose	5.00	*25.00*
		Nos. 9-11 (3)	75.00	*37.00*

The 1r surcharged 4c is fraudulent.

A5 A6

A7 A8

A9 A10

1881, Nov. 1 Engr. *Perf. 12*

12	A5	1c yellow brn	.40	.25
13	A6	2c lake	.40	.25
14	A7	5c blue	10.00	.50
15	A8	10c orange	.40	.25
16	A9	20c gray violet	.40	.25
17	A10	50c blue green	2.00	*3.00*
		Nos. 12-17 (6)	13.60	*4.50*

The 1c surcharged 3c, and 20c surcharged 5c are fraudulent.

For overprints see Nos. O1-O6.

No. 17 Surcharged in Black

1883, Apr.

18	A10	10c on 50c blue grn	50.00	30.00
a.		Double surcharge		

Dangerous forgeries exist.

A12 A13

A14 A15

1887

19	A12	1c blue green	.50	.40
20	A13	2c vermilion	1.00	.40
21	A14	5c blue	3.00	.50
22	A15	80c olive green	6.00	*15.00*
		Nos. 19-22 (4)	10.50	*16.30*

For overprints see Nos. O7-O10.

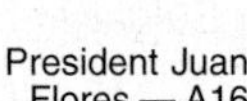

President Juan Flores — A16

1892

23	A16	1c orange	.30	1.00
24	A16	2c dk brown	.30	1.00
25	A16	5c vermilion	.30	1.00
26	A16	10c green	.30	1.00
27	A16	20c red brown	.30	1.00
28	A16	50c maroon	.30	*2.00*
29	A16	1s blue	.30	*4.00*
30	A16	5s purple	1.00	*8.00*
		Nos. 23-30 (8)	3.10	*19.00*

The issues of 1892, 1894, 1895 and 1896 were printed by the Hamilton Bank Note Co., New York, to the order of N. F. Seebeck, who held a contract for stamps with the government of Ecuador.

No. 30 in green is said to be an essay or color trial.

For surcharges and overprints see Nos. 31-37, O11-O17.

Nos. 29 and 30 Surcharged in Black

1893

Surcharge Measures 25½x2½mm

31	A16	5c on 1s blue	6.00	6.00
32	A16	5c on 5s purple	10.00	9.00
a.		Double surcharge		

Surcharge Measures 24x2¼mm

33	A16	5c on 1s blue	3.00	3.00
a.		Double surcharge, one inverted		
34	A16	5c on 5s purple	12.00	10.00
a.		Double surcharge, one invtd.		

Nos. 28-30 Surcharged in Black

35	A16	5c on 50c maroon	2.00	2.00
a.		Inverted surcharge	5.00	
36	A16	5c on 1s blue	2.50	2.00
37	A16	5c on 5s purple	10.00	10.00
		Nos. 31-37 (7)	45.50	42.00

Pres. Juan Flores — A19

38	A19	5c on 5s lake	4.00	4.00

It is stated that No. 38 was used exclusively as a postage stamp and not for telegrams.

Pres. Vicente Rocafuerte — A20

Dated "1894"

1894 Various Frames *Perf. 12*

39	A20	1c blue	.40	.40
40	A20	2c yellow brn	.40	.40
41	A20	5c green	.40	.40
b.		Perf. 14	6.00	2.00
42	A20	10c vermilion	.70	.60
43	A20	20c black	1.10	.70
44	A20	50c orange	6.00	2.00
45	A20	1s carmine	9.50	4.00
46	A20	5s dark blue	12.00	6.00
		Nos. 39-46 (8)	30.50	14.50

1895 Same, Dated "1895"

No.	Type	Description	Unused	Used
47	A20	1c blue	.90	.70
48	A20	2c yellow brn	.90	.70
49	A20	5c green	.70	.50
50	A20	10c vermilion	.70	.40
51	A20	20c black	1.00	1.00
52	A20	50c orange	3.50	2.25
53	A20	1s carmine	21.00	8.00
54	A20	5s dark blue	8.50	4.00
		Nos. 47-54 (8)	37.20	17.55

Reprints of the 2c, 10c, 50c, 1s and 5s of the 1894-95 issues are generally on thick paper. Original issues are on thin to medium thick paper. To distinguish reprints from originals, a comparison of paper thickness, paper color, gum, printing clarity and direction of paper weave is necessary. Value 20 cents each.

For overprints see Nos. 77-112, O20-O33, O50-O91.

A21

A22

A23

A24

A25

A26

A27

A28

1896 Wmk. 117

No.	Type	Description	Unused	Used
55	A21	1c dk green	.70	.60
56	A22	2c red	.70	.40
57	A23	5c blue	.70	.40
58	A24	10c bister brn	.60	*.90*
59	A25	20c orange	1.40	*2.00*
60	A26	50c dark blue	5.00	3.00
61	A27	1s yellow brn	4.00	*4.00*
62	A28	5s violet	14.00	5.50
		Nos. 55-62 (8)	27.10	*16.80*

Unwmk.

No.	Type	Description	Unused	Used
62A	A21	1c dk green	1.00	.40
62B	A22	2c red	1.10	.40
62C	A23	5c blue	1.10	.70
62D	A24	10c bister brn	.70	*1.40*
62E	A25	20c orange	6.00	5.50
62F	A26	50c dark blue	2.00	*2.75*
62G	A27	1s yellow brn	6.00	*8.00*
62H	A28	5s violet	15.00	6.00
		Nos. 62A-62H (8)	*32.90*	*25.15*

Reprints of Nos. 55-62H are on very thick paper, with paper weave direction vertical. Value 20 cents each.

For surcharges and overprints see Nos. 74, 76, 113-114, O34-O49.

Vicente Roca, Diego Noboa and José Olmedo — A28a

General Juan Francisco Elizalde — A28b

Perf. 11½

1896, Oct. 9 Unwmk. Litho.

No.	Type	Description	Unused	Used
63	A28a	1c rose	.55	.55
64	A28b	2c blue	.55	.55
65	A28a	5c green	.75	.75
66	A28b	10c ocher	.75	.75
67	A28a	20c red	1.10	*3.25*
68	A28b	50c violet	1.75	*4.75*
69	A28a	1s orange	3.25	*8.00*
		Nos. 63-69 (7)	8.70	*18.60*

Success of the Liberal Party in 1845 & 1895.

For overprints see Nos. 115-125.

A29

Black Surcharge

1896, Nov. *Perf. 12*

No.	Type	Description	Unused	Used
70	A29	1c on 1c ver, "1893-1894"	1.00	.60
a.		Inverted surcharge	2.50	2.00
b.		Double surcharge	8.00	7.00
71	A29	2c on 2c bl, "1893-1894"	2.00	1.75
a.		Inverted surcharge	4.00	3.50
72	A29	5c on 10c org, "1887-1888"	2.00	.60
a.		Inverted surcharge	4.00	1.75
b.		Double surcharge	7.00	4.00
c.		Surcharged "2cts"	1.00	.80
d.		"1893-1894"	6.00	5.00
73	A29	10c on 4c brn, "1887-1888"	2.00	1.10
a.		Inverted surcharge	4.00	1.75
b.		Double surcharge	6.00	3.50
c.		Double surcharge, one inverted		
d.		Surcharged "1 cto"	2.00	*2.75*
e.		"1891-1892"	17.00	13.50
		Nos. 70-73 (4)	7.00	4.05

Similar surcharges of type A29 include: Dated "1887-1888" — 1c on 1c blue green, 1c on 2c red, 1c on 4c brown, 1c on 10c yellow; 2c on 2c red, 2c on 10c yellow; 10c on 1c green.

Dated "1891-1892" — 1c on 1c blue green, 1c on 4c brown.

Dated "1893-1894" — 2c on 10c yellow; 10c on 1c vermilion, 10c on 10s black.

For overprints see Nos. O18-O19.

Nos. 59-60 Surcharged in Black or Red

1896, Oct. Wmk. 117

No.	Type	Description	Unused	Used
74	A25	5c on 20c orange	40.00	40.00
76	A26	10c on 50c dk bl (R)	50.00	50.00
a.		Double surcharge		

The surcharge is diag., horiz. or vert.

Nos. 39-54 Overprinted

On Issue of 1894

1897 Unwmk.

No.	Type	Description	Unused	Used
77	A20	1c blue	2.25	2.25
78	A20	2c yellow brn	1.90	1.30
79	A20	5c green	.90	.90
80	A20	10c vermilion	2.75	2.25
81	A20	20c black	3.00	2.75
82	A20	50c orange	6.50	3.25
83	A20	1s carmine	19.00	6.50
84	A20	5s dark blue	110.00	90.00
		Nos. 77-84 (8)	146.30	109.20

On Issue of 1895

No.	Type	Description	Unused	Used
85	A20	1c blue	6.00	5.50
86	A20	2c yellow brn	2.25	2.25
87	A20	5c green	1.90	1.60
88	A20	10c vermilion	7.00	6.00
89	A20	20c black	1.90	1.75
90	A20	50c orange	32.50	13.00
91	A20	1s carmine	14.50	7.50
92	A20	5s dark blue	14.50	14.50
		Nos. 85-92 (8)	80.55	52.10

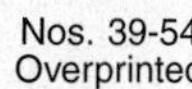

Nos. 39-54 Overprinted

On Issue of 1894

No.	Type	Description	Unused	Used
93	A20	1c blue	1.40	.90
94	A20	2c yellow brn	1.20	.75
95	A20	5c green	.60	.50
96	A20	10c vermilion	3.50	1.75
97	A20	20c black	3.75	2.50
98	A20	50c orange	7.00	2.75
99	A20	1s carmine	13.00	8.50
100	A20	5s dark blue	115.00	85.00
		Nos. 93-100 (8)	145.45	102.65

On Issue of 1895

No.	Type	Description	Unused	Used
101	A20	1c blue	3.25	1.60
102	A20	2c yellow brn	1.60	1.60
103	A20	5c green	1.75	1.00
104	A20	10c vermilion	5.50	4.50
105	A20	20c black	5.00	1.20
106	A20	50c orange	1.75	1.75
107	A20	1s carmine	8.00	7.00
108	A20	5s dark blue	9.50	9.50
		Nos. 101-108 (8)	36.35	28.15

Overprints on Nos. 77-108 are to be found reading upward from left to right and downward from left to right, as well as inverted.

Overprinted

1897 On Issue of 1894

No.	Type	Description	Unused	Used
109	A20	10c vermilion	—	—

On Issue of 1895

No.	Type	Description	Unused	Used
110	A20	2c yellow brn	—	—
111	A20	1s carmine	—	—
112	A20	5s dark blue	—	—

Nos. 56, 59 Overprinted like Nos. 93-108

1897, June Wmk. 117

No.	Type	Description	Unused	Used
113	A22	2c red	—	—
114	A25	20c orange	—	—

Many forged overprints on Nos. 77-114 exist, made on original stamps and reprints.

Stamps or Types of 1896 Overprinted in Black

1897 Unwmk. *Perf. 11½*

No.	Type	Description	Unused	Used
115	A28a	1c rose	3.75	3.75
116	A28b	2c blue	3.00	3.00
117	A28b	10c ocher	3.00	3.00
118	A28a	1s yellow	15.00	15.00
		Nos. 115-118 (4)	24.75	24.75

No. 63 Overprinted in Black

1897

No.	Type	Description	Unused	Used
119	A28a	1c rose	.60	.50

Nos. 63-66 Overprinted in Black

1897

No.	Type	Description	Unused	Used
122	A28a	1c rose	4.50	4.00
123	A28b	2c blue	4.50	4.00
124	A28a	5c green	4.50	4.00
125	A28b	10c ocher	4.50	4.00
a.		Double overprint	10.50	9.50
		Nos. 122-125 (4)	18.00	16.00

The 20c, 50c and 1s with this overprint in black and all values of the issue overprinted in blue are reprints.

Overprint Inverted

No.	Type	Description	Unused	Used
122a	A28a	1c	6.00	5.50
123a	A28b	2c	6.00	5.50
124a	A28a	5c	6.00	5.50
125b	A28b	10c	6.00	5.50

Coat of Arms — A33

1897, June 23 Engr. *Perf. 14-16*

No.	Type	Description	Unused	Used
127	A33	1c dk yellow grn	.35	.25
128	A33	2c orange red	.35	.25
129	A33	5c lake	.35	.25
130	A33	10c dk brown	.35	.25
131	A33	20c yellow	.45	.40
132	A33	50c dull blue	.45	*.65*
133	A33	1s gray	.90	*1.25*
134	A33	5s dark lilac	4.00	*5.00*
		Nos. 127-134 (8)	7.20	*8.30*

No. 135

No. 136

1899, May

No.	Type	Description	Unused	Used
135	A33	1c on 2c orange red	3.00	1.50
136	A33	5c on 10c brown	2.50	1.00
a.		Double surcharge		

Luis Vargas Torres A36

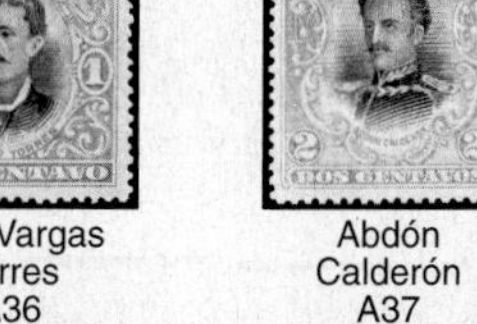

Abdón Calderón A37

Juan Montalvo A38

José Mejia A39

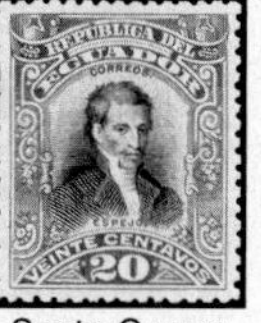

Santa Cruz y Espejo — A40

Pedro Carbo — A41

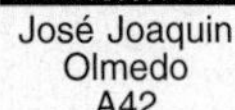

José Joaquin Olmedo A42

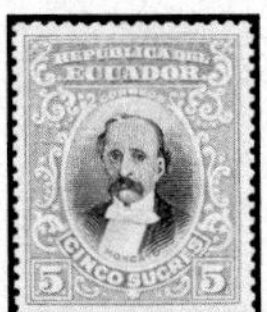

Pedro Moncayo A43

1899			**Perf. 12½-16**	
137	A36	1c gray blue & blk	.40	.25
a.		Horiz. pair, imperf. vert.		
138	A37	2c brown lil & blk	.40	.25
139	A38	5c lake & blk	.70	.25
140	A39	10c reddsh lil & blk	.70	.25
141	A40	20c green & blk	.70	.25
142	A41	50c lil rose & blk	1.75	.55
143	A42	1s ocher & blk	8.00	2.75
144	A43	5s lilac & blk	14.50	7.50
		Nos. 137-144 (8)	27.15	12.05

1901				
145	A36	1c scarlet & blk	.45	.25
146	A37	2c green & blk	.45	.25
147	A38	5c gray lil & blk	.45	.25
148	A39	10c dp blue & blk	.50	.25
149	A40	20c gray & blk	.50	.25
150	A41	50c lt blue & blk	1.75	.95
151	A42	1s brown & blk	6.00	2.75
152	A43	5s gray blk & blk	9.00	5.75
		Nos. 145-152 (8)	19.10	10.70

In July, 1902, following the theft of a quantity of stamps during a fire at Guayaquil, the Government authorized the governors of the provinces to handstamp their stocks. Many varieties of these handstamps exist.

Other control marks were used in 1907.

For overprints see Nos. O103-O106, O167.

A44

Surcharged on Revenue Stamp Dated 1901-1902

1903-06			**Perf. 14, 15**	
153	A44	1c on 5c gray lil ('06)	.75	.40
154	A44	1c on 20c gray ('06)	10.00	4.50
155	A44	1c on 25c yellow	1.50	.40
a.		Double surcharge		
156	A44	1c on 1s bl ('06)	77.50	50.00
157	A44	3c on 5c gray lil ('06)	10.00	4.00
158	A44	3c on 20c gray ('06)	25.00	15.00
159	A44	3c on 25c yel ('06)	24.00	15.00
159A	A44	3c on 1s blue ('06)	3.75	2.25
		Nos. 153-159A (8)	152.50	91.55

Counterfeits are plentiful.

See Nos. 191-197.

Capt. Abdón Calderón
A45 A46

1904, July 31			**Perf. 12**	
160	A45	1c red & blk	.45	.30
161	A45	2c blue & blk	.50	.35
162	A46	5c yellow & blk	1.90	1.00
163	A45	10c red & blk	6.00	2.00
164	A45	20c blue & blk	10.00	8.00
165	A46	50c yellow & blk	85.00	*120.00*
		Nos. 160-165 (6)	103.85	*131.65*

Centenary of the birth of Calderón.

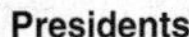

Presidents

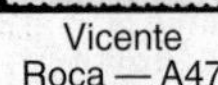

Vicente Roca — A47

Diego Noboa — A48

Francisco Robles — A49

José M. Urvina — A50

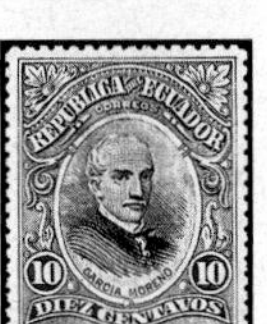

García Moreno — A51

Jerónimo Carrión — A52

Javier Espinoza A53

Antonio Borrero A54

1907, July			**Perf. 14, 15**	
166	A47	1c red & blk	1.00	.25
167	A48	2c pale blue & blk	2.00	.25
168	A49	3c orange & blk	3.00	.25
169	A50	5c lilac rose & blk	3.75	.25
170	A51	10c dp blue & blk	7.50	.25
171	A52	20c yellow grn & blk	10.00	.35
172	A53	50c violet & blk	22.50	.70
173	A54	1s green & blk	30.00	2.00
		Nos. 166-173 (8)	79.75	4.30

The stamps of the 1907 issue frequently have control marks similar to those found on the 1899 and 1901 issues. These marks were applied to distinguish the stamps issued in the various provinces and to serve as a check on local officials.

Locomotive — A55

García Moreno — A56

Gen. Eloy Alfaro — A57

Abelardo Moncayo — A58

Archer Harman — A59

James Sivewright — A60

Mt. Chimborazo A61

1908, June 25				
174	A55	1c red brown	1.10	*2.10*
175	A56	2c blue & blk	1.30	*2.25*
176	A57	5c claret & blk	2.75	*5.25*
177	A58	10c ocher & blk	1.75	*2.75*
178	A59	20c green & blk	1.75	*3.75*
179	A60	50c gray & blk	1.75	*3.75*
180	A61	1s black	3.50	*8.00*
		Nos. 174-180 (7)	13.90	*27.85*

Opening of the Guayaquil-Quito Railway.

José Mejía Vallejo — A62

Principal Exposition Building — A70

Designs: 2c, Francisco J. E. Santa Cruz y Espejo. 3c, Francisco Ascásubi. 5c, Juan Salinas. 10c, Juan Pio de Montúfar, el Marques de Selva Alegre. 20c, Carlos de Montúfar. 50c, Juan de Dios Morales. 1s, Manuel R. de Quiroga.

1909, Aug. 10			**Perf. 12**	
181	A62	1c green	.35	*.65*
182	A62	2c blue	.35	*.65*
183	A62	3c orange	.35	*.75*
184	A62	5c claret	.35	*.75*
185	A62	10c yellow brn	.45	*.75*
186	A62	20c gray	.45	*1.10*
187	A62	50c vermilion	.45	*1.10*
188	A62	1s olive grn	.45	*1.40*
189	A70	5s violet	1.25	*2.75*
		Nos. 181-189 (9)	4.45	*9.90*

National Exposition of 1909.

No. 187 Surcharged

1909				
190	A62	5c on 50c vermilion	.90	.75

Revenue Stamps Surcharged as in 1903

1910			**Perf. 14, 15**	
		Stamps Dated 1905-1906		
191	A44	1c on 5c green	2.25	1.75
192	A44	5c on 20c blue	9.50	2.00
193	A44	5c on 25c violet	18.00	3.50
		Stamps Dated 1907-1908		
194	A44	1c on 5c green	.40	.40
195	A44	5c on 20c blue	14.00	9.50
196	A44	5c on 25c violet	1.20	.40
		Stamp Dated 1909-1910		
197	A44	5c on 20c blue	*80.00*	*60.00*
		Nos. 191-197 (7)	*125.35*	*77.55*

Presidents

Roca — A71

Noboa — A72

Robles — A73

Urvina — A74

Moreno — A75

Borrero — A76

1911-28			**Perf. 12**	
198	A71	1c scarlet & blk	.80	.25
199	A71	1c orange ('16)	.80	.25
200	A71	1c lt blue ('25)	.40	.25
201	A72	2c blue & blk	1.10	.25
202	A72	2c green ('16)	1.10	.25
203	A72	2c dk violet ('25)	1.10	.25
204	A73	3c orange & blk ('13)	2.25	.30
205	A73	3c black ('15)	1.50	.25
206	A74	5c scarlet & blk	1.90	.25
207	A74	5c violet ('15)	1.90	.25
208	A74	5c rose ('25)	.70	.25
209	A74	5c dk brown ('28)	.70	.25
210	A75	10c dp blue & blk	2.25	.25
211	A75	10c dp blue ('15)	2.25	.25
212	A75	10c yellow grn ('25)	.70	.25
213	A75	10c black ('28)	1.60	.25
214	A76	1s green & blk	12.00	1.50
215	A76	1s orange & blk ('27)	8.00	.25
		Nos. 198-215 (18)	41.05	5.80

For overprints see Nos. 260-262, 264-265, O107-O122, O124-O134, O156-O157, O160-O162, O164-O166, O168-O173, O175-O178, O183-O184, O189, RA1.

A77

1912			**Perf. 14, 15**	
216	A77	1c on 1s green	1.00	1.00
217	A77	2c on 2s carmine	2.50	1.50
218	A77	2c on 5s dull blue	1.50	1.50
219	A77	2c on 10s yellow	5.00	5.00
a.		Inverted surcharge	16.00	12.00
		Nos. 216-219 (4)	10.00	9.00

No. 216 exists with narrow "V" and small "U" in "UN" and Nos. 217, 218 and 219 with "D" with serifs or small "O" in "DOS."

Enrique Váldez — A78

Jerónimo Carrión — A79

Javier Espinoza — A80

1915-17 ***Perf. 12***

No.	Type	Description	Unused	Used
220	A78	4c red & blk	.40	.25
221	A79	20c green & blk ('17)	3.50	.25
222	A80	50c dp violet & blk	6.00	.45
		Nos. 220-222 (3)	9.90	.95

For overprints see Nos. O123, O135, O163, O174.

Olmedo — A86

Monument to "Fathers of the Country" — A95

Laurel Wreath and Star — A104

Designs: 2c, Rafael Ximena. 3c, Roca. 4c, Luis F. Vivero. 5c, Luis Febres Cordero. 6c, Francisco Lavayen. 7c, Jorge Antonio de Elizalde. 8c, Baltazar Garcia. 9c, Jose de Antepara. 15c, Luis Urdaneta. 20c, Jose M. Villamil. 30c, Miguel Letamendi. 40c, Gregorio Escobedo. 50c, Gen. Antonio Jose de Sucre. 60c, Juan Illingworth. 70c, Roca. 80c, Rocafuerte. 1s, Simon Bolivar.

1920

No.	Type	Description	Unused	Used
223	A86	1c yellow grn	.35	.25
224	A86	2c carmine	.35	.25
225	A86	3c yellow brn	.35	.25
226	A86	4c myrtle green	.55	.25
227	A86	5c pale blue	.55	.25
228	A86	6c red orange	.90	.30
229	A86	7c brown	2.25	.75
230	A86	8c apple green	1.25	.35
231	A86	9c lake	4.25	1.50
232	A95	10c lt blue	1.50	.25
233	A86	15c dk gray	2.25	.35
234	A86	20c dk violet	2.25	.25
235	A86	30c brt violet	4.25	1.40
236	A86	40c dk brown	7.50	2.10
237	A86	50c dk green	5.25	.55
238	A86	60c dk blue	9.50	2.10
239	A86	70c bluish gray	16.00	4.75
240	A86	80c orange yel	16.50	4.75
241	A104	90c green	17.00	4.75
242	A86	1s pale blue	24.00	8.50
		Nos. 223-242 (20)	116.80	33.90

Cent. of the independence of Guayaquil.
For overprints and surcharges see Nos. 263, 274-292, O136-O155, O179-O182, O185-O188.

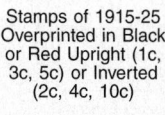

No. RA12 Overprinted in Black

1925

No.	Type	Description	Unused	Used
259	PT6	20c bister brown	4.00	1.50

Stamps of 1915-25 Overprinted in Black or Red Upright (1c, 3c, 5c) or Inverted (2c, 4c, 10c)

1926

No.	Type	Description	Unused	Used
260	A71	1c lt blue	12.50	10.50
261	A72	2c dk violet	12.50	10.50
262	A73	3c black (R)	12.50	10.50
263	A86	4c myrtle green	12.50	10.50
264	A74	5c rose	17.50	10.50
265	A75	10c yellow grn	17.50	10.50
		Nos. 260-265 (6)	85.00	63.00

Quito-Esmeraldas railway opening.
Upright overprints on 2c, 4c, 10c and inverted overprints on 1c, 3c, 5c sell for more.

Nos. RA10-RA12 Overprinted in Black

1927

No.	Type	Description	Unused	Used
266	PT6	1c olive green	.50	.25
a.		"POSTAI"	1.40	.85
b.		Double overprint	2.00	.85
c.		Inverted overprint	2.00	.85
267	PT6	2c deep green	.50	.25
a.		"POSTAI"	1.40	.85
b.		Double overprint	2.00	.85
268	PT6	20c bister brown	1.00	.25
a.		"POSTAI"	8.50	5.00
		Nos. 266-268 (3)	2.00	.75

Quito Post Office — A109

1927, June

No.	Type	Description	Unused	Used
269	A109	5c orange	.50	.25
270	A109	10c dark green	.70	.25
271	A109	20c violet	.80	.25
		Nos. 269-271 (3)	2.00	.75

Opening of new Quito P.O.
For overprint see No. O190.

No. RA12 Overprinted in Dark Blue

1928

No.	Type	Description	Unused	Used
273	PT6	20c bister brown	.50	.25
a.		Double overprint, one inverted	2.00	.70

See No. 339 for 10c with same overprint.

Nos. 235, 239-240 Ovptd. in Red Brown and Srchd. in Bluish Black

1928, July 8

No.	Type	Description	Unused	Used
274	A86	10c on 30c violet	16.00	16.00
275	A86	50c on 70c bluish gray	20.00	20.00
276	A86	1s on 80c org yel	22.50	22.50
		Nos. 274-276 (3)	58.50	58.50

Quito-Cayambe railway opening.

Stamps of 1920 Surcharged

1928, Oct. 9

No.	Type	Description	Unused	Used
277	A86	1c on 1c yel grn	15.00	15.00
278	A86	1c on 2c car	.30	.30
279	A86	2c on 3c yel brn	2.25	2.25
a.		Dbl. surch., one reading up	30.00	30.00
280	A86	2c on 4c myr grn	1.50	1.50
281	A86	2c on 5c lt blue	.60	.45
a.		Dbl. surch., one reading up	30.00	30.00
282	A86	2c on 7c brown	75.00	75.00
283	A86	5c on 6c red org	.40	.30
a.		"5 ctvos." omitted	37.50	37.50
284	A86	10c on 7c brown	1.25	1.25
285	A86	20c on 8c apple grn	.35	.30
a.		Double surcharge		
286	A95	40c on 10c blue	4.25	4.25
287	A86	40c on 15c dk gray	1.25	1.25
288	A86	50c on 20c dk vio	13.25	13.25
289	A86	1s on 40c dk brown	4.50	4.50
290	A86	5s on 50c dk green	5.25	5.25
291	A86	10s on 60c dk blue	19.50	19.50

With Additional Surcharge in Red

No.	Type	Description	Unused	Used
292	A86	10c on 2c on 7c brn	.55	.55
a.		Red surcharge double	30.00	30.00
		Nos. 277-292 (16)	145.20	144.90

National Assembly of 1928.
Counterfeit overprints exist of Nos. 277-291.

A111

Surcharged in Various Colors

1928, Oct. 31 ***Perf. 14***

No.	Type	Description	Unused	Used
293	A111	5c on 20c gray lil (Bk)	3.00	1.75
294	A111	10c on 20c gray lil (R)	3.00	1.75
295	A111	20c on 1s grn (O)	3.00	1.75
296	A111	50c on 1s grn (Bl)	3.75	1.40
297	A111	1s on 1s grn (V)	4.75	1.75
298	A111	5s on 2s red (G)	15.00	9.00
299	A111	10s on 2s red (Br)	18.00	12.00
a.		Black surcharge	15.00	10.00
		Nos. 293-299 (7)	50.50	29.40

Quito-Otavalo railway opening.
See Nos. 586-587.

No. RA11 Overprinted in Red

1929 ***Perf. 12***

No.	Type	Description	Unused	Used
302	PT6	2c deep green	.50	.25

There are two types of overprint on No. 302 differing slightly.

A112

1929 ***Red Overprint***

No.	Type	Description	Unused	Used
303	A112	1c dark blue	.50	.25
a.		Overprint reading down	.75	.50

See Nos. 586-587.

Plowing — A113

Cultivating Cacao — A114

Cacao Pod — A115

Growing Tobacco — A116

Exportation of Fruits — A117

Landscape — A118

Loading Sugar Cane — A119

Scene in Quito A120

Scene in Quito A121

Olmedo — A122

Monument to Simón Bolívar — A125

Designs: 2s, Sucre. 5s, Bolivar.

1930, Aug. 1 *Perf. 12½*

304	A113	1c yellow & car	.30	.25
305	A114	2c yellow & grn	.30	.25
306	A115	5c dp grn & vio brn	.35	.25
307	A116	6c yellow & red	.45	.25
308	A117	10c orange & ol grn	.45	.25
309	A118	16c red & yel grn	.55	.25
310	A119	20c ultra & yel	.90	.25
311	A120	40c orange & sepia	1.10	.35
312	A121	50c orange & sepia	1.10	.40
313	A122	1s dp green & blk	4.25	.45
314	A122	2s dk blue & blk	6.50	2.00
315	A122	5s dk violet & blk	11.50	3.00
316	A125	10s car rose & blk	40.00	6.50
		Nos. 304-316 (13)	67.75	14.45

Centenary of founding of republic.
For surcharges and overprints see Nos. 319-320, 331-338, RA25, RA33, RA43.

A126

A127

1933 **Red Overprint** *Perf. 15*

317 A126 10c olive brown 1.15 .25

Blue Overprint

318 A127 10c olive brown .70 .25
a. Inverted overprint 5.00 5.00

For overprint see No. 339.

Nos. 307, 309 Surcharged in Black

1933 *Perf. 12½*

319 A116 5c on 6c yellow & red 1.00 .25
320 A118 10c on 16c red & yel grn 2.00 .25
a. Inverted overprint 4.00 4.00

Landscape A128

Mt. Chimborazo A129

1934-45 *Perf. 12*

321	A128	5c violet	1.40	.55
322	A128	5c blue	1.40	.55
323	A128	5c dark brown	1.40	.55
323A	A128	5c slate blk ('45)	1.40	.55
324	A128	10c rose	1.40	.55
325	A128	10c dark green	1.40	.55
326	A128	10c brown	1.40	.55
327	A128	10c orange	1.40	.55
328	A128	10c olive green	1.40	.55
329	A128	10c gray blk ('35)	1.40	.55
329A	A128	10c red lilac ('44)	1.40	.55

Perf. 14

330 A129 1s carmine rose 1.60 .55
Nos. 321-330 (12) 17.00 6.60

Stamps of 1930 Srchd. or Ovptd. in various colors

1935 *Perf. 12½*

331	A116	5c on 6c (Bl)	.90	.35
332	A116	10c on 6c (G)	1.25	.35
333	A119	20c (R)	1.75	.35
334	A120	40c (G)	2.50	.35
335	A121	50c (G)	3.00	.45
336	A122	1s on 5s (Gold)	7.00	1.25
337	A122	2s on 5s (Gold)	9.50	1.75
338	A125	5s on 10s (Bl)	12.00	5.00
		Nos. 331-338,C35-C38 (12)	87.90	29.85

Unveiling of a monument to Bolivar at Quito, July 24, 1935.

A129a

1935, Oct. 13 **Photo.** *Perf. 11½x11*

338A	A129a	5c ultra & black	.25	.25
338B	A129a	10c org & blue	.25	.25
338C	A129a	40c dk car & red	.25	*.30*
338D	A129a	1S blue grn & red	.30	*.70*
338E	A129a	2S violet & red	.55	*1.20*
		Nos. 338A-338E,C38A-C38E (10)	4.35	*7.60*

Columbus Day. Nos. 338A-338E and C38A-C38E were prepared by the Sociedad Colombista Panamericana and were sold by the Ecuadorian post office through Oct. 30.

Telegraph Stamp Overprinted Diagonally in Red like No. 273

1935 *Perf. 14½*

339 A126 10c olive brown .75 .25

Map of Galápagos Islands A130

Galapagos Land Iguana A131

Galápagos Tortoise — A132

Charles R. Darwin — A133

Columbus A134

Island Scene A135

1936 *Perf. 14*

340	A130	2c black	1.00	.25
341	A131	5c olive grn	1.25	.25
342	A132	10c brown	2.40	.30
343	A133	20c dk violet	2.75	.45
344	A134	1s dk carmine	5.00	.85
345	A135	2s dark blue	7.75	1.40
		Nos. 340-345 (6)	20.15	3.50

Cent. of the visit of Charles Darwin to the Galápagos Islands, Sept. 17, 1835.
For overprints see Nos. O191-O195.

Tobacco Stamp Overprinted in Black

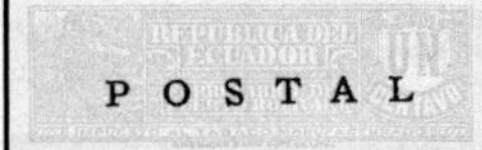

1936 *Rouletted 7*

346 PT7 1c rose red .50 .25
a. Horiz. pair, imperf. vert.
b. Double surcharge

No. 346 is similar to type PT7 but does not include "CASA CORREOS."

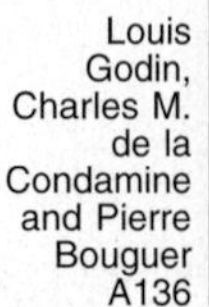

Louis Godin, Charles M. de la Condamine and Pierre Bouguer A136

Portraits: 5c, 20c, Antonio Ulloa, La Condamine and Jorge Juan.

1936 **Engr.** *Perf. 12½*

347	A136	2c deep blue	.50	.30
348	A136	5c dark green	.50	.30
349	A136	10c deep orange	.50	.30
350	A136	20c violet	.80	.30
351	A136	50c dark red	1.25	.30
		Nos. 347-351,C39-C42 (9)	6.60	2.60

Bicentenary of Geodesical Mission to Quito.

Independence Monument — A137

1936 *Perf. 13½x14*

352	A137	2c green	2.25	1.25
353	A137	5c dark violet	2.25	1.25
354	A137	10c carmine rose	2.25	1.25
355	A137	20c black	2.25	1.25
356	A137	50c blue	3.25	2.10
357	A137	1s dark red	3.75	3.25
		Nos. 352-357,C43-C50 (14)	50.50	41.35

1st Intl. Philatelic Exhibition at Quito.

Coat of Arms — A138

Overprint in Black or Red

1937 *Perf. 12½*

359 A138 5c olive green 2.00 .30
360 A138 10c dark blue (R) 2.00 .25

For overprint see No. 562.

Andean Landscape A139

Atahualpa, the Last Inca A140

Hat Weavers — A141

Coast Landscape A142

Gold Washing A143

1937, Aug. 19 *Perf. 11½*

361	A139	2c green	.50	.25
362	A140	5c deep rose	.50	.25
363	A141	10c blue	.50	.25
364	A142	20c deep rose	1.50	.30
365	A143	1s olive green	2.00	.35
		Nos. 361-365 (5)	5.00	1.40

For overprints see Nos. O196-O200.

"Liberty" Carrying Flag of Ecuador — A144

Engraved and Lithographed

1938, Feb. 22 *Perf. 12*

Center Multicolored

366	A144	2c blue	.25	.25
367	A144	5c violet	.35	.25
368	A144	10c black	.55	.25
369	A144	20c brown	.65	.25
370	A144	50c black	1.10	.25
371	A144	1s olive blk	1.75	.30
372	A144	2s dk brn	3.25	.55
		Nos. 366-372,C57-C63 (14)	22.40	4.50

US Constitution, 150th anniversary.
For overprints and surcharges see Nos. 413-415, 444-446, RA46, RA52.

A145

A146

A147

A148

Designs: 10c, Winged figure holding globe. 50c, Cactus, winged wheel. 1s, "Communications." 2s, "Construction."

Perf. 13, 13x13½

1938, Oct. 30 **Engr.**

373	A145	10c bright ultra	.40	.25
374	A146	50c deep red violet	.40	.25
375	A147	1s copper red	.70	.25
376	A148	2s dark green	1.10	.25
		Nos. 373-376 (4)	2.60	1.00

Progress of Ecuador Exhibition.
For overprints see Nos. C105-C113.

Parade of Athletes — A149

Runner — A150

Basketball — A151

Wrestlers A152

Diver A153

1939, Mar. *Perf. 12*

377	A149	5c	carmine rose	3.00	.55
378	A150	10c	deep blue	3.50	.65
379	A151	50c	gray olive	5.75	.85
380	A152	1s	dull violet	7.75	.85
381	A153	2s	dull olive green	12.50	.95
	Nos. 377-381,C65-C69 (10)			78.35	6.15

First Bolivarian Games (1938), Bogota.

Dolores Mission — A154

1939, June 16 *Perf. 12½x13*

382	A154	2c	blue green	.50	.25
383	A154	5c	rose red	.50	.25
384	A154	10c	ultra	.50	.25
385	A154	50c	yellow brown	1.20	.25
386	A154	1s	black	1.90	.25
387	A154	2s	purple	1.25	.40
	Nos. 382-387,C73-C79 (13)			11.25	3.40

Golden Gate International Exposition.
For surcharges see Nos. 429, 436.

Trylon and Perisphere — A155

1939, June 30

388	A155	2c	lt olive green	.80	.35
389	A155	5c	red orange	.80	.35
390	A155	10c	ultra	.80	.35
391	A155	50c	slate gray	1.10	.35
392	A155	1s	rose carmine	1.90	.35
393	A155	2s	black brown	2.25	.40
	Nos. 388-393,C80-C86 (13)			16.55	4.20

New York World's Fair.
For surcharge see No. 437.

Flags of the 21 American Republics — A156

1940 *Perf. 12*

394	A156	5c	dp rose & blk	1.00	.25
395	A156	10c	dk blue & blk	.40	.25
396	A156	50c	Prus green & blk	.60	.25
397	A156	1s	dp violet & blk	1.00	.30
	Nos. 394-397,C87-C90 (8)			8.30	2.75

Pan American Union, 50th anniversary.

Francisco J. E. Santa Cruz y Espejo — A157

1941, Dec. 15

398	A157	30c	blue	1.25	.25
399	A157	1s	red orange	2.50	.35
	Nos. 398-399,C91-C92 (4)			21.50	1.30

Exposition of Journalism held under the auspices of the Natl. Newspaper Men's Union.

Francisco de Orellana A158

Gonzalo Pizarro A159

View of Guayaquil A160

View of Quito — A161

1942, Jan. 30

400	A158	10c	sepia	.90	.35
401	A159	40c	deep rose	2.50	.35
402	A160	1s	violet	3.50	.35
403	A161	2s	dark blue	4.50	.45
	Nos. 400-403,C93-C96 (8)			23.45	3.35

400th anniv. of the discovery and exploration of the Amazon River by Orellana.

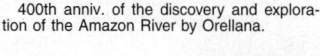

Remigio Crespo Toral — A162

1942 *Perf. 13½*

404	A162	10c	green	.60	.25
405	A162	50c	brown	1.00	.25
	Nos. 404-405,C97 (3)			2.85	1.00

Alfredo Baquerizo Moreno — A163

1942

406	A163	10c	green	.25	.25

Mt. Chimborazo A164

1942-47 *Perf. 12*

407	A164	30c	red brown	.60	.30
407A	A164	30c	lt blue ('43)	.60	.30
407B	A164	30c	red orange ('44)	.60	.30
407C	A164	30c	green ('47)	.60	.30
	Nos. 407-407C (4)			2.40	1.20

View of Guayaquil A165

1942-44

408	A165	20c	red	.55	.25
408A	A165	20c	deep blue ('44)	.55	.25

Gen. Eloy Alfaro — A166

Devil's Nose — A167

President Alfaro (1842-1912): 30c, Military College. 1s, Montecristi, Alfaro's birthplace.

1942

409	A166	10c	dk rose & blk	.60	.25
410	A167	20c	ol blk & red brn	.60	.25
411	A167	30c	ol gray & grn	.75	.25
412	A167	1s	slate & salmon	1.80	.25
	Nos. 409-412,C98-C101 (8)			20.15	4.40

Nos. 370-372 Overprinted in Red Brown

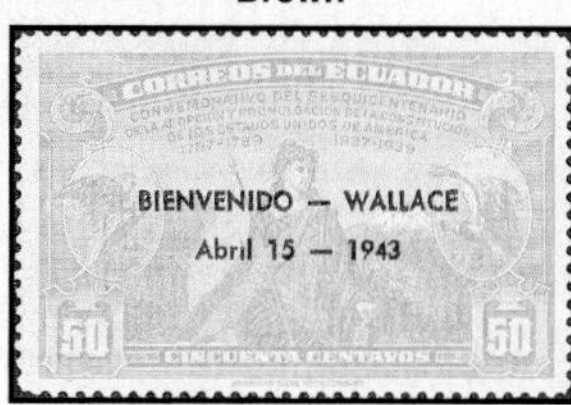

1943, Apr. 15 *Perf. 11½*

413	A144	50c	multicolored	.65	.65
414	A144	1s	multicolored	1.25	1.25
415	A144	2s	multicolored	2.75	2.75
	Nos. 413-415,C102-C104 (6)			14.65	10.25

Visit of US Vice-Pres. Henry A. Wallace.

"30 Centavos" — A170

1943 **Black Surcharge** *Perf. 12½*

416	A170	30c	on 50c red brn	1.00	.25
a.			Without bars	1.00	.25

Map Showing US and Ecuador — A171

1943, Oct. 9 *Perf. 12*

417	A171	10c	dull violet	.75	.50
418	A171	20c	red brown	.75	.50
419	A171	30c	orange	.75	.50
420	A171	50c	olive green	.90	.60
421	A171	1s	deep violet	1.00	.65
422	A171	10s	olive bister	8.25	5.25
	Nos. 417-422,C114-C118 (11)			32.70	15.10

Good will tour of Pres. Arroyo del Rio in 1942.

1944, Feb. 7

423	A171	10c	yellow green	.65	.45
424	A171	20c	rose pink	.65	.45
425	A171	30c	dark gray brown	.65	.45
426	A171	50c	deep red lilac	.65	.45
427	A171	1s	olive gray	1.00	.65
428	A171	10s	red orange	10.50	6.00
	Nos. 423-428,C119-C123 (11)			24.90	13.40

For surcharges see Nos. B1-B6.

No. 385 Surcharged in Black

1944 **Unwmk.** *Perf. 12½x13*

429	A154	30c	on 50c yel brn	2.00	.25

Archbishop Federico González Suárez, Birth Cent. — A172

1944 *Perf. 12*

430	A172	10c	deep blue	.40	.25
431	A172	20c	green	.40	.25
432	A172	30c	dk violet brn	.50	.25
433	A172	1s	dull violet	.90	.25
	Nos. 430-433,C124-C127 (8)			15.50	4.30

Air Post Stamps Nos. C76 and C83 Surcharged in Black

1944 *Perf. 12½x13*

434	AP15	30c	on 50c rose vio	.40	.25
435	AP16	30c	on 50c sl grn	.40	.25

Nos. 382 and 388 Surcharged in Black

1944-45

436	A154	5c	on 2c bl grn	.50	.25
a.			Double surcharge	4.00	
437	A155	5c	on 2c lt ol grn ('45)	.50	.25

Government Palace, Quito — A173

1944 **Engr.** *Perf. 11*

438	A173	10c	dark green	.50	.25
439	A173	30c	blue	.50	.25

See Nos. C128-C130, C221. For surcharges see Nos. 452, RAC1-RAC2.

Symbol of the Red Cross A174

1945, Apr. 25 *Perf. 12*

Cross in Rose

440 A174 30c bister brown 1.90 .35
441 A174 1s red brown 2.75 .45
442 A174 5s turq green 4.75 1.10
443 A174 10s scarlet 13.00 3.00
Nos. 440-443,C131-C134 (8) 58.40 14.75

International Red Cross, 80th anniversary.

Nos. 370 to 372 Overprinted in Dark Blue and Gold

1945, Oct. 2 *Perf. 11½*

Center Multicolored

444 A144 50c black .80 .70
a. Double overprint *22.50*
445 A144 1s olive black 1.40 1.40
446 A144 2s dark brown 2.75 2.50
a. Double overprint *22.50*
Nos. 444-446,C139-C141 (6) 10.45 8.25

Visit of Pres. Juan Antonio Rios of Chile.

General Antonio José de Sucre, 150th Birth Anniv. — A175

1945, Nov. 14 **Engr.** *Perf. 12*

447 A175 10c olive .55 .25
448 A175 20c red brown .55 .25
449 A175 40c olive gray .55 .25
450 A175 1s dark green 1.10 .25
451 A175 2s sepia 2.25 .75
Nos. 447-451,C142-C146 (10) 13.20 6.10

No. 438 Surcharged in Blue

1945 *Perf. 11*

452 A173 20c on 10c dark green .50 .25
a. Fancy bar omitted

Catalogue values for unused stamps in this section, from this point to the end of the section, are for Never Hinged items.

Map of Pan-American Highway and Arms of Loja — A176

1946, Apr. 22 **Engr.** *Perf. 12*

453 A176 20c red brown .60 .40
454 A176 30c bright green .60 .45
455 A176 1s bright ultra .60 .45
456 A176 5s deep red lilac 1.90 1.50
457 A176 10s scarlet 3.50 2.00
Nos. 453-457,C147-C151 (10) 14.55 7.95

Torch of Democracy — A177

Popular Suffrage A178

Flag of Ecuador — A179

Pres. José M. Velasco Ibarra — A180

1946, Aug. 9 **Unwmk.** *Perf. 12½*

458 A177 5c dark blue .25 .25
459 A178 10c Prus green .25 .25
460 A179 20c carmine .30 .25
461 A180 30c chocolate .45 .25
Nos. 458-461,C152-C155 (8) 3.45 2.20

Revolution of May 28, 1944, 2nd anniv.

"30 Ctvs." — A181

1946 **Black Surcharge**

462 A181 30c on 50c red brown .50 .25

For overprint see No. 484.

Nos. CO13-CO14 With Additional Ovpt. in Black

1946 *Perf. 11½*

463 AP7 10c chestnut .50 .25
464 AP7 20c olive black .50 .25

Instructor and Student — A182

1946, Sept. 16 *Perf. 12½*

465 A182 10c deep blue .40 .30
466 A182 20c chocolate .40 .30
467 A182 30c dark green .40 .30
468 A182 50c bluish blk .55 .45
469 A182 1s dark red 1.10 .75
470 A182 10s dark violet 6.50 1.40
Nos. 465-470,C156-C160 (11) 21.00 6.85

Campaign for adult education.

Mariana de Jesus Paredes y Flores — A183

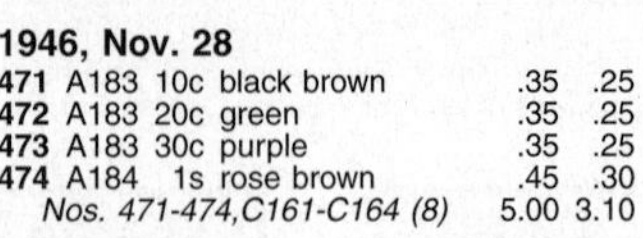

Urn — A184

1946, Nov. 28

471 A183 10c black brown .35 .25
472 A183 20c green .35 .25
473 A183 30c purple .35 .25
474 A184 1s rose brown .45 .30
Nos. 471-474,C161-C164 (8) 5.00 3.10

300th anniv. of the death of the Blessed Mariana de Jesus Paredes y Flores.

Pres. Vicente Rocafuerte A185

Jesuits' Church Quito A186

45c, 50c, 80c, F.J.E. de Santa Cruz y Espejo.

1947, Nov. 27 *Perf. 12*

475 A185 5c redsh brown .25 .25
476 A185 10c sepia .25 .25
477 A185 15c gray black .25 .25
478 A186 20c redsh brown .30 .25
479 A186 30c red violet .50 .25
480 A186 40c brt ultra .65 .25
481 A185 45c dk slate grn .80 .30
482 A185 50c olive black .85 .30
483 A185 80c orange red 1.20 .35
Nos. 475-483,C165-C171 (16) 8.60 4.20

For overprints and surcharges see Nos. 489, 496, 525-527, C215.

Type of 1946, Overprinted "POSTAL" in Black but Without Additional Surcharge

1948 **Engr.**

484 A181 10c orange .50 .25

Andrés Bello — A188

1948, Apr. 21 *Perf. 13*

485 A188 20c lt blue .30 .25
486 A188 30c rose carmine .30 .25
487 A188 40c blue green .30 .25
488 A188 1s black brown .60 .25
Nos. 485-488,C172-C174 (7) 3.20 1.75

83rd anniversary of the death of Andrés Bello (1781-1865), educator.

No. 480 Overprinted in Black

1948, May 24 *Perf. 12*

489 A186 40c bright ultra .60 .35

See No. C175.

Flagship of Columbus — A189

1948 *Perf. 14*

490 A189 10c dark blue green .50 .25
491 A189 20c brown .50 .25
492 A189 30c dark purple 1.20 .25
493 A189 50c deep claret 1.60 .25
494 A189 1s ultra 2.40 .40
495 A189 5s carmine 6.50 .80
Nos. 490-495,C176-C180 (11) 25.65 7.55

Issued to publicize the proposed Columbus Memorial Lighthouse near Ciudad Trujillo, Dominican Republic.

No. 483 Overprinted in Blue, "MANANA" Reading Down

1948 *Perf. 12*

496 A185 80c orange red .25 .25

Issued to publicize the National Fair of Today and Tomorrow, 1948. See No. C181.

Telegrafo I in Flight — A190

1948 **Engr.** *Perf. 12½*

497 A190 30c red orange .65 .25
498 A190 40c rose lilac .65 .25
499 A190 60c violet blue .65 .25
500 A190 1s brown red .65 .25
501 A190 3s brown 2.00 .35
502 A190 5s gray black 2.40 .35
Nos. 497-502,C182-C187 (12) 13.80 3.50

25th anniversary (in 1945) of the first postal flight in Ecuador.

Book and Pen — A191

1948, Oct. 12 **Unwmk.** *Perf. 14*

503 A191 10c deep claret .60 .25
504 A191 20c brown .60 .25
505 A191 30c dark green 1.25 .25
506 A191 50c red 2.00 .25
507 A191 1s purple 3.00 .30
508 A191 10s dull blue 8.00 1.00
Nos. 503-508,C188-C192 (11) 32.45 7.80

Campaign for adult education.

A192

Franklin D. Roosevelt and Two of "Four Freedoms" — A193

1948, Oct. 24 ***Perf. 12½***

509 A192 10c rose brn & gray .40 .30
510 A192 20c brn ol & bl .50 .40
511 A193 30c ol bis & car rose .50 .40
512 A193 40c red vio & sep .65 .40
513 A193 1s org brn & car .70 .50
Nos. 509-513,C193-C197 (10) 7.05 3.70

Maldonado and Map — A194

Riobamba Aqueduct A195

Maldonado on Bank of Riobamba A196

Pedro V. Maldonado A197

1948, Nov. 17 **Engr.** **Unwmk.**

514 A194 5c gray blk & ver .40 .25
515 A195 10c car & gray blk .50 .25
516 A196 30c bis brn & ultra .60 .25
517 A195 40c sage grn & vio .75 .25
518 A194 50c grn & car 1.00 .30
519 A197 1s brn & slate bl 1.25 .35
Nos. 514-519,C198-C201 (10) 8.10 2.65

Bicentenary of the death of Pedro Vicente Maldonado, geographer.

For overprints and surcharges see Nos. 537-540.

A198

Miguel de Cervantes Saavedra A199

1949, May 2 ***Perf. 12½x12***

520 A198 30c dk car rose & dp ultra .75 .25
521 A199 60c bis & brn vio 1.25 .30
522 A198 1s grn & rose car 1.75 .25
523 A199 2s gray blk & red brn 3.25 .30
524 A198 5s choc & aqua 6.50 1.25
Nos. 520-524,C202-C206 (10) 25.75 5.95

400th anniv. of the birth of Miguel de Cervantes Saavedra, novelist, playwright and poet.

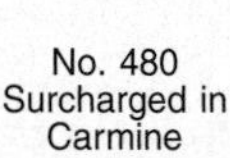

No. 480 Surcharged in Carmine

1949, June 15 ***Perf. 12***

525 A186 10c on 40c brt ultra .40 .25
526 A186 20c on 40c brt ultra .55 .25
a. Double surcharge
527 A186 30c on 40c brt ultra .55 .25
Nos. 525-527,C207-C209 (6) 3.05 1.50

2nd Natl. Eucharistic Cong., Quito, 6/49.
No. 526 exists se-tenant with No. 527.

Monument on Equator — A200

1949, June **Engr.** ***Perf. 12½x12***

528 A200 10c deep plum .40 .25

For overprint see No. 536.

No. 542 Surcharged in Black and Carmine

1949 ***Perf. 12x12½***

529 A203 10c on 50c green .55 .25
530 A203 20c on 50c green .55 .25
531 A203 30c on 50c green .65 .25
Nos. 529-531,C210-C213 (7) 6.05 2.25

Universal Postal Union, 75th anniversary.

Consular Service Stamps Surcharged in Black

Arms of Ecuador — R1

1949 ***Perf. 12***

532 R1 20c on 25c red brown .75 .25
533 R1 30c on 50c gray .75 .25

For other overprints and surcharges on type R1 see Nos. 544-549, 566-570, C214 C245, C249-C252, RA60-RA62, RA72.

Nos. RA49A and RA55 Overprinted in Black — a

1950 **Unwmk.** ***Perf. 12***

534 PT18 5c green .30 .25
535 PT21 5c blue .30 .25

Overprint 15mm on No. 534.

Nos. 528 and 517 to 519 Ovptd. or Srchd. in Black or Carmine

1950, Feb. 10 ***Perf. 12½x12***

536 A200 10c dp plum .50 .50

Perf. 12½

537 A195 20c on 40c sage grn & vio 1.00 1.00
538 A195 30c on 40c sage grn & vio 1.25 1.25
539 A194 50c grn & car 2.00 2.00
540 A197 1s brn & slate bl (C) 2.50 2.50

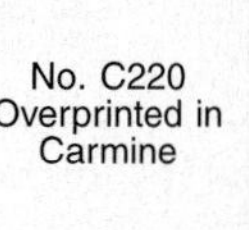

No. C220 Overprinted in Carmine

Overprint 15mm long

Perf. 11

541 A173 10s violet 6.00 3.00
Nos. 536-541,C216-C220 (11) 33.00 22.25

Nos. 536-541 publicize adult education.

San Pablo Lake — A203

Perf. 12x12½

1950, May **Engr.** **Unwmk.**

542 A203 50c green .50 .25

For surcharges see Nos. 529-531.

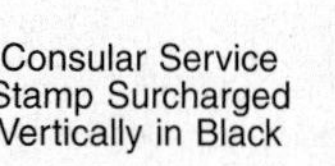

Consular Service Stamp Surcharged Vertically in Black

1950 ***Perf. 12***

544 R1 30c on 50c gray .50 .25

Consular Service Stamps Overprinted or Surcharged in Black

b

c

d

e

f

g

1951 **Unwmk.** ***Perf. 12***

545 R1 (b) 5c on 10c car rose .50 .25
546 R1 (c) 10c car rose .50 .25
547 R1 (d) 10c car rose .50 .25
548 R1 (e) 20c on 25c red brn .50 .25
549 R1 (e) 30c on 50c gray .50 .25
550 R2 (f) 40c on 25c blue .50 .25
551 R2 (g) 50c on 25c blue .50 .25
Nos. 545-551 (7) 3.50 1.75

See Nos. 552-554, C233-C234, C246-C248, RA67.

Consular Service Stamps Surcharged in Black

1951

552 R2 20c on 25c blue .50 .25
553 R2 30c on 25c blue .50 .25

Adult education. See Nos. C225-C226.

Consular Service Stamp Surcharged in Black

1951

554 R2 $0.30 on 50c car rose .50 .25

Reliquary of St. Mariana and Vatican — A204

Perf. 12½x12

1952, Feb. **Engr.** **Unwmk.**

555 A204 10c emer & red brn .90 .70
556 A204 20c dp bl & pur .90 .70
557 A204 30c car & bl grn .90 .70
Nos. 555-557,C227-C230 (7) 6.00 3.30

Issued to publicize the canonization of Mariana de Jesus Paredes y Flores.

Presidents Galo Plaza and Harry Truman — A205

2s, Pres. Plaza addressing US Congress.

1952, Mar. 26 ***Perf. 12***

558 A205 1s rose car & gray blk .70 .60
559 A205 2s dl bl & sepia 1.75 .90
Nos. 558-559,C231-C232 (4) 5.15 3.70

1951 visit of Pres. Galo Plaza y Lasso to the US.

R3

Fiscal Stamps Srchd. or Ovptd. Horiz. in Carmine or Black

Type of 1937 Overprinted Diagonally

1952 Unwmk. Engr. *Perf. 12*
560 R3 20c on 30c dp bl (C) .75 .25
561 R3 30c deep blue .75 .25
562 A138 50c purple .75 .25
Nos. 560-562 (3) 2.25 .75

For overprints and surcharge see Nos. RA68-RA69, RA71.

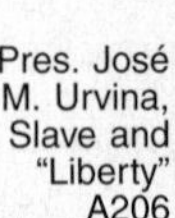

Pres. José M. Urvina, Slave and "Liberty" A206

Hyphen-hole Perf. 7x6½

1952 Litho.
563 A206 20c red & green .65 .45
564 A206 30c red & vio bl .80 .45
565 A206 50c blue & car 1.40 .45
Nos. 563-565,C236-C239 (7) 16.85 3.15

Centenary of abolition of slavery in Ecuador. Counterfeits exist.

Consular Service Stamps Surcharged in Black — h

1952-53 Unwmk. *Perf. 12*
566 R1 10c on 20s blue ('53) .75 .25
567 R1 20c on 10s gray ('53) .75 .25
568 R1 20c on 20s blue .75 .25
569 R1 30c on 10s gray ('53) .75 .25
570 R1 30c on 20s blue .75 .25
Nos. 566-570 (5) 3.75 1.25

Similar surcharges of 60c and 90c on the 20s blue are said to be bogus.

Teacher and Students — A207

New Citizens Voting — A208

Designs: 10c, Instructor with student. 30c, Teaching the alphabet.

1953, Apr. 13 Engr.
571 A207 5c lt bl .30 .25
572 A207 10c dk car rose .45 .25
573 A208 20c brt brn org .50 .25
574 A208 30c dp red lil .75 .25
Nos. 571-574,C240-C241 (6) 4.70 1.50

1952 adult education campaign.

A209

1953 Black Surcharge
575 A209 40c on 50c purple 1.00 .25

Cuicocha Lagoon — A210

Designs: 10c, Equatorial Line monument. 20c, Quininde countryside. 30c, Tomebamba river. 40c, La Chilintosa rock. 50c, Iliniza Mountains.

Frames in Black

1953 Engr. *Perf. 13x12½*
576 A210 5c brt bl .50 .50
577 A210 10c brt grn .50 .50
578 A210 20c purple .50 .50
579 A210 30c brown .50 .50
580 A210 40c orange .50 .50
581 A210 50c dp car .90 .50
Nos. 576-581 (6) 3.40 3.00

A211

Carlos Maria Cardinal de la Torre and arches.

1954, Jan. Photo. *Perf. 8½*
582 A211 30c blk & ver .65 .65
583 A211 50c blk & rose lil .65 .65
Nos. 582-583,C253-C255 (5) 3.80 2.35

1st anniv. of the elevation of Archbishop de la Torre to Cardinal.

A212

1954, Apr. 22
584 A212 30c blk & gray 1.40 1.40
585 A212 50c blk & yel 1.40 1.40
Nos. 584-585,C256-C260 (7) 6.75 4.80

Queen Isabella I (1451-1504) of Spain, 500th birth anniv.

Type of 1929 Overprint Larger, No Letterspacing

1954-55 Unwmk. *Perf. 12*
586 A112 5c ol grn ('55) .75 .25
587 A112 10c orange .75 .25

The normal overprint on Nos. 586-587 reads up. It also exists reading down.

Indian Messenger — A213

1954, Aug. 2 Litho. *Perf. 11*
588 A213 30c dk brn 1.00 .25

Day of the Postal Employee. See No. C263.

Products of Ecuador — A214

1954, Sept. 24 Photo.
589 A214 10c orange .40 .25
590 A214 20c vermilion .40 .25
591 A214 30c rose pink .40 .25
592 A214 40c dk gray grn .60 .25
593 A214 50c yel brn .80 .25
Nos. 589-593 (5) 2.60 1.25

José Abel Castillo — A215

Perf. 11½x11

1955, Oct. 19 Engr. Unwmk.
594 A215 30c olive bister .60 .25
595 A215 50c dk gray .60 .25
Nos. 594-595,C282-C286 (7) 10.20 2.10

30th anniv. of the 1st flight of the "Telegrafo I" and to honor Castillo, aviation pioneer.

Babahoyo River Los Rios — A216

Designs: 5c, Palms, Esmeraldas. 10c, Fishermen, Manabi. 30c, Guayaquil, Guayas. 50c, Pital River, El Oro. 70c, Cactus, Galapagos Isls. 80c, Orchids, Napo-Pastaza. 1s, Aguacate Mission, Zamora-Chinchipe. 2s, Jibaro Indian, Morona-Santiago.

1955-56 Photo. *Perf. 13*
596 A216 5c yel grn ('56) 1.50 .30
597 A216 10c blue ('56) 1.50 .30
598 A216 20c brown 1.50 .30
599 A216 30c dk gray 1.50 .30
600 A216 50c bl grn 1.50 .30
601 A216 70c ol ('56) 1.50 .30
602 A216 80c dp vio ('56) 3.75 .30
603 A216 1s org ('56) 2.00 .30
604 A216 2s rose red ('56) 3.75 .30
Nos. 596-604 (9) 18.50 2.70

See Nos. 620-630, 670, C288-C297, C310-C311.

Brother Juan Adam Schwarz, S. J. — A217

1956, Aug. 27 Engr. *Perf. 13½*
605 A217 5c yel grn .45 .25
606 A217 10c org red .45 .25
607 A217 20c lt vio .45 .25
608 A217 30c dk grn .45 .25
609 A217 40c blue .45 .25
610 A217 50c dp ultra .45 .25
611 A217 70c orange .45 .25
Nos. 605-611,C302-C305 (11) 5.55 2.75

Bicentennial of printing in Ecuador and honoring Brother Juan Adam Schwarz, S.J.

Andres Hurtado de Mendoza — A218

Gil Ramirez Davalos A219

Designs: 20c, Brother Vincent Solano.

1957, Apr. 7 Unwmk. *Perf. 12*
612 A218 5c dk bl, *pink* .65 .25
613 A219 10c grn, *grnsh* .65 .25
614 A218 20c choc, *buff* .65 .25
a. Souvenir sheet of 4, imperf. 3.50 3.50
Nos. 612-614,C312-C314 (6) 2.85 1.50

4th cent. of the founding of Cuenca.

No. 614a contains 2 5c gray & 2 20c brown red stamps in designs similar to #612, 614. It was printed on white ungummed paper.

A220

Design: 40c, 50c, 2s, Francisco Marcos, Gen. Pedro Alcantara Herran and Santos Michelena.

1957, Sept. 5 Engr. *Perf. 14½x14*
615 A220 40c yellow .40 .25
616 A220 50c ultra .40 .25
617 A220 2s dk red 1.00 .25
Nos. 615-617 (3) 1.80 .75

7th Postal Congress of the Americas and Spain (in 1955).

Souvenir Sheets

Various Railroad Scenes — A221

1957 Litho. *Perf. 10½x11*
618 A221 20c Sheet of 5 9.25 4.25
619 A221 30c Sheet of 5 9.25 4.25

Issued to commemorate the opening of the Quito-Ibarra-San Lorenzo railroad.

Nos. 618-619 contain 2 orange yellow, 1 ultramarine and 2 carmine stamps, each in a different design.

Scenic Type of 1955-56.

Designs as before, except: 40c, as 70c. 90c, as 80c. No. 629, San Pablo, Imbabura.

1957-58 Photo. *Perf. 13*
620 A216 5c light blue 1.75 .25
621 A216 10c brown 1.75 .25
622 A216 20c crimson rose 1.75 .25
623 A216 20c yel green 1.75 .25
624 A216 30c rose red 2.50 .25
625 A216 40c chalky blue 1.75 .25
626 A216 50c lt vio 2.50 .25
627 A216 90c brt ultra 1.75 .25
628 A216 1s dark brown 1.75 .25
629 A216 1s gray blk ('58) 1.75 .25
630 A216 2s brown 2.75 .25
Nos. 620-630 (11) 21.75 2.75

Blue and Yellow Macaw — A222

Birds: 20c, Red-breasted toucan. 30c, Condor. 40c, Black-tailed and sword-tailed hummingbirds.

Perf. 13½x13

1958, Jan. 7 Litho. Unwmk.

Birds in Natural Colors

634 A222 10c red brn 1.40 .25
635 A222 20c dk gray 1.40 .25
636 A222 30c brt yel grn 3.50 .25
637 A222 40c red org 3.50 .25
Nos. 634-637 (4) 9.80 1.00

Carlos Sanz de Santamaria A223

Richard M. Nixon and Flags — A224

No. 640, Dr. Ramon Villeda Morales, flags. 2.20s, José Carlos de Macedo Soares, horizontal flags.

1958 *Perf. 12*

Flags in Red, Blue, Yellow & Green

638 A223 1.80s dl vio .65 .25
639 A224 2s dk grn .65 .25
640 A224 2s dk brn .65 .25
641 A223 2.20s blk brn .65 .25
Nos. 638-641 (4) 2.60 1.00

Visits: Colombia's Foreign Minister Dr. Carlos Sanz de Santamaria; US Vice Pres. Nixon, May 9-10; Pres. Ramon Villeda Morales of Honduras; Brazil's Foreign Minister José Carlos de Macedo Soares. See Nos. C419-C421. For overprints and surcharges see Nos. 775-775C, C419-C421, C460.

Locomotive of 1908 A225

Garcia Moreno, Jose Caamano, L. Plaza and Eloy Alfaro — A226

Design: 50c, Diesel locomotive.

Perf. 13½x14, 14

1958, Aug. 9 Photo. Unwmk.

642 A225 30c brn blk .25 .25
643 A225 50c dk car .35 .25
644 A226 5s dk brn 1.75 .70
Nos. 642-644 (3) 2.35 1.20

Guayaquil-Quito railroad, 50th anniv.

Cardinal — A227

Birds: 30c, Andean cock-of-the-rock. 50c, Glossy cowbird. 60c, Red-fronted Amazon.

1958 Litho. *Perf. 13½x13*

Birds in Natural Colors

645 A227 20c bluish grn, blk & red 1.40 .25
646 A227 30c buff, blk & brt bl 1.65 .25
647 A227 50c org, blk & grn 1.90 .55
648 A227 60c pale rose, blk & bluish grn 3.75 .55
Nos. 645-648 (4) 8.70 1.60

UNESCO Building and Eiffel Tower, Paris — A228

1958, Nov. 3 Engr. *Perf. 12½*

649 A228 80c brown .50 .25

UNESCO Headquarters in Paris opening, Nov. 3.

Globe and Satellites — A229

1958, Dec. 20 Photo. *Perf. 14x13½*

650 A229 1.80s dark blue 1.00 .45

International Geophysical Year, 1957-58. For overprints see Nos. 718, C422.

Virgin of Quito — A230

1959, Sept. 8 Unwmk. *Perf. 13*

651 A230 5c ol grn .25 .25
652 A230 10c yel brn .25 .25
653 A230 20c purple .25 .25
654 A230 30c ultra .25 .25
655 A230 80c dk car rose .25 .25
Nos. 651-655 (5) 1.25 1.25

See No. C290. For surcharges and overprint see Nos. 695-699.

Uprooted Oak Emblem — A231

1960, Apr. 7 Litho. *Perf. 14x13*

656 A231 80c rose car & grn .25 .25

World Refugee Year, 7/1/59-6/30/60. For overprints see Nos. 709, 719, O205.

Great Anteater and Arms — A232

Animals: 40c, Tapir and map. 80c, Spectacled bear and arms. 1s, Puma and map.

1960, May 14 Photo. *Perf. 13*

657 A232 20c org, grn & blk .60 .25
658 A232 40c yel grn, bl grn & brn .90 .25
659 A232 80c bl, blk & red brn 1.50 .25
660 A232 1s Prus bl, plum & ocher 2.75 .60
Nos. 657-660 (4) 5.75 1.35

Founding of the city of Baeza, 4th cent. See Nos. 676-679.

Hotel Quito A233

No. 662, Dormitory, Catholic University. No. 663, Dormitory, Central University. No. 664, Airport, Quito. No. 665, Overpass on Highway to Quito. No. 666, Security Bank. No. 667, Ministry of Foreign Affairs. No. 668, Government Palace. No. 669, Legislative Palace.

Perf. 11x11½

1960, Aug. 8 Engr. Unwmk.

661 A233 1s dk pur & redsh brn .45 .25
662 A233 1s dk bl & brn .45 .25
663 A233 1s blk & red .45 .25
664 A233 1s dk bl & ultra .45 .25
665 A233 1s dk pur & dk car rose .45 .25
666 A233 1s blk & ol bis .45 .25
667 A233 1s dk pur & turq .45 .25
668 A233 1s dk bl & grn .45 .25
669 A233 1s blk & vio .45 .25
Nos. 661-669 (9) 4.05 2.25

11th Inter-American Conference, Quito. For surcharges see Nos. 700-708.

Type of Regular Issue, 1955-56

Souvenir Sheet

Design: Orchids, Napo-Pastaza.

1960 Photo. *Perf. 13*

Yellow Paper

670 Sheet of 2 5.00 5.00
a. A216 80c deep violet .85 .45
b. A216 90c deep green .85 .45

25th anniv. of Asociacion Filatelica Ecuatoriana. Marginal inscription in silver. Exists with silver inscription omitted.

"Freedom of Expression" — A234

Manabi Bridge A235

10c, "Freedom to vote." 20c, "Freedom to work." 30c, Coins, "Monetary stability."

1960, Aug. 29 Litho. *Perf. 13*

671 A234 5c dk bl .75 .25
672 A234 10c lt vio .75 .25
673 A234 20c orange .75 .25
674 A234 30c bluish grn .75 .25
675 A235 40c brn & bluish grn .75 .25
Nos. 671-675 (5) 3.75 1.25

Achievements of President Camilo Ponce Enriquez. See Nos. C370-C374.

Animal Type of 1960

Animals: 10c, Collared peccary. 20c, Kinkajou. 80c, Jaguar. 1s, Mountain coati.

Unwmk.

1961, July 13 Photo. *Perf. 13*

676 A232 10c grn, rose red & blk .55 .25
677 A232 20c vio, grnsh bl & brn 1.00 .25
678 A232 80c red org, dl yel & blk 1.60 .55
679 A232 1s brn, brt grn & org 2.10 .65
Nos. 676-679 (4) 5.25 1.70

Founding of the city of Tena, 400th anniv.

Graphium Pausianus A236

Butterflies: 30c, Papilio torquatus leptalea. 50c, Graphium molops molops. 80c, Battus lycidas.

1961, July 13 Litho. *Perf. 13½*

680 A236 20c pink & multi .65 .25
681 A236 30c lt ultra & multi 1.10 .25
682 A236 50c org & multi 1.25 .25
683 A236 80c bl grn & multi 2.25 .25
Nos. 680-683 (4) 5.25 1.00

See Nos. 711-713.

Galapagos Islands Nos. L1-L3 Overprinted in Black or Red

1961, Oct. 31 Photo. *Perf. 12*

684 A1 20c dk brn 1.00 .25
685 A2 50c violet 1.00 .25
686 A1 1s dk ol grn (R) 2.40 1.50
Nos. 684-686,C389-C391 (6) 12.05 3.25

Establishment of maritime biological stations on Galapagos Islands by UNESCO. Overprint arranged differently on 20c, 1s.

See Nos. C389-C391.

Daniel Enrique Proano School A237

Designs: 60c, Loja-Zamora highway, vert. 80c, Aguirre Abad College, Guayaquil. 1s, Army quarters, Quito.

Perf. 11x11½, 11½x11

1962, Jan. 10 Engr. Unwmk.

687 A237 50c dl bl & blk .45 .25
688 A237 60c ol grn & blk .45 .25
689 A237 80c org red & blk .45 .25
690 A237 1s rose lake & blk .45 .25
Nos. 687-690 (4) 1.80 1.00

Pres. Arosemena, Flags of Ecuador, US — A238

Designs (Arosemena and): 10c, Flags of Ecuador. 20c, Flags of Ecuador and Panama.

1963, July 1 Litho. *Perf. 14*

691 A238 10c buff & multi .25 .25
692 A238 20c multi .25 .25
693 A238 60c multi .25 .25
Nos. 691-693,C409-C411 (6) 2.60 1.60

Issued to commemorate Pres. Carlos J. Arosemena's friendship trip, July 1962.

Imperfs exist. Value $9.

Protection for The Family — A239

1963, July 9 Unwmk. *Perf. 14*

694 A239 10c ultra, red, gray & blk .25 .25

Social Insurance, 25th anniv. See No. C413.

No. 655 Ovptd. or Srchd. in Black or Blue

1963 Photo. *Perf. 13*
695 A230 10c on 80c dk car rose .25 .25
696 A230 20c on 80c dk car rose .25 .25
697 A230 50c on 80c dk car rose .25 .25
698 A230 60c on 80c dk car rose (Bl) .25 .25
699 A230 80c dk car rose .30 .25
Nos. 695-699 (5) 1.30 1.25

Nos. 661-669 Surcharged

1964, Apr. 20 Engr. *Perf. 11x11½*
700 A233 10c on 1s dk pur & redsh brn .40 .25
701 A233 10c on 1s dk pur & turq .40 .25
702 A233 20c on 1s dk bl & brn .40 .25
703 A233 20c on 1s dk bl & grn .40 .25
704 A233 30c on 1s dk pur & dk car rose .40 .25
705 A233 40c on 1s blk & ol bis .40 .25
706 A233 60c on 1s blk & red .40 .25
707 A233 80c on 1s dk bl & ultra .40 .25
708 A233 80c on 1s blk & vio .40 .25
Nos. 700-708 (9) 3.60 2.25

No. 656 Overprinted in Black or Light Ultramarine

1964 Litho. *Perf. 14x13*
709 A231 80c rose car & grn 4.50 1.25

Butterfly Type of 1961

Butterflies: Same as on Nos. 680, 682-683.

1964, June Litho. *Perf. 13½*
711 A236 20c brt grn & multi .75 .25
712 A236 50c sal pink & multi 1.50 .25
713 A236 80c lt red brn & multi 3.00 .25
Nos. 711-713 (3) 5.25 .75

Alliance for Progress Emblem, Agriculture and Industry A240

Designs: 50c, Emblem, gear wheels, mountain and seashore. 80c, Emblem, banana worker, fish, factory and ship.

1964, Aug. 26 Unwmk. *Perf. 12*
715 A240 40c bis brn & vio .25 .25
716 A240 50c red org & blk .25 .25
717 A240 80c bl & dk brn .40 .25
Nos. 715-717 (3) .90 .75

Issued to publicize the Alliance for Progress which aims to stimulate economic growth and raise living standards in Latin America.

No. 650 Overprinted in Red

1964 Photo. *Perf. 14x13½*
718 A229 1.80s dark blue 2.75 2.25

No. 656 Overprinted

1964, July Litho. *Perf. 14x13*
719 A231 80c block of 4 4.00 4.00

Organization of American States.

World Map and Banana Tree — A241

1964, Oct. 26 *Perf. 12½x12*
720 A241 50c dk brn, gray & gray ol .30 .25
721 A241 80c blk, org & gray ol .30 .25

Issued to publicize the Banana Conference, Oct.-Nov. 1964. See Nos. C427-C428a.

King Philip II of Spain and Map of Upper Amazon River A242

Designs (Map and): 20c, Juan de Salinas de Loyola. 30c, Hernando de Santillan.

1964, Dec. 6 Litho. *Perf. 13½*
722 A242 10c rose, blk & buff .30 .25
723 A242 20c bl grn, blk & buff .30 .25
724 A242 30c bl, blk & buff .30 .25
Nos. 722-724 (3) .90 .75

4th centenary of the establishment of the Royal High Court in Quito.

Pole Vaulting A243

1964, Dec. 16 *Perf. 14x13½*
725 A243 80c vio bl, yel grn & brn .35 .25

18th Olympic Games, Tokyo, Oct. 10-25. See Nos. C432-C434.

Peter Fleming and Two-toed Sloth — A244

Designs: 20c, James Elliot and armadillo. 30c, T. Edward McCully, Jr., and squirrel. 40c, Roger Youderian and deer. 60c, Nathaniel (Nate) Saint and plane over Napo River.

1965 Unwmk. *Perf. 13½*
726 A244 20c emerald & multi 1.00 .25
727 A244 30c yellow & multi 1.00 .25
728 A244 40c lilac & multi 1.00 .25
729 A244 60c multi 1.00 .25
730 A244 80c multi 1.00 .25
Nos. 726-730 (5) 5.00 1.25

Issued in memory of five American Protestant missionaries, killed by the Auca Indians, 1/8/56.

Issue dates: 80c, May 11; others, July 8.

Juan B. Vázquez and Benigno Malo College — A245

1965, June 6 Litho. *Perf. 14*
731 A245 20c blk, yel & vio bl .25 .25
732 A245 60c blk, red, yel & vio bl .25 .25
733 A245 80c blk, emer, yel & vio bl .25 .25
Nos. 731-733 (3) .75 .75

Centenary (in 1964) of the founding of Benigno Malo National College.

National Anthem, Juan Leon Mera and Antonio Neumane A246

1965, Aug. 10 Litho. *Perf. 13½*
734 A246 50c pink & blk .25 .25
735 A246 80c lt grn & blk .35 .25
736 A246 5s bis & blk .80 .35
737 A246 10s lt ultra & blk 1.40 .90
Nos. 734-737 (4) 2.80 1.75

Cent. of the national anthem. The name of the poet Juan Leon Mera is misspelled on the stamps.

For surcharges see Nos. 766C, 766H.

Torch and Athletes (Shot Put, Discus, Javelin and Hammer Throw) — A247

50c, 1s, Runners. 60c, 1.50s, Soccer.

1965, Nov. 20 *Perf. 12x12½*
738 A247 40c org, gold, & blk .25 .25
739 A247 50c org ver, gold & blk .25 .25
740 A247 60c bl, gold & blk .25 .25
741 A247 80c brt yel grn, gold & blk .45 .25
742 A247 1s lt vio, gold & blk .45 .25
743 A247 1.50s brt pink, gold & blk .75 .50
Nos. 738-743,C435-C440 (12) 6.25 3.75

Issued to publicize the 5th Bolivarian Games, held at Guayaquil and Quito.

For surcharges see Nos. 766B, 766D, C449.

Stamps of 1865 A248

1965, Dec. 30 Litho. *Perf. 13½*
Stamps of 1865 in Yellow, Ultramarine & Green
744 A248 80c rose red .35 .25
745 A248 1.30s rose lilac .40 .25
746 A248 2s chocolate .55 .25
747 A248 4s black .80 .25
a. Souv. sheet, #744-747, imperf. 4.00 4.00
Nos. 744-747 (4) 2.10 1.00

Cent. of Ecuadorian postage stamps.

The postal validity of some of the following sets has been questioned.

ITU Centenary — A248a

No. 748, Telstar. No. 748A, Syncom. No. 748B, Relay. No. 748C, Luna 3. No. 748D, Echo II. No. 748E, E. Branly, Marconi, Bell, E. Belin.

1966, Jan. 27 Litho. *Perf. 12x12½*
748 A248a 10c multi .25 .25
748A A248a 10c multi .25 .25
748B A248a 80c multi .25 .25
748C A248a 1.50s multi .40 .35
748D A248a 3s multi 2.00 1.25
f. Souv. sheet of 3, #748, 748B, 748D, perf. 14x12½ 15.00
748E A248a 4s multi 2.00 1.50
g. Souv. sheet of 3, #748A, 748C, 748E, perf. 14x12½ 15.00
Nos. 748-748E (6) 5.15 3.85

1.50s, 3s, 4s are airmail.

Nos. 748Df, 748Eg are printed on surface colored paper. Exist imperf. Value, each $18.

Space Exploration — A248b

10c, Edward White's space walk, June 8, 1965. 1s, Gemini 5, Aug. 21, 1965. 1.30s, Solar system. 2s, Charles Conrad, L. Gordon Cooper, Gemini 5, Aug. 21-29, 1965. 2.50s, Gemini 6. 3.50s, Alexei L. Leonov's space walk, Mar. 18, 1965.

1966, Jan. 27 *Perf. 12x12½*
749 A248b 10c multi .25 .25
749A A248b 1s multi .35 .25
749B A248b 1.30s multi .35 .25
749C A248b 2s multi 1.20 .65
749D A248b 2.50s multi 1.20 .65
749E A248b 3.50s multi 2.75 2.50
f. Souv. sheet of 3, #749, 749B, 749E, perf. 14x12½ 15.00 10.00
Nos. 749-749E (6) 6.10 4.55

1.30s, 2s, 2.50s, 3.50s are airmail.

No. 749Ef is printed on surface colored paper. Exists imperf. Value $15.

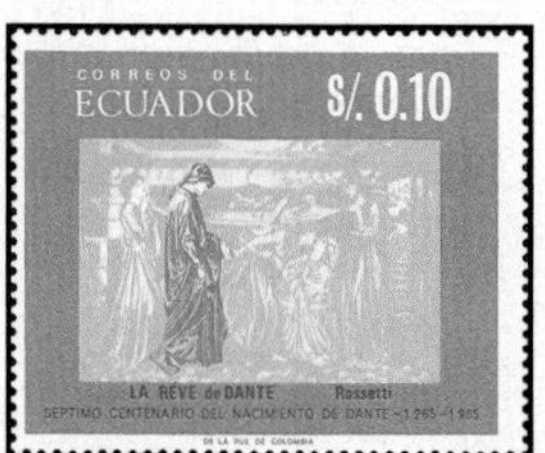

Dante's Dream by Rossetti — A248c

Designs: 80c, Dante and Beatrix by Holliday. 2s, Galileo Galilei, 400th birth cent., vert. 3s, Dante, 700th birth cent., vert.

1966, June *Perf. 13½x14, 14x13½*
750 A248c 10c multicolored .25 .25
750A A248c 80c multicolored .25 .25
750B A248c 2s multicolored 2.40 1.50

750C	A248c	3s multicolored	2.50	1.60
d.		Souv. sheet of 3, #750, 750A, 750C, perf. 12x12½	18.00	18.00
		Nos. 750-750C (4)	5.40	3.60

Nos. 750A-750B are airmail. No. 750Cd exists imperf. Value $18.

Pavonine Quetzal — A249

Birds: 50c, Blue-crowned motmot. 60c, Paradise tanager. 80c, Wire-tailed manakin.

1966, June 17 Litho. *Perf. 13½*

Birds in Natural Colors

751	A249	40c dl rose & blk	1.60	.25
751A	A249	50c sal & blk	1.60	.25
751B	A249	60c lt ocher & blk	1.60	.25
751C	A249	80c lt bl & blk	1.60	.25
		Nos. 751-751C,C441-C448 (12)	31.70	6.25

For surcharges see Nos. 766E-766F, C450, C455-C457.

Pope Paul VI — A249a

Pope Paul VI and: 1.30s, Nativity. 3.50s, Virgin of Merced.

1966, June 24 *Perf. 12½x12*

752	A249a	10c multicolored	.25	.25
752A	A249a	1.30s multicolored	.75	.35
752B	A249a	3.50s multicolored	2.25	.75
c.		Souv. sheet of 3, #752, perf. 14x13½, 752A-752B, perf. 12½x12	15.00	15.00
		Nos. 752-752B (3)	3.25	1.35

Nos. 752A-752B are airmail.

No. 752Bc is printed on surface colored paper. Exists imperf. Value $18.

Sir Winston Churchill, (1874-1965) — A249b

Famous Men: 10c, Dag Hammarskjold, vert. 1.50s, Albert Schweitzer, vert. 2.50s, John F. Kennedy, vert. 4s, Churchill, Kennedy.

Perf. 14x13½, 13½x14

1966, June 24

753	A249b	10c vio bl, brn & blk	.25	.25
753A	A249b	1s ver, bl & blk	.35	.25
753B	A249b	1.50s brn, lil rose & blk	.80	.30
753C	A249b	2.50s ver, bl & blk	2.00	1.00
753D	A249b	4s bl, blk & brn	2.25	1.50
e.		Souv. sheet of 3, #753, 753B, 753D	27.50	27.50
		Nos. 753-753D (5)	5.65	3.30

Nos. 753C-753D are airmail.

No. 753De is printed on surface colored paper. 10c stamp is perf. 14x13½, 1.50s is perf. 14x13½x14x12, 4s is perf. 12x12½x13x12½. Exists imperf. Value $27.50.

History of Summer Olympics — A249c

No. 754, Long jump. No. 754A, Wrestling. No. 754B, Discus, javelin. No. 754C, Chariot racing. No. 754D, High jump. No. 754E, Discus.

1966, June 27 *Perf. 12x12½*

754	A249c	10c multi	.25	.25
754A	A249c	10c multi	.25	.25
754B	A249c	80c multi	.50	.25
754C	A249c	1.30s multi	1.25	.45
754D	A249c	3s multi	2.00	.90
f.		Souv. sheet of 3, #754, 754B, 754D	12.00	5.00
754E	A249c	3.50s multi	3.25	1.10
g.		Souv. sheet of 3, #754A, 754C, 754E	12.50	5.00
		Nos. 754-754E (6)	7.50	3.20

Nos. 754C-754D are airmail.

Nos. 754Df, 754Eg are printed on surface colored paper.

Nos. 754Df and 754Eg exist imperf. Value $13.50.

1968 Winter Olympics, Grenoble — A249d

Designs: 10c, Speedskating. 1s, Ice hockey. 1.50s, Ski jumping. 2s, Cross country skiing. 2.50s, Downhill skiing. 4s, Figure skating.

1966, June 27 *Perf. 14*

755	A249d	10c multi	.25	.25
755A	A249d	1s multi	.40	.25
755B	A249d	1.50s multi	.60	.30
755C	A249d	2s multi	1.20	.45
755D	A249d	2.50s multi	1.60	1.25
755E	A249d	4s multi	2.00	1.50
f.		Souv. sheet of 3, #755, 755B, 755E, perf. 14x13½	8.00	6.00
		Nos. 755-755E (6)	6.05	4.00

Nos. 755B-755E are airmail.

No. 755Ef is printed on surface colored paper. Exists imperf. Value same as perf.

French-American Cooperation in Space — A249e

Designs: 1.50s, French satellite D-1, Mt. Gros observatory, vert. 4s, John F. Kennedy, satellites.

1966 *Perf. 13½x14, 14x13½*

756	A249e	10c multicolored	.25	.25
756A	A249e	1.50s multicolored	1.60	1.10
756B	A249e	4s multicolored	3.75	2.25
c.		Sheet of 3, #756-756B	15.00	12.00
		Nos. 756-756B (3)	5.60	3.60

Nos. 756A-756B are airmail.

No. 756Bc exists imperf. Value same as perf.

Italian Space Program — A249n

Designs: 10c, San Marco satellite. 1.30s, San Marco satellite, diff. 3.50s, Leonardo da Vinci, Moon, and Johannes Kepler.

1966 Litho. Unwmk. *Perf. 14*

757	A249n	10c multi	.25	.25
757A	A249n	1.30s multi	.75	.45
757B	A249n	3.50s multi	2.00	1.10
c.		Souvenir sheet of 3, #757, 757A, 757B	12.00	8.00
		Nos. 757- (3)	3.00	1.80

Nos. 757A and 757B are airmail. No. 757Bc is printed on paper with a gray pattern, and exists imperforate on paper printed with a green pattern.

Moon Exploration A249f

Designs: 10c, Surveyor. 80c, Luna 10. 1s, Luna 9. 2s, Astronaut flight trainer. 2.50s, Ranger 7. 3s, Lunar Orbiter 1.

1966 *Perf. 14*

758	A249f	10c multi	.25	.25
758A	A249f	80c multi	.25	.25
758B	A249f	1s multi	.25	.25
758C	A249f	2s multi	.80	.45
758D	A249f	2.50s multi	1.00	.75
758E	A249f	3s multi	1.20	.90
f.		Sheet of 3, #758, 758A, 758E	12.00	6.00
		Nos. 758-758E (6)	3.75	2.85

Nos. 758C-758E are airmail. Stamps in No. 758Ef have colored pattern in border.

No. 758Ef exists imperf. Value same as perf.

1968 Summer Olympics, Mexico City — A249g

Paintings by Mexican artists: 10c, Wanderer by Diego Rivera. 1s, Workers by Jose Orozco. 1.30s, Pres. Juarez by Orozco. 2s, Mother and Child by David Siqueiros. 2.50s, Two Women by Rivera. 3.50s, New Democracy by Siqueiros.

1967, Mar. 13 *Perf. 14*

759	A249g	10c multicolored	.25	.25
759A	A249g	1s multicolored	.55	.25
759B	A249g	1.30s multicolored	.80	.30
759C	A249g	2s multicolored	1.00	.50
759D	A249g	2.50s multicolored	1.20	.90
759E	A249g	3.50s multicolored	2.25	1.75
f.		Sheet of 3, #759, 759B, 759E	15.00	
		Nos. 759-759E (6)	6.05	3.95

Nos. 759B-759E are airmail.

No. 759f is printed on surface colored paper that differs slightly from Nos. 759-759E. Exists imperf. Value same as perf.

1968 Summer Olympics, Mexico City — A249h

No. 760, Soccer. No. 760A, Hurdles. No. 760B, Track. No. 760C, Fencing. No. 760D, High jump. No. 760E, Swimming.

1967, Mar. 13

760	A249h	10c multi	.25	.25
760A	A249h	10c multi	.25	.25
760B	A249h	80c multi	.25	.25
760C	A249h	1.50s multi	.75	.30
760D	A249h	3s multi	1.50	1.00
f.		Souv. sheet of 3, #760A, 760B, 760D	15.00	7.50
760E	A249h	4s multi	3.25	1.50
g.		Souv. sheet of 3, #760, 760C, 760E	12.00	7.00
		Nos. 760-760E (6)	6.25	3.55

Nos. 760C-760E are airmail.

Nos. 760f-760g are printed on surface colored paper. Exist imperf. Value same as perf.

4th Natl. Eucharistic Congress A249i

Paintings: 10c, Madonna and Child by unknown artist. 60c, Holy Family by Rodriguez. 80c, Madonna and Child by Samaniego. 1s, Good Shepherd by Samaniego. 1.50s, Assumption of the Virgin by Vargas. 2s, Man in Prayer by Santiago.

10s, Chalice, eucharist, church, wheat.

1967, May 10

761	A249i	10c multicolored	.25	.25
761A	A249i	60c multicolored	.55	.30
761B	A249i	80c multicolored	.80	.30
761C	A249i	1s multicolored	.80	.50
761D	A249i	1.50s multicolored	1.50	.75
761E	A249i	2s multicolored	2.50	.75
		Nos. 761-761E (6)	6.40	2.85

Souvenir Sheet

761F	A249i	10s multi	6.50	6.50

Nos. 761D-761E are airmail. Frames and inscriptions vary greatly.

No. 761F exists imperf. with an orange margin color. Value, same.

Madonna and Child Enthroned by Guido Reni A249j

Paintings of the Madonna and Child by: 40c, van Hemesen. 50c, Memling. 1.30s, Durer. 2.50s, Raphael. 3s, Murillo.

1967, May 25 *Perf. 14x13½*

762	A249j	10c multicolored	.25	.25
762A	A249j	40c multicolored	.25	.25
762B	A249j	50c multicolored	.25	.25
762C	A249j	1.30s multicolored	.70	.30

762D A249j 2.50s multicolored 1.75 .95
762E A249j 3s multicolored 2.75 1.20
Nos. 762-762E (6) 5.95 3.20

Nos. 762C-762E are airmail.

Portrait of a Young Woman by Rogier van der Weyden A249k

Designs: 1s, Helene Fourment by Rubens. 1.50s, Venetian Woman by Durer. 2s, Lady Sheffield by Gainsborough. 2.50s, Suzon by Manet. 4s, Lady with a Unicorn by Raphael.

1967, Sept. 9 ***Perf. 14x13½***
763 A249k 10c multicolored .25 .25
763A A249k 1s multicolored .55 .30
763B A249k 1.50s multicolored 1.20 .50
763C A249k 2s multicolored 1.60 .65
763D A249k 2.50s multicolored 2.40 .80
763E A249k 4s multicolored 2.75 1.25
f. Sheet of 3, #763, 763B, 763E, perf. 14 12.00 8.00
Nos. 763-763E (6) 8.75 3.75

Nos. 763B-763E are airmail.
Stamps in No. 763f have colored pattern in border. Exists imperf. Value same as perf.

John F. Kennedy, 50th Birth Anniv. A249l

JFK and: No. 764A, Dag Hammarskjold. 80c, Pope Paul VI. 1.30s, Konrad Adenauer. 3s, Charles de Gaulle. 3.50s, Winston Churchill.

Perf. 14x13½, 13½x14
1967, Sept. 11
764 A249l 10c lil, brn & bl .25 .25
764A A249l 10c yel, brn & sky bl .25 .25
764B A249l 80c yel, brn & sal .25 .25
764C A249l 1.30s yel, brn & pink 2.00 .75
764D A249l 3s yel, brn & yel grn 2.90 1.25
764E A249l 3.50s yel, brn & bl 4.00 1.75
Nos. 764-764E (6) 9.65 4.50

Souvenir Sheets

764F Sheet of 3 16.00 8.00
h. like #764, 35x27mm
i. like #764B, 35x27mm
j. like #764D, 35x27mm
764G Sheet of 3 16.00 8.00
k. like #764A, 35x27mm
l. like #764C, 35x27mm
m. like #764E, 35x27mm

Nos. 764C-764E are airmail. Nos. 764A-764E horiz. Stamps in Nos. 764F-764G have colored pattern in border.
Nos. 764F and 764G exist imperf. Values same as perf.

Christmas — A249m

Designs: No. 765A, Children's procession. 40c, Candlelight procession. 50c, Children singing. 60c, Processional. 2.50s, Christmas celebration.

1967, Dec. 29 ***Perf. 13x14***
765 A249m 10c multi .40 .25
765A A249m 10c multi .40 .25
765B A249m 40c multi .40 .25
765C A249m 50c multi .40 .25
765D A249m 60c multi .40 .25
765E A249m 2.50s multi 11.00 9.75
Nos. 765-765E (6) 13.00 11.00

No. 765E is airmail. See Nos. 768-768F.

Various Surcharges on Issues of 1956-66

1967-68
766 AP72 30c on 1.10s (C337) .35 .25
766A AP66 40c on 1.70s (C292) .35 .25
766B A247 40c on 3.50s (C438) .35 .25
766C A246 50c on 5s ('68) .35 .25
766D A247 80c on 1.50s .40 .25
766E A249 80c on 2.50s (C445) .40 .25
766F A249 1s on 4s (C447) .50 .25
766G AP66 1.30s on 1.90s (C293) .65 .55
766H A246 2s on 10s ('68) .80 .25
Nos. 766-766H,C449-C450 (11) 4.95 3.15

The surcharge on Nos. 766B-766C, 766E and 766G-766H includes "Resello." The obliteration of old denomination and arrangement of surcharges differ on each stamp.

Bust of Peñaherrera, Central University, Quito — A250

50c, Law books. 80c, Open book, laurel, horiz.

Perf. 12x12½, 12½x12
1967, Dec. 29 **Litho.**
767 A250 50c brt grn & blk .25 .25
767A A250 60c rose & blk .25 .25
767B A250 80c rose lil & blk .25 .25
Nos. 767-767B,C451-C452 (5) 1.35 1.25

Cent. (in 1964) of the birth of Dr. Victor Manuel Peñaherrera (1864-1932), author of the civil and criminal codes of Ecuador.

Christmas Type of 1967

Native Christian Art: 10c, Mourning of the Death of Christ, by Manuel Chili. 80c, Ascension of the Holy Virgin, vert. 1s, The Holy Virgin. 1.30s, Coronation of the Holy Virgin, by Bernardo Rodriguez, vert. 1.50s, Madonna and Child with the Heavenly Host, vert. 2s, Madonna and Child, by Manuel Samaniego, vert. 3s, Immaculate Conception, by Bernardo de Legranda, vert. 3.50s, Passion of Christ, by Chili, vert. 4s, The Holy Virgin of Quito, by de Legranda, vert.

1968 Jan. 19 ***Perf. 13½x14, 14x13½***
768 A249m 10c multi .25 .25
768A A249m 80c multi .25 .25
768B A249m 1s multi .25 .25
768C A249m 1.30s multi .25 .25
768D A249m 1.50s multi .50 .30
768E A249m 2s multi .80 .75
Nos. 768-768E (6) 2.30 2.05

Souvenir Sheet

Perf. 14

768F Sheet of 3 16.00 8.00
g. A249m 3s multicolored
h. A249m 3.50s multicolored
i. A249m 4s multicolored

Nos. 768C-768F are airmail. No. 768F exists imperf. Value same.

Tourism Year — A250a

20c, Woman from Otavalo. 30c, Colorado Indian. 40c, Petroglyph of a cat. 50c, Petroglyph of a mythological predator. 60c, Woman in a bazaar. 80c, 1s, 1.30s, Petroglyphs, diff. 1.50s, Colonial street, Quito. 2s, Amulet.

1968, Apr. 1 ***Perf. 13½x14***
769 A250a 20c multicolored .25 .25
769A A250a 30c multicolored .25 .25
769B A250a 40c multicolored .25 .25
769C A250a 50c multicolored .25 .25
769D A250a 60c multicolored .25 .25
769E A250a 80c multicolored .25 .25
769F A250a 1s multicolored .30 .25
769G A250a 1.30s multicolored .25 .25
769H A250a 1.50s multicolored .30 .25
769I A250a 2s multicolored .35 .25
Nos. 769-769I (10) 2.70 2.50

Eleventh Congress of the Confederation of Latin American Tourist Organizations (COTAL). Nos. 769G-769I are airmail.

Otto Arosemena Gomez — A251

Design: 1s, Page from the Constitution.

1968, May 9 **Litho.** ***Perf. 13½x14***
770 A251 80c lil & multi .25 .25
770A A251 1s multi .25 .25
Nos. 770-770A,C453-C454 (4) 1.05 1.00

First anniversary of the administration of Pres. Otto Arosemena Gomez.

Lions Emblem — A252

1968, May 24 **Litho.** ***Perf. 13½x14***
771 A252 80c multi .25 .25
771A A252 1.30s multi .25 .25
771B A252 2s pink & multi .30 .25
c. Souvenir sheet of 1 4.75 4.75
Nos. 771-771B (3) .80 .75

50th anniv. (in 1967) of Lions Intl.
No. 771c contains one 5s 39x49mm stamp. Exists imperf. Value same as perf.

Pope Paul VI, Visit to Latin America — A252a

39th Intl. Eucharistic Congress, Bogota, Colombia A252b

60c, Pope Paul VI, vert. 1s, Madonna by Botticelli. 1.30s, Pope Paul VI with flags of South American nations. 2s, Madonna and Child by Durer.

1969 ***Perf. 13½x14, 14x13½***
772 A252a 40c multicolored .25 .25
772A A252a 60c multicolored .35 .25
772B A252b 1s multicolored 1.10 .30
772C A252a 1.30s multicolored .80 .40
e. Souv. sheet of 3, #772, 772A, 772C, imperf. 4.00 2.50
772D A252b 2s multicolored 1.75 .75
f. Souv. sheet of 2, #772B, 772D, imperf. 4.75 2.50
Nos. 772-772D (5) 4.25 1.95

Nos. 772C-772D are airmail. Nos. 772-772f overprinted in silver with the national coat of arms.

Madonna with the Angel by Rogier van der Weyden A252c

Paintings by various artists showing the life of the Virgin Mary: 40c, Annunciation of the Lord, by van der Weyden. 60c, Presentation of the Lord, by van der Weyden. 1s, Holy Family, by Raphael. 1.30s, Adoration of the Shepherds, by Bonifazio Veronese. 2s, Adoration of the Magi, by van der Weyden

1969 ***Perf. 14x13½, 13½x14***
773 A252c 40c shown .25 .25
773A A252c 60c multi .25 .25
773B A252c 1s multi .35 .25
773C A252c 1.30s multi 1.25 .65
e. Souv. sheet of 2, #773B-773C, imperf. 5.75 2.50
773D A252c 2s multi 2.00 .80
f. Souv. sheet of 3, #773-773A, 773D, imperf. 5.75 2.50
Nos. 773-773D (5) 4.10 2.20

Nos. 773-773Df overprinted in silver with the national coat of arms. Sizing of No. 773Df stamps, side stamps are 25mm x 50mm; center stamp is 54.5mm x 50mm. Nos. 773C-773D are airmail.

Nos. C331 and C326 Surcharged in Violet and Dark Blue

a

b

1969, Jan. 10 ***Perf. 11½, 14x13½***
774 AP79 (a) 40c on 1.30s (V) .55 .25
774A AP76 (b) 50c on 1.30s (DBl) .55 .25

Types of 1958

No. 775 & 775B Srchd. and Ovptd. in Plum and Black

No. 775A Srchd. and Ovptd. in Plum and Black

No. 775C Overprinted in Red & Black

Design: Ignacio Luis Arcaya, Foreign Minister of Venezuela.

1969, Mar. Litho. *Perf. 12*
Flags in Red, Blue and Yellow

775 A223 50c on 2s sepia .30 .25
775A A223 80c on 2s sepia .30 .25
775B A223 1s on 2s sepia .30 .25
775C A223 2s sepia .30 .25
Nos. 775-775C,C455-C457 (7) 2.70 1.75

Nos. 775-775C were not issued without overprint. The obliteration of old denomination on No. 775A is a small square around a star. Overprint is plum, except for the black small coat of arms on right flag.

Map of Ecuador and Oriental Region — A253

Surcharge typographed in Dark Blue, Red Brown, Black or Lilac

1969 Litho. *Perf. 14*

776 A253 20c on 30c (DBl) .35 .25
776A A253 40c on 30c (RBr) .35 .25
777 A253 50c on 30c (DBl) .35 .25
778 A253 60c on 30c (DBl) .35 .25
778A A253 60c on 30c (Bk) .40 .40
778B A253 80c on 30c (DBl) — 20.00
779 A253 80c on 30c (Bk) .35 .25
780 A253 1s on 30c (L) .35 .25
780A A253 1s on 30c (DBl) 1.20 .80
781 A253 1.30s on 30c (Bk) .50 .25
782 A253 1.50s on 30c (Bk) .50 .25
783 A253 2s on 30c (DBl) .65 .25
784 A253 3s on 30c (DBl) .75 .25
784A A253 4s on 30c (DBl) 2.00 2.00
785 A253 4s on 30c (Bk) .80 .25
786 A253 5s on 30c (Bk) 1.00 .35
Nos. 776-786 (16) 9.90 26.30

Not issued without surcharge.

M. L. King, John and Robert Kennedy — A254

1969-70 Typo. *Perf. 12½*

787 A254 4s blk, bl, grn & buff .50 .25

Perf. 13½

788 A254 4s blk, lt bl & grn ('70) .50 .25

In memory of John F. Kennedy, Robert F. Kennedy and Martin Luther King, Jr.

Thecla Coronata — A255

Butterflies: 20c, Papilio zabreus. 30c, Heliconius chestertoni. 40c, Papilio pausanias. 50c, Pereute leucodrosime. 60c, Metamorpha dido. 80c, Morpho cypris. 1s, Catagramma astarte.

1970 Litho. *Perf. 12½*

789 A255 10c buff & multi 3.25 .45
790 A255 20c lt grn & multi 3.25 .45
791 A255 30c pink & multi 3.25 .45
792 A255 40c lt bl & multi 3.25 .25
793 A255 50c gold & multi 3.25 .25
794 A255 60c salmon & multi 3.25 .25
795 A255 80c silver & multi 3.25 .25
796 A255 1s lt grn & multi 3.25 .25

Same, White Background

Perf. 13½

797 A255 10c multi 3.25 .45
798 A255 20c multi 3.25 .45
799 A255 30c multi 3.25 .45
800 A255 40c multi 3.25 .25
801 A255 50c multi 3.25 .25
802 A255 60c multi 3.25 .25
803 A255 80c multi 3.25 .25
804 A255 1s multi 3.25 .25
Nos. 789-804,C461-C464 (20) 66.00 6.20

Surcharged Revenue Stamps — A256

1970, June 16 Litho. *Perf. 14*
Red Surcharge

805 A256 1s on 1s light blue .25 .25
806 A256 1.30s on 1s light blue .25 .25
807 A256 1.50s on 1s light blue .30 .30
808 A256 2s on 1s light blue .35 .25
809 A256 5s on 1s light blue .75 .30
810 A256 10s on 1s light blue 1.50 .55
Nos. 805-810 (6) 3.40 1.90

Surcharged Revenue Stamps — A257

1970 Typo. *Perf. 12*
Black Surcharge

811 A257 60c on 1s violet .30 .25
812 A257 80c on 1s violet .30 .25
813 A257 1s on 1s violet .30 .25
814 A257 1.10s on 1s violet .30 .25
815 A257 1.30s on 1s violet .30 .25
816 A257 1.50s on 1s violet .35 .25
817 A257 2s on 1s violet .35 .25
818 A257 2.20s on 1s violet .40 .25
819 A257 3s on 1s violet .50 .25
Nos. 811-819 (9) 3.10 2.25

1970

820 A257 1.10s on 2s green .30 .25
821 A257 1.30s on 2s green .30 .25
822 A257 1.50s on 2s green .35 .25
823 A257 2s on 2s green .35 .25
824 A257 3.40s on 2s green .50 .25
825 A257 5s on 2s green .75 .25
826 A257 10s on 2s green 1.25 .25
827 A257 20s on 2s green 2.10 .70
828 A257 50s on 2s green 5.00 2.25
Nos. 820-828 (9) 10.90 4.70

1970

829 A257 3s on 5s blue .50 .25
830 A257 5s on 5s blue .65 .35
831 A257 10s on 40s orange 1.25 .65
Nos. 829-831 (3) 2.40 1.25

In the surcharge applied to Nos. 811-831, the word "POSTAL" is not locked into horizontal and vertical position relative to the "1970". On some stamps the "P" is directly below the numeral "1", on others the "O" is below the "1". The top of "POSTAL" can vary from 1mm-8mm from the bottom of the date.

Arms of Zamora Chinchipe — A258

Design: 1s, Arms and flag of Esmeraldas.

1971 Litho. *Perf. 10½*

832 A258 50c pale yel & multi .25 .25
833 A258 1s sal & multi .25 .25
Nos. 832-833,C465-C469 (7) 3.50 2.00

Flags of Ecuador and Chile — A259

1971, Sept. *Perf. 12½*

840 A259 1.30s blk & multi .25 .25
Nos. 840,C481-C482 (3) .75 .75

Visit of Pres. Salvador Allende of Chile, Aug. 24.

Ismael Pérez Pazmiño — A260

1971, Sept. 16 *Perf. 12x11½*

841 A260 1s grn & multi .25 .25
Nos. 841,C485-C486 (3) .85 .75

"El Universo," newspaper founded by Ismael Pérez Pazmiño, 50th anniv.

CARE Package — A261

1971-72 *Perf. 12½*

842 A261 30c lilac ('72) .25 .25
843 A261 40c emerald ('72) .25 .25
844 A261 50c blue .25 .25
845 A261 60c carmine .25 .25
846 A261 80c lt brn ('72) .25 .25
Nos. 842-846 (5) 1.25 1.25

25th anniversary of CARE, a US-Canadian Cooperative for American Relief Everywhere.

Flags of Ecuador and Argentina — A262

1972 *Perf. 11½*

847 A262 1s blk & multi .25 .25
Nos. 847,C491-C492 (3) 1.00 .80

Visit of Lt. Gen. Alejandro Agustin Lanusse, president of Argentina, Jan. 25.

Jesus Giving Keys to St. Peter, by Miguel de Santiago — A263

Ecuadorian Paintings: 1.10s, Virgin of Mercy, Quito School. 2s, Virgin Mary, by Manuel Samaniego.

1972, Apr. 24 Litho. *Perf. 14x13½*

848 A263 50c black & multi .25 .25
849 A263 1.10s black & multi .35 .30
850 A263 2s black & multi .55 .50
a. Souvenir sheet of 3 2.50 2.50
Nos. 848-850,C494-C495 (5) 2.60 1.95

No. 850a contains 3 imperf. stamps similar to Nos. 848-850.

1972, May 4

Ecuadorian Statues: 50c, Our Lady of Sorrow, by Caspicara. 1.10s, Nativity, Quito School, horiz. 2s, Virgin of Quito, anonymous.

851 A263 50c blk & multi .25 .25
852 A263 1.10s blk & multi .35 .35
853 A263 2s blk & multi .50 .50
a. Souv. sheet of 3 2.90 2.40
Nos. 851-853,C496-C497 (5) 2.45 2.00

Letters of "Ecuador" 3mm high on Nos. 851-853, 7mm high on Nos. 848-850. No. 853a contains 3 imperf. stamps similar to Nos. 851-853.

A264

Designs: 30c, Gen. Juan Ignacio Pareja. 40c, Juan José Flores. 50c, Leon de Febres Cordero. 60c, Ignacio Torres. 70c, Francisco de Paula Santander. 1s, José M. Cordova.

1972, May 24 *Perf. 12½*

854 A264 30c blue & multi .25 .25
855 A264 40c blue & multi .25 .25
856 A264 50c blue & multi .25 .25
857 A264 60c blue & multi .25 .25
858 A264 70c blue & multi .25 .25
859 A264 1s blue & multi .25 .25
Nos. 854-859,C498-C503 (12) 5.90 4.10

Sesquicentennial of the Battle of Pichincha and the liberation of Quito.

A265

Designs: 2s, Woman Wearing Poncho. 3s, Striped poncho. 5s, Embroidered poncho. 10s, Metal vase.

1972, July Photo. *Perf. 13*

860 A265 2s multicolored .25 .25
861 A265 3s multicolored .50 .25
862 A265 5s multicolored .65 .40
863 A265 10s dp blue & multi 1.40 .90
a. Souvenir sheet of 4 4.00 4.00
Nos. 860-863,C504-C507 (8) 5.75 3.60

Handicraft of Ecuador. No. 863a contains 4 imperf. stamps similar to Nos. 860-863.

Sucre Statue, Santo Domingo — A266

1.80s, San Agustin Convent. 2.30s, Plaza de la Independencia. 2.50s, Bolivar statue, La Alameda. 4.75s, Chapel door.

1972, Dec. 6 Litho. *Perf. 11½*

864 A266 1.20s yel & multi .25 .25
865 A266 1.80s yel & multi .25 .25
866 A266 2.30s yel & multi .30 .25
867 A266 2.50s yel & multi .45 .25
868 A266 4.75s yel & multi .60 .30
Nos. 864-868,C518-C524 (12) 6.00 3.95

Sesquicentennial of the Battle of Pichincha.

Radar Station — A267

1973, Apr. 5 **Wmk. 367**

869 A267 1s multicolored .35 .25

Inauguration of earth telecommunications station, Oct. 19, 1972.

Blue-footed Boobies A268

Designs: 40c, Blue-faced booby. 50c, Oyster-catcher. 60c, California sea lions. 70c, Galapagos giant tortoise. 1s, California sea lion.

Wmk. 367, Unwmkd. (#872)

1973 **Litho.** ***Perf. 11½x12***

870 A268 30c shown .55 .25
871 A268 40c multicolored .55 .25
872 A268 50c multicolored .55 .25
873 A268 60c multicolored 1.10 .25
874 A268 70c multicolored 1.25 .25
875 A268 1s multicolored 1.75 .25
Nos. 870-875,C527-C528 (8) 9.95 2.00

Elevation of Galapagos Islands to a province of Ecuador.

Issue dates: 50c, Oct. 3; others Aug. 16.

Black-chinned Mountain Tanager — A269

Birds of Ecuador: 2s, Moriche oriole. 3s, Toucan barbet, vert. 5s, Masked crimson tanager, vert. 10s, Blue-necked tanager, vert.

Perf. 11x11½, 11½x11

1973, Dec. 6 **Litho.** **Unwmk.**

876 A269 1s brick red & multi .65 .25
877 A269 2s lt blue & multi 1.10 .25
878 A269 3s lt green & multi 1.10 .25
879 A269 5s pale lilac & multi 2.40 .65
880 A269 10s pale yel grn & multi 4.75 1.40
Nos. 876-880 (5) 10.00 2.80

Two souvenir sheets exist: one contains 2 imperf. stamps similar to Nos. 876-877 with yellow margin and black inscription; the other 3 stamps similar to Nos. 878-880; gray margin and black inscription including "Aereo." Both sheets dated "1972." Size: 143x84mm. Value, each $9.

Marco T. Varea, Botanist — A270

Portraits: 60c, Pio Jaramillo Alvarado, writer. 70c, Prof. Luciano Andrade M. No. 883, Marco T. Varea, botanist. No. 884, Dr. Juan Modesto Carbo Noboa, medical researcher. No. 885, Alfredo J. Valenzuela. No. 886, Capt. Edmundo Chiriboga G. 1.20s, Francisco Campos R., scientist. 1.80s, Luis Vernaza Lazarte, philanthropist.

1974 **Unwmk.** ***Perf. 12x11½***

881 A270 60c crimson rose .35 .25
882 A270 70c lilac .35 .25
883 A270 1s ultra .25 .25
884 A270 1s orange .25 .25
885 A270 1s emerald .25 .25
886 A270 1s brown .25 .25
887 A270 1.20s apple green .35 .25
889 A270 1.80s lt blue .40 .25
Nos. 881-889 (8) 2.45 2.00

Arcade A271

Designs: 30c, Monastery, entrance. 40c, Church. 50c, View of Church through gate, vert. 60c, Chapel, vert. 70c, Church and cemetery, vert.

Perf. 11½x12, 12x11½

1975, Feb. 4 **Litho.**

896 A271 20c yellow & multi .30 .25
897 A271 30c yellow & multi .30 .25
898 A271 40c yellow & multi .30 .25
899 A271 50c yellow & multi .30 .25
900 A271 60c yellow & multi .30 .25
901 A271 70c yellow & multi .30 .25
Nos. 896-901 (6) 1.80 1.50

Colonial Monastery, Tilipulo, Cotopaxi Province.

Angel Polibio Chaves, Founder of Bolivar Province — A272

Portrait: No. 903, Emilio Estrada Ycaza (1916-1961), archeologist.

1975 **Litho.** ***Perf. 12x11½***

902 A272 80c violet bl & lt bl .25 .25
903 A272 80c vermilion & pink .25 .25

Issue dates: No. 902, 2/21; No. 903, 3/25.

R. Rodriguez Palacios and A. Duran Quintero — A273

1975, Apr. 1 **Litho.** ***Perf. 12x11½***

910 A273 1s multicolored .25 .25
Nos. 910,C547-C548 (3) .85 .75

Meeting of the Ministers for Public Works of Ecuador and Colombia, July 27, 1973.

"Woman of Action" — A274

Design: No. 912, "Woman of Peace."

1975, June

911 A274 1s yellow & multi .35 .25
912 A274 1s blue & multi .45 .25

International Women's Year 1975.

Planes, Soldier and Ship — A275

1975, July 9 ***Perf. 11½x12***

913 A275 2s multicolored .40 .25

3 years of Natl. Revolutionary Government.

Hurdling — A276

Designs: Modern sports drawn Inca style.

1975, Sept. 11 **Litho.** ***Perf. 11½***

914 A276 20c shown .50 .35
915 A276 20c Chess .50 .35
916 A276 30c Basketball .50 .35
917 A276 30c Boxing .50 .35
918 A276 40c Bicycling .50 .35
919 A276 40c Steeplechase .50 .35
920 A276 50c Soccer .50 .35
921 A276 50c Fencing .50 .35
922 A276 60c Golf .50 .35
923 A276 60c Vaulting .50 .35
924 A276 70c Judo (standing) .50 .35
925 A276 70c Wrestling .50 .35
926 A276 80c Swimming .50 .35
927 A276 80c Weight lifting .50 .35
928 A276 1s Table Tennis .50 .35
929 A276 1s Paddle ball .50 .35
Nos. 914-929,C554-C558 (21) 11.35 6.85

3rd Ecuadorian Games.

Genciana A277

Ecuadorian plants — 20c, Phragmipedium caudatum, vert. 40c, Bromeliaceae cactaceae, vert. 50c, Cochlioda vulcanica. 60c, Odontoglossum hallii. 80c, Pitahaya flowering cactus. 1s, Odontoglossum cirrhosum.

Perf. 12x11½, 11½x12

1975, Nov. 18 **Litho.**

930 A277 20c multicolored .25 .25
931 A277 30c shown .25 .25
932 A277 40c multicolored .35 .25
933 A277 50c multicolored .35 .25
934 A277 60c multicolored .45 .25
935 A277 80c multicolored .45 .25
936 A277 1s multicolored .75 .25
Nos. 930-936,C559-C563 (12) 7.20 3.95

Venus, Chorrera Culture — A278

Female Mask, Tolita Culture — A279

Designs: 30c, Venus, Valdivia Culture. 40c, Seated man, Chorrera Culture. 50c, Man with poncho, Panzaleo Culture (late). 60c, Mythical head, Cashaloma Culture. 80c, Musician, Tolita Culture. No. 943, Chief Priest, Mantefia Culture. No. 945, Ornament, Tolita Culture. No. 946, Angry mask, Tolita Culture.

1976, Feb. 12 **Litho.** ***Perf. 11½***

937 A278 20c multicolored .40 .25
938 A278 30c multicolored .40 .25
939 A278 40c multicolored .40 .25
940 A278 50c multicolored .40 .25
941 A278 60c multicolored .40 .25
942 A278 80c multicolored .40 .25
943 A278 1s multicolored .40 .25
944 A279 1s multicolored .40 .25
945 A279 1s multicolored .40 .25
946 A279 1s multicolored .40 .25
Nos. 937-946,C568-C572 (15) 7.65 4.35

Archaeological artifacts.

Strawberries A280

1976, Mar. 30

947 A280 1s blue & multi .35 .25
Nos. 947,C573-C574 (3) 1.55 .90

25th Flower and Fruit Festival, Ambato.

Carlos Amable Ortiz (1859-1937) A281

No. 949, Sixto Maria Duran (1875-1947). No. 950, Segundo Cueva Celi (1901-1969). No. 951, Cristobal Ojeda Davila (1910-1952). No. 952, Luis Alberto Valencia (1918-1970).

1976, Mar. 15 **Litho.** ***Perf. 11½***

948 A281 1s ver & multi .35 .25
949 A281 1s orange & multi .35 .25
950 A281 1s lt green & multi .35 .25
951 A281 1s blue & multi .35 .25
952 A281 1s lt brn & multi .35 .25
Nos. 948-952 (5) 1.75 1.25

Ecuadorian composers and musicians.

Institute Emblem A282

1977, Aug. 15 **Litho.** ***Perf. 11½x12***

953 A282 2s multicolored .35 .25

11th General Assembly of Pan-American Institute of Geography and History, Quito, Aug. 15-30. See Nos. C597-C597a.

Hands Holding Rotary Emblem A283

1977, Aug. 31 **Litho.** ***Perf. 12***

954 A283 1s multicolored .25 .25
955 A283 2s multicolored .45 .25

Souvenir Sheets

Imperf

956 A283 5s multicolored 1.25 1.25
957 A283 10s multicolored 1.50 1.50

Rotary Club of Guayaquil, 50th anniv.

José Peralta — A284

Design: 2.40s, Peralta statue.

1977 Litho. *Perf. 11½*
958 A284 1.80s multi .25 .25
959 A284 2.40s multi .25 .25
Nos. 958-959,C609 (3) .90 .75

José Peralta (1855-1937), writer.

Blue-faced Booby A285

Galapagos Birds: 1.80s, Red-footed booby. 2.40s, Blue-footed boobies. 3.40s, Gull. 4.40s, Galapagos hawk. 5.40s, Map of Galapagos Islands and boobies, vert.

Perf. 11½x12, 12x11½
1977, Nov. 29 Litho.
960 A285 1.20s multi .45 .25
961 A285 1.80s multi .60 .25
962 A285 2.40s multi 1.00 .25
963 A285 3.40s multi 1.40 .25
964 A285 4.40s multi 2.10 .30
965 A285 5.40s multi 2.75 .30
Nos. 960-965 (6) 8.30 1.60

Dr. Corral Moscoso Hospital, Cuenca A286

1978, Apr. 12 Litho. *Perf. 11½x12*
966 A286 3s multicolored .30 .25
Nos. 966,C613-C614 (3) 1.95 1.00

Inauguration (in 1977) of Dr. Vicente Corral Moscoso Regional Hospital, Cuenca.

Surveyor Plane over Ecuador — A287

1978, Apr. 12 Litho. *Perf. 11½*
967 A287 6s multicolored .75 .35
Nos. 967,C619-C620 (3) 3.60 2.65

Military Geographical Institute, 50th anniv.

Latin-American Lions Emblem — A288

1978, May 24
968 A288 3s multi .60 .25
969 A288 4.20s multi .90 .25
Nos. 968-969,C621-C623 (5) 5.65 2.40

7th meeting of Latin American Lions, Jan. 25-29.

70th Anniversary Emblem — A289

1978, Sept. Litho. *Perf. 11½*
970 A289 4.20s gray & multi .55 .30

70th anniversary of Filanbanco (Philanthropic Bank). See No. C626.

Goalmouth and Net — A290

Designs: 1.80s, "Gauchito" and Games emblem, vert. 4.40s, "Gauchito," vert.

1978, Nov. 1 Litho. *Perf. 12*
971 A290 1.20s multi .25 .25
972 A290 1.80s multi .25 .25
973 A290 4.40s multi .65 .25
Nos. 971-973,C627-C629 (6) 3.35 2.05

11th World Cup Soccer Championship, Argentina, June 1-25.

Symbols for Male and Female — A291

1979, Feb. 15 Litho. *Perf. 12x11½*
974 A291 3.40s multi .55 .30

Inter-American Women's Commission, 50th anniversary.

Emblem A292

1979, June 21 Litho. *Perf. 11½x12*
975 A292 4.40s multi .45 .30
976 A292 5.40s multi .55 .30

Ecuadorian Mortgage Bank, 16th anniv.

Street Scene, Quito — A293

Perf. 12x11½
1979, Aug. 3 Litho. Unwmk.
977 A293 3.40s multi .35 .25
Nos. 977,C651-C653 (4) 8.00 3.70

Natl. heritage: Quito & Galapagos Islands.

Jose Joaquin de Olmedo (1780-1847), Physician — A294

1980, Apr. 29 Litho. *Perf. 12x11½*
978 A294 3s multi .35 .25
979 A294 5s multi .55 .40
Nos. 978-979,C662 (3) 2.15 1.30

First Pres. of Free State of Guayaquil, 1820.

Chief Enriquillo, Dominican Republic — A295

Indo-American Tribal Chiefs: 3.40s, Guaycaypuro, Venezuela. No. 982, Abayuba, Uruguay. No. 983, Atlacatl, Salvador.

Wmk. 367, Unwmkd. (#981-983)
1980, May 12
980 A295 3s multi .60 .25
981 A295 3.40s multi .75 .30
982 A295 5s multi 1.50 .45
983 A295 5s multi 1.50 .45
Nos. 980-983,C663-C678 (20) 39.85 9.70

King Juan Carlos and Queen Sofia, Visit to Ecuador A296

Perf. 11½x12
1980, May 18 Unwmk.
984 A296 3.40s multi .55 .30

See No. C679.

Cofan Indian, Napo Province — A297

3.40s, Zuleta man, Imbabura. 5s, Chota woman, Imbabura.

1980, June 10 Litho. *Perf. 12x11½*
985 A297 3s shown .45 .25
986 A297 3.40s multicolored .45 .25
987 A297 5s multicolored .70 .30
Nos. 985-987,C681-C684 (7) 7.10 4.55

Basilica, Our Lady of Mercy Church, Quito A298

1980, July 7 Litho. *Perf. 11½*
988 A298 3.40s shown .45 .25
989 A298 3.40s Balcony .45 .25
989A A298 3.40s Dome and cupolas .45 .25

Sizes: 91x116mm, 116x91mm
Imperf
990 A298 5s multi 1.75 1.60
990A A298 5s multi, horiz. 1.75 1.60
990B A298 5s multi 1.75 1.60
Nos. 988-990B,C685-C691 (13) 15.60 10.05

Virgin of Mercy, patron saint of Ecuadorian armed forces. No. 990 contains designs of Nos. C686, C685, 989. No. 990A contains designs of Nos. C688, C691, C690. No. 990B contains designs of Nos. C689, C687, 989A, 988.

Olympic Torch and Rings — A299

Perf. 12x11½
1980, July 19 Wmk. 395
991 A299 5s multi .70 .25
992 A299 7.60s multi .80 .30
Nos. 991-992,C695-C696 (4) 3.65 2.05

Souvenir Sheet
Imperf
993 A299 30s multi 6.75 6.75

22nd Summer Olympic Games, Moscow, July 19-Aug. 3.
No. 993 contains vignettes in designs of Nos. 991 and C695.

Coronation of Virgin of Cisne, 50th Anniv. — A300

1980 Litho. *Perf. 11½*
994 A300 1.20s shown .25 .25
995 A300 3.40s Different statue .50 .30

J.J. Olmedo, Father de Velasco, Flags of Ecuador and Riobamba, Constitution A301

1980, Sept. 20 Litho. *Perf. 11½*
996 A301 3.40s multi .25 .25
997 A301 5s multi .70 .40
Nos. 996-997,C700-C701 (4) 2.60 1.35

Souvenir Sheet
Imperf
998 A301 30s multi 3.00 3.00

Constitutional Assembly of Riobamba sesquicentennial. No. 998 contains vignettes in designs of #996-997.

Young Indian Girl — A302

Perf. 12x11½
1980, Oct. 9 Litho. Wmk. 395
999 A302 1.20s multi .25 .25
1000 A302 3.40s multi .50 .25
Nos. 999-1000,C703-C704 (4) 2.85 1.45

Democratic government, 1st anniversary.

OPEC Emblem A303

1980, Nov. 8 *Perf. 11½x12*

1001 A303 3.40s multi .50 .25

20th anniversary of OPEC. See No. C706.

Decorative Hedges, Capitol Gardens, Carchi A304

1980, Nov. 21 *Perf. 13*

1002 A304 3s multi .45 .25
Nos. 1002,C707-C708 (3) 3.60 1.55

Carchi province centennial.

Cattleya Maxima A305

Orchids: 3s, Comparattia speciosa. 3.40s, Cattleya iricolor.

1980, Nov. 22 *Perf. 11½x12*

1003 A305 1.20s shown .75 .25
1004 A305 3s multicolored 1.00 .30
1005 A305 3.40s multicolored 1.10 .35
Nos. 1003-1005,C709-C712 (7) 21.60 5.20

Souvenir Sheet

Imperf

1006 A305 20s multi 14.00 10.00

No. 1006 contains vignettes in designs of Nos. 1003-1005.

Pope John Paul II and Children — A306

1980, Dec. 27 *Perf. 12*

1007 A306 3.40s multi .60 .30
Nos. 1007,C715-C716 (3) 2.85 1.40

Christmas and visit of Pope John Paul II.

Carlos and Jorge Mantilla Ortega, Editors of El Comercio — A307

El Comercio Newspaper, 75th Anniv.: 3.40s, Editors Cesar & Carlos Mantilla Jacome.

1981, Jan. 6

1008 A307 2s multi .30 .25
1009 A307 3.40s multi .50 .25

Soldier on Map of Ecuador A308

1981, Mar. 10 **Litho.** *Perf. 13*

1010 A308 3.40s shown .30 .25
1011 A308 3.40s Pres. Roldos .30 .25
a. Pair, #1010-1011 1.40 .90

National defense.

Theodore E. Gildred and Ecuador I A309

1981, Mar. 31 **Litho.** *Perf. 13*

1012 A309 2s lt bl & blk .35 .25

Ecuador-US flight, 50th anniv.

A310

1981, Apr. 10

1013 A310 2s multi .45 .25

Octavio Cordero Palacios (1870-1930), humanist.

Radio Station HCJB, 50th Anniv. — A311

1981 **Litho.** *Perf. 13*

1014 A311 2s multi .30 .30
Nos. 1014,C721-C722 (3) 3.30 1.85

Virgin of Dolorosa A312

1981, Apr. 30 **Litho.** *Perf. 12*

1015 A312 2s shown .30 .25
1016 A312 2s San Gabriel College Church .30 .25

Miracle of the painting of the Virgin of Dolorosa at San Gabriel College, 75th anniv.

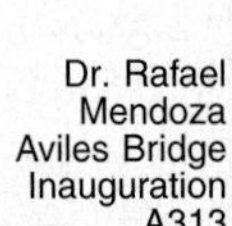

Dr. Rafael Mendoza Aviles Bridge Inauguration A313

1981, July 25 *Perf. 13*

1017 A313 2s multi .45 .25

Pablo Picasso (1881-1973), Painter — A313a

1981, Oct. 26 **Litho.** *Imperf.*

1017A A313a 20s multi 2.75 2.75
Nos. 1017A,C728-C731 (5) 9.30 7.50

No. 1017A contains design of No. C728, additional portrait.

World Food Day — A314

1981, Dec. 31 **Litho.** *Perf. 13½x13*

1018 A314 5s multi .60 .25

See No. C732

Transnave Shipping Co. 10th Anniv. — A315

1982, Jan. 21 **Litho.** *Perf. 13*

1019 A315 3.50s Freighter Isla Salango .60 .25

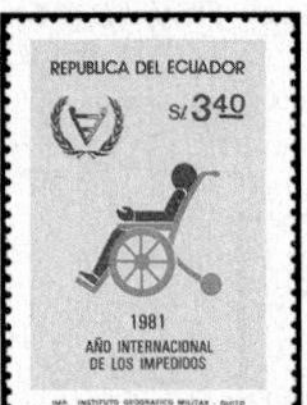

Intl. Year of the Disabled — A316

1982, Feb. 25

1020 A316 3.40s Man in wheel-chair .35 .25
Nos. 1020,C733-C734 (3) 1.95 1.10

Arch — A317

1982, May **Litho.** *Perf. 13*

1021 A317 2s shown .30 .25
1022 A317 3s Houses .45 .25

Miniature Sheet

Perf. 12½ on 2 Sides

1023 Sheet of 4, 18th cent. map of Quito 4.50 3.50
a.-d. A317 6s multi .90 .50

QUITEX '82, 4th Natl. Stamp Exhib., Quito, Apr. 16-22. No. 1023 contains 4 48x31mm stamps.

Juan Montalvo Birth Sesqui. — A318

1982 *Perf. 13*

1024 A318 2s Portrait .35 .25
1025 A318 3s Mausoleum .35 .25
Nos. 1024-1025,C735 (3) 1.95 1.15

American Air Forces Cooperation System — A319

1982

1026 A319 5s Emblem .55 .35

4th World Swimming Champ., Guayaquil A320

1982, July 30

1027 A320 1.80s Stadium .30 .25
1028 A320 3.40s Water polo .35 .25
Nos. 1027-1028,C736-C737 (4) 2.85 1.55

A321

1982, Dec. **Litho.** *Perf. 13*

1029 A321 5.40s shown .35 .25
1030 A321 6s Statue .45 .25

Juan L. Mera (1832-?), Writer, by Victor Mideros.

A322

1983, Mar. 28 **Litho.** *Perf. 13*

1031 A322 2s multi .45 .25

St. Teresa of Jesus of Avila (1515-82).

Sea Lions A323

Flamingoes A324

1983, June 17 Litho. *Perf. 13*

1032 A323 3s multi 1.40 .25
1033 A324 5s multi 2.25 .25

Ecuadorian rule over Galapagos Islds., sesqui. (3s); Charles Darwin (1809-1882).

Pres. Rocafuerte A325

Simon Bolivar A326

Perf. 13x13½

1983, Aug. 26 Litho. Wmk. 395

1034 A325 5s Statue .25 .25
1035 A325 20s Portrait .85 .35
1036 A326 20s Portrait .85 .35
Nos. 1034-1036 (3) 1.95 .95

Vicente Rocafuerte Bejarano, president, 1833-39 (Nos. 1034-1035).

A327

1983, Sept. 3

1037 A327 5s River .70 .25
1038 A327 10s Dam 1.10 .85

Size: 110x89mm

Imperf

1039 A327 20s Dam, river 3.50 2.50
Nos. 1037-1039 (3) 5.30 3.60

Paute hydroelectric plant opening. No. 1039 is airmail.

World Communication Year — A328

Wmk. 395

1983, Oct. 11 Litho. *Perf. 13*

1040 A328 2s multi .45 .30

World Communication Year.

A329

1983, Sept. Litho. *Perf. 13*

1041 A329 3s multi .45 .30

Cent. of Bolivar and El Oro Provinces (1984).

A330

1984, Mar. Litho. *Perf. 13*

1042 A330 15s Engraving .55 .45

Atahualpa (1497-1529), last Incan ruler.

A331

Christmas 1983 — A331a

Creche figures: No. 1043, Jesus & the teachers. No. 1044, Three kings. No. 1045, Holy Family. No. 1046, Priest.

Perf. 13½x13, 13x13½

1984, July 7 Litho.

1043 A331 5s multicolored .30 .25
1044 A331 5s multicolored .30 .25
1045 A331 5s multicolored .30 .25
1046 A331a 6s multicolored .30 .25
Nos. 1043-1046 (4) 1.20 1.00

Foreign Policy of Pres. Hurtado A332

State visits: 8s, Brazil. 9s, PRC. 24s, UN. 28s, USA. 29s, Venezuela. 37s, Latin American Economic Conf., Quito.

1984, July 10 *Perf. 13½x13*

1047 A332 8s multicolored .35 .25
1048 A332 9s multicolored .40 .25
1049 A332 24s multicolored 1.10 .75
1050 A332 28s multicolored 1.40 .80
1051 A332 29s multicolored 1.40 .80
1052 A332 37s multicolored 1.75 1.25
Nos. 1047-1052 (6) 6.40 4.10

Miguel Diaz Cueva (1884-1942), Lawyer A333

1984, Aug. 8 Litho. *Perf. 13½x13*

1053 A333 10s multicolored .75 .30

1984 Winter Olympics — A334

Designs: 2s, Emblem. 4s, Ice skating, right leg in air. 6s, Ice skating, left leg in air. 10s, Skiing. 20s, Figure skating.

Perf. 13x13½, 12x11½ (6s)

1984, Aug. 15

1054 A334 2s multi .35 .25
1055 A334 4s multi .35 .25
1056 A334 6s multi .35 .25
1057 A334 10s multi .65 .25
Nos. 1054-1057 (4) 1.70 1.00

Size: 90x100mm

Imperf

1057A A334 20s multi 40.00 17.50

No. 1057A is airmail.

Manned Flight Bicentenary A335

3s, Montgolfier. 6s, Charlier's balloon, Paris, 1789.
20s, Graf Zeppelin, Montgolfier.

1984, Aug. 15 *Perf. 13x13½*

1058 A335 3s multicolored .25 .25
1059 A335 6s multicolored .50 .25

Souvenir Sheet

1060 A335 20s multicolored 2.50 1.50

No. 1060 is airmail and contains one imperf. stamp (50x37mm).

SAN MATEO '83, Esmeraldas A336

8s, La Marimba folk dance. 15s, La Marimba, 8 dancers in white.

1984 Litho. *Perf. 13*

1061 A336 8s multi 1.75 .25

Size: 89x110mm

Imperf

1061A A336 15s multi 2.50 1.50

No. 1061A is airmail.

Jose Maria de Jesus Yerovi (b. 1824), 4th Archbishop of Quito — A337

1984

1062 A337 5s multi .45 .30

Canonization of Brother Miguel A338

Designs: 9s, Academy of Languages. 24s, Vatican City, vert. 28s, Home of Brother Miguel.

1984 Litho. *Perf. 13*

1063 A338 9s multi .35 .25
1064 A338 24s multi 1.00 .60

Imperf

Size: 110x90mm

1065 A338 28s multi 3.50 1.50
Nos. 1063-1065 (3) 4.85 2.35

No. 1065, airmail, has black control number.

State Visit of Pope John Paul II — A339

Designs: 1.60s, Papal arms. 5s, Blessing crowd. 9s, World map, itinerary. 28s, Pope waving. 29s, Portrait. 30s, Pope holding crosier.

1985, Jan. 23 Litho. *Perf. 13x13½*

1066 A339 1.60s multi .85 .25
1067 A339 5s multi .85 .25
1068 A339 9s multi .85 .25
1069 A339 28s multi 2.25 .40
1070 A339 29s multi 2.50 .40

Size: 90x109mm

Imperf

1071 A339 30s multi 8.00 6.00
Nos. 1066-1071 (6) 15.30 7.55

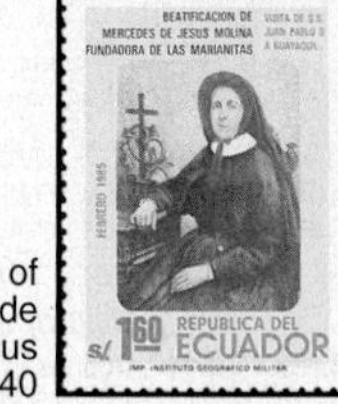

Beatification of Mercedes de Jesus Molina — A340

Paintings, sculpture: 1.60s, Portrait. 5s, Czestochowa Madonna. 9s, Alborada Madonna. 20s, Mercedes de Jesus, children.

1985, Jan. 23

1072 A340 1.60s multi .30 .25
1073 A340 5s multi .30 .25
1074 A340 9s multi .50 .25

Size: 90x110mm

Imperf

1075 A340 20s multi 3.00 3.00
Nos. 1072-1075 (4) 4.10 3.75

Visit of Pope John Paul II, birth bimillennium of the Virgin Mary.

Samuel Valarezo Delgado, Naturalist, Politician — A341

1985, Feb.

1076 A341 2s Bird .25 .25
1077 A341 3s Swordfish, tuna .25 .25
1078 A341 6s Portrait .40 .25
Nos. 1076-1078 (3) .90 .75

ESPANA '84, Madrid A342

Designs: 6s, Emblem. 10s, Spanish royal family. 15s, Retiro Park, exhibition site.

1985, Apr. 25 *Perf. 13½x13*

1079 A342 6s multi .30 .25
1080 A342 10s multi .50 .25

Size: 110x90mm

Imperf

1081 A342 15s multi 1.50 1.50

Dr. Pio Jaramillo Alvarado (1884-1968), Historian
A343

1985, May 17
1082 A343 6s multi .35 .25

Ingenio Valdez Sugar Refinery — A344

Designs: 50s, Sugar cane, emblem. 100s, Rafael Valdez Cervantes, founder.

1985, June **Litho.** ***Perf. 13***
1082A A344 50s multi 1.10 .50
1082B A344 100s multi 2.40 1.00

Size: 110x90mm

Imperf

1083 A344 30s multi 1.50 1.50
Nos. 1082A-1083 (3) 5.00 3.00

Chamber of Commerce, 10th Anniv.
A345

50s, Natl. and American Statues of Liberty.

1985, Aug. 15 ***Perf. 13½x13***
1084 A345 24s multicolored .80 .30
1085 A345 28s multicolored .90 .45

Size: 110x90mm

Imperf

1086 A345 50s multicolored 2.25 2.25
Nos. 1084-1086 (3) 3.95 3.00

Natl. Philatelic Assoc., AFE, 50th Anniv. — A346

1985, Aug. 25 ***Perf. 12***
1087 A346 25s AFE emblem .75 .45
1088 A346 30s No. 357, horiz. 1.10 .50

Guayaquil Fire Dept., 150th Anniv.
A347

6s, Steam fire pump, 1882. 10s, Fire Wagon, 1899. 20s, Anniv. emblem, natl. flag.

1985, Oct. 10 ***Perf. 13½x13***
1089 A347 6s multi .45 .25
1090 A347 10s multi .75 .25
1091 A347 20s multi 1.50 .75
Nos. 1089-1091 (3) 2.70 1.25

Natl. Infant Survival Campaign — A348

1985, Oct. ***Perf. 13x13½***
1092 A348 10s Boy, girl, tree .55 .30

1st Natl. Phil. Cong., Quito, Nov. 25-28 — A349

20th cent. illustrations, natl. cultural collection: 5s, Supreme Court, Quito, by J. M. Roura. 10s, Riobamba Cathedral, by O. Munaz. 15s, House of 100 Windows, by J. M. Roura, horiz. 20s, Rural cottage near Cuenca, by J. M. Roura.

No. 1097: a, Stampless cover, 1779, Riobamba. b, Hand press, 1864, Quito. c, Postrider, 1880, Cuenca. d, Monoplane, 1st airmail flight, 1919, Guayaquil.

1985, Nov. ***Perf. 13x13½, 13½x13***
1093 A349 5s multi .25 .25
1094 A349 10s multi .55 .25
1095 A349 15s multi .65 .40
1096 A349 20s multi .95 .50
Nos. 1093-1096 (4) 2.40 1.40

Souvenir Sheet

1097 Sheet of 4 1.25 1.25
a.-d. A349 5s, any single .25 .25

AFE, 50th anniv. No. 1097 contains 53x42mm stamps, perf. 13x12½ on 2 sides.

10th Bolivarian Games, Cuenca
A350

Designs: 10s, Boxing. 25s, Women's gymnastics. 30s, Discus.

1985, Nov. ***Perf. 13½x13***
1098 A350 10s multi .45 .25
1099 A350 25s multi .75 .30
1100 A350 30s multi .90 .45
Nos. 1098-1100 (3) 2.10 1.00

BAE Calderon, Navy Cent. — A351

Military anniv.: No. 1102, Fighter plane, Air Force 65th anniv. No. 1103, Army & paratroops emblems, Special Forces 30th anniv.

1985, Dec. ***Perf. 13x13½***
1101 A351 10s multi .50 .30
1102 A351 10s multi .50 .30
1103 A351 10s multi .50 .30
Nos. 1101-1103 (3) 1.50 .90

UN, 40th Anniv.
A352

1985, Oct. **Litho.** ***Perf. 13***
1104 A352 10s UN flag .50 .30
1105 A352 20s Natl. flag .50 .30

Size: 110x90mm

Imperf

1106 A352 50s UN Building 1.50 1.50
Nos. 1104-1106 (3) 2.50 2.10

No. 1106 is airmail.

Christmas — A353

Designs: 5s, Little girl riding donkey. 10s, Baked goods. 15s, Little boy riding donkey.

1985, Nov.
1107 A353 5s multicolored .25 .25
1108 A353 10s multicolored .50 .30
1109 A353 15s multicolored .70 .50

Size: 90x110mm

Imperf

1110 A353 30s like 5s 1.75 1.50
Nos. 1107-1110 (4) 3.20 2.55

Indigenous Flowers — A354

Designs: 24s, Embotrium grandiforum. 28s, Topobea sp. 29s, Befaria resinosa mutis.

1986, Feb.
1111 A354 24s multi 1.00 .30
1112 A354 28s multi 1.50 .30
1113 A354 29s multi 2.00 .40

Size: 110x90mm

Imperf

1114 A354 15s multi 6.50 3.50
Nos. 1111-1114 (4) 11.00 4.50

No. 1114 contains designs of Nos. 1111, 1113, 1112; black control number.

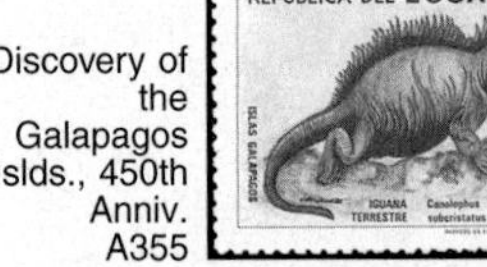

Discovery of the Galapagos Islds., 450th Anniv.
A355

Map of the Islands — A356

Designs: 10s, Land iguana. 20s, Sea lion. 30s, Frigate birds. 40s, Penguins. 50s, Giant tortoise. 100s, Charles Darwin. 200s, Bishop Tomas de Berlenga, discoverer.

1986, Feb. 12
1115 A355 10s multi .55 .30
1116 A355 20s multi 1.10 .65
1117 A355 30s multi 1.75 1.10
1118 A355 40s multi 2.25 1.50
1119 A355 50s multi 2.75 1.75
1120 A355 100s multi 5.50 3.75
1121 A355 200s multi 11.00 7.00

Perf. 12½ on 2 Sides

1122 A356 Sheet of 4 13.00 13.00
a.-d. 50s, any single 1.75 1.75
Nos. 1115-1122 (8) 37.90 29.05

No. 1122 contains 53x42mm stamps.

Inter-American Development Bank, 25th Anniv. — A357

5s, Antonio Ortiz Mena, pres. 1971-88. 10s, Felipe Herrera, pres. 1960-71. 50s, Emblem.

1986, Mar. 6
1123 A357 5s multicolored .45 .25
1124 A357 10s multicolored .65 .25
1125 A357 50s multicolored 1.25 .80
Nos. 1123-1125 (3) 2.35 1.30

Guayaquil Tennis Club, 75th Anniv.
A358

Designs: No. 1126, Emblem. No. 1127, Francisco Segura Cano, vert. No. 1128, Andres Gomez Santos, vert.

1986, Mar. 7
1126 A358 10s multicolored .55 .30
1127 A358 10s multicolored .55 .30
1128 A358 10s multicolored .55 .30
Nos. 1126-1128 (3) 1.65 .90

1986 World Cup Soccer Championships, Mexico — A359

1986, May 5
1129 A359 5s Shot .35 .25
1130 A359 10s Block .80 .25

An imperf. stamp exists picturing flags, player and emblem. Value $8.50.

Meeting of Presidents Cordero and Betancourt of Colombia, Feb. 1985
A360

1986 **Litho.** ***Perf. 13½x13***
1131 A360 20s Presidents .55 .30
1132 A360 20s Embracing .55 .30

Exports
A361

35s, No. 1137c, Shrimp. 40s, No. 1137b, Tuna. 45s, No. 1137a, Sardines. No. 1137d, MICIP emblem.

1986, Apr. 12
1133 A361 35s ultra & ver 1.10 .40
1134 A361 40s red & yel grn 1.10 .40
1135 A361 45s car & dk yel 1.25 .60

Perf. 12½ on 2 Sides

1137 Sheet of 4 2.50 2.50
a.-d. A361 10s, any single .40 .40
Nos. 1133-1137 (4) 5.95 3.90

No. 1137 contains 4 53x42mm stamps.

A362

La Condamine's First Geodesic Mission, 250th Anniv. — A363

Designs: 10s, La Condamine. 15s, Maldonado. 20s, Middle of the World, Quito.

No. 1141a, Triangulation map for determining equatorial meridian, 1736. No. 1141b, Partial map of the Maranon & Amazon Rivers, by Samuel Fritz, 1743-1744. No. 1141c, Base of measurement, Yaruqui plains. No. 1141d, Caraburo & Dyambaru Pyramids near Quito. No. 1141 has a continuous design.

1986, July 10 Litho. *Perf. 13½x13*

1138 A362 10s multicolored .45 .25
1139 A362 15s multicolored .55 .30
1140 A362 20s multicolored .65 .30
Nos. 1138-1140 (3) 1.65 .85

Souvenir Sheet

Perf. 12½ on 2 Sides

1141 A363 Sheet of 4 3.25 3.25
a.-d. 10s any single .45 .45

Chambers of Commerce A364

1986 Litho. *Perf. 13½x13*

1142 A364 10s Pichincha .35 .25
1143 A364 10s Cuenca .35 .25
1144 A364 10s Guayaquil .35 .25
Nos. 1142-1144 (3) 1.05 .75

Civil Service and Communications Ministry, 57th Anniv. — A365

Organization emblems: 5s, State railway. 10s, Post office. 15s, Communications. 20s, Ministry of Public Works.

1986, Dec. Litho. *Perf. 13x13½*

1145 A365 5s multicolored .25 .25
1146 A365 10s multicolored .35 .25
1147 A365 15s multicolored .65 .25
1148 A365 20s multicolored .75 .55
Nos. 1145-1148 (4) 2.00 1.30

A366

1987, Feb. 16 Litho. *Perf. 13x13½*

1149 A366 5s multi .45 .25

Chamber of Agriculture of the 1st Zone, 50th anniv.

Col. Luis Vargas Torres (d. 1887) — A367

Combat unit, c. 1885 — A367a

A367b

No. 1152a, Torres & his mother, Delfina. No. 1152b, Letter to Delfina written by Torres during imprisonment, 1882. No. 1152c, Arms of Ecuador & combat unit.

Litho. & Typo.

1988, Jan. 6 *Perf. 13*

1150 A367 50s yel grn, blk & gold 1.25 .80
1151 A367a 100s ver, gold & ultra 2.75 1.40

Size: 95x140mm

Perf. 12 on One or Two Sides

1152 A367b Block of 3 8.25 8.25
a.-c. 100s any single 1.50 1.50
Nos. 1150-1152 (3) 12.25 10.45

Sizes: Nos. 1152a, 1152c, 95x28mm, No. 1152b, 95x83mm.

Founding of Guayaquil, 450th Anniv. A368

15s, Street in Las Penas. 30s, Rafael Mendoza Aviles Bridge. 40s, Francisco de Orellana (c. 1490-1546), Spanish explorer, founder, & reenactment of landing, 1538.

1988, Feb. 19 Litho. *Perf. 13*

1153 A368 15s multi, vert. .30 .25
1154 A368 30s multi .55 .25
1155 A368 40s multi .65 .25
Nos. 1153-1155 (3) 1.50 .75

Social Security Foundation (IESS), 60th Anniv. A369

1988, Mar. 11

1156 A369 50s shown .90 .55
1157 A369 100s multi, diff. 1.90 1.10

Dr. Pedro Moncayo y Esparza (1807-1888), Author, Politician A370

Designs: 10s, Yaguarcocha Lake. 20s, Residence. 100s, Full-length portrait.

1988, Apr. 28 Litho. *Perf. 14x13½*

1158 A370 10s multicolored .25 .25
1159 A370 15s shown .35 .25
1160 A370 20s multicolored .35 .25

Size: 89x110mm

Imperf

1161 A370 100s multi 1.50 1.50
Nos. 1158-1161 (4) 2.45 2.25

A371

Avianca Airlines, 60th Anniv. — A372

10s, Junkers F-13. 20s, Dornier Wal seaplane. 30s, Ford 5AT trimotor. 40s, Boeing 247-D. 50s, Boeing 720-059B. 100s, Douglas DC-3. 200s, Boeing 727-200. 300s, Sikorsky S-38.

1988, May 12 Litho. *Perf. 14x13½*

1162 A371 10s shown .35 .25
1163 A371 20s multi .35 .25
1164 A371 30s multi .45 .25
1165 A371 40s multi .55 .25
1166 A371 50s multi .65 .45
1167 A371 100s multi 1.50 .60
1168 A371 200s multi 2.75 1.50
1169 A371 300s multi 4.75 2.00

Perf. 13½x14

1170 A372 500s shown 7.25 3.75
Nos. 1162-1170 (9) 18.60 9.30

San Gabriel College, 125th Anniv. A373

15s, Contemporary facility. 35s, College entrance, 19th cent.

1988, July 25 Litho. *Perf. 14x13½*

1171 A373 15s multicolored .25 .25
1172 A373 35s multicolored .75 .30

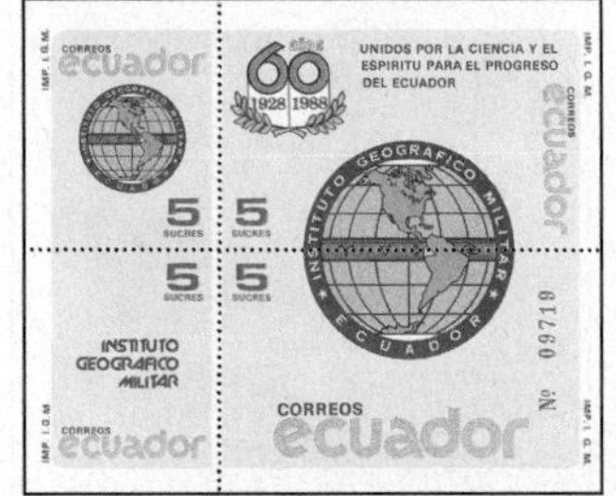

A374

Military Geographical Institute, 60th Anniv. A375

25s, Planetarium. 50s, Zeiss projector. 60s, Anniv. emblem. 500s, Creation, mural by E. Kingman.

1988, July 25 *Perf. 12½ on 2 Sides*

Size of No. 1173: 110x90mm

1173 A374 Block of 4 2.25 2.25
a.-d. 5s any single .30 .30

Perf. 13½

1174 A375 25s multi .55 .30
1175 A375 50s multi 1.00 .30
1176 A375 60s multi 1.25 .40
1177 A375 500s multi 7.75 3.75
Nos. 1173-1177 (5) 12.80 7.00

In 1996 Nos. 1174, 1183, 1265 were surcharged 800s, 2600s 400s respectively. Only a few sets were sold to the public. The balance were sold by postal employees at greatly inflated prices.

Salesian Brothers in Ecuador, Cent. A376

Designs: 10s, St. John Bosco (1815-88), vert. 50s, 1st Salesian Cong. in Ecuador. 100s, Bosco, Salesian Brothers monument and Andes Mountains.

1988, July 29 Litho. *Perf. 13½*

1178 A376 10s multi .25 .25
1179 A376 50s multi 1.00 .40

Size: 89x110mm

Imperf

1180 A376 100s multi 2.75 1.60
Nos. 1178-1180 (3) 4.00 2.25

Francisco Coello, Founder — A377

Social Services Council, Guayaquil, Cent. — A378

Designs: 20s, Eduardo Arosemena, 1st Director. 45s, Emblem.

No. 1184 — Flag: a, Emblem (upper left portion). b, Emblem (upper right portion). c, Emblem (lower left portion) and "100 ANOS." d, Emblem (lower right portion) and "DE TRADICION DE FE, AMPARO Y ESPERANZA."

1988, Nov. 24 Litho. *Perf. 13½x14*

1181 A377 15s shown .25 .25
1182 A377 20s multicolored .30 .25
1183 A377 45s multicolored .65 .25

Size: 110x90mm

Perf. 12½ on 2 Sides

1184 A378 Block of 4 1.75 1.75
a.-d. 10s any single .25 .25
Nos. 1181-1184 (4) 2.95 2.50

For surcharge see note following No. 1177.

A379

Azuay Bank, 75th Anniv. — A380

Perf. 14x13½, 13½x14

1989, Mar. 1 **Litho.**

1185 A379 20s shown .30 .25
1186 A379 40s multi, vert. .40 .25

Size: 90x110mm

Imperf

1187 A380 500s shown 11.00 2.75
Nos. 1185-1187 (3) 11.70 3.25

1988 Summer Olympics, Seoul — A381

Character trademark demonstrating sports.

1989, Mar. 20 ***Perf. 13½x14***

1188 A381 10s Running .30 .25
1189 A381 20s Boxing .30 .25
1190 A381 30s Cycling .50 .25
1191 A381 40s Shooting .50 .25
1192 A381 100s Diving 1.25 .65
1193 A381 200s Weight lifting 2.25 1.40
1194 A381 300s Tae kwon do 3.50 2.10

Size: 90x110mm

Imperf

1195 A381 200s Emblems 3.50 3.25
Nos. 1188-1195 (8) 12.10 8.40

RUMINAHUI '88 — A382

Designs: 50s, *Bird*, by Joaquin Tinta, vert. 70s, Matriz Church, Sangolqui. 300s, Monument to Ruminahui in Sangolqui, Pichincha.

Perf. 14x13½, 13½x14

1989, May 2 **Litho.** **Wmk. 395**

1196 A382 50s multi .90 .30
1197 A382 70s multi 1.25 .45

Size: 90x111mm

Imperf

1198 A382 300s multi 7.25 2.10
Nos. 1196-1198 (3) 9.40 2.85

Cantonization, 50th anniv.

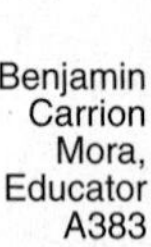

Benjamin Carrion Mora, Educator A383

50s, Portrait, vert. 70s, Loja landscape. 1000s, University. 200s, Portrait, diff.

Perf. 13½x14, 14x13½

1989, May 10 **Litho.**

1199 A383 50s multi .45 .25
1200 A383 70s multi .65 .25
1201 A383 1000s multi 10.50 5.25

Size: 110x90mm

Imperf

1202 A383 200s multi 2.00 2.00
Nos. 1199-1202 (4) 13.60 7.75

2nd Intl. Art Biennial A384

Prize-winning art: 40s, *The Gilded Frame*, by Myrna Baez. 70s, *Paraguay III*, by Carlos Colorabino, vert. 100s, Ordinance establishing the art exhibition. 180s, *Modulation 892*, by Julio Le Parc, vert.

Perf. 14x13½, 13½x14, Imperf. (100s)

1989, June 2 **Litho.**

Size of No. 1205: 110x90mm

1203 A384 40s multi .55 .25
1204 A384 70s multi 1.10 .25
1205 A384 100s multi 2.25 .75
1206 A384 180s multi 1.75 .95
Nos. 1203-1206 (4) 5.65 2.20

Guayaquil Chamber of Commerce, Cent. A385

50s, Founder Ignacio Molestina, vert. 200s, Flags. 300s, Headquarters. 500s, Flags, diff.

Perf. 13½x14, 14x13½, Imperf. (No. 1208)

1989, June 20 **Litho.**

Size of No. 1208: 110x91mm

1207 A385 50s multi .85 .35
1208 A385 200s multi 3.50 2.00
1209 A385 300s multi 2.50 2.25
1210 A385 500s multi 1.75 1.50
Nos. 1207-1210 (4) 8.60 6.10

French Revolution, Bicent. A386

20s, French natl. colors, anniv. emblem. 50s, Cathedral fresco. 100s, Rooster. 200s, Symbols of the revolution. 600s, Story board showing events of the revolution.

1989, July 11 ***Perf. 13½x14, 14x13½***

1211 A386 20s multi, vert. .25 .25
1212 A386 50s multi .55 .25
1213 A386 100s multi, vert. .90 .45

Size: 90x110mm

Imperf

1214 A386 200s multi, vert. 1.75 1.75
1215 A386 600s multi, vert. 6.75 6.75
Nos. 1211-1215 (5) 10.20 9.45

A387

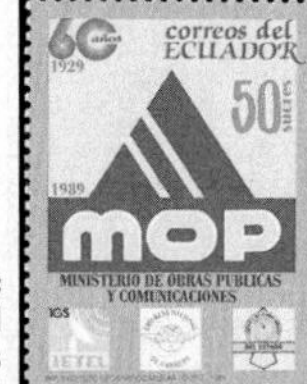

Ministry of Public Works and Communications A388

No. 1216a, MOP emblem, 2-lane roadway. No. 1216b, State railway emblem, train. No. 1216c, Postal service emblem, airmail cover. No. 1216d, Telecommunications (IETEL) emblem, wall telephone. No. 1217, MOP, IETEL, postal service & state railway emblems. 100s, IETEL emblem. 200s, MOP emblem.

1989, July 7 ***Perf. 12½ on 2 Sides***

1216 A387 Block of 4 2.00 2.00
a.-d. 50s any single .40 .40

Perf. 13½x14

1217 A388 50s shown .45 .25
1218 A388 100s multi .90 .55
1219 A388 200s multi 1.90 1.10
Nos. 1216-1219 (4) 5.25 3.90

MOP, 60th anniv.; national communications, 105th anniv. (No. 1216d, 100s).

A389

Designs: 10s, Medical volunteer, vert. 200s, Two volunteers.

1989, Sept. 14 **Litho.** ***Perf. 13½***

1220 A389 10s multi .25 .25
1221 A389 30s shown .25 .25
1222 A389 200s multi 2.00 .85
Nos. 1220-1222 (3) 2.50 1.35

Natl. Red Cross, Intl. Red Cross and Red Crescent Societies, 125th Annivs.

Juan Montalvo (1832-1889), Writer A390

Designs: 50s, Mausoleum, Ambato. 100s, Portrait (detail). No. 1225, Monument, Ambato. No. 1226, Portrait.

1989, Nov. 11 **Litho.** ***Perf. 14x13½***

1223 A390 50s multi .45 .25
1224 A390 100s multi 1.25 .65
1225 A390 200s multi 2.10 1.40

Size: 90x110mm

Imperf

1226 A390 200s multi 1.75 1.75
Nos. 1223-1226 (4) 5.55 4.05

America Issue A391

UPAE emblem and pre-Columbian pottery: 200s, La Tolita incensory, vert. 300s, Warrior (plate).

1990, Mar. 6 **Litho.** ***Perf. 13½***

1227 A391 200s multi 2.10 1.25
1228 A391 300s multi 3.25 2.00

Dated 1989.

Dr. Luis Carlos Jaramillo Leon, Founder A392

No. 1233a, Dr. Leon. Nos. 1230, 1233b, Federico Malo Andrade, honorary president. 130s, No. 1233c, Roberto Crespo Toral, 1st president. 200s, Alfonso Jaramillo Leon, founder.

1990, Jan. 17 **Litho.** ***Perf. 13½***

1229 A392 100s shown .90 .60
1230 A392 100s multicolored .90 .60
1231 A392 130s multicolored 1.25 .75
1232 A392 200s multicolored 1.75 1.25

Size: 91x38mm

Perf. 12½ Horiz. on 1 or 2 sides

1233 Block of 3 3.00 3.00
a.-c. A392 100s any single .50 .50
Nos. 1229-1233 (5) 7.80 6.20

Chamber of Commerce, 70th anniversary.

World Cup Soccer, Italy — A393

Designs: No. 1235, Soccer player. No. 1236, Map of Italy, trophy. No. 1237, Player, flags. No. 1238, World Cup Trophy.

1990, July 12 **Litho.** ***Perf. 13½***

1234 A393 100s shown .60 .25
1235 A393 200s multi 1.25 .60
1236 A393 300s multi 1.90 .90

Imperf

Size: 110x90mm

1237 A393 200s multi 1.75 1.75

Size: 60x90mm

1238 A393 300s multi 2.50 2.50
Nos. 1234-1238 (5) 8.00 6.00

Nos. 1235-1236, 1238 vert.

A394

Design: 200s, Church tower, book.

1990, June 12 ***Perf. 13½***

1239 A394 100s multi .70 .25
1240 A394 200s multi 1.25 .60

College of St. Mariana, cent.

A395

Tourism: No. 100s, No. 1244c, Iguana. 200s, No. 1244b, La Compania Church, Quito. 300s, No. 1244a, Old man from Vilcabamba. No. 1244d, Locomotive.

1990, Sept. 7 **Litho.** ***Perf. 13½***

1241 A395 100s multi .85 .25
1242 A395 200s multi, vert. 1.75 .55
1243 A395 300s multi 2.50 .75

Size: 111x90mm

Perf. 12½ on 2 sides

1244 Block of 4 7.50 3.25
a.-d. A395 100s any single .35 .25
Nos. 1241-1244 (4) 12.60 4.80

A396

National Census: 100s, No. 1248a, People and house. 200s, No. 1248b, Map. 300s, No. 1248c, Census breakdown, pencil.

1990, Sept. 1 *Perf. 13½*

1245	A396 100s multicolored	.60	.25
1246	A396 200s multi, horiz.	1.25	.55
1247	A396 300s multicolored	1.75	.75

Size: 109x88mm

Perf. 12½ on 2 sides

1248	Block of 3	1.90	1.90
a.-c.	A396 100s any single	.30	.30
	Nos. 1245-1248 (4)	5.50	3.45

A397

1990, Nov. 2 **Litho.** *Perf. 14*

1249	A397 200s Flags	1.25	.55
1250	A397 300s shown	1.90	.75

Organization of Petroleum Exporting Countries (OPEC), 30th anniv.

A398

Designs: No. 1251, Emblem. No. 1252, Four wooden parrots. No. 1253, Wooden parrots, diff.

1990, Oct. 31 *Perf. 13½x14*

1251	A398 200s multi	1.25	.55
1252	A398 300s multi	1.90	.75

Size: 92x110mm

Imperf

1253	A398 200s multi	2.10	2.10
	Nos. 1251-1253 (3)	5.25	3.40

Artisans' Organization, 25th anniv.

Flowers — A399

Wmk. 395

1990, Nov. 12 **Litho.** *Perf. 13½*

1254	A399 100s Sobralia	1.25	.25
1255	A399 100s Blakea, vert.	1.25	.25
1256	A399 100s Cattleya, vert.	1.25	.25
1257	A399 100s Loasa, vert.	1.25	.25
	Nos. 1254-1257 (4)	5.00	1.00

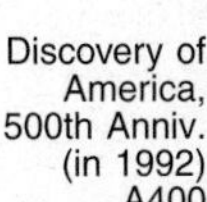

Discovery of America, 500th Anniv. (in 1992) A400

Designs: 100s, Ancient dwelling. 200s, Mangrove swamp.

1990, Dec. 31 **Litho.** *Perf. 13½*

1258	A400 100s multi	.70	.25
1259	A400 200s multi	1.60	.35

Natl. Union of Journalists, 50th Anniv. A401

Designs: 300s, Eugenio Espejo, writer. 400s, Union emblem.

1991, Feb. 28

1260	A401 200s shown	1.10	.70
1261	A401 300s multicolored	1.75	.80
1262	A401 400s multicolored	1.90	1.10
	Nos. 1260-1262 (3)	4.75	2.60

Radio Quito, 50th Anniv. A402

Designs: 200s, Man with microphone, vert. 500s, Family listening to radio.

1991, Apr. 10

1263	A402 200s multicolored	.85	.35
1264	A402 500s multicolored	1.75	.95

Dr. Pablo A. Suarez, Birth Cent. — A403

1991, Sept. 16 **Wmk. 395**

1265	A403 70s multicolored	.45	.25

Dated 1990.

For surcharge see note following No. 1177. Value $20.

America Issue A404

UPAEP emblem and: 200s, Columbus' ships. 500s, Columbus, landing in America.

1991, Oct. 18 **Litho.** *Perf. 13½x13*

1266	A404 200s multicolored	1.25	.65
1267	A404 500s multicolored	2.25	1.25

Cultural Artifacts — A405

Designs: 100s, Cat censer. 200s, Statue of old man's head. 300s, Zoomorphic statue.

Wmk. 395

1991, Nov. 14 **Litho.** *Perf. 13½*

1268	A405 100s multi	.50	.25
1269	A405 200s multi	1.00	.35
1270	A405 300s multi	1.75	.60
	Nos. 1268-1270 (3)	3.25	1.20

Dated 1990. See No. 1291.

A406

Design: 500s, Woman in profile.

1991 *Perf. 13*

1271	A406 300s shown	1.00	.55
1272	A406 500s multicolored	1.90	1.00

Day of Non-violence Toward Women.

Jacinto Jijon y Caamano, Archaeologist, Birth Cent. — A407

1991, Dec. 11 *Perf. 13½*

1273	A407 200s Portrait, vert.	.70	.35
1274	A407 300s shown	1.10	.55

Pres. Rodrigo Borja, Ecuador and Pres. Jaime Paz Zamora, Bolivia — A408

1991, Dec. 10 *Perf. 14x13½*

1275	A408 500s multicolored	2.00	1.00

Pres. Rodrigo Borja's Visit to the UN — A409

Designs: 1000s, Flags, world map.

Wmk. 395

1992, Jan. 24 **Litho.** *Perf. 14*

1276	A409 100s multicolored	.40	.25
1277	A409 1000s multicolored	3.00	1.60

Battle of Jambeli, 50th Anniv. — A410

No. 1278, Gunboat Calderon and Capt. Raphael Moran Valverde. No. 1279, Dispatch boat Atahualpa and Ens. Victor Naranjo Fiallo. No. 1280, Valverde, Fiallo and ships.

1992, Apr. 7

1278	A410 300s multicolored	.55	.40
1279	A410 500s multicolored	1.25	.90

Size: 110x90mm

Imperf

1280	A410 500s multicolored	2.75	2.40
	Nos. 1278-1280 (3)	4.55	3.70

Galapagos Islands Wildlife — A411

Designs: No. 1281, Giant tortoise. No. 1282, Galapagos penguin, vert. No. 1283, Zalophus californianus, vert. No. 1284, Swallow-tailed gull. No. 1285, Fregata minor. No. 1286, Land iguana.

1992, Apr. 9 **Litho.** *Perf. 13½*

1281	A411 100s multicolored	1.75	.80
1282	A411 100s multicolored	1.75	.80
1283	A411 100s multicolored	1.75	.80
1284	A411 100s multicolored	1.75	.80
1285	A411 100s multicolored	1.75	.80
1286	A411 100s multicolored	1.75	.80
	Nos. 1281-1286 (6)	10.50	4.80

Vicente Rocafuerte National College, 150th Anniv. (in 1991) A412

Designs: 400s, Vicente Rocafuerte.

Perf. 14x13½

1992, Apr. 29 **Litho.** **Wmk. 395**

1287	A412 200s shown	.85	.35
1288	A412 400s multicolored	1.40	.65

Eloy Alfaro (1842-1912), President — A413

Designs: 300s, Portrait, vert.

Perf. 13½x14, 14x13½

1992, Aug. 26 **Litho.** **Wmk. 395**

1289	A413 300s multicolored	.90	.70
1290	A413 700s multicolored	1.60	1.00

Cultural Artifacts Type of 1991

Designs: 400s, Ceremonial mask.

1992, Sept. 6 **Litho.** *Perf. 13½*

1291	A405 400s multi	1.40	.75

Dated 1990.

Discovery of America, 500th Anniv. A414

Designs: 200s, Sailing ship. 400s, Columbus, map, vert.

Wmk. 395

1992, Oct. 15 **Litho.** *Perf. 13½*

1292	A414 200s multi	.75	.50
1293	A414 400s multi	1.40	.85

Andres F. Cordova (b. 1892) A415

1992, Nov. 17 **Litho.** *Perf. 13½*

1294	A415 300s multicolored	1.10	.60

Beatification of Narcisa of Jesus — A416

1992, Nov. 30 *Perf. 13½*

1295	A416 100s multicolored	.45	.30

A417

Christmas: 300s, Infant Jesus of Saqueo, 18th cent. 600s, Stable scene, Infant Jesus asleep on hay.

1992, Dec. 14 ***Perf. 13½***
1296 A417 300s multicolored 1.10 .60
1297 A417 600s multicolored 1.90 1.25

A418

1992, Dec. 29
1298 A418 200s multicolored .80 .45

Father Juan de Velasco, Death Bicent.

Frogs — A419

No. 1299, Agalychnis spurelli. No. 1300, Atelopus bomolochos. No. 1301, Gastrotheca plumbea. No. 1302, Hyla picturata. No. 1303, Dendrobates sp. No. 1304, Sphaenorhyncus lacteus.

Perf. 13½x14
1993, Jan. 28 **Litho.** **Wmk. 395**
1299 A419 300s multi .85 .35
1300 A419 300s multi .85 .35
1301 A419 600s multi 2.00 .90
1302 A419 600s multi 2.00 .90
1303 A419 900s multi 2.75 1.40
1304 A419 900s multi 2.75 1.40
Nos. 1299-1304 (6) 11.20 5.30

A420

1993, Feb. 16 **Litho.** ***Perf. 13x13½***
1305 A420 300s blue .80 .25

J. Roberto Paez, (1893-1983), co-founder of social security.

Francisco Robles (1811-93) — A421

1993, Mar. 16 ***Perf. 13½x14***
1306 A421 500s No. 168 1.50 .55

National Police — A422

Perf. 13½x14
1993, Mar. 25 **Litho.** **Wmk. 395**
1307 A422 300s multicolored 1.00 .60

Pres. Jose Maria Velasco Ibarra (1893-1979) A423

Perf. 14x13½
1993, Mar. 31 **Litho.** **Wmk. 395**
1308 A423 500s multicolored 1.50 .55

Insects — A424

150s, Fulgora laternaria. 200s, Semiotus ligneus. 300s, Taeniotes pulverulenta. 400s, Danaus plexippus. 600s, Erotylus onagga. 700s, Xylocopa darwini.

Wmk. 395
1993, May 27 **Litho.** ***Perf. 13½***
1309 A424 150s multi .75 .25
1310 A424 200s multi 1.00 .25
1311 A424 300s multi 1.50 .45
1312 A424 400s multi 2.00 .60
1313 A424 600s multi 3.00 .95
1314 A424 700s multi 3.25 1.10
Nos. 1309-1314 (6) 11.50 3.60

A425

Wmk. 395
1993, May 31 **Litho.** ***Perf. 13½***
1315 A425 1000s multicolored 3.00 1.50

Pedro Fermin Cevallos Villacreces (1812-93), historian and founder of Academy of Language.

First Latin-American Children's Peace Assembly, Quito — A426

1993, June 7
1316 A426 300s multicolored .80 .45

Juan Benigno Vela Hervas (1843-97), Jurist A427

Perf. 13x13½
1993, July 8 **Litho.** **Wmk. 395**
1317 A427 2000s multicolored 5.00 3.00

Guillermo Bustamante, Birth Cent. A428

1993, Sept. 23 ***Perf. 13½***
1318 A428 1500s multicolored 4.00 1.75

University of Ecuador School of Medicine, 300th Anniv. A429

Perf. 14x13½
1993, Sept. 7 **Litho.** **Wmk. 395**
1319 A429 300s multicolored .80 .45

Maldonado-La Condamine Amazon Expedition, 250th Anniv. — A430

Designs: 150s, Cinchona cordifolia. 200s, Pedro V. Maldonado, 1500s, Charles La Condamine (1701-74), explorer.

1993, Aug. 20
1320 A430 150s multicolored .35 .25
1321 A430 200s multicolored .50 .25
1322 A430 1500s multicolored 4.25 2.10
Nos. 1320-1322 (3) 5.10 2.60

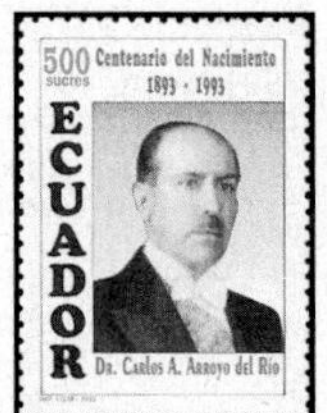

A431

Wmk. 395
1993, Nov. 27 **Litho.** ***Perf. 13***
1323 A431 500s multicolored 1.10 .55

Dr. Carlos A. Arroyo del Rio, birth cent.

Endangered Species — A432

400s, Dinomys branickii, horiz. 800s, Ara severa.

1993, Oct. 15 ***Perf. 13½x13, 13x13½***
1324 A432 400s multicolored 2.00 .60
1325 A432 800s multicolored 3.00 1.25

America issue.

Christmas A433

600s, Holy Family, 18th cent. Tagua miniatures. 900s, Mother and child, vert.

Wmk. 395
1993, Dec. 1 **Litho.** ***Perf. 13***
1326 A433 600s multicolored 1.40 .90
1327 A433 900s multicolored 2.25 1.40

Intl. Year of the Family — A434

Wmk. 395
1994, Jan. 18 **Litho.** ***Perf. 13***
1328 A434 300s grn, blk & org .40 .35

A435

1994, Jan. 25
1329 A435 500s multicolored 1.75 .90

Dr. Julio Tobar Donoso, birth cent.

Orchids — A436

No. 1330, Dracula hirtzii. No. 1331, Sobralia dichotoma. No. 1332, Encyclia pulcherrima. No. 1333, Lepanthes delhierroi. No. 1334, Masdevallia rosea. No. 1335, Telipogon andicola.

Wmk. 395
1994, Feb. 7 **Litho.** ***Perf. 13½***
1330 A436 150s multicolored .35 .25
1331 A436 150s multicolored .35 .25
1332 A436 300s multicolored .85 .40
1333 A436 300s multicolored .85 .40
1334 A436 600s multicolored 1.75 .90
1335 A436 600s multicolored 1.75 .90
Nos. 1330-1335 (6) 5.90 3.10

First Convention on the Conservation of Andean Orchids.

Federico Gonzalez Suarez (1844-1917) A437

1994, Apr. 12 ***Perf. 13***
1336 A437 200s multicolored .55 .25

Scouting in Ecuador — A438

1994, Jan. 11
1337 A438 400s multicolored 1.25 .60

Dr. Miguel Egas Cabezas (1823-94) A439

Wmk. 395

1994, Mar. 10 Litho. *Perf. 13*

1338 A439 100s multicolored .50 .25

Father Aurelio Espinosa, Birth Cent. — A440

1994, July 12

1339 A440 200s multicolored .70 .45

A441

Nos. 1341, 1343d, Mascot. 900s, Player. No. 1343: a, Emblem. b, "COPA MUNDIAL FUTBOL '94," emblem. c, "COPA MUNDIAL, USA 94."

Wmk. 395

1994, June 10 Litho. *Perf. 13*

1340 A441 300s shown 1.25 .60
1341 A441 600s Mascot 2.40 1.25
1342 A441 900s Soccer player 3.75 1.75

Perf. 12 on 2 Sides

1343 A441 600s Block of 4, #a.-d. 9.75 7.50
Nos. 1340-1343 (4) 17.15 11.10

1994 World Cup Soccer Championships, US. No. 1343 contains two 50x25mm stamps, two 50x51mm stamps.

Ecuador in Antarctica A442

1994, July 19 *Perf. 13*

1344 A442 600s Outpost 2.25 1.10
1345 A442 900s Ship, B/1 Orion 3.50 1.75

ILO, 75th Anniv. A443

1994 Litho. Wmk. 395 *Perf. 13*

1346 A443 100s multicolored .50 .25

Ecuadorian Culture Center, 50th Anniv. A444

700s, Benjamin Carrion, vert. 900s, Cultural center.

1994

1347 A444 700s multi 2.40 1.40
1348 A444 900s multi 3.50 1.60

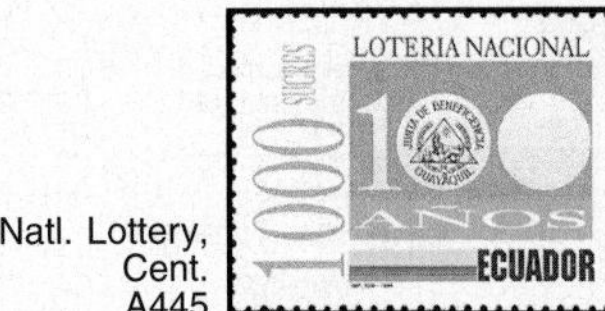

Natl. Lottery, Cent. A445

1994

1349 A445 1000s multicolored 3.75 1.75

Junior World Cycling Championships, Quito — A446

Design: No. 1351, Stylized cyclist, vert.

Wmk. 395

1994, June 22 Litho. *Perf. 13*

1350 A446 300s shown .75 .35
1351 A446 400s multi 1.00 .50

Postal Transportation A447

America Issue: No. 1352, Van, airplane, ship, horiz. No. 1353, Airplane, mail bag.

1994

1352 A447 600s multicolored .80 .40
1353 A447 600s multicolored 1.00 .50

Christmas — A448

No. 1354, Simulated stamp showing globe circled by envelope, horiz. No. 1355, Nativity.

1994

1354 A448 600s multicolored 1.10 .75
1355 A448 900s multicolored 1.60 .85

Juan Leon Mera, Death Cent.
A449 A450

Wmk. 395

1994, Dec. 21 Litho. *Perf. 13*

1356 A449 600s Mera's home 1.00 .65
1357 A450 900s multicolored 2.25 1.40

Gen. Antonio Jose de Sucre (1795-1830) — A451

Designs: 2000s, Portrait at right. 3000s, In military uniform.

Perf. 14x13½

1995, Mar. 14 Litho. Wmk. 395

1358 A451 1500s shown 3.75 1.75
1359 A451 2000s multi 5.00 2.50

Size: 80x105

Imperf

1360 A451 3000s multi 5.50 5.50
Nos. 1358-1360 (3) 14.25 9.75

Beatification of Josemaria Escriva, 3rd Anniv. — A452

1995, May 17 *Perf. 13x13½*

1361 A452 900s multicolored 1.50 .90

Gen. Eloy Alfaro (1842-1912), Alfarista Revolution, Cent. A453

1995, June 5 *Perf. 13½x13*

1362 A453 800s multicolored 1.40 .80

A454

Conflict Between Ecuador & Peru — A455

Designs: 200s, Soldier writing to children. 400s, Hand holding flag of Ecuador. 800s, Soldier in wilderness.

1995, July *Perf. 13½, 13 (#1364)*

1363 A454 200s multicolored .50 .25
1364 A455 400s multicolored 1.00 .45
1365 A454 800s multicolored 1.75 .90
Nos. 1363-1365 (3) 3.25 1.60

CARE, 50th Anniv. — A456

1995, July 14 *Perf. 13½*

1366 A456 400s Girl, vert. .60 .30
1367 A456 800s shown 1.75 1.00

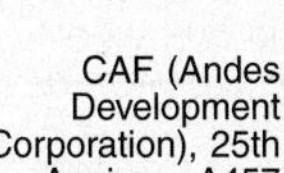

CAF (Andes Development Corporation), 25th Anniv. — A457

1995, Aug. 22 *Perf. 13*

1368 A457 1000s multicolored 3.00 1.25

Virgin of Cisne — A458

1995, Sept. 2 Litho. *Perf. 13*

1369 A458 500s multi .75 .50

A459

1995, Sept. 28

1370 A459 400s multicolored .85 .45

Natl. Institute of Children and Families (INNFA), 35th anniv.

UN, 50th Anniv. A460

Wmk. 395

1995, Oct. 6 Litho. *Perf. 13*

1371 A460 1000s bl, blk & bis 2.00 1.00

Intl. Decade for Natural Disaster Reduction A461

Civil defense emblem and: No. 1372, House surrounded by flood waters. No. 1373, Family leaving site of erupting volcano. No. 1374, People under table during earthquake. No. 1375, Couple planting seedlings on hillside. No. 1376, Man reading instruction booklet for natural disaster preparation.

1995, Oct. 11

1372 A461 1000s multicolored 2.00 1.00
1373 A461 1000s multicolored 2.00 1.00
1374 A461 1000s multicolored 2.00 1.00
1375 A461 1000s multicolored 2.00 1.00
1376 A461 1000s multicolored 2.00 1.00
Nos. 1372-1376 (5) 10.00 5.00

FAO, 50th Anniv. A462

1995, Oct. 16

1377 A462 1300s multicolored 2.75 1.50

Women's Culture Club, 50th Anniv. A463

1995, Oct. 20
1378 A463 1500s multicolored 2.75 1.50

29th Assembly of Inter-America Philatelic Federation, Quito — A464

1995, Nov. 11
1379 A464 1000s blue & red 1.75 1.00

A465

Christmas: 2000s, Santa, sleigh, reindeer on top of world. 2600s, Man on decorated horse, children.

Wmk. 395

1995, Dec. Litho. *Perf. 13*
1380 A465 2000s multicolored 5.00 2.40
1381 A465 2600s multicolored 6.00 2.40

A466

Indigenous Birds: No. 1382, Aglaiocercus kingi.

No. 1383: a, Coeligena torquata. b, Phaethornis superciliosus. c, Ocreatus underwoodii. d, Oreotrochilus chimborazo. e, Aglaiocercus coelestis.

1995, Dec.
1382 A466 1000s multicolored 2.25 .85
1383 A466 1000s Strip of 5, #a.-e. 11.25 6.25

Ecuadoran Air Force, 75th Anniv. A467

1995, Dec.
1384 A467 1000s multicolored 2.00 .95

Year of Folk Music — A468

2000s, Julio Jaramillo (1935-78), musician, composer. 3000s, Jaramillo, wall.

1996, Jan. 16 Litho. *Perf. 13*
1385 A468 2000s multicolored 3.75 2.00

Imperf

1386 A468 3000s multicolored 5.00 4.25

Advancement of Ecuador, 4 Year Program A469

Designs show symbols for: 1500s, Mail delivery. 2000s, Customs crossing. 2600s, Telecommunications. 3000p, Ports.

Wmk. 395

1996, July 23 Litho. *Perf. 13*
1387 A469 1000s multicolored 1.75 .80
1388 A469 1500s multicolored 2.75 1.25
1389 A469 2000s multicolored 3.25 1.75
1390 A469 2600s multicolored 4.50 1.90
a. Pair, #1388, #1390 8.00 8.00
b. Pair, #1389, #1390 8.50 8.50
1391 A469 3000s multicolored 5.50 3.00
a. Pair, #1387, #1391 8.00 8.00
b. Pair, #1389, #1391 9.50 9.50
Nos. 1387-1391 (5) 17.75 8.70
Nos. 1390a-1391b (4) 34.00 34.00

Nos. 1387-1391 were issued in strips of 2 each.

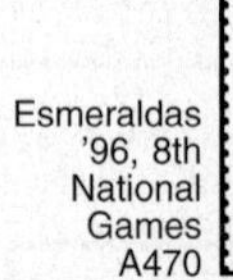

Esmeraldas '96, 8th National Games A470

Mascot depicting two sports on each stamp: No. 1392, Tennis, boxing. No. 1393, Basketball, socccer. 600s, Racketball, swimming. 800s, Weight lifting, karate. 1000s, Volleyball, gymnastics. 1200s, Athletics, judo. No. 1398, Chess, wrestling.

No. 1399, Mascot holding flag, emblem, surrounded by flags.

1996, July 30
1392 A470 400s multicolored .55 .25
1393 A470 400s multicolored .55 .25
1394 A470 600s multicolored .90 .45
a. Pair, #1392, #1394 1.50 1.50
1395 A470 800s multicolored 1.25 .60
a. Pair, #1394-1395 2.25 2.25
1396 A470 1000s multicolored 1.60 .75
a. Pair, #1393, #1396 2.40 2.40
b. Pair, #1395-1396 3.00 3.00
1397 A470 1200s multicolored 1.75 .95
1398 A470 2000s multicolored 3.25 1.40
Nos. 1392-1398 (7) 9.85 4.65
Nos. 1394a-1396b (4) 9.15 9.15

Size: 120x100mm

1399 A470 2000s multicolored 4.00 3.50

Nos. 1392-1396 were printed in strips of 2 each.

Civil Aviation, 50th Anniv. A471

1996, Aug. 8
1400 A471 2000s multicolored 3.00 1.25

1996 Summer Olympic Games, Atlanta A472

Atlanta Games emblem and: 1000s, Mascot carrying torch. No. 1402, Emblem of Olympic Committee of Ecuador. 3000s, Jefferson Perez, vert.

No. 1404, Perez, gold medalist, 20-kilometer walk, walking.

1996
1401 A472 1000s multicolored 2.00 .75
1402 A472 2000s multicolored 4.00 2.25
a. Pair, #1401-1402 6.00 6.00
1403 A472 3000s multicolored 5.00 2.50
Nos. 1401-1403 (3) 11.00 5.50

Size: 100x120mm

Imperf

1404 A472 2000s multicolored 4.50 3.50

Fight Against Drug Abuse — A473

1996 Litho. Wmk. 395 *Perf. 13*
1408 A473 2000s multicolored 4.00 2.00

Dr. Eduardo Salazar Gomez, Birth Cent. — A474

1996
1409 A474 1000s multicolored 2.50 1.25

Catholic University, Quito, 50th Anniv. — A475

Designs: 400s, Outside view of building, horiz. 800s, Entrance.

1996
1410 A475 400s multicolored .90 .45
1411 A475 800s multicolored 1.75 .85

Junior Chamber International A476

2000s, Children's faces, horiz.

1996
1412 A476 2000s multi 4.50 2.75
1413 A476 2600s shown 5.50 3.50

Catholic University, Quito, 50th Anniv. A477

1996, Nov.
1414 A477 2000s multicolored 4.00 2.00

The Universe Daily Newspaper, 75th Anniv. — A478

1996, Dec.
1415 A478 2000s multicolored 4.00 2.00

Private Technical University, Loja — A479

1996, Dec. 9
1416 A479 4700s multicolored 11.00 5.50

UNICEF, 50th Anniv. A480

1996, Dec. 11
1417 A480 2000s multicolored 4.50 2.25

Christmas A481

Children's paintings: 600s, Merry Chrismas All Over the World. 800s, World of Peace and Love. 2000s, Christmas.

1996, Dec. 19
1418 A481 600s multicolored 1.50 1.00
1419 A481 800s multicolored 2.00 1.25

Size: 51x31mm

Perf. 13½

1420 A481 2000s multicolored 5.00 2.50
Nos. 1418-1420 (3) 8.50 4.75

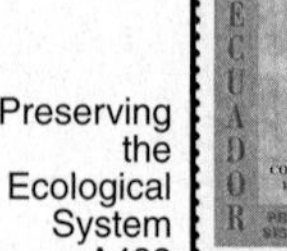

Preserving the Ecological System A482

America '95: 1000s, Voltur grypus. 1500s, Harpia harpyja, vert.

1996, Dec. 30 *Perf. 13*
1421 A482 1000s multicolored 2.50 1.50
1422 A482 1500s multicolored 3.75 2.00

Typical Children's Costumes — A483

America '96: No. 1423, "Bordando" girl, Zuleta. No. 1424, Girl from Otavalo.

1996, Dec. 30
1423 A483 2600s multicolored 5.00 1.75
1424 A483 2600s multicolored 5.00 4.25
a. Pair, #1423-1424 12.50 12.50

Mejia Natl. Institute, Cent. A484

Design: Jose Mejia Lequerica, building.

1997, Jan. 10

1425	A484	1000s multicolored	2.25	1.25

Army Polytechnical School, 75th Anniv. A485

Wmk. 395

1997, June 16 Typo. *Perf. 13*

1426	A485	400s multicolored	1.10	.75

Natl. Experimental College, Ambato, 50th Anniv. A486

1997, June 20

1427	A486	600s multicolored	1.50	1.00

Vicente Rocafuerte (1783-1847), First Constitutional President of Ecuador — A487

1997, July 1

1428	A487	400s multicolored	1.25	.75

49th Intl. Congress of the Americanists A488

1997, July 3

1429	A488	2000s multicolored	5.00	3.25

Butterflies A489

Designs: 400s, Actinote equatoria. 600s, Dismorphia amphione. 800s, Marpesia corinna. 2000s, Marpesia berania. 2600s, Morpho helenor.

1997, July 21

1430	A489	400s multicolored	1.25	.80
1431	A489	600s multicolored	1.50	1.00
1432	A489	800s multicolored	2.00	1.25
1433	A489	2000s multicolored	5.00	3.25
1434	A489	2600s multicolored	7.00	4.75
		Nos. 1430-1434 (5)	16.75	11.05

Air Club of Ecuador, 66th Anniv. A490

1997, July 23

1435	A490	2600s multicolored	6.00	3.00

Orchids — A491

400s, Epidendrum secundum. 600s, Epidendrum. 800s, Oncidium cultratrum. 2000s, Oncidium sp mariposa. 2600s, Pleurothalis corrulensis.

1997, Aug. 14 Litho. *Perf. 13*

1436	A491	400s multicolored	1.25	.80
1437	A491	600s multicolored	1.50	1.00
1438	A491	800s multicolored	2.00	1.25
1439	A491	2000s multicolored	5.00	3.25
1440	A491	2600s multicolored	7.00	4.75
		Nos. 1436-1440 (5)	16.75	11.05

Rocks and Minerals — A492

Designs: 400s, Quartz. 600s, Chalcopyrite. 800s, Gold. 2000s, Petrified wood. 2600s, Pyrite.

1997, Oct. 6 Litho. *Perf. 13*

1441	A492	400s multi	1.25	.80
1442	A492	600s multi	1.50	1.00
1443	A492	800s multi	2.00	1.25
1444	A492	2000s multi	5.00	3.25
1445	A492	2600s multi	7.00	4.75
		Nos. 1441-1445 (5)	16.75	11.05

A493

Christmas (Children's designs): 400s, Santa as postman delivering letters over world. 2600s, Star on Christmas tree reaching for letters, airplane under tree. 3000s, Child dreaming of angels carrying letters.

1997, Dec. 22 Litho. *Perf. 13*

1446	A493	400s multicolored	1.25	.80
1447	A493	2600s multicolored	7.00	4.75
1448	A493	3000s multicolored	8.25	5.50
		Nos. 1446-1448 (3)	16.50	11.05

America Issue — A494

Designs: 800s, Life of a Postman. 2000s, On bicycle.

1997, Dec. 29

1449	A494	800s multi	2.00	1.00
1450	A494	2000s multi	5.00	2.50

Intl. Women's Day — A495

Matilde Hidalgo de Procel (1889-1974), physician, social reformer.

1998, Mar. 6 Litho. *Perf. 13*

1451	A495	2000s multicolored	4.75	3.25

Dr. Misael Acosta Solis, Botanist — A496

Wmk. 395

1998, Apr. 22 Litho. *Perf. 13*

1452	A496	2000s multicolored	8.25	5.50

Organization of American States (OAS), 50th Anniv. A497

1998, Apr. 30

1453	A497	2600s multicolored	5.00	3.25

1998 World Cup Soccer Championships, France — A498

Designs: 2600s, Trophy, mascot, vert. 3000s, Two players, trophy.

1998, May

1454	A498	2000s multicolored	4.00	2.25
1455	A498	2600s multicolored	5.00	2.75
1456	A498	3000s multicolored	6.00	3.25
		Nos. 1454-1456 (3)	15.00	8.25

Flowers — A499

600s, Gypsophila paniculata. 800s, Banana flowers. 2000s, Roses. 2600s, Asters.

1998, June

1457	A499	600s multicolored	1.40	.60
1458	A499	800s multicolored	1.75	.90
1459	A499	2000s multicolored	4.00	2.25
1460	A499	2600s multicolored	5.00	2.75
		Nos. 1457-1460 (4)	12.15	6.50

Galapagos Flora — A500

Designs: 600s, Jasminocereus thouarsii. 1000s, Cordia lutea lamarck. 2600s, Momordica charantia.

1998, July

1461	A500	600s multicolored	1.10	.60
1462	A500	1000s multicolored	1.90	1.00
1463	A500	2600s multicolored	5.00	2.75
		Nos. 1461-1463 (3)	8.00	4.35

Tourism A501

Designs: 600s, St. Augustine Church, Quito. 800s, Monument to the Heroes of the Independence, Guayaquil. 2000s, Equator Monument, Quito. 2600s, Mojanda Lake.

1998, July

1464	A501	600s multi, vert.	1.25	.60
1465	A501	800s multi, vert.	1.50	.90
1466	A501	2000s multi	3.50	2.25
1467	A501	2600s multi	4.50	2.75
		Nos. 1464-1467 (4)	10.75	6.50

Emiliano Ortega Espinosa (1898-1974), Educator A502

Perf. 13¼x13, 13x13¼

1998 Litho. Wmk. 395

1468	A502	400s shown	.90	.50
1469	A502	4700s Portrait, vert.	11.00	8.25

Carlos Cueva Tamariz (1898-1991), Educator — A503

Perf. 13x13¼

1998, Nov. Litho. Wmk. 395

1470	A503	2600s multicolored	5.00	3.50

Radio Club of Guayaquil, 75th Anniv. — A504

Wmk. 395

1998, Nov. 20 Litho. *Perf. 13*

1471	A504	600s multicolored	1.25	.90

6th South American Games — A505

Designs: 400s, Mascot. 1000s, Games poster, tennis rackets, hurdles, sailing, hammer throw, bowling, boxing. 2600s, Mascot, parallel bars, wrestling, judo, fencing, running, swimming, shooting, cycling.

1998

1472	A505	400s multicolored	1.10	.50
1473	A505	1000s multicolored	1.90	1.00
1474	A505	2600s multicolored	5.00	2.75
		Nos. 1472-1474 (3)	8.00	4.25

Paintings by Eduardo Kingman (1913-85) A506

Designs: 600s, Ecuadoran Woman, vert. 800s, World Without Answers.

1998, Dec. 10

1475	A506	600s multicolored	1.25	.65
1476	A506	800s multicolored	1.90	1.00

Manuela Sáenz (1797-1856), Mistress of Simon Bolívar — A507

1999, Jan. 19

1477 A507 1000s multicolored 2.00 .95

America issue. Exists imperf.

Christmas A508

Children's drawings: 1000s, Santa posting letters on tree. 2600s, People holding up giant letter, vert. 3000s, Santas parachuting with letters, nativity scene, tree, vert.

1998, Dec. 22

1478 A508 1000s multicolored 1.75 .95
1479 A508 2600s multicolored 4.50 2.50
1480 A508 3000s multicolored 5.00 2.75
Nos. 1478-1480 (3) 11.25 6.20

Los Tayos Caves A509

Design: 1000s, Man in cave, vert.

1999, Feb. 25 Litho. ***Perf. 13***

1481 A509 1000s multi 1.75 .90
1482 A509 2600s shown 4.75 2.50

Napal, the Age of Wrath, by Oswaldo Guayasamin (1919-99) — A510

Wmk. 395

1999, May 12 Litho. ***Perf. 13***

1483 A510 2000s multicolored 4.25 2.10

Iberoamerica art exhibition.

Universal Day of Human Rights A511

1999, May 28

1484 A511 4000s multicolored 7.50 4.50

Eloy Alfaro Superior Military College, Cent. A512

5200s, Cannon, monument, flags, buildings. 9400s, Honor Guard, modern building.

1999, June 4

1485 A512 5200s multicolored 10.50 7.00
1486 A512 9400s multicolored 17.50 11.50

Puyo, 100th Anniv. — A513

Designs: a, Bromeliad. b, Ara chloroptera.

1999, June 2

1487 A513 4000s Pair, #a.-b. 14.50 10.00

Dr. Rafael Barahona Andrade (1827-98) A514

Perf. 13¼x13

1999, June 17 Litho. Wmk. 395

1488 A514 5200s multi 9.00 4.50

Generals — A515

Designs: 2000s, Manuel Antonio de Luzarraga y Echezurria (1776-1859). 4000s, Tomas Carlos Wright (1799-1868).

1999, Aug. 11 ***Perf. 13x13¼***

1489-1490 A515 Set of 2 11.00 6.00

Galapagos Islands Flora and Fauna A516

No. 1491, vert.: a, Phoenicopterus ruber. b, Buteo galapagoensis. c, Amblyrhynchus cristatus. d, Conolophus subcristatus. e, Opuntia galapageia. f, Pyrocephalus rubinus. g, Sula nebouxii. h, Sula dactylatra. i, Scalesia villosa. j, G. elephantopus abingdoni.

No. 1492: a, Brachycereus nesioticus. b, Dendroica petechia. c, Nannopterum harrisi. d, Tursiops truncatus. e, Pentaceraster cumingi. f, G. elephantopus porteri. g, Microlophus albemarlensis. h, Arctocephalus galapagoensis. i, Spheniscus mendiculus. j, Geospiza scandens.

Perf. 13x13¼, 13¼x13

1999, Sept. 3 Litho. Wmk. 395

1491 Strip of 10 90.00 75.00
a.-j. A516 7000s Any single 5.50 1.75
1492 Strip of 10 175.00 125.00
a.-j. A516 15,000s Any single 12.00 5.00

Intl. Year of Older Persons A517

Designs: No. 1493, 1000s, Hands of child and old person. No. 1494, 1000s, Emblem.

Perf. 13¼x13

1999, Sept. 22 Litho. Wmk. 395

1493-1494 A517 Set of 2 3.00 1.75

SOS Children's Villages, 50th Anniv. — A518

a, 2000s, Two children. b, 2000s, One child.

1999, Sept. 30

1495 A518 Pair, #a-b 5.00 2.50

America Issue, A World Without Arms — A519

No. 1496: a, World map. b, Tree, bird, Earth.

Perf. 13¼x13

1999, Dec. 11 Litho. Wmk. 395

1496 A519 4000s Pair, #a-b *14.50 10.00*

UPU, 125th Anniv. A520

Designs: 1000s, Ecuadorian Postal Service mascot, vert. 4000s, Dove with letter, vert. 8000s, UPU emblem.

Perf. 13¼x12¾

1999, Dec. 11 Litho. Wmk. 395

1497 A520 1000s multi .90 .45
1498 A520 4000s multi 3.50 1.75
1499 A520 8000s multi 7.00 4.00
Nos. 1497-1499 (3) 11.40 6.20

Ecuador as Secretary General of Permanent South Pacific Commission A521

Design: Le‡n Dormido.

Perf. 13x13¼

1999, Dec. 21 Litho. Wmk. 395

1500 A521 7000s multi *7.50 5.50*

Machala Tourism A522

Designs: No. 1501, Banana flower and city. No. 1502, vert.: a, Monument to banana plantation workers. b, City Hall.

1999, Dec. 28 ***Perf. 13¼x13, 13x13¼***

1501 A522 3000s multi *3.25 1.60*
1502 A522 3000s Pair, #a-b *6.50 3.25*

EMELEC Soccer Team — A523

No. 1503: a, Jorge Bolanos. b, Carlos Raffo. No. 1504, EMELEC team photo, 1957. No. 1505, Player, vert.

Perf. 13x13¼, 13¼x13

2000, Jan. 7 Litho.

1503 A523 1000s Pair, #a-b *3.00 2.25*
1504 A523 2000s multi *3.00 1.50*
1505 A523 2000s multi *3.00 1.50*

Guayas Philanthropic Society, 150th Anniv. A524

Designs: 1000s, Building. 2000s, Founder Juan Maria Martinez Coello. 4000s, Emblem.

Perf. 13¼x13

2000, Jan. 19 Litho. Wmk. 395

1506-1508 A524 Set of 3 *3.00 1.50*

Dual Nationality Day — A525

2000, Jan. 24 ***Perf. 13x13¼***

1509 A525 7000s multi *3.00 1.50*

Cuenca, World Heritage Site — A526

No. 1510: a, Buildings. b, Puente Roto and Tomebamba River. c, Church bell gable, Concepcion Monastery. d, Cathedral and city skyline. e, San José Church.

2000, Mar. 24 ***Perf. 13¼x13***

1510 Strip of 5 *7.00 6.00*
a.-e. A526 4000s Any single *.75 .50*

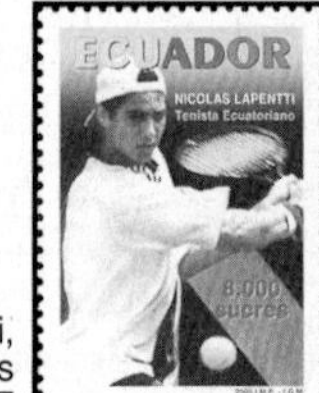

Nicolas Lapentti, Tennis Player — A527

2000, Mar. 26 ***Perf. 13x13¼***

1511 A527 8000s multi *3.00 1.50*

Birds — A528

No. 1512: a, Diglossa cyanea. b, Oreotrochilus chimborazo. c, Trogon personatus. d, Colibri coruscans. e, Atlapetes rufinucha.

2000, Apr. 7

1512 Horiz. strip of 5 *13.00 11.50*
a.-e. A528 8000s Any single *2.25 1.50*

Relocation of Riobamba, Bicent. A529

Designs: No. 1513, Mt. Chimborazo. No. 1514: a, Riobamba Cathedral. b, Statue of Pedro Vicente Maldonado.

2000, Apr. 13 ***Perf. 13¼x13, 13x13¼***
1513 A529 8000s multi *2.75 1.00*
1514 A529 8000s Pair, #a-b 5.25 3.50

Gen. Eloy Alfaro, Founder of Natl. Music Conservatory A530

2000, Apr. 19 ***Perf. 13x13¼***
1515 A530 10,000s multi *4.00 1.60*

Natl. Music Conservatory, cent.

Climbing of Mt. Everest by Ivan Vallejo Ricaurte A531

2000, May 23 ***Perf. 13¼x13***
1516 A531 8000s multi *3.50 2.00*

100 Cents=1 Dollar

Dolores Sucre Fiscal College, 50th Anniv. — A532

Perf. 13x13¼
2000 **Litho.** **Wmk. 395**
1517 A532 32c multi 2.50 1.25

Training Ship Guayas — A533

2000, July 5 ***Perf. 13x13¼***
1518 A533 68c multi 1.60 .80

Imperf

Size: 90x110mm

1519 A533 $1 multi 7.00 3.25

Battle of Jambeli, 59th Anniv., Navy Day — A534

2000 ***Perf. 13¼x13***
1520 A534 16c multi 1.50 .25

Guayaquil Civic Renovation A535

2000, July ***Perf. 13x13¼***
1521 A535 84c multi 7.50 3.75

Megaptera Novaeangliae — A536

2000, Aug. 3 ***Perf. 13¼x13***
1522 A536 84c multi 8.50 4.25

Imperf

Size: 90x110mm

1523 A536 $1 Two whales 11.50 5.75

American and Caribbean Dog Show, Quito A537

2000, Aug. ***Perf. 13¼x13***
1524 A537 68c multi 4.50 2.25

Guayaquil Tennis Club, 90th Anniv. A538

2000, Aug. **Wmk. 395**
1525 A538 84c multi 5.50 2.50

Alberto Spencer, Soccer Player — A539

2000 ***Perf. 13x13¼***
1526 A539 68c multi 5.00 2.50

Imperf

Size: 69x99mm

1527 A539 $1 Spencer, crowd 9.00 4.50

2000 Summer Olympics, Sydney — A540

Ecuadoran team emblem, Games emblem and: 32c Mascots. 68c, Runner Jefferson Perez Marchista. 84c, Weight lifter Boris Burov, Olympic flag, horiz.

2000, Sept. ***Perf. 13x13¼, 13¼x13***
1528-1530 A540 Set of 3 12.00 6.00

Salinas Yacht Club, 60th Anniv. A541

Designs: No. 1531a, Lighthouse, vert. Nos. 1531b, 1533, Sailboat, vert. 68c, Sailboats, fisherman, waterskier, scuba diver.

2000, Oct. ***Perf. 13x13¼***
1531 A541 32c Horiz. pair, #a-b 5.50 2.75

Perf. 13¼x13

1532 A541 68c multi 5.75 2.75

Imperf

Size: 69x100mm

1533 A541 $1 multi 9.00 4.50

Inter-American Development Bank, 40th Anniv. — A542

Designs: No. 1534a, 68c, No. 1536a, 25c, Salsipuedes Bridge, Felipe Herrera. No. 1534b, 68c, No. 1536b, 25c, Daule-Peripa Dam, Antonio Ortiz Mena. No. 1535a, 84c, No. 1536c, 25c, Enrique Iglesias, Ucubamba Water Treatment Plant. No. 1535b, 84c, No. 1536d, 25c, Bank emblem, History Museum, Quito.

2000, Oct. 27 ***Perf. 13¼x13***

Horiz. Pairs, #a-b

1534-1535 A542 Set of 2 20.00 10.00

Rouletted 14 on 2 sides

1536 A542 25c Sheet of 4, #a-d 7.50 3.75

Size of Nos. 1536a-1536b, 75x48mm; Nos. 1536c-1536d, 75x42mm.

National Union of Journalists A543

2000, Nov. 1 ***Perf. 13¼x13***
1537 A543 16c multi 1.25 .25

Civil Registry, Cent. — A544

No. 1538: a, People, flag, computer. b, Fingerprint, family.

2000, Oct. 27 ***Perf. 13x13¼***
1538 A544 68c Horiz. pair, #a-b 9.00 4.50

Mama Negra Festival, Latacunga — A545

No. 1539: a, Mama Negra with doll. b, Man in Moor King costume.

2000, Nov. ***Perf. 13x13¼***
1539 A545 32c Horiz. pair, #a-b 5.50 2.75

Imperf

Size: 100x68mm

1540 A545 $1 Mama Negra, doll, diff. 6.50 3.00

Ministry of Labor, 75th Anniv. — A546

2000, Nov. 15 ***Perf. 13x13¼***
1541 A546 68c multi 4.75 2.25

Intl. Fruits and Flowers Festival, Ambato, 50th Anniv. — A547

No. 1542, horiz.: Design inside "0" of 50 — a, Tungurahua Volcano. b, Aerial view of Ambato.

No. 1544, horiz.: Design inside "0" of 50 — a, Flower. b. Fruit.

2000, Nov. ***Perf. 13¾***
1542 A547 32c Vert. pair, #a-b 4.25 2.10
1543 A547 84c shown 5.75 2.75
1544 A547 84c Vert. pair, #a-b 12.00 6.00
Nos. 1542-1544 (3) 22.00 10.85

Imperf

Size: 68x100mm

1545 A547 $1 Ambato 6.25 3.00

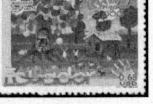

Christmas — A548

Children's art by — No. 1546, 68c: a, Giannina Rhor Isaias. b, Josue Remache Romero. No. 1547, 84c: a, Maria Cedeño Bazurtto. b, Juan Alban Salazar.

$1, Walther Carvache.

2000, Dec. 15 ***Perf. 13¼x13***

Horiz. Pairs, #a-b

1546-1547 A548 Set of 2 21.50 11.00

Imperf

Size: 100x69mm

1548 A548 $1 multi 6.25 3.00

Expoflores Flower Producer and Exporter Association A549

2000 ***Perf. 13x13¼***
1549 A549 68c multi 5.00 2.50

Man's Chapel, Guayasamin A550

2000 *Perf. 13¼x13*
1550 A550 16c multi 1.25 .25

Spanish Chamber of Commerce in Ecuador, 80th Anniv. — A551

2000, Dec. *Perf. 13x13¼*
1551 A551 16c multi 1.25 .25

Intl. Volunteers Year — A552

2000 **Wmk. 395**
1552 A552 16c multi 1.25 .25

Restoration of Bolivar Theater, Quito — A553

Designs: 16c, Piano, banquet room. 32c, Stage, orchestra, horiz.

2000, Dec. *Perf. 13x13¼, 13¼x13*
1553-1554 A553 Set of 2 3.75 1.75

Spondylus Princeps A554

2000, Dec. 16 *Perf. 13¾*
1555 A554 84c multi 6.00 3.00

Imperf

Size: 69x99mm

1556 A554 $1 multi 7.00 3.50

America Issue, Fight Against AIDS — A555

No. 1557: a, Strands. b, Earth.

2000 *Perf. 13x13¼*
1557 A555 84c Horiz. pair, #a-b 15.00 7.50

Guayas Province Red Cross, 90th Anniv. A556

2000 *Perf. 13¼x13*
1558 A556 16c multi 1.25 .60

Guayas Sports Federation, 78th Anniv. — A557

2000, Dec. *Perf. 13x13¼*
1559 A557 16c multi 1.25 .60

Landscapes A557a

Designs: No. 1559A, 16c, Andean region. No. 1559B, 16c, Pacific coast. 32c, Tourism emblem. 68c, Amazonia. 84c, Galápagos Islands.

Perf. 13¼x12¾

2001, Jan. 24 **Litho.** **Wmk. 395**

1559A	A557a 16c multi	1.25	.60
1559B	A557a 16c multi	1.25	.60
1559C	A557a 32c multi	2.50	1.10
1559D	A557a 68c multi	4.75	2.40
1559E	A557a 84c multi	4.75	2.40
	Nos. 1559A-1559E (5)	14.50	7.10

Guayas Soccer Team, 50th Anniv. A558

2001, Mar. 8 *Perf. 13¼x13*
1560 A558 68c multi 5.00 2.50

Census — A558a Census — A558b

Perf. 12¾x13¼

2001, Mar. 12 **Litho.** **Wmk. 395**
1560A A558a 68c multi 4.50 4.50
1560B A558b 68c multi 4.50 4.50
c. Horiz. pair, #1560A-1560B 10.00 10.00

Dr. Raúl Clemente Huerta A559

2001, Apr. 4 *Perf. 13¼x13*
1561 A559 68c multi 5.50 2.75

Dr. Antonio J. Quevedo, Birth Cent. A560

2001, Apr. 5 **Litho.**
1562 A560 84c multi 6.50 3.25

Military Geographic Institute A560a

No. 1562A: b, Soldier, building. c, Computer, printing press.

Perf. 13¼x12¾

2001, Apr. 11 **Litho.** **Wmk. 395**
1562A A560a 68c Vert. pair, #b-c 12.00 6.00

Automobile Club of Ecuador, 50th Anniv. A561

2001, May 15 **Wmk. 395**
1563 A561 84c multi 6.50 3.25

San Francisco de Peleusí Church, Azogues — A561a

Perf. 12¾x13¼

2001, May **Litho.** **Wmk. 395**
1563A A561a 84c multi 6.50 3.25

Women's Training Institute — A562

2001, Apr. 10 *Perf. 13x13¼*
1564 A562 84c multi 6.50 3.25

Intl. Women's Day A563

No. 1565: a, Woman, child, corn. b, Woman, emblem.

2001, Apr. 2 *Perf. 13¼x13*
1565 A563 84c Vert. pair, #a-b 12.50 6.25

Secular Education at Manuela Cañizares University, Cent. A564

2001, Mar. 29 **Wmk. 395**
1566 A564 84c multi 6.50 3.25

Ecuador Merchant Marines, Cent. — A565

2001, Jan. 2001 *Perf. 13x13¼*
1567 A565 16c multi 1.25 .60

Ambato Technical University, 32nd Anniv. A566

No. 1568: a, Building. b, Painting.

2001 *Perf. 13¼x13*
1568 A566 32c Vert. pair, #a-b 5.50 2.75

Galapagos Islands Scenes — A567

No. 1569: a, Española Island (shown). b, San Cristobal Island. c, Bartolome Island. d, Española Island, diff. e, Bartolome and Santiago Islands.
$1, Bird on rock, Española Island.

2001, Feb. 17 *Perf. 13¾*
1569 Horiz. strip of 5 6.00 3.00
a.-e. A567 16c Any single .50 .25

Imperf

Size: 100x70mm

1570 A567 $1 multi 8.00 4.00

Alexander von Humboldt (1769-1859), Naturalist — A568

Perf. 13x13¼

2001, June 14 **Litho.** **Wmk. 395**
1571 A568 84c multi 6.00 3.00

Ecuadorian Atomic Energy Commission A568a

2001, Aug. 3 Litho. *Perf. 12¾x13¼*

1571A A568a 70c multi 5.50 2.75

Lebanese Union, 80th Anniv. — A569

No. 1572: a, Building and emblem. b, Emblem.

2001, Aug. 30 *Perf. 13¼x13*

1572 A569 16c Horiz. pair, #a-b 3.00 1.50

Manta Port Authority — A570

No. 1573: a, Emblem. b, Ships in port.

2001, Sept. 28

1573 A570 68c Horiz. pair, #a-b 10.00 5.00

Esmereldas Province Tourism — A571

No. 1574: a, Beach. b, Musicians and dancers on beach.

2001

1574 A571 86c Horiz. pair, #a-b 12.50 6.25

Latin American Writers — A572

No. 1575: a, Claudia Lars (1899-1974), Salvadoran poet. b, Federico Proaño (1848-94), Ecuadoran journalist.

2001, Aug. 28 *Perf. 13x13¼*

1575 A572 86c Horiz. pair, #a-b 13.50 6.75

Andean Condor Preservation — A573

No. 1576: a, Condor and chick. b, Condor heads, FRAPZOO emblem.
$1, Condor in flight, FRAPZOO emblem.

2001, July 23 *Perf. 13x13¼*

1576 A573 86c Horiz. pair, #a-b 12.50 6.25

Imperf

Size: 68x99mm

1577 A573 $1 multi 7.50 3.75

Ecuador — Peru Peace Accords A574

No. 1578: a, Map of Ecuador and Peru. b, Soldier. c, Flags of military obeservers. d, Amazon River. e, Men in field.

2001, May 22 *Perf. 13¼x13*

1578 Horiz. strip of 5 22.50 11.00

a.-e. A574 68c Any single 4.00 2.00

Archidona Canton — A575

No. 1579: a, Phragmipedium orchid. b, Saimiri sciureus. c, B. macrophylla. d, Church. e, Kichwa Indian family.

2001, Apr. 28 *Perf. 13x13¼*

1579 Vert. strip of 5 30.00 15.00

a.-e. A575 84c Any single 5.00 2.40

Ecotourism in Baños A576

No. 1580: a, Orchid. b, Basilica, Baños. c, Tungurahua Volcano. d, Pailon del Diablo Waterfall. e, Statue of Virgin of Rosario de Agua Santa.
$1, Pailon del Diablo Waterfall, orchid.

2001 *Perf. 13¼x13*

1580 Horiz. strip of 5 27.50 13.50

a.-e. A576 86c Any single 5.00 2.40

Imperf

Size: 68x99mm

1581 A576 $1 multi 7.50 3.75

Guayas Educational Journalists Association, 30th Anniv. A577

Perf. 13¼x13

2001, Oct. 15 Litho. Wmk. 395

1582 A577 16c multi 1.25 .60

Foundation for Development of Cattle Ranching, 15th Anniv. — A578

2001, Aug. 15 *Perf. 13x13¼*

1583 A578 16c multi 1.25 .60

City Gates, Loja — A579

2001 *Perf. 13¼x13*

1584 A579 32c multi 2.50 1.25

Quito Municipal District Directorate of Security A580

2001, Nov. 26

1585 A580 68c multi 5.00 2.50

Salvador Bustamante Celi (1876-1935), Musician A581

2001

1586 A581 68c multi 5.50 2.75

Marcel Laniado de Wind (1927-98), First Pres. of Natl. Modernization Council — A582

2001, Aug. 6 *Perf. 13x13¼*

1587 A582 70c multi 5.50 2.75

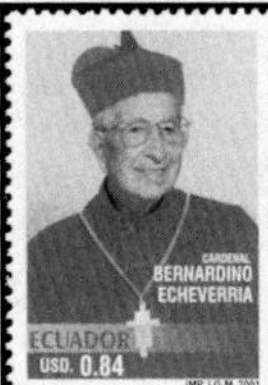

Bernardino Cardinal Echeverria (1912-2000) A583

2001, Nov. 14

1588 A583 84c multi 6.50 3.25

José Joaquin Olmedo (1780-1847), Statesman and Poet — A584

2001, Nov. 8

1589 A584 84c multi 6.50 3.25

El Angel Ecological Reserve — A585

No. 1590: a, Paja de Paramo. b, Frailejón.

2001 *Perf. 13¼x13*

1590 A585 16c Horiz. pair, #a-b 2.75 1.40

Yahuarcocha Race Track — A586

No. 1591: a, Race track and lake. b, Lake.

2001, Nov. 30

1591 A586 68c Horiz. pair, #a-b 10.00 5.00

World Food Day — A587

No. 1592: a, Wheat ears. b, Food baskets.

2001, Nov. 5

1592 A587 84c Horiz. pair, #a-b 12.50 6.25

Art of Voroshilov Bazante A588

No. 1593: a, Spatial composition. b, Abstract, artists name at LR. c, Urban landscape. d, Abstract, diff., "Abstracto" at UL, denomination at LL. e, Abstract, denomination at LR.

2001, Nov.

1593 Horiz. strip of 5 27.50 12.50

a.-e. A588 84c Any single 5.00 2.50

Wilson Popenoe Private Foundation A589

2001, Nov. 19 Litho. *Perf. 13¼x13*

1594 A589 16c multi 1.25 .60

FAO Food Program A590

2001, Aug. 15

1595 A590 84c multi 6.50 3.25

Rotary District 4400, 75th Anniv. — A591

2001, Nov. 30 *Perf. 13x13¼*

1596 A591 84c multi 6.50 3.25

Pres. Camilo Ponce Enriquez (1912-76) — A592

2001

1597 A592 84c multi 6.50 3.25

Pedro Vicente Maldonado (1702-48), Geographer A593

2001, Dec. 12
1598 A593 84c multi 6.50 3.25

Otonga Foundation — A595

No. 1599: a, Frog on branch. b, Mustela frenata.

2001, Oct. 31
1599 A595 16c Horiz. pair, #a-b 2.75 1.40

Tourism in Zaruma — A596

No. 1600: a, Virgen del Carmen. b, Orchid.

2001, Dec. 12 ***Perf. 13¼x13***
1600 A596 68c Horiz. pair, #a-b 10.00 5.00

Radio HCJB, 70th Anniv. — A597

No. 1601: a, Microphone. b, Announcer.

2001, Dec. 21
1601 A597 68c Horiz. pair, #a-b 10.00 5.00

Tennis A598

No. 1602: a, Davis Cup. b, K. Lapentti, G. Lapentti, L.A. Morejón, A. Intriago and R. Viver. c, Francisco Guzman and Miguel Olvera. d, Pancho Segura. e, Andres Gomez.

2001, Nov. 1
1602 Horiz. strip of 5 24.00 12.00
a.-e. A598 68c Any single 4.50 2.25

Church Paintings of Wilfrido Martínez — A599

No. 1603: a, San Francisco (artist's name is vert.). b, Guapulo. c, San Francisco (artist's name is horiz.). d, La Compania. e, El Rosario.

2002, Apr. 9 ***Perf. 13¾***
1603 Horiz. strip of 5 27.00 13.50
a.-e. A599 90c Any single 5.00 2.50

First Judicial Summit of the Americas, Quito A600

Perf. 13¼x13
2002, Jan. 8 Litho. Wmk. 395
1604 A600 68c multi 5.00 2.50

Union Club, Guayaquil — A601

2002, Apr. 25 ***Perf. 13x13¼***
1605 A601 90c multi 5.75 2.75

South American Soccer Confederation A602

Designs: 25c, Confederation Pres. Nicolás Leoz. 40c, Confederation emblem, soccer players. 70c, Emblem of Emelec team.

2002, Jan. 29
1606-1608 A602 Set of 3 10.00 5.00

World Conservation Union — A603

Designs: 70c, Fish, man's head. 85c, Leopard, man, horiz.
$1, Bird, animals, women and children, horiz.

2002, Feb. 21 ***Perf. 13x13¼, 13¼x13***
1609-1610 A603 Set of 2 11.50 5.75

Imperf

Size: 100x70mm

1611 A603 $1 multi 7.50 3.75

UN High Commissioner for Refugees — A604

Designs: 70c, Emblem. 85c, Child.
$1, Refugees carrying belongings, horiz.

2002, Feb. 28 ***Perf. 13x13¼***
1612-1613 A604 Set of 2 11.50 5.75

Imperf

Size: 100x70mm

1614 A604 $1 multi 7.50 3.75

Ecuadorian Educational Credit and Scholarship Institute — A605

No. 1615: a, Student using microscope. b, Emblem.

2002, Apr. 30 ***Perf. 13x13¼***
1615 A605 25c Horiz. pair, #a-b 3.00 1.50

Cuenca Soccer Team — A606

No. 1616: a, Team photo. b, Emblem, player dribbling.

2002, Apr. 19 ***Perf. 13¼x13***
1616 A606 25c Horiz. pair, #a-b 3.00 1.50

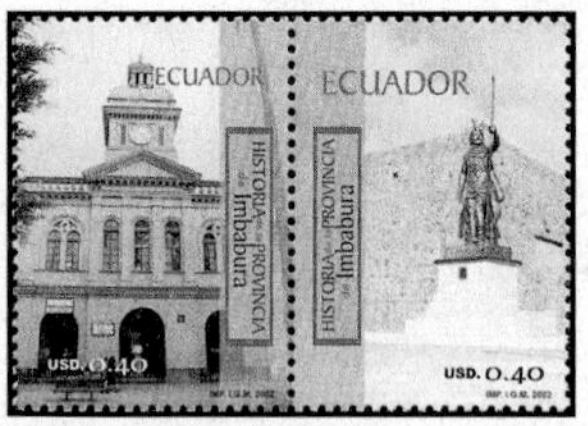

Imbabura Province History — A607

No. 1617: a, Building. b, Statue.

2002, Mar. 27 ***Perf. 13x13¼***
1617 A607 40c Horiz. pair, #a-b 6.00 3.00

Crucita — A608

No. 1618: a, Parachutist with sun on horizon. b, Prachutist above beach.

2002, Mar. 28 ***Perf. 13¼x13***
1618 A608 40c Horiz. pair, #a-b 6.00 3.00

Mountains A609

No. 1619: a, Mt. Altar (trees in foreground). b, Mt. Chimborazo. c, Mt. Carihuayrazo. d, Mt. Altar (lake in foreground). e, Mt. Cubillin.

2002, Apr. 19
1619 Horiz. strip of 5 29.00 15.00
a.-e. A609 90c Any single 5.00 2.25

Endangered Frogs A610

No. 1620: a, Atelopus bomolochos. b, Atelopus longirostris. c, Atelopus pachydermus. d, Atelopus arthuri. e, Atelopus sp.
$1, Atelopus ignescens.

2002, Mar. 25 ***Perf. 13¼x13***
1620 Horiz. strip of 5 29.00 15.00
a.-e. A610 $1.05 Any single 5.00 2.25

Imperf

Size: 100x70mm

1621 A610 $1 multi 10.00 8.00

National Anti-narcotics Police — A611

No. 1622: a, Policeman and dog. b, Emblem.

Perf. 13x13¼
2002, Apr. 23 Litho. Wmk. 395
1622 A611 40c Horiz. pair, #a-b 6.00 3.00

2002 World Cup Soccer Championships, Japan and Korea — A612

Designs: 90c, Ecuadorian Soccer Federation emblem, vert. $1.05, $2, Emblem, team photo, players in action.

2002, Apr. 28 ***Perf. 13x13¼, 13¼x13***
1623-1624 A612 Set of 2 9.00 4.50

Imperf

Size: 100x70mm

1625 A612 $2 multi 9.00 4.50

Dr. Servio Aguirre Villamagua, Forest Conservationist — A613

No. 1626: a, Aguirre. b, Plant.

2002, May 22 ***Perf. 13¼x13***
1626 A613 40c Horiz. pair, #a-b 4.00 2.00

Food and Agriculture Organization in Ecuador, 50th Anniv. A614

2002, May 30
1627 A614 $1.05 multi 5.00 2.50

Galapagos Islands Fauna A615

No. 1628: a, Grapsus grapsus. b, Conolophus subcristatus.
No. 1629, vert.: a, Sula sula websteri. b, Phoenicopterus ruber.
No. 1630, Amblyrhynchus cristatus.
No. 1631, vert.: a, Pair of Zalophus californianus wollebacki. b, One Zalophus californianus wollebacki.
No. 1632, Sula nebouxii excisa, vert.
No. 1633, vert.: a, Sula dactylatra granti. b, Emblem of Iberoamerican Summit on Tourism and Environment.
$2, Bird, tourists, tourist ship.

2002, May 31 ***Perf. 13¼x13, 13x13¼***
1628 A615 25c Horiz. pair, #a-b 3.00 1.50
1629 A615 40c Horiz. pair, #a-b 4.00 2.00
1630 A615 90c multi 6.00 3.00
1631 A615 90c Horiz. pair, #a-b 9.00 4.50
1632 A615 $1.05 multi 5.00 2.50
1633 A615 $1.05 Horiz. pair, #a-b 10.00 5.00
Nos. 1628-1633 (6) 37.00 18.50

Imperf
Size: 100x68mm
1634 A615 $2 multi 11.50 7.00

Ministry of Foreign Relations — A616

2002, June 5 ***Perf. 13x13¼***
1635 A616 90c multi 4.50 2.25

Army Polytechnic School, 80th Anniv. A617

2002, June 13 ***Perf. 13¼x13***
1636 A617 25c multi 1.75 .90

Military Engineers, Cent. A618

Designs: No. 1637, 40c, Castle of Engineering. No. 1638, 40c, Castle of Engineering, Military engineers in action, vert.
$2, Castle of Engineering, engineers in action, emblems of military groups.

Perf. 13¼x13, 13x13¼
2002, June 19
1637-1638 A618 Set of 2 4.00 2.00

Imperf
Size: 100x68mm
1639 A618 $2 multi 9.00 4.50

Dr. Alfredo Pérez Guerrero (1901-66), Academic — A619

2002, July 4 ***Perf. 13x13¼***
1640 A619 25c multi 1.75 .90

20th Anniv. of Ecuador's Second Place Finish In World Taekwondo Championships — A620

2002, July 18 ***Perf. 13¼x13***
1641 A620 40c multi 2.00 1.00

Orellana Province — A621

No. 1642: a, Three native men. b, Man in tree.

2002, July 30 **Wmk. 395**
1642 A621 25c Horiz. pair, #a-b 3.00 1.50

CARE in Ecuador, 40th Anniv. — A622

No. 1643: a, Two children. b, Boy.

2002, July 30 ***Perf. 13x13¼***
1643 A622 90c Horiz. pair, #a-b 9.00 4.50

Macará Region A623

2002, Aug. 10 ***Perf. 13¼x13***
1644 A623 40c multi 2.00 1.00

Intl. Organization for Migration, 50th Anniv. — A624

2002, Aug. 18 ***Perf. 13x13¼***
1645 A624 $1.05 multi 5.00 2.50

Quito Philharmonic Society, 50th Anniv. — A625

2002, Aug. 29
1646 A625 25c multi 1.75 .90

Comptroller General, 75th Anniv. — A625a

Perf. 13x13¼
2002, Sept. 26 **Litho.** **Wmk. 395**
1646A A625a 40c multi 2.00 1.00

Second World Meeting of Mountain People — A626

No. 1647 — Emblem of World Meeting and: a, Mountain. b, Group of people. c, Houses in valley. d, Town. e, Other emblems.

2002, Sept. 18
1647 Horiz. strip of 5 22.50 11.00
a.-e. A626 90c Any single 4.00 2.00

Pujili Dancer — A627

Perf. 13x13¼
2002, Oct. 14 **Litho.** **Wmk. 395**
1648 A627 $1.05 multi 5.00 2.50

Paintings of Milton Estrella Gavidia — A628

No. 1649 — Various paintings with background colors of: a, Blue violet. b, Brown violet. c, Olive green. d, Blue. e, Gray lilac.

Wmk. 395
2002, May 17 **Litho.** ***Perf. 13¾***
1649 Horiz. strip of 5 22.50 11.00
a.-e. A628 90c Any single 4.00 2.00

Paintings of Leonardo Hidalgo A629

No. 1650: a, La Dolorosa. b, El Hombre Cargando su Fruto. c, Frida Kahlo. d, El Hombre Fuerte del Mar. e, Jesus.

Wmk. 395
2002, Oct. 3 **Litho.** ***Perf. 13¾***
1650 Horiz. strip of 5 22.50 11.00
a.-e. A629 90c Any single 4.00 2.00

Pan-American Health Organization, Cent. — A630

2002, Dec. 2 ***Perf. 13¼x12¾***
1651 A630 $1.05 multi 5.00 2.50

Lo Nuestro Art Exhibition — A631

No. 1652: a, Wall with six works of art. b, Walls with 16 works of art.

2002, Dec. 15
1652 A631 25c Horiz. pair, #a-b 2.50 1.25

Catholic University, 40th Anniv. A632

2002, Dec. 18
1653 A632 40c multi 2.00 1.00

America Issue — UNESCO World Heritage Sites — A633

No. 1654: a, Cupola of San Blas Church, Cuenca. b, Society of Jesus Church, Quito.

2002, Dec. 18 ***Perf. 12¾x13¼***
1654 A633 25c Horiz. pair, #a-b 3.00 1.50

Dated 2001.

America Issue — Youth, Education and Literacy — A634

No. 1655: a, Students and blackboard. b, Toddler and books.

2002, Dec. 18 ***Perf. 13¼x12¾***
1655 A634 25c Horiz. pair, #a-b 3.00 1.50

Second Meeting of South American Presidents, Guayaquil — A635

No. 1656: a, Meeting emblem. b, Emblem, presidents and flags.

2003, Jan. 13
1656 A635 $1.05 Horiz. pair, #a-b 8.00 4.00

Papal Benediction for Ecuadorian Emigrants — A636

2003, Jan. 24 ***Perf. 12¾x13¼***
1657 A636 $1.05 multi 4.50 2.25

Size: 68x100mm
Imperf
1658 A636 $2 multi 9.00 4.50

World Vision — A637

2003, Feb. 6 *Perf. 12¾x13¼*

1659 A637 40c multi 1.90 .95

Intl. Women's Day — A638

2003, Mar. 8 **Wmk. 395**

1660 A638 $1.05 multi 5.00 2.50

Agustin Cueva Vallejo (1820-73), Physician — A639

2003, Mar. 13 **Litho.**

1661 A639 40c multi 1.90 .95

Blasco Moscoso Cuesta, Founder of Pichincha Sports Writers Association — A640

2003, Mar. 14

1662 A640 25c multi 1.50 .75

Cuenca Artisan Products A641

No. 1663: a, Azuay University domes. b, Tinware. c, Jewelry. d, Fireworks. e, Saddles.

No. 1664: a, Engraving. b, Metallurgy. c, Baskets. d, Embroidery. e, Ceramics.

$2, Assorted products.

2003, Mar. 27 *Perf. 13¼x12¾*

1663 Horiz. strip of 5 6.00 3.00
a.-e. A641 25c Any single 1.00 .50
1664 Horiz. strip of 5 22.50 11.00
a.-e. A641 $1.05 Any single 4.00 2.00

Size: 100x68mm

Imperf

1665 A641 $2 multi 9.00 4.50

Flora and Fauna A642

No. 1666: a, Curculionidae. b, Lycidae. c, Acridoidea. d, Aracnidae. e, Liliacea.

2003, Apr. 4 *Perf. 13¼x12¾*

1666 Horiz. strip of 5 22.50 11.00
a.-e. A642 $1.05 Any single 4.00 2.00

Military Geographic Institute, 75th Anniv. A643

Designs: No. 1667, 40c, No. 1669, $2, Painting by Eduardo Kingman. No. 1668, 40c, Institute emblem, vert.

Perf. 13¼x12¾, 12¾x13¼

2003, Apr. 11

1667-1668 A643 Set of 2 3.50 1.75

Size: 100x68mm

Imperf

1669 A643 $2 multi 9.00 4.50

Galápagos Marine Reserve — A644

Designs: 40c, Stylized butterfly.

No. 1671, $1.05, horiz.: a, Sphyrna lewini. b, Chelonia mydas agassisi.

No. 1672, $1.05, horiz.: a, Xanthichthys mento. b, Zanclus cornutus.

$2, Tubastrea coccinea, horiz.

Perf. 12¾x13¼, 13¼x12¾

2003, May 9

1670 A644 40c multi 1.75 .90

Horiz. Pairs, #a-b

1671-1672 A644 Set of 2 17.50 8.75

Size: 100x68mm

Imperf

1673 A644 $2 multi 9.00 4.50

Intl. Tourism Trade Fair of Ecuador A645

No. 1674: a, Monkey in tree. b, Birds. c, Embroidery. d, Mountain. e, Hat seller on beach.

2003, May 14 *Perf. 13¼x12¾*

1674 Vert. strip of 5 6.00 3.00
a.-e. A645 25c Any single 1.00 .50

Artifacts of Pre-Columbian Cultures — A646

No. 1675, 25c: a, Gold bell with monkey. b, Amphora.

No. 1676, 25c: a, Sculpture of a man. b, Three-footed pot.

Perf. 13x13¼

2003, May 16 **Litho.** **Wmk. 395**

Horiz. pairs, #a-b

1675-1676 A646 Set of 2 4.50 2.25

Central Bank of Ecuador A647

No. 1677, vert.: a, Tolita Culture mask. b, Guayaquil Historic Park.

$1.05, Pumapungo Museum.

Perf. 13x13¼, 13¼x13

2003, June 5 **Litho.**

1677 A647 25c Horiz. pair, #a-b 1.50 .75
1678 A647 $1.05 multi 2.75 1.40

Philately and Guayaquil A648

No. 1679, horiz.: a, British consular cover to Veracruz with British stamp and cancel. b, Stampless cover.

No. 1680, horiz.: a, SCADTA first flight cover. b, French consular cover to Lima with French stamps and cancels.

$1.05, Philatelic magazines.

$2, Guayaquil Philatelic Club emblem, Ecuadoran stamps, horiz.

2003, July 22 *Perf. 13¾*

1679 A648 40c Vert. pair, #a-b 3.25 1.60
1680 A648 40c Vert. pair, #a-b 3.25 1.60
1681 A648 $1.05 multi 4.00 2.00
Nos. 1679-1681 (3) 10.50 5.20

Size: 100x69mm

Imperf

1682 A648 $2 multi 9.00 4.50

Guayaquil Urban Renewal A649

No. 1683: a, Punta Cerro Santa Ana. b, Plaza Colón. c, Malecón Gardens. d, Crystal Palace. e, Plaza de San Francisco.

2003, July 26 *Perf. 13¼x13*

1683 Horiz. strip of 5 19.00 9.50
a.-e. A649 90c Any single 3.50 1.75

World Bird Festival A650

Designs: No. 1684, $1.05, Geranoaetus melanoleucus. No. 1685, $1.05, Harpia harpyja, vert.

2003, Sept. 2 *Perf. 13¼x13, 13x13¼*

1684-1685 A650 Set of 2 9.00 4.50

Zamora-Chinchipe Province, 50th Anniv. — A651

No. 1686: a, Shown. b, Eira barbara. c, Boa constrictor. d, Tapirus terrestris. e, Psophia crepitans.

2003, Nov. 7 *Perf. 13¼x13*

1686 Vert. strip of 5 6.00 3.00
a.-e. A651 25c Any single 1.00 .50

America Issue — Flora and Fauna — A652

No. 1687: a, Semnornis ramphastinus. b, Bomarea glaucescens.

Perf. 13x13¼

2003, Nov. 1 **Litho.** **Wmk. 395**

1687 A652 $1.05 Horiz. pair, #a-b 7.50 3.75

Selection of Quito as World Heritage Site, 25th Anniv. A653

Churches: 40c, El Sagrario. No. 1689a, La Compañia de Jesus. No. 1689b, Santa Barbara. $1.05, San Francisco, vert.

2003, Nov. 1 *Perf. 13¼x13, 13x13¼*

1688 A653 40c multi 1.25 .60
1689 A653 90c Horiz. pair, #a-b 6.00 3.00
1690 A653 $1.05 multi 3.75 1.90
Nos. 1688-1690 (3) 11.00 5.50

Christmas A654

Children's art by: No. 1691a, Stephanie Pacheco. No. 1691b, Sebastián Tejada. 40c, María Claudia Iturralde, vert. 90c, Luis Antonio Ortega. $1.05, Angel Andrés Castro, vert.

2003, Nov. 1

1691 A654 25c Horiz. pair, #a-b 1.90 .95
1692 A654 40c multi 1.50 .75
1693 A654 90c multi 3.50 1.75
1694 A654 $1.05 multi 3.75 1.90
Nos. 1691-1694 (4) 10.65 5.35

Treasures of Guayaquil Municipal Museum A655

No. 1695: a, Santiago de Guayaquil Act of Independence. b, Punaes ceremonial stone. c, Proclamation of Mariano Donoso. d, Tzantzas. e, Manteño-Huancavilca totem.

2003, Dec. 1 *Perf. 13¼x13*

1695 Horiz. strip of 5 7.00 3.50
a.-e. A655 40c Any single 1.25 .65

Selection of Galapagos Islands as World Heritage Site, 25th Anniv. — A656

No. 1696: a, Zalophus californianus wollebacki. b, Fregata minor palmerstoni. c, Sula nebouxxi excisa. d, Isla Bartolomé. e, Two Sula nebouxxi excisa shaped as "25."

2003, Nov. 26 *Perf. 13x13¼*

1696 Horiz. strip of 5 7.00 3.50
a.-e. A656 40c Any single 1.25 .65

Army Aviation Instruction, 50th Anniv. — A657

No. 1697, 40c: a, Mountain, airplanes, emblem. b, Airplane in flight, men on ground.
No. 1698, 40c, horiz.: a, Helicopter and soldiers. b, Airplanes, mountain, people.

2004, Jan. 21 ***Perf. 13x13¼, 13¼x13***
Horiz. pairs, #a-b

1697-1698 A657 Set of 2 6.00 3.00

Military Geographical Institute's Role in National Development — A658

2004, Apr. 14 ***Perf. 13¼x13***
1699 A658 $1.05 multi 3.25 1.90

Commander Rafael Morán Valverde, Military Hero — A659

2004, Apr. 5 ***Perf. 13x13¼***
1700 A659 $1.05 multi 3.75 1.90

Intl. Philately Day — A660

No. 1701: a, Ecuador #2, Greece #1. b, Cover with six stamps.
$2, Various stamps, tongs, magnifying glass, stamp catalogues.

2004, May 6 ***Perf. 13¼x13***
1701 A660 75c Horiz. pair, #a-b 6.00 3.00

Imperf
Size: 100x68mm

1702 A660 $2 multi 7.50 3.75

Ecuadorian Volleyball Federation A661

Perf. 13x13¼
2004, May 27 Litho. Wmk. 395
1703 A661 75c multi 3.00 1.50

2004 Miss Universe Pageant A662

2004, May 29 ***Perf. 13¾***
1704 A662 75c multi 3.00 1.50

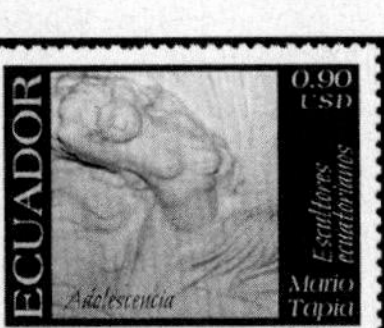

Sculpture by Mario Tapia A663

No. 1705: a, Adolescencia. b, Beato Chaminade. c, Delfin de Galapagos. d, Pelicano. e, Homenaje a Carlo Vidano.
$2, Similar to No. 1705b.

2004, June 1 ***Perf. 13¼x13***
1705 Horiz. strip of 5 16.00 8.00
a.-e. A663 90c Any single 2.25 1.10

Imperf
Size: 100x69mm

1706 A663 $2 multi 9.00 4.50

Pedro Vicente Maldonado (1704-48), Cartographer A664

2004, June 25 ***Perf. 13x13¼***
1707 A664 90c multi 3.00 1.50

Dr. Agustín Cueva Tamariz (1903-79) — A665

2004, June 30 **Litho.**
1708 A665 90c multi 3.00 1.50

34th General Assembly of the Organization of American States — A666

2004, July 4 **Wmk. 395**
1709 A666 75c multi 3.00 1.50

Dr. Angel Felicísmo Rojas (b. 1909), Writer — A667

2004, July 11
1710 A667 50c multi 2.00 1.00

Ecuadoran and Spanish Postal Money Orders A668

2004, Aug. 3 ***Perf. 13¼x13***
1711 A668 $1.05 multi 3.25 1.90

2004 Summer Olympics, Athens — A669

No. 1712 — 2004 Summer Olympics emblem, Ecuadoran Olympic Committee emblem and: a, 2004 Olympics mascots. b, Alexandra Escobar Guerrero.

2004, Aug. 3 ***Perf. 13x13¼***
1712 A669 $1.05 Horiz. pair, #a-b 7.50 3.75

Ecuador Orchid Association, 30th Anniv. — A670

Designs: 25c, Cattleya maxima. $1.05, Epidendrum bracteolatum.

2004, Sept. 30
1713-1714 A670 Set of 2 5.00 2.50

Guayaquil Symphony Orchestra — A671

Perf. 13x13¼
2004, Nov. 19 Litho. Wmk. 395
1715 A671 90c multi 3.00 1.50

Christmas — A672

Children's art: 40c, Christmas stocking with envelopes. $1.05, Santa Claus giving letter to Christmas tree, horiz.

2004, Dec. 12 ***Perf. 13x13¼, 13¼x13***
1716-1717 A672 Set of 2 5.00 2.50

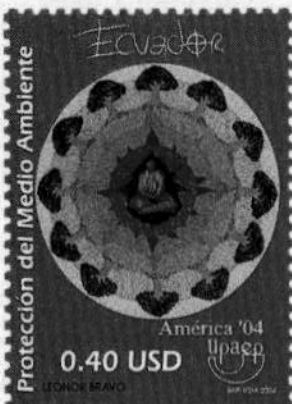

America Issue - Environmental Protection — A673

Designs: 40d, Buddha and trees. $1.05, Mother Earth.

2004, Dec. 23 ***Perf. 13x13¼***
1718-1719 A673 Set of 2 5.00 2.50

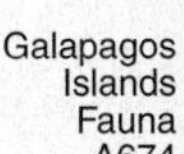

Galapagos Islands Fauna A674

Designs: 40c, Chelonoidis abingdonii. 90c, Amblyrhynchus cristatus, vert. $2.15, Sula granti. $3, Fregata magnifiscens.
$2, Creagrus furcatus, vert.

2005, Feb. 18 ***Perf. 13¼x13, 13x13¼***
1720-1723 A674 Set of 4 24.00 12.00

Imperf
Size: 68x98mm

1724 A674 $2 multi 7.50 3.75

El Mercurio Newspaper, 80th Anniv. A675

Designs: $1.25, Masthead. $2, Dr. Nicanor Merchan Bermeo, newspaper co-founder. $2.25, Miguel Merchan Ochoa.

2005, Mar. 4 ***Perf. 13¼x13, 13x13¼***
1725-1727 A675 Set of 3 22.50 11.00

Tourism A676

2005, Mar. 22 ***Perf. 13¼x13***
1728 A676 $3.75 multi 14.00 7.00

Ecuadorian Chess Federation, 25th Anniv. — A677

2005, Apr. 1 ***Perf. 13x13¼***
1729 A677 $1.25 multi 5.00 2.50

Ecuadorian Olympic Academy, 25th Anniv. — A678

Perf. 13x13¼

2005, June 20 Litho. Wmk. 395

1730 A678 $1.25 shown 5.00 2.50

Imperf

Size: 69x100mm

1731 A678 $2 Emblems 9.00 4.50

Rotary International, Cent. A679

Rotary emblem and: 40c, Man on Mt. Chimborazo. 90c, People on Mt. Cotopaxi. $2, Man on Mt. Shisha Pangma, Nepal.

2005, June 29 ***Perf. 13¼x13***

1732-1734 A679 Set of 3 12.50 6.25

Guayaquil Conference, 183rd Anniv. — A680

No. 1735 — Guayaquil Philatelic Club emblem and: a, José de San Martín, Argentina #1. b, Simón Bolívar, Venezuela #1.

$2, Bolívar, San Martín, monument.

2005, July 22 ***Perf. 13¼x13***

1735 A680 90c Horiz. pair, #a-b 7.50 3.75

Imperf

Size:98x68mm

1736 A680 $2 multi 9.00 4.50

Intl. Year of Books and Reading — A681

Perf. 13x13¼

2005, July 22 Litho. Wmk. 395

1737 A681 25c multi 1.25 .60

Dr. Juan Isaac Lovato Vargas (1904-2001), Judge — A682

Perf. 13¼x13

2005, July 28 Litho. Wmk. 395

1738 A682 $1.25 multi 6.00 3.00

Mountain and Eastern Cattleman's Association — A683

No. 1739 — Emblem and: a, Mountains. b, Head of cow.

2005, Aug. 4 ***Perf. 13x13¼***

1739 A683 40c Horiz. pair, #a-b 3.00 3.00

University Sports League of Quito, 75th Anniv. A684

No. 1740: a, University Sports League Stadium. b, 1969 University Sports League soccer team. c, Emblem. d, Children playing at school. e, Statue of emblem, League Country Club.

$2, Soccer shirt, vert.

2005, Aug. 4 ***Perf. 13¼x13***

1740 Horiz. strip of 5 8.00 4.00
a.-e. A684 40c Any single 1.40 .70

Imperf

Size: 68x98mm

1741 A684 $2 multi 9.00 4.50

15th Bolivarian Games, Armenia and Pereira A685

2005, Aug. 8 ***Perf. 13¼x13***

1742 A685 25c multi 1.25 .60

A686

Design: 1938 South American Swimming Champions, Trophy and Swimming Federation Emblem.

2005, Aug. 8 Litho.

1743 A686 25c multi 1.25 .60

First Ecuadoran victory in international sports competition.

Virgin of Cisne — A687

2005, Sept. 6 ***Perf. 13¾***

1744 A687 $1.25 multi 6.00 3.00

History of the Ecuadoran Army A688

No. 1745: a, Troops in Esmeraldas, 1916. b, Military school cadets, 1928. c, Cayambe Battalion. d, Arms and Grandsons of Gen. Eloy Alfaro. e, Imbabura Battalion.

$2, Battle for emancipation of Guayaquil.

2005, Sept. 15 ***Perf. 13¼x13***

1745 Horiz. strip of 5 8.00 4.00
a.-e. A688 40c Any single 1.00 .50

Imperf

Size: 98x67mm

1746 A688 $2 multi 9.00 4.50

Carchi Province Arms — A689

No. 1747: a, Tulcán Canton. b, Bolívar Canton.

No. 1748: a, Carchi Province. b, Huaca Canton. c, Mira Canton. d, Espejo Canton. e, Montúfar Canton.

2005, Sept. 26 ***Perf. 13x13¼***

1747 Horiz. pair 3.00 1.50
a.-b. A689 40c Either single 1.40 .70
1748 Horiz. strip of 5 7.50 3.75
a.-e. A689 40c Any single 1.40 .70

Tourism — A690

No. 1749: a, Cerro Santa Ana, Guayaquil. b, Esmereldas. c, Misahualli. d, Tsunki Shuar, Pastaza.

No. 1750: a, Cisne Church, Loja. b, Ingapirca Ruins. c, Seal, Galapagos Islands. d, Sea turtle, Galapagos Islands.

Perf. 13¼x13

2005, Sept. 26 Litho. Wmk. 395

1749 A690 30c Block of 4, #a-d 5.00 2.50
1750 A690 40c Block of 4, #a-d 6.50 3.25

St. Mariana de Jesús Paredes y Flores A691

2005, Oct. 19

1751 A691 25c multi 1.25 .60

Popes Reigning in 2005 — A692

No. 1752: a, $1.25, Pope John Paul II (1920-2005). b, $2, Pope Benedict XVI.

2005, Oct. 19

1752 A692 Horiz. pair, #a-b 12.50 6.25

Cenepa War With Peru, 10th Anniv. — A693

No. 1753: a, Mirage F1-JA airplanes. b, Cessna A-37B airplanes. c, Kfir-C2 airplanes. d, Lt. Col. Carlos Uscategui and airplane.

2005, Oct. 26

1753 A693 $1.25 Block of 4, #a-d 22.50 11.00

First Guayaquil to Cuenca Airmail Flight, 85th Anniv. — A694

No. 1754: a, 25c, Tail of Telegrafo I airplane, flight manager José Abel Castillo. b, $1, Front of Telegrafo I airplane, pilot Elia Liut.

2005, Nov. 12

1754 A694 Horiz. pair, #a-b 5.50 2.75

Ecuadorian Armed Forces in United Nations Peacekeeping Forces — A695

No. 1755: a, Female soldier. b, Two soldiers wearing helmets. c, Soldiers with flags. d, United Nations and Ecuadorian flags, beret of Peacekeeping forces.

2005, Nov. 25 ***Perf. 13x13¼***

1755 A695 75c Block of 4, #a-d 12.00 6.00

Christmas — A696

No. 1756 — Children's drawings by: a, Pamela Alejandra Castillo Rocha. b, Kira Cedeño. c, Silvia Moran Burgos. d, Carol Garcia.

2005, Nov. 25

1756 A696 $1.25 Block of 4, #a-d 22.50 11.00

19th Cent. Watercolors of Ecuadorians A697

No. 1757: a, Water bearer. b, Indian governor's wife. c, Dancer. d, Cuenca Indian. e, Municipal council piper. f, Indian carrying skyrockets. g, Woman (Mina gigante). h, Majordomo. i, Society woman (Chola pinganilla). j, Street sweeper.

2005, Nov. 30 ***Perf. 13¾***
1757 Block of 10 12.50 6.25
a.-j. A697 25c Any single 1.00 .50

Publication of Don Quixote, 400th Anniv. — A698

No. 1758 — Drawings of Don Quixote and: a, Windmills. b, Tree.

2005, Dec. 7 ***Perf. 13x13¼***
1758 A698 $2 Horiz. pair, #a-b 17.00 8.50

Colonial Religious Art — A699

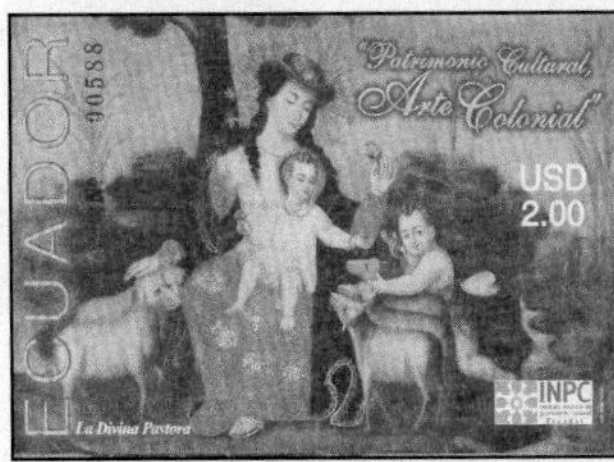

Colonial Religious Art — A700

No. 1759: a, St. Joseph and Baby Jesus. b, Resurrected Christ. c, Virgin of Quito. d, St. Augustine.
No. 1760: $2, The Divine Shepherd.

2005, Dec. 9
1759 A699 40c Block of 4, #a-d 6.00 3.00

Souvenir Sheet
Imperf
1760 A700 $2 multi 9.00 4.50

El Comercio Newspaper, Cent. (in 2006) A701

"100" and: No. 1761, Statue at LL, newspaper masthead. No. 1762a, Statue at LR. No. 1762b, Statue in "0." No. 1763, Statue in seal. No. 1764, Statue at LL, newspaper masthead, simulated perforations.

Perf. 13¼x13
2006, Jan. 2 **Litho.** **Wmk. 395**
1761 A701 40c multi 1.75 .85
1762 A701 40c Horiz. pair, #a-b 3.25 1.60

Size: 55x35mm
Perf. 13¾
1763 A701 50c multi 2.00 1.00
Nos. 1761-1763 (3) 7.00 3.45

Size: 100x69mm
Imperf
1764 A701 $2 multi 8.00 4.00

Dated 2006.

Quito Tourism A702

2006, Jan. 11 ***Perf. 13¼x13***
1765 A702 25c multi 1.25 .60

Dated 2005.

35th Latin American and Caribbean Lions' Club Forum, Quito — A703

Color of oceans: 90c, White. $2, Orange.

2006, Jan. 19 ***Perf. 13x13¼***
1766 A703 90c multi 4.00 2.00

Size: 68x99mm
Imperf
1767 A703 $2 multi 8.00 4.00

Biodiversity of Puyo A704

Designs: $1, Cromacris sp. $1.20, Desmodus rotundus.

2006, Mar. 22 ***Perf. 13¼x13***
1768-1769 A704 Set of 2 10.00 5.00

America Issue, Fight Against Poverty A705

Various Pre-Columbian Guayasamin figurines: 40c, 80c, $1, $1.20.

2006, Feb. 12
1770-1773 A705 Set of 4 14.50 7.25

Benito Juarez (1806-72), President of Mexico — A706

2006, Mar. 21 ***Perf. 13x13¼***
1774 A706 $1.20 multi 5.00 2.50

Manteña Raft A707

2006, Mar. 23 ***Perf. 13¼x13***
1775 A707 $1 multi 4.50 2.25

Straw Hat Makers A708

Designs: No. 1776, 40c, Hat maker. No. 1777, 40c, Hat maker wearing hat, vert.

2006, Apr. 8 ***Perf. 13¼x13, 13x13¼***
1776-1777 A708 Set of 2 3.75 1.90

Federation of University Students — A709

2006, Apr. 21 ***Perf. 13x13¼***
1778 A709 30c multi 1.25 .60

Miracle of Colegio San Gabriel, Cent. — A710

2006, Apr. 21 **Wmk. 395**
1779 A710 80c multi 3.75 1.90

Ibarra, 400th Anniv. A711

2006, Apr. 28 ***Perf. 13¼x13***
1780 A711 20c shown .80 .25

Size: 68x100mm
Imperf
1781 A711 $2.50 Painting, diff. 11.00 5.50

Baltazara Calderon — A712

2005, May 16 ***Perf. 13x13¼***
1782 A712 $1 multi 4.50 2.25

18th Cent. Military Uniforms A713

No. 1783: a, Compañia Fija de Quito. b, Dragones de Quito. c, Infanteria de Quito. d, Dragones de Guayaquil (gray horse). e, Dragones de Guayaquil (brown horse).

2006, May 18 ***Perf. 13¾***
1783 Horiz. strip of 5 4.25 2.10
a.-e. A713 20c Any single .70 .25

Mushrooms and Fauna of Podocarpus Park — A714

Designs: 20c, Basidiomicetes. 25c, Tremarctus ornatus. 90c, Harpya harpyja, vert.

Perf. 13¼x13, 13x13¼
2006, May 22 **Litho.** **Wmk. 395**
1784-1786 A714 Set of 3 6.00 3.00

Wolfgang Amadeus Mozart (1756-91), Composer A715

2006, May 31 ***Perf. 13¼x13***
1787 A715 20c multi .80 .25

UNICEF, 60th Anniv. A716

Designs: 75c, Child, butterfly, and sun. $1, Children and books.

Perf. 13¼x13
2006, June 1 **Litho.** **Wmk. 395**
1788-1789 A716 Set of 2 8.00 4.00

Eloy Alfaro Military School A717

2006, June 5
1790 A717 80c multi 3.75 1.90

Banco Pichincha, Cent. A718

Designs: No. 1791, 1906 1-sucre banknote. No. 1792 — First bank building: a, Denomination at left. b, Denomination at right.

2006, June 8

1791 A718 40c shown 1.80 .90
1792 A718 40c Horiz. pair, #a-b 3.75 1.90

2006 World Cup Soccer Championships, Germany — A719

FIFA emblem and: 40c, World Cup. 80c, 2006 World Cup emblem. $1, Mascot. $1.20, World Cup and flags of competing countries.

Perf. 13¼x13

2006, June 9 Litho. Wmk. 395

1793-1796 A719 Set of 4 14.50 7.25

World Cup Type of 2006

Perf. 13¼x13

2006, June 9 Litho. Wmk. 395

Stamps Without FIFA Emblem With Inscription "COPA MONDIAL de la FIFA"

1796A A719 40c Like #1793 *16.00 16.00*
1797 A719 80c Like #1794 *5.25 5.25*
1797A A719 $1 Like #1795 *6.75 6.75*
1797B A719 $1.20 Like #1795 *8.00 8.00*
Nos. 1796A-1797B (4) 36.00 36.00

2006 Litho. Wmk. 395 ***Imperf.***

Size: 60x40mm

Designs: No. 1797C, Like #1796. No. 1797D, Similar to #1796, but with scores of Ecuador team's first round victories.

1797C A719 $2 multi 8.00 4.00
1797D A719 $2 multi 8.00 4.00

A720

Plaza de Mayo Mothers of Argentina — A721

Perf. 13¼x13

2006, June 19 Litho. Wmk. 395

1798 A720 80c multi 3.75 1.90

Imperf

1799 A721 $2.50 multi 11.00 5.50

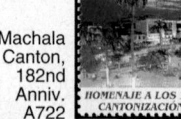

Machala Canton, 182nd Anniv. A722

2006, June 20 ***Perf. 13¼x13***

1800 A722 30c multi 1.25 .60

Machala Canton, 182nd Anniv. — A723

Flags of 2006 World Cup Soccer Championship participants, FIFA emblem and: No. 1801, Flag of Ecuador. No. 1802, Soccer shoes and ball.

2006 Litho. Wmk. 395 ***Imperf.***

1801 A723 $2 multi 8.00 4.00
1802 A723 $2 multi 8.00 4.00

2006 World Cup Soccer Championships, Germany.

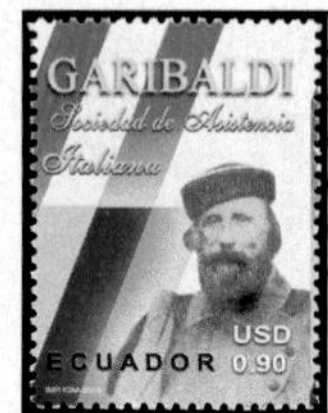

Garibaldi Italian Assistance Society — A724

2006, July 7 ***Perf. 13x13¼***

1803 A724 90c multi 4.00 2.00

Municipal Railroads A725

Designs: No. 1804, $1, Steam locomotive. No. 1805, $1, Steam locomotive, vert.

Perf. 13¼x13, 13x13¼

2006, July 20 Litho. Wmk. 395

1804-1805 A725 Set of 2 *8.00 8.00*

Souvenir Sheet

Municipal Railroads — A726

Wmk. 395

2006, July 20 Litho. ***Imperf.***

1806 A726 $2 multi 8.00 4.00

Simón Bolívar Experimental College — A727

Bolívar A728

2006, July 25 Litho. ***Perf. 13x13¼***

1807 A727 20c multi .80 .25

Imperf

1808 A728 $10 multi 40.00 20.00

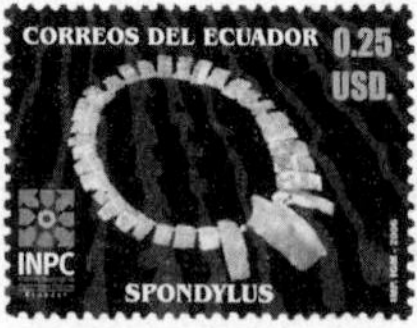

Spondylus Shell Carvings in National Institute of Cultural Heritage A729

Designs: 25c, Necklace.

No. 1810, vert.: a, Figurine of trader. b, Figurine of fishermen in boat.

2006, July 26 ***Perf. 13¼x13, 13x13¼***

1809 A729 25c multi 1.50 .75
1810 A729 $1 Horiz. pair, #a-b 8.00 8.00

Indian Postal Runner and Ecuador Post Emblem — A730

Background colors: 25c, White. 30c, Dark blue. 40c, Black. 60c, Beige. 80c, Olive green

2006, Aug. 5 ***Perf. 13x13¼***

1811-1815 A730 Set of 5 10.00 5.00

Ecuadorian Olympic Committee A731

2006, Aug. 15 Litho.

1816 A731 30c multi 1.25 .60

Writers — A732

Designs: $1, Jorge Icaza (1906-78). $1.20, Pablo Palacio (1906-47).

2006, Sept. 18 Wmk. 395

1817-1818 A732 Set of 2 10.00 5.00

Ecuadorian Food — A733

No. 1819: a, Bandera Manabi. b, Viche de Manabi.

2006, Sept. 23 ***Perf. 13¼x13***

1819 A733 $1 Horiz. pair, #a-b 8.50 4.25

Orchids — A734

No. 1820: a, Caucaea olivaceum. b, Cyrtochilum macranthum. c, Miltoniopsis vexillaria. d, Odontoglossum harryanum. e, Cyrtochilum pastasae. f, Cyrtochilum loxense. g, Cyrtochilum eduardii. h, Odontoglossum epidendroides. i, Cyrtochilum retusum. j, Cyrtochilum geniculatum.

$2, Cyrtochilum macranthum, diff.

2006, Sept. 29 ***Perf. 13x13¼***

1820 Block of 10 13.00 6.50
a.-j. A734 30c Any single 1.25 .60

Imperf

Size: 66x95mm

1821 A734 $2 multi 8.50 4.25

America Issue, Energy Conservation — A735

Background color: $1, Brown. $1.20, Blue.

2006, Oct. 4 ***Perf. 13¼x13***

1822-1823 A735 Set of 2 10.00 5.00

Natural Fiber Art, by Giti Neuman — A736

Designs: No. 1824, En la Ventana.

No. 1825: a, Forma en Movimiento. b, Caminantes.

No. 1826, horiz.: a, Caminando. b, Cabezas Huecas.

2006, Oct. 4 ***Perf. 13x13¼, 13¼x13***

1824 A736 30c multi 1.25 .60
1825 A736 30c Vert. pair, #a-b 2.75 1.40
1826 A736 30c Horiz. pair, #a-b 2.75 1.40
Nos. 1824-1826 (3) 6.75 3.40

Tourism in Otavalo A737

Designs: 25c, El Lechero tree. 30c, El Jordan Church. 75c, Young girl, vert. $1, Costume for El Coraza Festival, vert.

2006, Oct. 18 *Perf. 13¼x13, 13x13¼*
1827-1830 A737 Set of 4 10.50 5.25

Eruption of Tungurahua Volcano — A738

No. 1831: a, Ash cloud above volcano. b, Lava flowing down volcano.

2006, Oct. 20 *Perf. 13x13¼*
1831 A738 $1 Horiz. pair, #a-b 8.50 4.25

Urban Renewal of Guayaquil A739

No. 1832: a, Municipal Palace, denomination at left. b, Municipal Palace, denomination at right. c, Vulcan forge. d, José Joaquín de Olmedo Airport. e, Bus station.

2006, Oct. 24 *Perf. 13¼x13*
1832 Horiz. strip of 5 21.50 11.00
a.-e. A739 $1 Any single 3.75 1.90

Radio Station HCJB, 75th Anniv. A740

2006, Oct. 26 **Wmk. 395**
1833 A740 $1 multi 4.50 2.25

Millennium Development Objectives of the United Nations — A741

2006, Oct. 27 *Perf. 13¾*
1834 A741 $2 multi 8.50 4.25

Pres. Galo Plaza Lasso (1906-87) — A742

Designs: 40c, Photograph. 80c, Tree.

2006, Oct. 27 *Perf. 13x13¼*
1835-1836 A742 Set of 2 5.00 2.50

German Shepherd Breeding Association A743

2006, Oct. 28 **Litho.** *Perf. 13¼x13*
1837 A743 $1 multi 4.50 2.25

Military Parachuting, 50th Anniv. A744

Designs: 20c, Soldiers. 40c, Soldiers and airplane. 60c, Soldier and troop emblem. 80c, Paratrooper in air.

Perf. 13¼x13, 13x13¼
2006, Oct. 31 **Litho.** **Wmk. 395**
1838-1841 A744 Set of 4 8.50 4.25

Galapagos Islands Fauna — A745

No. 1842, horiz.: a, Sea turtle. b, Sea gull. c, Marine iguana. d, Blue-footed boobies. e, Sea lion.
80c, Flamingo. $1, Crab. $1.20, Fish.

2006, Nov. 1
1842 A745 30c Horiz. strip of 5, #a-e 6.50 3.25
1843 A745 80c multi 3.25 1.60
1844 A745 $1 multi 4.00 2.00
1845 A745 $1.20 multi 5.00 2.50
Nos. 1842-1845 (4) 18.75 9.35

Christmas — A746

2006, Nov. 28 *Perf. 13x13¼*
1846 A746 80c multi 3.25 1.60

Monsignor Juan I. Larrea Holguín (1927-2006) — A747

No. 1847: a, In bishop's robes. b, In judicial robes.

2006, Dec. 8 *Perf. 13¾*
1847 A747 40c Horiz. pair, #a-b 3.75 1.90

Freemasonry A748

Designs: 25c, Masonic altar, beehive. 40c, Compass and square.

2006, Dec. 11 *Perf. 13x13¼*
1848-1849 A748 Set of 2 3.00 1.50

Quito Zoo Animals — A749

No. 1850: a, Parrot. b, Frog.
No. 1851: a, Harpy eagle. b, Jaguar.
$2, Parrot on branch.

2006, Dec. 11 *Perf. 13x13¼*
1850 A749 60c Horiz. pair, #a-b 4.75 2.40
1851 A749 80c Horiz. pair, #a-b 6.50 3.25

Imperf

Size: 40x65mm

1852 A749 $2 multi 8.50 4.25

Erotic and Fertility Figurines — A750

Designs: 10c, Nursing mother. 20c, Copulating couple. $1.20, Pregnant woman. $2, Man with erect penis.

2006, Dec. 12 *Perf. 13x13¼*
1853-1856 A750 Set of 4 15.00 7.50

Admiral Juan Illingworth Naval Museum — A751

Emblem of Ecuador Navy and Illingworth: 20c, On rope ladder, 1880. 25c, As Marine Guard, 1854.

2006, Dec. 15 **Litho.**
1857-1858 A751 Set of 2 2.00 1.00

Colors of Ecuador Flag — A752

2006, Dec. 15 **Wmk. 395**
1859 A752 $10 multi 37.50 19.00

Postmen and Bicycles A753

Color of photograph: 20c, Gray brown. 40c, Gray blue. 80c, Red.

2006, Dec. 17 *Perf. 13¼x13*
1860-1862 A753 Set of 3 6.00 3.00

Pets A754

Designs: 25c, Puppy. 40c, Dog, vert. 50c, Cat with brown and blue eyes, vert. 80c, Dog running. $1, Cat with blue eyes, vert.

2006, Dec. 17 *Perf. 13¼x13, 13x13¼*
1863-1867 A754 Set of 5 12.00 6.00

Cuenca Biennale A755

Art by: 5c, Alexander Apóstol. 15c, Ricardo González Elias, vert.

2006, Dec. 20
1868-1869 A755 Set of 2 .55 .25

Independence Monument, 50th Anniv. — A756

No. 1870: a, Head of statue. b, Entire statue.

2006, Dec. 21 *Perf. 13¾*
1870 A756 20c Horiz. pair, #a-b 1.80 .90

Quito Fair — A757

Designs: No. 1871, Matador Manolo Caena.
No. 1872 — Matadors: a, Sebastián Castella. b, El Juli.
No. 1873, horiz. — Quito Bull Ring: a, At right. b, At left.
$3, Sculpture of Jesus, horiz.

Perf. 13x13¼, 13¼x13
2006, Dec. 27 **Litho.**
1871 A757 50c multi 2.50 1.25
1872 A757 50c Horiz. pair, #a-b 4.25 2.10
1873 A757 50c Horiz. pair, #a-b 4.25 2.10
Nos. 1871-1873 (3) 11.00 5.45

Litho. With Foil Application

Imperf

Size: 65x40mm

1874 A757 $3 multi 13.00 6.50

Pirates A758

No. 1875, vert.: a, Jolly Roger flag, ship, sea lions. b, Sea lions, ships. c, Ships, Jolly roger flag. d, Armed pirate on ship. e, Ship, Jolly Roger flag.

No. 1876: a, Map of Galapagos Islands, Jolly Roger flag, Sir Francis Drake. b, Ship, map, skull.

$1, Ship, map, skull, William Dampier.

Perf. 13x13¼, 13¼x13

2006, Dec. 27 **Litho.**

1875 A758 30c Horiz. strip of 5, #a-e 7.25 3.50
1876 A758 40c Horiz. pair, #a-b 3.75 1.90
1877 A758 $1 multi 5.00 2.50
Nos. 1875-1877 (3) 16.00 7.90

SEK International University, Quito A759

Perf. 13¼x13

2006, Dec. 29 **Wmk. 395**

1878 A759 10c multi .50 .40

Scouting, Cent. — A760

Scout emblem and: 25c, Circles. $2, Scout and circles.

Perf. 13x13¼

2007, Mar. 29 **Litho.** **Wmk. 395**

1879-1880 A760 Set of 2 8.00 4.00

Hispanic-American Poetry Festival — A761

2007, Apr. 19

1881 A761 10c multi .40 .30

Cuenca, 450th Anniv. — A762

Designs: 40c, Casa de los Arcos (Arch House). 75c, Vergel Plaza. 80c, Tomebamba River Gorge, horiz. $3, Cathedral of the Immaculate Conception.

2007, Apr. 27 *Perf. 13x13¼, 13¼x13*

1882-1885 A762 Set of 4 17.50 8.75

Prehistoric Animals — A763

Designs: No. 1886, 80c, Megatherium. No. 1887, 80c, Smilodon, horiz.

2007, May 10

1886-1887 A763 Set of 2 5.75 3.75

Beetles A764

Designs: No. 1888, Golopha eaucus.
No. 1889: a, Chrysophora chrysochlora. b, Dynastes hercules.

2007, May 10 *Perf. 13¼x13*

1888 A764 40c multi 1.50 .75
1889 A764 40c Horiz. pair, #a-b 3.00 1.50

Guayaquil Rotary Club, 80th Anniv. A765

2007, June 1 **Wmk. 395**

1890 A765 25c multi .90 .45

America Issue, Education For All — A766

Designs: 40c, Children on school bus. 80c, Girl doing geometry work. $1, Children flying kites, vert. $1.20, Student in wheelchair, vert. $2, Girl and handprints, vert.

2007, June 6 *Perf. 13¼x13, 13x13¼*

1891-1894 A766 Set of 4 12.00 6.00

Imperf

Size: 40x65mm

1895 A766 $2 multi 7.50 3.75

Naval Institute of Oceanography, 75th Anniv. — A767

Antarctic research: 10c, Penguin, ship. $3, Scientists and scientific equipment, horiz.

2007, July 18 *Perf. 13x13¼*

1896 A767 10c multi .40 .30

Perf. 12

Size: 52x32mm

1897 A767 $3 multi 11.00 5.50

Central Bank of Ecuador, 80th Anniv. — A768

2007, Aug. 28 *Perf. 12*

1898 A768 $2 multi 7.50 3.75

Guayaquil Firefighters A769

Various firefighters at fires: 5c, 10c, 15c, 25c, $1. 25c and $1 are horiz.

2007, Oct. 10 *Perf. 13x13¼, 13¼x13*

1899-1903 A769 Set of 5 5.50 2.75

Breast Cancer Prevention A770

2007, Oct. 15 *Perf. 13¼x13*

1904 A770 $3 multi 11.00 5.50

Guayaquil Tourism — A771

Designs: 5c, Las Peñas. 10c, Lighthouse, Santa Ana Hill. 15c, El Velero Bridge. 25c, Mercado Sur, horiz. $1, June 5 Bridge, horiz.

2007, Oct. 23 *Perf. 13x13¼, 13¼x13*

1905-1909 A771 Set of 5 5.50 2.25

Cuenca Chamber of Industries, 70th Anniv. A772

2007, Oct. 25 *Perf. 13¼x13*

1910 A772 $1.20 multi 4.25 2.10

Operation Smile A773

2007, Nov. 16 **Litho.**

1911 A773 $1 multi 3.75 1.90

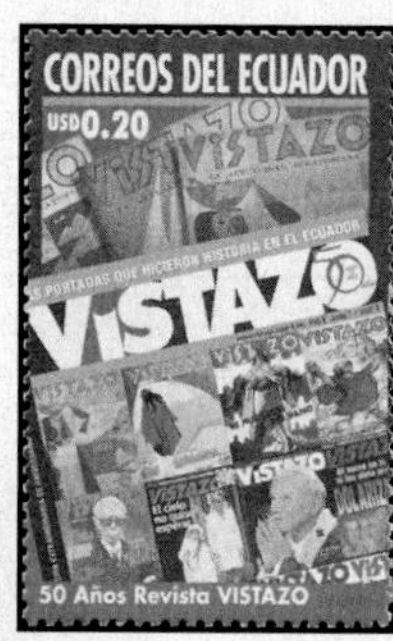

Vistazo Magazine, 50th Anniv. A774

2007, Nov. 29 *Perf. 12*

1912 A774 20c multi .75 .25

Galapagos Islands Fauna A775

Designs: 40c, Sea turtle. 80c, Penguin. $1, Dolphin. $1.20, Tropicbird.

2007, Nov. 30 *Perf. 13¼x13*

1913-1916 A775 Set of 4 12.00 6.00

Compare with type A780.

Comptroller General, 80th Anniv. A776

2007, Dec. 3 *Perf. 12*

1917 A776 20c multi .75 .25

2007 Pan American Games, Rio de Janeiro — A777

No. 1918 — Athletes and text noting gold medalists: a, Alexandra Escobar. b, Seledina Nieve. c, Jefferson Perez. d, Xavier Moreno. e, Under-18 soccer team.

2007, Dec. 18 *Perf. 13x13¼*

1918 Horiz. strip of 5 7.25 3.00
a.-e. A777 40c Any single 1.25 .60

Christmas — A778

No. 1919: a, The Annunciation. b, The Three Magi. c, Nativity. d, Flight into Egypt.

2007, Dec. 20 *Perf. 13¼x13*

1919 A778 20c Block of 4, #a-d 2.75 1.40

Guayas Province Transit Commission, 60th Anniv. — A779

Perf. 13x13¼

2008, Jan. 29 Litho. Wmk. 395
1920 A779 $1 multi 3.75 1.90

Galapagos Islands A780

Map of islands and: 40c, Pelecanus occidentalis. 80c, Aetobatus narinari. $1, Carcharhinus galapagensis. $1.20, San Cristóbal Windmill Project.

2008, Mar. 18 *Perf. 13¼x13*
1921-1924 A780 Set of 4 12.00 6.00

Compare with Type A775.

Free Maternity and Infant Care — A781

2008, Mar. 28 *Perf. 12*
1925 A781 $1 multi 3.75 1.90

Guayaquil Port Authority, 50th Anniv. A782

2008, Apr. 8
1926 A782 20c multi .75 .25

Tungurahua Chamber of Industry, 80th Anniv. — A783

Wmk. 395

2008, Apr. 24 Litho. *Perf. 12*
1927 A783 $3 multi 11.00 5.50

Father Carlos Crespi (1891-1982) — A784

2008, Apr. 30
1928 A784 $2 multi 7.25 3.00

Santiago de Guayaquil Medallion A785

2008, June 3
1929 A785 30c multi 1.10 .55

Intl. Philately Day.

Jorge Pérez Concha, Historian and Diplomat, Birth Cent. — A786

2008, June 4
1930 A786 $3 multi 11.00 5.50

Los Pinos College, Quito, 40th Anniv. A787

2008, June 6
1931 A787 20c multi .75 .25

Guayaquil-Quito Railway, Cent. — A788

Ecuador No. 174 and: 56c, Steam locomotive. $5, Steam locomotives, Gabriel García Moreno and Gen. Eloy Alfaro.

2008, June 23 *Perf. 12*
1932 A788 56c multi 2.00 1.00

Imperf

Size: 100x70mm

1933 A788 $5 multi 18.00 9.00

Polytechnic School of the Coast, 50th Anniv. — A789

Wmk. 395

2008, July 28 Litho. *Perf. 12*
1934 A789 32c multi 1.10 .55

Latin American Youth Year — A790

2008, Aug. 20
1935 A790 30c multi 1.10 .55

Ecuadorian Cacao — A791

No. 1936: a, Cacao pod, UL corner of #306. b, Cacao flower, UR corner of #306. c, Cacao processing, LL corner of #306. d, Cacao pods and beans, chocolate candy, LR corner of #306.

2008, Oct. 1 *Perf. 13¼x13*
1936 A791 56c Block of 4, #a-d 8.00 4.00

Meridiano Newspaper, 25th Anniv. — A792

2008, Oct. 22 *Perf. 13x13¼*
1937 A792 60c multi 2.00 1.00

Intl. Swimming Federation, Cent. A793

No. 1938: a, World Map. b, Ecuadorian swimmer.
30c, Swimmer from underwater.

2008, Oct. 31 *Perf. 13¼x13*
1938 A793 24c Horiz. pair, #a-b 1.25 .60
1939 A793 30c multi .70 .30

Office of the Procurator General, 80th Anniv. — A794

2008, Nov. 11 *Perf. 13x13¼*
1940 A794 25c multi .60 .25

Guayaquil Chamber of Construction, 40th Anniv. A795

2008, Nov. 27 *Perf. 13¼x13*
1941 A795 $1 multi 2.25 1.10

New Constitution — A796

Flag and: 32c, Sun behind clouds. $5, People, vert.

2008, Nov. 29 *Perf. 12*
1942 A796 32c multi .75 .30

Size: 66x95mm

Imperf

1943 A796 $5 multi 12.00 6.00

Santiago de Guayaquil Municipal Museum, Cent. A797

No. 1944: a, Old musuem building. b, New museum building with murals.
$2, Entrance to old musuem building.

2008, Dec. 16 *Perf. 13¼x13*
1944 A797 60c Horiz. pair, #a-b 3.00 1.50
1945 A797 $2 multi 5.00 2.50

Friendship Between Ecuador and Japan, 90th Anniv. — A798

No. 1945: a, Cotopaxi Volcano, Ecuador. b, Mt. Fuji, Japan.

2008, Dec. 17
1946 A798 30c Horiz. pair, #a-b 1.50 .75

America Issue, National Festivals — A799

No. 1947 — Festival of Sts. Peter and Paul: a, Dancers. b, Guitarist.
No. 1948, vert. — Diablada Pillareña: a, Figure with red mask. b, Figure with black mask.

2008, Dec. 23 *Perf. 13¼x13*
1947 A799 20c Horiz. pair, #a-b 1.00 .50

Perf. 13x13¼
1948 A799 $1 Horiz. pair, #a-b 5.00 2.50

Christmas A800

Various creche figurines of Holy Family and animals with background color of: 30c, Blue. No. 1949: a, Green. b, Yellow brown.

2008, Dec. 23 *Perf. 13¼x13*
1949 A800 30c multi .75 .30
1950 A800 80c Horiz. pair, #a-b 4.00 2.00

A801

A802

A803

A804

Jacchigua National Folk Ballet A805

Perf. 13¼x13
2009, Feb. 18 **Litho.** **Wmk. 395**
1951 Horiz. strip of 5 12.00 6.00
a. A801 $1 multi 2.00 1.00
b. A802 $1 multi 2.00 1.00
c. A803 $1 multi 2.00 1.00
d. A804 $1 multi 2.00 1.00
e. A805 $1 multi 2.00 1.00

Preservation of Polar Regions and Glaciers A806

Designs: 20c, Feet of polar bear. 80c, Earth in water.

2009, Mar. 31
1952-1953 A806 Set of 2 2.50 1.25

A807

Tourism — A808

Designs: No. 1954, Babahoyo River, Los Ríos Province. No. 1955, Ingapirca Ruins, Cañar Province. No. 1956, Rafters on Quijos River, Napo Province. No. 1957, Marimba group, Esmeraldas Province. $1.25, Tulcán cemetery, Carchi Province. $2, Train and Mt. Chimborazo, Chimborazo Province. $3, Alcea rosea flowers, Morona-Santiago Province. $5, Acrocinus longimanus, Sucumbíos Province.

No. 1962: a, Like #1954. b, Like #1957. c, Like #1958. d, Like #1955. e, Like #1959. f, Like #1956. g, Like #1960. h, Like #1961.

No. 1963: a, Equator Monument, Pichincha Province. b, Colorado Indians, Santo Domingo de los Tsáchilas Province. c, Los Frailes Beach, Manabí Province. d, Banana plantation, El Oro Province. e, Arctocephalus galapagoensis, Galápagos Province. f, Cuicocha Lake, Imbabura Province. g, Harpia harpyja, Pastaza Province. h, Shuar community, Orellana Province.

No. 1964: a, Bolívar and San Martín Monument, Guayas Province. b, The Lovers of Sumpa, Santa Elena Province. c, Pillaro devil, Tungurahua Province. d, Mt. Cotopaxi, Cotopaxi Province. e, Guaranga Indian Monument, Bolívar Province. f, Virgin of Cisne, Loja Province. g, Tomebamba River, Azuay Province. h, Leopardus pardalis, Zamora Province.

Perf. 13¼x13
2009 **Litho.** **Wmk. 395**
1954 A807 25c multi .60 .25
1955 A807 50c multi 1.25 .60
1956 A807 75c multi 1.75 .90
1957 A807 $1 multi 2.50 1.25
1958 A807 $1.25 multi 3.00 1.50
1959 A807 $2 multi 4.75 2.40
1960 A807 $3 multi 7.25 3.50
1961 A807 $5 multi 12.00 6.00
Nos. 1954-1961 (8) 33.10 16.40

Booklet Stamps
Self-Adhesive
Die Cut
Unwmk.

1962 Booklet pane of 8 + 2 labels 12.50
a.-b. A808 25c Either single .60 .25
c.-d. A808 50c Either single 1.25 .50
e.-f. A808 75c Either single 1.75 .75
g.-h. A808 $1 Either single 2.50 1.00
1963 Booklet pane of 8 + 2 labels 12.50
a.-b. A808 25c Either single .60 .25
c.-d. A808 50c Either single 1.25 .50
e.-f. A808 75c Either single 1.75 .75
g.-h. A808 $1 Either single 2.50 1.00
1964 Booklet pane of 8 + 2 labels 12.50
a.-b. A808 25c Either single .60 .25
c.-d. A808 50c Either single 1.25 .50
e.-f. A808 75c Either single 1.75 .75
g.-h. A808 $1 Either single 2.50 1.00
Nos. 1962-1964 (3) 37.50

Issued: Nos. 1954-1961, 4/29; Nos. 1962-1964, July.

See Nos. 1985-2000, 2021-2022.

Intl. Philately Day — A809

Perf. 13¼x13
2009, May 6 **Wmk. 395**
1965 A809 75c multi 1.75 .90

Icons of Santa Clara Monastery A810

No. 1966: a, Angel. b, Jesus Christ. c, Pensive child. d, Protective Virgin. e, Virgin of Quito.

2009, June 9 *Perf. 13x13¼*
1966 Horiz. strip of 5 12.00 6.00
a.-e. A810 $1 Any single 2.00 1.00

National Finance Corporation, 45th Anniv. A811

2009, June 22 *Perf. 13¼x13*
1967 A811 $1.25 multi 3.00 1.50

Ambato Electric Company, 50th Anniv. A812

2009, June
1968 A812 $1 multi 2.50 1.25

Paute-Molino Dam, 25th Anniv. A813

2009, July 22
1969 A813 $2 multi 5.00 2.50

El Telégrafo Newspaper, 125th Anniv. A814

2009, July 30 *Perf. 12*
1970 A814 $1.75 multi 4.25 2.10

Call for Independence, Bicent. — A815

Nos. 1971 and 1972 — Doves, butterflies, bell and: a, Open mouth. b, Monument.

2009, Aug. 14 *Perf. 13¼x13*
1971 A815 $3 Horiz. pair, #a-b 14.50 7.25

Souvenir Sheet
With Horizontal Blue Stripe Added to Middle of Stamps

1972 A815 $3 Sheet of 2, #a-b 14.50 7.25

Call for Independence, Bicent. — A816

Serpentine Die Cut 12½x12¼
2009, Aug. 14 **Litho.** **Unwmk.**
Self-Adhesive
Printed on Cork

1973 A816 $3.50 multi 8.50 4.25

Chinese Benevolent Society, Cent. — A817

No. 1974: a, Galápagos tortoise. b, Giant panda.

Perf. 13¼x13
2009, Aug. 18 **Wmk. 395**
1974 A817 25c Horiz. pair, #a-b 1.25 .60

Famous People A818

No. 1975: a, Carlos Silva Pareja (1909-68), musician. b, Tránsito Amaguaña (1909-2009), Indian rights advocate. c, Demetrio Aguilera Malta (1909-81), writer, diplomat. d, Carlos Zevallos Menéndez (1909-81), archaeologist. e, Humberto Salvador Guerra (1909-82), writer.

2009, Aug. 28 **Litho.**
1975 Horiz. strip of 5 3.00 1.50
a.-e. A818 25c Any single .50 .25

Ecuadorian Olympic Committee, 50th Anniv. A819

Designs: No. 1976, 25c, Shooting, cycling, equestrian, wrestling, archery, and basketball. No. 1977, 25c, Diving, running, weight lifting, tennis, boxing and soccer, vert.

2009, Oct. 17 *Perf. 13¼x13, 13x13¼*
1976-1977 A819 Set of 2 1.25 .60

Exportation of Cooperative Open Banking Information System A820

Perf. 13¼x13
2009, Nov. 5 **Litho.** **Wmk. 395**
1978 A820 50c multi 1.25 1.00

Loja National University, 150th Anniv. — A821

Wmk. 395
2009, Nov. 27 **Litho.** *Perf. 12*
1979 A821 $2 multi 5.00 2.50

Independence, Bicent. — A822

No. 1980: a, Juan Pío Montúfar (1758-1818), Chairman of Supreme Council of Government. b, José Mejía Lequerica (1777-1813), representative to Cortes of Cadiz. c, Eugenio Espejo (1747-95), journalist, medical pioneer. d, Manuela Cañizares (1769-1814), patriot. e, Bicentenary emblem.

2009, Nov. 28

1980	Horiz. strip of 5	9.00	4.50
a.-e.	A822 75c Any single	1.50	.75

A823

Charles Darwin (1809-82), Naturalist — A824

No. 1982 — Darwin and: a, Phoenicopterus ruber. b, Ardea herodias. c, Calandria galapagosa. d, Conolopus marthae. e, Sula granti. f, Rhincodon typus. g, Zalophus wollebaeki. h, Phalacrocorax harrisi. i, Geochelone nigra abingdoni. Nos. 1982a-1982h are 35x35mm, No. 1982i is 38mm diameter.

Perf. 13¾x14

2009, Nov. 30 Unwmk.

Granite Paper

1981	A823 $5 multi	12.00	6.00

Perf. 13¼ ($1), 13¾ ($2)

1982	A824 Sheet of 9	24.00	12.00
a.-h.	$1 Any single	2.00	1.00
i.	$2 multi	4.00	2.00

Christmas A825

Perf. 13¼x13

2009, Dec. 10 Wmk. 395

1983	A825 $1 multi	2.50	1.25

America Issue, Toys and Games — A826

No. 1984: a, Paddle and ball. b, Go-cart.

2009, Dec. 18

1984	A826 $1 Horiz. pair, #a-b	5.00	2.50

Tourism Type of 2009

Designs: No. 1985, The Lovers of Sumpa, Santa Elena Province. No. 1986, Colorado Indians, Santo Domingo de los Tsáchilas Province. No. 1987, Shuar community, Orellana Province. No. 1988, Guaranga Indian Monument, Bolívar Province. No. 1989, Banana plantation, El Oro Province. No. 1990, Virgin of Cisne, Loja Province. No. 1991, Pillaro devil, Tungurahua Province. No. 1992, Equator Monument, Pichincha Province. No. 1993, Cuicocha Lake, Imbabura Province. $1.75, Bolívar and San Martín Monument, Guayas Province. No. 1995, Tomebamba River, Azuay Province. No. 1996, Leopardus pardalis, Zamora Province. No. 1997, Los Frailes Beach, Manabí Province. No. 1998, Harpia harpyja, Pastaza Province. No. 1999, Arctocephalus galapagoensis, Galápagos Province. $5, Mt. Cotopaxi, Cotopaxi Province.

Wmk. 395, 377 (#1986-1987, 1989, 1992, 1993, 1997-1999)

2010-11 Litho. *Perf. 13¼x13*

1985	A807	25c multi	.50	.25
1986	A807	25c multi	.50	.25
1987	A807	25c multi	.50	.25
1988	A807	50c multi	1.00	.50
1989	A807	50c multi	1.00	.50
1990	A807	$1 multi	2.00	1.00
1991	A807	$1.25 multi	2.50	1.25
1992	A807	$1.25 multi	2.50	1.25
1993	A807	$1.25 multi	2.50	1.25
1994	A807	$1.75 multi	3.50	1.75
1995	A807	$2 multi	4.00	2.00
1996	A807	$2 multi	4.00	2.00
1997	A807	$2 multi	4.00	2.00
1998	A807	$3 multi	6.00	3.00
1999	A807	$3 multi	6.00	3.00
2000	A807	$5 multi	10.00	5.00
		Nos. 1985-2000 (16)	50.50	25.25

Issued: Nos. 1985, 1988, 1991, 1995, 1/20; Nos. 1990, 1994, 1996, 2000, 4/12; Nos. 1986, 1992, 1997, 1998, 9/30; Nos. 1987, 1989, 1993, 1999, 1/24/11.

Miniature Sheet

First Unmanned Ecuadorian Airship — A827

No. 2001: a, $1, Pilot with remote-control device (40x18mm). b, $1, Airship over coastline (40x18mm). c, $1, Airship and mountain (40x18mm). d, $3, Airship (115x42mm).

Wmk. 395

2010, Feb. 7 Litho. *Perf. 14*

2001	A827 Sheet of 4, #a-d	12.00	6.00

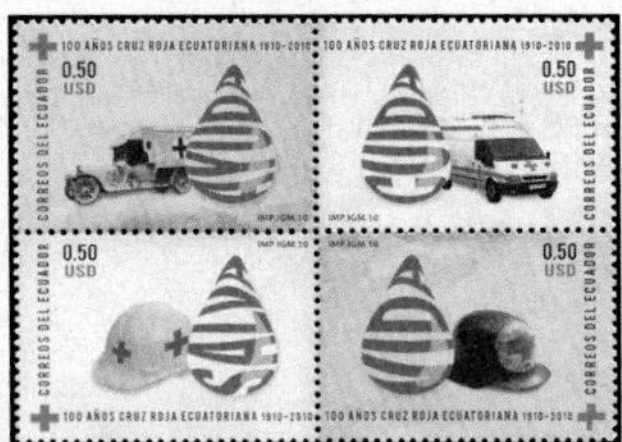

Ecuadorian Red Cross, Cent. — A828

No. 2002: a, Old ambulance, blood drop inscribed "Ayuda." b, New ambulance, blood drop inscribed "Cuida." c, Modern Red Cross hard hat, blood drop inscribed "Salva." d, Old Red Cross hard hat, blood drop inscribed "Vida."

Perf. 13¼x13

2010, Mar. 18 Wmk. 395

2002	A828 50c Block of 4, #a-d	4.00	2.00

Birds — A829

No. 2003: a, Tachycineta albiventer. b, Momotus momota. c, Semnornis ramphastinus. d, Aulacorhynchus haematopygus.

No. 2004, horiz.: a, Ramphocelus carbo. b, Tangara vitriolina.

2010, Apr. 16 Wmk. 395 *Perf. 14*

2003	A829 25c Block of 4, #a-d	2.00	1.00

Souvenir Sheet

Perf. 13¼x13

2004	A829 $1.50 Sheet of 2, #a-b	6.00	3.00

No. 2004 contains two 38x27mm stamps. Birdpex 2010, Antwerp, Belgium (No. 2004).

Tall Ships in Velas Sudamérica 2010 — A830

No. 2005, vert. (27x38mm) — Various knots, ships and flags: a, Cisne Branco, Brazil. b, Libertad, Argentina. c, Sagres, Portugal. d, Capitán Miranda, Uruguay. e, Europa, Netherlands. f, Esmerelda, Chile. g, Gloria, Colombia. h, Simón Bolívar, Venezuela. i, Cuauhtémoc, Mexico. j, Juan Sebastián Elcano, Spain.

$1, Training Ship Guayas, Ecuador.

Perf. 13x13¼

2010, May 7 Wmk. 377

2005	Block of 10	15.00	7.50
a.-j.	A830 75c Any single	1.50	.75

Perf. 12

2006	A830 $1 shown	2.00	1.00

Miniature Sheet

Manuela Sáenz (c. 1797-1856), Mistress of Simón Bolívar — A831

Litho. with Foil Application

2010, May 24 *Imperf.*

2007	A831 $3 multi	6.00	3.00

See Venezuela No. 1707.

2010 World Cup Soccer Championships, South Africa — A832

No. 2008 — Emblem of 2010 World Cup, soccer player, ball and: a, Lion. b, Elephant. c, Zebra.

$5, Mascot of 2010 World Cup, giraffe.

2010, June 9 Litho. *Perf. 13¼x13*

2008	Horiz. strip of 3	6.00	3.00
a.-c.	A832 $1 Any single	2.00	1.00

Souvenir Sheet

Imperf

2009	A832 $5 multi	10.00	5.00

No. 2009 contains one 45x36mm stamp with simulated perforations. Animals on No. 2009 have blurred appearance, but have a three-dimensional appearance when seen through 3-D glasses.

Creation of Tungurahua Province, 150th Anniv. A833

No. 2010: a, Atelopus ignescens. b, Mt. Tungurahua, flag at Parque de la Familia. c, Casa del Portal Museum.

Perf. 13¼x13

2010, July 1 Wmk. 377

2010	Horiz. strip of 3	1.50	.75
a.-c.	A833 25c Any single	.50	.25

Las Floristas, by Camilo Egas — A834

2010, July 21 *Perf. 12*

2011	A834 $1.25 multi	2.50	1.25

Campaign against illegal trafficking in historical objects.

Souvenir Sheet

Massacre of Patriots, Bicent. — A835

No. 2012: a, Soldier with sword threatening woman, man and child. b, Soldier threatening to shoot man.

2010, Aug. 2 *Perf. 13x13¼*

2012	A835 $2 Sheet of 2, #a-b, + central label	8.00	4.00

Souvenir Sheet

Philatelic Firsts of Ecuador — A836

No. 2013: a, First postmark of Ecuador, 1770, emblem of Philatelic Association of Ecuador. b, First Ecuadorian stamps (#2, 3, 5, 6), emblem of Intl. Federation of Philately. c, Cover from first SCADTA flight, 1928, emblem of 2010 Philatelic Association of Ecuador Expo.

2010, Aug. 25 *Perf. 13¼x13*

2013	A836 $1 Sheet of 3, #a-c	6.00	3.00

Philatelic Association of Ecuador, 75th anniv., and its admission to Intl. Federation of Philately.

Organization of Petroleum Exporting Countries, 50th Anniv. — A837

2010, Sept. 14 Wmk. 377 *Perf. 12*
2014 A837 50c multi 1.00 .50

Citigroup in Ecuador, 50th Anniv. A838

2010, Oct. 7 *Perf. 13¼x13*
2015 A838 $1 multi 2.00 1.00

General Directorate of Civil Registration, Identification and Certification — A839

2010, Oct. 29 Litho. *Perf. 12*
2016 A839 50c multi 1.00 .50

America Issue, National Symbols A840

No. 2017 — National: a, Flag. b, Coat of arms. c, Anthem.

2010, Nov. 24 *Perf. 13¼x13*
2017 Horiz. strip of 3 6.00 3.00
a.-c. A840 $1 Any single 2.00 1.00

Christmas — A841

2010, Dec. 3 *Perf. 13x13¼*
2018 A841 $2 multi 4.00 2.00

San José-La Salle College, Guayaquil, Cent. — A842

2010, Dec. 16 Litho. Wmk. 377
2019 A842 25c multi .50 .25

Children's Christmas Parade, Cuenca A843

2010, Dec. 21 *Perf. 13¼x13*
2020 A843 50c multi 1.00 .50

Tourism Type of 2009

No. 2021 — Galapagos Islands fauna: a, Fregata magnificens. b, Sula dactylatra. c, Spheniscidorme. d, Sula nebouxi. e, Conolophus subcristatus. f, Geochelone nigra. g, Chelonia mydas agassisi. h, Oxycirrhites typus.

No. 2022 — Galapagos Islands sites and fauna: a, Bartolomé Island, denomination at L. b, Bartolomé Island, denomination at R. c, Zoluphus wallebaeki, denomination at R. d, Zoluphus wallebaeki, denomination at L. e, Darwin's Arch, denomination at L. f, Darwin's Arch, denomination at R. g, Amblyrhynchus cristatus, denomination at L. h, Amblyrhynchus cristatus, denomination at R.

2011, Mar. 18 Unwmk. *Die Cut*
Self-Adhesive

2021 Booklet pane of 8 + 2 labels 10.00
a.-b. A808 25c Either single .50 .25
c.-d. A808 50c Either single 1.00 .50
e.-f. A808 75c Either single 1.50 .75
g.-h. A808 $1 Either single 2.00 1.00
i. Booklet pane of 8, #a-h, with lilac pane margins 10.00
2022 Booklet pane of 8 + 2 labels 10.00
a.-b. A808 25c Either single .50 .25
c.-d. A808 50c Either single 1.00 .50
e.-f. A808 75c Either single 1.50 .75
g.-h. A808 $1 Either single 2.00 1.00
i. Booklet pane of 8, #a-h, with lilac pane margins 10.00

Issued: Nos. 2021i, 2022i, 1/13/12. Nos. 2021 and 2022 have gray pane margins.

Souvenir Sheet

Postal Union of the Americas, Spain and Portugal (UPAEP), Cent. — A844

2011, Mar. 18 Wmk. 377 *Perf. 12*
2023 A844 $3 multi 6.00 3.00

Souvenir Sheet

Yuri Gagarin, First Man in Space, 50th Anniv. — A845

2011, May 6 *Perf. 13x13¼*
2024 A845 $5 multi 10.00 5.00

Intl. Year of Forests — A846

No. 2025, 50c: a, Chinchona officinalis. b, Ceiba tichistandra.
No. 2026, 75c, horiz.: a, Jacaranda sp. b, Prosopis sp.

2011, May 19 *Perf. 13x13¼, 13¼x13*
Horiz. pairs, #a-b
2025-2026 A846 Set of 2 5.00 2.50

Pichincha Chamber of Industries and Production, 75th Anniv. — A847

Wmk. 377
2011, June 16 Litho. *Perf. 12*
2027 A847 $2 multi 4.00 4.00

Christopher Columbus College, Guayaquil, Cent. A848

2011, July 7 *Perf. 13¼x13*
2028 A848 $1 multi 2.00 2.00

National Telecommunications Day — A849

No. 2029: a, First Bell telephone, 1876. b, Western Electric magneto wall telephone, 1894. c, Ericsson wall pay telephone, 1970. d, Apple iPhone, 2011.

2011, July 8
2029 A849 50c Block of 4, #a-d 4.00 4.00

Miniature Sheet

Seven Wonders of Quito — A850

No. 2030: a, Basilica of the National Vow. b, Virgin of the Panecillo. c, Chimbacalle Railway Station. d, San Francisco Convent. e, Independence Plaza. f, Church of the Society of Jesus. g, Sanctuary of the Virgin of El Quinche.

2011, Sept. 8
2030 A850 75c Sheet of 7, #a-g, + label 10.50 10.50

Quito, 2011 American Capital of Culture.

Yasuni- ITT Initiative — A851

No. 2031 — Reptiles: a, Chelonoidis denticulata. b, Anolis trachyderma. c, Thecadactylus solimoensis. d, Epicrates cenchria. e, Dendropsophus bifurcus. f, Osteocephalus taurinus. g, Ranitomeya ventrimaculata. h, Melanosuchus niger.

No. 2032: a, Clavija procera. b, Duguetia hadrantha. c, Hymenaea oblongifolia. d, Connarus ruber. e, Fungi. f, Theobroma speciosum. g, Brownea gradiceps. h, Apeiba membranacea.

Unwmk.
2011, Sept. 20 Litho. *Die Cut*
Self-Adhesive

2031 Booklet pane of 8 + 2 labels 10.00
a.-b. A851 25c Either single .50 .25
c.-d. A851 50c Either single 1.00 .50
e.-f. A851 75c Either single 1.50 .75
g.-h. A851 $1 Either single 2.00 1.00
2032 Booklet pane of 8 + 2 labels 10.00
a.-b. A851 25c Either single .50 .25
c.-d. A851 50c Either single 1.00 .50
e.-f. A851 75c Either single 1.50 .75
g.-h. A851 $1 Either single 2.00 1.00

See Nos. 2061-2062.

Intl. Year For People of African Descent — A852

No. 2033 — Musical instruments: a, Marimba. b, Guasá. c, Maracas. d, Cununos.

Perf. 13¼x13
2011, Sept. 26 Litho. Wmk. 395
2033 A852 $1 Block of 4, #a-d 8.00 4.00

Flowers — A853

Designs: 25c, Passiflora manicata. $2, Passiflora pinnatistipula. $3, Herrania balaensis. $5, Passiflora arborea.

Perf. 13x13¼
2011, Sept. 26 Litho. Wmk. 377
2034-2037 A853 Set of 4 20.50 20.50

Trains — A854 Railroad Stations — A855

No. 2038 — Locomotives: a, 1992 GEC Alsthon. b, 1900 Baldwin. c, 1900 Baldwin, diff. d, 1935 Baldwin. e, 1992 GEC Alsthon on hillside. f, Front of 1992 GEC Alsthon. g, 1953 Baldwin. h, Baldwin XXXX.

No. 2039 — Stations at: a, Machachi. b, Latacunga. c, Sibambe. d, Durán. e, El Tambo. f, Riobamba. g, Chimbacalle. h, Boliche.

2011, Oct. 3 Unwmk. *Die Cut*
Self-Adhesive

2038 Booklet pane of 8 + 2 labels 10.00
a.-b. A854 25c Either single .50 .25
c.-d. A854 50c Either single 1.00 .50
e.-f. A854 75c Either single 1.50 .75
g.-h. A854 $1 Either single 2.00 1.00
2039 Booklet pane of 8 + 2 labels 10.00
a.-b. A855 25c Either single .50 .25
c.-d. A855 50c Either single 1.00 .50
e.-f. A855 75c Either single 1.50 .75
g.-h. A855 $1 Either single 2.00 1.00

Exports — A856

No. 2040: a, Wicker basket. b, Chocolate. c, Wooden automobile. d, Hats. e, Textiles. f, Leather goods. g, Filigree. h, Tagua carvings.

Perf. 13¼x13

2011, Oct. 11 **Wmk. 395**

2040 A856 50c Block of 8, #a-h, + central label 8.00 8.00

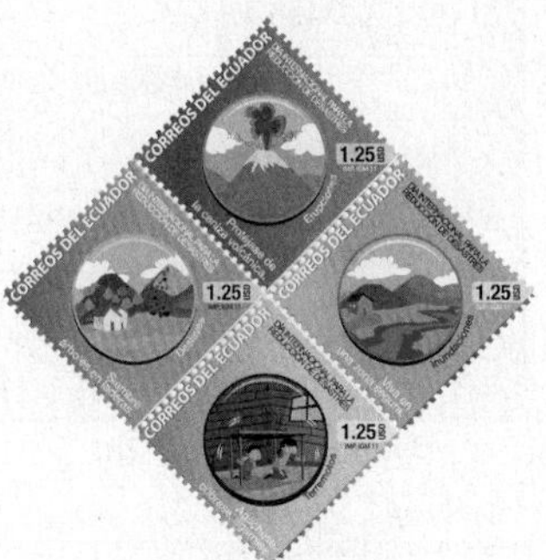

Intl. Day for Disaster Reduction — A857

No. 2041: a, Volcano eruption. b, Landslide. c, Flood, d, Earthquake.

2011, Oct. 12 ***Perf. 13¼***

2041 A857 $1.25 Block of 4, #a-d 10.00 10.00

Mail Boxes and Postal Transportation — A858

Designs: No. 2042, $1.75, 1928 mailbox, bicycle. No. 2043, $1.75, 2011 mailbox, motorcycle.

$5, Mailbox, Post Office Bay, Galápagos Islands, vert.

Perf. 13½x13¾

2011, Nov. 28 **Wmk. 377**

2042-2043 A858 Set of 2 7.00 7.00

Souvenir Sheet

Perf. 13x13¼

2044 A858 $5 multi 10.00 10.00

America issue. No. 2044 contains one 28x38mm stamp.

Christmas — A859

No. 2045: a, Holy Family. b, Angel.

2011, Nov. 29 ***Perf. 13½x13¾***

2045 A859 $1 Horiz. pair, #a-b 4.00 4.00

2011 Pan-American Games, Guadalajara, Mexico — A860

Emblem, sports equipment and athletes: a, Karate. b, Weight lifting. c, Kayaking. d, Boxing. e, Rollerblading.

2011, Nov. 30

2046 Horiz. strip of 5 2.50 2.50

a.-e. A860 25c Any single .50 .50

Guayaquil Chamber of Industries, 75th Anniv. — A861

2011, Dec. 14 **Wmk. 377**

2047 A861 $2 multi 4.00 4.00

Ecuador Cancer Society, 60th Anniv. — A862

2011, Dec. 19 ***Perf. 13¼x13***

2048 A862 75c multi 1.50 .75

Pres. Luis Cordero (1833-1912) A864

2012, Mar. 1 ***Perf. 13¾x13½***

2051 A864 $1 multi 2.00 2.00

Flowers — A865

Designs: $1, Barnadesia spinosa. $2, Bixa orellana. $3, Espeletia pycnophylla. $5, Brugmansia sanguinea.

Perf. 13½x13¾

2012, Mar. 28 **Unwmk.**

2052-2055 A865 Set of 4 22.00 22.00

Souvenir Sheets

Sinking of the Titanic, Cent. — A866

Designs: No. 2056, $4, Titanic, sepia-toned image. No. 2056, $4, Titanic and Olympic at dock.

Perf. 13¾x13½

2012, Apr. 20 **Wmk. 377**

2056-2057 A866 Set of 2 16.00 16.00

Bananas — A867

Perf. 13½x13¾

2012, May 17 **Litho.** **Wmk. 377**

2058 A867 $2 multi 4.00 4.00

Banco de Machala, 50th anniv.

Catholic University of Santiago, Guayaquil, 50th Anniv. A868

2012, May 31 ***Perf. 13¾***

2059 A868 $1 multi 2.00 2.00

Miniature Sheet

Guayaquil Tourist Attractions — A869

No. 2060: a, Hemiciclo la Rotonda (monument honoring meeting of Simón Bolívar and José de San Martín). b, Malecón del ío Guayas (Guayas River Walk). c, Metropolitan Cathedral. d, Torre del Reloj (Clock Tower). e, Malecón del Salado (Salado Walk). f, Edificio del Municipio (City Hall). g, Las Peñas Cerro Santa Ana (Santa Ana Hill).

2012, June 8 **Wmk. 377**

2060 A869 75c Sheet of 7, #a-g, + label 10.50 10.50

Yasuni-ITT Type of 2011

No. 2061 — Flora and fauna: a, Dasypodidae. b, Saimiri sciureus. c, Tettigoniidae. d, Automeris postalbida. e, Brownea sp. f, Aristolochia sp. g, Hypsiboas sp. h, Hypsiboas geographicus.

No. 2062 — Birds: a, Morphnus guianensis. b, Sarcorhamphus papa. c, Ara ararauna. d, Harpia harpyja. e, Trochilidae sp. f, Ramphastos tucanus. g, Pteroglossus pluricinctus. h, Pionus menstruus.

2012, June 11 **Unwmk.** ***Die Cut***

Self-Adhesive

2061 Booklet pane of 8 + 2 labels 10.00

a.-b. A851 25c Either single .50 .50

c.-d. A851 50c Either single 1.00 1.00

e.-f. A851 75c Either single 1.50 1.50

g.-h. A851 $1 Either single 2.00 2.00

2062 Booklet pane of 8 + 2 labels 10.00

a.-b. A851 25c Either single .50 .50

c.-d. A851 50c Either single 1.00 1.00

e.-f. A851 75c Either single 1.50 1.50

g.-h. A851 $1 Either single 2.00 2.00

Galapagos Islands Landscapes and Fauna — A870

No. 2063: a, Rocks in surf. b, Head of Amblyrhynchus cristatus. c, Numenius phaeopus. d, South Plaza Island. e. Pinnacle Rock, Bartolomé Island. f, Sula nebouxi. g, Chelonoidis sp. h, Kicker Rock (Leon Dormido), San Cristóbal Island.

No. 2064: a, Zalophus wollebaeki. b, Geospiza magnirostris. c, Sula granti. d, Fregata magnificens. e, Microlophus bivittatus. f, Spheniscus mendiculus. g, Anas bahamensis. h, Sphyrna lewini.

2012, July 11 **Unwmk.** ***Die Cut***

Self-Adhesive

Water Droplets on Blue Depicted in Frames Around Stamps

2063 Booklet pane of 8 10.00

a.-b. A870 25c Either single .50 .25

c.-d. A870 50c Either single 1.00 .50

e.-f. A870 75c Either single 1.50 .75

g.-h. A870 $1 Either single 2.00 1.00

i. Booklet pane of 8, #a-h, with pane margins depiciting rocks 10.00

2064 Booklet pane of 8 10.00

a.-b. A870 25c Either single .50 .25

c.-d. A870 50c Either single 1.00 .50

e.-f. A870 75c Either single 1.50 .75

g.-h. A870 $1 Either single 2.00 1.00

i. Booklet pane of 8, #a-h, with pane margins depiciting rocks 10.00

Issued: Nos. 2063i, 2064i, 10/8. See Nos. 2094-2095.

Guayas Sports Federation, 90th Anniv. A871

No. 2065: a, Shooting (tiro). b, Wrestling (lucha). c, Kayaking (canotaje). d, Boxing (boxeo). e, Weight lifting (pesas).

Perf. 13¾x13½

2012, July 25 **Wmk. 377**

2065 Horiz. strip of 5 5.00 2.50

a.-e. A871 50c Any single 1.00 .50

A872

Legacy of the Revolution of 1895 — A873

No. 2066: a, Ecuador #129, Matilde Huerta, first Ecuadoran female postal official, 1895. b, Bolívar College, Tulcán, first lay college, 1896. c, Civil Registration Law, 1900. d, School of Fine Arts, Quito, 1904. e, Opening of Guayaquil-Quito Railroad, 1908. f, Founding of Guayaquil Worker's Society, 1903. g, Creation of Independence Plaza, Quito, 1909. h, Map of South America, José Marti, Eloy Alfaro, and Augusto César Sandino, 1911.
$3, Alfaro, locomotive.

2012, July 31 ***Perf. 13¾x13½***
2066 A872 25c Sheet of 8, #a-h 4.00 2.00

Souvenir Sheet
Imperf

2067 A873 $3 multi 6.00 3.00

Enrique Gil Gilbert (1912-73), Writer A874

2012, Aug. 8 ***Perf. 13¾x13½***
2068 A874 $1 multi 2.00 1.00

Souvenir Sheet

Steamship Ecuador — A875

No. 2069 — Emblem of 2012 Ecuador Philatelic Society Stamp Exposition and: a, Ship's stern and flag. b, Ship's bow.

Litho. (Foil Application in Margin)
2012, Aug. 16 ***Perf. 13½x13¾***
2069 A875 $3 Sheet of 2, #a-b, gold inscription in sheet margin 12.00 6.00
c. As #2069, silver inscription in sheet margin 12.00 6.00
d. As #2069, red metallic inscription in sheet margin 12.00 6.00

Miniature Sheet

Moths — A876

No. 2070: a, Getta baetifica. b, Sematura diana. c, Xylophanes pyrrhus. d, Leucanella contempta.

Perf. 13¾x13½
2012, Aug. 28 **Litho.**
2070 A876 50c Sheet of 4, #a-d 4.00 2.00

Quito Chamber of Construction, 50th Anniv. — A877

Construction materials: No. 2071, $1, Timber (madera). No. 2072, $1, Bamboo (guadua). No. 2073, $1, Wattle (bahareque). No. 2074, $1, Compacted mud (tapial).

2012, Sept. 4 ***Perf. 13½x13¾***
2071-2074 A877 Set of 4 8.00 4.00

America Issue A878

Myths and legends: No. 2075, $2, Legend of Ayer. No. 2076, $2, Legend of the Rooster of the Cathedral, vert.

Perf. 13¾x13½, 13½x13¾
2012, Sept. 17
2075-2076 A878 Set of 2 8.00 4.00

Nelson Estupiñán Bass (1912-2002), Writer — A879

2012, Sept. 20 ***Perf. 13¾x13½***
2077 A879 $2 multi 4.00 2.00

Alexander von Humboldt (1769-1859), Naturalist A880

Denominations: 50c, $2.

2012, Sept. 26 **Wmk. 377**
2078-2079 A880 Set of 2 5.00 2.50

Friendship between Ecuador and Germany, 125th anniv.

A881

Trains — A882

No. 2080: a, Baldwin No. 3 Ingenio Valdez. b, Baldwin No. 2 Inés María. c, Baldwin No. 12 C.F.F.E. d, Baldwin No. 37 G&Q. e. Baldwin No. 7 G&Q. f, Baldwin No. 3 Quito-Esmeraldas train. g, Baldwin No. 2 Yaguachi train. h, Baldwin No. 1 Curaray train.
No. 2081: a, Baldwin No. 53. b, Gec Alsthom No. 2408. c, Gec Alsthom No. 2405. d, Baldwin No. 17. e, Baldwin No. 58. f, Gec Alsthom No. 2407 and station. g, Gec Alsthom No. 2404. h, Gec Alsthom No. 2407.
No. 2082: a, Baldwin No. 58, diff. b, Gec Alsthom No. 2404, diff. c, Gec Alsthom No. 2406. d, Baldwin No. 53, diff. e, Gec Alsthom No. 2402. f, Baldwin No. 58 on bridge. g, Baldwin No. 17, diff. h, Gec Alsthom No. 2405, diff.

2012, Oct. 8 **Unwmk.** ***Die Cut***
Self-Adhesive

2080		Booklet pane of 8	10.00	
a.-b.	A881	25c Either single	.50	.25
c.-d.	A881	50c Either single	1.00	.50
e.-f.	A881	75c Either single	1.50	.75
g.-h.	A881	$1 Either single	2.00	1.00
2081		Booklet pane of 8	10.00	
a.-b.	A882	25c Either single	.50	.25
c.-d.	A882	50c Either single	1.00	.50
e.-f.	A882	75c Either single	1.50	.75
g.-h.	A882	$1 Either single	2.00	1.00
2082		Booklet pane of 8	10.00	
a.-b.	A882	25c Either single	.50	.25
c.-d.	A882	50c Either single	1.00	.50
e.-f.	A882	75c Either single	1.50	.75
g.-h.	A882	$1 Either single	2.00	1.00

Jesuit Institutions A883

Schools: No. 2083, $1, Unidad Educativa Borja, 75th anniv. No. 2084, $1, Unidad Educativa San Felipe Neri, 175th anniv. No. 2085, $1.25, Colegio San Gabriel, 150th anniv.
$5, Jesuit church and emblem.

Perf. 13¾x13½
2012, Oct. 29 **Wmk. 377**
2083-2085 A883 Set of 3 6.50 3.25

Size: 100x70mm
Imperf

2086 A883 $5 multi 10.00 10.00

Permanent return of Jesuits to Ecuador, 150th anniv.

Renovation of Guayas Government Palace — A884

2012, Nov. 6 ***Perf. 13½x13¾***
2087 A884 $5 multi 10.00 10.00

Ecuadorian Army's Communications Group, 50th Anniv. — A885

No. 2088: a, Indian messenger. b, Men and wagon transporting radiotelegraphic station, 1924. c, Bicycle messengers, 1932. d, Communication transmission school building, 1942.

2012, Nov. 14
2088 Horiz. strip of 4 2.00 2.00
a.-d. A885 25c Any single .50 .50

Guayaquil Beneficence Council, 125th Anniv. — A886

2012, Nov. 27 ***Perf. 13¾x13½***
2089 A886 $3 multi 6.00 6.00

Miniature Sheet

Guayas Tourism — A887

No. 2090: a, Crucifix. b, Rock climbers. c, Fishermen in boats. d, Rice farmer. e, Cacao farmer. f, Sugar processing.

2012, Nov. 29
2090 A887 75c Sheet of 6, #a-f, + 2 labels 9.00 9.00

Christmas A888

Icons: No. 2091, $1, Bethlehem Portal, Concepción Monastery, Quito. No. 2092, $1, Mystery, Carmen Alto Monastery, Quito.

2012, Dec. 3 **Wmk. 377**
2091-2092 A888 Set of 2 4.00 4.00

Military Leaders A889

No. 2093: a, Gen. Eloy Alfaro (1842-1912). b, Col. Carlos Concha Torres (1864-1919). c, Col. Luis Vargas Torres (1855-87).

2012, Dec. 14 ***Rouletted 13½***
2093 Horiz. strip of 3 7.50 7.50
a.-c. A889 $1.25 Any single 2.50 2.50

Galapagos Islands Type of 2012

No. 2094: a, Rock with carving of face, Isla Floreana. b, Phoebastria irrorata. c, Carcharhinus galapagensis. d, Chelonia mydas. e, Pterophyllum scalare. f, Sleeping Lion Rock, San Cristóbal. g, Flower. h, Isla Plaza Sur.
No. 2095: a, Fregata magnificens. b, Post barrel, Post Office Bay, Isla Floreana. c, Camarhynchus pallidus. d, Pyrocephalus rubinus. e, Buteo galapagoensis. f, Isla

Bartolomé. g, Red reef fish. h, Vicente Roca Point.

2013, Jan. 16 Unwmk. *Die Cut*
Self-Adhesive

2094	Booklet pane of 8	10.00
a.-b.	A870 25c Either single	.50 .50
c.-d.	A870 50c Either single	1.00 1.00
e.-f.	A870 75c Either single	1.50 1.50
g.-h.	A870 $1 Either single	2.00 2.00
2095	Booklet pane of 8	10.00
a.-b.	A870 25c Either single	.50 .50
c.-d.	A870 50c Either single	1.00 1.00
e.-f.	A870 75c Either single	1.50 1.50
g.-h.	A870 $1 Either single	2.00 2.00

Miniature Sheet

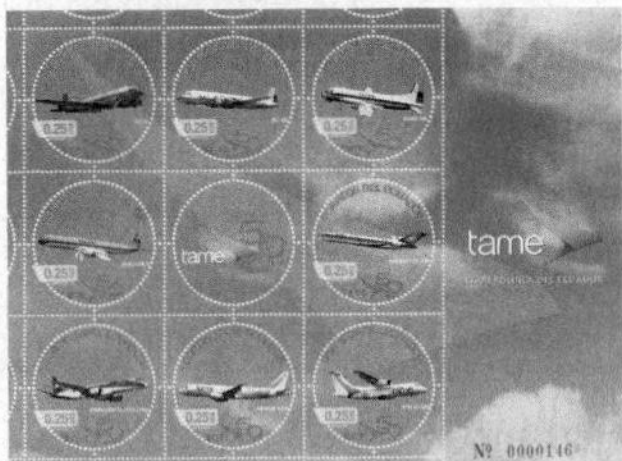

TAME Airlines, 50th Anniv. — A890

No. 2096: a, DC-3. b, DC-6B. c, Avro 748. d, Electra II. e, Boeing 727-200. f, Embraer E-190. g, Airbus A320. h, ATR 42-500.

2013, Feb. 8 Wmk. 377 *Perf. 13½*
2096 A890 25c Sheet of 8, #a-h, + central label 4.00 4.00

Hat Making — A891

No. 2097: a, Unfinished hats (orange panel). b, Hat maker (blue panel). c, Hat maker, diff. (red panel).

2013, Mar. 18 *Perf. 13¼*
2097 Horiz. strip of 3 3.00 3.00
a.-c. A891 50c Any single 1.00 1.00

Scout Group No. 14, Guayaquil, 50th Anniv. — A892

Litho. With Foil Application
Perf. 13½x13¾
2013, June 21 Wmk. 377
2098 A892 $1 multi 2.00 2.00

Launch of Pegasus NEE-01 (First Ecuadorian Satellite) A893

Perf. 13¾x13½
2013, June 28 Litho.
2099 A893 $2 multi 4.00 4.00

Diplomatic Relations Between Dominican Republic and Ecuador, 75th Anniv. — A894

2013, July 2 *Perf. 13½x13¾*
2100 A894 $1 multi 2.00 2.00

Popes Francis and Benedict XVI — A895

Litho. With Foil Application
2013, July 3 Wmk. 377
2101 A895 $5 multi 10.00 10.00

June 24, 2012 Death of Pinta Island Tortoise, Lonesome George — A896

Lonesome George and: $3, Surf spray. $25, Trees.

Litho. With Grit Affixed
Perf. 13½x13¼
2013, July 4 Unwmk.
2102 A896 $3 multi 6.00 6.00

Litho.
Wmk. 377
Size: 91x71mm
Imperf
2103 A896 $25 multi 50.00 50.00

Dr. Ricardo Descalzi (1912-90), Writer and Physician — A897

Perf. 13½x13¾
2013, Aug. 1 Litho. Wmk. 377
2104 A897 $3 multi 6.00 6.00

Volcanos A898

No. 2105: a, Mt. Chimborazo. b, Mt. Cotopaxi. c, Mt.Tungurahua.

Perf. 13¾x13½
2013, Aug. 21 Litho. Wmk. 377
2105 Horiz. strip of 3 1.50 1.50
a.-c. A898 25c Any single .50 .50

Flower With Black and White Faces, Dr. Martin Luther King, Jr. — A899

Perf. 13¾x13½
2013, Oct. 22 Litho. Wmk. 377
2106 A899 $1 multi 2.00 2.00

America issue (campaign against discrimination).

Royal Audience of Quito, 450th Anniv. — A900

Designs: 25c, Hernando de Santillán y Figueroa (1519-75), First President of the Royal Audience of Quito. $5, Map of the Royal Audience of Quito.

Perf. 13¾x13½
2013, Nov. 13 Litho. Wmk. 377
2107 A900 25c multi .50 .50

Size: 74x94mm
Imperf
2108 A900 $5 multi 10.00 10.00

Ecuadorian Presence in the Antarctic, 25th Anniv. — A901

No. 2109: a, Pygoscelis papua. b, Leptonychotes weddellii. c, Catharacta lonnbergi.

Wmk. 377
2013, Nov. 21 Litho. *Perf. 13½*
2109 Horiz. strip of 3 3.00 3.00
a.-c. A901 50c Any single 1.00 1.00

Miniature Sheet

Christmas — A902

No. 2110: a, Annunciation (Primer día). b, Visitation of St. Elizabeth (Segundo día). c, St. Joseph's dream (Tercer día). d, Journey to Bethlehem (Cuarto día). e, Arrival at the inn (Quinto día). f, Star of Bethlehem (Sexto día). g, Shepherds (Séptimo día). h, Angels (Octavo día). i, Holy Family (Noveno día).

Perf. 13½x13¼
2013, Nov. 29 Litho. Wmk. 377
2110 A902 25c Sheet of 9, #a-i 4.50 4.50

Intl. Year of Quinoa A903

No. 2111: a, Chenopodium quinoa. b, Amaranthus caudatus. c, Lupinus mutabilis.

Perf. 13¾x13½
2013, Dec. 16 Litho. Wmk. 377
2111 Horiz. strip of 3 12.00 12.00
a.-c. A903 $2 Any single 4.00 4.00

Imbabura Textile Mill — A904

No. 2112: a, Workers near weaving machines. b, Workers near machines with thread spools.

Rouletted 12¼
2014, Jan. 27 Litho. Wmk. 377
2112 A904 $1 Horiz. pair, #a-b 4.00 4.00

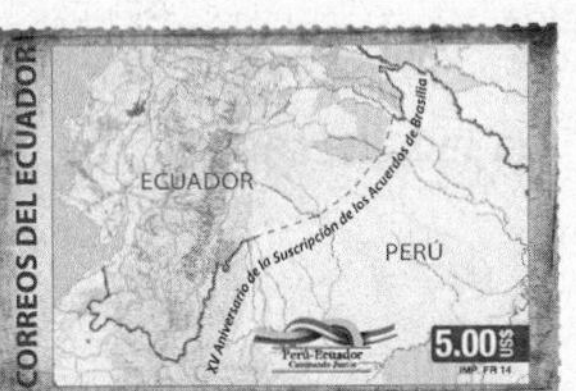

Resolution of Ecuador-Peru Border Dispute, 15th Anniv. — A905

Rouletted 12¼
2014, Jan. 30 Litho. Wmk. 377
2113 A905 $5 multi 10.00 10.00

Presidents of Ecuador — A906

No. 2114: a, Juan José Flores A. (1800-64). b, Vicente Rocafuerte B. (1783-1847). c, Vicente Roca R. (1792-1858). d, Diego Noboa A, (1789-1870). e, José M. Urbina V. (1808-91). f, Francisco Robles G. (1811-93). g, Gabriel García M. (1821-75). h, Jerónimo Carrión P. (1804-73). i, Javier Espinosa E. (1815-70). j, Antonio Borrero C. (1827-1911). k, Ignacio de Veintemilla V. (1828-1908). l, José M. Camaño (1837-1900). m, Antonio Flores J. (1833-1915). n, Luis Cordero C. (1833-1912). o, Eloy Alfaro D. (1842-1912). p, Leonidas Plaza G. (1865-1932). q, Lizardo García S. (1844-1937). r, Emilio Estrada C. (1855-1911). s, Alfredo Baquerizo M. (1859-1951). t, José L. Tamayo T. (1858-1947). u, Gonzalo S. córdova R. (1863-1928). v, Isidro Ayora C. (1879-1978). w, Juan D. Martínez M. (1875-1955). x, José M. Velasco I. (1893-1979). y, Aurelio Mosquera N. (1883-1939). z, Carlos A. Arroyo (1893-1969). aa, Mariano Suárez V. (1897-1980). ab, Carlos J. Arosemena T. (1888-1952). ac, Galo Plaza L. (1906-87). ad, Camilo Ponce E. (1912-76). ae, Carlos J. Arosemena M. (1919-2004). af, Otto Arosemena G. (1925-84). ag, Jaime Roldós A. (1940-81). ah, León Febres Cordero R. (1931-2008).

Perf. 13¾x13½
2014, Apr. 1 Litho. Wmk. 377
2114 Sheet of 34 + label 17.00 17.00
a.-ah. A906 25c Any single .50 .50

Hugo R. Chávez (1954-2013), President of Venezuela A907

Perf. 13¾x13½

2014, Apr. 14 Litho. Wmk. 377

2115 A907 50c multi 1.00 1.00

Parade of Tall Ships, Manabí — A908

No. 2116 — Ship and national flag: a, Cisne Branco, Brazil. b, Cuauhtémoc, Mexico. c, Gloria, Colombia. d, Libertad, Argentina. e, Esmerelda, Chile. f, Guayas, Ecuador. g, Simón Bolívar, Venezuela.

Perf. 13½x13¾

2014, May 3 Litho. Wmk. 377

2116 Sheet of 7 + label 10.50 10.50

a.-g. A908 75c Any single 1.50 1.50

Intl. Philately Day — A909

Magnifying glass over: $2, Ecuadorian stamps. $3, Text from *El Nacional.*

2014, May 22 Litho. *Perf. 13½x13¾*

2117 A909 $2 multi 4.00 4.00

Size: 90x70mm

Wmk. 395

Imperf

2118 A909 $3 multi 6.00 6.00

Regional Platform for Disaster Risk Reduction in the Americas, Guayaquil — A910

Perf. 13½x13¾

2014, May 27 Litho. Wmk. 377

2119 A910 $1 multi 2.00 2.00

2014 World Cup Soccer Championships, Brazil — A911

Designs: 50c, Stadium and stylized Ecuador soccer player. $3, Stylized Ecuador soccer player in stadium, Christ the Redeemer Statue, Rio de Janeiro, horiz. $5, Soccer player and field, horiz.

Perf. 13½x13¾, 13¾x13½

2014, June 18 Litho. Wmk. 377

2120-2121 A911 Set of 2 7.00 7.00

Size: 55x35mm

Imperf

2122 A911 $5 multi 10.00 10.00

Pancho Segura, Ecuadorian-born Tennis Player — A912

Designs: 25c, Segura on tennis court as young man. $5, Segura, tennis ball and racquet, Ecuadoran flag.

Perf. 13½x13¾

2014, July 25 Litho. Wmk. 377

2123-2124 A912 Set of 2 10.50 10.50

Intl. Year of Family Farming A913

Designs: 75c, Woman near tree. $1, Woman spinning yarn from wool. $2, Man pulling down cacao pod from tree.

Perf. 13¾x13½

2014, Aug. 11 Litho. Wmk. 377

2125-2127 A913 Set of 3 7.50 7.50

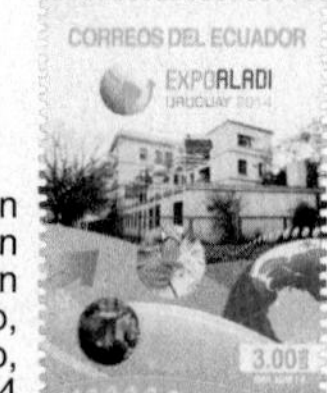

2014 Latin American Integration Association Expo, Montevideo, Uruguay — A914

Perf. 13½x13¾

2014, Aug. 28 Litho. Wmk. 377

2128 A914 $3 multi 6.00 6.00

Mural by Oswaldo Guayasamín — A915

No. 2129: a, Denomination at left. b, Denomination at right.

Perf. 13¾x13½

2014, Aug. 29 Litho. Wmk. 377

2129 A915 25c Horiz. pair, #a-b 1.00 1.00

Latin American Parliament, 50th anniv.

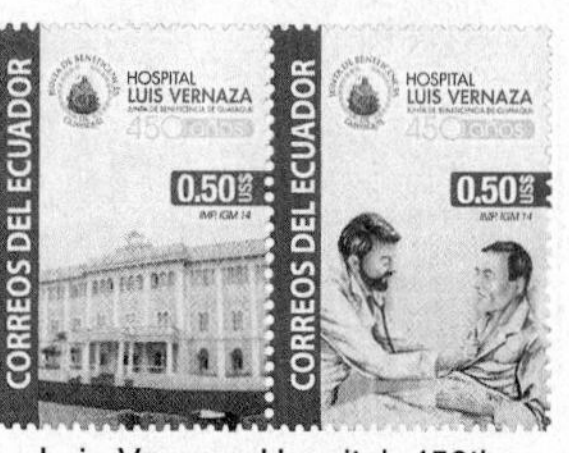

Luis Vernaza Hospital, 450th Anniv. — A916

No. 2130: a, Hospital building. b, Doctor examining patient.

Perf. 13½x13¾

2014, Sept. 10 Litho. Wmk. 377

2130 A916 50c Horiz. pair, #a-b 2.00 2.00

Miniature Sheet

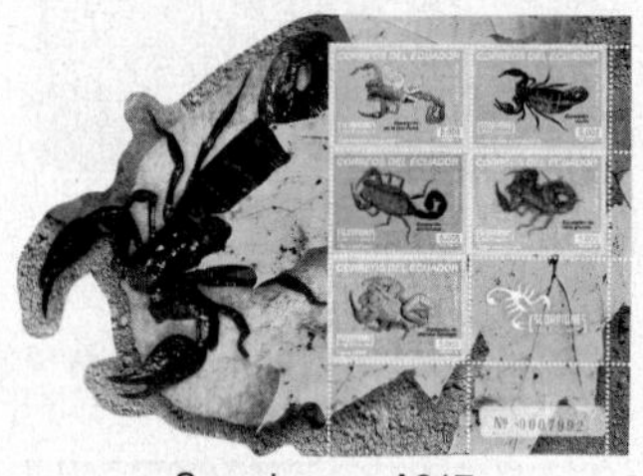

Scorpions — A917

No. 2131: a, Centruroides margaritatus. b, Teuthraustes atramentarius. c, Tityus asthenes. d, Tityus crassicauda. e, Tityus ythieri.

Perf. 13¾x13½

2014, Sept. 30 Litho. Wmk. 377

2131 A917 $5 Sheet of 5, #a-e, + label 50.00 50.00

Yachay University Buildings — A918

No. 2132: a, Capitular Building, b, Library.

Perf. 13¾x13½

2014, Oct. 21 Litho. Wmk. 377

2132 A918 $2 Horiz. pair, #a-b 8.00 8.00

Oryx Leucoryx, Vultur Gryphus, Flags of Ecuador and Qatar — A919

Litho. With Foil Application

Perf. 13½x13¾

2014, Oct. 22 Wmk. 377

2133 A919 $10 multi 20.00 20.00

See Qatar No. 1101.

Manuela Espejo (c. 1757-c. 1829), Writer — A920

Litho. With Foil Application

Perf. 13½x13¾

2014, Oct. 28 Wmk. 377

2134 A920 $5 metallic blue & blue 10.00 10.00

America issue.

Electricity Generation Projects — A921

Designs: 75c, Baba Dam. $1.25, Wind generators, Villonaco. $2, Mazar Dam.

Perf. 13½x13¾

2014, Oct. 31 Litho. Wmk. 377

2135-2137 A921 Set of 3 8.00 8.00

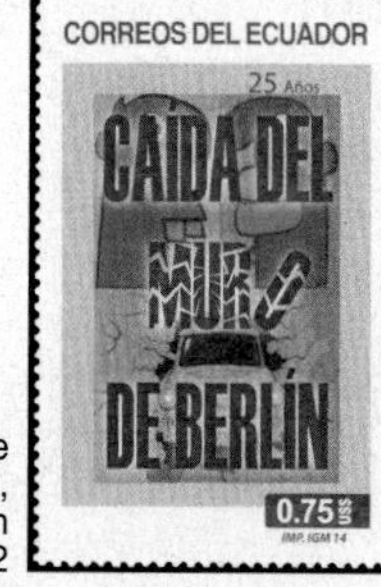

Fall of the Berlin Wall, 25th Anniv. — A922

Perf. 13¾x13½

2014, Nov. 10 Litho. Wmk. 377

2138 A922 75c multi 1.50 1.50

Christmas A923

Designs: 50c, Ivory creche figurines, 18th cent. $1, Wood carving of Infant Jesus, by Caspicara, vert.

Perf. 13¾x13½, 13½x13¾

2014, Nov. 25 Litho. Wmk. 377

2139-2140 A923 Set of 2 3.00 3.00

Miniature Sheet

Cuenca Tourist Attractions — A924

No. 2141: a, Rio Tomebamba. b, Mayor's office (Alcaldía). c, Benigno Malo College. d, Interamerican Artisans Center. e, New Cathedral. f, Azuay Provincial Court. g, Plaza de las Flores.

Perf. 13¾x13½

2014, Dec. 2 Litho. Wmk. 377

2141 A924 75c Sheet of 7, #a-g, + label 10.50 10.50

Miniature Sheet

First Ecuadorian Postage Stamps, 150th Anniv. — A925

No. 2142: a, Emilia Rivadeneira (1839-1916), engraver. b, Printing press, Ecuador #3. c, Printing press, Ecuador #2. d, Printing press, Ecuador #5. e, Manuel Rivadeneira (1814-94), printer.

Litho. With Foil Application

Perf. 13¾x13½

2015, Mar. 19 Wmk. 377

2142 A925 $5 Sheet of 5, #a-e, + 4 labels 50.00 50.00

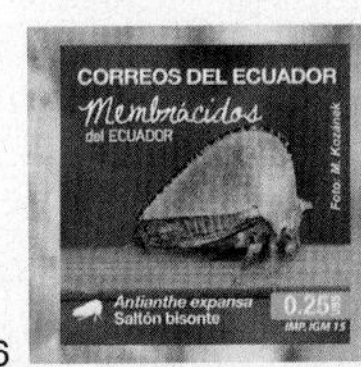

Insects — A926

No. 2143: a, Antianthe expansa. b, Heteronotus abbreviatus. c, Cyphonia clavata. d, Guayaquila gracilicornis. e, Stegaspis fronditia. f, Thuris depressus. g, Tritropidia galeata. h, Membracis mexicana.

Unwmk.

2015, Apr. 21 Litho. *Die Cut*

Self-Adhesive

2143 Booklet pane of 8 10.00
a.-b. A926 25c Either single .50 .50
c.-d. A926 50c Either single 1.00 1.00
e.-f. A926 75c Either single 1.50 1.50
g.-h. A926 $1 Either single 2.00 2.00

Pres. Sixto Durán Ballén and Dove — A927

Perf. 13½x13¾

2015, May 15 Litho. Wmk. 377

2144 A927 $1.25 multi 2.50 2.50

Insects — A928

No. 2145: a, Alchisme grossa. b, Membracis foliata. c, Cladonota apicalis. d, Cyphonia trifida. e, Adippe histrio.

Perf. 13½x13¾

2015, May 28 Litho. Wmk. 377

2145 Horiz. strip of 5 30.00 30.00
a.-e. A928 $3 Any single 6.00 6.00

Cattle — A929

Breeds: 75c, Aberdeen Angus. $1.25, Brahman. $3, Holstein Friesian.

Perf. 13½x13¾

2015, June 2 Litho. Wmk. 377

2146-2148 A929 Set of 3 10.00 10.00

Eradication of hoof-and-mouth disease in Ecuador.

Renovation of San Francisco Monastery, Quito — A930

Designs: 25c, Friar Jodoco Ricke baptizing indigenous people. 50c, Icon of Jesus, San Francisco Church. $1, San Francisco Church and Plaza. $1.75, Franciscan monk making beer. $2, Religious procession.

Perf. 13½x13¾

2015, June 11 Litho. Wmk. 377

2149-2153 A930 Set of 5 11.00 11.00

Birds — A931

Designs: 25c, Grallaria ridgelyi. 50c, Amazona lilacina. $1, Atlapetes pallidiceps. $2, Pyrrhura albipectus. $3, Chaetocercus berlepschi.

Perf. 13½x13¾

2015, June 16 Litho. Wmk. 377

2154-2158 A931 Set of 5 13.50 13.50

Visit of Pope Francis to Ecuador A932

Perf. 13¾x13½

2015, June 30 Litho. Wmk. 377

2159 A932 $3 multi 6.00 6.00

Litho. With Foil Application

Size: 100x70mm

Imperf

2160 A932 $5 Pope Francis, diff. 10.00 10.00

Official Registrar, 120th Anniv. A933

Perf. 13¾x13½

2015, Sept. 1 Litho. Wmk. 377

2161 A933 $1.50 multi 3.00 3.00

Famous People A934

No. 2162: a, Antonio Bastidas y Carranza (1615-81), poet. b, Raúl Clemente Huerta (1915-91), politician. c, Morayma Ofyr Carvajal (1915-51), writer. d, José Modesto Espinosa (1833-1915), writer. e, José Cuero y Caicedo (1735-1815), bishop of Quito.

Perf. 13¾x13½

2015, Sept. 22 Litho. Wmk. 377

2162 Horiz. strip of 5 12.50 12.50
a.-e. A934 $1.25 Any single 2.50 2.50

Miniature Sheet

ExpoAFE,150th Anniv. — A935

No. 2163: a, Argentina #594, flag of Argentina. b, Unissued Bolivia stamp of 1863, flag of Bolivia. c, Brazil #3252c, flag of Brazil. d, Canada #322, flag of Canada. e, Chile #348A, flag of Chile. f, Colombia #C56, flag of Colombia. g, Costa Rica #1, flag of Costa Rica. h, Cuba #432, flag of Cuba. i, Ecuador #306, flag of Ecuador. j, El Salvador #509, flag of El Salvador. k, Cover of *El Coleccionista Ecuatoriano,* emblem of Ecuadorian Philatelic Association. l, Block of six of Ecuador #2, ExpoAFE 80th anniv. emblem. m, Cover to Lima, emblem of ExpopAFE thematic stamp exhibition. n, Cover depicting airplane, emblem of FIAF thematic stamp exhibition. o, Postal card, FIAF emblem. p, Spain #345, flag of Spain. q, United States #C3a, flag of United States. r, Guatemala #21, flag of Guatemala. s, Mexico #246, flag of Mexico. t, Panama #214, flag of Panama. u, Paraguay #407, flag of Paraguay. v, Peru #C338, flag of Peru. w, St. Pierre & Miquelon #136, flag of St. Pierre & Miquelon. x, Uruguay #1167, flag of Uruguay. y, Venezuela #C9, flag of Venezuela.

Perf. 13½x13¾

2015, Sept. 29 Litho. Wmk. 377

2163 A935 Sheet of 25 37.50 37.50
a.-y. 75c Any single 1.50 1.50

Birds — A936

No. 2164: a, Tangara florida. b, Acropternis orthonyx. c, Pipreola jucunda. d, Pionopsitta pyrilia. e, Semnornis ramphastinus. f, Trogon chionurus. g, Pipra filicauda. h, Dacnis egregia.

No. 2165: a, Thryothorus nigricapillus. b, Neomorphus radiolosus. c, Phoenicircus nigricollis. d, Tangara gyrola. e, Aegolius harrisii. f, Grallaricula lineifrons. g, Melanopareia elegans. h, Piculus rivolii.

Unwmk.

2015, Oct. 20 Litho. *Die Cut*

Self-Adhesive

2164 Booklet pane of 8 10.00
a.-b. A936 25c Either single .50 .50
c.-d. A936 50c Either single 1.00 1.00
e.-f. A936 75c Either single 1.50 1.50
g.-h. A936 $1 Either single 2.00 2.00
2165 Booklet pane of 8 10.00
a.-b. A936 25c Either single .50 .50
c.-d. A936 50c Either single 1.00 1.00
e.-f. A936 75c Either single 1.50 1.50
g.-h. A936 $1 Either single 2.00 2.00

Don Quixote in Art — A937

No. 2166, $1 — Depictions of Don Quixote by: a, Carlos Monsalve. b, Ernesto Saá Sevilla.

No. 2167, $1.50 — Depictions of Don Quixote by: a, Oswaldo Viteri. b, Vilma Vargas.

No. 2168, $1.75, horiz. — Depictions of Don Quixote by: a, Joaquín Pinto. b, Karlomán Villota.

Perf. 13½x13¾, 13¾x13½

2015, Oct. 30 Litho. Wmk. 377

Horiz. Pairs, #a-b

2166-2168 A937 Set of 3 17.00 17.00

A938

A939

Tourism A940

No. 2169: a, Chelonia mydas. b, Vicugna vicugna. c, Paleosuchus trigonatus. d, Megaptera novaeangliae. e, Marine iguana.

$5, Tortoise, caiman, whale, condor.

No. 2171: a, Corallus batesii. b, San Rafael Waterfall. c, Dasyatis brevis. d, Gardner Bay Beach, Española Island, Galapagos Islands. e, Ceratophrys stolzmanni. f, Ship on Guayas River. g, Coeligena torquata. h, El Vado, Cuenca.

No. 2172: a, Hippocampus ingens. b, Amblyrhynchus cristatus. c, Prionurus laticlavius. d, Fregata magnificens. e, Spheniscus mendiculus. f, Boats near Isabela Island, Galapagos Islands. g, Roca Pináculo, Bartolomé Island, Galapagos Islands. h, Boats near Plaza Islands, Galapagos Islands.

Perf. 13¾x13½

2015, Nov. 11 Litho. Wmk. 377

2169 Horiz. strip of 5 10.00 10.00
a.-e. A938 $1 Any single 2.00 2.00

Imperf

2170 A939 $5 multi 10.00 10.00

Self-Adhesive

Unwmk.

Die Cut

2171 Booklet pane of 8 10.00
a.-b. A940 25c Either single .50 .50
c.-d. A940 50c Either single 1.00 1.00
e.-f. A940 75c Either single 1.50 1.50
g.-h. A940 $1 Either single 2.00 2.00
2172 Booklet pane of 8 10.00
a.-b. A940 25c Either single .50 .50
c.-d. A940 50c Either single 1.00 1.00
e.-f. A940 75c Either single 1.50 1.50
g.-h. A940 $1 Either single 2.00 2.00

Campaign to End Violence Against Women
A941

Perf. 13¾x13½

2015, Nov, 25 Litho. Wmk. 377

2173 A941 $5 multi 10.00 10.00

See Dominican Republic No. 1583, Guatemala No. 717, El Salvador No. 1747, Venezuela No. 1731.

Campaign Against Human Trafficking — A942

Perf. 13½x13¾

2015, Nov. 22 Litho. Wmk. 377

2174 A942 $1.50 multi 3.00 3.00

America Issue.

Christmas — A943

Perf. 13½x13¾

2015, Dec. 3 Litho. Wmk. 377

2175 A943 $2 multi 4.00 4.00

Yachay, City of Knowledge
A944

Perf. 13¾x13½

2016, Mar. 31 Litho. Wmk. 377

2176 A944 $2 multi 4.00 4.00

Amphibians
A945

No. 2177: a, Epipedobates anthonyi. b, Hyloscirtus princecharlesi, c, Oophaga sylvatica. d, Ceratophrys stolzmanni. e, Gastrotheca riobambae. f, Hyalinobatrachium aureoguttatum. g, Hypsiboas picturatus. h, Atelopus balios.

Unwmk.

2016, Mar. 31 Litho. *Die Cut*

Self-Adhesive

2177 Booklet pane of 8 10.00
a.-b. A945 25c Either single .50 .50
c.-d. A945 50c Either single 1.00 1.00
e.-f. A945 75c Either single 1.50 1.50
g.-h. A945 $1 Either single 2.00 2.00

Quito Central Lions Club, 70th Anniv. — A946

Perf. 13½x13¾

2016, Apr. 27 Litho. Wmk. 377

2178 A946 $5 multi 10.00 10.00

Ecuador Postal Service, 185th Anniv. — A947

No. 2179: a, Chasqui (relay messenger). b, Postman on bicycle. c, Postal worker on motorcycle. d, Old Quito Post Office, 185th anniv. emblem.

Perf. 13½x13¾

2016, May 25 Litho. Wmk. 377

2179 A947 10c Block of 4, #a-d .80 .80

Miniature Sheet

2016 Summer Olympics, Rio de Janeiro — A948

No. 2180: a, Swimming. b, Running, c, Weight lifting. d, Boxing.

Perf. 13¾x13½

2016, Aug. 16 Litho. Wmk. 377

2180 A948 $1.25 Sheet of 4, #a-d 10.00 10.00

Colegio Intisana, Quito, 50th Anniv. — A949

Perf. 13½x13¾

2016, Oct. 24 Litho. Wmk. 377

2181 A949 $2 multi 4.00 4.00

Jamaica Letter, by Simón Bolívar, 200th Anniv. (in 2015) — A950

No. 2182: a, Portrait of Bolívar, by Antonio Salguero. b, Jamaica Letter, ribbon in colors of Ecuadorian flag.

Perf. 13½x13¾

2016, Oct. 28 Litho. Wmk. 377

2182 A950 $10 Horiz. pair, #a-b 40.00 40.00

Coca Codo Sinclair Hydroelectric Project
A951

Designs: $1.25, Dam. $1.50, Compensating reservoir. $1.75, Generators.

Perf. 13¾x13½

2016, Oct. 25 Litho. Wmk. 377

2183-2185 A951 Set of 3 9.00 9.00

Flowers
A952

No. 2186: a, Cyrtocaucaea. b, Masdevallia. c, Hippeastrum sp. d, Gentianella hirculus. e, Bomarea caldasii.

Perf. 13¾x13½

2016, Nov. 12 Litho. Wmk. 395

2186 Horiz. strip of 5 10.00 10.00
a.-e. A952 $1 Any single 2.00 2.00

Third French-Ecuadorian Geodesic Mission — A953

No. 2187: a, Drawing of people near globe. b, Mt. Chimborazo.

Perf. 13¾x13½

2016, Nov. 14 Litho. Wmk. 377

2187 A953 10c Horiz. pair, #a-b .40 .40

Society for Protection of Children — A954

Perf. 13½x13¾

2016, Nov. 22 Litho. Wmk. 377

2188 A954 $5 multi 10.00 10.00

Santa Elena Petroleum Ancón Oil Well — A955

Perf. 13¾x13½

2016, Nov. 30 Litho. Wmk. 377

2189 A955 30c multi .60 .60

Christmas
A956

No. 2190: a, Shepherd and sheep, volcano. b, Star of Bethlehem, Andean village. c, Annunciation, Galapagos turtle. d, Three Magi in Ecuadorian Indian costumes. e, Afro-American Holy Family.

Perf. 13¾x13½

2016, Dec. 12 Litho. Wmk. 377

2190 Horiz. strip of 5 20.00 20.00
a.-e. A956 $2 Any single 4.00 4.00

Union of South American Nations Summit, Quito
A957

Perf. 13¾x13½

2016, Dec. 22 Litho. Wmk. 377

2191 A957 $3 multi 6.00 6.00

Ecuadorian Institute for Promotion of Exportation and Investment — A958

No. 2192: a, Dam, emblem for 2016 Ecuador Investment Summit. b, Spiral and "love life." c, Hats. d, Cacao pods. e, Onions, bananas, herbs, shrimp.

Perf. 13½x13¾

2016, Dec. 29 Litho. Wmk. 377

2192 Horiz. strip of 5 10.00 10.00
a.-e. A958 $1 Any single 2.00 2.00

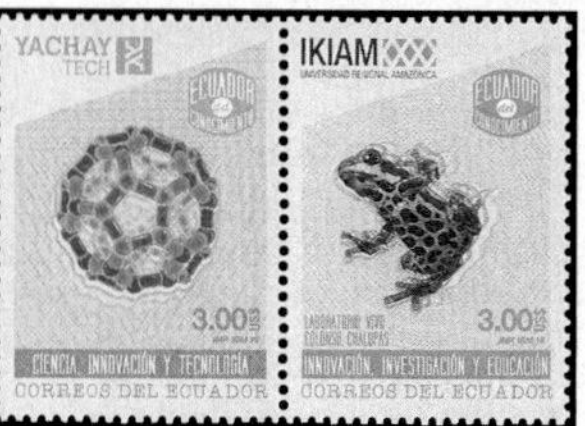

A959

Schools — A960

No. 2193: a, Hands, emblem of Ecuador University of Arts. b, Book, quill pen, emblem of National University of Ecuador.

No. 2194: a, Buckminsterfullerene molecule, emblem for Yachay Tech. b, Frog, emblem for Amazon Regional University.

Perf. 13½x13¾

2016, Dec. 30 Litho. Wmk. 377

2193 A959 $3 Horiz. pair, #a-b 12.00 12.00
2194 A960 $3 Horiz. pair, #a-b 12.00 12.00

Carnival, Guaranda — A961

No. 2195: a, Aerial view of Guaranda. b, Guitarist.

Perf. 13¾x13½

2017, Feb. 24 Litho.

2195 A961 $1 Horiz. pair, #a-b 4.00 4.00

Ants — A962

No. 2196: a, Atta cephalotes (Hormiga arriera). b, Eciton hamatum (Hormiga legionaria). c, Daceton armigerum (Hormiga cazadora). d, Acanthoponera minor (Conga enana). e, Ectatomma tuberculatum (Hormiga rugosa). f, Gigantiops destructor (Hormiga ojona). g, Neoponera villosa (Hormiga peluda). h, Cephalotes atratus (Cabezona negra).

No. 2197: a, Cephalotes spinosus (Hormiga paracaidista). b, Odontomachus hastatus (Hormiga mandibula). c, Pheidole xanthogaster (Hormiga zanahoria). d, Myrmelachista ruszkii (Hormiga limón). e, Leptogenys pucuna (Hormiga de Lattke). f, Eciton rapax (Hormiga rapaz). g, Paraponera clavata (Conga). h, Camponotus sericeiventris (Hormiga aterciopelada).

Unwmk.

2017, Mar. 31 Litho. ***Die Cut***

Self-Adhesive

2196 Booklet pane of 8 10.00
a.-b. A962 25c Either single .50 .50
c.-d. A962 50c Either single 1.00 1.00
e.-f. A962 75c Either single 1.50 1.50
g.-h. A962 $1 Either single 2.00 2.00
2197 Booklet pane of 8 10.00
a.-b. A962 25c Either single .50 .50
c.-d. A962 50c Either single 1.00 1.00
e.-f. A962 75c Either single 1.50 1.50
g.-h. A962 $1 Either single 2.00 2.00

Miniature Sheet

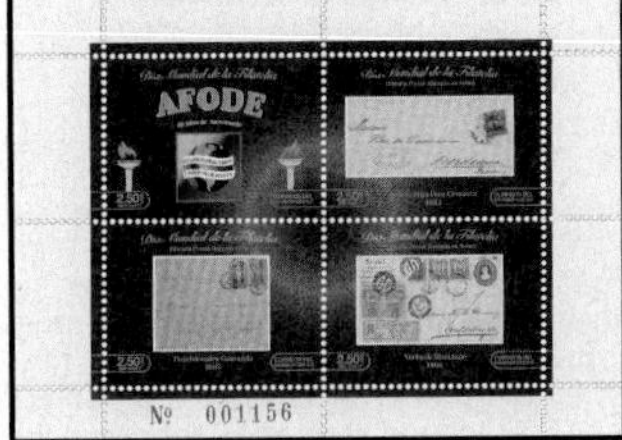
World Philately Day — A963

No. 2198: a, Emblem of Olympic and Sports Philatelic Association of Ecuador. b, 1883 cover with Ecuador #18. c, 1895 cover with Guaranda provisional surcharge stamps. d, 1896 cover with bisected Seebeck stamp and other Ecuador stamps.

Litho., Litho With Foil Application (#2198a)

Perf. 13¾x13½

2017, May 18 Wmk. 377

2198 A963 $2.50 Sheet of 4, #a-d 20.00 20.00

German School, Quito, Cent. A964

Perf. 13¼x13

2017, Oct. 3 Litho. Wmk. 377

2199 A964 $5 multi 10.00 10.00

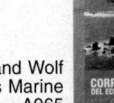

Darwin and Wolf Islands Marine Sanctuary — A965

No. 2200: a, Darwin Island and Darwin Arch. b, Sphyrna lewini. c, Rhincodon typus. d, Aetobatus narinari. e, Darwin Arch. f, Chelonia mydas. g, Delphinus delphis. h, Sula nebouxii.

Unwmk.

2017, Oct. 24 Litho. ***Die Cut***

Self-Adhesive

2200 Booklet pane of 8 10.00
a.-b. A965 25c Either single .50 .50
c.-d. A965 50c Either single 1.00 1.00
e.-f. A965 75c Either single 1.50 1.50
g.-h. A965 $1 Either single 2.00 2.00

Amazon Regional Economic Development Institute (ECORAE) — A966

No. 2201: a, Communication between Amazon cultures. b, Bridge, Morona-Santiago Province.

Perf. 13¼x13

2017, Nov. 2 Litho. Wmk. 377

2201 A966 $2.50 Horiz. pair, #a-b 10.00 10.00

A967

Tourism — A968

No. 2202: a, Train, Guamote Canton. b, Chimborazo Volcano. c, San Rafael Waterfall. d, San Lorenzo Beach. e, Negra Beach.

No. 2203: a, Caucaea nubigena. b, Handroanthus chrysanthus. c, Sula granti. d, Podocnemis expansa. e, Oreotrochilus. f, Cuyabeno River. g, Los Frailes Beach. h, San Francisco Church, Quito.

Perf. 13¼x13

2017 Litho. Wmk. 377

2202 Horiz. strip of 5 30.00 30.00
a.-e. A967 $3 Any single 6.00 6.00

Self-Adhesive

Unwmk.

Die Cut

2203 Booklet pane of 8 10.00
a.-b. A968 25c Either single .50 .50
c.-d. A968 50c Either single 1.00 1.00
e.-f. A968 75c Either single 1.50 1.50
g.-h. A968 $1 Either single 2.00 2.00

America issue. Issued: No. 2202, 12/27; No. 2203, 11/27.

Christmas — A969

Perf. 13x13¼

2017, Dec. 18 Litho. Wmk. 377

2204 A969 $2 multi 4.00 4.00

Eugenio Espejo National Prize — A970

Perf. 13x13¼

2017, Dec. 21 Litho. Wmk. 377

2205 A970 $10 multi 20.00 20.00

15th Interamerican Scout Jamboree, Ecuador — A971

Perf. 13x13¼

2017, Dec. 29 Litho. Wmk. 377

2206 A971 $5 multi 10.00 10.00

Souvenir Sheet

Locomotives — A972

No. 2207: a, Model of Sapucai locomotive. b, Baldwin steam locomotive.

Perf. 13¼x13

2018, Apr. 27 Litho. Wmk. 377

2207 A972 $2.50 Sheet of 2, #a-b, + 2 labels 10.00 10.00

See Paraguay No.

Spiders — A973

No. 2208: a, Micrathena pilaton. b, Patrera fulvastra.

No. 2209: a, Argiope argentata. b, Chrysometa tenuipes.

No. 2210: a, Micrathena raimondi. b, Micrathena pichincha.

$5, Linothele quori.

Perf. 13x13¼

2018, May 9 Litho. Wmk. 377

2208 Horiz. pair .80 .80
a.-b. A973 20c Either single .40 .40
2209 Horiz. pair 2.00 2.00
a.-b. A973 50c Either single 1.00 1.00
2210 Horiz. pair 8.00 8.00
a.-b. A973 $2 Either single 4.00 4.00
2211 A973 $5 multi 10.00 10.00
Nos. 2208-2211 (4) 20.80 20.80

A974

Domesticated Animals — A975

No. 2212: a, Lama glama. b, Cavia porcellus. c, Bos primigenius taurus. d, Ovis orientalis aries. e, Equus ferus caballus.

No. 2213: a, Anser anser. b, Gallus gallus. c, Canis lupus familiaris. d, Felis silvestris catus. e, Capra aegagrus hircus. f, Oryctolagus cuniculus. g, Equus ferus caballus. h, Lama glama.

Perf. 13¼x13

2018, May 18 Litho. Wmk. 377

2212 Horiz. strip of 5 20.00 20.00
a.-e. A974 $2 Any single 4.00 4.00

Self-Adhesive

Unwmk.

Die Cut

2213 Booklet pane of 8 10.00
a.-b. A975 25c Either single .50 .50
c.-d. A975 50c Either single 1.00 1.00
e.-f. A975 75c Either single 1.50 1.50
g.-h. A975 $1 Either single 2.00 2.00

University of Azuay, 50th Anniv. — A976

Designs: $3, Emblem. $5, Emblem and trees, horiz.

Perf. 13x13¼

2018, June 14 Litho. Wmk. 377

2214 A976 $3 multi 6.00 6.00

Imperf

Size: 96x71mm

2215 A976 $5 multi 10.00 10.00

Nelson Mandela (1918-2013), President of South Africa, and Flag of South Africa A977

Perf. 13¼x13

2018, July 18 Litho. Wmk. 377

2216 A977 $10 multi 20.00 20.00

Miniature Sheet

Diplomatic Relations Between Ecuador and Japan, Cent. — A978

No. 2217: a, Kinkaku-ji Temple, Kyoto, Japan. b, Torii, Itsukushima Shrine, Miyajima, Japan. c, Church of the Society of Jesus, Quito. d, Darwin's Arch, Galapagos Islands.

Wmk. 377

2018, Aug. 13 Litho. ***Perf. 13***

2217 A978 $2.50 Sheet of 4, #a-d 20.00 20.00

Volcanoes A979

No. 2218: a, Corazón Volcano. b, Imbabura Volcano. c, Cotacachi Volcano.

Wmk. 377

2018, Aug. 20 Litho. *Perf. 13*

2218 Horiz. strip of 3 12.00 12.00

a.-c. A979 $2 Any single 4.00 4.00

Souvenir Sheet

12th Latin American Botanical Congress, Quito — A980

Perf. 13¾x13½

2018, Aug. 29 Litho. Wmk. 377

2219 A980 $4 multi 8.00 8.00

A981

Green Tourism — A982

No. 2220: a, Amblyrhynchus cristatus. b, Mount Carihuairazo. c, Machalilla National Park. d, Paleosuchus trigonatus.

No. 2221: a, Zalophus wollebaeki. b, Isabela Island. c, Chalcostigma herrani. d, Espelitia plants, Páramo el Angel Ecological Reserve. e, Oophaga sylvatica. f, Cayapas Mataje Reserve. g, Cebuella pygmaea. h, Lake, Orellana Province.

Perf. 13¾x13½

2018, Sept. 13 Litho. Wmk. 377

2220 A981 $2 Block of 4, #a-d 16.00 16.00

Self-Adhesive

Die Cut

Unwmk.

2221 Booklet pane of 8 10.00

a.-b. A982 25c Either single .50 .50

c.-d. A982 50c Either single 1.00 1.00

e.-f. A982 75c Either single 1.50 1.50

g.-h. A982 $1 Either single 2.00 2.00

A983

A984

Image of the Motherland Mural, by Oswaldo Guayasamín A985

Perf. 13¾x13½

2018, Sept. 18 Litho. Wmk. 377

2222 Horiz. strip of 3 6.00 6.00

a. A983 $1 multi 2.00 2.00

b. A984 $1 multi 2.00 2.00

c. A985 $1 multi 2.00 2.00

Christmas A986

No. 2223: a, Buildings. b, Magi on camels. c, Holy Family. d, Angel with horn. e, Shepherd and sheep.

Perf. 13¾x13½

2018, Nov. 30 Litho. Wmk. 377

2223 Horiz. strip of 5 1.25 1.25

a.-e. A986 10c Any single .25 .25

Miniature Sheet

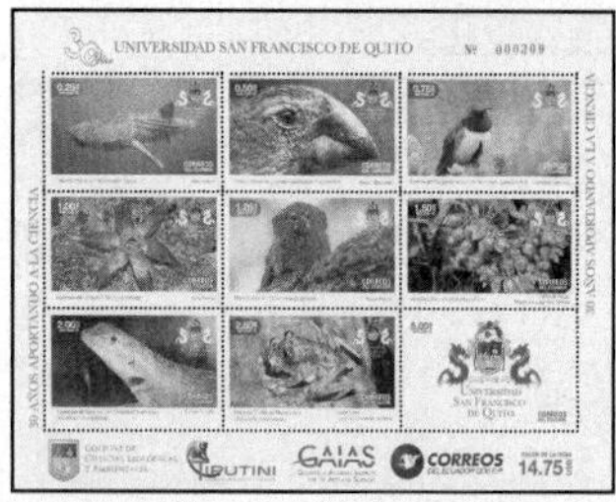

Scientific Contributions of San Francisco University, Quito — A987

No. 2224: a, 25c, Rhincodon typus. b, 50c, Geospiza magnirostri. c, 75c, Oreotrochilus cyanolaemus. d, $1, Tiputinia foetida. e, $1.25, Cebuella pygmaea. f, $1.50, Vaccinium floribundum. g, $2, Microlophus bivittatus. h, $2.50, Chimerella mariaelenae. i, $5, University crest.

Perf. 13½x13¾

2018, Dec. 11 Litho. Wmk. 377

2224 A987 Sheet of 9, #a-i 29.50 29.50

A988

Cotacachi-Cayapas Ecological Reserve, 50th Anniv. — A989

No. 2225: a, Podiceps occipitalis. b, Odocoileus virginiannus. c, Cuicocha Lake. d, Elaenia albiceps. e, Epidendrum jamiesonis.

No. 2226: a, Eira barbara. b, Tremarctos ornatus. c, Geranoaetus melanoleucus. d, Anisgomathus igniventris. e, Eriocnemis nigrivestis. f, Cerro Pilavo. g, Bomarea glaucenscens. h, Vaccinium floribundum.

Perf. 13¾x13½

2018, Dec. 27 Litho. Wmk. 377

2225 Horiz. strip of 5 30.00 30.00

a.-e. A988 $3 Any single 6.00 6.00

Self-Adhesive

Unwmk.

Die Cut

2226 Booklet pane of 8 10.00

a.-b. A989 25c Either single .50 .50

c.-d. A989 50c Either single 1.00 1.00

e.-f. A989 75c Either single 1.50 1.50

g.-h. A989 $1 Either single 2.00 2.00

National Development Plan — A990

Perf. 13¾x13½

2018 Litho. Wmk. 377

2227 A990 $5 multi 10.00 10.00

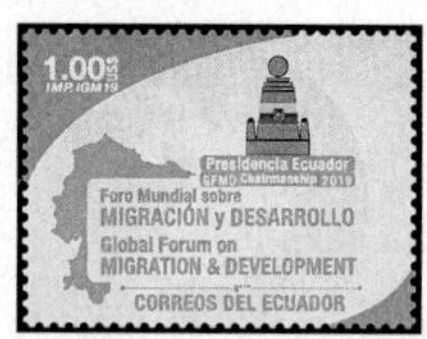

2019 Global Forum on Miigration and Development, Quito — A991

Perf. 13¾x13½

2019, Apr. 8 Litho. Wmk. 377

2228 A991 $1 multi 2.00 2.00

Birds — A992

No. 2229: a, Turdus fuscater. b, Zonotrichia capensis. c, Sicalis flaveola. d, Thraupis bonariensis. e, Mimus gilvus. f, Pyrocephalus rubinus. g, Diglossa sittoides. h, Notiochleidon cyanoleuca.

No. 2230: a, Sporophila luctuosa. b, Dendroica fusca. c, Thraupis episcopus. d, Zenaida auriculata. e, Camptostoma obsoletum. f, Patagona gigas. g, Pheucticus chrysogaster. h, Euphonia cyanocephala.

Unwmk.

2019, May 2 Litho. *Die Cut*

Self-Adhesive

2229 Booklet pane of 8 10.00

a.-b. A992 25c Either single .50 .50

c.-d. A992 50c Either single 1.00 1.00

e.-f. A992 75c Either single 1.50 1.50

g.-h. A992 $1 Either single 2.00 2.00

2230 Booklet pane of 8 10.00

a.-b. A992 25c Either single .50 .50

c.-d. A992 50c Either single 1.00 1.00

e.-f. A992 75c Either single 1.50 1.50

g.-h. A992 $1 Either single 2.00 2.00

Frogs — A993

No. 2231: a, Hyalinobatrachium pellucidum. b, Nymphargus anomalus. c, Nymphargus cochranae. d, Nymphargus grandisonae facing forward. e, Nymphargus griffithsi facing left. f, Sachatamia albomaculata. g, Sachatamia ilex. h, Overhead view of Teratohyla pulverata.

No. 2232: a, Centrolene ballux. b, Centrolene buckleyi. c, Centrolene condor. d, Centrolene heloderma. e, Chimerella mariaelenae. f, Espadarana callistomma. g, Espadarana prosoblepon. h, Overhead view of Hyalinobatrachium aureoguttatum.

No. 2233: a, Cochranella balionota. b, Cochranella litoralis. c, Cochranella mache. d, Nymphargus grandisonae facing right. e, Underside view of Hyalinobatrachium aureoguttatum. f, Underside view of Teratohyla pulverata. g, Underside view of Nymphargus griffithsi. h, Two Terarohyla spinosa.

Unwmk.

2019, May 29 Litho. *Die Cut*

Self-Adhesive

2231 Booklet pane of 8 10.00

a.-b. A993 25c Either single .50 .50

c.-d. A993 50c Either single 1.00 1.00

e.-f. A993 75c Either single 1.50 1.50

g.-h. A993 $1 Either single 2.00 2.00

2232 Booklet pane of 8 10.00

a.-b. A993 25c Either single .50 .50

c.-d. A993 50c Either single 1.00 1.00

e.-f. A993 75c Either single 1.50 1.50

g.-h. A993 $1 Either single 2.00 2.00

2233 Booklet pane of 8 10.00

a.-b. A993 25c Either single .50 .50

c.-d. A993 50c Either single 1.00 1.00

e.-f. A993 75c Either single 1.50 1.50

g.-h. A993 $1 Either single 2.00 2.00

Nos. 2231-2233 (3) 30.00

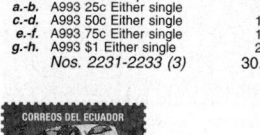

Paintings by Oswaldo Guayasamín (1919-99) — A994

No. 2234: a, Manos del Mendigo (Hands of a Beggar). b, Manos de la Ternura (Hands of Tenderness). c, Autoretrato (Self-portrait). d, Manos de la Oración (Hands in Prayer). e, Manos de la Esperanza (Hands of Hope).

Perf. 13½x13¾

2019, June 28 Litho. Wmk. 377

2234 Horiz. strip of 5 20.00 20.00

a.-e. A994 $2 Any single 4.00 4.00

SEMI-POSTAL STAMPS

Nos. 423-428 Surcharged in Carmine or Blue

1944, May 9 Unwmk. *Perf. 12*

B1 A171 10c + 10c yel grn (C) .60 .30

B2 A171 20c + 20c rose pink .60 .35

B3 A171 30c + 20c dk gray brn .60 .30

B4 A171 50c + 20c dp red lil 1.20 .60

B5 A171 1s + 50c ol gray (C) 2.00 1.00

B6 A171 10s + 2s red orange 7.00 3.50

Nos. B1-B6 (6) 12.00 6.00

The surtax aided Mendez Hospital.

AIR POST STAMPS

In 1928-30, the internal airmail service of Ecuador was handled by the Sociedad Colombo-Alemana de Transportes Aereos ("SCADTA") under government sanction. During this period SCADTA issued stamps which were the only legal franking for airmail service except that handled under contract with Pan American-Grace Airways. SCADTA issues are Nos. C1-C6, C16-C25, CF1-CF2.

Colombla Air Post Stamps of 1923 Surcharged in Carmine

"Provisional" at 45 degree Angle

Perf. 14x14½

1928, Aug. 28 Wmk. 116

C1 AP6 50c on 10c green 110.00 70.00

C2 AP6 75c on 15c car 210.00 160.00

C3 AP6 1s on 20c gray 70.00 42.50

C4 AP6 1⅕s on 30c blue 45.00 35.00

C5 AP6 3s on 60c brown 85.00 52.50

Nos. C1-C5 (5) 520.00 360.00

"Provisional" at 41 degree Angle

1929, Mar. 20

C1a AP6 50c on 10c green 125.00 110.00

C2a AP6 75c on 15c carmine 225.00 175.00

C3a AP6 1s on 20c gray 225.00 175.00

Nos. C1a-C3a (3) 575.00 460.00

C6	AP6	50c on 10c green	*700.00*	*1,700.*

A 75c on 15c carmine with "Cts." between the surcharged numerals exists. There is no evidence that it was regularly issued or used.

For overprints see Nos. CF1-CF1a.

Plane over River Guayas — AP1

Unwmk.

1929, May 5 Engr. *Perf. 12*

C8	AP1	2c black	.40	.25
C9	AP1	5c carmine rose	.40	.25
C10	AP1	10c deep brown	.40	.25
C11	AP1	20c dark violet	.90	.25
C12	AP1	50c deep green	1.60	.45
C13	AP1	1s dark blue	6.00	2.75
C14	AP1	5s orange yellow	25.00	11.00
C15	AP1	10s orange red	135.00	57.50
		Nos. C8-C15 (8)	169.70	72.70

Establishment of commercial air service in Ecuador. The stamps were available for all forms of postal service and were largely used for franking ordinary letters.

Nos. C13-C15 show numerals in color on white background. Counterfeits of No. C15 exist.

See Nos. C26-C31. For overprints and surcharge see Nos. C32-C38, C287, CO1-CO12.

Jesuit Church La Compania AP2

Mount Chimborazo AP3

Wmk. 127

1929, Apr. 1 Litho. *Perf. 14*

C16	AP2	50c red brown	4.50	2.25
C17	AP2	75c green	4.50	2.25
C18	AP2	1s rose	7.00	2.25
C19	AP2	1½s gray blue	7.00	2.25
C20	AP2	2s violet	11.50	4.50
C21	AP2	3s brown	11.50	4.50
C22	AP3	5s lt blue	50.00	15.00
C23	AP3	10s lt red	100.00	32.50
C24	AP3	15s violet	160.00	65.00
C25	AP3	25s olive green	225.00	75.00
		Nos. C16-C25 (10)	581.00	205.50

For overprint see No. CF2.

Plane Type of 1929

1930-44 Unwmk. Engr. *Perf. 12*

C26	AP1	1s carmine lake	6.50	.55
C27	AP1	1s green ('44)	1.00	.25
C28	AP1	5s olive green	10.00	3.75
C29	AP1	5s purple ('44)	2.00	.25
C30	AP1	10s black	30.00	5.50
C31	AP1	10s brt ultra ('44)	4.50	.30
		Nos. C26-C31 (6)	54.00	10.60

Nos. C26-C31 show numerals in color on white background.

For surcharge see No. C287.

Nos. C26, C28, C30 Ovptd. in Various Colors

1930, June 4

C32	AP1	1s car lake (Bk)	22.50	22.50
a.		Double ovpt. (R Br + Bk)	75.00	
C33	AP1	5s olive grn (Bl)	22.50	22.50
C34	AP1	10s black (R Br)	22.50	22.50
		Nos. C32-C34 (3)	67.50	67.50

Flight of Capt. Benjamin Mendez from Bogota to Quito, bearing a crown of flowers for the tomb of Grand Marshal Sucre.

Air Post Official Stamps of 1929-30 Ovptd. in Various Colors or Srchd. Similarly in Upper & Lower Case

1935, July 24

C35	AP1	50c deep green (Bl)	12.50	5.00
C36	AP1	50c olive brn (R)	12.50	5.00
C37	AP1	1s on 5s ol grn (Bk)	12.50	5.00
a.		Double surcharge	95.00	
C38	AP1	2s on 10s black (R)	12.50	5.00
		Nos. C35-C38 (4)	50.00	20.00

Unveiling of a monument to Bolívar at Quito, July 24th, 1935.

AP5

1935, Oct. 13 Photo. *Perf. 11½x11*

C38A	AP5	5c ultra & red	.25	*.30*
C38B	AP5	10c brown & black	.25	*.50*
C38C	AP5	50c green & red	.25	*.50*
C38D	AP5	1S carmine & blue	.80	*1.20*
C38E	AP5	5S gray grn & red	1.20	*2.40*
		Nos. C38A-C38E (5)	2.75	*4.90*

Columbus Day. Nos. 338A-338E and C38A-C38E were prepared by the Sociedad Colombista Panamericana and were sold by the Ecuadorian post office through Oct. 30. Nos. C38B-C38E exist imperf.

Geodesical Mission Issue

Type of Regular Issue and Nos. 349-351 Overprinted in Blue or Black

1936, July 3 *Perf. 12½*

C39	A136	10c deep orange (Bl)	.60	.25
C40	A136	20c violet (Bk)	.60	.25
C41	A136	50c dark red (Bl)	.60	.25
C42	A136	70c black	1.25	.35
		Nos. C39-C42 (4)	3.05	1.10

For surcharge see No. RA42.

Philatelic Exhibition Issue

Type of Regular Issue Overprinted "AEREA"

1936, Oct. 20 *Perf. 13½x14*

C43	A137	2c rose	5.00	5.00
C44	A137	5c brown orange	5.00	5.00
C45	A137	10c brown	5.00	5.00
C46	A137	20c ultra	5.00	5.00
C47	A137	50c red violet	5.00	5.00
C48	A137	1s green	5.00	5.00
		Nos. C43-C48 (6)	30.00	30.00

Condor and Plane — AP6

Perf. 13½

C49	AP6	70c orange brown	2.25	.50
C50	AP6	1s dull violet	2.25	.50

Nos. C43-C50 were issued for the 1st Intl. Phil. Exhib. at Quito.

Condor over "El Altar" — AP7

1937-46 *Perf. 11½, 12*

C51	AP7	10c chestnut	5.00	.25
C52	AP7	20c olive black	6.50	.25
C53	AP7	40c rose car ('46)	6.50	.25
C54	AP7	70c black brown	9.00	.25
C55	AP7	1s gray black	14.00	.25
C56	AP7	2s dark violet	24.00	.65
		Nos. C51-C56 (6)	65.00	1.90

Issue dates: 40c, Oct. 7; others, Aug. 19.

For overprints see Nos. 463-464, CO13-CO17.

Portrait of Washington, American Eagle and Flags — AP8

Engraved and Lithographed

1938, Feb. 9 *Perf. 12*

Center Multicolored

C57	AP8	2c brown	.40	.25
C58	AP8	5c black	.40	.25
C59	AP8	10c brown	.40	.25
C60	AP8	20c dark blue	.80	.25
C61	AP8	50c violet	1.75	.25
C62	AP8	1s black	3.25	.25
C63	AP8	2s violet	7.50	.90
		Nos. C57-C63 (7)	14.50	2.40

150th anniv. of the US Constitution.

In 1947, Nos. C61-C63 were overprinted in dark blue: "Primero la Patria!" and plane. These revolutionary propaganda stamps were later renounced by decree. Value $20.

For overprints see Nos. C102-C104, C139-C141.

No. RA35 Surcharged in Red

1938, Nov. 16 *Perf. 13½*

C64	PT12	65c on 3c ultra	.40	.25

A national airmail concession was given to the Sociedad Ecuatoriano de Transportes Aereos (SEDTA) in July, 1938. No. RA35 was surcharged for SEDTA postal requirements. SEDTA operated through 1940.

Army Horseman — AP9

Woman Runner — AP10

Tennis — AP11

Boxing — AP12

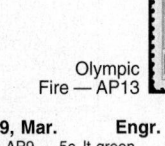

Olympic Fire — AP13

1939, Mar. Engr. *Perf. 12*

C65	AP9	5c lt green	1.60	.25
C66	AP10	10c salmon	2.25	.25
C67	AP11	50c redsh brown	11.50	.25
C68	AP12	1s black brown	13.50	.45
C69	AP13	2s rose carmine	17.00	1.10
		Nos. C65-C69 (5)	45.85	2.30

First Bolivarian Games (1938).

Plane over Chimborazo AP14

1939, May 1 *Perf. 13x12½*

C70	AP14	1s yellow brown	.40	.25
C71	AP14	2s rose violet	.70	.25
C72	AP14	5s black	1.90	.25
		Nos. C70-C72 (3)	3.00	.75

Golden Gate Bridge and Mountain Peak — AP15

1939 *Perf. 12½x13*

C73	AP15	2c black	.40	.25
C74	AP15	5c rose red	.40	.25
C75	AP15	10c indigo	.40	.25
C76	AP15	50c rose violet	.40	.25
C77	AP15	1s chocolate	.80	.25
C78	AP15	2s yellow brown	1.00	.25
C79	AP15	5s emerald	2.00	.25
		Nos. C73-C79 (7)	5.40	1.75

Golden Gate International Exposition.

For surcharge & overprint see Nos. 434, CO18.

Empire State Building and Mountain Peak — AP16

1939

C80	AP16	2c brown orange	.65	.30
C81	AP16	5c dark carmine	.65	.25
C82	AP16	10c indigo	.65	.30
C83	AP16	50c slate green	.65	.30
C84	AP16	1s deep orange	1.30	.30
C85	AP16	2s dk red violet	1.50	.30
C86	AP16	5s dark gray	3.50	.30
		Nos. C80-C86 (7)	8.90	2.05

New York World's Fair.

For surcharge see No. 435.

Map of the Americas and Airplane — AP17

1940, July 9

C87	AP17	10c red org & blue	.45	.25
C88	AP17	70c sepia & blue	.45	.25
C89	AP17	1s copper brn & blue	.90	.25
C90	AP17	10s black & blue	3.50	.95
		Nos. C87-C90 (4)	5.30	1.70

Pan American Union, 50th anniversary.

Journalism Type

1941, Dec. 15

C91	A157	3s rose carmine	5.75	.25
C92	A157	10s yellow orange	12.00	.45

See note after No. 399.

Old Map of South America Showing Amazon River — AP19

Panoramic View of Amazon River — AP20

Designs: 70c, Gonzalo de Pineda. 5s, Painting of the expedition.

1942, Jan. 30
C93 AP19 40c black & buff 1.90 .25
C94 AP19 70c olive 2.90 .25
C95 AP20 2s dark green 3.25 .25
C96 AP19 5s rose 4.00 1.10
Nos. C93-C96 (4) 12.05 1.85

See note after No. 403.

Remigio Crespo Toral Type

1942, Sept. 1 ***Perf. 13½***
C97 A162 10c dull violet 1.25 .50

Alfaro Types

70c, Gen. Eloy Alfaro. 1s, Devil's Nose. 3s, Military College. 5s, Montecristi, Alfaro's birthplace.

1943, Feb. 16 ***Perf. 12***
C98 A166 70c dk rose & blk 1.90 .25
C99 A167 1s ol blk & red brn 3.25 .75
C100 A167 3s ol gray & grn 4.50 1.10
C101 A167 5s slate & salmon 6.75 1.30
Nos. C98-C101 (4) 16.40 3.40

Nos. C61-C63 Overprinted in Red Brown

1943, Apr. 15 ***Perf. 11½***
Center Multicolored
C102 AP8 50c violet 2.75 1.50
C103 AP8 1s black 3.25 1.60
C104 AP8 2s violet 4.00 2.50
Nos. C102-C104 (3) 10.00 5.60

Visit of US Vice-Pres. Henry A. Wallace.

Nos. 374-376 Overprinted "AEREO LOOR A BOLIVIA JUNIO 11-1943" (like Nos. C111-C113)

1943, June 11 ***Perf. 13***
C105 A146 50c dp red violet .40 .25
C106 A147 1s copper red .60 .25
C107 A148 2s dark green .70 .25
Nos. C105-C107 (3) 1.70 .75

Visit of Pres. Eurique Penaranda of Bolivia. Vertical overprints on Nos. C105-C106.

Nos. 374-376 Overprinted "AEREO LOOR A PARAGUAY JULIO 5-1943" (like Nos. C111-C113)

1943, July 5
C108 A146 50c dp red violet .45 .25
a. Double overprint 75.00
C109 A147 1s copper red 1.10 .50
C110 A148 2s dark green 1.50 .70
Nos. C108-C110 (3) 3.05 1.45

Visit of Pres. Higinio Morinigo of Paraguay. Vertical overprints on Nos. C108-C109.

Nos. 374-376 Overprinted in Black

1943, July 23
C111 A146 50c dp red violet .45 .25
C112 A147 1s copper red .65 .25
C113 A148 2s dark green .75 .25
Nos. C111-C113 (3) 1.85 .75

Issued to commemorate the visit of President Isaias Medina Angarita of Venezuela. Vertical overprint on Nos. C111-C112.
See Nos. C105-C110.

President Arroyo del Rio Addressing US Congress — AP26

1943, Oct. 9 ***Perf. 12***
C114 AP26 50c dark brown 1.00 .50
C115 AP26 70c brt rose 1.30 .50
C116 AP26 3s dark blue 1.50 .65
C117 AP26 5s dark green 3.50 1.20
C118 AP26 10s olive black 13.00 4.25
Nos. C114-C118 (5) 20.30 7.10

Good will tour of Pres. Arroyo del Rio in 1942.
For surcharges see Nos. CB1-CB5.

1944, Feb. 7
C119 AP26 50c dp red lilac .90 .65
C120 AP26 70c red brown 1.75 .65
C121 AP26 3s turq green 1.75 .65
C122 AP26 5s brt ultra 2.90 1.40
C123 AP26 10s scarlet 3.50 1.60
Nos. C119-C123 (5) 10.80 4.95
Nos. C114-C123 (10) 31.10 12.05

Church of San Francisco, Quito — AP27

1944, Feb. 13
C124 AP27 70c turq green 1.90 .45
C125 AP27 1s olive 1.90 .45
C126 AP27 3s red orange 4.25 1.10
C127 AP27 5s carmine rose 5.25 1.30
Nos. C124-C127 (4) 13.30 3.30

Palace Type

1944 **Engr.** ***Perf. 11***
C128 A173 3s orange 1.00 .25
C129 A173 5s dark brown 1.75 .25
C130 A173 10s dark red 4.00 .25
Nos. C128-C130 (3) 6.75 .75

See No. C221. For overprints and surcharges see Nos. 541, C136-C138, C210-C213, C218-C220, C223-C224, C277-C279.

Red Cross Type

1945, Apr. 25 **Unwmk.** ***Perf. 12***
Cross in Rose
C131 A174 2s deep blue 4.00 1.10
C132 A174 3s green 4.50 1.25
C133 A174 5s dark violet 6.50 1.75
C134 A174 10s carmine rose 21.00 5.75
Nos. C131-C134 (4) 36.00 9.85

No. RA55 Surcharged in Black

1945, June 8
C135 PT21 40c on 5c blue 1.00 .25
a. Double surcharge 10.00

Counterfeits exist.

Nos. C128-C130 Overprinted in Green

1945, Sept. 6 ***Perf. 11***
C136 A173 3s orange 1.00 .50
a. Inverted overprint 50.00
b. Double overprint 50.00
C137 A173 5s dark brown 1.25 .65
C138 A173 10s dark red 3.25 1.25
Nos. C136-C138 (3) 5.50 2.40

Nos. C61-C63 Overprinted in Dark Blue and Gold like Nos. 444-446

1945, Oct. 2 ***Perf. 12***
Center Multicolored
C139 AP8 50c violet 1.40 .25
C140 AP8 1s black 1.60 1.50
C141 AP8 2s violet 2.50 1.90
Nos. C139-C141 (3) 5.50 3.65

Visit of Pres. Juan Antonio Rios of Chile.

Monument to Liberty — AP30

1945, Nov. 14 **Engr.**
C142 AP30 30c blue .45 .25
C143 AP30 40c rose carmine .45 .25
C144 AP30 1s dull violet 1.30 .55
C145 AP30 3s gray black 2.50 1.40
C146 AP30 5s purple brown 3.50 1.90
Nos. C142-C146 (5) 8.20 4.35

Gen. Antonio Jose de Sucre, 150th birth anniv.

Catalogue values for unused stamps in this section, from this point to the end of the section, are for Never Hinged items.

Highway Type

1946, Apr. 22 **Unwmk.**
C147 A176 1s carmine rose .65 .40
C148 A176 2s violet .80 .55
C149 A176 3s turq green 1.40 .60
C150 A176 5s red orange 1.75 .80
C151 A176 10s dark blue 2.75 .80
Nos. C147-C151 (5) 7.35 3.15

Revolution Types

1946, Aug. 9 ***Perf. 12½***
C152 A177 40c deep claret .25 .25
C153 A178 1s sepia .25 .25
C154 A179 2s indigo .60 .25
C155 A180 3s olive green 1.10 .45
Nos. C152-C155 (4) 2.20 1.20

National Union of Journalists, Initials and Quill Pen — AP36

1946, Sept. 16
C156 AP36 50c dull purple .75 .30
C157 AP36 70c dark green .90 .45
C158 AP36 3s red 1.50 .60
C159 AP36 5s indigo 2.00 .75
C160 AP36 10s chocolate 6.50 1.25
Nos. C156-C160 (5) 11.65 3.35

Campaign for adult education.

The Blessed Mariana Teaching Children — AP37

"Lily of Quito" — AP38

1946, Nov. 28 **Unwmk.**
C161 AP37 40c chocolate .30 .25
C162 AP37 60c deep blue .40 .35
C163 AP38 3s orange yellow .80 .60
C164 AP38 5s green 2.00 .85
Nos. C161-C164 (4) 3.50 2.05

300th anniv. of the death of the Blessed Mariana de Jesus Paredes y Flores.

Rocafuerte Type

60c-1.10s, Jual de Velasco. 1.30s-2s, Riobamba Irrigation Canal.

1947, Nov. 27 ***Perf. 12***
C165 A185 60c dark green .25 .25
C166 A185 70c purple .25 .25
C167 A185 1s black brown .25 .25
C168 A185 1.10s car rose .25 .25
C169 A185 1.30s deep blue .35 .25
C170 A185 1.90s olive bister 1.00 .25
C171 A185 2s olive green 1.20 .25
Nos. C165-C171 (7) 3.55 1.75

For overprints & surcharges see Nos. C175, C181, C207-C209, C215, C216-C217, C222, C235.

Bello Type

1948, Apr. 21 ***Perf. 13***
C172 A188 60c magenta .40 .25
C173 A188 1.30s dk blue grn .70 .25
C174 A188 1.90s dk rose car .60 .25
Nos. C172-C174 (3) 1.70 .75

No. C166 Overprinted in Black

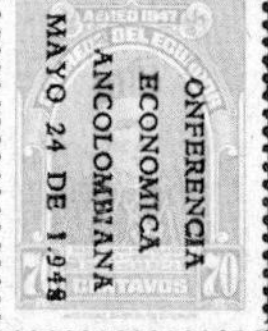

1948, May 24 ***Perf. 12***
C175 A185 70c purple .65 .35

Columbus — AP42

1948, May 26 ***Perf. 14***
C176 AP42 50c olive green .25 .25
C177 AP42 70c rose carmine .50 .40
C178 AP42 3s ultra 1.60 1.10
C179 AP42 5s brown 2.60 1.60
C180 AP42 10s deep violet 8.00 2.00
Nos. C176-C180 (5) 12.95 5.35

See note after No. 495.

No. C169 Overprinted in Carmine like No. 496 (MANANA reads up)

1948, Aug. 26 **Unwmk.** ***Perf. 12***
C181 A185 1.30s deep blue .40 .25

National Fair of Today and Tomorrow, 1948.

Elia Liut and Telegrafo I — AP43

1948, Sept. 10 ***Perf. 12½***
C182 AP43 60c rose red .80 .25
C183 AP43 1s green .80 .25
C184 AP43 1.30s deep claret .80 .25
C185 AP43 1.90s deep violet .80 .25
C186 AP43 2s dark brown 1.20 .30
C187 AP43 5s blue 2.40 .50
Nos. C182-C187 (6) 6.80 1.80

25th anniv. (in 1945) of the 1st postal flight in Ecuador.

Teacher and Pupils — AP44

1948, Oct. 12 *Perf. 14*

C188 AP44 50c violet 1.50 .50
C189 AP44 70c deep blue 1.50 .50
C190 AP44 3s dark green 2.50 1.00
C191 AP44 5s red 4.00 1.50
C192 AP44 10s brown 7.50 2.00
Nos. C188-C192 (5) 17.00 5.50

Campaign for adult education.

AP45

Franklin D. Roosevelt and Two of "Four Freedoms" — AP46

1948, Oct. 24 *Perf. 12½*

C193 AP45 60c emer & org brn .40 .25
C194 AP45 1s car rose & slate .60 .30
C195 AP46 1.50s grn & red brn .75 .55
C196 AP46 2s red & black .80 .30
C197 AP46 5s ultra & blk 1.75 .30
Nos. C193-C197 (5) 4.30 1.70

Maldonado Types

1948, Nov. 17

C198 A196 60c dp org & rose car .80 .25
C199 A197 90c red & gray blk .80 .25
C200 A196 1.30s pur & dp org 1.00 .25
C201 A197 2s dp bl & dull grn 1.00 .25
Nos. C198-C201 (4) 3.60 1.00

See note after No. 519.

Juan Montalvo and Cervantes AP47

Don Quixote — AP48

1949, May 2 **Engr.** *Perf. 12½x12*

C202 AP47 1.30s ol brn & ultra 3.00 2.50
C203 AP48 1.90s grn & rose car 1.00 .30
C204 AP47 3s vio & org brn 1.50 .30
C205 AP48 5s red & gray blk 2.75 .25
C206 AP47 10s red lil & aqua 4.00 .25
Nos. C202-C206 (5) 12.25 3.60

400th anniv. of the birth of Miguel de Cervantes Saavedra, novelist, playwright and poet, and the 60th anniv. of the death of Juan Montalvo (1832-89), Ecuadorean writer.
For surcharges see Nos. C225-C226.

No. C168 Surcharged in Blue

1949, June 15 *Perf. 12*

C207 A185 50c on 1.10s car rose .45 .25
C208 A185 60c on 1.10s car rose .45 .25
C209 A185 90c on 1.10s car rose .65 .25
Nos. C207-C209 (3) 1.55 .75

2nd Eucharistic Cong., Quito, June 1949.

No. C128 Surcharged in Black

1949, Oct. 11 *Perf. 11*

C210 A173 60c on 3s orange .75 .40
a. Double surcharge 30.00
C211 A173 90c on 3s orange .80 .30
C212 A173 1s on 3s orange 1.00 .40
C213 A173 2s on 3s orange 1.75 .40
Nos. C210-C213 (4) 4.30 1.50

"SUCRE(S)" in capitals on Nos. C212-C213.
75th anniv. of the UPU.

Consular Service Stamps Type of 1949 Surcharged in Black

1950 **Unwmk.** *Perf. 12*

C214 R1 60c on 50c gray .75 .25
a. Double surcharge 15.00

No. C170 Surcharged with New Value in Black

C215 A185 90c on 1.90s ol bis .75 .25

See Nos. 475-483, 532-533.

Nos. C168, C128-C129 and Type of 1944 Srchd. or Ovptd. in Black or Carmine

1950, Feb. 10 *Perf. 12*

C216 A185 50c on 1.10s 1.75 1.75
C217 A185 70c on 1.10s 2.25 1.75

Perf. 11

C218 A173 3s orange 3.25 3.00
C219 A173 5s dark brown (C) 5.00 2.50
C220 A173 10s violet (C) 7.50 3.00
Nos. C216-C220 (5) 19.75 12.00

Issued to publicize adult education.
For overprint see No. 541.

Govt. Palace Type of 1944

1950, May 15 **Engr.** *Perf. 11*

C221 A173 10s violet 2.00 .25

For surcharges see Nos. C277-C279.

No. C169 Surcharged with New Value in Black

1950 *Perf. 12*

C222 A185 90c on 1.30s dp blue .30 .25

See No. C235.

Nos. C128-C129 Overprinted in Black

20.000 Cruce
Línea Ecuatorial
PANAGRA
26-Julio-1951

1951, July 28 **Unwmk.** *Perf. 11*

C223 A173 3s orange 1.25 .90
C224 A173 5s dark brown 2.50 1.25

20,000th crossing of the equator by Pan American-Grace Airways planes.

Nos. C202-C203 Surcharged in Black

1951 **Unwmk.** *Perf. 12½x12*

C225 AP47 60c on 1.30s .30 .25
C226 AP48 1s on 1.90s .30 .25
a. Inverted surcharge 20.00

Issued to publicize adult education.

St. Mariana de Jesus — AP50

1952, Feb. 15 **Engr.**

C227 AP50 60c plum & aqua .60 .30
C228 AP50 90c dk grn & lt ultra .80 .30
C229 AP50 1s car & dk grn .90 .30
C230 AP50 2s indigo & rose lil 1.00 .30
Nos. C227-C230 (4) 3.30 1.20

Canonization of Mariana de Jesus Paredes y Flores.

Plaza Visit to US Issue

3s, as No. 558. 5s, as No. 559.

1952, Mar. 26 *Perf. 12*

C231 A205 3s lilac & bl grn .70 .45
C232 A205 5s red brn & ol gray 2.00 1.75
a. Souv. sheet of 2, #C231-C232 4.50 *9.00*

Consular Service Stamps Surcharged in Black

1952 **Unwmk.** *Perf. 12*

C233 R2 60c on 1s green .30 .25
C234 R2 1s on 1s green .30 .25

Type R2 illustrated above No. 545.

No. C169 Surcharged with New Value in Carmine

C235 A185 90c on 1.30s dp bl .30 .25
Nos. C233-C235 (3) .90 .75

See No. C222.

Pres. José M. Urvina and Allegory of Freedom — AP52

Hyphen-hole Perf. 7x6½

1952, Nov. 18 **Litho.**

C236 AP52 60c rose red & blue 3.50 .45
C237 AP52 90c lilac & red 3.50 .60
C238 AP52 1s orange & green 3.50 .30
C239 AP52 2s red brn & blue 3.50 .45
Nos. C236-C239 (4) 14.00 1.80

Centenary of abolition of slavery in Ecuador. Counterfeits exist.

Torch of Knowledge AP53

Design: 2s, Aged couple studying alphabet.

Unwmk.

1953, Apr. 13 **Engr.** *Perf. 12*

C240 AP53 1s dark blue 1.20 .25
C241 AP53 2s red orange 1.50 .25

1952 adult education campaign.

Globe Showing Part of Western Hemisphere AP54

1953, June 5 *Perf. 12½x12*

C242 AP54 60c orange yellow .30 .25
C243 AP54 90c dark blue .40 .30
C244 AP54 3s carmine .70 .45
Nos. C242-C244 (3) 1.40 1.00

Issued to publicize the crossing of the equator by the Pan-American highway.

Consular Service Stamps Surcharged in Black

a

b

1953-54 *Perf. 12*

C245 R1 (a) 60c on 2s brown .35 .25
C246 R2 (a) 60c on 5s sep ('54) .35 .25
C247 R2 (a) 70c on 5s sep ('54) .35 .25
C248 R2 (a) 90c on 50c car rose ('54) .35 .25
C249 R1 (b) 1s on 2s brown .35 .25
C250 R1 (a) 1s on 2s brn ('54) .35 .25
C251 R1 (a) 2s on 2s brn ('54) .65 .25
C252 R1 (a) 3s on 5s vio ('54) .90 .25
Nos. C245-C252 (8) 3.65 2.00

Surcharge is horizontal on Nos. C245-C248.

Carlos Maria Cardinal de la Torre — AP55

1954, Jan. 13 **Photo.** *Perf. 8½*

Center in Black

C253 AP55 60c rose lilac .50 .30
C254 AP55 90c green .80 .30
C255 AP55 3s orange 1.20 .45
Nos. C253-C255 (3) 2.50 1.05

1st anniv. of the elevation of Archbishop de la Torre to Cardinal.

Queen Isabella I — AP56

1954, Apr. 22

C256 AP56 60c dk grn & grn .50 .40
C257 AP56 90c lil rose .50 .40
C258 AP56 1s blk & pale lil .50 .40
C259 AP56 2s blk brn & pale bl .70 .40
C260 AP56 5s blk brn & sepia 1.75 .40
Nos. C256-C260 (5) 3.95 2.00

See note with No. 585.

Post Office, Guayaquil AP57

1954, May 19 Engr. *Perf. 12½x12*

Black Surcharge

C261	AP57	80c on 20c red	.30	.25
C262	AP57	1s on 20c red	.30	.25

25th anniversary of Pan American-Grace Airways' operation in Ecuador.

Plane, Gateway and Wheel — AP58

Unwmk.

1954, Aug. 2 Litho. *Perf. 11*

C263	AP58	80c blue	.35	.25

Day of the Postal Employee.

San Pablo Lagoon AP59

1954, Sept. 24 Photo.

C264	AP59	60c orange	.30	.25
C265	AP59	70c rose pink	.30	.25
C266	AP59	90c dp grn	.30	.25
C267	AP59	1s dk gray grn	.30	.25
C268	AP59	2s blue	.40	.25
C269	AP59	3s yel brn	.75	.25
		Nos. C264-C269 (6)	2.35	1.50

Glorification of Abdon Calderon Garaicoa AP60

Capt. Calderon — AP61

1954, Oct. 1

C270	AP60	80c rose pink	.45	.25
C271	AP61	90c blue	.45	.25

150th anniversary of the birth of Capt. Abdon Calderon Garaicoa.

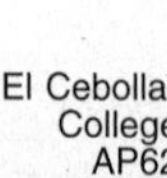

El Cebollar College AP62

Brother Miguel Instructing Boys — AP63

Designs: 90c, Francisco Febres Cordero (Brother Miguel). 2.50s, Tomb of Brother Miguel. 3s, Monument to Brother Miguel.

1954, Dec. 3 Unwmk. *Perf. 11*

C272	AP62	70c dk grn	.25	.25
C273	AP63	80c dk brn	.25	.25
C274	AP63	90c dk gray bl	.25	.25
C275	AP63	2.50s indigo	.45	.25
C276	AP62	3s lil rose	.55	.35
		Nos. C272-C276 (5)	1.75	1.35

Centenary of the birth of Francisco Febres Cordero (Brother Miguel).

No. C221 Surcharged in Various Colors

1955, May 25

C277	A173	1s on 10s vio (Bk)	.30	.25
C278	A173	1.70s on 10s vio (C)	.40	.25
C279	A173	4.20s on 10s vio (Br)	.65	.35
		Nos. C277-C279 (3)	1.35	.85

Denomination in larger type on No. C279. National Exhibition of Daily Periodicals.

"La Rotonda," Guayaquil, and Rotary Emblem AP64

Design: 90c, Eugenio Espejo hospital, Quito, and Rotary emblem.

1955, July 9 Engr. *Perf. 12½*

C280	AP64	80c dark brown	.30	.25
C281	AP64	90c dark green	.50	.35

50th anniv. of the founding of Rotary Intl.

José Abel Castillo AP65

2s, 5s, José Abel Castillo, Map of Ecuador.

1955, Oct. 19 *Perf. 11x11½*

C282	AP65	60c chocolate	1.10	.25
C283	AP65	90c light olive green	1.25	.25
C284	AP65	1s lilac	1.40	.25
C285	AP65	2s vermilion	1.75	.30
C286	AP65	5s ultra	3.50	.55
		Nos. C282-C286 (5)	9.00	1.60

See note after No. 595.

No. C29 Surcharged in Black

1955, Oct. 24 *Perf. 12*

C287	AP1	1s on 5s purple	.65	.25

A similar surcharge on No. C29, set in two lines with letters 5mm high and no X's or black-out line of squares, was privately applied.

San Pablo, Imbabura — AP66

50s, Rumichaca Caves. 1.30s, Virgin of Quito. 1.50s, Cotopaxi Volcano. 1.70s, Tungurahua Volcano, Tungurahua. 1.90s, Guanacos. 2.40s, Mat market. 2.50s, Ruins at Ingapirca. 4.20s, El Carmen, Cuenca, Azuay. 4.80s, Santo Domingo Church.

1956, Jan. 2 Photo. *Perf. 13*

C288	AP66	50c slate blue	2.75	.25
C289	AP66	1s ultra	2.75	.25
C290	AP66	1.30s crimson	4.25	.25
C291	AP66	1.50s dp grn	2.75	.25
C292	AP66	1.70s yel brn	1.75	.25
C293	AP66	1.90s olive	3.50	.25
C294	AP66	2.40s red org	3.75	.25
C295	AP66	2.50s violet	3.75	.25
C296	AP66	4.20s black	4.75	.25
C297	AP66	4.80s yel org	7.50	.30
		Nos. C288-C297 (10)	37.50	2.55

See Nos. C310-C311. For surcharges see Nos. 766A, 766G.

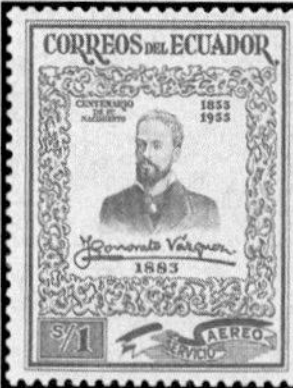

Honorato Vazquez — AP67

1956, May 28 Engr.

Various Portraits

C298	AP67	1s yellow green	.50	.25
C299	AP67	1.50s red	.50	.25
C300	AP67	1.70s bright blue	.50	.25
C301	AP67	1.90s slate blue	.50	.25
		Nos. C298-C301 (4)	2.00	1.00

Birth centenary (in 1955) of Honorato Vazquez, statesman.

Title Page of First Book — AP68

1956, Aug. 27 Unwmk. *Perf. 13½*

C302	AP68	1s black	.60	.25
C303	AP68	1.70s slate bl	.60	.25
C304	AP68	2s blk brn	.60	.25
C305	AP68	3s redsh brn	.60	.25
		Nos. C302-C305 (4)	2.40	1.00

Bicentenary of printing in Ecuador.

Hands Reaching for UN Emblem AP69

1956, Oct. 24 *Perf. 14*

C307	AP69	1.70s red org	1.10	.25

10th anniv. of the UN (in 1955).
See No. C319. For overprint see No. C426.

Coat of Arms and Basketball Player — AP70

Designs: 1.70s, Map of South America with flags and girl basketball players.

1956, Dec. 28 Photo. *Perf. 14½x14*

C308	AP70	1s red lilac	.65	.25
C309	AP70	1.70s deep green	1.00	.25

6th South American Women's Basketball Championship, Aug. 1956.

Scenic Type of 1956

1957, Jan. 2 *Perf. 13*

C310	AP66	50c bl grn	1.75	.25
C311	AP66	1s orange	1.75	.25

Type of Regular Issue, 1957

Designs: 50c, Map of Cuenca, 16th century. 80c, Cathedral of Cuenca. 1s, Modern City Hall.

Unwmk.

1957, Apr. 7 Photo. *Perf. 12*

C312	A219	50c brn, *cr*	.30	.25
a.		Souvenir sheet of 4	1.00	1.00
C313	A219	80c red, *bluish*	.30	.25
C314	A219	1s pur, *yel*	.30	.25
a.		Souvenir sheet of 3	2.00	2.00
		Nos. C312-C314 (3)	.90	.75

No. C312a contains 4 imperf. 50c stamps similar to No. 613, but inscribed "AEREO" and printed in green. The sheet is printed on white ungummed paper.

No. C314a contains 3 imperf. stamps in designs similar to Nos. C312-C314, but with colors changed to orange (50c), brown (80c), violet (1s). The sheet is printed on white ungummed paper.

Gabriela Mistral — AP71

Unwmk.

1957, Sept. 18 Litho. *Perf. 14*

C315	AP71	2s lt bl, blk & red	.55	.25

Issued to honor Gabriela Mistral (1889-1957), Chilean poet and educator.
See Nos. C406-C407.

Arms of Espejo, Carchi — AP72

Arms of Cantons: 2s, Montufar. 4.20s, Tulcan.

1957, Nov. 16 *Perf. 14½x13½*

Coat of Arms Multicolored

C316	AP72	1s carmine	.55	.25
C317	AP72	2s black	.55	.25
C318	AP72	4.20s ultra	1.00	.25
		Nos. C316-C318 (3)	2.10	.75

Province of Carchi.
See Nos. C334-C337, C355-C364, C392-C395. For surcharge see No. 766.

Redrawn UN Type of 1956

1957, Dec. 10 Engr. *Perf. 14*

C319	AP69	2s greenish blue	.55	.25

Honoring the UN. Dates, as on No. C307, are omitted; inscribed: "Homenaje a las Naciones Unidas."

Mater Dolorosa, San Gabriel College — AP73

No. C321, 1s, Door of San Gabriel College, Quito.

1958, Apr. 27 Engr. *Perf. 14*

C320	AP73	30c rose cl, *dp rose*	.30	.25
C321	AP73	30c rose cl, *dp rose*	.30	.25
a.		Pair, #C320-C321	.75	.60
C322	AP73	1s dk bl, *lt bl*	.30	.25
C323	AP73	1.70s dk bl, *lt bl*	.30	.25
a.		Pair, #C322-C323	.75	.60

Miracle of San Gabriel College, Quito, 50th anniv.

Rafael Maria Arizaga (1858-1933), Writer — AP74

1958, July 21 Litho.

C324	AP74	1s multi	.45	.30

See Nos. C343, C350, C412.

Daule River Bridge AP75

1958, July 25 Engr. *Perf. 13½x14*

C325	AP75	1.30s green	.50	.25

Issued to commemorate the opening of the River Daule bridge in Guayas province.
See Nos. C367-C369.

Basketball Player — AP76

1958, Sept. 1 Photo. *Perf. 14x13½*

C326	AP76	1.30s dk grn & lt brn	.55	.45

South American basketball championships.
For surcharge see No. 774A.

Symbolical of the Eucharist — AP77

Design: 60c, Cathedral of Guayaquil.

1958, Sept. 25 Litho. Unwmk.

C327	AP77	10c vio & buff	.40	.30
C328	AP77	60c org & vio brn	.40	.30
C329	AP77	1s brn & lt bl	.40	.30
		Nos. C327-C329 (3)	1.20	.90

Souvenir Sheet

Symbolical of the Eucharist — AP78

Perf. 13½x14

C330	AP78	Sheet of 4	2.75	2.25
a.-d.		40c dark blue, any single	.25	.25

3rd National Eucharistic Congress.

Stamps of 1865 and 1920 — AP79

Designs: 2s, Stamps of 1920 and 1948. 4.20s, Municipal museum and library.

1958, Oct. 8 Photo. *Perf. 11½*
Granite Paper

C331	AP79	1.30s grn & brn red	.35	.25
C332	AP79	2s bl & vio	.70	.30
C333	AP79	4.20s dk brn	.90	.40
		Nos. C331-C333 (3)	1.95	.95

National Philatelic Exposition (EXFIGUA), Guayaquil, Oct. 4-14.
For surcharge see No. 774.

Coat of Arms Type of 1957
Province of Imbabura

Arms of Cantons: 50c, Cotacachi. 60c, Antonio Ante. 80c, Otavalo. 1.10s, Ibarra.

1958, Nov. 9 Litho. *Perf. 14½x13½*
Coats of Arms Multicolored

C334	AP72	50c blk & red	.50	.25
C335	AP72	60c blk, bl & red	.50	.25
C336	AP72	80c blk & yel	.50	.25
C337	AP72	1.10s blk & red	.50	.25
		Nos. C334-C337 (4)	2.00	1.00

Charles V AP80

Engr. & Photo.
1958, Dec. 12 *Perf. 14x13½*

C338	AP80	2s brn red & dk brn	.45	.30
C339	AP80	4.20s dk gray & red brn	.55	.45

400th anniv. of the death of Charles V, Holy Roman Emperor.

Paul Rivet — AP81

1958, Dec. 29 Photo. *Perf. 11½*
Granite Paper

C340	AP81	1s brown	.45	.30

Issued in honor of Paul Rivet (1876-1958), French anthropologist.

1959, May 6

Portrait: 2s, Alexander von Humboldt.

C341	AP81	2s slate	.35	.25

Cent. of the death of Alexander von Humboldt, German naturalist and geographer.

Front Page of "El Telegrafo" — AP82

1959, Feb. Litho. *Perf. 13½*

C342	AP82	1.30s bl grn & blk	.35	.25

75th anniv. of Ecuador's oldest newspaper.

Portrait Type of 1958

José Luis Tamayo (1858-1947), lawyer.

1959, June 26 Unwmk. *Perf. 14*
Portrait Multicolored

C343	AP74	1.30s lt grn, bl & sal	.45	.30

El Sagrario & House of Manuela Canizares AP83

Condor — AP84

Designs: 80c, Hall at San Agustin. 1s, First words of the constitutional act. 2s, Entrance to Cuartel Real. 4.20s, Allegory of Liberty.

Unwmk.
1959, Aug. 28 Photo. *Perf. 14*

C344	AP83	20c ultra & lt brn	.25	.25
C345	AP83	80c brt bl & dp org	.25	.25
C346	AP83	1s dk red & dk ol	.25	.25
C347	AP84	1.30s brt bl & org	.25	.25
C348	AP84	2s ultra & org brn	.25	.25
C349	AP84	4.20s scar & brt bl	.65	.45
		Nos. C344-C349 (6)	1.90	1.70

Sesquicentennial of the revolution.

Portrait Type of 1958

1s, Alfredo Baquerizo Moreno (1859-1951), statesman.

1959, Sept. 26 Litho. *Perf. 14*

C350	AP74	1s gray, red & salmon	.45	.30

Pope Pius XII — AP85

1959, Oct. 9 Unwmk. *Perf. 14½*

C351	AP85	1.30s multi	.45	.30

Issued in memory of Pope Plus XII.

Flags of Argentina, Bolivia, Brazil, Guatemala, Haiti, Mexico and Peru — AP86

Flags of: 80c, Chile, Costa Rica, Cuba, Dominican Republic, Panama, Paraguay, United States. 1.30s, Colombia, Ecuador, Honduras, Nicaragua, Salvador, Uruguay, Venezuela.

1959, Oct. 12 *Perf. 13½.*

C352	AP86	50c multi	.25	.25
C353	AP86	80c yel, red & bl	.30	.25
C354	AP86	1.30s multi	.40	.25
		Nos. C352-C354 (3)	.95	.75

Organization of American States.
For overprints see Nos. C423-C425, CO19-CO21.

Arms of the Cantons Type of 1957
Province of Pichincha

10c, Rumiñahui. 40c, Pedro Moncayo. 1s, Mejia. 1.30s, Cayambe. 4.20s, Quito.

Perf. 14½x13½
1959-60 Unwmk. Litho.
Coat of Arms Multicolored

C355	AP72	10c blk & dk red ('60)	.50	.30
C356	AP72	40c blk & yel	.50	.30
C357	AP72	1s blk & brn ('60)	.50	.30
C358	AP72	1.30s blk & grn ('60)	.50	.30
C359	AP72	4.20s blk & org	.50	.30
		Nos. C355-C359 (5)	2.50	1.50

Province of Cotopaxi

40c, Pangua. 60c, Pujili. 70c, Saquisili. 1s, Salcedo. 1.30s, Latacunga.

1960 Coat of Arms Multicolored

C360	AP72	40c blk & car	.30	.25
C361	AP72	60c blk & bl	.30	.25
C362	AP72	70c blk & turq	.30	.25
C363	AP72	1s blk & red org	.30	.25
C364	AP72	1.30s blk & org	.35	.25
		Nos. C360-C364 (5)	1.55	1.25

Flags of American Nations — AP87

1960, Feb. 23 *Perf. 13x12½*

C365	AP87	1.30s multi	.30	.25
C366	AP87	2s multi	.30	.25

11th Inter-American Conference, Feb. 1960.

Bridge Type of 1958.

Bridges: No. C367, Juntas. No. C368, Saracay. 2s, Railroad bridge, Ambato.

1960 Litho. *Perf. 13½*

C367	AP75	1.30s chocolate	.30	.25

Photo. *Perf. 12½*

C368	AP75	1.30s emerald	.30	.25
C369	AP75	2s brown	.50	.25
		Nos. C367-C369 (3)	1.10	.75

Building of three new bridges.

Bahia-Chone Road — AP88

Pres. Camilo Ponce Enriquez AP89

Designs: 4.20s, Public Works Building, Cuenca. 5s, El Coca airport. 10s, New Harbor, Guayaquil.

1960, Aug. Litho. *Perf. 14*

C370	AP88	1.30s blk & dl yel	.30	.25
C371	AP88	4.20s rose car & lt grn	.45	.45
C372	AP88	5s dk brn & yel	.65	.55
C373	AP88	10s dk bl & bl	1.50	.55

Perf. 11x11½

C374	AP89	2s org brn & blk	2.25	.30
		Nos. C370-C374 (5)	5.15	2.10

Nos. C370-C374 publicize the achievements of Pres. Camilo Ponce Enriquez (1956-1960).
Issued: Nos. C370-C373, 8/24; No. C374, 8/31.

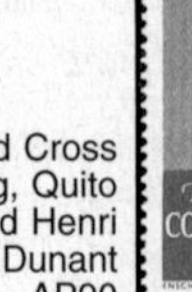

Red Cross Building, Quito and Henri Dunant AP90

1960, Oct. 5 Unwmk. *Perf. 13x14*

C375 AP90 2s rose vio & car .60 .25

Centenary (in 1959) of Red Cross idea.
For overprint see No. C408.

El Belen Church, Quito — AP91

1961, Jan. 14 *Perf. 12½*

C376 AP91 3s multi .50 .25

Ecuador's participation in the 1960 Barcelona Philatelic Congress.

Map of Ecuador and Amazon River System AP92

1961, Feb. 27 Litho. *Perf. 10½*

C377 AP92 80c salmon, claret & grn .35 .25
C378 AP92 1.30s gray, slate & grn .55 .25
C379 AP92 2s beige, red & grn .75 .25
Nos. C377-C379 (3) 1.65 .75

Amazon Week, and the 132nd anniversary of the Battle of Tarqui against Peru.

Juan Montalvo, Juan Leon Mera, Juan Benigno Vela — AP93

1961, Apr. 13 Unwmk. *Perf. 13*

C380 AP93 1.30s salmon & blk .50 .25

Centenary of Tungurahua province.

Hugo Ortiz G. — AP94

Design: No. C382, Ortiz monument.

1961, May 25 *Perf. 14x14½*

C381 AP94 1.30s grnsh bl, blk & yel .35 .25
C382 AP94 1.30s grnsh bl, pur, ol & brn .35 .25

Lt. Hugo Ortiz G., killed in battle 8/2/41.

Condor and Airplane Stamp of 1936 AP95

1.30s, Map of South America and stamp of 1865. 2s, Bolivar monument stamp of 1930.

Perf. 10½

1961, May 25 Litho. Unwmk.

Size: 41x28mm

C383 AP95 80c org & vio .50 .25

Size: 41x34mm

C384 AP95 1.30s bl, yel, ol & car .80 .35

Size: 40½x37mm

C385 AP95 2s car rose & blk 1.25 .35
Nos. C383-C385 (3) 2.55 .95

Third National Philatelic Exhibition, Quito, May 25-June 3, 1961.

Arms of Los Rios and Egret — AP96

1961, May 27 *Perf. 14½x13½*

Coat of Arms Multicolored

C386 AP96 2s bl & blk .50 .30

Centenary (in 1960) of Los Rios province.

Gabriel Garcia Moreno — AP97

1961, Sept. 24 Unwmk. *Perf. 12*

C387 AP97 1s bl, brn & buff .45 .25

Centenary of the restoration of national integrity.

Remigio Crespo Toral — AP98

1961, Nov. 3 Unwmk. *Perf. 14*

C388 AP98 50c multi .35 .25

Centenary of the birth of Remigio Crespo Toral, poet laureate of Ecuador.

Galapagos Islands Nos. LC1-LC3 Overprinted in Black or Red (Similar to #684-686)

"ESTACION DE BIOLOGIA MARITIMA DE GALAPAGOS" and " UNESCO 1961"

1961, Oct. 31 Photo. *Perf. 12*

C389 A1 1s dp bl 1.75 .25
a. "de Galapagos" on top line 6.00 6.00
C390 A1 1.80s rose vio 2.40 .40
a. UNESCO emblem omitted 6.00 6.00
C391 A1 4.20s blk (R) 3.50 .60
Nos. C389-C391 (3) 7.65 1.25

Establishment of maritime biological stations on Galapagos Islands by UNESCO.

Arms of the Cantons Type of 1957

Province of Tungurahua

50c, Pillaro. 1s, Pelileo. 1.30s, Baños. 2s, Ambato.

Perf. 14½x13½

1962, Mar. 30 Litho. Unwmk.

Coats of Arms Multicolored

C392 AP72 50c black .25 .25
C393 AP72 1s black .35 .25
C394 AP72 1.30s black .45 .25
C395 AP72 2s black .75 .25
Nos. C392-C395 (4) 1.80 1.00

AP99

Designs: 1.30s, 2s, Pres. Arosemena and Prince Philip, Arms of Ecuador and Great Britain and Equator Monument.

Perf. 14x13½

1962, Feb. 17 Wmk. 340

C396 AP99 1.30s bl, sepia, red & yel .30 .25
C397 AP99 2s multi .50 .25

Visit of Prince Philip, Duke of Edinburgh, to Ecuador, Feb. 17-20, 1962.

Mountain Farming — AP100

Perf. 12½

1963, Mar. 21 Unwmk. Litho.

C398 AP100 30c emer, yel & blk .30 .25
C399 AP100 3s dl red, grn & org .70 .25
C400 AP100 4.20s bl, blk & yel 1.10 .55
Nos. C398-C400 (3) 2.10 1.05

FAO "Freedom from Hunger" campaign.
Exist imperf. Value $32.50.

Mosquito and Malaria Eradication Emblem AP101

1963, Apr. 17 Unwmk. *Perf. 12½*

C401 AP101 50c multi .25 .25
C402 AP101 80c multi .25 .25
C403 AP101 2s multi .40 .25
Nos. C401-C403 (3) .90 .75

WHO drive to eradicate malaria.

Stagecoach and Jet Plane AP102

1963, May 7 Litho.

C404 AP102 2s org & car rose .40 .30
C405 AP102 4.20s claret & ultra .70 .50

1st Intl. Postal Conference, Paris, 1863.

Type of 1957 Inscribed "Islas Galapagos," Surcharged with New Value and Overprinted "Ecuador" in Black or Red

1963, June 19 Unwmk. *Perf. 14*

C406 AP71 5s on 2s gray, dk bl & red 1.10 .80
C407 AP71 10s on 2s gray, dk bl & red (R) 2.00 1.60

The basic 2s exists without surcharge and overprint. No. C407 exists with "ECUADOR" omitted, and with both "ECUADOR" and "10 SUCRES" double.

No. C375 Overprinted: "1863-1963/Centenario/de la Fundación/ de la Cruz Roja/Internacional"

1963, June 21 Photo. *Perf. 13x14*

C408 AP90 2s rose vio & car .40 .25

Intl. Red Cross, centenary.

Type of Regular Issue, 1963

Arosemena and: 70c, Flags of Ecuador. 2s, Flags of Ecuador, Panama. 4s, Flags of Ecuador, US.

1963, July 1 Litho. *Perf. 14*

C409 A238 70c pale bl & multi .25 .25
C410 A238 2s pink & multi .50 .25
C411 A238 4s lt bl & multi 1.10 .35
Nos. C409-C411 (3) 1.85 .85

Imperfs exist. Value $15.

Portrait Type of 1958

Portrait: 2s, Dr. Mariano Cueva (1812-82).

Unwmk.

1963, July 4 Litho. *Perf. 14*

C412 AP74 2s lt grn & multi .45 .25

Social Insurance Symbol — AP103

1963, July 9 Litho.

C413 AP103 10s brn & multi 1.10 .90

25th anniversary of Social Insurance.
Exists imperf. Value $9.

Mother and Child — AP104

1963, July 28 *Perf. 12½*

C414 AP104 1.30s org, dk bl & blk .30 .25
C415 AP104 5s gray, red & brn .60 .60

7th Pan-American and South American Pediatrics Congresses, Quito.

Simon Bolivar Airport, Guayaquil AP105

1963, July 25 *Perf. 14*

C416 AP105 60c gray .25 .25
C417 AP105 70c dl grn .30 .25
C418 AP105 5s brn vio .50 .35
Nos. C416-C418 (3) 1.05 .85

Opening of Simon Bolivar Airport, Guayaquil, July 15, 1962.
Exist imperf. Value $4.50.

Nos. 638, 640-641 Overprinted "AEREO"

1964 *Perf. 12*

Flags in National Colors

C419 A223 1.80s dl vio .60 .35
C420 A224 2s dk brn .60 .35
C421 A223 2.20s blk brn .60 .35
Nos. C419-C421 (3) 1.80 1.05

On 1.80s and 2.20s, "AEREO" is vertical, reading down.

No. 650 Overprinted in Gold: "FARO DE COLON / AEREO"

1964 Photo. *Perf. 14x13½*

C422 A229 1.80s dk bl 3.00 2.00

Nos. C352-C354 Overprinted

1964 Litho. *Perf. 13½*

C423	AP86	50c bl & multi	.80	.45
C424	AP86	80c yel & multi	.80	.45
C425	AP86	1.30s pale grn & multi	.80	.45
		Nos. C423-C425 (3)	2.40	1.35

No. C307 Overprinted: "DECLARACION / DERECHOS HUMANOS / 1964 / XV-ANIV"

Unwmk.

1964, Sept. 29 Engr. *Perf. 14*

C426	AP69	1.70s red org	.40	.25

15th anniversary (in 1963) of the Universal Declaration of Human Rights.

Banana Type

1964, Oct. 26 Litho. *Perf. 12½x12*

C427	A241	4.20s blk, bis & gray ol	.40	.30
C428	A241	10s blk, scar & gray ol	.70	.50
a.		Souv. sheet of 4	3.25	3.00

No. C428a contains imperf. stamps similar to Nos. 720-721 and C427-C428.

John F. Kennedy, Flag-draped Coffin and John Jr. — AP106

1964, Nov. 22 Litho. *Perf. 14*

C429	AP106	4.20s multi	1.25	.95
C430	AP106	5s multi	1.60	1.25
C431	AP106	10s multi	3.00	1.60
a.		Souv. sheet of 3	10.00	10.00
		Nos. C429-C431 (3)	5.85	3.80

President John F. Kennedy (1917-63).
No. C431a contains stamps similar to Nos. C429-C431, imperf.

Olympic Type

1.30s, Gymnast, vert. 1.80s, Hurdler. 2s, Basketball.

Perf. 13½x14, 14x13½

1964, Dec. 16 Unwmk.

C432	A243	1.30s vio bl, ver & brn	.45	.25
C433	A243	1.80s vio bl & multi	.45	.25
C434	A243	2s red & multi	.45	.25
a.		Souv. sheet of 4	3.25	3.25
		Nos. C432-C434 (3)	1.35	.75

No. C434a contains stamps similar to Nos. 725 and C432-C434, imperf.

Sports Type

Torch and Athletes: 2s, 3s, Diver, gymnast, wrestlers and weight lifter. 2.50s, 4s, Bicyclists. 3.50s, 5s, Jumpers.

1965, Nov. 20 Litho. *Perf. 12x12½*

C435	A247	2s bl, gold & blk	.60	.25
C436	A247	2.50s org, gold & blk	.60	.25
C437	A247	3s brt pink, gold & blk	.60	.25
C438	A247	3.50s lt vio, gold & bl	.65	.65
C439	A247	4s brt yel grn, gold & blk	.65	.25
C440	A247	5s red org, gold & blk	.75	.35
a.		Souv. sheet of 12	12.00	12.00
		Nos. C435-C440 (6)	3.85	2.00

No. C440a contains 12 imperf. stamps similar to Nos. 738-743 and C435-C440.
For surcharges see Nos. 766B, C449.

Bird Type

Birds: 1s, Yellow grosbeak. 1.30s, Black-headed parrot. 1.50s, Scarlet tanager. 2s, Sapphire quail-dove. 2.50s, Violet-tailed sylph. 3s, Lemon-throated barbet. 4s, Yellow-tailed oriole. 10s, Collared puffbird.

1966, June 17 Litho. *Perf. 13½*

Birds in Natural Colors

C441	A249	1s lt red brn & blk	1.10	.25
C442	A249	1.30s pink & blk	1.10	.25
C443	A249	1.50s pale grn & blk	1.10	.25
C444	A249	2s sal & blk	2.75	.45
C445	A249	2.50s lt yel grn & blk	2.75	.45
C446	A249	3s sal & blk	3.75	.65
C447	A249	4s gray & blk	5.00	.85
C448	A249	10s beige & blk	7.75	2.10
		Nos. C441-C448 (8)	25.30	5.25

For surcharges see Nos. 766E-766F, C450, C455-C457.

Nos. C436 and C443 Surcharged

1967

C449	A247	80c on 2.50s multi	.40	.35
C450	A249	80c on 1.50s multi	.40	.25

Old denomination on No. C449 is obliterated with heavy bar; the surcharge on No. C450 includes "Resello" and an ornament over old denomination.

Peñaherrera Monument, Quito — AP107

Design: 2s, Peñaherrera statue.

1967, Dec. 29 Litho. *Perf. 12x12½*

C451	AP107	1.30s blk & org	.30	.25
C452	AP107	2s blk & lt ultra	.30	.25

See note after No. 767B.

Arosemena Type

1.30s, Inauguration. 2s, Pres. Arosemena speaking in Punta del Este.

1968, May 9 Litho. *Perf. 13½x14*

C453	A251	1.30s multi	.25	.25
C454	A251	2s multi	.30	.25

No. C448 Srchd. in Plum, Dark Blue or Green

1969, Jan. 9 Litho. *Perf. 13½*

Bird in Natural Colors

C455	A249	80c on 10s beige (P)	.50	.25
C456	A249	1s on 10s beige (DBl)	.50	.25
C457	A249	2s on 10s beige (G)	.50	.25
		Nos. C455-C457 (3)	1.50	.75

"Operation Friendship" AP108

1969-70 Typo. *Perf. 13½*

C458	AP108	2s yel, blk, red & lt bl	.30	.25
a.		Perf. 12½	.30	.25
C459	AP108	2s bl, blk, car & yel ('70)	.30	.25

Friendship campaign. Medallion background on Nos. C458 and C458a is blue; on No. C459, yellow.
No. C459 exists imperf. Value $5.

No. 639 Surcharged in Gold "S/. 5 AEREO" and Bar

1969, Nov. 25 Litho. *Perf. 12*

C460	A224	5s on 2s multi	2.00	.75

Butterfly Type

Butterflies: 1.30s, Morpho peleides. 1.50s, Anartia amathea.

1970 Litho. *Perf. 12½*

C461	A255	1.30s multi	3.50	.25
C462	A255	1.50s pink & multi	3.50	.25

Same, White Background

1970 *Perf. 13½*

C463	A255	1.30s multi	3.50	.25
C464	A255	1.50s multi	3.50	.25

Arms Type

Provincial Arms and Flags: 1.30s, El Oro. 2s, Loja. 3s, Manabi. 5s, Pichincha. 10s, Guayas.

1971 Litho. *Perf. 10½*

C465	A258	1.30s pink & multi	.25	.25
C466	A258	2s multi	.35	.25
C467	A258	3s multi	.50	.30
C468	A258	5s multi	.65	.30
C469	A258	10s multi	1.25	.40
		Nos. C465-C469 (5)	3.00	1.50

Presentation of the Virgin — AP109

Art of Quito: 1.50s, Blessed Anne at Prayer. 2s, St. Theresa de Jesus. 2.50s, Altar of Carmen, horiz. 3s, Descent from the Cross. 4s, Christ of St. Mariana de Jesus. 5s, Shrine of St. Anthony. 10s, Cross of San Diego.

1971 *Perf. 11½*

Inscriptions in Black

C473	AP109	1.30s multi	.25	.25
C474	AP109	1.50s multi	.25	.25
C475	AP109	2s multi	.25	.25
C476	AP109	2.50s multi	.40	.25
C477	AP109	3s multi	.50	.25
C478	AP109	4s multi	.65	.25
C479	AP109	5s multi	.65	.35
C480	AP109	10s multi	1.25	.65
		Nos. C473-C480 (8)	4.20	2.50

Pres. Allende and Chilean Flag AP110

2.10s, Pres. José M. Velasco Ibarra of Ecuador, Pres. Salvador Allende of Chile, national flags.

1971, Aug. 24 *Perf. 12½*

C481	AP110	2s multi	.25	.25
C482	AP110	2.10s multi	.25	.25

Visit of Pres. Salvador Allende of Chile, Aug. 24.

Globe and Emblem AP111

1971

C483	AP111	5s black	1.10	.45
C484	AP111	5.50s dl pur & blk	1.10	.45

Opening of Postal Museum, Aug. 24, 1971.
Exist imperf. Value $7.50.

Pazmiño Type

1971, Sept. 16 *Perf. 12x11½*

C485	A260	1.50s grn & multi	.25	.25
C486	A260	2.50s grn & multi	.35	.25

AP112

Designs: 5s, Map of Americas. 10s, Converging roads and map. 20s, Map of Americas and Equator. 50s, Mountain road and monument on Equator.

1971 *Perf. 11½*

C487	AP112	5s org & multi	.80	.30
C488	AP112	10s org & blk	1.25	.55
C489	AP112	20s blk, bl & brt rose	2.00	1.00
C490	AP112	50s bl, blk & gray	3.25	1.50
		Nos. C487-C490 (4)	7.30	3.35

11th Pan-American Road Congress.
Issued: 5s, 10s, 50s, 11/15; 20s, 11/22.
No. C488 exists imperf. Value $8.

AP113

Design: 3s, Arms of Ecuador and Argentina. 5s, Presidents José M. Velasco Ibarra and Alejandro Agustin Lanusse.

1972

C491	AP113	3s blk & multi	.25	.25
C492	AP113	5s blk & multi	.50	.30

Visit of Lt. Gen. Alejandro Agustin Lanusse, president of Argentina, Jan. 25.

Flame, Scales, Map of Americas AP114

1972, Apr. 24 Litho. *Perf. 12½*

C493	AP114	1.30s bl & red	.50	.25

17th Conference of the Interamerican Federation of Lawyers, Quito, Apr. 24.

Religious Paintings Type of Regular Issue

Ecuadorian Paintings: 3s, Virgin of the Flowers, by Miguel de Santiago. 10s, Virgin of the Rosary, by Quito School.

1972, Apr. 24 *Perf. 14x13½*

C494	A263	3s blk & multi	.35	.35
C495	A263	10s blk & multi	1.10	.55
a.		Souv. sheet of 2, #C494-C495	1.90	1.90

1972, May 4

Ecuadorian Statues: 3s, St. Dominic, Quito School. 10s, St. Rosa of Lima, by Bernardo de Legarda.

C496	A263	3s blk & multi	.35	.35
C497	A263	10s blk & multi	1.00	.55
a.		Souv. sheet of 2, #C496-C497	2.50	2.10

Letters of "Ecuador" 3mm high on Nos. C496-C497, 7mm high on Nos. C494-C495.

Portrait Type

Designs (Generals, from Paintings): 1.30s, José Maria Saenz. 3s, Tomás Wright. 4s, Antonio Farfan. 5s, Antonio José de Sucre. 10s, Simon Bolivar. 20s, Arms of Ecuador.

1972, May 24

C498	A264	1.30s bl & multi	.25	.25
C499	A264	3s bl & multi	.25	.25
C500	A264	4s bl & multi	.35	.25
C501	A264	5s bl & multi	.55	.30

C502 A264 10s bl & multi 1.00 .55
C503 A264 20s bl & multi 2.00 1.00
Nos. C498-C503 (6) 4.40 2.60

Artisan Type

Handicraft of Ecuador: 2s, Woman wearing flowered poncho. 3s, Striped poncho. 5s, Poncho with roses. 10s, Gold sunburst sculpture.

1972, July Photo. *Perf. 13*
C504 A265 2s multi .25 .25
C505 A265 3s multi .50 .25
C506 A265 5s multi .80 .40
C507 A265 10s org red & multi 1.40 .90
a. Souv. sheet of 4, #C504-C507 4.00 4.00
Nos. C504-C507 (4) 2.95 1.80

Epidendrum Orchid — AP115

1972 Photo. *Perf. 12½*
C508 AP115 4s shown .90 .90
C509 AP115 6s Canna 1.40 1.40
C510 AP115 10s Jimson weed 2.00 2.00
a. Souv. sheet of 3, #C508-C510 6.00 6.00
Nos. C508-C510 (3) 4.30 4.30

Exists imperf.

Oil Drilling Towers — AP116

1972, Oct. 17 Litho. *Perf. 11½*
C511 AP116 1.30s bl & multi .50 .25

Ecuadorian oil industry.

Coat of Arms — AP117

Arms Multicolored

1972, Nov. 18 Litho. *Perf. 11½*
C512 AP117 2s black .25 .25
C513 AP117 3s black .25 .25
C514 AP117 4s black .30 .25
C515 AP117 4.50s black .30 .25
C516 AP117 6.30s black .75 .30
C517 AP117 6.90s black .75 .30
Nos. C512-C517 (6) 2.60 1.60

Pichincha Type

Designs: 2.40s, Corridor, San Agustin. 4.50s, La Merced Convent. 5.50s, Column base. 6.30s, Chapter Hall, San Agustin. 6.90s, Interior, San Agustin. 7.40s, Crucifixion, Cantuña Chapel. 7.90s, Decorated ceiling, San Agustin.

1972, Dec. 6 Wmk. 367
C518 A266 2.40s yel & multi .25 .25
C519 A266 4.50s yel & multi .45 .30
C520 A266 5.50s yel & multi .45 .30
C521 A266 6.30s yel & multi .60 .35
C522 A266 6.90s yel & multi .60 .35
C523 A266 7.40s yel & multi .90 .55
C524 A266 7.90s yel & multi .90 .55
Nos. C518-C524 (7) 4.15 2.65

UN Emblem — AP118

1973, Mar. 23 Unwmk.
C525 AP118 1.30s lt bl & blk .30 .25

25th anniversary of the Economic Committee for Latin America (CEPAL).

OAS Emblem — AP119

1973, Apr. 14 Wmk. 367
C526 AP119 1.50s multi .30 .25
a. Unwatermarked .30 .25

Day of the Americas and "Philately for Peace."

Bird Type

Designs: 1.30s, Blue-footed booby. 3s, Brown pelican.

1973 Unwmk. *Perf. 11½x11*
C527 A268 1.30s multi 2.10 .25
C528 A268 3s multi 2.10 .25

Presidents Lara and Caldera AP120

1973, June 15 Wmk. 367
C529 AP120 3s multi .45 .30

Visit of Venezuela Pres. Rafael Caldera, Feb. 5-7.

Silver Coin, 1934 — AP121

Ecuadorian Coins: 10s, Silver coin, obverse. 50s, Gold coin, 1928.

Unwmk.

1973, Dec. 14 Photo. *Perf. 14*
C530 AP121 5s multi .60 .40
C531 AP121 10s multi 1.00 .60
C532 AP121 50s multi 4.50 2.50
a. Souvenir sheet of 3 7.25 7.25
Nos. C530-C532 (3) 6.10 3.50

No. C532a contains one each of Nos. C530-C532; Dated "1972." Exists imperf. Value, same.

A gold marginal overprint was applied in 1974 to No. C532a (perf. and imperf.): "X Campeonato Mundial de Football / Munich - 1974." Value, each $75.

A carmine overprint was applied in 1974 to No. C532a (perf. and imperf.): "Seminario de Telecommunicaciones Rurales, / Septiembre-1974 / Quito-Ecuador" and ITU emblem. Value, each $10.

Globe, OPEC Emblem, Oil Derrick — AP122

1974, June 15 Litho. *Perf. 11½*
C533 AP122 2s multi .45 .30

Meeting of Organization of Oil Exporting Countries, Quito, June 15-24.

Ecuadorian Flag, UPU Emblem — AP123

1974, July 15 Litho. *Perf. 11½*
C534 AP123 1.30s multi .30 .25

Centenary of Universal Postal Union.

Two 25s souvenir sheets exist. These were sold on a restricted basis. Value, each $75.

Teodoro Wolf AP124

Capt. Edmundo Chiriboga AP125

1974 Litho. *Perf. 12x11½*
C535 AP124 1.30s blk & ultra .25 .25
C536 AP125 1.50s gray .30 .25

Teodoro Wolf, geographer; Edmundo Chiriboga, national hero.

Issued: No. C535, 11/29; No. C536, 12/4.

Congress Emblem AP126

1974, Dec. 8 Litho. *Perf. 11½x12*
C537 AP126 5s bl & multi .45 .30

8th Inter-American Postmasters' Cong., Quito.

Map of Americas and Coat of Arms — AP127

1975, Feb. 1 *Perf. 12x11½*
C538 AP127 3s bl & multi .45 .30

EXFIGUA Stamp Exhibition and 5th General Assembly of Federation Inter-Americana de Filatelia, Guayaquil, Nov. 1973.

Prominent Ecuadorians AP128

No. C539, Manuel J. Calle, Journalist. No. C540, Leopoldo Benites V., president of UN General Assembly, 1973-74; No. C541, Adolfo H. Simmonds G. (1892-1969), journalist; No. C542, Juan de Dios Martinez Mera, President of Ecuador, birth centenary.

1975 *Perf. 12x11½*
C539 AP128 5s lilac rose .60 .30
C540 AP128 5s gray .60 .30
C541 AP128 5s violet .60 .30
C542 AP128 5s blk & rose red .60 .30
Nos. C539-C542 (4) 2.40 1.20

Pres. Guillermo Rodriguez Lara — AP129

1975 Unwmk. *Perf. 12*
C546 AP129 5s vermilion & blk .60 .30

State visit of Pres. Guillermo Rodriguez Lara to Algeria, Romania and Venezuela.

Meeting Type of 1975

1.50s, Rafael Rodriguez Palacios & Argelino Duran Quintero meeting at border in Rumichaca. 2s, Signing border agreement.

1975, Apr. 1 Litho. *Perf. 12x11½*
C547 A273 1.50s multi .30 .25
C548 A273 2s multi .30 .25

Sacred Heart (Painting) AP130

Quito Cathedral AP131

Design: 2s, Monstrance.

1975, Apr. 28 Litho. *Perf. 12x11½*
C549 AP130 1.30s yel & multi .25 .25
C550 AP130 2s bl & multi .30 .25
C551 AP131 3s multi .40 .25
Nos. C549-C551 (3) .95 .75

3rd Bolivarian Eucharistic Congress, Quito, June 9-16, 1974.

J. Delgado Panchana with Trophy — AP132

J. Delgado Panchana Swimming AP133

Perf. 12x11½, 11½x12

1975, June 12 **Unwmk.**

C552 AP132 1.30s bl & multi .25 .25
C553 AP133 3s blk & multi .30 .25

Jorge Delgado Panchana, South American swimming champion, 1971 and 1974.

Sports Type of 1975

1975, Sept. 11 **Litho.** ***Perf. 11½***

C554 A276 1.30s Tennis .40 .25
C555 A276 2s Target shooting .55 .25
C556 A276 2.80s Volleyball .65 .25
C557 A276 3s Raft with sails .65 .25
C558 A276 5s Mask 1.10 .25
Nos. C554-C558 (5) 3.35 1.25

Flower Type of 1975

Designs: 1.30s, Pitcairnia pungens. 2s, Scarlet sage. 3s, Amaryllis. 4s, Opuntia quitense. 5s, Bomarea.

1975, Nov. 18 **Litho.** ***Perf. 11½x12***

C559 A277 1.30s multi .35 .25
C560 A277 2s multi .55 .25
C561 A277 3s multi .75 .40
C562 A277 4s multi 1.10 .55
C563 A277 5s multi 1.60 .75
Nos. C559-C563 (5) 4.35 2.20

Tail Assemblies and Emblem — AP134

Planes over Map of Ecuador — AP135

1975, Dec. 17 **Litho.** ***Perf. 11½***

C564 AP134 1.30s bl & multi .45 .30
C565 AP135 3s multi .55 .30

TAME, Military Transport Airline, 13th anniv.

Benalcázar Statue — AP136

1976, Feb. 6 **Litho.** ***Perf. 11½***

C566 AP136 2s multi .35 .25
C567 AP136 3s multi .35 .25

Sebastián de Benalcázar (1495-1550), Spanish conquistador, founder of Quito.

Archaeology Type of 1975

1.30s, Seated man, Carchi Culture. 2s, Funerary urn, Tuncahuan Culture. 3s, Priest, Bahia de Caraquez Culture. 4s, Snail's shell, Cuasmal Culture. 5s, Bowl supported by figurines, Guangala Culture.

1976, Feb. 12 **Litho.** ***Perf. 11½***

C568 A278 1.30s multi .35 .25
C569 A278 2s multi .45 .25
C570 A278 3s multi .65 .45
C571 A278 4s multi .95 .45
C572 A278 5s multi 1.25 .45
Nos. C568-C572 (5) 3.65 1.85

Fruit Type of 1976

1976, Mar. 30

C573 A280 2s Apples .40 .25
C574 A280 5s Rose .80 .40

Lufthansa Jet — AP137

1976, June 25 **Litho.** ***Perf. 12***

C575 AP137 10s bl & multi 1.50 .50

Lufthansa, 50th anniversary.

An imperf. 20s miniature sheet exists, similar to No. C575 enlarged, with overprinted black bar covering line below "Lufthansa." Size: 90x115mm.

Projected PO, Quito — AP138

1976, Aug. 10 **Litho.** ***Perf. 12***

C576 AP138 5s blk & multi .40 .25

Design for new General Post Office, Quito.

Fruit Peddler — AP139

No. C578, Longshoreman. No. C579, Cerros del Carmen & Santa Ana, hills of Guayaquil, horiz. No. C580, Sebastián de Belalcázar. No. C581, Francisco de Orellana. No. C582, Chief Guayas & his wife Quila.

1976, July 25

C577 AP139 1.30s red & multi .25 .25
C578 AP139 1.30s red & multi .25 .25
C579 AP139 1.30s red & multi .25 .25
C580 AP139 2s red & multi .25 .25
C581 AP139 2s red & multi .25 .25
C582 AP139 2s red & multi .25 .25
Nos. C577-C582 (6) 1.50 1.50

Founding of Guayaquil, 441st anniversary.

Emblem and Laurel AP140

1976, Aug. 9

C583 AP140 1.30s yel & multi .35 .25

Bolivarian Soc. of Ecuador, 50th anniv.

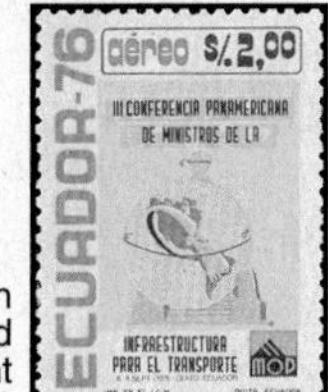

Western Hemisphere and Equator Monument AP141

1976, Sept. 6

C584 AP141 2s multi .35 .25

Souvenir Sheet
Imperf

C585 AP141 5s multi 4.00 4.00

3rd Conf. of Pan-American Transport Ministers, Quito, Sept. 6-11. No. C585 contains design similar to No. C584 with black denomination and red control number in margin.

Congress Emblem — AP142

1976, Sept. 27 **Litho.** ***Perf. 11½***

C586 AP142 1.30s bl & multi .40 .25
C587 AP142 3s bl & multi .50 .30

Souvenir Sheet
Imperf

C588 AP142 10s bl & multi 1.75 1.00

10th Inter-American Congress of the Construction Industry, Quito, Sept. 27-30.

George Washington AP143

American Bicentennial: 5s, Naval battle, Sept. 23, 1779, in which the Bonhomme Richard, commanded by John Paul Jones, defeated and captured the Serapis, British man-of-war, off Yorkshire coast, horiz.

1976, Oct. 18 **Litho.** ***Perf. 12***

C589 AP143 3s blk & multi .65 .30
C590 AP143 5s red brn & yel 1.25 .60

Dr. Hideyo Noguchi — AP144

1976 **Litho.** ***Perf. 11½***

C591 AP144 3s yel & multi .40 .25

Dr. Hideyo Noguchi (1876-1928), bacteriologist (at Rockefeller Institute). A 10s imperf. miniature sheet in same design exists without "Aereo." Size: 95x114mm. Value $6.

Luis Cordero — AP145

1976, Dec. **Litho.** ***Perf. 11½***

C592 AP145 2s multi .35 .25

Luis Cordero (1833-1912), president of Ecuador.

Mariuxi Febres Cordero — AP146

1976, Dec. ***Perf. 11½***

C593 AP146 3s multi .35 .25

Mariuxi Febres Cordero, South American swimming champion.

Flags and Monument AP147

1976, Nov. 9 ***Perf. 12***

C594 AP147 3s multi .35 .25

Miniature Sheet
Imperf

C595 AP147 5s multi 2.50 1.50

2nd Meeting of the Agriculture Ministers of the Andean Countries, Quito, Nov. 8-10.

Sister Catalina — AP148

1977, June 17 **Litho.** ***Perf. 12x11½***

C596 AP148 1.30s blk & pale salmon .45 .30

Sister Catalina de Jesus Herrera (1717-1795), writer.

Congress Hall, Quito — AP149

1977, Aug. 15 **Litho.** ***Perf. 12x11½***

C597 AP149 5s multi .60 .30
a. 10s souvenir sheet 2.00 2.00

11th General Assembly of Pan-American Institute of Geography and History, Quito, Aug. 15-30. No. C597a contains the designs of types A282 and AP149 without denominations and with simulated perforations.

Pres. Alfonso López Michelsen, Flag of Colombia — AP150

Designs: 5s, Pres. López Michelsen of Colombia, Pres. Alfredo Poveda Burbano of

Ecuador and aide. 7s, as 5s, vert. 9s, 10s, Presidents with aides.

1977, Sept. 13 *Perf. 12*

C598 AP150 2.60s multi .50 .25
C599 AP150 5s multi .75 .30
C600 AP150 7s multi .90 .40
C601 AP150 9s multi 1.25 .60

Imperf

C602 AP150 10s multi 1.25 1.00
Nos. C598-C602 (5) 4.65 2.55

Meeting of the Presidents of Ecuador and Colombia and Declaration of Putumayo, Feb. 25, 1977. Nos. C598-C602 are overprinted in multiple fluorescent, colorless rows: INSTITUTO GEOGRAFICO MILITAR GOBIERNO DEL ECUADOR.

Ceramic Figure, Tolita Culture AP151

9s, Divine Shepherdess, sculpture by Bernardo de Legarda. 11s, The Fruit Seller, sculpture by Legarda. 20s, Sun God, pre-Columbian gold mask.

1977, Aug. 24 *Perf. 12*

C603 AP151 7s gold & multi 1.20 .30
C604 AP151 9s gold & multi 1.50 .35
C605 AP151 11s gold & multi 2.00 .70
Nos. C603-C605 (3) 4.70 1.35

Souvenir Sheet
Gold Embossed
Imperf

C606 AP151 20s vio, bl, blk & gold 8.50 3.50

Central Bank of Ecuador, 50th anniversary. Nos. C603-C605 overprinted like Nos. C598-C602.

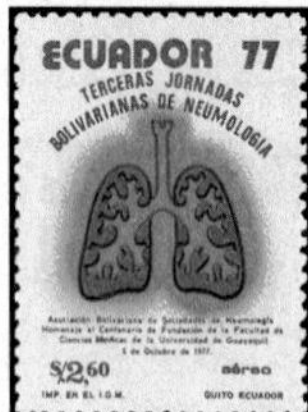

Lungs — AP152

1977, Oct. 5 Litho. *Perf. 12x11½*

C607 AP152 2.60s multi .35 .25

3rd Cong. of the Bolivarian Pneumonic Soc. and cent. of the founding of the medical faculty of the University of Guayaquil.

Brother Miguel, St. Peter's, Rome — AP153

1977

C608 AP153 2.60s multi .35 .25

Beatification of Brother Miguel.

Peralta Type

2.60s, Titles of works by Peralta & his bookmark.

1977 *Perf. 11½*

C609 A284 2.60s multi .40 .25

Broadcast Tower — AP154

1977, Dec. 2 Litho. *Perf. 12x11½*

C610 AP154 5s multi .45 .45

9th World Telecommunications Day.

Remigio Romero y Cordero (1895-1967), Poet — AP155

1978, Mar. 2 Litho. *Perf. 12½x11½*

C611 AP155 3s multi .40 .25
C612 AP155 10.60s multi .55 .30

Imperf

C612A AP155 10s multi 1.40 1.40
Nos. C611-C612A (3) 2.35 1.95

No. C612A contains a vignette similar to Nos. C611-C612.

Dr. Vicente Corral Moscoso — AP156

5s, Hospital emblem with Caduceus.

1978, Apr. 12 Litho. *Imperf.*

C613 AP156 5s multi .55 .25

Perf. 12x11½

C614 AP156 7.60s multi 1.10 .50

Inauguration (in 1977) of Dr. Vicente Corral Moscoso Regional Hospital, Cuenca.

Faces — AP157

Designs: 9s, Emblems and flags of Ecuador. 10s, 11s, Hands reaching for light.

1978, Mar. 17

C615 AP157 7s multicolored .70 .25
C616 AP157 9s multicolored 1.00 .25
C617 AP157 11s multicolored 1.25 .25

Imperf

C618 AP157 10s multicolored 1.25 1.25
Nos. C615-C618 (4) 4.20 2.00

Ecuadorian Social Security Institute, 50th anniv.

Geographical Institute Type

7.60s, Plane over map of Ecuador with mountains.

1978, Apr. 12 Litho. *Perf. 11½*

C619 A287 7.60s multi 1.10 .55

Imperf

C620 A287 10s multi 1.75 1.75

No. C620 contains 2 vignettes with simulated perforations in designs of Nos. 967 and C619.

Lions Type

1978 *Perf. 11½*

C621 A288 5s multi .75 .25
C622 A288 6.20s multi .90 .40

Imperf

C623 A288 10s multi 2.50 1.25
Nos. C621-C623 (3) 4.15 1.90

No. C623 contains a vignette similar to Nos. C621-C622.

San Martin — AP158

1978, Apr. 13 Litho. *Perf. 12*

C624 AP158 10.60s multi 1.60 .50

Imperf

C625 AP158 10s multi 1.75 1.75

Gen. José de San Martin (1778-1850), soldier and statesman. No. C625 contains a vignette similar to No. C624.

Bank Type

Design: 5s, Bank emblem.

1978, Sept. Litho. *Perf. 11½*

C626 A289 5s gray & multi .45 .30

Soccer Type

Designs: 2.60s, "Gauchito" and Games' emblem. 5s, "Gauchito." 7s, Soccer ball. 9s, Games' emblem, vert. 10s, Games' emblem.

1978, Nov. 1 *Perf. 12*

C627 A290 2.60s multi .30 .25
C628 A290 7s multi .80 .40
C629 A290 9s multi 1.10 .65

Imperf

C630 A290 5s blk & bl 6.00 6.00
C631 A290 10s blk & bl 6.00 6.00
Nos. C627-C631 (5) 14.20 13.30

Bernardo O'Higgins AP159

1978, Nov. 11 Litho. *Perf. 12x11½*

C632 AP159 10.60s multi .80 .30

Imperf

C633 AP159 10s multi 1.50 .90

Gen. Bernardo O'Higgins (1778-1842), Chilean soldier and statesman. No. C633 contains a vignette similar to No. C632.

Old Men of Vilcabamba AP160

1978, Nov. 11 *Perf. 12x11½*

C634 AP160 5s multi .50 .30

Vilcabamba, valley of longevity.

Humphrey AP161

1978, Nov. 27 Litho. *Perf. 12x11½*

C635 AP1615s multi .50 .30

Hubert H. Humphrey (1911-1978), Vice President of the US.

Virgin and Child — AP162

Children's Drawings: 4.60s, Holy Family. 6.20s, Candle and children.

1978

C636 AP162 2.20s multi .30 .25
C637 AP162 4.60s multi .50 .25
C638 AP162 6.20s multi .85 .40
Nos. C636-C638 (3) 1.65 .90

Christmas 1978.

Village, by Anibal Villacis AP163

Ecuadorian Painters: No. C640, Mountain Village, by Gilberto Almeida. No. C641, Bay, by Roura Oxandaberro. No. C642, Abstract, by Luis Molinari. No. C643, Statue, by Oswaldo Viteri. No. C644, Tools, by Enrique Tabara.

1978, Dec. 9 *Perf. 12*

C639 AP163 5s multi .60 .25
C640 AP163 5s multi .60 .25
C641 AP163 5s multi .60 .25
C642 AP163 5s multi .60 .25
C643 AP163 5s multi .60 .25
C644 AP163 5s multi .60 .25
Nos. C639-C644 (6) 3.60 1.50

House and Monument AP164

Design: 3.40s, Monument, vert.

1979, Feb. 27 Litho. *Perf. 12*

C645 AP164 2.40s multi .30 .25
C646 AP164 3.40s multi .30 .25

Imperf

C647 AP164 10s multi .90 .90
Nos. C645-C647 (3) 1.50 1.40

Sesquicentennial of Battle of Portete and Tarqui. No. C647 contains vignettes similar to Nos. C645-C646.

Fish and Ship — AP165

7s, Map of Ecuador & Galapagos showing territorial waters. 9s, Map of South America with west-coast territorial waters.

Perf. 12x11½, 11½x12

1979, July 23 Litho. Wmk. 367

C648	AP165	5s	multi	.75	.25
C649	AP165	7s	multi, horiz.	1.00	.35
C650	AP165	9s	multi	1.40	.50
	Nos. C648-C650 (3)			3.15	1.10

Declaration of 200-mile territorial limit, 25th anniversary.

National Heritage Type

Designs: 10.60s, Bells in Quito clock tower, horiz. 13.60s, Aerial view of Galapagos coast.

1979, Aug. 3 ***Perf. 12x11½***

C651	A293	10.60s	multi	1.25	.60
C652	A293	13.60s	multi	1.40	.75

Size: 115x91mm

Imperf

Unwmk.

C653	A293	10s	multi	5.00	2.10
	Nos. C651-C653 (3)			7.65	3.45

National heritage: Quito and Galapagos Islands. No. C653 contains vignettes similar to Nos. 977, C651-C652.

Flags of Ecuador and U.S. — AP166

1979, Aug. Wmk. 367 ***Perf. 11½x12***

C654	AP166	7.60s	multi	.50	.50
C655	AP166	10.60s	multi	.75	.75

Size: 115x91mm

Imperf

Unwmk.

C656	AP166	10s	multi	.90	.75
	Nos. C654-C656 (3)			2.15	2.00

5th anniv. of Ecuador-US Chamber of Commerce. No. C656 contains vignettes similar to Nos. C654-C655.

Smiling Girl, IYC Emblem — AP167

Perf. 12x11½

1979, Sept. 7 Litho. Wmk. 367

C657	AP167	10s	multi	.85	.40

International Year of the Child.

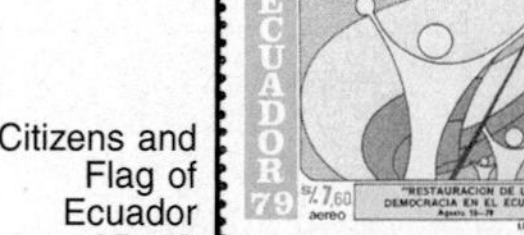

Citizens and Flag of Ecuador AP168

Design: 10.60s, Pres. Jaime Roldos Aguilera, flag of Ecuador, vert.

Perf. 11½

1979, Sept. 27 Litho. Unwmk.

C658	AP168	7.60s	multi	1.00	.45

Wmk. 367

C659	AP168	10.60s	multi	1.25	.40

Restoration of democracy to Ecuador.

Ecuador Coat of Arms, Olympic Rings and Eagle — AP169

Perf. 12x11½

1979, Nov. 23 Unwmk.

C660	AP169	28s	multi	2.00	1.25

5th National Games, Cuenca.

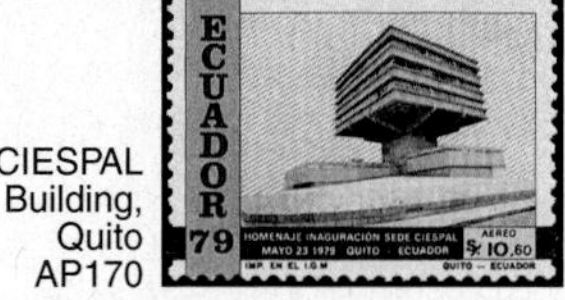

CIESPAL Building, Quito AP170

Perf. 11½x12½

1979, Dec. 26 Wmk. 367

C661	AP170	10.60s	multi	.80	.40

Opening of Ecuadorian Institute of Engineers building.

Olmedo Type

Perf. 12x11½

1980, Apr. 29 Litho. Unwmk.

C662	A294	10s	multi	1.25	.65

Tribal Chief Type

Indo-American Tribal Chiefs: No. C663, Cuauhtemoc, Mexico. No. C664, Lempira, Honduras. No. C665, Nicaragua. No. C666, Lambaré, Paraguay. No. C667, Urraca, Panama. No. C668, Anacaona, Haiti. #C669, Caupolican, Chile. No. C670, Tacun-Uman, Guatemala. No. C671, Calarca, Colombia. No. C672, Garabito, Costa Rica. No. C673, Hatuey, Cuba. No. C674, Cmarao, Brazil. No. C675, Tehuelche, Argentina. No. C676, Tupaj Katri, Bolivia. 17.80s, Sequoyah, US. 22.80s, Ruminahui, Ecuador.

Wmk. 367 (#C663, C667), Unwmkd.

1980, May 12

C663	A295	7.60s	multi	1.50	.35
C664	A295	7.60s	multi	1.50	.35
C665	A295	7.60s	multi	1.50	.35
C666	A295	10s	multi	1.90	.40
C667	A295	10s	multi	1.90	.40
C668	A295	10.60s	multi	1.90	.40
C669	A295	10.60s	multi	1.90	.40
C670	A295	10.60s	multi	1.90	.40
C671	A295	12.80s	multi	2.50	.55
C672	A295	12.80s	multi	2.50	.55
C673	A295	12.80s	multi	2.50	.55
C674	A295	13.60s	multi	2.50	.55
C675	A295	13.60s	multi	2.50	.55
C676	A295	13.60s	multi	2.50	.55
C677	A295	17.80s	multi	3.00	.65
C678	A295	22.80s	multi	3.50	1.25
	Nos. C663-C678 (16)			35.50	8.25

Royal Visit Type

Perf. 11½x12

1980, May 18 Unwmk.

C679	A296	10.60s	multi	.75	.40

Pichincha Provincial Development Council Building — AP171

1980, June 1 ***Perf. 12x11½***

C680	AP171	10.60s	multi	1.25	.60

Progress in Pichincha Province.

Indian Type

Designs: 7.60s, Salasaca boy, Tungurahua. 10s, Amula woman, Chimborazo. 10.60s, Canar woman, Canar. 13.60s, Colorado Indian, Pichincha.

1980, June 10 Litho. ***Perf. 12x11½***

C681	A297	7.60s	multi	1.00	.75
C682	A297	10s	multi	1.25	.85
C683	A297	10.60s	multi	1.50	.90
C684	A297	13.60s	multi	1.75	1.25
	Nos. C681-C684 (4)			5.50	3.75

Virgin of Mercy Type

Designs: No. C685, Cupola, cloisters. No. C686, Gold screen. No. C687, Quito from basilica tower. No. C688, Retable. No. C689, Pulpit. No. C690, Cupola. No. C691, Statue of Virgin.

1980, July 7 Litho. ***Perf. 11½***

C685	A298	7.60s	multi	1.00	.50
C686	A298	7.60s	multi	1.00	.50
C687	A298	7.60s	multi	1.00	.50
C688	A298	10.60s	multi	1.25	.60
C689	A298	10.60s	multi	1.25	.60
C690	A298	13.60s	multi	1.75	.90
C691	A298	13.60s	multi	1.75	.90
	Nos. C685-C691 (7)			9.00	4.50

Nos. C685-C691 are vert.

UPU Monument AP172

Design: 17.80s, Mail box, 1880.

1980, July 7 ***Perf. 12***

C692	AP172	10.60s	multi	1.50	.75
C693	AP172	17.80s	multi	2.50	1.25

Souvenir Sheet

C694	AP172	25s	multi	3.50	3.00

UPU membership cent. No. C694 contains designs of C692 and C693, horiz., perf. 11½.

Olympic Type.

Design: 10.60s, 13.60s, Moscow '80 emblem, Olympic rings.

Perf. 12x11½

1980, July 19 Wmk. 395

C695	A299	10.60s	multi	.90	.65
C696	A299	13.60s	multi	1.25	.85

Souvenir Sheet

C697	A299	30s	multi	7.00	7.00

No. C697 contains vignettes in designs of Nos. 991 and C695.

Marshal Sucre, by Marco Sales — AP173

1980

C698	AP173	10.60s	multi	.90	.60

Marshal Antonio Jose de Sucre, death sesquicentennial.

Rotary International, 75th Anniversary AP174

1980, Aug. 4 ***Perf. 11½***

C699	AP174	10s	multi	1.40	.50

Riobamba Type

Design: 7.60s, 10.60s, Monstrance, Riobamba Cathedral, vert.

1980, Sept. 20 Litho. ***Perf. 11½***

C700	A301	7.60s	multi	.70	.30
C701	A301	10.60s	multi	.95	.40

Souvenir Sheet

Imperf

C702	A301	30s	multi	2.25	2.25

No. C702 contains vignettes in designs of Nos. 996 and C701.

Democracy Type

7.60s, 10.60s, Pres. Aguilera and voter.

Perf. 12x11½

1980, Oct. 9 Litho. Wmk. 395

C703	A302	7.60s	multi	.90	.45
C704	A302	10.60s	multi	1.20	.50

Souvenir Sheet

Imperf

C705	A302	15s	multi	1.50	1.50

No. C705 contains vignettes in designs of Nos. 999 and C703.

OPEC Type

20th Anniversary of OPEC: 7.60s, Men holding OPEC emblem, vert.

1980, Nov. 8 ***Perf. 11½x12***

C706	A303	7.60s	multi	.60	.45

Carchi Province Type

10.60s, Governor's Palace, vert. 17.80s, Victory Museum, Central Square, vert.

1980, Nov. 21 ***Perf. 13***

C707	A304	10.60c	multi	1.25	.50
C708	A304	17.80s	multi	1.90	.80

Orchid Type

Designs: No. C709, Anguloa uniflora. No. C710, Scuticaria salesiana. C711, Helcia sanguinolenta, vert. No. C712, Anguloa virginalis.

Perf. 12x11½, 11½x12

1980, Nov. 22

C709	A305	7.60s	multi	2.25	.60
C710	A305	10.60s	multi	3.25	.35
C711	A305	50s	multi	5.75	1.10
C712	A305	100s	multi	7.50	2.25
	Nos. C709-C712 (4)			18.75	4.30

Souvenir Sheets

Imperf

C713	A305	20s	multi	7.50	5.25
C714	A305	20s	multi	7.50	5.25

Nos. C713-C714 contain vignettes in designs of Nos. C709, C711 and C710, C712 respectively.

Christmas Type

7.60s, Pope blessing crowd. 10.60s, Portrait.

1980, Dec. 27 ***Perf. 12***

C715	A306	7.60s	multi, vert.	1.00	.50
C716	A306	10.60s	multi, vert.	1.25	.60

Isidro Cueva — AP175

1980, Nov. 20 ***Perf. 13***

C717	AP175	18.20s	multi	2.50	1.25

Dr. Isidro Ayora Cueva, former president, birth centenary.

Simon Bolivar, by Marco Salas — AP176

1980, Dec. 17 *Perf. 11½*
C718 AP176 13.60s multi 2.00 1.00

Simon Bolivar death sesquicentennial.

Turtle, Galapagos Islands AP177

100s, Oldest Ecuadorian mail box, 1793.

1981, Feb. 12 **Litho.** *Perf. 13*
C719 AP177 50s multi 6.50 4.00
C720 AP177 100s multi, vert. 8.00 5.00

HCJB Type

1981 **Litho.** *Perf. 13*
C721 A311 7.60s Emblem, horiz. 1.25 .65
C722 A311 10.60s Emblem, diff. 1.75 .90

Soccer Players — AP178

1981, July 8
C723 AP178 7.60s Emblem .90 .45
C724 AP178 10.60s shown 1.20 .45
C725 AP178 13.60s World Cup 1.40 .75
Nos. C723-C725 (3) 3.50 1.65

Souvenir Sheets

C726 AP178 20s multi 3.50 3.50
C727 AP178 20s multi 3.50 3.50

1982 World Cup Soccer Championship. Nos. C726-C727 contain vignettes in designs of Nos. C723 and C725 respectively.

Picasso Type

7.60s, Still-life. 10.60s, First Communion, vert. 13.60s, Las Meninas, vert.

1981, Oct. 26 **Litho.** *Perf. 13*
C728 A313a 7.60s multi .90 .45
C729 A313a 10.60s multi 1.25 .60
C730 A313a 13.60s multi 1.40 .70

Size: 110x90mm

Imperf

C731 A313a 20s multi 3.00 3.00
Nos. C728-C731 (4) 6.55 4.75

No. C731 contains designs of Nos. C730, C729.

World Food Day Type

1981, Dec. 31 **Litho.** *Perf. 13x13½*
C732 A314 10.60s Farming, vert. 1.40 .70

IYD Type

Designs: No. C733, Emblem. No. C734, Man with crutch.

1982, Feb. 25 **Litho.** *Perf. 13*
C733 A316 7.60s multi .70 .30
C734 A316 10.60s multi .90 .55

Montalvo Type

1982 **Litho.** *Perf. 13*
C735 A318 5s Home, horiz. 1.25 .65

Swimming Type

1982, July 30
C736 A320 10.20s Emblem, vert. .95 .45
C737 A320 14.20s Diving, vert. 1.25 .60

Pres. Jaime Roldos, (1940-81), Mrs. Martha Roldos, Independence Monument, Quito — AP179

1983, May 25 **Litho.** *Perf. 12*
C738 AP179 13.60s multi .65 .50

Souvenir Sheet

Imperf

C739 AP179 20s multi 2.00 2.00

AIR POST SEMI-POSTAL STAMPS

Nos. C119-C123 Surcharged in Blue or Red

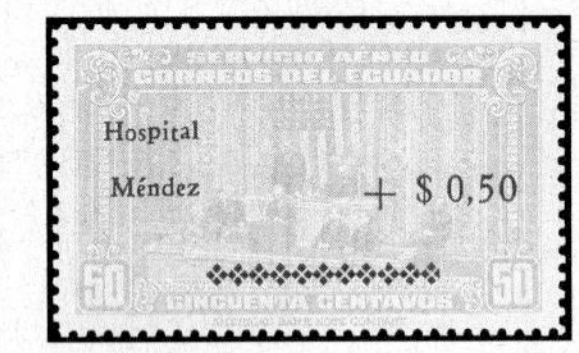

1944, May 9 **Unwmk.** *Perf. 12*
CB1 AP26 50c + 50c 7.00 3.50
CB2 AP26 70c + 30c 7.00 3.50
CB3 AP26 3s + 50c (R) 7.00 3.50
CB4 AP26 5s + 1s (R) 7.00 3.50
CB5 AP26 10s + 2s 7.00 3.50
Nos. CB1-CB5 (5) 35.00 17.50

The surtax aided Mendez Hospital.

AIR POST REGISTRATION STAMPS

Issued by Sociedad Colombo-Alemana de Transportes Aereos (SCADTA)

Nos. C3 and C3a Overprinted in Carmine

1928-29 **Wmk. 116** *Perf. 14x14½*
CF1 AP6 1s on 20c (#C3) 110.00 100.00
a. 1s on 20c (#C3a) ('29) 140.00 110.00

No. C18 Overprinted in Black

1929, Apr. 1 **Wmk. 127** *Perf. 14*
CF2 AP2 1s rose 85.00 55.00

AIR POST OFFICIAL STAMPS

Nos. C8-C15 Overprinted in Red or Black

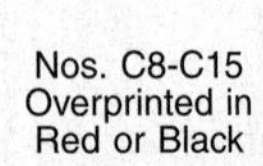

1929, May **Unwmk.** *Perf. 12*
CO1 AP1 2c black (R) 1.00 .50
CO2 AP1 5c carmine rose 1.00 .50
CO3 AP1 10c deep brown 1.00 .50
CO4 AP1 20c dark violet 1.00 .50
CO5 AP1 50c deep green 4.00 2.00
CO6 AP1 1s dark blue 4.00 2.00
a. Inverted overprint 240.00
CO7 AP1 5s orange yellow 18.00 7.75
CO8 AP1 10s orange red 210.00 75.00
Nos. CO1-CO8 (8) 240.00 88.75

Establishment of commercial air service in Ecuador.
Counterfeits of No. CO8 exist.
See Nos. CO9-CO12. For overprints and surcharges see No. C35.

1930, Jan. 9
CO9 AP1 50c olive brown 3.50 1.75
CO10 AP1 1s carmine lake 4.50 2.25
CO11 AP1 5s olive green 11.00 5.50
CO12 AP1 10s black 21.00 10.50
Nos. CO9-CO12 (4) 40.00 20.00

For surcharges and overprint see Nos. C32-C34, C36-C38.

Air Post Stamps of 1937 Overprinted in Black

1937, Aug. 19
CO13 AP7 10c chestnut .50 .25
CO14 AP7 20c olive black .50 .25
CO15 AP7 70c black brown .60 .25
CO16 AP7 1s gray black .70 .25
CO17 AP7 2s dark violet .70 .30
Nos. CO13-CO17 (5) 3.00 1.30

For overprints see Nos. 463-464.

No. C79 Overprinted in Black

1940, Aug. 1 *Perf. 12½x13*
CO18 AP15 5s emerald 2.00 .60

Catalogue values for unused stamps in this section, from this point to the end of the section, are for Never Hinged items.

Nos. C352-C354 Overprinted

1964 *Perf. 13½*
CO19 AP86 50c multi 2.00 .85
CO20 AP86 80c multi 2.00 .85
CO21 AP86 1.30s multi 2.00 .85
Nos. CO19-CO21 (3) 6.00 2.55

SPECIAL DELIVERY STAMPS

SD1

SD1a

1928 **Unwmk.** *Perf. 12*
E1 SD1 2c on 2c blue 8.00 *9.00*
a. "DOS CVTOS." inverted 35.00 *37.50*
E2 SD1a 5c on 2c blue 7.00 *9.00*
E3 SD1a 10c on 2c blue 7.00 6.00
a. "10 CENTAVOS" inverted 21.00 *25.00*
E4 SD1a 20c on 2c blue 10.00 9.00
E5 SD1a 50c on 2c blue 12.00 9.00
Nos. E1-E5 (5) 44.00 *42.00*

No. E1 surcharge reads "CTVOS". Nos. E2-E5 surcharge reads "CENTAVOS".

No. RA49A Surcharged in Red

1945
E6 PT18 20c on 5c green 3.00 2.00

LATE FEE STAMP

No. RA49A Surcharged in Black

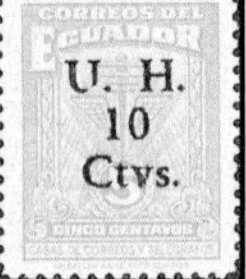

1945 **Unwmk.** *Perf. 12*
I1 PT18 10c on 5c green 1.00 1.00

POSTAGE DUE STAMPS

Numeral — D1

1896 **Engr.** **Wmk. 117** *Perf. 12*
J1 D1 1c blue green 6.00 *6.50*
J2 D1 2c blue green 6.00 *6.50*
J3 D1 5c blue green 6.00 *6.50*
J4 D1 10c blue green 6.00 *6.50*
J5 D1 20c blue green 6.00 *8.50*
J6 D1 50c blue green 6.00 *13.00*
J7 D1 100c blue green 6.00 *17.00*
Nos. J1-J7 (7) 42.00 *64.50*

Reprints are on very thick paper with distinct watermark and vertical paper-weave direction. Value 15c each.

Unwmk.

J8 D1 1c blue green *5.00* *6.00*
J9 D1 2c blue green *5.00* *6.00*
J10 D1 5c blue green *5.00* *6.00*
J11 D1 10c blue green *5.00* *6.00*
J12 D1 20c blue green *5.00* *7.50*
J13 D1 50c blue green *5.00* *10.50*
J14 D1 100c blue green *5.00* *15.00*
Nos. J8-J14 (7) 35.00 *57.00*

Coat of Arms — D2

1929
J15 D2 5c deep blue .40 .40
J16 D2 10c orange yellow .40 .40
J17 D2 20c red .60 .60
Nos. J15-J17 (3) 1.40 1.40

Numeral — D3

Perf. 13½

1958, Nov.	Unwmk.	Litho.	
J18 D3	10c bright lilac	.50	.40
J19 D3	50c emerald	.50	.40
J20 D3	1s maroon	.60	.40
J21 D3	2s red	.70	.40
	Nos. J18-J21 (4)	2.30	1.60

OFFICIAL STAMPS

Regular Issues of 1881 and 1887 Handstamped in Black

1886	Unwmk.	*Perf. 12*	
O1 A5	1c yellow brown	2.50	2.50
O2 A6	2c lake	3.00	3.00
O3 A7	5c blue	6.75	8.75
O4 A8	10c orange	5.25	3.25
O5 A9	20c gray violet	5.25	5.25
O6 A10	50c blue green	15.00	11.50
	Nos. O1-O6 (6)	37.75	34.25

1887			
O7 A12	1c green	3.25	2.50
O8 A13	2c vermilion	3.25	3.25
O9 A14	5c blue	5.25	2.50
O10 A15	80c olive green	17.50	10.00
	Nos. O7-O10 (4)	29.25	18.25

Nos. O1-O10 are known with red handstamp but these are believed to be speculative.

The overprint on the 1886-87 issues is handstamped and is found in various positions.

Flores — O1

1892		Carmine Overprint	
O11 O1	1c ultramarine	.25	.40
O12 O1	2c ultramarine	.25	.40
O13 O1	5c ultramarine	.25	.40
O14 O1	10c ultramarine	.25	.60
O15 O1	20c ultramarine	.25	.90
O16 O1	50c ultramarine	.25	.90
O17 O1	1s ultramarine	.35	1.00
	Nos. O11-O17 (7)	1.85	4.60

Arms — O1a

1894		
O18 O1a	1c slate green (R)	15.00
O19 O1a	2c lake (Bk)	20.00

Nos. O18 and O19 were not placed in use.

Rocafuerte — O2

Dated "1894"

1894		Carmine Overprint	
O20 O2	1c gray black	.60	1.00
O21 O2	2c gray black	.60	.60
O22 O2	5c gray black	.60	.60
O23 O2	10c gray black	.75	1.00
O24 O2	20c gray black	1.00	1.00
O25 O2	50c gray black	3.75	3.75
O26 O2	1s gray black	6.00	6.00
	Nos. O20-O26 (7)	13.30	13.95

Dated "1895"

1895		Carmine Overprint	
O27 O2	1c gray black	5.25	5.25
O28 O2	2c gray black	7.50	7.50
O29 O2	5c gray black	1.50	1.50
O30 O2	10c gray black	7.50	7.50
O31 O2	20c gray black	11.00	10.50
O32 O2	50c gray black	75.00	75.00
O33 O2	1s gray black	3.75	3.75
	Nos. O27-O33 (7)	111.50	111.00

Reprints of 1894-95 issues are on very thick paper with paper weave found both horizontal and vertical for all denominations. Values: Nos. O20-O26, 35c each; O27-O33, 20c each. Generally they are blacker than originals.

For overprints see Nos. O50-O91.

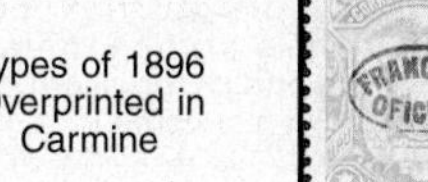

Types of 1896 Overprinted in Carmine

1896		Wmk. 117	
O34 A21	1c olive bister	1.00	1.00
O35 A22	2c olive bister	1.00	1.00
O36 A23	5c olive bister	1.00	1.00
O37 A24	10c olive bister	1.00	1.00
O38 A25	20c olive bister	1.00	1.00
O39 A26	50c olive bister	1.00	1.00
O40 A27	1s olive bister	3.00	3.00
O41 A28	5s olive bister	6.00	6.00
	Nos. O34-O41 (8)	15.00	15.00

Reprints of Nos. O34-O41 are on thick paper with vertical paper weave direction.

Unwmk.

O42 A21	1c olive bister	3.00	3.00
O43 A22	2c olive bister	3.00	3.00
O44 A23	5c olive bister	3.00	3.00
O45 A24	10c olive bister	3.00	3.00
O46 A25	20c olive bister	3.00	3.00
O47 A26	50c olive bister	3.00	3.00
O48 A27	1s olive bister	7.50	7.50
O49 A28	5s olive bister	10.50	10.50
	Nos. O42-O49 (8)	36.00	36.00

Reprints of Nos. O42-O49 all have overprint in black. Value 20 cents each.

Nos. O20-O26 Overprinted

1897-98			
O50 O2	1c gray black	20.00	20.00
O51 O2	2c gray black	35.00	35.00
O52 O2	5c gray black	200.00	200.00
O53 O2	10c gray black	30.00	30.00
O54 O2	20c gray black	20.00	20.00
O55 O2	50c gray black	35.00	35.00
O56 O2	1s gray black	55.00	55.00
	Nos. O50-O56 (7)	395.00	395.00

Nos. O20-O26 Overprinted

O57 O2	1c gray black	4.00	4.00
O58 O2	2c gray black	9.00	9.00
O59 O2	5c gray black	90.00	90.00
O60 O2	10c gray black	100.00	100.00
O61 O2	20c gray black	25.00	25.00
O62 O2	50c gray black	15.00	15.00
O63 O2	1s gray black	165.00	165.00
	Nos. O57-O63 (7)	408.00	408.00

Nos. O20-O26 Overprinted

O64 O2	1c gray black	40.00	40.00
O65 O2	2c gray black	40.00	40.00
O66 O2	5c gray black	40.00	40.00
O67 O2	10c gray black	40.00	40.00
O68 O2	20c gray black	40.00	40.00
O69 O2	50c gray black	40.00	40.00
O70 O2	1s gray black	40.00	40.00
	Nos. O64-O70 (7)	280.00	280.00

Nos. O27-O33 Overprinted in Black like Nos. O50-O56

O71 O2	1c gray black	20.00	20.00
O72 O2	2c gray black	20.00	20.00
O73 O2	5c gray black	20.00	20.00
O74 O2	10c gray black	20.00	20.00
O75 O2	20c gray black	30.00	30.00
O76 O2	50c gray black	275.00	275.00
O77 O2	1s gray black	100.00	100.00
	Nos. O71-O77 (7)	485.00	485.00

Nos. O27-O33 Overprinted

O78 O2	1c gray black	35.00	35.00
O79 O2	2c gray black	30.00	30.00
O80 O2	5c gray black	30.00	30.00
O81 O2	10c gray black	32.50	32.50
O82 O2	20c gray black	42.50	42.50
O83 O2	50c gray black	30.00	30.00
O84 O2	1s gray black	30.00	30.00
	Nos. O78-O84 (7)	230.00	230.00

Nos. O27-O33 Overprinted like #O64-O70

O85 O2	1c gray black	90.00	90.00
O86 O2	2c gray black	20.00	20.00
O87 O2	5c gray black	80.00	80.00
O88 O2	10c gray black	80.00	80.00
O89 O2	20c gray black	140.00	140.00
O90 O2	50c gray black	85.00	85.00
O91 O2	1s gray black	165.00	165.00
	Nos. O85-O91 (7)	660.00	660.00

Many forged overprints of Nos. O50-O91 exist, made on the original stamps and reprints.

O3

1898-99		*Perf. 15, 16*	
	Black Surcharge		
O92 O3	5c on 50c lilac	10.00	10.00
a.	Inverted surcharge	25.00	25.00
O93 O3	10c on 20s org	15.00	15.00
a.	Double surcharge	40.00	30.00
O94 O3	10c on 50c lilac	140.00	140.00
O95 O3	20c on 50c lilac	30.00	30.00
O96 O3	20c on 50s green	30.00	30.00
	Nos. O92-O96 (5)	225.00	225.00
	Green Surcharge		
O97 O3	5c on 50c lilac	10.00	10.00
a.	Double surcharge	5.00	
b.	Double surcharge, blk and grn	12.00	
c.	Same as "b," blk surch. invtd.	5.00	

1899		Red Surcharge	
O98 O3	5c on 50c lilac	10.00	10.00
a.	Double surcharge	20.00	
b.	Dbl. surch., blk and red	25.00	
O99 O3	20c on 50s green	15.00	15.00
a.	Inverted surcharge	40.00	
b.	Dbl. surch., red and blk	60.00	

Similar Surcharge in Black Value in Words in Two Lines

O100 O3	1c on 5c blue	650.00

Red Surcharge

O101 O3	2c on 5c blue	1,150.
O102 O3	4c on 20c blue	800.00

Types of Regular Issue of 1899 Ovptd. in Black

1899		*Perf. 14, 15*	
O103 A37	2c orange & blk	.70	1.60
O104 A39	10c orange & blk	.70	1.60
O105 A40	20c orange & blk	.50	2.50
O106 A41	50c orange & blk	.50	3.25
	Nos. O103-O106 (4)	2.40	8.95

For overprint see No. O167.

The above overprint was applied to remainders of the postage stamps of 1904 with the idea of increasing their salability. They were never regularly in use as official stamps.

Regular Issue of 1911-13 Overprinted in Black

1913		*Perf. 12*	
O107 A71	1c scarlet & blk	3.50	3.50
O108 A72	2c blue & blk	3.50	3.50
O109 A73	3c orange & blk	2.25	2.25
O110 A74	5c scarlet & blk	4.50	4.50
O111 A75	10c blue & blk	4.50	4.50
	Nos. O107-O111 (5)	18.25	18.25

Regular Issue of 1911-13 Overprinted

1916-17		Overprint 22x3½mm	
O112 A72	2c blue & blk	25.00	18.00
O113 A74	5c scarlet & blk	25.00	18.00
O114 A75	10c blue & blk	15.00	12.00
	Nos. O112-O114 (3)	65.00	48.00

Overprint 25x4mm

O115 A71	1c scarlet & blk	1.10	1.10
O116 A72	2c blue & blk	1.60	1.60
a.	Inverted overprint	5.00	5.00
O117 A73	3c orange & blk	1.00	1.00
O118 A74	5c scarlet & blk	1.60	1.60
O119 A75	10c blue & blk	1.60	1.60
	Nos. O115-O119 (5)	6.90	6.90

Same Overprint On Regular Issue of 1915-17

O120 A71	1c orange	1.40	1.40
O121 A72	2c green	1.40	1.40
O122 A73	3c black	2.25	2.25
O123 A78	4c red & blk	2.25	2.25
a.	Inverted overprint	15.00	
O124 A74	5c violet	1.40	1.40
O125 A75	10c blue	2.75	2.75
O126 A79	20c green & blk	15.00	15.00
	Nos. O120-O126 (7)	26.45	26.45

Regular Issues of 1911-17 Overprinted in Black or Red

O127 A71	1c orange	.90	.90
O128 A72	2c green	.70	.70
O129 A73	3c black (Bk)	.90	.90
O130 A73	3c black (R)	.90	.70
a.	Inverted overprint		
O131 A78	4c red & blk	.90	.90
O132 A74	5c violet	1.75	.90
O133 A75	10c blue & blk	4.50	1.75
O134 A75	10c blue	.90	.90
O135 A79	20c green & blk	4.50	1.75
	Nos. O127-O135 (9)	15.95	9.40

Regular Issue of 1920 Overprinted

1920

O136	A86	1c green	1.25	1.25
a.		Inverted overprint	17.00	—
O137	A86	2c carmine	1.00	1.00
O138	A86	3c yellow brn	1.25	1.25
O139	A86	4c dark green	2.00	2.00
a.		Inverted overprint	17.00	—
O140	A86	5c blue	2.00	2.00
O141	A86	6c orange	1.25	1.25
O142	A86	7c brown	2.00	2.00
O143	A86	8c yellow green	2.50	2.50
O144	A86	9c red	3.25	3.25
O145	A95	10c blue	2.00	2.00
O146	A86	15c gray	11.00	11.00
O147	A86	20c deep violet	14.50	14.50
O148	A86	30c violet	17.00	17.00
O149	A86	40c dark brown	21.00	21.00
O150	A86	50c dark green	14.50	14.50
O151	A86	60c dark blue	17.00	17.00
O152	A86	70c bluish gray	17.00	17.00
O153	A86	80c yellow	21.00	21.00
O154	A104	90c green	21.00	21.00
O155	A86	1s blue	45.00	45.00
		Nos. O136-O155 (20)	217.50	217.50

Cent. of the independence of Guayaquil.

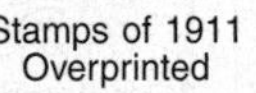
Stamps of 1911 Overprinted

1922

O156	A71	1c scarlet & blk	9.00	9.00
O157	A72	2c blue & blk	4.50	4.50

Revenue Stamps of 1919-1920 Overprinted like Nos. O156 and O157

1924

O158	PT3	1c dark blue	2.00	2.00
O159	PT3	2c green	12.50	12.50

Regular Issues of 1911-17 Overprinted

1924

O160	A71	1c orange	7.00	7.00
a.		Inverted overprint	15.00	

Overprinted in Black or Red

O161	A72	2c green	.60	.60
O162	A73	3c black (R)	.80	.80
O163	A78	4c red & blk	1.25	1.25
O164	A74	5c violet	1.25	1.25
O165	A75	10c deep blue	1.25	1.25
O166	A76	1s green & blk	7.00	7.00
		Nos. O160-O166 (7)	19.15	19.15

No. O106 with Additional Overprint

1924 ***Perf. 14, 15***

O167	A41	50c orange & blk	2.25	2.25

Nos. O160-O167 exist with inverted overprint.

No. 199 Overprinted

1924 ***Perf. 12***

O168	A71	1c orange	5.50	5.50

Regular Issues of 1911-25 Overprinted

1925

O169	A71	1c scarlet & blk	10.00	4.25
a.		Inverted overprint	15.00	
O170	A71	1c orange	.60	.60
a.		Inverted overprint	4.00	
O171	A72	2c green	.60	.60
a.		Inverted overprint	4.00	
O172	A73	3c black (Bk)	.60	.60
O173	A73	3c black (R)	1.10	1.10
O174	A78	4c red & blk	.60	.60
O175	A74	5c violet	.80	.80
O176	A74	5c rose	.80	.80
O177	A75	10c deep blue	.60	.60
		Nos. O169-O177 (9)	15.70	9.95

Regular Issues of 1916-25 Ovptd. Vertically Up or Down

1927, Oct.

O178	A71	1c orange	2.00	2.00
O179	A86	2c carmine	2.00	2.00
O180	A86	3c yellow brown	2.00	2.00
O181	A86	4c myrtle green	2.00	2.00
O182	A86	5c pale blue	2.00	2.00
O183	A75	10c yellow green	2.00	2.00
		Nos. O178-O183 (6)	12.00	12.00

Regular Issues of 1920-27 Overprinted

1928

O184	A71	1c lt blue	1.25	1.25
O185	A86	2c carmine	1.25	1.25
O186	A86	3c yellow brown	1.25	1.25
a.		Inverted overprint	5.00	
O187	A86	4c myrtle green	1.25	1.25
O188	A86	5c lt blue	1.25	1.25
O189	A75	10c yellow green	1.25	1.25
O190	A109	20c violet	11.00	2.50
a.		Overprint reading up	3.50	2.25
		Nos. O184-O190 (7)	18.50	10.00

The overprint is placed vertically reading down on No. O190.

Regular Issue of 1936 Overprinted in Black

1936 ***Perf. 14***

O191	A131	5c olive green	1.50	1.50
O192	A132	10c brown	1.50	1.50
O193	A133	20c dark violet	1.90	.70
O194	A134	1s dark carmine	2.25	1.10
O195	A135	2s dark blue	2.50	1.75
		Nos. O191-O195 (5)	9.65	6.55

The overprint is placed vertically reading up on No. O192.

Regular Postage Stamps of 1937 Overprinted in Black

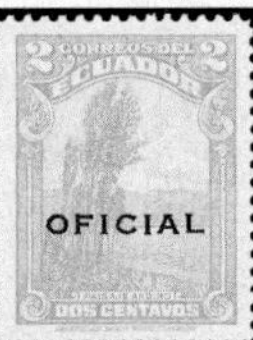

1937 ***Perf. 11½***

O196	A139	2c green	.40	.40
O197	A140	5c deep rose	.40	.40
O198	A141	10c blue	.40	.40
O199	A142	20c deep rose	.40	.40
O200	A143	1s olive green	.40	.40
		Nos. O196-O200 (5)	2.00	2.00

Catalogue values for unused stamps in this section, from this point to the end of the section, are for Never Hinged items.

Tobacco Stamp, Overprinted in Black

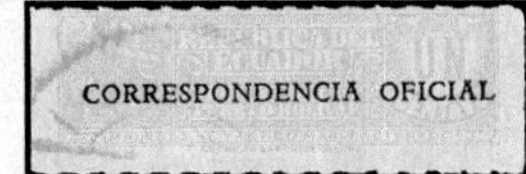

1946 **Unwmk.** ***Rouletted***

O201	PT7	1c rose red	1.75	1.75

Communications Building, Quito — O4

1947 **Unwmk.** **Litho.** ***Perf. 11***

O202	O4	30c brown	.60	.40
O203	O4	30c greenish blue	.60	.40
a.		Imperf., pair		
O204	O4	30c purple	.60	.40
		Nos. O202-O204 (3)	1.80	1.20

Nos. O202 to O204 overprinted "Primero la Patria!" and plane in dark blue were issued in August, 1947, by a revolutionary group. They were later repudiated by decree.

No. 719 with Additional Diagonal Overprint

1964 ***Perf. 14x13***

O205	A231	80c block of 4	6.00	6.00

The "OEA" overprint covers four stamps, the "oficial" overprint is applied to every stamp.

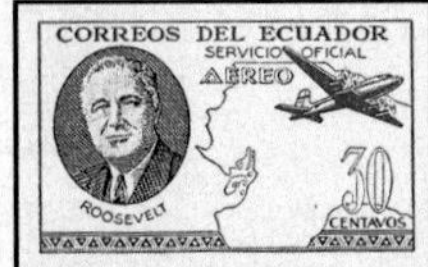

A set of 20 imperforate items in the above Roosevelt design, some overprinted with the initials of various government ministries, was released in 1949. Later that year a set of 8 miniature sheets, bearing the same design plus a marginal inscription, "Presidencia (or Vicepresidencia) de la Republica," and a frame-line were released. In the editors' opinion, information justifying the listing of these issues has not been received.

POSTAL TAX STAMPS

Roca — PT1

1920 **Unwmk.** ***Perf. 12***

RA1	PT1	1c orange	.75	.30

PT2

PT3

RA2	PT2	1c red & blue	1.10	.25
a.		"de" inverted	10.50	5.25
b.		Double overprint	10.00	.60
c.		Inverted overprint	10.00	.60
RA3	PT3	1c deep blue	1.25	.25
a.		Inverted overprint	6.00	1.00
b.		Double overprint	6.00	1.00

For overprints see Nos. O158-O159.

PT4

PT5

Red or Black Surcharge or Overprint

Stamp Dated 1911-1912

RA4	PT4	20c deep blue	—	30.00

Stamp Dated 1913-1914

RA5	PT4	20c deep blue (R)	2.25	.35

Stamp Dated 1917-1918

RA6	PT4	20c olive green (R)	6.50	.55
a.		Dated 1919-20	*25.00*	
RA7	PT5	1c on 2c green	.90	.25

Stamp Dated 1911-1912

RA8	PT5	1c on 5c green	.90	.25
a.		Double surcharge		

Stamp Dated 1913-1914

RA9	PT5	1c on 5c green	8.00	.55
a.		Double surcharge	12.00	4.00

On Nos. RA7, RA8 and RA9 the surcharge is found reading upward or downward.

For surcharges see Nos. RA15-RA16.

Post Office — PT6

1920-24 **Engr.**

RA10	PT6	1c olive green	.40	.25
RA11	PT6	2c deep green	.40	.25
RA12	PT6	20c bister brn ('24)	1.75	.25

RA13 PT6 2s violet 11.50 3.25
RA14 PT6 5s blue 20.00 5.75
Nos. RA10-RA14 (5) 34.05 9.75

For overprints and surcharge see Nos. 259, 266-268, 273, 302, RA17, RA28.

Revenue Stamps of 1917-18 Srchd. Vertically in Red reading up or down

1921-22

RA15 PT5 20c on 1c dk blue 55.00 6.50
RA16 PT5 20c on 2c green 55.00 6.50

No. RA12 Surcharged in Green

1924

RA17 PT6 2c on 20c bis brn .60 .25
a. Inverted surcharge 14.00 5.00
b. Double surcharge 4.00 2.00

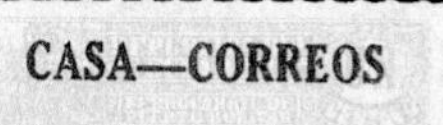

PT7

1924 *Rouletted 7*

RA18 PT7 1c rose red .90 .25
a. Inverted overprint 3.50

Similar Design, Eagle at left

Perf. 12

RA19 PT7 2c blue .90 .25
a. Inverted overprint 3.50 1.75

For overprints and surcharges see Nos. 346, O201, RA32, RA34, RA37, RA44-RA45, RA47.

PT8

Inscribed "Timbre Fiscal"

1924

RA20 PT8 1c yellow 4.50 .85
RA21 PT8 2c dark blue 1.40 .35

Inscribed "Region Oriental"

RA22 PT8 1c yellow .70 .30
RA23 PT8 2c dark blue 1.40 .35
Nos. RA20-RA23 (4) 8.00 1.85

Overprint on No. RA22 reads down or up.

Revenue Stamp Overprinted in Blue

1934

RA24 2c green .50 .25
a. Blue overprint inverted 3.50 1.75
b. Blue ovpt. dbl., one invtd. 4.00 1.25

Postage Stamp of 1930 Overprinted in Red

Perf. 12½

RA25 A119 20c ultra & yel .50 .25

Telegraph Stamp Overprinted in Red, like No. RA24, and Surcharged diagonally in Black

1934 *Perf. 14*

RA26 2c on 10c olive brn .70 .25
a. Double surcharge 5.50

Overprint Blue, Surcharge Red

RA27 2c on 10c olive brn .70 .25

PT9

1934-36 *Perf. 12*

RA28 PT9 2c green .60 .25
a. Both overprints in red ('36) .60 .25

Postal Tax stamp of 1920-24, overprinted in red "POSTAL" has been again overprinted "CASA de Correos y Teleg. de Guayaquil" in black.

PT10

Perf. 14½x14

1934 **Photo.** **Wmk. 233**

RA29 PT10 2c yellow green .50 .25

For the rebuilding of the GPO at Guayaquil.
For surcharge see No. RA31.

Symbols of Post and Telegraph Service PT11

1935

RA30 PT11 20c claret .50 .25

For the rebuilding of the GPO at Guayaquil.

No. RA29 Surcharged in Red and Overprinted in Black

1935

RA31 PT10 3c on 2c yel grn .40 .25
a. Double surcharge

Social and Rural Workers' Insurance Fund.

Tobacco Stamp Surcharged in Black

Seguro Social 3
del Campesino ctvs.

1936 **Unwmk.** *Rouletted 7*

RA32 PT7 3c on 1c rose red .60 .25
a. Lines of words reversed 2.00 .25
b. Horiz. pair, imperf. vert.

Issued for the Social and Rural Workers' Insurance Fund.

No. 310 Overprinted in Black

1936 *Perf. 12½*

RA33 A119 20c ultra & yel .60 .25
a. Double overprint

Tobacco Stamp Surcharged in Black

SEGURO SOCIAL 3
DEL CAMPESINO ctvs.

1936 *Rouletted 7*

RA34 PT7 3c on 1c rose red .60 .25

Social and Rural Workers' Insurance Fund.

Worker — PT12

1936 **Engr.** *Perf. 13½*

RA35 PT12 3c ultra .40 .25

Social and Rural Workers' Insurance Fund.
For surcharges see Nos. C64, RA36, RA53-RA54.

Surcharged in Black

1936

RA36 PT13 5c on 3c ultra .60 .25

This combines the 2c for the rebuilding of the post office with the 3c for the Social and Rural Workers' Insurance Fund.

National Defense Issue
Tobacco Stamp Surcharged in Black

1936 *Rouletted 7*

RA37 PT7 10c on 1c rose .90 .25
a. Double surcharge

Symbolical of Defense — PT14

1937-42 *Perf. 12½*

RA38 PT14 10c deep blue .90 .25

A 1s violet and 2s green exist in type PT14.
For surcharge see No. RA40.

Overprinted or Surcharged in Black

PT15

1937 **Engr. & Typo.** *Perf. 13½*

RA39 PT15 5c lt brn & red 2.00 .25
d. Inverted overprint 20.00

1942 *Perf. 12, 11½*

RA39A PT15 20c on 5c rose pink & red 75.00 20.00
RA39B PT15 20c on 1s yel brn & red 75.00 20.00
e. Surcharge omitted —
RA39C PT15 20c on 2s grn & red 75.00 20.00
Nos. RA39A-RA39C (3) 225.00 60.00

A 50c dark blue and red exists.

No. RA38 Surcharged in Red

1937 **Engr.** *Perf. 12½*

RA40 PT14 5c on 10c dp blue 1.10 .25

Map of Ecuador — PT16

1938 *Perf. 14x13½*

RA41 PT16 5c carmine rose .70 .25

Social and Rural Workers' Insurance Fund.

No. C42 Surcharged in Red

1938 *Perf. 12½*

RA42 A136 20c on 70c black 1.10 .25

No. 307 Surcharged in Red

1938

RA43 A116 5c on 6c yel & red .40 .25

This stamp was obligatory on all mail from Nov. 23rd to 30th, 1938. The tax was for the Intl. Union for the Control of Cancer.

Tobacco Stamp Surcharged in Black

POSTAL ADICIONAL
CINCO CENTAVOS

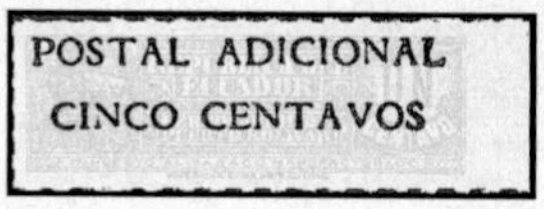

1939 *Rouletted*

RA44 PT7 5c on 1c rose .70 .25
a. Double surcharge
b. Triple surcharge

Tobacco Stamp Surcharged in Blue

CASAS DE CORREOS
Y TELEGRAFOS
CINCO CENTAVOS

1940

RA45 PT7 5c on 1c rose red 1.00 .25
a. Double surcharge 3.50 3.50

No. 370 Surcharged in Carmine

1940 *Perf. 11½*

RA46 A144 20c on 50c blk & multi .50 .25
  a. Double surcharge, one inverted

Tobacco Stamp Surcharged in Black

1940 *Rouletted*

RA47 PT7 20c on 1c rose red 6.00 .50

Farmer Plowing — PT17

1940 *Perf. 13x13½*

RA48 PT17 5c carmine rose .70 .25

Communication Symbols — PT18

1940-43 *Perf. 12*

RA49 PT18 5c copper brown .70 .25
RA49A PT18 5c green ('43) .70 .25

For overprint and surcharges see #534, E6, I1.

Pursuit Planes — PT19

1941 *Perf. 11½x13*

RA50 PT19 20c ultra 1.10 .25

The tax was used for national defense.

Warrior Shielding Women — PT20

1942-46 **Engr.** *Perf. 12*

RA51 PT20 20c dark blue 1.10 .25
RA51A PT20 40c blk brn ('46) 1.10 .25

The tax was used for national defense.
A 20c carmine, 20c brown and 30c gray exist lithographed in type PT20.

No. 370 Surcharged in Carmine

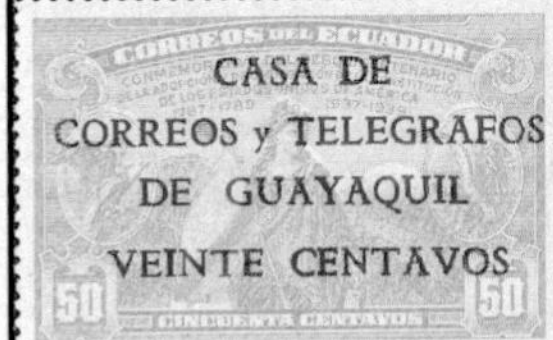

1942 *Perf. 11½*

RA52 A144 20c on 50c multi 1.10 .25
  a. Double surcharge 10.00

No. RA35 Surcharged in Red

1943 *Perf. 13½*

RA53 PT12 5c on 3c ultra .60 .25

No. RA53 with Additional Surcharge in Black

1943

RA54 PT12 5c on 5c on 3c ultra 1.10 .25

Peons — PT21

1943 *Perf. 12*

RA55 PT21 5c blue .90 .25

The tax was for farm workers.
For overprint & surcharge see #535, C135.

Revenue Stamp (as No. RA64) Overprinted or Surcharged in Black

1943 *Perf. 12½*

RA56 20c red orange *75.00* 1.50

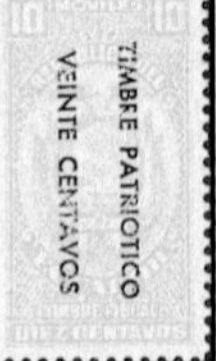

Revenue Stamp (as No. RA64) Overprinted or Surcharged in Black

1943 *Perf. 12*

RA57 20c on 10c orange 2.25 .25
  a. Double surcharge

Coat of Arms — PT22

1943 *Perf. 12½*

RA58 PT22 20c orange red .70 .25

The tax was for national defense.

No. RA58 Surcharged in Black

1944

RA59 PT22 30c on 20c org red .70 .25
  a. Double surcharge

Catalogue values for unused stamps in this section, from this point to the end of the section, are for Never Hinged items.

Consular Service Stamps Surcharged in Black

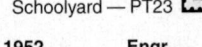

1951 **Unwmk.** *Perf. 12*

RA60 R1 20c on 1s red .60 .25
RA61 R1 20c on 2s brown .60 .25
RA62 R1 20c on 5s violet .60 .25
  Nos. RA60-RA62 (3) 1.80 .75

Teacher and Pupils in Schoolyard — PT23

1952 **Engr.** *Perf. 13*

RA63 PT23 20c blue green .60 .25

Revenue Stamp Overprinted — PT24

1952 *Perf. 12*

RA64 PT24 40(c) olive green 1.10 .25

For overprints & surcharges see #RA56-RA57

Woman Holding Flag — PT25

1953 *Perf. 12½*

RA65 PT25 40c ultra 1.25 .25

Telegraph Stamp Surcharged in Black — PT26

1954 **Unwmk.** *Perf. 13*

RA66 PT26 20c on 30c red brn 1.00 .25

Revenue Stamps Surcharged or Overprinted Horizontally in Black

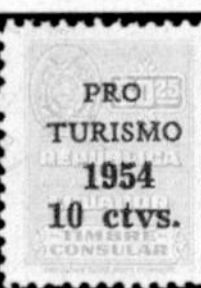

PT26a

PT26b

PT26c

1954 **Unwmk.** *Perf. 12*

RA67 PT26a 10c on 25c blue 1.25 .25
RA68 PT26b 10c on 50c org red 1.25 .25
RA69 PT26c 10c carmine 1.25 .25
  Nos. RA67-RA69 (3) 3.75 .75

Telegraph Stamp Surcharged — PT27

1954 *Perf. 13*

RA70 PT27 10c on 30c red brn 2.25 .25

Revenue Stamp Overprinted in Black

1954 *Perf. 12*

RA71 R3 20c olive black 1.75 .25

Consular Service Stamp Surcharged in Black

1954

RA72 R1 20c on 10s gray 1.75 .25

Young Student at Desk — PT28

Imprint: "Heraclio Fournier.-Vitoria"

1954 **Photo.** *Perf. 11*

RA73 PT28 20c rose pink 1.25 .25

See No. RA76.

Globe, Ship, Plane — PT29

1954 Engr. *Perf. 12*

RA74 PT29 10c dp magenta	2.25	.25

Soldier Kissing Flag — PT30

1955 Photo. *Perf. 11*

RA75 PT30 40c blue	2.25	.25

See No. RA77.

Types of 1954-55 Redrawn. Imprint: "Thomas de la Rue & Co. Ltd."

1957 Unwmk. *Perf. 13*

RA76 PT28 20c rose pink	1.10	.25
Perf. 14x14½		
RA77 PT30 40c blue	2.25	.25

No. RA77 is inscribed "Republica del Ecuador."

The above stamp is believed to have been used only for fiscal purposes.

AIR POST POSTAL TAX STAMPS

No. 438 Surcharged in Black or Carmine

1945 Unwmk. *Perf. 11*

RAC1 A173 20c on 10c dk grn	.75	.25
a. Pair, one without surcharge	90.00	
RAC2 A173 20c on 10c dk grn (C)	.75	.25

Obligatory on letters and parcel post carried on planes in the domestic service.

Liberty, Mercury and Planes PTAP1

1946 Engr. *Perf. 12*

RAC3 PTAP1 20c orange brown	.75	.25

GALAPAGOS ISLANDS

Issued for use in the Galapagos Islands (Columbus Archipelago), a province of Ecuador, but were commonly used throughout the country.

Catalogue values for unused stamps in this section are for Never Hinged items.

Sea Lions — A1

Map — A2

Design: 1s, Marine iguana.

Unwmk.

1957, July 15 Photo. *Perf. 12*

L1 A1 20c dark brown	1.50	.30
L2 A2 50c violet	1.00	.30
L3 A1 1s dull olive green	4.75	.80
Nos. L1-L3 (3)	7.25	1.40
Nos. L1-L3,LC1-LC3 (6)	18.50	3.65

125th anniv. of Ecuador's possession of the Galapagos Islands, and publicizing the islands.

See Nos. LC1-LC3. For overprints see Nos. 684-686, C389-C391.

GALAPAGOS AIR POST STAMPS

Type of Regular Issue

1s, Santa Cruz Island. 1.80s, Map of Galapagos archipelago. 4.20s, Galapagos giant tortoise.

Unwmk.

1957, July 19 Photo. *Perf. 12*

LC1 A1 1s deep blue	1.25	.30
LC2 A1 1.80s rose violet	2.50	.70
LC3 A1 4.20s black	7.50	1.25
Nos. LC1-LC3 (3)	11.25	2.25

For overprints see Nos. C389-C391.

Redrawn Type of Ecuador, 1956

1959, Jan. 3 Engr. *Perf. 14*

LC4 AP69 2s lt olive green	1.25	.70

Issued to honor the United Nations. See note after No. C407.

EGYPT

'ē-jəpt

LOCATION — Northern Africa, bordering on the Mediterranean and the Red Sea
GOVT. — Republic
AREA — 386,900 sq. mi.
POP. — 61,404,000 (1997 est.)
CAPITAL — Cairo

Modern Egypt was a part of Turkey until 1914 when a British protectorate was declared over the country and the Khedive was deposed in favor of Hussein Kamil under the title of sultan. In 1922 the protectorate ended and the reigning sultan was declared king of the new monarchy. Egypt became a republic on June 18, 1953. Egypt merged with Syria in 1958 to form the United Arab Republic. Syria left this union in 1961. In 1971 Egypt took the name of Arab Republic of Egypt.

40 Paras = 1 Piaster
1000 Milliemes = 100 Piasters = 1 Pound (1888)
1000 Milliemes = 1 Pound (1953)
1000 Milliemes = 100 Piasters = 1 Pound (1982)

Catalogue values for unused stamps in this country are for Never Hinged items, beginning with Scott 241 in the regular postage section, Scott B1 in the semi-postal section, Scott C38 in the airpost section, Scott CB1 in the airpost semi-postal section, Scott E5 in the special delivery section, Scott J40 in the postage due section, Scott M16 in the military stamps section, Scott O60 in the officials section, Scott N1 in the occupation section, Scott NC1 in the occupation airpost section, Scott NE1 in the occupation special delivery section, and Scott NJ1 in the occupation postage due section.

Watermarks

Wmk. 118 — Pyramid and Star

Wmk. 119 — Crescent and Star

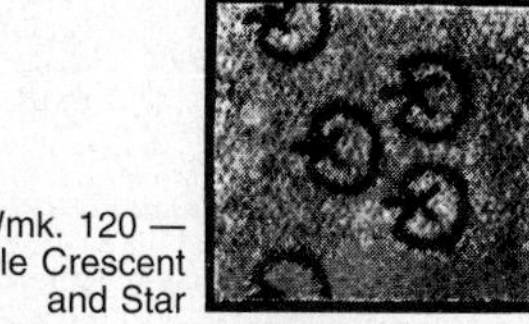
Wmk. 120 — Triple Crescent and Star

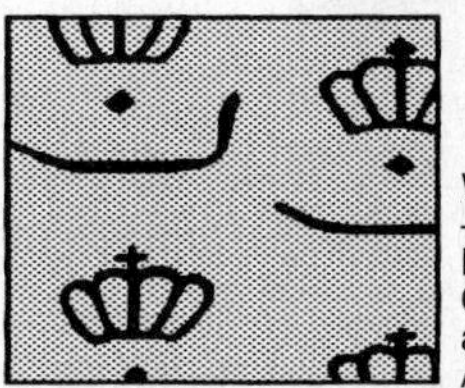
Wmk. 195 — Multiple Crown and Arabic F

"F" in watermark stands for Fuad.

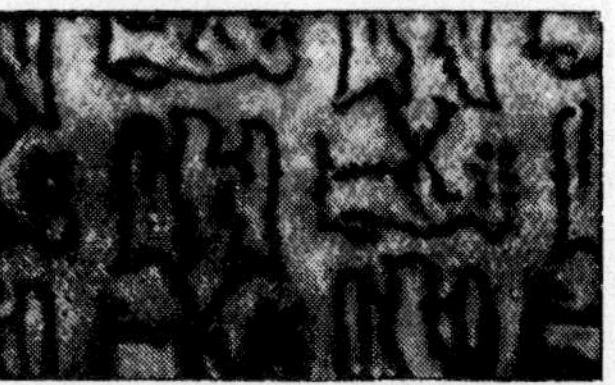
Wmk. 315 — Multiple Eagle

Wmk. 318 — Multiple Eagle and "Misr"

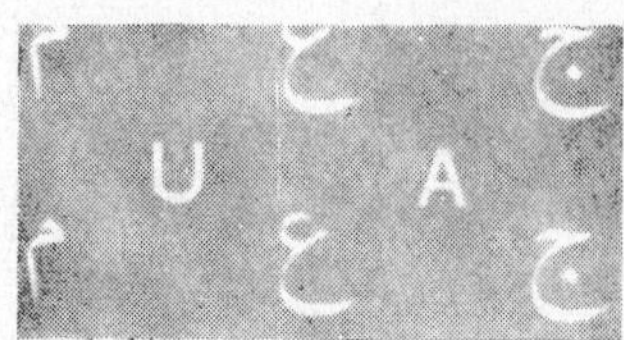

Wmk. 328 — U A R

Wmk. 342 — Coat of Arms, Multiple

Values for unused stamps are for examples with original gum as defined in the catalogue introduction. Very fine examples of Nos. 1-15 will have perforations that are clear of the framelines but with the design noticeably off center. Well centered stamps are extremely scarce and will command substantial premiums.

Turkish Numerals

١	٢	٣	٤	٥
1	2	3	4	5
٦	٧	٨	٩	٠
6	7	8	9	0

Turkish Suzerainty

A1

A2

A3

A4

A5

A6

A7

Surcharged in Black

Wmk. 118

1866, Jan. 1 Litho. *Perf. 12½*

1 A1 5pa greenish gray	62.50	37.50
a. Imperf., pair	250.00	
b. Pair, imperf. between	400.00	

No.	Type	Description	Unused	Used
c.		Perf. 12½x13	82.50	62.50
d.		Perf. 13	325.00	365.00
2	A2	10pa brown	75.00	37.50
a.		Imperf., pair	210.00	
b.		Pair, imperf. between	525.00	
c.		Perf. 13	290.00	*325.00*
d.		Perf. 12½x15	325.00	*350.00*
e.		Perf. 12½x13	100.00	62.50
3	A3	20pa blue	105.00	40.00
a.		Imperf., pair	300.00	
b.		Pair, imperf. between	500.00	
c.		Perf. 12½x13	140.00	95.00
d.		Perf. 13	575.00	375.00
4	A4	2pi yellow	125.00	52.50
a.		Imperf.	*150.00*	*125.00*
b.		Imperf. vert. or horiz., pair	500.00	425.00
c.		Perf. 12½x15	210.00	
d.		Diagonal half used as 1pi on cover		*3,000.*
e.		Perf. 12½x13, 13x12½	200.00	75.00
f.		Pair, imperf. between	625.00	525.00
5	A5	5pi rose	325.00	250.00
a.		Imperf.	425.00	375.00
b.		Imperf. vert. or horiz., pair	*1,250.*	
d.		Inscription of 10pi, imperf.	1,100.	950.00
e.		Perf. 12½x13, 13x12½	350.00	275.00
f.		As "d," perf. 12½x15	1,050.	1,000.
g.		Perf. 13	825.00	
6	A6	10pi slate bl	375.00	325.00
a.		Imperf.	*550.00*	450.00
b.		Pair, imperf. between	*2,500.*	
c.		Perf. 12½x13, 13x12½	550.00	550.00
d.		Perf. 13	*2,000.*	

Unwmk.

Typo.

No.	Type	Description	Unused	Used
7	A7	1pi rose lilac	80.00	5.50
a.		Imperf.	125.00	
b.		Horiz. pair, imperf. vert.	500.00	
c.		Perf. 12½x13, 13x12½	110.00	25.00
d.		Perf. 13	450.00	300.00
e.		Perf. 12½x15	*350.00*	
		Nos. 1-7 (7)	1,148.	748.00

Single imperforates of types A1-A10 are sometimes simulated by trimming wide-margined examples of perforated stamps.

No. 4d must be dated between July 16 and July 31, 1867.

Proofs of Nos. 1-7 are on smooth white paper, unwatermarked and imperforate. Proofs of No. 7 are on thinner paper than No. 7a.

Sphinx and Pyramid — A8

Perf. 15x12½

1867 Litho. Wmk. 119

No.	Type	Description	Unused	Used
8	A8	5pa orange	42.50	*11.00*
a.		Imperf.	250.00	—
b.		Horiz. pair, imperf between	190.00	
c.		Vert. pair, imperf between	—	
9	A8	10pa lilac ('69)	70.00	11.00
a.		10pa violet	95.00	14.00
b.		Half used as 5pa on newspaper piece		850.00
11	A8	20pa yel grn ('69)	135.00	14.00
a.		20pa blue green	135.00	17.00
13	A8	1pi rose red	27.50	1.10
a.		Imperf, pair	150.00	
b.		Pair, imperf. between	300.00	
d.		Rouletted	70.00	
e.		1pi lake red	175.00	32.50
14	A8	2pi blue	150.00	18.00
a.		Imperf.	325.00	
b.		Horiz. pair, imperf. vert.	500.00	
d.		Perf. 12½	275.00	
15	A8	5pi brown	375.00	200.00
		Nos. 8-15 (6)	800.00	255.10

There are 4 types of each value, so placed that any block of 4 contains all types.

A9

Clear Impressions

Thick Opaque Paper

Typographed by the Government at Boulac

Perf. 12½x13½ Clean-cut

1872 Wmk. 119

No.	Type	Description	Unused	Used
19	A9	5pa brown	10.00	5.50
20	A9	10pa lilac	9.00	3.75
21	A9	20pa blue	67.50	4.75
22	A9	1pi rose red	72.50	2.25
h.		Half used as 20pa on cover		750.00
23	A9	2pi dull yellow	100.00	15.00
j.		Half used as 1p on cover		1,200.
24	A9	2½pi dull violet	95.00	25.00
25	A9	5pi green	325.00	42.50
i.		Tête bêche pair	*8,000.*	
		Nos. 19-25 (7)	679.00	98.75

Perf. 13½ Clean-cut

No.	Type	Description	Unused	Used
19a	A9	5pa brown	27.50	10.00
20a	A9	10pa dull lilac	7.00	3.50
21a	A9	20pa blue	95.00	22.00
22a	A9	1pi rose red	95.00	4.00
23a	A9	2pi dull yellow	20.00	4.50
24a	A9	2½pi dull violet	800.00	225.00
25a	A9	5pi green	325.00	62.50

Litho.

No.	Type	Description	Unused	Used
21m	A9	20pa blue, perf. 12½x13½	160.00	80.00
21n	A9	20pa blue, perf. 13½	250.00	65.00
21p	A9	20pa blue, imperf.	—	
21q	A9	20pa blue, pair, imperf. between	—	2,000.
22m	A9	1pi rose red, perf. 12½x13½	550.00	20.00
22n	A9	1pi rose red, perf. 13½	875.00	50.00

A10

Blurred Impressions

Thinner Paper

Perf. 12½ Rough

1874-75 Typo. Wmk. 119

No.	Type	Description	Unused	Used
26	A10	5pa brown ('75)	22.50	3.75
e.		Imperf.	200.00	200.00
f.		Vert. pair, imperf. horiz.	1,000.	—
g.		Tête bêche pair	45.00	45.00
20b	A9	10pa gray lilac	16.00	3.75
g.		Tête bêche pair	225.00	225.00
21b	A9	20pa gray blue	105.00	4.00
k.		Half used as 10pa on cover		—
22b	A9	1pi vermilion	12.00	1.75
f.		Imperf.	—	150.00
g.		Tête bêche pair	150.00	125.00
23b	A9	2pi yellow	90.00	5.75
i.		Tête bêche pair	600.00	600.00
24b	A9	2½pi deep violet	9.25	6.25
e.		Imperf.	—	—
f.		Tête bêche pair	600.00	600.00
25b	A9	5pi yellow green	65.00	22.50
e.		Imperf.	400.00	—

No. 26f normally occurs tête-bêche.

Perf. 13½x12½ Rough

No.	Type	Description	Unused	Used
26c	A10	5pa brown	24.00	4.50
i.		Tête bêche pair	62.50	62.50
20c	A9	10pa gray lilac	37.50	3.50
i.		Tête bêche pair	225.00	*225.00*
21c	A9	20pa gray blue	11.00	3.75
h.		Pair, imperf. between	350.00	
22c	A9	1pi vermilion	90.00	3.25
i.		Tête bêche pair	500.00	500.00
23c	A9	2pi yellow	10.00	6.25
g.		Tête bêche pair	500.00	500.00
k.		Half used as 1pi on cover		*4,000.*

Perf. 12½x13½ Rough

No.	Type	Description	Unused	Used
23d	A9	2pi yellow ('75)	80.00	17.00
h.		Tête bêche pair	*1,250.*	
24d	A9	2½pi dp violet ('75)	80.00	20.00
i.		Tête bêche pair	*1,150.*	*800.00*
25d	A9	5pi yel grn ('75)	375.00	300.00

Nos. 24b, 24d Surcharged in Black

1879, Jan. 1 ***Perf. 12½ Rough***

No.	Type	Description	Unused	Used
27	A9	5pa on 2½pi dull vio	10.00	*12.00*
a.		Imperf.	450.00	450.00
b.		Tête bêche pair	*7,500.*	
c.		Inverted surcharge	125.00	75.00
d.		Perf. 12½x13½ rough	12.00	*12.00*
e.		As "d," tête bêche pair	7,500.	
f.		As "d," inverted surcharge	150.00	150.00
28	A9	10pa on 2½pi dull vio	12.50	12.50
a.		Imperf.	400.00	400.00
b.		Tête bêche pair	*2,500.*	
c.		Inverted surcharge	125.00	82.50
d.		Perf. 12½x13½ rough	17.00	17.00
e.		As "d," tête bêche pair	3,000.	
f.		As "d," inverted surcharge	150.00	125.00

A11

A12

A13

A14

A15

A16

1879-1902 Typo. ***Perf. 14x13½***

Ordinary Paper

No.	Type	Description	Unused	Used
29	A11	5pa brown	4.25	1.25
30	A12	10pa violet	57.50	5.00
31	A12	10pa lilac rose ('81)	70.00	10.00
32	A12	10pa gray ('82)	8.00	1.75
33	A12	10pa green ('84)	2.50	2.00
34	A13	20pa ultra	67.50	2.25
35	A13	20pa rose ('84)	22.00	1.25
36	A14	1pi rose	42.50	.30
37	A14	1pi ultra ('84)	5.75	.30
38	A15	2pi orange yel	42.50	1.50
39	A15	2pi orange brn	27.50	.50
40	A16	5pi green	77.50	11.50
41	A16	5pi gray ('84)	25.00	.50
		Nos. 29-41 (13)	452.50	38.10

Nos. 29-31, 35-41 imperf are proofs.

Nos. 37, 39, 41, exist on both ordinary and chalky paper. See *Scott Classic Specialized Catalogue of Stamps & Covers* for detailed listings.

For overprints see Nos. 42, O6-O7.

A17

1884, Feb. 1

No.	Type	Description	Unused	Used
42	A17	20pa on 5pi green	14.00	2.25
a.		Inverted surcharge	70.00	62.50
b.		Double surcharge	—	

A18

A19

A20

A21

A22

A23

1888-1906 Ordinary Paper

No.	Type	Description	Unused	Used
43	A18	1m pale brown ('02)	3.50	.25
44	A19	2m green ('02)	3.00	.25
45	A20	3m maroon ('92)	8.00	2.25
46	A20	3m yel org ('02)	5.75	.25
48	A22	5m carmine rose	6.50	.25
49	A23	10p purple ('89)	35.00	1.00
		Nos. 43-49 (6)	61.75	4.25

Chalky Paper

No.	Type	Description	Unused	Used
43a	A18	1m pale brown ('02)	4.00	.25
44a	A19	2m green ('02)	1.25	.25
46a	A20	3m yel org ('02)	3.00	.25
47	A21	4m brown red ('06)	4.75	.25
a.		Half used as 2m on cover		—
48b	A22	5m rose ('02)	3.00	.25
49b	A23	10p mauve ('02)	22.50	.55

Nos. 43-44, 47-48 imperf are proofs.

For overprints see Nos. O2-O5, O8-O10, O14-O15.

Boats on Nile A24

Cleopatra A25

Ras-el-Tin Palace A26

Giza Pyramids A27

Sphinx A28

Colossi of Thebes A29

Pylon of Karnak and Temple of Khonsu — A30

Citadel at Cairo — A31

Rock Temple of Abu Simbel — A32

Aswan Dam — A33

Perf. 13½x14

1914, Jan. 8 Wmk. 119

Chalk-surfaced Paper

No.	Type	Description	Unused	Used
50	A24	1m olive brown	1.25	*.80*
51	A25	2m dp green	3.75	.25
52	A26	3m orange	3.50	.50
53	A27	4m red	4.50	.75
54	A28	5m lake	4.25	.25
a.		Booklet pane of 6	250.00	
55	A29	10m dk blue	7.50	.40

Perf. 14

No.	Type	Description	Unused	Used
56	A30	20m olive grn	8.00	.70
57	A31	50m red violet	24.00	1.10
58	A32	100m black	25.00	1.40
59	A33	200m plum	42.50	4.00
		Nos. 50-59 (10)	124.25	10.15

All values of this issue exist imperforate on both watermarked and unwatermarked paper but are not known to have been issued in that condition.

See Nos. 61-69, 72-74. For overprints and surcharge see Nos. 60, 78-91, O11-O13, O16-O27, O30.

British Protectorate

No. 52 Surcharged

1915, Oct. 15

No.	Type	Description	Unused	Used
60	A26	2m on 3m orange	1.25	2.25
a.		Inverted surcharge	250.00	250.00

Scenic Types of 1914 and

Statue of Ramses II

A34 A35

1921-22 Wmk. 120 ***Perf. 13½x14***

Chalk-surfaced Paper

No.	Type	Description	Unused	Used
61	A24	1m olive brown	1.50	*3.00*
62	A25	2m dp green	9.00	4.75
63	A25	2m red ('22)	6.00	2.50
64	A26	3m orange	9.00	6.00
65	A27	4m green ('22)	8.00	*6.50*
66	A28	5m lake	7.00	1.75
67	A28	5m pink	14.00	.25
68	A29	10m dp blue	12.00	.70
69	A29	10m lake ('22)	3.50	.70
70	A34	15m indigo ('22)	10.00	.30
71	A35	15m indigo ('22)	40.00	5.00

Perf. 14

72 A30 20m olive green 12.50 .40
73 A31 50m maroon 10.00 1.25
74 A32 100m black 95.00 7.50
Nos. 61-74 (14) 237.50 40.60

For overprints see Nos. O28-O29.

Independent Kingdom

Stamps of 1921-22 Overprinted

1922, Oct. 10

78 A24 1m olive brown 1.50 1.10
a. Inverted overprint 475.00 450.00
b. Double overprint 225.00 —
79 A25 2m red 1.10 .65
a. Double overprint 225.00 —
80 A26 3m orange 2.25 1.10
81 A27 4m green 1.50 1.00
b. Inverted overprint 225.00 —
82 A28 5m pink 2.75 .25
83 A29 10m lake 2.75 .25
84 A34 15m indigo 5.75 1.10
85 A35 15m indigo 4.50 1.10

Perf. 14

86 A30 20m olive green 6.00 1.10
a. Inverted overprint 200.00 —
b. Double overprint 300.00 —
87 A31 50m maroon 9.00 1.10
a. Inverted overprint 400.00 500.00
88 A32 100m black 22.50 1.25
a. Inverted overprint 500.00 160.00
b. Double overprint 400.00 250.00
Nos. 78-88 (11) 59.60 10.00

Same Overprint on Nos. 58-59

Wmk. Crescent and Star (119)

90 A32 100m black 90.00 50.00
91 A33 200m plum 30.00 1.60

Proclamation of the Egyptian monarchy.
The overprint signifies "The Egyptian Kingdom, March 15, 1922." It exists in four types, one lithographed and three typographed on Nos. 78-87, but lithographed only on Nos. 88-91.

A36

King Fuad — A37

Wmk. 120

1923-24 Photo. *Perf. 13½*

Size 18x22½mm

92 A36 1m orange .35 .25
93 A36 2m black 1.10 .25
94 A36 3m brown 1.00 .65
a. Imperf., pair 225.00
95 A36 4m yellow grn .90 .50
96 A36 5m orange brn .45 .25
a. Imperf., pair 50.00
97 A36 10m rose 2.00 .25
98 A36 15m ultra 3.25 .25

Perf. 14

Size: 22x28mm

99 A36 20m dk green 6.25 .25
100 A36 50m myrtle grn 10.00 .25
101 A36 100m red violet 25.00 .55
102 A36 200m violet ('24) 45.00 2.00
a. Imperf., pair 325.00
103 A37 £1 ultra & dk vio ('24) 175.00 27.50
a. Imperf., pair 1,750.
Nos. 92-103 (12) 270.30 32.95

For overprints & surcharge see Nos. 167, O31-O38.

Thoth Carving Name of King Fuad — A38

1925, Apr. Litho. *Perf. 11*

105 A38 5m brown 11.00 6.00
106 A38 10m rose 22.50 12.50
107 A38 15m ultra 22.50 14.00
Nos. 105-107 (3) 56.00 32.50

International Geographical Congress, Cairo.
Nos. 106-107 exist with both white and yellowish gum.

Oxen Plowing A39

1926 Wmk. 195 *Perf. 13x13½*

108 A39 5m lt brown 3.00 2.00
109 A39 10m brt rose 2.75 2.00
110 A39 15m dp blue 3.00 2.00
111 A39 50m Prus green 14.00 5.00
112 A39 100m brown vio 22.50 8.00
113 A39 200m brt violet 32.50 17.50
Nos. 108-113 (6) 77.75 36.50

12th Agricultural and Industrial Exhibition at Gezira.
For surcharges see Nos. 115-117.

King Fuad — A40

Perf. 14x14½

1926, Apr. 2 Photo. Wmk. 120

114 A40 50p brn vio & red vio 140.00 22.50

58th birthday of King Fuad.
For overprint and surcharge see Nos. 124, 166.

Nos. 111-113 Surcharged

Perf. 13x13½

1926, Aug. 24 Wmk. 195

115 A39 5m on 50m Prus green 2.50 2.50
116 A39 10m on 100m brn vio 2.50 2.50
117 A39 15m on 200m brt vio 2.50 2.50
a. Double surcharge 300.00
Nos. 115-117 (3) 7.50 7.50

Ship of Hatshepsut — A41

1926, Dec. 9 Litho. *Perf. 13x13½*

118 A41 5m brown & blk 3.00 1.40
119 A41 10m dp red & blk 3.50 1.50
120 A41 15m dp blue & blk 4.00 1.50
Nos. 118-120 (3) 10.50 4.40

International Navigation Congress, Cairo.
For overprints see Nos. 121-123.

Nos. 118-120, 114 Overprinted — a

No. 114 Overprinted — b

1926, Dec. 21

121 A41 (a) 5m 300.00 250.00
122 A41 (a) 10m 300.00 250.00
123 A41 (a) 15m 300.00 250.00

Perf. 14x14½

Wmk. 120

124 A40 (b) 50p 1,600. *875.00*

Inauguration of Port Fuad opposite Port Said.
Nos. 121-123 have a block over "Le Caire" at lower left.
Forgeries of Nos. 121-124 exist.

Branch of Cotton A42

Perf. 13x13½

1927, Jan. 25 Wmk. 195

125 A42 5m dk brown & sl grn 1.75 .80
126 A42 10m dp red & slate grn 2.75 1.50
127 A42 15m dp blue & slate grn 3.50 1.50
Nos. 125-127 (3) 8.00 3.80

International Cotton Congress, Cairo.

King Fuad
A43 A44

A45

A46

Type I

Type II

Early printings of the seven values indicated were printed from plates with screens of vertical dots in the vignettes (type I). All values were printed later from plates with screens of diagonal dots (type II).

Perf. 13x13½

1927-37 Wmk. 195 Photo.

Type II

128 A43 1m orange .35 .25
a. Type I 3.25 .60
129 A43 2m black .35 .25
a. Type I 11.00 6.00
130 A43 3m olive brn .35 .55
a. Type I 2.50 1.00
131 A43 3m dp green ('30) .65 .25
132 A43 4m yellow grn 1.25 1.10
a. Type I 65.00 12.50
133 A43 4m brown ('30) 1.10 .55
134 A43 4m dp green ('34) .85 .40
135 A43 5m dk red brn ('29) .95 .40
a. Type I 3.50 1.00
136 A43 10m dk red ('29) 1.40 .25
a. 10m orange red, type I 2.50 .45
137 A43 10m purple ('34) 3.75 .25
138 A43 13m car rose ('32) 1.50 .40
139 A43 15m ultra 2.50 .25
a. Type I 12.00 .65
140 A43 15m dk violet ('34) 5.25 .25
141 A43 20m ultra ('34) 9.25 .30

Perf. 13½x14

142 A44 20m olive grn 3.25 .40
143 A44 20m ultra ('32) 7.50 .25
144 A44 40m olive brn ('32) 4.25 .25
145 A44 50m Prus green 3.50 .25
a. 50m greenish blue 6.00 .35
146 A44 100m brown vio 10.00 .35
a. 100m claret 14.00 .50
147 A44 200m deep violet 9.00 1.25

Printings of Nos. 142, 145 and 146, made in 1929 and later, were from new plates with stronger impressions and darker colors.

Perf. 13x13½

148 A45 500m choc & Prus bl, entirely photo ('32) 100.00 25.00
a. Frame litho, vignette photo 125.00 11.50
149 A46 £1 dk grn & org brn, entirely photo ('37) 125.00 8.25
a. Frame litho, vignette photo 140.00 7.00
Nos. 128-149 (22) 292.00 41.45

Statue of Amenhotep, Son of Hapu — A47

1927, Dec. 29 Photo. *Perf. 13½x13*

150 A47 5m orange brown 1.50 1.00
151 A47 10m copper red 2.00 1.00
152 A47 15m deep blue 3.25 1.00
Nos. 150-152 (3) 6.75 3.00

Statistical Congress, Cairo.

Imhotep — A48 Mohammed Ali Pasha — A49

1928, Dec. 15

153 A48 5m orange brown 1.10 .65
154 A49 10m copper red 1.25 .65

Intl. Congress of Medicine at Cairo and the cent. of the Faculty of Medicine at Cairo.

Prince Farouk — A50

1929, Feb. 11 **Litho.**

155 A50 5m choc & gray 2.00 1.40
156 A50 10m dull red & gray 3.00 1.50
157 A50 15m ultra & gray 3.00 1.50
158 A50 20m Prus blue & gray 3.50 1.50
Nos. 155-158 (4) 11.50 5.90

Ninth birthday of Prince Farouk.

Nos. 155-158 with black or brown centers are trial color proofs. They were sent to the UPU, but were never placed on sale to the public, although some are known used.

Tomb Fresco at El-Bersheh — A51

1931, Feb. 15 ***Perf. 13x13½***

163 A51 5m brown 1.50 1.00
164 A51 10m copper red 2.50 1.75
165 A51 15m dark blue 3.50 2.00
Nos. 163-165 (3) 7.50 4.75

14th Agricultural & Industrial Exhib., Cairo.

Nos. 114 and 103 Surcharged in Black

1932 **Wmk. 120** ***Perf. 14x14½***

166 A40 50m on 50p 20.00 3.00

Perf. 14

167 A37 100m on £1 250.00 190.00

Locomotive of 1852 — A52

Perf. 13x13½

1933, Jan. 19 **Litho.** **Wmk. 195**

168 A52 5m shown 14.00 8.00
169 A52 13m 1859 21.00 12.00
170 A52 15m 1862 21.00 12.00
171 A52 20m 1932 21.00 12.00
Nos. 168-171 (4) 77.00 44.00

International Railroad Congress, Heliopolis.

Commercial Passenger Airplane — A56

Dornier Do-X A57

Graf Zeppelin A58

1933, Dec. 20 **Photo.**

172 A56 5m brown 7.50 4.00
173 A56 10m brt violet 17.50 12.00
174 A57 13m brown car 20.00 15.00
175 A57 15m violet 20.00 13.00
176 A58 20m blue 25.00 20.00
Nos. 172-176 (5) 90.00 64.00

International Aviation Congress, Cairo.

A59 Khedive Ismail Pasha — A60

1934, Feb. 1 ***Perf. 13½***

177 A59 1m dp orange .60 *1.10*
178 A59 2m black .60 *1.10*
179 A59 3m brown .75 *1.25*
180 A59 4m blue green 1.25 .40
181 A59 5m red brown 1.40 .25
182 A59 10m violet 2.50 .35
183 A59 13m copper red 4.00 2.25
184 A59 15m dull violet 4.50 1.75
185 A59 20m ultra 3.00 .40
186 A59 50m Prus blue 9.50 .65
187 A59 100m olive grn 9.50 1.25
188 A59 200m dp violet 75.00 7.25

Perf. 13½x13

189 A60 50p brown 225.00 95.00
190 A60 £1 Prus blue 400.00 150.00
Nos. 177-190 (14) 737.60 263.00

10th Congress of UPU, Cairo.

King Fuad — A61

1936-37 ***Perf. 13½***

191 A61 1m dull orange .55 *.90*
192 A61 2m black 1.75 .25
193 A61 4m dk green 2.00 .25
194 A61 5m chestnut 1.40 .55
195 A61 10m purple ('37) 2.50 .35
196 A61 15m brown violet 2.75 .50
197 A61 20m sapphire 3.25 .35
Nos. 191-197 (7) 14.20 3.15

Entrance to Agricultural Building — A62

Agricultural Building — A63

Design: 15m, 20m, Industrial Building.

1936, Feb. 15 ***Perf. 13½x13***

198 A62 5m brown 1.75 1.25

Perf. 13x13½

199 A63 10m violet 2.00 1.50
200 A63 13m copper red 3.25 2.50
201 A63 15m dark violet 1.75 1.25
202 A63 20m blue 3.75 2.25
Nos. 198-202 (5) 12.50 8.75

15th Agricultural & Industrial Exhib., Cairo.

Signing of Treaty — A65

1936, Dec. 22 ***Perf. 11x11½***

203 A65 5m brown .80 .80
204 A65 15m dk violet 1.00 1.00
205 A65 20m sapphire 1.75 1.75
Nos. 203-205 (3) 3.55 3.55

Signing of Anglo-Egyptian Treaty, Aug. 26, 1936.

King Farouk — A66

1937-44 **Wmk. 195** ***Perf. 13x13½***

206 A66 1m brown org .30 .25
207 A66 2m vermilion .30 .25
208 A66 3m brown .30 .25
209 A66 4m green .30 .25
210 A66 5m red brown .50 .25
211 A66 6m lt yel grn ('40) .60 .25
212 A66 10m purple .30 .25
213 A66 13m rose car .60 .35
214 A66 15m dk vio brn .50 .25
215 A66 20m blue .75 .35
216 A66 20m lil gray ('44) .75 .25
Nos. 206-216 (11) 5.20 2.95

For overprints see Nos. 301, 303, 345, 348, 360E, N3, N6, N8, N22, N25, N27.

Medal for Montreux Conf. — A67

1937, Oct. 15 ***Perf. 13½x13***

217 A67 5m red brown .75 .55
218 A67 15m dk violet 1.25 1.10
219 A67 20m sapphire 1.50 1.25
Nos. 217-219 (3) 3.50 2.90

Intl. Treaty signed at Montreux, Switzerland, under which foreign privileges in Egypt were to end in 1949.

Eye of Ré — A68

1937, Dec. 8 ***Perf. 13x13½***

220 A68 5m brown 1.25 .80
221 A68 15m dk violet 1.50 .90
222 A68 20m sapphire 1.75 1.00
Nos. 220-222 (3) 4.50 2.70

15th Ophthalmological Congress, Cairo, December, 1937.

King Farouk, Queen Farida — A69

1938, Jan. 20 ***Perf. 11***

223 A69 5m red brown 6.50 5.00

Royal wedding of King Farouk and Farida Zulficar.

Inscribed: "11 Fevrier 1938"

1938, Feb. 11

224 A69 £1 green & sepia 200.00 *150.00*

King Farouk's 18th birthday.

No. 224 is valued CTO; postally used examples: Value, $300.

Cotton Picker — A70

1938, Jan. 26 ***Perf. 13½x13***

225 A70 5m red brown .75 .75
226 A70 15m dk violet 2.25 1.50
227 A70 20m sapphire 2.00 1.75
Nos. 225-227 (3) 5.00 4.00

18th International Cotton Congress at Cairo.

Pyramids of Giza and Colossus of Thebes A71

1938, Feb. 1 ***Perf. 13x13½***

228 A71 5m red brown 1.40 1.00
229 A71 15m dk violet 2.00 1.25
230 A71 20m sapphire 2.25 1.25
Nos. 228-230 (3) 5.65 3.50

Intl. Telecommunication Conf., Cairo.

Branch of Hydnocarpus — A72

1938, Mar. 21 ***Perf. 13x13½***

231 A72 5m red brown 1.50 1.25
232 A72 15m dk violet 2.25 1.25
233 A72 20m sapphire 2.50 1.25
Nos. 231-233 (3) 6.25 3.75

International Leprosy Congress, Cairo.

King Farouk and Pyramids — A73

King Farouk
A74 A75

Backgrounds: 40m, Hussan Mosque. 50m, Cairo Citadel. 100m, Aswan Dam. 200m, Cairo University.

1939-46 **Photo.** ***Perf. 14x13½***

No.	Type	Value	Color	Unused	Used
234	A73	30m	gray	.75	.25
a.		30m	slate gray	.75	.25
234B	A73	30m	ol grn ('46)	.80	.25
235	A73	40m	dk brown	.85	.25
236	A73	50m	Prus green	1.00	.25
237	A73	100m	brown vio	1.40	.50
238	A73	200m	dk violet	5.00	.50

Perf. 13½x13

No.	Type	Value	Color	Unused	Used
239	A74	50p	green & sep	11.00	4.00
240	A75	£1	dp bl & dk brn	26.00	7.00
			Nos. 234-240 (8)	46.80	13.00

For £1 with A77 portrait, see No. 269D. See Nos. 267-269D. For overprints see Nos. 310-314, 316, 355-358, 360, 363-364, N13-N19, N32-N38.

Catalogue values for unused stamps in this section, from this point to the end of the section, are for Never Hinged items.

King Fuad — A76

1944, Apr. 28 ***Perf. 13½x13***

No.	Type	Value	Color	Unused	Used
241	A76	10m	dk violet	.50	.25

8th anniv. of the death of King Fuad.

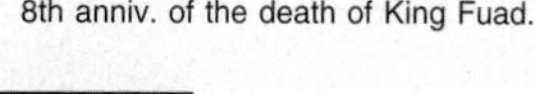

King Farouk — A77

1944-50 **Wmk. 195** ***Perf. 13x13½***

No.	Type	Value	Color	Unused	Used
242	A77	1m	yellow brn ('45)	.45	.25
243	A77	2m	red org ('45)	.45	.25
244	A77	3m	sepia ('46)	1.00	1.00
245	A77	4m	dp green ('45)	.45	.25
246	A77	5m	red brown ('46)	.45	.25
247	A77	10m	dp violet	.45	.25
247A	A77	13m	rose red ('50)	12.00	4.25
248	A77	15m	dk violet ('45)	1.25	.25
249	A77	17m	olive grn	1.25	.25
250	A77	20m	dk gray ('45)	1.40	.25
251	A77	22m	dp blue ('45)	1.40	.25
			Nos. 242-251 (11)	20.55	7.50

For overprints see Nos. 299-300, 302, 304-309, 343-344, 346-347, 349-354, 360B, 361-362, N1-N2, N4-N5, N7, N9-N12, N20-N21, N23-N24, N26, N28-N31.

King Farouk — A78

1945, Feb. 10 ***Perf. 13½x13***

No.	Type	Value	Color	Unused	Used
252	A78	10m	deep violet	.40	.25

25th birthday of King Farouk.

Khedive Ismail Pasha — A79

1945, Mar. 2 **Photo.**

No.	Type	Value	Color	Unused	Used
253	A79	10m	dark olive	.35	.25

50th anniv. of death of Khedive Ismail Pasha.

Flags of Arab Nations — A80

1945, July 29

No.	Type	Value	Color	Unused	Used
254	A80	10m	violet	.35	.25
255	A80	22m	dp yellow grn	.45	.25

League of Arab Nations Conference, Cairo, Mar. 22, 1945.

Flags of Egypt and Saudi Arabia A81

Perf. 13x13½

1946, Jan. 10 **Wmk. 195**

No.	Type	Value	Color	Unused	Used
256	A81	10m	dp yellow grn	.35	.25

Visit of King Ibn Saud, Jan. 1946.

Citadel, Cairo A82

1946, Aug. 9

No.	Type	Value	Color	Unused	Used
257	A82	10m	yel brn & dp yel grn	.40	.25

Withdrawal of British troops from Cairo Citadel, Aug. 9, 1946.

King Farouk and Inchas Palace, Cairo A83

2m, Prince Abdullah, Yemen. 3m, Pres. Bechara el-Khoury, Lebanon. 4m, King Abdul Aziz ibn Saud, Saudi Arabia. 5m, King Faisal II, Iraq. 10m, Amir Abdullah ibn Hussein, Jordan. 15m, Pres. Shukri el Kouatly, Syria.

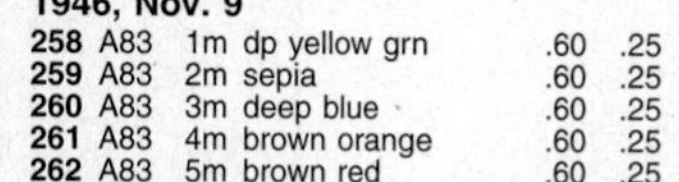

1946, Nov. 9

No.	Type	Value	Color	Unused	Used
258	A83	1m	dp yellow grn	.60	.25
259	A83	2m	sepia	.60	.25
260	A83	3m	deep blue	.60	.25
261	A83	4m	brown orange	.60	.25
262	A83	5m	brown red	.60	.25
263	A83	10m	dark gray	.75	.25
264	A83	15m	deep violet	.75	.25
			Nos. 258-264 (7)	4.50	1.75

Arab League Cong. at Cairo, May 28, 1946.

Parliament Building, Cairo — A84

1947, Apr. 7 **Photo.**

No.	Type	Value	Color	Unused	Used
265	A84	10m	green	.35	.25

36th conf. of the Interparliamentary Union, Apr. 1947.

Raising Egyptian Flag over Kasr-el-Nil Barracks — A85

1947, May 6 ***Perf. 13½x13***

No.	Type	Value	Color	Unused	Used
266	A85	10m	dp plum & yel grn	.40	.25

Withdrawal of British troops from the Nile Delta.

Farouk Types 1939 Redrawn and

King Farouk — A85a

1947-51 **Wmk. 195** ***Perf. 14x13½***

No.	Type	Value	Color	Unused	Used
267	A73	30m	olive green	.75	.25
268	A73	40m	dk brown	.60	.25
269	A73	50m	Prus grn ('48)	.90	.25
269A	A73	100m	dk brn vio ('49)	6.00	.90
269B	A73	200m	dk vio ('49)	14.00	1.40

Perf. 13½x13

No.	Type	Value	Color	Unused	Used
269C	A85a	50p	green & sep ('51)	27.50	9.50
269D	A75	£1	dp bl & dk brn ('50)	37.50	3.75
			Nos. 267-269D (7)	87.25	16.30

The king faces slightly to the left and clouds have been added in the sky on Nos. 267-269B. Backgrounds as in 1939-46 issue. Portrait on £1 as on type A77.

For overprints see Nos. 315, 359.

Field and Branch of Cotton — A86

Perf. 13½x13

1948, Apr. 1 **Wmk. 195**

No.	Type	Value	Color	Unused	Used
270	A86	10m	olive green	.65	.25

Intl. Cotton Cong. held at Cairo in Apr. 1948.

Map and Infantry Column — A87

1948, June 15 ***Perf. 11½x11***

No.	Type	Value	Color	Unused	Used
271	A87	10m	green	1.40	.25

Arrival of Egyptian troops at Gaza, 5/15/48.

Ibrahim Pasha (1789-1848) — A88

1948, Nov. 10 ***Perf. 13x13½***

No.	Type	Value	Color	Unused	Used
272	A88	10m	brn red & dp grn	.40	.25

Statue, "The Nile" A89

Protection of Industry and Agriculture — A90

Perf. 13x13½

1949, Mar. 1 **Photo.** **Wmk. 195**

No.	Type	Value	Color	Unused	Used
273	A89	1m	dk green	.40	.25
274	A89	10m	purple	1.00	.25
275	A89	17m	crimson	1.00	.25
276	A89	22m	deep blue	1.00	.45

Perf. 11½x11

No.	Type	Value	Color	Unused	Used
277	A90	30m	dk brown	1.50	.60
			Nos. 273-277 (5)	4.90	1.80

Souvenir Sheets

Photo. & Litho.

Imperf

No.	Description	Unused	Used
278	Sheet of 4	3.75	3.75
a.	A89 1m red brown	.75	.75
b.	A89 10m dark brown	.75	.75
c.	A89 17m brown orange	.75	.75
d.	A89 22m dark Prussian green	.75	.75
279	Sheet of 2	3.75	3.75
a.	A90 10m violet gray	1.60	1.60
b.	A90 30m red orange	1.60	1.60

16th Agricultural & Industrial Expo., Cairo.

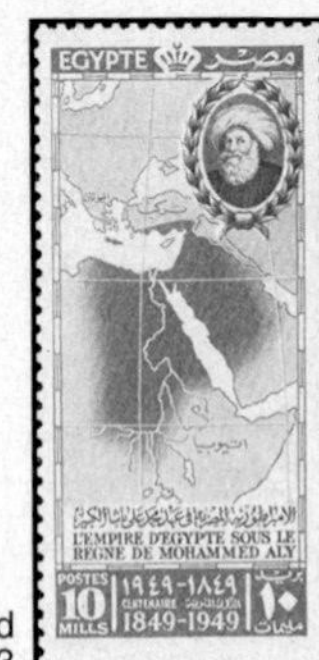

Mohammed Ali and Map — A93

Perf. 11½x11

1949, Aug. 2 Photo. Wmk. 195

280	A93	10m orange brn & grn	.60	.25

Centenary of death of Mohammed Ali.

Globe — A94

1949, Oct. 9 *Perf. 13½x13*

281	A94	10m rose brown	1.00	.60
282	A94	22m violet	2.00	.90
283	A94	30m dull blue	2.75	1.20
		Nos. 281-283 (3)	5.75	2.70

75th anniv. of the UPU.

Scales of Justice A95

1949, Oct. 14 *Perf. 13x13½*

284	A95	10m deep olive green	.40	.25

End of the Mixed Judiciary System, 10/14/49.

Desert Scene A96

1950, Dec. 27

285	A96	10m violet & red brn	.90	.75

Opening of the Fuad I Institute of the Desert.

Fuad I University A97

1950, Dec. 27

286	A97	22m dp green & claret	.90	.75

Founding of Fuad I University, 25th anniv.

Globe and Khedive Ismail Pasha A98

1950, Dec. 27

287	A98	30m claret & dp grn	.90	.75

75th anniv. of Royal Geographic Society of Egypt.

Picking Cotton — A99

1951, Feb. 24

290	A99	10m olive green	.40	.35

International Cotton Congress, 1951.

King Farouk and Queen Narriman — A100

1951, May 6 Photo. *Perf. 11x11½*

291	A100	10m green & red brn	3.00	2.25
a.		Souvenir sheet	17.50	*19.00*

Marriage of King Farouk and Narriman Sadek, May 6, 1951.

Stadium Entrance A101

Arms of Alexandria and Olympic Emblem — A102

King Farouk A103

1951, Oct. 5 *Perf. 13x13½, 13½x13*

292	A101	10m brown	1.10	1.10
293	A102	22m dp green	1.40	1.40
294	A103	30m blue & dp grn	1.40	1.40
a.		Souvenir sheet of 3, #292-294	14.00	*16.00*
		Nos. 292-294 (3)	3.90	3.90

Issued to publicize the first Mediterranean Games, Alexandria, Oct. 5-20, 1951.

Winged Figure and Map — A105

Designs: 22m, King Farouk and Map. 30m, King Farouk and Flag.

Dated "16 Oct. 1951"

1952, Feb. 11 *Perf. 13½x13*

296	A105	10m dp green	.75	.40
297	A105	22m plum & dp grn	1.00	.75
298	A105	30m green & brown	1.25	.95
a.		Souvenir sheet of 3, #296-298	14.00	14.00
		Nos. 296-298 (3)	3.00	2.10

Abrogation of the Anglo-Egyptian treaty.

Stamps of 1937-51 Overprinted in Various Colors

Perf. 13x13½

1952, Jan. 17 Wmk. 195

299	A77	1m yellow brown	.85	.25
300	A77	2m red org (Bl)	.35	.25
301	A66	3m brown (Bl)	.35	.50
302	A77	4m dp green (RV)	.35	.25
303	A66	6m lt yel grn (RV)	1.25	1.25
304	A77	10m dp vio (C)	.45	.25
305	A77	13m rose red (Bl)	1.75	1.60
306	A77	15m dk violet (C)	2.75	1.75
307	A77	17m olive grn (C)	2.00	.35
308	A77	20m dk gray (RV)	1.60	.35
309	A77	22m dp blue (C)	3.00	3.00

No. 244, the 3m sepia, exists with this overprint but was not regularly issued or used.

Same Overprint, 24½mm Wide, on Nos. 267 to 269B

310	A73	30m olive grn (DkBl)	3.75	.25
a.		Black overprint	2.25	1.00
311	A73	40m dk brown (G)	.90	.25
312	A73	50m Prus grn (C)	1.75	.25
313	A73	100m dk brn vio (C)	3.00	.50
314	A73	200m dk violet (C)	15.00	2.25

Same Overprint, 19mm Wide, on Nos. 269C-269D

315	A85a	50p grn & sep (C)	25.00	8.00
316	A75	£1 dp bl & dk brn (Bl)	45.00	9.00
		Nos. 299-316 (18)	109.10	30.30

The overprint translates: King of Egypt and the Sudan, Oct. 16, 1951.

Overprints in colors other than as listed are color trials.

Egyptian Flag — A106

Perf. 13½x13

1952, May 6 Photo. Wmk. 195

317	A106	10m org yel, dp bl & dp grn	1.00	.25
a.		Souvenir sheet of 1	7.50	5.25

Issued to commemorate the birth of Crown Prince Ahmed Fuad, Jan. 16, 1952.

"Dawn of New Era" A107

Symbolical of Egypt Freed — A108

Designs: 10m, "Egypt" with raised sword. 22m, Citizens marching with flag.

Dated: "23 Juillet 1952"

Perf. 13x13½, 13½x13

1952, Nov. 23

318	A107	4m dp green & org	.35	.25
319	A107	10m dp grn & cop brn	.35	.75
320	A108	17m brn org & dp grn	.75	.90
321	A108	22m choc & dp grn	1.25	.60
		Nos. 318-321 (4)	2.70	2.50

Change of government, July 23, 1952.

Republic

Farmer A109

Soldier A110

Mosque of Sultan Hassan — A111

Queen Nefertiti — A112

1953-56 *Perf. 13x13½*

322	A109	1m red brown	.50	.25
323	A109	2m dk lilac	.35	.25
324	A109	3m brt blue	.50	.45
325	A109	4m dk green	.35	.25
326	A110	10m dk brown *("Defence")*	.40	.40
327	A110	10m dk brown *("Defense")*	.80	.25
328	A110	15m gray	.55	.25
329	A110	17m dk grnsh blue	.75	.25
330	A110	20m purple	.35	.25

Perf. 13¼x13¾

331	A111	30m dull green	.35	.25
332	A111	32m brt blue	.90	.25
333	A111	35m violet ('55)	1.10	.25
334	A111	37m gldn brn ('56)	1.75	.60
335	A111	40m red brown	.90	.25
336	A111	50m violet brn	1.75	.25
337	A112	100m henna brn	2.75	.30
338	A112	200m dk grnsh blue	4.50	.75
339	A112	500m purple	12.00	1.75
340	A112	£1 dk grn, blk & red	22.50	3.25
		Nos. 322-340 (19)	53.05	10.50

Nos. 327-330 are inscribed "Defense."

See No. 490. For overprints and surcharges see Nos. 460, 500, N44-N56, N72.

Stamps of 1939-51 Overprinted in Black

1953 *Perf. 13x13½, 13½x13*

343	A77	1m yellow brn	.35	.25
344	A77	2m red orange	.35	.25
345	A66	3m brown	.75	.75
346	A77	3m sepia	.35	.25
347	A77	4m dp green	.35	.25
348	A66	6m lt yel grn	.35	.25
349	A77	10m dp violet	.35	.25
350	A77	13m rose red	1.00	1.00
351	A77	15m dk violet	.75	.25
352	A77	17m olive grn	.75	.25
353	A77	20m dk gray	.90	.25
354	A77	22m deep blue	1.25	.25
355	A73	30m ol grn (#267)	.75	.35

356 A73 50m Prus grn (#269) 1.20 .35
357 A73 100m dk brn vio (#269A) 2.00 .75
358 A73 200m dk vio (#269B) 7.50 1.60
359 A85a 50p grn & sepia 19.00 7.00
360 A75 £1 dp bl & dk brn (#269D) 24.00 4.75
Nos. 343-360 (18) 61.95 19.05

No. 206 with this overprint is a forgery.

Same Overprint on Nos. 300, 303-305, 311 and 314

360B A77 2m red orange .40 .25
360E A66 6m lt yel grn *35.00*
361 A77 10m dp violet 4.00 4.00
362 A77 13m rose red 1.25 .75
363 A73 40m dk brown 6.00 .75
364 A73 200m dk violet 4.00 .90
Nos. 360B,361-364 (5) 15.65 6.65

Practically all values of Nos. 343-364 exist with double overprint. Other values of the 1952 overprinted issue are known only with counterfeit bars.

Symbols of Electronic Progress A113

1953, Nov. 23 Photo. ***Perf. 13x13½***
365 A113 10m brt blue .75 .50

Electronics Exposition, Cairo, Nov. 23.

Crowd Acclaiming the Republic — A114

Design: 30m, Crowd, flag and eagle.

Perf. 13½x13
1954, June 18 **Wmk. 195**
366 A114 10m brown .55 .25
367 A114 30m deep blue .90 .60

Proclamation of the republic, 1st anniv.

Farmer — A115

1954-55 ***Perf. 13x13½***
368 A115 1m red brown .35 .25
369 A115 2m dark lilac .35 .25
370 A115 3m brt blue .35 .25
371 A115 4m dk green ('55) 1.25 .95
372 A115 5m dp car ('55) .35 .25
Nos. 368-372 (5) 2.65 1.95

For overprints see Nos. N39-N43.

Egyptian Flag, Map — A116

Design: 35m, Bugler, soldier and map.

1954, Nov. 4 ***Perf. 13½x13***
373 A116 10m rose vio & grn .50 .30
374 A116 35m ver, blk & bl grn .80 .70

Agreement of Oct. 19, 1954, with Great Britain for the evacuation of the Suez Canal zone by British troops.

Arab Postal Union Issue

Globe — A117

1955, Jan. 1
375 A117 5m yellow brn .60 .30
376 A117 10m green .60 .50
377 A117 37m violet 1.25 .95
Nos. 375-377 (3) 2.45 1.75

Founding of the Arab Postal Union, 7/1/54. For overprints see Nos. 381-383.

Paul P. Harris and Rotary Emblem — A118

35m, Globe, wings and Rotary emblem.

Perf. 13½x13
1955, Feb. 23 **Wmk. 195**
378 A118 10m claret 1.10 .35
379 A118 35m blue 1.50 .75

50th anniv. of the founding of Rotary Intl.

Nos. 375-377 Overprinted

1955, Nov. 1
381 A117 5m yellow brown 1.00 .80
382 A117 10m green 1.25 1.00
383 A117 37m violet 1.75 1.25
Nos. 381-383 (3) 4.00 3.05

Arab Postal Union Congress held at Cairo, Mar. 15, 1955.

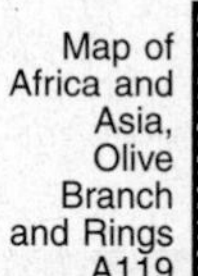

Map of Africa and Asia, Olive Branch and Rings A119

Globe, Torch, Dove and Olive Branch — A120

1956, July 29 ***Perf. 13x13½, 13½x13***
384 A119 10m chestnut & green .40 .25
385 A120 35m org yel & dull pur 1.00 .70

Afro-Asian Festival, Cairo, July, 1956.

Map of Suez Canal and Ship — A121

Perf. 11½x11
1956, Sept. 26 **Wmk. 195**
386 A121 10m blue & buff .60 .60

Nationalization of the Suez Canal, July 26, 1956. See No. 393.

Queen Nefertiti — A122

1956, Oct. 15 ***Perf. 13½x13***
387 A122 10m dark green 1.40 1.25

Intl. Museum Week (UNESCO), Oct. 8-14.

Egyptians Defending Port Said — A123

1956, Dec. 20 Litho. ***Perf. 11x11½***
388 A123 10m brown violet 1.00 .75

Honoring the defenders of Port Said.

No. 388 Overprinted in Carmine Rose

1957, Jan. 14
389 A123 10m brown violet 1.00 .60

Evacuation of Port Said by British and French troops, Dec. 22, 1956.

Old and New Trains A124

1957, Jan. 30 Photo. ***Perf. 13x13½***
390 A124 10m red violet & gray 1.10 1.00

100th anniv. of the Egyptian Railway System (in 1956).

Mother and Children A125

1957, Mar. 21
391 A125 10m crimson .90 .35

Mother's Day, 1957.

Battle Scene A126

Perf. 13x13½
1957, Mar. 28 **Wmk. 195**
392 A126 10m bright blue .40 .35

Victory over the British at Rosetta, 150th anniv.

Type of 1956; New Inscriptions in English

1957, Apr. 15 ***Perf. 11½x11***
393 A121 100m blue & yel grn 1.60 1.25

Reopening of the Suez Canal.
No. 393 is inscribed: "Nationalisation of Suez Canal Co. Guarantees Freedom of Navigation" and "Reopening 1957."

Map of Gaza Strip — A127

Perf. 13½x13
1957, May 4 Photo. **Wmk. 195**
394 A127 10m Prus blue 1.50 .70

"Gaza Part of Arab Nation."
For overprint see No. N57.

Al Azhar University A128

1957, Apr. 27 ***Perf. 13x13½***
New Arabic Date in Red
395 A128 10m brt violet .50 .40
396 A128 15m violet brown .80 .60
397 A128 20m dark gray 1.30 .90
Nos. 395-397 (3) 2.60 1.90

Millenary of Al Azhar University, Cairo.

Shepheard's Hotel, Cairo — A129

Perf. 13½x13
1957, July 20 **Wmk. 195**
398 A129 10m brt violet .70 .45

Reopening of Shepheard's Hotel, Cairo.

Gate, Palace and Eagle — A130

Perf. 11½x11

1957, July 22 **Wmk. 315**

399 A130 10m yellow & brown .70 .40

First meeting of New National Assembly.

Amasis I in Battle of Avaris, 1580 B.C. A131

Designs: No. 401, Sultan Saladin, Hitteen, 1187 A. D. No. 402, Louis IX of France in chains, Mansourah, 1250, vert. No. 403, Map of Middle East, Ein Galout, 1260. No. 404, Port Said, 1956.

Inscribed: "Egypt Tomb of Aggressors 1957"

1957, July 26 *Perf. 13x13½, 13½x13*

400	A131	10m	carmine rose	1.50	1.50
401	A131	10m	dk olive grn	1.50	1.50
402	A131	10m	brown violet	1.50	1.50
403	A131	10m	grnsh blue	1.50	1.50
404	A131	10m	yellow brown	1.50	1.50
			Nos. 400-404 (5)	7.50	7.50

No. 400 exists with Wmk. 195.

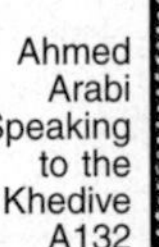

Ahmed Arabi Speaking to the Khedive A132

Perf. 13x13½

1957, Sept. 16 **Wmk. 315**

405 A132 10m deep violet .80 .25

75th anniversary of Arabi Revolution.

Hafez Ibrahim — A133

Portrait: No. 407, Ahmed Shawky.

1957, Oct. 14 *Perf. 13½x13*

406	A133	10m	dull red brn	.30	.25
407	A133	10m	olive green	.30	.25
a.			Pair, #406-407	1.00	*1.00*

25th anniv. of the deaths of Hafez Ibrahim and Ahmed Shawky, poets.

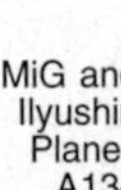

MiG and Ilyushin Planes A134

Design: No. 409, Viscount plane.

1957, Dec. 19 *Perf. 13x13½*

408	A134	10m	ultra	.70	.50
409	A134	10m	green	.70	.50
a.			Pair, #408-409	1.60	1.60

25th anniv. of the Egyptian Air Force and of Misrair, the Egyptian airline.

Pyramids, Dove and Globe A135

1957, Dec. 26 **Photo.** **Wmk. 315**

410	A135	5m	brown orange	.60	.40
411	A135	10m	green	.60	.30
412	A135	15m	brt violet	.50	.40
			Nos. 410-412 (3)	1.70	1.10

Afro-Asian Peoples Conf., Cairo, 12/26-1/2.

Farmer's Wife A136

Ramses II A137

1957-58 **Wmk. 315** *Perf. 13½*

413	A136	1m	blue green ('58)	.30	.25
414	A137	10m	violet	.30	.25

"Industry" — A138

1958 **Wmk. 318**

415	A136	1m	lt blue green	.30	.25
416	A138	5m	brown	.35	.25
417	A137	10m	violet	.60	.25
			Nos. 413-417 (5)	1.85	1.25

See Nos. 438-444, 474-488, 535. For overprints see Nos. N58-N63, N66-N68, N75, N77-N78.

Cyclists — A139

Perf. 13½x13

1958, Jan. 12 **Wmk. 315**

418 A139 10m lt red brown .65 .45

5th Intl. Bicycle Race, Egypt, Jan. 12-26.

Mustafa Kamel — A140

1958, Feb. 10 **Photo.** **Wmk. 318**

419 A140 10m blue gray .80 .25

50th anniversary of the death of Mustafa Kamel, orator and politician.

United Arab Republic

Linked Maps of Egypt and Syria — A141

Perf. 11½x11

1958, Mar. 22 **Wmk. 318**

436 A141 10m yellow & green .75 .25

Birth of United Arab Republic. See No. C90. See also Syria-UAR Nos. 1 and C1.

Cotton — A142

1958, Apr. 5 *Perf. 13½x13*

437 A142 10m Prussian blue .35 .25

Intl. Fair for Egyptian Cotton, Apr., 1958.

Types of 1957-58 Inscribed "U.A.R. EGYPT" and

Princess Nofret — A143

Designs: 1m, Farmer's wife. 2m, Ibn-Tulun's Mosque. 4m, 14th century glass lamp (design lacks "1963" of A217). 5m, "Industry" (factories and cogwheel). 10m, Ramses II. 35m, "Commerce" (eagle, ship and cargo).

1958 *Perf. 13½x14*

438	A136	1m	crimson	.30	.30
439	A138	2m	blue	.25	.25
440	A143	3m	dk red brown	.25	.25
441	A217	4m	green	.30	.25
442	A138	5m	brown	.30	.25
443	A137	10m	violet	.85	.30
444	A138	35m	lt ultra	3.75	.45
			Nos. 438-444 (7)	6.00	2.05

See Nos. 474-488, 532-533, N62-N68, N75-N78.

Qasim Amin — A144

1958, Apr. 23 *Perf. 13½x13*

445 A144 10m deep blue .60 .25

50th anniversary of the death of Qasim Amin, author of "Emancipation of Women."

Doves, Broken Chain and Globe — A145

1958, June 18

446 A145 10m violet .60 .25

5th anniv. of the republic and to publicize the struggle of peoples and individuals for freedom.

For overprint see No. N69.

Cement Industry — A146

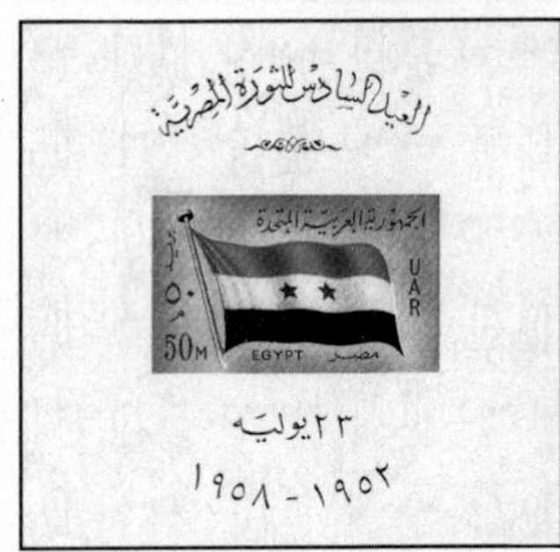

UAR Flag — A147

Industries: No. 448, Textile. No. 449, Iron & steel. No. 450, Petroleum (Oil). No. 451, Electricity and fertilizers.

Perf. 13½x13

1958, July 23 **Photo.** **Wmk. 318**

447	A146	10m	red brown	.40	.25
448	A146	10m	blue green	.40	.25
449	A146	10m	bright red	.40	.25
450	A146	10m	olive green	.40	.25
451	A146	10m	dark blue	.40	.25
a.			Strip of 5, #447-451	2.75	2.75

Souvenir Sheet

Imperf

452 A147 50m grn, dp car & blk 16.00 14.00

Revolution of July 23, 1952, 6th anniv.

Sayed Darwich — A148

1958, Sept. 15 *Perf. 13½x13*

453 A148 10m violet brown .50 .25

35th anniv. of the death of Sayed Darwich, Arab composer.

Hand Holding Torch, Broken Chain and Flag — A149

1958, Oct. 14 Photo. Wmk. 318

454 A149 10m carmine rose .40 .25

Establishment of the Republic of Iraq. See Syria-UAR No. 13.

Maps and Cogwheels — A150

1958, Dec. 8 ***Perf. 13x13½***

455 A150 10m blue .50 .25

Issued to publicize the Economic Conference of Afro-Asian Countries, Cairo, Dec. 8.

Ovptd. in Red in English and Arabic in 3 Lines "Industrial and Agricultural Production Fair"

1958, Dec. 9

456 A150 10m lt red brown .50 .25

Issued to publicize the Industrial and Agricultural Production Fair, Cairo, Dec. 9.

Dr. Mahmoud Azmy and UN Emblem A151

1958, Dec. 10

457 A151 10m dull violet .45 .25
458 A151 35m green 1.00 .75

10th anniv. of the signing of the Universal Declaration of Human Rights.
For overprints see Nos. N70-N71.

University Building, Sphinx, "Education" and God Thoth — A152

1958, Dec. 21 Photo. Wmk. 318

459 A152 10m grnsh black .40 .25

50th anniversary of Cairo University.

No. 337 Surcharged

1959, Jan. 20 Wmk. 195 ***Perf. 13½***

460 A112 55m on 100m henna brn 3.00 .75

For overprint see No. N72.

Emblem A153

1959, Feb. 2 ***Perf. 13x13½***

461 A153 10m lt olive green .35 .25

Afro-Asian Youth Conf., Cairo, Feb. 2.

See Syria UAR issues for stamps of designs A141, A149, A154, A156, A157, A162, A170, A172, A173, A179 with denominations in piasters (p).

Arms of UAR — A154

Perf. 13½x13

1959, Feb. 22 Photo. Wmk. 318

462 A154 10m green, blk & red .35 .25

First anniversary, United Arab Republic. See Syria UAR No. 17.

Nile Hilton Hotel A155

1959, Feb. 22 ***Perf. 13x13½***

463 A155 10m dark gray .35 .25

Opening of the Nile Hilton Hotel, Cairo.

Globe, Radio and Telegraph A156

1959, Mar. 1

464 A156 10m violet .40 .25

Arab Union of Telecommunications. See Syria-UAR Nos. C20-C21.

United Arab States Issue

Flags of UAR and Yemen A157

1959, Mar. 8

465 A157 10m sl grn, car & blk .35 .25

First anniversary of United Arab States. See Syria-UAR No. 16.

Oil Derrick and Pipe Line — A158

Perf. 13½x13

1959, Apr. 16 Litho. Wmk. 318

466 A158 10m lt bl & dk bl .65 .25

First Arab Petroleum Congress, Cairo.

Railroad A159

Designs: No. 468, Bus on highway. No. 469, River barge. No. 470, Ocean liner. No. 471, Telecommunications on map. No. 472, Stamp printing building, Heliopolis. No. 472A, Ship, train, plane and motorcycle mail carrier.

1959, July 23 Photo. ***Perf. 13x13½***

Frame in Gray

467	A159 10m maroon		1.10	.50
468	A159 10m green		1.10	.50
469	A159 10m violet		1.10	.50
470	A159 10m dark blue		1.10	.50
471	A159 10m dull purple		1.10	.50
472	A159 10m scarlet		1.10	.50
	Nos. 467-472 (6)		6.60	3.00

Souvenir Sheet

Imperf

472A A159 50m green & red *12.00 12.00*

No. 472A for the 7th anniv. of the Egyptian revolution of 1952 and was sold only with 5 sets of Nos. 467-472.

Globe, Swallows and Map — A160

1959, Aug. 8 ***Perf. 13½x13***

473 A160 10m maroon .40 .25

Convention of the Assoc. of Arab Emigrants in the US.

Types of 1953-58 without "Egypt" and

St. Simon's Gate, Bosra, Syria — A161

Designs: 1m, Farmer's wife. 2m, Ibn-Tulun's Mosque. 3m, Princess Nofret. 4m, 14th century glass lamp (design lacks "1963" of A217). 5m, "Industry" (factories and cogwheel). 10m, Ramses II. 15m, Omayyad Mosque, Damascus. 20m, Lotus vase, Tutankhamun treasure. 35m, Eagle, ship and cargo. 40m, Scribe statue. 45m, Saladin's citadel, Aleppo. 55m, Eagle, cotton and wheat. 60m, Dam and factory. 100m, Eagle, hand, cotton and grain. 200m, Palmyra ruins, Syria. 500m, Queen Nefertiti, inscribed "UAR" (no ovpt.).

Perf. 13½x14, 14x13½

1959-60 Wmk. 328 Photo.

474	A136	1m	vermilion	.25	.25
475	A138	2m	dp blue ('60)	.25	.25
476	A143	3m	maroon	.25	.25
477	A217	4m	green ('60)	.25	.25
478	A138	5m	black ('60)	.25	.25
479	A137	10m	dk ol grn	.30	.25
480	A138	15m	deep claret	.30	.25
481	A138	20m	crimson ('60)	.90	.25
482	A161	30m	brown vio	.65	.25
483	A138	35m	lt vio bl ('60)	.75	.25
484	A143	40m	sepia	1.10	.25
485	A161	45m	lil gray ('60)	2.25	.35
486	A138	55m	brt blue grn	2.00	.25
487	A138	60m	dp purple ('60)	2.75	.25
488	A138	100m	org & sl grn ('60)	2.25	.30
489	A161	200m	lt blue & mar	4.50	.50
490	A112	500m	dk gray & red ('60)	14.00	1.60
			Nos. 474-490 (17)	33.00	6.00

See Nos. 532-535.

Shield and Cogwheel — A162

Perf. 13½x13

1959, Oct. 20 Photo. Wmk. 328

491 A162 10m brt car rose .35 .25

Issued for Army Day, 1959. See Syria-UAR No. 32.

Cairo Museum A163

1959, Nov. 18 ***Perf. 13x13½***

492 A163 10m olive gray .40 .25

Centenary of Cairo museum.

Abu Simbel Temple of Ramses II — A164

1959, Dec. 22 ***Perf. 11x11½***

493 A164 10m lt red brn, *pnksh* .70 .30

Issued as propaganda to save historic monuments in Nubia threatened by the construction of Aswan High Dam.

Postrider, 12th Century A165

1960, Jan. 2 ***Perf. 13x13½***

494 A165 10m dark blue .35 .25

Issued for Post Day, Jan. 2.

Hydroelectric Power Station, Aswan Dam — A166

1960, Jan. 9

495 A166 10m violet blk .35 .25

Inauguration of the Aswan Dam hydroelectric power station, Jan. 9.

A167

10m, Arabic and English Description of Aswan High Dam. 35m, Architect's Drawing of Aswan High Dam.

1960, Jan. 9 ***Perf. 11x11½***

496 10m claret .75 .60
497 35m claret 1.10 .75
a. A167 Pair, #496-497 2.00 2.00

Start of work on the Aswan High Dam.

Symbols of Agriculture and Industry — A169

1960, Jan. 16 ***Perf. 13½x13***

498 A169 10m gray grn & sl grn .35 .25

Industrial and Agricultural Fair, Cairo.

Arms and Flag — A170

1960, Feb. 22 Photo. Wmk. 328

499 A170 10m green, blk & red .35 .25

2nd anniversary of the proclamation of the United Arab Republic.
See Syria-UAR No. 38.

No. 340 Overprinted in Red

1960 Wmk. 195 ***Perf. 13½***

500 A112 £1 dk grn, blk & red 19.00 4.25

"Art" — A171

Perf. 13½x13

1960, Mar. 1 Wmk. 328

501 A171 10m brown .35 .25

Issued to publicize the 3rd Biennial Exhibition of Fine Arts in Alexandria.

Arab League Center, Cairo A172

1960, Mar. 22 Photo. ***Perf. 13x13½***

502 A172 10m dull grn & blk .35 .25

Opening of Arab League Center and Arab Postal Museum, Cairo.
See Syria-UAR No. 40.

Refugees Pointing to Map of Palestine A173

1960, Apr. 7

503 A173 10m orange ver .55 .30
504 A173 35m Prus blue .80 .65

World Refugee Year, 7/1/59-6/30/60.
See Nos. N73-N74. See also Syria-UAR Nos. 43-44.

Weight Lifter — A174

Stadium, Cairo — A175

Sports: No. 506, Basketball. No. 507, Soccer. No. 508, Fencing. No. 509, Rowing. 30m, Steeplechase, horiz. 35m, Swimming, horiz.

Perf. 13½x13

1960, July 23 Photo. Wmk. 328

505 A174 5m gray .60 .30
506 A174 5m brown .60 .30
507 A174 5m dp claret .60 .30
508 A174 10m brt carmine .60 .30
509 A174 10m gray green .60 .30
a. Vert. or horiz. strip, #505-509 3.75
510 A174 30m purple .85 .50
511 A174 35m dark blue 1.10 .60
Nos. 505-511 (7) 4.95 2.60

Souvenir Sheet

Imperf

512 A175 100m car & brown 3.25 3.25

Nos. 505-511 for the 17th Olympic Games, Rome, Aug. 25-Sept. 11.

Dove and UN Emblem — A176

35m, Lights surrounding UN emblem, horiz.

Perf. 13½x13

1960, Oct. 24 Wmk. 328

513 A176 10m purple .25 .25
514 A176 35m brt rose .50 .30

15th anniversary of United Nations.

Abu Simbel Temple of Queen Nefertari — A177

Perf. 11x11½

1960, Nov. 14 Photo. Wmk. 328

515 A177 10m ocher, *buff* .80 .50

Issued as propaganda to save historic monuments in Nubia and in connection with the UNESCO meeting, Paris, Nov. 14.

Model Post Office A178

1961, Jan. 2 ***Perf. 13x13½***

516 A178 10m brt car rose .40 .25

Issued for Post Day, Jan. 2.

Eagle, Fasces and Victory Wreath — A179

1961, Feb. 22 ***Perf. 13½x13***

517 A179 10m dull violet .35 .25

3rd anniversary of United Arab Republic.
See Syria-UAR No. 50.

Wheat and Globe Surrounded by Flags — A180

1961, Mar. 21 Wmk. 328

518 A180 10m vermilion .35 .25

Intl. Agricultural Exhib., Cairo, 3/21-4/20.

Patrice Lumumba and Map — A181

1961, Mar. 30 ***Perf. 13½x13***

519 A181 10m black .35 .25

Africa Day, Apr. 15 and 3rd Conf. of Independent African States, Cairo, Mar. 25-31.

Reading Braille and WHO Emblem — A182

1961, Apr. 6 Photo.

520 A182 10m red brown .35 .25

WHO Day. See Nos. B21, N80.

Tower of Cairo — A183

1961, Apr. 11 ***Perf. 13½x13***

521 A183 10m grnsh blue .35 .25

Opening of the 600-foot Tower of Cairo, on island of Gizireh. See No. C95.

Arab Woman and Son, Palestine Map — A184

1961, May 15 Wmk. 328

522 A184 10m brt green .45 .30

Issued for Palestine Day.
See No. N79.

Symbols of Industry and Electricity A185

Chart and Workers — A186

No. 524, New buildings and family. No. 525, Ship, train, bus and radio. No. 526, Dam, cotton and field. No. 527, Hand holding candle and family.

1961, July 23 Photo. ***Perf. 13x13½***

523 A185 10m dp carmine .65 .30
524 A185 10m brt blue .65 .30
525 A185 10m dk vio brown .65 .30
526 A185 35m dk green .85 .40
527 A185 35m brt purple .85 .40
Nos. 523-527 (5) 3.65 1.70

Souvenir Sheet

Imperf

528 A186 100m red brown 4.00 3.75

9th anniv. of the revolution.

Map of Suez Canal and Ships — A187

Perf. 11½x11

1961, July 26 **Unwmk.**

529 A187 10m olive .50 .30

Suez Canal Co. nationalization, 5th anniv.

Various Enterprises of Misr Bank — A188

Perf. 13x13½

1961, Aug. 22 **Wmk. 328**

530 A188 10m red brn, *pnksh* .35 .25

The 41st anniversary of Misr Bank.

Flag, Ship's Wheel and Battleship — A189

1961, Aug. 29 **Photo.** ***Perf. 13½x13***

531 A189 10m deep blue .45 .25

Issued for Navy Day.

Type A136 Redrawn, Type A138, Type A217 and

Eagle of Saladin over Cairo — A190

Designs: 1m, Farmer's wife. 4m, 14th cent. glass lamp. 35m, "Commerce."

1961, Aug. 31 **Unwmk.** ***Perf. 11½***

532	A136	1m blue	.25	.25
533	A217	4m olive	.25	.25
534	A190	10m purple	.40	.25
535	A138	35m slate blue	.70	.25
		Nos. 532-535 (4)	1.60	1.00

Smaller of two Arabic inscriptions in new positions: 1m, at right above Egyptian numeral; 4m, upward to spot beside waist of lamp; 35m, upper left corner below "UAR." On 4m, "UAR" is 2mm deep instead of 1mm. "Egypt" omitted as in 1959-60.

UN Emblem, Book, Cogwheel, Corn — A191

Design: 35m, Globe and cogwheel, horiz.

Perf. 13½x13

1961, Oct. 24 **Photo.** **Wmk. 328**

536 A191 10m black & ocher .30 .25

537 A191 35m blue grn & brn .65 .35

UN Technical Assistance Program and 16th anniv. of the UN.

See Nos. N81-N82.

Trajan's Kiosk, Philae — A192

1961, Nov. 4 **Unwmk.** ***Perf. 11½***

Size: 60x27mm

538 A192 10m dp vio blue .85 .40

15th anniv. of UNESCO, and to publicize UNESCO's help in safeguarding the monuments of Nubia.

Palette, Brushes, Map of Mediterranean A193

1961, Dec. 14 **Wmk. 328** ***Perf. 13½***

539 A193 10m dk red brown .35 .25

Issued to publicize the 4th Biennial Exhibition of Fine Arts in Alexandria.

Atom and Educational Symbols — A194

1961, Dec. 18

540 A194 10m dull purple .35 .25

Issued to publicize Education Day.

See No. N83.

Arms of UAR A195

1961, Dec. 23 **Unwmk.** ***Perf. 11½***

541 A195 10m brt pink, brt grn & blk .35 .25

Victory Day. See No. N84.

Sphinx at Giza — A196

1961, Dec. 27 ***Perf. 11x11½***

542 A196 10m black .55 .35

Issued to publicize the "Sound and Light" Project, the installation of floodlights and sound equipment at the site of the Pyramids and Sphinx.

Post Office Printing Plant, Nasser City A197

1962, Jan. 2 **Photo.** ***Perf. 11½x11***

543 A197 10m dk brown .40 .25

Issued for Post Day, Jan. 2.

Map of Africa, King Mohammed V of Morocco and Flags — A198

1962, Jan. 4 ***Perf. 11x11½***

544 A198 10m indigo .35 .25

African Charter, Casablanca, 1st anniv.

Girl Scout Saluting and Emblem A199

Perf. 13x13½

1962, Feb. 22 **Wmk. 328**

545 A199 10m bright blue .95 .30

Egyptian Girl Scouts' 25th anniversary.

Arab Refugees, Flag and Map — A200

1962, Mar. 7 ***Perf. 13½x13***

546 A200 10m dark slate green .40 .25

5th anniv. of the liberation of the Gaza Strip.

See No. N85.

Mother and Child — A201

1962, Mar. 21 **Photo.**

547 A201 10m dk violet brn .40 .25

Issued for Arab Mother's Day, Mar. 21.

Map of Africa and Post Horn — A202

1962, Apr. 23 **Wmk. 328**

548 A202 10m crimson & ocher .40 .30

549 A202 50m dp blue & ocher .80 .55

Establishment of African Postal Union.

Cadets on Parade and Academy Emblem A203

1962, June 18 ***Perf. 13x13½***

550 A203 10m green .35 .25

Egyptian Military Academy, 150th anniv.

Malaria Eradication Emblem — A204

1962, June 20 ***Perf. 13½x13***

551 A204 10m dk brown & red .25 .25

552 A204 35m dk green & blue .70 .50

WHO drive to eradicate malaria.

See Nos. N87-N88.

Theodor Bilharz — A205

1962, June 24 ***Perf. 11x11½***

553 A205 10m brown orange .55 .25

Dr. Theodor Bilharz (1825-1862), German physician who first described bilharziasis, an endemic disease in Egypt.

Patrice Lumumba and Map of Africa — A206

1962, July 1 **Photo.** **Wmk. 342**

554 A206 10m rose & red .35 .25

Issued in memory of Patrice Lumumba (1925-61), Premier of Congo.

Hand on Charter — A207

1962, July 10 ***Perf. 11x11½***

555 A207 10m brt blue & dk brn .35 .25

Proclamation of the National Charter.

"Birth of the Revolution" A208

Symbolic Designs: No. 557, Proclamation (Scroll and book). No. 558, Agricultural Reform (Farm and crescent). No. 559, Bandung Conference (Dove, globe and olive branch). No. 560, Birth of UAR (Eagle and flag). No. 561, Industrialization (cogwheel, factory, ship and bus). No. 562, Aswan High Dam. No. 563, Social Revolution (Modern buildings and emblem). 100m, Arms of UAR, emblems of Afro-Asian and African countries and UN.

1962, July 23 ***Perf. 11½***

556 A208 10m brn, dk red brn & pink .40 .30
557 A208 10m dk blue & sepia .40 .30
558 A208 10m sepia & brt bl .40 .30
559 A208 10m olive & dk ultra .40 .30
560 A208 10m grn, blk & red .40 .30
561 A208 10m brn org & indigo .40 .30
562 A208 10m brn org & vio blk .40 .30
563 A208 10m orange & blk .40 .30
Nos. 556-563 (8) 3.20 2.40

Souvenir Sheets

Perf. 11½

564 A208 100m grn, pink, red & blk 2.75 2.50

10th anniv. of the revolution.
No. 564 exists imperf. Same value.

Mahmoud Moukhtar, Museum and Sculpture A209

1962, July 24 ***Perf. 11½x11***

565 A209 10m lt vio bl & olive .40 .25

Opening of the Moukhtar Museum, Island of Gezireh. The sculpture is "La Vestale de Secrets" by Moukhtar.

Flag of Algeria and Map of Africa Showing Algeria — A210

1962, Aug. 15 ***Perf. 11x11½***

566 A210 10m multicolored .35 .25

Algeria's independence, July 1, 1962.

Rocket, Arms of UAR and Atom Symbol — A211

1962, Sept. 1 Photo. Wmk. 342

567 A211 10m brt grn, red & blk .45 .25

Launching of UAR rockets.

Rifle and Target — A212

Map of Africa, Table Tennis Paddle, Net and Ball — A213

1962, Sept. 18 ***Perf. 11½***

568 A212 5m green, blk & red .55 .45
569 A213 5m green, blk & red .55 .45
a. Pair, #568-569 1.25 1.25
570 A212 10m bister, bl & dk grn .65 .55
571 A213 10m bister, bl & dk grn .65 .55
a. Pair, #570-571 1.50 1.50
572 A212 35m dp ultra, red & blk 1.50 1.50
573 A213 35m dp ultra, red & blk 1.50 1.50
a. Pair, #572-573 3.25 3.25
Nos. 568-573 (6) 5.40 5.00

38th World Shooting Championships and the 1st African Table Tennis Tournament. Types A212 and A213 are printed se-tenant at the base.

Dag Hammarskjold and UN Emblem — A214

Perf. 11½x11

1962, Oct. 24 Photo. Wmk. 342

Portrait in Slate Blue

574 A214 5m deep lilac .65 .25
575 A214 10m olive .75 .25
576 A214 35m deep ultra 1.10 .50
Nos. 574-576 (3) 2.50 1.00

Dag Hammarskjold, Secretary General of the UN, 1953-61, and 17th anniv. of the UN.
See Nos. N89-N91.

Queen Nefertari Crowned by Isis and Hathor — A215

1962, Oct. 31 ***Perf. 11½***

577 A215 10m blue & ocher 1.25 .40

Issued to publicize the UNESCO campaign to safeguard the monuments of Nubia.

Jet Trainer, Hawker Hart Biplane and College Emblem A216

1962, Nov. 2 ***Perf. 11½x11***

578 A216 10m bl, dk bl & crim .40 .25

25th anniversary of Air Force College.

14th Century Glass Lamp and "1963" — A217

1963, Feb. 20 ***Perf. 11x11½***

579 A217 4m dk brn, grn & car .35 .25

Issued for use on greeting cards.
See Nos. 441, 477, 533, N76, N92. For overprint see No. N65.

Yemen Flag and Hand with Torch — A218

1963, Mar. 14 Photo. Wmk. 342

580 A218 10m olive & brt car .45 .25

Establishment of Yemen Arab Republic.

Tennis Player, Pyramids and Globe A219

Perf. 11½x11

1963, Mar. 20 Unwmk.

581 A219 10m gray, blk & brn .75 .30

Intl. Lawn Tennis Championships, Cairo.

Cow, UN and FAO Emblems A220

Designs: 10m, Corn, wheat and emblems, vert. 35m, Wheat, corn and emblems.

Perf. 11½x11, 11x11½

1963, Mar. 21 Wmk. 342

582 A220 5m violet & dp org .45 .30
583 A220 10m ultra & yel .55 .30
584 A220 35m blue, yel & blk .75 .75
Nos. 582-584 (3) 1.75 1.35

FAO "Freedom from Hunger" campaign.
See Nos. N93-N95.

Centenary Emblem — A221

Design: 35m, Globe and emblem.

1963, May 8 Unwmk. ***Perf. 11x11½***

585 A221 10m lt blue, red & mar .30 .25
586 A221 35m lt blue & red .85 .85

Centenary of the Red Cross.
See Nos. N96-N97.

Arab Socialist Union Emblem A222

50m, Tools, torch & symbol of National Charter.

Wmk. 342

1963, July 23 Photo. ***Perf. 11½***

587 A222 10m slate & rose pink .35 .25

Souvenir Sheets

Perf. 11½

588 A222 50m vio bl & org yel 2.25 2.25

11th anniv. of the revolution and to publicize the Arab Socialist Union.
No. 588 exists imperf. Same value.

Television Station, Cairo, and Screen A223

1963, Aug. 1 ***Perf. 11½x11***

589 A223 10m dk blue & yel .35 .25

2nd Intl. Television Festival, Alexandria, 9/1-10.

Queen Nefertari — A224

Designs: 10m, Great Hypostyle Hall, Abu Simbel. 35m, Ramses in moonlight.

Size: 25x42mm (5m, 35m); 28x61mm (10m)

Wmk. 342

1963, Oct. 1 Photo. ***Perf. 11***

590 A224 5m brt vio blue & yel .65 .40
591 A224 10m gray, blk & red org .75 .45
592 A224 35m org yel & blk 1.60 .85
Nos. 590-592 (3) 3.00 1.70

UNESCO world campaign to save historic monuments in Nubia.
See Nos. N98-N100.

Swimmer and Map of Suez Canal — A225

1963, Oct. 15

593 A225 10m blue & sal rose .35 .25

Intl. Suez Canal Swimming Championship.

Ministry of Agriculture — A226

Perf. 11½x11

1963, Nov. 20 Wmk. 342

594 A226 10m multicolored .35 .25

50th anniv. of the Ministry of Agriculture.

Modern Building and Map of Africa and Asia A227

1963, Dec. 7

595 A227 10m multicolored .35 .25

Afro-Asian Housing Congress, Dec. 7-12.

Scales, Globe, UN Emblem A228

1963, Dec. 10

596	A228	5m dk green & yel	.30	.25
597	A228	10m blue, gray & blk	.35	.25
598	A228	35m rose red, pink & red	.85	.45
		Nos. 596-598 (3)	1.50	.95

15th anniv. of the Universal Declaration of Human Rights.
See Nos. N101-N103.

Sculpture, Arms of Alexandria and Palette with Flags — A229

1963, Dec. 12 *Perf. 11x11½*

599 A229 10m pale bl, dk bl & brn .35 .25

Issued to publicize the 5th Biennial Exhibition of Fine Arts in Alexandria.

Lion and Nile Hilton Hotel — A230

Vase, 13th Century — A231

Pharaoh Userkaf (5th Dynasty) A232

Designs: 1m, Long Necked Mamluke glass bottle, 14th century. 2m, Ivory headrest. 3m, Pharaonic calcite boat. 4m, Minaret and gate. 5m, Nile and Aswan High Dam. 10m, Eagle of Saladin over pyramids. 15m, Window, Ibn Tulun's mosque. No. 608, Mitwalli Gate, Cairo. 35m, Nefertari. 40m, Tower Hotel. 55m, Sultan Hassan's Mosque. 60m, Courtyard, Al Azhar University. 200m, Head of Ramses II. 500m, Funerary mask of Tutankhamun.

1964-67 Unwmk. Photo. *Perf. 11*

Size: Nos. 608, 612, 19x24mm; others, 24x29mm

600	A231	1m citron & ultra	.25	.25
601	A230	2m magenta & bis	.25	.25
602	A230	3m sal, org & bl	.25	.25
603	A235	4m och, blk & ultra	.35	.25
604	A230	5m brn & brt blue	.25	.25
a.		5m brown & dark blue	.50	.25
605	A231	10m green, dk brn & lt brn	.30	.25
606	A230	15m ultra & yel	.30	.25
607	A230	20m brn org & blk	.90	.25
608	A231	20m lt olive grn ('67)	1.60	.25
609	A231	30m yellow & brown	.75	.25
610	A231	35m sal, och & ultra	.90	.25
611	A231	40m ultra & yellow	1.75	.40
612	A231	55m brt red lil ('67)	2.00	.25
613	A231	60m grnsh bl & yel brn	1.25	.55

Wmk. 342

614	A232	100m dk vio brn & sl	3.50	.85
615	A232	200m bluish blk & yel brn	8.00	1.00
616	A232	500m ultra & dp org	17.50	3.25
		Nos. 600-616 (17)	40.10	9.05

Nos. 603 & N107 lack the vertically arranged dates which appear at lower right on No. 619.
See Nos. N104-N116.

HSN Commission Emblem — A233

Perf. 11x11½

1964, Jan. 10 Wmk. 342

617 A233 10m dull bl, dk bl & yel .35 .25

1st conf. of the Commission of Health, Sanitation and Nutrition.

Arab League Emblem — A234

1964, Jan. 13 *Perf. 11*

618 A234 10m brt green & blk .35 .25

1st meeting of the Heads of State of the Arab League, Cairo, January.
See No. N117.

Minaret at Night — A235

1964 Unwmk. *Perf. 11*

619 A235 4m emerald, blk & red .35 .25

Issued for use on greeting cards.
See Nos. 603, N107, N118.

Old and New Dwellings and Map of Nubia A236

Perf. 11½x11

1964, Feb. 27 Photo. Wmk. 342

620 A236 10m dull vio & yel .35 .25

Resettlement of Nubian population.

Map of Africa and Asia and Train A237

1964, Mar. 21

621 A237 10m dull bl, dk bl & yel .90 .50

Asian Railway Conference, Cairo, Mar. 21.

Ikhnaton and Nefertiti with Children — A238

1964, Mar. 21 *Perf. 11x11½*

622 A238 10m dk brown & ultra .90 .30

Issued for Arab Mother's Day, Mar. 21.

APU Emblem — A239

1964, Apr. 1 Photo. Wmk. 342

623 A239 10m org brn & bl, *sal* .35 .25

Permanent Office of the APU, 10th anniv.
See No. N119.

WHO Emblem — A240

1964, Apr. 7

624 A240 10m dk blue & red .35 .25

World Health Day (Anti-Tuberculosis).
See No. N120.

Statue of Liberty, World's Fair Pavilion and Pyramids A241

1964, Apr. 22 *Perf. 11½x11*

625 A241 10m brt green & ol, *grysh* .35 .25

New York World's Fair, 1964-65.

Nile and Aswan High Dam A242

1964, May 15 Unwmk. *Perf. 11½*

626 A242 10m black & blue .35 .25

The diversion of the Nile.

"Land Reclamation" — A243

A423a

Design: No. 628, "Electricity," Aswan High Dam hydroelectric station. No. 628A, Aswan High Dam before and after diversion of the Nile.

1964, July 23 *Perf. 11½*

627	A243	10m yellow & emer	.35	.25
628	A243	10m green & blk	.35	.25

Souvenir Sheet

Imperf

628A A243a 50m blue & black 2.00 2.00

Land reclamation and hydroelectric power due to the Aswan High Dam.

Map of Africa and 34 Flags — A244

1964, July 17 Photo.

629 A244 10m brn, brt bl & blk .40 .25

Assembly of Heads of State and Government of the Organization for African Unity at Cairo in July.

Jamboree Emblem — A245

Design: No. 631, Emblem of Air Scouts.

1964, Aug. 28 Unwmk. *Perf. 11½*

630 A245 10m red, grn & blk .60 .40
631 A245 10m green & red .60 .40
a. Pair, #630-631 2.50 2.50

The 6th Pan Arab Jamboree, Alexandria.

Flag of Algeria
A246

1964, Sept. 5 *Perf. 11½x11*

Flags in Original Colors

632 A246 10m Algeria .75 .40
633 A246 10m Iraq .75 .40
634 A246 10m Jordan .75 .40
635 A246 10m Kuwait .75 .40
636 A246 10m Lebanon .75 .40
637 A246 10m Libya .75 .40
638 A246 10m Morocco .75 .40
639 A246 10m Saudi Arabia .75 .40
640 A246 10m Sudan .75 .40
641 A246 10m Syria .75 .40
642 A246 10m Tunisia .75 .40
643 A246 10m UAR .75 .40
644 A246 10m Yemen .75 .40
Nos. 632-644 (13) 9.75 5.20

2nd meeting of the Heads of State of the Arab League, Alexandria, Sept. 1964.

World Map, Dove, Olive Branches and Pyramids — A247

1964, Oct. 5 *Perf. 11½*

645 A247 10m slate blue & yel .35 .25

Conference of Heads of State of Non-Aligned Countries, Cairo, Oct. 1964.

Pharaonic Athletes
A248

Designs from ancient decorations: 10m, Four athletes, vert. 35m, Wrestlers, vert. 50m, Pharaoh in chariot hunting.

Perf. 11½x11, 11x11½

1964, Oct. 10 Photo. Unwmk.

Sizes: 39x22mm, 22x39mm

646 A248 5m lt green & org .40 .25
647 A248 10m slate bl & lt brn .45 .25
648 A248 35m dull vio & lt brn 1.10 .75

Size: 58x24mm

649 A248 50m ultra & brn org 1.75 1.00
Nos. 646-649 (4) 3.70 2.25

18th Olympic Games Tokyo, Oct. 10-25.

Emblem, Map of Africa and Asia — A249

1964, Oct. 10 *Perf. 11x11½*

650 A249 10m violet & yellow .35 .25

First Afro-Asian Medical Congress.

Map of Africa, Communication Symbols — A250

1964, Oct. 24

651 A250 10m green & dp sepia .35 .25

Pan-African and Malagasy Posts and Telecommunications Cong., Cairo, Oct. 24-Nov. 6.

Horus and Facade of Nefertari Temple, Abu Simbel
A251

Ramses II — A252

Designs: 35m, A god holding rope of life, Abu Simbel. 50m, Isis of Kalabsha, horiz.

1964, Oct. 24 *Perf. 11½, 11x11½*

652 A251 5m grnsh bl & yel brn .70 .35
653 A252 10m sepia & brt yel 1.10 .40
654 A251 35m brown org & indigo 2.50 1.25
Nos. 652-654 (3) 4.30 2.00

Souvenir Sheet

Imperf

655 A252 50m olive & vio blk 15.00 15.00

"Save the Monuments of Nubia" campaign. No. 655 contains one horiz. stamp.

Emblems of Cooperation, Rural Handicraft and Women's Work — A253

Perf. 11½x11

1964, Dec. 8 Photo. Unwmk.

656 A253 10m yellow & dk blue .35 .25

25th anniv. of the Ministry of Social Affairs.

UN, UNESCO Emblems, Pyramids — A254

1964, Dec. 24 *Perf. 11x11½*

657 A254 10m ultra & yellow .35 .25

Issued for UNESCO Day.

Minaret, Mardani Mosque — A255

1965, Jan. 20 Photo. *Perf. 11*

658 A255 4m blue & dk brown .35 .25

Issued for use on greeting cards.
See No. N121.

Police Emblem over City — A256

Perf. 11x11½

1965, Jan. 25 Wmk. 342

659 A256 10m dp sepia & yellow .85 .40

Issued for Police Day.

Oil Derrick and Emblem — A257

1965, Mar. 16 Photo.

660 A257 10m dk brown & yellow .45 .25

5th Arab Petroleum Congress and the 2nd Arab Petroleum Exhibition.

Flags and Emblem of the Arab League — A258

Design: 20m, Arab League emblem, horiz.

1965, Mar. 22 Wmk. 342

661 A258 10m green, red & blk .80 .40
662 A258 20m ultra & brown 1.00 .55

20th anniversary of the Arab League.
See Nos. N122-N123.

Red Crescent and WHO Emblem — A259

1965, Apr. 7 Photo.

663 A259 10m blue & crimson .55 .35

World Health Day (Smallpox: Constant Alert).
See No. N124.

Dagger in Map of Palestine — A260

1965, Apr. 9 *Perf. 11x11½*

664 A260 10m black & red 1.50 .35

Deir Yassin massacre, Apr. 9, 1948.
See No. N125.

ITU Emblem, Old and New Communication Equipment — A261

1965, May 17 *Perf. 11½x11*

665 A261 5m violet blk & yel .40 .30
666 A261 10m red & yellow .65 .30
667 A261 35m dk blue, ultra & yel 1.75 .80
Nos. 665-667 (3) 2.80 1.40

Cent. of the ITU. See Nos. N126-N128.

Library Aflame and Lamp
A262

1965, June 7 Photo. Wmk. 342

668 A262 10m black, grn & red .60 .25

Burning of the Library of Algiers, 6/7/62.

Sheik Mohammed Abdo (1850-1905), Mufti of Egypt — A263

1965, July 11 *Perf. 11x11½*

669 A263 10m Prus blue & bis brn .35 .25

Pouring Ladle (Heavy Industry)
A264

President Gamal Abdel Nasser and Emblems of Arab League, African Unity Organization, Afro-Asian Countries and UN — A265

No. 670, Search for off-shore oil. No. 672, Housing, construction in Nasser City (diamond shaped).

1965, July 23 ***Perf. 11½***

670	A264	10m indigo & lt blue	.85	.50
671	A264	10m brown & yellow	.85	.50
672	A264	10m yel brn & blk	.85	.50
673	A265	100m lt green & blk	5.75	3.25
		Nos. 670-673 (4)	8.30	4.75

13th anniversary of the revolution.

The 100m was printed in sheets of six, consisting of two singles and two vertical pairs. Margins and gutters contain multiple UAR coat of arms in light green. Size: 240x330mm.

4th Pan Arab Games Emblem A266

Map and Emblems of Previous Games — A267

No. 675, Swimmers Zeitun & Abd el Gelil, arms of Alexandria. 35m, Race horse "Saadoon."

Perf. 11½x11; 11½ (#676)

1965, Sept. 2 **Photo.** **Wmk. 342**

674	A266	5m blue & red	.40	.40
675	A266	10m dp blue & dk brn	.65	.30
676	A267	10m org brn & dp bl	.80	.45
677	A266	35m green & brown	1.40	1.00
		Nos. 674-677 (4)	3.25	2.15

4th Pan Arab Games, Cairo, Sept. 2-11. No. 675 for the long-distance swimming competition at Alexandria, a part of the Games.

Map of Arab Countries, Emblem of Arab League and Broken Chain A268

1965, Sept. 13 **Photo.** ***Perf. 11½***

678	A268	10m brown & yellow	.40	.25

3rd Arab Summit Conf., Casablanca, 9/13.

Land Forces Emblem and Sun — A269

Perf. 11x11½

1965, Oct. 20 **Wmk. 342**

679	A269	10m bister brn & blk	.65	.30

Issued for Land Forces Day.

Map of Africa, Torch and Olive Branches — A270

1965, Oct. 21 ***Perf. 11½***

680	A270	10m dull pur & car rose	.40	.25

Assembly of Heads of State of the Organization for African Unity.

Ramses II, Abu Simbel, and ICY Emblem A271

Pillars, Philae, and UN Emblem — A272

Designs: 35m, Two Ramses II statues, Abu Simbel and UNESCO emblem. 50m, Cartouche of Ramses II and ICY emblem, horiz.

Wmk. 342

1965, Oct. 24 **Photo.** ***Perf. 11½***

681	A271	5m yellow & slate grn	1.00	.50
682	A272	10m blue & black	2.00	.50
683	A271	35m dk violet & yel	3.75	2.00
		Nos. 681-683 (3)	6.75	3.00

Souvenir Sheet

Imperf

684	A272	50m brt ultra & dk brn	5.00	4.00

Intl. cooperation in saving the Nubian monuments. No. 684 also for the 20th anniv. of the UN. No. 684 contains one 42x25mm stamp.

Al-Maqrizi, Buildings and Books A273

Perf. 11½x11

1965, Nov. 20 **Photo.** **Wmk. 342**

685	A273	10m olive & dk slate grn	.40	.25

Ahmed Al-Maqrizi (1365-1442), historian.

Flag of UAR, Arms of Alexandria and Art Symbols — A274

1965, Dec. 16 ***Perf. 11x11½***

686	A274	10m multicolored	.40	.25

6th Biennial Exhibition of Fine Arts in Alexandria, Dec. 16, 1965-Mar. 31, 1966.

Parchment Letter, Carrier Pigeon and Postrider A275

1966, Jan. 2 **Wmk. 342** ***Perf. 11½***

687	A275	10m multicolored	.80	.25
		Nos. 687,CB1-CB2 (3)	8.30	6.50

Post Day, Jan. 2.

Lamp and Arch — A276

1966, Jan. 10 **Unwmk.** ***Perf. 11***

688	A276	4m violet & dp org	.40	.25

Issued for use on greeting cards.

Exhibition Poster — A277

Perf. 11x11½

1966, Jan. 27 **Wmk. 342**

689	A277	10m lt blue & blk	.40	.25

Industrial Exhibition, Jan. 29-Feb.

Arab League Emblem — A278

1966, Mar. 22 **Photo.** **Wmk. 342**

690	A278	10m brt yellow & pur	.40	.25

Arab Publicity Week, Mar. 22-28.

Printed Page and Torch — A279

1966, Mar. 25 ***Perf. 11x11½***

691	A279	10m dp orange & sl blue	.40	.25

Centenary of the national press.

Traffic Signal at Night — A280

1966, May 4 **Photo.** **Wmk. 342**

692	A280	10m green & red	.85	.25

Issued for Traffic Day.

Hands Holding Torch, Flags of UAR & Iraq — A281

1966, May 26 ***Perf. 11x11½***

693	A281	10m dp claret, rose red & brt grn	.40	.25

Friendship between UAR and Iraq.

Workers and UN Emblem A282

Perf. 11½x11

1966, June 1 **Photo.** **Wmk. 342**

694	A282	5m blue grn & blk	.35	.25
695	A282	10m brt rose lil & grn	.40	.25
696	A282	35m orange & black	1.25	.85
		Nos. 694-696 (3)	2.00	1.35

50th session of the ILO.

Mobilization Dept. Emblem, People and City — A283

1966, June 30 ***Perf. 11x11½***
697 A283 10m dull pur & brn .35 .25

Population sample, May 31-June 16.

"Salah el Din," Crane and Cogwheel A284

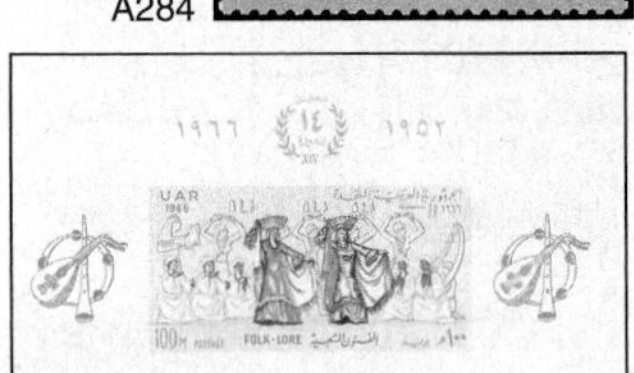

Present-day Basket Dance and Pharaonic Dance — A285

No. 699, Transfer of first stones of Abu Simbel. No. 700, Development of Sinai (map of Red Sea area and Sinai Peninsula). No. 701, El Maadi Hospital and nurse with patient.

Wmk. 342
1966, July 23 **Photo.** ***Perf. 11½***

698	A284	10m orange & multi	.65	.30
699	A284	10m brt green & multi	.65	.30
700	A284	10m yellow & multi	.65	.30
701	A284	10m lt blue & multi	.65	.30
		Nos. 698-701 (4)	2.60	1.20

Souvenir Sheet
Imperf
702 A285 100m multicolored 5.00 3.75

14th anniv. of the revolution.

Suez Canal Headquarters, Ships and Map of Canal — A286

1966, July 26 ***Perf. 11½***
703 A286 10m blue & crimson 1.10 .50

Suez Canal nationalization, 10th anniv.

Cotton, Farmers with Plow and Tractor A287

Perf. 11½x11
1966, Sept. 9 **Photo.** **Wmk. 342**

704	A287	5m shown	.35	.25
705	A287	10m Rice	.35	.25
706	A287	35m Onions	1.10	.90
		Nos. 704-706 (3)	1.80	1.40

Issued for Farmer's Day.

WHO Headquarters, Geneva — A288

Designs: 10m, UN refugee emblem. 35m, UNICEF emblem.

Perf. 11½x11
1966, Oct. 24 **Wmk. 342**

707	A288	5m olive & brt pur	.40	.25
708	A288	10m orange & brt pur	.40	.25
709	A288	35m lt blue & brt pur	.90	.80
		Nos. 707-709 (3)	1.70	1.30

21st anniversary of the United Nations.
See Nos. N129-N131.

World Map and Festival Emblem A289

1966, Nov. 8 **Photo.**
710 A289 10m brt purple & yellow .55 .25

5th Intl. Television Festival, Nov. 1-10.

Arms of UAR, Rocket and Pylon A290

1966, Dec. 23 **Wmk. 342** ***Perf. 11½***
711 A290 10m brt grn & car rose .55 .25

Issued for Victory Day.
See No. N132.

Jackal A291

35m, Alabaster head from Tutankhamun treasure.

1967, Jan. 2 **Photo.**

712	A291	10m slate, yel & brn	1.50	.35
713	A291	35m bl, dk vio & ocher	2.75	.70

Issued for Post Day, Jan. 2.

Carnations — A292

1967, Jan. 10 **Unwmk.** ***Perf. 11***
714 A292 4m citron & purple .50 .25

Issued for use on greeting cards.

Workers Planting Tree — A293

Perf. 11x11½
1967, Mar. 15 **Wmk. 342**
715 A293 10m brt green & blk vio .40 .25

Issued to publicize the Tree Festival.

Gamal el-Dine el-Afaghani and Arab League Emblem — A294

1967, Mar. 22 **Photo.** **Wmk. 342**
716 A294 10m dp green & dk brn .40 .25

Arab Publicity Week, Mar. 22-28.
See No. N133.

Census Emblem, Man, Woman and Factory A295

1967, Apr. 23 ***Perf. 11½x11***
717 A295 10m black & dp org .40 .25

First industrial census.

Brickmaking Fresco, Tomb of Rekhmire, Thebes, 1504-1450 B.C. — A296

1967, May 1 **Photo.** **Wmk. 342**
718 A296 10m olive & orange .55 .30

Issued for Labor Day, 1967.
See No. N134.

Ramses II and Queen Nefertari — A297

Design: 35m, Shooting geese, frieze from tomb of Atet at Meidum, c. 2724 B. C.

Perf. 11½x11
1967, June 7 **Photo.** **Wmk. 342**

719	A297	10m multicolored	1.00	.50
720	A297	35m dk green & org	4.25	1.40
		Nos. 719-720,C113-C115 (5)	13.60	6.15

Issued for International Tourist Year, 1967.

President Nasser, Crowd and Map of Palestine A298

1967, June 22 ***Perf. 11½***
721 A298 10m dp org, yel & ol 2.75 1.50

Issued to publicize Arab solidarity for "the defense of Palestine."

Souvenir Sheet

National Products — A299

1967, July 23 **Wmk. 342** ***Imperf.***
722 A299 100m multicolored 4.00 3.50

15th anniv. of the revolution.

Salama Higazi — A300

Perf. 11x11½
1967, Oct. 14 **Photo.** **Wmk. 342**
723 A300 20m brown & dk blue .80 .40

50th anniversary of the death of Salama Higazi, pioneer of Egyptian lyric stage.

Stag on Ceramic Disk A301

Design: 55m, Apse showing Christ in Glory, Madonna and Saints, Coptic Museum, and UNESCO Emblem.

1967, Oct. 24 ***Perf. 11½***

724	A301	20m dull rose & dk bl	.95	.40
725	A301	55m dk slate grn & yel	1.75	.85
		Nos. 724-725,C117 (3)	4.20	2.15

22nd anniv. of the UN.

Savings Bank and Postal Authority Emblems A302

1967, Oct. 31 ***Perf. 11½x11***
726 A302 20m sal pink & dk blue .60 .30

International Savings Day.

Rose — A303

Unwmk.

1967, Dec. 15 Photo. *Perf. 11*

727 A303 5m green & rose lilac .50 .25

Issued for use on greeting cards.

Pharaonic Dress — A304

Designs: Various pharaonic dresses from temple decorations.

Perf. 11x11½

1968, Jan. 2 Wmk. 342

728 A304 20m brown, grn & buff 1.40 .35
729 A304 55m lt grn, yel & sepia 2.25 .85
730 A304 80m dk brn, bl & brt rose 3.75 1.25
Nos. 728-730 (3) 7.40 2.45

Issued for Post Day, Jan. 2.
See Nos. 752-755.

Aswan High Dam and Power Lines — A305

1968, Jan. 9

731 A305 20m yel, bl & dk brn .35 .25

1st electricity generated by the Aswan Hydroelectric Station.

Alabaster Vessel, Tutankhamun Treasure — A306

Capital of Coptic Limestone Pillar A307

Perf. 11x11½, 11½

1968, Jan. 20 Photo. Wmk. 342

732 A306 20m dk ultra, yel & brn .75 .30
733 A307 80m lt grn, dk pur & ol grn 1.60 1.00

2nd International Festival of Museums.

Girl, Moon and Paint Brushes — A308

1968, Feb. 15 *Perf. 11x11½*

734 A308 20m brt blue & black .40 .30

7th Biennial Exhibition of Fine Arts, Alexandria, Feb. 15.

Cattle and Veterinarian — A309

Perf. 11½x11

1968, May 4 Photo. Wmk. 342

735 A309 20m brown, yel & grn .75 .25

8th Arab Veterinary Congress, Cairo.

Human Rights Flame — A310

Perf. 11x11½

1968, July 1 Photo. Wmk. 342

736 A310 20m citron, crim & grn .50 .25
737 A310 60m sky blue, crim & grn 1.00 .90

International Human Rights Year, 1968.

Open Book with Symbols of Science, Victory Election Result A311

Workers, Cogwheel with Coat of Arms and Open Book — A312

1968, July 23 *Perf. 11½*

738 A311 20m rose red & sl grn .50 .25

Souvenir Sheet

Imperf

739 A312 100m lt grn, org & pur 3.25 3.00

16th anniversary of the revolution.

Imhotep and WHO Emblem A313

No. 741, Avicenna and WHO emblem.

Perf. 11½x11

1968, Sept. 1 Photo. Wmk. 342

740 A313 20m blue, yel & brn 1.10 .55
741 A313 20m yellow, bl & brn 1.10 .55
a. Pair, #740-741 3.00 3.00

20th anniv. of the WHO. Nos. 740-741 printed in checkerboard sheets of 50 (5x10).

Table Tennis — A314

Perf. 11x11½

1968, Sept. 20 Photo. Wmk. 342

742 A314 20m lt green & dk brn .90 .35

First Mediterranean Table Tennis Tournament, Alexandria, Sept. 20-27.

Factories and Fair Emblem A315

1968, Oct. 20 Wmk. 342 *Perf. 11½*

743 A315 20m bl gray, red & sl bl .45 .25

Cairo International Industrial Fair.

Temples of Philae — A316

Refugees, Map of Palestine, Refugee Year Emblem A317

55m, Temple at Philae & UNESCO emblem.

1968, Oct. 24 Photo.

744 A316 20m multicolored 1.25 .30
745 A317 30m multicolored 1.75 .85
746 A317 55m lt blue, yel & blk 3.00 1.10
Nos. 744-746 (3) 6.00 2.25

Issued for United Nations Day, Oct. 24.

Egyptian Boy Scout Emblem — A318

1968, Nov. 1

747 A318 10m dull org & vio bl .80 .30

50th anniversary of Egyptian Boy Scouts.

Pharaonic Sports A319

Design: 30m, Pharaonic sports, diff.

1968, Nov. 1

748 A319 20m pale ol, pale sal & blk .80 .25
749 A319 30m pale blue, buff & pur 1.25 .75

19th Olympic Games, Mexico City, 10/12-27.

Aly Moubarak — A320

1968, Nov. 9 *Perf. 11½*

750 A320 20m green, brn & bister .55 .25

Aly Moubarak (1823-93), founder of the modern educational system in Egypt.

Lotus — A321

1968, Dec. 11 Photo. Wmk. 342

751 A321 5m brt blue, grn & yel .55 .25

Issued for use on greeting cards.

Ramses IV — A322

Pharaonic Dress: No. 753, Ramses III. No. 754, Girl carrying basket on her head. 55m, Queen of the New Empire in transparent dress.

1969, Jan. 2 Photo. *Perf. 11½*

752 A322 5m blue & multi .75 .30
753 A322 20m blue & multi 1.25 .50
754 A322 20m blue & multi 1.50 .60
755 A322 55m blue & multi 3.75 1.75
Nos. 752-755 (4) 7.25 3.15

Issued for Post Day, Jan. 2.

Hefni Nassef — A323

Portrait: No. 757, Mohammed Farid.

Perf. 11x11½

1969, Mar. 2 Photo. Wmk. 342

756 A323 20m purple & brown .55 .30
757 A323 20m emerald & brown .55 .30
a. Pair, #756-757 1.25 1.25

50th anniv. of the death of Hefni Nassef (1860-1919) writer and government worker, and Mohammed Farid (1867-1919), lawyer and Speaker of the Nationalist Party.

Teacher and Children — A324

1969, Mar. 2 ***Perf. 11x11½***

758 A324 20m multicolored .55 .25

Arab Teacher's Day.

ILO Emblem and Factory Chimneys — A325

1969, Apr. 11 Photo. Wmk. 342

759 A325 20m brown, ultra & car .55 .25

50th anniv. of the ILO.

A326

Design: Flag of Algeria, Africa Day and Tourist Year Emblems.

Perf. 11½x11

1969, May 25 Litho. Wmk. 342

760 A326 10m Algeria .95 .55
761 A326 10m Botswana .95 .55
762 A326 10m Burundi .95 .55
763 A326 10m Cameroun .95 .55
764 A326 10m Cent. Afr. Rep. .95 .55
765 A326 10m Chad .95 .55
766 A326 10m Congo (Brazzaville) .95 .55
767 A326 10m Congo (Kinshassa) .95 .55
768 A326 10m Dahomey .95 .55
769 A326 10m Equatorial Guinea .95 .55
770 A326 10m Ethiopia .95 .55
771 A326 10m Gabon .95 .55
772 A326 10m Gambia .95 .55
773 A326 10m Ghana .95 .55
774 A326 10m Guinea .95 .55
775 A326 10m Ivory Coast .95 .55
776 A326 10m Kenya .95 .55
777 A326 10m Lesotho .95 .55
778 A326 10m Liberia .95 .55
779 A326 10m Libya .95 .55
780 A326 10m Malagasy .95 .55
781 A326 10m Malawi .95 .55
782 A326 10m Mali .95 .55
783 A326 10m Mauritania .95 .55
784 A326 10m Mauritius .95 .55
785 A326 10m Morocco .95 .55
786 A326 10m Niger .95 .55
787 A326 10m Nigeria .95 .55
788 A326 10m Rwanda .95 .55
789 A326 10m Senegal .95 .55
790 A326 10m Sierra Leone .95 .55
791 A326 10m Somalia .95 .55
792 A326 10m Sudan .95 .55
793 A326 10m Swaziland .95 .55
794 A326 10m Tanzania .95 .55
795 A326 10m Togo .95 .55
796 A326 10m Tunisia .95 .55
797 A326 10m Uganda .95 .55
798 A326 10m UAR .95 .55
799 A326 10m Upper Volta .95 .55
800 A326 10m Zambia .95 .55
Nos. 760-800 (41) 38.95 22.55

El Fetouh Gate, Cairo A327

Sculptures from the Egyptian Museum, Cairo — A328

Millenary of Cairo — A329

No. 802, Al Azhar University. No. 803, The Citadel. No. 805, Sculptures, Coptic Museum. No. 806, Glass plate and vase, Fatimid dynasty, Islamic Museum.

No. 807: a, Islamic coin. b, Fatimist era jewelry. c, Copper vase. d, Coins and plaque.

Perf. 11½x11

1969, July 23 Photo. Wmk. 342

801 A327 10m dk brown & multi .55 .25
802 A327 10m green & multi .55 .25
803 A327 10m blue & multi .55 .25

Perf. 11½

804 A328 20m yellow grn & multi .95 .40
805 A328 20m dp ultra & multi .95 .40
806 A328 20m brown & multi .95 .40
Nos. 801-806 (6) 4.50 1.95

Souvenir Sheet

807 A329 Sheet of 4 15.00 14.00
a. 20m dark blue & multi 2.50 2.00
b. 20m lilac & multi 2.50 2.00
c. 20m yellow & multi 2.50 2.00
d. 20m dark green & multi 2.50 2.00

Millenium of the founding of Cairo.

African Development Bank Emblem — A330

Perf. 11x11½

1969, Sept. 10 Photo. Wmk. 342

808 A330 20m emerald, yel & vio .40 .25

African Development Bank, 5th anniv.

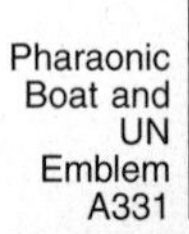

Pharaonic Boat and UN Emblem A331

Temple of Philae Inundated and UNESCO Emblem A332

Design: 5m, King and Queen from Abu Simbel Temple and UNESCO Emblem (size: 21x38mm).

Perf. 11x11½, 11½x11

1969, Oct. 24 Photo. Wmk. 342

809 A332 5m brown & multi .45 .30
810 A331 20m yellow & ultra 1.40 .55

Perf. 11½

811 A332 55m yellow & multi 1.60 .75
Nos. 809-811 (3) 3.45 1.60

Issued for United Nations Day.

Ships of 1869 and 1967 and Maps of Africa and Suez Canal — A333

1969, Nov. 15 ***Perf. 11½x11***

812 A333 20m lt blue & multi 1.50 .55

Centenary of the Suez Canal.

Cairo Opera House and Performance of Aida — A334

1969, Nov. 15

813 A334 20m multicolored 1.00 .45

Centenary of the Cairo Opera House.

Crowd with Egyptian and Revolutionary Flags — A335

1969, Nov. 15 ***Perf. 11½x11***

814 A335 20m brt grn, dull lil & red 1.00 .45

Revolution of 1919.

Ancient Arithmetic and Computer Cards A336

Perf. 11½x11

1969, Dec. 17 Photo. Wmk. 342

815 A336 20m multicolored .55 .30

Intl. Congress for Scientific Accounting, Cairo, Dec. 17-19.

Poinsettia — A337

1969, Dec. 24 Unwmk. ***Perf. 11***

816 A337 5m yellow, grn & car .30 .25

Issued for use on greeting cards.

Sakkara Step Pyramid — A338

El Fetouh Gate, Cairo — A339

Fountain, Sultan Hassan Mosque, Cairo — A340

King Khafre (Ruled c. 2850 B.C.) A341

Designs: 5m, Al Azhar Mosque. 10m, Luxor Temple. 50m, Qaitbay Fort, Alexandria.

Wmk. 342 (20m, £1), Unwmkd.
Photo.; Engr. (20m, 55m)

1969-70 ***Perf. 11***

817 A338 1m multi ('70) .30 *.40*
818 A338 5m multi ('70) .50 .25
819 A338 10m multi ('70) .50 .25
820 A339 20m dark brown 2.25 .35
821 A338 50m multi ('70) 2.25 .50
822 A340 55m slate green 3.50 .30

Perf. 11½

Photo. & Engr.

823 A341 £1 org & sl grn ('70) 40.00 9.50
Nos. 817-823 (7) 49.30 11.55

See Nos. 889-891, 893-897, 899, 901-902, 904.

Veiled Women, by Mahmoud Said — A342

Perf. 11x11½

1970, Jan. 2 Photo. Wmk. 342

824 A342 100m blue & multi 3.50 3.00

Post Day. Sheet of 8 with 2 panes of 4.

Parliament, Scales, Globe and Laurel — A343

1970, Feb. 2 ***Perf. 11½x11***

825 A343 20m blue, vio bl & ocher .75 .25

Intl. Conf. of Parliamentarians on the Middle East Crisis, Cairo, Feb. 2-5.

Map of Arab League Countries, Flag and Emblem A344

Perf. 11½x11

1970, Mar. 22 Photo. Wmk. 342

826 A344 30m brn org, grn & dk pur .65 .40

Arab League, 25th anniv. See No. B42.

Mena House and Sheraton Hotel — A345

1970, Mar. 23

827 A345 20m olive, org & bl .55 .25

Centenary of Mena House and the inauguration of the Cairo Sheraton Hotel.

Manufacture of Medicine — A346

1970, Apr. 20

828 A346 20m brown, yel & bl 1.25 .35

Production of medicines in Egypt, 30th anniv.

Mermaid — A347

1970, Apr. 20 ***Perf. 11x11½***

829 A347 20m orange, blk & ultra .65 .25

8th Biennial Exhibition of Fine Arts, Alexandria, March 12.

Misr Bank and Talaat Harb — A348

1970, May 7 Photo. Wmk. 342

830 A348 20m multicolored .65 .25

50th anniversary of Misr Bank.

ITU Emblem — A349

1970, May 17 ***Perf. 11x11½***

831 A349 20m dk brn, yel & dull bl .65 .25

World Telecommunications Day.

UPU Headquarters, Bern — A350

1970, May 20 ***Perf. 11½x11***

832 A350 20m multicolored .80 .35

Inauguration of the UPU Headquarters in Bern. See No. C128.

Basketball Player and Map of Africa — A351

UPU, UN and U.P.A.F. Emblems A352

No. 834, Soccer player, map of Africa & cup, horiz.

Perf. 11x11½, 11½x11

1970, May 25 Photo. Wmk. 342

833 A351 20m lt blue, yel & brn 1.25 .40
834 A351 20m yellow & multi .80 .35
835 A352 20m ocher, grn & blk .70 .25
Nos. 833-835 (3) 2.75 1.00

Africa Day. No. 833 also for the 5th African basketball championship for men; No. 834 the annual African Soccer championship; No. 835 publicizes the African Postal Union seminar.

Fist and Freed Bird — A353

1970, July 23 Photo. ***Perf. 11***

836 A353 20m lt green, org & blk .95 .25

Souvenir Sheet

Imperf

837 A353 100m lt blue, dp org & blk 3.25 2.40

18th anniv. of the revolution.

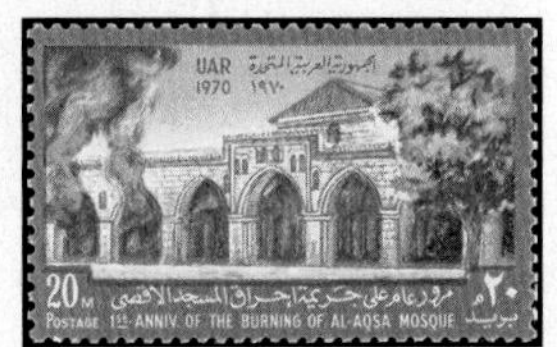

Al Aqsa Mosque on Fire — A354

1970, Aug. 21 Wmk. 342 ***Perf. 11***

838 A354 20m multicolored 1.25 .40
839 A354 60m brt blue & multi 2.75 1.60

1st anniv. of the burning of Al Aqsa Mosque, Jerusalem.

Standardization Emblems — A355

1970, Oct. 14 Wmk. 342 ***Perf. 11***

840 A355 20m yellow, ultra & grn .75 .25

World Standards Day and 25th anniv. of the Intl. Standardization Organization, ISO.

UN Emblem, Scales and Dove — A356

Temple at Philae A357

Child, Education Year and UN Emblems A358

Designs: 10m, UN emblem. No. 845, 2nd Temple at Philae (denomination at left).

Perf. 11 (5m), 11½ (others)

1970, Oct. 24 Photo. Wmk. 342

841 A356 5m lt bl, rose lil & sl .25 .25
842 A357 10m yel, brn & lt bl .25 .25
843 A358 20m slate & multi .65 .30
844 A357 55m brn, bl & ocher 1.10 .75
845 A357 55m brn, bl & ocher 1.10 .75
a. Strip of 3, #842, 844-845 4.00 4.00
Nos. 841-845,B43 (6) 4.25 3.10

25th anniv. of the UN. No. 843 also for Intl. Education Year; Nos. 842, 844-845, the work of UNESCO in saving the Temples of Philae. No. 845a printed in sheets of 35 (15 No. 842, 10 each Nos. 844-845). Nos. 844-845 show continuous picture of the Temples at Philae.

Gamal Abdel Nasser — A359

1970, Nov. 6 Wmk. 342 ***Perf. 11***

846 A359 5m sky blue & blk .25 .25
847 A359 20m gray green & blk .55 .25
Nos. 846-847,C129-C130 (4) 4.55 2.15

Gamal Abdel Nasser (1918-70), Pres. of Egypt.

Medical Association Building — A360

No. 849, Old & new National Library. No. 850, Egyptian Credo (Nasser quotation). No. 851, Engineering Society, old & new buildings. No. 852, Government Printing Offices, old & new buildings.

1970, Dec. 20 Photo. ***Perf. 11***

848 A360 20m yel, grn & brn .80 .40
849 A360 20m green & multi .80 .40
850 A360 20m lt blue & brn .80 .40
851 A360 20m blue, yel & brn .80 .40
852 A360 20m blue, yel & brn .80 .40
a. Strip of 5, #848-852 4.50 4.25

50th anniv. of Egyptian Medical Assoc. (No. 848); cent. of Natl. Library (No. 849); Egyptian Engineering Assoc. (No. 851); sesqui. of Government Printing Offices (No. 852).

Map and Flags of UAR, Libya, Sudan A361

1970, Dec. 27 ***Perf. 11½***

853 A361 20m lt grn, car & blk .75 .25

Signing of the Charter of Tripoli affirming the unity of UAR, Libya & the Sudan, 12/27/70.

Qalawun Minaret — A362

Designs (Minarets): 10m, As Saleh. 20m, Isna. 55m, Al Hakim.

1971, Jan. 2 Wmk. 342 ***Perf. 11***

854 A362 5m green & multi .60 .25
855 A362 10m green & multi 1.25 .40
856 A362 20m green & multi 2.50 .80
857 A362 55m green & multi 4.00 2.25
a. Strip of 4, #854-857 + label 10.00 9.00

Post Day, 1971.
See Nos. 905-908, 932-935.

Gamal Abdel Nasser A363

Design: Nos. 860a-860b, Portrait facing right.

Photogravure and Engraved

1971 Wmk. 342 ***Perf. 11½***

858 A363 200m brn vio & dk bl 5.00 1.25
859 A363 500m blue & black 12.00 3.25

Souvenir Sheet

Imperf

860 Sheet of 2 13.00 13.00
a. A363 100m lt green & black 4.00 2.75
b. A363 200m blue & black 6.00 4.50

No. 860 commemorates inauguration of the Aswan High Dam, which is shown in margin.

Issued: No. 860, 1/15; Nos. 858-859, 2/1.

See No. 903.

Cotton and Globe A364

1971, Mar. 6 Photo. *Perf. 11½x11*
861 A364 20m lt grn, blue & brn .65 .25

Egyptian cotton.

Arab Countries, and Arab Postal Union Emblem A365

1971, Mar. 6 Wmk. 342
862 A365 20m lt bl, org & sl grn .65 .25

9th Arab Postal Cong., Cairo, 3/6-25. See No. C131.

Cairo Fair Emblem — A366

1971, Mar. 6 *Perf. 11x11½*
863 A366 20m plum, blk & org .65 .25

Cairo International Fair, March 2-23.

Nesy Ra, Apers Papyrus and WHO Emblem A367

Perf. 11½x11
1971, Apr. 30 Photo. Wmk. 342
864 A367 20m yellow bis & pur 1.25 .30

World Health Organization Day.

Gamal Abdel Nasser — A368

1971, May 1 *Perf. 11*
865 A368 20m purple & bl gray .90 .30
866 A368 55m blue & purple 2.75 .95

Map of Africa, Telecommunications Symbols — A369

1971, May 17 *Perf. 11½x11*
867 A369 20m blue & multi .65 .25

Pan-African telecommunications system.

Wheelwright A370

Hand Holding Wheat and Laurel A371

Candle Lighting Africa — A372

Perf. 11x11½
1971, July 23 Photo. Wmk. 342
868 A370 20m yellow & multi .60 .25
869 A371 20m tan, grn & ocher .60 .25

Souvenir Sheet

Imperf

870 A372 100m blue & multi 6.00 4.75

19th anniv. of the July Revolution. No. 870 contains one stamp with simulated perforations in gold.

Arab Postal Union Emblem A373

1971, Aug. 3 *Perf. 11½*
871 A373 20m black, yel & grn .65 .25

25th anniv. of the Conf. of Sofar, Lebanon, establishing the APU. See No. C135.

Arab Republic of Egypt

Three Links A374

Perf. 11½x11
1971, Sept. 28 Photo. Wmk. 342
872 A374 20m gray, org brn & blk .65 .30

Confederation of Arab Republics (Egypt, Syria and Libya). See No. C136.

Gamal Abdel Nasser — A375

1971, Sept. 28 *Perf. 11x11½*
873 A375 5m slate grn & vio brn .45 .25
874 A375 20m violet brn & ultra .65 .25
875 A375 30m ultra & brown 1.25 .75
876 A375 55m brown & emerald 2.10 1.10
Nos. 873-876 (4) 4.45 2.35

Death of Pres. Gamal Abdel Nasser, 1st anniv.

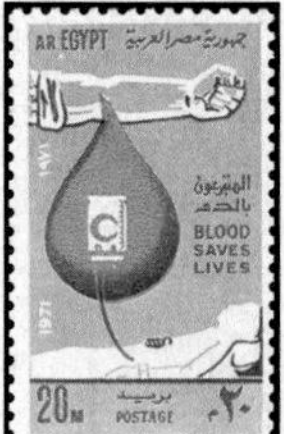

Blood Donation — A376

1971, Oct. 24
877 A376 20m green & carmine 1.10 .25

"Blood Saves Lives."

Princess Nursing Child, UNICEF Emblem A377

Submerged Pillar, Philae, UNESCO Emblem A379

Equality Year Emblem A378

Perf. 11x11½, 11½x11
1971, Oct. 24 Photo. Wmk. 342
878 A377 5m buff, blk & org brn .55 .30
879 A378 20m red brn, grn, yel & blk .90 .30
880 A379 55m black, lt bl, yel & brn 2.25 .30
Nos. 878-880,C137 (4) 5.45 1.35

UN Day. No. 878 honors UN Intl. Children's Fund; No. 879 for Intl. Year Against Racial Discrimination; No. 880 honors UNESCO.

Postal Traffic Center, Alexandria A380

1971, Oct. 31 *Perf. 11½x11*
881 A380 20m blue & bister 1.00 .30

Opening of Postal Traffic Center in Alexandria.

Sunflower — A381

1971, Nov. 13 *Perf. 11*
882 A381 5m lt blue & multi .45 .25

For use on greeting cards.

Abdalla El Nadim — A382

1971, Nov. 14 *Perf. 11x11½*
883 A382 20m green & brown .65 .25

Abdalla El Nadim (1845-1896), journalist, publisher, connected with Orabi Revolution.

Section of Earth's Crust, Map of Africa on Globe A383

1971, Nov. 27 *Perf. 11½x11*
884 A383 20m ultra, yel & brn 1.25 .25

75th anniv. of Egyptian Geological Survey and Intl. Conference, Nov. 27-Dec. 1.

Postal Union Emblem, Letter and Dove A384

55m, African Postal Union emblem and letter.

1971, Dec. 2
885 A384 5m multicolored .45 .25
886 A384 20m olive, blk & org .90 .25
887 A384 55m red, blk & blue 2.00 1.10
Nos. 885-887,C138 (4) 4.75 2.00

10th anniversary of African Postal Union.

Money and Safe Deposit Box A385

1971, Dec. 23 *Perf. 11½*
888 A385 20m rose, brn & grn .85 .30

70th anniversary of Postal Savings Bank.

Types of 1969-70, 1971 Inscribed "A. R. Egypt" and

Ramses II — A385a

Designs as before and: No. 894, King Citi I. No. 897, View of Alexandria. No. 898, Queen Nefertari. No. 900, Sphinx and Middle Pyramid. 100m, Cairo Mosque. 200m, Head of Pharaoh Userkaf.

Wmk. 342 (892A, 901-904)
1972-76 Photo. Unwmk. *Perf. 11*

889	A338	1m	multi	.25	.25
890	A338	1m	dk brn ('73)	.30	.25
891	A338	5m	multi	.40	.25
892	A385a	5m	olive ('73)	.45	.25
892A	A385a	5m	bister ('76)	.45	.25
893	A338	10m	multi	.70	.25
894	A338	10m	lt brn ('73)	.70	.25
895	A339	20m	olive	1.10	.25
896	A339	20m	purple ('73)	1.10	.25
897	A338	50m	multi	2.25	.30
898	A385a	50m	dull bl ('73)	2.25	.30
899	A340	55m	red lilac	4.00	.90
900	A340	55m	green ('74)	2.00	.50

901 A339 100m lt blue, dp org & blk 3.00 .70

Perf. 11½

Photo. & Engr.

902 A341 200m yel grn & brn 6.75 1.50
903 A363 500m bl & choc 17.50 4.00
904 A341 £1 org & sl grn 32.50 9.00
Nos. 889-904 (17) 75.70 19.45

Minaret Type of 1971

5m, West Minaret, Nasser Mosque. 20m, East Minaret, Nasser Mosque. 30m, Minaret, Al Gawli Mosque. 55m, Minaret, Ibn Tulun Mosque.

Wmk. 342

1972, Jan. 2 Photo. *Perf. 11*

905 A362 5m dk green & multi .45 .25
906 A362 20m dk green & multi 1.25 .25
907 A362 30m dk green & multi 2.75 .50
908 A362 55m dk green & multi 3.75 1.50
a. Strip of 4, #905-908 + label 11.00 3.50

Post Day, 1972.

Police Emblem and Activities — A386

1972, Jan. 25 *Perf. 11½*

909 A386 20m dull blue, brn & yel 2.25 .35

Police Day 1972.

UNESCO, UN and Book Year Emblems — A387

1972, Jan. 25 *Perf. 11x11½*

910 A387 20m lt yel grn, vio bl & yel 1.10 .25

International Book Year 1972.

Alexandria Biennale A388

1972, Feb. 15 Wmk. 342 *Perf. 11½*

911 A388 20m black, brt rose & yel .85 .30

9th Biennial Exhibition of Fine Arts, Alexandria, Mar., 1972.

Fair Emblem — A389

1972, Mar. 5 *Perf. 11x11½*

912 A389 20m blue, org & yel grn 1.10 .30

International Cairo Fair.

Abdel Moniem Riad — A390

1972, Mar. 21 Photo. Wmk. 342

913 A390 20m blue & brown 1.25 .30

In memory of Brig. Gen. Abdel Moniem Riad (1919-1969), military hero.

Bird Feeding Young A391

1972, Mar. 21 *Perf. 11½*

914 A391 20m yellow & multi 1.00 .25

Mother's Day.

Tutankhamun — A392

Design: 55m, Back of chair with king's name and symbols of eternity.

1972, May 22 Unwmk.

915 A392 20m gray, blk & ocher 2.25 .65
916 A392 55m purple & yellow 6.25 1.75
Nos. 915-916,C142-C143 (4) 28.50 13.40

Discovery of the tomb of Tutankhamun by Howard Carter & Lord Carnarvon, 50th anniv. See No. C144.

Queen Nefertiti A393

Wmk. 342

1972, May 22 Photo. *Perf. 11½*

917 A393 20m red, blk & gold 1.25 .30

Soc. of the Friends of Art, 50th anniv.

Map of Africa — A394

1972, May 25 *Perf. 11x11½*

918 A394 20m purple, bl & brn .75 .30

Africa Day.

Atom Symbol, "Faith and Science" A395

Design: No. 920, Egyptian coat of arms.

1972, July 23 *Perf. 11½*

919 A395 20m blue, claret & blk 1.10 .30
920 A395 20m ol grn, gold & blk 1.10 .30

20th anniversary of the revolution.

Boxing, Olympic and Motion Emblems — A396

Designs (Olympic and Motion Emblems and): 10m, Wrestling. 20m, Basketball.

1972, Aug. 17 *Perf. 11½x11*

921 A396 5m blue & multi .35 .25
922 A396 10m yellow & multi .50 .25
923 A396 20m ver & multi .60 .30
Nos. 921-923,C149-C152 (7) 6.65 3.70

20th Olympic Games, Munich, 8/26-9/11.

Flag of Confederation of Arab Republics — A397

1972, Sept. 1 Wmk. 342 *Perf. 11½*

924 A397 20m carmine, bis & blk .85 .30

Confederation of Arab Republics, 1st anniv.

Red Crescent, TB and UN Emblems — A398

Heart and WHO Emblem A399

Refugees, UNRWA Emblem, Map of Palestine — A400

Design: 55m, Inundated Temple of Philae, UNESCO emblem.

Perf. 11x11½ (#925), 11½ (#926, 928), 11 (#927)

1972, Oct. 24 Photo.

925 A398 10m brn org, red & bl .55 .30
926 A399 20m green, yel & blk 1.00 .40
927 A400 30m lt bl, pur & lt brn 3.00 .75
928 A399 55m brn, gold & bluish gray 3.25 1.00
Nos. 925-928 (4) 7.80 2.45

UN Day. No. 925 is for the 14th Regional Tuberculosis Conf., Cairo, 1972; No. 926 World Health Month; No. 927 publicizes aid to refugees and No. 928 the UN campaign to save the Temples at Philae.

Morning Glory — A401

1972, Oct. 24 *Perf. 11*

929 A401 10m yel, lilac & grn .65 .25

For use on greeting cards.

"Seeing Eye" A402

1972, Nov. 30 *Perf. 11½*

930 A402 20m multicolored 1.00 .25

Social Work Day.

Sculling Race, View of Luxor — A403

1972, Dec. 17 Wmk. 342 *Perf. 11*

931 A403 20m blue & brown 1.40 .40

3rd Nile Intl. Rowing Festival, Dec. 1972.

Minaret Type of 1971

10m, Al Maridani, 1338. 20m, Bashtak, 1337. 30m, Qusun, 1330. 55m, Al Gashankir, 1306.

1973, Jan. 2

Frame in Bright Yellow Green

932 A362 10m multicolored .80 .25
933 A362 20m multicolored 1.25 .30
934 A362 30m multicolored 2.75 .75
935 A362 55m multicolored 3.75 2.00
a. Strip of 4, #932-935 + Label 11.00 10.00

Post Day, 1973.

Cairo Fair Emblem A404

Perf. 11½x11

1973, Mar. 21 Photo. Wmk. 342

936 A404 20m gray & multi .55 .25

International Cairo Fair.

Family — A405

1973, Mar. 21 ***Perf. 11x11½***
937 A405 20m multicolored .65 .25

Family planning.

Sania Girls' School and Hoda Sharawi A406

Perf. 11½x11
1973, July 15 Photo. Wmk. 342
938 A406 20m ultra & green .65 .25

Centenary of education for girls and 50th anniversary of the Egyptian Women's Union, founded by Hoda Sharawi.

Rifaa el Tahtawi — A407

1973, July 15 ***Perf. 11x11½***
939 A407 20m brt green, ol & brn .70 .30

Centenary of the death of Rifaa el Tahtawi, champion of democracy and principal of language school.

Omar Makram A408

Abdel Rahman al Gabarti, Historian A409

"Reconstruction and Battle" — A410

No. 941, Mohamed Korayem, martyr.

1973, July 23
940 A408 20m yel grn, bl & brn .65 .30
941 A408 20m lt grn, bl & brn .65 .30
942 A409 20m ocher & brown .65 .30
Nos. 940-942 (3) 1.95 .90

Souvenir Sheet

Imperf

943 A410 110m gold, bl & blk 3.25 3.00

Revolution establishing the republic, 21st anniv.

Grain, Cow, FAO Emblem A411

Perf. 11½x11
1973, Oct. 24 Wmk. 342
944 A411 10m brn, dk bl & yel grn .65 .25

10th anniv. of the World Food Org.

Inundated Temples at Philae A412

1973, Oct. 24 ***Perf. 11½***
945 A412 55m blue, pur & org 4.00 1.40

UNESCO campaign to save the temples at Philae.

Bank Building A413

1973, Oct. 24
946 A413 20m brn org, grn & blk .75 .30

75th anniv. of the National Bank of Egypt.

Rose — A414

1973, Oct. 24 ***Perf. 11***
947 A414 10m blue & multi .55 .25

For use on greeting cards.

Human Rights Flame — A415

Perf. 11x11½
1973, Dec. 8 Photo. Wmk. 342
948 A415 20m yel grn, dk bl & car .75 .25

25th anniversary of the Universal Declaration of Human Rights.

Taha Hussein — A416

1973, Dec. 10
949 A416 20m dk blue, brn & emer .75 .25

Dr. Taha Hussein (1893-1973), "Father of Education" in Egypt, writer, philosopher.

Pres. Sadat, Flag and Battle of Oct. 6 — A417

1973, Dec. 23 ***Perf. 11x11½***
950 A417 20m yellow, blk & red 1.25 .60

October War against Israel (crossing of Suez Canal by Egyptian forces, Oct. 6, 1973). See No. 959.

WPY Emblem and Chart — A418

1974, Mar. 21 Wmk. 342 ***Perf. 11***
951 A418 55m org, grn & dk bl 1.10 .50

World Population Year.

Cairo Fair Emblem — A419

1974, Mar. 21 Photo.
952 A419 20m blue & multi .65 .25

Cairo International Fair.

Nurse and Medal of Angels of Ramadan 10 — A420

1974, May 15 ***Perf. 11½***
953 A420 55m multicolored 2.00 .65

Nurses' and World Hospital Day.

Workers, Relief Carving from Queen Tee's Tomb, Sakhara — A421

1974, May 15 ***Perf. 11***
954 A421 20m yellow, blue & brn .85 .30

Workers' Day.

Pres. Sadat, Troops Crossing Suez Canal — A422

"Reconstruction," Map of Suez Canal and New Building — A423

Sheet of Aluminum A424

Design: 110m, Pres. Sadat's "October Working Paper," symbols of science and development.

1974, July 23 Photo. ***Perf. 11x11½***
955 A422 20m multicolored .75 .40
956 A423 20m blue, gold & blk .75 .40

Perf. 11½

957 A424 20m plum & silver .75 .40
Nos. 955-957 (3) 2.25 1.20

Souvenir Sheet

Imperf

958 A424 110m green & multi 3.75 3.75

22nd anniv. of the revolution establishing the republic and for the end of the October War. No. 958 contains one 52x59mm stamp.

Pres. Sadat and Flag — A425

Perf. 11x11½
1974, Oct. 6 Wmk. 342
959 A425 20m yellow, blk & red 1.50 .75

1st anniv. of Battle. See No. 950.

Palette and Brushes A426

1974, Oct. 6 ***Perf. 11½***

960 A426 30m purple, yel & blk 1.00 .40

6th Exhibition of Plastic Art.

Teachers and Pupils — A427

1974, Oct. 6 ***Perf. 11x11½***

961 A427 20m multicolored .75 .25

Teachers' Day.

Souvenir Sheet

UPU Monument, Bern — A428

1974, Oct. 6 ***Imperf.***

962 A428 110m gold & multi 5.50 5.00

Cent. of the UPU.

Emblems, Cogwheel and Calipers — A429

Refugee Camp under Attack and UN Refugee Organization Emblem — A430

Child and UNICEF Emblem A431

Temple of Philae — A432

1974, Oct. 24 ***Perf. 11½, 11x11½***

963 A429 10m black, bl & yel .55 .25
964 A430 20m dp org, bl & blk .85 .25
965 A431 30m green, bl & brn 1.25 .40
966 A432 55m black, bl & yel 3.00 .85
Nos. 963-966 (4) 5.65 1.75

UN Day. World Standards Day (10m); Palestinian refugee repatriation (20m); Family Planning (30m); Campaign to save Temple of Philae (55m).

Calla Lily — A433

1974, Nov. 7 ***Perf. 11***

967 A433 10m ultra & multi .55 .25

For use on greeting cards.

10m-coins, Smokestacks and Grain — A434

1974, Nov. 7 ***Perf. 11½x11***

968 A434 20m yel grn, dk bl & sil .60 .25

International Savings Day.

Organization Emblem and Medical Services — A435

1974, Nov. 7 ***Perf. 11½***

969 A435 30m vio, red & gold .90 .30

Health Insurance Organization, 10th anniv.

Mustafa Lutfy El Manfalouty A436

Abbas Mahmoud El Akkad A437

Perf. 11x11½

1974, Dec. 8 **Photo.** **Wmk. 342**

970 A436 20m blue blk & brn .55 .30
971 A437 20m brown & bl blk .55 .30
a. Pair, #970-971 1.30 1.30

Arab writers; El Manfalouty (1876-1924) and El Akkad (1889-1964).

Goddess Maat Facing God Thoth — A438

Fish-shaped Vase — A439

Pharaonic Golden Vase — A440

Sign of Life, Mirror — A441

Wmk. 342

1975, Jan. 2 **Photo.** ***Perf. 11½***

972 A438 20m silver & multi 1.00 .30
973 A439 30m multicolored 1.25 .30
974 A440 55m multicolored 1.75 1.00
975 A441 110m blue & multi 3.00 1.75
Nos. 972-975 (4) 7.00 3.35

Post Day 1975. Egyptian art works from 12th-5th centuries B.C.

Om Kolthoum — A442

Perf. 11½

1975, Mar. 3 **Photo.** **Unwmk.**

976 A442 20m brown .85 .25

In memory of Om Kolthoum, singer.

Crescent, Globe, Al Aqsa and Kaaba — A443

1975, Mar. 25

977 A443 20m multicolored .85 .25

Mohammed's Birthday.

Cairo Fair Emblem — A444

Perf. 11x11½

1975, Mar. 25 **Wmk. 342**

978 A444 20m multicolored .65 .25

International Cairo Fair.

Kasr El Ainy Hospital WHO Emblem A445

Perf. 11½x11

1975, May 7 **Photo.** **Wmk. 342**

979 A445 20m dk brown & blue .85 .25

World Health Organization Day.

Children Reading Book — A446

Children and Line Graph — A447

1975, May 7 ***Perf. 11x11½***

980 A446 20m multicolored 1.00 .40
981 A447 20m multicolored 1.00 .40

Science Day.

Suez Canal, Globe, Ships, Pres. Sadat — A448

1975, June 5 ***Perf. 11½***
982 A448 20m blue, brn & blk .85 .30
Nos. 982,C166-C167 (3) 5.35 2.90

Reopening of the Suez Canal, June 5.

Belmabgoknis Flowers — A449

1975, July 30 Photo. Wmk. 342
983 A449 10m green & blue .65 .25

For use on greeting cards.

Sphinx and Pyramids Illuminated — A450

Rural Electrification — A451

Map of Egypt with Tourist Sites — A452

1975, July 23
984 A450 20m black, org & grn .75 .25
985 A451 20m dk blue & brown .75 .25

Perf. 11
986 A452 110m multicolored 5.75 5.00
Nos. 984-986 (3) 7.25 5.50

23rd anniversary of the revolution establishing the republic. No. 986 printed in sheets of 6 (2x3). Size: 71x80mm.

Volleyball — A453

No. 988, Running. No. 989, Torch and flag bearers. No. 990, Basketball. No. 991, Soccer.

1975, Aug. 2 Photo. ***Perf. 11x11½***
987 A453 20m shown .90 .45
988 A453 20m multicolored .90 .45
989 A453 20m multicolored .90 .45
990 A453 20m multicolored .90 .45
991 A453 20m multicolored .90 .45
a. Strip of 5, #987-991 5.75 5.75

6th Arab School Tournament.

Egyptian Flag and Tanks A454

1975 Photo. Unwmk. ***Perf. 11½***
992 A454 20m multicolored 1.40 .40

Two-line Arabic Inscription in Bottom Panel, "M" over "20"
992A A454 20m multicolored 1.40 .40

No. 992 for 2nd anniv. of October War against Israel, "The Spark;" No. 992A, the Intl. Symposium on October War against Israel 1973, Cairo University, Oct. 27-31.

Issue dates: No. 992, Oct. 6; No. 992A, Oct. 24.

Arrows Pointing to Fluke, and Emblems A455

Submerged Wall and Sculpture, UNESCO Emblem A456

Perf. 11x11½
1975, Oct. 24 Wmk. 342
993 A455 20m multicolored .95 .40
994 A456 55m multicolored 2.50 1.25

UN Day. 20m for Intl. Conf. on Schistosomiasis (Bilharziasis); 55m for UNESCO help in saving temples at Philae. See Nos. C169-C170.

Pharaonic Gate, University Emblem — A457

1975, Nov. 15 Photo. Wmk. 342
995 A457 20m multicolored .55 .25

Ain Shams University, 25th anniversary.

Al Biruni — A458

Arab Philosophers: No. 997, Al Farabi and lute. No. 998, Al Kanady, book and compass.

1975, Dec. 23 Photo. ***Perf. 11x11½***
996 A458 20m blue, brn & grn 1.50 .50
997 A458 20m blue, brn & grn 1.50 .50
998 A458 20m blue, brn & grn 1.50 .50
Nos. 996-998 (3) 4.50 1.50

Ibex (Prow) — A459

Post Day (from Tutankhamun's Tomb): 30m, Lioness. 55m, Cow's head (Goddess Hawthor). 110m, Hippopotamus' head (God Horus).

1976, Jan. 2 Unwmk. ***Perf. 11½***
999 A459 20m multicolored 4.75 2.00

Wmk. 342
1000 A459 30m brown, gold & ultra 7.50 2.50
1001 A459 55m multicolored 12.50 6.50
1002 A459 110m multicolored 18.00 13.50
Nos. 999-1002 (4) 42.75 24.50

Lake, Aswan Dam, Industry and Agriculture — A460

Perf. 11½x11
1976, Jan. 27 Photo. Wmk. 342
1003 A460 20m multicolored .90 .25

Filling of lake formed by Aswan High Dam.

Fair Emblem — A461

1976, Mar. 15 ***Perf. 11x11½***
1004 A461 20m orange & purple .50 .25

9th International Cairo Fair, Mar. 8-27.

Commemorative Medal — A462

1976, Mar. 15 Wmk. 342
1005 A462 20m olive, yel & blk .60 .25

11th Biennial Exhibition of Fine Arts, Alexandria.

Hands Shielding Invalid A463

1976, Apr. 7 Photo. ***Perf. 11½***
1006 A463 20m dk grn, lt grn & yel .65 .30

Founding of Faithfulness and Hope Society.

Eye and WHO Emblem A464

1976, Apr. 7
1007 A464 20m dk brn, yel & grn .85 .25

World Health Day: "Foresight prevents blindness."

Pres. Sadat, Legal Department Emblem — A465

Perf. 11½x11
1976, May 15 Photo. Wmk. 342
1008 A465 20m olive & multi .65 .30

Centenary of State Legal Department.

Scales of Justice — A466

1976, May 15 ***Perf. 11x11½***
1009 A466 20m carmine, blk & grn .60 .30

5th anniversary of Rectification Movement.

Al-Ahram Front Page, First Issue A467

Perf. 11½x11

1976, June 25 Photo. Wmk. 342

1010 A467 20m bister & multi .65 .30

Centenary of Al-Ahram newspaper.

World Map, Pres. Sadat and Emblems — A468

1976, July 23 ***Perf. 11x11½***

1011 A468 20m bl, blk & yel .85 .35

Size: 240x216mm

Imperf

1012 A468 110m bl, brn & yel 7.00 6.75

24th anniv. of the revolution. No. 1012 design is similar to No. 1011.

Scarborough Lily — A469

1976, Sept. 10 Photo. ***Perf. 11***

1013 A469 10m multicolored .55 .25

For use on greeting cards.

Reconstruction of Sinai by Irrigation — A470

Abu Redice Oil Wells and Refinery — A471

Unknown Soldier, Memorial Pyramid for October War — A472

1976, Oct. 6 ***Perf. 11x11½***

1014 A470 20m multicolored .85 .40

1015 A471 20m multicolored .85 .40

Size: 65x77mm

1016 A472 110m grn, bl & blk 7.50 7.00

October War against Israel, 3rd anniv.

Papyrus with Children's Animal Story — A473

Al Aqsa Mosque, Palestinian Refugees — A474

55m, Isis, from Philae Temple, UNESCO emblem, vert. 110m, UNESCO emblem & "30."

Perf. 11½, 11½x11

1976, Oct. 24 Photo. Wmk. 342

1017 A473 20m dk bl, bis & brn .65 .30

1018 A474 30m brn, grn & blk .80 .35

1019 A473 55m dk blue & bister 1.50 .50

1020 A474 110m lt grn, vio bl & red 2.50 1.40

Nos. 1017-1020 (4) 5.45 2.55

30th anniversary of UNESCO.

Census Chart A475

1976, Nov. 22 Photo. ***Perf. 11½x11***

1021 A475 20m multicolored .65 .25

10th General Population and Housing Census.

A476

Nile and commemorative medal.

1976, Nov. 22 ***Perf. 11x11½***

1022 A476 20m green & brown .65 .25

Geographical Soc. of Egypt, cent. (in 1975).

A477

Post Day: 20m, Akhnaton. 30m, Akhnaton's daughter. 55m, Nefertiti, Akhnaton's wife. 110m, Akhnaton, front view.

1977, Jan. 2 Photo. ***Perf. 11x11½***

1023 A477 20m multicolored .65 .30

1024 A477 30m multicolored .65 .35

1025 A477 55m multicolored 1.10 .55

1026 A477 110m multicolored 3.50 1.50

Nos. 1023-1026 (4) 5.90 2.70

Policeman, Emblem and Emergency Car — A478

Perf. 11½x11

1977, Feb. 25 Photo. Wmk. 342

1027 A478 20m multicolored 1.10 .30

Police Day.

Map of Africa, Arab League Emblem — A479

1977, Mar 7 ***Perf. 11x11½***

1028 A479 55m multicolored .90 .50

First Afro-Arab Summit Conference, Cairo.

Fair Emblem, Pharaonic Ship A480

1977, Mar. 7 ***Perf. 11½x11***

1029 A480 20m green, blk & red .65 .30

10th International Cairo Fair.

King Faisal — A481

1977, Mar. 22 Photo. ***Perf. 11x11½***

1030 A481 20m indigo & brown .65 .25

King Faisal Ben Abdel-Aziz Al Saud of Saudi Arabia (1906-1975).

Healthy and Crippled Children — A482

1977, Apr. 12 Wmk. 342

1031 A482 20m multicolored .95 .30

National campaign to fight poliomyelitis.

APU Emblem, Members' Flags A483

1977, Apr. 12 ***Perf. 11½***

1032 A483 20m blue & multi .45 .25

1033 A483 30m gray & multi .65 .25

25th anniv. of Arab Postal Union (APU).

Children's Village A484

Perf. 11½x11

1977, May 7 Photo. Wmk. 342

1034 A484 20m multicolored .55 .35

1035 A484 55m multicolored 1.25 .70

Inauguration of Children's Village, Cairo.

Loom, Spindle and Factory A485

1977, May 7

1036 A485 20m multicolored .55 .25

Egyptian Spinning and Weaving Company, El Mehalla el Kobra, 50th anniv.

Satellite, Globe, ITU Emblem — A486

1977, May 17 ***Perf. 11x11½***

1037 A486 110m dk blue & multi 2.00 .50

World Telecommunications Day.

Flag and "25" A487

Egyptian Flag and Eagle — A488

Perf. 11½x11

1977, July 23 Photo. Wmk. 342

1038 A487 20m silver, car & blk .65 .25

Perf. 11x11½

1039 A488 110m multicolored 3.00 3.00

25th anniversary of July 23rd Revolution. No. 1039 printed in sheets of six. Size: 75x83mm.

Saad Zaghloul — A489

Perf. 11x11½

1977, Aug. 23 Photo. Wmk. 342

1040 A489 20m dk green & dk brn .40 .25

Saad Zaghloul, leader of 1919 Revolution, 50th death anniversary.

Archbishop Capucci, Map of Palestine — A490

1977, Sept. 1

1041 A490 45m emerald & blue 1.10 .50

Palestinian Archbishop Hilarion Capucci, jailed by Israel in 1974.

Bird-of-Paradise Flower — A491

1977, Sept. 3

1042 A491 10m multicolored .45 .25

For use on greeting cards.

Proclamation Greening the Land — A492

Perf. 11x11½

1977, Sept. 25 Photo. Wmk. 342

1043 A492 20m multicolored .50 .25

Agrarian Reform Law, 25th anniversary.

Soldier, Tanks, Medal of Oct. 6 A493

Anwar Sadat — A494

1977, Oct. 6 *Perf. 11½x11*

1044 A493 20m multicolored .55 .25

Unwmk.

Perf. 11

1045 A494 140m dk brn, gold & red 8.50 8.50

October War against Israel, 4th anniv. No. 1045 printed in sheets of 16.

Refugees Looking at Al Aqsa Mosque A495

Goddess Taueret and Spirit of Flight (Horus) A496

Mural Relief, Temple of Philae — A497

Wmk. 342

1977, Oct. 24 Photo. *Perf. 11*

1046 A495 45m grn, red & blk .80 .35
1047 A496 55m dp blue & yel 1.50 .45
1048 A497 140m ol bis & dk brn 2.50 1.25
Nos. 1046-1048 (3) 4.80 2.05

United Nations Day.

Electric Trains, First Egyptian Locomotive — A498

1977, Oct. 22

1049 A498 20m multicolored 1.75 .40

125th anniversary of Egyptian railroads.

Film and Eye A499

1977, Nov. 16 *Perf. 11½x11*

1050 A499 20m gray, blk & gold .75 .25

50th anniversary of Egyptian cinema.

Natural Gas Well and Refinery — A500

1977, Nov. 17 Photo.

1051 A500 20m multicolored 1.25 .30

National Oil Festival, celebrating the acquisition of Sinai oil wells.

Pres. Sadat and Dome of the Rock A501

Perf. 11½x11

1977, Dec. 31 Photo. Wmk. 342

1052 A501 20m green, brn & blk .60 .25
1053 A501 140m green, blk & brn 2.00 .80

Pres. Sadat's peace mission to Israel.

Ramses II — A502

Post Day: 45m, Queen Nefertari, bas-relief.

1978, Jan. 2 *Perf. 11½*

1054 A502 20m green, blk & gold .85 .40
1055 A502 45m orange, blk & ol 1.75 .90

Post Day 1978.

Water Wheels, Fayum — A503

Flying Duck, from Floor in Ikhnaton's Palace A504

5m, Birdhouse, 10m, Statue of Horus. 20m, 30m, Al Rifa'i Mosque, Cairo. 50m, Monastery, Wadi al-Natrun. 55m, Ruins of Edfu Temple. 70m, 80m, Bridge of Oct. 6. 85m, Medum pyramid. 100m, Facade, El Morsi Mosque, Alexandria. 200m, Column, Alexandria, Sphinx. 500m, Arabian stallion.

Wmk. 342, Unwmkd. (30m, 70m, 80m)

1978-85 *Perf. 11½*

1056 A503 1m slate blue .25 .25
a. Unwmkd. ('79) .25 .25
b. 1m gray ('83) .25 .25
c. 1m gray, unwmkd. ('83) .25 .25
1057 A503 5m bister brn .25 .25
a. 5m dull brn, unwmkd. .25 .25
1058 A503 10m brt green .25 .25
a. Unwmkd. ('79) .25 .25
1059 A503 20m dk brown .25 .25
b. Unwmkd. ('79) .25 .25
1059A A503 30m sepia .60 .50
c. Wmk. 342 ('82) — —
1060 A503 50m Prus blue .25 .25
a. Unwmkd. ('79) .25 .25
b. Unwmkd., brt blue ('87) .25 .25
1061 A503 55m olive .25 .25
1062 A503 70m olive ('79) .40 .25
1062A A503 80m olive ('82) .50 .30
1063 A503 85m dp purple .70 .30
a. Unwmkd. ('85) .70 .35
1064 A503 100m brown .95 .30
a. Unwmkd. ('85) 1.25 .40
1065 A503 200m bl & indigo 2.25 .80
a. Unwmkd. ('85) 2.25 .85
1066 A504 500m multicolored 7.00 2.00
a. Unwmkd. ('85) 7.00 2.00
1067 A504 £1 multicolored 11.00 4.00
a. Unwmkd. ('85) 11.00 4.00
Nos. 1056-1067 (14) 24.90 9.95

Issued: 500m, £1, 2/27/78; 70m, 8/22/79; others, 7/23/78.

Fair Emblem and Wheat A505

1978, Mar. 15 *Perf. 11½*

1072 A505 20m multicolored .45 .25

11th Cairo International Fair, Mar. 11-25.

Emblem, Kasr El Ainy School A506

1978, Mar. 18 *Perf. 11½x11*

1073 A506 20m lt blue, blk & gold .55 .25

Kasr El Ainy School of Medicine, 150th anniv.

A507

No. 1074, Soldiers and Emblem. No. 1075, Youssef El Sebai.

1978, Mar. 30 *Perf. 11x11½*

1074 20m multicolored .50 .30
1075 20m bister brown .50 .30
a. A507 Pair, #1074-1075 1.25 1.25

Youssef El Sebai, newspaper editor, assassinated on Cyprus and in memory of the commandos killed in raid on Cyprus.

Biennale Medal, Statue for Entrance to Port Said A509

1978, Apr. 1 *Perf. 11½*

1076 A509 20m blue, grn & blk .55 .25

12th Biennial Exhibition of Fine Arts, Alexandria.

Child with Smallpox, UN Emblem A510

1978, Apr. 7 Photo. *Perf. 11½*

1077 A510 20m multicolored .55 .35

Eradication of smallpox.

Heart & Arrow, UN Emblem — A511

1978, Apr. 7 **Wmk. 342**
1078 A511 20m multicolored .55 .35

Fight against hypertension.

Anwar Sadat — A512

1978, May 15 **Photo.** ***Perf. 11½x11***
1079 A512 20m grn, brn & gold .65 .30

7th anniversary of Rectification Movement.

Social Security Emblem — A513

1978, May 16 ***Perf. 11***
1080 A513 20m lt green & dk brn .35 .25

General Organization of Insurance and Pensions (Social Security), 25th anniversary.

New Cities on Map of Egypt — A514

Map of Egypt and Sudan, Wheat — A515

Wmk. 342

1978, July 23 **Photo.** ***Perf. 11½***
1081 A514 20m multicolored .85 .30
1082 A515 45m multicolored 1.75 .50

26th anniversary of July 23rd revolution.

Symbols of Egyptian Ministries — A516

1978, Aug. 28 **Photo.** ***Perf. 11½x11***
1083 A516 20m multicolored .65 .30

Centenary of Egyptian Ministerial System.

Pres. Sadat and "Spirit of Egypt" Showing Way — A517

1978, Oct. 6 **Photo.** ***Perf. 11x11½***
1084 A517 20m multicolored .85 .30

October War against Israel, 5th anniv.

Fight Against Racial Discrimination Emblem — A518

Kobet al Sakra Mosque, Refugee Camp A519

Dove and Human Rights Emblem — A520

UN Day: 55m, Sanctuary of Isis at Philae and UNESCO emblem, horiz.

Perf. 11, 11½ (45m)

1978, Oct. 24 **Photo.** **Wmk. 342**
1085 A518 20m multicolored .45 .25
1086 A519 45m multicolored .90 .50
1087 A518 55m multicolored 1.00 .60
1088 A520 140m multicolored 2.25 1.00
Nos. 1085-1088 (4) 4.60 2.35

Pilgrims, Mt. Arafat and Holy Kaaba — A521

1978, Nov. 7 **Photo.** ***Perf. 11***
1089 A521 45m multicolored 1.00 .40

Pilgrimage to Mecca.

Tahtib Horse Dance — A522

1978, Nov. 7
1090 A522 10m multicolored .50 .25
1091 A522 20m multicolored .50 .25

For use on greeting cards.

UN Emblem, Globe and Grain A523

1978, Nov. 11 **Photo.** ***Perf. 11½***
1092 A523 20m green, dk bl & yel .45 .25

Technical Cooperation Among Developing Countries Conf., Buenos Aires, Sept. 1978.

Pipes, Map and Emblem of Sumed Pipeline A524

1978, Nov. 11
1093 A524 20m brown, bl & yel .65 .25

Inauguration of Sumed pipeline from Suez to Alexandria, 1st anniversary.

Mastheads — A525

1978, Dec. 24 ***Perf. 11x11½***
1094 A525 20m brown & black .65 .25

El Wakea el Masriya newspaper, 150th anniv.

Abu el Walid — A526

1978, Dec. 24
1095 A526 45m brt grn & indigo .85 .30

800th death anniv. of Abu el Walid ibn Rashid.

Helwan Observatory and Sky — A527

1978, Dec. 30 **Wmk. 342**
1096 A527 20m multicolored .95 .35

Helwan Observatory, 75th anniversary.

Second Daughter of Ramses II A528

Ramses Statues, Abu Simbel, and Cartouches — A529

1979, Jan. 2 **Photo.** ***Perf. 11***
1097 A528 20m brown & yellow .65 .30

Perf. 11½x11

1098 A529 140m multicolored 2.25 .80

Post Day 1979.

Book, Reader and Globe A530

Perf. 11½x11

1979, Feb. 1 **Photo.** **Wmk. 342**
1099 A530 20m yel grn & brn .45 .25

Cairo 11th International Book Fair.

Wheat, Globe, Fair Emblem — A531

Perf. 11x11½
1979, Mar. 17 Photo. Unwmk.
1100 A531 20m blue, org & blk .50 .25

12th Cairo International Fair, Mar.-Apr.

Skull, Poppy, Agency Emblem — A532

1979, Mar. 20 ***Perf. 11***
1101 A532 70m multicolored 1.90 .65

Anti-Narcotics General Administration, 50th anniv.

Isis Holding Horus — A533

1979, Mar. 21
1102 A533 140m multicolored 3.25 1.00

Mother's Day.

World Map and Book — A534

Perf. 11x11½
1979, Mar. 22 Wmk. 342
1103 A534 45m yellow, bl & brn .55 .25

Cultural achievements of the Arabs.

Pres. Sadat's Signature, Peace Doves A535

Wmk. 342
1979, Mar. 31 Photo. ***Perf. 11½***
1104 A535 70m brt green & red 1.25 .45
1105 A535 140m yel grn & red 2.25 1.00

Signing of Peace Treaty between Egypt and Israel, Mar. 26.

1979, May 26 Photo. ***Perf. 11½***
1106 A535 20m yellow & dk brn .55 .30

Return of Al Arish to Egypt.

Honeycomb with Food Symbols A536

1979, May 15
1107 A536 20m multicolored .35 .25

8th anniversary of movement to establish food security.

Coins, 1959, 1979 A537

Perf. 11½x11
1979, June 1 Wmk. 342 Photo.
1108 A537 20m yellow & gray .45 .25

25th anniversary of the Egyptian Mint.

Egypt No. 1104 under Magnifying Glass — A538

1979, June 1 ***Perf. 11***
1109 A538 20m green, blk & brn .55 .25

Philatelic Society of Egypt, 50th anniversary.

Book, Atom Symbol, Rising Sun — A539

"23 July," "Revolution" and "Peace" — A540

Perf. 11½x11
1979, July 23 Wmk. 342
1110 A539 20m multicolored .50 .25

Miniature Sheet

Imperf
1111 A540 140m multicolored 3.75 3.75

27th anniversary of July 23rd revolution.

Musicians — A541

1979, Aug. 22 ***Perf. 11½***
1112 A541 10m multicolored .25 .25

For use on greeting cards.

Dove over Map of Suez Canal A542

Wmk. 342
1979, Oct. 6 Photo. ***Perf. 11½***
1113 A542 20m blue & brown .65 .30

October War against Israel, 6th anniv.

Prehistoric Mammal Skeleton, Map of Africa — A543

Perf. 11½x11
1979, Oct. 9 Photo. Wmk. 342
1114 A543 20m multicolored 2.00 .35

Egyptian Geological Museum, 75th anniv.

T Square on Drawing Board — A544

1979, Oct. 11 ***Perf. 11***
1115 A544 20m multicolored .65 .25

Engineers Day.

Human Rights Emblem Over Globe — A545

Boy Balancing IYC Emblem — A546

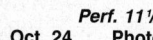

Perf. 11½
1979, Oct. 24 Photo. Unwmk.
1116 A545 45m multicolored .65 .30
1117 A546 140m multicolored 1.50 1.25

UN Day and Intl. Year of the Child.

International Savings Day — A547

1979, Oct. 31
1118 A547 70m multicolored 1.00 .45

A548

Design: Shooting championship emblem.

1979, Nov. 16
1119 A548 20m multicolored .65 .25

20th International Military Shooting Championship, Cairo.

International Palestinian Solidarity Day — A549

1979, Nov. 29 ***Perf. 11x11½***
1120 A549 45m multicolored .85 .30

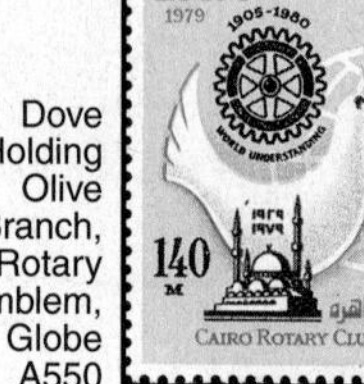

Dove Holding Olive Branch, Rotary Emblem, Globe A550

1979, Dec. 3 Photo. ***Perf. 11½***
1121 A550 140m multicolored 1.60 1.00

Rotary Intl., 75th anniv,; Cairo Rotary Club, 50th anniv.

Arms Factories, 25th Anniversary — A551

Perf. 11½x11
1979, Dec. 23 Photo. Wmk. 342
1122 A551 20m lt olive grn & brn .55 .25

Aly El Garem (1881-1949) — A552

Poets: No. 1124, Mahmoud Samy El Baroudy (1839-1904).

1979, Dec. 25 ***Perf. 11x11½***

1123	A552 20m dk brn & yel brn		.50	.30
1124	A552 20m brn & dk brn		.50	.30
a.	Pair, #1123-1124		1.25	1.25

Pharaonic Capital — A553

Post Day: Various Pharaonic capitals.

1980, Jan. 2 **Unwmk.** ***Perf. 11½***

1125	A553 20m multicolored	.45	.30
1126	A553 45m multicolored	.65	.65
1127	A553 70m multicolored	1.00	.75
1128	A553 140m multicolored	2.75	1.50
a.	Strip of 4, #1125-1128	6.50	.650

Golden Goddess of Writing, Fair Emblem — A554

1980, Feb. 2 **Photo.** ***Perf. 11½***

1129 A554 20m multicolored 1.10 .25

12th Cairo Intl. Book Fair, Jan. 24-Feb. 4.

Exhibition Catalogue and Medal — A555

1980, Feb. 2

1130 A555 20m multicolored .60 .30

13th Biennial Exhibition of Fine Arts, Alexandria.

13th Cairo International Fair — A556

1980, Mar. 8 **Photo.** ***Perf. 11x11½***

1131 A556 20m multicolored .60 .25

Kiosk of Trajan — A557

a, Kiosk of Trajan. b, Temple of Korasy, entry at right. c, Temple of Ksalabsha, carvings on frame. d, Temple of Philae, 5 columns..

1980, Mar. 10 ***Perf. 11½***

1132	Strip of 4 + label	5.50	5.50
a.-d.	A557 70m, any single	1.10	.85

UNESCO campaign to save Nubian monuments, 20th anniversary. Shown on stamps are Temples of Philae, Kalabsha, Korasy.

Physicians' Day — A558

1980, Mar. 18 ***Perf. 11x11½***

1133 A558 20m multicolored .60 .25

Rectification Movement, 9th Anniversary — A559

Perf. 11½x11

1980, May 15 **Photo.** **Wmk. 342**

1134 A559 20m multicolored .60 .25

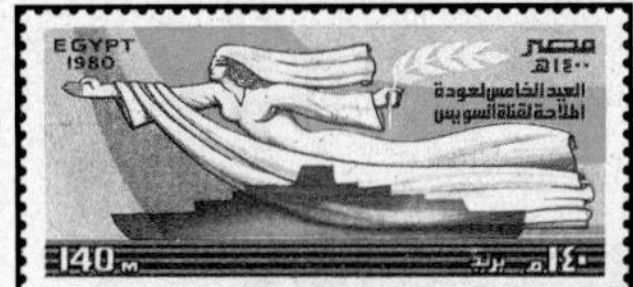

Re-opening of Suez Canal, 5th Anniversary — A560

1980, June 5 ***Perf. 11½***

1135 A560 140m multicolored 1.50 1.00

Prevention of Cruelty to Animals Week A561

1980, June 5

1136 A561 20m lt yel grn & gray .85 .25

Industry Day A562

Perf. 11½x11

1980, July 12 **Photo.** **Wmk. 342**

1137 A562 20m multicolored .55 .25

Leaf with Text A563

Family Protection Emblem — A564

1980, July 23 ***Perf. 11½***

1138 A563 20m multicolored .60 .25

Souvenir Sheet

Imperf

1139 A564 140m multicolored 3.75 3.75

July 23rd Revolution, 28th anniv.; Social Security Year.

Erksous Seller and Nakrazan Player — A565

Perf. 11½

1980, Aug. 8 **Unwmk.** **Photo.**

1140 A565 10m multicolored .50 .25

For use on greeting cards.

October War Against Israel, 7th Anniv. — A566

1980, Oct. 6 **Litho.**

1141 A566 20m multicolored .75 .25

Islamic and Coptic Columns A567

International Telecommunications Union Emblem — A568

Wmk. 342

1980, Oct. 24 **Photo.** ***Perf. 11½***

1142	A567 70m multicolored	.80	.60
1143	A568 140m multicolored	1.60	1.25

UN Day. Campaign to save Egyptian monuments (70m), Intl. Telecommunications Day (140m).

Hegira (Pilgrimage Year) A569

1980, Nov. 9 **Litho.** ***Perf. 11x11½***

1144 A569 45m multicolored .70 .30

Opening of Suez Canal Third Branch A570

Perf. 11½x11

1980, Dec. 16 **Photo.** **Wmk. 342**

1145 A570 70m multicolored 1.10 .60

Mustafa Sadek El-Rafai (1880-1927), Writer — A571

No. 1147, Ali Mustafa Mousharafa (1898-1950), mathematician (with glasses). No. 1148, Ali Ibrahim (1880-1947), surgeon.

1980, Dec. 23 ***Perf. 11x11½***

1146	A571	20m green & brown	.50	.30
1147	A571	20m green & brown	.50	.30
1148	A571	20m green & brown	.50	.30
a.		Strip of 3, #1146-1148	2.00	2.00

See Nos. 1178-1179.

Ladybug Scarab Emblem — A572

Perf. 11½

1981, Jan. 2 Photo. Unwmk.

1149	A572	70m shown	1.25	.50
1150	A572	70m Scarab, reverse	1.25	.50

Post Day.

von Stephan, UPU — A573

Perf. 11x11½

1981, Jan. 7 Wmk. 342

1151	A573	140m grnsh bl & dk brn	1.75	.70

Heinrich von Stephan (1831-97), founder of UPU.

13th Cairo International Book Fair — A574

1981, Feb. 1 ***Perf. 11½x11***

1152	A574	20m multicolored	.60	.25

14th Cairo International Fair, Mar. 14-28 — A575

Perf. 11x11½

1981, Mar. 14 Photo. Wmk. 342

1153	A575	20m multicolored	.60	.25

Rural Electrification Authority, 10th Anniversary — A576

1981, Mar. 18

1154	A576	20m multicolored	.60	.25

Veterans' Day — A577

1981, Mar. 26

1155	A577	20m multicolored	.60	.25

Intl. Dentistry Conf., Cairo — A578

Perf. 11x11½

1981, Apr. 14 Photo. Wmk. 342

1156	A578	20m red & olive	.60	.25

Trade Union Emblem — A579

Perf. 11x11½

1981, May 1 Photo. Wmk. 342

1157	A579	20m brt blue & dk brn	.60	.25

International Confederation of Arab Trade Unions, 25th anniv.

Nurses' Day — A580

1981, May 12

1158	A580	20m multicolored	.60	.25

Irrigation Equipment (Electrification Movement) — A581

1981, May 15 ***Perf. 11½***

1159	A581	20m multicolored	.60	.25

Air Force Day — A582

Perf. 11x11½

1981, June 30 Photo. Wmk. 342

1160	A582	20m multicolored	.60	.25

A583

Designs: No. 1161, Flag Surrounding Map of Suez Canal. No. 1162, Emblems.

Wmk. 342

1981, July 23 Photo. ***Perf. 11½***

1161	A583	20m multicolored	.60	.25
1162	A583	20m multicolored	.60	.25

July 23rd Revolution, 29th anniv.; Social Defense Year.

Lotus — A584

Wmk. 342

1981, July 29 Photo. ***Perf. 11***

1163	A584	10m multicolored	.60	.25

For use on greeting cards.

Kemal Ataturk — A585

1981, Aug. 10 ***Perf. 11x11½***

1164	A585	140m dp bluish grn, brn	2.25	1.25

Orabi Revolution Centenary — A586

20m, Orabi Pasha, Leader of Egyptian Force.

Perf. 11x11½

1981, Sept. 9 Photo. Wmk. 342

1165	A586	20m dp bluish grn, brn	.60	.25

A587

1981, Sept. 14

1166	A587	45m ochre, blk, brn	.85	.25

World Muscular Athletics Championships, Cairo.

A588

Perf. 11x11½

1981, Sept. 26 Photo. Wmk. 342

1167	A588	45m multicolored	.60	.25

Ministry of Industry and Mineral Resources, 25th anniv.

20th Intl. Occupational Health Congress, Cairo — A589

1981, Sept. 28 ***Perf. 11½x11***

1168	A589	20m multicolored	.60	.25

October War Against Israel, 8th Anniv. A590

1981, Oct. 6

1169	A590	20m multicolored	.65	.25

World Food Day A591

13th World Telecommunications Day — A592

EGYPT 1981 45M

Intl. Year of the Disabled — A593

Fight Against Apartheid A594

Perf. 11½x11, 11x11½

1981, Oct. 24 Photo. Wmk. 342

1170	A591	10m	multicolored	.45	.25
1171	A592	20m	multicolored	.60	.25
1172	A593	45m	multicolored	.80	.55
1173	A594	230m	multicolored	3.75	1.10
	Nos. 1170-1173 (4)			5.60	2.15

United Nations Day.

Pres. Anwar Sadat (1917-81) — A595

Perf. 11x11½

1981, Nov. 14 Unwmk.

1174	A595	30m	multicolored	1.25	.75
1175	A595	230m	multicolored	5.50	3.00

Establishment of Shura Council — A596

Perf. 11½x11

1981, Dec. 12 Photo. Wmk. 342

1176 A596 45m purple & yellow .60 .30

Agricultural Credit and Development Bank, 50th Anniv. — A597

1981, Dec. 15 ***Perf. 11x11½***

1177 A597 20m multicolored .50 .25

Famous Men Type of 1980

30m, Ali el-Ghayati (1885-1956), journalist. 60m, Omar Ebn sl-Fared (1181-1234), Sufi poet.

Perf. 11x11½

1981, Dec. 21 Photo. Wmk. 342

1178	A571	30m	green & brown	.40	.30
1179	A571	60m	green & brown	.65	.45
a.	Pair, #1178-1179			1.50	1.50

20th Anniv. of African Postal Union A598

1981, Dec. 21 ***Perf. 11½x11***

1180 A598 60m multicolored .95 .35

14th Cairo Intl. Book Fair — A599

1982, Jan. 28

1181 A599 3p brown & yellow .65 .25

Arab Trade Union of Egypt, 25th Anniv. — A600

1982, Jan. 30

1182 A600 3p multicolored .45 .25

Khartoum Branch of Cairo University, 25th Anniv. A601

Perf. 11½x11

1982, Mar. 4 Wmk. 342

1183 A601 6p blue & green .75 .35

15th Cairo Intl. Fair — A602

1982, Mar. 13 ***Perf. 11x11½***

1184 A602 3p multicolored .60 .25

50th Anniv. of Al-Ghardaka Marine Biological Station — A603

Fish of the Red Sea: 10m, Lined butterfly fish. 30m, Blue-banded sea perch. 60m, Bat-fish. 230m, Blue-spotted boxfish.

1982, Apr. 24 Litho. ***Perf. 11½x11***

1185	10m multicolored		.90	.60
1186	30m multicolored		1.10	.70
1187	60m multicolored		1.50	.90
1188	230m multicolored		3.50	2.00
a.	A603 Block of 4, #1185-1188		7.50	7.50

Liberation of the Sinai — A604

1982, Apr. 25 Photo. ***Perf. 11x11½***

1189 A604 3p multicolored .65 .25

50th Anniv. of Egypt Air A605

1982, May 7 Photo. ***Perf. 11½x11***

1190 A605 23p multicolored 3.25 2.25

Minaret — A606

Al Azhar Mosque — A607

a, shown. b, Two terraces. c, Three terraces. d, Two turrets at top.

Perf. 11x11½

1982, June 28 Photo. Wmk. 342

1191	Strip of 4 + label	5.00	5.00
a.-d.	A606 6p any single, multi	.75	.55

Souvenir Sheet

Unwmk. ***Imperf.***

1192 A607 23p multicolored 6.25 6.25

Al Azhar Mosque millennium.
No. 1192 airmail.

Dove — A608

Flower in Natl. Colors — A609

Perf. 11x11½

1982, July 23 Photo. Wmk. 342

1193 A608 3p multicolored .50 .25

Souvenir Sheet

Imperf

1194 A609 23p multicolored 4.00 4.00

30th anniv. of July 23rd Revolution.

World Tourism Day A610

Design: Sphinx, pyramid of Cheops, St. Catherine's Tower.

Perf. 11½x11

1982, Sept. 27 Photo. Wmk. 342

1195 A610 23p multicolored 3.50 2.25

October War Against Israel, 9th Anniv. A611

1982, Oct. 6

1196 A611 3p Memorial, map .65 .25

Biennale of Alexandria Art Exhibition — A612

1982, Oct. 17 ***Perf. 11x11½***

1197 A612 3p multicolored .60 .25

10th Anniv. of UN Conference on Human Environment — A613

2nd UN Conference on Peaceful Uses of Outer Space, Vienna, Aug. 9-21 — A614

Scouting Year A615

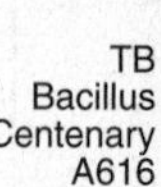

TB Bacillus Centenary A616

Perf. 11½x11, 11½ (A615)

1982, Oct. 24

1198	A613	3p multicolored	.50	.35
1199	A614	6p multicolored	.80	.55
1200	A615	6p multicolored	1.10	.55
1201	A616	8p multicolored	1.25	.75
		Nos. 1198-1201 (4)	3.65	2.20

United Nations Day.

50th Anniv. of Air Force A617

1982, Nov. 2 ***Perf. 11½x11***

1202 A617 3p Jet, plane .70 .25

Ahmed Chawki (1868-1932) and Hafez Ibrahim (1871-1932), Poets — A618

Perf. 11½x11

1982, Nov. 25 Photo. Wmk. 342

1203 A618 6p multicolored .65 .50

Natl. Research Center, 25th Anniv. — A619

1982, Dec. 12 Photo. ***Perf. 11x11½***

1204 A619 3p red & blue .70 .30

50th Anniv. of Arab Language Society A620

1982, Dec. 25 ***Perf. 11½x11***

1205 A620 6p multicolored .80 .50

Year of the Aged — A621

1982, Dec. 25 ***Perf. 11x11½***

1206 A621 23p multicolored 3.25 2.00

Post Day A622

1983, Jan. 2 ***Perf. 11½***

1207 A622 3p multicolored .60 .25

15th Cairo Intl. Book Fair — A623

Perf. 11x11½

1983, Jan. 25 Photo. Wmk. 342

1208 A623 3p blue & red .65 .25

Police Day A624

1983, Jan. 25 ***Perf. 11½x11***

1209 A624 3p multicolored .65 .25

16th Cairo Intl. Fair — A625

Perf. 11x11½

1983, Mar. 2 Photo. Wmk. 342

1210 A625 3p multicolored .65 .30

5th UN African Map Conf., Cairo — A626

1983, Mar. 2

1211 A626 3p lt green & blue .70 .30

African Ministers of Transport, Communications and Planning, 3rd Conference — A627

1983, Mar. 8 ***Perf. 11½x11***

1212 A627 23p green & blue 1.75 1.00

Victory in African Soccer Cup — A628

1983, Mar. 20 ***Perf. 11x11½***

1213	A628	3p Heading	.55	.30
1214	A628	3p Kick	.55	.30
a.		Pair, #1213-1214	1.25	1.25

World Health Day and Natl. Blood Donation Campaign — A629

Perf. 11x11½

1983, Apr. 2 Photo. Wmk. 342

1215 A629 3p olive & red .70 .25

Org. of African Trade Union Unity A630

Perf. 11½x11

1983, Apr. 21 Photo. Wmk. 342

1216 A630 3p multicolored .65 .30

1st Anniv. of Sinai Liberation — A631

1983, Apr. 25 ***Perf. 11x11½***

1217 A631 3p multicolored .70 .30

75th Anniv. of Entomology Society — A632

3p, Emblem (Holy Scarab).

1983, May 23

1218 A632 3p blue & black .70 .30

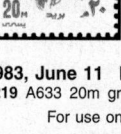

Chrysanthemums A633

1983, June 11 Photo. ***Perf. 11½x11***

1219 A633 20m green & org red .40 .25

For use on greeting cards.

5th African Handball Championship, Cairo — A634

Perf. 11½x11

1983, July 22 Photo. Wmk. 342

1220 A634 6p brown & dk grn .65 .30

31st Anniv. of Revolution A635

1983, July 23 ***Perf. 11½***

1221 A635 3p multicolored .45 .25

Simon Bolivar (1783-1830) — A636

1983, Aug. ***Perf. 11x11½***

1222 A636 23p brown & dull grn 1.75 1.00

Centenary of Arrival of Natl. Hero Orabi in Ceylon A637

3p, Map, Orabi, El-Zahra School.

Perf. 11½x11

1983, Aug. 25 Photo. Wmk. 342

1223 A637 3p multicolored .55 .25

Islamic Vase, Museum Building A638

1983, Sept. 14 Photo. ***Perf. 11½x11***

1224 A638 3p yel brn & dk brn .85 .30

Reopening of Islamic Museum.

October War Against Israel, 10th Anniv. — A639

1983, Oct. 6 *Perf. 11½*
1225 A639 3p multicolored .70 .25

2nd Pharaonic Race — A640

1983, Oct. 17 *Perf. 11½*
1226 A640 23p multicolored 2.25 1.25

United Nations Day — A641

1983, Oct. 24 **Photo.** *Perf. 11*
1227 A641 3p IMO, ships, horiz. .60 .25
1228 A641 6p ITU, UPU .75 .50
1229 A641 6p FAO, UN, grain .75 .50
1230 A641 23p UN, ocean 2.50 1.75
Nos. 1227-1230 (4) 4.60 3.00

4th World Karate Championship, Cairo — A642

1983, Nov. **Photo.** *Perf. 13*
1231 A642 3p multicolored .70 .30

Intl. Palestinian Cooperation Day — A643

1983, Nov. 29 **Photo.** *Perf. 13x13½*
1232 A643 6p Dome of the Rock 1.00 .30

75th Anniv. of Faculty of Fine Arts, Cairo A644

1983, Nov. 30 *Perf. 13*
1233 A644 3p multicolored .55 .25

75th Anniv. of Cairo University — A645

1983, Nov. 30 *Perf. 11x11½*
1234 A645 3p multicolored .55 .25
a. Perf. 13¼x12¾

Intl. Egyptian Society of Mother and Child Care A646

1983, Nov. 30 *Perf. 11½x11*
1235 A646 3p multicolored .55 .25

Org. of African Unity, 20th Anniv. — A647

Perf. 11x11½
1983, Dec. 20 **Photo.** **Wmk. 342**
1236 A647 3p multicolored .55 .25

World Heritage Convention, 10th Anniv. — A648

1983, Dec. 24
1237 A648 Strip of 3 2.25 2.25
a. 3p Wood carving, Islamic .70 .45
b. 3p Coptic tapestry .70 .45
c. 3p Ramses II Thebes .70 .45

Post Day A649

Restored Forts: 6p, Quatbay. 23p, Mosque, Salah El-Din.

1984, Jan. 2 *Perf. 13*
1238 A649 6p multicolored .80 .45
1239 A649 23p multicolored 2.50 1.25

Misr Insurance Co., 50 Anniv. A650

1984, Jan. 14 *Perf. 11½x11*
1240 A650 3p multicolored .55 .30

16th Cairo Intl. Book Fair — A651

Perf. 13½x13
1984, Jan. 26 **Photo.** **Wmk. 342**
1241 A651 3p multicolored .55 .25

17th Cairo Intl. Fair A652

Perf. 11½x11
1984, Mar. 10 **Photo.** **Wmk. 342**
1242 A652 3p multicolored .55 .30

25th Anniv. of Asyut University — A653

1984, Mar. 10 *Perf. 11x11½*
1243 A653 3p multicolored .55 .25

75th Anniv. of Cooperative Unions — A654

1984, Mar. 17
1244 A654 3p multicolored .55 .25

World Theater Day — A655

Mahmoud Mokhtar (1891-1934), Sculptor — A656

Perf. 11x11½, 11½x11
1984, Mar. 27 **Photo.** **Unwmk.**
1245 A655 3p Masks .55 .25
1246 A656 3p Pride of the Nile .55 .25

World Health Day and Fight Against Polio — A657

Perf. 11½x11
1984, Apr. 7 **Photo.** **Wmk. 342**
1247 A657 3p Polio vaccine 1.00 .30

2nd Anniv. of Sinai Liberation — A658

1984, Apr. 25
1248 A658 3p Doves, map .55 .25

Africa Day A659

Perf. 12½x13½
1984, May 25 **Photo.** **Wmk. 342**
1249 A659 3p Map, UN emblem .55 .25

Satellite, Waves — A660

1984, May 31 *Perf. 11x11½*
1250 A660 3p multicolored .55 .25

Radio broadcasting in Egypt, 50th anniv.

Carnations — A661

1984, June 1
1251 A661 2p red & green .45 .25

For use on greeting cards.

Intl. Cairo Arab Arts Biennale — A662

1984, June 1 *Perf. 13½x12½*
1252 A662 3p multicolored .55 .25

July Revolution, 32nd Anniv. — A663

3p, Atomic energy, agriculture.

Wmk. 342
1984, July 23 **Photo.** *Perf. 11*
1253 A663 3p multicolored .55 .25

A664

1984 Summer Olympics: a, Boxing. b, Basketball. c, Volleyball. d, Soccer.

1984, July 28

1254 Strip of 4 + label 5.75 5.75
a.-d. A664 3p any single .45 .25

Size: 130x80mm

Imperf

1255 A664 30p like No. 1254 4.25 4.25

A665

Wmk. 342

1984, Aug. 13 Photo. *Perf. 11*

1256 A665 3p bl & multi .55 .25
1257 A665 23p grn & multi 2.50 1.40

2nd Genl. Conference of Egyptians Abroad, Aug. 11-15, Cairo.

Youth Hostels, 30th Anniv. — A666

Perf. 11x11½

1984, Sept. 22 Photo. Wmk. 342

1258 A666 3p Youths, emblem .55 .25

Egypt Tour Co., 50th Anniv. — A667

1984, Sept. 27

1259 A667 3p Emblem, sphinx .60 .25

October War Against Israel, 11th Anniv. — A668

1984, Oct. 6

1260 A668 3p Map, eagle .55 .25

Egypt-Sudan Unity — A669

1984, Oct. 12

1261 A669 3p Map of Nile, arms .55 .25

UN Day — A670

Perf. 13½x12½

1984, Oct. 24 Photo. Wmk. 342

1262 A670 3p UNICEF Emblem, child .55 .25

UN campaign for infant survival.

Tanks, Emblem — A671

1984, Nov. 10

1263 A671 3p multicolored .60 .25

Military Equipment Exhibition, Cairo, Nov. 10-14.

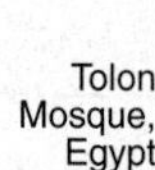

Tolon Mosque, Egypt A672

1984, Dec. 23 Photo. *Perf. 11½x11*

1264 A672 3p multicolored .65 .25

Ahmed Ebn Tolon (A.D. 835-884), Gov. of Egypt, founder of Kataea City.

A673

1984, Dec. 23 *Perf. 11x11½*

1265 A673 3p multicolored .55 .25

Kamel el-Kilany (1897-1959), author.

Globe and Congress Emblem — A674

Perf. 11x11½

1984, Dec. 26 Photo. Wmk. 342

1266 A674 3p lt blue, ver & blk .65 .25

29th Intl. Congress on the History of Medicine, Dec. 27, 1984-Jan. 1, 1985, Cairo.

Academy of the Arts, 25th Anniv. A675

1984, Dec. 31 *Perf. 13*

1267 A675 3p Emblem in spotlights .60 .25

A676

Design: Pharaoh Receiving Message, Natl. Postal Museum, Cairo.

1985, Jan. 2 *Perf. 11½x11*

1268 A676 3p brown, lt bl & ver .65 .25

Postal Museum, 50th anniv.

Intl. Union of Architects, 15th Conference, Jan. 14-Feb. 15 — A677

1985, Jan. 20

1269 A677 3p multicolored .60 .25

Seated Pharaonic Scribe — A678

1985, Jan. 22 *Perf. 11x11½*

1270 A678 3p brt org & dk blue grn .70 .30

17th Intl. Book Fair, Jan. 22-Feb. 3, Cairo.

Wheat, Cogwheels, Fair Emblem — A679

1985, Mar. 9 *Perf. 13½x13*

1271 A679 3p multicolored .60 .25

18th Intl. Fair, Mar. 9-22, Cairo.

Return of Sinai to Egypt, 3rd Anniv. — A680

1985, Apr. 25 Wmk. 342 Litho.

1272 A680 5p multicolored 1.00 .30

Ancient Artifacts — A681

A681a

Designs: 1p, God Mout, limestone sculpture, 360-340 B.C. 2p, No. 1281, Five wading birds, bas-relief. 3p, No. 1276, Seated statue, Ramses II, Temple of Luxor. No. 1276A, Vase. 8p, 15p, Slave bearing votive fruit offering, mural. 10p, Double-handled flask. 11p, Sculpted head of woman. No. 1282, Pitcher. 30p, 50p, Decanter. 35p, Temple of Karnak carved capitals. £1, Mosque.

1985-90 Photo. Unwmk. *Perf. 11½*

1273	A681	1p	brown olive	.40	.25
1274	A681	2p	brt grnsh bl	.40	.25
1275	A681	3p	yel brn	.40	.25
1276	A681	5p	dk violet	.50	.25
1276A	A681	5p	lemon	.40	.25
1277	A681	8p	pale ol grn, sep & brn	.75	.25
1278	A681	10p	dk vio & bl	.60	.25
1279	A681	11p	dk violet	.90	.30
1280	A681	15p	pale yel, sep & brn	1.40	.30
1281	A681	20p	yel grn	.60	.30
1282	A681	20p	dk grn & yel	.60	.30
1283	A681	30p	ol bis & buff	.70	.30
1284	A681	35p	sep & pale yel	1.00	.60
1285	A681	50p	pur & buff	1.25	.50
1285A	A681a	£1	brn & buff	3.00	1.25
1286	A681a	£2	sepia & yel	6.00	2.00
	Nos. 1273-1286 (16)			18.90	7.60

Issued: 1p, 2p, 3p, No. 1276, 8p, 11p, 15p, 5/1/85; 35p, 7/7/85; No. 1281, 4/1/86; 10p, 10/1/89; £2, 12/1/89; No. 1282, 2/1/90; 30p, 50p, 2/5/90; £1, 2/8/90; No. 1276A, 12/15/90.

No. 1276A is 18x23mm.

No. 1278 exists dated "1990."

See Nos. 1467, 1470, 1472.

Helwan University School of Music, 50th Anniv. A682

1985, May 15
1287 A682 5p multicolored .75 .30

El-Moulid Bride, Folk Doll — A683

1985
1288 A683 2p orange & multi .50 .25
1289 A683 5p red & multi .60 .30

Festivals 1985. Issued: 2p, 6/11; 5p, 8/10. For use on greeting cards.

A684

Winning teams: a, b, Cairo Sports Stadium. c, El-Zamalek Club, white uniform, 1983. d, Natl. Club, red uniform, 1984. e, El-Mokawiloon Club (Arab Contractor Club), orange uniform, 1984.

1985, June 17 ***Perf. 13½x13***
1290 Strip of 5 5.50 5.50
a.-e. A684 5p any single .80 .50

1985 Africa Cup Soccer Championships. Cairo Sports Stadium, 25th anniv. Nos. 1290a-1290b have continuous design.

A685

1985, July 23 ***Perf. 11½x11***
1291 A685 5p blue, brn & yel .80 .30

Egyptian Television, 25th anniv. Egyptian Revolution, 33rd anniv.

Suez Canal Reopening, 10th Anniv. — A686

Perf. 13x13½
1985, July 23 Litho. Wmk. 342
1292 A686 5p multicolored .80 .30

Egyptian Revolution, 33rd anniv.

Ahmed Hamdi Memorial Underwater Tunnel — A687

1985, July 23 ***Perf. 13½x13***
1293 A687 5p blue, vio & org .60 .25

Egyptian Revolution, 33rd anniv.

Souvenir Sheet

Aswan High Dam, 25th Anniv. — A688

Wmk. 342
1985, July 23 Photo. ***Imperf.***
1294 A688 30p multicolored 4.00 4.00

Heart, Map, Olive Laurel, Conference Emblem — A689

1985, Aug. 10 Litho. ***Perf. 13½x13***
1295 A689 15p multicolored 1.25 .85

Egyptian Emigrants, 3rd general conference, Aug. 10-14, Cairo.

Natl. Tourism Ministry, 50th Anniv. — A690

1985, Sept. 10 ***Perf. 13x13½***
1296 A690 5p multicolored .55 .30

October War Against Israel, 12th Anniv. — A691

1985, Oct. 6
1297 A691 5p multicolored .60 .30

Air Scouts Assoc., 30th Anniv. — A692

1985, Oct. 15 Photo. ***Perf. 11½***
1298 A692 5p Emblem .80 .30

UN Day, Meteorology Day — A693

5p, UN emblem, weather map.

1985, Oct. 24
1299 A693 5p multicolored .55 .25

UN, 40th Anniv. — A694

1985, Oct. 24
1300 A694 15p multicolored 1.25 .85

Intl. Youth Year — A695

1985, Oct. 24
1301 A695 5p multicolored .55 .25

A696

1985, Oct. 24
1302 A696 15p blue & int blue 1.25 .85

Intl. Communications Development Program.

2nd Intl. Dentistry Conference — A697

Emblem, hieroglyphics of Hassi Raa, 1st known dentist.

1985, Oct. 29 ***Perf. 11x11½***
1303 A697 5p beige & pale bl vio .75 .30

Emblem, Squash Player — A698

1985, Nov. 18 Photo. ***Perf. 11½***
1304 A698 5p multicolored .65 .25

1985 World Squash Championships, Nov. 18-Dec. 4.

A699

1985, Nov. 2 Litho. ***Perf. 13½x13***
1305 A699 5p multicolored .55 .30

4th Intl. Conference on the Biography and Sunna of Mohammed.

A700

1985, Dec. 1 Photo. ***Perf. 11x11½***
1306 A700 5p multicolored .55 .25

1st Conference on the Development of Vocational Training.

Natl. Olympic Committee, 75th Anniv. — A701

1985, Dec. 28 Photo. ***Perf. 13x13½***
1307 A701 5p multicolored .60 .30

18th Intl. Book Fair, Cairo — A702

1986, Jan. 21 ***Perf. 11x11½***
1308 A702 5p Pharaonic scribe .55 .25

CODATU III — A703

1986, Jan. 26 ***Perf. 11½***
1309 A703 5p lt ol grn, ver & grnsh bl .55 .25

3rd Intl. Conference on Urban Transportation in Developing Countries, Cairo.

Central Bank, 25th Anniv. — A704

1986, Jan. 30 ***Perf. 13x13½***
1310 A704 5p multicolored .55 .25

Cairo Postal Traffic Center Inauguration — A705

1986, Jan. 30 ***Perf. 11½x11***
1311 A705 5p blue & dk brown .55 .25

Pharaonic Mural, Btah Hotteb's Tomb at Saqqara A706

1986, Feb. 27 Photo. ***Perf. 11½x11***
1312 A706 5p yel, gldn brn & brn .70 .35

Faculty of Commerce, Cairo Univ., 75th anniv.

Cairo Intl. Fair, Mar. 8-21 — A707

1986, Mar. 8 Litho. ***Perf. 13½x13***
1313 A707 5p multicolored .55 .25

Queen Nefertiti, Sinai — A708

Perf. 13x13½
1986, Apr. 25 Litho. Wmk. 342
1314 A708 5p multicolored .70 .30

Return of the Sinai to Egypt, 4th anniv.

Ministry of Health, 50th Anniv. — A709

1986, Apr. 10 ***Perf. 13½x13***
1315 A709 5p multicolored .55 .30

1986 Census — A710

1986, May 26 Photo. ***Perf. 11½***
1316 A710 15p brn, grnsh bl & yel bis 1.00 .50

Egypt, Winner of African Soccer Cup — A711

No. 1317, English inscription below cup. No. 1318, Arabic inscription below cup.

1986, May 31 ***Perf. 13½x13***
1317 A711 5p multicolored .65 .45
1318 A711 5p multicolored .65 .45
a. Pair, #1317-1318 1.50 1.50

Festivals, Roses — A712

1986, June 2 ***Perf. 11½***
1319 A712 5p multicolored .55 .25

For use on greeting cards.

World Environment Day — A713

15p, Emblem, smokestacks.

1986, June 5 ***Perf. 13½x13***
1320 A713 15p multicolored 1.25 .50

July 23rd Revolution, 34th Anniv. A714

1986, July 23 Litho. ***Perf. 13***
1321 A714 5p gray grn, scar & yel bis .60 .25

6th African Roads Conference, Cairo, Sept. 22-26 — A715

Perf. 13½x13
1986, Sept. 21 Litho. Wmk. 342
1322 A715 15p multicolored 1.25 .55

October War Against Israel, 13th Anniv. A716

1986, Oct. 6 Litho. ***Perf. 13***
1323 A716 5p multicolored 1.00 .30

Engineers' Syndicate, 40th Anniv. A717

1986, Oct. 11 Photo. ***Perf. 11½***
1324 A717 5p lt blue, brn & pale grn .55 .25

Workers' Cultural Education Assoc., 25th Anniv. — A718

1986, Oct. 11 ***Perf. 11x11½***
1325 A718 5p orange & rose vio .55 .25

Intl. Peace Year — A719

1986, Oct. 24
1326 A719 5p blue, grn & pale sal .55 .25

First Oil Well in Egypt, Cent. — A720

1986, Nov. 7 Photo. ***Perf. 11½***
1327 A720 5p dull grn, blk & pale yel .65 .25

UN Child Survival Campaign A721

1986, Nov. 20 Litho. ***Perf. 13***
1328 A721 5p multicolored .60 .25

Ahmed Amin, Philosopher A722

1986, Dec. 20 ***Perf. 11½***
1329 A722 5p pale grn, pale yel & brn .55 .25

National Theater, 50th Anniv. — A723

1986, Dec. 20 ***Perf. 13½x13***

1330 A723 5p multicolored .55 .25

Post Day A724

Step Pyramid, Saqqara, King Zoser.

Perf. 13x13½

1987, Jan. 2 **Litho.** **Wmk. 342**

1331 A724 5p multicolored .65 .30

19th Intl. Book Fair, Cairo A725

1987, Jan. 25 **Litho.** ***Perf. 13***

1332 A725 5p multicolored .60 .30

5th World Conference on Islamic Education A726

Wmk. 342

1987, Mar. 8 **Litho.** ***Perf. 13***

1333 A726 5p multicolored .55 .25

20th Intl. Fair, Cairo — A727

5p, Good workers medal.

1987, Mar. 21 **Photo.** ***Perf. 11½***

1334 A727 5p multicolored .55 .25

Veteran's Day A728

1987, Mar. 26

1335 A728 5p multicolored .55 .30

Intl. Gardens Inauguration, Nasser City — A729

1987, Mar. 30 **Litho.** ***Perf. 13***

1336 A729 15p multicolored 1.10 .60

World Health Day A730

No. 1337, Mother feeding child. No. 1338, Oral rehydration therapy.

1987, Apr. 7 **Photo.** ***Perf. 11½***

1337 A730 5p multicolored .55 .30

Litho.

Perf. 13

1338 A730 5p multicolored .55 .30

A731

Natl. Team Victory at 1986 Intl. Soccer Championships — A732

Trophies: No. 1339a, Al Ahly Cup. No. 1339b, National Cup. No. 1339c, Al Zamalek Cup. No. 1340, Natl. flag, Cairo Stadium and trophies pictured on No. 1339.

1987, Apr. 19 **Litho.** ***Perf. 13½x13***

1339 Strip of 3 1.75 1.75

a.-c. A731 5p any single .55 .30

Size: 115x85mm

Imperf

1340 A732 30p multicolored 4.00 4.00

A733

Salah El Din Citadel, Pharoah's Is., Sinai.

1987, Apr. 25

1341 A733 5p sky blue & lt brown .65 .30

Return of the Sinai to Egypt, 5th anniv.

Festivals — A734

1987, May 21 **Photo.** ***Perf. 11½***

1342 A734 5p Dahlia .55 .25

Cultural Heritage Exhibition — A735

1987, June 17 **Litho.** ***Perf. 13x13½***

1343 A735 15p multicolored 1.00 1.00

Tourism Year — A736

a, Column and Sphinx, Alexandria. b, St. Catherine's Monastery, Mt. Sinai. c, Colossi of Thebes. d, Temple of Theban Triad, Luxor.

1987, June 18

1344 Block of 4 5.25 5.25

a.-d. A736 15p any single 1.10 .90

See No. C187.

Loyalty Day A737

1987, June 26 ***Perf. 13***

1345 A737 5p multicolored .55 .25

General Intelligence Service, 32nd anniv.

Industry-Agriculture Exhibition — A738

1987, July 23 **Photo.** ***Perf. 11½***

1346 A738 5p grn, dull org & blk .55 .25

Intl. Year of Shelter for the Homeless A739

1987, Sept. 2 **Litho.** ***Perf. 13***

1347 A739 5p multicolored .55 .25

World Architects' Day.

Aida, Performed at Al Ahram Pyramid, Giza A740

Radamis and troops returning from Ethiopia.

1987, Sept. 21

1348 A740 15p multicolored 1.50 .65

Size: 70x70mm

Imperf

1349 A740 30p multicolored 10.00 10.00

Greater Cairo Subway Inauguration — A741

1987, Sept. 27 ***Perf. 13x13½***

1350 A741 5p multicolored 1.20 .30

Industry Day A742

1987, Oct. 1 ***Perf. 13***

1351 A742 5p multicolored .55 .25

Battle of Hettin, 800th Anniv. — A743

1987, Oct. 6 Photo. ***Perf. 11x11½***
1352 A743 5p multicolored .70 .30

UPU Emblem A744

Perf. 11½
1987, Oct. 24 Unwmk. Photo.
1353 A744 5p multicolored .55 .25

UN Executive Council, 40th anniv.; UPU Consultative Council, 30th anniv.

16th Art Biennial of Alexandria A745

1987, Nov. 7 Litho. ***Perf. 13½x13***
1354 A745 5p multicolored .55 .25

Second Intl. Defense Equipment Exhibition, Cairo, Nov. 9-13 — A746

Perf. 13x13½
1987, Nov. 9 Litho. Unwmk.
1355 A746 5p multicolored .60 .25

2nd Pan-Arab Congress on Anaesthesia and Intensive Care — A747

Unwmk.
1987, Dec. 1 Litho. ***Perf. 13***
1356 A747 5p multicolored .65 .30

Intl. Orthopedic and Traumatology Conference A748

1987, Dec. 1 ***Perf. 13½x13***
1357 A748 5p gray, red brn & bl .55 .25

Selim Hassan (1887-1961), Egyptologist, and Hieroglyphs A749

Abdel Hamid Badawi (1887-1965), Jurist, and Scales of Justice — A750

Perf. 13½x13
1987, Dec. 30 Litho. Unwmk.
1358 A749 5p multicolored .55 .25
1359 A750 5p multicolored .55 .25

Stamp Day 1988 — A751

Pyramids of the Pharaohs and: a, Cheops. b, Chefren. c, Mycerinus. No. 1360 has a continuous design.

1988, Jan. 2
1360 A751 Strip of 3 5.50 5.50
a.-c. 15p, any single 1.40 .90

Afro-Asian Peoples Solidarity Organization, 30th Anniv. — A752

1988, Jan. 10 ***Perf. 13x13½***
1361 A752 15p multicolored 1.00 .55

20th Intl. Book Fair, Cairo — A753

1988, Jan. 26 ***Perf. 13½x13***
1362 A753 5p multicolored .55 .25

Martrans (Natl. Shipping Line), 25th Anniv. A754

Unwmk.
1988, Mar. 3 Litho. ***Perf. 13***
1363 A754 5p multicolored .85 .25

Cairo Intl. Fair A755

1988, Mar. 12 Photo. ***Perf. 11½x11***
1364 A755 5p multicolored .55 .25

World Health Day 1988: Diabetes — A756

Perf. 11x11½
1988, Apr. 7 Photo. Unwmk.
1365 A756 5p multicolored .55 .25

Prince, Fig Tree — A757

1988, Apr. 17 ***Perf. 11½***
1366 A757 5p grn, brn org & brn .55 .25

1988 Festival. For use on greeting cards.

African Postal Union, 25th Anniv. — A758

1988, Apr. 23 Litho. ***Perf. 13x13½***
1367 A758 15p brt blue 1.00 1.00

Oppose Racial Discrimination — A759

1988, May 25 Photo. ***Perf. 11½***
1368 A759 5p multicolored .50 .25

Taw Fek-Hakem (1902-1987), Playwright, Novelist — A760

1988, Aug. 5 Photo. ***Perf. 11½***
1369 A760 5p brt grn bl & org brn .60 .25

See Nos. 1383-1384, 1479-1480, 1486, 1500-1502, 1543-1546.

Faculty of Art Education, 50th Anniv. A761

Perf. 11½
1988, Sept. 10 Photo. Unwmk.
1370 A761 5p multicolored .50 .25

A762

1988 Summer Olympics, Seoul — A763

1988, Sept. 17 Litho. ***Perf. 13***
1371 A762 15p multicolored 1.25 1.25

Size: 96x91mm
Imperf.
1372 A763 30p multicolored 6.25 6.25

No. 1371 is airmail.

October War Against Israel, 15th Anniv. — A764

Perf. 13x13½

1988, Oct. 6 Litho. Unwmk.

1373 A764 5p multicolored .55 .35

A765

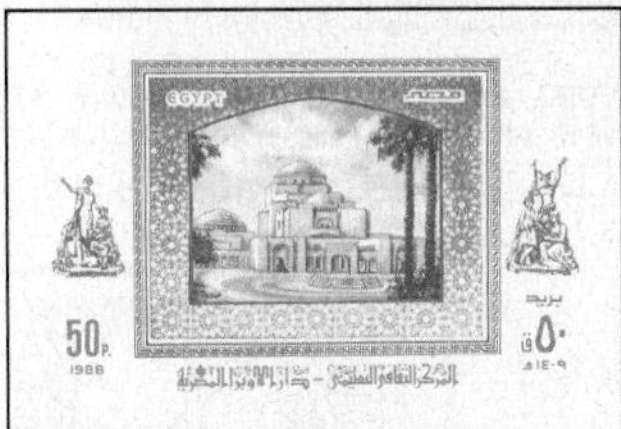

Opening of the Opera House — A766

1988, Oct. 10 ***Perf. 11½***

1374 A765 5p multicolored .55 .30

Size: 112x75mm

Imperf

1375 A766 50p multicolored 3.50 3.50

Intl. Red Cross and Red Crescent Organizations, 125th Annivs. — A767

Perf. 11½

1988, Oct. 24 Photo. Unwmk.

1376 A767 5p green, blk & red .50 .25

WHO, 40th Anniv. — A768

1988, Oct. 24 ***Perf. 11x11½***

1377 A768 20p multicolored 1.25 1.10

Naguib Mahfouz, 1988 Nobel Prize Winner for Literature — A769

1988, Nov. 7 Litho. ***Perf. 13x13½***

1378 A769 5p multicolored .50 .25

See No. C190.

Arab Scouting Organization, 75th Anniv. — A770

1988, Nov. 10

1379 A770 25p multicolored 1.25 1.25

Return of Taba to Egypt — A771

1988, Nov. 15

1380 A771 5p multicolored .50 .25

Intl. Conference on Orthopedic Surgery, Cairo, Nov. 15-18 — A772

1988, Nov. 15 Photo. ***Perf. 11½x11***

1381 A772 5p pale yel, brt yel grn & brn .60 .25

A773

1988, Dec. 3 ***Perf. 11½***

1382 A773 5p multicolored .50 .25

Ministry of Agriculture, 75th anniv.

A774

Famous Men: No. 1383, Mohamed Hussein Hekal (1888-1956), author, politician. No. 1384, Ahmed Lotfi El Sayed (1872-1963), educator, politician.

Perf. 13½x13

1988, Dec. 29 Litho. Unwmk.

1383 A774 5p green & red brn .45 .25

1384 A774 5p green & red brn .45 .25

a. Pair, #1383-1384 1.00 1.00

Stamp Day — A775

Statues: 5p, Statue of K. Abr, a priest, 5th cent. No. 1386, Queen Nefert, 4th Dynasty. No. 1387, King Ra Hoteb, 4th Dynasty.

1989, Jan. 2

1385 A775 5p multicolored .50 .30

1386 A775 25p multicolored 1.60 1.00

1387 A775 25p multicolored 1.60 1.00

a. Pair, #1386-1387 3.50 3.50

Nos. 1385-1387 (3) 3.70 2.30

A776

1989, Jan. 10

1388 A776 5p dull green .55 .25

Jawaharlal Nehru (1889-1964), 1st Prime Minister of independent India.

Nile Hilton Hotel, 30th Anniv. — A777

1989, Feb. 22 Litho. ***Perf. 13x13½***

1389 A777 5p multicolored .45 .25

Return of Taba to Egypt A778

Unwmk.

1989, Mar. 15 Litho. ***Perf. 13***

1390 A778 5p multicolored .45 .25

2nd Stage of Cairo Subway A779

1989, Apr. 12 Litho. ***Perf. 13***

1391 A779 5p multicolored 1.00 .30

Lantern — A780

1989, May 4 Photo. ***Perf. 11½***

1392 A780 5p multicolored .45 .25

1989 Festival. For use on greeting cards.

1st Arab Olympic Day A781

1989, May 24

1393 A781 5p tan, blk & dull grn .50 .25

Interparliamentary Union, Cent. — A782

Pyramids and the Parliament Building, Cairo.

1989, June 29 Litho. ***Perf. 13x13½***

1394 A782 25p shown 1.60 1.25

Size: 87x76mm

Imperf

1395 A782 25p multi, diff. 2.75 2.75

French Revolution, Bicent. — A783

1989, July 14 Photo. ***Perf. 11½***

1396 A783 25p multicolored 1.50 1.25

No. 1396 is an airmail issue.

African Development Bank, 25th Anniv. — A784

Perf. 11½

1989, Oct. 1 Photo. Unwmk.

1397 A784 10p multicolored .45 .25

A785

October War Against Israel, 16th Anniv. — A786

1989, Oct. 6 ***Perf. 13***

1398	Strip of 3	1.50	1.50
a.	A785 10p shown	.50	.25
b.	A786 10p shown	.50	.25
c.	A785 10p Battle scene	.50	.25

See No. 1424.

Aga Khan Award for Architecture A788

Perf. 11½

1989, Oct. 15 Photo. Unwmk.

1400 A788 35p multicolored 1.25 .60

Natl. Health Insurance Plan, 25th Anniv. A789

1989, Oct. 24

1401 A789 10p blk, gray & ver .50 .25

World Post Day — A790

1989, Oct. 24 ***Perf. 11x11½***

1402 A790 35p blue, blk & brt yel 1.00 .50

Statues of Memnon, Thebes — A791

Perf. 11½

1989, Nov. 12 Photo. Unwmk.

1403 A791 10p lt vio, blk & brt yel grn .50 .25

Intl. Cong. & Convention Assoc. (ICCA) annual convention, Nov. 11-18, Cairo.

Cairo University School of Agriculture, Cent. — A792

1989, Nov. 15

1404 A792 10p pale grn, blk & brt yel .45 .25

Cairo Intl. Conference Center — A793

1989, Nov. 20 ***Perf. 11½x11***

1405 A793 5p multicolored .45 .25

Road Safety Soc., 20th Anniv. — A794

1989, Nov. 20 ***Perf. 11½***

1406 A794 10p multicolored .45 .25

Alexandria University, 50th Anniv. — A795

1989, Nov. 30 ***Perf. 11x11½***

1407 A795 10p pale blue & tan .45 .25

Portrait of Pasha, Monument in Opera Square, Cairo A796

Perf. 11½x11

1989, Dec. 31 Photo. Unwmk.

1408 A796 10p multicolored .45 .25

Ibrahim Pasha (d. 1838), army commander from 1825 to 1828.

Famous Men

A797 A798

1989, Dec. 31 ***Perf. 11x11½***

1409 A797 10p grn & dk ol grn .45 .25

1410 A798 10p golden brown .45 .25

Abd El-Rahman El-Rafei (b. 1889), historian (No. 1409); Abdel Kader El Mazni (b. 1889), man of letters (No. 1410).

See Nos. 1431-1432.

Statue of Priest Ranofr — A799

Relief Sculpture of Betah Hoteb — A800

1990, Jan. 2 ***Perf. 13½x13***

1411	A799 30p multicolored	1.00	.40
1412	A800 30p multicolored	1.00	.40
a.	Pair, #1411-1412	2.75	2.75

Stamp Day.

Arab Cooperation Council, 1st Anniv. — A801

Perf. 13x13½

1990, Feb. 16 Photo. Unwmk.

1413 A801 10p multicolored .45 .25

1414 A801 35p multicolored 1.25 .60

Emblem, Conference Center — A802

Perf. 13½x13

1990, Mar. 10 Litho. Unwmk.

1415 A802 10p brt yel grn, red & blk .50 .25

Size: 80x59mm

Imperf

1416 A802 30p multicolored 1.50 1.50

African Parliamentary Union 13th general conference, Mar. 10-15.

Road Safety Emblems — A803

1990, Mar. 19 Photo. ***Perf. 11x11½***

1417 A803 10p multicolored .60 .25

Intl. Conference on Road Safety & Accidents in Developing Countries, Mar. 19-22.

Egyptian Wild Daisies — A804

1990, Apr. 24 ***Perf. 11½***

1418 A804 10p multicolored .45 .25

1990 Festival. For use on greeting cards.

Sinai Liberation, 8th Anniv. A805

1990, Apr. 25

1419 A805 10p blue, blk & yel grn .50 .25

World Cup Soccer Championships, Italy — A806

1990, May 26 Litho. ***Perf. 13½x13***

1420 A806 10p multicolored .40 .25

Souvenir Sheet

Imperf

1421 A806 50p Flags, trophy 2.25 2.25

World Basketball Championships, Argentina — A807

1990, Aug. 8 ***Perf. 13x13½***

1422 A807 10p multicolored .50 .25

Natl. Population Council, 5th Anniv. — A808

1990, Sept. 15 ***Perf. 13½x13***
1423 A808 10p brown & yel grn .50 .25

October War Against Israel Type

1990, Oct. 6 **Litho.** ***Perf. 13x13½***
1424 Strip of 3 1.75 1.75
a. A785 10p Bunker, tank .40 .25
b. A786 10p like #1398b .40 .25
c. A785 10p Troops with flag, flame thrower .40 .25

Egyptian Postal Service, 125th Anniv. — A809

1990, Oct. 9
1425 A809 10p lt blue, blk & red .50 .25

Dar El Eloum Faculty, Cent. A810

1990, Oct. 13 **Litho.** ***Perf. 13***
1426 A810 10p multicolored .45 .25

UN Development Program, 40th Anniv. — A811

ITU, 125th Anniv. — A812

1990, Oct. 24 ***Perf. 11½***
1427 A811 30p yel, bl grn & yel grn .90 .30

Perf. 13
1428 A812 30p multicolored .90 .30

UN Day.

Ras Mohammed Natl. Park — A813

Designs: a, Crown butterfly fish. b, Lionfish. c, Twobar anemone fish. d, Grouper.

1990, Dec. 22 **Litho.** ***Perf. 13***
1429 A813 Block of 4 3.50 3.50
a.-b. 10p any single .50 .30
c.-d. 20p any single .80 .40

Day of the Disabled — A814

1990. Dec. 15 **Photo.** ***Perf. 11***
1430 A814 10p multicolored .50 .25

Mohamed Fahmy Abdel Meguid Bey, Medical Reformer A815

Nabaweya Moussa (1890-1951), Educator A816

Perf. 11x11½

1990, Dec. 30 **Unwmk.**
1431 A815 10p Prus bl, brn & org .40 .25
1432 A816 10p grn, org brn & blk .40 .25

Stamp Day — A817

1991, Jan. 1 **Litho.** ***Perf. 13½x13***
1433 A817 5p No. 1 .30 .25
1434 A817 10p No. 2 .45 .25
1435 A817 20p No. 3 .60 .40
a. Strip of 3, #1433-1435 1.75 1.75

See Nos. 1443-1446, 1459-1460.

Veterinary Surgeon Syndicate, 50th Anniv. — A818

1991, Feb. 28 **Photo.** ***Perf. 11½***
1436 A818 10p multicolored .45 .25

Syndicate of Journalists, 50th Anniv. — A819

1991, Apr. **Photo.** ***Perf. 11½***
1437 A819 10p multicolored .40 .25

Narcissus — A820

1991, Apr. 13
1438 A820 10p multicolored .40 .25

1991 Festival. For use on greeting cards.

Giza Zoo, Cent. — A821

1991, June 15 **Litho.** ***Imperf.***
Size: 80x63mm
1439 A821 50p multicolored 4.00 4.00

Mahmoud Mokhtar (1891-1934), Sculptor — A822

Mohamed Nagi (1888-1956), Painter — A823

Perf. 13x13½, 13½x13

1991, June 11 **Litho.**
1440 A822 10p multicolored .40 .25
1441 A823 10p multicolored .40 .25

Faculty of Engineering — A824

1991, June 30 ***Perf. 13x13½***
1442 A824 10p multicolored .40 .25

Stamp Day Type

Designs: No. 1443, No. 5. No. 1444, No. 4. No. 1445, No. 7. No. 1446, Sphinx, pyramid, No. 6.

1991, July 23 ***Perf. 13***
1443 A817 10p orange & blk .40 .25
1444 A817 10p yellow & blk .40 .25
1445 A817 10p lilac & blk .40 .25
a. Strip of 3, #1443-1445 1.40 1.40

Size: 80x60mm

Imperf
1446 A817 50p multicolored 2.25 1.75
Nos. 1443-1446 (4) 3.45 2.50

Mohamed Abdel el Wahab, Musician A825

1991, Aug. 28 ***Perf. 13***
1447 A825 10p multicolored .55 .25

5th Africa Games, Cairo — A826

No. 1448, Karate, judo. No. 1449, Table tennis, field hockey, tennis. No. 1450, Running, gymnastics, swimming. No. 1451, Soccer, basketball, shooting. No. 1452, Boxing, wrestling, weightlifting. No. 1453, Handball, cycling, volleyball. No. 1454, Games mascot, vert. No. 1455, Mascot, emblem, torch.

Perf. 13x13½

1991, Sept. **Litho.** **Unwmk.**
1448 A826 10p multicolored .40 .25
1449 A826 10p multicolored .40 .25
a. Pair, #1448-1449 .90 .90
1450 A826 10p multicolored .40 .25
1451 A826 10p multicolored .40 .25
a. Pair, #1450-1451 .90 .90
1452 A826 10p multicolored .40 .25
1453 A826 10p multicolored .40 .25
a. Pair, #1452-1453 .90 .90

Perf. 13½x13
1454 A826 10p multicolored .45 .25

Size: 80x60mm

Imperf
1455 A826 50p multicolored 1.75 1.75
Nos. 1448-1455 (8) 4.60 3.50

Intl. Statistics Institute, 48th Session A827

1991, Sept. 9
1456 A827 10p multicolored .40 .25

Opening of Dar Al Eftaa Religious Center — A828

1991, Oct. 1 Litho. *Perf. 13*

1457 A828 10p multicolored .40 .25

October War Against Israel, 18th Anniv. — A829

1991, Oct. 6 *Perf. 13x13½*

1458 A829 10p multicolored .55 .25

Stamp Day Type

Designs: 10p, No. 6. £1, Stamp exhibition emblem, hieroglyphics, pyramids, sphinx.

1991, Oct. 7 *Perf. 13*

1459 A817 10p blue & black .50 .25

Size: 90x60mm

Imperf

1460 A817 £1 multicolored *5.50 5.50*

Natl. Philatelic Exhibition, Cairo, 10/7-12 (No. 1460). No. 1460 sold only with £1 admission ticket at exhibition.

Ancient Artifacts Type of 1985

Perf. 11½x11

1990-92 Unwmk. Photo.

Size: 18x23mm

1467 A681 10p like #1278 .60 .25
1470 A681 30p like #1283 1.00 1.00
1472 A681 50p like #1285 1.75 1.75
Nos. 1467-1472 (3) 3.35 3.00

Issued: 10p, 1/20/90; 30p, 9/1/91; 50p, 7/11/92.

United Nations Day — A830

No. 1477, Brick hands housing people. No. 1478, Woman learning to write, fingerprint, vert.

Perf. 13x13½, 13½x13

1991, Oct. 24 Litho.

1476 A830 10p shown .40 .25
1477 A830 10p multicolored .40 .25
1478 A830 10p multicolored .40 .25
Nos. 1476-1478 (3) 1.20 .75

Famous Men Type of 1988

Inscribed "1991"

Designs: No. 1479, Dr. Zaki Mubarak (1891-1952), writer and poet. No. 1480, Abd El Kader Hamza (1879-1941), journalist.

1991, Dec. 23 Photo. *Perf. 13½x13*

1479 A760 10p olive brown .40 .25
1480 A760 10p gray .40 .25

A831

Post Day — A832

1992, Jan. 2 Litho. *Perf. 13*

1481 A831 10p shown .40 .25
1482 A831 45p Bird mosaic 1.00 1.00

Perf. 14

1483 A832 70p shown 1.75 1.75
Nos. 1481-1483 (3) 3.15 3.00

Nos. 1482-1483 are airmail.

Police Day — A833

1992, Jan. 25 *Perf. 14*

1484 A833 10p multicolored .40 .25

25th Cairo Intl. Fair A834

1992, Feb. 15 Litho. *Perf. 14*

1485 A834 10p multicolored .40 .25

Famous Men Type of 1988

Inscribed "1992"

10p, Sayed Darwish (1882-1923), musician.

1992, Mar. 17 Photo. *Perf. 14x13½*

1486 A760 10p dull org & olive .40 .25

Festivals — A835

1992, Mar. 18 *Perf. 11½*

1487 A835 10p Egyptian hoopoe .40 .25

For use on greeting cards.

World Health Day A836

1992, Apr. 20 Litho. *Perf. 13*

1488 A836 10p multicolored .50 .25

Aswan Dam, 90th Anniv. A837

1992, July Litho. *Perf. 13*

1489 A837 10p No. 487 .50 .25

20th Arab Scout Jamboree — A838

1992, July 10 *Perf. 13x13½*

1490 A838 10p multicolored .50 .25

A839

70p, Summer Games' emblem.

1992, July 20 *Perf. 13½x13*

1491 A839 10p multicolored .45 .25

Size: 80x60mm

Imperf

1492 A839 70p multicolored 5.00 2.50

1992 Summer Olympics, Barcelona.

El Helal Magazine, Cent. — A840

1992, Sept. 14 Litho. *Perf. 13½x13*

1493 A840 10p multicolored .45 .25

Alexandria World Festival — A841

1992, Sept. 27 *Perf. 13x13½*

1494 A841 70p multicolored 1.60 1.60

Congress of Federation of World and American Travel Companies, Cairo — A842

1992, Sept. 20

1495 A842 70p multicolored 1.50 1.50

World Post Day A843

1992, Oct. 9 Litho. *Perf. 13*

1496 A843 10p dk bl, lt bl & blk .45 .25

Children's Day — A844

1992, Oct. 24 Litho. *Perf. 13½x13*

1497 A844 10p multicolored .55 .25

Intl. Conference on Food, Agriculture and World Health A845

1992, Oct. 24 *Perf. 13*

1498 A845 70p multicolored 1.50 1.50

A846

1992, Nov. 21 *Perf. 13½x13*

1499 A846 10p multicolored .50 .25

20th Arab Scout Conference, Cairo.

Famous Men Type of 1988

Inscribed "1992"

No. 1500, Talaat Harb, economist. No. 1501, Mohamed Taymour, writer. No. 1502, Dr. Ahmed Zaki Abu Shadi (with glasses), physician & poet.

1992, Dec. 23 Photo. *Perf. 13½x13*

1500	A760	10p blue & brown	.40	.25
1501	A760	10p citron & blue gray	.40	.25
1502	A760	10p citron & blue gray	.40	.25
a.		Pair, #1501-1502	.90	.90
		Nos. 1500-1502 (3)	1.20	.75

A847

Pharaohs: 10p, Sesostris I. 45p, Amenemhet III. 70p, Hur I.

1993, Jan. 2 Litho. *Perf. 13½x13*

1503	A847	10p brown & yellow	.45	.25
1504	A847	45p brown & yellow	.75	.65
1505	A847	70p brown & yellow	1.20	1.00
a.		Strip of 3, #1503-1505	3.00	3.00

Post Day.

25th Intl. Book Fair, Cairo — A848

1993, Jan. 26 Litho. *Perf. 13½x13*

1506	A848	15p multicolored	.40	.25

A849

A849a

A849b

A849c

A849d

A849e

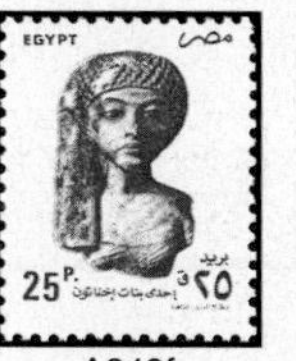

A849f

A849g

A849h

Artifacts: A849, Bust. A849a, Sphinx. A849b, Bust of princess. A849c, Ramses II. A849d, Queen Ti. A849e, Horemheb. A849f, As A849b. A849g, Amenhotep III. £1, Head of a woman. £2, Woman wearing headdress. £5, Pharaonic capital.

Photo., Litho. (#1511)

1993-99 Unwmk. *Perf. 11½x11,*

1507	A849	5p multi	.55	.25
1508	A849a	15p brn & bis	.55	.25
1509	A849a	15p brn & bis	.30	.25
1510	A849b	25p brn & org brn	.35	.25
1511	A849c	55p blk & bl	.90	.50

Size: 21x25mm

Perf. 11¼

1512	A849	5p dp cl & brick red	.50	.25
1513	A849d	5p brown	.30	.25
a.		Wmk. 342	.30	.25
1514	A849a	15p brn & bis	.50	.25
1515	A849e	20p blk & gray	.30	.25
a.		Wmk. 342	.30	.25
1516	A849f	25p brn & org brn	.70	.30
1517	A849f	25p black brown	.30	.25
1518	A849c	55p blk & lt bl	.60	.60
1519	A849g	75p blk & brn	.90	.80

Perf. 11½

1520	A849h	£1 slate & blk	2.25	2.25
1521	A849h	£2 brn & grn	5.00	5.00
1521A	A849h	£5 brn & gold	10.00	10.00
		Nos. 1507-1521A (16)	24.00	21.70

Warning: Avoid using watermark fluid on Nos. 1513-1513a and 1515-1515a. Images will be adversely affected.

Body of Sphinx on Nos. 1509, 1514 stops above value, and extends through value on No. 1508.

Issued: Nos. 1507-1508, 2/1; No. 1509, 3/10; £1, £2, 4/1; No. 1511, 7/1/93; £5, 8/1/93; Nos. 1512, 1514, 1518, 10/30/94; No. 1516, 6/25/94; 20p, 2/1/97; 75p, 3/25/97; No. 1517, 1998; Nos. 1513a, 1515a, 1999.

See Nos. C204-C206.

Architects' Association, 75th Anniv. — A850

1993, Feb. 28 Litho. *Perf. 13x13½*

1522	A850	15p multicolored	.45	.25

New Building for Ministry of Foreign Affairs A851

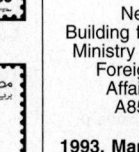

1993, Mar. 15 *Perf. 13*

1523	A851	15p multicolored	.45	.25
1524	A851	80p multicolored	1.50	1.50

Diplomacy Day (No. 1523). No. 1524 is airmail.

Feasts — A852

1993, Mar. 20 Litho. *Perf. 13x13½*

1525	A852	15p Opuntia	.45	.25

For use on greeting cards.

Newspaper, Le Progres Egyptien, Cent. — A853

1993, Apr. 15 Litho. *Perf. 13x13½*

1526	A853	15p multicolored	.40	.25

A854

1993, May 15 Litho. *Perf. 13½x13*

1527	A854	15p multicolored	.50	.25

World Telecommunications Day.

A855

1993, June 15 Litho. *Perf. 13½x13*

1528	A855	15p multicolored	.45	.25

UN Conference on Human Rights, Vienna.

Organization of African Unity — A856

1993, June 26 *Perf. 13*

1529	A856	15p yel grn & multi	.45	.25
1530	A856	80p red violet & multi	1.10	1.10

No. 1530 is airmail.

World PTT Conference, Cairo — A857

1993, Sept. 4 Litho. *Perf. 13*

1531	A857	15p multicolored	.45	.25

Salah El-Din El Ayubi (1137-1193), Dome of the Rock — A858

1993, Sept. 4

1532	A858	55p multicolored	1.10	1.10

A859

1993, Oct. 6

1533	A859	15p multicolored	.50	.25

October War Against Israel, 20th Anniv.

A860

1993, Oct. 12 *Perf. 13½x13*

1534	A860	15p cream & multi	.45	.25
1535	A860	55p silver & multi	1.10	.55
1536	A860	80p gold & multi	1.50	.85

Imperf

Size: 90x70mm

1537	A860	80p multicolored	2.00	2.00
		Nos. 1534-1537 (4)	5.05	3.65

Pres. Mohamed Hosni Mubarak, Third Term.

Reduction of Natural Disasters A861

1993, Oct. 24 Litho. *Perf. 13*

1538	A861	80p multicolored	1.10	1.10

Electricity in Egypt, Cent. — A862

1993, Oct. 24 ***Perf. 13½x13***

1539 A862 15p multicolored .45 .25

Intl. Conference on Big Dams, Cairo — A863

1993, Nov. 19 **Litho.** ***Perf. 13***

1540 A863 15p multicolored .45 .25

35th Military Intl. Soccer Championship — A864

1993, Dec. 1 **Litho.** ***Perf. 13x13½***

1541 A864 15p orange & multi .40 .25
1542 A864 15p Trophy, emblem .40 .25

9th Men's Junior World Handball Championship (No. 1542).

Famous Men Type of 1988

Inscribed "1993"

No. 1543, Abdel Azis Al-Bishry. No. 1544, Mohammad Farid Abu Hadid. No. 1545, Mahmud Beyram el-Tunsi. No. 1546, Ali Moubarak.

1993, Dec. 25 ***Perf. 13½x13***

1543 A760 15p blue .40 .25
1544 A760 15p blue black .40 .25
1545 A760 15p light violet .40 .25
1546 A760 15p green .40 .25
Nos. 1543-1546 (4) 1.60 1.00

Post Day — A865

15p, Amenhotep III. 55p, Queen Hatshepsut. 80p, Thutmose III.

1994, Jan. 2

1547 A865 15p multicolored .45 .25
1548 A865 55p multicolored 1.10 .30
1549 A865 80p multicolored 1.75 .40
Nos. 1547-1549 (3) 3.30 .95

Congress of Egyptian Sedimentary Geology Society — A866

1994, Jan. 4 **Litho.** ***Perf. 13x13½***

1550 A866 15p multicolored .45 .25

Birds A867

1994, Mar. 3 **Litho.** ***Perf. 13***

1551 A867 Block of 4, #a.-d. 2.75 2.75
a. 15p Egyptian swallow .45 .30
b. 15p Fire crest .45 .30
c. 15p Rose-ringed parrot .45 .30
d. 15p Goldfinch .45 .30

Festivals 1994.

Arab Scouting, 40th Anniv. — A868

1994, Mar. 25 ***Perf. 13½x13***

1552 A868 15p multicolored .45 .25

27th Cairo Intl. Fair — A869

1994, Apr. 9 **Litho.** ***Perf. 13½x13***

1553 A869 15p multicolored .45 .25

A870

1994, Apr. 15 **Litho.** ***Perf. 13***

1554 A870 15p green & brown .45 .25

1994 African Telecommunications Exhibition, Cairo.

A871

1994, Apr. 30 **Litho.** ***Perf. 13***

1555 A871 15p grn, blk & blue .45 .25

Natl. Afforestation Campaign.

5th Arab Energy Conference, Cairo. — A872

1994, July 5 **Litho.** ***Perf. 13***

1556 A872 15p multicolored .45 .25

Signing of Washington Accord for Palestinian Self-Rule in Gaza and Jericho — A873

1994, May 4 **Litho.** ***Perf. 13***

1557 A873 15p multicolored .60 .25

18th Biennial Art Exhibition, Alexandria — A874

1994, May 21

1558 A874 15p yel, blk & gray .45 .25

Organization of African Unity — A875

1994, May 25

1559 A875 15p multicolored .45 .25

Natl. Reading Festival — A876

1994, June 15

1560 A876 15p multicolored .45 .25

ILO, 75th Anniv. — A877

1994, June 28 **Litho.** ***Perf. 13½x13***

1561 A877 15p multicolored .45 .25

Intl. Conference on Population and Development, Cairo — A878

15p, Conference, UN emblems. 80p, Drawings, hieroglyphics, conference emblem.

1994, Sept. 5 **Litho.** ***Perf. 13***

1562 A878 15p multi .45 .25
1563 A878 80p multi, vert. 1.10 .75

No. 1563 is airmail.

World Junior Squash Championships — A879

1994, Sept. 14 **Litho.** ***Perf. 13***

1564 A879 15p multicolored .45 .25

World Post Day A880

1994, Oct. 9 **Litho.** ***Perf. 13***

1565 A880 15p multicolored .50 .25

Intl. Red Cross & Red Crescent Societies, 75th Anniv. — A881

1994, Oct. 24

1566 A881 80p multicolored 1.50 .90

Akhbar El-Yom Newspaper, 50th Anniv. — A882

1994, Nov. 11
1567 A882 15p multicolored .45 .25

African Field Hockey Club Championships — A883

1994, Nov. 14 Litho. *Perf. 13*
1568 A883 15p multicolored .45 .25

A884

Opera Aida, by Verdi — A885

1994, Nov. 26
1569 A884 15p multicolored .45 .25

Imperf

Size: 58x69mm

1570 A885 80p multicolored 2.25 2.25

No. 1570 is airmail.

Intl. Olympic Committee, Cent. — A886

1994, Dec. 10 *Perf. 13*
1571 A886 15p multicolored .45 .25

Egyptian Youth Hostels Assoc., 40th Anniv. — A887

1994, Dec. 24
1572 A887 15p multicolored .45 .25

Intl. Speed Ball Federation, 10th Anniv. — A888

1994, Dec. 25
1573 A888 15p multicolored .45 .25

African Development Bank, 30th Anniv. — A889

1994, Dec. 26
1574 A889 15p multicolored .45 .25

Opening of Suez Canal, 125th Anniv. — A890

Design: 80p, Map, inaugural ceremony.

1994, Dec. 27
1575 A890 15p multicolored .65 .25
1576 A890 80p multicolored 1.25 .75

No. 1576 is airmail.

Famous Men — A891

No. 1577, Hassan Fathy, engineer. No. 1578, Mahmoud Taimour, writer.

1994, Dec. 29
1577 A891 15p multicolored .40 .25
1578 A891 15p multicolored .40 .25

Post Day — A892

15p, Statue of Akhenaton. 55p, Golden mask of King Tutankhamun. 80p, Statue of Nefertiti.

1995, Jan. 2 Litho. *Perf. 13½x13*
1579 A892 15p multicolored .50 .25
1580 A892 55p multicolored 1.10 .40
1581 A892 80p multicolored 1.50 .50
Nos. 1579-1581 (3) 3.10 1.15

World Tourism Organization, 20th Anniv. — A893

1995, Jan. 2 *Perf. 13x13½*
1582 A893 15p multicolored .45 .25

Festivals — A894

1995, Feb. 25 Litho. *Perf. 13x13½*
1583 A894 15p multicolored .45 .25

For use on greeting cards.

Egyptian Women's Day — A895

1995, Mar. 16 Litho. *Perf. 13x13½*
1584 A895 15p multicolored .45 .25

Arab League, 50th Anniv. — A896

1995, Mar. 22 *Perf. 13½x13*
1585 A896 15p blue & multi .45 .25
1586 A896 55p green & multi .75 .75

Sheraton Hotel, Cairo, 25th Anniv. — A897

1995, Mar. 28 *Perf. 13x13½*
1587 A897 15p multicolored .45 .25

Misr Bank, 75th Anniv. — A898

1995, May 7 Litho. *Perf. 13½x13*
1588 A898 15p multicolored .50 .25

World Telecommunications Day — A899

1995, May 31 *Perf. 13x13½*
1589 A899 80p multicolored 1.00 .50

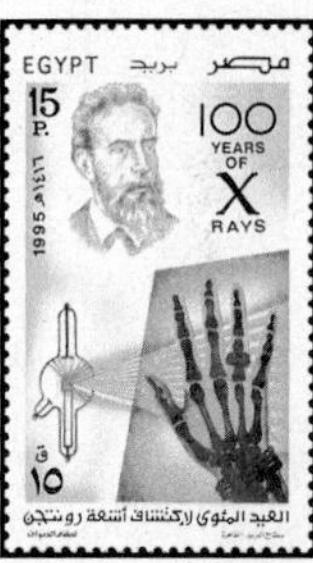

Wilhelm Roentgen (1845-1923), Discovery of the X-Ray, Cent. — A900

1995, May Litho. *Perf. 13½x13*
1590 A900 15p multicolored .50 .25

Membership in World Heritage Committee, 20th Anniv. (in 1994) — A901

Artifacts from the Shaft of Luxor: No. 1591, Goddess Hathor. No. 1592, God Atoum. 80p, God Amon and Horemheb.

1995, July 23 Litho. *Perf. 13½x13*
1591 15p multicolored .45 .25
1592 15p multicolored .45 .25
a. A901 Pair, #1591-1592 1.10 1.10
1593 A901 80p multicolored 1.10 1.10
Nos. 1591-1593 (3) 2.00 1.60

No. 1592a is a continuous design. No. 1593 is airmail.

21st Intl. Conference on Pediatrics, Cairo A902

1995, Sept. 10 Litho. *Perf. 13*

1594 A902 15p multicolored .50 .25

Intl. Ozone Day — A903

1995, Sept. 16 Litho. *Perf. 13x12½*

1595 A903 15p green & multi .45 .25
1596 A903 55p brown & multi .90 .45
1597 A903 80p blue & multi 1.40 .55
Nos. 1595-1597 (3) 2.75 1.25

See Nos. 1622-1623.

World Tourism Day A904

1995, Sept. 25 *Perf. 12½x13*

1598 A904 15p multicolored 1.00 .25

Government Printing House, 175th Anniv. — A905

1995, Sept. 27

1599 A905 15p multicolored .45 .25

Sun Verticality on Abu Simbel Temple A906

1995, Oct. 22 Litho. *Perf. 12½x13*

1600 A906 15p multicolored .95 .30

Opening of New Esna Dam — A907

1995, Nov. 25 *Perf. 12½*

1601 A907 15p multicolored .75 .30

Egyptian Engineers Assoc., 75th Anniv. A908

1995, Dec. 20 *Perf. 13*

1602 A908 15p multicolored .45 .25

A909

Famous entertainers.

1995, Dec. 9 Litho. *Perf. 13x12½*

1603 A909 15p Abdel Halim Hafez .40 .25
1604 A909 15p Youssef Wahbi .40 .25
1605 A909 15p Naquib el-Rihani .40 .25
Nos. 1603-1605 (3) 1.20 .75

A910

1995, Dec. 23 Litho. *Perf. 13x12½*

1606 A910 15p multicolored .45 .25

Motion Pictures, cent.

Post Day A911

Ancient paintings: 55p, Man facing right. 80p, Man facing left. 100p, Playing flute, dancers.

1996, Jan. 2 Litho. *Perf. 13½x13*

1607 55p multicolored 1.10 .60
1608 80p multicolored 1.50 .90
a. A911 Pair, Nos. 1607-1608 2.75 2.75

Imperf

Size: 88x72mm

1609 A911 100p multicolored 3.00 3.00

Nos. 1607-1608 are airmail.

Feasts — A912

1996, Feb. 15 *Perf. 12½*

1610 A912 15p Blue convolvulus .45 .25
1611 A912 15p Red poppies .45 .25
a. Pair, No. 1610-1611 .95 .95

For use on greeting cards.

A913

1996, Mar. 13 Litho. *Perf. 13x12½*

1612 A913 15p pink & multi .40 .25
1613 A913 80p brown & multi .90 .60

Summit of Peace Makers, Sharm al-Sheikh. No. 1613 is airmail.

A914

1996, Mar. 16

1614 A914 15p multicolored .45 .25

29th Intl. Fair, Cairo.

Egyptian Geological Survey, Cent. A915

1996, Mar. 18 *Perf. 12½x13*

1615 A915 15p multicolored .45 .25

A916

1996, Apr. 11 Litho. *Perf. 13x12½*

1616 A916 15p blue & multi .45 .25
1617 A916 80p pink & multi .95 .50

Signing of African Nuclear Weapon-Free Zone Treaty.

A917

1996, Apr. 20 Litho. *Perf. 13x12½*

1618 A917 15p multicolored .45 .25

Egyptian Society of Accountants and Auditors, 50th anniv.

General Census — A918

1996, May 4

1619 A918 15p multicolored .45 .25

A919

1996 Summer Olympics, Atlanta: 15p, Atlanta 1996 emblem. £1, Emblem surrounded by sports pictograms.

1996, July 15 Litho. *Perf. 13x12½*

1620 A919 15p lilac & multi .50 .25

Size: 63x103mm

Imperf

1621 A919 £1 black & multi 2.75 2.75

No. 1621 is airmail.

Intl. Ozone Day Type of 1995

1996, Sept. 16 Litho. *Perf. 13x12½*

1622 A903 15p pink & multi .40 .25
1623 A903 80p gray & multi 1.10 .55

No. 1623 is airmail.

A920

1996, Sept. 19

1624 A920 80p multicolored .75 .45

2nd Alexandria World Festival.

A921

1996, Sept. 21

1625 A921 15p grn, blk & bl .45 .25

Scientific Research and Technology Academy, 25th anniv.

A922

1996, Oct. 7 *Perf. 12½x13*

1626 A922 15p multicolored .50 .25

Opening of 2nd Line of Greater Cairo Subway System.

Rowing Festival A923

1996, Sept. 27
1627 A923 15p multicolored .75 .25

Intl. Tourism Day. See Nos. C215-C216.

Courts of the State Council, 50th Anniv. A924

1996, Nov. 2 Litho. *Perf. 12½x13*
1628 A924 15p blue & claret .45 .25

A925

1996, Nov. 4 *Perf. 13x12½*
1629 A925 15p yel, blk & blue .40 .25

25th World Conference of Intl. Federation of Training and Development Organizations.

A926

Cairo Economic Summit (MENA): £1, Graph, earth, gear, olive branch, wheat.

1996, Nov. 12 Litho. *Perf. 13x12½*
1630 A926 15p shown .45 .25

Size: 65x45mm

Imperf

1631 A926 £1 multicolored 1.75 1.75

No. 1631 is airmail.

A927

1996, Nov. 13 *Perf. 13x12½*
1632 A927 15p multicolored .45 .25

1996 World Food Summit, Rome.

A928

National Day of El-Gharbia Governorate: Al Sayd Ahmed El-Badawy mosque, Tanta.

1996, Nov. 16
1633 A928 15p multicolored .45 .25

A929

Famous artists: No. 1634, Ali El-Kassar. No. 1635, George Abyad. No. 1636, Mohamed Kareem. No. 1637, Fatma Roshdi.

1996, Dec. 28 Litho. *Perf. 13x12½*
1634 A929 20p black .45 .25
1635 A929 20p red brown .45 .25
1636 A929 20p brown .45 .25
1637 A929 20p black .45 .25
Nos. 1634-1637 (4) 1.80 1.00

See Nos. 1666-1669.

A930

1997, Jan. 2
1638 A930 20p multicolored .45 .25

Size: 61x80mm

Imperf

1639 A930 £1 multicolored 2.00 2.00

Post Day; Discovery of Tutankhamun's tomb, 75th anniv.
No. 1639 is airmail.

Police Day A931

1997, Jan. 25 Litho. *Perf. 13x13½*
1640 A931 20p multicolored .45 .25

Feasts — A932

1997, Feb. 1 *Perf. 13*
1641 A932 20p Pink asters .40 .25
1642 A932 20p White asters .40 .25
a. Pair, #1641-1642 .95 .95

For use on greeting cards.

World Civil Defense Day A933

1997, Mar. 10 Litho. *Perf. 13x13½*
1643 A933 20p multicolored .45 .25

30th Cairo Intl. Fair — A934

1997, Mar. 19 *Perf. 13½x13*
1644 A934 20p multicolored .45 .25

Mahmoud Said, Photographer, Artist, Birth Cent. — A935

The City, By Mahmoud Said — A936

1997, Apr. 12 Litho. *Perf. 12½*
1645 A935 20p multicolored .45 .25

Size: 80x60mm

Imperf

1646 A936 £1 multicolored 1.25 1.25

No. 1646 is airmail.

Institute of African Research and Studies, 50th Anniv. — A937

1997, May 27 Litho. *Perf. 13*
1647 A937 75p multicolored .65 .65

New Headquarters of State Information Service — A938

1997, Aug. 16 Litho. *Perf. 12½*
1648 A938 20p multicolored .45 .25

A939

£1, Mascot, soccer ball, playing field, emblems.

1997, Sept. 4 *Perf. 13x12½*
1649 A939 20p multicolored .45 .25
1650 AP81 75p multicolored .70 .65

Size: 75x55mm

Imperf

1651 A939 £1 multicolored 1.75 1.75

Nos. 1650-1651 are airmail. Under 17 FIFA World Soccer Championships, Egypt.

A940

1997, Sept. 16 *Perf. 13*
1652 A940 20p lt bl grn & multi .60 .30
1653 A940 £1 pink & multi 1.60 1.25

Montreal Protocol on Substances that Deplete the Ozone Layer, 10th anniv. No. 1653 is airmail.

Completion of Second Stage of Metro Line No. 2 — A941

1997, Sept. 27 *Perf. 12½x13*
1654 A941 20p multicolored .45 .25

Premiere in Egypt of Opera Aida, by Verdi, 125th Anniv. A942

1997, Oct. 12 *Perf. 13*
1655 A942 20p multicolored .60 .25

Size: 80x75mm

Imperf

1656 A942 £1 like #1655 4.00 4.00

No. 1656 is airmail.

Queen Nefertari — A943

1997, Oct. 25 Litho. *Perf. 13*
1657 A943 £1 multicolored 1.25 1.25
a. Perf. 14¼x14 — —

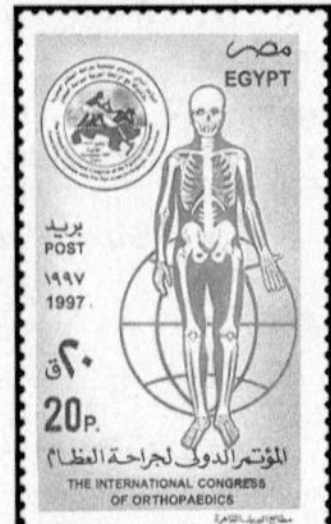
A944

1997, Nov. 17 Litho. *Perf. 13*

1658	A944	20p multicolored	.50	.25

Intl. Congress of Orthopedics, Cairo.

A945

Designs: 20p, Goddess Selket. £1, Scarab, baboon pendant.

1997, Nov. 22 *Perf. 13x12½*

1659	A945	20p black & gold	.50	.25

Size: 73x62mm

Imperf

1660	A945	£1 multicolored	1.50	1.50

No. 1660 is airmail. Discovery of King Tutanhkamen's tomb, 75th anniv.

Inauguration of Nubia Monument Museum — A946

1997, Nov. 23 *Perf. 13*

1661	A946	20p multicolored	.95	.25

Arab Land Bank, 50th Anniv. — A947

1997, Dec. 10 *Perf. 12½*

1662	A947	20p multicolored	.60	.25

5th Pan Arab Congress on Anesthesia and Intensive Care — A948

1997, Dec. 9 Litho. *Perf. 13*

1663	A948	20p multicolored	.45	.25

El Salaam Canal — A949

1997, Dec. 28

1664	A949	20p multicolored	.60	.25

Liberation of Sinai, 15th anniv.

Famous Artists Type of 1996 and

A950

1997, Dec. 23 Litho. *Perf. 13x12½*

1665	A950	20p blue	.40	.25
1666	A929	20p Zaky Tolaimat	.40	.25
1667	A929	20p Ismael Yassen	.40	.25
1668	A929	20p Zaky Roustom	.40	.25
1669	A929	20p Soliman Naguib	.40	.25
a.		Strip of 5, #1665-1669	2.00	2.00

A951

Post Day: 20p, King Tutankhamun's guard. 75p, King Ramses III. £1, Cover of King Tutankhamun's coffin.

1998, Jan. 2 *Perf. 13*

1670	A951	20p multicolored	.45	.25
1671	A951	75p multicolored	1.10	.65

Size: 26x43mm

1672	A951	£1 multicolored	1.75	.85

Nos. 1671-1672 are airmail.

Feasts — A952

1998, Jan. 20

1673	20p multicolored	.40	.25
1674	20p multicolored	.40	.25
a.	A952 Pair, #1673-1674	.80	.80

For use on greeting cards.

Intl. Cairo Fair — A954

1998, Mar. 11 Litho. *Perf. 13*

1675	A954	20p multicolored	.50	.25

Natl. Bank of Egypt, Cent. — A955

1998, Mar. 12

1676	A955	20p multicolored	.50	.25

Tutankhamun A956

Thutmose IV A957

1998 Litho. *Perf. 13½x12½*

1677	A956	£2 pink & multi	1.75	1.75
1677A	A956	£2 Like #1677, with white background	—	—
b.		Perf. 14x14¼	—	—
1678	A957	£5 purple & black	5.00	3.75
		Nos. 1677-1678 (3)	6.75	5.50

Issued: £2, 4/23; £5, 3/23.

A958

1998, Apr. 14 *Perf. 13*

1679	A958	20p green & multi	.45	.25
1680	A958	75p blue & multi	1.10	.75

Size: 70x52mm

Imperf

1681	A958	£1 Natl. flags, map, trophy	1.50	1.00

Egypt, winners of 21st African Cup of Nations soccer competition.
Nos. 1680-1681 are airmail.

Egyptian Satellite "Nile Sat" — A959

1998, May 30 Litho. *Perf. 13*

1682	A959	20p multicolored	.50	.25

World Environment Day — A960

1998, June 5

1683	A960	20p shown	.60	.25

Size: 43x62mm

Imperf

1684	A960	£1 Fauna, emblems	3.75	3.75

No. 1684 is airmail.

A961

1998, June 14

1685	A961	20p blue & black	.40	.25
1686	A961	£1 yel, grn & blk	1.10	.80

Dr. Ahmed Zewail, winner of Franklin Institute award.
No. 1686 is airmail.

A962

Imam Sheikh Mohamed Metwalli Al-Shaarawi.

1998, July 15

1687	A962	20p buff & multi	.40	.25
1688	A962	£1 green & multi	1.10	.80

No. 1688 is airmail.

Day of the Nile Flood — A963

1998, Sept. 12 Litho. *Perf. 13*

1689	A963	20p multicolored	.50	.25

A964

1998, Sept. 30 Litho. *Perf. 13*

1690	A964	20p multicolored	.50	.25

Chemistry Administration, cent.

October War Against Israel, 25th Anniv. — A965

1998, Oct. 6 Litho. *Perf. 13*
1691 A965 20p multicolored .60 .25

Size: 50x70mm

Imperf

1692 A965 £2 like No. 1691 3.25 3.25

No. 1692 is airmail.

Egyptian Survey Authority, Cent. — A966

1998, Oct. 15 *Perf. 13*
1693 A966 20p multicolored .50 .25

Cairo University, 90th Anniv. — A967

1998, Dec. 7 Litho. *Perf. 13*
1694 A967 20p multicolored .50 .25

A968

1998, Dec. 17 Litho. *Perf. 13*
1695 A968 20p multicolored .45 .25

Egyptian trade unions, cent.

A970

Post Day (19th Dynasty): 20p, Queen Nefertari, Goddess Isis. 125p, God Osiris, Goddess Isis.

1999, Jan. 2 Litho. *Perf. 13*
1696 A970 20p multicolored .50 .25

Size: 41x61mm

Imperf

1697 A970 125p multicolored 2.00 2.00

No. 1697 is airmail.

Feasts — A971

1999, Jan. 5 *Perf. 13*
1698 20p multicolored 1.00 .30
1699 20p multicolored .40 .25
a. A971 Pair, #1698-1699 1.75 *1.75*

For use on greeting cards.

Intl. Women's Day — A973

1999, Mar. 7 Litho. *Perf. 13*
1700 A973 20p multicolored .50 .25

Cairo Intl. Fair — A974

1999, Mar. 9
1701 A974 20p multicolored .50 .25

Opening of Metro Line Beneath Nile River — A975

1999, Apr. Litho. *Perf. 13*
1702 A975 20p multicolored .60 .25

A976

UPU, 125th Anniv. — A977

1999, Apr. 21
1703 A976 20p shown .45 .25
1704 A976 £1 multi 1.25 .85
1705 A977 125p shown 1.50 1.20

Size: 50x70mm

Imperf

1706 A977 125p multi 2.10 2.10
Nos. 1703-1706 (4) 5.30 4.40

Nos. 1704-1706 are airmail.

A978

1999, May 8 *Perf. 13*
1707 A978 20p green & multi .45 .25
1708 A978 125p buff, red & multi 1.25 1.00

Geneva Conventions, 50th anniv. No. 1708 is airmail.

A980

1999, May 20 Litho. *Perf. 13x12¾*
1710 A980 20p green & multi .45 .25
1711 A980 £1 buff & multi .95 .85

African Development Bank, 35th Meeting, Cairo. No. 1711 is airmail.

16th Men's Handball World Championship — A981

20p, Stylized player with ball, pyramids. 1£, Mascot with ball, Sphinx, pyramids, globe. 125p, Mascot with ball, goalie, pyramids.

1999, June 1 *Perf. 13*
1712 A981 20p multicolored .45 .25
1713 A981 £1 multicolored .90 .85
1714 A981 125p multicolored 1.10 1.00
Nos. 1712-1714 (3) 2.45 2.10

Nos. 1713-1714 are airmail.

Goddess Selket — A982

1999, June 23 Litho. *Perf. 13*
1715 A982 25p multicolored .40 .25

See Nos. 1750, 1754.

SOS Children's Village, 50th Anniv. — A983

1999, June 23 *Perf. 12¾x13¼*
1716 A983 20p grn, blk & blue .45 .25
1717 A983 125p pale yel, blk & bl 1.25 1.10

No. 1717 is airmail.

A984

No. 1718, Sameera Moussa (1917-52), Physicist. No. 1719, Aisha Abdul Rahman (1913-98), writer. No. 1720, Ahmed Eldemerdash Touny (1907-97), member of Intl. Olympic Committee.

1999 Litho. *Perf. 13x12¾*
1718 A984 20p multicolored .45 .25
1719 A984 20p multicolored .45 .25
1720 A984 20p multicolored .45 .25
Nos. 1718-1720 (3) 1.35 .75

Issued: Nos. 1718-1719, 7/23; No. 1720, 8/13.

See Nos. 1730-1733.

A985

1999, Oct. 5 Litho. *Perf. 13x12¾*
1721 A985 20p org & multi .45 .25
1722 A985 £1 silver & multi .90 .85
1723 A985 125p gold & multi 1.10 1.00

Imperf

1724 A985 125p multicolored 2.00 2.00
Nos. 1721-1724 (4) 4.45 4.10

Pres. Hosni Mubarak, 4th term. Nos. 1722-1724 are airmail.

A986

1999, Nov. 15 Litho. *Perf. 13¼x13*

Background Color

1725 A986 20p green .45 .25
1726 A986 £1 red vio .90 .85
1727 A986 125p purple 1.10 1.00
Nos. 1725-1727 (3) 2.45 2.10

Intl. Year of the Elderly. Nos. 1726-1727 are airmail.

A987

1999, Nov. 20
1728 A987 20p multi .50 .25

Children's Day.

Famous People Type of 1999

No. 1730, Farid El Attrash (1913-76), singer, movie star. No. 1731, Laila Mourad (1918-95), singer, movie star. No. 1732, Anwar Wagdi (1911-55), actor, director. No. 1733, Asia Dagher (1901-86), actor, producer.

1999, Dec. 30 Litho. ***Perf. 13x12¾***

1730	A984	20p lt bl & blk	.40	.25
1731	A984	20p lt bl & blk	.40	.25
1732	A984	20p lt bl & blk	.40	.25
1733	A984	20p lt bl & blk	.40	.25
		Nos. 1730-1733 (4)	1.60	1.00

Millennium A989

20p, "1999" & "2000." 125p, Countdown of years. £2, Holy Family, Virgin Tree.

2000, Jan. 1 ***Perf. 13x12¾***

1734	A989	20p multi	.45	.25
1735	A989	125p multi	1.25	1.10

Size: 70x50mm

Imperf

1736	A989	£2 multi, horiz.	4.00	4.00
		Nos. 1734-1736 (3)	5.70	5.35

Nos. 1735-1736 are airmail.

A990

Post Day — A991

2000, Jan. 2 ***Perf. 13¼x12¾***

1737	A990	20p multi	.50	.25
1738	A991	20p multi	.50	.25
a.		Pair, #1737-1738	1.25	1.25

Size: 70x50mm

Imperf

1739	A991	125p Chariot, horiz.	2.00	2.00
		Nos. 1737-1739 (3)	3.00	2.50

Ain Shams University, 50th Anniv. — A992

2000, Jan. 3 ***Perf. 13¼x13***

1740 A992 20p multi .50 .25

Festivals

A993 A994

2000, Jan. 5 ***Perf. 13x13¼***

1741	A993	20p multi	.40	.25
1742	A994	20p multi	.40	.25
a.		Pair, #1741-1742	.90	.90

For use on greeting cards.

A995

2000, Jan. 20 ***Perf. 13¼x13***

1743 A995 20p multi .50 .25

Islamic Development Bank, 25th anniv.

A996

2000, Feb. 28 ***Perf. 13¼x12¾***

1744 A996 125p multi 1.25 1.25

Common Market for Eastern and Southern Africa Economic Conference.

Death of Om Kolthoum, 25th Anniv. — A997

2000, Mar. 11 ***Perf. 13¼x13***

1745 A997 20p multi .50 .25

8th Intl. Congress of Egyptologists — A998

2000, Mar. 28 ***Perf. 13x13¼***

1746 A998 20p multi .50 .25

Europe-Africa Summit, Cairo — A999

2000, Apr. 3 ***Perf. 13¼x13***

1747 A999 125p multi 1.25 1.25

Group of 15 Developing Nations, 10th Summit, Cairo — A1000

Perf. 12¾x13¼

2000, June 19 **Litho.**

1748 A1000 125p multi 1.25 1.25

Goddess Selket Type of 1999 and

Scene from 20th Dynasty A1003

Nofret, Wife of Rahotep A1004

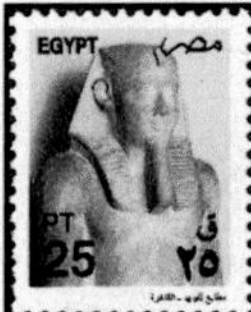

King Seostris A1005

Princess Merit Aton A1006

20th Dynasty — A1007

Pyramid at Snefru A1008

Wife of Sheikh-el-Balad A1009

King Psusennes I A1010

King Tutankhamun A1011

Obelisk of Ramses II A1011a

Temple of Karnak A1012

Perf. 12¾x13¼, 11¼ (#1750A, 1752-1755, 1757), 11x11½ (#1758-1760), 13¼x12¾ (#1756, 1761, 1763)

Photo., Litho. (#1750, 1750A, 1751, 1754, 1754A, 1761, 1763)

2000-2002

1750	A982	10p multi, type I	.40	.25
1750A	A982	10p multi, Type II	*3.00*	*3.00*
1751	A1003	10p multi	.40	.25
1752	A1004	20p multi	.40	.25
a.		With dot pattern in headdress and on chest and face ('07)	—	—
1753	A1005	25p multi	.40	.25
1754	A982	30p multi, Type I	.60	.45
1754A	A982	30p multi, Type II	—	—
1755	A1006	30p multi	.50	.35
1756	A1007	50p multi	.65	.45
1757	A1008	£1 multi	.60	.25
1758	A1009	110p multi	1.25	.95
1759	A1010	125p multi	1.40	1.00
1760	A1011	150p multi	1.75	1.25
1761	A1011a	225p multi	2.75	2.00
1763	A1012	£5 multi	5.75	5.50
a.		Perf. 14x14¼	—	—
		Nos. 1750-1763 (15)	19.85	16.20

Issued: 20p, 6/25; No. 1750, 3/25/01; No. 1750A, 2001 (?); 30p, 6/11/01. Nos. 1751, 1755, 225p, 5/25/02; 110p, 6/4/02; 125p, 6/20/02; 150p, 6/15/02; £5, 6/1/02. 30p, 50p, £1, 6/30/02.

Type I (Nos. 1750, 1754), has "Goddess" in smaller type than "Silakht." Type II (No. 1750A, 1754A), has "Goddess" and "Silakht" in type the same height.

Intl. Day Against Drug Abuse — A1013

Perf. 12¾x13¼

2000, June 26 **Litho.**

1764 A1013 20p multi .50 .25

See No. 1796.

Natl. Insurance Company, Cent. — A1014

125p, Emblem, building, horiz.

Perf. 13¼x12¾

2000, Aug. 20 **Litho.**

1765 A1014 20p shown .50 .25

Imperf

Size: 96x75mm

1766 A1014 125p multi 2.25 2.25

2000 Summer Olympics, Sydney
A1015

Background colors: 20p, Light blue. 125p, Pink.

2000, Sept. 9 ***Perf. 13¼x12¾***
1767-1768 A1015 Set of 2 1.75 1.50

No. 1768 is airmail.

Productive Cooperative Union, 25th Anniv. — A1016

2000, Sept. 15 ***Perf. 12¾x13¼***
1769 A1016 20p multi .50 .25

Opening of Fourth Stage of Second Cairo Subway Line — A1017

2000, Oct. 7
1770 A1017 20p multi .60 .25

World Post Day — A1018

2000, Oct. 9
1771 A1018 125p multi 1.40 1.40

Solidarity with Palestinians — A1019

Palestinian Authority flag and: 20p, Dome of the Rock, Jerusalem, vert. No. 1773, 125p, shown. No. 1774, 125p, Dome of the Rock, father and boy, vert.

Perf. 13¼x12¾, 12¾x13¼
2000, Nov. 29
1772-1774 A1019 Set of 3 3.25 3.25

No. 1774 is airmail.

Opening of El-Ferdan Railway Bridge — A1020

2000, Dec. 2 ***Perf. 12¾x13¼***
1775 A1020 20p multi .70 .25

Disabled Person's Day — A1021

2000, Dec. 9 ***Perf. 13¼x12¾***
1776 A1021 20p multi .50 .25

Opening of Al-Azhar Professorial Building — A1022

2000, Dec. 10 ***Perf. 12¾x13¼***
1777 A1022 20p multi .50 .25

Famous Egyptians
A1023

No. 1778: a, Karem Mahmoud, artist (yellow background). b, Mahmoud El-Miligi, artist (green background). c, Mohamed Fawzi, musician (pink background). d, Hussein Riyad, artist (lilac background). e, Abdel Wares Asser, artist (light blue background).

2000, Dec. 24 ***Perf. 13¼x12¾***
1778 Horiz. strip of 5 2.00 2.00
a.-e. A1023 20p Any single .40 .25

Feasts — A1024

a, Red and yellow flowers. b, Purple flowers.

Perf. 12¾x13¼
2000, Dec. 23 **Litho.**
1779 A1024 20p Pair, #a-b .90 .90

For use on greeting cards.

Jerusalem, City of Peace — A1025

2001, Jan. 1 ***Imperf.***
1780 A1025 £2 multi 2.00 2.00

Post Day — A1026

Ancient Egyptian art: 20p, 8 standing figures. No. 1782, 125p, 3 large standing figures.

2001, Jan. 2 ***Perf. 12¾x13¼***
1781-1782 A1026 Set of 2 1.75 1.75

Imperf

Size: 80x60mm

1783 A1026 125p Chariot 2.00 2.00

No. 1782 is airmail.

Arab Labor Organization, 36th Anniv. — A1027

Perf. 13¼x12¾
2001, Feb. 10 **Litho.**
1784 A1027 20p multi .50 .25

Postal Savings Bank, Cent. — A1028

2001, Mar. 1
1785 A1028 20p multi .50 .25

Natl. Council for Women, 1st Anniv. — A1029

Background colors: 30p, Pink. 125p, Blue.

2001, Mar. 16 ***Perf. 12¾x13¼***
1786-1787 A1029 Set of 2 2.00 1.40

No. 1787 is airmail.

Cairo Intl. Fair — A1030

2001, Mar. 21 ***Perf. 13¼x12¾***
1788 A1030 30p multi .50 .25

Helwan University, 25th Anniv. — A1031

2001, May 4 ***Perf. 12¾x13¼***
1789 A1031 30p multi .50 .25

Inauguration of Alexandria Library — A1032

2001, May 20
1790 A1032 125p multi 1.40 1.25

African Conference on the Future of Children
A1033

Background color: 30p, Blue. 125p, Red.

2001, May 28 ***Perf. 13¼x12¾***
1791-1792 A1033 Set of 2 1.75 1.40

No. 1792 is airmail.

World Environment Day — A1034

2001, June 5 **Litho.** ***Perf. 13¼x12¾***
1793 A1034 125p multi 1.40 1.25

World Military Soccer Championships A1035

Designs: 30p, Emblem. 125p, Emblem and map.

Perf. 13¼x12¾

2001, June 21 **Litho.**
1794-1795 A1035 Set of 2 1.75 1.50

Intl. Day Against Drug Abuse Type of 2000

2001, June 26 ***Perf. 12¾x13¼***
1796 A1013 30p multi .50 .25

Egypt's Victory in World Military Soccer Championships — A1036

2001, July 6 **Litho.** ***Imperf.***
1797 A1036 125p multi 1.75 1.75

Egyptian Railways, 150th Anniv. — A1037

2001, July 12 ***Perf. 12¾x13¼***
1798 A1037 30p multi .75 .25

Poets — A1038

No. 1799: a, Aziz Abaza Pasha (1898-73), blue background. b, Ahmed Rami (1892-1981), pink background.

2001, July 28 ***Perf. 13¼x12¾***
1799 A1038 30p Horiz. pair, #a-b .80 .80

Intl. Volunteers Year — A1039

2001, Aug. 18
1800 A1039 125p multi 1.40 1.10

Ismailia Folklore Festival — A1040

2001, Aug. 20
1801 A1040 30p multi .60 .25

Satellite Telecommunications Ground Stations, 25th Anniv. — A1041

2001, Sept. 8 ***Perf. 12¾x13¼***
1802 A1041 30p multi .60 .25

Year of Dialogue Among Civilizations A1042

Designs: No. 1803, 125p, Emblem. No. 1804, 125p, UN emblem, globe, symbols of various civilizations, horiz.

Perf. 13¼x12¾, 12¾x13¼

2001, Oct. 9
1803-1804 A1042 Set of 2 3.00 2.50

Opening of Suez Canal Bridge — A1043

No. 1805: a, 30p, Bridge, ship. b, 125p, Bridge, road.
No. 1806, Bridge, ship and flags of Egypt and Japan.

2001, Oct. 10 ***Perf. 12¾x13¼***
1805 A1043 Horiz. pair, #a-b 1.75 1.75

Imperf

Size: 81x60mm

1806 A1043 125p multi 2.00 2.00

Ancient Gold Masks — A1044

Designs: No. 1807, 30p, Mask of San Xing Dui, China, green background. No. 1808, 30p, Funerary mask of King Tutankhamun, brown background.

2001, Oct. 12 ***Perf. 12¾x13¼***
1807-1808 A1044 Set of 2 .80 .60

See People's Republic of China 3141-3142.

Opening of Azhar Tunnels, Cairo — A1045

2001, Oct. 28 ***Perf. 13¼x12¾***
1809 A1045 30p multi .60 .25

El-Menoufia University, 25th Anniv. — A1046

2001, Nov. 25
1810 A1046 30p multi .60 .25

Feasts — A1047

No.1811: a, Black and white bird on branch. b, Sea gulls. c, Parrot. d, Blue bird on branch.

2001, Dec. 5
1811 A1047 30p Block of 4, #a-d 2.50 2.00

For use on greeting cards.

Musicians — A1048

No. 1812: a, Zakaria Ahmed (1896-1961) with scarf around neck (4). b, Riyadh El-Sonbati (1908-81) with glasses with rectangular lenses (3). c, Mahmoud El-Sherif (1912-90) (2). d, Mohamed El-Kasabgi (1898-1966) with glasses with round lenses (1). Stamp numbers, shown in parentheses, are found at the bottom center in Arabian script.

2001, Dec.
1812 A1048 30p Horiz. strip of 4 2.00 1.40

Painting From Tomb of Anhur Khawi — A1049

Painting from Tomb of Irinefer — A1050

2002, Jan. 2 **Litho.** ***Perf. 12¾x13¼***
1813 A1049 30p multi .45 .25

Imperf

Size: 79x60mm

1814 A1050 125p multi 2.25 2.25

Post Day.

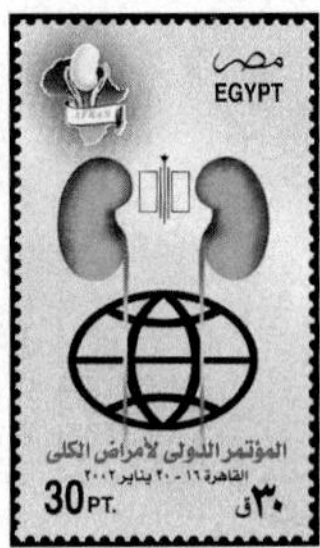

Intl. Nephrology Congress A1051

2002, Jan. 16 **Litho.** ***Perf. 13¼x12¾***
1815 A1051 30p multi .45 .25

Police Day, 50th Anniv. A1052

2002, Jan. 25 ***Perf. 12¾x13¼***
1816 A1052 30p multi .45 .25

Imperf

Size: 79x50mm

1817 A1052 30p multi 1.60 1.50

Return of Sinai to Egypt, 20th Anniv. — A1053

2002, Apr. 25 ***Perf. 13¼x12¾***
1818 A1053 30p multi .60 .25

Cairo Bank, 50th Anniv. — A1054

2002, May 15
1819 A1054 30p multi .50 .25

Weight Lifters — A1055

No. 1820: a, Ibrahim Shams, 1948 (weights over head). b, Khidre el Touney, 1936 (weights at knees).

2002, June 1
1820 A1055 30p Horiz. pair, #a-b .80 .80

Al Akhbar Newspaper, 50th Anniv. — A1056

2002, June 15 ***Perf. 12¾x13¼***
1821 A1056 30p multi .45 .25

Nos. 318-321 and Egyptian Arms — A1057

2002, July 23 **Litho.** ***Imperf.***
1822 A1057 125p multi 1.40 1.40

July 23rd Revolution, 50th anniv.

Aswan Dam, Cent. — A1058

No. 1823: a, Dam. b, Dam and buildings.

2002, Aug. 15 ***Perf. 12¾x13¼***
1823 A1058 30p Horiz. pair, #a-b .90 .90

Intl. Day for Preservation of the Ozone Layer — A1059

2002, Sept. 16 ***Perf. 13¼x12¾***
1824 A1059 125p multi 1.40 1.25

18th Intl. Conference on Road Safety, Cairo — A1060

2002, Sept. 22
1825 A1060 30p multi .50 .25

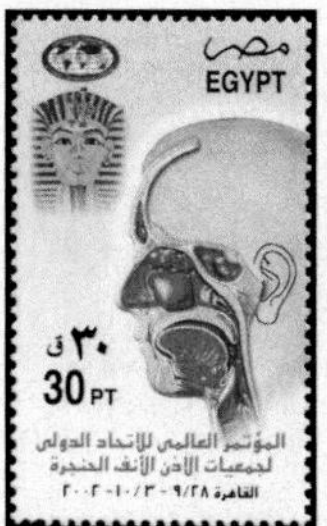

A1061

2002, Sept. 28
1826 A1061 30p multi .50 .25

17th Congress of Intl. Federation of Otorhinolaryngological Societies, Cairo.

World Post Day — A1062

2002, Oct. 9
1827 A1062 125p multi 1.10 1.10

Opening of Alexandria Library — A1063

Ancient Alexandria Library — A1064

Designs: 30p, Library exterior. 125p, Pillar, sun on horizon, vert.

Perf. 12¾x13¼, 13¼x12¾
2002, Oct. 16
1828-1829 A1063 Set of 2 1.75 1.50

Size: 60x80mm
Imperf
1830 A1064 125p multi 1.60 1.60

Hassan Faek, Actor — A1065

Aziza Amir, Actress — A1066

Farid Shawki, Actor — A1067

Mary Mounib, Actress — A1068

2002, Nov. 23 ***Perf. 13¼x12¾***
1831 Horiz. strip of 4 1.75 1.60
a. A1065 30p tan & black .40 .25
b. A1066 30p tan & black .40 .25
c. A1067 30p tan & black .40 .25
d. A1068 30p tan & black .40 .25

A1069

A1070

A1071

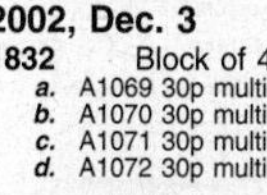

Birds — A1072

2002, Dec. 3 ***Perf. 13¼x12¾***
1832 Block of 4 1.75 1.60
a. A1069 30p multi .40 .25
b. A1070 30p multi .40 .25
c. A1071 30p multi .40 .25
d. A1072 30p multi .40 .25

Egyptian Museum, Cent. — A1073

125p, Entrance, statue of Cheops.

2002, Dec. 11 ***Perf. 12¾x13¼***
1833 A1073 30p shown .50 .25

Size: 80x60mm
Imperf
1834 A1073 125p multi 1.40 1.40

Opening of Aswan Suspension Bridge — A1074

No. 1835: a, Bridge and support cables. b, Bridge towers.

2002, Dec. 17 ***Perf. 12¾x13¼***
1835 A1074 30p Horiz. pair, #a-b .90 .90

Suez Canal University, 25th Anniv. — A1075

2002, Dec. 29 ***Perf. 13¼x12¾***
1836 A1075 30p multi .45 .25

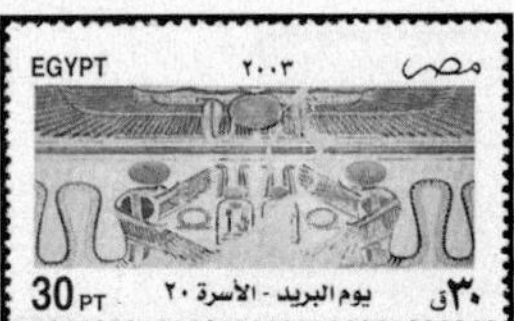

Toshka Land Reclamation Project — A1076

2002, Dec. 31 ***Perf. 12¾x13¼***
1837 A1076 30p multi .45 .25

A1077

A1078

Post Day — A1079

2003, Jan. 2
1838 A1077 30p multi .45 .25
1839 A1078 30p multi .45 .25
1840 A1079 125p multi 1.10 1.00
Nos. 1838-1840 (3) 2.00 1.50

Cairo Intl. Communications and Information Technology Fair — A1080

2003, Jan. 12 Litho. ***Perf. 13¼x12¾***
1841 A1080 30p multi .50 .25

Intl. Nile Children's Song Festival — A1081

Background color: 30p, Brown. 125p, Green.

2003, Jan. 28 ***Perf. 12¾x13¼***
1842-1843 A1081 Set of 2 1.50 1.25

Intl. Table Tennis Championships — A1082

Background color: 30p, Blue. 125p, Orange.

2003, Feb. 3
1844-1845 A1082 Set of 2 1.50 1.25

Tenth Intl. Building and Construction Conference A1083

Background color: 30p, Orange. 125p, Blue.

2003, Apr. 1 ***Perf. 13¼x12¾***
1846-1847 A1083 Set of 2 1.50 1.10

Arab Lawyer's Union, 60th Anniv. — A1084

Background color: 30p, Blue. 125p, Lilac.

2003, Apr. 25 ***Perf. 12¾x13¼***
1848-1849 A1084 Set of 2 1.40 1.10

Inauguration of First Phase of Smart Village Project — A1085

Denomination color: 30p, White. 125p, Yellow. £1, White.

2003, July 1 ***Perf. 12¾x13¼***
1850-1851 A1085 Set of 2 1.50 1.50

Size: 79x59mm

Imperf

1852 A1085 £1 multi 1.50 1.50

Writers — A1086

No. 1853: a, Ihsan Abdul Qudous (1919-90) (wearing checked tie). b, Youssef Idris (1927-91) (wearing solid tie).

2003, July 28 ***Perf. 13¼x12¾***
1853 A1086 30p Horiz. pair, #a-b .90 .90

African Men's Basketball Championships A1087

Background color: 30p, Black. 125p, Blue.

2003, Aug. 12
1854-1855 A1087 Set of 2 1.50 1.10

Natl. Institute of Astronomical and Geophysical Research, Cent. — A1088

2003, Sept. 7 ***Perf. 12¾x13¼***
1856 A1088 30p multi .60 .30

World Tourism Day — A1089

Denomination color: 30p, White. 125p, Red.

Perf. 12¾x13¼

2003, Sept. 27 **Litho.**
1857-1858 A1089 Set of 2 1.50 1.10

Egypt's Bid for Hosting 2010 World Cup Soccer Championships — A1090

Designs: 30p, Emblem, vert. 125p, Emblem, funerary mask of King Tutankhamun.

Perf. 13¼x12¾, 12¾x13¼

2003, Sept. 27
1859-1860 A1090 Set of 2 1.50 1.10

October War Against Israel, 30th Anniv. — A1091

2003, Oct. 6 ***Perf. 13¼x12¾***
1861 A1091 30p multi 1.00 .30

World Post Day — A1092

2003, Oct. 9
1862 A1092 125p multi 1.00 .80

National Bar Association, 91st Anniv. — A1093

2003, Oct. 30
1863 A1093 30p multi .60 .25

Festivals — A1094

No. 1864: a, Pink orchids. b, White rose. c, Red rose. d, Sunflower.

2003, Nov. 23 ***Perf. 14***
1864 A1094 30p Block of 4, #a-d 1.50 1.50

For use on greeting cars.

Film Directors — A1095

No. 1865: a, Salah Abou Seif (balding man with open collar). b, Kamal Selim (round eyeglasses) c, Henri Barakat (square eyeglasses). d, Hassan El Emam.

2003, Dec. 1 ***Perf. 13¼x12¾***
1865 A1095 30p Horiz. strip of 4, #a-d 1.50 1.50

El Gomhoreya Newspaper, 50th Anniv. — A1096

2003, Dec. 7
1866 A1096 30p multi .50 .25

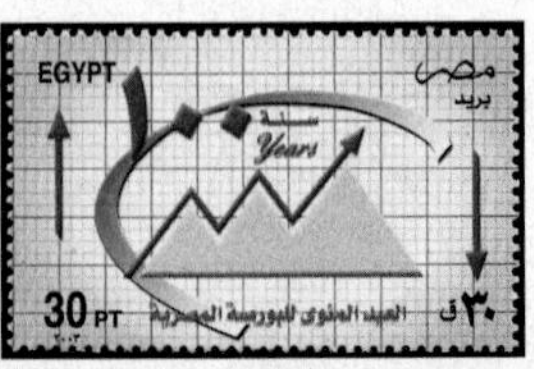

Cairo Bourse, Cent. — A1097

2003, Dec. 7 ***Perf. 12¾x13¼***
1867 A1097 30p multi .45 .25

Mrs. Suzanne Mubarak, Emblems of Fifth E-9 Ministerial Review Meeting and UNESCO — A1098

Background color: 30p, Blue. 125p, Orange. £2, Blue.

Perf. 12¾x13¼

2003, Dec. 18 **Litho.**

1868-1869	A1098	Set of 2	1.50	1.10

Imperf

Size: 79x60mm

1870	A1098	£2 multi	2.00	2.00

Delta International Bank, 25th Anniv. — A1099

Background color: 30p, Green. 125p, Blue. £2, Green and blue, horiz.

2004, Jan. 1 ***Perf. 12¾x13¼***

1871-1872	A1099	Set of 2	1.40	1.00

Imperf

Size: 80x60mm

1873	A1099	£2 multi	2.00	2.00

Post Day A1100

Denominations: 30p, 125p.

2004, Jan. 2 ***Perf. 12¾x13¼***

1874-1875	A1100	Set of 2	1.50	1.25

Eighth Intl. Telecommunications Conference — A1101

2004, Jan. 17

1876	A1101	30p multi	.80	.30

Treasures of Egypt A1102

No. 1877: a, Sinai. b, Pyramids at dusk. c, Egyptian Bedouin. d, Red Sea corals. e, Suez Canal, Ferdinand-Marie de Lesseps, Khedive Ismail. f, Ramadan lanterns. g, Nile felucca. h, White Western Desert. i, Maydum Pyramid.

No. 1878: a, St. Catherine Monastery, Sinai. b, Icon of Sts. Paul and Anthony. c, Mosque of Muhammad Ali. d, Lamp, Old Cairo. e, Emblem of Sultan Qaytbay. f, Minaret, Cairo. g, Mosque of al-Azhar. h, Coptic priest and icon, Cairo. i, Ben Ezra Synagogue.

No. 1879: a, Ankh. b, Rosetta Stone. c, Sarcophagus of Ahmes Meritamun. d, Stela of Amenmhat. e, Sphinx. f, Udjat. g, Canopic jars of Tutankhamun. h, Cartouche of Tutankhamun. i, Egyptian scribe.

No. 1880: a, Sphinx, diff. b, Queen Nefertiti. c, Tutankhamun.

2004, Jan. 22 **Litho.** ***Perf. 13x13¼***

1877	Booklet pane of 9	2.25	—
a.-i.	A1102 30p Any single	.40	.25
1878	Booklet pane of 9	8.25	—
a.-i.	A1102 125p Any single	.90	.80

Litho. & Embossed, Litho. & Embossed With Foil Application (£10)

1879	Booklet pane of 9	13.50	—
a.-i.	A1102 £2 Any single	1.50	1.25

Perf. 13¼

1880	Booklet pane of 3	15.00	—
a.-b.	A1102 £5 Either single, 38x51mm	3.75	3.75
c.	A1102 £10 gold & multi, 38x51mm	7.00	7.00
	Complete booklet, #1877-1880	39.00	

Complete booklet sold for £80.

Morkos Hanna — A1103

Ahmed Lotfi — A1104

Mahmoud Abu el Nasr — A1105

Abd el Aziz Fahmy — A1106

Ibrahim el Helbawi — A1107

Makram Ebeid — A1108

Mohammad Naguib el Gharabli — A1109

Mohammad Bassiouni A1110

Mohammad Hafez Ramadan A1111

Mohammad Abu Shadi — A1112

Mahmoud Fahmi Goundia — A1113

Kamel Youssof Saleh — A1114

Abd el Hamid Abd el Hakk — A1115

Mohammad Ali Allouba — A1116

Kamel Sedki Beck — A1117

Bar Association Emblem — A1118

Abd el Rahman el Rafei — A1119

Abd el Fattah el Shalkany A1120

Mohammad Sabri Abu Alam — A1121

Omar Omar — A1122

Sameh Ashour — A1123

Ahmed el Khawaga A1124

Abd el Aziz el Shorgabi A1125

Mostafa el Baradei — A1126

2004, Feb. **Litho.** ***Perf. 13¼x12¾***

1881	Block of 25	8.75	8.75
a.	A1103 30p bright blue & black	.35	.25
b.	A1104 30p bright blue & black	.35	.25
c.	A1105 30p bright blue & black	.35	.25
d.	A1106 30p bright blue & black	.35	.25
e.	A1107 30p bright blue & black	.35	.25
f.	A1108 30p pink & black	.35	.25
g.	A1109 30p pink & black	.35	.25
h.	A1110 30p pink & black	.35	.25
i.	A1111 30p pink & black	.35	.25
j.	A1112 30p pink & black	.35	.25
k.	A1113 30p orange & black	.35	.25
l.	A1114 30p orange & black	.35	.25
m.	A1115 30p orange & black	.35	.25
n.	A1116 30p orange & black	.35	.25
o.	A1117 30p orange & black	.35	.25
p.	A1118 30p green & multi	.35	.25
q.	A1119 30p green & black	.35	.25
r.	A1120 30p green & black	.35	.25
s.	A1121 30p green & black	.35	.25
t.	A1122 30p green & black	.35	.25
u.	A1118 30p dark blue & multi	.35	.25
v.	A1123 30p dark blue & black	.35	.25
w.	A1124 30p dark blue & black	.35	.25
x.	A1125 30p dark blue & black	.35	.25
y.	A1126 30p dark blue & black	.35	.25

National Bar Association, 92nd anniv.

IBM Corporation in Egypt, 50th Anniv. — A1127

2004, Feb. 24

1882 A1127 30p multi .60 .25

Cairo Rotary Club, 75th Anniv. — A1128

2004, Mar. 11

1883 A1128 30p multi .60 .25

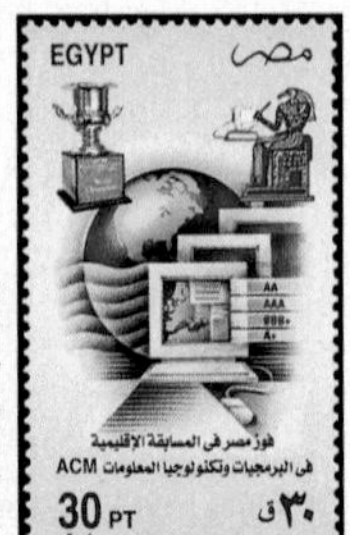

Egyptian Victory in Regional Computer Programming and Information Technology Competition A1129

2004, Mar. 15

1884 A1129 30p multi .60 .25

National Women's Day — A1130

Background colors: 30p, Blue. 125p, Red orange.

2004, Mar. 16 **Litho.**

1885-1886 A1130 Set of 2 1.50 1.00

Anti-Narcotics General Administration, 75th Anniv. — A1131

2004, Mar. 20 ***Perf. 12¾x13¼***

1887 A1131 30p multi .75 .30

Imperf

Size: 80x60mm

1888 A1131 125p multi 1.50 1.50

Orphan's Day — A1132

2004, Apr. 2 ***Perf. 13¼x12¾***

1889 A1132 30p multi .60 .25

Compare with Types A1169 and A1199.

Telecom Africa Fair and Conference, Cairo — A1133

2004, May 4 ***Perf. 12¾x13¼***

1890 A1133 30p multi .60 .25

Egyptian Philatelic Society, 75th Anniv. — A1134

Designs: 30p, Emblem. 125p, Emblem, stamp, magnifying glass, tongs.

2004, May 20 ***Perf. 13¼x12¾***

1891 A1134 30p multi .60 .25

Imperf

Size: 80x60mm

1892 A1134 125p multi 1.50 1.50

State Information Service, 50th Anniv. — A1135

2004, May 30 ***Perf. 12¾x13¼***

1893 A1135 30p multi .75 .25

Tenth Radio and Television Festival, Cairo — A1136

Designs: 30p, Festival emblem, green background. £1, Fesitval emblem, brown background. 125p, Sphinx, festival emblem, film, horiz.

£2, Like 125p, horiz.

Perf. 13¼x12¾, 12¾x13¼

2004, June 1

1894-1896 A1136 Set of 3 2.00 2.00

Imperf

Size: 80x60mm

1897 A1136 £2 multi 2.00 2.00

Pres. Hosni Mubarak, "Education for All" Arab Regional Conference Emblem — A1137

Stylized Children, Emblems A1138

Perf. 12¾x13¼, 13¼x12¾

2004, June 1

1898	A1137 30p yel & multi	.35	.25
1899	A1137 125p red org & multi	.60	.60
1900	A1138 125p multi	.60	.60
	Nos. 1898-1900 (3)	1.55	1.45

Imperf

Size: 80x60mm

1901 A1137 £2 blue & multi 1.75 1.75

Construction and Housing Bank, 25th Anniv. — A1139

2004, June 24 ***Perf. 13¼x12¾***
1902 A1139 30p multi .60 .25

2004 Summer Olympics, Athens — A1140

Background color: 30p, Gray. 150p, Orange yellow.

Perf. 13¼x12¾
2004, Aug. 13 **Litho.**
1903-1904 A1140 Set of 2 1.50 1.40

Scouting in Egypt, 90th Anniv. — A1141

2004, Aug. 15 ***Perf. 12¾x13¼***
1905 A1141 30p multi .80 .30

14th Intl. Folklore Festival, Ismailia — A1142

2004, Aug. 24 ***Perf. 13¼x12¾***
1906 A1142 30p multi .70 .25

Administrative Attorneys, 50th Anniv. — A1143

2004, Sept. 16 ***Perf. 13¼x12¾***
1907 A1143 30p multi .60 .25

Imperf

Size: 60x80mm

1908 A1143 £1 multi 1.50 1.50

Egyptian National Archives, 50th Anniv. — A1144

2004, Sept. 20 ***Perf. 12¾x13¼***
1909 A1144 30p multi .75 .25

Light and Hope Society, 50th Anniv. — A1145

2004, Sept. 26
1910 A1145 30p multi .70 .25

General Arab Journalists Union, 10th Conference A1146

2004, Oct. 2 ***Perf. 13¼x12¾***
1911 A1146 125p multi 1.00 .80

Telecom Egypt, 150th Anniv. A1146a

2004, Oct. 3 **Litho.** ***Perf. 12¾x13¼***
1911A A1146a 30p multi *18.50 18.50*

No. 1911A was withdrawn from sale after a few days as anniversary emblem was incorrect.

Military Production Day, 50th Anniv. — A1147

2004, Oct. 6 ***Perf. 12¾x13¼***
1912 A1147 30p multi .90 .30

World Post Day — A1148

2004, Oct. 9
1913 A1148 150p multi 1.10 1.00

Egyptian Youth Hostels Association, 50th Anniv. — A1149

2004, Oct. 20 ***Perf. 13¼x12¾***
1914 A1149 30p multi .80 .25

Rose — A1150

Songbird A1151

Perf. 12¾x13¼
2004, Nov. 10 **Litho.**
1915 A1150 30p multi .50 .25

Perf. 13¼x12¾
1916 A1151 30p multi .50 .25

24th Arab Scouting Congress — A1152

2004, Nov. 27 ***Perf. 12¾x13¼***
1917 A1152 30p multi .65 .25

Arab Scouting Organization, 50th Anniv. — A1153

2004, Dec. 4
1918 A1153 30p multi .65 .25

Islamic Art Museum Foundation, Cent. — A1154

2004, Dec. 15 ***Perf. 13¼x12¾***
1919 A1154 30p multi .65 .25

FIFA (Fédération Internationale de Football Association), Cent. — A1155

2004, Dec. 15 ***Perf. 12¾x13¼***
1920 A1155 150p multi 1.25 1.00

Fekri Abaza (1896-1979), Journalist A1156

Abd El Rahman El Sharqawi (1920-87), Journalist A1157

2004, Dec. 28 ***Perf. 13¼x12¾***
1921 A1156 30p multi .40 .25
1922 A1157 30p multi .40 .25

Telecom Egypt, 150th Anniv. — A1158

Color of central panel: 30p, White. 125p, Gray.

2004, Dec. 30 ***Perf. 12¾x13¼***
1923-1924 A1158 Set of 2 1.50 1.10

First Sale of Natural Gas to Jordan — A1159

2005, Jan. 1
1925 A1159 30p multi .90 .30

Post Day — A1160

2005, Jan. 2 ***Perf. 13¼x12¾***
1926 A1160 30p multi .80 .30

Opening of Om El Massrean — El Moneib Subway Line, Cairo — A1161

2005, Jan. 16 *Perf. 12¾x13¼*
1927 A1161 30p multi .65 .30

Imperf

Size: 80x59mm

1928 A1161 150p multi 1.40 1.40

Police Day — A1162

Pres. Hosni Mubarak and flag stripes aligned: 30p, Vertically. £1, Horizontally.

2005, Jan. 25 *Perf. 13¼x12¾*
1929 A1162 30p multi .60 .25

Imperf

Size: 80x59mm

1930 A1162 £1 multi 1.25 1.25

El Mohandes Insurance Company, 25th Anniv. — A1163

2005, Jan. 26 *Perf. 13¼x12¾*
1931 A1163 30p multi .65 .30

9th Intl. Telecommunications and Information Conference, Cairo — A1164

2005, Feb. 1
1932 A1164 30p multi .65 .25

7th University Youth Week — A1165

2005, Feb. 5
1933 A1165 30p multi .65 .25

Rotary International, Cent. — A1166

2005, Feb. 23 **Litho.**
1934 A1166 30p multi .75 .30

38th Intl. Fair, Cairo — A1167

2005, Mar. 15
1935 A1167 30p multi .50 .25

Arab League, 60th Anniv. — A1168

2005, Mar. 22
1936 A1168 30p multi .55 .25

Orphan's Day — A1169

2005, Apr. 2
1937 A1169 30p multi .70 .30

Compare with Types A1132 and A1199. See also Nos. 2035, 2053.

Heliopolis Foundation, Cent. — A1170

2005, May 5 *Perf. 12¾x13¼*
1938 A1170 30p multi .65 .25

National Center of Social and Criminological Research, 50th Anniv. — A1171

2005, May 22 **Litho.** *Perf. 13¼x12¾*
1939 A1171 30p multi .70 .30

Egyptian-European Association Agreement, 1st Anniv. — A1172

2005, June 1
1940 A1172 150p multi .90 .50

World Environment Day — A1173

2005, June 5 *Perf. 12¾x13¼*
1941 A1173 30p multi .80 .30

World Summit on the Information Society, Tunis — A1174

2005, July 31 **Litho.** *Perf. 13¼x12¾*
1942 A1174 150p multi 1.40 1.40

Ministry of Youth, 50th Anniv. — A1175

Background colors: 30p, Green. 125p, Olive green.

2005, Aug. 13
1943-1944 A1175 Set of 2 1.25 1.10

Presidential Elections A1176

2005, Sept. 7
1945 A1176 30p multi .65 .30

13th World Psychiatry Congress, Cairo — A1177

Designs: 30p, Emblem. 150p, Emblem and funerary mask of King Tutankhamun, horiz.

2005, Sept. 10 *Perf. 13¼x12¾*
1946 A1177 30p multi .65 .30

Imperf

Size: 80x60mm

1947 A1177 150p multi 1.90 1.90

World Literacy Day — A1178

2005, Sept. 24 *Perf. 12¾x13¼*
1948 A1178 30p multi .70 .30

Re-election of Pres. Hosni Mubarak A1179

2005, Sept. 27 *Perf. 13¼x12¾*
1949 A1179 30p multi .60 .25

Mohamed El-Baradei, Director General of Intl. Atomic Energy Agency — A1180

Background colors: 30p, Blue green. 150p, Rose lilac.

2005, Oct. 8

1950-1951 A1180 Set of 2 1.75 1.50

Awarding of 2005 Nobel Peace Prize to El-Baradei and IAEA.

World Post Day — A1181

Denominations: 30p, 150p.

2005, Oct. 9

1952-1953 A1181 Set of 2 1.40 1.25

Intl. Year of Sports and Physical Education A1182

2005, Oct. 24

1954 A1182 150p multi 1.25 1.00

United Nations, 60th Anniv. — A1183

2005, Oct. 24 ***Perf. 12¾x13¼***

1955 A1183 150p multi 1.25 1.00

Festivals A1184

2005, Nov. 1 ***Perf. 13¼x12¾***

1956 A1184 30p multi .70 .30

Alexandria Biennale, 50th Anniv. — A1185

2005, Dec. 1

1957 A1185 30p multi .65 .30

K-8 Training Airplane — A1186

Denominations: 30p, 150p.

Perf. 12¾x13¼

2005, Dec. 26 **Litho.**

1958-1959 A1186 Set of 2 2.00 1.50

Saved Mekawi, Musician A1187

Mohamed El Mogi (1923-95), Musician A1188

Kamal El Taweel, Composer A1189

Ali Ismael (1921-75), Composer A1190

Mohamed Roshdi, Folk Singer — A1191

2005, Dec. 31 ***Perf. 13¼x12¾***

1960 Horiz. strip of 5 1.75 1.75
- *a.* A1187 30p green & multi .30 .25
- *b.* A1188 30p blue & multi .30 .25
- *c.* A1189 30p lilac & black .30 .25
- *d.* A1190 30p org & black .30 .25
- *e.* A1191 30p brt org & black .30 .25

Post Day — A1192

2006, Jan. 2

1961 A1192 30p multi .75 .30

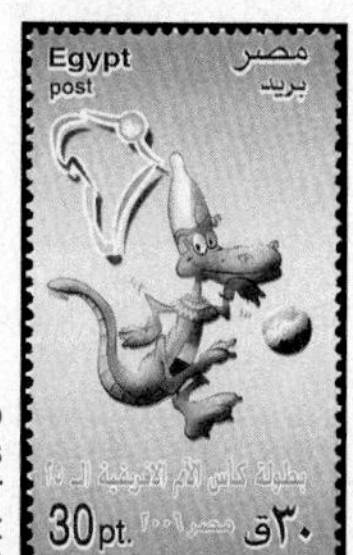

25th Africa Cup of Nations Soccer Tournament A1193

2006, Jan. 20

1962 A1193 30p multi .60 .25

Arab University Youth Week — A1194

2006, Feb. 4 ***Perf. 12¾x13¼***

1963 A1194 30p multi .55 .25

Intl. Telecommunications, Information and Networking Exhibition, Cairo — A1195

2006, Feb. 5 ***Perf. 13¼x12¾***

1964 A1195 30p multi .55 .25

Pres. Hosni Mubarak Holding African Cup of Nations — A1196

2006, Feb. 10 ***Perf. 12¾x13¼***

1965 A1196 30p multi .75 .35

Size: 80x60mm

Imperf

1966 A1196 150p multi 1.75 1.60

Information and Decision Support Center, 20th Anniv. — A1197

2006, Mar. 27 ***Perf. 13¼x12¾***

1967 A1197 30p multi .55 .25

Total Solar Eclipse of March 29, 2006 — A1198

2006, Mar. 29 ***Perf. 12¾x13¼***

1968 A1198 30p multi .55 .35

Size: 82x60mm

Imperf

1969 A1198 150p multi 2.25 1.90

Orphan's Day — A1199

2006, Apr. 2 ***Perf. 13¼x12¾***

1970 A1199 30p multi .70 .30

Compare with types A1132 and A1169. See also Nos. 2035, 2053.

Gamal Hemdan (1928-93), Geographical Historian A1200

2006, Apr. 16

1971 A1200 30p lilac & black .55 .30

Abd El-Rahman ibn Khaldun (1332-1406), Historian
A1201

2006, May 27
1972 A1201 30p multi .70 .30

World Environment Day — A1202

Designs: 30p, Stone pillar in White Desert. 150p, Trees in desert.

2006, June 5 ***Perf. 12¾x13¼***
1973-1974 A1202 Set of 2 1.50 1.25

Diplomatic Relations Between Egypt and People's Republic of China, 50th Anniv. — A1203

No. 1975, £1.50: a, Abu Simbel Temple, Egypt. b, South Gate Pavilion, China.

2006, July 13 Litho. ***Perf. 12***
1975 A1203 Horiz. pair, #a-b, + central label 1.75 1.75
c. Souvenir sheet, #1975 *25.00 25.00*

Military Academy Headquarters, Heliopolis, 50th Anniv. — A1204

2006, July 19 ***Perf. 12¾x13¼***
1976 A1204 30p multi .70 .30

Nationalization of the Suez Canal, 50th Anniv. — A1205

2006, July 26 ***Perf. 13¼x12¾***
1977 A1205 30p multi .55 .25

World Post Day — A1206

Denominations: 30p, 150p.

2006, Oct. 9
1978-1979 A1206 Set of 2 1.50 1.25

China - Africa Summit — A1206a

No. 1979A: b, Chinese mask. c, African mask.

2006, Nov. 5 Litho. ***Perf. 12***
1979A A1206a Horiz. pair with central label 2.25 2.25
b.-c. £1.50 Either single .80 .60

National Housing Census — A1207

2006, Nov. 21 Litho. ***Perf. 13¼x13***
1980 A1207 30p multi .55 .25

Al-Ahram Newspaper — A1208

No. 1981: a, Newspaper headquarters. b, Newspaper emblem.
150p, Headquarters and emblem.

2006, Nov. 26 ***Perf. 13x13¼***
1981 A1208 30p Horiz. pair, #a-b, + central label 1.00 1.00

Imperf

Size: 80x60mm

1982 A1208 150p multi 1.00 1.00

Egyptian Initiative to Support Lebanon — A1209

2006, Dec. 27 ***Perf. 13x13¼***
1983 A1209 150p multi 1.00 1.00

Feasts — A1210

2006, Dec. 30
1984 A1210 30p multi .45 .25

Post Day — A1211

2007, Jan. 2
1985 A1211 30p multi .45 .25

Ali El Kassar (1888-1957), Artist — A1212

2007, Jan. 15 ***Perf. 13¼x13***
1986 A1212 30p multi .45 .25

Automobile and Touring Club of Egypt — A1213

2007, Jan. 14 Litho. ***Perf. 12¾x13¼***
1987 A1213 30p multi .55 .30

Imperf

Size: 80x60mm

1988 A1213 150p multi 1.50 1.50

Police Day — A1214

2007, Jan. 25 ***Perf. 12¾x13¼***
1989 A1214 30p multi .55 .30

Imperf

Size: 80x60mm

1990 A1214 150p multi 1.00 1.00

Rededication of National Library — A1215

2007, Feb. 25 ***Perf. 12¾x13¼***
1991 A1215 30p multi .55 .30

Arabic Language Academy, 75th Anniv. — A1216

2007, Mar. 17 ***Perf. 13¼x12¾***
1992 A1216 30p multi .55 .30

World Health Day — A1217

2007, Apr. 7 Litho. ***Perf. 12¾x13¼***
1993 A1217 30p multi .55 .30

Egyptian Trade Union Federation, 50th Anniv. — A1218

2007, May 1 ***Perf. 13¼x12¾***
1994 A1218 30p multi .45 .25

Egypt Air, 75th Anniv. — A1219

Anniversary emblem and: 30p, Biplane. 150p, Biplane and jet.

2007, May 7 ***Perf. 12¾x13¼***
1995-1996 A1219 Set of 2 1.00 .75

Return of Sinai to Egypt, 25th Anniv. — A1220

No. 1997: a, Monastery of St. Catherine. b, Salah el Din Castle. c, Sharm el-Sheikh. d, Oasis of Nabq.

2007, Apr. 25 Litho. ***Perf. 12¾x13¼***
1997 A1220 30p Block of 4, #a-d 1.90 1.25

Mevlana Jalal ad-Din Rumi (1207-73), Islamic Philosopher A1221

2007, May 8 ***Perf. 13¼x12¾***
1998 A1221 150p multi .55 .30

World Environment Day — A1222

Designs: 30p, Sinai baton blue butterfly. 150p, Melting ice, horiz.

Perf. 13¼x12¾, 12¾x13¼
2007, June 5
1999-2000 A1222 Set of 2 1.50 .75

Scouting, Cent. — A1223

2007, June 6 ***Perf. 12¾x13¼***
2001 A1223 150p multi 1.25 .80

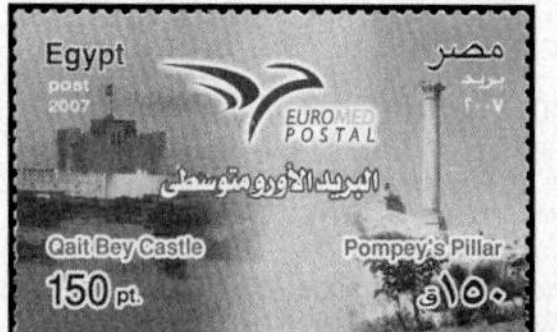

EuroMed Postal Conference, Marseille, France — A1224

2007, July 9
2002 A1224 150p multi 1.10 .75

Diplomatic Relations Between Egypt and Nepal, 50th Anniv. — A1225

2007, July 16
2003 A1225 150p multi 1.10 .75

Egyptian Air Force, 75th Anniv. — A1226

2007, Oct. 14 Litho. ***Perf. 13x13¼***
2004 A1226 30p multi .55 .25

A1227

11th Arab Games — A1228

2007, Oct. 26 Litho. ***Perf. 13¼x12¾***
2005 A1227 150p multi 1.25 .90

Imperf
Size: 95x75mm
2006 A1228 150p multi 1.25 1.00

Assiut University, 50th Anniv. — A1229

2007, Nov. 27 ***Perf. 13¼x12¾***
2007 A1229 30p brn & blk .45 .25

Hafez Ibrahim (1872-1932), Poet — A1230

Ahmed Shawky (1868-1932), Poet — A1231

2007, Dec. 16
2008 A1230 30p multi .45 .25
2009 A1231 30p multi .45 .25

A 150p stamp issued in December 2007 depicting riders on horses on a beach with a se-tenant label was created exclusively for the Utopia Resort in Marsa Alam. The resort sold the stamps to its guests.

Egyptian Handball Federation, 50th Anniv. — A1232

2007, Dec. 30
2010 A1232 30p multi .50 .25

Musicians — A1233

2008, Jan. 1 ***Perf. 12¾x13¼***
2011 A1233 30p multi .45 .25

Post Day — A1234

2008, Feb. 7 Litho. ***Imperf.***
2012 A1234 150p multi 1.00 1.00

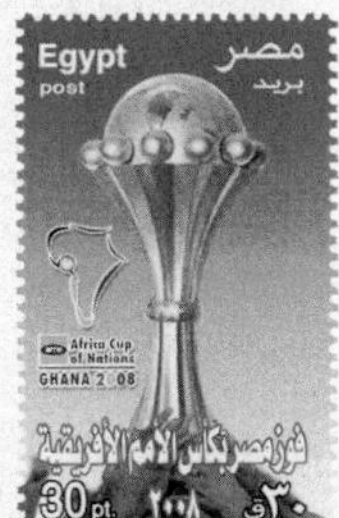

Africa Cup of Nations Soccer Championships, Ghana — A1235

2008, Feb. 10 ***Perf. 13¼x13***
2013 A1235 30p multi .45 .25

Wadi El-Hitan UNESCO World Heritage Site — A1236

No. 2014: a, Whale bones on ground. b, Reconstructed whale skeleton.

2008, Feb. 10 ***Perf. 13x13¼***
2014 Horiz. pair with central label 1.00 1.00
a.-b. A1236 30p Either single .45 .25

Cairo University, Cent. — A1237

2008, Apr. 14 ***Perf. 13¼x13***
2015 A1237 30p multi .45 .25

Land Mine Clearance in Northwest Egypt — A1238

No. 2016 — Map and: a, Amputee surrounded by land mines. b, Hand, "no land mines" symbol, vert.

Perf. 13x13¼, 13¼x13 (#2016b)
2008, Apr. 22
2016 A1238 150p Pair, #a-b 1.10 1.10

Telecom Africa Conference A1239

2008, May 12 ***Perf. 13¼x13***
2017 A1239 30p multi .45 .25

World Environment Day — A1240

Background colors: 30p, Blue. 150p, Lilac.

2008, June 5
2018-2019 A1240 Set of 2 1.00 .70

Faculty of Fine Arts, Cent. — A1241

No. 2020 — Background color: a, 30p, Blue. b, 150p, Green.

2008, June 21 Litho. *Perf. 13¼x13*
2020 A1241 Horiz. pair, #a-b 1.25 1.25

Pan African Postal Union Plenipotentiary Conference, Cairo — A1242

2008, June 28 *Perf. 13x13¼*
2021 A1242 150p multi 1.25 .60

Egypt Air Joining Star Alliance — A1243

2008, July 11
2022 A1243 150p multi 1.25 .85

Alexandria, 2008 Islamic Cultural Capital — A1244

2008, July 26
2023 A1244 150p multi .85 .60

Arab Post Day — A1245

No. 2024 — Emblem and: a, World map, pigeon. b, Camel caravan.

2008, Aug. 3
2024 Horiz. pair 2.00 2.00
a.-b. A1245 150p Either single .75 .60

24th Universal Postal Union Congress, Geneva, Switzerland — A1246

2008, Aug. 4 Litho. *Perf. 12¾x13¼*
2025 A1246 150p multi 1.00 .75

Men's Sports Education Faculty, 50th Anniv. — A1247

2008, Oct. 15 Litho. *Perf. 13¼x13*
2026 A1247 30p multi .50 .30

Postech 2008 Intl. Postal Technology Conference, Sharm El-Sheikh — A1248

Map and: 30p, Queen Nefertari holding Postech 2008 emblem. 150p, Statue of King Tutankhamun, hand holding Postech emblem.

Perf. 12¾x13¼

2008, Nov. 17 Litho.
2027-2028 A1248 Set of 2 1.40 .90

Egyptian Cooperative Movement, Cent. — A1249

2008, Dec. 22 *Perf. 13¼x12¾*
2029 A1249 30p multi .45 .25

Natl. Telecommunications Institute, 25th Anniv. — A1250

2008, Dec. 31 *Perf. 12¾x13¼*
2030 A1250 30p multi .55 .30

Natl. Sports Council — A1251

2009, Mar. 3 *Perf. 13¼x12¾*
2031 A1251 150p multi .95 .75

Constitutional Judiciary, 40th Anniv. — A1252

Designs: 30p, Emblem, text below. 150p, Emblem, text at right, horiz.

2009, Mar. 7 *Perf. 13¼x12¾*
2032 A1252 30p multi .65 .40

Size:80x60mm

Imperf

2033 A1252 150p multi 1.00 1.00

Intl. Francophone Day — A1253

2009, Mar. 20 *Perf. 12¾x13¼*
2034 A1253 150p multi .95 .55

Orphan's Day — A1254

2009, Apr. 3 *Perf. 13¼x12¾*
2035 A1254 150p multi 1.00 .60

Compare with Types A1132, A1169 and A1199. See also No. 2053.

Intl. Labor Organization, 90th Anniv. — A1255

2009, Apr. 21 *Perf. 12¾x13¼*
2036 A1255 150p multi .90 .60

Suzanne Mubarak Women's International Peace Movement A1256

2009, May 14 *Perf. 13¼x12¾*
2037 A1256 150p multi .75 .55

Yehia Hakki (1905-92), Writer — A1257

2009, May 11 Litho. *Perf. 12¾x13¼*
2038 A1257 150p multi .95 .55

Nobel Laureates From Africa — A1258

No. 2039: a, Ahmed Zewail, Chemistry, 1999. b, Bishop Desmond Tutu, Peace, 1984. c, Wangari Maathai, Peace 2004. d, Anwar al-Sadat, Peace, 1978. e, Naguib Mahfouz, Literature, 1988. f, Allan M. Cormack, Physiology or Medicine, 1979. g, Nelson Mandela, Peace, 1993. h, Wole Soyinka, Literature, 1986. i, Sydney Brenner, Physiology or Medicine, 2002. j, F.W. de Klerk, Peace, 1993. k, Nadine Gordimer, Literature, 1991. l, Max Theiler, Physiology or Medicine, 1951. m, Mohamed El Baradei, Peace, 2005. n, Albert Luthuli, Peace, 1960. o, Kofi Annan, Peace, 2001. p, J.M. Coetzee, Literature, 2003.

2009, June 9
2039 Sheet of 16, #a-p, + 9 labels 22.50 22.50
a.-p. A1258 150p Any single .95 .75

Fourth Extraordinary Session of the Pan-African Postal Union Plenipotentiary Conference, Cairo.

Fifteenth Non-Aligned Movement Summit, Sharm el-Sheikh A1259

2009, July 15 *Perf. 13¼x12¾*
2040 A1259 150p multi .55 .55

Opening of Mubarak Public Library, Damanhour — A1260

2009, May 7 Litho. *Perf. 13x13¼*
2041 A1260 150p multi .95 .70

Jerusalem, Capital of Arab Culture — A1261

2009, Aug. 3 ***Perf. 13¼x13***
2042 A1261 150p multi .95 .75

FIFA Under-20 World Cup Soccer Championships, Egypt — A1262

No. 2042 — Tournament emblem, trophy and flag of participating team: a, Paraguay. b, Brazil. c, Uruguay. d, Germany. e, Nigeria. f, South Korea. g, Venezuela. h, Ghana. i, United Arab Emirates. j, South Africa. k, Egypt. l, Spain. m, Italy. n, Hungary. o, Czech Republic. p, Costa Rica.

2009, Oct. 5 ***Perf. 13x13¼***
2043 Sheet of 16, #a-p, + 9 labels 19.50 19.50
a.-p. A1262 150p Any single .95 .75

Fourth Ministerial Conference of Forum on China-African Cooperation, Sharm El Sheikh — A1263

2009, Nov. 8
2044 A1263 150p multi .95 .75

Fourth Meeting of Internet Governance Forum, Sharm El Sheikh — A1264

2009, Nov. 15
2045 A1264 150p multi .95 .75

Luxor Governate — A1264a

2009, Dec. 9 Litho. ***Perf. 12¾x13¼***
2045A A1264a 250p multi 1.25 1.25

Egyptian Society of Political Economy, Statistics and Legislation, Cent. — A1265

2009, Dec. 19
2046 A1265 150p multi .95 .95

Pharmaceutical Industry Drug Holding Company, 75th Anniv. — A1266

Background colors: 30p, Pink, yellow and pale green. 150p, Green.

2009, Dec. 19 ***Perf. 13¼x13***
2047-2048 A1266 Set of 2 .95 .95

Egyptian Stock Exchange, 125th Anniv. — A1267

Stock Exchange Building with anniversary emblem at left in: 30p, Gold and white. 150p, Gold (75x30mm).

2009, Dec. 21 ***Perf. 13x13¼***
2049-2050 A1267 Set of 2 .95 .95

Pan-African Postal Union, 30th Anniv. — A1268

2010, Jan. 18
2051 A1268 150p multi .85 .85

National Council for Women, 10th Anniv. — A1269

2010, Mar. 16
2052 A1269 30p multi .65 .65

Orphan's Day — A1270

2010, Jan. 4 Litho. ***Perf. 13¼x12¾***
2053 A1270 30p multi .55 .55

Compare with Types A1132, A1169 and A1199. See also No. 2035.

Edfu Temple — A1271

2010, Jan. 5 ***Perf. 12¾x13¼***
2054 A1271 250p multi 1.50 1.50

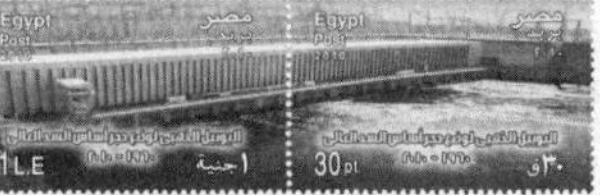

Aswan High Dam, 50th Anniv. — A1272

No. 2055 — Part of dam: a, 30p. b, £1.

2010, Jan. 15
2055 A1272 Horiz. pair, #a-b 1.50 1.50

Arab League Center, 50th Anniv. — A1273

2010, Mar. 22
2056 A1273 200p multi 1.25 1.25

Egyptian Soccer Team, 2010 Winner of African Cup of Nations — A1274

No. 2057 — Pyramid, African Cup of Nations, tournament emblems and: a, 30p, Crocodile mascot. b, 200p, Eagle mascot. c, 250p, Antelope mascot.

No. 2058, 250p, Soccer players, African Cup of nations, years of Egyptian championships, horiz.

2010, Jan. 31 Litho. ***Perf. 13¼x12¾***
2057 A1274 Horiz. strip of 3, #a-c 4.50 4.50

Size: 80x60mm

Imperf

2058 A1274 250p multi 1.50 1.50

Egyptian Gazette, 130th Anniv. — A1275

2010, Apr. 20 ***Perf. 13¼x12¾***
2059 A1275 30p multi .55 .55

Egypt Pavilion, Expo 2010, Shanghai — A1276

2010, May 1 Litho. ***Perf. 12¾x13¼***
2060 A1276 £2.50 multi 1.75 1.75

Opening of Road to Red Sea — A1277

2010, May 27 ***Perf. 13¼x12¾***
2061 A1277 £1 multi .95 .95

Tawfiq al-Hakim (1898-1987), Writer — A1279

World Environment Day — A1278

2010, June 5 ***Perf. 12¾x13¼***
2062 A1278 £2.50 multi 1.50 1.50

2010, June 6 Litho. ***Perf. 13¼x12¾***
2063 A1279 150p multi .95 .95

Second Egyptian Post Innovation Meeting.

Reading for All, 20th Anniv. — A1280

2010, June 21
2064 A1280 £1 multi .95 .95

Egyptian Television, 50th Anniv. — A1281

2010, July 21
2065 A1281 £1.50 multi 1.25 1.25

Alexandria, 2010 Captial of Arab Tourism — A1282

2010, July 22 ***Perf. 12¾x13¼***
2066 A1282 150p multi 1.25 1.25

2010 Asia-Pacific Broadcasting Union Robotics Competition, Cairo — A1283

2010, Sept. 19
2067 A1283 £2.50 multi 1.50 1.50

2010 Euromed Postal Conference, Alexandria — A1284

2010, Sept. 28
2068 A1284 £2.50 multi 1.75 1.75

Alabaster Canopic Jar — A1285

2010, Oct. 8 ***Perf. 13¼x12¾***
2069 A1285 £2.50 multi 1.75 1.75

See Slovakia No. 601.

Second Arab University Games, Cairo — A1286

2010, Oct. 17 ***Perf. 13¼x12¾***
2070 A1286 30p multi .55 .55

World Statistics Day — A1287

2010, Oct. 20
2071 A1287 30p multi .55 .55

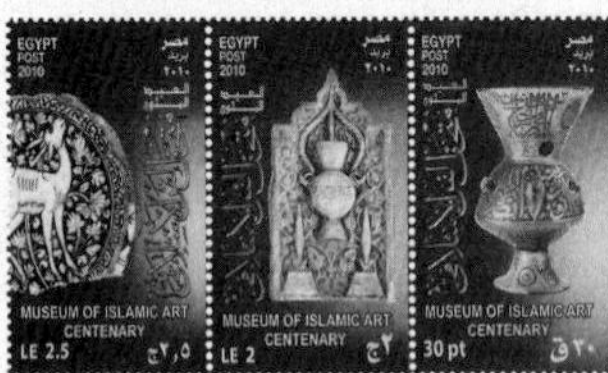

Reopening of Museum of Islamic Art, Cairo — A1288

No. 2072: a, 30p, Goblet. £2, Bas-relief. £2.50, Plate with antelope design.

2010, Oct. 25
2072 A1288 Horiz. strip of 3, #a-c 2.50 2.50

Egyptian Olympic Committee, Cent. — A1289

2010, Dec. 11
2073 A1289 30p multi .60 .60

Information and Decision Support Center, 25th Anniv. — A1290

2010, Dec. 20 ***Perf. 12¾x13¼***
2074 A1290 30p multi .55 .55

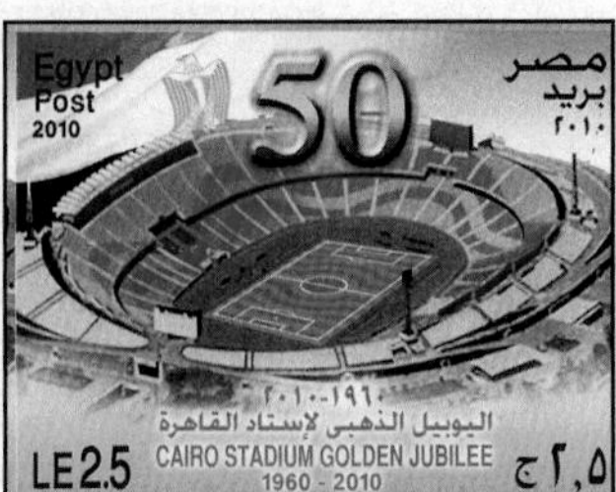

Cairo Stadium, 50th Anniv. — A1291

2010, Dec. 30 ***Imperf.***
2075 A1291 £2.50 multi 1.50 1.50

Post Day A1292

No. 2076 — Egyptian stamps: a, #3. b, #57. c, #107. d, #183. e, #271. f, #321. g, #386. h, #389. i, #873. j, #C1.

2011, Jan. 2 ***Perf. 13***
2076 Block of 10 5.50 5.50
a.-h. A1292 30p Any single .40 .30
i. A1292 £2 multi 1.00 .75
j. A1292 £2.50 multi 1.25 1.00

Cairo Tower, 50th Anniv. — A1293

No. 2077 — Tower: a, 30p, In daylight. b, £2.50, At night.

2011, Apr. 11 ***Perf. 13¼x12¾***
2077 A1293 Horiz. pair, #a-b 2.25 2.25

World Environment Day — A1294

2011, June 5
2078 A1294 £2.50 multi 1.50 1.50

War Academy, 200th Anniv. — A1295

2011, July 20 ***Perf. 12¾x13¼***
2079 A1295 30p multi .80 .80

Rivers — A1296

No. 2080: a, 30p, Pyramids, Nile River. b, 30p, Downtown Singapore, Singapore River. c, £2, Ancient Egyptian boat, Nile River. d, £2, Modern boat, Singapore River. e, £2.50, Cairo skyline, yellow flowers, Nile River. f, £2.50, Singapore buildings, pink flowers, Singapore River.

2011, Oct. 17
2080 A1296 Block of 6, #a-f 3.25 3.25

See Singapore Nos. 1513-1515.

Post Day — A1297

No. 2081: a, Dove, flowers, Egypt Post emblem. b, Post office, air mail envelopes. c, Eye of Horus, flowers, Egypt Post emblem.

2012, Jan. 2 ***Perf. 13¼x12¾***
2081 A1297 £2.50 Horiz. strip of 3, #a-c 2.50 2.50

Temple — A1297a

2011 **Litho.** ***Perf. 11¼***
2081D A1297a £2.50 multi — —

January 25 Revolution, 1st Anniv. — A1298

2012, Jan. 25 ***Imperf.***
2082 A1298 £2.50 multi .85 .85

Pope Shenouda III of Alexandria (1923-2012) — A1299

2012, Mar. 17 ***Imperf.***
2083 A1299 £5 multi 1.75 1.75

Diplomatic Relations Between Egypt and Azerbaijan, 20th Anniv. — A1300

No. 2084: a, Arches and Maiden Tower, Baku, Azerbaijan. b, Sphinx and Pyramids, Egypt.

2012, May 28 ***Perf. 12¾x13¼***
2084 A1300 £2.50 Horiz. pair, #a-b 1.75 1.75

Environment Day — A1301

2012, June 5 ***Perf. 13¼x12¾***
2085 A1301 £2 multi .70 .70

A1302

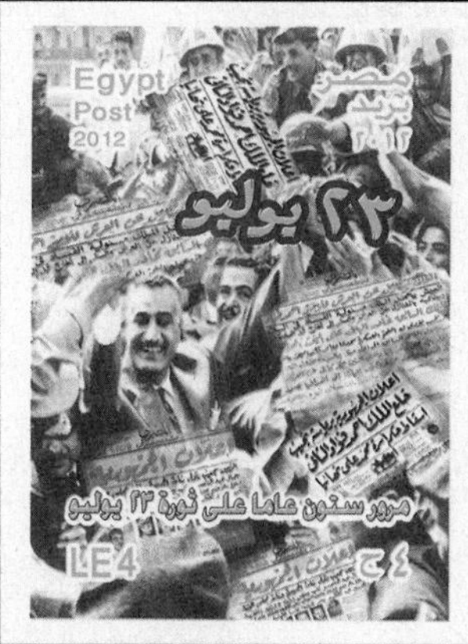

Overthrow of King Farouk by Gamal Abdel Nasser, 60th Anniv. — A1303

2012, July 23 ***Perf. 12¾x13¼***
2086 A1302 £2 multi .65 .65

Imperf

2087 A1303 £4 multi 1.40 1.40

2012 Summer Olympics, London — A1304

No. 2088 — Mascot and: a, Cycling. b, Running. c, Emblem of 2012 Summer Olympics. d, Basketball. e, Soccer.

2012, July 27 ***Perf. 13¼x12¾***
2088 Horiz. strip of 5 4.25 4.25
a.-e. A1304 £2.50 Any single .85 .85

Arab Postal Day — A1305

2012, Aug. 3 ***Perf. 12¾x13¼***
2089 A1305 £3 multi 1.00 1.00

Festivals — A1306

No. 2090: a, Rider on blue gray horse, heads of white and black horses. b, Two riders, black horse, head of brown horse. c, Rider on brown horse.

2012, Aug. 18 ***Perf. 13¼x12¾***
2090 A1306 £1 Horiz. strip of 3, #a-c 1.00 1.00

Lawyers Trade Union, Cent. — A1307

2012, Sept. 12 ***Perf. 12¾x13¼***
2091 A1307 £1 multi .35 .35

Tourism and Sustainable Energy — A1308

2012, Sept. 27 ***Perf. 13¼x12¾***
2092 A1308 £1 multi .35 .35

Helwan University Art Education Faculty, 75th Anniv. — A1309

2012, Nov. 12 **Litho.**
2093 A1309 £2 multi .65 .65

Post Day — A1310

No. 2094: a, Ancient Egyptian art with Isis seated at right, envelopes. b, Lotus flowers. funerary mask of King Tutankhamun. c, Anceint Egyptian art with Isis seated at left.

2013, Jan. 2 ***Perf. 13¼x13***
2094 A1310 £3 Horiz. strip of 3, #a-c 3.00 3.00

January 25th Revolution, 2nd Anniv. — A1311

2013, Jan. 25 ***Perf. 13x13¼***
2095 A1311 £1 multi .30 .30

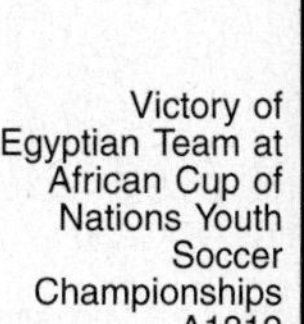

Victory of Egyptian Team at African Cup of Nations Youth Soccer Championships A1312

2013, Apr. 24 ***Perf. 13¼x13***
2096 A1312 £3 multi .90 .90

Return of Sinai to Egypt, 31st Anniv. — A1313

No. 2097 — Various tourist attractions and Sinai Peninsula map showing: a, Northwestern section. b, Northeastern section. c, Southwestern section. d, Southeastern section.

2013, Apr. 25 ***Perf. 13x13¼***
2097 A1313 £2 Block of 4, #a-d 2.40 2.40

World Environment Day — A1314

2013, June 5 ***Perf. 13¼x13***
2098 A1314 £3 multi .85 .85

July 23rd Revolution, 61st Anniv. — A1315

2013, July 23 **Litho.** ***Perf. 12¾x13¼***
2099 A1315 £3 multi .85 .85

Day of the Nile Inundation — A1316

2013, Aug. 25 **Litho.** ***Imperf.***
2100 A1316 £4 multi 1.25 1.25

Intl. Islamic Council for Da'wa and Relief — A1317

Perf. 13¼x12¾

2013, Sept. 21 **Litho.**
2101 A1317 £2 multi .60 .60

World Tourism Day — A1318

Perf. 13¼x12¾

2013, Sept. 27 **Litho.**
2102 A1318 £3 multi .90 .90

A1319

October War Against Israel, 40th Anniv. — A1320

2013, Oct. 6 Litho. *Perf. 12¾x13¼*
2103 A1319 £1 multi .30 .30
2104 A1320 £4 multi 1.25 1.25

Sculptures of Egyptian Pharaohs
A1321 A1322

Designs: Nos. 2105, 2106, Thutmosis III. £1, Senusret I. £3, Ramesses II. £4, Akhenaten.

2013, Oct. 7 Litho. *Perf. 11¼*
2105 A1321 50p org & multi .25 .25
2106 A1321 50p grn & multi .25 .25

Perf. 11x11½
2107 A1322 £1 multi .30 .30
2108 A1322 £3 lil & multi .90 .90
2108A A1322 £3 blue & multi — —
2109 A1322 £4 brn & multi 1.25 1.25
2109A A1322 £4 rose brn & multi — —
Nos. 2105-2109A (7) 2.95 2.95

World Post Day — A1323

2013, Oct. 9 Litho. *Perf. 12¾x13¼*
2110 A1323 £4 multi 1.25 1.25

Tourists on Horseback, Utopia Resort, Marsa Alam — A1324

Old Town, Hurghada — A1325

Madinat Makadi Resort, Hurghada — A1326

Perf. 12¾x13¼
2013, Dec. 17 Litho.
2111 A1324 £4 multi 1.25 1.25
2112 A1325 £4 multi 1.25 1.25
2113 A1326 £4 multi 1.25 1.25
Nos. 2111-2113 (3) 3.75 3.75

Nile Meter, by M. Sabry — A1327

2014, Jan. 2 Litho. *Imperf.*
2114 A1327 £4 multi 1.25 1.25

Post Day.

January 25th Revolution, 3rd Anniv. — A1328

2014, Jan. 25 Litho. *Perf. 12¾x13¼*
2115 A1328 £2 multi .60 .60

Intl. Women's Day — A1329

2014, Mar. 8 Litho. *Perf. 12¾x13¼*
2116 A1329 £2 multi .60 .60

World Heritage Day — A1330

No. 2117: a, Two women. b, Men and camel. c, Men playing board game. d, Man, pottery in windows.

2014, Apr. 18 Litho. *Perf. 12¾x13¼*
2117 A1330 £1 Block of 4 #a-d 1.25 1.25

Diversion of the Nile River, 50th Anniv. — A1331

2014, May 15 Litho. *Imperf.*
2118 A1331 £4 multi 1.10 1.10

African Regional Postal Training Center — A1332

2014, June 1 Litho. *Perf. 12¾x13¼*
2119 A1332 £2 multi .55 .55

Day of the African Child — A1333

Perf. 12¾x13¼
2014, June 17 Litho.
2120 A1333 £3 multi .85 .85

Euromed Postal Emblem and Mediterranean Sea — A1334

2014, July 9 Litho. *Perf. 13x13¼*
2121 A1334 £4 multi 1.10 1.10

July 23rd Revolution, 62nd Anniv. — A1335

2014, July 23 Litho. *Perf. 13¼x13*
2122 A1335 £2 multi .55 .55

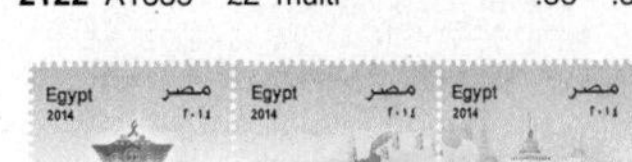

Start of Construction on Second Suez Canal — A1336

No. 2123: a, Suez Canal emblem, ship, map of northern portion of canal. b, Map of central portion of canal, ships near locks of Panama Canal. c, Map of southern portion of canal, Administration building, ship.

2014, Aug. 5 Litho. *Perf. 13¼x13*
2123 A1336 £2 Horiz. strip of 3, #a-c *55.00 37.50*

No. 2123 was withdrawn shortly after the error in stamp design (the Suez Canal has no locks) was made known to Egypt Post.

General Arab Insurance Federation, 50th Anniv. — A1337

50th anniversary emblem: No. 2124, Above map of Arab countries. No. 2125, To left of map of Arab countries.

2014, Sept. 1 Litho. *Perf. 13¼x13*
2124 A1337 £4 multi 1.10 1.10

Imperf
Size: 90x70mm
2125 A1337 £4 multi 1.10 1.10

Start of Construction on New Suez Canal — A1338

No. 2126: a, Map of canal, Adminisration Building, ship in canal. b, Map of canal, ship approaching canal. c, Suez Canal emblem, ship in canal.

2014, Sept. 16 Litho. *Perf. 13¼x13*
2126 A1338 £2 Horiz. strip of 3, #a-c 1.75 1.75

No. 2126 replaces the hastily withdrawn No. 2123. First day covers of No. 2126 show the Aug. 5 first day cancel of No. 2123, though the stamps were printed after the discovery of the design error on No. 2123.

Shali Siwa Oasis — A1339

Perf. 12¾x13¼
2014, Sept. 27 Litho.
2127 A1339 £4 multi 1.10 1.10

October War Against Israel, 41st Anniv. — A1340

2014, Oct. 6 Litho. *Perf. 12¾x13¼*
2128 A1340 £2 multi .55 .55

World Post Day — A1341

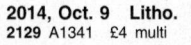

2014, Oct. 9 Litho. *Perf. 13¼x12¾*
2129 A1341 £4 multi 1.10 1.10

Scouting in Egypt, Cent. — A1342

2014, Oct. 15 Litho. ***Perf. 12¾x13¼***
2130 A1342 £1.25 multi .35 .35

Arabic Calligraphy — A1343

2014, Dec. 6 Litho. ***Imperf.***
2131 A1343 £5 multi 1.40 1.40

Central Agency for Public Mobilization and Statistics, Cent. — A1344

2014, Dec. 8 Litho. ***Perf. 13¼x12¾***
2132 A1344 £3 multi .85 .85

Birds — A1345

No. 2133, £1.25: a, Palm dove. b, Hoopoe. c, Roller. d, Bee-eater. e, Sooty falcon. f, Golden oriole.

Perf. 13¼x12¾
2014, Dec. 10 Litho.
2133 A1345 Block of 6, #a-f, + 3 central labels 2.10 2.10

Re-opening of National Theater — A1346

Perf. 12¾x13¼
2014, Dec. 20 Litho.
2134 A1346 £1.50 multi .45 .45

Amenhotep, Son of Hapu — A1347

2015 Litho. ***Perf. 11¼***
2135 A1347 £3 multi .85 .85

A1348

Egyptian Post, 150th Anniv. — A1349

2015, Jan. 2 Litho. ***Perf. 12¾x13¼***
2136 A1348 £1.50 multi .45 .45

Imperf
2137 A1349 £4 multi 1.10 1.10

January 25 Revolution, 4th Anniv. — A1350

2015, Jan. 25 Litho. ***Perf. 12¾x13¼***
2138 A1350 £2 multi .55 .55

Faten Hamama (1931-2015), Actress — A1351

2015, Mar. 8 Litho. ***Perf. 13¼x12¾***
2139 A1351 £3 black .80 .80

Egypt Economic Development Conference — A1352

Perf. 12¾x13¼
2015, Mar. 13 Litho.
2140 A1352 £2 multi .55 .55

26th Arab Summit, Sharm el-Sheikh A1353

Perf. 13¼x12¾
2015, Mar. 23 Litho.
2141 A1353 £3 multi .80 .80

International Telecommunication Union, 150th Anniv. — A1354

2015, May 17 Litho. ***Perf. 12¾x13¼***
2142 A1354 £4 multi 1.10 1.10

Dar al-Ifta al-Misriyyah Educational Institute, 120th Anniv. — A1355

2015, June 1 Litho. ***Perf. 12¾x13¼***
2143 A1355 £2 multi .55 .55

July 23rd Revolution, 63rd Anniv. — A1356

2015, July 23 Litho. ***Perf. 12¾x13¼***
2144 A1356 £2 multi .55 .55

Campaign to Save the Nile River — A1357

2015, July 25 Litho. ***Perf. 12¾x13¼***
2145 A1357 £2 multi .55 .55

A1358

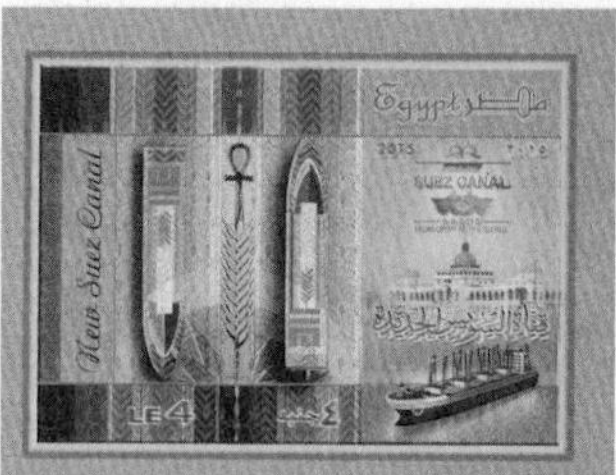

New Suez Canal — A1359

2015, Aug. 6 Litho. ***Perf. 12¾x13¼***
2146 Horiz. strip of 3 2.40 2.40
a. A1358 £3 lilac & multi .80 .80
b. A1358 £3 beige & multi .80 .80
c. A1358 £3 lt blue green & multi .80 .80

Imperf
2147 A1359 £4 multi 1.10 1.10

Poets — A1360

No. 2148: a, Fouad Hadad (1927-85). b, Salah Jaheen (1930-86). c, Abd el Rahman El Abnody (1938-2015).

Perf. 13¼x12¾
2015, Aug. 10 Litho.
2148 A1360 £2 Horiz. strip of 3, #a-c 1.60 .80

Food and Agricultural Organization, 70th Anniv. — A1361

2015, Oct. 1 Litho. ***Perf. 12¾x13¼***
2149 A1361 £3 multi .80 .40

October War With Israel, 42nd Anniv. — A1362

2015, Oct. 6 Litho. ***Perf. 12¾x13¼***
2150 A1362 £2 multi .50 .25

A1363

Federation of Afro-Asian Insurers and Reinsurers, 50th Anniv. — A1364

2015, Oct. 12 Litho. *Perf. 13¼x12¾*
2151 A1363 £4 multi 1.00 .50

Imperf

2152 A1364 £4 multi 1.00 .50

World Statistics Day — A1365

2015, Oct. 20 Litho. *Perf. 12¾x13¼*
2153 A1365 £3 multi .75 .35

Yacht "Mahrousa," 150th Anniv. — A1366

Perf. 12¾x13¼

2015, Dec. 15 Litho.
2154 A1366 £2 multi .55 .55

Al-Ahram Newspaper, 140th Anniv. — A1367

Perf. 13¼x12¾

2015, Dec. 20 Litho.
2155 A1367 £2 multi .55 .55

Helwan University Faculty of Applied Arts, 175th Anniv. — A1368

Perf. 12¾x13¼

2015, Dec. 31 Litho.
2156 A1368 £2 multi .55 .55

A1369

First Egyptian Postage Stamps, 150th Anniv. — A1370

No. 2157: a, Egypt #4-7, dove, boat. b, Egyptian man on donkey. c, Egypt #1-3, Egyptian man on camel.

£4, Emblem of Philatelic Society of Egypt, dove, boat, train, mail carrier on bicycle, mail box.

2016, Jan. 1 Litho. *Perf. 13¼x12¾*
2157 A1369 £2 Horiz. strip of 3, #a-c 1.60 1.60

Imperf

2158 A1370 £4 multi 1.10 1.10

Syndicate of Journalists, 75th Anniv. — A1371

Perf. 13¼x12¾

2016, Mar. 31 Litho.
2159 A1371 £3 multi .70 .70

Famous Men — A1372

No. 2160: a, United Nations emblem and Boutros Boutros-Ghali (1922-2016), United Nations Secretary-General. b, Muhammad Husayn Haykal (1888-1956), Minister of Education.

2016, May 31 Litho. *Perf. 13¼x12¾*
2160 A1372 £2 Horiz. pair, #a-b .90 .90

World Day to Combat Drugs — A1373

Perf. 12¾x13¼

2016, June 26 Litho.
2161 A1373 £2 multi .45 .45

Egypt Nos. 356, 374, 386, 388 and 393 — A1374

2016, July 23 Litho. *Imperf.*
2162 A1374 £4 multi .90 .90

July 23 Revolution, 64th anniv.

Arab Postal Day — A1375

No. 2163 — Area behind denomination in: a, White. b, Green.

2016, Aug. 3 Litho. *Perf. 12¾x13¼*
2163 A1375 £3 Horiz. pair, #a-b 1.40 1.40

Gezera Youth Center — A1376

Perf. 13¼x12¾

2016, Aug. 15 Litho.
2164 A1376 £2 multi .45 .45

Relocation of Abu Simbel Temples, 50th Anniv. — A1377

No. 2165: a, Moving of statues. b, Man wearing glasses. c, Face of Ramesses II statue.

Perf. 13¼x12¾

2016, Aug. 18 Litho.
2165 A1377 £2 Horiz. strip of 3, #a-c 1.40 1.40

World Tourism Day — A1378

No. 2166: a, Hanging Church, Cairo. b, Al-Moez Street, Cairo. c, Philae Temple, Aswan. d, Qaitbay Castle, Alexandria.

Perf. 12¾x13¼

2016, Sept. 27 Litho.
2166 A1378 £2 Block of 4, #a-d 1.90 1.90

October War Against Israel, 43rd Anniv. — A1379

2016, Oct. 6 Litho. *Perf. 12¾x13¼*
2167 A1379 £2 multi .45 .45

Egyptian Parliament, 150th Anniv. — A1380

2016, Oct. 22 Litho. *Perf. 12¾x13¼*
2168 A1380 £2 multi + label .45 .45

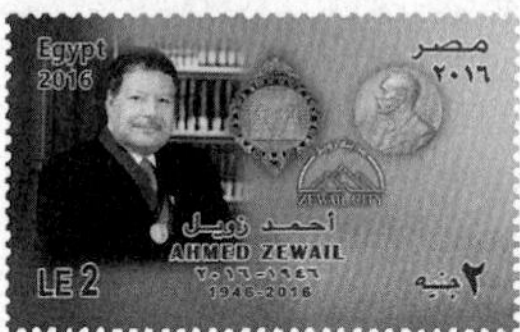

Ahmed Zewail (1946-2016), 1999 Nobel Laureate in Chemistry — A1381

2016, Oct. 25 Litho. *Perf. 12¾x13¼*
2169 A1381 £2 multi .45 .45

Actors — A1382

No. 2170: a, Mahmoud Abd El-Aziz (1946-2016). b, Nour El-Sherif (1946-2015). c, Ahmed Zaki (1949-2005).

Perf. 13¼x12¾ Syncopated

2016, Nov. 27 Litho.
2170 A1382 £2 Horiz. strip of 3, #a-c .70 .70

Miniature Sheet

Giza Zoo, 125th Anniv. — A1383

No. 1383: a, Barbary sheep. b, Giraffe. c, Elephant. d, Crocodile. e, Hippopotamus. f, Pelicans. g, Lion. h, Tiger.

2016, Dec. 2 Litho. *Perf. 12¾x13¼*
2171 A1383 £2 Sheet of 8, #a-h 1.90 1.90

World Day of the Arabic Language — A1384

No. 2172: a, £1, Arabic calligraphy. b, £2, Arabic calligraphy, diff., circle arc at left. c, £2, Arabic calligraphy, diff., circle arc at right.

2016, Dec. 18 Litho. *Perf. 11½*
2172 A1384 Horiz. strip of 3, #a-c .55 .55

National Circus, 50th Anniv. — A1385

2016, Dec. 25 Litho. *Imperf.*
2173 A1385 £4 multi .45 .45

Dendera Temple — A1385a

Perf. 12¾x13¼
2017, Nov. 19 Litho.
2176 A1385a £5 multi .60 .60

Central Agency for Public Mobilization and Statistics A1386

Perf. 13¼x12¾ Syncopated
2017, Apr. 10 Litho.
2177 A1386 £2 multi .25 .25

Modern Egypt Heritage, 150th Anniv. — A1387

Perf. 12¾x13¼ Syncopated
2017, July 5 Litho.
2178 A1387 £2 multi .25 .25

July 23 Revolution, 65th Anniv. — A1388

Perf. 12¾x13¼ Syncopated
2017, July 23 Litho.
2179 A1388 £4 multi .45 .45

General Sports Union for Businesses, 50th Anniv. — A1389

Perf. 13¼x12¾ Syncopated
2017, Sept. 14 Litho.
2180 A1389 £2 multi .25 .25

Forum on Heavenly Religions, Sharm el Sheikh — A1390

Perf. 13¼x12¾ Syncopated
2017, Sept. 28 Litho.
2181 A1390 £4 multi .45 .45

October War Against Israel, 44th Anniv. — A1391

Perf. 12¾x13¼ Syncopated
2017, Oct. 6 Litho.
2182 A1391 £2 multi .25 .25

No. 2182 has simulated perfs to look like a label is attached.

A1392

Discovery of Abu Simbel Temples, 200th Anniv. — A1393

Perf. 12¾x13¼ Syncopated
2017, Oct. 21 Litho.
2183 A1392 £4 multi .45 .45

Size: 90x70mm
Imperf
2184 A1393 £5 multi .60 .60

Egyptian Women's Year — A1394

Perf. 12¾x13¼ Syncopated
2017, Dec. 10 Litho.
2185 A1394 £2 multi .25 .25

The National Post Organization of Egypt has declared as "illegal" miniature sheets of 3 depicting Renaissance painters and miniature sheets of 4 depicting Coins, Napoleonic Wars, High Speed Trains, and the 2018 Winter Olympics.

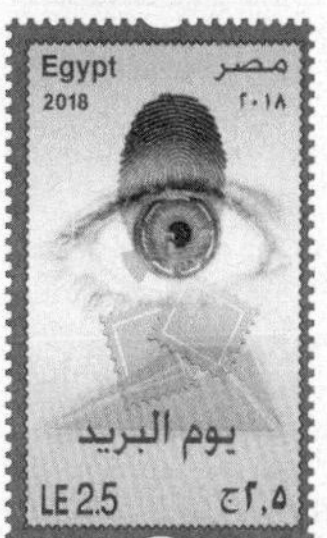

Post Day — A1395

Perf. 13¼x12¾ Syncopated
2018, Jan. 2 Litho.
2186 A1395 £2.50 multi .30 .30

2018 World Cup Soccer Championships, Russia — A1396

Designs: £2.50, World Cup trophy, silhouette of soccer player dribbling ball. £5, World Cup trophy, soccer ball, player kicking ball, horiz.

Perf. 13¼x12¾ Syncopated
2018, June 14 Litho.
2187 A1396 £2.50 multi .30 .30

Size: 90x70mm
Imperf
2188 A1395 £5 multi .55 .55

Luxor Temple — A1397

2018, Sept. 12 Litho. *Perf. 11¼*
2189 A1397 £2.50 multi .30 .30

October War Against Israel, 45th Anniv. — A1398

Perf. 12¾x13¼ Syncopated
2018, Oct. 6 Litho.
2190 A1398 £4 multi .45 .45

Ministry of Culture, 60th Anniv. — A1399

2018, Oct. 14 Litho. *Perf. 12¾x13¼*
2191 A1399 £2.50 multi .30 .30

Post Day — A1400

Perf. 12¾x13¼ Syncopated
2019, Jan. 2 Litho.
2192 A1400 £3 multi .35 .35

Cairo International Book Fair, 50th Anniv. — A1401

2019, Jan. 23 Litho. *Perf. 12¾x13¼*
2193 A1401 £2.50 multi .30 .30

Egyptian Chairmanship of African Union — A1402

Perf. 12¾x13¼ Syncopated
2019, Feb. 10 Litho.
2194 A1402 £4 multi .45 .45

National Institute of Oceanography and Fisheries, Cent. — A1403

Perf. 12¾x13¼ Syncopated
2019, Feb. 12 Litho.
2195 A1403 £3 multi .35 .35

International Women's Day — A1405

Perf. 13¼x12¾ Syncopated
2019, Mar. 8 Litho.
2198 A1405 £4 multi .50 .50

Saad Zaghloul (1859-1927), Leader of 1919 Egyptian Revolution and Prime Minister — A1406

Perf. 12¾x13¼ Syncopated

2019, Mar. 9 **Litho.**

2199 A1406 £4 multi .50 .50

Return of Sinai to Egypt, 37th Anniv. — A1407

Perf. 13¼x12¾ Syncopated

2019, Apr. 25 **Litho.**

2200 A1407 £4 multi .50 .50

Labor Day — A1408

Perf. 13¼x12¾ Syncopated

2019, May 1 **Litho.**

2201 A1408 £5 multi .60 .60

World Telecommunications Day — A1410

Perf. 13¼x12¾ Syncopated

2019, May 17 **Litho.**

2203 A1410 £5 multi .60 .60

World Environment Day — A1411

Perf. 13¼x12¾ Syncopated

2019, June 5 **Litho.**

2204 A1411 £4 multi .50 .50

A1412

Africa Cup of Nations Soccer Tournament, Egypt — A1413

No. 2205 — Silhouettes of Egyptian buildings and: a, Flags of African countries on map of Africa, emblem of African Cup of Nations. b, Arabic text in red, "2019" in violet. c, Mascot and African Cup of Nations.

Perf. 13¼x12¾ Syncopated

2019, June 21 **Litho.**

2205 A1412 £4 Horiz. strip of 3, #a-c 1.50 1.50

Imperf

2206 A1413 £5 multi .60 .60

Traditional Costumes — A1414

No. 2207 — Euromed Postal emblem and: a, Man and woman dancing, ship's wheel and anchor. b, Women in robes. c, Women in ancient Egyptian costumes.

Perf. 13¼x12¾ Syncopated

2019, July 8 **Litho.**

2207 A1414 £4 Horiz. strip of 3, #a-c 1.50 1.50

July 23rd Revolution, 67th Anniv. — A1415

Perf. 13¼x12¾ Syncopated

2019, July 23 **Litho.**

2208 A1415 £4 multi .50 .50

Egyptian Team's Victory at World Under-19 Handball Championships — A1416

Perf. 12¾x13¼ Syncopated

2019, Aug. 16 **Litho.**

2209 A1416 £5 multi .60 .60

Egyptian Philatelic Society, 90th Anniv. — A1417

Perf. 13¼x12¾ Syncopated

2019, Sept. 9 **Litho.**

2210 A1417 £5 multi .65 .65

Egypt as Host of African Space Agency — A1418

Perf. 13¼x12¾ Syncopated

2019, Sept. 19 **Litho.**

2211 A1418 £5 multi .65 .65

Cairo University School of Law, 150th Anniv. — A1419

Perf. 13¼x12¾ Syncopated

2019, Sept. 23 **Litho.**

2212 A1419 £5 multi .65 .65

Opening of the Suez Canal, 150th Anniv. — A1420

Perf. 13¼x12¾ Syncopated

2019, Oct. 3 **Litho.**

2213 A1420 £5 multi .65 .65

October War Against Israel, 46th Anniv. — A1421

Perf. 13¼x12¾ Syncopated

2019, Oct. 6 **Litho.**

2214 A1421 £5 multi .65 .65

World Post Day — A1422

Perf. 12¾x13¼ Syncopated

2019, Oct. 9 **Litho.**

2215 A1422 £5 multi .65 .65

Dome of the Rock, Jerusalem, Doves, and Flag of Palestinian Authority — A1423

Perf. 12¾x13¼ Syncopated

2019, Oct. **Litho.**

2216 A1423 £5 multi .65 .65

Supreme Constitutional Court, 50th Anniv. — A1424

Perf. 13¼x12¾ Syncopated

2019, Oct. **Litho.**

2217 A1424 £5 multi .65 .65

SEMI-POSTAL STAMPS

Catalogue values for unused stamps in this section are for Never Hinged items.

Princess Ferial — SP1

Perf. 13½x14

1940, May 17 **Photo.** **Wmk. 195**

B1 SP1 5m + 5m copper brown 4.50 1.25

No. B1 Overprinted in Green

1943, Nov. 17

B2 SP1 5m + 5m 14.00 9.00

a. Arabic date "1493" 300.00 300.00

The surtax on Nos. B1 and B2 was for the children's fund.

First Postage Stamp of Egypt SP2

King Fuad SP3

No. B4, Khedive Ismail Pasha. No. B6, King Farouk.

Perf. 13¼x13½

1946, Feb. 28 Wmk. 195

B3	SP2	1m + 1m gray	.40	.25
B4	SP3	10m + 10m violet	.50	.25
B5	SP3	17m + 17m brown	.50	.40
B6	SP3	22m + 22m yel grn	.75	.60
a.		Souv. sheet, #B3-B6, perf. 8½	85.00	85.00
b.		As "a," imperf.	85.00	85.00
		Nos. B3-B6 (4)	2.15	1.50

80th anniv. of Egypt's 1st postage stamp. Nos. B6a, B6b measure 129x171mm.

Goddess Hathor, King Men-kau-Re (Mycerinus) and Jackalheaded Goddess — SP7

Ramesseum, Thebes — SP8

Queen Nefertiti SP9

Funerary Mask of King Tutankhamun SP10

Perf. 13½x13¼, 13¼x13½

1947, Mar. 9 Wmk. 195

B9	SP7	5m + 5m slate	1.75	.80
B10	SP8	15m + 15m dp blue, perf. 13¼x13½	2.00	1.00
B11	SP9	30m + 30m henna brn	2.50	1.75
B12	SP10	50m + 50m brown	3.50	2.25
		Nos. B9-B12 (4)	9.75	5.80

Intl. Exposition of Contemporary Art, Cairo.

Boy Scout Emblem — SP11

Scout Emblems: 20m+10m, Sea Scouts. 35m+15m, Air Explorers.

1956, July 25 Photo. *Perf. 13½x13*

B13	SP11	10m + 10m green	1.00	.55
B14	SP11	20m + 10m ultra	1.50	.85
B15	SP11	35m + 15m blue	2.00	1.25
		Nos. B13-B15 (3)	4.50	2.65

2nd Arab Scout Jamboree, Alexandria-Aboukir, 1956.

Souvenir sheets, perf. and imperf., contain one each of Nos. B13-B15. Size: 118x158mm. Values: $1,750 unused each, $1,100 used each.

Ambulance — SP12

1957, May 13 *Perf. 13x13½*

B16	SP12	10m + 5m rose red	.80	.55

50th anniv. of the Public Aid Society.

United Arab Republic

Eye and Map of Africa, Europe and Asia — SP13

Perf. 13½x13

1958, Mar. 1 Photo. Wmk. 318

B17	SP13	10m + 5m orange	1.25	1.00

1st Afro-Asian Cong. of Ophthalmology, Cairo.

The surtax was for centers to aid the blind.

Postal Emblem — SP14

1959, Jan. 2

B18	SP14	10m + 5m bl grn, red & blk	.40	.30

Post Day. The surtax went to the social fund for postal employees.

See Syria UAR issues No. B1 for similar stamp with denominations in piasters (p).

Children and UN Emblem — SP15

1959, Oct. 24 Wmk. 328

B19	SP15	10m + 5m brown lake	.60	.30
B20	SP15	35m + 10m dk blue	.90	.40

Issued for International Children's Day and to honor UNICEF.

Braille Type of Regular Issue, 1961

1961, Apr. 6 *Perf. 13½x13*

B21	A182	35m + 15m yel & brn	.80	.50

Arab League Building, Cairo, and Emblem — SP16

1962, Mar. 22 Photo. Wmk. 328

B22	SP16	10m + 5m gray	.60	.40

Arab Publicity Week, Mar. 22-28.

See No. N86.

Postal Emblem — SP17

Stamp of 1866 — SP18

1963, Jan. 2 Wmk. 342 *Perf. 11½*

B23	SP17	20m +10m brt grn, red & blk	1.25	1.25
B24	SP18	40m +20m blk & brn org	1.75	1.75
B25	SP18	40m +20m brn org & blk	1.75	1.75
a.		Pair, #B24-B25	4.00	4.00
		Nos. B23-B25 (3)	4.75	4.75

Post Day, Jan. 2 and 1966 exhibition of the FIP.

Arms of UAR and Pyramids SP19

1964, Jan. 2 Wmk. 342 *Perf. 11*

B26	SP19	10m + 5m org yel & grn	1.75	1.00
B27	SP19	80m + 40m grnsh bl & blk	3.00	1.75
B28	SP19	115m + 55m org brn & blk	4.00	2.25
		Nos. B26-B28 (3)	8.75	5.00

Issued for Post Day. Jan. 2.

Type of 1963 and

SP20

Postal Emblem — SP20a

No. B30, Emblem of Postal Secondary School. 80m+40m, Postal emblem, gear-wheel, laurel wreath.

Perf. 11½

1965, Jan. 2 Unwmk. Photo.

B29	SP20	10m + 5m lt grn & car	1.00	.50
B30	SP20	10m + 5m ultra, car & blk	1.00	.50
a.		Pair, #B29-B30	2.50	2.00
B31	SP20a	80m + 40m rose, brt grn & blk	2.75	2.00
		Nos. B29-B31 (3)	4.75	3.00

Issued for Post Day, Jan. 2. No. B31 also publicizes the Stamp Centenary Exhibition.

Souvenir Sheet

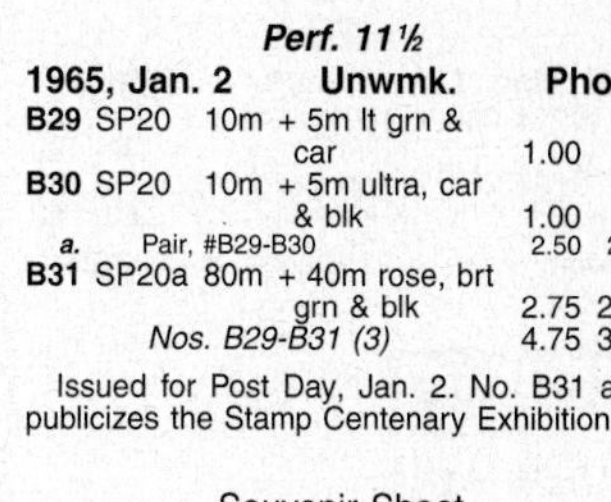

Stamps of Egypt, 1866 — SP21

1966, Jan. 2 Wmk. 342 *Imperf.*

B32	SP21	140m + 60m blk, sl bl & rose	4.50	4.50

Post Day, 1966, and cent. of the 1st Egyptian postage stamps.

Pharaonic "Mediator" — SP22

Design: 115m+40m, Pharaonic guard.

1967, Jan. 2 Wmk. 342 *Perf. 11½*

B33	SP22	80m + 20m multi	3.75	2.75
B34	SP22	115m + 40m multi	6.00	3.50

Issued for Post Day, Jan. 2.

Grand Canal, Doges' Palace, Venice, and Santa Maria del Fiore, Florence — SP23

115m+30m, Piazetta and Campanile, Venice, and Palazzo Vecchio, Florence.

Perf. 11½x11

1967, Dec. 9 Photo. Wmk. 342

B35	SP23	80m + 20m grn, yel & brn	1.75	1.25
B36	SP23	115m + 30m ol, yel & sl bl	2.75	2.00

The surtax was to help save the cultural monuments of Venice and Florence, damaged in the 1966 floods.

Boy and Girl — SP24

Design: No. B38, Five children and arch.

Wmk. 342

1968, Dec. 11 Photo. *Perf. 11*

B37 SP24 20m + 10m car, bl & lt brn .80 .60
B38 SP24 20m + 10m vio bl, sep & lt grn .80 .60

Children's Day & 22nd anniv. of UNICEF.

Emblem and Flags of Arab League — SP25

1969, Mar. 22 *Perf. 11x11½*

B39 SP25 20m + 10m multi .80 .60

Arab Publicity Week, Mar. 22-28.

Refugee Family SP26

1969, Oct. 24 Photo. *Perf. 11½*

B40 SP26 30m + 10m multi .80 .60

Issued for United Nations Day.

Men of Three Races, Human Rights Emblem SP27

1970, Mar. 21 *Perf. 11½x11*

B41 SP27 20m + 10m multi 1.00 .75

Issued to publicize the International Day for the Elimination of Racial Discrimination.

Arab League Type

1970, Mar. 22 Wmk. 342

B42 A344 20m + 10m bl, grn & brn .90 .60

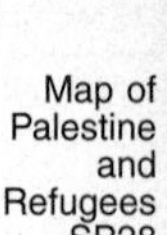

Map of Palestine and Refugees SP28

Perf. 11½x11

1970, Oct. 24 Photo. Wmk. 342

B43 SP28 20m + 10m multi .90 .80

25th anniv. of the UN and to draw attention to the plight of the Palestinian refugees.

Arab Republic of Egypt

Blind Girl, WHO and Society Emblems — SP29

1973, Oct. 24 Photo. *Perf. 11x11½*

B44 SP29 20m + 10m blue & gold .85 .75

25th anniv. of WHO and for the Light and Hope Soc., which educates and helps blind girls.

Map of Africa, OAU Emblem — SP30

Perf. 11x11½

1973, Dec. 8 Photo. Wmk. 342

B45 SP30 55m + 20m multi 2.25 1.50

Organization for African Unity, 10th anniv.

Social Work Day Emblem — SP31

1973, Dec. 8

B46 SP31 20m + 10m multi .75 .65

Social Work Day.

Jihan al Sadat Consoling Wounded Man — SP32

1974, Mar. 21 Wmk. 342 *Perf. 11*

B47 SP32 20m + 10m multi 1.25 .90

Faithfulness and Hope Society.

Afghan Solidarity SP33

Wmk. 342

1981, July 15 Photo. *Perf. 11½*

B48 SP33 20m + 10m multi 1.00 .75

Size: 30x25mm

1981 Photo. *Perf. 11½*

B49 SP33 20m + 10m multi 4.25 3.75

Map of Sudan, Dunes, Dead Tree — SP34

1986, Mar. 25 Photo. *Perf. 13x13½*

B50 SP34 15p + 5p multi 1.75 1.25

Fight against drought and desertification of the Sudan. Surtax for drought relief.

Organization of African Unity, 25th Anniv. — SP35

1988, May 25 Litho. *Perf. 13*

B51 SP35 15p +10p multi 1.25 1.00

AIR POST STAMPS

Mail Plane in Flight AP1

Perf. 13x13½

1926, Mar. 10 Wmk. 195 Photo.

C1 AP1 27m deep violet 32.50 32.50

1929, July 17

C2 AP1 27m orange brown 10.00 2.50

Zeppelin Issue

No. C2 Surcharged in Blue or Violet

1931, Apr. 6

C3 AP1 50m on 27m (Bl) 90.00 77.50
a. "1951" instead of "1931" 125.00 115.00
C4 AP1 100m on 27m (V) 90.00 *82.50*

Airplane over Giza Pyramids AP2

1933-38 Litho. *Perf. 13x13½*

C5 AP2 1m orange & blk .30 .50
C6 AP2 2m gray & blk .80 1.50
C7 AP2 2m org red & blk ('38) 2.75 2.00
C8 AP2 3m ol brn & blk .60 .35
C9 AP2 4m green & blk .90 .90
C10 AP2 5m dp brown & blk .75 .25
C11 AP2 6m dk green & blk 1.50 1.25
C12 AP2 7m dk blue & blk 1.25 1.00
C13 AP2 8m violet & blk .80 .25
C14 AP2 9m dp red & blk 2.00 1.50
C15 AP2 10m violet & brn .75 .70
C16 AP2 20m dk green & brn .60 .25
C17 AP2 30m dull blue & brn .75 .25
C18 AP2 40m dp red & brn 15.00 .60
C19 AP2 50m orange & brn 13.00 .25
C20 AP2 60m gray & brn 6.00 1.10
C21 AP2 70m dk blue & bl grn 3.50 1.00
C22 AP2 80m ol brn & bl grn 3.50 1.00
C23 AP2 90m org & bl grn 4.00 1.00
C24 AP2 100m vio & bl grn 9.00 .80
C25 AP2 200m dp red & bl grn 15.00 1.75
Nos. C5-C25 (21) 82.75 18.20

See Nos. C34-C37. For overprint see No. C38.

Type of 1933

1941-43 Photo.

C34 AP2 5m copper brn ('43) .30 .30
C35 AP2 10m violet .55 .30
C36 AP2 25m dk vio brn ('43) .55 .30
C37 AP2 30m green .70 .30
Nos. C34-C37 (4) 2.10 1.20

Catalogue values for unused stamps in this section, from this point to the end of the section, are for Never Hinged items.

No. C37 Overprinted in Black

1946, Oct. 1

C38 AP2 30m green .85 .40
a. Double overprint 425.00 —
b. Inverted overprint 425.00 —

Middle East Intl. Air Navigation Congress, Cairo, Oct. 1946.

King Farouk, Delta Dam and DC-3 Plane AP3

Perf. 13x13½

1947, Feb. 19 Photo. Wmk. 195

C39 AP3 2m red orange .30 *.85*
C40 AP3 3m dk brown .30 *1.00*
C41 AP3 5m red brown .30 .30
C42 AP3 7m dp yellow org .60 .30
C43 AP3 8m green .60 *.90*
C44 AP3 10m violet .60 .30
C45 AP3 20m brt blue .90 .30
C46 AP3 30m brown violet 1.20 .30
C47 AP3 40m carmine rose 2.00 .75
C48 AP3 50m Prus green 2.50 .85
C49 AP3 100m olive green 5.00 2.50
C50 AP3 200m dark gray 11.00 5.00
Nos. C39-C50 (12) 25.30 13.35

For overprints see Nos. C51-C64, C67-C89, NC1-NC30.

Nos. C49 and C50 Surcharged in Black

1948, Aug. 23

C51 AP3 13m on 100m .60 .55
C52 AP3 22m on 200m .85 *.85*
a. Date omitted

Inaugural flights of "Services Aeriens Internationaux d'Egypte" from Cairo to Athens and Rome, Aug. 23, 1948.

Nos. C39 to C50 Overprinted in Various Colors

Overprint 27mm Wide

1952, Jan. Wmk. 195 *Perf. 13x13½*

C53 AP3 2m red orange (Bl) .45 .30
C54 AP3 3m dark brown (R) 1.60 1.25
C55 AP3 5m red brown .55 .55
C56 AP3 7m dp yel org (Bl) .85 .50
C57 AP3 8m green (R) 2.50 1.60
C58 AP3 10m violet (G) 1.75 1.60
C59 AP3 20m brt blue (R) 4.25 2.50
C60 AP3 30m brown vio (G) 1.90 1.60
C61 AP3 40m carmine rose 4.00 2.50

C62	AP3	50m Prus green (R)	4.25	2.75
C63	AP3	100m olive green	7.50	3.75
C64	AP3	200m dark gray (R)	15.00	7.50
		Nos. C53-C64 (12)	44.60	26.40

See notes after No. 316.

Delta Dam and Douglas DC-3 — AP4

1953 **Photo.**

C65	AP4	5m red brown	.60	.60
C66	AP4	15m olive green	1.50	1.25

For overprints see Nos. NC31-NC32.

Nos. C39-C49 Overprinted in Black

1953

C67	AP3	2m red orange	3.00	3.00
C68	AP3	3m dk brown	1.25	1.25
C69	AP3	5m red brown	1.60	1.60
C70	AP3	7m dp yellow org	.60	.60
C71	AP3	8m green	2.00	2.00
C72	AP3	10m violet	*32.50*	*37.50*
C73	AP3	20m brt blue	2.10	.60
C74	AP3	30m brown violet	3.00	1.60
C75	AP3	40m carmine rose	3.00	1.90
C76	AP3	50m Prus green	5.00	2.00
C77	AP3	100m olive green	9.25	4.75
C77A	AP3	200m gray	*55.00*	

No. C77A is in question. It is not known postally used.

Nos. C53-C64 Overprinted in Black with Three Bars to Obliterate Portrait

1953

C78	AP3	2m red orange	.90	.50
C79	AP3	3m dark brown	1.90	1.60
C80	AP3	5m red brown	.50	.35
C82	AP3	8m green	1.10	*2.50*
C83	AP3	10m violet	.90	*2.00*
C85	AP3	30m brown violet	2.00	2.00
C87	AP3	50m Prus green	4.25	1.60
C88	AP3	100m olive green	6.25	3.75
C89	AP3	200m dark gray	12.50	12.50
		Nos. C78-C89 (9)	30.30	26.80

Practically all values of Nos. C67-C89 exist with double overprint. The 7m, 20m and 40m with this overprint have been considered forgeries. Values: 7m, $8 mint and used; 20m, $5 mint and used; 40m, $20 mint, $25 used.

United Arab Republic
Type of Regular Issue

Perf. 11½x11

1958, Mar. 22 **Photo.** **Wmk. 318**

C90	A141	15m ultra & red brn	.65	.30

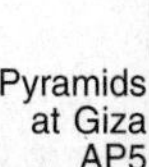

Pyramids at Giza AP5

Al Azhar University AP6

Designs: 15m, Colossi of Memnon, Thebes. 90m, St. Catherine Monastery, Mt. Sinai.

1959-60 **Wmk. 328** ***Perf. 13x13½***

C91	AP5	5m bright red	.35	.25
C92	AP5	15m dk dull violet	.40	.35
C93	AP6	60m dk green	.95	.60
C94	AP5	90m brown car ('60)	2.00	1.25
		Nos. C91-C94 (4)	3.70	2.45

Nos. C91-C93 exist imperf. See Nos. C101, C105, NC33.

Tower of Cairo Type, Redrawn

1961, May 1 ***Perf. 13½x13***

C95	A183	50m bright blue	1.10	.55

Top inscription has been replaced by two airplanes.

Weather Vane, Anemometer and UN World Meteorological Organization Emblem — AP7

Perf. 11½x11

1962, Mar. 23 **Photo.** **Unwmk.**

C96	AP7	60m yellow & dp blue	2.00	1.00

2nd World Meteorological Day, Mar. 23.

Patrice Lumumba and Map of Africa — AP8

Perf. 13½x13

1962, July 1 **Wmk. 328**

C97	AP8	35m multicolored	.65	.40

Patrice Lumumba (1925-61), Premier of Congo.

Maritime Station, Alexandria — AP9

Designs: 30m, International Airport, Cairo. 40m, Railroad Station, Luxor.

1963, Mar. 18 ***Perf. 13x13½***

C98	AP9	20m dark brown	.70	.30
C99	AP9	30m carmine rose	.95	.40
C100	AP9	40m black	1.50	1.00
		Nos. C98-C100 (3)	3.15	1.70

Type of 1959-60 and

Temple of Queen Nefertari, Abu Simbel AP10

Arch and Tower of Cairo — AP11

Designs: 80m, Al Azhar University seen through arch. 140m, Ramses II, Abu Simbel.

Perf. 11½x11, 11x11½

1963-65 **Photo.** **Wmk. 342**

C101	AP6	80m vio blk & brt bl	3.75	1.60
C102	AP10	115m brown & yel	4.00	1.50
C103	AP10	140m pale vio, blk & org red	4.00	2.00

Unwmk.

C104	AP11	50m yel brn & brt bl	2.25	1.00
C105	AP6	80m vio bl & lt bl	3.75	1.60
		Nos. C101-C105 (5)	17.75	7.70

Issued: 50m, 11/2/64; No. C105, 2/13/65; others, 10/24/63.
See Nos. NC34-NC36.

Weather Vane, Anemometer and WMO Emblem — AP12

Perf. 11½x11

1965, Mar. 23 **Wmk. 342**

C106	AP12	80m dk blue & rose lil	2.75	1.50

Fifth World Meteorological Day.
See No. NC37.

Game Board from Tomb of Tutankhamun — AP13

1965, July 1 **Photo.** **Unwmk.**

C107	AP13	10m yellow & dk blue	2.00	.45

See No. NC38.

Temples at Abu Simbel — AP14

1966, Apr. 28 **Wmk. 342** ***Perf. 11½***

C108	AP14	20m multicolored	1.10	.55
C109	AP14	80m multicolored	2.50	1.75

Issued to commemorate the transfer of the temples of Abu Simbel to a hilltop, 1963-66.

Scout Camp and Jamboree Emblem AP15

1966, Aug. 10 ***Perf. 11½x11***

C110	AP15	20m olive & rose	1.60	.50

7th Pan-Arab Boy Scout Jamboree, Good Daim, Libya, Aug. 12.

St. Catherine Monastery, Mt. Sinai — AP16

1966, Nov. 30 **Photo.** **Wmk. 342**

C111	AP16	80m multicolored	2.25	1.75

St. Catherine Monastery, Sinai, 1400th anniv.

Cairo Airport AP17

1967, Apr. 26 ***Perf. 11½x11***

C112	AP17	20m sky bl, sl grn & lt brn	1.00	.40

Hotel El Alamein and Map of Nile Delta AP18

Intl. Tourist Year: 80m, The Virgin's Tree, Virgin Mary and Child. 115m, Fishing in the Red Sea.

1967, June 7 **Wmk. 342** ***Perf. 11½***

C113	AP18	20m dull pur, sl grn & dl org	1.10	.50
C114	AP18	80m blue & multi	2.50	1.50
C115	AP18	115m brown, org & bl	4.75	2.25
		Nos. C113-C115 (3)	8.35	4.25

Oil Derricks, Map of Egypt AP19

1967, July 23 **Photo.**

C116	AP19	50m org & bluish blk	1.25	.85

15th anniversary of the revolution.

Type of Regular Issue, 1967

Design: 80m, Back of Tutankhamun's throne and UNESCO emblem.

1967, Oct. 24 **Wmk. 342** ***Perf. 11½***

C117	A301	80m blue & yellow	1.50	.90

Koran — AP20

1968, Mar. 25 **Wmk. 342** ***Perf. 11½***

C118	AP20	30m lilac, bl & yel	1.25	1.00
C119	AP20	80m lilac, bl & yel	2.25	1.25
a.		Pair, #C118-C119 + label	4.50	3.50

1400th anniv. of the Koran. Nos. C118-C119 are printed in miniature sheets of 4 containing 2 each of Nos. C118-C119.

St. Mark and St. Mark's Cathedral — AP21

1968, June 25 **Wmk. 342** ***Perf. 11½***

C120	AP21	80m brt grn, dk brn & dp car	1.75	1.00

Martyrdom of St. Mark, 1900th anniv. and the consecration of St. Mark's Cathedral, Cairo.

AP22

Design: No. C121, Map of United Arab Airlines and Boeing 707. No. C122, Ilyushin 18 and routes of United Arab Airlines.

1968-69 Photo. *Perf. 11½x11*

C121 AP22 55m blue, ocher & car 1.75 .90
C122 AP22 55m bl, yel & vio blk ('69) 1.25 .90

1st flights of a Boeing 707 and an Ilyushin 18 for United Arab Airlines.

Mahatma Gandhi, Arms of India and UAR — AP23

1969, Sept. 10 *Perf. 11x11½*

C123 AP23 80m lt blue, ocher & brn 4.00 1.75

Mohandas K. Gandhi (1869-1948), leader in India's fight for independence.

Imam El Boukhary — AP24

1969, Dec. 27 Photo. Wmk. 342

C124 AP24 30m lt ol & dk brn .70 .25

1100th anniv. of the death of the Imam El Boukhary (824-870), philosopher and writer.

Azzahir Beybars Mosque AP25

1969, Dec. 27 Engr. *Perf. 11½x11*

C125 AP25 30m red lilac .70 .25

700th anniv. of the founding of the Azzahir Beybars Mosque, Cairo.

Lenin (1870-1924) — AP26

Perf. 11x11½

1970, Apr. 22 Photo. Wmk. 342

C126 AP26 80m lt grn & brn 2.00 1.25

Phantom Fighters and Destroyed Factory AP27

1970, May 1 *Perf. 11½x11*

C127 AP27 80m yel, grn & dk vio brn 2.00 1.00

Issued to commemorate the destruction of the Abu-Zaabal factory by Israeli planes.

UPU Type of Regular Issue

1970, May 20 Photo. Wmk. 342

C128 A350 80m multicolored 1.40 .85

Nasser and Burial Mosque — AP28

1970, Nov. 6 Wmk. 342 *Perf. 11*

C129 AP28 30m olive & blk 1.00 .40
C130 AP28 80m brown & blk 2.75 1.25

Gamal Abdel Nasser (1918-70), Pres. of Egypt.

Postal Congress Type

Perf. 11½x11

1971, Mar. 6 Photo. Wmk. 342

C131 A365 30m lt ol, org & sl grn .90 .45

Nasser, El Rifaei and Sultan Hussein Mosques AP29

Designs: 85m, Nasser and Ramses Square, Cairo. 110m, Nasser, Sphinx and pyramids.

Perf. 11½x11

1971, July 1 Photo. Wmk. 342

C132 AP29 30m multicolored 2.50 .80
C133 AP29 85m multicolored 4.50 1.25
C134 AP29 110m multicolored 5.75 2.50
Nos. C132-C134 (3) 12.75 4.55

APU Type of Regular Issue

1971, Aug. 3 Wmk. 342 *Perf. 11½*

C135 A373 30m brown, yel & bl 1.40 .50

Arab Republic of Egypt Confederation Type

Perf. 11½x11

1971, Sept. 28 Photo. Wmk. 342

C136 A374 30m gray, sl grn & dk pur 1.25 .50

Al Aqsa Mosque and Woman AP30

Wmk. 342

1971, Oct. 24 Photo. *Perf. 11½*

C137 AP30 30m bl, yel, brn & grn 1.75 .45

25th anniv. of the UN (in 1970) and return of Palestinian refugees.

Postal Union Type

30m, African Postal Union emblem & letter.

1971, Dec. 2 *Perf. 11½x11*

C138 A384 30m green, blk & bl 1.40 .40

Aida, Triumphal March AP31

1971, Dec. 23 Wmk. 342 *Perf. 11½*

C139 AP31 110m dk brn, yel & sl grn 5.75 3.00

Centenary of the first performance of the opera Aida, by Giuseppe Verdi.

Globe, Glider, Rocket Club Emblem — AP32

1972, Feb. 11 *Perf. 11x11½*

C140 AP32 30m blue, ocher & yel 1.50 .50

International Aerospace Education Conference, Cairo, Jan. 11-13.

St. Catherine's Monastery on Fire — AP33

Perf. 11½x11

1972, Feb. 15 Unwmk.

C141 AP33 110m dp car, org & blk 4.75 4.00

The burning of St. Catherine's Monastery in Sinai Desert, Nov. 30, 1971.

Tutankhamun in Garden — AP34

Tutankhamun, from 2nd Sarcophagus — AP35

Design: No. C143, Ankhesenamun.

1972, May 22 Photo. *Perf. 11½*

C142 110m brn org, bl & grn 10.00 5.50
C143 110m brn org, bl & grn 10.00 5.50
a. AP34 Pair, #C142-C143 26.00 22.50

Souvenir Sheet

Imperf

C144 AP35 200m gold & multi 32.50 32.50

50th anniv. of the discovery of the tomb of Tutankhamun.

Souvenir Sheet

Flag of Confederation of Arab Republics — AP36

1972, July 23 Photo. *Imperf.*

C145 AP36 110m gold, dp car & blk 4.50 4.25

20th anniversary of the revolution.

Temples at Abu Simbel AP37

Designs: 30m, Al Azhar Mosque and St. George's Church. 110m, Pyramids at Giza.

1972 Wmk. 342 *Perf. 11½x11*

C146 AP37 30m blue, brn & buff 2.50 .40
C147 AP37 85m bl, brn & ocher 3.50 1.75
C148 AP37 110m multicolored 5.25 1.75
Nos. C146-C148 (3) 11.25 3.90

Issued: Nos. C146, C148, 11/22; No. C147, 8/1.

Olympic Type of Regular Issue

Olympic and Motion Emblems and: No. C149, Handball. No. C150, Weight lifting. 50m, Swimming. 55m, Gymnastics. All vertical.

1972, Aug. 17 *Perf. 11x11½*

C149 A396 30m multicolored .80 .40
C150 A396 30m yellow & multi .80 .40
C151 A396 50m blue & multi 1.60 1.00
C152 A396 55m multicolored 2.00 1.10
Nos. C149-C152 (4) 5.20 2.90

Champollion, Rosetta Stone, Hieroglyphics — AP38

1972, Oct. 16

C153 AP38 110m gold, grn & blk 7.50 2.50

Sesquicentennial of the deciphering of Egyptian hieroglyphics by Jean-François Champollion.

World Map, Telephone, Radar, ITU Emblem — AP39

1973, Mar. 21 Photo. *Perf. 11*

C154 AP39 30m lt bl, dk bl & blk .90 .25

5th World Telecommunications Day.

Karnak Temple, Luxor — AP40

1973, Mar. 21
C155 AP40 110m dp ultra, blk & rose 4.75 2.50

Sound and light at Karnak.

Hand Dripping Blood and Falling Plane — AP41

1973, May 1 ***Perf. 11x11½***
C156 AP41 110m multicolored 6.25 3.00

Israeli attack on Libyan civilian plane, Feb. 1973.

WMO Emblem, Weather Vane — AP42

1973, Oct. 24 ***Perf. 11x11½***
C157 AP42 110m blue, gold & pur 3.00 1.75

Cent. of intl. meteorological cooperation.

Refugees, Map of Palestine AP43

1973, Oct. 24 ***Perf. 11½***
C158 AP43 30m dk brn, yel & bl 1.60 .50

Plight of Palestinian refugees.

INTERPOL Emblem — AP44

Perf. 11x11½

1973, Dec. 8 Photo. Wmk. 342
C159 AP44 110m black & multi 3.75 2.00

Intl. Criminal Police Organization, 50th anniv.

Postal and UPU Emblems — AP45

Post Day (UPU Emblems and): 30m, APU emblem. 55m, African Postal Union emblem. 110m, UPU emblem.

Size: 26x46½mm

1974, Jan. 2 Unwmk. ***Perf. 11***
C160 AP45 20m gray, red & blk .45 .25
C161 AP45 30m sal, blk & pur .65 .25
C162 AP45 55m emerald, blk & brt mag 1.25 .85

Size: 37x37½mm

Perf. 11½

C163 AP45 110m lt bl, blk & gold 1.75 1.50
Nos. C160-C163 (4) 4.10 2.85

Solar Bark of Khufu (Cheops) — AP46

Wmk. 342

1974, Mar. 21 Photo. ***Perf. 11½***
C164 AP46 110m blue, gold & brn 3.75 2.25

Solar Bark Museum.

Hotel Meridien AP47

1974, Oct. 6 ***Perf. 11½x11***
C165 AP47 110m multicolored 2.25 1.25

Opening of Hotel Meridien, Cairo.

Suez Canal Type of 1975

1975, June 5 ***Perf. 11½***
C166 A448 30m bl, yel grn & ind 1.75 .60
C167 A448 110m indigo & blue 2.75 2.00

Irrigation Commission Emblem — AP48

1975, July 20
C168 AP48 110m orange & dk grn 2.25 1.25

9th Intl. Congress on Irrigation and Drainage, Moscow, and 25th anniv. of the Intl. Commission on Irrigation and Drainage.

Refugees and UNWRA Emblem — AP49

Woman and IWY Emblem — AP50

Perf. 11x11½

1975, Oct. 24 Photo. Wmk. 342
C169 AP49 30m multicolored 1.40 .50

Unwmk.

C170 AP50 110m olive, org & blk 3.50 2.00

UN Day. 30m publicizes UN help for refugees; 110m is for Intl. Women's Year 1975.

Step Pyramid, Sakhara, and Entrance Gate AP51

Designs: 45m, 60m, Plane over Giza Pyramids. 140m, Plane over boats on Nile.

Perf. 11½x11

1978-82 Photo. Wmk. 342
C171 AP51 45m yel & brown .60 .25
b. Unwatermarked — —
C171A AP51 60m olive 2.00 1.00
c. Unwatermarked — —
C172 AP51 115m blue & brn 1.10 .55
C173 AP51 140m blue & pur 2.00 1.00
C173A AP51 185m bl, sep & gray brn 5.00 2.25
Nos. C171-C173A (5) 10.70 5.05

Issued: 60m, 1/15/82; 185m, 1982; others, 1/1/78.

Flyer and UN ICAO Emblem — AP52

Perf. 11x11½

1978, Dec. 30 Photo. Wmk. 342
C174 AP52 140m blue, blk & brn 2.50 1.25

75th anniversary of 1st powered flight.

Seeing Eye Medallion AP53

Perf. 11½x11

1981, Oct. 1 Photo. Wmk. 342
C175 AP53 230m multicolored 2.50 1.25

Hilton Ramses Hotel Opening — AP54

Perf. 11x11½

1982, Mar. 15 Photo. Wmk. 342
C176 AP54 18½p multi 2.00 1.00

Temple of Horus, Edfu AP55

Designs: 15p, like 6p. 18½p, 25p, Statue of Akhnaton, Thebes, hieroglyphics, vert. 23p, 30p, Giza pyramids.

Perf. 11½x11, 11x11½

1985 Photo. Wmk. 342
C177 AP55 6p lt blue & dk bl grn 1.00 .40
C178 AP55 15p grnsh bl & brn 1.75 .50
a. Unwatermarked — —
C179 AP55 18½p grn, sep & dp yel 2.00 1.25
C180 AP55 23p grnsh bl, sep & yel bis 2.50 1.50
C181 AP55 25p lt bl, sep & yel bis 2.10 .95
a. Unwmkd. ('87) 2.75 1.10
C182 AP55 30p grnsh bl, sep & org yel 2.10 .85
a. Unwmkd. ('87) 2.75 1.10
Nos. C177-C182 (6) 11.45 5.45

Issued: 6p, 18½p, 23p, 3/1; 15p, 25p, 30p, 5/1.

See No. C236.

Post Day — AP56

Narmer Board, oldest known hieroglyphic inscriptions: No. C183a, Tablet obverse. No. C183b, Reverse.

1986, Jan. 2 Photo. ***Perf. 13½x13***
C183 AP56 Pair 2.50 2.50
a.-b. 15p any single 1.10 1.00

Map, Jet, AFRAA Emblem AP57

1986, Apr. 7 Photo. ***Perf. 11½***
C184 AP57 15p blue, yel & blk 1.25 .50

African Airlines Assoc., 18th General Assembly, Cairo, Apr. 7-10.

World Food Day AP58

UNESCO, 40th Anniv. — AP59

Perf. 13½x13, 13x13½

1986, Oct. 24		**Litho.**	
C185 AP58 15p multicolored		1.00	1.00
C186 AP59 15p multicolored		1.00	1.00

UN Day.

Tourism Year — AP60

Design: Column and Sphinx in Alexandria, St. Catherine's Monastery in Mt. Sinai, Colossi of Thebes and Temple of Theban Triad in Luxor.

Unwmk.

1987, Sept. 30 Litho. ***Imperf.***

Size: 140x90mm

C187 AP60 30p multicolored	4.25	4.25

See No. 1344.

Palestinian Uprising — AP61

1988, Sept. 28 Litho. ***Perf. 12x13½***

C188 AP61 25p multicolored	1.60	1.40

UN Day AP62

1988, Oct. 20 Litho. ***Perf. 13x13½***

C189 AP62 25p multicolored	1.60	1.40

Nobel Prize Type of 1988

1988, Nov. 7

C190 A769 25p multicolored	1.60	1.40

Arab Cooperation Council — AP63

1989, May 10 Litho. ***Perf. 13½x13***

C191 AP63 25p Flags	1.25	.55

Size: 89x80mm

Imperf

C192 AP63 50p Flags, seal	3.50	3.50

Architecture and Art — AP64

1989-91	**Photo.**	***Perf. 11x11½***	
C193 AP64 20p Balcony		.75	.45
C194 AP64 25p Brazier		1.10	.60
C195 AP64 35p shown		1.25	.75
C196 AP64 45p Tapestry		1.60	.75
C197 AP64 45p like #C195		1.40	.40
C198 AP64 50p Stag (dish)		2.00	1.00
C199 AP64 55p 4 animals (plate)		1.90	.90
C200 AP64 60p like #C198		2.25	1.25
C201 AP64 65p like #C198		2.50	1.50
C202 AP64 70p like #C193		2.50	1.50
C203 AP64 85p like #C199		3.00	1.75
Nos. C193-C203 (11)		20.25	10.85

Issued: 35p, 60p, 10/1/89; 55p, 1/1/90; No. C197, C202, 1/25/91; 65p, 85p, 7/20/91; others, 4/1/89.

AP65

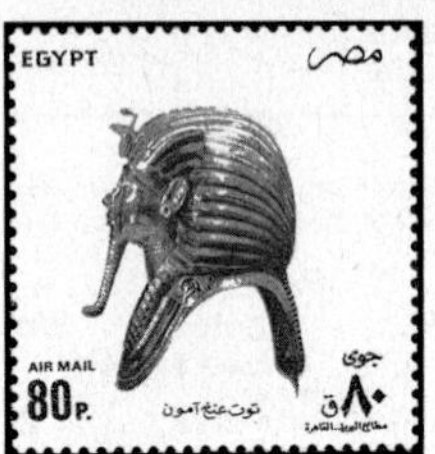

Funerary Mask of King Tutankhamun — AP66

King Tutankhamun AP66a

No. C205, 21mm between "EGYPT" and Arabic text at top.

No. C205A, 17mm between "Egypt" and Arabic text at top ('00).

1993-2000	**Litho.**	***Perf. 11½***	
C204 AP65 55p black & sepia		2.00	.95
C205 AP66 80p black & drab		3.25	1.25
C205A AP66 80p black & sepia		—	—

Photo.

Perf. 11x11¼

C206 AP66a £1 black & brown		1.50	1.25
b. Wmk. 342		2.00	1.25
Nos. C204-C206 (4)		6.75	3.45

Issued: 55p, 80p, 3/1/93; £1, 1997; No. C206b, 1999.

See No. C231.

ICAO, 50th Anniv. — AP67

1994, Sept. 16 Litho. ***Perf. 13***

C207 AP67 80p multicolored	1.00	.45

Intl. Year of the Family — AP68

1994, Oct. 24 Litho. ***Perf. 13***

C208 AP68 80p multicolored	1.50	1.00

Arab League for Education, Culture, & Science Organization — AP69

1995, July 25 Litho. ***Perf. 13x13½***

C209 AP69 55p multicolored	.80	.50

UN Organizations, 50th Anniv. — AP70

Perf. 12½x13, 13x12½

1995, Oct. 24	**Litho.**	
C210 AP70 80p UN	2.00	1.00
C211 AP70 80p FAO	2.00	1.00
C212 AP70 80p UNESCO, vert.	2.00	1.00
Nos. C210-C212 (3)	6.00	3.00

Arab Summit, Cairo — AP71

1996, June 21 Litho. ***Perf. 13x12½***

C213 AP71 55p multicolored	.70	.30

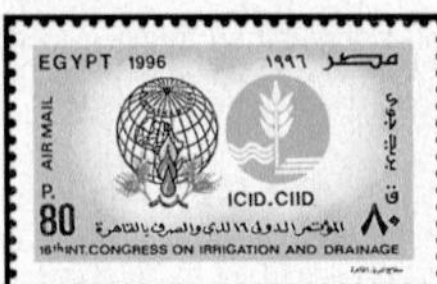

16th Intl. Conference on Irrigation and Drainage, Cairo — AP72

1996, Sept. 15 Litho. ***Perf. 12½x13***

C214 AP72 80p multicolored	1.10	1.10

Intl. Tourism Day — AP73

1996, Sept. 27 ***Perf. 13***

C215 AP73 80p multicolored	1.50	.60

Arabian Horse Day — AP74

1996, Sept. 27 ***Perf. 13x12½***

C216 AP74 55p grn, blk & gray	1.00	.35

World Post Day — AP75

1996, Oct. 9 Litho. ***Perf. 13x12½***

C217 AP75 80p multicolored	1.25	.60

AP76

1996, Oct. 24

C218 AP76 55p multicolored	.70	.40

Cairo, Arab cultural capital of 1996.

UNICEF, 50th Anniv. — AP77

1996, Oct. 24

C219 AP77 80p multicolored	1.10	.55

World Meteorological Day — AP78

1997, Mar. 23 Litho. ***Perf. 13x12½***

C220 AP78 £1 multicolored	1.75	1.00

Thutmose III — AP79

1997, Mar. 25 Photo. *Perf. 11x11½*
C221 AP79 75p blk, bl & gray 1.10 1.10

Heinrich von Stephan (1831-97) — AP80

1997, Apr. 15 Litho. *Perf. 13*
C222 AP80 £1 multicolored 1.60 1.25

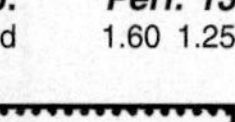

AP81

1997, Sept. 11
C223 AP81 £1 multicolored 1.00 .90

98th Intl. Parliamentary Conference, Cairo.

AP82

1997, Sept. 10 Litho. *Perf. 13*
C224 AP82 75p multicolored 1.00 .90

1997 Egyptian Team, top medal winners of 8th Pan Arab Games, Beirut, Lebanon.

AP83

1997, Sept. 27 *Perf. 13x12½*
C225 AP83 £1 multicolored 1.90 1.00

Sarabas (180-211), mumified Egyptian.

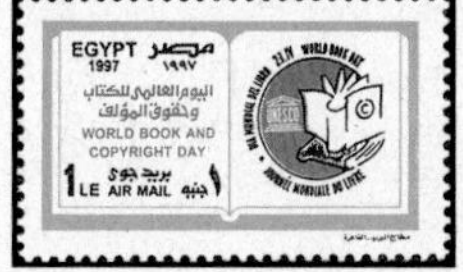
World Book and Copyright Day AP84

1997, Oct. 24 Litho. *Perf. 12½x13*
C226 AP84 £1 multicolored 1.75 1.00

African Ministries of Transport and Communications, 11th Conference — AP85

1997, Nov. 22 Litho. *Perf. 13x12½*
C227 AP85 75p multicolored .80 .70

Arab Scout Movement, 85th Anniv. — AP86

1997, Nov. 24 *Perf. 12½x13*
C228 AP86 75p multicolored 1.00 .90

8th G-15 Summit Meeting — AP87

1998, May 11 Litho. *Perf. 13*
C229 AP87 £1 multicolored 1.10 .90

Lighthouse of Alexandria AP88

1998, May 20 Litho. *Perf. 13*
C230 AP88 £1 multicolored 1.75 1.00

King Tut Type of 1997

1998, July 25 Litho. *Perf. 11x11¼*
C231 AP66a 125p Tutankhamun 1.75 1.25
a. Wmk. 342 ('99) 5.50 4.00

Arab Post Day — AP90

1998, Aug. 3 *Perf. 13*
C232 AP90 £1 multicolored 1.10 .90

World Post Day — AP91

1998, Oct. 9 Litho. *Perf. 13*
C233 AP91 125p multicolored 1.40 1.25

67th Interpol Meeting, Cairo — AP92

1998, Oct. 22
C234 AP92 125p multicolored 1.40 1.25

AP93

1998, Oct. 24
C235 AP93 125p multicolored 1.40 1.25

Universal Declaration of Human Rights, 50th anniv.

Statue of Akhnaton Type of 1985

1998 Litho. *Perf. 13*
C236 AP55 25p lt bl, brn & tan 1.75 1.00

AP94

1999, Oct. 12 Litho. *Perf. 13x12¾*
C237 AP94 125p multicolored 2.25 1.75

Performance of opera "Aida" at the Pyramids.

AP95

1999, Oct. 16
C238 AP95 125p multicolored 2.50 1.75

Discovery of the Rosetta Stone, bicent.

World Tourism Day — AP96

Perf. 13¼x12¾

2000, Sept. 27 Litho.
C239 AP96 125p multi 1.50 1.25

Awarding of Nobel Prize for Chemistry to Dr. Ahmed Zewail — AP97

1999, Dec. 10 *Imperf.*
C240 AP97 125p multi 2.00 2.00

UN High Commissioner for Refugees, 50th Anniv. — AP98

2000, Dec. 13
C241 AP98 125p multi 1.50 1.25

AIR POST SEMI-POSTAL STAMPS

Catalogue values for unused stamps in this section are for Never Hinged items.

United Arab Republic

Pharaonic Mail Carriers and Papyrus Plants SPAP1

Design: 115m+55m, Jet plane, world map and stamp of Egypt, 1926 (No. C1).

Wmk. 342

1966, Jan. 2 Photo. *Perf. 11½*

CB1 SPAP1 80m + 40m multi 3.25 2.75
CB2 SPAP1 115m + 55m multi 4.25 3.50
a. Pair, #CB1-CB2 10.00 8.00

Post Day, Jan. 2.

SPECIAL DELIVERY STAMPS

Motorcycle Postman — SD1

Perf. 13x13½

1926, Nov. 28 Photo. Wmk. 195

E1 SD1 20m dark green 35.00 9.50

1929, Sept.

E2 SD1 20m brown red & black 6.75 1.75

Inscribed "Postes Expres"

1943-44 Litho.

E3 SD1 26m brn red & gray blk 6.75 *6.75*
E4 SD1 40m dl brn & pale gray ('44) 6.00 4.00

For overprints see Nos. E5, NE1.

Catalogue values for unused stamps in this section, from this point to the end of the section, are for Never Hinged items.

No. E4 Overprinted in Black

1952, Jan. Overprint 27mm Wide

E5 SD1 40m dl brn & pale gray 3.50 2.00

See notes after No. 316.

POSTAGE DUE STAMPS

D1

Wmk. Crescent and Star (119)

1884, Jan. 1 Litho. *Perf. 10½*

J1 D1 10pa red 57.50 9.50
a. Horiz. pair, imperf. vert. 175.00
J2 D1 20pa red 175.00 50.00
J3 D1 1pi red 145.00 52.50
J4 D1 2pi red 240.00 12.50
J5 D1 5pi red 20.00 *65.00*
Nos. J1-J5 (5) 637.50 189.50

1886, Aug. 1 Unwmk.

J6 D1 10pa red 75.00 17.50
a. Horiz. pair, imperf. vert. 150.
J7 D1 20pa red 260.00 50.00
J8 D1 1pi red 37.50 10.00
a. Pair, imperf. between 225.00 150.00
J9 D1 2pi red 37.50 5.00
a. Pair, imperf. between 200.00
Nos. J6-J9 (4) 410.00 82.50

D2

1888, Jan. 1 *Perf. 11½*

J10 D2 2m green 22.50 *27.50*
a. Horiz. pair, imperf. between 250.00 225.00
J11 D2 5m rose red 45.00 27.50
J12 D2 1pi blue 145.00 40.00
a. Pair, imperf. between 325.00
J13 D2 2pi yellow 155.00 20.00
J14 D2 5pi gray 240.00 210.00
a. Period after "PIASTRES" 325.00 250.00
Nos. J10-J14 (5) 607.50 325.00

Excellent counterfeits of #J1-J14 are plentiful.

There are 4 types of each of Nos. J1-J14, so placed that any block of 4 contains all types.

D3

Perf. 14x13½

1889 Wmk. 119 Typo.

J15 D3 2m green 10.00 .70
a. Half used as 1m on cover 400.00
J16 D3 4m maroon 3.75 .70
J17 D3 1pi ultra 7.75 .70
J18 D3 2pi orange 7.50 1.00
a. Half used as 1p on cover —
Nos. J15-J18 (4) 29.00 3.10

Nos. J15-J18 exist on both ordinary and chalky paper. Imperf. examples of Nos. J15-J17 are proofs.

Black Surcharge

Type I — D4

1898

J19 D4 3m on 2pi orange 2.10 *6.25*
a. Inverted surcharge 67.50 *90.00*
b. Pair, one without surcharge —
f. Double surcharge 250.00 —

There are two types of this surcharge. In type I, the spacing between the last two Arabic characters at the right is 2mm. In type II, this spacing is 3mm, and there is an added sign on top of the second character from the right. See *Scott Classic Specialized Catalogue of Stamps & Covers* for detailed listing.

D5

D6

1921 Wmk. 120 *Perf. 14x13½*

J20 D5 2m green 3.75 *6.75*
J21 D5 4m vermilion 7.50 *19.00*
J22 D6 10m deep blue 12.50 *25.00*
Nos. J20-J22 (3) 23.75 50.75

1921-22

J23 D5 2m vermilion 1.00 *2.25*
J24 D5 4m green 6.00 2.00
J25 D6 10m lake ('22) 6.50 1.50
Nos. J23-J25 (3) 13.50 5.75

Nos. J18, J23-J25 Overprinted

1922, Oct. 10 Wmk. 119

J26 D3 2pi orange 7.50 *10.50*
a. Overprint right side up 32.50 *32.50*

Wmk. 120

J27 D5 2m vermilion 1.00 *3.25*
J28 D5 4m green 1.60 *3.25*
J29 D6 10m lake 2.75 2.00
Nos. J26-J29 (4) 12.85 19.00

Overprint on Nos. J26-J29 is inverted.

Arabic Numeral — D7

Perf. 13x13½

1927-56 Litho. Wmk. 195

Size: 18x22½mm

J30 D7 2m slate .85 .50
J31 D7 2m orange ('38) 1.00 1.10
J32 D7 4m green .85 .55
J33 D7 4m ol brn ('32) 8.00 5.25
J34 D7 5m brown 4.25 1.10
J35 D7 6m gray grn ('41) 2.75 2.10
J36 D7 8m brn vio 1.60 .65
J37 D7 10m brick red ('29) 1.25 .35
a. 10m deep red 1.90 1.00
J38 D7 12m rose lake ('41) 1.90 *3.75*
J38A D7 20m dk red ('56) 2.50 2.50

Perf. 13½x14

Size: 22x28mm

J39 D7 30m purple 5.25 3.75
Nos. J30-J39 (11) 30.20 21.60

See Nos. J47-J59. For overprints see Nos. J40-J46, NJ1-NJ7.

Catalogue values for unused stamps in this section, from this point to the end of the section, are for Never Hinged items.

Postage Due Stamps and Type of 1927 Overprinted in Various Colors

1952, Jan. 16 *Perf. 13x13½*

J40 D7 2m orange (Bl) 1.60 1.60
J41 D7 4m green 1.60 1.60
J42 D7 6m gray grn (RV) 1.90 1.90
J43 D7 8m brn vio (Bl) 2.50 2.50
J44 D7 10m dl rose (Bl) 4.25 3.50
a. 10m brown red (Bk) 4.00 3.75
J45 D7 12m rose lake (Bl) 2.10 2.10

Perf. 14

J46 D7 30m purple (C) 3.50 3.50
Nos. J40-J46 (7) 17.45 16.70

See notes after No. 316.

United Arab Republic

1960 Wmk. 318 *Perf. 13x13½*

Size: 18x22½mm

J47 D7 2m orange 1.00 1.00
J48 D7 4m light green 1.50 1.50
J49 D7 6m green 2.50 2.50
J50 D7 8m brown vio 5.00 5.00
J51 D7 12m rose brown 12.00 10.00
J52 D7 20m dull rose brn 2.00 .50

Perf. 14

Size: 22x28mm

J53 D7 30m violet 12.00 6.00
Nos. J47-J53 (7) 36.00 26.50

1962 Wmk. 328 *Perf. 13x13½*

Size: 18x22½mm

J54 D7 2m salmon 1.00 1.00
J55 D7 4m light green 1.50 1.50
J56 D7 10m red brown 2.50 2.50
J57 D7 12m rose brown 5.00 5.00
J58 D7 20m dull rose brn 11.00 11.00

Perf. 14

Size: 22x28mm

J59 D7 30m light violet 16.00 16.00
Nos. J54-J59 (6) 37.00 37.00

D8

1965 Unwmk. Photo. *Perf. 11*

J60 D8 2m org & vio blk 1.25 1.00
J61 D8 8m lt bl & dk bl 1.50 1.50
J62 D8 10m yel & emer 2.25 1.50
J63 D8 20m lt bl & vio blk 2.75 2.25
J64 D8 40m org & emer 4.75 2.00
Nos. J60-J64 (5) 12.50 8.25

MILITARY STAMPS

The "British Forces" and "Army post" stamps were special issues provided at a reduced rate for the purchase and use by the British military forces in Egypt and their families for ordinary letters sent to Great Britain and Ireland by a concessionary arrangement made with the Egyptian government. From Nov. 1, 1932 to Feb. 29, 1936, in order to take advantage of the concessionary rate, it was mandatory to use #M1-M11 by affixing them to the backs of envelopes. An "Egypt Postage Prepaid" handstamp was applied to the face of the envelopes. Envelopes bearing these stamps were to be posted only at British military post boxes. Envelopes bearing the 1936-39 "Army Post" stamps (#M12-M15, issued by the Egyptian Postal Administration) also were sold at the concessionary rate and also were to be posted only at British military post boxes. The "Army Post" stamps were withdrawn in 1941, but the concession continued without the use of special stamps. The concession was finally canceled in 1951.

Imperf examples of Nos. M1-M4, M6, M9 (without overprint) and M10 are proofs.

M1

Unwmk.

1932, Nov. 1 Typo. *Perf. 11*

M1 M1 1pi red & blue 70.00 4.50

For similar design see No. M3.

M2

1932, Nov. 26 Typo. *Perf. 11½*

M2 M2 3m blk, *sage grn* 57.50 *80.00*

See Nos. M4, M6, M10.

M3

1933, Aug. Typo. *Perf. 11*

M3 M3 1pi red & blue 47.50 1.10

Camel Type of 1932

1933, Nov. 13 Typo. *Perf. 11½*

M4 M2 3m brown lake 40.00 *57.50*

M4

1934, June 1 Photo. *Perf. 14½x14*

M5 M4 1pi bright carmine 40.00 1.25

See Nos. M7-M8. For overprint and surcharge see Nos. M9, M11.

Camel Type of 1932

1934, Nov. 17 Typo. *Perf. 11½*

M6 M2 3m deep blue 30.00 *30.00*

Type of 1934

1934, Dec. 5 Photo. *Perf. 14½x14*

M7 M4 1pi green 6.00 6.00

Type of 1934

1935, Apr. 24 *Perf. 13½x14*

M8 M4 1pi bright carmine 2.90 *3.75*

Type of 1934 Overprinted in Red

1935, May 6 *Perf. 14*
M9 M4 1pi ultramarine 350.00 275.00

Camel Type of 1932

1935, Nov. 23 Typo. *Perf. 11½*
M10 M2 3m vermilion 30.00 *45.00*

No. M8 Surcharged

1935, Dec. 16 Photo. *Perf. 13½x14*
M11 M4 3m on 1pi brt car 40.00 *100.00*

Fuad Type of 1927

Inscribed "Army Post" — M5

1936, Mar. 1 Wmk. 195
M12 M5 3m green 2.50 2.50
M13 M5 10m carmine 7.00 .25

King Farouk — M6

1939, Dec. 16 *Perf. 13x13½*
M14 M6 3m green 6.00 *12.00*
M15 M6 10m carmine rose 8.00 .25

Catalogue values for unused stamps in this section, from this point to the end of the section, are for Never Hinged items.

United Arab Republic

Arms of UAR and Military Emblems — M7

Perf. 11x11½
1971, Apr. 15 Photo. Wmk. 342
M16 M7 10m purple .75 .50

OFFICIAL STAMPS

O1

Wmk. Crescent and Star (119)
1893, Jan. 1 Typo. *Perf. 14x13½*
O1 O1 orange brown 3.75 .25

No. O1 exists on ordinary and chalky paper. Imperf. examples of No. O1 are proofs.

Regular Issues of 1884-93 Overprinted

1907
O2 A18 1m brown 2.40 .35
O3 A19 2m green 4.25 .25
O4 A20 3m orange 4.75 1.25
O5 A22 5m car rose 7.75 .25
O6 A14 1pi ultra 4.75 .25
O7 A16 5pi gray 17.00 6.00
Nos. O2-O7 (6) 40.90 8.35

Nos. O2-O3, O5-O7 imperf. are proofs.

No. 48 Overprinted

1913
O8 A22 5m carmine rose 9.50 .70
a. Inverted overprint 90.00
b. No period after "S" 65.00 19.00

Regular Issues Overprinted

1914-15 On Issues of 1888-1906
O9 A19 2m green 5.00 *10.00*
a. Inverted overprint 42.50 42.50
b. Double overprint 450.00
c. No period after "S" 16.00 16.00
O10 A21 4m brown red 7.50 5.50
a. Inverted overprint 225.00 160.00

On Issue of 1914
O11 A24 1m olive brown 2.50 *5.00*
a. No period after "S" 14.00 *30.00*
O12 A26 3m orange 3.75 *6.00*
a. No period after "S" 16.00 *30.00*
O13 A28 5m lake 4.75 2.75
a. No period after "S" 17.50 *26.00*
b. Two periods after "S" 17.50 *26.00*
Nos. O9-O13 (5) 23.50 29.25

Regular Issues Overprinted

1915, Oct. On Issues of 1888-1906
O14 A19 2m green 5.50 *5.00*
a. Inverted overprint 24.00 24.00
b. Double overprint 30.00
O15 A21 4m brown red 11.00 *11.00*

On Issue of 1914
O16 A28 5m lake 15.00 1.75
a. Pair, one without overprint 325.00
Nos. O14-O16 (3) 31.50 17.75

Nos. 50, 63, 52, 67 Overprinted

1922 Wmk. 120
O17 A24 1m olive brown 4.25 *16.00*
O18 A25 2m red 10.00 *24.00*
O19 A26 3m orange 77.50 *150.00*
O20 A28 5m pink 21.00 6.00
Nos. O17-O20 (4) 112.75 196.00

Regular Issues of 1921-22 Overprinted

1922
O21 A24 1m olive brn 1.50 *3.25*
O22 A25 2m red 2.00 *4.50*
O23 A26 3m orange 3.25 *5.00*
O24 A27 4m green 7.00 *9.00*
a. Two periods after "H" none after "S" 175.00 175.00
O25 A28 5m pink 4.00 1.00
a. Two periods after "H" none after "S" 75.00 75.00
O26 A29 10m deep blue 7.00 *8.00*
O27 A29 10m lake ('23) 10.00 4.00
a. Two periods after "H" none after "S" 100.00 100.00
O28 A34 15m indigo 8.00 7.00
O29 A35 15m indigo 160.00 160.00
a. Two periods after "H" none after "S" 250.00 250.00
O30 A31 50m maroon 20.00 18.00

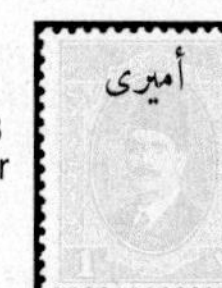
Regular Issue of 1923 Overprinted in Black or Red

1924 *Perf. 13½x14*
O31 A36 1m orange 2.10 *2.25*
O32 A36 2m gray (R) 2.75 *3.50*
O33 A36 3m brown 6.75 *6.75*
O34 A36 4m yellow green 8.50 8.50
O35 A36 5m orange brown 2.00 1.05
O36 A36 10m rose 5.50 4.00
O37 A36 15m ultra 9.25 6.75

Perf. 14
O38 A36 50m myrtle green 25.00 13.50
Nos. O31-O38 (8) 61.85 46.30

O2

Perf. 13x13½
1926-35 Litho. Wmk. 195
Size: 18½x22mm
O39 O2 1m lt orange 1.05 .55
O40 O2 2m black .70 .40
O41 O2 3m olive brn 2.00 1.35
O42 O2 4m lt green 1.75 1.60
O43 O2 5m brown 2.10 .55
O44 O2 10m dull red 5.25 .55
O45 O2 10m brt vio ('34) 3.00 .60
O46 O2 15m dp blue 5.25 1.25
O47 O2 15m brown vio ('34) 5.25 1.10
O48 O2 20m dp blue ('35) 5.50 1.60

Perf. 13½
Size: 22½x27½mm
O49 O2 20m olive green 7.50 2.75
O50 O2 50m myrtle green 10.00 2.00
Nos. O39-O50 (12) 49.35 14.30

O3

1938, Dec. Size: 22½x19mm
O51 O3 1m orange .35 .35
O52 O3 2m red .35 .35
O53 O3 3m olive brown 1.60 1.60
O54 O3 4m yel green 1.00 1.00
O55 O3 5m brown .50 .50
O56 O3 10m brt violet .60 .60
O57 O3 15m rose violet 1.60 1.60
O58 O3 20m blue 1.60 1.60

Perf. 14x13½
Size: 26½x22mm
O59 O3 50m myrtle green 3.75 3.00
Nos. O51-O59 (9) 11.35 10.60

Catalogue values for unused stamps in this section, from this point to the end of the section, are for Never Hinged items.

Nos. O51 to O59 Overprinted in Various Colors

Overprint 19mm Wide

1952, Jan. *Perf. 13x13½*
O60 O3 1m orange (Br) 2.10 2.10
O61 O3 2m red (Br) 2.10 2.10
O62 O3 3m olive brn (Bl) 2.50 2.50
O63 O3 4m yel green (Bl) 2.50 2.50
O64 O3 5m brown (Bl) 2.50 2.50
O65 O3 10m brt violet (Bl) 2.50 2.50
O66 O3 15m rose violet (Bl) 3.00 3.00
O67 O3 20m blue 3.75 3.75

Overprint 24½mm Wide
Perf. 14x13½
O68 O3 50m myrtle grn (RV) 8.00 8.00
Nos. O60-O68 (9) 28.95 28.95

See notes after No. 316.

United Arab Republic

O4

Perf. 13x13½
1959 Litho. Wmk. 318
O69 O4 10m brown violet .65 .25
O70 O4 35m chalky blue 1.75 .30

1962-63 Wmk. 328
O71 O4 1m orange ('63) .30 .30
O72 O4 4m yel grn ('63) .60 .60
O73 O4 5m brown .60 .25
O74 O4 10m dk brown .75 .30
O75 O4 35m dark blue 2.25 .50
O76 O4 50m green 3.50 .60
O77 O4 100m violet ('63) 7.00 1.75
O78 O4 200m rose red ('63) 15.00 8.00
O79 O4 500m gray ('63) 22.50 15.00
Nos. O71-O79 (9) 52.50 27.30

Arms of UAR — O5

Perf. 11½x11
1966-68 Unwmk. Photo.
O80 O5 1m ultra .25 .25
O81 O5 4m brown .25 .25
O82 O5 5m olive .30 .25
O83 O5 10m brown blk 1.00 .35
O84 O5 20m magenta .60 .30
O85 O5 35m dk purple 1.00 .35
O86 O5 50m orange 1.10 .45
O87 O5 55m dk purple 1.10 .45

Wmk. 342
O88 O5 100m brt grn & brick red 2.25 1.00
O89 O5 200m blue & brick red 4.50 2.00
O90 O5 500m olive & brick red 10.00 6.25
Nos. O80-O90 (11) 22.35 11.90

1969 Wmk. 342
O91 O5 10m magenta 1.10 .65

Arab Republic of Egypt

Arms of Egypt — O6

Wmk. 342
1972, June 30 Photo. *Perf. 11*
O92 O6 1m black & vio blue .30 .25
a. 1m black & light blue ('75) .25 .25
O93 O6 10m black & car .65 .30
a. 10m black & rose red ('76) .25 .25
O94 O6 20m black & olive .90 .40
O95 O6 50m black & orange .60 .55
O96 O6 55m black & purple 3.00 1.00

1973
O97 O6 20m lilac & sepia .90 .40
a. 20m purple & light brown ('76) 2.50 .75
O98 O6 70m black & grn ('79) .85 .45

1982 Photo. Unwmk. *Perf. 11*
O99 O6 30m purple & brown .60 .30
O100 O6 60m black & orange .70 .30
O101 O6 80m black & green .95 .35
Nos. O92-O101 (10) 9.45 4.30

Issued: 30m, 2/12; 60m, 2/24; 80m, 2/18.

Arms of Egypt — O7

1985-89 Photo. *Perf. 11½*
Size: 21x25mm

O102 O7 1p vermilion .25 .25
O103 O7 2p brown .25 .25
O104 O7 3p sepia .25 .25
O105 O7 5p orange yel .35 .30
O106 O7 8p green .70 .35
O107 O7 10p brown olive .25 .25
O108 O7 15p dull violet 1.50 .70
O109 O7 20p blue .85 .80
O110 O7 25p red 1.50 1.00
O111 O7 30p dull violet .90 .70
O112 O7 50p green 2.25 2.25
O113 O7 60p myrtle green 2.00 1.40
Nos. O102-O113 (12) 11.05 8.50

Issued: 1p, 3p, 5p, 8p, 15p, 5/1/85; 20p, 50p, 4/88; 10p, 30p, 60p, 12/1/89; 2p, 25p, 1989.

1991-99 Wmk. 342 *Perf. 11½x11*
Size: 18x22mm

O114 O7 5p orange yellow .25 .25
O115 O7 10p brown violet .25 .25
O116 O7 15p brown .25 .25
O117 O7 20p blue .35 .25
O118 O7 20p violet .25 .25
O119 O7 25p purple .45 .25
O120 O7 30p dk violet .50 .25
O121 O7 50p green .80 .60
O122 O7 55p red .70 .55
O123 O7 75p brown .75 .55
O124 O7 £1 green blue 1.25 .75
O125 O7 £2 green 2.50 1.50
Nos. O114-O125 (12) 8.30 5.70

Issued: 10p, 30p, 7/1/91; 50p, 12/1/91; 55p, 4/1/93; £1, £2, 3/22/94; No. O123, 75p, 2/1/97; No. O118, 4/11/99.

Arms Type of 1985-89
Perf. 11½x11

2001-02? Photo. Unwmk.
Size: 18x22mm

O126 O7 5p orange yellow — —
O127 O7 10p brown 2.75 .50
O128 O7 20p dark blue — —
O129 O7 25p purple — —
O130 O7 30p violet 3.75 .60
O131 O7 75p olive brown — —
O132 O7 £1 greenish blue — —

Issued: Nos. O126-O129, O131-O132, 3/25/01; No. O130, 2002?.

Arms Type of 1985-89
Perf. 11½x11

2018, Aug. 16 Photo. Unwmk.
Size: 18x22mm

O133 O7 50p brown .25 .25
O134 O7 £2.50 Prus blue .30 .30
O135 O7 £3 blksh pur .35 .35
O136 O7 £4 dark brown .45 .45
O137 O7 £5 green .55 .55
Nos. O133-O137 (5) 1.90 1.90

OCCUPATION STAMPS

Catalogue values for unused stamps in this section are for Never Hinged items.

For Use in Palestine

Stamps of 1939-46 Overprinted in Red, Green or Black — a

Perf. 13x13½, 13½x13

1948, May 15 Wmk. 195

N1 A77 1m yellow brn (G) .35 .35
N2 A77 2m red org (G) .35 .35
N3 A66 3m brown (G) .35 .35
N4 A77 4m dp green .35 .35
N5 A77 5m red brown (Bk) .35 .35
N6 A66 6m lt yel grn (Bk) .35 .35
N7 A77 10m dp violet .35 .35
N8 A66 13m rose car (G) 2.00 *2.50*
N9 A77 15m dk violet .45 .45
N10 A77 17m olive green .45 .45
N11 A77 20m dk gray .45 .45
N12 A77 22m deep blue .50 .50
N13 A74 50pi green & sep 30.00 30.00
N14 A75 £1 dp bl & dk brn 50.00 50.00

The two lines of the overprint are more widely separated on Nos. N13 and N14.

Nos. 267-269, 237 and 238 Ovptd. in Red — b

Perf. 14x13½

N15 A73 30m olive green 1.25 1.25
N16 A73 40m dark brown 1.60 1.60
N17 A73 50m Prus green 3.00 3.00
N18 A73 100m brown violet 5.00 5.00
N19 A73 200m dark violet 15.00 15.00
Nos. N1-N19 (19) 112.15 112.65

Overprint arranged to fit size of stamps.

Nos. N1-N19 Overprinted in Black with Three Bars to Obliterate Portrait

Perf. 13x13½, 13½x13, 14x13½

1953 Wmk. 195

N20 A77 1m yellow brown .70 .70
N21 A77 2m red orange .70 .70
N22 A66 3m brown .70 .70
N23 A77 4m deep green .70 .70
N24 A77 5m red brown .70 .70
N25 A66 6m lt yel grn .80 .80
N26 A77 10m deep violet .85 .85
N27 A66 13m rose carmine .90 .90
N28 A77 15m dark violet .95 .95
N29 A77 17m olive green .95 .95
N30 A77 20m dark gray 1.10 1.10
N31 A77 22m deep blue 1.45 1.45
N32 A73 30m olive green 1.45 1.45
N33 A73 40m dark brown 2.60 2.60
N34 A73 50m Prus green 8.00 8.00
N35 A73 100m brown violet 17.00 17.00
N36 A73 200m dark violet 40.00 40.00
N37 A74 50pi green & sepia 80.00 75.00
N38 A75 £1 dp bl & dk brn 170.00 170.00
Nos. N20-N38 (19) 329.55 324.55

Regular Issue of 1953-55 Overprinted Type "a" in Blue or Red

1954-56 *Perf. 13x13½*

N39 A115 1m red brown .45 .45
N40 A115 2m dark lilac .45 .45
N41 A115 3m brt blue (R) .45 .45
N42 A115 4m dark green (R) .45 .45
N43 A115 5m deep carmine .45 .45
N44 A110 10m dark brown .45 .45
N45 A110 15m gray (R) .45 .45
N46 A110 17m dk grnsh bl (R) .45 .45
N47 A110 20m purple (R) ('54) .60 .60

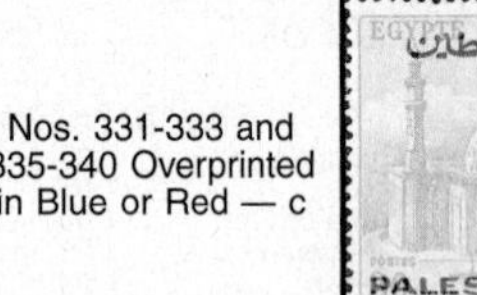

Nos. 331-333 and 335-340 Overprinted in Blue or Red — c

Perf. 13½

N48 A111 30m dull green (R) .85 .85
N49 A111 32m brt blue (R) .95 .95
N50 A111 35m violet (R) 1.25 1.25
N51 A111 40m red brown 1.90 1.90
N52 A111 50m violet brown 2.25 2.25
N53 A112 100m henna brown 5.50 5.50
N54 A112 200m dk grnsh bl (R) 20.00 20.00
N55 A112 500m purple (R) 70.00 70.00
N56 A112 £1 dk grn, blk & red (R) ('56) 115.00 115.00
Nos. N39-N56 (18) 221.90 221.90

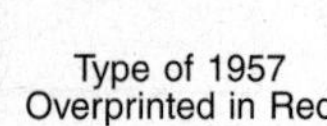

Type of 1957 Overprinted in Red — d

1957 Wmk. 195 *Perf. 13½x13*

N57 A127 10m blue green 5.00 5.00

Nos. 414-417 Overprinted Type "d" in Red

1957-58 Wmk. 315 *Perf. 13½*

N58 A137 10m violet 3.00 3.00

Wmk. 318

N59 A136 1m lt bl grn ('58) .60 .60
N60 A138 5m brown ('58) .60 .60
N61 A137 10m violet ('58) .90 .90
Nos. N58-N61 (4) 5.10 5.10

United Arab Republic

Nos. 438-444 Overprinted in Red or Green

Perf. 13½x14

1958 Wmk. 318 Photo.

N62 A136 1m crimson .35 .35
N63 A138 2m blue .35 .35
N64 A143 3m dk red brn (G) .35 .35
N65 A217 4m green .35 .35
N66 A138 5m brown .35 .35
N67 A137 10m violet .45 .35
N68 A138 35m lt ultra 3.50 3.25
Nos. N62-N68 (7) 5.70 5.35

Freedom Struggle Type of 1958 Overprint in Red

1958 *Perf. 13½x13*

N69 A145 10m dark brown 2.00 2.00

Declaration of Human Rights Type of 1958 Overprinted in Green

1958 *Perf. 13x13½*

N70 A151 10m rose violet 3.00 3.00
N71 A151 35m red brown 8.00 8.00

No. 460 Overprinted in Green

1959 Wmk. 195 *Perf. 13½*

N72 A112 55m on 100m henna brn 4.00 4.00

World Refugee Year Type "PALESTINE" Added in English and Arabic to Stamps of Egypt

OS1

1960 Wmk. 328 *Perf. 13x13½*

N73 OS1 10m orange brown .75 .75
N74 OS1 35m dk blue gray 1.75 1.50

Type of Regular Issue 1957-63

1960 *Perf. 13½x14*

N75 A136 1m brown orange .35 .35
N76 A217 4m olive gray .35 .35
N77 A138 5m dk dull pur .35 .35
N78 A137 10m dk olive grn .35 .35
Nos. N75-N78 (4) 1.40 1.40

Palestine Day Type

1961, May 15 *Perf. 13½x13*

N79 A184 10m purple 1.00 1.00

WHO Day Type

1961 Wmk. 328 *Perf. 13½x13*

N80 A182 10m blue 1.25 .75

U.N.T.A.P. Type

1961, Oct. 24

N81 A191 10m dk blue & org .50 .50
N82 A191 35m vermilion & blk .75 .75

Education Day Type

1961, Dec. 18 Photo. *Perf. 13½*

N83 A194 10m red brown .50 .50

Victory Day Type

1961, Dec. 23 Unwmk. *Perf. 11½*

N84 A195 10m brn org & brn .40 .40

Gaza Strip Type
Perf. 13½x13

1962, Mar. 7 Wmk. 328

N85 A200 10m red brown .40 .40

Arab Publicity Week Type

1962, Mar. 22 *Perf. 13½x13*

N86 SP16 10m dark purple .30 .30

Anti-Malaria Type

1962, June 20 Photo.

N87 A204 10m brn & dk car rose .45 .45
N88 A204 35m black & yellow .55 .55

Hammarskjold Type
Perf. 11½x11

1962, Oct. 24 Wmk. 342
Portrait in Slate Blue

N89 A214 5m bright rose .35 .35
N90 A214 10m brown .45 .45
N91 A214 35m blue .75 .75
Nos. N89-N91 (3) 1.55 1.55

Lamp Type of Regular Issue
Perf. 11x11½

1963, Feb. 20 Unwmk.

N92 A217 4m dk brn, org & ultra .35 .35

"Freedom from Hunger" Type
Perf. 11½x11, 11x11½

1963, Mar. 21 Wmk. 342

N93 A220 5m lt grn & dp org .35 .35
N94 A220 10m olive & yellow .45 .45
N95 A220 35m dull pur, yel & blk .65 .65
Nos. N93-N95 (3) 1.45 1.45

Red Cross Centenary Type

Designs: 10m, Centenary emblem, bottom panel added. 35m, Globe and emblem, top and bottom panels added.

1963, May 8 Unwmk. *Perf. 11x11½*

N96 A221 10m dk blue & crim .35 .35
N97 A221 35m crim & dk blue .60 .60

"Save Abu Simbel" Type, 1963

1963, Oct. 15 Wmk. 342 *Perf. 11*

N98 A224 5m black & yellow .40 .40
N99 A224 10m gray, blk & yellow .50 .50
N100 A224 35m org yel & violet 1.25 .95
Nos. N98-N100 (3) 2.15 1.85

Human Rights Type

1963, Dec. 10 Photo. *Perf. 11½x11*

N101 A228 5m dk brown & yellow .35 .35
N102 A228 10m dp claret, gray & blk .40 .40
N103 A228 35m lt grn, pale grn & blk .95 .95
Nos. N101-N103 (3) 1.70 1.70

Types of Regular Issue

1964 Unwmk. *Perf. 11*

N104 A231 1m citron & lt vio .40 .40
N105 A230 2m orange & slate .40 .40
N106 A230 3m blue & ocher .40 .40
N107 A235 4m ol gray, ol, brn & rose .40 .40
N108 A230 5m rose & brt blue .40 .40
a. 5m rose & dark blue 1.25 1.25
N109 A231 10m ol, rose & brn .40 .40
N110 A230 15m lilac & yellow .50 .50
N111 A230 20m brown blk & ol .80 .80
N112 A231 30m dp org & ind 1.60 1.60
N113 A231 35m buff, ocher & emer 1.40 1.40
N114 A231 40m ultra & emer 1.75 1.75
N115 A231 60m grnsh bl & brn org 2.50 2.50

Wmk. 342

N116 A232 100m bluish blk & yel brn 3.50 3.50
Nos. N104-N116 (13) 14.45 14.45

Arab League Council Type

1964, Jan. 13 Photo.

N117 A234 10m olive & black .35 .35

Minaret Type

1964 Unwmk. *Perf. 11*

N118 A235 4m ol, red brn & red .35 .35

Arab Postal Union Type

1964, Apr. 1 Wmk. 342 *Perf. 11*

N119 A239 10m emer & ultra, *lt grn* .35 .35

WHO Type

1964, Apr. 7

N120 A240 10m violet blk & red .35 .35

Minaret Type

1965, Jan. 20 Unwmk. *Perf. 11*

N121 A255 4m green & dk brn .35 .35

Arab League Type

1965, Mar. 22 Wmk. 342 *Perf. 11*

N122 A258 10m green, red & blk .35 .35
N123 A258 20m green & brown .35 .35

World Health Day Type

1965, Apr. 7 Wmk. 342 *Perf. 11*

N124 A259 10m brt green & crim .35 .35

Massacre Type

1965, Apr. 9 Photo.

N125 A260 10m slate blue & red .60 .60

ITU Type

1965, May 17 Wmk. 342 *Perf. 11*

N126 A261 5m sl grn, sl bl & yel .40 .40
N127 A261 10m car, rose red & gray .50 .50
N128 A261 35m vio bl, ultra & yel 1.40 .95
Nos. N126-N128 (3) 2.30 1.85

United Nations Type

5m, WHO Headquarters Building, Geneva. 10m, UN Refugee emblem. 35m, UNICEF emblem.

1966, Oct. 24 Wmk. 342 *Perf. 11*

N129 A288 5m rose & brt pur .35 .35
N130 A288 10m yel brn & brt pur .40 .40
N131 A288 35m brt green & brt pur .80 .80
Nos. N129-N131 (3) 1.55 1.55

Victory Day Type

Wmk. 342

1966, Dec. 23 Photo. *Perf. 11½*

N132 A290 10m olive & car rose .40 .40

Arab Publicity Week Type

Perf. 11x11½

1967, Mar. 22 Photo. Wmk. 342

N133 A294 10m vio blue & brn .35 .35

Labor Day Type

Perf. 11½x11

1967, May 1 Photo. Wmk. 342

N134 A296 10m olive & sepia .35 .35

OCCUPATION AIR POST STAMPS

Catalogue values for unused stamps in this section are for Never Hinged items.

Nos. C39-C50 Overprinted Type "b" in Black, Carmine or Red

Perf. 13x13½

1948, May 15 Wmk. 195

NC1 AP3 2m red org (Bk) .75 .75
NC2 AP3 3m dk brn (C) .75 .75
NC3 AP3 5m red brn (Bk) .75 .75
NC4 AP3 7m dp yel org (Bk) 1.05 1.05
NC5 AP3 8m green (C) 1.05 1.05
NC6 AP3 10m violet 1.20 1.20
NC7 AP3 20m brt bl 1.90 1.90
NC8 AP3 30m brn vio (Bk) 4.50 4.50
NC9 AP3 40m car rose (Bk) 3.00 3.00
NC10 AP3 50m Prus grn 4.00 4.00
NC11 AP3 100m olive grn 6.75 6.75
NC12 AP3 200m dark gray 34.00 34.00
Nos. NC1-NC12 (12) 59.70 59.70

Nos. NC1-NC12 Overprinted in Black with Three Bars to Obliterate Portrait

1953

NC13 AP3 2m red org 1.90 1.90
NC14 AP3 3m dk brn 1.20 1.20
NC15 AP3 5m red brn 20.00 20.00
NC16 AP3 7m dp yel org 1.25 1.25
NC17 AP3 8m green 3.75 3.75
NC18 AP3 10m violet 3.75 3.75
NC19 AP3 20m brt bl 3.75 3.75
NC20 AP3 30m brn vio 3.75 3.75
NC21 AP3 40m car rose 6.75 6.75
NC22 AP3 50m Prus grn 28.00 28.00
NC23 AP3 100m olive grn 115.00 115.00
NC24 AP3 200m dk gray 15.00 15.00
Nos. NC13-NC24 (12) 204.10 204.10

Nos. NC1-NC3, NC6, NC10, NC11 with Additional Overprint in Various Colors

1953

NC25 AP3 2m red org (Bk + Bl) 1.00 1.00
NC26 AP3 3m dk brn (Bk + RV) 19.00 19.00
NC27 AP3 5m red brn (Bk) 2.75 2.75
NC28 AP3 10m vio (R + G) 28.00 28.00
NC29 AP3 50m Prus grn (R + RV) 8.75 8.75
NC30 AP3 100m ol grn (R + Bk) 62.50 62.50
Nos. NC25-NC30 (6) 122.00 122.00

Nos. C65-C66 Overprinted Type "b" in Black or Red

1955 Wmk. 195 *Perf. 13x13½*

NC31 AP4 5m red brn 7.00 5.75
NC32 AP4 15m ol grn (R) 10.00 8.25

United Arab Republic

OAP1

Designs: 80m, Al Azhar University. 115m, Temple of Queen Nefertari, Abu Simbel. 140m, Ramses II, Abu Simbel.

Perf. 11½x11

1963, Oct. 24 Photo. Wmk. 342

NC33 OAP1 80m blk & brt bl 2.50 2.50
NC34 OAP1 115m blk & yel 3.50 3.50
NC35 OAP1 140m bl, ultra & org red 4.00 4.00
Nos. NC33-NC35 (3) 10.00 10.00

Cairo Tower Type, 1964

1964, Nov. 2 Unwmk. *Perf. 11x11½*

NC36 AP11 50m dl vio & lt bl 1.25 1.25

World Meteorological Day Type

1965, Mar. 23 Wmk. 342 *Perf. 11*

NC37 AP12 80m dk bl & org 3.00 3.00

Tutankhamun Type of 1965

1965, July 1 Photo. *Perf. 11*

NC38 AP13 10m brn org & brt grn 1.75 1.75

OCCUPATION SPECIAL DELIVERY STAMP

Catalogue values for unused stamps in this section are for Never Hinged items.

No. E4 Overprinted Type "b" in Carmine

1948 Wmk. 195 *Perf. 13x13½*

NE1 SD1 40m dl brn & pale gray 12.50 12.50

OCCUPATION POSTAGE DUE STAMPS

Catalogue values for unused stamps in this section are for Never Hinged items.

Postage Due Stamps of Egypt, 1927-41, Overprinted Type "a" in Black or Rose

1948 Wmk. 195 *Perf. 13x13½*

NJ1 D7 2m orange 2.25 *2.40*
NJ2 D7 4m green (R) 1.60 *2.00*
NJ3 D7 6m gray green 1.60 *2.00*
NJ4 D7 8m brown violet 1.60 *2.00*
NJ5 D7 10m brick red 1.60 *2.00*
NJ6 D7 12m rose lake 1.60 *2.00*

Overprinted Type "b" in Red

Perf. 14

Size: 22x28mm

NJ7 D7 30m purple 5.00 *9.00*
Nos. NJ1-NJ7 (7) 15.25 *21.40*

ELOBEY, ANNOBON & CORISCO

ˌel-ə-ˈbā, ˌan-ə-ˈbän and kə-ˈris-ˌₒkō

LOCATION — A group of islands near the Guinea Coast of western Africa.

GOVT. — Spanish colonial possessions administered as part of the Continental Guinea District. A second district under the same governor-general included Fernando Po.

AREA — 13¾ sq. mi.

POP. — 2,950 (estimated 1910)

CAPITAL — Santa Isabel

100 Centimos = 1 Peseta

King Alfonso XIII — A1

1903 Unwmk. Typo. *Perf. 14*

Control Numbers on Back

1 A1 ¼c carmine .75 .55
2 A1 ½c dk violet .75 .55
3 A1 1c black .75 .55
4 A1 2c red .75 .55
5 A1 3c dk green .75 .55
6 A1 4c dk blue grn .75 .55
7 A1 5c violet .75 .55
8 A1 10c rose lake 1.50 1.60
9 A1 15c orange buff 4.50 1.75
10 A1 25c dark blue 7.75 6.00
11 A1 50c red brown 9.00 10.50
12 A1 75c black brn 9.00 *14.50*
13 A1 1p orange red 15.00 *20.00*
14 A1 2p chocolate 40.00 *60.00*
15 A1 3p dp olive grn 60.00 *75.00*
16 A1 4p claret 140.00 100.00
17 A1 5p blue green 165.00 110.00
18 A1 10p dull blue 300.00 165.00
Nos. 1-18 (18) 757.00 568.20
Set, never hinged 1,500.

Dated "1905"

1905 Control Numbers on Back

19 A1 1c carmine 1.25 .70
20 A1 2c dp violet 5.00 .70
21 A1 3c black 1.25 .70
22 A1 4c dull red 1.25 .70
23 A1 5c dp green 1.25 .70
24 A1 10c blue grn 4.50 .90
25 A1 15c violet 5.00 4.75
26 A1 25c rose lake 5.00 4.75
27 A1 50c orange buff 9.00 7.25
28 A1 75c dark blue 9.00 7.25
29 A1 1p red brown 18.50 16.00
30 A1 2p black brn 20.00 22.50
31 A1 3p orange red 20.00 23.00
32 A1 4p dk brown 150.00 72.50
33 A1 5p bronze grn 160.00 80.00
34 A1 10p claret 350.00 225.00
Nos. 19-34 (16) 761.00 467.40
Set, never hinged 1,500.

Nos. 19-22 Surcharged in Black or Red

1906

35 A1 10c on 1c rose (Bk) 11.50 6.50
a. Inverted surcharge 11.50 6.50
b. Value omitted 30.00 16.00
c. Frame omitted 16.00 7.50
d. Double surcharge 11.50 6.50
e. Surcharged "15 cents" 30.00 16.00
f. Surcharged "25 cents" 52.50 22.50
g. Surcharged "50 cents" 37.50 22.50
h. "1906" omitted 17.50 7.50
36 A1 15c on 2c dp vio (R) 11.50 6.50
a. Frame omitted 12.50 6.50
b. Surcharged "25 cents" 16.00 9.00
c. Inverted surcharge 11.50 6.50
d. Double surcharge 11.50 6.50
37 A1 25c on 3c blk (R) 11.50 6.50
a. Inverted surcharge 11.50 6.50
b. Double surcharge 11.50 6.50
c. Surcharged "15 cents" 16.00 6.50
d. Surcharged "50 cents" 25.00 11.00
38 A1 50c on 4c red (Bk) 11.50 6.50
a. Inverted surcharge 11.50 6.50
b. Value omitted 35.00 17.50
c. Frame omitted 17.50 8.00
e. Double surcharge 11.50 6.50
f. "1906" omitted 17.50 8.00
g. Surcharged "10 cents" 32.50 16.00
h. Surcharged "25 cents" 32.50 16.00
Nos. 35-38 (4) 46.00 26.00

Eight other surcharges were prepared but not issued: 10c on 50c, 75c, 1p, 2p and 3p; 15c on 50c and 5p; 50c on 5c.

Exist with surcharges in different colors; #35 in blue, red or violet, #36 in black or violet, #37 in black or violet, #38 in blue, violet or red. Value, set of 10, $135.

King Alfonso XIII — A2

1907 Control Numbers on Back

39 A2 1c dk violet .50 .45
40 A2 2c black .50 .45
41 A2 3c red orange .50 .45
42 A2 4c dk green .50 .45
43 A2 5c blue green .50 .45
44 A2 10c violet 5.50 5.50
45 A2 15c carmine 1.60 1.75
46 A2 25c orange 1.60 1.75
47 A2 50c blue 1.60 1.75
48 A2 75c brown 6.00 2.75
49 A2 1p black brn 9.00 4.75
50 A2 2p orange red 12.00 8.00
51 A2 3p dk brown 12.00 9.00
52 A2 4p bronze grn 18.00 8.50

53	A2	5p claret	22.00	10.00
54	A2	10p rose	45.00	27.50
		Nos. 39-54 (16)	136.80	83.50
		Set, never hinged	350.00	

Stamps of 1907 Surcharged

1908-09 **Black Surcharge**

55	A2	5c on 3c red org ('09)	2.25	1.25
56	A2	5c on 4c dk grn ('09)	2.25	1.25
57	A2	5c on 10c violet	4.50	5.00
58	A2	25c on 10c violet	30.00	15.00
		Nos. 55-58 (4)	39.00	22.50

1910 **Red Surcharge**

59	A2	5c on 1c dark violet	1.75	.90
60	A2	5c on 2c black	1.75	.90

Nos. 55-60 exist with surcharge inverted (value set, $125 unused or used); with double surcharge, one black, one red (value set, $300 unused or used); with "PARA" omitted (value set, $150.00 unused or used)

The same 5c surcharge was also applied to Nos. 45-54, but these were not issued (value set, $250).

In 1909, stamps of Spanish Guinea replaced those of Elobey, Annobon and Corisco.

Revenue stamps surcharged as above were unauthorized although some were postally used.

For postally valid examples similar to the item shown above see Rio de Oro Nos. 44-45 and Spanish Guinea Nos. 98-101C.

For revenue stamps with the arms at the left surcharged for postal use see Spanish Guinea Nos. 8A-8J.

EPIRUS

i-ˈpī-rəs

LOCATION — A region of southeastern Europe, now divided between Greece and Albania.

During the First Balkan War (1912-13), this territory was occupied by the Greek army, and the local Greek majority wished to be united with Greece. Italy and Austria-Hungary favored its inclusion in the newly created Albania, however, which both powers expected to dominate. Greek forces were withdrawn subsequently in early 1914. The local population resisted inclusion in Albania and established the Autonomous Republic of Northern Epirus on Feb. 28, 1914. Resistance to Albanian control continued until October, when Greece reoccupied the country. Northern Epirus was administered as an integral part of Greece, and it was expected that Greece's annexation of the territory would become official following World War I. Instead, in 1916, Italian pressure and its own military reverses in Anatolia caused Greece to withdraw from Epirus and to formally cede the territory to Albania.

100 Lepta = 1 Drachma

Chimarra Issue

Double-headed Eagle, Skull and Crossbones — A1

Handstamped

1914, Feb. 10 Unwmk. *Imperf.*

Control Mark in Blue

Without Gum

1 A1 1 l black & blue *475.00* 250.00
a. Tête-bêche pair 3,000.
2 A1 5 l blue & red *475.00* 250.00
3 A1 10 l red & blk *475.00* 250.00
4 A1 25 l blue & red *475.00* 250.00
Nos. 1-4 (4) *1,900.* 1,000.

All values exist without control mark. This mark is a solid blue oval, about 12x8mm, containing the colorless Greek letters "SP," the first two letters of Spiromilios, the Chimarra commander.

All four exist with denomination inverted and the 1 l, 5 l and 10 l with denomination double.

The values above are for the first printing on somewhat transparent shiny, white, thin, wove paper, which is sometimes known as "rice paper."

A second printing was made from original handstamps, on similar thin wove paper, but not transluscent, known as "Spetsiotis Reprints." Value, unused or canceled to order, each $55. Later printings were made from original handstamps on other papers, generally thicker and whiter, sometimes surfaced. Value, unused or canceled to order, each $45.

Values above are for genuine stamps expertized by knowledgeable authorities. Most of the stamps offered as Nos. 1-4 in the marketplace are forgeries. Most resemble the stamps from the second reprinting, but the designs differ in details of the lettering, monogram and skull. Such forgeries have only nominal commercial value.

Some experts question the official character of this issue.

Argyrokastro Issues

Stamps of Turkey surcharged "AUTONOMOUS EPIRUS" and new denominations in several formats in Greek currency.

On Turkish stamps of 1908

No. 4A

No. 4B

1914, Mar. 2

4A A19 1d on 2½pi (#137) 11.00 12.50
4B A19 2d on 2½pi (#137) 11.00 12.50

No. 4C

No. 4D

4C A19 5d on 25pi (#140) 80.00 92.50
4D A19 5d on 50pi (#141) 127.50 140.00

On Turkish stamps of 1909-10

4E A21 5 l on 5pa (#151) 80.00 —

No. 4F

No. 4G

4F A21 5 l on 10pa (#152) 3.50 *4.00*
4G A21 10 l (oval "O") on 20pa (#153) 2.50 *2.75*
a. Double surcharge 80.00

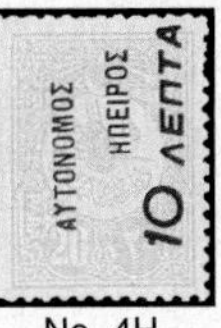

No. 4H

No. 4I

4H A21 10 l (round "O") on 20pa (#153) 2.50 *2.75*
a. Double surcharge 80.00
4I A21 20 l on 1pi (#154) 2.50 *2.75*
a. Double surcharge 80.00

No. 4J

No. 4K

4J A21 25 l on 1pi (#154) 2.50 *2.75*
a. Double surcharge 80.00
4K A21 40 l on 2pi (#155) 3.50 *3.75*

No. 4L

No. 4M

4L A21 80 l on 2pi (#155) 3.50 *3.75*
4M A21 1d on 5pi (#157) 13.00 *14.00*

No. 4N

No. 4O

4N A21 2d on 5pi (#157) 13.00 14.00
4O A21 5d on 10pi (#158) 80.00 *92.50*
a. Double surcharge
4P A21 5d on 10pa (#152) 135.00 *170.00*
4Q A21 5d on 20pa (#153) 135.00 *170.00*
4R A21 5d on 1pi (#154) 135.00 *170.00*
4RR A21 5d on 2½pi (#156) 135.00 *170.00*
4S A21 5d on 50pi (#160) 135.00 *170.00*

On Turkish stamps of 1909-11 (with "Béhié")

4T A21 5 l on 10pa (#161) 80.00
4U A21 10 l (oval "O") on 20pa (#162) 80.00
4V A21 10 l (round "O") on 20pa (#162) 80.00
4W A21 20 l on 1pi (#163) 80.00
4X A21 25 l on 1pi (#163) 80.00
4Y A21 40 l on 2pi (#164) 80.00
4Z A21 80 l on 2pi (#164) 80.00
4AA A21 5d on 10pa (#161) 135.00
4BB A21 5d on 20pa (#162) 135.00
4CC A21 5d on 1pi (#163) 135.00
4CA A21 5d on 2pi (#164) 135.00

On Turkish Printed Matter stamps of 1910-11

No. 4DD

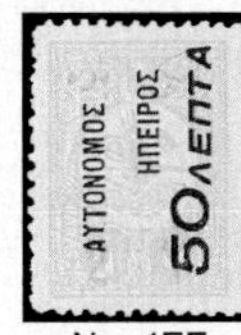

No. 4EE

4DD A21 30 l on 2pa on 5pa (#P67) 87.50
4EE A21 50 l on 2pa on 5pa (#P67) 87.50

No. 4FF

4FF A21 30 l on 2pa (#P68) 2.50 *2.75*
4GG A21 50 l on 2pa (#P68) 2.50 *2.75*

Provisional Government Issues

Infantryman with Rifle
A2 A3

Serrate Roulette 13½

1914, Mar. Litho.

5 A2 1 l orange .50 1.00
a. Imperf., pair 60.00
6 A2 5 l green .50 1.00
a. Imperf., pair 60.00
7 A3 10 l carmine .50 1.00
8 A3 25 l deep blue .50 1.00
9 A2 50 l brown 1.50 1.50
10 A2 1d violet 2.25 2.50
11 A2 2d blue 14.00 14.00
12 A2 5d gray green 18.00 19.00
Nos. 5-12 (8) 37.75 41.00

Issue dates: 10 l, 25 l, Mar. 5; balance of set, Mar. 26.

Flag of Epirus — A5

1914, Aug. 28

15 A5 1 l brown & blue .35 *.40*
16 A5 5 l green & blue .35 *.40*
17 A5 10 l rose red & blue .40 *.65*
18 A5 25 l dk blue & blue 1.00 1.10
19 A5 50 l violet & blue 1.00 1.10
20 A5 1d carmine & blue 5.75 *6.50*
21 A5 2d orange & blue 1.50 *2.25*
b. Double impression, one inverted *1,000.*
22 A5 5d dk green & blue 9.50 11.00
a. Double impression 1,000.
Nos. 15-22 (8) 19.85 *23.40*

Nos. 16 and 21 exist with the blue color inverted.

Koritsa Issue

A7

1914, Sept. 25

26 A7 25 l dk blue & blue 6.00 5.25
27 A7 50 l violet & blue 12.00 *13.50*

Nos. 26 and 27 were issued at Koritsa (Korce) to commemorate that city's occupation by Epirot forces.

Chimarra Issues

King Constantine I — A8

1914, Oct.

28 A8 1 l yellow green 135.00 77.50
29 A8 2 l red 120.00 42.50
30 A8 5 l dark blue 120.00 77.50
31 A8 10 l orange brown 80.00 30.00
32 A8 20 l carmine 87.50 62.50
33 A8 25 l gray blue 115.00 77.50
33A A8 50 l yellow green 170.00 90.00
33B A8 1d carmine 170.00 90.00
33C A8 2d pale yellow green 255.00 125.00
33D A8 5d orange brown 425.00 290.00
Nos. 28-33D (10) 1,678. 962.50

Nos. 28-33D were printed by Papachrysanthou, Athens. The papermaker's watermark "PARCHIMINE JOHANNOT" appears on some stamps in the set.

1911-23 Issues of Greece Overprinted

1914, Aug. 24 *Perf. Perf. 11 ½*

34 A24 1 l green 55.00 62.50
35 A25 2 l carmine 45.00 52.50
36 A24 3 l vermilion 45.00 52.50
37 A26 5 l green 45.00 52.50
38 A24 10 l carmine 60.00 65.00
39 A25 20 l slate 80.00 87.50
40 A25 25 l blue 175.00 185.00
41 A26 50 l violet brn 220.00 225.00
Nos. 34-41 (8) 725.00 782.50

The 2 l and 3 l are engraved stamps of the 1911-21 issue; the others are lithographed stamps of the 1912-23 issue.

Overprint reads: "Greek Chimarra 1914."

Stamps of this issue are with or without a black monogram (S.S., for S. Spiromilios) in manuscript. Counterfeits are plentiful.

Moschopolis Issue

Arms A9

Ancient Epirot Coins/Medals A10

1914, Sept.		**Engr.**	*Perf. 14 ½*	
42 A9	1 l	yellow brown	.75	*3.50*
43 A9	2 l	black	.75	*3.50*
44 A9	3 l	yellow	.75	*3.50*
45 A9	5 l	green	.75	*3.50*
46 A9	10 l	red	.75	*3.50*
47 A9	25 l	deep blue	.75	*3.50*
48 A9	30 l	violet	.75	*3.50*
49 A9	40 l	olive gray	.75	*3.50*
50 A9	50 l	violet black	.75	*3.50*
51 A10	1d	yellow brown & olive	5.00	*11.50*
52 A10	2d	carmine & gray	6.00	*11.50*
53 A10	3d	gray green & red brown	5.00	*11.50*
54 A10	5d	olive & yellow brown	5.00	*11.50*
55 A10	10d	orange & blue	5.00	*14.50*
56 A10	25d	violet & black	5.00	*20.00*
		Nos. 42-56 (15)	37.75	*112.00*

Nos. 42-56 were privately printed in early 1914. In June 1914, the Epirots occupied Moschopolis (Voskopoj), and these stamps were authorized for use by the local military commander in Sept. After the occupation of Moschopolis by Greek forces in Nov., remaining stocks of this issue were sent to Athens, where they were destroyed in 1931.

All values exist imperf., and all but the 5 l and 10 l stamps exist in different colors. For details, see the *Scott Classic Specialized Catalogue of Stamps and Covers.*

The 1d exists with center omitted. Value $100. The 1d, 2d, 10d and 25d exist with center inverted. Values, each $65.

Stamps of the following designs were locals, privately produced. Issued primarily for propaganda and for philatelic purposes, their postal use is in dispute. The 1917 and 1920 designs are fantasy items, created long after Epirus was annexed by Albania.

From 1914: 1st design, 3 varieties. 2nd design, 6 varieties. 3rd design, 7 varieties.

From 1917: 4th design, 8 varieties, + 1 surcharged; perforated and imperforate.

From 1920: 5th design, 4 varieties.

OCCUPATION STAMPS

Issued under Greek Occupation

Greek Occupation Stamps of 1913 Overprinted Horizontally

Serrate Roulette 13½

1914-15		**Black Overprint**		**Unwmk.**
N1 O1	1 l	brown	.90	.90
b.		Inverted overprint	25.00	25.00
c.		Double overprint	25.00	25.00
d.		Double overprint, one inverted	25.00	25.00
N2 O2	2 l	red	.90	.90
b.		2 l rose	1.35	1.35
c.		As #N2, inverted overprint	25.00	25.00
d.		As "b", inverted overprint	32.50	32.50
e.		As #N2, double overprint	26.00	*32.50*
f.		As "b", double overprint	32.50	32.50
g.		As #N2, double overprint, one inverted	25.00	25.00
N4 O2	3 l	orange	.90	.90
b.		Inverted overprint	20.00	17.50
c.		Double overprint	20.00	17.50
d.		Double overprint, one inverted	26.00	26.00
N5 O1	5 l	green	2.50	2.50
b.		Inverted overprint	37.50	37.50
N6 O1	10 l	rose red	3.00	3.00
a.		Inverted overprint	52.50	52.50
b.		Double overprint	52.50	52.50
N7 O1	20 l	violet	7.00	7.00
a.		Inverted overprint	52.50	52.50
b.		Double overprint	87.50	67.50
N8 O2	25 l	pale blue	3.00	3.25
N9 O1	30 l	gray green	14.50	15.00
N10 O2	40 l	indigo	19.50	21.00
N11 O1	50 l	dark blue	22.00	24.00
N12 O2	1d	violet brown	140.00	150.00
a.		Inverted overprint	325.00	*225.00*
b.		Double overprint	400.00	*300.00*
		Nos. N1-N12 (11)	214.20	228.45

Red Overprint

N1a O1	1 l	brown	5.75
N2a O2	2 l	red	5.75
N4a O2	3 l	orange	5.75
N5a O1	5 l	green	5.75

Nos. N1a-N5a were not issued. Exist canceled.

Regular Issues of Greece, 1911-23, Ovptd. Reading Up

On Issue of 1911-21

1916				**Engr.**
N17 A24	3 l	vermilion	11.50	11.50
a.		Overprint reading down	15.00	
N18 A26	30 l	carmine rose	52.50	40.00
a.		Overprint reading down	225.00	
N18B A25	40 l	dark blue	—	—
N19 A27	1d	ultra	85.00	85.00
N20 A27	2d	vermilion	95.00	95.00
N21 A27	3d	carmine rose	130.00	130.00
N22 A27	5d	ultra	—	—
a.		Double overprint	1,300.	—
b.		Overprint reading down	725.00	
		Nos. N17-N22 (6)	374.00	361.50

On Issue of 1912-23

1916				**Litho.**
N23 A24	1 l	green	2.75	2.75
b.		Overprint reading down	10.00	
N24 A25	2 l	carmine	2.75	2.75
a.		Double overprint	13.00	
b.		Overprint reading down	10.00	
N25 A24	3 l	vermilion	2.75	2.75
a.		Double overprint	13.00	
b.		Overprint reading down	15.00	
N26 A26	5 l	green	2.75	2.75
a.		Double overprint	15.00	
b.		Overprint reading down	15.00	
N27 A24	10 l	carmine	2.75	2.75
a.		Double overprint	15.00	
b.		Overprint reading down	15.00	
N28 A25	20 l	slate	2.75	2.75
a.		Double overprint	17.50	
N29 A25	25 l	blue	3.75	3.75
a.		Double overprint	30.00	
N30 A26	30 l	rose	22.00	22.00
a.		Overprint reading down	250.00	
N31 A25	40 l	indigo	16.50	16.50
a.		Overprint reading down	475.00	
N32 A26	50 l	violet brown	26.50	26.50
		Nos. N23-N32 (10)	85.25	85.25

In each sheet, there are two varieties in the overprint. For listings, see the *Scott Classic Catalogue.*

Counterfeits exist of Nos. N1-N32.

Postage stamps issued in 1940-41, during Greek occupation, are listed under Greece.

EQUATORIAL GUINEA

ˌē-kwə-ˈtō-ē-əl ˈgi-nē

LOCATION — Gulf of Guinea, West Africa
GOVT. — Republic
AREA — 10,832 sq. mi.
POP. — 465,746 (1999 est.)
CAPITAL — Malabo

The Spanish provinces Fernando Po and Rio Muni united and became independent as the Republic of Equatorial Guinea, Oct. 12, 1968.

100 Centimos = 1 Peseta
100 centimos = 1 ekuele, bipkwele is plural (1973)
100 centimes = 1 CFA franc (1985)

Catalogue values for all unused stamps in this country are for Never Hinged items.

Clasped Hands and Laurel — A1

Unwmk.

1968, Oct. 12		**Photo.**	*Perf. 13*	
1 A1	1p	dp bl, gold & sep	.35	.35
2 A1	1.50p	dk grn, gold & brn	.35	.35
3 A1	6p	cop red, gold & brn	.35	.35
		Nos. 1-3 (3)	1.05	1.05

Attainment of independence, Oct. 12, 1968.

Pres. Francisco Macias Nguema — A2

1970, Jan. 27			*Perf. 13x12½*	
4 A2	50c	dl org, brn & crim	.25	.25
5 A2	1p	pink, grn & lil	.25	.25
6 A2	1.50p	pale ol, brn & bl grn	.25	.25
7 A2	2p	buff, grn & ol	.25	.25
8 A2	2.50p	pale grn, dk grn & dk bl	.30	.25
9 A2	10p	bis, Prus bl & vio brn	1.00	.25
10 A2	25p	gray, blk & brn	2.10	.25
		Nos. 4-10 (7)	4.40	1.75

Pres. Macias Nguema and Cock — A3

1971, Apr.		**Photo.**	*Perf. 13*	
11 A3	3p	lt bl & multi	.25	.25
12 A3	5p	buff & multi	.30	.25
13 A3	10p	pale lilac & multi	.75	.25
14 A3	25p	pale grn & multi	1.50	.35
		Nos. 11-14 (4)	2.80	1.10

2nd anniv. of independence, Oct. 12, 1970.

Torch, Bow and Arrows — A4

1972		**Photo.**	*Perf. 11½*	
15 A4	50p	ocher & multi	1.50	.55

"3rd Triumphal Year."

Upon achieving independence from Spain in 1968, Francisco Macias Nguema was elected the first president of Equatorial Guinea. By May 1971, Nguema controlled a government that essentially performed no functions except internal security. From 1972 to 1979, the country's main post office was padlocked and completely inoperative. Nonetheless, European agents continued to produce postage stamps for Equatorial Guinea that were promoted by so-called press releases from Madrid, Spain.

With the exception of Nos. 16-25, the editors question whether any of the stamps described below could have reached Equatorial Guinea or been placed on sale in that country. As such, they do not meet the criteria for listing in the Scott catalogue. See the Catalogue Listing Policy section in the catalogue introduction for additional details.

Apollo 15, set of seven, 1p, 3p, 5p, 8p, 10p, airmail 15p, 25p, plus two airmail semi-postal gold foil perf. 200p+25p, imperf. 250p+50p, and two souv. sheets, perf. 25p+200p, imperf. 50p+250p, issued Jan. 28. Nos. 7201-7211.

1972 Winter Olympics, Sapporo, set of seven, 1p, 2p, 3p, 5p, 8p, airmail 15p, 50p, plus two airmail semi-postal gold foil perf., imperf., 200p+25p, 250p+50p, and two souv. sheets, perf. 200p+25p, imperf. 250p+50p, issued Feb. 3, 1972. Nos. 7212-7222.

Christmas, paintings, set of seven, 1p, 3p, 5p, 8p, 10p, airmail 15p, 25p, plus two airmail semi-postal gold foil perf. 200p+25p, imperf. 250p+50p, and two souv. sheets, perf. 25p+200p, imperf. 50p+250p (Virgin and Child by da Vinci, Murillo, Raphael, Mabuse, van der Weyden, Durer), issued Feb. 20. Nos. 7223-7233.

Easter, set of seven, 1p, 3p, 5p, 8p, 10p, airmail 15p, 25p, plus two airmail semi-postal gold foil perf., imperf., 200p+25p, 250p+50p (designs by Velazquez and El Greco), two souv. sheets, perf. (25p, 200p), and imperf. 250p+50p, issued Apr. 28. Nos. 7234-7244.

1972 Summer Olympics, Munich, set of seven, 1p, 2p, 3p, 5p, 8p, airmail 15p, 50p, plus two airmail semi-postal souv. sheets, perf. 200p+25p, imperf. 250p+50p, and presentation folder with two gold foil, perf. 200p+25p, imperf. 250p+50p, issued May 5, 1972. Nos. 7245-7255.

Gold Medal Winners, Sapporo, set of seven, 1p, 2p, 3p, 5p, 8p, airmail 15p, 50p, plus 12 airmail semi-postal gold foil perf. 200p+25p (6), imperf. 250p+50p (6), imperf. souv. sheet 250p+50p, and perf. souv. sheet of two (25p, 200p), issued May 25. Nos. 7256-7276.

Black Gold Medal Winners, Munich, set of seven, 1p, 2p, 3p, 5p, 8p, airmail 15p, 50p, plus 18 gold foil airmail semi-postal perf. 200p+25p (9), imperf. 250p+50p (9), and two souv. sheets, perf. 200p+25p, imperf. 250p+50p, issued June 26. Nos. 7277-72103.

Olympic Games, Regatta in Kiel and Oberschleissheim, set of seven, 1p, 2p, 3p, 5p, 8p, airmail 15p, 50p, plus four airmail semi-postal gold foil, perf. 200p+25p (2), imperf. 250p+50p (2), and two souv. sheets, perf. 200p+25p, imperf. 250p+50p, issued July 25. Nos. 72104-72116.

1972 Summer Olympics, Munich, set of seven, 1p, 2p, 3p, 5p, 8p, airmail 15p, 50p, plus two airmail semi-postal souv. sheets, perf. 200p+25p, imperf, 250p+50p, issued Aug. 10, 1972; and 20 gold foil, perf. 200p+25p (10), imperf. 250+50p (10), issued Aug. 17. Nos. 72117-72145.

Olympic Equestrian Events, set of seven, 1p, 2p, 3p, 5p, 8p, airmail 15p, 50p, plus two airmail semi-postal souv. sheets, perf. 200p+25p, imperf. 250p+50p, two gold foil, perf. 200p+25p, imperf. 250p+50p, four gold foil souv. sheets of two, 200p+25p (2 perf., 2 imperf.), and 16 souv. sheets, perf. 200p+25p (8), imperf. 250p+50p (8), issued Aug. 24. Nos. 72146-72176.

Japanese Railroad Cent. (locomotives), set of seven, 1p, 3p, 5p, 8p, 10p, airmail 15p, 25p, plus 2 airmail semi-postal souv. sheets, perf. 200p+25p, imperf. 250p+50p, 11 gold foil souv. sheets of 1, perf. 200p+25p (9), imperf. 200p+25p (2), and 2 souv. sheets of 2, perf., imperf., 200p+25p, issued Sept. 21. Nos. 72177-72198.

Gold Medal Winners, Munich, set of seven, 1p, 2p, 3p, 5p, 8p, airmail 15p, 50p, plus two airmail semi-postal souv. sheets, perf. 200p+25p, imperf. 250p+50p, and four gold foil souv. sheets, perf. 200p+25p (2), imperf. 250p+50p (2), issued Oct. 30. Nos. 72199-72211.

Christmas and 500th Birth Anniv. of Lucas Cranach, Madonnas and Christmas seals, set of seven, 1p, 3p, 5p, 8p, 10p, airmail 15p, 25p (Giotto, Schongauer, Fouquet, de Morales, Fini, David, Sassetta), plus two airmail semi-postal souv. sheets, perf. 200p+25p, imperf. 250p+50p, 12 gold foil souv. sheets, perf. 200p+25p (6), imperf. 250p+50p (6), two souv. sheets of two, perf., imperf., 200p+25p, and ovptd. 200p+25p stamp, issued Nov. 22. Nos. 72212-72234.

American and Russian Astronaut Memorial, set of seven, 1p, 3p, 5p, 8p, 10p, airmail 15p, 25p, plus two airmail semi-postal souv. sheets, perf. 200p+25p, imperf. 250p+50p, and four gold foil ovptd. "Apollo 16 and 17" perf. 200p+25p (2), imperf. 250p+50p (2), issued Dec. 14. Nos. 72235-72247.

United Natl. Workers' Party Emblem — A5

1973	**Litho.**	***Perf. 13½x13***	
16 A5	1p multi	.25	.25
17 A5	1.50p multi	.25	.25
18 A5	2p multi	.25	.25
19 A5	4p multi	.30	.25
20 A5	5p multi	.40	.25
	Nos. 16-20 (5)	1.45	1.25

Natl. Independence, 4th Anniv. — A6

Pres. Macias Nguema and: 1.50p, Agriculture. 2p, 4p, Education. 3p, 5p, Natl. defense.

1973		***Perf. 13½***	
21 A6	1.50p multi	.25	.25
22 A6	2p multi	.25	.25
23 A6	3p multi	.35	.25
24 A6	4p multi	.40	.25
25 A6	5p multi	.60	.35
	Nos. 21-25 (5)	1.85	1.35

1973

Transatlantic Yacht Race, set of seven, 1p, 2p, 3p, 5p, 8p, airmail 15p, 50p, and two airmail semi-postal souv. sheets, perf. 200p+25p, imperf. 250p+50p, issued Jan. 22. Nos. 7301-7309.

Renoir paintings, set of seven, 1p, 2p, 3p, 5p, 8p, airmail 15p, 50p, plus two airmail semi-postal gold foil, perf. 200p+25p, imperf. 250p+50p, and two souv. sheets, perf. 200p+25p, imperf. 250p+50p, issued Feb. 22. Nos. 7310-7320.

Conquest of Venus (spacecraft), set of seven, 1p, 3p, 5p, 8p, 10p, airmail 5p, 25p, and two airmail semi-postal souv. sheets, perf. 200p+25p, imperf. 250p+50p, issued Mar. 22. Nos. 7321-7329.

Apollo 11-17 Flights, gold foil airmail semi-postal souv. sheets, perf. 200p+25p (7), 250p+50p (7), and four souv. sheets of two, perf. 200p+25p (2), imperf. 250p+50p (2), issued Mar. 22. Nos. 7330-7347.

Easter, paintings, set of seven, 1p, 3p, 5p, 8p, 10p, airmail 15p, 25p (Verrocchio, Perugino, Tintoretto, Witz, Pontormo), plus two airmail semi-postal souv. sheets, perf. 200p+25p, imperf. 250p+50p, and four gold foil issue of 1972 souv. sheets ovptd., perf. 200p+25p (2), imperf. 250p+50p (2), issued Apr. 25. Nos. 7348-7360.

Copernicus, 500th birth anniv. (US and USSR space explorations), four gold foil airmail semi-postal souv. sheets, perf. 200p+25p (2), imperf. 250p+50p (2), issued May 15. Nos. 7361-7364.

Tour de France bicycle race, set of seven, 1p, 2p, 3p, 5p, 8p, airmail 15p, 50p, and two airmail semi-postal souv. sheets, perf. 200p+25p, imperf. 250p+50p, issued May 22. Nos. 7365-7373.

Paintings, set of seven, 1p, 2p, 3p, 5p, 8p, airmail 15p, 50p, and two airmail semi-postal souv. sheets, 200p+25p, imperf. 250p+50p, issued June 29. Nos. 7374-7382.

1974 World Cup Soccer Championships, Munich, set of nine, 5c, 10c, 15c, 20c, 25c, 55c, 60c, airmail 5p, 70p, and two airmail souv. sheets, perf. 130p, imperf. 200p, issued Aug. 30. Nos. 7383-7393.

Rubens paintings, set of seven, 1p, 2p, 3p, 5p, 8p, airmail 15p, 50p, and two airmail semi-postal souv. sheets, perf. (25p, 200p), imperf. (50p, 250p), issued Sept. 23. Nos. 7394-73102.

1974 World Cup Soccer Championships, Munich, four gold foil airmail souv. sheets, perf. 130e (2), imperf. 200e (2), and two souv. sheets of two, perf. 130e, imperf. 200e, issued Oct. 24. Nos. 73103-73108.

Christmas, paintings, set of seven, 1p, 3p, 5p, 8p, 10p, airmail 15p, 25p, and two airmail semi-postal souv. sheets, perf. 200p+25p, imperf. 250p+50p (Nativity, by van der Weyden, Bosco, de Carvajal, Mabuse, Lucas Jordan, P. Goecke, Maino, Fabriano, Lochner), issued Oct. 30. Nos. 73109-73117.

Apollo Program and J.F. Kennedy, two gold foil airmail semi-postals, perf. 200p+25p, imperf. 250p+50p, and two souv. sheets, perf. 200p+25p, imperf. 250p+50p, issued Nov. 10. Nos. 73118-73121.

World Cup Soccer (famous players), set of nine, 30c, 35c, 40c, 45c, 50c, 65c, 70c, airmail 8p, 60p, and two airmail souv. sheets, perf. 130p, imperf. 200p, issued Nov. 20. Nos. 73122-73132.

Princess Anne's Wedding, six gold foil airmail souv. sheets, perf., imperf., two sheets of one, each 250e, one sheet of two 250e, issued Dec. 17. Nos. 73133-73141.

Pablo Picasso Memorial (Blue Period paintings), set of seven, 30c, 35c, 40c, 45c, 50c, airmail 8e, 60e, and two airmail souv. sheets, perf. 130e, imperf. 200e, issued Dec. 20. Nos. 73142-73150.

1974

Copernicus, 500th birth anniv., set of seven, 5c, 10c, 15c, 20c, 4e, airmail 10e, 70e, two airmail souv. sheets, perf. 130e, imperf. 200e, issued Feb. 8, 1974; eight gold foil airmail souv. sheets, perf. 130e (3), 250e, imperf. 200e (3), 300e, and four souv. sheets of two, perf. 250e (2), imperf. 250e (2), issued Apr. 10. Nos. 7401-7421.

World Cup Soccer Championships (final games), set of nine, 75c, 80c, 85c, 90c, 95c, 1e, 1.25e, airmail 10e, 50e, and two airmail souv. sheets, perf. 130e, imperf. 200e, issued Feb. 28. Nos. 7422-7432.

Easter, paintings, set of seven, 1p, 3p, 5p, 8p, 10p, airmail 15p, 25p (Fra Angelico, Castagno, Allori, Multscher, della Francesca, Pleydenwurff, Correggio), and two airmail semi-postal souv. sheets, perf. 200p+25p, imperf. 250p+50p, issued Mar. 27. Nos. 7433-7441.

Holy Year 1975 (famous churches), set of seven, 5c, 10c, 15c, 20c, 3.50e, airmail 10e, 70e, and two airmail souv. sheets, perf. 130e, imperf. 200e, issued Apr. 11. Nos. 7442-7450.

World Cup Soccer (contemporary players), set of nine, 1.50, 1.75, 2, 2.25, 2.50, 3, 3.50e, airmail 10, 60e, and 2 airmail souv. sheets of 2, perf. (2x65e), imperf. (2x100e), issued Apr. 30. Nos. 7451-7461.

UPU Cent. (transportation from messenger to rocket), set of seven, 60c, 70c, 80c, 1e, 1.50e, airmail 30e, 50e, and two airmail souv. sheets, perf. 225e, imperf. (150e, 150e), issued May 30; three airmail deluxe souv. sheets, 130e, and 2x130e, issued June 8. Nos. 7462-7472A.

Picasso Memorial (Pink Period paintings), set of seven, 55c, 60c, 65c, 70c, 75c, airmail 10e, 50e, and two airmail souv. sheets, perf. 130e, imperf. 200e, issued June 28. Nos. 7473-7481.

World Cup Soccer Championships, gold foil airmail souv. sheets, four sheets of one, 130e (2), 250e (2), two sheets of two (2x130e; 2x250e), issued July 8. Nos. 7482-7487.

Aleksander Solzhenitsyn, two gold foil airmail souv. sheets, perf. 250e, imperf. 300e, issued July 25. Nos. 7488-7489.

Opening of American West, set of seven, 30c, 35c, 40c, 45c, 50c, airmail 8p, 60p, and two souv. sheets, perf. 130p, imperf. 200p, issued July 30. Nos. 7490-7498.

Flowers, set of 14, 5c, 10c, 15c, 20c, 25c, 1p, 3p, 5p, 8p, 10p, airmail 5p, 15p, 25p, 70p, and 4 airmail souv. sheets, perf. 130p, 25p+200p, imperf. 200p, 50p+250p, issued Aug. 20. Nos. 7499-74116.

Christmas, set of seven, 60c, 70c, 80c, 1e, 1.50e, airmail 30e, 50e, and two souv. sheets, perf. 225e, imperf. 300e, issued Sept. 16. Nos. 74117-74125.

Barcelona Soccer Team, 75th anniv., set of seven, 1e, 3e, 5e, 8e, 10e, airmail 15e, 60e, miniature sheet of seven plus label, two airmail souv. sheets, perf. 200e, imperf. 300e, and two gold foil airmail souv. sheets, perf., imperf., 200e each, issued Sept. 25. Nos. 74126-74137.

UPU Cent. and ESPANA 75, set of seven, 1.25e, 1.50e, 1.75e, 2e, 2.25e, airmail 35e, 60e, and 2 airmail souv. sheets, perf. 225e, imperf. 300e, issued Oct. 9; 6 gold foil sheets, perf. 250e, 250e, 2x250e, imperf. 300e, 300e, 2x300e, issued Oct. 14. Nos. 74138-74152.

Nature Protection

Australian Animals, set of seven, 80c, 85c, 90c, 95c, 1e, airmail 15e, 40e, and two airmail souv. sheets, perf. 130e, imperf. 200e, issued Oct. 25. Nos. 74153-74161.

African Animals, set of seven, 55c, 60c, 65c, 70c, 75c, airmail 10e, 70e, and two airmail souv. sheets, perf. 130e, imperf. 200e, issued Nov. 6. Nos. 74162-74170.

Australian and South American Birds, set of 14, 1.25p, 1.50p, 1.75p, 2p, 2.25p, 2.50p, 2.75p, 3p, 3.50p, 4p, airmail 20p, 25p, 30p, 35p, and four souv. sheets, perf. 130p (2), imperf. 200p (2), issued Nov. 26. Nos. 74171-74188.

Endangered Species, set of 15, 10c, 15c, 20c, 25c, 30c, 35c, 40c, 45c, 50c, 55c, 60c, 1e, 2e, airmail 10e, 70e, se-tenant in sheet of 15, issued Dec. 17. Nos. 74189-74203.

Monkeys, various species, set of 16, 5c, 10c, 15c, 20c, 25c, 30c, 35c, 40c, 45c, 50c, 55c, 60c, 1e, 2e, airmail 10e, 70e, se-tenant in sheet of 16, issued Dec. 27. Nos. 74204-74219.

Cats, various species, set of 16, 5c, 10c, 15c, 20c, 25c, 30c, 35c, 40c, 45c, 50c, 55c, 60c, 1e, 2e, airmail 10e, 70e, se-tenant in sheet of 16, issued Dec. 27. Nos. 74220-74235.

Fish, various species, set of 16, 5c, 10c, 15c, 20c, 25c, 30c, 35c, 40c, 45c, 50c, 55c, 60c, 1e, 2e, airmail 10e, 70e, se-tenant in sheet of 16, issued Dec. 27. Nos. 74236-74251.

Butterflies, various species, set of 16, 5c, 10c, 15c, 20c, 25c, 30c, 35c, 40c, 45c, 50c, 55c, 60c, 1e, 2e, airmail 10e, 70e, se-tenant in sheet of 16, issued Dec. 27. Nos. 74252-74267.

1975

Picasso Memorial (paintings from last period), set of seven, 5c, 10c, 15c, 20c, 25c, airmail 5e, 70e, and two souv. sheets, perf. 130e, imperf. 200e, issued Jan. 27. Nos. 7501-7509.

ARPHILA 75 Phil. Exhib., Paris, 8 gold foil airmail souv. sheets: perf. 3 sheets of 1 250e, 1 sheet of 2 250e, imperf. 3 sheets of 1 300e, 1 sheet of 2 300e, issued Jan. 27. Nos. 7510-7517.

Easter and Holy Year 1975, set of seven, 60c, 70c, 80c, 1e, 1.50e, airmail 30e, 50e, and two airmail souv. sheets, perf. 225e, imperf. 300e, issued Feb. 15. Nos. 7518-7526.

1976 Winter Olympics, Innsbruck, set of 11, 5c, 10c, 15c, 20c, 25c, 30c, 35c, 40c, 45c, 25e, 70e, two airmail souv. sheets, perf. 130e, imperf. 200e, and two gold foil airmail souv. sheets, 1 sheet of 1 250e, 1 sheet of 2 250e, issued Mar. 10. Nos. 7527-7541.

Don Quixote, set of seven, 30c, 35c, 40c, 45c, 50c, airmail 25e, 60e, and two airmail souv. sheets, perf. 130e, imperf. 200e, issued Apr. 4. Nos. 7542-7550.

American Bicent. (1st issue), set of nine, 5c, 20c, 40c, 75c, 2e, 5e, 8e, airmail 25e, 30e, and two airmail souv.

sheets, perf. 130e, imperf. 200e, issued Apr. 30. Nos. 7551-7561.

American Bicent. (2nd issue), set of nine, 10c, 30c, 50c, 1e, 3e, 6e, 10e, airmail 12e, 40e, and two airmail souv. sheets, perf. 130e, imperf. 200e, issued Apr. 30. Nos. 7562-7572.

American Bicent. (Presidents), set of 18, 5c, 10c, 20c, 30c, 40c, 50c, 75c, 1e, 2e, 3e, 5e, 6e, 8e, 10e, airmail 12e, 25e, 30e, 40e, four airmail souv. sheets, perf. 225e (2), imperf. 300e (2), and six embossed gold foil airmail souv. sheets, perf. 200e, 200e, 2x200e, imperf. 300e, 300e, 2x300e, issued July 4. Nos. 7573-75100.

Bull Fight, set of seven, 80c, 85c, 90c, 95c, 8e, airmail 35e, 40e, and two airmail souv. sheets, perf. 130e, imperf. 200e, issued May 26. Nos. 75101-75109.

Apollo-Soyuz Space Project, set of 11, 1e, 2e, 3e, 5e, 5.50e, 7e, 7.50e, 9e, 15e, airmail 20e, 30e, and two airmail souv. sheets, perf. 225e, imperf. 300e, issued June 20, 1975; airmail souv. sheet, perf. 250e, issued July 17. Nos. 75110-75123.

Famous Painters, Nudes, set of 16, 5c, 10c, 15c, 20c, 25c, 30c, 35c, 40c, 45c, 50c, 55c, 60c, 1e, 2e, airmail 10e, 70e (Egyptian Greek, Roman, Indian art, Goes, Durer, Liss, Beniort, Renoir, Gauguin, Stenlen, Picasso, Modigliani, Matisse, Padua), se-tenant in sheet of 16, and 20 airmail embossed gold foil souv. sheetlets, perf. 200p+25p (10), imperf. 250p+50p (10), issued Aug. 10. Nos. 75124-75159.

Conquerors of the Sea, set of 14, 30c, 35c, 40c, 45c, 50c, 55c, 60c, 65c, 70c, 75c, airmail 8p, 10p, 50p, 60p, and four airmail souv. sheets, perf. 130p (2), imperf. 200p (2), issued Sept. 5. Nos. 75160-75177.

Christmas and Holy Year, 1975, set of seven, 60c, 70c, 80c, 1e, 1.50e, airmail 30e, 50e (Jordan, Barocci, Vereycke, Rubens, Mengs, Del Castillo, Cavedone), two airmail souv. sheets, perf. 225e, imperf. 300e, plus four embossed gold foil souv. sheets, perf. 200e (2), imperf. 300e (2), and two gold foil miniature sheets of two, perf. 200e+200e, imperf. 300e+300e, issued Oct. Nos. 75178-75192.

President Macias, IWY, set of eight, 1.50e, 3e, 3.50e, 5e, 7e, 10e, airmail 100e, 300e, and two imperf. airmail souv. sheets (world events), 100e (US 2c Yorktown), 300e, issued Dec. 25. Nos. 75193-75202.

1976

Cavalry Uniforms, set of seven, 5c, 10c, 15c, 20c, 25c, airmail 5p, 70p, and two airmail souv. sheets, perf. 130p, imperf. 200p, issued Feb. 2. Nos. 7601-7609.

1976 Winter Olympics, Innsbruck, set of 11, 50c, 55c, 60c, 65c, 70c, 75c, 80c, 85c, 90c, airmail 35e, 60e, and two airmail souv. sheets, perf. 130e, imperf. 200e, issued Feb. Nos. 7610-7622.

1976 Summer Olympics, Montreal, Ancient to Modern Games, set of seven, 50c, 60c, 70c, 80c, 90c, airmail 35e, 60e, and two airmail souv. sheets, perf. 225e, imperf. 300e, issued Feb. Nos. 7623-7631.

1976 Summer Olympics, Montreal, set of seven, 50c, 60c, 70c, 80c, 90c, airmail 30e, 60e, plus two airmail souv. sheets, perf. 225e, imperf. 300e, four embossed gold foil airmail souv. sheets, per. 250e (2), imperf. 300e (2), and two imperf. miniature sheets of two, perf. 2x250e, imperf. 2x300e, issued Mar. 5. Nos. 7632-7646.

El Greco, paintings, set of seven, 1e, 3e, 5e, 8e, 10e, airmail 15e, 25e, and two airmail semi-postal souv. sheets, perf. 200e+25e, imperf. 250e+50e, issued Apr. 5. Nos. 7647-7655.

1976 Summer Olympics, modern games, set of 11, 50c, 55c, 60c, 65c, 70c, 75c, 80c, 85c, 90c, airmail 35e, 60e, plus two airmail souv. sheets, perf. 225e, imperf. 300e, four embossed gold foil airmail souv. sheets, perf. 250e (2), imperf. 300e (2), and two miniature sheets of two, perf. 2x250e, imperf. 2x300e, issued May 7. Nos. 7656-7674.

UN 30th Anniv., airmail souv. sheet, 250e, issued June. No. 7675.

Contemporary Automobiles, set of seven, 1p, 3p, 5p, 8p, 10p, airmail 15p, 25p, and two airmail semi-postal souv. sheets, perf. 200p+25p, imperf. 250p+50p, issued June 10. Nos. 7675-7684.

Nature Protection

European Animals, set of seven, 5c, 10c, 15c, 20c, 25c, airmail 5p, 70p, and two airmail souv. sheets, perf. 130p, imperf. 200p, issued July 1. Nos. 7685-7693.

Asian Animals, set of seven, 30c, 35c, 40c, 45c, 8p, airmail 50c, 60p, and two airmail souv. sheets, perf. 130p, imperf. 200p, issued Sept. 20. Nos. 7694-74102.

Asian Birds, set of seven, 55c, 60c, 65c, 70c, 75c, airmail 10p, 50p, and two airmail souv. sheets, perf. 130p, imperf. 200p, issued Sept. 20. Nos. 76103-76111.

European Birds, set of seven, 5c, 10c, 15c, 20c, 25c, airmail 5p, 70p, and two airmail souv. sheets, perf. 130p, imperf. 200p, issued Sept. 20. Nos. 76112-76120.

North American Birds, set of seven, 80c, 85c, 90c, 95c, 1p, airmail 15p, 40p, and two airmail souv. sheets, perf. 130p, imperf. 200p, issued Sept. 20. Nos. 76121-76129.

Motorcycle Aces, set of 16, two each 1e, 2e, 3e, 4e, 5e, 10e, 30e, 40e, in se-tenant blocks of eight diff. values, issued July 22. Nos. 76130-76145.

1976 Summer Olympics, Montreal, set of five, 10e, 25e se-tenant strip of 3, airmail 200e, and imperf. airmail souv. sheet, 300e, issued Aug. 7. Nos. 76146-76151.

South American Flowers, set of seven, 30c, 35c, 40c, 45c, 50c, airmail 8p, 60p, and two airmail souv. sheets, perf. 130p, imperf. 200p, issued Aug. 16. Nos. 76152-76160.

Oceania, set of seven, 80c, 85c, 90c, 95c, 1p, airmail 15p, 40p, and two airmail souv. sheets, perf. 130p, imperf. 200p, issued 1976. Nos. 76161-76169.

1977

Butterflies, set of seven, 80c, 85c, 90c, 95c, 8e, airmail 35e, 40e, and two airmail souv. sheets, perf. 130e, imperf. 200e, issued Jan. Nos. 7701-7709.

Madrid Real, 75th Anniv., set of nine, 2e, 4e, 5e, 8e, 10e, 15e, airmail 20e, 35e, 150e, issued Jan. Nos. 7710-7718.

Ancient Carriages, set of 16, 5c, 10c, 15c, 20c, 25c, 30c, 35c, 40c, 45c, 50c, 55c, 60c, 1e, 2e, airmail 10e, 70e, issued Feb. Nos. 7719-7734.

Chinese Art, set of seven, 60c, 70c, 80c, 1e, 1.50e, airmail 30e, 50e, and two airmail souv. sheets, perf. 130e, imperf. 200e, issued Feb. Nos. 7735-7743.

African Masks, set of seven, 5c, 10c, 15c, 20c, 25c, airmail 5e, 70e, and two airmail souv. sheets, perf. 130e, imperf. 200e, issued Mar. Nos. 7744-7752.

North American Animals, set of seven, 1.25e, 1.50e, 1.75e, 2e, 2.25e, airmail 20e, 50e, and two airmail souv. sheets, perf. 130e, imperf. 200e, issued 1977. Nos. 7753-7761.

World Cup Soccer Championships, Argentina '78 (famous players), set of eight, 2e, 4e, 5e, 8e, 10e, 15e, airmail 20e, 35e, and two airmail souv. sheets, perf. 150e, imperf. 250e, issued July 25. Nos. 7762-7771.

World Cup Soccer (famous teams), se-tenant set of eight, 2e, 4e, 5e, 8e, 10e, 15e, airmail 20e, 35e, and two gold foil embossed souv. sheets, 500e (AMPHILEX '77, Cutty Sark, Concorde), airmail 500e (World Cup), issued Aug. 25.Nos. 7772-7781.

Napoleon, Life and Battle Scenes, se-tenant sheet of 16, 5c, 10c, 15c, 20c, 25c, 30c, 35c, 40c, 45c, 50c, 55c, 60c, 1e, 2e, airmail 10e, 70e, issued Aug. 20. Nos. 7782-7797.

Napoleon, Military Uniforms, se-tenant sheet of 16, 5c, 10c, 15c, 20c, 25c, 30c, 35c, 40c, 45c, 50c, 55c, 60c, 1e, 2e, airmail 10e, 70e, issued Aug. 20. Nos. 7798-77113.

South American Animals, set of seven, 2.50e, 2.75e, 3e, 3.50e, 4e, airmail 25e, 35e, and two airmail souv. sheets, perf. 130e, imperf. 200e, issued Aug. Nos. 77114-77122.

USSR Space Program, 20th Anniv., set of eight, 2e, 4e, 5e, 8e, 10e, 15e, airmail 20e, 35e, and two airmail souv. sheets, imperf. 150e, perf. 250e, issued Dec. 15. Nos. 77123-77132.

1978

Ancient Sailing Ships, set of 12, 5c, 10c, 15c, 20c, 25c, airmail 5e, 70e, also 5e, 10e, 20e, 25e, 70e, plus four airmail souv. sheets, perf. 150e, 225e, imperf. 250e, 300e, and two embossed gold foil airmail souv. sheets, perf., imperf., 500e, issued Jan. 6. Nos. 7801-7818.

1980 Winter Olympics, Lake Placid, set of five, 5e, 10e, 20e, 25e, airmail 70e, two airmail souv. sheets, perf. 150e, imperf. 250e, and two embossed gold foil airmail souv. sheets, perf., imperf., 500e, issued Jan. 17. Nos. 7819-7827.

1980 Summer Olympics, Moscow, set of eight, 2e, 3e, 5e, 8e, 10e, 15e, airmail 30e, 50e, two airmail souv. sheets, perf. 150e, imperf. 250e, and two embossed gold foil airmail souv. sheets, perf., imperf., 500e, issued Jan. 17. Nos. 7828-7839.

1980 Summer Olympic Water Games, Tallinn, set of five, 5e, 10e, 20e, 25e, airmail 70e, two airmail souv. sheets, perf. 150e, imperf. 250e, and two embossed gold foil airmail souv. sheets, perf., imperf., 500e, issued Jan. 17. Nos. 7840-7848.

Eliz. II Coronation, 25th Anniv., set of eight, 2e, 5e, 8e, 10e, 12e, 15e, airmail 30e, 50e, and two airmail souv. sheets, perf. 150e, imperf. 250e, issued Apr. 25. Nos. 7849-7858.

English Knights of 1200-1350 A.D., set of seven, 5e, 10e, 15e, 20e, 25e, airmail 15e, 70e, and two airmail souv. sheets, perf. 130e, imperf. 200e, issued Apr. 25. Nos. 7859-7867.

Old Locomotives, set of seven, 1e, 2e, 3e, 5e, 10e, airmail 25e, 70e, and two airmail souv. sheets, perf. 150e, imperf. 250e, issued Aug. Nos. 7868-7876.

Prehistoric Animals, set of seven, 30e, 35e, 40e, 45e, 50e, airmail 25e, 60e, and airmail souv. sheets, 130e, 200e, issued Aug. Nos. 7877-7884, 7884A.

Francisco Goya, "Maja Vestida," airmail souv. sheet, 150e, issued Aug. No. 7885.

Peter Paul Rubens — UNICEF, airmail souv. sheet, 250e, issued Aug. No. 7886.

Europa — CEPT — Europhila '78, airmail souv. sheet, 250e, issued Aug. No. 7887.

30th Intl. Stamp Fair, Riccione, airmail souv. sheet, 150e, issued Aug. Nos. 7888.

Eliz. II Coronation, 25th anniv., airmail souv. sheet of three, 150e, issued

CEPT, airmail souv. sheet, 250e, issued Aug. Nos. 7890.

World Cup Soccer Championships, Argentina '78 and Spain '82, airmail souv. sheet, 150e, issued Aug. Nos. 7891.

Christmas, Titian painting, "The Virgin," airmail souv. sheet, 150e, issued Aug. Nos. 7892.

Natl. Independence, 5th Anniv. (in 1973) — A7

1979			*Perf. 13x13½*	
26	A7	1e Ekuele coin	1.10	.25

Natl. Independence, 5th Anniv. (in 1973) — A8

1e, Port Bata. 1.50e, State Palace. 2b, Central Bank, Bata. 2.50b, Nguema Biyogo Bridge. 3b, Port, palace, bank, bridge.

1979					
27	A8	1e	multicolored	.25	.25
28	A8	1.50e	multicolored	.25	.25
29	A8	2b	multicolored	.30	.30
30	A8	2.50b	multicolored	.35	.35
31	A8	3b	multicolored	.60	.60
			Nos. 27-31 (5)	1.75	1.75

Pres. Nguema — A9

1979			*Perf. 13½x13*	
32	A9	1.50e multi	.50	.35

United Natl. Workers's Party (PUNT), 3rd Congress.

Independence Martyrs — A10

1e, Enrique Nvo. 1.50e, Salvador Ndongo Ekang. 2b, Acacio Mane.

1979

33	A10	1e multicolored	.30	.30
34	A10	1.50e multicolored	.35	.35
35	A10	2b multicolored	.45	.45
		Nos. 33-35 (3)	1.10	1.10

Agricultural Experiment Year A11

1979 ***Perf. 13x13½***

36	A11	1e multi	.65	.25
37	A11	1.50e multi, diff.	.95	.35

Independence Martyrs — A12 Natl. Coat of Arms — A13

5b, Obiang Esono Nguema. 15b, Fermando Nvara Engonga. 25b, Ela Edjodjomo Mangue. 35b, Obiang Nguema Mbasogo, president. 50b, Hipolito Micha Eworo.

1981, Mar. Photo. ***Perf. 13½x12½***

38	A12	5b multicolored	.40	.25
39	A12	15b multicolored	.40	.25
40	A12	25b multicolored	.40	.25
41	A12	35b multicolored	.55	.25
42	A12	50b multicolored	.80	.30
43	A13	100b multicolored	1.60	.45
		Nos. 38-43 (6)	4.15	1.75

Dated 1980.

Christmas 1980 A14

1981, Mar. 30 ***Perf. 13½***

44	A14	8b Cathedral, infant	.30	.25
45	A14	25b Bells, youth	.35	.25

Dated 1980.

Souvenir Sheet

Pres. Obiang Nguema Mbasogo — A15

1981, Aug. 30 **Litho.** ***Imperf.***

46	A15	400b multi	5.00	2.25

State Visit of King Juan Carlos of Spain — A16

50b, Government reception. 100b, Arrival at airport. 150b, King, Pres. Mbasogo, vert.

Perf. 13x13½, 13½x13

1981, Nov. 30

47	A16	50b multicolored	.90	.25
48	A16	100b multicolored	1.75	.50
49	A16	150b multicolored	2.75	.75
		Nos. 47-49 (3)	5.40	1.50

State Visit of Pope John Paul II — A17

100b, Papal and natl. arms. 200b, Pres. Mbasogo greeting Pope. 300b, Pope, vert.

1982, Feb. 18

50	A17	100b multicolored	1.50	.80
51	A17	200b multicolored	3.25	1.60
52	A17	300b multicolored	4.75	2.40
		Nos. 50-52 (3)	9.50	4.80

Christmas 1981 A18

1982, Feb. 25 **Photo.**

53	A18	100b Carolers, vert.	1.25	.40
54	A18	150b Magi, African youth	1.90	.70

Dated 1981.

1982 World Cup Soccer Championships, Spain — A19

40b, Emblem. 60b, Naranjito character trademark. 100b, World Cup trophy. 200b, Players, palm tree, emblem.

1982, June 13 ***Perf. 13½***

55	A19	40b multicolored	.45	.25
56	A19	60b multicolored	.70	.35
57	A19	100b multicolored	1.25	.60
58	A19	200b multicolored	2.50	1.10
		Nos. 55-58 (4)	4.90	2.30

Fauna A20

1983, Feb. 4 **Litho.**

59	A20	40b Gorilla	.75	.25
60	A20	60b Hippopotamus	1.25	.40
61	A20	80b Atherurus africanus	1.75	.50
62	A20	120b Felis pardus	2.75	.75
		Nos. 59-62 (4)	6.50	1.90

Dated 1982.

Christmas 1982 A21

1983, Feb. 25 **Photo.**

63	A21	100b Stars	.95	.35
64	A21	200b King offering frankincense	2.25	.75

Dated 1982.

World Communications Year — A22

Designs: 150b, Postal runner. 200b, Microwave station, drummer.

1983, July 18 **Litho.**

65	A22	150b multicolored	1.00	.45
66	A22	200b multicolored	2.25	.80

Banana Trees A23

1983, Oct. 8

67	A23	300b shown	3.25	1.00
68	A23	400b Forest, vert.	4.50	1.40

Christmas 1983 A24

Designs: 80b, Folk dancer, musical instruments. 100b, Holy Family.

1984

69	A24	80b multicolored	1.00	.35
70	A24	100b multicolored	1.25	.50

Dated 1983.

Constitution of State Powers — A25

Scales of justice, fundamental lawbook and various maps.

1984, Feb. 15

71	A25	50b Annobon and Bioko	.60	.30
72	A25	100b Mainland regions	1.40	.65

Inscription at the UR on No. 71 reads "Region Insular". No. 71 also exists with inscription reading "Regiones Insulares".

Turtle Hunting, Rio Muni — A26

1984, May 1

73	A26	125b Hunting Whales, horiz.	1.75	.75
74	A26	150b shown	2.00	.85

World Food Day — A27

1984, Sept.

75	A27	60b Papaya	1.25	.50
76	A27	80b Malanga	1.50	.65

Abstract Wood-Carved Figurines and Art — A28

Designs: 25b, *Black Gazelle* and *Anxiety.* 30b, *Black Gazelle,* diff., and *Woman.* 60b, *Man and woman,* vert. 75b, *Poster,* vert. 100b, *Mother and Child,* vert. 150b, *Man and Woman,* diff., and *Bust of a Woman.*

1984, Nov. 15

77	A28	25b multi	.25	.25
78	A28	30b multi	.35	.25
79	A28	60b multi	.75	.35
80	A28	75b multi	1.00	.40
81	A28	100b multi	1.50	.50
82	A28	150b multi	2.00	.90
		Nos. 77-82 (6)	5.85	2.65

Christmas A29

60b, Mother and child, vert. 100b, Musical instruments.

1984, Dec. 24

83	A29	60b multicolored	.75	.25
84	A29	100b multicolored	1.25	.55

Immaculate Conception Missions, Cent. — A30

50fr, Emblem, vert. 60fr, Map, nun and youths, vert. 80fr, First Guinean nuns. 125fr, Missionaries landing at Bata Beach, 1885.

1985, Apr. ***Perf. 14***

85	A30	50fr multi	.45	.25
86	A30	60fr multi	.60	.25
87	A30	80fr multi	.90	.30
88	A30	125fr multi	1.40	.60
		Nos. 85-88 (4)	3.35	1.40

Jose Mavule Ndjong, First Postmaster A31

1985, July ***Perf. 13½***

89	A31	50fr Postal emblem, vert.	1.00	.25
90	A31	80fr shown	1.75	.55

Equatorial Guinea Postal Service.

Christmas A32

Designs: 40fr, Nativity. 70fr, Folk band, dancers, mother and child.

1985, Dec.
91 A32 40fr multicolored .65 .25
92 A32 70fr multicolored 1.10 .35

Nature Conservation — A33

15fr, Crab, snail. 35fr, Butterflies, bees, birds. 45fr, Flowering plants. 65fr, Spraying and harvesting cacao.

1985
93 A33 15fr multicolored .30 .25
94 A33 35fr multicolored .85 .30
95 A33 45fr multicolored .85 .30
96 A33 65fr multicolored 1.25 .45
Nos. 93-96 (4) 3.25 1.30

Folklore — A34

10fr, Ndowe dance, Mekuyo, horiz. 50fr, Fang dance, Mokom. 65fr, Cacha Bubi, Bisila. 80fr, Fang dance, Ndong-Mba.

1986, Apr. 15
97 A34 10fr multicolored .25 .25
98 A34 50fr multicolored .60 .25
99 A34 65fr multicolored .90 .30
100 A34 80fr multicolored 1.00 .40
Nos. 97-100 (4) 2.75 1.20

A35

1986 World Cup Soccer Championships, Mexico: Various soccer plays.

1986, June 25
101 A35 50fr multi, horiz. .30 .25
102 A35 100fr multi, horiz. .80 .30
103 A35 150fr multi 1.25 .45
104 A35 200fr multi 1.60 .60
Nos. 101-104 (4) 3.95 1.60

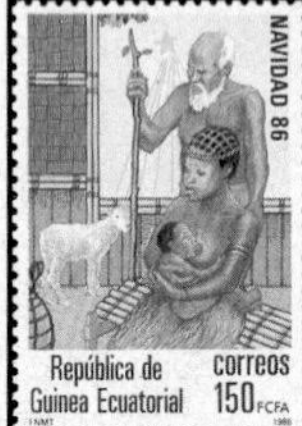

Christmas — A36

Designs: 100fr, Musical instruments, horiz. 150fr, Holy Family, lamb.

1986, Dec. 12
105 A36 100fr multicolored 1.10 .35
106 A36 150fr multicolored 1.60 .60

Conf. of the Union of Central African States — A37

Designs: 80fr, Flags, map. 100fr, Emblem, map, horiz.

1986, Dec. 29
107 A37 80fr multicolored .90 .35
108 A37 100fr multicolored 1.25 .40

Campaign Against Hunger A38

1987, June 5
109 A38 60fr Chicken .65 .25
110 A38 80fr Fish .95 .35
111 A38 100fr Wheat 1.25 .45
Nos. 109-111 (3) 2.85 1.05

Intl. Peace Year A39

1987, July 15 Litho. *Perf. 13½*
112 A39 100fr shown .85 .40
113 A39 200fr Hands holding dove 1.90 .80

Stamp Day 1987 A40

1987, Oct. 5 Litho. *Perf. 13½*
114 A40 150fr shown 1.25 .50
115 A40 300fr Posting envelope 2.25 .90

Christmas 1987 — A41

Mother and child (wood carvings).

1987, Dec. 22 Litho. *Perf. 13½*
116 A41 80fr multi 1.00 .35
117 A41 100fr multi, diff. 1.40 .45

Climbing Palm Tree — A42

75fr, Woman carrying fish. 150fr, Chopping down trees.

1988, May 4 Litho. *Perf. 13½*
118 A42 50fr shown .45 .25
119 A42 75fr multicolored .65 .35
120 A42 150fr multicolored 1.40 .65
Nos. 118-120 (3) 2.50 1.25

Democratic Party — A43

40fr, Crest. 75fr, Torch, motto, horiz. 100fr, Torch, flag, weaving, horiz.

1988, Nov. 16
121 A43 40fr multicolored .40 .25
122 A43 75fr multicolored .65 .30
123 A43 100fr multicolored .95 .40
Nos. 121-123 (3) 2.00 .95

Cultural Revolution Day — A44

Geometric shapes.

1988, June 4
124 A44 35fr shown .40 .25
125 A44 50fr Squares, sphere .60 .25
126 A44 100fr Bird 1.00 .40
Nos. 124-126 (3) 2.00 .90

Christmas — A45

1988, Dec. 22
127 A45 50fr shown .55 .25
128 A45 100fr Mother and child 1.20 .40

Natl. Independence, 20th Anniv. — A46

Designs: 10fr, Lumber on truck. 35fr, Folk dancers. 45fr, Officials on dais.

1989, Apr. 14 Litho. *Perf. 14*
129 A46 10fr multicolored .35 .25
130 A46 35fr multicolored .40 .35
131 A46 45fr multicolored .55 .40
Nos. 129-131 (3) 1.30 1.00

Youths Bathing, Ilachi Falls — A47

25fr, Waterfall in the jungle. 60fr, Boy drinking from fruit, boys swimming at Luba Beach.

1989, July 7 *Perf. 13½*
132 A47 15fr shown .45 .25
133 A47 25fr multicolored .50 .25
134 A47 60fr multicolored .75 .40
Nos. 132-134 (3) 1.70 .90

1st Congress of the Democratic Party of Equatorial Guinea A48

1989, Oct. 23 Litho. *Perf. 13½*
135 A48 25fr shown .35 .25
136 A48 35fr Torch, vert. .60 .25
137 A48 40fr Pres. Nguema, vert. .70 .25
Nos. 135-137 (3) 1.65 .75

Christmas — A49

1989, Dec. 18 Litho. *Perf. 13½*
138 A49 150fr shown 1.60 .50
139 A49 300fr Nativity, horiz. 2.00 .75

Boy Scouts A50

Designs: 100fr, Lord Baden-Powell. 250fr, Salute. 350fr, Bugler.

1990, Mar. 23 Litho. *Perf. 13*
140 A50 100fr multi 1.50 .50
141 A50 250fr multi 3.50 1.10
142 A50 350fr multi 4.75 1.50
Nos. 140-142 (3) 9.75 3.10

World Cup Soccer Championships, Italy — A51

Designs: 100fr, Soccer player, map. 250fr, Goalkeeper. 350fr, Trophy.

1990, June 8 Litho. *Perf. 13*
143 A51 100fr multicolored .60 .35
144 A51 250fr multicolored 1.50 .65
145 A51 350fr multicolored 2.00 1.00
Nos. 143-145 (3) 4.10 2.00

Musical Instruments of the Ndowe People — A52

Instruments of the: 250fr, Fang. 350fr, Bubi.

1990, June 19
146 A52 100fr multicolored .50 .30
147 A52 250fr multicolored 1.50 .75
148 A52 350fr multicolored 2.00 1.00
Nos. 146-148 (3) 4.00 2.05

Discovery of America, 500th Anniv. (in 1992) A53

Designs: 170fr, Arrival in New World. 300fr, Columbus' fleet.

1990, Oct. 10

149 A53 170fr multicolored 2.00 .60
150 A53 300fr multicolored 2.50 1.00

Christmas — A54

1990, Dec. 23 Litho. ***Perf. 13½***

151 A54 170fr shown 1.00 .45
152 A54 300fr Bubi tribesman 2.00 .90

1992 Summer Olympics, Barcelona A55

1991, Apr. 22 Litho. ***Perf. 13½x14***

153 A55 150fr Tennis 1.25 .75
154 A55 250fr Cycling 2.25 1.25

Souvenir Sheet

155 A55 500fr Equestrian 20.00 20.00

La Maja Desnuda by Goya A56

Designs: 250fr, Eve by Durer, vert. 350fr, The Three Graces by Rubens, vert.

1991, May 6 Litho. ***Perf. 14***

156 A56 100fr shown 1.50 .50
157 A56 250fr multicolored 2.75 1.00
158 A56 350fr multicolored 3.75 1.25
Nos. 156-158 (3) 8.00 2.75

Madrillus Sphinx — A57

1991, July 1 Litho. ***Perf. 13½x14***

159 A57 25fr shown 2.50 1.25
160 A57 25fr Face 2.50 1.25
161 A57 25fr Seated 2.50 1.25
162 A57 25fr Walking, horiz. 2.50 1.25
Nos. 159-162 (4) 10.00 5.00

World Wildlife Fund.

Discovery of America, 500th Anniv. A58

Captains, ships: 150fr, Vicente Yanez Pinzon, Nina. 260fr, Martin Alonso Pinzon, Pinta. 350fr, Christopher Columbus, Santa Maria.

1991 Litho. ***Perf. 13½x14***

163 A58 150fr multicolored 1.50 .60
164 A58 250fr multicolored 2.75 1.00
165 A58 350fr multicolored 3.75 1.50
Nos. 163-165 (3) 8.00 3.10

Locomotives — A59

150fr, Electric, Japan, 1932. 250fr, Steam, US, 1873. 500fr, Steam, Germany, 1841.

1991, Sept. 10

166 A59 150fr multicolored 1.00 .50
167 A59 250fr multicolored 2.50 .75

Souvenir Sheet

168 A59 500fr multicolored 22.50 22.50

1992 Summer Olympics, Barcelona A60

1992, Feb. 12 Litho. ***Perf. 13½x14***

169 A60 200fr Basketball 1.75 .75
170 A60 300fr Swimming 2.50 1.10

Souvenir Sheet

171 A60 400fr Baseball 22.50 22.50

Souvenir Sheet

Discovery of America, 500th Anniv. — A61

Columbus: a, 300fr, Departing from Palos, Spain. b, 500fr, Landing in New World.

1992, Apr. 8

172 A61 Sheet of 2, #a.-b. 22.50 22.50

Motion Pictures, Cent. A61a

Scenes from movies: 100fr, Humphrey Bogart, Ingrid Bergman, Dooley Wilson in "Casablanca," 1942. 250fr, "Viridiana," 1961. 350fr, Laurel and Hardy in "Sons of the Desert," 1933.

1992, Sept. Litho. ***Perf. 14***

172C A61a 100fr multicolored 1.00 .65
172D A61a 250fr multicolored 1.50 1.00
172E A61a 350fr multicolored 2.50 1.50
Nos. 172C-172E (3) 5.00 3.15

Mushrooms A62

75fr, Termitomyces globulus. 125fr, Termitomyces le testui. 150fr, Termitomyces robustus.

1992, Nov. Litho. ***Perf. 14x13½***

173 A62 75fr multicolored 1.00 .25
174 A62 125fr multicolored 1.50 .50
175 A62 150fr multicolored 2.00 .65
Nos. 173-175 (3) 4.50 1.40

A62a

Wildlife Protection: 150fr, Halcyon malimbicus. 250fr, Corythaeola cristata. 500fr, Mariposa nymphalidae, horiz.

1992 Litho. ***Perf. 14x13½***

175A A62a 150fr multicolored 2.50 1.00
175B A62a 250fr multicolored 4.25 1.50

Souvenir Sheet

Perf. 13½x14

175C A62a 500fr multicolored 25.00 25.00

Virgin and Child with Virtuous Saints, by Claudio Coello (c. 1635-1693) — A63

Paintings, by Jacob Jordaens (1593-1678): 300fr, Apollo Conquering Marsias. 400fr, Meleager and Atalanta.

1993, Mar. Litho. ***Perf. 13½x14***

176 A63 200fr multicolored 2.25 .75
177 A63 300fr multicolored 3.00 1.10

Souvenir Sheet

178 A63 400fr multicolored 20.00 20.00

1992 Olympic Gold Medalists A64

Designs: 100fr, Quincy Watts, 400-meter dash, US. 250fr, Martin Lopez Zubero, swimming, Spain. 350fr, Petra Kronberger, women's slalom, Austria. 400fr, Flying Dutchman class yachting, Spain.

1993 Litho. ***Perf. 13½x14***

179 A64 100fr multicolored .90 .35
180 A64 250fr multicolored 2.25 .75
181 A64 350fr multicolored 3.25 1.00
182 A64 400fr multicolored 4.00 1.25
Nos. 179-182 (4) 10.40 3.35

Scene from Romeo and Juliet, by Tchaikovsky — A65

Design: 200fr, Scene from Faust, by Charles-Francois Gounod (1818-93).

1993, June Litho. ***Perf. 13½x14***

183 A65 100fr multicolored 1.40 .40
184 A65 200fr multicolored 2.40 .65

First Ford Gasoline Engine, Cent. A66

1993 ***Perf. 13½x14, 14x13½***

185 A66 200fr First Ford vehicle 2.00 .75
186 A66 300fr Ford Model T 2.75 1.00
187 A66 400fr Henry Ford, vert. 4.00 1.25
Nos. 185-187 (3) 8.75 3.00

25th Anniv. of Independence — A67

Designs: 150fr, Pres. Obiang Nguema Mbasogo, vert. 250fr, Cargo ship, map, communications . 300fr, Hydroelectric plant, Riaba. 350fr, Bridge.

Perf. 14x13½, 13½x14

1993, Oct. 12 Litho.

188 A67 150fr multicolored 1.10 .50
189 A67 250fr multicolored 1.90 .75
190 A67 300fr multicolored 2.50 .85
191 A67 350fr multicolored 3.00 .95
Nos. 188-191 (4) 8.50 3.05

1994 World Cup Soccer Championships, US — A68

Designs: 200fr, German team, 1990 champions. 300fr, Rose Bowl Stadium, Pasadena, Calif. 500fr, Player kicking ball, vert.

1994 Litho. ***Perf. 13½x14, 14x13½***

192 A68 200fr multicolored 1.35 .50
193 A68 300fr multicolored 1.90 .70
194 A68 500fr multicolored 3.50 1.20
Nos. 192-194 (3) 6.75 2.40

First Manned Moon Landing, 25th Anniv. A69

Designs: 500fr, Lunar module, Eagle. 700fr, "Buzz" Aldrin, Michael Collins, Neil Armstrong. 900fr, Footprint on moon, astronaut.

1994 ***Perf. 13½x14***

195 A69 500fr multicolored 2.75 1.10
196 A69 700fr multicolored 4.25 1.50
197 A69 900fr multicolored 6.50 2.00
Nos. 195-197 (3) 13.50 4.60

Dinosaurs A70

Designs: 300fr, Chasmosaurus. 500fr, Tyrannosaurus rex. 700fr, Triceratops. 800fr, Styracosaurus, deinonychus.

1994

198 A70 300fr multicolored 2.00 .65
199 A70 500fr multicolored 3.25 1.10
200 A70 700fr multicolored 6.00 1.60
Nos. 198-200 (3) 11.25 3.35

Souvenir Sheet

201 A70 800fr multicolored 21.00 21.00

Famous Men
A71

Designs: 300fr, Jean Renoir (1894-1979), French film director. 500fr, Ferdinand de Lesseps (1805-94), French diplomat, promoter of Suez Canal. 600fr, Antoine de Saint Exupery (1900-44), French aviator, writer. 700fr, Walter Gropius (1883-1969), architect.

1994 Litho. *Perf. 13½x14*

202 A71 300fr multicolored 2.25 .75
203 A71 500fr multicolored 3.75 1.40
204 A71 600fr multicolored 4.50 1.50
205 A71 700fr multicolored 5.50 2.00
Nos. 202-205 (4) 16.00 5.65

Establishment of The Bauhaus, 75th anniv. (No. 205).

Minerals
A72

1994 Litho. *Perf. 13½x14*

206 A72 300fr Aurichalcite 2.50 .90
207 A72 400fr Pyromorphite 3.50 1.25
208 A72 600fr Fluorite 5.00 1.75
209 A72 700fr Halite 6.00 2.00
Nos. 206-209 (4) 17.00 5.90

Domestic Animals
A73

Designs: a, Cat. b, Dog. c, Pig.

1995 Litho. *Perf. 13½x14*

210 Strip of 3, #a.-c. 8.50 8.50
a.-c. A73 500fr Any single 1.60 1.40

Butterflies & Orchids
A74

a, Hypolimnas salmacis. b, Myrina silenus. c, Palla ussheri. d, Pseudacraea boisduvali.

1995

211 Strip of 4, #a.-d. 14.00 14.00
a.-d. A74 400fr Any single 2.75 1.50

Anniversaries — A75

Designs: a, 350fr, End of World War II, 50th Anniv. b, 450fr, UN, 50th anniv. c, 600fr, Sir Rowland Hill, birth bicent.

1995 Litho. *Perf. 13½x14*

212 Strip of 3, #a.-c. 11.00 11.00
a. A75 350fr multi 2.50 1.25
b. A75 450fr multi 3.25 1.50
c. A75 600fr multi 4.00 2.25

Trains
A76

Designs: No. 213a, English steam engine. b, German diesel engine. c, Japanese Shinkansen train.
800fr, Swiss electric locomotive.

1995

213 Strip of 3, #a.-c. 13.00 13.00
a.-c. A76 500fr Any single 2.75 2.25

Souvenir Sheet

214 A76 800fr multicolored 11.00 11.00

Formula 1 Driving Champions
A77

Designs: a, Juan Manuel Fangio. b, Ayrton Senna. c, Jim Clark. d, Jochen Rindt.

1995 Litho. *Perf. 14*

215 Strip of 4, #a.-d. 12.00 12.00
a.-d. A77 400fr Any single 2.25 1.50

Motion Pictures, Cent.
A78

Designs: a, Marilyn Monroe. b, Elvis Presley. c, James Dean. d, Vittorio de Sica.

1996 Litho. *Perf. 14*

216 Strip of 4, #a.-d. 9.00 9.00
a.-d. A78 350fr Any single 1.50 1.50

Famous People
A79

Designs: a, Alfred Nobel (1833-96), inventor, philanthropist. b, Anton Bruckner (1824-96), composer. c, Abraham and Three Angels, by Giovanni B. Tiepolo (1696-1770).
800fr, Family of Charles IV, by Francisco de Goya, (1746-1828).

1996

217 Strip of 3, #a.-c. 13.50 13.50
a.-c. A79 500fr Any single 2.75 2.00

Souvenir Sheet

218 A79 800fr multicolored 8.00 7.75

Chess
A80

Designs: a, World Chess Festival for youth and children, Minorca, Spain. b, Women's World Chess Championship, Jaén, Spain. c, Men's World Chess Championship, Karpov versus Kamsky, Elista, Kalmyk. d, Chess Olympiad, Yerevan, Armenia.

1996 *Perf. 14*

219 Strip of 4, #a.-d. 14.00 14.00
a.-d. A80 400fr Any single 3.00 1.50

1996 Summer Olympic Games, Atlanta
A81

Designs: a, Olympic Stadium, Athens, 1896. b, Cycling. c, Tennis. d, Equestrian show jumping.

1996 Litho. *Perf. 14*

220 Strip of 4, #a.-d. 10.00 10.00
a.-d. A81 400fr Any single 1.75 1.50

Ships
A82

Designs: a, Paddle steamer with sails, 19th cent. b, Bark "Galatea," 1896. c, Modern ferry.

1996

221 Strip of 3, #a.-c. 12.00 12.00
a.-c. A82 500fr Any single 2.75 2.00

Franz Schubert (1797-1828), Composer — A83

Miguel de Cervantes (1547-1616), Novelist — A84

Designs: a, shown. b, Chinese Lunar New Year, 1997, (Year of the Ox). c, Johannes Brahms (1833-97), composer.

1997, Apr. 23 Litho. *Perf. 14*

222 Strip of 3, #a.-c. 10.00 10.00
a.-c. A83 500fr Any single 2.50 2.00

Souvenir Sheet

223 A84 800fr multicolored 11.00 11.00

Mushrooms — A85

a, Sparassis laminosa. b, Amanita pantherina. c, Morchella esculenta. d, Aleuria aurantia.

1997

224 Strip of 4, #a.-d. 13.50 13.50
a.-d. A85 400fr Any single 2.25 1.75

1998 World Cup Soccer Championships, France — A86

Designs: a, Players with ball on field. b, Stadium. c, Kicking ball.

1997 Litho. *Perf. 14*

225 Strip of 3, #a.-c. 7.00 7.00
a.-c. A86 300fr Any single 1.50 1.10

Fauna
A88

a, Snake. b, Snail. c, Turtle. d, Monitor lizard.

1998 Litho. *Perf. 14*

230 Strip of 4, #a.-d. 14.00 14.00
a.-d. A88 400fr Any single 2.25 1.50

A89

Military Uniforms: a, Alsace Regiment, French Infantry, 18th cent. b, English Marine, 18th cent. c, Georgian Hussars Regiment, Russian Calvary, 18th cent. d, Prussian Artillery, 19th cent.

1998

231 Strip of 4, #a.-d. 10.00 10.00
a.-d. A89 400fr Any single 1.75 1.50

A90

Easter (Museum paintings): a, Crucifixion of Christ, by Velázquez. b, Adoration of the Magi, by Rubens. c, Holy Family, by Michelangelo.

1999 Litho. *Perf. 14*

232 Strip of 3, #a.-c. 10.00 10.00
a.-c. A90 500fr Any single 2.25 2.00

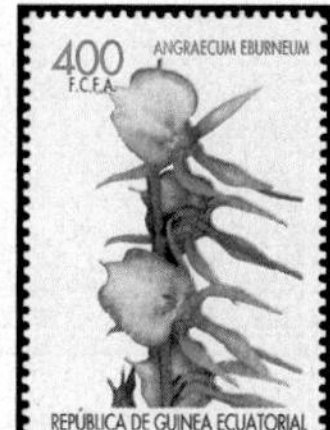

Orchids — A91

Designs: a, Angraecum eburneum. b, Paphiopedilum insigne. c, Ansellia africana. d, Cattleya leopoldii.

1999

233 Strip of 4, #a.-d. 16.00 16.00
a.-d. A91 400fr Any single 3.00 1.50

Birth and Death Anniversaries
A92

No. 234: a, 750fr, Portrait of Frederic Chopin (1810-49), by Eugene Delacroix. b, 100fr, Christ Crowned With Thorns, by Anthony Van Dyck (1599-1641). c, 250fr, Portrait of Johann Wolfgang von Goethe (1749-1832), by Joseph Carl Stieler. d, 500fr, Jacques-Etienne Montgolfiere (1745-1799) and balloon.

1999 Litho. *Perf. 14x13¾*

234 Horiz. strip of 4, #a-d 11.00 11.00
a. A92 750fr multi 4.00 3.00
b. A92 100fr multi .45 .35
c. A92 250fr multi 1.25 1.10
d. A92 500fr multi 2.75 2.00

Parrots — A93

No. 235: a, Aratinga guarouba. b, Ara ambigua. c, Anodorhynchus hyacinthinus.
800fr, Alisterus amboinensis.

1999

235 Vert. strip of 3, #a-c 13.00 13.00
a.-c. A93 500fr any single 3.00 2.25

Souvenir Sheet

236 A93 800fr multi 11.00 11.00

Economic and Monetary Community of Central Africa Week (CEMAC) — A93a

Designs: 100fr, Map of Africa, flags of member nations.

1999 Litho. *Perf. 14½*

236A A93a 100fr multi —

An additional stamp was issued in this set. The editors would like to examine any example.

Locomotives — A94

No. 237: a, Swiss. b, German. c, Japanese.

2000 Litho. *Perf. 13¾x14*

237 Horiz. strip of 3 12.00 12.00
a.-c. A94 500fr Any single 3.00 2.50

Souvenir Sheet

238 A94 800fr AVE Train 7.25 7.25

Butterflies A95

a, Fabriciana niobe. b, Palaeochrysophanus hippothoe. c, Inachis io. d, Apatura iris.

2000

239 Horiz. strip of 4 16.00 16.00
a.-d. A95 400fr Any single 3.00 1.75

UPU, 125th Anniv. (in 1999) A96

2000 Litho. *Perf. 13¾*

240 A96 400fr multi 3.00 2.60

Mushrooms A97

No. 241: a, Gyroporus cyanescens. b, Terfezia arenaria. c, Battarrea stevenii. d, Amanita muscaria.

2001 Litho. *Perf. 13¾*

241 Horiz. strip of 4 12.00 12.00
a.-d. A97 400fr Any single 2.25 1.75

Fire Trucks A98

No. 242: a, Truck, 1915. b, Tanker, 1943. c, Ladder truck, 1966. d, Merryweather pumper, 1888.

2001

242 Horiz. strip of 4 13.00 13.00
a.-d. A98 400fr Any single 2.50 2.00

Soldiers — A99

No. 243: a, Infantry officer, 1700. b, Harquebusier, 1534. c, Musketeer, 17th cent. d, Fusilier, 1815.

2001 Litho. *Perf. 14x13¾*

243 Horiz. strip of 4 12.00 12.00
a.-d. A99 400fr Any single 2.50 1.75

Prehistoric Animals A100

No. 244: a, Carnotaurus sastrei. b, Iberomesornis romerali. c, Troodon.
800fr, Diplodocus carnegiei.

2001 *Perf. 13¾x14*

244 Horiz. strip of 3 12.00 12.00
a.-c. A100 500fr Any single 3.00 2.50

Souvenir Sheet

245 A100 800fr multi 10.00 10.00

Millennium A101

Designs: No. 246, 200fr, Intl. Conference Center. No. 247, 200fr, Offshore petroleum exploration. No. 248, 200fr, Women's Plaza, Malabo.
400fr, Statue at Intl. Conference Center, vert.

2001 Litho. *Perf. 13¾x14*

246-248 A101 Set of 3 10.50 10.50

Souvenir Sheet

Perf. 14x13¾

249 A101 400fr multi 7.75 7.75

Flora — A102

No. 250: a, Alstonia congensis. b, Harongana madagascariensis. c, Caloncoba glauca. d, Cassia occidentalis.

2002 *Perf. 14x13¾*

250 Horiz. strip of 4 12.00 12.00
a.-d. A102 400fr Any single 2.60 2.10

Automobiles — A103

No. 251: a, 1924 Rochet Schneider 20,000. b, 1930 Bugatti T49. c, 1931 Ford Model A. d, 1925 Alfa Romeo RLSS.

2002 *Perf. 13¾x14*

251 Vert. strip of 4 12.00 12.00
a.-d. A103 400fr Any single 2.60 2.10

Butterflies A104

No. 252: a, Papilio menestheus canui. b, Papilio policenes. c, Papilio tynderaeus. d, Papilio zalmoxis.

2002

252 Strip of 4 12.00 12.00
a.-d. A104 400fr Any single 2.60 2.10

Famous Men A105

No. 253: a, Victor Hugo (1802-85), writer. b, Santiago Ramón y Cajal (1852-1934), histologist. c, Emile Zola (1840-1902), writer.

2002

253 Horiz. strip of 3 7.25 7.25
a.-c. A105 400fr Any single 1.90 1.75

2002 World Cup Soccer Championships, Japan and Korea — A106

No. 254: a, Player with yellow shirt with knee on ground. b, Stadium. c, Player with yellow shirt on ground.

2002

254 Horiz. strip of 3 11.00 11.00
a.-c. A106 500fr Any single 3.00 2.75

Souvenir Sheet

2002 Chess Olympiad, Bled, Slovenia — A107

2002

255 A107 800fr multi 7.50 7.50

Anniversaries and Events — A108

No. 256: a, Painting by Henri de Toulouse-Lautrec (1864-1901). b, Year of Dialogue Among Civilizations. c, Giuseppe Verdi (1813-1901), composer.

2004 ? Litho. *Perf. 14x13¾*

256 Vert. strip of 3 8.00 8.00
a.-c. A108 400fr Any single 2.50 2.50

Dated 2001. Stamps did not appear in philatelic market until 2004.

Anniversaries and Events — A109

No. 257: a, Tour de France bicycle race, cent. b, Painting by Vincent van Gogh (1853-90). c, Wright Brothers and Wright Flyer.

2004 ? *Perf. 13¾x14*

257 Horiz. strip of 3 10.00 10.00
a. A109 400fr multi 2.75 2.75
b. A109 500fr multi 3.25 3.25
c. A109 600fr multi 4.00 4.00

Dated 2003. Stamps did not appear in philatelic market until 2004.

Minerals A110

2004 ?

258 Vert. strip of 4 12.00 12.00
a. A110 400fr Realgar 2.25 2.25
b. A110 450fr Gypsum 2.75 2.75
c. A110 550fr Red quartz 3.25 3.25
d. A110 600fr Chrysoberyl 3.50 3.50

Dated 2003. Stamps did not appear in philatelic market until 2004.

Lighthouses A111

Designs: a, Marina Lighthouse, Luba, Equatorial Guinea. b, La Plata Lighthouse, Spain. c, Prodecao Lighthouse, Luba. d, Torre de Hércules, Spain.

2004 ? *Perf. 14x13¾*

259 Horiz. strip of 4 12.50 12.50
a. A111 400fr multi 2.50 2.50
b. A111 450fr multi 2.75 2.75
c. A111 550fr multi 3.00 3.00
d. A111 600fr multi 3.75 3.75

Dated 2003. Stamps did not appear in philatelic market until 2004.

Space Shuttle Columbia Accident — A112

No. 260: a, Rocket lift-off. b, Rocket on launch pad. c, Flight crew patch.
1000fr, View of earth from outer space.

2004 ?

260 Vert. strip of 3 10.50 10.50
a. A112 500fr multi 3.00 3.00
b. A112 600fr multi 3.25 3.25
c. A112 700fr multi 3.75 3.75

Souvenir Sheet

261 A112 1000fr multi 8.00 8.00

Dated 2003. Stamps did not appear in philatelic market until 2004.

Motorcycles — A113

No. 262: a, 1944-47 Soriano Tigre. b, 1970 Derbi 50 Grand Prix. c, 1938 DKW 250 with sidecar.
1000fr, Harley-Davidson VRSCA V-Rod.

2004 ? ***Perf. 13¾x14***

262 Horiz. strip of 3 8.50 8.50
a. A113 450fr multi 2.00 2.00
b. A113 500fr multi 2.50 2.50
c. A113 550fr multi 3.00 3.00

Souvenir Sheet

263 A113 1000fr multi 7.50 7.50

Dated 2003. Stamps did not appear in philatelic market until 2004.

Souvenir Sheet

Wedding of Spanish Prince Felipe and Letizia Ortiz Rocasolano — A114

2004 **Litho.** ***Perf. 13¾x14***

264 A114 1400fr multi 11.00 11.00

2004 Summer Olympics, Athens A115

2004

265 Horiz. strip of 4 10.00 10.00
a. A115 400fr Basketball 1.90 1.90
b. A115 450fr Track 2.25 2.25
c. A115 550fr Tennis 2.75 2.75
d. A115 600fr Cycling 3.00 3.00

2004 Anniversaries A116

No. 266: a, FIFA (Fédération Internationale de Football Association), cent. b, Pablo Neruda (1904-73), poet. c, Anton Dvorak (1841-1904), composer.

2005 ? **Litho.** ***Perf. 14x13¾***

266 Vert. strip of 3 10.00 10.00
a. A116 450fr multi 2.75 2.75
b. A116 500fr multi 3.00 3.00
c. A116 550fr multi 3.50 3.50

Dated 2004. Stamps did not appear in philatelic marketplace until 2005.

Airplanes A117

No. 267: a, Concorde. b, Airbus A340-600. c, Boeing 747-400. d, Eurofighter C-16 Typhoon.

2005 ? ***Perf. 13¾x14***

267 Vert. strip of 4 11.00 11.00
a. A117 400fr multi 2.00 2.00
b. A117 450fr multi 2.50 2.50
c. A117 500fr multi 2.75 2.75
d. A117 600fr multi 3.25 3.25

Dated 2004. Stamps did not appear in philatelic marketplace until 2005.

Churches — A118

No. 268: a, Cathedral, Pisa, Italy. b, Notre-Dame-la-Grande Church, Poitiers, France. c, Speyer Cathedral, Germany. d, Cathedral, Santiago de Compostela, Spain.

2005 ***Perf. 14x13¾***

268 Horiz. strip of 4 12.00 12.00
a. A118 400fr multi 2.00 2.00
b. A118 450fr multi 2.50 2.50
c. A118 550fr multi 3.00 3.00
d. A118 600fr multi 3.25 3.25

Paintings by Salvador Dali (1904-89) — A119

Various unnamed paintings.

2005 ***Perf. 14x13¾***

269 Vert. strip of 3 10.00 10.00
a. A119 500fr multi 2.50 2.50
b. A119 600fr multi 3.00 3.00
c. A119 700fr multi 3.50 3.50

Souvenir Sheet

270 A119 1000fr multi 9.00 9.00

Art and Architecture — A120

No. 271: a, Statue of African Woman, Malabo. b, Building, Bioko Sur. c, Eyi Muan Ndong, troubador.

2005 **Litho.** ***Perf. 13¾x14***

271 Horiz. strip of 3 8.00 8.00
a. A120 450fr multi 2.25 2.25
b. A120 550fr multi 2.60 2.60
c. A120 600fr multi 3.00 3.00

Trains A121

No. 272: a, Tren Basculante. b, Tren Talgo Pendular. c, Tren Electrotrén. d, Tren T. A. F.

2005

272 Strip of 4 11.00 11.00
a. A121 400fr multi 2.10 2.10
b. A121 450fr multi 2.25 2.25
c. A121 550fr multi 3.00 3.00
d. A121 600fr multi 3.25 3.25

Publication of Don Quixote, 400th Anniv. — A122

No. 273: a, Emblem. b, Don Quixote and Sancho Panza riding. c, Quixote catching falling Panza. d, Quixote on horse, windmill.

2005 ***Perf. 14x13¾***

273 Horiz. strip of 4 11.00 11.00
a. A122 400fr multi 2.10 2.10
b. A122 450fr multi 2.25 2.25
c. A122 550fr multi 3.00 3.00
d. A122 600fr multi 3.25 3.25

Famous People A123

No. 274: a, Christopher Columbus (1451-1506), explorer. b, Federico García Lorca (1898-1936), poet. c, Wolfgang Amadeus Mozart (1756-91), composer.

2006 ***Perf. 13¾x14***

274 Horiz. strip of 3 11.00 11.00
a. A123 450fr multi 3.00 3.00
b. A123 550fr multi 3.50 3.50
c. A123 600fr multi 3.75 3.75

Pope Benedict XVI A124

No. 275: a, Coat of Arms. b, St. Peter's Basilica.
1000fr, Pope Benedict XVI.

2006

275 Vert. pair 6.00 6.00
a. A124 450fr multi 2.50 2.50
b. A124 550fr multi 3.50 3.50

Souvenir Sheet

276 A124 1000fr multi 7.00 7.00

Tourism A125

No. 277: a, Road from Boloko to Luba. b, Malabo Intl. Airport Terminal. c, Sculpture, Avenida de Juan Pablo II. d, National Parliament.

2006 **Litho.** ***Perf. 13¾x14***

277 Strip of 4 12.00 12.00
a. A125 400fr multi 2.40 2.40
b. A125 450fr multi 2.60 2.60
c. A125 550fr multi 3.25 3.25
d. A125 600fr multi 3.50 3.50

Spain, 2006 World Basketball Champions A126

No. 278: a, Emblem of Spanish Basketball Federation. b, Basketball and hoop. c, Players.

2006 ***Perf. 14x13¾***

278 Vert. strip of 3 10.00 10.00
a. A126 450fr multi 2.50 2.50
b. A126 550fr multi 3.25 3.25
c. A126 600fr multi 3.50 3.50

Christmas A127

No. 279 — Baby and: a, People and drummer. b, People. c, People and airplane.

2006 ***Perf. 13¾x14***

279 Horiz. strip of 3 9.00 9.00
a. A127 450fr multi 2.25 2.25
b. A127 550fr multi 3.00 3.00
c. A127 600fr multi 3.25 3.25

European Economic Community, 50th Anniv. — A128

No. 280: a, Orchard, Spain. b, Mountain, France. c, Farm fields, Italy. d, Village, Germany.

2007 **Litho.** ***Perf. 13¾x14***

280 Horiz. strip of 4 13.00 13.00
a. A128 400fr multi 2.25 2.25
b. A128 500fr multi 2.75 2.75
c. A128 550fr multi 3.00 3.00
d. A128 600fr multi 3.25 3.25

Locomotives in Madrid Train Museum — A129

No. 281: a, Steam locomotive 242F-2009. b, Diesel locomotive 1615. c, Electric locomotive 6101. d, Talgo II train.
1000fr, Steam locomotive, diff.

2007

281 Strip of 4 13.00 13.00
a. A129 450fr multi 2.25 2.25
b. A129 550fr multi 2.75 2.75

c. A129 600fr multi 3.50 3.50
d. A129 650fr multi 3.75 3.75

Souvenir Sheet

282 A129 1000fr multi 5.75 5.75

Native Toys A130

2007 Litho. *Perf. 13¾x14*

283 Horiz. strip of 4 10.00 10.00
a. A130 400fr Airplane 2.00 2.00
b. A130 450fr Car 2.40 2.40
c. A130 500fr Scooter 2.60 2.60
d. A130 550fr Songo game 3.00 3.00

Flora A131

No. 284: a, Artocarpus communis. b, Hibiscus sabdariffa. c, Spathodea campanulata. d, Theobroma cacao.

2007 Litho. *Perf. 13¾x14*

284 Horiz. strip of 4 12.00 12.00
a. A131 400fr multi 2.25 2.25
b. A131 450fr multi 2.60 2.60
c. A131 550fr multi 3.25 3.25
d. A131 600fr multi 3.50 3.50

African Children A132

No. 285: a, Child and basket. b, Five children and toy cars. c, Six children and net.

2008 Litho. *Perf. 13¾*

285 Horiz. strip of 3 8.50 8.50
a. A132 400fr multi 2.50 2.50
b. A132 450fr multi 2.75 2.75
c. A132 500fr multi 3.00 3.00

2008 African Cup of Nations Soccer Championships, Ghana — A133

No. 286 — Emblem and: a, Soccer ball and player's foot. b, Soccer ball being caught. c, Goalie. d, Goalie, diff.

2008

286 Horiz. strip of 4 12.00 12.00
a. A133 400fr multi 2.50 2.50
b. A133 450fr multi 2.75 2.75
c. A133 500fr multi 3.00 3.00
d. A133 600fr multi 3.50 3.50

Flora and Fauna A134

No. 287: a, Sitatunga. b, Passiflora quadrangularis. c, Pachylobus edulis.

2008

287 Horiz. strip of 3 8.00 8.00
a. A134 450fr multi 2.25 2.25
b. A134 500fr multi 2.60 2.60
c. A134 600fr multi 3.00 3.00

Intl. Year of Planet Earth A135

No. 288: a, Seedlings. b, Parched earth. c, Waterfall.

2008

288 Horiz. strip of 3 7.50 7.50
a. A135 400fr multi 2.25 2.25
b. A135 450fr multi 2.40 2.40
c. A135 550fr multi 2.75 2.75

Declaration of the Rights of Children, 50th Anniv. — A136

No. 289: a, Child drinking glass of milk. b, Children playing with ball. c, Children reading. d, Child coloring.

2009, Mar. 27 Litho. *Perf. 14x13¾*

289 Horiz. strip of 4 11.00 11.00
a. A136 400fr multi 2.00 2.00
b. A136 500fr multi 2.75 2.75
c. A136 550fr multi 3.00 3.00
d. A136 600fr multi 3.25 3.25

Women's Soccer A137

No. 290: a, Cheering crowd. b, Soccer ball hitting net. c, Players battling for ball. d, Corner of field.

2009, May 14 Litho. *Perf. 13¾*

290 Vert. strip of 4 13.00 13.00
a. A137 450fr multi 2.50 2.50
b. A137 550fr multi 3.00 3.00
c. A137 600fr multi 3.25 3.25
d. A137 650fr multi 3.50 3.50

Medicinal Plants — A138

No. 291: a, Asystasia gangetica. b, Bryophyllum pinnatum. c, Solanum torvum. 1000fr, Cassia alata.

2009, Aug. 14

291 Vert. strip of 3 10.00 10.00
a. A138 400fr multi 2.75 2.75
b. A138 450fr multi 3.25 3.25
c. A138 550fr multi 3.75 3.75

Souvenir Sheet

292 A138 1000fr multi 7.25 7.25

Christmas — A139

No. 293 — Paintings: a, Birth of Christ, by Federico Barocci. b, Adoration of the Kings, by J. B. Maíno. c, Adoration of the Shepherds, by Maíno. d, Nativity, by Master of Sopetrán.

2009, Sept. 25

293 Horiz. strip of 4 11.00 11.00
a. A139 400fr multi 2.00 2.00
b. A139 450fr multi 2.75 2.75
c. A139 500fr multi 3.00 3.00
d. A139 550fr multi 3.25 3.25

Paintings by Joaquin Sorolla y Bastida A140

No. 294: a, Paseo a Orillas del Mar. b, El Balandrito. c, La Hora del Baño. d, Self-portrait.

Perf. 13¾x13¼

2010, Mar. 15 Litho.

294 Horiz. strip of 4 14.00 14.00
a. A140 475fr multi 2.75 2.75
b. A140 575fr multi 3.50 3.50
c. A140 625fr multi 3.75 3.75
d. A140 675fr multi 4.00 4.00

Architecture — A141

No. 295: a, La Paz Medical Center, Bata. b, Gepetrol Building, Malabo. c, Gecotel Building, Bata. d, Central African Economic and Monetary Community Parliament Building, Malabo.

2010, June 15

295 Horiz. strip of 4 14.00 14.00
a. A141 475fr multi 2.75 2.75
b. A141 575fr multi 3.50 3.50
c. A141 625fr multi 3.75 3.75
d. A141 675fr multi 4.00 4.00

2010 World Cup Soccer Championships, South Africa — A142

No. 296: a, Emblem of 2010 tournament. b, Mascot. c, World Cup. d, Colors of Spain, World Cup champions.

2010 Litho. *Perf. 13¼x13¾*

296 Horiz. strip of 4 14.00 14.00
a. A142 475fr multi 2.75 2.75
b. A142 575fr multi 3.50 3.50
c. A142 625fr multi 3.75 3.75
d. A142 675fr multi 4.00 4.00

Miniature Sheet

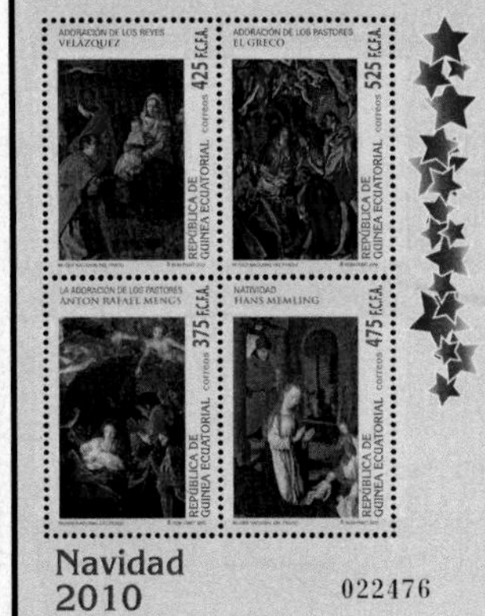

Christmas — A143

No. 297: a, 375fr, Adoration of the Shepherds, by Anton Rafael Mengs. b, 425fr, Adoration of the Magi, by Diego Velázquez. c, 475fr, Nativity, by Hans Memling. d, 525fr, Adoration of the Shepherds, by El Greco.

2010

297 A143 Sheet of 4, #a-d 12.00 12.00

Intl. Women's Day, Cent. A144

No. 298 — Stylized woman as: a, Doctor. b, Police officer. c, Chemist. d, Chef.

2011 *Perf. 13¾x14*

298 Horiz. strip of 4 16.00 16.00
a. A144 525fr black 3.25 3.25
b. A144 625fr green 3.75 3.75
c. A144 675fr red violet 4.25 4.25
d. A144 725fr blue 4.50 4.50

Intl. Year of Chemistry — A145

No. 299 — Emblem and: a, Chemical glassware. b, Molecular model and textbook. c, Children in school. d, Water.

2011 *Perf. 14x13¾*

299 Horiz. strip of 4 16.00 16.00
a. A145 525fr multi 3.25 3.25
b. A145 625fr multi 3.75 3.75
c. A145 675fr multi 4.25 4.25
d. A145 725fr multi 4.50 4.50

Gustavo Adolfo Bécquer (1836-70), Poet — A146

No. 300: a, Drawing of Woman. b, Windows of Veruela Monastery. c, Portrait of Bécquer by his brother, Valeriano.

2011

300 Horiz. strip of 3 11.00 11.00
a. A146 525fr multi 3.00 3.00
b. A146 625fr multi 3.75 3.75
c. A146 675fr multi 4.00 4.00

Christmas A147

No. 301 — Christmas-themed paintings by: a, Nicolás Francés. b, Fra Angelico. c, Luca di Tommè. d, Jaume Serra.

2011 *Perf. 13¾x14*

301 Horiz. strip of 4 13.00 13.00
a. A147 525fr multi 2.60 2.60
b. A147 625fr multi 3.00 3.00
c. A147 675fr multi 3.25 3.25
d. A147 725fr multi 3.50 3.50

Paintings by Juan Gris (1887-1927) A148

Various paintings.

2012 ***Perf. 14x13¾***

302	Horiz. strip of 4	12.00	12.00
a.	A148 525fr multi	2.40	2.40
b.	A148 625fr multi	2.75	2.75
c.	A148 675fr multi	3.00	3.00
d.	A148 725fr multi	3.25	3.25

Spices — A149

No. 303: a, Xylopia aethiopica. b, Piper guineense. c, Capsicum frutescens. d, Zingiber officinale.

2012

303	Horiz. strip of 4	12.00	12.00
a.	A149 525fr multi	2.40	2.40
b.	A149 625fr multi	2.75	2.75
c.	A149 675fr multi	3.00	3.00
d.	A149 725fr multi	3.25	3.25

Sports A150

No. 304: a, Gymnastics. b, Table tennis. c, Running. d, Kayaking.

2012 ***Perf. 14x13¾***

304	Horiz. strip of 4	12.00	12.00
a.	A150 525fr multi	2.40	2.40
b.	A150 625fr multi	2.75	2.75
c.	A150 675fr multi	3.00	3.00
d.	A150 725fr multi	3.25	3.25

Christmas A151

No. 305 — Religious painting by: a, Pietro de Lignis. b, Francisco and Rodrigo de Osona. c, Pietro da Cortona. d, Hans Memling.

2012 ***Perf. 14x13¾***

305	Horiz. strip of 4	12.00	12.00
a.	A151 525fr multi	2.40	2.40
b.	A151 625fr multi	2.75	2.75
c.	A151 675fr multi	3.00	3.00
d.	A151 725fr multi	3.25	3.25

Tourist Areas A152

No. 306: a, Sipopo. b, Luba. c, Mbini. d, Bata.

2013 ***Perf. 13¾x13¼***

306	Horiz. strip of 4	12.00	12.00
a.	A152 550fr multi	2.50	2.50
b.	A152 600fr multi	2.75	2.75
c.	A152 650fr multi	3.00	3.00
d.	A152 700fr multi	3.25	3.25

Intl. Red Cross, 150th Anniv. A153

No. 307: a, Students in classroom. b, Man carrying large pot on head. c, Red Cross worker. d, Flags on building.

2013 ***Perf. 13¾x14***

307	Horiz. strip of 4	12.00	12.00
a.	A153 550fr multi	2.50	2.50
b.	A153 600fr multi	2.75	2.75
c.	A153 650fr multi	3.00	3.00
d.	A153 700fr multi	3.25	3.25

Pope John XXIII (1881-1963) A154

No. 307: a, Pope John XXIII. b, Pope John XXIII, diff. c, Pope John XXIII, diff. d, Arms of Pope John XXIII.

2013 ***Perf. 13¼x13¾***

308	Horiz. strip of 4	12.00	12.00
a.	A154 550fr multi	2.60	2.60
b.	A154 600fr multi	2.75	2.75
c.	A154 650fr multi	3.00	3.00
d.	A154 700fr multi	3.50	3.50

Christmas — A155

No. 308: a, Nativity. b, Adoration of the Magi. c, Nativity, diff. d, Nativity, diff.

2013 ***Perf. 13¼x13¾***

309	Horiz. strip of 4	12.00	12.00
a.	A155 550fr multi	2.60	2.60
b.	A155 600fr multi	2.75	2.75
c.	A155 650fr multi	3.00	3.00
d.	A155 700fr multi	3.50	3.50

Bolondo-Mbini Bridge — A156

Various views of bridge.

2014 **Litho.** ***Perf. 13¼x13¾***

310	Horiz. strip of 4	11.50	11.50
a.	A156 600fr multi	2.50	2.50
b.	A156 650fr multi	2.75	2.75
c.	A156 700fr multi	3.00	3.00
d.	A156 750fr multi	3.25	3.25

Intl. Year of Family Farms A157

No. 311: a, Hands leveling earth. b, Woman tending cows. c, Woman tending goats. d, Farmer inspecting crops.

2014 **Litho.** ***Perf. 13¾x13¼***

311	Horiz. strip of 4	11.50	11.50
a.	A157 600fr multi	2.50	2.50
b.	A157 650fr multi	2.75	2.75
c.	A157 700fr multi	3.00	3.00
d.	A157 750fr multi	3.25	3.25

Religious Paintings by El Greco (1541-1614) A158

No. 312: a, St. Andrew and St. Francis. b, Christ Carrying the Cross. c, St. Peter. d, The Disrobing of Christ.

2014 **Litho.** ***Perf. 13¼x13¾***

312	Horiz. strip of 4	11.50	11.50
a.	A158 600fr multi	2.50	2.50
b.	A158 650fr multi	2.75	2.75
c.	A158 700fr multi	3.00	3.00
d.	A158 750fr multi	3.25	3.25

Christmas A159

No. 313: a, Adoration of the Shepherds, by Bartolomé Esteban Murillo. b, Adoration of the Magi, by Peter Paul Rubens. c, Adoration of the Magi, by Luis de Morales. d, Adoration of the Shepherds, by de Morales.

2014 **Litho.** ***Perf. 13¼x13¾***

313	Horiz. strip of 4	11.50	11.50
a.	A159 600fr multi	2.50	2.50
b.	A159 650fr multi	2.75	2.75
c.	A159 700fr multi	3.00	3.00
d.	A159 750fr multi	3.25	3.25

Sipopo Congress Center, Malabo — A160

No. 314: a, Seats and video screen in meeting hall (29x41mm). b, Seats in auditorium (29x41mm). c, Building exterior (29x41mm). d, Building entrance (58x41mm).

2015 **Litho.** ***Perf. 13¼x13¾***

314	Horiz. strip of 4	14.50	14.50
a.	A160 650fr multi	2.25	2.25
b.	A160 700fr multi	2.40	2.40
c.	A160 750fr multi	2.60	2.60
d.	A160 2100fr multi	7.25	7.25

Paintings of Women by Federico de Madrazo y Kuntz (1815-94) — A161

No. 315 — Various women wearing: a, Blue dress. b, White dress. c, Lilac dress. d, Black dress.

2015 **Litho.** ***Perf. 13¾***

315	Horiz. strip of 4	9.25	9.25
a.	A161 600fr multi	2.00	2.00
b.	A161 650fr multi	2.25	2.25
c.	A161 700fr multi	2.40	2.40
d.	A161 750fr multi	2.60	2.60

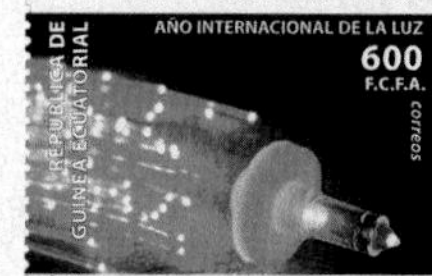

International Year of Light — A162

No. 316: a, Fiber optic cord connector. b, Ends of optical fibers. c, Ends of optical fibers, diff. d, Close-up of ends of bound optical fibers.

2015 **Litho.** ***Perf. 13¾x13¼***

316	Horiz. strip of 4	8.75	8.75
a.	A162 600fr multi	2.00	2.00
b.	A162 650fr multi	2.10	2.10
c.	A162 700fr multi	2.25	2.25
d.	A162 750fr multi	2.40	2.40

Christmas — A163

No. 317 — Various Nativity paintings by unknown artists from: a, Prado, Madrid. b, Museum of Fine Arts, Bilbao. c, Prado, diff. d, Museum of Fine Arts, diff.

2015 **Litho.** ***Perf. 13¼x13¾***

317	Horiz. strip of 4	8.75	8.75
a.	A163 600fr multi	2.00	2.00
b.	A163 650fr multi	2.10	2.10
c.	A163 700fr multi	2.25	2.25
d.	A163 750fr multi	2.40	2.40

Paintings by Hieronymus Bosch (c.1450-1516) A164

No. 318 — Details of paintings: a, Garden of Earthly Delights (left panel). b, Garden of Earthly Delights (center panel). c, The Hay Wagon (center panel). d, St. John the Baptist in the Wilderness.

2016 **Litho.** ***Perf. 13¾***

318	Horiz. strip of 4	8.75	8.75
a.	A164 600fr multi	2.00	2.00
b.	A164 650fr multi	2.25	2.25
c.	A164 700fr multi	2.40	2.40
d.	A164 750fr multi	2.60	2.60

Miguel de Cervantes (1547-1616), Writer — A165

No. 319 — Various paintings from Prado Museum, Madrid.

2016 **Litho.** ***Perf. 13¾***

319	Horiz. strip of 4	8.75	8.75
a.	A165 600fr multi	2.00	2.00
b.	A165 650fr multi	2.25	2.25
c.	A165 700fr multi	2.40	2.40
d.	A165 750fr multi	2.60	2.60

Flora and Fauna A166

No. 320: a, Hibisco (hibiscus). b, Geranio de la jungla (jungle geranium). c, Pangolín arborícola (tree pangolin). d, Barbasco guineano (Vogel's tephrosia).

2016 Litho. *Perf. 13¾x14*

320	Horiz. strip of 4	8.75	8.75
a.	A166 600fr multi	1.90	1.90
b.	A166 650fr multi	2.10	2.10
c.	A166 700fr multi	2.25	2.25
d.	A166 750fr multi	2.40	2.40

Christmas — A167

Various paintings depicting the Nativity from the Prado Museum, Madrid.

2016 Litho. *Perf. 14x13¾*

321	Horiz. strip of 4	8.75	8.75
a.	A167 600fr multi	1.90	1.90
b.	A167 650fr multi	2.10	2.10
c.	A167 700fr multi	2.25	2.25
d.	A167 750fr multi	2.40	2.40

International Year for Sustainable Tourism for Development — A168

No. 322: a, Bicyclist walking bicycle. b, Boat near dock. c, Cyclist on trail. d, Canoers.

2017 Litho. *Perf. 13¾*

322	Horiz. strip of 4	9.50	9.50
a.	A168 600fr multi	2.10	2.10
b.	A168 650fr multi	2.25	2.25
c.	A168 700fr multi	2.40	2.40
d.	A168 750fr multi	2.60	2.60

Paintings by Bartolomé Esteban Murillo (1617-82) — A169

No. 323: a, Leander and St. Bonaventure. b, Saints Justa and Rufina. c, Christ the Good Shepherd. d, Immaculate Conception.

2017 Litho. *Perf. 13¾*

323	Horiz. strip of 4	9.50	9.50
a.	A169 600fr multi	2.10	2.10
b.	A169 650fr multi	2.25	2.25
c.	A169 700fr multi	2.40	2.40
d.	A169 750fr multi	2.60	2.60

Malabo National Park A170

No. 324: a, Bridge. b, Sculptures. c, Island. d, Park entrance.

2017 Litho. *Perf. 13¾*

324	Horiz. strip of 4	10.00	10.00
a.	A170 600fr multi	2.25	2.25
b.	A170 650fr multi	2.40	2.40
c.	A170 700fr multi	2.60	2.60
d.	A170 750fr multi	2.75	2.75

Christmas — A171

Various unattributed Nativity paintings from the Prado Museum.

2017 Litho. *Perf. 13¾*

325	Horiz. strip of 4	10.00	10.00
a.	A171 600fr multi	2.25	2.25
b.	A171 650fr multi	2.40	2.40
c.	A171 700fr multi	2.60	2.60
d.	A171 750fr multi	2.75	2.75

Paintings by Tintoretto (1518-94) A172

No. 326: a, Christ Washing the Feet of His Disciples. b, The Queen of Sheba and Solomon. c, Susanna and the Elders. d, Esther Before Ahasuerus.

2018 Litho. *Perf. 13¾*

326	Horiz. strip of 4	9.75	9.75
a.	A172 600fr multi	2.10	2.10
b.	A172 650fr multi	2.40	2.40
c.	A172 700fr multi	2.50	2.50
d.	A172 750fr multi	2.75	2.75

A173

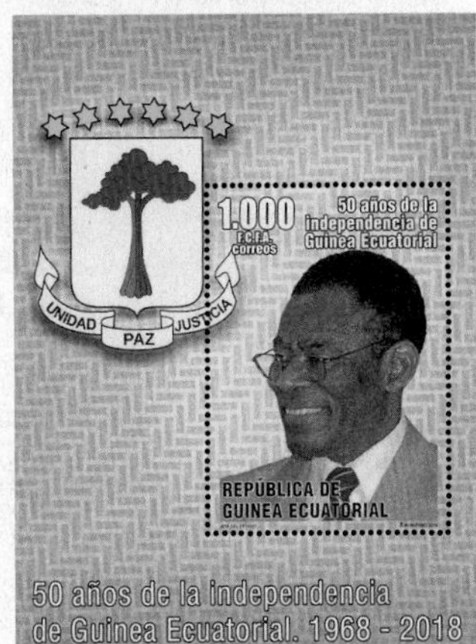

Independence, 50th Anniv. — A174

No. 326: a, Mongomo Basilica. b, Coat of arms of Equatiorial Guinea. c, Presidential Palace. d, President Teodoro Obiang Nguema Mbasogo.

1000fr, Pres. Obiang, diff.

2018 Litho. *Perf. 13¾*

327	Horiz. strip of 4	9.75	9.75
a.	A173 600fr multi	2.10	2.10
b.	A173 650fr multi	2.40	2.40
c.	A173 700fr multi	2.50	2.50
d.	A173 750fr multi	2.75	2.75

Souvenir Sheet

Perf. 13¾x13½

328	A174 1000fr multi	3.50	3.50

Items Made by Artisans — A175

No. 329: a, Decorated gourds. b, Comb. c, Basket. d, Carved wooden shelf.

2018 Litho. *Perf. 13¾*

329	Horiz. strip of 4	9.50	9.50
a.	A175 600fr multi	2.10	2.10
b.	A175 650fr multi	2.25	2.25
c.	A175 700fr multi	2.40	2.40
d.	A175 750fr multi	2.60	2.60

Christmas — A176

Various unnamed works of religious art from the Prado, Madrid.

2018 Litho. *Perf. 13¾*

330	Horiz. strip of 4	9.50	9.50
a.	A176 600fr multi	2.10	2.10
b.	A176 650fr multi	2.25	2.25
c.	A176 700fr multi	2.40	2.40
d.	A176 750fr multi	2.60	2.60

SPECIAL DELIVERY STAMPS

Archer with Crossbow — SD1

1971, Oct. 12 Photo. *Perf. 12½x13*

E1	SD1 4p blue & multi	.75	.25
E2	SD1 8p rose & multi	1.25	.35

3rd anniversary of independence.

ERITREA

ˌer-ə-ˈtrē-ə

LOCATION — In northeast Africa, bordering on the Red Sea, Sudan, Ethiopia and Djibouti.
GOVT. — Independent state
AREA — 45,300 (?) sq. mi.
POP. — 3,984,723 (1999 est.)
CAPITAL — Asmara

Formerly an Italian colony, Eritrea was incorporated as a State of Italian East Africa in 1936.

Under British occupation (1941-52) until it became part of Ethiopia as its northernmost region. Eritrea became independent May 24, 1993.

100 Centesimi = 1 Lira
100 cents = 1 birr (1991)
100 cents = 1 nakfa (1997)

Catalogue values for unused stamps in this country are for Never Hinged items, beginning with Scott 200 in the regular postage section.

All used values to about 1916 are for postally used stamps. From 1916-1934, used values in italics are for postally used stamps. CTO's, for stamps valued postally used, sell for about the same as unused, hinged stamps.

Watermark

Wmk. 140 — Crown

Stamps of Italy Overprinted

a

b

1892 Wmk. 140 *Perf. 14*

Overprinted Type "a" in Black

1	A6	1c bronze grn	6.00	12.00
a.		Inverted overprint	725.00	750.00
b.		Double overprint	2,150.	
		Never hinged	*3,200.*	
c.		Vert. pair, one without overprint	4,800.	
		Never hinged	*7,250.*	
2	A7	2c org brn	3.75	6.00
a.		Inverted overprint	725.00	750.00
b.		Double overprint	2,150.	
		Never hinged	*3,200.*	
3	A33	5c green	75.00	16.00
a.		Inverted overprint	*9,500.*	*4,275.*
		Never hinged	*13,500.*	

Overprinted Type "b" in Black

4	A17	10c claret	100.00	15.00
5	A17	20c orange	185.00	12.00
6	A17	25c blue	675.00	50.00
7	A25	40c brown	7.50	*27.50*
8	A26	45c slate grn	7.50	*30.00*
9	A27	60c violet	7.50	60.00
10	A28	1 l brn & yel	37.50	*75.00*
11	A38	5 l bl & rose	300.00	500.00
		Nos. 1-11 (11)	1,405.	*803.50*
		Set, never hinged	*3,600.*	

1895-99

Overprinted type "a" in Black

12	A39	1c brown ('99)	12.50	9.00
13	A40	2c org brn ('99)	3.00	1.85
14	A41	5c green	3.00	1.90
a.		Inverted overprint	500.00	*4,500.*

Overprinted type "b" in Black

15	A34	10c claret ('98)	3.00	1.90
16	A35	20c orange	3.00	2.50
17	A36	25c blue	3.00	3.75
18	A37	45c olive grn	24.00	*22.00*
		Nos. 12-18 (7)	51.50	*42.90*
		Set, never hinged	130.00	

1903-28

Overprinted type "a" in Black

19	A42	1c brown	1.25	1.10
a.		Inverted overprint	125.00	100.00
20	A43	2c orange brn	1.25	.55
21	A44	5c blue green	35.00	.50
22	A45	10c claret	40.00	.55
23	A45	20c orange	6.00	1.10
24	A45	25c blue	340.00	13.75
a.		Double overprint	*1,400.*	—
25	A45	40c brown	375.00	22.00
26	A45	45c olive grn	6.00	*7.50*
27	A45	50c violet	135.00	25.00
28	A46	75c dk red & rose ('28)	85.00	6.00

29 A46 1 l brown & grn 5.00 .75
30 A46 1.25 l bl & ultra ('28) 37.50 3.00
31 A46 2 l dk grn & org ('25) 85.00 *100.00*
32 A46 2.50 l dk grn & org ('28) 250.00 75.00
33 A46 5 l blue & rose 24.00 *35.00*
Nos. 19-33 (15) 1,426. 291.80
Set, never hinged 3,700.

Surcharged in Black

1905

34 A45 15c on 20c orange 100.00 18.50
Never hinged 250.00

1908-28

Overprinted type "a" in Black

35 A48 5c green .90 .85
36 A48 10c claret ('09) .90 .85
37 A48 15c slate ('20) 17.00 11.00
38 A49 20c green ('25) 24.50 11.00
39 A49 20c lilac brn ('28) 8.50 3.00
40 A49 25c blue ('09) 5.00 2.00
41 A49 30c gray ('25) 24.00 15.00
42 A49 40c brown ('16) 75.00 30.00
43 A49 50c violet ('16) 30.00 1.60
44 A49 60c brown car ('18) 21.00 *21.50*
a. Printed on both sides *2,000.*
45 A49 60c brown org ('28) 135.00 *240.00*
46 A51 10 l gray grn & red ('16) 340.00 *625.00*
Nos. 35-46 (12) 681.80 *961.80*
Set, never hinged 1,970.

See No. 53.

A1

Government Building at Massaua — A2

1910-29 Unwmk. Engr. *Perf. 13½*

47 A1 15c slate 500.00 24.00
a. Perf. 11 ('29) 50.00 *55.00*
Never hinged 125.00
48 A2 25c dark blue 12.50 *13.50*
a. Perf. 12 925.00 925.00

For surcharges see Nos. 51-52.

A3

Farmer Plowing — A4

1914-28

49 A3 5c green 2.50 *2.00*
a. Perf. 11 ('28) 250.00 75.00
Never hinged 625.00
50 A4 10c carmine 12.00 *13.50*
a. Perf. 11 ('28) 21.00 *42.50*
Never hinged 52.50
b. Perf. 13½x14 55.00 55.00

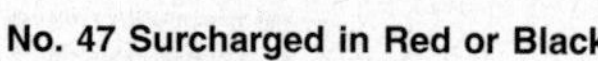

No. 47 Surcharged in Red or Black

1916

51 A1 5c on 15c slate (R) 8.50 *13.00*
52 A1 20c on 15c slate 3.75 3.75
a. "CEN" for "CENT" 27.50 30.00
b. "CENT" omitted 160.00 160.00
c. "ENT" 44.00 *44.00*
Set, never hinged 31.00

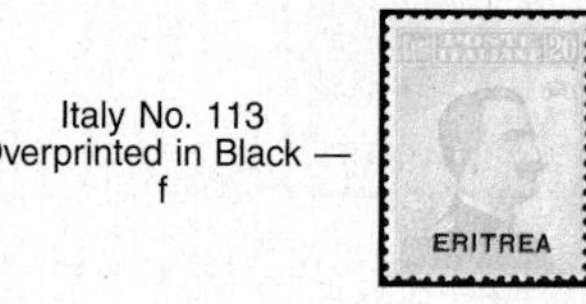

Italy No. 113 Overprinted in Black — f

1921 Wmk. 140 *Perf. 14*

53 A50 20c brown orange 3.75 *11.00*
Never hinged 9.00

Victory Issue

Italian Victory Stamps of 1921 Overprinted type "f" 13mm long

1922

54 A64 5c olive green 1.90 *6.00*
55 A64 10c red 1.90 *5.50*
56 A64 15c slate green 1.90 *8.50*
57 A64 25c ultra 1.90 *8.50*
Nos. 54-57 (4) 7.60 *28.50*
Set, never hinged 27.00

Somalia Nos. 10-16 Overprinted In Black g

1922 Wmk. 140

58 A1 2c on 1b brn 5.00 *14.75*
a. Pair, one missing "ERITREA" 2,450.
59 A1 5c on 2b bl grn 5.00 *10.25*
60 A2 10c on 1a claret 5.00 2.25
61 A2 15c on 2a brn org 5.00 2.25
62 A2 25c on 2½a blue 5.00 2.25
63 A2 50c on 5a yellow 20.00 10.25
a. "ERITREA" double *950.00*
64 A2 1 l on 10a lilac 20.00 18.50
a. "ERITREA" double *1,850.* 950.00
b. Pair, one missing "ERITREA" *3,750.*
Nos. 58-64 (7) 65.00 *60.50*
Set, never hinged 160.00

See Nos. 81-87.

Propagation of the Faith Issue

Italy Nos. 143-146 Overprinted

1923

65 A68 20c ol grn & brn org 11.00 *45.00*
66 A68 30c claret & brn org 11.00 *45.00*
67 A68 50c vio & brn org 7.00 *52.50*
68 A68 1 l bl & brn org 7.00 *82.50*
Nos. 65-68 (4) 36.00 *225.00*
Set, never hinged 90.00

Fascisti Issue

Italy Nos. 159-164 Overprinted in Red or Black — j

1923 Unwmk. *Perf. 14*

69 A69 10c dk green (R) 12.00 *17.00*
70 A69 30c dk violet (R) 12.00 *17.00*
71 A69 50c brown carmine 12.00 *23.50*

Wmk. 140

72 A70 1 l blue 12.00 *42.50*
73 A70 2 l brown 12.00 *52.50*
74 A71 5 l black & blue (R) 12.00 *80.00*
Nos. 69-74 (6) 72.00 *232.50*
Set, never hinged 180.00

Manzoni Issue

Italy Nos. 165-170 Overprinted in Red

1924 *Perf. 14*

75 A72 10c brown red & blk 12.00 *62.50*
76 A72 15c blue grn & blk 12.00 *62.50*
77 A72 30c black & slate 12.00 *62.50*
78 A72 50c org brn & blk 12.00 *62.50*
79 A72 1 l blue & blk 75.00 *375.00*
80 A72 5 l violet & blk 375.00 *2,750.*
Nos. 75-80 (6) 498.00 *3,375.*
Set, never hinged 1,240.

On Nos. 79 and 80 the overprint is placed vertically at the left side.

Somalia Nos. 10-16 Overprinted type "g" in Blue or Red

1924

Bars over Original Values

81 A1 2c on 1b brn 17.00 *22.50*
a. Pair, one without "ERITREA" *2,750.*
82 A1 5c on 2b bl grn (R) 17.00 *14.00*
83 A2 10c on 1a rose red 8.50 *12.00*
84 A2 15c on 2a brn org 8.50 *13.50*
a. Pair, one without "ERITREA" 2,750.
b. "ERITREA" inverted 1,950. *2,000.*
85 A2 25c on 2½a bl (R) 8.50 *8.50*
a. Double surcharge 1,475.
86 A2 50c on 5a yellow 8.50 *16.00*
87 A2 1 l on 10a lil (R) 8.50 *22.50*
Nos. 81-87 (7) 76.50 *109.00*
Set, never hinged 195.00

Stamps of Italy, 1901-08 Overprinted type "j" in Black

1924

88 A42 1c brown 8.50 *8.75*
a. Inverted overprint 250.00
b. Vertical pair, one without ovpt. 1,850.
89 A43 2c orange brown 6.25 *7.50*
b. Vertical pair, one without ovpt. 1,850.
90 A48 5c green 8.50 *8.75*
Nos. 88-90 (3) 23.25 *25.00*
Set, never hinged 60.00

Victor Emmanuel Issue

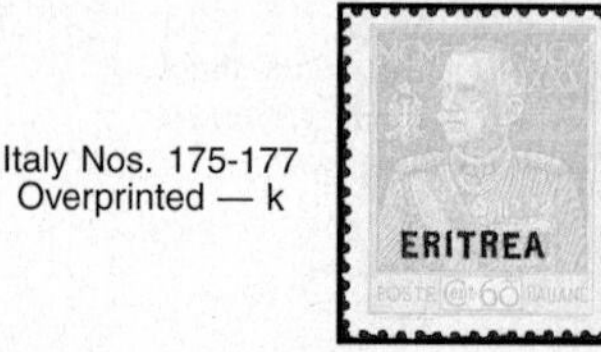

Italy Nos. 175-177 Overprinted — k

1925-26 Unwmk. *Perf. 11*

91 A78 60c brown car 2.25 *9.25*
a. Perf. 13½ 12.50 37.50
92 A78 1 l dark blue 2.25 *14.50*
a. Perf. 13½ *24,000.* *9,300.*
Never hinged *36,000.*

Perf. 13½

93 A78 1.25 l dk blue ('26) 4.00 *32.50*
a. Perf. 11 8.00 *40.00*
Nos. 91-93 (3) 8.50 *56.25*
Set, never hinged 21.50

Saint Francis of Assisi Issue

Italian Stamps of 1926 Overprinted

1926 Wmk. 140 *Perf. 14*

94 A79 20c gray green 2.40 *14.00*
95 A80 40c dark violet 2.40 *14.00*
96 A81 60c red violet 2.40 *25.00*

Overprinted in Red

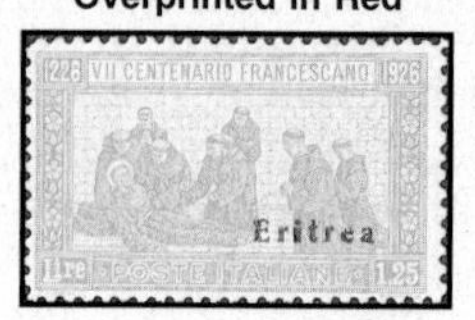

Unwmk. *Perf. 11*

97 A82 1.25 l dark blue 2.40 *36.00*

Perf. 14

98 A83 5 l + 2.50 l ol grn 8.00 *72.50*
Nos. 94-98 (5) 17.60 *161.50*
Set, never hinged 42.50

Italian Stamps of 1926 Overprinted type "f" in Black

1926 Wmk. 140 *Perf. 14*

99 A46 75c dk red & rose 70.00 20.00
a. Double overprint 450.00
100 A46 1.25 l blue & ultra 40.00 20.00
101 A46 2.50 l dk green & org 175.00 72.50
Nos. 99-101 (3) 285.00 112.50
Set, never hinged 710.00

Volta Issue

Type of Italy, 1927, Overprinted — o

1927

102 A84 20c purple 6.50 *35.00*
103 A84 50c deep orange 9.50 *23.50*
a. Double overprint 160.00
104 A84 1.25 l brt blue 14.00 *57.50*
Nos. 102-104 (3) 30.00 *116.00*
Set, never hinged 75.00

Italian Stamps of 1925-28 Overprinted type "a" in Black

1928-29

105 A86 7½c lt brown ('29) 24.00 *72.50*
106 A86 50c brt violet 87.50 65.00
Set, never hinged 270.00

Italian Stamps of 1927-28 Overprinted type "f"

1928-29

107 A86 50c brt violet 72.50 *60.00*
Never hinged 175.00

Unwmk. *Perf. 11*

107A A85 1.75 l deep brown 95.00 47.50
Never hinged 240.00

Italy No. 192 Overprinted type "o"

1928 Wmk. 140 *Perf. 14*

108 A85 50c brown & slate 24.00 12.00
Never hinged 60.00

Monte Cassino Issue

Types of 1929 Issue of Italy Overprinted in Red or Blue

1929				*Perf. 14*
109	A96	20c dk green (R)	6.50	*18.50*
110	A96	25c red orange (Bl)	6.50	*18.50*
111	A98	50c + 10c crim (Bl)	6.50	*23.50*
112	A98	75c + 15c ol brn (R)	6.50	*23.50*
113	A96	1.25 l + 25c dl vio (R)	14.50	*42.50*
114	A98	5 l + 1 l saph (R)	14.50	*47.50*

Overprinted in Red

Unwmk.

115	A100	10 l + 2 l gray brn	14.50	*70.00*
		Nos. 109-115 (7)	69.50	*244.00*
		Set, never hinged	170.00	

Royal Wedding Issue

Type of Italian Stamps of 1930 Overprinted

1930				Wmk. 140
116	A101	20c yellow green	2.60	*7.50*
117	A101	50c + 10c dp org	1.90	*9.25*
118	A101	1.25 l + 25c rose red	1.90	*19.00*
		Nos. 116-118 (3)	6.40	*35.75*
		Set, never hinged	17.50	

Lancer — A5

Scene in Massaua A6

2c, 35c, Lancer. 5c, 10c, Postman. 15c, Lineman. 25c, Askari (infantryman). 2 l, Railroad viaduct. 5 l, Asmara Deghe Selam. 10 l, Camels.

1930	Wmk. 140	Litho.		*Perf. 14*
119	A5	2c brt bl & blk	4.75	*20.00*
120	A5	5c dk vio & blk	8.00	2.40
121	A5	10c yel brn & blk	8.00	1.25
122	A5	15c dk grn & blk	8.00	1.60
123	A5	25c gray grn & blk	8.00	1.25
124	A5	35c red brn & blk	12.50	*35.00*
125	A6	1 l dk bl & blk	8.00	1.25
126	A6	2 l choc & blk	12.50	*35.00*
127	A6	5 l ol grn & blk	24.00	*52.50*
128	A6	10 l dl bl & blk	32.50	*100.00*
		Nos. 119-128 (10)	126.25	*250.25*
		Set, never hinged	300.00	

Ferrucci Issue

Types of Italian Stamps of 1930 Overprinted type "f" in Red or Blue

1930				
129	A102	20c violet (R)	5.25	*5.25*
130	A103	25c dk green (R)	5.25	*5.25*
131	A103	50c black (R)	5.25	*12.00*
132	A103	1.25 l dp blue (R)	5.25	*18.00*
133	A104	5 l + 2 l dp car (Bl)	17.00	*37.50*
		Nos. 129-133 (5)	38.00	*78.00*
		Set, never hinged	95.00	

Virgil Issue

Types of Italian Stamps of 1930 Overprinted in Red or Blue

1930				Photo.
134	A106	15c violet black	1.00	*9.50*
135	A106	20c org brn	1.00	*3.75*
136	A106	25c dark green	1.00	*3.75*
137	A106	30c lt brown	1.00	*3.75*
138	A106	50c dull violet	1.00	*3.75*
139	A106	75c rose red	1.00	*7.50*
140	A106	1.25 l gray blue	1.00	*9.50*

		Unwmk.		**Engr.**
141	A106	5 l + 1.50 l dk vio	6.75	*47.50*
142	A106	10 l + 2.50 l ol brn	6.75	*72.50*
		Nos. 134-142 (9)	20.50	*161.50*
		Set, never hinged	46.80	

Saint Anthony of Padua Issue

Types of Italian Stamps of 1931 Overprinted type "f" in Blue, Red or Black

1931		Photo.		Wmk. 140
143	A116	20c brown (Bl)	2.00	*18.00*
144	A116	25c green (R)	2.00	*7.00*
145	A118	30c gray brn (Bl)	2.00	*7.00*
146	A118	50c dl violet (Bl)	2.00	*7.00*
147	A120	1.25 l slate bl (R)	3.00	*40.00*

		Unwmk.		**Engr.**
148	A121	75c black (R)	3.00	*19.00*
149	A122	5 l + 2.50 l dk brn (Bk)	6.75	*80.00*
		Nos. 143-149 (7)	20.75	*178.00*
		Set, never hinged	44.00	

Victor Emmanuel III — A13

1931		Photo.		Wmk. 140
150	A13	7½c olive brown	1.40	*5.25*
151	A13	20c slate bl & car	1.40	.25
152	A13	30c ol grn & brn vio	1.40	.25
153	A13	40c bl & yel grn	2.40	.50
154	A13	50c bis brn & ol	1.40	.25
155	A13	75c carmine rose	4.75	.25
156	A13	1.25 l vio & indigo	5.75	5.25
157	A13	2.50 l dull green	5.75	12.00
		Nos. 150-157 (8)	24.25	24.00
		Set, never hinged	60.00	

Camel A14

Temple Ruins — A18

Designs: 2c, 10c, Camel. 5c, 15c, Shark fishery. 25c, Baobab tree. 35c, Pastoral scene. 2 l, African elephant. 5 l, Eritrean man. 10 l, Eritrean woman.

1934		Photo.		Wmk. 140
158	A14	2c deep blue	2.40	*4.75*
159	A14	5c black	4.00	.40
160	A14	10c brown	4.00	.35
161	A14	15c orange brn	4.75	*1.60*
162	A14	25c gray green	4.00	.35
163	A14	35c purple	12.50	*9.50*
164	A18	1 l dk blue gray	.80	.35
165	A14	2 l olive black	35.00	3.25
166	A18	5 l carmine rose	19.00	6.50
167	A18	10 l red orange	27.50	*22.50*
		Nos. 158-167 (10)	113.95	*49.55*
		Set, never hinged	275.00	

Abruzzi Issue

Types of 1934 Issue Overprinted in Black or Red

1934				
168	A14	10c dull blue (R)	22.50	*29.00*
169	A14	15c blue	16.00	*29.00*
170	A14	35c green (R)	9.50	*29.00*
171	A18	1 l copper red	9.50	*29.00*
172	A14	2 l rose red	27.50	*29.00*
173	A18	5 l purple (R)	19.00	*57.50*
174	A18	10 l olive grn (R)	19.00	*70.00*
		Nos. 168-174 (7)	123.00	*272.50*
		Set, never hinged	293.00	

Grant's Gazelle A22

1934				Photo.
175	A22	5c ol grn & brn	5.50	*22.50*
176	A22	10c yel brn & blk	5.50	*22.50*
177	A22	20c scar & indigo	5.50	*20.00*
178	A22	50c dk vio & brn	5.50	*20.00*
179	A22	60c org brn & ind	5.50	*27.50*
180	A22	1.25 l dk bl & grn	5.50	*47.50*
		Nos. 175-180 (6)	33.00	*160.00*
		Set, never hinged	80.00	

Second Colonial Arts Exhibition, Naples. See Nos. C1-C6.

Catalogue values for unused stamps in this section, from this point to the end of the section, are for Never Hinged items.

Between 1981 and 1986 unofficial labels appeared showing such non-Eritrean subjects as the British royal weddings, Queen Mother, Queen's birthday, and the Duke & Duchess of York. These labels are not listed.

In 1978, two sets of stamps were issued for use within liberated areas of Eritrea and to publicize the liberation effort. A May 26 set of 5c, 10c, 80c and 1b commemorated the 8th anniv. of the Eritrean People's Liberation Front (EPLF). An August 1 set of 80c, 1b, 1.50b featured the Future of Eritrea theme. A September 1, 1991 set of 5c, 15c and 20c was issued with a Freedom Fighter design in orange and black almost identical to design A24. Although the 80c from the 1st 1978 issue was available at the Asmara post office in late 1992 and early 1993, there is no evidence that any of these stamps were available at the time of independence. Thus these stamps are more properly considered locals and provisionals.

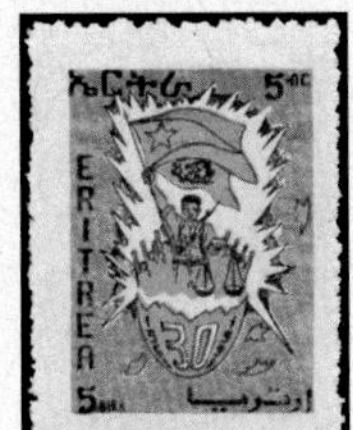

A23

Designs: Freedom fighter with EPLF flags.

1991, Jan. 16		Typo.		*Perf. 11 rough*
192	A23	5c lt bl, blk & org	*30.00*	*40.00*
193	A23	15c pale green, blk & org	*30.00*	*40.00*
194	A23	20c pale yel, blk & org	*30.00*	*40.00*
195	A23	3b silver, blk & org	*25.00*	*25.00*
196	A23	5b gold, blk & org	*25.00*	*25.00*

See footnotes following No. 199.

A24

1993, Feb. 1		Litho.		*Perf. 10*
197	A24	5c lt bl, blk & org	*25.00*	*25.00*
198	A24	15c pale grn, blk & org	*25.00*	*25.00*
199	A24	20c pale yel, blk & org	*25.00*	*25.00*

Nos. 192-199 commemorate 30 years of the war for national liberation.

Nos. 192-199 were issued for local use, and became valid for international mail on Sept. 13, 1993.

Referendum for Independence A25

Designs: 15c, Placing ballot in box. 60c, Group of arrows pointing right, one pointing left. 75c, Signs indicating "yes" & "no." 1b, Candle burning. 2b, Peace dove, horn over country map.

Perf. 14x15

1993, Apr. 22		Litho.		Wmk. 373
200	A25	15c multicolored	*1.50*	*1.50*
201	A25	60c multicolored	*2.75*	*2.75*
202	A25	75c multicolored	*4.00*	*4.00*
203	A25	1b multicolored	*7.50*	*7.50*
204	A25	2b multicolored	*10.00*	*10.00*
		Nos. 200-204 (5)	*25.75*	*25.75*

Natl. Flag — A26

1993		Litho.		*Perf. 11 rough*
		Blue Border		
205	A26	5c multicolored	*2.50*	*.50*
206	A26	20c multicolored	—	—
207	A26	35c multicolored	*4.25*	*2.00*
208	A26	50c multicolored	*11.00*	*2.50*
209	A26	70c multicolored	*3.50*	*3.50*
210	A26	80c multicolored	*3.50*	*4.00*

The border of the 40c, No. 215, is similar to that of this issue but it was issued with next set. And the type face of the "0.40" matches that set.

1994		Litho.		*Perf. 11 rough*
		Color of Border		
211	A26	5c brown	*2.00*	*1.50*
212	A26	15c red	*2.00*	*1.50*
213	A26	20c gold	*15.00*	—
214	A26	25c lt blue	*2.00*	*1.50*
215	A26	40c blue	*15.00*	*15.00*
216	A26	60c yellow	*3.00*	*2.00*
217	A26	70c purple	*3.00*	*2.25*
218	A26	3b light green	*7.50*	*6.00*
219	A26	5b silver	*9.00*	*6.00*

Flag & Map — A27

1994, Sept. 2 Litho. *Perf. 13½x14*
Color of Border

220 A27 5c deep yellow *.45* .40
221 A27 10c yellow green *.50* .45
222 A27 20c salmon *.70* .65
223 A27 25c red *1.25* 1.25
224 A27 40c lilac rose *1.40* 1.25
225 A27 60c blue green *1.50* 1.25
226 A27 70c dark green *1.60* 1.50
227 A27 1b yellow *1.60* 1.50
228 A27 2b orange *1.75* 1.50
229 A27 3b blue violet *1.90* 1.75
230 A27 5b red lilac *2.25* 2.00
231 A27 10b pale violet *3.75* 3.50
Nos. 220-231 (12) *18.65* 17.00

See Nos. 277A-277D.

World Tourism Organization, 20th Anniv. — A29

Perf. 14x13½, 13½x14
1995, Jan. 2 Litho.

232 A29 10c Fishing from boat *1.50* 1.50
233 A29 35c Monument, vert. *1.50* 1.50
234 A29 85c Winding road *3.00* 3.00
235 A29 2b Stone dwelling, vert. *5.00* 5.00
Nos. 232-235 (4) *11.00* 11.00

Fish — A30

Designs: 30c, Horned butterflyfish. 55c, Gonochaetodon larvatus. 70c, Shrimp lobster. 1b, Bluestripe snapper.

1995, Apr. 1 *Perf. 14x13½*

236 A30 30c multicolored *.60* .60
237 A30 55c multicolored *.85* .85
238 A30 70c multicolored *1.25* 1.25
239 A30 1b multicolored *1.50* 1.50
Nos. 236-239 (4) *4.20* 4.20

Independence Day — A31

Designs: 25c, Breaking chains, mountain, buildings, animals. 40c, Raising natl. flag, vert. 70c, Three men, holding natl. flag, sword, vert. 3b, Natl. flag, fireworks, vert.

Perf. 14x13½, 13½x14
1995, May 23 Litho.

240 A31 25c multicolored *.40* .40
241 A31 40c multicolored *.45* .45
242 A31 70c multicolored *.70* .70
243 A31 3b multicolored *1.40* 1.40
Nos. 240-243 (4) *2.95* 2.95

Future Development Plan — A32

1995, Aug. 28 Litho. *Perf. 13*

244 A32 60c Building bridge *.60* .60
245 A32 80c Trees *.75* .75
246 A32 90c Rural village *.90* .90
247 A32 1b Camels *1.00* 1.00
Nos. 244-247 (4) *3.25* 3.25

A33

1995, Oct. 23 *Perf. 13½x14*

248 A33 40c shown *.30* .30
249 A33 60c Tree, emblem *.40* .40
250 A33 70c Dove, "50," emblem *.50* .50
251 A33 2b like No. 248 *2.25* 2.25
Nos. 248-251 (4) *3.45* 3.45

UN, 50th anniv.

A34

COMESA, Committee for Economic Growth and Development in Southern Africa: 40c, Map of African member countries. 50c, Tree with country names on branches. 60c, Emblem, 3b, Emblem surrounded by country flags, horiz.

1995, Oct. 2 *Perf. 13½x14, 14x13½*

252 A34 40c multicolored *.30* .30
253 A34 50c multicolored *.50* .50
254 A34 60c multicolored *.60* .60
255 A34 3b multicolored *2.25* 2.25
Nos. 252-255 (4) *3.65* 3.65

FAO, 50th Anniv. — A35

5c, Food bowl with world map on it, spoon. 25c, Men with tractor. 80c, Mother bird feeding chicks. 3b, Vegetables in horn of plenty.

1995, Dec. 18 Litho. *Perf. 13x14*

256 A35 5c multicolored *.40* .40
257 A35 25c multicolored *.40* .40
258 A35 80c multicolored *.80* .80
259 A35 3b multicolored *2.50* 2.50
Nos. 256-259 (4) *4.10* 4.10

Endangered Fauna — A36

No. 260: a, Green monkey. b, Aardwolf. c, Dugong. d, Maned rat.

Beisa oryx: No. 261: a, With young. b, One facing left. c, Two with heads together. d, One facing right.

White-eyed gull: No. 262: a, Preening. b, In flight. c, Two standing. d, One facing right.

1996, July 15 Litho. *Perf. 14*

260-262 A36 3b Set of 3 strips 26.00 26.00

Nos. 260-262 were each issued in sheets of 12 stamps, containing three strips of four stamps, Nos. a.-d. No. 261 for World Wildlife Fund.

Martyrs Day — A37

1996, June 17 Litho. *Perf. 13½x14*

263 A37 40c People, flag .40 .40
264 A37 60c At grave .40 .40
265 A37 70c Mother, child .80 .80
266 A37 80c Planting crops 1.00 1.00
Nos. 263-266 (4) 2.60 2.60

1996 Summer Olympic Games, Atlanta A38

No. 267, Cycling. No. 268, Basketball, vert. No. 269, Volleyball, vert. No. 270, Soccer.

No. 271, vert: a, Volleyball. b, Laurel wreath. c, Basketball. d, Torch. e, Cycling, yellow shirt. f, Torch, diff. g, Cycling, green shirt. h, Gold medal. i, Soccer.

Each 10b: No. 272, Soccer, vert. No. 273, Cycling, vert.

1996, Nov. 20 Litho. *Perf. 14*

267-270 A38 3b Set of 4 7.50 7.50
271 A38 2b Sheet of 9, #a.-i. 11.00 11.00

Souvenir Sheets

272-273 A38 Set of 2 11.00 11.00

UNICEF, 50th Anniv. A39

UNICEF emblem and: 40c, Mother with child. 55c, Nurse helping child. 60c, Weighing baby. 95c, Boy with one leg walking with crutch.

1996, Dec. 9 Litho. *Perf. 14x13½*

274 A39 40c multicolored .45 .45
275 A39 55c multicolored .45 .45
276 A39 60c multicolored 1.00 1.00
277 A39 95c multicolored 1.00 1.00
Nos. 274-277 (4) 2.90 2.90

Flag and Map Type of 1994 Redrawn With Islands Added on Map at Lower Right

1996, Dec. 25 Litho. *Perf. 13½x14*
Color of Border

277A A27 20c salmon — —
277B A27 40c lilac rose — —
277C A27 60c blue green — —
277D A27 3b blue violet — —

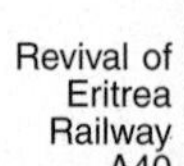

Revival of Eritrea Railway A40

Designs: 40c, Repairing track. 55c, Steam train arriving at station. 60c, Train shuttle transporting people. 95c, Train tunnel.

1997, Jan. 10

278 A40 40c multicolored .50 .50
279 A40 55c multicolored .50 .50
280 A40 60c multicolored .50 .50
281 A40 95c multicolored 1.50 1.50
Nos. 278-281 (4) 3.00 3.00

National Service A41

40c, Service members, speaker's platform, flags, vert. 55c, People looking over mountainside, vert. 60c, People digging ditches. 95c, Man standing on mountain top, overlooking valley, lake.

1996, Dec. 28 *Perf. 13½x14, 14x13½*

282 A41 40c multicolored .75 .75
283 A41 55c multicolored .75 .75
284 A41 60c multicolored 1.25 1.25
285 A41 95c multicolored 2.00 2.00
Nos. 282-285 (4) 4.75 4.75

Butterflies and Moths A42

1b, Pieris napi. 2b, Heliconius melpomerie. 4b, Ornithoptera goliath. 8b, Heliconius astraea.

No. 290, vert, each 3b: a, Psaphis eusehemoides. b, Papilio brookiana. c, Parnassius charitonius. d, Morpho cypris. e, Dariaus plexippus. f, Precis octavia. g, Teinopalpus imperialis. h, Samia gloreri. i, Automeris nyctimene.

No. 291, each 3b: a, Papilio polymnestar. b, Ornithoptera paradiseo. c, Graphium marcellus. d, Panaxia quadripunctaria. e, Cardui japonica. f, Papilio childrence. g, Philosamea cynthis. h, Actias luna. i, Heticopis acit.

Each 10b: No. 292, Papilio glaucus. No. 293, Parnassius phoebus.

1997, June 16 Litho. *Perf. 14*

286-289 A42 Set of 4 12.00 12.00

Sheets of 9

290-291 A42 3b Set of 2 Sheets, #a.-i. 30.00 30.00

Souvenir Sheets

292-293 A42 10b Set of 2 Sheets 15.00 15.00

Environmental Protection — A43

1997, Aug. 15 Litho. *Perf. 14x13½*

294 A43 60c Irrigation .90 .90
295 A43 90c Reforestation .90 .90
296 A43 95c Preventing erosion 2.00 2.00
Nos. 294-296 (3) 3.80 3.80

Marine Life A44

No. 297, each 3n: a, Sergeant major, white tipped reef shark. b, Hawksbill turtle, devil ray (e). c, Surgeonfish. d, Red sea houndfish, humpback whale (a, g). e, Devil ray (b, f, h). f, Devil ray (e, c), two-banded clownfish. g, Long-nosed butterflyfish. h, Red sea houndfish (g), yellow sweetlips (i). i, White moray eel.

No. 298, each 3n: a, Masked butterflyfish. b, Suckerfish (a), whale shark (a). c, Sunrise dottyback, bluefin trevally. d, Moon wrasse (a), purple moon angel (a), two-banded anemonefish. e, Lionfish (b, f). f, White tipped shark, sand diver fish. g, Golden jacks (d), lunar tailed grouper. h, Batfish (e, i). i, Black triggerfish.

Each 10n: No. 299, Powder-blue surgeonfish. No. 300, Twin-spot wrasse.

1997, Dec. 29 Litho. *Perf. 14*
Sheets of 9, #a.-i.

297-298 A44 Set of 2 20.00 20.00

Souvenir Sheets

299-300 A44 Set of 2 Sheets 12.50 12.50

A45

Natl. Constitution: 10c, Speaker, crowd seated beneath tree. 40c, Dove, scales of justice. 85c, Hands holding constitution.

1997, Oct. 24 Litho. *Perf. 13½x14*

301-303 A45 Set of 3 3.50 3.50

A46

Birds — No. 304, each 3n: a, African darter (b, d, e). b, White-headed vulture (e). c, Egyptian vulture (f). d, Yellow-billed hornbill (g). e, Helmeted guineafowl (d, f). f, Secretary bird (d, e, i). g, Martial eagle (h). h, Bateleur eagle (i). i, Red-billed queleas.

No. 305, each 3n: a, Black-headed weaver. b, Abyssinian roller (c, f). c, Abyssinian ground hornbill (b, e, f). d, Lichtenstein's sandgrouse. e, Erckel's francolin (d, g, h). f, Arabian bustard (e, i). g, Chestnut-backed finch-lark. h, Desert lark. i, Bifasciated lark.

Each 10n: #306, Peregrine falcon. #307, Hoopoe.

1998, Mar. 16 Litho. *Perf. 14*
Sheets of 9, #a.-i.

304-305 A46 Set of 2 25.00 25.00

Souvenir Sheets

306-307 A46 Set of 2 Sheets 12.00 12.00

Dwellings — A47

1998, July 1 Litho. *Perf. 13½x14*

308 A47 50c Highlanders 1.50 1.50
309 A47 60c Lowlanders 1.50 1.50
310 A47 85c Danakils (Afars) 1.50 1.50
Nos. 308-310 (3) 4.50 4.50

Traditional Hair Styles — A48

1998, Nov. 23 Litho. *Perf. 13½x14*

311 A48 10c Cunama .30 .30
312 A48 50c Tignnys .60 .60
313 A48 85c Bilen 1.00 1.00
314 A48 95c Tigre 1.25 1.25
Nos. 311-314 (4) 3.15 3.15

Dated 1997.

A49

Traditional Musical Instruments: 15c, Chirawata. 60c, Imbilta, malaket, shambeko. 75c, Kobero. 85c, K'rar.

1998, Dec. 28 Litho. *Perf. 13½x14*

315 A49 15c multicolored .35 .35
316 A49 60c multicolored .60 .60
317 A49 75c multicolored .80 .80
318 A49 85c multicolored 1.00 1.00
Nos. 315-318 (4) 2.75 2.75

A50

1999, May 25 Litho. *Perf. 13¼x14*

319 A50 60c green & multi .60 .60
320 A50 1n red & multi 1.00 1.00
321 A50 3n blue & multi 4.00 4.00
Nos. 319-321 (3) 5.60 5.60

Independence, 8th Anniv.

1997 Introduction of Nakfa Currency — A51

Bank notes: 10c, 1 Nakfa. 60c, 5 Nakfa. 80c, 10 Nakfa. 1n, 20 Nakfa. 2n, 50 Nakfa. 3n, 100 Nakfa.

1999, Nov. 8 Litho. *Perf. 13¼*

322 A51 10c multicolored .45 .45
323 A51 60c multicolored .60 .60
324 A51 80c multicolored .75 .75
325 A51 1n multicolored 1.00 1.00
326 A51 2n multicolored 2.00 2.00
327 A51 3n multicolored 3.50 3.50
Nos. 322-327 (6) 8.30 8.30

Natl. Union of Eritrean Women, 20th Anniv. A52

Designs: 5c, Woman and child, vert. 10c, Three women. 25c, Women and flag. 1n, Woman with binoculars.

Perf. 13¼x14, 14x13¼
1999, Nov. 26

328 A52 5c multicolored .35 .35
329 A52 10c multicolored .35 .35
330 A52 25c multicolored .50 .50
331 A52 1n multicolored .75 .75
Nos. 328-331 (4) 1.95 1.95

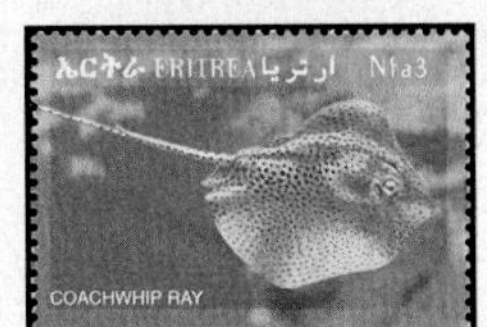

A53

Marine Life A54

No. 332, each 3n: a, Coachwhip ray. b, Sulfur damselfish. c, "Gray moray." d, Sabre squirrelfish. e, Rusty parrotfish. f, "Striped eel catfish."

No. 333, each 3n: a, Spangled emperor. b, Devil scorpionfish. c, Crown squirrelfish. d, Vanikoro sweeper. e, Sergeant major. f, Giant manta.

No. 334, each 3n: a, Chilomycterus spilostylus. b, Dascyllus marginatus. c, Balistapus undulatus. d, Pomacanthus semicirculatus. e, Rhinecanthus assasi. f, Millepora.

No. 335, each 3n: a, Epinephalus fasciata. b, Pygoplites diacanthus. c, Cephalopholis miniata. d, Centropyge eibli. e, Ostracion cubicus. f, Heniochus acuminatus.

Each 10n: No. 336, Centropyge flavissimus. No. 337, Larabicus quadrilineatus. No. 338, Anthias squamipinnis. 15n, Pomacanthus maculosus.

2000, Apr. 17 Litho. *Perf. 14*
Sheets of 6, #a.-f.

332-333 A53 Set of 2 13.50 13.50
334-335 A54 Set of 2 13.50 13.50

Souvenir Sheets

336-338 A54 Set of 3 15.00 15.00
339 A54 15n multi 6.00 6.00

Illustrations on Nos. 332c and 332f were switched.

A55

Flag and: 5c, Man with sword. 10c, Ship Denden Assab. 25c, Independence Day festivities. 60c, Soldiers and barracks. 1n, Finger, heart and map. 2n, People under tree. 3n, Ballot box. 5n, Eritrean seal, military plane, tank, ship. 7n, Seal. 10n, Ten-nakfa note.

Perf. 13¾x13¼
2000, Mar. 17 Litho.
Denominations in Sans-Serif Type

340-349 A55 Set of 10 16.00 16.00

See Nos. 363A-363F.

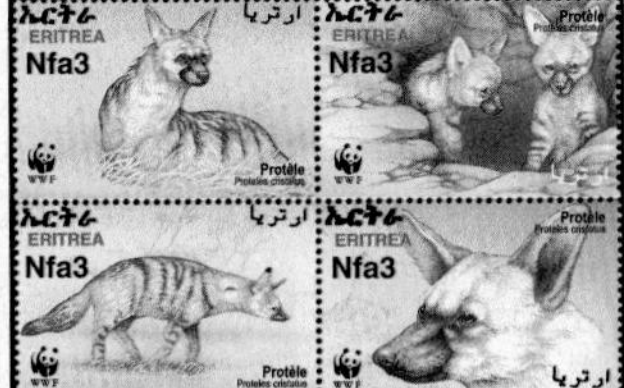

Worldwide Fund for Nature (WWF) — A56

Proteles cristatus: a, Laying down. b. Pair in den. c, Walking. d, Close-up.

2001, Oct. 1 Litho. *Perf. 14*

350 A56 3n Block or strip of 4, #a-d 4.50 4.50

Wild Animals — A57

No. 351, 3n: a, Salt's dik-dik. b, Klipspringer. c, Greater kudu. d, Soemmering's gazelle. e, Dorcas gazelle. f, Somali wild ass.

No. 352, 3n: a, Aardvark. b, Black-backed jackal. c, Striped hyena. d, Spotted hyena. e, East African leopard. f, African elephant.

2001, Oct. 29 Sheets of 6, #a-f

351-352 A57 Set of 2 10.00 10.00

Struggle for Independence, 10th Anniv. — A58

Designs: 20c, Women, flag, jewelry. 60c, Doves, stylized flag, vert. 1n, Bees, honeycomb, flag, vert. 3n, Men with sticks, vert.

Perf. 13x13¼, 13¼x13
2001, May 23 Litho.

353-356 A58 Set of 4 3.00 3.00

Liberation of Nakfa, 25th Anniv. A59

Designs: 50c, Denden. 1n, Town of Nakfa, 1977 (77x27mm). 3n, First Organizational Congress of the Eritrean People's Liberation Front (77x27mm).

2002, Mar. 23 Litho. *Perf. 14x13¼*

357-359 A59 Set of 3 2.00 2.00

Martyr's Day — A60

Designs: 1n, People and map. 2n, Hand, map of Badma area, and flag. 3n, Map and ship. 5n, Dove, map and dead man (49x29mm, triangular).

Perf. 14x13¼, 13½ (5n)
2002, June 20

360-363 A60 Set of 4 4.50 4.50

Type of 2000 Redrawn

Flag and: 30c, People under tree. 45c, Man with sword. 50c, Independence Day festivities. 60c, Soldiers and barracks. 75c, Ship Denden Assab. 3n, Ballot box.

2002, Oct. 21 Litho. *Perf. 13¼x14¼*
Denominations in Serifed Type

363A A55 30c multi — —
363B A55 45c multi — —
363C A55 50c multi — —
363D A55 60c multi — —
363E A55 75c multi — —
363F A55 3n multi — —

Denominations on Nos. 340-349 are in sans-serif type.

Dr. Fred C. Hollows (1929-93), Ophthalmologist A61

Designs: 50c, Portrait. 1n, Hollows wearing ophthalmological equipment. 2n, Hollows with man.

2003, Feb. 10 *Perf. 13¼x14*

364-366 A61 Set of 3 2.00 2.00

Eritrea — People's Republic of China Diplomatic Relations, 10th Anniv. A62

2003, May 24 *Perf. 12*

367 A62 4.50n multi 2.50 2.50

Eritrean postal authorities have declared "illegal" the following items:

Sheetlet of nine 5n stamps depicting Trains;

Sheetlets of nine 3n stamps depicting Marilyn Monroe (two different), Dogs, The Beatles "Yellow Submarine," September 11 firefighters, Brigitte Bardot, Grace Kelly, Sophia Loren, Golf etiquette, Sexy actresses, Sexy models, Boris Vallejo nudes, Dorian Cleavenger, Michael Möbius, Olivia, Ricky Carralero, Concorde;

Sheetlets of six stamps with various denominations depicting Lighthouses (with Rotary emblem) (two different), Hopper paintings (two different), Vettriano paintings (two different), Marilyn Monroe (two different), Elvgren pin-ups (two different), Teddy bears (two different);

Sheetlets of six 3n stamps depicting Van Gogh paintings, Paintings of nudes;

Sheetlets of five 3n stamps depicting Corot paintings, Pisarro paintings, Renoir paintings, Elvis Presley, Marilyn Monroe;

Sheetlets of four stamps with various denominations depicting Pandas (with Scouting emblem), Crocodiles (with Scouting emblem), Buffalos (with Rotary emblem), Elephants (with Rotary emblem), Monkeys (with Scouting emblem), Lizards (with Scouting emblem), Snakes (with Scouting Emblem), Turtles (with Rotary emblem), Wild cats (with Scouting emblem), Birds of prey (with Rotary emblem), Fowl (with Rotary emblem), Parrots (with Scouting emblem), Penguins (with Rotary emblem), Fish (with Rotary emblem), Marine life (with Scouting emblem), Mushrooms (with Rotary emblem), Butterflies (with Scouting emblem), Bees (with Scouting emblem), Spiders (with Scouting emblem);

Sheetlets of four 3n stamps depicting Dinosaurs (with Scouting emblem), Dinosaurs (with Rotary emblem) Elephants (with Scouting emblem), Elephants (with Rotary emblem), Horses (with Scouting emblem), Horses (with Rotary emblem), Birds (with Scouting emblem), Birds (with Rotary emblem), Penguins (with Scouting emblem), Penguins (with Rotary emblem), Orchids (with Scouting emblem), Orchids (with Rotary emblem), Butterflies (with Scouting emblem), Butterflies (with Rotary emblem), Cars (with Scouting emblem), Cars (with Rotary emblem), Motorcycles (with Scouting emblem), Motorcycles (with Rotary emblem), Trains (with Scouting emblem), Trains (with Rotary emblem);

Sheetlets of three 5n stamps depicting Dinosaurs (with Rotary emblem) (two different), Pandas;

Strips of three 5n stamps depicting Steam trains (four different);

Souvenir sheet with one 8n stamp depicting Steam Trains (with Rotary emblem) (two different), Dinosaurs (with Rotary emblem), Pandas (with Scouting emblem), Elephants (with Scouting emblem), Tigers (with Scouting emblem), Birds of prey (with Scouting emblem);

Souvenir sheets with one 5n stamp depicting Marilyn Monroe (six different), Lighthouses (with Rotary emblem) (four different), Teddy bears (four different), Hopper paintings (two different), Vettriano paintings (two different).

Eritrean Railway A63

Independence Celebrations A63a

Massawa A63b

2003 **Litho.** *Perf. 14x13¼*

Denomination Color

368	A63	5c	Prussian blue	.25	.25
369	A63	10c	greenish blk	.25	.25
370	A63	15c	lilac	.25	.25
371	A63	35c	violet	.25	.25
372	A63	50c	orange	.25	.25
373	A63	90c	olive green	.25	.25
374	A63	1n	red	.25	.25
375	A63	2n	blue violet	.55	.55
376	A63	10n	red	2.75	2.75
376A	A63a	50n	white	12.00	12.00
376B	A63b	75n	white	18.00	18.00
376C	A63	100n	white	24.00	24.00
			Nos. 368-376C (12)	59.05	59.05

Issued: 50n, 75n, 100n, 8/29.

Liberation of Massawa, 14th Anniv. A64

Designs: 40c, Tanks as fountains. 50c, Boat with soldiers.

No. 379: a, 3n, Crashed airplane, people, soldiers in shallow water. b, 3n, Tank, soldier, flag, boat. c, 4n, People, buildings at shore.

2004

377-378 A64 Set of 2 1.00 1.00

Miniature Sheet

379 A64 Sheet of 3, #a-c 4.00 4.00

Man and Camels — A65

Man and Cattle A66

Highland Woman, Child and Camel — A67

2004, July 12 **Litho.** *Perf. 12*

Frame Color

380	A65	20c	violet blue	.25	.25
381	A65	25c	red violet	.25	.25
382	A65	40c	brown	.25	.25
383	A66	50c	red	.25	.25
384	A66	55c	green	.25	.25
385	A66	60c	light blue	.25	.25
386	A67	80c	olive green	.50	.50
387	A67	1n	orange	.50	.50
388	A67	4.50n	blue	1.25	1.25
			Nos. 380-388 (9)	3.75	3.75

A68

A69

Monuments and Statues — A70

Perf. 13¼x14, 14x13¼

2006, Jan. 5 **Litho.**

389	A68	1.50n	multi	.25	.25
390	A69	6n	multi	.80	.80
391	A70	25n	multi	3.50	3.50
			Nos. 389-391 (3)	4.55	4.55

China - Africa Cooperation Forum, Beijing — A71

2006, Nov. 3 **Litho.** *Perf. 12*

392 A71 7n multi .95 .95

African Soccer Confederation, 50th Anniv. — A72

Anniversary emblem and: 3n, Eritrean soccer players and flags. 5n, Soccer field. 10n, Soccer players in action.

2007, May 29 **Litho.** *Perf. 13x13¼*

393-395 A72 Set of 3 2.40 2.40

Soldiers Carrying Flag — A73

2008, Dec. 31 **Litho.** *Perf. 14x13¼*

Denomination Color

396	A73	15c	dark blue	.25	.25
397	A73	35c	green	.25	.25
398	A73	50c	orange	.25	.25
399	A73	70c	red	.25	.25
400	A73	75c	blue	.25	.25
401	A73	90c	brown	.25	.25
402	A73	1.50n	red violet	.25	.25
403	A73	2n	indigo	.25	.25
404	A73	3n	org yellow	.40	.40
405	A73	5n	gray	.65	.65
406	A73	10n	yel green	1.25	1.25
			Nos. 396-406 (11)	4.30	4.30

Eritrean National Festival A74

Ethnic groups in costume: 5c, Afars. 10c, Bilens. 30c, Hedarebs. 95c, Kunamas. 1n, Naras. 1.50n, Rashaidas. 4n, Sahos. 7n, Tigres. 8n, Tigrinyas.

2010, Nov. 15

407-415 A74 Set of 9 4.25 4.25

Independence, 20th Anniv. — A75

Designs: 70c, Eritrean flag, stylized people defining border. 95c, Map of Eritrea, hand holding torch, vert. 8n, Map of Africa, flag of Eritrea, vert.

2011, Mar. 24 *Perf. 14x13¼, 13¼x14*

416-418 A75 Set of 3 2.00 2.00

Eritrean Martyr's Day, 20th Anniv. — A76

Designs: 80c, Eritreans and woman holding shining square. 9n, Woamn and child lighting candles

2011, June 17 *Perf. 13¾x13¼*

419-420 A76 Set of 2 2.10 2.10

Eritrean Armed Struggle, 50th Anniv. — A77

Designs: 1.50n, Arm holding rifle, "50," flame, stylized people. 7n, Flame, arms holding rifles.

2011, Sept. 3 *Perf. 13¼x14*

421-422 A77 Set of 2 1.75 1.75

Miniature Sheet

Diplomatic Relations Between Eritrea and People's Republic of China, 20th Anniv. — A78

No. 423: a, 1n, Mosque, Nakfa, Eritrea. b, 1n, Harbor, Massawa, Eritrea. c, 1.50n, Pagoda and bridge, Yan'an, People's Republic of China. d, 1.50n, Harbor, Qingdao, People's Republic of China. e, 7n, Buildings, Asmara, Eritrea. f, 7n, Camels. g, 10n, Buildings, Datong, People's Republic of China. h, 10n, Antelopes.

2013, May 27 Litho. *Perf. 12*

423	A78	Block of 8, #a-h	8.50	8.50
i.		Souvenir sheet of 8, #423a-423h	8.50	8.50

Gelaalo A79

2013, June 27 Litho. *Perf. 13x13¼*

Frame Color

424	A79	55c orange yellow	.50	.50
425	A79	60c green	.55	.55
426	A79	70c purple	.60	.60
427	A79	80c blue	.70	.70
428	A79	90c red	.80	.80
429	A79	95c olive yellow	.85	.85
430	A79	1.50n yellow brown	1.40	1.40
431	A79	50n light blue	42.50	42.50
		Nos. 424-431 (8)	47.90	47.90

Operation Fenkil, 25th Anniv. — A80

Designs: 3n, Soldiers watching man in water. 7n, Tank in Massawa. 10n, Soldiers watching people in boats.

Perf. 13¼x13¾

2015, Feb. 10 Litho.

432-434	A80	Set of 3	4.25	4.25

A81

Liberation of Eritrea, 25th Anniv. A82

2016 Litho. *Perf. 14x14¼*

435	A81	7n multi	1.40	1.40
436	A82	8n multi	1.60	1.60

Souvenir Sheet

Liberation of Eritrea, 25th Anniv. — A83

No. 437: a, 3n, Eritrean flag. b, 4n, Flagbearer and camel's head. c, 5n, Body of camel.

2016 Litho. *Perf. 14x13½*

437	A83	Sheet of 3, #a-c	2.75	2.75

SEMI-POSTAL STAMPS

Many issues of Italy and Italian Colonies include one or more semipostal denominations. To avoid splitting sets, these issues are generally listed as regular postage, airmail, etc., unless all values carry a surtax.

Italy Nos. B1-B3 Overprinted type "f"

1915-16 Wmk. 140 *Perf. 14*

B1	SP1	10c + 5c rose	4.00	*16.00*
a.		"EPITREA"	32.50	*45.00*
b.		Inverted overprint	800.00	800.00
B2	SP2	15c + 5c slate	32.50	*27.50*
B3	SP2	20c + 5c orange	4.75	*35.00*
a.		"EPITREA"	80.00	*110.00*
b.		Inverted overprint	800.00	800.00
c.		Pair, one without ovpt.	—	*4,500.*
		Nos. B1-B3 (3)	41.25	*78.50*
		Set, never hinged	102.00	

No. B2 Surcharged

1916

B4	SP2	20c on 15c+5c slate	32.50	*35.00*
		Never hinged	80.00	
a.		"EPITREA"	80.00	*110.00*
b.		Pair, one without overprint	2,000.	

Counterfeits exist of the minor varieties of Nos. B1, B3-B4.

Holy Year Issue
Italy Nos. B20-B25 Overprinted in Black or Red

1925 *Perf. 12*

B5	SP4	20c + 10c dk grn & brn	4.00	*24.00*
B6	SP4	30c + 15c dk brn & brn	4.00	*27.50*
a.		Double overprint		
B7	SP4	50c + 25c vio & brn	4.00	*24.00*
B8	SP4	60c + 30c dp rose & brn	4.00	*32.50*
a.		Inverted overprint		
B9	SP8	1 l + 50c dp bl & vio (R)	4.00	*40.00*
B10	SP8	5 l + 2.50 l org brn & vio (R)	4.00	*60.00*
		Nos. B5-B10 (6)	24.00	*208.00*
		Set, never hinged	60.00	

Colonial Institute Issue

"Peace" Substituting Spade for Sword — SP1

1926 Typo. *Perf. 14*

B11	SP1	5c + 5c brown	1.20	*9.50*
B12	SP1	10c + 5c olive grn	1.20	*9.50*
B13	SP1	20c + 5c blue grn	1.20	*9.50*
B14	SP1	40c + 5c brown red	1.20	*9.50*
B15	SP1	60c + 5c orange	1.20	*9.50*
B16	SP1	1 l + 5c blue	1.20	*20.00*
		Nos. B11-B16 (6)	7.20	*67.50*
		Set, never hinged	18.00	

The surtax of 5c on each stamp was for the Italian Colonial Institute.

Italian Semi-Postal Stamps of 1926 Overprinted

1927 Unwmk. *Perf. 11½*

B17	SP10	40c + 20c dk brn & blk	4.00	*45.00*
B18	SP10	60c + 30c brn red & ol brn	4.00	*45.00*
B19	SP10	1.25 l + 60c dp bl & blk	4.00	*65.00*
B20	SP10	5 l + 2.50 l dk grn & blk	6.50	*100.00*
		Nos. B17-B20 (4)	18.50	*255.00*
		Set, never hinged	46.00	

The surtax on these stamps was for the charitable work of the Voluntary Militia for Italian National Defense.

Fascism and Victory — SP2

1928 Wmk. 140 Typo. *Perf. 14*

B21	SP2	20c + 5c blue grn	3.25	*14.00*
B22	SP2	30c + 5c red	3.25	*14.00*
B23	SP2	50c + 10c purple	3.25	*24.00*
B24	SP2	1.25 l + 20c dk blue	4.00	*32.50*
		Nos. B21-B24 (4)	13.75	*84.50*
		Set, never hinged	34.00	

The surtax was for the Society Africana d'Italia, whose 46th anniv. was commemorated by the issue.

Types of Italian Semi-Postal Stamps of 1928 Overprinted type "f"

1929 Unwmk. *Perf. 11*

B25	SP10	30c + 10c red & blk	4.75	*27.50*
B26	SP10	50c + 20c vio & blk	4.75	*30.00*
B27	SP10	1.25 l + 50c brn & bl	7.25	*52.50*
B28	SP10	5 l + 2 l olive grn & blk	7.25	*100.00*
		Nos. B25-B28 (4)	24.00	*210.00*
		Set, never hinged	60.00	

Surtax for the charitable work of the Voluntary Militia for Italian Natl. Defense.

Types of Italian Semi-Postal Stamps of 1930 Overprinted type "f" in Black or Red

1930 *Perf. 14*

B29	SP10	30c + 10c dk grn & bl grn (Bk)	35.00	*65.00*
B30	SP10	50c + 10c dk grn & vio	35.00	*100.00*
B31	SP10	1.25 l + 30c ol brn & red brn	35.00	*100.00*
B32	SP10	5 l + 1.50 l ind & grn	120.00	*275.00*
		Nos. B29-B32 (4)	225.00	*540.00*
		Set, never hinged	560.00	

Surtax for the charitable work of the Voluntary Militia for Italian Natl. Defense.

Agriculture — SP3

1930 Photo. Wmk. 140

B33	SP3	50c + 20c ol brn	4.00	*25.00*
B34	SP3	1.25 l + 20c dp bl	4.00	*25.00*
B35	SP3	1.75 l + 20c green	4.00	*27.50*
B36	SP3	2.55 l + 50c purple	9.50	*45.00*
B37	SP3	5 l + 1 l dp car	9.50	*67.50*
		Nos. B33-B37 (5)	31.00	*190.00*
		Set, never hinged	76.00	

Italian Colonial Agricultural Institute, 25th anniv. The surtax aided that institution.

AIR POST STAMPS

Desert Scene AP1

Design: 80c, 1 l, 2 l, Plane and globe.

Wmk. Crowns (140)

1934, Oct. 17 Photo. *Perf. 14*

C1	AP1	25c sl bl & org red	5.50	*22.50*
C2	AP1	50c grn & indigo	5.50	*20.00*
C3	AP1	75c brn & org red	5.50	*20.00*
C4	AP1	80c org brn & ol grn	5.50	*22.50*
C5	AP1	1 l scar & ol grn	5.50	*27.50*
C6	AP1	2 l dk bl & brn	5.50	*47.50*
		Nos. C1-C6 (6)	33.00	*160.00*
		Set, never hinged	81.00	

Second Colonial Arts Exhibition, Naples.

Plowing AP3

Plane and Cacti
AP6

Designs: 25c, 1.50 l, Plowing. 50c, 2 l, Plane over mountain pass. 60c, 5 l, Plane and trees. 75c, 10 l, Plane and cacti. 1 l, 3 l, Bridge.

1936 **Photo.**
C7 AP3 25c deep green 4.75 *4.75*
C8 AP3 50c dark brown 3.25 .35
C9 AP3 60c brn org 6.50 *16.00*
C10 AP6 75c org brn 4.75 1.60
C11 AP3 1 l deep blue 1.60 .35
C12 AP3 1.50 l purple 6.50 .85
C13 AP3 2 l gray blue 6.50 *3.25*
C14 AP3 3 l copper red 25.00 27.50
C15 AP3 5 l green 19.00 8.00
C16 AP6 10 l rose red 45.00 27.50
Nos. C7-C16 (10) 122.85 90.15
Set, never hinged 300.00

AIR POST SEMI-POSTAL STAMPS

King Victor Emmanuel III — SPAP1

1934 **Wmk. 140** **Photo.** ***Perf. 14***
CB1 SPAP1 25c + 10c 9.50 *27.50*
CB2 SPAP1 50c + 10c 9.50 *27.50*
CB3 SPAP1 75c + 15c 9.50 *27.50*
CB4 SPAP1 80c + 15c 9.50 *27.50*
CB5 SPAP1 1 l + 20c 9.50 *27.50*
CB6 SPAP1 2 l + 20c 9.50 *27.50*
CB7 SPAP1 3 l + 25c 27.50 *125.00*
CB8 SPAP1 5 l + 25c 27.50 *125.00*
CB9 SPAP1 10 l + 30c 27.50 *125.00*
CB10 SPAP1 25 l + 2 l 27.50 *125.00*
Nos. CB1-CB10 (10) 167.00 *665.00*
Set, never hinged 410.00

65th birthday of King Victor Emmanuel III and the nonstop flight from Rome to Mogadiscio. Used values are for stamps canceled to order.

AIR POST SEMI-POSTAL OFFICIAL STAMP

Type of Air Post Semi-Postal Stamps, 1934, Overprinted in Black

1934 **Wmk. 140** ***Perf. 14***
CBO1 SPAP1 25 l + 2 l cop red *2,800.*
Never hinged *5,500.*

SPECIAL DELIVERY STAMPS

Special Delivery Stamps of Italy, Overprinted type "a"

1907 **Wmk. 140** ***Perf. 14***
E1 SD1 25c rose red 24.00 20.00
Never hinged 60.00
a. Double overprint — —

1909
E2 SD2 30c blue & rose 145.00 *240.00*
Never hinged 375.00

1920
E3 SD1 50c dull red 4.00 *24.00*
Never hinged 10.00

"Italia"
SD1

1924 **Engr.** **Unwmk.**
E4 SD1 60c dk red & brn 6.50 *24.00*
a. Perf. 13½ 14.00 *40.00*
E5 SD1 2 l dk blue & red 17.50 *27.50*
Set, never hinged 59.00

For surcharges see Nos. E6-E8.

Nos. E4 and E5 Surcharged in Dark Blue or Red

v

w

1926
E6 SD1 70c on 60c (Bl) 6.50 *16.00*
E7 SD1 2.50 l on 2 l (R) 17.50 *27.50*
Set, never hinged 60.00

Type of 1924 Surcharged in Blue or Black

1927-35 ***Perf. 11***
E8 SD1 1.25 l on 60c dk red & brn (Bl) 16.00 4.00
Never hinged 40.00
a. Perf. 14 (Bl) ('35) 110.00 24.00
Never hinged 275.00
b. Perf. 11 (Bk) ('35) *9,500.* 1,250.
Never hinged *14,500.*
c. Perf. 14 (Bk) ('35) 400.00 65.00
Never hinged 1,000.

AUTHORIZED DELIVERY STAMP

Authorized Delivery Stamp of Italy, No. EY2, Overprinted Type "f" in Black

1939-41 **Wmk. 140** ***Perf. 14***
EY1 AD2 10c dk brown ('41) .80
Never hinged 2.00
a. 10c reddish brown 27.50 *47.50*
Never hinged 72.50

On No. EY1a, which was used in Italian East Africa, the overprint hits the figures "10." On No. EY1, which was sold in Rome, the overprint falls above the 10's.

POSTAGE DUE STAMPS

Postage Due Stamps of Italy Overprinted type "a" at Top

1903 **Wmk. 140** ***Perf. 14***
J1 D3 5c buff & mag 24.00 *47.50*
a. Double overprint 550.00
J2 D3 10c buff & mag 16.00 *47.50*
J3 D3 20c buff & mag 16.00 *32.50*
J4 D3 30c buff & mag 24.00 *35.00*
J5 D3 40c buff & mag 80.00 *72.50*
J6 D3 50c buff & mag 87.50 72.50
J7 D3 60c buff & mag 24.00 *72.50*
J8 D3 1 l blue & mag 16.00 *40.00*
J9 D3 2 l blue & mag 200.00 *180.00*
J10 D3 5 l blue & mag 325.00 340.00
J11 D3 10 l blue & mag 3,600. 875.00
Never hinged 7,200.
Set, #J1-J10, never hinged 1,600.

Same with Overprint at Bottom

1920-22
J1b D3 5c buff & magenta 4.75 *16.00*
c. Numeral and ovpt. inverted 550.00 550.00
J2a D3 10c buff & magenta 8.00 *16.00*
J3a D3 20c buff & magenta 950.00 475.00
J4a D3 30c buff & magenta 65.00 65.00
J5a D3 40c buff & magenta 47.50 52.50
J6a D3 50c buff & magenta 24.00 *47.50*
J7a D3 60c buff & magenta 24.00 *47.50*
J8a D3 1 l blue & magenta 40.00 47.50
J9a D3 2 l blue & magenta 1,900. 1,450.
J10a D3 5 l blue & magenta 475.00 350.00
J11a D3 10 l blue & magenta 47.50 *100.00*
Set, never hinged 7,125.

1903 **Wmk. 140**
J12 D4 50 l yellow 875.00 300.00
J13 D4 100 l blue 475.00 180.00
Set, never hinged 2,700.

1927
J14 D3 60c buff & brown 160.00 *240.00*
Never hinged 325.00

Postage Due Stamps of Italy, 1934, Overprinted type "j" in Black

1934
J15 D6 5c brown .80 *16.00*
J16 D6 10c blue .80 *3.25*
J17 D6 20c rose red 4.00 *4.75*
a. Inverted overprint — —
J18 D6 25c green 4.00 *6.50*
J19 D6 30c red orange 4.00 *16.00*
J20 D6 40c black brown 4.00 *16.00*
J21 D6 50c violet 4.00 2.40
J22 D6 60c black 8.00 *24.00*
J23 D7 1 l red orange 4.00 3.25
a. Inverted overprint 550.00 —
J24 D7 2 l green 16.00 *47.50*
J25 D7 5 l violet 28.00 *55.00*
J26 D7 10 l blue 32.50 *65.00*
J27 D7 20 l carmine rose 40.00 *72.50*
a. Inverted overprint 550.00 —
Nos. J15-J27 (13) 150.10 *332.15*
Set, never hinged 375.00

PARCEL POST STAMPS

These stamps were used by affixing them to the way bill so that one half remained on it following the parcel, the other half staying on the receipt given the sender. Most used halves are right halves. Complete stamps were obtainable canceled, probably to order. Both unused and used values are for complete stamps.

Parcel Post Stamps of Italy, 1914-17, Overprinted type "j" in Black on Each Half

1916 **Wmk. 140** ***Perf. 13½***
Q1 PP2 5c brown 145.00 *225.00*
Q2 PP2 10c deep blue *2,600.* *4,250.*
Never hinged 5,250.
Q3 PP2 25c red 290.00 *350.00*
Q4 PP2 50c orange 72.50 *225.00*
Q5 PP2 1 l violet 145.00 *225.00*
Q6 PP2 2 l green 110.00 *225.00*
Q7 PP2 3 l bister 875.00 *625.00*
Q8 PP2 4 l slate 875.00 *625.00*
Set #Q1, Q3-Q8, never hinged 5,200.

Halves Used, Each

Q1	4.25
Q2	85.00
Q3	5.50
Q4	3.00
Q5	3.00
Q6	8.50
Q7	19.00
Q8	19.00

Overprinted type "f" on Each Half

1917-24
Q9 PP2 5c brown 3.25 *8.00*
Q10 PP2 10c deep blue 3.25 *8.00*
Q11 PP2 20c black 3.25 *8.00*
Q12 PP2 25c red 3.25 *8.00*
Q13 PP2 50c orange 6.50 *12.00*
Q14 PP2 1 l violet 6.50 *12.00*
Q15 PP2 2 l green 6.50 *12.00*
Q16 PP2 3 l bister 6.50 *12.00*
Q17 PP2 4 l slate 6.50 *20.00*
Q18 PP2 10 l rose lil ('24) 87.50 *190.00*
Q19 PP2 12 l red brn ('24) 240.00 *375.00*
Q20 PP2 15 l olive grn ('24) 240.00 *375.00*
Q21 PP2 20 l brn vio ('24) 325.00 *525.00*
Nos. Q9-Q21 (13) 938.00 *1,565.*
Set, never hinged 1,860.

Halves Used, Each

Q9	1.20
Q10	1.20
Q11	1.20
Q12	1.20
Q13	1.20
Q14	1.20
Q15	1.60
Q16	4.25
Q17	4.25
Q18	8.50
Q19	12.50
Q20	12.50
Q21	17.00

Parcel Post Stamps of Italy, 1927-39, Overprinted type "f" on Each Half

1927-37
Q21A PP3 10c dp blue ('37) *8,750.* 1,250.
Never hinged *13,500.*
Q22 PP3 25c red ('37) 550.00 72.50
Q23 PP3 30c ultra ('29) 4.00 *24.00*
Q24 PP3 50c org ('36) 725.00 47.50
Q25 PP3 60c red ('29) 4.00 *24.00*
Q26 PP3 1 l brn vio ('36) 325.00 47.50
a. 1 l lilac 400.00 47.50
Q27 PP3 2 l grn ('36) 325.00 47.50
Q28 PP3 3 l bister 9.50 *40.00*
Q29 PP3 4 l gray 9.50 *40.00*
Q30 PP3 10 l rose lil ('36) 525.00 800.00
Q31 PP3 20 l lilac brn ('36) 525.00 800.00
Nos. Q22-Q31 (10) 3,002.
Set, never hinged 6,000.
Nos. Q21A-Q31 (11) 3,193.

Halves Used, Each

Q21A	27.50
Q22	1.20
Q23	.65
Q24	1.70
Q25	.85
Q26	1.25
Q26a	1.25
Q27	1.25
Q28	1.25
Q29	1.25
Q30	37.50
Q31	37.50

ESTONIA

e-'stō-nē-ə

LOCATION — Northern Europe, bordering on the Baltic Sea and the Gulf of Finland
GOVT. — Independent republic
AREA — 17,462 sq. mi.
POP. — 1,408,523 (1999 est.)
CAPITAL — Tallinn

Formerly a part of the Russia empire, Estonia declared its independence in 1918. In 1940 it was incorporated in the Union of Soviet Socialist Republics.

Estonia declared the restoration of its independence from the USSR on Aug. 20, 1991. Estonian independence was recognized by the Soviet Union on Sept. 6, 1991.

100 Kopecks = 1 Ruble (1918, 1991)
100 Penni = 1 Mark (1919)
100 Sents = 1 Kroon (1928, 1992)

Catalogue values for unused stamps in this country are for Never Hinged items, beginning with Scott 200 in the regular postage section, Scott B60 in the semi-postal section, and Scott F1 in the registration section.

Watermark

Wmk. 207 — Arms of Finland in the Sheet

Watermark covers a large part of sheet.

A1

A2

1918-19 Unwmk. Litho. *Imperf.*

1 A1 5k pale red .95 .80
2 A1 15k bright blue .95 .80
3 A2 35p brown ('19) .80 .80
a. Printed on both sides 200.00
b. 35p olive 80.00 80.00
4 A2 70p olive grn ('19) 1.60 *2.00*
Nos. 1-4 (4) 4.30 4.40

Nos. 1-4 exist privately perforated.

Russian Stamps of 1909-17 Handstamped in Violet or Black

1919, May 7 *Perf. 14, 14½x15, 13½*

8 A14 1k orange *8,000.* *8,000.*
9 A14 2k green 45.00 *45.00*
10 A14 3k red 52.50 *52.50*
11 A14 5k claret 45.00 *45.00*
12 A15 10k dk bl (Bk) 85.00 *85.00*
13 A15 10k dk bl 500.00 *500.00*
14 A14 10k on 7k lt bl *2,400.* *2,400.*
15 A11 15k red brn & bl 67.50 *67.50*
16 A11 25k grn & vio 80.00 *80.00*
17 A11 35k red brn & grn 7,000. *7,000.*
18 A8 50k vio & grn 190.00 190.00
19 A9 1r pale brn, brn & org 325.00 325.00
20 A13 10r scar, yel & gray *12,000.* *12,000.*

Imperf

21 A14 1k orange 62.50 *62.50*
22 A14 2k green *2,000.* *2,000.*
23 A14 3k red 85.00 85.00
24 A9 1r pale brn, brn & red org *475.00* *475.00*
25 A12 3½r mar & grn *2,000.* *2,000.*
26 A13 5r dk bl, grn & pale bl *2,750.* *2,750.*

Provisionally issued at Tallinn. This overprint has been extensively counterfeited. Values are for genuine examples competently expertized.
No. 20 is always creased.

Gulls — A3

1919, May 13 *Imperf.*

27 A3 5p yellow 2.50 *5.50*

A4

A5

A6

A7

Viking Ship — A8

1919-20 *Perf. 11½*

28 A4 10p green .45 .80

Imperf

29 A4 5p orange .25 .25
30 A4 10p green .25 .25
31 A5 15p rose .25 .30
32 A6 35p blue .25 .30
33 A7 70p dl vio ('20) .25 .30
34 A8 1m bl & blk brn 4.25 1.60
a. Gray granite paper ('20) 1.60 .80
35 A8 5m org yel & blk 6.25 4.75
a. Gray granite paper ('20) 3.25 1.25
36 A8 15m yel grn & vio ('20) 4.00 2.40
37 A8 25m ultra & blk brn ('20) 6.50 5.50
Nos. 28-37 (10) 22.70 16.45
Set, never hinged 32.50

The 5m exists with inverted center. Not a postal item.
See Nos. 76-77. For surcharges see Nos. 55, 57.

Skyline of Tallinn — A9

1920-24 Pelure Paper *Imperf.*

39 A9 25p green .30 .40
40 A9 25p yellow ('24) .30 .30
41 A9 35p rose .40 .40
42 A9 50p green ('21) .60 .25
43 A9 1m vermilion 1.25 .80
44 A9 2m blue .80 .40
45 A9 2m ultramarine 1.00 1.25
46 A9 2.50m blue 1.25 .80
Nos. 39-46 (8) 5.90 4.60
Set, never hinged 16.50

Nos. 39-46 with sewing machine perforation are unofficial.
For surcharge see No. 56.

Stamps of 1919-20 Surcharged

1920 *Imperf.*

55 A5 1m on 15p rose .50 .50
56 A9 1m on 35p rose .70 .80
57 A7 2m on 70p dl vio .85 .80
Nos. 55-57 (3) 2.05 2.10
Set, never hinged 4.25

Weaver A10

Blacksmith A11

1922-23 Typo. *Imperf.*

58 A10 ½m orange ('23) 2.75 *8.00*
59 A10 1m brown ('23) 4.75 *11.00*
60 A10 2m yellow green 4.75 *8.00*
61 A10 2½m claret 5.50 *8.00*
62 A11 5m rose 8.00 8.00
63 A11 9m red ('23) 12.00 *24.00*
64 A11 10m deep blue 5.50 *16.00*
Nos. 58-64 (7) 43.25 83.00
Set, never hinged 110.00

1922-25 *Perf. 14*

65 A10 ½m orange ('23) 1.25 .80
66 A10 1m brown ('23) 2.40 .80
67 A10 2m yellow green 2.40 .40
68 A10 2½m claret 4.75 .80
69 A10 3m blue green ('24) 2.00 .40
70 A11 5m rose 2.75 .40
71 A11 9m red ('23) 4.75 1.60
72 A11 10m deep blue 6.00 .40
73 A11 12m red ('25) 6.00 1.75
74 A11 15m plum ('25) 8.00 1.40
75 A11 20m ultra ('25) 22.00 .80
Nos. 65-75 (11) 62.30 9.55
Set, never hinged 130.00

See No. 89. For surcharges see Nos. 84-88.

Viking Ship Type of 1920

1922, June 8 *Perf. 14x13½*

76 A8 15m yel grn & vio 20.00 .80
77 A8 25m ultra & blk brn 20.00 3.25
Set, never hinged 80.00

Map of Estonia — A13

1923-24 Paper with Lilac Network

78 A13 100m ol grn & bl 24.00 3.50

Paper with Buff Network

79 A13 300m brn & bl ('24) 80.00 17.50
Set, never hinged 210.00

For surcharges see Nos. 106-107.

National Theater, Tallinn — A14

Paper with Blue Network

1924, Dec. 9 *Perf. 14x13½*

81 A14 30m violet & blk 10.00 4.00

Paper with Rose Network

82 A14 70m car rose & blk 15.00 8.00
Set, never hinged 50.00

For surcharge see No. 105.

Vanemuine Theater, Tartu — A15

Paper with Lilac Network

1927, Oct. 25

83 A15 40m dp bl & ol brn 10.00 3.50
Never hinged 20.00

Stamps of 1922-25 Surcharged in New Currency in Red or Black

1928 *Perf. 14*

84 A10 2s yellow green 1.25 1.25
85 A11 5s rose red (B) 1.25 1.25
86 A11 10s deep blue 2.40 1.25
a. Imperf., pair *2,000.* *16,000.*
87 A11 15s plum (B) 3.75 1.25
88 A11 20s ultra 3.75 1.25
Nos. 84-88 (5) 12.40 6.25
Set, never hinged 30.00

10th anniversary of independence.

3rd Philatelic Exhibition Issue
Blacksmith Type of 1922-23

1928, July 6

89 A11 10m gray 3.00 *6.00*
Never hinged 6.00

Sold only at Tallinn Philatelic Exhibition. Exists imperf. Value $1,000.

Arms — A16

Paper with Network in Parenthesis

1928-40 *Perf. 14, 14½x14*

90 A16 1s dk gray (bl) .50 .25
a. Thick gray-toned laid paper ('40) 10.00 *27.50*
91 A16 2s yel grn (org) .50 .25
92 A16 4s grn (brn) ('29) 1.10 .25
93 A16 5s red (grn) .70 .25
a. 5 feet on lowest lion 45.00 32.50
94 A16 8s vio (buff) ('29) 2.75 .25
95 A16 10s lt bl (lilac) 1.75 .25
96 A16 12s crimson (grn) 1.75 .25
97 A16 15s yel (blue) 2.75 .25
98 A16 15s car (gray) ('35) 12.00 1.50
99 A16 20s slate bl (red) 3.75 .25
100 A16 25s red vio (grn) ('29) 9.00 .25
101 A16 25s bl (brn) ('35) 10.00 1.50
102 A16 40s red org (bl) ('29) 5.75 .80
103 A16 60s gray (brn) ('29) 10.00 .80
104 A16 80s brn (bl) ('29) 12.00 1.60
Nos. 90-104 (15) 74.30 8.70
Set, never hinged 160.00

Types of 1924 Issues Surcharged

1930, Sept. 1 *Perf. 14x13½*

Paper with Green Network

105 A14 1k on 70m car & blk 16.00 5.50

Paper with Rose Network

106 A13 2k on 300m brn & bl 32.50 16.00

Paper with Blue Network

107 A13 3k on 300m brn & bl 60.00 27.50
Nos. 105-107 (3) 108.50 49.00
Set, never hinged 215.00

University Observatory
A17

University of Tartu
A18

Paper with Network as in Parenthesis

1932, June 1 *Perf. 14*

108 A17 5s red (yellow) 6.00 .80
109 A18 10s light bl (lilac) 4.00 .80
110 A17 12s car (blue) 10.00 4.00
111 A18 20s dk bl (green) 6.00 1.60
Nos. 108-111 (4) 26.00 7.20
Set, never hinged 57.50

University of Tartu tercentenary.

Narva Falls — A19

1933, Apr. 1 Photo. *Perf. 14x13½*

112 A19 1k gray black 6.50 3.00
Never hinged 14.00

See No. 149.

Ancient Bard Playing Harp — A20

Paper with Network as in Parenthesis

1933, May 29 Typo. *Perf. 14*

113 A20 2s green (orange) 1.60 .30
114 A20 5s red (green) 2.75 .30
115 A20 10s blue (lilac) 3.50 .30
Nos. 113-115 (3) 7.85 .90
Set, never hinged 17.00

Tenth National Song Festival.
Nos. 113-115 exist imperf. Value $125.

Woman Harvester — A21

1935, Mar. 1 Engr. *Perf. 13½*

116 A21 3k black brown .80 *6.50*
Never hinged 1.75

Pres. Konstantin Päts — A22

1936-40 Typo. *Perf. 14*

117 A22 1s chocolate .80 .40
118 A22 2s yellow green .80 .40
119 A22 3s dp org ('40) 8.00 8.00
120 A22 4s rose vio 1.60 .80
121 A22 5s lt blue grn 2.00 .40
122 A22 6s rose lake 1.60 .40
123 A22 6s dp green ('40) 40.00 *55.00*
124 A22 10s greenish blue 2.00 .40
125 A22 15s crim rose ('37) 2.40 .40
126 A22 15s dp bl ('40) 4.00 3.25
127 A22 18s dp car ('39) 17.50 6.25
128 A22 20s brt vio 4.00 .40
129 A22 25s dk bl ('38) 12.00 1.60
130 A22 30s bister ('38) 18.00 1.60
131 A22 30s ultra ('39) 24.00 6.25
132 A22 50s org brn 8.75 1.60
133 A22 60s brt pink 20.00 5.50
Nos. 117-133 (17) 167.45 92.65
Set, never hinged 340.00

St. Brigitta Convent Entrance
A23

Ruins of Convent, Pirita River
A24

Front View of Convent — A25

Seal of Convent — A26

Paper with Network as in Parenthesis

1936, June 10 *Perf. 13½*

134 A23 5s green (buff) .60 *1.60*
135 A24 10s blue (lil) .60 *1.60*
136 A25 15s red (org) 1.75 *4.75*
137 A26 25s ultra (brn) 3.00 *8.00*
Nos. 134-137 (4) 5.95 *15.95*
Set, never hinged 12.00

St. Brigitta Convent, 500th anniversary.

Harbor at Tallinn — A27

1938, Apr. 11 Engr. *Perf. 14*

138 A27 2k blue .80 *8.00*
Never hinged 1.75

Friedrich R. Faehlmann
A28

Friedrich R. Kreutzwald
A29

1938, June 15 Typo. *Perf. 13½*

139 A28 5s dark green .40 *.80*
140 A29 10s deep brown .40 *.80*
141 A29 15s dark carmine .80 *5.50*
142 A28 25s ultra 1.25 *7.25*
a. Sheet of 4, #139-142 10.00 *80.00*
Nos. 139-142 (4) 2.85 *14.35*
Set, never hinged 8.00

Society of Estonian Scholars centenary.

Hospital at Pärnu — A30

Beach Hotel — A31

1939, June 20 Typo. *Perf. 14x13½*

144 A30 5s dark green 1.60 1.60
145 A31 10s deep red violet .80 1.60
146 A30 18s dark carmine 1.25 *5.50*
147 A31 30s deep blue 1.60 *7.25*
a. Sheet of 4, #144-147 16.00 *87.50*
Nos. 144-147 (4) 5.25 15.95
Set, never hinged 11.00

Cent. of health resort and baths at Pärnu.

Narva Falls Type of 1933

1940, Apr. 15 **Engr.**

149 A19 1k slate green 1.40 *12.00*
Never hinged 2.75

The sky consists of heavy horizontal lines and the background consists of horizontal and vertical lines.

Carrier Pigeon and Plane — A32

1940, July 30 **Typo.**

150 A32 3s red orange .25 .25
151 A32 10s purple .25 .25
152 A32 15s rose brown .25 .25
153 A32 30s dark blue 1.60 1.25
Nos. 150-153 (4) 2.35 2.00
Set, never hinged 4.75

Centenary of the first postage stamp.
The 15s exists imperf. Value $6.25.

Catalogue values for unused stamps in this section, from this point to the end of the section, are for Never Hinged items.

Natl. Arms — A40

1991, Oct. 1 Litho. *Perf. 13x12½*

200 A40 5k salmon & red .30 .30
201 A40 10k lt grn & dk bl grn .30 .30
202 A40 15k lt bl & dk bl .30 .30
203 A40 30k vio & gray .35 .35
204 A40 50k org & brn .40 .40
205 A40 70k pink & purple .50 .50
206 A40 90k pur & rose lilac .60 .60

Size: 20½x27mm
Engr.
Perf. 12½ Horiz.

207 A40 1r dark brown .75 .75
208 A40 2r lt bl & dk bl 1.50 1.50
Nos. 200-208 (9) 5.00 5.00

See Nos. 211-213, 215, 216, 230, 299-301, 314-314A, 317, 333-334, 339-340. For surcharge, see No. 217.

A41

Perf. 13½x14, 14x13½

1991, Nov. 1 **Litho.**

209 A41 1.50r Flag, vert. 1.10 1.10
210 A41 2.50r shown 1.90 1.90

National Arms — A42

1992, Mar. 16 Litho. *Perf. 13x12½*

211 A42 E (1r) lemon .25 .25
212 A42 I (20r) blue green .85 .85
213 A42 A (40r) blue 1.90 1.90
Nos. 211-213 (3) 3.00 3.00

No. 211 was valid for postage within Estonia. No. 212 was valid for postage within Europe. No. 213 was valid for overseas mail. See Nos. 214, 219, 220, 224-229.

Arms Types of 1991-1992 and

No. 202 Surcharged

Natl. Arms — A42a

Perf. 14, 13x12½ (#214, 217, 219-220)

1992-96

214 A42 E (10s) orange .25 .25
215 A40 10s blue & gray .25 .25
216 A40 50s gray & brt bl .25 .25
a. Perf. 13x13¼ —
217 A40 60s on 15k #202 .25 .25
218 A40 60s lilac & olive .25 .25
219 A42 I (1k) emerald .75 .75
220 A42 A (2k) violet blue 1.50 1.50
221 A42a 5k bis & red vio 1.25 1.25
a. 5k yel orange & red violet 2.75 2.75
222 A42a 10k turq blue & dp ol 2.50 2.50
223 A42a 20k pale lilac & slate grn 4.25 4.25
Nos. 214-223 (10) 11.50 11.50

Coil Stamps
Engr.
Size: 20½x27mm
Perf. 12½ Horiz.

224 A42 X (10s) brown .30 .30
225 A42 X (10s) olive .30 .30
226 A42 X (10s) black .30 .30
227 A42 Z (30s) red lilac .30 .30
228 A42 Z (30s) red .30 .30
229 A42 Z (30s) dark blue .30 .30

Litho.

230 A40 60s lilac brown .30 .30
Nos. 224-230 (7) 2.10 2.10

Issued: Nos. 214, 219-220, 6/22; No. 224, 8/29; No. 225, 9/25; No. 226, 10/31; No. 227, 11/16; No. 228, 12/1; No. 229, 12/22; No. 230, 1/8/93; No. 217, 3/5/93; 10s, 50s, 3/23 1993; 10k, 5/25/93; 5k, 7/7/93; No. 218, 8/5/93; 20k, 9/8/93; No. 221a, 9/19/96; No. 216a, 3/5/96.
See note after No. 213. Nos. 224-229 were valid for postage within Estonia.
See No. F1.

A44

Birds of the Baltic shores.

1992, Oct. 3 Litho. & Engr. *Perf. 13*
Booklet Stamps

231 A44 1k Pandion haliaetus .65 *.65*
232 A44 1k Limosa limosa .65 *.65*
233 A44 1k Mergus merganser .65 *.65*
234 A44 1k Tadorna todorna .65 *.65*
a. Booklet pane of 4, #231-234 2.60 2.60

See Latvia Nos. 332-335a, Lithuania Nos. 427-430a and Sweden Nos. 1975-1978a.

A45

1992, Dec, 15 Litho. *Perf. 14*

235 A45 30s gray & multi .30 .30
236 A45 2k light brown & multi .70 .70

Christmas.
Exist on ordinary and fluorescent paper. Values are for former. Value for set on fluorescent paper, $30.

Friendship
A46

1993, Feb. 8 Litho. *Perf. 14*
237 A46 1k multicolored .30 .30
a. Booklet pane of 6 1.80

See Finland No. 906.

First Republic, 75th Anniv. — A47

1993, Feb. 16 *Perf. 13x13½*
238 A47 60s black & multi .25 .25
239 A47 1k violet & multi .25 .25
240 A47 2k blue & multi .50 .50
Nos. 238-240 (3) 1.00 1.00

First Baltic Sea Games — A48

60s, Wrestling. 1k +25s, Viking ship, map. 2k, Shot put with rock.

1993, June 9 Litho. *Perf. 13½x14*
241 A48 60s multi .25 .25
242 A48 1k +25s multi .30 .30
243 A48 2k multi .45 .45
Nos. 241-243 (3) 1.00 1.00

Tallinn Castle — A49

Designs: 1k, Toolse Castle. No. 245, Paide Castle, vert. No. 246, Purtse Castle. No. 247, Haapsalu Castle and Cathedral. 2.70k, Narva Fortress. 2.90k, Haapsalu Cathedral. 3k, Monks' Tower, Kiiu. 3.20k, Rakvere Castle. 4k, Kuressaare Castle. 4.80k, Viljandi Castle.

1993-97 Litho. *Perf. 14*
244 A49 1k gray & black .45 .45
245 A49 2k tan & brown .45 .45
246 A49 2.50k lt vio & dk vio .55 .55
247 A49 2.50k gray .55 .55
248 A49 2.70k lt blue & dk blue .55 .55
249 A49 2.90k lt grn & dk grn .60 .60
250 A49 3k rose & brown .60 .60
251 A49 3.20k lt grn & dk grn .85 .85
252 A49 4k lt gray vio & gray vio .90 .90
253 A49 4.80k dull org & brn .95 .95
Nos. 244-253 (10) 6.45 6.45

Issued: 1k, 2/22/94; 2k, 10/12/93; 2.70k, 12/10/93; 2.90k, 12/23/93; 3k, 3/31/94; 3.20, 12/28/94; 4k, 9/20/94; No. 246, 1/25/96; 247, 7/25/96; 4.80k, 1/21/97.

First Estonian Postage Stamp, 75th Anniv. — A50

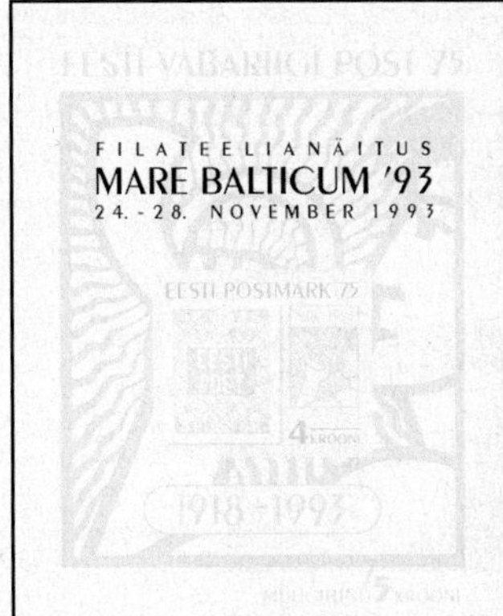

No. 260a

1993, Nov. 13 Litho. *Perf. 14*
259 A50 1k multicolored .40 .40

Souvenir Sheet
Imperf

260 A50 4k multicolored 3.00 3.00
a. Ovptd. in sheet margin 11.50 11.50

No. 260 sold for 5k.

Christmas A51

80s, Haapsalu Cathedral. 2k, Tallinn Church.

1993, Nov. Litho. *Perf. 14*
261 A51 80s red .25 .25
262 A51 2k blue, vert. .40 .40

See Nos. 279-280.

Lydia Koidula — A52

1993, Dec. 14 Litho. *Perf. 14*
263 A52 1k multicolored .35 .35

1994 Winter Olympics, Lillehammer — A53

1994, Jan. 26
264 A53 1k +25s Ski jumping .40 .40
265 A53 2k Speed skating .50 .50

Festival Badges — A54

1k+25s, Tartu, 1869. 2k, Tallinn, 1923. 3k, Tallinn, 1969.
15k, Anniversary badge.

1994, May 31 Litho. *Perf. 13½x14*
266 A54 1k +25s olive & multi .25 .25
267 A54 2k blue & brown .45 .45
268 A54 3k brown, buff & bister .60 .60
Nos. 266-268 (3) 1.30 1.30

Souvenir Sheet

269 A54 15k multicolored 3.00 3.00

All Estonian Song Festival, 125th anniv.

Flying Squirrel — A55

1994, June 27 Litho. *Perf. 13½x14*
270 A55 1k shown .40 .40
271 A55 2k On leafy branch .50 .50
272 A55 3k In fir tree .85 .85
273 A55 4k With young 1.10 1.10
Nos. 270-273 (4) 2.85 2.85

World Wildlife Fund.

A56

Europa (Estonian Inventions): 1k, Rotating horizontal millstones, by Aleksander Mikiver. 2.70k, First mini-camera, by Walter Zapp.

1994, July 19
274 A56 1k multicolored *.25 .25*
275 A56 2.70k multicolored *.50 .50*

Folk Costumes — A57

1994, Aug. 23 Litho. *Perf. 14*
276 A57 1k Jamaja .25 .25
277 A57 1k Mustjala .25 .25

See Nos. 286-287, 303-304, 325-326, 347-348, 369-370, 476-477, 497-498, 524-525.

Estonian Art Museum, 75th Anniv. — A58

1994, Sept. 27 Litho. *Perf. 13½*
278 A58 1.70k multicolored .35 .35

Christmas Type of 1993

Designs: 1.20k, Ruhnu Church, vert. 2.50k, Urvaste Church.

1994, Nov. 15 Litho. *Perf. 14*
279 A51 1.20k brown .30 .30
280 A51 2.50k green .55 .55

For surcharge see No. B63.

Intl. Year of the Family — A59

1994, Oct. 18
281 A59 1.70k multicolored .40 .40

A60

Gustavus II Adolphus (1594-1632), King of Sweden.

1994, Dec. 9
282 A60 2.50k lilac 1.00 1.00

Matsalu Nature Reserve — A61

1995, Jan. 26 Litho. *Perf. 14*
283 A61 1.70k Branta leucopsis .35 .35
284 A61 3.20k Anser anser .60 .60

FAO, 50th Anniv. — A62

Farm Laborer's Family at Table, by Efraim Allsalu.

1995, Feb. 28 Litho. *Perf. 14*
285 A62 2.70k multicolored .55 .55

Folk Costumes Type of 1994

1995, Mar. 30 Litho. *Perf. 14*
286 A57 1.70k Muhu couple .40 .40
287 A57 1.70k Three Muhu girls .40 .40

A63

Via Baltica Highway Project: Nos. 288, 289a, Beach Hotel, Parnu. No. 289b, Castle, Bauska, Latvia. No. 289c, Kaunas, Lithuania.

1995, Apr. 20 Litho. *Perf. 14*
288 A63 1.70k multicolored .45 .45

Souvenir Sheet

289 A63 3.20k Sheet of 3, #a.-c. 2.00 2.00

See Latvia Nos. 394-395, Lithuania Nos. 508-509.

A64

1995, Apr. 20 Litho. *Perf. 14*
290 A64 2.70k multicolored *.75 .75*

Europa. Liberation of Nazi Concentration Camps, 50th anniv.

UN, 50th Anniv. — A65

1995, June 1 Litho. *Perf. 14*
291 A65 4k multicolored .75 .75

Pakri Lighthouse A66

1995, July 5 Litho. *Perf. 14*
292 A66 1.70k multicolored .45 .45

See Nos. 309, 318, 338, 356, 388-389, 408, 434, 452, 501-502.

Vanemuine Theater, 125th Anniv. — A67

1995, Aug. 14 Litho. *Perf. 14*
293 A67 1.70k multicolored .45 .45

Louis Pasteur (1822-95) A68

1995, Sept. 20 Litho. *Perf. 14*
294 A68 2.70k multicolored .60 .60

Miniature Sheet

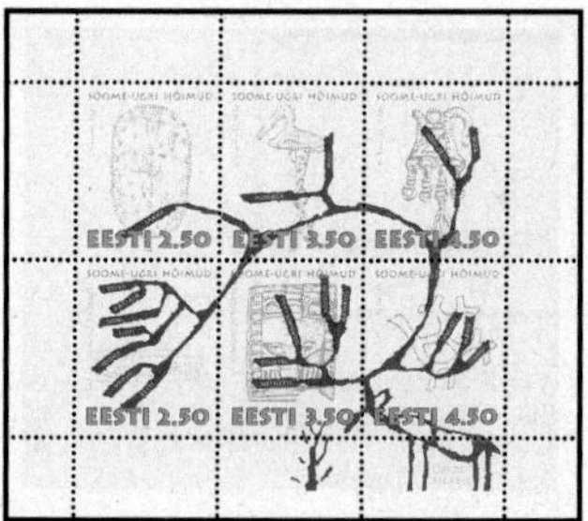
Finno-Ugric Peoples — A69

Ethnographic object, languages: a, 2.50k, Drawing on shaman's drum, Saami. b, 3.50k, Duck-shaped brooch, Mordva, Mari. c, 4.50k, Duck-feet necklace pendant, Udmurdi, Komi. d, 2.50k, Khanty band ornament, Ungari, Mansi, Handi. e, 3.50k, Bronze amulet, Neenetsi, Eenetsi, Nganassaani, Solkupi, Kamassi. f, 4.50k, Karelian writing on birchbark, Eesti, Vadia, Soome, Liivi, Isuri, Karjala, Vespa.

1995, Oct. 17 Litho. *Perf. 14*
295 A69 Sheet of 6, #a.-f. 4.00 4.00

Aleksander Kunileid (1845-75), Composer — A70

1995, Nov. 1 Engr. *Perf. 12½ Horiz.*
296 A70 2k dark blue black .45 .45

Christmas — A71

Churches: 2k, St. Martin's, Türi. 3.50k, Charles' Church of the Toompea Congregation, Tallinn.

1995, Nov. 15 Litho. *Perf. 14*
297 A71 2k yellow orange .55 .55
298 A71 3.50k dull carmine .95 .95

See Nos. 315-316, 331.

Natl. Arms Type of 1991

1995, Oct. 26 Litho. *Perf. 14*
299 A40 20s blue green & black .25 .25
300 A40 30s gray & magenta .25 .25
301 A40 80s lilac & blue black .25 .25
a. Perf. 13 .25 .25
Nos. 299-301 (3) .75 .75

No. 301a issued in 1996.

Submarine *Lembit* — A72

1996, Feb. 29 Litho. *Perf. 14*
302 A72 2.50k multicolored .65 .65

See No. 308, 328.

Folk Costume Type of 1994

1996, Mar. 26 Litho. *Perf. 14*
303 A57 2.50k Emmaste .65 .65
304 A57 2.50k Reigi .65 .65

A73

Designs: a, 2.50k, First gold medal, 1896. b, 3.50k, Alfred Neuland, weight lifter, first to win gold medal for Estonia, 1920. c, 4k, Cyclist.

1996, Apr. 25 Litho. *Perf. 14*
305 A73 Sheet of 3, #a.-c. 2.00 2.00

Modern Olympic Games, Cent. & 1996 Summer Olympics, Atlanta.

A74

Europa: Marie Under (1883-1980), poet.

1996, May 10
306 A74 2.50k multicolored *1.00 1.00*

Radio, Cent. — A75

1996, June 27 Litho. *Perf. 14*
307 A75 3.50k Guglielmo Marconi .90 .90

Ship Type of 1996

Design: Icebreaker, Suur Toll.

1996, Aug. 30 Litho. *Perf. 14*
308 A72 2.50k multicolored .65 .65

Lighthouse Type of 1995

1996, Sept. 25 Litho. *Perf. 14*
309 A66 2.50k Vaindloo .70 .70

Estonian Narrow Gauge Railway, Cent. — A76

Designs: 3.20k, Class Gk steam locomotive. 3.50k, DeM 1 diesel motor wagon. 4.50k, Class Sk steam locomotive.

1996, Oct. 17 Litho. *Perf. 14*
310 A76 3.20k multicolored .70 .70
311 A76 3.50k multicolored .75 .75
312 A76 4.50k multicolored .85 .85
Nos. 310-312 (3) 2.30 2.30

See No. 397.

Christmas A77

1996, Nov. 27 Litho. *Perf. 14*
313 A77 2.50k multicolored .60 .60

Natl. Arms Type of 1991

1996-97 *Perf. 14*
314 A40 3.30k lilac and claret 1.25 1.25

Perf. 13x13¼
314A A40 3.30k blue & lt claret 1.25 1.25

Issued: No. 314, 12/2; No. 314A, 12/10/97.

Church Type of 1995

Christmas: 3.30k, Harju-Madise Church. 4.50k, Holy Spirit Church, Tallinn.

1996, Dec. 12
315 A71 3.30k blue .70 .70
316 A71 4.50k pink .85 .85

Natl. Arms Type of 1991

1996, Oct. 24 Litho. *Perf. 13½*
317 A40 2.50k grn & dark grn 1.25 1.25

Lighthouse Type of 1995

1997, Feb. 11 Litho. *Perf. 14*
318 A66 3.30k Ruhnu .75 .75

Tallinn Zoo — A78

a, Haliaeetus pelagicus. b, Mustela lutreola. c, Aegypius monachus. d, Panthera pardus orientalis. e, Diceros bicornis. f, Capra cylindricornis.

1997, Mar. 26 Litho. *Perf. 14*
319 A78 3.30k Sheet of 6, #a.-f. 3.50 3.50

Heinrich von Stephan (1831-97), Founder of UPU — A79

1997, Apr. 8 Litho. *Perf. 14*
320 A79 7k black & bister 1.25 1.25

Goldspinners Fairy Tale — A80

1997, May 5 Litho. *Perf. 14*
321 A80 4.80k multicolored *1.00 1.00*

Europa.

A81

No. 323: a, like #322. b, Linijkugis, 17th cent. c, Kurenas, 16th cent.

1997, May 10
322 A81 3.30k multicolored .70 .70

Perf. 14x14½
323 A81 4.50k Sheet of 3, #a.-c. 5.25 5.25

Maasilinn ship, 16th cent.
See Latvia Nos. 443-444, Lithuania Nos. 571-572.

Folk Costume Type of 1994

1997, June 10 Litho. *Perf. 14*
325 A57 3.30k Ruhnu .55 .55
326 A57 3.30k Vormsi .55 .55

One Kroon Coin — A82

1997, June 12 Litho. *Perf. 14*
327 A82 50k bl grn, blk & gray 9.00 9.00

See Nos. 345, 363, 391.

Ship Type of 1996

Design: Four-masted barkentine, Tormilind.

1997, July 2
328 A72 5.50k multicolored .90 .90

Stone Bridge, Tartu — A83

1997, Sept. 16 Litho. *Perf. 14*
329 A83 3.30k multicolored .65 .65

Wastne Testament, Estonian Bible Translation, 1686 — A84

1997, Oct. 14 Litho. *Perf. 14*
330 A84 3.50k multicolored .65 .65

Church Type of 1995

Christmas: St. Anne's, Halliste.

1997, Nov. 27 Litho. *Perf. 14*
331 A71 3.30k brown .65 .65

Christmas A85

1997, Dec. 3
332 A85 2.90k Elves .60 .60

Natl. Arms Type of 1991

1998, Jan. 19 Litho. *Perf. 13x13½*
333 A40 3.10k lt violet & rose .60 .60
334 A40 3.60k lt blue & ultra .70 .70
a. 3.60k gray & vio bl .80 .80

Issued: No. 334a, 8/4/98.

1998 Winter Olympic Games, Nagano — A86

1998, Jan. 28 Litho. *Perf. 14*
335 A86 3.60k multicolored .70 .70

Republic of Estonia, 80th Anniv. — A87

1998, Feb. 6 Litho. *Imperf.*
336 A87 7k Proclamation, arms 1.40 1.40

Eduard Wiiralt (1898-1954), Print Artist — A88

Various sections of print, "Hell," showing faces: a, 3.60k, shown. b, 3.60k, Explosion coming from center figure. c, 5.50k, Cat on top of one figure's head. d, 5.50k, Faces within faces.

1998, Feb. 18 *Perf. 14*
337 A88 Sheet of 4, #a.-d. 4.00 4.00

Lighthouse Type of 1995

1998, Mar. 12 Litho. *Perf. 14*
338 A66 3.60k Kunda .70 .70

Natl. Arms Type of 1991

1998, Mar. 16 *Perf. 13*
339 A40 10s grn bl & brn blk .25 .25
340 A40 4.50k pale orange & brick red .80 .80

Issued: 10s, 3/25/97; 4.50k, 3/16/98.

A88a

1998, Apr. 16 Litho. *Perf. 14*
341 A88a 7k multicolored 1.30 1.30

1998 World Cup Soccer Championship, France.

St. John's Day — A89

1998, May 5 Litho. *Perf. 14*
342 A89 5.20k multi *1.25 1.25*

Europa.

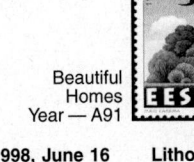

Use of Lübeck Charter in Tallinn, 750th Anniv. — A90

1998, June 1
343 A90 4.80k multicolored .95 .95

Beautiful Homes Year — A91

1998, June 16 Litho. *Perf. 14*
344 A91 3.60k multicolored .85 .85

One Kroon Coin Type of 1997

1998, June 18
345 A82 25k green, gray & black 4.75 4.75

A92

1998, Aug. 4 Litho. *Perf. 14*
346 A92 5.50k multicolored 1.00 1.00

470 Class World Yachting Championships.

Folk Costume Type of 1994

1998, Aug. 21 Litho. *Perf. 14*
347 A57 3.60k Kihnu couple .65 .65
348 A57 3.60k Kihnu family .65 .65

A93

1998, Sept. 3
349 A93 3.60k yel, blue & blk .70 .70

Juhan Jaik (1899-1948), author.

Tallinn Zoo — A94

Design: Panthera tigris altaica.

1998, Sept. 17
350 A94 3.60k multicolored .70 .70

See No. 357.

Estonian Post, 80th Anniv. — A95

1998, Oct. 22 Litho. *Perf. 14*
351 A95 3.60k multicolored .75 .75

Military Aid from Finland, 90th Anniv. — A96

1998, Nov. 5 Litho. *Perf. 14*
352 A96 4.50k Freedom Cross .85 .85

Christmas A97

1998, Nov. 26 Litho. *Perf. 14*
353 A97 3.10k Santa, child, vert. .60 .60
354 A97 5k shown .90 .90

Friedrich Robert Faehlmann, Founder of Learned Estonian Society, Birth Bicent. — A98

1998, Dec. 2
355 A98 3.60k multicolored .70 .70

Lighthouse Type of 1995

1999, Jan. 20 Litho. *Perf. 14*
356 A66 3.60k Vilsandi .70 .70

Tallinn Zoo Type of 1998

1999, Feb. 18 Litho. *Perf. 14*
357 A94 3.60k Uncia uncia .70 .70

Council of Europe, 50th Anniv. — A99

1999, Mar. 24 Litho. *Perf. 14*
358 A99 5.50k multicolored 1.00 1.00

Estonian Pres. Lennart Meri, 70th Birthday A100

1999, Mar. 29
359 A100 3.60k multicolored .70 .70

Tolkuse Bog — A101

1999, Apr. 27 Litho. *Perf. 14*
360 A101 5.50k multicolored *1.25 1.25*

Europa.

Bank of Estonia, 80th Anniv. — A102

1999, May 3 Litho. *Perf. 14*
361 A102 5k multicolored 1.00 1.00

Olustvere Manor — A103

1999, June 1
362 A103 3.60k multicolored .70 .70

See Nos. 395, 414, 433, 456, 490, 520, 551, 562, 603, 627, 648.

One Kroon Coin Type of 1997

1999, June 18 Litho. *Perf. 14*
363 A82 100k bl, bister & blk 17.00 17.00

Estonian Natl. Anthem — A104

1999, June 30 Litho. *Perf. 14*
364 A104 3.60k multicolored .70 .70

No. 364 is printed se-tenant with label.

Tower on Suur Munamägi, Highest Point in Baltic Countries A105

1999, July 17
365 A105 5.20k multicolored 1.00 1.00

A106

Families holding hands and: 3.60k, Estonian flag.

No. 367: a, like #366. b, Latvian flag. c, Lithuanian flag.

1999, Aug. 23 Litho. *Perf. 14*
366 A106 3.60k multicolored .70 .70

Souvenir Sheet

367 A106 5.50k Sheet of 3, #a.-c. 3.00 3.00

Baltic Chain, 10th Anniv.

See Latvia Nos.493-494, Lithuania Nos. 639-640.

A107

1999, Sept. 23 Litho. *Perf. 14x13¾*
368 A107 7k multicolored 1.40 1.40

UPU, 125th Anniv.

Folk Costumes Type of 1994

1999, Oct. 12 Litho. *Perf. 13¾x14*
369 A57 3.60k Setu couple .65 .65
370 A57 5k Setu man, boy .90 .90

Three Lions — A108

Perf. 13x13¼, 13¾x14 (#371, 373, 374, 378-382)

1999-2002 **Litho.**

371 A108 10s brn & dk brn .30 .30
372 A108 30s lt bl & dk bl .30 .30
a. Perf. 13¾x14 .30 .30
373 A108 30s blue & slate blue, dated 2003 .30 .30
374 A108 50s ol & dk grn .30 .30
375 A108 1k brn & fawn .30 .30
376 A108 2k gray .50 .50
377 A108 3.60k sky bl & dk bl .75 .75
a. Bright blue green ('00) .75 .75
378 A108 4.40k grn & bl grn 1.00 .80
a. Inscribed "2001" 1.00 .80
b. Inscribed "2002" 1.00 .80
379 A108 4.40k bl grn & brt bl grn, wide 2001 date 1.00 .30
380 A108 4.40k Prus bl & lt bl, narrow 2001 date 1.00 .30
381 A108 4.40k grn & lt grn, dated 2002 1.00 .30
382 A108 4.40k grn & apple grn, dated 2002 1.00 .30
382A A108 4.40k ol grn & apple grn, dated 2003 1.00 .35
382B A108 5k grn & lt grn, dated "2001" 1.30 1.30
a. Inscribed "2002" 1.20 1.20
b. Inscribed "2004" .75 .75
382C A108 6k bis & yel 1.50 1.50
382D A108 6.50k bis & org 1.50 1.50
382E A108 8k lake & pink 1.75 1.75
Nos. 371-382E (17) 14.80 11.15

Issued: 30s, 2k, 11/4; No. 377, 10/22; No. 377a, 3/31/00; No. 378, 8/21/00; 6k, 10/12/00; 6.50k, 10/5/00; 8k, 10/19/00; No. 372a: 4/17/01; 1k, 5k, 8/28/01; 10s, 2/2/02. 50s, 1/7/03; No. 373, 3/11/03; No. 379, 4/17/01; No. 380, 9/24/01; No. 381, 2/2/02; No. 382, 11/14/02; No. 382A, 3/11/03.

The background color of No. 379 is bolder than that on No. 380.

See Nos. 467, 472-474.

Christmas A109

1999, Nov. 25 **Litho.** ***Perf. 14x13¾***
383 A109 3.10k multicolored .60 .60

A110

1999, Nov. 25 ***Perf. 13¾x14***
384 A110 7k multicolored 1.25 1.25

1st public Christmas tree in Tallinn, 1441.

Christmas Lottery A110a

1999, Dec. 1 **Litho.** ***Perf. 14x13¾***
384A A110a 3.10k + 1.90k multi 1.75 1.75

A111

1999, Dec. 14 **Litho.** ***Perf. 13¾x14***
385 A111 5.50k Millennium 1.10 1.10

2000 Census — A112

2000, Jan. 5
386 A112 3.60k multicolored .70 .70

Tartu Peace Treaty, 80th Anniv. — A113

2000, Feb. 2 **Litho.** ***Perf. 14x13¾***
387 A113 3.60k multi .70 .70

Lighthouse Type of 1995

2000, Feb. 25
388 A66 3.60k Ristna .65 .65
389 A66 3.60k Kopu .65 .65
a. Pair, #388-389 1.30 1.30

Congress, 10th Anniv. — A114

2000, Mar. 9 ***Perf. 13¾x14***
390 A114 3.60k multi .65 .65

One Kroon Coin Type of 1997

2000, Mar. 14 ***Perf. 14x13¾***
391 A82 10k red, sil & blk 1.75 1.75

Cornflower (Natl. Flower) — A115

2000, Apr. 7
392 A115 4.80k multi .85 .85

Natl. Book Year — A116

2000, Apr. 22 ***Perf. 13¾x14***
393 A116 3.60k multi .65 .65

First book printed in Estonian language, 475th anniv.

Europa, 2000
Common Design Type

2000, May 9
394 CD17 4.80k multi *1.25 1.25*

Manor Type of 1999

2000, May 23 **Litho.** ***Perf. 14x13¾***
395 A103 3.60k Palmse Hall .70 .70

Tallinn Zoo — A117

2000, June 13 **Litho.** ***Perf. 14x13¾***
396 A117 3.60k Naemorhedus caudatus .70 .70

Railway Type of 1996

4.50k, Viljandi-Tallinn Railway, cent.

2000, June 30
397 A76 4.50k multi .80 .80

9th Intl. Finno-Ugric Congress A118

2000, Aug. 1
398 A118 5k multi 1.00 1.00

2000 Summer Olympics, Sydney — A119

2000, Sept. 5 **Litho.** ***Perf. 13¾x14***
399 A119 8k multi 1.50 1.50

Folk Costume Type of 1994

Designs: 4.40k, Hargla. 8k, Polva.

2000, Sept. 12
400-401 A57 Set of 2 2.25 2.25

August Mälk (1900-87), Writer — A120

2000, Sept. 20 ***Perf. 14x13¾***
402 A120 4.40k multi .80 .80

Lake Peipus Fish — A121

No. 403: a, Osmerus eperlanus spirinchus. b, Stizostedion lucioperka.

2000, Oct. 25
403 Horiz. pair + central label 2.50 2.50
a.-b. A121 6.50k Any single 1.10 1.10

See Russia No. 6607.

Souvenir Sheet

Estonian Bookplates, Cent. — A122

Various bookplates. Denominiations in: a, LR. b, UR.

2000, Nov. 11 ***Perf. 13¾x14***
404 A122 6k Sheet of 2, #a-b 2.25 2.25

Christmas A123

3.60k, Horn and bow. 6k, Ornament.

2000, Nov. 29 ***Perf. 14x13¾***
405-406 A123 Set of 2 1.60 1.60

Erki Nool, Olympic Decathlon Champion A124

2001, Jan. 10 **Litho.** ***Perf. 14x13¾***
407 A124 4.40k multi .75 .75

Lighthouse Type of 1995

2001, Jan. 24
408 A66 4.40k Mohni .80 .80

Valentine's Day — A125

2001, Feb. 6 **Litho.** ***Perf. 13¾x14***
409 A125 4.40k multi .80 .80

Stenbock House, Seat of Government A126

2001, Feb. 20 ***Perf. 14x13¾***
410 A126 6.50k multi 1.10 1.10

Souvenir Sheet

Paintings of Johann Köler (1826-99) — A127

No. 411: a, Girl on the Spring, 1858-62. b, Eve of the Pomegranate, 1879-80.

2001, Feb. 27
411 A127 4.40k Sheet of 2, #a-b 1.50 1.50

European Year of Languages A128

2001, Mar. 6
412 A128 4.40k multi .85 .85

Vanellus Vanellus A129

2001, Apr. 4 ***Perf. 12¾x13***
413 A129 4.40k multi .85 .85

See No. 435.

Manor Type of 1999

2001, Apr. 17 ***Perf. 14x13¾***
414 A103 4.40k Laupa Hall .80 .80

Europa — A130

2001, May 9 ***Perf. 13¾x14***
415 A130 6.50k multi *1.30 1.30*

Kalev Sports Association, Cent. — A131

2001, May 24
416 A131 6.50k multi 1.25 1.25

Pärnu, 750th Anniv. — A132

2001, June 5 Litho. ***Perf. 14x13¾***
417 A132 4.40k multi .85 .85

Illustrations from Pokuland, by Edgar Valter — A133

Characters and — No. 418: a, Lake. b, Owl. c, Crane. d, Bird in nest.

No. 419: a, Fence. b, Flowers. c, Dog. d, Moon.

2001, June 19
418 Booklet pane of 4 2.75
a.-d. A133 3.60k Any single .75 .75
419 Booklet pane of 4 3.75
a.-d. A133 4.40k Any single .90 .90
Booklet, #418-419 7.25

Entire booklet sold for 35k, 3k of which went to the Pokuland Project of the Estonian Nature Fund.

Restoration of Independence, 10th Anniv. — A134

2001, Aug. 7 ***Perf. 13¾x14***
420 A134 4.40k multi .85 .85

Establishment of St. Mary's Land, 800th Anniv. — A135

2001, Aug. 15 ***Perf. 14x13¾***
421 A135 6.50k multi 1.25 1.25

Resumption of Issuing Stamps, 10th Anniv. — A136

2001, Sept. 4 ***Perf. 13¾x14***
422 A136 4.40k #200 .85 .85

Baltic Coast Landscapes A137

Designs: 4.40k, No. 424a, Lahemaa. No. 424b, Vidzeme. No. 424c, Palanga.

2001, Sept. 15 ***Perf. 14x13¾***
423 A137 4.40k multi .90 .90

Souvenir Sheet
Perf. 13¼x13½

424 Sheet of 3 3.50 3.50
a.-c. A137 6k Any single 1.10 1.10

No. 424 contains three 35x29mm stamps. See Lithuania Nos.

See Latvia Nos. 534-535, Lithuania Nos. 698-699.

Tallinn Zoo — A138

2001, Oct. 4 ***Perf. 14x13¾***
425 A138 4.40k Alligator sinensis .90 .90

Estonia 26/9 Racing Car — A139

2001, Oct. 23
426 A139 6k multi 1.15 1.15

Folk Costume Type of 1994

Designs: 4.40k, Paistu woman. 7.50k, Tarvastu man.

2001, Nov. 7 Litho. ***Perf. 13¾x14***
427-428 A57 Set of 2 2.25 2.25

A140

Christmas A141

Perf. 13¾x14, 14x13¾

2001, Nov. 22
429 A140 3.60k multi .70 .70
430 A141 6.50k multi 1.40 1.40

Radio Broadcasting in Estonia, 75th Anniv. — A142

2001, Dec. 4 ***Perf. 14x13¾***
431 A142 4.40k multi .90 .90

2002 Winter Olympics, Salt Lake City — A143

2002, Jan. 10 Litho. ***Perf. 14x13¾***
432 A143 8k multi 1.40 1.40

Manor Type of 1999

2002, Jan. 22
433 A103 4.40k Sangaste Hall .80 .80

Lighthouse Type of 1995

2002, Feb. 20
434 A66 4.40k Laidunina .80 .80

Bird Type of 2001

Design: Passer domesticus and Passer montanus.

2002, Mar. 7 ***Perf. 12¾x13***
435 A129 4.40k multi .80 .80

Spring Flowers — A144

2002, Mar. 20 ***Perf. 14x13¾***
436 A144 4.40k multi .80 .80

Estonian Puppet Theater, 50th Anniv. — A145

2002, Mar. 27 ***Perf. 13¾x14***
437 A145 4.40k multi + label .80 .80

PTO-4 Training Airplane — A146

2002, Apr. 10 ***Perf. 14x13¾***
438 A146 6k multi 1.10 1.10

Andrus Veerpalu, Gold Medalist at 2002 Winter Olympics A147

2002, Apr. 12
439 A147 4.40k multi .80 .80

Tartu University Anniversaries — A148

No. 440: a, Main building, 1806-09, founding act of 1632. b, University Library, 1982, text from Biblia Latina.

2002, Apr. 24
440 A148 4.40k Horiz. pair, #a-b, + central label 2.25 2.25

Europa A149

2002, May 9 ***Perf. 12¾x13***
441 A149 6.50k multi *1.60 1.60*

Re-adoption of Constitution, 10th Anniv. — A150

2002, May 23 ***Perf. 13¾x14***
442 A150 4.40k multi .80 .80

Adoption of Lübeck Charter by Town of Rakvere, 700th Anniv. — A151

2002, June 5

443 A151 4.40k multi .80 .80

Souvenir Sheet

Re-introduction of the Kroon, 10th Anniv. — A152

No. 444 — Portraits from bank notes: a, Lydia Koidula, poet. b, Carl Rober Jakobson, journalist.

2002, June 10 ***Perf. 14x13¾***

444 A152 4.40k Sheet of 2, #a-b 2.00 2.00

Souvenir Sheet

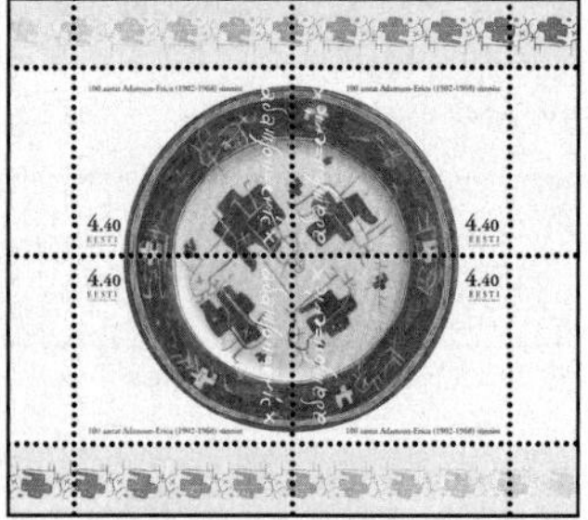

Adamson-Eric (1902-68), Painter — A153

Denomination at: a, LL. b, LR. c, UL. d, UR.

2002, Aug. 8 Litho. ***Perf. 14x13¾***

445 A153 4.40k Sheet of 4, #a-d 3.00 3.00

Sus Scrofa A154

2002, Aug. 21 ***Perf. 12¾x13***

446 A154 4.40k multi .80 .80

Limestone, Estonia's National Stone A155

2002, Sept. 18

447 A155 4.40k multi .80 .80

Folk Costume Type of 1994

Designs: 4.40k, Kolga-Jaani women. 5.50k, Suure-Jaani boy and girl.

2002, Oct. 1 ***Perf. 13¾x14***

448-449 A57 Set of 2 1.60 1.60

A156

Christmas — A157

Perf. 14x13¾, 13¾x14

2002, Nov. 20 Litho.

450 A156 3.60k Reindeer .60 .60

451 A157 6.50k Christmas tree 1.15 1.15

Lighthouse Type of 1995

2003, Jan. 15 ***Perf. 14x13¾***

452 A66 4.40k Keri .80 .80

Anton Hansen Tammsaare (1878-1940), Novelist — A158

2003, Jan. 30 Litho. ***Perf. 14x13¾***

453 A158 4.40k multi .80 .80

Pica Pica A159

2003, Feb. 13 ***Perf. 12¾x13***

454 A159 4.40k multi .80 .80

See Nos. 485, 509, 540, 566, 595, 625.

Spring Flowers — A160

No. 455: a, Tulips. b, Helleborus purpurascens. c, Narcissus poeticus. d, Crocus vernus.

2003, Mar. 20 ***Perf. 13¾x14***

455 A160 4.40k Sheet of 4, #a-d 7.00 7.00

e. Booklet pane, like #455, without date in margin 3.25 —

Complete booklet, #455e 3.25

See No. 484.

Manor Type of 1999

2003, Apr. 9 ***Perf. 14x13¾***

456 A103 4.40k Alatskivi Hall .80 .80

Pres. Arnold Rüütel, 75th Birthday — A161

2003, Apr. 24

457 A161 4.40k multi + label .90 .90

Europa — A162

2003, May 8 ***Perf. 13¾x14***

458 A162 6.50k multi *1.60 1.60*

Tartu University Botanical Gardens, Bicent. — A163

2003, June 11 Litho. ***Perf. 14x13¾***

459 A163 4.40k multi .90 .90

14th Junior World Orienteering Championships A164

2003, June 27

460 A164 7.50k multi 1.25 1.25

Circumnavigation of Adam Johann von Krusenstern (1770-1846) — A165

2003, Aug. 6 ***Perf. 12½***

461 A165 8k multi 1.40 1.40

Phoca Hispida A166

2003, Aug. 27 ***Perf. 12¾x13***

462 A166 4.40k multi .80 .80

Adm. Fabian Gottlieb von Bellingshausen (1778-1852) — A167

2003, Sept. 10

463 A167 8k multi 1.75 1.75

Ancient Trade Routes — A168

Map and: No. 464, 6.50k, Silver coin of Prince Volodymyr Sviatoslavovych, Slavic warship with sail. No. 465, 6.50k, Arrival of Scandinavian Seamen, coin of Danish King Svend Estridsen.

2003, Sept. 10 ***Perf. 11½***

464-465 A168 Set of 2 2.10 2.10

See Ukraine No. 524.

Three Lions Type of 1999-2002

2003-04 Litho. ***Perf. 13¾x14***

467 A108 20s blk & gray .30 .30

472 A108 4.40k ol grn & apple grn .80 .80

473 A108 5k dk grn & apple grn, dated 2004 .90 .90

474 A108 5.50k dk grn & yel grn 1.00 1.00

Issued: 20s, 4.40k, 8/22; 5k, 1/20/04; 5.50k, 3/25/04.

Folk Costume Type of 1994

Designs: 4.40k, Aksi woman and girl. 6.50k, Otepää man, woman and girl.

2003, Oct. 9 Litho. ***Perf. 13¾x14***

476-477 A57 Set of 2 1.90 1.90

A169

Christmas A170

2003, Nov. 26 ***Perf. 14x13¾***

478 A169 3.60k multi .70 .70

479 A170 6k multi .90 .90

Souvenir Sheet

Friedrich Reinhold Kreutzwald (1803-82), Writer — A171

No. 480: a, 4.40k, Illustration by Kristjan Raud of "Voyage to the End of the World," from "Kalevipoeg," by Kreutzwald. b, 6.50k, Portrait of Kreutzwald.

2003, Dec. 4 ***Perf. 13x12¾***

480 A171 Sheet of 2, #a-b 2.10 2.10

Lighthouse Type of 1995

2004, Jan. 7 Litho. ***Perf. 14x13¾***

481 A66 4.40k Sorgu .85 .85

Canis Lupus A172

2004, Feb. 3 ***Perf. 12¾x13***
482 A172 4.40k multi .85 .85

Voyage Around Cape Horn of the Hioma, 150th Anniv. — A173

2004, Feb. 18 ***Perf. 13¾x14***
483 A173 8k multi 1.50 1.50

Spring Flowers Type of 2003

No. 484: a, Viola riviniana. b, Anemone nemorosa. c, Hepatica nobilis. d, Trollius europaeus.

2004, Mar. 17
484 A160 4.40k Sheet of 4, #a-d 3.25 3.25
e. Booklet pane, like #484 without date in margin 3.25
Complete booklet, #484e 3.25

Bird Type of 2003

2004, Apr. 6 ***Perf. 12¾x13***
485 A159 4.40k Ciconia ciconia .80 .80

Admission to European Union A174

2004, May 1 ***Perf. 13¼x13***
486 A174 6.50k multi 1.25 1.25

Europa — A175

2004, May 4 ***Perf. 13***
487 A175 6.50k multi *1.25 1.25*

Tallinn Town Hall, 600th Anniv. A176

2004, May 13 Litho. ***Perf. 12¾x13***
488 A176 4.40k multi .80 .80

Consecration of Estonian Flag, 120th Anniv. — A177

2004, June 4 ***Perf. 13¾x14***
489 A177 4.40k multi .80 .80

Manor Type of 1999

2004, June 15 ***Perf. 14x13¾***
490 A103 4.40k Vasalemma Hall .80 .80

Admission to NATO — A178

2004, June 28 ***Perf. 13¾x14***
491 A178 6k multi 1.10 1.10

2004 Summer Olympics, Athens — A179

2004, July 15 Litho. ***Perf. 13¾x14***
492 A179 8k multi 1.40 1.40

Dragon Class Yachting European Championships — A180

2004, Aug. 17 ***Perf. 14x13¾***
493 A180 6k multi 1.10 1.10

Taraxacum Officinale — A181

Serpentine Die Cut 12½

2004, Sept. 14 **Self-Adhesive**
494 A181 30s multi .40 .40

See Nos. 547, 560, 572.

County Arms — A182

2004, Sept. 28 **Self-Adhesive**
495 A182 4.40k Harjumaa .80 .80
496 A182 4.40k Hiiumaa .80 .80

See Nos. 506-507, 518-519, 532-533, 536, 552, 561, 573, 588, 594, 608.

Folk Costumes Type of 1994

Designs: 4.40k, Viru-Jaagupi boy and girl. 7.50k, Jõhvi woman and girl.

2004, Oct. 5 Litho. ***Perf. 13¾x14***
497-498 A57 Set of 2 2.10 2.10

A183

Christmas A184

2004, Nov. 23 ***Perf. 13¾x14***
499 A183 4.40k multi .90 .90

Perf. 14x13¾
500 A184 6.50k multi 1.00 1.00

Lighthouse Type of 1995

Norrby Lighthouse with: 4.40k, White top, vert. 6.50k, Red top, vert.

2005, Jan. 11 Litho. ***Perf. 14***
501-502 A66 Set of 2 1.75 1.75

Castor Fiber A185

2005, Jan. 25 ***Perf. 12¾x13***
503 A185 4.40k multi .70 .70

Rotary International, Cent. — A186

2005, Feb. 11 ***Perf. 13¾x14***
504 A186 8k multi 1.25 1.25

Flag Over Pikk Hermann Tower, Tallinn — A187

Serpentine Die Cut 12½

2005, Feb. 22 **Self-Adhesive**
505 A187 5k multi .90 .90

See Nos. 530, 559, 574.

County Arms Type of 2004

2005 **Self-Adhesive** **Litho.**
506 A182 4.40k Ida-Virumaa .80 .80
507 A182 4.40k Järvamaa .80 .80

Issued: No. 506, 3/8; No. 507, 3/15.

Souvenir Sheet

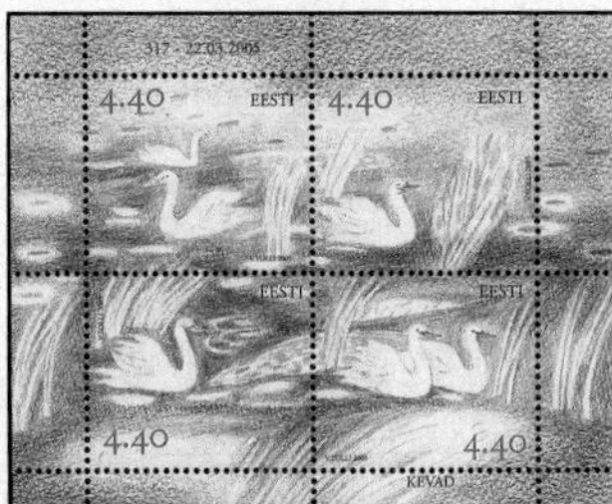
Spring — A188

No. 508: a, Two swans, denomination at UL. b, One swan, denomination at UL. c, One swan, denomination at LL. d, Two swans, denomination at LR.

2005, Mar. 22 Litho. ***Perf. 14x13¾***
508 A188 4.40k Sheet of 4, #a-d 2.75 2.75

Bird Type of 2003

2005, Apr. 5 ***Perf. 12¾x13***
509 A159 4.40k Accipiter gentilis .80 .80

Mother's Day — A189

2005, Apr. 20 ***Perf. 14x13¾***
510 A189 4.40k multi .80 .80

Europa — A190

Designs: 6k, Vegetable wrap. 6.50k, Tomato, carrots, egg yolk, parsley, fish, onion, beet.

2005, May 3
511-512 A190 Set of 2 *2.25 2.25*

Eduard Tubin (1905-82), Composer A191

2005, May 18
513 A191 6k multi 1.00 1.00

Intl. Children's Day — A192

No. 514: a, Birds. b, Butterflies.

2005, June 1 ***Perf. 13¼x13¾***
514 A192 4.40k Horiz. pair, #a-b, + central label 1.50 1.50

Orchids — A193

Designs: 4.40k, Epipactis palustris. 8k, Epipogium aphyllum.

2005, June 16 Litho. ***Perf. 13¾x14***
515-516 A193 Set of 2 2.50 2.50

Restoration of St. John's Cathedral, Tartu — A194

2005, June 29
517 A194 4.40k multi .80 .80

Tartu, 975th anniv.

County Arms Type of 2004

Serpentine Die Cut 12½

2005 **Self-Adhesive** **Litho.**
518 A182 4.40k Jõgevamaa .75 .75
519 A182 4.40k Läänemaa .75 .75

Issued: No. 518, 7/5; No. 519, 7/8.

Manor Type of 1999

2005, July 12 ***Perf. 14x13¾***
520 A103 4.40k Kiltsi Hall .75 .75

St. Catherine's Church, Karja — A195

2005, Sept. 20

521 A195 4.40k multi .75 .75

Souvenir Sheet

Sculptures by Amandus Adamson (1855-1929) — A196

No. 522: a, Igavesti Voidutsev Armastus, 1889. b, Lüüriline Muusika, 1891. c, Memento Mori, 1907. d, Koit ja Hämarik, 1895.

2005, Oct. 12 ***Perf. 13½***

522 A196 650s Sheet of 4, #a-d 4.00 4.00

Dogs — A197

No. 523: a, Kazakh hound (Kasaahi hurt). b, Estonian hound (Eesti hagijas).

2005, Oct. 19 ***Perf. 14x13¾***

523 A197 6.50k Horiz. pair, #a-b 2.10 2.10

See Kazakhstan No. 495.

Folk Costumes Type of 1994

Designs: 4.40k, Ambla man, woman and girl. 8k, Türi women.

2005, Oct. 28 ***Perf. 13¾x14***

524-525 A57 Set of 2 2.25 2.25

New Year's Goat — A198

Adoration of the Magi — A199

2005, Nov. 22

526 A198 4.40k multi .80 .80
527 A199 8k sil & red lil 1.45 1.45

Christmas and New Year's Day.

Due to the postponed conversion to the euro, originally scheduled for Jan. 1, 2007, Estonian stamps issued between 2006 and 2010 show denominations in kroons and the at-that-time-uncirculating euros.

Europa Stamps, 50th Anniv. — A200

CEPT emblem and: 6k, Superimposed letters. 6.50k, Map of Europe.

2006, Jan. 4 Litho. ***Perf. 14x13¾***

528 A200 6k multi .95 .95

Souvenir Sheet

529 A200 6.50k multi 1.00 1.00

Flag Over Pikk Hermann Tower Type of 2005 With Euro Denominations Added

2006, Jan. 11 ***Die Cut Perf. 12½***

Self-Adhesive

530 A187 11k multi 1.75 1.75

2006 Winter Olympics, Turin, Italy — A201

2006, Jan. 18 ***Perf. 14x13¾***

531 A201 8k multi 1.25 1.25

County Arms Type of 2004 With Euro Denominations Added

2006 ***Die Cut Perf. 12½***

Self-Adhesive

532 A182 4.40k Lääne-Virumaa .70 .70
533 A182 4.40k Polvamaa .70 .70

Issued: No. 532, 1/25; No. 533, 2/8.

Alces Alces A202

2006, Feb. 1 ***Perf. 12¾x13***

534 A202 4.40k multi .75 .75

Opening of KUMU Art Museum — A203

2006, Feb. 17 Litho. ***Perf. 13¾x14***

535 A203 4.40k multi .75 .75

County Arms Type of 2004 With Euro Denominations Added

2006, Mar. 8 ***Die Cut Perf. 12½***

Self-Adhesive

536 A182 4.40k Pärnumaa .85 .85

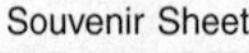

Souvenir Sheet

National Opera, Cent. — A204

No. 537: a, Characters from Vikerlased, first opera staged in 1928. b, Ballerina.

2006, Mar. 27 ***Perf. 13¾x14***

537 A204 6.50k Sheet of 2, #a-b, + central label 2.25 2.25

A205

Gold Medalists at 2006 Winter Olympics — A206

No. 539: a, Andrus Veerpalu. b, Kristina Smigun.

2006, Mar. 30 ***Perf. 14x13¾***

538 A205 4.40k multi .75 .75

Souvenir Sheet

539 A206 8k Sheet of 2, #a-b 2.50 2.50

Bird Type of 2003 With Euro Denominations Added

2006, Apr. 5 ***Perf. 12¾x13***

540 A159 4.40k multi .75 .75

Lighthouses A207

Designs: 4.40k, Tallinn Bay lower lighthouse. 6.50k, Tallinn Bay upper lighthouse.

2006, Apr. 12 ***Perf. 13¾x14***

541-542 A207 Set of 2 1.75 1.75

See Nos. 564, 587, 624.

Estonian Shooting Sport Federation, 75th Anniv. — A208

2006, Apr. 26

543 A208 4.40k car & sil .75 .75

Europa — A209

2006, May 3

544 A209 6.50k multi 1.25 1.25

Confectionery Industry in Estonia, Bicent. A210

2006, May 18 ***Perf. 14x13¾***

545 A210 4.40k multi .75 .75

Posthorns — A211

2006, May 22 ***Die Cut Perf. 10***

Self-Adhesive

546 A211 4.40k gray brn + label .75 .75

Labels could be personalized.
See No. 563.

Flower Type of 2004 with Euro Denominations Added

2006, May 24 ***Die Cut Perf. 12½***

Self-Adhesive

547 A181 30s Hepatica nobilis .35 .35

Souvenir Sheet

Tori Stud Farm, 150th Anniv. — A212

No. 548: a, Three horses, denomination at UL. b, Pony and three horses, denomination at UR.

2006, June 7 ***Perf. 14x13¾***

548 A212 4.40k Sheet of 2, #a-b 1.40 1.40

Victory Day — A213

2006, June 23

549 A213 4.40k multi .75 .75

20th Intl. Organ Music Festival, Tallinn — A214

2006, July 28 Litho. ***Perf. 14x13¾***

550 A214 4.40k multi .75 .75

Manor Type of 1999 With Added Euro Denomination

2006, Aug. 16

551 A103 4.40k Taagepera Hall .75 .75

County Arms Type of 2004 With Added Euro Denomination

2006, Sept. 6 ***Die Cut Perf. 12½***

Self-Adhesive

552 A182 4.40k Raplamaa .75 .75

St. Lawrence's Church, Noo — A215

2006, Sept. 20 ***Perf. 13¾x14***

553 A215 4.40k multi .75 .75

Betti Alver (1906-89), Writer — A216

2006, Oct. 11 ***Perf. 13***
554 A216 4.40k multi .75 .75

Antarctic Wildlife — A217

No. 555 — Estonian and Chilean flags and: a, Aptenodytes forsteri. b, Balaenoptera acutorostrata.

2006, Oct. 25 ***Perf. 13½***
555 A217 8k Pair, #a-b 2.50 2.50

See Chile No. 1468.

A218

Christmas — A219

2006, Nov. 22 Litho. ***Perf. 13¾x14***
556 A218 4.40k multi .70 .70
557 A219 6k multi .95 .95

Lotte From Gadgetville A220

2007, Jan. 4 ***Perf. 14x13¾***
558 A220 4.40k multi .85 .85

Flag Over Pikk Hermann Tower Type of 2005 With Euro Denomination Added

2007, Jan. 11 ***Die Cut Perf. 12½***
Self-Adhesive
559 A187 5k tan & multi .85 .85

Flower Type of 2004 With Euro Denomination Added

2007, Jan. 17 ***Die Cut Perf. 12½***
Self-Adhesive
560 A181 30s Leucanthemum vulgare .30 .30

County Arms Type of 2004 With Euro Denomination Added

2007, Jan. 25 ***Die Cut Perf. 12½***
Self-Adhesive
561 A182 4.40k Saaremaa .85 .85

Manor Type of 1999 With Euro Denomination Added

2007, Feb. 14 ***Perf. 14x13¾***
562 A103 5.50k Sagadi Hall .95 .95

Posthorns Type of 2006

2007, Feb. 22 ***Die Cut Perf. 10***
Self-Adhesive
563 A211 5.50k bl grn + label 1.00 1.00

Labels could be personalized.

Lighthouse Type of 2006

2007, Mar. 8 ***Perf. 14x13¾***
564 A207 6k Juminda, horiz. 1.00 1.00

Meles Meles A221

2007, Mar. 22 ***Perf. 12¾x13***
565 A221 4.40k multi .90 .90

Bird Type of 2003 With Euro Denomination Added

2007, Apr. 5 ***Perf. 12¾x13***
566 A159 4.40k Cygnus bewickii .90 .90

Miniature Sheet

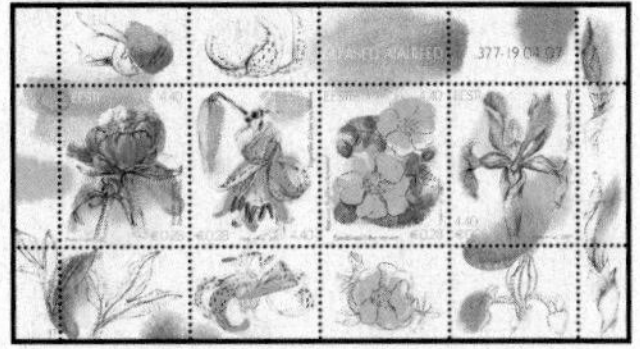
Summer Flowers — A222

No. 567: a, Paeonia officinalis. b, Lilium lancifolium. c, Rosa ecae Golden Chersonese. d, Iris latifolia.

2007, Apr. 19 ***Perf. 13¾x14***
567 A222 4.40k Sheet of 4, #a-d 3.25 3.25

Europa — A223

2007, May 3 ***Perf. 12½***
568 A223 20.50k multi 3.50 3.50

Scouting, cent.

Intl. Children's Day — A224

2007, June 1 Litho. ***Perf. 13½***
569 A224 10k multi 1.75 1.75

Souvenir Sheet

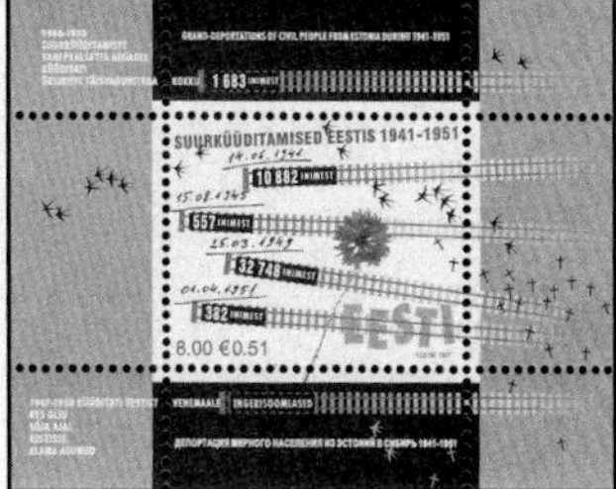
1941-51 Deportation of Estonians — A225

2007, June 14 ***Perf. 13***
570 A225 8k multi 1.40 1.40

Pirita Convent, 600th Anniv. — A226

2007, June 15 Litho. ***Perf. 12½***
571 A226 5.50k multi 1.00 1.00

Flower Type of 2004 With Euro Denominations Added

2007, July 2 ***Die Cut Perf. 12½***
Self-Adhesive
572 A181 1.10k Centaurea phrygia .30 .30

County Arms Type of 2004 With Euro Denominations Added

2007, July 2 **Self-Adhesive**
573 A182 5.50k Tartumaa 1.00 1.00

Flag Over Pikk Hermann Tower Type of 2005 With Euro Denominations Added

2007, Aug. 1 **Self-Adhesive**
574 A187 10k multi 1.75 1.75

Hellenurme Mill — A227

2007, Aug. 9 ***Perf. 14x13¾***
575 A227 5.50k multi 1.00 1.00

Hirvepark Demonstration, 20th Anniv. — A228

2007, Aug. 23 ***Perf. 14x14¼***
576 A228 5.50k multi 1.00 1.00

Souvenir Sheet

Matthias Johann Eisen (1857-1934), Folklorist — A229

2007, Sept. 14 ***Imperf.***
577 A229 10k multi 1.75 1.75

No. 577 has simulated perforations.

Ragnar Nurkse (1907-59), Economist — A230

2007, Oct. 5 ***Perf. 13***
578 A230 10k multi 1.75 1.75

St. John's Church, Kanepi — A231

2007, Oct. 11 ***Perf. 13¾x14***
579 A231 5.50k multi 1.00 1.00

Arms of Viljandi — A232

2007, Oct. 25 Litho. ***Perf. 13¾x14***
580 A232 5.50k multi 1.00 1.00

A233

Christmas A234

Die Cut Perf. 11¼ Syncopated
2007, Nov. 22 **Self-Adhesive**
581 A233 5.50k multi .90 .90
582 A234 8k multi 1.40 1.40

Post Horn — A235

2008 Litho. *Die Cut Perf. 12½*
Self-Adhesive

583 A235 5.50k brt orange 1.00 1.00
584 A235 6.50k brt yel green 1.15 1.15
585 A235 9k blue 1.60 1.60
Nos. 583-585 (3) 3.75 3.75

Issued: 5.50k, 1/10; 6.50k, 3/6; 9k, 4/1.
See Nos. 600, 638, 649, 658-662, 675-677, 682-684, 696-697, 708, 719-721.

Gustav Ernesaks (1908-93), Composer A236

2008, Jan. 17 Litho. *Perf. 13*
586 A236 5.50k multi 1.00 1.00

Lighthouse Type of 2006

2008, Jan. 24 *Perf. 14x13¾*
587 A207 5.50k Mehikoorma, horiz. 1.00 1.00

County Arms Type of 2004 With Euro Denominations Added

2008, Feb. 7 *Die Cut Perf. 12½*
Self-Adhesive
588 A182 5.50k Valgamaa 1.00 1.00

Plecotus Auritus A237

2008, Feb. 14 *Perf. 12¾x13*
589 A237 5.50k multi 1.00 1.00

Oak Tree — A238

2008, Feb. 23 *Perf. 13*
590 A238 5.50k multi 1.00 1.00

Republic of Estonia, 90th anniv.

Kristjan Palusalu (1908-87), Olympic Wrestling Gold Medalist — A239

2008, Mar. 10 *Perf. 12½*
591 A239 10k multi 1.75 1.75

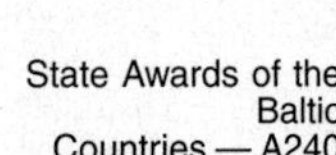

State Awards of the Baltic Countries — A240

Designs: Nos. 592, 593a, Order of the National Coat of Arms, Estonia. No. 593b, Order of Three Stars, Latvia. No. 593c, Order of Vytautas the Great, Lithuania.

2008, Mar. 15 Litho. *Perf. 13¾*
592 A240 5.50k multi 1.00 1.00

Souvenir Sheet

593 A240 10k Sheet of 3, #a-c, + label 5.25 5.25

See Latvia Nos. 701-702, Lithuania Nos. 862-863.

County Arms Type of 2004 With Euro Denominations Added

2008, Mar. 27 *Die Cut Perf. 12½*
Self-Adhesive
594 A182 5.50k Viljandimaa 1.00 1.00

Bird Type of 2003 With Euro Denomination Added

2008, Apr. 3 *Perf. 12¾x13*
595 A159 5.50k Tetrao tetrix 1.10 1.10

Europa A241

2008, Apr. 30 *Perf. 14x14¼*
596 A241 9k multi 1.60 1.60

Otto Strandman (1875-1941), Statesman — A242

2008, May 9 Litho. *Perf. 13¾x14*
597 A242 5.50k brown 1.00 1.00

Wavy Lines — A243

2008, May 22 *Serpentine Die Cut 10*
Self-Adhesive
598 A243 9k multi + label 1.75 1.75

The label shown is generic. Labels could be personalized for a fee.

Peasant War at Mahtra, 150th Anniv. — A244

2008, May 31 *Perf. 14x13¾*
599 A244 5.50k multi 1.00 1.00

Posthorn Type of 2008
Die Cut Perf. 12½
2008, May 31 Litho.
Self-Adhesive
600 A235 50s gray .35 .35

2008 Summer Olympics, Beijing — A245

2008, Aug. 8 Litho. *Perf. 13¾x14*
601 A245 9k multi 1.60 1.60

Polma Windmill A246

2008, Aug. 28 *Perf. 14x13¾*
602 A246 5.50k multi 1.00 1.00

Manor Type of 1999 With Euro Denomination Added

2008, Sept. 18 Litho. *Perf. 14x13¾*
603 A103 5.50k Kalvi Hall 1.00 1.00

Gerd Kanter, Olympic Discus Champion A247

2008. Sept. 25 *Perf. 13½*
604 A247 5.50k multi 1.00 1.00

Church of the Holy Cross, Audru — A248

2008, Oct. 16 Litho. *Perf. 13¾x14*
605 A248 5.50k multi 1.00 1.00

County Arms Type of 2004 With Euro Denominations Added

2008, Oct. 30 *Die Cut Perf. 12½*
Self-Adhesive
606 A182 5.50k Vorumaa 1.00 1.00

Estonia Post, 90th Anniv. — A249

2008, Nov. 13 *Perf. 13¾x14*
607 A249 5.50k multi 1.00 1.00

Christmas A250

Designs: 5.50k, Gift on skis. 9k, Snowman on gift.

Die Cut Perf. 11¼ Syncopated
2008, Nov. 20 Litho.
Booklet Stamps Self-Adhesive

608 A250 5.50k multi .90 .90
a. Booklet pane of 10 8.25
609 A250 9k multi 1.60 1.60
a. Booklet pane of 10 13.50

Souvenir Sheet

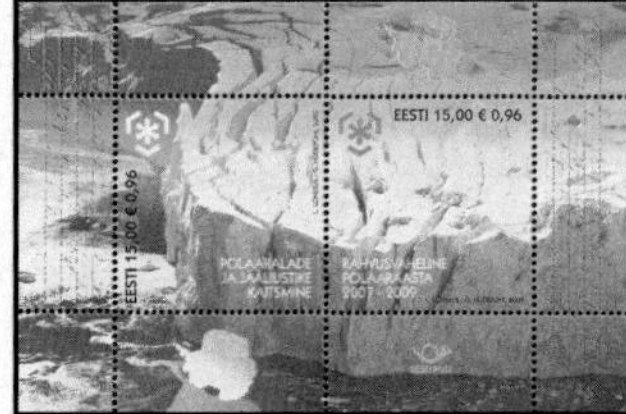

International Polar Year — A251

No. 610 — Antarctic glacier with snowflake emblem in: a, White. b, Blue.

2009, Jan. 15 Litho. *Perf. 13x12¾*
610 A251 15k Sheet of 2, #a-b 5.50 5.50

Battle of Paju, 90th Anniv. A252

2009, Jan. 29 *Perf. 12¾x13*
611 A252 5.50k multi 1.00 1.00

Gen. Johan Laidoner (1884-1953) — A253

2009, Feb. 12 Litho. *Perf. 13*
612 A253 5.50k multi 1.00 1.00

Ants Piip (1884-1942), Prime Minister — A254

2009, Feb. 26 *Perf. 14*
613 A254 5.50k maroon 1.00 1.00

Pres. Lennart Meri (1929-2006) A255

2009, Mar. 26 Litho. *Perf. 14*
614 A255 5.50k blue 1.00 1.00

Estonian National Museum, Cent. — A256

2009, Apr. 14 *Perf. 13*
615 A256 5.50k multi 1.00 1.00

Estonian Parliament, 90th Anniv. — A257

2009, Apr. 23 ***Perf. 14***
616 A257 5.50k multi 1.00 1.00

Europa — A258

No. 617: a, Galaxies and hexagonal cells. b, Galaxy and hexagonal cells at left.

2009, May 5 Litho. ***Perf. 13¾x14***
617 A258 9k Horiz. pair, #a-b 3.25 3.25

Intl. Year of Astronomy.

Räpina Paper Mill, 275th Anniv. — A259

2009, May 14
618 A259 5.50k multi 1.00 1.00

Estonian Flag, 125th Anniv. — A260

Die Cut Perf. 11¼ Syncopated
2009, June 5
Booklet Stamp Self-Adhesive
619 A260 9k multi 1.50 1.50
a. Booklet pane of 10 15.00

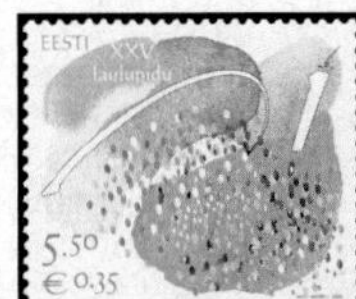

25th Song Festival — A261

2009, June 18 ***Perf. 14x13¾***
620 A261 5.50k multi 1.00 1.00

Alexander Church, Narva, 125th Anniv. — A262

2009, July 10 Litho. ***Perf. 13¾x14***
621 A262 5.50k multi *1.50 1.50*

Ursus Arctos A263

2009, Sept. 10 ***Perf. 12¾x13***
622 A263 5.50k multi 1.00 1.00

First Track and Field Competition in Estonia, Cent. — A264

2009, Sept. 22 ***Perf. 14x13¾***
623 A264 5.50k multi 1.10 1.10

Lighthouse Type of 2006

2009, Sept. 24 ***Perf. 14x13¾***
624 A207 5.50k Hara Tuletorn, horiz. 1.10 1.10

Bird Type of 2003 With Euro Denomination Added

2009, Oct. 8 Litho. ***Perf. 12¾x13***
625 A159 5.50k Strix aluco 1.10 1.10

Windmill, Angla — A265

2009, Oct. 22 ***Perf. 13¾x14***
626 A265 5.50k multi 1.10 1.10

Manor Type of 1999 With Euro Denomination Added

2009, Nov. 5 ***Perf. 14x13¾***
627 A103 5.50k Saku Hall 1.10 1.10

A266

Christmas A267

Die Cut Perf. 11¼ Syncopated
2009, Nov. 19
Booklet Stamps Self-Adhesive
628 A266 5.50k multi .95 .95
a. Booklet pane of 10 9.50
629 A267 9k multi 1.60 1.60
a. Booklet pane of 10 16.00

Fabric Design — A268

Die Cut Perf. 11¼ Syncopated
2010, Jan. 7 **Litho.**
Booklet Stamp Self-Adhesive
630 A268 50k orange & multi 8.50 8.50
a. Booklet pane of 10 85.00

See Nos. 646, 650.

Jüri Jaakson (1870-1942), Politician — A269

2010, Jan. 15 ***Perf. 14***
631 A269 5.50k multi .95 .95

2010 European Figure Skating Championships, Tallinn — A270

2010, Jan. 19 ***Perf. 12¾x13***
632 A270 9k multi 1.50 1.50
a. Tete-beche pair 3.00 3.00

Tartu Peace Treaty, 90th Anniv. A271

2010, Feb. 2 ***Perf. 13***
633 A271 5.50k multi 1.00 1.00

Post Horn Type of 2008

2010, Feb. 4 ***Die Cut Perf. 12½***
Self-Adhesive
634 A235 9k deep blue 1.50 1.50

Dated 2010. Compare with No. 585.

2010 Winter Olympics, Vancouver — A272

2010, Feb. 4 ***Perf. 14***
635 A272 9k multi 1.60 1.60

Platanthera Bifolia — A273

2010, Feb. 19
636 A273 5.50k multi 1.00 1.00

Estonia Pavilion, Expo 2010, Shanghai A274

2010, Mar. 11
637 A274 9k multi 1.50 1.50

Posthorn Type of 2008
Die Cut Perf. 12½
2010, Mar. 23 **Litho.**
Self-Adhesive
638 A235 5.50k bright pink 1.00 1.00

St. Catherine's Church, Pärnu — A275

2010, Mar. 23 ***Perf. 13¾x14***
639 A275 6.50k multi 1.10 1.10

Juhan Kukk (1885-1942), State Elder — A276

2010, Apr. 13
640 A276 5.50k olive brown 1.00 1.00

Lighthouses Type of 2006

Designs: 6.50k, Suurupi front lighthouse. 8k, Suurupi rear lighthouse.

2010, Apr. 22
641-642 A207 Set of 2 2.50 2.50

Europa — A277

Children's book illustrations: No. 643, 9k, Family of mice, by Jüri Mildeberg. No. 644, 9k, Skaters in snow, by Viive Noor.

2010, May 6 ***Perf. 14x13¾***
643-644 A277 Set of 2 2.50 2.50

Bird Type of 2003 With Euro Denominations Added

2010, May 13 ***Perf. 12¾x13***
645 A159 5.50k Lanius collurio 1.00 1.00

Fabric Design Type of 2010
Die Cut Perf. 11¼ Syncopated
2010, June 1
Booklet Stamp Self-Adhesive
646 A268 26k brt yel grn & multi 4.50 4.50
a. Booklet pane of 10 45.00

Intl. Children's Day — A278

2010, June 1 **Litho.**
Booklet Stamp Self-Adhesive
647 A278 5.50k multi 1.00 1.00
a. Booklet pane of 10 10.00

Manor Type of 1999 With Euro Denominations Added

2010, Aug. 5 Litho. *Perf. 14x13¾*
648 A103 5.50k Suuremõisa Hall .95 .95

Posthorn Type of 2008

2010, Aug. 18 *Die Cut Perf. 12*
Self-Adhesive
649 A235 9k bright yellow 1.50 1.50

Fabric Design Type of 2010

Die Cut Perf. 11¼ Syncopated
2010, Aug. 18
Booklet Stamp
Self-Adhesive
650 A268 26k lilac & multi 4.50 4.50
a. Booklet pane of 10 45.00

Tallinn, 2011 European Capital of Culture — A279

2010, Sept. 9 Litho.
Self-Adhesive
651 A279 5.50k multi 1.00 1.00

Eliomys Quercinus A280

2010, Sept. 23 *Perf. 12¾x13*
652 A280 5.50k multi .75 .75

A281

A282

A283

Worldwide Fund for Nature (WWF) — A284

Various views of Triturus cristatus.

2010, Oct. 14 *Perf. 14x13¾*
653 Horiz. strip of 4 6.50 6.50
a. A281 9k multi 1.60 1.60
b. A282 9k multi 1.60 1.60
c. A283 9k multi 1.60 1.60
d. A284 9k multi 1.60 1.60
e. Sheet of 8 stamps with two tete-beche strips 13.00 13.00

Lennuk, by Nikolai Triik — A285

2010, Nov. 17 Litho. *Perf. 14*
654 A285 9k multi 1.60 1.60

A286

Christmas — A287

Die Cut Perf. 11¼ Syncopated
2010, Nov. 25
Booklet Stamps
Self-Adhesive
655 A286 5.50k multi .95 .95
a. Booklet pane of 10 9.50
656 A287 9k multi 1.60 1.60
a. Booklet pane of 10 16.00

Stamps in No. 655a are tete-beche in relation to adjacent stamps. Vertical pairs of stamps in No. 656a are tete-beche.

100 Cents = 1 Euro

Introduction of Euro Currency A288

Die Cut Perf. 11¼ Syncopated
2011, Jan. 1
Booklet Stamp
Self-Adhesive
657 A288 €1 multi 2.75 2.75
a. Booklet pane of 10 27.50

Post Horn Type of 2008 with Euro Denominations Only

2011, Jan. 3 *Die Cut Perf. 12½*
Self-Adhesive
658 A235 1c orange .25 .25
659 A235 5c salmon pink .25 .25
660 A235 10c lilac .25 .25
661 A235 50c blue 1.40 1.40
662 A235 65c green 1.75 1.75
Nos. 658-662 (5) 3.90 3.90

New Year 2011 (Year of the Rabbit) A289

2011, Feb. 3 Litho. *Perf. 12¾x13*
663 A289 58c multi 1.60 1.60

Friedebert Tuglas (1886-1971), Writer — A290

2011, Mar. 2 *Perf. 13¾x14*
664 A290 58c multi 1.60 1.60

Villem Reiman (1861-1917), Historian — A291

2011, Mar. 9
665 A291 35c multi 1.00 1.00

Peony A292

2011, Mar. 24 *Perf. 13x12¾*
666 A292 58c multi 1.75 1.75

Printed in sheets of 4 having each stamp rotated 90 degrees in relation to each other.

Folk Costumes — A293

Designs: 35c, Man and woman from Rapla. 58c, Two women from Joelähtme.

2011, Apr. 14 *Perf. 13¾x14*
667-668 A293 Set of 2 2.50 2.50

Hirundo Rustica A294

2011, Apr. 21 *Perf. 12¾x13*
669 A294 35c multi 1.00 1.00

Europa A295

Designs: No. 670, 58c, Elk in forest. No. 671, 58c, Cut logs.

2011, Apr. 28 *Perf. 13*
670-671 A295 Set of 2 3.00 3.00

Intl. Year of Forests.

Souvenir Sheet

Struve Geodetic Arc — A296

No. 672 — Map of arc and: a, Friedrch Georg Wilhelm Struve (1793-1864), astronomer. b, Tartu Observatory.

2011, May 6 *Perf. 14x13¾*
672 A296 58c Sheet of 2, #a-b 3.25 3.25

Lepus Europaeus A297

2011, May 19 *Perf. 12¾x13*
673 A297 35c multi 1.00 1.00

Vergi Lighthouse A298

2011, June 2 *Perf. 14x13¾*
674 A298 35c multi 1.00 1.00

Posthorn Type of 2008 With Euro Denominations Only

2011 *Die Cut Perf. 12½*
Self-Adhesive
675 A235 35c brt yel grn 1.00 1.00
676 A235 58c lt purple 1.75 1.75
677 A235 58c green 1.60 1.60

Issued: 35c, No. 676, 6/2. No. 677, 8/25.

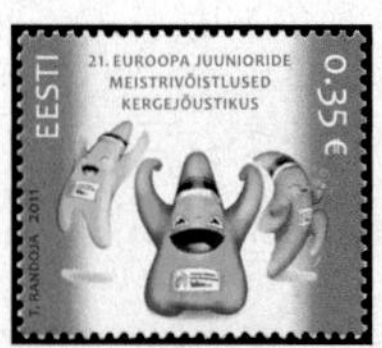

21st European Junior Track and Field Championships, Tallinn — A299

2011, July 20 Litho. *Perf. 14x13¾*
678 A299 35c multi 1.00 1.00

Restoration of Independence, 20th Anniv. — A300

2011, Aug. 20 ***Perf. 13¾x14¼***
679 A300 35c multi 1.00 1.00

St. Margaret's Church, Karuse — A301

2011, Aug. 25 ***Perf. 14x13¾***
680 A301 35c multi 1.00 1.00

Friedrich Karl Akel (1871-1941), State Elder — A302

2011, Sept. 5 ***Perf. 13¾x14***
681 A302 35c brown 1.00 1.00

Posthorn Type of 2008 With Euro Denominations Only

2011 ***Die Cut Perf. 12½***
Self-Adhesive

682 A235 10c sage green .30 .30
683 A235 35c cerise .95 .95
684 A235 45c rose 1.25 1.25
Nos. 682-684 (3) 2.50 2.50

Issued: 10c, 45c, 11/1; 35c, 9/15.

Heinrich Mark (1911-2004), Prime Minister — A303

2011, Sept. 30 ***Perf. 13¾x14***
685 A303 35c blue .95 .95

Michael Andreas Barclay de Tolly (1761-1818), Military Leader — A304

2011, Oct. 20 ***Perf. 14x13¾***
686 A304 €1 multi 2.75 2.75

10-Cent and 2-Euro Coins — A305

Die Cut Perf. 11¼ Syncopated
2011, Nov. 1
Booklet Stamp
Self-Adhesive

687 A305 €2.10 multi 5.50 5.50
a. Booklet pane of 10 55.00

Market, Painting by Henn-Olavi Roode (1924-74) A306

2011, Nov. 17 ***Perf. 14***
688 A306 €1 multi 2.75 2.75

Christmas — A307

Die Cut Perf. 11¼ Syncopated
2011, Nov. 24
Booklet Stamps
Self-Adhesive

689 A307 45c Angel 1.25 1.25
a. Booklet pane of 10 12.50
690 A307 €1 Ornament 2.75 2.75
a. Booklet pane of 10 27.50

Vertical pairs of stamps in Nos. 689a and 690a are tete-beche.

Oskar Luts (1887-1953), Writer — A308

2012, Jan. 7 **Litho.** ***Perf. 13***
691 A308 45c multi 1.25 1.25

Population and Housing Census — A309

Die Cut Perf. 11¼x11½ Syncopated
2012, Jan. 12 **Self-Adhesive**
692 A309 45c multi 1.25 1.25

New Year 2012 (Year of the Dragon) A310

2012, Jan. 23 ***Perf. 12¾x13***
693 A310 €1.10 multi 3.00 3.00

Capreolus Capreolus A311

2012, Feb. 16 ***Perf. 12¾x13***
694 A311 45c multi 1.25 1.25

Heino Eller (1887-1970), Composer A312

2012, Mar. 7 ***Perf. 14x13¾***
695 A312 45c multi 1.25 1.25

Posthorn Type of 2008 With Euro Denominations Only

2012, Mar. 29 ***Die Cut Perf. 12½***
Self-Adhesive
Dated "2012"

696 A235 10c dull blue green .25 .25
697 A235 50c pale yel grn 1.40 1.40

Compare Nos. 696 and 750.

Personalized Stamp — A313

Die Cut Perf. 8¾ Syncopated
2012, Mar. 29 **Self-Adhesive**
698 A313 45c multi 1.25 1.25

The generic vignette shown, depicting a map of Saaremaa, could be personalized for an additional fee.
See Nos. 773, 901.

Folk Costumes — A314

Designs: 45c, Woman and girl from Hageri. €1, Woman from Nissi.

2012, Apr. 14 **Litho.** ***Perf. 13¾x14***
699-700 A314 Set of 2 4.00 4.00

Charadrius Dubius A315

2012, Apr. 19 ***Perf. 12¾x13***
701 A315 45c multi 1.25 1.25

Johannes Pääsuke (1892-1918), Creator of First Estonian Film in 1912 — A316

2012, Apr. 30
702 A316 45c multi 1.25 1.25

Europa A317

Inscriptions: No. 703, €1, "wild est." No. 704, €1, "smart est."

2012, May 3 ***Perf. 14x13¾***
703-704 A317 Set of 2 5.25 5.25

Church of St. Simeon and the Prophet Anne, Tallinn — A318

2012, May 17 ***Perf. 13¾x14***
705 A318 45c multi 1.25 1.25

2012 Summer Olympics, London A319

2012, June 1 ***Perf. 14x13¾***
706 A319 €1.10 multi 2.75 2.75

Martin Klein (1884-1947), First Estonian Olympic Medalist — A320

2012, July 13 ***Perf. 14x14¼***
707 A320 €1 multi 2.50 2.50

Posthorn Type of 2008 With Euro Denominations Only

2012, Aug. 10 ***Die Cut Perf. 12½***
Self-Adhesive

708 A235 45c citron 1.25 1.25

One-Euro Coin — A321

Die Cut Perf. 11¼ Syncopated
2012, Aug. 10 **Self-Adhesive**
709 A321 €1 multi 2.60 2.60

Amanita Virosa — A322

2012, Aug. 30 ***Perf. 13¾x14***
710 A322 45c red & black 1.25 1.25

Käsmu Lighthouse A323

2012, Sept. 13 *Perf. 14x13¾*
711 A323 45c multi 1.25 1.25

Jaan Teemant (1872-1941), State Elder — A324

2012, Sept. 24 *Perf. 13¾x14*
712 A324 45c brown 1.25 1.25

Railway Bridges A325

Train and: Nos. 713, 714a, Narva Bridge, Estonia. No. 714b, Carnikava Bridge, Latvia. No. 714c, Lyduvenai Bridge, Lithuania.

2012, Oct. 25 *Perf. 13¼*
713 A325 45c multi 1.25 1.25

Souvenir Sheet

714 A325 €1 Sheet of 3, #a-c 8.00 8.00

See Latvia Nos. 815-816, Lithuania Nos. 985-986.

Scouting in Estonia, Cent. — A326

2012, Nov. 7 *Perf. 14x13¾*
715 A326 45c multi 1.25 1.25

Still Life with Mandolin, by Lepo Mikko — A327

2012, Nov. 16 *Perf. 14*
716 A327 €1.10 multi 3.00 3.00

Santa Claus on Skis — A328

Poinsettia A329

Die Cut Perf. 11¼ Syncopated

2012, Nov. 22 **Self-Adhesive**
717 A328 45c multi 1.25 1.25
718 A329 €1 multi 2.60 2.60

Christmas.

Posthorn Type of 2008 With Euro Denominations Only Self-Adhesive

2013, Jan. 10 ***Die Cut Perf. 12½***
719 A235 5c light blue .30 .30
720 A235 50c green 1.40 1.40
721 A235 65c red violet 1.75 1.75
Nos. 719-721 (3) 3.45 3.45

Kiipsaare Lighthouse A330

2013, Jan. 31 *Perf. 14x13¾*
722 A330 45c multi 1.25 1.25

New Year 2013 (Year of the Snake) A331

2013, Feb. 8 *Perf. 12¾x13*
723 A331 €1.10 multi 3.00 3.00

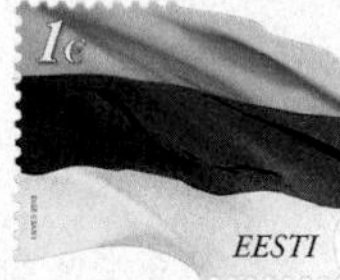
Estonian Flag — A332

Die Cut Perf. 11¼ Syncopated

2013, Feb. 22
Self-Adhesive
724 A332 €1 multi 2.60 2.60
a. Dated "2014" 2.75 2.75

See No. 754.
Issued No. 724a, 5/22/14.

Perdix Perdix A333

2013, Mar. 7 *Perf. 12¾x13*
725 A333 45c multi 1.25 1.25

Arms of Sindi — A333a

Die Cut Perf. 12½

2013, Mar. 28 **Litho.**
Self-Adhesive
725A A333a 45c multi 1.75 1.75

Folk Costumes — A334

Man and woman from: 45c, Kihelkonna. €1, Karja.

2013, Apr. 12 *Perf. 13¾x14*
726-727 A334 Set of 2 4.00 4.00

Icebreaker "Tarmo" — A335

2013, Apr. 25 *Perf. 14x13¾*
728 A335 €1 multi 2.75 2.75

Europa — A336

No. 729 — Postal vehicles: a, Horse-drawn stagecoach, 1840s. b, Modern van.

2013, May 2 **Litho.**
729 A336 €1 Horiz. pair, #a-b 5.25 5.25

Souvenir Sheet

Estcube-1 Satellite — A337

2013, May 2
730 A337 €1.10 multi 3.00 3.00

Kuressaare, 450th Anniv. A338

2013, May 8 *Perf. 14x14¼*
731 A338 45c multi 1.40 1.40

Kaarel Eenpalu (1888-1942), State Elder and Prime Minister — A339

2013, May 28 *Perf. 13¾x14*
732 A339 45c dk brn violet 1.25 1.25

Mustela Nivalis A340

2013, June 6 *Perf. 12¾x13*
733 A340 45c multi 1.25 1.25

St. Catherine's Church, Voru — A341

2013, July 24 *Perf. 13¾x14*
734 A341 45c multi 1.25 1.25

Souvenir Sheet

Cultural Heritage Year — A342

2013, Aug. 3 *Perf.*
735 A342 €1.10 multi 3.00 3.00

Finn Class Sailing World Championships, Tallinn — A343

2013, Aug. 23 *Perf. 14¼x13¾*
736 A343 €1.10 multi 3.00 3.00

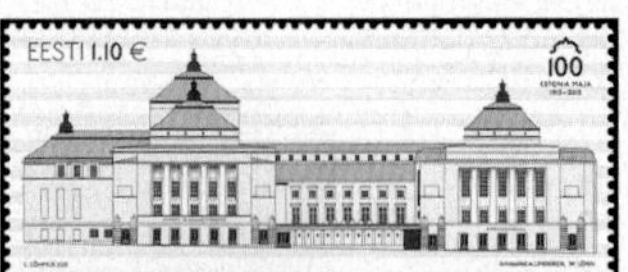
Estonia Theater and Concert House, Tallinn, Cent. — A344

2013, Sept. 6 *Perf. 13*
737 A344 €1.10 multi 3.00 3.00

Amanita Phalloides — A345

2013, Sept. 12 *Perf. 13¾x14*
738 A345 45c multi 1.25 1.25

Raimond Valgre (1913-49), Composer — A346

2013, Oct. 7 Litho. *Perf. 13*
739 A346 45c multi 1.25 1.25

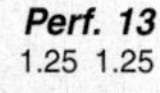

Arms of Moisaküla — A347

Die Cut Perf. 12½
2013, Oct. 31 Litho.
Self-Adhesive
740 A347 45c sil & black 1.50 1.50

Regular Postal Services in Estonia, 375th Anniv. A348

Perf. 14¼x13¾
2013, Nov. 13 Litho.
741 A348 45c multi 1.50 1.50

Aadu (Ado) Birk (1883-1942), Prime Minister — A349

2013, Nov. 14 Litho. *Perf. 13¾x14*
742 A349 45c dull brown 1.25 1.25

After Dinner, by Elmar Kits (1913-72) A350

2013, Nov. 15 Litho. *Perf. 14*
743 A350 €1.10 multi 2.50 2.50

A351

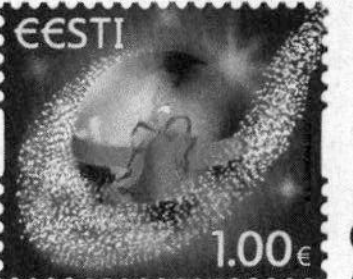

Christmas A352

Serpentine Die Cut 11¼ Syncopated
2013, Nov. 22 Litho.
Self-Adhesive
744 A351 45c multi 1.25 1.25
745 A352 €1 multi 2.75 2.75

Estonian Olympic Committee, 90th Anniv. — A353

2013, Dec. 9 Litho. *Perf. 13¾x14*
746 A353 45c multi 1.50 1.50

Jaan Tonisson (1888-c. 1941), Prime Minister — A354

2013, Dec. 20 Litho. *Perf. 13¾x14*
747 A354 45c brown 1.25 1.25

2014 Winter Olympics, Sochi, Russia — A355

2014, Jan. 16 Litho. *Perf. 14x13¾*
748 A355 €1.10 multi 3.00 3.00

New Year 2014 (Year of the Horse) A356

2014, Jan. 31 Litho. *Perf. 12¾x13*
749 A356 €1.10 multi 3.00 3.00

Post Horn Type of 2008 With Euro Denomination Only
Die Cut Perf. 12½
2014, Feb. 19 Litho.
Self-Adhesive
Dated "2014"
750 A235 10c brt bl grn .35 .35
a. Dated "2015" .35 .35

Issued: No. 750a, 10/16/15. Compare with No. 696.

Estonian History Museum, 150th Anniv. A357

2014, Feb. 19 Litho. *Perf. 12¾x13*
751 A357 45c multi 1.25 1.25

Pres. Konstantin Päts (1874-1956) A358

2014, Feb. 21 Litho. *Perf. 13¾x14*
752 A358 45c blue 1.25 1.25

Arms of Voru — A359

Die Cut Perf. 12½
2014, Mar. 5 Litho.
Self-Adhesive
753 A359 45c multi 1.25 1.25

Estonian Flag Type of 2013
Die Cut Perf. 11¼ Syncopated
2014, Mar. 5 Litho.
Self-Adhesive
754 A332 €2 multi 5.50 5.50
754a Dated "2018" 4.75 4.75

Issued: No. 754a, 6/27/18.

Alcedo Atthis A360

2014, Mar. 20 Litho. *Perf. 12¾x13*
755 A360 45c multi 1.25 1.25

Folk Costumes — A361

Designs: 45c, Man and woman from Mihkli. €1, Women from Vigala.

2014, Apr. 12 Litho. *Perf. 13¾x14*
756-757 A361 Set of 2 4.00 4.00

Juhan Liiv (1864-1913), Poet — A362

2014, Apr. 30 Litho. *Perf. 13*
758 A362 45c multi 1.25 1.25

Inachis Io — A363

Serpentine Die Cut 12½
2014, May 2 Litho.
Booklet Stamp
Self-Adhesive
759 A363 45c multi 1.40 1.40
a. Booklet pane of 4 5.60

Europa A364

Musical instruments: No. 760, €1, Väikekannel (zither). No. 761, €1, Lootspill (accordion).

2014, May 8 Litho. *Perf. 14x13¾*
760-761 A364 Set of 2 5.00 5.00

Erinaceus Europaeus A365

2014, May 30 Litho. *Perf. 12¾x13*
762 A365 45c multi 1.25 1.25

Estonian Herdbook, Cent. A366

2014, July 19 Litho. *Perf. 14x13½*
Textured and Flocked Granite Paper
763 A366 €1 multi 2.75 2.75

Baltic Chain Demonstration, 25th Anniv. — A367

Designs: 55c, Man and child.
No. 765: a, Five adults and one child. b, Three women. c, Like #764

2014, Aug. 23 Litho. *Perf. 13¼*
764 A367 55c multi 1.50 1.50
Souvenir Sheet
765 A367 €1 Sheet of 3, #a-c 8.00 8.00

See Latvia Nos. 883-884; Lithuania No. 1031.

Souvenir Sheet

Tallinn Zoo, 75th Anniv. — A368

No. 766: a, Gypaetus barbatus. b, Panthera pardus orientalis.

Perf. 14¼x13¾
2014, Aug. 25 Litho.
766 A368 55c Sheet of 2, #a-b 3.00 3.00

Estonian Academy of Arts, Cent. — A369

2014, Sept. 1 Litho. *Perf. 14x13¾*
767 A369 55c multi 1.50 1.50

Inocybe Erubescens A370

2014, Sept. 11 Litho. *Perf. 13¾x14*
768 A370 55c red & black 1.40 1.40

Arms of Saue — A371

Die Cut Perf. 12½
2014, Sept. 11 Litho.
Self-Adhesive
769 A371 55c multi 1.40 1.40

1-Euro and 20-Cent Coins — A372

Die Cut Perf. 11¼ Syncopated
2014, Oct. 2 Litho.
Self-Adhesive
770 A372 €1.20 multi 3.00 3.00

Lighthouses A373

Designs: 55c, Northern Soru Lighthouse. €1.30, Southern Soru Lighthouse.

2014, Oct. 17 Litho. *Perf. 13¾x14*
771-772 A373 Set of 2 5.00 5.00

Personalized Stamp Type of 2012
Die Cut Perf. 8¾ Syncopated
2014, Nov. 17 Litho.
Self-Adhesive
773 A313 55c multi 1.40 1.40

The generic vignette, depicting a map of Hüumaa, could be personalized for an additional fee.

Courtyard, by Herbert Lukk (1892-1919) A374

2014, Nov. 17 Litho. *Perf. 14*
774 A374 €1.30 multi 3.50 3.50

Christmas A375

Christmas tree, ornaments and: 55c, Ribbon. €1.20, Pine cone.

Die Cut Perf. 11¼ Syncopated
2014, Nov. 20 Litho.
Self-Adhesive
775-776 A375 Set of 2 4.50 4.50

Jüri Uluots (1890-1945), Prime Minister — A376

2015, Jan. 13 Litho. *Perf. 13¾x14*
777 A376 55c blue 1.25 1.25

Johannes Kotkas (1915-88), Wrestler — A377

2015, Feb. 3 Litho. *Perf. 12½*
778 A377 55c multi 1.25 1.25

New Year 2015 (Year of the Ram) A378

2015, Feb. 19 Litho. *Perf. 12¾x13*
779 A378 €1.30 multi 3.00 3.00

Eduard Vilde (1865-1933), Writer — A379

2015, Mar. 4 Litho. *Perf. 13*
780 A379 55c multi 1.25 1.25

Arms of Elva — A380

Die Cut Perf. 12½
2015, Mar. 12 Litho.
Self-Adhesive
781 A380 55c multi 1.25 1.25

Souvenir Sheet

Seal and Map of Baltic Sea — A381

2015, Mar. 12 Litho. *Perf.*
782 A381 €2.55 multi 6.25 6.25

Folk Costumes — A382

Designs: 55c, Man, woman and girl from Lihula. €1.20, Women from Kirbla.

2015, Apr. 14 Litho. *Perf. 13¾x14*
783-784 A382 Set of 2 4.00 4.00

Europa A383

Designs: No. 785, €1.20, Toy horses. No. 786, €1.20, Stuffed animals.

2015, May 6 Litho. *Perf. 14*
785-786 A383 Set of 2 5.50 5.50

Pernis Apivorus A384

2015, May 21 Litho. *Perf. 12¾x13*
787 A384 55c multi 1.25 1.25

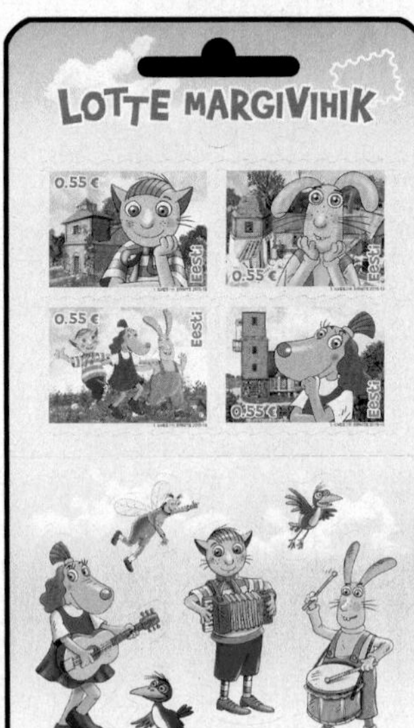

Characters From Animated Film *Lotte From Gadgetville* — A385

No. 788: a, Bruno the Kitten. b, Albert the Bunny. c, Bruno, Albert and Lotte. d, Lotte the Puppy.

Serpentine Die Cut 5x6
2015, May 30 Litho.
Self-Adhesive
788 A385 Booklet pane of 4 + 6 stickers 5.50
a.-d. 55c Any single 1.35 1.35

Giraffe With Head Above Cloud — A386

Serpentine Die Cut 5x6
2015, June 4 Litho.
Booklet Stamp
Self-Adhesive
789 A386 €1.20 multi 2.75 2.75
a. Booklet pane of 4 11.00

Aleksander Warma (1890-1970), Prime Minister — A387

2015, June 22 Litho. *Perf. 13¾x14*
790 A387 55c Prus grn 1.25 1.25

European Under-23 Track and Field Championships, Tallinn — A388

2015, July 1 Litho. *Perf. 14x13¾*
791 A388 55c multi 1.25 1.25

Estonian Business Innovations — A389

No. 792: a, Fortumo. b, GrabCAD. c, Skype. d, TransferWise.

Die Cut Perf. 12½
2015, July 6 Litho.
Self-Adhesive
792 A389 Booklet pane of 4 12.00
a.-d. €1.30 Any single 3.00 3.00

Lutra Lutra A390

2015, Aug. 25 Litho. *Perf. 12¾x13*
793 A390 55c multi 1.35 1.35

Arms of Paide — A391

Die Cut Perf. 12½

2015, Sept. 10 **Litho.**

Self-Adhesive

794 A391 55c multi 1.25 1.25

Cortinarius Rubellus — A392

2015, Sept. 10 **Litho.** ***Perf. 13¾x14***

795 A392 55c multi 1.35 1.35

Tahkuna Lighthouse A393

2015, Oct. 16 **Litho.** ***Perf. 14x13¾***

796 A393 55c multi 1.25 1.25

Penny Black, 175th Anniv. — A394

2015, Nov. 13 **Litho.** ***Perf. 13½***

797 A394 55c multi 1.25 1.25

A Girl and the Moon, by Karl Pärsimägi (1902-42) — A395

2015, Nov. 17 **Litho.** ***Perf. 14***

798 A395 55c multi 1.25 1.25

A396

Christmas — A397

Die Cut Perf. 11¼ Syncopated

2015, Nov. 19 **Litho.**

Self-Adhesive

799 A396 55c multi 1.25 1.25
800 A397 €1.20 multi 2.60 2.60

Arthur Joachim von Oettingen (1836-1920), Meteorologist, and Tartu University Meteorological Observatory — A398

2015, Dec. 2 **Litho.** ***Perf. 14¼x13¾***

801 A398 65c multi 1.60 1.60

Tartu University Meteorological Observatory, 150th anniv.

Paul Keres (1916-75), Chess Player — A399

2016. Jan. 7 **Litho.** ***Perf. 12½***

802 A399 65c multi 1.50 1.50

Souvenir Sheet

Tolkuse Bog — A400

2016, Feb. 2 **Litho.** ***Perf. 13***

803 A400 €3.05 multi 7.25 7.25

New Year 2016 (Year of the Monkey) A401

2016, Feb. 8 **Litho.** ***Perf. 12¾x13***

804 A401 €1.50 multi 3.25 3.25

Arms of Keila — A402

Die Cut Perf. 12½

2016, Feb. 10 **Litho.**

Self-Adhesive

805 A402 65c multi 1.40 1.40

Posthorn — A403

Die Cut Perf. 12½

2016, Feb. 10 **Litho.**

Self-Adhesive

806 A403 €1.40 multi 3.00 3.00
a. Dated "2017" 3.00 3.00

Issued: No. 806a, 1/18/17.

See Nos. 816-818, 832-833.

Parus Major A404

2016, Feb. 17 **Litho.** ***Perf. 12¾x13***

807 A404 65c multi 1.40 1.40

Architecture — A405

No. 808: a, Tartu University Narva College, Narva (magenta background). b, Snail Tower, Tartu (green background). c, Estonian Embassy, Beijing (yellow brown background). d, Rotermann Quarter, Tallinn (turquoise green background).

2016, Mar. 17 **Litho.** ***Perf. 14***

808 A405 65c Block of 4, #a-d 6.00 6.00
e. Booklet pane of 4, #808a-808d 6.00 —
Complete booklet, #808e 6.00

August Rei (1886-1963), Chairman of Estonian National Council — A406

2016, Mar. 22 **Litho.** ***Perf. 13¾x14***

809 A406 65c brown 1.50 1.50

Otepää, 900th Anniv. — A407

2016, Apr. 1 **Litho.** ***Perf. 13¼x12¾***

810 A407 65c multi 1.50 1.50

Folk Costumes — A408

Designs: 65c, Man and woman from Audru. €1.50, Girl and woman from Tostamaa.

2016, Apr. 14 **Litho.** ***Perf. 13¾x14***

811-812 A408 Set of 2 5.00 5.00

Self-Portrait of Ants Laikmaa (1866-1942), Painter — A409

2016, May 5 **Litho.** ***Perf. 12¾x13***

813 A409 65c multi 1.50 1.50

A410

Europa A411

2016, May 9 **Litho.** ***Perf. 14***

814 A410 €1.40 multi 3.25 3.25
815 A411 €1.40 multi 3.25 3.25

Think Green Issue.

Posthorn Type of 2016

Die Cut Perf. 12½

2016, May 19 **Litho.**

Self-Adhesive

Background Color

816 A403 5c yel & pale yel .25 .25
817 A403 20c mag & pale mag .45 .45
818 A403 40c brt grn & pale grn .90 .90
Nos. 816-818 (3) 1.60 1.60

2016 Summer Olympics, Rio de Janeiro — A412

2016, June 9 **Litho.** ***Perf. 13¾x14¼***

819 A412 €1.50 multi 3.50 3.50

Souvenir Sheet

Oil Shale Mining in Estonia, Cent. — A413

Perf. 13¼x13½

2016, June 15 **Litho.**

820 A413 €2.95 multi 6.75 6.75

2016 Veterans' World Orienteering Championships, Tallinn and Harju County — A414

2016, Aug. 5 Litho. *Perf. 12¾x13*
821 A414 €1.50 multi 3.50 3.50

Tonis Kint (1896-1991), Deputy Prime Minister of Exile Government A415

2016, Aug. 17 Litho. *Perf. 13¾x14*
822 A415 65c blue green 1.50 1.50

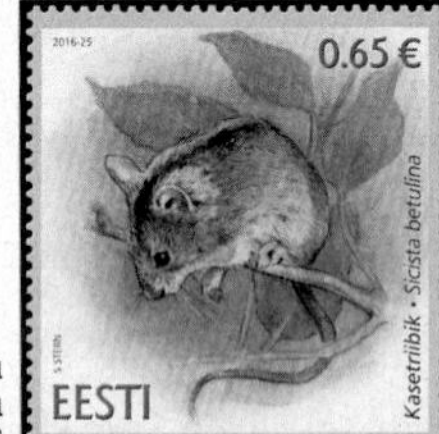

Sicista Betulina A416

2016, Aug. 25 Litho. *Perf. 12¾x13*
823 A416 65c multi 1.50 1.50

Amanita Muscaria — A417

2016, Sept. 8 Litho. *Perf. 13¾x14*
824 A417 65c multi 1.50 1.50

National Museum — A418

2016, Oct. 1 Litho. *Perf. 13*
825 A418 €1.50 multi 3.50 3.50

Virtsu Lighthouse A419

2016, Oct. 27 Litho. *Perf. 14x13¾*
826 A419 65c multi 1.50 1.50

Baltic Assembly, 25th Anniv. — A420

2016, Nov. 8 Litho. *Perf. 13½*
Stamp With White Frame
827 A420 65c multi 1.50 1.50

Souvenir Sheet
Stamp With Multicolored Frame
828 A420 €1.40 multi 3.25 3.25

See Latvia Nos. 948-949, Lithuania Nos. 1088-1089.

Fish Above Karlova, by Valve Janov (1921-2003) A421

2016, Nov. 17 Litho. *Perf. 14*
829 A421 65c multi 1.50 1.50

Cookies A422

Stylized Christmas Tree A423

Die Cut Perf. 13½x14
2016, Nov. 18 Litho.
Self-Adhesive
830 A422 65c multi 1.50 1.50
831 A423 €1.40 multi 3.25 3.25

Christmas. No. 830 is impregnated with a gingerbread scent.

Posthorn Type of 2016
Die Cut Perf. 12½
2017, Jan. 18 Litho.
Self-Adhesive
Background Color
832 A403 10c org & pale org .30 .30
833 A403 65c bl grn & pale bl 1.50 1.50

New Year 2017 (Year of the Rooster) A424

2017, Jan. 28 Litho. *Perf. 12¾x13*
834 A424 €1.50 multi 3.50 3.50

Streptopelia Turtur — A425

2017, Feb. 9 Litho. *Perf. 12¾x13*
835 A425 65c multi 1.50 1.50

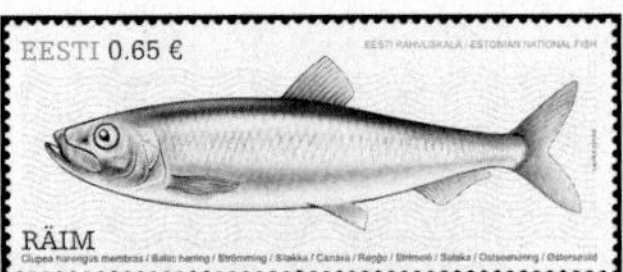

Baltic Herring — A426

2017, Feb. 23 Litho. *Perf. 13*
836 A426 65c multi 1.50 1.50

Ships Built in Estonia — A427

No. 837: a, Patrol 4500 WP patrol vessel. b, AC600PVDB fish feeding barge. c, Saare 46 yacht. d, Koidula ferry.

2017, Mar. 30 Litho. *Perf. 14*
837 A427 65c Block of 4, #a-d 6.00 6.00
e. Booklet pane of 4, #837a-837d 6.00 —
Complete booklet, #837e 6.00

No. 837 was printed in sheets containing two blocks that are tete-beche in relation to each other.

Souvenir Sheet

Figure Skating in Estonia, Cent. — A428

2017, Apr. 15 Litho. *Perf. 13¼*
838 A428 €3.05 multi + 2 labels 7.00 7.00

Lions Clubs International, Cent. — A429

2017, Apr. 29 Litho. *Perf. 13*
839 A429 65c multi 1.50 1.50

Europa A430

Designs: No. 840, €1.40, Keila-Joa Castle, lion. No. 841, €1.40, Maarjamäe Castle, eagle.

2017, May 8 Litho. *Perf. 12¾x13*
840-841 A430 Set of 2 6.50 6.50

Estonian Presidency of the European Union Council in 2017 — A431

2017, May 13 Litho. *Perf. 14¼x14*
842 A431 €1.40 multi 3.25 3.25

Statue of Martin Luther — A432

2017, May 27 Litho. *Perf. 13¾x14*
843 A432 65c multi 1.50 1.50

Protestant Reformation, 500th anniv.

Republic of Estonia, Cent. (in 2018) — A433

Die Cut Perf. 11¼ Syncopated
2017, June 1 Litho.
Self-Adhesive
844 A433 €1.50 multi 3.50 3.50

Gustav Boesberg (1867-1922), Weight Lifter — A434

2017, June 19 Litho. *Perf. 12½*
845 A434 65c multi 1.50 1.50

Constitution of Republic of Estonia, 25th Anniv. — A435

2017, June 28 Litho. *Perf. 14x13¾*
846 A435 65c multi 1.50 1.50

World Orienteering Championships, Estonia — A436

2017, July 1 Litho. *Perf. 13¾x14*
847 A436 €1.50 multi 3.50 3.50

Landscape with a Red Cloud, by Konrad Mägi (1878-1925) — A437

2017, Aug. 25 Litho. ***Perf. 12¾x13***
848 A437 €1.50 multi 3.75 3.75

Orjaku Lighthouses A438

Designs: 65c, Lighthouse 26mm tall. €1.40, Lighthouse 29mm tall.

2017, Sept. 8 Litho. ***Perf. 13¾x14***
849-850 A438 Set of 2 5.00 5.00

Lynx Lynx A439

2017, Sept. 11 Litho. ***Perf. 12¾x13***
851 A439 65c multi 1.60 1.60

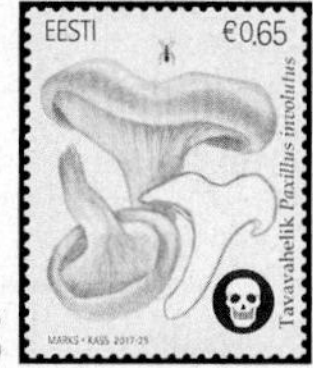

Paxillus Involutus — A440

2017, Sept. 21 Litho. ***Perf. 13¾x14***
852 A440 65c multi 1.60 1.60

Pres. Kersti Kaljulaid — A441

2017, Oct. 10 Litho. ***Perf. 13¾x14***
853 A441 65c multi 1.50 1.50

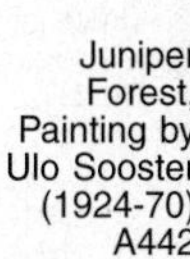

Juniper Forest, Painting by Ulo Sooster (1924-70) A442

2017, Nov. 17 Litho. ***Perf. 14***
854 A442 65c multi 1.60 1.60

Trees — A443

Designs: No. 855, Picea abies. No. 856, Sorbus aucuparia.

2017, Nov. 24 Litho. ***Perf. 14***
855 A443 €1.40 multi 3.50 3.50
a. Tete-beche pair 7.00 7.00
856 A443 €1.40 multi 3.50 3.50
a. Tete-beche pair 7.00 7.00

See Romania Nos. 6031-6032.

Miniature Sheet

Christmas — A444

No. 857: a, Bells and cinnamon sticks (43x34mm). b, Two Christmas ornaments on tree (27x31mm). c, Christmas tree with ornaments (33x47mm). d, Snowman and gifts (28x32mm).

2017, Nov. 24 Litho. ***Die Cut***
Self-Adhesive
857 A444 Sheet of 4 + 4 stickers, 2 etiquettes 7.00
a.-d. 75c Any single 1.75 1.75

No. 857 is impregnated with a cinnamon scent.

2018 Winter Olympics, PyeongChang, South Korea — A445

2018, Jan. 12 Litho. ***Perf. 13x12¾***
858 A445 €1.50 multi 3.75 3.75

Estonian Defense League, Cent. A446

2018, Jan. 26 Litho. ***Perf. 14x14¼***
859 A446 65c multi 1.60 1.60

New Year 2018 (Year of the Dog) A447

2018, Feb. 16 Litho. ***Perf. 12¾x13***
860 A447 €1.50 multi 3.75 3.75

Republic of Estonia, Cent. — A448

Die Cut Perf. 12¾x12½
Etched on Silver Foil
2018, Feb. 22 Self-Adhesive
861 A448 €10 silver 25.00 25.00

No. 861 was sold as a single stamp in a protective plastic box.

Flag of Estonia and Centenary Emblem — A449

Die Cut Perf. 11¼ Syncopated
2018, Mar. 15 Litho.
Self-Adhesive
862 A449 €1.40 multi 3.50 3.50

Tetrao Urogallus A450

2018, Mar. 29 Litho. ***Perf. 12¾x13***
863 A450 65c multi 1.60 1.60

Research Vessel Mare — A451

2018, Apr. 5 Litho. ***Perf. 14x13¾***
864 A451 65c multi 1.60 1.60

Estonian Maritime Museum, 50th anniv.

Estonian Ballet, Cent. A452

2018, Apr. 29 Litho. ***Perf. 12¾x13***
865 A452 65c gold & blk 1.60 1.60

Europa A453

Bridges in Tartu: No. 866, €1.40, Stone bridge. No. 867, €1.40, Arch bridge.

2018, May 3 Litho. ***Perf. 14***
866-867 A453 Set of 2 6.50 6.50

Pres. Arnold Rüütel — A454

2018, May 5 Litho. ***Perf. 13¾x14***
868 A454 65c cobalt & blue 1.50 1.50

Arms of Tallinn — A455

Die Cut Perf. 12½
2018, May 30 Litho.
Self-Adhesive
869 A455 65c multi 1.60 1.60

Manilaiu Lighthouse A456

2018, June 7 Litho. ***Perf. 14x13¾***
870 A456 65c multi 1.50 1.50

Estonia No. 1 — A457

2018, July 13 Litho. ***Perf. 13¾x14***
871 A457 65c multi 1.60 1.60

First Estonian postage stamps, cent.

Kadriorg Palace, Tallinn, 300th Anniv. — A458

2018, July 22 Litho. ***Perf. 13¾x14***
872 A458 65c multi 1.60 1.60

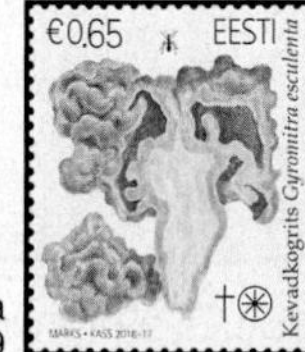

Gyromitra Esculenta — A459

2018, Aug. 23 Litho. ***Perf. 13¾x14***
873 A459 65c multi 1.50 1.50

Litwinsky House, Tel Aviv A460

2018, Aug. 28 Litho. ***Perf. 14x13¾***
874 A460 €1.50 multi 3.50 3.50

See Israel No. 2192.

Souvenir Sheet

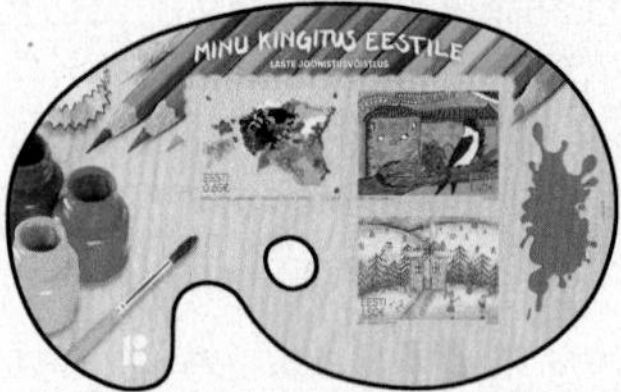

Winning Art in Children's Stamp Design Contest — A461

No. 875: a, Map of Estonia, by Tartu kindergarten students. b, Barn swallow, by Emeli Matjusenko. c, Windmill, by Ann-Elisbeth Sang.

Serpentine Die Cut 5x6

2018, Sept. 1 Litho.

Self-Adhesive

875 A461 Sheet of 3 8.25
a. 65c multi 1.50 1.50
b. €1.40 multi 3.25 3.25
c. €1.50 multi 3.50 3.50

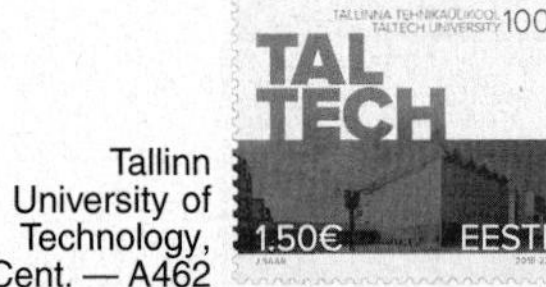

Tallinn University of Technology, Cent. — A462

2018, Sept. 17 Litho. *Perf. 14x13¾*
876 A462 €1.50 multi 3.50 3.50

Souvenir Sheet

Automobiles From 1933 Tallinn-Monte Carlo Rally — A463

No. 877: a, Hotchkiss AM 80S. b, GAZ-M20 Pobeda.

2018, Sept. 18 Litho. *Perf. 14x13¾*
877 A463 €1.50 Sheet of 2, #a-b 7.00 7.00

Canis Aureus A464

2018, Oct. 18 Litho. *Perf. 12¾x13*
878 A464 65c multi 1.50 1.50

Estonian Postal Service, Cent. — A465

Perf. 13¾x14¼

2018, Nov. 12 Litho.
879 A465 65c multi 1.50 1.50

Estonian Paintings — A466

No. 880: a, Truu Valvur, by Johann Köler (1826-99). b, Merikapsad, by Konrad Mägi (1878-1925). c, Pühapäev, by Felix Randel (1901-77). d, Comédie-Française, by Karin Luts (1904-93).

2018, Nov. 17 Litho. *Perf. 12¾x13*
880 A466 €1.50 Block or horiz. strip of 4, #a-d 14.00 14.00

Estonian Spelling Dictionary, Cent. — A467

2018, Nov. 20 Litho. *Perf. 14x13¾*
881 A467 65c multi 1.50 1.50

Christmas A468

Die Cut Perf. 13½x14

2018, Nov. 23 Litho.

Self-Adhesive

882 A468 €1.50 multi 3.50 3.50

No. 882 is impregnated with a pine scent.

Toomas Hendrik Ilves, 4th President of Estonia — A469

2018, Dec. 20 Litho. *Perf. 13¾x14*
883 A469 65c blue 1.50 1.50

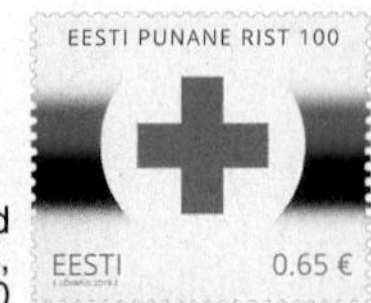

Estonian Red Cross, Cent. — A470

2019, Jan. 24 Litho. *Perf. 14x13¾*
884 A470 65c multi 1.50 1.50

Arms of Narva-Joesuu A471

Die Cut Perf. 12½

2019, Jan. 31 Litho.

Self-Adhesive

885 A471 65c sil & multi 1.50 1.50

New Year 2019 (Year of the Pig) A472

2019, Feb. 5 Litho. *Perf. 12¾x13*
886 A472 €1.50 gold & multi 3.50 3.50

Tallinn Cathedral School, 700th Anniversary — A473

No. 887: a, St. Mary's Cathedral. b, St. Mary's Cathedral school house and crest.

2019, Feb. 11 Litho. *Perf. 13¼*
887 A473 €1.50 Sheet of 2, #a-b 7.00 7.00

Vello Agori (1894-1944), Cartoonist — A474

Perf. 14¼x13¾

2019, Feb. 20 Litho.
888 A474 65c multi 1.50 1.50

Tallinn University, Cent. A475

Perf. 14¼x13¾

2019, Feb. 22 Litho.
889 A475 65c multi 1.50 1.50

Osmussaare Lighthouse A476

2019, Mar. 14 Litho. *Perf. 13¾x14*
890 A476 65c multi 1.50 1.50

Hepatica Nobilis — A477

Serpentine Die Cut 6x7

2019, Mar. 28 Litho.

Self-Adhesive

891 A477 65c multi 1.50 1.50

Parliament of Estonia, Cent. — A478

2019, Apr. 24 Litho. *Perf. 13¾x14*
892 A478 65c multi 1.50 1.50

Europa A479

Map of Estonia and Hirundo rustica: No. 893, €1.40, Head. No. 894, €1.40, In flight.

2019, Apr. 25 Litho. *Perf. 14x13¾*
893-894 A479 Set of 2 6.50 6.50

Estonian Bank, Cent. A480

2019, May 3 Litho. *Perf. 14*
895 A480 65c multi 1.50 1.50

Johann Voldemar Jannsen (1819-90), Journalist — A481

2019, May 16 Litho. *Perf. 13*
896 A481 65c multi 1.50 1.50

Metrosert (Central Office of Metrology), Cent. A482

2019, May 20 Litho. *Perf. 14*
897 A482 65c multi 1.50 1.50

Estonian Patent Office, Cent. — A483

2019, May 23 Litho. *Perf. 13¾*
898 A483 65c multi 1.50 1.50

Battle of Lyndanisse, by Märt Bormeister (1916-91) — A484

2019, May 30 Litho. *Perf. 12¾x13*

899 A484 €1.50 multi 3.50 3.50

First mention of Tallinn, 800th anniv.

Battle of Cesis, Cent. A485

2019, June 21 Litho. *Perf. 14*

900 A485 65c multi 1.50 1.50

Personalized Stamp Type of 2012

Die Cut Perf. 8¾ Syncopated

2019, July 5 Litho.

Self-Adhesive

901 A313 65c multi 1.50 1.50

The generic vignette depicting a map of Muhu could be personalized for an additional fee.

Souvenir Sheet

Estonian Song Festival, 150th Anniv. — A486

2019, July 5 Litho. *Perf. 13½*

On Cotton-faced Paper

902 A486 €10 multi 22.50 22.50

Galerina Marginata — A487

2019, Aug. 29 Litho. *Perf. 13¾x14*

903 A487 65c multi 1.50 1.50

Souvenir Sheet

Fire Fighting in Estonia, Cent. — A488

No. 904: a, Fire truck and female fire fighters, 1939. b, Fireman and helicopter fighting forest fire.

2019, Sept. 6 Litho. *Perf. 14*

904 A488 Sheet of 2 6.50 6.50

a.-b. €1.50 Either single 3.25 3.25

Talpa Europaea A489

2019, Sept. 11 Litho. *Perf. 12¾x13*

905 A489 65c multi 1.40 1.40

SEMI-POSTAL STAMPS

Assisting Wounded Soldier — SP1

Offering Aid to Wounded Hero — SP2

1920, June Unwmk. Litho. *Imperf.*

B1 SP1 35p + 10p red & ol grn .50 *2.00*

B2 SP2 70p + 15p dp bl & brn .50 *2.00*

Surcharged

1920

B3 SP1 1m on No. B1 .35 .30

B4 SP2 2m on No. B2 .35 .30

Nurse and Wounded Soldier — SP3

1921, Aug. 1 *Imperf.*

B5 SP3 2½ (3½)m org, brn & car 2.00 *8.00*

B6 SP3 5 m ultra, brn & car 2.00 *8.00*

1922, Apr. 26 *Perf. 13½x14*

B7 SP3 2½ (3½)m org, brn & car 2.00 *8.00*

a. Vert. pair, imperf. horiz. 30.00 *95.00*

B8 SP3 5 m ultra, brn & car 2.00 *8.00*

a. Vert. pair, imperf. horiz. 30.00 *95.00*

Nos. B5-B8 Overprinted

1923, Oct. 8 *Imperf.*

B9 SP3 2½ (3½)m 60.00 *160.00*

B10 SP3 5 m 60.00 *160.00*

Perf. 13½x14

B11 SP3 2½ (3½)m 60.00 *160.00*

a. Vert. pair, imperf. horiz. 300.00 *1,000.*

B12 SP3 5 m 60.00 *160.00*

a. Vert. pair, imperf. horiz. 300.00 *1,000.*

Nos. B9-B12 (4) 240.00 *640.00*

Excellent forgeries are plentiful.

Nos. B7 and B8 Surcharged

1926, June 15

B13 SP3 5 (6)m on #B7 3.75 *9.50*

a. Vert. pair, imperf. horiz. 32.50 *120.00*

B14 SP3 10 (12)m on #B8 4.50 *9.50*

a. Vert. pair, imperf. horiz. 32.50 *120.00*

Nos. B5-B14 had the franking value of the lower figure. They were sold for the higher figure, the excess going to the Red Cross Society.

Kuressaare Castle SP4

Tartu Cathedral SP5

Tallinn Castle SP6

Narva Fortress SP7

View of Tallinn — SP8

Laid Paper

Perf. 14½x14

1927, Nov. 19 Typo. Wmk. 207

B15 SP4 5m + 5m bl grn & ol, *grysh* .60 *9.50*

B16 SP5 10m + 10m dp bl & brn, *cream* .60 *9.50*

B17 SP6 12m + 12m rose red & ol grn, *bluish* .60 *9.50*

Perf. 14x13½

B18 SP7 20m + 20m bl & choc, *gray* .60 *9.50*

B19 SP8 40m + 40m org brn & slate, *buff* .60 *9.50*

Nos. B15-B19 (5) 3.00 *47.50*

The money derived from the surtax was donated to the Committee for the commemoration of War for Liberation.

Red Cross Issue

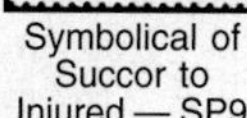

Symbolical of Succor to Injured — SP9

Symbolical of "Light of Hope" — SP10

1931, Aug. 1 Unwmk. *Perf. 13½*

B20 SP9 2s + 3s grn & car 10.00 9.50

B21 SP10 5s + 3s red & car 10.00 9.50

B22 SP10 10s + 3s lt bl & car 10.00 9.50

B23 SP9 20s + 3s dk bl & car 12.00 *20.00*

Nos. B20-B23 (4) 42.00 48.50

Set, never hinged 85.00

Nurse and Child SP11

Taagepera Sanatorium SP12

Lorraine Cross and Flower — SP13

Paper with Network as in Parenthesis

1933, Oct. 1 *Perf. 14, 14½*

B24 SP11 5s + 3s ver (grn) 8.00 *8.00*

B25 SP12 10s + 3s lt bl & red (vio) 8.00 *8.00*

B26 SP13 12s + 3s rose & red (grn) 10.00 *12.00*

B27 SP12 20s + 3s dk bl & red (org) 12.00 *16.00*

Nos. B24-B27 (4) 38.00 44.00

Set, never hinged 75.00

The surtax was for a fund to combat tuberculosis.

Coats of Arms

Narva — SP14

Pärnu — SP15

Tartu — SP16

Tallinn — SP17

Paper with Network as in Parenthesis

1936, Feb. 1 *Perf. 13½*

B28 SP14 10s + 10s grn & ultra (gray) 2.50 *8.00*

B29 SP15 15s + 15s car & bl (gray) 4.00 *12.00*

B30 SP16 25s + 25s gray bl & red (brn) 4.50 *16.00*

B31 SP17 50s + 50s blk & dl org (ol) 18.00 *52.50*

Nos. B28-B31 (4) 29.00 *88.50*

Set, never hinged 57.50

Paide SP18

Rakvere SP19

Valga SP20

Viljandi SP21

Paper with Network as in Parenthesis

1937, Jan. 2 *Perf. 13½x14*

B32 SP18 10s + 10s grn (gray) 2.50 *9.50*

B33 SP19 15s + 15s red brn (gray) 3.50 *9.50*

B34 SP20 25s + 25s dk bl (lil) 4.00 *14.50*

B35	SP21 50s + 50s dk vio (gray)	10.00	*24.00*
	Nos. B32-B35 (4)	20.00	*57.50*
	Set, never hinged	40.00	

Baltiski — SP22

Võru — SP23

Haapsalu SP24

Kuressaare SP25

Designs are the armorial bearings of various cities

1938, Jan. 21

Paper with Gray Network

B36	SP22 10s + 10s dk brn	2.00	*8.00*
B37	SP23 15s + 15s car & grn	2.00	*12.00*
B38	SP24 25s + 25s dk bl & car	4.00	*20.00*
B39	SP25 50s + 50s blk & org yel	12.00	*40.00*
a.	Sheet of 4, #B36-B39	30.00	*95.00*
	Nos. B36-B39 (4)	20.00	*80.00*
	Set, never hinged	40.00	

Annual charity ball, Tallinn, Jan. 2, 1938.

Viljandimaa SP27

Pärnumaa SP28

Tartumaa SP29

Harjumaa SP30

Designs are the armorial bearings of various cities

1939, Jan. 10 ***Perf. 13½***

Paper with Gray Network

B41	SP27 10s + 10s dk bl grn	2.00	*8.00*
B42	SP28 15s + 15s carmine	2.00	*8.00*
B43	SP29 25s + 25s dk blue	6.00	*20.00*
B44	SP30 50s + 50s brn lake	16.00	*47.50*
a.	Sheet of 4, #B41-B44	45.00	*175.00*
	Nos. B41-B44 (4)	26.00	*83.50*
	Set, never hinged	52.50	

Võrumaa SP32

Järvamaa SP33

Läänemaa SP34

Saaremaa SP35

Designs are the armorial bearings of various cities

1940, Jan. 2 **Typo.** ***Perf. 13½***

Paper with Gray Network

B46	SP32 10s + 10s dp grn & ultra	2.00	*12.00*
B47	SP33 15s + 15s dk car & ultra	2.00	*16.00*
B48	SP34 25s + 25s dk bl & scar	3.00	*24.00*
B49	SP35 50s + 50s ocher & ultra	8.00	*32.50*
	Nos. B46-B49 (4)	15.00	*84.50*
	Set, never hinged	30.00	

Catalogue values for unused stamps in this section, from this point to the end of the section, are for Never Hinged items.

1992 Summer Olympics, Barcelona — SP40

1992, June 22 **Litho.** ***Perf. 14***

B60	SP40 1r +50k red	.40	.40
B61	SP40 3r +1.50r green	1.75	1.75
B62	SP40 5r +2.50r blue & blk	.80	.80
	Nos. B60-B62 (3)	2.95	2.95

While face values are shown in kopecks and rubles, the stamps were sold in the new currency at the rate of 1 ruble = 10 sents.

No. 280 Surcharged

1994, Nov. 18 **Litho.** ***Perf. 14***

B63	A51 2.50k +20k green	6.00	6.00

Surtax for benefit of survivors of sinking of ferry "Estonia."

Haliaeetus Albicilla — SP41

1995, Aug. 29 **Litho.** ***Perf. 14***

B64	SP41 2k +25k black & blue	.45	.45

Surtax for Keep the Estonian Sea Clean Assoc.

UNICEF, 60th Anniv. SP42

2006, June 1 **Litho.** ***Perf. 13½***

B65	SP42 4.40k +1k multi	1.00	1.00

AIR POST STAMPS

Airplane AP1

Unwmk.

1920, Mar. 13 **Typo.** ***Imperf.***

C1	AP1 5m yel, blk & lt grn	2.50	*6.50*
	Never hinged	7.00	

No. C1 Overprinted "1923" in Red

1923, Oct. 1

C2	AP1 5m multicolored	8.00	*32.50*
	Never hinged	16.00	

No. C1 Surcharged in Red

1923, Oct. 1

C3	AP1 15m on 5m multi	16.00	*47.50*
	Never hinged	32.50	

Pairs of No. C1 Surcharged in Black or Red

1923, Oct.

C4	AP1 10m on 5m+5m (B)	10.00	*35.00*
C5	AP1 20m on 5m+5m	20.00	*55.00*
C6	AP1 45m on 5m+5m	60.00	*200.00*

Rough Perf. 11½

C7	AP1 10m on 5m+5m (B)	*650.00*	*1,600.*
C8	AP1 20m on 5m+5m	*275.00*	*725.00*
	Nos. C4-C8 (5)	*1,015.*	*2,615.*
	Set, never hinged	*1,850.*	

The pairs comprising Nos. C7 and C8 are imperforate between. Forged surcharges and perforations abound. Authentication is required.

Monoplane in Flight — AP2

Designs: Various views of planes in flight.

1924, Feb. 12 ***Imperf.***

C9	AP2 5m yellow & blk	1.60	*8.00*
C10	AP2 10m blue & blk	1.60	*8.00*
C11	AP2 15m red & blk	1.60	*8.00*
C12	AP2 20m green & blk	1.60	*8.00*
C13	AP2 45m violet & blk	1.60	*16.00*
	Nos. C9-C13 (5)	8.00	*48.00*
	Set, never hinged	16.00	

The paper is covered with a faint network in pale shades of the frame colors. There are four varieties of the frames and five of the pictures.

1925, July 15 ***Perf. 13½***

C14	AP2 5m yellow & blk	1.25	*8.00*
C15	AP2 10m blue & blk	1.25	*8.00*
C16	AP2 15m red & blk	1.25	*8.00*
C17	AP2 20m green & blk	1.25	*8.00*
C18	AP2 45m violet & blk	1.25	*16.00*
	Nos. C14-C18 (5)	6.25	*48.00*
	Set, never hinged	12.00	

Counterfeits of Nos. C1-C18 are plentiful.

REGISTRATION STAMP

Catalogue values for unused stamps in this section are for Never Hinged items.

Arms Type of 1992

1992, Mar. 16 **Litho.** ***Perf. 13x12½***

F1	A42 R (10r) pink & red	*.60*	*.60*

OCCUPATION STAMPS

Issued under German Occupation

For Use in Tartu (Dorpat)

Russian Stamps of 1909-12 Surcharged

1918 **Unwmk.** ***Perf. 14x14½***

N1	A15 20pf on 10k dk bl	40.00	*160.00*
N2	A8 40pf on 20k bl & car	40.00	*160.00*
	Set, never hinged	250.00	

Forged overprints exist.

Estonian Arms and Swastika — OS1

Perf. 11½

1941, Aug. **Typo.** **Unwmk.**

N3	OS1 15k brown	8.00	*16.00*
N4	OS1 20k green	5.50	*14.50*
N5	OS1 30k dark blue	5.50	*14.50*
	Nos. N3-N5 (3)	19.00	*45.00*
	Set, never hinged	45.00	

Exist imperf. Value, set $200.

Nos. N3-N5 were issued on both ordinary paper with colorless gum and thick chalky paper with yellow gum. Value, set on chalky paper $22.50.

OCCUPATION SEMI-POSTAL STAMPS

Castle Tower, Tallinn — OSP1

Designs: 20k+20k, Stone Bridge, Tartu, horiz. 30k+30k, Narva Castle, horiz. 50k+50k, Tallinn view, horiz. 60k+60k, Tartu University. 100k+100k, Narva Castle, close view.

Paper with Gray Network

Perf. 11½

1941, Sept. 29 **Photo.** **Unwmk.**

NB1	OSP1 15k + 15k dk brn	.60	*4.75*
NB2	OSP1 20k + 20k red lil	.60	*4.75*
NB3	OSP1 30k + 30k dk bl	.60	*4.75*
NB4	OSP1 50k + 50k bluish grn	.70	*9.50*
NB5	OSP1 60k + 60k car	1.00	*8.00*
NB6	OSP1 100k + 100k gray	1.50	*9.50*
	Nos. NB1-NB6 (6)	5.00	*41.25*
	Set, never hinged	10.00	

Nos. NB1-NB6 exist imperf. Value, set unused $70, used $200.

A miniature sheet containing one each of Nos. NB1-NB6, imperf., exists in various colors. Value, mint $40, used $60. It was not postally valid. Reproductions are common.

ETHIOPIA

ˌē-thē-ˈō-pē-ə

(Abyssinia)

LOCATION — Northeastern Africa
GOVT. — Republic (1988)
AREA — 426,260 sq. mi.
POP. — 59,680,383 (1999 est.)
CAPITAL — Addis Ababa

During the Italian occupation (1936-1941) Nos. N1-N7 were used, also stamps of Italian East Africa, Eritrea and Somalia.

During the British administration (1941-42) stamps of Great Britain and Kenya were used when available.

16 Guerche = 1 Menelik Dollar or 1 Maria Theresa Dollar
100 Centimes = 1 Franc (1905)
40 Paras = 1 Piaster (1908)
16 Mehalek = 1 Thaler or Talari (1928)
100 Centimes = 1 Thaler (1936)
100 Cents = 1 Ethiopian Dollar (1946)
100 Cents = 1 Birr (1978)

Catalogue values for unused stamps in this country are for Never Hinged items, beginning with Scott 247 in the regular postage section, Scott B6 in the semi-postal section, Scott C18 in the airpost section, Scott E1 in the special delivery section, and Scott J57 in the postage due section.

Watermarks

Wmk. 140 — Crown

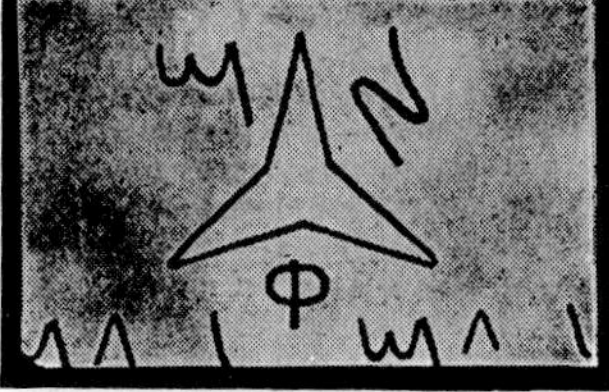

Wmk. 282 — Ethiopian Star and Amharic Characters, Multiple

Excellent forgeries of Nos. 1-86 exist.

Very Fine examples of Nos. 1-86 and J1-J42 will have perforations touching the design on one or more sides due to the narrow spacing of the stamps on the plates and imperfect perforating methods. Stamps with margins clear on all sides are scarce and command high premiums.

On March 9, 1894 Menelik II awarded Alfred Ilg a concession to develop a railway, including postal service. Ilg's stamps, Nos. 1-79, were valid locally and to Djibouti. Mail to other countries had to bear stamps of Obock, Somali Coast, etc.

Ethiopia joined the UPU Nov. 1, 1908.

Menelik II
A1

Lion of Judah
A2

Amharic numeral "8"

Perf. 14x13½

1895, Jan. Unwmk. Typo.

No.	Type	Description	Unused	Used
1	A1	¼g green	4.00	6.00
2	A1	½g red	3.50	5.00
3	A1	1g blue	3.50	5.00
4	A1	2g dark brown	3.00	6.00
5	A2	4g lilac brown	3.00	6.00
6	A2	8g violet	3.00	6.00
7	A2	16g black	4.00	6.00
		Nos. 1-7 (7)	24.00	40.00

For 4g, 8g and 16g stamps of type A1, see Nos. J3a, J4a and J7a.

Earliest reported use is Jan. 29, 1895.

Forged cancellations are plentiful.

For overprints see Nos. 8-86, J8-J28, J36-J42. For surcharges see Nos. 94-100, J29-J35.

Nos. 1-7 Handstamped in Violet or Blue

Overprint 9¼x2½mm, Serifs on "E"

1901, July 18

No.	Type	Description	Unused	Used
8	A1	¼g green	27.50	27.50
9	A1	½g red	27.50	27.50
10	A1	1g blue	27.50	27.50
11	A1	2g dark brown	27.50	27.50
12	A2	4g lilac brown	32.50	32.50
13	A2	8g violet	47.50	47.50
14	A2	16g black	60.00	60.00
		Nos. 8-14 (7)	250.00	250.00

Violet overprints were issued July 18, 1901, for postal use, while the blue overprints were issued in Jan. 5 1902 for philatelic purposes. The blue overprints were not used in the mails. Values for unused stamps are for examples with blue overprints. The blue overprints became valid for postage in 1908 only. Unused stamps with violet overprints are worth much more.

Overprints 8¼mm wide are unofficial reproductions.

Nos. 1-7 Handstamped in Violet, Blue or Black

Overprint 11x3mm, Low Colons

1902, Apr. 1

No.	Type	Description	Unused	Used
15	A1	¼g green	14.00	14.00
16	A1	½g red	14.00	14.00
17	A1	1g blue	14.00	14.00
18	A1	2g dark brown	14.00	14.00
19	A2	4g lilac brown	24.00	24.00
20	A2	8g violet	30.00	30.00
21	A2	16g black	55.00	55.00
		Nos. 15-21 (7)	165.00	165.00

The handstamp reads "Bosta" (Post).

Overprints 10¾mm and 11mm wide with raised colons are unofficial reproductions.

Nos. 1-7 Handstamped in Black

1903, Jan. 9 Overprint 16x3¾mm

No.	Type	Description	Unused	Used
22	A1	¼g green	14.00	14.00
23	A1	½g red	20.00	20.00
24	A1	1g blue	22.50	22.50
25	A1	2g dark brown	22.50	22.50
26	A2	4g lilac brown	35.00	35.00
27	A2	8g violet	50.00	50.00
28	A2	16g black	70.00	70.00
		Nos. 22-28 (7)	234.00	234.00

The handstamp reads "Malekt." (Also "Melekt," message).

Original stamps have blurred colons. Unofficial reproductions have clean colons.

Nos. 22-28 have black overprints only. All other colors are fakes.

Nos. 1-7 Handstamped in Violet or Blue

Overprint 18¼mm Wide

1904, Dec.

No.	Type	Description	Unused	Used
36	A1	¼g green	30.00	30.00
37	A1	½g red	30.00	
38	A1	1g blue	40.00	
39	A1	2g dark brown	40.00	
40	A2	4g lilac brown	55.00	
41	A2	8g violet	100.00	
42	A2	16g black	140.00	
		Nos. 36-42 (7)	435.00	

The handstamp reads "Malekathe" (message). This set was never issued.

Preceding Issues Surcharged with New Values in French Currency in Blue, Violet, Rose or Black

a

b

On Nos. 1-7

1905, Jan. 1 Overprint 3mm High

No.	Type	Description	Unused	Used
43	A1 (a)	5c on ¼g	10.00	10.00
44	A1 (a)	10c on ½g	10.00	10.00
45	A1 (a)	20c on 1g	10.00	10.00
46	A1 (a)	40c on 2g	11.00	11.00
47	A2 (a)	80c on 4g	21.00	21.00
48	A2 (b)	1.60fr on 8g	22.50	22.50
49	A2 (b)	3.20fr on 16g	40.00	40.00
		Nos. 43-49 (7)	124.50	124.50

Nos. 48-49 exist with period or comma.

1905, Feb.

On No. 8, "Ethiopie" in Blue

No.	Type	Description	Unused	Used
50	A1 (a)	5c on ¼g	150.00	150.00

On No. 15, "Bosta" in Black

No.	Type	Description	Unused	Used
51	A1 (a)	5c on ¼g	100.00	100.00

On No. 22, "Malekt" in Black

No.	Type	Description	Unused	Used
52	A1 (a)	5c on ¼g	75.00	75.00

Unofficial reproductions exist of Nos. 50, 51, 52. The 5c on No. 36, 10c, 20c, 40c, 80c, and 1.60fr surcharges exist as unofficial reproductions only.

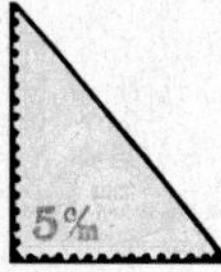

c

d

1905 On No. 2

No.	Type	Description	Unused	Used
54	A1 (c)	5c on half of ½g	10.00	10.00

On No. 21, "Bosta" in Black

No.	Type	Description	Unused	Used
55	A2 (d)	5c on 16g blk	200.00	100.00

On No. 55, "Bosta" is in black.

On No. 28, "Malekt" in Black

No.	Type	Description	Unused	Used
56	A2 (d)	5c on 16g blk	250.00	250.00
		Nos. 54-56 (3)	460.00	360.00

No. 54 issued in March. Nos. 55-56 issued Mar. 30.

The overprints and surcharges on Nos. 8 to 56 inclusive were handstamped, the work being very roughly done.

As is usual with handstamped overprints and surcharges there are many inverted and double, but most of them are fakes or unofficial reproductions.

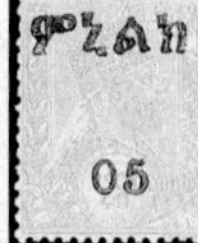

Surcharged with New Values in Various Colors and in Violet

Overprint 14¾x3½mm

1906, Jan. 1

No.	Type	Description	Unused	Used
57	A1	5c on ¼g green	12.50	12.50
58	A1	10c on ½g red	15.00	15.00
59	A1	20c on 1g blue	15.00	15.00
60	A1	40c on 2g dk brn	15.00	15.00
61	A2	80c on 4g lilac brn	22.50	22.50
62	A2	1.60fr on 8g violet	35.00	35.00
63	A2	3.20fr on 16g black	90.00	90.00
		Nos. 57-63 (7)	205.00	205.00

Two types of the 4-character overprint ("Menelik"): 14x¾x3½mm and 16x4mm.

Surcharged in Violet Brown

1906, July 1 Overprint 16x4¼mm

No.	Type	Description	Unused	Used
64	A1	5c on ¼g grn	12.50	12.50
a.		Surcharged "20"	110.00	110.00
65	A1	10c on ½g red	12.50	12.50
66	A1	20c on 1g blue	22.50	22.50
67	A1	40c on 2g dk brn	22.50	22.50
68	A2	80c on 4g lil brn	35.00	35.00
69	A2	1.60fr on 8g vio	35.00	35.00
70	A2	3.20fr on 16g blk	75.00	75.00
		Nos. 64-70 (7)	215.00	215.00

The control overprint reads "Menelik."

Surcharged in Violet

e

f

1907, June 21

No.	Type	Description	Unused	Used
71	A1 (e)	¼ on ¼g grn	8.75	8.75
72	A1 (e)	½ on ½g red	8.75	8.75
73	A1 (f)	1 on 1g blue	11.00	11.00
74	A1 (f)	2 on 2g dk brn	12.00	12.00
a.		Surcharged "40"	65.00	
75	A2 (f)	4 on 4g lil brn	13.00	13.00
a.		Surcharged "80"	57.50	
76	A2 (f)	8 on 8g vio	25.00	25.00
77	A2 (f)	16 on 16g blk	30.00	30.00
		Nos. 71-77 (7)	108.50	108.50

Nos. 71-72 are also found with stars farther away from figures.

The control overprint reads "Dagmawi" ("Second"), meaning Emperor Menelik II.

On stamps with "1" in surcharge, genuine examples have straight serifs, forgeries have curved serifs.

Nos. 2, 23 Surcharged in Bluish Green

1908, Aug. 14

No.	Type	Description	Unused	Used
78	A1	1pi on ½g red (#2)	15.00	15.00
79	A1	1pi on ½g red (#23)	*1,150.*	—

Official reproductions exist. Value, set $25.

Forgeries exist.

The surcharges on Nos. 57-78 are handstamped and are found double, inverted, etc.

Surcharged in Black

1908, Nov. 1

No.	Type	Description	Unused	Used
80	A1	¼p on ¼g grn	2.25	2.25
81	A1	½p on ½g red	2.25	2.25
82	A1	1p on 1g blue	2.75	2.75
83	A1	2p on 2g dk brn	5.00	5.00
84	A2	4p on 4g lil brn	7.50	7.50
85	A2	8p on 8g vio	14.00	14.00
86	A2	16p on 16g blk	18.00	18.00
		Nos. 80-86 (7)	51.75	51.75

Surcharges on Nos. 80-85 are found double, inverted, etc. Forgeries exist.

These are the 1st stamps valid for international mail.

King Solomon's Throne — A3

Menelik in Native Costume — A4

Menelik in Royal Dress — A5

1909, Jan. 29 *Perf. 11½*

No.	Type	Description	Unused	Used
87	A3	¼g blue green	.70	.60
88	A3	½g rose	.75	.75
89	A3	1g green & org	4.50	1.50
90	A4	2g blue	3.00	1.75
91	A4	4g green & car	5.00	4.00
92	A5	8g ver & dp grn	9.00	7.00
93	A5	16g ver & car	15.00	10.00
		Nos. 87-93 (7)	37.95	25.60

For overprints see Nos. 101-115, J43-J49, J55-J56. For surcharges see Nos. 116-119.

Nos. 1-7 Handstamped and Surcharged in ms.

1911, Oct. 1 *Perf. 14x13½*

No.	Type	Description	Unused	Used
94	A1	¼g on ¼g grn	85.00	
95	A1	½g on ½g red	85.00	
96	A1	1g on 1g blue	85.00	
97	A1	2g on 2g dk brn	85.00	
98	A2	4g on 4g lil brn	85.00	
99	A2	8g on 8g violet	85.00	
100	A2	16g on 16g black	85.00	
		Nos. 94-100 (7)	595.00	

Nos. 94-100 were produced as a philatelic speculation by the postmaster at Dire-Dawa. The overprint is abbreviated from "Affranchissement Exceptionnel Faute Timbres" (Special Franking Lacking Stamps). The overprints and surcharges were applied to stamps on cover and then canceled. These covers were then sold to dealers in Europe. No. 98 is known postally used on a small number of commercial covers.

Nos. 94-100 without surcharge are forgeries.

Stamps of 1909 Handstamped in Violet or Black

Nos. 101-102

Nos. 104-107

1917, Mar. 30 *Perf. 11½*

No.	Type	Description	Unused	Used
101	A3	¼g blue grn (V)	7.50	9.00
102	A3	½g rose (V)	7.50	9.00
104	A4	2g blue (Bk)	10.00	9.50
105	A4	4g grn & car (Bk)	15.00	15.00
106	A5	8g ver & dp grn (Bk)	25.00	22.50
107	A5	16g ver & car (Bk)	40.00	45.00
		Nos. 101-107 (6)	105.00	110.00

Coronation of Empress Zauditu and appointment of Prince Tafari as Regent and Heir to the throne.

Exist with overprint inverted and double.

Stamps of 1909 Overprinted in Blue, Black or Red

Nos. 108-111

Nos. 112-115

1917, Apr. 5-Oct. 1

No.	Type	Description	Unused	Used
108	A3	¼g blue grn (Bl)	1.25	1.25
109	A3	½g rose (Bl)	1.25	1.25
110	A3	1g grn & org (Bl)	2.25	2.25
111	A4	2g blue (R)	82.50	87.25
112	A4	2g blue (Bk)	1.25	1.25
113	A4	4g grn & car (Bl)	1.25	1.25
a.		Black overprint	11.00	11.00
114	A5	8g ver & dp grn (Bl)	1.25	1.25
115	A5	16g ver & car (Bl)	2.25	2.25
		Nos. 108-115 (8)	93.25	98.00

Coronation of Empress Zauditu.

Nos. 108-115 all exist with double overprint, inverted overprint, double overprint, one inverted, and various combinations.

Nos. 114-115 with Additional Surcharge

k

l

m

n

1917, May 28

No.	Type	Description	Unused	Used
116	A5 (k)	¼g on 8g	3.00	3.00
117	A5 (l)	½g on 8g	3.00	3.00
118	A5 (m)	1g on 16g	8.00	8.00
119	A5 (n)	2g on 16g	10.00	9.00
		Nos. 116-119 (4)	24.00	23.00

Nos. 116-119 all exist with the numerals double and inverted and No. 116 with the Amharic surcharge missing.

Sommering's Gazelle — A6

Prince Tafari — A9

Cathedral of St. George A12

Empress Waizeri Zauditu — A18

¼g, Giraffes. ½g, Leopard. 2g, Prince Tafari, diff. 4g, Prince Tafari, diff. 8g, White rhinoceros. 12g, Somali ostriches. 1t, African elephant. 2t, Water buffalo. 3t, Lions. 5t, 10t, Empress Zauditu.

1919, June 16 **Typo.** *Perf. 11½*

No.	Type	Description	Unused	Used
120	A6	⅛g violet & brn	.25	.25
121	A6	¼g bl grn & drab	.25	.25
122	A6	½g scar & ol grn	.25	.25
123	A9	1g rose lil & gray grn	.25	.25
124	A9	2g dp ultra & fawn	.25	.25
125	A9	4g turq bl & org	.25	*2.50*
126	A12	6g lt blue & org	.25	.25
127	A12	8g ol grn & blk brn	.35	.25
128	A12	12g red vio & gray	.50	.30
129	A12	1t rose & gray blk	.90	.40
130	A12	2t black & brown	2.50	
131	A12	3t grn & dp org	2.50	1.90
132	A18	4t brn & lil rose	3.00	2.50
133	A18	5t carmine & gray	4.00	4.00
134	A18	10t gray grn & bis	8.00	5.25
		Nos. 120-134 (15)	23.50	
		Nos. 120-129,131-134 (14)		18.25

No. 130 was not issued.

For overprints see Nos. J50-J54. For surcharges see Nos. 135-154.

Reprints have brownish gum that is cracked diagonally. Originals have smooth, white gum. Reprints exist imperf. and some values with inverted centers. Value for set, unused or canceled, $5.

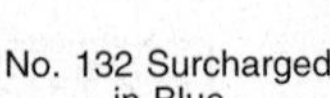

No. 132 Surcharged in Blue

1919, July

No.	Type	Description	Unused	Used
135	A18	4g on 4t brn & lil rose	3.00	3.00

Nos. 135-154

The Amharic surcharge indicates the new value and, therefore, varies on Nos. 135-154. There are numerous defective letters and figures, several types of the "2" of "½," the errors "guerhce," "gnerche," etc.

Many varieties of surcharge, such as double, inverted, lines transposed or omitted, and inverted "2" in "½," exist.

There are many irregularly produced settings in imitation of Nos. 136-154 which differ slightly from the originals. These may be essays or proofs.

Stamps of 1919 Surcharged

1921

No.	Type	Description	Unused	Used
136	A6	½g on ⅛g vio & brn	1.00	1.00
137	A6	1g on ¼g grn & db	2.50	1.00
138	A9	2g on 1g lil brn & gray grn	1.00	1.50
139	A18	2g on 4t brn & lil rose	35.00	30.00
140	A6	2½g on ½g scar & ol grn	1.00	*1.50*
141	A9	4g on 2g ultra & fawn	1.00	*1.25*
		Nos. 136-141 (6)	41.50	36.25

Forgeries of No. 139 exist.

Stamps and Type of 1919 Surcharged

1925-26

No.	Type	Description	Unused	Used
142	A12	½g on 1t rose & gray blk ('26)	1.25	1.25
a.		Without colon ('26)	12.50	12.50
143	A18	½g on 5t car & gray ('26)	1.50	1.50
144	A12	1g on 6g bl & org	1.25	1.25
145	A12	1g on 12g lil & gray	*450.00*	*400.00*
146	A12	1g on 3t grn & org ('26)	22.50	16.00
147	A18	1g on 10t gray grn & bis ('26)	1.50	*1.50*
		Nos. 142-147 (6)	478.00	421.50

On No. 142 the surcharge is at the left side of the stamp, reading upward. On No. 142a it is at the right, reading downward. The two surcharges are from different, though similar, settings. On No. 146 the surcharge is at the right, reading upward. See note following No. 154.

Type of 1919 Srchd.

1925, Oct.

No.	Type	Description	Unused	Used
147A	A12	1g on 12g lil & gray	*400.00*	

Forgeries exist.

Nos. 126-128 Srchd.

1926

No.	Type	Description	Unused	Used
148	A12	½g on 8g	3.00	1.25
149	A12	1g on 6g	80.00	50.00
150	A12	1g on 12g	*350.00*	
		Nos. 148-150 (3)	433.00	51.25

The Amharic line has 7 (½g) or 6 characters (1g).

Nos. 126-128, 131 Srchd.

1925-27

No.	Type	Description	Unused	Used
151	A12	½g on 8g ('27)	1.50	1.50
152	A12	1g on 6g ('27)	60.00	40.00
153	A12	1g on 12g ('27)	5.00	1.50
154	A12	1g on 3t	375.00	
		Nos. 151-154 (4)	441.50	43.00

The Amharic line has 7 (½g) or 4 characters (1g). No. 152 has the lines closer together than do the others.

Forgeries of No. 154 exist.

Ras Tafari — A22

Empress Zauditu — A23

1928, Sept. 5 Typo. *Perf. 13½x14*

No.	Type	Description	Unused	Used
155	A22	⅛m org & lt bl	.65	1.40
156	A23	¼m ind & red org	.40	*1.40*
157	A22	½m gray grn & blk	.65	1.40
158	A23	1m dk car & blk	.40	*1.40*
159	A22	2m dk bl & blk	.40	*1.40*
160	A23	4m yel & olive	.40	*1.40*
161	A22	8m vio & olive	1.00	1.40
162	A23	1t org brn & vio	1.10	1.40
163	A22	2t grn & bister	1.75	3.25
164	A23	3t choc & grn	2.75	3.75
		Nos. 155-164 (10)	9.50	18.20

For overprints and surcharges see Nos. 165-209, 217-230, C1-C10.

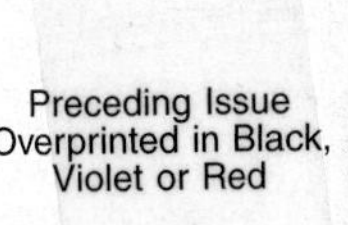

Preceding Issue Overprinted in Black, Violet or Red

1928, Sept. 1

No.	Type	Description	Unused	Used
165	A22	⅛m (Bk)	1.75	3.25
166	A23	¼m (V)	1.75	3.25
167	A22	½m (V)	1.75	3.25
168	A23	1m (V)	1.75	3.25
169	A22	2m (R)	1.75	3.25
170	A23	4m (Bk)	1.75	3.25
171	A22	8m (R)	1.75	3.25
172	A23	1t (Bk)	1.75	3.25
173	A22	2t (R)	2.75	3.25
174	A23	3t (R)	4.00	3.25
		Nos. 165-174 (10)	20.75	32.50

Opening of General Post Office, Addis Ababa.

Exist with overprint inverted, double, double, one inverted, etc.

Nos. 155, 157, 159, 161, 163 Handstamped in Violet, Red or Black

1928, Oct. 7

No.	Type	Description	Unused	Used
175	A22	⅛m (V)	2.10	8.00
176	A22	½m (R)	2.10	8.00
177	A22	2m (R)	2.10	10.00
178	A22	8m (Bk)	2.10	10.00
179	A22	2t (V)	2.10	10.00
		Nos. 175-179 (5)	10.50	46.00

Crowning of Prince Tafari as king (Negus) on Oct. 7, 1928.

Nos. 175-177 exist with overprint vertical, inverted, double, etc.

Forgeries exist.

Nos. 155-164 Overprinted in Red or Green

1930, Apr. 3

No.	Type	Description	Unused	Used
180	A22	⅛m org & lt bl (R)	.25	.25
181	A23	¼m ind & red org (G)	.50	.50
182	A22	½m gray grn & blk (R)	.25	.25
183	A23	1m dk car & blk (G)	.55	.55
184	A22	2m dk bl & blk (R)	.55	.55
185	A23	4m yel & ol (R)	.85	.85
186	A22	8m vio & ol (R)	1.60	1.60
187	A23	1t org brn & vio (R)	4.50	4.50
188	A22	2t grn & bis (R)	5.50	5.50
189	A23	3t choc & grn (R)	8.00	8.00
		Nos. 180-189 (10)	22.55	22.55

Proclamation of King Tafari as King of Kings of Abyssinia under the name "Haile Selassie."

A similar overprint, set in four vertical lines, was printed on all denominations of the 1928 issue. It was not considered satisfactory and was rejected. The trial impressions were not placed on sale to the public, but some stamps reached private hands and have been passed through the post.

Nos. 155-164 Overprinted in Red or Olive Brown

1930, Apr. 3

No.	Type	Description	Unused	Used
190	A22	⅛m orange & lt bl	.50	.50
191	A23	¼m ind & red org (OB)	.55	.55
192	A22	½m gray grn & blk	1.40	1.40
193	A23	1m dk car & blk (OB)	.55	.55
194	A22	2m dk blue & blk	.55	.55
195	A23	4m yellow & ol	1.00	1.00
196	A22	8m violet & ol	1.60	1.60
197	A23	1t org brn & vio	4.50	4.50
198	A22	2t green & bister	5.50	5.50
199	A23	3t chocolate & grn	8.00	8.00
		Nos. 190-199 (10)	24.15	24.15

Proclamation of King Tafari as Emperor Haile Selassie.

All stamps of this series exist with "H" of "HAILE" omitted and with many other varieties.

Nos. 155-164 Handstamped in Violet or Red

1930, Nov. 2

No.	Type	Description	Unused	Used
200	A22	⅛m (V)	1.10	1.10
201	A23	¼m (V)	1.10	1.10
202	A22	½m (R)	1.10	1.10
203	A23	1m (V)	1.10	1.10
204	A22	2m (R)	1.10	1.10
205	A23	4m (V)	1.10	1.10
206	A22	8m (V or R)	1.90	1.90
207	A23	1t (V)	3.00	3.00
208	A22	2t (V or R)	4.50	4.50
209	A23	3t (V or R)	6.50	6.50
		Nos. 200-209 (10)	22.50	22.50

Coronation of Emperor Haile Selassie, Nov. 2, 1930.

Haile Selassie Coronation Monument, Symbols of Empire — A24

1930, Nov. Engr. *Perf. 12½*

No.	Type	Description	Unused	Used
210	A24	1g orange	1.00	1.00
211	A24	2g ultra	1.00	1.00
212	A24	4g violet	1.00	1.00
213	A24	8g dull green	1.00	1.00
214	A24	1t brown	1.25	1.25
215	A24	3t green	2.00	2.00
216	A24	5t red brown	2.00	2.00
		Nos. 210-216 (7)	9.25	9.25

Coronation of Emperor Haile Selassie.

Issued: 4g, 11/2; others, 11/23.

Reprints of Nos. 210 to 216 exist. Colors are more yellow and the ink is thicker and slightly glossy. Ink on the originals is dull and granular. Value 50c each.

Nos. 158-160, 164 Surcharged in Green, Red or Blue

Type I Type II

1931 *Perf. 13½x14*

No.	Type	Description	Unused	Used
217	A23	⅛m on 1m	.55	1.00
218	A22	⅛m on 2m (R)	.55	1.00
219	A23	⅛m on 4m	.55	1.00
220	A23	¼m on 1m (Bl)	.55	1.00
221	A22	¼m on 2m (R)	1.60	2.10
222	A23	¼m on 4m	1.60	2.10
225	A23	½m on 1m (Bl)	1.60	2.10
226	A22	½m on 2m (R)	1.60	2.10
227	A23	½m on 4m, type II	1.60	2.10
a.		½m on 4m, type I	15.00	15.00
228	A23	½m on 3t (R)	13.00	16.00
230	A22	1m on 2m (R)	2.25	2.75
		Nos. 217-230 (11)	25.45	33.25

The ½m on ⅛m orange & light blue and ½m on ¼m indigo & red orange were clandestinely printed and never sold at the post office.

No. 230 with double surcharge in red and blue is a color trial.

Many varieties exist.

Issued: 1m, Apr.; others, 3/20.

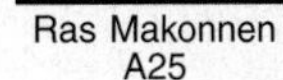

Ras Makonnen A25

Empress Menen A27

View of Hawash River and Railroad Bridge A26

Designs: 2g, 8g, Haile Selassie (profile). 4g, 1t, Statue of Menelik II. 3t, Empress Menen (full face). 5t, Haile Selassie (full face).

Perf. 12½, 12x12½, 12½x12

1931, June 27 Engr.

No.	Type	Description	Unused	Used
232	A25	⅛g red	.50	.80
233	A26	¼g olive green	.50	.80
234	A25	½g dark violet	.50	.80
235	A27	1g red orange	.50	.80
236	A27	2g ultra	.50	.80
237	A25	4g violet	.80	1.60
238	A27	8g blue green	2.50	3.00
239	A25	1t chocolate	24.00	10.00
240	A27	3t yellow green	7.00	7.00
241	A27	5t red brown	13.00	13.00
		Nos. 232-241 (10)	49.80	38.60

For overprints see Nos. B1-B5. For surcharges see Nos. 242-246.

Reprints of Nos. 232-236, 238-240 are on thinner and whiter paper than the originals. On originals the ink is dull and granular. On reprints, heavy, caked and shiny. Value 50c each.

Nos. 232-236 Surcharged in Blue or Carmine

1936, Jan. 29 *Perf. 12x12½, 12½x12*

No.	Type	Description	Unused	Used
242	A25	1c on ⅛g red	2.50	2.50
243	A26	2c on ¼g ol grn (C)	2.50	2.50
244	A25	3c on ½g dk vio	2.50	2.50
245	A27	5c on 1g red org	5.00	5.00
246	A27	10c on 2g ultra (C)	6.00	5.00
		Nos. 242-246 (5)	18.50	17.50

Catalogue values for unused stamps in this section, from this point to the end of the section, are for Never Hinged items.

Haile Selassie I — A32

1942, Mar. 23 Litho. *Perf. 14x13½*

No.	Type	Description	Unused	Used
247	A32	4c lt bl grn, ind & blk	.80	.40
248	A32	10c rose, indigo & blk	2.50	.75
249	A32	20c dp ultra, ind & blk	5.00	1.25
		Nos. 247-249 (3)	8.30	2.40

Haile Selassie I — A33

1942-43 Unwmk.

No.	Type	Description	Unused	Used
250	A33	4c lt bl grn & indigo	.90	.25
251	A33	8c yel org & indigo	1.00	.25
252	A33	10c rose & indigo	1.25	.25
253	A33	12c dull vio & indigo	1.25	.30
254	A33	20c dp ultra & indigo	2.00	.50
255	A33	25c dull grn & indigo	2.50	.70
256	A33	50c dull brn & indigo	4.75	1.25
257	A33	60c lilac & indigo	7.25	1.50
		Nos. 250-257 (8)	20.90	5.00

Issued: 25c, 50c, 60c, 4/1/43; others, 6/22/42.

For surcharges see Nos. 258-262, 284, C18-C20.

Nos. 250-254 Surcharged in Black or Brown

1943, Nov. 3

258	A33	5c on 4c	65.00	—
259	A33	10c on 8c	65.00	—
260	A33	15c on 10c	65.00	—
261	A33	20c on 12c (Br)	65.00	—
262	A33	30c on 20c (Br)	65.00	—
		Nos. 258-262 (5)	325.00	

Restoration of the Obelisk in Myazzia Place, Addis Ababa, and the 13th anniv. of the coronation of Emperor Haile Selassie.

Nos. 258-262 were almost entirely sold to collectors. Used examples are mostly CTO. Only 10 postally used examples are known.

No. 258 exists with inverted "5" in surcharge. Value $150. On No. 262, "3" is surcharged on "2" of "20" to make "30."

Approximately 40 sets exist with a somewhat different handstamped surcharge. Value, set *$2,000.* Forgeries exist.

Palace of Menelik II A34

Menelik II — A35

Statue — A36

50c, Mausoleum. 65c, Menelik II (with scepter).

1944, Dec. 31 Litho. *Perf. 10½*

263	A34	5c green	1.25	.65
264	A35	10c red lilac	2.25	1.10
265	A36	20c deep blue	4.00	2.25
266	A34	50c dull purple	5.25	2.25
267	A35	65c bister brown	9.25	3.50
		Nos. 263-267 (5)	22.00	9.75

Cent. of the birth of Menelik II, 8/18/44. Printed on gum-impregnated paper.

Unissued Semi-Postal Stamps Overprinted in Carmine

Nurse & Baby — A39

Various Designs Inscribed "Croix Rouge"

1945, Aug. 7 Photo. *Perf. 11½*

268	A39	5c brt green	.90	1.50
269	A39	10c brt red	1.10	1.50
270	A39	25c brt blue	1.10	1.50
271	A39	50c dk yellow brn	5.00	7.00
272	A39	1t brt violet	7.50	9.00
		Nos. 268-272 (5)	15.60	20.50

Nos. 268-272 without overprint were ordered printed in Switzerland before Ethiopia fell to the invading Italians, so were not delivered to Addis Ababa. After the country's liberation, the set was overprinted "V" and issued for ordinary postage. These stamps exist without overprint, but were not issued. Value, set $17.50.

Some values exist inverted or double. Forged overprints exist.

For surcharges see Nos. B11-B15, B36-B40.

Lion of Judah — A44

Menelik II — A45

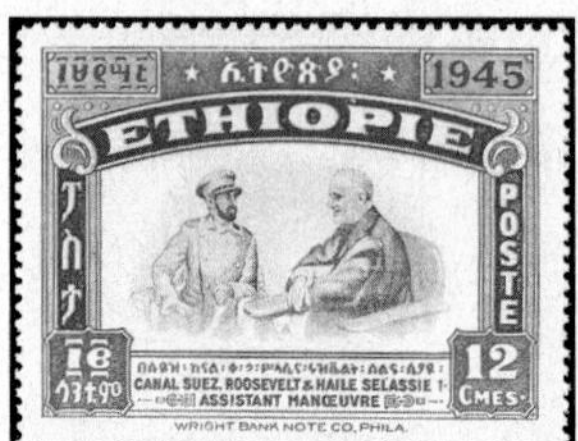

Mail Transport, Old and New A46

Designs: 50c, Old Post Office, Addis Ababa. 70c, Menelik II and Haile Selassie.

1947, Apr. 18 Engr. *Perf. 13*

273	A44	10c yellow org	3.50	2.00
274	A45	20c deep blue	5.75	2.25
275	A46	30c orange brn	9.50	3.75
276	A46	50c dk slate grn	22.50	7.50
277	A46	70c red violet	37.50	14.00
		Nos. 273-277 (5)	78.75	29.50

50th anniv. of Ethiopia's postal system.

Haile Selassie and Franklin D. Roosevelt — A49

Design: 65c, Roosevelt and US Flags.

Engraved and Photogravure

1947, May 23 Unwmk. *Perf. 12½*

278	A49	12c car lake & bl grn	1.60	2.25
279	A49	25c dk blue & rose	3.00	3.50
280	A49	65c blk, red & dp bl	6.00	7.50
		Nos. 278-280,C21-C22 (5)	45.60	51.25

King Sahle Selassie Reclining A50

King Sahle Selassie — A52

Design: 30c, View of Ankober.

1947, May 1 Engr. *Perf. 13*

281	A50	20c deep blue	2.00	2.40
282	A50	30c dark purple	4.00	4.00
283	A52	$1 deep green	10.00	8.00
		Nos. 281-283 (3)	16.00	14.40

150th anniversary of Selassie dynasty.

No. 255 Surcharged in Orange

1947, July 14 *Perf. 14x13½*

284	A33	12c on 25c	95.00	95.00

Amba Alaguie A53

Designs: 2c, Trinity Church. 4c, Debra Sina. 5c, Mecan, near Achanguie. 8c, Lake Tana. 12c, 15c, Parliament Building, Addis Ababa. 20c, Aiba, near Mai Cheo. 30c, Bahr Bridge over Blue Nile. 60c, 70c, Canoe on Lake Tana. $1, Omo Falls. $3, Mt. Alamata. $5, Ras Dashan Mountains.

Perf. 13x13½

1947-53 Engr. Wmk. 282

285	A53	1c rose violet	.25	.25
286	A53	2c blue violet	.25	.25
a.		Unwatermarked ('51)	37.50	15.00
287	A53	4c green	.35	.25
288	A53	5c dark green	.35	.25
289	A53	8c deep orange	.65	.25
290	A53	12c red	.80	.25
290A	A53	15c dk ol brn ('53)	.75	.25
291	A53	20c blue	1.10	.40
292	A53	30c orange brown	1.90	.55
292A	A53	60c red ('51)	2.25	.95
293	A53	70c rose lilac	3.25	.70
294	A53	$1 dk carmine rose	5.25	.70
295	A53	$3 bright blue	14.00	2.75
296	A53	$5 olive	22.50	5.50
		Nos. 285-296 (14)	53.65	13.30

Issue dates: 15c, May 25, 1953; 60c, Feb. 10, 1951; others, Aug. 23, 1947.

Shades exist.

For overprints see Nos. 355-356. For surcharges see Nos. B6-B10, B16-B20.

Empress Waizero Menen and Emperor Haile Selassie A54

1949, May 5 Wmk. 282 *Perf. 13*

297	A54	20c blue	1.75	.85
298	A54	30c yellow org	1.75	1.10
299	A54	50c purple	4.50	1.75
300	A54	80c green	4.50	2.75
301	A54	$1 red	9.00	4.50
		Nos. 297-301 (5)	21.50	10.95

Central ornaments differ on each denomination.

8th anniv. of Ethiopia's liberation from Italian occupation.

Dejach Balcha Hospital A55

Abuna Petros — A56

Designs: 20c, Haile Selassie raising flag. 30c, Lion of Judah statue. 50c, Empress Waizero Menen, Haile Selassie and building.

Perf. 13x13½, 13½x13

1950, Nov. 2 Engr. Wmk. 282

302	A55	5c purple	1.10	.65
303	A56	10c deep plum	3.50	1.60
304	A56	20c deep carmine	4.50	1.60
305	A56	30c green	9.50	3.25
306	A55	50c deep blue	13.50	6.50
		Nos. 302-306 (5)	32.10	13.60

20th anniv. of the coronation of Emperor Haile Selassie and Empress Menen.

Abbaye Bridge — A57

1951, Jan. 1 Unwmk. *Perf. 14*

308	A57	5c dk green & dk brn	4.25	1.60
309	A57	10c dp orange & blk	6.50	2.75
310	A57	15c dp blue & org brn	11.00	4.50
311	A57	30c olive & lil rose	16.00	6.50
312	A57	60c brown & dp bl	22.50	8.50
313	A57	80c purple & green	32.50	12.50
		Nos. 308-313 (6)	92.75	36.35

Opening of the Abbaye Bridge over the Blue Nile.

Tomb of Ras Makonnen A58

1951, Mar. 2 Center in Black

314	A58	5c dark green	3.25	1.10
315	A58	10c deep ultra	3.25	1.60
316	A58	15c blue	5.50	2.75
317	A58	30c claret	11.00	3.25
318	A58	80c rose carmine	17.00	5.50
319	A58	$1 orange brown	22.50	8.50
		Nos. 314-319 (6)	62.50	22.70

55th anniversary of the Battle of Adwa.

Emperor Haile Selassie — A59

1952, July 23 *Perf. 13½*

320	A59	5c dark green	.55	.55
321	A59	10c red orange	.85	.55
322	A59	15c black	1.10	.55
323	A59	25c ultra	1.75	.85
324	A59	30c violet	2.75	1.10
325	A59	50c rose red	3.50	1.10
326	A59	65c chocolate	9.00	2.75
		Nos. 320-326 (7)	19.50	7.45

60th birthday of Haile Selassie.

Open Road to Sea A60

Designs: 25c, 50c, Road and broken chain. 65c, Map. 80c, Allegory: Reunion. $1, Haile Selassie raising flag. $2, Ethiopian flag and seascape. $3, Haile Selassie addressing League of Nations.

Wmk. 282

1952, Sept. 11 Engr. *Perf. 13*

327	A60	15c brown carmine	.85	.60
328	A60	25c red brown	1.10	1.00
329	A60	30c yellow brown	2.00	1.10
330	A60	50c purple	3.00	1.25
331	A60	65c gray	5.75	1.60
332	A60	80c blue green	6.50	2.25
333	A60	$1 rose carmine	13.00	3.00

334 A60 $2 deep blue 22.50 5.00
335 A60 $3 magenta 47.50 7.50
Nos. 327-335 (9) 102.20 23.30

Issued to celebrate Ethiopia's federation with Eritrea, effected Sept. 11, 1952.

Haile Selassie and New Ethiopian Port A61

15c, 30c, Haile Selassie on deck of ship.

1953, Oct. 4

337 A61 10c red & dk brn 4.75 2.75
338 A61 15c blue & dk grn 5.00 2.75
339 A61 25c orange & dk brn 9.00 5.00
340 A61 30c red brn & dk grn 16.00 8.00
341 A61 50c purple & dk brn 25.00 9.00
Nos. 337-341 (5) 59.75 27.50

Federation of Ethiopia and Eritrea, 1st anniv.

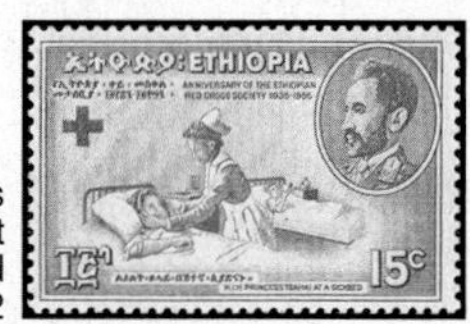

Princess Tsahai at a Sickbed A62

Perf. 13x13½

1955, July 8 Engr. Wmk. 282

Cross Typo. in Red

342 A62 15c choc & ultra 2.50 1.25
343 A62 20c green & orange 3.75 1.50
344 A62 30c ultra & green 6.25 1.90
Nos. 342-344 (3) 12.50 4.65

Ethiopian Red Cross, 20th anniv.
For surcharges see Nos. B33-B35.

Promulgating the Constitution — A63

Bishops' Consecration by Archbishop — A64

25c, Kagnew Battalion. 35c, Reunion with the Motherland. 50c, "Progress." 65c, Empress Waizero Menen & Emperor Haile Selassie.

Perf. 12½

1955, Nov. 3 Unwmk. Engr.

345 A63 5c green & choc 1.25 .55
346 A64 20c carmine & slate grn 2.50 .90
347 A64 25c magenta & gray 3.50 1.40
348 A63 35c brown & red org 4.75 1.75
349 A64 50c dk brn & ultra 7.00 2.50
350 A64 65c violet & car 9.75 4.00
Nos. 345-350 (6) 28.75 11.10

Silver jubilee of the coronation of Emperor Haile Selassie and Empress Waizero Menen.

Emperor Haile Selassie and Fair Emblem — A65

1955, Nov. 5 Wmk. 282

351 A65 5c green & ol grn 1.00 .35
352 A65 10c car & dp ultra 1.50 .40
353 A65 15c vio blk & grn 2.00 .60
354 A65 50c mag & red brn 3.00 2.00
Nos. 351-354 (4) 7.50 3.35

Silver Jubilee Fair, Addis Ababa.

Nos. 291 and 292A Overprinted

1960, Apr. 7 ***Perf. 13x13½***

355 A53 20c blue 1.75 1.25
356 A53 60c red 3.00 2.40

WRY, July 1, 1959-June 30, 1960.
The 60c without serifs is a trial printing.

Map of Africa, "Liberty" and Haile Selassie — A66

Perf. 13½

1960, June 14 Engr. Unwmk.

357 A66 20c orange & green .85 .85
358 A66 80c orange & violet 2.75 .85
359 A66 $1 orange & maroon 2.75 1.10
Nos. 357-359 (3) 6.35 2.80

2nd Conf. of Independent African States at Addis Ababa. Issued in sheets of 10.

Emperor Haile Selassie — A67

1960, Nov. 2 Wmk. 282 ***Perf. 14***

360 A67 10c brown & blue .85 .85
361 A67 25c violet & emerald 1.10 1.10
362 A67 50c dk bl & org yel 2.75 2.75
363 A67 65c slate grn & sal pink 4.25 4.25
364 A67 $1 indigo & rose vio 5.00 5.00
Nos. 360-364 (5) 13.95 13.95

30th anniv. of the coronation of Emperor Haile Selassie.

Africa Hall, UN Economic Commission for Africa — A68

1961, Apr. 15 Wmk. 282 ***Perf. 14***

365 A68 80c ultra 2.75 1.40

Africa Freedom Day, Apr. 15. Sheets of 10.

Map of Ethiopia, Olive Branch A69

1961, May 5 ***Perf. 13x13½***

366 A69 20c green .40 .40
367 A69 30c violet blue .60 .45
368 A69 $1 brown 3.25 1.40
Nos. 366-368 (3) 4.25 2.25

20th anniv. of Ethiopia's liberation from Italian occupation.

African Wild Ass A70

1961, June 16 Wmk. 282 ***Perf. 14***

369 A70 5c shown 1.10 .25
370 A70 15c Eland 1.10 .25
371 A70 25c Elephant 1.25 .40
372 A70 35c Giraffe 3.00 .50
373 A70 50c Beisa 3.00 .50
374 A70 $1 Lion 6.00 1.50
Nos. 369-374 (6) 15.45 3.40

Issued in sheets of 10. Used values are for CTO's.

Emperor Haile Selassie and Empress Waizero Menen — A71

1961, July 27 Unwmk. ***Perf. 11***

375 A71 10c green .85 .45
376 A71 50c violet blue 1.50 .80
377 A71 $1 carmine rose 3.25 1.60
Nos. 375-377 (3) 5.60 2.85

Golden wedding anniv. of the Emperor and Empress.

Warlike Horsemanship (Guks) — A72

15c, Hockey. 20c, Bicycling. 30c, Soccer. 50c, 1960 Olympic marathon winner, Abebe Bikila.

Photogravure and Engraved

1962, Jan. 14 ***Perf. 12x11½***

378 A72 10c yel grn & car .50 .35
379 A72 15c pink & dk brn .85 .60
380 A72 20c red & black 1.00 .70
381 A72 30c ultra & dl pur 1.10 .85
382 A72 50c yellow & green 1.75 1.00
Nos. 378-382 (5) 5.20 3.50

Third Africa Football (soccer) Cup, Addis Ababa, Jan. 14-22.

Malaria Eradication Emblem, World Map and Mosquito — A73

Wmk. 282

1962, Apr. 7 Engr. ***Perf. 13½***

383 A73 15c black .30 .25
384 A73 30c purple .55 .25
385 A73 60c red brown 1.20 .65
Nos. 383-385 (3) 2.05 1.15

WHO drive to eradicate malaria.

Abyssinian Ground Hornbill A74

Birds: 15c, Abyssinian roller. 30c, Bateleur, vert. 50c, Double-toothed barbet, vert. $1, Didric cuckoo.

Perf. 11½

1962, May 5 Unwmk. Photo.

Granite Paper

386 A74 5c multicolored .85 .25
387 A74 15c emer, brn & ultra 1.10 .50
388 A74 30c lt brn, blk & red 2.25 .85
389 A74 50c multicolored 4.50 1.10
390 A74 $1 multicolored 9.00 2.50
Nos. 386-390 (5) 17.70 5.20

See Nos. C77-C81, C97-C101, C107-C111.

Assab Hospital A75

15c, School at Assab. 20c, Church at Massawa. 50c, Mosque at Massawa. 60c, Assab port.

Wmk. 282

1962, Sept. 11 Engr. ***Perf. 13½***

391 A75 3c purple .25 .25
392 A75 15c dark blue .25 .25
393 A75 20c green .30 .25
394 A75 50c brown .55 .30
395 A75 60c carmine rose .85 .50
Nos. 391-395 (5) 2.20 1.55

Federation of Ethiopia and Eritrea, 10th anniv.

King Bazen, Madonna and Stars over Bethlehem — A76

15c, Ezana, obelisks & temple. 20c, Kaleb & sailing fleet. 50c, Lalibela, rock-church and frescoes, vert. 60c, King Yekuno Amlak & Abuna Tekle Haimanot preaching in Ankober. 75c, King Zara Yacob & Maskal celebration. $1, King Lebna Dengel & battle against Mohammed Gragn.

Perf. 14½

1962, Nov. 2 Unwmk. Photo.

396 A76 10c multicolored .30 .25
397 A76 15c multicolored .50 .25
398 A76 20c multicolored .50 .25
399 A76 50c multicolored .85 .25
400 A76 60c multicolored 1.10 .50
401 A76 75c multicolored 1.75 .85
402 A76 $1 multicolored 2.25 1.25
Nos. 396-402 (7) 7.25 3.60

32nd anniv. of the coronation of Emperor Haile Selassie and to commemorate ancient kings and saints.

Map of Ethiopian Telephone Network — A77

Designs: 50c, Radio mast and waves. 60c, Telegraph pole and rising sun.

Perf. 13½x14

1963, Jan. 1 Engr. Wmk. 282

403 A77 10c dark red .50 .25
404 A77 50c ultra 1.10 .50
405 A77 60c brown 1.75 .60
Nos. 403-405 (3) 3.35 1.35

10th anniv. of the Imperial Board of Telecommunications.

Wheat Emblem — A78

1963, Mar. 21 Unwmk. *Perf. 13½*

No.	Type	Description	Unused	Used
406	A78	5c deep rose	.25	.25
407	A78	10c rose carmine	.25	.25
408	A78	15c violet blue	.25	.25
409	A78	30c emerald	1.25	.25
		Nos. 406-409 (4)	2.00	1.00

FAO "Freedom from Hunger" campaign.

Abuna Salama — A79

Spiritual Leaders: 15c, Abuna Aregawi. 30c, Abuna Tekle Haimanot. 40c. Yared. 60c, Zara Yacob.

1964, Jan. 3 Unwmk. *Perf. 13½*

No.	Type	Description	Unused	Used
410	A79	10c blue	.55	.25
411	A79	15c dark green	.85	.25
412	A79	30c brown red	1.10	.50
413	A79	40c dark blue	1.60	.75
414	A79	60c brown	2.75	1.60
		Nos. 410-414 (5)	6.85	3.35

Queen of Sheba — A80

Ethiopian Empresses: 15c, Helen. 50c, Seble Wongel. 60c, Mentiwab. 80c, Taitu, consort of Menelik II.

Granite Paper

1964, Mar. 2 Photo. *Perf. 11½*

No.	Type	Description	Unused	Used
415	A80	10c multicolored	.85	.30
416	A80	15c multicolored	.85	.30
417	A80	50c multicolored	1.60	.85
418	A80	60c multicolored	2.75	1.10
419	A80	80c multicolored	4.50	1.60
		Nos. 415-419 (5)	10.55	4.15

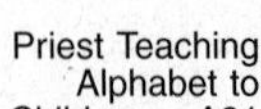

Priest Teaching Alphabet to Children — A81

10c, Classroom. 15c, Woman learning to read. 40c, Students in chemistry laboratory. 60c, Graduation procession.

1964, June 1 Unwmk. *Perf. 11½*

Granite Paper

No.	Type	Description	Unused	Used
420	A81	5c brown	.25	.25
421	A81	10c emerald	.25	.25
422	A81	15c rose vio, vert.	.25	.25
423	A81	40c vio blue, vert.	1.00	.30
424	A81	60c dark pur, vert.	1.50	.55
		Nos. 420-424 (5)	3.25	1.60

Issued to publicize education.

Eleanor Roosevelt (1884-1962) — A82

1964, Oct. 11 Photo.

Granite Paper

Portrait in Slate Blue

No.	Type	Description	Unused	Used
425	A82	10c yellow bister	.25	.25
426	A82	60c orange brown	1.10	.75
427	A82	80c green & gold	1.75	1.00
		Nos. 425-427 (3)	3.10	2.00

King Serse Dengel and View of Gondar, 1563 A83

Ethiopian Leaders: 10c, King Fasiladas and Gondar in 1632. 20c, King Yassu the Great and Gondar in 1682. 25c, Emperor Theodore II and map of Ethiopia. 60c, Emperor John IV and Battle of Gura, 1876. 80c, Emperor Menelik II and Battle of Adwa, 1896.

1964, Dec. 12 Photo. *Perf. 14½x14*

No.	Type	Description	Unused	Used
428	A83	5c multicolored	.30	.25
429	A83	10c multicolored	.30	.25
430	A83	20c multicolored	.55	.25
431	A83	25c multicolored	.85	.25
432	A83	60c multicolored	1.60	1.10
433	A83	80c multicolored	1.60	1.10
		Nos. 428-433 (6)	5.20	3.20

Ethiopian Rose — A84

Flowers: 10c, Kosso tree. 25c, St.-John's-wort. 35c, Parrot's-beak. 60c, Maskal daisy.

1965, Mar. 30 *Perf. 12x13½*

No.	Type	Description	Unused	Used
434	A84	5c multicolored	.30	.25
435	A84	10c multicolored	.30	.25
436	A84	25c multicolored	.85	.55
437	A84	35c multicolored	1.20	1.20
438	A84	60c green, yel & org	2.25	1.60
		Nos. 434-438 (5)	4.90	3.85

ITU Emblem, Old and New Communication Symbols — A85

Perf. 13½x14½

1965, May 17 Litho. Unwmk.

No.	Type	Description	Unused	Used
439	A85	5c blue, indigo & yel	.25	.25
440	A85	10c blue, indigo & org	.55	.25
441	A85	60c blue, indigo & lil rose	2.00	.95
		Nos. 439-441 (3)	2.80	1.45

Cent. of the ITU.

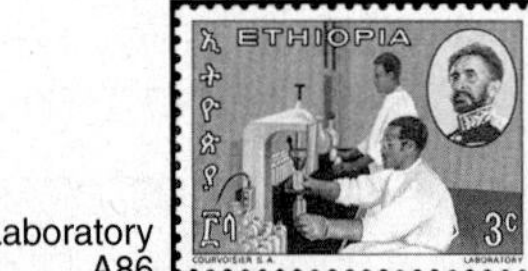

Laboratory A86

Designs: 5c, Textile spinning mill. 10c, Sugar factory. 20c, Mountain road. 25c, Autobus. 30c, Diesel locomotive and bridge. 35c, Railroad station, Addis Ababa.

1965, July 19 Photo. *Perf. 11½*

Granite Paper

Portrait in Black

No.	Type	Description	Unused	Used
442	A86	3c sepia	.30	.25
443	A86	5c dull pur & buff	.30	.25
444	A86	10c black & gray	.30	.25
445	A86	20c green & pale yel	.30	.25
446	A86	25c dk brown & yel	.55	.30
447	A86	30c maroon & gray	.85	.30
448	A86	35c dk blue & gray	.85	.50
		Nos. 442-448 (7)	3.45	2.10

For overprints see Nos. 609-612.

ICY Emblem A87

1965, Oct. 24 Unwmk. *Perf. 11½*

Granite Paper

No.	Type	Description	Unused	Used
449	A87	10c blue & red brn	.50	.25
450	A87	50c dp blue & red brn	1.40	.75
451	A87	80c vio blue & red brn	2.25	1.10
		Nos. 449-451 (3)	4.15	2.10

International Cooperation Year, 1965.

National Bank Emblem A88

Designs: 10c, Commercial Bank emblem. 60c, Natl. and Commercial Bank buildings.

1965, Nov. 2 Photo. *Perf. 13*

No.	Type	Description	Unused	Used
452	A88	10c dp car, blk & indigo	.45	.25
453	A88	30c ultra, blk & indigo	1.00	.40
454	A88	60c black, yel & indigo	1.50	.65
		Nos. 452-454 (3)	2.95	1.30

Natl. and Commercial Banks of Ethiopia.

"Light and Peace" Press Building A89

1966, Apr. 5 Engr. *Perf. 13*

No.	Type	Description	Unused	Used
455	A89	5c pink & black	.25	.25
456	A89	15c lt yel grn & blk	.60	.25
457	A89	30c orange yel & blk	1.10	.55
		Nos. 455-457 (3)	1.95	1.05

Opening of the "Light and Peace" Printing Press building.

Kabaro Drum — A90

Musical Instruments: 10c, Bagana harp. 35c, Messenko guitar. 50c, Krar lyre. 60c, Wachent flutes.

1966, Sept. 9 Photo. *Perf. 13½*

No.	Type	Description	Unused	Used
458	A90	5c brt green & blk	.30	.25
459	A90	10c dull blue & blk	.30	.25
460	A90	35c orange yel & blk	1.10	.85
461	A90	50c yellow & blk	1.75	1.10
462	A90	60c rose car & blk	2.75	1.60
		Nos. 458-462 (5)	6.20	4.05

Emperor Haile Selassie — A91

1966, Nov. 1 Unwmk. *Perf. 12*

No.	Type	Description	Unused	Used
463	A91	10c black, gold & grn	.30	.25
464	A91	15c black, gold & dp car	.55	.25
465	A91	40c black & gold	1.10	.85
		Nos. 463-465 (3)	1.95	1.35

50 years of leadership of Emperor Haile Selassie.

UNESCO Emblem and Map of Africa A92

Wmk. 282

1966, Nov. 30 Litho. *Perf. 13½*

No.	Type	Description	Unused	Used
466	A92	15c blue car & blk	.50	.25
467	A92	60c olive, brn & dk bl	1.10	.85

20th anniv. of UNESCO.

WHO Headquarters, Geneva — A93

1966, Nov. 30

No.	Type	Description	Unused	Used
468	A93	5c olive, ultra & brn	.80	.25
469	A93	40c brown, pur & emer	1.25	.85

Opening of WHO Headquarters, Geneva.

Expo '67 Ethiopian Pavilion and Columns of Axum (Replica) — A94

Perf. 12x13½

1967, May 2 Photo. Unwmk.

No.	Type	Description	Unused	Used
470	A94	30c brt blue & multi	.75	.30
471	A94	45c multicolored	1.00	.40
472	A94	80c gray & multi	1.25	.60
		Nos. 470-472 (3)	3.00	1.30

EXPO '67, Intl. Exhibition, Montreal, Apr. 28-Oct. 27, 1967.

Diesel Train and Map — A95

1967, June 7 Photo. *Perf. 12*

No.	Type	Description	Unused	Used
473	A95	15c multicolored	1.10	.55
474	A95	30c multicolored	2.75	1.50
475	A95	50c multicolored	4.25	2.25
		Nos. 473-475 (3)	8.10	4.30

Djibouti-Addis Ababa railroad, 50th anniv.

Papilionidae Aethiops — A96

Various Butterflies.

Perf. 13½x13

1967, June 30 Photo. Unwmk.

476 A96 5c buff & multi .60 .25
477 A96 10c lilac & multi 2.00 .40
478 A96 20c multicolored 2.75 .75
479 A96 35c blue & multi 4.75 1.50
480 A96 40c multicolored 7.75 2.00
Nos. 476-480 (5) 17.85 4.90

Emperor Haile Selassie and Lion of Judah A97

1967, July 21 ***Perf. 11½***

Granite Paper

481 A97 10c dk brn, emer & gold .45 .25
482 A97 15c dk brn, yel & gold .80 .25
483 A97 $1 dk brn, red & gold 3.50 1.50
Nos. 481-483 (3) 4.75 2.00

Souvenir Sheet

484 A97 $1 dk brn, pur & gold 16.00 22.50

75th birthday of Emperor Haile Selassie.

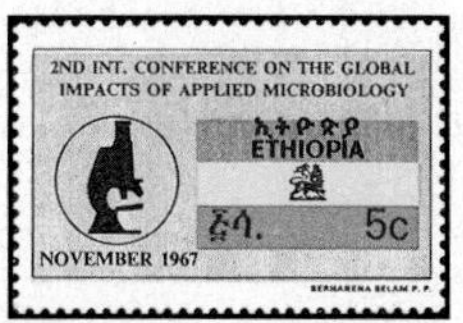

Microscope and Ethiopian Flag — A98

1967, Nov. 6 Litho. ***Perf. 13***

Flag in Grn, Yel, Red & Blk

485 A98 5c blue .25 .25
486 A98 30c ocher .55 .30
487 A98 $1 violet 1.75 1.10
Nos. 485-487 (3) 2.55 1.65

2nd Intl. Conf. on the Global Impact of Applied Microbiology, Addis Ababa, 11/6-12.

Wall Painting from Debre Berhan Selassie Church, Gondar, 17th Century — A99

ITY Emblem and: 25c, Votive throne from Atsbe Dera, 4th Cent. B.C., vert. 35c, Prehistoric cave painting, Harar Province. 50c, Prehistoric stone tools, Melke Kontoure, vert.

1967, Nov. 20 Photo. ***Perf. 14½***

488 A99 15c multicolored 3.00 1.40
489 A99 25c yel grn, buff & blk 3.25 1.40
490 A99 35c green, brn & blk 3.00 1.75
491 A99 50c yellow & blk 5.50 2.75
Nos. 488-491 (4) 14.75 7.30

International Tourist Year, 1967.

A100

Crosses of Lalibela: 5c, Processional Bronze Cross, Biet-Maryam Church. 10c, Processional copper cross. 15c, Copper cross, Biet-Maryam church. 20c, Lalibela-style cross. 50c, Chiseled copper cross, Madhani Alem church.

1967, Dec. 7 Photo. ***Perf. 14½***

Crosses in Silver

492 A100 5c yellow & blk .30 .25
493 A100 10c red orange & blk .30 .25
494 A100 15c violet & blk .40 .25
495 A100 20c brt rose & blk .65 .25
496 A100 50c orange yel & blk 2.00 .60
Nos. 492-496 (5) 3.65 1.60

A101

Designs: 10c, Emperor Theodore (1818?-1868). 20c, Emperor Theodore and lions, horiz. 50c, Imperial crown.

Perf. 14x13½

1968, Apr. 18 Litho. Unwmk.

497 A101 10c lt vio, ocher & brn .50 .25
498 A101 20c lilac, brn & dk vio .85 .50
499 A101 50c dk grn, org & rose cl 1.75 1.10
Nos. 497-499 (3) 3.10 1.85

Human Rights Flame A102

1968, May 31 Unwmk. ***Perf. 14½***

500 A102 15c pink, red & blk .55 .55
501 A102 $1 lt bl, brt bl & blk 2.40 2.40

International Human Rights Year, 1968.

Shah Mohammed Reza Pahlavi, Emperor and Flags — A103

1968, June 3 Litho. ***Perf. 13½***

502 A103 5c multicolored .25 .25
503 A103 15c multicolored .30 .30
504 A103 30c multicolored 1.25 1.25
Nos. 502-504 (3) 1.80 1.80

Visit of Shah Mohammed Riza Pahlavi of Iran.

Emperor Haile Selassie Appealing to League of Nations, 1935 — A104

35c, African Unity Building and map of Africa. $1, World map, symbolizing intl. relations.

1968, July 22 Photo. ***Perf. 14x13½***

505 A104 15c bl, red, blk & gold .40 .25
506 A104 35c blk, emer, red & gold .75 .75
507 A104 $1 dk bl, lil, blk & gold 2.50 2.75
Nos. 505-507 (3) 3.65 3.75

Ethiopia's struggle for peace. Issued with tabs on bottom row. Value, set $10.

WHO Emblem A105

Perf. 14x13½

1968, Aug. 30 Litho. Unwmk.

508 A105 15c brt green & blk .50 .35
509 A105 60c red lilac & blk 1.75 1.90

20th anniv. of the WHO.

Abebe Bikila, Marathon Runner A106

1968, Oct. 12 ***Perf. 11½***

510 A106 10c shown .25 .25
511 A106 15c Soccer .40 .40
512 A106 20c Boxing .50 .50
513 A106 40c Basketball 1.25 1.25
514 A106 50c Bicycling 1.90 1.90
Nos. 510-514 (5) 4.30 4.30

19th Olympic Games, Mexico City, 10/12-27.

Arrussi Woman — A107

Regional Costumes: 15c, Man from Gemu Gefa. 20c, Gojam man. 30c, Kefa man. 35c, Harar woman. 50c, Ilubabor grass coat. 60c, Woman from Eritrea.

Perf. 13½x13

1968, Dec. 10 Photo. Unwmk.

515 A107 5c silver & multi .65 .25
516 A107 15c silver & multi .65 .25
517 A107 20c silver & multi .65 .25
518 A107 30c silver & multi .85 .55
519 A107 35c silver & multi .85 .65
520 A107 50c silver & multi 1.75 1.10
521 A107 60c silver & multi 2.25 1.60
Nos. 515-521 (7) 7.65 4.65

See Nos. 575-581.

Message Stick and Amharic Postal Emblem A108

1969, Mar. 10 Litho. ***Perf. 14***

522 A108 10c emerald, blk & brn .75 .70
523 A108 15c yellow, blk & brn .75 .70
524 A108 35c multicolored 1.40 1.25
Nos. 522-524 (3) 2.90 2.65

Ethiopian postal service, 75th anniv.

ILO Emblem A109

1969, Apr. 11 Litho. ***Perf. 14½***

525 A109 15c orange & blk .50 .50
526 A109 60c emerald & blk 2.00 2.00

50th anniv. of the ILO.

Dove, Red Cross, Crescent, Lion and Sun Emblems A110

1969, May 8 Wmk. 282 ***Perf. 13***

527 A110 5c lt ultra, blk & red .25 .25
528 A110 15c lt ultra, grn & red .65 .65
529 A110 30c lt ultra, vio bl & red 1.40 1.40
Nos. 527-529 (3) 2.30 2.30

League of Red Cross Societies, 50th anniv.

Endybis Silver Coin, 3rd Century — A111

Ancient Ethiopian Coins: 10c, Gold of Ezana, 4th cent. 15c, Gold of Kaleb, 6th cent. 30c, Bronze of Armah, 7th cent. 40c, Bronze of Wazena, 7th cent. 50c, Silver of Gersem, 8th cent.

1969, June 19 Photo. ***Perf. 14½***

530 A111 5c ultra, blk & sil .30 .25
531 A111 10c brt red, blk & gold .50 .45
532 A111 15c brown, blk & gold .80 .70
533 A111 30c dp car, blk & brnz 1.10 1.25
534 A111 40c dk green, blk & brnz 1.60 1.10
535 A111 50c dp violet, blk & sil 1.75 1.75
Nos. 530-535 (6) 6.05 5.50

Zebras and Tourist Year Emblem A112

Designs: 10c, Camping. 15c, Fishing. 20c, Water skiing. 25c, Mountaineering, vert.

Perf. 13x13½, 13½x13

1969, Aug. 29 Litho. Unwmk.

536 A112 5c multicolored .30 .30
537 A112 10c multicolored .55 .30
538 A112 15c multicolored .85 .55
539 A112 20c multicolored .85 .85
540 A112 25c multicolored 1.75 1.10
Nos. 536-540 (5) 4.30 3.10

International Year of African Tourism.

Stylized Bird and UN Emblem A113

UN 25th anniv.: 30c, Stylized flowers, UN and peace emblems, vert. 60c, Stylized bird, UN emblem and plane.

1969, Oct. 24 Unwmk. ***Perf. 11½***

541 A113 10c lt blue & multi .25 .25
542 A113 30c lt blue & multi .80 .80
543 A113 60c lt blue & multi 2.00 2.00
Nos. 541-543 (3) 3.05 3.05

Ancient Cross and Holy Family
A114

Designs: Various ancient crosses.

Perf. 14½x13½

1969, Dec. 10 Photo.

544 A114 5c black, yel & dk bl .25 .25
545 A114 10c black & yellow .25 .55
546 A114 25c black, yel & grn 1.10 1.10
547 A114 60c black & ocher 2.75 2.25
Nos. 544-547 (4) 4.35 4.15

Ancient Figurines — A115

Ancient Ethiopian Pottery: 20c, Vases, Yeha period, 4th-3rd centuries B.C. 25c, Vases and jugs, Axum, 4th-6th centuries A.D. 35c, Bird-shaped jug and jugs, Matara, 4th-6th centuries A.D. 60c, Decorated pottery, Adulis, 6th-7th centuries A.D.

1970, Feb. 6 Photo. *Perf. 14½*

548 A115 10c black & multi .65 .55
549 A115 20c black & multi .65 .55
550 A115 25c black & multi .65 .55
551 A115 35c black & multi 1.40 1.25
552 A115 60c black & multi 2.50 2.25
Nos. 548-552 (5) 5.85 5.15

Medhane Alem Church — A116

Rock Churches of Lalibela, 12th-13th Centuries: 10c, Bieta Emmanuel. 15c, The four Rock Churches of Lalibela. 20c, Bieta Mariam. 50c, Bieta Giorgis.

1970, Apr. 15 Unwmk. *Perf. 13*

553 A116 5c brown & multi .30 .25
554 A116 10c brown & multi .30 .25
555 A116 15c brown & multi .50 .40
556 A116 20c brown & multi .75 .65
557 A116 50c brown & multi 1.80 1.50
Nos. 553-557 (5) 3.65 3.05

Sailfish Tang
A117

Tropical Fish: 10c, Undulate triggerfish. 15c, Orange butterflyfish. 25c, Butterflyfish. 50c, Imperial Angelfish.

1970, June 19 Photo. *Perf. 12½*

558 A117 5c multicolored .25 .25
559 A117 10c multicolored .25 .25
560 A117 15c multicolored .60 .60
561 A117 25c multicolored 1.50 1.50
562 A117 50c multicolored 3.00 3.00
Nos. 558-562 (5) 5.60 5.60

Education Year Emblem — A118

1970, Aug. 14 Unwmk. *Perf. 13½*

563 A118 10c multicolored .25 .25
564 A118 20c gold, ultra & emer .45 .45
565 A118 50c gold, emer & org 1.40 1.40
Nos. 563-565 (3) 2.10 2.10

Issued for International Education Year.

Map of Africa — A119

30c, Flag of Organization of African Unity. 40c, OAU Headquarters, Addis Ababa.

1970, Sept. 21 Photo. *Perf. 13½*

566 A119 20c multicolored .30 .30
567 A119 30c multicolored .60 .60
568 A119 40c green & multi .85 .85
Nos. 566-568 (3) 1.75 1.75

Africa Unity Day and Organization of African Unity.

Emperor Haile Selassie — A120

1970, Oct. 30 Unwmk. *Perf. 14½*

569 A120 15c Prus bl & multi .30 .30
570 A120 50c multicolored 1.00 1.00
571 A120 60c multicolored 1.75 1.75
Nos. 569-571 (3) 3.05 3.05

Coronation, 40th anniv.

Buildings — A121

1970, Dec. 30 Litho. *Perf. 13½*

572 A121 10c ver & multi .30 .30
573 A121 50c brown & multi 1.10 1.10
574 A121 80c multicolored 1.75 1.75
Nos. 572-574 (3) 3.15 3.15

Opening of new Posts, Telecommunications and General Post Office buildings.

Costume Type of 1968

Regional Costumes: 5c, Warrior from Begemdir and Semien. 10c, Woman from Bale. 15c, Warrior from Welega. 20c,Woman from Shoa. 25c, Man from Sidamo. 40c, Woman from Tigre. 50c, Man from Welo.

1971, Feb. 17 Photo. *Perf. 11½*
Granite Paper

575 A107 5c gold & multi .30 .30
576 A107 10c gold & multi .30 .30
577 A107 15c gold & multi .55 .50
578 A107 20c gold & multi .60 .60
579 A107 25c gold & multi .85 .85
580 A107 40c gold & multi 1.10 1.10
581 A107 50c gold & multi 2.25 2.25
Nos. 575-581 (7) 5.95 5.90

Plane's Tail with Emblem — A122

Designs: 10c, Ethiopian scenes. 20c, Nose of Boeing 707. 60c, Pilots in cockpit, and engine. 80c, Globe with routes shown.

1971, Apr. 8 *Perf. 14½x14*

582 A122 5c multicolored .30 .30
583 A122 10c multicolored .30 .30
584 A122 20c multicolored .60 .60
585 A122 60c multicolored 1.25 1.25
586 A122 80c multicolored 2.00 2.00
Nos. 582-586 (5) 4.45 4.45

Ethiopian Airlines, 25th anniversary. Issued with tabs on bottom row. Value, set $11.

Fountain of Life, 15th Century Gospel Book — A123

Ethiopian Paintings: 10c, King David, 15th cent. manuscript. 25c, St. George, 17th cent. painting on canvas. 50c, King Lalibela, 18th cent. painting on wood. 60c, Yared singing before King Kaleb. Mural in Axum Cathedral.

1971, June 15 Photo. *Perf. 11½*
Granite Paper

587 A123 5c tan & multi .25 .25
588 A123 10c pale sal & multi .25 .25
589 A123 25c lemon & multi .60 .60
590 A123 50c yellow & multi 1.60 1.60
591 A123 60c gray & multi 2.50 2.50
Nos. 587-591 (5) 5.20 5.20

Black and White Heads, Globes
A124

Designs: 60c, Black and white hand holding globe. 80c, Four races, globes.

1971, Aug. 31 Unwmk.

592 A124 10c org, red brn & blk .30 .30
593 A124 60c green, bl & blk 1.75 1.75
594 A124 80c bl, org, yel & blk 2.75 2.75
Nos. 592-594 (3) 4.80 4.80

Intl. Year Against Racial Discrimination.

Emperor Menelik II and Reading of Treaty of Ucciali
A125

Contemporary Paintings: 30c, Menelik II on horseback gathering the tribes. 50c, Ethiopians and Italians in Battle of Adwa. 60c, Menelik II and Taitu at head of their armies.

1971, Oct. 20 Litho. *Perf. 13½*

595 A125 10c multicolored .35 .35
596 A125 30c multicolored .95 .95
597 A125 50c multicolored 1.40 1.40
598 A125 60c multicolored 2.40 2.40
Nos. 595-598 (4) 5.10 5.10

75th anniversary of victory of Adwa over the Italians, March 1, 1896.

Two telephones, 1897, Menelik II and Ras Makonnen — A126

Designs: 10c, Haile Selassie Broadcasting and Map of Ethiopia. 30c, Ethiopians around television set. 40c, Telephone microwave circuits. 60c, Map of Africa on globe and telephone dial.

1971, Nov. 2

599 A126 5c brown & multi .30 .30
600 A126 10c yellow & multi .30 .30
601 A126 30c vio bl & multi .30 .30
602 A126 40c black & multi .85 .85
603 A126 60c vio bl & multi 2.25 2.25
Nos. 599-603 (5) 4.00 4.00

Telecommunications in Ethiopia, 75th anniv.

UNICEF Emblem, Mother and Child — A127

UNICEF Emblem and: 10c, Children drinking milk. 15c, Man holding sick child. 30c, Kindergarten class. 50c, Father and son.

1971, Dec. 15 Unwmk.

604 A127 5c yellow & multi .30 .30
605 A127 10c pale brn & multi .30 .30
606 A127 15c rose & multi .30 .30
607 A127 30c violet & multi .85 .85
608 A127 50c green & multi 1.60 1.60
Nos. 604-608 (5) 3.35 3.35

25th anniv. of UNICEF.

Nos. 445-448 Overprinted

1972, Jan. 28 Photo. *Perf. 11*
Portrait in Black

609 A86 20c grn & pale yel .55 .55
610 A86 25c dk brn & yel .85 .85
611 A86 30c maroon & gray 3.50 3.50
612 A86 35c dk blue & gray 3.50 3.50
Nos. 609-612 (4) 8.40 8.40

1st meeting of UN Security Council in Africa.

River Boat on Lake Haik — A128

1972, Feb. 7 Litho. *Perf. 11½*
Granite Paper

613 A128 10c shown .30 .30
614 A128 20c Boats on Lake Abaya .55 .55
615 A128 30c on Lake Tana .85 .85
616 A128 60c on Baro River 1.75 1.75
Nos. 613-616 (4) 3.45 3.45

Proclamation of Cyrus the Great — A129

1972, Mar. 28 Photo. *Perf. 14x14½*

617 A129 10c red & multi .50 .50
618 A129 60c emerald & multi 2.00 2.00
619 A129 80c gray & multi 3.00 3.00
Nos. 617-619 (3) 5.50 5.50

2500th anniversary of the founding of the Persian empire by Cyrus the Great.

Houses, Sidamo Province A130

Ethiopian Architecture: 10c, Tigre Province. 20c, Eritrea Province. 40c, Addis Ababa. 80c, Shoa Province.

1972, Apr. 11 Litho. *Perf. 13½*

620 A130 5c black & multi .30 .30
621 A130 10c black, gray & brn .30 .30
622 A130 20c black & multi .65 .65
623 A130 40c black, bl grn & brn 1.10 1.10
624 A130 80c black, brn & red brn 2.75 2.75
Nos. 620-624 (5) 5.10 5.10

Hands Holding Map of Ethiopia — A131

10c, Hands shielding Ethiopians. 25c, Map of Africa, hands reaching for African Unity emblem. 50c, Brown & white hands clasped, UN emblem. 60c, Hands protecting dove. Each denomination shows different portrait of the Emperor.

Perf. 14½x14

1972, July 21 Litho. Unwmk.

625 A131 5c scarlet & multi .35 .35
626 A131 10c ultra & multi .35 .35
627 A131 25c vio bl & multi .60 .60
628 A131 50c lt blue & multi 1.25 1.25
629 A131 60c brown & multi 1.50 1.50
Nos. 625-629 (5) 4.05 4.05

80th birthday of Emperor Haile Selassie.

Running, Flags of Mexico, Japan, Italy — A132

1972, Aug. 25 *Perf. 13½x13*

630 A132 10c shown .35 .35
631 A132 30c Soccer .80 .80
632 A132 50c Bicycling 1.75 1.75
633 A132 60c Boxing 2.25 2.25
Nos. 630-633 (4) 5.15 5.15

20th Olympic Games, Munich, Germany, Aug. 26-Sept. 11.

Open Bible, Cross and Orbit A133

Designs: 50c, First and 1972 headquarters of the British and Foreign Bible Society, vert. 80c, First Amharic Bible.

1972, Sept. 25 Photo. *Perf. 13½*

634 A133 20c deep red & multi .60 .60
635 A133 50c deep red & multi 1.10 1.10
636 A133 80c deep red & multi 2.75 2.75
Nos. 634-636 (3) 4.45 4.45

United Bible Societies World Assembly, Addis Ababa, Sept. 1972.

Security Council Meeting A134

Designs: 60c, Building where Security Council met. 80c, Map of Africa with flags of participating members.

1972, Nov. 1 Litho. *Perf. 13½*

637 A134 10c lt bl & vio bl .25 .25
638 A134 60c multicolored 1.10 1.10
639 A134 80c multicolored 1.75 1.75
Nos. 637-639 (3) 3.10 3.10

First United Nations Security Council meeting, Addis Ababa, Jan. 28-Feb. 4, 1972.

Fish in Polluted Sea A135

Designs: 30c, Fisherman, beacon, family. 80c, Polluted seashore.

1973, Feb. 23 Photo. *Perf. 13½*

640 A135 20c gold & multi .75 .50
641 A135 30c gold & multi 1.00 .85
642 A135 80c gold & multi 2.25 2.00
Nos. 640-642 (3) 4.00 3.35

World message from the sea, Ethiopian anti-pollution campaign.

INTERPOL and Ethiopian Police Emblems — A136

50c, INTERPOL emblem & General Secretariat, Paris. 60c, INTERPOL emblem.

1973, Mar. 20 Photo. *Perf. 13½*

643 A136 40c dull orange & blk 1.25 1.25
644 A136 50c blue, blk & yel 1.75 1.75
645 A136 60c dk carmine & blk 2.00 2.00
Nos. 643-645 (3) 5.00 5.00

50th anniversary of International Criminal Police Organization (INTERPOL).

Virgin of Emperor Zara Yaqob — A137

Ethiopian Art: 15c, Crucifixion, Zara Yaqob period. 30c, Virgin and Child, from Entoto Mariam Church. 40c, Christ, contemporary mosaic. 80c, The Evangelists, contemporary bas-relief.

1973, May 15 Photo. *Perf. 11½*
Granite Paper

646 A137 5c brown & multi .30 .30
647 A137 15c dp blue & multi .55 .55
648 A137 30c gray grn & multi .85 .85
649 A137 40c multicolored 1.10 1.10
650 A137 80c slate & multi 2.75 2.75
Nos. 646-650 (5) 5.55 5.55

Free African States in 1963 and 1973 A138

Designs (Map of Africa and): 10c, Flags of OAU members. 20c, Symbols of progress. 40c, Dove and people. 80c, Emblems of various UN agencies.

1973 May 25 *Perf. 14½x14*

651 A138 5c red & multi .25 .25
652 A138 10c ol gray & multi .30 .30
653 A138 20c green & multi .50 .50
654 A138 40c sepia & multi 1.10 1.10
655 A138 80c lt blue & multi 2.75 2.75
Nos. 651-655 (5) 4.90 4.90

OAU, 10th anniv.

Scouts Saluting Ethiopian and Scout Flags — A139

Designs: 15c, Road and road sign. 30c, Girl Scout reading to old man. 40c, Scout and disabled people. 60c, Ethiopian Boy Scout.

1973, July 10 Photo. *Perf. 11½*
Granite Paper

656 A139 5c blue & multi .30 .30
657 A139 15c lt green & multi .55 .55
658 A139 30c yellow & multi .85 .85
659 A139 40c crimson & multi 1.10 1.10
660 A139 60c violet & multi 2.75 2.75
Nos. 656-660 (5) 5.55 5.55

24th Boy Scout World Conference, Nairobi, Kenya, July 16-21.

WMO Emblem A140

50c, WMO emblem, anemometer. 60c, Weather satellite over earth, WMO emblem.

1973, Sept. 4 Photo. *Perf. 13½*

661 A140 40c black, bl & dl bl 1.10 1.10
662 A140 50c dull blue & blk 1.25 1.25
663 A140 60c dull blue & multi 1.90 1.90
Nos. 661-663 (3) 4.25 4.25

Cent. of intl. meteorological cooperation.

Printed with tabs at top of sheet inscribed in Amharic and tabs at bottom with "ETHIOPIA."

Ras Makonnen, Duke of Harar — A141

5c, Old wall of Harar. 20c, Operating room. 40c, Boy Scouts learning 1st aid & hospital. 80c, Prince Makonnen & hospital.

1973, Nov. 1 Unwmk. *Perf. 14½*

664 A141 5c gray & multi .30 .30
665 A141 10c red brn & multi .30 .30
666 A141 20c green & multi .60 .60
667 A141 40c brown red & multi 1.10 1.10
668 A141 80c ultra & multi 2.75 2.75
Nos. 664-668 (5) 5.05 5.05

Opening of Ras Makonnen Memorial Hospital.

Human Rights Flame — A142

Perf. 11½

1973, Nov. 16 Photo. Unwmk.
Granite Paper

669 A142 40c yel, gold & dk grn .70 .70
670 A142 50c lt grn, gold & dk grn 1.00 1.00
671 A142 60c org, gold & dk grn 1.25 1.25
Nos. 669-671 (3) 2.95 2.95

25th anniversary of the Universal Declaration of Human Rights.

Emperor Haile Selassie — A143

1973, Nov. 5 Photo. *Perf. 11½*

672 A143 5c yellow & multi .35 .30
673 A143 10c brt blue & multi .35 .30
674 A143 15c green & multi .45 .40
675 A143 20c dull yel & multi .55 .40
676 A143 25c multicolored .65 .40
677 A143 30c multicolored .80 .40
678 A143 35c multicolored .85 .40
679 A143 40c ultra & multi .95 .40
680 A143 45c multicolored 1.10 .50
681 A143 50c orange & multi 1.25 .50
682 A143 55c magenta & multi 1.60 .85
683 A143 60c multicolored 1.75 1.10
684 A143 70c red org & multi 2.10 1.25
685 A143 90c brt vio & multi 2.75 1.40
686 A143 $1 multicolored 3.25 1.90
687 A143 $2 orange & multi 6.25 3.25
688 A143 $3 multicolored 10.50 5.00
689 A143 $5 multicolored 17.00 8.25
Nos. 672-689 (18) 52.50 27.00

Wicker Furniture A144

Designs: Various wicker baskets, wall hangings, dinnerware.

1974, Jan. 31 Photo. *Perf. 11½*
Granite Paper

690 A144 5c violet bl & multi .25 .25
691 A144 10c violet bl & multi .30 .30
692 A144 30c violet bl & multi .60 .60
693 A144 50c violet bl & multi .95 .95
694 A144 60c violet bl & multi 1.20 1.20
Nos. 690-694 (5) 3.30 3.30

Cow, Calf, Syringe — A145

Designs: 15c, Inoculation of cattle. 20c, Bullock and syringe. 50c, Laboratory technician, cow's head, syringe. 60c, Map of Ethiopia, cattle, syringe.

1974, Feb. 20 Litho. *Perf. 13½x13*

695 A145 5c sepia & multi .25 .25
696 A145 15c ultra & multi .40 .40
697 A145 20c ultra & multi .50 .50
698 A145 50c orange & multi 1.40 1.40
699 A145 60c gold & multi 1.75 1.75
Nos. 695-699 (5) 4.30 4.30

Campaign against cattle plague.

Umbrella Makers A146

Designs: 30c, Weaving. 50c, Child care. 60c, Foundation headquarters.

1974, Apr. 17 Photo. *Perf. 14½*

700 A146 10c lt lilac & multi .30 .30
701 A146 30c multicolored .50 .50
702 A146 50c multicolored 1.00 1.00
703 A146 60c blue & multi 1.25 1.25
Nos. 700-703 (4) 3.05 3.05

20th anniv. of Haile Selassie Foundation.

Ceremonial Robe — A147

Designs: Ceremonial robes.

1974, June 26 Litho. *Perf. 13*

704 A147 15c multicolored .40 .40
705 A147 25c ocher & multi .60 .60
706 A147 35c green & multi 1.10 1.10
707 A147 40c lt brown & multi 1.25 1.25
708 A147 60c gray & multi 2.50 2.50
Nos. 704-708 (5) 5.85 5.85

World Population Statistics — A148

Designs: 50c, "Larger families-lower living standard." 60c, Rising population graph.

1974, Aug. 19 Photo. *Perf. 14½*

709 A148 40c yellow & multi .85 .85
710 A148 50c violet & multi .85 .85
711 A148 60c green & multi .85 .85
Nos. 709-711 (3) 2.55 2.55

World Population Year 1974.

UPU Emblem, Letter Carrier's Staff — A149

UPU Emblem and: 50c, Letters and flags. 60c, Globe. 70c, Headquarters, Bern.

1974, Oct. 9 Photo. *Perf. 11½*
Granite Paper

712 A149 15c yellow & multi .30 .30
713 A149 50c multicolored .85 .85
714 A149 60c ultra & multi 1.25 1.10
715 A149 70c multicolored 1.25 1.25
Nos. 712-715 (4) 3.65 3.50

Centenary of Universal Postal Union.

Celebration Around "Damara" Pillar — A150

5c, Site of Gishen Mariam Monastery. 20c, Cross and festivities. 80c, Torch (Chibos) Parade.

1974, Dec. 17 Photo. *Perf. 14x14½*

716 A150 5c yellow & multi .30 .30
717 A150 10c yellow & multi .30 .30
718 A150 20c yellow & multi .30 .30
719 A150 80c yellow & multi 1.75 1.75
Nos. 716-719 (4) 2.65 2.65

Meskel Festival, Sept. 26-27, commemorating the finding in the 4th century of the True Cross, of which a fragment is kept at Gishen Mariam Monastery in Welo Province.

Precis Clelia — A151

Butterflies: 25c, Charaxes achaemenes. 45c, Papilio dardanus. 50c, Charaxes druceanus. 60c, Papilio demodocus.

1975, Feb. 18 Photo. *Perf. 12x12½*

720 A151 10c silver & multi .60 .40
721 A151 25c gold & multi .90 .75
722 A151 45c purple & multi 1.75 1.75
723 A151 50c green & multi 2.75 2.75
724 A151 60c brt blue & multi 3.50 3.00
Nos. 720-724 (5) 9.50 8.65

Adoration of the Kings — A152

10c, Baptism of Jesus. 15c, Jesus teaching in the Temple. 30c, Jesus giving sight to the blind. 40c, Crucifixion. 80c, Resurrection.

Granite Paper

1975, Apr. 23 Photo. *Perf. 11½*

725 A152 5c brown & multi .30 .30
726 A152 10c black & multi .30 .30
727 A152 15c dk brown & multi .30 .30
728 A152 30c dk brown & multi .60 .60
729 A152 40c black & multi 1.10 1.10
730 A152 80c slate & multi 2.25 2.25
Nos. 725-730 (6) 4.85 4.85

Murals from Ethiopian churches.

Wild Animals A153

1975, May 27 Photo. *Perf. 11½*
Granite Paper

731 A153 5c Warthog .60 .60
732 A153 10c Aardvark .60 .60
733 A153 20c Semien wolf .85 .85
734 A153 40c Gelada baboon 1.75 1.75
735 A153 80c Civet 4.25 4.25
Nos. 731-735 (5) 8.05 8.05

"Peace," Dove, Globe, IWY Emblem — A154

50c, Symbols of development. 90c, Equality between men and women.

1975, June 30 Litho. *Perf. 14x14½*

736 A154 40c blue & black .60 .60
737 A154 50c salmon & multi .85 .85
738 A154 90c multicolored 1.75 1.75
Nos. 736-738 (3) 3.20 3.20

International Women's Year 1975.

Postal Museum A155

Various interior views of Postal Museum.

1975, Aug. 19 Photo. *Perf. 13x12½*

739 A155 10c ocher & multi .35 .30
740 A155 30c pink & multi .65 .50
741 A155 60c multicolored 1.50 1.10
742 A155 70c lt green & multi 1.75 1.25
Nos. 739-742 (4) 4.25 3.15

Ethiopian Natl. Postal Museum, opening.

Map of Ethiopia and Sun — A156

1975, Sept. 11 Photo. *Perf. 11½*
Granite Paper

743 A156 5c lilac & multi .25 .25
744 A156 10c ultra & multi .25 .25
745 A156 25c brown & multi .35 .35
746 A156 50c yellow & multi .90 .90
747 A156 90c brt green & multi 1.75 1.75
Nos. 743-747 (5) 3.50 3.50

1st anniv. of Ethiopian revolution.

UN Emblem A157

1975, Oct. 24 Photo. *Perf. 11½*

748 A157 40c lilac & multi .85 .85
749 A157 50c multicolored .85 .85
750 A157 90c blue & multi 1.75 1.75
Nos. 748-750 (3) 3.45 3.45

United Nations, 30th anniversary.

Regional Hair Styles — A158

1975, Dec. 15 Photo. *Perf. 11½*

751 A158 5c Ilubabor .30 .30
752 A158 15c Arusi .40 .40
753 A158 20c Eritrea .60 .60
754 A158 30c Bale .85 .85
755 A158 35c Kefa 1.00 1.00
756 A158 50c Begemir 1.40 1.40
757 A158 60c Shoa 1.75 1.75
Nos. 751-757 (7) 6.30 6.30

See Nos. 832-838.

Delphinium Wellbyi — A159

Flowers: 10c, Plectocephalus varians. 20c, Brachystelma asmarensis, horiz. 40c, Ceropegia inflata. 80c, Erythrina brucei.

1976, Jan. 15 Photo. *Perf. 11½*

758 A159 5c multicolored .35 .35
759 A159 10c multicolored .40 .40
760 A159 20c multicolored .60 .60
761 A159 40c multicolored 1.50 1.50
762 A159 80c multicolored 2.50 2.50
Nos. 758-762 (5) 5.35 5.35

Goalkeeper, Map of Africa, Games' Emblem A160

Designs: Various scenes from soccer, map of Africa and ball.

1976, Feb. 27 Photo. *Perf. 14½*

763 A160 5c orange & multi .30 .30
764 A160 10c yellow & multi .30 .30
765 A160 25c lilac & multi .60 .60
766 A160 50c green & multi 1.10 1.10
767 A160 90c brt grn & multi 2.25 2.25
Nos. 763-767 (5) 4.55 4.55

10th African Cup of Nations, Addis Ababa and Dire Dawa, Feb. 29-Mar. 14.

Telephones, 1876 and 1976 — A161

Designs: 60c, Alexander Graham Bell. 90c, Transmission tower.

1976, Mar. 10 Litho. *Perf. 12x13½*

768 A161 30c lt ocher & multi .55 .55
769 A161 60c emerald & multi 1.10 1.10
770 A161 90c ver, blk & buff 1.75 1.75
Nos. 768-770 (3) 3.40 3.40

Centenary of first telephone call by Alexander Graham Bell, Mar. 10, 1876.

Ethiopian Jewelry — A162

Designs: Women wearing various kinds of Ethiopian jewelry.

Granite Paper

1976, May 14 Photo. *Perf. 11½*

771 A162 5c blue & multi .30 .30
772 A162 10c plum & multi .30 .30
773 A162 20c gray & multi .60 .60
774 A162 40c green & multi .90 .90
775 A162 80c orange & multi 1.75 1.75
Nos. 771-775 (5) 3.85 3.85

Boxing — A163

Designs (Montreal Olympic Emblem and): 80c, Runner and maple leaf. 90c, Bicycling.

1976, July 15 Litho. *Perf. 12½x12*

776 A163 10c multicolored .30 .30
777 A163 80c brt red, blk & grn 1.75 1.75
778 A163 90c brt red & multi 1.75 1.75
Nos. 776-778 (3) 3.80 3.80

21st Olympic Games, Montreal, Canada, July 17-Aug. 1.

Hands Holding Map of Ethiopia — A164

1976, Aug. 5 Photo. *Perf. 14½*

779 A164 5c rose & multi .25 .25
780 A164 10c olive & multi .30 .25
781 A164 25c orange & multi .40 .30
782 A164 50c multicolored .95 .70
783 A164 90c dk blue & multi 1.75 1.40
Nos. 779-783 (5) 3.65 2.90

Development through cooperation.

Revolution Emblem: Eye and Map A165

1976, Sept. 9 Photo. *Perf. 13½*

784 A165 5c multicolored .30 .30
785 A165 10c multicolored .30 .30
786 A165 25c multicolored .30 .30
787 A165 50c yellow & multi .90 .90
788 A165 90c green & multi 1.25 1.25
Nos. 784-788 (5) 3.05 3.05

2nd anniversary of the revolution.

Sunburst Around Crest — A166

1976, Sept. 13 Photo. *Perf. 11½*

789 A166 5c green, gold & blk .25 .25
790 A166 10c org, gold & blk .25 .25
791 A166 15c grnsh bl, gold & blk .55 .25
792 A166 20c lilac, gold & blk .55 .25
793 A166 25c brt grn, gold & blk .55 .25
794 A166 30c car, gold & blk .55 .55
795 A166 35c yel, gold & blk .85 .55
796 A166 40c ol, gold & blk .85 .55
797 A166 45c brt grn, gold & blk .85 .55
798 A166 50c car rose, gold & blk 1.10 .85
799 A166 55c ultra, gold & blk 1.10 .85
800 A166 60c fawn, gold & blk 1.10 .85
801 A166 70c rose, gold & blk 1.75 .90
802 A166 90c blue, gold & blk 1.75 .90
803 A166 $1 dull grn, gold & blk 2.25 .90
804 A166 $2 gray, gold & blk 4.50 1.75
805 A166 $3 brn vio, gold & blk 7.00 2.75
806 A166 $5 slate bl, gold & blk 11.00 4.50
Nos. 789-806 (18) 36.80 17.70

Denomination Expressed as "BIRR"

1983, June 16

806A A166 1b dull grn, gold & blk 7.50 2.25
806B A166 2b gray, gold & blk 20.00 4.50
806C A166 3b brn vio, gold & blk 25.00 6.25

Plane Over Man with Donkey — A167

10c, Globe showing routes. 25c, Crew and passengers forming star. 50c, Propeller and jet engine. 90c, Airplanes surrounding map of Ethiopia.

1976, Oct. 28 Litho. *Perf. 12x12½*

807 A167 5c dull bl & multi .30 .30
808 A167 10c lilac & multi .30 .30
809 A167 25c multicolored .40 .40
810 A167 50c orange & multi 1.25 1.25
811 A167 90c olive & multi 2.00 2.00
Nos. 807-811 (5) 4.25 4.25

Ethiopian Airlines, 30th anniversary.

Tortoises — A168

Reptiles: 20c, Chameleon. 30c, Python. 40c, Monitor lizard. 80c, Nile crocodiles.

1976, Dec. 15 Photo. *Perf. 14½*

812 A168 10c multicolored .40 .40
813 A168 20c multicolored .60 .60
814 A168 30c multicolored .90 .90
815 A168 40c multicolored 1.25 1.25
816 A168 80c multicolored 2.75 2.75
Nos. 812-816 (5) 5.90 5.90

Hand Holding Makeshift Hammer — A169

Designs: 5c, Hands holding bowl and plane dropping food. 45c, Infant with empty bowl, and bank note. 60c, Map of affected area, footprints and tire tracks. 80c, Film strip, camera and Ethiopian sitting between eggshells.

1977, Jan. 20 Litho. *Perf. 12½*

817 A169 5c multicolored .40 .40
818 A169 10c multicolored .40 .40
819 A169 45c multicolored .85 .85
820 A169 60c multicolored .85 .85
821 A169 80c multicolored 1.60 1.60
Nos. 817-821 (5) 4.10 4.10

Ethiopian Relief and Rehabilitation Commission for drought and disaster areas.

Elephant and Ruins, Axum, 7th Century A170

Designs: 10c, Ibex and temple, 5th century, B.C., Yeha. 25c, Megalithic dolmen and pottery, Sourre Kabanawa. 50c, Awash Valley, stone axe, Acheulean period. 80c, Omo Valley, hominid jawbone.

1977, Mar. 15 Photo. *Perf. 13½*

822 A170 5c gold & multi .35 .35
823 A170 10c gold & multi .35 .35
824 A170 25c gold & multi .55 .55
825 A170 50c gold & multi 1.00 1.00
826 A170 80c gold & multi 1.40 1.40
Nos. 822-826 (5) 3.65 3.65

Archaeological sites and finds in Ethiopia.

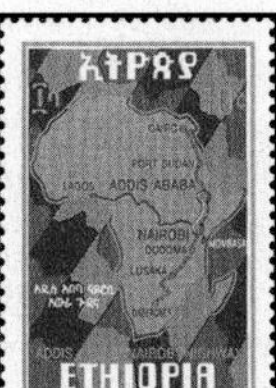

Map of Africa with Trans-East Highway — A171

1977, Mar. 30 *Perf. 14*

827 A171 10c gold & multi .30 .30
828 A171 20c gold & multi .30 .30
829 A171 40c gold & multi .85 .85
830 A171 50c gold & multi .85 .85
831 A171 60c gold & multi 1.10 1.10
Nos. 827-831 (5) 3.40 3.40

Addis Ababa to Nairobi Highway and projected highways to Cairo, Egypt, and Gaborone, Botswana.

Hairstyle Type of 1975

1977, Apr. 28 Photo. *Perf. 11½*

832 A158 5c Welega .30 .30
833 A158 10c Gojam .30 .30
834 A158 15c Tigre .30 .30
835 A158 20c Harar .60 .60
836 A158 25c Gemu Gefa .60 .60
837 A158 40c Sidamo 1.10 1.10
838 A158 50c Welo 1.10 1.10
Nos. 832-838 (7) 4.30 4.30

Addis Ababa A172

Towns of Ethiopia: 10c, Asmara. 25c, Harar. 50c, Jima. 90c, Dese.

1977, June 20 Photo. *Perf. 14½*

839 A172 5c silver & multi .30 .30
840 A172 10c silver & multi .30 .30
841 A172 25c silver & multi .30 .30
842 A172 50c silver & multi .85 .85
843 A172 90c silver & multi 1.25 1.25
Nos. 839-843 (5) 3.00 3.00

Terebratula Abyssinica A173

Fossil Shells: 10c, Terebratula subalata. 25c, Cuculloea lefeburiaua. 50c, Ostrea plicatissima. 90c, Trigonia cousobrina.

1977, Aug. 15 Photo. *Perf. 14x13½*

844 A173 5c multicolored .75 .30
845 A173 10c multicolored 1.25 .30
846 A173 25c multicolored 1.50 .60
847 A173 50c multicolored 2.50 1.10
848 A173 90c multicolored 4.00 1.75
Nos. 844-848 (5) 10.00 4.05

Fractured Imperial Crown — A174

Designs: 10c, Symbol of the Revolution (spade, axe, torch). 25c, Warriors, hammer and sickle, map of Ethiopia. 60c, Soldier, farmer and map. 80c, Map and emblem of revolutionary government.

1977, Sept. 9 Litho. *Perf. 15*

849 A174 5c multicolored .30 .30
850 A174 10c multicolored .30 .30
851 A174 25c multicolored .55 .55
852 A174 60c multicolored .85 .85
853 A174 80c multicolored 1.10 1.10
Nos. 849-853 (5) 3.10 3.10

Third anniversary of the revolution.

Cicindela Petitii — A175

Insects: 10c, Heliocopris dillonii. 25c, Poekilocerus vignaudii. 50c, Pepsis heros. 90c, Pepsis dedjaz.

1977, Sept. 30 Photo. *Perf. 14x13½*

854 A175 5c multicolored .40 .30
855 A175 10c multicolored .50 .30
856 A175 25c multicolored 1.00 .60
857 A175 50c multicolored 2.50 1.75
858 A175 90c multicolored 3.75 2.90
Nos. 854-858 (5) 8.15 5.85

Lenin, Globe, Map of Ethiopia and Emblem — A176

1977, Nov. 15 Litho. *Perf. 12*

859 A176 5c orange & multi .40 .30
860 A176 10c multicolored .40 .30
861 A176 25c salmon & multi .40 .30
862 A176 50c lt blue & multi 1.00 .85
863 A176 90c yellow & multi 1.25 1.10
Nos. 859-863 (5) 3.45 2.85

60th anniv. of Russian October Revolution.

Chondrostoma Dilloni — A177

Salt-water Fish: 10c, Ostracion cubicus. 25c, Serranus summana. 50c, Serranus luti. 90c, Tetraodon maculatus.

1978, Jan. 20 Litho. *Perf. 15½*

864 A177 5c multicolored .65 .65
865 A177 10c multicolored .75 .75
866 A177 25c multicolored 1.25 1.25
867 A177 50c multicolored 2.25 2.25
868 A177 90c multicolored 4.00 4.00
Nos. 864-868 (5) 8.90 8.90

Domestic Animals — A178

1978, Mar. 27 Litho. *Perf. 13½x14*

No.	Type	Description	Unused	Used
869	A178	5c Cattle	.25	.25
870	A178	10c Mules	.25	.25
871	A178	25c Goats	.60	.55
872	A178	50c Dromedaries	1.25	1.25
873	A178	90c Horses	1.75	1.75
		Nos. 869-873 (5)	4.10	4.05

Weapons and Shield, Map of Ethiopia — A179

"Call of the Motherland." (Map of Ethiopia and): 10c, Civilian fighters. 25c, Map of Africa. 60c, Soldiers. 80c, Red Cross nurse and wounded man.

1978, May 13 Litho. *Perf. 15½*

No.	Type	Description	Unused	Used
874	A179	5c multicolored	.25	.25
875	A179	10c multicolored	.30	.30
876	A179	25c multicolored	.30	.30
877	A179	60c multicolored	.90	.90
878	A179	80c multicolored	1.25	1.25
		Nos. 874-878 (5)	3.00	3.00

Bronze Ibex, 5th Century B.C. — A180

Ancient Bronzes: 10c, Lion, Yeha, 5th cent. B.C., horiz. 25c, Lamp with ibex attacked by dog, Matara, 1st cent. B.C. 50c, Goat, Axum, 3rd cent. A.D., horiz. 90c, Ax, chisel and sickle, Yeha, 5th-4th centuries B.C.

1978, June 21 Litho. *Perf. 15½*

No.	Type	Description	Unused	Used
879	A180	5c multicolored	.25	.25
880	A180	10c multicolored	.30	.30
881	A180	25c multicolored	.60	.60
882	A180	50c multicolored	.90	.90
883	A180	90c multicolored	1.75	1.75
		Nos. 879-883 (5)	3.80	3.80

See Nos. 1024-1027.

Globe and Argentina '78 Emblem A181

20c, Soccer player kicking ball. 30c, Two players embracing, net and ball. 55c, World map and ball. 70c, Soccer field, vert.

Perf. 14x13½, 13½x14

1978, July 19 Litho.

No.	Type	Description	Unused	Used
884	A181	5c multicolored	.30	.30
885	A181	20c multicolored	.60	.50
886	A181	30c multicolored	.60	.60
887	A181	55c multicolored	1.10	1.10
888	A181	70c multicolored	1.75	1.75
		Nos. 884-888 (5)	4.35	4.25

11th World Cup Soccer Championship, Argentina, June 1-25.

Map of Africa, Oppressed African — A182

Namibia Day: 10c, Policeman pointing gun. 25c, Sniper with gun. 60c, African caught in net. 80c, Head of free man.

1978, Aug. 25 *Perf. 12½x13½*

No.	Type	Description	Unused	Used
889	A182	5c multicolored	.25	.25
890	A182	10c multicolored	.30	.30
891	A182	25c multicolored	.60	.60
892	A182	60c multicolored	1.10	1.10
893	A182	80c multicolored	1.25	1.25
		Nos. 889-893 (5)	3.50	3.50

Soldiers, Guerrilla and Jets A183

Design: 1b, People looking toward sun, crushing snake, flags.

1978, Sept. 8 Photo. *Perf. 14*

No.	Type	Description	Unused	Used
894	A183	80c multicolored	1.10	1.10
895	A183	1b multicolored	1.75	1.75

4th anniversary of revolution.

Hand and Globe with Tools — A184

Designs: 15c, Symbols of energy, communications, education, medicine, agriculture and industry. 25c, Cogwheels and world map. 60c, Globe and hands passing wrench. 70c, Flying geese and turtle over globe.

1978, Nov. 14 Litho. *Perf. 12x12½*

No.	Type	Description	Unused	Used
896	A184	10c multicolored	.25	.25
897	A184	15c multicolored	.30	.30
898	A184	25c multicolored	.60	.50
899	A184	60c multicolored	1.10	1.00
900	A184	70c multicolored	1.25	1.10
		Nos. 896-900 (5)	3.50	3.15

Technical Cooperation Among Developing Countries Conference, Buenos Aires, Argentina, Sept. 1978.

Human Rights Emblem — A185

1978, Dec. 7 Photo. *Perf. 12½x13½*

No.	Type	Description	Unused	Used
901	A185	5c multicolored	.25	.25
902	A185	15c multicolored	.30	.30
903	A185	25c multicolored	.30	.30
904	A185	35c multicolored	.60	.60
905	A185	1b multicolored	1.75	1.75
		Nos. 901-905 (5)	3.20	3.20

Declaration of Human Rights, 30th anniv.

Broken Chain, Anti-Apartheid Emblem — A186

1978, Dec. 28 Litho. *Perf. 12½x12*

No.	Type	Description	Unused	Used
906	A186	5c multicolored	.25	.25
907	A186	20c multicolored	.30	.30
908	A186	30c multicolored	.60	.60
909	A186	55c multicolored	.85	.85
910	A186	70c multicolored	1.25	1.25
		Nos. 906-910 (5)	3.25	3.25

Anti-Apartheid Year.

Stele from Osole — A187

Ancient Carved Stones, Soddo Region: 10c, Anthropomorphous stele, Gorashino. 25c, Leaning stone, Wado. 60c, Round stones, Ambeut. 80c, Bas-relief, Tiya.

1979, Jan. 25 *Perf. 14*

No.	Type	Description	Unused	Used
911	A187	5c multicolored	.25	.25
912	A187	10c multicolored	.30	.30
913	A187	25c multicolored	.30	.30
914	A187	60c multicolored	1.25	1.25
915	A187	80c multicolored	1.25	1.25
		Nos. 911-915 (5)	3.35	3.35

Cotton Plantation A188

Shemma Industry: 10c, Women spinning cotton yarn. 20c, Man reeling cotton. 65c, Weaver. 80c, Shemma (Natl. dress).

1979, Mar. 15 Litho. *Perf. 15½*

No.	Type	Description	Unused	Used
916	A188	5c multicolored	.25	.25
917	A188	10c multicolored	.30	.30
918	A188	20c multicolored	.60	.60
919	A188	65c multicolored	1.25	1.25
920	A188	80c multicolored	1.75	1.75
		Nos. 916-920 (5)	4.15	4.15

Ethiopian Trees — A189

1979, Apr. 26 Photo. *Perf. 13½x14*

No.	Type	Description	Unused	Used
921	A189	5c Grar	.25	.25
922	A189	10c Weira	.30	.30
923	A189	25c Tidh	.60	.40
924	A189	50c Shola	.85	.85
925	A189	90c Zigba	1.75	1.50
		Nos. 921-925 (5)	3.75	3.30

Agricultural Development A190

Revolutionary Development Campaign: 15c, Industry. 25c, Transportation and communication. 60c, Education and health. 70c, Commerce.

1979, July 3 Litho. *Perf. 12x12½*

No.	Type	Description	Unused	Used
926	A190	10c multicolored	.25	.25
927	A190	15c multicolored	.30	.30
928	A190	25c multicolored	.30	.30
929	A190	60c multicolored	.85	.85
930	A190	70c multicolored	1.25	1.25
		Nos. 926-930 (5)	2.95	2.95

IYC Emblem — A191

Intl. Year of the Child: 15c, Adults leading children. 25c, Adult helping child. 60c, IYC emblem surrounded by children. 70c, Adult and children embracing.

1979, Aug. 16 Litho. *Perf. 12x12½*

No.	Type	Description	Unused	Used
931	A191	10c multicolored	.30	.30
932	A191	15c multicolored	.30	.30
933	A191	25c multicolored	.60	.60
934	A191	60c multicolored	1.10	1.10
935	A191	70c multicolored	1.75	1.75
		Nos. 931-935 (5)	4.05	4.05

Guerrilla Fighters — A192

15c, Soldiers. 25c, Map of Africa within cogwheel, star. 60c, Students with book, torch. 70c, Family, hammer & sickle emblem.

1979, Sept. 11 Photo. *Perf. 14*

No.	Type	Description	Unused	Used
936	A192	10c multicolored	.30	.30
937	A192	15c multicolored	.30	.30
938	A192	25c multicolored	.60	.60
939	A192	60c multicolored	1.10	1.10
940	A192	70c multicolored	1.75	1.75
		Nos. 936-940 (5)	4.05	4.05

Fifth anniversary of revolution.

Telephone Receiver — A193

Telecom Emblem and: 5c, Symbolic waves. 35c, Satellite beaming to earth. 45c, Dish antenna. 65c, Television cameraman.

1979, Sept. 20 Photo. *Perf. 11½*

No.	Type	Description	Unused	Used
941	A193	5c multicolored	.30	.30
942	A193	30c multicolored	.60	.60
943	A193	35c multicolored	.60	.60
944	A193	45c multicolored	.85	.85
945	A193	65c multicolored	1.25	1.25
		Nos. 941-945 (5)	3.60	3.60

3rd World Telecommunications Exhibition, Geneva, Sept. 20-26.

Incense Container — A194

1979, Nov. 15 Litho. *Perf. 15*

No.	Type	Description	Unused	Used
946	A194	5c shown	.30	.30
947	A194	10c Vase	.60	.60
948	A194	25c Earthenware cover	.85	.85
949	A194	60c Milk container	1.25	1.25
950	A194	80c Storage container	1.75	1.75
		Nos. 946-950 (5)	4.75	4.75

Wooden Grain Bowl — A195

1980, Jan. 3 Litho. ***Perf. 13½x13***

951 A195 5c shown .30 .30
952 A195 30c Chair, stool .85 .85
953 A195 35c Mortar, pestle .85 .85
954 A195 45c Buckets 1.25 1.25
955 A195 65c Storage jars 1.75 1.75
Nos. 951-955 (5) 5.00 5.00

Lappet-faced Vulture — A196

Birds of Prey: 15c, Long-crested hawk eagle. 25c, Secretary bird. 60c, Abyssinian long-eared owl. 70c, Lanner falcon.

1980, Feb. 12 ***Perf. 13½x14***

956 A196 10c multicolored .60 .60
957 A196 15c multicolored .85 .85
958 A196 25c multicolored 1.25 1.25
959 A196 60c multicolored 2.90 2.90
960 A196 70c multicolored 4.50 4.50
Nos. 956-960 (5) 10.10 10.10

Fight Against Cigarette Smoking — A197

1980, Apr. 7 Photo. ***Perf. 13x13½***

961 A197 20c shown .60 .60
962 A197 60c Cigarette 1.25 1.25
963 A197 1b Respiratory system 1.75 1.75
Nos. 961-963 (3) 3.60 3.60

"110" and Lenin House Museum A198

Lenin, 110th "Birthday" (Paintings): 15c, In hiding. 20c, As a young man. 40c, Returning to Russia. 1b, Speaking on the Goelro Plan.

1980, Apr. 22 Litho. ***Perf. 12x12½***

964 A198 5c multicolored .30 .30
965 A198 15c multicolored .30 .30
966 A198 20c multicolored .30 .30
967 A198 40c multicolored .85 .85
968 A198 1b multicolored 1.75 1.75
Nos. 964-968 (5) 3.50 3.50

Grévy's Zebras A199

Designs: 15c, Gazelles. 25c, Wild hunting dogs. 60c, Swayne's hartebeests. 70c, Cheetahs.

1980, June 10 Litho. ***Perf. 12½x12***

969 A199 10c shown .30 .30
970 A199 15c multi .60 .60
971 A199 25c multi .85 .85
972 A199 60c multi 2.25 2.25
973 A199 70c multi 3.00 3.00
Nos. 969-973 (5) 7.00 7.00

Runner, Moscow '80 Emblem — A200

1980, July 19 Photo. ***Perf. 11½x12***

974 A200 30c shown .85 .85
975 A200 70c Cycling 1.25 1.25
976 A200 80c Boxing 1.75 1.75
Nos. 974-976 (3) 3.85 3.85

22nd Summer Olympic Games, Moscow, July 19-Aug. 3.

Removing Blindfold — A201

40c, Revolutionary. 50c, Woman breaking chain. 70c, Russian & Ethiopian flags.

1980, Sept. 10 Photo. ***Perf. 14x13½***

977 A201 30c shown .60 .50
978 A201 40c multicolored .60 .60
979 A201 50c multicolored .85 .85
980 A201 70c multicolored 1.25 1.25
Nos. 977-980 (4) 3.30 3.20

6th anniversary of revolution.

Bamboo Folk Craft — A202

Designs: 5c, Bamboo food basket. 15c, Hand basket. 25c, Stool. 35c, Fruit basket. 1b, Lamp shade.

1980, Oct. 23 Litho. ***Perf. 14***

981 A202 5c multi .30 .30
982 A202 15c multi .30 .30
983 A202 25c multi .60 .60
984 A202 35c multi .85 .85
985 A202 1b multi 1.75 1.75
Nos. 981-985 (5) 3.80 3.80

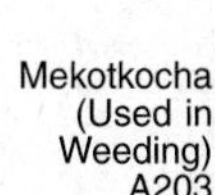

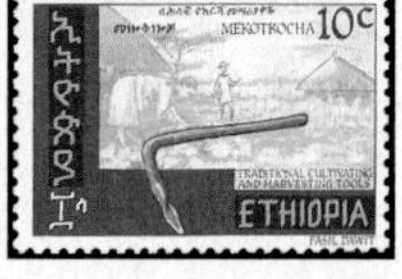

Mekotkocha (Used in Weeding) A203

Traditional Harvesting Tools: 15c, Layda (grain separator). 40c, Mensh (fork). 45c, Mededekia (soil turner). 70c, Mofer & Kenber (plow and yoke).

1980, Dec. 18 Litho. ***Perf. 12½x12***

986 A203 10c multicolored .30 .25
987 A203 15c multicolored .30 .30
988 A203 40c multicolored .60 .60
989 A203 45c multicolored .85 .85
990 A203 70c multicolored 1.25 1.25
Nos. 986-990 (5) 3.30 3.25

Baro River Bridge Opening A204

1981, Feb. 28 Photo. ***Perf. 13½x13***

991 A204 15c Canoes and ferry .30 .30
992 A204 65c Bridge construction 1.25 1.25
993 A204 1b shown 2.25 2.25
Nos. 991-993 (3) 3.80 3.80

Semien National Park — A205

World Heritage Year: 5c, Wawel Castle, Poland. 15c, Quito Cathedral, Ecuador. 20c, Old Slave Quarters, Goree Island, Senegal. 30c, Mesa Verde Indian Village, US. 1b, L'Anse aux Meadows excavation, Canada.

Perf. 11x11½, 11½x11

1981, Mar. 10 Photo.

994 A205 5c multicolored .30 .30
995 A205 15c multicolored .30 .30
996 A205 20c multicolored .55 .55
997 A205 30c multicolored .60 .60
998 A205 80c multicolored 1.75 1.75
999 A205 1b multicolored 2.25 2.25
Nos. 994-999 (6) 5.75 5.75

1981, June 16 Photo.

10c, Biet Medhanialem Church, Ethiopia. 15c, Nahanni Natl. Park, Canada. 20c, Yellowstone River Lower Falls, U.S. 30c, Aachen Cathedral, Germany. 80c, Kicker Rock, San Cristobal Island, Ecuador. 1b, The Lizak corridor, Holy Cross Chapel, Cracow, Poland.

1000 A205 10c multi .30 .30
1001 A205 15c multi .30 .30
1002 A205 20c multi .60 .60
1003 A205 30c multi .85 .80
1004 A205 80c multi 1.75 1.75
1005 A205 1b multi, vert. 2.25 2.25
Nos. 1000-1005 (6) 6.05 6.00

Ancient Drinking Vessel A206

Designs: 25c, Spice container. 35c, Jug. 40c, Cooking pot holder. 60c, Animal figurine.

1981, May 5 Litho. ***Perf. 12½x12***

1006 A206 20c shown .30 .30
1007 A206 25c multicolored .30 .30
1008 A206 35c multicolored .60 .60
1009 A206 40c multicolored .85 .85
1010 A206 60c multicolored 1.25 1.25
Nos. 1006-1010 (5) 3.30 3.30

Intl. Year of the Disabled — A207

1981, July 16 Photo. ***Perf. 11½x12***

1011 A207 5c Prostheses .25 .25
1012 A207 15c Boys writing .30 .30
1013 A207 20c Activities .60 .50
1014 A207 40c Knitting .85 .85
1015 A207 1b Weaving 1.75 1.75
Nos. 1011-1015 (5) 3.75 3.65

7th Anniv. of Revolution A208

1981, Sept. 10 ***Perf. 14***

1016 A208 20c Children's Center .30 .30
1017 A208 60c Heroes' Center .85 .85
1018 A208 1b Serto Ader (state newspaper) 1.75 1.75
Nos. 1016-1018 (3) 2.90 2.90

World Food Day — A209

Designs: 5c, Wheat airlift. 15c, Plowing. 20c, Malnutrition. 40c, Agriculture education. 1b, Cattle, corn.

1981, Oct. 15 Litho. ***Perf. 13½x12½***

1019 A209 5c multi .25 .25
1020 A209 15c multi .25 .25
1021 A209 20c multi .30 .30
1022 A209 40c multi .85 .85
1023 A209 1b multi 1.75 1.75
Nos. 1019-1023 (5) 3.40 3.40

Ancient Bronze Type of 1978

Designs: 15c, Bird shaped pitcher. 45c, Tsenatsil (musical instrument). 50c, Pitcher with large handle on top. 70c, Pot.

1981, Dec. 15 Litho. ***Perf. 14x13½***

1024 A180 15c multi .30 .30
1025 A180 45c multi .85 .85
1026 A180 50c multi .85 .85
1027 A180 70c multi 1.25 1.25
Nos. 1024-1027 (4) 3.25 3.25

Horn Artifacts — A210

Designs: 10c, Tobacco containers. 15c, Cup. 40c, Tej container. 45c, Goblet. 70c, Spoons.

1982, Feb. 18 Photo. ***Perf. 12x12½***

1028 A210 10c multi .25 .25
1029 A210 15c multi .30 .30
1030 A210 40c multi .85 .85
1031 A210 45c multi .85 .85
1032 A210 70c multi 1.25 1.25
Nos. 1028-1032 (5) 3.50 3.50

Coffee Cultivation A211

1982, May, 6 Photo. ***Perf. 13½***

1033 A211 5c Plants .25 .25
1034 A211 15c Bushes .30 .30
1035 A211 25c Mature bushes .50 .45
1036 A211 35c Picking beans .85 .80
1037 A211 1b Drinking coffee 2.00 1.75
Nos. 1033-1037 (5) 3.90 3.55

1982 World Cup — A212

Various soccer plays.

Perf. 13½x12½

1982, June 10 Litho.

1038 A212 5c multicolored .25 .25
1039 A212 15c multicolored .30 .30
1040 A212 20c multicolored .50 .50
1041 A212 40c multicolored .85 .85
1042 A212 1b multicolored 1.75 1.75
Nos. 1038-1042 (5) 3.65 3.65

TB Bacillus Centenary A213

1982, July 12 Litho. ***Perf. 13½x12½***

1043 A213 15c Cow .30 .30
1044 A213 20c Magnifying glass .30 .30
1045 A213 30c Koch, microscope .60 .60
1046 A213 35c Koch .65 .65
1047 A213 80c Man coughing 1.75 1.75
Nos. 1043-1047 (5) 3.60 3.60

8th Anniv. of Revolution — A214

Designs: Symbols of justice.

1982, Sept. 10 ***Perf. 12½x13½***

1048 A214 80c multicolored 1.25 1.25
1049 A214 1b multicolored 1.75 1.75

World Standards Day — A215

1982, Oct. 14 Litho. ***Perf. 13½x12½***

1050 A215 5c Hand, foot, square .30 .30
1051 A215 15c Scales .30 .30
1052 A215 20c Rulers .35 .35
1053 A215 40c Weights .60 .60
1054 A215 1b Emblem 1.75 1.75
Nos. 1050-1054 (5) 3.30 3.30

10th Anniv. of UN Conference on Human Environment A216

5c, Wildlife conservation. 15c, Environmental health and settlement. 20c, Forest protection. 40c, Natl. literacy campaign. 1b, Soil and water conservation.

1982, Dec. 13 Litho. ***Perf. 12***

1055 A216 5c multicolored .25 .25
1056 A216 15c multicolored .30 .30
1057 A216 20c multicolored .40 .40
1058 A216 40c multicolored .85 .85
1059 A216 1b multicolored 1.90 1.90
Nos. 1055-1059 (5) 3.70 3.70

Cave of Sof Omar A217

Various views.

1983, Feb. 10 Photo. ***Perf. 13½***

1060 A217 5c multicolored .25 .25
1061 A217 10c multicolored .30 .30
1062 A217 15c multicolored .30 .30
1063 A217 70c multicolored 1.25 1.25
1064 A217 80c multicolored 1.25 1.25
Nos. 1060-1064 (5) 3.35 3.35

A218

1983, Apr. 29 Photo. ***Perf. 14***

1065 A218 80c multicolored 1.25 1.25
1066 A218 1b multicolored 1.75 1.75

25th Anniv. of Economic Commission for Africa.

A219

Perf. 12½x11½

1983, June 3 Photo.

1067 A219 85c Emblem 1.25 1.25
1068 A219 1b Lighthouse, ship 2.25 2.25

25th Anniv. of Intl. Maritime Org.

WCY — A220

Designs: 25c, UPU emblem. 55c, Dish antenna, emblems. 1b, Bridge, tunnel.

1983, July 22 Litho.

1069 A220 25c multi .55 .55
1070 A220 55c multi .85 .85
1071 A220 1b multi 2.75 2.75
Nos. 1069-1071 (3) 4.15 4.15

9th Anniv. of Revolution — A221

1983, Sept. 10 Litho. ***Perf. 14½***

1072 A221 25c Dove .30 .30
1073 A221 55c Star .85 .85
1074 A221 1b Emblems 1.25 1.25
Nos. 1072-1074 (3) 2.40 2.40

Musical Instruments — A222

1983, Oct. 17 Litho. ***Perf. 12½x13½***

1075 A222 5c Hura .25 .25
1076 A222 15c Dinke .30 .30
1077 A222 20c Meleket .60 .60
1078 A222 40c Embilta 1.25 1.25
1079 A222 1b Tom 1.75 1.75
Nos. 1075-1079 (5) 4.15 4.15

Charaxes Galawadiwosi A223

15c, Epiphora elianae. 55c, Batuana rougeoti. 1b, Achaea saboeareginae.

1983, Dec. 13 Photo. ***Perf. 14***

1080 A223 10c shown .85 .85
1081 A223 15c multicolored 1.25 1.25
1082 A223 55c multicolored 2.75 2.75
1083 A223 1b multicolored 3.50 3.50
Nos. 1080-1083 (4) 8.35 8.35

Intl. Anti-Apartheid Year (1983) — A224

Perf. 13½x12½

1984, Feb. 10 Litho.

1084 A224 5c multicolored .25 .25
1085 A224 15c multicolored .30 .30
1086 A224 20c multicolored .60 .60
1087 A224 40c multicolored .85 .85
1088 A224 1b multicolored 2.25 2.25
Nos. 1084-1088 (5) 4.25 4.25

Local Flowers — A225

5c, Protea gaguedi. 25c, Sedum epidendrum. 50c, Echinops amplexicaulis. 1b, Canarina eminii.

1984, Apr. 13 Litho. ***Perf. 13½***

1089 A225 5c multi .30 .30
1090 A225 25c multi .85 .85
1091 A225 50c multi 1.75 1.75
1092 A225 1b multi 3.00 3.00
Nos. 1089-1092 (4) 5.90 5.90

Traditional Houses — A226

1984, June 13 Photo.

1093 A226 15c Konso .30 .30
1094 A226 65c Dorze 1.25 1.25
1095 A226 1b Harer 1.75 1.75
Nos. 1093-1095 (3) 3.30 3.30

10th Anniv. of the Revolution A227

1984, Sept. 10 Photo. ***Perf. 11½***

1096 A227 5c Sept. 12, 1974 .40 .40
1097 A227 10c Mar. 4, 1975 .40 .40
1098 A227 15c Apr. 20, 1976 .40 .40
1099 A227 20c Feb. 11, 1977 .50 .50
1100 A227 25c Mar. 1978 .65 .65
1101 A227 40c July 8, 1980 1.20 1.20
1102 A227 45c Dec. 17, 1980 1.60 1.50
1103 A227 50c Sept. 15, 1980 1.75 1.75
1104 A227 70c Sept. 18, 1981 2.40 2.40
1105 A227 1b June 6, 1983 2.75 2.75
Nos. 1096-1105 (10) 12.05 11.95

Traditional Sports A228

1984, Dec. 7 Photo. ***Perf. 14***

1106 A228 5c Gugs .25 .25
1107 A228 25c Tigil .40 .40
1108 A228 50c Genna .95 .95
1109 A228 1b Gebeta 1.75 1.75
Nos. 1106-1109 (4) 3.35 3.35

Birds — A229

Designs: 5c, Francolinus harwoodi. 15c, Rallus rougetti. 80c, Merops pusillus. 85c, Malimbus rubriceps.

1985, Jan. 4 Photo. ***Perf. 14½***

1110 A229 5c multi .30 .30
1111 A229 15c multi .85 .85
1112 A229 80c multi 3.00 3.00
1113 A229 85c multi 3.00 3.00
Nos. 1110-1113 (4) 7.15 7.15

Indigenous Fauna A230

20c, Hippopotamus amphibius. 25c, Litocranius walleri. 40c, Sylvicapra grimmia. 1b, Rhynchotragus guentheri.

1985, Feb. 4 Litho. ***Perf. 12½x12***

1114 A230 20c multicolored .85 .85
1115 A230 25c multicolored 1.00 1.00
1116 A230 40c multicolored 2.00 2.00
1117 A230 1b multicolored 3.50 3.50
Nos. 1114-1117 (4) 7.35 7.35

Freshwater Fish — A231

10c, Barbus degeni. 20c, Labeo cylindricus. 55c, Protopterus annectens. 1b, Alestes dentex.

1985, Apr. 3 ***Perf. 13½***

1118 A231 10c multicolored .50 .25
1119 A231 20c multicolored .90 .50
1120 A231 55c multicolored 2.10 1.20
1121 A231 1b multicolored 3.25 2.50
Nos. 1118-1121 (4) 6.75 4.45

Medicinal Plants A232

10c, Securidaca longepedunculata. 20c, Plumbago zeylanicum. 55c, Brucea antidysenteric. 1b, Dorstenia barminiana.

1985, May 23 ***Perf. 11½x12½***

1122 A232 10c multicolored .30 .30
1123 A232 20c multicolored .30 .30
1124 A232 55c multicolored .85 .85
1125 A232 1b multicolored 2.25 2.25
Nos. 1122-1125 (4) 3.70 3.70

Ethiopian Red Cross Soc., 50th Anniv. — A233

1985, Aug. 6 Litho. ***Perf. 13½x13***

1126 A233 35c multicolored .60 .60
1127 A233 55c multicolored .85 .85
1128 A233 1b multicolored 2.25 2.25
Nos. 1126-1128 (3) 3.70 3.70

Ethiopian Revolution, 11th Anniv. A234

10c, Kombolcha Mills, Welo Region. 80c, Muger Cement Factory, Mokoda, Shoa. 1b, Relocating famine and drought victims.

1985, Sept. 10 Litho. ***Perf. 13½***

1129 A234 10c multicolored .30 .30
1130 A234 80c multicolored 1.75 1.75
1131 A234 1b multicolored 2.25 2.25
Nos. 1129-1131 (3) 4.30 4.30

UN 40th Anniv. — A235

1985, Nov. 22 Litho. ***Perf. 13½x14***

1132 A235 25c multicolored .90 .75
1133 A235 55c multicolored 1.75 1.50
1134 A235 1b multicolored 3.25 2.50
Nos. 1132-1134 (3) 5.90 4.75

Anti-Polio Campaign A236

Designs: 5c, Boy, prosthesis. 10c, Boy on crutches. 20c, Nurse, boy. 55c, Man, sewing machine. 1b, Nurse, mother, child.

1986, Jan. 10 Litho. ***Perf. 11½x12½***

1135 A236 5c multi .75 .25
1136 A236 10c multi .30 .30
1137 A236 20c multi .60 .50
1138 A236 55c multi 1.10 1.10
1139 A236 1b multi 2.75 2.75
Nos. 1135-1139 (5) 5.50 4.90

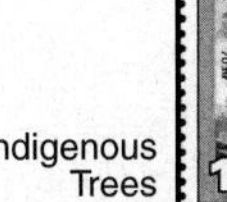

Indigenous Trees A237

10c, Millettia ferruginea. 30c, Syzygium guineense. 50c, Cordia africana. 1b, Hagenia abyssinica.

1986, Feb. 10 ***Perf. 13½x14½***

1140 A237 10c multicolored .35 .35
1141 A237 30c multicolored .60 .60
1142 A237 50c multicolored .90 .90
1143 A237 1b multicolored 2.25 2.25
Nos. 1140-1143 (4) 4.10 4.10

Spices — A238

10c, Zingiber officinale rosc. 15c, Ocimum bacilicum. 55c, Sinapsis alba. 1b, Cuminum cyminum.

1986, Mar. 10 ***Perf. 13½***

1144 A238 10c multicolored .60 .60
1145 A238 15c multicolored .60 .60
1146 A238 55c multicolored 1.25 1.25
1147 A238 1b multicolored 2.75 2.75
Nos. 1144-1147 (4) 5.20 5.20

Current Coins, Obverse and Reverse A239

1986, May 9 Litho. ***Perf. 13½x14***

1148 A239 5c 1-cent .30 .30
1149 A239 10c 25-cent .30 .30
1150 A239 35c 5-cent .85 .85
1151 A239 50c 50-cent 1.25 1.25
1152 A239 1b 10-cent 2.25 2.25
Nos. 1148-1152 (5) 4.95 4.95

Discovery of 3.5 Million Year-old Hominid Skeleton, "Lucy" — A240

1986, July 4 ***Perf. 13½***

1153 A240 2b multicolored 6.50 6.50

Ethiopian Revolution, 12th Anniv. — A241

Designs: 20c, Military service. 30c, Tiglachin monument. 55c, Delachin Exhibition emblem. 85c, Food processing plant, Merti.

1986, Sept. 10 Litho. ***Perf. 14***

1154 A241 20c multicolored .40 .40
1155 A241 30c multicolored .65 .65
1156 A241 55c multicolored 1.10 1.10
1157 A241 85c multicolored 1.40 1.40
Nos. 1154-1157 (4) 3.55 3.55

Ethiopian Airlines, 40th Anniv. — A242

1986, Oct. 14

1158 A242 10c DC-7 .30 .30
1159 A242 20c DC-3 .60 .60
1160 A242 30c Personnel, jet tail .85 .85
1161 A242 40c Engine .85 .85
1162 A242 1b DC-7, map 2.25 2.25
Nos. 1158-1162 (5) 4.85 4.85

Intl. Peace Year — A243

1986, Nov. 13 ***Perf. 13½***

1163 A243 10c multicolored .30 .30
1164 A243 80c multicolored 2.00 2.00
1165 A243 1b multicolored 2.25 2.25
Nos. 1163-1165 (3) 4.55 4.55

UN Child Survival Campaign — A244

10c, Breast feeding. 35c, Immunization. 50c, Hygiene. 1b, Growth monitoring.

1986, Dec. 11 ***Perf. 12½***

1166 A244 10c multi .30 .30
1167 A244 35c multi .85 .85
1168 A244 50c multi 1.25 1.10
1169 A244 1b multi 2.25 2.00
Nos. 1166-1169 (4) 4.65 4.25

Umbrellas A245

1987, Feb. 10 ***Perf. 13½***

1170 A245 35c Axum .85 .85
1171 A245 55c Negele-Borena 1.25 1.25
1172 A245 1b Jimma 1.75 1.75
Nos. 1170-1172 (3) 3.85 3.85

Artwork by Afewerk Tekle (b. 1932) A246

Designs: 50c, Defender of His Country — Afar, stained glass window. 2b, Defender of His Country — Adwa, painting.

1987, Mar. 19 Litho. ***Perf. 13½***

1173 A246 50c multicolored 1.50 1.00
1174 A246 2b multicolored 5.50 4.50

Stained Glass Windows by Afewerk Tekle — A247

1987, June 16 Photo. ***Perf. 11½x12***

Granite Paper

1175 A247 50c multicolored *4.00 2.00*

Size: 26x38mm

1176 A247 80c multicolored *5.00 2.75*
1177 A247 1b multicolored *7.50 .40*
Nos. 1175-1177 (3) *16.50 5.15*

Struggle of the African People.
Sold out in Addis Ababa on date of issue.

Simien Fox A248

1987, June 29 Litho. ***Perf. 13½***

1178 A248 5c multicolored .25 .25
1179 A248 10c multicolored .25 .25
1180 A248 15c multicolored .35 .25
1181 A248 20c multicolored .45 .30
1182 A248 25c multicolored .60 .30
1183 A248 45c multicolored 1.00 .85
1184 A248 55c multicolored 1.25 .85
Nos. 1178-1184 (7) 4.15 3.05

For overprints see Nos. 1234-1237. For similar design see A294a.

Ethiopian Revolution, 13th Anniv. A249

Designs: 5c, Constitution, freedom of press. 10c, Popular elections. 80c, Referendum. 1b, Bahir Dar Airport, map.

1987, Sept. 10 ***Perf. 12½***

1185 A249 5c multi .65 .65
1186 A249 10c multi .65 .40
1187 A249 80c multi 1.75 1.75
1188 A249 1b multi 2.25 2.25
Nos. 1185-1188 (4) 5.30 5.05

Addis Ababa, Cent. A251

"100" and views: 5c, Emperor Menelik II, Empress Taitu and city. 10c, Traditional buildings. 80c, Central Addis Ababa. 1b, Aerial view of city.

1987, Sept. 7 ***Perf. 13½***

1193 A251 5c multicolored .30 .30
1194 A251 10c multicolored .30 .30
1195 A251 80c multicolored 1.75 1.75
1196 A251 1b multicolored 2.25 2.25
Nos. 1193-1196 (4) 4.60 4.60

Wooden Spoons A252

1987, Nov. 30

1197 A252 85c Hurso, Harerge 1.25 1.25
1198 A252 1b Borena, Sidamo 1.75 1.75

Intl. Year of Shelter for the Homeless A253

10c, Village revitalization program. 35c, Resettlement program. 50c, Urban improvement. 1b, Cooperative and government housing.

1987, Dec. 12 Litho. ***Perf. 13***

1199 A253 10c multicolored .30 .30
1200 A253 35c multicolored .60 .60
1201 A253 50c multicolored .85 .85
1202 A253 1b multicolored 1.25 1.25
Nos. 1199-1202 (4) 3.00 3.00

October Revolution, Russia, 70th Anniv. (in 1987) — A254

Painting: 1b, Lenin receiving Workers' Council delegates in the Smolny Institute.

1988, Feb. 17 ***Perf. 12½x12***

1203 A254 1b multicolored 2.25 2.00

Traditional Hunting Methods and Prey — A255

Designs: 85c, Bow and arrow. 1b, Double-pronged spear.

1988, Mar. 30 Litho. *Perf. 13½*

1204 A255 85c multi 1.75 1.75
1205 A255 1b multi 3.00 3.00

A256

1988, May 6

1206 A256 85c multicolored 1.25 1.25
1207 A256 1b multicolored 1.75 1.75

Intl. Red Cross and Red Crescent Organizations, 125th annivs.

A257

1988, June 7 Photo. *Perf. 11½x12*

1208 A257 2b multicolored 3.00 2.75

Organizaton of African Unity, 25th anniv.

Ethiopian Revolution, 14th Anniv. A258

Design: Various details of *The Victory of Ethiopia,* six-panel mural by Afewerk Tekle (b. 1932) in the museum of the Heroes Center, Debre Zeit — 10c, Jet over farm, vert. 20c, Farm workers on road, vert. 35c, Allegory of unity, vert. 55c, Jet over industry. 80c, Steel works. 1b, Weaving.

1988, June 28 Litho. *Perf. 13½x13*

1209 A258 10c multi .30 .30
1210 A258 20c multi .30 .30
1211 A258 35c multi .60 .60
1212 A258 55c multi .85 .85
1213 A258 80c multi 1.25 1.25
1214 A258 1b multi 1.25 1.25
Nos. 1209-1214 (6) 4.55 4.55

Nos. 1209-1211 vert.

Women, Bracelets and Maps A259

1988, July 27 Litho. *Perf. 13x13½*

1215 A259 15c Sidamo .30 .30
1216 A259 85c Arsi 1.25 1.25
1217 A259 1b Harerge 1.75 1.75
Nos. 1215-1217 (3) 3.30 3.30

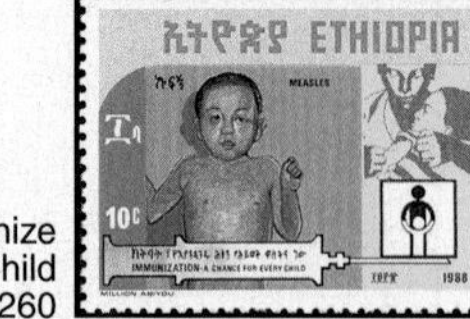

Immunize Every Child A260

1988, June 14 Litho. *Perf. 13x13½*

1218 A260 10c Measles .30 .30
1219 A260 35c Tetanus .60 .60
1220 A260 50c Whooping cough .85 .85
1221 A260 1b Diphtheria 1.75 1.75
Nos. 1218-1221 (4) 3.50 3.50

Intl. Fund for Agricultural Development (IFAD), 10th Anniv. — A261

1988, Aug. 16 *Perf. 13½*

1222 A261 15c Monetary aid .30 .30
1223 A261 85c Farming activities 1.25 1.25
1224 A261 1b Harvest 1.75 1.75
Nos. 1222-1224 (3) 3.30 3.30

People's Democratic Republic of Ethiopia, 1st Anniv. — A262

5c, 1st Session of the natl. Shengo (congress). 10c, Mengistu Haile-Mariam, 1st president of the republic. 80c, Natl. crest, flag & crowd. 1b, State assembly building.

1988, Sept. 9 *Perf. 14*

1225 A262 5c multicolored .30 .30
1226 A262 10c multicolored .30 .30
1227 A262 80c multicolored 1.25 1.25
1228 A262 1b multicolored 1.75 1.75
Nos. 1225-1228 (4) 3.60 3.60

Bank Notes A263

1988, Nov. 10 Photo. *Perf. 13*

1229 A263 5c 1-Birr .30 .30
1230 A263 10c 5-Birr .30 .30
1231 A263 20c 10-Birr .50 .50
1232 A263 75c 50-Birr 1.40 1.40
1233 A263 85c 100-Birr 1.75 1.75
Nos. 1229-1233 (5) 4.25 4.25

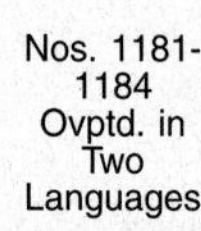

Nos. 1181-1184 Ovptd. in Two Languages

1988, Dec. 1 Litho. *Perf. 13½*

1234 A248 20c multicolored *4.75 4.50*
1235 A248 25c multicolored *6.25 5.50*
1236 A248 45c multicolored *12.50 10.50*
1237 A248 55c multicolored *13.00 11.00*
Nos. 1234-1237 (4) 36.50 31.50

Intl. Day for the Fight Against AIDS.

WHO, 40th Anniv. A264

1988, Dec. 30 Litho. *Perf. 14*

1238 A264 50c multicolored .85 .85
1239 A264 65c multicolored 1.10 1.10
1240 A264 85c multicolored 1.25 1.25
Nos. 1238-1240 (3) 3.20 3.20

Traditional Musical Instruments A265

1989, Feb. 9 *Perf. 13x13½*

1241 A265 30c Gere .55 .55
1242 A265 40c Fanfa .55 .55
1243 A265 50c Chancha .85 .85
1244 A265 85c Negareet 1.25 1.25
Nos. 1241-1244 (4) 3.20 3.20

Ethiopian Shipping Lines, 25th Anniv. A266

1989, Mar. 27 Litho. *Perf. 14*

1245 A266 15c *Abyot* .30 .30
1246 A266 30c *Wolwol* .60 .60
1247 A266 55c *Queen of Sheba* 1.25 1.25
1248 A266 1b *Abbay Wonz* 1.75 1.75
Nos. 1245-1248 (4) 3.90 3.90

Birds — A267

10c, Yellow-fronted parrot. 35c, White-winged cliff chat. 50c, Yellow-throated seed eater. 1b, Black-headed forest oriole.

1989, May 18 Litho. *Perf. 13½x13*

1249 A267 10c multicolored .30 .30
1250 A267 35c multicolored .85 .85
1251 A267 50c multicolored 1.25 1.25
1252 A267 1b multicolored 2.25 2.25
Nos. 1249-1252 (4) 4.65 4.65

Production of Early Manuscripts — A268

Designs: 5c, Preparing vellum. 10c, Ink horns, pens. 20c, Scribe. 75c, Book binding. 85c, Illuminated manuscript.

1989, June 16 Litho. *Perf. 13½*

1253 A268 5c multi .30 .30
1254 A268 10c multi .30 .30
1255 A268 20c multi .35 .35
1256 A268 75c multi 1.25 1.25
1257 A268 85c multi 1.50 1.50
Nos. 1253-1257 (5) 3.70 3.70

Indigenous Wildlife — A269

1989, July 18

1258 A269 30c Greater kudu .85 .85
1259 A269 40c Lesser kudu .95 .95
1260 A269 50c Roan antelope 1.25 1.25
1261 A269 85c Nile lechwe 1.75 1.75
Nos. 1258-1261 (4) 4.80 4.80

People's Democratic Republic of Ethiopia, 2nd Anniv. A270

Designs: 15c, Melka Wakana Hydroelectric Power Station. 75c, Adea Berga Dairy Farm. 1b, Pawe Hospital.

1989, Sept. 8

1262 A270 15c multicolored .30 .25
1263 A270 75c multicolored 1.25 1.25
1264 A270 1b multicolored 2.00 2.00
Nos. 1262-1264 (3) 3.55 3.50

African Development Bank, 25th Anniv. — A271

1989, Nov. 10 Litho. *Perf. 13½x13*

1265 A271 20c multicolored .30 .30
1266 A271 80c multicolored 1.25 1.25
1267 A271 1b multicolored 1.75 2.00
Nos. 1265-1267 (3) 3.30 3.55

Pan-African Postal Union, 10th Anniv. — A272

1990, Jan. 18 Litho. *Perf. 13½*

1268 A272 50c multicolored .75 .75
1269 A272 70c multicolored 1.25 1.25
1270 A272 80c multicolored 1.50 1.75
Nos. 1268-1270 (3) 3.50 3.75

UNESCO World Literacy Year — A273

15c, Illiterate man holding newspaper upside down. 85c, Adults learning alphabet in school. 1b, Literate man holding newspaper upright.

1990, Mar. 13

1271 A273 15c multicolored .40 .40
1272 A273 85c multicolored 1.40 1.40
1273 A273 1b multicolored 1.75 1.75
Nos. 1271-1273 (3) 3.55 3.55

Abebe Bikila, Marathon Runner A274

5c, Race. 10c, Flag bearer, Olympic team. 20c, Race, Rome Olympics. 75c, Race, Tokyo Olympics. 85c, Bikila, trophies, vert.

1990, Apr. 17

1274 A274 5c multicolored .30 .30
1275 A274 10c multicolored .30 .30
1276 A274 20c multicolored .60 .60
1277 A274 75c multicolored 1.25 1.25
1278 A274 85c multicolored 1.75 1.75
Nos. 1274-1278 (5) 4.20 4.20

Flag — A275

1990, Apr. 30 Litho. *Perf. 13½x13*

1279 A275 5c multicolored .30 .30
1280 A275 10c multicolored .30 .30
1281 A275 15c multicolored .30 .30
1282 A275 20c multicolored .40 .30
1283 A275 25c multicolored .50 .30
1284 A275 30c multicolored .60 .30
1285 A275 35c multicolored .70 .30
1286 A275 40c multicolored .80 .30
1287 A275 45c multicolored .85 .60
1288 A275 50c multicolored 1.00 .60
1289 A275 55c multicolored 1.00 .60
1290 A275 60c multicolored 1.25 .60
1291 A275 70c multicolored 1.25 .85
1292 A275 80c multicolored 1.25 .85
1293 A275 85c multicolored 1.25 .85
1294 A275 90c multicolored 1.25 .85
1295 A275 1b multicolored 1.75 1.25
1296 A275 2b multicolored 3.50 2.25
1297 A275 3b multicolored 5.50 4.50
Nos. 1279-1297 (19) 23.75 16.20

Dated 1989.

Sowing of Teff A276

Designs: 10c, Harvesting. 20c, Threshing. 75c, Storage, preparation. 85c, Consumption.

1990, May 18 Litho. *Perf. 13½*

1298 A276 5c shown .30 .30
1299 A276 10c multi .30 .30
1300 A276 20c multi .30 .30
1301 A276 75c multi 1.25 1.25
1302 A276 85c multi 1.75 1.75
Nos. 1298-1302 (5) 3.90 3.90

Walia Ibex — A277

1990, June 18 *Perf. 14x13½*

1303 A277 5c multi .75 .35
1304 A277 15c multi 1.40 .75
1305 A277 20c multi 2.25 1.10
1306 A277 1b multi, horiz. 8.00 4.25
Nos. 1303-1306 (4) 12.40 6.45

World AIDS Day A278

Designs: 15c, Stages of disease. 85c, Education. 1b, Causes, preventatives.

1991, Jan. 31 Litho. *Perf. 14*

1307 A278 15c multi .30 .30
1308 A278 85c multi 1.50 1.50
1309 A278 1b multi 2.25 2.25
Nos. 1307-1309 (3) 4.05 4.05

Intl. Decade for Natural Disaster Reduction A279

Map of disaster-prone African areas and: 5c, Volcano. 10c, Earthquake. 15c, Drought. 30c, Flood. 50c, Red Cross health education. 1b, Red Cross assisting fire victims.

1991, Apr. 9 Litho. *Perf. 14*

1310 A279 5c multicolored .30 .30
1311 A279 10c multicolored .30 .30
1312 A279 15c multicolored .30 .30
1313 A279 30c multicolored .60 .60
1314 A279 50c multicolored 1.10 1.10
1315 A279 1b multicolored 2.25 2.25
Nos. 1310-1315 (6) 4.85 4.85

The Cannon of Tewodros A280

Designs: 15c, Villagers receiving cannon 85c, Warriors leaving with cannon. 1b, Hauling cannon up mountainside.

1991, June 18 Litho. *Perf. 13½*

1316 A280 15c multicolored .40 .40
1317 A280 85c multicolored 1.50 1.50
1318 A280 1b multicolored 2.25 1.75
Nos. 1316-1318 (3) 4.15 3.65

Fish A281

5c, Lacepede. 15c, Black-finned butterflyfish. 80c, Regal angelfish. 1b, Bleeker.

1991, Sept. 6 Litho. *Perf. 13½*

1319 A281 5c multi .50 .50
1320 A281 15c multi .50 .50
1321 A281 80c multi 2.25 2.25
1322 A281 1b multi 2.75 2.75
Nos. 1319-1322 (4) 6.00 6.00

A282

Traditional Ceremonial Robes: Various robes.

1992, Jan. 1 Litho. *Perf. 13½x14*

1323 A282 5c yellow & multi .30 .30
1324 A282 15c orange & multi .30 .30
1325 A282 80c yel green & multi 1.75 1.75
1326 A282 1b blue & multi 2.00 2.00
Nos. 1323-1326 (4) 4.35 4.35

A283

Flowers: 5c, Cissus quadrangularis. 15c, Delphinium dasycaulon. 80c, Epilobium hirsutum. 1b, Kniphofia foliosa.

1992, Mar. 5 Litho. *Perf. 13½x14*

1327 A283 5c multicolored .30 .30
1328 A283 15c multicolored .40 .40
1329 A283 80c multicolored 2.00 1.75
1330 A283 1b multicolored 2.50 2.00
Nos. 1327-1330 (4) 5.20 4.45

Traditional Homes A284

1992, May 14 Litho. *Perf. 12½x12*

1331 A284 15c Afar .30 .30
1332 A284 35c Anuak .60 .60
1333 A284 50c Gimira .90 .90
1334 A284 1b Oromo 2.25 1.75
Nos. 1331-1334 (4) 4.05 3.55

A285

Pottery.

1992, July 7 Litho. *Perf. 13x13½*

1335 A285 15c Cover .30 .30
1336 A285 85c Jug 1.25 1.25
1337 A285 1b Tall jar 2.00 2.00
Nos. 1335-1337 (3) 3.55 3.55

A286

1992, Sept. 29 *Perf. 14x13½*

1338 A286 20c multicolored .30 .30
1339 A286 80c multicolored 1.25 1.25
1340 A286 1b multicolored 2.00 1.75
Nos. 1338-1340 (3) 3.55 3.30

Pan-African Rinderpest campaign.

Musical Instruments A287

1993, Feb. 16 Litho. *Perf. 14x13½*

1341 A287 15c Catchel .30 .30
1342 A287 35c Huldudwa .55 .55
1343 A287 50c Dita .85 .85
1344 A287 1b Atamo 1.75 1.75
Nos. 1341-1344 (4) 3.45 3.45

Birds — A288

Designs: 15c, Banded barbet. 35c, Ruppell's chat. 50c, Abyssinian catbird. 1b, White-billed starling.

1993, Apr. 22 Litho. *Perf. 14x13½*

1345 A288 15c multi .30 .30
1346 A288 35c multi .75 .75
1347 A288 50c multi 1.00 1.00
1348 A288 1b multi 2.00 2.00
Nos. 1345-1348 (4) 4.05 4.05

Animals A289

Designs: 15c, Honey badger. 35c, Spotted necked otter. 50c, Rock hyrax. 1b, White-tailed mongoose.

1993, May 14 *Perf. 13½x14*

1349 A289 15c multi .30 .30
1350 A289 35c multi .60 .60
1351 A289 50c multi 1.00 1.00
1352 A289 1b multi 2.00 2.00
Nos. 1349-1352 (4) 3.90 3.90

Herbs — A290

Designs: 5c, Caraway seed. 15c, Garlic. 80c, Turmeric. 1b, Capsicum peppers.

1993, June 10 *Perf. 14x13½*

1353 A290 5c multi .60 .60
1354 A290 15c multi .75 .75
1355 A290 80c multi 1.40 1.40
1356 A290 1b multi 1.50 1.50
Nos. 1353-1356 (4) 4.25 4.25

Butterflies A291

20c, Papilio echeriodes. 30c, Papilio rex. 50c, Graphium policenes. 1b, Graphium leonidas.

1993, July 9 Litho. *Perf. 14x13½*

1357 A291 20c multicolored 1.00 .85
1358 A291 30c multicolored .85 .85
1359 A291 50c multicolored 1.40 1.40
1360 A291 1b multicolored 2.50 2.50
Nos. 1357-1360 (4) 5.75 5.60

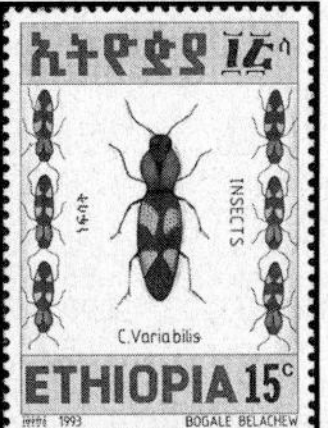

Insects — A292

Designs: 15c, C. Variabilis. 35c, Lycus trabeatus. 50c, Malachius bifasciatus. 1b, Homoeogryllus xanthographus.

1993, Aug. 10

1361	A292	15c multi	.60	.60
1362	A292	35c multi	.60	.60
1363	A292	50c multi	.85	.85
1364	A292	1b multi	1.75	1.75
		Nos. 1361-1364 (4)	3.80	3.80

Trees A293

15c, Euphorbia ampliphylla. 35c, Erythrina brucei. 50c, Dracaena steudneri. 1b, Allophylus abyssinicus.

1993, Oct. 12 Litho. *Perf. 13½x14*

1365	A293	15c multicolored	.30	.30
1366	A293	35c multicolored	.30	.30
1367	A293	50c multicolored	.30	.30
1368	A293	1b multicolored	1.00	1.00
		Nos. 1365-1368 (4)	1.90	1.90

Lakes A294

1993, Dec. 14

1369	A294	15c Wonchi	.35	.30
1370	A294	35c Zuquala	.50	.30
1371	A294	50c Ashengi	.70	.50
1372	A294	1b Tana	1.25	1.00
		Nos. 1369-1372 (4)	2.80	2.10

Simien Fox A294a

Rough Perf. 13½

1994, Jan. 18 Litho.

Color of Border

1372A	A294a	5c violet	—	—
1372B	A294a	10c brown	—	—
1372C	A294a	15c lemon	—	—
1372D	A294a	20c salmon	—	—
1372E	A294a	40c pale rose	—	—
1372F	A294a	55c dull green	—	—
1372G	A294a	60c dark blue	—	—
1372H	A294a	80c bright blue	—	—
1372I	A294a	85c gray green	—	—
1372J	A294a	1b bright green	—	—
		Nos. 1372A-1372J	—	3.65

Nos. 1372A-1372J have rough perforations and a poor quality printing impression. Dated "1991."

See Nos. 1393A-1393T.

A295

Transitional government: 15c, First anniversary of EPRDF's control of Addis Ababa. 35c, Transition Conference. 50c, National, regional elections. 1b, Coat of arms of Transitional Government.

1994, Mar. 31 Litho. *Perf. 14*

1373	A295	15c multicolored	.30	.30
1374	A295	35c multicolored	.30	.30
1375	A295	50c multicolored	.40	.40
1376	A295	1b multicolored	.75	.75
		Nos. 1373-1376 (4)	1.75	1.75

A296

1994, May 17 *Perf. 13½*

1377	A296	15c blue & multi	.30	.30
1378	A296	85c green & multi	.50	.50
1379	A296	1b violet & multi	.75	.75
		Nos. 1377-1379 (3)	1.55	1.55

Intl. Year of the Family.

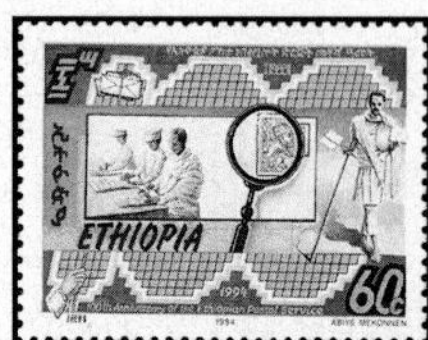

Ethiopian Postal Service, Cent. A297

Designs: 60c, Early, modern postal workers, Scott Type A1. 75c, Early letter carriers. 80c, Older building, methods of transportation. 85c, People, mail buses. 1b, Modern methods of transportation, modern high-rise building.

1994, July 4 Litho. *Perf. 13½*

1380	A297	60c multicolored	.75	.55
1381	A297	75c multicolored	.90	.60
1382	A297	80c multicolored	1.15	.70
1383	A297	85c multicolored	1.20	.75
1384	A297	1b multicolored	1.45	1.05
a.		Souvenir sheet, #1380-1384 + label	10.00	8.00
		Nos. 1380-1384 (5)	5.45	3.65

Enset Plant — A298

1994, Aug. 3

1385	A298	10c shown	.25	.25
1386	A298	15c Young plants, hut	.35	.30
1387	A298	25c Root, women processing leaves	.40	.35
1388	A298	50c Mature plants	.75	.40
1389	A298	1b Uses as food	1.50	.65
		Nos. 1385-1389 (5)	3.25	1.95

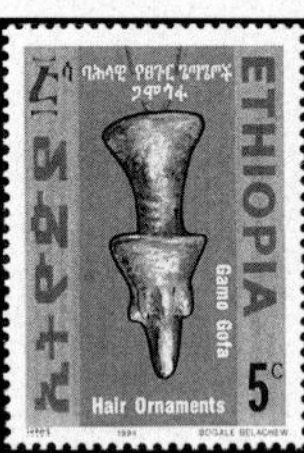

Hair Ornaments A299

1994, Sept. 2

1390	A299	5c Gamo gofa	.40	.30
1391	A299	15c Sidamo	.50	.35
1392	A299	80c Gamo gofa, diff.	.80	.60
1393	A299	1b Wello	1.10	.85
		Nos. 1390-1393 (4)	2.80	2.10

Simien Fox Type of 1994

Size: 39x25mm

Color of Border

1994, Oct. 18 Litho. *Perf. 14*

1393A	A294a	5c dull lilac	—	*.35*
1393B	A294a	10c brown	—	*.45*
1393C	A294a	15c lemon	—	*.55*
1393D	A294a	20c salmon	—	*.65*
1393E	A294a	25c lemon	—	*.75*
1393F	A294a	30c yel brn	—	*1.00*
1393G	A294a	35c orange	—	*1.25*
1393H	A294a	40c pale rose	—	*1.50*
1393I	A294a	45c pale red org	—	*1.75*
1393J	A294a	50c rose lilac	—	*2.00*
1393K	A294a	55c pale grn	—	*2.25*
1393L	A294a	60c dark blue	—	*2.50*
1393M	A294a	65c pale lilac	—	*2.75*
1393N	A294a	70c brt grn	—	*3.00*
1393O	A294a	75c pale bl grn	—	*3.25*
1393P	A294a	80c bright blue	—	*3.50*
1393Q	A294a	85c dk grnsh blue	—	*3.75*
1393R	A294a	90c pale brn	—	*4.00*
1393S	A294a	1b grnsh blue	—	*5.00*
1393T	A294a	2b yel brn	—	*9.00*
		Nos. 1393A-1393T (20)		*49.25*
		Nos. 1393A-1393T	—	

Nos. 1393A-1393T have sharp impressions, Questa imprint, clean perforations. Dated "1993."

For overprints see Nos. 1393U-1393X, 1396A-1396D.

Nos. 1393L, 1393P-1393Q, 1393S Ovptd. in Blue

1994, Oct. 20 Litho. *Perf. 14*

1393U	A294a	60c on #1393L	—	—
1393V	A294a	80c on #1393P	—	—
1393W	A294a	85c on #1393Q	—	—
1393X	A294a	1b on #1393S	—	—

UNFPA, 50th anniv.

ICAO, 50th Anniv. A300

1994, Dec. 7 Litho. *Perf. 13½*

1394	A300	20c mag, lt bl & yel	.40	.40
1395	A300	80c yel & lt bl	.60	.60
1396	A300	1b dk bl, lt bl & yel	.90	.90
		Nos. 1394-1396 (3)	1.90	1.90

Nos. 1393M-1393O, 1393R Ovptd.

1994, Dec. 20 Litho. *Perf. 14*

1396A	A294a	65c on #1393M	—	—
1396B	A294a	70c on #1393N	—	—
1396C	A294a	75c on #1393O	—	—
1396D	A294a	90c on #1393R	—	—

African Development Bank, 30th anniv.

Baskets for Serving Food A301

1995, June 7 Litho. *Perf. 13½*

1397	A301	30c Erbo	.30	.25
1398	A301	70c Sedieka	.50	.50
1399	A301	1b Tirar	.85	.85
		Nos. 1397-1399 (3)	1.65	1.60

Traditional Hair Styles — A302

1995, July 5 Litho. *Perf. 13½*

1400	A302	25c Kuncho	.40	.40
1401	A302	75c Gamme	.60	.60
1402	A302	1b Sadulla	1.00	1.00
		Nos. 1400-1402 (3)	2.00	2.00

FAO, 50th Anniv. A303

1995, Aug. 29 Litho. *Perf. 13½*

1403	A303	20c green & multi	.75	.65
1404	A303	80c blue & multi	1.25	1.00
1405	A303	1b brown & multi	1.50	1.25
		Nos. 1403-1405 (3)	3.50	2.90

Cultivating Tools A304

1995, Sept. 7

1406	A304	15c Dangora	.60	.60
1407	A304	35c Gheso	.60	.60
1408	A304	50c Akafa	.60	.60
1409	A304	1b Ankasse	1.10	1.10
		Nos. 1406-1409 (4)	2.90	2.90

UN, 50th Anniv. — A305

1995, Oct. 18 Litho. *Perf. 13½*

Color of UN Emblem

1410	A305	20c black	.40	.30
1411	A305	80c bister	.85	.65
1412	A305	1b blue	1.00	.85
		Nos. 1410-1412 (3)	2.25	1.80

Intergovernmental Authority on Drought and Development (IGADD), 10th Anniv. — A306

Flags of member nations and: 15c, Seedling being planted in arid region. 35c, People carrying supplies through desert. 50c, Person picking fruit. 1b, Map of member nations.

1995, Dec. 27 Litho. *Perf. 13½*

1413	A306	15c multicolored	.45	.35
1414	A306	35c multicolored	.55	.45
1415	A306	50c multicolored	.70	.60
1416	A306	1b multicolored	1.10	1.00
		Nos. 1413-1416 (4)	2.80	2.40

Victory at Battle of Adwa, Cent. — A307

Designs: 40c, Battle sites. 50c, Map of Africa focused at Ethiopia. 60c, Troops, ship. 70c, Warriors, soldiers in two battle scenes. 80c, Italians surrendering, Ethiopian troops, cannons. 1b, Emperor Menelik II, constitution, Empress Taitu.

1996, Mar. 2 Litho. *Perf. 13½x14½*

1417	A307	40c multicolored	.35	.35
1418	A307	50c multicolored	.40	.35
1419	A307	60c multicolored	.60	.45
1420	A307	70c multicolored	.75	.55
1421	A307	80c multicolored	1.00	.80
1422	A307	1b multicolored	1.40	1.10
a.		Souvenir sheet, #1417-1422	5.50	5.50
		Nos. 1417-1422 (6)	4.50	3.60

UN Volunteers, 25th Anniv. A308

Designs: 20c, People, temporary housing huts. 30c, Planting seedlings. 50c, Instructing students. 1b, Caring for infant.

1996, June 6 Litho. *Perf. 13½*

1423	A308	20c multicolored	.25	.25
1424	A308	30c multicolored	.35	.25
1425	A308	50c multicolored	.50	.40
1426	A308	1b multicolored	1.40	1.25
		Nos. 1423-1426 (4)	2.50	2.15

1996 Summer Olympic Games, Atlanta A310

1996, Aug. 1 Litho. *Perf. 12½x12*

Overprint in Black

1427	A310	15c Boxing	.30	.30
1428	A310	20c Swimming	.30	.30
1429	A310	40c Cycling	.30	.30
1430	A310	85c Athletics	.60	.60
1431	A310	1b Soccer	.90	.90
		Nos. 1427-1431 (5)	2.40	2.40

Nos. 1427-1431 were originally prepared for the 1984 Summer Olympic Games in Los Angeles, but were not released due to the Soviet-led boycott. Nos. 1427-1431 exist without overprint. Value, set $100.

A311

UNICEF, 50th Anniv.: 10c, Emblems. 15c, Mother, child receiving vaccination. 25c, Woman carrying water, boy drinking from faucet. 50c, Children studying. 1b, Mother breastfeeding infant.

1996, Sept. 10 Litho. *Perf. 13½*

1432	A311	10c multicolored	.35	.35
1433	A311	15c multicolored	.40	.35
1434	A311	25c multicolored	.50	.40
1435	A311	50c multicolored	.85	.65
1436	A311	1b multicolored	1.40	1.05
		Nos. 1432-1436 (5)	3.50	2.80

A312

Creation of Federal Democratic Republic of Ethiopia: 10c, People discussing new Constitution, approved Dec. 8, 1994. 20c, Ballot boxes, hand placing ballot in box. 30c, Marking ballot, placing into box, tower building, items from country's environment. 40c, Building, ballot, assembly hall. 1b, Natl. flag, transition of power.

1996, Dec. 26 Litho. *Perf. 13½*

1437	A312	10c multicolored	.30	.30
1438	A312	20c multicolored	.40	.30
1439	A312	30c multicolored	.50	.30
1440	A312	40c multicolored	.60	.30
1441	A312	1b multicolored	.75	.60
		Nos. 1437-1441 (5)	2.55	1.80

Traditional Baskets — A313

1997, Feb. 20 Litho. *Perf. 13½*

1442	A313	5c Jimma	.40	.40
1443	A313	15c Wello	.40	.40
1444	A313	80c Welega	1.00	1.00
1445	A313	1b Shewa	1.25	1.25
		Nos. 1442-1445 (4)	3.05	3.05

Traditional Baskets A314

1997, May 22 Litho. *Perf. 13½*

1446	A314	35c Arssi	.40	.40
1447	A314	65c Gojam	.60	.50
1448	A314	1b Harer	1.25	1.00
		Nos. 1446-1448 (3)	2.25	1.90

See Nos. 1464-1466.

UN Decade Against Drug Abuse & Illicit Trafficking A315

1997, Sept. 9 Litho. *Perf. 14*

1449	A315	20c green & multi	.60	.60
1450	A315	80c brown & multi	.60	.60
1451	A315	1b blue & multi	1.00	.85
		Nos. 1449-1451 (3)	2.20	2.05

Historic Buildings, Addis Ababa A316

45c, Bitwoded Haile Giorgis' house. 55c, Alfred Ilg's house, vert. 3b, Menelik's Elfign.

Perf. 14½x14, 14x14½

1997, Dec. 23 Litho.

1452	A316	45c multicolored	.30	.30
1453	A316	55c multicolored	.45	.45
1454	A316	3b multicolored	1.50	1.50
		Nos. 1452-1454 (3)	2.25	2.25

Addis Ababa's Oldest Historical Buildings A317

Designs: 60c, Ras Biru W/Gabriel's house. 75c, Sheh Hojele Alhassen's house. 80c, Fitawrari H/Giorgis Dinegde's house. 85c, Etege Taitu Hotel. 1b, Dejazmach Wube Atnafseged's house.

1997, Dec. 30 Litho. *Perf. 14½x14*

1455	A317	60c multicolored	.55	.45
1456	A317	75c multicolored	.60	.55
1457	A317	80c multicolored	.70	.60
1458	A317	85c multicolored	.75	.70
1459	A317	1b multicolored	1.15	.90
		Nos. 1455-1459 (5)	3.75	3.20

Pan African Postal Union, 18th Anniv. A318

Union's emblem and wildlife: 45c, Deculla bushback. 55c, Soemmering's gazelle. 1b, Defassa waterbuck. 2b, Black buffalo.

1998, Mar. 25 Litho. *Perf. 14½x14*

1460	A318	45c multicolored	.50	.35
1461	A318	55c multicolored	.55	.45
1462	A318	1b multicolored	1.00	.65
1463	A318	2b multicolored	2.00	1.25
		Nos. 1460-1463 (4)	4.05	2.70

Traditional Basket Type of 1997

1998, May 21 Litho. *Perf. 13½*

1464	A314	45c Gonder	.45	.35
1465	A314	55c Harere	.55	.35
1466	A314	3b Tigray	2.00	1.25
		Nos. 1464-1466 (3)	3.00	1.95

Golden-Backed Woodpecker A319

1998, Jan. 12 Photo. *Perf. 11½*

Granite Paper

Panel Color

1467	A319	5c green blue	.45	.30
1468	A319	10c yellow	.45	.30
1469	A319	15c blue	.45	.30
1470	A319	20c light brown	*15.00*	.30
1471	A319	25c violet	.45	.30
1472	A319	30c light blue	.45	.30
1473	A319	35c salmon rose	.45	.30
1474	A319	40c lilac	.45	.30
1475	A319	45c green	.45	.30
1476	A319	50c salmon	.45	.35
1477	A319	55c blue	.45	.35
1478	A319	60c brick red	.45	.40
1479	A319	65c light gray	.45	.45
1480	A319	70c bright yellow	.45	.50
1481	A319	75c pale violet	.70	.65
1482	A319	80c apple green	.75	.70
1483	A319	85c gray	.80	.75
1484	A319	90c orange	.90	.80
1485	A319	1b yellow green	1.25	.95
1486	A319	2b pale rose	1.50	1.25
1487	A319	3b lilac rose	2.50	2.00
1488	A319	5b bister	3.50	3.00
1489	A319	10b orange yellow	7.00	6.00
		Nos. 1467-1489 (23)	39.75	20.85

Agreement for Return of Axum Obelisk from Italy — A320

45c, Map of Italy, pieces of obelisk. 55c, Obelisk in Rome. 3b, Map of E. Africa, obelisk, ruins of Axum.

1998, Sept. 3 Litho. *Perf. 13½*

1490	A320	45c multicolored	.50	.30
1491	A320	55c multicolored	.60	.40
1492	A320	3b multicolored	2.50	1.50
		Nos. 1490-1492 (3)	3.60	2.20

Ethiopia-Djibouti Railway, Cent. — A321

Designs: 45c, Men carrying rails during construction. 55c, Early steam train, CFE 404. 1b, Terminal building. 2b, Modern train, BB 1212.

1998, Nov. 24 Litho. *Perf. 11½*

Granite Paper

1493	A321	45c multicolored	.55	.35
1494	A321	55c multicolored	.70	.45
1495	A321	1b multicolored	1.20	.75
1496	A321	2b multicolored	2.50	1.25
		Nos. 1493-1496 (4)	4.95	2.80

Universal Declaration of Human Rights, 50th Anniv. A322

1998, Dec. 23 Litho. *Perf. 13x13½*

1497	A322	45c red & multi	.45	.25
1498	A322	55c yellow & multi	.45	.30
1499	A322	1b green & multi	.75	.50
1500	A322	2b blue & multi	1.10	.75
		Nos. 1497-1500 (4)	2.75	1.80

Mother Teresa (1910-97) — A323

Various portraits.

1999, Mar. 9 Litho. *Perf. 13½x13*

1501	A323	45c brown & multi	.60	.60
1502	A323	55c green & multi	.60	.60
1503	A323	1b yel org & multi	1.00	.75
1504	A323	2b blue & multi	2.00	1.75
		Nos. 1501-1504 (4)	4.20	3.70

Intl. Year of the Ocean A324

1999, May 6 Litho. *Perf. 13½x13¼*

1505	A324	45c black & multi	.60	.30
1506	A324	55c red & multi	.75	.30
1507	A324	1b blue & multi	1.00	.60
1508	A324	2b green & multi	2.25	1.25
		Nos. 1505-1508 (4)	4.60	2.45

World Environment Day — A325

1999, June 17 Litho. *Perf. 13½*

1509	A325	45c pink & multi	.55	.30
1510	A325	55c vio & multi	.70	.40
1511	A325	1b yel org & multi	1.10	.70
1512	A325	2b grn & multi	1.90	1.00
		Nos. 1509-1512 (4)	4.25	2.40

National Parks — A326

45c, Abijata, Shalla Lakes. 70c, Nechisar. 85c, Bale Mountains. 2b, Awash.

Perf. 13¾x13¼, 13¼x13¾

1999, Sept. 8 Litho.

1513	A326	45c multi, vert.	.50	.50
1514	A326	70c multi, vert.	.80	.70
1515	A326	85c multi, vert.	1.25	.90
1516	A326	2b multi	3.00	1.50
		Nos. 1513-1516 (4)	5.55	3.60

See Nos. 1521-1524.

UPU, 125th Anniv. — A327

1999, Oct. 28 *Perf. 13¼x13*

1517	A327	20c multicolored	.50	.50
1518	A327	80c multicolored	.70	.35
1519	A327	1b multicolored	.75	.60
1520	A327	2b multicolored	1.50	.85
		Nos. 1517-1520 (4)	3.45	2.30

National Parks Type of 1999

Designs: 50c, Omo, vert. 70c, Mago, vert. 80c, Yangudi-Rassa, vert. 2b, Gambella.

1999, Nov. 30 Litho. *Perf. 13¼*

1521-1524 A326 Set of 4 5.00 3.00

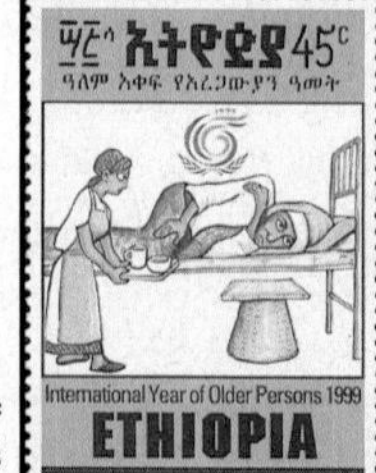

Intl. Year of Older Persons A328

45c, Woman attending to sick man. 70c, Older people gardening. 85c, Four men, bench. 2b, Older man, two young people.

1999, Dec. 30 *Perf. 13¾x13¼*

1525-1528 A328 Set of 4 4.50 3.50

Alexander Pushkin, Writer, Birth Bicent. (in 1999) — A329

Various portraits: 45c, 70c, 85c, 2b.

2000, Mar. 9 Litho. *Perf. 13¾x13¼*

1529-1532 A329 Set of 4 3.25 2.25

Worldwide Fund for Nature (WWF) — A330

Grevy's zebra: a, Grazing. b, Running. c, Resting. d, Head.

2001, Jan. 30 Litho. *Perf. 13¼x13¾*

1533	Strip of 4	*4.25*	*3.50*
a.	A330 45c multi	*.40*	*.30*
b.	A330 55c multi	*.50*	*.40*
c.	A330 1b multi	*.80*	*.70*
d.	A330 3b multi	*2.50*	*2.25*

Operation Sunset — A331

Designs: 45c, President Meles Zenawi, Parliament. 55c, Soldiers, flag ceremony. 1b, People, house. 2b, Agriculture, construction.

2000, June 27 *Perf. 13¾*

1534-1537 A331 Set of 4 4.50 2.50

Flags A332

Designs: 25c, Harar Region. 30c, Oromia Region. 50c, Amhara Region. 60c, Tigre Region. 70c, Benishangi Region. 80c, Somalia Region. 90c, Peoples of the South Region. 95c, Gambella Region. 1b, Afar Region. 2b, Ethiopia.

2000, Oct. 26 *Perf. 13¼x13¾*

1538-1547 A332 Set of 10 7.00 4.50

Afro Ayigeba, Cross of St. Lalibela A333

2000, Apr. 27 *Perf. 13¾x13¼*

1548 A333 4b multi 2.50 2.25

Menelik's Bushbuck A334

Perf. 13¾x13¼

2000, June 19 Litho.

Frame Color

1548A	A334	5c dk Prus blue	*2.00*	.25
1549	A334	10c lilac	*2.00*	.25
1549A	A334	15c blue	*2.00*	.25
1549B	A334	20c yellow bister	*2.00*	.25
1549C	A334	25c purple	*2.00*	.25
1549D	A334	30c lt Prus blue	*2.00*	.25
1549E	A334	35c brt red	*2.00*	.25
1549F	A334	40c lilac	*2.00*	.25
1549G	A334	45c emerald	*2.00*	.25
1549H	A334	50c red	*2.25*	.25
1549I	A334	55c blue	*2.50*	.25
1549J	A334	60c yellow orange	*2.50*	.25
1549K	A334	65c deep blue	*2.50*	.25
1549L	A334	70c dull blue	*2.50*	.25
1549M	A334	75c orange yellow	*3.00*	.35
1549N	A334	80c carmine	*3.00*	.35
1549O	A334	85c light blue	*3.00*	.40
1550	A334	90c ocher	*3.00*	.40
1551	A334	1b green	*4.00*	.50
1552	A334	2b red violet	*9.00*	.75
1553	A334	3b purple	*16.00*	.90
1554	A334	5b dark carmine	*27.50*	1.75
1555	A334	10b light carmine	*37.50*	4.00
		Nos. 1548A-1555 (23)	136.25	12.90

Haile Gebreselassie, Runner — A335

Gebreselassie: No. 1557, 50c, Running. No. 1557A, 60c, Running, diff. No. 1557B, 90c, Running, diff. No. 1558, 2b, With arms raised.

2000, Nov. 9 Litho. *Perf. 13½*

1557-1558 A335 Set of 4 3.50 2.00

World Meteorological Organization, 50th Anniv. — A336

Color of inscriptions: 40c, Gray. 75c, Green. 85c, Brown. 2b, Blue.

2000, Oct. 10 Litho. *Perf. 13½*

1559-1562 A336 Set of 4 3.00 2.00

Addis Ababa University, 50th Anniv. — A337

2000, Nov. 30 *Perf. 13½x14¼*

1563 A337 4b multi 3.25 2.75

UN High Commissioner for Refugees, 50th Anniv. — A338

Frame color: 40c, Brown. 75c, Green. 85c, Blue. 2b, Gold.

2000 Dec. 14 *Perf. 13½x14*

1564-1567 A338 Set of 4 4.00 2.50

Freshwater Fish — A340

Designs: 45c, Catfish. 55c, Tilapia. 3b, Nile perch.

2001, July 26 Litho. *Perf. 14¼*

1572-1574 A340 Set of 3 3.50 1.75

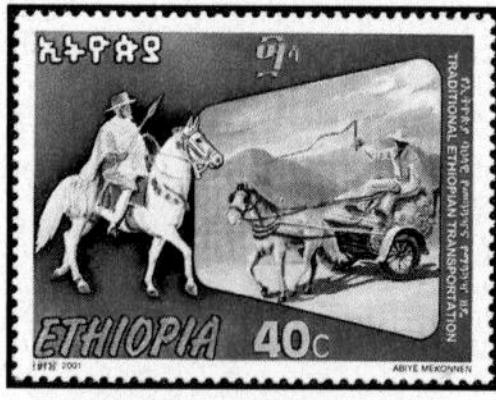

Traditional Means of Transportation — A341

Designs: 40c, Man on horseback, horse-drawn cart. 60c, Camel caravan. 1b, Man on horseback, horse carrying load. 2b, Man on donkey, donkeys carrying goods.

2001, Aug. 30 *Perf. 13¼x13½*

1575-1578 A341 Set of 4 4.25 2.25

Year of Dialogue Among Civilizations A342

Color of country name: 25c, Light blue. 75c, White. 1b, Light yellow. 2b, Pink.

2001, Oct. 9 *Perf. 14*

1579-1582 A342 Set of 4 3.50 2.25

Birds — A343

Designs: 50c, White-tailed swallow. 60c, Spot-breasted plover. 90c, Abyssinian long-claw. 2b, Prince Ruspoli's turaco.

2001, Nov. 29 *Perf. 14¼*
1583-1586 A343 Set of 4 5.00 3.00

Traditional Beehives A344

Various beehives: 40c, 70c, 90c, 2b.

2002, Jan. 24 **Litho.** *Perf. 14*
1587-1590 A344 Set of 4 4.50 3.50

Traditional Grain Storage — A345

Designs: 30c, Gota. 70c, Bekollo Gotera. 1b, Gotera. 2b, Gotera, diff.

2002, Mar. 28 *Perf. 13½x14*
1591-1594 A345 Set of 4 4.50 3.50

Lions Club Intl. — A346

Lions Club Intl. emblem and: 45c, Quality emblem. 55c, Woman at pump. 1b, Eye doctor treating patient. 2b, Man in wheelchair.

2002, Apr. 26 **Litho.** *Perf. 13x13¼*
1595-1598 A346 Set of 4 4.50 4.00

Trees A347

Designs: 50c, Acacia abyssinica. 60c, Boswellia papyrifera, vert. 90c, Aningeria adolfi-freiderici, vert. 2b, Prunus africana, vert.

Perf. 13½x13¼, 13¼x13½
2002, June 27
1599-1602 A347 Set of 4 4.50 4.00

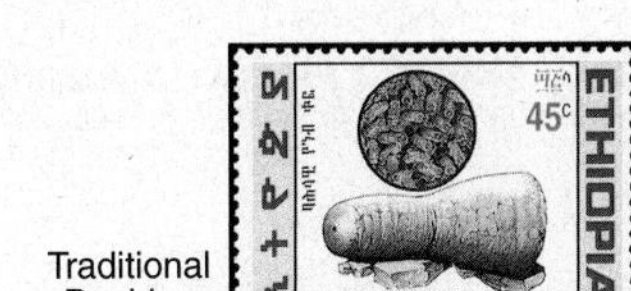

Traditional Beehives A348

Various beehives with panel colors of: 45c, Pink. 55c, Yellow. 1b, Light blue. 2b, Light green.

2002, Sept. 19 **Litho.** *Perf. 13¼x13*
1603-1606 A348 Set of 4 4.50 3.50

Granite — A349

Designs: 45c, Sidamo. 55c, Harrar. 1b, Tigray. 2b, Wollega.

2002, Oct. 24 *Perf. 13x13¼*
1607-1610 A349 Set of 4 4.50 4.00

Konso Waka A350

Various wooden sculptures with background colors of: 40c, Green. 60c, Blue. 1b, Yellow. 2b, Red.

2002, Nov. 28 *Perf. 14*
1611-1614 A350 Set of 4 4.00 2.00

Menelik's Bushbuck — A351

2002, Dec. 12 *Perf. 13½x13¾*

Frame Color

No.	Type	Value	Color	Unused	Used
1615	A351	5c	brt grn blue	.30	.25
1616	A351	10c	lilac	.30	.25
1617	A351	15c	bright blue	.30	.25
1618	A351	20c	brn orange	.30	.25
1619	A351	25c	purple	.30	.25
1620	A351	30c	bright blue	.30	.25
1621	A351	35c	carmine	.30	.25
1622	A351	40c	purple	.30	.25
1623	A351	45c	emerald	.30	.25
1624	A351	50c	red	.30	.25
1625	A351	55c	blue	.30	.25
1626	A351	60c	bright yel	.40	.25
1627	A351	65c	red	.40	.25
1628	A351	70c	light blue	.40	.25
1629	A351	75c	bright yel	.45	.35
1630	A351	80c	carmine	.45	.35
1631	A351	85c	bright blue	.60	.40
1632	A351	90c	orange brn	.60	.40
1633	A351	95c	green	.60	.40
1634	A351	1b	red violet	.70	.50
1635	A351	2b	purple	1.00	.75
1636	A351	3b	blue	1.25	.90
1637	A351	5b	dull red	2.25	1.50
1638	A351	10b	light green	6.50	3.00
1639	A351	20b	rose pink	11.00	6.00
			Nos. 1615-1639 (25)	29.90	18.05

Oil Crops A352

Designs: 40c, Abyssinian mustard. 60c, Linseed. 3b, Niger seed.

2002, Dec. 31 **Litho.** *Perf. 13¼x13*
1640-1642 A352 Set of 3 3.00 2.00

Pan-African Postal Union, 23rd Anniv. — A353

Background color: 20c, Green. 80c, Blue green. 1b, Orange brown. 2b, Purple.

2003, Feb. 18 *Perf. 13x13¼*
1643-1646 A353 Set of 4 3.00 2.00

Opals — A354

Designs: 45c, Milk opal. 60c, Brown precious opal. 95c, Fire opal. 2b, Yellow precious opal.

2003, May 8 *Perf. 14*
1647-1650 A354 Set of 4 4.00 2.00

Emperor Tewodros's Amulet — A355

Various views with frame color of: 40c, Green. 60c, Yellow orange. 3b, Red.

2003, Sept. 4 **Litho.** *Perf. 13x13¼*
1651-1653 A355 Set of 3 4.50 2.50

Flowers — A356

Designs: 45c, Kniphofia isoetfolia. 55c, Kniphofia insignis. 1b, Crinum bambusetum. 2b, Crinum abyssinicum, horiz.

2003, Nov. 27 **Litho.** *Perf. 13x13¼*
1654-1657 A356 Set of 4 3.00 2.00

Konso Terracing System A357

Designs: 40c, Village, crops. 60c, Man and woman, ears of grains. 1b, Terraces, tool. 2b, Farmers working on terraces, crops.

2003, Dec. 30 *Perf. 13¼x13¾*
1658-1661 A357 Set of 4 3.00 2.00

Amaranths A358

Designs: 20c, Seeds. 80c, White amaranth. 1b, Red amaranth. 2b, Amaranth bread.

2004, Mar. 11 **Litho.** *Perf. 13¼x14*
1662-1665 A358 Set of 4 3.00 2.00

Marble A359

Designs: 25c, Sabian multicolored marble. 75c, Eshet blue marble. 1b, Sabian rose green marble. 2b, Sabian purple marble.

2004, July 27 *Perf. 14*
1666-1669 A359 Set of 4 2.25 2.25

FIFA (Fédération Internationale de Football Association), Cent. — A360

Soccer field, "100" and: 5c, FIFA emblem. 95c, Old soccer ball. 1b, Cleats. 2b, Modern soccer ball.

2004, Sept. 7 **Litho.** *Perf. 14*
1670-1673 A360 Set of 4 2.25 2.25

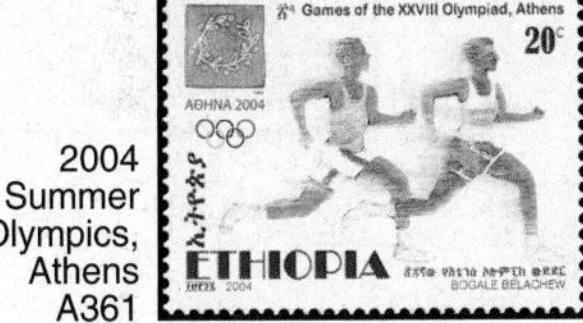

2004 Summer Olympics, Athens A361

Designs: 20c, Track. 35c, Hammer throw. 45c, Boxing. 3b, Cycling.

2004, Dec. 7
1674-1677 A361 Set of 4 2.25 2.25

Gesho — A362

Designs: 40c, Chopped plant. 60c, Plants, horiz. 1b, Cut logs. 2b, Branch with berries.

2004, Dec. 28
1678-1681 A362 Set of 4 2.25 2.25

Black Rhinoceros A363

2005, June 20 Litho. *Perf. 14*

Background Color

1682	A363	5c bright blue	.25	.25
1683	A363	10c lilac	.25	.25
1684	A363	15c dark blue	.25	.25
1685	A363	20c bister	1.00	1.00
1686	A363	25c dark purple	1.00	1.00
1687	A363	30c blue	1.00	1.00
1688	A363	35c red	1.00	1.00
1689	A363	40c purple	1.00	1.00
1690	A363	45c green	1.00	1.00
1691	A363	4b bright red	4.25	4.25
		Nos. 1682-1691 (10)	11.00	11.00

Sabean Inscriptions — A364

Various inscriptions with background colors of: 15c, Green. 40c, Red, vert. 45c, Orange, vert. 3b, Blue, vert.

Perf. 13¾x14, 14x13¾

2005, Aug. 20 Litho.
1692-1695 A364 Set of 4 2.00 2.00

Surma Hairstyles A365

Various hairstyles with background colors of: 15c, Red. 40c, Green. 45c, Blue. 3b, Lilac.

2005, Dec. 20 *Perf. 14x13¾*
1696-1699 A365 Set of 4 2.00 2.00

Flowers A366

Designs: 45c, Chlorophytum neghellense. 55c, Aloe bertemariae, vert. 3b, Aloe schelpei, vert.

Perf. 13¾x14, 14x13¾

2006, June 6 Litho.
1700-1702 A366 Set of 3 2.00 2.00

Ethiopian Airlines, 60th Anniv. A367

Designs: 15c, Douglas C-47A Dakota III. 40c, Douglas DC-6B Super Cloudmaster. 45c, Boeing 720-060B. 1b, Boeing 767-300ER. 2b, Boeing 787 Dreamliner.

2006, Sept. 28 *Perf. 13x13¼*
1703-1707 A367 Set of 5 2.00 2.00

Intl. Year of Deserts and Desertification — A368

Emblem and: 15c, United Nations emblem. 40c, Map of Ethiopia showing desertification vulnerability. 45c, Map of Africa showing climate types. 3b, Map of world showing climate types.

2006, Oct. 31 *Perf. 14x13½*
1708-1711 A368 Set of 4 2.00 2.00

Ethiopian Millennium A369

Panel color: 40c, Pink. 60c, Buff. 3b, Green.

2007, Nov. 15 Litho. *Perf. 13¾*
1712-1714 A369 Set of 3 2.00 2.00

Minerals A370

Designs: 40c, Gypsum. 60c, Quartz. 1b, Ambo sandstone. 2b, Feldspar.

2007, Dec. 25 *Perf. 14*
1715-1718 A370 Set of 4 2.00 2.00

Onslaught Martyrs Memorial A371

Designs: 40c, Martyrs Memorial Center. 60c, Emblem of Association for the Erection of the Martyrs Memorial Monument, vert. 3b, Woman, jail cell, gun, vert.

2008, Aug. 26 Litho. *Perf. 14*
1719-1721 A371 Set of 3 3.00 3.00

Catha Edulis — A372

Designs: 45c, Red leaves. 55c, Harvesting of plant. 3b, Plant.

2008, Sept. 8 *Perf. 13¾*
1722-1724 A372 Set of 3 3.00 3.00

Diplomatic Relations Between Ethiopia and India, 60th Anniv. A373

"60" and: 30c, Ethiopian and Indian flowers. 70c, Rock church, Lalibela, and Taj Mahal, India. 3b, Symbols of India and Ethiopia.

2008, Dec. 30 Litho. *Perf. 14x13¼*
1725-1727 A373 Set of 3 3.00 3.00

Pan-African Tsetse and Trypanosomiasis Eradication Campaign A374

Designs: 15c, Campaign emblem. 40c, Tsetse fly. 45c, Tsetse fly and blood drop, horiz. 3b, Tsetse fly, cow, silhouette of human, map of Africa, horiz.

Perf. 13½x14, 14x13½

2009, July 21 Litho.
1728-1731 A374 Set of 4 3.00 3.00

Addis Ababa Monuments — A375

Designs: 45c, Arat Kilo, Miazia 27 Square Monument. 55c, Sidist Kilo, Yekatit 12 Square Monument. 3b, Abune Petros Monument, vert.

2009, Sept. 17 Litho. *Perf. 13¾*
1732-1734 A375 Set of 3 3.00 3.00

Eradication of Rinderpest in Ethiopia A376

Designs: 15c, First laboratory in Addis Ababa where rinderpest vaccine was produced. 40c, Certificate from World Organization for Animal Health. 45c, Dead cattle. 3b, Dr. Alemework Beyene, monument to Dr. Engueda Johannes, veterinarians.

2009, Dec. 31 *Perf. 14*
1735-1738 A376 Set of 4 3.00 3.00

Pan-African Postal Union, 30th Anniv. — A377

Background color: 45c, Green. 55c, Yellow. 3b, Rose.

2010, Apr. 6 Litho. *Perf. 13¼x14*
1739-1741 A377 Set of 3 3.00 3.00

Writers — A378

Designs: No. 1742, 1b, Tsegaye Gebremedhin (1936-2006). No. 1743, 1b, Dr. Sindehu Gebru (1915-2009). No. 1744, 1b, Dr. Haddis Alemayehu (1910-2003). No. 1745, 1b, Dr. Kebede Michael (1915-98).

2010, Aug. 6 *Perf. 14*
1742-1745 A378 Set of 4 3.25 3.25

Ethiopian Red Cross, 75th Anniv. A379

75th anniversary emblem and: 45c, Ambulance, Red Cross workers and truck. 55c, Bags of blood, boy receiving transfusion. 1b, Amharic letters, vert. 2b, Red Cross building.

2010, Oct. 12 Litho. *Perf. 14*
1746-1749 A379 Set of 4 3.00 3.00

Mosques A380

Designs: 20c, Goze Mosque. 80c, Al-Nejashi Mosque. 3b, Sheh Hussein Mosque, Dire.

2011, May 24 Litho. *Perf. 14*
1750-1752 A380 Set of 3 3.00 3.00

Monasteries and Churches — A381

Designs: 35c, Zoz Amba St. George's Monastery, Gonder. 65c, Meskele Kiristonse Church, Wollo, vert. 3b, Debre Damo Abuna Aregawi Monastery, Tigrai, vert.

2011, June 9
1753-1755 A381 Set of 3 3.00 3.00

Bridges A382

Designs: 20c, Tezeke Bridge No. 3. 80c, Hidassie Bridge. 1b, Beshela River Bridge. 2b, Blue Nile Bridge.

2011, Sept. 2 Litho. *Perf. 14x13¼*
1756-1759 A382 Set of 4 3.00 3.00

Martyr's Monuments A383

Designs: 40c, Amhara Region Martyr's Monument, Bahir Dar. 60c, Oromo Martyr's Monument, Adama. 3b, Tigrai Region Martyr's Monument, Mekelle, horiz.

2011, Sept. 9 *Perf. 13¼x13, 13x13¼*
1760-1762 A383 Set of 3 3.00 3.00

Coffee Ceremony A384

Designs: 20c, Coffee pots. 80c, Preparation of coffee. 1b, Bean roasting. 2b, Pouring of coffee into cups.

2011, Dec. 20 ***Perf. 13¼x14***
1763-1766 A384 Set of 4 3.00 3.00

Medicinal Plants A385

Designs: 20c, Lippia adoensis. 35c, Artemisia absinthium. 45c, Thymus schimperi. 3b, Ocimum lamiifolium.

2012, Apr. 10 ***Perf. 14x13¼***
1767-1770 A385 Set of 4 3.00 3.00

Addis Ababa Monuments — A386

Designs: 40c, Lion of Judah Monument. 60c, Ras Mekonen Monument. 1b, Lion of Judah Monument, vert. 2b, Menelik II Monument, vert.

2012, July 5 ***Perf. 14x13¼, 13¼x14***
1771-1774 A386 Set of 4 3.00 3.00

Writers — A387

Designs: 20c, Temesgen Gebre. 80c, Hiruy Woldeslassie. 1b, Yoftahe Nigussie. 2b, Afework Gebreyesus.

2012, Sept. 7 ***Perf. 13¼x14***
1775-1778 A387 Set of 4 3.00 3.00

Addis Ababa, 125th Anniv. (in 2011) — A388

Various views of Addis Ababa: 15c, 35c, 2b, 4b.

Perf. 13¾x13½
2013, Aug. 20 **Litho.**
1779-1782 A388 Set of 4 4.00 4.00
Dated 2012.

Rift Valley Sites A393

Designs: 25c, Sulfur deposits, Dallol. 30c, Brine ponds, Dallol. 35c, Salt deposits, Dallol. 45c, Erta Ale Volcano erupting. 65c, Ash plume over Erta Ale Volcano. 4b, Erta Ale caldera.

2014, Aug. 26 **Litho.** ***Perf. 14***
1799-1804 A393 Set of 6 4.00 4.00

African Union, 50th Anniv. — A389

African Union emblem, "50," and: 10c, Year of Pan-Africanism emblem, building. 40c, Building, diff. 2b, Assembly hall. 4b, Map of Africa, doves, airplane, road, farm field.

2013, Dec. 3 **Litho.** ***Perf. 13¼x14***
1783-1786 A389 Set of 4 4.00 4.00

Ethio Telecom A390

Designs: 10c, Man holding wireless telephone console. 40c, Woman holding mobile telephone, woman using wall-mounted telephone, old dial telephone, vert. 2b, Man and woman using computer. 4b, Satellite, satellite dish, map, vert.

Perf. 14x13¼, 13¼x14
2014, May 13 **Litho.**
1787-1790 A390 Set of 4 4.00 4.00

Traditional Costumes of Southern Ethiopian People A391

Map and costumes of the: 15c, Karo. 35c, Erbore. 2b, Hamer. 4b, Daasanach.

2014, May 27 **Litho.** ***Perf. 14x13¼***
1791-1794 A391 Set of 4 4.00 4.00

Ethiopian Orthodox Tewahedo Churches and Monasteries — A392

Designs: 50c, Orra Kidanemihiret Zege (monastery), Tana Island. 1b, Kibran Gebriel (monastery), Tana Island. 2b, Debrebirihan Silassie (church), Gonder, vert. 3b, Tsion Mariam Church, Axum.

Perf. 14x13¼, 13¼x14
2014, June 12 **Litho.**
1795-1798 A392 Set of 4 4.50 4.50

University of Gondar, 60th Anniv. — A394

Designs: 5c, Millennium Steps, Referral Hospital, Health team training group on horses in 1964, new campus. 45c, President's office. 2b, Main gate. 4b, 60th anniv. emblem, vert.

2014, Dec. 2 **Litho.** ***Perf. 13½***
1805-1808 A394 Set of 4 3.50 3.50

Ethiopian Airlines A395

Designs: 15c, Boeing 777-F6N cargo plane. 35c, Boeing 777-200R passenger plane. 2b, Ethiopian Airlines Star Alliance jet. 4b, Boeing 787 Dreamliner.

2014, Dec. 25 **Litho.** ***Perf. 13x13¼***
1809-1812 A395 Set of 4 *3.50 3.50*
1812a Booklet pane of 16, 4 each #1809-1812, perf. 13x13¼ on 3 sides *15.00* —
Complete booklet, #1812a *15.00*

Ethiopian Visual Artists Association — A396

Painters and their works: 10c, Yegezu Bisrat (1926-79). 40c, Emealaf Hiruy (1907-71). 2b, Belachew Yimer (1869-1957). 4b, Agegnehu Engida (1905-50).

2015, Nov. 10 **Litho.** ***Perf. 13¼***
1813-1816 A396 Set of 4 *3.50 3.50*

Ethiopian postal officials have declared as "illegal" sheets of 9 dated "2016" depicting Ferrari automobiles, Michael Schumacher, National Hockey League stars, Soccer stars, Cristiano Ronaldo, Crocodile, Fish, Tigers, Roses, and Nudes, sheets of 9 dated "2009" depicting Pandas, sheets of 6 dated "2009" depicting Chimpanzees, sheets of 5 dated "2015" depicting Netherlands 2018 World Cup soccer players, and sheets of 4 dated "2009" depicting Pandas and Chimpanzees.

Ethiopian National Archives and Libraries Agency, 70th Anniv. — A397

Designs: 10c, Sea of Computs. 15c, Ethiopian Cultural Medicine Book. 25c, Letter from Ethiopian King Theodros to Queen Victoria of Great Britain, 19th cent. 1b, Four Gospels Bible, 14th cent. 2b, Book of Enoch, 15th cent., horiz. 3b, National Archives, horiz.

Perf. 13¼x13½, 13½x13¼
2016, Jan. 28 **Litho.**
1817-1822 A397 Set of 6 *3.50 3.50*

Palaces — A398

Designs: 10c, Emperor Menelik Palace, Fit Ber Gate. 40c, Emperor Menelik Palace, Entoto. 2b, Guenete Leul Palace and gate, Addis Ababa. 4b, National Palace, Addis Ababa.

Perf. 13¼x13½
2016, Feb. 18 **Litho.**
1823-1826 A398 Set of 4 *3.50 3.50*

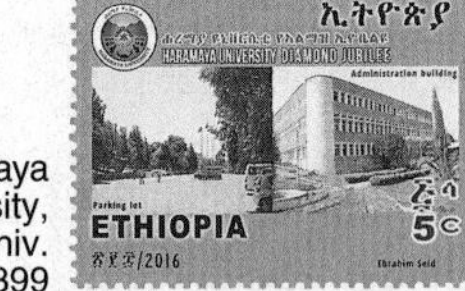

Haramaya University, 60th Anniv. A399

Designs: 5c, Parking lot and Administration building. 45c, Agricultural research plot, dairy production. 2b, Main gate. 4b, 60th anniv. emblem, vert.

Perf. 13½x13¼, 13¼x13½
2016, Apr. 21 **Litho.**
1827-1830 A399 Set of 4 *3.50 3.50*

Waterfalls A400

Designs: 10c, Habera River Falls, Bale. 40c, Sor Waterfalls, Ilu Abba Bora. 2b, Blue Nile Falls, Gojam. 4b, Ajora Falls, Wolaitta.

Perf. 13½x13¼
2016, June 14 **Litho.**
1831-1834 A400 Set of 4 *3.50 3.50*

Ministry of Urban Development and Housing — A401

Designs: 50c, Building under construction. 1b, Housing complexes and bricks. 2b, Main office. 3b, Emblem.

Perf. 13½x13¼
2016, Sept. 28 **Litho.**
1835-1838 A401 Set of 4 *3.50 3.50*

Snakes A402

Designs: 50c, Ethiopian house snake. 1b, Abyssinian house snake. 2b, Ethiopian blind snake. 3b, Ethiopian mountain adder.

2016, Oct. 27 **Litho.** ***Perf. 13½x13¼***
1839-1842 A402 Set of 4 *3.50 3.50*

Defeat of Italy In East African Campaign, 75th Anniv. — A403

Designs: No. 1843, 1b, People on gallows, statue at left, monuments, four Ethiopians in foreground, green frame. No. 1844, 1b, Four Ethiopians, monument at center, green frame. No. 1845, 1b, Ethiopians planting flag in ground, monument, train, dam, tractor, red frame. No. 1846, 1b, Eight Ethiopians, monument at center, gray green frame. No. 1847, 1b, Six Ethiopians, monument at center, blue frame. 1.50b, Two Ethiopians, monument at center, blue frame.

2016, Nov. 6 Litho. ***Perf. 13½x13¾***
1843-1848 A403 Set of 6 *4.00 4.00*

Fish A404

Map and: 5c, Labeobarbus marcophtalmus. 45c, Labeobarbus gorguari. 1b, Labeobarbus acutirostris. 5b, Labeobarbus osseensis.

Perf. 13½x13¼
2017, Mar. 21 Litho.
1849-1852 A404 Set of 4 *3.50 3.50*

Dated 2016.

Gates of Harar A405

Designs: 15c, Buda Gate. 35c, Fellana Gate. 1b, Senga Gate. 2b, Showa Gate. 3b, Erer Gate.

Perf. 13¾x13½
2017, Aug. 24 Litho.
1853-1857 A405 Set of 5 *3.50 3.50*

Commercial Bank of Ethiopia, 75th Anniv. — A406

75th anniversary emblem and: 40c, Tefera Degefe, first general manager of bank. 50c, State Bank of Ethiopia Building, horiz. 60c, Former headquarters, 1964, horiz. 2b, Bank builiding, automatic teller machine, mobile banking application on cell phone, computer and credit card reader. 3b, Bank emblem, train, ship, dam, wheat and factory.

Perf. 13¾x13¼, 13¼x13¾
2018, Apr. 26 Litho.
1858-1862 A406 Set of 5 *3.50 3.50*

Churches A407

Designs: 5c, Narga Selassie Church, Bahar Dar. 45c, Adadi Maryam Church, Oromia. 2b, Medhane Alem Kesho Church, Tigray. 4b, Maryam Korkor Church, Tigray.

2018, June 5 Litho. ***Perf. 13½x13¼***
1863-1866 A407 Set of 4 *3.50 3.50*

Ethiopia-Djibouti Electrified Railway — A408

Designs: 50c, Train. 1b, Station. 2b, Trains on multiple tracks. 3b, Construction of railway.

Perf. 13¼x13½
2018, Aug. 31 Litho.
1867-1870 A408 Set of 4 *3.50 3.50*
1870a Souvenir sheet of 4, #1867-1870 *3.50 3.50*

Diplomatic Relations Between Ethiopia and Russia, 120th Anniv. — A409

Designs: 50c, Balcha Safo (1863-1936), Ethiopian military commander, Nikolay S. Leontiev (1862-1910), Russian military officer, and Balcha Hospital. 1b, Musical instruments of Ethiopia and Russia. 2b, Castle of Fasilides, Ethiopia, and Castle of Nizhny Novgorod, Russia, horiz. 3b, Ethiopian jebena (coffee pot), and tagine and Russian Khokhloma bowls, horiz.

Perf. 14¼x14, 14x14¼
2018, Dec. 28 Litho.
1871-1874 A409 Set of 4 .45 .45

Birds A410

Designs: 40c, White-bellied go-away bird. 50c, Long-tailed nightjar. 60c, Dusky turtle dove. 2b, Black-billed barbet. 3b, Red-fronted tinker bird.

2019, Jan. 24 Litho. ***Perf. 13½***
1875-1879 A410 Set of 5 .50 .50

Animals — A411

Designs: 50c, Aardwolves. 1b, Striped hyenas. 5b, Spotted hyenas.

2019, Feb. 14 Litho. ***Perf. 14***
1880-1882 A411 Set of 3 .45 .45

SEMI-POSTAL STAMPS

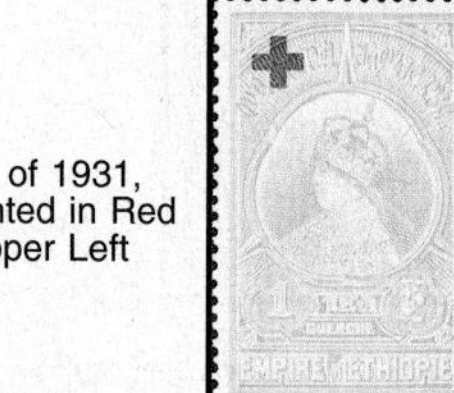

Types of 1931, Overprinted in Red at Upper Left

Perf. 12x12½, 12½x12
1936, Feb. 24 Unwmk.

B1	A27	1g light green	.60	1.00
B2	A27	2g rose	.60	1.00
B3	A25	4g blue	.60	1.00
B4	A27	8g brown	.85	1.50
B5	A25	1t purple	.85	1.50
		Nos. B1-B5 (5)	3.50	6.00

Nos. B1-B5 were sold at twice face value, the surtax going to the Red Cross.

Catalogue values for unused stamps in this section, from this point to the end of the section, are for Never Hinged items.

Nos. 289, 290, 292-294 Surcharged in Blue

Perf. 13x13½
1949, June 13 Wmk. 282

B6	A53	8c + 8c deep org	2.50	2.50
B7	A53	12c + 5c red	2.50	2.50
B8	A53	30c + 15c org brn	4.00	4.00
B9	A53	70c + 70c rose lilac	25.00	25.00
B10	A53	$1 + 80c dk car rose	32.50	32.50
		Nos. B6-B10 (5)	66.50	66.50

No. B10 exists with "80+" error.
See Nos. B16-B20.

Type A39 Surcharged in Red or Carmine

Perf. 11½
1950, May 8 Unwmk. Photo.
Various Designs
Inscribed "Croix Rouge"

B11	A39	5c + 10c brt grn	.85	1.60
B12	A39	10c + 10c brt red	1.10	1.60
B13	A39	25c + 10c brt bl	2.25	3.25
B14	A39	50c + 10c dk yel brn	6.50	5.50
B15	A39	1t + 10c brt vio	11.00	13.50
		Nos. B11-B15 (5)	21.70	25.45

The surtax was for the Red Cross.

The surcharge includes two dots which invalidate the original surtax. The original surcharge with uneven cross was red, a 1951 printing with even cross was carmine. Forgeries exist.

Nos. B6-B10 Overprinted in Black

Perf. 13x13½
1951, Nov. 17 Wmk. 282

B16	A53	8c + 8c dp org	.70	.70
B17	A53	12c + 5c red	.70	.70
B18	A53	30c + 15c org brn	1.25	1.25
B19	A53	70c + 70c rose lilac	12.00	12.00
B20	A53	$1 + 80c dk car rose	20.00	20.00
		Nos. B16-B20 (5)	34.65	34.65

No. B20 exists with "80 +" error.

Tree, Staff and Snake — SP1

Wmk. 282
1951, Nov. 25 Engr. ***Perf. 13***
Lower Panel in Red

B21	SP1	5c + 2c dp bl grn	.50	.25
B22	SP1	10c + 3c orange	.55	.30
B23	SP1	15c + 3c dp bl	.85	.50
B24	SP1	30c + 5c red	1.60	1.10
B25	SP1	50c + 7c red brn	4.50	2.75
B26	SP1	$1 + 10c purple	9.00	4.50
		Nos. B21-B26 (6)	17.00	9.40

The surtax was for anti-tuberculosis work.

1958, Dec. 1
Lower Panel in Red

B27	SP1	20c + 3c dl pur	.75	.75
B28	SP1	25c + 4c emerald	1.10	1.10
B29	SP1	35c + 5c rose vio	1.50	1.50
B30	SP1	60c + 7c vio bl	2.75	2.75
B31	SP1	65c + 7c violet	5.00	5.00
B32	SP1	80c + 9c car rose	9.00	9.00
		Nos. B27-B32 (6)	20.10	20.10
		Nos. B21-B32 (12)	37.10	29.50

The surtax was for anti-tuberculosis work.

Nos. B21-B32 were the only stamps on sale from Dec. 1-25, 1958.

Type of Regular Issue, 1955, Overprinted and Surcharged

Engr.; Cross Typo. in Red
1959, May 30 Wmk. 282

B33	A62	15c + 2c olive bister & rose red	.70	.70
B34	A62	20c + 3c vio & emer	.85	.85
B35	A62	30c + 5c rose car & grnsh bl	1.25	1.25
		Nos. B33-B35 (3)	2.80	2.80

Cent. of the Intl. Red Cross idea. Surtax for the Red Cross.

The overprint includes the cross, "RED CROSS CENTENARY" and date in two languages. The surcharge includes the date in Amharic and the new surtax. The surcharge was applied locally.

Design A39 Surcharged

Perf. 11½
1960, May 7 Photo. Unwmk.

B36	A39	5c + 1c brt green	.85	.85
B37	A39	10c + 2c brt red	1.25	1.25
B38	A39	25c + 3c brt blue	1.60	1.60
B39	A39	50c + 4c dk yel brn	2.75	2.75
B40	A39	1t + 5c brt vio	6.50	6.50
		Nos. B36-B40 (5)	12.95	12.95

25th anniversary of Ethiopian Red Cross. Forgeries exist.

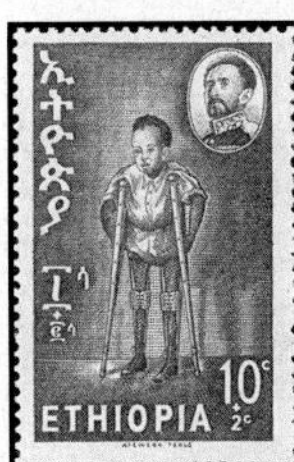

Crippled Boy on Crutches — SP2

Wmk. 282

1963, July 23 Engr. *Perf. 13½*

B41	SP2	10c + 2c ultra	.30	.30
B42	SP2	15c + 3c red	.55	.55
B43	SP2	50c + 5c brt green	1.10	1.10
B44	SP2	60c + 5c red lilac	2.25	2.25
		Nos. B41-B44 (4)	4.20	4.20

The surtax was to aid the disabled.

AIR POST STAMPS

Regular Issue of 1928 Handstamped in Violet, Red, Black or Green

Perf. 13½x14

1929, Aug. 17 Unwmk.

C1	A22	⅛m orange & lt bl	1.50	*2.00*
C2	A23	¼m ind & red org	1.50	*2.00*
C3	A22	½m gray grn & blk	1.50	*2.75*
C4	A23	1m dk car & blk	1.50	*2.75*
C5	A22	2m dk blue & blk	1.50	*2.75*
C6	A23	4m yellow & olive	1.50	*2.75*
C7	A22	8m violet & olive	1.50	*2.75*
C8	A23	1t org brn & vio	2.75	*4.25*
C9	A22	2t green & bister	4.25	*5.25*
C10	A23	3t choc & grn	4.25	*5.25*
		Nos. C1-C10 (10)	21.75	*32.50*

The overprint signifies "17 August 1929-Airplane of the Ethiopian Government." The stamps commemorate the arrival at Addis Ababa of the 1st airplane of the Ethiopian Government.

There are 3 types of the overprint: (I) 19½mm high; "colon" at right of bottom word. (II) 20mm high; same "colon." (III) 19½mm high; no "colon." Many errors exist.

Symbols of Empire, Airplane and Map — AP1

1931, June 17 Engr. *Perf. 12½*

C11	AP1	1g orange red	.25	*.50*
C12	AP1	2g ultra	.25	*.50*
C13	AP1	4g violet	.25	*.80*
C14	AP1	8g blue green	.80	*1.40*
C15	AP1	1t olive brown	1.60	*2.10*
C16	AP1	2t carmine	2.75	*8.00*
C17	AP1	3t yellow green	4.00	*9.00*
		Nos. C11-C17 (7)	9.90	*22.30*

Nos. C11 to C17 exist imperforate.

Reprints of C11 to C17 exist. Paper is thinner and gum whiter than the originals and the ink is heavy and shiny. Originals have ink that is dull and granular. Reprints usually sell at about one-third of above values.

Catalogue values for unused stamps in this section, from this point to the end of the section, are for Never Hinged items.

Nos. 250, 255 and 257 Surcharged in Black

a

b

Perf. 14x13½

1947, Mar. 20 Unwmk.

C18	A33 (a)	12c on 4c	77.50	77.50
a.		"26-12-46"	275.00	
C19	A33 (b)	50c on 25c	72.50	72.50
a.		"26-12-46"	275.00	
C20	A33 (b)	$2 on 60c	125.00	125.00
a.		"26-12-46"	340.00	
		Nos. C18-C20 (3)	275.00	275.00
		Set, hinged	175.00	

Resumption of airmail service, 12/29/46.

Franklin D. Roosevelt AP2

Design: $2, Haile Selassie.

Engraved and Photogravure

1947, May 23 *Perf. 12½*

C21	AP2	$1 dk purple & sepia	12.50	14.00
C22	AP2	$2 carmine & dp blue	22.50	24.00

Farmer Plowing AP3

Designs: 10c, 25c, Zoquala, extinct volcano. 30c, 35c, Tesissat Falls, Abai River. 65c, 70c, Amba Alaguie. $1, Sacala, source of Nile. $3, Gorgora and Dembia, Lake Tana. $5, Magdala, former capital. $10, Ras Dashan, mountain peak.

Perf. 13x13½

1947-55 Wmk. 282 Engr.

C23	AP3	8c purple brown	.30	.30
C24	AP3	10c bright green	.30	.30
C25	AP3	25c dull pur ('52)	.45	.30
C26	AP3	30c orange yellow	.85	.30
C27	AP3	35c blue ('55)	.95	.45
C28	AP3	65c purple ('55)	1.10	.80
C29	AP3	70c red	1.25	.55
C30	AP3	$1 deep blue	1.60	.80
C31	AP3	$3 rose lilac	6.50	4.25
C32	AP3	$5 red brown	13.00	5.50
C33	AP3	$10 rose violet	27.50	13.50
		Nos. C23-C33 (11)	53.80	27.05

For overprints see Nos. C64-C70.

UPU Monument, Bern — AP4

1950, Apr. 3 Unwmk. *Perf. 12½*

C34	AP4	5c green & red	1.00	.50
C35	AP4	15c dk sl grn & car	1.50	1.10
C36	AP4	25c org yel & grn	2.75	1.10
C37	AP4	50c carmine & ultra	4.50	3.25
		Nos. C34-C37 (4)	9.75	5.95

75th anniv. of the UPU.

No. C34 exists in the colors of Nos. C35-C37. These are considered to be trial color proofs.

Convair Plane over Mountains AP5

Engraved and Lithographed

1955, Dec. 30 Unwmk. *Perf. 12½*

Center Multicolored

C38	AP5	10c gray green	1.25	.30
C39	AP5	15c carmine	1.60	.80
C40	AP5	20c violet	2.50	1.25
		Nos. C38-C40 (3)	5.35	2.35

10th anniversary of Ethiopian Airlines.

Promulgating the Constitution — AP6

Perf. 14x13½

1956, July 16 Engr. Wmk. 282

C41	AP6	10c redsh brn & ultra	.60	.70
C42	AP6	15c dk car rose & ol grn	.95	1.00
C43	AP6	20c blue & org red	1.25	1.00
C44	AP6	25c purple & green	1.40	1.60
C45	AP6	30c dk grn & red brn	2.40	2.50
		Nos. C41-C45 (5)	6.60	6.80

25th anniversary of the constitution.

Aksum AP7

Ancient Capitals: 10c, Lalibela. 15c, Gondar. 20c, Mekele. 25c, Ankober.

1957, Feb. 7 *Perf. 14*

Centers in Green

C46	AP7	5c red brown	.75	.40
C47	AP7	10c rose carmine	.75	.40
C48	AP7	15c red orange	.90	.50
C49	AP7	20c ultramarine	1.40	.70
C50	AP7	25c claret	2.10	1.00
		Nos. C46-C50 (5)	5.90	3.00

Amharic "A" — AP8

Designs: Various Amharic characters and views of Addis Ababa. The characters, arranged by values, spell Addis Ababa.

1957, Feb. 14 Engr.

Amharic Letters in Scarlet

C51	AP8	5c ultra, *sal pink*	.35	.35
C52	AP8	10c ol grn, *pink*	.35	.35
C53	AP8	15c dl pur, *yel*	.55	.35
C54	AP8	20c grn, *buff*	.90	.40
C55	AP8	25c plum, *pale bl*	2.50	.55
C56	AP8	30c red, *pale grn*	1.75	.60
		Nos. C51-C56 (6)	6.40	2.60

70th anniversary of Addis Ababa.

Map, Rock Church at Lalibela and Obelisk AP9

1958, Apr. 15 Wmk. 282 *Perf. 13½*

C57	AP9	10c green	.50	.50
C58	AP9	20c rose red	1.10	1.10
C59	AP9	30c bright blue	1.75	1.10
		Nos. C57-C59 (3)	3.35	2.70

Conf. of Independent African States, Accra, Apr. 15-22.

Map of Africa and UN Emblem AP10

1958, Dec. 29 *Perf. 13*

C60	AP10	5c emerald	.25	.25
C61	AP10	20c carmine rose	.55	.25
C62	AP10	25c ultramarine	.75	.55
C63	AP10	50c pale purple	1.50	.75
		Nos. C60-C63 (4)	3.05	1.80

1st session of the UN Economic Conf. for Africa, opened in Addis Ababa Dec. 29.

Nos. C23-C29 Overprinted

Perf. 13x13½

1959, Aug. 16 Engr. Wmk. 282

C64	AP3	8c purple brown	.50	.30
C65	AP3	10c brt green	.70	.35
C66	AP3	25c dull purple	1.05	.40
C67	AP3	30c orange yellow	1.15	.60
C68	AP3	35c blue	1.40	.65
C69	AP3	65c purple	2.25	1.00
C70	AP3	70c red	2.75	1.25
		Nos. C64-C70 (7)	9.80	4.55

30th anniv. of Ethiopian airmail service.

Ethiopian Soldier and Map of Congo — AP11

Perf. 11½

1962, July 23 Unwmk. Photo.

Granite Paper

C71	AP11	15c org, bl, brn & grn	.30	.25
C72	AP11	50c pur, bl, brn & grn	.90	.50
C73	AP11	60c red, bl, brn & grn	1.60	.65
		Nos. C71-C73 (3)	2.80	1.40

2nd anniv. of the Ethiopian contingent of the UN forces in the Congo and in honor of the 70th birthday of Emperor Haile Selassie.

Globe with Map of Africa — AP12

1963, May 22 **Granite Paper**

C74 AP12 10c magenta & blk .60 .30
C75 AP12 40c emerald & blk 1.10 .55
C76 AP12 60c blue & blk 1.75 .85
Nos. C74-C76 (3) 3.45 1.70

Conf. of African heads of state for African Unity, Addis Ababa.

Bird Type of Regular Issue

Birds: 10c, Black-headed forest oriole. 15c, Broad-tailed paradise whydah, vert. 20c, Lammergeier, vert. 50c, White-checked touraco. 80c, Purple indigo bird.

1963, Sept. 12 ***Perf. 11½***
Granite Paper

C77 A74 10c multicolored .75 .25
C78 A74 15c multicolored .90 .25
C79 A74 20c blue, blk & ocher 1.75 .60
C80 A74 50c lemon & multi 2.60 1.10
C81 A74 80c ultra, blk & brn 5.00 1.90
Nos. C77-C81 (5) 11.00 4.10

Swimming AP13

Sport: 10c, Basketball, vert. 15c, Javelin. 80c, Soccer game in stadium.

Perf. 14x13½

1964, Sept. 15 **Litho.** **Unwmk.**

C82 AP13 5c multicolored .30 .25
C83 AP13 10c multicolored .40 .25
C84 AP13 15c multicolored .85 .55
C85 AP13 80c multicolored 2.25 1.10
Nos. C82-C85 (4) 3.80 2.15

18th Olympic Games, Tokyo, Oct. 10-25.

Queen Elizabeth II and Emperor Haile Selassie — AP14

1965, Feb. 1 **Photo.** ***Perf. 11½***
Granite Paper

C86 AP14 5c multicolored .30 .30
C87 AP14 35c multicolored .85 .55
C88 AP14 60c multicolored 1.10 .85
Nos. C86-C88 (3) 2.25 1.70

Visit of Queen Elizabeth II, Feb. 1-8.

Koka Dam and Power Plant — AP15

Designs: 15c, Sugar cane field. 50c, Blue Nile Bridge. 60c, Gondar castles. 80c, Coffee tree. $1, Cattle at water hole. $3, Camels at well. $5, Ethiopian Air Lines jet plane.

1965, July 19 **Unwmk.** ***Perf. 11½***
Granite Paper
Portrait in Black

C89 AP15 15c vio brn & buff .30 .30
C90 AP15 40c vio bl & lt bl .50 .40
C91 AP15 50c grn & lt bl .80 .45
C92 AP15 60c claret & yel 1.30 .70
C93 AP15 80c grn, yel & red 1.75 .80
C94 AP15 $1 brn & lt bl 1.90 .95
C95 AP15 $3 claret & pink 6.50 2.40
C96 AP15 $5 ultra & lt bl 14.00 4.50
Nos. C89-C96 (8) 27.05 10.50

Bird Type of Regular Issue

Birds: 10c, White-collared kingfisher. 15c, Blue-breasted bee-eater. 25c, African paradise flycatcher. 40c, Village weaver. 60c, White-collared pigeon.

1966, Feb. 15 **Photo.** ***Perf. 11½***
Granite Paper

C97 A74 10c dull yel & multi .85 .25
C98 A74 15c lt blue & multi .85 .25
C99 A74 25c gray & multi 1.75 .55
C100 A74 40c pink & multi 3.50 .85
C101 A74 60c multicolored 4.50 1.10
Nos. C97-C101 (5) 11.45 3.00

Black Rhinoceros — AP16

Animals: 10c, Leopard. 20c, Black-and-white colobus (monkey). 30c, Mountain nyala. 60c, Nubian ibex.

1966, June 20 **Litho.** ***Perf. 13***

C102 AP16 5c dp grn, blk & gray .55 .30
C103 AP16 10c grn, blk & ocher .55 .55
C104 AP16 20c cit, blk & grn 1.10 .55
C105 AP16 30c yel grn, blk & ocher 1.75 .85
C106 AP16 60c yel grn, blk & dk brn 4.50 1.60
Nos. C102-C106 (5) 8.45 3.85

Bird Type of Regular Issue

Birds: 10c, Blue-winged goose, vert. 15c, Yellow-billed duck. 20c, Wattled ibis. 25c, Striped swallow. 40c, Black-winged lovebird, vert.

1967, Sept. 29 **Photo.** ***Perf. 11½***
Granite Paper

C107 A74 10c lt ultra & multi .55 .25
C108 A74 15c green & multi .85 .25
C109 A74 20c yellow & multi 1.10 .55
C110 A74 25c salmon & multi 2.25 .55
C111 A74 40c pink & multi 4.50 1.10
Nos. C107-C111 (5) 9.25 2.70

SPECIAL DELIVERY STAMPS

Catalogue values for unused stamps in this section are for Never Hinged items.

Motorcycle Messenger — SD1

Addis Ababa Post Office SD2

Unwmk.

1947, Apr. 24 **Engr.** ***Perf. 13***

E1 SD1 30c orange brown 5.00 1.25
E2 SD2 50c blue 9.00 3.50

1954-62 **Wmk. 282**

E3 SD1 30c org brown ('62) 4.50 1.25
E4 SD2 50c blue 5.50 1.25

POSTAGE DUE STAMPS

Very Fine examples of Nos. J1-J42 will have perforations touching the design on one or more sides.

Nos. 1-4 and unissued values Overprinted

Perf. 14x13½

1896, June 10 **Unwmk.**
Black Overprint

J1 A1 ¼g green 1.45
J2 A1 ½g red 1.45
J3 A1 4g lilac brown 1.00
a. Without overprint 1.00
J4 A1 8g violet 1.00
a. Without overprint 1.00

Red Overprint

J5 A1 1g blue 1.45
J6 A1 2g dark brown 1.45
J7 A1 16g black 1.00
a. Without overprint 1.00
Nos. J1-J7 (7) 8.80

Nos. J1-J7 were not issued. Forgeries exist.

Nos. 1-7 Handstamped in Various Colors

a

1905, Apr.

J8 A1 (a) ¼g green 55.00 55.00
J9 A1 (a) ½g red 55.00 55.00
J10 A1 (a) 1g blue 55.00 55.00
J11 A1 (a) 2g dk brown 55.00 55.00
J12 A2 (a) 4g lilac brown 55.00 55.00
J13 A2 (a) 8g violet 55.00 55.00
J14 A2 (a) 16g black 55.00 55.00
Nos. J8-J14 (7) 385.00 385.00

b

1905, Aug.

J15 A1 (b) ¼g green 55.00 55.00
J16 A1 (b) ½g red 55.00 55.00
J17 A1 (b) 1g blue 55.00 55.00
J18 A1 (b) 2g dark brown 55.00 55.00
J19 A2 (b) 4g lilac brown 55.00 55.00
J20 A2 (b) 8g violet 55.00 55.00
J21 A2 (b) 16g black 55.00 55.00
Nos. J15-J21 (7) 385.00 385.00

Excellent forgeries of Nos. J8-J42 exist.

Nos. 1-7 Handstamped in Blue or Violet

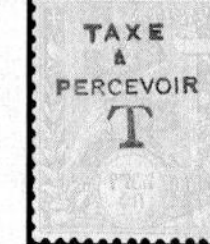

1905, Sept.

J22 A1 ¼g green 14.50 14.50
J23 A1 ½g red 14.50 14.50
J24 A1 1g blue 14.50 14.50
J25 A1 2g dark brown 14.50 14.50
J26 A2 4g lilac brown 14.50 14.50
J27 A2 8g violet 21.00 21.00
J28 A2 16g black 25.00 25.00
Nos. J22-J28 (7) 118.50 118.50

Nos. J22-J27 exist with inverted overprint, also No. J22 with double overprint.
Forgeries exist.

With Additional Surcharge of Value Handstamped as on Nos. 71-77

1907, July 1

J29 A1 (e) ¼ on ¼g grn 14.00 14.00
J30 A1 (e) ½ on ½g red 14.00 14.00
J31 A1 (f) 1 on 1g blue 14.00 14.00
J32 A1 (f) 2 on 2g dk brown 14.00 14.00
J33 A2 (f) 4 on 4g lilac brn 14.00 14.00
J34 A2 (f) 8 on 8g violet 14.00 14.00
J35 A2 (f) 16 on 16g blk 22.50 22.50
Nos. J29-J35 (7) 106.50 106.50

Nos. J30-J35 exist with inverted surcharge. Nos. J30, J33-J35 exist with double surcharge.

Nos. 1-7 Handstamped in Black

1908, Dec. 1

J36 A1 ¼g green 1.40 1.25
J37 A1 ½g red 1.40 1.25
J38 A1 1g blue 1.40 1.25
J39 A1 2g dark brown 1.75 1.50
J40 A2 4g lilac brown 2.50 2.50
J41 A2 8g violet 5.50 6.25
J42 A2 16g black 17.50 20.00
Nos. J36-J42 (7) 31.45 34.00

Nos. J36 to J42 exist with inverted overprint and Nos. J36, J37, J38 and J40 with double overprint.
Forgeries of Nos. J36-J56 exist.

Same Handstamp on Nos. 87-93

1912, Dec. 1 ***Perf. 11½***

J43 A3 ¼g blue green 1.75 1.25
J44 A3 ½g rose 1.75 1.50

1913, July 1

J45 A3 1g green & org 6.00 4.25
J46 A4 2g blue 7.00 6.00
J47 A4 4g green & car 11.00 7.00
J48 A5 8g ver & dp grn 14.00 11.00
J49 A5 16g ver & car 35.00 27.50
Nos. J43-J49 (7) 76.50 58.50

Nos. J43-J49, all exist with inverted, double and double, one inverted overprint.

Same Handstamp on Nos. 120-124 in Blue Black

1925-27 ***Perf. 11½***

J50 A6 ⅛g violet & brn *18.00 18.00*
J51 A6 ¼g bl grn & db *18.00 18.00*
J52 A6 ½g scar & ol grn *20.00 20.00*
J53 A9 1g rose lil & gray grn *20.00 20.00*
J54 A9 2g dp ultra & fawn *20.00 20.00*
Nos. J50-J54 (5) *96.00 96.00*

Same Handstamp on Nos. 110, 112

1917 (?)

J55 A3 (i) 1g green & org *30.00 30.00*
J56 A4 (j) 2g blue *30.00 30.00*

The status of Nos. J55-J56 is questioned.

Catalogue values for unused stamps in this section, from this point to the end of the section, are for Never Hinged items.

D2

Perf. 11½

1951, Apr. 2 **Unwmk.** **Litho.**

J57 D2 1c emerald .35 .25
J58 D2 5c rose red .75 .25
J59 D2 10c violet 1.40 .55
J60 D2 20c ocher 2.00 1.25
J61 D2 50c bright ultra 3.75 2.75
J62 D2 $1 rose lilac 7.75 3.75
Nos. J57-J62 (6) 16.00 8.80

Nos. J57-J62 were reissued in 1968 on slightly yellowish paper.

OCCUPATION STAMPS

Issued under Italian Occupation

100 Centesimi = 1 Lira

OS1

Emperor Victor Emmanuel III — OS2

1936 **Wmk. 140** ***Perf. 14***

N1 OS1 10c org brn 16.00 9.50
N2 OS1 20c purple 14.50 4.00
N3 OS2 25c dark green 9.50 .80

N4 OS2 30c dark brown 9.50 1.60
N5 OS2 50c rose car 4.00 .40
N6 OS1 75c deep orange 36.00 8.00
N7 OS1 1.25 l deep blue 36.00 12.00
Nos. N1-N7 (7) 125.50 36.30
Set, never hinged 300.00

Issued: Nos. N3-N5, May 22; others Dec. 5.
For later issues see Italian East Africa.

FALKLAND ISLANDS

ˈfol-klənd ˈī-lənds

LOCATION — A group of islands about 300 miles east of the Straits of Magellan at the southern limit of South America
GOVT. — British Crown Colony
AREA — 4,700 sq. mi.
POP. — 2,607 (1996)
CAPITAL — Stanley

Dependencies of the Falklands are South Georgia and South Sandwich. In March 1962, three other dependencies — South Shetland Islands, South Orkneys and Graham Land—became the new separate colony of British Antarctic Territory. In 1985 South Georgia and the South Sandwich Islands became a separate colony.

12 Pence = 1 Shilling
20 Shillings = 1 Pound
100 Pence = 1 Pound (1971)

Catalogue values for unused stamps in this country are for Never Hinged items, beginning with Scott 97 in the regular postage section, Scott B1 in the semi-postal section, Scott J1 in the postage due section, Scott 1L1 in Falkland Island Dependencies regular issues, Scott 1LB1 in Falkland Island Dependencies semi-postals, and Scott 2L1, 3L1, 4L1, 5L1 in the Issues for Separate Islands.

Values for unused stamps are for examples with original gum as defined in the catalogue introduction.

Nos. 1-4, 7-8, and some printings of Nos. 5-6, exist with straight edges on one or two sides, being the imperforate margins of the sheets. This occurs in 24 out of 60 stamps. Catalogue values are for stamps with perforations on all sides.

Queen Victoria — A1

1878-79 Unwmk. Engr. *Perf. 14*
1 A1 1p claret 850.00 500.00
2 A1 4p dark gray ('79) 1,400. 200.00
3 A1 6p green 125.00 85.00
4 A1 1sh bister brown 85.00 80.00

1883-95 Wmk. 2
5 A1 1p brt claret ('94) 130.00 95.00
a. 1p claret 425.00 190.00
b. Horiz. pair, imperf. vert. *90,000.*
c. 1p red brown ('91) 375.00 95.00
d. Diag. half of #5c used as ½p on cover *4,600.*
6 A1 4p ol gray ('95) 16.00 27.50
a. 4p gray black 875.00 100.00
b. 4p olive gray black ('89) 200.00 65.00
c. 4p brownish black ('94) 1,300. 400.00

No. 6c has watermark reversed.
For surcharge see No. 19E.

1886 Wmk. 2 Sideways
7 A1 1p claret 95.00 65.00
a. 1p brownish claret 125.00 80.00
b. Diagonal half of #7a used as ½p on cover *4,250.*
8 A1 4p olive gray 525.00 60.00
a. 4p pale gray black 850.00 90.00

For surcharge see No. 19.

1891-1902 Wmk. 2
9 A1 ½p green ('92) 19.00 18.00
a. ½p blue green 30.00 29.00
10 A1 ½p yel green ('99) 3.75 3.50
11 A1 1p orange brown 130.00 85.00
a. Diagonal half used as ½p on cover *4,250.*
11B A1 1p pale red ('99) 9.00 3.50
12 A1 1p org red ('02) 17.50 4.75
a. 1p Venetian red ('95) 32.50 20.00
13 A1 2p magenta ('96) 7.00 14.00
14 A1 2½p deep blue ('94) 275.00 160.00
15 A1 2½p ultra ('94) 50.00 14.00
a. 2½p pale ultra ('98) 70.00 20.00
b. 2½p dull blue 350.00 35.00
c. 2½p deep ultra ('01) 50.00 42.50
d. 2½p pale chalky ultra 275.00 60.00
16 A1 6p yellow ('96) 55.00 52.50
a. 6p orange ('92) 325.00 225.00
17 A1 9p ver ('95) 60.00 60.00
a. 9p salmon ('96) 65.00 65.00
18 A1 1sh gray brn ('95) 80.00 65.00
a. 1sh bis brn ('96) 75.00 55.00
Nos. 9-18 (11) 706.25 480.25

Nos. 7 and 5a Surcharged in Black

1891 Wmk. 2 Sideways
19 A1 ½p on half of 1p, #7 725.00 360.00
d. Unsevered pair 4,000. 1,600.

Wmk. 2
19E A1 ½p on half of 1p, #5a 825.00 325.00
f. Unsevered pair 5,000. 1,800.

Genuine used bisects should be canceled with a segmented circular cork cancel. Any other cancel must be linked by date to known mail ship departures. This surcharge exists on "souvenir" bisects, including examples of No. 11, and can be found inverted, double and sideways.

A3

A4

1898 Wmk. 1
20 A3 2sh6p dark blue 290.00 290.00
21 A4 5sh brown red 260.00 260.00

A5

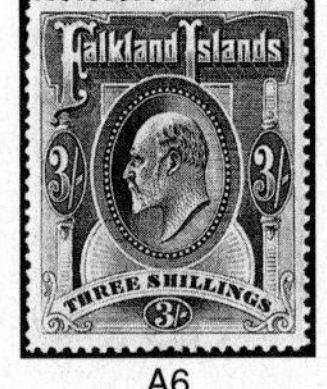
A6

King Edward VII

1904-07 Wmk. 3 *Perf. 14*
22 A5 ½p yellow green 9.00 1.75
23 A5 1p red, wmk. sideways ('07) 1.50 *4.50*
a. Wmk. upright ('04) 17.00 1.75
24 A5 2p dull vio ('04) 25.00 *24.00*
25 A5 2½p ultramarine 35.00 10.00
a. 2½p deep blue 300.00 200.00
26 A5 6p orange ('05) 50.00 *57.50*
27 A5 1sh bis brn ('05) 50.00 40.00
28 A6 3sh gray green 180.00 160.00
29 A6 5sh dull red ('05) 240.00 160.00
Nos. 22-29 (8) 590.50 457.75

A7

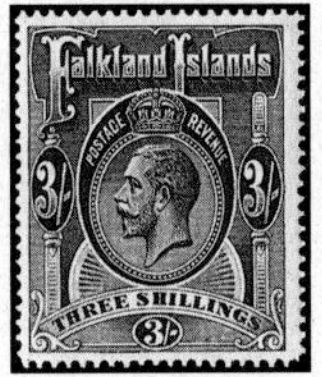
A8

King George V

1912-14 *Perf. 13¾x14, 14 (#36-40)*
30 A7 ½p yel grn 3.00 3.75
31 A7 1p red 5.50 2.75
32 A7 2p brn vio 30.00 24.00
33 A7 2½p deep ultra 27.50 25.00
34 A7 6p orange 17.50 *22.50*
35 A7 1sh bis brn 40.00 37.50
36 A8 3sh dark green 100.00 100.00
37 A8 5sh brown red 120.00 120.00
38 A8 5sh plum ('14) 300.00 300.00
39 A8 10sh red, *green* 200.00 *275.00*
40 A8 £1 black, *red* 550.00 *600.00*
Nos. 30-40 (11) 1,394. *1,511.*

For overprints see Nos. MR1-MR3.

1921-29 Wmk. 4 *Perf. 14*
41 A7 ½p yellow green 3.50 *4.50*
42 A7 1p red ('24) 6.00 2.10
43 A7 2p brown vio ('23) 26.00 8.50
44 A7 2½p dark blue 24.00 *20.00*
a. 2½p Prussian blue ('29) *375.00* *550.00*
45 A7 2½p vio, *yel* ('23) 6.00 *42.50*
46 A7 6p orange ('25) 11.00 *45.00*
47 A7 1sh bister brown 24.00 *57.50*
48 A8 3sh dk green ('23) 100.00 *190.00*
Nos. 41-48 (8) 200.50 *370.10*

Some specialists call into question No. 44a. The editors would like to see authenticated evidence of its existence.

No. 43 Surcharged

1928
52 A7 2½p on 2p brn vio *1,300.* *1,400.*
a. Double surcharge *60,000.*

Beware of forged surcharges.

King George V — A9

1929-31 *Perf. 14*
54 A9 ½p green 1.40 *4.25*
55 A9 1p scarlet 4.50 .90
56 A9 2p gray 6.00 3.75
57 A9 2½p blue 6.00 2.50
58 A9 4p deep orange 23.00 15.00
59 A9 6p brown violet 24.00 19.00
60 A9 1sh black, *green* 32.50 *37.50*
a. 1sh black, *emerald* *27.50* *37.50*
61 A9 2sh6p red, *blue* 70.00 70.00
62 A9 5sh green, *yel* 105.00 *120.00*
63 A9 10sh red, *green* 225.00 *275.00*

Wmk. 3
64 A9 £1 black, *red* 350.00 425.00
Nos. 54-64 (11) 847.40 972.90

Issue dates: 4p, 1931, others, Sept. 2.

Romney Marsh Ram — A10

Iceberg A11

Whaling Ship — A12

Port Louis A13

Map of the Islands A14

South Georgia A15

Blue Whale A16

Government House A17

Battle Memorial — A18

King Penguin — A19

Coat of Arms — A20

King George V — A21

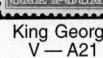

1933, Jan. 2 Wmk. 4 *Perf. 12*
65 A10 ½p grn & blk 4.00 *13.00*
66 A11 1p dl red & blk 3.75 2.75
67 A12 1½p lt bl & blk 21.00 *27.50*
68 A13 2p ol brn & blk 17.50 *32.50*
69 A14 3p dl vio & blk 28.00 *35.00*
70 A15 4p org & blk 26.00 *28.00*
71 A16 6p gray & blk 75.00 *95.00*
72 A17 1sh ol grn & blk 75.00 *100.00*
73 A18 2sh6p dp vio & blk 250.00 *400.00*
74 A19 5sh yel & blk 950.00 *1,500.*
a. 5sh yel org & blk 3,250. *3,750.*
75 A20 10sh lt brn & blk 850.00 *1,500.*
76 A21 £1 rose & blk 2,500. *3,500.*
Nos. 65-76 (12) 4,800. *7,234.*

Cent. of the permanent occupation of the islands as a British colony.

Common Design Types pictured following the introduction.

Silver Jubilee Issue

Common Design Type

1935, May 7 *Perf. 11x12*
77 CD301 1p car & blue 3.50 .50
78 CD301 2½p ultra & brn 12.50 2.25
79 CD301 4p indigo & grn 24.00 8.00
80 CD301 1sh brn vio & ind 15.00 4.00
Nos. 77-80 (4) 55.00 14.75
Set, never hinged 75.00
Set , Ovptd. "SPECIMEN" *500.00*

Coronation Issue
Common Design Type

1937, May 12 ***Perf. 11x11½***
81 CD302 ½p deep green .25 .25
82 CD302 1p dark carmine .75 *.55*
83 CD302 2½p deep ultra 1.90 *1.50*
Nos. 81-83 (3) 2.90 *2.30*
Set, never hinged 4.00
Set , Ovptd. "SPECIMEN" *450.00*

Whale Jawbones (Centennial Monument) — A22

Nos. 85, 86A, Black-necked swan. Nos. 85B, 86, Battle memorial. 2½p, 3p, Flock of sheep. 4p, Upland goose. 6p, R.R.S. "Discovery II." 9p, R.R.S. "William Scoresby." 1sh, Mt. Sugar Top. 1sh3p, Turkey vultures. 2sh6p, Gentoo penguins. 5sh, Sea lions. 10sh, Deception Island. £1, Arms of Colony.

1938-46 ***Perf. 12***
84 A22 ½p green & blk .25 .75
85 A22 1p red & black 2.50 1.00
a. 1p rose carmine & black 22.50 1.00
85B A22 1p dk vio & blk ('41) 2.00 2.00
86 A22 2p dk vio & blk 1.30 1.00
86A A22 2p rose car & black ('41) 1.40 *4.50*
87 A22 2½p ultra & blk 1.00 .50
87A A22 3p blue & blk ('41) 5.50 *8.50*
c. 3p dp blue & blk 12.50 4.50
88 A22 4p rose vio & black 2.75 2.00
89 A22 6p sepia & blk 7.50 4.25
90 A22 9p sl bl & blk 15.00 6.00
91 A22 1sh lt dl blue 30.00 19.00
92 A22 1sh3p car & blk 2.00 1.60
93 A22 2sh6p gray black 40.00 22.50
94 A22 5sh org brn & ultra 75.00 95.00
a. 5sh yel brown & indigo 650.00 150.00
95 A22 10sh org & blk 100.00 65.00
96 A22 £1 dk vio & blk 75.00 75.00
Nos. 84-96 (16) 361.20 308.60
Set, never hinged 600.00
Set , perf. "SPECIMEN" *2,500.*

Issued: Nos. 85B, 86A, 3p, 7/14/41; 1sh3p, 12/10/46; No. 94a, 1942; others, 1/3/38.

See Nos. 101-102. For overprints see Nos. 2L1-2L8, 3L1-3L8, 4L1-4L8.

Catalogue values for unused stamps in this section, from this point to the end of the section, are for Never Hinged items.

Peace Issue
Common Design Type
Perf. 13½x14

1946, Oct. 7 **Engr.** **Wmk. 4**
97 CD303 1p purple .35 *.80*
98 CD303 3p deep blue .55 .55

Silver Wedding Issue
Common Design Types

1948, Nov. 1 **Photo.** ***Perf. 14x14½***
99 CD304 2½p bright ultra 2.10 1.10

Engr.; Name Typo.
Perf. 11½x11
100 CD305 £1 purple 110.00 75.00

Types of 1938-46

2½p, Upland goose. 6p, R.R.S. "Discovery II."

Perf. 12
1949, June 15 **Engr.** **Wmk. 4**
101 A22 2½p dp blue & black 7.50 *8.50*
102 A22 6p gray black 6.75 5.50

UPU Issue
Common Design Types
Engr.; Name Typo. on 3p, 1sh3p

1949, Oct. 10 ***Perf. 13½, 11x11½***
103 CD306 1p violet 1.75 1.10
104 CD307 3p indigo 5.00 5.00
105 CD308 1sh3p green 3.50 2.50
106 CD309 2sh blue 3.75 8.50
Nos. 103-106 (4) 14.00 17.10

Sheep A35

Arms of the Colony — A36

Designs: 1p, R.M.S. Fitzroy. 2p Upland goose. 2½p, Map. 4p, Auster plane. 6p, M.S.S. John Biscoe. 9p, "Two Sisters" peaks. 1sh, Gentoo penguins. 1sh 3p, Kelp goose and gander. 2sh 6p, Sheep shearing. 5sh, Battle memorial. 10sh, Sea lion and clapmatch. £1, Hulk of "Great Britain."

Perf. 13½x13, 13x13½
1952, Jan. 2 **Engr.** **Wmk. 4**
107 A35 ½p green 1.25 *1.00*
108 A35 1p red 2.40 .55
109 A35 2p violet 4.50 *3.00*
110 A35 2½p ultra & blk 2.00 .70
111 A36 3p deep ultra 2.25 *1.10*
112 A35 4p claret 12.50 1.75
113 A35 6p yellow brn 12.00 1.10
114 A35 9p orange yel 9.00 2.25
115 A36 1sh black 24.00 1.10
116 A35 1sh3p red orange 18.00 *7.00*
117 A36 2sh6p olive 22.50 *12.50*
118 A36 5sh red violet 20.00 *11.00*
119 A35 10sh gray 30.00 *20.00*
120 A35 £1 black 40.00 *27.00*
Nos. 107-120 (14) 200.40 *90.05*

Coronation Issue
Common Design Type

1953, June 4 ***Perf. 13½x13***
121 CD312 1p car & black .90 *1.50*

Types of 1952 with Portrait of Queen Elizabeth II

1955-57 ***Perf. 13½x13, 13x13½***
122 A35 ½p green ('57) 1.00 *1.50*
123 A35 1p red ('57) 1.25 1.25
124 A35 2p violet ('56) 3.25 *4.75*
125 A35 6p light brown 9.00 .70
126 A35 9p ocher ('57) 10.50 *17.00*
127 A36 1sh black 12.00 2.50
Nos. 122-127 (6) 37.00 *27.70*

Marsh Starling A37

Birds: ½p, Falkland Islands Thrush. 1p, Dominican gull. 2p, Gentoo penguins. 3p, Upland geese. 4p, Steamer ducks. 5½p, Rock-hopper penguin. 6p, black-browed albatross. 9p, Silver grebe. 1sh, Pied oystercatchers. 1sh3p, Yellow-billed teal. 2sh, Kelp geese, 5sh, King shag. 10sh, Guadelupe caracara. £1, Black-necked swan.

Perf. 13½x13
1960, Feb. 10 **Engr.** **Wmk. 314**
Center in Black
128 A37 ½p green 5.00 2.25
a. Wmk. sideways ('66) .45 .40
129 A37 1p rose red 3.00 2.00
130 A37 2p blue 4.50 1.25
131 A37 2½p bister brn 2.50 1.00
132 A37 3p olive 1.25 .50
133 A37 4p rose car 1.50 1.25
134 A37 5½p violet 3.25 2.50
135 A37 6p sepia 3.50 .30
136 A37 9p orange 2.50 1.25
137 A37 1sh dull purple 1.25 .40
138 A37 1sh3p ultra 12.50 *14.00*
139 A37 2sh brown car 30.00 2.50
140 A37 5sh grnsh blue 27.50 11.00
141 A37 10sh rose lilac 42.60 22.00
142 A37 £1 yellow org 45.00 27.00
Nos. 128-142 (15) 185.85 89.20

Morse Key — A38

1962, Oct. 5 **Photo.** ***Perf. 11½x11***
143 A38 6p dp org & dk red .85 .50
144 A38 1sh brt ol grn & dp green .95 .50
145 A38 2sh brt ultra & violet 1.25 *1.75*
Nos. 143-145 (3) 3.05 2.75

Falkland Islands radio station, 50th anniv.

Freedom from Hunger Issue
Common Design Type

1963, June 4 ***Perf. 14x14½***
146 CD314 1sh ultramarine 10.50 2.50

Red Cross Centenary Issue
Common Design Type
Wmk. 314

1963, Sept.2 **Litho.** ***Perf. 13***
147 CD315 1p black & red 2.00 .75
148 CD315 1sh ultra & red 16.00 4.75

Shakespeare Issue
Common Design Type

1964, Apr. 23 **Photo.** ***Perf. 14x14½***
149 CD316 6p black 1.60 .50

H.M.S. Glasgow A39

6p, H.M.S. Kent. 1sh, H.M.S. Invincible. 2sh, Falkland Islands Battle Memorial, vert.

1964, Dec. 8 **Engr.** ***Perf. 13***
150 A39 2½p ver & black 9.00 3.75
151 A39 6p blue & black .55 .30
a. "Glasgow" vignette *30,000.*
152 A39 1sh carmine & blk .55 *1.00*

Perf. 13x14
153 A39 2sh dk blue & blk .55 .75
Nos. 150-153 (4) 10.65 5.80

Battle of the Falkland Islands between the British and German navies, 50th anniv.

ITU Issue
Common Design Type
Perf. 11x11½

1965, May 26 **Litho.** **Wmk. 314**
154 CD317 1p blue & dl dk bl .50 .40
155 CD317 2sh lilac & dl yel 6.25 2.75

Intl. Cooperation Year Issue
Common Design Type

1965, Oct. 25 ***Perf. 14½***
156 CD318 1p blue grn & claret 1.25 .40
157 CD318 1sh lt violet & grn 4.75 1.25

Churchill Memorial Issue
Common Design Type

1966, Jan. 24 **Photo.** ***Perf. 14***
Design in Black, Gold and Carmine Rose
158 CD319 ½p bright blue .75 *2.25*
159 CD319 1p green 2.00 .30
160 CD319 1sh brown 5.50 3.00
161 CD319 2sh violet 4.50 4.00
Nos. 158-161 (4) 12.75 9.55

Human Rights Flame and Globe A40

Perf. 14x14½
1968, July 4 **Photo.** **Wmk. 314**
162 A40 2p brt rose & multi .40 .25
163 A40 6p brt green & multi .45 .25
164 A40 1sh orange & multi .55 .30
165 A40 2sh ultra & multi .65 .35
Nos. 162-165 (4) 2.05 1.15

International Human Rights Year.

Dusty Miller — A41

Falkland Islands flora: 1½p, Pig vine, horiz. 2p, Pale maiden. 3p, Dog orchid. 3½p, Sea cabbage, horiz. 4½p, Vanilla daisy. 5½p, Arrowleaf marigold, horiz. 6p, Diddle-dee, horiz. 1sh, Scurvy grass, horiz. 1sh6p, Prickly burr. 2sh, Fachine. 3sh, Lavender. 5sh, Felton's flower, horiz. £1, Yellow orchid.

1968, Oct. 9 **Photo.** ***Perf. 14***
166 A41 ½p multicolored .25 *1.75*
167 A41 1½p multicolored .45 .25
168 A41 2p multicolored .60 .25
169 A41 3p multicolored 6.00 1.00
170 A41 3½p multicolored .35 *1.00*
171 A41 4½p multicolored 1.60 *2.00*
172 A41 5½p multicolored 1.60 *2.00*
173 A41 6p multicolored .85 *.30*
174 A41 1sh multicolored 1.00 *1.50*
175 A41 1sh6p multicolored 5.00 *15.00*
176 A41 2sh multicolored 5.50 6.25
177 A41 3sh multicolored 7.75 8.00
178 A41 5sh multicolored 27.00 13.00
179 A41 £1 multicolored 11.50 3.25
Nos. 166-179 (14) 69.45 55.55

See Nos. 210-222. For surcharges see Nos. 197-209.

Beaver DHC 2 Seaplane A42

Designs: 6p, Norseman seaplane. 1sh, Auster plane. 2sh, Falkland Islands arms.

1969, Apr. 8 **Litho.** ***Perf. 14***
180 A42 2p multicolored .45 .30
181 A42 6p multicolored .65 .35
182 A42 1sh multicolored .65 .40
183 A42 2sh multicolored 1.20 *2.00*
Nos. 180-183 (4) 2.95 3.05

21st anniv. of Government Air Service.

Bishop Stirling A43

2p, Holy Trinity Church, 1869. 6p, Christ Church Cathedral, 1969. 2sh, Bishop's miter.

1969, Oct. 30 ***Perf. 14***
184 A43 2p emerald & black .40 .60
185 A43 6p red orange & black .50 .60
186 A43 1sh lilac & black .50 .60
187 A43 2sh yellow & multi .60 .75
Nos. 184-187 (4) 2.00 2.55

Consecration of Waite Hocking Stirling (1829-1923), as first Bishop of the Bishopric of the Falkland Islands, cent.

Gun Emplacement — A44

2p, Volunteer on horseback, vert. 1sh, Volunteer in dress uniform, vert. 2sh, Defense Force badge.

Perf. 13½x13, 13x13½

1970, Apr. 30 Litho. Wmk. 314

188 A44 2p ultra & multi 1.15 .70
189 A44 6p multicolored 1.40 .80
190 A44 1sh buff & multi 2.25 .80
191 A44 2sh yellow & multi 3.25 1.00
Nos. 188-191 (4) 8.05 3.30

Falkland Islands Defense Force, 50th anniv.

The Great Britain, 1843 A45

The Great Britain in: 4p, 1845. 9p, 1876. 1sh, 1886. 2sh, 1970.

1970, Oct. 30 Litho. *Perf. 14½*

192 A45 2p lemon & multi 1.00 .50
193 A45 4p lilac & multi 1.25 .90
194 A45 9p bister & multi 1.50 .90
195 A45 1sh org brn & multi 1.50 .90
196 A45 2sh multicolored 2.00 1.10
Nos. 192-196 (5) 7.25 4.30

Nos. 166-178 Surcharged

1971, Feb. 15 Photo. *Perf. 14*

197 A41 ½p on ½p multi .40 .40
198 A41 1p on 1½p multi .25 .25
a. 5p on 1½p (error) 750.00
199 A41 1½p on 2p multi .35 .35
200 A41 2p on 3p multi .55 .55
201 A41 2½p on 3½p multi .30 .30
202 A41 3p on 4½p multi .35 .35
203 A41 4p on 5½p multi .40 .40
204 A41 5p on 6p multi .70 .70
205 A41 6p on 1sh multi 6.00 7.00
206 A41 7½p on 1sh6p multi 8.00 8.00
207 A41 10p on 2sh multi 8.00 3.50
208 A41 15p on 3sh multi 3.50 2.75
209 A41 25p on 5sh multi 4.50 3.75
Nos. 197-209 (13) 33.30 28.30

Flower Type of 1968
"p" instead of "d"

Designs as before. 1p, 2½p, 4p, 5p, 6p, 25p, horizontal.

Wmk. 314, Sideways on Vert. Stamps

1972, June 1 *Perf. 14*

210 A41 ½p Dusty miller .75 *4.75*
a. Wmk. upright ('74) *15.00* *32.50*
b. Wmk. 373 ('75) 3.25 *3.50*
211 A41 1p Pig vine .40 .40
212 A41 1½p Pale maiden .55 *4.50*
213 A41 2p Dog orchid 6.00 1.50
a. Wmk. upright ('74) 30.00 3.25
214 A41 2½p Sea cabbage .70 *4.50*
215 A41 3p Vanilla daisy .75 *1.40*
216 A41 4p Arrowleaf marigold 1.00 *1.10*
217 A41 5p Diddle-dee 1.10 .75
218 A41 6p Scurvy grass 18.00 9.50
a. Wmk. sideways ('74) 2.10 *2.50*
219 A41 7½p Prickly burr 2.00 3.75
220 A41 10p Fachine 10.00 4.00
221 A41 15p Lavender 4.00 4.50
222 A41 25p Felton's flower 8.00 6.00
Nos. 210-222 (13) 53.25 46.65

Silver Wedding Issue, 1972
Common Design Type

Design: Queen Elizabeth II, Prince Philip, Romney Marsh sheep and giant sea lions.

1972, Nov 20 Photo. *Perf. 14x14½*

223 CD324 1p sl grn & multi .30 .30
224 CD324 10p ultra & multi .70 *.85*

Princess Anne's Wedding Issue
Common Design Type

1973, Nov. 14 Litho. *Perf. 14*

225 CD325 5p lilac & multi .25 .25
226 CD325 15p citron & multi .45 .35

Fur Seals A46

Tourist Publicity: 4p, Trout fishing. 5p, Rockhopper penguins. 15p, Military starling.

1974, Mar. 6 Litho. Wmk. 314

227 A46 2p lt ultra & multi 2.25 2.00
228 A46 4p brt blue & multi 3.25 1.50
229 A46 5p yellow & multi 10.50 2.50
230 A46 15p lt ultra & multi 12.00 5.00
Nos. 227-230 (4) 28.00 11.00

Early 19th Cent. Mail Coach, UPU Emblem — A47

UPU Cent.: 5p, Packet, 1841. 8p, First British mail planes, 1911. 16p, Catapult mail, 1920's.

1974, July 31 *Perf. 14*

231 A47 2p multicolored .25 .25
232 A47 5p multicolored .30 *.45*
233 A47 8p multicolored .35 *.55*
234 A47 16p multicolored .55 *.75*
Nos. 231-234 (4) 1.45 *2.00*

Churchill, Parliament and Big Ben A48

Design: 20p, Churchill and warships.

1974, Nov. 30 *Perf. 13x13½*

235 A48 16p multicolored 1.00 1.00
236 A48 20p multicolored 1.50 1.50
a. Souvenir sheet of 2, #235-236 8.00 8.00

Sir Winston Churchill (1874-1965).

HMS Exeter A49

Battleships: 6p, HMNZS Achilles. 8p, Admiral Graf Spee. 16p, HMS Ajax.

1974, Dec. 13 *Perf. 14*

237 A49 2p multicolored 2.50 1.75
238 A49 6p multicolored 4.25 3.50
239 A49 8p multicolored 5.25 4.50
240 A49 16p multicolored 10.00 14.00
Nos. 237-240 (4) 22.00 23.75

35th anniv. of the Battle of the River Plate between British ships and the German battleship Graf Spee.

Seal and Flag Badge — A50

7½p, Coat of arms, 1925. 10p, Arms, 1948. 16p, Arms (Falkland Islands Dependencies), 1952.

1975, Oct. 28 Litho. Wmk. 373

241 A50 2p multicolored 1.00 .50
242 A50 7½p multicolored 1.60 1.50
243 A50 10p multicolored 1.75 1.75
244 A50 16p multicolored 2.50 *3.25*
Nos. 241-244 (4) 6.85 7.00

Falkland Islands heraldic arms, 50th anniv.

½p-Coin and Trout A51

New Coinage: 5½p, 1p-coin and gentoo penguins, 8p, 2p-coin and upland geese. 10p, 5p-coin and black-browed albatross. 16p, 10p-coin and sea lions.

1975, Dec. 31 Litho. Wmk. 373

245 A51 2p copper & multi .75 .50
246 A51 5½p copper & multi 1.75 1.50
247 A51 8p copper & multi 2.00 1.75
248 A51 10p silver & multi 2.50 2.00
249 A51 16p silver & multi 3.00 3.00
Nos. 245-249 (5) 10.00 8.75

Gathering Sheep — A52

Sheep Farming: 7½p, Shearing. 10p, Dipping sheep. 20p, Motor Vessel Monsunen collecting wool.

1976, Apr. 28 Litho. *Perf. 13½*

250 A52 2p multicolored .90 .75
251 A52 7½p multicolored 1.25 1.25
252 A52 10p multicolored 1.60 1.60
253 A52 20p multicolored 2.50 *3.50*
Nos. 250-253 (4) 6.25 7.10

Prince Philip, 1957 Visit A53

11p, Queen, ampulla and spoon. 33p, Queen awaiting anointment, and Knights of the Garter.

1977, Feb. 7 *Perf. 13½x14*

254 A53 6p multicolored .35 .35
a. Booklet pane of 4, wmk. 314 6.00
b. Single stamp from #254a 1.50 *4.00*
255 A53 11p multicolored .60 .60
a. Booklet pane of 4 2.40
256 A53 33p multicolored 1.50 1.50
a. Booklet pane of 4 6.00
Nos. 254-256 (3) 2.45 2.45

25th anniv. of the reign of Elizabeth II.

Map of West and East Falkland with Communications Centers — A54

Telecommunications: 11p, Ship to shore communications at Fox Bay. 40p, Globe with Telex tape and telephone.

1977, Oct. 24 Litho. *Perf. 14½x14*

257 A54 3p yel brown & multi .90 .25
258 A54 11p lt ultra & multi 1.60 .60
259 A54 40p rose & multi 2.50 2.00
Nos. 257-259 (3) 5.00 2.85

A.E.S., 1957-1974 — A55

Designs: Mail ships.

1978, Jan. 25 Wmk. 373 *Perf. 14*
No Date Inscription

260 A55 1p shown .25 .25
261 A55 2p Darwin, 1957-75 .35 .25
262 A55 3p Merak-N 1951-53 .25 *1.50*
263 A55 4p Fitzroy, 1936-57 .25 *1.50*
264 A55 5p Lafonia 1936-41 .25 *.30*
265 A55 6p Fleurus, 1924-33 .30 *.40*
266 A55 7p S.S. Falkland, 1914-34 .40 *2.75*
267 A55 8p Oravia, 1900-12 .45 *1.25*
268 A55 9p Memphis, 1890-97 .45 *1.00*
269 A55 10p Black Hawk, 1873-80 .60 .50
270 A55 20p Foam, 1963-72 1.00 *1.50*
271 A55 25p Fairy, 1857-61 1.00 *3.25*
272 A55 50p Amelia, 1852-54 1.50 *3.50*
273 A55 £1 Nautilus, 1846-48 2.50 *5.50*
274 A55 £3 Hebe, 1842-46 9.00 *13.00*
Nos. 260-274 (15) 18.55 *36.45*

The 1p, 3p, 5p, 6p and 10p were also issued in booklet panes of 4.

For overprints see Nos. 352-353.

1982, Dec. 1 Inscribed "1982"

260a A55 1p shown .40 *2.00*
261a A55 2p Darwin, 1957-75 .50 *2.00*
262a A55 3p Merak-N 1951-53 .60 *2.00*
263a A55 4p Fitzroy, 1936-57 .60 *2.00*
264a A55 5p Lafonia 1936-41 .70 *2.00*
265a A55 6p Fleurus, 1924-33 .70 *2.00*
266a A55 7p S.S. Falkland, 1914-34 .75 *2.00*
267a A55 8p Oravia, 1900-12 .75 *2.00*
268a A55 9p Memphis, 1890-97 .80 *2.00*
269a A55 10p Black Hawk, 1873-80 .85 *2.00*
270a A55 20p Foam, 1963-72 1.50 *3.25*
271a A55 25p Fairy, 1857-61 1.50 *3.25*
272a A55 50p Amelia, 1852-54 1.75 *4.00*
273a A55 £1 Nautilus, 1846-48 3.25 *5.00*
274a A55 £3 Hebe, 1842-46 5.00 *10.00*
Nos. 260a-274a (15) 19.65 *45.50*

Elizabeth II Coronation Anniversary Issue
Souvenir Sheet
Common Design Type

1978, June 2 Unwmk. *Perf. 15*

275 Sheet of 6 4.00 *5.50*
a. CD326 25p Red Dragon of Wales .60 .85
b. CD327 25p Elizabeth II .60 .85
c. CD328 25p Hornless ram .60 .85

No. 275 contains 2 se-tenant strips of Nos. 275a-275c, separated by horizontal gutter with commemorative and descriptive inscriptions.

Short Sunderland Mark III — A56

Design: 33p, Plane in flight and route Southampton to Stanley.

1978, Apr. 28 Wmk. 373 *Perf. 14*

276 A56 11p multicolored 2.75 2.25
277 A56 33p multicolored 4.00 3.25

First direct flight Southampton, England to Stanley, Falkland Islands, 26th anniv.

First Fox Bay PO and No. 1 — A57

Designs: 11p, Second Stanley Post Office and #2. 15p, New Island Post Office and #3. 22p, 1st Stanley Post Office and #4.

1978, Aug. 8 Litho. *Perf. 13½x13*

278	A57	3p multicolored	.25	.25
279	A57	11p multicolored	.30	*.40*
280	A57	15p multicolored	.40	.50
281	A57	22p multicolored	.70	*.85*
		Nos. 278-281 (4)	1.65	2.00

Falkland Islands postage stamps, cent.

Macrocystis Pyrifera — A58

Kelp: 7p, Durvillea. 11p, Lessoniae, horiz. 15p, Callophyllis, horiz. 25p, Iridea.

1979, Feb. 19 Litho. *Perf. 14*

282	A58	3p multicolored	.40	.40
283	A58	7p multicolored	.45	.45
284	A58	11p multicolored	.55	.55
285	A58	15p multicolored	.80	.80
286	A58	25p multicolored	.95	1.10
		Nos. 282-286 (5)	3.15	3.30

Britten-Norman Islander over Map — A59

Opening of Stanley Airport: 11p, Fokker F27 over map. 15p, Fokker F28 over Stanley. 25p, Cessna 172 Skyhawk, Islander and Fokkers F27, F28 over runway.

1979, May 1 Litho. *Perf. 13½*

287	A59	3p multicolored	.45	.25
288	A59	11p multicolored	.85	.65
289	A59	15p multicolored	1.00	.65
290	A59	25p multicolored	1.50	1.00
		Nos. 287-290 (4)	3.80	2.55

Rowland Hill and No. 121 A60

Sir Rowland Hill (1795-1879), originator of penny postage, and: 11p, Falkland Islands No. 1, vert. 25p, Penny Black. 33p, Falkland Islands No. 37, vert.

1979, Aug. 27 *Perf. 14*

291	A60	3p multicolored	.25	.25
292	A60	11p multicolored	.40	.40
293	A60	25p multicolored	.75	.75
		Nos. 291-293 (3)	1.40	1.40

Souvenir Sheet

294	A60	33p multicolored	1.50	1.50

Mail Delivery by Air, UPU Emblem A61

UPU Membership Cent. (Modes of Mail Delivery): 11p, Horseback. 25p, Schooner Gwendolin.

1979, Nov. 26

295	A61	3p multicolored	.25	.25
296	A61	11p multicolored	.45	*.55*
297	A61	25p multicolored	.65	*1.10*
		Nos. 295-297 (3)	1.35	*1.90*

Commerson's Dolphin — A62

Designs: 3p, Peale's porpoise, vert. 7p, Hour-glass dolphin. 11p, Spectacled porpoise, vert. 15p, Dusky dolphin. 25p, Killer whale.

1980, Feb. 25 Wmk. 373 *Perf. 14*

298	A62	3p multicolored	.40	.40
299	A62	6p shown	.60	.60
300	A62	7p multicolored	.60	.60
301	A62	11p multicolored	.70	.70
302	A62	15p multicolored	.80	.80
303	A62	25p multicolored	.90	*1.50*
		Nos. 298-303 (6)	4.00	4.60

Miniature Sheet

A63

Designs: a, Falkland Islands Cancel, 1878. b, New Islds., 1915. c, Falklands Islds., 1901. d, Port Stanley, 1935. e, Port Stanley airmail, 1952. f, Fox Bay, 1934.

1980, May 6 Litho. *Perf. 14*

304	A63	Sheet of 6	1.60	1.60
a.-f.		11p any single	.25	.25

London 1980 Intl. Stamp Exhib., May 6-14.

Queen Mother Elizabeth Birthday

Common Design Type

1980, Aug. 4 Litho. *Perf. 14*

305	CD330	11p multicolored	.40	.40

Striated Caracara A64

Designs: 11p, Red-backed buzzard. 15p, Crested caracara. 25p, Cassin's falcon.

1980, Aug. 11 Wmk. 373 *Perf. 13½*

306	A64	3p shown	.60	.30
307	A64	11p multicolored	.75	.55
308	A64	15p multicolored	.85	.65
309	A64	25p multicolored	1.00	1.00
		Nos. 306-309 (4)	3.20	2.50

Port Egmont, Early Settlement — A65

1980, Dec. 22 Litho. *Perf. 14*

310	A65	3p Stanley	.25	.25
311	A65	11p shown	.35	.35
312	A65	25p Port Louis	.75	.75
313	A65	33p Mission House, Keppel Island	.95	.95
		Nos. 310-313 (4)	2.30	2.30

Polwarth Sheep A66

1981, Jan. 19 Litho. *Perf. 14*

314	A66	3p shown	.25	.25
315	A66	11p Frisian cow and calf	.35	.30
316	A66	25p Horse	.70	*1.00*
317	A66	33p Welsh collies	.80	*1.25*
		Nos. 314-317 (4)	2.10	2.80

Map of Falkland Islands, Bowles and Carver, 1779 A67

10p, Hawkin's Mainland, 1773. 13p, New Isles, 1747. 15p, French & British Islands. 25p, Falklands, 1771. 26p, Falklands, 1764.

1981, May 22 Litho. *Perf. 14*

318	A67	3p shown	.25	.25
319	A67	10p multicolored	.30	.35
320	A67	13p multicolored	.35	.35
321	A67	15p multicolored	.45	.35
322	A67	25p multicolored	.60	.50
323	A67	26p multicolored	.65	.50
		Nos. 318-323 (6)	2.60	2.30

Royal Wedding Issue

Common Design Type

1981, July 22 Litho. *Perf. 13½x13*

324	CD331	10p Bouquet	.25	.25
325	CD331	13p Charles	.40	.45
326	CD331	52p Couple	1.00	1.00
		Nos. 324-326 (3)	1.65	1.70

Duke of Edinburgh's Awards, 25th Anniv. — A68

1981, Sept. 28 Litho. *Perf. 14*

327	A68	10p Spinning	.25	.25
328	A68	13p Camping	.25	.25
329	A68	15p Kayaking	.35	.35
330	A68	26p Duke of Edinburgh	.55	.55
		Nos. 327-330 (4)	1.40	1.40

The Holy Virgin, by Guido Reni (1575-1642) A69

Christmas: 3p, Adoration of the Holy Child, 16th cent. Dutch. 13p, Holy Family in an Italian Landscape, 17th cent. Italian.

1981, Nov. 9 Litho. *Perf. 14*

331	A69	3p multicolored	.25	.25
332	A69	13p multicolored	.50	.50
333	A69	26p multicolored	.75	.75
		Nos. 331-333 (3)	1.50	1.50

This set was issued Nov. 2 in London by the Crown Agents.

Rock Cod — A70

Designs: Shelf fish — 5p, Falkland herring, horiz. 15p, Patagonian hake, horiz. 25p, Southern blue whiting, horiz. 26p, Gray-tailed skate.

1981, Dec. 7

334	A70	5p multicolored	.25	.25
335	A70	13p shown	.30	*.35*
336	A70	15p multicolored	.35	*.40*
337	A70	25p multicolored	.55	*.75*
338	A70	26p multicolored	.55	*.75*
		Nos. 334-338 (5)	2.00	*2.50*

Shipwrecks — A71

Designs: 5p, Lady Elizabeth, 1913. 13p, Capricorn, 1882. 15p, Jhelum, 1870. 25p, Snowsquall, 1864. 26p, St. Mary, 1890.

1982, Feb. 15 Wmk. 373 *Perf. 14½*

339	A71	5p multicolored	.35	.35
340	A71	13p multicolored	.45	.45
341	A71	15p multicolored	.50	.50
342	A71	25p multicolored	.70	.70
343	A71	26p multicolored	.70	.70
		Nos. 339-343 (5)	2.70	2.70

Sesquicentennial of Charles Darwin's Visit — A72

1982, Apr. 19 Litho. *Perf. 14*

344	A72	5p Darwin	.45	.45
345	A72	17p Microscope	.55	.55
346	A72	25p Warrah	.85	.85
347	A72	34p Beagle	1.10	1.10
		Nos. 344-347 (4)	2.95	2.95

Princess Diana Issue

Common Design Type

1982, July 5 Wmk. 373 *Perf. 13*

348	CD333	5p Arms	.30	.30
349	CD333	17p Diana	.60	.60
350	CD333	37p Wedding	.90	.90
351	CD333	50p Portrait	1.15	1.15
		Nos. 348-351 (4)	2.95	2.95

Nos. 264, 271 Overprinted

1982, Oct. 7 Litho. *Perf. 14*

352	A55	5p multicolored	.25	*.30*
353	A55	25p multicolored	.50	*1.00*

12th Commonwealth Games, Brisbane, Australia, Sept. 30-Oct. 9.

Tussock Bird — A73

Designs: 10p, Black-chinned siskin. 13p, Grass wren. 17p, Black-throated finch. 25p, Falkland-correndera pipit. 34p, Dark-faced ground-tyrant.

1982, Dec. 6 *Perf. 15x14½*

354	A73	5p shown	.40	.40
355	A73	10p multicolored	.50	.50
356	A73	13p multicolored	.50	.50
357	A73	17p multicolored	.50	.50
358	A73	25p multicolored	.60	.60
359	A73	34p multicolored	.70	.70
		Nos. 354-359 (6)	3.20	3.20

British Occupation Sesquicentennial — A74

1p, Raising the Standard, Port Louis, 1833. 2p, Chelsea pensioners & barracks, 1849. 5p, Wool trade, 1874. 10p, Ship repairing trade, 1850-90. 15p, Government House, early 20th cent. 20p, Battle of the Falkland Islands, 1914. 25p, Whalebone Arch centenary, 1933. 40p, Contribution to World War II effort, 1939-45. 50p, Visit of Duke of Edinburgh, 1957. £1, Royal Marines, 1933, 1983, vert. £2, Queen Elizabeth II.

1983, Jan. 1 Litho. *Perf. 14*

No.	Type	Description	Unused	Used
360	A74	1p multi, vert.	.35	.35
361	A74	2p multi	.40	.40
362	A74	5p multi, vert.	.40	.40
363	A74	10p multi	.55	.70
364	A74	15p multi	.55	.80
365	A74	20p multi, vert.	.75	1.25
366	A74	25p multi	.75	1.25
367	A74	40p multi, vert.	.80	1.25
368	A74	50p multi	.95	1.25
369	A74	£1 multi	1.25	1.75
370	A74	£2 multi, vert.	2.50	3.00
		Nos. 360-370 (11)	9.25	12.40

For surcharges see Nos. 402-403.

A75

1983, Mar. 14

No.	Type	Description	Unused	Used
371	A75	5p No. 69	.25	.25
372	A75	17p No. 65	.45	.45
373	A75	34p No. 75, vert.	.70	1.00
374	A75	50p No. 370, vert.	.90	1.00
		Nos. 371-374 (4)	2.30	2.70

Commonwealth Day.

First Anniv. of Liberation A76

1983, June 14 Wmk. 373 *Perf. 14*

No.	Type	Description	Unused	Used
375	A76	5p Army	.30	.30
376	A76	13p Merchant Navy	.40	.40
377	A76	17p Royal Air Force	.60	.60
378	A76	50p Royal Navy	1.20	1.75
a.		Souvenir sheet of 4, #375-378	2.50	2.75
		Nos. 375-378 (4)	2.50	3.05

Local Fruit A77

1983, Oct. 10 Litho. *Perf. 14*

No.	Type	Description	Unused	Used
379	A77	5p Diddle dee	.25	.25
380	A77	17p Tea berries	.35	.40
381	A77	25p Mountain berries	.50	.60
382	A77	34p Native strawberries	.70	.80
		Nos. 379-382 (4)	1.80	2.05

Britten-Norman Islander — A78

Designs: 13p, DHC-2 Beaver. 17p, Noorduyn Norseman. 50p, Auster.

1983, Nov. 14 Litho. *Perf. 14*

No.	Type	Description	Unused	Used
383	A78	5p shown	.25	.25
384	A78	13p multicolored	.35	.40
385	A78	17p multicolored	.45	.50
386	A78	50p multicolored	1.00	1.25
		Nos. 383-386 (4)	2.05	2.40

Green Spider A79

Insects and Spiders: 2p, 7p, Ichneumon-Fly. 3p, Brocade Moth. 4p, Black Beetle. 5p, Fritillary. 6p, Green Spider, diff. 8p, Ochre Shoulder. 9p, Clocker Weevil. 10p, Hover Fly. 20p, Weevil. 25p, Metallic Beetle. 50p, Camel Cricket. £1, Beauchene Spider. £3, Southern Painted Lady.

1984, Jan. 1 Litho. *Perf. 14*

No.	Type	Description	Unused	Used
387	A79	1p shown	.30	.80
388	A79	2p multicolored	2.75	2.50
a.		Inscribed "1986"	4.00	3.25
389	A79	3p multicolored	.65	.85
390	A79	4p multicolored	.50	.85
391	A79	5p multicolored	.50	.85
392	A79	6p multicolored	.50	.85
393	A79	7p multicolored	.50	.70
394	A79	8p multicolored	.50	.70
395	A79	9p multicolored	.50	.70
396	A79	10p multicolored	.50	.70
397	A79	20p multicolored	2.75	1.10
398	A79	25p multicolored	.65	1.10
399	A79	50p multicolored	1.10	1.75
400	A79	£1 multicolored	1.40	2.50
401	A79	£3 multicolored	4.00	6.50
		Nos. 387-401 (15)	17.10	22.45

Nos. 364, 366 Surcharged

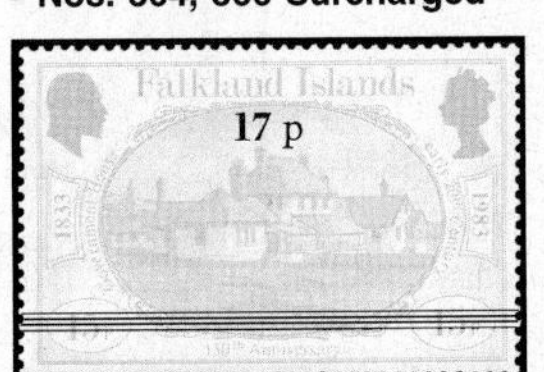

1984, Jan. 3 Litho. *Perf. 14*

No.	Type	Description	Unused	Used
402	A74	17p on 15p multi	.65	.90
403	A74	22p on 25p multi	.35	.45

Lloyd's List Issue

Common Design Type

Designs: 6p, Wavertree. 17p, Port Stanley, 1910. 22p, Oravia. 52p, Cunard Countess.

1984, May 7 Wmk. 373 *Perf. 14½*

No.	Type	Description	Unused	Used
404	CD335	6p multi	.60	.50
405	CD335	17p multi	.90	.65
406	CD335	22p multi	.90	.75
407	CD335	52p multi	1.10	1.75
		Nos. 404-407 (4)	3.50	3.65

Great Grebe — A80

1984, Aug. 6 *Perf. 14½x14*

No.	Type	Description	Unused	Used
408	A80	17p shown	1.25	1.25
409	A80	22p Silver grebe	1.50	1.50
410	A80	52p Rolland's grebe	2.25	3.25
		Nos. 408-410 (3)	5.00	6.00

See Nos. 450-453.

1984 UPU Congress A81

1984, June 25 Litho. *Perf. 14*

No.	Type	Description	Unused	Used
411	A81	22p Emblem, jet, ship	.60	.75

Wildlife Conservation A82

1984, Nov. 5 Litho. *Perf. 14½*

No.	Type	Description	Unused	Used
412	A82	6p Birds	1.00	1.00
413	A82	17p Plants	.90	.70
414	A82	22p Mammals	1.00	.80
415	A82	52p Marine Life	1.60	2.25
a.		Souvenir sheet of 4, #412-415	7.00	7.75
		Nos. 412-415 (4)	4.50	4.75

Camber Railway, 1915-1927 A83

1985, Feb. 18 Litho. *Perf. 14*

No.	Type	Description	Unused	Used
416	A83	7p multicolored	.35	.35
417	A83	22p multicolored	.65	.65
418	A83	27p multicolored	.70	.85

Size: 77x26mm

No.	Type	Description	Unused	Used
419	A83	54p multicolored	1.40	1.75
		Nos. 416-419 (4)	3.10	3.60

Queen Mother 85th Birthday

Common Design Type

Designs: 7p, Commonwealth Visitor's Reception. 22p, With Prince Charles, Mark Phillips, Princess Anne. 27p, 80th birthday celebration. 54p, Holding Prince Henry. £1, In coach with Princess Diana.

Perf. 14½x14

1985, June 7 Litho. Wmk. 384

No.	Type	Description	Unused	Used
420	CD336	7p multicolored	.35	.35
421	CD336	22p multicolored	.90	.70
422	CD336	27p multicolored	1.00	1.00
423	CD336	54p multicolored	1.10	1.60
		Nos. 420-423 (4)	3.35	3.65

Souvenir Sheet

No.	Type	Description	Unused	Used
424	CD336	£1 multicolored	4.00	3.00

Mount Pleasant Airport Opening A84

Designs: 7p, Pioneer camp, docked ship. 22p, Construction site. 27p, Runway layout. 54p, Aircraft landing.

1985, May 12 Litho. *Perf. 14½*

No.	Type	Description	Unused	Used
425	A84	7p multicolored	.75	.40
426	A84	22p multicolored	1.00	1.00
427	A84	27p multicolored	1.30	1.30
428	A84	54p multicolored	1.75	2.40
		Nos. 425-428 (4)	4.80	5.10

Captain J. McBride, HMS Jason, 1765 — A85

18th-19th century naval explorers: 22p, Commodore J. Byron, HMS Dolphin and Tamar, 1765. 27p, Vice-Adm. R. Fitzroy, HMS Beagle, 1831. 54p, Adm. Sir B.J. Sulivan, HMS Philomel, 1842.

1985, Sept. 23

No.	Type	Description	Unused	Used
429	A85	7p multicolored	.75	.45
430	A85	22p multicolored	1.25	.90
431	A85	27p multicolored	1.35	1.15
432	A85	54p multicolored	2.50	2.25
		Nos. 429-432 (4)	5.85	4.75

Philibert Commerson (1727-1773), Commerson's Dolphin — A86

Naturalists, endangered species: 22p, Rene Primevere Lesson (1794-1849), kelp. 27p, Joseph Paul Gaimard (1796-1858), diving petrel. 54p, Charles Darwin (1803-1882), Calceolaria darwinii.

1985, Nov. 4 *Perf. 14½*

No.	Type	Description	Unused	Used
433	A86	7p multicolored	.85	.30
434	A86	22p multicolored	1.10	1.10
435	A86	27p multicolored	2.00	2.00
436	A86	54p multicolored	2.25	2.25
		Nos. 433-436 (4)	6.20	5.65

Seashells A87

Designs: 7p, Painted keyhole limpet. 22p, Magellanic volute. 27p, Falkland scallop. 54p, Rough thorn drupe.

1986, Feb. 10 Wmk. 384 *Perf. 14½*

No.	Type	Description	Unused	Used
437	A87	7p multicolored	.95	.95
438	A87	22p multicolored	1.50	1.50
439	A87	27p multicolored	1.60	1.90
440	A87	54p multicolored	2.75	3.25
		Nos. 437-440 (4)	6.80	7.60

Queen Elizabeth II 60th Birthday

Common Design Type

Designs: 10p, With Princess Margaret at St. Paul's, Waldenbury, 1932. 24p, Christmas broadcast from Sandringham, 1958. 29p, Order of the Thistle, St. Giles Cathedral, Edinburgh, 1962. 45p, Royal reception on the Britannia, US visit, 1976. 58p, Visiting Crown Agents' offices, 1983.

1986, Apr. 21 Litho. *Perf. 14x14½*

No.	Type	Description	Unused	Used
441	CD337	10p scar, blk & sil	.30	.30
442	CD337	24p ultra, blk & sil	.55	.65
443	CD337	29p green & multi	.60	.85
444	CD337	45p violet & multi	1.25	1.40
445	CD337	58p rose vio & multi	1.25	1.75
		Nos. 441-445 (5)	3.95	4.95

AMERIPEX '86 — A88

SS Great Britain's arrival in the Falkland Isls., Cent.: 10p, Maiden voyage, crossing the Atlantic, 1845. 24p, Wreck in Sparrow Cove, 1937. 29p, Refloating wreck, 1970. 58p, Restored vessel, Bristol, 1986.

1986, May 22

No.	Type	Description	Unused	Used
446	A88	10p multicolored	.50	.50
447	A88	24p multicolored	.60	.90
448	A88	29p multicolored	.75	1.10
449	A88	58p multicolored	1.10	2.25
a.		Souvenir sheet of 4, #446-449	3.75	3.75
		Nos. 446-449 (4)	2.95	4.75

Bird Type of 1984

Rockhopper Penguins.

1986, Aug. 25 Wmk. 373 *Perf. 14½*

No.	Type	Description	Unused	Used
450	A80	10p Adult	1.00	.75
451	A80	24p Adults swimming	1.90	1.90
452	A80	29p Adults, diff.	2.10	2.10
453	A80	58p Adult and young	3.25	4.25
		Nos. 450-453 (4)	8.25	9.00

Wedding of Prince Andrew and Sarah Ferguson — A90

Various photographs: 17p, Presenting Queen's Polo Cup, Windsor, 1986. 22p, Open carriage, wedding. 29p, Andrew wearing military fatigues.

1986, Nov. 10 Wmk. 384 *Perf. 14½*
454 A90 17p multicolored .70 .70
455 A90 22p multicolored .90 .90
456 A90 29p multicolored 1.25 1.25
Nos. 454-456 (3) 2.85 2.85

Royal Engineers, 200th Anniv. A91

10p, Surveying Sapper Hill. 24p, Explosives disposal. 29p, Boxer Bridge, Pt. Stanley. 58p, Postal services, Stanley Airport.

1987, Feb. 9 Litho. *Perf. 14½*
457 A91 10p multicolored 1.35 .90
458 A91 24p multicolored 2.40 1.50
459 A91 29p multicolored 2.10 *2.50*
460 A91 58p multicolored 3.50 *4.25*
Nos. 457-460 (4) 9.35 9.15

Seals A92

Designs: 10p, Southern sea lion. 24p, Falkland fur seal. 29p, Southern elephant seal. 58p, Leopard seal.

1987, Apr. 27
461 A92 10p multicolored 1.25 1.25
462 A92 24p multicolored 2.00 2.00
463 A92 29p multicolored 2.25 2.25
464 A92 58p multicolored 3.00 *4.50*
Nos. 461-464 (4) 8.50 10.00

Hospitals A93

Designs: 10p, Victorian Cottage Home, c. 1912. 24p, King Edward VII Memorial Hospital, c. 1914. 29p, Churchill Wing, 1953. 58p, Prince Andrew Wing, 1987.

1987, Dec. 8 *Perf. 14*
465 A93 10p multicolored .65 .50
466 A93 24p multicolored 1.10 .90
467 A93 29p multicolored 1.25 1.00
468 A93 58p multicolored 2.00 1.50
Nos. 465-468 (4) 5.00 3.90

Fungi — A94

10p, Suillus luteus. 24p, Mycena. 29p, Camarophyllus adonis. 58p, Gerronema schusteri.

1987, Sept. 14 Litho. *Perf. 14½*
469 A94 10p multicolored 2.50 1.75
470 A94 24p multicolored 3.50 3.00
471 A94 29p multicolored 4.00 3.50
472 A94 58p multicolored 5.00 *5.50*
Nos. 469-472 (4) 15.00 13.75

1940 Morris Truck, Fitzroy A95

Classic automobiles: 24p, 1929 Citroen Kegresse, San Carlos. 29p, 1933 Ford 1-Ton Truck, Port Stanley. 58p, 1935 Ford Model T Saloon, Darwin.

1988, Apr. 11 Litho. *Perf. 14*
473 A95 10p multicolored .65 .35
474 A95 24p multicolored 1.10 .65
475 A95 29p multicolored 1.25 .75
476 A95 58p multicolored 1.90 1.50
Nos. 473-476 (4) 4.90 3.25

Geese A96

1988, July 25
477 A96 10p Kelp 2.50 .60
478 A96 24p Upland 3.25 .90
479 A96 29p Ruddy-headed 3.50 1.10
480 A96 58p Ashy-headed 5.75 2.50
Nos. 477-480 (4) 15.00 5.10

Lloyds of London, 300th Anniv.
Common Design Type

Designs: 10p, Lloyd's Nelson Collection silver service. 24p, Hydroponic Gardens, horiz. 29p, Supply ship A.E.S., horiz. 58p, Wreck of the Charles Cooper near the Falklands, 1866.

1988, Nov. 14 Litho. Wmk. 373
481 CD341 10p multicolored .45 .45
482 CD341 24p multicolored .85 .85
483 CD341 29p multicolored 1.75 1.05
484 CD341 58p multicolored 2.40 1.50
Nos. 481-484 (4) 5.45 3.85

Ships of Cape Horn A97

Designs: 1p, Padua. 2p, Priwall, vert. 3p, Passat. 4p, Archibald Russell, vert. 5p, Pamir, vert. 6p, Mozart. 7p, Pommern. 8p, Preussen. 9p, Fennia. 10p, Cassard. 20p, Lawhill. 25p, Garthpool. 50p, Grace Harwar. £1, Criccieth Castle. £3, Cutty Sark, vert. £5, Flying Cloud.

1989, Feb. 28
485 A97 1p multicolored 1.75 .85
486 A97 2p multicolored 1.40 1.40
a. Wmk. 384 1.20 1.20
487 A97 3p multicolored 1.40 1.40
a. Wmk. 384 1.20 1.20
488 A97 4p multicolored 2.40 .85
489 A97 5p multicolored 2.40 .85
490 A97 6p multicolored 1.90 1.90
a. Wmk. 384 1.90 1.90
491 A97 7p multicolored 2.40 .95
492 A97 8p multicolored 2.40 .95
493 A97 9p multicolored 1.90 1.90
a. Wmk. 384 2.50 2.50
494 A97 10p multicolored 2.40 .95
495 A97 20p multicolored 3.50 1.90
496 A97 25p multicolored 3.75 1.90
497 A97 50p multicolored 4.25 3.00
498 A97 £1 multicolored 5.00 4.75
a. Wmk. 384 6.00 6.00
499 A97 £3 multicolored 15.00 10.00
500 A97 £5 multicolored 27.50 11.50
Nos. 485-500 (16) 79.35 45.05

Nos. 486a, 487a, 490a, 493a, 498a are dated "1991."

Whales — A98

1989, May 15 Wmk. 384 *Perf. 14*
501 A98 10p Southern right 1.50 .85
502 A98 24p Minke 2.50 1.25
503 A98 29p Humpback 3.25 2.00
504 A98 58p Blue 4.75 3.00
Nos. 501-504 (4) 12.00 7.10

Sports Assoc. Activities A99

Children's drawings.

1989, Sept. 16
505 A99 5p Gymkhana .30 .30
506 A99 10p Steer Riding .35 .35
507 A99 17p Sheep shearing .55 .55
508 A99 24p Dog trial .70 .70
509 A99 29p Horse racing .95 .95
510 A99 45p Sack race 1.25 1.25
Nos. 505-510 (6) 4.10 4.10

Battles — A100

Commanders, ships and ship crests: 10p, Vice-Adm. Sturdee, HMS *Invincible*. 24p, Vice-Adm. Von Spee, SMS *Scharnhorst*. 29p, Commodore Harwood, HMS *Ajax*. 58p, Capt. Langsdorff, *Admiral Graff Spee*.

1989, Dec. 8 *Perf. 14x13½*
511 A100 10p multicolored 1.35 .35
512 A100 24p multicolored 2.25 .80
513 A100 29p multicolored 2.25 1.00
514 A100 58p multicolored 3.25 2.50
Nos. 511-514 (4) 9.10 4.65

Battle of the Falklands, 75th anniv. (10p, 24p); Battle of the River Plate, 50th anniv. (29p, 58p).

Emblems and Presentation Spitfires, 1940 — A101

Designs: 12p, No. 92 Squadron, whole plane. 26p, No. 611 Squadron. 31p, No. 92 Squadron, close up of cockpit. 62p, Spitfires scramble.

£1, Battle of Britain.

1990, May 3 Wmk. 373 *Perf. 14*
515 A101 12p multicolored 1.00 1.00
516 A101 26p multicolored 1.40 1.40
517 A101 31p multicolored 1.75 1.75
518 A101 62p multicolored 3.00 3.00
Nos. 515-518 (4) 7.15 7.15

Souvenir Sheet

519 A101 £1 multicolored 7.00 7.00

Stamp World London '90.

For souvenir sheet similar to No. 519, see No. 530.

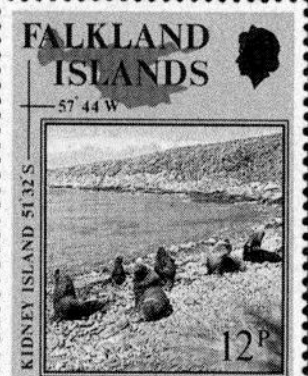

A102

1990, Apr. 1 Wmk. 384 *Perf. 14½*
520 A102 12p Kidney Is. .80 .55
521 A102 26p Beauchene Is. 1.25 .55
522 A102 31p Bird Is. 1.50 1.25
523 A102 62p Elephant Jason Is. 2.25 2.75
Nos. 520-523 (4) 5.80 5.10

Nature reserves and bird sanctuaries.

Queen Mother, 90th Birthday
Common Design Types

26p, Queen Mother in Dover. £1, Steering the "Queen Elizabeth," 1946.

1990, Aug. 4 Wmk. 384 *Perf. 14x15*
524 CD343 26p multicolored 1.00 1.00

Perf. 14½
525 CD344 £1 multicolored 3.75 3.75

A103

Designs: 12p, Black browed albatross. 26p, Adult bird. 31p, Adult, chick. 62p, Bird in flight.

Wmk. 384
1990, Oct. 3 Litho. *Perf. 14*
526 A103 12p multicolored 1.00 .75
527 A103 26p multicolored 1.90 1.25
528 A103 31p multicolored 2.25 1.50
529 A103 62p multicolored 3.50 3.50
Nos. 526-529 (4) 8.65 7.00

Battle of Britain Type of 1990 inscribed "SECOND VISIT OF / HRH THE DUKE OF EDINBURGH"
Souvenir Sheet

1991, Mar. 7
530 A101 £1 multicolored 13.00 13.00

Orchids — A104

Designs: 12p, Gavilea australis. 26p, Codonorchis lessonii. 31p, Chlorea gaudichaudii. 62p, Gavilea littoralis.

1991, Mar. 18 Wmk. 373
531 A104 12p multi 1.60 1.00
532 A104 26p multi 1.90 1.50
533 A104 31p multi 2.25 1.75
534 A104 62p multi 3.50 *4.00*
Nos. 531-534 (4) 9.25 8.25

King Penguin — A105

2p, Two adults crossing bills. 6p, Two adults, one brooding. 12p, Adult with two young. 20p, Adult swimming. 31p, Adult feeding young. 62p, Two adults, diff.

1991, Aug. 26 **Wmk. 384**

535	A105	2p multi	1.10	1.10
536	A105	6p multi	1.60	1.60
537	A105	12p multi	2.00	2.00
538	A105	20p multi	2.25	2.25
539	A105	31p multi	2.25	2.25
540	A105	62p multi	3.25	3.25
		Nos. 535-540 (6)	12.45	12.45

World Wildlife Fund.

Falkland Islands Bisects, Cent. A106

1991, Sept. 10 **Wmk. 384** ***Perf. 14½***

541	A106	12p #9, #15	1.00	.90
542	A106	26p On cover	1.90	1.50
543	A106	31p Unsevered pair	1.50	1.50
544	A106	62p S.S. Isis	2.50	*3.25*
		Nos. 541-544 (4)	6.90	7.15

Discovery of America, 500th Anniv. (in 1992) — A107

Sailing ships: 14p, STV Eye of the Wind. 29p, STV Soren Larsen. 34p, Nina, Santa Maria, Pinta. 68p, Columbus and Santa Maria.

1991, Dec. 12 **Wmk. 373** ***Perf. 14***

545	A107	14p multicolored	.90	.90
546	A107	29p multicolored	2.00	1.75
547	A107	34p multicolored	2.25	2.00
548	A107	68p multicolored	3.50	*4.25*
		Nos. 545-548 (4)	8.65	8.90

World Columbian Stamp Expo '92, Chicago and Genoa '92 Intl. Philatelic Exhibitions.

Queen Elizabeth II's Accession to the Throne, 40th Anniv.

Common Design Type

1992, Feb. 6

549	CD349	7p multicolored	.65	.50
550	CD349	14p multicolored	.90	.90
551	CD349	29p multicolored	1.00	1.10
552	CD349	34p multicolored	1.40	1.40
553	CD349	68p multicolored	2.00	2.00
		Nos. 549-553 (5)	5.95	5.90

Christ Church Cathedral, Cent. — A108

Designs: 14p, Laying foundation stone. 29p, Interior, 1920. 34p, Bishop's chair. 68p, Without tower c. 1900, horiz.

1992, Feb. 21 **Wmk. 384** ***Perf. 14½***

554	A108	14p multicolored	1.00	.75
555	A108	29p multicolored	2.00	1.25
556	A108	34p multicolored	2.25	1.50
557	A108	68p multicolored	3.00	2.75
		Nos. 554-557 (4)	8.25	6.25

A109

Designs: 22p, Capt. John Davis using backstaff. 29p, Capt. Davis working on chart. 34p, Queen Elizabeth I, Queen Elizabeth II. 68p, The Desire sights Falkland Islands.

1992, Aug. 14 **Wmk. 373**

558	A109	22p multicolored	1.60	1.10
559	A109	29p multicolored	2.00	1.50
560	A109	34p multicolored	2.10	1.90
561	A109	68p multicolored	3.50	*5.00*
		Nos. 558-561 (4)	9.20	9.50

First sighting of Falkland Islands by Capt. John Davis, 400th anniv.

Falkland Islands Defense Force and West Yorkshire Regiment — A110

7p, Private, Falkland Islands Volunteers, 1892. 14p, Officer, Falkland Islands Defense Corps, 1914. 22p, Officer, Falkland Islands Defense Force, 1920. 29p, Private, Falkland Islands Defense Force, 1939-45. 34p, Officer, West Yorkshire Regiment, 1942. 68p, Private, West Yorkshire Regiment, 1942.

1992, Oct. 1 ***Perf. 14***

562	A110	7p multicolored	.60	.60
563	A110	14p multicolored	.90	.90
564	A110	22p multicolored	1.25	.90
565	A110	29p multicolored	1.50	1.25
566	A110	34p multicolored	1.90	1.60
567	A110	68p multicolored	3.00	*3.75*
		Nos. 562-567 (6)	9.15	9.00

Gulls and Terns A111

Designs: 15p, South American tern. 31p, Pink breasted gull. 36p, Dolphin gull. 72p, Dominican gull.

Perf. 14x14½

1993, Jan. 2 **Litho.** **Wmk. 384**

568	A111	15p multicolored	1.40	1.00
569	A111	31p multicolored	1.90	1.50
570	A111	36p multicolored	2.50	2.25
571	A111	72p multicolored	3.50	*5.50*
		Nos. 568-571 (4)	9.30	10.25

Souvenir Sheet

Visit of Liner QE II to Falkland Islands — A112

Wmk. 373

1993, Jan. 22 **Litho.** ***Perf. 14***

572	A112	£2 multicolored	10.00	10.00

Royal Air Force, 75th Anniv.

Common Designs Type

Designs: No. 573, Lockheed Tristar. No. 574, Lockheed Hercules. No. 575, Boeing Vertol Chinook. No. 576, Avro Vulcan.

No. 577a, Hawker Siddeley Andover. b, Westland Wessex. c, Panavia Tornado F3. d, McDonnell Douglas Phantom.

Wmk. 373

1993, Apr. 3 **Litho.** ***Perf. 14***

573	CD350	15p multicolored	1.15	1.15
574	CD350	15p multicolored	1.15	1.15
575	CD350	15p multicolored	1.15	1.15
576	CD350	15p multicolored	1.15	1.15
		Nos. 573-576 (4)	4.60	4.60

Souvenir Sheet of 4

577	CD350	36p #a.-d.	6.25	6.25

Fisheries A113

Designs: 15p, Short-finned squid. 31p, Stern haul of whiptailed hake. 36p, Fishery Patrol Vessel Falklands Protector. 72p, Aerial surveillance by Britten-Norman Islander.

Wmk. 384

1993, July 1 **Litho.** ***Perf. 14***

578	A113	15p multicolored	.85	.85
579	A113	31p multicolored	1.75	1.75
580	A113	36p multicolored	2.10	2.10
581	A113	72p multicolored	3.25	*5.00*
		Nos. 578-581 (4)	7.95	9.70

Launch of SS Great Britain, 150th Anniv. — A114

Perf. 14x13½

1993, July 19 **Litho.** **Wmk. 384**

582	A114	8p In drydock, Bristol	.80	.50
583	A114	£1 At sea	4.25	*5.50*

Cruise Ships and Penguins A115

16p, Explorer. 34p, Rockhopper penguins. 39p, World Discoverer. 78p, Columbus Caravelle.

Wmk. 373

1993, Oct. 1 **Litho.** ***Perf. 14***

584	A115	16p multicolored	1.60	.80
585	A115	34p multicolored	2.50	1.60
586	A115	39p multicolored	2.75	2.00
587	A115	78p multicolored	3.75	*7.50*
		Nos. 584-587 (4)	10.60	11.90

Pets — A116

Perf. 14x14½

1993, Dec. 1 **Litho.** **Wmk. 384**

588	A116	8p Pony	.90	.90
589	A116	16p Lamb	1.10	1.10
590	A116	34p Puppy, kitten	2.25	1.50

Perf. 14½x14

591	A116	39p Kitten, vert.	2.75	2.00
592	A116	78p Collie, vert.	3.75	*5.75*
		Nos. 588-592 (5)	10.75	11.25

Ovptd. with Hong Kong '94 Emblem

1994, Feb. 18

593	A116	8p on #588	1.00	*1.25*
594	A116	16p on #589	1.25	*1.50*
595	A116	34p on #590	2.75	*3.00*
596	A116	39p on #591	3.00	*4.00*
597	A116	78p on #592	4.00	*6.50*
		Nos. 593-597 (5)	12.00	*16.25*

Inshore Marine Life A117

Designs: 1p, Goose barnacles, vert. 2p, Painted shrimp. 8p, Common limpet. 9p, Mullet. 10p, Sea anemones. 20p, Rock eel. 25p, Spider crab. 50p, Lobster krill, vert. 80p, Falkland skate. £1, Centollon crab. £3, Rock cod. £5, Octopus, vert.

Wmk. 384

1994, Apr. 4 **Litho.** ***Perf. 14***

598	A117	1p multicolored	1.00	.75
599	A117	2p multicolored	1.75	.75
600	A117	8p multicolored	2.00	1.00
601	A117	9p multicolored	2.00	1.00
602	A117	10p multicolored	2.00	.75
603	A117	20p multicolored	2.75	1.00
604	A117	25p multicolored	2.75	1.00
605	A117	50p multicolored	2.75	2.75
606	A117	80p multicolored	2.75	2.75
607	A117	£1 multicolored	2.75	3.00
a.		Souv. sheet of 1, wmk. 373	6.75	6.75
608	A117	£3 multicolored	12.00	8.00
609	A117	£5 multicolored	18.00	14.00
		Nos. 598-609 (12)	52.50	36.75

No. 607a for return of Hong Kong to China. Issued 7/1/97.

See No. 671.

Founding of Stanley, 150th Anniv. A118

9p, Blacksmith's shop, dockyard, Sir James Clark Ross, explorer. 17p, James Leith Mody, 1st colonial chaplain, home at 21 Fitzroy Road. 30p, Stanley cottage, Dr. Henry J. Hamblin, 1st colonial surgeon. 35p, Pioneer row, Sergeant Major Henry Felton. 40p, Government House, Governor R. C. Moody R.E. 65p, View of Stanley, Edward Stanley, 14th Earl of Derby, Secretary of State for Colonies.

Wmk. 373

1994, July 1 **Litho.** ***Perf. 14***

610	A118	9p multicolored	.85	.75
611	A118	17p multicolored	1.25	1.00
612	A118	30p multicolored	2.00	1.25
613	A118	35p multicolored	2.25	1.75
614	A118	40p multicolored	2.50	2.00
615	A118	65p multicolored	3.00	*3.50*
		Nos. 610-615 (6)	11.85	10.25

Methods of Transportation — A119

17p, Tristar over Gypsy Cove. 35p, Cruise ship, Sea Lion Island. 40p, FIGAS Islander, Pebble Island Beach. 65p, Land Rover, Volunteer Beach.

Wmk. 384

1994, Oct. 24 **Litho.** ***Perf. 14***

616	A119	17p multicolored	1.10	.75
617	A119	35p multicolored	2.10	1.50
618	A119	40p multicolored	2.75	2.75
619	A119	65p multicolored	3.25	*4.25*
		Nos. 616-619 (4)	9.20	9.25

South American Missionary Society, 150th Anniv. — A120

Designs: 5p, Mission House, Keppel Island. 17p, Thomas Bridges, compiler of Yahgan dictionary. 40p, Fuegian Indians. 65p, Schooner Allen Gardiner, Capt. Allen Gardiner.

1994, Dec. 1

620	A120	5p multicolored	.30	.30
621	A120	17p multicolored	.85	.85
622	A120	40p multicolored	1.75	1.75
623	A120	65p multicolored	2.75	*3.50*
		Nos. 620-623 (4)	5.65	6.40

Flowering Shrubs — A121

Designs: 9p, Lupinus arboreus. 17p, Boxwood. 30p, Fuchsia magellanica. 35p, Berberis ilicifolia. 40p, Gorse. 65p, Veronica.

Perf. 14½x14

1995, Jan. 3 Litho. Wmk. 384

624	A121	9p multicolored	.90	.65
625	A121	17p multicolored	1.10	.80
626	A121	30p multicolored	1.45	1.45
627	A121	35p multicolored	1.75	1.45
628	A121	40p multicolored	1.90	1.60
629	A121	65p multicolored	3.25	4.25
		Nos. 624-629 (6)	10.35	10.20

Shore Birds A122

Designs: 17p, Magellanic oystercatcher. 35p, Rufous chested dotterel. 40p, Black oystercatcher. 65p, Two banded plover.

Wmk. 373

1995, Mar. 1 Litho. *Perf. 13½*

630	A122	17p multicolored	1.75	.90
631	A122	35p multicolored	2.50	1.50
632	A122	40p multicolored	2.75	1.75
633	A122	65p multicolored	4.00	7.00
		Nos. 630-633 (4)	11.00	11.15

End of World War II, 50th Anniv.

Common Design Types

17p, Falkland Islands Victory Parade contingent. 35p, Governor Sir Alan Wolsey Cardinall on Bren gun carrier. 40p, HMAS Esperance Bay, 1942. 65p, HMS Exeter, 1939.

£1, Reverse of War Medal 1939-45.

Wmk. 373

1995, May 8 Litho. *Perf. 14*

634	CD351	17p multicolored	1.50	.90
635	CD351	35p multicolored	2.40	1.50
636	CD351	40p multicolored	2.75	2.00
637	CD351	65p multicolored	4.75	*5.50*
		Nos. 634-637 (4)	11.40	9.90

Souvenir Sheet

638	CD352	£1 multicolored	7.25	7.25

Transporting Peat — A123

Wmk. 384

1995, Aug. 1 Litho. *Perf. 14*

639	A123	17p Ox, cart	.80	.80
640	A123	35p Horse, cart	1.75	1.25
641	A123	40p Tractor, sledge	2.00	1.50
642	A123	65p Truck, peat bank	3.50	*4.00*
		Nos. 639-642 (4)	8.05	7.55

Miniature Sheet of 6

Wildlife — A124

Designs: a, Kelp geese. b, Albatross. c, Cormorants. d, Magellanic penguins. e, Fur seals. f, Rockhopper penguins.

1995, Sept. 11

643	A124	35p #a.-f.	19.00	19.00

No. 643 is a continuous design.

Wild Animals A125

1995, Nov. 6 Wmk. 373

644	A125	9p Rabbit	1.00	.90
645	A125	17p Hare	1.60	1.10
646	A125	35p Guanaco	2.50	1.75
647	A125	40p Fox	3.00	2.00
648	A125	65p Otter	4.00	*5.00*
		Nos. 644-648 (5)	12.10	10.75

Visit by Princess Anne A126

Princess Anne and: 9p, Government House. 19p, San Carlos Cemetery. 30p, Christ Church Cathedral. 73p, Goose Green.

1996, Jan. 30 *Perf. 14½*

649	A126	9p multicolored	1.00	.60
650	A126	19p multicolored	1.35	1.00
651	A126	30p multicolored	1.75	1.50
652	A126	73p multicolored	6.00	*7.50*
		Nos. 649-652 (4)	10.10	10.60

Queen Elizabeth II, 70th Birthday

Common Design Type

Various portraits of Queen, scenes from Falkland Islands: 17p, Steeple Jason. 40p, Ship, KV Tamar. 45p, New Island with shipwreck on beach. 65p, Community School.

£1, Queen in formal dress at Sandringham Ball.

1996, Apr. 21 *Perf. 13½*

653	CD354	17p multicolored	.90	.70
654	CD354	40p multicolored	2.25	1.35
655	CD354	45p multicolored	2.40	1.90
656	CD354	65p multicolored	3.00	2.25
		Nos. 653-656 (4)	8.55	6.20

Souvenir Sheet

657	CD354	£1 multicolored	5.00	5.00

CAPEX '96 A127

Mail delivery: 9p, Horseback, 1890. 40p, Norseman floatplane. 45p, Inter-island ship. 76p, Beaver floatplane.

£1, LMS Jubilee Class 4-6-0 locomotive.

1996, June 8 Wmk. 384 *Perf. 14*

658	A127	9p multicolored	.90	.65
659	A127	40p multicolored	2.40	1.50
660	A127	45p multicolored	2.50	1.60
661	A127	76p multicolored	3.50	*4.00*
		Nos. 658-661 (4)	9.30	7.75

Souvenir Sheet

662	A127	£1 multicolored	4.25	4.25

No. 662 contains one 48x32mm stamp.

Beaked Whales — A128

Designs: 9p, Southern bottlenose whale. 30p, Cuvier's beaked whale. 35p, Straptoothed beaked whale. 75p, Gray's beaked whale.

Wmk. 373

1996, Sept. 2 Litho. *Perf. 14*

663	A128	9p multicolored	.80	.60
664	A128	30p multicolored	1.60	1.50
665	A128	35p multicolored	1.90	1.75
666	A128	75p multicolored	4.00	4.00
		Nos. 663-666 (4)	8.30	7.85

Magellanic Penguins — A129

Designs: 17p, Two adults. 35p, Young in nest. 40p, Chick, adult. 65p, Swimming.

Wmk. 373

1997, Jan. 2 Litho. *Perf. 14*

667	A129	17p multicolored	2.00	.75
668	A129	35p multicolored	3.00	1.25
669	A129	40p multicolored	3.25	1.50
670	A129	65p multicolored	4.50	3.25
		Nos. 667-670 (4)	12.75	6.75

Fish Type of 1994

Souvenir Sheet

Wmk. 373

1997, Feb. 3 Litho. *Perf. 14*

671	A117	£1 Smelt	5.50	5.50

Hong Kong '97.

Ferns — A130

Perf. 14½x14

1997, Mar. 3 Litho. Wmk. 373

672	A130	17p Coral	1.75	.60
673	A130	35p Adder's tongue	2.50	1.25
674	A130	40p Fuegian tall	2.50	1.50
675	A130	65p Small fern	3.50	3.00
		Nos. 672-675 (4)	10.25	6.35

Lighthouses — A131

Designs: 9p, Bull Point. 30p, Cape Pembroke. £1, Cape Meredith.

Wmk. 373

1997, July 1 Litho. *Perf. 14*

676	A131	9p multi	3.25	1.00
677	A131	30p multi	4.50	2.00
678	A131	£1 multi	10.50	5.00
		Nos. 676-678 (3)	18.25	8.00

Queen Elizabeth II and Prince Philip, 50th Wedding Anniv. — A132

No. 679, Queen holding flowers. No. 680, Prince with horse. No. 681, Queen riding in open carriage. No. 682, Prince in uniform. No. 683, Queen in red coat & hat, Prince. No. 684, Princes William and Harry on horseback.

£1.50, Queen, Prince riding in open carriage.

1997 Wmk. 384 *Perf. 14½x14*

679		9p multicolored	1.00	.75
680		9p multicolored	1.00	.75
a.	A132	Pair, #679-680	2.75	2.75
681		17p multicolored	1.75	1.00
682		17p multicolored	1.75	1.00
a.	A132	Pair, #681-682	4.00	4.00
683		40p multicolored	3.00	1.50
684		40p multicolored	3.00	1.50
a.	A132	Pair, #683-684	8.00	8.00
		Nos. 679-684 (6)	11.50	6.50

Souvenir Sheet

685	A132	£1.50 multicolored	9.00	9.00

Endangered Species — A133

Designs: 17p, Phalcoboenus australis. 19p, Otaria flavescens. 40p, Calandrinia feltonii. 73p, Aplochiton zebra.

Wmk. 373

1997, Oct. 16 Litho. *Perf. 14½*

686	A133	17p multicolored	3.75	1.75
687	A133	19p multicolored	2.75	2.25
688	A133	40p multicolored	4.50	3.00
689	A133	73p multicolored	7.50	*8.50*
		Nos. 686-689 (4)	18.50	15.50

Fire Service in Falkland Islands, Cent. — A134

Equipment, manufacturer: 9p, Greenwich Gem, Merryweather & Son. 17p, Hatfield trailer pump, Merryweather & Son. 40p, Godiva trailer pump, Coventry Climax. 65p, Water tender type B, Carmichael Bedford.

Wmk. 384

1998, Feb. 26 Litho. *Perf. 14½*

690	A134	9p multicolored	3.25	1.50
691	A134	17p multicolored	3.75	1.50
692	A134	40p multicolored	6.00	3.00
693	A134	65p multicolored	8.00	*9.25*
		Nos. 690-693 (4)	21.00	15.25

Diana, Princess of Wales (1961-97)

Common Design Type

Portraits: a, Looking left. b, In red dress. c, Hand on cheek. d, Investigating land mines.

Perf. 14½x14

1998, Mar. 31 Wmk. 373

694	CD355	30p Sheet of 4, #a-d	5.00	5.00

No. 694 sold for £1.20 + 20p, with surtax from international sales being donated to the Princess Diana Memorial Fund and surtax from national sales being donated to designated local charity.

Birds A135

1p, Tawny-throated dotterel. 2p, Hudsonian godwit. 5p, Eared dove. No. 698, Great grebe. No. 699, Roseate spoonbill. 10p, Southern lapwing. 16p, Buff-necked ibis. 17p, Astral parakeet. 30p, Ashy-headed goose. 35p, American kestrel. 65p, Red-legged shag. 88p, Red shoveler. £1, Red-fronted coot. £3, Chilean flamingo. £5, Fork-tailed flycatcher.

Wmk. 373

1998, July 14 Litho. *Perf. 14*

695	A135	1p multicolored	1.00	*1.25*
696	A135	2p multicolored	1.00	*1.25*
697	A135	5p multicolored	1.00	*1.25*
698	A135	9p multicolored	1.50	1.00
699	A135	9p multicolored	6.00	*9.50*
700	A135	10p multicolored	2.25	1.00
701	A135	16p multicolored	2.25	2.25

702 A135 17p multicolored 1.25 *2.25*
a. Booklet pane, 2 #699, 8 #702 + 2 labels 22.00
Complete booklet, #702a 22.00
703 A135 30p multicolored 2.50 1.75
704 A135 35p multicolored 3.00 *4.00*
Complete booklet, 6 #704 18.00
705 A135 65p multicolored 4.00 2.50
706 A135 88p multicolored 4.25 *6.25*
707 A135 £1 multicolored 4.50 4.50
708 A135 £3 multicolored 11.00 *15.00*
709 A135 £5 multicolored 15.00 *22.50*
Nos. 695-709 (15) 60.50 76.25

Boats — A136

Boat, country flag, year: 17p, Penelope, Germany, 1926. 35p, Ilen, Italy, 1926. 40p, Weddell, Chile, 1940. 65p, Lively, Scotland, 1940.

Wmk. 373

1998, Sept. 30 Litho. *Perf. 14*
710 A136 17p multicolored 2.50 1.00
711 A136 35p multicolored 3.50 2.00
712 A136 40p multicolored 3.75 2.25

Size: 29x18mm

713 A136 65p multicolored 5.50 *6.00*
Nos. 710-713 (4) 15.25 11.25

FIGAS (First Medivac Air Ambulance Service), 50th Anniv. — A137

17p, Man carrying patient, airplane. £1, Airplane, map of Islands, float plane.

Wmk. 373

1998, Dec. 1 Litho. *Perf. 14*
714 A137 17p multicolored 3.00 1.25
715 A137 £1 multicolored 12.50 12.50

Military Uniforms — A138

Uniform, background location: 17p, Marine Private, 1776, The Block House at Port Egmont, Saunders Island. 30p, Marine Officer, 1833, Port Louis, East Falkland. 35p, Royal Marine Corporal, 1914, HMS Kent. 65p, Royal Marine Bugler, 1976, Government House.

Wmk. 373

1998, Dec. 8 Litho. *Perf. 14½*
716 A138 17p multicolored 3.00 1.00
717 A138 30p multicolored 4.00 2.50
718 A138 35p multicolored 4.25 2.50
719 A138 65p multicolored 6.50 *9.50*
Nos. 716-719 (4) 17.75 15.50

St. Mary's Church, Cent. A139

Designs: 17p, Inside view. 40p, Outside view. 75p, Laying cornerstone, 1899.

Wmk. 373

1999, Feb. 12 Litho. *Perf. 14*
720 A139 17p multi 2.40 .90
721 A139 40p multi 3.75 3.00
722 A139 75p multi 7.75 *2.75*
Nos. 720-722 (3) 13.90 6.65

Australia '99, World Stamp Expo A140

25p, HMS Beagle. 35p, HMAS Australia. 40p, SS Canberra. No. 726, SS Great Britain. No. 727, All-England Eleven visit Australia, 1861-62.

1999, Mar. 5 Wmk. 384
723 A140 25p multicolored 3.25 2.00
724 A140 35p multicolored 3.50 2.50
725 A140 40p multicolored 4.75 2.75
726 A140 50p multicolored 4.50 *7.00*
727 A140 50p multicolored 4.50 *7.00*
a. Pair, #726-727 9.00 *14.00*
Nos. 723-727 (5) 20.50 21.25

1999 Visit of HRH Prince of Wales — A141

Perf. 14x13½

1999, Mar. 13 Litho. Wmk. 384
728 A141 £2 multicolored 16.00 16.00

Wedding of Prince Edward and Sophie Rhys-Jones

Common Design Type

Perf. 13¾x14

1999, June 15 Litho. Wmk. 384
729 CD356 80p Separate portraits 6.00 6.00
730 CD356 £1.20 Couple 8.00 8.00

PhilexFrance '99, World Philatelic Exhibition — A142

Designs: 35p, French cruiser, Jeanne d'Arc, Port Stanley, 1931. 40p, CAMS 37/11 Flying Boat's first flight.
£1, CAMS 37 Flying Boat over Port Stanley, 1931.

1999, June 21 Wmk. 373 *Perf. 14*
731 A142 35p multicolored 5.25 5.25
732 A142 40p multicolored 5.75 5.75

Souvenir Sheet

733 A142 £1 multicolored 13.00 *14.00*

No. 733 contains one 48x31mm stamp.

Queen Mother's Century

Common Design Type

Queen Mother: 9p, With King George VI at Port of London. 20p, With Queen Elizabeth at Women's Institute, Sandringham. 30p, With Princes Charles, William and Harry at Clarence House, 95th birthday. 67p, As Colonel-in-Chief of the Queen's Royal Hussars.
£1.40, With Ernest Shackleton, Robert F. Scott and Edward A. Wilson.

Wmk. 384

1999, Aug. 18 Litho. *Perf. 13½*
734 CD358 9p multi 2.00 1.00
735 CD358 20p multi 3.00 1.50
736 CD358 30p multi 3.50 1.75
737 CD358 67p multi 5.50 *8.00*
Nos. 734-737 (4) 14.00 12.25

Souvenir Sheet

738 CD358 £1.40 multi 16.00 16.00

For overprint see No. 767.

Waterfowl A143

Perf. 14¼x14½

1999, Sept. 9 Litho. Wmk. 384
739 A143 9p Chiloe wigeon 2.50 1.75
740 A143 17p Crested duck 3.25 2.00
741 A143 30p Brown pintail 4.00 3.25
742 A143 35p Silver teal 4.25 3.50
743 A143 40p Yellow billed teal 4.75 4.00
744 A143 65p Flightless steamer duck 7.00 *9.50*
Nos. 739-744 (6) 25.75 24.00

California Gold Rush A144

Designs: 9p, Vicar of Bray, 1999. 35p, Gold panning, 1849. 40p, Gold rocking cradle, 1849. 80p, Vicar of Bray, 1849.
£1, Vicar of Bray in San Francisco Harbor, 1849.

Wmk. 373

1999, Nov. 3 Litho. *Perf. 14*
745 A144 9p multicolored 1.10 1.10
746 A144 35p multicolored 4.25 4.25
747 A144 40p multicolored 4.75 4.75
748 A144 80p multicolored 10.00 *12.00*
Nos. 745-748 (4) 20.10 22.10

Souvenir Sheet

Perf. 13¾

749 A144 £1 multicolored 15.00 15.00

No. 749 contains one 48x31mm stamp.

Millennium A145

Designs: No. 750, Kelp gull. No. 751, Upland goose. No. 752, Christchurch Cathedral. No. 753, Night heron. No. 754, King penguin. No. 755, Christmas at home.

1999, Dec. 6 *Perf. 14x14½*
750 A145 9p multicolored 2.75 2.75
751 A145 9p multicolored 2.75 2.75
752 A145 9p multicolored 2.75 2.75
753 A145 30p multicolored 4.75 4.75
754 A145 30p multicolored 4.75 4.75
755 A145 30p multicolored 4.75 4.75
Nos. 750-755 (6) 22.50 22.50

Visit of Princess Alexandra A146

Designs: 9p, Princess in patterned dress, trees. £1, Princess in blue dress, trees.

Perf. 13¼x13¾

2000, Feb. 1 Litho. Wmk. 373
756 A146 9p multicolored 2.00 2.00
757 A146 £1 multicolored 9.50 9.50

Sir Ernest Shackleton (1874-1922), Polar Explorer — A147

17p, Ship Endurance, discovery of the Caird Coast. 45p, Endurance trapped in pack ice. 75p, Shackleton, Chilean tugboat Yelcho.

2000, Feb. 10 Wmk. 373 *Perf. 14*
758 A147 17p multicolored 5.00 2.00
759 A147 45p multicolored 8.50 4.50
760 A147 75p multicolored 12.50 *14.00*
Nos. 758-760 (3) 26.00 20.50

See British Antarctic Territory Nos. 285-287, South Georgia and South Sandwich Islands Nos. 254-256.

British Monarchs — A148

a, Elizabeth I. b, James II. c, George I. d, William IV. e, Edward VIII. f, Elizabeth II.

2000, Feb. 29 Wmk. 373 *Perf. 14*
761 A148 40p Sheet of 6, #a.-f. 17.00 17.00

The Stamp Show 2000, London.

Prince William, 18th Birthday

Common Design Type

William: 10p, As toddler with fireman's helmet, vert. 20p, In checked suit and in navy suit, vert. 37p, With blue shirt. 43p, In gray suit and in navy suit holding flowers. 50p, As child with dog.

Perf. 13¾x14¼, 14¼x13¾

2000, June 21 Litho. Wmk. 373

Stamps with White Border

762 CD359 10p multi 1.50 1.25
763 CD359 20p multi 2.10 1.50
764 CD359 37p multi 3.00 2.75
765 CD359 43p multi 4.00 3.00
Nos. 762-765 (4) 10.60 8.50

Souvenir Sheet

Stamps Without White Border

Perf. 14¼

766 Sheet of 5 14.00 14.00
a. CD359 10p multi 1.00 1.00
b. CD359 20p multi 1.50 1.50
c. CD359 37p multi 2.50 2.50
d. CD359 43p multi 3.00 3.00
e. CD359 50p multi 5.00 5.00

No. 738 Ovptd. in Gold

Wmk. 384

2000, Aug. 4 Litho. *Perf. 13½*
767 CD358 £1.40 multi 17.00 17.00

Bridges A149

Bridges over: 20p, Malo River. 37p, Bodie Creek. 43p, Fitzroy River.

2000, Oct. 16 *Perf. 14¼x14½*
768-770 A149 Set of 3 17.00 17.00

Christmas — A150

Designs: 10p, Shepherd, sheep. 20p, Shepherds, sheep, angel. 33p, Holy family, shepherds, Magus, donkey, sheep. 43p, Angel, two Magi. 78p, Camel.

2000, Nov. 1 **Wmk. 373**
771-775 A150 Set of 5 15.50 15.50
775a Souvenir sheet, #771-775 17.50 17.50

Sunrises and Sunsets A151

Various photos: 10p, 20p, 37p, 43p.

2001, Jan. 10 ***Perf. 14½x14¼***
776-779 A151 Set of 4 15.00 15.00

Souvenir Sheet

New Year 2001 (Year of the Snake) — A152

Birds: a, Striated caracara. b, Mountain hawk eagle.

Perf. 14½x14¼
2001, Feb. 1 **Litho.** **Wmk. 373**
780 A152 37p Sheet of 2, #a-b 10.50 *12.00*

Hong Kong 2001 Stamp Exhibition.

Age of Victoria — A153

Designs: 3p, Falkland Islands #1. 10p, S.S. Great Britain, horiz. 20p, Stanley Harbor, 1888, horiz. 43p, Cape Pembroke Lighthouse, telephones, 1897. 93p, Royal Marines, 1900. £1.50, Queen Victoria, by Franz Xavier Winterhalter, 1859.

£1, Funeral procession for Queen Victoria.

2001, May 24 ***Perf. 14***
781-786 A153 Set of 6 24.50 24.50

Souvenir Sheet

787 A153 £1 multi 10.50 10.50

Royal Navy Connections to Falkland Islands — A154

Designs: 10p, Welfare, ship that made first recorded landing, 1690. 17p, HMS Invincible, ship in Battle of the Falklands, 1914. 20p, HMS Exeter, ship in Battle of the River Plate, 1939. 37p, SN.R6 Hovercraft, 1967. 43p, Antarctic patrol ship HMS Protector and Wasp helicopter, 1955. 68p, Desire, ship that made first sighting, 1592.

2001, July 24
788-793 A154 Set of 6 27.50 27.50

Carcass Island and its Flora and Fauna — A155

No. 794, 37p: a, Yellow violet. b, Tussac bird.

No. 795, 43p: a, Carcass Island settlement. b, Black-crowned night heron.

Wmk. 373
2001, Sept. 28 **Litho.** ***Perf. 13¾***
Pairs, #a-b
794-795 A155 Set of 2 19.00 19.00

Gentoo Penguins — A156

Designs: 10p, Birds flapping wings. 33p, Feeding young. 37p, Bird with beak open. 43p, Four birds walking.

2001, Oct. 26 ***Perf. 14½x14¼***
796-799 A156 Set of 4 10.00 10.00

Falkland Islands Company, 150th Anniv. A157

Designs: 10p, Company coat of arms, and gathering of cattle. 20p, Company flag, and ship Amelia. 43p, Manager F. E. Cobb, and company buildings. £1, Sheep farmer William Wickham Bertrand, sheep dip.

Wmk. 373
2002, Jan. 10 **Litho.** ***Perf. 14***
800-803 A157 Set of 4 16.00 16.00

Reign Of Queen Elizabeth II, 50th Anniv. Issue
Common Design Type

Designs: Nos. 804, 808a, 20p, Princess Elizabeth reading, 1945. Nos. 805, 808b, 37p, In 1977. Nos. 806, 808c, 43p, Holding Prince Charles, 1949. Nos. 807, 808d, 50p, At Garter ceremony, 1994. No. 808e, 50p, 1955 portrait by Annigoni (38x50mm).

Perf. 14¼x14½, 13¾ (#808e)
2002, Feb. 6 **Litho.** **Wmk. 373**
With Gold Frames
804 CD360 20p multicolored 1.75 1.00
805 CD360 37p multicolored 2.25 2.00
806 CD360 43p multicolored 3.50 3.50
807 CD360 50p multicolored 4.00 4.00
Nos. 804-807 (4) 11.50 10.50

Souvenir Sheet
Without Gold Frames
808 CD360 Sheet of 5, #a-e 11.50 11.50

Falkland Islands War, 20th Anniv. — A158

No. 809, 22p: a, HMS Hermes, 1982. b, Fishery patrol vessel, 2002.

No. 810, 40p: a, Troops landing, 1982. b, Mine clearing, 2002.

No. 811, 45p: a, RAF Harrier on HMS Hermes, 1982. b, RAF Tristar, 2002.

Wmk. 373
2002, June 14 **Litho.** ***Perf. 14***
Horiz. pairs, #a-b
809-811 A158 Set of 3 20.00 20.00

Queen Mother Elizabeth (1900-2002)
Common Design Type

Designs: 22p, Wearing hat and scarf (black and white photograph). 25p, Wearing blue hat with polka dots. Nos. 814, 816a, 95p, Wearing feathered hat (black and white photograph). Nos. 815, 816b, £1.20, Wearing blue hat.

Wmk. 373
2002, Aug. 5 **Litho.** ***Perf. 14¼***
With Purple Frames
812 CD361 22p multicolored 1.00 1.00
813 CD361 25p multicolored 1.25 1.25
814 CD361 95p multicolored 5.00 5.00
815 CD361 £1.20 multicolored 6.75 6.75
Nos. 812-815 (4) 14.00 14.00

Souvenir Sheet
Without Purple Frames
Perf. 14½x14¼
816 CD361 Sheet of 2, #a-b 14.50 14.50

Worldwide Fund for Nature (WWF) — A159

Penguins: 36p, Rockhopper. 40p, Magellanic. 45p, Gentoo. 70p, Macaroni.

Wmk. 373
2002, Aug. 30 **Litho.** ***Perf. 14¼***
817-820 A159 Set of 4 11.50 11.50
a. Horiz. strip of 4, #817-820 13.00 13.00

West Point Island and its Flora and Fauna — A160

No. 821, 40p: a, Felton's flower. b, Black-browed albatross.

No. 822, 45p: a, Rockhopper penguin. b, Island settlement.

Perf. 14¼x14½
2002, Oct. 31 **Litho.** **Wmk. 373**
Horiz. Pairs, #a-b
821-822 A160 Set of 2 15.00 15.00

Visit of Prince Andrew — A161

No. 823: a, 22p, In uniform. b, £1.52, In suit and tie.

2002, Nov. 11 ***Perf. 13¼x13½***
823 A161 Horiz. pair, #a-b 14.50 14.50

Shepherds' Houses — A162

Designs: 10p, Gun Hill shanty, Little Chartres. 22p, Paragon House, Lafonia. 45p, Dos Lomas, Lafonia. £1, Old House, Shallow Bay Farm.

Wmk. 373
2003, Mar. 31 **Litho.** ***Perf. 14***
824-827 A162 Set of 4 12.00 12.00

Head of Queen Elizabeth II
Common Design Type
Wmk. 373
2003, June 2 **Litho.** ***Perf. 13¾***
828 CD362 £2 multi 9.00 9.00

Prince William, 21st Birthday
Common Design Type

Color photographs: a, In suit at right. b, With Prince Harry at left.

Wmk. 373
2003, June 21 **Litho.** ***Perf. 14¼***
829 Horiz. pair 13.50 13.50
a.-b. CD364 95p Either single 5.50 5.50

Birds — A163

Designs: 1p, Chiloe widgeon. 2p, Dolphin gull, vert. 5p, Falkland flightless steamer duck. 10p, Black-throated finch, vert. 22p, White-tufted grebe. 25p, Rufous-chested dotterel, vert. 45p, Upland goose. 50p, Dark-faced ground-tyrant, vert. 95p, Black-crowned night heron. £1, Red-backed hawk, vert. £3, Black-necked swan. £5, Short-eared owl, vert.

Perf. 13x13¼, 13¼x13
2003, July 21 **Litho.** **Wmk. 373**
830 A163 1p multi .60 *1.25*
831 A163 2p multi .90 *1.50*
832 A163 5p multi 1.25 *1.50*
833 A163 10p multi 1.50 1.50
834 A163 22p multi 1.75 1.25
835 A163 25p multi 2.00 1.25
836 A163 45p multi 2.50 2.00
837 A163 50p multi 3.00 3.00
838 A163 95p multi 4.25 *5.25*
839 A163 £1 multi 4.50 *5.25*
840 A163 £3 multi 12.00 *13.00*
841 A163 £5 multi 18.00 *20.00*
Nos. 830-841,C1 (13) 54.75 59.25

See Nos. 917-919, C1.

Bird Life International A164

Black-browed albatross: No. 842, Adult on nest, facing right. No. 843, Chick. 40p, Heads of two adults, vert. £1, Adult on nest, facing left, vert.

16p, In flight.

Perf. 14¼x13¾, 13¾x14¼
2003, Sept. 26
842 A164 22p multi 1.75 1.75
a. Perf. 14¼x14½ 1.75 1.75
843 A164 22p multi 1.75 1.75
a. Perf. 14¼x14½ 1.75 1.75
844 A164 40p multi 2.75 2.75
a. Perf. 14½x14¼ 2.75 2.75
845 A164 £1 multi 7.25 7.25
a. Perf. 14½x14¼ 7.25 7.25
Nos. 842-845 (4) 13.50 13.50

Souvenir Sheet
846 Sheet, #842a-846a 16.50 16.50
a. A164 16p multi, perf. 14¼x14½ 1.40 1.40

New Island and its Flora and Fauna A165

No. 847, 40p: a, Striated caracara. b, Lady's slipper.
No. 848, 45p: a, Stone Cottage. b, King penguin.

Wmk. 373

2003, Oct. 24 Litho. *Perf. 13¾*
Pairs, #a-b

847-848 A165 Set of 2 18.00 18.00

Christmas — A166

Various depictions of Pale maiden flower: 16p, 30p, 40p, 95p.

2003, Nov. 3 *Perf. 14x14¼*
849-852 A166 Set of 4 16.50 16.50

Sheep Farming A167

Designs: 19p, Traditional hand shearing. 22p, Driving the sheep. 45p, Big House, Hill Cove. 70p, The early years. £1, Wool collection, SS Fitzroy.

Unwmk.

2004, Apr. 30 Litho. *Perf. 14*
853-857 A167 Set of 5 22.50 22.50

Wildlife Conservation in Falkland Islands, 25th Anniv. — A168

Designs: 20p, Man planting tussac grass. 24p, People cleaning beach. 50p, Satellite tracking of rockhopper penguins. £1, Weighing of albatross chick.

2004, June 17 Litho. *Perf. 14*
858-861 A168 Set of 4 18.00 18.00

Sir Rowland Hill (1795-1879) and Falkland Islands Postage Stamps — A169

Hill and: 24p, #20. 50p, #74. 75p, #94. £1, #151a.

2004, Aug. 31 Litho. *Perf. 13¼*
862-865 A169 Set of 4 19.00 19.00

Sea Lion Island and its Flora and Fauna — A170

No. 866, 42p: a, King cormorant. b, Dog orchid.
No. 867, 50p: a, Magellanic penguin. b, Sea Lion Lodge.

2004, Sept. 15 *Perf. 13¾*
Pairs, #a-b

866-867 A170 Set of 2 19.50 19.50
866c As #866a, dated "2005" 2.25 —
866d As #866b, dated "2005" 2.25 —
866e Pair, #866c-866d 7.00 —

Owls — A171

Designs: 18p, Head of short-eared owl. 45p, Short-eared owl. 50p, Barn owl in flight. £1.50, Barn owl.
£2, Barn owl in flight, horiz.

2004, Oct. 25
868-871 A171 Set of 4 18.00 18.00

Souvenir Sheet

872 A171 £2 multi 12.00 12.00

Battle of the Falkland Islands, 90th Anniv. A172

No. 873: a, HMS Kent, HMS Inflexible, half of HMS Carnarvon, half of HMS Cornwall. b, British Navy flag, HMS Glasgow, half of HMS Carnarvon, half of HMS Cornwall, half of HMS Invincible. c, Medals, half of HMS Invincible.
No. 874: a, Medals, half of SMS Scharnhorst. b, German imperial war ensign, SMS Dresden, half of SMS Scharnhorst, half of SMS Leipzig. c, SMS Nürnberg, SMS Gneisenau, half of SMS Leipzig.

2004, Dec. 8 Litho. *Perf. 14*
873 Horiz. strip of 3 9.50 9.50
a.-c. A172 24p Any single 2.40 1.90
874 Horiz. strip of 3 17.50 17.50
a.-c. A172 50p Any single 4.25 3.25

Camber Railway, 90th Anniv. — A173

Designs: 3p, Old track bed. 24p, Kerr Stuart Wren Class locomotive at Camber Depot, horiz. 50p, Kerr Stuart Wren Class locomotive Falkland Islands Express, horiz. £2, Camber sailing wagon.

2005, Feb. 28 *Perf. 13¾*
875-878 A173 Set of 4 17.00 17.00

Wedding of Prince Charles and Camilla Parker Bowles A174

Designs: 24p, Couple. 50p, Couple in formal wear, vert.
£2, Couple, Windsor Castle.

2005, Apr. 29 *Perf. 14*
879-880 A174 Set of 2 5.00 5.00

Souvenir Sheet

881 A174 £2 multi 10.50 10.50

End of World War II, 60th Anniv. — A175

No. 882, 24p: a, Walrus reconnaissance seaplane. b, Presentation Spitfire X4616.
No. 883, 80p: a, HMS Exeter at Port Stanley. b, Governor, King Edward Memorial Hospital staff, Rear Admiral Harwood and Capt. Bell.
No. 884, £1: a, Fitzroy. b, HMS William Scoresby.

Perf. 13¼x13½

2005, June 29 Litho.
Horiz. Pairs, #a-b

882-884 A175 Set of 3 28.00 28.00

Maritime Heritage A176

Designs: 24p, Snow Squall escaping CSS Tuscaloosa, 1863. No. 886, 55p, Jhelum, 1870. No. 887, 55p, Charles Cooper, 1866. £1.20, SS Imo colliding with the Mont Blanc, Halifax Harbor, 1917.

2005, Aug. 29 Litho. *Perf. 14*
885-888 A176 Set of 4 13.00 13.00

Pebble Island and its Flora and Fauna — A177

No. 889, 45p: a, Gentoo penguin. b, Falkland lavender.
No. 890, 55p: a, Pebble Island Lodge. b, Black-necked swan.

2005, Sept. 12 *Perf. 13¾*
Pairs, #a-b

889-890 A177 Set of 2 14.00 14.00

Souvenir Sheet

The Fall of Nelson, Battle of Trafalgar, 21 October 1805, by Denis Dighton — A178

2005, Oct. 21
891 A178 £2 multi 12.00 12.00

Battle of Trafalgar, bicent.

Hans Christian Andersen (1805-75), Author — A179

Stories: 18p, The Little Mermaid. 30p, The Snowman. 45p, The Ugly Duckling. £1, Thumbelina.

2005, Oct. 28 *Perf. 14*
892-895 A179 Set of 4 11.50 11.50

Stanley Infant and Junior School, 50th anniv.

Black-crowned Night Heron — A180

Designs: 24p, Head. 55p, Bird on one leg. 80p, Juvenile standing. £1, Head of juvenile.

2006, Feb. 10 Litho. *Perf. 13¾*
896-899 A180 Set of 4 13.00 13.00

Queen Elizabeth II, 80th Birthday — A181

Queen wearing: 24p, Yellow hat. 55p, Green hat. 80p, Blue hat. £1, Red hat.
£2, Tiara and white hat, horiz.

2006, Apr. 21 *Perf. 14*
900-903 A181 Set of 4 13.00 13.00

Souvenir Sheet

904 A181 £2 multi 11.00 11.00

SS Great Britain — A182

View of: 24p, Bow. 55p, Stern. £1.50, Deck and masts.

2006, May 19 *Perf. 13¾x13¼*
905-907 A182 Set of 3 13.00 13.00

Birds A183

Designs: No. 908, 25p, Gentoo penguin chicks. No. 909, 25p, King cormorants. No. 910, 60p, King penguin. No. 911, 60p, Wandering albatross.

2006, Aug. 30 Litho. *Perf. 14¼x14*
908-911 A183 Set of 4 11.00 11.00

Bleaker Island and its Flora and Fauna — A184

No. 912, 50p: a, Woolly Falkland ragwort. b, Macaroni penguin.
No. 913, 60p: a, The Outlook and sheep. b, Long-tailed meadowlark.

2006, Sept. 18 *Perf. 13¼x13*
Pairs, #a-b

912-913 A184 Set of 2 15.00 15.00

Victoria Cross, 150th Anniv. — A185

Designs: Nos. 914, 916a, 60p, Lt. Col. H. Jones. Nos. 915, 916b, 60p, Sgt. Ian McKay. No. 916c, £1, Victoria Cross.

2006, Nov. 11 ***Perf. 13¼***

Stamps With White Frames

914-915 A185 Set of 2 7.00 7.00

Souvenir Sheet

Stamps Without White Frames

916 A185 Sheet of 3, #a-c 7.00 7.00

Bird Type of 2003

Designs: 20p, Black-browed albatross, vert. 25p, Rufous-chested dotterel, vert. £5, Short-eared owl, vert.

Perf. 13¼x13

2006, Nov. 15 **Litho.** **Unwmk.**

917 A163 20p multi 2.50 2.00
918 A163 25p multi 2.75 2.50
919 A163 £5 multi 22.50 *24.00*
Nos. 917-919 (3) 27.75 28.50

Nos. 918-919 differ from Nos. 835 and 841 by having less color around the Queen's head. Nos. 917-919 are dated "2006."

Worldwide Fund for Nature (WWF) A186

Striated caracara: 25p, Heads of two birds. 50p, Bird in flight. 60p, Bird standing. 85p, Bird eating shellfish.

2006, Dec. 20 **Litho.** ***Perf. 13¾***

920-923 A186 Set of 4 10.00 10.00
923a Miniature sheet, 4 each #920-923 47.50 47.50

Fisheries, 20th Anniv. A187

Designs: 3p, Fishermen at sea. 11p, Fishing boat at night. 25p, Fishermen leaving boat. 30p, Japanese jigger. 60p, Fishery protection boat Dorada. £1.05, Trawler transferring fish to a freezer container ship.

2007, Feb. 24 ***Perf. 14¼***

924-929 A187 Set of 6 13.50 13.50

HMS Plymouth A188

HMS Plymouth: 25p, Joining Falkland Islands Task Force. 40p, Supporting SBS. 60p, Under attack by Argentine fighters. £1.05, Docked at Port Stanley.

2007, Mar. 27

930-933 A188 Set of 4 17.50 17.50

Souvenir Sheet

Falkland Islands War, 25th Anniv. — A189

No. 934: a, Avro Vulcan prototype VX770. b, Avro Vulcan XM597. c, Avro Vulcan XM607. d, Vulcan in the Sky Project.

2007, May 25 **Litho.** ***Perf. 13¼***

934 A189 60p Sheet of 4, #a-d 14.00 14.00

Miniature Sheets

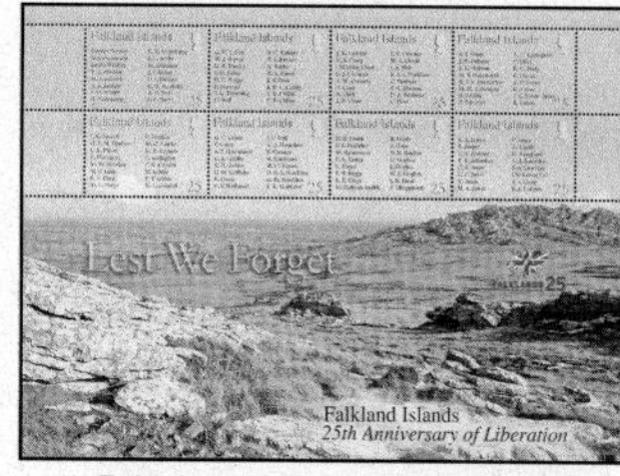

British and Falkland Islander Casualties of the Falkland Islands War — A190

No. 935, 25p — Casualties beginning with: a, Doreen Bonner. b, G. W. J. Batt. c, J. R. Carlyle. d, S. J. Dixon. e, I. R. Farrell. f, G. C. Grace. g, R. R. Heath. h, A. S. James.

No. 936, 60p: a, D. Lee. b, P. B. McKay. c, G. T. Nelson. d, J. B. Pashley. e, M. Sambles. f, D. A. Strickland. g, R. G. Thomas. h, P. A. West.

2007, June 14 **Litho.** ***Perf. 14¼***

Sheets of 8, #a-h

935-936 A190 Set of 2 30.00 30.00

Scouting, Cent. — A191

Designs: 10p, Scouts on ladder of RRS Discovery. 20p, Dignitaries on ship's deck. 25p, Dignitaries, diff. £2, RRS Discovery.

2007, July 23 **Litho.** ***Perf. 13½x13¼***

937-940 A191 Set of 4 12.00 12.00

Voyage of RRS Discovery from Falkland Islands for presentation to British Scout Association, 70th anniv.

Princess Diana (1961-97) — A192

2007, Aug. 31 ***Perf. 14***

941 A192 60p multi 3.75 3.75

Printed in sheets of 8 stamps + 2 labels.

Saunders Island and its Flora and Fauna — A193

No. 942, 50p: a, Rockhopper penguin. b, Dusty miller.

No. 943, 55p: a, Crested caracara. b, Earliest British settlement at Port Egmont.

2007, Sept. 28 **Litho.** ***Perf. 13¾***

Pairs, #a-b

942-943 A193 Set of 2 15.00 15.00

A194

2007, Nov. 20 **Litho.** ***Perf. 14***

944 A194 £1 multi 6.00 6.00

Wedding of Queen Elizabeth II and Prince Philip, 60th Anniv.

Polar Explorers and Their Ships A195

Explorers and ships: 4p, James Weddell (1787-1834), and Jane. 25p, James Clark Ross (1800-62), and HMS Erebus. 85p, William Spiers Bruce (1867-1921), and Scotia. £1.61, James Marr (1902-65), and Discovery II.

2008, Apr. 7

945-948 A195 Set of 4 13.00 13.00

Southern Elephant Seals A196

Designs: 27p, Seal pup. 55p, Male and female. 65p, Seals play fighting. £1.10, Seal and tussock bird.

2008, July 15 **Litho.** ***Perf. 14***

949-952 A196 Set of 4 14.00 14.00

Aircraft A197

Designs: 1p, Taylorcraft Auster Mk 5. 2p, Boeing 747-300. 5p, De Havilland Canada DHC-6 Twin Otter. 10p, Lockheed C-130 Hercules. 27p, De Havilland Canada DHC-2 Beaver. 55p, Airbus A320. 65p, Lockheed L-1011-385-3 Tristar C2. 90p, Avro Vulcan B2. £1, Britten-Norman BN-2 Islander. £2, Panavia Tornado F3. £3, De Havilland Canada DHC-7-110 Dash 7. £5, BAE Sea Harrier.

2008, Aug. 1 **Litho.** ***Perf. 14***

953 A197 1p multi .40 *.75*
954 A197 2p multi .40 *.75*
955 A197 5p multi .75 .85
956 A197 10p multi .90 .90
957 A197 27p multi 1.75 1.75
958 A197 55p multi 2.25 2.25
959 A197 65p multi 2.75 2.75
960 A197 90p multi 3.50 3.50
961 A197 £1 multi 4.00 4.00
962 A197 £2 multi 7.25 *8.00*
963 A197 £3 multi 10.00 *11.00*
964 A197 £5 multi 16.00 *18.00*
Nos. 953-964 (12) 49.95 54.50

Souvenir Sheet

Stamps With Royal Air Force 90th Anniv. Emblem Added

965 Sheet of 4 14.50 14.50
a. A197 10p Like #956 .40 .40
b. A197 65p Like #959 2.60 2.60
c. A197 90p Like #960 3.50 3.50
d. A197 £2 Like #962 8.00 8.00

Port Louis, 175th Anniv. — A198

Designs: 27p, Sailor raising British flag. 65p, Royal Marines, British flag.

£2, Capt. Onslow of HMS Clio, British flag.

2008, Sept. 22 **Litho.** ***Perf. 14***

966-967 A198 Set of 2 4.75 4.75

Souvenir Sheet

968 A198 £2 multi 9.00 9.00

Islands and Rocks A199

Designs: 22p, The Slipper. 40p, Kidney Island. 60p, Stephens Bluff and Castle Rock. £1, The Colliers.

2008, Oct. 1 **Litho.** ***Perf. 13¾***

969-972 A199 Set of 4 10.00 10.00

See Nos. 986-989, 1025-1028.

Retirement of Queen Elizabeth 2 as Ocean Liner — A200

Designs: 23p, Launch of Queen Elizabeth 2. 27p, Service of Queen Elizabeth 2 as troop ship in Falkland Islands War. 65p, Queen Elizabeth 2, Palm Jumeirah, Dubai. £2, Queen Elizabeth 2 (70x34mm).

2008, Nov. 21 **Litho.** ***Perf. 13¼***

973-976 A200 Set of 4 13.00 13.00

Charles Darwin (1809-82), Naturalist — A201

Designs: 4p, Darwin seated. 27p, Warrah. 65p, HMS Beagle in Berkeley Sound, 1834. £1.10, Darwin encountering a Magellanic penguin.

2009, Apr. 23 **Litho.** ***Perf. 14***

977-980 A201 Set of 4 8.00 8.00

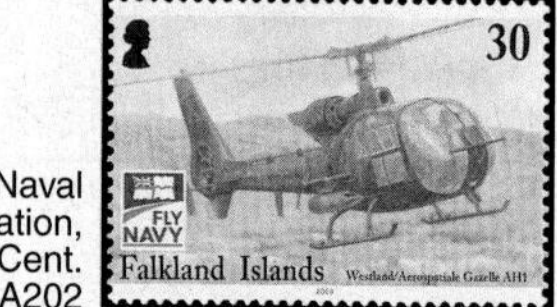

Naval Aviation, Cent. A202

Royal Navy aircraft and ships: 30p, Westland/Aerospatiale Gazelle AH1 helicopter.

50p, Westland Lynx HAS2 helicopter. 65p, Westland Wessex HU5 helicopter. £1.10, Westland Sea King HAS5 helicopter. £2, BAe Sea Harrier, HMS Hermes.

2009, May 7 Litho. *Perf. 14*
981-984 A202 Set of 4 11.00 11.00

Souvenir Sheet

985 A202 £2 multi 7.50 7.50

Islands and Rocks Type of 2008

Designs: 27p, Seal Rocks. 40p, Beauchene Island. 65p, Jason East Cay, Steeple Jason. £1.50, Horse Block.

2009, Aug. 14 Litho. *Perf. 13¾*
986-989 A199 Set of 4 11.50 11.50

Albatrosses A203

Designs: 22p, Black-browed albatross. 27p, Gray-headed albatross. 60p, Light-mantled sooty albatross. 90p, Wandering albatross.

2009, Oct. 19 Litho. *Perf. 13¾*
990-993 A203 Set of 4 8.50 8.50

Cobb's Wren A204

Designs: Nos. 994, 998a, 27p, Wren on seaweed. Nos. 995, 998b, 65p, Wrens at nest. Nos. 996, 998c, 90p, Wren on rock. Nos. 997, 998d, £1.10, Two wrens.

2009, Nov. 10 *Perf. 13¾*

Stamps With WWF Emblem

994-997 A204 Set of 4 10.00 10.00
997a Sheet of 16, 4 each #994-997 52.50 52.50

Souvenir Sheet

Stamps With Falklands Conservation Emblem

998 A204 Sheet of 4, #a-d 10.00 10.00

Ships Named HMS Exeter A205

Ship used from: 4p, 1931-42. 20p, 1931-42, with helicopter. 30p, 1980-2009, with helicopter. £1.66, 1980-2009, with helicopter, diff.

2009, Dec. 8 Litho. *Perf. 14*
999-1002 A205 Set of 4 7.50 7.50

Skies in Four Seasons A206

Designs: 27p, Carcass Island in spring. 55p, Beach on New Island in summer. 65p, Rainbow over Stanley in autumn. £1.10, Islands in winter.

2010, Jan. 25 Litho. *Perf. 13*
1003-1006 A206 Set of 4 8.00 8.00

Restoration of the SS Great Britain A207

SS Great Britain: 27p, On pontoon near jetty in Stanley. 50p, Beached at Sparrow Cove. 65p, Bow. £1.10, Mast and rigging.

2010, Apr. 12 *Perf. 13¼*
1007-1010 A207 Set of 4 8.00 8.00

Miniature Sheet

Battle of Britain, 70th Anniv. — A208

No. 1011 — Airplanes: a, Hawker Hurricane P2961. b, Supermarine Spitfire P9398. c, Hawker Hurricane P3854. d, Supermarine Spitfire P7350. e, Hawker Hurricane V6665. f, Supermarine Spitfire L1035. g, Hawker Hurricane P3576. h, Supermarine Spitfire X4620.

2010, May 7 Litho. *Perf. 14x14¼*
1011 A208 65p Sheet of 8, #a-h 15.00 15.00

London 2010 Festival of Stamps.

Birds A209

Designs: Nos. 1012, 1016a, 27p, Sooty shearwater. Nos. 1013, 1016b, 70p, White-chinned petrel. Nos. 1014, 1016c, 95p, Southern giant petrel. Nos. 1015, 1016d, £1.15, Greater shearwater.

2010, July 8 Litho. *Perf. 13¾*

Stamps With White Frames

1012-1015 A209 Set of 4 9.50 9.50

Souvenir Sheet

Stamps Without White Frames

1016 A209 Sheet of 4, #a-d 11.50 11.50

Flowering Shrubs A210

Designs: 27p, Fuchsia. 70p, Boxwood. 95p, Gorse. £1.15, Honeysuckle.

2010, Oct. 27 Litho. *Perf. 13¼x13*
1017-1020 A210 Set of 4 10.00 10.00

Royal Air Force Search and Rescue Force, 70th Anniv. — A211

Anniversary emblem and: 27p, Helicopter on ground. 70p, Helicopter in flight. 95p, Crew in helicopter cockpit. £1.15, Helicopter in flight with open door.

2011, Mar. 9 *Perf. 13¼*
1021-1024 A211 Set of 4 10.00 10.00

Islands and Rocks Type of 2008

Designs: 3p, Bird Island. 27p, Eddystone Rock. 70p, Round Island and Sail Rock. £1.71, Direction Island.

2011, Apr. 11 *Perf. 13¼x13*
1025-1028 A199 Set of 4 8.50 8.50

Wedding of Prince William and Catherine Middleton — A212

2011, Apr. 29 *Perf. 13¼*
1029 A212 £2 multi 6.75 6.75

Worldwide Fund for Nature (WWF) — A213

Southern sea lions: 27p, Males and females on beach. 40p, Pod in water. 70p, Males on beach. £1.15, Head.

2011, May 30 *Perf. 13¾*
1030-1033 A213 Set of 4 8.75 8.75
1033a Miniature sheet of 16, 4 each #1030-1033 35.00 35.00

Queen Elizabeth II, 85th Birthday — A214

Queen Elizabeth II wearing: 27p, Red violet hat with flower. 30p, Fur hat. 70p, White hat with pink and white ribbons. £1.50, White hat with feather.

2011, June 11 *Perf. 13¾*
1034-1037 A214 Set of 4 8.50 8.50

Souvenir Sheet

Queen Elizabeth II — A215

2011, Aug. 8 Litho. *Perf. 14¼x15*
1038 A215 £2 multi 6.75 6.75

Commonwealth Parliamentary Association, cent.

Wildlife A216

Designs: 27p, Gentoo penguins. 70p, Leopard seal. 95p, Gonatus squid. £1.15, Gentoo penguins, diff.

2011, Nov. 16 *Perf. 13¾*
1039-1042 A216 Set of 4 10.00 10.00

Marine Life A217

Designs: 27p, Sea anemone. 50p, Jellyfish. 70p, Starfish. £1.15, Nudibranch.

2012, Apr. 11 *Perf. 13¼x13½*
1043-1046 A217 Set of 4 8.00 8.00

Reign of Queen Elizabeth II, 60th Anniv. — A218

Photograph of Queen Elizabeth II in: 27p, 1952. 30p, 1977. 70p, 2002. £1.71, 2012. £3, Queen Elizabeth II wearing tiara, 1955.

2012, May 10 *Perf. 13½x13¼*
1047-1050 A218 Set of 4 9.00 9.00

Souvenir Sheet

Perf. 13¼

1051 A218 £3 multi 9.00 9.00

No. 1051 contains one 30x48mm stamp.

Liberation of the Falkland Islands, 30th Anniv. — A219

Designs: No. 1052, 30p, Ferry MV Concordia Bay. No. 1053, 30p, Liberation Monument, Stanley. No. 1054, 75p, School, Stanley. No. 1055, 75p, Wind turbines. £1, Sign and houses near Stanley Harbor. £1.20, Children and penguins.

2012, June 14 *Perf. 14*
1052-1057 A219 Set of 6 12.50 12.50

Coastal Landscapes — A220

Designs: 30p, Surf Bay, East Falkland Island. 75p, Cliffs, New Island. £1, Mountain, Steeple Jason Island. £1.20, Deaths Head and Grave Cove, West Falkland Island.

2012, July 12 ***Perf. 13***
1058-1061 A220 Set of 4 9.25 9.25

Sinking of the P.S.N.C. Oravia, Cent. A221

Designs: 30p, Oravia at sea. 75p, Passengers and crew wearing life vests. £1, Passengers filling lifeboats. £1.20 Oravia and the Samson.

2012, Aug. 28 ***Perf. 14***
1062-1065 A221 Set of 4 12.00 12.00

Souvenir Sheet

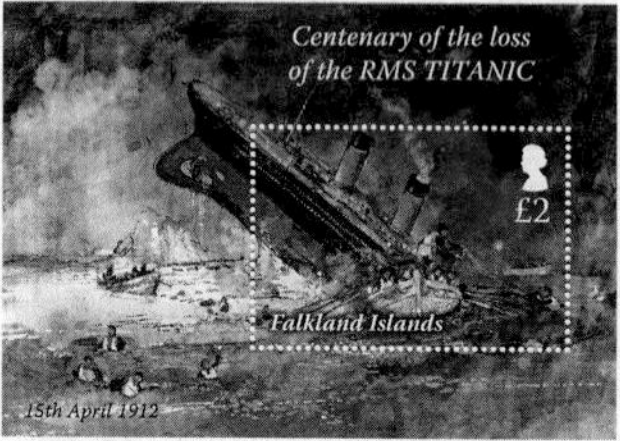

Sinking of the Titanic, Cent. — A222

2012, Aug. 28 ***Perf. 14x14¾***
1066 A222 £2 multi 9.00 9.00

Dolphins and Whales — A223

Designs: 1p, Southern right whale dolphins. 2p, Minke whale. 5p, Peale's dolphin. 10p, Dusky dolphin. 30p, Southern right whale. 50p, Fin whale. 75p, Hourglass dolphin. £1, Long-finned pilot whale. £1.20, Killer whales. £2, Sperm whale. £3.50, Commerson's dolphin. £5, Sei whale.

2012, Nov. 9 ***Perf. 13¼***

1067	A223	1p multi	.25	.25
1068	A223	2p multi	.25	.25
1069	A223	5p multi	.25	.25
1070	A223	10p multi	.30	.30
1071	A223	30p multi	.95	.95
1072	A223	50p multi	1.60	1.60
1073	A223	75p multi	2.40	2.40
1074	A223	£1 multi	3.25	3.25
1075	A223	£1.20 multi	4.00	4.00
1076	A223	£2 multi	6.50	6.50
1077	A223	£3.50 multi	11.00	11.00
1078	A223	£5 multi	14.00	14.00
	Nos. 1067-1078 (12)		44.75	44.75

See No. 1172.

Color in Nature — A224

No. 1079: a, Night heron. b, Diddle-dee berries.

No. 1080: a, Short-eared owl. b, Scurvy grass flowers.

2012, Dec. 14 ***Perf. 13***
1079 Pair 2.00 2.00
a.-b. A224 30p Either single 1.00 1.00
1080 Pair 4.50 4.50
a.-b. A224 75p Either single 2.25 2.25

See Nos. 1108-1109, 1122-1123, 1136-1137.

2013 Referendum on Political Status A225

Map, of Falkland Island, hand and ballot box with denomination color of: 3p, Deep blue. 40p, Red violet. 75p, Green. £1.76, Red brown.
£3, Purple.

2013, Feb. 15
1081-1084 A225 Set of 4 8.75 8.75

Souvenir Sheet
Perf. 13½x13¼
1085 A225 £3 multi 9.00 9.00

No. 1085 contains one 56x45mm stamp.

Wildlife A226

Designs: 30p, Johnny rook. 75p, Rockhopper penguins. £1, Rockhopper penguin swimming. £1.20, Lobster krill.

2013, Mar. 28 ***Perf. 13¾***
1086-1089 A226 Set of 4 10.00 10.00

Lady Margaret Thatcher (1925-2013), British Prime Minister — A227

Lady Thatcher: 30p, And husband, Denis arriving at 10 Downing Street, 1979. 75p, Inspecting Falkland Islands minefield, 1983. £1, With flag at celebration of 10th anniversary of Falkland Islands liberation, 1992. £1.20, Holding Falkland Islands coin commemorating 25th anniversary of the liberation, 2007.

2013, May 16 ***Perf. 13¾***
1090-1093 A227 Set of 4 10.00 10.00

Sir Rex Hunt (1926-2012), Governor of Falkland Islands — A228

Falkland Islands coat of arms and Hunt: 30p, As Civil Commissioner, 1982. 75p, In uniform next to Governor's car. £1, With flag of Falkland Islands, 1992. £1.20, Talking to Queen Elizabeth II, 2000.

2013, June 11 ***Perf. 14***
1094-1097 A228 Set of 4 10.00 10.00

Coronation of Queen Elizabeth II, 60th Anniv. — A229

Queen Elizabeth II: 30p, Wearing coronation gown. 75p, With crown and orb. £1, Waving. £1.20, With Prince Philip.

2013, July 22 ***Perf. 13½x13¼***
1098-1101 A229 Set of 4 10.00 10.00

Shallow Marine Surveys Group A230

Marine life: Nos. 1102, 1106a, 30p, Saffron sea cucumber. Nos. 1103, 1106b, 75p, Stalked jellyfish. Nos. 1104, 1106c, £1, Scythe-edged serolis. Nos. 1105, 1106d, £1.20, Naked sea urchin.
No. 1107a, £1, Painted shrimp, vert.

2013, Aug. 29 ***Perf. 13¼x13½***

Stamps With White Frames
1102-1105 A230 Set of 4 10.50 10.50

Stamps Without White Frames
1106 A230 Strip of 4, #a-d 10.50 10.50

Souvenir Sheet
Perf. 13½x13¼
1107 A230 Sheet of 3 (see footnote) 9.75 9.75
a. A230 £1 multi 3.25 3.25

No. 1107 contains No. 1107a, Ascension No. 1104a and South Georgia and South Sandwich Islands No. 485a. This sheet was sold in Ascension, Falkland Islands and South Georgia and South Sandwich Islands.

Color in Nature Type of 2012

No. 1108: a, Macaroni penguin. b, Purple cap fungi.
No. 1109: a, Crested duck. b, Southern painted lady butterfly.

2013, Oct. 3 ***Perf. 13¼***
1108 Pair 1.90 1.90
a.-b. A224 30p Either single .95 .95
1109 Pair 4.80 4.80
a.-b. A224 75p Either single 2.40 2.40

Wildlife A231

Designs: 30p, King penguin and chick. 75p, Gaptooth lanternfish. £1, Southern sea lion. £1.20, King penguins, diff.

2014, Mar. 25 **Litho.** ***Perf. 13¼***
1110-1113 A231 Set of 4 11.00 11.00

Mushrooms A232

Designs: 30p, False chanterelle. 75p, Red wax cap. £1, Clustered domecap. £1.20, Shaggy inkcap.

2014, Apr. 15 **Litho.** ***Perf. 13¼***
1114-1117 A232 Set of 4 10.00 10.00

Royal Christenings A233

Photograph from christening of: 30p, Queen Elizabeth II. 75p, Prince Charles. £1, Prince William. £1.20, Prince George.

2014, May 21 **Litho.** ***Perf. 13¼***
1118-1121 A233 Set of 4 10.00 10.00

Color in Nature Type of 2012

No. 1122: a, King penguins. b, Marsh marigolds.
No. 1123: a, Black oystercatcher. b, Vanilla daisies.

2014, Sept. 16 **Litho.** ***Perf. 13¼***
1122 Pair 2.00 2.00
a.-b. A224 30p Either single 1.00 1.00
1123 Pair 5.00 5.00
a.-b. A224 75p Either single 2.50 2.50

Battle of the Falkland Islands, Cent. — A234

Designs: 30p, SMS Scharnhorst. 75p, HMS Invincible. £1, British and German flags, poppies. £1.20, Sailor, Battle of the Falkland Islands Monument.

2014, Dec. 8 **Litho.** ***Perf. 13¾***
1124-1127 A234 Set of 4 10.00 10.00

Type 42 Destroyers — A235

Designs: 30p, HMS Sheffield. 75p, HMS Exeter. £1, HMS Liverpool. £1.20, HMS Edinburgh.

2014, Dec. 22 **Litho.** ***Perf. 14***
1128-1131 A235 Set of 4 9.00 9.00

Birds — A236

Adult and chicks: 30p, Pied oystercatchers. 75p, Gentoo penguins. £1, Black-browed albatrosses. £1.20, Falkland skuas.

2015, Feb. 11 **Litho.** ***Perf. 13¾***
1132-1135 A236 Set of 4 10.00 10.00

Color in Nature Type of 2012

No. 1136: a, Black-throated finch. b, Fuegian ferns.
No. 1137: a, Dolphin gulls. b, Yellow daisies.

2015, May 12 **Litho.** ***Perf. 13¼***
1136 Pair 1.90 1.90
a.-b. A224 30p Either single .95 .95
1137 Pair 4.50 4.50
a.-b. A224 75p Either single 2.25 2.25

Magna Carta, 800th Anniv. A237

Designs: 30p, King John, Magna Carta and barons. 75p, Courtroom. £1, Gilbert House, Stanley. £1.20, King John, arms of Falkland Islands.

2015, June 15 Litho. *Perf. 14*
1138-1141 A237 Set of 4 10.50 10.50

Wildlife A238

Designs: 30p, Magellanic penguin. 75p, Falkland sprats. £1, Falkland skua. £1.20, Heads of two magellanic penguins.

2015, Aug. 21 Litho. *Perf. 13¾*
1142-1145 A238 Set of 4 10.00 10.00

Queen Elizabeth II, Longest-Reigning British Monarch — A239

Queen Elizabeth II and events during her reign: 30p, Publications reporting on her coronation, 1953. 75p, Arrival of first Land Rovers in the Falkland Islands, 1950s. £1, Coach used for Golden Jubilee, 2012. £1.25, Falkland Islands referendum, 2013.

2015, Sept. 9 Litho. *Perf. 14*
1146-1149 A239 Set of 4 10.00 10.00

Elephant Seal Research Group, 20th Anniv. — A240

No. 1150, 30p: a, Seal in water. b, Researcher with equipment near seal.
No. 1151, 75p: a, Pod of seals on beach. b, Researcher approaching seal.
No. 1152, £1: a, Seal and penguins. b, Researcher holding measuring stick above seal.

2015, Nov. 30 Litho. *Perf. 13*
Horiz. Pairs, #a-b
1150-1152 A240 Set of 3 12.50 12.50

Clouds — A241

Designs: 31p, Asperitas. 76p, Altocumulus. £1.01, Altocumulus lenticularis. £1.22, Cumulonimbus and Stratocumulus.

2015, Dec. 9 Litho. *Perf. 13¼*
1153-1156 A241 Set of 4 9.75 9.75

Birds of Prey — A242

Designs: No. 1157, 31p, Barn owl. No. 1158, 31p, Short-eared owl. No. 1159, 76p, Red-backed buzzard. No. 1160, 76p, Crested caracara. £1.01, Peregrine falcon. £1.22, Striated caracara.

2016, Jan. 13 Litho. *Perf. 13¾*
1157-1162 A242 Set of 6 13.00 13.00

Items at Historic Dockyard Museum — A243

Designs: 31p, Traditional horse gear. 76p, Peat-burning stove. £1.01, Warrah skull. £1.22, Antarctic exploration hut.

2016, Mar. 30 Litho. *Perf. 13¾*
1163-1166 A243 Set of 4 9.50 9.50

Queen Elizabeth II, 90th Birthday — A244

Photographs of Queen Elizabeth from: 31p, 1977. 76p, 1982. £1.01, 1953. £1.22, 2014. £3, Queen Elizabeth II in 1962.

2016, Apr. 21 Litho. *Perf. 14*
1167-1170 A244 Set of 4 9.75 9.75

Souvenir Sheet

1171 A244 £3 multi 9.00 9.00

Dolphins and Whales Type of 2012

2016, Aug. 1 Litho. *Perf. 13¼*
1172 A223 31p Southern right whale .85 .85

Endemic Plants A245

Designs: No. 1173, 31p, Falkland rock-cress. No. 1174, 31p, Lady's slipper. No. 1175, 76p, False-plantain. No. 1176, 76p, Silvery buttercup. No. 1177, £1.01, Snakeplant. No. 1178, £1.01, Falkland nassauvia.
No. 1179, 66p: a, Like No. 1173. b, Like No. 1174. c, Like No. 1175. d, Like No. 1176. e, Like No. 1177. f, Like No. 1178.

2016, Nov. 21 Litho. *Perf. 13¾*
1173-1178 A245 Set of 6 11.00 11.00

Miniature Sheet

1179 A245 66p Sheet of 6, #a-f 10.00 10.00

No. 1179 has cream colored margins around the stamps.

Shipwrecks A246

Designs: 31p, Acteon. 76p, Charles Cooper. £1.01, Afterglow. £1.22, Capricorn.

2017, Mar. 27 Litho. *Perf. 13*
1180-1183 A246 Set of 4 8.25 8.25

See Nos. 1213-1216, 1244-1247.

Falkland Islands Journal, 50th Anniv. — A247

Journal cover from: 31p, 2010. 76p, 2013r. £1.01, 2014. £1.22, 2016.

2017, July 5 Litho. *Perf. 13½x13¼*
1184-1187 A247 Set of 4 8.50 8.50

A248

Birds — A249

Designs: 1p, Tussacbird. 2p, Long-tailed meadowlark. 5p, Black-chinned siskin. 10p, Falkland pipit, above white flowers. 20p, Cobb's wren. 50p, White-bridled finch. 76p, Falkland thrush. £1, Two-banded plover. £1.20, Falkland grass wren. £2, Dark-faced ground tyrant. £3.50, Rufous-chested dotterel. £5, Magellanic snipe.
(31p), Falkland pipit, above red flowers.

2017, Aug. 14 Litho. *Perf. 13*

1188	A248	1p	multi	.25	.25
1189	A248	2p	multi	.25	.25
1190	A248	5p	multi	.25	.25
1191	A248	10p	multi	.30	.30
1192	A248	20p	multi	.55	.55
1193	A248	50p	multi	1.40	1.40
1194	A248	76p	multi	2.00	2.00
1195	A248	£1	multi	2.75	2.75
1196	A248	£1.20	multi	3.25	3.25
1197	A248	£2	multi	5.25	5.25
1198	A248	£3.50	multi	9.25	9.25
1199	A248	£5	multi	13.50	13.50
	Nos. 1188-1199 (12)			39.00	39.00

Booklet Stamp
Self-Adhesive

Serpentine Die Cut 13

1200	A249 (31p) multi		.85	.85
a.	Booklet pane of 10		8.50	
b.	Dated "2019"		.80	.80
c.	Booklet pane of 10 #1200b		8.00	

Issued: No. 1200b, 8/6/19. No. 1200b sold for 32p on day of issue.

Falkland Islands Fisheries, 30th Anniv. — A250

Designs: 31p, Toothfish and CFL Hunter. 76p, FPV Protegat and fishery RIB. £1.01, Argos Vigo and Frank Wild. £1.22, Robin M. Lee and Falkland calamari.

2017, Oct. 23 Litho. *Perf. 13½x13¼*
1201-1204 A250 Set of 4 8.75 8.75

70th Wedding Anniversary of Queen Elizabeth II and Prince Philip A251

Photograph of Queen Elizabeth II and Prince Philip from: 31p, 1952. 76p, 1961. £1.22, 1972. £1.78, 2016.

2017, Nov. 20 Litho. *Perf. 13¼x13*
1205-1208 A251 Set of 4 11.00 11.00

Christ Church Cathedral, Stanley, 125th Anniv. A252

Various views of Cathedral: 31p, 76p, £1.01, £1.22.

2017, Dec. 18 Litho. *Perf. 13¼x13*
1209-1212 A252 Set of 4 9.00 9.00

Shipwrecks Type of 2017

Designs: 31p, Glengowan. 76p, Jhelum. £1.01, Golden Chance. £1.22, Lady Elizabeth.

2018, Mar. 2 Litho. *Perf. 13*
1213-1216 A246 Set of 4 9.25 9.25

Wildlife A253

Designs: 31p, Macaroni penguin on nest. 76p, Euphausiid krill. £1.01, Southern sea lion. £1.22, Two Macaroni penguins.

2018, Apr. 18 Litho. *Perf. 13*
1217-1220 A253 Set of 4 9.00 9.00

Royal Air Force, Cent. A254

Designs: 31p, Hawker Siddeley Nimrod MR2. 76p, McDonnell Douglas F-4 Phantom. £1.22, Hawker Siddeley Harrier GR.3. £1.92, Eurofighter Typhoon.

2018, July 2 Litho. *Perf. 13¼x13½*
1221-1224 A254 Set of 4 11.00 11.00

Wedding of Prince Harry and Meghan Markle A255

Designs: 31p, Engagement photograph. 75p, Couple at ANZAC Day service. £1.10, Couple at altar on wedding day. £1.22, Couple leaving wedding.
£3, Couple kissing, vert.

Perf. 13¼x13½
2018, Aug. 14 Litho.
1225-1228 A255 Set of 4 8.25 8.25

Souvenir Sheet
Perf. 13½x13¼

1229 A255 £3 multi 7.75 7.75

Migratory Birds A256

No. 1230 — Southern rockhopper penguin and map of: a, 31p, South America and Northern Patagonian Shelf. b, 76p, Southern tip of South America and the Falkland Islands.

No. 1231 — Sooty shearwater and map of: a, £1.01, North America, Europe and Northern Africa. b, £1.22, South America, Falkland Islands and Southern Africa.

2018, Oct. 18 Litho. *Perf. 13¼x13½*

1230 A256 Vert. pair, #a-b 2.75 2.75
1231 A256 Vert. pair, #a-b 5.75 5.75

Old Fox Bay Post Office, Cent. A257

Fox Bay cancel and: 31p, 1940s photograph of Post Office. 76p, Old post office scales. £1.01, Princess Anne mailing postcard, old postmark box. £1.22, Old Post Office and Museum.

Perf. 13¼x13½

2018, Nov. 28 Litho.

1232-1235 A257 Set of 4 8.50 8.50

Falkland Islands Government Air Service, 70th Anniv. — A258

Airplanes: 31p, Auster 4. 76p, Norseman V. £1.01, DHC-2 Beaver. £1.22, BN-2B-26 Islander.

Perf. 13¼x13½

2018, Dec. 19 Litho.

1236-1239 A258 Set of 4 8.50 8.50

Landscapes — A259

Photographs: 31p, Quarry Point, Fox Bay, by Carli Sudder. 76p, New Island, by Georgina Strange. £1.01, Road to Nowhere, Port Howard, by Maria Forman. £1.22, Towards Albemarle, by Ben Cockwell.

2018, Dec. 28 Litho. *Perf. 13¼*

1240-1243 A259 Set of 4 8.50 8.50

Shipwrecks Type of 2017

Designs: 31p, Lily. 76p, Plym. £1.01, Philomel. £1.22, Protector.

2019, Mar. 4 Litho. *Perf. 13*

1244-1247 A246 Set of 4 8.75 8.75

D-Day, 75th Anniv. A260

Designs: 32p, Troops looking at graffiti on side of their glider. 78p, Airplanes for invasion on runway in England. £1.04, Soldiers landing on Utah Beach. £1.26, Tank in water after leaving landing craft,

2019, June 6 Litho. *Perf. 13¼x13½*

1248-1251 A260 Set of 4 8.75 8.75

Feathers A261

Feathers of: No. 1252, 32p, Striated caracara. No. 1253, 32p, Black-browed albatross. No. 1254, 78p, Yellow-billed teal. No. 1255, 78p, Barn owl. No. 1256, £1.26, Black-crowned night heron. No. 1257, £1.26, King penguin.

2019, Aug. 5 Litho. *Perf. 13¼x13½*

1252-1257 A261 Set of 6 11.50 11.50

Cancer Support and Awareness Fund Emblem and Peter Collins — A262

Stephen Jaffray Memorial Medical Emergency Assistance Fund Emblem and Stephen Jaffray (1970-92) A263

2019, Dec. 6 Litho. *Perf. 13*

1258 A262 78p multi 2.10 2.10
1259 A263 78p multi 2.10 2.10

Land Rovers A264

Designs: 32p, Series I 88-inch. 78p, Series I hard top. £1.26, Series IIA roadless traction forest rover. £1.96, Series IIB forward control.

2019, Dec. 20 Litho. *Perf. 13*

1260-1263 A264 Set of 4 11.50 11.50

SEMI-POSTAL STAMPS

Catalogue values for unused stamps in this section are for Never Hinged items.

Rebuilding after Conflict with Argentina — SP1

Wmk. 373

1982, Sept. 13 Litho. *Perf. 11*

B1 SP1 £1 + £1 Battle sites 3.00 3.00

Liberation of Falkland Islands, 10th Anniv. — SP2

Designs: 14p+6p, San Carlos Cemetery. 29p+11p, 1982 War Memorial, Port Stanley. 34p+16p, South Atlantic Medal. 68p+32p, Government House, Port Stanley.

Wmk. 373

1992, June 14 Litho. *Perf. 14*

B2 SP2 14p + 6p multicolored 1.00 *1.60*
B3 SP2 29p + 11p multicolored 1.75 2.00
B4 SP2 34p + 16p multicolored 2.00 2.25
B5 SP2 68p + 32p multicolored 2.75 *3.50*
a. Souvenir sheet of 4, #B2-B5 8.50 8.50
Nos. B2-B5 (4) 7.50 9.35

Surtax for Soldiers', Sailors' and Airmen's Families Association.

AIR POST STAMPS

Bird Type of 2003

Design: Rockhopper penguins, vert.

Booklet Stamp

Serpentine Die Cut 6x6½ Syncopated

2003, Sept. 19 Litho.

Self-Adhesive

C1 A163 (40p) multi 2.50 2.50
a. Booklet pane of 8 20.00

Penguins — AP1

Designs: No. C2, (55p), King penguin. No. C3, (55p), Macaroni penguin. No. C4, (55p), Magellanic penguin. No. C5, (55p), Rockhopper penguin. No. C6, (55p), Gentoo penguin. No. C7, (55p), Albino rockhopper penguin.

2008, Dec. 1 Litho. *Perf. 13¼*

C2-C7 AP1 Set of 6 19.00 19.00
C7a Souvenir sheet, #C2-C7 19.00 19.00

Penguins — AP2

Designs: Nos. C8, C14a, (70p), King penguin. Nos. C9, C14b, (70p), Macaroni penguin. Nos. C10, C14c, (70p), Rockhopper penguins. Nos. C11, C14d, (70p), Albino and normal rockhopper penguins. Nos. C12, C14e, (70p), Magellanic penguin. Nos. C13, C14f, (70p), Gentoo penguins.

2010, Sept. 29 Litho. *Perf. 13¾*

Stamps With White Frames

C8-C13 AP2 Set of 6 13.50 13.50

Stamps Without White Frames

C14 AP2 (70p) Sheet of 6, #a-f 13.50 13.50

Albino and Normal Rockhopper Penguins AP3

Gentoo Penguins AP4

Magellanic Penguin AP5

Rockhopper Penguins AP6

King Penguins AP7

Macaroni Penguins AP8

2013, Nov. 21 Litho. *Perf. 13¼*

Stamps With White Frames

C15 AP3 (65p) multi 2.10 2.10
C16 AP4 (65p) multi 2.10 2.10
C17 AP5 (65p) multi 2.10 2.10
C18 AP6 (65p) multi 2.10 2.10
C19 AP7 (65p) multi 2.10 2.10
C20 AP8 (65p) multi 2.10 2.10
Nos. C15-C20 (6) 12.60 12.60

Souvenir Sheet

Stamps Without White Frames

C21 Sheet of 6 14.00 *16.00*
a. AP3 (65p) multi 2.25 *2.60*
b. AP4 (65p) multi 2.25 *2.60*
c. AP5 (65p) multi 2.25 *2.60*
d. AP6 (65p) multi 2.25 *2.60*
e. AP7 (65p) multi 2.25 *2.60*
f. AP8 (65p) multi 2.25 *2.60*

POSTAGE DUE STAMPS

Catalogue values for unused stamps in this section are for never hinged items.

Penguin — D1

Perf. 14½x14

1991, Jan. 7 Litho. Wmk. 373

J1 D1 1p lilac rose & lake .25 *.60*
J2 D2 2p buff & brown org .25 *.60*
J3 D1 3p yel & orange yel .25 *.60*
J4 D1 4p lt bl grn & dk bl grn .25 *.60*
J5 D1 5p sky blue & Prus bl .25 *.60*
J6 D1 10p lt blue & dk blue .35 *.70*
J7 D1 20p lt violet & dk vio .90 *1.50*
J8 D1 50p brt yel grn & dk yel green 2.00 *3.00*
Nos. J1-J8 (8) 4.50 *8.20*

Penguins D2

Various penguins.

2005, Dec. 2 Litho. *Perf. 13¾*

J9 D2 1p multi .25 .25
J10 D2 3p multi .25 .25
J11 D2 5p multi .25 .25
J12 D2 10p multi .45 .45
J13 D2 20p multi .85 .85
J14 D2 50p multi 1.90 1.90
J15 D2 £1 multi 3.75 3.75
J16 D2 £2 multi 7.50 7.50
J17 D2 £3 multi 11.00 11.00
J18 D2 £5 multi 17.00 17.00
Nos. J9-J18 (10) 43.20 43.20

WAR TAX STAMPS

Regular Issue of 1912-14 Overprinted

1918-20 **Wmk. 3** ***Perf. 14***

MR1	A7	½p	dp ol grn	.55	*7.25*
MR2	A7	1p	org ver ('19)	.55	*4.00*
a.			Double overprint	*4,250.*	
MR3	A7	1sh	bis brn	6.50	*52.50*
a.			Pair, one without overprint	18,000.	
b.			Double ovpt., one albino	2,250.	
c.			1sh brn, thick grayish paper ('20)	6.00	50.00
d.			As "c," double ovpt., one albino	2,000.	
			Nos. MR1-MR3 (3)	7.60	*63.75*

No. MR3a probably is caused by a foldover and is not constant.

FALKLAND ISLANDS DEPENDENCIES

Catalogue values for unused stamps in this section are for Never Hinged items.

Map of Falkland Islands — A1

Engr., Center Litho. in Black

1946, Feb. 1 **Wmk. 4** ***Perf. 12***

1L1	A1	½p	yellow green	1.10	*3.50*
1L2	A1	1p	blue violet	1.30	*2.00*
1L3	A1	2p	deep carmine	1.30	*2.60*
1L4	A1	3p	ultramarine	1.90	*5.25*
1L5	A1	4p	deep plum	2.40	*5.00*
1L6	A1	6p	orange yellow	3.75	*5.25*
1L7	A1	9p	brown	2.25	*4.00*
1L8	A1	1sh	rose violet	3.00	*4.50*
			Nos. 1L1-1L8 (8)	17.00	*32.10*

Nos. 1L1-1L8 were reissued in 1948, printed on more opaque paper with the lines of the map finer and clearer. Value for set, unused or used $130.

See No. 1L13.

Common Design Types pictured following the introduction.

Peace Issue

Common Design Type

1946, Oct. 4 ***Perf. 13½x14***

1L9	CD303	1p	purple	.50	.50
1L10	CD303	3p	deep blue	.80	.50

Silver Wedding Issue

Common Design Types

1948, Dec. 6 **Photo.** ***Perf. 14x14½***

1L11	CD304	2½p	brt ultra	1.75	*3.25*

Perf. 11½x11

Engr.

1L12	CD305	1sh	blue violet	2.50	*2.75*

Type of 1946

1949, Mar. 6 ***Perf. 12***

Center Litho. in Black

1L13	A1	2½p	deep blue	9.00	4.25

UPU Issue

Common Design Types

Engr.; Name Typo. on 2p, 3p

1949, Oct. 10 ***Perf. 13½, 11x11½***

1L14	CD306	1p	violet	1.10	*4.00*
1L15	CD307	2p	deep carmine	5.00	4.00
1L16	CD308	3p	indigo	3.75	2.25
1L17	CD309	6p	red orange	4.75	4.25
			Nos. 1L14-1L17 (4)	14.60	14.50

Coronation Issue

Common Design Type

1953, June 4 ***Perf. 13½x13***

1L18	CD312	1p	purple & black	1.80	1.40

John Biscoe — A2

Trepassey — A3

Ships: 1½p, Wyatt Earp. 2p, Eagle. 2½p, Penola. 3p, Discovery II. 4p, William Scoresby. 6p, Discovery. 9p, Endurance. 1sh, Deutschland. 2sh, Pourquoi-pas? 2sh6p, Français. 5sh, Scotia. 10sh, Antarctic. £1, Belgica.

1954, Feb. 1 **Engr.** ***Perf. 12½***

Center in Black

1L19	A2	½p	blue green	.25	*2.00*
1L20	A3	1p	sepia	1.75	1.50
1L21	A3	1½p	olive	2.00	1.75
1L22	A3	2p	rose red	1.25	2.50
1L23	A3	2½p	yellow	1.25	.35
1L24	A3	3p	ultra	1.25	.35
1L25	A3	4p	red violet	3.00	1.75
1L26	A2	6p	rose violet	3.50	1.75
1L27	A2	9p	black	3.50	2.00
1L28	A3	1sh	org brown	3.50	2.00
1L29	A3	2sh	lilac rose	18.00	10.00
1L30	A2	2sh6p	blue gray	19.00	7.00
1L31	A2	5sh	violet	40.00	7.50
1L32	A3	10sh	brt blue	55.00	18.00
1L33	A2	£1	black	85.00	47.50
			Nos. 1L19-1L33 (15)	238.25	105.95

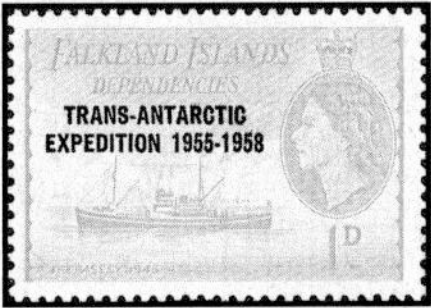

Nos. 20, 23-24, 26 Ovptd. in Black

1956, Jan 30 **Center in Black**

1L34	A3	1p	sepia	.30	.30
1L35	A3	2½p	yellow	.55	.55
1L36	A3	3p	ultramarine	.65	.65
1L37	A2	6p	rose violet	.75	.75
			Nos. 1L34-1L37 (4)	2.25	2.25

Trans-Antarctic Expedition, 1955-1958.

A4

1p, Map of Dependencies. 2p, Shag Rocks. 3p, Bird and Willis Islands. 4p, Gulbrandsen Lake. 5p, King Edward Point. 6p, Shackleton's Memorial Cross. 7p, Shackleton's grave. 8p, Grytviken Church. 9p, Coaling Hulk "Louise". 10p, Clerke Rocks. 20p, Candlemas Island. 25p, Twitcher Rock, Cook Island. 50p, "John Biscoe". £1, "Bransfield". £3, "Endurance".

Wmk. 373

1980, May 5 **Litho.** ***Perf. 13½***

1L38	A4	1p	multicolored	.25	.25
1L39	A4	2p	multicolored	.25	.25
1L40	A4	3p	multicolored	.25	.25
1L41	A4	4p	multicolored	.25	.25
1L42	A4	5p	multicolored	.25	.25
1L43	A4	6p	multicolored	.25	.25
1L44	A4	7p	multicolored	.25	.25
1L45	A4	8p	multicolored	.25	.25
1L46	A4	9p	multicolored	.25	.30
1L47	A4	10p	multicolored	.25	.30
1L48	A4	20p	multicolored	.45	.55
1L49	A4	25p	multicolored	.60	.70
1L50	A4	50p	multicolored	1.10	1.25
1L51	A4	£1	multicolored	2.25	2.75
1L52	A4	£3	multicolored	5.50	7.00
			Nos. 1L38-1L52 (15)	12.40	14.85

Nos. 38-50 exist dated 1984; issued May 3, 1984. Value, set $16.

1985, Nov. 18 **Wmk. 384**

1L48a	A4	20p	3.25	*4.50*
1L49a	A4	25p	3.25	*4.50*
1L50a	A4	50p	3.25	*4.50*
1L51a	A4	£1	3.25	*4.50*
1L52a	A4	£3	7.50	6.50
		Nos. 1L48a-1L52a (5)	20.50	*24.50*

Magellanic Clubmoss — A5

Designs: 6p, Alpine cat's-tail. 7p, Greater burnet. 11p, Antarctic bedstraw. 15p, Brown rush. 25p, Antarctic hair grass.

1981, Feb. 5 **Litho.** ***Perf. 14***

1L53	A5	3p	shown	.25	.25
1L54	A5	6p	multicolored	.25	.25
1L55	A5	7p	multicolored	.25	.25
1L56	A5	11p	multicolored	.35	.35
1L57	A5	15p	multicolored	.45	.45
a.			Brown missing	*3,750.*	
1L58	A5	25p	multicolored	.65	.65
			Nos. 1L53-1L58 (6)	2.20	2.20

Royal Wedding Issue

Common Design Type

1981, July 22 **Litho.** ***Perf. 14***

1L59	CD331	10p	Bouquet	.25	.25
1L60	CD331	13p	Charles	.35	.35
1L61	CD331	52p	Couple	.85	.85
			Nos. 1L59-1L61 (3)	1.45	1.45

Reindeer in Spring — A6

1982, Jan. 29 **Litho.** ***Perf. 14***

1L62	A6	5p	shown	.25	*.60*
1L63	A6	13p	Autumn	.35	*.75*
1L64	A6	25p	Winter	.45	*1.00*
1L65	A6	26p	Late winter	.50	*1.00*
			Nos. 1L62-1L65 (4)	1.55	*3.35*

Gamasellus Racovitzai — A7

10p, Alaskozetes antarcticus. 13p, Cryptopygus antarcticus. 15p, Notiomaso australis. 25p, Hydromedion sparsutum. 26p, Parochlus steinenii.

1982, Mar. 16 **Litho.** ***Perf. 14***

1L66	A7	5p	shown	.25	.25
1L67	A7	10p	multicolored	.25	.35
1L68	A7	13p	multicolored	.30	.40
1L69	A7	15p	multicolored	.35	.40
1L70	A7	25p	multicolored	.40	.50
1L71	A7	26p	multicolored	.45	.50
			Nos. 1L66-1L71 (6)	2.00	2.40

Princess Diana Issue

Common Design Type

1982, July 1 **Litho.** ***Perf. 13½x14***

1L72	CD333	5p	Arms	.25	.25
1L73	CD333	17p	Diana	.35	.45
a.			Perf. 13.5	2.50	*2.75*
1L74	CD333	37p	Wedding	.90	.90
1L75	CD333	50p	Portrait	1.00	1.00
			Nos. 1L72-1L75 (4)	2.50	2.60

Crustacea — A8

5p, Euphausia superba. 17p, Glyptonotus antarcticus. 25p, Epimeria monodon. 34p, Serolis pagenstecheri.

Perf. 14½x14

1984, Mar. 23 **Wmk. 373**

1L76	A8	5p	multicolored	.30	.30
1L77	A8	17p	multicolored	.40	.40
1L78	A8	25p	multicolored	.70	.70
1L79	A8	34p	multicolored	1.10	1.10
			Nos. 1L76-1L79 (4)	2.50	2.50

Manned Flight Bicentenary — A9

Designs: 5p, Westland Whirlwind. 13p, Westland Wasp. 17p, Saunders-Roe Walrus. 50p, Auster.

1983, Dec. 23 **Litho.** ***Perf. 14***

1L80	A9	5p	multicolored	.25	.25
1L81	A9	13p	multicolored	.45	.45
1L82	A9	17p	multicolored	.55	.55
1L83	A9	50p	multicolored	1.75	1.75
			Nos. 1L80-1L83 (4)	3.00	3.00

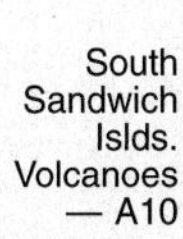

South Sandwich Islds. Volcanoes — A10

6p, Zavodovski Island. 17p, Mt. Michael, Saunders Island. 22p, Bellingshausen Island. 52p, Bristol Island.

1984, Nov. 8 **Wmk. 373** ***Perf. 14½***

1L84	A10	6p	multicolored	.60	.60
1L85	A10	17p	multicolored	1.40	1.40
1L86	A10	22p	multicolored	2.00	2.00
1L87	A10	52p	multicolored	3.50	3.50
			Nos. 1L84-1L87 (4)	7.50	7.50

Albatrosses — A11

7p, Diomedea chrysostoma. 22p, Diomedea melanophris. 27p, Diomedea exulans. 54p, Phoebetria palpebrata.

1985, May 5 **Wmk. 384** ***Perf. 14½***

1L88	A11	7p	multicolored	.80	.80
1L89	A11	22p	multicolored	2.25	2.25
1L90	A11	27p	multicolored	2.50	2.50
1L91	A11	54p	multicolored	4.75	4.75
			Nos. 1L88-1L91 (4)	10.30	10.30

Queen Mother 85th Birthday

Common Design Type

Designs: 7p, 14th birthday celebration. 22p, With Princess Anne, Lady Sarah Armstrong-Jones, Prince Edward. 27p, Queen Mother. 54p, Holding Prince Henry. £1, On the Britannia.

1985, June 23 ***Perf. 14½x14***

1L92	CD336	7p	multicolored	.25	.25
1L93	CD336	22p	multicolored	.75	.75
1L94	CD336	27p	multicolored	1.00	1.00
1L95	CD336	54p	multicolored	2.00	2.00
			Nos. 1L92-1L95 (4)	4.00	4.00

Souvenir Sheet

1L96	CD336	£1	multicolored	4.00	4.00

Falkland Islands Naturalists Type of 1985

Naturalists, endangered species: 7p, Dumont d'Urville (1790-1842), kelp. 22p, Johann Reinhold Forster (1729-1798), king penguin. 27p, Johann Georg Adam Forster (1754-1794), tussock grass. 54p, Sir Joseph Banks (1743-1820), dove prion.

1985, Nov. 4 *Perf. 13½x14*

1L97 A86 7p multicolored .75 .75
1L98 A86 22p multicolored 1.60 1.60
1L99 A86 27p multicolored 2.00 2.00
1L100 A86 54p multicolored 3.75 3.75
Nos. 1L97-1L100 (4) 8.10 8.10

SEMI-POSTAL STAMP

Rebuilding Type of Falkland Islands

Wmk. 373

1982, Sept. 13 Litho. *Perf. 11*

1LB1 SP1 £1 Map of So. Georgia 2.75 2.75

ISSUES FOR THE SEPARATE ISLANDS

Graham Land

Nos. 84, 85B, 86A, 87A, 88-91 Overprinted in Red

1944, Feb. 12 Wmk. 4 *Perf. 12*

2L1 A22 ½p green & black .45 *2.25*
2L2 A22 1p dk vio & black .45 *1.10*
2L3 A22 2p rose car & blk .55 *1.10*
2L4 A22 3p deep bl & blk .55 *1.10*
2L5 A22 4p rose vio & blk 1.90 1.75
2L6 A22 6p brown & black 19.00 2.75
2L7 A22 9p slate bl & blk 1.25 *1.50*
2L8 A22 1sh dull blue 1.25 *1.50*
Nos. 2L1-2L8 (8) 25.40 *13.05*

South Georgia

1944, Apr. 3 Wmk. 4 *Perf. 12*

3L1 A22 ½p green & black .35 *2.25*
3L2 A22 1p dark vio & blk .35 *1.10*
3L3 A22 2p rose car & blk .55 *1.10*
3L4 A22 3p deep bl & blk .55 *1.10*
3L5 A22 4p rose vio & blk 1.90 1.75
3L6 A22 6p brown & black 19.00 2.50
3L7 A22 9p slate bl & blk 1.25 *1.50*
3L8 A22 1sh dull blue 1.25 *1.50*
Nos. 3L1-3L8 (8) 25.20 *12.80*

South Orkneys

1944, Feb. 21 Wmk. 4 *Perf. 12*

4L1 A22 ½p green & black .45 *2.25*
4L2 A22 1p dark vio & blk .45 *1.10*
4L3 A22 2p rose car & blk .75 *1.10*
4L4 A22 3p deep bl & blk .75 *1.10*
4L5 A22 4p rose vio & blk 1.75 1.75
4L6 A22 6p brown & black 19.00 2.50
4L7 A22 9p slate bl & blk 1.25 *1.50*
4L8 A22 1sh dull blue 1.25 *1.50*
Nos. 4L1-4L8 (8) 25.65 *12.80*

South Shetlands

1944 Wmk. 4 *Perf. 12*

5L1 A22 ½p green & black .45 *2.25*
5L2 A22 1p dark vio & blk .45 *1.10*
5L3 A22 2p rose car & blk .55 *1.10*
5L4 A22 3p deep bl & blk .55 *1.10*
5L5 A22 4p rose vio & blk 1.25 1.75
5L6 A22 6p brown & black 19.00 2.50
5L7 A22 9p slate bl & blk 1.25 *1.50*
5L8 A22 1sh dull blue 1.25 *1.50*
Nos. 5L1-5L8 (8) 24.75 *12.80*

FAR EASTERN REPUBLIC

'fär 'ē-stərn ri-'pə-blik

LOCATION — In Siberia east of Lake Baikal
GOVT. — Republic
AREA — 900,745 sq. mi.
POP. — 1,560,000 (approx. 1920)
CAPITAL — Chita

A short-lived independent government was established here in 1920.

100 Kopecks = 1 Ruble

Watermark

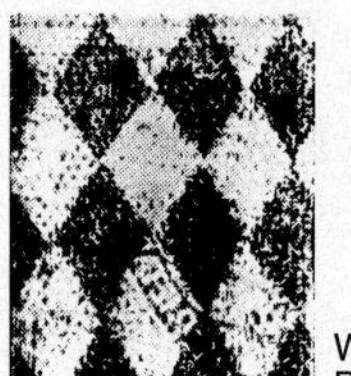

Wmk. 171 — Diamonds

Vladivostok Issue

Russian Stamps Surcharged or Overprinted

a

b

c

On Stamps of 1909-17

Perf. 14, 14½x15, 13½

1920 **Unwmk.**

2 A14(a) 2k green 10.00 *15.00*
3 A14(a) 3k red 10.00 10.00
4 A11(b) 3k on 35k red brn & grn 40.00 *50.00*
5 A15(a) 4k carmine 10.00 *12.00*
6 A11(b) 4k on 70k brn & org 10.00 *15.00*
8 A11(b) 7k on 15k red brn & bl 2.00 2.00
a. Inverted surcharge 100.00
b. Pair, one ovptd. "DBP" only 100.00
9 A15(a) 10k dark blue 100.00 75.00
a. Overprint on back 125.00
10 A12(c) 10k on 3½r mar & lt grn 25.00 25.00
11 A11(a) 14k blue & rose 50.00 35.00
12 A11(a) 15k red brn & bl 35.00 25.00
13 A8(a) 20k blue & car 150.00 100.00
14 A11(b) 20k on 14k bl & rose 10.00 *8.00*
a. Surcharge on back 30.00
15 A11(a) 25k green & vio 25.00 20.00
16 A11(a) 35k red brn & grn 75.00 50.00
17 A8(a) 50k brn vio & grn 10.00 *12.00*
18 A9(a) 1r pale brn, dk brn & org *700.00 700.00*

On Stamps of 1917

Imperf

21 A14(a) 1k orange 25.00 10.00
22 A14(a) 2k gray grn 20.00 10.00
23 A14(a) 3k red 20.00 10.00
25 A11(b) 7k on 15k red brn & dp bl 2.00 *5.00*
a. Pair, one without surcharge *100.00*
b. Pair, one ovptd. "DBP" only *100.00*
26 A12(c) 10k on 3½r mar & lt grn 30.00 15.00
27 A9(a) 1r pale brn, brn & red org 50.00 *20.00*

On Stamps of Siberia 1919

Perf. 14, 14½x15

30 A14(a) 35k on 2k green 5.00 *8.00*
a. "DBP" on back 25.00 *50.00*

Imperf

31 A14(a) 35k on 2k green 35.00 25.00
32 A14(a) 70k on 1k orange 6.00 6.00

Counterfeit surcharges and overprints abound, including digital forgeries.

On Russia Nos. AR2, AR3

Perf. 14½x15

Wmk. 171

35 PF1 1k on 5k green, *buff* 30.00 25.00
36 PF1 2k on 10k brown, *buff* 40.00 30.00

The letters on these stamps resembling "DBP," are the Russian initials of "Dalne Vostochnaya Respublika" (Far Eastern Republic).

Chita Issue

A2

A2a

1921 Unwmk. Typo. *Imperf.*

38 A2 2k gray green 1.50 1.50
39 A2a 4k rose 3.00 3.00
40 A2 5k claret 3.00 3.00
41 A2a 10k blue 2.50 2.50
Nos. 38-41 (4) 10.00 10.00

For overprints see Nos. 62-65.

Blagoveshchensk Issue

A3

1921 Litho. *Imperf.*

42 A3 2r red 3.00 2.00
43 A3 3r dark green 3.00 2.00
44 A3 5r dark blue 3.00 2.00
a. Tête bêche pair 50.00 15.00
45 A3 15r dark brown 3.00 2.00
46 A3 30r dark violet 3.00 2.00
a. Tête bêche pair 35.00 15.00
Nos. 42-46 (5) 15.00 10.00

Remainders of Nos. 42-46 were canceled in colored crayon or by typographed bars. These sell for half of foregoing values.

Chita Issue

A4

A5

1922 Litho. *Imperf.*

49 A4 1k orange 1.00 *.85*
50 A4 3k dull red .40 *.45*
51 A5 4k dp rose & buff .40 *.45*
52 A4 5k orange brown .80 .45
53 A4 7k light blue 1.50 *1.50*
a. Perf. 11½ 2.00 2.50
b. Rouletted 9 3.00 3.00
c. Perf. 11½x rouletted 6.50 6.50
54 A5 10k dk blue & red .60 *.65*
55 A4 15k dull rose .80 *1.10*
56 A5 20k blue & red .80 *1.10*
57 A5 30k green & red org 1.25 *1.10*
58 A5 50k black & red org 3.00 *2.25*
Nos. 49-58 (10) 10.55 *9.90*

The 4k exists with "4" omitted. Value $100.

Vladivostok Issue

Stamps of 1921 Overprinted in Red

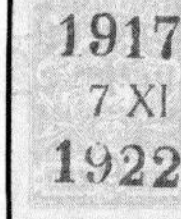

1922 *Imperf.*

62 A2 2k gray green 35.00 25.00
a. Inverted overprint 250.00
63 A2a 4k rose 35.00 25.00
a. Inverted overprint 250.00
b. Double overprint 250.00
64 A2 5k claret 35.00 35.00
a. Inverted overprint 100.00
b. Double overprint 350.00
65 A2a 10k blue 35.00 35.00
a. Inverted overprint 250.00
Nos. 62-65 (4) 140.00 120.00

Russian revolution of Nov. 1917, 5th anniv.

Once in the setting the figures "22" of 1922 have the bottom stroke curved instead of straight. Value, each $75.

No. 63 exists in a block with overprints missing on some stamps.

Vladivostok Issue

Russian Stamps of 1922-23 Surcharged in Black or Red

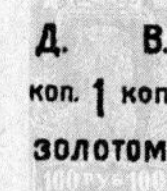

1923 *Imperf.*

66 A50 1k on 100r red .40 *1.00*
a. Inverted surcharge 60.00
67 A50 2k on 70r violet .40 *.75*
68 A49 5k on 10r blue (R) .40 *.75*
69 A50 10k on 50r brown .90 *1.25*
a. Inverted surcharge 250.00

Perf. 14½x15

70 A50 1k on 100r red .90 *1.25*
Nos. 66-70 (5) 3.00 *5.00*

OCCUPATION STAMPS

Issued under Occupation of General Semenov

Chita Issue

Russian Stamps of 1909-12 Surcharged

a

b

c

1920 Unwmk. ***Perf. 14, 14x15½***

N1	A15 (a)	1r on 4k car	150.00	*100.00*
N2	A8 (b)	2r50k on 20k bl & car	40.00	30.00
N3	A14 (c)	5r on 5k clar	25.00	*50.00*
a.		Double surcharge	200.00	
N4	A11 (a)	10r on 70k brn & org	20.00	*25.00*
		Nos. N1-N4 (4)	235.00	*205.00*

FAROE ISLANDS

'far-,ü 'i-lənds

(The Faroes)

LOCATION — North Atlantic Ocean
GOVT. — Self-governing part of Kingdom of Denmark
AREA — 540 sq. mi.
POP. — 41,059 (1999 est.)
CAPITAL — Thorshavn

100 Ore = 1 Krone

Catalogue values for unused stamps in this country are for Never Hinged items, beginning with Scott 7.

Denmark No. 97 Handstamp Surcharged

1919, Jan. Typo. *Perf. 14x14½*

1	A16 2o on 5o green	1,400.	475.00

Counterfeits of surcharge exist.
Denmark No. 88a, the bisect, was used with Denmark No. 97 in Faroe Islands Jan. 3-23, 1919.

Denmark Nos. 220, 224, 238A, 224C Surcharged in Blue or Black

Nos. 2, 5-6

No. 3

No. 4

1940-41 Engr. *Perf. 13*

2	A32 20o on 1o ('41)	40.00	110.00
3	A32 20o on 5o ('41)	40.00	35.00
4	A30 20o on 15o (Bk)	60.00	22.50
5	A32 50o on 5o (Bk)	275.00	90.00
6	A32 60o on 6o (Bk)	125.00	*250.00*
	Nos. 2-6 (5)	540.00	507.50
	Set, never hinged	1,150.	

Issued during British administration.

Catalogue values for unused stamps in this section, from this point to the end of the section, are for Never Hinged items.

Map of Islands, 1673 — A1

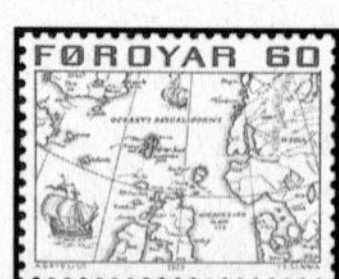
Map of North Atlantic, 1573 — A2

West Coast, Sandoy — A3

Vidoy and Svinoy, by Eyvindur Mohr — A4

Designs: 200o, like 70o. 250o, 300o, View of Streymoy and Vagar. 450o, Houses, Nes, by Ruth Smith. 500o, View of Hvitanes and Skalafjordur, by S. Joensen-Mikines.

Unwmk.

1975, Jan. 30 Engr. *Perf. 13*

7	A1 5o sepia	.25	.25
8	A2 10o emer & dark blue	.25	.25
9	A1 50o graysh green	.25	.25
10	A2 60o brown & dark blue	.80	.80
11	A3 70o vio bl & slate grn	.80	.80
12	A2 80o ocher & dark blue	.45	.45
13	A1 90o red brown	.80	.80
14	A2 120o brt bl & dark bl	.60	.40
15	A3 200o vio bl & slate grn	.60	.60
16	A3 250o multicolored	.60	.60
17	A3 300o multicolored	5.00	1.60

Photo.

Perf. 12½x13

18	A4 350o multicolored	.80	.80
19	A4 450o multicolored	.80	.80
20	A4 500o multicolored	1.00	1.00
	Nos. 7-20 (14)	13.00	9.40

Faroe Boat — A5

Faroe Flag — A6

Faroe Mailman — A7

Perf. 12½x13, 12 (A6)

1976, Apr. 1 Engr.; Litho. (A6)

21	A5 125o copper red	1.60	1.25
22	A6 160o multicolored	.45	.45
23	A7 800o olive	1.75	1.25
	Nos. 21-23 (3)	3.80	2.95

Faroe Islands independent postal service, Apr. 1, 1976.

Motor Fishing Boat — A8

Faroese Fishing Vessels and Map of Islands: 125o, Inland fishing cutter. 160o, Modern seine fishing vessel. 600o, Deep-sea fishing trawler.

1977, Apr. 28 Photo. *Perf. 14½x14*

24	A8 100o green & black	4.50	3.75
25	A8 125o carmine & black	.65	.65
26	A8 160o blue & black	.90	.65
27	A8 600o brown & black	1.60	1.10
	Nos. 24-27 (4)	7.65	6.15

Common Snipe A9

Photogravure & Engraved

1977, Sept. 29 *Perf. 14½x14*

28	A9 70o shown	.25	.25
29	A9 180o Oystercatcher	.55	.55
30	A9 250o Whimbrel	.65	.65
	Nos. 28-30 (3)	1.45	1.45

North Coast, Puffins — A10

Mykines Village — A11

Mykines Island: 140o, Coast. 150o, Aerial view. 180o, Map.

Perf. 13x13½, 13½x13

1978, Jan. 26 Photo.

Size: 21x28mm, 28x21mm

31	A10 100o multicolored	.25	.25
32	A11 130o multicolored	.45	.45
33	A11 140o multicolored	.55	.55
34	A10 150o multicolored	.55	.55

Size: 37x26mm

Perf. 14½x14

35	A11 180o multicolored	.55	.55
	Nos. 31-35 (5)	2.35	2.35

Sea Birds — A12

Lithographed and Engraved

1978, Apr. 13 *Perf. 12x12½*

36	A12 140o Gannets	.45	.45
37	A12 180o Puffins	.55	.55
38	A12 400o Guillemots	1.40	1.10
	Nos. 36-38 (3)	2.40	2.10

Old Library — A13

1978, Dec. 7 *Perf. 13*

39	A13 140o shown	.45	.45
40	A13 180o New library	.55	.55

Completion of New Library Building.

Girl Guide, Tent and Fire — A14

1978, Dec. 7 Photo. *Perf. 13½*

41	A14 140o multicolored	.45	.45

Faroese Girl Guides, 50th anniversary.

Ram — A15

Lithographed and Engraved

1979, Mar. 19 *Perf. 12*

42	A15 25k multicolored	6.00	6.00

Denmark No. 88a — A16

Europa: 180o, Faroe Islands No. 1.

1979, May 7 *Perf. 12½*

43	A16 140o yellow & blue	*.45*	*.45*
44	A16 180o rose, grn & blk	*.55*	*.55*

Girl Wearing Festive Costume — A17

Children's Drawings and IYC Emblem: 150o, Fisherman. 200o, Two friends.

1979, Oct. 1 *Perf. 12*

45	A17 110o multicolored	.45	.45
46	A17 150o multicolored	.45	.45
47	A17 200o multicolored	.55	.55
	Nos. 45-47 (3)	1.45	1.45

International Year of the Child.

Sea Plantain — A18

1980, Mar. 17 Photo. *Perf. 12x11½*

48	A18 90o shown	.25	.25
49	A18 110o Glacier buttercup	.45	.45
50	A18 150o Purple saxifrage	.55	.55
51	A18 200o Starry saxifrage	.55	.55
52	A18 400o Lady's mantle	.90	.90
	Nos. 48-52 (5)	2.70	2.70

Europa — A19

Europa: 150o, Jakob Jakobsen (1864-1918), linguist. 200o, Venceslas Ulricus Hammershaimb (1819-1909), theologian, linguist and folklorist.

1980, Oct. 6 Engr. *Perf. 11½*

53	A19 150o dull green	*.40*	*.40*
54	A19 200o dull red brown	*.60*	*.60*

Perf. 13 bicolored examples of Nos. 53-54 are rejected stamps never put on sale that were to have been burned, but which escaped destruction.

Coat of Arms, Virgin and Child, Gothic Pew Gable — A20

Kirkjubour Pew Gables, 15th Century: 140o, Norwegian coat of arms, John the Baptist. 150o, Christ's head, St. Peter. 200o, Hand in halo, Apostle Paul.

Photo. & Engr.

1980, Oct. 6 ***Perf. 13½***

55 A20 110o multicolored .45 .45
56 A20 140o multicolored .45 .45
57 A20 150o multicolored .45 .45
58 A20 200o multicolored .55 .55
Nos. 55-58 (4) 1.90 1.90

See Nos. 102-105, 389-392

A21

Sketches of Old Torshavn by Ingalzur Reyni.

1981, Mar. 2 **Engr.**

59 A21 110o dark green .45 .45
60 A21 140o black .45 .45
61 A21 150o dark brown .45 .45
62 A21 200o dark blue .55 .55
Nos. 59-62 (4) 1.90 1.90

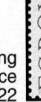

The Ring Dance A22

Europa: 200o, The garter dance.

1981, June 1 **Engr.** ***Perf. 13x14***

63 A22 150o pale rose & grn *.35 .35*
64 A22 200o pale yel grn & dk brn *.55 .55*

Rune Stones, 800-1000 AD — A23

Historic Writings: 1k, Folksong, 1846. 3k, Sheep Letter excerpt, 1298. 6k, Seal and text, 1533. 10k, Titlepage from Faeroae et Faeroa, by Lucas Jacobson Debes, library.

Photo. & Engr.

1981, Oct. 19 ***Perf. 11½***

65 A23 10o multicolored .25 .25
66 A23 1k multicolored .25 .25
67 A23 3k multicolored 1.00 .65
68 A23 6k multicolored 1.60 1.25
69 A23 10k multicolored 2.75 2.75
Nos. 65-69 (5) 5.85 5.15

Nos. 70-80 not assigned.

Europa 1982 — A24

1.50k, Viking North Atlantic routes. 2k, Viking house foundation.

1982, Mar. 15 **Engr.** ***Perf. 13½***

81 A24 1.50k dk blue & blue .45 .45
82 A24 2k gray & blk .55 .55

View of Gjogv, by Ingalvur av Reyni A25

1982, June 7 **Litho.** ***Perf. 12½x13***

83 A25 180o shown .45 .45
84 A25 220o Hvalvik 1.00 .75
85 A25 250o Kvivik .65 .65
Nos. 83-85 (3) 2.10 1.85

Ballad of Harra Paetur and Elinborg — A26

Scenes from the medieval ballad of chivalry.

1982, Sept. 27 **Litho.**

86 A26 220o multicolored .65 .65
87 A26 250o multicolored .75 .75
88 A26 350o multicolored 1.00 1.00
89 A26 450o multicolored 1.20 1.20
Nos. 86-89 (4) 3.60 3.60

Cargo Ships A27

1983, Feb. 21 **Litho.** ***Perf. 14x14½***

90 A27 220o Arcturus, 1856 .65 .65
91 A27 250o Laura, 1882 .90 .90
92 A27 700o Thyra, 1866 2.00 2.00
Nos. 90-92 (3) 3.55 3.55

Chessmen, by Pol i Buo (1791-1857) — A28

1983, May 2 **Engr.** ***Perf. 13 Vert.***

Booklet Stamps

93 250o King 2.25 2.25
94 250o Queen 2.25 2.25
a. Bklt. pane of 6, 3 each #93-94 16.00
b. A28 Pair, #93-94 5.50 5.50

Europa 1983 — A29

Nobel Prizewinners in Medicine: 250o, Niels R. Finsen (1860-1903), ultraviolet radiation pioneer. 400o, Alexander Fleming (1881-1955), discoverer of penicillin.

1983, June 6 **Engr.** ***Perf. 12x11½***

95 A29 250o dark blue *.65 .65*
96 A29 400o red brown *1.10 1.10*

A30

1983, Sept. 19 **Litho.** ***Perf. 12½x13***

97 A30 250o Tusk .65 .65
98 A30 280o Haddock .85 .85
99 A30 500o Halibut 1.60 1.60
100 A30 900o Catfish 2.50 2.50
Nos. 97-100 (4) 5.60 5.60

Souvenir Sheet

Traditional Costumes — A31

Various national costumes.

1983, Nov. 4 **Litho.** ***Perf. 12***

101 A31 Sheet of 3 10.00 11.00
a.-c. 250o multicolored 2.75 2.75

Nordic House Cultural Center opening. Margin shows Scandinavian flags.

Pew Gables Type of 1980

Designs: 250o, John, shield with three crowns. 300o, St. Jacob, shield with crossed keys. 350o, Thomas, shield with crossbeam. 400o, Judas Taddeus, Toulouse cross halo.

Photo. & Engr.

1984, Jan. 30 ***Perf. 14x13½***

102 A20 250o lil, pur & dk brn .75 .75
103 A20 300o red brn, dk buff & dk brn .85 .85
104 A20 350o blk, lt gray & dk brn 1.00 1.00
105 A20 400o ol grn, pale yel & dk brn 1.10 1.10
Nos. 102-105 (4) 3.70 3.70

Europa (1959-84) A33

1984, Apr. 2 **Engr.** ***Perf. 13½***

106 A33 250o red *.60 .60*
107 A33 500o dark blue *1.40 1.40*

Sverri Patursson (1871-1960), Writer — A34

Poets: 2.50k, Joannes Patursson (1866-1946). 3k, J. H. O. Djurhuus (1881-1948). 4.50k, H.A. Djurhuus (1883-1951).

1984, May 28 **Engr.** ***Perf. 13½***

108 A34 2k olive green .55 .55
109 A34 2.50k red .65 .65
110 A34 3k dark blue .85 .85
111 A34 4.50k violet 1.25 1.25
Nos. 108-111 (4) 3.30 3.30

Faroese Smack (Fishing Boat) — A35

Perf. 12½x13, 13x12½

1984, Sept. 10 **Engr.**

112 A35 280o shown .75 .75
113 A35 300o Fishermen, vert. .85 .85
114 A35 12k Helmsman, vert. 3.75 3.75
Nos. 112-114 (3) 5.35 5.35

Fairytale Illustrations by Elinborg Lutzen — A36

Designs: No. 115, Beauty of the Veils. No. 116, Veils, diff. No. 117, Girl Shy Prince. No. 118, The Glass Sword. No. 119, Little Elin. No. 120, The Boy and the Ox.

1984, Oct. 29 **Litho.** ***Perf. 13 Vert.***

Booklet Stamps

115 A36 140o multicolored 5.00 5.00
116 A36 280o multicolored 5.00 5.00
117 A36 280o multicolored 5.00 5.00
118 A36 280o multicolored 5.00 5.00
119 A36 280o multicolored 5.00 5.00
120 A36 280o multicolored 5.00 5.00
a. Booklet pane of 6, #115-120 30.00

View of Torshavn and the Forts, by Edward Dayes A37

Dayes' Landscapes, 1789: 280o, Skaeling. 550o, View Towards the North Seen from the Hills Near Torshavn in Stremoy, Faroes. 800o, The Moving Stones in Eysturoy, Faroes.

Litho. & Engr.

1985, Feb. 4 ***Perf. 13***

121 A37 250o multicolored .65 .65
122 A37 280o multicolored .85 .85
123 A37 550o multicolored 2.00 2.00
124 A37 800o multicolored 2.50 2.50
Nos. 121-124 (4) 6.00 6.00

Europa 1985 — A38

Children taking music lessons.

1985, Apr. 1 **Litho.** ***Perf. 13½x14½***

125 A38 280o multicolored *.85 .85*
126 A38 550o multicolored *1.90 1.90*

Paintings, Faroese Museum of Art A39

Designs: 280o, The Garden, Hoyvik, 1973, by Thomas Arge (1942-78). 450o, Self-Portrait, 1952, by Ruth Smith (1913-58), vert. 550o, Winter's Day in Nolsoy, 1959, by Steffan Danielsen (1922-76).

Litho. & Engr.

1985, June 3 ***Perf. 12½***

127 A39 280o multicolored 1.25 1.25
128 A39 450o multicolored 1.75 1.75
129 A39 550o multicolored 2.50 2.50
Nos. 127-129 (3) 5.50 5.50

Lighthouses — A40

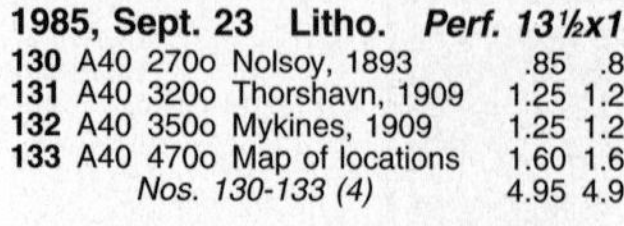

1985, Sept. 23 Litho. *Perf. 13½x14*

130	A40 270o Nolsoy, 1893	.85	.85
131	A40 320o Thorshavn, 1909	1.25	1.25
132	A40 350o Mykines, 1909	1.25	1.25
133	A40 470o Map of locations	1.60	1.60
	Nos. 130-133 (4)	4.95	4.95

Passenger Aviation in the Faroes, 22nd Anniv. A41

Designs: No. 134, Douglas DC-3. No. 135, Fokker Friendship. No. 136, Boeing 737. No. 137, Interisland LM-IKB. No. 138, Helicopter Snipan.

Perf. 13½ Horiz.

1985, Oct. 28 Photo.

Booklet Stamps

134	A41 300o multicolored	2.75	2.75
135	A41 300o multicolored	2.75	2.75
136	A41 300o multicolored	2.75	2.75
137	A41 300o multicolored	2.75	2.75
138	A41 300o multicolored	2.75	2.75
a.	Booklet pane of 5, #134-138	14.00	14.00

Skrimsla, Ancient Folk Ballad — A42

Designs: No. 139, Peasant in woods. No. 140, Meets Giant. No. 141, Giant loses game. No. 142, Giant grants Peasant's wish.

1986, Feb. 3 Litho. *Perf. 12½x13*

139	A42 300o multicolored	.80	.80
140	A42 420o multicolored	1.20	1.20
141	A42 550o multicolored	1.40	1.40
142	A42 650o multicolored	1.60	1.60
	Nos. 139-142 (4)	5.00	5.00

Europa 1986 — A43

1986, Apr. 7 Litho. *Perf. 13½*

143	A43 3k shown	*1.60*	*1.60*
144	A43 5.50k Sea pollution	*2.25*	*2.25*

Amnesty Intl., 25th Anniv. — A44

Winning design competition artwork.

1986, June 2 *Perf. 14x13½*

145	A44 3k Olivur vid Neyst	1.25	1.25
146	A44 4.70k Eli Smith	1.90	1.90
147	A44 5.50k Ranna Kunoy	2.40	2.40
	Nos. 145-147 (3)	5.55	5.55

Nos. 145-146 horiz.

Souvenir Sheet

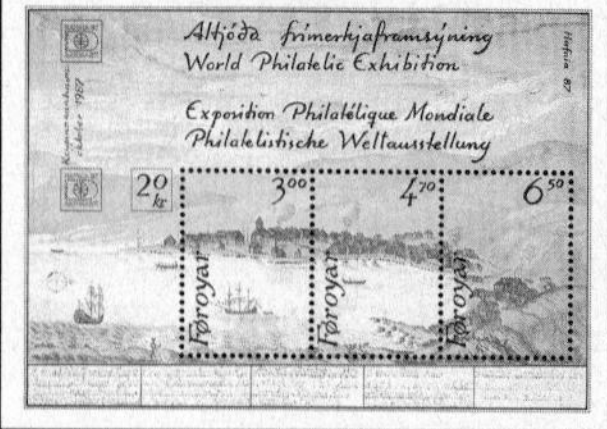

HAFNIA '87, Copenhagen — A45

Design: East Bay of Torshavn, watercolor, 1782, by Christian Rosenmeyer (1728-1802).

1986, Aug. 29 Litho. *Perf. 13x13½*

148	A45 Sheet of 3	8.75	8.75
a.	3k multicolored	2.75	2.75
b.	4.70k multicolored	2.75	2.75
c.	6.50k multicolored	2.75	2.75

Sold for 20k.

Old Stone Bridges A46

2.70k, Glyvrar on Eysturoy. 3k, Leypanagjogv on Vagar, vert. 13k, Skaelinger on Streymoy.

Perf. 13½x14½, 14½x13½

1986, Oct. 13 Engr.

149	A46 2.70k dp brown vio	1.75	1.75
150	A46 3k bluish blk	1.40	1.40
151	A46 13k gray green	3.00	3.00
	Nos. 149-151 (3)	6.15	6.15

Farmhouses — A47

Traditional architecture: 300o, Depil on Borooy, 1814. 420o, Depil, diff. 470o, Frammi vio Gjonna on Streymoy, c. 1814. 650o, Frammi, diff.

1987, Feb. 9 Engr. *Perf. 13x14½*

152	A47 300o pale blue & blue	.90	.90
153	A47 420o buff & brown	1.40	1.40
154	A47 470o pale grn & dp grn	1.75	1.75
155	A47 650o pale gray & black	2.25	2.25
	Nos. 152-155 (4)	6.30	6.30

Europa 1987 — A48

Nordic House.

1987, Apr. 6 *Perf. 13x14*

156	A48 300o Exterior	*.85*	*.85*
157	A48 550o Interior	*1.90*	*1.60*

Fishing Trawlers A49

Designs: 3k, Joannes Patursson. 5.50k, Magnus Heinason. 8k, Sjurdarberg.

1987, June 1 Litho. *Perf. 14x13½*

158	A49 3k multi	.90	.90
159	A49 5.50k multi	1.90	1.90
160	A49 8k multi	4.00	4.00
	Nos. 158-160 (3)	6.80	6.80

Hestur (Horse) Island A50

Litho. & Engr.

1987, Sept. 7 *Perf. 13*

161	A50 270o Map	.80	.80
162	A50 300o Seaport	.75	.75
163	A50 420o Bird cliff	1.60	1.60
164	A50 470o Pasture, sheep	1.75	1.75
165	A50 550o Seashore	1.75	1.75
	Nos. 161-165 (5)	6.65	6.65

Nos. 161, 163 and 165 vert.

Collages by Zacharias Heinesen A51

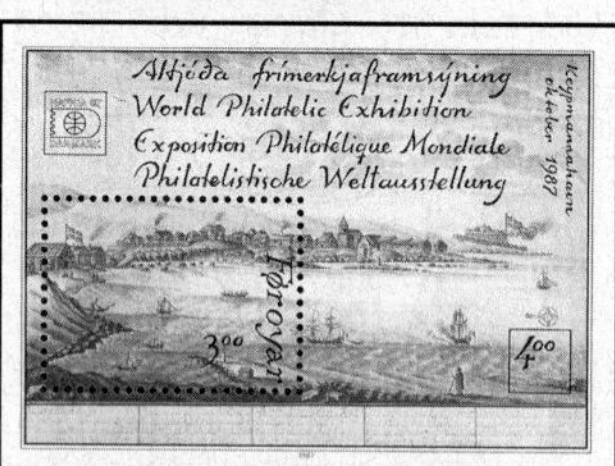

West Bay of Torshavn, Watercolor by Rosenmeyer — A52

1987, Oct. 16 Litho. *Perf. 13½x14*

166	A51 4.70k Eystaravag	1.25	1.25
167	A51 6.50k Vestarvag	1.75	1.75

Souvenir Sheet

Perf. 13½x13

168	A52 3k multicolored	3.50	3.50

HAFNIA '87. Sold for 4k.

Flowers — A53

Designs: 2.70k, Bellis perennis. 3k, Dactylorchis maculata. 4.70k, Potentilla erecta. 9k, Pinguicula vulgaris.

1988, Feb. 8 Litho. *Perf. 11½*

Granite Paper

169	A53 2.70k multicolored	1.10	1.10
170	A53 3k multicolored	.65	.65
171	A53 4.70k multicolored	1.75	1.75
172	A53 9k multicolored	2.50	2.50
	Nos. 169-172 (4)	6.00	6.00

Europa — A54

Communication and transport: 3k, Satellite dish, satellite. 5.50k, Fork lift, crane, ship.

1988, Apr. 11 Photo. *Perf. 11½*

173	A54 3k multicolored	*.90*	*.90*
174	A54 5.50k multicolored	*1.50*	*1.50*

A55

Writers: 270o, Jorgen-Frantz Jacobsen (1900-38). 300o, Christian Matras (b. 1900). 470o, William Heinesen (b. 1900). 650o, Hedin Bru (1901-87).

1988, June 6 Engr. *Perf. 13½*

175	A55 270o myrtle green	1.40	1.40
176	A55 300o rose lake	.85	.85
177	A55 470o dark blue	2.00	2.00
178	A55 650o brown black	2.25	2.25
	Nos. 175-178 (4)	6.50	6.50

A56

Text, illustrations and cameo portraits of organizers: 3k, Announcement and Djoni Geil, Enok Baerentsen and H.H. Jacobsen. 3.20k, Meeting, Rasmus Effersoe, C.L. Johannesen and Samal Krakusteini. 12k, Oystercatcher and lyrics of *Now the Hour Has Come,* by poet Sverri Patursson (1871-1960), Just A. Husum, Joannes Patursson and Jens Olsen.

Granite Paper

1988, Sept. 5 Photo. *Perf. 12*

179	A56 3k multicolored	.80	.80
180	A56 3.20k multicolored	1.20	1.20
181	A56 12k multicolored	4.50	4.50
	Nos. 179-181 (3)	6.50	6.50

1888 Christmas meeting to preserve cultural traditions and the natl. language, cent.

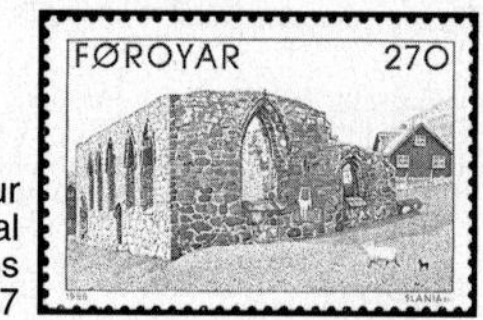

Kirkjubour Cathedral Ruins A57

270o, Exterior. 300o, Arch. 470o, Crucifixion, bas-relief. 550o, Interior.

1988, Oct. 17 Engr. *Perf. 13*

182	A57 270o dark green	1.40	1.40
183	A57 300o dark bl, vert.	1.10	1.10
184	A57 470o dark brn, vert.	1.60	1.60
185	A57 550o dark violet	1.60	1.60
	Nos. 182-185 (4)	5.70	5.70

Havnar Church, Torshavn, 200th Anniv. A58

Designs: 350o, Church exterior. 500o, Crypt, vert. 15k, Bell, vert.

1989, Feb. 6 Engr. *Perf. 13*

186	A58 350o dark green	1.00	1.00
187	A58 500o dark brown	1.75	1.75
188	A58 15k deep blue	3.50	3.50
	Nos. 186-188 (3)	6.25	6.25

Folk Costumes — A59

Photo. & Engr.

1989, Apr. 10 *Perf. 13½*

189 A59 350o Man 1.00 1.00
190 A59 600o Woman 2.00 2.00

Europa 1989 — A60

Wooden children's toys.

1989, Apr. 10 Photo. *Perf. 12x11½*

Granite Paper

191 A60 3.50k Boat *1.00 1.00*
192 A60 6k Horse *1.50 1.50*

Island Games, July 5-13 — A61

1989, June 5 Photo. *Perf. 12½*

Granite Paper

193 A61 200o Rowing .75 .75
194 A61 350o Handball 1.25 1.25
195 A61 600o Soccer 1.75 1.75
196 A61 700o Swimming 2.25 2.25
Nos. 193-196 (4) 6.00 6.00

A62

Bird cliffs of Suduroy.

1989, Oct. 2 Engr. *Perf. 14x13½*

197 A62 320o Tvoran 1.00 1.00
198 A62 350o Skuvanes 1.40 1.40
199 A62 500o Beinisvord 1.75 1.75
200 A62 600o Asmundarstakkur 2.00 2.00
Nos. 197-200 (4) 6.15 6.15

A63

Modern fish factory (filleting station): 3.50k, Unloading fish. 3.70k, Cleaning and sorting. 5k, Filleting. 7k, Packaged frozen fish.

1990, Feb. 5 Litho. *Perf. 14x13½*

201 A63 3.50k multi 1.00 1.00
202 A63 3.70k multi 1.00 1.00
203 A63 5k multi 1.25 1.25
204 A63 7k multi 2.00 2.00
Nos. 201-204 (4) 5.25 5.25

Europa 1990 — A64

Post offices.

1990, Apr. 9 Litho. *Perf. 13½x14*

205 A64 3.50k Gjogv *1.00 1.00*
206 A64 6k Klaksvik *1.75 1.75*

Souvenir Sheet

Recognition of the Merkid, Flag of the Faroes, by the British, 50th Anniv. — A65

Designs: a, Flag. b, Fishing trawler *Nyggjaberg,* disappeared, 1942. c, Sloop *Saana,* sunk by the Germans, 1942.

1990, Apr. 9 Photo. *Perf. 12*

Granite Paper

207 A65 Sheet of 3 4.50 4.50
a.-c. 3.50k any single 1.60 1.60

Whales A66

Designs: 320o, Mesoplodon bidens. 350o, Balaena mysticetus. 600o, Eubalaena glacialis. 700o, Hyperoodon ampullatus.

1990, June 6 Photo. *Perf. 11½*

Granite Paper

208 A66 320o multi 1.25 1.25
209 A66 350o multi 1.50 1.50
210 A66 600o multi 2.25 2.25
211 A66 700o multi 2.50 2.50
Nos. 208-211 (4) 7.50 7.50

Nolsoy Island by Steffan Danielsen A67

1990, Oct. 8 Photo. *Perf. 11½*

Granite Paper

212 A67 50o shown .25 .25
213 A67 350o Coastline 1.10 1.10
214 A67 500o Town 1.50 1.50
215 A67 1000o Coastline, cliffs 3.00 3.00
Nos. 212-215 (4) 5.85 5.85

Flora and Fauna — A68

3.70k, Plantago lanceolata. 4k, Rumex longifolius. 4.50k, Amara aulica. 6.50k, Lumbricus terrestris.

1991, Feb. 4 Litho. *Perf. 13*

216 A68 3.70k multi 1.00 1.00
217 A68 4k multi 1.20 1.20
218 A68 4.50k multi 1.50 1.50
219 A68 6.50k multi 2.00 2.00
Nos. 216-219 (4) 5.70 5.70

Europa — A69

Designs: 3.70k, Weather satellite. 6.50k, Celestial navigation.

1991, Apr. 4 Litho. *Perf. 13*

220 A69 3.70k multicolored *1.00 1.00*
221 A69 6.50k multicolored *1.75 1.75*

Town of Torshavn, 125th Anniv. — A70

1991, Apr. 4 *Perf. 14x13½*

222 A70 3.70k Town Hall 1.25 1.25
223 A70 3.70k View of town 1.25 1.25

Birds — A71

1991, June 3 Litho. *Perf. 13½*

224 A71 3.70k Rissa tridactyla 1.20 1.20
225 A71 3.70k Sterna paradisaea 1.20 1.20
a. Bklt. pane, 3 each #224-225 9.00

Village of Saksun A72

Design: 650o, Cliffs of Vestmanna.

1991, June 3

226 A72 370o shown 1.00 1.00
227 A72 650o multicolored 1.75 1.75

Samal Joensen-Mikines (1906-1979), Painter — A73

Designs: 340o, Funeral Procession. 370o, The Farewell. 550o, Handanagarthur. 1300o, Winter morning.

1991, Oct. 7 Litho. *Perf. 13½*

228 A73 340o multi 1.00 1.00
229 A73 370o multi 1.10 1.10
230 A73 550o multi 1.60 1.60
231 A73 1300o multi 3.75 3.75
Nos. 228-231 (4) 7.45 7.45

Mail Boats A74

1992, Feb. 10 Litho. *Perf. 13½x14*

232 A74 200o Ruth .70 .70
233 A74 370o Ritan 1.00 1.00
234 A74 550o Sigmundur 1.50 1.50
235 A74 800o Masin 2.50 2.50
Nos. 232-235 (4) 5.70 5.70

Europa A75

Designs: 3.70k, Map of North Atlantic, Viking ship. 6.50k, Map of Central Atlantic region, one of Columbus' ships.

1992, Apr. 6 Litho. *Perf. 13½x14*

236 A75 3.70k multicolored *1.10 1.10*
237 A75 6.50k multicolored *2.00 2.00*

Souvenir Sheet

238 A75 Sheet of 2, #236-237 *8.50 8.50*

First landing in the Americas by Leif Erikson (No. 236). Discovery of America by Christopher Columbus, 500th anniv. (No. 237).
See Iceland Nos. 749-751.

Seals A76

Designs: No. 239, Halichoerus grypus. No. 240, Phoca vitulina.

1992, June 9 Litho. *Perf. 14x13½*

239 A76 3.70k multi 1.40 1.40
240 A76 3.70k multi 1.40 1.40
a. Bklt. pane, 3 #239, 3 #240 *17.50*

Minerals — A77

1992, June 9 Photo. *Perf. 12*

Granite Paper

241 A77 370o Stilbite 1.25 1.25
242 A77 650o Mesolite 2.25 2.25

Traditional Houses A78

1992, Oct. 5 Litho. *Perf. 13½*

243 A78 3.40k Hja Glyvra Hanusi 1.00 1.00
244 A78 3.70k I Nordragotu 1.10 1.10
245 A78 6.50k Blasastova 2.00 2.00
246 A78 8k Jakupsstova 2.40 2.40
Nos. 243-246 (4) 6.50 6.50

Nordic House Entertainers — A79

1993, Feb. 8 Litho. *Perf. 13½*

247 A79 400o Dancers 1.10 1.10
248 A79 400o Pianist 1.10 1.10
249 A79 400o Trio 1.10 1.10
a. Souv. sheet, #247-249, perf 12½ 4.00 4.00
Nos. 247-249 (3) 3.30 3.30

Village of Gjogv A80

1993, Apr. 5

250 A80 4k View toward sea 1.50 1.50
251 A80 4k Ravine, village 1.50 1.50
a. Booklet pane, 3 each #250-251 9.00

Europa — A81

Sculptures by Hans Pauli Olsen: 4k, Movement. 7k, Reflection.

1993, Apr. 5

252 A81	4k multicolored		*1.50*	*1.50*
253 A81	7k multicolored		*2.00*	*2.00*

Horses — A82

Perf. 13½x13, 13x13½

1993, June 7 **Engr.**

254 A82	400o shown	1.10	1.10
255 A82	20k Mare, foal, horiz.	5.50	5.50

Butterflies A83

1993, Oct. 4 **Litho.** ***Perf. 14½***

256 A83	350o Apamea zeta	1.10	1.10
257 A83	400o Hepialus humuli	1.25	1.25
258 A83	700o Vanessa atalanta	2.10	2.10
259 A83	900o Perizoma albulata	2.75	2.75
	Nos. 256-259 (4)	7.20	7.20

Fish — A84

Designs: 10o, Gasterosteus aculeatus. 4k, Neocyttus helgae. 7k, Salmo trutta fario. 10k, Hoplostethus atlanticus.

1994, Feb. 7 **Litho.** ***Perf. 14½***

260 A84	10o multi	.25	.25
261 A84	4k multi	1.25	1.25
262 A84	7k multi	2.25	2.25
263 A84	10k multi	3.00	3.00
	Nos. 260-263 (4)	6.75	6.75

Voyages of St. Brendan (484-577) A85

Europa: 4k, St. Brendan on island with sheep, Irish monks in boat. 7k, St. Brendan, monks sailing past volcano.

1994, Apr. 18 **Litho.** ***Perf. 14½x14***

264 A85	4k multicolored	*1.25*	*1.25*
265 A85	7k multicolored	*2.40*	*2.00*
a.	Miniature sheet of 2, #264-265	*4.50*	*4.50*

Nos. 264-265 have designers name below the design. Stamps in No. 265a do not.

See Iceland Nos. 780-781; Ireland Nos. 923-924.

Sheepdogs — A86

Design: No. 267, Dog watching over sheep.

1994, June 6 **Litho.** ***Perf. 13½***

266 A86	4k multicolored	1.40	1.40

Size: 39x25mm

267 A86	4k multicolored	1.40	1.40
a.	Booklet pane, 3 each #266-267	8.50	
	Complete booklet, #267a	9.50	

School of Navigation A87

Designs: 3.50k, Man using sextant, schooner. 7k, Ship, man at computer.

1994, June 6

268 A87	3.50k multicolored	1.00	1.00
269 A87	7k multicolored	2.50	2.50

Brusajokil's Lay — A88

Scenes, verses of the ballad: 1k, Ship at sea. 4k, Asbjorn entering Brusajokil's cave. 6k, Ormar with cat, trolls. 7k, Ormar pulling Brusajokil's beard.

1994, Sept. 19 **Litho.** ***Perf. 14***

270 A88	1k multicolored	.35	.35
271 A88	4k multicolored	1.40	1.40
272 A88	6k multicolored	1.75	1.75
273 A88	7k multicolored	2.25	2.25
	Nos. 270-273 (4)	5.75	5.75

Twelve Days of Christmas A89

No. 274, Goats, men, deer, hides. No. 275, Ducks, cattle, sheep, horses, banners, barrels.

1994, Oct. 31 **Litho.** ***Perf. 14x13***

274 A89	4k multicolored	1.10	1.10
275 A89	4k multicolored	1.10	1.10
a.	Bklt. pane, 3 each #274-275	7.00	
	Complete booklet, #275a	7.00	

Leafhoppers — A90

Designs: 50o, Ulopa reticulata. 4k, Streptanus sordidus. 5k, Anoscopus flavostriatus. 13k, Macrosteles alpinus.

1995, Feb. 6 **Litho.** ***Perf. 14***

276 A90	50o multicolored	.25	.25
277 A90	4k multicolored	1.60	1.60
278 A90	5k multicolored	1.60	1.60
279 A90	13k multicolored	4.50	4.50
	Nos. 276-279 (4)	7.95	7.95

Tourism A91

1995, Apr. 10 **Litho.** ***Perf. 13½x14***

280 A91	4k Village of Famjin	1.50	1.50
281 A91	4k Vatnsdalur valley	1.50	1.50

Peace & Freedom A92

Europa: 4k, Island couple, "Vidar, vali og baldur." 7k, Couple looking toward sun, "Liv og livtrasir."

1995, Apr. 10 ***Perf. 13x14***

282 A92	4k multicolored	*1.20*	*1.20*
283 A92	7k multicolored	*2.50*	*2.50*

Nordic Art — A93

Designs: 2k, Museum of Art, Torshavn. 4k, Woman, by Frimod Joensen, vert. 5.50k, Self-portrait, by Joensen, vert.

Perf. 13½x14, 14x13½

1995, June 12 **Litho.**

284 A93	2k multicolored	.65	.65
285 A93	4k multicolored	1.40	1.40
286 A93	5.50k multicolored	1.90	1.90
	Nos. 284-286 (3)	3.95	3.95

Corvus Corax A94

Designs: No. 287, Black raven. No. 288, White-speckled raven.

1995, June 12 ***Perf. 13½x14***

287 A94	4k multicolored	1.40	1.40
288 A94	4k multicolored	1.40	1.40
a.	Booklet pane, 5 each #287-288	14.00	
	Complete booklet, #288a	14.00	

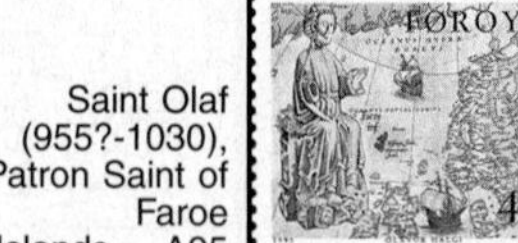

Saint Olaf (955?-1030), Patron Saint of Faroe Islands — A95

Litho. & Engr.

1995, Sept. 12 ***Perf. 13½x13***

289 A95	4k multicolored	1.60	1.60

See Aland Islands No. 119.

Early Folk Life A95a

4k, Dairy maids carrying buckets. 6k, Peasants fleecing sheep. 15k, Schooners, saltfish being brought ashore, vert.

1995, Sept. 12 **Engr.** ***Perf. 12½***

290 A95a	4k dark green	1.50	1.50
291 A95a	6k dark brn, vert.	2.25	2.25
292 A95a	15k dark blue	5.00	5.00
	Nos. 290-292 (3)	8.75	8.75

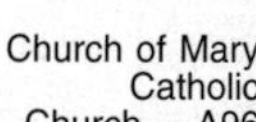

Church of Mary Catholic Church — A96

Designs: No. 293, Stained glass window. No. 294, Exterior view of church.

1995, Nov. 9 **Litho.** ***Perf. 13½***

293 A96	4k multicolored	1.40	1.40
294 A96	4k multicolored	1.40	1.40
a.	Booklet pane, 5 ea #293-294	14.00	
	Complete booklet, #294a	14.00	

Rocky Coastline — A97

1996, Jan. 1 **Litho.** ***Perf. 14***

295 A97	4.50k multicolored	1.40	1.40

Seaweed — A98

4k, Ptilota plumosa. 5.50k, Fucus spiralis. 6k, Ascophyllum nodosum. 9k, Laminaria hyperborea.

1996, Feb. 12 ***Perf. 15***

296 A98	4k multicolored	1.10	1.10
297 A98	5.50k multicolored	1.40	1.40
298 A98	6k multicolored	1.60	1.60
299 A98	9k multicolored	2.75	2.75
	Nos. 296-299 (4)	6.85	6.85

Birds — A99

Designs: No. 300, Laxia curvirostra. No. 301, Bombycilla garrulus.

1996, Apr. 15 **Litho.** ***Perf. 14x15***

300 A99	4.50k multicolored	1.40	1.40
301 A99	4.50k multicolored	1.40	1.40
a.	Booklet pane, 5 ea #300-301	14.00	
	Complete booklet, #301a	14.00	

See Nos. 313-314.

A100

Europa (Wives of Faroese Seamen): 4.50k, Woman standing beside sea coast. 7.50k, Portrait of a woman, vert.

1996, Apr. 15 ***Perf. 15x14½, 14½x15***

302 A100	4.50k multicolored	*1.50*	*1.50*
303 A100	7.50k multicolored	*2.00*	*2.00*

A101

Nordatlantex '96 (Children's drawings): a, Boy playing with hoop, stick, by Bugvi. b, Two girls on steet, road sign, by Gudrid. c, Girl on bicycle, car on street, by Herborg.

1996, June 7 Litho. *Perf. 14½*
Souvenir Sheet of 3

304 A101 4.50k #a.-c. 3.50 3.50

A102

Sea bed off the Faroes.

Litho. & Engr.
1996, June 7 *Perf. 13*

305 A102 10k violet & multi 2.50 2.50
306 A102 16k green & multi 4.00 4.00

See Nos. 319-320, 343, 377-378.

Janus Kamban (b. 1913), Sculptor, Graphic Artist A103

Works of art: 4.50k, Flock of Sheep. 6.50k, Fisherman on the Way Home. 7.50k, View from Tórshavn's Old Quarter.

1996, Sept. 16 Litho. *Perf. 14*

307 A103 4.50k multicolored 1.40 1.40
308 A103 6.50k multicolored 1.60 1.60
309 A103 7.50k multicolored 2.25 2.25
Nos. 307-309 (3) 5.25 5.25

A104

Christian's Church, Klaksvík — A105

Designs: No. 310, Exterior. No. 311, Interior, altar fresco.

1996, Nov. 4 Litho. *Perf. 14x15*

310 A104 4.50k multi 1.40 1.40
311 A105 4.50k multi 1.40 1.40
a. Booklet pane, 6 #310, 4 #311 14.00
Complete booklet, #311a 14.00

Christmas.

Souvenir Sheet

Reign of Queen Margaret II, 25th Anniv. — A106

1997, Jan. 14 Litho. *Perf. 14½*

312 A106 4.50k multicolored 1.25 1.25

Bird Type of 1996

Designs: No. 313, Pyrrhula pyrrhula. No. 314, Carduelis flammea.

1997, Feb. 17 Litho. *Perf. 14x15*

313 A99 4.50k multi 1.25 1.25
314 A99 4.50k multi 1.25 1.25
a. Booklet pane, 5 each #313-314 12.50 —
Complete booklet, #314a 12.50

Mushrooms — A107

Designs: 4.50k, Hygrocybe helobia. 6k, Hygrocybe chlorophana. 6.50k, Hygrocybe virginea. 7.50k, Hygrocybe psittacina.

1997, Feb. 17 *Perf. 14½*

315 A107 4.50k multicolored 1.10 1.10
316 A107 6k multicolored 1.60 1.60
317 A107 6.50k multicolored 1.60 1.60
318 A107 7.50k multicolored 2.00 2.00
Nos. 315-318 (4) 6.30 6.30

Map Type of 1996
Litho. & Engr.
1997, May 20 *Perf. 13*

319 A102 11k red & multi 2.90 2.90
320 A102 18k claret & multi 4.50 4.50

Europa — A108

Legends illustrated by William Heinesen: 4.50k, The Temptations of Saint Anthony. 7.50k, The Merman sitting at bottom of sea eating fish bait.

1997, May 20 Litho. *Perf. 14½*

321 A108 4.50k multicolored *1.40 1.40*
322 A108 7.50k multicolored *2.25 2.25*

Kalmar Union, 600th Anniv. — A109

1997, May 20 Engr. *Perf. 12½*

323 A109 4.50k deep blue violet 1.50 1.50

A110

Barbara, Film Shot in Faroe Islands (Scenes from film): 4.50k, Danish theologian Poul Aggerso arriving at Faroe Islands. 6.50k, Barbara and Poul. 7.50k, Barbara with men on boat. 9k, Barbara in row boat, sailing ship.

1997, Sept. 15 Litho. *Perf. 14*

324 A110 4.50k multicolored 1.25 1.25
325 A110 6.50k multicolored 1.60 1.60
326 A110 7.50k multicolored 2.00 2.00
327 A110 9k multicolored 2.25 2.25
Nos. 324-327 (4) 7.10 7.10

A111

Hvalvik church.

1997, Sept. 15

328 A111 4.50k Interior 1.25 1.25
329 A111 4.50k Exterior 1.25 1.25
a. Booklet pane, 5 each #328-329 12.50 —
Complete booklet, #329a 12.50

Birds — A112

1998, Feb. 23 Litho. *Perf. 14x14½*

330 A112 4.50k Sturnus vulgaris 1.25 1.25
331 A112 4.50k Turdus merula 1.25 1.25
a. Bklt. pane, 5 each #330-331 12.50
Complete booklet, #331a 12.50

A113

Scenes from the Sigurd poem "Brynhild's Ballad": 4.50k, King Buole, daughter Brynhild. 6.50k, Sigurd riding through wall of fire on horseback. 7.50k, Sigurd, Brynhild together. 10k, Guthrun alone leading horse.

1998, Feb. 23 *Perf. 14*

332 A113 4.50k multicolored 1.25 1.25
333 A113 6.50k multicolored 1.60 1.60
334 A113 7.50k multicolored 1.90 1.90
335 A113 10k multicolored 2.50 2.50
Nos. 332-335 (4) 7.25 7.25

Europa — A114

1998, May 18 Litho. *Perf. 14*

336 A114 4.50k Parade *1.25 1.25*
337 A114 7.50k Processional *1.25 1.25*

Olavsoka, Natl. Festival of Faroe Islands.

A115

1998, May 18 *Perf. 14½*

338 A115 7.50k multicolored 1.90 1.90

UN Declaration of Human Rights, 50th anniv.

Intl. Year of the Ocean A116

Toothed whales: 4k, Lagenorhynchus acutus. 4.50k, Orcinus orca. 7k, Tursiops truncatus. 9k, Delphinapterus leucas.

1998, May 18 *Perf. 14½x14*

339 A116 4k multicolored 1.00 1.00
340 A116 4.50k multicolored 1.10 1.10
341 A116 7k multicolored 1.75 1.75
342 A116 9k multicolored 2.25 2.25
Nos. 339-342 (4) 6.10 6.10

Map Type of 1996
Litho. & Engr.
1998, Sept. 14 *Perf. 13*

343 A102 14k multicolored 3.75 3.75

Frederickschurch A117

Designs: No. 344, Exterior, coastline. No. 345, Interior.

1998, Sept. 14 Litho. *Perf. 14*

344 A117 4.50k multi 1.25 1.25
345 A117 4.50k multi 1.25 1.25
a. Bklt. pane, 5 each #344-345 12.50
Complete booklet, #345a 12.50

A118

Paintings by Hans Hansen (1920-70): 4.50k, Fell-field, 1966. 5.50k, Village Interior, 1965. 6.50k, Portrait of Farmer Ólavur í Utistovu from Mikladalur, 1968. 8k, Self-portrait, 1968.

Perf. 13½x14, 14x13½
1998, Sept. 14

346 A118 4.50k multi 1.25 1.25
347 A118 5.50k multi 1.50 1.50
348 A118 6.50k multi, vert. 1.60 1.60
349 A118 8k multi, vert. 2.25 2.25
Nos. 346-349 (4) 6.60 6.60

Birds — A119

Designs: No. 350, Passer domesticus. No. 351, Troglodytes troglodytes.

1999, Feb. 22 Litho. *Perf. 13½*

350 A119 4.50k multi 1.25 1.25
351 A119 4.50k multi 1.25 1.25
a. Bklt. pane, 5 each #350-351 12.50
Complete booklet, #351a 12.50

Ships Named "Smyril" A120

1999, Feb. 22 *Perf. 14½x14*

352 A120 4.50k 1895 1.25 1.25
353 A120 5k 1932 1.40 1.40
354 A120 8k 1967 2.25 2.25
355 A120 13k 1975 3.50 3.50
Nos. 352-355 (4) 8.40 8.40

Northern Islands A121

1999, May 25 Litho. *Perf. 13½*

356 A121 50o Kalsoy .25 .25
357 A121 100o Vithoy .25 .25
358 A121 400o Svinoy 1.10 1.10
359 A121 450o Fugloy 1.25 1.25

360 A121 600o Kunoy 1.60 1.60
361 A121 800o Borthoy 2.10 2.10
Nos. 356-361 (6) 6.55 6.55

See Nos. 383-386.

Waterfalls — A122

Europa: 6k, Svartifossur. 8k, Foldarafossur.

1999, May 25 ***Perf. 14x14½***
362 A122 6k multicolored *1.60 1.60*
363 A122 8k multicolored *2.25 2.25*

Abstract Paintings of Ingálvur av Reyni — A123

1999, Sept. 27 **Litho.** ***Perf. 12½***
364 A123 4.50k Bygd 1.25 1.25
365 A123 6k Húsavik 1.60 1.60
366 A123 8k Reytt regn 2.10 2.10
367 A123 20k Genta 5.25 5.25
Nos. 364-367 (4) 10.20 10.20

Bible Stories — A124

1999, Sept. 27 ***Perf. 14½x14***
368 A124 450o John 1:1-5 1.25 1.25
a. Booklet pane of 6 7.50
Complete booklet, #368a 7.50
369 A124 600o Luke 1:26-28 1.60 1.60
a. Booklet pane of 6 10.00
Complete booklet, #369a 10.00

See Nos. 387-388, 407-408.

A125

Christianity in the Faroes, 1000th Anniv.: 4.50k, Man on rocks in ocean. 5.50k, Monk with cross, man with sword. 8k, People, flags. 16k, Cross in sky.

Perf. 13½x13¼
2000, Feb. 21 **Litho.**
370 A125 4.50k multi 1.25 1.25
371 A125 5.50k multi 1.40 1.40
372 A125 8k multi 2.10 2.10
373 A125 16k multi 4.25 4.25
Nos. 370-373 (4) 9.00 9.00

A126

School and: No. 374, Sanna av Skarthi, Anna Suffia Rasmussen, wives of founders. No. 375, Rasmus Rasmussen (1871-1962), Símun av Skarthi (1872-1942), school founders.

2000, Feb. 21
374 A126 4.50k multi 1.25 1.25
375 A126 4.50k multi 1.25 1.25
a. Bklt. pane, 4 ea #374-375 10.00
Complete booklet, #375a 10.00

Faroese Folk High School, cent.

Europa, 2000
Common Design Type

2000, May 9 **Litho.** ***Perf. 13¼x13***
376 CD17 8k multi *2.40 2.40*

Map Type of 1996
Litho. & Engr.

2000, May 22 ***Perf. 13¼x13***
377 A102 15k multi 3.75 3.75
378 A102 22k multi 5.75 5.75

Stampin' The Future Children's Stamp Design Contest Winners A127

Art by: 4k, Katrin Mortensen. 4.50k, Sigga Andreassen. 6k, Steingrímur Joensen. 8k, Dion Dam Frandsen.

2000, May 22 **Litho.** ***Perf. 13x13¼***
379 A127 4k multi 1.10 1.10
380 A127 4.50k multi 1.25 1.25
381 A127 6k multi 1.60 1.60
382 A127 8k multi 2.25 2.25
Nos. 379-382 (4) 6.20 6.20

Island Type of 1999

2000, Sept. 18 **Litho.** ***Perf. 13½***
383 A121 200o Skúvoy .65 .65
384 A121 650o Hestoy 1.60 1.60
385 A121 750o Koltur 1.90 1.90
386 A121 1000o Nólsoy 2.50 2.50
Nos. 383-386 (4) 6.65 6.65

Bible Story Type of 1999

2000, Sept. 18 **Litho.** ***Perf. 13x13¼***
387 A124 4.50k Micah 5:1 1.25 1.25
a. Booklet pane of 6 7.50
Booklet, #387a 7.50
388 A124 6k John 1:14 1.60 1.60
a. Booklet pane of 6 10.00
Booklet, #388a 10.00

Pew Gables Type of 1980

Kirkjubour pew gables: 430o, St. Andrew with cross. 650o, St. Bartholomew. 800o, Unknown apostle. 18k, Unknown apostle, diff.

Photo. & Engr.

2001, Feb. 12 ***Perf. 12¾x12½***
389 A20 450o multi 1.25 1.25
390 A20 650o multi 1.60 1.60
391 A20 800o multi 2.10 2.10
392 A20 18k multi 4.50 4.50
Nos. 389-392 (4) 9.45 9.45

Faroese Red Cross, 75th Anniv. A128

Designs: 4.50k, Old person. 6k, Relief worker.

2001, Feb. 12 **Litho.** ***Perf. 14½x14***
393 A128 4.50k multi 1.25 1.25
a. Booklet pane of 6 7.50
Booklet, #393a 7.50
394 A128 6k multi 1.60 1.60
a. Booklet pane of 6 10.00
Booklet, #394a 10.00

Souvenir Sheet

Faroe Islands Postal Service, 25th Anniv. — A129

No. 395: a, Boat for interisland mail transport, 19th cent. b, Tórshavn post office, 1906. c, Simon Pauli Poulsen (Morkabóndin), mail carrier.

Photo. & Engr.

2001, Apr. 1 ***Perf. 13x13¼***
395 A129 4.50k Sheet of 3, #a-c 5.00 5.00

Nordic Myths and Legends About Light and Darkness — A130

No. 396: a, The Death of Hogni. b, The Tree of the Year. c, The Harp. d, Gram and Grane. e, The Ballad of Nornagest. f, Gudrun's Evil Magic.

Litho. with Foil Application

2001, Apr. 1 ***Perf. 13½x13¼***
396 A130 6k Sheet of 6, #a-f 10.00 10.00

Hafnia 2001 Philatelic Exhibition, Copenhagen.

Paintings by Zacharias Heinesen A131

Designs: 4k, The Artist's Mother, 1992. 4.50k, Úti á Reyni, 1974. 10k, Ur Vágunum, 2000. 15k, Sunrise, 1975.

2001, June 11 **Litho.** ***Perf. 13¼x13***
397 A131 4k multi 1.10 1.10
398 A131 4.50k multi 1.25 1.25
399 A131 10k multi 2.75 2.75
400 A131 15k multi 4.00 4.00
Nos. 397-400 (4) 9.10 9.10

Europa A132

Hydroelectric power stations: 6k, Fossáverkith. 8k, Eithisverkith.

2001, June 11 ***Perf. 13x13½***
401 A132 6k multi *1.60 1.60*
402 A132 8k multi *2.25 2.25*

Whales — A133

Designs: 4.50k, Physeter macrocephalus. 6.50k, Balaenoptera physalus. 9k, Balaenoptera musculus. 20k, Balaenoptera borealis.

Perf. 13¾x13¼
2001, Sept. 17 **Litho.**
403 A133 4.50k multi 1.25 1.25
404 A133 6.50k multi 1.60 1.60
405 A133 9k multi 2.25 2.25
406 A133 20k multi 5.50 5.50
Nos. 403-406 (4) 10.60 10.60

Bible Stories Type of 1999

2001, Sept. 17 ***Perf. 13***
407 A124 5k Luke 2:34-35 1.40 1.40
a. Booklet pane of 6 8.50 —
Booklet, #407a 8.50
408 A124 6.50k Matthew 2:18 1.60 1.60
a. Booklet pane of 6 10.00 —
Booklet, #408a 10.00

Mollusks — A134

Designs: 5k, Sepiola atlantica. 7k, Modiolus modiolus. 7.50k, Polycera faeroensis. 18k, Buccinum undatum.

2002, Feb. 11 **Litho.** ***Perf. 13***
409 A134 5k multi 1.40 1.40
410 A134 7k multi 1.75 1.75
411 A134 7.50k multi 1.90 1.90
412 A134 18k multi 4.50 4.50
Nos. 409-412 (4) 9.55 9.55

Portions of the designs were applied by a thermographic process producing a shiny, raised effect.

Souvenir Sheet

Viking Voyages — A135

No. 413: a, Navigation tool. b, Viking sailor on boat. c, Viking boat.

Litho. & Engr.

2002, Feb. 11 ***Perf. 13***
413 A135 6.50k Sheet of 3, #a-c 5.00 5.00

Europa A136

Designs: 6.50k, Clowns. 8k, Various circus performers.

2002, Apr. 8 **Litho.** ***Perf. 13¼x13½***
414 A136 6.50k multi *1.60 1.60*
415 A136 8k multi *2.10 2.10*

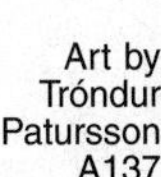

Art by Tróndur Patursson
A137

Designs: 5k, Bládypi. 6.50k, Kosmiska Rúmith.

2002, Apr. 8

416 A137 5k multi 1.40 1.40
417 A137 6.50k multi 1.60 1.60
a. Booklet pane of 8, 4 each #416-417 13.00 —
Booklet, #417a 13.00

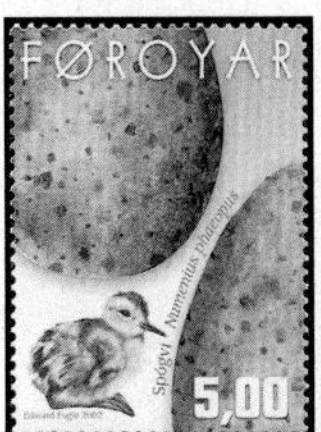

Eggs and Chicks — A138

Designs: 5k, Numenius phaeopus. 7.50k, Gallinago gallinago. 12k, Haematopus ostralegus. 20k, Pluvialis apricaria.

2002, June 17 ***Perf. 14x14½***

418 A138 5k multi 1.40 1.40
419 A138 7.50k multi 1.90 1.90
420 A138 12k multi 3.00 3.00
421 A138 20k multi 5.25 5.25
Nos. 418-421 (4) 11.55 11.55

Souvenir Sheet

Faroese Representative Council, 150th Anniv. — A139

Designs: 5k, Royal book and seal. 6.50k, Royal book, Protocol of 1852.

2002, June 17 ***Perf. 14***

422 A139 Sheet of 2, #a-b 4.00 4.00

Falco Columbarius Subaesalon — A140

Litho. & Embossed

2002, Sept. 23 ***Perf. 13¼***

423 A140 30k multi 8.25 8.25

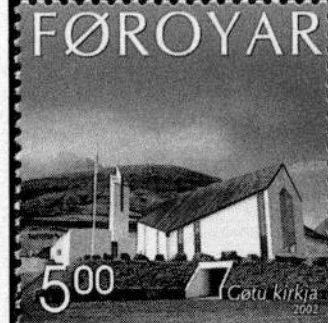

Gota Church — A141

2002, Sept. 23 Litho. ***Perf. 12½***

424 A141 5k Exterior 1.40 1.40
425 A141 6.50k Interior 1.60 1.60
a. Booklet pane, 5 each #424-425 15.00 —
Booklet, #425a 15.00

Souvenir Sheet

Intl. Council for the Exploration of the Sea, Cent. — A142

No. 426: a, Micromesistius poutassou and island. b, Exploration ship Magnus Heinason and fish.

Litho. & Engr.

2002, Sept. 23 ***Perf. 13***

426 A142 8k Sheet of 2, #a-b 4.50 4.50

See Denmark Nos. 1237-1238, Greenland Nos. 401-402.

Opening of Vagár-Streymoy Tunnel, Nov. 2002 — A143

Designs: No. 427, Wheeled tunneling machine at right. No. 428, Workers in red uniforms at left.

2003, Feb. 24 Litho. ***Perf. 13¼x13***

427 A143 5k multi 1.40 1.40
428 A143 5k multi 1.40 1.40
a. Booklet pane, 5 each #427-428 14.00 —
Complete booklet, #428a 14.00

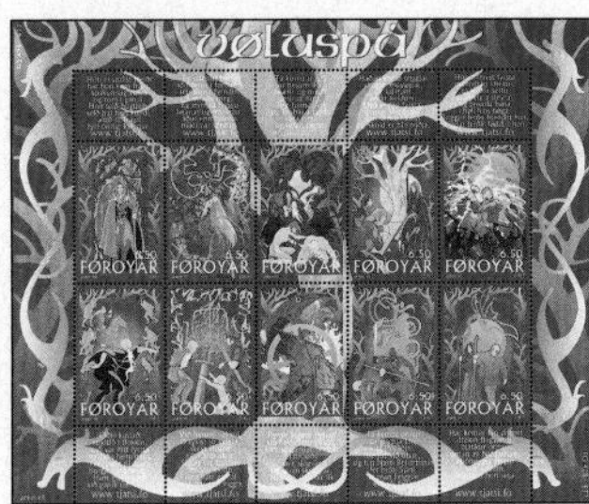

Voluspá, Ancient Norse Poem — A144

No. 429: a, Seeress Heid holding staff. b, Heid sees animal and man in vision. c, Nude man and woman. d, Scribe and horseman. e, Battle between group with swords and man with hammer. f, Horseman and warriors. g, Men, large sword. h, Longboat. i, Attack on man holding spear, fire. j, Two figures with staffs, winged serpent.

2003, Feb. 24 ***Perf. 14***

429 A144 Sheet of 10 17.50 17.50
a.-j. 6.50k Any single 1.60 1.60

Europa — A145

Poster art for Nordic House: 6.50k, Fish Tree, by Astrid Andreasen, 1991. 8k, Ceramics by Guthrith Poulsen, 1997.

2003, Apr. 14 ***Perf. 13½x13¼***

430 A145 6.50k multi *1.60 1.60*
431 A145 8k multi *2.10 2.10*

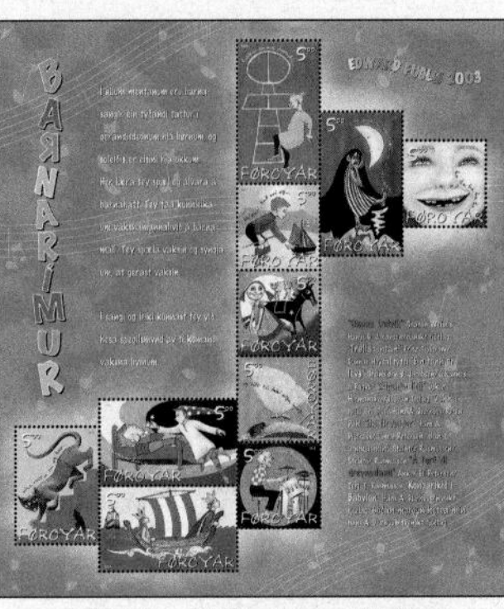

Children's Songs — A146

No. 432: a, Woman playing hopscotch (26x44mm). b, Boy on rocks, moon (26x44mm). c, Girl with missing teeth (26x26mm). d, Boy with toy sailboat (26x26mm). e, Cat, horse and girl (26x26mm). f, Butterfly and fly (26x26mm). g, Girl in bed, boy with stars (44x26mm). h, Cat on stairs, mouse (26x36mm). i, Man playing drums (26x26mm). j, King and queen in longboat (44x26mm).

Perf. 13¼, 13¼x13¼x13¼x14 (#432g, 432j), 13¼x14 (#432h)

2003, Apr. 14

432 A146 Sheet of 10 14.00 14.00
a.-j. 5k Any single 1.25 1.25

Small Towns
A147

2003, June 10 Litho. ***Perf. 13x13¼***

433 A147 5k Bour 1.40 1.40
434 A147 5k Gásadalur 1.40 1.40

Communities With Post Offices 100 Years Old — A148

No. 435: a, Fuglafjorthur. b, Strendur. c, Sandur. d, Eithi. e, Vestmanna. f, Vágur. g, Mithvágur. h, Hvalba.

2003, June 10 ***Perf. 13¼x13***

435 A148 Sheet of 8 11.00 11.00
a.-h. 5k Any single 1.25 1.25

Theologians — A149

Designs: 5k, Jesper Rasmussen Brochmand (1585-1652). 6.50k, Thomas Kingo (1634-1703).

2003, Sept. 22 ***Perf. 13x13¼***

436 A149 5k multi 1.40 1.40
437 A149 6.50k multi 1.60 1.60
a. Booklet pane, 5 each #436-437 15.00 —
Complete booklet, #437a 15.00

Souvenir Sheet

Dancing in the Inn's Smoking Room, by Emil Krause — A150

Litho. & Engr.

2003, Sept. 22 ***Perf. 12¼***

438 A150 25k multi 7.50 7.50

100th Faroese stamp engraved by Czeslaw Slania.

Islands Type of 1999

2004, Jan. 26 Litho. ***Perf. 13½***

439 A121 550o Stóra Dímun 1.40 1.40
440 A121 700o Lítla Dímun 1.90 1.90

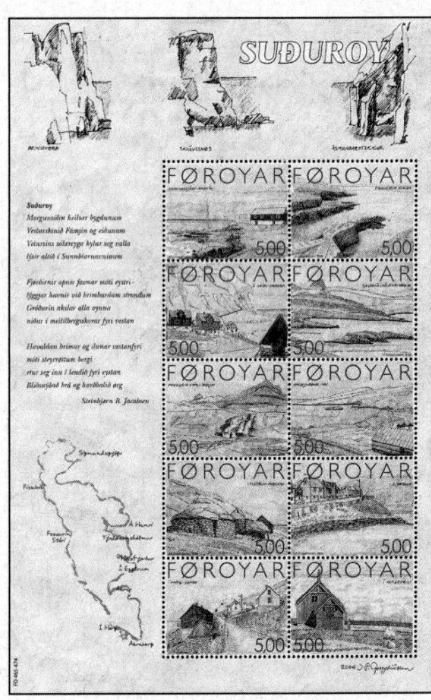

Suthuroy Island — A151

No. 441: a, Sigmundargjogv, Sandvik. b, Fiskieithi, Hvalba. c, A Hamri, Frothba. d, Tjaldavíkshólmur, Oravík. e, Fossurin Stóri, Fámjin. f, Hovsfjorthur, Hov. g, I Eystrum, Porkeri. h, A Okrum. i, I Horg, Sumba. j, I Akrabergi.

2004, Jan. 26 ***Perf. 13x13¼***

441 A151 5k Sheet of 10, #a-j 14.00 14.00

1854 Cruise of Yacht "Maria" — A152

No. 442: a, Gáshólmur and Tindhólmur. b, Framvith "Diamantunum." c, Hús av tí betra slagnum. d, Mylingur sunnanífrá. e, Mylingur northanífrá. f, Kalsoyggin northanífrá. g, Raetha teir infoddu. h, Sunnari endi av Kunoynni.

2004, Mar. 26 Litho. ***Perf. 13***

442 A152 6.50k Sheet of 8, #a.-h. 14.00 14.00

Souvenir Sheet

Norse Gods — A153

No. 443: a, Thor, in boat, fighting Midgard serpent. b, Ran in fishing net.

2004, Mar. 26

443 A153 6.50k Sheet of 2, #a.-b. 4.50 4.50

Souvenir Sheet

Wedding of Crown Prince Frederik and Mary Donaldson — A154

Litho. & Photo.

2004, May 14 *Perf. 13¼*

444 A154 Sheet of 2 + central label 4.00 4.00
a. 5k Couple facing right 1.60 1.60
b. 6.50k Couple facing left 2.25 2.25

See Denmark No. 1275 and Greenland Nos. 429-430.

Soccer Organization Centenaries A155

Soccer players and emblems of: 5k, Klaksvík and Tórshavn teams. 6.50k, FIFA (Fédération Internationale de Football Association).

2004, May 24 Litho. *Perf. 13¼x13*

445 A155 5k multi 1.40 1.40
446 A155 6.50k multi 1.60 1.60
a. Booklet pane, 4 each #445-446 12.00 —
Complete booklet, #446a 12.00

Europa A156

Designs: 6.50k, Tourists in gorge, Hestur. 8k, Tourists at shore, Stóra Dímun.

2004, May 24 *Perf. 13x13¼*

447 A156 6.50k multi *1.60 1.60*
448 A156 8k multi *2.25 2.25*

Churches A157

2004, Sept. 20 Litho. *Perf. 13¼x13*

449 A157 5.50k Vágur 1.40 1.40
450 A157 7.50k Tvoroyri 2.00 2.00
a. Booklet pane, 4 each #449-450 14.00 —
Complete booklet, #450a 14.00

Poems by Janus Djurhuus (1881-1948) — A158

No. 451: a, Atlantis. b, Grímur Kamban. c, Gandkvaethi Tróndar. d, Til Foroya I-III. e, Mín sorg. f, Loki. g, I búri og Slatur. h, Heimferth Nólsoyar Páls. i, Móses á Sinai fjalli. j, Cello.

2004, Sept. 20 *Perf. 13*

451 A158 Sheet of 10 20.00 20.00
a.-j. 7.50k Any single 2.00 2.00

Souvenir Sheet

Life of the Vikings — A159

No. 452: a, Men tending sheep. b, Men with farm implements. c, Women weaving and woman milking cow.

Litho. & Engr.

2005, Feb. 7 *Perf. 13*

452 A159 Sheet of 3 6.00 6.00
a.-c. 7.50k Any single 2.00 2.00

Miniature Sheet

Vágar Island — A160

No. 453: a, Víkar. b, Gásadalur. c, Bour. d, Slaettanes. e, Kvígandalsá. f, Sorvágur. g, Sandavágur. h, Vatnsoyrar. i, Fjallavatn. j, Mithvágur.

2005, Feb. 7 Litho. *Perf. 13x13¼*

453 A160 Sheet of 10 15.00 15.00
a.-j. 5.50k Any single 1.50 1.50

Lepus Timidus — A161

2005, Apr. 18 *Perf. 13¼x13½*

454 A161 5.50k shown 1.60 1.60
455 A161 5.50k Brown fur 1.60 1.60
a. Booklet pane, 4 each #454-455 13.00 —
Complete booklet, #455a 13.00

Europa — A162

Various traditional foods with: 7.50k, Brown panel. 10k, Green panel.

2005, Apr. 18 *Perf. 13¼x13*

456 A162 7.50k multi *2.00 2.00*
457 A162 10k multi *2.75 2.75*

Worldwide Fund for Nature (WWF) A163

Petrels: 8.50k, Oceanodroma leucorhoa. 9k, Hydrobates pelagicus. 12k, Oceanodroma leucorhoa on ground. 20k, Hydrobates pelagicus on ground.

2005, June 6 *Perf. 13*

458 A163 8.50k multi 1.60 1.60
459 A163 9k multi 2.75 2.75
460 A163 12k multi 3.25 3.25
461 A163 20k multi 5.50 5.50
Nos. 458-461 (4) 13.10 13.10

Miniature Sheet

Landscapes by Jógvan Waagstein (1879-1949) — A164

No. 462: a, Path and wall at LL, denomination in red, year date in black in grass. b, Path and wall at LL, denomination in white, year date in black on wall. c, Stone hut at left, denomination in red, year date in black. d, Path at right, denomination in red, year date in black. e, Two large rocks at right, denomination in red, year date in black. f, Rocks at LL, denomination in red, year date in white. g, Path at center, denomination in white, year date in black on path. h, Buildings at LL, denomination in red, year date in black in path. i, Churches, denomination in white, year date in black in water.

2005, Sept. 19 Litho. *Perf. 14x14¼*

462 A164 Sheet of 9 17.00 17.00
a.-i. 7.50k Any single 1.90 1.90

End of British Occupation In World War II, 60th Anniv. A165

Soldiers with: 5.50k, Arms. 9k, Children.

2005, Sept. 19 *Perf. 14*

463 A165 5.50k pale blue & blk 1.40 1.40
464 A165 9k pale yel & blk 2.40 2.40

Christmas — A166

Ballads: 5.50k, Jólavísan. 7.50k, Rudisar Vísa.

2005, Nov. 7 *Perf. 13½x13¼*

465 A166 5.50k multi 1.40 1.40
466 A166 7.50k multi 2.00 2.00
a. Booklet pane, 5 each #465-466 17.00 —
Complete booklet, #466a 17.00

Villages A167

2006, Feb. 13 Litho. *Perf. 13¾*

467 A167 7k Sythrugota 1.90 1.90
468 A167 12k Fuglafjorthur 2.50 2.50
469 A167 20k Leirvík 5.00 5.00
Nos. 467-469 (3) 9.40 9.40

Miniature Sheet

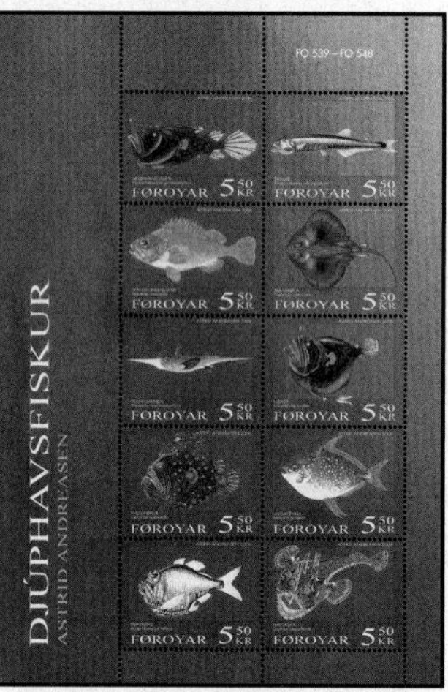

Fish — A168

No. 470: a, Himantolophus groenlandicus. b, Gonostoma elongatum. c, Sebastes mentella. d, Neoraja caerulea. e, Rhinochimaera atlantica. f, Linophryne lucifer. g, Ceratias holboelli. h, Lampris guttatus. i, Argyropelecus olfersi. j, Lophius piscatorius.

2006, Feb. 13 *Perf. 14*

470 A168 Sheet of 10 15.00 15.00
a.-j. 5.50k Any single 1.40 1.40

Souvenir Sheet

Norse Folklore — A169

No. 471: a, Norns surrounding sleeping child. b, Sea ghost.

2006, Mar. 29 *Perf. 13*

471 A169 7.50k Sheet of 2, #a-b 4.00 4.00

Miniature Sheet

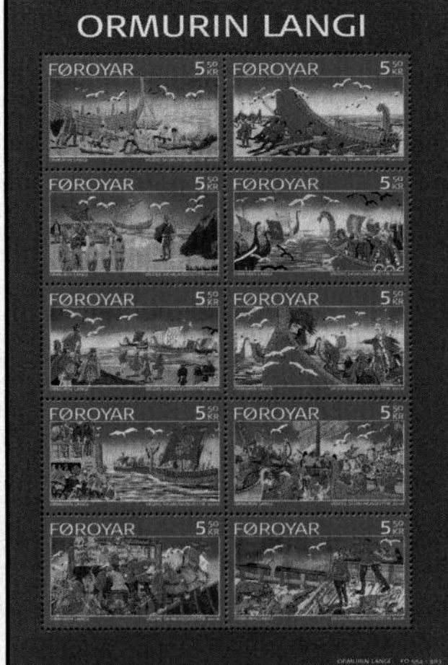

Ballad of the Long Serpent, by Jens Christian Djurhuus — A170

No. 472: a, Building of ship. b, Launch of ship. c, King on throne. d, King's fleet at sea (brown ship at LL, blue ship at LR). e, King and sailors on shore. f, King pointing. g, Ship with red sail at R. h, Battle scene (injured men falling into water). i, Battle scene (men with shields jumping from ship to ship). j, Dead men on ship's deck.

2006, Mar. 29 ***Perf. 13¼x13***

472 A170 Sheet of 10 15.00 15.00
a.-j. 5.50k Any single 1.40 1.40

Opening of Northoy Tunnel — A171

Tunnel and: No. 473, Fish. No. 474, Canoe.

2006, June 12 ***Perf. 13¼***

473 A171 5.50k multi 1.40 1.40
474 A171 5.50k multi 1.40 1.40
a. Booklet pane, 4 each #473-474 11.00 —
Complete booklet, #474a 11.00

Europa A172

2006, June 12 ***Perf. 13¾***

475 A172 7.50k shown 2.00 2.00
476 A172 10k Hands, diff. 2.75 2.75

Miniature Sheet

Sandoy Island — A173

No. 477: a, Sunnan fyri Skopun. b, Dalur. c, Soltuvík. d, Skálavík. e, Skopun. f, Sandur. g, Skarvanes. h, Húsavík.

2006, Sept. 18 Litho. ***Perf. 13x13¼***

477 A173 Sheet of 8 16.00 16.00
a.-h. 7.50k Any single 2.00 2.00

Sandur Church A174

Designs: 5.50k, Building exterior, steeple cross. 7.50k, Interior.

2006, Sept. 18 ***Perf. 14***

478 A174 5.50k multi 1.40 1.40
479 A174 7.50k multi 2.00 2.00
a. Booklet pane, 4 each #478-479 14.00 —
Complete booklet, #479a 14.00

Wave Energy A175

2007, Feb. 12 Litho. ***Perf. 12½x13***

480 A175 7.50k multi 2.00 2.00

Art From 1838 La Recherche Expedition A176

Art by Barthélemy Lauvergne: 5.50k, La Recherche off Nólsoy. 7.50k, Skaelingsfjall.

2007, Feb. 12

481 A176 5.50k multi 1.40 1.40
482 A176 7.50k multi 2.00 2.00
a. Booklet pane, 4 each #481-482 12.00 —
Complete booklet, #482a 12.00

Miniature Sheet

Legend of the Seal Woman — A177

No. 483: a, Man, head of white seal. b, Woman and seals in ring. c, Man, nude woman, seals. d, Man and nude woman seated on chest. e, Ship and two seals. f, Children, seal woman nursing child. g, Seal woman and man. h, Sleeping man and seal woman with hands open. i, Man and dead seals. j, Seal woman.

2007, Feb. 12 ***Perf. 14***

483 A177 Sheet of 10 15.00 15.00
a.-j. 5.50k Any single 1.50 1.50

Miniature Sheet

The Old Man and His Sons, Novel by Hethin Brú — A178

No. 484: a, Ketil cutting whale's throat. b, Men carrying injured Klávus on log. c, Kálvur and fiancee, Klávusardóttir with pot and kettle. d, Ketil and Kálvur in fishing boat. e, Ketil's wife arguing with daughter-in-law. f, Ketil catching flying northern fulmars. g, Kálvur and stone fence. h, Ketil, Kálvur and cow.

2007, Apr. 10 Litho. ***Perf. 13x12½***

484 A178 Sheet of 8 16.00 16.00
a.-h. 7.50k Any single 2.00 2.00

Europa — A179

Design: 5.50k, Scout holding bird. 10k, Tent.

2007, Apr. 10

485 A179 5.50k multi 1.40 1.40
486 A179 10k multi 2.75 2.75

Scouting, cent.

Souvenir Sheet

Bible Translators — A180

No. 487: a, Jákup Dahl (1878-1944). b, Kristian O. Videro (1906-91). c, Victor Danielsen (1894-1961).

2007, June 11 Litho. ***Perf. 13x12½***

487 A180 Sheet of 3 5.00 5.00
a.-c. 5.50k Any single 1.60 1.60

Domesticated Birds — A181

Designs: 9k, Chickens and rooster. 20k, Ducks. 25k, Geese.

2007, June 11 ***Perf. 12½x13***

488 A181 9k multi 2.40 2.40
489 A181 20k multi 5.00 5.00
490 A181 25k multi 6.50 6.50
Nos. 488-490 (3) 13.90 13.90

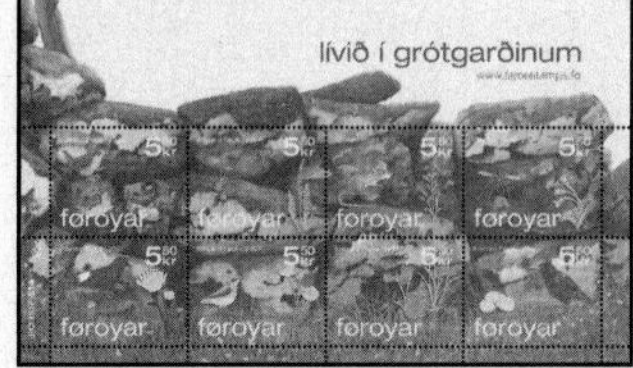

Hoyvík — A182

2007, Oct. 1 ***Perf. 13½***

491 A182 7.50k multi 2.00 2.00

Wooden Religious Statues of Kirkjubour Cathedral — A183

2007, Oct. 1 ***Perf. 13x12½***

492 A183 5.50k Jesus 1.40 1.40
493 A183 7.50k Mary 2.00 2.00
a. Booklet pane, 4 each #492-493 14.00 —
Complete booklet, #493a 14.00

Miniature Sheet

Stone Fence and Wildlife — A184

No. 494: a, Bird, worm. b, Two red beetles, fern. c, Mouse, purple flowers. d, Mosquito, pink flowers. e, Large black and white bird, dandelions. f, Bird with black wings, buttercups. g, Earwigs, grass. h, Bird and eggs.

2007, Oct. 1 ***Perf. 13½x14¼***

494 A184 Sheet of 8 12.00 12.00
a.-h. 5.50k Any single 1.40 1.40

Klaksvík, Cent. — A185

Litho. & Embossed

2008, Feb. 11 ***Perf. 14***

495 A185 5.50k multi 1.40 1.40

Tinganes A186

2008, Feb. 11 Litho. ***Perf. 13¼***

496 A186 14k multi 3.50 3.50

Hoydalar Tuberculosis Sanatorium, Cent. — A187

Lungs and: 5.50k, Patients, buildings. 9k, Dr. Vilhelm Magnussen examining patient, child.

2007, Feb. 11 ***Perf. 12½x13***

497 A187 5.50k multi 1.40 1.40
498 A187 9k multi 2.50 2.50
a. Booklet pane, 4 each #497-498 16.00
Complete booklet, #498a 16.00

Miniature Sheet

Prints by Elinborg Lützens — A188

No. 499: a, Houses below mountain. b, Milk maids (30x30mm). c, Houses. d, Underwater scene. e, Chicken (30x30mm). f, Person and bird near wooden bucket.

2008, Feb. 11 ***Perf. 13¼***

499 A188 Sheet of 6 16.00 16.00
a.-f. 10k Any single 2.60 2.60

Souvenir Sheet

Mythical Places — A189

No. 500: a, Alvheyggur. b, Klovningasteinur.

2008, Mar. 27 Litho. ***Perf. 12½x13***

500 A189 Sheet of 2	4.00	4.00
a.-b. 7.50k Either single	2.00	2.00

Caltha Palustris A190

2008, May 19 ***Perf. 13¼***

501 A190 30k multi	8.00	8.00

Europa A191

Designs: 550o, Heart and "Teg." 750o, Posthorn with "@" symbol and "Hey."

2008, May 19 ***Perf. 13¼x13***

502 A191 550o multi	1.40	1.40
503 A191 750o multi	2.00	2.00

Miniature Sheet

Famous People — A192

No. 504: a, Niels Winther (1822-92), politician and newspaper publisher. b, Súsanna Helena Patursson (1864-1916), writer and newspaper publisher. c, Rasmus C. Effersoe (1857-1916), writer and newspaper editor. d, Jógvan Poulsen (1854-1941), religious and school book writer. e, Frithrikur Petersen (1853-1917), poet. f, Andreas Christian Evensen (1874-1917), magazine publisher and school book writer.

2008, May 19 ***Perf. 13½x13¼***

504 A192 Sheet of 6	9.00	9.00
a.-f. 5.50k Any single	1.40	1.40

Miniature Sheet

Ferns — A193

No. 505: a, Gymnocarpium dryopteris. b, Polypodium vulgare. c, Dryopteris dilatata. d, Asplenium adiantum-nigrum. e, Athyrium filix-femina. f, Dryopteris filix-mas. g, Cystopteris fragilis. h, Phegopteris connectilis. i, Polystichum lonchitis. j, Asplenium trichomanes.

2008, Sept. 22 Litho. ***Perf. 13x13½***

505 A193 Sheet of 10	25.00	25.00
a.-j. 800o Any single	2.40	2.40

Christmas — A194

2008, Sept. 22 ***Perf. 13x12½***

506 A194 6k shown	1.60	1.60
507 A194 10k Wooden cross	2.75	2.75
a. Booklet pane of 8, 4 each #506-507	17.00	—
Complete booklet, #507a	17.00	

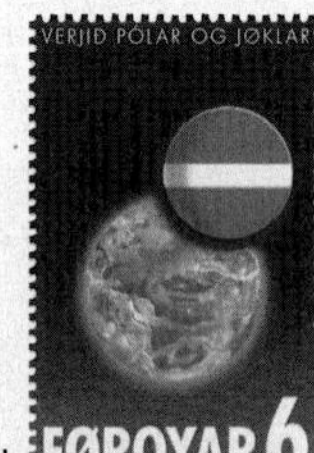

Global Warming — A195

Designs: 6k, Earth and "No entry" sign. 8k, Earth in shape of water droplet.

2009, Feb. 23 Litho. ***Perf. 13¾x14***

508 A195 6k multi	1.60	1.60
509 A195 8k multi	2.10	2.10
a. Souvenir sheet, #508-509	3.75	3.75

Portions of the designs were applied by a thermographic process producing a shiny raised effect.

Miniature Sheet

Scenes From *The Lost Musicians,* by William Heinesen — A196

No. 510: a, People, stylized harp. b, Ring of silhouetted dancers. c, Woman on roof of house, kneeling people and standing woman near house. d, Silhouetted man approaching woman on park bench. e, Women and seated cellist. f, Violinist and two silhoutted men. g, Man in bed. h, People in rowboat.

2009, Feb. 23 ***Perf. 13½***

510 A196 Sheet of 8	19.00	19.00
a.-h. 8k Any single	2.25	2.25

Europa — A197

Designs: 10k, Trollhovdi Island and Saturn. 12k, Heygadrangur Island, Jupiter and one of its moons, Europa.

2009, May 25 Litho. ***Perf. 13x12½***

511 A197 10k multi	2.75	2.75
512 A197 12k multi	3.25	3.25

Intl. Year of Astronomy.

Miniature Sheet

Geological Formation of the Faroe Islands — A198

No. 513: a, Large volcano spewing lava, trees. b, Smaller volcano spewing ash, dead tree, lava on landscape. c, Map of area 60 million years ago. d, Map of area 15 million years ago. e, Map of Faroe Isands, map of Faroe Islands and area nearby. f, Glacier, rock pinnacles.

2009, May 25 ***Perf. 12½x13***

513 A198 Sheet of 6	18.00	18.00
a.-f. 10k Any single	3.00	3.00

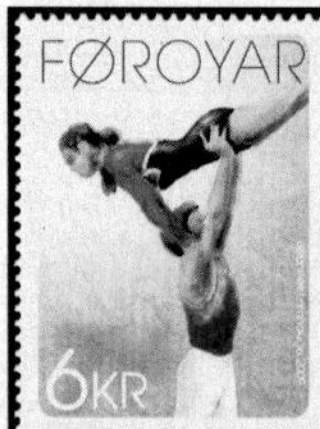

Thorshavn Gymnastics Club, Cent. — A199

Gymnasts: 6k, Male lifting female. 10k, Female doing handstand. 26k, Male on rings.

2009, May 25 ***Perf. 14***

514 A199 6k multi	1.75	1.75
515 A199 10k multi	3.00	3.00
516 A199 26k multi	7.75	7.75
Nos. 514-516 (3)	12.50	12.50

Serpentine Die Cut 14

Booklet Stamps

Self-Adhesive

517 A199 6k multi	2.00	2.00
518 A199 10k multi	3.00	3.00
a. Booklet pane of 8, 4 each #517-518	20.00	

Leynar — A200

2009, Sept. 16 ***Perf. 12¾***

519 A200 10k multi	3.00	3.00

Rock Pigeons A201

Designs: 14k, Two pigeons on rocks. 36k, Head of pigeon, two pigeons in flight.

2009. Sept. 16 ***Perf. 13***

520 A201 14k multi	4.00	4.00
521 A201 36k multi	11.00	11.00

Altarpiece at Vestmanna Church — A202

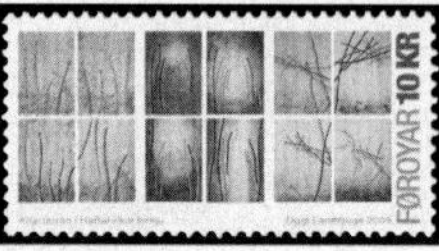

Altarpiece at Hattarvik Church A203

2009, Sept. 16 ***Perf. 13¾x13¼***

522 A202 6k multi	1.75	1.75
a. Perf. 13¾ vert.	1.75	1.75
523 A203 10k multi	3.25	3.25
a. Perf. 14¼x13¾ on 3 sides	3.25	3.25
b. Booklet pane of 8, 4 each #522a, 523a	20.00	—
Complete booklet, #523b	20.00	

Christmas.

Globicephala Melas — A204

2010, Feb. 22 Litho. ***Perf. 14¾***

524 A204 50k multi	15.00	15.00

Marine Flora and Fauna — A205

Various photographs.

2010, Feb. 22 ***Perf. 13¼x13½***

525 A205 1k multi	.35	.35
526 A205 6k multi	1.75	1.75
527 A205 8k multi	2.50	2.50
528 A205 12k multi	3.50	3.50
Nos. 525-528 (4)	8.10	8.10

Butterflies and Moths A206

Designs: 6k, Inachis io. 8k, Vanessa cardui. 14k, Agrius convolvuli. 16k, Acherontia atropos.

2010, Feb. 22 ***Perf. 13x12¾***

529 A206 6k multicolored 1.75 1.75
530 A206 8k multicolored 2.50 2.50
531 A206 14k multicolored 4.25 4.25
532 A206 16k multicolored 5.00 5.00
Nos. 529-532 (4) 13.50 13.50

Souvenir Sheet

Aquaculture — A207

No. 533: a, Fish, net. b, Fisherman holding net.

Perf. 14¼x14½

2010, Mar. 24 **Litho.**

533 A207 Sheet of 2 6.00 6.00
a.-b. 10k Either single 3.00 3.00

Paintings by Eli Smith — A208

Various paintings.

2010, Apr. 26 ***Perf. 14½***

534 A208 18k multicolored 5.50 5.50
535 A208 24k multicolored 7.50 7.50

Europa A209

Scenes from children's books: 10k, A Dog, A Cat and A Mouse, by Bárthur Oskarsson. 12k, Moss Mollis's Journey, by Janus á Húsagarthi.

2010, Apr. 26 ***Perf. 13¾***

536 A209 10k multicolored 3.00 3.00
537 A209 12k multicolored 3.50 3.50

Booklet Stamps
Self-Adhesive
Serpentine Die Cut 14

538 A209 10k multicolored 3.00 3.00
539 A209 12k multicolored 3.50 3.50
a. Booklet pane of 8, 4 each #538-539 26.00 26.00

Jens Christian Svabo (1746-1824), Writer and Lexicographer — A210

Writings of Svabo and Svabo: 6k, Holding walking stick. 12k, At desk. 14k, Holding book. 22k, With sheaf of papers, pen and inkwell.

Perf. 13¼x13¾

2010, Sept. 20 **Litho. & Engr.**

540 A210 6k multicolored 1.75 1.75
541 A210 12k multicolored 3.75 3.75
542 A210 14k multicolored 4.50 4.50
543 A210 22k multicolored 7.00 7.00
Nos. 540-543 (4) 17.00 17.00

Vegetables — A211

2010, Sept. 20 **Litho.** ***Perf. 13x13¼***

544 A211 6k Potatoes 1.75 1.75
545 A211 8k Turnips 2.50 2.50

Christmas — A212

Carols: 6k, My Little Sweet Brownie (Lítla Fitta Nissa Mín). 10k, In My Early Childhood (A Barnaárum Ungu).

2010, Sept. 20 ***Perf. 13x12½***

546 A212 6k multicolored 1.75 1.75
547 A212 10k multicolored 3.25 3.25
a. Booklet pane of 8, 4 each #546-547 20.00 —
Complete booklet, #547a 20.00

See Nos. 570-571, 592-593.

Intl. Women's Day, Cent. A213

2011, Feb. 21 **Litho.** ***Perf. 14***

548 A213 10k multicolored 3.00 3.00

Traditional Women's Professions — A214

Designs: 6k, Nurses with patient and child. 16k, Midwives holding babies.

2011, Feb. 21 ***Perf. 13x13¼***

549 A214 6k multicolored 1.75 1.75
550 A214 16k multicolored 5.00 5.00

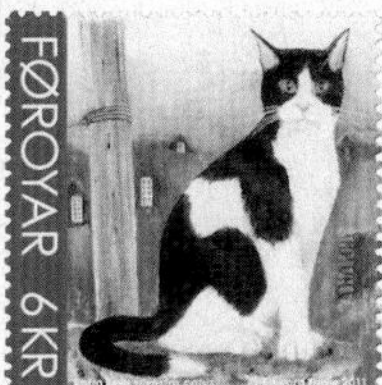

Cats — A215

Color of cat: 6k, Black and white. 10k, Brown and white.

2011, Feb. 21 ***Perf. 13¾***

551 A215 6k multicolored 1.75 1.75
552 A215 10k multicolored 3.25 3.25

Booklet Stamps
Self-Adhesive
Serpentine Die Cut 14

553 A215 6k multicolored 1.75 1.75
554 A215 10k multicolored 3.25 3.25
a. Booklet pane of 8, 4 each #553-554 20.00

Souvenir Sheet

Legend of Annika od Dímun — A216

No. 555 — Annika: a, With chalice. b, With guards. c, With bound hands in water.

2011, Feb. 21 ***Perf. 14¾***

555 A216 Sheet of 3 9.00 9.00
a.-c. 10k Any single 3.00 3.00

Paintings by Bergithe Johannessen (1905-95) — A217

Designs: 2k, Skerjut Strond (Glowing Beach). 24k, Ur Nólsoy (From Nólsoy).

2011, Apr. 26 ***Perf. 12½x13***

556 A217 2k multicolored .65 .65
557 A217 24k multicolored 7.50 7.50

Paintings by Frida Zachariassen (1912-92) — A218

Designs: 6k, Urtagardhur (The Garden). 26k, Kona (Woman).

2011, Apr. 26 ***Perf. 13***

558 A218 6k multicolored 1.75 1.75
559 A218 26k multicolored 7.50 7.50

Europa A219

Tree plantations on: 10k, Tórshavn. 12k, Kunoy, vert.

2011, Apr. 26 ***Perf. 12½***

560 A219 10k multicolored 3.25 3.25
561 A219 12k multicolored 3.75 3.75

Intl. Year of Forests.

Flowers — A220

Designs: 14k, Silene dioica. 20k, Geranium sylvaticum.

2011, Apr. 26 ***Perf. 13¼***

562 A220 14k multicolored 4.50 4.50
563 A220 20k multicolored 6.00 6.00

Berries — A221

Designs: 50o, Juniperus communis subsp. alpina. 6.50k, Empetrum nigrum. subsp. hermaphroditum.

2011, Sept. 1 **Litho.** ***Perf. 12¾x13½***

564 A221 50o multicolored .25 .25
565 A221 6.50k multicolored 2.00 2.00

Stóridrangur — A222

2011, Sept. 28 ***Perf. 12½x13***

566 A222 10.50k multicolored 3.25 3.25

Old Motor Vehicles A223

Designs: No. 567, Black Ford TT truck, first vehicle on Faroe Islands. No. 568, Red Morris bus. No. 569, White De Luxe Model, automobile built on Faroe Islands.

2011, Sept. 28 ***Perf. 13½x12¾***

567 A223 13k multicolored 4.00 4.00
568 A223 13k multicolored 4.00 4.00
569 A223 13k multicolored 4.00 4.00
a. Souvenir sheet of 3, #567-569 12.50 12.50
Nos. 567-569 (3) 12.00 12.00

Christmas Type of 2010

Carols: 6.50k, I Can't Wait for Christmas to Come (Eg Eri So Spent Til Jóla). 10.50k, I Rejoice Every Christmas Eve (Eg Gledist So Hvort Jólakvold).

2011, Sept. 28 ***Perf. 13x12½***

570 A212 6.50k multi 2.00 2.00
571 A212 10.50k multi 3.25 3.25
a. Booklet pane of 8, 4 each #570-571 21.00 —
Complete booklet, #571a 21.00

Reign of Queen Margrethe II, 40th Anniv. — A224

Litho. & Engr.

2012, Jan. 4 ***Perf. 13¼***

572 A224 10.50k multicolored 3.00 3.00
a. Souvenir sheet of 1 3.00 3.00

Extinct Animals — A225

Designs: 13k, Pinguinis impennis. 21k, Dímun sheep (Ovis aries), horiz.

2012, Feb. 20 Litho. *Perf. 13¼x13*

573 A225 13k multicolored 4.00 4.00

Perf. 13x13¼

574 A225 21k multicolored 6.00 6.00

Sea Anemones A226

Various sea anemones.

2012, Feb. 20 *Perf. 14*

575	A226	3k multi	.90	.90
576	A226	6.50k multi	2.00	2.00
577	A226	8.50k multi	2.40	2.40
578	A226	10.50k multi	3.00	3.00
		Nos. 575-578 (4)	8.30	8.30

Booklet Stamps Self-Adhesive

Serpentine Die Cut 14

579	A226	6.50k multi	2.00	2.00
580	A226	10.50k multi	3.00	3.00
a.		Booklet pane of 8, 4 each #579-580	20.00	

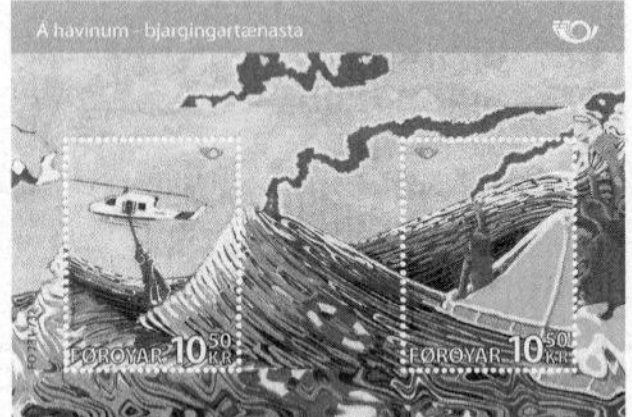

Sea Rescue — A227

No. 581: a, Helicopter. b, Life raft.

2012, Mar. 21 *Perf. 14¼x13½*

581 A227 Sheet of 2 6.00 6.00
a.-b. 10.50k Either single 3.00 3.00

Europa — A228

Designs: 6.50k, Tourists on boat near Suthuroy Island cliffs. 10.50k, Hikers on rocks.

2012, Apr. 30 *Perf. 12½x13*

582 A228 6.50k multi 2.00 2.00
583 A228 10.50k multi 3.00 3.00

Monsters A229

Designs: 6.50k, Gryla. 11k, Marra. 17k, Nithagrísur. 19k, Fjorutroll.

2012, Apr. 30 *Perf. 13*

584	A229	6.50k multi	2.00	2.00
585	A229	11k multi	3.25	3.25
586	A229	17k multi	4.75	4.75
587	A229	19k multi	5.50	5.50
		Nos. 584-587 (4)	15.50	15.50

Old Pharmacy, Klaksvík — A230

2012, Sept. 24 *Perf. 12½x13*

588 A230 8.50k multi 2.40 2.40

Contemporary Art — A231

Designs: 13k, Mr. Walker on the Faroes, by Jan Hafström. 21k, Egg Procession, by Edward Fuglo.

2012, Sept. 24 *Perf. 13*

589 A231 13k multicolored 3.50 3.50
590 A231 21k multicolored 5.75 5.75

Miniature Sheet

Legend of Regin the Blacksmith — A232

No. 591: a, Hjordis attends to dying husband, Sigmund, on battlefield. b, Sigurd on horse. c, Regin hammering sword. d, Sigurd on horseback encounters Odin. e, Sigurd attacks serpent. f, Birds watching Sigurd cooking serpent's heart.

Litho., Litho & Embossed (#591e)

2012, Sept. 24 *Perf. 13¼x13*

591 A232 Sheet of 6 20.00 20.00
a.-f. 11k Any single 3.25 3.25

Christmas Type of 2010

Carols: 6.50k, Why is Everything So Cozy Tonight? (Hví Man Tadh Vera?) 12.50k, Silent Night (Gledhilig Jól).

2012, Sept. 24 Litho. *Perf. 13x12½*

592	A212	6.50k multi	2.00	2.00
593	A212	12.50k multi	4.00	4.00
a.		Booklet pane of 8, 4 each #592-593	24.00	24.00
		Complete booklet, #593a	24.00	24.00

Lambs — A233

2013, Feb. 25 *Perf. 13¼x13¾*

594 A233 12.50k multi 4.00 4.00

Crustaceans — A234

Designs: 7k, Cancer pagurus. 9k, Chaceon affinis. 23k, Pandalus borealis. 34k, Nephrops norvegicus.

2013, Feb. 25 *Perf. 12½x13*

595	A234	7k multi	2.50	2.50
596	A234	9k multi	3.25	3.25
597	A234	23k multi	8.00	8.00
598	A234	34k multi	12.00	12.00
		Nos. 595-598 (4)	25.75	25.75

Miniature Sheet

Traditional Faroese Rowboat — A235

No. 599: a, Tollur og homluband (oarlock and strap, 26x23mm). b, Arar (oars, 66x23mm). c, Rodhur og rodhurarmur (rudder, 26x23mm). d, Kumpass (compass, 26x23mm). e, Seksmannafar (hull of six-man boat, 66x23mm). f, Kaggi (barrel, 26x23mm). g, Eyskar (bailing scoop, 26x23mm). h, Mastur og vrá vidh segli (mast and sail, 66x23mm). i, Nogla og togendi (bung and rope, 26x23mm).

Litho. & Engr.

2013, Feb. 25 *Perf. 13¼*

599 A235 Sheet of 9 20.00 20.00
a.-i. 7k Any single 2.00 2.00

Soren Kierkegaard (1813-55), Philosopher A266

2013, Mar. 4 *Perf. 12¼*

600 A266 35k multi 11.00 11.00

Europa A267

Designs: 7k, Postal van. 12.50k, Postal truck.

2013, Apr. 29 Litho. *Perf. 14*

601 A267 7k multi 2.25 2.25
602 A267 12.50k multi 4.00 4.00

Booklet Stamps Self-Adhesive

Serpentine Die Cut 14

603	A267	7k multi	2.25	2.25
604	A267	12.50k multi	4.00	4.00
a.		Booklet pane of 8, 4 each #603-604	27.00	

Rodents — A268

Designs: 11k, Rattus norvegicus. 12.50k, Mus domesticus.

2013, Apr. 29 *Perf. 13¾x13¼*

605 A268 11k multi 3.50 3.50
606 A268 12.50k multi 4.00 4.00

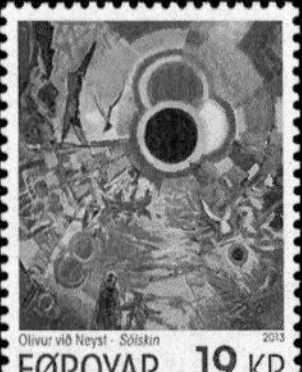

Paintings by Olivur Vith Neyst — A269

Designs: 19k, Sólskin (Sunshine). 38k, Vestaravág (West Harbor).

2013, Sept. 23 *Perf. 12½*

607 A269 19k multi 5.50 5.50
608 A269 38k multi 11.00 11.00

Souvenir Sheet

Nordafar Fishery, Foroyinghavn, Greenland — A270

No. 609: a, Fishing boat, white building in background. b, Fishermen on dock. c, Fishing boats, red buildings in background.

Perf. 13¼x13¾

2013, Sept. 23 Litho. & Engr.

609 A270 Sheet of 3 8.50 8.50
a.-c. 9k Any single 2.75 2.75

See Greenland No. 652.

Christmas — A271

Designs: 7k, Manger. 12.50k, Holy Family.

2013, Sept. 23 Litho. *Perf. 12¾*

610	A271	7k multi	2.25	2.25
611	A271	12.50k multi	3.75	3.75
a.		Booklet pane of 8, 4 each #610-611	24.00	—
		Complete booklet, #611a	24.00	

See Nos. 632-633, 651-652.

Rosa Mollis — A272

2014, Feb. 26 Litho. *Perf. 12½x13*

612 A272 14.50k multi 4.75 4.75

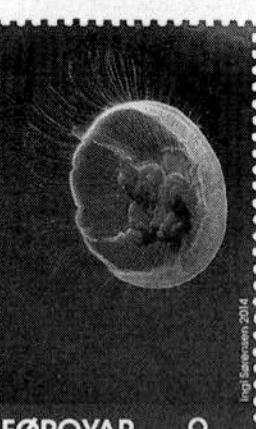

Jellyfish — A273

Designs: 8k, Aurelia aurita. 15.50k, Cyanea capillata. 18.50k, Pelagia noctiluca. 26k, Beroe cucumis.

2014, Feb. 26 Litho. *Perf. 13*

613	A273	8k multi	2.50	2.50
614	A273	15.50k multi	4.75	4.75
615	A273	18.50k multi	5.75	5.75
616	A273	26k multi	7.50	7.50
		Nos. 613-616 (4)	20.50	20.50

Souvenir Sheet

Legend of the Lady of Húsavik — A274

No. 617: a, Woman holding horn of Viking chief. b, Woman and nykur (mythical beast). c, Woman on throne.

2014, Feb. 26 Litho. *Perf. 13x13½*

617	A274	Sheet of 3	10.00	10.00
a.-c.		10k Any single	3.25	3.25

Souvenir Sheet

Ferry MS Norröna — A275

No. 618: a, Ship's stern. b, Ship's bow.

2014, Mar. 17 Litho. *Perf. 13x13¼*

618	A275	Sheet of 2	9.00	9.00
a.-b.		14.50k Either single	4.25	4.25

Europa A276

Designs: 14.50k, Faroese Symphony Orchestra. 19.50k, Bass players, vert.

2014, Apr. 28 Litho. *Perf. 13x13¼*

619	A276 14.50k multi	4.50	4.50

Perf. 13¼x13

620	A276 19.50k multi	6.00	6.00

Lighthouses — A277

Designs: 14.50k, Akraberg Lighthouse. 15.50k, Dímun Lighthouse. 17k, Toftir Lighthouse.

2014, Apr. 28 Litho. *Perf. 14*

621	A277 14.50k multi	4.50	4.50
622	A277 15.50k multi	4.75	4.75
623	A277 17k multi	5.25	5.25
	Nos. 621-623 (3)	14.50	14.50

Booklet Stamps
Self-Adhesive
Serpentine Die Cut 14

624	A277 14.50k multi	4.50	4.50
625	A277 15.50k multi	4.75	4.75
626	A277 17k multi	5.25	5.25
a.	Booklet pane of 6, 2 each #624-626	29.00	
	Nos. 624-626 (3)	14.50	14.50

Prince Henrik, 80th Birthday A278

Perf. 13½x13¼
2014, June 11 Litho.

627	A278 14.50k multi	4.50	4.50

Booklet Stamp
Self-Adhesive
Die Cut Perf. 13½x13¼

628	A278 14.50k multi	4.50	4.50
a.	Booklet pane of 4	18.00	

Roger Casement, Boats, Congolese Natives, and Daniel J. Danielsen — A279

Perf. 13¼x13½
2014, Sept. 24 Litho.

629	A279 25k multi	7.50	7.50

Danielsen (1871-1916), missionary to the Congo, and documenter of human rights abuses reported on in Casement's 1904 report to the British Government.

Captain Vilhelm Reinert-Joensen (1891-1949), Ships Used in D-Day Invasion — A280

Perf. 13¼x13½
2014, Sept. 24 Litho.

630	A280 26k multi	7.50	7.50

D-Day, 70th anniv.

Miniature Sheet

World War I, Cent. — A281

No. 631: a, Newspaper headlines, map of Europe, man in rowboat. b, Children, ration coupons, national leaders of the World War I combattants. c, Faroese boat attacked by German submarine, map of Faroe islands and British Isles. d, Map of Vimy Ridge, Faroese-Canadian soldier Christian L. Petersen, soldiers.

Perf. 13¼x13½
2014, Sept. 24 Litho.

631	A281	Sheet of 4	10.00	10.00
a.-d.		8k Any single	2.50	2.50
e.		Like #631, with "In Memoriam" and poppies added in red in sheet margin	9.00	9.00

Issued: No. 631e, 5/13/15.

Christmas Type of 2013

Designs: 8k, Angels. 14.50k, Shepherds.

2014, Sept. 24 Litho. *Perf. 12¾*

632	A271 8k multi	2.50	2.50
633	A271 14.50k multi	4.50	4.50
a.	Booklet pane of 8, 4 each #632-633	28.00	—
	Complete booklet, #633a	28.00	

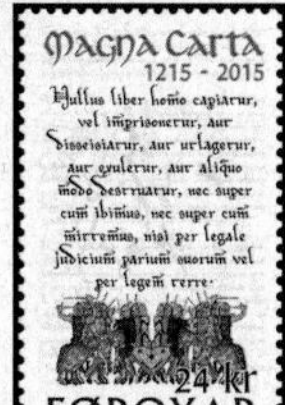

Magna Carta, 800th Anniv. — A282

2015, Feb. 23 Litho. *Perf. 13½*

634	A282 24k multi	7.00	7.00

Woman Suffrage, Cent. A283

2015, Feb. 23 Litho. *Perf. 13x13¼*

635	A283 36k multi	11.00	11.00

Opening of New Terminal at Vagar Airport A284

Designs: 8.50k, Airplanes on ground. 15k, New terminal.

2015, Feb. 23 Litho. *Perf. 13x13¼*

636	A284 8.50k multi	2.60	2.60
637	A284 15k multi	4.50	4.50
a.	Booklet pane of 8, 4 each #636-637	28.50	—
	Complete booklet, #637a	28.50	

Miniature Sheet

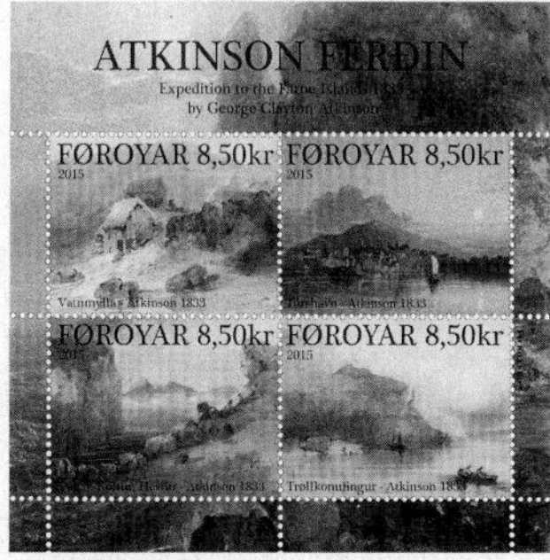

1833 Expedition of George Clayton Atkinson to Faroe Islands — A285

No. 638 — Paintings by Thomas Miles Richarson of: a, Vatnmylla (watermill). b, Tórshavn. c, Waterfall on Vágar, Koltur and Hestur Islands. d, Trollkonufingur.

2015, Feb. 23 Litho. *Perf. 13x13¼*

638	A285	Sheet of 4	10.50	10.50
a.-d.		8.50k Any single	2.60	2.60

March 20, 2015 Total Solar Eclipse A286

Eclipse at: 17k, Right. 19k, Left.

2015, Mar. 11 Litho. *Perf. 12*

639	A286 17k multi	5.00	5.00
640	A286 19k multi	5.75	5.75
a.	Souvenir sheet of 2, #639-640	11.00	11.00

Booklet Stamps
Self-Adhesive
Die Cut Perf. 11½

641	A286 17k multi	5.00	5.00
a.	Booklet pane of 4	20.00	
642	A286 19k multi	5.75	5.75
a.	Booklet pane of 4	23.00	

Faroe Islands Flag, 75th Anniv. — A287

Designs: 11k, Arne Vatnhamar holding Faroe Islands flag on Mt. Everest. 12k, Map and flag of Faroe Islands.

2015, Apr. 14 Litho. *Perf. 13½*

643	A287 11k multi	3.50	3.50
644	A287 12k multi	3.75	3.75

Europa — A288

Old toys: 17k, Rag doll. 22k, Hoop made of ram's horn.

2015, Apr. 14 Litho. *Perf. 13½*

645	A288 17k multi	5.25	5.25
646	A288 22k multi	6.75	6.75

Knitted Art by Randi Samsonsen — A289

2015, Sept. 28 Litho. *Perf. 13x12¾*

647	A289 17k multi	5.25	5.25

FØROYAR 17 KR

H. N. Jacobsen's Bookstore, 150th Anniv. A290

Designs: 17k, Bookstore exterior. 26k, Bookstore interior, book covers, bindery machinery.

2015, Sept. 28 Litho. *Perf. 12½*

648	A290 17k multi	5.25	5.25
649	A290 26k multi	8.00	8.00

Souvenir Sheet

Christian Artifacts of the Viking Era — A291

No. 650 — Inscriptions: a, Krossteinur úr Olansgardhi í Skúvoy (stone with crucifix from Olansgardhi). b, Botnur úr laggadhum traeílati (cross on wooden bucket bottom). c, Vadhsteinur vidh ihogdum St. Hanskrossi (stone fishing sinkers with St. Hans crucifix).

Litho. & Engr.
2015, Sept. 28 *Perf. 12¾x13*

650	A291	Sheet of 3	11.50	11.50
a.-c.		12k Any single	3.75	3.75

Christmas Type of 2013

Designs: 8.50k, Magi on camels. 17k, Holy Family fleeing to Egypt.

2015, Sept. 28 Litho. *Perf. 12¾*

651	A271 8.50k multi	2.60	2.60
652	A271 17k multi	5.25	5.25
a.	Booklet pane of 8, 4 each #651-652	32.00	—
	Complete booklet, #652a	32.00	

Oystercatchers in Flight — A292

Perf. 13¼x13¾

2016, Feb. 22 **Litho.**

653 A292 17k multi 5.25 5.25

Grounding of the Westerbeek off Lopra, 274th Anniv. — A293

Designs: 17k, Chest and the Westerbeek. 19k, Grounding of the Westerbeek.

Perf. 13¾x13½

2016, Feb. 22 **Litho.**

654 A293 17k multi 5.25 5.25
655 A293 19k multi 5.75 5.75
a. Souvenir sheet of 2, #654-655 11.00 11.00

Fire Fighting Equipment A294

Designs: 1k, Fire pump, 1776. 15k, 1948 Bedford K fire truck. 19k, 1937 Triangle fire truck.

2016, Feb. 22 **Litho.** ***Perf. 13***

656 A294 1k multi .30 .30
657 A294 15k multi 4.75 4.75
658 A294 19k multi 5.75 5.75
Nos. 656-658 (3) 10.80 10.80

Booklet Stamps
Self-Adhesive

Serpentine Die Cut 13¼

659 A294 1k multi .30 .30
660 A294 15k multi 4.75 4.75
661 A294 19k multi 5.75 5.75
a. Booklet pane of 6, 2 each #659-661 22.00
Nos. 659-661 (3) 10.80 10.80

Faroe Islands Mailboxes A295

Designs: 9k, Blue Postverk Foroya mailbox used 1976-present. 17k, Red Danish Postal Service mailbox used until 1976.

2016, Apr. 1 **Litho.** ***Perf. 14¼***

662 A295 9k multi 2.75 2.75

Souvenir Sheet

663 Sheet of 2, #662, 663a 8.00 8.00
a. A295 17k multi 5.25 5.25

Postverk Foroya (Faroe Islands Postal Service), 40th anniv.

Foods in Faroese Drying Shed — A296

2016, Apr. 26 **Litho.** ***Perf. 13½***

664 A296 9k multi 2.75 2.75

Nólsoyar Páll (1766-1808 or 1809), National Hero — A297

Litho. & Engr.

2016, Apr. 26 ***Perf. 13***

665 A297 24k blk & brn lake 7.50 7.50

A298

Europa A299

2016, May 9 **Litho.** ***Perf. 13½x13***

666 A298 9k green 2.75 2.75
667 A299 17k multi 5.25 5.25

Booklet Stamps
Self-Adhesive

Serpentine Die Cut 13¾

667A A298 9k green 2.75 2.75
667B A299 17k multi 5.25 5.25
c. Booklet pane of 6, 3 each #667A-667B 24.00

Think Green Issue.

Cod A300

Litho. & Engr.

2016, Sept. 26 ***Perf. 13x13¼***

668 A300 50k multi 15.00 15.00

A square of tanned cod skin with engraved text is affixed to No. 668. The square of cod skin has a fish odor and may detach from the stamp if soaked.

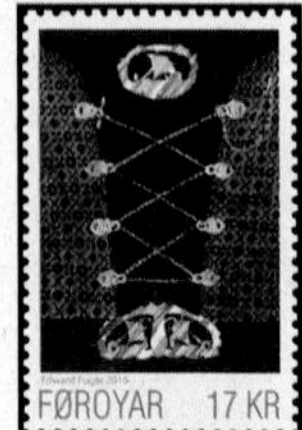

Traditional Woman's Blouse A301

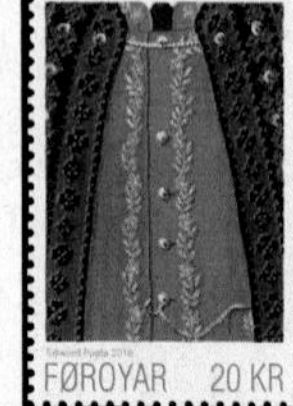

Traditional Men's Waistcoat A302

2016, Sept. 26 **Litho.** ***Perf. 13x13½***

669 A301 17k multi 5.25 5.25
670 A302 20k multi 6.00 6.00

Booklet Stamps
Self-Adhesive

Serpentine Die Cut 14x13¾

670A A301 17k multi 5.25 5.25
670B A302 20k multi 6.00 6.00
c. Booklet pane of 6, 3 each #670A-670B 34.00

Miniature Sheet

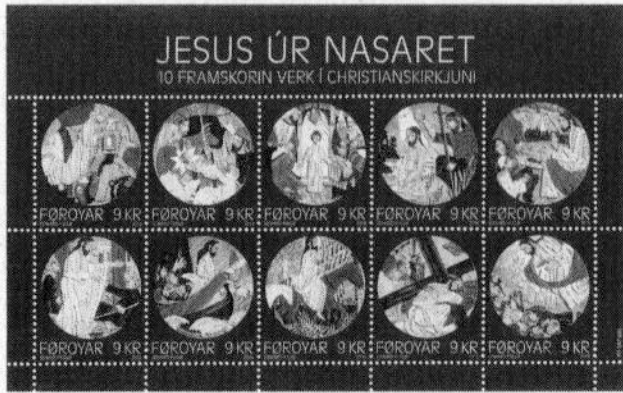

Life of Jesus — A303

No. 671 — Wood carvings by Edward Fuglo depicting: a, Annunciation. b, Adoration of the Shepherds. c, Jesus as child in temple. d, Baptism of Jesus. e, Jesus feeding the multitude. f, Jesus healing lepers. g, Jesus calming storm at sea. h, Entry into Jerusalem. i, Jesus carrying cross. j, Resurrection.

2016, Sept. 26 **Litho.** ***Perf. 13x12½***

671 A303 Sheet of 10 27.50 27.50
a.-j. 9k Any single 2.75 2.75

House Near Skorá River Waterfall — A304

2017, Feb. 27 **Litho.** ***Perf. 13***

672 A304 9.50k multi 2.75 2.75

Leitisvatn Lake — A305

Lakeside: 17k, Cliffs. 19k, Buildings.

Perf. 13½x13¼

2017, Feb. 27 **Litho.**

673 A305 17k multi 5.00 5.00
674 A305 19k multi 5.50 5.50

Booklet Stamps
Self-Adhesive

Serpentine Die Cut 9

674A A305 17k multi 5.00 5.00
674B A305 19k multi 5.50 5.50
c. Booklet pane of 6, 3 each #674A-674B 32.00

Somateria Mollissima Faeroensis — A306

Eider facing: 18k, Right. 27k, Left.

Perf. 13½x13¾

2017, Feb. 27 **Litho.**

675 A306 18k multi 5.25 5.25
676 A306 27k multi 7.75 7.75

Miniature Sheet

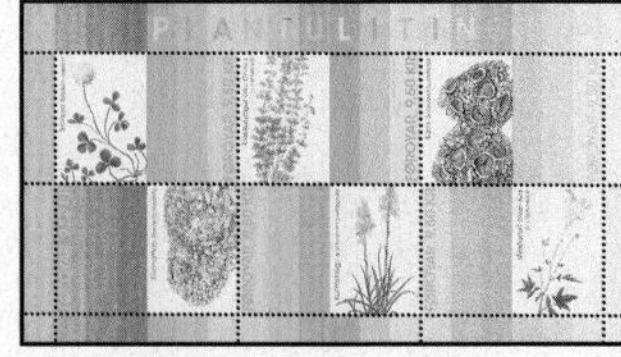

Natural Dyes — A307

No. 677: a, Trifolium repens. b, Erica cinerea. c, Ochrolechia tartarea. d, Parmelia saxatilis. e, Narthecium ossifragum. f, Filipendula ulmaria.

2017, Feb. 27 **Litho.** ***Perf. 13x12½***

677 A307 Sheet of 6 16.50 16.50
a.-f. 9.50k Any single 2.75 2.75

Europa — A308

Legend of the Princess of Nólsoy: 9.50k, Ship and castle. 17k, Ship, Princess and her husband.

2017, May 15 **Litho.** ***Perf. 14***

678 A308 9.50k multi 3.00 3.00
679 A308 17k multi 5.25 5.25

Booklet Stamps
Self-Adhesive

Serpentine Die Cut 13½

680 A308 9.50k multi 3.00 3.00
681 A308 17k multi 5.25 5.25
a. Booklet pane of 6, 3 each #680-681 25.00

Items From 1817 Visit to Faroe Islands of Hans Christan Lyngbye (1782-1837), Botanist — A309

Designs: 9.50k, Carex lyngbyei. 13k, Illustrations of seaweeds from Lyngbye's book, *Tentamen Hydrophytologiae Danicae*, horiz. 19k, Illustrations by Lyngbye of Faroese baptismal fonts and rocking stones, horiz. 22k, Seaweed from Lyngbye's herbarium, horiz.

2017, May 15 **Litho.** ***Perf. 13¼x13***

682 A309 9.50k multi 3.00 3.00

Perf. 13x13¼

683 A309 13k multi 4.00 4.00
684 A309 19k multi 5.75 5.75
685 A309 22k multi 6.75 6.75
Nos. 682-685 (4) 19.50 19.50

Souvenir Sheet

Queen Margrethe II and Prince Henrik, 50th Wedding Anniversary — A310

2017, May 15 **Litho.** ***Perf. 13½***

686 A310 50k gold & multi 15.00 15.00

See Denmark No. 1777, Greenland No. 754.

Legend of the Seven Swans A311

Designs: 9.50k, Men turning into swans. 19k, Woman near stake.

Perf. 13¾x13¼

2017, Sept. 8 Litho. & Engr.

687 A311 9.50k multi 3.00 3.00
688 A311 19k multi 6.00 6.00
a. Souvenir sheet of 2, #687-688 9.00 9.00

Traditional Clothing — A312

Designs: 9.50k, Women's dress, apron and shoes. 17k, Men's breeches, stockings and shoes.

2017, Oct. 2 Litho. *Perf. 12¾x13½*

689 A312 9.50k multi 3.00 3.00
690 A312 17k multi 5.50 5.50

Booklet Stamps
Self-Adhesive

Serpentine Die Cut 13¾

691 A312 9.50k multi 3.00 3.00
692 A312 17k multi 5.50 5.50
a. Booklet pane of 6, 3 each #691-692 26.00

Martin Luther Nailing 95 Theses to Church Door — A313

2017, Oct. 2 Litho. *Perf. 13¼x13*

693 A313 18k multi 5.75 5.75
a. Souvenir sheet of 1 5.75 5.75

Protestant Reformation, 500th anniv.

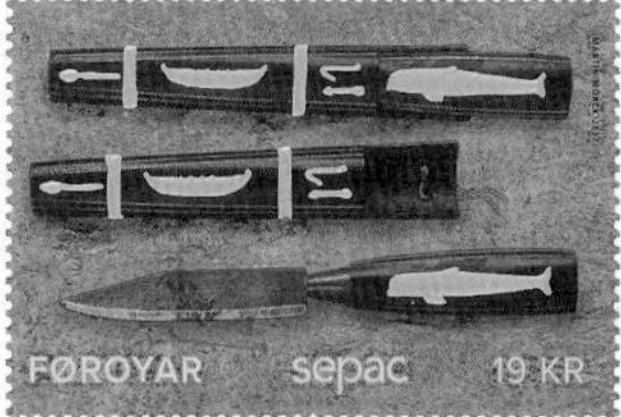

Faroese Knives and Sheaths — A314

Litho. & Embossed With Foil Application

2017, Oct. 2 *Perf. 13¼x13*

Inscribed "sepac"

694 A314 19k gold & multi 6.00 6.00

Souvenir Sheet
Without "sepac" Inscription

695 A314 19k gold & multi 6.00 6.00

Hans C. Müller (1818-97), First Postal Agent for Denmark in the Faroe Islands — A315

2018, Feb. 26 Litho. *Perf. 13½*

696 A315 18k multi 6.00 6.00

Seabird Fowling — A316

Designs: 10k, Man carrying fowling net. 44k, Men fowling in boat.

2018, Feb. 26 Engr. *Perf. 12¾x13*

697 A316 10k deep claret 3.25 3.25
698 A316 44k dp vio blue 14.50 14.50

Lakes — A317

Designs: 10k, Sandsvatn Lake. 20k, Toftavatn Lake.

Perf. 13½x13¾

2018, Feb. 26 Litho.

699 A317 10k multi 3.25 3.25
700 A317 20k multi 6.50 6.50

Booklet Stamps
Self-Adhesive

Serpentine Die Cut 9

701 A317 10k multi 3.25 3.25
702 A317 20k multi 6.50 6.50
a. Booklet pane of 6, 3 each #701-702 29.50

Miniature Sheet

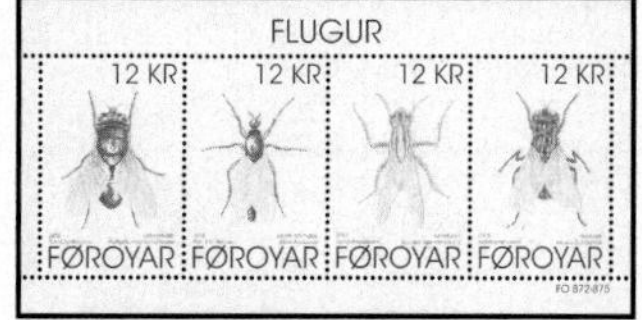

Flies — A318

No. 703: a, Protophormia terraenovae. b, Bibio pomonae. c, Scatophaga stercoraria. d, Musca domestica.

Perf. 13½x13¼

2018, Feb. 26 Litho.

703 A318 Sheet of 4 16.00 16.00
a.-d. 12k Any single 4.00 4.00

Scomber Scombrus — A319

2018, Apr. 23 Litho. *Perf. 13¾x13¼*

704 A319 18k multi 6.00 6.00

Recreational Vehicles and Large Wave Near Torshavn — A320

2018, Apr. 23 Litho. *Perf. 13½x13¼*

705 A320 20k multi 6.50 6.50

Celtic Quaternary Knot — A321

Gate to the World, Sculpture by 7-9-13 Art Group A322

2018, Apr. 23 Litho. *Perf. 13¼x13*

706 A321 14k multi 4.50 4.50

Perf. 13x13¼

707 A322 22k multi 7.25 7.25

Town of Fuglafjordhur, cent.

Europa A323

Designs: 10k, Streymin Bridge. 18k, Sandá River Bridge.

2018, Apr. 23 Litho. *Perf. 13x13¼*

708 A323 10k multi 3.25 3.25
709 A323 18k multi 6.00 6.00

Booklet Stamps
Self-Adhesive

Die Cut Perf. 13x12½

710 A323 10k multi 3.25 3.25
711 A323 18k multi 6.00 6.00
a. Booklet pane of 6, 3 each #710-711 28.00

Souvenir Sheet

Tórshavn Actors' Association, Cent. — A324

No. 712 — Masks and: a, Three actors. b, Five actors.

2018, Apr. 23 Litho. *Perf. 14*

712 A324 Sheet of 2 12.50 12.50
a.-b. 19k Either single 6.25 6.25

Miniature Sheet

End of World War I, Cent. — A325

No. 713: a, Soldiers and map of battle lines of 100 Day Offensive in France. b, Airplanes, ambulance, wounded soldier and Red Cross nurses. c, Dove and soldiers. d, Dove, soldier, woman at cemetery.

Perf. 13¼x13¾

2018, Sept. 24 Litho.

713 A325 Sheet of 4 13.00 13.00
a.-d. 10k Any single 3.25 3.25

Regin Dahl (1918-2007), Poet and Musician — A326

2018, Sept. 24 Litho. *Perf. 13x12¾*

714 A326 28k multi 8.75 8.75

Traditional Clothing — A327

Designs: 18k, Woman wearing bonnet. 20k, Man wearing hat.

Perf. 12¾x13½

2018, Sept. 24 Litho.

715 A327 18k multi 5.75 5.75
716 A327 20k multi 6.25 6.25

Booklet Stamps
Self-Adhesive

Serpentine Die Cut 14x13¾

717 A327 18k multi 5.75 5.75
718 A327 20k multi 6.25 6.25
a. Booklet pane of 6, 3 each #717-718 36.00

Christmas — A328

Icon of: 10k, Angel and gannet. 18k, Madonna and Child.

Litho. & Embossed

2018, Sept. 24 *Perf. 13*

719 A328 10k gold & multi 3.25 3.25
720 A328 18k gold & multi 5.75 5.75

Souvenir Sheet

1919 Provisional Stamp, Cent. — A329

No. 721: a, Surcharging device (21x28mm). b, Essays of handwritten surcharge (63x28mm).

2019, Jan. 11 Litho. ***Perf. 13¼x13½***

721 A329 Sheet of 2 7.00 7.00
a.-b. 11k Either single 3.50 3.50

Old Farmhouse, Kirkjubour A330

Litho. & Silk-Screened

2019, Feb. 25 ***Perf. 13***

722 A330 19k multi 5.75 5.75

Detail From 1539 Nautical Map by Olaus Magnus (1490-1557) — A331

Various map details.

2019, Feb. 25 Litho. ***Perf. 13***

723 A331 11k multi 3.50 3.50
724 A331 17k multi 5.25 5.25
725 A331 27k multi 8.25 8.25
a. Souvenir sheet of 3, #723-725, perf. 13 on 3 sides 17.00 17.00
Nos. 723-725 (3) 17.00 17.00

Lakes — A332

Designs: Nos. 726, 728, Lake Leynar. No. 727, 729, Lake Eidhi.

Perf. 13½x13¼

2019, Feb. 25 Litho.

726 A332 19k multi 5.75 5.75
727 A332 19k multi 5.75 5.75

Booklet Stamp
Self-Adhesive

Serpentine Die Cut 9

728 A332 19k multi 5.75 5.75
729 A332 19k multi 5.75 5.75
a. Booklet pane of 6, 3 each #728-729 34.50

First Man on the Moon, 50th Anniv. — A333

2019, Apr. 29 Litho. ***Perf. 13¾***

730 A333 17k multi 5.25 5.25

1896 Drawings of Water Mills by Daniel Bruun (1856-1931) A334

Mill in: 11k, Sandágerdhi. 35k, Frodhba.

Perf. 13½x13¾

2019, Apr. 29 Litho. & Engr.

731 A334 11k multi 3.50 3.50
732 A334 35k multi 10.50 10.50

Europa A335

Cepphus grylle faeroeensis: 19k, Two on rock. 26k, One in water.

2019, Apr. 29 Litho. ***Perf. 13***

733 A335 19k multi 5.75 5.75
734 A335 26k multi 7.75 7.75

Booklet Stamp
Self-Adhesive

Die Cut Perf. 13x12¾

735 A335 19k multi 5.75 5.75
a. Booklet pane of 6 34.50

Souvenir Sheet

Venceslaus Ulricus Hammershaimb (1819-1909), Theologian, Linguist, and Folklorist — A336

No. 736: a, Faroese Anthology, by Hammershaimb. b, Hammershaimb. c, The Native Tongue, sculpture by Janus Karnban, and alphabet of Hammershaimb's orthography.

2019, Apr. 29 Litho. ***Perf. 13x13¼***

736 A336 Sheet of 3 14.50 14.50
a. 11k multi 3.50 3.50
b. 17k multi 5.25 5.25
c. 19k multi 5.75 5.75

Souvenir Sheet

Labels Created for Fatherless Children's Fund — A337

No. 737: a, Flag of Faroe Islands. b, Mother and child.

2019, June 3 Litho. ***Perf. 13¼***

737 A337 Sheet of 2 14.00 14.00
a. 11k multi 3.50 3.50
b. 35k multi 10.50 10.50

Children's Aid Foundation, 77th anniv.; flag of the Faroe Islands, cent.

Smacks Johanna and Westward Ho — A338

2019, Sept. 23 Litho. ***Perf. 13¼***

738 A338 11k multi 3.25 3.25

Sculpture of Elinborg Lützen, by Pauli Olsen — A339

2019, Sept. 23 Litho. ***Perf. 13¼x13***

739 A339 55k multi 16.00 16.00

Lützen (1919-95), graphic artist.

Chasubles A340

Chasuble from church in: 11k, Sandvík. 19k, Funning.

2019, Sept. 23 Litho. ***Perf. 13¼x13***

740 A340 11k multi 3.25 3.25
741 A340 19k multi 5.50 5.50

FERNANDO PO

fər-ˈnan-ˌdō ˈpō

LOCATION — An island in the Gulf of Guinea off west Africa.
GOVT. — Former province of Spain
AREA — 800 sq. mi.
POP. — 62,612 (1960)
CAPITAL — Santa Isabel

Together with the islands of Elobey, Annobon and Corisco, Fernando Po came under the administration of Spanish Guinea. Postage stamps of Spanish Guinea were used until 1960.

The provinces of Fernando Po and Rio Muni united Oct. 12, 1968, to form the Republic of Equatorial Guinea.

100 Centimos = 1 Escudo = 2.50 Pesetas
100 Centimos = 1 Peseta
1000 Milesimas = 100 Centavos = 1 Peso (1882)

Catalogue values for unused stamps in this country are for Never Hinged items, beginning with Scott 181 in the regular postage section and Scott B1 in the semi-postal section.

Isabella II — A1

1868	**Unwmk.**	**Typo.**		*Perf. 14*
1	A1	20c brown	350.00	140.00
a.		20c red brown	525.00	140.00

No. 1 is valued in the grade of fine, as illustrated. Examples with very fine centering are uncommon and sell for more.

Forgeries exist.

Alfonso XII — A2

1879		**Centimos de Peseta**		
2	A2	5c green	52.50	15.00
3	A2	10c rose	40.00	15.00
4	A2	50c blue	90.00	15.00
		Nos. 2-4 (3)	182.50	45.00

1882-89		**Centavos de Peso**		
5	A2	1c green	9.50	5.50
6	A2	2c rose	18.00	8.75
7	A2	5c gray blue	60.00	12.00
8	A2	10c dk brown ('89)	82.50	6.75
		Nos. 5-8 (4)	170.00	33.00

Nos. 5-7 Handstamp Surcharged in Blue, Black or Violet — a

1884-95				
9	A2	50c on 1c green ('95)	120.00	19.00
11	A2	50c on 2c rose	32.00	6.00
12	A2	50c on 5c blue ('87)	150.00	25.00
		Nos. 9-12 (3)	302.00	50.00

Values above are for examples surcharged in black. Stamps surcharged in violet or blue are worth about 25% more.

Inverted and double surcharges exist. No. 12 exists overprinted in carmine. Value $100.

King Alfonso XIII — A4

1894-97				*Perf. 14*
13	A4	⅛c slate ('96)	22.00	3.00
14	A4	2c rose ('96)	15.50	2.50
15	A4	5c blue grn ('97)	16.00	2.50
16	A4	6c dk violet ('96)	13.00	3.00
17	A4	10c blk vio ('94)	450.00	115.00
17A	A4	10c dark brown ('94)	30.00	5.00
18	A4	10c lake ('95)	50.00	8.75
19	A4	10c org brn ('96)	10.50	2.50
20	A4	12½c dk brown ('96)	11.50	3.00
21	A4	20c slate bl ('96)	11.50	3.00
22	A4	25c claret ('96)	23.00	3.00
		Nos. 13-22 (10)	623.00	146.25

Most exist imperf. Value, set, pairs Nos. 13-16 and Nos. 18-22, $2,500.

Stamps of 1894-97 Handstamped in Blue, Black or Red

b

c

Type "b" Surcharge

1896-98				
22A	A4	5c on ⅛c slate (Bl)	100.00	27.50
23	A4	5c on 2c rose (Bl)	50.00	16.50
23A	A4	5c on 6c dk vio (Bl)	180.00	45.00
24	A4	5c on 10c brn vio (Bl)	180.00	45.00
24A	A4	5c on 10c org brn (Bl)	180.00	45.00
24B	A4	5c on 10c dk brn (Bk)	67.50	27.50
25	A4	5c on 12½c brn (Bl)	37.50	13.00
a.		Black surcharge	37.50	13.00
25B	A4	5c on 20c sl bl (R)	180.00	45.00
25C	A4	5c on 25c claret (Bk)	180.00	35.00
		Nos. 22A-25C (9)	1,155.	299.50

Type "c" Surcharge

26	A4	5c on ⅛c slate (Bk)	32.50	6.75
27	A4	5c on 2c rose (Bl)	32.50	6.75
a.		Black surcharge	32.50	6.75
28	A4	5c on 5c green (R)	160.00	22.00
29	A4	5c on 6c dk vio (R)	23.00	14.00
a.		Violet surcharge	24.00	15.50
30	A4	5c on 10c org brn (Bk)	210.00	27.50
30A	A4	5c on 10c dk brn (Bk)	160.00	26.00
30B	A4	5c on 10c lake (Bl)	400.00	110.00
31	A4	5c on 12½c brn (R)	70.00	11.00
32	A4	5c on 20c sl bl (R)	40.00	10.50
33	A4	5c on 25c claret (Bk)	37.50	11.00
a.		Blue surcharge	37.50	13.50
		Nos. 26-33 (10)	1,166.	245.50

Exist surcharged in other colors.

Type "a" Srch. in Blue or Black

1898-99				
34	A4	50c on 2c rose	92.50	11.50
35	A4	50c on 10c brn vio	220.00	33.00
36	A4	50c on 10c lake	230.00	33.00
37	A4	50c on 10c org brn	220.00	33.00
38	A4	50c on 12½c brn (Bk)	190.00	22.00

The "a" surch. also exists on ⅛c, 5c & 25c. Values, $325, $225 and $210, respectively.

Revenue Stamps Privately Handstamped in Blue

Arms
A5 A6

1897-98				*Imperf.*
39	A5	5c on 10c rose	28.00	12.50
40	A6	10c rose	24.00	11.00

Revenue Stamps Handstamped in Black or Red

A7

A8

A9

Arms — A9a

1899				*Imperf.*
41	A7	15c on 10c grn	45.00	23.00
a.		Blue surcharge, vert.	39.00	21.00
42	A8	10c on 25c grn	120.00	65.00
43	A9	15c on 25c grn	190.00	120.00
43A	A9a	15c on 25c grn (R)	*1,800.*	*1,100.*
b.		Black surcharge	*1,800.*	*1,100.*

Surcharge on No. 41 is either horizontal, inverted or vertical.

On No. 42 "CORREOS" is ovptd. in red.

On Nos. 43A and 43Ab, the signature is always in black.

King Alfonso XIII — A10

Double-lined shaded letters at sides.

1899				*Perf. 14*
44	A10	1m orange brn	2.40	.45
45	A10	2m orange brn	2.40	.45
46	A10	3m orange brn	2.40	.45
47	A10	4m orange brn	2.40	.45
48	A10	5m orange brn	2.40	.45
49	A10	1c black vio	2.40	.45
50	A10	2c dk blue grn	2.40	.45
51	A10	3c dk brown	2.40	.45
52	A10	4c orange	13.00	1.10
53	A10	5c carmine rose	2.50	.45
54	A10	6c dark blue	2.50	.45
55	A10	8c gray brn	8.00	.45
56	A10	10c vermilion	5.25	.45
57	A10	15c slate grn	5.25	.45
58	A10	20c maroon	14.50	1.10
59	A10	40c violet	100.00	19.00
60	A10	60c black	100.00	19.00
61	A10	80c red brown	100.00	19.00
62	A10	1p yellow grn	325.00	92.50
63	A10	2p slate blue	325.00	95.00
		Nos. 44-63 (20)	1,020.	252.55

Nos. 44-63 exist imperf. Value for set, $3,500.

See Nos. 66-85. For surcharges see Nos. 64-65, 88-88B.

1900		**Surcharged type "a"**		
64	A10	50c on 20c maroon	16.00	2.50
a.		Blue surcharge	32.00	4.75
		Surcharged type "b"		
64B	A10	5c on 20c maroon	300.00	40.00
		Surcharged type "c"		
65	A10	5c on 20c maroon	9.50	2.40
		Nos. 64-65 (3)	325.50	44.90

1900		**Dated "1900"**		
		Solid letters at sides.		
66	A10	1m black	3.00	.50
67	A10	2m black	3.00	.50
68	A10	3m black	3.00	.50
69	A10	4m black	3.00	.50
70	A10	5m black	3.00	.50
71	A10	1c green	3.00	.50
72	A10	2c violet	3.00	.50
73	A10	3c rose	3.00	.50
74	A10	4c black brn	3.00	.50
75	A10	5c blue	3.00	.50
76	A10	6c orange	3.00	.50
77	A10	8c bronze grn	3.00	.50
78	A10	10c claret	3.00	.50
79	A10	15c dk violet	3.00	.50
80	A10	20c olive brn	3.00	.50
81	A10	40c brown	7.75	2.25
82	A10	60c green	16.50	2.50
83	A10	80c dark blue	17.50	3.75
84	A10	1p red brown	110.00	30.00
85	A10	2p orange	190.00	62.50
		Nos. 66-85 (20)	386.75	108.50
		Set, never hinged	750.00	

Nos. 66-85 exist imperf. Value, set *$3,500.*

Revenue Stamps Overprinted or Surcharged with Handstamp in Red or Black

A11

A12

1900				*Imperf.*
86	A11	10c blue (R)	37.50	17.50
87	A12	5c on 10c blue	100.00	40.00
		Set, never hinged	175.00	

Nos. 52 and 80 Surcharged type "a" in Violet or Black

1900				
88	A10	50c on 4c orange (V)	14.00	4.00
a.		Green surcharge	22.50	12.00
88B	A10	50c on 20c ol brn	14.00	3.50
		Set, never hinged	37.50	

A13

1901				*Perf. 14*
89	A13	1c black	2.60	.90
90	A13	2c orange brn	2.60	.90
91	A13	3c dk violet	2.60	.90
92	A13	4c lt violet	2.60	.90
93	A13	5c orange red	1.60	.90
94	A13	10c violet brn	1.60	.90
95	A13	25c dp blue	1.75	.90
96	A13	50c claret	2.60	.90
97	A13	75c dk brown	2.00	.90
98	A13	1p blue grn	60.00	7.50
99	A13	2p red brown	40.00	10.00
100	A13	3p olive grn	400.00	14.00
101	A13	4p dull red	40.00	14.00

102 A13 5p dk green 47.50 14.00
103 A13 10p buff 115.00 40.00
Nos. 89-103 (15) 722.45 107.60
Set, never hinged 850.00

Dated "1902"

1902 **Control Numbers on Back**

104 A13 5c dk green 2.60 .45
105 A13 10c slate 2.90 .50
106 A13 25c claret 6.25 1.00
107 A13 50c violet brn 15.00 3.25
108 A13 75c lt violet 15.00 3.25
109 A13 1p car rose 18.50 4.00
110 A13 2p olive grn 40.00 9.50
111 A13 5p orange red 57.50 20.00
Nos. 104-111 (8) 157.75 41.95
Set, never hinged 250.00

Exist imperf. Value for set, *$1,500.*

A14

Dated "1903"

1903 ***Perf. 14***
Control Numbers on Back

112 A14 ¼c dk violet .45 .25
113 A14 ½c black .45 .25
114 A14 1c scarlet .45 .25
115 A14 2c dk green .45 .30
116 A14 3c blue grn .45 .30
117 A14 4c violet .45 .30
118 A14 5c rose lake .50 .30
119 A14 10c orange buff .60 .45
120 A14 15c blue green 2.50 1.00
121 A14 25c red brown 2.75 1.25
122 A14 50c black brn 4.50 2.00
123 A14 75c carmine 16.50 3.50
124 A14 1p dk brown 25.00 6.00
125 A14 2p dk olive grn 32.50 7.50
126 A14 3p claret 32.50 7.50
127 A14 4p dark blue 40.00 12.50
128 A14 5p dp dull blue 60.00 16.00
129 A14 10p dull red 130.00 27.50
Nos. 112-129 (18) 350.05 87.15
Set, never hinged 600.00

Dated "1905"

1905 **Control Numbers on Back**

136 A14 1c dp violet .40 .30
137 A14 2c black .40 .30
138 A14 3c vermilion .40 .30
139 A14 4c dp green .40 .30
140 A14 5c blue grn .45 .35
141 A14 10c violet 1.60 .75
142 A14 15c car lake 1.60 .75
143 A14 25c orange buff 12.50 2.25
144 A14 50c green 8.00 2.75
145 A14 75c red brown 11.00 7.50
146 A14 1p dp gray brn 12.50 7.50
147 A14 2p carmine 20.00 12.50
148 A14 3p deep brown 32.50 14.00
149 A14 4p bronze grn 40.00 18.00
150 A14 5p claret 62.50 25.00
151 A14 10p deep blue 90.00 35.00
Nos. 136-151 (16) 294.25 127.55
Set, never hinged 600.00

King Alfonso XIII — A15

1907 **Control Numbers on Back**

152 A15 1c blue black .30 .25
153 A15 2c car rose .30 .25
154 A15 3c dp violet .40 .25
155 A15 4c black .40 .25
156 A15 5c orange buff .40 .25
157 A15 10c maroon 2.00 .80
158 A15 15c bronze grn .55 .35
159 A15 25c dk brown 65.00 15.00
160 A15 50c blue green .45 .30
161 A15 75c vermilion .45 .30
162 A15 1p dull blue 3.00 .60
163 A15 2p brown 11.00 4.00
164 A15 3p lake 11.00 4.00
165 A15 4p violet 11.00 4.00
166 A15 5p black brn 11.00 4.00
167 A15 10p orange brn 11.00 4.00
Nos. 152-167 (16) 128.25 38.60
Set, never hinged 350.00

No. 157 Handstamp Surcharged in Black, Blue or Red

1908

168 A15 5c on 10c mar (Bk) 2.75 2.00
a. Blue surcharge 10.00 5.50
b. Red surcharge 30.00 10.00
169 A15 25c on 10c mar (Bk) 60.00 20.00
Set, never hinged 77.50

The surcharge on Nos. 168-169 exist inverted, double, etc. The surcharge also exists on other stamps.

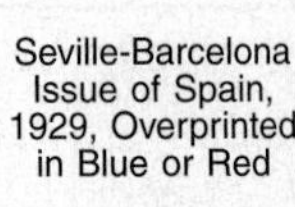

Seville-Barcelona Issue of Spain, 1929, Overprinted in Blue or Red

1929 ***Perf. 11***

170 A52 5c rose lake .25 .25
171 A53 10c green (R) .25 .25
a. Perf. 14 .65 .65
172 A50 15c Prus bl (R) .25 .25
173 A51 20c purple (R) .25 .25
174 A50 25c brt rose .25 .25
175 A52 30c black brn .25 .25
176 A53 40c dk blue (R) .45 .45
177 A51 50c dp orange 1.00 1.00
178 A52 1p blue blk (R) 3.75 3.75
179 A53 4p deep rose 20.00 20.00
180 A53 10p brown 25.00 25.00
Nos. 170-180 (11) 51.70 51.70
Set, never hinged 100.00

Catalogue values for unused stamps in this section, from this point to the end of the section, are for Never Hinged items.

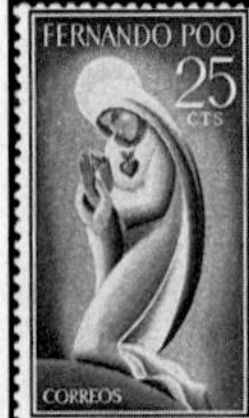

Virgin Mary — A16

1960 **Unwmk.** **Photo.** ***Perf. 13x12½***

181 A16 25c dull gray vio .40 .25
182 A16 50c brown olive .40 .25
183 A16 75c violet brn .40 .25
184 A16 1p orange ver .40 .25
185 A16 1.50p lt blue grn .40 .25
186 A16 2p red lilac .40 .25
187 A16 3p dark blue 4.00 .80
188 A16 5p lt red brn .65 .25
189 A16 10p lt olive grn .80 .30
Nos. 181-189 (9) 7.85 2.85

Tricorn and Windmill from "The Three-Cornered Hat" by Falla — A17

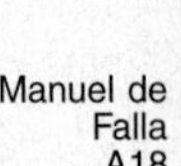

Manuel de Falla A18

1960 ***Perf. 13x12½, 12½x13***

190 A17 35c slate green .60 .60
191 A18 80c Prus green .70 .70

Issued to honor Manuel de Falla (1876-1946), Spanish composer.
See Nos. B1-B2.

Map of Fernando Po — A19

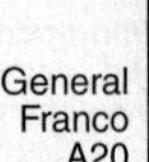
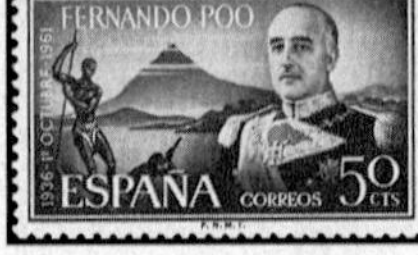

General Franco A20

Designs: 70c, Santa Isabel Cathedral.

Perf. 13x12½, 12½x13
1961, Oct. 1 **Photo.** **Unwmk.**

192 A19 25c gray violet .35 .35
193 A20 50c olive brown .35 .35
194 A19 70c brt green .40 .40
195 A20 1p red orange .45 .45
Nos. 192-195 (4) 1.55 1.55

25th anniv. of the nomination of Gen. Francisco Franco as Chief of State.

Ocean Liner A21

Design: 50c, S.S. San Francisco.

1962, July 10 ***Perf. 12½x13***

196 A21 25c dull violet .30 .30
197 A21 50c gray olive .35 .35
198 A21 1p orange brn .35 .35
Nos. 196-198 (3) 1.00 1.00

Mailman — A22

Mail Transport Symbols A23

Perf. 13x12½, 12½x13
1962, Nov. 23 **Unwmk.**

199 A22 15c dark green .30 .30
200 A23 35c lilac rose .35 .35
201 A22 1p brown .35 .35
Nos. 199-201 (3) 1.00 1.00

Issued for Stamp Day.

Fetish — A24

1963, Jan. 29 ***Perf. 13x12½***

202 A24 50c olive gray .30 .30
203 A24 1p deep magenta .35 .35

Issued to help victims of the Seville flood.

Nuns A25

Design: 50c, Nun and child, vert.

Perf. 12½x13, 13x12½
1963, July 6 **Photo.** **Unwmk.**

204 A25 25c bright lilac .30 .30
205 A25 50c dull green .35 .35
206 A25 1p red orange .35 .35
Nos. 204-206 (3) 1.00 1.00

Issued for child welfare.

Child and Arms A26

1963, July 12 ***Perf. 12½x13***

207 A26 50c brown olive .30 .30
208 A26 1p carmine rose .35 .35

Issued for Barcelona flood relief.

Governor Chacon A27

Orange Blossoms — A28

1964, Mar. 6 ***Perf. 12½x13, 13x12½***

209 A27 25c violet black .30 .30
210 A28 50c dark olive .35 .35
211 A27 1p brown red .35 .35
Nos. 209-211 (3) 1.00 1.00

Issued for Stamp Day 1963.

Men in Dugout Canoe — A29

Design: 50c, Pineapple.

1964, June 1 **Photo.** ***Perf. 13x12½***

212 A29 25c purple .30 .30
213 A28 50c dull olive .35 .35
214 A29 1p deep claret .35 .35
Nos. 212-214 (3) 1.00 1.00

Issued for child welfare.

Ring-necked Francolin — A30

Designs: 15c, 70c, 3p, Ring-necked francolin. 25c, 1p, 5p, Two mallards. 50c, 1.50p, 10p, Head of great blue touraco.

1964, July 1

215 A30 15c chestnut .30 .30
216 A30 25c dull violet .30 .30
217 A30 50c dk olive grn .30 .30
218 A30 70c green .30 .30
219 A30 1p brown orange .35 .30
220 A30 1.50p grnsh blue .40 .35
221 A30 3p violet blue .65 .35
222 A30 5p dull purple 1.60 .40
223 A30 10p bright green 2.40 1.00
Nos. 215-223 (9) 6.60 3.60

The Three Kings A31

Designs: 50c, 1.50p, Caspar, vert.

Perf. 13x12½, 12½x13

1964, Nov. 23 **Unwmk.**

224 A31 50c green .35 .35
225 A31 1p orange ver .40 .35
226 A31 1.50p deep green .45 .35
227 A31 3p ultra 1.75 1.40
Nos. 224-227 (4) 2.95 2.45

Issued for Stamp Day, 1964.

Boy — A32

Woman Fruit Picker — A33

1.50p, Girl learning to write, and church.

1964, Mar. 1 **Photo.** ***Perf. 13x12½***

228 A32 50c indigo .30 .30
229 A33 1p dark red .35 .30
230 A33 1.50p grnsh blue .40 .35
Nos. 228-230 (3) 1.05 .95

Issued to commemorate 25 years of peace.

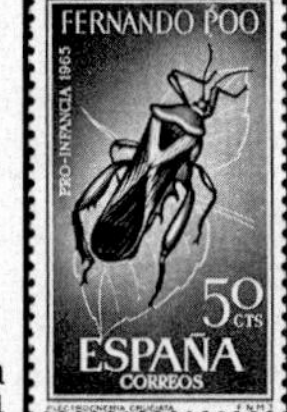
Plectrocnemia Cruciata — A34

Design: 1p, Metopodontus savagei, horiz.

Perf. 13x12½, 12½x13

1965, June 1 **Photo.** **Unwmk.**

231 A34 50c slate green .45 .35
232 A34 1p rose red .45 .35
233 A34 1.50p Prus blue .45 .35
Nos. 231-233 (3) 1.35 1.05

Issued for child welfare.

Pole Vault A35

Arms of Fernando Po — A36

Perf. 12½x13, 13x12½

1965, Nov. 23 **Photo.** **Unwmk.**

234 A35 50c yellow green .30 .30
235 A36 1p brt org brn .35 .30
236 A35 1.50p brt blue .40 .35
Nos. 234-236 (3) 1.05 .95

Issued for Stamp Day, 1965.

Children Reading A37

1.50p, St. Elizabeth of Hungary, vert.

Perf. 12½x13, 13x12½

1966, June 1 **Photo.** **Unwmk.**

237 A37 50c dark green .30 .30
238 A37 1p brown red .35 .30
239 A37 1.50p dark blue .35 .35
Nos. 237-239 (3) 1.00 .95

Issued for child welfare.

White-nosed Monkey — A38

Stamp Day: 40c, 4p, Head of moustached monkey, vert.

1966, Nov. 23 **Photo.** ***Perf. 13***

240 A38 10c dk blue & yel .35 .30
241 A38 40c lt brn, bl & blk .40 .30
242 A38 1.50p ol bis, brn org & blk .45 .40
243 A38 4p sl grn, brn org & blk .55 .45
Nos. 240-243 (4) 1.75 1.45

Flowers — A39

Designs: 40c, 4p, Six flowers.

1967, June 1 **Photo.** ***Perf. 13***

244 A39 10c brt car & pale grn .30 .30
245 A39 40c red brn & org .35 .30
246 A39 1.50p red lil & lt red brn .40 .35
247 A39 4p dk blue & lt grn .45 .40
Nos. 244-247 (4) 1.50 1.35

Issued for child welfare.

Linsang — A40

Stamp Day: 1.50p, Needle-clawed galago, vert. 3.50p, Fraser's scaly-tailed flying squirrel.

1967, Nov. 23 **Photo.** ***Perf. 13***

248 A40 1p black & bister .35 .30
249 A40 1.50p brown & olive .40 .35
250 A40 3.50p rose lake & dl grn .50 .40
Nos. 248-250 (3) 1.25 1.05

Stamp of 1868, No. 1, and Arms of San Carlos A41

Fernando Po No. 1 and: 1.50p, Arms of Santa Isabel. 2.50p, Arms of Fernando Po.

1968, Feb. 4 **Photo.** ***Perf. 13***

251 A41 1p brt plum & brn org .30 .30
252 A41 1.50p dp blue & brn org .40 .30
253 A41 2.50p brn & brn org .50 .40
Nos. 251-253 (3) 1.20 1.00

Centenary of the first postage stamp.

Signs of the Zodiac — A42

1968, Apr. 25 **Photo.** ***Perf. 13***

254 A42 1p Libra .30 .30
255 A42 1.50p Leo .40 .35
256 A42 2.50p Aquarius .50 .40
Nos. 254-256 (3) 1.20 1.05

Issued for child welfare.

SEMI-POSTAL STAMPS

Catalogue values for unused stamps in this section are for Never Hinged items.

Types of Regular Issue, 1960

Designs: 10c+5c, Manuel de Falla. 15c+5c, Dancers from "Love, the Magician."

Perf. 12½x13, 13x12½

1960 **Photo.** **Unwmk.**

B1 A18 10c + 5c maroon .35 .30
B2 A17 15c + 5c dk brn & bister .35 .35

The surtax was for child welfare.

Whale SP1

Design: Nos. B4, B6, Harpooning whale.

1961 ***Perf. 12½x13***

B3 SP1 10c + 5c rose brown .35 .30
B4 SP1 20c + 5c dk slate grn .35 .30
B5 SP1 30c + 10c olive brn .40 .30
B6 SP1 50c + 20c dark brn .45 .30
Nos. B3-B6 (4) 1.55 1.20

Issued for Stamp Day, 1960.

Hand Blessing Woman — SP2

Design: 25c+10c, Boy making sign of the cross, and crucifix.

1961, June 21 ***Perf. 13x12½***

B7 SP2 10c + 5c rose brn .40 .30
B8 SP2 25c + 10c gray vio .40 .30
B9 SP2 80c + 20c dk grn .50 .35
Nos. B7-B9 (3) 1.30 .95

The surtax was for child welfare.

Ethiopian Tortoise SP3

Stamp Day: 25c+10c, 1p+10c, Native carriers, palms and shore.

1961, Nov. 23 ***Perf. 12½x13***

B10 SP3 10c + 5c rose red .35 .30
B11 SP3 25c + 10c dk pur .40 .30
B12 SP3 30c + 10c vio brn .40 .30
B13 SP3 1p + 10c red org .50 .40
Nos. B10-B13 (4) 1.65 1.30

FIJI

'fē-ˌjē

LOCATION — Group of 332 islands (106 inhabited) in the South Pacific Ocean east of Vanuatu
GOVT. — Independent nation in British Commonwealth
AREA — 7,078 sq. mi.
POP. — 812,918 (1999 est.)
CAPITAL — Suva

A British colony since 1874, Fiji became fully independent in 1970.

12 Pence = 1 Shilling
20 Shillings = 1 Pound
100 Cents = 1 Dollar (1872-74, 1969)

Syncopated Perforations

Type A (1st stamp #873): On shorter sides, the seventh hole from the larger side is an oval hole equal in width to three holes.

Catalogue values for unused stamps in this country are for Never Hinged items, beginning with Scott 137 in the regular postage section and Scott B1 in the semi-postal section.

Values for unused stamps are for examples with original gum as defined in the catalogue introduction except for Nos. 1-10 which are valued without gum. Additionally, Nos. 1-10 are valued with roulettes showing on two or more sides, but expect small faults that do not detract from the appearance of the stamps. Very few examples of Nos. 1-10 will be found free of faults, and these will command substantial premiums.

Watermark

Wmk. 17 — FIJI POSTAGE Across Center Row of Sheet

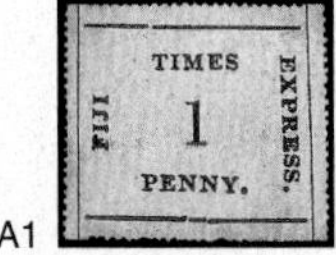

A1

1870 Unwmk. Typeset *Rouletted*
Thin Quadrille Paper

1	A1	1p black, *pink*	4,500.	4,750.
2	A1	3p black, *pink*	5,500.	5,000.
a.		Comma after "EXPRESS"	*8,000.*	*8,000.*
3	A1	6p black, *pink*	3,000.	3,000.
5	A1	1sh black, *pink*	2,250.	2,500.

1871 Thin Vertically Laid Paper

6	A1	1p black, *pink*	1,250.	2,100.
7	A1	3p black, *pink*	1,900.	3,400.
8	A1	6p black, *pink*	1,600.	2,100.
9	A1	9p black, *pink*	3,400.	4,000.
10	A1	1sh black, *pink*	1,900.	1,900.

This service was established by the *Fiji Times*, a weekly newspaper, for the delivery of the newspaper. Since there was no postal service to the other islands, delivery of letters to agents of the newspaper on the islands was offered to the public.

Nos. 1-5 were printed in the same sheet, one horizontal row of 6 of each (6p, 1sh, 1p, 3p). Nos. 6-10 were printed from the same plate with three 9p replacing three 3p.

Most used examples have pen cancels.

Up to three sets of imitations exist. One on pink laid paper, pin-perforated, measuring 22½x16mm. Originals measure 22½x18½mm. A later printing was made on pink wove paper.

Forgeries also exist plus fake cancellations.

Crown and "CR" (Cakobau Rex)

A2 A3

A4

1871 Typo. Wmk. 17 *Perf. 12½*
Wove Paper

15	A2	1p blue	62.50	140.00
16	A3	3p green	125.00	400.00
17	A4	6p rose	170.00	325.00
		Nos. 15-17 (3)	357.50	865.00

Sheets of 50 (10x5).

For overprints and surcharges see Nos. 18-39.

Forgeries exist.

Stamps of 1871 Surcharged in Black

1872, Jan. 13

18	A2	2c on 1p blue	60.00	*65.00*
19	A3	6c on 3p green	90.00	90.00
20	A4	12c on 6p rose	125.00	90.00
		Nos. 18-20 (3)	275.00	245.00

Nos. 18-20 with Additional Overprint in Black

b

c

1874, Oct. 10

21	A2(b)	2c on 1p blue	1,250.	340.00
a.		No period after "R"	3,250.	1,150.
22	A2(c)	2c on 1p blue	1,150.	300.00
a.		Invtd. "A" instead of "V"	3,250.	1,500.
b.		Period after "R" is a Maltese Cross	3,250.	1,500.
c.		No period after "R"	3,250.	1,500.
d.		Round raised period after "V"	3,250.	1,500.
e.		Round raised period after "V" and "R"	3,250.	1,500.
23	A3(b)	6c on 3p green	3,250.	1,000.
a.		No period after "R"	5,500.	2,000.
24	A3(c)	6c on 3p green	2,750.	750.00
a.		Inverted "A"	5,500.	1,900.
b.		Period after "R" is a Maltese Cross	5,250.	2,000.
c.		No period after "R"	5,500.	2,000.
d.		Round raised period after "V"	5,500.	2,000.
e.		Round raised period after "V" and "R"	5,500.	2,000.
25	A4(b)	12c on 6p rose	1,050.	275.00
a.		"V.R." inverted	7,500.	
b.		No period after "R"	3,000.	1,150.
26	A4(c)	12c on 6p rose	1,000.	250.00
a.		Inverted "A"	3,000.	1,200.
b.		Period after "R" is a Maltese Cross	3,000.	1,200.
c.		"V.R." inverted	—	6,250.
d.		No period after "R"	3,000.	1,225.
e.		Round raised period after "V"	3,000.	1,225.
f.		Round raised period after "V" and "R"	3,000.	1,225.

Forged overprints exist on both forged stamps and on genuine stamps.

Types "b" and "c" were in the same sheet.

Nos. 23-26 with Additional Surcharge in Black or Red

1875

27	A3(b)	2p on 6c on 3p	2,750.	800.00
a.		Period btwn. "2" and "d"	4,750.	1,600.
b.		"V.R." double	5,500.	4,500.
c.		No period after "R"	4,750.	1,600.
28	A3(b)	2p on 6c on 3p (R)	900.00	325.00
a.		Period btwn. "2" and "d"	2,250.	850.00
b.		No period after "R"	2,250.	900.00
29	A3(c)	2p on 6c on 3p	1,900.	600.00
a.		Inverted "A"	4,750.	1,600.
b.		Period after "R" is a Maltese Cross	4,750.	1,600.
c.		No period after "2d"	4,750.	1,600.
d.		No period after "R"	4,750.	1,600.
e.		Round raised period after "V"	4,750.	1,600.
f.		Round raised period after "V" and "R"	4,750.	1,600.
30	A3(c)	2p on 6c on 3p (R)	750.00	250.00
a.		Inverted "A"	2,400.	850.00
b.		Period after "R" is a Maltese Cross	2,400.	875.00
c.		No period after "2d"	2,400.	875.00
d.		No period after "R"	2,400.	875.00
e.		Round raised period after "V"	2,400.	875.00
f.		Round raised period after "V" and "R"	2,400.	875.00
31	A4(b)	2p on 12c on 6p	3,250.	1,000.
a.		Period btwn. "2" and "d"		
b.		No period after "2d"		
c.		"2d, VR" double		5,500.
32	A4(c)	2p on 12c on 6p	3,000.	900.00
a.		Inverted "A"	4,500.	1,400.
b.		No period after "2d"	—	2,250.
c.		"2d, VR" double		5,500.
d.		Round raised period after "R"	—	1,250.
f.		As "a," with raised period after "V"	3,000.	1,000.

Forged overprints exist on both forged stamps and on genuine stamps.

Types of 1871 Overprinted or Surcharged in Black

e

f

1876, Jan. 31 Unwmk.
Wove Paper

33	A2(e)	1p ultramarine	60.00	60.00
a.		Inverted surcharge		
b.		Dbl. impression of stamp	1,000.	
c.		Horiz. pair, imperf vert.	1,000.	
34	A3(e+f)	2p on 3p dk grn	60.00	*65.00*
a.		Dbl. surch. "Two Pence"		
35	A4(e)	6p rose	70.00	65.00
b.		Surcharge inverted		
c.		Dbl. impression of stamp	2,750.	
		Nos. 33-35 (3)	190.00	190.00

1877 Laid Paper

36	A2(e)	1p ultramarine	32.50	*50.00*
a.		Horiz. pair, imperf. vert.	1,000.	
37	A3(e+f)	2p on 3p dk grn	80.00	*85.00*
b.		Perf 10	400.00	
c.		Perf 11	375.00	
d.		Horiz. pair, imperf. vert.	1,100.	
e.		Horiz. pair, imperf. between	1,000.	
38	A3(e+f)	4p on 3p lilac	110.00	27.50
a.		Horiz. pair, imperf. vert.	1,000.	
39	A4(e)	6p rose	60.00	40.00
a.		Horiz. pair, imperf. vert.	800.00	
		Nos. 36-39 (4)	282.50	202.50

Many of the preceding stamps are known imperforate. They are printer's waste and were never issued.

A12

A13

Queen Victoria

A14 A15

Perf. 10-13½ & Compound

1878-90 Wove Paper Typo.

40	A12	1p ultra ('79)	20.00	20.00
a.		1p blue	65.00	6.50
41	A12	2p green	45.00	1.75
b.		2p ultramarine (error)	*40,000.*	
42	A12	4p brt vio ('90)	16.00	9.00
a.		4p mauve	40.00	12.00
43	A13	6p brt rose ('80)	16.00	4.75
a.		Printed on both sides	2,500.	2,000.
44	A14	1sh yel brn ('81)	60.00	12.50
a.		1sh deep brown	100.00	32.50

Litho. & Typo.

45	A15	5sh blk & red brn ('82)	75.00	50.00
		Nos. 40-45 (6)	232.00	98.00

No. 41b was not put on sale. All examples were supposed to be destroyed.

A quantity of No. 45 was sold as remainders, canceled-to-order with the following Suva dates: 15.DEC.00; 22.DE.1900; 28.DEC.1900; 12.DEC.01; 15.DEC.01; 16.DE.1901; 21.JUN.02; 15.DEC.02; 15. DE. 1902; and 21.DE.1902. Examples so canceled are worth less than postally used examples.

No. 45 imperf was sold only as a remainder, canceled "Suva, 15.DEC.00."

A late printing of the 5sh, made from an electrotyped plate, exists in gray black and red orange, perf 10, differing from No. 45 in many details. It was also sold only as a remainder, canceled "Suva, 15.DEC.00." It is scarce.

For surcharges see Nos. 46-52.

Nos. 40-45 exist with sheetmaker's watermark. Watermarked stamps are scarcer than unwatermarked.

1881-90 *Perf. 10*

40d	A12	1p ultramarine	32.50	3.00
40e	A12	1p blue	65.00	3.25
41d	A12	2p yellow green	45.00	1.00
41e	A12	2p blue green	55.00	6.00
42d	A12	4p mauve	85.00	75.00
43d	A13	6p bright rose	30.00	32.50
43e	A13	6p pale rose	75.00	32.50
44d	A14	1sh pale yel brown	100.00	32.50
44e	A14	1sh deep brown	100.00	32.50

Surcharged type "f" in Black

1878-90 Typo.

46	A12	2p on 3p green	12.00	*42.50*
47	A12	4p on 1p vio ('90)	75.00	60.00
48	A12	4p on 2p lilac ('83)	100.00	16.00
		Nos. 46-48 (3)	187.00	118.50

Nos. 40-43 Surcharged in Black

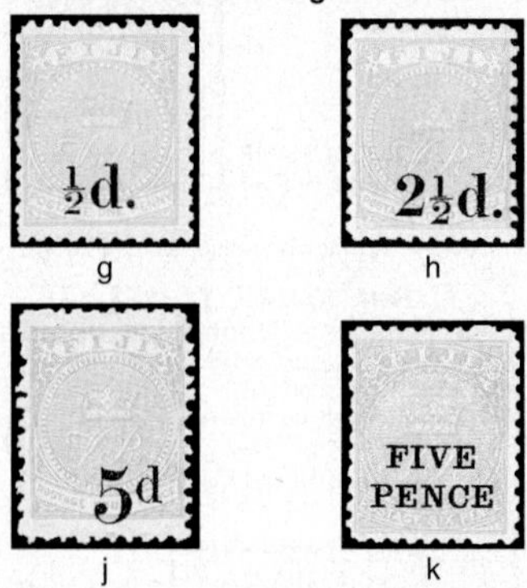

g h j k

1891-92 *Perf. 10*

49	A12(g)	½p on 1p ('92)	62.50	*80.00*
50	A12(h)	2½p on 2p	52.50	*55.00*
a.		Wider space (2mm) between "2" and "½"	140.00	*150.00*
51	A12(j)	5p on 4p ('92)	62.50	*80.00*
52	A13(k)	5p on 6p ('92)	67.50	*75.00*
a.		"FIVE" and "PENCE" 3mm apart	75.00	*85.00*
		Nos. 49-52 (4)	245.00	*290.00*

No. 50a resulted from loose type, sometimes printing narrow, sometimes wide. Intermediate spacing is known.

A18

A20

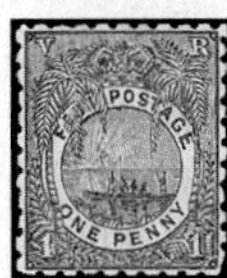

Fijian Canoe — A19

1891-96 ***Perf. 10-12 & Compound***

53 A18 ½p grnsh blk ('92) 2.75 7.00
a. ½p gray 3.75 7.00
54 A19 1p black ('93) 22.50 7.50
55 A19 1p lilac rose ('96) 22.50 1.10
56 A19 2p green ('93) 9.00 .85
a. Perf. 10x12 ('94) 800.00 425.00
57 A20 2½ red brown 8.75 5.50
58 A19 5p ultra ('93) 25.00 8.00
Nos. 53-58 (6) 90.50 29.95

Perf. 10

53d A18 p slate gray 6.75 10.00
54d A19 1p black 30.00 6.00
56d A19 2p green 145.00 22.50
57d A20 2½p brown 60.00 30.00
58d A19 5p ultramarine 125.00 65.00

Edward VII — A22

1903, Feb. 1 **Wmk. 2** ***Perf. 14***

59 A22 ½p gray grn & pale grn 3.25 2.25
60 A22 1p vio & blk, *red* 20.00 .65
61 A22 2p vio & orange 4.50 1.40
62 A22 2½p vio & ultra, *bl* 15.00 1.75
63 A22 3p vio & red vio 1.60 *4.00*
64 A22 4p violet & blk 1.60 *2.75*
65 A22 5p vio & green 1.60 *2.50*
66 A22 6p vio & car rose 1.60 *2.00*
67 A22 1sh grn & car rose 18.50 *85.00*
68 A22 5sh green & blk 85.00 *170.00*
69 A22 £1 gray & ultra 400.00 *500.00*
Revenue cancel 75.00
Nos. 59-68 (10) 152.65 *272.30*

Numerals of 2p, 4p, 6p and 5sh of type A22 are in color on plain tablet.

1904-12 **Ordinary Paper** **Wmk. 3**

70 A22 ½p grn & pale grn ('04) 18.50 3.25
70A A22 ½p green ('08) 15.00 3.50
71 A22 1p vio & blk, *red* ('04) 40.00 .25
72 A22 1p carmine ('06) 25.00 .25
73 A22 2½p ultra ('10) 7.50 *10.00*

Chalky Paper

74 A22 6p violet ('10) 30.00 *50.00*
75 A22 1sh grn & car rose ('09) 32.50 *42.50*
76 A22 1sh blk, *grn* ('11) 11.00 *16.00*
77 A22 5sh grn & scar, *yel* ('11) 75.00 *105.00*
78 A22 £1 vio & blk, *red* ('12) 360.00 300.00
Nos. 70-77 (9) 254.50 *230.75*

George V — A23

Die I

For description of Dies I and II see "Dies of British Colonial Stamps" in Table of Contents.

1912-23 **Ordinary Paper**

79 A23 ¼p brown ('16) 2.75 .40
80 A23 ½p green 4.50 1.10
81 A23 1p scarlet 3.75 .50
a. 1p carmine ('16) 2.25 .75
82 A23 2p gray ('14) 2.00 .25
83 A23 2½p ultra ('14) 3.50 3.75
84 A23 3p violet, *yel* 4.50 *12.50*
a. Die II ('21) 3.25 *30.00*
85 A23 4p blk & red, *lem* ('21) 24.00 *22.50*
a. Die II ('23) 3.25 *35.00*

Chalky Paper

86 A23 5p dl vio & ol grn ('14) 5.50 *12.50*
87 A23 6p dl vio & red vio ('14) 2.40 *6.00*
88 A23 1sh black, *green* 1.30 *14.50*
a. 1sh black, *blue green,* ol back 3.25 *11.00*
b. 1sh black, *emerald* ('21) 5.50 *67.50*
c. Die II ('22) 3.25 *37.50*
89 A23 2sh 6p blk & red, *blue* 37.50 *35.00*
90 A23 5sh grn & scar, *yellow* 37.50 *45.00*
91 A23 £1 vio & blk, *red* 300.00 325.00
a. Die II ('21) 300.00 325.00
Revenue cancel 52.50

Surface-colored Paper

92 A23 1sh black, *green* 1.25 *14.50*
Nos. 79-90,92 (13) 130.45 *168.50*

Numerals of ¼p, 1½p, 2p, 4p, 6p, 2sh, 2sh6p and 5sh of type A23 are in color on plain tablet.

For overprints see Nos. MR1-MR2.

Die II

1922-27 **Wmk. 4** **Ordinary Paper**

93 A23 ¼p dark brown 3.75 *27.50*
94 A23 ½p green 1.10 *1.50*
95 A23 1p rose red 6.00 1.00
96 A23 1p violet ('27) 1.40 .25
97 A23 1½p rose red ('27) 4.50 1.50
98 A23 2p gray 1.40 .25
a. "2d" and value tablet omitted 27,500.
99 A23 3p ultra ('23) 3.00 1.20
100 A23 4p blk & red, *yel* 16.00 7.00
101 A23 5p dl vio & ol grn 1.75 *2.25*
102 A23 6p dl vio & red violet 2.40 1.50

Chalky Paper

103 A23 1sh blk, *emerald* 14.00 2.75
104 A23 2sh vio & ultra, *bl* ('27) 30.00 *72.50*
105 A23 2sh6p blk & red, *bl* 12.50 *35.00*
106 A23 5sh grn & scar, *yellow* 55.00 *90.00*
Nos. 93-106 (14) 152.80 *244.20*

The only known example of No. 98a is the center stamp of an unused block of nine.

Common Design Types pictured following the introduction.

Silver Jubilee Issue
Common Design Type

1935, May 6 ***Perf. 13½x14***

110 CD301 1½p car & blue 1.00 *10.00*
111 CD301 2p gray blk & ultra 1.50 .50
112 CD301 3p blue & brown 2.75 *5.50*
113 CD301 1sh brt vio & indigo 15.00 *18.00*
Nos. 110-113 (4) 20.25 34.00
Set, never hinged 30.00

Coronation Issue
Common Design Type

1937, May 12 ***Perf. 11x11½***

114 CD302 1p dark violet .45 *1.25*
115 CD302 2p gray black .45 *2.25*
116 CD302 3p indigo .45 *2.25*
Nos. 114-116 (3) 1.35 *5.75*
Set, never hinged 2.00

Outrigger Canoe — A24

Fijian Village — A25

Outrigger Canoe A26

Map of Fiji Islands A27

Government Buildings — A27a

Canoe and Arms of Fiji — A28

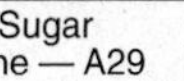

Sugar Cane — A29

Spear Fishing at Night — A30

Arms of Fiji — A31

Suva Harbor — A32

River Scene — A33

Fijian House — A34

Papaya Tree — A35

Bugler — A36

8p, 1sh5p, 1sh6p, Arms of Fiji.

Perf. 13½, 12½ (1p)

1938-55 **Engr.** **Wmk. 4**

117 A24 ½p green .25 1.00
c. Perf. 14 ('41) 16.00 6.75
d. Perf. 12 ('48) .80 *3.00*
118 A25 1p blue & brn .40 .25
119 A26 1½p rose car (empty canoe) 12.00 .50
120 A27 2p grn & org brn (no "180 degree") 40.00 .50
121 A27a 2p mag & grn .45 *.80*
a. Perf. 12 ('46) 1.25 .90

Perf. 12½, 13x12 (6p), 14 (8p)

122 A28 3p dp ultra .80 .40
123 A29 5p rose red & blue 32.50 13.00
124 A29 5p rose red & yel grn .25 .40
125 A27 6p blk (no "180 degree") 45.00 16.00
126 A31 8p rose car 1.40 *3.50*
a. Perf. 13 ('50) 1.25 *3.50*
127 A30 1sh black & yel 1.50 .90

Perf. 14

128 A31 1sh5p car & blk .25 .25
128A A31 1sh6p ultra 2.75 3.50
b. Perf. 13 ('55) 1.10 *20.00*

Perf. 12½

129 A32 2sh vio & org 2.25 .55
130 A33 2sh6p brn & grn 4.00 2.00
131 A34 5sh dk vio & grn 4.00 2.50
131A A35 10sh emer & brn org 27.50 *52.50*
131B A36 £1 car & ultra 37.50 *65.00*
Nos. 117-131B (18) 212.80 *163.55*

Issued: 1sh5p, 6/13/40; 5p, 10/1/40; No. 121, 5/19/42; 8p, 11/15/48; 10sh, £1, 3/13/50; 1sh6p, 8/1/50; others, 4/5/38.

Types of 1938-40 Redrawn

Man in Canoe — A36a

180 Degree Added to the Lower Right Hand Corner of the Design — A36b

Perf. 13½ (1½p, 2p, 6p), 14 (2½p)

1940-49 **Wmk. 4**

132 A36a 1½p rose carmine 1.00 3.00
a. Perf. 12 ('49) .80 1.60
b. Perf. 14 ('42) 14.50 22.50
133 A36b 2p grn & org brn ("180 degree") 12.50 17.50
134 A36b 2½p grn & org brn .50 1.25
a. Perf. 12 ('48) .80 .60
b. Perf. 13½ ('42) .55 1.00
135 A36b 6p blk ("180 degree") 2.50 2.00
a. Perf. 12 ('47) 1.40 1.50
Nos. 132-135 (4) 16.50 23.75

Issued: 2½p, Jan. 6, 1942; others Oct. 1, 1940.

No. 133 Surcharged in Black

1941, Feb. 10 ***Perf. 13½***

136 A27 2½p on 2p grn & org brn 1.50 1.00
Never hinged 2.50

Catalogue values for unused stamps in this section, from this point to the end of the section, are for Never Hinged items.

Peace Issue
Common Design Type

1946, Aug. 17 ***Perf. 13½***

137 CD303 2½p bright green .25 *1.50*
138 CD303 3p deep blue .50 .25

Silver Wedding Issue
Common Design Types

1948, Dec. 17 **Photo.** ***Perf. 14x14½***

139 CD304 2½p dark green .70 2.50

Engr.; Name Typo.

Perf. 11½x11

140 CD305 5sh blue violet 17.50 9.00

UPU Issue
Common Design Types
Engr.; Name Typo. on 3p, 8p
Perf. 13½, 11x11½

1949, Oct. 10 Wmk. 4

No.	Type	Denom.	Description	Unused	Used
141	CD306	2p	red violet	.35	.75
142	CD307	3p	indigo	2.25	7.50
143	CD308	8p	dp carmine	.35	*4.50*
144	CD309	1sh6p	blue	.40	*3.00*
			Nos. 141-144 (4)	3.35	15.75

Coronation Issue
Common Design Type

1953, June 2 *Perf. 13½x13*

No.	Type	Denom.	Description	Unused	Used
145	CD312	2½p	dk green & blk	1.00	.60
			Nos. 145 (1)	1.00	.60

Type of 1938-40 with Portrait of Queen Elizabeth II Inscribed: "Royal Visit 1953"

1953, Dec. 16 *Perf. 13*

No.	Type	Denom.	Description	Unused	Used
146	A31	8p	carmine lake	.65	.35

Visit of Queen Elizabeth II and the Duke of Edinburgh, 1953.

Types of 1938-50 with Portrait of Queen Elizabeth II, and

A39

Loading Copra A40

Designs: 1sh6p, Sugar cane train. 2sh, Bananas for export. 5sh, Gold industry.

Perf. 11½ (A24, A27, A39); 11½x11 (A40); 12 (A27, 2p); 12½ (A30, A33, A35, A36); 13 (A31)

1954-56 Engr.

No.	Type	Denom.	Description	Unused	Used
147	A24	½p	green	1.00	*1.60*
148	A39	1p	grnsh blue	1.90	.25
149	A39	1½p	brown	3.00	.70
150	A27a	2p	mag & green	1.35	.40
151	A39	2½p	blue vio	3.25	.25
152	A40	3p	purple & brn	5.00	.25
154	A27	6p	black	2.75	.90
155	A31	8p	carmine lake	8.50	1.90
156	A30	1sh	black & yel	3.25	.25
157	A40	1sh6p	grn & dp ultra	17.00	1.05
158	A40	2sh	brt car & blk	5.00	.65
159	A33	2sh6p	brn & bl grn	1.90	.25
160	A40	5sh	dp ultra & yel	8.50	1.30
161	A35	10sh	emer & brn org	8.00	*15.00*
162	A36	£1	car & ultra	35.00	11.00
			Nos. 147-162 (15)	105.40	35.75

Issued: 2p, 1sh, 2sh6p, 2/1/54; ½p, 6p, 8p, 10sh, £1, 7/1/54; 1p, 6/1/56; 1½p, 2½p, 3p, 1sh6p, 2sh, 5sh, 10/1/56.

Types of 1954-56 and

Nautilus Shells — A41

Hibiscus — A42

Kandavu Parrot A43

½p, 2p, 2½p, Queen Elizabeth II (A39). 1p, Queen, turtles in bottom panels. 6p, Fijian beating drum (lali). 10p, Yaqona ceremony. 1sh, South Pacific map. 2sh6p, Nadi Airport. 10sh, Cutting sugar cane. £1, Arms of Fiji.

Perf. 11½ (A39, A41); 11½x11 (A40); 14½x14 (A42); 14x14½ (A43)
Engr. (A39, A40, A41); others Photo.

1959-63 Wmk. 4

No.	Type	Denom.	Description	Unused	Used
163	A39	½p	green ('61)	.25	*2.60*
164	A41	1p	dk blue ('62)	3.75	2.60
165	A41	1½p	dk brown ('62)	3.75	2.60
166	A39	2p	crim rose ('61)	1.60	.25
167	A39	2½p	brown org ('62)	3.25	*5.00*
168	A40	6p	blk & car rose ('61)	1.90	.25
169	A42	8p	gray, red, yel & grn ('61)	.55	.30
170	A40	10p	car & brn ('63)	2.60	.65
171	A40	1sh	dk bl & bl ('61)	1.60	.25
172	A40	2sh6p	pur & blk ('61)	9.50	.25
173	A43	4sh	dk grn, red, bl & emer	3.00	1.30
174	A40	10sh	sep & emer ('61)	2.75	1.30
175	A40	£1	org & blk ('61)	5.75	3.75
			Nos. 163-175 (13)	40.25	21.10

Issued: 4sh, 7/13; 8p, 8/1; ½p, 2p, 6p, 1sh, 2sh6p, 10sh, £1, 11/14; 1p, 1½p, 2½p, 12/3; 10p, 4/1.

For type overprinted see No. 205.

Types of 1954-63 and

Elizabeth II — A44

1sh6p, 180th meridian and Intl. Date Line. 2sh, White orchids. 5sh, Orange dove.

Perf. 11½ (A41); 12½ (A44); 11½x11 (A40); 14x14½ (A43)
Engr. (A40, A41); others Photo.

1962-67 Wmk. 314

No.	Type	Denom.	Description	Unused	Used
176	A41	1p	dark blue ('64)	1.00	*3.75*
177	A39	2p	crim rose ('65)	.50	.25
178	A44	3p	rose cl & multi	.25	.25
179	A40	6p	blk & car rose ('64)	1.50	.25
180	A42	9p	ultra, red, yel & grn ('63)	.90	.65
181	A40	10p	car & brn ('64)	.60	.50
182	A40	1sh	dk bl & bl ('66)	2.25	.45
183	A43	1sh6p	dk bl & multi	1.50	.60
184	A42	2sh	gold, yel grn & grn	10.00	3.50
185	A40	2sh6p	pur & blk ('65)	5.50	1.25
186	A43	4sh	grn & multi, wmk. sideways ('67)	4.25	1.00
a.			As #186, wmk. upright ('64)	7.50	2.00
b.			4sh dark green & multi ('66)	6.00	2.50
187	A43	5sh	dk gray, yel & red	10.00	.35
188	A40	10sh	sep & emer ('64)	7.50	2.50
189	A40	£1	org & blk ('64)	14.00	7.00
			Nos. 176-189 (14)	59.75	22.30

Issued: 3p, 1sh6p, 2sh, 5sh, 12/3; 9p, No. 186a, 4/1; 1p, 10p, 10sh, 1/14; 6p, £1, 6/9; 2p, 2sh6p, 8/3; No. 186b, 3/1; No. 186, 2/16.

Nos. 178 and 171 Overprinted

1963, Feb. 1

No.	Type	Denom.	Description	Unused	Used
196	A44	3p	multicolored	.50	.35
197	A40	1sh	dark blue & blue	.65	.35

Visit of Elizabeth II & Prince Philip, Feb. 3.

Freedom from Hunger Issue
Common Design Type

1963, June 4 Photo. *Perf. 14x14½*

No.	Type	Denom.	Description	Unused	Used
198	CD314	2sh	ultramarine	3.50	2.25

Running A45

9p, Throwing the discus, vert. 1sh, Field hockey, vert. 2sh6p, Women's high jump.

Perf. 14½x14, 14x14½

1963, Aug. 6 Wmk. 314

No.	Type	Denom.	Description	Unused	Used
199	A45	3p	yel, blk & brn	.45	.25
200	A45	9p	violet, blk & brn	.45	1.00
201	A45	1sh	green, blk & brn	.45	.25
202	A45	2sh6p	blue, blk & brn	1.10	.95
			Nos. 199-202 (4)	2.45	2.45

1st So. Pacific Games, Suva, 8/29-9/7.

Red Cross Centenary Issue
Common Design Type

1963, Sept. 2 Litho. *Perf. 13*

No.	Type	Denom.	Description	Unused	Used
203	CD315	2p	black & red	1.00	.30
204	CD315	2sh	ultra & red	2.25	2.50

Type of 1959-63 Overprinted

1963, Dec. 2 Engr. *Perf. 11½x11*

No.	Type	Denom.	Description	Unused	Used
205	A40	1sh	dark blue & blue	1.00	.35

Opening of the Commonwealth Pacific (telephone) Cable service, COMPAC.

Fiji Scout Badge — A46

Scouts of India, Fiji and Europe Tying Knot — A47

1964, Aug. 3 Photo. *Perf. 12½*

No.	Type	Denom.	Description	Unused	Used
206	A46	3p	multicolored	.50	.50
207	A47	1sh	ocher & purple	.65	.65

50th anniv. of the founding of the Fiji Boy Scouts.

Amphibian "Aotearoa," 1939 — A48

Map of Fiji and Tonga Islands and Plane A49

Design: 6p, Heron plane.

1964, Oct. 24 *Perf. 12½, 14½*

No.	Type	Denom.	Description	Unused	Used
208	A48	3p	brt red & black	.50	.35
209	A48	6p	ultra & red	.85	.85
210	A49	1sh	grnsh blue & black	.85	.85
			Nos. 208-210 (3)	2.20	2.05

Fiji-Tonga airmail service, 25th anniv.

ITU Issue
Common Design Type
Perf. 11x11½

1965, May 17 Litho. Wmk. 314

No.	Type	Denom.	Description	Unused	Used
211	CD317	3p	blue & rose red	.50	.30
212	CD317	2sh	yel & bister	1.50	.75

Intl. Cooperation Year Issue
Common Design Type

1965, Oct. 25 *Perf. 14½*

No.	Type	Denom.	Description	Unused	Used
213	CD318	2p	blue grn & claret	.35	.25
214	CD318	2sh6p	lt vio & grn	1.60	1.00

Churchill Memorial Issue
Common Design Type

1966, Jan. 24 Photo. *Perf. 14*
Design in Black, Gold and Carmine Rose

No.	Type	Denom.	Description	Unused	Used
215	CD319	3p	brt blue	.75	.25
216	CD319	9p	green	1.10	1.25
217	CD319	1sh	brown	1.10	.25
218	CD319	2sh6p	violet	1.45	1.25
			Nos. 215-218 (4)	4.40	3.00

World Cup Soccer Issue
Common Design Type

1966, July 1 Litho. *Perf. 14*

No.	Type	Denom.	Description	Unused	Used
219	CD321	2p	multicolored	.30	.25
220	CD321	2sh	multicolored	1.40	.35

H.M.S. Pandora and Split Island, Rotuma A50

Designs: 10p, Rotuma chiefs, Pandora, and Rotuma's position in Pacific. 1sh6p, Rotuma islanders welcoming Pandora.

1966, Aug. 29 Photo. *Perf. 14x13*

No.	Type	Denom.	Description	Unused	Used
221	A50	3p	multicolored	.40	.25
222	A50	10p	multicolored	.40	.25
223	A50	1sh6p	multicolored	.65	.95
			Nos. 221-223 (3)	1.45	1.45

175th anniv. of the discovery of Rotuma, a group of eight islands forming part of the colony of Fiji.

WHO Headquarters Issue
Common Design Type

1966, Sept. 20 Litho. *Perf. 14*

No.	Type	Denom.	Description	Unused	Used
224	CD322	6p	multicolored	1.45	.30
225	CD322	2sh6p	multicolored	3.25	3.00
			Nos. 224-225 (2)	4.70	3.30

Woman Runner A51

Designs: 9p, Shot put, vert. 1sh, Diver.

1966, Dec. 8 Photo. *Perf. 14x14½*

No.	Type	Denom.	Description	Unused	Used
226	A51	3p	ol, black & lt brn	.25	.25
227	A51	9p	brt blue, blk & brn	.35	.35
228	A51	1sh	blue green & multi	.40	.40
			Nos. 226-228 (3)	1.00	1.00

2nd South Pacific Games, Noumea, New Caledonia, Dec. 8-18.

Military Band A52

Intl. Tourist Year: 9p, Reef diving. 1sh, Beqa fire walkers. 2sh, Liner Oriana and Mt. Rama volcano.

1967, Oct. 20 *Perf. 14x13*

No.	Type	Denom.	Description	Unused	Used
229	A52	3p	multi & gold	.60	.25
230	A52	9p	multi & silver	.30	.25
231	A52	1sh	multi & gold	.30	.25
232	A52	2sh	multi & silver	.60	.30
			Nos. 229-232 (4)	1.80	1.05

Admiral Bligh, H.M.S. Providence and Old Map of "Feejee" A53

Designs: 1sh, Bligh's longboat being chased by double canoe and map of Fiji Islands. 2sh6p, Bligh's tomb, St. Mary's Cemetery, Lambeth, London.

Perf. 15x14, 12½x13 (1sh)

1967, Dec. 7 Photo. Wmk. 314

Size: 35x21mm

233	A53	4p emer, blk & yel	.25	.25

Size: 54x20mm

234	A53	1sh brt bl, brn org & blk	.40	.25

Size: 35x21mm

235	A53	2sh6p sepia & multi	.40	.30
		Nos. 233-235 (3)	1.05	.80

150th anniv. of the death of Adm. William Bligh (1754-1817), captain of the Bounty and principal discoverer of the Fiji Islands.

Simmonds "Spartan" Seaplane — A54

Designs: 6p, Fiji Airways Hawker-Siddeley H748 and emblems of various airlines. 1sh, Fokker "Southern Cross," Capt. Charles Kingsford-Smith, his crew and Southern Cross constellation. 2sh, Lockheed Altair "Lady Southern Cross."

Perf. 14x14½

1968, June 5 Wmk. 314

236	A54	2p green & black	.25	.25
237	A54	6p brt blue, car & blk	.25	.25
238	A54	1sh dp violet & green	.30	.25
239	A54	2sh org brn & dk blue	.50	.25
		Nos. 236-239 (4)	1.30	1.00

40th anniv. of the first Trans-Pacific Flight through Fiji under Capt. Charles Kingsford-Smith.

Fijian Bures — A55

Eastern Reef Heron — A56

1p, Passion fruit flowers. 2p, Nautilus pompilius shell. 4p, Hawk moth. 6p, Reef butterflyfish. 9p, Bamboo raft (bilibili). 10p, Tiger moth. 1sh, Black marlin. 1sh6p, Orange-breasted honey eaters. 2sh, Ringed sea snake, horiz. 2sh6p, Outrigger canoes (takia), horiz. 3sh, Golden cowrie shell. 4sh, Emperor gold mine and gold ore. 5sh, Bamboo orchids, horiz. 10sh, Tabua (ceremonial whale's tooth). £1, Coat of Arms and Queen Elizabeth II, horiz.

Perf. 13½ (A55), 14 (A56)

1968, July 15 Photo. Wmk. 314

240	A55	½p multicolored	.25	.25
241	A55	1p multicolored	.25	.25
242	A55	2p multicolored	.25	.25
243	A56	3p multicolored	.45	.25
244	A55	4p multicolored	.95	1.60
245	A55	6p multicolored	.30	.25
246	A55	9p multicolored	.25	1.60
247	A55	10p multicolored	1.50	.25
248	A56	1sh multicolored	.25	.25
249	A56	1sh6p multicolored	5.50	4.50
250	A56	2sh multicolored	.90	1.60
251	A56	2sh6p multicolored	.90	.30
252	A55	3sh multicolored	1.90	4.75
253	A56	4sh multicolored	4.25	2.25
254	A56	5sh multicolored	2.40	1.25
255	A56	10sh multicolored	1.25	2.40
256	A56	£1 red & multi	1.50	2.40
		Nos. 240-256 (17)	23.05	24.40

See Nos. 260-276.

WHO Emblem, Map of Fiji and Nurses — A57

WHO Emblem and: 9p, Medical team loading patient on stretcher on dinghy and medical ship "Vuniwai." 3sh, People playing on beach.

1968, Dec. 9 Litho. *Perf. 14*

257	A57	3p blue green & multi	.25	.25
258	A57	9p brt blue & multi	.40	.40
259	A57	3sh dk blue & multi	.60	.60
		Nos. 257-259 (3)	1.25	1.25

WHO, 20th anniv.

Types of 1968
Values in Cents and Dollars

Designs: 1c, Passion fruit flowers. 2c, Nautilus pompilius shell. 3c, Reef heron. 4c, Hawk moth. 5c, Reef butterflyfish. 6c, Fijian bures. 8c, Bamboo raft. 9c, Tiger moth. 10c, Black marlin. 15c, Orange-breasted honey-eater. 20c, Ringed sea snake, horiz. 25c, Outrigger canoes (takia), horiz. 30c, Golden cowrie shell. 40c Emperor gold mine and gold ore. 50c, Bamboo orchids, horiz. $1, Tabua (ceremonial whale's tooth). $2, Coat of Arms and Queen Elizabeth II, horiz.

Perf. 13½ (A55), 14 (A56)

1969, Jan. 13 Photo. Wmk. 314

260	A55	1c multicolored	.25	.25
261	A55	2c multicolored	.25	.25
262	A56	3c multicolored	1.25	1.00
263	A55	4c multicolored	1.50	1.00
264	A55	5c multicolored	.25	.25
265	A55	6c multicolored	.25	.25
266	A55	8c multicolored	.25	.25
267	A55	9c multicolored	1.50	*2.25*
268	A56	10c multicolored	.25	.25
269	A56	15c multicolored	6.50	6.00
270	A56	20c multicolored	1.25	.80
271	A56	25c multicolored	1.00	.25
272	A55	30c multicolored	3.50	1.50
273	A56	40c multicolored	7.50	4.00
274	A56	50c multicolored	2.00	.25
275	A56	$1 multicolored	1.50	.40
276	A56	$2 red & multi	3.00	1.50
		Nos. 260-276 (17)	32.00	20.45

For overprints & surcharges see Nos. 286-288, B5-B6.

Nos. 274 and 275 exist on glazed paper. Values, set: $15 unused, $5 used.

Fiji Soldiers and Map of Solomon Islands A58

Designs: 10c, Flags of Fiji Military Force, soldiers in full and battle dress. 25c, Cpl. Sefanaia Sukanaivalu and Victoria Cross.

1969, June 23 Wmk. 314 *Perf. 14*

277	A58	3c emerald & multi	.50	.25
278	A58	10c red & multi	.55	.25
279	A58	25c black & multi	.85	.45
		Nos. 277-279 (3)	1.90	.95

25th anniv. of the Fiji Military Forces campaign in the Solomon Islands and of the posthumous award of the Victoria Cross to Cpl. Sefanaia Sukanaivalu.

Yachting — A59

Designs: 4c, Javelin. 20c, Winners and South Pacific Games medal.

1969, Aug. 18 Photo. *Perf. 14½x14*

280	A59	4c red, brown & blk	.30	.30
281	A59	8c blue & black	.40	.40
282	A59	20c ol grn, blk & ocher	.50	.50
		Nos. 280-282 (3)	1.20	1.20

3rd South Pacific Games, Port Moresby, Papua New Guinea, Aug. 13-23.

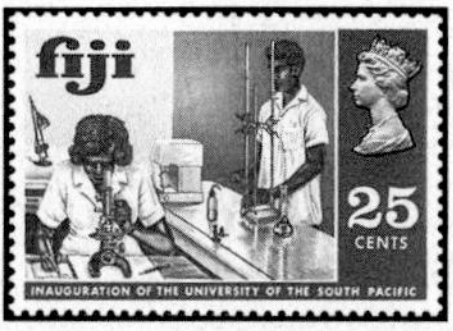

Students in Laboratory — A60

2c, Map of South Pacific and mortarboard. 8c, Site of University at Royal New Zealand Air Force Seaplane Station, Laucala Bay, RNZAF badge and Sunderland flying boat.

1969, Nov. 10 *Perf. 14x14½*

283	A60	2c multicolored	.25	.25
284	A60	8c red & multi	.35	.35
285	A60	25c dk green & multi	.80	.75
		Nos. 283-285 (3)	1.40	1.35

Inauguration of the University of the South Pacific, Laucala Bay, Suva.

Nos. 261, 268 and 271 Overprinted

1970, Mar. 4 *Perf. 13½, 14*

286	A55	2c multicolored	.30	*.40*
287	A56	10c multicolored	.40	.30
288	A55	25c multicolored	.80	.80
		Nos. 286-288 (3)	1.50	1.50

Visit of Queen Elizabeth II, Prince Philip and Princess Anne, Mar. 4-5.

Nuns Sitting under Chaulmoogra Tree, and Chaulmoogra Fruit — A61

Designs: 10c, Paintings by Semisi Maya (former patient). No. 290, Cascade, vert. No. 291, Sea urchins, vert. 30c, Aerial view of Makogai Hospital.

Perf. 14x14½, 14½x14

1970, May 25 Photo. Wmk. 314

289	A61	2c brt pink & multi	.25	.55
290	A61	10c gray green & blk	.50	.55
291	A61	10c blue, car & blk	.50	.55
	a.	Pair, #290-291	1.00	1.10
292	A61	30c orange & multi	1.00	.60
		Nos. 289-292 (4)	2.25	2.25

Closing of the Leprosy Hospital on Makogai Island in 1969.

Abel Tasman and Ship's Log, 1643 — A62

3c, Capt. James Cook & "Endeavour." 8c, Capt. William Bligh & longboat, 1789. 25c, Man of Fiji & Fijian ocean-going canoe.

1970, Aug. 18 Litho. *Perf. 13x12½*

293	A62	2c blue green & multi	.75	.55
294	A62	3c gray green & multi	1.25	.55
295	A62	8c multicolored	1.25	.45
296	A62	25c dull lilac & multi	.75	.45
		Nos. 293-296 (4)	4.00	2.00

Discoverers and explorers of Fiji Islands.

King Cakobau and Cession Stone at Lavuka A63

Designs: 3c, Chinese, Fijian, Indian and European children. 10c, Prime Minister Ratu Sir Kamisese Mara and flag of Fiji. 25c, Fijian male dancer and Indian female dancer.

1970, Oct. 10 Wmk. 314 *Perf. 14*

297	A63	2c multicolored	.25	.25
298	A63	3c multicolored	.25	.25
299	A63	10c multicolored	1.10	.25
300	A63	25c multicolored	.30	.30
		Nos. 297-300 (4)	1.90	1.05

Fijian independence.

Fiji Nos. 1 and 3 — A64

15c, Fiji #15, 44, 59, 81, 127, 166. 20c, Fiji Times Office, Levuka, & G. P. O., Suva.

1970, Nov. 2 Photo. *Perf. 14½x14*

Size: 35x21mm

301	A64	4c multicolored	.30	.25

Size: 60x21½mm

302	A64	15c multicolored	.75	.30

Size: 35x21mm

303	A64	20c multicolored	.75	.30
		Nos. 301-303 (3)	1.80	.85

Centenary of first postage stamps of Fiji.

Gray-backed White Eyes — A65

Yellow-breasted Musk Parrots — A66

Designs: 1c, Cirrhopetalum umbellatum. 2c, Cardinal honey eaters. 3c, Calanthe furcata.4c, Bulbophyllum. 6c, Phaius tancarvilliae. 8c,Blue-crested broadbills. 10c, Acanthephippiumvitiense. 15c, Dendrobium tokai. 20c, Slaty flycatchers. 25c, Kandavu honey eaters. 30c, Dendrobium gordonii. 50c, White-throated pigeon. $1, Collared lories (kula). $2, Dendrobium platygastrium. (Orchids shown on 1c, 3c, 4c, 6c, 10c, 15c, 30c, $2.)

Wmk. 314 Upright

1971-72 Litho. *Perf. 13½x14*

305	A65	1c blk & multi ('72)	.25	.30
306	A65	2c carmine & multi	.45	.25
307	A65	3c multi ('72)	.85	.25
308	A65	4c blk & multi ('72)	.65	1.75
309	A65	5c brown & multi	.35	.25
310	A65	6c lt bl & multi ('72)	4.75	6.00
311	A65	8c black & multi	.35	.25
312	A65	10c multi ('72)	.35	.25
313	A65	15c multi ('72)	4.75	1.00
314	A65	20c gray & multi	1.35	.30

Perf. 14

315	A66	25c sepia & multi	3.75	.25
316	A66	30c grn & multi ('72)	8.75	.85
317	A66	40c blue & multi	4.00	.45
318	A66	50c gray & multi	2.60	.45
319	A66	$1 red & multi	3.50	.85
320	A66	$2 multi ('72)	2.75	8.00
		Nos. 305-320 (16)	39.45	21.45

Issued: 5c, 20c, 40c, 50c, 8/6; 2c, 8c, 25c, $1, 11/22; 1c, 10c, 30c, $2, 1/4; 3c, 4c, 6c, 15c, 6/23.

1972-74 Wmk. 314 Sideways

306c	A65	2c ('73)	.40	*9.00*
307a	A65	3c ('73)	2.25	.50
308a	A65	4c ('73)	5.50	.85
309a	A65	5c ('73)	7.75	3.75
310a	A65	6c ('73)	9.75	1.40
311a	A65	8c ('73)	3.50	.80
313a	A65	15c ('73)	5.00	2.50
314a	A65	20c	13.50	2.10
315a	A66	25c ('73)	1.75	.95
317a	A66	40c ('74)	2.75	*9.50*

318a A66 50c ('74) 2.75 *4.00*
319a A66 $1 2.75 *4.50*
320a A66 $2 2.75 *4.50*
Nos. 306c-320a (13) 60.40 44.35

Issued: 20c, $1, $2, 11/17; 3c, 5c, 3/8; 4c, 6c, 8c, 15c, 25c, 4/11; 2c, 12/12; 40c, 50c, 3/15.

1975-77 Wmk. 373

305b A65 1c 1.00 *4.50*
306d A65 2c .80 *4.50*
307b A65 3c .45 *4.50*
308b A65 4c ('76) 3.50 .25
309b A65 5c 1.30 *4.75*
310b A65 6c ('76) 2.90 .25
311b A65 8c ('76) .35 .25
312b A65 10c .40 *2.50*
313b A65 15c ('76) 2.60 .50
314b A65 20c ('77) 3.75 .60
316b A66 30c ('76) 5.00 1.10
317b A66 40c ('76) 4.50 .65
318b A66 50c ('76) 3.00 .65
319b A66 $1 ('76) 3.00 1.05
320b A66 $2 ('76) 1.45 1.05
Nos. 305b-320b (15) 34.00 27.10

Issued: 1c, 2c, 3c, 5c, 10c, 4/9; 20c, 7/15; others, 9/3.

Women's Basketball — A67

1971, Sept. 6 Wmk. 314 *Perf. 14*

321 A67 8c shown .25 .25
322 A67 10c Running .50 .50
323 A67 25c Weight lifting 1.00 .95
Nos. 321-323 (3) 1.75 1.70

4th South Pacific Games, Papeete, French Polynesia, Sept. 8-19.

Community Education — A68

Designs: 4c, Public health. 50c, Economic growth (farm scenes).

1972, Feb. 7

324 A68 2c bright rose & multi .25 .25
325 A68 4c gray & multi .25 .25
326 A68 50c bright blue & multi 1.05 1.05
Nos. 324-326 (3) 1.55 1.55

South Pacific Commission, 25th anniv.

Arts Festival Emblem — A69

1972, Apr. 10

327 A69 10c blue, org & black .40 .40

South Pacific Festival of Arts, May 6-20.

Silver Wedding Issue, 1972

Common Design Type

Queen Elizabeth II, Prince Philip, flowers, shells.

1972, Nov. 20 Photo. *Perf. 14x14½*

328 CD324 10c slate grn & multi .25 .25
329 CD324 25c red lilac & multi .45 .45
a. Blue omitted *550.00*

On No. 329a, Prince Philip's coat is brown instead of blue.

Rugby — A70

1973, Mar. 9 Litho. *Perf. 14*

330 A70 2c shown .40 .40
331 A70 8c Tackle .80 .80
332 A70 25c Kicking ball 1.05 1.05
Nos. 330-332 (3) 2.25 2.25

60th anniversary of Fiji Rugby Union.

Forestry Development — A71

Development projects: 8c, Irrigation of rice field. 10c, Low income housing. 25c, Highway construction.

1973, July 23 *Perf. 14*

333 A71 5c multicolored .25 *.45*
334 A71 8c multicolored .35 .25
335 A71 10c multicolored .40 .25
336 A71 25c multicolored .70 *.75*
Nos. 333-336 (4) 1.70 1.70

Holy Family — A72

Festivals: 10c, Diwali (Candles; Indian New Year). 20c, Id-Ul-Fitar (Friendly greeting and mosque; Moslem, Ramadan). 25c, Chinese New Year (dragon dance).

1973, Oct. 26 *Perf. 14x14½*

337 A72 3c blue & multi .30 .25
338 A72 10c purple & multi .30 .25
339 A72 20c emerald & multi .55 *.60*
340 A72 25c red & multi .55 *.60*
Nos. 337-340 (4) 1.70 1.70

Festivals celebrated by various groups in Fiji.

Runners — A73

1974, Jan. 7

341 A73 3c shown .40 .25
342 A73 8c Boxing .40 .25
343 A73 50c Lawn bowling 1.20 *1.50*
Nos. 341-343 (3) 2.00 2.00

10th British Commonwealth Games, Christchurch, N.Z., Jan. 24-Feb. 2.

Centenary of Cricket in Fiji — A74

Designs: 3c, Bowler. 25c, Batsman and wicketkeeper. 40c, Fielder, horiz.

Perf. 14x14½, 14½x14

1974, Feb. 21 Litho.

344 A74 3c multicolored 1.10 .25
345 A74 25c multicolored 1.35 .25
346 A74 40c multicolored 1.60 *2.25*
Nos. 344-346 (3) 4.05 2.75

Mailman and UPU Emblem A75

UPU Emblem and: 8c, Loading mail on ship. 30c, Post office and truck. 50c, Jet.

1974, May 22 Wmk. 314 *Perf. 14*

347 A75 3c orange & multi .25 .25
348 A75 8c multicolored .30 .25
349 A75 30c lt blue & multi .45 .40
350 A75 50c multicolored .90 *1.00*
Nos. 347-350 (4) 1.90 1.90

Centenary of the Universal Postal Union.

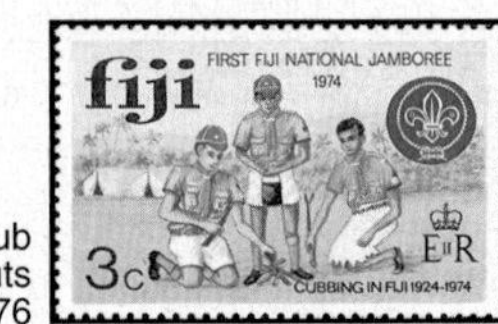

Cub Scouts A76

Designs: 10c, Boy Scouts reading map. 40c, Scouts and Fiji flag, vert.

1974, Aug. 30

351 A76 3c multicolored .25 .25
352 A76 10c multicolored .50 .25
353 A76 40c multicolored 1.25 1.80
Nos. 351-353 (3) 2.00 2.30

First National Boy Scout Jamboree, Lautoka, Viti Levu Island.

Cakobau Club and Flag — A77

King Cakobau, Queen Victoria A78

Design: 50c, Signing ceremony at Levuka.

1974, Oct. 9 Litho. *Perf. 13½x13*

354 A77 3c multicolored .25 .25
355 A78 8c multicolored .25 .25
356 A78 50c multicolored .60 .60
Nos. 354-356 (3) 1.10 1.10

Deed of Cession, cent. and 4th anniv. of independence.

Diwali, Hindu Festival of Lights — A79

Designs: 15c, Id-Ul-Fitar (women exchanging greetings under moon). 25c, Chinese New Year (girl twirling streamer, and fireworks). 30c, Christmas (man and woman singing hymns, and star).

1975, Oct. 31 Wmk. 373 *Perf. 14*

357 A79 3c black & multi .25 .25
358 A79 15c black & multi .45 .25
359 A79 25c black & multi .85 .25
360 A79 30c black & multi 1.10 1.90
a. Souvenir sheet of 4, #357-360 4.50 4.50
Nos. 357-360 (4) 2.65 2.65

Festivals celebrated by various groups in Fiji.

Steam Locomotive No. 21 — A80

Sugar mill trains: 15c, Diesel locomotive No. 8. 20c, Diesel locomotive No. 1. 30c, Free passenger train.

1976, Jan. 26 Litho. *Perf. 14½*

361 A80 4c yellow & multi .45 .25
362 A80 15c salmon & multi .85 .40
363 A80 20c multicolored .95 1.00
364 A80 30c blue & multi 1.20 1.80
Nos. 361-364 (4) 3.45 3.45

Fiji Blind Society and Rotary Emblems A81

Rotary Intl. of Fiji, 40th Anniv.: 25c, Ambulance and Rotary emblems.

Perf. 13x13½

1976, Mar. 26 Wmk. 373

365 A81 10c lt green, brn, ultra .25 .25
366 A81 25c multicolored .65 .65

De Havilland Drover — A82

Planes: 15c, BAC One-Eleven. 25c, Hawker-Siddeley 748. 30c, Britten Norman Trislander.

1976, Sept. 1 Litho. *Perf. 14*

367 A82 4c multicolored .60 .25
368 A82 15c multicolored 1.10 1.10
369 A82 25c multicolored 1.25 1.25
370 A82 30c multicolored 1.40 *1.75*
Nos. 367-370 (4) 4.35 4.35

Fiji air service, 25th anniversary.

Queen's Visit, 1970 — A83

Designs: 25c, King Edward's Chair. 30c, Queen wearing cloth-of-gold supertunica.

1977, Feb. 7 Litho. *Perf. 14x13½*

371 A83 10c silver & multi .25 .25
372 A83 25c silver & multi .30 .25
373 A83 30c silver & multi .40 .30
Nos. 371-373 (3) .95 .80

25th anniv. of reign of Elizabeth II.

World Map, Sinusoidal Projection — A84

Design: 30c, Map showing Fiji Islands.

Wmk. 373

1977, Apr. 12 Litho. *Perf. 14½*

374 A84 4c multicolored .25 .25
375 A84 30c multicolored .60 .60

First Joint Council of Ministers Conference of the European Economic Community (EEC) and of African, Caribbean and Pacific States (ACP).

Hibiscus A85

1977, Aug. 27 Wmk. 373 *Perf. 14*

376 A85 4c red .25 .25
377 A85 15c orange .25 .25
378 A85 30c pink .45 .30
379 A85 35c yellow .75 *.90*
Nos. 376-379 (4) 1.70 1.70

Fiji Hibiscus Festival, 21st anniversary.

Drua, Double Canoe A86

Canoes: 15c, Tabilai. 25c, Takia, dugout outrigger canoe. 40c, Camakau.

1977, Nov. 7 Litho. *Perf. 14½*

380 A86 4c multicolored .25 .25
381 A86 15c multicolored .35 .30
382 A86 25c multicolored .50 .45
383 A86 40c multicolored .60 *.70*
Nos. 380-383 (4) 1.70 1.70

Elizabeth II Coronation Anniversary Issue

Common Design Types
Souvenir Sheet

Unwmk.

1978, Apr. 21 Litho. *Perf. 15*

384 Sheet of 6 1.75 1.75
a. CD326 25c White hart of Richard II .25 .25
b. CD327 25c Elizabeth II .25 .25
c. CD328 25c Banded iguana .25 .25

No. 384 contains 2 se-tenant strips of Nos. 348a-348c, separated by horizontal gutter.

Southern Cross on Naselai Beach — A87

4c, Fiji Defence Force surrounding Southern Cross. 25c, Wright Flyer. 30c, Bristol F2B.

1978, June 26 Wmk. 373 *Perf. 14½*

385 A87 4c multicolored .25 .25
386 A87 15c multicolored .40 .30
387 A87 25c multicolored .75 .60
388 A87 30c multicolored 1.10 .75
Nos. 385-388 (4) 2.50 1.90

50th anniv. of Kingsford-Smith's Trans-Pacific flight, May 31-June 10, 1928 (4c, 15c); 75th anniv. of Wright brothers' first powered flight, Dec. 17, 1903 (25c); 60th anniv. of Royal Air Force, Apr. 1, 1918 (30c).

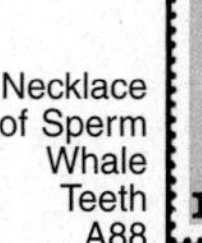

Necklace of Sperm Whale Teeth A88

Fiji artifacts: 4c, Wooden oil dish in shape of man, vert. 25c, Twin water bottles. 30c, Carved throwing club (Ula), vert.

1978, Aug. 14 Litho. *Perf. 14*

389 A88 4c multicolored .25 .25
390 A88 15c multicolored .25 .25
391 A88 25c multicolored .30 .30
392 A88 30c multicolored .45 .45
Nos. 389-392 (4) 1.25 1.25

Christmas Wreath and Candles A89

Festivals: 15c, Diwali (oil lamps). 25c, Id-Ul-Fitr (fruit, coffeepot and cups). 40c, Chinese New Year (paper dragon).

1978, Oct. 30 *Perf. 14*

393 A89 4c multicolored .25 .25
394 A89 15c multicolored .25 .25
395 A89 25c multicolored .35 .35
396 A89 40c multicolored .55 .55
Nos. 393-396 (4) 1.40 1.40

Banded Iguana A90

Endangered species and Wildlife Fund emblem: 15c, Tree frog. 25c, Long-legged warbler. 30c, Pink-billed parrot finch.

1979, Mar. 19 Litho. Wmk. 373

397 A90 4c multicolored 1.25 .50
398 A90 15c multicolored 2.00 1.00
399 A90 25c multicolored 8.75 1.50
400 A90 30c multicolored 8.75 5.00
Nos. 397-400 (4) 20.75 8.00

Indian Women Making Music A91

15c, Indian men sitting around kava bowl. 30c, Indian sugar cane, houses. 40c, Sailing ship Leonidas, map of South Pacific.

1979, May 11 Wmk. 373 *Perf. 14*

401 A91 4c multicolored .25 .25
402 A91 15c multicolored .25 .25
403 A91 30c multicolored .35 .35
404 A91 40c multicolored .50 .50
Nos. 401-404 (4) 1.35 1.35

Arrival of Indians as indentured laborers, cent.

Soccer A92

Games Emblem and: 15c, Rugby. 30c, Tennis. 40c, Weight lifting.

1979, July 2 Litho. *Perf. 14*

405 A92 4c multicolored .30 .25
406 A92 15c multicolored .40 .30
407 A92 30c multicolored .80 .65
408 A92 40c multicolored .95 1.25
Nos. 405-408 (4) 2.45 2.45

6th South Pacific Games.

Old Town Hall, Suva A93

2c, Dudley Church, Suva. 3c, Telecommunications building, Suva. 4c, 5c, Lautoka Mosque. 6c, GPO, Suva. 8c, 12c, Levuka Public School. 10c, Visitors' Bureau, Suva. 15c, Colonial War Memorial Hospital Suva. 18c, Labasa Sugar Mill. 20c, Rewa Bridge, Nausori. 30c Sacred Heart Cathedral, Suva. 35c Grand Pacific Hotel, Suva. 45c, Shiva Temple, Suva. 50c Serua Island Village. $1, Solo Lighthouse. $2, Baker memorial Hall, Nausori. $5, Government House.

Without Inscribed Date, except #411B (1991)

Chalky Paper (#409-411, 414, 416, 418-419, 425)

Ordinary Paper (#412-413, 415, 417, 420-424)

1979-94 Wmk. 373 *Perf. 14*

409 A93 1c multicolored .30 .60
a. Ordinary paper 1.75 2.00
b. Inscribed "1994" 2.00 3.00
410 A93 2c multicolored .90 .75
a. Ordinary paper 1.75 2.00
b. Inscribed "1983" 1.00 .50
c. Inscribed "1986" 1.50 .25
d. Inscribed "1991" .75 .75
e. Inscribed "1993" 3.50 3.50
f. Inscribed "1994" 1.00 1.50
411 A93 3c multicolored .75 .75
a. Ordinary paper 2.00 2.00
b. Inscribed "1993" 4.50 4.50
411B A93 4c multicolored 1.50 1.50
a. Inscribed "1993" 6.00 6.00
b. Inscribed "1994" 3.50 5.50
412 A93 5c multicolored .25 .25
a. Inscribed "1983" .60 .25
413 A93 6c multicolored .25 .75
a. Inscribed "1983" .30 .25
414 A93 10c multicolored .40 .25
a. Ordinary paper 2.00 1.75
b. Inscribed "1991" 2.75 3.00
415 A93 12c multicolored .40 2.75
a. Inscribed "1993" 3.50 4.00
b. Inscribed "1994" 2.00 3.50
416 A93 15c multicolored .75 .60
a. Ordinary paper 1.75 1.75
b. Inscribed "1991" 3.50 3.00
417 A93 18c multicolored .30 .25
418 A93 20c multicolored 1.00 .30
a. Ordinary paper 2.50 2.00
b. Inscribed "1993" 3.75 3.75
c. Inscribed "1994" 3.50 3.50
419 A93 30c multi, vert. 1.25 .50
a. Ordinary paper .60 1.75
420 A93 35c multicolored .60 *1.50*
421 A93 45c multicolored .45 .45
422 A93 50c multicolored .60 .40
a. Inscribed "1994" 3.50 4.00

Perf. 14x13½, 13½x14

Size: 45x29mm, 29x45mm (#423)

423 A93 $1 multi, vert. 1.50 *2.50*
424 A93 $2 multicolored 1.50 *1.75*
425 A93 $5 multicolored 2.50 *2.75*
Nos. 409-425 (18) 15.20 18.60

Issued: 5c, 6c, 12c, 18c, 35c-$2, 12/22/80; No. 411B, 11/1991; others, 11/11/79.

1986-92 Wmk. 384

With Date Inscription

1986

410g A93 2c multicolored 1.25 1.25
413B A93 8c multicolored 4.50 4.50

1988

410h A93 2c multicolored 1.00 1.00
411h A93 3c multicolored 1.00 1.00
411Bh A93 4c multicolored 1.00 1.00
418h A93 20c multicolored 2.00 2.00

1990

414i A93 10c multicolored 1.50 1.50
418i A93 20c multicolored 2.00 2.00

1991

409j A93 1c multicolored 1.75 3.50
410j A93 2c multicolored 1.00 1.00
411j A93 3c multicolored 1.75 1.75
411Bj A93 4c multicolored 1.00 1.00
414j A93 10c multicolored 2.00 2.00
416j A93 15c multicolored 1.00 1.00
420j A93 35c multicolored 2.75 2.75
422j A93 50c multicolored 3.75 3.75
423j A93 $1 multi, vert. 9.00 9.00

1992

409k A93 1c multicolored 2.00 2.00
411k A93 3c multicolored 3.75 3.75
411Bk A93 4c multicolored 3.75 3.75
416k A93 15c multicolored 2.75 2.75
418k A93 20c multicolored 5.50 5.50
420k A93 35c multicolored 5.50 5.50
422k A93 50c multicolored 5.50 5.50
423k A93 $1 multi, vert. 11.00 11.00

Southern Cross, 1873, London 1980 Emblem A94

1980, Apr. 28 Wmk. 373 *Perf. 13½*

426 A94 6c shown .25 .25
427 A94 20c Levuka, 1910 .35 .25
428 A94 45c Matua, 1936 .70 .50
429 A94 50c Oronsay, 1951 .70 *1.00*
Nos. 426-429 (4) 2.00 2.00

London 80 Intl. Stamp Exhib., May 6-14.

Sovi Bay A95

Designs: 20c, Yanuca Island, evening scene. 45c, Dravuni Beach. 50c, Wakaya Island.

1980, Aug. 18 *Perf. 13½x14*

430 A95 6c shown .25 .25
431 A95 20c multicolored .25 .25
432 A95 45c multicolored .40 .40
433 A95 50c multicolored .40 .40
Nos. 430-433 (4) 1.30 1.30

Opening of Parliament, 1979 — A96

1980, Oct. 6 Litho. *Perf. 13*

434 A96 6c shown .25 .25
435 A96 20c Coat of arms, vert. .35 .25
436 A96 45c Fiji flag .50 .50
437 A96 50c Elizabeth II, vert. .60 .65
Nos. 434-437 (4) 1.70 1.65

Independence, 10th anniversary.

Coastal Scene, by Semisi Maya A97

Intl. Year of the Disabled: Paintings and portrait of disabled artist Semisi Maya.

1981, Apr. 21 Wmk. 373 *Perf. 14*

438 A97 6c shown .25 .25
439 A97 35c Underwater Scene .35 .35
440 A97 50c Maya Painting, vert. .45 .45
441 A97 60c Peacock, vert. .50 .50
Nos. 438-441 (4) 1.55 1.55

Royal Wedding Issue

Common Design Type

1981, July 22 Wmk. 373 *Perf. 14*

442 CD331 6c Bouquet .25 .25
443 CD331 45c Charles .40 .25
444 CD331 $1 Couple .70 *.85*
Nos. 442-444 (3) 1.35 1.35

Operator Assistance Center — A98

35c, Microwave station, map. 50c, Satellite earth station. 60c, Cableship Retriever.

1981, Aug. 7 Litho. *Perf. 14*

445	A98	6c shown	.25	.25
446	A98	35c multicolored	.50	.50
447	A98	50c multicolored	.60	.60
448	A98	60c multicolored	.75	.75
		Nos. 445-448 (4)	2.10	2.10

World Food Day — A99

1981, Sept. 21 Litho. *Perf. 14½x14*

449	A99	20c multicolored	.45	.25

Ratu Sir Lala Sukuna, First Legislative Council Speaker — A100

Designs: 35c, Mace, flag. 50c, Suva Civic Center.
60c, Emblem, participants' flags.

1981, Oct. 19 Litho. *Perf. 14*

450	A100	6c shown	.25	.25
451	A100	35c multicolored	.40	.40
452	A100	50c multicolored	.60	.60
		Nos. 450-452 (3)	1.25	1.25

Souvenir Sheet

453	A100	60c multicolored	1.10	1.10

27th Commonwealth Parliamentary Assoc. Conf., Suva.

World War II Aircraft A101

6c, Bell P-39 Aircobra. 18c, Consolidated PBY-5 Catalina. 35c, Curtiss P-40 Warhawk. 60c, Short Singapore.

1981, Dec. 7 Litho. *Perf. 14*

454	A101	6c multi	1.50	.25
455	A101	18c multi	2.40	.30
456	A101	35c multi	3.25	.65
457	A101	60c multi	3.50	5.00
		Nos. 454-457 (4)	10.65	6.20

Scouting Year A102

1982, Feb. 22 Litho. *Perf. 14½*

458	A102	6c Building	.35	.25
459	A102	20c Sailing, vert.	.60	.35
460	A102	45c Campfire	.75	.50
461	A102	60c Baden-Powell, vert.	1.00	1.00
		Nos. 458-461 (4)	2.70	2.10

Disciplined Forces — A103

Designs: 12c, UN checkpoint. 30c, Construction project. 40c, Police, car. 70c, Navy ship.

1982, May 10 Wmk. 373 *Perf. 14*

462	A103	12c multicolored	.60	.25
463	A103	30c multicolored	.70	.55
464	A103	40c multicolored	2.00	1.00
465	A103	70c multicolored	2.00	*3.50*
		Nos. 462-465 (4)	5.30	5.30

1982 World Cup A104

Designs: 6c, Fiji Soccer Assoc. emblem. 18c, Flag, ball. 50c, Stadium. 90c, Emblem.

1982, June 15 Litho. *Perf. 14*

466	A104	6c multicolored	.25	.25
467	A104	18c multicolored	.35	.25
468	A104	50c multicolored	.85	.50
469	A104	90c multicolored	1.25	1.60
		Nos. 466-469 (4)	2.70	2.60

Princess Diana Issue

Common Design Type

1982, July 1 *Perf. 14½x14*

470	CD333	20c Arms	.35	.35
471	CD333	35c Diana	.50	.35
472	CD333	45c Wedding	.65	.50
473	CD333	$1 Portrait	1.75	1.75
		Nos. 470-473 (4)	3.25	2.95

October Royal Visit — A105

1982, Nov. 1 Litho. *Perf. 14*

474	A105	6c Duke of Edinburgh	.30	.30
475	A105	45c Elizabeth II	1.10	1.10

Souvenir Sheet

476		Sheet of 3	3.50	3.50
c.		A105 $1 Britannia	1.00	1.00

No. 476 contains Nos. 474-475 and 476c.

Christmas A106

Designs: 6c, Holy Family. 20c, Adoration of the Kings. 35c, Carolers.
$1, Faith, from The Three Virtues, by Raphael.

1982, Nov. 22 *Perf. 14x14½*

477	A106	6c multi	.25	.25
478	A106	20c multi	.40	.40
479	A106	35c multi	.70	.70
		Nos. 477-479 (3)	1.35	1.35

Souvenir Sheet

480	A106	$1 multi	2.00	2.00

Red-throated Lory — A107

Parrots: 40c, Blue-crowned lory. 55c, Sulphur-breasted musk parrot. 70c, Red-breasted musk parrot.

1983, Feb. 14 Litho. *Perf. 14*

481	A107	20c shown	2.00	.30
482	A107	40c multicolored	2.50	.60
483	A107	55c multicolored	3.00	1.75
484	A107	70c multicolored	3.25	*5.25*
		Nos. 481-484 (4)	10.75	7.90

A108

Designs: 8c, Traditional house. 25c, Barefoot firewalkers. 50c, Sugar cane crop. 80c, Kava Yagona ceremony.

1983, Mar. 14

485	A108	8c multicolored	.25	.25
486	A108	25c multicolored	.30	.30
487	A108	50c multicolored	.50	.50
488	A108	80c multicolored	.65	.65
		Nos. 485-488 (4)	1.70	1.70

Commonwealth Day.

Manned Flight Bicentenary — A109

1983, July 18 Wmk. 373 *Perf. 14*

489	A109	8c Montgolfiere, 1783	.45	.25
490	A109	20c Wright Flyer	.55	.35
491	A109	25c DC-3	.65	.40
492	A109	40c DeHavilland Comet	1.00	.70
493	A109	50c Boeing 747	1.15	.85
494	A109	58c Columbia space shuttle	1.35	1.00
		Nos. 489-494 (6)	5.15	3.55

Cordia Subcordata — A110

Flowers: 25c, Gmelina vitiensis. 40c, Carruthersia scandens. $1, Amylotheca insularum.

1983, Sept. 26 Litho. *Perf. 14*

495	A110	8c shown	.25	.25
496	A110	25c multicolored	.45	.30
497	A110	40c multicolored	.55	.45
498	A110	$1 multicolored	.90	1.15
		Nos. 495-498 (4)	2.15	2.15

See Nos. 505-508.

Earth Satellite Station, Fijian Playing Lali — A111

Perf. 14x13½

1983, Nov. 7 Wmk. 373

499	A111	50c multicolored	.75	.75

Dacryopinax Spathularia A112

Various fungi: 15c, Podoscypha involuta. 40c, Lentinus squarrosulus. 50c, Scleroderma flavidum. $1, Phillipsia domingensis.

1984, Jan. 9 *Perf. 14x13½, 13½x14*

500	A112	8c shown	1.25	.25
501	A112	15c multicolored	1.50	.45
502	A112	40c multicolored	2.50	1.10
503	A112	50c multicolored	2.50	1.50
504	A112	$1 multicolored	3.75	3.50
		Nos. 500-504 (5)	11.50	6.80

Flower Type of 1983

Designs: 15c, Pseuderanthemum laxiflorum. 20c, Storkiella vitiensis. 50c, Paphia vitiensis. 70c, Elaeocarpus storkii.

1984 Litho. *Perf. 14x14½*

505	A110	15c multicolored	.40	.25
506	A110	20c multicolored	.50	.30
507	A110	50c multicolored	.70	.80
508	A110	70c multicolored	.80	*1.05*
		Nos. 505-508 (4)	2.40	2.40

Lloyd's List Issue

Common Design Type

Perf. 14½x14

1984, May 7 Wmk. 373

509	CD335	8c Tui Lau on reef	.80	.25
510	CD335	40c Tofua	1.50	.90
511	CD335	55c Canberra	1.50	1.50
512	CD335	60c Suva Wharf	1.50	2.25
		Nos. 509-512 (4)	5.30	4.90

Souvenir Sheet

1984 UPU Congress — A113

1984, June 14 Litho. *Perf. 14½*

513	A113	25c Map	2.50	2.50

Ausipex '84 — A114

Designs: 8c, Yalavou cattle. 25c, Wailoa Power Station, vert. 40c, Boeing 737. $1, Cargo ship Fua Kavenga.

Perf. 14x14½

1984, Sept. 17 **Wmk. 373**

514 A114 8c multicolored .25 .25
515 A114 25c multicolored .50 .55
516 A114 40c multicolored 1.90 .95
517 A114 $1 multicolored 1.50 *2.40*
Nos. 514-517 (4) 4.15 4.15

No. 515 is perf. 14½x14

Christmas A115

Designs: 8c, Church on hill. 20c, Sailing. 25c, Santa, children, tree. 40c, Going to church. $1, Family, tree, vert.

1984, Nov. 5 **Litho.** ***Perf. 14***

518 A115 8c multicolored .25 .25
519 A115 20c multicolored .50 .25
520 A115 25c multicolored .50 .25
521 A115 40c multicolored .50 .60
522 A115 $1 multicolored .95 *1.35*
Nos. 518-522 (5) 2.70 2.70

Butterflies A116

Designs: 8c, Monarch. 25c, Common eggfly. 40c, Long-tailed blue, vert. $1, Meadow argus, vert.

1985, Feb. 4 ***Perf. 14***

523 A116 8c multicolored 2.00 .25
524 A116 25c multicolored 3.25 .80
525 A116 40c multicolored 4.00 1.40
526 A116 $1 multicolored 5.75 *6.50*
Nos. 523-526 (4) 15.00 8.95

EXPO '85, Tsukuba, Japan — A117

Designs: 20c, Outrigger canoe, Toberua Island. 25c, Wainivula Falls. 50c, Mana Island. $1, Sawa-I-Lau Caves.

1985, Mar. 18 **Litho.** ***Perf. 14***

527 A117 20c multi .90 .40
528 A117 25c multicolored 1.20 .50
529 A117 50c multicolored 1.35 1.25
530 A117 $1 multicolored 1.60 *2.50*
Nos. 527-530 (4) 5.05 4.65

Queen Mother 85th Birthday Issue

Common Design Type

Designs: 8c, Holding Prince Andrew. 25c, With Prince Charles. 40c, On Oaks Day, Epsom Races. 50c, Holding Prince Henry. $1, In Royal Wedding Cavalcade, 1981.

Perf. 14½x14

1985, June 7 **Wmk. 384**

531 CD336 8c multicolored .25 .25
532 CD336 25c multicolored .40 .40
533 CD336 40c multicolored 1.00 .80
534 CD336 50c multicolored 1.00 *1.20*
Nos. 531-534 (4) 2.65 2.65

Souvenir Sheet

535 CD336 $1 multicolored 3.50 3.50

Shallow Water Fish A118

Designs: 40c, Horned squirrel fish. 50c, Yellow-banded goatfish. 55c, Fairy cod. $1, Peacock rock cod.

1985, Sept. 23 ***Perf. 14½***

536 A118 40c multicolored 1.50 .75
537 A118 50c multicolored 1.75 1.00
538 A118 55c multicolored 2.00 1.50
539 A118 $1 multicolored 2.75 *4.50*
Nos. 536-539 (4) 8.00 7.75

Sea Birds — A119

Designs: 15c, Collared petrel. 20c, Lesser frigate bird. 50c, Brown booby. $1, Crested tern.

1985, Nov. 4 ***Perf. 14***

540 A119 15c multi 2.50 .45
541 A119 20c multi 2.50 .50
542 A119 50c multi 4.75 4.00
543 A119 $1 multi 7.25 *8.00*
Nos. 540-543 (4) 17.00 12.95

Queen Elizabeth II 60th Birthday Issue

Common Design Type

20c, With the Duke of York at the Royal Tournament, 1936. 25c, On Buckingham Palace balcony, wedding of Princess Margaret and Anthony Armstrong-Jones, 1960. 40c, Inspecting the Guard of Honor, Suva, 1982. 50c, State visit to Luxembourg, 1976. $1, Visiting Crown Agents' offices, 1983.

Perf. 14x14½

1986, Apr. 21 **Wmk. 384**

544 CD337 20c scar, blk & sil .40 .30
545 CD337 25c ultra & multi .40 .30
546 CD337 40c green & multi .65 .50
547 CD337 50c violet & multi .75 .75
548 CD337 $1 rose vio & multi .80 *1.15*
Nos. 544-548 (5) 3.00 3.00

Intl. Peace Year — A120

1986, June 23 **Wmk. 373** ***Perf. 14½***

549 A120 8c shown .50 .25
550 A120 40c Dove .85 *1.10*

Halley's Comet — A121

Designs: 25c, Newton's reflector telescope. 40c, Comet over Lomaiviti. $1, Comet nucleus, Giotto probe.

1986, July 7 ***Perf. 13½***

551 A121 25c multicolored 2.00 .55
552 A121 40c multicolored 2.25 .95
553 A121 $1 multicolored 2.75 *5.50*
Nos. 551-553 (3) 7.00 7.00

Reptiles and Amphibians — A122

1986, Aug. 1 ***Perf. 14½***

554 A122 8c Ground frog 1.05 .25
555 A122 20c Burrowing snake 1.50 .30
556 A122 25c Spotted gecko 1.50 .35
557 A122 40c Crested iguana 1.60 .85
558 A122 50c Blotched skink 1.60 *2.50*
559 A122 $1 Speckled skink 2.00 *5.50*
Nos. 554-559 (6) 9.25 9.75

Ancient War Clubs — A123

1986, Nov. 10 **Wmk. 384** ***Perf. 14***

560 A123 25c Gatawaka .95 .35
561 A123 40c Siriti 1.25 .60
562 A123 50c Bulibuli 1.40 *1.60*
563 A123 $1 Culacula 2.50 *3.00*
Nos. 560-563 (4) 6.10 5.55

Cone Shells — A124

1987, Feb. 26 **Litho.** ***Perf. 14x14½***

564 A124 15c Weasel 1.25 .25
565 A124 20c Pertusus 1.25 .30
566 A124 25c Admiral 1.40 .30
567 A124 40c Leaden 1.50 1.00
568 A124 50c Imperial 1.75 *2.25*
569 A124 $1 Geography 2.00 *5.00*
Nos. 564-569 (6) 9.15 9.10

Souvenir Sheet

Tagimoucia Flower — A125

1987, Apr. 23 **Wmk. 373** ***Perf. 14½***

570 A125 $1 multicolored 4.75 3.75

No. 570 Overprinted

1987, June 13

571 A125 $1 multicolored *40.00 40.00*

Intl. Year of Shelter for the Homeless A126

Designs: 55c, Hut. 70c, Government housing.

1987, July 20 ***Perf. 14***

572 A126 55c multicolored .65 .65
573 A126 70c multicolored .85 .85

Beetles — A127

Designs: 20c, Bulbogaster ctenostomoides. 25c, Paracupta flaviventris. 40c, Cerambyrhynchus schoenherri. 50c, Rhinoscapha lagopyga. $1, Xixuthrus heros.

1987, Sept. 7 **Wmk. 384**

574 A127 20c multicolored 2.50 .45
575 A127 25c multicolored 2.50 .55
576 A127 40c multicolored 3.00 1.75
577 A127 50c multicolored 3.25 *3.50*
578 A127 $1 multicolored 4.00 *8.50*
Nos. 574-578 (5) 15.25 14.75

Christmas — A128

Designs: 8c, Holy Family, vert. 40c, Shepherds see star. 50c, Three Kings follow star. $1, Adoration of the Magi.

1987, Nov. 19

579 A128 8c multicolored 1.00 .25
580 A128 40c multicolored 2.25 .65
581 A128 50c multicolored 2.75 1.50
582 A128 $1 multicolored 3.75 *5.00*
Nos. 579-582 (4) 9.75 7.40

World Expo '88, Apr. 30-Oct. 30, Brisbane, Australia A129

1988, Apr. 27 **Litho.** ***Perf. 14***

583 A129 30c Windsurfing 1.60 1.60

Intl. Council of Women, Cent. A130

1988, June 14

584 A130 45c Fiji Nouna 1.30 1.30

Pottery A131

Designs: 9c, Lapita (bowl). 23c, Kuro (cooking pot). 58c, Saqa (Priest drinking vessel). 63c, Saqa, diff. 69c, Ramarama (oil lamp). 75c, Tall Kuro, vert.

Wmk. 384, 373 (69c)

1988, Aug. 29 Litho. *Perf. 13½*

585 A131 9c multicolored .25 .25
586 A131 23c multicolored .40 .25
587 A131 58c multicolored .80 .80
588 A131 63c multicolored .90 .90
589 A131 69c multicolored .95 *1.00*
590 A131 75c multicolored 1.10 *1.20*
Nos. 585-590 (6) 4.40 4.40

Fiji Tree Frog — A132

1988, Oct. 3 Wmk. 384 *Perf. 14*

591 A132 18c multi 4.50 3.00
592 A132 23c multi, diff. 5.00 3.00
593 A132 30c multi, diff. 5.75 5.75
594 A132 45c multi, diff. 6.50 *10.00*
Nos. 591-594 (4) 21.75 21.75

World Wildlife Fund.

Indigenous Flowering Plants — A133

Designs: 9c, Dendrobium mohlianum. 30c, Dendrobium cattilare. 45c, Degeneria vitiensis. $1, Degeneria roseiflora.

1988, Nov. 21 Wmk. 373

595 A133 9c multicolored .85 .25
596 A133 30c multicolored 1.25 .45
597 A133 45c multicolored .95 *1.35*
598 A133 $1 multicolored 1.75 *2.75*
Nos. 595-598 (4) 4.80 4.80

Intl. Red Cross and Red Crescent Orgs., 125th Anniv. — A134

Designs: 58c, Battle of Solferino, 1859. 63c, Jean-Henri Dunant, vert. 69c, Medicine. $1, Anniv. emblem, vert.

1989, Feb. 6 Wmk. 384

599 A134 58c multicolored 1.75 1.00
600 A134 63c multicolored 1.75 1.10
601 A134 69c multicolored 2.25 1.40
602 A134 $1 multicolored 2.75 1.90
Nos. 599-602 (4) 8.50 5.40

Epic Voyage of William Bligh A135

Designs: 45c, Plans (line drawing) of the Bounty's launch. 58c, Diary and inscription on artifacts "The cup I eat my miserable allowance out of." 80c, Silhouette, lightning, quote "O Almighty God, relieve us. . ." $1, Map of Bligh's Islands, launch and compass rose.

1989, Apr. 28 *Perf. 14½*

603 A135 45c multicolored 2.10 .70
604 A135 58c multicolored 2.25 1.50
605 A135 80c multicolored 3.50 3.25
606 A135 $1 multicolored 4.75 3.50
Nos. 603-606 (4) 12.60 8.95

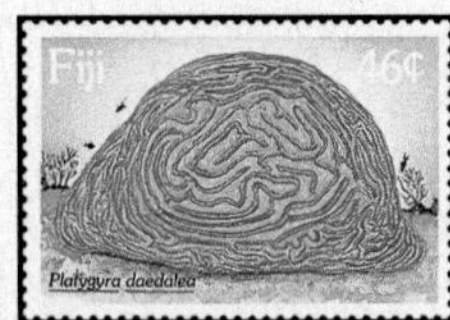

Coral A136

Designs: 46c, Platygyra daedalea. 60c, Caulastrea furcata. 75c, Acropora echinata. 90c, Acropora humilis.

1989, Aug. 21 Wmk. 373 *Perf. 14*

607 A136 46c multicolored 2.00 1.00
608 A136 60c multicolored 2.50 2.00
609 A136 75c multicolored 3.00 2.50
610 A136 90c multicolored 3.75 3.00
Nos. 607-610 (4) 11.25 8.50

Nos. 609-610 vert.

1990 World Cup Soccer Championships, Italy — A137

Various Fijian soccer players.

1989, Sept. 25 Wmk. 384 *Perf. 14½*

611 A137 35c shown 1.35 .75
612 A137 63c multi, diff. 2.40 2.40
613 A137 70c multi, diff. 2.60 2.60
614 A137 85c multi, diff. 2.90 3.00
Nos. 611-614 (4) 9.25 8.75

Christmas A138

Designs: 9c, Church service. 45c, *Delonix regia* tree. $1, Holy family. $1.40, Tree, Fijian children.

1989, Nov. 1 Wmk. 373

615 A138 9c multicolored .40 .25
616 A138 45c multicolored 1.00 .25
617 A138 $1 multicolored 2.00 2.10
618 A138 $1.40 multicolored 2.25 3.00
Nos. 615-618 (4) 5.65 5.60

Fish A139

Designs: 50c, Mangrove jack. 70c, Orange-spotted therapon perch. 85c, Spotted scat. $1, Flagtail.

1990, Apr. 23 Litho. Wmk. 384

619 A139 50c multicolored 2.60 1.00
620 A139 70c multicolored 3.50 3.50
621 A139 85c multicolored 3.75 3.75
622 A139 $1 multicolored 4.25 4.25
Nos. 619-622 (4) 14.10 12.50

Souvenir Sheet

Stamp World London '90 — A140

1990, May 1

623 A140 Sheet of 2 12.50 9.50
a. $1 No. 243 3.75 2.60
b. $2 No. 249 8.00 6.00

Soil Conservation — A141

50c, Vertiver grass contours. 70c, Mulching. 90c, Contour cultivation. $1, Proper land use.

1990, July 23 Litho. Wmk. 373

625 A141 50c multi 1.25 .65
626 A141 70c multi 1.75 1.75
627 A141 90c multi 1.90 *2.25*
628 A141 $1 multi, vert. 2.00 *2.50*
Nos. 625-628 (4) 6.90 7.15

Trees — A142

25c, Dacrydium nidulum. 35c, Decussocarpus vitiensis. $1, Agathis vitiensis. $1.55, Santalum yasi.

1990, Oct. 2

629 A142 25c multi .90 .25
630 A142 35c multi 1.00 .35
631 A142 $1 multi 3.00 3.00
632 A142 $1.55 multi 4.25 *5.50*
Nos. 629-632 (4) 9.15 9.10

Christmas — A143

Christmas carols: 10c, Hark! The Herald Angels Sing. 35c, Silent Night. 65c, Joy to the World! $1, The Race that Long in Darkness Pined.

1990, Nov. 26 Wmk. 373 *Perf. 14*

633 A143 10c multicolored .40 .25
634 A143 35c multicolored 1.00 .35
635 A143 65c multicolored 1.60 *1.75*
636 A143 $1 multicolored 2.50 *2.75*
Nos. 633-636 (4) 5.50 5.10

Scenic Views — A144

Designs: 35c, Sigatoka sand dunes. 50c, Monu, Monuriki Islands. 65c, Ravilevu Nature Reserve. $1, Colo-I-Suva Forest Park.

1991, Feb. 25 Wmk. 384

637 A144 35c multicolored 1.35 .35
638 A144 50c multicolored 2.25 1.25
639 A144 65c multicolored 2.60 *2.75*
640 A144 $1 multicolored 4.00 *4.50*
Nos. 637-640 (4) 10.20 8.85

Discovery of Rotuma Island, Bicent. A145

Designs: 54c, HMS Pandora. 70c, Map of Rotuma Island. 75c, Natives. $1, Mt. Solroroa, Uea Island.

1991, Aug. 8 Wmk. 373 *Perf. 14*

641 A145 54c multicolored 2.75 1.25
642 A145 70c multicolored 3.00 3.00
643 A145 75c multicolored 3.00 3.00
644 A145 $1 multicolored 4.75 4.75
Nos. 641-644 (4) 13.50 12.00

Crabs A146

Designs: 38c, Scylla serrata. 54c, Metopograpsus messor. 96c, Parasesarma erythrodactyla. $1.65, Cardisoma carnifex.

1991, Sept. 26 *Perf. 14½x14*

645 A146 38c multicolored 1.15 .45
646 A146 54c multicolored 1.75 .75
647 A146 96c multicolored 2.90 2.75
648 A146 $1.65 multicolored 4.00 5.50
Nos. 645-648 (4) 9.80 9.45

Christmas A147

Designs: 11c, Mary, Joseph travelling to Bethlehem. 75c, Manger scene. 96c, Jesus being blessed at temple in Jerusalem. $1, Baby Jesus.

1991, Oct. 31 Wmk. 384 *Perf. 14*

649 A147 11c multicolored .65 .25
650 A147 75c multicolroed 2.00 .75
651 A147 96c multicolored 2.10 2.50
652 A147 $1 multicolored 2.25 2.50
Nos. 649-652 (4) 7.00 6.00

No. 649 exists with wmk. 373.

Air Pacific, 40th Anniv. A148

Airplanes: 54c, Dragon Rapide, Harold Gatty, founder. 75c, Douglas DC3. 96c, ATR 42. $1.40, Boeing 767.

1991, Nov. 18 *Perf. 14½*

653 A148 54c multicolored 2.40 1.25
654 A148 75c multicolored 3.25 2.50
655 A148 96c multicolored 3.50 3.50
656 A148 $1.40 multicolored 4.75 *5.00*
Nos. 653-656 (4) 13.90 12.25

Expo '92, Seville A149

Designs: 27c, Traditional dance and costumes. 75c, Faces of people. 96c, Train and gold bars. $1.40, Cruise ship in port.

Perf. 14½x14

1992, Mar. 23 Litho. Wmk. 373

657 A149 27c multicolored .75 .50
658 A149 75c multicolored 1.75 1.75
659 A149 96c multicolored 8.25 5.50
660 A149 $1.40 multicolored 8.75 8.25
Nos. 657-660 (4) 19.50 16.00

Inter-Islands Shipping — A150

1992, June 22 ***Perf. 14***

661 A150 38c Tabusoro 2.75 .75
662 A150 54c Degei II 3.25 1.50
663 A150 $1.40 Dausoko 5.50 4.50
664 A150 $1.65 Nivanga 5.50 4.50
Nos. 661-664 (4) 17.00 11.25

1992 Summer Olympics, Barcelona — A151

1992, July 30 ***Perf. 13½***

665 A151 20c Running 1.00 .25
666 A151 86c Yachting 3.00 2.50
667 A151 $1.34 Swimming 3.50 4.00
668 A151 $1.50 Judo 3.50 4.00
Nos. 665-668 (4) 11.00 10.75

Levuka A152

30c, European War Memorial. 42c, Map. 59c, Beach Street. 77c, Sacred Heart Church, vert. $2, Deed of Cession Site, vert.

1992, Sept. 21 ***Perf. 14½***

669 A152 30c multicolored .45 .30
670 A152 42c multicolored .65 .50
671 A152 59c multicolored .95 .95
672 A152 77c multicolored 1.20 *1.25*
673 A152 $2 multicolored 2.50 *2.75*
Nos. 669-673 (5) 5.75 5.75

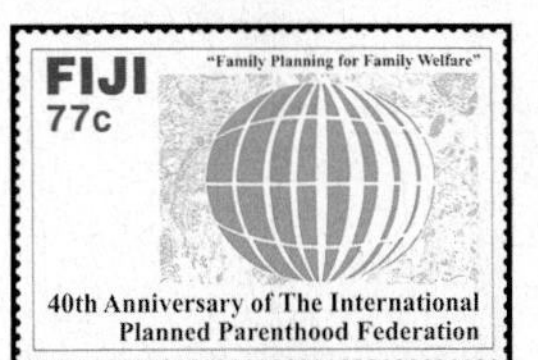

Intl. Planned Parenthood Federation, 40th Anniv. — A153

1992, Nov. 2 ***Perf. 15x14½***

674 A153 77c Globe 1.35 1.00
675 A153 $2 Family 3.50 3.50

Christmas — A154

Bible interpretations: 12c, "God so loved the world..." 77c, "We love because God first loved us." 83c, "It is more blessed to give..." $2, "Every good gift..."

1992, Nov. 17

676 A154 12c multicolored .75 .25
677 A154 77c multicolored 2.25 1.75
678 A154 83c multicolored 2.50 2.00
679 A154 $2 multicolored 4.00 5.50
Nos. 676-679 (4) 9.50 9.50

Peace Corps in Fiji, 25th Anniv. A155

Designs: 59c, Voluntary service. 77c, Fiji/US friendship. $1, Education. $2, Income generating business through volunteer help.

Wmk. 373

1993, Feb. 22 **Litho.** ***Perf. 14½***

680 A155 59c multicolored 1.40 .75
681 A155 77c multicolored 1.90 1.00
682 A155 $1 multicolored 2.00 1.50
683 A155 $2 multicolored 3.50 5.00
Nos. 680-683 (4) 8.80 8.25

Hong Kong Rugby Sevens — A156

Designs: 77c, Players performing traditional Cibi Dance. $1.06, Two players, map of Fiji, Hong Kong, and Australia. $2, Stadium, players in scrum.

Perf. 14x15

1993, Mar. 26 **Litho.** **Wmk. 384**

684 A156 77c multicolored 1.75 1.50
685 A156 $1.06 multicolored 4.00 2.50
686 A156 $2 multicolored 4.25 5.50
Nos. 684-686 (3) 10.00 9.50

Royal Air Force, 75th Anniv.

Common Design Type

Designs: 59c, Gloster Gauntlet. 77c, Armstrong Whitworth Whitley. 83c, Bristol F2b. $2, Hawker Tempest.

No. 691: a, Vickers Vildebeest. b, Handley Page Hampden. c, Vickers Vimy. d, British Aerospace Hawk.

1993, Apr. 1 ***Perf. 14***

687 CD350 59c multicolored 1.50 .75
688 CD350 77c multicolored 1.75 1.40
689 CD350 83c multicolored 2.25 1.75
690 CD350 $2 multicolored 3.50 4.75
Nos. 687-690 (4) 9.00 8.65

Souvenir Sheet of 4

691 CD350 $1 #a.-d. 8.75 8.75
e. Overprinted in sheet margin 9.75 9.75

Overprint on No. 691e is exhibition emblem for Hong Kong '94.

Nudibranchs A157

12c, Chromodoris fidelis. 42c, Halgerda carlsoni. 53c, Chromodoris lochi. 83c, Glaucus atlanticus. $1, Phyllidia bourguini. $2, Hexabranchus sanguineus.

Wmk. 373

1993, July 27 **Litho.** ***Perf. 14***

692 A157 12c multicolored .80 .25
693 A157 42c multicolored 1.60 .50
694 A157 53c multicolored 1.75 1.00
695 A157 83c multicolored 2.50 2.25
696 A157 $1 multicolored 2.90 2.25
697 A157 $2 multicolored 4.00 *6.50*
Nos. 692-697 (6) 13.55 12.75

Tropical Fruit — A158

Wmk. 373

1993, Oct. 25 **Litho.** ***Perf. 13½***

698 A158 30c Mango 1.90 .50
699 A158 42c Guava 2.10 1.00
700 A158 $1 Lemon 3.75 3.00
701 A158 $2 Soursop 6.00 8.00
Nos. 698-701 (4) 13.75 12.50

Souvenir Sheet

Hong Kong '94 — A159

Butterflies: a, Caper white. b, Blue branded king crow. c, Vagrant. d, Glasswing.

Perf. 14½x13

1994, Feb. 18 **Litho.** **Wmk. 373**

702 A159 $1 Sheet of 4, #a.-d. 9.00 9.00

Easter A160

59c, The Last Supper. 77c, The Crucifixion. $1, The Resurrection. $2, Jesus showing his wounds to his disciples.

Perf. 14x15, 15x14

1994, Mar. 31 **Litho.** **Wmk. 373**

703 A160 59c multi 1.35 .50
704 A160 77c multi, vert. 1.75 .75
705 A160 $1 multi 2.00 1.75
706 A160 $2 multi, vert. 3.75 5.25
Nos. 703-706 (4) 8.85 8.25

Edible Seaweeds A161

42c, Codium bulbopilum. 83c, Coulerpa racemosa. $1, Hypnea pannosa. $2, Gracilaria.

Wmk. 384

1994, June 6 **Litho.** ***Perf. 14***

707 A161 42c multicolored 1.10 .40
708 A161 83c multicolored 2.25 1.60
709 A161 $1 multicolored 2.75 1.90
710 A161 $2 multicolored 4.00 6.25
Nos. 707-710 (4) 10.10 10.15

Souvenir Sheet

White-Collared Kingfisher — A162

Designs: a, On branch. b, In flight.

Wmk. 373

1994, Aug. **Litho.** ***Perf. 13½***

711 A162 $1.50 Sheet of 2, #a.-b. 11.50 11.50
c. Overprinted in sheet margin 11.50 11.50

Overprint on No. 711c consists of exhibition emblem and "JAKARTA '95."

Issued: #711, 8/16; #711c, 8/19.

Souvenir Sheet

Singpex '94 — A163

Neoveitchia storckii: a, Complete tree. b. Fruits, inflorescence.

1994, Aug. 31 **Wmk. 384** ***Perf. 14***

712 A163 $1.50 Sheet of 2, #a.-b. 9.00 9.00

First Catholic Missionaries in Fiji, 150th Anniv. — A164

Designs: 23c, Father Ioane Batita. 31c, Local catechist. 44c, Sacred Heart Cathedral. 63c, Lomary Church. 81c, Pope Gregory XVI. $2, Pope John Paul II.

Wmk. 373

1994, Dec. 16 **Litho.** ***Perf. 14***

713 A164 23c multicolored .50 .25
714 A164 31c multicolored .60 .25
715 A164 44c multicolored .80 .60
716 A164 63c multicolored 1.10 1.00
717 A164 81c multicolored 1.50 1.50
718 A164 $2 multicolored 4.00 *4.75*
Nos. 713-718 (6) 8.50 8.35

Souvenir Sheet

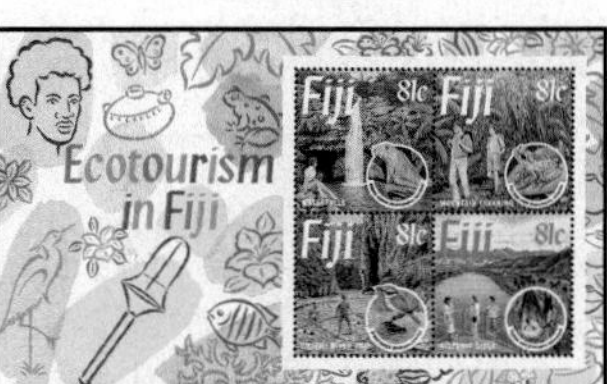

Ecotourism in Fiji — A165

Designs: a, Waterfalls, banded iguana. b, Mountain trekking, Fiji tree frog. c, Bilibili River trip, kingfisher. d, Historic sites, flying fox.

Wmk. 373

1995, Mar. 27 **Litho.** ***Perf. 14***

719 A165 81c Sheet of 4, #a.-d. 8.25 8.25

End of World War II, 50th Anniv.

Common Design Types

Designs: 13c, Fijian regiment guarding crashed Japanese Zero Fighter. 63c, Kameli Airstrip, Solomon Islands, built by Fijian regiment. 87c, Corp. Sukanaivalu VC, Victoria Cross. $1.12, HMS Fiji.

$2, Reverse side of War Medal 1939-45.

Wmk. 373

1995, May 8 **Litho.** ***Perf. 13½***

720 CD351 13c multicolored 1.25 .25
721 CD351 63c multicolored 2.75 1.75
722 CD351 87c multicolored 3.25 2.75
723 CD351 $1.12 multicolored 3.75 3.25
Nos. 720-723 (4) 11.00 8.00

Souvenir Sheet

Perf. 14

724 CD352 $2 multicolored 6.50 6.50

Birds — A166

1c, Red-headed parrotfinch. 2c, Golden whistler. 3c, Ogea flycatcher. 4c, Peale's pigeon. 6c, Blue-crested broadbill. 13c, Island thrush. 23c, Many-colored fruit dove. 31c, Mangrove heron. 44c, Purple swamphen. 63c, Fiji goshawk. 81c, Kadavu fantail. 87c, Collared lory. $1, Scarlet robin. $2, Peregrine falcon. $3, Barn owl. $5, Yellow-breasted musk parrot.

1995 Litho. Wmk. 373 *Perf. 13*

725	A166	1c multi	1.00	1.75
726	A166	2c multi	1.00	1.75
727	A166	3c multi	1.00	1.75
728	A166	4c multi	1.00	1.75
729	A166	6c multi	1.00	1.75
730	A166	13c multi	.75	.25
731	A166	23c multi	.75	.30
732	A166	31c multi	.85	.35
733	A166	44c multi	1.00	.40
734	A166	63c multi	1.50	.50
735	A166	81c multi	1.75	.65
736	A166	87c multi	2.00	.75
737	A166	$1 multi	2.00	.85
738	A166	$2 multi	3.00	1.75
739	A166	$3 multi	4.25	3.75
739A	A166	$5 multi	4.50	*5.50*
		Nos. 725-739A (16)	27.35	23.80

Issued: 13c, 23c, 31c, 44c, 63c, 81c, $2, $3, 7/25; 1c, 2c, 3c, 4c, 6c, 87c, $1, $5, 11/7.

See No. 1011.

For surcharges, see Nos. 1149-1160, 1191-1197C, 1214-1223A, 1249-1254G, 1314-1317, 1346-1347, 1353-1356, 1370-1371, 1407A-1407B.

Souvenir Sheet

Singapore '95 — A167

Orchids: a, Arundina graminifolia. b, Phaius tankervilliae.

Wmk. 373

1995, Sept. 1 Litho. *Perf. 14*

740 A167 $1 Sheet of 2, #a.-b. 7.50 7.50

Independence, 25th Anniv. — A168

Designs: 81c, Pres. Kamisese Mara, Parliament Building. 87c, Fijian youth. $1.06, Playing rugby. $2, Air Pacific Boeing 747.

Wmk. 373

1995, Oct. 4 Litho. *Perf. 14*

741	A168	81c multicolored	1.50	1.10
742	A168	87c multicolored	1.35	1.35
743	A168	$1.06 multicolored	2.10	2.25
744	A168	$2 multicolored	4.25	*4.50*
		Nos. 741-744 (4)	9.20	9.20

Christmas — A169

Paintings: 10c, Praying Madonna with the Crown of Stars, from Correggio Workshop. 63c, Madonna and Child with Crowns on porcelain. 87c, The Holy Virgin with the Holy Child and St. John, after Titian. $2, The Holy Family and St. John, from Rubens Workshop.

Wmk. 373

1995, Nov. 22 Litho. *Perf. 13*

745	A169	10c multicolored	.30	.25
746	A169	63c multicolored	1.20	1.00
747	A169	87c multicolored	1.60	1.50
748	A169	$2 multicolored	3.50	3.75
		Nos. 745-748 (4)	6.60	6.50

Arrival of Banabans in Fiji, 50th Anniv. A170

Perf. 14x14½, 14½x14

1996, Jan. 24 Litho. Wmk. 373

749	A170	81c Trolling lure	2.25	1.25
750	A170	87c Canoes	2.50	1.25
751	A170	$1.12 Warrior, vert.	2.75	2.00
752	A170	$2 Frigate bird, vert.	5.25	7.00
		Nos. 749-752 (4)	12.75	11.50

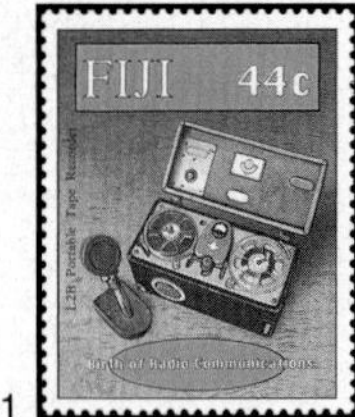

A171

Radio, Cent.: 44c, L2B portable tape recorder. 63c, Fiji Broadcasting Center. 81c, Communications satellite in orbit. $3, Marconi.

Wmk. 373

1996, Mar. 11 Litho. *Perf. 14½*

753	A171	44c multicolored	.90	.50
754	A171	63c multicolored	1.25	.75
755	A171	81c multicolored	1.60	1.25
756	A171	$3 multicolored	5.25	*6.50*
		Nos. 753-756 (4)	9.00	9.00

A172

Ancient Chinese artifacts: 63c, Bronze monster mask and ring, c. 450 BC. 81c, Archer, 210 BC. $1, Plate, Hsuan Te Period, 1426-35. $2, Central Asian horseman, dated 706.

30c, Yan Deng Mountain.

Wmk. 384

1996, Apr. 25 Litho. *Perf. 13½*

757	A172	63c multicolored	1.25	.50
758	A172	81c multicolored	1.60	1.00
759	A172	$1 multicolored	2.00	1.50
760	A172	$2 multicolored	3.50	*4.25*
		Nos. 757-760 (4)	8.35	7.25

Souvenir Sheet

Perf. 13½x13

761 A172 30c multicolored 2.50 2.50

No. 761 contains one 48x76mm stamp.

CHINA '96, 9th Asian Intl. Philatelic Exhibition.

A173

Wmk. 373

1996, June 18 Litho. *Perf. 14*

762	A173	31c Hurdling	.65	.25
763	A173	63c Judo	1.50	1.00
764	A173	87c Sailboarding	2.10	1.75
765	A173	$1.12 Swimming	2.40	*2.50*
		Nos. 762-765 (4)	6.65	5.50

Souvenir Sheet

766 A173 $2 Athlete, 1896 3.75 3.75

Modern Olympic Games, cent.

A174

31c, Computerized telephone exchange, horiz. 44c, Mail being unloaded, horiz. 81c, Manual switchboard operator. $1, Mail delivery.

No. 771: a, #117. b, #527.

1996, July 1

767	A174	31c multicolored	.60	.35
768	A174	44c multicolored	.85	.75
769	A174	81c multicolored	1.20	*1.50*
770	A174	$1 multicolored	2.10	2.10
		Nos. 767-770 (4)	4.75	4.70

Souvenir Sheet of 2

771 A174 $1.50 #a.-b. 8.25 8.25

Creation of independent Postal, Telecommunications Companies.

UNICEF, 50th Anniv. A175

Designs: 81c, "Our children, our future." 87c, Village scene. $1, "Living in harmony the world over." $2, "Their future."

Wmk. 384

1996, Aug. 13 Litho. *Perf. 14*

772	A175	81c multicolored	2.00	1.50
773	A175	87c multicolored	2.00	1.50
774	A175	$1 multicolored	2.10	1.60
775	A175	$2 multicolored	3.25	*4.75*
		Nos. 772-775 (4)	9.35	9.35

Nadi Intl. Airport, 50th Anniv. A176

Designs: 31c, First airplane in Fiji, 1921. 44c, Nadi Airport commences Commercial Operations, 1946. 63c, First jet in Fiji, 1959. 87c, Airport entrance. $1, Control tower, 1996. $2, Global positioning system, first commercial use, 1994.

Wmk. 373

1996, Oct. 1 Litho. *Perf. 14*

776	A176	31c multicolored	.80	.35
777	A176	44c multicolored	1.00	.50
778	A176	63c multicolored	1.60	1.15
779	A176	87c multicolored	1.75	1.60
780	A176	$1 multicolored	2.10	1.90
781	A176	$2 multicolored	3.50	5.00
		Nos. 776-781 (6)	10.75	10.50

Christmas — A177

Scene from the Christmas story and native story or scene: 13c, Angel Gabriel & Mary, beating of Lali. 81c, Shepherds with sheep, Fijian canoe. $1, Wise men on camels, multiracial Fiji. $3, Mary, Christ Child in stable, blowing of conch shell.

1996, Nov. 20 Wmk. 373

782	A177	13c multicolored	.50	.25
783	A177	81c multicolored	1.90	1.00
784	A177	$1 multicolored	2.10	1.50
785	A177	$3 multicolored	6.25	7.25
		Nos. 782-785 (4)	10.75	10.00

Hong Kong '97 A178

Cattle: a, Brahman. b, Freisian (Holstein). c, Hereford. d, Fiji draught bullock.

1997, Feb. 12

786 A178 $1 Sheet of 4, #a.-d. 8.50 8.50

Souvenir Sheet

Black-Faced Shrikebill — A179

1997, Feb. 21 *Perf. 14x15*

787 A179 $2 multicolored 4.25 4.25

Singpex '97.

Orchids — A180

Designs: 81c, Dendrobium biflorum. 87c, Dendrobium dactylodes. $1.06, Spathoglottis pacifica. $2, Dendrobium macropus.

Wmk. 384

1997, Apr. 22 Litho. *Perf. 14*

788	A180	81c multicolored	2.40	1.50
789	A180	87c multicolored	2.40	1.50
		Wmk. 373		
790	A180	$1.06 multicolored	2.75	2.50
791	A180	$2 multicolored	4.50	4.50
		Nos. 788-791 (4)	12.05	10.00

Souvenir Sheet

Hawksbill Turtle — A181

Designs: a, 63c, Female laying eggs. b, 81c, Baby turtles emerging from nest. c, $1.06 Young turtles in water. d, $2, One adult in water, coral.

1997, May 26 Wmk. 373

792 A181 Sheet of 4, #a.-d. 10.00 10.00

Coral A182

Designs: 63c, Branching hard coral 87c, Massive hard coral. $1, Soft coral, sinularia. $3, Soft coral, dendronephthya.

Wmk. 373

1997, July 16 Litho. *Perf. 14*

No.	Type	Description	Unused	Used
793	A182	63c multicolored	1.25	.50
794	A182	87c multicolored	1.90	1.00
795	A182	$1 multicolored	2.10	1.50
796	A182	$3 multicolored	5.25	*7.50*
		Nos. 793-796 (4)	10.50	10.50

Fijian Monkey-faced Bat — A183

63c, With nose pointed downward. 81c, Hanging below flower. $2, Between leaves on tree branch.

Perf. 13½

1997, Oct. 15 Litho. Unwmk.

No.	Type	Description	Unused	Used
797	A183	44c multicolored	1.00	.50
798	A183	63c multicolored	1.40	.75
799	A183	81c multicolored	1.75	1.15
800	A183	$2 multicolored	3.50	*4.50*
a.		Sheet, 2 each #797-800	15.50	15.50
		Nos. 797-800 (4)	7.65	6.90

World Wildlife Fund.

Christmas A184

Designs: 13c, Angel, shepherd. 31c, Birth of Jesus. 87c, Magi. $3, Madonna and Child.

Perf. 14x14½

1997, Nov. 18 Wmk. 373

No.	Type	Description	Unused	Used
801	A184	13c multicolored	.35	.25
802	A184	31c multicolored	.75	.25
803	A184	87c multicolored	1.75	.85
804	A184	$3 multicolored	4.25	*5.75*
		Nos. 801-804 (4)	7.10	7.10

A185

1997 Rugby World Cup Sevens Champions: a, 50c, Waisale Serevi, captain, highest point scorer. b, 50c, Taniela Qauqau. c, 50c, Jope Tuikabe. d, 50c, Leveni Duvuduvukula. e, 50c, Inoke Maraiwai. f, 50c, Aminiasi Naituyaga. g, 50c, Lemeki Koroi. h, 50c, Marika Vunibaka, highest try scorer. i, 50c, Luke Erenavula. j, 50c, Manasa Bari. k, $1, Entire team.

Wmk. 373

1997, Oct. 30 Litho. *Perf. 14*

No.	Type	Description	Unused	Used
805	A185	Sheet of 11, #a.-k.	14.50	14.50

No. 805k is 53x39mm.

A186

Chief's Traditional Costumes: 81c, War dress. 87c, Formal dress. $1.12, Presentation dress. $2, Highland war dress.

Wmk. 373

1998, Jan. 20 Litho. *Perf. 14*

No.	Type	Description	Unused	Used
806	A186	81c multicolored	1.25	.75
807	A186	87c multicolored	1.25	1.00
808	A186	$1.12 multicolored	1.50	1.50
809	A186	$2 multicolored	2.75	*3.50*
		Nos. 806-809 (4)	6.75	6.75

Asian and Pacific Decade of Disabled Persons, 1993-2000 A187

63c, Mastering modern technology. 87c, Assisting the will to overcome. $1, Using natural born skills. $2, Competing to win.

Wmk. 373

1998, Mar. 18 Litho. *Perf. 13*

No.	Type	Description	Unused	Used
810	A187	63c multicolored	1.25	.60
811	A187	87c multicolored	1.50	.75
812	A187	$1 multicolored	1.50	1.40
813	A187	$2 multicolored	2.75	*4.25*
		Nos. 810-813 (4)	7.00	7.00

Royal Air Force, 80th Anniv.

Common Design Type of 1993 Re-Inscribed

Designs: 44c, R34 Airship. 63c, Handley Page Heyford. 87c, Supermarine Swift FR.5. $2, Westland Whirlwind.

No. 818: a, Sopwith Dolphin. b, Avro 504K. c, Vickers Warwick V. d, Shorts Belfast.

1998, Apr. 1 *Perf. 13½x14*

No.	Type	Description	Unused	Used
814	CD350	44c multicolored	1.00	.50
815	CD350	63c multicolored	1.25	.75
816	CD350	87c multicolored	1.75	1.50
817	CD350	$2 multicolored	3.00	3.00
		Nos. 814-817 (4)	7.00	5.75

Souvenir Sheet of 4

No.	Type	Description	Unused	Used
818	CD350	$1 #a.-d.	7.00	7.00

Diana, Princess of Wales (1961-97)

Common Design Type

Design: No. 819, Wearing plaid jacket.

No. 820: a, Wearing blue jacket. b, In high-collared blouse. c, Holding flowers.

1998, Mar. 31 Litho. *Perf. 14x14½*

No.	Type	Description	Unused	Used
819	CD355	81c multicolored	1.00	1.00
820	CD355	81c Sheet of 4, #819, a.-c.	4.25	4.25

No. 820 sold for $3.24 + 50c, with surtax from international sales being donated to the Princess Diana Memorial Fund and surtax from national sales being donated to designated local charity.

Sperm Whale A188

Designs: 81c, Adult, calf. 87c, Breaching. $2, Sperm whale tooth.

Wmk. 373

1998, June 22 Litho. *Perf. 14*

No.	Type	Description	Unused	Used
821	A188	63c shown	1.75	.75
822	A188	81c multi	1.90	1.00
823	A188	87c multi	2.25	1.25
824	A188	$2 multi	3.00	*4.00*
a.		Souvenir sheet	5.50	5.50
		Nos. 821-824 (4)	8.90	7.00

16th Commonwealth Games, Kuala Lumpur, Malaysia — A189

Designs: 44c, Athletics. 63c, Lawn bowls. 81c, Javelin. $1.12, Weight lifting.

$2, Waisale Serevi, rugby sevens.

Wmk. 384

1998, Sept. 11 Litho. *Perf. 14*

No.	Type	Description	Unused	Used
825	A189	44c multi	.85	.35
826	A189	63c multi	1.00	.50
827	A189	81c multi	1.40	1.15
828	A189	$1.12 multi	1.75	*2.50*
		Nos. 825-828 (4)	5.00	4.50

Souvenir Sheet

No.	Type	Description	Unused	Used
829	A189	$2 multi	4.25	4.25

Maritime Heritage A190

Designs: 13c, Takia, hollowed-out log with outrigger. 44c, Camakau, sailing canoe. 87c, Drua, twin-hulled sailing canoe. $3, MV Pioneer motor yacht.

$1.50, Camakau, map of Fiji.

Wmk. 384

1998, Oct. 26 Litho. *Perf. 13½*

No.	Type	Description	Unused	Used
830	A190	13c multicolored	.45	.25
831	A190	44c multicolored	.75	.35
832	A190	87c multicolored	1.40	1.00
833	A190	$3 multicolored	5.00	*6.00*
		Nos. 830-833 (4)	7.60	7.60

Souvenir Sheet

No.	Type	Description	Unused	Used
834	A190	$1.50 multicolored	3.75	3.75

Australia '99, World Stamp Expo (#834).

See Nos. 843-847.

Christmas A191

Children's drawings: 13c, "Jesus in a Manger." 50c, "A Time for Family and Friends." $1, "What Christmas Means to Me," vert. $2, "The Joy of Christmas," vert.

1998, Nov. 23 Wmk. 373

No.	Type	Description	Unused	Used
835	A191	13c multicolored	.50	.25
836	A191	50c multicolored	1.20	.45
837	A191	$1 multicolored	2.00	1.10
838	A191	$2 multicolored	2.60	*4.50*
		Nos. 835-838 (4)	6.30	6.30

Traditional Dances — A192

Designs: 13c, Vakamalolo (women's sitting dance). 81c, Mekeiwau (club dance). 87c, Seasea (women's fan dance). $3, Meke ni yaqona (Kava serving dance).

Wmk. 373

1999, Jan. 20 Litho. *Perf. 14½*

No.	Type	Description	Unused	Used
839	A192	13c multicolored	.75	.25
840	A192	81c multicolored	1.75	1.25
841	A192	87c multicolored	1.75	1.25
842	A192	$3 multicolored	5.25	*6.75*
		Nos. 839-842 (4)	9.50	9.50

Maritime Heritage Type of 1998

Designs: 63c, SS Toufua, 1920-30's. 81c, MF Adi Beti, 1920-30's. $1, SS Niagara, 1920-30's. $2, MV Royal Viking Sun, 1990's.

$1.50, SS. Makatea, 1920's.

1999, Mar. 19 Wmk. 384 *Perf. 13½*

No.	Type	Description	Unused	Used
843	A190	63c multicolored	1.60	.50
844	A190	81c multicolored	1.75	.75
845	A190	$1 multicolored	1.90	1.50
846	A190	$2 multicolored	3.00	*4.00*
		Nos. 843-846 (4)	8.25	6.75

Souvenir Sheet

No.	Type	Description	Unused	Used
847	A190	$1.50 multicolored	4.00	4.00

Australia '99, World Stamp Exhibition (#847).

Souvenir Sheet

Ducks — A193

a, Wandering whistling. b, Pacific black.

1999, Apr. 27 Wmk. 373

No.	Type	Description	Unused	Used
848	A193	$2 Sheet of 2, #a.-b.	6.25	6.25

IBRA '99, Intl. Philatelic Exhibition, Nuremberg.

Orchids — A194

Designs: 44c, Calanthe ventilabrum. 63c, Dendrobium prasinum. 81c, Dendrobium macrophyllum. $3, Dendrobium tokai.

1999, June 28

No.	Type	Description	Unused	Used
849	A194	44c multicolored	1.00	.50
850	A194	63c multicolored	1.25	.90
851	A194	81c multicolored	1.75	1.00
852	A194	$3 multicolored	4.00	*5.00*
		Nos. 849-852 (4)	8.00	7.40

1st Manned Moon Landing, 30th Anniv.

Common Design Type

13c, Astronaut waves goodbye. 87c, Stage 3 fires towards moon. $1, Aldrin walks on lunar surface. $2, Command module fires towards earth.

$2, Looking at earth from moon.

Perf. 14x13¾

1999, July 20 Wmk. 384

No.	Type	Description	Unused	Used
853	CD357	13c multicolored	.60	.25
854	CD357	87c multicolored	1.35	1.10
855	CD357	$1 multicolored	1.45	1.25
856	CD357	$2 multicolored	2.60	2.60
		Nos. 853-856 (4)	6.00	5.20

Souvenir Sheet

Perf. 14

No.	Type	Description	Unused	Used
857	CD357	$2 multicolored	3.25	3.25

No. 857 contains one circular stamp 40mm in diameter.

Queen Mother's Century

Common Design Type

Queen Mother: 13c, Visiting Hull to see bomb damage. 63c, With Prince Charles. 81c, As Colonel-in-Chief of Light Infantry. $3, With Prince Charles at Clarence House.

$2, With crowd on Armistice Day.

Wmk. 384

1999, Aug. 18 Litho. *Perf. 13½*

No.	Type	Description	Unused	Used
858	CD358	13c multicolored	.80	.50
859	CD358	63c multicolored	1.25	.75
860	CD358	81c multicolored	2.00	1.75
861	CD358	$3 multicolored	4.00	*5.50*
		Nos. 858-861 (4)	8.05	8.50

Souvenir Sheet

No.	Type	Description	Unused	Used
862	CD358	$2 multicolored	4.75	4.75

UPU, 125th Anniv. A195

Sugar Mills rolling stock: 50c, Diesel locomotive. 87c, Steam locomotive. $1, Diesel locomotive, diff. $2, Free passenger train.

Wmk. 373

1999, Oct. 26 Litho. ***Perf. 13¾***

863 A195 50c multicolored .85 .40
864 A195 87c multicolored 1.25 .75
865 A195 $1 multicolored 1.40 1.10
866 A195 $2 multicolored 2.50 *3.75*
Nos. 863-866 (4) 6.00 6.00

Christmas — A196

Designs: 13c, Giving gifts. 31c, Angels and star. 63c, Bible, Magi, Holy family. 87c, Joseph, mary, donkey, vert. $1, Mary, Jesus, animals, vert. $2, Children, Santa, vert.

Perf. 13¼x13

1999, Nov. 29 Litho. Wmk. 373

867 A196 13c multicolored .25 .25
868 A196 31c multicolored .60 .35
869 A196 63c multicolored .95 .50
870 A196 87c multicolored 1.15 .75
871 A196 $1 multicolored 1.30 .85
872 A196 $2 multicolored 2.25 *3.50*
Nos. 867-872 (6) 6.50 6.20

Millennium A197

Designs: No. 873, Outstretched hands, islands (arch at top). No. 874, Map, flag (arch at right). No. 875, Globe, warrior beating lali, temple (arch at bottom). No. 876, Globe, drua, red line (arch at left).

No. 877: a, Fiji petrel (arch at top). b, Crested iguana, islands (arch at top). c, Red prawns (arch at bottom). d, Tagimaucia (arch at bottom).

Perf. 13¼ Syncopated Type A

Litho. with Foil Application

2000, Jan. 1 Unwmk.

873 A197 $5 gold & multi 7.00 7.00
874 A197 $5 gold & multi 7.00 7.00
875 A197 $5 gold & multi 7.00 7.00
876 A197 $5 gold & multi 7.00 7.00
Nos. 873-876 (4) 28.00 28.00

Souvenir Sheet

877 A197 $10 Sheet of 4, #a-d 60.00 60.00

Beetles — A198

Designs: 15c, Paracupta sulcata. 87c, Agrilus sp. $1.06, Cyphogastra abdominalis. $2, Paracupta sp.

Perf. 13¾x14

2000, Mar. 14 Litho. Wmk. 373

878 A198 15c multi .40 .25
879 A198 87c multi 1.20 .75
880 A198 $1.06 multi 1.45 *1.50*
881 A198 $2 multi 2.40 *3.00*
Nos. 878-881 (4) 5.45 5.50

Sesame Street — A199

No. 882: a, Big Bird. b, Oscar the Grouch. c, Cookie Monster. d, Grover. e, Elmo. f, Ernie. g, Zoe. h, The Count. i, Bert.

No. 883, Big Bird, Elmo and Ernie, horiz. No. 884, Cookie Monster, Bert and Ernie, horiz.

Perf. 14½x14¾

2000, Apr. 20 Litho. Wmk. 373

882 A199 50c Sheet of 9, #a-i 7.75 7.75

Souvenir Sheets

Perf. 14¾x14½

883 A199 $2 multi 3.25 3.25
884 A199 $2 multi 3.25 3.25

The Stamp Show 2000, London (#882).

Pres. Ratu Sir Kamisese Mara, 80th Birthday — A200

President with: 15c, Lumberjack, timber truck. 81c, Women. $1, Workers in cane field. $3, Ships.

2000, May 13 ***Perf. 14x13¾***

885 A200 15c multi .35 .25
886 A200 81c multi .95 .65
887 A200 $1 multi 1.05 .75
888 A200 $3 multi 4.50 5.00
Nos. 885-888 (4) 6.85 6.65

Prince William, 18th Birthday

Common Design Type

William: Nos. 889, 893a, As child, wearing fireman's helmet, vert. Nos. 890, 893b, Wearing navy suit, vert. Nos. 891, 893c, Wearing scarf. Nos. 892, 893d, Wearing suit and wearing blue shirt. No. 893e, As child, wearing camouflage and beret.

Perf. 13¾x14¼, 14¼x13¾

2000, June 21 Wmk. 373

Stamps With White Border

889 CD359 $1 multi 1.35 1.35
890 CD359 $1 multi 1.35 1.35
891 CD359 $1 multi 1.35 1.35
892 CD359 $1 multi 1.35 1.35
Nos. 889-892 (4) 5.40 5.40

Souvenir Sheet

Stamps Without White Border

Perf. 14¼

893 CD359 $1 Sheet of 5, #a-e 7.50 7.50

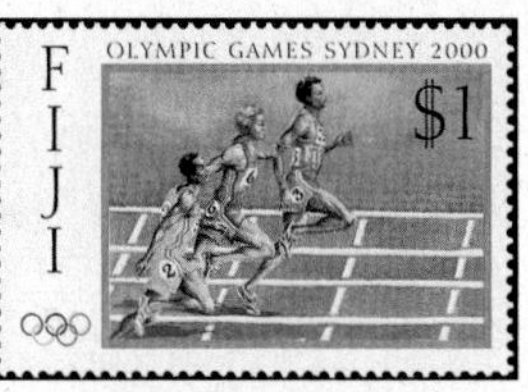

2000 Summer Olympics, Sydney — A201

Wmk. 373

2000, Aug. 8 Litho. ***Perf. 13¾***

894 A201 44c Swimming, vert. .75 .50
895 A201 87c Judo, vert. 1.15 .75
896 A201 $1 Running 1.25 1.25
897 A201 $2 Windsurfing 2.25 2.90
Nos. 894-897 (4) 5.40 5.40

Souvenir Sheet

Alsmithia Longipes — A202

No. 898: a, Red frond at R. b, Red frond at L. c, Yellow frond. d, Fruit.

Wmk. 373

2000, Sept. 12 Litho. ***Perf. 13½***

898 A202 $1 Sheet of 4, #a-d 6.50 6.50

Lapita Pottery Shards and Discovery Sites — A203

44c, Yanuca Island. 63c, Mago Island. $1, Ugaga Island. $2, Sigatoka sand dunes.

2000, Oct. 24 ***Perf. 13¾***

899-902 A203 Set of 4 5.75 5.75

Christmas A204

Designs: 15c, Jungle. 81c, Cliffside trail. 87c, Coastal village. $3, Outrigger canoe.

2000, Nov. 21

903-906 A204 Set of 4 6.25 6.25

Souvenir Sheet

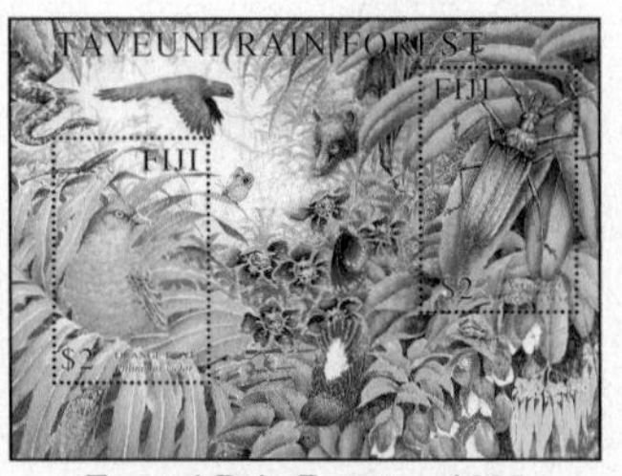

Taveuni Rain Forest — A205

Designs: a, Orange dove. b, Xixuthrus heyrovskyi.

Perf. 13¾x13½

2001, Feb. 1 Litho. Unwmk.

907 A205 $2 Sheet of 2, #a-b 6.00 6.00

Moths A206

Designs: 17c, Macroglossum hirundo vitiensis. 48c, Hippotion celerio. 69c, Gnathothlibus erotus eras. 89c, Theretra pinastrina intersecta. $1.17, Deilephila placida torenia. $2, Psilogramma jordana.

2001, Mar. 20 ***Perf. 13¼x13***

908-913 A206 Set of 6 6.75 6.75

Souvenir Sheet

Gallus Gallus — A207

Designs: a, Hen. b, Rooster.

2001, May 22 ***Perf. 13¾x14***

914 A207 $2 Sheet of 2, #a-b 7.00 7.00

Society for Prevention of Cruelty — A208

Designs: 34c, Girl, cat. 96c, Boy, dogs. $1.23, Girl, cat, diff. $2, Boy, dog.

Perf. 14x13¾

2001, June 26 Litho. Unwmk.

915-918 A208 Set of 4 6.50 6.50

Pigeons — A209

Designs: 69c, White-throated. 89c, Pacific, vert. $1.23, Peal's, vert. $2, Rock.

2001, July 20 ***Perf. 14x14¾, 14¾x14***

919-922 A209 Set of 4 7.25 7.25

Westpac Pacific Bank, 100th Anniv. in Fiji — A210

Bank office in: 48c, 1901. 96c, 1916. $1, 1934. $2, 2001.

2001, Aug. 10 ***Perf. 13¼x13¾***
923-926 A210 Set of 4 5.00 5.00

Fish A211

Designs: 50c, Yellowfin tuna. 96c, Wahoo. $1.17, Dolphin fish. $2, Pacific blue marlin.

2001, Aug. 23
927-930 A211 Set of 4 5.50 5.50

Christmas A212

Designs: 17c, Angel appears to Mary. 34c Nativity. 48c, Adoration of the shepherds. 69c, Adoration of the Magi. 89c, Flight to Egypt. $2, Fijian Chirst child.

2001, Oct. 29 Litho. ***Perf. 13¾x13¼***
931-936 A212 Set of 6 6.75 6.75

Colonial Financial Services Group, 125th Anniv. in Fiji — A213

Designs: 17c, Bank office. 48c, Women using automatic teller machine. $1, Suva Private Hospital. $3, Hoisting of British flag.

2001, Nov. 16 Litho. ***Perf. 13¼***
937-940 A213 Set of 4 6.75 6.75

Air Pacific, 50th Anniv. — A214

No. 941: a, De Havilland Drover. b, Hawker Siddley HS-748. c, Douglas DC-10-30. d, Boeing 747-200.

2001, Nov. 30 Litho. ***Perf. 13***
941 Horiz. strip of 4 7.50 7.50
a. A214 89c multi 1.50 1.50
b. A214 96c multi 1.75 1.75
c. A214 $1 multi 1.75 1.75
d. A214 $2 multi 2.25 2.25

Spices — A215

Designs: 69c, Pepper. 89c, Nutmeg. $1, Vanilla. $2, Cinnamon.

2002, Mar. 12 Litho. ***Perf. 13¼***
942-945 A215 Set of 4 6.25 6.25

Souvenir Sheet

Balaka Palm — A216

Palm and: a, Bird, butterfly, beetle. b, Lizard, butterfly

2002, Apr. 29
946 A216 $2 Sheet of 2, #a-b 6.75 6.75

Freshwater Fish — A217

Designs: 48c, Redigobius sp. 96c, Spotted flagtail. $1.23, Silverstripe mudskipper. $2, Snakehead gudgeon.

2002, May 13
947-950 A217 Set of 4 6.50 6.50

Fruit — A218

Designs: 25c, Breadfruit. 34c, Wi. $1, Jakfruit. $3, Avocado.

2002, July 25 Litho. ***Perf. 13¾x13¼***
951-954 A218 Set of 4 6.25 6.25

Murex Shells — A219

Designs: 69c, Saul's murex. 96c, Caltrop murex. $1, Purple Pacific drupe. $2, Ramose murex.

2002, Aug. 20 ***Perf. 13¾***
955-958 A219 Set of 4 7.00 7.00

Fiji Goshawk A220

Designs: 48c, Goshawk and eggs. 89c, Chicks in nest. $1, Juvenile on branch. $3, Adult.

2002, Sept. 10
959-962 A220 Set of 4 8.25 8.25

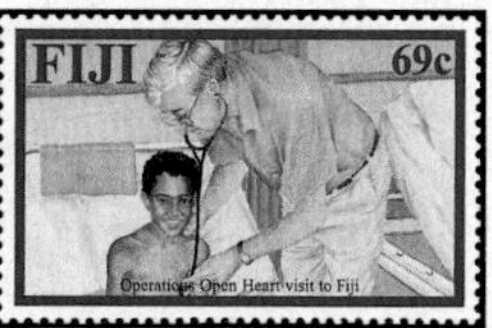

2002 Operation Open Heart Visit to Fiji — A221

Designs: 34c, Doctors performing operation, vert. 69c, Doctor listening to patient's heart with stethoscope. $1.17, Technician administering echocardiogram. $2, Administration of anesthesia to patient, vert.

2002, Oct. 30 ***Perf. 13¼***
963-966 A221 Set of 4 7.25 7.25

Fiji Natural Artesian Water — A222

Designs: 25c, Bottle of water, flowers, vert. 48c, Bottling plant. $1, Delivery truck. $3, Children with bottled water, vert.

2002, Nov. 5
967-970 A222 Set of 4 7.50 7.50

Christmas — A223

Designs: 17c, Christian church. 89c, Mosque. $1, Hindu temple. $3, Christian church, diff.

2002, Nov. 20
971-974 A223 Set of 4 7.50 7.50

Post Fiji, Ltd. Improvements — A224

Designs: 48c, General Post Office. 96c, Post Fiji Mail Center. $1, Post Fiji Logistics Center. $2, Smart Mail.

2003, Mar. 19 Litho. ***Perf. 13¼***
975-978 A224 Set of 4 6.75 6.75

Souvenir Sheet

Intl. Year of Fresh Water — A225

No. 979: a, Top of waterfall, flowers. b, Base of waterfall, butterfly.

2003, Apr. 22
979 A225 $2 Sheet of 2, #a-b 7.25 7.25

2003 South Pacific Games, Suva — A226

Designs: 10c, Track athlete with arms raised. 14c, Baseball. 20c, Netball. No. 983, $5, Shot put.
No. 984, $5, Flags of participating nations, venues, volleyball players.

2003 ***Perf. 13¼***
980-983 A226 Set of 4 7.25 7.25

Size: 120x85mm

Imperf

984 A226 $5 multi 6.75 6.75

Issued: Nos. 980-983, 5/26; No. 984, 6/28.

Fish A227

Siganus uspi: 58c, Fish, crab and coral. 83c, Two fish and coral. $1.15, Two fish, coral, and other fish species. $3, Fish and coral.

2003, Aug. 12 ***Perf. 13¼***
985-988 A227 Set of 4 8.50 8.50

Bird Life International A228

Designs: 41c, Long-legged warbler. 60c, Silktail. $1.07, Red-throated lorikeet. $3, Pink-billed parrot finch.

2003, Sept. 16
989-992 A228 Set of 4 13.00 13.00

Geckos
A229

Designs: 83c, Pacific slender-toed gecko. $1.07, Indopacific tree gecko. $1.15, Mann's gecko. $2, Voracious gecko.

2003, Oct. 21 Litho. *Perf. 13¼*
993-996 A229 Set of 4 9.75 9.75

Christmas — A230

Children's art: 18c, Children, Christmas tree. 41c, Children, flag of Fiji. 58c, Children, Santa Claus, reindeer pulling sleighs, vert. 83c, Santa Claus on chimney, gifts, children, Christmas tree, vert. $1.07, Children with candles, Christmas tree, vert. $1.15, Santa Claus, children, bell, rainbow, vert.
$1.41, Handshake.

2003, Nov. 26 Litho. *Perf. 13¼*
997-1002 A230 Set of 6 7.25 7.25

Souvenir Sheet
1003 A230 $1.41 multi 3.50 3.50

Tagimoucia — A231

2003, Dec. 1 Litho. *Perf. 14½x14*
1004 A231 50c multi + label *5.00 5.00*

Sold in sheets of 10 stamps + 10 labels that could be personalized for $15 per sheet.

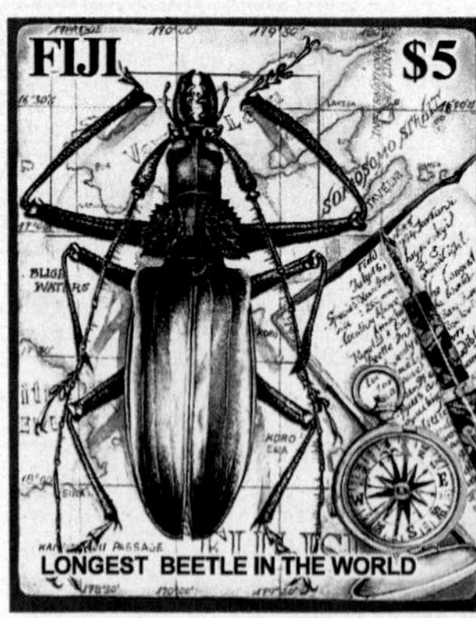

Xixuthrus Heyrovskyi, Longest Beetle in the World — A232

2003, Feb. 27 *Imperf.*
1005 A232 $5 multi 7.50 7.50

Miniature Sheet

Worldwide Fund for Nature (WWF) — A233

No. 1006: a, 58c, Skipjack tuna. b, 83c, Albacore tuna. c, $1.07, Yellowfin tuna. d, $3, Bigeye tuna.

2004, Apr. 7 *Perf. 13¼*
1006 A233 Sheet of 4, #a-d 8.50 8.50
e. Like #1006, with artist's name at LL of each stamp 8.50 8.50

Land Snails
A234

Designs: 18c, Malleated placostyle. 41c, Kandavu placostyle. $1.15, Fragile orpiella. $3, Thin Fijian placostyle.

2004, May 28
1007-1010 A234 Set of 4 7.25 7.25

Bird Type of 1995 and

No. 1011A

Perf. 13¼x13
2004, June 26 Unwmk.
1011 A166 18c Island thrush 1.90 1.90
1011A A166 4c on 18c #1011 *250.00 250.00*

No. 1011A issued Aug. 2008. Surcharge on No. 1011A exists only inverted. Values are for stamps with surcharge at top, as shown. Value, with surcharge centered $400.

Coral Reef Shrimp — A235

Designs: 58c, Boxer shrimp. 83c, Bumblebee shrimp. $1.07, Mantis shrimp. $3, Anemone shrimp.

2004, June 30 *Perf. 13¼*
1012-1015 A235 Set of 4 7.25 7.25

Birds
A236

Designs: 41c, Wandering tattler. 58c, Whimbrel. $1.15, Pacific golden plover. $3, Bristle-thighed curlew.

2004, July 28
1016-1019 A236 Set of 4 10.00 10.00

2004 Summer Olympics, Athens
A237

Designs: 41c, Swimming. 58c, Judo, vert. $1.40, Weight lifting, vert. $2, Makelesi Bulikiobo, runner.

2004, Aug. 12
1020-1023 A237 Set of 4 7.25 7.25

Musket Cove to Port Vila Yacht Race, 25th Anniv. — A238

Various yachts: 83c, $1.07, $1.15, $2. $1.07 and $2 are vert.

2004, Sept. 18 *Perf. 14¼*
1024-1027 A238 Set of 4 8.00 8.00
1027a Souvenir sheet of 1 4.25 4.25

See Vanuatu Nos. 858-861.

Souvenir Sheet

Coconut Crab — A239

2004, Oct. 20 Litho. *Perf. 14*
1028 A239 $5 multi 7.50 7.50

Papilio Schmeltzii — A240

Designs: 58c, Newly-emerged adult, vert. 83c, Larva. $1.41, Adult. $3, Pupa, vert.

Perf. 14x14½, 14½x14
2004, Nov. 10
1029-1032 A240 Set of 4 9.50 9.50

Christmas
A241

Designs: 18c, Annunciation. 58c, Infant in manger. $1.07, Madonna and child. $3, Adoration of the Shepherds.

2004, Dec. 1 Litho. *Perf. 13¼*
1033-1036 A241 Set of 4 9.00 9.00

Birds — A242

No. 1037: a, Little heron. b, Great white egret. c, White-faced heron. d, Pacific reef heron.

2005, Jan. 26
1037 Horiz. strip of 4 9.25 9.25
a.-d. A242 $1 Any single 2.25 2.25

Flowers For Perfume — A243

Designs: 58c, Cananga odorata. $1.15, Euodia hortensis. $1.41, Pandanus tecorius. $2, Santalum yasi.

2005, Feb. 20 *Perf. 14x14½*
1038-1041 A243 Set of 4 7.50 7.50

Peregrine Falcons — A244

Designs: 41c, Head of falcon. 83c, Adult at nest. $1.07, Chicks. $3, Adult on rock.

2005, Mar. 14 Litho. *Perf. 14½x14*
1042-1045 A244 Set of 4 9.50 9.50

Triggerfish — A245

Designs: 58c, Whitebanded triggerfish. 83c, Yellow-spotted triggerfish. $1.15, Orange-lined triggerfish. $2, Clown triggerfish.

2005, Apr. 27
1046-1049 A245 Set of 4 8.00 8.00

European Philatelic Cooperation, 50th Anniv. (in 2006) — A246

Color of arches: 58c, Red. 83c, Blue green. $1.41, Purple. $4, Yellow bister.

2005, June 1 *Perf. 13¾*
1050-1053 A246 Set of 4 10.00 10.00
1053a Souvenir sheet, #1050-1053 10.00 10.00

Europa stamps, 50th anniv. (in 2006).

Miniature Sheet

End of World War II, 60th Anniv. — A247

No. 1054: a, HMNZS Achilles. b, Japanese Yokosuka E14Y "Glen" over Suva Harbor. c, Fijian South Pacific Scouts in Solomon Islands. d, USS Chicago. e, Patrol vessel HMS

Viti. f, British Prime Minister Winston Churchill. g, HMS Hood. h, Dambusters Raid. i, German King Tiger tank in Ardennes. j, Gen. Dwight D. Eisenhower.

2005, June 27 Litho. *Perf. 13¾*
1054 A247 83c Sheet of 10, #a-j 12.75 12.75

Game Fish A248

Designs: 41c, Great barracuda. 58c, Narrow-barred Spanish mackerel. $1.07, Giant trevally. $3, Indo-Pacific sailfish.

2005, July 27 Litho. *Perf. 14½x14*
1055-1058 A248 Set of 4 8.75 8.75

Pope John Paul II (1920-2005) A249

2005, Aug. 18 *Perf. 14*
1059 A249 $1 multi 2.50 2.50

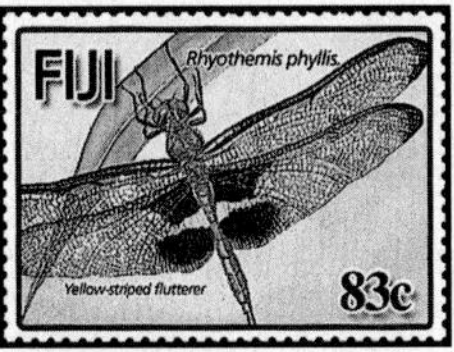

Dragonflies — A250

Designs: 83c, Yellow-striped flutterer. $1.07, Agrionoptera insignis. $1.15, Green skimmer. $2, Common percher.

2005, Aug. 30 Litho. *Perf. 13¼*
1060-1063 A250 Set of 4 7.50 7.50

Albert Einstein (1879-1955), Physicist — A251

Einstein: 83c, As a child. $1.07, In 1905. $1.15, And blackboard. $2, And galaxies.

2005, Sept. 27 Litho. *Perf. 14¼x14*
1064-1067 A251 Set of 4 9.25 9.25

Intl. Year of Physics.

Root Crops — A252

Designs: 41c, Manihot utilissima. 83c, Ipomoea satatas. $1.41, Colocasia esculenta. $2, Dioscorea sativa.

2005, Oct. 13 *Perf. 13¼*
1068-1071 A252 Set of 4 7.25 7.25

Tall Ships A253

Designs: 83c, Eliza of Province. $1.15, Elbe. $1.41, HMS Rosario. $2, L'Astrolabe.

2005, Nov. 21 Litho. *Perf. 14x14¼*
1072-1075 A253 Set of 4 9.00 9.00

Barn Owls — A254

Owl: 18c, And eggs. $1.15, Juvenile. $1.41, With prey. $2, Perched.

2006, Jan. 10 Litho. *Perf. 14¼x14*
1076-1079 A254 Set of 4 9.75 9.75

Platymantis Vitianus — A255

Various depictions: 50c, 83c, $1.15, $2.

2006, Feb. 8 Litho. *Perf. 14x14¼*
1080-1083 A255 Set of 4 8.00 8.00

Skinks A256

Designs: 18c, Pygmy snake-eyed skink. 58c, Brown-tailed copper striped skink. $1.15, Pacific black skink. $3, Pacific blue-tailed skink.

2006, Mar. 22
1084-1087 A256 Set of 4 7.50 7.50

Queen Elizabeth II, 80th Birthday A257

Designs: 50c, As child. 65c, Wearing tiara. 90c, Wearing blue hat. $3, Wearing blue hat, diff.

No. 1092: a, Like 65c. b, Like 90c.

2006, Apr. 21 Litho. *Perf. 14*
With White Frames
1088-1091 A257 Set of 4 7.00 7.00

Souvenir Sheet
Without White Frames
1092 A257 $2 Sheet of 2, #a-b 5.75 5.75

Miniature Sheet

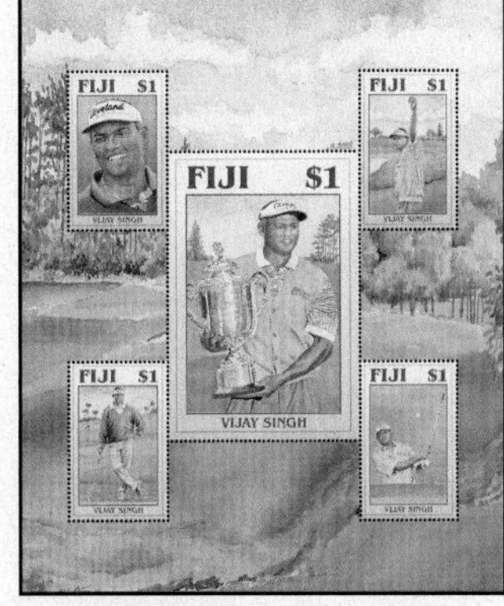

Vijay Singh, Golfer — A258

No. 1097 — Singh: a, Head. b, With arm raised. c, Leaning on golf club. d, Hitting ball from sand trap. e, Holding trophy (60x87mm).

Perf. 14x14¼
2006, May 26 Litho. Unwmk.
1097 A258 $1 Sheet of 5, #a-e 8.50 8.50

2006 World Cup Soccer Championships, Germany — A259

Various players: 65c, 90c, $1.20, $2.

2006, June 9 *Perf. 14¼x14*
1098-1101 A259 Set of 4 7.50 7.50

Souvenir Sheet

Purple Swamphen — A260

No. 1102: a, Swamphen and flowers. b, Swamphen on nest.

2006, July 20 *Perf. 14½x14*
1102 A260 $2 Sheet of 2, #a-b 6.50 6.50

Extinct Species A261

Designs: 50c, Brachylophus vitiensis. $1.10, Natunaornis gigoura, vert. $1.20, Vitirallus watlingi, vert. $1.50, Platymantis megabotoniviti.

Perf. 14x14¼, 14¼x14
2006, Aug. 15 Litho.
1103-1106 A261 Set of 4 7.00 7.00

Phasmids — A262

Designs: 10c, Hermarchus apollonius. $1.10, Cotylosoma dipneusticum. $1.20, Chitoniscus feejeeanus. $2, Graeffea crouanii.

2006, Sept. 7 *Perf. 14½x14*
1107-1110 A262 Set of 4 7.00 7.00

Honey Production A263

Designs: 18c, Bees and honeycomb. 40c, Apiarist examining honeycomb, horiz. $1, Woman and beehives, horiz. $3, Man and bottle of honey.

2006, Oct. 16 *Perf. 14x14½, 14½x14*
1111-1114 A263 Set of 4 7.50 7.50

Christmas A264

Flowering plants: 18c, Decaspermum vitiense. 65c, Quisqualis indica. 90c, Mussaendra raiateensis. $3, Delonix regia.

2006, Dec. 5 *Perf. 14x14½*
1115-1118 A264 Set of 4 7.50 7.50

Anemonefish — A265

Designs: 18c, Spine-cheek anemonefish. 60c, Pink anemonefish. 90c, Orange-fin anemonefish. $3, Dusky anemonefish.

Perf. 14½x14, 14x14½
2006, Nov. 7 Litho.
1119-1122 A265 Set of 4 7.50 7.50

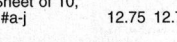

Souvenir Sheet

Thalassina Anomala — A266

2007, Jan. 24 *Perf. 13½*
1123 A266 $4 multi 5.50 5.50

Traditional Architecture — A267

Designs: 20c, Coastal dwelling. 65c, Inland dwelling. $1.10, Temple, Bau. $3, Lauan-style house.

2007, Mar. 20 Litho. *Perf. 13¼*
1124-1127 A267 Set of 4 7.25 7.25

Freshwater Gobies — A268

Designs: 20c, Sicyopterus lagocephalus. $1.10, Stiphodon rutilaureus. $1.20, Sicyopus zosterophorum. $2, Stiphodon sp.

2007, Apr. 5 Litho. *Perf. 13¼*
1128-1131 A268 Set of 4 6.25 6.25

Birds Introduced to Fiji — A269

Designs: 50c, Red-vented bulbul. 65c, Spotted dove, horiz. $1.50, Australian magpie, horiz. $2, Java sparrow.

2007, May 22
1132-1135 A269 Set of 4 7.50 7.50

Scouting, Cent. A270

Designs: 50c, Scout in kayak, hand holding compass. 90c, Three Scouts wearing helmets, hands tying knot. No. 1138, $1.50, Scout in harness climbing, Scout saluting. $2, Scout writing observation notes, hands tying neckerchief.

No. 1140, $1.50, vert.: a, Scout emblem. b, Lord Robert Baden-Powell.

2007, July 9 *Perf. 13¾*
1136-1139 A270 Set of 4 7.00 7.00

Souvenir Sheet

1140 A270 $1.50 Sheet of 2, #a-b 4.75 4.75

Snails A271

Designs: 40c, Clithon diadema. 90c, Neritina variegata. $1.20, Fijidoma maculata. $2, Neritina squamaepicta.

2007, Aug. 18 *Perf. 14x14¼*
1141-1144 A271 Set of 4 6.50 6.50

Orchids — A272

Designs: 20c, Liparis layardii. 65c, Dendrobium catillare, horiz. $1.10, Dendrobium mohlianum, horiz. $3, Glomera montana.

Perf. 14¼x14, 14x14¼
2007, Aug. 21
1145-1148 A272 Set of 4 7.25 7.25

Nos. 725 and 729 Surcharged

No. 1149

No. 1150

Methods, Types and Watermarks As Before

2006-08
1149 A166 1c on 6c #729 1.50 1.50
1150 A166 1c on 6c #729 *7.00 7.00*

No. 1149 exists with inverted surcharge. Value, $90. No. 1149 also exists with double surcharge, one inverted. Value, $150. No. 1149 also exists with normal surcharge shifted 75% upward. Value, $50.

No. 1151

No. 1152

No. 1152c

1151 A166 2c on 1c #725 *4.50 4.50*
1152 A166 2c on 1c #725, larger font *2.50 2.50*
c. 1½mm gap between "2" and "c" (position 67) *60.00 60.00*

No. 1152 exists with normal surcharge shifted 50% upward. Value, $50.

No. 1152A

No. 1152Ab

No. 1152Ac

1152A A166 2c on 1c #725, 4mm between "c" and obliterator *200.00 200.00*
b. 5mm between "c" and obliterator *200.00 200.00*
c. 3mm between "c" and obliterator —

No. 1152Ab exists with inverted surcharge. Value, $375.

No. 1153

No. 1153a

No. 1153c

1153 A166 2c on 6c #729, 4mm between "c" and obliterator 1.25 1.25
a. 5mm between "c" and obliterator 1.25 1.25
c. 1½mm gap between "2" and "c" (position 57) *60.00 60.00*

No. 1153a exists with inverted surcharge. Value, $110. No. 1153a also exists with double surcharge, one inverted. Value, $150.

No. 1153B

No. 1154

No. 1154A

1153B A166 2c on 6c #729 *550.00 550.00*
1154 A166 3c on 1c #725 1.25 1.25
1154A A166 3c on 1c #725, larger font *650.00 650.00*

No. 1154 exists with inverted surcharge. Value, $275. No. 1154 exists with double surcharge, one inverted. Value, $225.

No. 1155

No. 1155a

1155 A166 4c on 1c #725 1.50 1.50
a. 1½mm gap between "4" and "c" (position 57) *60.00 60.00*

No. 1156

No. 1156a

1156 A166 4c on 6c #729, 4mm between "c" an obliterator 1.25 1.25
a. 5mm between "c" and obliterator 1.25 1.25

No. 1156a exists with inverted surcharge. Value, $110. No. 1156a also exists with double surcharge, one inverted. Value, $150. No. 1156a also exists with normal surcharge shifted 75% upward and 50% upward. Values, each $50.

No. 1156B

No. 1157

1156B A166 6c on 6c #729 *650.00 650.00*
1157 A166 18c on 6c #729, 4mm between "c" and obliterator *6.50 6.50*

No. 1157 exists with double surcharge, one with normal 4mm between "c" and obliterator and the other with 2½mm between "c" and obliterator. One surcharge is shifted 75% upward. Half of the errors have the normal separation between "c" and obliterator at top and half have it at bottom. Each error variety is equally scarce. Value, each $130. No. 1157 exists with double surcharge, both with 4mm between "c" and obliterator. Value, $150.

No. 1157 also exists with normal surcharge shifted 75% upward but with no second surcharge. Value, $50.

No. 1158

No. 1158a

1158 A166 18c on 6c #729, 2½mm between "c" and obliterator *11.00 11.00*
a. 4mm between "c" and obliterator *22.00 22.00*

No. 1158 exists with double surcharge. Value, $150. No. 1158 also exists with double surcharge, both inverted. Value, $225.

No. 1159

No. 1159a

1159 A166 20c on 6c #729, 2½mm between "c" and obliterator *6.50 6.50*
a. 4mm between "c" and obliterator *14.50 14.50*

No. 1159 exists with inverted surcharge. Value, $110.

No. 1160

No. 1160a

No. 1160b

1160 A166 20c on 6c #729, 4mm between "c" and obliterator *30.00 30.00*
a. 1 ½mm between "c" and obliterator *60.00 60.00*
b. No gap between "c" and obliterator *475.00 475.00*
Nos. 1149-1160 (16) 2,125. 2,125.

No. 1160a exists with double surcharge. Value, $150.

Issued: No. 1149, 5/30/07; No. 1150, 9/19/07; No. 1151, 4/3; No. 1152, 11/13; No. 1152A, July 2007, No. 1152Ab, 8/20/08; Nos. 1153, 1153B 2/19/07; No. 1153a, 2/27/07; No. 1154, 3/13; No. 1155, 6/27; No. 1156, 6/6/07; No. 1156a, 2/19/08; No. 1156B, Feb. 2007; No. 1157, 6/8; No. 1158, 9/8; No. 1158a, Aug. 2007; No. 1159, 1/19/07; No. 1159a, Jan. 2007; No. 1160, 3/8/07; No. 1160a, 4/12/08.

Fish A273

Designs: 50c, Coronation trout. 90c, Roving coral trout. $1.50, Squaretail coral trout. $2, Chinese footballer.

2007, Oct. 15 Litho. *Perf. 13¼*
1161-1164 A273 Set of 4 7.75 7.75

Butterflies — A274

Designs: 20c, Polyura caphontis. $1.10, Hypolimnas bolina, horiz. $1.20, Doleschallia bisaltide, horiz. $2, Danaus hamata.

2007, Nov. 20 Litho. *Perf. 13¼*
1165-1168 A274 Set of 4 6.00 6.00

Souvenir Sheet

Barred-winged Rail — A275

No. 1169: a, Head of adult. b, Chick.

2007, Dec. 3
1169 A275 $2 Sheet of 2, #a-b 5.50 5.50

National Medals — A276

Designs: 50c, Medal of the Order of Fiji. 65c, Member of the Order of Fiji. $1.20, Officer of the Order of Fiji. $2, Companion of the Order of Fiji.

2008, Feb. 20 Litho. *Perf. 13¼*
1170-1173 A276 Set of 4 6.25 6.25

Souvenir Sheet

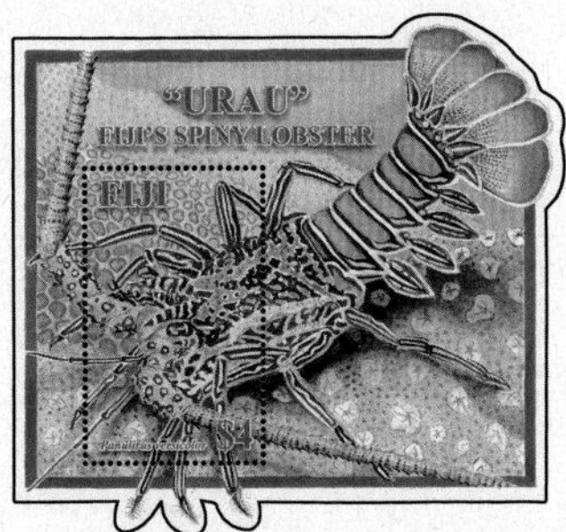
Spiny Lobster — A277

2008, Apr. 22 Litho. *Perf. 14x14½*
1174 A277 $4 multi 5.25 5.25

First Trans-Pacific Flight of the Southern Cross, 80th Anniv. — A278

Southern Cross: 20c, Over Fiji. 90c, In Albert Park, Suva. $1.50, Surrounded by police guard. $2, With crew.

2008, June 13 *Perf. 13½*
1175-1178 A278 Set of 4 5.75 5.75

2008 Summer Olympics, Beijing A279

Designs: 20c, Bamboo, Running. 65c, Dragon, Judo. 90c, Lanterns, Shooting. $1.50, Carp, Swimming.

2008, May 5 Litho. *Perf. 13¼*
1179-1182 A279 Set of 4 4.25 4.25

Red-breasted Musk Parrot Varieties — A280

Prosopeia tabuensis: 65c, Koroensis. 90c, Atrogularis, horiz. $1.50, Taviunensis, horiz. $2, Splendens.

2008, Mar. 25 Litho. *Perf. 13½*
1183-1186 A280 Set of 4 6.75 6.75

Humpback Whales — A281

Humpback whale: 20c, Pair underwater. 50c, Breaching water's surface. $1.10, Reentering water. $3, Flukes.

2008, July 17 Litho. *Perf. 14½x14*
1187-1190 A281 Set of 4 6.00 6.00

Nos. 729-731 Surcharged Like Nos. 1149-1160

No. 1191

No. 1191A

No. 1191Ab

Methods, Perfs and Watermarks As Before

2007-09
1191 A166 1c on 13c #730, 5mm between "c" and obliterator 1.50 1.50
b. 4mm between "c" and obliterator (positions 3 and 89) *50.00 50.00*
1191A A166 1c on 23c #731, 4mm between "c" and obliterator 1.00 1.00
b. 5mm between "c" and obliterator 1.00 1.00
c. Pair, Nos. 1191Ab and 1191A (positions 3 and 89) *50.00 50.00*

No. 1191 exists with double surcharge, one inverted. Value, $150. No. 1191 exists with double surcharge: one upright with "XX" obliterator, the other inverted with "xxx" obliterator. Value, $175. No. 1191A exists with inverted surcharge. Value, $160. No. 1191A exists with a "2c" surcharge having a 1 ½mm gap between the "2" and the "c" (position 57). Value, $100. No. 1191Ab exists with inverted surcharge. Value, $160. No. 1191Ab also exists with double surcharge, one inverted. Value, $175.

No. 1191C

No. 1192

1191C A166 2c on 6c #729 *175.00 175.00*
d. 1 ½mm gap between "2" and "c" (position 57) —
1192 A166 2c on 6c #729 *175.00 175.00*
c. 2 ½mm gap between pair of double bars of obliterator *400.00 400.00*
d. 4mm between "c" and obliterator *325.00 325.00*

No. 1192 exists with obliterator of three double bars and with obliterator of four double bars. Value, each $500. No. 1192 exists with obliterator of two double bars and a single bar. Value, $400. No. 1192 exists with obliterator omitted. Value, $750.

No. 1192A

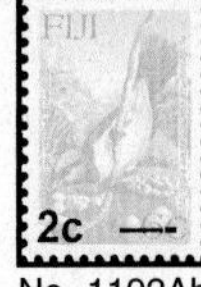
No. 1192Ab

No. 1193 No. 1193a

No. 1193B

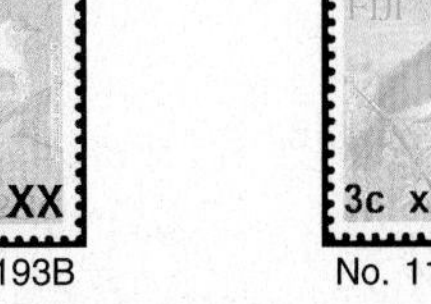
No. 1193C

1192A A166 2c on 6c #729 *175.00 175.00*
b. Short obliterator *250.00 250.00*
e. 4 ½mm obliterator *250.00 250.00*
f. 12 ½mm obliterator *250.00 250.00*
1193 A166 2c on 13c #730, 5 mm between "c" and obliterator 1.50 1.50
a. 4mm between "c" and obliterator (positions 3 and 89) *50.00 50.00*
1193B A166 2c on 23c #731, 5 mm between "c" and obliterator *125.00 125.00*
a. 4mm between "c" and obliterator (positions 3 and 89) *200.00 200.00*
1193C A166 3c on 13c #730 *175.00 175.00*

No. 1192A has an 8mm obliterator. Two lines comprise the obliterator on No. 1192Ab: one long, one short. The obliterator on No. 1192Af extends into the right margin and must be collected with right selvage attached to show the entire obliterator.

No. 1193 exists with double surcharge, one inverted. Value, $150. No. 1193 exists with double surcharge: one upright with "XX" obliterator, the other inverted with "xxx" obliterator. Value, $175. No. 1193 exists with a period after the "2c." Value, $500.

No. 1194

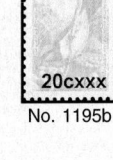

No. 1194a

No. 1195

No. 1195b

1194 A166 4c on 13c #730, 5mm between "c" and obliterator 1.50 1.50
a. 4mm between "c" and obliterator (positions 3 and 89) *50.00 50.00*
b. 1 ½mm gap between "4" and "c" *225.00 225.00*
1195 A166 20c on 6c #729 *100.00 100.00*
b. No gap between "c" and obliterator *550.00 550.00*

No. 1194 exists with double surcharge, one inverted at top of stamp. Value, $200. No. 1194 exists with double surcharge, one inverted in center of stamp. Value, $200.

No. 1195A

1195A A166 20c on 23c #731 *400.00 400.00*
- *c.* 3½mm between "c" and obliterator *400.00 400.00*

No. 1195A exists with normal surcharge shifted 75% upward. Value, $300. No. 1195A also exists with inverted surcharge. Value, $350. No. 1195A also exists with "c" of surcharge omitted. Value, $400.

No. 1196

No. 1196a

1196 A166 20c on 23c #731 2.00 2.00
- *a.* No gap between "c" and obliterator (position 70) *35.00 35.00*

No. 1196 exists with inverted surcharge. Value, $90. No. 1196 also exists with double surcharge and with double surcharge, one inverted. Value, each $150. No. 1196 also exists surcharged on gum side only; the surcharge is always inverted. Value, $200. No. 1196 also exists surcharged on both sides. Value, $180.

No. 1197

No. 1197a

No. 1197d

No. 1197e

No. 1197f

1197 A166 20c on 23c #731, 1½mm between "c" and obliterator 200.00 200.00
- *a.* 2½mm between "c" and obliterator *90.00 90.00*
- *d.* 3mm between "c" and obliterator *100.00 100.00*
- *e.* 4mm between "c" and obliterator *90.00 90.00*
- *f.* 5mm between "c" and obliterator *175.00 175.00*

No. 1197 exists with surcharge shifted 75% upward. Value, $175. No. 1197d exists with inverted surcharge. Value, $150.

No. 1197B

No. 1197C

1197B A166 20c on 23c #731 *35.00 35.00*
- *a.* No gap between "c" and obliterator (positions 70 and 79) *100.00 100.00*
- *c.* 3mm between "c" and obliterator *70.00 70.00*

1197C A166 20c on 23c #731 *175.00 175.00*
- *a.* No gap between "c" and obliterator *450.00 450.00*

Nos. 1191-1197C (15) *1,743. 1,743.*

No. 1197B exists with inverted surcharge. Value, $150. No. 1197C exists with inverted surcharge. Value, $350. No 1197C exists with obliterator of two double bars with a dash between them. Value, $450.

Issued: No. 1191, 8/22/08; No. 1191A, 12/18/08; No. 1191Ab, 1/23/09; No. 1191C, 1192, 1192A, 2/19/07; Nos. 1193, 1194, 8/20/08; No. 1195, 4/28/08; No. 1195A, Apr. 2008; Nos. 1196, 4/12/08; Nos. 1197, 1197a, 1197d, 1197e, 1197f. Apr. 2008; 1197B, 4/12/08; 1197C, Apr. 2008.

Bananas — A282

Various banana varieties: 65c, $1.10, $1.20, $2.

2008, Sept. 23 Litho. *Perf. 14x14½*

1198-1201 A282 Set of 4 5.50 5.50

Eels A283

Designs: 50c, Anguilla obscura. 90c, Anguilla marmorata. $1.50, Anguilla obscura, diff. $2, Gymnothorax potyuranodon.

2008, Oct. 15 *Perf. 14½x14*

1202-1205 A283 Set of 4 5.50 5.50

Christmas — A284

Various choirs: 20c, 50c, 65c, $3.

2008, Dec. 10 Litho. *Perf. 14½x14*

1206-1209 A284 Set of 4 4.50 4.50

Fruit Doves — A285

Designs: 50c, Many-colored fruit dove. 65c, Crimson-crowned fruit dove. 90c, Whistling dove. $3, Orange dove.

2009, Feb. 17 Litho. *Perf. 14x14½*

1210-1213 A285 Set of 4 5.50 5.50

Nos. 729-731 Surcharged Like Nos. 1149-1160

No. 1214

No. 1214B

No. 1215

No. 1215A

Methods, Perfs and Watermarks As Before

2009-12

1214 A166 1c on 13c #730 *45.00 45.00*
- *a.* 2½mm gap between "c" and obliterator (positions 3 and 89) *120.00 120.00*

1214B A166 1c on 13c #730, small font *90.00 90.00*

1215 A166 1c on 23c #731 1.25 1.25
- *b.* 2½mm gap between "c" and obliterator (positions 3 and 89) *50.00 50.00*

1215A A166 1c on 23c #731, small font 1.00 1.00

No. 1215 exists with inverted surcharge. Value, $90. No. 1215A exists with inverted surcharge. Value, $90. No. 1215A also exists with "xx" obliterator (position 70). Value, $300.

No. 1216

No. 1216A

No. 1216B

No. 1216D

1216 A166 2c on 6c #729 *100.00 100.00*
- *e.* 2½mm gap between "c" and obliterator (positions 3 and 89) *175.00 175.00*

1216A A166 2c on 13c #730 *45.00 45.00*
- *c.* 2½mm gap between "c" and obliterator (positions 3 and 89) *120.00 120.00*

1216B A166 2c on 23c #731 *175.00 175.00*

1216D A166 2c on 13c #730, small font *175.00 175.00*

No. 1216D has a 2½mm gap between "c" and obliterator.

No. 1217

No. 1217A

1217 A166 2c on 23c #731 *20.00 20.00*
- *b.* 2½mm between "c" and obliterator (positions 3 and 89) *50.00 50.00*

1217A A166 2c on 23c #731, small font *1.00 1.00*

No. 1217 exists with inverted surcharge. Value, $175. No. 1217A exists with inverted surcharge. Value, $90. No. 1217A also exists with double surcharge, one inverted. Value, $120. No. 1217A also exists with "xx" obliterator (position 70). Value, $300.

No. 1218

No. 1218A

1218 A166 3c on 23c #731 *45.00 45.00*
- *b.* 2½mm between "c" and obliterator (positions 3 and 89) *140.00 140.00*

1218A A166 3c on 23c #731, small font *1.00 1.00*

No. 1218 exists with "3" of surcharge omitted. Most of the known singles have irregular perforations from being roughly removed from sheets. Value thus, $100. Errors with intact perforations are extremely scarce. Value, $300. Value of single error in pair with normal stamp, $350.

No. 1218A exists with double surcharge. Value, $150. No. 1218A exists with inverted surcharge. Value, $100. No. 1218A exists with double surcharge, one inverted. Value, $130. No. 1218A exists with "xx" obliterator (position 70). Value, $300.

No. 1219

No. 1219B

No. 1220

No. 1220B

No. 1220C

No. 1220D

1219 A166 4c on 6c #729 *70.00 70.00*
- *a.* 2½mm between "c" and obliterator (positions 3 and 89) *100.00 100.00*

1219B A166 40c on 6c #729 *100.00 100.00*
- *a.* No gap between "c" and obliterator (position 70) *200.00 200.00*

1219C A166 4c on 6c #729, small font *85.00* 85.00

1220 A166 4c on 13c #730 *45.00 45.00*
- *a.* 2½mm gap between "c" and obliterator (positions 3 and 89) *120.00 120.00*

1220B A166 5c on 13c #730 *160.00 130.00*

1220C A166 4c on 13c #730, small font *90.00 90.00*

1220D A166 40c on 13c #730 *400.00 400.00*
- *a.* No gap between "c" and obliterator (position 70) — —

Nos. 1219 and 1219a exist with inverted surcharge. Value, each $200. No. 1219C exists with inverted surcharge. Value, $175. No. 1219C also exists with double surcharge, one inverted. Value, $225. No. 1220C exists with inverted surcharge. Value, $100.

No. 1221

No. 1222

No. 1222A

No. 1222C

1221 A166 4c on 23c #731 *90.00 90.00*
a. 4mm between "c" and obliterator (positions 3 and 89) *250.00 250.00*
1222 A166 4c on 23c #731 1.50 1.50
b. 2½mm between "c" and obliterator (positions 3 and 89) *50.00 50.00*
1222A A166 4c on 23c #731, small font 1.00 1.00
1222C A166 50c on 23c #731 *300.00 300.00*
a. No gap between "c" and obliterator (position 70) *1,000.*

No. 1221 exists with inverted surcharge. Value, $150.

No. 1222 exists with inverted surcharge. Value, $90. No. 1222 exists with double surcharge, one inverted. Value, $130. No. 1222 exists with double surcharge, one with normal 4mm between "c" and obliterator and the other with 2½mm between "c" and obliterator. Value, $150.

No. 1222A exists with inverted surcharge. Value, $100. No. 1222A exists with double surcharge, one inverted. Value, $120. No. 1222A exists with double surcharge. Value, $150.

No. 1223

No. 1223b

No. 1223c

No. 1223A

1223 A166 5c on 23c #731, 4mm between "c" and obliterator 1.50 1.50
b. 2½mm between "c" and obliterator (positions 3 and 89) *50.00 50.00*
c. No obliterator *325.00 325.00*
1223A A166 5c on 23c #731, small font 1.00 1.00
Nos. 1214-1223A (23) 1,644. 1,614.

No. 1223 exists with surcharge shifted 50% upward. Value, $60. No. 1223 also exists with inverted surcharge and with double surcharge, one inverted. Values, $100 and $150, respectively. No. 1223A exists with inverted surcharge. Value, $90.

On Nos. 1215, 1217, 1218, 1219, 1222 and 1223, the "c" and obliterator are 4mm apart.

Issued: Nos. 1214, 1215, 1215b, Mar. 10; Nos. 1215A, 1217A, 1218A, 8/5/10; No. 1216A, Mar. 30; Nos. 1216, 1216B, Mar.; Nos. 1217, 1217b, Mar. 30; No. 1218, Aug. 27; No. 1219, 1220, 1221, 1222, Mar. 10; No. 1222A, 8/3/10; No. 1223, July 8; No. 1223A, 8/6/10.

Weddings in Fiji — A286

Designs: 20c, Chinese wedding. 40c, Muslim wedding. $1.50, Indian wedding. $3, Fijian wedding, vert.

Perf. 14½x14, 14x14½

2009, Aug. 17 Litho. Unwmk.
1224-1227 A286 Set of 4 6.00 6.00

Passion Fruit — A287

Designs: 20c, Passiflora foetida. 65c, Passiflora edulis (yellow green). $1.20, Passiflora maliformis. $2, Passiflora edulis (purple).

2009, Sept. 29 ***Perf. 14x14¼***
1228-1231 A287 Set of 4 6.00 6.00

Souvenir Sheet

People's Republic of China, 60th Anniv. — A288

2009, Oct. 1 ***Perf. 13¼***
1232 A288 $5 multi 6.00 6.00

Ferns — A289

Designs: 20c, Cyathea lunulata. 40c, Asplenium australasicum. $1.50, Diplazium proliferum. $3, Nephrolepsis biserrata.

2009, Dec. 15 ***Perf. 14x14½***
1233-1236 A289 Set of 4 6.00 6.00

Snakes — A290

Designs: 20c, Yellow-bellied sea snake. 90c, Fiji burrowing snake. $1.10, Banded sea krait. $2, Pacific boa.

2010, Mar. 30 Litho. ***Perf. 14½x14***
1237-1240 A290 Set of 4 4.50 4.50

Peonies — A291

No. 1241: a, 20c, Pink peony. b, 40c, Red peony.

2010, Apr. 8 Litho. ***Perf. 13¼***
1241 A291 Horiz. pair, #a-b 13.00 13.00

Raiateana Knowlesi — A292

No. 1242: a, 20c, Newly-emerged insect. b, $1.50, Mature insect.

Perf. 14x14½

2010, June 30 Unwmk.
1242 A292 Vert. pair, #a-b 2.00 2.00

A293

A294

A295

Worldwide Fund for Nature (WWF) — A296

2010, Oct. 27 ***Perf. 14¼x14***
1243 Horiz. strip of 4 9.00 9.00
a. A293 $2 multi 2.25 2.25
b. A294 $2 multi 2.25 2.25
c. A295 $2 multi 2.25 2.25
d. A296 $2 multi 2.25 2.25

Fruit — A297

Designs: 20c, Citrus maxima. 40c, Barringtinia edulis. 65c, Pometia pinnata. $1.20, Musa troglogytarum. $10, Syzygium malacensis.

2010, Dec. 2 ***Perf. 14¼***
1244-1248 A297 Set of 5 14.50 14.50

No. 1249

No. 1249A

1c XX
No. 1249Ab

20c xxx
No. 1254

20c xxx
No. 1254a

20c XX
No. 1254C

No. 1254G

Methods, Perfs and Watermarks As Before

2011-14
1249 A166 1c on 31c #732 1.00 1.00
c. 3½mm between "c" and obliterator *75.00 75.00*
d. 1½mm between "c" and obliterator *125.00 125.00*
e. 4mm between "c" and obliterator, larger font *50.00 50.00*
f. 2¼mm between "c" and obliterator *100.00 100.00*
g. 2½mm between "c" and obliterator *75.00 75.00*
1249A A166 1c on 31c #732 *80.00 80.00*
b. Extra large "XX" (position 51) *275.00 275.00*
1250 A166 2c on 31c #732 1.00 1.00
a. 4mm between "c" and obliterator *95.00 95.00*
b. 3mm between "c" and obliterator (positions 3 and 89) *185.00 185.00*
1251 A166 3c on 31c #732 1.00 1.00
1252 A166 4c on 31c #732 1.00 1.00
a. 4mm between "c" and obliterator *95.00 95.00*
b. 3mm between "c" and obliterator (positions 3 and 89) *185.00 185.00*
1253 A166 5c on 31c #732 1.00 1.00
a. 3½mm between "c" and obliterator *75.00 75.00*
b. 1½mm between "c" and obliterator *100.00 100.00*
c. 2¼mm between "c" and obliterator *100.00 100.00*
1254 A166 20c on 31c #732 2.00 2.00
a. Larger font *50.00 50.00*
b. As "a," 2½mm between "c" and obliterator *100.00 100.00*
d. As No. 1254, no gap between "c" and obliterator (position 70) *35.00 35.00*
f. As "a," no gap between "c" and obliterator *250.00 300.00*
h. 3¾mm btwn "c" and obliterator *180.00 180.00*
1254C A166 20c on 31c #732 *125.00 125.00*
1254E A166 40c on 31c #732 3.00 3.00
a. No gap between "c" and obliterator *50.00 50.00*
1254G A166 20c on 31c #732 *180.00 180.00*
a. No gap between "c" and obliterator *225.00 225.00*
Nos. 1249A-1254G (10) 395.00 395.00

Nos. 1249-1253 have 2½mm between "c" and obliterator. No. 1249A has 3½mm spacing. Nos. 1249Ab, 1254, 1254a, 1254E and 1254G have 1½mm spacing.

No. 1249 exists with inverted surcharge. Value, $90. No. 1249 exists with double surcharge. Value, $120; and with double surcharge, one inverted, value, $130. No.

1249A exists with denomination omitted (position 77). Value, $500.

No. 1250 exists with inverted surcharge. Value, $90. No. 1250 exists with double surcharge. Value, $120. No. 1250 exists with double surcharge, one inverted. Value, $130. No. 1250a exists with double surcharge. Value, $200.

No. 1251 exists with inverted surcharge. Value, $100. No. 1251 exists with double surcharge. Value, $120. No. 1251 exists with double surcharge, one inverted. Value, $130. No. 1251 exists with surcharge shifted 50% upward. Value, $50. No. 1252 exists with inverted surcharge. Value, $90. No. 1252 exists with double surcharge. Value, $120. No. 1252 with double surcharge, one inverted. Value, $130.

No. 1253 exists with inverted surcharge. Value, $90. No. 1253 exists with double surcharge, with double surcharge, one shifted 50% upward, and with double surcharge, one inverted, value, each $130. No. 1253 exists with surcharge shifted 50% upward. Value, $50.

No. 1254 exists with inverted surcharge. Value, $100. No. 1254 exists with double surcharge. Value, $65. No. 1254 exists with double surcharge, one with large "20," the other with small "20." Value, $175. No. 1254 exists with double surcharge, one inverted: one with large "20," the other with small "20." Value, $175. No. 1254 exists with double surcharge, one inverted (top surcharge inverted, bottom shifted 50% upward). Value, $110. No. 1254 exists with surcharge shifted 50% upward. Value, $50. No. 1254 exists with double surcharge, one shifted 50% upward. Value, $100. No. 1254 exists with double surcharge, one shifted 50% upward; both with no gap between "c" and obliterator. Value, $300. No. 1254a exists with surcharge shifted 50% upward. Value, $80. No. 1254a exists with surcharge inverted and shifted 50% upward. Value, $130. No. 1254f exists with surcharge shifted 50% upward. Value, $250.

No. 1254E exists with inverted surcharge. Value, $90. No. 1254E exists with double surcharge. Value, $120. No. 1254E exists with double surcharge, one inverted. Value, $130. No. 1254E exists with surcharge shifted 45% upward. Value, $50.

No. 1254G exists with inverted surcharge. Value, $225. No. 1254G also exists with "c" of "20c" omitted. Value, $325.

Issued: No. 1249, 6/6; No. 1249A, 7/30/14; Nos. 1250, 1253, 3/24; No. 1250a, 3/2014; No. 1251, 7/8; No. 1252, 5/20; No. 1252a, 2/2014; No. 1254, 5/4; Nos. 1254a, 1254b, 2011; No. 1254d, 5/4; Nos. 1254E, 1254Ea, 12/7/12.

Souvenir Sheet

Wedding of Prince William and Catherine Middleton — A298

Perf. 14¾x14¼

2011, Apr. 29 Litho. Wmk. 406
1255 A298 $10 multi 11.50 11.50

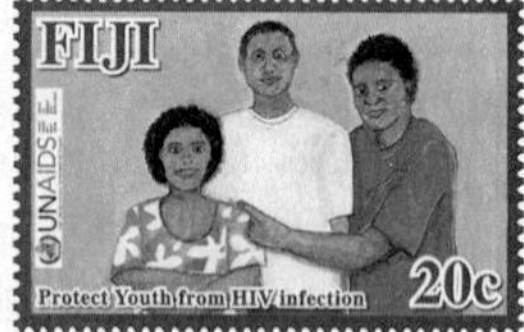

Campaign Against AIDS — A299

People, UNAIDS emblem and slogan: 20c, Protect youth from HIV infection. 40c, Zero new HIV infections, vert. 65c, Stop mothers & babies from being infected with HIV, vert. $5, Zero discrimination.

Perf. 14½x14, 14x14½

2011, June 22 Unwmk.
1256-1259 A299 Set of 4 7.25 7.25

Frangipani Flowers — A300

Designs: 50c, Plumeria rubra bud. 90c, Plumeria rubra f. rubra flower. $1.50, Plumeria rubra f. lutea. $3, Plumeria obtusa.

2011, July 12 *Perf. 14½x14*
1260-1263 A300 Set of 4 6.75 6.75

Pomegranate Tree Branches and Birds — A301

No. 1264: a, 65c, Bird on branch. b, $1.20, Bird in flight near branch.

2011, Aug. 15 *Perf. 13¼x13¾*
1264 A301 Horiz. pair, #a-b 2.25 2.25

No. 1264 was printed in sheets containing three pairs.

War Clubs A302

Designs: 20c, Saulaki vividrasa. 65c, Cali. $1.20, Totokia. $10, I ula tavatava.

2011, Aug. 15 *Perf. 14½x14*
1265-1268 A302 Set of 4 14.00 14.00

Intl. Year of Volunteers — A303

Volunteers for: 40c, St. John Ambulance Association. 90c, Suva City Council, vert. $1.10, Red Cross, vert. $10, National Blood Bank.

Perf. 14½x14, 14x14½

2011, Nov. 25
1269-1272 A303 Set of 4 14.50 14.50

Christmas — A304

Designs: 20c, Fijian with gift box. 65c, Fijian with pottery. $1.20, Fijian with necklace. $2, Holy Family.

2011, Dec. 16 *Perf. 14½x14*
1273-1276 A304 Set of 4 4.50 4.50

New Year 2012 (Year of the Dragon) A305

2012, Jan. 23 *Perf. 14¼*
1277 A305 $3 multi 3.50 3.50

No. 1277 was printed in sheets of 4.

Endangered Flora — A306

Designs: 20c, Fijian acmopyle. 65c, Lau fan palm. $1.20, Cycad. $2, Fiji magnolia.

2012, Apr. 26 *Perf. 14½x14*
1278-1281 A306 Set of 4 4.50 4.50

Intl. Year of Sustainable Energy For All — A307

Designs: 20c, Water power. 50c, Biomass. $1.20, Wind energy. $3, Solar power.

2012, June 25
1282-1285 A307 Set of 4 5.50 5.50

A308

A309

A310

Worldwide Fund for Nature (WWF) A311

2012, July 11 *Perf. 14¼x14*
1286 Horiz. strip of 4 9.00 9.00
a. A308 $2 multi 2.25 2.25
b. A309 $2 multi 2.25 2.25
c. A310 $2 multi 2.25 2.25
d. A311 $2 multi 2.25 2.25

Christmas — A312

Designs: 20c, Journey to Bethlehem. 40c, Holy Family. 65c, Adoration of the Shepherds. $1.20, Adoration of the Shepherds, diff. $5, Adoration of the Magi.

2012, Dec. 14 Litho. *Perf. 14½x14*
1287-1291 A312 Set of 5 8.50 8.50

Birth of Prince George of Cambridge A313

Prince George and: 40c, Duke and Duchess of Cambridge. 65c, Duchess of Cambridge. $1.20, Duke and Duchess of Cambridge, diff. $5, Duke of Cambridge.

2013, Aug. 28 Litho. *Perf. 13½*
1292-1295 A313 Set of 4 7.75 7.75

Mangrove Protection A314

Designs: 50c, Mangroves. 65c, Mangrove, jellyfish, starfish. $1.20, Fish and underwater root system of mangrove. $10, People planting mangroves.

2013, Oct. 30 Litho. *Perf. 13½*
1296-1299 A314 Set of 4 13.50 13.50

Christmas — A315

Bell-shaped Christmas ornament with: 40c, Cathedral. 65c, Flowers. $1.20, Fijian family walking on beach. $3, Fijian children with Christmas gifts.

2013, Dec. 2 Litho. *Perf. 13½*
1300-1303 A315 Set of 4 5.75 5.75

Submarine Cable Between Fiji and Vanuatu — A316

No. 1304: a, Workers, ship and cable with floats. b, Diver examining cable. c, Electronic cables plugged into machine.

Litho. With Foil Application

2014, Jan. 15 *Perf. 14½x14*

1304 Horiz. strip of 6 + central label, #1304a-1304c, Vanuatu #1070a-1070c 14.50 14.50
a. A316 65c multi .70 .70
b. A316 $1.20 multi 1.25 1.25
c. A316 $6 multi 6.50 6.50

No. 1304 sold for $13.30 in Fiji and 750v in Vanuatu. See Vanuatu No. 1070.

Sharks A317

Designs: 50c, Blacktip reef shark. 90c, Silky shark. $1.20, Oceanic whitetip shark. $5, Bigeye thresher shark.

2014, July 28 **Litho.** *Perf. 13¾x13¼*
1305-1308 A317 Set of 4 8.25 8.25

Grand Pacific Hotel, Cent. A318

Designs: 40c, Hotel driveway and entrance. 65c, Sofas and tables. 90c, Swimming pool. $1.20, Dining area. $5, Entrance, diff.

2014, Aug. 8 **Litho.** *Perf. 13¾x13¼*
1309-1313 A318 Set of 5 8.75 8.75

Nos. 732-733 Surcharged

No. 1313A

No. 1314

No. 1314b

No. 1315

No. 1315B

No. 1316

No. 1317

Methods, Perfs and Watermarks As Before

2014-15

1313A A166 1c on 44c #733 4.00 4.00
b. 2¼mm between "c" and obliterator 50.00 50.00
c. 4¼mm between "c" and obliterator 40.00 40.00
1314 A166 20c on 44c #733 1.50 1.50
a. No gap between "c" and obliterator (position 70) 50.00 50.00
b. Large "20" 30.00 30.00
c. As "b," no gap between "c" and obliterator (positions 70 and 79) 75.00 75.00
d. As "b," 3mm between "c" and obliterator (positions 31, 41, 61, 71, 81 and 91) 50.00 50.00
e. 3¾mm between "c" and obliterator (position 3) 175.00 175.00
1315 A166 40c on 44c #733 2.00 2.00
a. No gap between "c" and obliterator (position 70) 60.00 60.00
1315B A166 50c on 3c #727 450.00 450.00
c. No gap between "c" and obliterator (position 70) — —
1316 A166 50c on 31c #732 6.00 6.00
a. No gap between "c" and obliterator (position 70) 50.00 50.00
1317 A166 50c on 44c #733 3.00 3.00
a. No gap between "c" and obliterator (position 70) 65.00 65.00
Nos. 1313A-1317 (6) 466.50 466.50

No. 1313A exists with double surcharge. Value, $120. No. 1313A also exists with inverted surcharge. Value, $110.

No. 1314 exists with surcharge shifted 50% upward. Value, $25. No. 1314 exists with surcharge inverted. Value, $60. No. 1314a exists with surcharge shifted 50% upward. Value, $75. No. 1314b exists with surcharge inverted. Value, $100. No. 1314b exists with double surcharge. Value, $120.

No. 1315 exists with surcharge shifted 50% upward. Value, $25. No. 1315a exists with surcharge shifted 50% upward. Value, $80.

No. 1316 exists with double surcharge. Value, $70. Nos. 1316 and 1316a exist with inverted surcharge. Value, both $120.

No. 1317 exists with surcharge shifted 50% upward. Value, $30. No. 1317a exists with surcharge shifted 50% upward. Value, $90.

Issued: No. 1313A, 8/28/15; No. 1314, 6/11; No. 1314b, 7/31; Nos. 1315, 1317, 6/10. No. 1316, 3/5.

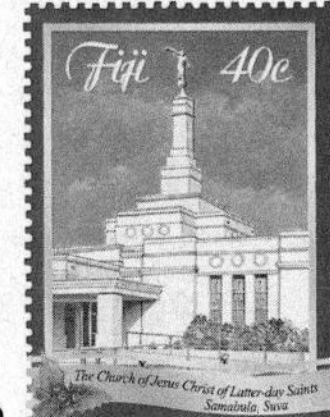

Christmas — A319

Houses of worship: 40c, The Church of Jesus Christ of Latter-day Saints, Suva. 65c, Holy Redeemer Anglican Church, Levuka. $3, Baker Memorial Methodist Church, Nausori. $10, St. Francis Xavier Church, Navunibitu.

Perf. 13½

2014, Dec. 4 **Litho.** **Unwmk.**
1320-1323 A319 Set of 4 14.00 14.00

Souvenir Sheet

Blue Coral — A320

No. 1324 — Heliopora coerulea: a, 65c. b, $5.

Perf. 13½x13¼

2015, Feb. 23 **Litho.**
1324 A320 Sheet of 2, #a-b 5.50 5.50

Fiji Flying Fox — A321

Fiji flying fox: 40c, Head. 65c, In flight, horiz. 90c, Head, horiz. $10, Hanging from tree.

Perf. 13¼x13¾, 13¾x13¼

2015, Apr. 30 **Litho.**
1325-1328 A321 Set of 4 13.50 13.50

Levuka UNESCO World Heritage Site A322

Designs: 50c, Fiji Times Building, Beach Street, c. 1894. 65c, Sacred Heart Church, c. 1902, vert. 90c, Levuka Public School, c. 1884, vert. $5, Public Office, Nasova, c. 1877-82.

2015, June 16 **Litho.** *Perf. 13½*
1329-1332 A322 Set of 4 6.75 6.75

Voyages of Uto Ni Yalo Outrigger Canoe A323

Uto Ni Yalo: 40c, Near shore with white and black sails. 65c, Near Sydney Harbour Bridge and Sydney Opera House. $1.50, Near Golden Gate Bridge. $10, Near shore with red and black sails.

Perf. 13¾x13¼

2015, Aug. 31 **Litho.**
1333-1336 A323 Set of 4 11.50 11.50

Medicinal Plants A324

Designs: 40c, Scaevola sericea. 65c, Vigna marina. 90c, Ipomoea pes-caprae subsp. brasiliensis. $1.20, Clerodendrum inerme. $5, Morinda citrifolia.

2015, Oct. 21 **Litho.** *Perf. 13¾x13¼*
1337-1341 A324 Set of 5 7.75 7.75

Christmas — A325

Archangels: 40c, St. Uriel. 65c, St. Gabriel. 90c, St. Raphael. $10, St. Michael.

2015, Dec. 7 **Litho.** *Perf. 13¼x13¾*
1342-1345 A325 Set of 4 11.50 11.50

Nos. 735 Surcharged

Nos. 734 Surcharged

Methods, Perfs. and Watermarks As Before

2015-16

1346 A166 1c on 81c #735 7.50 10.00
a. 2¼mm between and obliterator (positions 1 and 2) 125.00 125.00
b. 4¼mm between "c" and obliterator (position 51) 175.00 175.00
1347 A166 20c on 63c #734 20.00 20.00
a. No gap between "c" and obliterator (position 70) 120.00 120.00
b. 3¼mm between "c" and obliterator (position 3) 120.00 120.00
c. Large "20" 120.00 120.00

No. 1346 has 3¼mm between "c" and obliterator. No. 1347 has 1½mm between "c" and obliterator.

Issued: No. 1346, 1/29/16; No. 1347, 12/31.

New Year 2016 (Year of the Monkey) A326

No. 1348: a, Macaca arctoides, bananas. b, Rhinopithecus, peonies. c, Rhesus macaque, coconut palm trees. d, White-headed langur, hibiscus flowers.

Perf. 13½x13¼

2016, Mar. 30 **Litho.** **Unwmk.**
1348 Horiz. strip of 4 + central label 11.50 11.50
a. A326 38c multi .40 .40
b. A326 47c multi .45 .45
c. A326 85c multi .85 .85
d. A326 $10 multi 9.75 9.75

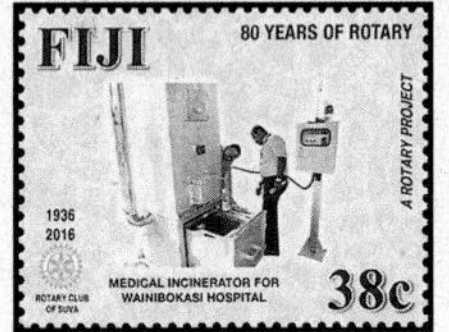

Rotary International in Fiji, 80th Anniv. — A327

Designs: 38c, Medical incinerator for Wainibokasi Hospital. 62c, Dialysis machine for Kidney Foundation of Fiji, vert. $1.04, Emergency Response Kit label, vert. $5, Braille machine for Fiji Society for the Blind.

Perf. 13½x13¼, 13¼x13½

2016, May 19 **Litho.** **Unwmk.**
1349-1352 A327 Set of 4 6.75 6.75

No. 733 Surcharged

No. 1353

No. 1354

No. 1355

No. 1356

Methods, Perfs. and Watermarks As Before

2016

1353 A166 3c on 44c #733 3.00 3.00
1354 A166 4c on 44c #733 3.00 3.00
1355 A166 5c on 44c #733 3.00 3.00
1356 A166 23c on 44c #733 4.50 4.50
Nos. 1353-1356 (4) 13.50 13.50

No. 1355 exists with double surcharge. Value, $800.

Issued: No. 1353, 6/13; No. 1354, 6/15; No. 1355, 8/26; No. 1356, 10/25.

Thatched Structures at Navala Village A328

Designs: 38c, Dwelling. 47c, Home for the elderly. 85c, Meeting house. $10, Chief's home.

Perf. 13½x13¼

2016, July 27 Litho. Unwmk.

1357-1360 A328 Set of 4 11.50 11.50

Flowers — A329

Designs: 47c, Pink Hibiscus rosa-sinensis. 58c, Abelmoschus esculentus (okra). 85c, Red Hibiscus rosa-sinensis. $1.04, Thespesia populnea. $15, Hibiscus tiliaceus.

Perf. 13¼x13½

2016, Aug. 12 Litho. Unwmk.

1361-1365 A329 Set of 5 17.50 17.50

Christmas A330

Designs: 40c, Carolers. 90c, People preparing lovo for feast. $1.20, Family going to church. $10, Exchanging gifts.

Perf. 13½x13¼

2016, Dec. 5 Litho. Unwmk.

1366-1369 A330 Set of 4 12.00 12.00

No. 733 Surcharged

No. 1370

50c XX

No. 1371

Methods, Perfs. and Watermarks As Before

2016-17

1370 A166 2c on 44c #733 *3.00 3.00*
a. 1½mm btwn "c" and obliterator *75.00 75.00*
1371 A166 50c on 44c #733 *24.00 24.00*

Issued: No. 1370, 2016; No. 1371, 2017. Compare No. 1371 with No. 1317.
No. 1370 has a standard gap of 2¼mm between the "c" and the obliterator.

New Year 2017 (Year of the Rooster) — A331

Designs: 85c, Rooster and red hibiscus flower. $1.20, Hen and yellow frangipani flower. $3, Rooster and palm trees. $15, Rooster and tree blossoms.

Perf. 13¼x13½

2017, Feb. 10 Litho. Unwmk.

1372-1375 A331 Set of 4 19.50 19.50

Great Sea Reef A332

Designs: 62c, Branching coral. 85c, Boulders. $1.04, Soft coral. $15, Plate coral.

Perf. 13½x13¼

2017, May 19 Litho. Unwmk.

1376-1379 A332 Set of 4 17.00 17.00

National Women's Expo A333

Women and: 40c, Pottery. 62c, Boxes, baskets and handbags. $1.14, Pottery, baskets and textiles. $10, Textiles, bowls and kitchen utensils.

Perf. 13½x13¼

2017, June 14 Litho. Unwmk.

1380-1383 A333 Set of 4 12.00 12.00

Sigatoka Sand Dunes A334

Designs: 40c, Vegetation surrounding the dunes. 85c, People trekking through the dunes. $1.14, Dunes overlooking the Pacific Ocean. $5, Team training at the dunes.

Perf. 13½x13¼

2017, Sept. 28 Litho. Unwmk.

1384-1387 A334 Set of 4 7.25 7.25

2017 United Nations Climate Change Conference, Bonn — A335

Designs: 40c, Drua. 62c, People planting mangroves. $1.40, Traditional Fijian houses. $10, Workers in sugar cane field.

Perf. 13½

2018, Feb. 5 Litho. Unwmk.

1388-1391 A335 Set of 4 12.50 12.50

New Year 2018 (Year of the Dog) — A336

Various dogs: 38c, 50c, $1.04, $10.

2018, Feb. 28 Litho. *Perf. 14½*

1392-1395 A336 Set of 4 12.00 12.00

Peace Corps in Fiji, 50th Anniv. A337

Various Peace Corps workers and Fijians: 40c, $1.14, $2, $10.

2018, Mar. 28 Litho. *Perf. 14½*

1396-1399 A337 Set of 4 13.50 13.50

Reptiles A338

Designs: 38c, Giant forest gecko. 40c, Fiji barred tree skink. $1.63, Gau banded iguana. $5, Ono I Lau skink.

2018, July 13 Litho. *Perf. 13½*

1400-1403 A338 Set of 4 7.25 7.25

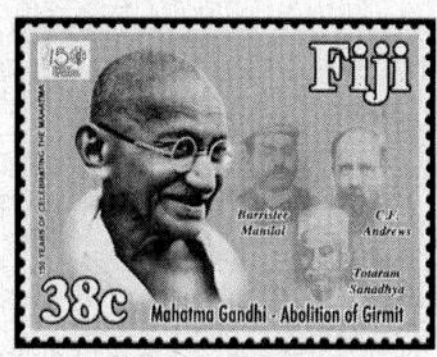

Mohandas K. Gandhi (1869-1948), Indian Nationalist Leader — A339

Gandhi and: 38c, Manilal Doctor (1881-1956), Indian barrister assisting Indians in Fiji, Charles Freer Andrews (1871-1940), social reformer in India, and Totaram Sanadhya (1876-1947), indentured Indian laborer working in Fiji. 50c, Devanagari script and pencil. 90c, Doves. $15, Drua.

Perf. 13½

2018, Dec. 20 Litho. Unwmk.

1404-1407 A339 Set of 4 16.00 16.00

Nos. 729 and 733 Surcharged

No. 1407A

No. 1407B

Methods, Perfs. and Watermarks As Before

2018-19 ?

1407A A166 3c on 6c #729 *425.00 425.00*
1407B A166 40c on 44c #733 *30.00 30.00*
c. 1¼mm btwn "c" and "XX." *125.00 125.00*

Issued: No. 1407A, 2019 ?; No. 1407B, Sept. 2018. Compare No. 1407B with No. 1315.
The issue date of No. 1407A is uncertain and may have been as early as 2007.

New Year 2019 (Year of the Pig) — A340

Designs: 38c, Flower, bananas and orange and red pig. 40c, Flowers and blue pig. $1.20, Dove, trees and red pig. $10, Trees and green pig.

Perf. 14½

2019, Feb. 2 Litho. Unwmk.

1408-1411 A340 Set of 4 11.50 11.50

International Labor Organization, Cent. — A341

Designs: 40c, Five workers. 90c, Worker wearing face mask. $1.15, Child playing with blocks. $10, People on arrows surrounding globe.

Perf. 14¼

2019, May Litho. Unwmk.

1412-1415 A341 Set of 4 11.50 11.50

Morris Hedstrom Ltd., 150th Anniv. in Fiji — A342

Designs: Inscribed: 50c, The Voyage — MH Copra Boat. 65c, They Way We Were. 85c, Steeped in History. $1.50, Way Back When. $5, The Birth of a Legacy.

Perf. 14x13½

2019, July Litho. Unwmk.

1416-1420 A342 Set of 5 8.00 8.00

SEMI-POSTAL STAMPS

Catalogue values for unused stamps in this section are for Never Hinged items.

Children at Play — SP1

Rugby Player — SP2

Perf. 13x13½

1951, Sept. 17 Engr. Wmk. 4

B1 SP1 1p + 1p brown .30 *1.60*
B2 SP2 2p + 1p deep green .55 *1.10*

Bamboo River Raft — SP3

Design: 2½p+½p, Cross of Lorraine.

1954, Apr. 1 *Perf. 11x11½*

B3 SP3 1½p + ½p green & brn .25 *1.10*
B4 SP3 2½p + ½p black & org .30 .30

Nos. 269 and 272 Surcharged

1972, Dec. 4 Photo. *Perf. 14, 13½*

B5	A56	15c + 5c multi	.40	.35
B6	A55	30c + 10c multi	1.10	.35

Indian Boy, Map of Fiji SP4

Map of Fiji and: 15c+2c, European girl. 30c+3c, Chinese girl. 40c+4c, Fijian boy.

Wmk. 373

1979, Sept. 17 Litho. *Perf. 14½*

B7	SP4	4c + 1c multicolored	.25	.25
B8	SP4	15c + 2c multicolored	.25	.25
B9	SP4	30c + 3c multicolored	.40	.40
B10	SP4	40c + 4c multicolored	.60	.60
		Nos. B7-B10 (4)	1.50	1.50

The surtax was for IYC fund.

Iliesa Delana, Gold Medalist at 2012 Paralympic Games — SP5

Delana: 40c+10c, High jumping. 65c+10c, Standing and waving flag of Fiji, vert. $1.20+10c, Wearing gold medal, vert. $2+10c, Going around track waving flag of Fiji.

2013, Mar. 7 *Perf. 14½x14, 14x14½*

B11-B14	SP5	Set of 4	5.25	5.25

Surtax for Fiji Paralympic Committee.

POSTAGE DUE STAMPS

D1

D2

D3

1917 Unwmk. Typeset *Perf. 11*
Laid Papers; Without Gum

J1	D1	½p black	1,450.	500.00
J2	D2	½p black	550.00	300.00
a.		Narrow setting	500.00	150.00
J3	D3	1p black	575.00	150.00
a.		Narrow setting	350.00	150.00
J4	D3	2p black	325.00	80.00
a.		Narrow setting	1,350.	650.00
J5	D3	3p black	675.00	125.00
J6	D3	4p black	1,600.	575.00
a.		Strip of 8, 3 #J3, 1 ea. #J1 and #J6, and 3 #J5	*19,000.*	
		Nos. J1-J6 (6)	5,175.	1,730.

There were two printings of this issue. In the first printing, the 2d was printed in sheets of 84 (7x12), and the other four values were printed together in sheets of 96 (8x12), with each row consisting of three 1p, one ½p, one 4p and three 3p values. Setenant multiples exist. Sheets were not perforated on the margins, so that marginal stamps were not perforated on the outer edge. Examples from the first printing are 25mm wide (including margins).

In the second printing, the ½p, 1p and 2p were printed in separate sheets of 84 (7x12). The clichés were set a little closer, so that examples of this printing are 23mm wide.

D4

Perf. 14

1918, June 1 Typo. Wmk. 3

J7	D4	½p black	3.25	*30.00*
J8	D4	1p black	3.75	*5.50*
J9	D4	2p black	3.50	*8.00*
J10	D4	3p black	3.50	*60.00*
J11	D4	4p black	6.50	*30.00*
		Nos. J7-J11 (5)	20.50	*133.50*

D5

1940 Wmk. 4 *Perf. 12½*

J12	D5	1p bright green	9.00	*72.50*
J13	D5	2p bright green	17.50	*72.50*
J14	D5	3p bright green	20.00	*80.00*
J15	D5	4p bright green	20.00	*85.00*
J16	D5	5p bright green	24.00	*90.00*
J17	D5	6p bright green	25.00	*90.00*
J18	D5	1sh dk carmine	25.00	*115.00*
J19	D5	1sh6p dk carmine	25.00	*175.00*
		Nos. J12-J19 (8)	165.50	*780.00*
		Set, never hinged	295.00	

WAR TAX STAMPS

Regular Issue of 1912-16 Overprinted

Die I

1916 Wmk. 3 *Perf. 14*

MR1	A23	½p green	1.90	*7.50*
a.		Inverted overprint	700.00	
b.		Double overprint		
MR2	A23	1p scarlet	4.00	.80
a.		1p carmine	42.50	27.50
b.		Pair, one without ovpt.	*8,000.*	
c.		Inverted overprint	800.00	

Most examples of No. MR2b are within horiz. strips of 12.

FINLAND

ˈfin-lənd

(Suomi)

LOCATION — Northern Europe bordering on the Gulfs of Bothnia and Finland
GOVT. — Republic
AREA — 130,119 sq. mi.
POP. — 5,147,349 (1997)
CAPITAL — Helsinki

Finland was a Grand Duchy of the Russian Empire from 1809 until December 1917, when it declared its independence.

100 Kopecks = 1 Ruble
100 Pennia = 1 Markka (1866)
100 Cents = 1 Euro (2002)

Catalogue values for unused stamps in this country are for Never Hinged items, beginning with Scott 220 in the regular postage section, Scott B39 in the semi-postal section, Scott C2 in the air post section, Scott M1 in the military stamp section, and Scott Q6 in the parcel post section.

Unused stamps are valued with original gum as defined in the catalogue introduction except for Nos. 1-3B which are valued without gum. Used values for Nos. 1-3B are for pen-canceled examples. Very fine examples of the serpentine rouletted issues, Nos. 4-13c, will have roulettes cutting the design slightly on one or more sides and will have all "teeth" complete and intact. Stamps with roulettes clear of the design on all four sides are extremely scarce and sell for substantial premiums. Stamps with teeth entirely missing or with several short roulettes are worth much less. See *Scott Classic Specialized Catalogue* for values for used stamps with one or two short roulettes.

Watermarks

Wmk. 121 — Multiple Swastika

Wmk. 208 — Post Horn

Wmk. 168 — Wavy Lines and Letters

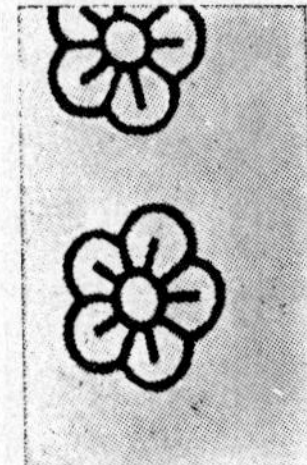

Wmk. 273 — Roses

Wmk. 363 — Tree Stump

Syncopated Perforations

Type A (1st stamp #1065): On one longer side, groups of five holes are separated by an oval hole equal in width to eight holes.

Type B (1st stamp, #1142): On the top groups of 3 holes at left and right and a middle group of 4 holes separated by rectangular perforations equal in width to 4 holes.

Issues under Russian Empire

Coat of Arms — A1

1856-58 Unwmk. Typo. *Imperf.*
Small Pearls in Post Horns
Wove Paper

1	A1	5k blue	*6,750.*	1,600.
		Pen and town cancellation		1,900.
		Town cancellation		3,250.
a.		Tête bêche pair	*80,000.*	*80,000.*
		Pen and town cancellation		*75,000.*
2	A1	10k rose	9,000.	400.
		Pen and town cancellation		575.
		On cover		1,850.
		Town cancellation		925.
		On cover		2,850.
a.		Tête bêche pair	*80,000.*	*65,000.*
		Pen and town cancellation		*75,000.*

Cut to shape

1	A1	5k blue	150.
		Pen and town cancellation	200.
		Town cancellation	250.
2	A1	10k rose	65.
		Pen and town cancellation	90.
		Town cancellation	100.

Wide Vertically Laid Paper

2C	A1	10k rose ('58)	—	1,400.
		Pen and town cancellation		1,800.
		Town cancellation		2,500.
d.		Tête bêche pair		—

Cut to shape

2C	A1	10k rose	200.
		Pen and town cancellation	250.
		Town cancellation	300.

Narrow Vertically Laid Paper

2C	A1	10k carmine	625.
		Pen and town cancellation	800.
		Town cancellation	1,100.

The wide vertically laid paper has 13-14 distinct lines per 2 centimeters. The narrow laid paper has lines that sometimes are indistinct.

A 5k blue with small pearls exists on narrow vertically laid paper. It is rare. Value $16,250 used.

Stamps on diagonally laid paper are envelope cut squares. Envelope cut squares also exist on unwatermarked wove paper.

Large Pearls in Post Horns

1858 Wove Paper

3	A1	5k blue	*11,000.*	1,800.
		Pen and town cancellation		1,550.
		Town cancellation		2,500.
a.		Tête bêche pair		*60,000.*
		Pen and town cancellation		*65,000.*

Cut to shape

3	A1	5k blue	125.00
		Pen and town cancellation	150.00
		Town cancellation	200.00

1859 Wide Vertically Laid Paper

3B	A1	5k blue	—	*18,000.*
		Pen and town cancellation		*25,000.*

Cut to shape

3B	A1	5k blue	2,000.
		Pen and town cancellation	*2,500.*

Reprints of Nos. 2 and 3, made in 1862, are on brownish paper, on vertically laid paper, and in tête bêche pairs on normal and vertically laid paper. Reprints of 1871, 1881 and 1893 are on yellowish or white paper. Value for least costly of each, $85.

In 1956, Nos. 2 and 3 were reprinted for the Centenary with post horn watermark and gum. Value, $85 each.

Values for rouletted stamps with one or two short teeth are considerably less than the values shown, which are for stamps with all teeth full and intact. See the *Scott Classic Specialized Catalogue* for greater detail. Stamps with several short teeth or teeth entirely missing sell for very small percentages of the values shown.

Coat of Arms — A2

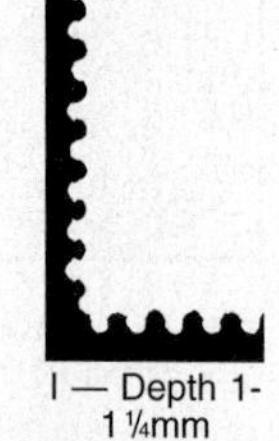

I — Depth 1-1¼mm

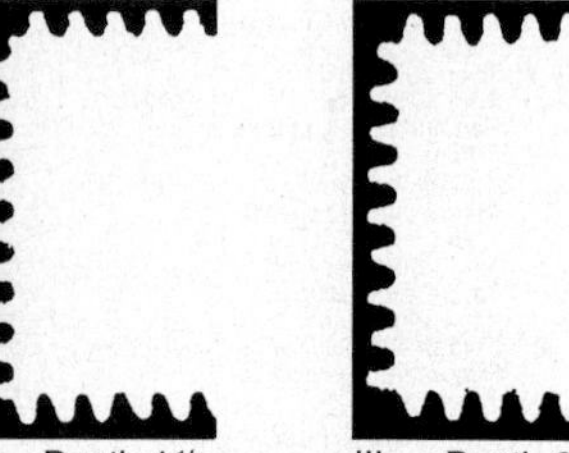

II — Depth 1½-1¾mm

III — Depth 2-2¼mm

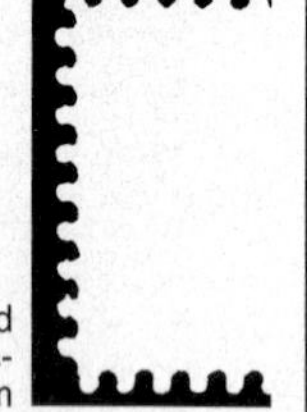

IV — Shovel-shaped teeth. Depth 1¼-1½mm

Wove Paper

1860 *Serpentine Roulette 7½, 8*

4	A2	5k blue, *bluish,* I	850.00	200.00
a.		Roulette II	850.00	225.00
b.		Perf. vert.		
5	A2	10k rose, *pale rose,* I	575.00	57.50
a.		Roulette II	1,150.	160.00

A3

A4

1866-74 *Serpentine Roulette*

6	A3	5p pur brn, *lil,* I ('73)	375.00	170.00
a.		Roulette II		5,000.
b.		5p red brn, *lil,* III ('71)	350.00	180.00
7	A3	8p blk, *grn,* III ('67)	275.00	225.00
a.		Ribbed paper, III ('72)	1,150.	925.00
b.		Roulette II ('74)	340.00	275.00
c.		As "b," ribbed paper ('74)	340.00	225.00
d.		Roulette I ('73)	525.00	325.00
e.		As "d," ribbed paper	1,050.	400.00
f.		Serpentine roulette 10½ ('67)		*13,500.*
8	A3	10p blk, *yel,* III ('70)	675.00	350.00
a.		10p blk, *buff,* II	1,000.	550.00
b.		10p blk, *buff,* I ('73)	750.00	375.00
9	A3	20p bl, *bl,* III	575.00	57.50
a.		Roulette II	575.00	90.00
b.		Roulette I ('73)	675.00	115.00
c.		Roulette IV ('74)	—	*1,150.*
d.		Perf. horiz.		—
e.		Printed on both sides (40p blue on back)		*10,500.*
10	A3	40p rose, *lil rose,* III	525.00	67.50
a.		Ribbed paper, III ('73)	675.00	200.00
b.		Roulette II	525.00	85.00
c.		As "b," ribbed paper ('73)	675.00	170.00
d.		Roulette I	750.00	170.00
e.		As "d," ribbed paper	675.00	115.00
f.		Roulette IV	—	*2,275.*
g.		As "f," ribbed paper	—	—
h.		Serpentine roulette 10½		—
11	A4	1m yel brn, III ('67)	2,250.	850.00
a.		Roulette II	2,850.	1,700.

Nos. 7f and 10h are private roulettes and are also known in compound serpentine roulette 10½ and 7½.

Nos. 4-11 were reprinted in 1893 on thick wove paper. Colors differ from originals. Roulette type IV. Value for Nos. 4-5, each $40, Nos. 6-10, each $50. Value for No. 11, $55.

Thin or Thick Laid Paper

12	A3	5p red brn, *lil,* III	290.00	160.00
a.		Roulette II	300.00	300.00
b.		Roulette I	290.00	300.00
d.		5p blk, *buff,* roul. III (error)		*20,000.*
e.		Tête bêche pair		*17,500.*
13	A3	10p black, *buff,* III	675.00	290.00
a.		10p black, *yel,* II	850.00	290.00
b.		10p black, *yel,* I	1,150.	750.00
c.		10p red brown, *lil,* III (error)	*8,000.*	*7,000.*

Forgeries of No. 13c exist.

A5

1875 *Perf. 14x13½*

16	A5	32p lake	2,400.	425.00

Forgeries exist of No. 16 that have been created by perforating cut squares.

1875-82 *Perf. 11*

17	A5	2p gray	62.50	70.00
18	A5	5p orange	140.00	15.00
a.		5p yellow org	160.00	18.00
19	A5	8p blue green	300.00	90.00
a.		8p yellow green	275.00	70.00
20	A5	10p brown ('81)	700.00	70.00
21	A5	20p ultra	175.00	3.50
a.		20p blue	175.00	5.00
b.		20p Prussian blue	400.00	45.00
c.		Tête bêche pair		3,500.
22	A5	25p car ('79)	350.00	17.00
a.		25p rose ('82)	475.00	75.00
23	A5	32p carmine	400.00	60.00
a.		32p rose	450.00	62.50
24	A5	1m violet ('77)	1,000.	160.00
		Nos. 17-24 (8)	3,128.	485.50

A souvenir card issued in 1974 for NORDIA 1975 reproduced a block of four of the unissued "1 MARKKAA" design.

Nos. 19, 23 were reprinted in 1892-93, perf. 12½. Value $25.00 each. They exist imperf.

1881-83 *Perf. 12½*

25	A5	2p gray	20.00	20.00
a.		Imperf., pair	600.00	600.00
26	A5	5p orange	62.50	6.25
a.		Tête bêche pair	8,250.	4,750.
b.		Imperf. vert., pair		*800.00*
c.		Imperf. horiz., pair		*800.00*
27	A5	10p brown	100.00	27.00
28	A5	20p ultra	65.00	2.00
a.		20p blue	65.00	2.00
b.		Tête bêche pair	—	2,500.
c.		Imperf., pair	—	
29	A5	25p rose ('82)	55.00	12.00
a.		25p carmine	55.00	21.00
b.		Tête bêche pair	*15,000.*	—
30	A5	1m violet ('82)	450.00	55.00
		Nos. 25-30 (6)	752.50	122.25

Nos. 27-29 were reprinted in 1893 in deeper shades, perf. 12½. Value $40 each.

Most examples of No. 28c are from printer's waste.

1881 *Perf. 11x12½*

26d	A5	5p orange	450.00	90.00
27a	A5	10p brown	925.00	225.00
28d	A5	20p ultra	575.00	42.50
28e	A5	20p blue	575.00	42.50
29c	A5	25p rose	675.00	190.00
29d	A5	25p carmine	650.00	125.00
30a	A5	1m violet		1,450.

1881 *Perf. 12½x11*

26e	A5	5p orange	450.00	90.00
27b	A5	10p brown	—	325.00
28f	A5	20p ultra	575.00	45.00
28g	A5	20p blue	575.00	45.00
29e	A5	25p rose	—	290.00
29f	A5	25p carmine	575.00	115.00

1885 *Perf. 12½*

31	A5	5p emerald	20.00	8.00
a.		5p yellow green	24.00	1.10
b.		Tête bêche pair	*14,000.*	*11,000.*
32	A5	10p carmine	30.00	3.50
a.		10p rose	50.00	3.50
33	A5	20p orange	35.00	.65
a.		20p yellow	47.50	2.50
b.		Tête bêche pair	—	3,500.
34	A5	25p ultra	70.00	4.25
a.		25p blue	70.00	3.00
35	A5	1m gray & rose	37.50	25.00
36	A5	5m grn & rose	500.00	500.00
37	A5	10m brn & rose	625.00	750.00

Denomination on No. 35 is spelled "MARKKA". Denomination on Nos. 36-37 is spelled "MARKKAA",

A6

1889-92 *Perf. 12½*

38	A6	2p slate ('90)	.75	*1.25*
39	A6	5p green ('90)	40.00	.50
40	A6	10p carmine ('90)	70.00	.50
a.		10p rose ('90)	90.00	.75
b.		Imperf.	110.00	
41	A6	20p orange ('92)	95.00	.50
a.		20p yellow ('89)	95.00	1.25
42	A6	25p ultra ('91)	80.00	.85
a.		25p blue	80.00	1.15
43	A6	1m slate & rose ('92)	6.00	3.25
a.		1m brnsh gray & rose ('90)	35.00	4.00
44	A6	5m grn & rose ('90)	32.50	*77.50*
45	A6	10m brn & rose ('90)	40.00	*90.00*
		Nos. 38-45 (8)	364.25	*174.35*

The 2p slate, perf. 14x13, is believed to be an essay.

See Nos. 60-63.

See Russia for types similar to A7-A18.

Finnish stamps have "dot in circle" devices or are inscribed "Markka," "Markkaa," "Pen." or "Pennia."

Imperial Arms of Russia

A7 A8 A9

A10

A11

Laid Paper

1891-92 **Wmk. 168** *Perf. 14½x15*

46	A7	1k org yel	6.50	*11.00*
47	A7	2k green	6.50	*11.00*
48	A7	3k carmine	12.00	*18.00*
49	A8	4k rose	14.00	18.00
50	A7	7k dark blue	8.00	2.25
51	A8	10k dark blue	17.50	*18.00*
52	A9	14k blue & rose	20.00	*30.00*
53	A8	20k blue & car	20.00	24.00
54	A9	35k vio & grn	30.00	*60.00*
55	A8	50k vio & grn	35.00	42.50

Perf. 13½

56	A10	1r brn & org	90.00	67.50
57	A11	3½r blk & gray	325.00	*550.00*
a.		3½r black & yellow (error)	*15,000.*	*18,000.*
58	A11	7r blk & yel	250.00	*350.00*
		Nos. 46-58 (13)	834.50	*1,202.*

Forgeries of Nos. 57, 57a, 58 exist.

Type of 1889-90
Wove Paper

1895-96 **Unwmk.** *Perf. 14x13*

60	A6	5p green	.80	.50
61	A6	10p carmine	.80	.50
62	A6	20p orange	.80	.50
b.		Imperf.	160.00	—
63	A6	25p ultra	1.25	.70
a.		25p blue	1.25	.70
b.		Imperf.	125.00	—
		Nos. 60-63 (4)	3.65	2.20

A12

A13

A14

A15

1901 **Litho.** *Perf. 14½x15*

Chalky Paper

64	A12	2p yellow	6.00	8.00
65	A12	5p green	12.50	2.00
66	A13	10p carmine	27.50	3.25
67	A12	20p dark blue	70.00	1.50
68	A14	1m violet & grn	350.00	10.00

Perf. 13½

69	A15	10m black & gray	325.00	350.00
		Nos. 64-69 (6)	791.00	374.75

Imperf sheets of 10p and 20p, stolen during production, were privately perforated 11½ to defraud the P.O. Uncanceled imperfs. of Nos. 65-68 are believed to be proofs.

See Nos. 70-75, 82.

Types of 1901 Redrawn

No. 64

No. 70

2p. On No. 64, the "2" below "II" is shifted slightly leftward. On No. 70, the "2" is centered below "II."

No. 65

No. 71

5p. On No. 65, the frame lines are very close. On No. 71, a clear white space separates them.

Nos. 66, 67 Nos. 72, 73

10p, 20p. On Nos. 66-67, the horizontal central background lines are faint and broken. On Nos. 72-73, they are clear and solid, though still thin.

20p. On No. 67, "H" close to "2" with period midway. On No. 73 they are slightly separated with period close to "H."

No. 68 Nos. 74, 74a

1m. On No. 68, the "1" following "MARKKA" lacks serif at base. On Nos. 74-74a, this "1" has serif.

No. 69 No. 75

10m. On No. 69, the serifs of "M" and "A" in top and bottom panels do not touch. On No. 75, the serifs join.

Perf. 14¼x14¾, 14¼x14

1901-14 Typo. Ordinary Paper

70 A12 2p orange 1.00 1.50
71 A12 5p green 2.00 .60
a. Perf 14¼x14 ('06) 3.50 .75
Never hinged 4.00
72 A13 10p carmine 14.00 .60
a. Perf 14¼x14 ('07) 90.00 .95
Never hinged 92.50
b. Background inverted, perf 14¼x14¾ 17.50 5.00
c. Background inverted, perf 14¼x14 95.00 2.75
73 A12 20p dark blue 10.00 .60
a. Perf 14¼x14 ('06) 82.50 1.25
Never hinged 115.00
74 A14 1m lil & grn, perf. 14¼x14 ('14) 1.10 .60
a. 1m violet & blue green, perf. 14¼x14¾ ('02) 10.00 .90
Never hinged 22.50
Nos. 70-74 (5) 28.10 3.90
Set, never hinged 45.00

Perf. 13½

75 A15 10m blk & drab ('03) 160.00 60.00
Never hinged 275.00

Imperf Pairs

70a A12 2p 375.00 525.00
71b A12 5p 100.00 200.00
72d A13 10p 110.00 225.00
73b A12 20p 200.00 225.00
74b A14 1m 190.00 210.00
Nos. 70a-74b (5) 975.00 1,385.

A16 A17 A18

1911-16 *Perf. 14, 14¼x14¾*

77 A16 2p orange .30 .90
78 A16 5p green .35 .40
a. Imperf. —
b. Perf. 14¼x14¾ 1,400. 140.00
Never hinged 675.00
79 A17 10p rose ('15) .30 .75
a. Imperf. 110.00 225.00
b. Perf. 14¼x14¾ ('16) 3.50 5.50
Never hinged 9.50
80 A16 20p deep blue .40 .60
a. Imperf. 180.00 140.00
b. Perf. 14¼x14¾ 27.50 3.50
Never hinged 21.00
81 A18 40p violet & blue .40 .40
a. Perf. 14¼x14¾ 6,000. 4,000.
Nos. 77-81 (5) 1.75 3.05
Set, never hinged 3.00

There are three minor types of No. 79. Values are for the least expensive type.

Perf. 14½

82 A15 10m blk & grnsh gray ('16) 160.00 210.00
Never hinged 275.00
a. Horiz. pair, imperf. vert. 3,900.

Republic
Helsinki Issue

Arms of the Republic — A19

Type I

Type II

Two types of the 40p.
Type I — Thin figures of value.
Type II — Thick figures of value.

Perf. 14, 14¼x14¾

1917-30 Unwmk.

83 A19 5p green .35 .35
84 A19 5p gray ('19) .35 .35
85 A19 10p rose .35 .45
a. Imperf., pair 250.00 400.00
86 A19 10p green ('19) 1.50 .55
a. Perf. 14¼x14¾ 3,000.
87 A19 10p brt blue ('21) .40 .45
88 A19 20p buff .40 .50
89 A19 20p rose ('20) .40 .45
90 A19 20p brown ('24) 1.00 .90
a. Perf. 14¼x14¾ .65 25.00
Never hinged 1.50
91 A19 25p blue .40 .45
92 A19 25p lt brn ('19) .40 .40
93 A19 30p green ('23) .40 .55
94 A19 40p violet (I) .40 .35
a. Perf. 14¼x14¾ 400.00 27.50
Never hinged 850.00
95 A19 40p bl grn (II) ('29) .50 3.00
a. Type I ('24) 14.00 6.00
Never hinged 30.00
b. Perf. 14¼x14¾ 1.25 21.00
Never hinged 2.50
96 A19 50p orange brn .45 .45
97 A19 50p dp blue ('19) 4.00 .45
a. Perf. 14¼x14¾ 2,200.
98 A19 50p green ('21) 4.50 .40
a. Perf. 14¼x14¾ .40 1.50
Never hinged .50
99 A19 60p red vio ('21) .60 .40
a. Imperf., pair — —
100 A19 75p yellow ('21) .40 .75
101 A19 1m dull rose & blk 16.00 .30
102 A19 1m red org ('25) 9.00 30.00
a. Perf. 14 ('30) .25 550.00
Never hinged .65
103 A19 1½m bl grn & red vio ('29) .25 2.50
a. Perf. 14¼x14¾ .40 1.25
Never hinged .65
104 A19 2m green & blk ('21) 3.50 .70
105 A19 2m dk blue & ind ('22) 2.50 .45
a. Perf. 14¼x14¾ .65 4.00
Never hinged 1.50
106 A19 3m blue & blk ('21) 25.00 .50
107 A19 5m red vio & blk 17.50 .45
108 A19 10m brn & gray blk, perf. 14 1.00 1.25
a. 10m light brown & black, perf. 14¼x14¾ ('29) 3.50 400.00
Never hinged 7.00
110 A19 25m dull red & yel ('21) .90 26.00
Nos. 83-108,110 (27) 92.45 73.35
Set, never hinged 260.00

Examples of a 2½p gray of this type exist. They are proofs from the original die which were distributed through the UPU. No plate was made for this denomination.

See Nos. 127-140, 143-152. For surcharge and overprints see Nos. 119-126, 153-154.

Vasa Issue

Arms of the Republic — A20

1918 Litho. *Perf. 11½*

111 A20 5p green .75 1.25
112 A20 10p red .75 1.25
113 A20 30p slate 1.25 4.50
114 A20 40p brown vio .70 1.75
115 A20 50p orange brn .75 5.00
116 A20 70p gray brown 2.25 32.50
117 A20 1m red & gray .75 2.50
118 A20 5m red violet & gray 45.00 125.00
Nos. 111-118 (8) 52.20 173.75
Set, never hinged 100.00

Nos. 111-118 exist imperforate but were not regularly issued in that condition.

Sheet margin examples, perf. on 3 sides, imperf. on margin side, were sold by post office.

Stamps and Type of 1917-29 Surcharged

1919 *Perf. 14*

119 A19 10p on 5p green .50 .55
120 A19 20p on 10p rose .50 .55
121 A19 50p on 25p blue 1.00 .55
122 A19 75p on 20p orange .50 .85
Nos. 119-122 (4) 2.50 2.50
Set, never hinged 5.50

Stamps and Type of 1917-29 Surcharged

Nos. 123-125

No. 126

1921

123 A19 30p on 10p green .65 .65
124 A19 60p on 40p red violet 3.75 1.25
125 A19 90p on 20p rose .40 .50
126 A19 1½m on 50p blue 1.40 .50
a. Thin "2" in "½" 12.50 11.00
b. Imperf., pair 300.00 500.00
Nos. 123-126 (4) 6.20 2.90
Set, never hinged 13.00

Arms Type of 1917-29

Perf. 14, 14¼x14¾

1925-29 Wmk. 121

127 A19 10p ultra ('27) .50 2.75
128 A19 20p brown .50 2.00
129 A19 25p brn org ('29) 1.00 90.00
130 A19 30p yel green .40 .95
a. Perf. 14¼x14¾ 7.00 1.50
Never hinged 7.50
131 A19 40p blue grn (I) ('26) 9.50 1.40
a. Perf. 14¼x14¾ ('26) 9.50 1.40
Never hinged 15.00
b. Type II ('28) 140.00 82.50
Never hinged 290.00
c. As "b," perf. 14¼x14¾ ('28) 9.50 1.40
Never hinged 25.00
132 A19 50p gray grn ('26) 1.25 .80
a. Perf. 14¼x14¾ ('26) .55 .55
Never hinged 2.00
133 A19 60p red violet .40 .95
134 A19 1m dp orange 7.00 .40
a. Perf. 14¼x14¾ 100.00 1.25
Never hinged 250.00

Perf. 14¼x14¾

135 A19 1½m blue grn & red vio ('26) 6.25 .60
a. Perf. 14 ('26) 60.00 .50
Never hinged 150.00
136 A19 2m dk blue & indigo ('27) 1.00 .50
a. Perf. 14 1.00 .50
Never hinged 2.25
137 A19 3m chlky blue & blk ('26) 1.00 .50
138 A19 5m red violet & blk ('27) .50 .50
a. Perf. 14 1.25 .50
Never hinged 2.75
139 A19 10m lt brn & blk ('27) 4.00 32.50
140 A19 25m dp org & yel ('27) 20.00 400.00
Nos. 127-140 (14) 53.30 533.85
Set, never hinged 100.00

No. 130a is not known cancelled during the period in which it was valid for postal use.

A21

Wmk. 208

1927, Dec. 6 Typo. *Perf. 14*

141 A21 1½m deep violet .30 .60
142 A21 2m deep blue .30 2.00

10th anniv. of Finnish independence.

Arms Type of 1917-29

Perf. 14, 14¼x14¾

1927-29 Wmk. 208

143 A19 20p lt brown ('29) 2.00 40.00
144 A19 40p bl grn (II) ('28) .40 .65
145 A19 50p gray grn ('28) .40 .75
146 A19 1m dp orange .40 1.00
a. Imperf., pair 115.00 200.00
b. Perf. 14 1.25 1.25
147 A19 1½m bl grn & red vio ('28) 3.00 .70
a. Perf. 14 1,000. 26.00
148 A19 2m dk bl & ind ('28) .45 .65
149 A19 3m chlky bl & blk .50 .65
a. Perf. 14 1.60 5.00
150 A19 5m red vio & blk ('28) .50 .60
151 A19 10m lt brown & blk 2.00 35.00
152 A19 25m brown org & yel 2.25 400.00
Nos. 143-152 (10) 11.90 480.00
Set, never hinged 30.00

Nos. 146-147 Overprinted

1928, Nov. 10 Litho. Wmk. 208

153 A19 1m deep orange 10.00 19.00
154 A19 1½m bl grn & red vio 10.00 19.00
Set, never hinged 35.00

Nos. 153 and 154 were sold exclusively at the Helsinki Philatelic Exhibition, Nov. 10-18, 1928, and were valid only during that period.

S. S. "Bore" Leaving Turku — A23

Turku Cathedral — A24

Turku Castle — A25

Wmk. 208

1929, May 22 Typo. *Perf. 14*

155 A23 1m olive green 1.50 5.00
156 A24 1½m chocolate 2.25 4.00
157 A25 2m dark gray .45 4.50
Nos. 155-157 (3) 4.20 13.50
Set, never hinged 13.00

Founding of the city of Turku (Abo), 700th anniv.

A26

1930-46 Unwmk. *Perf. 14*

No.	Type	Value	Description	Unused	Used
158	A26	5p	chocolate	.50	*.50*
159	A26	10p	dull violet	.50	.50
160	A26	20p	yel grn	.50	*.50*
161	A26	25p	yel brn	.50	.50
162	A26	40p	blue grn	2.00	.25
163	A26	50p	yellow	.50	.50
164	A26	50p	blue grn ('32)	.45	.45
b.			Imperf., pair	150.00	*200.00*
165	A26	60p	dark gray	.50	*.65*
165A	A26	75p	dp org ('42)	.55	*.75*
166	A26	1m	red org	.50	.50
166B	A26	1m	yel grn ('42)	.50	.50
167	A26	1.20m	crimson	.55	*1.75*
168	A26	1.25m	yel ('32)	.50	.50
169	A26	1½m	red vio	2.00	.50
170	A26	1½m	car ('32)	.50	.50
170A	A26	1½m	sl ('40)	.50	.50
170B	A26	1.75m	org yel ('40)	.90	.70
171	A26	2m	indigo	.50	.50
172	A26	2m	dp vio ('32)	6.00	.50
173	A26	2m	car ('36)	.50	.50
			Complete booklet, panes of 4 #161, 164, 166, 168, 173	5.75	
173B	A26	2m	yel org ('42)	.50	.50
173C	A26	2m	blue grn ('45)	.50	.50
174	A26	2½m	brt blue ('32)	4.75	.55
174A	A26	2½m	car ('42)	.50	.50
174B	A26	2.75m	rose vio ('40)	.50	.50
175	A26	3m	olive blk	35.00	.65
175B	A26	3m	car ('45)	1.00	.50
175C	A26	3m	yel ('45)	.50	*.80*
176	A26	3½m	brt bl ('36)	9.00	.50
176A	A26	3½m	olive ('42)	.50	.50
176B	A26	4m	olive ('45)	1.10	.50
176C	A26	4½m	saph ('42)	.50	.50
176D	A26	5m	saph ('45)	.50	.50
176E	A26	5m	pur ('45)	1.50	.50
j.			Imperf., pair	150.00	*200.00*
176F	A26	5m	yel ('46)	1.25	.55
k.			Imperf., pair	150.00	*200.00*
176G	A26	6m	car ('45)	1.20	.50
m.			Imperf., pair	200.00	*275.00*
176H	A26	8m	pur ('46)	.50	.50
176I	A26	10m	saph ('45)	1.75	.50
			Nos. 158-176I (38)	80.00	21.10

See Nos. 257-262, 270-274, 291-296, 302-304. For surcharges and overprints see Nos. 195-196, 212, 221-222, 243, 250, 275, M2-M3.

Stamps of types A26-A29 overprinted "ITA KARJALA" are listed under Karelia, Nos. N1-N15.

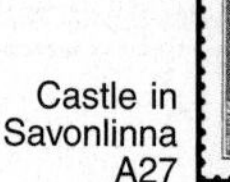

Castle in Savonlinna A27

Lake Saima — A28

Woodchopper A29

1930 Engr.

No.	Type	Description	Unused	Used
177	A27	5m blue	1.50	*.65*
178	A28	10m gray lilac	55.00	4.75
179	A29	25m black brown	1.00	.50
		Nos. 177-179 (3)	57.50	5.90
		Set, never hinged	150.00	

See Nos. 205, 305. For overprint see No. C1.

Elias Lönnrot — A30

Seal of Finnish Literary Society — A31

1931, Jan. 1 Typo.

No.	Type	Description	Unused	Used
180	A30	1m olive brown	2.50	*5.75*
181	A31	1½m dull blue	12.50	6.25
		Never hinged	45.00	

Centenary of Finnish Literary Society.

A32

1931, Feb. 28

No.	Type	Description	Unused	Used
182	A32	1½m red	2.75	*9.50*
		Never hinged	6.00	
183	A32	2m blue	2.75	*11.50*
		Never hinged	6.00	

1st use of postage stamps in Finland, 75th anniv.

Nos. 162-163 Surcharged

1931, Dec.

No.	Type	Description	Unused	Used
195	A26	50p on 40p blue grn	2.75	1.20
		Never hinged	8.50	
196	A26	1.25m on 50p yellow	4.00	3.50
		Never hinged	13.00	

Svinhufvud — A33

1931, Dec. 15

No.	Type	Description	Unused	Used
197	A33	2m gray blue & blk	1.50	*3.25*
		Never hinged	5.25	

Pres. Pehr Eyvind Svinhufvud, 70th birthday.

Lake Saima Type of 1930

1932-43 Re-engraved

No.	Type	Description	Unused	Used
205	A28	10m red violet ('43)	.70	.50
		Never hinged	1.60	
a.		10m dark violet	20.00	.70
		Never hinged	40.00	

On Nos. 205 and 205a the lines of the islands, the clouds and the foliage are much deeper and stronger than on No. 178.

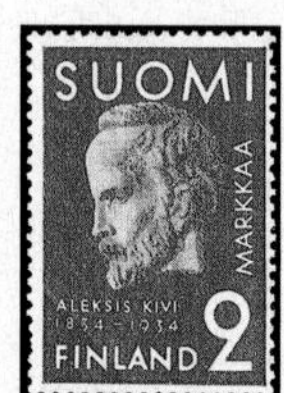

Alexis Kivi — A34

1934, Oct. 10 Typo.

No.	Type	Description	Unused	Used
206	A34	2m red violet	2.25	*4.50*
		Never hinged	5.50	

Alexis Kivi, Finnish poet (1834-1872).

Bards Reciting the "Kalevala" A35

Goddess Louhi, As Eagle Seizing Magic Mill — A36

Kullervo — A37

1935, Feb. 28 Engr.

No.	Type	Description	Unused	Used
207	A35	1¼m brown lake	2.00	*2.50*
		Never hinged	4.00	
208	A36	2m black	4.50	2.00
		Never hinged	12.50	
209	A37	2½m blue	3.00	3.00
		Never hinged	10.00	
		Nos. 207-209 (3)	9.50	7.50
		Set, never hinged	26.50	

Cent. of the publication of the "Kalevala" (Finnish National Epic).

No. 170 Surcharged in Black

1937, Feb.

No.	Type	Description	Unused	Used
212	A26	2m on 1½m car	8.00	1.40
		Never hinged	14.00	

Gustaf Mannerheim — A38

1937, June 4 Photo. *Perf. 14*

No.	Type	Description	Unused	Used
213	A38	2m ultra	1.00	*1.45*
		Never hinged	2.50	

70th birthday of Field Marshal Baron Carl Gustaf Mannerheim, June 4th, 1937.

Swede-Finn Co-operation in Colonization A39

1938, June 1

No.	Type	Description	Unused	Used
214	A39	3½m dark brown	.90	*2.75*
		Never hinged	3.00	

Tercentenary of the colonization of Delaware by Swedes and Finns.

Early Post Office — A40

Designs: 1¼m, Mail delivery in 1700. 2m, Modern mail plane. 3½m, Helsinki post office.

1938, Sept. 6 Photo. *Perf. 14*

No.	Type	Description	Unused	Used
215	A40	50p green	.35	.55
		Never hinged	.65	
216	A40	1¼m dk blue	1.15	*3.25*
		Never hinged	3.25	
217	A40	2m scarlet	1.15	1.25
		Never hinged	6.25	
218	A40	3½m slate black	3.25	*8.00*
		Never hinged	8.75	
		Nos. 215-218 (4)	5.90	13.05
		Set, never hinged	19.00	

300th anniv. of the Finnish Postal System.

Margin strips of each denomination (3 of No. 215, 2 each of Nos. 216, 217, 218) were pasted on to advertising sheets and stapled into a booklet. Value, $120.

Post Office, Helsinki — A44

1939-42 Photo.

No.	Type	Description	Unused	Used
219	A44	4m brown black	.40	*.45*
		Never hinged	1.10	

Engr.

No.	Type	Description	Unused	Used
219A	A44	7m black brn ('42)	.50	*.45*
		Never hinged	1.90	
219B	A44	9m rose lake ('42)	.60	.50
		Never hinged	1.60	
		Nos. 219-219B (3)	1.50	1.40
		Set, never hinged	3.50	

See No. 248.

Catalogue values for unused stamps in this section, from this point to the end of the section, are for Never Hinged items.

University of Helsinki — A45

1940, May 1 Photo.

No.	Type	Description	Unused	Used
220	A45	2m dp blue & blue	.75	*.90*

300th anniv. of the founding of the University of Helsinki.

Nos. 168 and 173 Surcharged in Black

1940, June 16 Typo.

No.	Type	Description	Unused	Used
221	A26	1.75m on 1.25m yel	4.00	*3.25*
222	A26	2.75m on 2m carmine	10.00	.90

President Kallio Reviewing Military Band — A46

1941, May 24 Engr.

No.	Type	Description	Unused	Used
223	A46	2.75m black	.75	*1.00*

Pres. Kyösti Kallio (1873-1940).

Castle at Viborg — A47

1941, Aug. 30 Typo.

No.	Type	Description	Unused	Used
224	A47	1.75m yellow orange	.50	*.60*
225	A47	2.75m rose violet	.50	*.60*
226	A47	3.50m blue	.90	*1.25*

Field Marshal Mannerheim — A48

1941, Dec. 31 Engr. Wmk. 273

227	A48	50p dull green	1.75	*2.75*
228	A48	1.75m deep brown	1.75	*2.75*
229	A48	2m dark red	2.75	2.75
230	A48	2.75m dull vio brn	2.75	2.75
231	A48	3.50m deep blue	1.75	*2.00*
232	A48	5m slate blue	1.75	*2.00*
		Nos. 227-232 (6)	12.50	*15.00*

Pres. Risto Ryti — A49

233	A49	50p dull green	1.60	*2.25*
234	A49	1.75m deep brown	1.60	*2.25*
235	A49	2m dark red	1.60	*2.25*
236	A49	2.75m dull vio brn	1.60	*3.50*
237	A49	3.50m deep blue	1.60	*2.25*
238	A49	5m slate blue	1.60	*2.25*
		Nos. 233-238 (6)	9.60	*14.75*

Types A48-A49 overprinted "ITA KARJALA" are listed under Karelia, Nos. N16-N27.

Häme Bridge, Tampere A50

South Harbor, Helsinki — A51

1942 Unwmk.

239	A50	50m dull brown vio	3.25	.45
240	A51	100m indigo	5.00	.40

See No. 350.

Altar and Open Bible — A52

17th Century Printer — A53

1942, Oct. 10

241	A52	2.75m dk brown	.90	*1.40*
242	A53	3.50m violet blue	1.00	*3.50*

300th anniv. of the printing of the 1st Bible in Finnish.

No. 174B Surcharged in Black

1943, Feb. 1

243 A26 3.50m on 2.75m rose vio .85 .70

Minna Canth (1844-96), Author and Playwright — A54

1944, Mar. 20

244 A54 3.50m dk olive grn .60 *1.00*

Pres. P. E. Svinhufvud — A55

1944, Aug. 1

245 A55 3.50m black .90 *1.25*

Death of President Svinhufvud (1861-1944).

K. J. Stahlberg — A56

1945, May 16 Engr. *Perf. 14*

246 A56 3.50m brown vio .60 *.75*

80th birthday of Dr. K. J. Stahlberg.

Castle in Savonlinna A57

1945, Sept. 4

247	A57	15m lilac rose	2.75	.60
248	A44	20m sepia	1.75	.60

For a 35m of type A57, see No. 280.

Jean Sibelius — A58

1945, Dec. 8

249 A58 5m dk slate green 1.00 .55

Jean Sibelius (1865-1957), composer.

No. 176E Surcharged in Black

1946, Mar. 16

250 A26 8(m) on 5m purple .75 .50

Victorious Athletes — A59

1946, June 1 Engr. *Perf. 13½*

251 A59 8m brown violet .60 *.75*

3rd Sports Festival, Helsinki, June 27-30, 1946.

Lighthouse at Uto — A60

1946, Sept. 19

252 A60 8m deep violet .75 *.70*

250th anniv. of the Finnish Department of Pilots and Lighthouses.

Post Bus — A61

1946-47 Unwmk. *Perf. 14*

253	A61	16m gray black	.85	*.75*
253A	A61	30m gray black ('47)	3.00	.50

Issue dates: 16m, Oct. 16, 30m, Feb. 10.

Old Town Hall, Porvoo — A62

Cathedral, Porvoo — A63

1946, Dec. 3

254	A62	5m gray black	.60	*.75*
255	A63	8m deep claret	.60	*.75*

600th anniv. of the founding of the city of Porvoo (Borga).

Waterfront, Tammisaari A64

1946, Dec. 14

256 A64 8m grnsh black .60 *.75*

400th anniv. of the founding of the town of Tammisaari (Ekenas).

Lion Type of 1930

1947 Typo. *Perf. 14*

257	A26	2½m dark green	.65	.50
258	A26	3m slate gray	.75	.50
259	A26	6m deep orange	2.00	.50
260	A26	7m carmine	1.50	.45
261	A26	10m purple	5.00	.45
262	A26	12m deep blue	4.50	.45
		Nos. 257-262 (6)	14.40	2.85

Issued: 3m, 6/9; 7m, 12m, 2/10; others, 1/20.

Pres. Juho K. Paasikivi — A65

1947, Mar. 15 Engr.

263 A65 10m gray black .65 .50

Postal Savings Emblem — A66

1947, Apr. 1

264 A66 10m brown violet .50 .50

60th anniv. of the foundation of the Finnish Postal Savings Bank.

Ilmarinen, the Plowman — A67

1947, June 2

265 A67 10m gray black .50 .50

2nd year of peace following WW II.

Girl and Boy Athletes — A68

1947, June 2

266 A68 10m bright blue .70 *.75*

Finnish Athletic Festival, Helsinki, June 29-July 3, 1947.

Wheat and Savings Bank Assoc. Emblem — A69

1947, Aug. 21

267 A69 10m red brown .80 *.75*

Finnish Savings Bank Assoc., 125th anniv.

Sower — A70

1947, Nov. 1

268 A70 10m gray black .75 .70

150th anniv. of Finnish Agricultural Societies.

Koli Mountain and Lake Pielisjärvi A71

1947, Nov. 1

269 A71 10m indigo .90 *.75*

60th anniv. of the Finnish Touring Assoc.

Lion Type of 1930

1948 Typo. *Perf. 14*

270	A26	3m dark green	4.50	.45
271	A26	6m yellow green	1.25	.65
272	A26	9m carmine	1.25	.50

273 A26 15m dark blue 8.00 .50
274 A26 24m brown lake 2.75 .50
Nos. 270-274 (5) 17.75 2.60

Issued: 3m, 2/9; 24m, 4/26; others, 9/13.

No. 261 Surcharged in Black

1948, Feb. 9
275 A26 12(m) on 10m purple 2.00 .50

Statue of Michael Agricola — A72

12m, Agricola translating New Testament.

1948, Oct. 2 Engr. *Perf. 14*
276 A72 7m rose violet 1.25 *2.25*
277 A72 12m gray blue 1.25 *2.25*

400th anniv. of publication of the Finnish translation of the New Testament, by Michael Agricola.

Sveaborg Fortress A73

1948, Oct. 15
278 A73 12m deep green 1.60 *2.00*

200th anniv. of the construction of Sveaborg Fortress on the Gulf of Finland.

Post Rider — A74

1948, Oct. 27
279 A74 12m green 9.00 *17.50*

Helsinki Philatelic Exhibition. Sold only at exhibition for 62m, of which 50m was entrance fee.

Castle Type of 1945

1949
280 A57 35m violet 9.00 .50

Sawmill and Cellulose Plant — A75

Pine Tree and Globe — A76

1949, June 15
281 A75 9m brown 3.00 *4.50*
282 A76 15m dull green 3.00 *4.50*

Issued to publicize the Third World Forestry Congress, Helsinki, July 10-20, 1949.

Woman with Torch — A77

1949, July 16 Engr. *Perf. 14*
283 A77 5m dull green 5.50 *11.50*
284 A77 15m red *(Worker)* 5.50 *11.50*

50th anniv. of the Finnish labor movement.

Harbor of Lappeenranta (Willmanstrand) — A78

Raahe (Brahestad) — A79

1949
285 A78 5m dk blue grn 2.00 1.50
286 A79 9m brown carmine 2.00 *2.00*
287 A78 15m brt blue *(Kristi-inan-kaupunki)* 2.75 *4.50*
Nos. 285-287 (3) 6.75 8.00

300th anniv. of the founding of Willmanstrand, Brahestad and Kristinestad (Kristiinankaupunki).
Issued: 5m, 8/6; 9m, 8/13; 15m, 7/30.

Technical High School Badge — A80

1949, Sept. 13
288 A80 15m ultra 1.40 *1.60*

Founding of the technical school, cent.

Hannes Gebhard — A81

1949, Oct. 2
289 A81 15m dull green 1.40 *1.60*

Establishment of Finnish cooperatives, 50th anniv.

Finnish Lake Country — A82

1949, Oct. 8
290 A82 15m blue 1.40 *1.60*

75th anniv. of the UPU.

Lion Type of 1930

1950, Jan. 9 Typo. *Perf. 14*
291 A26 8m brt green 2.25 1.75
292 A26 9m red orange 2.40 .60
293 A26 10m violet brown 7.25 .50
294 A26 12m scarlet 2.00 .50
295 A26 15m plum 25.00 .50
296 A26 20m deep blue 10.00 .50
Nos. 291-296 (6) 48.90 4.35

Forsell's Map of Old Helsinki — A83

J. A. Ehrenstrom and C. L. Engel — A84

City Hall — A85

1950, June 11 Engr.
297 A83 5m emerald 1.00 *.90*
298 A84 9m brown 1.25 *1.50*
299 A85 15m deep blue .90 *1.10*
Nos. 297-299 (3) 3.15 3.50

400th anniv. of the founding of Helsinki.

J. K. Paasikivi — A86

1950, Nov. 27
300 A86 20m deep ultra .70 .50

80th birthday of Pres. J. K. Paasikivi.

View of Kajaani — A87

1951, July 7 Unwmk. *Perf. 14*
301 A87 20m red brown 2.00 *1.00*

Tercentenary of Kajaani.

Lion and Chopper Types of 1930

1952, Jan. 18 Typo.
302 A26 10m emerald 4.50 .40
303 A26 15m red 4.25 .45
304 A26 25m blue 7.00 .40

Engr.
305 A29 40m black brown 4.25 .50
Nos. 302-305 (4) 20.00 1.75

Arms of Pietarsaari — A88

1952, June 19 Unwmk. *Perf. 14*
306 A88 25m blue 1.40 1.10

300th anniv. of the founding of Pietarsaari (Jacobstad).

Rooftops of Vaasa — A89

1952, Aug. 3
307 A89 25m brown 2.25 1.10

Centenary of the burning of Vaasa.

Chess Symbols — A90

1952, Aug. 10
308 A90 25m gray 3.00 *3.00*

10th Chess Olympics, Helsinki, 8/10-31/52.

Torch Bearers — A91

1953, Jan. 27
309 A91 25m blue 1.60 1.10

Temperance movement in Finland, cent.

Air View of Hamina (Fredrikshamn) A92

1953, June 20
310 A92 25m dk gray green 2.10 1.10

Tercentenary of Hamina.

Ivar Wilskman — A93

1954, Feb. 26
311 A93 25m blue 1.10 1.00

Centenary of the birth of Prof. Ivar Wilskman, "father of gymnastics in Finland."

Arms of Finland — A94

1954-59 *Perf. 11½*
312 A94 1m red brown ('55) .40 .25
313 A94 2m green ('55) .40 .25
314 A94 3m deep orange .40 .25
314A A94 4m gray ('58) .75 .50
315 A94 5m violet blue .80 .25
316 A94 10m blue green 1.25 .25
a. Bklt. pane of 5 (vert. strip) 22.50 22.50
Complete booklet, #316a 25.00
317 A94 15m rose red 4.50 .25
318 A94 15m yellow org ('57) 8.25 .25
319 A94 20m rose lilac 14.00 .25
320 A94 20m rose red ('56) 2.40 .25
321 A94 25m deep blue 4.50 .25

322 A94 25m rose lilac ('59) 12.00 .25
323 A94 30m lt ultra ('56) 2.40 .25
Nos. 312-323 (13) 52.05 3.50

See Nos. 398, 400-405A, 457-459A, 461A-462, 464-464B.

"In the Outer Archipelago" A95

1954, July 21 ***Perf. 14***
324 A95 25m black .90 .70

Cent. of the birth of Albert Edelfelt, painter.

J. J. Nervander A96

1955, Feb. 23
325 A96 25m blue 1.70 1.00

150th anniv. of the birth of J. J. Nervander, astronomer and poet.

Composite of Finnish Public Buildings — A97

1955, Mar. 30 **Engr.** ***Perf. 14***
326 A97 25m gray 17.00 *24.00*

Sold for 125m, which included the price of admission to the Natl. Postage Stamp Exhibition, Helsinki, Mar. 30-Apr. 3, 1955.

Bishop Henrik with Foot on Lalli, his Murderer — A98

25m, Arrival of Bishop Henrik and monks.

1955, May 19
327 A98 15m rose brown 1.25 1.00
328 A98 25m green 1.25 1.00

Adoption of Christianity in Finland, 800th anniv.

Conference Hall, Helsinki — A99

1955, Aug. 25
329 A99 25m bluish green 1.25 *2.00*

44th conf. of the Interparliamentarian Union, Helsinki, Aug. 25-31, 1955.

Sailing Vessel and Merchant A100

1955, Sept. 2
330 A100 25m sepia 2.40 2.10

350th anniv. of founding of Oulu.

Town Hall, Lahti — A101

1955, Nov. 1 ***Perf. 14x13½***
331 A101 25m violet blue 1.50 *2.50*

50th anniversary of founding of Lahti.

Radio Sender, Map of Finland — A102

Designs: 15m, Otto Nyberg. 25m, Telegraph wires and pines under snow.

Inscribed: Lennatin 1855-1955 Telegrafen

1955, Dec. 10 ***Perf. 14***
332 A102 10m green 3.00 *2.40*
333 A102 15m dull violet 3.00 1.25
334 A102 25m lt ultra 4.50 2.00
Nos. 332-334 (3) 10.50 5.65

Cent. of the telegraph in Finland.

A103

1956, Jan. 26 **Unwmk.** ***Perf. 14***
335 A103 25m Lighthouse, Porkkala Peninsula 1.10 *1.40*

Return of the Porkkala Region to Finland by Russia, Jan. 1956.

A104

30m, 50m, Church at Lammi. 40m, House of Parliament. 60m, Fortress of Olavinlinna (Olofsborg).

1956-57 ***Perf. 11½***
336 A104 30m gray olive 1.25 .30
337 A104 40m dull purple 2.75 .30
338 A104 50m gray ol ('57) 8.25 .30
338A A104 60m pale pur ('57) 12.00 .30
Nos. 336-338A (4) 24.25 1.20

Issued: 30m, 3/4; 40m, 3/11; 50m, 3/3; 60m, 4/7. See Nos. 406-408A.

Johan V. Snellman — A105

1956, May 12 **Engr.** ***Perf. 14***
339 A105 25m dk violet brn .85 *1.00*

Johan V. Snellman (1806-81), statesman.

Gymnast and Athletes — A106

1956, June 28
340 A106 30m violet blue 1.60 1.25

Finnish Gymnastic and Sports Games, Helsinki, June 28-July 1, 1956.

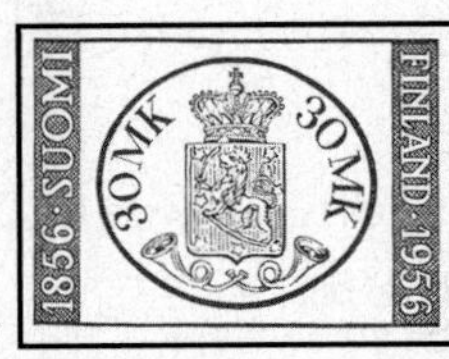

A107

Wmk. 208

1956, July 7 **Typo.** ***Rouletted***
341 A107 30m deep ultra 4.00 *6.50*
a. Tête bêche pair 10.00 *15.00*
b. Pane of 10 50.00 *75.00*

Issued to publicize the FINLANDIA Philatelic Exhibition, Helsinki, July 7-15, 1956.

Printed in sheets containing four 2x5 panes, with white margins around each group. The stamps in each double row are printed tete-beche, making the position of the watermark differ in the vertical row of each pane of ten.

Sold for 155m, price including entrance ticket to exhibition.

Town Hall at Vasa — A108

Unwmk.

1956, Oct. 2 **Engr.** ***Perf. 14***
342 A108 30m bright blue 1.60 1.25

350th anniversary of Vasa.

Northern Countries Issue

Whooper Swans — A108a

1956, Oct. 30 ***Perf. 12½***
343 A108a 20m rose red 1.50 1.40
344 A108a 30m ultra 5.00 1.40

See footnote after Denmark No. 362.

University Clinic, Helsinki A109

1956, Dec. 17 ***Perf. 11½***
345 A109 30m dull green 1.75 1.10

Public health service in Finland, bicent.

Scout Sign, Emblem and Globe — A110

1957, Feb. 22 ***Perf. 14***
346 A110 30m ultra 3.00 1.40

50th anniversary of Boy Scouts.

Arms Holding Hammers and Laurel — A111

Design: 20m, Factories and cogwheel.

1957 **Engr.** ***Perf. 13½***
347 A111 20m dark blue 1.10 1.10
348 A111 30m carmine 2.50 1.40

50th anniv.: Central Fed. of Finnish Employers (20m, issued 9/27); Finnish Trade Union Movement (30m, issued 4/15).

"Lex" from Seal of Parliament — A112

1957, May 23 ***Perf. 14***
349 A112 30m olive gray 1.50 1.10

50th anniv. of the Finnish parliament.

Harbor Type of 1942

1957 **Unwmk.** ***Perf. 14***
350 A51 100m grnsh blue 12.50 .35

Ida Aalberg — A114

1957, Dec. 4 ***Perf. 14***
351 A114 30m vio gray & mar 1.50 *.90*

Birth cent. of Ida Aalberg, Finnish actress.

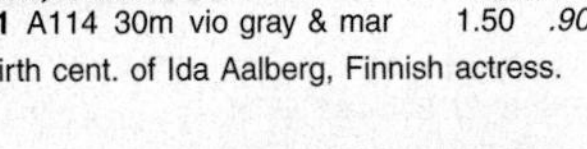

Arms of Finland A115

1957, Dec. 6 ***Perf. 11½***
352 A115 30m blue 1.40 *1.00*

40th anniv. of Finland's independence.

Jean Sibelius — A116

1957, Dec. 8 ***Perf. 14***
353 A116 30m black 2.75 1.10

Jean Sibelius (1865-1957), composer.

Ski Jump — A117

Design: 30m, Skier, vert.

1958, Feb. 1 **Engr.** ***Perf. 11½***
354 A117 20m slate green 1.10 *1.60*
355 A117 30m blue 1.10 .80

Nordic championships of the Intl. Ski Federation, Lahti.

"March of the Bjorneborgienses," by Edelfelt — A118

1958, Mar. 8

356 A118 30m violet gray 1.75 .95

400th anniv. of the founding of Pori (Bjorneborg).

South Harbor, Helsinki A119

1958, June 2 Unwmk. *Perf. 11½*

357 A119 100m bluish green 17.50 .35

See No. 410.

Seal of Jyväskylä Lyceum A120

1958, Oct. 1 *Perf. 11½*

358 A120 30m rose carmine 1.75 1.10

Cent. of the founding of the 1st Finnish secondary school.

Chrismon and Globe — A121

1959, Jan. 19

359 A121 30m dull violet .75 .65

Finnish Missionary Society, cent.

Diet at Porvoo, 1809 — A122

1959, Mar. 22 *Perf. 11½*

360 A122 30m dk blue gray .75 .65

150th anniv. of the inauguration of the Diet at Porvoo.

Saw Cutting Log — A123

1959, May 13 Engr.

361 A123 10m shown .95 .95

362 A123 30m Forest .95 .95

No. 361 for the cent. of the establishment of the 1st steam saw-mill in Finland; No. 362, the cent. of the Dept. of Forestry.

Pyhakoski Power Station — A124

1959, May 24

363 A124 75m gray 5.75 .40

See No. 409.

Oil Lamp — A125

1959, Dec. 19

364 A125 30m blue .90 .75

Cent. of the liberation of the country trade.

Woman Gymnast A126

1959, Nov. 14 Unwmk.

365 A126 30m rose lilac 1.10 .75

Finnish women's gymnastics and the cent. of the birth of Elin Oihonna Kallio, pioneer of Finnish women's physical education.

Arms of Six New Towns — A127

1960, Jan. 2 *Perf. 14*

366 A127 30m light violet 1.75 1.00

Issued to commemorate the founding of new towns in Finland: Hyvinkaa, Kouvola, Riihimaki, Rovaniemi, Salo and Seinajoki.

Type of 1860 Issue A128

1960, Mar. 25 Typo. *Rouletted 4½*

367 A128 30m blue & gray 5.50 9.75

Cent. of Finland's serpentine roulette stamps, and in connection with HELSINKI 1960, 40th anniv. exhib. of the Federation of Philatelic Societies of Finland, Mar. 25-31. Sold only at the exhibition for 150m including entrance ticket.

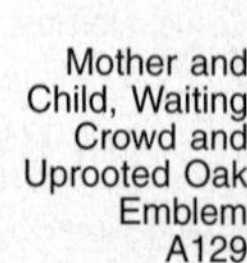

Mother and Child, Waiting Crowd and Uprooted Oak Emblem A129

1960, Apr. 7 Engr. *Perf. 11½*

368 A129 30m rose claret .80 .80

369 A129 40m dark blue .80 .80

World Refugee Year, 7/1/59-6/30/60.

Johan Gadolin — A130

1960, June 4 *Perf. 11½*

370 A130 30m dark brown 1.10 .75

Bicent. of the birth of Gadolin, chemist.

Hj. Nortamo — A131

1960, June 13 Unwmk.

371 A131 30m gray green 1.10 .75

Cent. of the birth of Hj. Nortamo (Hjalmar Nordberg), writer.

Symbolic Tree and Cuckoo A132

1960, June 18

372 A132 30m vermilion 1.40 .80

Karelian Natl. Festival, Helsinki, June 18-19.

Geodetic Instrument A133

Design: 30m, Aurora borealis and globe.

1960, July 26 Unwmk. *Perf. 13½*

373 A133 10m blue & pale brn 1.00 .65

374 A133 30m ver & rose car 1.25 .65

12th General Assembly of the Intl. Union of Geodesy and Geophysics, Helsinki.

Urho Kekkonen — A134

1960, Sept. 3 Engr. *Perf. 11½*

375 A134 30m violet blue .90 .40

Issued to honor President Urho Kekkonen on his 60th birthday.

Common Design Types pictured following the introduction.

Europa Issue, 1960

Common Design Type

1960, Sept. 19 *Perf. 13½*

Size: 30½x21mm.

376 CD3 30m dk bl & Prus bl *.90* .90

377 CD3 40m dk brn & plum *.80* *.90*

A 30m gray similar to No. 376 was printed with simulated perforations in a non-valid souvenir sheet privately released in London for STAMPEX 1961.

Uno Cygnaeus — A135

1960, Oct. 13 *Perf. 11½*

378 A135 30m dull violet .80 .80

150th anniv. of the birth of Pastor Uno Cygnaeus, founder of elementary schools.

"Pommern" and Arms of Mariehamn A136

1961, Feb. 21 *Perf. 11½*

379 A136 30m grnsh blue 2.75 2.00

Centenary of the founding of Mariehamn.

Lake and Rowboat A137

Turku Castle — A138

1961 Engr. Unwmk.

380 A137 5m green .40 .30

381 A138 125m slate green 20.00 .35

See Nos. 399, 411.

Postal Savings Bank Emblem — A139

1961, May 24

382 A139 30m Prus green .75 .45

75th anniv. of Finland's Postal Savings Bank.

Symbol of Standardization — A140

1961, June 5 Litho. *Perf. 14x13½*

383 A140 30m dk sl grn & org .75 .45

Meeting of the Intl. Organization for Standardization (ISO), Helsinki, June 5.

Juhani Aho — A141

Perf. 11½

1961, Sept. 11 Unwmk. Engr.

384 A141 30m red brown .75 .65

Juhani Aho (1861-1921), writer.

Various Buildings — A142

1961, Oct. 16 ***Perf. 11½***
385 A142 30m slate .75 .65

150 years of the Central Board of Buildings.

Arvid Jarnefelt A143

1961, Nov. 16
386 A143 30m deep claret .75 .65

Cent. of the birth of Arvid Jarnefelt, writer.

Bank of Finland — A144

1961, Dec. 12 **Engr.** ***Perf. 11½***
387 A144 30m brown violet .75 .65

150th anniversary of Bank of Finland.

First Finnish Locomotive A145

30m, Steam locomotive & timber car. 40m, Diesel locomotive & passenger train.

1962, Jan. 31 **Unwmk.** ***Perf. 11½***
388 A145 10m gray green 1.75 .60
389 A145 30m violet blue 2.50 .60
390 A145 40m dull red brown 6.00 .60
Nos. 388-390 (3) 10.25 1.80

Centenary of the Finnish State Railways.

Mora Stone — A146

1962, Feb. 15
391 A146 30m gray brown .75 .70

Issued to commemorate 600 years of political rights of the Finnish people.

Senate Place, Helsinki A147

1962, Apr. 8 **Unwmk.** ***Perf. 11½***
392 A147 30m violet brown .75 .70

Sesquicentennial of the proclamation of Helsinki as capital of Finland.

Customs Emblem A148

1962, Apr. 11
393 A148 30m red .75 .70

Finnish Board of Customs, sesquicentennial.

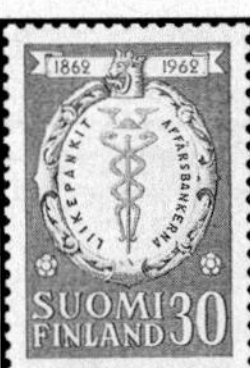

Staff of Mercury — A149

1962, May 21 **Engr.**
394 A149 30m bluish green .65 .60

Cent. of the 1st commercial bank in Finland.

Santeri Alkio — A150

1962, June 17 **Unwmk.** ***Perf. 11½***
395 A150 30m brown carmine 1.20 .80

Cent. of the birth of Santeri Alkio, writer and pioneer of the young people's societies in Finland.

Finnish Labor Emblem and Conveyor Belt — A151

1962, Oct. 19
396 A151 30m chocolate .75 .40

National production progress.

Survey Plane and Compass — A152

1962, Nov. 14
397 A152 30m yellow green .95 .75

Finnish Land Survey Board, 150th anniv.

Types of 1954-61 and

House of Parliament — A152a

Church at Lammi — A152b

Fortress of Olavinlinna — A152c

Log Floating A153

Parainen Bridge — A154

Farm on Lake Shore — A155

Aerial View of Punkaharju — A155a

A155b

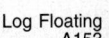

Ristikallio in Kuusamo A156

1963-67 **Engr.** ***Perf. 11½***

398	A94	5p	vio blue	.50	.25
a.	Booklet pane of 2 (vert. pair)			22.50	20.00
b.	Bklt. pane of 2 (horiz. pair)			12.00	10.00
399	A137	5p	green	.50	.25
400	A94	10p	blue grn	2.00	.25
a.	Booklet pane of 2 (vert. pair)			22.50	20.00
401	A94	15p	yel org	4.25	.25
402	A94	20p	rose red	3.00	.25
a.	Booklet pane of 2 (vert. pair)			24.00	
	Complete booklet, #398a, 400a, 402a			85.00	
b.	Bklt. pane, 2 #400, 1 #402 + label; horiz. strip			45.00	35.00
	Complete booklet, #398b, 402b			100.00	
c.	Bklt. pane, 2 #398, 2 #400, 1 #402; horiz. strip			3.50	3.50
	Complete booklet, #402c			5.00	
403	A94	25p	rose lilac	4.00	.25
404	A94	30p	lt ultra	6.00	.25
404A	A94	30p	blue gray ('65)	6.25	.25
405	A94	35p	blue	1.50	.25
405A	A94	40p	ultra ('67)	1.75	.35
406	A152a	40p	dull pur	3.50	.35
407	A152b	50p	gray olive	5.75	.50
408	A152c	60p	pale pur	8.25	.50
408A	A152c	65p	pale pur ('67)	1.20	.25
409	A124	75p	gray	2.25	.50
410	A119	1m	bluish grn	2.00	.25
411	A138	1.25m	slate grn	2.00	.50
412	A153	1.50m	dk grnsh gray	2.00	.25
413	A154	1.75m	blue	2.00	.50
414	A155	2m	grn ('64)	12.00	.25
414A	A155a	2.50m	ultra & yel grn ('67)	11.00	.65
414B	A155b	2.50m	ultra, dk grn & yel grn ('69)	8.00	.40
415	A156	5m	dk slate grn ('64)	21.00	.50
	Nos. 398-415 (23)			110.70	8.00

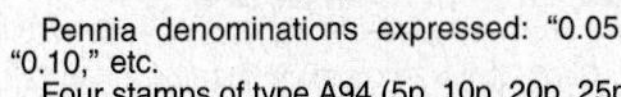

Pennia denominations expressed: "0.05," "0.10," etc.

Four stamps of type A94 (5p, 10p, 20p, 25p) come in two types: I. Four vertical lines in "O" of SUOMI. II. Three lines in "O."

For similar designs see Nos. 457-470A.

Mother and Child — A157

1963, Mar. 21 **Unwmk.** ***Perf. 11½***
416 A157 40p red brown .55 .40

FAO "Freedom from Hunger" campaign.

"Christ Today" — A158

Design: 10p, Crown of thorns and medieval cross of consecration.

1963, July 30 **Engr.** ***Perf. 11½***
417 A158 10p maroon .50 .45
418 A158 30p dark green .50 .45

4th assembly of the Lutheran World Federation, Helsinki, July 30-Aug. 8.

Europa Issue, 1963

Common Design Type

1963, Sept. 16 **Size: 30x20mm**
419 CD6 40p red lilac *1.25* .55

Assembly Building, Helsinki A159

1963, Sept. 18
420 A159 30p violet blue .70 .40

Representative Assembly of Finland, cent.

Convair Metropolitan A160

Design: 40p, Caravelle jetliner.

1963, Nov. 1
421 A160 35p slate green 1.00 .60
422 A160 40p brt ultra 1.10 .50

40th anniversary of Finnish air traffic.

M. A. Castrén — A161

1963, Dec. 2 **Unwmk.**
423 A161 35p violet blue .70 .45

Matthias Alexander Castrén (1813-52), ethnologist and philologist.

Stone Elk's Head, 2000 B.C. — A162

1964, Feb. 5 **Litho.** ***Perf. 14***
424 A162 35p ocher & slate grn .70 .45

Cent. of the Finnish Artists' Association. The soapstone sculpture was found at Huittinen.

Emil Nestor Setälä — A163

1964, Feb. 27 Engr. *Perf. 11½*

425 A163 35p dk red brown .80 .50

Emil Nestor Setälä (1864-1946), philologist, minister of education and foreign affairs and chancellor of Abo University.

Staff of Aesculapius A164

1964, June 13 Unwmk. *Perf. 11½*

426 A164 40p slate green 1.10 .45

18th General Assembly of the World Medical Association, Helsinki, June 13-19, 1964.

Ice Hockey — A165

1965, Jan. 4 Engr.

427 A165 35p dark blue 1.10 .60

World Ice Hockey Championships, Finland, March 3-14, 1965.

Design from Centenary Medal — A166

1965, Feb. 6 Unwmk. *Perf. 11½*

428 A166 35p olive gray .70 .40

Centenary of communal self-government in Finland.

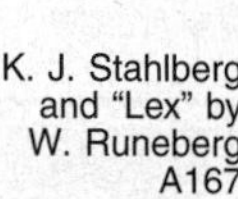

K. J. Stahlberg and "Lex" by W. Runeberg A167

1965, Mar. 22 Engr.

429 A167 35p brown .70 .40

Kaarlo Juho Stahlberg (1865-1952), 1st Pres. of Finland.

International Cooperation Year Emblem A168

1965, Apr. 2 Litho. *Perf. 14*

430 A168 40p bis, dull red, blk & grn .70 .40

UN International Cooperation Year.

"Fratricide" by Gallen-Kallela A169

35p, Girl's Head by Akseli Gallen-Kallela.

1965, Apr. 26 *Perf. 13½x14*

431 A169 25p multicolored 1.40 .65
432 A169 35p multicolored 1.40 .65

Centenary of the birth of the painter Aksell Gallen-Kallela.

Sibelius, Piano and Score — A170

Design: 35p, Musical score and bird.

1965, May 15 Engr. *Perf. 11½*

433 A170 25p violet 1.40 .80
434 A170 35p dull green 1.40 .40

Jean Sibelius (1865-1957), composer.

Antenna for Satellite Telecommunication — A171

1965, May 17

435 A171 35p blue .70 .50

Cent. of the ITU.

"Winter Day" by Pekka Halonen — A172

Perf. 14x13½

1965, Sept. 23 Litho. Unwmk.

436 A172 35p gold & multi .70 .40

Centenary of the birth of the painter Pekka Halonen.

Europa Issue, 1965

Common Design Type

Engraved and Lithographed

1965, Sept. 27 *Perf. 13½x14*

437 CD8 40p bister, red brn, dk bl & grn *1.25* *.55*

"Growth" — A173

1966, May 11 Litho. *Perf. 14*

438 A173 35p vio blue & blue .70 .40

Centenary of the promulgation of the Elementary School Decree.

Old Post Office — A174

1966, June 11 Litho. *Perf. 14*

439 A174 35p ocher, yel, dk bl & blk 4.50 *7.00*

Cent. of the 1st postage stamps in Finnish currency, and in connection with the NORDIA Stamp Exhibition, Helsinki, June 11-15. The stamp was sold only to buyers of a 1.25m exhibition entrance ticket.

UNESCO Emblem and World Map — A175

Lithographed and Engraved

1966, Oct. 9 *Perf. 14*

440 A175 40p grn, yel, blk & brn org .65 .30

20th anniv. of UNESCO.

Finnish Police Emblem — A176

1966, Oct. 15

441 A176 35p dp ultra, blk & sil .65 .30

Issued to honor the Finnish police.

Insurance Sesquicentennial Medal — A177

1966, Oct. 28 Engr. & Photo.

442 A177 35p mar, ol & blk .65 .30

150th anniv. of the Finnish insurance system.

UNICEF Emblem A178

1966, Nov. 14

443 A178 15p lt ultra, pur & grn .30 .30

Activities of UNICEF.

"FINEFTA," Finnish Flag and Circle — A179

1967, Feb. 15 Engr. *Perf. 14*

444 A179 40p ultra .65 .30

European Free Trade Association, EFTA. See note after Denmark No. 431.

Windmill and Arms of Uusikaupunki A180

Lithographed and Engraved

1967, Apr. 19 *Perf. 14*

445 A180 40p multicolored .65 .30

350th anniv. of Uusikaupunki (Nystad).

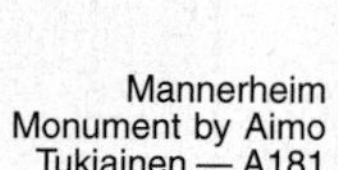

Mannerheim Monument by Aimo Tukiainen — A181

1967, June 4 *Perf. 14*

446 A181 40p violet & multi .65 .30

Cent. of the birth of Field Marshal Carl Gustav Emil Mannerheim.

Double Mortise Corner — A182

1967, June 16 Litho. & Photo.

447 A182 40p multicolored .65 .30

Issued to honor Finnish settlers in Sweden.

Watermark of Thomasböle Paper Mill — A183

1967, Sept. 6 *Perf. 14*

448 A183 40p olive & black .65 .30

300th anniv. of the Finnish paper industry.

Martin Luther, by Lucas Cranach A184

Photogravure and Engraved

1967, Nov. 4 *Perf. 14*

449 A184 40p bister & brown .65 .30

450th anniversary of the Reformation.

"Wood and Water" Globe and Flag — A185

Designs (Globe, Flag and): 25p, Flying swan. 40p, Ear of wheat.

1967, Dec. 5 *Perf. 11½*

450 A185 20p green & blue .65 .30
451 A185 25p ultra & blue .65 .30
452 A185 40p magenta & bl .65 .30
Nos. 450-452 (3) 1.95 .90

50th anniv. of Finland's independence.

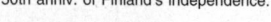

Zachris Topelius and Blue Bird — A186

1968, Jan. 14 Litho. *Perf. 14*

453 A186 25p blue & multi 1.10 .50

Topelius (1818-98), writer and educator.

Skiers and Ski Lift — A187

1968, Feb. 19 Photo. *Perf. 14*

454 A187 25p multicolored .85 .70

Winter Tourism in Finland.

Paper Making, by Hannes Autere — A188

1968, Mar. 12 Litho. Wmk. 363

455 A188 45p dk red, brn & org .70 .45

Finnish paper industry and 150th anniv. of the oldest Finnish paper mill, Tervakoski, whose own watermark was used for this stamp.

World Health Organization Emblem A189

Lithographed and Photogravure

1968, Apr. 6 Unwmk. *Perf. 14*

456 A189 40p red org, dk blue & gold .65 .30

To honor World Health Organization.

Lion Type of 1954-58 and

Market Place and Mermaid Fountain, Helsinki A190

Keuru Wooden Church, 1758 — A191

Häme Bridge, Tampere A192

Finnish Arms from Grave of King Gustav Vasa, 1581 — A194

A194a

25p, Post bus. 30p, Aquarium-Planetarium, Tampere. No. 463, P.O., Tampere. No. 465, National Museum, Helsinki, vert. No. 467A, like 70p. 1.30m, Helsinki railroad station.

Engr. (type A94, except #459A); Litho. (#459A, 465 & type A190); Engr. & Litho. (others)

Perf. 11½; 12½ (#466, 467A); 13 (#465); 13½ (#470); 14 (#463, 470A)

1968-78

457	A94	1p	lt red brn	.40	*.50*
458	A94	2p	gray green	.40	*.65*
459	A94	4p	gray	.50	*.65*
459A	A94	5p	violet blue	2.00	*3.00*
460	A192	25p	multi ('71)	.50	.25
461	A191	30p	multi ('71)	1.25	.25
461A	A94	35p	dull org ('74)	.55	*.40*
b.			Bklt. pane of 4, #459A, 461A, 400, 464A + label	2.50	2.50
			Complete booklet, #461b	3.50	
462	A94	40p	org ('73)	.90	.65
a.			Bklt. pane of 3, #462, 2 #404A + 2 labels	6.00	*8.00*
			Complete booklet, #462a	8.00	
463	A192	40p	multi ('73)	1.00	.25
464	A94	50p	lt ultra ('70)	3.00	.25
c.			Bklt. pane of 5, #401, 403, 464, 2 #459A + 5 labels	13.00	*14.50*
			Complete booklet, #464c	14.00	
464A	A94	50p	rose lake ('74)	.80	.25
d.			Bklt. pane of 4, #400, 464A, 2 #402 + label	1.75	1.75
			Complete booklet, #464Ad	2.00	
464B	A94	60p	blue ('73)	1.10	.25
465	A191	60p	multi ('73)	1.25	.25
466	A190	70p	multi ('73)	.95	.25
467	A191	80p	multi ('70)	5.25	.25
467A	A190	80p	multi ('76)	.50	.50
468	A192	90p	multi	2.00	.50
469	A191	1.30m	multi ('71)	1.25	.50
470	A194	10m	multi ('74)	5.25	.50
470A	A194a	20m	multi ('78)	11.00	.50
	Nos. 457-470A (20)			39.85	10.60

Issued: 5p, 6/72.

Infantry Monument, Vaasa — A195

Designs: 25p, War Memorial (cross), Hietaniemi Cemetery. 40p, Soldier, 1968.

1968, June 4 Photo. *Perf. 14*

471 A195 20p lt violet & multi 1.10 .35

472 A195 25p lt blue & multi 1.10 .35

473 A195 40p orange & multi 1.10 .35

Nos. 471-473 (3) 3.30 1.05

To honor Finnish national defense.

Camping Ground A196

1968, June 10 Litho.

474 A196 25p multicolored .60 .40

Issued to publicize Finland for summer vacations.

Paper, Pulp and Pine — A197

Lithographed and Embossed

1968, July 2 Unwmk. *Perf. 14*

475 A197 40p multicolored .70 .40

Finnish wood industry.

Mustola Lock, Saima Canal — A198

1968, Aug. 5 Litho. *Perf. 14*

476 A198 40p multicolored .70 .40

Opening of the Saima Canal.

Oskar Merikanto and Pipe Organ — A199

1968, Aug. 5 Unwmk.

477 A199 40p vio, silver & lt brn 1.10 .40

Centenary of the birth of Oskar Merikanto, composer.

Ships in Harbor and Emblem of Central Chamber of Commerce A200

1968, Sept. 13 Litho. *Perf. 14*

478 A200 40p lt bl, brt bl & blk .70 .40

Publicizing economic development and for the 50th anniv. of the Central Chamber of Commerce of Finland.

Welder — A201

1968, Oct. 11 Litho. *Perf. 14*

479 A201 40p blue & multi .70 .40

Finnish metal industry.

Lyre, Students' Emblem — A202

Lithographed and Engraved

1968, Nov. 24 *Perf. 14*

480 A202 40p ultra, vio bl & gold .70 .40

Issued to publicize the work of the student unions in Finnish social life.

Nordic Cooperation Issue

Five Ancient Ships — A203

1969, Feb. 28 Engr. *Perf. 11½*

481 A203 40p lt ultra 2.00 .40

50th anniv. of the Nordic Society and centenary of postal cooperation among the northern countries. The design is taken from a coin found at the site of Birka, an ancient Swedish town. See also Denmark Nos. 454-455, Iceland Nos. 404-405, Norway Nos. 523-524 and Sweden Nos. 808-810.

Town Hall and Arms of Kemi — A203a

1969, Mar. 5 Photo. *Perf. 14*

482 A203a 40p multicolored .70 .40

Centenary of the town of Kemi.

Europa Issue, 1969

Common Design Type

1969, Apr. 28 Photo. *Perf. 14*

Size: 30x20mm

483 CD12 40p dl rose, vio bl & dk bl *3.50 .75*

ILO Emblem A204

Lithographed and Engraved

1969, June 2 *Perf. 11½*

484 A204 40p dp rose & vio blue .70 .40

50th anniv. of the ILO.

Armas Järnefelt — A205

1969, Aug. 14 Photo. *Perf. 14*

485 A205 40p multicolored 1.40 .40

Järnefelt (1869-1958), composer and conductor. Portrait on stamp by Vilho Sjöström.

Emblems and Flag — A206

1969, Sept. 19 Photo. *Perf. 14*

486 A206 40p lt bl, blk, grn & lil .70 .40

Publicizinge the importance of National and International Fairs in Finnish economy.

Johannes Linnankoski — A207

1969, Oct. 18 Litho.

487 A207 40p dk brn red & multi .70 .40

Linnankoski (1869-1913), writer.

Educational Symbols A208

Lithographed and Engraved

1969, Nov. 24 *Perf. 11½*

488 A208 40p gray, vio & grn .70 .40

Centenary of the Central School Board.

DC-8-62 CF Plane and Helsinki Airport — A209

1969, Dec. 22 Photo. *Perf. 14*
489 A209 25p sky blue & multi 1.10 .75

Golden Eagle — A210

1970, Feb. 10 Litho. *Perf. 14*
490 A210 30p multicolored 3.50 1.10

Year of Nature Conservation, 1970.

Swatches in Shape of Factories A211

1970, Mar. 9 Litho. *Perf. 14*
491 A211 50p multicolored .85 .40

Finnish textile industry.

Molecule Diagram and Factories A212

1970, Mar. 26 Photo. *Perf. 14*
492 A212 50p multicolored .85 .40

Finnish chemical industry.

UNESCO Emblem and Lenin — A213

Atom Diagram and Laurel — A214

UN Emblem and Globe — A215

1970 Litho. and Engr.
493 A213 30p gold & multi .70 .40
494 A214 30p red & multi .70 .40

Photogravure and Gold Embossed

495 A215 50p bl, vio bl & gold .70 .40
Nos. 493-495 (3) 2.10 1.20

25th anniv. of the UN. No. 493 also publicizes the UNESCO-sponsored Lenin Symposium, Tampere, Apr. 6-10. No. 494 also publicizes the Nuclear Data Conf. of the Atomic Energy Commission, Otaniemi (Helsinki), June 15-19.

Issued: No. 493, 4/6; No. 494, 6/15; No. 495, 10/24.

Handicapped Volleyball Player — A216

1970, June 27 Litho. *Perf. 14*
496 A216 50p orange, red & blk 1.00 .40

Issued to publicize the position of handicapped civilians and war veterans in society and their potential contributions to it.

Meeting of Auroraseura Society — A217

1970, Aug. 15 Photo. *Perf. 14*
497 A217 50p multicolored .70 .40

200th anniv. of the Auroraseura Soc., dedicated to the study of Finnish history, geography, economy and language. The design of the stamp is after a painting by Eero Jarnefelt.

Uusikaarlepyy Arms, Church and 17th Cent. Building A218

Design: No. 499, Arms of Kokkola, harbor, Sports Palace and 17th century building.

1970 *Perf. 14*
498 A218 50p multicolored .70 .40
499 A218 50p multicolored .70 .40

Towns of Uusikaarlepyy and Kokkola, 350th anniv.

Issued: No. 498, Aug. 21; No. 499, Sept. 17.

Urho Kekkonen, Medal by Aimo Tukiainen — A219

1970, Sept. 3 Litho. & Engr.
500 A219 50p ultra, sil & blk .70 .40

70th birthday of Pres. Urho Kekkonen.

Globe, Maps of US, Finland, USSR — A220

Lithographed and Gold Embossed

1970, Nov. 2
501 A220 50p blk, bl, pink & gold .70 .40

Strategic Arms Limitation Talks (SALT) between the US & USSR, Helsinki, 11/2-12/18.

Pres. Paasikivi by Essi Renavall — A221

1970, Nov. 27 Photo. *Perf. 14*
502 A221 50p gold, brt bl & slate .70 .40

Centenary of the birth of Juho Kusti Paasikivi (1870-1956), President of Finland.

Cogwheels A222

1971, Jan. 28 Litho. *Perf. 14*
503 A222 50p multicolored .70 .40

Finnish industry.

Europa Issue, 1971

Common Design Type

1971, May 3 Litho. *Perf. 14*
Size: 30x20mm
504 CD14 50p dp rose, yel & blk *5.00* .75

Tornio Church — A223

1971, May 12 Litho. *Perf. 14*
505 A223 50p multicolored 1.00 .40

350th anniversary of the town of Tornio.

Front Page, January 15, 1771 — A224

1971, June 1 Litho. *Perf. 14*
506 A224 50p multicolored .70 .40

Bicentenary of the Finnish press.

Athletes in Helsinki Stadium A225

50p, Running & javelin in Helsinki Stadium.

1971, July 5 Litho. *Perf. 14*
507 A225 30p multicolored 1.50 .85
508 A225 50p multicolored 2.50 .85

European Athletic Championships.

Sailboats A226

1971, July 14
509 A226 50p multicolored 1.25 .60

International Lightning Class Championships, Helsinki, July 14-Aug. 1.

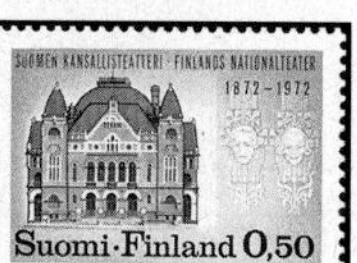

Silver Tea Pot, Guild's Emblem, Tools — A227

1971, Aug. 6
510 A227 50p lilac & multi .70 .40

600th anniv. of Finnish goldsmiths' art.

"Plastic Buttons and Houses" A228

Photogravure and Embossed

1971, Oct. 20 *Perf. 14*
511 A228 50p multicolored .70 .40

Finnish plastics industry.

Europa Issue 1972

Common Design Type

1972, May 2 Litho. *Perf. 14*
Size: 20x30mm
512 CD15 30p dk red & multi *2.50* *.70*
513 CD15 50p lt brn & multi *4.50* *.70*

Finnish National Theater A229

1972, May 22. Litho. *Perf. 14*
514 A229 50p lt violet & multi .70 .40

Centenary of the Finnish National Theater, founded by Kaarlo and Emilie Bergbom.

Globe, US and USSR Flags — A230

1972, June 2
515 A230 50p multicolored 1.25 .40

Strategic Arms Limitation Talks (SALT), final meeting, Helsinki, Mar. 28-May 26; treaty signed, Moscow, May 26.

Map and Arms of Aland — A231

1972, June 9
516 A231 50p multicolored 3.25 .85

1st Provincial Meeting of Aland, 50th anniv.

Training Ship Suomen Joutsen — A232

1972, June 19
517 A232 50p orange & multi 1.25 .40

Tall Ships' Race 1972, Helsinki, Aug. 20.

Costume from Perni, 12th Cent. — A233

No. 519, Couple, Tenhola, 18th cent. No. 520, Girl, Nastola, 19th cent. No. 521, Man, Voyni, 19th cent. No. 522, Lapps, Inari, 19th cent.

1972, Nov. 19 Litho. *Perf. 13*

518 A233 50p shown	2.50	.65
519 A233 50p multicolored	2.50	.65
520 A233 50p multicolored	2.50	.65
521 A233 50p multicolored	2.50	.65
522 A233 50p multicolored	2.50	.65
a. Strip of 5, #518-522	12.50	14.50
Complete booklet, 2 each #518-522	30.00	

Regional costumes.

See Nos. 533-537.

Circle Surrounding Map of Europe — A234

1972, Dec. 11 *Perf. 14x13½*
523 A234 50p multicolored 2.25 .55

Preparatory Conference on European Security and Cooperation.

Book, Finnish and Soviet Colors — A235

Litho.; Gold Embossed

1973, Apr. 6 *Perf. 14*
524 A235 60p gold & multi .55 .40

Soviet-Finnish Treaty of Friendship, 25th anniv.

Kyösti Kallio (1873-1940), Pres. of Finland — A236

1973, Apr. 10 Litho. *Perf. 13*
525 A236 60p multicolored .55 .40

Europa Issue 1973

Common Design Type

1973, Apr. 30 Photo. *Perf. 14*
Size: 31x21mm
526 CD16 60p bl, brt bl & emer 1.25 .55

Nordic Cooperation Issue

Nordic House, Reykjavik A236a

1973, June 26 Engr. *Perf. 12½*

527 A236a 60p multicolored	1.00	.40
528 A236a 70p multicolored	1.00	.40

A century of postal cooperation among Denmark, Finland, Iceland, Norway and Sweden, and in connection with the Nordic Postal Conference, Reykjavik.

Map of Europe, "EUROPA" as a Maze — A237

Litho. & Embossed

1973, July 3 *Perf. 13*
529 A237 70p multicolored .75 .40

Conference for European Security and Cooperation, Helsinki, July 1973.

Paddling A238

1973, July 18 Litho. *Perf. 14*
530 A238 60p multicolored .75 .40

Canoeing World Championships, Tampere, July 26-29.

Radiosonde, WMO Emblem — A239

1973, Aug. 6 Litho. *Perf. 14*
531 A239 60p multicolored .55 .40

Cent. of intl. meteorological cooperation.

Eliel Saarinen and Design for Parliament, Helsinki A240

1973, Aug. 20 *Perf. 12½x13*
532 A240 60p multicolored .55 .40

Eliel Saarinen (1873-1950), architect.

Costume Type of 1972

Designs: No. 533, Woman, Kaukola. 534, Woman, Jaaski. No. 535, Married couple, Koivisto. No. 536, Mother and son, Sakyla. No. 537, Girl, Hainavesi.

1973, Oct. 10 Litho. *Perf. 13*

533 A233 60p multicolored	2.75	.40
534 A233 60p multicolored	2.75	.40
535 A233 60p multicolored	2.75	.40
536 A233 60p multicolored	2.75	.40
537 A233 60p multicolored	2.75	.40
a. Strip of 5, #533-537	16.00	19.00

Regional costumes.

DC10-30 Jet — A241

1973, Nov. 1 Litho. *Perf. 14*
538 A241 60p multicolored .80 .40

50th anniv. of regular air service, Finnair.

Santa Claus in Reindeer Sleigh — A242

1973, Nov. 15 Litho. *Perf. 14*
539 A242 30p multicolored .95 .40

Christmas 1973.

"The Barber of Seville" A243

1973, Nov. 21
540 A243 60p multicolored .55 .40

Centenary of opera in Finland.

Production of Porcelain Jug — A244

1973, Nov. 23
541 A244 60p blue & multi .55 .40

Finnish porcelain.

Nurmi, by Waino Aaltonen — A245

1973, Dec. 11
542 A245 60p multicolored .85 .40

Paavo Nurmi (1897-1973), runner, Olympic winner, 1920-1924-1928.

Arms, Map and Harbor of Hanko — A246

1974, Jan. 10 Litho. *Perf. 14*
543 A246 60p blue & multi .75 .40

Centenary of the town of Hanko.

Ice Hockey A247

1974, Mar. 5 Litho. *Perf. 14*
544 A247 60p multicolored .90 .40

European and World Ice Hockey Championships, held in Finland.

Seagulls (7 Baltic States) A248

1974, Mar. 18 *Perf. 12½*
545 A248 60p multicolored 1.00 .40

Protection of marine environment of the Baltic Sea.

Goddess of Freedom, by Waino Aaltonen — A249

1974, Apr. 29 Litho. *Perf. 13x12½*
546 A249 70p sil & multi *5.00 .50*

Europa.

Ilmari Kianto and Old Pine — A250

1974, May 7 *Perf. 13*
547 A250 60p multicolored .55 .40

Ilmari Kianto (1874-1970), writer.

Society Emblem, Symbol A251

Lithographed and Embossed

1974, June 12 *Perf. 13½x14*
548 A251 60p gold & multi .55 .40

Centenary of Adult Education.

Grid — A252

1974, June 14 Litho. *Perf. 14x13½*
549 A252 60p multicolored .55 .40

Rationalization Year in Finland, dedicated to economic and business improvements.

UPU Emblem — A253

1974, Oct. 10 Litho. *Perf. 13½x14*

550 A253 60p multicolored	.55	.40
551 A253 70p multicolored	.55	.40

Centenary of Universal Postal Union.

Elves Distributing Gifts — A254

1974, Nov. 16 Litho. *Perf. 14x13½*
552 A254 35p multicolored 1.75 .35

Christmas 1974.

Concrete Bridge and Granite Bridge, Aunessilta — A255

Litho. & Engr.

1974, Dec. 17 ***Perf. 14***

553 A255 60p multicolored 1.25 .70

Royal Finnish Directorate of Roads and Waterways, 175th anniversary.

Coat of Arms, 1581 — A256

Chimneyless Log Sauna — A256a

Cheese Frames A257

Carved Wooden Distaffs A258

Kirvu Weather Vane A258a

1.50m, Wood-carved high drinking bowl, 1542.

Perf. 11½; 14 (2m, 5m)

1975-90					**Engr.**
555	A256	10p	red lil ('78)	.25	*.50*
a.	Bklt. pane of 4 (#555, 2 #556, #559) + label			2.25	2.25
	Complete booklet, #555a			2.50	
b.	Bklt. pane of 5 (2 #555, #557, #563, #564)			2.50	2.25
	Complete booklet, #555b			5.00	
c.	As "a," no label			2.50	2.50
	Complete booklet, #555c			3.00	
d.	Perf. 13x12½			.35	.25
556	A256	20p	olive ('77)	.40	*.30*
a.	20p yellow bister ('85)			1.10	1.40
b.	As "a," perf. 13x12½			1.25	1.25
557	A256	30p	car ('77)	2.25	1.50
557A	A256	30p	car, litho.	5.50	3.00
558	A256	40p	orange	.40	.30
a.	Perf. 13x12½			1.75	1.50
559	A256	50p	green ('76)	.50	.30
a.	Perf. 13x12½			2.00	1.25
560	A256	60p	blue	.60	.30
a.	Perf. 13x12½			2.50	1.50
561	A256	70p	sepia	.50	.25
562	A256	80p	dl red & bl grn ('76)	.50	.50
a.	Perf. 13x12½			4.25	4.00
563	A256	90p	vio bl ('77)	.45	.40
564	A256	1.10m	yellow ('79)	.45	.35
565	A256	1.20m	dk blue ('79)	.70	.60
566	A258	1.50m	multi ('76)	1.10	.25

Litho.

567	A256a	2m	multi ('77)	1.25	.30

Lithographed and Engraved

568	A257	2.50m	multi ('76)	1.25	.50
a.	Perf. 14			2.25	1.00
569	A258	4.50m	multi ('76)	2.40	.40
a.	Perf. 14			3.25	2.50
570	A258a	5m	multi ('77)	2.25	.30
	Nos. 555-570 (17)			20.75	10.05

Some denominations of design A256 exist in up to three engraving types.

Nos. 560a and 562a was only issued within the booklet panes Nos. 713a and 715a.

Issued: No. 557A, 6/3/80; No. 560a, 7/25/88; No. 555d, 7/25/89; No. 562a, 3/1/90; No. 558a, 8/18/94; No. 568a, 12/28/88; No. 569a, 9/26/88; No. 556b, 4/3/98.

See Nos. 629, 631-633, 711-715, 861.

Finland No. 16 — A259

Lithographed and Typographed

1975, Apr. 26 ***Perf. 13***

571 A259 70p multicolored 2.75 4.50

Nordia 75 Philatelic Exhibition, Helsinki, Apr. 26-May 1. Sold only at exhibition for 3m including entrance ticket.

Girl Combing Hair, by Magnus Enckell — A260

Europa: 90p, The Washerwomen, by Tyko Sallinen (1879-1955).

1975, Apr. 28 **Litho.** ***Perf. 13x12½***

572 A260 70p gray & multi *2.50 .40*

573 A260 90p tan & multi *2.50 .40*

Balance of Justice, Sword of Legality — A261

1975, May 7 ***Perf. 14***

574 A261 70p vio blue & multi .55 .40

Sesquicentennial of State Economy Comptroller's Office.

Rescue Boat and Sinking Ship — A262

1975, June 2 **Litho.** ***Perf. 14***

575 A262 70p multicolored .85 .40

12th Intl. Salvage Conf., Finland, stressing importance of coordinating sea, air and communications resources in salvage operations.

Safe and Unsafe Levels of Drugs — A263

1975, July 21 **Litho.** ***Perf. 14***

576 A263 70p multicolored .55 .40

Importance of pharmacological studies and for the 6th Intl. Pharmacology Cong., Helsinki.

Olavinlinna Castle A264

1975, July 29 ***Perf. 13***

577 A264 70p multicolored .55 .40

500th anniversary of Olavinlinna Castle.

Swallows over Finlandia Hall — A265

1975, July 30

578 A265 90p multicolored .70 .40

European Security and Cooperation Conference, Helsinki, July 30-Aug. 1. (The swallows of the design represent freedom, mobility and continuity.) See No. 709.

"Men and Women Working for Peace" — A266

1975, Oct. 24 **Litho.** ***Perf. 13x12½***

579 A266 70p multicolored .55 .40

International Women's Year 1975.

"Continuity and Growth" — A267

1975, Oct. 29 ***Perf. 13***

580 A267 70p brown & multi .55 .40

Industrial Art and for the centenary of the Finnish Society of Industrial Art.

Boys as Three Kings and Herod — A268

1975, Nov. 8 ***Perf. 14***

581 A268 40p blue & multi 1.10 .35

Christmas 1975.

Top Border of State Debenture A269

Lithographed and Engraved

1976, Jan. 9 ***Perf. 11½***

582 A269 80p multicolored .55 .40

Centenary of State Treasury.

Glider over Lake Region A270

1976, Jan. 13 **Litho.** ***Perf. 14***

583 A270 80p multicolored .90 .40

15th World Glider Championships, Rayskala, June 13-27.

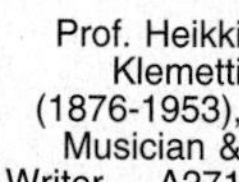

Prof. Heikki Klemetti (1876-1953), Musician & Writer — A271

1976, Feb. 14 **Litho.** ***Perf. 13***

584 A271 80p green & multi .55 .40

Map with Areas of Different Dialects — A272

1976, Mar. 10 **Litho.** ***Perf. 13***

585 A272 80p multicolored .55 .40

Finnish Language Society, centenary.

Aino Ackté, by Albert Edelfelt — A273

1976, Apr. 23

586 A273 70p yellow & multi .70 .40

Aino Ackté (1876-1944), opera singer.

Europa Issue

Knife from Voyri, Sheath and Belt — A274

1976, May 3 **Litho.** ***Perf. 13***

587 A274 80p violet bl & multi *3.25 .50*

Radio and Television A275

1976, Sept. 9 **Litho.** ***Perf. 13***

588 A275 80p multicolored .55 .40

Radio broadcasting in Finland, 50th anniv.

Christmas Morning Ride to Church A276

1976, Oct. 23 **Litho.** ***Perf. 14***

589 A276 50p multicolored .90 .40

Christmas 1976.

Turku Chapter Seal (Virgin and Child) A277

1976, Nov. 1 Litho. ***Perf. 12½***
590 A277 80p buff, brn & red .55 .40

Cathedral Chapter of Turku, 700th anniv.

Alvar Aalto, Finlandia Hall, Helsinki A278

1976, Nov. 4
591 A278 80p multicolored .55 .40

Hugo Alvar Henrik Aalto (1898-1976), architect.

Ice Dancers — A280

1977, Jan. 25 Litho. ***Perf. 13***
592 A280 90p multicolored .65 .40

European Figure Skating Championships, Finland, Jan. 25-29.

Five Water Lilies — A281

Photogravure and Engraved

1977, Feb. 2 ***Perf. 12½***
593 A281 90p brt green & multi 1.00 .40
594 A281 1m ultra & multi 1.00 .40

Nordic countries cooperation for protection of the environment and 25th Session of Nordic Council, Helsinki, Feb. 19.

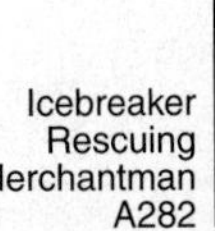

Icebreaker Rescuing Merchantman A282

1977, Mar. 2 Litho. ***Perf. 13***
595 A282 90p multicolored 1.00 .40

Winter navigation between Finland and Sweden, centenary.

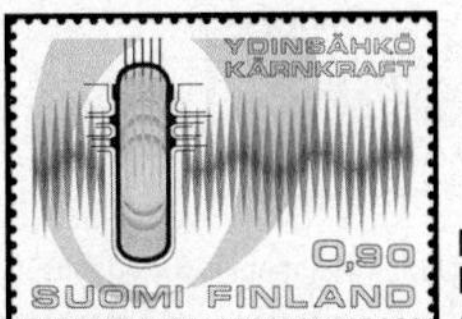

Nuclear Reactor A283

1977, Mar. 3 ***Perf. 12½x13***
596 A283 90p multicolored .55 .40

Opening of nuclear power station on Hästholmen Island.

Europa Issue

Autumn Landscape, Northern Finland — A284

1977, May 2 Litho. ***Perf. 12½x13***
597 A284 90p multicolored *3.25 .45*

Tree, Birds and Nest — A285

1977, May 4 ***Perf. 13x12½***
598 A285 90p multicolored .55 .40

75th anniversary of cooperative banks.

Orthodox Church, Valamo Cloister — A286

1977, May 31 Litho. ***Perf. 14***
599 A286 90p multicolored .55 .40

Consecration festival of new Orthodox Church at Valamo Cloister, Heinävesi; 800th anniversary of introduction of orthodoxy in Karelia and of founding of Valamo Cloister.

Paavo Ruotsalainen (1777-1852), Lay Leader of Pietists in Finland — A287

1977, July 8 Litho. ***Perf. 13***
600 A287 90p multicolored .55 .40

People Fleeing Fire and Water — A288

1977, Sept. 14 Litho. ***Perf. 14***
601 A288 90p multicolored .55 .40

Civil defense for security.

Volleyball — A289

1977, Sept. 15
602 A289 90p multicolored .70 .40

European Women's Volleyball Championships, Finland, Sept. 29-Oct. 2.

Children Bringing Water for Sauna — A290

1977, Oct. 25
603 A290 50p multicolored 1.10 .40

Christmas 1977.

Finnish Flag — A291

1977, Dec. 5 Litho. ***Perf. 14***

Size: 31x21mm

604 A291 80p multicolored .70 .40

Size: 37x25mm

Perf. 13

605 A291 1m multicolored 1.00 .40

Finland's declaration of independence, 60th anniv.

Wall Telephone, 1880, New Telephone — A292

1977, Dec. 9 ***Perf. 14***
606 A292 1m multicolored .60 .40

Centenary of first telephone in Finland.

Harbor, Sunila Factory, Kotka Arms — A293

1978, Jan. 2 Litho. ***Perf. 14***
607 A293 1m multicolored .60 .40

Centenary of founding of Kotka.

Paimio Sanitarium by Alvar Aalto — A294

Europa: 1.20m, Hvittrask studio house, 1902, horiz.

1978, May 2 Litho. ***Perf. 13***
608 A294 1m multicolored *7.50 1.00*
609 A294 1.20m multicolored *9.50 11.50*

Rural Bus Service A295

1978, June 8 Litho. ***Perf. 14***
610 A295 1m multicolored .60 .40

Eino Leino and Eagle — A296

1978, July 6 Litho. ***Perf. 13***
611 A296 1m multicolored .60 .40

Eino Leino (1878-1926), poet.

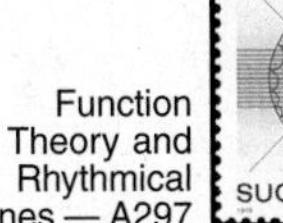

Function Theory and Rhythmical Lines — A297

1978, Aug. 15 Litho. ***Perf. 14***
612 A297 1m multicolored .60 .40

ICM 78, International Congress of Mathematicians, Helsinki, Aug. 15-23.

Child Feeding Birds — A298

1978, Oct. 23 Litho. ***Perf. 14***
613 A298 50p multicolored 1.00 .40

Christmas 1978.

A299

1979, Jan. 2 Litho. ***Perf. 13***
614 A299 1.10m multicolored .75 .40

International Year of the Child.

Runner — A300

1979, Feb. 7 Litho. ***Perf. 14***
615 A300 1.10m multicolored .55 .40

8th Orienteering World Championships, Finland, Sept. 1-4.

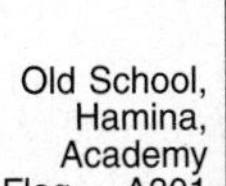

Old School, Hamina, Academy Flag — A301

1979, Mar. 20 Litho. ***Perf. 14***
616 A301 1.10m multicolored .55 .40

200th anniv. of Finnish Military Academy.

A302

Design: Turku Cathedral and Castle, Prinkkala house, Brahe statue.

1979, Mar. 31
617 A302 1.10m multicolored .55 .40

Streetcar, Helsinki — A303

1979, May 2 Litho. *Perf. 14*
618 A303 1.10m multi .55 .30

Non-polluting urban transportation.

View of Tampere, 1779 — A304

1979, May 2
619 A304 90p multicolored .55 .40

View of Tampere, 1979 — A305

1979, Oct. 1 *Perf. 13*
620 A305 1.10m multicolored .55 .40

Bicentenary of founding of Tampere.

Optical Telegraph, 1796, Map of Islands A306

Europa: 1.10m, Letter of Queen Christina to Per Brahe, 1638, establishing postal service.

1979, May 2 *Perf. 13*
621 A306 1.10m multi *3.00 .80*
622 A306 1.30m multi, horiz. *4.50 1.40*

Shops and Merchants' Signs — A307

1979, Sept. 26 *Perf. 14*
623 A307 1.10m multicolored .55 .40

Business and industry regulation centenary.

Old and New Cars, Street Crossing A308

1979, Oct. 1
624 A308 1.10m multicolored .55 .40

Road safety.

Elves Feeding Horse — A309

1979, Oct. 24
625 A309 60p multicolored .90 .40

Christmas 1979.

Korppi House, Lapinjarvi A310

Farm houses, First Row: Syrjala House, Tammela, 2 stamps in continuous design; Murtovaara House, Valtimo; Antila House, Lapua. Second row: Lofts, Pohjanmaa; Courtyard gate, Kanajarvi House, Kalvola; Main door, Havuselka House, Kauhajoki; Maki-Rasinpera House and dinner bell tower; Gable and eaves, Rasula Kuortane granary.

1979, Oct. 27 Litho. *Perf. 13*
626 Booklet pane of 10 8.00 6.00
a.-j. A310 1.10m single stamp .60 .35
Complete booklet, #626 8.00

See design A349a.

Type of 1975 and

Kauhaneva Swamp A315

Hame Castle, Hameenlinna A316

Windmill, Harrstrom A318

Multiharju Forest, Seitseminen Natl. Park — A319

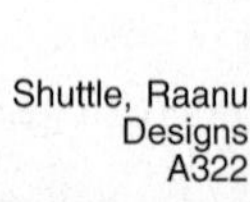

Shuttle, Raanu Designs A322

Kaspaikka Towel Design — A323

Bridal Rug, Teisko, 1815 — A324

Iron-forged Door, Hollola Church — A325

Iron Fish Spear c. 1100 — A326

Design: 1.80m, Eastern Gulf natl. park.

Litho. & Engr., Litho., Engr.

1979-98 *Perf. 14, 11½ (A256, A318)*

627	A315	70p	multicolored	.40	.25
628	A316	90p	brown red	.30	.30
629	A256	1m	red brown	.40	.30
a.			Perf. 13x12½ ('98)	1.25	1.25
630	A318	1m	bl & red brn	.40	.30
631	A256	1.30m	dk green	.60	.60
631A	A256	1.30m	dk green, litho.	1.00	1.10
b.			Booklet pane, #555-556, 557A, 560, 631A	3.00	3.00
			Complete booklet, #631Ab	6.00	
632	A256	1.40m	purple	.65	.60
633	A256	1.50m	grnsh blue	.80	.80
634	A319	1.60m	multicolored	1.20	.40
635	A315	1.80m	multicolored	2.00	.50
636	A322	3m	multicolored	1.40	.40
637	A323	6m	multicolored	2.50	.30
638	A324	7m	multicolored	3.00	.60
639	A325	8m	multicolored	3.50	.40
640	A326	9m	blk & dk bl	4.00	.90
			Nos. 627-640 (15)	22.15	7.75

Coil Stamps

Perf. 11½ Vert.

641 A316 90p brown red .85 1.00

Perf. 12½ Horiz.

642 A318 1m blue & red brn 1.10 .50

Issued: 3m, 10/27/79; 6m, 4/9/80; No. 629, 1/2/81; 70p, 1/12/81; 90p, 9/1/82; 1.60m, 2/8/82; 7m, 2/15/82; No. 631, 1/3/83; Nos. 630, 642, 1/12/83; 1.80m, 8m, 2/10/83; 1.40m, 9m, 1/2/84; 1.50m, 1/2/85; No. 631A, 11/1/85.

Maria Jotuni (1880-1943), Writer — A327

1980, Apr. 9 Litho.
643 A327 1.10m multicolored .55 .40

Frans Eemil Sillanpaa (1888-1964), Writer — A328

Europa: 1.30m, Artturi Ilmari Virtanen (1895-1973), chemist, vert.

1980, Apr. 28 *Perf. 13*
644 A328 1.10m multicolored *2.25 .40*
645 A328 1.30m multicolored *2.50 1.25*

Pres. Urho Kekkonen, 80th Birthday — A329

1980, Sept. 3 Litho. *Perf. 13*
646 A329 1.10m multicolored .55 .40

Nordic Cooperation Issue

Back-piece Harness, 19th century A330

1980, Sept. 9 *Perf. 14*
647 A330 1.10m shown .55 .40
648 A330 1.30m Collar harness, vert. .55 .40

Biathlon A331

1980, Oct. 17 Litho. *Perf. 14*
649 A331 1.10m multicolored .55 .40

World Biathlon Championship, Lahti, Feb. 10-15, 1981.

Pull the Roller, Weighing out the Salt — A332

Christmas 1980 (Traditional Games): 1.10m, Putting out the shoemaker's eye.

1980, Oct. 27
650 A332 60p multicolored 1.10 .50
651 A332 1.10m multicolored 1.10 .50

Boxing Match — A333

1981, Feb. 28 Litho. *Perf. 14*
652 A333 1.10m multicolored .45 .40

European Boxing Championships, Tampere, May 2-10.

Glass Blowing A334

1981, Mar. 12
653 A334 1.10m multicolored .45 .40

Glass industry, 300th anniversary.

Mail Boat Furst Menschikoff, 1836 — A335

Litho & Engr.

1981, May 6 *Perf. 13*
654 A335 1.10m brown & tan 3.25 4.50

Nordia '81 Stamp Exhibition, Helsinki, May 6-10. Sold only at exhibition for 3m including entrance ticket.

Europa Issue

Rowing to Church A336

Design: 1.50m, Midsummer's Eve dance.

1981, May 18 Litho. *Perf. 13*
655 A336 1.10m shown *.75 .30*
656 A336 1.50m multicolored *1.50 .50*

Traffic Conference Emblem — A337

1981, May 26 **Litho.** ***Perf. 14***
657 A337 1.10m multicolored .45 .40

European Conference of Ministers of Transport, May 25-28.

Boy and Girl Riding Pegasus A338

1981, June 11
658 A338 1m multicolored .45 .40

Youth associations centenary.

Intl. Year of the Disabled — A339

1981, Sept. 2 **Litho.** ***Perf. 13***
659 A339 1.10m multicolored .45 .40

Christmas 1981 — A340

70p, Children, Christmas tree. 1.10m, Decorating tree, vert.

1981, Oct. 27 **Litho.** ***Perf. 14***
660 A340 70p multicolored .85 .30
661 A340 1.10m multicolored .85 .30

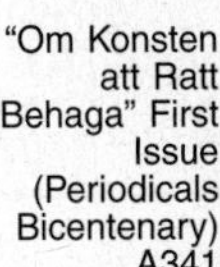

"Om Konsten att Ratt Behaga" First Issue (Periodicals Bicentenary) A341

1982, Jan. 15
662 A341 1.20m multicolored .45 .40

Kuopio Bicentenary — A343

1982, Mar. 4 **Litho.** ***Perf. 14***
664 A343 1.20m multicolored .45 .40

Score, String Instrument Neck — A344

1982, Mar. 11 ***Perf. 13***
665 A344 1.20m multicolored 1.20 .45

Centenaries of Sibelius Academy of Music and Helsinki Orchestra.

Electric Power Plant Centenary A345

1982, Mar. 15 ***Perf. 14***
666 A345 1.20m multicolored .85 .40

Gardening A346

1982, Apr. 16 **Litho.** ***Perf. 14***
667 A346 1.10m multicolored .45 .40

Europa — A347

1.20m, Publication of Abckiria (1st Finnish book), 1543 (Sculpture of Mikael Agricola, translator, by Oskari Jauhiainen, 1951). 1.50m, Turku Academy, 1st Finnish university (Turku Academy Inaugural Procession, 1640, after Albert Edelfelt).

1982, Apr. 29 **Litho.** ***Perf. 13x12½***
668 A347 1.20m multicolored *1.50* .45

Size: 47x31mm

Perf. 12½

669 A347 1.50m multicolored *1.90* .60

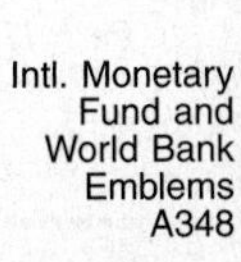

Intl. Monetary Fund and World Bank Emblems A348

1982, May 12 ***Perf. 14***
670 A348 1.60m multicolored .55 .50

IMF Interim Committee and IMF-WB Joint Development Committee Meeting, Helsinki, May 12-14.

75th Anniv. of Unicameral Parliament A349

2.40m, Future, by Waino Aaltonen, Parliament.

1982, May 25
671 A349 2.40m ultra & blk .85 .70

Manor Houses A349a

1st Row: a, Kuitia, Parainen, 1490. b, Louhisaari, Askainen, 1655. c, Frugard, Joroinen, 1780. d, Jokioinen, 1798. e, Moisio, Elimaki, 1820.

2nd Row: f, Sjundby, Siuntio, 1560. g, Fagervik, Inkoo, 1773. h, Mustio, Karjaa, 1792. i, Fiskars, Pohja, 1818. j, Kotkaniemi, Vihti, 1836.

1982, June 14 **Litho.** ***Perf. 13x13½***
672 Booklet pane of 10 12.00 12.00
a.-j. A349a 1.20m single stamp 1.20 .50
Complete booklet, #672 12.00 12.00

See design A310.

Christmas 1982 — A350

Designs: 90p, Feeding forest animals. 1.20m, Children eating porridge.

1982, Oct. 25
673 A350 90p multi .70 .40
674 A350 1.20m multi .70 .40

Nordic Cooperation A351

1.20m, Panning for gold. 1.30m, Kitkajoki River rapids.

1983, Mar. 24 **Litho.** ***Perf. 14***
675 A351 1.20m multi .55 .40
676 A351 1.30m multi .55 .40

World Communications Year — A352

1.30m, Postal services. 1.70m, Sound waves, optical cables.

1983, Apr. 9 **Litho.** ***Perf. 13***
677 A352 1.30m multi .55 .40
678 A352 1.70m multi .65 .45

Europa 1983 A353

1.30m, Flash smelting method. 1.70m, Temppeliaukio Church.

1983, May 2 **Litho.** ***Perf. 12½x13***
679 A353 1.30m multicolored *5.00* *.45*
680 A353 1.70m multicolored *6.00* *.90*

Pres. Lauri Kristian Relander (1883-1942) — A354

1983, May 31 **Litho.** ***Perf. 14***
681 A354 1.30m multicolored .45 .40

Running — A355

1983, June 6
682 A355 1.20m Javelin, horiz. .45 .40
683 A355 1.30m shown .45 .40

First World Athletic Championships, Helsinki, Aug. 7-14.

Toivo Kuula (1883-1918), Composer — A356

1983, July 7 ***Perf. 14***
684 A356 1.30m multicolored .55 .40

Christmas 1983 — A357

Childrens drawings: 1m, Santa, reindeer, sled and gifts by Eija Myllyviita. 1.30m, Two candles by Camilla Lindberg.

Engr., Litho.

1983, Nov. 4 ***Perf. 12, 14***
685 A357 1m dark blue .85 .40
686 A357 1.30m multi, vert. .85 .40

A358

1983, Nov. 25 **Litho.** ***Perf. 14***
687 A358 1.30m brt blue & blk .45 .40

President Mauno Henrik Koivisto, 60th birthday.

A360

1.10m, Letters (2nd class rate). 1.40m, Automated sorting (1st class rate), vert.

1984, Mar. 1 **Engr.** ***Perf. 12***
689 A360 1.10m multicolored .90 .50

Photo. & Engr.

690 A360 1.40m multicolored .70 .50

Inauguration of Nordic postal rates.

Museum Pieces — A361 | Work and Skill — A362

Designs: No. 691, Pottery, 3200 B.C.; Silver chalice, 1416; Crossbow, 16th cent. No. 692, Kaplan hydraulic turbine.

1984, Apr. 30 Litho. *Perf. 13½*

691 A361 1.40m multicolored .50 .40
692 A362 1.40m multicolored .50 .40

Europa (1959-84) A363

1984, May 7 *Perf. 12½x13*

693 A363 1.40m multicolored *4.00* .25
694 A363 2m multicolored *4.00* .80

Dentistry — A364

1984, Aug. 27 Litho. *Perf. 14*

695 A364 1.40m Dentist, teeth .80 .50

Astronomy A365

Design: Observatory, planets, sun.

1984, Sept. 12

696 A365 1.10m multicolored 1.00 .55

Aleksis Kivi (1934-72), Writer — A366

Design: Song of my Heart.

1984, Oct. 10 Litho. *Perf. 14*

697 A366 1.40m blk & dull mauve .80 .40

Christmas 1984 — A367

Design: Father Christmas, brownie.

Litho. & Engr.

1984, Nov. 30 *Perf. 12*

698 A367 1.10m multicolored 1.40 .40

Common Law of 1734 — A368

1984, Dec. 6 *Perf. 14*

699 A368 2m Statute Book 1.20 .70

25th Anniv. of EFTA — A369

1985, Feb. 2 Litho.

700 A369 1.20m multicolored .50 .40

100th Anniv. of Society of Swedish Literature in Finland A370

Design: Johan Ludvig Runeberg.

1985, Feb. 5 Litho.

701 A370 1.50m multicolored .50 .35

Icon — A371

1985, Feb. 18 Litho. *Perf. 11½x12*

702 A371 1.50m multicolored .50 .40

Order of St. Sergei and St. Herman, 100th anniv.

150th Anniv. of Kalevala — A372

Designs: 1.50m, Pedri Shemeikka. 2.10m, Larin Paraske.

Litho. & Engr.

1985, Feb. 28 *Perf. 13x12½*

703 A372 1.50m multicolored .80 .40
704 A372 2.10m multicolored 1.20 .75

Mermaid and Sea Lions — A373

Litho. & Engr.

1985, May 15 *Perf. 13*

705 A373 1.50m multicolored 4.50 *6.25*

NORDIA 1985 philatelic exhibition, May 15-19. Sold for 10m, which included admission ticket.

A374

Finnish Banknote Cent.: banknotes of 1886, 1909, 1922, 1945 and 1955.

Photo. & Engr.

1985, May 18 *Perf. 11½*

706 A374 Booklet pane of 8 7.50 7.50
a.-h. 1.50m any single .90 .70
Complete booklet, #706 7.50

A375

Europa: 1.50m, Children playing the recorder. 2.10m, Excerpt "Ramus Virens Olivarum" from the "Piae Cantiones," 1582.

1985, June 17 Litho. *Perf. 13*

707 A375 1.50m multicolored *5.50* *.50*
708 A375 2.10m multicolored *6.50* *1.10*

Security Conference Type of 1975

1985, June 19 Litho.

709 A265 2.10m multicolored .75 .60

European Security and Cooperation Conference, 10th Anniv.

Provincial Arms, Count's Seal — A376

1985, Sept. 5 Litho. *Perf. 14*

710 A376 1.50m multicolored 1.20 .35

Provincial Administration Established by Count Per Brahe, 350th Anniv.

Arms Type of 1975 and

Kerimaki Church A376a

Urho Kekkonen Natl. Park — A376b

Tulip Damask Table Cloth, 18th Cent. A377 | Postal Service A377a

Brown Bear — A377b

Perf. 11½, 13x12½ (2m)

1985-90 Engr.

711 A256 1.60m vermilion .80 .60
712 A256 1.70m black 1.20 .50
a. Bklt. pane, #558, 560, 2 each #555, 556a, 712 + 2 labels 9.00 *11.00*
Complete booklet, #712a 10.00
713 A256 1.80m ol grn 1.25 .70
a. Bklt. pane, 2 ea #555d, 560a, 713b 3.50 3.00
Complete booklet, #713a 3.50
b. Perf. 13x12½ 2.50 1.50
714 A256 1.90m brt orange 1.10 .30
715 A256 2m blue grn, bklt. stamp 2.50 .90
a. Bklt. pane, #562a, 2 ea #715, 555d 7.00 7.00
Complete booklet, #715a 7.00

Litho. *Perf. 14*

716 A376a 2.20m multi 1.10 .30
717 A376b 2.40m multi 1.40 .40
718 A377 12m multi 7.00 1.00

Litho. & Engr.

Perf. 13x12½

719 A377b 50m blk, grn & lt red brn 24.00 8.50
Nos. 711-719 (9) 40.35 13.20

No. 712a contains two labels inscribed to publicize FINLANDIA '88.

Issued: 12m, 9/13/85; 1.60m, 1/2/86; 1.70m, 1/2/87; No. 712a, 8/10/87; 1.80m, 1/4/88; 2.20m, 2.40m, 1/20/88; No. 713b, 7/25/88; 1.90m, 1/2/89; 2m, 1/19/90; 50m, 8/30/89.

Booklet Stamps

No. 720, Telephone, mailbox. No. 721, Postal truck, transport plane. No. 722, Transport plane, fork lift. No. 723, Postman delivering letter. No. 724, Woman accepting letter.

Perf. 12½ on 3 Sides

1988, Feb. 1 **Litho.**

720 A377a 1.80m multi 1.50 .50
721 A377a 1.80m multi 1.50 .50
722 A377a 1.80m multi 1.50 .50
723 A377a 1.80m multi 1.50 .50
724 A377a 1.80m multi 1.50 .50
a. Bklt. pane, 2 each #720-724 16.00 10.50
Complete booklet, #724a 16.00
Nos. 720-724 (5) 7.50 2.50

Nos. 721-722 and 723-724 printed se-tenant in continuous designs. No. 724c sold for 14m to households on mainland Finland. Each household entitled to buy 2 booklets at discount price from Feb. 1 to May 31, with coupon.

Miniature Sheet

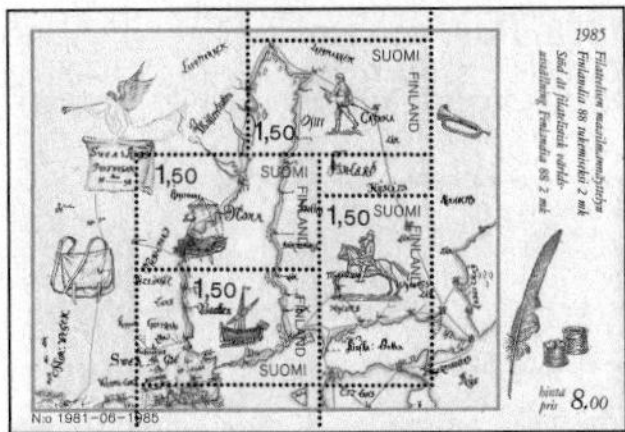

Postal Map, 1698 — A378

Designs: a, Postman on foot. b, Postal Map, 1698. c, Sailing vessel, diff. d, Postrider, vert.

Litho. & Engr.

1985, Oct. 16 ***Perf. 14***

728 A378 Sheet of 4 8.00 10.00
a.-d. 1.50m any single 2.00 2.50

FINLANDIA '88, 350th anniv. of Finnish Postal Service, founded in 1638 by Gov.-Gen. Per Brahe. Sheet sold for 8m.

Intl. Youth Year — A379

1985, Nov. 1 **Litho.** ***Perf. 13***

729 A379 1.50m multicolored .70 .35

Christmas — A380

No. 730, Bird, tulips. No. 731, Cross of St. Thomas, hyacinths.

1985, Nov. 29 ***Perf. 14***

730 A380 1.20m multicolored 1.10 .40
731 A380 1.20m multicolored 1.10 .40

Natl. Geological Society, Cent. — A390

1986, Feb. 8 **Litho.** ***Perf. 14***

732 A390 1.30m Orbicular granite .90 .40
733 A390 1.60m Rapaviki 1.00 .40
734 A390 2.10m Veined gneiss 1.25 .60
Nos. 732-734 (3) 3.15 1.40

Europa 1986 A391

1.60m, Saimaa ringed seal. 2.20m, Environmental conservation.

1986, Apr. 10 ***Perf. 12½x13***

735 A391 1.60m multicolored *2.50 .40*
736 A391 2.20m multicolored *5.50 .80*

Conference Palace, Baghdad, 1982 — A392

Natl. Construction Year. b, Lahti Theater, 1983. c, Kuusamo Municipal Offices, 1978. d, Hamina Court Building, 1983. e, Finnish Embassy, New Delhi, 1986. f, Western Sakyla Daycare Center, 1980.

1986, Apr. 19 ***Perf. 14***

737 Booklet pane of 6 5.75 6.00
a.-f. A392 1.60m, any single .90 .70
Complete booklet, #737 5.75

Nordic Cooperation Issue 1986 — A393

Sister towns.

1986, May 27 **Litho.** ***Perf. 14***

738 A393 1.60m Joensuu .70 .40
739 A393 2.20m Jyvaskyla .90 .75

Souvenir Sheet

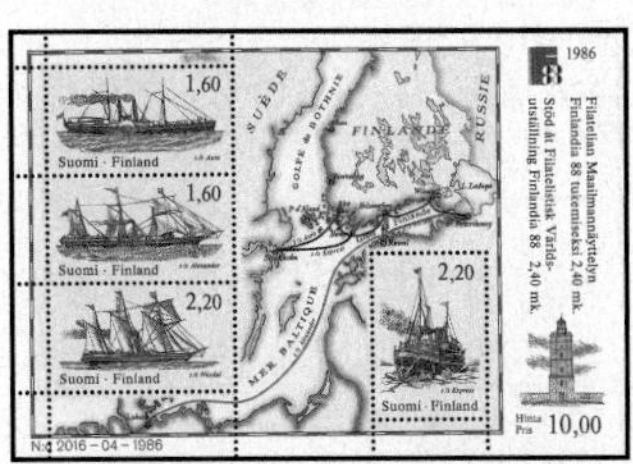

FINLANDIA '88 — A394

Postal ships: a, Iron paddle steamer Aura, Stockholm-St. Petersburg, 1858. b, Screw vessel Alexander, Helsinki-Tallinn-Lubeck, 1859. c, Steamship Nicolai, Helsinki-Tallinn-St. Petersburg, 1858. d, 1st Ice steamship Express II, Helsinki-Stockholm, 1877-98, vert.

Litho. & Engr.

1986, Aug. 29 ***Perf. 13***

740 A394 Sheet of 4 14.00 14.00
a.-b. 1.60m, any single 3.25 3.25
c.-d. 2.20m, any single 3.25 3.25

Sold for 10k.

Pierre-Louis Moreau de Maupertuis (1698-1759) — A395

1986, Sept. 5 **Litho.** ***Perf. 12½x13***

741 A395 1.60m multicolored .80 .40

Lapland Expedition, 250th anniv., proved Earth's poles are flattened.
See France No. 2016.

Urho Kaleva Kekkonen (1900-86), Pres. — A396

1986, Sept. 30 **Engr.** ***Perf. 14***

742 A396 5m black 2.25 2.00

Intl. Peace Year — A397

1986, Oct. 13 **Litho.** ***Perf. 13***

743 A397 1.60m multicolored .70 .40

A398

Christmas A399

Photo. & Engr.

1986, Oct. 31 ***Perf. 12***

744 1.30m Denomination at L .70 .45
745 1.30m Denomination at R 1.50 .40
a. A398 Pair, #744-745 3.00 2.40
746 A399 1.60m Elves 1.25 .40
Nos. 744-746 (3) 3.45 1.25

No. 745a has a continuous design.

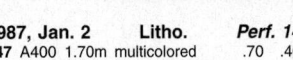

Postal Savings Bank, Cent. — A400

1987, Jan. 2 **Litho.** ***Perf. 14***

747 A400 1.70m multicolored .70 .40

Natl. Tourism, Cent. — A401

1987, Feb. 4 **Litho.** ***Perf. 14***

748 A401 1.70m Winter .65 .40
749 A401 2.30m Summer .85 .60

A402

1987, Feb. 4 ***Perf. 14***

750 A402 1.40m multicolored .70 .40

Metric system in Finland, cent.

A403

1987, Feb. 17 **Litho.** ***Perf. 14***

751 A403 2.10m multicolored 1.10 .50

Leevi Madetoja (1887-1947), composer.

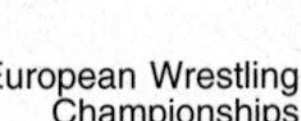

European Wrestling Championships A404

1987, Feb. 17

752 A404 1.70m multicolored .80 .40

1987 World Bowling Championships A405

1987, Apr. 13

753 A405 1.70m multicolored .80 .40

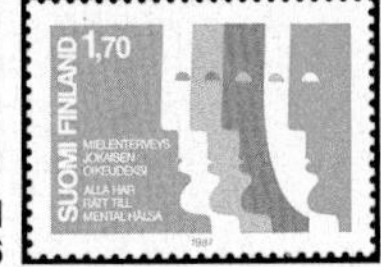

Mental Health — A406

1987, Apr. 13

754 A406 1.70m multicolored .70 .40

Souvenir Sheet

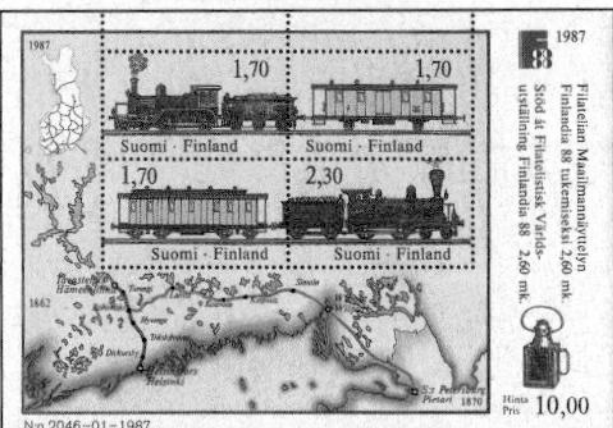

FINLANDIA '88 — A407

Locomotives and mail cars: a, Steam locomotive, 6-wheeled tender. b, 4-window mail car. c, 7-window mail car.

Litho. & Engr.

1987, May 8 ***Perf. 12½x13***

755 A407 Sheet of 4 15.00 15.00
a.-c. 1.70m any single 4.00 4.00
d. 2.30m multicolored 4.00 4.00

Sold for 10m.

Europa 1987 A408

Modern architecture: 1.70m, Tampere Main Library, 1986, designed by Raili and Reima Pietila. 2.30m, Stoa Monument, Helsinki, c. 1981, by sculptor Hannu Siren.

1987, May 15 **Litho.** ***Perf. 13***

756 A408 1.70m multicolored *5.25 .25*
757 A408 2.30m multicolored *5.25 .90*

Natl. Art Museum, Ateneum, Cent. — A409

Paintings: a, Strawberry Girl, by Nils Schillmark (1745-1804). b, Still-life on a Lady's Work Table, by Ferdinand von Wright (1822-1906). c, Old Woman with Basket, by Albert

Edelfelt (1854-1906). d, Boy and Crow, by Akseli Gallen-Kallela (1865-1931). e, Late Winter, by Tyko Sallinen (1879-1955).

1987, May 15

758 Booklet pane of 5 8.50 8.50
a.-e. A409 1.70m any single 1.60 .90
Complete booklet, #758 9.00

A410

1987, Aug. 12 ***Perf. 14***

759 A410 1.70m multicolored .70 .40

European Physics Soc. 7th gen. conf., Helsinki, Aug. 10-14.

A411

1987, Oct. 12

760 A411 1.70m ultra, sil & pale lt gray .70 .40

Size: 30x41mm

761 A411 10m dark ultra, lt blue & sil 4.00 2.00

Natl. independence, 70th anniv.

Ylppo, Child and Lastenlinna Children's Hospital A412

1987, Oct. 27

762 A412 1.70m multicolored .70 .40

Arvo Ylppo (b. 1887), pediatrics pioneer.

Christmas — A413

Design: 1.40m, Santa Claus, youths, horiz.

1987, Oct. 30

763 A413 1.40m multi 1.00 .40
764 A413 1.70m shown 1.00 .40

Finnish News Agency (STT), Cent. — A414

1987, Nov. 1

765 A414 2.30m multicolored .95 .80

A415

1988, Jan. 5 Litho. ***Perf. 14***

766 A415 1.80m blk, chalky blue & brt blue .80 .40

Lauri "Tahko" Pihkala (1888-1981), promulgator of sports and physical education.

A416

1988, Mar. 14 Litho.

767 A416 1.40m multicolored .70 .40

Meteorological Institute, 150th anniv.

Settlement of New Sweden in America, 350th Anniv. — A417

Design: 17th Century European settlers negotiating with 3 American Indians, map of New Sweden, the Swedish ships Kalmar Nyckel and Fogel Grip, based on an 18th cent. illustration from a Swedish book about the American Colonies.

Litho. & Engr.

1988, Mar. 29 ***Perf. 13***

768 A417 3m multicolored 1.25 .80

See US No. C117 and Sweden No. 1672.

FINLANDIA '88, June 1-12, Helsinki Fair Center — A418

Agathon Faberge (1876-1951), famed philatelist, & rarities from his collection.

Booklet Stamp

1988, May 2 Litho. ***Perf. 13***

769 A418 5m Pane of 1+2 labels 14.00 *17.50*
Complete booklet, #769 15.00

350th Anniv. of the Finnish Postal Service. No. 769 sold for 30m to include the price of adult admission to the exhibition.

Achievements of Finnish Athletes at the 1988 Winter Olympics, Calgary — A419

Design: Matti Nykanen, gold medalist in all 3 ski jumping events at the '88 Games.

1988, Apr. 6 ***Perf. 14***

770 A419 1.80m multicolored .90 .40

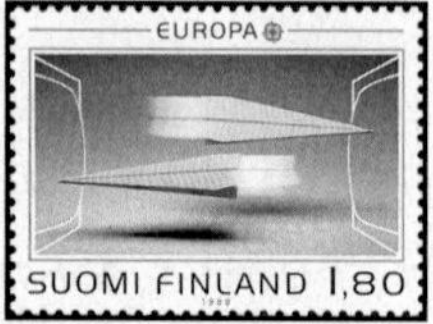
Europa 1988 A420

Communication and transport: 2.40m, Horse-drawn tram, 1890.

1988, May 23 Litho. ***Perf. 13***

771 A420 1.80m shown *5.00 .25*
772 A420 2.40m multicolored *5.00 .90*

Souvenir Sheet

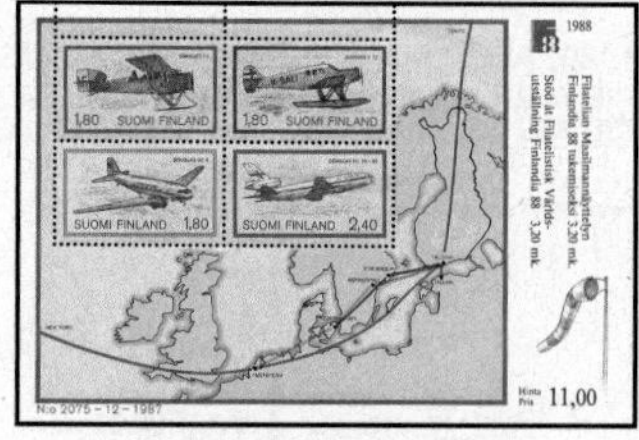
FINLANDIA '88 — A421

1st airmail flights: a, Finnish air force Breguet 14 biplane transporting mail from Helsinki to Tallinn, Feb. 12, 1920. b, AERO Junkers F-13 making 1st airmail night flight from Helsinki to Copenhagen, May 15, 1930. c, AERO Douglas DC-3, 1st intl. route, Helsinki-Norrkoping-Copenhagen-Amsterdam, 1947. d, Douglas DC 10-30, 1975-88, inauguration of Helsinki-Beijing route, June 2, 1988.

Litho. & Engr.

1988, June 2 ***Perf. 13½***

773 A421 Sheet of 4 15.00 16.00
a.-c. 1.80m any single 3.75 4.00
d. 2.40m multicolored 3.75 4.00

Sold for 11m.

Turku Fire Brigade, 150th Anniv. — A422

Design: 1902 Horse-drawn, steam-driven fire pump, preserved at the brigade.

1988, Aug. 15 Litho. ***Perf. 14***

774 A422 2.20m multicolored .95 .55

A423

Missale Aboense, the 1st printed book in Finland, 500th anniv.

1988, Aug. 17

775 A423 1.80m multicolored .90 .40

A424

Finnish Postal Service, 350th Anniv.: No. 776, Postal tariff issued by Queen Christina of Sweden, Sept. 6, 1638. No. 777, Postal cart, c. 1880. #778, Leyland Sherpa 185 mail van, 1976. No. 779, Malmi P.O. interior. #780, Skier using mobile telephone, c. 1970. No. 781, Telecommunications satellite in orbit.

Booklet Stamps

1988, Sept. 6 Litho. ***Perf. 13***

776 A424 1.80m multicolored .90 .65
777 A424 1.80m multicolored .90 .65
778 A424 1.80m multicolored .90 .65
779 A424 1.80m multicolored .90 .65
780 A424 1.80m multicolored .90 .65
781 A424 1.80m multicolored .90 .65
a. Booklet pane of 6, #776-781 5.50 6.50
Complete booklet, #781a 5.50

Children's Playgroups (Preschool) A425

1988, Oct. 10 ***Perf. 14***

782 A425 1.80m multicolored .80 .40

Christmas A426

1988, Nov. 4 Litho.

783 A426 1.40m multicolored 1.40 .35
784 A426 1.80m multicolored 1.75 .55

Hameenlinna Township, 350th Anniv. — A427

Design: Market square, coat of arms and 17th century plan of the town.

1989, Jan. 19 Litho.

785 A427 1.90m multicolored .80 .40

1989 Nordic Ski Championships, Lahti, Feb. 17-26 — A428

1989, Jan. 25

786 A428 1.90m multicolored .80 .40

Salvation Army in Finland, Cent. — A429

1989, Feb. 6 Litho.

787 A429 1.90m multicolored .80 .40

Photography, 150th Anniv. — A430

1.50m, Photographer, box camera, c.1900.

1989, Feb. 6

788 A430 1.50m brn, buff, cream .75 .55

31st Intl. Physiology Congress, Basel, July 9-14 — A431

Design: Congress emblem, silhouettes of Robert Tigerstedt and Ragnar Granit, eye, flowmeter measuring flow of blood through heart, color-sensitive retinal cells and microelectrode.

1989, Mar. 2

789 A431 1.90m multicolored .80 .40

Sports — A432

1989, Mar. 10 **Booklet Stamps**

790	A432	1.90m Skiing	1.00	.50
791	A432	1.90m Jogging	1.00	.50
792	A432	1.90m Cycling	1.00	.50
793	A432	1.90m Canoeing	1.00	.50
a.		Booklet pane of 4, #790-793	4.25	4.25
		Complete booklet, #793a	4.50	

Souvenir Sheet

Finnish Kennel Club, Cent. — A433

Dogs: a, Lapponian herder. b, Finnish spitz. c, Karelian bear dog. d, Finnish hound.

1989, Mar. 17 **Litho.** ***Perf. 14***

794	A433	Sheet of 4	4.00	4.00
a.-d.		1.90m any single	1.00	.70

Europa — A434

1989, Mar. 31 ***Perf. 13***

795	A434	1.90m Hopscotch	*2.50*	*.25*
796	A434	2.50m Sledding	*2.50*	*.65*

A435

Nordic Cooperation Year: Folk Costumes.

1989, Apr. 20 ***Perf. 14***

797	A435	1.90m Sakyla (man)	1.10	.45
798	A435	2.50m Veteli (woman)	1.10	.65

Finnish Pharmacies, 300th Anniv. — A436

Foxglove, distilling apparatus, mortar, flask.

1989, June 2 **Litho.**

799	A436	1.90m multicolored	.90	.35

A437

1989, June 2

800	A437	1.90m multicolored	.90	.35

Savonlinna Municipal Charter, 350th anniv.

Helsinki Zoo, Cent. — A438

No. 801, Panthera uncia. No. 802, Capra falconeri

1989, June 12

801	A438	1.90m multi	.90	.45
802	A438	2.50m multi	1.10	.70

Vocational Training, 150th Anniv. — A439

Interparliamentary Union, Cent. — A440

Council of Europe, 40th Anniv. — A441

1989, Sept. 4 **Litho.** ***Perf. 14***

803	A439	1.50m multicolored	.70	.70
804	A440	1.90m multicolored	.90	.35
805	A441	2.50m multicolored	1.25	.90
		Nos. 803-805 (3)	2.85	1.95

Admission of Finland to the Council of Europe (2.50m).

A442

1989, Oct. 9 **Litho.**

806	A442	1.90m multicolored	.90	.35

Hannes Kolehmainen (1889-1966) winning the 5000-meter race at the Stockholm Olympics, 1912.

A443

1989, Oct. 20

807	A443	1.90m multicolored	.90	.35

Continuing Education in Finland, cent.

A444

Christmas: 1.90m, Sodankyla Church, Siberian jays in snow.

1989, Nov. 3

808	A444	1.50m shown	1.10	.40
809	A444	1.90m multicolored	1.10	.40

A445

1990, Jan. 19 **Litho.** ***Perf. 13x13½***

810	A445	1.90m multicolored	1.40	1.10
811	A445	2.50m multicolored	1.60	1.25

Incorporation of the State Posts and Telecommunications Services.

Emblem of the corporation was produced by holography. Soaking may affect the design.

Musical Soc. of Turku and Finnish Orchestras, 200th Annivs. A446

1990, Jan. 26 ***Perf. 14***

812	A446	1.90m multicolored	1.10	.40

Disabled Veteran's Assoc., 50th Anniv. — A447

1990, Mar. 13 **Litho.**

813	A447	2m multicolored	.90	.35

End of the Winter (Russo-Finnish) War, 50th Anniv. — A448

1990, Mar. 13

814	A448	2m blue	.90	.35

University of Helsinki, 350th Anniv. — A449

University crest and: 2m, Queen Christina on horseback. 3.20m, Degree ceremony procession in front of the main university building.

1990, Mar. 26 **Litho.** ***Perf. 13***

815	A449	2m multicolored	.85	.40
816	A449	3.20m multicolored	1.25	.70

Europa 1990 A450

Post Offices: 2m, Lapp man, P.O. at Nuvvus, Mt. Nuvvus Ailigas. 2.70m, Turku main P.O.

1990, Mar. 26 ***Perf. 12½x13***

817	A450	2m multicolored	*6.00*	*.25*
818	A450	2.70m multicolored	*6.00*	*.65*

Rural Postal Service and Address Reform, Cent. — A451

1990, Apr. 19 **Litho.** ***Perf. 13***

819	A451	2m multicolored	.90	.35

"Ali Baba and the Forty Thieves" A452

"Story of the Great Musician" A453

"Story of the Giants, the Witches and the Daughter of the Sun" A454

"The Golden Bird, the Golden Horse and the Princess" A455

"Lamb Brother" A456

"The Snow Queen" A457

Fairy tale illustrations by Rudolf Koivu.

Booklet Stamps

Perf. 14 on 3 sides

1990, Aug. 29 **Litho.**

820	A452	2m multicolored	1.60	.65
821	A453	2m multicolored	1.60	.65
822	A454	2m multicolored	1.60	.65
823	A455	2m multicolored	1.60	.65
824	A456	2m multicolored	1.60	.65
825	A457	2m multicolored	1.60	.65
a.		Booklet pane of 6, #820-825	10.00	8.00
		Complete booklet, #825a	10.00	

Souvenir Sheet

Horse Care — A458

a, Feeding. b, Riding. c, Watering. d, Currying.

1990, Oct. 10 **Litho.** ***Perf. 14***

826	A458	Sheet of 4	4.50	4.25
a.-d.		2m any single	1.10	.75

Christmas A459

1990, Nov. 2

827 A459 1.70m Santa's elves 1.70 .40
828 A459 2m Santa, reindeer 1.70 .40

Provincial Flowers

A460

A460a

A460b A460c

A460d

A460e

A460f A460g

A460h

A460i

A460j

A460k

2m, Wood anemone. 2.10m, Rowan. 2.70m, Heather. 2.90m, Sea buckthorn. 3.50m, Oak. No. 834, Globeflower. No. 835, Hepatica. No. 836, Iris. No. 838, Rosebay willowherb. No. 839, Labrador tea. No. 840, Karelian rose. No. 841, Daisy. No. 842, Water lily. No. 843, Bird cherry. No. 844, Harebell. No. 845, Cowslip.

1990-99 ***Perf. 13x12½***

829 A460 2m multi 1.10 .25
830 A460 2.10m multi 1.10 .25
831 A460 2.70m multi 1.40 .40
832 A460 2.90m multi 1.50 .40
833 A460 3.50m multi 2.00 .50
834 A460a 2 multi 2.25 .50
835 A460b 1 multi 2.50 .30
Nos. 829-835 (7) 11.85 2.60

Self-Adhesive

Die Cut

836 A460c 2 multi 2.25 .30
a. Booklet pane of 20 45.00 27.50
837 A460 2.10m like #830 1.40 .30
838 A460d 1 multi 2.50 .35
839 A460e 1 multi 2.50 .35
a. Booklet pane of 10 24.50 7.50
840 A460f 1 multi 2.50 .40
841 A460g 1 multi 2.50 .35
842 A460h 1 multi 2.50 .35
843 A460i 1 multi 2.50 .45
844 A460j 1 multi 2.50 .45
845 A460k 1 multi 2.50 .45
Nos. 836-845 (10) 23.65 3.75

Issued: 2m, 2.70m, 1/19/90; No. 830, 2.90m, 3.50m, 2/5/90; 2.10m, 1991; Nos. 834-835, 3/2/92; No. 838, 10/9/92; No. 836, 3/1/93; No. 839, 6/14/93; No. 840, 5/5/94; No. 841, 3/15/95; No. 842, 6/3/96; No. 843, 3/18/97; No. 844, 3/12/98; No. 845, 4/28/99.

No. 834 sold for 1.60m, No. 836 sold for 1.90m, Nos. 835, 838 for 2.10m, Nos. 839-840 for 2.30m, Nos. 841-844 sold for 2.80m, No. 845 sold for 3m at time of release.

Nos. 837-838, 840-845 issued in sheets of 10. Nos. 836a and 839a were issued as complete booklets. The peelable backing serves as a booklet cover.

The numbers on the stamps represent the class of mail for which each was intended at time of release.

A461

1991, Mar. 1 ***Perf. 14***

846 A461 2.10m multicolored 1.10 .40

World Hockey Championships, Turku.

A462

1991, Mar. 1

847 A462 2.10m Cooking class .80 .40

Home economics teacher education, cent.

Sauna Type of 1977 and

Birds — A463

No. 848, Great tit. No. 849, Wagtail. No. 850, Aegolius funereus. No. 850A, Phoenicurus phoenicurus. No. 851, Chaffinches. No. 852, Robin. No. 856, Bullfinch. No. 857, Waxwing. No. 859, Dendrocopos leucotos.

Perf. 13x12½, 14 (#861)

1991-99 **Litho.**

Booklet Stamps (#848-859)

848 A463 10p multi .40 .35
849 A463 10p multi .40 .25
850 A463 10p multi .90 .60
850A A463 20p multi 10.00 5.00
851 A463 60p multi 6.00 .65
852 A463 60p multi 7.00 1.25
856 A463 2.10m multi .90 .40
a. Bklt. pane, #851, 2 each #848, 856 7.50 7.50
Complete booklet, #856a 8.00
857 A463 2.10m multi .90 .40
a. Bklt. pane, #852, 2 each #849, 857 6.25 6.25
Complete booklet, #857a 6.75
859 A463 2.30m multi 1.00 .50
a. Booklet pane of #850A, 2 each #850, #859 + 1 label 7.50 7.50
Complete booklet, #859a 8.00

Sheet Stamp

861 A256a 4.80m multi 2.00 1.25
Nos. 848-861 (10) 29.50 10.65

Issued: Nos. 848, 851, 856, 3/20/91; Nos. 849, 852, 857, 4/22/92; Nos. 850, 850A, 859, 6/4/93. 861, 7/1/99.

"SUOMI" is in upper left on Nos. 849, 852, 857.

Fishing — A464

Designs: a, Fly fisherman, trout. b, Perch, bobber. c, Crayfish, trap. d, Trawling for herring. e, Stocking powan.

1991, Mar. 20 ***Perf. 14***

863 Booklet pane of 5 6.00 6.00
a.-e. A464 2.10m any single 1.20 .45
Complete booklet, #863 6.50

Tourism — A465

2.10m, Seurasaari Island. 2.90m, Steamship, Lake Saimaa.

1991, June 4 **Litho.** ***Perf. 14***

864 A465 2.10m multi 1.00 .25
865 A465 2.90m multi 1.10 .70

Europa A466

European map and: 2.10m, Human figures. 2.90m, Satellites, dish antennae.

1991, June 7 **Litho.** ***Perf. 12½x13***

866 A466 2.10m multicolored *5.50* *.25*
867 A466 2.90m multicolored *5.50* *.70*

Alfred W. Finch (1854-1930) A467

Designs: 2.10m, Iris, ceramic vase. 2.90m, Painting, The English Coast at Dover.

1991, Sept. 7 **Litho.** ***Perf. 13***

868 A467 2.10m multicolored 1.10 .25
869 A467 2.90m multicolored 2.25 .70

See Belgium No. 1410.

Finnish Candy Industry, Cent. — A468

1991, Sept. 17 **Photo.** ***Perf. 11½***

870 A468 2.10m multicolored 1.00 .50

Souvenir Sheets

Children's Stamp Designs — A469

a, Sun. b, Rainbow. c, Cows grazing.

1991, Sept. 17 **Litho.** ***Perf. 13½***

871 A469 Sheet of 3 3.00 3.00
a.-c. 2.10m any single 1.00 .65

Skiing — A470

Color of skisuit: a, red. b, green. c, yellow. d, blue.

1991, Oct. 4 ***Perf. 14***

872 A470 Sheet of 4 4.00 4.00
a.-d. 2.10m any single 1.00 .65

Town Status for Iisalmi, Cent. — A471

1991, Oct. 18 **Litho.** ***Perf. 14***

873 A471 2.10m multicolored .90 .50

Christmas A472

1.80m, Santa, animals carrying candles. 2.10m, Reindeer pulling Santa's sleigh.

1991, Nov. 1 **Litho.** ***Perf. 14***

874 A472 1.80m multi 1.75 .45
875 A472 2.10m multi, vert. 1.75 .45

Chemists' Club, Finnish Chemists' Society, Cent. — A473

1991, Nov. 1

876 A473 2.10m multi 1.10 .40
877 A473 2.10m multi, diff. 1.10 .40
a. Pair, #876-877 + label 3.00 3.00

Second and third vertical branches merge while second and third branches below almost touch in the upper left part of camphor molecular structure on No. 877. Nos. 876-877 are designed to produce a three dimensional effect when viewed together.

1992 Olympic Games A474

Designs: No. 878, Skier, Albertville. No. 879, Swimmer, Barcelona.

1992, Feb. 4 **Litho.** ***Perf. 14***

878 A474 2.10m multicolored 1.00 .40
879 A474 2.90m multicolored 1.40 .75

Expo '92, Seville — A475

1992, Mar. 20 **Litho.** ***Perf. 14***

880 A475 3.40m multicolored 1.50 .75

Conference on Security and Cooperation in Europe, Helsinki A476

1992, Mar. 20 ***Perf. 14½x15***

881 A476 16m multicolored 6.00 3.50

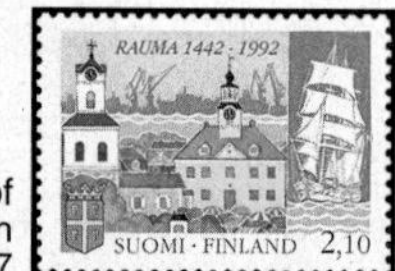

Town of Rauma, 550th Anniv. — A477

1992, Mar. 27 ***Perf. 14***

882 A477 2.10m multicolored 1.40 .40

Healthy Brains — A478

1992, Mar. 27

883 A478 3.50m multicolored 1.40 1.00

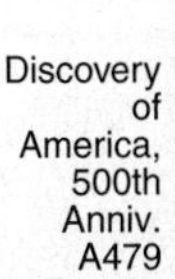

Discovery of America, 500th Anniv. A479

Designs: No. 884, Santa Maria, map. No. 885, Map, Columbus.

1992, May 8 Litho. *Perf. 12½x13*

884 A479 2.10m multicolored *2.25 .30*
885 A479 2.10m multicolored *2.25 .30*
a. Pair, #884-885 *4.50 5.00*

Europa.

Finnish Technology A480

Hologram of trees and: 2.10m, Drawing of blowing machine. 2.90m, Schematic of electronic circuits. 3.40m, Triangles and grid.

1992, May 8 *Perf. 13x12½*

886 A480 2.10m multicolored 1.10 .60
887 A480 2.90m multicolored 1.40 .75
888 A480 3.40m multicolored 1.75 1.20
Nos. 886-888 (3) 4.25 2.55

First Finnish patent granted, sesqui. (No. 886), Finnish chairmanship of Eureka (No. 887), Government Technology Research Center, 50th anniv. (No. 888).

Nos. 886-888 have holographic images. Soaking in water may affect the hologram.

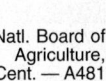

Natl. Board of Agriculture, Cent. — A481

Design: Currant harvesting.

1992, June 4 Litho. *Perf. 14*

889 A481 2.10m multicolored 1.00 .40

Finnish Women A482

No. 890, Aurora Karamzin (1808-1902), founder of Deaconesses' Institution of Helsinki. No. 891, Baroness Sophie Mannerheim (1863-1928), reformer of nursing education. No. 892, Laimi Leidenius (1877-1938), physician and educator. No. 893, Miina Sillanpaa (1866-1952), Minister for social affairs. No. 894, Edith Sodergran (1892-1923), poet. No. 895, Kreeta Haapasalo (1813-1893), folk singer.

Litho. & Engr.

1992, June 8 *Perf. 14*

Booklet Stamps

890 A482 2.10m multicolored 1.00 .55
891 A482 2.10m multicolored 1.00 .55
892 A482 2.10m multicolored 1.00 .55
893 A482 2.10m multicolored 1.00 .55
894 A482 2.10m multicolored 1.00 .55
895 A482 2.10m multicolored 1.00 .55
a. Booklet pane of 6, #890-895 6.00 7.25
Complete booklet, #895a 6.00

Child's Painting A483

Independence, 75th Anniv. — A484

1992, Oct. 5 Litho. *Perf. 13*

896 A483 2.10m multicolored 1.00 .40

Souvenir Sheet

Perf. 13½

897 A484 2.10m multicolored 1.90 1.20

Nordia '93 — A485

Illustrations depicting "Moomin" characters, by Tove Jansson: No. 898, Winter scene, ice covered bridges. No. 899, Winter scene in forest. No. 900, Boats in water. No. 901, Characters on beach.

Perf. 13 on 3 Sides

1992, Oct. 9 Litho.

Booklet Stamps

898 A485 2.10m multicolored 2.75 .55
899 A485 2.10m multicolored 2.75 .55
900 A485 2.10m multicolored 2.75 .55
901 A485 2.10m multicolored 2.75 .55
a. Booklet pane of 4, #898-901 11.00 11.50
Complete booklet, #901a 11.00

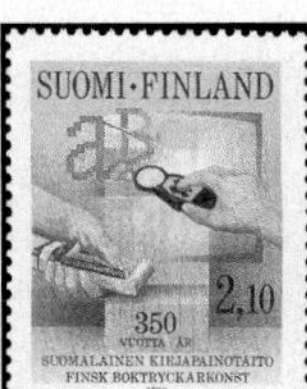

A486

1992, Oct. 20 Litho. *Perf. 13*

902 A486 2.10m multicolored 1.00 .40

Printing in Finland, 350th anniv.

Christmas A487

Designs: 1.80m, Church of St. Lawrence, Vantaa. 2.10m, Stained glass window of nativity scene, Karkkila Church, vert.

1992, Oct. 30 Litho. *Perf. 14*

903 A487 1.80m multicolored 1.25 .45
904 A487 2.10m multicolored 1.25 .45

Central Chamber of Commerce, 75th Anniv. — A488

1993, Feb. 8 Litho. *Perf. 14*

905 A488 1.60m multicolored .75 .50

Friendship A489

1993, Feb. 8 Litho. *Perf. 14*

906 A489 1 multicolored 2.50 .40
a. Booklet pane of 5 + label 14.00 7.50
Complete booklet, 2 #906a 28.00

No. 906 sold for 2m at time of release. See note following No. 845.

See Estonia No. 237.

Alopex Lagopus — A490

a, Adult with winter white coat. b, Face, full view, winter white coat. c, Mother, kits, summer coat. d, Two on rock, summer coat.

1993, Mar. 19 Litho. *Perf. 12½x13*

907 A490 Block of 4 5.50 5.50
a.-d. 2.30m Any single 1.40 .45

World Wildlife Fund.

Sculptures A491

Europa: 2m, Rumba, by Martti Aiha. 2.90m, Complete Works, by Kari Caven.

1993, Apr. 26 *Perf. 13*

908 A491 2m multicolored *1.90 .25*
909 A491 2.90m multicolored *1.40 .60*

Organized Philately in Finland, Cent. — A492

Design: Rosa pimpinellifolia.

1993, May 6 *Perf. 13x12½*

910 A492 2.30m multicolored 1.10 .70

Vyborg Castle, 700th Anniv. A493

1993, May 6 *Perf. 13½*

911 A493 2.30m multicolored 2.00 .40

Tourism A494

1993, May 7 *Perf. 13x12½*

912 A494 2.30m Naantali 1.00 .25
913 A494 2.90m Imatra 1.25 .70

550th anniv. of Naantali (No. 912).

A495

Independent Finland Defense Forces, 75th Anniv.: 2.30m, Finnish landscape in form of soldier's silhouette. 3.40m, UN checkpoint of Finnish battalion, Middle East.

1993, June 4 Litho. *Perf. 14*

914 A495 2.30m multicolored .85 .25
915 A495 3.40m multicolored 1.40 1.00

A496

Art by Martta Wendelin (1893-1986): No. 916, Boy on skis, 1936. No. 917, Mother, daughter knitting, 1931. No. 918, Children building snowman, 1931. No. 919, Mother, children at fence, 1935. #920, Girl with lamb, 1936.

Booklet Stamps

1993, June 14 Litho. *Perf. 12½x13*

916 A496 2.30m multicolored 1.50 .45
917 A496 2.30m multicolored 1.50 .45
918 A496 2.30m multicolored 1.50 .45
919 A496 2.30m multicolored 1.50 .45
920 A496 2.30m multicolored 1.50 .45
a. Booklet pane of 5, #916-920 7.50 8.00
Complete booklet, #920a 9.50

Water Birds — A497

No. 921, Flock of gavia arctica. No. 922, Pair of gavia arctica. No. 923, Mergus merganser. No. 924, Anas platyrhynchos. No. 925, Mergus serrator.

Perf. 12½x13 on 3 or 4 Sides

1993, Sept. 20 Litho.

Booklet Stamps

921 A497 2.30m multicolored 1.10 .75
922 A497 2.30m multicolored 1.10 .75

Size: 26x40mm

923 A497 2.30m multicolored 1.10 .75
924 A497 2.30m multicolored 1.10 .75
925 A497 2.30m multicolored 1.10 .75
a. Booklet pane of 5, #921-925 5.50 5.50
Complete booklet, #925a 7.50

Physical Education in Finnish Schools, 150th Anniv. — A498

1993, Oct. 8 *Perf. 14*

926 A498 2.30m multicolored .90 .35

Souvenir Sheet

New Opera House, Helsinki — A499

Operas and ballet: a, 2.30m, Ostrobothnians, by Leevi Madetoja. b, 2.30m, The Faun (four dancers), by Claude Debussy. c, 2.90m, Giselle, by Adolphe Adam. d, 3.40m, The Magic Flute, by Wolfgang Amadeus Mozart.

1993, Oct. 8 ***Perf. 13***

927 A499 Sheet of 4 6.00 7.00
a.-b. 2.30m Either single 1.10 .70
c. 2.90m multi 1.75 1.75
d. 3.40m multi 1.75 *2.25*

Christmas — A500

Designs: 1.80m, Christmas tree, elves. 2.30m, Three angels.

1993, Nov. 5 **Litho.** ***Perf. 14***

928 A500 1.80m multi 1.25 .40
a. Booklet pane of 10 16.00 16.00
Complete booklet, #928a 16.00
929 A500 2.30m multi 1.25 .40

Pres. Mauno Koivisto, 70th Birthday — A501

1993, Nov. 25

930 A501 2.30m multicolored .80 .40

Friendship — A502

Moomin characters: No. 931, Two standing. No. 932, Seven running.

1994, Jan. 27 **Litho.** ***Perf. 12½x13***

Booklet Stamps

931 A502 1 multicolored 2.50 .40
932 A502 1 multicolored 2.50 .40
a. Bklt. pane, 4 each #931-932 20.00 10.00
Complete booklet, #932a 20.00

Nos. 931-932 each sold for 2.30m at time of release. See note following No. 845.

Souvenir Sheet

Intl. Olympic Committee, Cent. — A503

Winter Olympics medalists from Finland: a, Marja-Liisa Kirvesniemi, Marjo Matikainen, cross-country skiing. b, Clas Thunberg, speed skating. c, Veikko Kankkonen, ski jumping. d, Veikko Hakulinen, cross-country skiing.

1994, Jan. 27 ***Perf. 13***

933 A503 4.20m Sheet of 4, #a-d 8.00 9.50

See No. 939.

A504

Waino Aaltonen (1894-1966), Sculptor — A505

1994, Mar. 8

934 A504 2m "Peace" 1.00 .40
935 A505 2m "Muse" 1.00 .40
a. Pair, #934-935 2.10 2.10

Postal Service Civil Servants' Federation, Cent. — A506

1994, Mar. 11

936 A506 2.30m multicolored .85 .45

Finnish Technology A507

Europa: 2.30m, Paper roll, nitrogen fixation, safety lock, ice breaker MS Fennica. 4.20m, Radiosonde, fishing lure, mobile phone, wind power plant.

1994, Mar. 18

937 A507 2.30m multicolored *1.40 .25*
938 A507 4.20m multicolored *1.90 1.10*

Olympic Athlete Type of 1994

Souvenir Sheet

Finnish athletes: a, Riitta Salin, Pirjo Haggman, runners. b, Lasse Viren, runner. c, Tiina Lillak, javelin thrower. d, Pentti Nikula, pole vaulter.

1994, May 5 **Litho.** ***Perf. 13***

939 A503 4.20m Sheet of 4, #a-d 8.00 8.00

European Track & Field Championships, Finlandia '95.

Finlandia '95, Helsinki — A508

Coccinella septempunctata.

1994, May 10 ***Perf. 13½x13***

940 A508 16m multicolored 9.00 8.00

See Nos. 962, 1009.

Miniature Sheet

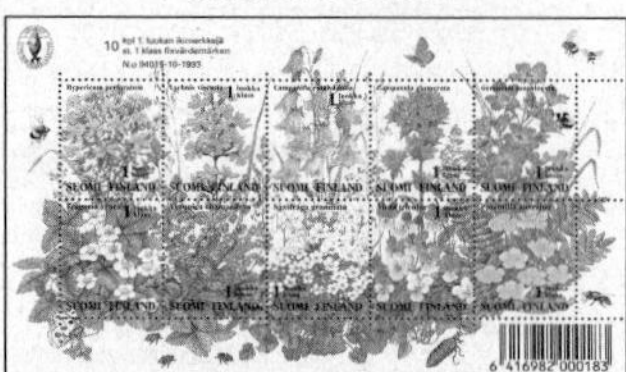

Wildflowers — A509

Designs: a, Hypericum perforatum (b). b, Lychnis viscaria. c, Campanula rotundifolia. d, Campanula glomerata. e, Geranium sanguineum (d). f, Fragaria vesca. g, Veronica chamaedrys (f, h). h, Saxifraga granulata (c, i). i, Viola tricolor (j). j, Potentilla anserina.

1994, June 1 ***Perf. 12***

941 A509 1 Sheet of 10 25.00 22.50
a.-j. Any single 2.50 .40

No. 941 sold for 23m at time of release. See note following No. 845.

Finland-Sweden Track and Field Meet — A510

No. 942, Seppo Raty, Finland, javelin. No. 943, Patrick Sjoberg, Sweden, high jump.

1994, Aug. 26 **Litho.** ***Perf. 12½***

Booklet Stamps

942 A510 2.40m multicolored 1.10 .60
943 A510 2.40m multicolored 1.10 .60
a. Booklet pane, 2 each #942-943 4.50 4.50
Complete booklet, #943a 4.50

See Sweden Nos. 2091-2092.

Population Registers, 450th Anniv. — A511

1994, Sept. 1

944 A511 2.40m multicolored 1.10 .35

Intl. Year of the Family — A512

1994, Sept. 1

945 A512 3.40m multicolored 1.40 .90

Souvenir Sheet

Letter Writing Day — A513

Dog Hill Kids in the Post Office: a, At Post Office window. b, Standing in doorway, mail cart. c, Blowing horn, pig. d, Putting letters in mailbox.

1994, Oct. 7 **Litho.** ***Perf. 14***

946 A513 2.80m Sheet of 4, #a-d 5.00 5.00

Christmas A514

2.10m, Reindeer, bullfinches on antlers. 2.80m, Elves among snow-covered trees.

1994, Nov. 4

947 A514 2.10m multi 1.25 .25
a. Booklet pane of 10 16.00 16.00
Complete booklet, #947a 18.00
948 A514 2.80m multi, vert. 1.40 .50

Greetings — A515

"Dog Hill Kids," sending/receiving greetings: No. 949, Delivering mail to Moon, spaceman. No. 950, Cat writing letter, clown. No. 951, Receiving mail from postman, baby. No. 952, Writing in bed, friend. No. 953, Winter scene at mailbox, characters at beach. No. 954, On bus, girl friend. No. 955, Standing at microphone with guitar, fan. No. 956, Baby in play pen, teddy bear.

Perf. 13 on 3 Sides

1995, Jan. 30 **Litho.**

Booklet Stamps

949 A515 2.80m multicolored 1.75 .75
950 A515 2.80m multicolored 1.75 .75
951 A515 2.80m multicolored 1.75 .75
952 A515 2.80m multicolored 1.75 .75
953 A515 2.80m multicolored 1.75 .75
954 A515 2.80m multicolored 1.75 .75
955 A515 2.80m multicolored 1.75 .75
956 A515 2.80m multicolored 1.75 .75
a. Booklet pane, #949-956 14.00 14.00
Complete booklet, 956a 14.00

Nos. 949-952 are printed tete beche with Nos. 953-956. Soaking in water may affect the holographic images on Nos. 949-956.

Souvenir Sheet

Team Sports — A516

a, Paivi Ikola, pesapallo. b, Jari Kurri, ice hockey. c, Jari Litmanen, soccer. d, Lea Hakala, basketball.

1995, Jan. 30 ***Perf. 13***

957 A516 3.40m Sheet of 4, #a-d 7.00 7.00

See No. 961.

Membership in European Union — A517

1995, Jan. 30 ***Perf. 14***

958 A517 3.50m multicolored 1.75 .90

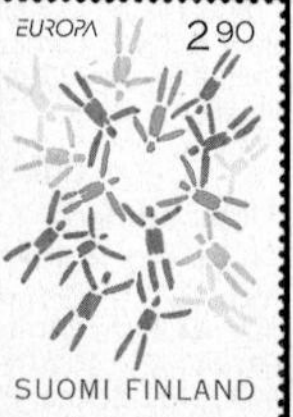

Peace & Liberty — A518

Europa: 2.90m, Stylized parachutists.

1995, Mar. 1 Litho. *Perf. 14*

959 A518 2.90m multicolored *1.90 .45*

Endangered Species — A519

Designs: a, Felis lynx. b, Lake, forest. c, Rocks, lake. d, Pusa hispida.

1995, Mar. 1 *Perf. 13*

960 Block of 4 5.50 5.50
a.-d. A519 2.90m Any single 1.40 1.00

Nos. 960a-960b, 960c-960d are continuous designs. See Russia No. 6249.

Athlete Type of 1995
Souvenir Sheet

Motor sports drivers in cars, on motorcycles: a, Timo Makinen. b, Juha Kankkunen. c, Tommi Ahvala. d, Heikki Mikkola.

1995, May 10 Litho. *Perf. 13*

961 A516 3.50m Sheet of 4, #a.-d. 6.50 6.50

Insect Type of 1994

1995, May 11

962 A508 19m Geotrupes stercorarius 12.50 12.50

Tourism — A520

Designs: 2.80m, Linnanmaki amusement park, Helsinki. 2.90m, Town of Mantyharju.

1995, May 12

963 A520 2.80m multicolored 1.75 .50
964 A520 2.90m multicolored 1.75 .70

Town of Loviisa, 250th Anniv. — A521

1995, June 30 Litho. *Perf. 14*

965 A521 3.20m multicolored 1.40 1.00

Intl. Union of Forestry Research Organizations, 20th World Congress, Tampere — A522

Designs: No. 966, Betula pendula. No. 967, Pinus sylvestris. No. 968, Picea abies. No. 969, Research, tree grown from needle.

Perf. 14 on 2 or 3 Sides

1995, Aug. 8 Litho.

Booklet Stamps

966 A522 2.80m multicolored 1.25 .50
967 A522 2.80m multicolored 1.25 .50
968 A522 2.80m multicolored 1.25 .50
969 A522 2.80m multicolored 1.25 .50
a. Booklet pane of 4, #966-969 5.25 5.25
Complete booklet, #969a 5.25

Wilhelm Roentgen (1845-1923), Discovery of the X-Ray, Cent. — A523

1995, Aug. 8 *Perf. 14*

970 A523 4.30m multicolored 1.90 1.25

Cats — A525

Designs: No. 972, Somali. No. 973, Siamese. No. 974, Norwegian forest. No. 975, Persian. No. 976, European domestic female. No. 977, Three kittens, frog.

1995, Oct. 9 Litho. *Perf. 13½*

972 A525 2.80m multi 1.75 .65
973 A525 2.80m multi 1.75 .65
974 A525 2.80m multi 1.75 .65
975 A525 2.80m multi 1.75 .65

Size: 59x35mm

976 A525 2.80m multi 1.75 .65
977 A525 2.80m multi 1.75 .65
a. Booklet pane of 6, #972-977 11.00
Complete booklet, #977a 11.00

UN, 50th Anniv. — A526

1995, Oct. 20 *Perf. 14*

978 A526 3.40m multicolored 1.40 .90

A527

Christmas A528

1995, Nov. 3 Litho. *Perf. 14*

979 A527 2m Santa on skates 1.10 .25
980 A528 2.80m Poinsettias 1.10 .60

Letter Stamps — A529

1996, Feb 2 Litho. *Perf. 13½x14*

Booklet Stamps

981 A529 1m "M" .65 .65
982 A529 1m "O" .65 .65
983 A529 1m "I" .65 .65
984 A529 1m "H" .65 .65
985 A529 1m "E" .65 .65
986 A529 1m "J" .65 .65
987 A529 1m "A" .65 .65
988 A529 1m "N" .65 .65
989 A529 1m "T" .65 .65
990 A529 1m "P" .65 .65
991 A529 1m "U" .65 .65
992 A529 1m "S" .65 .65
a. Booklet pane of 12, #981-992 7.75 7.75
Complete booklet, No. 992a 7.75

UNICEF, 50th Anniv. — A530

1996, Feb. 2 *Perf. 14*

993 A530 2.80m multicolored 1.10 .55

Women's Gymnastics in Finland, Cent. — A531

1996, Feb. 26 Litho. *Perf. 13*

994 A531 2.80m multicolored 1.10 .55

Woman Suffrage, 90th Anniv. A532

Litho. & Engr.

1996, Mar. 8 *Perf. 13*

995 A532 3.20m multicolored *1.25 .75*

Europa.

Cinema, Cent. — A533

Finnish films: No. 996, "Juha," 1937. No. 997, "Laveata Tieta," 1931. No. 998, "Tuntematon Sotilas," 1935. No. 999, Oldest known photo of a motion picture show, 1896. No. 1000, "Jäniksen Vuosi," 1977. No. 1001, "Valkoinen Peura," 1952. No. 1002, "Kaikki Rakastavat," 1935. No. 1003, "Varjoja Paratiisissa," 1986.

1996, Apr. 1 Litho. *Perf. 14x13½*

Booklet Stamps

996 A533 2.80m multicolored 1.40 .70
997 A533 2.80m multicolored 1.40 .70
998 A533 2.80m multicolored 1.40 .70
999 A533 2.80m multicolored 1.40 .70
1000 A533 2.80m multicolored 1.40 .70
1001 A533 2.80m multicolored 1.40 .70
1002 A533 2.80m multicolored 1.40 .70
1003 A533 2.80m multicolored 1.40 .70
a. Bklt. pane of 8, #996-1003 11.50 11.50
Complete booklet, #1003a 11.50

Radio, Cent. — A534

1996, Apr. 25 *Perf. 14*

1004 A534 4.30m multicolored 1.80 1.10

1996 Summer Olympic Games, Atlanta — A535

1996, June 3 Litho. *Perf. 12 Vert.*

Booklet Stamps

1005 A535 3.40m Kayaking 1.75 1.75
1006 A535 3.40m Sailing 1.75 1.75
1007 A535 3.40m Rowing 1.75 1.75
1008 A535 3.40m Swimming 1.75 1.75
a. Booklet pane of 4, #1005-1008 7.00 7.00
Complete booklet, #1008a 9.00

Insect Type of 1994

1996, July 1 Litho. *Perf. 13*

1009 A508 19m Dytiscus marginalis 11.00 11.00

Shore Birds — A536

No. 1010, Gallinago gallinago. No. 1011, Haematopus ostralegus. No. 1012, Scolopax rusticola. No. 1013, Vanellus vanellus. No. 1014, Numenius arquata.

Perf. 13½ on 3 Sides

1996, Sept. 6 Litho. & Engr.

1010 A536 2.80m multicolored 1.40 .70
1011 A536 2.80m multicolored 1.40 .70
1012 A536 2.80m multicolored 1.40 .70
1013 A536 2.80m multicolored 1.40 .70

Size: 30x52mm

1014 A536 2.80m multicolored 1.40 .70
a. Sheet of 5, #1010-1014 7.00 7.00

Finnish Comic Strips — A537

No. 1015, "Professor Itikainen" examining plant with magnifying glass, by Ilmari Vainio. No. 1016, "Pekka Puupää (Peter Blockhead)" taking letter from mailbox, by Ola Fogelberg. No. 1017, "Joonas" holding drawing pencil, by Veikko Savolainen. No. 1018, "Mämmilä" wearing helmet, by Tarmo Koivisto. No. 1019, "Rymy-Eetu" smoking pipe, by Erkki Tanttu. No. 1020, "Kieku" writing letter, by Asmo Alho. No. 1021, "Pikku Risunen" with animal, by Riitta Uusitalo. No. 1022, "Kiti" holding up pencil, by Kati Kovács.

1996, Oct. 9 Litho. *Perf. 13½*

Booklet Stamps

1015 A537 2.80m black & red 1.40 .75
1016 A537 2.80m black & red 1.40 .75
1017 A537 2.80m red & black 1.40 .75
1018 A537 2.80m black & red 1.40 .75
1019 A537 2.80m black & red 1.40 .75
1020 A537 2.80m red & black 1.40 .75
1021 A537 2.80m red & black 1.40 .75
1022 A537 2.80m red & black 1.40 .75
a. Bklt. pane of 8, #1015-1022 11.00 11.00
Complete booklet, #1022a 11.00

Christmas A538

2m, Snowman, Santa, gnome playing musical instruments. 2.80m, Rabbit, reindeer watching northern lights. 3.20m, Santa reading letters.

1996, Nov. 1 Litho. *Perf. 14*

1023 A538 2m multi 1.75 .50
1024 A538 2.80m multi 1.75 .55
1025 A538 3.20m multi, vert. 2.75 .85
Nos. 1023-1025 (3) 6.25 1.90

Greetings Stamps — A539

End of 19th cent.: No. 1026, Two angels. No. 1027, Flowers in basket. No. 1028, Hand reaching through garland, bluebird. No. 1029, Boy, girl dancing. No. 1030, Boy, envelope, shamrocks. No. 1031, Clasping hands through heart-shaped garlands. No. 1032, Roses. No. 1033, Angel.

Perf. 13x12½ on 3 Sides

1997, Jan. 30 **Litho.**

Booklet Stamps

1026	A539 1 multicolored	2.50	.65
1027	A539 1 multicolored	2.50	.65
1028	A539 1 multicolored	2.50	.65
1029	A539 1 multicolored	2.50	.65
1030	A539 1 multicolored	2.50	.65
1031	A539 1 multicolored	2.50	.65
1032	A539 1 multicolored	2.50	.65
1033	A539 1 multicolored	2.50	.65
a.	Bklt. pane of 8, #1026-1033	20.00	20.00
	Complete booklet, #1033a	20.00	

Nos. 1026-1033 sold for 2.80m on day of issue.

Number on stamp represents class of mail.

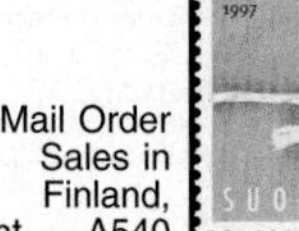

Mail Order Sales in Finland, Cent. — A540

1997, Jan. 30 ***Perf. 13½x14***

1034	A540 2.80m multicolored	1.10	.45

1997 Ice Hockey World Championships, Helsinki — A541

1997, Jan. 30

1035	A541 2.80m multicolored	1.20	.50

On each stamp from the right vertical row of the sheet, No. 1035 exists without the thin, curved black line at the center right edge of the stamp. Value, single stamp $3.00.

Lepus Timidus A542

1997, Mar. 4 **Litho.** ***Perf. 14***

1036	A542 2.80m multicolored	1.10	.40

Saami Folktale, "Girl Who Turned into a Golden Merganser" — A543

Europa: 3.20m, Duck, girl, prince. 3.40m, Girl falling into crevice.

1997, Mar. 4 ***Perf. 13***

1037	A543 3.20m multicolored	*1.50*	*.50*
1038	A543 3.40m multicolored	*2.00*	*1.00*

Paavo Nurmi (1897-1973), Winner of 9 Olympic Gold Medals — A544

1997, Mar. 18 ***Perf. 14***

1039	A544 3.40m multicolored	1.40	1.20

Southwest Archipelago Natl. Park — A545

Litho. & Engr.

1997, Apr. 25 ***Perf. 14***

1040	A545 4.30m multicolored	1.75	1.10

Tango — A546

1997, May 19 **Litho.**

1041	A546 1 multicolored	2.50	.40
	Complete booklet of 5	12.50	

No. 1041 sold for 2.80m on day of release. Number on stamp represents class of mail.

A547

Sailing Ships: No. 1042, Astrid. No. 1043, Jacobstads Wapen. No. 1044, Tradewind. No. 1045, Merikokko. No. 1046, Suomen Joutsen. No. 1047, Sigyn.

Booklet Stamps

1997, May 19 ***Perf. 13½***

1042	A547 2.80m multicolored	1.25	.60
1043	A547 2.80m multicolored	1.25	.60
1044	A547 2.80m multicolored	1.25	.60
1045	A547 2.80m multicolored	1.25	.60

Size: 48x25½mm

1046	A547 2.80m multicolored	1.25	.60
1047	A547 2.80m multicolored	1.25	.60
a.	Booklet pane of 6, #1042-1047	7.50	
	Complete booklet, #1047a	7.50	

Pres. Martti Ahtisaari, 60th Birthday A548

1997, June 23 **Litho.** ***Perf. 14***

1048	A548 2.80m multicolored	1.10	.40

Independence, 80th Anniv. — A549

Four seasons: No. 1049, Spring, lily-of-the-valley (natl. flower). No. 1050, Summer, white clouds. No. 1051, Fall, colorful leaves. No. 1052, Winter, snow crystals.

Perf. 13x12½ on 2 or 3 Sides

1997, June 23 **Booklet Stamps**

1049	A549 2.80m multicolored	1.10	.65
1050	A549 2.80m multicolored	1.10	.65
1051	A549 2.80m multicolored	1.10	.65
1052	A549 2.80m multicolored	1.10	.65
a.	Booklet pane, #1049-1052	4.50	4.50
	Complete booklet, #1052a	4.50	

Souvenir Sheet

A550

Grus Grus (Cranes): a, With young. b, With frog. c, Performing mating dance. d, In flight.

1997, Aug. 19 **Litho.** ***Perf. 14***

1053	A550 2.80m Sheet of 4, #a.-d.	5.00	5.00

A551

Finnish Writers Assoc. (Covers from books): No. 1054, "Seven Brothers," by Aleksis Kivi. No. 1055, "Sinuhe the Egyptian," by Mika Waltari. No. 1056, "Täällä Pohjantähden alla I," by Väinö Linna. No. 1057, "Hyvästi Iijoki," by Kalle Päätalo. No. 1058, "Haukka, minum rakkaani," by Kaari Utrio. No. 1059, "Juhannustanssit," by Hannu Salama. No. 1060, "Manillaköysi," by Veijo Meri. No. 1061, "Uppo-Nalle ja Kumma," by Elina Karjalainen.

Booklet Stamps

1997, Oct. 9 **Litho.** ***Perf. 14¼, 14½***

1054	A551 2.80m multicolored	1.25	.75
1055	A551 2.80m multicolored	1.25	.75
1056	A551 2.80m multicolored	1.25	.75
1057	A551 2.80m multicolored	1.25	.75
1058	A551 2.80m multicolored	1.25	.75
1059	A551 2.80m multicolored	1.25	.75
1060	A551 2.80m multicolored	1.25	.75
1061	A551 2.80m multicolored	1.25	.75
a.	Booklet pane, #1054-1061	10.00	10.00
	Complete booklet, #1061a	10.00	

No. 1056 exists perf 14½x14¼. The other values also should exist thus. The editors would like to examine such stamps.

Christmas A552

Designs: 2m, Village. 2.80m, Candelabra, vert. 3.20m, Church, vert.

1997, Oct. 31

1062	A552 2m multi	1.00	.40
1063	A552 2.80m multi	1.00	.40
1064	A552 3.20m multi	1.25	.65
	Nos. 1062-1064 (3)	3.25	1.45

Wildlife A553

2nd, Stizostedion lucioperca. 1st, Turdus merula.

Die Cut Perf. 10 Horiz. Syncopated

1998, Jan. 15 **Litho.**

Self-Adhesive

Coil Stamps

1065	A553 2 multicolored	2.75	.40
1066	A553 1 multicolored	2.00	.35

Nos. 1065-1066 were valued at 2.40m and 2.80m, respectively, on date of issue. Number on stamp represents class of mail.

See Nos. 1099-1100.

A554

Moomin Cartoon Characters, by Tove Jansson: No. 1067, Boy Moomin drawing with pad and pencil. No. 1068, Girl Moomin in sunshine. No. 1069, Organ grinder. No. 1070, Boy Moomin giving flower to girl Moomin.

1998, Jan. 15 ***Perf. 13 on 3 Sides***

Booklet Stamps

1067	A554 1 multicolored	2.90	.60
1068	A554 1 multicolored	2.90	.60
1069	A554 1 multicolored	2.90	.60
1070	A554 1 multicolored	2.90	.60
a.	Booklet pane, #1067-1070	12.00	12.00
	Complete booklet, #1070a	12.00	

Nos. 1067-1070 each sold for 2.80m on day of issue. Number on stamp represents class of mail.

See No. 1127.

A555

1998, Feb. 3 ***Perf. 14***

1071	A555 2.80m multicolored	1.20	.30

Finnish Federation of Nurses, cent.

A556

Valentine's Day Surprise Stamps. (Designs beneath scratch-off heart): a, Musical notes, two dogs. b, Elephant, mouse and flowers. c, Puppy, sealed envelope. d, Kittens, kittens hugging. e, Dog with nose in air, bouquet of flowers. f, Flowers, two rodents.

1998, Feb. 3 ***Perf. 12***

1072	1 Sheet of 6	15.00	9.50
a.-f.	A556 Any single, unscratched	2.50	.75

Nos. 1072a-1072f were each valued at 2.80m on day of issue. Number on stamp represents class of mail. Unused values are for singles with attached selvage. Inscriptions are shown in selvage above or below each stamp.

Each stamp bears a heart-shaped, golden scratch-off overlay. Values are for unscratched examples. Scratched stamps, with hearts partially or fully removed, sell for about 20 percent less.

Tussilago Farfara — A557

1998, Mar. 27 **Litho.** ***Perf. 14***

1073	A557 2.80m multi	1.20	.30

National Festivals A558

Europa: 3.20m, Boy and girl, balloons, "Vappu" (May Day). 3.40m, Boy and girl in a dream floating over water, Midsummer Festival.

1998, Mar. 27 ***Perf. 14x14½***

1074	A558 3.20m multicolored	*2.00*	*.30*
1075	A558 3.40m multicolored	*2.75*	*.80*

Finnish Marine Research Institute, 80th Anniv. — A559

Designs: 2.80m, Research vessel, "Aranda." 3.20m, "Vega," chart showing route of Nils Adolf Erik Nordenskjold's expedition.

Litho. & Engr.

1998, May 7 *Perf. 14x13*

1076 A559 2.80m multicolored 1.40 .40
1077 A559 3.20m multicolored 1.50 .60

First Performance of National Anthem, 150th Anniv. — A560

1998, May 7 *Perf. 13*

1078 A560 5m multicolored 2.00 1.00

Puppies A561

No. 1079, Bernese Mountain dog. No. 1080, Puli. No. 1081, Boxer. No. 1082, Bichon Frisé. No. 1083, Finnish lapphound. No. 1084, Wire-haired dachshund. No. 1085, Scottish cairn terrier. No. 1086, Labrador retriever.

Perf. 13½x13 on 2 or 3 Sides

1998, June 4 **Litho.**

Booklet Stamps

1079 A561 1 multicolored 2.50 .60
1080 A561 1 multicolored 2.50 .60
1081 A561 1 multicolored 2.50 .60
1082 A561 1 multicolored 2.50 .60
1083 A561 1 multicolored 2.50 .60
1084 A561 1 multicolored 2.50 .60
1085 A561 1 multicolored 2.50 .60
1086 A561 1 multicolored 2.50 .60
a. Booklet pane, #1079-1086 20.00 20.00
Complete booklet, #1086a 20.00

Nos. 1079-1086 each sold for 2.80m on day of issue. Number on stamp represents class of mail.

Owls — A562

Designs: a, Bubo bubo. b, Wing of bubo bubo. c, Bubo bubo, aegolius funereus. d, Strix nebulosa. e, Nyctea scandiaca.

1998, Sept. 4 **Litho.** *Perf. 13½*

1087 Sheet of 5 + label 6.00 6.00
a.-e. A562 3m any single 1.20 1.20

No. 1087b is 52x27mm; Nos. 1087c-1087d, 26x44mm; No. 1087e, 30x44mm.

See No. 1113.

Cycling — A563

1998, Sept. 4 *Perf. 14*

1088 A563 3m multicolored 1.25 1.25

Finnish Design — A564

No. 1089, Savoy vases, by Alvar Aalto. No. 1090, Karuselli chair, by Yrjö Kukkapuro. No. 1091, Tasaraita knitwear, designed by Annika Rimala for Marimekko. No. 1092, Kilta tableware set, by Kaj Franck. No. 1093, Cast iron pot, by Timo Sarpaneva. No. 1094, Carelia cutlery set, by Bertel Gardberg.

Perf. 13½ on 3 Sides

1998, Oct. 9 **Litho.**

Booklet Stamps

1089 A564 3m multicolored 1.40 .75
1090 A564 3m multicolored 1.40 .75
1091 A564 3m multicolored 1.40 .75
1092 A564 3m multicolored 1.40 .75
1093 A564 3m multicolored 1.40 .75
1094 A564 3m multicolored 1.40 .75
a. Booklet pane, #1089-1094 8.00 8.00
Complete booklet, #1094a 8.00

Nos. 1090-1091, 1093-1094 are 29x34mm.

Christmas A565

Designs: 2m, Christmas tree, children, vert. 3m, Children, dog riding sled. 3.20m, Winter scene of cottage in center of island.

1998, Oct. 30 *Perf. 14*

1095 A565 2m multicolored 1.25 .55
1096 A565 3m multicolored 1.40 .40
1097 A565 3.20m multicolored 1.50 .65
Nos. 1095-1097 (3) 4.15 1.60

Souvenir Sheet

Mika Häkkinen, Formula 1 Driving Champion — A566

1999, Jan. 15 *Perf. 13½*

1098 A566 3m multicolored 3.00 3.00

Native Wildlife Type of 1998

2, Salmo salar. 1, Luscinia svecica.

Coil Stamps

Die Cut Perf. 10 Horiz. Syncopated

1999, Jan. 27 **Litho.**

Self-Adhesive

1099 A553 2 multi 2.00 .60

Die Cut Perf. 10 Vert. Syncopated

1100 A553 1 multi, vert. 2.75 .60

Nos. 1099-1100 were valued at 2.40m and 3m, respectively, on day of issue. Number on stamp represents class of mail.

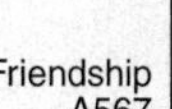

Friendship A567

Animals' tails: No. 1101, Zebra, lion. No. 1102, Dog, cat.

Booklet Stamps

Serpentine Die Cut Perf. 13 Horiz.

1999, Jan. 27 **Self-Adhesive**

1101 A567 3m multicolored 1.25 1.20
1102 A567 3m multicolored 1.25 1.20
a. Bklt. pane, 3 each #1101-1102 8.50 8.00

No. 1102a is a complete booklet.

Finnish Labor Movement, Cent. — A568

1999, Jan. 27 *Perf. 13½*

1103 A568 4.50m multicolored 1.80 1.80

Finland's Roads — A569

No. 1104, Snow-covered landscape, Arctic Ocean Road. No. 1105, Freeway interchanges, Jyväsjtkä Lakeshore Road. No. 1106, Raippaluoto Bridge. No. 1107, Wooded drive, Kitee.

1999, Feb. 15 **Litho.** *Perf. 14 Horiz.*

Booklet Stamps

1104 A569 3m multicolored 1.25 .75
a. Perf. 12¾ horiz. *75.00* *13.00*
1105 A569 3m multicolored 1.25 .75
a. Perf. 12¾ horiz. *75.00* *13.00*
1106 A569 3m multicolored 1.25 .75
a. Perf. 12¾ horiz. *75.00* *13.00*
1107 A569 3m multicolored 1.25 .75
a. Booklet pane, #1104-1107 5.00
Complete booklet, #1107a 6.00
b. Perf. 12¾ horiz. *75.00* *13.00*
c. Booklet pane, #1104a, 1105a, 1106a, 1107b *300.00* *300.00*
Complete booklet, #1107c *325.00*

A570

Women's Kalevala-style brooches: a, Horse clasp. b, Bird clasp. c, Virusmäki clasp.

1999, Feb. 15 *Perf. 13½x14*

1108 Sheet of 3 3.75 3.75
a.-c. A570 3m any single 1.25 1.10

1st Publication of Legend of the Kalevala, 150th Anniv.

Crocus Vernus — A571

1999, Mar. 15 *Perf. 13x13½*

1109 A571 3m multi 1.25 .60

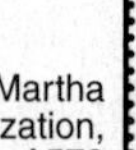

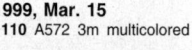

Martha Organization, Cent. — A572

1999, Mar. 15 *Perf. 13½x13*

1110 A572 3m multicolored 1.25 .60

Europa A573

Designs: 2.70m, Esplanade Park. 3.20m, Ruissalo Park.

1999, Mar. 15 *Perf. 13½x14*

1111 A573 2.70m multi *1.75* *.50*
1112 A573 3.20m multi *3.00* *.60*

Bird Type of 1998

Designs: a, Luscinia luscinia. b, Cuculus canorus. c, Botaurus stellaris. d, Caprimulgus europaeus. e, Crex crex.

1999, May 18 *Perf. 13½*

1113 Sheet of 5 + label 6.00 6.00
a.-e. A562 3m any single 1.10 .75

No. 1113b is 25x43mm. No. 1113c is 45x30mm. No. 1113d-1113e are 26x37mm.

Finland's Presidency of European Union — A574

1999, July 1 **Litho.** *Perf. 13¾x13½*

1114 A574 3.50m multicolored 1.40 .60

Finnish Entertainers A575

a, Harmony Sisters, Vera (1914-97), Maire (1916-95) & Raija (1918-97) Valtonen. b, Olavi Virta (1915-72), singer. c, Georg Malmstén (1902-81), composer, conductor. d, Topi Kärki (1915-22), composer, and Reino (Repe) Helismaa (1913-65), lyricist. e, Tapio Rautavaara (1915-79), singer. f, Esa Parkarinen (1911-89), musician, actor.

Perf. 13¼ on 3 Sides

1999, Sept. 6 **Litho.**

1115 Booklet pane of 6 8.50
a.-f. A575 3.50m any single 1.40 .75
Complete booklet, #1115 8.50

Nos. 1115a, 1115d are each 60x34mm.

Finnish Commercial Product Design — A576

a, Fiskars cutting tools. b, Zoel/Versoul guitars. c, Ergo II/Silenta hearing protectors. d, Ponsse Cobra HS 10 tree harvester. e, Suunto compass. f, Exel Avanti QLS ski pole.

Perf. 13¼ on 3 Sides

1999, Oct 8 **Litho.**

1116 Booklet pane of 6 8.00
a.-f. A576 3.50m any single 1.40 .75
Complete booklet, #1116 10.50

Size of b, c, e, f: 30x35mm.

"The Nativity," by Giorgio di Chirico (1888-1978) A577

Rabbits, Birds — A578

Design: 2.50m, Santa Claus, vert.

1999, Nov. 5 ***Perf. 14***

1117 A578 2.50m multicolored .90 .40
1118 A577 3m multicolored 1.20 1.20
1119 A578 3.50m multicolored 1.60 .60
Nos. 1117-1119 (3) 3.70 2.20

Christmas. See Italy Nos. 2314-2315.

Sveaborg Fortress — A579

2000, Jan. 12 Litho. ***Perf. 13¾x13½***

1120 A579 7.20m multi 3.00 1.75

Helsinki, 450th Anniv. A580

Designs: No. 1121, Baltic herring market (designer's name at UL).

No. 1122: a, Museum of Contemporary Art (blue building), vert. b, Cathedral, Senate Square (green building). c, Finlandia Hall (orange building). d, Glass Palace Film and Media Center (red building), vert.

No. 1123: a, Quest for the Lost Crown, Sveaborg Fortress (children and arch), vert. b, Like No. 1121, no designer's name. c, Forces of Light City Festival. d, Cellist at outdoor concert, Kaivopuisto Park.

2000, Jan. 12 ***Perf. 14***

1121 A580 3.50m multi 1.40 .70

Perf. 14½x14¾ (vert. stamps), 14¾x14½

1122 Booklet pane of 4 6.50 6.50
a.-d. A580 3.50m Any single 1.60 1.60
1123 Booklet pane of 4 6.50 6.50
a.-d. A580 3.50m Any single 1.60 1.60
Complete booklet, #1122-1123 13.00

Valentine's Day — A581

Designs: a, Earth as backpack. b, Painters on ladder. c, Birds in balloon. d, Alien with magnet. e, Boy with heart-shaped balloon. f, Polar bear and igloo.

Perf. 13x12¾ on 3 sides

2000, Jan. 12

1124 Bklt. pane of 6 + 4 labels 8.50
a.-f. A581 3.50m Any single 1.40 .70
Complete booklet, #1124 8.50

Souvenir Sheet of 2

Tommi Mäkinen, 1999 Rally World Champion — A582

a, Mäkinen behind wheel. b, Race car.

2000, Mar. 3 ***Perf. 13x13¼***

1125 A582 3.50m #a.-b. 3.00 3.00

Caltha Palustris — A583

2000, Mar. 15 ***Perf. 13¾x13¼***

1126 A583 3.50m multi 1.40 .70

Easter.

Moomin Type of 1998

a, Rat with broom looking at Moomins. b, Moomin with uniform, figures sprouting from ground. c, Moomin with hat in forest. d, Moomin with hat, children, in front of stove.

Perf. 13x12¾ on 3 Sides

2000, Mar. 15

1127 Booklet pane of 4 27.50 27.50
a.-d. A554 1 Any single 6.50 2.50
Complete booklet, #1127 30.00 12.00
e. As #1127, perf. 13¼ on 3 sides 12.00
f.-i. As #a-d, perf. 13¼ on 3 sides 2.75 .65
Booklet, #1127e 12.50

Nos. 1127a-1127d sold for 3.50m on day of issue. Number on stamp represents class of mail.

Issued: No. 1127e, 7/10/00.

Jubilee Year — A584

Turku Cathedral: a, Nave. b, Woman, votive candles. c, Christ on the Mount of Transfiguration, alterpiece. d, Infant baptism.

2000, Mar. 15 Litho. ***Perf. 14 Vert.***

1128 Booklet pane of 4 6.00 3.50
a.-d. A584 3.50m Any single 1.50 .60
Complete booklet, #1128 6.00

Europa, 2000

Common Design Type

2000, May 9 ***Perf. 13¼x13***

1129 CD17 3.50m multi 2.00 .60

Provincial Flowers

Spring Anemone A585

Blue Cornflower A586

Pulsatilla Patens — A587

Die Cut Perf. 13x12½

2000-01 **Litho.**

Booklet Stamps Self-Adhesive

1130 A585 1 multi 2.50 .50
a. Booklet pane of 10 16.00

Die Cut Perf. 14¾x13½

1131 A586 1 multi 2.50 .50
1132 A587 1 multi 2.50 .50
a. Booklet pane, 5 each #1131-1132 25.00

Number on stamp represents class of mail. No. 1130 sold for 3.50m at time of release. Nos. 1131-1132 each sold for 3.60m on day of issue. No. 1132a was issued in two printings. The white box containing the stamps on the original printing is 114mm wide and on the 2003 printing, the box is 110mm wide.

Issued: No. 1130, 5/9. Nos. 1131-1132, 5/16/01.

Souvenir Sheet

Science — A595

Designs: a, Children, molecuar model (triangular stamp). b, Man's face, DNA strand (rhomboid stamp). c, Man's face, Sierpinski triangles (square stamp).

2000, May 30 ***Perf. 14¼***

1140 A595 3.50m Sheet of 3, #a.-c. 4.25 4.25

No. 1140 has holographic image. Soaking in water may affect the hologram.

Finnish Design — A596

No. 1141: a, Rug, by Akseli Gallen-Kallela (1865-1931). b, Pearl Bird, by Birger Kaipiainen (1915-88). c, Pot, by Kyllikki Salmenhaara (1915-81). d, Leaf, by Tapio Wirkkala (1915-85). e, Detail from damask, by Dora Jung (1906-80). f, Glass vase, by Valter Jung (1879-1946).

Perf. 13¼ on 3 Sides

2000, Sept. 5 **Litho.**

1141 Booklet pane of 6 8.00 8.00
a.-f. A596 3.50m Any single 1.50 1.00
Booklet, #1141 8.00

Size of b, c, e, f: 30x35mm.

Coregonus Lavaretus A597

Lagopus Lagopus A598

Coil Stamps

Die Cut Perf. 10 Horiz. Syncopated

2000, Sept. 5 **Self-Adhesive**

1142 A597 2 multi 2.50 .50
1143 A598 1 multi 2.50 .50

Nos. 1142-1143 sold for 3m and 3.50m respectively on day of sale.

On modern stamps bearing the "denominations" "1" or "2," the number represents the class of mail.

Christmas A599

2.50m, Costumed Tiernapojat carol singers. 3.50m, Bullfinch on door ornament, vert.

Serpentine Die Cut 14¼

2000, Nov. 3 **Photo.**

Self-Adhesive

1144-1145 A599 Set of 2 3.00 .90

Litho.

Serpentine Die Cut 13¾

1146 A599 3.50m multi + label 7.00 5.25

No. 1146 issued in sheets of 20 that sold for 120m, together with a separate sheet of stickers that could be affixed on the label. The labels attached to the stamps are separated by a row of interrupted serpentine die cutting. Labels could be personalized with photographs taken at some sale sites.

European Year of Languages A600

2001, Jan. 17 **Litho.** ***Perf. 13¼***

1147 A600 1 multi 2.50 .75

No. 1147 sold for 3.50m on day of sale.

World Ski Championships, Lahti — A601

No. 1148: a, Ski jumper Janne Ahonen (yellow helmet). b, Skier Mika Myllylä.

2001, Jan. 17

1148 A601 3.50m Horiz. pair, #a-b 2.75 2.75

Valentine's Day — A602

No. 1149: a, Oval wreath. b, Basket of flowers, letter. c, Heart-shaped wreath. d, Bouquet of flowers, letter. e, Flowers, tea set. f, Flowers, heart-shaped pastry.

Serpentine Die Cut 11½x11¾ on 3 Sides

2001, Jan. 17 **Photo.**

Self-Adhesive

1149 Booklet pane of 6 15.00 10.00
a.-f. A602 1 Any single 2.50 .75
Booklet, #1149 15.00

Nos. 1149a-1149f each sold for 3.50m on day of issue.

Souvenir Sheet

Donald Duck Comics in Finland, 50th Anniv. — A603

No. 1150: a, Mickey Mouse, Donald Duck, Santa Claus, Goofy. b, First comics, silhouette of boy. c, Tin soldier with Finnish flag, Chip and Dale (25x30mm). d, Finnish epic hero Väinämöinien, silhouette of Donald Duck. e, Helsinki Cathedral, Donald Duck.

Perf. 7¾ on 3 or 4 Sides

2001, Mar. 13 **Litho.**

1150 A603 1 Sheet of 5, #a-e 12.50 8.00

Nos. 1150a-1150e sold for 3.50m each on day of issue.

Santa Claus and Sleigh — A604

2001-04 ***Serpentine Die Cut 14½x14***

Self-Adhesive

1151 A604 1 multi 2.50 .75
a. Serpentine die cut 13¾x13¼ ('04) 2.75 .80

No. 1151 sold for 3.60m on day of issue. No. 1151a sold for 65c on day of issue.
No. 1151, 4/2/01. No. 1151a, 12/04.

Europa A605

2001, Apr. 2 ***Perf. 13x13½***

1152 A605 5.40m multi *3.00 3.00*

Easter — A606

No. 1153: a, Chick. b, Decorated egg.

2001, Apr. 2 ***Perf. 13¼***

1153 A606 3.60m Horiz. pair, #a-b 2.75 2.50

Souvenir Sheet

Verla Mill, UNESCO World Heritage Site — A607

Denominations in: a, UL. b, UR. c, LL. d, LR.

2001, Apr. 2

1154 A607 3.60m Sheet of 4, #a-d 5.50 4.00

Orienteering World Championships, Tampere — A608

2001, May 16

1155 A608 3.60m multi 1.75 .75

Values are for stamps with surrounding selvage.

Souvenir Sheet

Woodpeckers — A609

No. 1156: a, Dendrocopos minor (32x36mm). b, Picoides tridactylus (29x36mm). c, Dendrocopos leucotos (32x42mm). d, Dendrocopos major (29x42mm). e, Picus canus (32x41mm). f, Dryocopus martius (29x41mm).

Perf. 14½x14¼ on 2, 3 or 4 Sides

2001, May 16

1156 A609 3.60m Sheet of 6, #a-f 10.00 8.00

Marine Life — A610

No. 1157: a, Lampetra fluviatilis. b, Aspius aspius. c, Coregonus albula.

Die Cut Perf. 10 Horiz. Syncopated

2001, Sept. 6 **Photo.**

Self-Adhesive

Coil Stamps

1157 Horiz. strip of 3 7.00 5.00
a.-c. A610 2 Any single 2.25 .35

Nos. 1157a-1157c were sold in boxes of 100 stamps that sold at a discount price of 270m on day of sale. The franking value on the day of sale for each stamp was 3m.

Birds A611

No. 1158: a, Parus caeruleus. b, Motacilla alba. c, Oriolus oriolus.

Die Cut Perf. 10 Horiz. Syncopated

2001, Sept. 6 **Photo.**

Self-Adhesive

Coil Stamps

1158 Horiz. strip of 3 7.00 4.75
a.-c. A611 1 Any single 2.25 .35

Nos. 1158a-1158c were sold in boxes of 100 stamps that sold at a discount price of 330m on day of sale. The franking value on the day of sale for each stamp was 3.60m.

History of Gulf of Finland A612

No. 1159: a, Utö Lighthouse. b, Wreck of the St. Mikael. c, Diver exploring St. Mikael. d, Opossum shrimp, isopod. e, Ship's cabin and nautical chart (32x55mm).

Perf. 13¼x13¾ on 2 or 3 Sides

2001, Sept. 6 **Litho.**

1159 Booklet pane of 5 12.50 9.50
a.-e. A612 1 Any single 2.50 1.00
Booklet, #1159 12.50

Nos. 1159a-1159e each sold for 3.60m on day of sale.
See No. 1177.

Christmas A613

Designs: 2.50m, Elf reading Santa's book, candle. 3.60m, Elf delivering package on sled, horiz.

Serpentine Die Cut 14¼

2001, Oct. 26 **Photo.**

Self-Adhesive

1160 A613 2.50m multi 1.10 .40
1161 A613 3.60m multi 1.40 .65

Slightly larger examples of Nos. 1160-1161 serpentine die cut 14 are known on first day and other covers produced by the postal service. They were not sold unused to the public.

100 Cents = 1 Euro (€)

Flowers — A614

National Symbols A615

Heraldic Lion — A616

Type A614 — No. 1162, Myosotis scorpioides: a, Forty-one flowers. b, Four flowers, five buds. c, One flower, four buds. d, Entire plant. e, Five flowers.

No. 1163, Convallaria majallis: a, Leaf, stem with five flowers. b, Two leaves, stem with eight flowers. c, Two flowers. d, Two leaves, stem with five flowers. e, Entire plants.

Type A615: 50c, Swan, vert. 60c, Birch. 1, Flag and bird. 90c, Kymintehtaalta, by Victor Westerholm. €1.30, Granite cliff. €2.50, Spruce. €3.50, Pine.

Die Cut Perf. 15

2002, Jan. 1 **Photo.**

Self-Adhesive

1162 Vert. strip of 5 .80 .80
a.-e. A614 5c Any single .25 .25
f. As #1162, die cut perf 14 .80
g.-k. A614 5c Any single, die cut perf 14 .25 .25

Die Cut Perf. 14

1163 Vert. strip of 5 1.75 1.75
a.-e. A614 10c Any single .35 .25
1164 A615 50c multi 1.60 .40
1165 A615 60c multi 2.00 .40

Die Cut Perf. 13¾

1166 A615 1 multi 2.50 .40
a. Booklet pane of 10 25.00
Booklet, #1166a 25.00

Die Cut Perf. 14¾x15

1167 A615 90c multi 3.00 .65

Die Cut Perf. 12 Syncopated

1168 A616 €1 blue & multi 3.25 .65

Die Cut Perf. 14¾x15

1169 A615 €1.30 multi 4.00 1.20
a. Die cut perf 14 ('04) 4.50 1.20

Die Cut Perf. 14

1170 A615 €2.50 multi 8.00 1.25
1171 A615 €3.50 multi 11.00 1.75

Die Cut Perf. 12 Syncopated

1172 A616 €5 red & multi 16.00 5.00
Nos. 1162-1172 (11) 53.90 14.25

No. 1166 sold for 60c on day of issue.

Die cut perf 14 examples of No. 1167 exist on first day and other covers produced by the postal service. They were not sold unused to the public.

No. 1169a issued 7/04. No. 1169a has a duller blue panel and a duller black denomination than that found on No. 1169, and a die cut perf. 14 version of No. 1169 that was available only on first day covers with 1/1/02 cancels, and which was not made available to the public unused. Nos. 1169 and 1169a were produced by different printers.

Nos. 1162f-1162k were printed and put on first day and other covers in 2002 but were not sold to the public until 2006.

See Nos. 1179-1180, 1383-1384.

Easter — A617

Die Cut Perf. 14

2002, Mar. 6 **Photo.**

Self-Adhesive

1173 A617 60c multi 1.90 .75

Souvenir Sheet

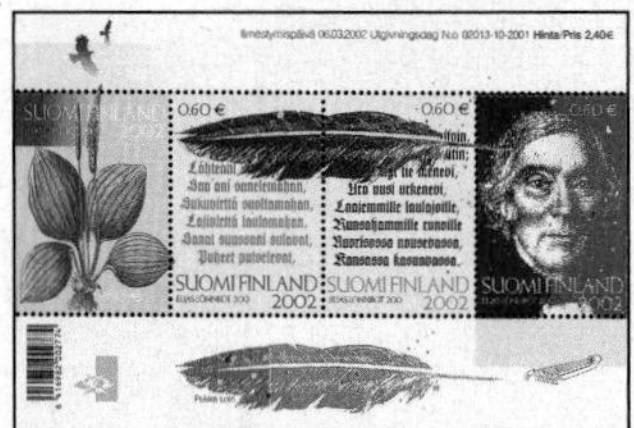

Elias Lönnrot (1802-84), Botanist, Linguist — A618

No. 1174: a, Plantain. b, Opening lines of "Kalevala" (denomination at UL). c, Closing lines of "Kalevala" (denomination at UR). d, Portrait.

Perf. 13¼ on 3 or 4 Sides

2002, Mar. 6 Litho.

1174 A618 60c Sheet of 4, #a-d 7.50 5.50

Souvenir Sheet

Old Rauma, UNESCO World Heritage Site — A619

Denominations at: a, UL. b, UR. c, LL. d, LR.

2002, Mar. 6 ***Perf. 13½***

1175 A619 60c Sheet of 4, #a-d 7.50 5.50

Europa — A620

2002, Apr. 15 ***Perf. 13***

1176 A620 60c multi *2.50 1.25*

Gulf of Finland Type of 2001

No. 1177: a, Birds, fish. b, Sailboat, plankton. c, Flounder on sea bed. d, Shrimp, herring. e, Tvärminne Zoological Station, ship, isopod, oceanographic equipment, mussels (32x55mm).

Perf. 13¼x13¾ on 2 or 3 Sides

2002, Apr. 15

1177 Booklet pane of 5 12.50 9.00
a.-e. A612 1 Any single 2.50 1.25
Booklet, #1177 12.50

Nos. 1177a-1177e each sold for 60c on day of issue.

Sibelius Monument, Helsinki, by Eila Hiltunen A621

2002, May 3 ***Perf. 13***

1178 A621 60c multi 1.90 .50

National Symbols Type of 2002 Without Finland Post Emblem

Designs: 60c, Juniperus communis. 1, Reindeer in Lapland.

Die Cut Perf. 14

2002, Oct. 9 Photo.

Self-Adhesive

1179 A615 60c multicolored 1.90 .50
1180 A615 1 multicolored 2.50 .50

No. 1180 sold for 60c on day of issue.

Christmas A622

Designs: 45c, Horse-drawn sleigh. 60c, Angel with trumpet, vert.

Serpentine Die Cut 14¼

2002, Nov. 1 Self-Adhesive

1181-1182 A622 Set of 2 3.75 1.50

Fish — A623

No. 1183: a, Abramis brama. b, Salmo trutta lacustris. c, Esox lucius.

Syncopated Die Cut Perf. 10 Horiz.

2003, Jan. 15 Self-Adhesive

Coil Stamps

1183 Horiz. strip of 3 8.00 8.00
a.-c. A623 2 Any single 2.50 2.50

Nos. 1183a-1183c were sold in boxes of 100 that sold at a discount price of €47 on day of issue. The franking value on the day of issue for each stamp was 50c.

Birds — A624

No. 1184: a, Cuculus canorus. b, Alauda arvensis. c, Perisoreus infaustus.

Syncopated Die Cut Perf. 10 Horiz.

2003, Jan. 15 Self-Adhesive

Coil Stamps

1184 Horiz. strip of 3 8.00 8.00
a.-c. A624 1 Any single 2.50 2.50

Nos. 1184a-1184c were sold in boxes of 100 that sold at a discount price of €57 on day of issue. The franking value on the day of issue for each stamp was 60c.

Viivi and Wagner, by Jussi Tuomola — A625

No. 1185: a, Viivi and Wagner running. b, Viivi and Wagner dancing. c, Viivi writing love letter. d, Wagner and Viivi in bed. e, Viivi and Wagner kissing. f, Wagner reading love letter.

Serpentine Die Cut 11½x11¾ on 3 Sides

2003, Jan. 15 Self-Adhesive

1185 Booklet pane of 6 15.00
a.-f. A625 1 Any single 2.50 1.25
Booklet, #1185 15.00

Nos. 1185a-1185f each sold for 60c on day of issue.

Ice Hockey World Championships — A626

2003, Mar. 3 Litho. ***Perf. 13¼x13¾***

1186 A626 65c multi 2.00 .75

St. Bridget (1303-73) — A627

2003, Mar. 3 ***Perf. 13***

1187 A627 65c multi 2.00 .75

Viola Wittrockiana — A628

Die Cut Perf. 13¾x14

2003, Mar. 3 Photo.

Self-Adhesive

1188 A628 65c multi 2.00 1.25

Fighting Wood Grouses, by Ferdinand von Wright — A629

2003, Mar. 3 ***Die Cut Perf. 13¾***

Self-Adhesive

1189 A629 90c multi 3.00 1.25

Airplanes A630

No. 1190: a, Super Caravelle. b, Airbus 320. c, Junkers Ju 52/3m. d, Douglas DC-3.

Perf. 14x14½ on 3 Sides

2003, Mar. 3

1190 Booklet pane of 4 + 4 etiquettes 8.00 —
a.-d. A630 65c Any single 2.00 1.00
Complete booklet, #1190 8.00

Finnair, 80th anniv.; Powered flight, cent.

Europa A631

No. 1191 — Posters by Lasse Hietala: a, Woman with newspaper. b, Hearts.

2003, May 7 Litho. ***Perf. 13¾x13¼***

1191 A631 Pair *4.25 3.75*
a.-b. 65c Either single 1.90 1.50

Souvenir Sheet

Flora and Fauna Seen in Summer — A632

No. 1192: a, Moth, flowers (35x29mm). b, Dragonfly, grasshopper (44x35mm). c, Grasshopper, caterpillar, thistle (35x25mm). d, Frog, flowers, butterfly, insects (44x36mm). e, Magpie, snail, flowers (35x46mm). f, Hedgehog, bee, ant, spider, flowers (44x29mm).

Perf. 14½ on 2 or 3 Sides

2003, May 7

1192 A632 Sheet of 6 12.00 10.00
a.-f. 65c Any single 2.00 1.75

Moomins A633

No. 1193: a, Moomin ancestors. b, Moomins around stove. c, Moomin standing on hands in water. d, Moomin and fox. e, Moomin looking at film negative. f, Moomin with hat, flowers.

Serpentine Die Cut 11½x11¾ on 3 Sides

2003, May 7 Photo.

Self-Adhesive

1193 Booklet pane of 6 15.00 —
a.-f. A633 1 Any single 2.50 .75
Complete booklet, #1193 15.00

Nos. 1193a-1193f each sold for 65c on day of issue.

Cupid A634

Serpentine Die Cut 11½ Syncopated

2003, May 14 Litho.

Self-Adhesive

1194 A634 1 multi 2.50 1.50

No. 1194 could be personalized. It sold for 65c on day of issue.

Lingonberries — A635

Serpentine Die Cut 14

2003, Sept. 10 Photo.

Self-Adhesive

1195 A635 65c multi 2.00 .75

Philanthropists A636

No. 1196: a, Juho (1852-1913) and Maria (1858-1923) Lallukka. b, Emil Aaltonen (1869-1949), vert. c, Heikki Huhtamäki (1900-70), vert. d, Antti (1883-1962) and Jenny Wihuri. e, Alfred Kordelin (1868-1917), vert. f, Amos Anderson (1878-1961), vert.

Perf. 13¼x13¾, 13¾x13¼ on 3 Sides

2003, Sept. 10 Litho.

1196 Booklet pane of 6 15.00 15.00
a.-f. A636 65c Any single 2.50 2.50
Complete booklet, #1196 11.50

Lighthouses — A637

No. 1197: a, Bengtskär. b, Russarö. c, Rönnskär. d, Harmaja Grahara. e, Söderskär.

2003, Sept. 10 ***Perf. 13¼x13¾***

1197 A637 Sheet of 5 12.50 9.50
a.-e. 1 Any single 2.50 .85

Nos. 1197a-1197e sold for 65c on day of issue. Size of No. 1197a, 28x45mm; Nos. 1197b-1197e, 21x36mm.

Christmas A638

Designs: 45c, Elf mailing letter. 65c, Elf with ginger biscuit on baking pan, vert.

Serpentine Die Cut 14x14¼, 14¼x14

2003, Oct. 31 Photo.

Self-Adhesive

1198-1199 A638 Set of 2 4.00 2.10

Slightly larger versions of No. 1198 with a serpentine die cutting of 13¼x13¾ and of No. 1199 with a serpentine die cutting of 13¾x13¼ exist only on first day and other covers produced by the postal service. They were not sold unused to the public.

Apples A639

Serpentine Die Cut 11½ Syncopated

2003, Oct. 31 Litho.

Self-Adhesive

1200 A639 1 multi 2.50 1.50

No. 1200 could be personalized. It sold for 65c on day of issue.

Pres. Tarja Halonen, 60th Birthday — A640

2003, Dec. 1 Litho. ***Perf. 13***

1201 A640 65c multi 2.00 .75

Linnaea Borealis — A641

Die Cut Perf. 14

2004, Jan. 14 Photo.

Self-Adhesive

1202 A641 30c multi 1.00 .60

Souvenir Sheet

Johan Ludvig Runeberg (1804-77), Poet — A642

No. 1203: a, Title page of *Tales of Ensign Stahl.* b, Sven Dufva with gun. c, Illustration for "Our Country." d, Sculpture of Runeberg.

Perf. 13½x13¼ on 3 or 4 Sides

2004, Jan. 14 Litho.

1203 A642 65c Sheet of 4, #a-d 8.00 6.00

Jean Sibelius (1865-1957), Composer A643

No. 1204: a, Satu, and Sibelius, paintings by Akseli Gallen-Kallela. b, Hands of Sibelius on piano keyboard. c, Swans, musical score by Sibelius.

No. 1205: a, Sibelius' house, Ainola. b, Sibelius and wife, Aino. c, Score of "Voces Intimae."

Die Cut Perf. 10 Horiz. Syncopated

2004, Jan. 14 Photo.

Coil Stamps

Self-Adhesive

1204 Horiz. strip of 3 12.00 —
a.-c. A643 2 Any single 3.00 1.50
1205 Horiz. strip of 3 12.00
a.-c. A643 1 Any single 3.00 1.50

Nos. 1204a-1204c each sold for 55c on day of issue and have two short syncopations; Nos. 1205a-1205c each sold for 65c on day of issue, and have one large syncopation.

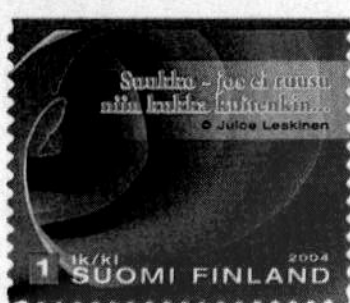

Love — A644

Text and: a, Rose. b, Man kissing. c, Woman's eye. d, Man and woman embracing. e, Elderly woman. f, Hand pulling petal from daisy.

Serpentine Die Cut 11½x11¾ on 3 Sides

2004, Jan. 14 Self-Adhesive

1206 Booklet pane of 6 15.00 —
a.-f. A644 1 Any single 2.50 .75

Nos. 1206a-1206f each sold for 65c on day of issue.

Ursus Arctos — A645

2004, Mar. 1 ***Die Cut Perf. 14***

Self-Adhesive

1207 A645 2 multi 2.25 1.00
a. Pale yellow background, animal name 8mm long 4.00 4.00

No. 1207 sold for 55c on day of issue. No. 1207 has a pale pink background and animal name is 6mm long.

Issued: No. 1207a, 2009.

Rose — A646

2004, Mar. 1 Booklet Stamp

Self-Adhesive

1208 A646 1 multi 2.50 1.40
a. Booklet pane of 10 25.00

No. 1208 sold for 65c on day of issue. Booklet pane was sold folded.

Easter Flowers — A647

Die Cut Perf. 14

2004, Mar. 1 Self-Adhesive Litho.

1209 A647 65c multi 2.00 .60

Heraldic Lion Type of 2002

Die Cut Perf. 12 Syncopated

2004, Mar. 1 Self-Adhesive

1210 A616 €3 multi 9.50 3.75

Swallows A648

Orchid A649

Serpentine Die Cut 11½ Syncopated

2004, Mar. 26 Self-Adhesive

1211 A648 1 multi 2.50 2.00
1212 A649 1 multi 2.50 2.00

Nos. 1211-1212 each sold for 65c on day of issue, and they could be personalized.

Souvenir Sheet

Norse Gods — A650

No. 1213: a, Head of Luonnotar (33x30mm). b, Luonnotar with arms extended (22x42mm).

Perf. 14¼x14½ (#1213a), 14½x14 (#1213b)

2004, Mar. 26

1213 A650 65c Sheet of 2, #a-b 6.25 6.25

Forest Animals — A651

No. 1214: a, Red squirrel (40x40mm). b, Raven (40x31mm). c, Variable hare (40x34mm). d, Stoat (40x37mm). e, Lizard (40x34mm). f, Red fox (40x40mm).

Perf. 13¼x14 on 2 or 3 Sides

2004, Apr. 28

1214 A651 Sheet of 6 14.00 11.50
a.-f. 65c Any single 2.25 1.25

Fragaria Vesca — A652

Die Cut Perf. 14

2004, Apr. 28 Photo.

Self-Adhesive

1215 A652 65c multi 2.00 1.40

Luxembourg Gardens, by Albert Edelfelt (1854-1905) A653

2004, Apr. 28 Self-Adhesive

1216 A653 1 multi 2.50 .75

No. 1216 sold for 65c on day of issue.

Europa — A654

No. 1217: a, People around campfire. b, Family in rowboat.

2004, Apr. 28 Litho. ***Perf. 13***

1217 A654 65c Horiz. pair, #a-b *4.00 3.75*

Snufkin and Moomintroll A655

Litho. & Embossed

2004, Sept. 8 ***Perf. 13***

Flocked Paper

1218 A655 1 multi *7.00* 2.00

No. 1218 sold for 65c on day of issue.

Shipwreck Treasures A656

No. 1219: a, Tankard. b, Fabric seal. c, Gold watch. d, Powder keg. e, Figurehead (23x40mm).

Perf. 14¼x13 on 3 or 4 Sides

2004, Sept. 8

1219 Booklet pane of 5 12.50 8.00
a.-e. A656 1 Any single 2.50 1.60
Complete booklet, #1219 12.50

Stamps sold for 65c each on day of issue.

Souvenir Sheet

Sammallahdenmäki, UNESCO World Heritage Site — A657

No. 1220: a, Stone wall and trees. b, Lichen-covered rocks.

2004, Sept. 8 Litho. ***Perf. 14¾x14¼***

1220 A657 65c Sheet of 2, #a-b 4.00 3.75

Rights of the Child — A658

No. 1221: a, Two girls. b, Boy painting.

2004, Oct. 29 ***Perf. 13***

1221 A658 65c Horiz. pair, #a-b 6.25 3.75

Christmas A659

Designs: 45c, Boy writing Santa Claus. 65c, Christmas tree branch, candle, ornaments, vert.

Serpentine Die Cut 13¼x13¾, 13¾x13¼

2004, Oct. 29 **Photo.**

Self-Adhesive

1222-1223 A659 Set of 2 3.50 2.50

Rotary International, Cent. — A660

2005, Jan. 14 Litho. ***Perf. 13***

1224 A660 65c blue & gold 2.00 1.00

Lahti, Cent. — A661

No. 1225: a, Sibelius Concert Hall. b, Illuminated radio towers.

2005, Jan. 14

1225 A661 65c Pair, #a-b 4.00 3.25

Oulo, 400th Anniv. — A662

No. 1226: a, Child with pail and shovel. b, Woman riding bicycle.

2005, Jan. 14

1226 A662 65c Horiz. pair, #a-b 4.00 3.25

Publishing of First Finnish Almanac, 300th Anniv. — A663

Die Cut Perf. 14

2005, Jan. 14 **Photo.**

Self-Adhesive

1227 A663 65c multi 2.00 .75

Children's Toys — A664

No. 1228: a, Stuffed lion and tiger. b, Stuffed elephant and dog. c, Airplane, train and car. d, Stuffed bear and rabbit.

Serpentine Die Cut 9¼x8½ on 3 Sides

2005, Jan. 14 **Self-Adhesive**

1228 Booklet pane of 4 10.00 —
a.-d. A664 1 Any single 2.50 1.25

Stamps sold for 65c each on day of issue.

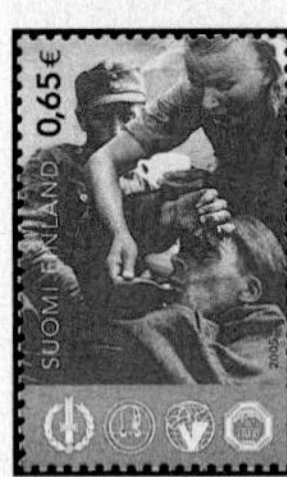

End of Winter War, 65th Anniv. — A665

2005, Mar. 2 Litho. ***Perf. 13***

1229 A665 65c multi 2.00 1.25

Easter — A666

2005, Mar. 2 ***Serpentine Die Cut 14***

Self-Adhesive

1230 A666 65c multi 2.00 1.00

Apple Blossom — A667

Die Cut Perf. 14

2005, Mar. 2 **Photo.**

Booklet Stamp

Self-Adhesive

1231 A667 1 multi 2.50 1.40
a. Booklet pane of 10 25.00

No. 1231 sold for 65c on day of issue.

Door Decoration, by Eliel Saarinen A668

Copper Stove Door — A669

Chair Back — A670

Stained Glass Window, by Olga Gummerus-Ehrström — A671

Dining Room — A672

Exterior of Hvitträsk A673

Die Cut Perf. 10 Horiz. Syncopated

2005, Mar. 2 **Litho.**

Self-Adhesive

Coil Stamps

1232 Horiz. strip of 3 10.00
a. A668 2 multi 2.75 .90
b. A669 2 multi 2.75 .90
c. A670 2 multi 2.75 .90
1233 Horiz. strip of 3 10.00
a. A671 1 multi 2.75 .90
b. A672 1 multi 2.75 .90
c. A673 1 multi 2.75 .90

Hvitträsk, home and studio of architects Eliel Saarinen, Armas Lindgren and Herman Gesellius. Nos. 1232a-1232c each sold for 55c on day of issue and have two short syncopations. Nos. 1233a-1233c each sold for 65c on day of issue and have one large syncopation.

Miniature Schnauzer A674

Serpentine Die Cut 11½ Syncopated

2005, Apr. 6

1234 A674 1 multi 2.50 1.90

Sold for 65c on day of issue. Sheets could be personalized.

Europa — A675

No. 1235 — Plates with: a, Whitefish and beetroot tartare on lettuce. b, Sauteed reindeer and grouse breast.

2005, May 11 ***Perf. 13***

1235 A675 65c Pair, #a-b *4.00 3.50*

Souvenir Sheet

Golf — A676

No. 1236: a, Man driving ball (44x31mm). b, Boy holding flag, vert. (30x44mm). c, Boy putting, vert. (33x44mm). d, Putter and golf ball (44x32mm).

Perf. 13¼ on 3 or 4 Sides

2005, May 11

1236 A676 65c Sheet of 4, #a-d 8.00 6.50

World Track Championships, Helsinki — A677

Serpentine Die Cut 12½

2005, May 11 **Self-Adhesive**

1237 A677 65c multi 2.00 1.00

Buses in Finland, Cent. A678

Die Cut Perf. 14

2005, May 11 **Photo.**

Self-Adhesive

1238 A678 65c brown & black 2.00 1.00

Horses — A679

No. 1239: a, Icelandic horse with saddle. b, White Welsh Mountain pony. c, New Forest pony with blanket. d, Shetland Pony.

Serpentine Die Cut 9¼x8½ on 3 Sides

2005, May 11 Self-Adhesive

1239 Booklet pane of 4 10.00
a.-d. A679 1 Any single 2.50 1.00

Stamps sold for 65c each on day of issue.

Cloudberries — A680

Die Cut Perf. 14

2005, Sept. 7 Photo.

Self-Adhesive

1240 A680 1 multi 2.50 1.40

Sold for 65c on day of issue.

Fruits I, by Kari Huhtamo A681

Die Cut Perf. 11½ Syncopated

2005, Sept. 7 Litho.

Self-Adhesive

1241 A681 90c multi 3.00 2.00

Sheets could be personalized.

Souvenir Sheet

Petäjävesi Church, UNESCO World Heritage Site — A682

No. 1242: a, Bell tower (26x47mm). b, Church (34x39mm). c, Angel (26x39mm). d, Chandelier (27x39mm).

2005, Sept. 7 Litho. *Perf. 13*

1242 A682 65c Sheet of 4, #a-d 8.00 6.00

Icebreakers — A683

No. 1243: a, Urho, 1975. b, Otso, 1986. c, Fennica, 1993. d, Botnica, 1998.

2005, Sept. 7 *Perf. 13¼ Horiz.*

1243 Booklet pane of 4 10.00 —
a.-d. A683 1 Any single 2.50 1.00

Each stamp sold for 65c on day of issue.

Souvenir Sheet

Imperial Winter Egg, by Carl Fabergé — A684

No. 684: a, Flowers in egg. b, Frost detail of egg.

Litho. & Embossed with Foil Application

2005, Oct. 28 *Perf. 13*

1244 A684 €3.50 Sheet of 2, #a-b 22.50 20.00

A limited quantity of 2,500 numbered sheets, which sold for €30, exist. Value, $100.

Christmas — A685

Designs: 50c, Santa Claus reading letters. 1, Santa Claus and wife dancing, horiz.

Serpentine Die Cut 13¾x13¼, 13¼x13¾

2005, Oct. 28 Photo.

Self-Adhesive

1245-1246 A685 Set of 2 4.00 1.50

No. 1246 sold for 65c on day of issue.

Postal Employees Union, Cent. — A686

2006, Jan. 11 Litho. *Perf. 13*

1247 A686 65c multi 2.00 .75

Heart — A687

2006, Jan. 11 *Die Cut*

Self-Adhesive

1248 A687 65c bright pink 2.00 .75

Renaming of Helsinki University Library as National Library of Finland — A688

2006, Jan. 11 *Die Cut Perf. 14x13¾*

Self-Adhesive

1249 A688 1 multi 2.50 1.40

Sold for 65c on day of issue.

Forest in Winter — A689

2006, Jan. 11 Photo.

Self-Adhesive

1250 A689 1 multi 2.50 1.40

Sold for 65c on day of issue.

Taxis, Cent. — A690

No. 1251: a, Women passengers in taxi, 1906. b, Driver standing in front of 1929 Chevrolet taxi. c, Driver leaning on 1957 Pobeda taxi. d, Driver on phone at taxi stand next to Mercedes-Benz taxi.

Serpentine Die Cut 11¼ Vert.

2006, Jan. 11 Litho.

Self-Adhesive

1251 Booklet pane of 4 8.00 —
a.-d. A690 65c Any single 2.00 .75

Souvenir Sheet

Johan Vilhelm Snellman (1806-81), Philosopher — A691

No. 1252: a, Caricature of Snellman, masthead of his newspaper "Saima." b, Snellman's portrait on 1940 five thousand mark note. c, Snellman and European railway map. d, Ilmarinen, first Finnish locomotive, and European railway map.

2006, Jan. 11 *Perf. 13¼x13¾*

1252 A691 65c Sheet of 4, #a-d 8.00 8.00

Parliament, Cent. — A692

Serpentine Die Cut 14

2006, Feb. 3 Litho.

Self-Adhesive

1253 A692 1 multi 2.50 1.40

Sold for 65c on day of sale.

Flag — A693

2006, Mar. 1 Self-Adhesive

1254 A693 1 multi 2.50 1.40

Sold for 65c on day of sale.

Lilacs — A694

Die Cut Perf. 13¾x14

2006, Mar. 1 Photo.

Self-Adhesive

1255 A694 1 multi 2.50 1.40

Sold for 65c on day of sale.

Easter — A695

2006, Mar. 1 Litho. *Die Cut*

Self-Adhesive

1256 A695 65c multi 2.00 1.00

Fortune Teller, by Helene Schjerfbeck — A696

Die Cut Perf. 13¾x14

2006, Mar. 1 Photo.

Self-Adhesive

1257 A696 95c multi 3.00 2.25

Bil-Bol Poster A697

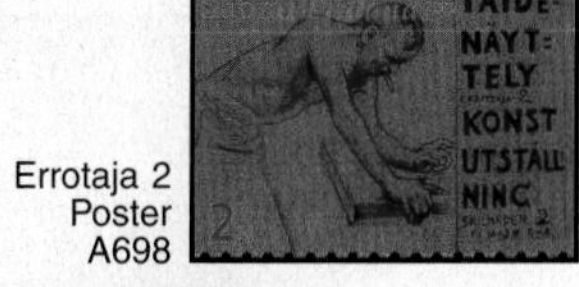

Errotaja 2 Poster A698

Concert Finnois Poster A699

Madonna A700

Self-Portrait A701

Home of Artist Akseli Gallen-Kallela, Tarvaspää — A702

Die Cut Perf. 10 Horiz. Syncopated

2006, Mar. 1 **Self-Adhesive**

Coil Stamps

1258	Horiz. strip of 3	6.75	—
a.	A697 2 multi	2.25	2.25
b.	A698 2 multi	2.25	2.25
c.	A699 2 multi	2.25	2.25

Die Cut Perf. 10 Vert. Syncopated

1259	Vert. strip of 3	6.75	—
a.	A700 1 multi	2.25	.75
b.	A701 1 multi	2.25	.75
c.	A702 1 multi	2.25	.75

Akseli Gallen-Kallela (1865-1931), artist. Nos. 1258a-1258c each sold for 55c and Nos. 1259a-1259c each sold for 65c on day of issue.

Souvenir Sheet

Norse Mythology — A703

No. 1260 — Fairy tale book cover illustrations by Rudolf Koivu: a, Fairy. b, Fairy dancing with Santa Claus, vert.

Perf. 13½x13¼, 13¼x13½ (#1260b)

2006, Mar. 29 **Litho.**

1260 A703 65c Sheet of 2, #a-b 4.00 4.00

Europa A704

2006, May 4 ***Perf. 13***

1261 A704 65c multi 2.00 1.00

Vaasa, 400th Anniv. — A705

2006, May 4

1262 A705 1 multi 2.50 1.00

Sold for 65c on day of issue.

A706

Serpentine Die Cut 10 Syncopated

2006, May 4 **Booklet Stamp**

Self-Adhesive

1263	A706 1 multi	2.50	1.50
a.	Booklet pane of 8	20.00	

No. 1263 sold for 65c on day of issue. Design portion of stamp could be personalized.

Summer Activities A707

No. 1264: a, Woman fishing. b, Children making flower garlands. c, Man making sauna whisk. d, Woman weeding flower garden.

Serpentine Die Cut 11¼ Vert.

2006, May 4 **Self-Adhesive**

1264	Booklet pane of 4	10.00	
a.-d.	A707 1 Any single	2.50	1.00

Nos. 1264a-1264d each sold for 65c on day of issue.

Cats — A708

No. 1265: a, Striped house cat. b, British shorthair (gray cat). c, Ragdoll cat (brown and white). d, Chocolate Persian cat.

2006, May 4 **Self-Adhesive**

1265	Booklet pane of 4	10.00	
a.-d.	A708 1 Any single	2.50	1.00

Nos. 1265a-1265d each sold for 65c on day of issue.

Suomenlinna (Sveaborg) Fortress, Helsinki — A709

No. 1266: a, Ship without oars. b, Ship with oars facing fortress. c, Ship with oars, windmill.

Litho. & Engr.

2006, May 4 ***Perf. 13x12¾***

1266	A709 Booklet pane of 3	7.50	—
a.-c.	1 Any single	2.50	1.00
	Complete booklet, #1266	7.50	

Nos. 1266a-1266c each sold for 65c on day of issue. See Sweden No. 2530.

Blueberries and Blueberry Pie — A710

Die Cut Perf. 14

2006, Aug. 24 **Photo.**

Self-Adhesive

1267 A710 1 multi 2.50 1.40

Sold for 70c on day of issue.

Miniature Sheet

Family Life — A711

No. 1268: a, Family watching television. b, Woman writing letter to husband.

2006, Aug. 24 ***Die Cut***

Self-Adhesive

1268 A711 1 Sheet of 2, #a-b 5.00 2.50

Nos. 1268a-1268b each sold for 70c on day of issue.

Newspaper Journalism — A712

Die Cut Perf. 14

2006, Sept. 22 **Litho.**

Self-Adhesive

1269 A712 70c multi 2.25 1.00

Points, Textile Art by Ritva Puotila — A713

Serpentine Die Cut 11½ Syncopated

2006, Sept. 22 **Self-Adhesive**

1270 A713 1 multi 2.50 1.75

Sold for 70c on day of issue.

Dryas Octopetala A714

Serpentine Die Cut 14

2006, Sept. 22 **Photo.**

Self-Adhesive

1271 A714 1 multi 2.50 1.00

Sold for 70c on day of issue.

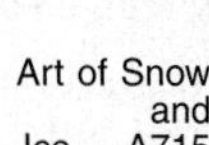

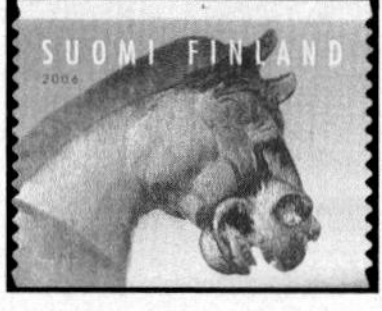

Art of Snow and Ice — A715

No. 1272: a, Horse. b, Kemi Snow Castle. c, Wall of ice tiles. d, Snowball lantern.

Serpentine Die Cut 11¾ Vert.

2006, Sept. 22 **Self-Adhesive**

1272	Booklet pane of 4	10.00	
a.-d.	A715 1 Any single	2.50	2.50

Nos. 1272a-1272d each sold for 70c on day of issue. Denominations are printed in thermographic ink that changes color when warmed.

Miniature Sheet

Finnish Postage Stamps, 150th Anniv. — A716

No. 1273: a, 70c, Heraldic lion and fleurons in white. b, 95c, Part of vignette of type A1. c, €1.40, Heraldic lion in gold, fleurons in red.

Litho. & Embossed With Foil Application

2006, Oct. 27 ***Perf. 13½x13***

1273 A716 Sheet of 3, #a-c 9.50 9.50

A717

Christmas — A718

Serpentine Die Cut 13¼x13¾

2006, Oct. 27 **Photo.**

Self-Adhesive

1274 A717 50c multi 1.40 .90

Serpentine Die Cut 13¾x13¼

1275 A718 1 multi 2.75 .90

No. 1275 sold for 70c on day of issue.

Television Broadcasting in Finland, 50th Anniv. — A719

Die Cut Perf. 14

2007, Jan. 24 **Litho.**

Self-Adhesive

1276 A719 70c multi 2.25 1.50

Faces — A720

2007, Jan. 24 **Self-Adhesive**

1277 A720 70c multi 2.25 1.50

Winter Landscape, Haminalahti, by Ferdinand von Wright A721

2007, Jan. 24 **Photo.**

Booklet Stamp

Self-Adhesive

1278 A721 1 multi 2.50 1.50
a. Booklet pane of 10 25.00

Sold for 70c on day of issue.

Sun Setting Over Flower Field — A722

2007, Jan. 24 **Litho.**

Self-Adhesive

1279 A722 €1.40 multi 4.50 3.00

Souvenir Sheet

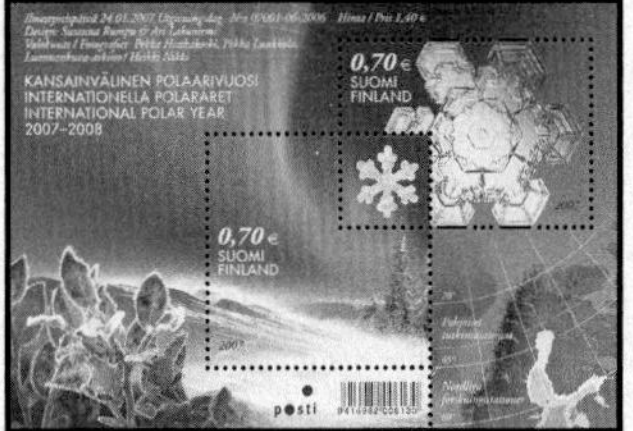
Intl. Polar Year — A723

No. 1280: a, Snowflake. b, Aurora borealis.

Perf. 13 Syncopated (#1280a), 13 (#1280b)

Litho. With Hologram Affixed

2007, Jan. 24

1280 A723 70c Sheet of 2, #a-b + label 4.50 4.00

Truck Transport — A724

No. 1281: a, Log truck. b, Milk truck. c, Dump truck. d, Tractor trailer.

Serpentine Die Cut 12¼ Horiz.

2007, Jan. 24 **Litho.**

Self-Adhesive

1281 Booklet pane of 4 9.00 6.00
a.-d. A724 70c Any single 2.25 1.40

Central Organization of Finnish Trade Unions — A725

2007, Mar. 7 ***Perf. 13***

1282 A725 70c multi 2.25 1.50

Soccer Association of Finland, Cent. — A726

2007, Mar. 7 ***Die Cut***

Self-Adhesive

1283 A726 70c multi 2.25 1.50

Easter — A727

2007, Mar. 7 ***Die Cut Perf. 14***

Self-Adhesive

1284 A727 1 multi 2.50 1.50

Sold for 70c on day of issue. Portions of design were applied by a thermographic process producing a shiny, raised effect.

Lilium Enchantment A728

2007, Mar. 7 **Litho.**

Booklet Stamp

Self-Adhesive

1285 A728 1 multi 2.50 1.50
a. Booklet pane of 10 25.00

No. 1285 sold for 70c on day of issue.

Souvenir Sheet

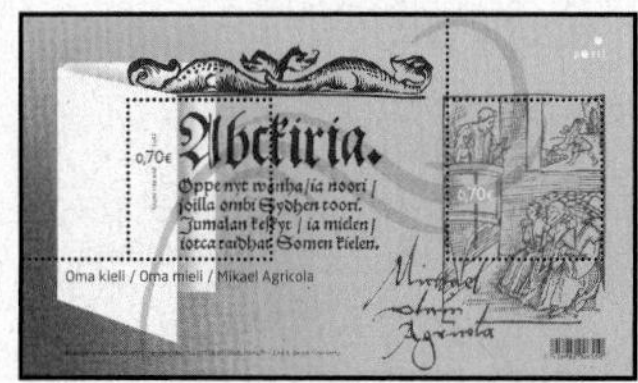
Bishop Michael Agricola (1509-57) — A729

No. 1286: a, Text and open book. b, Agricola preaching.

2007, Mar. 7 ***Perf. 13½***

1286 A729 70c Sheet of 2, #a-b 4.50 4.00

Tampere Cathedral, Cent. — A730

2007, May 9 ***Perf. 13¼***

1287 A730 70c multi 2.25 1.25

Europa — A731

No. 1288: a, Scouts on sailboat. b, Scouts around campfire.

2007, May 9 ***Perf. 12½x13***

1288 A731 Horiz. pair 4.50 4.50
a.-b. 70c Either single 2.25 2.25

Scouting, cent.

Helsinki Public Transportation — A732

No. 1289: a, Commuter train in station. b, Tram on street. c, Subway train on bridge. d. People in Kamppi Bus Station.

Serpentine Die Cut 12¼ Horiz.

2007, May 9 **Self-Adhesive**

1289 Booklet pane of 4 10.00 8.00
a.-d. A732 1 Any single 2.50 1.50

Nos. 1289a-1289d each sold for 70c on day of issue.

Moomins A733

No. 1290: a, Little My in water. b, Moomintroll running across rocks. c, Moominpappa at typewriter. d, Snork Maiden picking flowers. e, Moominmamma making pancakes. f, Snufkin amid flowers.

Serpentine Die Cut 11¾ Vert.

2007, May 9 **Photo.**

Self-Adhesive

1290 Booklet pane of 6 15.00
a.-f. A733 1 Any single 2.50 1.25

Nos. 1290a-1290f each sold for 70c on day of issue.

Souvenir Sheet

2007 Eurovision Song Contest, Helsinki — A734

No. 1291: a, Eurovision Song Contest emblem. b, Finnish singers Laila Kinnunen, Marion Rung, Kirka Babitzin and Katri Helena. c, 2006 Finnish contest-winning band, Lordi. d, Lead singer of Lordi.

Litho. With Foil Application

2007, May 9 ***Die Cut***

Self-Adhesive

1291 A734 70c Sheet of 4, #a-d 9.00 9.00

A735

Serpentine Die Cut 11½ Syncopated

2007, Aug. 24 **Litho.**

Self-Adhesive

1292 A735 1 multi 2.50 1.25

No. 1292 sold for 70c on day of issue. Design portion of stamp could be personalized.

Home Furnishings — A736

No. 1293 — Picture frame and: a, Empire-style chair, "Porvoo Garland" wallpaper, 19th cent. (country name at LR). b, Paimio chair, "2+3" wallpaper, 20th cent. (country name at LL).

Die Cut Perf. 14

2007, Aug. 24 **Litho.**

Self-Adhesive

1293 Pair 5.00
a.-b. A736 1 Either single 2.50 1.25

Nos. 1293a-1293b each sold for 70c on day of issue.

Raspberries and Raspberry Cake — A737

Die Cut Perf. 14

2007, Aug. 24 **Photo.**

Self-Adhesive

Booklet Stamp

1294 A737 1 multi 2.50 1.25

No. 1294 sold for 70c on day of issue.

Finnish Olympic Committee, Cent. — A738

2007, Aug. 24 **Litho.**

Self-Adhesive

Booklet Stamp

1295 A738 1 multi 2.50 1.25

No. 1295 sold for 70c on day of issue.

Butterflies — A739

No. 1296: a, Apatura iris. b, Scolitantides orion. c, Colias palaeno.

Die Cut Perf. 10 Vert., Syncopated at Right

2007, Aug. 24 **Self-Adhesive**

Coil Stamps

1296 Vert. strip of 3 7.50
a.-c. A739 1 Any single 2.50 2.50

Nos. 1296a-1296c had a franking value of 70c on day of issue. A roll of 100 stamps sold for €68.

Miniature Sheet

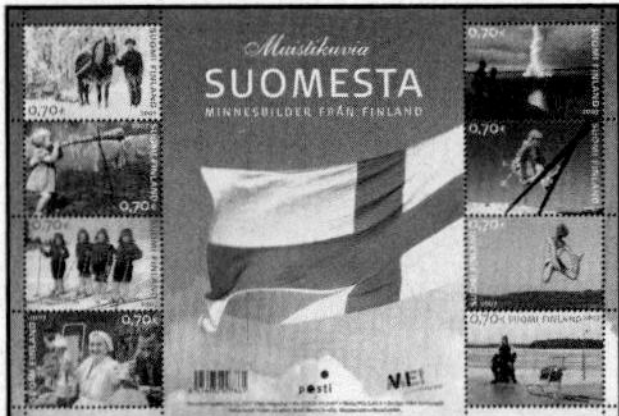

Independence, 90th Anniv. — A740

No. 1297 — Photographs of people at work and play: a, Man and horse hauling wood. b, Girl blowing horn. c, Four boys with skis. d, People at coffee break. e, People near bonfire. f, Boy ski jumping. g, Boy diving. h, Ice fisherman. Nos. 1297a-1297d are black and white photos.

2007, Nov. 2 ***Perf. 13¼***

1297 A740 Sheet of 8 18.00 16.50
a.-h. 70c Any single 2.25 1.50

Souvenir Sheet

Woodwork — A741

No. 1298: a, Zitan armchair with dragon design, China (denomination at left). b, Modern Finnish bowls (denomination at right).

2007, Nov. 2 ***Perf. 13¼x14¼***

1298 A741 Sheet of 2 4.50 4.50
a.-b. 70c Either single 2.25 1.75

See Hong Kong Nos. 1298-1299.

A742

Christmas — A743

Serpentine Die Cut 13¼x13¾

2007, Nov. 2 **Photo.**

Self-Adhesive

1299 A742 55c multi 1.75 1.25

Serpentine Die Cut 13¾x13¼

1300 A743 1 multi 2.50 1.75

No. 1300 sold for 70c on day of issue.

A744 A745

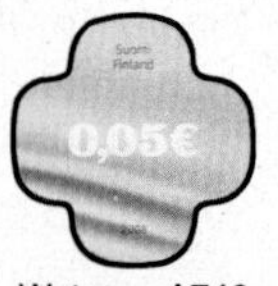

Water — A746

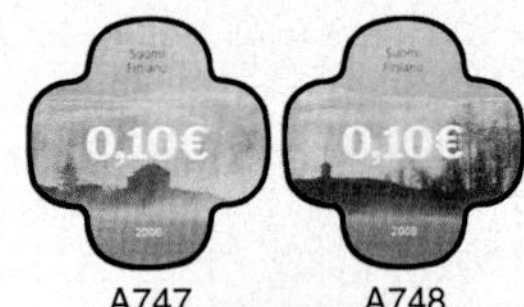

A747 A748

Islands — A749

2008, Jan. 24 **Photo.** ***Die Cut***

Self-Adhesive

1301 Horiz. strip of 3 .45
a. A744 5c multi .25 .25
b. A745 5c multi .25 .25
c. A746 5c multi .25 .25
1302 Horiz. strip of 3 .90
a. A747 10c multi .30 .30
b. A748 10c multi .30 .30
c. A749 10c multi .30 .30

Souvenir Sheet

Helsinki University of Technology, Cent. — A750

No. 1303: a, Robot. b, University building.

2008, Jan. 24 **Litho.** ***Perf. 13½x13¼***

1303 A750 Sheet of 2 5.00 4.25
a.-b. 1 Any single 2.50 1.25

Nos. 1303a-1303b each sold for 70c on day of issue.

Miniature Sheet

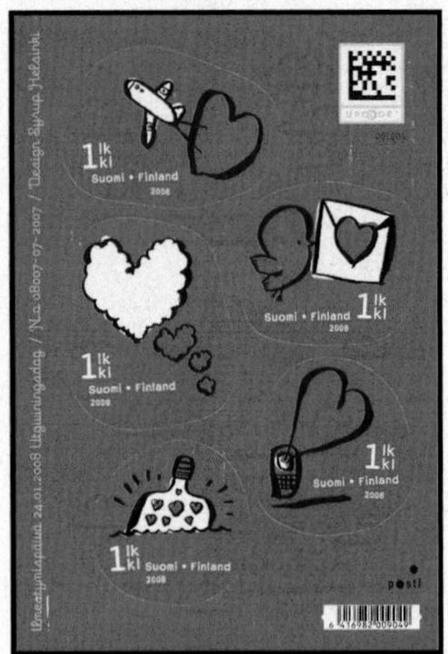

Love — A751

No. 1304: a, Airplane pulling heart banner. b, Carrier pigeon with envelope. c, Heart-shaped smoke signals. d, Heart and cell phone. e, Bottle with hearts.

2008, Jan. 24 ***Die Cut***

Self-Adhesive

1304 A751 Sheet of 5 12.50 10.50
a.-e. 1 Any single 2.50 1.25

Nos. 1304a-1304e each sold for 70c on day of issue.

Miniature Sheet

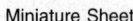

Snow Sports — A752

No. 1305: a, Matti Räty in yellow ski suit. b, Antti Autti (snowboarder) in air in red ski suit. c, Tapio Saarimaki in red ski suit. d, Tanja Poutiainen in white and green ski suit.

Litho. With Three-Dimensional Plastic Affixed

Serpentine Die Cut 9 Syncopated

2008, Jan. 24 **Self-Adhesive**

1305 A752 Sheet of 4 10.00 9.00
a.-d. 1 Any single 2.50 1.25

Nos. 1305a-1305d each sold for 70c on day of issue.

Clock and Lamp on Desk — A753

Die Cut Perf. 13¾

2008, Feb. 27 **Litho.**

Booklet Stamp

Self-Adhesive

1306 A753 €1.05 multi 3.50 2.60
a. Booklet pane of 10 35.00

Finnish Book Publishers Association, 150th Anniv. — A754

Serpentine Die Cut 13¼

2008, Feb. 27 **Self-Adhesive**

1307 A754 1 multi 2.50 1.75

No. 1307 sold for 70c on day of issue.

Lathyrus Odoratus — A755

Die Cut Perf. 13¾

2008, Feb. 27 **Photo.**

Self-Adhesive

1308 A755 1 multi 2.50 1.75

No. 1308 sold for 70c on the day of issue and has Braille dots applied by a thermographic process.

Easter — A756

Litho. With Foil Application

Serpentine Die Cut 13¾

2008, Feb. 27 **Self-Adhesive**

1309 A756 1 multi 2.50 1.75

No. 1309 sold for 70c on day of issue.

Fauna Associated With Weather Forecasting Folk Beliefs — A757

No. 1310: a, Perch. b, Lambs. c, Frogs. d, Swallows. e, Snail.

Serpentine Die Cut 12¼ Horiz.

2008, Feb. 27 **Litho.**

Self-Adhesive

1310 Booklet pane of 5 12.50 11.00
a.-e. A757 1 Any single 2.50 1.25

Nos. 1310a-1310e each sold for 70c on day of issue.

Souvenir Sheet

Mythical Places — A758

No. 1311: a, Cliff resembling human face, Astuvansalmi. b, Amber carving of head found at Astuvansalmi.

2008, Mar. 27 ***Perf. 13½***

1311 A758 Sheet of 2 4.75 4.25
a.-b. 70c Either single 2.25 2.00

Europa — A759

No. 1312 — Handwritten letters and portraits by Pekka Halonen of: a, Himself. b, His wife, Maija.

2008, May 9 ***Perf. 13***

1312 A759 Horiz. pair 5.25 5.25
a.-b. 70c Either single 2.50 2.10

Kvarken Archipelago UNESCO World Heritage Site — A760

Serpentine Die Cut 13¾

2008, May 9 **Self-Adhesive**

1313 A760 €1.50 blk & red 5.50 4.50

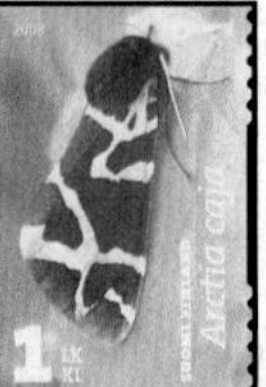

Moths — A761

No. 1314: a, Arctia caja. b, Aglia tau. c. Deilephila elpenor.

Die Cut Perf. 10 Syncopated

2008, May 9 **Photo.**

Coil Stamps

Self-Adhesive

1314 Vert. strip of 3 7.75 7.00
a.-c. A761 1 Any single 2.50 1.25

Nos. 1314a-1314c each sold for 70c on day of issue.

Psychedelic Art — A762

No. 1315: a, Melting mushrooms and teardrops. b, Guitars. c, Flying fish. d, Flowers and woman's legs in high heels. e, Six balloons.

Serpentine Die Cut 12½ Horiz.

2008, May 9 Litho.

Self-Adhesive

1315 Booklet pane of 5 13.00
a.-e. A762 1 Any single 2.60 1.25

Nos. 1315a-1315e each sold for 70c on day of issue.

Modern Art — A763

No. 1316: a, Sinistä ja Punaista, by Sam Vanni. b, Merirosvolaiva, by Kimmo Kaivanto. c, Hiljaisuuden Kuuntelija, by Juhani Linnovaara. d, Odotan Kevään Tuloa, by Göran Augustson. e, Minä, by Carolus Enckell. f, Pöytä, by Reino Hietanen.

Serpentine Die Cut 11¾ Vert.

2008, May 9 Self-Adhesive

1316 Booklet pane of 6 16.00 14.00
a.-f. A763 1 Any single 2.60 1.25

Nos. 1316a-1316f each sold for 70c on day of issue.

Personalized Stamp — A764

Serpentine Die Cut 10

2008, Sept. 5 Litho.

Self-Adhesive

1317 A764 1 multi 2.50 2.00

No. 1317 sold for 80c on day of issue. The generic design portion of the stamp shown could be personalized.

Dogs — A765

No. 1318: a, Spitz with open mouth, facing forward. b, Rough collie, with open mouth, facing right. c, Boxer, facing left. d, Finnish hound, facing left. e, Cavalier King Charles spaniel, facing right. f, Jack Russell terrier, looking over shoulder.

Serpentine Die Cut 11¾ Vert.

2008, Sept. 5 Self-Adhesive

1318 Booklet pane of 6 15.00 13.50
a.-f. A765 1 Any single 2.50 1.25

Nos. 1318a-1318f each sold for 80c on day of issue.

Souvenir Sheet

Mika Waltari (1908-79), Writer — A766

No. 1319: a, Waltari. b, Cover of Waltari's book, *Komisario Palmun Erehyds.*

2008, Sept. 5 ***Perf. 14x13½***

1319 A766 Sheet of 2 5.00 4.50
a.-b. 80c Either single 2.50 2.25

Souvenir Sheet

Kimi Räikkönen, 2007 Formula 1 Racing Champion — A767

No. 1320: a, Räikkönen (24x30mm). b, Räikkönen's Ferrari Formula 1 race car (74x30mm).

Die Cut Perf. 11x11½ on 2 Sides (#1320a), 11½ Vert. (#1320b)

2008, Sept. 5 Self-Adhesive

1320 A767 Sheet of 2 5.00 4.50
a.-b. 1 Either single 2.50 2.25

Nos. 1320a-1320b each sold for 80c on day of issue.

Souvenir Sheet

Adolf Erik Nordenskiöld (1832-1901), Arctic Explorer — A768

No. 1321: a, Nordenskiöld (29x34mm). b, Ship Sofia (58x34mm).

Litho. & Engr.

2008, Oct. 20 ***Perf. 13x13¼***

1321 A768 Sheet of 2 5.00 4.50
a.-b. 1 Either single 2.50 2.25

Nos. 1321a-1321b each sold for 80c on day of issue. See Greenland Nos. 527-528.

A769

A770

Christmas A771

Die Cut Perf. 14

2008, Nov. 6 Litho.

Self-Adhesive

1322 A769 60c multi 1.75 .75

Serpentine Die Cut 13¼x13¾

Photo.

1323 A770 1 multi 2.75 2.75

Printed On Plastic

Die Cut Perf. 13¾

1324 A771 1 multi 3.00 2.00
Nos. 1322-1324 (3) 7.50 5.50

On day of issue, Nos. 1323 and 1324 each sold for 80c.

Pres. Martti Ahtisaari, 2008 Nobel Peace Laureate A772

2008, Dec. 10 Litho. ***Perf. 13***

1325 A772 80c light blue 2.50 1.25

Hospital Work — A773

2009, Jan. 22 Litho. ***Perf. 13***

1326 A773 80c multi 2.25 1.75

Pallas-Yllästunturi National Park — A774

2009, Jan. 22 ***Die Cut Perf. 14***

Self-Adhesive

1327 A774 1 multi 2.50 1.40

No. 1327 sold for 80c on day of issue and has Braille dots applied in varnish.

Peony — A775

Die Cut Perf. 14

2009, Jan. 22 Photo.

Self-Adhesive

1328 A775 €1.10 multi 3.00 2.25

Children's Dream Occupations A776

No. 1329 — Child dressed as: a, Policeman. b, Doctor. c, Firefighter. d, Skier. e, Construction worker.

Serpentine Die Cut 12¼ Vert.

2009, Jan. 22 Litho.

Self-Adhesive

1329 Booklet pane of 5 12.50 10.00
a.-e. A776 1 Any single 2.50 1.40

Nos. 1329a-1329e each sold for 80c on day of issue.

Miniature Sheet

Finland as Grand Duchy of Russia, 200th Anniv. — A777

No. 1330: a, Tsar Alexander I (1777-1825), facing left with blue sash. b, Count Georg Magnus Sprengtporten (1740-1819), with red sash and gold epaulets. c, Count Carl Erik Mannerheim (1759-1837), without epaulets. d, Count Gustaf Mauritz Armfelt (1757-1814), facing right, with blue sash. Names are on sheet margin.

Litho. & Embossed With Foil Application

2009, Jan. 22 ***Perf. 13¾***

1330 A777 80c Sheet of 4, #a-d 9.00 9.00

Miniature Sheet

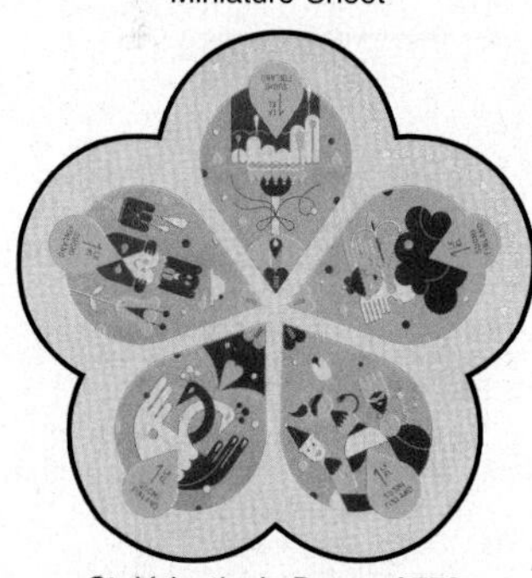

St. Valentine's Day — A778

No. 1331: a, Birthday cake and candle. b, Cupid. c, Three people, flower. d, Swans. e, Teddy bear hugging heart.

2009, Jan. 22 Litho. ***Die Cut***

Self-Adhesive

1331 A778 1 Sheet of 5, #a-e 12.50 10.00

Nos. 1331a-1331e each sold for 80c on day of issue.

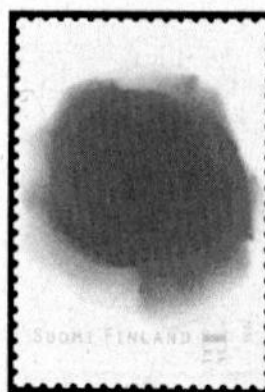

Rose — A779

Die Cut Perf. 14

2009, Mar. 18 Litho.

Self-Adhesive

1332 A779 1 multi 2.50 2.00

No. 1332 sold for 80c on day of issue.

Easter — A780

2009, Mar. 18 Self-Adhesive

1333 A780 1 multi 2.50 2.00

No. 1333 sold for 80c on day of issue.

Souvenir Sheet

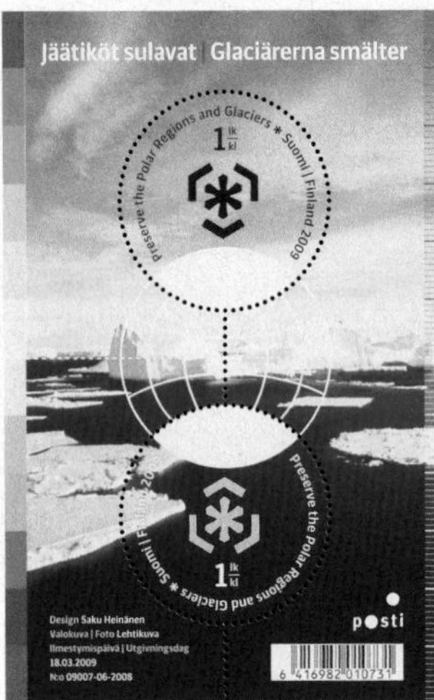

Preservation of Polar Regions and Glaciers — A781

No. 1334: a, Sky, blue emblem. b, Sea and ice, silver emblem.

Litho. With Foil Application

2009, Mar. 18 ***Perf.***

1334 A781 Sheet of 2 5.00 3.75
a.-b. 1 Either single 2.50 1.90

Nos. 1334a-1334b each sold for 80c on day of issue.

Greetings A782

No. 1335: a, Gift and tulips. b, Chocolate-covered strawberries, cake. c, Flowers. d, Coffee cup, letter and rose. e, Dove and apples.

Serpentine Die Cut 10¼ Horiz.

2009, Mar. 18 **Litho.**

Self-Adhesive

1335 Booklet pane of 5 + 5 labels 12.50
a.-e. A782 1 Any single 2.50 1.25

Nos. 1335a-1335e each sold for 80c on day of issue.

Europa — A783

No. 1336: a, Lake, birds, Moon, stars and other heavenly bodies. b, Lake, comet, Saturn, stars and other heavenly bodies.

2009, May 6 ***Perf. 13***

1336 A783 Horiz. pair 5.00 5.00
a.-b. 80c Either single 2.50 1.75

Intl. Year of Astronomy.

Sauna — A784

No. 1337: a, Towels, scrubber, bucket of birch branches (55x23mm). b, People in sauna (55x23mm). c, Waterside sauna (55x23mm). d, Birch whisk (27x45mm). e, Water tubs and window (27x45mm).

Serpentine Die Cut 11¾ Horiz.

2009, May 6 **Self-Adhesive**

1337 Booklet pane of 5 12.50
a.-e. A784 1 Any single 2.50 1.40

Nos. 1337a-1337e each sold for 80c on day of issue. No. 1337d is impregnated with a birch scent.

Moomins — A785

No. 1338: a, Moomin carrying purse. b, Moominpappa with hat holding paper. c, Little My holding large pair of glasses. d, Moomin at mirror. e, Moomin and Snufkin fishing. f, Moominpappa slipping down hill.

Serpentine Die Cut 11¾ Horiz.

2009, May 6 **Self-Adhesive**

1338 Booklet pane of 6 15.00
a.-f. A785 1 Any single 2.50 1.25

Nos. 1338a-1338f each sold for 80c on day of issue.

Miniature Sheet

Women's Fashion — A786

No. 1339: a, Dress by Anna and Tuomas Laitinen (30x45mm). b, Dress by Jasmin Santanen (30x45mm). c, Handbag by Lumi (30x35mm). d, Red shoes by Minna Parikka (30x25mm). e, Shoes by Julia Lundsten (30x30mm).

Serpentine Die Cut 14¼x13¾

2009, May 6 **Self-Adhesive**

1339 A786 Sheet of 5 12.50 9.50
a.-e. 1 Any single 2.50 1.25

Nos. 1339a-1339e each sold for 80c on day of issue.

Gustavian Style Clock, Table and Candle Holder — A787

Die Cut Perf. 13¾

2009, Sept. 9 **Litho.**

Self-Adhesive

1340 A787 1 multi 2.50 1.25
a. Booklet pane of 10 25.00

No. 1340 sold for 80c on day of issue.

Aurora Borealis — A788

No. 1341 — Various pictures of Aurora Borealis taken at: a, 65 degrees, 1 minute, 17.03 seconds north; 25 degrees, 39 minutes, 31.26 seconds east. b, 65 degrees, 57.16 seconds north; 25 degrees, 39 minutes, 41.01 seconds east. c, 67 degrees, 45 minutes, 2.44 seconds north; 23 degrees, 36 minutes, 41.53 seconds east.

Die Cut Perf. 10 Vert., Syncopated at Right

2009, Sept. 9 **Self-Adhesive**

Coil Stamps

1341 Vert. strip of 3 7.50
a.-c. A788 1 Any single 2.50 1.25

Nos. 1341a-1341c each sold for 80c on day of issue.

Paintings of Flowers — A789

No. 1342: a, Snapdragons, by Helene Schjerfbeck. b, Blooming Irises, by Wäinö Aaltonen. c, Burnet Roses, by Eero Järnefelt. d, Lone Calla, by Ester Helenius. e, Amaryllis, by Birger Carlstedt. f, Still Life with Carnations, by Tuomas von Boehm.

Serpentine Die Cut 11¾ Horiz.

2009, Sept. 9 **Self-Adhesive**

1342 Booklet pane of 6 15.00
a.-f. A789 1 Any single 2.50 1.25

Nos. 1342a-1342f each sold for 80c on day of issue.

Wreath — A790

Girl and Basket of Apples — A791

Amaryllis A792

Personalized Stamp — A793

Die Cut Perf. 14

2009, Nov. 6 **Litho.**

Self-Adhesive

1343 Horiz. pair 3.75
a. A790 60c multi 1.75 .50
b. A791 60c multi 1.75 .50
1344 A792 1 multi 2.50 2.25

Serpentine Die Cut 11½x11¾ Syncopated

1345 A793 1 multi 2.50 2.25

Nos. 1344 and 1345 each sold for 80c on day of issue. The generic design portion of No. 1345, shown, could be personalized.

Antennaria Dioica — A794

Die Cut Perf. 11 Syncopated

2010, Jan. 25 **Litho.**

Self-Adhesive

1346 A794 1 multi 2.75 2.25

No. 1346 sold for 80c on day of issue.

Miniature Sheet

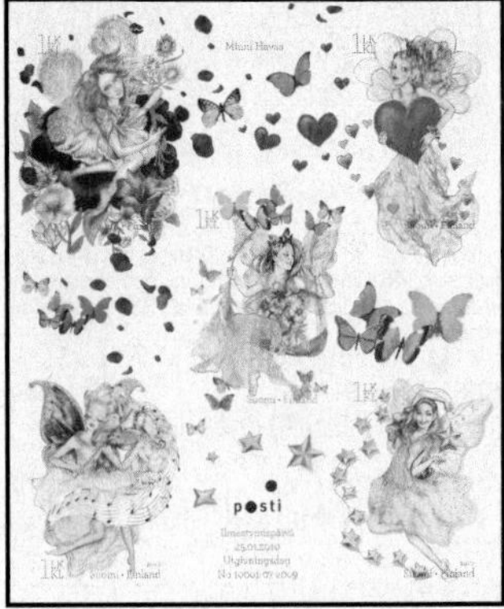

Fairies — A795

No. 1347 — Fairy: a, Holding flowers. b, Holding heart. c, On swing. d, Holding violin. e, With stars.

Serpentine Die Cut 14½x14

Litho. & Silk-screened

2010, Jan. 25 **Self-Adhesive**

1347 A795 Sheet of 5 13.50 10.50
a.-e. 1 Any single 2.50 1.25

Nos. 1347a-1347e each sold for 80c on day of issue.

Rock Stars A796

No. 1348: a, Eppu Normaali (45x33mm). b, Yö (41x31mm). c, Popeda (40x28mm). d, Dingo (44x33mm). e, Maarit (34x41mm). f, Mamba (38x36mm).

Die Cut Perf. 8½

2010, Jan. 25 **Litho.**

Self-Adhesive

1348 Booklet pane of 6 17.00 12.50
a.-f. A796 1 Any single 3.25 2.10

Nos. 1348a-1348f each sold for 80c on day of issue.

A797

Easter — A798

Serpentine Die Cut 12½

2010, Mar. 8 **Litho. & Embossed**

Self-Adhesive

1349 A797 1 multi 11.00 8.50

Litho.

Die Cut Perf. 14

1350 A798 1 multi 2.75 2.25

Nos. 1349 and 1350 each sold for 80c on day of issue.

Rural Life — A799

No. 1351: a, Mussels, children lifting caught fish. b, Children on swing, strawberries, flowers, horse in meadow. c, Farmer on tractor, farmhouses. d, Milk cans, girl milking cow. e, Musicians and dancers.

Serpentine Die Cut 10¼ Horiz.

2010, Mar. 8 Litho.

Self-Adhesive

1351 Booklet pane of 5 13.50 10.00
a.-e. A799 1 Any single 2.50 1.25

Nos. 1351a-1351e each sold for 80c on day of issue.

Famous Women — A800

No. 1352: a, Ritva-Liisa Pohjalainen, jewelry and clothing designer. b, Elina Haavio-Mannila, sociologist. c, Aira Samulin, dance instructor. d, Maria-Liisa Nevala, director of National Theater. e, Laila Hirvisaari, writer. f, Leena Palotie (1952-2010), geneticist.

Serpentine Die Cut 11 Horiz. Syncopated

Litho. & Silk-screened

2010, Mar. 8 Self-Adhesive

1352 Booklet pane of 6 17.00 12.00
a.-f. A800 1 Any single 2.75 1.40

Nos. 1352a-1352f each sold for 80c on day of issue.

Vegetables A801

No. 1353: a, Tomato (38x33mm). b, Onions (47x34mm). c, Pumpkin (34x36mm). d, Cucumber (27x43mm). e, Eggplant (42x41mm). f, Carrot (29x44mm). g, Broccoli (43x35mm). h, Potato (40x30mm).

2010, Mar. 8 Litho. *Die Cut*

Self-Adhesive

1353 Booklet pane of 8 22.00
a.-h. A801 1 Any single 2.75 1.40

Nos. 1353a-1353h each sold for 80c on day of issue.

Souvenir Sheet

Kotka Harbor — A802

No. 1354: a, Vellamo Maritime Center, museum ship Tarmo, crane. b, Sailboat, Wooden Boat Center, vert.

2010, Mar. 24 *Perf. 13¾*

1354 A802 Sheet of 2 5.50 5.50
a.-b. 1 Either single 2.75 2.10

Nos. 1354a-1354b each sold for 80c on day of issue.

Europa — A803

No. 1355 — Children, books, characters and background in: a, Orange. b, Blue green.

2010, May 4 *Perf. 14x13¼*

1355 A803 Horiz. pair 4.75 4.25
a.-b. 80c Either single 2.25 1.50

Personalized Stamp — A804

Serpentine Die Cut 11¾ Syncopated

2010, May 4 Self-Adhesive

1356 A804 1 multi 2.75 1.40

No. 1356 sold for 80c on day of issue. The generic design part of the stamp shown could be personalized.

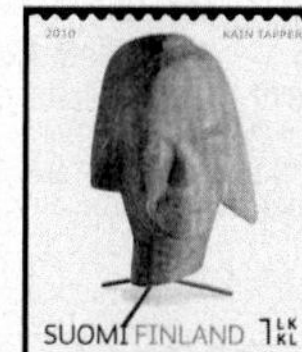

Sculpture — A805

No. 1357: a, Hymy, by Kain Tapper (28x33mm). b, Hefaistos, by Laila Pullinen (28x33mm). c, Cyclist, by Pekka Aarnio (28x33mm). d, Construction, by Kari Huhtamo (28x33mm). e, Salvos, by Mauno Hartman, horiz. (56x29mm). f, Joy, by Miina Akkijyrkka, horiz. (56x29mm).

Serpentine Die Cut 11¾ Horiz.

2010, May 4 Self-Adhesive

1357 Booklet pane of 6 17.00 13.00
a.-f. A805 1 Any single 2.75 2.10

Nos. 1357a-1357f each sold for 80c on day of issue.

Souvenir Sheet

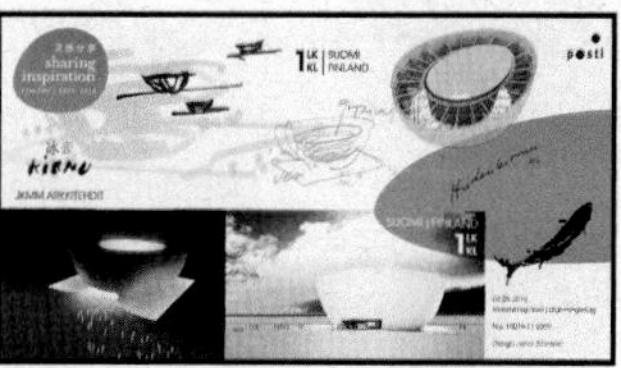

Finnish Pavilion, Expo 2010, Shanghai — A806

No. 1358: a, Aerial view of model and drawing. b, Side view of model.

Serpentine Die Cut 4½ At Bottom

2010, May 4 Self-Adhesive

1358 A806 Sheet of 2 5.50 4.25
a.-b. 1 Either single 2.75 2.10

Nos. 1358a-1358b each sold for 80c on day of issue.

Miniature Sheet

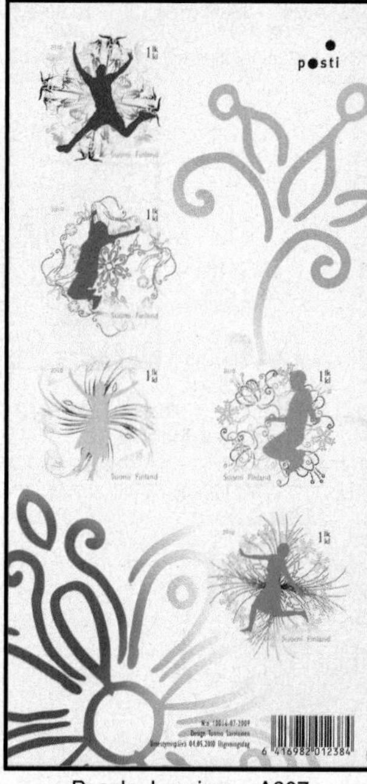

People Jumping — A807

No. 1359 — Jumpers in: a, Purple. b, Red. c, Yellow. d, Blue. e, Green.

2010, May 4 *Serpentine Die Cut 5*

Self-Adhesive

1359 A807 Sheet of 5 13.50 10.50
a.-e. 1 Any single 2.60 2.10

Nos. 1359a-1359e each sold for 80c on day of issue.

Torronsuo National Park — A808

Die Cut Perf. 14

2010, Sept. 13 Litho.

Self-Adhesive

1360 A808 1 multi 2.75 2.10

No. 1360 sold for 75c on day of issue.

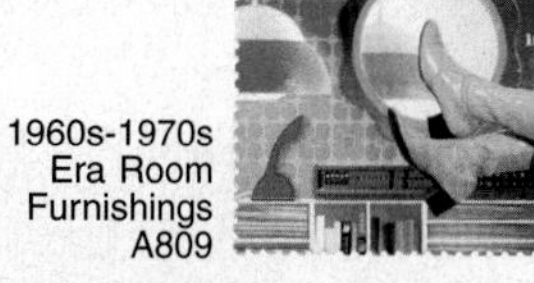

1960s-1970s Era Room Furnishings A809

2010, Sept. 13 Booklet Stamp

Self-Adhesive

1361 A809 1 multi 2.75 2.10
a. Booklet pane of 10 27.50

No. 1361 sold fo 75c on day of issue.

Souvenir Sheet

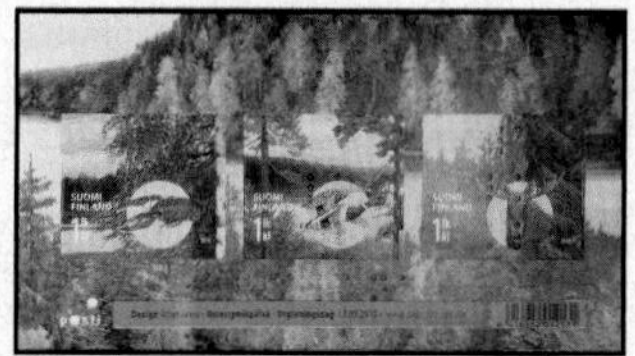
Autumn — A810

No. 1362 — Forest and: a, Crayfish. b, Ducks. c, Elk.

Serpentine Die Cut 12¾x13¼ Syncopated

Litho. & Silk-screened

2010, Sept. 13 Self-Adhesive

1362 A810 Sheet of 3 8.25 6.50
a.-c. 1 Any single 2.75 2.10

On day of issue, Nos. 1362a-1362c each sold for 75c.

Santa Claus — A811

Reindeer and Moon — A812

Sleigh of Santa Claus Over Lapland A813

No. 1365: a, Star and Santa Claus with sack. b, Poinsettias, ribbon and bell. c, Sleigh of Santa Claus over church. d, Heart-shaped wreath. e, Reindeer and Aurora Borealis.

Die Cut Perf. 14

2010, Nov. 5 Litho.

Self-Adhesive

1363 Horiz. pair 3.50 3.25
a. A811 55c multi 1.75 1.60
b. A812 55c multi 1.75 1.60
1364 A813 1 multi 2.75 2.10

Souvenir Sheet

1365 Sheet of 5 8.50 7.75
a. A811 55c multi 1.60 1.50
b. A811 55c multi 1.60 1.50
c. A813 55c multi 1.60 1.50
d. A811 55c multi 1.60 1.50
e. A811 55c multi 1.60 1.50

Christmas. No. 1364 sold for 75c on day of issue. See Japan No. 3269.

Birch Bud A814

Birch Leaves A815

2011, Jan. 24 Litho. *Die Cut*

Self-Adhesive

1366 A814 20c multi .60 .55
1367 A815 30c multi .90 .85

Flag of Finland A816

2011, Jan. 24 Litho. & Embossed

Self-Adhesive

1368 A816 2 gray & blue 2.50 1.75

No. 1368 sold for 60c on day of issue.

Birds and Flowers — A817

No. 1369: a, Bird on branch, country name in red circle. b, Bird in flight, country name in blue circle. c, Flowers, country name in red circle. d, Bird on branch, country name in blue circle. e, Bird in flight, country name in red circle.

Serpentine Die Cut 10¼ Horiz.

2011, Jan. 24 Litho.

Self-Adhesive

1369		Booklet pane of 5	12.50	8.00
a.-e.	A817	2 Any single	2.50	1.60

Nos. 1369a-1369e each sold for 60c on day of issue.

Mailboxes — A818

No. 1370: a, Mailbox mounted on tire. b, Snow-covered mailbox. c, Child opening mailbox. d, Mailbox next to sauna. e, Mailbox with posthorn and Finnish lion.

Die Cut Perf. 10 Vert. Syncopated at Right

2011, Jan. 24 Self-Adhesive

Coil Stamps

1370		Strip of 5	12.50	8.50
a.-e.	A818	2 Any single	2.50	1.75

Nos. 1370a-1370e each sold for 60c on day of issue.

Miniature Sheet

Finnish National Opera, Cent. — A819

No. 1371: a, Male and female performers dancing, men in helmets. b, Man with hat and red ribbon, vert. c, Male and female performers in embrace. d, Woman in red dress in water, vert.

Serpentine Die Cut 15½ Horiz.

2011, Jan. 24 Self-Adhesive

1371	A819	Sheet of 4	10.00	6.50
a.-d.		2 Any single	2.50	1.60

Nos. 1371a-1371d each sold for 60c on day of issue.

Miniature Sheet

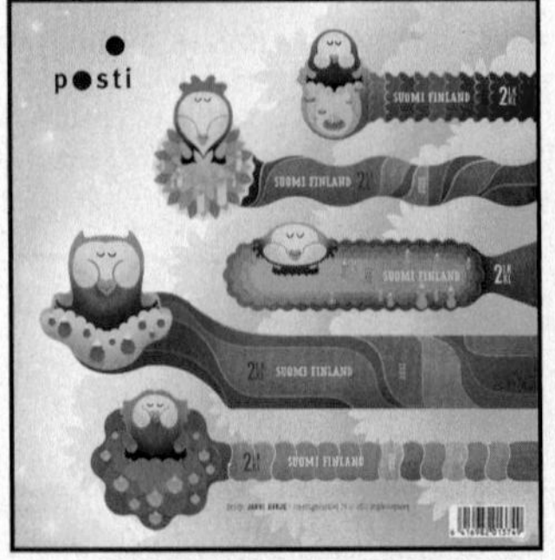

Birds in Trees — A820

No. 1372 — Various stylized birds with tree leaves in: a, Green (53x24mm). b, Blue (64x32mm). c, Orange (70x20mm). d, Yellow brown (89x39mm). e, Red violet (78x31mm).

2011, Jan. 24 *Die Cut*

Self-Adhesive

1372	A820	Sheet of 5	12.50	8.00
a.-e.		2 Any single	2.50	1.60

Nos. 1372a-1372e each sold for 60c on day of issue.

Tulips — A821

2011, Apr. 1 *Die Cut Perf. 13¾*

Self-Adhesive

1373	A821	2 multi	2.50	1.75

No. 1373 sold for 60c on day of issue.

Dahlias — A822

2011, Apr. 1 *Die Cut*

Self-Adhesive

Color of Country Name

1374	A822	1 red violet	2.75	.75
1375	A822	1 gray green	2.75	.75
a.		Horiz. pair, #1374-1375	5.50	

Nos. 1374-1375 each sold for 75c on day of issue.

Miniature Sheet

Kitchen — A823

No. 1376: a, Lamp, counter, pitcher, stove with pots (32x22mm, serpentine die cut 10x10¾). b, Bottles with stoppers (19x46mm, serpentine die cut 9¾x10). c, Hand dropping seasonings into bowl (24x32mm, serpentine die cut 10x10¼). d, Cup, saucer, bowl with lid (22x32mm, serpentine die cut 9½x10¼). e, Cup, eggs in bowl (24x32mm, serpentine die cut 9¾x10).

2011, Apr. 1 *Serpentine Die Cut*

Self-Adhesive

1376	A823	Sheet of 5	12.50	8.50
a.-e.		2 Any single	2.50	1.60

Nos. 1376a-1376e each sold for 60c on day of issue.

Government Buildings — A824

No. 1377: a, House of the Estates, Helsinki, 1890. b, Finnish Embassy, New Delhi, India, 1985. c, Helsinki Music Center, 2011. d, Government Palace, Helsinki, 1828. e, Malmi Airport, Helsinki, 1938. f, Finnish Forest Research Institute Research Center, Joensuu, 2004.

2011, Apr. 1 *Die Cut Perf. 13¼*

Self-Adhesive

1377		Booklet pane of 6	15.00	10.50
a.-f.	A824	2 Any single	2.50	1.75

Nos. 1377a-1377f each sold for 60c on day of issue.

National Council of Women, Cent. A825

No. 1378 — Comic strip characters Maisa and Kaarina, by Tiina Paju and Sari Luhtanen: a, Holding star-tipped wands. b, Knitting blanket with stars. c, Playing tennis. d, Posing and taking picture. e, Wearing stars on dresses. f, Placing star on cake.

2011, Apr. 1 *Serpentine Die Cut 11*

Self-Adhesive

1378		Booklet pane of 6	15.00	10.50
a.-f.	A825	2 Any single	2.50	1.75

Nos. 1378a-1378f each sold for 60c on day of issue.

Europa — A826

No. 1379 — Trees in: a, Spring and summer. b, Autumn and winter.

2011, May 6 *Perf. 12¾x13¼*

Self-Adhesive

1379	A826	Horiz. pair	5.00	3.00
a.-b.		2 Either single	2.50	1.25

Intl. Year of Forests. Nos. 1379a-1379b each sold for 60c on day of issue.

Moomin — A827

Mymble — A828

Little My — A829

Moominmamma and Moomin — A830

Hemulen A831

Hattifatteners A832

2011, May 6 *Die Cut*

Self-Adhesive

1380		Booklet pane of 6	15.00	10.00
a.	A827	2 multi	2.50	1.60
b.	A828	2 multi	2.50	1.60
c.	A829	2 multi	2.50	1.60
d.	A830	2 multi	2.50	1.60
e.	A831	2 multi	2.50	1.60
f.	A832	2 multi	2.50	1.60

Nos. 1380a-1380f each sold for 60c on day of issue.

Souvenir Sheet

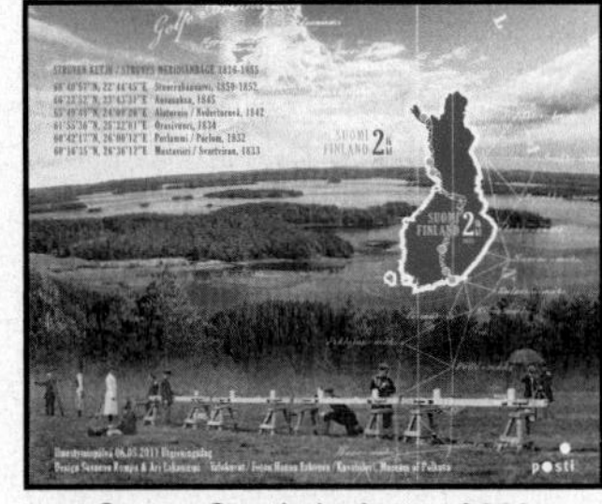

Struve Geodetic Arc — A833

No. 1381: a, Land, water, geodetic arc triangulations. b, Map of Finland with path of triangulations.

2011, May 6 *Die Cut*

Self-Adhesive

1381	A833	Sheet of 2	5.00	3.50
a.-b.		2 Either single	2.50	1.75

Nos. 1381a-1381b each sold for 60c on day of issue.

Miniature Sheet

Tree of Happiness — A834

No. 1382: a, Balloons and gifts (32mm diameter). b, Birds on branch (32mm diameter). c, Cake with Finnish flags (34x29mm oval). d, Bird in birdhouse (34x29mm oval). e, Boy and girl on branch (32mm diameter).

2011, May 6 *Die Cut*

Self-Adhesive

1382	A834	Sheet of 5	12.50	8.50
a.-e.		2 Any single	2.50	1.60

Nos. 1382a-1382e each sold for 60c on day of issue.

Heraldic Lion Type of 2002

Die Cut Perf. 12 Syncopated

2011, Sept. 5 Litho.

Self-Adhesive

1383	A616	€2 green & multi	5.75	5.50
1384	A616	€4 pur & multi	11.50	11.00

Souvenir Sheet

Juhani Aho (1861-1921), Writer — A835

No. 1385: a, Stack of paper, trees. b, Aho on skis.

Litho. & Embossed

2011, Sept. 5 *Perf. 13½*

Self-Adhesive

1385	A835	Sheet of 2	5.00	3.50
a.-b.		2 Either single	2.50	1.75

Nos. 1385a-1385b each sold for 60c on day of issue.

Miniature Sheet

Finnish Comics, Cent. — A836

No. 1386: a, Kili ja Possu, by Olavi Vikainen, 1950s. b, Unto Uneksija, by Joonas (Veikko Savolainen), 1960s. c, Herra Kerhonen, by Gösta Thilén, 1930s. d, Antti Puuhaara, by Aarne Nopsanen, 1940s. e, Janne Ankkanen, by Ola Fogelberg, 1910s. f, Olli Pirteä, by Hjalmar Löfving, 1920s.

Die Cut Perf. 8½

2011, Sept. 5 Litho.

Self-Adhesive

1386 A836 Sheet of 6 15.00 10.00
a.-f. 2 Any single 2.50 2.00

Nos. 1386a-1386f each sold for 60c on day of issue.

Houses with Snow-covered Roofs — A837

2011, Nov. 7 *Die Cut Perf. 14*

Booklet Stamp

Self-Adhesive

1387 A837 1 multi 2.75 2.10
a. Booklet pane of 10 + 10 etiquettes 27.50

No. 1387 sold for 75c on day of issue.

Personalized Stamp — A838

Serpentine Die Cut 11¾ Syncopated

2011, Nov. 7 Self-Adhesive

1388 A838 2 multi 2.50 1.75

No. 1388 sold for 60c on day of issue. The generic design part of the stamp shown could be personalized.

A839

Christmas — A840

Die Cut Perf. 14

2011, Nov. 7 Self-Adhesive

1389 A839 55c multi 1.75 1.50
1390 A840 2 multi 2.50 1.75

No. 1390 sold for 60c on day of issue.

Miniature Sheet

A841

No. 1391: a, Birds on wire. b, Girl with watering can. c, Hearts. d, Girl and dog. e, Woman blowing heart-shaped bubbles. f, Heart-shaped door and key.

2012, Jan. 23 *Die Cut Perf. 13¼x13*

Self-Adhesive

1391 A841 Sheet of 6 15.00 9.50
a.-f. 2 Any single 2.50 1.20

Nos. 1391a-1391f each sold for 60c on day of issue.

Miniature Sheet

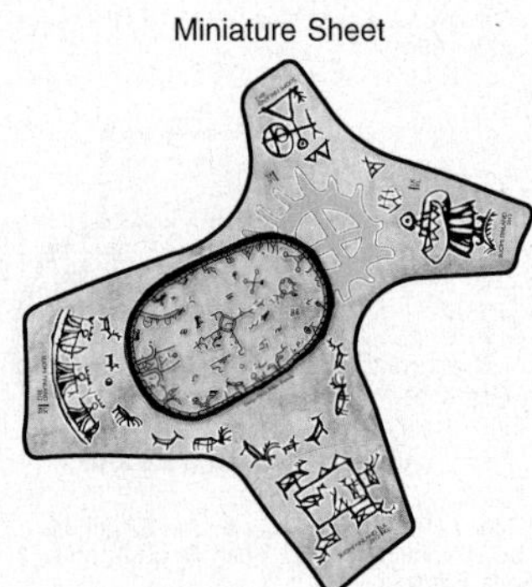

Sami Culture — A842

No. 1392: a, Stick-figure man holding forked stick. b, Stick figure of woman. c, Reindeer at sides of rectangle. d, Three daughters of Sami's mother god and reindeer. Stamps are of various sizes.

2012, Jan. 23 *Die Cut*

Self-Adhesive

1392 A842 Sheet of 4 11.00 8.00
a.-d. 1 Any single 2.75 2.00

Nos. 1392a-1392d each sold for 75c on day of issue.

The School Girl II — A843

Green Apples and Champagne Glass — A844

Self-Portrait on Black — A845

Silk Shoes A846

Die Cut Perf. 13, 12¾x13¼ (#1393b), 13¼ (#1393c)

2012, Jan. 23 Self-Adhesive

1393 Booklet pane of 4 11.00 8.00
a. A843 1 multi 2.75 2.00
b. A844 1 multi 2.75 2.00
c. A845 1 multi 2.75 2.00
d. A846 1 multi 2.75 2.00

Paintings by Helene Schjerfbeck (1862-1946). Nos. 1393a-1393d each sold for 75c on day of issue.

Winning Designs in Future City Stamp Design Contest A847

Designs: No. 1394, Hands, by Varpu Kangas. No. 1395, Shapes and dots, by Kangas. No. 1396, Future City is Diversity, by Chloé Chapeaublanc. No. 1397, Buildings, balloons, and inverted umbrella on tree branch, by Sini Henttonen. No. 1398, Children's drawingin red, blue, and black, by Daniel Kallström, vert. No. 1399, Children's drawing of animal under sun, by Elias Ollila, vert. No. 1400, Rabbits, by Katja Hynninen. No. 1401, Cat's head and heavy man on bicycle, by Ville Korhonen.

Booklet Stamps

Serpentine Die Cut 8¾x9 (#1394, 1400), Rectangle and Arc Die Cut (#1395-1396), Arc Die Cut 12¾ (#1397, 1401), Sawtooth Die Cut 15½x15¼ (#1398-1399)

2012, Jan. 23 Self-Adhesive

1394 A847 1 multi 2.75 2.75
1395 A847 1 multi 2.75 2.75
a. Booklet pane of 2, #1394-1395 5.50 4.00
1396 A847 1 multi 2.75 2.75
1397 A847 1 multi 2.75 2.75
a. Booklet pane of 2, #1396-1397 5.50 4.00
1398 A847 1 multi 2.75 2.75
1399 A847 1 multi 2.75 2.75
a. Booklet pane of 2, #1398-1399 5.50 4.00
1400 A847 1 multi 2.75 2.75
1401 A847 1 multi 2.75 2.75
a. Booklet pane of 2, #1400-1401 5.50 4.00
Complete booklet, #1395a, 1397a, 1399a, 1401a 22.00 16.00
Nos. 1394-1401 (8) 22.00 22.00

Nos. 1394-1401 each sold for 75c on day of issue.

Wedding Rings — A848

Die Cut Perf. 14

2012, Mar. 5 Litho. & Engr.

Self-Adhesive

1402 A848 1 multi 2.75 2.00

No. 1402 sold for 75c on day of issue.

Easter A849

Serpentine Die Cut 8¼ Vert.

2012, Mar. 5 Litho.

Self-Adhesive

1403 A849 1 multi 2.75 2.00

No. 1403 sold for 75c on day of issue.

Souvenir Sheet

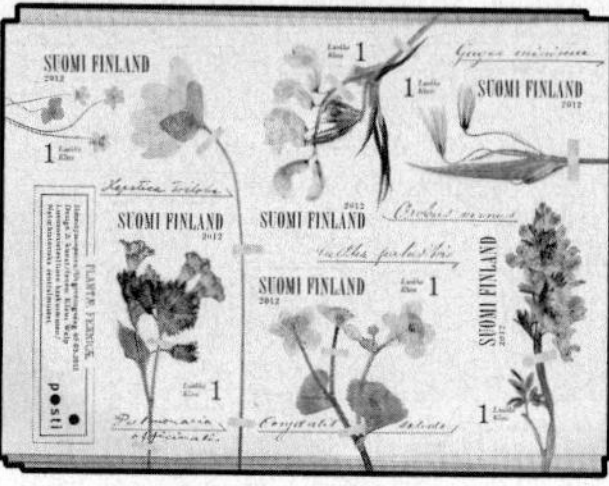

Flowers — A850

No. 1404: a, Hepatica triloba (three small yellow flowers at L, large yellow flower at R, denomination al LL). b, Orobus virnus (six yellow and white flowers on stem, denomination at UR), vert. c, Gagea minima (two partially opened buds, denomination at UL). d, Pulmonaria officinalis (four purple flowers, denomination at LR), vert. e, Caltha palastris (yellow flowers, denoimination at UR). f, Corydalis solida (cluster of purple flowers, denomination at LL), vert.

2012, Mar. 5 *Die Cut Perf. 10*

Self-Adhesive

1404 A850 Sheet of 6 17.00 12.00
a.-f. 1 Any single 2.75 2.00

Nos. 1404a-1404f each sold for 75c on day of issue.

Intl. Women's Day A851

No. 1405: a, Woman and hearts. b, Women's hands with glasses of fruit, vert. c, Women's legs and shoes, vert. d, Women and musical notes.

2012, Mar. 5 *Die Cut Perf. 12½*

Self-Adhesive

1405 Booklet pane of 4 11.00 8.00
a.-d. A851 1 Any single 2.75 2.00

Nos. 1405a-1405d each sold for 75c on day of issue.

Railroads in Finland, 150th Anniv. — A852

No. 1406: a, Train engineer, steam locomotive. b, Train, ticket. c, Railroad warning sign, train in snow. d, Passenger car and passengers at platform, clock. e, Railway worker, modern train. f, Train, lake, statue.

Serpentine Die Cut 9½ Horiz.

2012, Mar. 5 Self-Adhesive

1406 Booklet pane of 6 17.00 12.00
a.-f. A852 1 Any single 2.75 2.00

Nos. 1406a-1406f each sold for 75c on day of issue.

2012 Men's Ice Hockey World Cup Tournament, Finland and Sweden
A853

2012, Mar. 21 ***Die Cut Perf. 14***
Self-Adhesive

1407 A853 1 multi 2.75 2.00

No. 1407 sold for 75c on day of issue.

Souvenir Sheet

Rescue Boats — A854

No. 1408: a, Jenny Wihuri (red and white boat). b, Merikarhu (green, orange and white boat).

2012, Mar. 21 ***Perf. 13½x13***
Self-Adhesive

1408 A854 Sheet of 2 5.50 4.00
a.-b. 1 Either single 2.75 2.00

Nos. 1408a-1408b each sold for 75c on day of issue.

Europa — A855

No. 1409: a, Ship on lake. b, People at beach.

2012, May 7 ***Perf. 13¼x12¾***
Self-Adhesive

1409 A855 1 Vert. pair, #a-b 5.50 3.75

Nos. 1409a-1409b each sold for 75c on day of issue.

Bothnian Sea National Park — A856

2012, May 7 ***Die Cut Perf. 14***
Self-Adhesive

1410 A856 1 multi 2.75 2.00

No. 1410 sold for 75c on day of issue.

A857

Sunflowers — A858

2012, May 7 ***Die Cut Perf. 17***
Self-Adhesive

1411 A857 1 multi 2.75 2.00
1412 A858 1 multi 2.75 2.00

Nos. 1411-142 each sold for 75c on day of issue.

A859

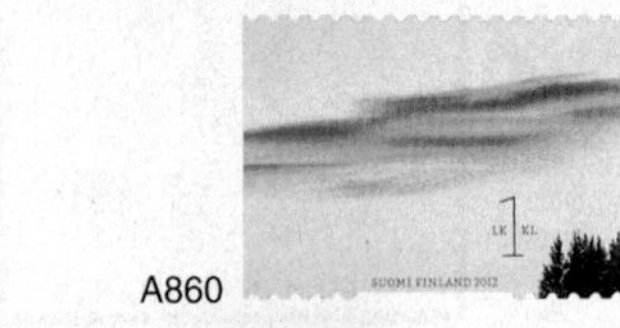
A860

Clouds
A861

Die Cut Perf. 10 Horiz., Syncopated at Bottom

2012, May 7 **Self-Adhesive**
Coil Stamps

1413 Horiz. strip of 3 8.25
a. A859 1 multi 2.75 1.40
b. A860 1 multi 2.75 1.40
c. A861 1 multi 2.75 1.40

Nos. 1413a-1413c each sold for 75c on day of issue.

Souvenir Sheet

Disabled Athletes — A862

No. 1414: a, Leo-Pekka Tahti, cyclist. b, Saana-Maria Sinisalo, archer.

Die Cut Perf. 11¼x11½
Litho. & Silk-screened

2012, May 7 **Self-Adhesive**

1414 A862 1 Sheet of 2, #a-b 5.50 4.00

Nos. 1414a-1414b each sold for 75c on day of issue.

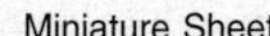
Miniature Sheet

Autumn Dreams — A863

No. 1415: a, Hot-air balloon (36x46mm). b, Moon, lanterns in tree (37x39mm). c, Flying geese (28x36mm). d, Scarecrow and hay rolls (29x46mm). e, Girl feeding carrots to horse (44x34mm).

Serpentine Die Cut 4 to 7

2012, Sept. 3 **Litho.**
Self-Adhesive

1415 A863 Sheet of 5 13.50 10.00
a.-e. 1 Any single 2.60 2.00

On day of issue, Nos. 1415a-1415e each sold for 80c.

Recording Stars of the 1990s
A864

No. 1416: a, Kaija Koo. b, Jari Sillanpää. c, Laura Voutilainen. d, Yölintu. e, Agents. f, Anna Eriksson.

2012, Sept. 3 ***Die Cut Perf. 8½***
Self-Adhesive

1416 Booklet pane of 6 17.00 12.00
a.-f. A864 1 Any single 2.75 2.00

On day of issue, Nos. 1416a-1416f each sold for 80c.

Pets — A865

No. 1417: a, Cat, inscriptions in red. b, White rabbit facing left. c, Gray rabbit facing right. d, Dachshund puppy, year date at LR. e, Jack Russell terrier puppy, year date at LL. f, Kitten, inscriptions in green.

Serpentine Die Cut 11¾ Horiz.

2012, Sept. 3 **Self-Adhesive**

1417 Booklet pane of 6 17.00 12.00
a.-f. A865 1 Any single 2.75 2.00

On day of issue, Nos. 1417a-1417f each sold for 80c.

Christmas Tree — A866

Stable Lantern — A867

2012, Nov. 5 ***Serpentine Die Cut 9½***
Self-Adhesive

1418 A866 60c multi 1.75 1.60

Serpentine Die Cut 10

1419 A867 1 multi 2.75 1.75

Christmas. No. 1419 sold for 80c on day of issue.

Sledders
A868

Self-Adhesive

2013, Jan. 21 ***Die Cut Perf. 14***

1420 A868 1 multi 2.75 1.40

No. 1420 sold for 80c on day of issue.

Coilostylis Parkinsoniana
A869

Self-Adhesive

2013, Jan. 21 ***Die Cut Perf. 14***

1421 A869 €1.10 multi 2.75 1.40

See No. 1442.

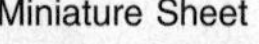
Miniature Sheet

St.Valentine's Day — A870

No. 1422: a, Polar bears. b, Whale. c, Parrots. d, Elephants. e, Chameleon. f, Monkey.

2013, Jan. 21 ***Die Cut***
Self-Adhesive

1422 A870 Sheet of 6 + 4 labels 17.00 12.00
a.-f. 1 Any single 2.75 2.00

Nos. 1422a-1422f each sold for 80c on day of issue.

Actors and Actresses — A871

No. 1427: a, Ritva Valkama. b, Esko Salminen. c, Outi Mäenpää. d, Martti Suosalo. e, Krista Kosonen. f, Aku Hirviniemi.

Die Cut Perf. 6¾ Vert. Syncopated

2013, Mar. 4
Self-Adhesive

1423 Booklet pane of 6 17.00 12.00
a.-f. A871 1 Any single 2.75 2.00

Finnish Actors Federation, cent. On day of issue, Nos. 1423a-1423f each sold for 80c.

Easter Rooster — A872

2013, Mar. 8 ***Die Cut Perf. 14***
Self-Adhesive

1424 A872 1 multi 2.75 2.00

No. 1424 sold for 80c on day of issue.

Roses — A873

2013, Mar. 8 **Self-Adhesive**

1425 A873 1 multi 2.75 2.00

No. 1425 sold for 80c on day of issue.

Blackberries A874

Gooseberry A875

Red Currants A876

Die Cut Perf. 10 Horiz. Syncopated
2013, Mar. 8 **Self-Adhesive**
Coil Stamps

1426 Horiz. strip of 3 8.50 6.00
a. A874 1 multi 2.75 2.00
b. A875 1 multi 2.75 2.00
c. A876 1 multi 2.75 2.00

On day of issue, Nos. 1426a-1426c each sold for 80c.

A877

A878

A879

Outhouses A880

2013, Mar. 8 ***Die Cut Perf. 12***
Self-Adhesive

1427 Booklet pane of 4 11.50
a. A877 2 multi 2.75 2.00
b. A878 2 multi 2.75 2.00
c. A879 2 multi 2.75 2.00
d. A880 2 multi 2.75 2.00

On day of issue, Nos. 1527a-1527d each sold for 70c.

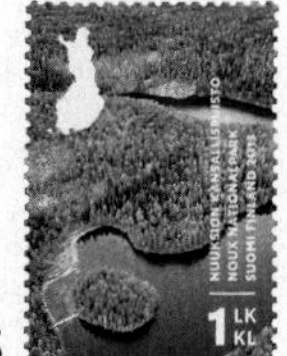
Flower Bouquet — A881

2013, May 6 ***Die Cut Perf. 14***
Self-Adhesive

1428 A881 1 multi 2.75 1.40

No. 1428 sold for 80c on day of issue.

Nuuksio Natl. Park — A882

2013, May 6 **Litho.**
Self-Adhesive

1429 A882 1 multi 2.75 1.40

No. 1429 sold for 80c on day of issue.

2012 Ford Transit Connect Mail Van — A883

1933 Volvo LV-70 Mail Truck A884

2013, May 6 ***Die Cut Perf. 12½x13¼***
Self-Adhesive

1430 Horiz. pair 5.50
a. A883 1 multi 2.75 2.00
b. A884 1 multi 2.75 2.00

Europa. On day of issue, Nos. 1430a-1430b each sold for 80c.

Miniature Sheet

Odd Finnish Sports and Activities — A885

No. 1431: a, Man carrying wife. b, Boot throwing. c, Air guitarist. d, Woman pushing man in milk cart. e, Man sitting on ant hill. f, Swamp soccer.

2013, May 6 ***Die Cut Perf. 10***
Self-Adhesive

1431 A885 Sheet of 6 + 6 etiquettes 17.50
a.-f. 1 Any single 2.75 2.00

On day of issue, Nos. 1431a-1431f each sold for 80c.

Moomins — A886

No. 1432: a, Moominpappa holding drink (red background, 30x34mm). b, Moomintroll jumping (blue background, 33x31mm). c, Moominmamma with purse (green background, 33x34mm). d, Little My with basket on head (yellow orange background, 32x33mm). e, Snorkmaiden and piece of paper (red violet background, 30x35mm). f, Snufkin (brown orange background, 32x36mm).

2013, May 6 ***Die Cut***
Self-Adhesive

1432 Booklet pane of 6 + 6 etiquettes 17.00
a.-f. A886 1 Any single 2.75 2.00

On day of issue, Nos. 1432a-1432f each sold for 80c.

Personalized Stamp — A891

Serpentine Die Cut 11¾ Syncopated
2013, Aug. 12 **Litho.**
Self-Adhesive

1437 A891 1 black 4.50 4.50

No. 1437 had a franking value of 85c on the day of issue. The vignette shown for No. 1437 is a generic image depicting a Volvo PV 444 police vehicle and is one of ten different police vehicles depicted in the image portion of stamps in a sheet of ten stamps having the same common "frame" that sold for €16.50. Customers purchasing sheets of No. 1437 could also download vignette images from an online library of images on the stamp creation website or use their own downloaded images.

Pres. Sauli Niinistö, 65th Birthday A895

Die Cut Perf. 12 Syncopated
2013, Aug. 23 **Litho.**
Self-Adhesive

1441 A895 1 blk & gray 2.75 1.40

No. 1441 sold for 85c on day of issue.

Coilostylis Parkinsoniana Type of 2013
Die Cut Perf. 14
2013, Aug. 23 **Litho.**
Self-Adhesive

1442 A869 €1.20 multi 2.75 1.40

Souvenir Sheet

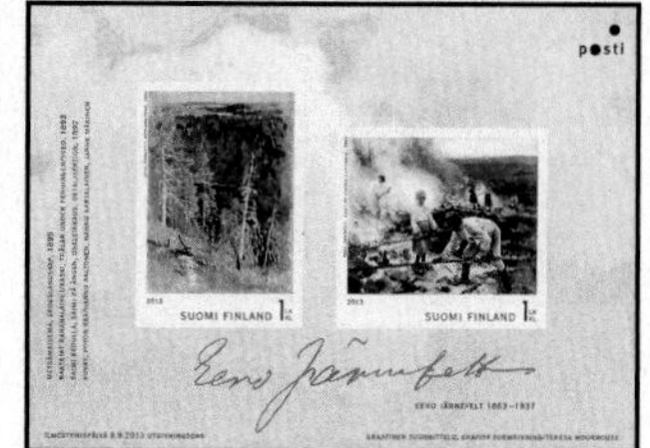
Paintings by Eero Järnefelt (1863-1937) — A896

No. 1443: a, Metsämaisema (Forest Scene) (34x49mm). b, Raatajat Rahanalaiset (Under the Yoke - Burning the Brushwood) (44x40mm).

Serpentine Die Cut 14½
2013, Sept. 9 **Litho.**
Self-Adhesive

1443 A896 Sheet of 2 5.50 4.25
a.-b. 1 Either single 2.75 2.10

On day of issue, Nos. 1443a-1443b each sold for 85c.

Postcrossing — A897

No. 1444 — Stylized postal card and: a, Hand holding pencil. b, Blackboard. c, Heart-shaped Earth. d, Open mouth.

Serpentine Die Cut 12¼
2013, Sept. 9 **Litho.**
Self-Adhesive

1444 Booklet pane of 4 + 4 etiquettes 11.00
a.-d A897 1 Any single 2.75 1.10

On day of issue Nos. 1444a-1444d each sold for 85c.

Miniature Sheet

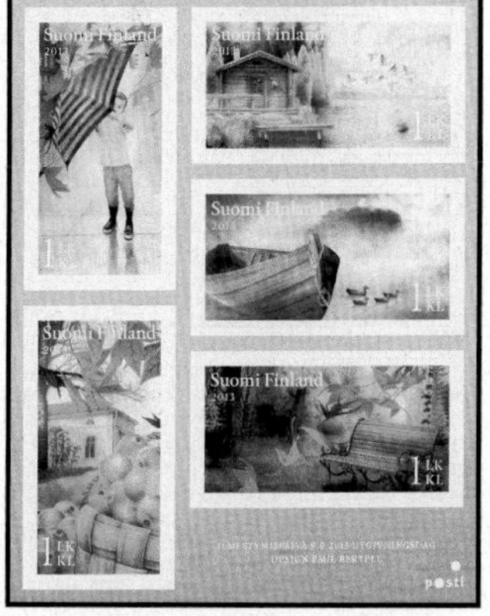
Autumn Scenes — A898

No. 1445: a, Boy with umbrella, falling leaves. b, Lakeside sauna, geese in flight, buoy, horiz. c, Rowboat and ducks, horiz. d, Apples in basket, house, falling leaves. e, Park bench, falling leaves, horiz.

Serpentine Die Cut 14x14¼, 14¼x14
2013, Sept. 9 **Litho.**
Self-Adhesive

1445 A898 Sheet of 5 11.50
a.-e. 1 Any single 2.25 2.25

On day of issue, Nos. 1445a-1445e each sold for 85c.

Miniature Sheet

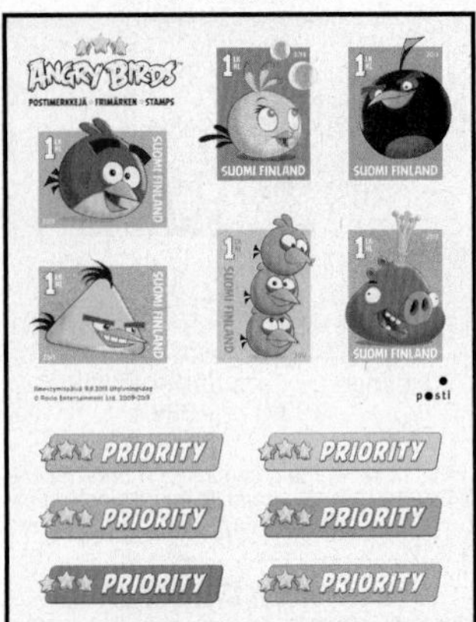

Angry Birds Characters — A899

No. 1446: a, Red Bird. b, Pink Bird, vert. c, Black Bird, vert. d, Yellow Bird. e, Blue Birds, vert. f, King Pig, vert.

Die Cut Perf. 8¼

2013, Sept. 9 **Litho.**

Self-Adhesive

1446 A899 Sheet of 6 + 6 etiquettes 13.50
a.-f. 1 Any single 2.25 2.25

On day of issue, Nos. 1446a-1446f each sold for 85c.

Finnish Parliament, 150th Anniv. — A900

Die Cut Perf. 14

2013, Sept. 17 **Litho.**

Self-Adhesive

1447 A900 1 multi 2.40 2.40

No. 1447 sold for 85c on day of issue.

Finnish School System — A901

No. 1448: a, Girl receiving school lunch, apple, lettuce, pitcher and plate. b, Boy receiving medical examination, posture diagrams. c, Girl practicing writing on blackboard, letters in Finnish alphabet. d, Uno Cygnaeus (1810-88), founder of Finnish school system, map of Finland. e, Children in physical education class, children skiing. f, Teacher watching boys writing at desk, orrery, sun and planet.

Die Cut Perf. 6¾ Horiz. At Top

2013, Nov. 14 **Litho.**

Self-Adhesive

1448 Booklet pane of 6 13.50
a.-f. A901 1 Any single 2.25 2.25

On day of issue, Nos. 1448a-1448f each sold for 85c.

Children Hugging A902

Angel A903

Boy with Christmas Trees — A904

Die Cut Perf. 14

2013, Nov. 4 **Litho.**

Self-Adhesive

1449 A902 65c multi 1.75 1.75
1450 A903 2 multi 2.00 2.00
1451 A904 1 multi 2.25 2.25
Nos. 1449-1451 (3) 6.00 6.00

Christmas. On day of issue, No. 1450 sold for 75c; No. 1451, 85c.

Snowmen A905

Serpentine Die Cut 10¼

2014, Jan. 20 **Litho.**

Self-Adhesive

1452 A905 1 multi 2.75 2.75

No. 1452 sold for €1 on day of issue.

Miniature Sheet

Teddy Bears — A906

No. 1453: a, Teddy bear writing with quill pen. b, Teddy bear pushing another on sled, horiz. c, Two Teddy bears and flower. d, Two Teddy bears dancing. e, Teddy bear sleeping in slipper, horiz. f, Two Teddy bears playing musical instruments.

Serpentine Die Cut 16

2014, Jan. 20 **Litho.**

Self-Adhesive

1453 A906 Sheet of 6 + 4 stickers 16.50
a.-f. 1 Any single 2.75 2.75

Nos. 1453a-1453f each sold for €1 on day of issue.

Castles — A907

No. 1454: a, Turun Linna (Turku Castle) (34x50mm). b, Hämeen Linna (Häme Castle) (34x50mm). c, Raaseporin Linna (Raseborg Castle) (34x50mm). d, Suomenlinna (Sveaborg Fortress) (34x58mm). e, Olavinlinna (Olavinlinna Castle) (34x50mm). f, Kastelholma (Kastelholma Castle) (50x34mm).

Die Cut Perf. 7½

2014, Jan. 20 **Litho.**

Self-Adhesive

1454 Booklet pane of 6 16.50
a.-f. A907 1 Any single 2.75 2.75

Nos. 1454a-1454f each sold for €1 on day of issue.

Souvenir Sheet

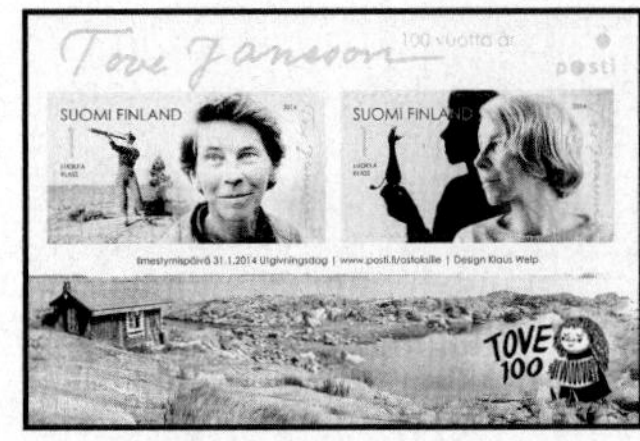

Tove Jansson (1914-2001), Creator of *Moomins* Characters — A908

No. 1456: a, Jansson with telescope. b, Silhouette of Jansson and Moomin character, Sniff.

Die Cut Perf. 12½

2014, Jan. 31 **Litho.**

Self-Adhesive

1455 A908 Sheet of 2 5.50
a.-b. 1 Either single 2.75 2.75

Nos. 1455a-1455b each sold for €1 on day of issue.

Easter A909

Die Cut Perf. 9¾ Horiz.

2014, Mar. 3 **Litho.**

Self-Adhesive

1456 A909 1 multi 2.75 2.75

No. 1456 sold for €1 on day of issue.

Sami Jauhojärvi and Iivo Niskanen, 2014 Winter Olympic Cross-Country Team Sprint Gold Medalists — A909a

Serpentine Die Cut 11¾ Syncopated

2014, Mar. 3 **Litho.**

Self-Adhesive

1456A A909a 1 multi 5.00 5.00

No. 1456A was printed in sheets of 10 that sold for €18. No. 1456 had a franking value of €1 on day of issue.

Fruits and Blossoms — A910

No. 1457: a, Pears (light green background). b, Apples (yellow background). c, Cherries (pink background).

Die Cut Perf. 10 Vert. Syncopated

2014, Mar. 3 **Litho.**

Coil Stamps

Self-Adhesive

1457 Vert. strip of 3 7.50
a.-c. A910 2 Any single 2.50 2.50

Nos. 1457a-1457c each sold for 90c on day of issue.

A911

Congratulations A912

No. 1458: a, Cat, cake with strawberries. b, Butterflies and flower. c, Squirrel and flowers. d, Strrawberries, blueberries and flower. e, Basket of flowers.

Serpentine Die Cut 13¾x13½ (A911), 14½x15¼ (A912)

2014, Mar. 3 **Litho.**

Self-Adhesive

1458 Booklet pane of 5 14.00
a.-b. A911 1 Either single 2.75 2.75
c.-e. A912 1 Any single 2.75 2.75

Nos. 1458a-1458e each sold for €1 on day of issue.

Souvenir Sheet

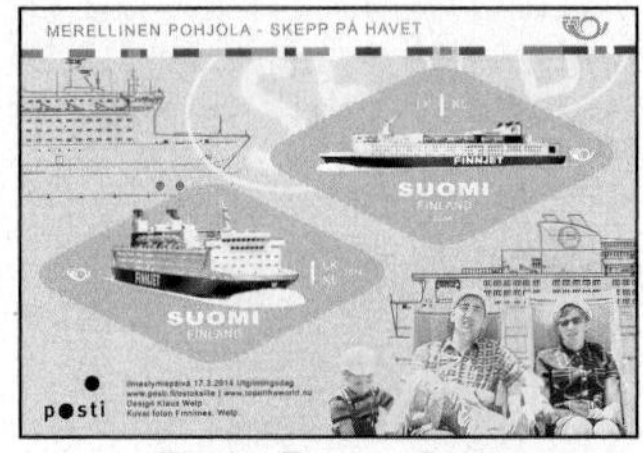

Finnjet Ferry — A913

No. 1459 — Ferry with posthorn at: a, Left. b, Right.

Serpentine Die Cut 13½

2014, Mar. 17 **Litho.**

Self-Adhesive

1459 A913 Sheet of 2 5.50
a.-b. 1 Either single 2.75 2.75

Nos. 1459a-1459b each sold for €1 on day of issue.

Violas — A914

2014, May 5 Litho. ***Die Cut Perf. 14***

Self-Adhesive

1460 A914 1 multi 2.75 2.75

No. 1460 sold for €1 on day of issue.

Linnansaari National Park — A915

2014, May 5 Litho. ***Die Cut Perf. 14***

Self-Adhesive

1461	A915 1 multi		2.75	2.75

No. 1461 sold for €1 on day of issue.

Europa A916

No. 1462: a, Man playing accordion. b, Woman playing kantele.

Irregular Serpentine Die Cut

2014, May 5 Litho.

Self-Adhesive

1462	Horiz. pair	5.50	
a.-b.	A916 1 Either single	2.75	2.75

Nos. 1462a-1462b each sold for €1 on day of issue.

A917

A918

A919

A920

A921

A922

Die Cut Perf. 13½

2014, May 5 Litho.

Self-Adhesive

1463	Booklet pane of 6	16.50	
a.	A917 1 multi	2.75	2.75
b.	A918 1 multi	2.75	2.75
c.	A919 1 multi	2.75	2.75
d.	A920 1 multi	2.75	2.75
e.	A921 1 multi	2.75	2.75
f.	A922 1 multi	2.75	2.75

Nos. 1463a-1463f each sold for €1 on day of issue.

Miniature Sheet

Caricatures of Dudesons Television Show Cast Members — A923

No. 1464 — Dudeson: a, On snowboard. b, With red cap. c, Wearing shirt with target. d, Running naked, holding book.

Crenellated Die Cut 5

2014, Sept. 1 Litho.

Self-Adhesive

1464	A923 Sheet of 4	11.00	
a.-d.	1 Any single	2.75	2.75

Nos. 1464a-1464d each sold for €1 on day of issue.

A924

A925

A926

Watercolors of Yards and Gardens by Urpo Martikainen A927

Die Cut Perf. 13

2014, Sept. 8 Litho.

Self-Adhesive

1465	Booklet pane of 4	11.00	
a.	A924 1 multi	2.75	2.75
b.	A925 1 multi	2.75	2.75
c.	A926 1 multi	2.75	2.75
d.	A927 1 multi	2.75	2.75

Nos. 1465a-1465d each sold for €1 on day of issue.

Celestial and Meteorological Objects — A928

No. 1466: a, Saturn (45x40mm). b, Moon (36x36mm). c, Sun (40x38mm). d, Cloud and lightning bolt (40x51mm). e, Earth and Moon (35x41mm). f, Comet (40x45mm). g, Cloud (48x42mm). h, Rainbow (40x38mm).

Serpentine Die Cut 9¼ on 1 or 2 Sides

2014, Sept. 8 Litho.

Self-Adhesive

1466	Booklet pane of 8	22.00	
a.-h.	A928 1 Any single	2.75	2.75

Nos. 1466a-1466h each sold for €1 on day of issue.

Souvenir Sheet

Art by Tom of Finland (Touko Laaksonen) (1920-91) — A929

No. 1467: a, Man wearing police cap smoking cigarette (43x32mm). b, Man's head between legs of another man (45x33mm). c, Man's head and buttocks (36x33mm).

Die Cut Perf. 5½

2014, Sept. 8 Litho.

Self-Adhesive

1467	Sheet of 3	8.25	
a.-c.	A929 1 Any single	2.75	2.75

Nos. 1467a-1467c each sold for €1 on day of issue.

A930

A931

A932

A933

A934

A935

A936

A937

A938

Bridges A939

Die Cut Perf. 8½ Horiz.

2014, Oct. 23 Litho.

Coil Stamps

Self-Adhesive

1468	A930 1 multi + etiquette	2.50	2.50
1469	A931 1 multi + etiquette	2.50	2.50
1470	A932 1 multi + etiquette	2.50	2.50
1471	A933 1 multi + etiquette	2.50	2.50
1472	A934 1 multi + etiquette	2.50	2.50
1473	A935 1 multi + etiquette	2.50	2.50
1474	A936 1 multi + etiquette	2.50	2.50
1475	A937 1 multi + etiquette	2.50	2.50
1476	A938 1 multi + etiquette	2.50	2.50
1477	A939 1 multi + etiquette	2.50	2.50
a.	Horiz. strip of 10, #1468-1477, + 10 etiquettes	25.00	
	Nos. 1468-1477 (10)	25.00	25.00

On day of issue, Nos. 1468-1477 had a franking value of €1. A complete roll of 100 stamps sold for €97.50 on the day of issue,

Changes in Everyday Items — A940

No. 1478: a, Computer keyboard, computer storage disks, computer, dial telephone, computer chip, television, computer mouse, compact disk and video cassette tapes (54x30mm). b, Potatoes, olives, cookies, cracker, sushi, shrimp, fish, pizza slice (54x30mm). c, Satellite, vacuum cleaner, chest freezer, coffee maker, stove, refrigerator, toaster, washing machine (54x30mm). d, Hay bales, cattle, tractor, storage shed, boarded windows, apartment house, automobiles, house (54x30mm). e, Radio, phonograph record, cassette tape player and headphones, mirrored ball, aerosol cans, electronic piano, dresses, make-up (54x30mm). f, Automobiles, rowboat, bus, scooter, sled, bicycle, cart, train (44x35mm).

2014, Oct. 23 Litho. ***Die Cut***

Self-Adhesive

1478	Booklet pane of 6	15.00	
a.-f.	A940 1 Any single	2.50	2.50

Nos. 1478a-1478f each sold for €1 on day of issue.

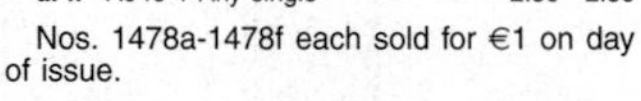

A941

Christmas — A942

Die Cut Perf. 13

2014, Oct. 23 Litho.

Self-Adhesive

1479	A941 75c multi	1.90	1.90
1480	A942 1 multi	2.50	2.50

No. 1480 sold for €1 on day of issue.

Christmas — A942a

Serpentine Die Cut 11½ Syncopated

2014, Nov. 17 **Litho.**

Self-Adhesive

1480A A942a 1 multi — —

No. 1480A had a franking value of €1 on day of issue and was printed in sheets of 10 that sold for €18.

Marigold IceUnity Synchronized Skating Team — A943

Die Cut Perf. 14

2015, Jan. 19 **Litho.**

Self-Adhesive

Textured Paper

1481 A943 1 multi 2.25 2.25

No. 1481 sold for €1 on day of issue.

Miniature Sheet

St. Valentine's Day — A944

No. 1482 — Smiling: a, Snowflakes. b, Trees, snowflakes and bird. c, Mouse and snow angel. d, Birds in nest. e, Berry plants. f, Fox and rabbit.

Serpentine Die Cut 7

2015, Jan. 19 **Litho.**

Self-Adhesive

1482 A944 Sheet of 6 + 6 etiquettes 13.50
a.-f. 1 Any single 2.25 2.25

Nos. 1482a-1482f each sold for €1 on day of issue.

Artists' Association of Finland, 150th Anniv. A945

No. 1483: a, Line Form, by Anneli Hilli (36x36mm). b, Point, by Mika Natri (36x36mm). c, Artist's Rollercoaster, by Marjo Suikkanen (36x40mm). d, Dance from the Bride, by Mayumi Niiranen-Hisatomi (32x40mm oval). e, Flight, by Laura Konttinen (36x30mm). f, You Will Know Them By Their Fruits, by Kalevi Karlsson (36x30mm).

Serpentine Die Cut 10¼

2015, Jan. 19 **Litho.**

Self-Adhesive

1483 Booklet pane of 6 + 6 etiquettes 13.50
a.-f. A945 1 Any single 2.25 2.25

Nos. 1483a-1483f each sold for €1 on day of issue.

Flowers A946

Die Cut Perf. 13¾

2015, Mar. 2 **Litho.**

Self-Adhesive

1484 A946 1 multi 2.50 2.50

No. 1484 sold for €1.10 on day of issue.

Easter — A947

Serpentine Die Cut 8¾

2015, Mar. 2 **Litho.**

Self-Adhesive

1485 A947 1 multi 2.50 2.50

No. 1485 sold for €1.10 on day of issue.

Student's Cap — A948

Die Cut Perf. 14¼

2015, Mar. 2 **Litho.**

Self-Adhesive

1486 A948 1 multi 2.50 2.50

No. 1486 sold for €1.10 on day of issue.

A949

A950

A951

International Women's Day — A952

2015, Mar. 2 **Litho.** ***Die Cut***

Self-Adhesive

1487 Booklet pane of 4 10.00
a. A949 1 multi 2.50 2.50
b. A950 1 multi 2.50 2.50
c. A951 1 multi 2.50 2.50
d. A952 1 multi 2.50 2.50

Nos. 1487a-1487d each sold for €1.10 on day of issue.

Souvenir Sheet

Toivo Kärki (1915-92), Composer — A953

No. 1488 — Kärki and: a, Record album (44mm diameter). b, Score (45x32mm). c, Accordion, silhouette of man and woman (45x32mm).

Die Cut (#1488a), Die Cut Perf. 5¼

2015, Mar. 2 **Litho.**

Self-Adhesive

1488 A953 Sheet of 3 7.50
a.-c. 1 Any single 2.50 2.50

Nos. 1488a-1488c each sold for €1.10 on day of issue.

Rugosa Roses — A954

Orchids A955

Die Cut Perf. 13¾

2015, May 8 **Litho.**

Self-Adhesive

1489 Horiz. pair 4.50
a. A954 2 multi 2.25 2.25
b. A955 2 multi 2.25 2.25

Nos. 1489a-1489b each sold for €1 on day of issue.

Swan A956

Litho. With Foil Application

2015, May 8 ***Die Cut Perf. 13½***

Self-Adhesive

1490 A956 1 multi 2.50 2.50

A957

Moomin Toys A958

Serpentine Die Cut 9¾

2015, May 8 **Self-Adhesive** **Litho.**

1491 Horiz. pair 5.00
a. A957 1 multi 2.50 2.50
b. A958 1 multi 2.50 2.50

Europa. Nos. 1491a-1491b each sold for €1.10 on day of issue.

Miniature Sheet

Sights of Summer — A959

No. 1492: a, Strawberry, ladybug and ant (22x30mm). b, Man and woman in rowboat (62x30mm). c, Bicycle (41x30mm). d, Woman with ice cream cone (30x50mm). e, Woman diving into water (30x45mm).

Serpentine Die Cut 9¼x11 (#1492a), 7½x6¼ (#1492b), 8x8¼ (#1492c), 7x6½ (#1492d), 7x7¼ (#1492e)

2015, May 8 **Self-Adhesive** **Litho.**

1492 A959 Sheet of 5 12.50
a.-e. 1 Any single 2.50 2.50

Nos. 1492a-1492e each sold for €1.10 on day of issue.

Man Pushing Lawnmower — A959a

Serpentine Die Cut 11½ Syncopated

2016, Mar. 30 **Litho.**

Self-Adhesive

1492F A959a 1 multi — —

No. 1492F had a franking value of €1.20 on day of issue and was printed in sheets of 10 that sold for €15.

Miniature Sheet

Scenes From Imaginary Town — A960

No. 1493: a, Woman riding giraffe (20x33mm). b, Woman with shopping bag (38x21mm). c, Sailboat and swan (30mm diameter). d, House and horse (41x24mm). e, Rabbits in front of building with clock (34x21mm). f, Birds and flowers in pots (18x35mm).

Serpentine Die Cut 7¾ on 2 Opposite Sides, Die Cut (#1493c, 1493d)

2015, Sept. 11 Litho.

Self-Adhesive

1493 A960 Sheet of 6 15.00
a.-f. 1 Any single 2.50 2.50

Nos. 1493a-1493f each sold for €1.10 on day of issue.

Miniature Sheet

Art — A961

No. 1494: a, Horse running. b, Head and arm of woman. c, Woman unzipping dress. d, Woman's legs with high-heeled shoes.

Litho. With Foil Application

Serpentine Die Cut 6¾

2015, Sept. 11 Self-Adhesive

1494 A961 Sheet of 4 10.00
a.-d. 1 Any single 2.50 2.50

Nos. 1494a-1494d each sold for €1.10 on day of issue.

A962

A963

Jean Sibelius (1865-1957), Composer A964

Serpentine Die Cut 10¼

2015, Sept. 11 Litho.

Self-Adhesive

1495 Booklet pane of 3 + 3 etiquettes 7.50
a. A962 1 multi 2.50 2.50
b. A963 1 multi 2.50 2.50
c. A964 1 multi 2.50 2.50

Nos. 1495a-1495c each sold for €1.10 on day of issue.

The Rasmus A965

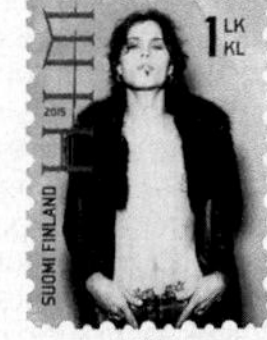

HIM A966

Apocalyptica A967

Children of Bodom A968

Hanoi Rocks — A969

Nightwish A970

Serpentine Die Cut 10¼x10 (#1496a-1496b), 9¾x10 (#1496c), 10¼x9½ (#1496d), 9½x10 (#1496e), 10¼x9¼ (#1496f)

2015, Sept. 11 Litho.

Self-Adhesive

1496 Booklet pane of 6 + 6 etiquettes 15.00
a. A965 1 multi 2.50 2.50
b. A966 1 multi 2.50 2.50
c. A967 1 multi 2.50 2.50
d. A968 1 multi 2.50 2.50
e. A969 1 multi 2.50 2.50
f. A970 1 multi 2.50 2.50

Rock bands. Nos. 1496a-1496f each sold for €1.10 on day of issue.

Finnish Design — A971

No. 1497: a, Marimekko Kukkuluuruu fabric design, by Sanna Annukka (28x45mm). b, Ultima Thule drinking glass, by Tapio Wirkkala (27x27mm). c, Block lamp, by Harri Koskinen (32x27mm). d, Paratiisi plate, by Birger Kaipiainen (27x33mm). e, Mademoiselle lounge chair, by Ilmari Tapiovaara (28x45mm). f, Solifer moped, by Richard Lindh (36x27mm).

Die Cut Perf. 13¼

2015, Sept. 11 Litho.

1497 Booklet pane of 6 15.00
a.-f. A971 1 Any single 2.50 2.50

Nos. 1497a-1497f each sold for €1.10 on day of issue.

Pertti Kurikan Nimipäivät A972

Die Cut Perf. 11½ Syncopated

2015, Apr. 28 Litho.

Self-Adhesive

1498 A972 1 multi 2.50 2.50

Eurovision Song Contest. No. 1498 sold for €1.10 on day of issue.

Tomatoes A973

Basil A974

Peppers — A975

Die Cut Perf. 9¾ Vert. Syncopated

2015, Nov. 6 Litho.

Coil Stamps

Self-Adhesive

1499 A973 1 multi + etiquette 2.50 2.50
1500 A974 1 multi + etiquette 2.50 2.50
1501 A975 1 multi + etiquette 2.50 2.50
a. Vert. strip of 3, #1499-1501, + 3 etiquettes 7.50
Nos. 1499-1501 (3) 7.50 7.50

Nos. 1499-1501 each sold for €1.10 on day of issue.

Miniature Sheet

Craft Items — A976

No. 1502: a, Purse made of tree bark (40x36mm). b, Crocheted square (35x35mm). c, Socks (32x50mm). d, Dancing shoes (38x35mm). e, Mushroom-shaped wooden stool (37x34mm).

Various Die Cuts

2015, Nov. 6 Litho.

Self-Adhesive

1502 A976 Sheet of 5 12.50
a.-e. 1 Any single 2.50 2.50

On day of issue, Nos. 1502a-1502e each sold for €1.10.

Father and Son Dragging Christmas Tree Past Church — A977

Child Looking at Christmas Ornament — A978

Die Cut Perf. 11 Syncopated

2015, Nov. 6 Litho.

Self-Adhesive

1503 A977 1 multi 2.50 2.50

Booklet Stamp

1504 A978 80c multi 1.90 1.90
a. Booklet pane of 20 38.00

No. 1503 sold for €1.10 on day of issue and was printed in sheets of 10 + 10 etiquettes.

Victory of Finnish Team in World Junior Ice Hockey Championships — A979

Die Cut Perf. 11½ Syncopated

2016, Jan. 15 Litho.

Self-Adhesive

1505 A979 1 multi 2.40 2.40

No. 1505 sold for €1.10 on day of issue.

Snowflake — A980

Litho. With Holographic Foil

Die Cut Perf. 9¾ Horiz.

2016, Jan. 22 Self-Adhesive

1506 A980 1 multi + etiquette 2.40 2.40

No. 1506 sold for €1.10 on day of issue.

Karelian Pasties — A981

Serpentine Die Cut 8 Syncopated

2016, Jan. 22 Litho.

Self-Adhesive

1507 A981 1 multi + etiquette 2.40 2.40

No. 1507 sold for €1.10 on day of issue.

Deer and Bird A982

Birds A983

Horse and Dog A984

Bird and Butterfly — A985

Cat and Dog A986

Serpentine Die Cut 6½

2016, Jan. 22 Litho.

Self-Adhesive

1508 Booklet pane of 5 + 5 etiquettes 12.00
a. A982 1 multi 2.40 2.40
b. A983 1 multi 2.40 2.40
c. A984 1 multi 2.40 2.40
d. A985 1 multi 2.40 2.40
e. A986 1 multi 2.40 2.40

On day of issue, Nos. 1508a-1508e each sold for €1.10.

Rabbit and Easter Basket — A987

Die Cut Perf. 13¾

2016, Feb. 26 Litho.

Self-Adhesive

1509 A987 1 multi + etiquette 2.60 2.60

No. 1509 sold for €1.20 on day of issue.

Siberian Iris — A988

Die Cut Perf. 13¾

2016, Feb. 26 Litho.

Self-Adhesive

1510 A988 1 multi 2.60 2.60

No. 1510 sold for €1.20 on day of issue.

Nuuksio National Park — A989

Birch Tree A990

Die Cut Perf. 11 Horiz.

2016, Feb. 26 Litho.

Self-Adhesive

1511 A989 €1.30 multi + etiquette 3.00 3.00
1512 A990 €1.30 multi + etiquette 3.00 3.00
a. Horiz. pair, #1511-1512, + 2 etiquettes 6.00

Wings of Thoughts A991

Die Cut Perf. 13¾

2016, Feb. 26 Litho.

Self-Adhesive

1513 A991 €1.80 multi 4.00 4.00

See Nos. 1537, 1554.

Package With Legs — A992

Bird Carrying Letter A993

Angel Blowing Trumpet A994

Birthday Cake — A995

Boot and Flowers — A996

2016, Feb. 26 Litho. *Die Cut*

Self-Adhesive

1514 Booklet pane of 5 + 5 etiquettes and 5 stickers 13.00
a. A992 1 multi 2.60 2.60
b. A993 1 multi 2.60 2.60
c. A994 1 multi 2.60 2.60
d. A995 1 multi 2.60 2.60
e. A996 1 multi 2.60 2.60

On day of issue, Nos, 1514a-1514e each sold for €1.20.

This stamp and many other stamps having the same gray panel at bottom were released on Apr. 8, 2016. The stamps, each with a coat of arms of a region or city of Finland, were printed using the Finland Post apparatus used to create personalized stamps. Apparently only coats of arms were printed in the vignette area and no personalized stamps could be created by customers using other vignette images and this gray panel. Even though Finland Post sold these items as "regional stamps," there is no indication that the stamps were sold only in the region of the coat of arms on each stamp, or that the stamps were valid only in those regions. Each stamp was printed in sheets of ten that sold for €15. The coat of arms of the city of Vaasa is shown in the image above.

Feather A997

Die Cut Perf. 13¾

2016, May 6 Litho.

Self-Adhesive

1515 A997 50c multi 1.10 1.10

Europa A998

Serpentine Die Cut 12¼ Syncopated

2016, May 6 Litho.

Self-Adhesive

1516 A998 1 multi + etiquette 2.75 2.75

Think Green Issue.
No. 1516 sold for €1.20 on day of issue.

Vacation Scenes A999

No. 1517: a, Woman's crossed feet in sandals, women in park. b, Feet of skateboarder, buildings and cranes. c, Men and women, umbrella and bicycle. d, People at beach. e, Woman at market stall.

2016, May 6 Litho. *Die Cut Perf. 13*

Self-Adhesive

1517 Booklet pane of 5 + 5 etiquettes 14.00
a.-e. A999 1 Any single 2.75 2.75

Nos. 1517a-1517e each sold for €1.20 on day of issue.

A1000

A1001

A1002

A1003

Barns A1004

Die Cut Perf. 9¼ Syncopated

2016, May 6 Litho.

Self-Adhesive

1518 Booklet pane of 5 + 5 etiquettes 14.00
a. A1000 1 multi 2.75 2.75
b. A1001 1 multi 2.75 2.75
c. A1002 1 multi 2.75 2.75
d. A1003 1 multi 2.75 2.75
e. A1004 1 multi 2.75 2.75

Nos. 1518a-1518e each sold for €1.20 on day of issue.

Worldwide Fund for Nature (WWF) — A1005

No. 1519: a, Pusa hispida saimensis. b, Nehalennia speciosa. c, Anser erythropus.

Serpentine Die Cut 4¼ at Top

2016, Sept. 9 Litho.

Self-Adhesive

1519 Vert. strip of 3 + 3 etiquettes 8.25
a.-c. A1005 1 Any single + etiquette 2.75 2.75

Nos. 1519a-1519c each sold for €1.20 on day of issue.

Mushrooms A1006

No. 1520: a, Russula paludosa. b, Tricholoma matsutake. c, Craterellus cornucopioides. d, Cantharellus cibarius. e, Lactarius deterrimus.

Serpentine Die Cut 14¼x13¾

2016, Sept. 9 Litho.

Self-Adhesive

1520 Booklet pane of 5 + 5 etiquettes 14.00
a.-e. A1006 1 Any single 2.75 2.75

Nos. 1520a-1520e each sold for €1.20 on day of issue.

People Enjoying Nature A1007

No. 1521: a, Flower picking. b, Ice fishing. c, Berry harvesting. d, Boating. e, Camping. f, Skiing.

Die Cut Perf. 8¾ on 1 Side

2016, Sept. 9 Litho.

Self-Adhesive

1521 Booklet pane of 6 + 6 etiquettes 16.50
a.-f. A1007 1 Any single 2.75 2.75

Nos. 1521a-1521f each sold for €1.20 on day of issue.

Miniature Sheet

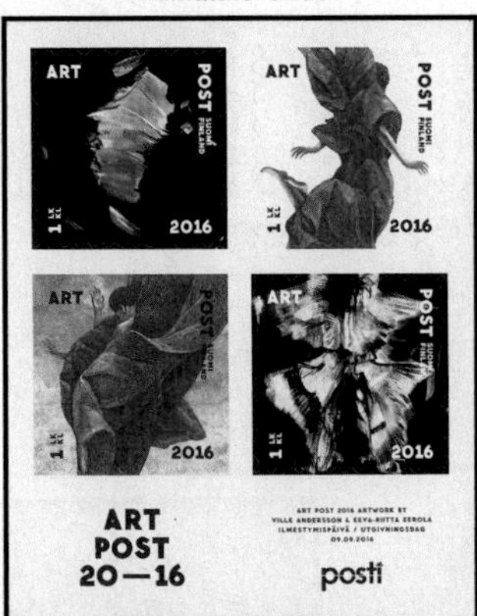

Art by Ville Andersson and Eeva-Riitta Eerola — A1008

Various unnamed works, as shown.

Serpentine Die Cut 6¾

2016, Sept. 9 Litho.

Self-Adhesive

1522 A1008 Sheet of 4 11.00
a.-d. 1 Any single 2.75 2.75

Nos. 1522a-1522d each sold for €1.20 on day of issue.

Kirkonvarkaus Bridge — A1009

Serpentine Die Cut 11½ Syncopated

2016, Sept. 19 Litho.

Self-Adhesive

1523 A1009 1 multi — —

No. 1523 had a franking value of €1.20 and was printed in sheets of 10 that sold for €20.

Flag of Finland and Candles A1010

Serpentine Die Cut 11½ Syncopated

2016, Nov. 4 Litho.

Self-Adhesive

1524 A1010 (€1.20) multi — —

No. 1524 was printed in sheets of 10 that sold for €15.

Church, Soini A1011

Wooden Pauper Statue, Soini — A1012

Wooden Pauper Statue, Alajärvi — A1013

Church, Alajärvi — A1014

Church, Hauho A1015

Wooden Pauper Statue, Hauho A1016

Sawtooth Die Cut 6

2016, Nov. 10 Litho.

Self-Adhesive

1525	Booklet pane of 6	16.00	
a.	A1011 (€1.20) multi	2.60	2.60
b.	A1012 (€1.20) multi	2.60	2.60
c.	A1013 (€1.20) multi	2.60	2.60
d.	A1014 (€1.20) multi	2.60	2.60
e.	A1015 (€1.20) multi	2.60	2.60
f.	A1016 (€1.20) multi	2.60	2.60

Reindeer A1017

Girl and Squirrel With Cookies A1018

Snow-covered House A1019

Die Cut Perf. 7¾

2016, Nov. 10 Litho.

Self-Adhesive

1526 A1017 (90c) multi 1.90 1.90

Die Cut Perf. 7¾x7½

1527 A1018 (€1.20) multi 2.60 2.60

Die Cut Perf. 14

1528 A1019 (€1.30) multi 2.75 2.75
Nos. 1526-1528 (3) 7.25 7.25

Etiquettes are found to the sides of No. 1528 in the sheet margin.

Flag of Finland A1020

Die Cut Perf. 5¾ Horiz.

2017, Jan. 20 Litho.

Self-Adhesive

1529 A1020 (€1.20) multi 2.60 2.60

Snow Castle A1021

Die Cut Perf. 8¾ Horiz.

2017, Jan. 20 Litho.

Self-Adhesive

1530 A1021 (€1.20) multi 2.60 2.60

Europa.

Hearts A1022

No. 1531: a, One heart. b, Four hearts. c, 39 hearts. d, Two hearts upright. e, Two hearts sideways.

Die Cut Perf. 9½ Vert.

2017, Jan. 20 Litho.

Self-Adhesive

1531 Booklet pane of 5 13.00
a.-e. A1022 (€1.20) Any single 2.60 2.60

Souvenir Sheet

Lions Clubs International, Cent. — A1023

No. 1532 — Various Lions pins and Lions International emblem, with map of Finland at: a, LL. b, UL.

Die Cut Perf. 12¾x12¼

2017, Jan. 20 Litho.

Self-Adhesive

1532 A1023 Sheet of 2 5.25
a.-b. (€1.20) Either single 2.60 2.60

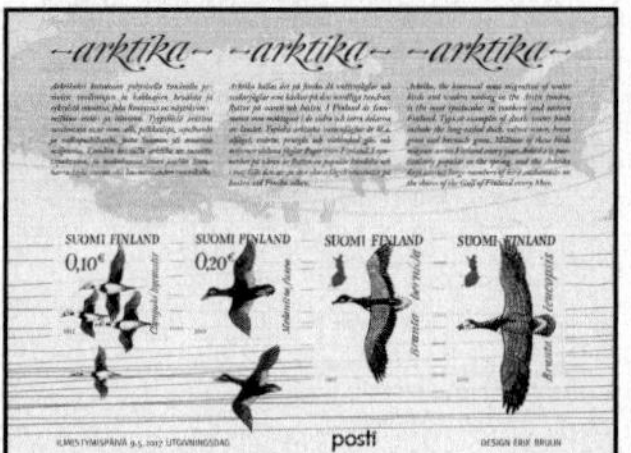

Flowers in Cup A1024

Die Cut Perf. 12½

2017, Feb. 24 Litho.

Self-Adhesive

1533 A1024 (€1.20) multi 2.60 2.60

Pussy Willows — A1025

Die Cut Perf. 8½x8¼

2017, Feb. 24 Litho.

Self-Adhesive

1534 A1025 (€1.20) multi 2.60 2.60

Carousel — A1026

Die Cut Perf. 8½x8¼

2017, Feb. 24 Litho.

Self-Adhesive

1535 A1026 (€1.20) multi 2.60 2.60

Fishermen in Boat — A1027

Reflection of Clouds in Lake A1028

Swans A1029

Die Cut Perf. Horiz.

2017, Feb. 24 Litho.

Self-Adhesive

1536	Vert. strip of 3 + 3 etiquettes	8.25	
a.	A1027 (€1.30) multi + etiquette	2.75	2.75
b.	A1028 (€1.30) multi + etiquette	2.75	2.75
c.	A1029 (€1.30) multi + etiquette	2.75	2.75

Wings of Thoughts Type of 2016

Die Cut Perf. 13¾

2017, Mar. 11 Litho.

Self-Adhesive

1537 A991 €2 multi — —

Miniature Sheet

Arctic Birds — A1030

No. 1538: a, Clangula hyemalis (27x27mm). b, Melanitta fusca (27x27mm). c, Branta bernicla (27x39mm). d, Branta leucopsis (27x39mm).

Die Cut Perf. 13¼

2017, May 9 **Litho.**

Self-Adhesive

1538 A1030 Sheet of 4 6.75
a. 10c multi .25 .25
b. 20c multi .45 .45
c.-d. (€1.30) Either single 3.00 3.00

Nos. 1538a and 1538b were each printed in sheets of 15.

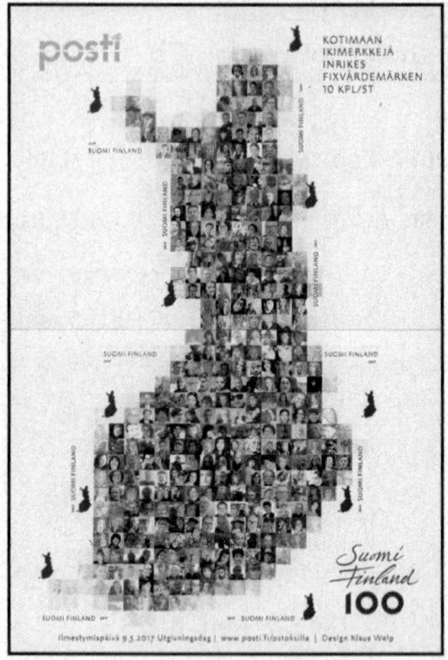

Faces of People Making Up Map of Finland — A1031

No. 1539 — Approximate areas of map of Finland: a, Northwestern Lappi Province. b, Northeastern Lappi Province, vert. c, Southwestern Lappi Province and upper Gulf of Bothnia, vert. d, Southeastern Lappi Province and northeastern Oulu Province, vert. e, Southwestern Oulu Province and northern Vaasa Province. f, Eastern Oulu Province. g, Southern Vaasa Province and northern Turku ja Pori Province. h, Mikkeli Province and southern Kuopio and Pohjois-Karjala Provinces. i, Aland Islands and Southern Turku ja Pori Province. j, Uusimaa and Kymi Provinces.

2017, May 9 Litho. ***Die Cut Perf. 13***

Self-Adhesive

1539 A1031 Booklet pane of 10 30.00
a.-j. (€1.30) Any single 3.00 3.00

Independence, cent.

Sauna — A1032

Sauna — A1033

Sauna — A1034

Sauna — A1035

Sauna Bucket and Birch Branch Whisk — A1036

Die Cut Perf. 6 Horiz.

2017, May 24 **Litho.**

Self-Adhesive

1540 Booklet pane of 5 15.00
a. A1032 (€1.30) multi 3.00 3.00
b. A1033 (€1.30) multi 3.00 3.00
c. A1034 (€1.30) multi 3.00 3.00
d. A1035 (€1.30) multi 3.00 3.00
e. A1036 (€1.30) multi 3.00 3.00

See Aland Islands Nos. 396-397.

A1037

A1038

A1039

A1040

Moomin Characters — A1041

Die Cut Perf. 7 Horiz.

2017, May 24 **Litho.**

Self-Adhesive

1541 Booklet pane of 5 + 5 etiquettes 16.50
a. A1037 (€1.40) multi 3.25 3.25
b. A1038 (€1.40) multi 3.25 3.25
c. A1039 (€1.40) multi 3.25 3.25
d. A1040 (€1.40) multi 3.25 3.25
e. A1041 (€1.40) multi 3.25 3.25

Souvenir Sheets

A1042

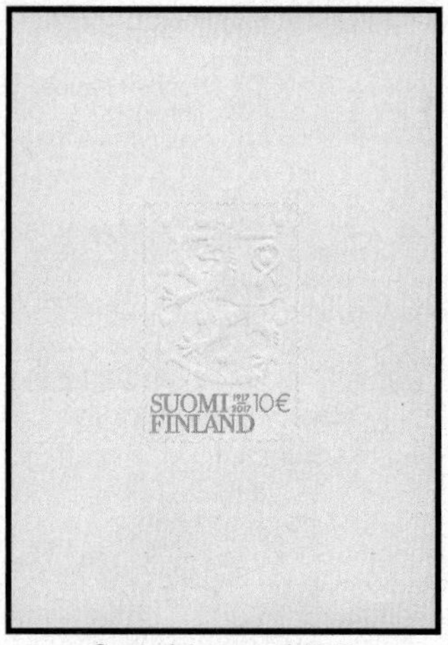

Coat of Arms — A1043

Die Cut Perf. 10

2017, May 24 **Litho.**

Self-Adhesive

1542 A1042 Sheet of 2 6.00
a. (€1.30) green 3.00 3.00
b. (€1.30) blue 3.00 3.00

Souvenir Sheet

Embossed With Foil Application

Die Cut Perf. 13¼

1543 A1043 €10 gold 22.50 22.50

Independence, cent. Finlandia 2017 Stamp Exhibition, Tampere (No. 1542).

Children's Art A1044

Serpentine Die Cut 11½ Syncopated

2017, May 24 **Litho.**

Self-Adhesive

1544 A1044 (€1.30) multi — —

Pres. Mauno Koivisto (1923-2017) A1045

Die Cut Perf. 13¾

2017, June 9 **Litho.**

Self-Adhesive

1545 A1045 (€1.30) multi 3.00 3.00

2017 Tall Ship Races, Turku A1046

Serpentine Die Cut 11½ Syncopated

2017, July 20 **Litho.**

Self-Adhesive

1546 A1046 (€1.30) multi — —

A1047

A1048

Figurines A1049

Die Cut Perf. 8½

2017, Sept. 6 **Litho.**

Self-Adhesive

1547 Strip of 3 9.75
a. A1047 (€1.30) multi 3.25 3.25
b. A1048 (€1.30) multi 3.25 3.25
c. A1049 (€1.30) multi 3.25 3.25

City Parks — A1050

No. 1548 — Park in: a, Porvoo. b, Hämeenlinna. c, Turku.

Die Cut Perf. 10¼

2017, Sept. 6 **Litho.**

Self-Adhesive

1548 Strip of 3 9.75
a.-c. A1050 (€1.30) Any single 3.25 3.25

Flower in Spring A1051

Boat on Shore in Summer A1052

Lake in Autumn A1053

Ice in Winter A1054

Die Cut Perf. 9½ Horiz.

2017, Sept. 6 Litho.

Coil Stamps

Self-Adhesive

1549	A1051	(€1.30) multi		3.25	3.25
1550	A1052	(€1.30) multi		3.25	3.25
1551	A1053	(€1.30) multi		3.25	3.25
1552	A1054	(€1.30) multi		3.25	3.25
a.	Horiz. strip of 4, #1549-1552			13.00	
	Nos. 1549-1552 (4)			13.00	13.00

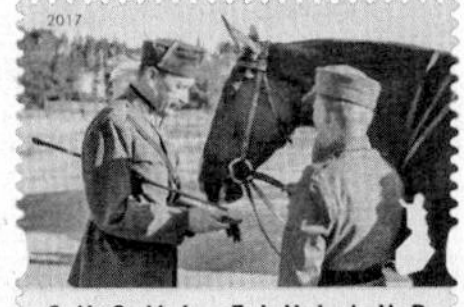

Baron Carl Gustaf Emil Mannerheim (1867-1951), President of Finland — A1055

Serpentine Die Cut 11½ Syncopated

2017, Sept. 6 Litho.

Self-Adhesive

1553 A1055 (€1.30) multi — —

Wings of ThoughtsType of 2016

Die Cut Perf. 13¾

2017, Oct. 2 Litho.

Self-Adhesive

1554 A991 €2.10 multi — —

Presidential Palace, Helsinki — A1056

President Sauli Niinistö, His Three Predecessors and Their Spouses — A1057

Woman in Dressing Room — A1058

Pres. Niinistö Shaking Hands — A1059

Formal Ball A1060

Children Watching Pres. Niinistö Shaking Hands — A1061

Serpentine Die Cut 9 Syncopated

2017, Nov. 3 Litho.

Self-Adhesive

1555	Booklet pane of 6		21.00	
a.	A1056 (€1.40) multi		3.50	3.50
b.	A1057 (€1.40) multi		3.50	3.50
c.	A1058 (€1.40) multi		3.50	3.50
d.	A1059 (€1.40) multi		3.50	3.50
e.	A1060 (€1.40) multi		3.50	3.50
f.	A1061 (€1.40) multi		3.50	3.50

Independence of Finland, cent.

Snow Queen — A1062

Die Cut Perf. 14¾x14

2017, Nov. 3 Litho.

Self-Adhesive

1556 A1062 (€1.40) multi 3.50 3.50

Candles in Christmas Tree A1063

Man and Squirrels Holding Candles A1064

Die Cut Perf. 14½x14¾

2017, Nov. 3 Litho.

Self-Adhesive

1557 A1063 (95c) multi 2.25 2.25

Die Cut Perf. 14¾x14

1558 A1064 (€1.40) multi 3.50 3.50

Christmas.

Souvenir Sheet

Zacharias Topelius (1818-98), Writer — A1065

No. 1559: a, Portrait of Topelius by Albert Edelfelt (39x36mm). b, Cradle and Angel Guardians, painting by Rudolf Koivu (39x29mm).

Die Cut Perf. 6½

2018, Jan. 24 Litho.

Self-Adhesive

1559	A1065	Sheet of 2	7.00	
a.-b.		(€1.40) Either single	3.50	3.50

A1066

A1067

A1068

A1069

St. Valentine's Day — A1070

Die Cut Perf. 13x12¾

2018, Jan. 24 Litho.

Self-Adhesive

1560	Booklet pane of 5	17.50	
a.	A1066 (€1.40) multi	3.50	3.50
b.	A1067 (€1.40) multi	3.50	3.50
c.	A1068 (€1.40) multi	3.50	3.50
d.	A1069 (€1.40) multi	3.50	3.50
e.	A1070 (€1.40) multi	3.50	3.50

Aurora Borealis — A1071

Reindeer — A1072

Die Cut Perf. 8½ Horiz.

2018, Jan. 24 Litho.

Self-Adhesive

1561	Horiz. pair	7.50	
a.	A1071 (€1.50) multi + etiquette	3.75	3.75
b.	A1072 (€1.50) multi + etiquette	3.75	3.75

Worldwide Fund for Nature (WWF) A1073

No. 1562: a, Vulpes lagopus. b, Bubo scandiacus. c, Salmo salar.

Die Cut Perf. 8½ Horiz.

2018, Feb. 28 Litho.

Self-Adhesive

1562	Vert. strip of 3	10.50	
a.-c.	A1073 (€1.40) Any single	3.50	3.50

A1074

A1075

Easter A1076

Die Cut Perf. 12½

2018, Feb. 28 Litho.

Self-Adhesive

1563	Vert. strip of 3	10.50	
a.	A1074 (€1.40) multi	3.50	3.50
b.	A1075 (€1.40) multi	3.50	3.50
c.	A1076 (€1.40) multi	3.50	3.50

Wooden Bridge, Humppila — A1077

Wooden Bridge, Suomussalmi — A1078

Serpentine Die Cut 7 Horiz.

2018, May 9 Litho.

Self-Adhesive

1564	Horiz. pair	7.00	
a.	A1077 (€1.50) multi	3.50	3.50
b.	A1078 (€1.50) multi	3.50	3.50

Europa.

Gerbera Daisies A1079

Daisies and Harebells A1080

Peonies A1081

Hydrangeas A1082

Poppies A1083

Die Cut Perf. 15¼x14¾

2018, May 9 Litho.

Self-Adhesive

1565	Horiz. strip of 5	17.50	
a.	A1079 (€1.50) multi	3.50	3.50
b.	A1080 (€1.50) multi	3.50	3.50

c. A1081 (€1.50) multi 3.50 3.50
d. A1082 (€1.50) multi 3.50 3.50
e. A1083 (€1.50) multi 3.50 3.50

1918 Airplane — A1084

2018 Airplane — A1085

1918 Soldier — A1086

2018 Soldier — A1087

1918 Ship — A1088

2018 Ship — A1089

Die Cut Perf. 8¼ Horiz.

2018, June 4 Litho.

Self-Adhesive

1566 Booklet pane of 6 21.00
a. A1084 (€1.50) multi 3.50 3.50
b. A1085 (€1.50) multi 3.50 3.50
c. A1086 (€1.50) multi 3.50 3.50
d. A1087 (€1.50) multi 3.50 3.50
e. A1088 (€1.50) multi 3.50 3.50
f. A1089 (€1.50) multi 3.50 3.50

Finnish Defense Forces, cent.

Fish A1090

No. 1567: a, Sander lucioperca. b, Coregonus albula.

Die Cut Perf. 12½ Horiz. at Bottom

2018, June 6 Litho.

Self-Adhesive

1567 Horiz. pair 7.00
a.-b. A1090 (€1.50) Either single 3.50 3.50

A1091

A1092

A1093

A1094

A1095

Popular Foods and Beverages — A1096

Sawtooth Die Cut 9¾

2018, June 6 Litho.

Self-Adhesive

1568 Booklet pane of 6 21.00
a. A1091 (€1.50) multi 3.50 3.50
b. A1092 (€1.50) multi 3.50 3.50
c. A1093 (€1.50) multi 3.50 3.50
d. A1094 (€1.50) multi 3.50 3.50
e. A1095 (€1.50) multi 3.50 3.50
f. A1096 (€1.50) multi 3.50 3.50

Miniature Sheet

Traditional Costumes — A1097

No. 1569: a, Woman wearing bonnet (37x25mm). b, Brooch (25x30mm). c, Tasseled scarf and jacket (25x30mm). d, Skirt with horizontal stripes (37x25mm). e, Skirt with vertical stripes (37x25mm). f, Bottom of skirt, stockings and shoes (25x30mm).

Sawtooth Die Cut 5¾x6, 6x6½

2018, June 6 Litho.

Self-Adhesive

1569 A1097 Sheet of 6 21.00
a.-f. (€1.50) Any single 3.50 3.50

Grafitti by EGS on Building, Melbourne, Australia — A1098

Grafitti by EGS on Truck, St. Petersburg, Russia — A1099

Serpentine Die Cut 6¾ Horiz.

2018, Sept. 12 Litho.

Self-Adhesive

1570 Horiz. pair 7.00
a. A1098 (€1.50) multi 3.50 3.50
b. A1099 (€1.50) multi 3.50 3.50

Seven-spot Ladybug A1100

Whooper Swans A1101

Brown Bears A1102

Lily of the Valley A1103

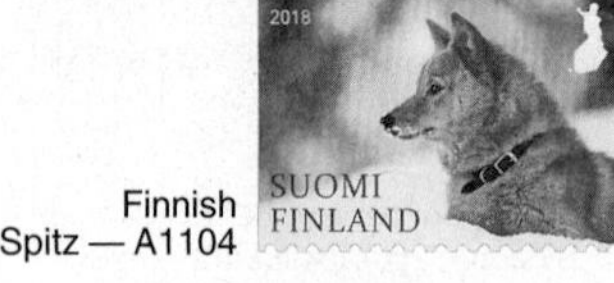

Finnish Spitz — A1104

Die Cut Perf. 9½ Horiz.

2018, Sept. 12 Litho.

Coil Stamps

Self-Adhesive

1571 Horiz. strip of 5 17.50
a. A1100 (€1.50) multi 3.50 3.50
b. A1101 (€1.50) multi 3.50 3.50
c. A1102 (€1.50) multi 3.50 3.50
d. A1103 (€1.50) multi 3.50 3.50
e. A1104 (€1.50) multi 3.50 3.50

Finnish national flora and fauna.

Park in Pori — A1105

Park in Hanko A1106

Park in Kotka — A1107

Die Cut Perf. 10¼

2018, Sept. 12 Litho.

Self-Adhesive

1572 Vert. strip of 3 10.50
a. A1105 (€1.50) multi 3.50 3.50
b. A1106 (€1.50) multi 3.50 3.50
c. A1107 (€1.50) multi 3.50 3.50

Souvenir Sheet

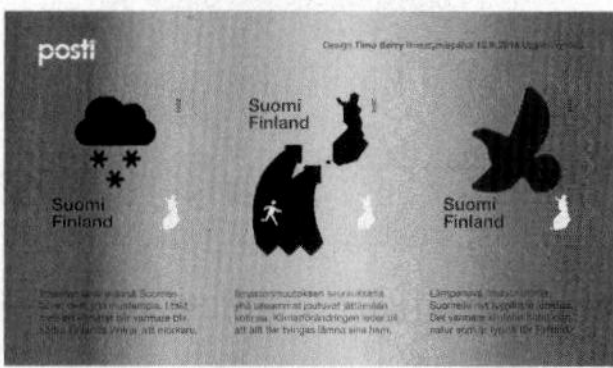

Climate Change — A1108

No. 1573 — Silhouette of: a, Cloud and snowflakes. b, Arrows and map of Finalnd. c, Bird.

Litho. & Silk-Screened

2018, Sept. 12 ***Sawtooth Die Cut 4***

Self-Adhesive

1573 A1108 Sheet of 3 10.50
a.-c. (€1.50) Any single 3.50 3.50

Parts of the designs of Nos. 1573a-1573c were printed with thermographic ink, which changes color when warmed.

Rowanberries in Snow — A1109

Die Cut Perf. 8½ Horiz.

2018, Nov. 7 Litho.

Self-Adhesive

1574 A1109 (€1.50) multi 3.50 3.50

Ice Skates A1110

Die Cut Perf. 13x13½

2018, Nov. 7 Litho.

Self-Adhesive

1575 A1110 (€1.60) multi 3.75 3.75

Ornament on Christmas Tree Branch A1111

Candles — A1112

Die Cut Perf. 13½x13¼

2018, Nov. 7 Litho.

Self-Adhesive

1576 A1111 (€1.05) multi 2.40 2.40

Die Cut Perf. 13¼x13½

1577 A1112 (€1.50) multi 3.50 3.50

Christmas.

Ice Fishing A1113

Swimming in Ice Water — A1114

Die Cut Perf. 8¾ Horiz.

2019, Jan. 23 **Litho.**

Self-Adhesive

1578	Horiz. pair	7.00	
a.	A1113 (€1.50) multi	3.50	3.50
b.	A1114 (€1.50) multi	3.50	3.50

Sharing of Joy A1115

No. 1579: a, Woman writing post card, white cat. b, Two women walking dogs. c, Two women swimming. d, Two women having tea. e, Woman and child on sled. f, Man giving flower to woman.

2019, Jan. 23 **Litho.** ***Die Cut***

Self-Adhesive

1579	Booklet pane of 6	21.00	
a.-f.	A1115 (€1.50) Any single	3.50	3.50

Miniature Sheet

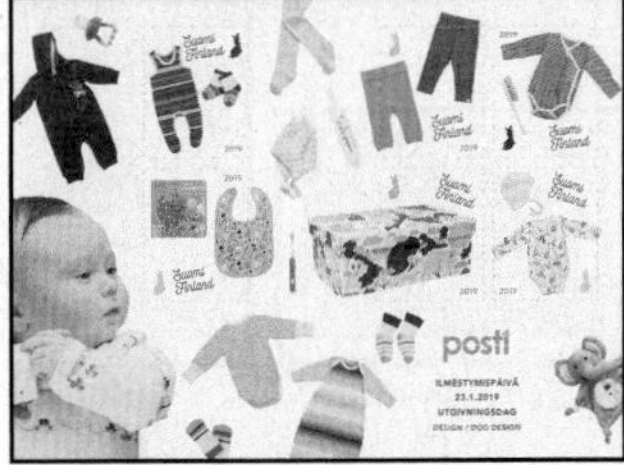

Layette Items — A1116

No. 1580: a, Striped baby onesie with snaps, socks. b, Two pairs of pants. c, Long sleeve baby onesie, hair brush. d, Children's book, bib. e, Storage box. f, Long sleeve baby onesie with animal print, bonnet.

Sawtooth Die Cut 17½

2019, Jan. 23 **Litho.**

Self-Adhesive

1580 A1116	Sheet of 6	21.00	
a.-f.	(€1.50) Any single	3.50	3.50

A1117

Easter A1118

Reversed Die Cut Perf. 4¾ Horiz.

2019, Mar. 13 **Litho.**

Self-Adhesive

1581	Horiz. pair	7.00	
a.	A1117 (€1.50) multi	3.50	3.50
b.	A1118 (€1.50) multi	3.50	3.50

Girl Singing Karaoke A1119

Boy Eating Sushi A1120

Die Cut Perf. 11x11¼

2019, Mar. 13 **Litho.**

Self-Adhesive

1582	Horiz. pair	7.50	
a.	A1119 (€1.60) multi	3.75	3.75
b.	A1120 (€1.60) multi	3.75	3.75

Dog With Floral Headdress A1121

Jewelry With Flowers A1122

Floral Wreath A1123

Die Cut Perf. 11½ Horiz.

2019, Mar. 13 **Litho.**

Self-Adhesive

1583	Vert. strip of 3	10.50	
a.	A1121 (€1.50) multi	3.50	3.50
b.	A1122 (€1.50) multi	3.50	3.50
c.	A1123 (€1.50) multi	3.50	3.50
d.	Booklet pane of 15, 5 each #1583a-1583c	52.50	

Miniature Sheet

Helsinki Central Railroad Station — A1124

No. 1584: a, Lamps on statues on exterior wall. b, Main entrance, horiz. c, Aerial view of station, horiz. d, Clock tower.

Die Cut Perf. 7 Syncopated

2019, Mar. 13 **Litho.**

Self-Adhesive

1584 A1124	Sheet of 4	14.00	
a.-d.	(€1.50) Any single	3.50	3.50

Cygnus Cygnus
A1125 A1126

Die Cut Perf. 13¼

2019, May 8 **Litho.**

Self-Adhesive

1585	Vert. pair	7.50	
a.	A1125 (€1.50) multi	3.50	3.50
b.	A1126 (€1.50) multi	3.50	3.50

Europa.

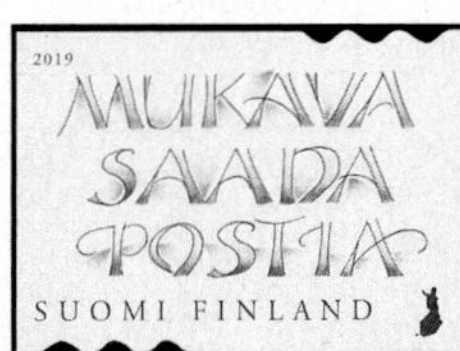

Calligraphy by Marja-Liisa Neuvonen — A1127

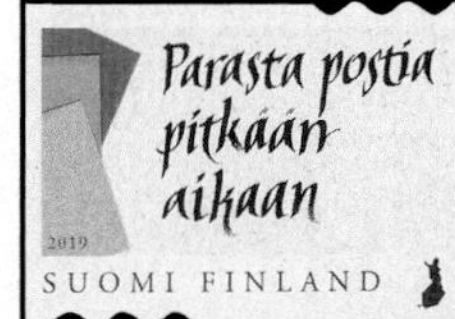

Calligraphy by Taru Tarvainen — A1128

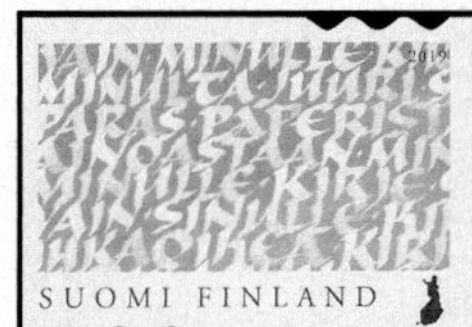

Calligraphy by Taru Tarvainen — A1129

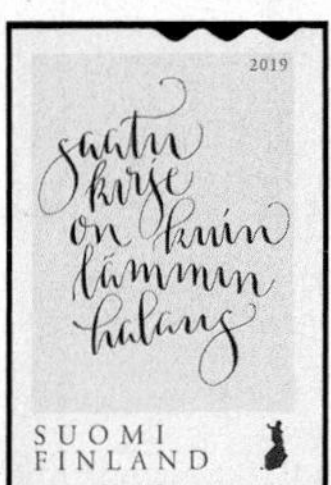

Calligraphy by Maarit Ali-Marttila-Olkkola — A1130

Calligraphy by Iiris Lyra — A1131

Serpentine Die Cut 4 Horiz.

2019, May 8 **Litho.**

Self-Adhesive

1586	Booklet pane of 5	17.50	
a.	A1127 (€1.50) multi	3.50	3.50
b.	A1128 (€1.50) multi	3.50	3.50
c.	A1129 (€1.50) multi	3.50	3.50
d.	A1130 (€1.50) multi	3.50	3.50
e.	A1131 (€1.50) multi	3.50	3.50

Rose on Letter A1132

Flowers in Wagon A1133

Sunflower on Typewriter A1134

Tulips in Watering Can A1135

Roses in Tea Cup A1136

Rose on Books A1137

Die Cut Perf. 12¼

2019, May 8 **Litho.**

Self-Adhesive

1587	Booklet pane of 6	21.00	
a.	A1132 (€1.50) multi	3.50	3.50
b.	A1133 (€1.50) multi	3.50	3.50
c.	A1134 (€1.50) multi	3.50	3.50
d.	A1135 (€1.50) multi	3.50	3.50
e.	A1136 (€1.50) multi	3.50	3.50
f.	A1137 (€1.50) multi	3.50	3.50

Rantapuisto Park and Siltasaari Island, Heinola A1138

Park Along Loimijoki River, Forssa A1139

Kuopio Cathedral A1140

Die Cut Perf. 10¼

2019, June 5 **Litho.**

Self-Adhesive

1588	Vert. strip of 3	10.50	
a.	A1138 (€1.50) multi	3.50	3.50
b.	A1139 (€1.50) multi	3.50	3.50
c.	A1140 (€1.50) multi	3.50	3.50
d.	Booklet pane of 15, 5 each #1588a-1588c	52.50	

A1141

A1142

A1143

A1144

A1145

Moomin Characters A1146

Die Cut Perf. 5¼ Horiz.

2019, June 5 Litho.

Self-Adhesive

1589 Booklet pane of 6 21.00
a. A1141 (€1.50) multi 3.50 3.50
b. A1142 (€1.50) multi 3.50 3.50
c. A1143 (€1.50) multi 3.50 3.50
d. A1144 (€1.50) multi 3.50 3.50
e. A1145 (€1.50) multi 3.50 3.50
f. A1146 (€1.50) multi 3.50 3.50

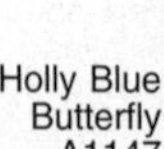

Holly Blue Butterfly A1147

Finnhorse — A1148

European Perch A1149

Silver Birch Trees A1150

Granite Stones — A1151

Die Cut Perf. 9½ Horiz. (horiz. stamps), Die Cut Perf. 9½ Vert. (vert. stamps)

2019, June 5 Litho.

Coil Stamps Self-Adhesive

1590 A1147 (€1.50) multi 3.50 3.50
1591 A1148 (€1.50) multi 3.50 3.50
1592 A1149 (€1.50) multi 3.50 3.50
1593 A1150 (€1.50) multi 3.50 3.50
1594 A1151 (€1.50) multi 3.50 3.50
a. Coil strip of 5, #1590-1594 17.50
Nos. 1590-1594 (5) 17.50 17.50

SEMI-POSTAL STAMPS

Arms — SP1

Unwmk.

1922, May 15 Typo. *Perf. 14*

B1 SP1 1m + 50p gray & red .90 *10.00*
Never hinged 2.00
a. Perf. 13x13½ *11.00*
Never hinged *22.50*

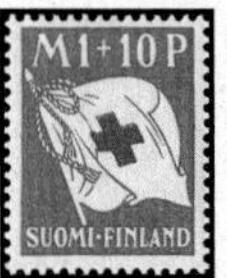
Red Cross Standard SP2

Symbolic SP3

Ship of Mercy — SP4

1930, Feb. 6

B2 SP2 1m + 10p red org & red 1.75 *11.50*
Never hinged 4.50
B3 SP3 1½m + 15p grysh grn & red 1.10 *11.50*
Never hinged 3.25
B4 SP4 2m + 20p dk bl & red 3.00 *50.00*
Never hinged 6.25
Nos. B2-B4 (3) 5.85 *73.00*
Set, never hinged 14.00

The surtax on this and subsequent similar issues was for the benefit of the Red Cross Society of Finland.

Church in Hattula — SP5

Designs: 1½m+15p, Castle of Hameenlinna. 2m+20p, Fortress of Viipuri.

1931, Jan. 1 Cross in Red Engr.

B5 SP5 1m + 10p gray grn 1.90 *14.00*
Never hinged 4.25
B6 SP5 1½m + 15p lil brn 11.50 *16.50*
Never hinged 35.00
B7 SP5 2m + 20p dull bl 1.90 *35.00*
Never hinged 3.50
Nos. B5-B7 (3) 15.30 *65.50*
Set, never hinged 42.50

SP8

1931, Oct. 15 Typo. *Rouletted 4, 5*

B8 SP8 1m + 4m black 12.50 *45.00*
Never hinged 20.00

The surtax was to assist the Postal Museum of Finland in purchasing the Richard Granberg collection of entire envelopes.

Helsinki University Library SP9

Nikolai Church at Helsinki SP10

2½m+25p, Parliament Building, Helsinki.

1932, Jan. 1 *Perf. 14*

B9 SP9 1¼m + 10p ol bis & red 1.50 *12.50*
Never hinged 4.75
B10 SP10 2m + 20p dp vio & red .40 *6.50*
Never hinged 1.00
B11 SP9 2½m + 25p lt blue & red 1.00 *25.00*
Never hinged 2.50
Nos. B9-B11 (3) 2.90 *44.00*
Set, never hinged 8.25

Bishop Magnus Tawast SP12

Michael Agricola SP13

Design: 2½m+25p, Isacus Rothovius.

1933, Jan. 20 Engr.

B12 SP12 1¼m + 10p blk brn & red 3.25 *16.00*
Never hinged 11.00
B13 SP13 2m + 20p brn vio & red 1.25 *4.50*
Never hinged 2.75
B14 SP13 2½m + 25p indigo & red 1.25 *8.75*
Never hinged 2.75
Nos. B12-B14 (3) 5.75 *29.25*
Set, never hinged 16.50

Evert Horn — SP15

Designs: 2m+20p, Torsten Stalhandske. 2½m+25p, Jakob (Lazy Jake) de la Gardie.

1934, Jan. Cross in Red

B15 SP15 1¼m + 10p brown 1.10 *4.50*
Never hinged 2.75
B16 SP15 2m + 20p gray lil 2.10 *8.00*
Never hinged 11.00
B17 SP15 2½m + 25p gray 1.10 *4.50*
Never hinged 2.75
Nos. B15-B17 (3) 4.30 *17.00*
Set, never hinged 16.50

Mathias Calonius — SP18

Designs: 2m+20p, Henrik C. Porthan. 2½m+25p, Anders Chydenius.

1935, Jan. 1 Cross in Red

B18 SP18 1¼m + 15p brown .90 *3.25*
Never hinged 2.10
B19 SP18 2m + 20p gray lil 2.00 *5.75*
Never hinged 5.75
B20 SP18 2½m + 25p gray bl .75 *3.25*
Never hinged 1.75
Nos. B18-B20 (3) 3.65 *12.25*
Set, never hinged 9.60

Robert Henrik Rehbinder — SP21

2m+20p, Count Gustaf Mauritz Armfelt. 2½m+25p, Count Arvid Bernard Horn.

1936, Jan. 1 Cross in Red

B21 SP21 1¼m + 15p dk brn .75 *2.40*
Never hinged 1.35
B22 SP21 2m + 20p vio brn 3.00 *7.25*
Never hinged 9.00
B23 SP21 2½m + 25p blue .75 *3.50*
Never hinged 1.60
Nos. B21-B23 (3) 4.50 *13.15*
Set, never hinged 12.00

Type "Uusimaa" SP24

Type "Turunmaa" SP25

Design: 3½m+35p, Type "Hameenmaa."

1937, Jan. 1 Cross in Red

B24 SP24 1¼m + 15p brown .70 *3.00*
Never hinged 2.00
B25 SP25 2m + 20p brn lake 13.00 9.00
Never hinged 50.00
B26 SP24 3½m + 35p indigo 1.00 *3.50*
Never hinged 2.75
Nos. B24-B26 (3) 14.70 15.50
Set, never hinged 54.00

Aukuste Makipeska — SP27

Designs: 1¼m+15p, Robert Isidor Orn. 2m+20p, Edward Bergenheim. 3½m+35p, Johan Mauritz Nordenstam.

1938, Jan. 5 Cross in Red Engr.

B27 SP27 50p + 5p dk grn .50 *1.35*
Never hinged .95
B28 SP27 1¼m + 15p dk brn .80 *2.25*
Never hinged 2.00
B29 SP27 2m + 20p rose lake 7.00 *7.50*
Never hinged 15.00
B30 SP27 3½m + 35p dk blue .55 *3.50*
Never hinged 1.25
Nos. B27-B30 (4) 8.85 *14.60*
Set, never hinged 19.00

Skiing — SP31

Designs: 2m+1m, Ski jumper. 3.50m+1.50m, Skier.

1938, Jan. 18

B31 SP31 1.25m + 75p sl grn 3.00 *13.00*
Never hinged 7.50
B32 SP31 2m + 1m dk car 3.00 *13.00*
Never hinged 7.50
B33 SP31 3.50m + 1.50m dk blue 3.00 *13.00*
Never hinged 7.50
Nos. B31-B33 (3) 9.00 *39.00*
Set, never hinged 22.50

Ski championships held at Lahti.

Soldier — SP34

1938, May 16

B34 SP34 2m + ½m blue 1.40 *5.00*
Never hinged 4.00

Victory of the White Army over the Red Guards. The surtax was for the benefit of the members of the Union of the Finnish Front.

Battlefield at Solferino SP35

1939, Jan. 2 Cross in Scarlet

B35 SP35 50p + 5p dk grn .85 *2.10*
Never hinged 1.75
B36 SP35 1¼m + 15p dk brn 1.00 *2.75*
Never hinged 1.50
B37 SP35 2m + 20p lake 14.00 *17.50*
Never hinged 32.50
B38 SP35 3½m + 35p dk bl .85 *3.50*
Never hinged 1.75
Nos. B35-B38 (4) 16.70 25.85
Set, never hinged 37.50

Intl. Red Cross Soc., 75th anniv.

Catalogue values for unused stamps in this section, from this point to the end of the section, are for Never Hinged items.

Soldiers with Crossbows — SP36

1¼m+15p, Cavalryman. 2m+20p, Soldier of Charles XII of Sweden. 3½m+35p, Officer and soldier of War with Russia, 1808-1809.

1940, Jan. 3 Cross in Red

B39 SP36 50p + 5p dk grn 1.40 *1.75*
B40 SP36 1¼m + 15p dk brn 3.50 3.00
B41 SP36 2m + 20p lake 5.50 3.50
B42 SP36 3½m + 35p dp ultra 3.50 *4.25*
Nos. B39-B42 (4) 13.90 12.50

The surtax aided the Finnish Red Cross.

Arms of Finland — SP40

1940, Feb. 15 Litho.

B43 SP40 2m +2m indigo .50 *1.75*

The surtax was given to a fund for the preservation of neutrality.

Mason — SP41

1.75m+15p, Farmer plowing. 2.75m+25p, Mother and child. 3.50m+35p, Finnish flag.

1941, Jan. 2 Cross in Red Engr.

B44 SP41 50p + 5p green .60 .55
B45 SP41 1.75m + 15p brown 1.75 *2.40*
B46 SP41 2.75m + 25p brn car 9.00 *9.50*
B47 SP41 3.50m + 35p dp ultra 2.00 *3.25*
Nos. B44-B47 (4) 13.35 15.70

See Nos. B65-B68.

Soldier's Emblem — SP45

1941, May 24 Unwmk.

B48 SP45 2.75m + 25p brt ultra .85 1.25

The surtax was for the aid of the soldiers who fought in the Russo-Finnish War.

Aland Arms — SP46

Coats of Arms: 1.75m+15p, Nyland. 2.75m+25p, Finland's first arms. 3.50m+35p, Karelia. 4.75m+45p, Satakunta.

1942, Jan. 2 ***Perf. 14***

Cross in Red

B49 SP46 50p + 5p green 1.40 1.25
B50 SP46 1.75m + 15p brown 2.10 *3.25*
B51 SP46 2.75m + 25p dark red 4.50 *3.25*
B52 SP46 3.50m + 35p deep ultra 3.50 *4.25*
B53 SP46 4.75m + 45p dk sl grn 2.75 *3.50*
Nos. B49-B53 (5) 14.25 *15.50*

The surtax aided the Finnish Red Cross.

Lapland Arms — SP51

Coats of Arms: 2m+20p, Hame. 3.50m+35p, Eastern Bothnia. 4.50m+45p, Savo.

Cross in Red

1943, Jan. 6 Inscribed "1943"

B54 SP51 50p + 5p green .70 *1.40*
B55 SP51 2m + 20p brown 1.50 *2.25*
B56 SP51 3.50m + 35p dark red 1.75 *2.25*
B57 SP51 4.50m + 45p brt ultra 4.25 *9.50*
Nos. B54-B57 (4) 8.20 *15.40*

The surtax aided the Finnish Red Cross.

Soldier's Helmet and Sword — SP55

Mother and Children — SP56

1943, Feb. 1 ***Perf. 13***

B58 SP55 2m + 50p dk brown .70 *1.20*
B59 SP56 3.50m + 1m brown red .70 *1.20*

The surtax was for national welfare.

Red Cross Train — SP57

2m+50p, Ambulance. 3.50m+75p, Red Cross Hospital, Helsinki. 4.50m+1m, Hospital plane.

1944, Jan. 2 Cross in Red ***Perf. 14***

B60 SP57 50p + 25p green .45 *.50*
B61 SP57 2m + 50p sepia .85 *1.50*
B62 SP57 3.50m + 75p ver .70 *1.25*
B63 SP57 4.50m + 1m brt ultra 1.75 *4.75*
Nos. B60-B63 (4) 3.75 *8.00*

The surtax aided the Finnish Red Cross.

Symbols of Peace — SP61

1944, Dec. 1

B64 SP61 3.50m + 1.50m dk red brn .55 *1.10*

The surtax was for national welfare.

Type of 1941 Inscribed "1945"

1945, May 2 Photo. & Engr.

Cross in Red

B65 SP41 1m + 25p green .40 *.50*
B66 SP41 2m + 50p brown .40 *1.00*
B67 SP41 3.50m + 75p brn car .40 *.70*
B68 SP41 4.50m + 1m dp ultra .85 *2.40*
Nos. B65-B68 (4) 2.05 4.60

The surtax was for the Finnish Red Cross.

Wrestling — SP62

2m+1m, Gymnast. 3.50m+1.75m, Runner. 4.50m+2.25m, Skier. 7m+3.50m, Javelin thrower.

1945, Apr. 16 Engr. ***Perf. 13½***

B69 SP62 1m + 50p bluish grn .40 *1.20*
B70 SP62 2m + 1m dp red .40 *1.20*
B71 SP62 3.50m + 1.75m dull vio .40 *1.20*
B72 SP62 4.50m + 2.25m ultra .75 *1.50*
B73 SP62 7m + 3.50m dull brn 1.00 *2.50*
Nos. B69-B73 (5) 2.95 7.60

Fishing — SP67

Designs: 3m+75p, Churning. 5m+1.25m, Reaping. 10m+2.50m, Logging.

Engraved; Cross Typo. in Red

1946, Jan. 7

B74 SP67 1m + 25p dull grn .55 *.70*
B75 SP67 3m + 75p lil brn .55 *.70*
B76 SP67 5m + 1.25m rose red .55 *.70*
a. Red cross omitted *850.00* 850.00
B77 SP67 10m + 2.50m ultra .70 *1.25*
Nos. B74-B77 (4) 2.35 *3.35*

The surtax was for the Finnish Red Cross.

Nurse and Children — SP71

Design: 8m+2m, Doctor examining infant.

1946, Sept. 2 Engr.

B78 SP71 5m + 1m green .50 *.75*
B79 SP71 8m + 2m brown vio .50 *.75*

The surtax was for the prevention of tuberculosis.

Nos. B78 and B79 Surcharged with New Values in Black

1947, Apr. 1

B80 SP71 6m + 1m on 5m + 1m .75 *1.10*
B81 SP71 10m + 2m on 8m + 2m .75 *1.10*

The surtax was for the prevention of tuberculosis.

SP73

Medical Examination of Infants — SP74

Designs: 10m+2.50m, Infant held by the feet. 12m+3m, Mme. Alli Paasikivi and a child. 20m+5m, Infant standing.

1947, Sept. 15 Engr.

B82 SP73 2.50m + 1m green .55 *1.40*
B83 SP74 6m + 1.50m dk red .70 *2.10*
B84 SP74 10m + 2.50m red brn 1.10 *2.10*
B85 SP73 12m + 3m dp blue 1.40 *2.75*
B86 SP74 20m + 5m dk red vio 2.10 *3.50*
Nos. B82-B86 (5) 5.85 *11.85*

The surtax was for the prevention of tuberculosis.

For surcharges see Nos. B91-B93.

Zachris Topelius — SP78

7m+2m, Fredrik Pacius. 12m+3m, Johan L. Runeberg. 20m+5m, Fredrik Cygnaeus.

Engraved; Cross Typo. in Red

1948, May 10 Unwmk. *Perf. 14*

B87 SP78 3m + 1m green .50 .75
B88 SP78 7m + 2m rose red .65 1.50
B89 SP78 12m + 3m brt blue .75 1.50
B90 SP78 20m + 5m dk vio .90 2.00
Nos. B87-B90 (4) 2.80 5.75

The surtax was for the Finnish Red Cross.

Nos. B83, B84 and B86 Surcharged with New Values and Bars in Black

1948, Sept. 13 Engr. *Perf. 13½*

B91 SP74 7m + 2m on #B83 2.25 3.50
B92 SP74 15m + 3m on #B84 2.25 3.50
B93 SP74 24m + 6m on #B86 2.50 5.25
Nos. B91-B93 (3) 7.00 12.25

The surtax was for the prevention of tuberculosis.

Tying Birch Boughs — SP79

9m+3m, Bathers in Sauna house. 15m+5m, Rural bath house. 30m+10m, Cold plunge in lake.

Engraved; Cross Typo. in Red

1949, May 5 *Perf. 13½x14*

B94 SP79 5m + 2m dull grn .50 .80
B95 SP79 9m + 3m dk car .90 1.40
B96 SP79 15m + 5m dp blue .90 1.40
B97 SP79 30m + 10m dk vio brn 2.00 3.25
Nos. B94-B97 (4) 4.30 6.85

The surtax was for the Finnish Red Cross.

Wood Anemone — SP83

1949, June 2 Engr.

Inscribed: "1949"

B98 SP83 5m + 2m shown .80 1.10
B99 SP83 9m + 3m Wild rose 1.00 1.25
B100 SP83 15m + 5m Coltsfoot 1.00 1.50
Nos. B98-B100 (3) 2.80 3.85

The surtax was for the prevention of tuberculosis.

Similar to Type of 1949

Designs: 5m+2m, Water lily. 9m+3m, Pasqueflower. 15m+5m, Bell flower cluster.

1950, Apr. 1 Inscribed: "1950"

B101 SP83 5m + 2m emer 3.25 2.75
B102 SP83 9m + 3m rose car 2.40 2.00
B103 SP83 15m + 5m blue 2.40 2.00
Nos. B101-B103 (3) 8.05 6.75

The surtax was for the prevention of tuberculosis.

Hospital Entrance, Helsinki SP84

Blood Donor's Medal SP86

Design: 12m+3m, Giving blood.

Engraved; Cross Typo. in Red

1951, Mar. 17 Unwmk. *Perf. 14*

B104 SP84 7m + 2m chocolate 1.10 2.10
B105 SP84 12m + 3m bl vio 1.75 2.75
B106 SP86 20m + 5m car 2.00 3.50
Nos. B104-B106 (3) 4.85 8.35

The surtax was for the Finnish Red Cross.

Capercaillie — SP87

Designs: 12m+3m, European cranes. 20m+5m, Caspian terns.

1951, Oct. 26 Engr.

B107 SP87 7m + 2m dk grn 3.75 4.00
B108 SP87 12m + 3m rose brn 3.75 4.00
B109 SP87 20m + 5m blue 3.75 4.00
Nos. B107-B109 (3) 11.25 12.00

The surtax was for the prevention of tuberculosis.

Diver — SP88

Soccer Players SP89

No. B112, Stadum, Helsinki. No. B113, Runners.

1951-52

B110 SP88 12m + 2m rose car 2.10 1.75
B111 SP89 15m + 2m grn ('52) 2.50 2.25
B112 SP88 20m + 3m deep blue 2.10 2.00
B113 SP89 25m + 4m brn ('52) 2.75 3.00
Nos. B110-B113 (4) 9.45 9.00

XV Olympic Games, Helsinki, 1952. The surtax was to help finance the games.

Issued: B110, B112, 11/16; B111, B113, 2/15/52.

Margin blocks of four of each denomination were cut from regular or perf-through-margin sheets and pasted by the selvage, overlapping, in a printed folder to create a kind of souvenir booklet. Value $60.

Field Marshal Mannerheim — SP90

Engraved; Cross Typo. in Red

1952, Mar. 4

B114 SP90 10m + 2m gray 2.40 2.50
B115 SP90 15m + 3m rose vio 2.40 2.50
B116 SP90 25m + 5m blue 2.40 2.50
Nos. B114-B116 (3) 7.20 7.50

The surtax was for the Red Cross.

Great Titmouse — SP91

Designs: 15m+3m, Spotted flycatchers and nest. 25m+5m, Swift.

1952, Dec. 4 Engr.

B117 SP91 10m + 2m green 3.75 3.50
B118 SP91 15m + 3m plum 3.75 3.50
B119 SP91 25m + 5m dp blue 3.75 3.50
Nos. B117-B119 (3) 11.25 10.50

The surtax was for the prevention of tuberculosis.

See Nos. B148-B150.

European Red Squirrel SP92

No. B121, Brown bear. No. B122, European elk.

Unwmk.

1953, Nov. 16 Engr. *Perf. 14*

B120 SP92 10m + 2m red brn 3.75 4.25
B121 SP92 15m + 3m violet 3.75 4.25
B122 SP92 25m + 5m dk grn 3.75 4.25
Nos. B120-B122 (3) 11.25 12.75

Surtax for the prevention of tuberculosis.

Children Receiving Parcel from Welfare Worker — SP93

Designs: 15m+3m, Aged woman knitting. 25m+5m, Blind basket-maker and dog.

Engraved; Cross Typo. in Red

1954, Mar. 8 *Perf. 11½*

B123 SP93 10m + 2m dk ol grn 1.50 2.00
B124 SP93 15m + 3m dk blue 1.50 2.00
B125 SP93 25m + 5m dk brown 1.50 2.00
Nos. B123-B125 (3) 4.50 6.00

The surtax was for the Finnish Red Cross.

Bumblebees, Dandelions — SP94

15m+3m, Butterfly. 25m+5m, Dragonfly.

Engraved; Cross Typo. in Red

1954, Dec. 7 *Perf. 14*

B126 SP94 10m + 2m brown 2.75 2.10
B127 SP94 15m + 3m carmine 3.25 2.75
B128 SP94 25m + 5m blue 3.25 2.75
Nos. B126-B128 (3) 9.25 7.60

The surtax was for the prevention of tuberculosis.

European Perch — SP95

Designs: 15m+3m, Northern pike. 25m+5m, Atlantic salmon.

Engraved; Cross Typo. in Red

1955, Sept. 26 *Perf. 14*

B129 SP95 10m + 2m dl grn 2.00 2.10
B130 SP95 15m + 3m vio brn 2.50 2.10
B131 SP95 25m + 5m dk bl 3.25 2.10
Nos. B129-B131 (3) 7.75 6.30

Surtax for the Anti-Tuberculosis Society.

Gen. von Dobeln in Battle of Juthas, 1808 — SP96

Illustrations by Albert Edelfelter from J. L. Runeberg's "Tales of Ensign Stal": 15m+3m, Col. J. Z. Duncker holding flag. 25m+5m, Son of fallen Soldier.

Engraved; Cross Typo. in Red

1955, Nov. 24

B132 SP96 10m + 2m dp ultra 1.75 2.00
B133 SP96 15m + 3m dk red brn 1.75 2.00
B134 SP96 25m + 5m green 1.75 2.00
Nos. B132-B134 (3) 5.25 6.00

The surtax was for the Red Cross.

Waxwing — SP97

Birds: 20m+3m, Eagle owl. 30m+5m, Mute swan.

Engraved; Cross Typo. in Red

1956, Sept. 25 *Perf. 11½*

B135 SP97 10m + 2m dl red brn 2.10 1.25
B136 SP97 20m + 3m bl grn 2.75 2.10
B137 SP97 30m + 5m blue 3.75 2.10
Nos. B135-B137 (3) 8.60 5.45

Surtax for the Anti-Tuberculosis Society.

Pekka Aulin — SP98

Portraits: 10m+2m, Leonard von Pfaler. 20m+3m, Gustaf Johansson. 30m+5m, Viktor Magnus von Born.

Engraved; Cross Typo. in Red

1956, Nov. 26 Unwmk.

B138 SP98 5m + 1m grysh grn 1.00 1.25
B139 SP98 10m + 2m brown 1.50 1.50
B140 SP98 20m + 3m mag 2.25 2.25
B141 SP98 30m + 5m lt ultra 2.25 2.25
Nos. B138-B141 (4) 7.00 7.25

The surtax was for the Red Cross.

Wolverine (Glutton) — SP99

20m+3m, Lynx. 30m+5m, Reindeer.

Engraved; Cross Typo. in Red

1957, Sept. 5 *Perf. 11½*

B142 SP99 10m + 2m dull purple 2.00 1.50
B143 SP99 20m + 3m sepia 3.00 2.40
B144 SP99 30m + 5m dark blue 3.00 2.40
Nos. B142-B144 (3) 8.00 6.30

The surtax was for the Anti-Tuberculosis Society. See Nos. B160-B165.

Red Cross Flag — SP100

1957, Nov. 25 **Engr.** *Perf. 14*

Cross in Red

B145 SP100 10m + 2m ol grn 1.75 2.40
B146 SP100 20m + 3m maroon 2.00 3.50
B147 SP100 30m + 5m dull blue 2.00 3.50
Nos. B145-B147 (3) 5.75 9.40

80th anniv. of the Finnish Red Cross.

Type of 1952

Flowers: 10m+2m, Lily of the Valley. 20m+3m, Red clover. 30m+5m, Hepatica.

Engraved; Cross Typo. in Red

1958, May 5 **Unwmk.** *Perf. 14*

B148 SP91 10m + 2m green 2.40 1.60
B149 SP91 20m + 3m lilac rose 2.75 2.60
B150 SP91 30m + 5m ultra 3.00 2.60
Nos. B148-B150 (3) 8.15 6.80

Surtax for the Anti-Tuberculosis Society.

Raspberry — SP101

20m+3m, Cowberry. 30m+5m, Blueberry.

Engraved; Cross Typo. in Red

1958, Nov. 20 *Perf. 11½*

B151 SP101 10m + 2m orange 2.40 1.75
B152 SP101 20m + 3m red 2.75 2.25
B153 SP101 30m + 5m dk blue 2.75 2.25
Nos. B151-B153 (3) 7.90 6.25

The surtax was for the Red Cross.

Daisy — SP102

20m+5m, Primrose. 30m+5m, Cornflower.

Engraved; Cross Typo. in Red

1959, Sept. 7 **Unwmk.**

B154 SP102 10m + 2m green 4.00 2.00
B155 SP102 20m + 3m lt brown 4.50 3.00
B156 SP102 30m + 5m blue 4.50 3.00
Nos. B154-B156 (3) 13.00 8.00

Surtax for the Anti-Tuberculosis Society.

Reindeer SP103

No. B158, Lapp & lasso. No. B159, Mountains.

Engraved; Cross Typo. in Red

1960, Nov. 24 *Perf. 11½*

B157 SP103 10m + 2m dk gray 1.50 1.50
B158 SP103 20m + 3m gray vio 2.25 2.25
B159 SP103 30m + 5m rose vio 2.25 2.25
Nos. B157-B159 (3) 6.00 6.00

The surtax was for the Red Cross.

Animal Type of 1957

Designs: 10m+2m, Muskrat. 20m+3m, Otter. 30m+5m, Seal.

Engr.; Cross at right, Typo. in Red

1961, Sept. 4

B160 SP99 10m + 2m brn car 1.75 1.40
B161 SP99 20m + 3m slate bl 2.50 2.00
B162 SP99 30m + 5m bl grn 2.50 2.00
Nos. B160-B162 (3) 6.75 5.40

Surtax for the Anti-Tuberculosis Society.

Animal Type of 1957

Designs: 10m+2m, Hare. 20m+3m, Pine marten. 30m+5m, Ermine.

Engraved; Cross Typo. in Red

1962, Oct. 1

B163 SP99 10m + 2m gray 1.90 1.90
B164 SP99 20m + 3m dl red brn 2.50 2.25
B165 SP99 30m + 5m vio bl 2.50 2.25
Nos. B163-B165 (3) 6.90 6.40

The surtax was for the Anti-Tuberculosis Society.

Cross and Outstretched Hands SP104

Engraved; Cross Typo. in Red

1963, May 8 **Unwmk.** *Perf. 11½*

B166 SP104 10p + 2p red brn .75 1.00
B167 SP104 20p + 3p violet 1.25 1.50
B168 SP104 30p + 5p green 1.25 1.50
Nos. B166-B168 (3) 3.25 4.00

The surtax was for the Red Cross.

Attending the Wounded SP105

Red Cross Activities: 25p+4p, Hospital ship. 35p+5p, Prisoner-of-war health examination. 40p+7p, Gift parcel distribution.

Engraved; Cross Typo. in Red

1964, May 26 *Perf. 11½*

B169 SP105 15p + 3p vio bl 1.25 .70
B170 SP105 25p + 4p green 1.50 1.10
B171 SP105 35p + 5p vio brn 1.50 1.10
B172 SP105 40p + 7p dk ol grn 1.50 1.10
Nos. B169-B172 (4) 5.75 4.00

The surtax was for the Red Cross.

Finnish Spitz — SP106

Designs: 25p+4p, Karelian bear dog. 35p+5p, Finnish hunting dog.

Engraved; Cross Typo. in Red

1965, May 10 *Perf. 11½*

B173 SP106 15p + 3p org brn 2.00 1.50
B174 SP106 25p + 4p black 3.00 2.25
B175 SP106 35p + 5p gray brn 3.00 2.25
Nos. B173-B175 (3) 8.00 6.00

Surtax for Anti-Tuberculosis Society.

Artificial Respiration — SP107

First Aid: 25p+4p, Skin diver rescuing occupants of submerged car. 35p+5p, Helicopter rescue in winter.

1966, May 7 **Litho.** *Perf. 14*

B176 SP107 15p + 3p multi 1.10 1.25
B177 SP107 25p + 4p multi 1.25 1.50
B178 SP107 35p + 5p multi 1.25 1.50
Nos. B176-B178 (3) 3.60 4.25

The surtax was for the Red Cross.

Birch — SP108

Trees: 25p+4p, Pine. 40p+7p, Spruce.

1967, May 12 **Litho.** *Perf. 14*

B179 SP108 20p + 3p multi 1.00 1.00
B180 SP108 25p + 4p multi 1.00 1.00
B181 SP108 40p + 7p multi 1.00 1.00
Nos. B179-B181 (3) 3.00 3.00

Surtax for Anti-Tuberculosis Society. See Nos. B185-B187.

Horse-drawn Ambulance SP109

25p+4p, Ambulance, 1967. 40p+7p, Red Cross.

Cross in Red

1967, Nov. 24 **Litho.** *Perf. 14*

B182 SP109 20p + 3p dl yel, grn & blk 1.10 1.10
B183 SP109 25p + 4p vio & blk 1.10 1.10
B184 SP109 40p + 7p dk grn, blk & dk ol 1.10 1.10
Nos. B182-B184 (3) 3.30 3.30

The surtax was for the Red Cross.

Tree Type of 1967

Trees: 20p+3p, Juniper. 25+4p, Aspen. 40p+7p, Chokecherry.

1969, May 12 **Litho.** *Perf. 14*

B185 SP108 20p + 3p multi .90 1.10
B186 SP108 25p + 4p multi .90 1.10
B187 SP108 40p + 7p multi .90 1.10
Nos. B185-B187 (3) 2.70 3.30

Surtax for Anti-Tuberculosis Society.

"On the Lapp's Magic Rock" SP110

Designs: 30p+6p, Juhani blowing horn on Impivaara Rock, vert. 50p+10p, The Pale Maiden. The designs are from illustrations by Askeli Gallen-Kallelas for "The Seven Brothers" by Aleksis Kivi.

1970, May 8 **Litho.** *Perf. 14*

B188 SP110 25p + 5p multi .70 .70
B189 SP110 30p + 6p multi .85 .90
B190 SP110 50p + 10p multi .85 .90
Nos. B188-B190 (3) 2.40 2.50

The surtax was for the Red Cross.

Cutting and Loading Timber SP111

Designs: 30p+6p, Floating logs downstream. 50p+10p, Sorting logs at sawmill.

1971, Apr. 25 **Litho.** *Perf. 14*

B191 SP111 25p + 5p multi .90 1.00
B192 SP111 30p + 6p multi .90 1.00
B193 SP111 50p + 10p multi 1.00 1.00
Nos. B191-B193 (3) 2.80 3.00

Surtax for Anti-Tuberculosis Society.

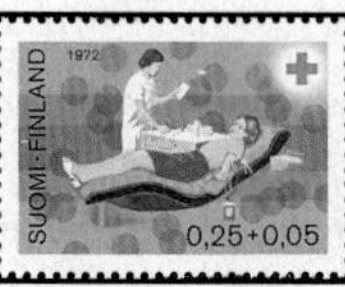

Blood Donor and Nurse SP112

30p+6p, Blood research (microscope, slides), vert. 50p+10p, Blood transfusion.

1972, Oct. 23

B194 SP112 25p + 5p multi .70 .85
B195 SP112 30p + 6p multi 1.10 1.10
B196 SP112 50p + 10p multi 1.10 1.10
Nos. B194-B196 (3) 2.90 3.05

Surtax was for the Red Cross.

Girl with Lamb, by Hugo Simberg — SP113

Paintings: 40p+10p, Summer Evening, by Vilho Sjöström. 60p+15p, Woman at Mountain Fountain, by Juho Rissanen.

1973, Sept. 12 **Litho.** *Perf. 13x12½*

B197 SP113 30p + 5p multi 1.25 1.25
B198 SP113 40p + 10p multi 1.75 1.75
B199 SP113 60p + 15p multi 1.75 1.75
Nos. B197-B199 (3) 4.75 4.75

Surtax for the Finnish Anti-Tuberculosis Assoc. Birth centenaries of featured artists.

Morel SP114

Mushrooms: 50p+10p, Chanterelle. 60p+15p, Boletus edulis.

1974, Sept. 24 **Litho.** *Perf. 12½x13*

B200 SP114 35p + 5p multi 2.50 1.50
B201 SP114 50p + 10p multi 2.25 1.50
B202 SP114 60p + 15p multi 2.25 1.50
Nos. B200-B202 (3) 7.00 4.50

Finnish Red Cross.

Echo, by Ellen Thesleff (1869-1954) SP115

Paintings: 60p+15p, Hilda Wiik, by Maria Wiik (1853-1928). 70p+20p, At Home (old woman in chair), by Helene Schjerfbeck (1862-1946).

1975, Sept. 30 Litho. *Perf. 13x12½*
B203 SP115 40p + 10p multi 1.10 1.10
B204 SP115 60p + 15p multi 1.25 1.25
B205 SP115 70p + 20p multi 1.25 1.25
Nos. B203-B205 (3) 3.60 3.60

Finnish Red Cross. In honor of International Women's Year paintings by women artists were chosen.

Disabled Veterans' Emblem SP116

Lithographed and Photogravure

1976, Jan. 15 *Perf. 14*
B206 SP116 70p + 30p multi .80 .80

The surtax was for hospitals for disabled war veterans.

Wedding Procession SP117

Designs: 70p+15p, Wedding dance, vert. 80p+20p, Bride, groom, matron and pastor at wedding dinner.

1976, Sept. 15 Litho. *Perf. 13*
B207 SP117 50p + 10p multi .85 .95
B208 SP117 70p + 15p multi 1.10 1.10
B209 SP117 80p + 20p multi 1.10 1.10
Nos. B207-B209 (3) 3.05 3.15

Surtax for Anti-Tuberculosis Society.

Disaster Relief SP118

Designs: 80p+15p, Community work. 90p+20p, Blood transfusion service.

1977, Jan. 19 Litho. *Perf. 14*
B210 SP118 50p + 10p multi .65 .65
B211 SP118 80p + 15p multi .80 .80
B212 SP118 90p + 20p multi .80 .80
Nos. B210-B212 (3) 2.25 2.25

Finnish Red Cross centenary.

Long-distance Skiing SP119

Design: 1m+50p, Ski jump.

1977, Oct. 5 Litho. *Perf. 13*
B213 SP119 80p + 40p multi 2.50 3.75
B214 SP119 1m + 50p multi 2.00 2.00

Surtax was for World Ski Championships, Lahti, Feb. 17-26, 1978.

Saffron Milkcap SP120

Edible Mushrooms: 80p+15p, Parasol, vert. 1m+20p, Gypsy.

1978, Sept. 13 Litho. *Perf. 13*
B215 SP120 50p + 10p multi 1.75 1.10
B216 SP120 80p + 15p multi 2.00 2.00
B217 SP120 1m + 20p multi 2.00 2.00
Nos. B215-B217 (3) 5.75 5.10

Surtax was for Red Cross. See Nos. B221-B223.

Pehr Kalm, 1716-1779 SP121

Finnish Scientists: 90p+15p, Title page of Pehr Adrian Gadd's (1727-97) book, vert. 1.10m+20p, Petter Forsskal (1732-63).

Perf. 12½x13, 13x12½
1979, Sept. 26 Litho.
B218 SP121 60p + 10p multi .65 .80
B219 SP121 90p + 15p multi .85 .85
B220 SP121 1.10m + 20p multi .85 .85
Nos. B218-B220 (3) 2.35 2.50

Surtax for Finnish Anti-Tuberculosis Assoc.

Mushroom Type of 1978

Edible Mushrooms: 60p+10p, Woolly milk-cap. 90p+15p, Orange-cap boletus, vert. 1.10m+20p, Russula paludosa.

1980, Apr. 19 Litho. *Perf. 13*
B221 SP120 60p + 10p multi 1.50 1.10
B222 SP120 90p + 15p multi 2.00 2.00
B223 SP120 1.10m + 20p multi 2.00 2.00
Nos. B221-B223 (3) 5.50 5.10

Surtax was for Red Cross.

Fuchsia — SP122

No. B225, African violet. No. B226, Geranium.

1981, Aug. 24 Litho. *Perf. 13*
B224 SP122 70p + 10p shown 1.10 1.10
B225 SP122 1m + 15p multi 1.10 1.10
B226 SP122 1.10m + 20p multi 1.10 1.10
Nos. B224-B226 (3) 3.30 3.30

Surtax for Finnish Anti-Tuberculosis Assoc.

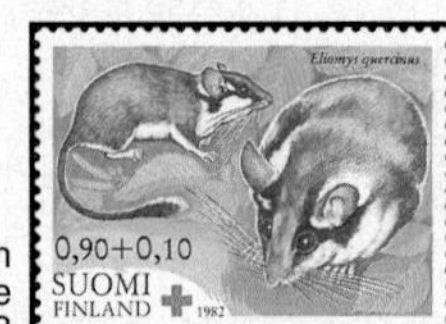

Garden Dormouse SP123

No. B228, Flying squirrels. No. B229, European minks.

1982, Aug. 16 Litho. *Perf. 13*
B227 SP123 90p + 10p shown 1.10 1.00
B228 SP123 1.10m + 15p multi 1.10 1.10
B229 SP123 1.20m + 20p multi 1.25 1.10
Nos. B227-B229 (3) 3.45 3.20

Surtax was for Red Cross. No. B228 vert.

Forest and Wetland Plants SP124

1m+20p, Chickweed wintergreen. 1.20m+25p, Marsh violet. 1.30m+30p, Marsh marigold.

1983, July 7 Litho. *Perf. 13*
B230 SP124 1m + 20p multi 1.00 1.00
B231 SP124 1.20m + 25p multi 1.00 1.00
B232 SP124 1.30m + 30p multi 1.00 1.00
Nos. B230-B232 (3) 3.00 3.00

Surtax for Finnish Anti-Tuberculosis Assoc.

Globe Puzzle — SP125

2m+40p, Symbolic world communication.

1984, May 28 Litho. *Perf. 13*
B233 SP125 1.40m + 35p multi .80 .75
B234 SP125 2m + 40p multi 1.25 1.10

Surtax for Red Cross.

Butterflies SP126

No. B235, Anthocharis cardamines. No. B236, Nymphalis antiopa. No. B237, Parnassius apollo.

1986, May 22 Litho. *Perf. 13*
B235 SP126 1.60m + 40p multi 1.25 .85
B236 SP126 2.10m + 45p multi 1.90 1.50
B237 SP126 5m + 50p multi 4.00 4.00
Nos. B235-B237 (3) 7.15 6.35

Surtax for Red Cross.

Festivals SP127

Designs: No. B238, Christmas. No. B239, Easter. No. B240, Midsummer.

1988, Mar. 14 Litho. *Perf. 13*
B238 SP127 1.40m +40p multi 1.10 .85
B239 SP127 1.80m +45p multi 1.25 .90
B240 SP127 2.40m +50p multi 1.25 1.25
Nos. B238-B240 (3) 3.60 3.00

Surtax for the Red Cross.

Heodes virgaureae on Goldrod Plant SP128

Butterflies and plants: No. B242, *Agrodiaetus amandus* on meadow vetchling. No. B243, *Inachis io* on tufted vetch.

1990, Apr. 6 Photo. *Perf. 12x11½*
B241 SP128 1.50m +40p multi 1.00 1.00
B242 SP128 2m +50p multi 1.25 1.25
B243 SP128 2.70m +60p multi 1.50 1.50
Nos. B241-B243 (3) 3.75 3.75

Surtax for the natl. Red Cross Soc.

Paintings by Helene Schjerfbeck — SP129

Designs: No. B244a, The Little Convalescent, No. B244b, Green Still-Life.

1991, Mar. 8 Litho. *Perf. 13*
B244 SP129 Pair 3.00 3.00
a.-b. 2.10m +50p any single 1.40 1.40

Surtax for philately.

Butterflies SP130

No. B245, Xestia brunneopicta. No. B246, Acerbia alpina. No. B247, Baptria tibiale.

Litho. & Embossed

1992, Apr. 22 *Perf. 13*
B245 SP130 1.60m +40p multi .90 .90
B246 SP130 2.10m +50p multi 1.20 1.20
B247 SP130 5m +60p multi 2.25 2.75
Nos. B245-B247 (3) 4.35 4.85

Surtax for Finnish Red Cross. Embossed "Arla 100" in braille for Arla Institute, training center for the blind, cent.

Autumn Landscape of Lake Pielisjarvi, by Eero Jarnefelt — SP131

a, Tree-covered hill. b, Lake shoreline.

1993, Mar. 19 Litho. *Perf. 13*
B248 SP131 2.30m + 70p Pair, #a.-b. 3.00 3.00

Surtax for philately.

Finnhorses SP132

Designs: No. B249, Draft horses. No. B250, Trotter. No. B251, War horses, vert.

1994, Mar. 11 Litho. *Perf. 13*
B249 SP132 2m +40p multi 1.00 1.00
B250 SP132 2.30m +50p multi 1.50 1.50
B251 SP132 4.20m +60p multi 2.25 2.25
Nos. B249-B251 (3) 4.75 4.75

Surtax for Finnish Red Cross.

Paintings, by Albert Edelfelt (1854-1905) — SP133

No. B252, Playing Boys on the Shore. No. B253, Queen Blanche.

1995, Mar. 1 Litho. *Perf. 13½*
B252 2.40m +60p multi 2.25 1.50

Size: 22x31mm

B253 2.40m +60p multi 2.25 1.50
a. SP133 Pair, #B252-B253 4.50 4.50

Surtax for philately.

Chickens SP134

Designs: No. B254, Chicks. No. B255, Hens. No. B256, Rooster, vert.

1996, Mar. 18 Litho. *Perf. 13*

B254	SP134 2.80m +60p multi	1.90	2.40
B255	SP134 3.20m +70p multi	1.90	1.90
B256	SP134 3.40m +70p multi	2.00	3.50
	Nos. B254-B256 (3)	5.80	7.80

Surtax for Finnish Red Cross.

The Aino Myth, by Akseli Gallen-Kallela (1865-1931) SP135

Designs: No. B257, Väinämöinen proposing marriage to Aino in forest. No. B258, Aino jumping into water to escape Väinämöinen. No. B259, Aino at shore for bath.

1997, Sept. 5 Litho. *Perf. 13½x13*

Booklet Stamps

B257	SP135 2.80m +60p multi	2.25	2.25
B258	SP135 2.80m +60p multi	2.25	2.25
B259	SP135 2.80m +60p multi	2.25	2.25
a.	Booklet pane, #B257-B259	6.75	6.75
	Complete booklet, #B259a	6.75	

No. B258 is 33x46mm.

Surtax for philately.

Pigs — SP136

2.80m+60p, Sow, piglets. 3.20m+70p, Three piglets. 3.40m+70p, Pig's head.

1998, Mar. 12 Litho. *Perf. 13*

B260	SP136 2.80m +60p multi	1.60	1.60
B261	SP136 3.20m +70p multi	1.90	1.90
B262	SP136 3.40m +70p multi	2.00	2.00
	Nos. B260-B262 (3)	5.50	5.50

Surtax for Finnish Red Cross.

Paintings by Hugo Simberg (1873-1917) SP137

a, Garden of Death. b, Wounded Angel.

Perf. 13¼x13¾

1999, Sept. 24 Litho.

B263	Booklet pane of 2	4.25	4.25
a.-b.	SP137 3.50m +50p any single	2.00	
	Complete booklet, #B263	4.25	

Surtax for philately.

Cow and Calf — SP138

Perf. 13¾x13¼

2000, Mar. 15 Litho.

B264	SP138 3.50m +70p Bull, vert.	1.50	1.20

Perf. 13¼x13¾

B265	SP138 4.80m +80p shown	2.25	2.00

Surtax for Finnish Red Cross.

Post Horn SP139

2010, May 4 Litho. *Perf. 14½x14¼*

B266	SP139 1 +5c multi	2.75	2.60

No. B266 had a franking value of 80c on day of issue. Surtax for construction of Finland's first solar energy plant.

No. 769 Surcharged in Silver and Black

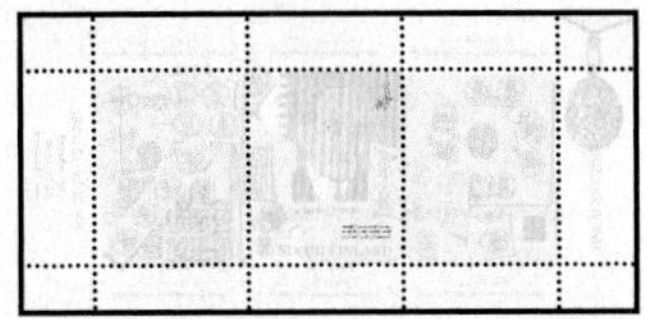

Methods and Perfs. As Before

2017, May 24

B267	A418 (€1.30) on 5m + (€28.70) booklet pane of 1 + 2 labels	—	—
	Complete booklet, #B267	—	

No. B267 had a franking value of €1.30. The surtax was for Finlandia 2017 International Philatelic Exhibition, as it does not appear that the purchase of the booklet for €30 included the price of admission to the exhibition, as was the case with No. 789 in 1988. The booklet was sold in a numbered envelope that included a postcard.

AIR POST STAMPS

No. 178 Overprinted in Red

1930, Sept. 24 Unwmk. *Perf. 14*

C1	A28 10m gray lilac	140.00	*290.00*
a.	1830 for 1930	2,500.	*12,000.*

Overprinted expressly for use on mail carried in "Graf Zeppelin" on return flight from Finland to Germany on Sept. 24, 1930, after which trip the stamps ceased to be valid for postage. Forgeries are almost always on No. 205, rather than No. 178.

Catalogue values for unused stamps in this section, from this point to the end of the section, are for Never Hinged items.

Douglas DC-2 — AP1

1944 Engr.

C2	AP1 3.50m dark brown	.70	*1.40*

Air Transport Service anniv, 1923-43.

Douglas DC-6 Over Winter Landscape — AP2

1950, Feb. 13

C3	AP2 300m blue	17.50	7.00

Available also for ordinary postage.

Redrawn

1958, Jan. 20 *Perf. 11½*

C4	AP2 300(m) blue	32.50	.80

On No. C4 "mk" is omitted.

See Nos. C9-C9a.

Convair 440 over Lakes — AP3

1958, Oct. 31 Unwmk. *Perf. 11½*

C5	AP3 34m blue	1.25	.75

No. C5 Surcharged

1959, Apr. 5

C6	AP3 45m on 34m blue	2.50	2.25

C7

C8

1959, Nov. 2

C7	AP3 45m blue	3.00	1.50

1963, Feb. 15

C8	AP3 45p blue	2.00	.40

On No. C7 the denomination is "45." On No. C8 it is "0.45."

DC-6 Type, Comma After "3" — AP5

Type I — 16 lines in numeral "0"
Type II — 13 lines in numeral "0"

1963, Oct. 10

C9	AP5 3m blue, Type II ('73)	3.25	.30
a.	Type I	40.00	.40

Convair Type of 1958

1970, July 15

C10	AP3 57p ultra	2.00	1.25

MILITARY STAMPS

Catalogue values for unused stamps in this section are for Never Hinged items.

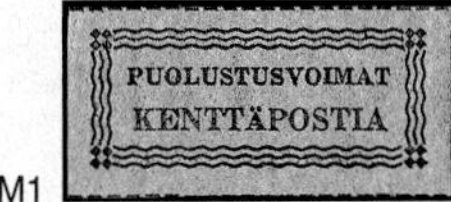

M1

Unwmk.

1941, Nov. 1 Typo. *Imperf.*

M1	M1 (4m) blk, *dk org*	.80	*.90*

#M1 has simulated roulette printed in black.

Type of 1930-46 Overprinted in Black

1943, Oct. 16 *Perf. 14*

M2	A26 2m deep orange	.65	*1.10*
M3	A26 3½m greenish blue	.65	*1.10*

Post Horn and Sword — M2

1943, July 1 Size: 29½x19½mm

M4	M2 (2m) green	.90	.75
M5	M2 (3m) rose violet	1.10	.75

1944, Feb. 16 Size: 20x16mm

M6	M2 (2m) green	.75	.60
M7	M2 (3m) rose violet	.75	.60

Post Horns and Arms of Finland — M3

1963, Sept. 26 Litho. *Perf. 14*

M8	M3 violet blue	*160.00*	*175.00*

Used during maneuvers Sept. 30-Oct. 5, 1963. Valid from Sept. 26.

No. M8 Overprinted "1983"

1983, Apr. 20

M9	M3 violet blue	*250.00*	*175.00*

Used during maneuvers Apr. 24-30.

PARCEL POST STAMPS

AUTOPAKETTI
0025290
1 mk
N:o 6 BILPAKET

PP1

Wmk. Rose & Triangles Multiple

Rouletted 6 on 2 or 3 Sides

1949-50 Typo.

Q1	PP1	1m brt grn & blk	1.90	*5.00*
Q2	PP1	5m red & blk	20.00	*32.50*
Q3	PP1	20m org & blk	30.00	*55.00*
Q4	PP1	50m bl & blk ('50)	12.00	*17.50*
Q5	PP1	100m brn & blk ('50)	12.50	*17.50*
		Nos. Q1-Q5 (5)	76.40	*127.50*
		Set, never hinged	130.00	

Catalogue values for unused stamps in this section, from this point to the end of the section, are for Never Hinged items.

Mail Bus — PP2

1952-58 Unwmk. Engr. *Perf. 14*

Q6	PP2 5m car rose	6.25	5.50
Q7	PP2 20m orange	25.00	11.00
Q8	PP2 50m blue ('54)	37.50	17.50
Q9	PP2 100m brn ('58)	50.00	37.50
	Nos. Q6-Q9 (4)	118.75	71.50

AUTOPAKETTI 0,05
BUSSPAKET

Mail Bus — PP3

1963 ***Perf. 12***

Q10	PP3	5p red & blk	3.50	5.00
Q11	PP3	20p org & blk	18.00	8.50
Q12	PP3	50p blue & blk	10.50	8.25
Q13	PP3	1m brn & blk	14.50	8.75
		Nos. Q10-Q13 (4)	46.50	30.50

Nos. Q1-Q13 were issued only in booklets: panes of 6 for Nos. Q1-Q5, 10 for Nos. Q6-Q9 and 5 for Nos. Q10-Q13.

Used values are for regular postal or mail-bus cancels. Pen strokes, cutting or other cancels sell for half as much.

1981 SISU Bus — PP4

Photo. & Engr.

1981, Dec. 7 ***Perf. 12 Horiz.***

Q14	PP4	50p dk bl & blk	2.75	*5.75*
Q15	PP4	1m dk brn & blk	3.25	*5.75*
Q16	PP4	5m grn & blk	4.00	*16.00*
Q17	PP4	10m red & blk	7.25	*32.50*
		Nos. Q14-Q17 (4)	17.25	*60.00*

Parcel post stamps invalid after Jan. 9, 1985.

ALAND ISLANDS

LOCATION — A group of 6,554 islands at the mouth of the Gulf of Bothnia, between Finland and Sweden.
GOVT. — Province of Finland
AREA — 590 sq. mi.
POP. — 23,761
CAPITAL — Mariehamn

The province of Aland was awarded to Finland in 1921 by the League of Nations. The Swedish language is spoken and the province has a considerable amount of self-determination.

Catalogue values for unused stamps in this country are for Never Hinged items.

Most Aland Island issues exist favor canceled, and used values are for such cancellations. Postally used examples are worth 30 to 40% more than the values shown.

Gaff-rigged Sloop — A1

Aland Flag — A2

Midsummer Pole — A3

Landscapes — A4

Map of Scandinavia — A5

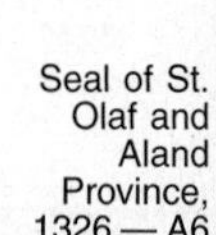

Seal of St. Olaf and Aland Province, 1326 — A6

Artifacts — A7

Sea Birds — A8

Gothic Tower, Jomala Church, 12th Cent. — A9

Mariehamn Town Hall, Designed by Architect Lars Sonck — A9a

Designs: 1.50m, Statue of Frans Petter von Knorring, vicar from 1834 to 1875, and St. Michael's Church, Finstrom, 12th cent. 1.60m, Burial site, clay hands. 1.70m, Somateria mollissima. 2.20m, Bronze Staff of Finby, apostolic decoration. 2.30m, Aythya fuligula. 5m, Outer Aland Archipelago. 8m, Farm and windmill. 12m, Melantha fusca. 20m, Ancient court site, contemporary monument.

1984-90 **Engr.** **Unwmk.** ***Perf. 12***

1	A1	10p magenta	.25	.25
2	A1	20p brown olive	.25	.25
3	A1	50p bright green	.35	.25
4	A1	1.10m deep blue	.70	.70
5	A1	1.20m black	.55	.50
6	A1	1.30m dark green	1.00	.60

Litho.

Perf. 14, 13x14 (#8)

7	A2	1.40m multi	.75	.30
8	A9	1.40m multi	2.00	1.20
9	A3	1.50m multi, I	2.00	1.00
9A	A3	1.50m multi, II	1.00	.80
10	A9	1.50m multi	2.00	1.25

Perf. 13, 14 (#13)

11	A7	1.60m multi, vert.	2.00	1.75
12	A8	1.70m multi	8.00	8.00
13	A9a	1.90m multi	2.00	1.50
14	A4	2m multi	2.00	2.00
15	A7	2.20m multi, vert.	2.00	1.00
16	A8	2.30m multi	4.00	4.00
17	A5	3m multi	3.50	1.50
18	A4	5m multi, horiz.	3.00	2.75
19	A4	8m multi, horiz.	5.50	3.75

Litho. & Engr.

20	A6	10m multi	5.50	4.00

Litho.

21	A8	12m multi	8.00	8.00
22	A7	20m multi	10.50	10.50
		Nos. 1-22 (23)	66.85	55.85

On No. 9A (type II) "Aland" is 10½mm long, figure support is 2mm wide, pole supports are thinner, diagonal black highlighting lines in pole greenery and horizontal black line on support under the man removed.

Issued: Nos. 2-4, 7, 17, 20, 3/1/84; Nos. 1, 5, 6, 9, 1/2/85; Nos. 14, 18-19, 9/16/85; Nos. 11, 15, 22, 4/4/86; Nos. 12, 16, 21, 1/2/87; No. 8, 8/26/88; No. 13, 1/2/89; No. 10, 9/4/89; No. 9A, 5/21/90.

See Nos. 39-42, 87-92, 178-179, 195-196.

A10

Bark Pommern and car ferries, Mariehamn West Harbor

1984, Mar. 1 **Litho.** ***Perf. 14***

23	A10	2m multicolored	8.50	3.00

A11

1986, Jan. 2 **Litho.** ***Perf. 14***

24	A11	1.60m multicolored	3.00	2.00

1986 Nordic Orienteering Championships, Aug. 30-31.

Onningeby Artists' Colony, Cent. — A12

Design: Pallette, pen and ink drawing of Onningeby landscape, 1891, by Victor Westerholm (1860-1919), founder.

1986, Sept. 1 **Litho.**

25	A12	3.70m multicolored	3.00	*2.00*

Mariehamn Volunteer Fire Brigade, Cent. — A13

1987, Apr. 27 **Litho.** ***Perf. 14***

26	A13	7m multicolored	4.00	3.00

Farjsund Bridge, 50th Anniv., Rebuilt in 1980 — A14

1987, Apr. 27 **Engr.** ***Perf. 13x13½***

27	A14	1m greenish black	.75	.60

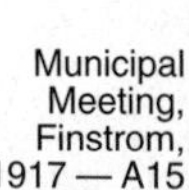

Municipal Meeting, Finstrom, 1917 — A15

1987, Aug. 20 **Litho.** ***Perf. 14***

28	A15	1.70m multicolored	1.00	1.00

Movement for reunification with Sweden, 70th anniv.

Loading of Mail Barrels on Sailboat, Post Office, Eckero — A16

1988, Jan. 4 **Litho.** ***Perf. 14***

29	A16	1.80m multicolored	3.00	2.50

Postal Service, 350th anniv. From Feb. I to May 31, Alanders were entitled to buy 20 stamps for 28m with a discount coupon.

New Aland Farm School, Horse-Drawn Plow — A17

1988, Mar. 29 **Litho.** ***Perf. 14***

30	A17	2.20m multicolored	2.25	*1.75*

Haga Farm School, cent.; Aland Farm School, 75th anniv.; 50th anniv. of experimental farming on Aland.

Sailing Ships — A18

Designs: 1.80m, Albanus, 1904, vert. 2.40m, Ingrid, c. 1900. 11m, Pamir, c. 1900.

1988, June 4 **Litho.** ***Perf. 13***

31	A18	1.80m multi	2.50	1.50
32	A18	2.40m multi	4.00	4.00
33	A18	11m multi	10.00	10.00
		Nos. 31-33 (3)	16.50	15.50

Type of 1988 and

Orchids — A19

Fish A20

Handicrafts A21

Fresco, St. Anna's Church of Kumlinge A22

Mammals A23

Geological Formations
A24 A25

Designs: 10p, Boulder field, Geta. No. 35, *Dactylorhiza sambucina*. No. 36, *Clupea harengus membras*. No. 37, *Erinaceus europauus*. No. 38, Drumlin, Finstrom. 1.70m, St. Andrew Church, Lumparland. No. 40, Vardo Church. No. 41, Hammarland Church. No. 42, Sottunga Church. No. 43, *Esox lucius*. No. 45, Diabase dike, Sottunga, Basskar. 2.10m, *Sciurus vulgaris*. 2.50m, *Cephalanthera longifolia*. No. 48, *Platichthys flesus*. No. 49, Pillow lava, Kumlinge, western Varpskar. No. 50, *Capreolus capreolus*. No. 51, Rouche Moutonne, Roda Kon, Lumparn. 6m, Folded gneiss, Sottunga, Gloskar. 13m, Tapestry, 1793. 14m, *Cypripedium calceolus*.

Perf. 13, 14 (Nos. 39-42, 44, 53), 15x14½ (10p, Nos. 38, 45, 49, 51-52)

1989-94 Litho.

No.	Type	Value	Color	Unused	Used
34	A25	10p	multicolored	.25	.25
35	A19	1.50m	multicolored	1.40	2.25
36	A20	1.50m	multicolored	1.60	1.20
37	A23	1.60m	multicolored	1.40	1.00
38	A25	1.60m	multicolored	1.50	1.10
39	A9	1.70m	multicolored	1.50	1.20
40	A9	1.80m	multicolored	1.40	1.10
41	A9	1.80m	multicolored	1.25	1.25
42	A9	1.80m	multicolored	1.25	1.25
43	A20	2m	multicolored	1.60	1.20
44	A22	2m	multicolored	1.10	.90
45	A24	2m	multicolored	.90	.80
46	A23	2.10m	multicolored	1.40	1.00
47	A19	2.50m	multicolored	2.00	2.00
48	A20	2.70m	multicolored	1.60	1.20
49	A24	2.70m	multicolored	1.25	1.00
50	A23	2.90m	multicolored	1.60	1.10
51	A25	2.90m	multicolored	2.50	1.75
52	A24	6m	multicolored	2.50	2.50
53	A21	13m	multicolored	6.75	5.75
54	A19	14m	multicolored	9.00	9.00
			Nos. 34-54 (21)	43.75	38.80

Issued: 2.50m, 14m, No. 35, 4/10/89; 2.70m, No. 36, 43, 3/1/90; 13m, 4/19/90; 1.70m, No. 44, 9/10/90; 1.60m, 2.10m, No. 50, 3/3/91; No. 40, 10/9/91; No. 41 10/5/92; Nos. 45, 49, 52, 9/3/93; No. 42, 10/8/93; 10p, Nos. 38, 51, 2/1/94.

See Nos. 96, 102, 105.

Educational System of the Province, 350th Anniv. — A33

1989, May 31 Litho. *Perf. 14*

57 A33 1.90m multicolored 1.50 .90

Souvenir Sheet

1991 Aland Island Games — A34

a, Volleyball. b, Shooting. c, Soccer. d, Running.

1991, Apr. 5 Litho. *Perf. 13x12½*

58 A34 2.10m Sheet of 4, #a.-d. 5.00 5.00

Autonomy of Aland, 70th Anniv. — A35

1991, June 4 *Perf. 13*

59 A35 16m multicolored 8.25 6.25

Kayaking A36

1991, June 4 *Perf. 14*

60 A36 2.10m shown 1.25 .75
61 A36 2.90m Cycling 1.75 1.25

Rev. Frans Peter Von Knorring (1792-1875), Educator — A37

Cape Horn Congress, Mariehamn, June 8-11 — A38

1992, Mar. 2 Litho. *Perf. 13*

62 A37 2 multicolored 1.40 1.00

Litho. & Engr.

Perf. 13½x14

63 A38 1 multicolored 3.00 2.25

No. 62 sold for 1.60m, No. 63 for 2.10m.

On stamps bearing the "denominations" "1" or "2," the number represents the class of mail.

Lighthouses A39

1992, May 8 Litho. *Perf. 13*

Booklet Stamps

No.	Type	Value	Design	Unused	Used
64	A39	2.10m	Ranno	7.75	4.50
65	A39	2.10m	Salskar	7.75	4.50
66	A39	2.10m	Lagskar	7.75	4.50
67	A39	2.10m	Market	7.75	4.50
a.			Booklet pane of 4, #64-67	30.00	22.50

First Aland Provincial Parliament, 70th Anniv. — A40

1992, June 8 Litho. *Perf. 13*

68 A40 3.40m multicolored 1.75 1.75

Joel Pettersson (1892-1937), Painter — A41

Designs: 2.90m, Landscape from Lemland. 16m, Self-Portrait.

1992, June 8

69 A41 2.90m multicolored 1.50 1.25
70 A41 16m multicolored 8.50 7.00

Arms of Aland — A42

1993, Mar. 1 Litho. *Perf. 14*

71 A42 1.60m gray, sepia & blue 1.20 .90

Autonomy Act, Jan. 1.

Souvenir Sheet

Autonomous Postal Administration — A43

Designs: a, Inscriptions from old letter canceled in Kastelholm, vert. b, Mariehamn post office. c, Ferry, mail truck. d, New post office emblem, vert.

Perf. 12½x13, 14 (#b.-c.)

1993, Mar. 1 Litho., Engr. (#b.-c.)

72 A43 1.90m Sheet of 4, #a.-d. 3.00 3.00

Fiddler, Jan Karlsgarden Museum — A44

2.30m, Boat Shed, Jan Karlsgarden Museum.

Perf. 13x12½, 12½x13

1993, May 7 Litho.

73 A44 2m multicolored 1.40 1.00
74 A44 2.30m multi, horiz. 1.40 1.00

Folk Dresses — A45

Clothing from: 1.90m, Saltvik. 3.50m, Brando, Eckero, Mariehamn. 17m, Finstrom.

1993, June 1 *Perf. 12½*

No.	Type	Value	Color	Unused	Used
75	A45	1.90m	multicolored	1.25	1.25
76	A45	3.50m	multicolored	2.00	1.50
77	A45	17m	multicolored	9.00	6.75
			Nos. 75-77 (3)	12.25	9.50

Butterflies A46

No. 78, Melitaea cinxia. No. 79, Quercusia querqus. No. 80, Parnassius mnemosyne. No. 81, Hesperia comma.

Perf. 14 on 3 Sides

1994, Mar. 1 Litho.

Booklet Stamps

No.	Type	Value	Color	Unused	Used
78	A46	2.30m	multicolored	1.60	1.25
79	A46	2.30m	multicolored	1.60	1.25
80	A46	2.30m	multicolored	1.60	1.25
81	A46	2.30m	multicolored	1.60	1.25
a.			Booklet pane, 2 each #78-81	13.00	*11.00*
			Nos. 78-81 (4)	6.40	5.00

A47

Europa, Inventions and Discoveries: 2.30m, Diagram showing transmission of von Willebrand's Disease, discovered by E. A. von Willebrand. 2.90m, Purification of heparin, by Erik Jorpes.

1994, May 5 Litho. *Perf. 13*

82 A47 2.30m multicolored *2.75 2.25*
83 A47 2.90m multicolored *1.90 1.60*

Types of 1989-93 and

Ice Age Survivors — A48

Fossils — A49

Sea Birds — A50

Bronze Age — A51

Stone Age — A52

Ships — A53

Lichens — A54

Primula Veris — A55

30p, Saduria entomon, mysis relicta. 40p, Trilobita asaphus. 1.80m, Sterna paradisaea. No. 87, Church of Mariehamn. No. 88, Church of Eckerö. No. 89, St. Bridget's Church, Lemland. No. 90, Church of St. John the Baptist, Sund. No. 91, St. George Church, Geta. No. 92, Church of Brando. No. 93, Bronze sword, bronze dagger. No. 94, Ship tumulus grave. No. 95, Larus canus. 2.30m, Pitcher of Kallskar. No. 97, Pottery. No. 98, Myoxocephalus quadricornis. 2.60m, Larus marinus. No. 100, Stone tools. No. 101, SS Thornbury. 3.40m, Erratic boulders. 3.50m, SS Osmo. 4.30m, Phoca hispida. 7m, Potholes. 9m, Gastropoda euomophalus. 18m, Settlement. 2, Hypogmnia physodes. 1, Xanthoria parietina.

Perf. 13 (A48, A50, A52, A54), 15x14½ (No. 89), 14½x15 (Nos. 101-103, 105), 14½ (40p, Nos. 88, 93-94, 96), 14 (Nos. 87, 90-92), 15 (No. 106)

1994-2000 **Engr.**

84	A48	30p	multi	.25	.25
85	A49	40p	multi	.25	.50
86	A50	1.80m	multi	.80	.70
87	A9	1.90m	multi	1.00	.90
88	A9	1.90m	multi	1.00	.90
89	A9	1.90m	multi	.75	.90
90	A9	2m	multi	1.25	1.00
91	A9	2m	multi	1.25	1.25
92	A9	2m	multi	1.25	1.00
93	A51	2m	multi	.85	.75
94	A51	2.20m	multi, vert.	1.00	.85
95	A50	2.20m	multi, vert.	.90	.70
96	A24	2.30m	multi	1.10	1.00
97	A52	2.40m	multi, vert.	1.90	1.50
98	A48	2.40m	multi	1.50	.90
99	A50	2.60m	multi	1.25	.90
100	A52	2.80m	multi, vert.	1.50	1.20
101	A53	2.80m	multi	1.10	1.00
102	A24	3.40m	multi, horiz.	1.75	1.50
103	A53	3.50m	multi	1.75	2.25
104	A48	4.30m	multi	2.25	1.90
105	A24	7m	multi, horiz.	3.25	2.75
106	A49	9m	multi	5.00	4.00
107	A52	18m	multi	9.25	6.00

Perf. 13

107A	A54	2	multi	1.10	.90
107B	A54	1	multi	1.10	.90

Self-Adhesive

Serpentine Die Cut Perf. 10

108	A55	2.40m	multi	1.00	1.10
	Nos. 84-108 (27)			45.35	37.50

No. 108 was issued in sheets of 10.

Nos. 107A-107B sold for 2m and 2.40m, respectively, on day of issue.

Issued: Nos. 97, 100, 18m, 8/16/94; No. 90, 10/7/94; 2.30m, 3.40m, 7m, 1/2/95; No. 91, 9/15/95; 40p, No. 92, 9m, 10/9/96; 30p, No. 98, 4.30m, 2/3/97; Nos. 101, 103, 9/8/97; No. 87, 10/9/97; No. 88, 10/9/98; Nos. 93-94, 2/1/99; No. 108, 4/28/99; Nos. 107A-107B, 9/25/99; No. 89, 10/8/99; 1.80m, No. 95, 2.60m, 1/3/00.

Cargo Vessels — A58

Perf. 14 on 3 Sides

1995, Mar. 1 **Litho.**

Booklet Stamps

109	A58	2.30m	Skuta	1.10	1.25
110	A58	2.30m	Sump	1.10	1.25
111	A58	2.30m	Storbat	1.10	1.25
112	A58	2.30m	Jakt	1.10	1.25
a.			Booklet pane, 2 each #109-112	9.00	*11.00*
			Complete booklet, #112a	9.50	
	Nos. 109-112 (4)			4.40	5.00

Entry into European Union — A59

1995, Mar. 1 **Litho.** ***Perf. 13x14***

113 A59 2.90m multicolored 1.50 *1.75*

Europa — A60

Design: 2.90m, Dove, island in sea.

1995, May 5 **Litho.** ***Perf. 13x14***

114	A60	2.80m	shown	*1.40*	*1.25*
115	A60	2.90m	multicolored	*1.40*	*1.25*

Tourism — A61

1995, May 12

116	A61	2	Golf	1.00	1.20
117	A61	1	Fishing	1.25	.75

Nos. 116-117 sold for value 2m and 2.30m, respectively.

Optimist Dinghy World Championships — A62

1995, June 2 **Litho.** ***Perf. 13½x14***

118 A62 3.40m multicolored 1.75 1.50

St. Olaf (995?-1030), Patron Saint of Aland — A63

Litho. & Engr.

1995, Sept. 15 ***Perf. 13½x13***

119 A63 4.30m multicolored 2.25 2.00

See Faroe Islands No. 289

A64

Greeting Stamps (stylized designs): No. 120, Fish with natl. flag, "Hälsningar fran Aland." No. 121, Yellow bird with flower, "Grattis."

1996, Feb. 14 **Litho.** ***Perf. 13x14***

120	A64	1	multicolored	1.20	1.00
121	A64	1	multicolored	1.20	.80

Nos. 120-121 had a face value of 2.30m on day of issue.

A65

Eagle owl (bubo bubo): No. 122, Landing on tree branch over lake. No. 123, Perched on branch over lake. No. 124, Male, darker feathers. No. 125, Female, lighter feathers.

Booklet Stamps

1996, Mar. 1 ***Perf. 14 on 3 Sides***

122	A65	2.40m	multicolored	1.20	1.25
123	A65	2.40m	multicolored	1.20	1.25
124	A65	2.40m	multicolored	1.20	1.25
125	A65	2.40m	multicolored	1.20	1.25
a.			Booklet pane, 2 ea #122-125	9.00	10.00
			Complete booklet, No. 125a	9.50	
	Nos. 122-125 (4)			4.80	5.00

World Wildlife Fund.

Famous Women A66

Europa: 2.80m, Sally Salminen (1906-76), writer. 2.90m, Fanny Sundström (1883-1944), politician.

1996, May 6 **Litho.** ***Perf. 14x13***

126	A66	2.80m	multicolored	*1.40*	*2.00*
127	A66	2.90m	multicolored	*1.40*	*2.00*

A67

1996, June 7 **Litho.** ***Perf. 13½x14***

128 A67 2.40m multicolored 1.25 1.10

Aland '96 Song and Music Festival.

A68

"Haircut," by Karl Emanuel Jansson (1846-74).

1996, June 7 ***Perf. 13***

129 A68 18m multicolored 9.00 8.00

Spring Flowers — A69

Designs: No. 130, Tussilago farfara. No. 131, Hepatica nobilis. No. 132, Anemone nemorosa. No. 133, Anemone ranunculoides.

1997, Feb. 3 **Litho.** ***Perf. 14***

Booklet Stamps

130	A69	2.40m	multicolored	1.10	1.10
131	A69	2.40m	multicolored	1.10	1.10
132	A69	2.40m	multicolored	1.10	1.10
133	A69	2.40m	multicolored	1.10	1.10
a.			Booklet pane, 2 each #130-133	9.00	*10.00*
			Complete booklet, #133a	9.50	

A70

1997, May 3 **Litho.** ***Perf. 14x13½***

134 A70 3.40m multicolored 1.50 1.25

1st Floorball World Championships, Aland.

Europa — A71

Devil's Dance with Clergyman's Wife.

1997, May 9 ***Perf. 13x14***

135 A71 2.90m multicolored *2.50* *1.25*

Kalmar Union, 600th Anniv. — A72

Design: Kastelholm Castle, arms of Lord High Chancellor Bo Jonsson Grip.

1997, May 30 **Litho.** ***Perf. 14x13***

136 A72 2.40m multicolored 1.25 1.10

Souvenir Sheet

Autonomy, 75th Anniv. — A73

1997, June 9 ***Perf. 13***

137 A73 20m multicolored 10.00 *11.00*

No. 137 contains a holographic image. Soaking in water may affect the hologram.

Horticulture A74

1998, Feb. 2 **Litho.** ***Perf. 14½x15***

138	A74	2m	Apples	.75	.75
139	A74	2.40m	Cucumbers	1.10	.85

Youth Activities A75

No. 140, Riding moped. No. 141, Computer. No. 142, Listening to music. No. 143, Aerobics.

1998, Mar. 28 ***Perf. 14 on 3 Sides***

Booklet Stamps

140	A75	2.40m multicolored	1.10	1.25
141	A75	2.40m multicolored	1.10	1.25
142	A75	2.40m multicolored	1.10	1.25
143	A75	2.40m multicolored	1.10	1.25
a.		Booklet pane, 2 each #140-143	9.00	*10.00*
		Complete booklet, #143a	9.50	

Midsummer Celebration in Aland — A76

1998, Apr. 27 **Litho.** ***Perf. 14***

144 A76 4.20m multicolored *1.75 1.50*

Europa.

Passenger Ferry — A77

1998, May 8 ***Perf. 14½***

145 A77 2.40m multicolored 1.25 1.00

Intl. Year of the Ocean — A78

1998, May 8

146 A78 6.30m multicolored 2.75 2.10

ATP Senior Tour of Champions Tennis Tournament, Mariehamn A79

Serpentine Die Cut

1998, June 25 **Litho.**

Self-Adhesive

147 A79 2.40m multicolored 1.25 1.40

Issued in sheets of 10.

Scouting — A80

1998, Aug. 1 ***Perf. 14***

148 A80 2.80m multicolored 1.25 1.00

Foyers — A81

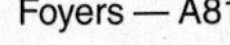

Homesteads: 1.60m, Seffers. 2m, Labbas. 2.90m, Abras.

1998, Sept. 11 **Litho.** ***Perf. 14½***

149	A81	1.60m multicolored	.75	.70
150	A81	2m multicolored	.90	.70
151	A81	2.90m multicolored	1.25	.85
		Nos. 149-151 (3)	2.90	2.25

18th Century Furniture Ornamentation A82

Perf. 14 on 3 Sides

1999, Feb. 1 **Litho.**

Booklet Stamps

152	A82	2.40m Wardrobe	1.50	1.25
153	A82	2.40m Distaff	1.50	1.25
154	A82	2.40m Chest	1.50	1.25
155	A82	2.40m Spinning wheel	1.50	1.25
a.		Booklet pane, 2 each #152-155	12.00	
		Complete booklet, #155a	12.50	

Passage of Cape Horn by Grain Ships Pamir & Passat, 50th Anniv. A83

1999, Mar. 19 **Litho.** ***Perf. 14½***

156 A83 3.40m multicolored 1.50 1.50

Beginning with No. 157, denominations are indicated on many stamps in both Markkas and Euros. The value shown is in Markkas.

Nature Reserve, Kökar — A84

1999, Apr. 28 **Litho.** ***Perf. 13***

157 A84 2.90m multicolored *1.25 1.20*

Europa.

Match Sailboat Racing — A85

1999, Aug. 5 **Litho.** ***Perf. 14½x15***

158 A85 2.70m multicolored 1.10 1.00

UPU, 125th Anniv. A86

1999, Sept. 25

159 A86 2.90m multicolored 1.20 1.00

Finnish Cross-Country Championships, Mariehamn — A87

1999, Oct. 9 **Litho.** ***Perf. 14¾x14½***

160 A87 3.50m multicolored 1.40 1.20

Souvenir Sheet

Peace Symbol, Aland Flag — A88

Background colors: a, Yellow. b, Red. c, Blue. d, White.

Litho. & Embossed

2000, Jan. 3 ***Perf. 13***

161 A88 3.40m Sheet of 4, #a.-d. 6.00 6.00

Elk — A89

Elk in: No. 162, Spring. No. 163, Summer. No. 164, Autumn. No. 165, Winter.

Perf. 11¾on 3 sides

2000, Mar. 1 **Litho.**

Booklet Stamps

162	A89	2.60m multicolored	1.10	1.10
163	A89	2.60m multicolored	1.10	1.10
164	A89	2.60m multicolored	1.10	1.10
165	A89	2.60m multicolored	1.10	1.10
a.		Block of 4, #162-165	4.50	4.50
b.		Booklet pane, 2 #165a	9.00	*10.50*
		Complete booklet, #165b	9.50	

Europa, 2000

Common Design Type

2000, May 9 ***Perf. 13***

166 CD17 3m multicolored *2.00 1.10*

A90

Self-Adhesive

Coil Stamp

2000, June 9 ***Die Cut Perf. 13x13¼***

167 A90 2.60m multicolored 1.75 1.40

Gymnastics Festival, Mariehamn.

A91

2000, July 21 **Litho.** ***Perf. 13½x13¼***

168 A91 3.40m multicolored 1.50 1.20

Cutty Sark Tall Ships race to Mariehamn.

Vikings From Aland — A92

2000, July 28

169 A92 4.50m multicolored 2.00 1.75

Recreation of Viking market, Saltvik.

Architecture by Hilda Hongell (1867-1952) A93

2000, Aug. 25 ***Perf. 13¼x13¾***

170	A93	3.80m shown	1.75	1.25
171	A93	10m House, diff.	4.75	4.00

Christianity, 2000th Anniv. — A94

2000, Oct. 9 ***Perf. 13***

172 A94 3m multicolored 1.40 1.10

Church Type of 1984-90 and

Swamp Plants — A95

Swamp plants: 1.90m, Equisetum fluviatile. 2.80m, Lycopodium annotinum. 3.50m, Polypodium vulgare.

Churches: No. 179, Föglö Church, Föglö. 2m, Kökar Church, Kökar.

Perf. 13x13¼, 13 (#178)

2000-01 **Litho.**

177	A95	1.90m multicolored	1.00	1.10
178	A9	2m multicolored	1.25	1.00
179	A9	2m multicolored	.90	.70
180	A95	2.80m multicolored	1.25	1.40
182	A95	3.50m multicolored	1.75	1.90
		Nos. 177-182 (5)	6.15	6.10

These stamps are part of an ongoing definitive set. Numbers have been reserved for additional stamps.

Issued: 2m, 10/9; 1.90m, 2.80m, 3.50m, 1/2/01; No. 179, 10/9/01.

Worldwide Fund for Nature (WWF) — A100

Polysticta stelleri: a, Pair in flight. b, Pair on rock. c, Pair in water. d, Male in water.

Perf. 13¼ on 3 sides

2001, Jan. 2 **Litho.**

Booklet Stamps

185	A100	Block of 4	5.00	5.50
a.-d.		2.70m any single	1.25	1.40
e.		Booklet pane, 2 #185	10.00	*11.00*
		Booklet, #185e	11.00	

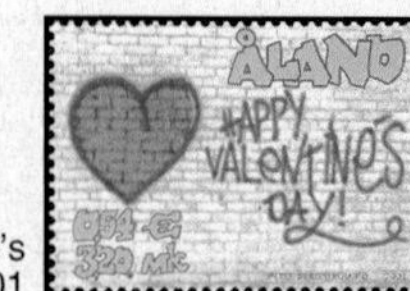

Valentine's Day — A101

2001, Feb. 14 *Perf. 14½x14¾*
186 A101 3.20m multicolored 1.40 1.10

Europa A102

2001, May 9 Litho. *Perf. 14½x14¾*
187 A102 3.20m multi *1.60 1.25*

Windmills A103

Windmill types: 3m, Archipelago. 7m, Timbered, horiz. 20m, Nest, horiz.

Perf. 13¾x14¼, 14¼x13¾
2001, June 8
188-190 A103 Set of 3 13.00 11.50

Puppies — A104

Designs: 2, Golden retriever. 1, Wire-haired dachshund.

2001, Sept. 3 *Perf. 13¼*
191-192 A104 Set of 2 2.75 2.00

Nos. 191-192 sold for 2.30m and 2.70m respectively on day of issue.

100 Cents = 1 Euro (€)

Church Type of 1998 with Euro Denominations and

Fauna — A105

Post Terminal — A106

Mushrooms A107

Designs: 5c, Coronella austriaca. 10c, Chanterelle mushroom. 35c, Saltviks Church. 40c, Kumlinge Church. 50c, King Bolete mushroom. 70c, Triturus cristatus. €1, Post Terminal. €2.50, Parasol mushroom.

Perf. 12½, 13 (#193, 196), 13¼ (#198), 14¾x14 (#195)

2002-03 **Litho.**

193	A105	5c multi	.25	.25
194	A107	10c multi	.30	.30
195	A9	35c multi	1.00	1.00
196	A9	40c multi	1.10	1.10
197	A107	50c multi	1.75	1.40
198	A105	70c multi	2.00	1.50
199	A106	€1 multi	2.75	2.10
200	A107	€2.50 multi	8.75	6.00
		Nos. 193-200 (8)	17.90	13.65

Issue dates: 5c, 70c, 1/2/02; €1, 2/28/02; 35c, 10/9/02; 10c, 50c, €2.50, 1/2/03. No. 196, 10/9/03.

Introduction of the Euro — A108

2002, Jan. 2 Litho. *Perf. 12½*
201 A108 60c multi 1.60 1.25

St. Canute's Day — A109

2002, Jan. 2
202 A109 €2 multi 3.75 3.25

Cuisine — A110

Flowers and: a, Gravlax, boiled potatoes. b, Fried herring, beets, mashed potatoes. c, Black bread, cheese, butter. d, Pancake with prune sauce and whipped cream, coffee.

Perf. 13½x13¼ on 3 Sides
2002, Feb. 28 **Litho.**

203	A110	Block of 4	7.00	5.50
a.-d.		1 Any single	1.75	1.40
e.		Booklet pane, 2 #203	14.00	
		Booklet, #203e	14.00	

Nos. 203a-203d each sold for 55c on day of issue.

Europa — A111

2002, May 3 *Perf. 13¼*
204 A111 40c multi *1.40 1.00*

Radar II, Sculpture by Stefan Lindfors A112

2002, May 3 *Perf. 13*
205 A112 €3 multi 8.00 7.00

"My Aland," by Lill Lindfors A113

2002, Aug. 12 Litho. *Perf. 13¼*
206 A113 90c multi 2.50 2.00

Iron Age Artifacts — A114

Designs: No. 207, 2, Buckle found in Persby. No. 208, 1, Ornamental pin found in Syllöda.

2002, Sept. 2 *Perf. 13x13¼*
207-208 A114 Set of 2 3.00 2.75

Nos. 207-208 sold for 45c and 55c respectively on day of issue.

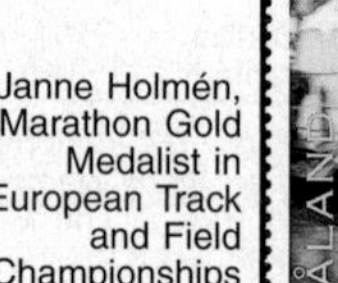

Janne Holmén, Marathon Gold Medalist in European Track and Field Championships A115

2002, Nov. 1 *Perf. 12½*
209 A115 1 multi 1.75 1.50

Sold for 55c on day of issue.

House Cats — A116

2003, Mar. 14 Litho. *Perf. 13¼*
210 A116 2 Tovis 1.25 .85
211 A116 1 Randi, horiz. 1.75 .95

Nos. 210-211 sold for 45c and 55c respectively on day of issue.

Landscape in Summer, by Elin Danielson-Gambogi (1861-1919) — A117

No. 212: a, Woman at fence. b, Tree without leaves. c, Sun. d, Boat.

2003, Mar. 28 *Perf. 14 Vert.*
Booklet Stamps

212	A117	Horiz. strip of 4	6.25	6.25
a.-d.		1 Any single	1.50	1.50
e.		Booklet pane, 2 #212	12.50	12.50
		Complete booklet, #212e	13.00	

Nos. 212a-212d each sold for 55c on day of issue.

Europa — A118

2003, May 9 *Perf. 13¼*
213 A118 45c multi *1.25 1.00*

Museum Ship "Pommern," Cent. A119

2003, June 6 ***Die Cut Perf. 9¼x9½***
Booklet Stamp
Self-Adhesive

214	A119 55c multi		1.50	1.40
a.		Booklet pane of 4	12.00	12.00
		Complete booklet, 2 #214a	25.00	

Mark and Stephen Levengood on Beach — A120

2003, June 18 *Perf. 12½*
215 A120 55c multi 1.50 1.40

Aland Folk Music Association, 50th Anniv. — A121

2003, Aug. 1 *Perf. 14¼*
216 A121 €1.10 buff & black 3.00 2.25

St. Lucia's Day Celebrations A122

2003, Oct. 9 Litho. *Perf. 12½*
217 A122 60c multi 1.60 1.50

Mammals — A123

Designs: 20c, Mustela erminea. 60c, Vulpes vulpes. €3, Martes martes.

2004, Feb. 2 Litho. *Perf. 14½x14¼*

218	A123	20c multi	.65	.60
219	A123	60c multi	2.00	1.50
220	A123	€3 multi	8.75	7.75
		Nos. 218-220 (3)	11.40	9.85

Souvenir Sheet

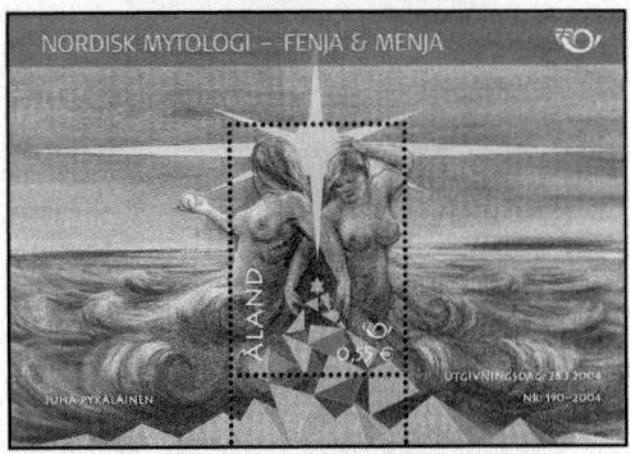

Norse Gods Fenja and Menja — A124

2004, Mar. 26 *Perf. 14¼x14¾*
221 A124 55c multi 2.25 2.40

Aland Flag, 50th Anniv. — A125

Serpentine Die Cut 12½
2004, Apr. 23 **Booklet Stamp**
Self-Adhesive

222 A125 1 multi 2.00 1.75
a. Booklet pane of 4 8.00 6.75
Complete booklet, 2 #222a 20.00

No. 222a was reprinted in 2007 with a hole for a pegboard hook. See No. 296.

Finnish Pres. Mauno Koivisto and Guests on Boat — A126

2004, Apr. 23 *Perf. 12½*
223 A126 90c multi 2.50 2.50

Europa — A127

2004, May 10 *Perf. 13¾x14¼*
224 A127 75c multi *2.00 1.75*

Destruction of Bomarsund Fortress, 150th Anniv. — A128

No. 225: a, Fortress, six ships in harbor. b, Fortress, three ships in harbor. c, Three soldiers in foreground. d, Six soldiers in foreground.

2004, June 9 *Perf. 13*
225 Booklet pane of 4 8.50 8.50
a.-d. A128 75c Any single 2.10 2.10
Complete booklet, 2 #225 18.00

2004 Summer Olympics, Athens A183

2004, Aug. 13 **Litho.** *Perf. 14¼*
226 A183 80c multi 2.25 2.25

Landscapes A184

Designs: 2, Storklynkan, Brändö. 1, Prästgardsnäset Nature Reserve, Finström.

2004, Aug. 13 *Perf. 12½*
227-228 A184 Set of 2 3.00 3.00

Nos. 227-228 sold for 50c and 60c respectively on day of issue.
See Nos. 252-253, 260.

Christmas A185

2004, Oct. 8 *Perf. 14½x14¾*
229 A185 45c multi 2.50 1.75

Birds — A186

Designs: 15c, Phalacrocorax carbo sinensis. 65c, Cygnus cygnus. €4, Ardea cinerea, vert.

2005, Jan. 14 **Litho.** *Perf. 13¼*
230 A186 15c multi .55 .55
231 A186 65c multi 1.75 1.75
232 A186 €4 multi 11.00 9.00
Nos. 230-232 (3) 13.30 11.30

Automobiles — A187

No. 233: a, 1928 Oakland Sport Cabriolet. b, 1939 Ford V8. c, 1957 Buick Super 4D HT. d, 1964 Volkswagen 1200.

2005, Mar. 4 *Perf. 13¼ Horiz.*
Booklet Stamps

233 Vert. strip of 4 7.00 7.25
a.-d. A187 1 Any single 1.75 1.75
e. Booklet pane, 2 #233 14.00 —
Complete booklet, #233e 14.00

Stamps sold for 60c each on day of issue.

Europa A188

2005, Apr. 29 *Perf. 13¼*
234 A188 90c multi *2.50 2.10*

Walpurgis Night Bonfire A189

Serpentine Die Cut 12½
2005, Apr. 29 **Booklet Stamp**
Self-Adhesive

235 A189 2 multi 1.50 1.40
a. Booklet pane of 4 5.75
Complete booklet, 2 #235a 11.50

Stamp sold for 50c on day of issue.

Tennis Player Bjorn Borg — A190

2005, May 26 *Perf. 12½*
236 A190 55c multi 1.50 1.50

Mr. Black and Mr. Smith at Bomarsund, by Fritz von Dardel A191

2005, Aug. 12 **Litho.** *Perf. 13¾*
237 A191 €1.30 multi 3.50 3.50

Schooner Linden — A192

2005, Aug. 26 *Perf. 13¼*
238 A192 60c multi 1.75 1.75

Landscapes Type of 2004

Designs: 70c, Pine tree on Sandö Island. 80c, Cliffs, Gröndal.

2005, Aug. 26 *Perf. 12½*
239-240 A184 Set of 2 4.00 4.00

Christmas — A193

Litho. with Hologram Applied
2005, Oct. 10 *Perf. 13*
241 A193 45c multi 1.50 1.40

Stars in hologram differ on each stamp.

Beetles A194

Designs: 40c, Potosia cuprea. 65c, Coccinella septempunctata. €2, Oryctes nasicornis.

Litho. & Embossed
2006, Jan. 2 *Perf. 13½*
242 A194 40c multi 1.10 1.10
243 A194 65c multi 1.75 1.60
244 A194 €2 multi 5.25 4.75
Nos. 242-244 (3) 8.10 7.45

Woman Suffrage in Finland, Cent. — A195

2006, Mar. 8 **Litho.** *Perf. 12½*
245 A195 85c multi 2.50 2.25

Demilitarization of Aland, 150th Anniv. — A196

2006, Mar. 29 *Perf. 13¾*
246 A196 €1.50 multi 4.00 3.75

Souvenir Sheet

Lettesgubbe, Mythological Being — A197

2006, Mar. 29 *Perf. 12½x13*
247 A197 85c multi 2.50 3.00

Europa — A198

2006, May 4
248 A198 €1.30 multi 3.50 3.50

A199

Serpentine Die Cut 10 Syncopated

2006, May 26

249 A199 1 multi 1.75 1.50
a. Booklet pane of 8 14.00 14.50

No. 249 sold for 65c on day of issue. Design portion of stamp could be personalized at €10.40 per booklet with a minimum purchase of three booklets. The label design shown is a generic vignette. Other generic vignettes were created for sale at stamp shows beginning in 2008.

Tattoos — A200

No. 250: a, Tribal tattoo on man's biceps. b, Sailor's tattoo on man's forearm. c, Flower tattoo, on woman's torso.

2006, Sept. 7 ***Perf. 14 Vert.***

Booklet Stamps

250 Horiz. strip of 3 5.25 5.25
a.-c. A200 65c Any single 1.75 1.75
d. Booklet pane, 3 #250 16.00
Complete booklet, #250d 16.00

Fishing Boat From Television Film Directed by Ake Lindman A201

2006, Aug. 4 Litho. ***Perf. 12½***

251 A201 75c multi 2.00 1.75

Landscapes Type of 2004

Designs: 55c, Foggy grove, windmill and houses, Söderby, Lemland. €1.20, Rocks, Norra Essvik, Sottunga.

2006, Aug. 4

252-253 A184 Set of 2 4.75 4.50

Christmas A202

Litho. With Holograms Affixed

2006, Oct. 9 ***Perf. 13***

254 A202 (50c) multi 1.40 1.40

Flowers A203

Designs: 80c, Tripolium vulgare. 90c, Lythrum salicaria. €5, Angelica archangelica.

2007, Feb. 1 Litho. ***Perf. 12½x13***

255 A203 80c multi 2.50 2.00
256 A203 90c multi 2.75 2.50
257 A203 €5 multi 13.50 13.00
Nos. 255-257 (3) 18.75 17.50

Mail Planes A204

Designs: 2, Junkers F13. 1, Saab 340.

2007, Mar. 1 ***Perf. 12½***

258-259 A204 Set of 2 3.50 3.25

No. 258 sold for 55c, and No. 259 sold for 70c on day of issue.

Landscapes Type of 2004

2007, Mar. 13

260 A184 2 Skaftö, Kumlinge 1.60 1.50

Sold for 55c on day of issue.

Untitled Painting by Tove Jansson A205

2007, Apr. 18 ***Perf. 13¼x13¾***

261 A205 85c multi 2.40 2.40

Europa — A206

2007, May 9 ***Perf. 12½x13¼***

262 A206 70c multi 2.00 1.75

Scouting, cent.

Contemporary Crafts — A207

Designs: No. 263, Bridal crown, by Titti Sundblom. No. 264, Floral textile design, by Maria Korpi-Gordon and Adam Gordon. No. 265, Cups, bowl and plate, by Judy Kuyitunen.

2007, May 18 ***Perf. 13 Horiz.***

Booklet Stamps

263 A207 1 multi 2.00 2.25
264 A207 1 multi 2.00 2.25
265 A207 1 multi 2.00 2.25
a. Booklet pane, 3 each #263-265 18.00 18.50
Complete booklet, #265a 18.00

Nos. 263-265 each sold for 70c on day of issue.

A208

Serpentine Die Cut 10 Syncopated

2007, June 7 Booklet Stamp

Self-Adhesive

266 A208 1 multi 2.00 1.75
a. Booklet pane of 8 16.00 14.00
Complete booklet, #266a 16.00

No. 266 sold for 70c on day of issue. Design portion of stamp could be personalized at €10.40 per booklet with a minimum purchase of three booklets.

Emigration to America A209

2007, Aug. 9 Litho. ***Perf. 13¼x12½***

267 A209 75c multi 2.25 2.10

Kjusan, Hammarland A210

2007, Oct. 1 ***Perf. 12½***

268 A210 1 multi 2.10 2.00

No. 268 sold for 70c on day of issue.

Christmas — A211

2007, Oct. 9 ***Perf. 14***

269 A211 (50c) multi 1.75 1.40

Fish A212

Designs: 45c, Perca fluviatilis. €4.50, Sander lucioperca.

2008, Feb. 1 Litho. ***Perf. 13¼x13***

270 A212 45c multi 1.75 1.50
271 A212 €4.50 multi 14.50 13.50

Souvenir Sheet

Mythical Princess Signhild at Drottningkleven — A213

Perf. 12½x13¼

2008, Mar. 27 Litho.

272 A213 (85c) multi 3.00 3.00

Badhusberget, Mariehamn — A214

Langvikshagen, Lumparland — A215

2008, Apr. 15 ***Perf. 13x12½***

273 A214 (70c) multi 2.40 2.25
274 A215 (70c) multi 2.40 2.25

2008 Summer Olympics, Beijing A216

2008, May 9 ***Perf. 13¾***

275 A216 (90c) multi 3.00 3.00

Europa A217

2008, May 9 ***Perf. 13¼x13***

276 A217 €1 multi 3.50 3.25

Lighthouses A218

No. 277: a, Marhällan Lighthouse. b, Gustaf Dalén Lighthouse. c, Kökarsören Lighthouse. d, Bogskär Lighthouse.

Litho., Litho & Engr (#277c-277d)

2008, June 6 ***Perf. 12¾ on 3 Sides***

Booklet Stamps

277 Block or strip of 4 10.00 9.75
a.-d. A218 (75c) Any single 2.50 2.40
e. Booklet pane, 2 #277 20.00 —
Complete booklet, #277e 20.00

Within the booklet pane, stamps in one row are tete-beche in relation to stamps in the adjacent row.

Gravel Road and Profiles of Marcus Grönholm, Rally Driver, and Christoph Treier, Trainer
A219

2008, July 26 Litho. *Perf. 13½*
278 A219 (90c) multi 2.75 2.50

Particles of granite were applied to portions of the design using a thermographic process.

Aland Peasant Bride, by Karl Emanuel Jansson — A220

2008, Aug. 15 *Perf. 13x13¼*
279 A220 €1.50 multi 5.00 4.75

Christmas A221

Litho. With Hologram Applied
2008, Oct. 9 *Perf. 13¾x13¼*
280 A221 (55c) multi 1.50 1.25

Personalized Stamp — A222

Serpentine Die Cut 10 Syncopated
2008, Oct. 9 Litho.
Booklet Stamp
Self-Adhesive

281 A222 (75c) multi 2.00 1.75
a. Booklet pane of 8 16.00 14.00
Complete booklet, #281a 16.00

The generic design portion of the stamp shown could be personalized. Other generic vignettes were created for sale at stamp shows in 2009 and 2010.

1810 Boundary Post — A223

Litho. & Embossed With Foil Application
2009, Jan. 22 *Perf. 14¼*
282 A223 (80c) multi 2.25 2.00

Souvenir Sheet

Electricity on Aland Islands, Cent. — A224

Litho. & Embossed
2009, Jan. 22 *Perf. 12½x13¼*
283 A224 €2 black 6.00 6.50

Writers — A225

No. 284: a, Ulla-Lena Lundberg and ship. b, Anni Blomqvist (1909-90), sailboat and dock-side shack. c, Valdemar Nyman (1904-98), flowers, cattle.

2009, Mar. 21 Litho. *Perf. 13 Horiz.*
Booklet Stamps

284 Vert. strip of 3 6.75 7.00
a.-c. A225 (80c) Any single 2.25 2.25
d. Booklet pane, 3 #284 21.00 —
Complete booklet, #284d 21.00

Movie Theaters in Aland, Cent. — A226

2009, Apr. 6 *Perf. 12½x13¼*
285 A226 €1.60 multi 4.50 4.00

Divers at Plus Shipwreck A227

2009, May 8
286 A227 (75c) multi 2.25 2.10

Europa A228

2009, May 8 *Perf. 13*
287 A228 (80c) multi 2.25 2.25

Intl. Year of Astronomy. Star-shaped holes are die cut in stamp.

Passenger Ferries A229

Designs: (75c), SS Viking. (80c), New Viking Line ferry, 2009.

2009, June 1 Litho. *Perf. 13*
288-289 A229 Set of 2 4.75 4.50

See Nos. 301-302, 311-312, 325-326, 339, 347, 351-352.

Personalized Stamp — A230

Booklet Stamp
Serpentine Die Cut 10 Syncopated
2009, June 27 Self-Adhesive

290 A230 (90c) multi 2.75 2.50
a. Booklet pane of 8 22.00
Complete booklet, #290a 22.00

The generic design portion of the stamp shown could be personalized.

Cliffs, Föglö A231

Islets, Saltvik A232

2009, Sept. 16 *Perf. 12½*
291 A231 (75c) multi 2.40 2.00
292 A232 (80c) multi 2.50 2.25

Honeymoon Cabin of Finland President Martti Ahtisaari A233

2009, Sept. 29 *Perf. 13x12½*
293 A233 (90c) multi 2.75 2.50

Christmas A234

Poinsettia and: (60c), Man and woman. (90c), Woman with scroll.

2009, Oct. 9 *Perf. 13¾*
294-295 A234 Set of 2 4.75 4.25

Flag Type of 2004 Inscribed "Inrikes"
Serpentine Die Cut 12½
2009, July 1 Litho.
Booklet Stamp
Self-Adhesive

296 A125 (75c) multi 2.10 2.10
a. Booklet pane of 4 8.50
Complete booklet, 2 #296a 17.00

Mail Jetty at Eckerö, Painting by Victor Westerholm — A235

2010, Jan. 4 *Perf. 13*
297 A235 (80c) multi 2.60 1.50

Jesus Christ, Painting by Warner Sallman — A236

Litho. With Foil Application
2010, Mar. 24 *Perf. 14x14¼*
298 A236 (90c) multi 2.75 1.60

Souvenir Sheet

Kobba Klintar Pilot Station — A237

2010, Mar. 24 Litho. *Perf. 12½*
299 A237 (90c) multi 2.75 3.00

Europa — A238

2010, Apr. 19 *Perf. 12½x13*
300 A238 (85c) multi 2.50 1.50

Ferries Type of 2009

Designs: 75c, MS Skandia. €3.50, MS Prinsessan.

2010, May 3 Litho. *Perf. 13*
301-302 A229 Set of 2 12.50 12.00

Plastic Toys Made By Plasto — A239

No. 303: a, Scooter. b, Dump truck. c, Ducks.

2010, May 10 *Perf. 13¾ Horiz.*
Booklet Stamps

303 Vert. strip of 3 7.50 8.00
a.-c. A239 (85c) Any single 2.50 2.60
d. Booklet pane, 3 #303 22.50 23.00
Complete booklet, #303d 22.50

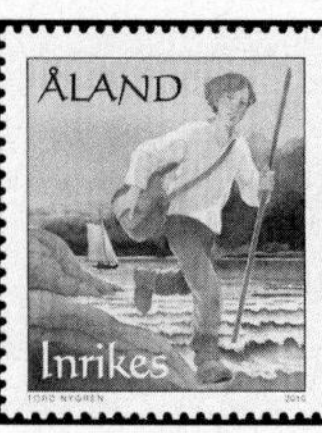

Farmhand Delivering Mail — A240

2010, June 12 *Perf. 12½x13¼*
304 A240 (75c) multi 2.25 2.00

Personalized Stamp — A241

2010, June 12 *Perf. 12½*
305 A241 (85c) black 2.50 2.25

No. 305 was printed in sheets of 8. The generic design portion of the stamp shown could be personalized for an extra fee.

Stained-Glass Windows — A242

Stained-glass window from church in Jomala: 80c, St. Olaf. €1.60, St. Olaf and other figures, horiz.

2010, Aug. 30 **Litho.** *Perf. 13*
306 A242 80c multi 2.75 2.40

Souvenir Sheet

307 A242 €1.60 multi 5.25 5.50

See Macao Nos. 1317-1318.

Shoreline, Eckerö A243

Cliffs, Sund A244

2010, Sept. 16 *Perf. 12½*
308 A243 80c multi 2.40 2.25
309 A244 (85c) multi 2.40 2.40

Christmas A245

2010, Oct. 8 *Perf. 13*
310 A245 (65c) multi 1.90 1.75

Ferries Type of 2009

Designs: 80c, MS Alandia. €1.50, MS Apollo.

2011, Feb. 1 **Litho.** *Perf. 13*
311-312 A229 Set of 2 6.75 6.25

Souvenir Sheet

Princess Maria Alexandrovna of Russia (1824-80) — A246

2011, Feb. 21 *Perf.*
313 A246 €1 multi 3.00 3.25

City of Mariehamn, 150th anniv. A limited edition of No. 313 with gold embossing sold for €15. See Russia No. 7255.

Georg August Wallin (1811-52), Explorer of Arabia — A247

2011, Apr. 1 *Perf. 14x14¼*
314 A247 (90c) multi 2.75 2.50

Europa A248

2011, May 9 *Perf. 13*
315 A248 (85c) multi 2.75 2.50

Intl. Year of Forests.

Comic Book Superheroes Created by Paul Gustafson (1916-77) A249

No. 316: a, The Arrow. b, Fantom of the Fair. c, Alias the Spider.

2011, May 9 *Perf. 13*

Booklet Stamps

316 Horiz. strip of 3 8.50 8.00
a.-c. A249 (90c) Any single 2.75 2.60
d. Tete-beche block of 6 18.00 18.00
e. Booklet pane of 3 #316 25.00 24.00
Complete booklet, #316e 25.00

Champagne Bottles From 1840s Shipwreck A250

2011, June 3 **Litho.** *Perf. 13½*
317 A250 (90c) multi 2.75 2.50

Chips Ab Potato Chips — A251

2011, June 7 *Perf. 13¾*
318 A251 85c multi 2.60 2.50

Strömma Apples — A252

2011, June 7 **Litho.**
319 A252 5c shown .25 .25
320 A252 €4 Apples, diff. 12.50 12.50

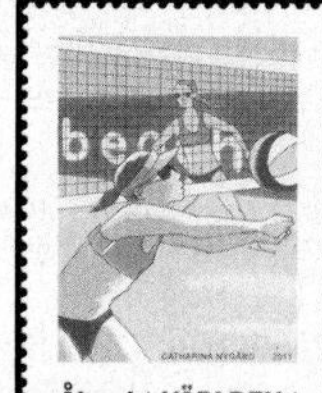

Personalized Stamp — A253

2011, Aug. 16 *Perf. 13¾x14¼*
321 A253 (95c) blk & grn 3.00 3.00

No. 321 was printed in sheets of 8. The generic design portion of the stamp shown could be personalized for an extra fee.

Kökar A254

Jomala A255

2011, Sept. 28 **Litho.** *Perf. 12½*
322 A254 (85c) multi 2.50 2.25
323 A255 (90c) multi 2.60 2.40

Christmas A256

2011, Oct. 7 *Perf. 14½*
324 A256 (55c) multi 1.60 1.40

Ferries Type of 2009

Designs: 55c, SS Birger Jarl. (75c), MS Sally Albatross.

2012, Feb. 1 *Perf. 13¼*
325-326 A229 Set of 2 3.75 3.50

No. 326 is inscribed "Lokalpost."

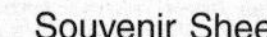

Souvenir Sheet

Fishermen at Sea — A257

2012, Mar. 21 *Perf. 13¼x13*
327 A257 (€1) multi 2.75 3.00

Sinking of the Titanic, Cent. — A258

2012, Apr. 16 *Perf. 12¾x13¼*
328 A258 €1.80 multi 5.00 4.75

See Belgium No. 2562.

The Man at the Wheel, Sculpture by Emil Cedercreutz A259

Litho. & Engr.

2012, Apr. 26 *Perf. 13¼x13*
329 A259 €3 multi 8.50 8.25

Europa A260

2012, May 9 **Litho.** *Perf. 13¾*
330 A260 (95c) multi 2.75 2.00

Personalized Stamp — A261

2012, June 4 *Perf. 14¼x13¾*
331 A261 (95c) multi 2.75 2.00

Printed in sheets of 8. The design portion of this stamp could be personalized. The design shown is a generic vignette. Other generic vignettes were created for sale at stamp shows beginning in 2013.

Dragonflies A262

Designs: (75c), Aeshna cyanea. (95c), Sympetrum sanguineum.

2012, June 4 ***Perf. 14¼***
332-333 A262 Set of 2 4.75 4.75

No. 332 is inscribed "Lokalpost;" No. 333, "Europa."

Architecture — A263

No. 334: a, Miramar. b, Societetshusen. c, Badhotellet.

2012, Aug. 23 ***Perf. 13¾ Horiz.***
Booklet Stamps

334	Vert. strip of 3	8.00	8.50
a.-c.	A263 (€1) Any single	2.60	2.75
d.	Booklet pane of 9, 3 each #334a-334c	24.00	—
	Complete booklet, #334d	24.00	

Nos. 334a-334c are each inscribed "Världen."

Public Transportation — A264

Designs: No. 335, (95c), 1954 Volvo L224 bus. No. 336, (95c), 1924 Ford TT bus.

2012, Sept. 19 ***Perf. 13¾x13½***
335-336 A264 Set of 2 5.50 5.25

No. 335 is inscribed "Inrikes." No. 336 is inscribed "Europa."

Christmas A265

2012, Oct. 9 ***Perf. 13***
337 A265 (60c) multi 1.75 1.75

Yearning, Painting by Guy Frisk — A266

2013, Jan. 15 ***Perf. 13¾x13¼***
338 A266 (€1.10) multi 3.25 3.00

Aland Art Museum, 50th anniv.

Ferries Type of 2009

Design: (80c), SS Alandsfärjan.

2013, Feb. 19 ***Perf. 13***
339 A229 (80c) multi 2.25 2.25

Worldwide Fund for Nature (WWF) — A267

No. 340: a, Gavia arctica. b, Gavia stellata. c, Podiceps auritus. d, Podiceps cristatus.

2013, Apr. 5 ***Perf. 12½x12¾***
Booklet Stamps

340	A267 Block of 4	11.00	11.50
a.-d.	(€1) Any single	2.75	2.75
e.	Booklet pane of 8, 2 each #340a-340d	22.00	23.00
	Complete booklet, #340e	22.00	

Europa A268

2013, May 6 ***Perf. 13¾x13¼***
341 A268 (€1) multi 2.75 2.75

Personalized Stamp — A269

2013, May 6 ***Perf. 12½***
342 A269 (€1.10) ol grn & blk 3.25 3.00

No. 342 was printed in sheets of 8. The generic design portion of the stamp shown could be personalized for an extra fee. Other generic vignettes were created for sale at stamp shows beginning in 2014.

Water Lilies A270

Designs: (€1), Nymphaea alba. €2.50, Nuphar lutea.

2013, June 4 ***Perf. 13x13¼***
343-344 A270 Set of 2 9.50 9.50

Crowd at Rockoff Music Festival A271

Woman at Island in the Sun Music Festival — A272

2013, July 12 **Litho.** ***Perf. 13¾***
345 A271 (80c) multi 2.10 2.10
346 A272 (€1.10) multi 3.25 3.00

Ferries Type of 2009

Design: €2, MS Princess Anastasia.

2013, Aug. 5 **Litho.** ***Perf. 13***
347 A229 €2 multi 5.50 5.50

See Russia No. 7468.

Inachis Io — A273

2013, Aug. 20 **Litho.** ***Perf. 13¾***
348 A273 (€1.10) multi 3.00 3.00

Christmas A274

Paintings by Pinturicchio: No. 349, Adoration of the Magi. No. 350, Nativity.

2013, Nov. 8 **Litho.** ***Perf. 13¼x13¾***
349 A274 (65c) multi 1.75 1.75
350 A274 65c multi 1.75 1.75

No. 350 was printed in sheets of 8 + central label. See Vatican City Nos. 1549-1550.

Ferries Type of 2009

Designs: No. 351, MS Birka Princess. No. 352, MS Viking Grace.

2014, Feb. 7 **Litho.** ***Perf. 13¾***
351 A229 (€1.10) multi 3.00 3.00
352 A229 (€1.10) multi 3.00 3.00

No. 351 is inscribed "Inrikes"; No. 352, "Europa."

Mariehamn Theater Society, Cent. — A275

2014, Feb. 7 **Litho.** ***Perf. 13¼***
353 A275 €1.50 multi 4.25 4.25

Souvenir Sheet

Bridge of a Freighter and Horizon — A276

2014, Mar. 17 **Litho.** ***Perf. 13¼***
354 A276 €3 multi 8.25 8.25

Grand Piano of Alie Lindberg (1849-1933), Concert Pianist — A277

2014, May 8 **Litho.** ***Perf. 13¼x13***
355 A277 (€1.10) multi 3.00 3.00

Europa.

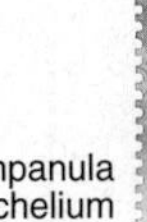

Campanula Trachelium A278

2014, May 8 **Litho.** ***Perf. 12½***
356 A278 (€1.10) multi 3.00 3.00

Kenta Sandvik, Weight Lifter A279

2014, May 31 **Litho.** ***Perf. 13x13¼***
357 A279 (90c) multi 2.50 2.50

Personalized Stamp — A280

2014, May 31 **Litho.** ***Perf. 12½***
358 A280 (€1.10) multi 3.00 3.00

No. 358 was printed in sheets of 8. The generic design portion of the stamp shown could be personalized for an extra fee. Other generic vignettes were created for sale at stamp shows beginning in 2015.

Robert Helenius, Professional Boxer, and Family on Aland Island — A281

2014, June 9 **Litho.** ***Perf. 13x13¼***
359 A281 €2.30 multi 6.25 6.25

Musical Groups of the 1960s — A282

No. 360: a, Hitch Hikers. b, Stockdoves. c, Anacondas.

2014, Aug. 25 **Litho.** ***Perf. 13x12¼***
Booklet Stamps

360	Vert. strip of 3	7.25	7.25
a.-c.	A282 (90c) Any single	2.40	2.40
d.	Booklet pane of 9, 3 each #360a-360c	22.00	—
	Complete booklet, #360d	22.00	

Christmas A283

Litho. With Foil Application

2014, Oct. 9 ***Perf. 13¾x13¼***
361 A283 (70c) multi 1.75 1.75

New Year 2015 (Year of the Ram) A284

No. 362: a, Ram, ewe and lamb. b, Ram's head.

Litho. & Engr.

2014, Nov. 5 *Perf. 13x12¾*

362	A284 Pair	4.00	4.00
a.-b.	80c Either single	2.00	2.00

Printed in sheets containing two pairs.

Ships A285

Designs: 85c, Schooner Lemland. (€1.20), Barquentine Leo.

2015, Feb. 2 **Litho.** *Perf. 13x13¼*

363-364	A285 Set of 2	4.75	4.75

See Nos. 377-378.

Campanula Persicifolia A286

2015, Apr. 10 **Litho.** *Perf. 14¼*

365	A286 85c multi	1.90	1.90

Midvinterblot, Painting by Carl Larsson (1853-1919) — A287

2015, Apr. 10 **Litho.** *Perf. 14x14¼*

366	A287 €3 multi	6.75	6.75

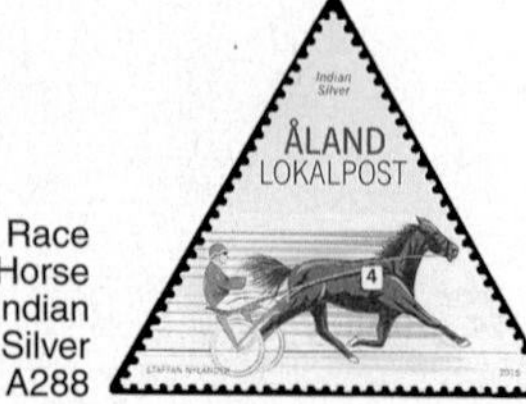

Race Horse Indian Silver A288

2015, May 1 **Litho.** *Perf. 14*

367	A288 (95c) multi	2.25	2.25

Europa A289

2015, May 8 **Litho.** *Perf. 14¼*

368	A289 (€1.20) multi	2.75	2.75

Personalized Stamp — A290

2015, May 8 **Litho.** *Perf. 12½*

369	A290 (€1.20) multi	2.75	2.75

Printed in sheets of 8. The design portion of this stamp could be personalized. The design shown is a generic vignette.

Julius Sundblom (1865-1945), Politician — A291

2015, June 22 **Litho.** *Perf. 13*

370	A291 (€1.20) multi	2.75	2.75

Silver Jewelry — A292

Designs: (€1.20), Buckle from Aland Islands. €2, Brooch from Bern, Switzerland.

Litho. & Embossed

2015, Sept. 3 *Perf. 13*

371	A292 (€1.20) multi	2.75	2.75
372	A292 €2 multi	4.50	4.50

See Switzerland Nos. 1568-1569.

Dogs — A293

No. 373: a, Finnish hound (Finsk stövare). b, Gray Norwegian elkhound (Norsk älghund gra). c, Wire-haired dachshund (Strävharig tax).

2015, Sept. 3 **Litho.** *Perf. 13*

Booklet Stamps

373	Horiz. strip of 3	8.25	8.25
a.-c.	A293 (€1.20) Any single	2.75	2.75
d.	Booklet pane of 9, 3 each #373a-373c	25.00	—
	Complete booklet, #373d	25.00	

A294

Christmas A295

2015, Oct. 9 **Litho.** *Perf. 13*

374	A294 (70c) multi	1.60	1.60
375	A295 (€1.20) multi	2.75	2.75

Aland Sea Rescue Society, 50th Anniv. — A296

2015, Oct. 30 **Litho.** *Perf. 13*

376	A296 (95c) multi	2.10	2.10

Ships Type of 2015

Designs: 10c, Brig Altai. €10, Barque Pehr Brahe.

2016, Feb. 2 **Litho.** *Perf. 13x13¼*

377-378	A285 Set of 2	22.00	22.00

Buckthorn Dessert Made by Chef Michael Björklund A297

2016, Mar. 18 **Litho.** *Perf. 14¼*

379	A297 (€1.30) multi	3.00	3.00

Witch Trials, 350th Anniv. — A298

2016, Apr. 8 **Litho.** *Perf. 13*

380	A298 (€1.30) multi	3.00	3.00

A299

Europa A300

2016, May 9 **Litho.** *Perf. 13*

381	A299 (€1.30) multi	3.00	3.00
382	A300 (€1.30) multi	3.00	3.00

Think Green Issue.

Medicinal Plants — A301

No. 383: a, Hyoscyamus niger. b, Digitalis purpurea. c, Tanacetum vulgare.

2016, May 9 **Litho.** *Perf. 12 Horiz.*

Booklet Stamps

383	Vert. strip of 3	9.00	9.00
a.-c.	A301 (€1.30) Any single	3.00	3.00
d.	Booklet pane of 9, 3 each #383a-383c	27.00	—
	Complete booklet, #383d	27.00	

Lilla Aland Chair Designed by Carl Malmsten — A302

2016, May 27 **Litho.** *Perf. 11½*

384	A302 €2.50 multi	5.75	5.75

House and Brudhäll Harbor, by Björn Ulvaeus A303

2016, July 8 **Litho.** *Perf. 11½*

385	A303 (€1.30) multi	3.00	3.00

Apple and Blossom A304

2016, Aug. 12 **Litho.** *Perf. 12½*

386	A304 (€1.30) multi	3.00	3.00

Elves Decorating Christmas Tree — A305

Elf, Reindeer and Gifts — A306

2016, Oct. 10 **Litho.** *Perf. 13*

387	A305 (70c) multi	1.60	1.60
388	A306 (€1.30) multi	3.00	3.00

Christmas.

Souvenir Sheet

New Year 2017 (Year of the Rooster) — A307

No. 389 — Rooster and: a, Flower. b, Rowboat.

2016, Nov. 11 **Litho.** ***Perf. 13***

389 A307 Sheet of 2 9.00 9.00
a.-b. €2 Either single 4.50 4.50

Mermerus A308

Mariehamn A309

2017, Feb. 2 **Litho.** ***Perf. 13x13¼***

390 A308 20c multi .45 .45
391 A309 (€1.10) multi 2.40 2.40

Personalized Stamp — A310

2017, Mar. 14 **Litho.** ***Perf. 12½***

392 A310 (€1.30) multi 3.00 3.00

No. 392 was printed in sheets of 8. The generic design portion of the stamp shown could be personalized for an extra fee.

Pinus Sylvestris and Salvadora Oleoides A311

2017, Mar. 14 **Litho.** ***Perf. 13x13¼***

393 A311 (€1.30) multi 3.00 3.00

Cultural Diversity.

Kastelholm Castle A312

2017, May 9 **Litho.** ***Perf. 13x13¼***

394 A312 (€1.40) multi 3.25 3.25

Europa.

Independence of Finland, Cent. — A313

Litho. & Embossed With Foil Application

2017, May 24 ***Perf. 13x13¼***

395 A313 €5 multi 11.50 11.50

Sauna Bench, Bucket and Whisk A314

Exterior of Sauna A315

2017, May 24 **Litho.** ***Perf. 13¼x13½***

396 A314 (€1.40) multi 3.25 3.25
397 A315 (€1.40) multi 3.25 3.25
a. Souvenir sheet of 2, #396-397 6.50 6.50

See Finland No. 1540.

Handcrafted Jewelry Made From Recycled Items — A316

2017, Aug. 17 **Litho.** ***Perf. 13x13¼***

398 A316 €1 multi 2.40 2.40

Mammals A317

No. 399: a, Lepus timidus. b, Mustela nivalis. c, Nyctereutes procyonoides.

Perf. 14¼x14½

2017, Sept. 15 **Litho.**

Booklet Stamps

399 Horiz. strip of 3 8.00 8.00
a.-c. A317 (€1.10) Any single 2.60 2.60
d. Booklet pane of 9, 3 each #399a-399c 24.00 —
Complete booklet, #399d 24.00

A318

Gingerbread Houses A319

2017, Oct. 9 **Litho.** ***Perf. 13¼***

400 A318 (70c) multi 1.60 1.60
401 A319 (€1.40) multi 3.25 3.25

Christmas.

Souvenir Sheet

New Year 2018 (Year of the Dog) — A320

No. 402 — China dog at: a, Right. b, Left.

2017, Nov. 10 **Litho.** ***Perf. 13¼x13***

402 A320 €1 Sheet of 2, #a-b 4.75 4.75

Clipper Ship Albania A321

Schooner Atlas A322

2018, Feb. 1 **Litho.** ***Perf. 12***

403 A321 (€1.30) multi 3.25 3.25
404 A322 €3 multi 7.50 7.50

Salmo Salar A323

2018, Mar. 13 **Litho.** ***Perf. 11½***

405 A323 (€1.50) sil & multi 3.75 3.75

Bomarsund Bridge — A324

2018, May 9 **Litho.** ***Perf. 12***

406 A324 (€1.50) multi 3.50 3.50

Europa.

Spray of Wave Hitting Rocks A325

2018, May 9 **Litho.** ***Perf. 12***

407 A325 (€1.50) multi 3.50 3.50

Apis Mellifera A326

2018, May 28 **Litho.** ***Perf. 13¼***

408 A326 (€1.50) gold & multi 3.50 3.50

Motorcycles — A327

No. 409: a, 2011 Victory Cross Country. b, 1919 Harley-Davidson F1000CC. c, 1944 Indian Chief. d, 1980 Harley-Davidson Chopper.

2018, May 28 **Litho.** ***Perf. 13¼***

Booklet Stamps

409 A327 Block of 4 14.00 14.00
a.-d. (€1.50) Any single 3.50 3.50
e. Booklet pane of 8, 2 each #409a-409d 28.00 —
Complete booklet, #409e 28.00

A328

Fireworks A329

2018, Sept. 18 **Litho.** ***Perf. 13***

410 A328 (€1.50) multi 3.50 3.50
411 A329 €4 multi 9.25 9.25

Christmas

A330 A331

Litho. With Hologram Affixed

2018, Oct. 9 ***Perf. 13¼***

412 A330 (80c) red & multi 1.90 1.90
413 A331 (€1.50) gold & multi 3.50 3.50

Souvenir Sheet

New Year 2019 (Year of the Pig) — A332

No. 414 — Apples and: a, Entire pig. b, Head of sow.

2018, Nov. 1 **Litho.** ***Perf. 12***

414 A332 Sheet of 2 9.00 9.00
a.-b. €2 Either single 4.50 4.50

Ships A333

Designs: €1.40, Schooner Vineta. €1.60, Barque Parma.

2019, Feb. 1 **Litho.** ***Perf. 12***

415-416 A333 Set of 2 7.00 7.00

Ice Skaters — A334

2019, Mar. 8 **Litho.** ***Perf. 12***

417 A334 €1.20 multi 2.75 2.75

Small Boat Transatlantic Voyage Captained by Uno Ekblom (1905-55), 80th Anniv. — A335

2019, Mar. 8 **Litho.** ***Perf. 12***
418 A335 €1.60 multi 3.75 3.75

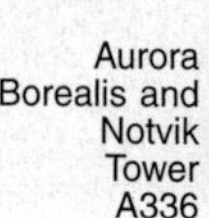

Aurora Borealis and Notvik Tower A336

2019, Mar. 8 **Litho.** ***Perf. 14***
419 A336 €1.70 multi 4.00 4.00

Haliaeetus Albicilla A337

2019, May 9 **Litho.** ***Perf. 13***
420 A337 (€1.40) multi 3.25 3.25

Europa.

Jonesas Farmhouse, Onningeby A338

2019, May 9 **Litho.** ***Perf. 14x14¼***
421 A338 (€1.70) multi 4.00 4.00

Postcrossing A339

2019, June 7 **Litho.** ***Perf. 13¾***
422 A339 (€1.80) multi 4.25 4.25

Values are for stamps with surrounding selvage.

House, Sailboat and Signature of Lasse Holm, Composer — A340

2019, June 7 **Litho.** ***Perf. 13***
423 A340 €6 multi 14.00 14.00

ALAND ISLANDS

SEMI-POSTAL STAMPS

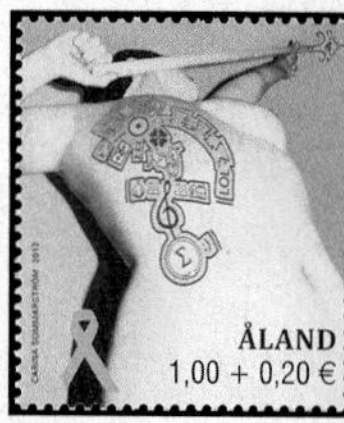

Campaign Against Breast Cancer — SP1

2012, Oct. 1 **Litho.** ***Perf. 13½x13¾***
B1 SP1 €1+20c multi 3.25 3.25

Surtax for Aland Cancer Society.

Sculpture of Gnome by Hakan Sandberg SP2

2013, Sept. 2 **Litho.** ***Perf. 13¾x13½***
B2 SP2 €1+20c multi 3.25 3.25

Surtax for Aland Cancer Society.

Zero Tolerance Program Against Drug Abuse — SP3

Litho. & Embossed

2014, Apr. 11 ***Perf. 14¾***
B3 SP3 €1.10 +20c black 3.75 3.75

FIUME

'fyü-ˌ(ˌ)mā

LOCATION — A city and surrounding territory on the Adriatic Sea
GOVT. — Formerly a part of Italy
AREA — 8 sq. mi.
POP. — 44,956 (estimated 1924)

Fiume was under Hapsburg rule after 1466 and was transferred to Hungarian control after 1870. Of mixed Italian and Croatian population and strategically important, it was Hungary's only international seaport. Following World War I, Fiume was disputed between Italy and the newly created Kingdom of the Serbs, Croats and Slovenes (later Yugoslavia). A force of Allied troops occupied the city in Nov. 1918, while its future status was negotiated at the Paris Peace Conference.

In Sept. 1919, the Italian nationalist poet Gabriele d'Annunzio organized his legionnaires and seized Fiume, together with the islands of Arbe, Carnaro and Veglia, in the name of Italy. D'Annunzio established an autonomous administration, which soon came into conflict with the Italian government. There followed several years of instability, with three Italian interventions after 1920. In Jan. 1924, the Treaty of Rome between Italy and Yugoslavia established formal Italian sovereignty over Fiume, and Fiume stamps were replaced by those of Italy after March 31, 1924.

100 Filler = 1 Korona
100 Centesimi = 1 Corona (1919)
100 Centesimi = 1 Lira

See note on FIUME-KUPA Zone, Italian Occupation, after Yugoslavia No. NJ22.

The overprints on Nos. 1-23a have been extensively forged. Even the inexpensive values are difficult to find with genuine overprints. Forgeries of many later issues also exist, most created for the packet trade in the 1920s. Values are for genuine stamps. Collectors should be aware that stamps sold "as is" are likely to be forgeries, and unexpertized collections should be assumed to consist of mostly forged stamps. Education plus working with knowledgeable dealers is mandatory in this collecting area. More valuable stamps should be expertized.

Hungarian Stamps of 1916-18 Typograph Overprinted, Bold Sans Serif Letters

1918, Dec. 2 **Wmk. 137** ***Perf. 15***

On Stamps of 1916

Colored Numerals

1A A9 20f gray brown 5,500. 3,000.

Hungarian Stamps of 1916-18 Typograph Overprinted

On Stamps of 1916

White Numerals

1	A8	10f rose	7,250.	7,250.
b.		Handstamped overprint	75.00	35.00
2	A8	15f violet	40.00	30.00

Value for No. 1a is for handstamped overprint. Value for No. 2 is for typographed overprint.

On Stamps of 1916-18

Colored Numerals

3	A9	2f	brown orange	4.00	2.40
4	A9	3f	red violet	4.00	2.40
5	A9	5f	green	4.00	2.40
6	A9	6f	grnsh blue	4.00	2.40
7a	A9	10f	rose red, *from*	50.00	20.00
8	A9	15f	violet	4.00	2.40
9	A9	20f	gray brown	3.00	1.50
10	A9	25f	deep blue	12.00	3.00
11	A9	35f	brown	7.50	4.00
12a	A9	40f	olive green, *from*	30.00	17.50

White Numerals

13	A10	50f	red vio & lil	5.00	3.00
14	A10	75f	brt bl & pale bl	10.00	4.00
15	A10	80f	grn & pale grn	10.00	3.00
16	A10	1k	red brn & claret	30.00	7.50
17	A10	2k	ol brn & bis	5.00	3.00
18	A10	3k	dk vio & ind	40.00	20.00
19	A10	5k	dk brn & lt brn	145.00	40.00
20a	A10	10k	vio brn & vio, *from*	400.00	175.00

Inverted or double overprints exist on most of Nos. 4-15.

On Stamps of 1918

21	A11	10f	scarlet	3.00	3.00
22	A11	20f	dark brown	2.50	2.00
23a	A12	40f	olive green	17.50	17.50

The overprint on Nos. 3-23a was applied by 2 printing plates and 6 handstamps. Values are for the less costly. Values of Nos. 7a, 12a, 20a and 23a are for handstamps. See the *Scott Specialized Catalogue of Stamps and Covers* for detailed listings.

Postage Due Stamps of Hungary, 1915-20 Ovptd. & Surcharged in Black

1919, Jan.

24	D1	45f on 6f green & red	15.00	10.00
25	D1	45f on 20f green & red	40.00	10.00
		Set, never hinged	138.00	

Hungarian Savings Bank Stamp Surcharged in Black

A2

1919, Jan. 29

26	A2	15f on 10f dk violet	22.00	17.00
		Never hinged	55.00	

Overprints on Nos. 24-26 are typographed.

No. 26 also exists with double surcharge, one black and one red, and with one violet and one black.

"Italy" — A3

Italian Flag on Clock-Tower in Fiume — A4

"Revolution" A5

Sailor Raising Italian Flag at Fiume (1918) A6

Nos. 30-43 exist on three types of paper: (A) grayish, porous paper, printed in sheets of 70 stamps (Jan, Feb. printings); (B) translucent or semi-translucent good quality white paper, printed in sheets of 70 stamps (March printing); and (C) good quality medium white paper, plain and opaque, sometimes grayish or yellowish, printed in sheets of 100 (April printing). Values are for the least expensive variety. See the *Scott Specialized Catalogue of Stamps and Covers* for detailed listings.

Perf. 11½

1919, April **Unwmk.** **Litho.**

27	A3	2c	dull blue	1.50	1.50
28	A3	3c	gray brown	1.50	1.50
29	A3	5c	yellow green	1.50	1.50
30a	A4	10c	rose	17.50	9.00
31	A4	15c	violet	1.50	1.50
32a	A4	20c	emerald green	2.50	*3.00*
33	A5	25c	dark blue	2.25	1.50
34	A6	30c	deep violet	2.25	1.50
35	A5	40c	brown	2.25	2.25
36	A5	45c	orange	2.25	2.25
37	A6	50c	yellow green	2.25	1.50
38	A6	60c	claret	2.25	1.50
39	A6	1cor	brown orange	3.75	2.25
40	A6	2cor	brt blue	3.75	2.25
41	A6	3cor	orange red	4.50	2.25
42	A6	5cor	deep brown	22.00	22.00
43a	A6	10cor	olive green	45.00	*75.00*
			Nos. 27-43a (17)	118.50	132.25

The earlier printings of Jan. and Feb. are on thin grayish paper, the Mar. printing is on semi-transparent white paper, all in sheets of 70. An Apr. printing is on white paper of medium thickness in sheets of 100. Part-perf. examples of most of this series are known.

For surcharges see Nos. 58, 60, 64, 66-69.

A7

A8

A9

A10

1919, July 28 *Perf. 11½*

No.	Type	Description	Unused	Used
46	A7	5c yellow green	2.00	2.00
47	A8	10c rose	2.00	2.00
48	A9	30c violet	7.75	2.50
49	A10	40c yellow brown	2.00	*2.00*
50	A10	45c orange	8.00	5.50
51	A9	50c yellow green	8.00	5.50
52	A9	60c claret	7.75	5.40
a.		Perf. 13x12½	140.00	
		Never hinged	200.00	
b.		Perf. 10½	320.00	
		Never hinged	825.00	
53	A9	10cor olive green	8.00	*15.00*
a.		Perf. 13x12½	50.00	*72.50*
		Never hinged	125.00	
b.		Perf. 10½	320.00	*225.00*
		Never hinged	825.00	
		Nos. 46-53 (8)	45.50	39.90
		Set, never hinged	115.00	

Five other denominations (25c, 1cor, 2cor, 3cor and 5cor) were not officially issued. Some examples of the 25c are known canceled.

For surcharges see Nos. 59, 61-63, 65, 70.

Stamps and Types of 1919 Handstamp Surcharged

1919-20

No.	Type	Description	Unused	Used
58	A4	5c on 20c grn ('20)	2.00	2.00
59	A9	5c on 25c blue	2.00	2.00
60	A5	10c on 45c orange	2.50	2.00
61	A9	15c on 30c vio ('20)	2.00	2.00
62	A10	15c on 45c orange	2.00	2.00
63	A9	15c on 60c cl ('20)	2.00	2.00
64	A6	25c on 50c yel grn ('20)	9.75	*24.00*
65	A9	25c on 50c yel grn ('20)	2.00	2.00
66	A6	55c on 1cor brn org	30.00	30.00
67	A6	55c on 2cor brt bl	5.00	*7.00*
68	A6	55c on 3cor org red	5.00	6.00
69	A6	55c on 5cor dp brn	5.00	6.00
70	A9	55c on 10cor ol grn	24.00	27.50
		Nos. 58-70 (13)	93.25	*114.50*
		Set, never hinged	235.00	

Semi-Postal Stamps of 1919 Surcharged

a

b

First Setting
Surcharge letters thin and small.

1919-20

No.	Type	Description	Unused	Used
73	SP6(a)	5c on 5c grn	2.00	2.00
74	SP6(a)	10c on 10c rose	2.00	2.00
75	SP6(a)	15c on 15c gray	2.00	2.00
76	SP6(a)	20c on 20c org	2.00	2.00
78	SP7(b)	45c on 45c ol grn	2.50	2.50
79	SP7(b)	60c on 60c rose	2.50	2.50
80	SP7(b)	80c on 80c vio	4.00	4.00
81	SP7(b)	1cor on 1cor sl	4.00	4.00
82	SP8(a)	2cor on 2cor red brn	4.00	4.00
83	SP8(a)	3cor on 3cor blk brn	5.00	5.00
84	SP8(a)	5cor on 5cor yel brn	6.00	6.00

Second Setting
Surcharge letters bold, 2.5mm between "Cent." and figures of value, 5c-25c; overprint larger, 45c-10cor.

1920, Feb.5

No.	Type	Description	Unused	Used
73A	SP6(a)	5c on 5c grn	2.00	2.00
74A	SP6(a)	10c on 10c rose	24.00	5.00
75A	SP6(a)	15c on 15c gray	2.00	2.00
76A	SP6(a)	20c on 20c org	2.00	2.00
77	SP9(a)	25c on 25c bl ('20)	2.00	2.00
78A	SP7(b)	45c on 45c ol grn	2.50	2.50
79A	SP7(b)	60c on 60c rose	2.50	2.50
80A	SP7(b)	80c on 80c vio	2.00	2.00
81A	SP7(b)	1cor on 1cor sl	2.50	2.50
82A	SP8(a)	2cor on 2cor red brn	17.00	20.00
83A	SP8(a)	3cor on 3cor blk brn	35.00	22.00
84A	SP8(a)	5cor on 5cor yel brn	24.00	50.00
85	SP8(a)	10cor on 10cor dk vio ('20)	2.50	2.50

Third Setting, Milano Printing (new plates)
5c and 10c: 2mm spacing between "Cent." and denominations; 15c: new color; 45c: surcharge with bold letters.

1920, Apr. 5

No.	Type	Description	Unused	Used
73B	SP6(a)	5c on 5c grn	2.00	2.00
74B	SP6(a)	10c on 10c rose	2.00	2.00
75B	SP6(a)	15c on 15c gray	4.00	4.00

Gabriele d'Annunzio — A11

1920, Sept. 12 **Typo.** ***Perf. 11½***
Pale Buff Background

No.	Type	Description	Unused	Used
86	A11	5c green	3.00	3.00
87	A11	10c carmine	3.00	3.00
88	A11	15c dark gray	3.00	3.00
89	A11	20c orange	3.00	3.00
90	A11	25c dark blue	3.00	3.00
91	A11	30c red brown	3.00	3.00
92	A11	45c olive gray	5.00	5.00
93	A11	50c lilac	5.00	5.00
94	A11	55c bister	5.00	5.00
95	A11	1 l black	17.50	*25.00*
96	A11	2 l red violet	17.50	*25.00*
97	A11	3 l dark green	17.50	*25.00*
98	A11	5 l brown	65.00	45.00
99	A11	10 l gray violet	17.50	*25.00*
		Nos. 86-99 (14)	168.00	*178.00*
		Set, never hinged	415.00	

The background print, pale buff, also exists doubly printed or shifted on several denominations.

Counterfeits of Nos. 86 to 99 are plentiful.

For overprints see Nos. 134-148.

Severing the Gordian Knot — A12

Designs: 10c, Ancient emblem of Fiume. 20c, Head of "Fiume." 25c, Hands holding daggers.

1920, Sept. 12

No.	Type	Description	Unused	Used
100	A12	5c green	35.00	25.00
a.		Imperf.	135.00	
b.		Horiz. pair, imperf. between	400.00	—
101	A12	10c deep rose	22.50	22.50
a.		Imperf.	87.50	
102	A12	20c brown orange	35.00	22.50
103	A12	25c indigo	22.50	*47.50*
a.		Imperf.	155.00	
b.		Double impression, imperf.	1,225.	
c.		Horiz. pair, imperf. between	550.00	
d.		25c blue	80.00	*80.00*
e.		As "d," imperf.	340.00	
f.		As "d," horiz. pair, imperf. between	1,200.	
		Nos. 100-103 (4)	115.00	117.50
		Set, never hinged	280.00	

Anniv. of the occupation of Fiume by d'Annunzio. They were available for franking the correspondence of the legionnaires on the day of issue only, Sept. 12, 1920.

Counterfeits of Nos. 100-103 are plentiful. Genuine stamps have a slight projection on the right side of the second vertical stroke of the "U" of "FIUME", and the basal serif of the "I" of "FIUME" projects more on the left than the right.

For overprints and surcharges see Nos. 104-133, E4-E9.

Nos. 100-103 Overprinted or Surcharged in Black or Red

1920, Nov. 20

No.	Type	Description	Unused	Used
104	A12	1c on 5c green	2.40	2.40
a.		Inverted overprint	55.00	55.00
b.		Double overprint	200.00	
105	A12	2c on 25c indigo (R)	2.40	2.40
a.		Inverted overprint	55.00	55.00
b.		Double overprint	72.50	72.50
c.		2c on 25c blue (R)	80.00	80.00
106	A12	5c green	20.00	2.40
a.		Inverted overprint	47.50	47.50
b.		Double overprint	72.50	72.50
107	A12	10c rose	20.00	2.40
a.		Inverted overprint	55.00	55.00
b.		Double overprint	72.50	72.50
108	A12	15c on 10c rose	2.40	2.40
a.		Inverted overprint	65.00	65.00
b.		Double overprint	72.50	72.50
109	A12	15c on 20c brn org	2.40	*2.40*
a.		Inverted overprint	65.00	65.00
b.		Double overprint	72.50	72.50
110	A12	15c on 25c indigo (R)	2.40	*2.40*
a.		Inverted overprint	65.00	65.00
b.		Double overprint	72.50	72.50
c.		15c on 25c blue (R)	225.00	225.00
111	A12	20c brn org	2.40	2.40
a.		Inverted overprint	27.50	27.50
b.		Double overprint	125.00	125.00
112	A12	25c indigo (R)	2.40	2.40
a.		Inverted overprint	24.00	24.00
b.		25c blue (R)	8.00	8.00
113	A12	25c indigo (Bk)	175.00	175.00
a.		Inverted overprint	450.00	350.00
b.		25c blue (Bk)	240.00	240.00
c.		As "b,", inverted overprint	725.00	
114	A12	25c on 10c rose	2.40	4.75
a.		Double overprint	72.50	72.50
115	A12	50c on 20c brn org	5.00	2.40
a.		Double overprint	72.50	72.50
116	A12	55c on 5c green	21.00	4.75
a.		Inverted overprint	95.00	95.00
b.		Double overprint	72.50	72.50
117	A12	1 l on 10c rose	47.50	40.00
a.		Inverted overprint	275.00	275.00
b.		Double overprint	275.00	
118	A12	1 l on 25c indigo (R)	100.00	100.00
a.		1 l on 25c blue (R)	600.00	600.00
b.		As "a," inverted overprint	875.00	725.00
119	A12	2 l on 5c green	47.50	40.00
a.		Inverted overprint	325.00	
b.		Double overprint	200.00	
120	A12	5 l on 10c rose	225.00	*240.00*
a.		Inverted overprint	725.00	725.00
b.		Double overprint	725.00	
121	A12	10 l on 20c brn org	700.00	550.00
a.		Inverted overprint	1,600.	800.00
b.		Double overprint	1,600.	800.00
		Nos. 104-121 (18)	1,380.	1,179.
		Set, never hinged	3,850.	

The Fiume Legionnaires of d'Annunzio occupied the islands of Arbe and Veglia in the Gulf of Carnaro Nov. 13, 1920-Jan. 5, 1921.

Varieties of overprint or surcharge exist for most of Nos. 104-121.

Nos. 113, 117-121, 125, 131 have a backprint.

Nos. 106-107, 111, 113, 115-116 Overprinted or Surcharged at top

1920, Nov. 28

No.	Type	Description	Unused	Used
122	A12	5c green	35.00	24.00
123	A12	10c rose	45.00	*52.50*
124	A12	20c brown org	87.50	52.50
125	A12	25c deep blue	52.50	*52.50*
126	A12	50c on 20c brn org	95.00	52.50
127	A12	55c on 5c green	95.00	52.50
		Nos. 122-127 (6)	410.00	286.50
		Set, never hinged	1,000.	

The overprint on Nos. 122-125 comes in two widths: 11mm and 14mm. Values are for the 11mm width.

Nos. 106-107, 111, 113, 115-116 Overprinted or Surcharged at top

1920, Nov. 28

No.	Type	Description	Unused	Used
128	A12	5c green	35.00	24.00
129	A12	10c rose	45.00	*52.50*
130	A12	20c brown orange	87.50	52.50
131	A12	25c deep blue	52.50	*52.50*
132	A12	50c on 20c brn org	95.00	52.50
133	A12	55c on 5c green	95.00	52.50
		Nos. 128-133 (6)	410.00	286.50
		Set, never hinged	1,000.	

Nos. 86-99 Overprinted

1921, Feb. 2
"Provvisorio" 20mm wide
Space between lines 3mm
Pale Buff Background

No.	Type	Description	Unused	Used
134	A11	5c green	2.40	2.40
a.		Inverted overprint	27.50	27.50
b.		Double overprint	52.50	52.50
135	A11	10c carmine	2.40	2.40
a.		Inverted overprint	27.50	27.50
b.		Double overprint	52.50	52.50
136	A11	15c dark gray	2.40	*2.40*
a.		Inverted overprint	27.50	27.50
b.		Double overprint	52.50	52.50
137	A11	20c orange	4.00	4.00
a.		Inverted overprint	27.50	27.50
b.		Double overprint	27.50	27.50
138	A11	25c dark blue	4.00	4.00
a.		Inverted overprint	27.50	27.50
b.		Double overprint	52.50	52.50
139	A11	30c red brown	4.00	4.00
a.		Inverted overprint	27.50	27.50
b.		Double overprint	27.50	27.50
140	A11	45c olive gray	2.40	2.40
a.		Inverted overprint	55.00	55.00
b.		Double overprint	40.00	40.00
141	A11	50c lilac	4.00	4.00
a.		Inverted overprint	27.50	27.50
142	A11	55c bister	4.00	4.00
a.		Inverted overprint	16.00	16.00
143	A11	1 l black	145.00	*180.00*
a.		Inverted overprint	350.00	350.00
144	A11	2 l red violet	95.00	95.00
145	A11	3 l dark green	95.00	95.00
146	A11	5 l brown	95.00	95.00
147	A11	10 l gray violet	95.00	95.00

With Additional Surcharge

148 A11 1 l on 30c red brown 2.50 2.50
a. Inverted overprint 27.50 27.50
b. Double overprint 55.00 55.00
Nos. 134-148 (15) 557.10 592.10
Set, never hinged 1,400.

Most of Nos. 134-143, 148 and E10-E11 exist with inverted or double overprint.
See Nos. E10-E11.

Second Printing, Milan "Provvisorio" 21mm wide Space between overprint lines 4mm

1921, Dec. 18

148A A11 5c yellow green 50.00 *57.50*
Never hinged 125.00
On cover 300.00
148B A11 10c carmine 135.00 40.00
Never hinged 340.00
On cover 300.00
c. Vert. pair, imperf. between *650.00*

First Constituent Assembly

Nos. B4-B15 Overprinted

1921, Apr. 24

149 SP6 5c blue green 6.50 4.75
150 SP6 10c rose 6.50 4.75
a. Inverted overprint 65.00 65.00
151 SP6 15c gray 6.50 4.75
152 SP6 20c orange 6.50 4.75
153 SP7 45c olive green 17.50 12.00
154 SP7 60c car rose 17.50 12.00
a. Inverted overprint 47.50 47.50
155 SP7 80c brt violet 27.50 24.00

With Additional Overprint "L"

156 SP7 1 l on 1cor dk slate 32.50 *35.00*
a. Inverted overprint 80.00 80.00
157 SP8 2 l on 2cor red brn 120.00 4.25
a. Inverted overprint 325.00 160.00
158 SP8 3 l on 3cor black brn 120.00 *130.00*
159 SP8 5 l on 5cor yel brn 120.00 4.25
160 SP8 10 l on 10cor dk vio 175.00 175.00
a. Inverted overprint 475.00 400.00
Nos. 149-160 (12) 656.00 415.50
Set, never hinged 1,625.

The overprint exists inverted on several denominations.

Second Constituent Assembly

"Constitution" Issue of 1921 With Additional Overprint "1922"

1922

161 SP6 5c blue green 4.75 3.25
a. Inverted overprint 24.00 24.00
162 SP6 10c rose 2.40 *2.40*
a. Inverted overprint 24.00 24.00
b. Double overprint, one inverted 40.00 40.00
163 SP6 15c gray 20.00 12.00
164 SP6 20c orange 2.40 2.40
a. Inverted overprint 32.50 32.50
b. Double overprint 40.00 40.00
c. Double overprint, one inverted — —
165 SP7 45c olive grn 13.00 12.00
a. Double overprint 40.00 40.00
166 SP7 60c car rose 2.40 *3.25*
167 SP7 80c brt violet 2.40 *3.25*
168 SP7 1 l on 1cor dk slate 2.40 *2.40*
a. Inverted overprint 55.00 55.00
b. Double overprint 40.00 40.00
169 SP8 2 l on 2cor red brn 20.00 16.00
170 SP8 3 l on 3cor blk brn 2.50 *3.25*
171 SP8 5 l on 5cor yel brn 2.50 *3.25*
Nos. 161-171 (11) 74.75 63.45
Set, never hinged 170.00

Nos. 161-171 have the overprint in heavier type than Nos. 149-160 and "IV" in Roman instead of sans-serif numerals.
The overprint exists inverted or double on almost all values.

Venetian Ship — A16

Roman Arch — A17

St. Vitus — A18

Rostral Column — A19

1923, Mar. 23 ***Perf. 11½***

Pale Buff Background

172 A16 5c blue green 2.40 2.40
173 A16 10c violet 2.40 2.40
174 A16 15c brown 2.40 2.40
175 A17 20c orange red 2.40 2.40
176 A17 25c dark gray 2.40 2.40
177 A17 30c dark green 2.40 2.40
178 A18 50c dull blue 2.40 2.40
179 A18 60c rose 4.00 *4.00*
180 A18 1 l dark blue 4.00 *4.00*
181 A19 2 l violet brown 65.00 20.00
182 A19 3 l olive bister 55.00 45.00
183 A19 5 l yellow brown 55.00 52.50
Nos. 172-183 (12) 199.80 142.30
Set, never hinged 465.00

Nos. 172-183 Overprinted

1924, Feb. 22

Pale Buff Background

184 A16 5c blue green 2.40 *12.00*
a. Inverted overprint 20.00 *40.00*
b. Double overprint 130.00
185 A16 10c violet 2.40 *12.00*
a. Inverted overprint 16.00 *40.00*
186 A16 15c brown 2.40 *12.00*
a. Inverted overprint 17.00 *40.00*
187 A17 20c orange red 2.40 *12.00*
a. Inverted overprint 21.00 *40.00*
b. Double overprint 260.00
188 A17 25c dk gray 2.40 *12.00*
189 A17 30c dk green 2.40 *12.00*
a. Inverted overprint 42.50
190 A18 50c dull blue 2.40 *12.00*
a. Inverted overprint 42.50 42.50
191 A18 60c red 2.40 *12.00*
a. Inverted overprint 87.50
192 A18 1 l dark blue 2.40 *12.00*
a. Inverted overprint 21.00 *40.00*
193 A19 2 l violet brown 4.00 *32.50*
a. Inverted overprint 130.00 *160.00*
194 A19 3 l olive 6.00 *40.00*
195 A19 5 l yellow brown 6.00 *40.00*
Nos. 184-195 (12) 37.60 *220.50*
Set, never hinged 80.00

The overprint exists inverted on almost all values.

Nos. 172-183 Overprinted

1924, Mar. 1

Pale Buff Background

196 A16 5c blue green 2.40 *20.00*
197 A16 10c violet 2.40 *20.00*
198 A16 15c brown 2.40 *20.00*
199 A17 20c orange red 2.40 *20.00*
200 A17 25c dark gray 2.40 *20.00*
201 A17 30c dark green 2.40 *20.00*
202 A18 50c dull blue 2.40 *20.00*
203 A18 60c red 2.40 *20.00*
204 A18 1 l dark blue 2.40 *20.00*
205 A19 2 l violet brown 4.00 *27.50*
206 A19 3 l olive 4.00 *27.50*
207 A19 5 l yellow brown 4.00 *27.50*
Nos. 196-207 (12) 33.60 *262.50*
Set, never hinged 62.50

Postage stamps of Fiume were superseded by stamps of Italy.

SEMI-POSTAL STAMPS

Semi-Postal Stamps of Hungary, 1916-17 Overprinted

1918, Dec. 2 **Wmk. 137** ***Perf. 15***

B1 SP3 10f + 2f rose 8.00 8.00
a. Inverted overprint 72.50 40.00
b. Double overprint 240.00 120.00
B2 SP4 15f + 2f dl vio 8.00 8.00
a. Inverted overprint 145.00 40.00
b. Double overprint 145.00 47.50
B3 SP5 40f + 2f brn car 14.50 8.00
a. Inverted overprint 87.50 37.50
Nos. B1-B3 (3) 30.50 24.00
Set, never hinged 72.50

Examples of Nos. B1-B3 with overprint handstamped sell for higher prices.

Statue of Romulus and Remus Being Suckled by Wolf — SP6

Venetian Galley — SP7

Church of St. Mark's, Venice — SP8

Perf. 11½

1919, May 18 **Unwmk.** **Typo.**

B4 SP6 5c +5 l bl grn 47.50 32.50
B5 SP6 10c +5 l rose 47.50 32.50
B6 SP6 15c +5 l dk gray 47.50 32.50
B7 SP6 20c +5 l orange 47.50 32.50
B8 SP7 45c +5 l ol grn 47.50 32.50
B9 SP7 60c +5 l car rose 47.50 32.50
B10 SP7 80c +5 l lilac 47.50 32.50
B11 SP7 1cor +5 l dk slate 47.50 32.50
B12 SP8 2cor +5 l red brn 47.50 32.50
B13 SP8 3cor +5 l blk brn 47.50 32.50
B14 SP8 5cor +5 l yel brn 47.50 32.50
B15 SP8 10cor +5 l dk vio 47.50 32.50
Nos. B4-B15 (12) 570.00 390.00
Set, never hinged 1,450.

200th day of peace. The surtax aided Fiume students in Italy. "Posta di Fiume" is printed on the back of Nos. B4-B16.
The surtax is shown on the stamps as "LIRE 5" but actually was 5cor.
For surcharges and overprints see Nos. 73-76, 78-85, 149-171, J15-J26.

Dr. Antonio Grossich — SP9

1919, Sept. 20

B16 SP9 25c + 2 l blue 3.25 3.25
Never hinged 8.00

Surtax for the Dr. Grossich Foundation.
For overprint and surcharge, see No. 77.

SPECIAL DELIVERY STAMPS

1916 Special Delivery Stamp of Hungary Overprinted

1918, Dec. 2 **Wmk. 137** ***Perf. 15***

Typographed Overprint

E1 SD1 2f gray green & red 4.75 4.75
Never hinged 12.00
a. Double overprint 190.00 175.00

Handstamped overprints sell for more.

SD3

Perf. 11½

1920, Sept. 12 **Unwmk.** **Typo.**

E2 SD3 30c slate blue 25.00 25.00
E3 SD3 50c rose 25.00 25.00
Set, never hinged 125.00

For overprints see Nos. E10-E11.

Nos. 102 and 100 Surcharged

1920, Nov.

E4 A12 30c on 20c brn org 190.00 175.00
a. Inverted overprint 625.00
b. Double overprint 625.00
E5 A12 50c on 5c green 290.00 125.00
a. Inverted overprint 1,000.
b. Double overprint 1,000.
c. Double overprint, one inverted 1,100.

Nos. E4-E5 have a backprint.

Same Surcharge as on Nos. 124, 122

E6 A12 30c on 20c brn org 275.00 180.00
E7 A12 50c on 5c green 210.00 180.00
a. Double overprint 950.00

Overprint on Nos. E6-E7 is 11mm wide.

Same Surcharge as on Nos. 130, 128

E8 A12 30c on 20c brn org 275.00 180.00
E9 A12 50c on 5c green 210.00 180.00
a. Double overprint 950.00 950.00
Nos. E4-E9 (6) 1,450. 1,020.
Set, never hinged 2,900.

Overprint on Nos. E8-E9 is 17mm wide.

Nos. E2 and E3 Overprinted

1921, Feb. 2

E10 SD3 30c slate blue 11.00 12.00
a. Inverted overprint 120.00 120.00
b. Double overprint 40.00 40.00
E11 SD3 50c rose 15.00 12.00
a. Inverted overprint 27.50 27.50
b. Double overprint 105.00 105.00
Set, never hinged 62.50

Fiume in 16th Century
SD4

1923, Mar. 23 *Perf. 11, 11½*

E12 SD4 60c rose & buff 24.00 24.00
E13 SD4 2 l dk bl & buff 24.00 24.00
Set, never hinged 120.00

Nos. E12-E13 Overprinted

1924, Feb. 22

E14 SD4 60c car & buff 3.25 *20.00*
E15 SD4 2 l dk bl & buff 3.25 *20.00*
a. Inverted overprint 130.00 *160.00*
Set, never hinged 16.00

Nos. E12-E13 Overprinted

1924, Mar. 1

E16 SD4 60c car & buff 4.00 *80.00*
E17 SD4 2 l dk bl & buff 4.00 *80.00*
Set, never hinged 20.00

POSTAGE DUE STAMPS

Postage Due Stamps of Hungary, 1915-1916, Overprinted

1918, Dec. **Wmk. 137** *Perf. 15*

J1c D1 6f green & black 190.00 105.00
d. Double overprint — 1,450.
J2c D1 12f green & black 180.00 72.50
d. Double overprint 1,450.
J3c D1 50c green & black 65.00 35.00
d. Double overprint 1,450.

J4c D1 1f green & red 40.00 24.00
d. Inverted overprint 425.00
e. Double overprint 525.00 190.00
J5 D1 2f green & red 6.50 6.50
a. Inverted overprint 52.50 45.00
b. Double overprint 175.00
J6c D1 5f green & red 40.00 47.50
d. Inverted overprint 320.00 440.00
e. Double overprint 525.00 525.00
J7 D1 6f green & red 6.50 6.50
a. Inverted overprint 25.00 25.00
b. Double overprint 27.50
J8c D1 10f green & red 32.50 32.50
d. Inverted overprint 475.00 475.00
J9 D1 12f green & red 6.50 6.50
J10c D1 15f green & red 32.50 32.50
d. Inverted overprint 800.00
e. Double overprint 440.00 440.00
J11 D1 20f green & red 6.50 6.50
a. Double overprint 45.00 32.50
J12c D1 30f green & red 32.50 32.50
d. Inverted overprint 900.00
e. Double overprint 950.00 950.00
Nos. J1c-J12 (12) 638.50 407.50
Set, never hinged 1,275.

Overprint was applied by press or handstamp. Six minor varieties of the handstamp exist. Some are sought by specialists at much higher values. Excellent forgeries exist. For more detailed listings, see *Scott Classic Specialized Catalogue of Stamps and Covers 1840-1940.*

Eagle — D2

Perf. 11½

1919, July 28 **Unwmk.** **Typo.**

J13 D2 2c brown 2.40 2.40
J14 D2 5c brown 2.40 2.40
Set, never hinged 12.00

Semi-Postal Stamps of 1919 Overprinted and Surcharged

1921, Mar. 21

J15 SP6 2c on 15c gray 6.50 6.50
J16 SP6 4c on 10c rose 4.75 4.75
J17 SP9 5c on 25c blue 4.75 4.75
J18 SP6 6c on 20c orange 4.75 4.75
J19 SP6 10c on 20c orange 6.50 6.50

Nos. B8-B11 Surcharged

J20 SP7 20c on 45c ol grn 2.40 *4.75*
J21 SP7 30c on 1cor dk slate 12.00 *12.00*
J22 SP7 40c on 80c violet 4.75 *6.50*
J23 SP7 50c on 60c car 4.75 *6.50*
J24 SP7 60c on 45c ol grn 2.40 *4.75*
J25 SP7 80c on 45c ol grn 2.40 *4.75*

Surcharged like Nos. J15-J19

J26 SP8 1 l on 2cor red brown 24.00 *24.00*
Nos. J15-J26 (12) 79.95 *90.50*
Set, never hinged 190.00

See note below No. 85 regarding settings of "Valore Globale" overprint.

NEWSPAPER STAMPS

Newspaper Stamp of Hungary, 1914, Overprinted like Nos. 1-23

1918, Dec. 2 **Wmk. 137** *Imperf.*

P1 N5 (2f) orange 4.75 3.25
Never hinged 15.00
a. Inverted overprint 55.00 52.50
b. Double overprint 210.00 190.00

Handstamped overprints sell for more.

Eagle
N1

1919 **Unwmk.** *Perf. 11½*

P2 N1 2c deep buff 9.50 *14.50*

Re-engraved

P3 N1 2c deep buff 9.50 *14.50*
Set, never hinged 48.00

In the re-engraved stamp the top of the "2" is rounder and broader, the feet of the eagle show clearly and the diamond at bottom has six lines instead of five.

Steamer — N2

1920, Sept. 12

P4 N2 1c gray green 4.00 3.25
Never hinged 10.00
a. Imperf 24.00 24.00

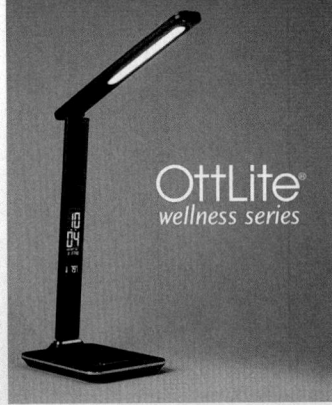

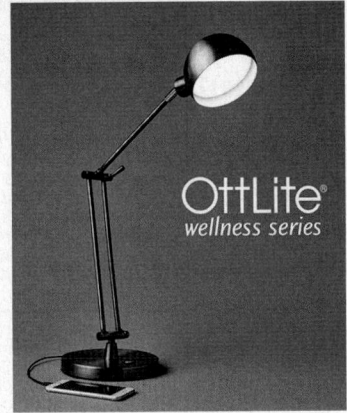

FRANCE

'fran(t)s

LOCATION — Western Europe
GOVT. — Republic
AREA — 210,033 sq. mi.
POP. — 58,978,172 (1999 est.)
CAPITAL — Paris

100 Centimes = 1 Franc
100 Cents = 1 Euro (2002)

Catalogue values for unused stamps in this country are for Never Hinged items, beginning with Scott 299 in the regular postage section, Scott B42 in the semi-postal section, Scott C18 in the airpost section, Scott CB1 in the airpost semi-postal section, Scott J69 in the postage due section, Scott M10 in the military stamps section, Scott 1O1 in the section for official stamps for the Council of Europe, Scott 2O1 for the section for UNESCO, Scott S1 for franchise stamps, Scott N27 for occupation stamps, and Scott 2N1 for AMG stamps.

Watermarks

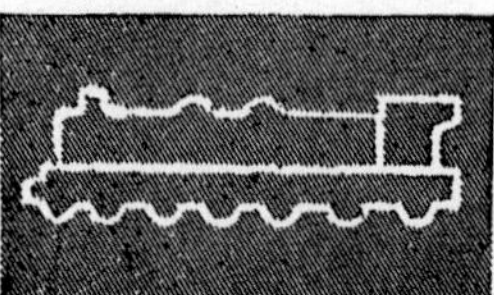

Wmk. 407

Ceres — A1

FORTY CENTIMES

Type I Type II

1849-50 Typo. Unwmk. *Imperf.*

1 A1 10c bis, *yelsh* ('50) 1,500. 210.00
- a. 10c dark bister, *yelsh* 1,825. 240.00
- b. 10c greenish bister 2,350. 600.00
- d. As #1, tête beche pair *85,000.* *18,000.*

2 A1 15c grn, *grnsh* 21,500. 800.00
- a. 15c yellow green, *grnsh* *20,000.* 700.00
- c. Tête bêche pair —

3 A1 20c blk, *yelsh* 340.00 34.00
- a. 20c black 375.00 50.00
- b. 20c black, *buff* 1,100. 135.00
- c. Tête bêche pair *9,250.* *6,500.*

4 A1 20c dark blue *2,400.*
- a. 20c blue, *bluish* *2,050.*
- b. 20c blue, *yelsh* *2,750.*
- c. Tête bêche pair *60,000.*

6 A1 25c lt bl, *bluish* 5,400. 30.00
- a. 25c blue, *bluish* ('50) 5,400. 30.00
- b. 25c blue, *yelsh* 6,250. 40.00
- c. Tête bêche pair 155,000. 12,500.

7 A1 40c org, *yelsh* (I) ('50) 2,950. 360.00
- a. 40c org ver, *yelsh* (I) 3,500. 475.00
- b. 40c orange, *yelsh* (II) 20,750. 5,250.
- c. Pair, types I and II 31,000. 12,500.
- g. Vertical half used as 20c on cover *260,000.*

8 A1 1fr ver, *yelsh* 92,500. 13,750.
- a. 1fr dull orange red 95,000. 17,000.
- c. 1fr pale ver ("Vervelle") 20,000.
- d. As "c," tête bêche pair 450,000.

9 A1 1fr lt car 8,750. 650.00
- a. Tête bêche pair 200,000. 23,250.
- b. 1fr brown carmine 10,000. 800.00
- c. 1fr dark carmine, *yelsh* 12,250. 1,075.

No. 4 was printed but not yet gummed when the rate change to 25c made them unnecessary. An essay with a red "25" surcharge on No. 4 was rejected.

An ungummed sheet of No. 8c was found in 1895 among the effects of Anatole A. Hulot, the printer. It was sold to Ernest Vervelle, a Parisian dealer, by whose name the stamps are known.

See Nos. 329-329e, 612-613, 624.

Nos. 1, 4a, 6a, 7 and 13 are of similar designs and colors to French Colonies Nos. 9, 11, 12, 14, and 8. There are numerous shades of each. Identification by those who are not experts can be difficult, though cancellations can be used as a guide for used stamps.

Because of the date of issue the Colonies stamps are similar in shades and papers to the perforated French stamps, Nos. 23a, 54, 57-59, and are not as clearly printed. Except for No. 13, unused, the French Colonies stamps sell for much less than the values shown here for properly identified French versions.

Expertization of these stamps is recommended.

1862 Re-issue

- *1g* A1 10c bister 435.
- *2d* A1 15c yellow green 560.
- *3d* A1 20c black, *yellowish* 375.
- *4d* A1 20c blue 340.
- *6d* A1 25c blue 400.
- *7d* A1 40c orange (I) 575.
- *7e* A1 40c orange (II) *11,000.*
- h. Pair, types I and II *15,000.*
- *9d* A1 1fr pale lake 600.

The re-issues are fine impressions in lighter colors and on whiter paper than the originals. An official imitation of the essay, 25c on 20c blue, also in a lighter shade and on whiter paper, was made at the same time as the re-issues.

President Louis Napoleon — A2

Inscribed: "REPUB FRANC"

1852

10 A2 10c pale bister, *yelsh* *30,000.* 450.00
- a. 10c dark bister, *yelsh* *30,000.* 525.00

11 A2 25c blue, *bluish* 2,450. 32.50
- b. 25c dark blue, *bluish* 2,900. 50.00

1862 Re-issue

- *10b* A2 10c bister 525.00
- *11a* A2 25c blue 350.00

The re-issues are in lighter colors and on whiter paper than the originals.

Emperor Napoleon III — A3

Die I. The curl above the forehead directly below "R" of "EMPIRE" is made up of two lines very close together, often appearing to form a single thick line. There is no shading across the neck.

Die II. The curl is made of two distinct, more widely separated lines. There are lines of shading across the upper neck.

Inscribed: "EMPIRE FRANC"

1853-60 *Imperf.*

12 A3 1c ol grn, *pale bl* ('60) 165.00 62.50
- a. 1c bronze grn, *pale bluish* 155.00 67.50

13 A3 5c grn, *grnsh* (I) ('54) 630.00 62.50

14 A3 10c bis, *yelsh* (I) 360.00 6.50
- a. 10c yellow, *yelsh* (I) 1,200. 27.50
- b. 10c bister brn, *yelsh* (I) 450.00 18.50
- c. 10c bister, *yelsh* (II) ('60) 450.00 19.00

15 A3 20c bl, *bluish* (I) ('54) 150.00 1.35
- a. 20c dark bl, *bluish* (I) 220.00 1.35
- b. 20c milky blue (I) 225.00 10.00
- c. 20c blue, *lilac* (I) 4,250. 62.50
- d. 20c blue, *bluish* (II) ('60) 285.00 4.00
- e. Half used as 10c on cover *16,000.*
- f. Tête bêche pair *155,000.*

16 A3 20c bl, *grnsh* (II) 5,250. 150.00
- a. 20c blue, *greenish* (I) 4,250. 100.00

17 A3 25c bl, *bluish* (I) 2,050. 165.00

18 A3 40c org, *yelsh* (I) 2,000. 10.00
- a. 40c org ver, *yellowish* 2,850. 16.00
- b. Half used as 20c on cover *110,000.*

19 A3 80c lake, *yelsh* (I) ('54) 2,800. 40.00
- a. Tête bêche pair 340,000. 22,000.
- b. Half used as 40c on cover *50,000.*

20 A3 80c rose, *pnksh* (I) ('60) 1,875. 42.50
- a. Tête-bêche pair 49,500. 10,000.

21 A3 1fr lake, *yelsh* (I) 7,450. 2,475.
- a. Tête bêche pair 300,000. 135,000.

Most values of the 1853-60 issue are known privately rouletted, pin-perf., perf. 7 and percé en scie.

1862 Re-issue

- *17c* A3 25c blue (I) 450.
- *19c* A3 80c lake (I) 1,800.
- *21c* A3 1fr lake (I) 1,500.
- d. Tête bêche pair *27,500.*

The re-issues are in lighter colors and on whiter paper than the originals.

1862-71 *Perf. 14x13½*

22 A3 1c ol grn, *pale bl* (II) 140.00 30.00
- a. 1c bronze grn, *pale bl* (II) 140.00 35.00
- On cover 175.00
- On cover, single franking 325.00

23 A3 5c yel grn, *grnsh* (I) 190.00 10.00
- a. 5c deep green, *grnsh* (I) 225.00 12.50

24 A3 5c grn, *pale bl* ('71) (I) 1,800. 110.00

25 A3 10c bis, *yelsh* (II) 1,350. 3.75
- a. 10c yel brn, *yelsh* (II) 1,750. 8.50

26 A3 20c bl, *bluish* (II) 200.00 1.25
- a. Tête bêche pair (II) 4,000. 1,000.

27 A3 40c org, *yelsh* (I) 1,200. 6.50

28 A3 80c rose, *pnksh* (I) 1,100. 30.00
- a. 80c bright rose, *pinkish* (I) 1,300. 35.00
- c. Tête bêche pair (I) *17,500.* *7,750.*

No. 26a imperf is from a trial printing.

A4 A5

Napoleon III — A6

1863-70 *Perf. 14x13½*

29 A4 1c brnz grn, *pale bl* ('70) 37.50 16.00
- a. 1c olive green, *pale blue* 37.50 16.00

30 A4 2c red brn, *yelsh* 105.00 25.00
- b. Half used as 1c on cover *36,000.*

31 A4 4c gray 165.00 37.50
- a. Tete beche pair *17,500.* *11,000.*
- d. Half used as 2c on cover *50,000.*

32 A5 10c bis, *yelsh* ('67) 215.00 5.00
- c. Half used as 5c on cover with other stamps *3,750.*

33 A5 20c bl, *bluish* ('67) 175.00 1.55
- c. Half used as 10c on cover *62,500.*
- e. 20c dark blue ('67) 275.00 3.25
- No gum 140.00
- On cover, single franking 4.00

34 A5 30c brn, *yelsh* ('67) 625.00 12.50
- a. 30c dk brn, *yellowish* 1,000. 30.00

35 A5 40c pale org, *yelsh* 700.00 8.00
- a. 40c org, *yelsh* ('68) 700.00 8.00
- c. Half used as 20c on cover *35,000.*

36 A5 80c rose, *pnksh* ('68) 800.00 20.00
- a. 80c carmine, *yellowish* 950.00 24.00
- d. Half used as 40c on cover *42,500.*
- e. Quarter used as 20c on cover *50,000.*

37 A6 5fr gray lil, *lav* ('69) *6,000.* 750.00

Values for blocks of 4
Original Issue Imperfs

31c	A4	4c gray	270.00	—
32b	A5	10c bis, *yelsh*	360.00	—
33b	A5	20c bl, *bluish*	270.00	—
36c	A5	80c rose, *pnksh*	—	—
37b	A6	5fr gray lil, *lav*	*7,800.*	

Imperfs, "Rothschild" Re-issue
Paper Colors are the Same

- *29b* A4 1c olive green 1,050.
- *30a* A4 2c pale red brown 200.00
- *31b* A4 4c pale gray 185.00
- *32a* A5 10c pale bister 160.00
- *33a* A5 20c pale blue 250.00
- *34c* A5 30c pale brown 190.00
- *35b* A5 40c pale orange 225.00
- *36b* A5 80c rose 400.00

The re-issues constitute the "Rothschild Issue." These stamps were authorized exclusively for the banker to use on his correspondence. Used examples exist.

Ceres

A7 A8

A9

A10

A11

Bordeaux Issue

On the lithographed stamps, except for type I of the 20c, the shading on the cheek and neck is in lines or dashes, not in dots. On the typographed stamps the shading is in dots. The 2c, 5c, 10c and 20c (types II and III) occur in two or more types. The most easily distinguishable are:

2c — Type A. To the left of and within the top of the left "2" are lines of shading composed of dots.

2c — Type B. These lines of dots are replaced by solid lines.

5c — Type A. The head and hairline merge with the background of the medallion, without a distinct separation.

5c — Type B. A white line separates the contour of the head and hairline from the background of the medallion.

10c — Type A. The inner frame lines are of the same thickness as all other frame lines.

10c — Type B. The inner frame lines are much thicker than the others.

Three Types of the 20c.

A9 — The inscriptions in the upper and lower labels are small and there is quite a space between the upper label and the circle containing the head. There is also very little shading under the eye and in the neck.

A10 — The inscriptions in the labels are similar to those of the first type, the shading under the eye and in the neck is heavier and the upper label and circle almost touch.

A11 — The inscriptions in the labels are much larger than those of the two preceding types, and are similar to those of the other values of the same type in the set.

1870-71 Litho. *Imperf.*

38 A7 1c ol grn, *pale bl* 125.00 100.00
a. 1c bronze green, *pale blue* 160.00 155.00
39 A7 2c red brn, *yelsh* (B) 225.00 225.00
a. 2c brick red, *yelsh* (B) 800.00 700.00
b. 2c chestnut, *yelsh* (B) 1,350. 700.00
c. 2c chocolate, *yelsh* (A) 750.00 700.00
40 A7 4c gray 250.00 200.00
41 A8 5c yel grn, *grnsh* (B) 250.00 160.00
a. 5c grn, *grnsh* (B) 325.00 175.00
b. 5c emerald, *greenish* (B) 3,500. 1,250.
c. 5c yellowish green, *greenish* (A) 2,400. 3,250.
42 A8 10c bis, *yelsh* (A) 825.00 60.00
a. 10c bister, *yellowish* (B) 825.00 90.00
43 A9 20c bl, *bluish* 21,500. 550.00
a. 20c dark blue, *bluish* 25,000. 725.00
44 A10 20c bl, *bluish* 950.00 45.00
a. 20c dark blue, *bluish* 1,150. 85.00
b. 20c ultra, *bluish* 20,000. 3,100.
45 A11 20c bl, *bluish* ('71) 825.00 16.00
a. 20c ultra, *bluish* 2,200. 675.00
46 A8 30c brn, *yelsh* 325.00 200.00
a. 30c blk brn, *yelsh* 1,750. 675.00
47 A8 40c org, *yelsh* 425.00 100.00
a. 40c yel orange, *yelsh* 1,250. 225.00
b. 40c red orange, *yelsh* 625.00 190.00
c. 40c scarlet, *yelsh* 1,250. 675.00
48 A8 80c rose, *pinkish* 600.00 250.00
a. 80c dull rose, *pinkish* 600.00 275.00

All values of the 1870 issue are known privately rouletted, pin-perf and perf. 14.

See Nos. 50-53.

A12

Dark Blue Surcharge

1871 Typo. *Perf. 14x13½*

49 A12 10c on 10c bister 1,400.
a. Pale blue surcharge 1,900.

No. 49 was never placed in use. Counterfeits exist.

A13

Two types of the 40c as in the 1849-50 issue.

1870-73 Typo. *Perf. 14x13½*

50 A7 1c ol grn, *pale bl* 40.00 11.50
a. 1c bronze grn, *pale bl* ('72) 47.50 14.00
51 A7 2c red brn, *yelsh* ('70) 80.00 13.50
52 A7 4c gray ('70) 250.00 40.00
53 A7 5c yel grn, *pale bl* ('72) 150.00 7.50
a. 5c green 150.00 7.50
54 A13 10c bis, *yelsh* 540.00 55.00
a. Tête beche pair *5,500.* *2,250.*
b. Half used as 5c on cover *4,500.*
55 A13 10c bis, *rose* ('73) 265.00 9.50
a. Tête bêche pair 3,750. 1,750.
56 A13 15c bis, *yelsh* ('71) 300.00 4.50
a. Tête bêche pair *37,500.* *12,000.*
57 A13 20c dl bl, *bluish* 225.00 6.75
a. 20c bright blue, *bluish* 350.00 8.00
b. Tête bêche pair 3,750. 1,450.
c. Half used as 10c on cover *55,000.*
d. Quarter used as 5c on cover *52,500.*
58 A13 25c bl, *bluish* ('71) 110.00 1.10
a. 25c dk bl, *bluish* 135.00 1.10
b. Tête bêche pair *6,750.* *3,000.*
59 A13 40c org, *yelsh* (I) 475.00 6.00
a. 40c orange yel, *yelsh* (I) 575.00 9.00
b. 40c orange, *yelsh* (II) 3,150. 130.00
c. 40c orange yel, *yelsh* (II) 3,150. 130.00
d. Pair, types I and II *6,500.* 525.00
f. Half used as 20c on circular *20,000.*
g. Half used as 20c on cover *40,000.*

No. 58 exists in three main plate varieties, differing in one or another of the flower-like corner ornaments.

Margins on this issue are extremely small.

Nos. 54, 57 and 58 were reprinted imperf. in 1887. See note after No. 37.

Imperf.

50b A7 1c 270.00
51a A7 2c 350.00
52a A7 4c 450.00
53b A7 5c yel grn, *pale bl* 260.00
55b A13 10c 350.00
56b A13 15c 375.00

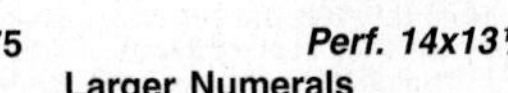

A14

1872-75 *Perf. 14x13½*

Larger Numerals

60 A14 10c bis, *rose* ('75) 325.00 11.00
a. Cliché of 15c in plate of 10c *3,750.* *4,250.*
b. Pair, #60, 60a *6,750.* *8,500.*
61 A14 15c bister ('73) 320.00 3.25
62 A14 30c brn, *yelsh* 550.00 5.25
63 A14 80c rose, *pnksh* 640.00 11.50

Imperf.

62a A14 30c 475.00
63a A14 80c 650.00

Peace and Commerce ("Type Sage") — A15

Type I. The "N" of "INV" is under the "B" of "REPUBLIQUE."

Type II. The "N" of "INV" is under the "U" of "REPUBLIQUE."

Type I

1876-78 *Perf. 14x13½*

64 A15 1c grn, *grnsh* 125.00 70.00
65 A15 2c grn, *grnsh* 1,425. 240.00
66 A15 4c grn, *grnsh* 145.00 55.00
67 A15 5c grn, *grnsh* 650.00 45.00
68 A15 10c grn, *grnsh* 800.00 21.00
69 A15 15c gray lil, *grysh* 800.00 17.50
70 A15 20c red brn, *straw* 575.00 17.50
71 A15 20c bl, *bluish* *27,500.*
72 A15 25c ultra, *bluish* *7,750.* 55.00
73 A15 30c brn, *yelsh* 425.00 8.25
74 A15 40c red, *straw* ('78) 600.00 35.00
75 A15 75c car, *rose* 950.00 12.50
76 A15 1fr brnz grn, *straw* 925.00 10.00

No. 71 was never put into use.

The reprints of No. 71 are type II. They are imperforate or with forged perforation.

For overprints and surcharges see Offices in China Nos. 1-17, J7-J10, J20-J22, Offices in Egypt, Alexandria 1-15, Port Said 1-17, Offices in Turkish Empire 1-7, Cavalle 1-8, Dedeagh 1-8, Port Lagos 1-5, Vathy 1-9, Offices in Zanzibar 1-33, 50-54, French Morocco 1-8, and Madagascar 14-27.

Imperf.

64a A15 1c 150.00
65a A15 2c 1,000.
66a A15 4c 160.00
67a A15 5c 525.00
68a A15 10c 575.00
69a A15 15c 575.00
70a A15 20c 375.00
73a A15 30c 275.00
74a A15 40c 250.00
75a A15 75c 550.00
76a A15 1fr 400.00

Beware of French Colonies Nos. 24-29.

Type II

1876-77 *Perf. 14x13½*

77 A15 2c grn, *grnsh* 115.00 19.00
78 A15 5c grn, *grnsh* 25.00 .60
a. Imperf. 175.00
79 A15 10c grn, *grnsh* 1,100. 240.00
80 A15 15c gray lil, *grysh* 675.00 1.90
81 A15 25c ultra, *bluish* 425.00 1.00
a. 25c blue, *bluish* 475.00 1.50
b. Pair, types I & II *60,000.* *17,500.*
c. Imperf. 325.00
82 A15 30c yel brn, *yelsh* 82.50 1.40
a. 30c brown, *yellowish* 90.00 1.40
b. Imperf. 525.00
83 A15 75c car, *rose* ('77) 1,775. 110.00
84 A15 1fr brnz grn, *straw* ('77) 145.00 7.50
a. Imperf. 1,100.

Beware of French Colonies Nos. 31, 35.

1877-80

86 A15 1c blk, *lil bl* 3.75 1.65
a. 1c black, *gray blue* 3.75 1.65
b. Imperf. 75.00
87 A15 1c blk, *Prus bl* ('80) *11,000.* *4,350.*

Values for No. 87 are for examples with the perfs touching the design on at least one side.

88 A15 2c brn, *straw* 4.50 1.90
a. 2c brown, *yellow* 4.50 1.90
b. Imperf. 210.00
89 A15 3c yel, *straw* ('78) 200.00 42.50
a. Imperf. 150.00
90 A15 4c claret, *lav* 5.00 1.90
a. 4c vio brown, *lavender* 8.25 4.50
b. Imperf. 60.00
91 A15 10c blk, *lavender* 35.00 1.00
a. 10c black, *rose lilac* 37.50 1.00
b. 10c black, *lilac* 37.50 1.00
c. Imperf. 70.00
92 A15 15c blue ('78) 22.50 .60
a. Imperf. 95.00
b. 15c blue, *bluish* 435.00 15.00
93 A15 25c blk, *red* ('78) 1,075. 25.00
a. Imperf. 675.00
94 A15 35c blk, *yel* ('78) 525.00 35.00
a. 35c blk, *yel org* 525.00 35.00
b. Imperf. 250.00
95 A15 40c red, *straw* ('80) 90.00 2.10
a. Imperf. 240.00
96 A15 5fr vio, *lav* 440.00 70.00
a. As #96, imperf. 750.00

b. 5fr red lilac, *lavender* 650.00 100.00

Beware of French Colonies Nos. 38-40, 42, 44.

1879-90

97 A15 3c gray, *grysh* ('80) 3.00 1.65
a. Imperf. 67.50
98 A15 20c red, *yel grn* 37.50 4.25
a. 20c red, *deep green* ('84) 72.50 6.00
b. Imperf. 100.00
99 A15 25c yel, *straw* 340.00 5.00
a. Imperf. 250.00
100 A15 25c blk, *pale rose* ('86) 72.50 1.00
a. Imperf. 155.00
101 A15 50c rose, *rose* ('90) 210.00 2.65
a. 50c carmine, *rose* 225.00 3.50
102 A15 75c dp vio, *org* ('90) 215.00 35.00
a. 75c deep violet, *yellow* 265.00 45.00
Nos. 97-102 (6) 878.00 49.55

Beware of French Colonies No. 43.

1892 Quadrille Paper

103 A15 15c blue 12.50 .35
a. Imperf. 175.00

1898-1900 Ordinary Paper

104 A15 5c yel grn 16.00 1.30
a. Imperf. 82.50

Type I

105 A15 5c yel grn 14.00 1.30
a. Imperf. 575.00
106 A15 10c blk, *lavender* 21.00 2.50
a. Imperf. 275.00
107 A15 50c car, *rose* 200.00 30.00
108 A15 2fr brn, *azure* ('00) 110.00 40.00
b. Imperf. 2,250.
Nos. 104-108 (5) 361.00 75.10

See No. 226.

Reprints of A15, type II, were made in 1887 and left imperf. See note after No. 37. Value for set of 27, $4,000.

Liberty, Equality, Fraternity A16

"The Rights of Man" A17

Liberty and Peace A18

1900-29 *Perf. 14x13½*

109 A16 1c gray .55 .40
110 A16 2c violet brn .70 .25
111 A16 3c orange .45 .45
a. 3c red 19.00 7.50
112 A16 4c yellow brn 3.00 1.60
113 A16 5c green 2.00 .35
b. Booklet pane of 10 330.00
114 A16 7½c lilac ('26) .60 .45
115 A16 10c lilac ('29) 4.00 .60
116 A17 10c carmine 25.00 1.50
a. Numerals printed separately 24.00 10.00
117 A17 15c orange 8.00 .60
118 A17 20c brown vio 55.00 9.25
119 A17 25c blue 125.00 1.65
a. Numerals printed separately 115.00 9.25
120 A17 30c violet 70.00 6.00
121 A18 40c red & pale bl 15.00 .85
122 A18 45c grn & bl ('06) 29.00 2.10
123 A18 50c bis brn & gray 100.00 1.65
124 A18 60c vio & ultra ('20) 1.00 1.15

125	A18	1fr	claret & ol grn	26.50	.85
126	A18	2fr	gray vio & yel	625.00	75.00
127	A18	2fr	org & pale bl ('20)	42.50	.60
128	A18	3fr	vio & bl ('25)	27.50	7.50
129	A18	3fr	brt vio & rose ('27)	55.00	2.80
130	A18	5fr	dk bl & buff	85.00	5.00
131	A18	10fr	grn & red ('26)	125.00	17.00
132	A18	20fr	mag & grn ('26)	200.00	37.50
			Nos. 109-132 (24)	1,626.	175.10

In the 10c and 25c values, the first printings show the numerals to have been impressed by a second operation, whereas, in later printings, the numerals were inserted in the plates. Two operations were used for all 20c and 30c, and one operation for the 15c.

No. 114 was issued precanceled only. Values for precanceled stamps in first column are for those which have not been through the post and have original gum. Values in the second column are for postally used, gumless stamps.

See Offices in China Nos. 34, 40-44, Offices in Crete 1-5, 10-15, Offices in Egypt, Alexandria 16-20, 26-30, 77, 84-86, Port Said 18-22, 28-32, 83, 90-92, Offices in Turkish Empire 21-26, 31-33, Cavalle 9, Dedeagh 9.

For overprints and surcharge see Nos. 197, 246, C1-C2, M1, P7. Offices in China 57, 62-65, 71, 73, 75, 83-85, J14, J27, Offices in Crete 17-20, Offices in Egypt, Alexandria 31-32, 34-35, 40-48, 57-64, 66, 71-73, Port Said 33, 35-40, 43, 46-57, 59, 65-71, 73, 78-80, Offices in Turkish Empire 35-38, 47-49, Cavalle 13-15, Dedeagh 16-18, Offices in Zanzibar 39, 45-49, 55, Offices in Morocco 11-15, 20-22, 26-29, 35-41, 49-54, 72-76, 84-85, 87-89, B6.

Imperf.

109a	A16	1c		55.00	
110a	A16	2c		67.50	60.00
111b	A16	3c		55.00	
112a	A16	4c		150.00	
113a	A16	5c		75.00	
116b	A17	10c	#116 or 116a	235.00	*135.00*
117a	A17	15c		190.00	*165.00*
119b	A17	25c	#119 or 119a	500.00	
121a	A18	40c		190.00	*155.00*
122a	A18	45c		260.00	
123a	A18	50c		375.00	*375.00*
124a	A18	60c		525.00	
125a	A18	1fr		250.00	*225.00*
126a	A18	2fr	No gum	*1,300.*	
127a	A18	2fr		475.00	
128a	A18	3fr		*725.00*	500.00
129a	A18	3fr		425.00	
130a	A18	5fr		950.00	

Flat Plate & Rotary Press

The following stamps were printed by both flat plate and rotary press: Nos. 109-113, 144-146, 163, 166, 168, 170, 175, 177-178, 185, 192 and P7.

"Rights of Man" — A19

1902

133	A19	10c	rose red	32.50	.90
134	A19	15c	pale red	11.00	.60
135	A19	20c	brown violet	82.50	14.00
136	A19	25c	blue	100.00	2.25
137	A19	30c	lilac	250.00	14.50
			Nos. 133-137 (5)	476.00	32.25

Imperf.

133a	A19	10c	rose red	450.00	*275.00*
134a	A19	15c	pale red	450.00	*325.00*
135a	A19	20c	brown violet	800.00	*475.00*
136a	A19	25c	blue	950.00	*625.00*
137a	A19	30c	lilac	*1,100.*	675.00

See Offices in China Nos. 35-39, Offices in Crete 6-10, Offices in Egypt, Alexandria 21-25, 81-82, Port Said 23-27, 87-88, Offices in Turkish Empire 26-30, Cavalle 10-11, Dedeagh 10-11.

For overprints and surcharges see Nos. M2, Offices in China 45, 58-61, 66-70, 76-82, J15-J16, J28-J30, Offices in Crete 16, Offices in Egypt, Alexandria 33, 36-39, 49-50, 52-56, 65, 67-70, B1-B4, Port Said 34, 41-42, 44-45, 57, 60-64, 77, 74-77, B1-B4, Offices in Turkish Empire 34, 39, Cavalle 12, Dedeagh 15, Offices in Zanzibar 40-44, 56-59, Offices in Morocco 16-19, 30-34, 42-48, 77-83, 86, B1-B5, B7, B9.

Sower — A20

1903-38

138	A20	10c	rose	8.00	.40
139	A20	15c	slate grn	4.00	.25
b.			Booklet pane of 10	450.00	
140	A20	20c	violet brn	67.50	1.90
141	A20	25c	dull blue	75.00	1.40
142	A20	30c	violet	175.00	5.25
143	A20	45c	lt violet ('26)	6.00	1.90
144	A20	50c	dull blue ('21)	27.50	1.40
145	A20	50c	gray grn ('26)	6.25	1.25
146	A20	50c	vermilion ('26)	1.25	.25
a.			Booklet pane of 10	40.00	
147	A20	50c	grnsh bl ('38)	1.00	.35
148	A20	60c	lt vio ('24)	6.25	2.10
149	A20	65c	rose ('24)	3.00	1.75
150	A20	65c	gray grn ('27)	6.50	2.10
151	A20	75c	rose lil ('26)	5.25	.60
152	A20	80c	ver ('25)	26.50	9.50
153	A20	85c	ver ('24)	13.50	3.25
154	A20	1fr	dull blue ('26)	6.00	.75
			Nos. 138-154 (17)	438.50	34.40
			Set, never hinged	940.00	

See Nos. 941, 942A. For surcharges and overprints see Nos. 229-230, 232-233, 236, 256, B25, B29, B32, B36, B40, M3-M4, M6, Offices in Turkish Empire 46, 54.

Imperf.

138a	A20	10c		175.00	
139a	A20	15c		140.00	55.00
140a	A20	20c		300.00	160.00
141a	A20	25c		350.00	
142a	A20	30c		625.00	
144a	A20	50c		140.00	
145a	A20	50c		125.00	
146b	A20	50c	No gum	70.00	
147a	A20	50c		67.50	
149a	A20	65c		300.00	
151a	A20	75c		450.00	
154a	A20	1fr		*1,000.*	

Ground — A21

1906, Apr. 13

With Ground Under Feet of Figure

155	A21	10c	red	2.50	1.75
a.			Imperf, pair, no gum	275.00	225.00
			As "a," with gum	450.00	

No Ground — A22

TEN AND THIRTY-FIVE CENTIMES

Type I — Numerals and letters of the inscriptions thin.

Type II — Numerals and letters thicker.

No Ground Under the Feet

1906-37

156	A22	1c	olive bis ('33)	.25	.30
157	A22	2c	dk grn ('33)	.25	.30
158	A22	3c	ver ('33)	.25	.30
159	A22	5c	green ('07)	1.50	.25
a.			Imperf., pair	40.00	30.00
b.			Booklet pane of 10	100.00	
160	A22	5c	orange ('21)	1.25	.30
a.			Booklet pane of 10	72.50	
161	A22	5c	cerise ('34)	.25	.25
162	A22	10c	red (II) ('07)	1.50	.25
a.			Imperf., pair	37.50	115.00
b.			10c red (I) ('06)	8.25	1.00
c.			As #162b, imperf., pair	37.50	115.00
d.			Booklet pane of 10 (I)	125.00	
e.			Booklet pane of 10 (II)	75.00	
f.			Booklet pane of 6 (II)	240.00	
163	A22	10c	grn (II) ('21)	1.00	.55
a.			10c green (I) ('27)	32.50	37.50
b.			Booklet pane of 10 (I, "Phena")	350.00	
c.			Booklet pane of 10 (I, "Mineraline")	3,200.	
164	A22	10c	ultra ('32)	1.40	.25
165	A22	15c	red brn ('26)	.25	.25
a.			Booklet pane of 10	27.50	
166	A22	20c	brown	3.00	.65
a.			Imperf., pair	82.50	100.00
b.			20c black brown	6.00	2.00
167	A22	20c	red vio ('26)	.25	.25
a.			Booklet pane of 10	7.50	
168	A22	25c	blue	2.40	.25
a.			Booklet pane of 10	37.50	
b.			Imperf, pair (dark blue)	45.00	60.00
169	A22	25c	yel brn ('27)	.25	.25
a.			25c red brown	.30	.25
170	A22	30c	orange	13.50	1.40
a.			Imperf, pair	200.00	175.00
171	A22	30c	red ('21)	6.50	2.25
172	A22	30c	cerise ('25)	1.25	.80
a.			Booklet pane of 10	13.50	
b.			Imperf, pair	575.00	
173	A22	30c	lt blue ('25)	3.75	.60
a.			Booklet pane of 10	35.00	
b.			Imperf, pair	2,200.	
174	A22	30c	cop red ('37)	.25	.30
a.			Booklet pane of 10	9.00	
175	A22	35c	vio (II) ('07)	8.25	.90
a.			Imperf, pair	150.00	120.00
b.			35c violet (I) ('06)	150.00	7.50
c.			As "b," Imperf, pair, no gum	*575.00*	
176	A22	35c	grn ('37)	.50	.55
a.			Imperf, pair	750.00	
177	A22	40c	olive ('25)	1.40	.55
b.			Booklet pane of 10	30.00	
178	A22	40c	ver ('26)	2.50	.80
a.			Booklet pane of 10	25.00	
179	A22	40c	violet ('27)	2.00	.90
180	A22	40c	lt ultra ('28)	1.25	.50
181	A22	1.05fr	ver ('25)	9.50	5.25
182	A22	1.10fr	cerise ('27)	11.50	2.50
183	A22	1.40fr	cerise ('26)	20.00	22.50
184	A22	2fr	Prus grn ('31)	14.00	1.75
			Nos. 156-184 (29)	109.95	45.95
			Set, never hinged	225.00	

The 10c and 35c, type I, were slightly retouched by adding thin white outlines to the sack of grain, the underside of the right arm and the back of the skirt. It is difficult to distinguish the retouches except on clearly-printed copies. The white outlines were made stronger on the stamps of type II.

Stamps of types A16, A18, A20 and A22 were printed in 1916-20 on paper of poor quality, usually grayish and containing bits of fiber. This is called G. C. (Grande Consommation) paper.

Nos. 160, 162b, 163, 175b and 176 also exist imperf.

See Nos. 241-241b. For surcharges and overprint see Nos. 227-228, 234, 238, 240, 400, B1, B24, B28, B31, B35, B37, B39, B41, M5, P8, Offices in Turkish Empire 40-45, 52, 55.

Louis Pasteur — A23

1923-26

185	A23	10c	green	.55	.30
a.			Booklet pane of 10	15.00	
186	A23	15c	green ('24)	1.40	.30
187	A23	20c	green ('26)	2.75	.90
188	A23	30c	red	.90	*1.50*
189	A23	30c	green ('26)	.55	.50
190	A23	45c	red ('24)	1.90	2.10
191	A23	50c	blue	4.50	.50
192	A23	75c	blue ('24)	3.75	1.00
a.			Imperf., pair	250.00	
193	A23	90c	red ('26)	11.00	3.50
194	A23	1fr	blue ('25)	21.00	.50
195	A23	1.25fr	blue ('26)	25.00	8.00
196	A23	1.50fr	blue ('26)	5.25	.50
			Nos. 185-196 (12)	78.55	19.60
			Set, never hinged	150.00	

Nos. 185, 188 and 191 were issued to commemorate the cent. of the birth of Pasteur.

For surcharges and overprint see Nos. 231, 235, 257, B26, B30, B33, C4.

No. 125 Overprinted in Blue

1923, June 15

197	A18	1fr	claret & ol grn	440.00	500.00
			Never hinged	825.00	

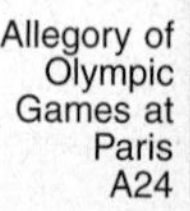

Allegory of Olympic Games at Paris A24

The Trophy A25

Milo of Crotona — A26

Victorious Athlete — A27

1924, Apr. 1 ***Perf. 14x13½, 13½x14***

198	A24	10c	gray grn & yel grn	2.25	1.25
199	A25	25c	rose & dk rose	3.00	.80
200	A26	30c	brn red & blk	9.50	11.00
201	A27	50c	ultra & dk bl	26.00	5.75
			Nos. 198-201 (4)	40.75	18.80
			Set, never hinged	125.00	

Imperf Singles

198a	A24	10c	1,000.	
199a	A25	25c	1,000.	*725.*
200a	A26	30c	1,000.	
201a	A27	50c	1,000.	1,000.

8th Olympic Games, Paris.

Pierre de Ronsard (1524-85), Poet — A28

1924, Oct. 6 ***Perf. 14x13½***

219	A28	75c	blue, *bluish*	1.90	1.40
			Never hinged	2.75	

"Light and Liberty" Allegory A29

Majolica Vase — A30

Potter Decorating Vase — A31

Terrace of Château A32

1924-25 ***Perf. 14x13½, 13½x14***

220	A29	10c	dk grn & yel ('25)	.55	.75
221	A30	15c	ind & grn ('25)	.55	.85
a.			Imperf.	*400.00*	
			Never hinged	*640.00*	
222	A31	25c	vio brn & garnet	.80	.50
223	A32	25c	gray bl & vio ('25)	1.60	.65
a.			Imperf.	*450.00*	150.00
			Never hinged	*700.00*	
224	A31	75c	indigo & ultra	3.50	2.25
225	A29	75c	dk bl & lt bl ('25)	18.00	6.50
a.			Imperf.	*375.00*	
			Never hinged	*650.00*	
			Nos. 220-225 (6)	25.00	11.50
			Set, never hinged	52.50	

Intl. Exhibition of Decorative Modern Arts at Paris, 1925.

Philatelic Exhibition Issue
Souvenir Sheet

A32a

1925, May 2 ***Perf. 14x13½***

226 A32a Sheet of 4, A15 II 1,100. 1,100.
Never hinged 3,750.
a. Imperf. sheet 5,000. 1,750.
Never hinged 7,750.
b. 5fr carmine, perf. 125.00 140.00
Never hinged 225.00
c. 5fr carmine, imperf. 900.00
Never hinged 1,325.

These were on sale only at the Intl. Phil. Exhib., Paris, May, 1925. Size: 140x220mm.

Nos. 148-149, 152-153, 173, 175, 181, 183, 192, 195 Surcharged

1926-27

227 A22 25c on 30c lt bl .25 .50
a. Pair, one without surcharge 1,050. 925.00
228 A22 25c on 35c vio .25 .50
a. Double surcharge 525.00 350.00
b. Pair, one without surcharge 550.00 *925.00*
229 A20 50c on 60c lt vio ('27) 1.40 1.10
a. Pair, one without surcharge 525.00 *925.00*
230 A20 50c on 65c rose ('27) .75 .55
a. Inverted surcharge *1,225.* *1,400.*
b. Pair, one without surcharge 675.00 *925.00*
231 A23 50c on 75c blue 3.25 1.50
232 A20 50c on 80c ver ('27) 1.25 1.10
a. Pair, one without surcharge 475.00 *925.00*
233 A20 50c on 85c ver ('27) 2.25 1.00
234 A22 50c on 1.05fr ver 1.25 .75
a. Pair, one without surcharge 475.00 *925.00*
235 A23 50c on 1.25fr blue 2.75 2.25
a. Pair, one without surcharge 525.00 *925.00*
236 A20 55c on 60c lt vio 125.00 52.50
238 A22 90c on 1.05fr ver ('27) 2.25 2.75
a. Pair, one without surcharge *1,000.* 925.00
240 A22 1.10fr on 1.40fr cer 1.00 1.10
a. Pair, one without surcharge 575.00 *925.00*
Nos. 227-240 (12) 141.65 65.60
Set, never hinged 275.00

Issue dates: Nos. 229-230, 232-234, 1927.

No. 236 is known only precanceled. See second note after No. 132.

Nos. 229, 230, 234, 238 and 240 have three bars instead of two. The 55c surcharge has thinner, larger numerals and a rounded "c." Width, including bars, is 17mm, instead of 13mm.

The 55c was used only precanceled at the Magasins du Louvre department store in Paris, August 1926.

Strasbourg Exhibition Issue
Souvenir Sheet

A32b

1927, June 4

241 A32b Sheet of 2 1,000. 1,000.
Never hinged 2,300.
a. 5fr light ultra (A22) 250.00 250.00
Never hinged 400.00
b. 10fr carmine rose (A22) 250.00 250.00
Never hinged 400.00

Sold at the Strasbourg Philatelic Exhibition as souvenirs. Size: 111x140mm.

Marcelin Berthelot (1827-1907), Chemist and Statesman — A33

1927, Sept. 7

242 A33 90c dull rose 1.90 .60
Never hinged 3.00

For surcharge see No. C3.

Lafayette, Washington, S. S. Paris and Airplane "Spirit of St. Louis" — A34

1927, Sept. 15

243 A34 90c dull red 1.25 1.75
a. Value omitted 2,000. 1,725.
244 A34 1.50fr deep blue 4.00 2.50
a. Value omitted 1,450.
Set, never hinged 10.00

Visit of American Legionnaires to France, September, 1927. Exist imperf.

Joan of Arc — A35

1929, Mar.

245 A35 50c dull blue 1.90 .25
Never hinged 2.75
a. Booklet pane of 10 50.00
b. Imperf. 140.00

500th anniv. of the relief of Orleans by the French forces led by Joan of Arc.

No. 127 Overprinted in Blue

1929, May 18

246 A18 2fr org & pale bl 600.00 600.00
Never hinged 1,325.

Sold exclusively at the Intl. Phil. Exhib., Le Havre, May, 1929, for 7fr, which included a 5fr admission ticket.

Excellent counterfeits of No. 246 exist.

Reims Cathedral — A37

Die I, II, III

Die IV

Die I Die II Die III

Die I — The window of the 1st turret on the left is made of 2 lines. The horizontal line of the frame surrounding 3F is continuous.

Die II — Same as Die I but the line under 3F is not continuous.

Die III — Same as Die II but there is a deeply cut line separating 3 and F.

Die IV — Same as Die III but the window of the first turret on the left is made of three lines.

Mont-Saint-Michel — A38

Die I

Die II

Die I — The line at the top of the spire is broken.

Die II — The line is unbroken.

Port of La Rochelle A39

Dies I & II

Die III

Die I — The top of the "E" of "POSTES" has a serif. The oval of shading inside the "0" of "10 fr" and the outer oval are broken at their bases.

Die II — The same top has no serif. Interior and exterior of "0" broken as in Die I.

Die III — Top of "E" has no serif. Interior and exterior of "0" complete.

Pont du Gard, Nimes A40

Dies I & II

Die III

Die I — Shading of the first complete arch in the left middle tier is made of horizontal lines. Size 36x20¾mm. Perf. 13½.

Die II — Same, size 35½x21mm. Perf. 11.

Die III — Shading of same arch is made of three diagonal lines. Thin paper. Perf. 13.

1929-33 **Engr.** ***Perf. 11, 13, 13½***

247 A37 3fr dk gray ('30) (I) 62.50 2.40
Never hinged 115.00
247A A37 3fr dk gray ('30) (II) 125.00 3.50
Never hinged 200.00
247B A37 3fr dk gray ('30) (III) 375.00 24.00
Never hinged 600.00
248 A37 3fr bluish sl ('31) (IV) 60.00 2.40
Never hinged 115.00
249 A38 5fr brn ('30) (I) 24.00 4.25
Never hinged 40.00
250 A38 5fr brn ('31) (II) 21.00 .75
Never hinged 32.50
251 A39 10fr lt ultra (I) 95.00 15.00
Never hinged 160.00
251A A39 10fr ultra (II) 140.00 26.00
Never hinged 225.00
252 A39 10fr dk ultra ('31) (III) 70.00 6.50
Never hinged 140.00
253 A40 20fr red brn (I) 275.00 40.00
Never hinged 500.00
254 A40 20fr brt red brn ('30) (II) 1,000. 350.00
Never hinged 1,650.
254A A40 20fr org brn ('31) (III) 250.00 35.00
Never hinged 450.00
Nos. 247-254A (12) 2,498. 509.80

View of Algiers A41

1929, Jan. 1 **Typo.**

255 A41 50c blue & rose red 2.40 .50
Never hinged 5.50

Cent. of the 1st French settlement in Algeria.

Nos. 146 and 196 Overprinted

1930, Apr. 23 ***Perf. 14x13½***

256 A20 50c vermilion 3.00 3.25
257 A23 1.50fr blue 20.00 14.50
Set, never hinged 47.50

Intl. Labor Bureau, 48th Congress, Paris.

Colonial Exposition Issue

Fachi Woman — A42

French Colonials A43

1930-31 **Typo.** ***Perf. 14x13½***

258 A42 15c gray black 1.10 .30
259 A42 40c dark brown 2.40 .30
260 A42 65c dark red .65 .25
a. Booklet pane of 10 12.50
261 A42 1.50fr deep blue 9.00 .65

Perf. 13½

Photo.

262 A43 1.50fr dp blue ('31) 45.00 2.75
Nos. 258-262 (5) 58.15 4.25
Set, never hinged 125.00

No. 260 has two types: type 1 shows four short downward hairlines near top of head, type 2 has no lines. Booklet stamps are type 2.

Arc de Triomphe A44

1931 **Engr.** ***Perf. 13***

263 A44 2fr red brown 40.00 1.25
Never hinged 80.00

Peace with Olive Branch — A45

1932-39 **Typo.** ***Perf. 14x13½***

264 A45 30c dp green 1.00 .55
265 A45 40c brt violet .30 .30
266 A45 45c yellow brown 1.75 1.00
267 A45 50c rose red .25 .25
a. Imperf., pair 140.00
b. Booklet pane of 10 5.50
268 A45 55c dull vio ('37) .60 .25
269 A45 60c ocher ('37) .30 .25
270 A45 65c violet brown .50 .50
271 A45 65c brt ultra ('37) .25 .25
a. Booklet pane of 10 7.00
272 A45 75c olive green .25 .30
273 A45 80c orange ('38) .25 .25
274 A45 90c dk red 32.50 2.00
275 A45 90c brt green ('38) .25 .25
276 A45 90c ultra ('38) .90 .25
a. Booklet pane of 10 8.50
277 A45 1fr orange 3.25 .25
278 A45 1fr rose pink ('38) 3.25 .50
279 A45 1.25fr brown ol 75.00 4.75

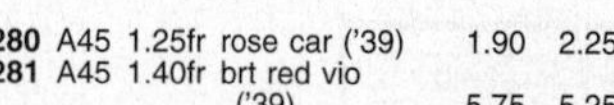

280 A45 1.25fr rose car ('39) 1.90 2.25
281 A45 1.40fr brt red vio ('39) 5.75 5.25
282 A45 1.50fr deep blue .30 .30
283 A45 1.75fr magenta 4.00 .50
Nos. 264-283 (20) 132.55 20.20
Set, never hinged 275.00

The 50c is found in 4 types, differing in the lines below belt and size of "c."

For surcharges and overprints see Nos. 298, 333, 401-403, 405-409, M7-M9, S1.

Le Puy-en-Velay — A46

1933 **Engr.** ***Perf. 13***

290 A46 90c rose 3.00 1.10
Never hinged 5.75

Aristide Briand A47

Paul Doumer A48

Victor Hugo — A49

1933, Dec. 11 **Typo.** ***Perf. 14x13½***

291 A47 30c blue green 17.00 8.00
292 A48 75c red violet 27.50 1.90
293 A49 1.25fr claret 6.00 2.25
Nos. 291-293 (3) 50.50 12.15
Set, never hinged 110.00

Dove and Olive Branch — A50

1934, Feb. 20

294 A50 1.50fr ultra 50.00 15.00
Never hinged 95.00

Joseph Marie Jacquard — A51

1934, Mar. 14 **Engr.** ***Perf. 14x13***

295 A51 40c blue 3.00 1.10
Never hinged 4.50

Jacquard (1752-1834), inventor of an improved loom for figured weaving.

Jacques Cartier A52

1934, July 18 ***Perf. 13***

296 A52 75c rose lilac 30.00 2.25
297 A52 1.50fr blue 50.00 4.25
Set, never hinged 210.00

Cartier's discovery of Canada, 400th anniv.

No. 279 Surcharged

1934, Nov. ***Perf. 14x13½***

298 A45 50c on 1.25fr brn ol 3.75 .65
Never hinged 7.00

Catalogue values for unused stamps in this section, from this point to the end of the section, are for Never Hinged items.

Breton River Scene A53

1935, Feb. **Engr.** ***Perf. 13***

299 A53 2fr blue green 70.00 1.00
Hinged 32.50

S. S. Normandie A54

1935, Apr.

300 A54 1.50fr dark blue 29.00 2.00
Hinged 14.00
a. 1.50fr pale blue ('36) 145.00 19.00
Hinged 55.00
b. 1.50fr blue green ('36) *30,000.* *12,500.*
Hinged *19,000.*
c. 1.50fr turquoise ('36) 400.00 40.00
Hinged 275.00

Maiden voyage of the transatlantic steamship, the "Normandie."

Benjamin Delessert A55

1935, May 20

301 A55 75c blue green 47.50 1.75
Hinged 17.50

Opening of the International Savings Bank Congress, May 20, 1935.

View of St. Trophime at Arles — A56

1935, May 3

302 A56 3.50fr dark brown 70.00 4.25
Hinged 27.50

Victor Hugo (1802-85) — A57

1935, May 30 ***Perf. 14x13***

303 A57 1.25fr magenta 8.25 2.00
Hinged 4.00

Cardinal Richelieu — A58

1935, June 12 ***Perf. 13***

304 A58 1.50fr deep rose 70.00 1.75
Hinged 20.00

Tercentenary of the founding of the French Academy by Cardinal Richelieu.

Jacques Callot — A59

1935, Nov. ***Perf. 14x13***

305 A59 75c red 19.00 .75
Hinged 10.00

300th anniv. of the death of Jacques Callot, engraver.

André Marie Ampère (1775-1836), Scientist, by Louis Boilly — A60

1936, Feb. 27 ***Perf. 13***

306 A60 75c brown 37.50 2.00
Hinged 17.50

Windmill at Fontvielle, Immortalized by Daudet — A61

1936, Apr. 27

307 A61 2fr ultra 5.75 .40
Hinged 3.00

Publication, in 1866, of Alphonse Daudet's "Lettres de mon Moulin," 75th anniv.

Pilâtre de Rozier and his Balloon A62

1936, June 4

308 A62 75c Prus blue 37.50 2.75
Hinged 19.00

150th anniversary of the death of Jean Francois Pilâtre de Rozier, balloonist.

Rouget de Lisle — A63

"La Marseillaise" — A64

1936, June 27

309 A63 20c Prus green 5.75 2.00
Hinged 3.25
310 A64 40c dark brown 11.50 3.25
Hinged 5.50

Cent. of the death of Claude Joseph Rouget de Lisle, composer of "La Marseillaise."

Canadian War Memorial at Vimy Ridge
A65

1936, July 26

311 A65 75c henna brown 25.00 2.00
Hinged 9.50
312 A65 1.50fr dull blue 32.50 9.50
Hinged 16.00

Unveiling of the Canadian War Memorial at Vimy Ridge, July 26, 1936.

A66

Jean Léon Jaurès
A67

1936, July 30

313 A66 40c red brown 5.75 1.40
Hinged 4.00
314 A67 1.50fr ultra 32.50 3.75
Hinged 13.00

Assassination of Jean Léon Jaurès (1859-1914), socialist and politician.

Herald — A68

Allegory of Exposition
A69

1936, Sept. 15 Typo. *Perf. 14x13½*

315 A68 20c brt violet 1.00 .50
Hinged .30
316 A68 30c Prus green 4.00 1.75
Hinged 2.40
317 A68 40c ultra 2.50 .50
Hinged 1.00
318 A68 50c red orange 2.25 .25
Hinged 1.00
319 A69 90c carmine 25.00 7.50
Hinged 11.00
320 A69 1.50fr ultra 67.50 4.00
Hinged 30.00
Nos. 315-320 (6) 102.25 14.50

Publicity for the 1937 Paris Exposition.

"Peace"
A70

1936, Oct. 1 Engr. *Perf. 13*

321 A70 1.50fr blue 27.50 4.00
Hinged 12.50

Skiing
A71

1937, Jan. 18

322 A71 1.50fr dark blue 14.00 1.75
Hinged 7.00

Intl. Ski Meet at Chamonix-Mont Blanc.

Pierre Corneille, Portrait by Charles Le Brun — A72

1937, Feb. 15

323 A72 75c brown carmine 3.75 1.40
Hinged 1.90

300th anniv. of the publication of "Le Cid."

Paris Exposition Issue

Exposition Allegory
A73

1937, Mar. 15

324 A73 1.50fr turq blue 4.00 1.25
Hinged 2.25

Jean Mermoz (1901-36), Aviator
A74

Memorial to Mermoz — A75

1937, Apr. 22

325 A74 30c dk slate green 1.00 .55
Hinged .50
326 A75 3fr dark violet 13.50 3.75
Hinged 6.25
a. 3fr violet 15.00 4.50
Hinged 6.75

Electric Train
A76

Streamlined Locomotive
A77

1937, May 31

327 A76 30c dk green 1.40 1.75
Hinged 1.00
328 A77 1.50fr dk ultra 15.00 8.25
Hinged 7.25

13th International Railroad Congress.

Intl. Philatelic Exhibition Issue
Souvenir Sheet

Ceres Type A1 of 1849-50 — A77a

1937, June 18 Typo. *Perf. 14x13½*

329 A77a Sheet of 4 700.00 300.00
Lightly hinged in margins 360.00
a. 5c ultra & dark brown 90.00 47.50
b. 15c red & rose red 90.00 47.50
c. 30c ultra & rose red 90.00 47.50
d. 50c red & dark brown 90.00 47.50
e. Sheet of 4, imperf 3,000.
Lightly hinged in margins 2,350.

Issued in sheets measuring 150x220mm.

The sheets were sold only at the exhibition in Paris, a ticket of admission being required for each sheet purchased.

René Descartes, by Frans Hals — A78

1937, June Engr. *Perf. 13*

Inscribed "Discours sur la Méthode"

330 A78 90c copper red 3.25 1.40
Hinged 1.90

Inscribed "Discours de la Méthode"

331 A78 90c copper red 11.00 1.75
Hinged 5.50

3rd centenary of the publication of "Discours de la Méthode" by René Descartes.

France Congratulating USA — A79

1937, Sept. 17

332 A79 1.75fr ultra 4.50 2.00
Hinged 2.50

150th anniv. of the US Constitution.

No. 277 Surcharged in Red

1937, Oct. *Perf. 14x13½*

333 A45 80c on 1fr orange 1.90 .85
Hinged .80
a. Inverted surcharge *1,225.*
Hinged *825.00*

Mountain Road at Iseran
A80

1937, Oct. 4 Engr. *Perf. 13*

334 A80 90c dark green 3.75 .30
Hinged 1.90

Issued in commemoration of the opening of the mountain road at Iseran, Savoy.

Ceres — A81

1938-40 Typo. *Perf. 14x13½*

335 A81 1.75fr dk ultra 1.40 .55
Hinged .55
336 A81 2fr car rose ('39) .30 .30
Hinged .25
337 A81 2.25fr ultra ('39) 15.00 1.10
Hinged 8.00
338 A81 2.50fr green ('39) 3.00 .50
Hinged 1.25
339 A81 2.50fr vio blue ('40) 1.25 .75
Hinged .65
340 A81 3fr rose lilac ('39) 1.25 .50
Hinged .55
Nos. 335-340 (6) 22.20 3.70

For surcharges see Nos. 397-399.

Léon Gambetta (1838-82), Lawyer and Statesman — A82

1938, Apr. 2 Engr. *Perf. 13*

341 A82 55c dark violet .55 .40
Hinged .35

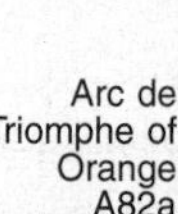

Arc de Triomphe of Orange A82a

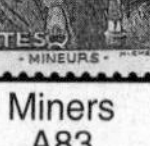

Miners A83

Keep and Gate of Vincennes A86

Palace of the Popes, Avignon A84

Medieval Walls of Carcassonne — A85

Port of St. Malo — A87

1938

342 A82a 2fr brown black 1.75 1.25
Hinged .55
343 A83 2.15fr violet brn 9.50 1.00
Hinged 4.75
344 A84 3fr car brown 26.50 5.00
Hinged 12.50
345 A85 5fr deep ultra 1.50 .40
Hinged .75
346 A86 10fr brown, *blue* 3.25 1.90
Hinged 1.50
347 A87 20fr dk blue grn 80.00 19.00
Hinged 37.50
Nos. 342-347 (6) 122.50 28.55

For surcharges see Nos. 410-413.

Clément Ader, Air Pioneer A88

1938, June 16

348 A88 50fr ultra (thin paper) 150.00 65.00
Hinged 95.00
a. 50fr dark ultra (thick paper) 175.00 77.50
Hinged 100.00

For surcharge, see No. 414.

Soccer Players A89

1938, June 1

349 A89 1.75fr dark ultra 29.00 13.50
Hinged 13.50

World Cup Soccer Championship.

Costume of Champagne Region — A90

1938, June 13

350 A90 1.75fr dark ultra 7.50 4.50
Hinged 3.75

Tercentenary of the birth of Dom Pierre Pérignon, discoverer of the champagne process.

Jean de La Fontaine — A91

1938, July 8

351 A91 55c dk blue green 1.00 .80
Hinged .65

Jean de La Fontaine (1621-1695) the fabulist.

Seal of Friendship and Peace, Victoria Tower and Arc de Triomphe A92

1938, July 19

352 A92 1.75fr ultra 1.25 .80
Hinged .65

Visit of King George VI and Queen Elizabeth of Great Britain to France.

Mercury — A93

1938-42 Typo. *Perf. 14x13½*

353 A93 1c dark brn ('39) .25 .25
Hinged .25
354 A93 2c slate grn ('39) .25 .25
Hinged .25
355 A93 5c rose .25 .25
Hinged .25
356 A93 10c ultra .25 .25
Hinged .25
357 A93 15c red orange .25 .25
Hinged .25
358 A93 15c org brn ('39) 1.00 .50
Hinged .55
359 A93 20c red violet .25 .25
Hinged .25
360 A93 25c blue green .25 .25
Hinged .25
361 A93 30c rose red ('39) .25 .25
Hinged .25
362 A93 40c dk violet ('39) .25 .25
Hinged .25
363 A93 45c lt green ('39) .80 .50
Hinged .50
364 A93 50c deep blue ('39) 4.00 .40
Hinged 2.25
365 A93 50c dk green ('41) .55 .35
Hinged .30
366 A93 50c grnsh blue ('42) .25 .25
Hinged .25
367 A93 60c red org ('39) .25 .25
Hinged .25
368 A93 70c magenta ('39) .25 .25
Hinged .25
369 A93 75c dk org brn ('39) 7.50 2.50
Hinged 3.75
Nos. 353-369 (17) 16.85 7.25

No. 366 exists imperforate. See Nos. 455-458. For overprints and surcharge see Nos. 404, 499-502.

Self-portrait — A95

1939, Mar. 15 Engr. *Perf. 13*

370 A95 2.25fr Prussian blue 8.25 3.50
Hinged 3.50

Paul Cézanne (1839-1906), painter.

Georges Clemenceau and Battleship Clemenceau — A96

1939, Apr. 18

371 A96 90c ultra 1.00 .75
Hinged .50

Laying of the keel of the warship "Clemenceau," Jan. 17, 1939.

Statue of Liberty, French Pavilion, Trylon and Perisphere A97

1939-40

372 A97 2.25fr ultra 17.00 6.50
Hinged 8.00
373 A97 2.50fr ultra ('40) 22.50 9.50
Hinged 8.50

New York World's Fair.

A98

Design: Joseph Nicéphore Niepce and Louis Jacques Mandé Daguerre.

1939, Apr. 24

374 A98 2.25fr dark blue 16.00 7.00
Hinged 7.00

Centenary of photography.

Iris — A99

1939-44 Typo. *Perf. 14x13½*

375 A99 80c red brown ('40) .25 .25
Hinged .25
376 A99 80c yellow grn ('44) .25 .25
Hinged .25
377 A99 1fr green 1.00 .25
Hinged .55
378 A99 1fr crimson ('40) .40 .35
Hinged .25
a. Booklet pane of 10 7.50
379 A99 1fr grnsh blue ('44) .25 .25
Hinged .25
380 A99 1.20fr violet ('44) .25 .25
Hinged .25
381 A99 1.30fr ultra ('40) .25 .25
Hinged .25
382 A99 1.50fr red org ('41) .25 .25
Hinged .25
383 A99 1.50fr henna brn ('44) .25 .25
Hinged .25
384 A99 2fr violet brn ('44) .25 .25
Hinged .25
385 A99 2.40fr car rose ('44) .25 .25
Hinged .25
386 A99 3fr orange ('44) .25 .25
Hinged .25
387 A99 4fr ultra ('44) .25 .25
Hinged .25
Nos. 375-387 (13) 4.15 3.35

Pumping Station at Marly A100

1939 Engr. *Perf. 13*

388 A100 2.25fr brt ultra 25.00 5.00
Hinged 11.00

France's participation in the International Water Exposition at Liège.

St. Gregory of Tours — A101

1939, June 10

389 A101 90c red .90 .55
Hinged .50

14th centenary of the birth of St. Gregory of Tours, historian and bishop.

"The Oath of the Tennis Court" by Jacques David A102

1939, June 20

390 A102 90c deep slate green 3.50 1.90
Hinged 1.90

150th anniversary of French Revolution.

Cathedral of Strasbourg — A103

1939, June 23

391 A103 70c brown carmine 1.50 1.00
Hinged .75

500th anniv. of the completion of Strasbourg Cathedral.

Porte Chaussée, Verdun A104

1939, June 23

392 A104 90c black brown 1.00 .80
Hinged .80

23rd anniv. of the Battle of Verdun.

View of Pau
A105

1939, Aug. 25
393 A105 90c brt rose, *gray bl* 1.25 1.25
Hinged .80

Maid of Languedoc
A106

Bridge at Lyons
A107

1939
394 A106 70c black, *blue* .50 .40
Hinged .40
395 A107 90c dull brown vio 1.00 *1.25*
Hinged .90

Imperforates
Nearly all French stamps issued from 1940 onward exist imperforate. Officially 20 sheets, ranging from 25 to 100 subjects, were left imperforate.

Georges Guynemer (1894-1917), World War I Ace — A108

1940, Nov. 7
396 A108 50fr ultra 16.00 9.00
Hinged 8.00

Stamps of 1938-39 Surcharged in Carmine

1940-41 ***Perf. 14x13½***
397 A81 1fr on 1.75fr dk ultra .30 .30
Hinged .25
398 A81 1fr on 2.25fr ultra ('41) .30 .30
Hinged .25
399 A81 1fr on 2.50fr grn ('41) 1.40 1.40
Hinged .65
Nos. 397-399 (3) 2.00 2.00

Stamps of 1932-39 Surcharged in Carmine, Red (#408) or Black (#407)

1940-41 ***Perf. 13, 14x13½***
400 A22 30c on 35c grn ('41) .30 .30
Hinged .25
401 A45 50c on 55c dl vio ('41) .30 .30
Hinged .25
a. Inverted surcharge 1,000.
402 A45 50c on 65c brt ultra ('41) .30 .30
Hinged .25
403 A45 50c on 75c ol grn ('41) .30 .30
Hinged .25
404 A93 50c on 75c dk org brn ('41) .30 .30
Hinged .25
405 A45 50c on 80c org ('41) .30 .30
Hinged .25
406 A45 50c on 90c ultra ('41) .30 .30
Hinged .25
a. Inverted surcharge 550.00
b. "05" instead of "50" 9,000. 6,400.
407 A45 1fr on 1.25fr rose car (Bk) ('41) .30 .30
Hinged .25
408 A45 1fr on 1.40fr brt red vio (R) ('41) .40 .40
Hinged .25
a. Double surcharge 1,600.
409 A45 1fr on 1.50fr dk bl ('41) 1.40 1.40
Hinged .25
410 A83 1fr on 2.15fr vio brn .40 .40
Hinged .25
411 A85 2.50fr on 5fr dp ultra ('41) .40 .40
Hinged .25
a. Double surcharge 350.00 190.00
412 A86 5fr on 10fr brn, *bl* ('41) 1.90 1.90
Hinged 1.00
413 A87 10fr on 20fr dk bl grn ('41) 1.60 1.60
Hinged 1.00
414 A88 20fr on 50fr dk ultra (#348a) ('41) 70.00 37.50
Hinged 29.00
a. 20fr on 50fr ultra, thin paper (#348) 75.00 50.00
Nos. 400-414 (15) 78.50 46.00

Issued: No. 410, 1940; others, 1941

Marshal Pétain — A109

1941 ***Perf. 13***
415 A109 40c red brown .40 .25
416 A109 80c turq blue .45 .40
417 A109 1fr red .25 .25
418 A109 2.50fr deep ultra 1.40 1.10
Nos. 415-418 (4) 2.50 2.00

For No. 417 with surcharge, see No. B111.

Frédéric Mistral — A110

1941, Feb. 20 ***Perf. 14x13***
419 A110 1fr brown lake .25 .25

Issued in honor of Frédéric Mistral, poet and Nobel prize winner for literature in 1904.

Beaune Hospital
A111

View of Angers
A112

Ramparts of St. Louis, Aiguesmortes — A113

1941
420 A111 5fr brown black .35 .25
421 A112 10fr dark violet .60 .45
422 A113 20fr brown black 1.10 .80
Nos. 420-422 (3) 2.05 1.50

Inscribed "Postes Francaises"

1942
Imprint: "FELTESSE" at right
423 A111 15fr brown lake .60 .40

A114

A115

Marshal Pétain — A116

1941-42 **Typo.** ***Perf. 14x13½***
427 A114 20c lilac ('42) .25 .25
428 A114 30c rose red .25 .25
429 A114 40c ultra .25 .25
431 A115 50c dp green .25 .25
432 A115 60c violet ('42) .25 .25
433 A115 70c saph ('42) .25 .25
434 A115 70c orange ('42) .25 .25
435 A115 80c brown .25 .25
436 A115 80c emerald ('42) .25 .25
437 A115 1fr rose red .25 .25
438 A115 1.20fr red brn ('42) .25 .25
439 A116 1.50fr rose .25 .25
440 A116 1.50fr dl red brn ('42) .25 .25
a. Booklet pane of 10 2.75
441 A116 2fr blue grn ('42) .25 .25
443 A116 2.40fr rose red ('42) .25 .25
444 A116 2.50fr ultra .25 .55
445 A116 3fr orange .25 .25
446 A115 4fr ultra ('42) .25 .25
447 A115 4.50fr dk green ('42) .25 .25
Nos. 427-447 (19) 4.75 5.05

Nos. 431 to 438 measure 16½x20½mm.

No. 440 was forged by the French Underground ("Defense de la France") and used to frank clandestine journals, etc., from Feb. to June, 1944. The forgeries were ungummed, both perf. 11½ and imperf., with a back handstamp covering six stamps and including the words: "Atelier des Faux."

For surcharge see No. B134.

A117

A118

1942 **Engr.** ***Perf. 14x13***
448 A115 4fr brt ultra .25 .25
449 A115 4.50fr dark green .25 .25
450 A117 5fr Prus green .25 .25

Perf. 13
451 A118 50fr black 3.00 3.00
Nos. 448-451 (4) 3.75 3.75

Nos. 448 and 449 measure 18x21½mm.

Jules Massenet — A119

1942, June 22 ***Perf. 14x13***
452 A119 4fr Prus green .25 .25

Jules Massenet (1842-1912), composer.

Stendhal (Marie Henri Beyle) — A120

1942, Sept. 14 ***Perf. 13***
453 A120 4fr blk brn & org red .40 .40

Stendhal (1783-1842), writer.

André Blondel — A121

1942, Sept. 14
454 A121 4fr dull blue .40 .40

André Eugène Blondel (1863-1938), physicist.

Mercury Type of 1938-42

Inscribed "Postes Françaises"

1942 ***Perf. 14x13½***

455 A93 10c ultra	.25	.25
456 A93 30c rose red	.25	.25
457 A93 40c dark violet	.25	.25
458 A93 50c turq blue	.25	.25
Nos. 455-458 (4)	1.00	1.00

Town-Hall Belfry, Arras — A122

1942, Dec. 8 **Engr.** ***Perf. 13***

459 A122 10fr green .25 .25

Coats of Arms

Lyon — A123

1943 **Typo.** ***Perf. 14x13½***

460 A123 5fr shown	.30	.30
461 A123 10fr Brittany	.40	.40
462 A123 15fr Provence	1.75	1.10
463 A123 20fr Ile de France	1.40	1.20
Nos. 460-463 (4)	3.85	3.00

Antoine Lavoisier (1743-94), French Scientist — A127

1943, July 5 **Engr.** ***Perf. 14x13***

464 A127 4fr ultra .25 .25

Lake Lerie and Meije Dauphiné Alps A128

1943, July 5 ***Perf. 13***

465 A128 20fr dull gray grn .75 .75

Nicolas Rolin, Guigone de Salins and Hospital of Beaune A129

1943, July 21

466 A129 4fr blue .25 .25

500th anniv. of the founding of the Hospital of Beaune.

Arms of Flanders — A130

1944, Mar. 27 **Typo.** ***Perf. 14x13½***

467 A130 5fr shown	.25	.25
468 A130 10fr Languedoc	.25	.25
469 A130 15fr Orleans	.60	.55
470 A130 20fr Normandy	1.00	.85
Nos. 467-470 (4)	2.10	1.90

Edouard Branly — A134

1944, Feb. 21 **Engr.** ***Perf. 14x13***

471 A134 4fr ultra .25 .25

Cent. of the birth of Edouard Branly, electrical inventor.

Early Postal Car A135

1944, June 10 ***Perf. 13***

472 A135 1.50fr dark blue green .55 .45

Cent. of France's traveling postal service.

Chateau de Chenonceaux — A136

1944, June 10

473 A136 15fr lilac brown	.60	.45
a. 15fr black brown	10.50	3.00
b. 15fr black	100.00	55.00

See No. 496.

Claude Chappe — A137

1944, Aug. 14 ***Perf. 14x13***

474 A137 4fr dark ultra .25 .25

150th anniv. of the invention of an optical telegraph by Claude Chappe (1763-1805).

Arc de Triomphe — OS2

Unwmk.

1944, Oct. 9 **Litho.** ***Perf. 11***

475	OS2	5c brt red violet	.25	.25
476	OS2	10c lt gray	.25	.25
476A	OS2	25c brown	.25	.25
476B	OS2	50c olive bis	.25	.25
476C	OS2	1fr pck green	.25	.25
476D	OS2	1.50fr rose pink	.25	.25
476E	OS2	2.50fr purple	.25	.25
476F	OS2	4fr ultra	.25	.25
476G	OS2	5fr black	.25	.25
476H	OS2	10fr yellow org	27.50	21.00
		Nos. 475-476H (10)	29.75	23.25

Nos 475-476H were printed by the U.S. Bureau of Engaving and Printing and were intended to be used by an Allied Military government, which was expected to administer the liberated areas of France. Instead, the Allies recognized the authority of Gen. de Gaulle's Provisional Government over these territories, and these stamps were transferred to the Free French in July, 1944. They were put on sale in liberated areas as the Allied armies advanced, and on Oct. 9, they were officially issued in Paris.

See Nos. 523A-523J.

Gallic Cock A138

Marianne A139

1944 **Litho.** ***Perf. 12***

477	A138	10c yellow grn	.25	.25
478	A138	30c dk rose vio	.30	.35
479	A138	40c blue	.25	.25
480	A138	50c dark red	.25	.25
481	A139	60c olive brown	.25	.25
482	A139	70c rose lilac	.25	.25
483	A139	80c yellow grn	.90	.90
484	A139	1fr violet	.25	.25
485	A139	1.20fr dp carmine	.25	.25
486	A139	1.50fr deep blue	.25	.25
487	A138	2fr indigo	.25	.25
488	A139	2.40fr red orange	1.10	1.10
489	A139	3fr dp blue grn	.25	.25
490	A139	4fr grnsh blue	.25	.25
491	A139	4.50fr black	.25	.25
492	A139	5fr violet blue	3.75	3.75
493	A138	10fr violet	4.50	4.25
494	A138	15fr olive brown	4.25	4.25
495	A138	20fr dk slate grn	3.75	3.75
		Nos. 477-495 (19)	21.55	21.35

Nos. 477-495 were issued first in Corsica after the Allied landing, and released in Paris Nov. 15, 1944.

Chateau Type Inscribed "RF"

1944, Oct. 30 **Engr.** ***Perf. 13***

496 A136 25fr black .75 .55

Thomas Robert Bugeaud — A141

1944, Nov. 20

497 A141 4fr myrtle green .25 .25

Battle of Isly, Aug. 14th, 1844.

Church of St. Denis A142

1944, Nov. 20

498 A142 2.40fr brown carmine .30 .30

800th anniv. of the Church of St. Denis.

Type of 1938-42, Overprinted in Black

Inscribed "Postes Francaises"

1944 ***Perf. 14x13½***

499 A93 10c ultra	.25	.25
500 A93 30c rose red	.25	.25
501 A93 40c dark violet	.25	.25
502 A93 50c grnsh blue	.25	.25
Nos. 499-502 (4)	1.00	1.00

The overprint "RF" in various forms, with or without Lorraine Cross, was also applied to stamps of the French State at Lyon and fourteen other cities.

French Forces of the Interior and Symbol of Liberation — A143

1945, Jan.

503 A143 4fr dark ultra .30 .30

Issued to commemorate the Liberation.

Stamps of the above design, and of one incorporating "FRANCE" in the top panel, were printed by photo. in England during WW II upon order of the Free French Government. They were not issued. There are 3 values in each design; 25c green, 1fr red, 2.50fr blue. Value: set, above design, $100; set inscribed "FRANCE," $600.

Marianne — A144

Perf. 11½x12½

1944-45 **Engr.** **Unwmk.**

504	A144	10c ultra	.25	.25
505	A144	30c bister	.25	.25
506	A144	40c indigo	.25	.25
507	A144	50c red orange	.25	.25
508	A144	60c chalky blue	.25	.25
509	A144	70c sepia	.25	.25
510	A144	80c deep green	.25	.25
511	A144	1fr lilac	.25	.25
512	A144	1.20fr dk ol grn	.25	.25
513	A144	1.50fr rose ('44)	.25	.25
514	A144	2fr dk brown	.25	.25
515	A144	2.40fr red	.25	.25
516	A144	3fr brt ol grn	.25	.25
517	A144	4fr brt ultra	.25	.25
518	A144	4.50fr slate gray	.25	.25
519	A144	5fr brt orange	.25	.25
520	A144	10fr yellow grn	.25	.25
521	A144	15fr lake	.25	.25
522	A144	20fr brown org	1.10	1.10
523	A144	50fr deep purple	2.90	2.40
		Nos. 504-523 (20)	8.50	8.00

The 2.40fr exists imperf. in a miniature sheet of 4 which was not issued. Value: never hinged $6,500; unused $4,500.

Compare with type A1759. See Nos. 4905, 4909.

Arc de Triomphe Type of 1944

1945, Feb. 12 **Litho.** ***Perf. 11***

Denominations in Black

523A	OS2	30c orange	.25	.25
523B	OS2	40c pale gray	.25	.25
523C	OS2	50c olive bis	.25	.25
523D	OS2	60c violet	.25	.25
523E	OS2	80c emerald	.25	.25
523F	OS2	1.20fr brown	.25	.25
523G	OS2	1.50fr vermilion	.25	.25
523H	OS2	2fr yellow	.25	.25
523I	OS2	2.40fr dark rose	.25	.25
523J	OS2	3fr brt red violet	.25	.25
		Nos. 523A-523J (10)	2.50	2.50

Coat of Arms A145

Ceres A146

Marianne — A147

1945-47 Typo. *Perf. 14x13½*

No.	Type	Value	Color	Unused	Used
524	A145	10c	brown black	.25	.25
525	A145	30c	dk blue grn	.25	.25
526	A145	40c	lilac rose	.25	.25
527	A145	50c	violet blue	.25	.25
528	A146	60c	brt ultra	.25	.25
530	A146	80c	brt green	.25	.25
531	A146	90c	dull grn ('46)	.65	.55
532	A146	1fr	rose red	.25	.25
533	A146	1.20fr	brown black	.25	.25
534	A146	1.50fr	rose lilac	.25	.25
535	A147	1.50fr	rose pink	.25	.25
536	A147	2fr	myrtle green	.25	.25
536A	A146	2fr	lt bl grn ('46)	.25	.25
537	A147	2.40fr	scarlet	.30	.30
538	A146	2.50fr	brown ('46)	.25	.25
539	A147	3fr	sepia	.25	.25
540	A147	3fr	dp rose ('46)	.25	.25
541	A147	4fr	ultra	.25	.25
541A	A147	4fr	violet ('46)	.25	.25
541B	A147	4.50fr	ultra ('47)	.25	.25
542	A147	5fr	lt green	.25	.25
542A	A147	5fr	rose pink ('47)	.25	.25
543	A147	6fr	brt ultra	.35	.25
544	A147	6fr	crim rose ('46)	1.60	.90
545	A147	10fr	red orange	.45	.30
546	A147	10fr	ultra ('46)	1.20	.75
547	A147	15fr	brt red vio	3.00	1.60
			Nos. 524-547 (27)	12.55	9.65

No. 531 is known only precanceled. See second note after No. 132.

Due to a reduction of the domestic postage rate, No. 542A was sold for 4.50fr.

Compare with type A1814. See Nos. 576-580, 594-602, 614, 615, 650-654, 4906, 4908. For surcharges see Nos. 589, 610, 706, Reunion 270-276, 278, 285, 290-291, 293, 295.

1945-46 Engr. *Perf. 14x13*

No.	Type	Value	Color	Unused	Used
548	A147	4fr	dark blue	.25	.25
549	A147	10fr	dp blue ('46)	1.10	.55
550	A147	15fr	brt red vio ('46)	6.75	1.75
551	A147	20fr	blue grn ('46)	1.00	.55
552	A147	25fr	red ('46)	6.75	1.50
			Nos. 548-552 (5)	15.85	4.60

Nos. 548-552 have "GANDON" at lower right in design, and no inscription below design.

Marianne — A148

1945 Engr. *Perf. 13*

No.	Type	Value	Color	Unused	Used
553	A148	20fr	dark green	1.00	.90
554	A148	25fr	violet	1.10	1.10
555	A148	50fr	red brown	1.50	1.50
556	A148	100fr	brt rose car	10.00	5.50
			Nos. 553-556 (4)	13.60	9.00

CFA

French stamps inscribed or surcharged "CFA" and new value are listed under Réunion at the end of the French listings.

Arms of Metz
A149

Arms of Strasbourg
A150

1945, Mar. 3 *Perf. 14x13*

No.	Type	Value	Color	Unused	Used
557	A149	2.40fr	dull blue	.25	.25
558	A150	4fr	black brown	.25	.25

Liberation of Metz and Strasbourg.

A151

Design: Costumes of Alsace and Lorraine and Cathedrals of Strasbourg and Metz.

1945, May 16 *Perf. 13*

No.	Type	Value	Color	Unused	Used
559	A151	4fr	henna brown	.25	.25

Liberation of Alsace and Lorraine. See No. 4907.

World Map Showing French Possessions — A152

1945, Sept. 17

No.	Type	Value	Color	Unused	Used
560	A152	2fr	Prussian blue	.25	.25

No. B193 Surcharged in Black

1946 *Perf. 14x13½*

No.	Type	Value	Color	Unused	Used
561	SP147	3fr on 2fr+1fr	red org	.25	.25

Arms of Corsica — A153

1946 Unwmk. Typo. *Perf. 14x13½*

No.	Type	Value	Design	Unused	Used
562	A153	10c	shown	.25	.25
563	A153	30c	Alsace	.25	.25
564	A153	50c	Lorraine	.25	.25
565	A153	60c	County of Nice	.25	.25
			Nos. 562-565 (4)	1.00	1.00

For surcharges see Reunion Nos. 268-269.

Reaching for "Peace" — A157

Holding the Dove of Peace — A158

1946, July 29 Engr. *Perf. 13*

No.	Type	Value	Color	Unused	Used
566	A157	3fr	Prussian green	.25	.25
567	A158	10fr	dark blue	.25	.25

Peace Conference of Paris, 1946.

Vézelay
A159

Luxembourg Palace — A160

Rocamadour
A161

Pointe du Raz, Finistère
A162

1946 Unwmk. *Perf. 13*

No.	Type	Value	Color	Unused	Used
568	A159	5fr	rose violet	.25	.25
569	A160	10fr	dark blue	.25	.25
570	A161	15fr	dk violet brn	3.50	.55
571	A162	20fr	slate gray	1.00	.25
			Nos. 568-571 (4)	5.00	1.30

See Nos. 591-592. For surcharges see Reunion Nos. 277, 279.

Globe and Wreath — A163

1946, Nov.

No.	Type	Value	Color	Unused	Used
572	A163	10fr	dark blue	.25	.25

Gen. conf. of UNESCO, Paris, 1946.

Cannes
A164

Stanislas Square, Nancy
A165

1946-48 Engr. *Perf. 13*

No.	Type	Value	Color	Unused	Used
573	A164	6fr	rose red	1.10	.40
574	A165	25fr	black brown	3.00	.25
575	A165	25fr	dark blue ('48)	10.00	.90
			Nos. 573-575 (3)	14.10	1.55

For surcharges see Reunion Nos. 280-281.

Ceres & Marianne Types of 1945

1947 Unwmk. Typo. *Perf. 14x13½*

No.	Type	Value	Color	Unused	Used
576	A146	1.30fr	dull blue	.25	.25
577	A147	3fr	green	1.50	.25
578	A147	3.50fr	brown red	.60	.30
579	A147	5fr	blue	.25	.25
580	A147	6fr	carmine	.25	.25
			Nos. 576-580 (5)	2.85	1.30

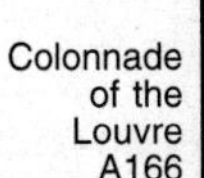

Colonnade of the Louvre
A166

La Conciergerie, Paris Prison — A167

La Cité, Oldest Section of Paris
A168

Place de la Concorde
A169

1947, May 7 Engr. *Perf. 13*

No.	Type	Value	Color	Unused	Used
581	A166	3.50fr	chocolate	.30	.30
582	A167	4.50fr	dk slate gray	.30	.30
583	A168	6fr	red	.85	.85
584	A169	10fr	bright ultra	.85	.85
			Nos. 581-584 (4)	2.30	2.30

12th UPU Cong., Paris, May 7-July 7. See No. 5035a.

Auguste Pavie — A170

1947, May 30

No.	Type	Value	Color	Unused	Used
585	A170	4.50fr	sepia	.30	.25

Cent. of the birth of Auguste Pavie, French pioneer in Laos.

Francois Fénelon — A171

1947, July 12

No.	Type	Value	Color	Unused	Used
586	A171	4.50fr	chocolate	.30	.25

Issued to honor Francois de Salignac de la Mothe-Fénelon, prelate and writer.

Fleur-de-Lis and Double Carrick Bend — A172

1947, Aug. 2 Unwmk.

No.	Type	Value	Color	Unused	Used
587	A172	5fr	brown	.30	.25

6th World Boy Scout Jamboree held at Moisson, Aug. 9th-18th, 1947.

Captured Patriot — A173

1947, Nov. 10 Engr. *Perf. 13*

No.	Type	Value	Color	Unused	Used
588	A173	5fr	sepia	.40	.35

No. 576 Surcharged in Carmine

1947, Nov. Typo. *Perf. 14x13½*
589 A146 1fr on 1.30fr dull blue .25 .25

View of Conques — A174

1947, Dec. 18 Engr. *Perf. 13*
590 A174 15fr henna brown 3.50 .70

For surcharge see Reunion No. 282.

Types of 1946-47

1948 Re-engraved
591 A160 12fr rose carmine 2.50 .45
592 A160 15fr bright red .60 .40
593 A174 18fr dark blue 3.50 .40
Nos. 591-593 (3) 6.60 1.25

"FRANCE" substituted for inscriptions "RF" and "REPUBLIQUE FRANCAISE."

Marianne Type of 1945

1948-49 Typo. *Perf. 14x13½*
594 A147 2.50fr brown 2.75 1.25
595 A147 3fr lilac rose .25 .25
596 A147 4fr lt blue grn .25 .25
597 A147 4fr brown org 2.50 .90
598 A147 5fr lt blue grn .60 .25
599 A147 8fr blue .30 .25
600 A147 10fr brt violet .25 .25
601 A147 12fr ultra ('49) 2.50 .25
602 A147 15fr crim rose ('49) .85 .25
a. Booklet pane of 10 150.00
Nos. 594-602 (9) 10.25 3.90

No. 594 known only precanceled. See second note after No. 132.

François René de Chateaubriand — A175

1948, July 3 Engr. *Perf. 13*
603 A175 18fr dark blue .30 .25

Vicomte de Chateaubriand (1768-1848).

Philippe François M. de Hautecloque (Gen. Jacques Leclerc) — A176

1948, July 3
604 A176 6fr gray black .30 .25

See Nos. 692-692A.

Chaillot Palace A177

A178

1948, Sept. 21
605 A177 12fr carmine rose .35 .30
606 A178 18fr indigo .35 .30

Meeting of the UN General Assembly, Paris, 1948.

Genissiat Dam A179

1948, Sept. 21
607 A179 12fr carmine rose .85 .75

Paul Langevin — A180

1948, Nov. 17 *Perf. 14x13*
608 A180 5fr shown .50 .25
609 A180 8fr Jean Perrin .50 .25

Placing of the ashes of physicists Langevin (1872-1946) and Perrin (1870-1942) in the Pantheon.

No. 580 Surcharged with New Value and Bars in Black

1949, Jan. *Perf. 14x13½*
610 A147 5fr on 6fr carmine .25 .25

Arctic Scene — A181

1949, May 2 *Perf. 13*
611 A181 15fr indigo .30 .25

French polar explorations.

Types of 1849 and 1945

1949, May 9 Engr. *Imperf.*
612 A1 15fr red 3.00 3.00
613 A1 25fr deep blue 3.00 3.00

Perf. 14x13
614 A147 15fr red 3.00 3.00
615 A147 25fr deep blue 3.00 3.00
a. Strip of 4, #612-615 + label 14.00 12.00
Nos. 612-615 (4) 12.00 12.00

Cent. of the 1st French postage stamps.

Arms of Burgundy — A182

Arms: 50c, Guyenne (Aquitania). 1fr, Savoy. 2fr, Auvergne. 4fr, Anjou.

1949, May 11 Typo. *Perf. 14x13½*
616 A182 10c blue, red & yel .25 .25
617 A182 50c blue, red & yel .25 .25
618 A182 1fr brown & red .40 .25
619 A182 2fr green, yel & red .40 .25
620 A182 4fr blue, red & yel .30 .25
Nos. 616-620 (5) 1.60 1.25

See Nos. 659-663, 694-699, 733-739, 782-785. For surcharges see Reunion Nos. 283-284, 288-289, 297, 301, 305, 311.

Collegiate Church of St. Barnard and Dauphiné Arms A183

1949, May 14 Engr. *Perf. 13*
621 A183 12fr red brown .30 .25

600th anniv. of France's acquisition of the Dauphiné region.

US and French Flags, Plane and Steamship A184

1949, May 14
622 A184 25fr blue & carmine .45 .35

Franco-American friendship.

Cloister of St. Wandrille Abbey A185

1949, May 18
623 A185 25fr deep ultra .30 .25

See No. 649. For surcharge see Reunion No. 287.

Type of 1849 Inscribed "1849-1949" in Lower Margin

1949, June 1
624 A1 10fr brown orange 55.00 40.00
a. Sheet of 10 700.00 450.00

Cent. of the 1st French postage stamp.

No. 624 has wide margins, 40x52mm from perforation to perforation. Sold for 110fr, which included cost of admission to the Centenary Intl. Exhib., Paris, June 1949.

Claude Chappe — A186

15fr, François Arago & André M. Ampère. 25fr, Emile Baudot. 50fr, Gen. Gustave A. Ferrié.

Inscribed: "C.I.T.T. PARIS 1949"

1949, June 13 Unwmk. *Perf. 13*
625 A186 10fr vermilion .75 .70
626 A186 15fr sepia .75 .70
627 A186 25fr deep claret 1.90 1.90
628 A186 50fr deep blue 3.75 2.75
Nos. 625-628 (4) 7.15 6.05

International Telegraph and Telephone Conference, Paris, May-July 1949.

Jean Racine — A187

1949
629 A187 12fr sepia .30 .25

Death of Jean Racine, dramatist, 250th anniv.

Abbey of St. Bertrand de Comminges A188

Meuse Valley, Ardennes A189

Mt. Gerbier de Jonc, Vivarais A190

1949 Engr.
630 A188 20fr dark red .25 .25
631 A189 40fr Prus green 12.50 .25
632 A190 50fr sepia 2.10 .25
Nos. 630-632 (3) 14.85 .75

For surcharge see Reunion No. 286.

A191

1949, Oct. 18
633 A191 15fr deep carmine .25 .25

50th anniv. of the Assembly of Presidents of Chambers of Commerce of the French Union.

UPU Allegory A192

1949, Nov. 7
634 A192 5fr dark green .25 .25
635 A192 15fr deep carmine .30 .25
636 A192 25fr deep blue 1.00 .90
Nos. 634-636 (3) 1.55 1.40

UPU, 75th anniversary.

Raymond Poincaré — A193

1950, May 27 Unwmk. *Perf. 13*
637 A193 15fr indigo .30 .25

Charles Péguy and Cathedral at Chartres A194

François Rabelais — A195

1950, June

638 A194 12fr dk brown .30 .25
639 A195 12fr red brown .60 .45

Chateau of Chateaudun — A196

1950, Nov. 25

640 A196 8fr choc & bis brn .55 .40

Madame Récamier A197

Marie de Sévigné A198

1950

641 A197 12fr dark green .45 .40
642 A198 15fr ultra .45 .40

See footnote after No. 4642.

Palace of Fontainbleau — A199

1951, Jan. 20

643 A199 12fr dark brown .75 .60

Jules Ferry — A200

1951, Mar. 17

644 A200 15fr bright red .40 .40

Hands Holding Shuttle A201

1951, Apr. 9

645 A201 25fr deep ultra .75 .45

Intl. Textile Exposition, Lille, April-May, 1951.

Jean-Baptiste de la Salle — A202

1951, Apr. 28

646 A202 15fr chocolate .45 .35

300th anniv. of the birth of Jean-Baptiste de la Salle, educator and saint.

Map and Anchor A203

1951, May 12

647 A203 15fr deep ultra .60 .30

50th anniv. of the creation of the French colonial troops.

Vincent d'Indy A204

1951, May 15

648 A204 25fr deep green 1.50 1.50

Vincent d'Indy, composer, birth cent.

Abbey Type of 1949

1951

649 A185 30fr bright blue 4.00 3.25

Marianne Type of 1945-47

1951 Typo. *Perf. 14x13½*

650 A147 5fr dull violet .30 .25
651 A147 6fr green 4.75 .45
652 A147 12fr red orange .70 .25
653 A147 15fr ultra .25 .25
a. Booklet pane of 10 60.00
654 A147 18fr cerise 15.00 1.20
Nos. 650-654 (5) 21.00 2.40

A205

Design: Professors Nocard, Bouley and Chauveau; gate at Lyons school.

1951, June 8 Engr. *Perf. 13*

655 A205 12fr red violet .60 .40

Issued to honor Veterinary Medicine.

A206

Design: Gen. Picqué, Cols. Roussin and Villemin; Val de Grace Dome.

1951, June 17 Unwmk.

656 A206 15fr red brown .75 .40

Issued to honor Military Medicine.

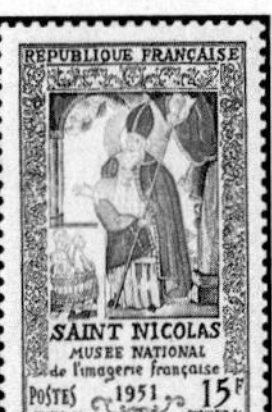

St. Nicholas, by Jean Didier — A207

1951, June 23

657 A207 15fr ind, dp claret & org 1.00 .75

Chateau Bontemps, Arbois A208

1951, June 23

658 A208 30fr indigo .75 .25

For surcharge see Reunion No. 296.

Arms Type of 1949

Arms of: 10c, Artois. 50c, Limousin. 1fr, Béarn. 2fr, Touraine. 3fr, Franche-Comté.

1951, June Typo. *Perf. 14x13½*

659 A182 10c red, vio bl & yel .25 .25
660 A182 50c green, red & blk .25 .25
661 A182 1fr blue, red & yel .25 .25
662 A182 2fr vio bl, red & yel .60 .25
663 A182 3fr red, vio bl & yel .45 .30
Nos. 659-663 (5) 1.80 1.30

Seal of Paris — A209

Unwmk.

1951, July 7 Engr. *Perf. 13*

664 A209 15fr dp bl, dk brn & red .55 .30

2,000th anniv. of the founding of Paris.

Maurice Noguès and Globe — A210

1951, Oct. 13

665 A210 12fr indigo & blue .70 .60

Maurice Nogues, aviation pioneer.

Charles Baudelaire A211

Poets: 12fr, Paul Verlaine. 15fr, Arthur Rimbaud.

1951, Oct. 27

666 A211 8fr purple .70 .45
667 A211 12fr gray .70 .45
668 A211 15fr dp green .70 .45
Nos. 666-668 (3) 2.10 1.35

Georges Clemenceau, Birth Cent. — A212

1951, Nov. 11

669 A212 15fr black brown .55 .35

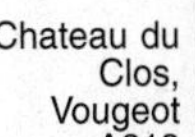

Chateau du Clos, Vougeot A213

1951, Nov. 17

670 A213 30fr blk brn & brn 5.25 1.75

Chaillot Palace and Eiffel Tower A214

1951, Nov. 6

671 A214 18fr red .90 .60
672 A214 30fr deep ultra 1.50 1.50

Opening of the Geneva Assembly of the United Nations, Paris, Nov. 6, 1951.

Observatory, Pic du Midi — A215

Abbaye aux Hommes, Caen — A216

1951, Dec. 22

673 A215 40fr violet 4.50 .25
674 A216 50fr black brown 4.00 .25

For surcharge see Reunion No. 294.

Marshal Jean de Lattre de Tassigny, 1890-1952 A217

1952, May 8 Unwmk. *Perf. 13*

675 A217 15fr violet brown .75 .45

See No. 717.

Gate of France, Vaucouleurs — A218

1952, May 11

676 A218 12fr brown black 1.00 .75

Flags and Monument at Narvik, Norway A219

1952, May 28

677 A219 30fr violet blue 2.50 1.75

Battle of Narvik, May 27, 1940.

Chateau de Chambord
A220

1952, May 30
678 A220 20fr dark purple .45 .25

For surcharge see Reunion No. 292.

Assembly Hall, Strasbourg
A221

1952, May 31
679 A221 30fr dark green 6.50 4.50

Issued to honor the Council of Europe.

Monument, Bir-Hacheim Cemetery — A222

1952, June 14
680 A222 30fr rose lake 3.00 1.75

10th anniv. of the defense of Bir-Hacheim.

Abbey of the Holy Cross, Poitiers — A223

1952, June 21
681 A223 15fr bright red .40 .40

14th cent. of the foundation of the Abbey of the Holy Cross at Poitiers.

A224

Design: Leonardo da Vinci, Amboise Chateau and La Signoria, Florence.

1952, July 9
682 A224 30fr deep ultra 7.00 5.25

Leonardo da Vinci, 500th birth anniv.

Garabit Viaduct
A225

1952, July 5
683 A225 15fr dark blue .45 .45

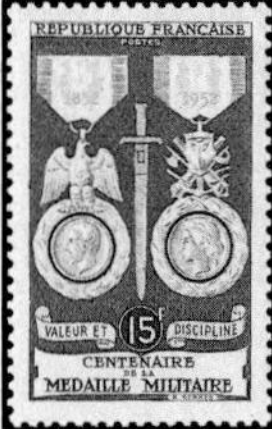

Sword and Military Medals, 1852-1952 — A226

1952, July 5
684 A226 15fr choc, grn & yel .45 .40

Cent. of the creation of the Military Medal.

Dr. René Laennec — A227

1952, Nov. 7
685 A227 12fr dark green .60 .45

Versailles Gate, Painted by Utrillo
A228

1952, Dec. 20
686 A228 18fr violet brown 2.25 1.50

Publicity for the restoration of Versailles Palace. See No. 728.

Mannequin — A229

1953, Apr. 24 **Unwmk.** ***Perf. 13***
687 A229 30fr blue blk & rose vio .75 .30

Dressmaking industry of France.

Gargantua of François Rabelais
A230

Célimène from The Misanthrope
A231

Figaro, from the Barber of Seville — A232

Hernani of Victor Hugo — A233

1953
688 A230 6fr dp plum & car .25 .25
689 A231 8fr indigo & ultra .25 .25
690 A232 12fr vio brn & dk grn .25 .25
691 A233 18fr vio brn & blk brn .50 .25
Nos. 688-691 (4) 1.25 1.00

For surcharge see Reunion No. 298.

Type of 1948

Inscribed "Général Leclerc Maréchal de France"

1953-54
692 A176 8fr red brown .75 .60
692A A176 12fr dk grn & gray grn ('54) 2.25 1.50

Issued to honor the memory of General Jacques Leclerc.

Map and Cyclists, 1903-1953
A234

1953, July 26
693 A234 12fr red brn, ultra & blk 1.75 1.10

50th anniv. of the Bicycle Tour de France.

Arms Type of 1949

50c, Picardy. 70c, Gascony. 80c, Berri. 1fr, Poitou. 2fr, Champagne. 3fr, Dauphiné.

1953 **Typo.** ***Perf. 14x13½***
694 A182 50c blue, yel & red .25 .25
695 A182 70c red, blue & yel .25 .25
696 A182 80c blue, red & yel .25 .25
697 A182 1fr black, red & yel .25 .25
698 A182 2fr brown, bl & yel .30 .25
699 A182 3fr red, blue & yel .45 .25
Nos. 694-699 (6) 1.75 1.50

Swimming
A235

1953, Nov. 28 **Engr.** ***Perf. 13***
700 A235 20fr shown 1.90 .25
701 A235 25fr Track 10.50 .25
702 A235 30fr Fencing 1.90 .25
703 A235 40fr Canoe racing 11.00 .25
704 A235 50fr Rowing 6.00 .25
705 A235 75fr Equestrian 30.00 11.00
Nos. 700-705 (6) 61.30 12.25

For surcharges see Reunion Nos. 299-300.

No. 654 Surcharged with New Value and Bars in Black

1954 ***Perf. 14x13½***
706 A147 15fr on 18fr cerise .40 .25

Farm Woman
A236

Gallic Cock
A237

1954 **Typo.**
707 A236 4fr blue .25 .25
708 A236 8fr brown red 4.75 1.00
709 A237 12fr cerise 3.00 .55
710 A237 24fr blue green 16.00 3.25
Nos. 707-710 (4) 24.00 5.05

Nos. 707-710 are known only precanceled. See second note after No. 132.

See Nos. 833-834, 840-844, 910-913, 939, 952-955. For surcharges see Reunion Nos. 324, 326-327.

Tapestry and Gobelin Workshop — A238

Designs: 30fr, Book manufacture. 40fr, Porcelain and glassware. 50fr, Jewelry and metalsmith's work. 75fr, Flowers and perfumes.

1954, May 6 **Engr.** ***Perf. 13***
711 A238 25fr red brn car & blk brn 9.50 .45
712 A238 30fr dk grn & lil gray 1.10 .25
713 A238 40fr dk brn, vio brn & org brn 3.50 .25
714 A238 50fr brt ultra, dl grn & org brn 1.10 .25
715 A238 75fr dp car & magenta 11.00 1.10
Nos. 711-715 (5) 26.20 2.30

For surcharges see Reunion Nos. 303-304.

Entrance to Exhibition Park — A239

1954, May 22
716 A239 15fr blue & dk car .30 .25

Founding of the Fair of Paris, 50th anniv.

De Lattre Type of 1952

1954, June 5
717 A217 12fr vio bl & indigo 1.50 .75

Allied Landings
A240

1954, June 5
718 A240 15fr scarlet & ultra 1.75 .90

The 10th anniversary of the liberation.

View of Lourdes
A241

Street Corner, Quimper — A242

Views: 8fr, Seine valley, Les Andelys. 10fr, Beach at Royan. 18fr, Cheverny Chateau. 20fr, Beach, Gulf of Ajaccio.

1954
719 A241 6fr ultra, ind & dk grn .30 .25
720 A241 8fr brt blue & dk grn .30 .25
721 A241 10fr aqua & org brn .25 .25
722 A242 12fr rose vio & dk vio .30 .25
723 A241 18fr bl, dk grn & ind 2.50 .50
724 A241 20fr blk brn, bl grn & red brn 2.25 .25
Nos. 719-724 (6) 5.90 1.75

See No. 873. For surcharges see Reunion Nos. 302, 306-310. See footnote after No. 4642.

Abbey Ruins, Jumièges — A243

1954, June 13

725 A243 12fr vio bl, ind & dk grn 1.50 .75

13th centenary of Abbey of Jumièges.

St. Philibert Abbey, Tournus — A244

1954, June 18

726 A244 30fr indigo & blue 4.00 3.00

1st conf. of the Intl. Center of Romance Studies.

View of Stenay A245

1954, June 26

727 A245 15fr dk brn & org brn .70 .30

Acquisition of Stenay by France, 300th anniv.

Versailles Type of 1952

1954, July 10

728 A228 18fr dp bl, ind & vio brn 7.50 4.50

Villandry Chateau A246

1954, July 17

729 A246 18fr dk bl & dk bl grn 4.00 3.00

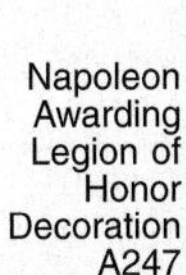

Napoleon Awarding Legion of Honor Decoration A247

1954, Aug. 14

730 A247 12fr scarlet 1.20 .75

150th anniv. of the 1st Legion of Honor awards at Camp de Boulogne.

Cadets Marching Through Gateway A248

1954, Aug. 1

731 A248 15fr vio gray, dk bl & car 1.00 1.00

150th anniversary of the founding of the Military School of Saint-Cyr.

Allegory — A249

1954, Oct. 4

732 A249 30fr indigo & choc 4.00 3.00

Issued to publicize the fact that the metric system was first introduced in France.

Arms Type of 1949

Arms: 50c, Maine. 70c, Navarre. 80c, Nivernais. 1fr, Bourbonnais. 2fr, Angoumois. 3fr, Aunis. 5fr, Saintonge.

1954 Typo. *Perf. 14x13½*

733 A182 50c multicolored .25 .25
734 A182 70c green, red & yel .25 .25
735 A182 80c blue, red & yel .25 .25
736 A182 1fr red, blue & yel .25 .25
737 A182 2fr black, red & yel .25 .25
738 A182 3fr brown, red & yel .25 .25
739 A182 5fr blue & yellow .25 .25
Nos. 733-739 (7) 1.75 1.75

Duke de Saint-Simon — A250

1955, Feb. 5 Engr. *Perf. 13*

740 A250 12fr dk brn & vio brn .45 .30

Louis de Rouvroy, Duke de Saint-Simon (1675-1755).

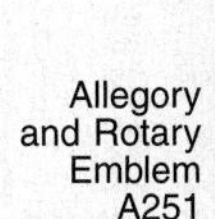

Allegory and Rotary Emblem A251

1955, Feb. 23

741 A251 30fr vio bl, bl & org 2.00 .75

50th anniv. of Rotary International.

Marianne — A252

1955-59 Typo. *Perf. 14x13½*

751 A252 6fr fawn 2.00 1.40
752 A252 12fr green 2.40 1.10
a. Bklt. pane of 10 + 2 labels 30.00
753 A252 15fr carmine .25 .25
a. Booklet pane of 10 10.00
754 A252 18fr green ('58) .25 .25
755 A252 20fr ultra ('57) .30 .25
756 A252 25fr rose red ('59) 1.00 .25
a. Booklet pane of 8 40.00
b. Booklet pane of 10 30.00
Nos. 751-756 (6) 6.20 3.50

No. 751 was issued in coils of 1,000.

No. 752 was issued in panes of 10 stamps and two labels with marginal instructions for folding to form a booklet.

Nos. 754-755 are found in two types, distinguished by the numerals. On the 18fr there is no serif at left of base of the "1" on the 1st type. The 2nd type has a shorter "1" with no serifs at base. On the 20fr the 2nd type has a well formed "2" and the horiz. lines of the "F" of the denomination are longer and of equal length.

No. 756 also in two types, distinguished by border width. On the 1st type, the border is thicker than the width of the letters. On the 2nd type, the border is thinner than the width of the letters.

For surcharges see Reunion Nos. 330-331.

Philippe Lebon, Inventor of Illuminating Gas A253

Inventors: 10fr, Barthélemy Thimonnier, sewing machine. 12fr, Nicolas Appert, canned foods. 18fr, Dr. E. H. St. Claire Deville, aluminum. 25fr, Pierre Martin, steel making. 30fr, Bernigaud de Chardonnet, rayon.

1955, Mar. 5 Engr. *Perf. 13*

757 A253 5fr dk vio bl & bl .70 .60
758 A253 10fr dk brn & org brn .70 .60
759 A253 12fr dk green .90 .70
760 A253 18fr dk vio bl & ind 2.25 1.40
761 A253 25fr dk brnsh pur & vio 2.50 1.50
762 A253 30fr rose car & scar 2.50 1.50
Nos. 757-762 (6) 9.55 6.30

St. Stephen Bridge, Limoges A254

1955, Mar. 26 Unwmk. *Perf. 13*

763 A254 12fr yel brn & dk vio brn 1.20 1.00

Gloved Model in Place de la Concorde — A255

1955, Mar. 26

764 A255 25fr blk brn, vio bl & blk .75 .25

French glove manufacturing. See footnote after No. 4642.

Jean Pierre Claris de Florian A256

1955, Apr. 2

765 A256 12fr blue green .60 .40

200th anniv. of the birth of Jean Pierre Claris de Florian, fabulist.

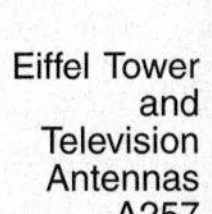

Eiffel Tower and Television Antennas A257

1955, Apr. 16

766 A257 15fr indigo & ultra .75 .70

French advancement in television.

Wire Fence and Guard Tower A258

1955, Apr. 23

767 A258 12fr dk gray bl & brn blk .75 .60

10th anniv. of the liberation of concentration camps.

Electric Train A259

1955, May 11

768 A259 12fr blk brn & slate bl 1.60 1.10

Issued to publicize the electrification of the Valenciennes-Thionville railroad line.

Jacquemart of Moulins — A260

1955, May 28

769 A260 12fr black brown 1.40 1.00

Jules Verne and Nautilus A261

1955, June 3

770 A261 30fr indigo 6.00 3.75

50th anniv. of the death of Jules Verne.

Auguste and Louis Lumière and Motion Picture Projector A262

1955, June 12

771 A262 30fr rose brown 5.25 3.25

Invention of motion pictures, 60th anniv.

Jacques Coeur and His Mansion at Bourges A263

1955, June 18

772 A263 12fr violet 1.90 1.20

5th centenary of the death of Jacques Coeur (1395?-1456), French merchant.

Corvette "La Capricieuse" — A264

1955, July 9

773 A264 30fr aqua & dk blue 3.75 3.25

Centenary of the voyage of La Capricieuse to Canada.

Bordeaux A265

Designs: 8fr, Marseille. 10fr, Nice. 12fr, Valentre bridge, Cahors. 18fr, Uzerche. 25fr, Fortifications, Brouage.

1955, Oct. 15

774	A265	6fr carmine lake	.25	.25
775	A265	8fr indigo	.45	.25
776	A265	10fr dp ultra	.25	.25
777	A265	12fr violet & brn	.25	.25
778	A265	18fr bluish grn & ind	.60	.25
779	A265	25fr org brn & red brn	.75	.25
		Nos. 774-779 (6)	2.55	1.50

See Nos. 838-839. For surcharges see Reunion Nos. 312-317, 323.

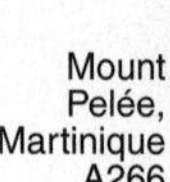

Mount Pelée, Martinique A266

1955, Nov. 1
780 A266 20fr dk & lt purple 2.40 .25

Gérard de Nerval — A267

1955, Nov. 11
781 A267 12fr lake & sepia .40 .25

Centenary of the death of Gérard de Nerval (Labrunie), author.

Arms Type of 1949

Arms of: 50c, County of Foix. 70c, Marche. 80c, Roussillon. 1fr, Comtat Venaissin.

Perf. 14x13½
1955, Nov. 19 Typo. Unwmk.

782	A182	50c multicolored	.25	.25
783	A182	70c red, blue & yel	.25	.25
784	A182	80c brown, yel & red	.25	.25
785	A182	1fr blue, red & yel	.25	.25
		Nos. 782-785 (4)	1.00	1.00

Concentration Camp Victim and Monument — A268

1956, Jan. 14 Engr. *Perf. 13*
786 A268 15fr brn blk & red brn .45 .40

Natl. memorial for Nazi deportation victims erected at the Natzwiller Struthof concentration camp in Alsace.

Belfry at Douai — A269

1956, Feb. 11
787 A269 15fr ultra & indigo .40 .40

Col. Emil Driant A270

1956, Feb. 21
788 A270 15fr dark blue .30 .25

40th anniv. of the death of Col. Emil Driant during the battle of Verdun.

Trench Fighting — A271

1956, Mar. 3
789 A271 30fr indigo & dk olive 1.50 1.25

40th anniversary of Battle of Verdun.

A272

A272a

A272b

A272c

Scientists: 12fr, Jean Henri Fabre, Entomology. 15fr, Charles Tellier, Refrigeration. 18fr, Camille Flammarion, Popular Astronomy. 30fr, Paul Sabatier, Catalytic Chemistry.

1956, Apr. 7

790	A272	12fr vio brn & org brn	.75	.40
791	A272a	15fr vio bl & int blk	.75	.40
792	A272b	18fr brt ultra	1.40	1.25
793	A272c	30fr Prus grn & dk grn	3.50	2.00
		Nos. 790-793 (4)	6.40	4.05

Grand Trianon, Versailles A273

1956, Apr. 14
794 A273 12fr vio brn & gray grn 1.10 .75

For similar stamp with euro denominations, see No. 5449a.

Symbols of Latin American and French Culture A274

1956, Apr. 21
795 A274 30fr brown & red brn 1.60 1.40

Issued in recognition of the friendship between France and Latin America.

"The Smile of Reims" and Botticelli's "Spring" A275

1956, May 5
796 A275 12fr black & green .60 .40

Issued to emphasize the cultural and artistic kinship of Reims and Florence.

Leprosarium and Maltese Cross — A276

1956, May 12
797 A276 12fr sepia, red brn & red .40 .35

Issued in honor of the Knights of Malta.

St. Yves de Treguier A277

1956, May 19
798 A277 15fr bluish gray & blk .35 .25

St. Yves, patron saint of lawyers.

Marshal Franchet d'Esperey — A278

1956, May 26
799 A278 30fr deep claret 2.25 1.40

Centenary of the birth of Marshal Louis Franchet d'Esperey.

Miners Monument — A279

1956, June 2
800 A279 12fr violet brown .45 .40

Town Montceau-les-Mines, 100th anniv.

Basketball — A280

Sports: 40fr, Pelota (Jai alai). 50fr, Rugby. 75fr, Mountain climbing.

1956, July 7

801	A280	30fr gray vio & blk	1.10	.25
802	A280	40fr brown & vio brn	4.00	.25
803	A280	50fr rose vio & vio	1.50	.25
804	A280	75fr indigo, grn & bl	9.00	1.75
		Nos. 801-804 (4)	15.60	2.50

For surcharges see Reunion Nos. 318-321.

Europa Issue

"Rebuilding Europe" — A281

Perf. 13½x14
1956, Sept. 15 Typo. Unwmk.
805 A281 15fr rose & rose lake .75 .25

Perf. 13
Engr.
806 A281 30fr lt blue & vio bl 4.50 .75

Issued to symbolize the cooperation among the six countries comprising the Coal and Steel Community.

No. 805 measures 21x35½mm, No. 806 measures 22x35½mm.

Dam at Donzère-Mondragon — A282

Cable Railway to Pic du Midi — A283

Rhine Port of Strasbourg A284

1956, Oct. 6 Engr. *Perf. 13*

807	A282	12fr gray vio & vio brn	1.10	.90
808	A283	18fr indigo	2.25	1.50
809	A284	30fr indigo & dk blue	9.50	4.50
		Nos. 807-809 (3)	12.85	6.90

French technical achievements.

Antoine-Augustin Parmentier — A285

1956, Oct. 27

810 A285 12fr brn red & brn .65 .45

Parmentier, nutrition chemist, who popularized the potato in France.

Petrarch — A286

Portraits: 12fr, J. B. Lully. 15fr, J. J. Rousseau. 18fr, Benjamin Franklin. 20fr, Frederic Chopin. 30fr, Vincent van Gogh.

1956, Nov. 10

811	A286	8fr green	.60	.45
812	A286	12fr claret	.60	.45
813	A286	15fr dark red	.90	.45
814	A286	18fr ultra	1.90	1.50
815	A286	20fr brt violet	2.40	1.50
816	A286	30fr brt grnsh blue	4.75	2.25
		Nos. 811-816 (6)	11.15	6.60

Famous men who lived in France.

Pierre de Coubertin and Olympic Stadium A287

1956, Nov. 24

817 A287 30fr dk blue gray & pur 1.50 .90

Issued in honor of Baron Pierre de Coubertin, founder of the modern Olympic Games.

Homing Pigeon A288

1957, Jan. 12

818 A288 15fr dp ultra, ind & red brn .40 .25

Victor Schoelcher — A289

1957, Feb. 16 **Engr.**

819 A289 18fr lilac rose .45 .40

Issued in honor of Victor Schoelcher, who freed the slaves in the French Colonies.

Sèvres Porcelain A290

1957, Mar. 23 **Unwmk.** ***Perf. 13***

820 A290 30fr ultra & vio blue .60 .40

Bicentenary of the porcelain works at Sèvres (in 1956).

Gaston Planté and Storage Battery A291

Designs: 12fr, Antoine Béclère and X-ray apparatus. 18fr, Octave Terrillon, autoclave, microscope and surgical instruments. 30fr, Etienne Oemichen and early helicopter.

1957, Apr. 13

821	A291	8fr gray blk & dp cl	.30	.25
822	A291	12fr dk bl, blk & emer	.35	.25
823	A291	18fr rose red & mag	1.00	.90
824	A291	30fr green & slate grn	2.10	1.60
		Nos. 821-824 (4)	3.75	3.00

Uzès Chateau A292

1957, Apr. 27

825 A292 12fr slate bl & bis brn .40 .40

Jean Moulin — A293

Portraits: 10fr, Honoré d'Estienne d'Orves. 12fr, Robert Keller. 18fr, Pierre Brossolette. 20fr, Jean-Baptiste Lebas.

1957, May 18

826	A293	8fr violet brown	.90	.30
827	A293	10fr black & vio bl	.90	.30
828	A293	12fr brown & sl grn	1.00	.35
829	A293	18fr purple & blk	1.40	1.10
830	A293	20fr Prus bl & dk bl	1.40	.90
		Nos. 826-830 (5)	5.60	2.95

Issued in honor of the heroes of the French Underground of World War II.

See Nos. 879-882, 915-919, 959-963, 990-993.

Le Quesnoy — A294

1957, June 1

831 A294 8fr dk slate green .25 .25

See No. 837.

Symbols of Justice A295

1957, June 1

832 A295 12fr sepia & ultra .25 .25

French Cour des Comptes, 150th anniv.

Farm Woman Type of 1954

1957-59 ***Perf. 14x13½***

833	A236	6fr orange	.25	.25
833A	A236	10fr brt green ('59)	.40	.25
834	A236	12fr red lilac	.25	.25
		Nos. 833-834 (3)	.90	.75

Nos. 833-834 issued without precancellation.

Symbols of Public Works A296

1957, June 20 **Engr.** ***Perf. 13***

835 A296 30fr sl grn, brn & ocher 1.50 1.00

Brest A297

1957, July 6

836 A297 12fr gray grn & brn ol .90 .75

Scenic Types of 1955, 1957

Designs: 15fr, Le Quesnoy. 35fr, Bordeaux. 70fr, Valentre bridge, Cahors.

1957, July 19 **Unwmk.**

837	A294	15fr dk bl grn & sep	.25	.25
838	A265	35fr dk bl grn & sl grn	2.90	.90
839	A265	70fr black & dull grn	16.00	1.60
		Nos. 837-839 (3)	19.15	2.75

For surcharge see Reunion No. 322.

Gallic Cock Type of 1954

1957 **Typo.** ***Perf. 14x13½***

840	A237	5fr olive bister	.25	.25
841	A237	10fr bright blue	1.50	.25
842	A237	15fr plum	1.25	.50
843	A237	30fr bright red	9.00	2.10
844	A237	45fr green	19.00	9.00
		Nos. 840-844 (5)	31.00	12.10

Nos. 840-844 are known only precanceled. See second note after No. 132.

Leo Lagrange and Stadium A298

1957, Aug. 31 **Engr.** ***Perf. 13***

845 A298 18fr lilac gray & blk .40 .40

Intl. University Games, Paris, 8/31-9/8.

"United Europe" — A299

1957, Sept. 16

846	A299	20fr red brown & green	*.40*	*.30*
847	A299	35fr dk brown & blue	*.90*	*.75*

A united Europe for peace and prosperity.

Auguste Comte — A300

1957, Sept. 14

848 A300 35fr brown red & sepia .40 .25

Centenary of the death of Auguste Comte, mathematician and philosopher.

Roman Amphitheater, Lyon — A301

1957, Oct. 5 ***Perf. 13***

849 A301 20fr brn org & brn vio .40 .25

2,000th anniv. of the founding of Lyon.

Sens River, Guadeloupe A302

Beynac-Cazenac, Dordogne — A303

Designs: 10fr, Elysee Palace. 25fr, Chateau de Valencay, Indre. 35fr, Rouen Cathedral. 50fr, Roman Ruins, Saint-Remy. 65fr, Evian-les-Bains.

1957, Oct. 19

850	A302	8fr green & lt brn	.25	.25
851	A302	10fr dk ol bis & vio brn	.25	.25
852	A303	18fr indigo & dk brn	.25	.25
853	A302	25fr bl gray & vio brn	.55	.25
854	A303	35fr car rose & lake	.25	.25
855	A302	50fr ol grn & ol bister	.35	.25
856	A302	65fr dk blue & indigo	.60	.30
		Nos. 850-856 (7)	2.50	1.80

See Nos. 907-909. See footnote after No. 4642. For overprint and surcharges see No. 1O1, Reunion Nos. 325, 328-329, 332-334.

Nicolaus Copernicus — A304

Portraits: 10fr, Michelangelo. 12fr, Miguel de Cervantes. 15fr, Rembrandt. 18fr, Isaac Newton. 25fr, Mozart. 35fr, Johann Wolfgang von Goethe.

1957, Nov. 9 **Engr.** ***Perf. 13***

857	A304	8fr dark brown	.65	.30
858	A304	10fr dark green	.65	.45
859	A304	12fr dark purple	.65	.45
860	A304	15fr brown & org brn	.80	.60
861	A304	18fr deep blue	1.10	.80
862	A304	25fr lilac & claret	1.25	.90
863	A304	35fr blue	1.50	1.00
		Nos. 857-863 (7)	6.60	4.50

Louis Jacques Thénard A305

1957, Nov. 30 **Unwmk.**

864	A305	15fr ol bis & grnsh blk	.40	.30

Centenary of the death of L. J. Thenard, chemist, and the founding of the Charitable Society of the Friends of Science.

Dr. Philippe Pinel — A306

French Physicians: 12fr, Fernand Widal. 15fr, Charles Nicolle. 35fr, René Leriche.

1958, Jan. 25

865	A306	8fr brown olive	.65	.45
866	A306	12fr brt vio blue	.65	.45
867	A306	15fr deep blue	1.00	.50
868	A306	35fr black	1.40	.80
		Nos. 865-868 (4)	3.70	2.20

Joseph Louis Lagrange — A307

French Scientists: 12fr, Urbain Jean Joseph Leverrier. 15fr, Jean Bernard Leon Foucault. 35fr, Claude Louis Berthollet.

1958, Feb. 15 ***Perf. 13***

869	A307	8fr blue & vio blue	.65	.35
870	A307	12fr sepia & gray	.75	.35
871	A307	15fr slate grn & grn	1.40	.60
872	A307	35fr maroon & cop red	1.75	.90
		Nos. 869-872 (4)	4.55	2.20

Lourdes Type of 1954

1958

873	A241	20fr grnsh bl & ol	.30	.25

Le Havre A308

Maubeuge — A309

Designs: 18fr, Saint-Die. 25fr, Sete.

1958, Mar. 29 **Engr.** ***Perf. 13***

874	A308	12fr ol grn & car rose	.55	.35
875	A309	15fr brt purple & brn	.60	.35
876	A309	18fr ultra & indigo	.90	.65
877	A308	25fr dk bl, bl grn & brn	1.25	.65
		Nos. 874-877 (4)	3.30	2.00

Reconstruction of war-damaged cities.

French Pavilion, Brussels A310

1958, Apr. 12

878	A310	35fr brn, dk grn & bl	.30	.25

Issued for the Universal and International Exposition at Brussels.

Heroes Type of 1957

8fr, Jean Cavaillès. 12fr, Fred Scamaroni. 15fr, Simone Michel-Levy. 20fr, Jacques Bingen.

1958, Apr. 19

879	A293	8fr violet & black	.60	.45
880	A293	12fr ultra & green	.60	.45
881	A293	15fr brown & gray	1.50	.85
882	A293	20fr olive & ultra	1.25	.85
		Nos. 879-882 (4)	3.95	2.60

Issued in honor of the heroes of the French Underground in World War II.

Bowling A311

Sports: 15fr, Naval joust. 18fr, Archery, vert. 25fr, Breton wrestling, vert.

1958, Apr. 26

883	A311	12fr rose & brown	.75	.75
884	A311	15fr bl, ol gray & grn	1.00	.75
885	A311	18fr green & brown	1.75	1.00
886	A311	25fr brown & indigo	2.50	1.75
		Nos. 883-886 (4)	6.00	4.25

Senlis Cathedral — A312

1958, May 17

887	A312	15fr ultra & indigo	.40	.25

Bayeux Tapestry Horsemen A313

1958, June 21

888	A313	15fr blue & carmine	.35	.25

Common Design Types pictured following the introduction.

Europa Issue, 1958

Common Design Type

1958, Sept. 13 **Engr.** ***Perf. 13***

Size: 22x36mm

889	CD1	20fr rose red	.40	.25
890	CD1	35fr ultra	1.25	.30

Foix Chateau A314

1958, Oct. 11

891	A314	15fr ultra, grn & ol brn	.40	.25

City Halls, Paris and Rome A315

1958, Oct. 11

892	A315	35fr gray, grnsh bl & rose red	.40	.25

Issued to publicize the cultural ties between Rome and Paris and the need for European unity.

UNESCO Building, Paris A316

Design: 35fr, Different view of building.

1958, Nov. 1 ***Perf. 13***

893	A316	20fr grnsh blue & ol bis	.25	.25
894	A316	35fr dk sl grn & red org	.25	.25

UNESCO Headquarters in Paris opening, Nov. 3.

Soldier's Grave in Wheat Field — A317

1958, Nov. 11

895	A317	15fr dk green & ultra	.30	.25

40th anniv. of the World War I armistice.

Arms of Marseille — A318

Cities: 70c, Lyon. 80c, Toulouse. 1fr, Bordeaux. 2fr, Nice. 3fr, Nantes. 5fr, Lille. 15fr, Algiers.

1958-59 **Typo.** ***Perf. 14x13½***

896	A318	50c dk blue & ultra	.25	.25
897	A318	70c multicolored	.25	.25
898	A318	80c red, blue & yel	.25	.25
899	A318	1fr dk bl, yel & red	.25	.25
900	A318	2fr dk bl, red & grn	.25	.25
901	A318	3fr multicolored	.25	.25
902	A318	5fr dk brown & red	.25	.25
903	A318	15fr multi ('59)	.25	.25
		Nos. 896-903 (8)	2.00	2.00

See Nos. 938, 940, 973, 1040-1042, 1091-1095, 1142-1144. For surcharges see Reunion Nos. 336, 345-346, 350-351, 353.

Arc de Triomphe and Flowers — A319

1959, Jan. 17 **Engr.** ***Perf. 13***

904	A319	15fr brn, bl, grn, cl & red	.40	.30

Paris Flower Festival.

Symbols of Learning and Medal A320

1959, Jan. 24 ***Perf. 13***

905	A320	20fr lake, blk & vio	.25	.25

Sesquicentennial of the Palm Leaf Medal of the French Academy.

Charles de Foucauld A321

1959, Jan. 31

906	A321	50fr dp brn, bl & mar	.40	.30

Issued to honor Father Charles de Foucauld, explorer and missionary of the Sahara.

Type of 1957

Designs: 30fr, Elysee Palace. 85fr, Evian-les Bains. 100fr, Sens River, Guadeloupe.

1959, Feb. 10

907	A302	30fr dk slate green	2.00	.25
908	A302	85fr deep claret	3.00	.30
909	A302	100fr deep violet	25.00	.30
		Nos. 907-909 (3)	30.00	.85

Gallic Cock Type of 1954

1959 **Typo.** ***Perf. 14x13½***

910	A237	8fr violet	.40	.25
911	A237	20fr yellow grn	1.50	.50
912	A237	40fr henna brn	3.25	1.60
913	A237	55fr emerald	15.00	6.00
		Nos. 910-913 (4)	20.15	8.35

Nos. 910-913 were issued with precancellation. See second note after No. 132. See Nos. 952-955.

Miners' Tools and School A322

1959, Apr. 11 **Engr.** ***Perf. 13***

914	A322	20fr red, blk & blue	.25	.25

175th anniv. of the National Mining School.

Heroes Type of 1957

Portraits: No. 915, The five martyrs of the Buffon school. No. 916, Yvonne Le Roux. No. 917, Médéric-Védy. No. 918, Louis Martin-Bret. 30fr, Gaston Moutardier.

1959, Apr. 25 **Engr.** ***Perf. 13***

915	A293	15fr black & vio	.30	.25
916	A293	15fr mag & rose vio	.30	.30
917	A293	20fr green & grnsh bl	.30	.25
918	A293	20fr org brn & brn	.45	.30
919	A293	30fr magenta & vio	.50	.40
		Nos. 915-919 (5)	1.85	1.50

Dam at Foum el Gherza A323

Marcoule Atomic Center — A324

Designs: 30fr, Oil field at Hassi Messaoud, Sahara. 50fr, C. N. I. T. Building (Centre National des Industries et des Techniques).

1959, May 23

920	A323 15fr olive & grnsh bl	.30	.25
921	A324 20fr brt car & red brn	.40	.40
922	A324 30fr dk blue, brn & grn	.40	.40
923	A323 50fr ol grn & sl blue	.65	.45
	Nos. 920-923 (4)	1.75	1.50

French technical achievements.

Marceline Desbordes-Valmore — A325

1959, June 20

924 A325 30fr blue, brn & grn .25 .25

Centenary of the death of Marceline Desbordes-Valmore, poet.

Pilots Goujon and Rozanoff A326

1959, June 13

925 A326 20fr lt blue & org brn .40 .40

Issued in honor of Charles Goujon and Col. Constantin Rozanoff, test pilots.

Tancarville Bridge A327

1959, Aug. 1 Engr. *Perf. 13*

926 A327 30fr dk blue, brn & ol .40 .25

Marianne and Ship of State — A328

1959, July Typo. *Perf. 14x13½*

927 A328 25fr black & red .30 .25

See Nos. 942, 3521, 4410a, 4513. For surcharge see No. B336.

Jean Jaures — A329

1959, Sept. 12 Engr. *Perf. 13*

928 A329 50fr chocolate .40 .25

Jean Jaures, socialist leader, birth cent.

Europa Issue, 1959

Common Design Type

1959, Sept. 19

Size: 22x36mm

929	CD2 25fr bright green	.30	.25
930	CD2 50fr bright violet	1.10	.55

Blood Donors A330

1959, Oct. 17 Engr.

931 A330 20fr magenta & gray .25 .25

French-Spanish Handshake — A331

1959, Oct. 24 *Perf. 13*

932 A331 50fr blue, rose car & org .45 .30

300th anniv. of the signing of the Treaty of the Pyrenees.

Polio Victim Holding Crutches — A332

1959, Oct. 31

933 A332 20fr dark blue .25 .25

Vaccination against poliomyelitis.

Henri Bergson — A333

1959, Nov. 7

934 A333 50fr lt red brown .35 .25

Henri Bergson, philosopher, birth cent.

Avesnes-sur-Helpe — A334

Design: 30fr, Perpignan.

1959, Nov. 14

935	A334 20fr sepia & blue	.40	.25
936	A334 30fr brn, dp claret & bl	.40	.25

New NATO Headquarters, Paris — A335

1959, Dec. 12

937 A335 50fr green, brn & ultra .45 .30

10th anniv. of the NATO.

Types of 1958-59 and

Farm Woman A336

Sower A337

Designs: 5c, Arms of Lille. 15c, Arms of Algiers. 25c, Marianne and Ship of State.

Perf. 14x13½

1960-61 Unwmk. Typo.

938	A318	5c dk brown & red	2.60	.25
939	A336	10c brt green	.25	.25
940	A318	15c red, ultra, yel & grn	.50	.25
941	A337	20c grnsh bl & car rose	.25	.25
942	A328	25c ver & ultra	1.60	.25
b.		Booklet pane of 8	27.50	
c.		Booklet pane of 10	32.50	
942A	A337	30c gray & ultra ('61)	1.10	.30
		Nos. 938-942A (6)	6.30	1.55

See Nos. 707-708, 833-834 for the Farm Woman type (A336), but with no decimals in denominations.

For surcharges see Reunion Nos. 337-338, 341. For overprint see Algeria No. 286.

Laon Cathedral A338

Kerrata Gorge — A339

Designs: 30c, Fougères Chateau. 50c, Mosque, Tlemcen. 65c, Sioule Valley. 85c, Chaumont Viaduct. 1fr, Cilaos Church, Reunion.

1960, Jan. 16 Engr. *Perf. 13*

943	A338 15c blue & indigo	.25	.25
944	A338 30c blue, sepia & grn	1.75	.25
945	A339 45c brt vio & ol gray	.60	.25
946	A339 50c sl grn & lt cl	1.20	.25
947	A338 65c sl grn, bl & blk brn	1.10	.25
948	A338 85c blue, sep & grn	1.75	.25
949	A339 1fr vio bl, bl & grn	2.50	.25
	Nos. 943-949 (7)	9.15	1.75

For surcharges see Reunion Nos. 335, 340, 342. For overprint see Algeria Nos. 288-289.

Pierre de Nolhac A340

1960, Feb. 13

950 A340 20c black & gray .45 .30

Centenary of the birth of Pierre de Nolhac, curator of Versailles and historian.

Museum of Art and Industry, Saint-Etienne — A341

1960, Feb. 20

951 A341 30c brn, car & slate .45 .30

Gallic Cock Type of 1954

1960 Typo. *Perf. 14x13½*

952	A237 8c violet	.40	.25
953	A237 20c yellow grn	1.90	.30
954	A237 40c henna brn	7.50	1.75
955	A237 55c emerald	24.00	11.00
	Nos. 952-955 (4)	33.80	13.30

Nos. 952-955 were issued only precanceled. See second note after No. 132. See Nos. 910-913.

View of Cannes A342

1960, Mar. 5 Engr. *Perf. 13*

956 A342 50c red brn & lt grn .45 .40

Meeting of European municipal administrators, Cannes, Mar., 1960.

Woman of Savoy and Alps A343

Woman of Nice and Shore A344

1960 Unwmk. *Perf. 13*

957	A343 30c slate green	.50	.40
958	A344 50c brn, yel & rose	.50	.30

Cent. of the annexation of Nice and Savoy.

Heroes Type of 1957

Portraits: No. 959, Edmund Debeaumarché. No. 960, Pierre Massé. No. 961, Maurice Ripoche. No. 962, Leonce Vieljeux. 50c, Abbé René Bonpain.

1960, Mar. 26

959	A293 20c bister & blk	1.10	.90
960	A293 20c pink & rose cl	1.10	.90
961	A293 30c vio & brt vio	1.50	.90
962	A293 30c sl bl & brt bl	2.10	1.75
963	A293 50c sl grn & red brn	2.40	2.10
	Nos. 959-963 (5)	8.20	6.55

Issued in honor of the heroes of the French Underground of World War II.

"Education" and Children A345

1960, May 21 Engr. *Perf. 13*

964 A345 20c rose lilac, pur & blk .25 .25

1st secondary school in Strasbourg, 150th anniv.

Blois Chateau A346

View of La Bourboule A347

1960, May

965	A346 30c dk bl, sep & grn	.60	.45
966	A347 50c ol brown, car & grn	.60	.35

Lorraine Cross — A348

1960, June 18
967 A348 20c red brn, dk brn & yel grn .45 .25

20th anniv. of the French Resistance Movement in World War II.

Marianne — A349

1960, June 18 Typo. *Perf. 14x13½*
968 A349 25c lake & gray .25 .25
a. Booklet pane of 8 4.50
b. Booklet pane of 10 3.50

See Nos. 3522, 4410b, 4514. For surcharge see Reunion No. 339. For overprint see Algeria No. 287.

Jean Bouin and Stadium A350

1960, July 9 Engr. *Perf. 13*
969 A350 20c blue, mag & ol gray .35 .25

17th Olympic Games, Rome, 8/25-9/11.

Europa Issue, 1960
Common Design Type

1960, Sept. 17 *Perf. 13*
Size: 36x22mm
970 CD3 25c green & bluish grn .25 .25
971 CD3 50c maroon & red lilac .25 .25

Lisieux Basilica A351

1960, Sept. 24 *Perf. 13*
972 A351 15c blue, gray & blk .25 .25

Arms Type of 1958-59
Design: Arms of Oran.

1960, Oct. 15 Typo. *Perf. 14x13½*
973 A318 5c red, bl, yel & emer .25 .25

Madame de Stael by François Gerard — A352

1960, Oct. 22 Engr. *Perf. 13*
974 A352 30c dull claret & brn .35 .25

Madame de Stael (1766-1817), writer.

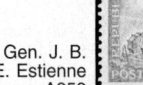

Gen. J. B. E. Estienne A353

1960, Nov. 5
975 A353 15c lt lilac & black .35 .25

Centenary of the birth of Gen. Jean Baptiste Eugene Estienne.

Marc Sangnier and Youth Hostel at Bierville A354

1960, Nov. 5
976 A354 20c blue, blk & lilac .25 .25

Issued to honor Marc Sangnier, founder of the French League for Youth Hostels.

Badge of Order of Liberation — A355

1960, Nov. 14 Engr. *Perf. 13*
977 A355 20c black & brt green .40 .25

Order of Liberation, 20th anniversary.

Lapwings A356

Birds: 30c, Puffin. 45c, European teal. 50c, European bee-eaters.

1960, Nov. 12
978 A356 20c multicolored .25 .25
979 A356 30c multicolored .25 .25
980 A356 45c multicolored .60 .45
981 A356 50c multicolored .55 .40
Nos. 978-981 (4) 1.65 1.35

Issued to publicize wildlife protection.

André Honnorat A357

1960, Nov. 19
982 A357 30c blue, blk & green .30 .25

Honnorat, statesman, fighter against tuberculosis and founder of the University City of Paris, an intl. students' community.

St. Barbara and Medieval View of School A358

1960, Dec. 3 Engr.
983 A358 30c red, bl & ol brn .30 .25

St. Barbara School, Paris, 500th anniv.

"Mediterranean" by Aristide Maillol — A359

1961, Feb. 18 Unwmk. *Perf. 13*
984 A359 20c carmine & indigo .25 .25

Aristide Maillol, sculptor, birth cent.

Marianne by Cocteau — A360

1961, Feb. 23
985 A360 20c blue & carmine .25 .25

A second type has an extra inverted V-shaped mark (a blue flag top) at right of hair tip. Value unused $2.25, used 35 cents.
See Nos. 3523, 4410c, 4515.
For surcharge see Reunion No. 357.

Paris Airport, Orly A361

1961, Feb. 25
986 A361 50c blk, dk bl, & bluish grn .45 .25

Inauguration of new facilities at Orly airport.

George Méliès and Motion Picture Screen A362

1961, Mar. 11
987 A362 50c pur, indigo & ol bis .50 .35

Cent. of the birth of George Méliès, motion picture pioneer.

Jean Baptiste Henri Lacordaire — A363

1961, Mar. 25 *Perf. 13*
988 A363 30c lt brown & black .30 .25

Cent. of the death of the Dominican monk Lacordaire, orator and liberal Catholic leader.

A364

1961, Mar. 25
989 A364 30c grn, red brn & red .25 .25

Introduction of tobacco use into France, fourth centenary. By error stamp portrays Jan Nicquet instead of Jean Nicot.

Heroes Type of 1957

Portraits: No. 990, Jacques Renouvin. No. 991, Lionel Dubray. No. 992, Paul Gateaud. No. 993, Mère Elisabeth.

1961, Apr. 22
990 A293 20c blue & lilac .75 .35
991 A293 20c gray grn & blue .75 .35
992 A293 30c brown org & blk 1.40 .65
993 A293 30c violet & blk .90 .80
Nos. 990-993 (4) 3.80 2.15

Bagnoles-de-l'Orne — A365

1961, May 6
994 A365 20c olive, ocher, bl & grn .25 .25

Dove, Olive Branch and Federation Emblem — A366

1961, May 6
995 A366 50c brt bl, grn & mar .30 .25

World Federation of Ex-Service Men.

Deauville in 19th Century A367

1961, May 13 Engr.
996 A367 50c rose claret 1.25 .90

Centenary of Deauville.

La Champmeslé A368

French actors: No. 998, Talma. No. 999, Rachel. No. 1000, Gérard Philipe. No. 1001, Raimu.

1961, June 10 Unwmk. *Perf. 13*
Dark Carmine Frame
997 A368 20c choc & yel grn .60 .25
998 A368 30c brown & crimson .60 .35
999 A368 30c yel grn & sl grn .65 .35
1000 A368 50c olive & choc 1.10 .45
1001 A368 50c bl grn & red brn 1.10 .45
Nos. 997-1001 (5) 4.05 1.85

Issued to honor great French actors and in connection with the Fifth World Congress of the International Federation of Actors.

Mont-Dore, Snowflake and Cable Car — A369

1961, July 1
1002 A369 20c orange & rose lilac .25 .25

Pierre Fauchard — A370

1961, July 1

1003 A370 50c dk green & blk .40 .30

Bicentenary of the death of Pierre Fauchard, 1st surgeon dentist.

St. Theobald's Church, Thann — A371

1961, July 1

1004 A371 20c sl grn, vio & brn .45 .25

800th anniversary of Thann.

Europa Issue, 1961

Common Design Type

1961, Sept. 16 *Perf. 13*

Size: 35x22mm

1005 CD4 25c vermilion .25 .25
1006 CD4 50c ultramarine .25 .25

Beach and Sailboats, Arcachon A372

Designs: 15c, Saint-Paul, Maritime Alps. 45c, Sully-sur-Loire Chateau. 50c, View of Cognac. 65c, Rance Valley and Dinan. 85c, City hall and Rodin's Burghers, Calais. 1fr, Roman gates of Lodi, Medea, Algeria.

1961, Oct. 9 **Engr.** *Perf. 13*

1007 A372 15c blue & purple .25 .25
1008 A372 30c ultra, sl grn & lt brn .25 .25
1009 A372 45c vio bl, red brn & grn .25 .25
1010 A372 50c grn, Prus bl & sl .75 .25
1011 A372 65c red brn, sl grn & bl .25 .25
1012 A372 85c sl grn, sl & red brn .35 .25
1013 A372 1fr dk bl, sl & bis 3.50 .25
Nos. 1007-1013 (7) 5.60 1.75

For surcharges see Reunion Nos. 347-348. For overprint see Algeria No. 290.

Blue Nudes, by Matisse — A373

Paintings: 50c, "The Messenger," by Braque. 85c, "The Cardplayers," by Cézanne. 1fr, "The 14th July," by Roger de La Fresnaye.

1961, Nov. 10 *Perf. 13x12*

1014 A373 50c dk brn, bl, blk & gray 2.25 1.20
1015 A373 65c grn, vio, & ultra 3.75 1.90
1016 A373 85c blk, brn, red & ol 1.50 1.10
1017 A373 1fr multicolored 3.00 1.90
Nos. 1014-1017 (4) 10.50 6.10

Liner France A374

1962, Jan. 11 **Engr.** *Perf. 13*

1018 A374 30c dk blue, blk & car .60 .35

New French liner France.

Skier Going Downhill — A375

1962, Jan. 27 *Perf. 13*

1019 A375 30c shown .25 .25
1020 A375 50c Slalom .35 .25

Issued to publicize the World Ski Championships, Chamonix, Feb. 1962.

Maurice Bourdet — A376

1962, Feb. 17

1021 A376 30c slate .30 .25

60th anniv. of the birth of Maurice Bourdet, radio commentator and resistance hero.

Pierre-Fidele Bretonneau — A377

1962, Feb. 17

1022 A377 50c brt lilac & blue .35 .25

Centenary of the death of Pierre-Fidele Bretonneau, physician.

Chateau and Bridge, Laval, Mayenne — A378

1962, Feb. 24

1023 A378 20c bis brn & slate grn .25 .25

Gallic Cock — A379

1962-65 *Perf. 13*

1024 A379 25c ultra, car & brn .25 .25
a. Bklt. pane of 4 (horiz. strip) 2.50
1024B A379 30c gray grn, red & brn ('65) .85 .25
c. Booklet pane of 5 5.00
d. Booklet pane of 10 10.00

No. 1024 was also issued on experimental luminescent paper in 1963. Value $750.

See Nos. 3524, 4410d, 4516.

Ramparts of Vannes A380

Dunkirk — A381

Paris Beach, Le Touquet A381a

1962 **Engr.** *Perf. 13*

1025 A380 30c dark blue .60 .50
1026 A381 95c grn, bis & red lil .75 .40
1027 A381a 1fr grn, red brn & bl .40 .25
Nos. 1025-1027 (3) 1.75 1.15

No. 1026 for the 300th anniv. of Dunkirk.

Stage Setting and Globe A382

1962, Mar. 24 **Unwmk.**

1028 A382 50c sl grn, ocher & mag .40 .25

International Day of the Theater, Mar. 27.

Memorial to Fighting France, Mont Valerien A383

Resistance Heroes' Monument, Vercors — A384

Design: 50c, Ile de Sein monument.

1962, Apr. 7

1029 A383 20c olive & slate grn .50 .40
1030 A384 30c bluish black .60 .45
1031 A384 50c blue & indigo .75 .60
Nos. 1029-1031 (3) 1.85 1.45

Issued to publicize memorials for the French Underground in World War II.

Malaria Eradication Emblem and Swamp — A385

1962, Apr. 14 **Engr.**

1032 A385 50c dk blue & dk red .35 .25

WHO drive to eradicate malaria.

Nurses with Child and Hospital — A386

1962, May 5 **Unwmk.** *Perf. 13*

1033 A386 30c bl grn, gray & red brn .25 .25

National Hospital Week, May 5-12.

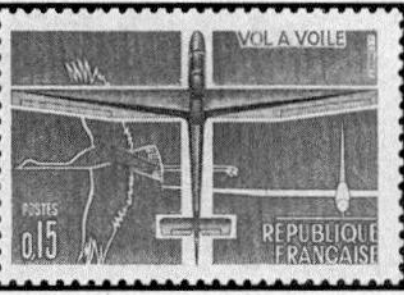

Glider A387

20c, Planes showing development of aviation.

1962, May 12

1034 A387 15c orange red & brn .30 .25
1035 A387 20c lil rose & rose cl .35 .25

Issued to publicize sports aviation.

School Emblem — A388

1962, May 19 **Engr.**

1036 A388 50c mar, ocher & dk vio .40 .25

Watchmaker's School at Besançon, cent.

Louis XIV and Workers Showing Modern Gobelin A389

1962, May 26 **Unwmk.** *Perf. 13*

1037 A389 50c ol, sl grn & car .40 .25

Gobelin tapestry works, Paris, 300th anniv.

Blaise Pascal A390

1962, May 26

1038 A390 50c slate grn & dp org .40 .25

Blaise Pascal (1623-1662), mathematician, scientist and philosopher.

Palace of Justice, Rennes A391

1962, June 12
1039 A391 30c blk, grysh bl & grn 1.00 .75

Arms Type of 1958-59

5c, Amiens. 10c, Troyes. 15c, Nevers.

1962-63 Typo. *Perf. 14x13½*
1040 A318 5c ver, ultra & yel .25 .25
1041 A318 10c red, ultra & yel ('63) .25 .25
1042 A318 15c ver, ultra & yel .25 .25
Nos. 1040-1042 (3) .75 .75

Phosphor Tagging

In 1970 France began to experiment with luminescence. Phosphor bands have been added to Nos. 1041, 1143, 1231, 1231C, 1292A-1294B, 1494-1498, 1560-1579B, etc.

Rose — A392

Design: 30c, Old-fashioned rose.

1962, Sept. 8 Engr. *Perf. 13*
1043 A392 20c ol, grn & brt car .45 .30
1044 A392 30c dk sl grn, ol & car .55 .40

Europa Issue, 1962
Common Design Type

1962, Sept. 15
Size: 36x22mm
1045 CD5 25c violet .25 .25
1046 CD5 50c henna brown .35 .25

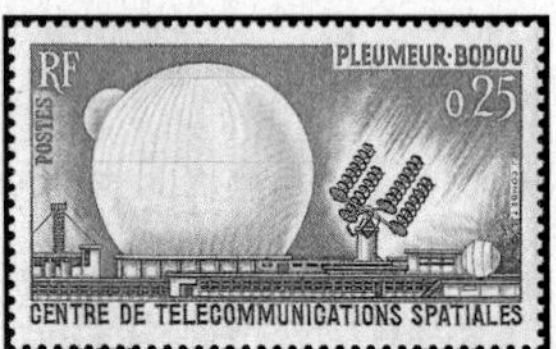
Space Communications Center, Pleumeur-Bodou, France — A394

Telstar, Earth and Television Set — A395

1962, Sept. 29 Engr. *Perf. 13*
1047 A394 25c gray, yel & grn .25 .25
1048 A395 50c dk bl, grn & ultra .40 .30

1st television connection of the US and Europe through Telstar satellite, July 11-12.
For surcharges see Reunion Nos. 343-344.

"Bonjour Monsieur Courbet" by Gustave Courbet — A396

Paintings: 65c, "Madame Manet on Blue Sofa," by Edouard Manet. 1fr, "Guards officer on horseback," by Theodore Géricault, vert.

1962, Nov. 9 *Perf. 13x12, 12x13*
1049 A396 50c multicolored 2.25 1.50
1050 A396 65c multicolored 2.25 1.40
1051 A396 1fr multicolored 4.50 2.00
Nos. 1049-1051 (3) 9.00 4.90

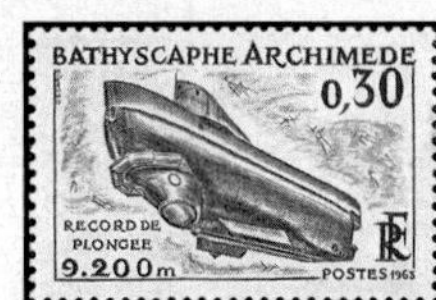
Bathyscaph "Archimede" — A397

1963, Jan. 26 Unwmk. *Perf. 13*
1052 A397 30c dk blue & blk .25 .25

French deep-sea explorations.

Flowers and Nantes Chateau A398

1963, Feb. 11
1053 A398 30c vio bl, car & sl grn .25 .25

Nantes flower festival.

St. Peter, Window at St. Foy de Conches A399

50c, Jacob Wrestling with the Angel, by Delacroix.

1963, Mar. 2 *Perf. 12x13*
1054 A399 50c multicolored 2.40 1.50
1055 A399 1fr multicolored 3.25 2.25

See Nos. 1076-1077.

Hungry Woman and Wheat Emblem A400

1963, Mar. 21 Engr. *Perf. 13*
1056 A400 50c slate grn & brn .40 .25

FAO "Freedom from Hunger" campaign.

Cemetery and Memorial, Glières — A401

Design: 50c, Memorial, Ile de la Cité, Paris.

1963, Mar. 23 Unwmk. *Perf. 13*
1057 A401 30c dk brown & olive .40 .30
1058 A401 50c indigo .40 .30

Heroes of the resistance against the Nazis.

Beethoven, Birthplace at Bonn and Rhine A402

No. 1060, Emile Verhaeren, memorial at Roisin & residence. No. 1061, Giuseppe Mazzini, Marcus Aurelius statue & Via Appia, Rome. No. 1062, Emile Mayrisch, Colpach Chateau & blast furnace, Esch. No. 1063, Hugo de Groot, Palace of Peace, The Hague & St. Agatha Church, Delft.

1963, Apr. 27 Unwmk. *Perf. 13*
1059 A402 20c ocher, sl & brt grn .30 .25
1060 A402 20c purple, blk & mar .30 .25
1061 A402 20c maroon, sl & ol .30 .25
1062 A402 20c mar, dk brn & ocher .30 .25
1063 A402 30c dk brn, vio & ocher .30 .25
Nos. 1059-1063 (5) 1.50 1.25

Issued to honor famous men of the European Common Market countries.

Hotel des Postes and Stagecoach, 1863 — A403

1963, May 4
1064 A403 50c grayish black .35 .25

1st Intl. Postal Conference, Paris, 1863.

Lycée Louis-le-Grand, Belvédère, Panthéon and St. Etienne du Mont Church — A404

1963, May 18
1065 A404 30c slate green .30 .25

400th anniversary of the Jesuit Clermont secondary school, named after Louis XIV.

St. Peter's Church and Ramparts, Caen A405

1963, June 1 Unwmk. *Perf. 13*
1066 A405 30c gray blue & brn .25 .25

Radio Telescope, Nançay — A406

1963, June 8 Engr.
1067 A406 50c dk bl & dk brn .45 .35

Amboise Chateau A407

Saint-Flour — A408

Designs: 50c, Côte d'Azur Varoise. 85c, Vittel. 95c, Moissac.

1963, June 15
1068 A407 30c slate, grn & bis .25 .25
1069 A407 50c dk grn, dk bl & hn brn .30 .25
1070 A408 60c ultra, dk grn & hn brn .40 .25
1071 A407 85c dk grn, yel grn & brn 1.00 .25
1072 A408 95c brnsh black .60 .25
Nos. 1068-1072 (5) 2.55 1.25

For surcharge see Reunion No. 355.

Water Skiing Slalom A409

1963, Aug. 31 Unwmk. *Perf. 13*
1073 A409 30c sl grn, blk & car .30 .25

World Water Skiing Championships, Vichy.

Europa Issue, 1963
Common Design Type

1963, Sept. 14
Size: 36x22mm
1074 CD6 25c red brown .25 .25
1075 CD6 50c green .35 .25

Art Type of 1963

Designs: 85c, "The Married Couple of the Eiffel Tower," by Marc Chagall. 95c, "The Fur Merchants," window, Chartres Cathedral.

1963, Nov. 9 Engr. *Perf. 12x13*
1076 A399 85c multicolored 1.10 .90
1077 A399 95c multicolored .50 .40

Philatec Issue
Common Design Type

1963, Dec. 14 Unwmk. *Perf. 13*
1078 CD118 25c dk gray, sl grn & dk car .25 .25

For surcharge see Reunion No. 349.

Radio and Television Center, Paris A411

1963, Dec. 15 Engr.
1079 A411 20c org brn, slate & ol .25 .25

A412

Design: Fire Brigade Insignia, Symbols of Fire, Water and Civilian Defense.

1964, Feb. 8 Engr. *Perf. 13*
1082 A412 30c blue, org & red .40 .25

Issued to honor the fire brigades and civilian defense corps.

Handicapped Laboratory Technician — A413

1964, Feb. 22 Unwmk. *Perf. 13*
1083 A413 30c blue grn, org brn & brn .25 .25

Rehabilitation of the handicapped.

John II the Good (1319-64) by Girard d'Orleans A414

1964, Apr. 25 *Perf. 12x13*
1084 A414 1fr multicolored 1.10 .75

Stamp of 1900 A415

Mechanized Mail Handling A416

Designs: No. 1086, Stamp of 1900, Type A17. No. 1088, Telecommunications.

1964, May 9 *Perf. 13*
1085 A415 25c bister & dk car .25 .25
1086 A415 25c bister & blue .25 .25
1087 A416 30c blk, bl & org brn .25 .25
1088 A416 30c blk, car rose & bluish grn .25 .25
a. Strip of 4, #1085-1088 + label 1.10 1.00

Printed in sheets of 20 stamps, containing five No. 1088a. The label shows the Philatec emblem in green.

Type of Semi-Postal Issue
with "25e ANNIVERSAIRE" added

1964, May 9
1089 SP208 25c multicolored .25 .25

25th anniversary, night airmail service.

Madonna and Child from Rose Window of Notre Dame A417

1964, May 23 *Perf. 12x13*
1090 A417 60c multicolored .50 .40

Notre Dame Cathedral, Paris, 800th anniv.

Arms Type of 1958-59

Arms: 1c, Niort. 2c, Guéret. 12c, Agen. 18c, Saint-Denis, Réunion. 30c, Paris.

1964-65 Typo. *Perf. 14x13½*
1091 A318 1c vio blue & yel .25 .25
1092 A318 2c emer, vio bl & yel .25 .25
1093 A318 12c black, red & yel .25 .25
1094 A318 18c multicolored .25 .25
1095 A318 30c vio bl & red ('65) .30 .25
a. Booklet pane of 10 15.00
Nos. 1091-1095 (5) 1.30 1.25

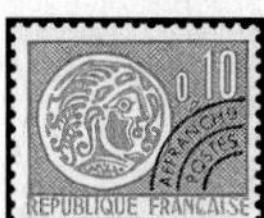
Gallic Coin — A418

Perf. 13½x14
1964-66 Typo. Unwmk.
1096 A418 10c emer & bister .75 .25
1097 A418 15c org & bister ('66) .30 .25
1098 A418 25c lilac & brn .45 .25
1099 A418 50c brt blue & brn .85 .75
Nos. 1096-1099 (4) 2.35 1.50

Nos. 1096-1099 are known only precanceled. See second note after No. 132. See Nos. 1240-1242, 1315-1318, 1421-1424.

Postrider, Rocket and Radar Equipment — A419

1964, June 5 Engr. *Perf. 13*
1100 A419 1fr brn, dk red & dk bl 17.50 13.50

Sold for 4fr, including 3fr admission to PHILATEC. Issued in sheets of 8 stamps and 8 labels (2x8 subjects with labels in horizontal rows 1, 4, 5, 8; stamps in rows 2, 3, 6, 7). Commemorative inscriptions on side margins. Value $150.

Caesar's Tower, Provins — A420

Chapel of Notre Dame du Haut, Ronchamp A421

1964-65
1101 A421 40c sl grn, dk brn & brn ('65) .25 .25
1102 A420 70c slate, grn & car .30 .25
1103 A421 1.25fr brt bl, sl grn & ol .70 .25
Nos. 1101-1103 (3) 1.25 .75

The 40c was issued in vertical coils in 1971. Every 10th coil stamp has a red control number printed twice on the back.

For surcharges see Reunion Nos. 352, 361.

Mandel — A422

1964, July 4 Unwmk. *Perf. 13*
1104 A422 30c violet brown .25 .25

Georges Mandel (1885-1944), Cabinet minister, executed by the Nazis.

Judo — A423

1964, July 4
1105 A423 50c dk blue & vio brn .25 .25

18th Olympic Games, Tokyo, 10/10-25/64.

Champlevé Enamel from Limoges, 12th Century A424

Design: No. 1107, The Lady (Claude Le Viste?) with the Unicorn, 15th cent. tapestry.

1964 *Perf. 12x13*
1106 A424 1fr multicolored .75 .50
1107 A424 1fr multicolored .40 .30

No. 1106 shows part of an enamel sepulchral plate portraying Geoffrey IV, Count of Anjou and Le Maine (1113-1151), who was called Geoffrey Plantagenet.

Issue dates: No. 1106, July 4. No. 1107, Oct. 31.

Paris Taxis Carrying Soldiers to Front, 1914 A425

1964, Sept. 5 Unwmk. *Perf. 13*
1108 A425 30c black, blue & red .25 .25

50th anniversary of Battle of the Marne.

Europa Issue, 1964
Common Design Type

1964, Sept. 12 Engr.
Size: 22x36mm
1109 CD7 25c dk car, dp ocher & grn .25 .25
1110 CD7 50c vio, yel grn & dk car .25 .25

Cooperation Issue
Common Design Type

1964, Nov. 6 Unwmk. *Perf. 13*
1111 CD119 25c red brn, dk brn & dk bl .25 .25

Joux Chateau — A427

1965, Feb. 6 Engr.
1112 A427 1.30fr redsh brn, brn red & dk brn .90 .25

"The English Girl from the Star" by Toulouse-Lautrec — A428

St. Paul on the Damascus Road, Window, Cathedral of Sens — A429

Leaving for the Hunt — A430

Apocalypse Tapestry, 14th Century A431

"The Red Violin" by Raoul Dufy — A432

Designs: No. 1115, "August" miniature of Book of Hours of Jean de France, Duc de Berry ("Les Très Riches Heures du Duc de Berry"), painted by Flemish brothers, Pol, Hermant and Jannequin Limbourg, 1411-16. No. 1116, Scene from oldest existing set of French tapestries, showing the Winepress of the Wrath of God (Revelations 14: 19-20).

1965 *Perf. 12x13, 13x12*

1113 A428 1fr multicolored .40 .30
1114 A429 1fr multicolored .40 .30
1115 A430 1fr multicolored .30 .30
1116 A431 1fr multicolored .30 .30
1117 A432 1fr blk, pink & car .30 .30
Nos. 1113-1117 (5) 1.70 1.50

No. 1114 issued to commemorate the 800th anniversary of the Cathedral of Sens.

Issued: No. 1113, 3/12; No. 1114, 6/5; No. 1115, 9/25; No. 1116, 10/30; No. 1117, 11/6.

Returning Deportees, 1945 — A433

1965, Apr. 1 **Unwmk.** ***Perf. 13***

1118 A433 40c Prussian green .45 .25

20th anniv. of the return of people deported during World War II.

House of Youth and Culture, Troyes A434

1965, Apr. 10 **Engr.**

1119 A434 25c ind, brn & dk grn .25 .25

20th anniv. of the establishment of recreational cultural centers for young people.

Woman Carrying Flowers — A435

1965, Apr. 24 **Unwmk.** ***Perf. 13***

1120 A435 60c dk grn, dp org & ver .30 .25

Tourist Campaign of Welcome & Amiability.

Flags of France, US, USSR and Great Britain Crushing Swastika — A436

1965, May 8

1121 A436 40c black, car & blue .30 .25

20th anniv. of victory in World War II.

Telegraph Key, Syncom Satellite and Pleumeur-Bodou Station — A437

1965, May 17

1122 A437 60c dk blue, brn & blk .30 .25

Centenary of the ITU.

Croix de Guerre — A438

1965, May 22 **Engr.**

1123 A438 40c red, brn & brt grn .35 .25

50th anniv. of the Croix de Guerre medal.

Cathedral of Bourges — A439

Moustiers-Sainte-Marie — A440

Views: 30c, Road and tunnel, Mont Blanc. 60c, Aix-les-Bains, sailboat. 75c, Tarn Gorge, Lozère mountains. 95c, Vendée River, man poling boat, and windmill. 1fr, Prehistoric stone monuments, Carnac.

1965

1124 A439 30c bl, vio bl & brn vio .25 .25
1125 A439 40c gray bl & redsh brn .25 .25
1126 A440 50c grn, bl gray & bis .25 .25
1127 A439 60c blue & red brn .45 .25
1128 A439 75c brown, bl & grn .75 .60
1129 A440 95c brown, grn & bl 4.50 .75
1130 A440 1fr gray, grn & brn .75 .25
Nos. 1124-1130 (7) 7.20 2.60

No. 1124 for the opening of the Mont Blanc Tunnel. No. 1125 (Bourges Cathedral) was issued in connection with the French Philatelic Societies Federation Congress, held at Bourges.

Issued: 40c, June 5; 50c, June 19; 30c, 60c, July 17; others, July 10.

For surcharges see Reunion Nos. 354, 362, 365.

Europa Issue, 1965

Common Design Type

1965, Sept. 25 ***Perf. 13***

Size: 36x22mm

1131 CD8 30c red .25 .30
1132 CD8 60c gray .45 .25

Planting Seedling — A441

1965, Oct. 2

1133 A441 25c slate grn, yel grn & red brn .25 .25

National reforestation campaign.

Etienne Régnault, "Le Taureau" and Coast of Reunion — A442

1965, Oct. 2

1134 A442 30c indigo & dk car .25 .25

Tercentenary of settlement of Reunion.

Atomic Reactor and Diagram, Symbols of Industry, Agriculture and Medicine — A443

1965, Oct. 9

1135 A443 60c brt blue & blk .50 .30

Atomic Energy Commission, 20th anniv.

Air Academy and Emblem A444

1965, Nov. 6 ***Perf. 13***

1136 A444 25c dk blue & green .35 .30

Air Academy, Salon-de-Provence, 50th anniv.

French Satellite A-1 Issue

Common Design Type

Design: 60c, A-1 satellite.

1965, Nov. 30 **Engr.** ***Perf. 13***

1137 CD121 30c Prus bl, brt bl & blk .25 .25
1138 CD121 60c blk, Prus bl & brt bl .40 .25
a. Strip of 2, #1137-1138 + label .65 .65

Launching of France's 1st satellite, 11/26/65.

For surcharges see Reunion Nos. 358-359.

Arms of Auch — A446

Cities: 20c, Saint-Lô. 25c, Mont-de-Marsan.

Typographed, Photogravure (20c)

1966 ***Perf. 14x13; 14 (20c)***

1142 A446 5c blue & red .25 .25
1143 A446 20c vio bl, sil, gold & red .25 .25
1144 A446 25c red brown & ultra .30 .25
Nos. 1142-1144 (3) .80 .75

The 5c and 20c were issued in sheets and in vertical coils. In the coils, every 10th stamp has a red control number on the back.

For surcharges see Reunion Nos. 360-360A.

French Satellite D-1 Issue

Common Design Type

1966, Feb. 18 **Engr.** ***Perf. 13***

1148 CD122 60c blue blk, grn & cl .25 .25

Horses from Bronze Vessel of Vix — A448

"The Newborn" by Georges de La Tour — A449

The Baptism of Judas (4th Century Bishop of Jerusalem) — A450

"The Moon and the Bull" Tapestry by Jean Lurçat A451

"Crispin and Scapin" by Honoré Daumier — A452

1966 ***Perf. 13x12, 12x13***

1149 A448 1fr multicolored .40 .35
1150 A449 1fr multicolored .40 .35
1151 A450 1fr multicolored .40 .35
1152 A451 1fr multicolored .40 .30
1153 A452 1fr multicolored .40 .30
Nos. 1149-1153 (5) 2.00 1.65

The design of No. 1149 is a detail from a 6th century B.C. vessel, found in 1953 in a grave near Vix, Cote d'Or.

The design of No. 1151 is from a stained glass window in the 13th century Sainte-Chapelle, Paris.

No. 1150 exists in an imperf, ungummed souv. sheet with 2 progressive die proofs, issued for benefit of the Postal Museum, and not postally valid. Value $2.

Issued: No. 1149, 3/26; No. 1150, 6/25; No. 1151, 10/22; No. 1152, 11/19; No. 1153, 12/10.

Chessboard, Knight, Emblems for King and Queen — A453

1966, Apr. 2 **Engr.** ***Perf. 13***
1154 A453 60c sepia, gray & dk vio bl .45 .30

Issued to publicize the Chess Festival.

Rhone Bridge, Pont-Saint-Esprit — A454

1966, Apr. 23 **Unwmk.** ***Perf. 13***
1155 A454 25c black & dull blue .25 .25

St. Michael Slaying the Dragon — A455

1966, Apr. 30 **Litho. & Engr.**
1156 A455 25c multicolored .25 .25

Millenium of Mont-Saint-Michel.

Stanislas Leszczynski, Lunéville Chateau — A456

1966, May 6 **Engr.**
1157 A456 25c slate, grn & brn .25 .25

200th anniv. of the reunion of Lorraine and Bar (Barrois) with France.

St. Andrew's and Sèvre River, Niort — A457

1966, May 28 **Engr.** ***Perf. 13***
1158 A457 40c brt bl, indigo & grn .30 .25

Bernard Le Bovier de Fontenelle and 1666 Meeting Room A458

1966, June 4
1159 A458 60c dk car rose & brn .30 .25

300th anniversary, Académie des Sciences.

William the Conqueror, Castle and Norman Ships — A459

1966, June 4
1160 A459 60c brown red & dp bl .40 .30

900th anniversary of Battle of Hastings.

Tracks, Globe and Eiffel Tower A460

1966, June 11
1161 A460 60c dk brn, car & dull bl .50 .25

19th International Railroad Congress.

Oléron Bridge A461

1966, June 20
1162 A461 25c Prus bl, brn & bl .25 .25

Issued to commemorate the opening of Oléron Bridge, connecting Oléron Island in the Bay of Biscay with the French mainland.

Europa Issue, 1966
Common Design Type

1966, Sept. 24 **Engr.** ***Perf. 13***
Size: 22x36mm
1163 CD9 30c Prussian blue .25 .25
1164 CD9 60c red .30 .25

Vercingetorix at Gergovie, 52 B.C. — A462

Bishop Remi Baptizing King Clovis, 496 A.D. — A463

Design: 60c, Charlemagne attending school (page holding book for crowned king).

1966, Nov. 5 ***Perf. 13***
1165 A462 40c choc, grn & gray bl .30 .25
1166 A463 40c dk red brn & blk .30 .25
1167 A463 60c pur, rose car & brn .30 .25
Nos. 1165-1167 (3) .90 .75

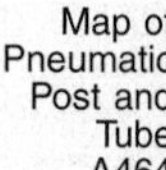
Map of Pneumatic Post and Tube A464

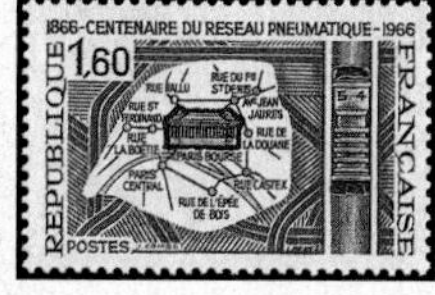

1966, Nov. 11
1168 A464 1.60fr mar & indigo .60 .30

Centenary of Paris pneumatic post system.

Val Chateau — A465

1966, Nov. 19 **Engr.** ***Perf. 13***
1169 A465 2.30fr dk bl, sl grn & brn 1.50 .25

Rance Power Station A466

1966, Dec. 3
1170 A466 60c dk bl, sl grn & brn .45 .25

Tidal power station in the estuary of the Rance River on the English Channel.

European Broadcasting Union Emblem — A467

1967, Mar. 4 **Engr.** ***Perf. 13***
1171 A467 40c dk blue & rose brn .25 .25

3rd Intl. Congress of the European Broadcasting Union, Paris, Mar. 8-22.

Father Juniet's Gig by Henri Rousseau — A468

Francois I by Jean Clouet A469

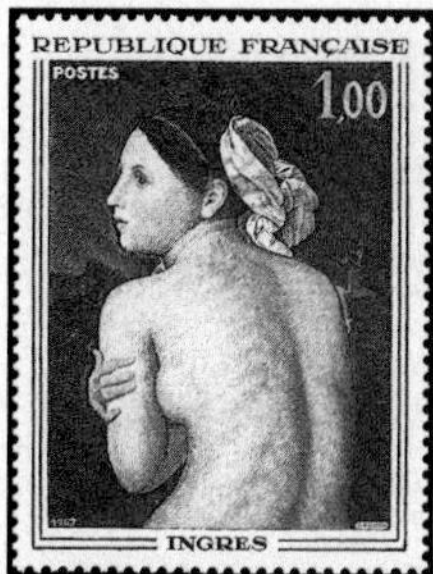

The Bather by Jean-Dominique Ingres — A470

St. Eloi, the Goldsmith, at Work — A471

1967 **Engr.** ***Perf. 13x12, 12x13***
1172 A468 1fr multicolored .30 .25
1173 A469 1fr multicolored .30 .25
1174 A470 1fr multicolored .30 .25
1175 A471 1fr multicolored .30 .25
Nos. 1172-1175 (4) 1.20 1.00

The design of No. 1175 is from a 16th century stained glass window in the Church of Sainte Madeleine, Troyes.

Issued: No. 1172, 4/15; No. 1173, 7/1; No. 1174, 9/9; No. 1175, 10/7.

Snow Crystal and Olympic Rings — A472

1967, Apr. 22 **Photo.** ***Perf. 13***
1176 A472 60c brt & lt blue & red .35 .25

Issued to publicize the 10th Winter Olympic Games, Grenoble, Feb. 6-18, 1968.

French Pavilion, EXPO '67 — A473

1967, Apr. 22 **Engr.**
1177 A473 60c dull bl & bl grn .35 .30

Intl. Exhibition EXPO '67, Montreal, Apr. 28-Oct. 27, 1967.

For surcharge see Reunion No. 363.

Europa Issue, 1967
Common Design Type

1967, Apr. 29 **Size: 22x36mm**
1178 CD10 30c blue & gray .25 .25
1179 CD10 60c brown & lt blue .30 .25

Great Bridge, Bordeaux A474

1967, May 8
1180 A474 25c olive, blk & brn .25 .25

Nungesser, Coli and "L'Oiseau Blanc" A475

1967, May 8
1181 A475 40c slate, dk & lt brn .30 .25

40th anniv. of the attempted transatlantic flight of Charles Nungesser and François Coil, French aviators.

Gouin House, Tours — A476

1967, May 13 Engr. *Perf. 13*
1182 A476 40c vio bl, red brn & red .30 .25

Congress of the Federation of French Philatelic Societies in Tours.

Ramon and Alfort Veterinary School A477

1967, May 27
1183 A477 25c brn, dp bl & yel grn .25 .25

200th anniv. of the Alfort Veterinary School and to honor Professor Gaston Ramon (1886-1963).

Robert Esnault-Pelterie, Diamant Rocket and A-1 Satellite — A478

1967, May 27
1184 A478 60c slate & vio blue .30 .25

Issued to honor Robert Esnault-Pelterie (1881-1957), aviation and space expert.

City Hall, Saint-Quentin A479

Saint-Germain-en-Laye — A480

Views: 60c, Clock Tower, Vire. 75c, Beach, La Baule, Brittany. 95c, Harbor, Boulogne-sur-Mer. 1fr, Rodez Cathedral. 1.50fr, Morlaix; old houses, grotesque carving, viaduct.

1967
1185 A479 50c bl, sl bl & brn .25 .25
1186 A479 60c dp bl, sl bl & dk red brn .30 .25
1187 A480 70c rose car, red brn & bl .30 .25
1188 A480 75c multicolored 1.10 .60
1189 A480 95c sky bl, lil & sl grn 1.10 .60
1190 A479 1fr indigo & bl gray .45 .25
1191 A479 1.50fr brt bl, brt grn & red brn .90 .35
Nos. 1185-1191 (7) 4.40 2.55

Issued: 1fr, 1.50fr, June 10; 70c, June 17; 50c, 60c, 95c, July 8; 75c, July 24.

Orchids — A481

1967, July 29 Engr. *Perf. 13*
1192 A481 40c dp car, brt pink & pur .50 .40

Orleans flower festival.

Scales of Justice, City and Harbor A482

1967, Sept. 4
1193 A482 60c dk plum, dl bl & ocher .50 .30

9th Intl. Accountancy Cong., Paris, 9/6-12.

Cross of Lorraine, Soldiers and Sailors — A483

1967, Oct. 7 Engr. *Perf. 13*
1194 A483 25c brn, dp ultra & bl .25 .25

25th anniv. of the Battle of Bir Hacheim.

Marie Curie, Bowl Glowing with Radium A484

1967, Oct. 23 Engr. *Perf. 13*
1195 A484 60c dk blue & ultra .30 .25

Marie Curie (1867-1934), scientist who discovered radium and polonium, Nobel prize winner for physics and chemistry.

Lions Emblem A485

1967, Oct. 28
1196 A485 40c dk car & vio bl .70 .40

50th anniversary of Lions International.
For surcharge see Reunion No. 364.

Marianne (by Cheffer) — A486

1967, Nov. 4 Engr.
1197 A486 25c dark blue .25 .25
1198 A486 30c bright lilac .25 .25
a. Booklet pane of 5 6.00
b. Booklet pane of 10 12.00

Coils (vertical) of Nos. 1197 and 1231 show a red number on the back of every 10th stamp.
See Nos. 1230-1231C, 3525, 4410e, 4517.
For surcharges see Reunion Nos. 367-368, 389.
Stamps of various colors and printing methods with denomination of €1 were limited printings sold in 2010. See footnote after No.3478.

King Philip II (Philip Augustus) at Battle of Bouvines A487

Designs: No. 1200, Election of Hugh Capet as King, horiz. 60c, King Louis IX (St. Louis) holding audience for the poor.

1967, Nov. 13 Engr. *Perf. 13*
1199 A487 40c gray & black .30 .25
1200 A487 40c dp bluish grn & blue .30 .25
1201 A487 60c grn & dk red brn .40 .25
Nos. 1199-1201 (3) 1.00 .75

Commemorative Medal — A488

1968, Jan. 6 Engr. *Perf. 13*
1202 A488 40c dk slate grn & bis .25 .25

50th anniversary of postal checking service.

Various Road Signs — A489

1968, Feb. 24
1203 A489 25c lil, red & dk bl grn .25 .25

Issued to publicize road safety.

Prehistoric Paintings, Lascaux Cave — A490

Arearea (Merriment) by Paul Gauguin — A491

The Dance by Emile Antoine Bourdelle A492

Portrait of the Model by Auguste Renoir A493

1968 Engr. *Perf. 13x12, 12x13*
1204 A490 1fr multicolored .50 .30
1205 A491 1fr multicolored .50 .30
1206 A492 1fr car & gray olive .50 .30
1207 A493 1fr multicolored .50 .30
Nos. 1204-1207 (4) 2.00 1.20

Issued: No. 1204, 4/13; No. 1205, 9/21; No. 1206, 10/26; No. 1207, 11/9.

Audio-visual Institute, Royan — A494

1968, Apr. 13 *Perf. 13*
1208 A494 40c slate grn, brn & Prus bl .25 .25

5th Conference for World Cooperation with the theme of teaching living languages by audio-visual means.

Europa Issue, 1968
Common Design Type

1968, Apr. 27 Size: 36x22mm
1209 CD11 30c brt red lil & ocher .25 .25
1210 CD11 60c brown & lake .60 .30

Alain René Le Sage — A495

1968, May 4
1211 A495 40c blue & rose vio .25 .25

Alain René Le Sage (1668-1747), novelist and playwright.

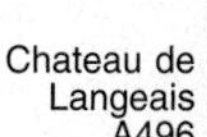

Chateau de Langeais
A496

1968, May 4

1212 A496 60c slate bl, grn & red brn .65 .30

Pierre Larousse
A497

1968, May 11 **Engr.** ***Perf. 13***

1213 A497 40c rose vio & brown .25 .25

Pierre Larousse (1817-75), grammarian, lexicographer and encyclopedist.

Gnarled Trunk and Fir Tree — A498

1968, May 18 **Engr.** ***Perf. 13***

1214 A498 25c grnsh bl, brn & grn .25 .25

Twinning of Rambouillet Forest in France and the Black Forest in Germany.

Map of Papal Enclave, Valréas, and John XXII Receiving Homage
A499

1968, May 25

1215 A499 60c brn, bis brn & pur .40 .25

Papal enclave at Valréas, 650th anniv.

Louis XIV, Arms of France and Flanders
A500

1968, June 29

1216 A500 40c rose car, gray & lemon .25 .25

300th anniv. of the Treaty of Aachen which reunited Flanders with France.

Martrou Bridge, Rochefort
A501

1968, July 20

1217 A501 25c sky bl, blk & dk red brn .25 .25

Letord Lorraine Bimotor Plane over Map of France
A502

1968, Aug. 17 **Engr.** ***Perf. 13***

1218 A502 25c brt blue, indigo & red .40 .25

1st regularly scheduled air mail route in France from Paris to St. Nazaire, 50th anniv.

Tower de Constance, Aigues-Mortes
A503

1968, Aug. 31

1219 A503 25c red brn, sky bl & olive bister .25 .25

Bicentenary of the release of Huguenot prisoners from the Tower de Constance, Aigues-Mortes.

Cathedral and Pont Vieux, Beziers
A504

1968, Sept. 7 **Engr.** ***Perf. 13***

1220 A504 40c ind, bis & grn .95 .30

"Victory" over White Tower of Salonika — A505

1968, Sept. 28

1221 A505 40c red lilac & plum .25 .25

50th anniv. of the armistice on the eastern front in World War I, Sept. 29, 1918.

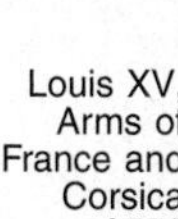

Louis XV, Arms of France and Corsica
A506

1968, Oct. 5 ***Perf. 13***

1222 A506 25c ultra, grn & blk .25 .25

Return of Corsica to France, 200th anniv.

Relay Race
A507

1968, Oct. 12

1223 A507 40c ultra, brt grn & ol brn .40 .25

19th Olympic Games, Mexico City, 10/12-27.

Polar Camp with Helicopter, Plane and Snocat Tractor — A508

1968, Oct. 19

1224 A508 40c Prus bl, lt grnsh bl & brn red .30 .25

20 years of French Polar expeditions.
For surcharge see Reunion No. 366.

Leon Bailby, Paris Opera Staircase and Hospital Beds — A509

1968, Oct. 26

1225 A509 40c ocher & maroon .25 .25

50th anniv. of the "Little White Beds" children's hospital fund.

"Victory" over Arc de Triomphe and Eternal Flame — A510

1968, Nov. 9 **Engr.** ***Perf. 13***

1226 A510 25c dk car rose & dp blue .25 .25

50th anniv. of the armistice which ended World War I.

Death of Bertrand Du Guesclin at Chateauneuf-de-Randon, 1380 — A511

No. 1228, King Philip IV (the Fair) and first States-General assembly, 1302, horiz. 60c, Joan of Arc leaving Vaucouleurs, 1429.

1968, Nov. 16

1227 A511 40c green, ultra & brn .30 .25
1228 A511 40c cop red, grn & gray .30 .25
1229 A511 60c vio bl, sl bl & bis .40 .30
Nos. 1227-1229 (3) 1.00 .80

See No. 1260.

Marianne Type of 1967

1969-70 **Engr.** ***Perf. 13***

1230 A486 30c green .35 .25
a. Booklet pane of 10 8.50
1231 A486 40c deep carmine .45 .25
a. Booklet pane of 5 (horiz. strip) 7.50
b. Booklet pane of 10 8.50
d. With label ('70) .50 .25

Typo. ***Perf. 14x13***

1231C A486 30c blue green .25 .25
Nos. 1230-1231C (3) 1.05 .75

No. 1231d was issued in sheets of 50 with alternating labels showing coat of arms of Perigueux, arranged checkerwise, to commemorate the inauguration of the Perigueux stamp printing plant.

The 40c coil is noted after No. 1198.

Church of Brou, Bourg-en-Bresse — A512

Views: 80c, Vouglans Dam, Jura. 85c, Chateau de Chantilly. 1.15fr, Sailboats in La Trinité-sur-Mer harbor.

1969 **Engr.** ***Perf. 13***

1232 A512 45c olive, bl & red brn .25 .25
1233 A512 80c ol bis, brn red & dk brn .40 .25
1234 A512 85c sl grn, dl bl & gray .75 .50
1235 A512 1.15fr brt bl, gray grn & brn .75 .50
Nos. 1232-1235 (4) 2.15 1.50

"February" Bas-relief from Amiens Cathedral
A513

Philip the Good, by Roger van der Weyden
A514

Sts. Savin and Cyprian before Ladicius, Mural, St. Savin, Vienne — A515

The Circus, by Georges Seurat
A515a

1969 ***Perf. 12x13***

1236 A513 1fr dk green & brn .40 .25
1237 A514 1fr multicolored .40 .25
1238 A515 1fr multicolored .40 .25
1239 A515a 1fr multicolored .40 .25
Nos. 1236-1239 (4) 1.60 1.00

Issue dates: No. 1236, Feb. 22; No. 1237, May 3; No. 1238, June 28; No. 1239, Nov. 8.

Gallic Coin Type of 1964-66

1969 Typo. *Perf. 13½x14*

1240 A418 22c brt green & vio .30 .25
1241 A418 35c red & ultra .85 .40
1242 A418 70c ultra & red brn 3.75 1.75
Nos. 1240-1242 (3) 4.90 2.40

Nos. 1240-1242 are known only precanceled. See note after No. 132.

Hautefort Chateau A516

1969, Apr. 5 Engr. *Perf. 13*

1243 A516 70c blue, slate & bister .40 .25

Irises A517

1969, Apr. 12 Photo.

1244 A517 45c multicolored .35 .25

3rd Intl. Flower Show, Paris, 4/23-10/5.

Europa Issue, 1969

Common Design Type

1969, Apr. 26 Engr. *Perf. 13*

Size: 36x22mm

1245 CD12 40c carmine rose .25 .25
1246 CD12 70c Prussian blue .30 .25

Albert Thomas and Thomas Memorial, Geneva A518

1969, May 10 Engr. *Perf. 13*

1247 A518 70c brn, ol bis & ind .40 .25

ILO, 50th anniv., and honoring Thomas (1878-1932), director of the ILO (1920-32).

Garigliano Battle Scene, 1944 — A519

1969, May 10

1248 A519 45c black & violet .40 .30

25th anniv. of the Battle of the Garigliano against the Germans.

Chateau du Marché, Chalons-sur-Marne A520

1969, May 24

1249 A520 45c bis, dull bl & grn .40 .30

Federation of French Philatelic Societies, 42nd congress.

Parachutists over Normandy Beach — A521

1969, May 31

1250 A521 45c dk blue & vio bl .85 .40

Landing of Special Air Service and Free French commandos in Normandy, June 6, 1944, 25th anniv.

Monument of the French Resistance, Mt. Mouchet — A522

1969, June 7

1251 A522 45c dk grn, slate & ind .60 .45

25th anniv. of the battle of Mt. Mouchet between French resistance fighters and the Germans, June 2 and 10, 1944.

French Troops Landing in Provence — A523

1969, Aug. 23 Engr. *Perf. 13*

1252 A523 45c slate & blk brn .75 .45

25th anniv. of the landing of French and American forces in Provence, Aug. 15, 1944.

Russian and French Aviators — A524

1969, Oct. 18 Engr. *Perf. 13*

1253 A524 45c slate, dp bl & car .75 .45

Issued to honor the French aviators of the Normandy-Neman Squadron who fought on the Russian Front, 1942-45.

Kayak on Isère River A525

1969, Aug. 2 Engr. *Perf. 13*

1254 A525 70c org brn, ol & dk bl .40 .25

Intl. Canoe and Kayak Championships, Bourg-Saint-Maurice, Savoy, July 31-Aug. 6.

Napoleon as Young Officer and his Birthplace, Ajaccio — A526

1969, Aug. 16

1255 A526 70c brt grnsh bl, ol & rose vio .40 .25

Napoleon Bonaparte (1769-1821).
For surcharge see Reunion No. 370.

Drops of Water and Diamond — A527

1969, Sept. 27

1256 A527 70c blk, dp bl & brt grn .40 .25

European Water Charter.

Mediterranean Mouflon — A528

1969, Oct. 11

1257 A528 45c ol, blk & org brn .60 .50

Issued to publicize wildlife protection.

Central School of Arts and Crafts A529

1969, Oct. 18

1258 A529 70c dk grn, yel grn & org .40 .25

Inauguration of the Central School of Arts and Crafts at Chatenay-Malabry.

Nuclear Submarine "Le Redoutable" — A530

1969, Oct. 25

1259 A530 70c dp bl, grn & sl grn .40 .25

Type of 1968 and

Henri IV and Edict of Nantes — A531

Designs: No. 1260, Pierre Terrail de Bayard wounded at Battle of Brescia (after a painting in Versailles). No. 1262, Louis XI, Charles the Bold and map of France.

1969, Nov. 8 Engr. *Perf. 13*

1260 A511 80c brn, bister & blk .45 .25
1261 A531 80c blk & vio bl .45 .25
1262 A531 80c ol, dp grn & dk red brn .45 .25
Nos. 1260-1262 (3) 1.35 .75

"Firecrest" and Alain Gerbault — A532

1970, Jan. 10 Engr. *Perf. 13*

1263 A532 70c ind, brt bl & gray .45 .30

Completion of Alain Gerbault's trip around the world aboard the "Firecrest," 1923-29, 40th anniv.

Gendarmery Emblem, Mountain Climber, Helicopter, Motorcyclists and Motorboat — A533

1970, Jan. 31

1264 A533 45c sl grn, dk bl & brn .80 .40

National Gendarmery, founded 1791.

Field Ball Player — A534

1970, Feb. 21 Engr. *Perf. 13*

1265 A534 80c slate green .45 .40

7th Intl. Field Ball Games, Feb. 26-Mar. 8.

Alphonse Juin and Church of the Invalides — A535

1970, Feb. 28

1266 A535 45c gray bl & dk brn .35 .25

Issued to honor Marshal Alphonse Pierre Juin (1888-1967), military leader.

Aerotrain A536

1970, Mar. 7

1267 A536 80c purple & gray .45 .40

Introduction of the aerotrain, which reaches a speed of 320 miles per hour.

Pierre Joseph Pelletier, Joseph Bienaimé Caventou, Quinine Formula and Cell — A537

1970, Mar. 21 Engr. *Perf. 13*
1268 A537 50c slate grn, sky bl & dp car .35 .25

Discovery of quinine, 150th anniversary.

Pink Flamingos — A538

1970, Mar. 21
1269 A538 45c olive, gray & pink .35 .25

European Nature Conservation Year, 1970.

Diamant B Rocket and Radar — A539

1970, Mar. 28
1270 A539 45c bright green .50 .25

Space center in Guyana and the launching of the Diamant B rocket, Mar. 10, 1970.

Europa Issue, 1970

Common Design Type

1970, May 2 Engr. *Perf. 13*
Size: 36x22mm
1271 CD13 40c deep carmine .25 .25
1272 CD13 80c sky blue .40 .25

Annunication, by Primitive Painter of Savoy, 1480 — A540

The Triumph of Flora, by Jean Baptiste Carpeaux — A541

Diana Returning from the Hunt, by François Boucher — A542

Dancer with Bouquet, by Edgar Degas A543

1970 *Perf. 12x13, 13x12*
1273 A540 1fr multicolored .50 .35
1274 A541 1fr red brown .50 .35
1275 A542 1fr multicolored .50 .35
1276 A543 1fr multicolored .50 .35
Nos. 1273-1276 (4) 2.00 1.40

Issued: No. 1273, 5/9; No. 1274, 7/4; No. 1275, 10/10; No. 1276, 11/14.

Arms of Lens, Miner's Lamp and Pit Head A544

1970, May 16 Engr. *Perf. 13*
1277 A544 40c scarlet .25 .25

43rd Natl. Congress of the Federation of French Philatelic Societies, Lens, May 14-21.

Diamond Rock, Martinique A545

Haute Provence Observatory and Spiral Nebula — A546

Designs: 95c, Chancelade Abbey, Dordogne. 1fr, Gosier Islet, Guadeloupe.

1970, June 20 Engr. *Perf. 13*
1278 A545 50c sl grn, brt bl & plum .30 .25
1279 A545 95c lt ol, car & brn .80 .80
1280 A545 1fr sl grn, brt bl & dk car rose .90 .25
1281 A546 1.30fr dk bl, vio bl & dk grn 1.10 .90
Nos. 1278-1281 (4) 3.10 2.20

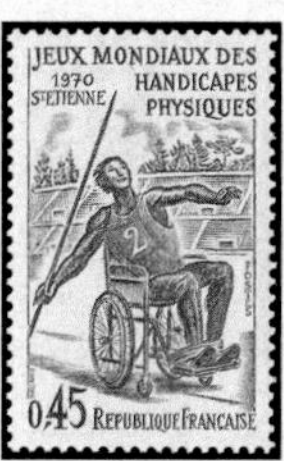

Hand Reaching for Freedom — A547

1970, June 27
1282 A547 45c vio bl, bl & bister .40 .25

Liberation of concentration camps, 25th anniv.

Handicapped Javelin Thrower — A548

1970, June 27
1283 A548 45c rose car, ultra & emer .40 .25

Issued to publicize the International Games of the Handicapped, St. Etienne, June 1970.

Pole Vault — A549

1970, Sept. 11 Engr. *Perf. 13*
1284 A549 45c car, bl & indigo .45 .25

First European Junior Athletic Championships, Colombes, Sept. 11-13.

Royal Salt Works, Arc-et-Senans — A550

1970, Sept. 26
1285 A550 80c bl, brn & dk grn .70 .65

Restoration of the 18th cent. Royal Salt Works buildings, by Claude Nicolas Ledoux (1736-1806) at Arc-et-Senans, for use as a center for studies of all aspects of future human life.

Armand Jean du Plessis, Duc de Richelieu — A551

Designs: No. 1287, Battle of Fontenoy, 1745. No. 1288, Louis XIV and Versailles.

1970, Oct. 17 Engr. *Perf. 13*
1286 A551 45c blk, sl & car rose .50 .30
1287 A551 45c org, brn & indigo .50 .30
1288 A551 45c sl grn, lem & org brn .50 .30
Nos. 1286-1288 (3) 1.50 .90

UN Headquarters in New York and Geneva — A552

1970, Oct. 24 Engr. *Perf. 13*
1289 A552 80c ol, dp ultra & dk pur .40 .25

25th anniversary of the United Nations.

View of Bordeaux and France No. 43 — A553

1970, Nov. 7
1290 A553 80c vio bl & gray bl .40 .25

Centerary of the Bordeaux issue.

Col. Denfert-Rochereau and Lion of Belfort, by Frederic A. Bartholdi — A554

1970, Nov. 14
1291 A554 45c dk bl, ol & red brn .40 .25

Centenary of the siege of Belfort during Franco-Prussian War.

Marianne (by Bequet) — A555

1971-74 Typo. *Perf. 14x13*
1292 A555 45c sky blue .30 .25
1292A A555 60c green ('74) .50 .25

For surcharges see Reunion Nos. 371, 397-398.

Engr. *Perf. 13*
1293 A555 50c rose carmine .30 .25
a. Bklt. pane of 5 (horiz. strip) 5.00
b. Booklet pane of 10 10.00
1294 A555 60c green ('74) 4.00 .25
a. Booklet pane of 10 65.00
1294B A555 80c car rose ('74) .50 .25
c. Booklet pane of 5 9.00
d. Booklet pane of 10 12.00
Nos. 1293-1294B (3) 4.80 .75

Nos. 1294 and 1294B issued also in vertical coils with control number on back of every 10th stamp.

No. 1293 issued only in booklets and in vertical coils with red control number on back of every 10th stamp.

See Nos. 1494-1498, 3526, 4410f, 4518.

St. Matthew, Sculpture from Strasbourg Cathedral A556

Winnower, by François Millet A557

The Dreamer, by Georges Rouault A558

1971 Engr. *Perf. 12x13*

1295 A556 1fr dark red brown .50 .40
1296 A557 1fr multicolored .50 .40
1297 A558 1fr multicolored .50 .40
Nos. 1295-1297 (3) 1.50 1.20

Issued: No. 1295, 1/23; No. 1296, 4/3; No. 1297, 6/5.

Figure Skating Pair A560

1971, Feb. 20 Engr. *Perf. 13*

1299 A560 80c vio bl, sl & aqua .50 .30

World Figure Skating Championships, Lyons, Feb. 23-28.

Underwater Exploration — A561

1971, Mar. 6

1300 A561 80c blue blk & bl grn .45 .25

International Exhibition of Ocean Exploration, Bordeaux, Mar. 9-14.

Cape Horn Clipper "Antoinette" and Solidor Castle, Saint-Malo — A562

1971, Apr. 10 Engr. *Perf. 13*

1301 A562 80c blue, pur & slate .80 .45

For surcharge see Reunion No. 372.

Pyrenean Chamois — A563

1971, Apr. 24 Engr. *Perf. 13*

1302 A563 65c bl, dk brn & brn ol .50 .30

National Park of Western Pyrenees.

Europa Issue, 1971

Common Design Type and

Santa Maria della Salute, Venice A564

1971, May 8 Engr. *Perf. 13*

1303 A564 50c blue gray & ol bis .30 .25

Size: 36x22mm

1304 CD14 80c rose lilac .45 .40

Cardinal, Nobleman and Lawyer — A565

Storming of the Bastille — A566

Design: No. 1306, Battle of Valmy.

1971

1305 A565 45c bl, rose red & pur .45 .30
1306 A565 45c bl, ol bis & brn red .50 .30
1307 A566 65c dk brn, gray bl & mag .65 .45
Nos. 1305-1307 (3) 1.60 1.05

No. 1305 commemorates the opening of the Estates General, May 5, 1789; No. 1306, Battle of Valmy (Sept. 20, 1792) between French and Prussian armies; 65c, Storming of the Bastille, Paris, July 14, 1789.

Issued: No. 1305, 5/8; No. 1306, 9/18; 65c, 7/10.

Grenoble A568

1971, May 29 Engr. *Perf. 13*

1308 A568 50c ocher, lil & rose red .35 .25

44th Natl. Cong. of the Federation of French Philatelic Societies, Grenoble, May 30-31.

"Rural Family Aid" Shedding Light on Village — A569

1971, June 5

1309 A569 40c vio, bl & grn .25 .25

Aid for rural families.

For surcharge see Reunion No. 373.

Chateau and Fort de Sedan A570

Pont d'Arc, Ardèche Gorge — A571

Views: 60c, Sainte Chapelle, Riom. 65c, Fountain and tower, Dole. 90c, Tower and street, Riquewihr.

1971 Engr. *Perf. 13*

1310 A571 60c black, grn & bl .30 .25
1311 A571 65c lil, ocher & blk .55 .25
1312 A571 90c grn, vio brn & red brn .55 .25
1313 A570 1.10fr sl grn, Prus bl & brn .65 .45
1314 A571 1.40fr sl grn, bl & dk brn .75 .25
Nos. 1310-1314 (5) 2.80 1.45

Issued: 60c, 6/19; 65c, 90c, 7/3; 1.10fr, 1.40fr, 6/12.

For surcharges see Reunion Nos. 374, 381.

Gallic Coin Type of 1964-66

1971, July 1 Typo. *Perf. 13½x14*

1315 A418 26c lilac & brn .30 .25
1316 A418 30c lt brown & brn .35 .25
1317 A418 45c dull green & brn 1.20 .40
1318 A418 90c red & brown 1.50 .75
Nos. 1315-1318 (4) 3.35 1.65

Nos. 1315-1318 are known only precanceled. See second paragraph after No. 132.

Bourbon Palace A572

1971, Aug. 28 Engr. *Perf. 13*

1319 A572 90c violet blue .50 .35

59th Conf. of the Interparliamentary Union.

Embroidery and Tool Making A573

1971, Oct. 16

1320 A573 90c brn red, brt lil & cl .50 .30

40th anniv. of the first assembly of presidents of artisans' guilds.

For surcharge see Reunion No. 375.

Reunion Chameleon A574

1971, Nov. 6 Photo. *Perf. 13*

1321 A574 60c brn, yel, grn & blk .65 .45

Nature protection.

De Gaulle Issue

Common Design Type and

De Gaulle in Brazzaville, 1944 — A576

Designs: No. 1324, De Gaulle entering Paris, 1944. No. 1325, Pres. de Gaulle, 1970.

1971, Nov. 9 Engr.

1322 CD134 50c black .65 .45
1323 A576 50c ultra .65 .45
1324 A576 50c rose red .65 .45
1325 CD134 50c black .65 .45
a. Strip of 4, #1322-1325 + label 3.00 2.50
Nos. 1325a (1) 3.00 2.50

1st anniv. of the death of Charles de Gaulle.

See Reunion Nos. 377, 380.

Antoine Portal and first Session of Academy — A577

1971, Nov. 13

1326 A577 45c dk purple & mag .40 .25

Sesquicentennial of the founding of the National Academy of Medicine; Baron Antoine Portal was first president.

L'Etude, by Jean Honoré Fragonard A578

Women in Garden, by Claude Monet A579

St. Peter Presenting Pierre de Bourbon, by Maitre de Moulins A580

Boats, by André Derain — A581

1972 Engr. *Perf. 12x13, 13x12*

1327 A578 1fr black & multi .50 .40
1328 A579 1fr slate grn & multi 1.00 .50
1329 A580 2fr dk brown & multi 1.25 1.00
1330 A581 2fr yellow & multi 1.25 1.00
Nos. 1327-1330 (4) 4.00 2.90

Issued: No. 1327, 1/22; No. 1328, 6/17; No. 1329, 10/14; No. 1330, 12/16.

Map of South Indian Ocean, Penguin and Ships — A582

1972, Jan. 29 *Perf. 13*

1331 A582 90c black, bl & ocher .50 .30

Bicentenary of discovery of the Crozet and Kerguelen Islands.

Slalom and Olympic Emblems A583

1972, Feb. 7

1332 A583 90c dk olive & dp car .50 .30

11th Winter Olympic Games, Sapporo, Japan, Feb. 3-13.

Hearts, UN Emblem, Caduceus and Pacemaker A584

1972, Apr. 8 Engr. *Perf. 13*

1333 A584 45c dk car, org & gray .35 .25

"Your heart is your health," world health month.

Red Deer, Sologne Plateau — A585

Charlieu Abbey A585a

Bazoches-du-Morvand Chateau — A586

Saint-Just Cathedral, Narbonne A587

1972 *Perf. 13*

1334 A585 1fr ocher & red brn .50 .25
1335 A585a 1.20fr sl & dull brn .65 .25
1336 A586 2fr sl grn, blk & red brn 1.00 .25
1337 A587 3.50fr bl, gray ol & car rose 1.50 .45
Nos. 1334-1337 (4) 3.65 1.20

Issued: 1fr, 9/10; 1.20fr, 4/29; 2fr, 9/9; 3.50fr, 4/8.
For surcharge see Reunion No. 388.

Eagle Owl — A588

Nature protection: 60c, Salmon, horiz.

1972

1338 A588 60c grn, ind & brt bl 1.50 .60
1339 A588 65c sl, ol brn & sep .80 .50

Issue dates: 60c, May 27; 65c, Apr. 15.

Europa Issue
Common Design Type and

Aix-la-Chapelle Cathedral — A589

1972, Apr. 22 Engr. *Perf. 13*

1340 A589 50c yel, vio brn & dk ol .25 .25

Photo.
Size: 22x36mm

1341 CD15 90c red org & multi .50 .35
Nos. 1341 (1) .50 .35

Bouquet Made of Hearts and Blood Donors' Emblem — A590

1972, May 5 Engr.

1342 A590 40c red .30 .25

20th anniv. of the Blood Donors Association of Post and Telecommunications Employees.
For surcharge see Reunion No. 383.

Newfoundlander "Côte d'Emeraude" A591

1972, May 6

1343 A591 90c org, vio bl & sl grn .75 .55

Cathedral, Saint-Brieuc A592

1972, May 20

1344 A592 50c lilac rose .35 .25

45th Congress of the Federation of French Philatelic Societies, Saint-Brieuc, May 21-22.

Hand Holding Symbol of Postal Code A593

1972, June 3 Typo. *Perf. 14x13*

1345 A593 30c green, blk & car .25 .25
1346 A593 50c car, blk & yel .30 .25

Introduction of postal code system.
For surcharges see Reunion Nos. 384-385.

Old and New Communications A594

1972, July 1 Engr. *Perf. 13*

1347 A594 45c slate & vio blue .40 .25

21st Intl. Congress of P.T.T. (Post, Telegraph & Telephone) Employees, Paris, 7/1-7.

Hurdler and Olympic Rings A595

1972, July 8

1348 A595 1fr deep olive .50 .25

20th Olympic Games, Munich, 8/26-9/11.

Hikers and Mt. Aigoual — A596

1972, July 15 Photo. *Perf. 13*

1349 A596 40c brt rose & multi .75 .30

Intl. Year of Tourism and 25th anniv. of the Natl. Hikers Association.

Bicyclist — A597

1972, July 22 Engr.

1350 A597 1fr gray, brn & lil 1.20 .60

World Bicycling Championships, Marseille, July 29-Aug. 2.

"Incroyables and Merveilleuses," 1794 — A598

French History: 60c, Bonaparte at the Arcole Bridge. 65c, Egyptian expedition (soldiers and scientists finding antiquities; pyramids in background).

1972 Engr. *Perf. 13*

1351 A598 45c ol, dk grn & car rose .40 .30
1352 A598 60c red, blk & ind .65 .35
1353 A598 65c ocher, ultra & choc .65 .35
Nos. 1351-1353 (3) 1.70 1.00

. Issued: 45c, Oct. 7; 60c, 65c, Nov. 11.

Champollion, Rosetta Stone with Key Inscription — A599

1972, Oct. 14

1354 A599 90c vio bl, brn red & blk .50 .30

Sesquicentennial of the deciphering of hieroglyphs by Jean-François Champollion.

St. Teresa, Portal of Notre Dame of Alençon A600

1973, Jan. 6 Engr. *Perf. 13*

1355 A600 1fr Prus blue & indigo .50 .30

Centenary of the birth of St. Teresa of Lisieux, the Little Flower (Thérèse Martin, 1873-1897), Carmelite nun.

Anthurium (Martinique) — A601

1973, Jan. 20 **Photo.**
1356 A601 50c gray & multi .35 .25

Colors of France and Germany Interlaced — A602

1973, Jan. 22
1357 A602 50c multicolored .40 .25

10th anniv. of the Franco-German Cooperation Treaty. See Germany No. 1101.

Polish Immigrants — A603

1973, Feb. 3 **Engr.** ***Perf. 13***
1358 A603 40c slate grn, dp car & brn .40 .25

50th anniversary of Polish immigration into France, 1921-1923.

Last Supper, St. Austremoine Church, Issoire — A604

Kneeling Woman, by Charles Le Brun A605

Angel, Wood, Moutier-D'Ahun — A606

Lady Playing Archlute, by Antoine Watteau A607

1973 **Engr.** ***Perf. 12x13***
1359 A604 2fr brown & multi 1.25 .75
1360 A605 2fr dk red & yel 1.25 .75
1361 A606 2fr ol brn & vio brn 1.25 .75
1362 A607 2fr black & multi 1.25 .75
Nos. 1359-1362 (4) 5.00 3.00

Issued: No. 1359, 2/10; No. 1360, 4/28; No. 1361, 5/26; No. 1362, 9/22.

Tuileries Palace, Telephone Relays A608

Oil Tanker, Francis I Lock A609

Airbus A300-B A610

1973
1363 A608 45c ultra, sl grn & bis .30 .25
1364 A609 90c plum, blk & bl .55 .25
1365 A610 3fr dk brn, bl & blk 1.25 .65
Nos. 1363-1365 (3) 2.10 1.15

French technical achievements.
Issued: 45c, 5/15; 90c, 10/27; 3fr, 4/7.

Europa Issue 1973
Common Design Type and

City Hall, Brussels, CEPT Emblem — A611

1973, Apr. 14 **Engr.** ***Perf. 13***
1366 A611 50c brt pink & choc .40 .25

Photo.
Size: 36x22mm
1367 CD16 90c slate grn & multi 1.25 .75

Masonic Lodge Emblem A612

1973, May 12 **Engr.** ***Perf. 13***
1368 A612 90c magenta & vio bl .50 .30

Bicentenary of the Free Masons of France.

Guadeloupe Raccoon A613

White Storks A614

1973
1369 A613 40c lilac, sepia & olive .35 .25
1370 A614 60c blk, aqua & org red .50 .25

Nature protection.
Issue dates: 40c, June 23; 60c, May 12.

Tourist Issue

Doubs Waterfall A615

Clos-Lucé, Amboise A617

Palace of Dukes of Burgundy, Dijon A616

Design: 90c, Gien Chateau.

1973 **Engr.** ***Perf. 13***
1371 A615 60c multicolored .30 .25
1372 A616 65c red & purple .30 .25
1373 A616 90c Prus bl, ind & brn .40 .25
1374 A617 1fr ocher, bl & sl grn .45 .25
Nos. 1371-1374 (4) 1.45 1.00

Issued: 60c, 9/8; 65c, 5/19; 90c, 8/18; 1fr, 6/23.
For surcharge see Reunion No. 387.

Academy Emblem — A618

1973, May 26
1375 A618 1fr lil, slate grn & red .50 .30

Academy of Overseas Sciences, 50th anniv.

Racing Car and Clocks A619

1973, June 2
1376 A619 60c dk brown & blue .50 .30

24-hour automobile race at Le Mans, 50th anniv.

Five-master France II — A620

1973, June 9
1377 A620 90c ultra, Prus bl & ind .90 .45

For surcharge see Reunion No. 386.

Tower and Square, Toulouse — A621

1973, June 9
1378 A621 50c purple & red brn .30 .25

46th Congress of the Federation of French Philatelic Societies, Toulouse, June 9-12.

Dr. Armauer G. Hansen — A622

1973, Sept. 29 **Engr.** ***Perf. 13***
1379 A622 45c grn, dk ol & ocher .30 .25

Centenary of the discovery of the Hansen bacillus, the cause of leprosy.

Ducretet and his Transmission Diagram — A623

1973, Oct. 6
1380 A623 1fr yel grn & magenta .40 .30

75th anniversary of the first transmission of radio signals from the Eiffel Tower to the Pantheon by Eugene Ducretet (1844-1915).

Molière as Sganarelle — A624

1973, Oct. 20

1381 A624 1fr dk red & olive brn .45 .30

Moliere (Jean-Baptiste Poquelin; 1622-1673), playwright and actor.

Pierre Bourgoin and Philippe Kieffer A625

1973, Oct. 27

1382 A625 1fr red, rose cl & vio bl .45 .30

Pierre Bourgoin (1907-70), and Philippe Kieffer (1899-1963), heroes of the Free French forces in World War II.

Napoleon, Jean Portalis and Palace of Justice, Paris — A626

Exhibition Halls — A627

The Coronation of Napoleon, by Jean Louis David — A628

1973 Engr. *Perf. 13*

1383 A626 45c blue, choc & gray .40 .30
1384 A627 60c ol, sl grn & brn .40 .40
1385 A628 1fr sl grn, ol & claret .55 .40
Nos. 1383-1385 (3) 1.35 1.10

History of France. 45c, for the preparation of the Code Napoleon; 60c, Napoleon's encouragement of industry; 1fr, his coronation.

Issued: 45c, 11/3; 60c, 11/24; 1fr, 11/12.

Eternal Flame, Arc de Triomphe — A629

1973, Nov. 10

1386 A629 40c pur, vio bl & red .40 .30

50th anniv. of the Eternal Flame at the Arc de Triomphe, Paris.

Weather Vane — A630

1973, Dec. 1

1387 A630 65c ultra, blk & grn .40 .30

50th anniv. of the Dept. of Agriculture.

Human Rights Flame and Man — A631

1973, Dec. 8 Engr. *Perf. 13*

1388 A631 45c car, org & blk .30 .25

25th anniversary of the Universal Declaration of Human Rights.

Postal Museum — A632

1973, Dec. 19

1389 A632 50c maroon & bister .30 .25

Opening of new post and philately museum, Paris.

ARPHILA 75 Emblem A633

1974, Jan. 19 Engr. *Perf. 13*

1390 A633 50c brn, bl & brt lil .30 .25

ARPHILA 75 Philatelic Exhibition, Paris, June 1975.

For surcharge see Reunion No. 390.

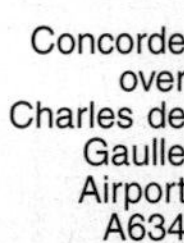

Concorde over Charles de Gaulle Airport A634

Turbotrain T.G.V. 001 A635

Phenix Nuclear Power Station A636

1974 Engr. *Perf. 13*

1391 A634 60c pur & ol gray .40 .30
1392 A635 60c multicolored .85 .40
1393 A636 65c multicolored .40 .30
Nos. 1391-1393 (3) 1.65 1.00

French technical achievements.

Issued: No. 1391, 3/18; No. 1392, 8/31; 65c, 9/21.

Cardinal Richelieu, by Philippe de Champaigne — A637

Painting by Joan Miró A638

Canal du Loing, by Alfred Sisley — A639

"In Honor of Nicolas Fouquet," Tapestry by Georges Mathieu A640

Engr., Photo. (#1395, 1397)

1974 *Perf. 12x13, 13x12*

1394 A637 2fr multicolored 1.25 1.00
1395 A638 2fr multicolored 1.25 1.00
1396 A639 2fr multicolored 1.25 1.00
1397 A640 2fr multicolored 1.25 1.00
Nos. 1394-1397 (4) 5.00 4.00

Nos. 1394-1397 are printed in sheets of 25 with alternating labels publicizing "ARPHILA 75," Paris, June 6-16, 1975.

Issued: No. 1394, 3/23; No. 1395, 9/14; No. 1396, 11/9; No. 1397, 11/16.

For surcharges see Reunion Nos. 391-394.

French Alps and Gentian A641

1974, Mar. 30 Engr. *Perf. 13*

1398 A641 65c vio blue & gray .40 .25

Centenary of the French Alpine Club.

Europa Issue 1974

"Age of Bronze," by Auguste Rodin — A642

"Air," by Aristide Maillol A643

1974, Apr. 20 *Perf. 13*

1399 A642 50c brt rose lil & blk .30 .25
1400 A643 90c olive & brown .55 .40

Sea Rescue — A644

1974, Apr. 27

1401 A644 90c multicolored .50 .30

Reorganized sea rescue organization.

For surcharge see Reunion No. 395.

Council Building, View of Strasbourg and Emblem — A645

1974, May 4 Engr. *Perf. 13*

1402 A645 45c indigo, bister & bl .30 .25

25th anniversary of the Council of Europe.

Tourist Issue

View of Salers A646

Basilica of St. Nicolas de Porte — A647

Seashell over Corsica — A648

Design: 1.10fr, View of Lot Valley.

1974 Engr. *Perf. 13*

1403 A646 65c yel grn & choc .25 .25
1404 A646 1.10fr choc & sl grn .45 .30
1405 A647 2fr gray & lilac .80 .30
1406 A648 3fr multicolored 1.00 .40
Nos. 1403-1406 (4) 2.50 1.25

Issued: 65c, 6/22; 1.10fr, 9/7; 2fr, 10/12; 3fr, 5/11.

Bison
A649

Giant Armadillo of Guyana
A650

1974

1407 A649 40c bis, choc & bl .35 .25
1408 A650 65c slate, olive & grn .35 .25

Nature protection.
Issued: No. 1407, 5/25; No. 1408, 10/19.

Americans Landing in Normandy and Arms of Normandy — A651

General Marie-Pierre Koenig — A652

Order of the French Resistance — A653

1974

1409 A651 45c grn, rose & ind .80 .50
1410 A652 1fr multicolored .50 .35
1411 A653 1fr multicolored .65 .50
Nos. 1409-1411 (3) 1.95 1.35

30th anniversary of the liberation of France from the Nazis. Design of No. 1410 includes diagram of battle of Bir-Hakeim and Free French and Bir-Hakeim memorials.

Issued: 45c, 6/8; No. 1410, 5/25; No. 1411, 11/23.

See No. B478.

Pfister House, 16th Century, Colmar — A654

1974, June 1

1412 A654 50c multicolored .25 .25

47th Congress of the Federation of French Philatelic Societies, Colmar, May 30-June 4.

Chess
A655

1974, June 8

1413 A655 1fr dk brown & multi .50 .30

21st Chess Olympiad, Nice, June 6-30.

Facade with Statue of Louis XIV, and 1675 Medal — A656

1974, June 15

1414 A656 40c indigo, bl & brn .30 .25

300th anniversary of the founding of the Hotel des Invalides (Home for poor and sick officers and soldiers).

Peacocks Holding Letter, and Globe — A657

1974, Oct. 5 **Engr.** ***Perf. 13***

1415 A657 1.20fr ultra, dp grn & dk car .50 .30

Centenary of Universal Postal Union.
For surcharge see Reunion No. 396.

Copernicus and Heliocentric System — A658

1974, Oct. 12

1416 A658 1.20fr multicolored .50 .25

500th anniversary of the birth of Nicolaus Copernicus (1473-1543), Polish astronomer.

Tourist Issue

Palace of Justice, Rouen
A659

Saint-Pol-de-Leon
A660

Chateau de Rochechouart — A661

1975 **Engr.** ***Perf. 13***

1417 A659 85c multicolored .50 .30
1418 A660 1.20fr bl, bis & choc .50 .30
1419 A661 1.40fr brn, ind & grn .60 .30
Nos. 1417-1419 (3) 1.60 .90

Issued: 85c, 1/25; 1.20fr, 1/18; 1.40fr, 1/11.

Snowy Egret — A662

1975, Feb. 15 **Engr.** ***Perf. 13***

1420 A662 70c brt blue & bister .40 .30

Nature protection.

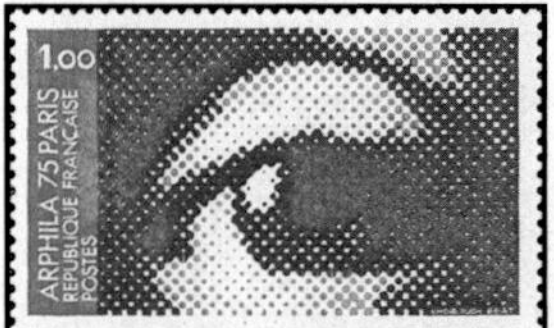

Gallic Coin — A663

1975, Feb. 16 **Typo.** ***Perf. 13½x14***

1421 A663 42c orange & mag .90 .45
1422 A663 48c lt bl & red brn 1.00 .70
1423 A663 70c brt pink & red 1.75 1.00
1424 A663 1.35fr lt green & brn 2.40 1.25
Nos. 1421-1424 (4) 6.05 3.40

Nos. 1421-1424 are known only precanceled. See second note after No. 132. See Nos. 1460-1463, 1487-1490.

The Eye — A664

Ionic Capital — A665

Graphic Art — A666

Ceres — A667

1975 **Engr.** ***Perf. 13***

1425 A664 1fr red, pur & org .45 .30
1426 A665 2fr grn, sl grn & mag .80 .55
1427 A666 3fr dk car & ol grn 1.25 .90
1428 A667 4fr red, sl grn & bis 1.60 1.25
Nos. 1425-1428 (4) 4.10 3.00

Souvenir Sheet

1429 Sheet of 4 7.50 7.50
a. A664 2fr dp car & slate blue 1.00 1.00
b. A665 3fr brt bl, sl bl & dp car 1.40 1.40
c. A666 4fr slate blue, brt bl & plum 2.00 2.00
d. A667 6fr brt bl, sl bl & plum 2.50 2.50

ARPHILA 75, Intl. Philatelic Exhibition, Paris, 6/6-16. Issued: 1fr, 3/1; 2fr, 3/22; 3fr, 4/19; 4fr, 5/17; No. 1429, 4/2.

Pres. Georges Pompidou — A668

1975, Apr. 3 **Engr.** ***Perf. 13***

1430 A668 80c black & gray .40 .25

Georges Pompidou (1911-74), President of France, 1969-74.

Paul as Harlequin, by Picasso — A669

Europa; 1.20fr, Woman on Balcony, by Kees van Dongen

1975, Apr. 26 **Photo.** ***Perf. 13***

1431 A669 80c multi .45 .35
1432 A669 1.20fr multi, horiz. .80 .70

Machines, Globe, Emblem
A670

1975, May 3 **Engr.**

1433 A670 1.20fr blue, blk & red .50 .30

World Machine Tool Exhib., Paris, 6/7-26.

Senate Assembly Hall
A671

1975, May 24 **Engr.** ***Perf. 13***

1434 A671 1.20fr olive & dk car .50 .30

Centenary of the Senate of the Republic.

Meter Convention Document, Atom Diagram and Waves — A672

1975, May 31

1435 A672 1fr multicolored .50 .30

Cent. of Intl. Meter Convention, Paris, 1875.

Metro Regional Train
A673

"Gazelle" Helicopter
A674

1975

1436 A673 1fr blue & brt bl .55 .30
1437 A674 1.30fr vio bl & grn .60 .40

French technical achievements.
Issue dates: 1fr, June 21; 1.30fr, May 31.

Youth and Flasks, Symbols of Study and Growth — A675

1975, June 21

1438 A675 70c red pur & blk .30 .25

Student Health Foundation.

People's Theater, Bussang, and Maurice Pottecher
A676

1975, Aug. 9 Engr. *Perf. 13*

1439 A676 85c multicolored .35 .25

80th anniversary of the People's Theater at Bussang, founded by Maurice Pottecher.

Regions of France

Central France
A677

Aquitaine
A678

Limousin
A679

Picardy
A680

Burgundy
A681

Loire
A682

Guyana
A683

Auvergne
A684

Poitou-Charentes
A685

Southern Pyrenees
A686

Pas-de-Calais — A687

1975-76 Engr. *Perf. 13*

1440 A677 25c blue & yel grn .25 .25
1441 A678 60c multicolored .25 .25
1442 A679 70c multicolored .50 .35
1443 A680 85c bl, grn & org .70 .35
1444 A681 1fr red, yel & mar .70 .35
1445 A682 1.15fr bl, bis & grn .70 .35
1446 A683 1.25fr multicolored .65 .50
1447 A684 1.30fr dk bl & red .85 .50
1448 A685 1.90fr sl, ol & Prus bl 1.00 .50
1449 A686 2.20fr multicolored 1.10 1.00
1450 A687 2.80fr car, bl & blk 1.40 1.00
Nos. 1440-1450 (11) 8.10 5.40

Issued: 85c, 11/15; 1fr, 10/25; 1.15fr, 9/6; 1.30fr, 10/4/75; 1.90fr, 12/6; 2.80fr, 12/13; 25c, 1/31/76; 2.20fr, 1/10/76; 60c, 5/22/76; 70c, 5/29/76; 1.25fr, 10/16/76.

A690

French Flag, F.-H. Manhes, Jean Verneau, Pierre Kaan

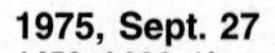

1975, Sept. 27

1453 A690 1fr multicolored .60 .30

Liberation of concentration camps, 30th anniversary. F.-H. Manhes (1889-1959), Jean Verneau (1890-1944) and Pierre Kaan (1903-1945) were French resistance leaders, imprisoned in concentration camps.

A691

Monument, by Joseph Riviere.

1975, Oct. 11

1454 A691 70c multicolored .45 .30

Land Mine Demolition Service, 30th anniversary. Monument was erected in Alsace to honor land mine victims.

Symbols of Suburban Living
A692

1975, Oct. 18

1455 A692 1.70fr brown, bl & grn .75 .50

Creation of new towns.

Women and Rainbow — A693

1975, Nov. 8 Photo.

1456 A693 1.20fr silver & multi .50 .40

International Women's Year 1975.

Saint-Nazaire Bridge — A694

1975, Nov. 8 Engr.

1457 A694 1.40fr bl, ind & grn .60 .30

French and Russian Flags — A695

1975, Nov. 22

1458 A695 1.20fr bl, red & ocher .50 .30

Franco-Soviet diplomatic relations, 50th anniv.

Frigate Melpomene
A696

1975, Dec. 6

1459 A696 90c multicolored 1.00 .50

Gallic Coin Type of 1975

1976, Jan. 1 Typo. *Perf. 13½x14*

1460 A663 50c lt green & brn 1.00 .65
1461 A663 60c lilac & brn 1.60 .95
1462 A663 90c orange & brn 2.00 1.25
1463 A663 1.60fr violet & brn 3.75 1.90
Nos. 1460-1463 (4) 8.35 4.75

Nos. 1460-1463 are known only precanceled. See second note after No. 132.

Lintel, St. Genis des Fontaines Church
A697

Venus of Brassempouy (Paleolithic) — A698

"The Joy of Life," by Robert Delaunay
A699

Ramses II, from Abu Simbel Temple, Egypt — A700

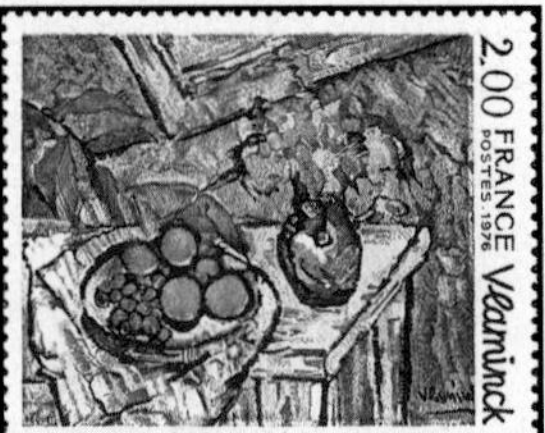

Still Life, by Maurice de Vlaminck — A701

1976 Engr. *Perf. 13*

1464	A697	2fr blue & slate bl	1.10	.60
1465	A698	2fr dk brn & yel	1.10	.60

Photo. *Perf. 12½x13*

1466	A699	2fr multicolored	1.10	.60

Engr. *Perf. 13x12½*

1467	A700	2fr multicolored	.80	.50

Perf. 13

1468	A701	2fr multicolored	.80	.50
		Nos. 1464-1468 (5)	4.90	2.80

Issued: No. 1464, 1/24; No. 1465, 3/6; No. 1466, 7/24; No. 1467, 9/4; No. 1468, 12/18.

Tourist Issue

Chateau Fort de Bonaguil A702

Lodève Cathedral — A703

Biarritz A704

Thiers — A705

Ussel — A706

Chateau de Malmaison A707

1976 Engr. *Perf. 13*

1469	A702	1fr multicolored	.35	.25
1470	A703	1.10fr violet blue	.40	.25
1471	A704	1.40fr multicolored	.60	.25
1472	A705	1.70fr multicolored	.60	.25
1473	A706	2fr multicolored	.90	.25
1474	A707	3fr multicolored	1.10	.25
		Nos. 1469-1474 (6)	3.95	1.50

Issued: 1fr, 2fr, 7/10; 1.10fr, 11/13; 1.40fr, 9/25; 1.70fr, 10/9; 3fr, 4/10.

Destroyers, Association Emblem A708

1976, Apr. 24

1475	A708	1fr vio bl, mag & lem	.50	.30

Naval Reserve Officers Assoc., 50th anniv.

Gate, Rouen — A709

1976, Apr. 24

1476	A709	80c olive gray & sal	.35	.25

49th Congress of the Federation of French Philatelic Societies, Rouen, Apr. 23-May 2.

Young Person — A710

1976, Apr. 27

1477	A710	60c bl grn, ind & car	.35	.25

JUVAROUEN 76, International Youth Philatelic Exhibition, Rouen, Apr. 25-May 2.

Europa Issue

Ceramic Pitcher, Strasbourg, 18th Century A711

1.20fr, Sevres porcelain plate & CEPT emblem.

1976, May 8 Photo. *Perf. 13*

1478	A711	80c multicolored	.30	.30
1479	A711	1.20fr multicolored	.65	.55

Count de Vergennes and Benjamin Franklin — A712

1976, May 15 Engr. *Perf. 13*

1480	A712	1.20fr multicolored	.50	.30

American Bicentennial.

Battle of Verdun Memorial — A713

1976, June 12 Engr.

1481	A713	1fr multicolored	.45	.25

Battle of Verdun, 60th anniversary.

Communication A714

1976, June 12 Photo.

1482	A714	1.20fr multicolored	.50	.40

Troncais Forest — A715

1976, June 19 Engr.

1483	A715	70c green & multi	.35	.25

Protection of the environment.

Cross of Lorraine — A716

1976, June 19

1484	A716	1fr multicolored	.50	.25

Association of Free French, 30th anniv.

Symphonie Communications Satellite — A717

1976, June 26 Photo.

1485	A717	1.40fr multicolored	.65	.50

French technical achievements.

Gallic Coin Type of 1975

1976, July 1 Typo. *Perf. 13½x14*

1487	A663	52c ver & dk brn	.40	.30
1488	A663	62c vio & dk brn	1.00	.70
1489	A663	95c tan & dk brn	1.00	.90
1490	A663	1.70fr dk bl & dk brn	2.75	1.40
		Nos. 1487-1490 (4)	5.15	3.30

Nos. 1487-1490 are known only precanceled. See second note after No. 132.

Paris Summer Festival — A719

1976, July 10 Engr.

1491	A719	1fr multicolored	.50	.30

Summer festival in Tuileries Gardens, Paris.

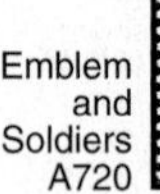

Emblem and Soldiers A720

1976, July 8

1492	A720	1fr blk, dp bl & mag	.50	.25

Officers Reserve Corps, centenary.

Sailing A721

1976, July 17

1493	A721	1.20fr blue, blk & vio	.50	.25

21st Olympic Games, Montreal, Canada, July 17-Aug. 1.

Marianne Type of 1971-74

1976 Typo. *Perf. 14x13*

1494	A555	80c green	.40	.25

Engr. *Perf. 13*

1495	A555	80c green	1.25	.50
a.		Booklet pane of 10	15.00	
1496	A555	1fr carmine rose	.50	.25
a.		Booklet pane of 5	4.00	
b.		Booklet pane of 10	8.00	
		Nos. 1495-1496 (2)	1.75	.75

No. 1495 issued in booklets only. "POSTES" 6mm long on Nos. 1292A and 1494; 4mm on others.

Nos. 1494, 1496 were issued untagged in 1977.

Coil Stamps

1976, Aug. 1 Engr. *Perf. 13 Horiz.*

1497	A555	80c green	.80	.55
1498	A555	1fr carmine rose	.80	.55

Red control number on back of every 10th stamp.

Woman's Head, by Jean Carzou — A722

1976, Sept. 18 Engr. *Perf. 13x12½*

1499	A722	2fr multicolored	.90	.65

Old and New Telephones A723

1976, Sept. 25 **Engr.** ***Perf. 13***
1500 A723 1fr multicolored .50 .25

Centenary of first telephone call by Alexander Graham Bell, Mar. 10, 1876.

Festival Emblem and Trophy, Pyrenees, Hercules and Pyrène — A724

1976, Oct. 2
1501 A724 1.40fr multicolored .65 .40

10th Intl. Tourist Film Festival, Tarbes, 10/4-10.

Police Emblem — A725

1976, Oct. 9 **Engr.** ***Perf. 13***
1502 A725 1.10fr ultra, red & ol .50 .30

National Police, help and protection.

Atomic Particle Accelerator, Diagram A726

1976, Oct. 22 **Photo.**
1503 A726 1.40fr multicolored .75 .45

European Center for Nuclear Research (CERN).

"Exhibitions" — A727

1976, Nov. 20 **Engr.** ***Perf. 13***
1504 A727 1.50fr multicolored .75 .50

Trade Fairs and Exhibitions.

Abstract Design A728

1976, Nov. 27 **Photo.**
1505 A728 1.10fr multicolored .50 .40

Customs Service.

Atlantic Museum, Port Louis — A729

1976, Dec. 4 **Engr.**
1506 A729 1.45fr grnsh bl & olive .60 .50

Regions of France

Réunion A730

Martinique A731

Franche-Comté A732

Brittany A733

Languedoc-Roussillon — A734

Rhône-Alps A735

Champagne-Ardennes A736

Alsace A737

Photo. (1.45fr, 1.50fr, 2.50fr); Engr.

1977 ***Perf. 13***
1507 A730 1.45fr grn & lil rose .65 .40
1508 A731 1.50fr multicolored .65 .60
1509 A732 2.10fr multicolored .90 .65
1510 A733 2.40fr multicolored 1.10 .35
1511 A734 2.50fr multicolored 1.10 .85
1512 A735 2.75fr Prus blue 1.40 .80
1513 A736 3.20fr multicolored 1.40 .80
1514 A737 3.90fr multicolored 2.50 1.50
Nos. 1507-1514 (8) 9.70 5.95

Issued: 1.45fr, 2/5; 1.50fr, 1/29; 2.10fr, 1/8; 2.40fr, 2/19; 2.50fr, 1/15; 2.75fr, 1/22; 3.20fr, 4/16; 3.90fr, 2/26.

Pompidou Cultural Center — A738

1977, Feb. 5 **Engr.** ***Perf. 13***
1515 A738 1fr multicolored .35 .25

Inauguration of the Georges Pompidou National Center for Art and Culture, Paris.

Dunkirk Harbor A739

1977, Feb. 12
1516 A739 50c multicolored .25 .25

Expansion of Dunkirk harbor facilities.

Bridge at Mantes, by Corot — A740

Virgin and Child, by Rubens A741

Tridimensional Design, by Victor Vasarely — A742

Head and Eagle, by Pierre-Yves Tremois A743

1977 **Engr.** ***Perf. 13x12½***
1517 A740 2fr multicolored .95 .75

Perf. 12x13
1518 A741 2fr multicolored 1.10 .75

Perf. 12½x13
1519 A742 3fr sl grn & pale lil 1.25 .75

Photo.
1520 A743 3fr dark red & blk 1.40 1.25
Nos. 1517-1520 (4) 4.70 3.50

Issue dates: No. 1517, Feb. 12; No. 1518, Nov. 5; No. 1519, Apr. 7; No. 1520, Sept. 17.

Hand Holding Torch and Sword — A744

1977, Mar. 5 **Engr.** ***Perf. 13***
1521 A744 80c ultra & multi .45 .30

"France remembers its dead."

Pisces — A745

Zodiac Signs: 58c, Cancer. 61c, Sagittarius. 68c, Taurus. 73c, Aries. 78c, Libra. 1.05fr, Scorpio. 1.15fr, Capricorn. 1.25fr, Leo. 1.85fr, Aquarius. 2fr, Virgo. 2.10fr, Gemini.

1977-78 **Engr.** ***Perf. 13***
1522 A745 54c violet blue .65 .30
1523 A745 58c emerald 1.00 .40
1524 A745 61c brt blue .55 .30
1525 A745 68c deep brown .85 .35
1526 A745 73c rose carmine 1.50 .80
1527 A745 78c vermilion .65 .35
1528 A745 1.05fr brt lilac 1.50 .75
1529 A745 1.15fr orange 2.25 1.40
1530 A745 1.25fr lt olive grn 1.25 .60
1531 A745 1.85fr slate grn 2.75 1.25
1532 A745 2fr blue green 3.00 1.75
1533 A745 2.10fr lilac rose 1.65 1.00
Nos. 1522-1533 (12) 17.60 9.25

Issued: 54c, 68c, 1.05fr, 1.85fr, 4/1/77; others, 1978.

Nos. 1522-1533 are known only precanceled. See second note after No. 132.

Village in Provence A746

Europa: 1.40fr, Brittany port.

1977, Apr. 23
1534 A746 1fr multicolored .45 .25
1535 A746 1.40fr multicolored 1.00 .35

Flowers and Gardening A747

1977, Apr. 23 **Engr.** ***Perf. 13***
1536 A747 1.70fr multicolored .80 .50

National Horticulture Society, centenary.

Symbolic Flower A748

1977, May 7
1537 A748 1.40fr multicolored .65 .40

Intl. Flower Show, Nantes, May 12-23.

Battle of Cambray A749

1977, May 14
1538 A749 80c multicolored .40 .30

Capture of Cambray and the incorporation of Cambresis District into France, 300th anniv.

Carmes Church, School, Map of France — A750

1977, May 14
1539 A750 1.10fr multicolored .50 .30

Catholic Institutes in France.

Modern Constructions A751

1977, May 21
1540 A751 1.10fr multicolored .50 .30

European Federation of the Construction Industry.

Annecy Castle A752

1977, May 28
1541 A752 1fr multicolored .50 .30

Congress of the Federation of French Philatelic Societies, Annecy, May 28-30.

Tourist Issue

Abbey, Pont-à-Mousson — A753

Abbey Tower, Saint-Amand-les-Eaux A754

Collegiate Church of Dorat A755

Fontenay Abbey A756

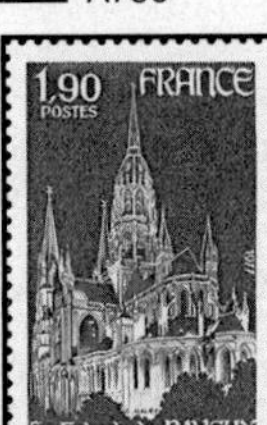
Bayeux Cathedral — A757

Chateau de Vitré A758

1977	**Engr.**	***Perf. 13***	
1542 A753	1.25fr multicolored	.50	.30
1543 A754	1.40fr multicolored	.50	.30
1544 A755	1.45fr multicolored	.55	.35
1545 A756	1.50fr multicolored	.55	.25
1546 A757	1.90fr black & yel	.75	.30
1547 A758	2.40fr black & yel	.80	.30
	Nos. 1542-1547 (6)	3.65	1.80

Issued: 1.25fr, 10/1; 1.40fr, 9/17; 1.45fr, 7/16; 1.50fr, 6/4; 1.90fr, 7/9; 2.40fr, 9/24.

Polytechnic School and "X" — A759

1977, June 4 **Engr.** ***Perf. 13***
1548 A759 1.70fr multicolored .70 .30

Relocation at Palaiseau of Polytechnic School, founded 1794.

Soccer and Cup — A760

1977, June 11
1549 A760 80c multicolored .60 .40

Soccer Cup of France, 60th anniversary.

De Gaulle Memorial A761

Photo. & Embossed

1977, June 18
1550 A761 1fr gold & multi 1.00 .40

5th anniversary of dedication of De Gaulle memorial at Colombey-les-Deux-Eglises.

Stylized Map of France — A762

1977, June 18 **Engr.** ***Perf. 13***
1551 A762 1.10fr ultra & red .50 .30

French Junior Chamber of Commerce.

Battle of Nancy — A763

1977, June 25
1552 A763 1.10fr blue & slate .60 .40

Battle of Nancy between the Dukes of Burgundy and Lorraine, 500th anniversary.

Arms of Burgundy — A764

1977, July 2
1553 A764 1.25fr ol brn & slate grn .55 .25

Annexation of Burgundy by the French Crown, 500th anniversary.

Association Emblem A765

1977, July 8
1554 A765 1.40fr ultra, olive & red .65 .25

French-speaking Parliamentary Association.

Red Cicada — A766

1977, Sept. 10 **Photo.** ***Perf. 13***
1555 A766 80c multicolored .40 .30

Nature protection.

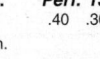

French Handicrafts A767

1977, Oct. 1 **Engr.** ***Perf. 13***
1556 A767 1.40fr multicolored .40 .45

French craftsmen.

Industry and Agriculture — A768

1977, Oct. 22
1557 A768 80c brown & olive .30 .25

Economic & Social Council, 30th anniv.

Table Tennis A769

1977, Dec. 17 **Engr.** ***Perf. 13***
1558 A769 1.10fr multicolored 1.25 .75

French Table Tennis Federation, 50th anniv., and French team, gold medal winner, Birmingham.

Abstract, by Roger Excoffon — A770

1977, Dec. 17 ***Perf. 13x12½***
1559 A770 3fr multicolored 1.40 1.00

Sabine, after David — A771

1977-78	**Engr.**	***Perf. 13***	
1560 A771	1c slate	.25	.25
1561 A771	2c brt violet	.25	.25
1562 A771	5c slate green	.25	.25
1563 A771	10c red brown	.25	.25
1564 A771	15c Prus blue	.25	.25
1565 A771	20c brt green	.25	.25
1566 A771	30c orange	.25	.25
1567 A771	50c red lilac	.25	.25
1568 A771	80c green	.50	.25
a.	Booklet pane of 10	10.00	

1569	A771	80c olive	.50	.25
1570	A771	1fr red	.60	.25
a.		Booklet pane of 5	7.00	
b.		Booklet pane of 10	10.00	
1571	A771	1fr green	.50	.25
a.		Booklet pane of 10	7.00	
1572	A771	1.20fr red	.55	.25
a.		Booklet pane of 5	5.00	
b.		Booklet pane of 10	8.50	
1573	A771	1.40fr brt blue	1.00	.25
1574	A771	1.70fr grnsh blue	.75	.25
1575	A771	2fr emerald	.90	.25
1576	A771	2.10fr lilac rose	1.00	.25
1577	A771	3fr dark brown	1.25	.25
		Nos. 1560-1577 (18)	9.55	4.50

Issued: Nos. 1560-1567, 1573, 1575, 1577, 4/3/78; Nos. 1568, 1570, 12/19/77; Nos. 1569, 1571, 1572, 1574, 1576, 6/5/78.

Coil Stamps

1978 *Perf. 13 Horiz.*

1578	A771	80c bright green	1.10	.90
1579	A771	1fr bright green	1.50	.90
1579A	A771	1fr bright red	1.10	.90
1579B	A771	1.20fr bright red	1.10	.90
		Nos. 1578-1579B (4)	4.80	3.60

See Nos. 1658-1677, 3527, 4410g, 4520, 5336-5343.

For similar design inscribed "REPUBLIQUE FRANCAISE" see type A900.

Percheron, by Jacques Birr A772

Osprey — A773

1978 **Photo.** *Perf. 13*

1580 A772 1.70fr multicolored 1.00 .80

Engr.

1581 A773 1.80fr multicolored .90 .50

Nature protection.

Issue dates: 1.70fr, Jan. 7; 1.80fr, Oct. 14.

Tournament, 1662, Etching — A774

Institut de France and Pont des Arts, Paris, by Bernard Buffet — A776

Horses, by Yves Brayer — A777

1978 **Engr.** *Perf. 12x13*

1582 A774 2fr black 1.00 .80

Perf. 13x12

1584	A776	3fr multicolored	1.40	1.25
1585	A777	3fr multicolored	1.40	1.25
		Nos. 1582-1585 (3)	3.80	3.30

Issued: 2fr, 1/14; No. 1584, 2/4; No. 1585, 12/9.

Communications School and Tower — A778

1978, Jan. 19 **Engr.** *Perf. 13*

1586 A778 80c Prussian blue .40 .25

Natl. Telecommunications School, cent.

Swedish and French Flags, Map of Saint Barthelemy A779

1978, Jan. 19

1587 A779 1.10fr multicolored .55 .25

Centenary of the reunion with France of Saint Barthelemy Island, West Indies.

Regions of France

Ile de France — A780

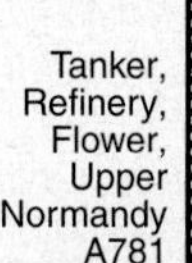

Tanker, Refinery, Flower, Upper Normandy A781

Lower Normandy A782

1978 **Photo.** *Perf. 13*

1588 A780 1fr red, blue & blk .45 .25

Engr.

1589 A781 1.40fr multicolored .60 .30

Photo.

1590	A782	1.70fr multicolored	.80	.30
		Nos. 1588-1590 (3)	1.85	.85

Issued: 1fr, 3/4; 1.40fr, 1/21; 1.70fr, 3/31.

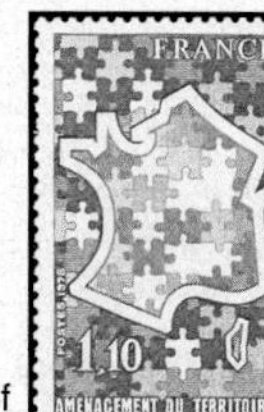

Stylized Map of France — A788

1978, Feb. 11 **Engr.** *Perf. 13*

1596 A788 1.10fr violet & green .45 .25

Program of administrative changes, 15th anniv.

Young Stamp Collector — A789

1978, Feb. 25

1597 A789 80c multicolored .35 .25

JUVEXNIORT, Youth Philatelic Exhibition, Niort, Feb. 25-March 5.

Tourist Issue

Verdon Gorge — A790

Saint-Saturnin Church — A792

Pont Neuf, Paris A791

Our Lady of Bec-Hellouin Abbey — A793

Chateau D'Esquelbecq — A794

Aubazine Abbey A795

Fontevraud Abbey A796

1978 **Engr.** *Perf. 13*

1598	A790	50c multicolored	.25	.25
1599	A791	80c multicolored	.35	.25
1600	A792	1fr black	.45	.25
1601	A793	1.10fr multicolored	.50	.25
1602	A794	1.10fr multicolored	.50	.25
1603	A795	1.25fr carmine & brn	.60	.30
1604	A796	1.70fr multicolored	.80	.30
		Nos. 1598-1604 (7)	3.45	1.85

Issued: 1.25fr, 2/18; 50c, 3/6; No. 1601, 3/26; 80c, 5/27; 1fr, 6/10; 1.70fr, 6/3; No. 1602, 6/17.

See No. 5035b.

Fish and Corals — A797

1978, Apr. 15 **Photo.** *Perf. 13*

1605 A797 1.25fr multicolored .80 .70

Port Cros National Park, 15th anniversary.

Flowers, Butterflies and Houses — A798

1978, Apr. 22 **Engr.** *Perf. 13*

1606 A798 1.70fr multicolored 1.25 .50

Beautification of France campaign, 50th anniv.

Hands Shielding Source of Heat and Light A799

1978, Apr. 22

1607 A799 1fr multicolored .50 .25

Energy conservation.

World War I Memorial near Lens — A800

1978, May 6

1608 A800 2fr lemon & magenta .50 .30

Colline Notre Dame de Lorette memorial of World War I.

Fountain of the Innocents, Paris — A801

Europa: 1.40fr, Flower Park Fountain, Paris.

1978, May 6

1609 A801 1fr multicolored .40 .25
1610 A801 1.40fr multicolored .75 .30

Maurois Palace, Troyes — A802

1978, May 13

1611 A802 1fr multicolored .45 .25

51st Congress of the Federation of French Philatelic Societies, Troyes, May 13-15.

Roland Garros Tennis Court and Player — A803

1978, May 27

1612 A803 1fr multicolored 1.00 .40

Roland Garros Tennis Court, 50th anniv.

Hand and Plant — A804

1978, Sept. 9 Engr. *Perf. 13*

1613 A804 1.30fr brown, red & grn .50 .25

Encouragement of handicrafts.

Printing Office Emblem — A805

1978, Sept. 23

1614 A805 1fr multicolored .50 .25

National Printing Office, established 1538.

Fortress, Besançon, and Collegiate Church, Dole — A806

Valenciennes and Maubeuge — A807

1978

1615 A806 1.20fr multicolored .55 .25
1616 A807 1.20fr multicolored .55 .25

Reunion of Franche-Comté and Valenciennes and Maubeuge with France, 300th anniversary.

Issued: No. 1615, 9/23; No. 1616, 9/30.

Sower Type of 1906-1937 and Academy Emblem — A808

1978, Oct. 7

1617 A808 1fr multicolored .45 .30

Academy of Philately, 50th anniversary.

Gymnasts, Strasbourg Cathedral, Storks — A809

1978, Oct. 21

1618 A809 1fr multicolored .50 .30

19th World Gymnastics Championships, Strasbourg, Oct. 23-26.

Various Sports — A810

1978, Oct. 21

1619 A810 1fr multicolored .50 .30

Sports for all.

Polish Veterans' Monument — A811

1978, Nov. 11

1620 A811 1.70fr multicolored .75 .45

Polish veterans of World War II.

Railroad Car and Monument, Compiègne Forest, Rethondes — A812

1978, Nov. 11 Engr. *Perf. 13*

1621 A812 1.20fr indigo .60 .30

60th anniversary of World War I armistice.

Handicapped People — A813

1978, Nov. 18

1622 A813 1fr multicolored .45 .25

Rehabilitation of the handicapped.

Human Rights Emblem A814

1978, Dec. 9 Engr. *Perf. 13*

1623 A814 1.70fr dk brown & blue .80 .40

30th anniversary of Universal Declaration of Human Rights.

Child and IYC Emblem A815

1979, Jan. 6 Engr. *Perf. 13*

1624 A815 1.70fr multicolored 1.25 .80

International Year of the Child.

"Music," 15th Century Miniature — A816

1979, Jan. 13 *Perf. 13x12½*

1625 A816 2fr multicolored 1.00 .80

Diana Taking a Bath, d'Ecouen Castle A817

Church at Auvers-on-Oise, by Vincent Van Gogh — A818

Head of Marianne, by Salvador Dali A819

Fire Dancer from The Magic Flute, by Chaplain Midy A820

1979 Photo. *Perf. 12½x13*

1626 A817 2fr multicolored 1.00 .80
1627 A818 2fr multicolored 1.50 .80
1628 A819 3fr multicolored 1.50 1.00
1629 A820 3fr multicolored 1.50 1.00
Nos. 1626-1629 (4) 5.50 3.60

Issued: No. 1626, 9/22; No. 1627, 10/27; No. 1628, 11/19; No. 1629, 11/26.

Orange Agaric — A821

Mushrooms: 83c, Death trumpet. 1.30fr, Olive wood pleurotus. 2.25fr, Cauliflower claveria.

1979, Jan. 15 Engr. *Perf. 13*

1630 A821 64c orange .40 .25
1631 A821 83c brown .40 .25
1632 A821 1.30fr yellow bister .85 .40
1633 A821 2.25fr brown purple 1.25 .85
Nos. 1630-1633 (4) 2.90 1.75

Nos. 1630-1633 are known only precanceled. See second note after No. 132.

Victor Segalen A822

1979, Jan. 20

1634 A822 1.50fr multicolored .60 .30

Physician, explorer and writer (1878-1919).

Hibiscus and Palms — A823

1979, Feb. 3

1635 A823 35c multicolored .25 .25

International Flower Festival, Martinique.

Buddha, Stupas, Temple of Borobudur A824

1979, Feb. 24

No.	Type	Denom.	Description	Unused	Used
1636	A824	1.80fr	ol & slate grn	.85	.40

Save the Temple of Borobudur, Java, campaign.

Boy, by Francisque Poulbot (1879-1946) A825

1979, Mar. 24 **Photo.**

No.	Type	Denom.	Description	Unused	Used
1637	A825	1.30fr	multicolored	.60	.25

Tourist Issue

Chateau de Maisons, Laffitte A826

Bernay and St. Pierre sur Dives Abbeys — A827

View of Auray — A827a

Steenvorde Windmill — A828

Wall Painting, Niaux Cave A829

Royal Palace, Perpignan A830

1979 **Engr.** ***Perf. 13***

No.	Type	Denom.	Description	Unused	Used
1638	A826	45c	multicolored	.45	.25
1639	A827	1fr	multicolored	.45	.25
1640	A827a	1fr	multicolored	.55	.25
1641	A828	1.20fr	multicolored	.65	.25
1642	A829	1.50fr	multicolored	.70	.40
1643	A830	1.70fr	multicolored	.75	.60
			Nos. 1638-1643 (6)	3.55	2.00

Issued: 45c, 10/6; No. 1639, 6/16; No. 1640, 6/30; 1.20fr, 6/12; 1.50fr, 7/9; 1.70fr, 4/21.

Honey Bee A831

1979, Mar. 31 **Engr.** ***Perf. 13***

No.	Type	Denom.	Description	Unused	Used
1644	A831	1fr	multicolored	.50	.30

Nature protection.

St. Germain des Prés Abbey A832

1979, Apr. 21

No.	Type	Denom.	Description	Unused	Used
1645	A832	1.40fr	multicolored	.60	.30

Simoun Mail Monoplanes, 1935, and Map of Mail Routes — A833

Europa: 1.70fr, Floating spheres used on Seine during siege of Paris, 1870.

1979, Apr. 28

No.	Type	Denom.	Description	Unused	Used
1646	A833	1.20fr	multicolored	.75	.35
1647	A833	1.70fr	multicolored	1.00	.50

Ship and View of Nantes A834

1979, May 5 **Engr.** ***Perf. 13***

No.	Type	Denom.	Description	Unused	Used
1648	A834	1.20fr	multicolored	.55	.30

52nd National Congress of French Philatelic Societies, Nantes, May 5-7.

Royal Palace, 1789 — A835

1979, May 19

No.	Type	Denom.	Description	Unused	Used
1649	A835	1fr	car rose & pur	.45	.25

European Elections A836

1979, May 19 **Photo.** ***Perf. 13***

No.	Type	Denom.	Description	Unused	Used
1650	A836	1.20fr	multicolored	.55	.25

European Parliament, 1st direct elections, June 10.

Joan of Arc Monument A837

1979, May 24 **Engr.**

No.	Type	Denom.	Description	Unused	Used
1651	A837	1.70fr	brt lilac rose	.70	.40

Joan of Arc, the Maid of Orleans (1412-1431).

Felix Guyon and Catheters A840

1979, June 23

No.	Type	Denom.	Description	Unused	Used
1652	A840	1.80fr	sepia & blue	.80	.35

Felix Guyon (1831-1920), urologist.

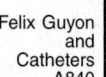

Lantern Tower, La Rochelle — A841

Towers: 88c, Chartres Cathedral. 1.40fr, Bourges Cathedral. 2.35fr, Amiens Cathedral.

1979, Aug. 13 **Engr.** ***Perf. 13***

No.	Type	Denom.	Description	Unused	Used
1653	A841	68c	vio brn & blk	.35	.25
1654	A841	88c	ultra & blk	.40	.25
1655	A841	1.40fr	gray grn & blk	.65	.50
1656	A841	2.35fr	dull brn & blk	1.10	.60
			Nos. 1653-1656 (4)	2.50	1.60

Nos. 1653-1656 are known only precanceled. See second note after No. 132. See Nos. 1684-1687, 1719-1722, 1814-1817.

Telecom '79 — A842

1979, Sept. 22

No.	Type	Denom.	Description	Unused	Used
1657	A842	1.10fr	multicolored	.45	.25

3rd World Telecommunications Exhibition.

Sabine Type of 1977-78

1979-81 **Engr.** ***Perf. 13***

No.	Type	Denom.	Description	Unused	Used
1658	A771	40c	brown ('81)	.25	.25
1659	A771	60c	red brn ('81)	.25	.25
1660	A771	70c	violet blue	.35	.25
1661	A771	90c	brt lilac ('81)	.45	.30
1662	A771	1fr	gray olive	.45	.25
1663	A771	1.10fr	green	.50	.25
1664	A771	1.20fr	green ('80)	.40	.25
1665	A771	1.30fr	rose red	.55	.25
1666	A771	1.40fr	rose red ('80)	.60	.25
1667	A771	1.60fr	purple	.75	.30
1668	A771	1.80fr	ocher	.80	.50
1669	A771	3.50fr	lt ol grn ('81)	1.40	.60
1670	A771	4fr	brt car ('81)	1.60	.40
1671	A771	5fr	brt grnsh bl ('81)	2.00	.30
			Nos. 1658-1671 (14)	10.35	4.40

Coil Stamps

1979-80 ***Perf. 13 Horiz.***

No.	Type	Denom.	Description	Unused	Used
1674	A771	1.10fr	green	1.25	.60
1675	A771	1.20fr	green ('80)	.70	.50
1676	A771	1.30fr	rose red	1.25	.60
1677	A771	1.40fr	rose red ('80)	.45	.40
			Nos. 1674-1677 (4)	3.65	2.10

Lorraine Region — A845

1979, Nov. 10

No.	Type	Denom.	Description	Unused	Used
1678	A845	2.30fr	multicolored	1.00	.30

Gears A847

1979, Nov. 17 ***Perf. 13***

No.	Type	Denom.	Description	Unused	Used
1680	A847	1.80fr	multicolored	.80	.30

Central Technical School of Paris, 150th anniv.

Judo Throw A848

1979, Nov. 24 **Engr.**

No.	Type	Denom.	Description	Unused	Used
1681	A848	1.60fr	multicolored	.75	.40

World Judo Championships, Paris, Dec.

Violins — A849

1979, Dec. 10

No.	Type	Denom.	Description	Unused	Used
1682	A849	1.30fr	multicolored	.60	.35

Eurovision A850

1980, Jan. 12 **Engr.** ***Perf. 13x13½***

No.	Type	Denom.	Description	Unused	Used
1683	A850	1.80fr	multicolored	.90	.70

Tower Type of 1979

Designs: 76c, Chateau d'Angers. 99c, Chateau de Kerjean. 1.60fr, Chateau de Pierrefonds. 2.65fr, Chateau de Tarascon.

1980, Jan. 21 **Engr.**

No.	Type	Denom.	Description	Unused	Used
1684	A841	76c	grnsh bl & blk	.35	.30
1685	A841	99c	slate grn & blk	.45	.30
1686	A841	1.60fr	red & blk	.75	.55
1687	A841	2.65fr	brn org & blk	1.25	.65
			Nos. 1684-1687 (4)	2.80	1.80

Nos. 1684-1687 are known only precanceled. See second note after No. 132.

Self-portrait, by Albrecht Dürer, Philexfrance '82 Emblem — A851

Woman Holding Fan, by Ossip Zadkine A852

Abstract, by Raoul Ubak — A853

Hommage to J.S. Bach, by Jean Picart Le Doux — A854

Peasant, by Louis Le Nain A855

Woman with Blue Eyes, by Modigliani A856

Abstract, by Hans Hartung A857

Engraved, Photogravure (#1691, 1694)

1980 ***Perf. 12½x13, 13x12½***

1688	A851	2fr multicolored	1.00	.80
1689	A852	3fr multicolored	1.40	1.00
1690	A853	3fr multicolored	1.40	1.00
1691	A854	3fr multicolored	1.40	1.00
1692	A855	3fr multicolored	1.40	1.00
1693	A856	4fr multicolored	1.75	1.25
1694	A857	4fr ultra & black	1.75	1.25
		Nos. 1688-1694 (7)	10.10	7.30

Issued: No. 1688, 6/7; No. 1689, 1/19; No. 1690, 2/2; No. 1691, 9/20; No. 1693, 10/26; No. 1692, 11/10; No. 1694, 12/20.

Giants of the North Festival — A858

1980, Feb. 16 ***Perf. 13***

1695 A858 1.60fr multicolored .75 .30

French Cuisine — A859

1980, Feb. 23

1696 A859 90c red & lt brown .60 .40

Woman Embroidering A860

Photogravure and Engraved

1980, Mar. 29 ***Perf. 13***

1697 A860 1.10fr multicolored .50 .30

Fight Against Cigarette Smoking — A861

1980, Apr. 5 **Photo.** ***Perf. 13***

1698 A861 1.30fr multicolored .50 .25

Aristide Briand — A862

Europa: 1.80fr, St. Benedict.

1980, Apr. 26 **Engr.** ***Perf. 13***

1699	A862	1.30fr multicolored	.60	.30
1700	A862	1.80fr red & red brown	.85	.50

Aristide Briand (1862-1932), prime minister, 1909-1911, 1921-1922; St. Benedict, patron saint of Europe.

Liancourt, College, Map of Northwestern France — A863

1980, May 19 **Engr.** ***Perf. 13***

1701 A863 2fr dk green & pur .80 .30

National College of Arts and Handicrafts (founded by Larochefoucauld Liancourt) bicentenary.

Cranes, Town Hall Tower, Dunkirk — A864

1980, May 24

1702 A864 1.30fr multicolored .60 .25

53rd Natl. Congress of French Federation of Philatelic Societies, Dunkirk, May 24-26.

Tourist Issue

Chateau de Maintenon A866

Cordes A865

Montauban A867

St. Peter's Abbey, Solesmes A868

Puy Cathedral A869

1980 **Engr.** ***Perf. 13***

1703	A865	1.50fr multicolored	.55	.30
1704	A866	2fr multicolored	.80	.30
1705	A867	2.30fr multicolored	1.00	.30
1706	A868	2.50fr multicolored	1.25	.30
1707	A869	3.20fr multicolored	1.40	.50
		Nos. 1703-1707 (5)	5.00	1.70

Issued: No. 1703, 4/5; No. 1704, 6/7; No. 1705, 5/7; No. 1706, 9/20; No. 1707, 5/12.

Graellsia Isabellae A870

1980, May 31 **Photo.**

1708 A870 1.10fr multicolored .70 .30

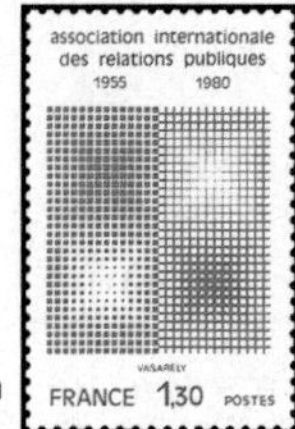

Association Emblem — A871

1980, June 10 **Photo.**

1709 A871 1.30fr red & blue .55 .25

Intl. Public Relations Assoc., 25th anniv.

Marianne, French Architecture A872

1980, June 21 **Engr.**

1710 A872 1.50fr bluish & gray blk .70 .30

Heritage Year.

Earth Sciences A873

1980, July 5

1711 A873 1.60fr dk brown & red .70 .50

International Geological Congress.

Rochambeau's Landing — A874

1980, July 15

1712 A874 2.50fr multicolored 1.10 .50

Rochambeau's landing at Newport, R.I. (American Revolution), bicentenary.

Message of Peace, by Yaacov Agam — A875

1980, Oct. 4 Photo. *Perf. 11½x13*
1713 A875 4fr multicolored 1.75 1.00

French Golf Federation A876

1980, Oct. 18 Engr.
1714 A876 1.40fr multicolored .60 .30

Comedie Francaise, 300th Anniversary A877

1980, Oct. 18
1715 A877 2fr multicolored .75 .40

Charles de Gaulle — A878

1980, Nov. 10 Photo. *Perf. 13*
1716 A878 1.40fr multicolored .90 .50

40th anniversary of De Gaulle's appeal of June 18, and 10th anniversary of his death.

Guardsman — A879

1980, Nov. 24 Engr. *Perf. 13*
1717 A879 1.70fr multicolored .80 .45

Rambouillet Chateau A880

1980, Dec. 6 Engr. *Perf. 13*
1718 A880 2.20fr multicolored 1.00 .35

Tower Type of 1979

Designs: 88c, Imperial Chapel, Ajaccio. 1.14fr, Astronomical Clock, Besancon. 1.84fr, Coucy Castle ruins. 3.05fr, Font-de-Gaume cave drawing, Les Eyzies de Tayac.

1981, Jan. 11 Engr. *Perf. 13*
1719 A841 88c dp mag & blk .40 .25
1720 A841 1.14fr ultra & blk .55 .30
1721 A841 1.84fr dk green & blk .85 .50
1722 A841 3.05fr brn red & blk 1.40 .80
Nos. 1719-1722 (4) 3.20 1.85

Nos. 1719-1722 are known only precanceled. See second note after No. 132.

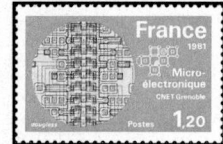

Microelectronics — A881

1981 Photo.
1723 A881 1.20fr shown .55 .30
1724 A881 1.20fr Biology .55 .30
1725 A881 1.40fr Energy .65 .30
1726 A881 1.80fr Marine exploration .85 .50
1727 A881 2fr Telemetry .90 .65
Nos. 1723-1727 (5) 3.50 2.05

Issue dates: No. 1723, 2/5; others, 3/28.

Abstract, by Albert Gleizes A882

1981, Feb. 28 *Perf. 12½x13*
1728 A882 4fr multicolored 1.75 .90

The Footpath by Camille Pissaro — A883

1981, Apr. 18 Engr. *Perf. 13x12½*
1729 A883 2fr multicolored 1.00 .80

Child Watering Smiling Map of France — A884

1981, Mar. 14 Engr. *Perf. 13*
1730 A884 1.40fr multicolored .65 .25

Sully Chateau, Rosny-sur-Seine — A885

1981, Mar. 21
1731 A885 2.50fr multicolored 1.10 .40

Tourist Issue

Roman Temple, Nimes — A886

1981, Apr. 11 Engr. *Perf. 13*
1732 A886 1.70fr multicolored .85 .30

Church of St. Jean, Lyon — A887

St. Anne d'Auray Basilica — A888

1981
1733 A887 1.40fr dk red & dk brn .65 .30
1734 A888 2.20fr blue & black 1.00 .40

Issue dates: 1.40fr, May 30; 2.20fr, July 4.

Vaucelles Abbey A889

Notre Dame of Louviers A890

1981
1735 A889 2fr red & black .90 .40
1736 A890 2.20fr red brn & dk brn 1.00 .50
Nos. 1732-1736 (5) 4.40 1.90

Issue dates: 2fr, Sept. 19; 2.20fr, Sept. 26.

Europa Issue

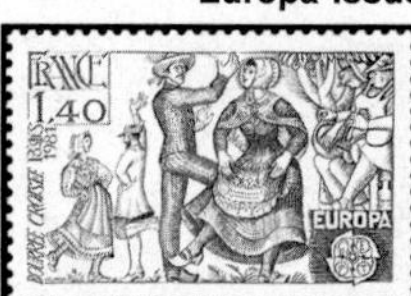

Folkdances A891

1981, May 4 *Perf. 13*
1737 A891 1.40fr Bouree .65 .25
1738 A891 2fr Sardane 1.00 .40

Bookbinding — A892

1981, Apr. 4 *Perf. 13*
1739 A892 1.50fr olive & car rose .70 .40

Cadets — A893

1981, May 16
1740 A893 2.50fr multicolored 1.00 .30

Military College at St. Maixent centenary.

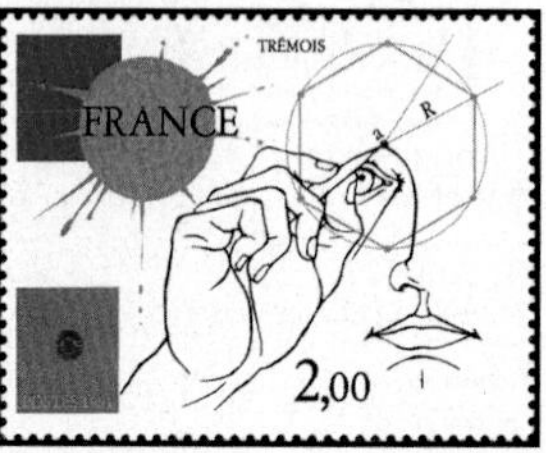

Man Drawing Geometric Diagram — A894

1981, May 23 Photo.
1741 A894 2fr shown 1.00 .75
1742 A894 2fr Faces 1.00 .75
a. Pair, #1741-1742 + label 2.50 2.00

PHILEXFRANCE '82 Stamp Exhibition, Paris, June 11-21, 1982.

Theophraste Renaudot and Emile de Girardin — A895

1981, May 30 Engr.
1743 A895 2.20fr black & red 1.00 .30

350th anniversary of La Gazette (founded by Renaudot), and death centenary of founder of Le Journal (de Girardin).

Public Gardens, Vichy — A896

1981, June 6
1744 A896 1.40fr multicolored .65 .30

54th National Congress of French Federation of Philatelic Societies, Vichy.

Higher National College for Commercial Studies Centenary A897

1981, June 20 *Perf. 13*
1745 A897 1.40fr multicolored .65 .30

Sea Shore Conservation — A898

1981, June 20
1746 A898 1.60fr multicolored .75 .55

World Fencing Championship, Clermont-Ferrand, July 2-13 — A899

1981, June 27
1747 A899 1.80fr multicolored .85 .45

Sabine, after David — A900

1981, Sept. 1 **Engr.**
1755 A900 1.40fr green .70 .25
1756 A900 1.60fr red .80 .25
1757 A900 2.30fr blue 1.40 .85
Nos. 1755-1757 (3) 2.90 1.35

Coil Stamps

1981 **Engr.** ***Perf. 13 Horiz.***
1758 A900 1.40fr green .75 .50
1759 A900 1.60fr red .75 .50

Highway Safety ("Drink or Drive") A901

1981, Sept. 5 ***Perf. 13***
1768 A901 1.60fr multicolored .75 .30

45th Intl. PEN Club Congress — A902

1981, Sept. 19 ***Perf. 13***
1769 A902 2fr multicolored 1.00 .35

Jules Ferry, Statesman — A903

1981, Sept. 26 ***Perf. 12½x13***
1770 A903 1.60fr multicolored .75 .35

Free compulsory public school centenary.

Natl. Savings Bank Centenary A904

1981, Sept. 21 **Photo.** ***Perf. 13***

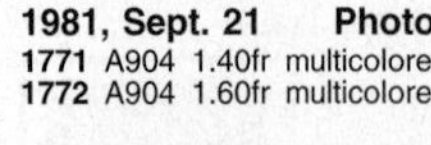

1771 A904 1.40fr multicolored .65 .25
1772 A904 1.60fr multicolored .75 .25

The Divers, by Edouard Pignon — A905

1981, Oct. 3 ***Perf. 13x12½***
1773 A905 4fr multicolored 1.75 .90

Alleluia, by Alfred Manessier A906

1981, Dec. 19 **Photo.** ***Perf. 12x13***
1774 A906 4fr multicolored 1.75 .90

Tourist Issue

Saint-Emilion — A907

Crest — A908

1981 **Engr.** ***Perf. 13x12½***
1775 A907 2.60fr dk red & lt ol grn 1.10 .25

Perf. 13

1776 A908 2.90fr dk green 1.20 .25

Issued: No. 1775, 10/10; No. 1776, 11/28.

150th Anniv. of Naval Academy A909

1981, Oct. 17 ***Perf. 13***
1777 A909 1.40fr multicolored .65 .30

A910

St. Hubert Kneeling before the Stag, 15th cent. sculpture.

1981, Oct. 24
1778 A910 1.60fr multicolored .75 .30

Museum of hunting and nature.

A911

V. Schoelcher, J. Jaures, J. Moulin, the Pantheon.

1981, Nov. 2
1779 A911 1.60fr blue & dull pur .75 .30

Intl. Year of the Disabled A912

1981, Nov. 7
1780 A912 1.60fr multicolored .75 .25

Men Leading Cattle, 2nd Cent. Roman Mosaic — A913

1981, Nov. 14 ***Perf. 13x12***
1781 A913 2fr multicolored 1.00 .75

Virgil's birth bimillennium.

Martyrs of Chateaubriant A914

1981, Dec. 12 **Engr.** ***Perf. 13***
1782 A914 1.40fr multicolored .70 .25

Liberty, after Delacroix — A915

1982 **Engr.** ***Perf. 13***
1783 A915 5c dk green .25 .25
1784 A915 10c dull red .25 .25
1785 A915 15c brt rose lilac .35 .35
1786 A915 20c brt green .25 .25
1787 A915 30c orange .25 .25
1788 A915 40c brown .25 .25
a. Bklt. pane of 5, 4 No. 1784, No. 1788 ('87) 1.00
1789 A915 50c lilac .25 .25
1790 A915 60c lt red brn .30 .25
1791 A915 70c ultra .35 .25
1792 A915 80c lt olive grn .35 .25
1793 A915 90c brt lilac .40 .25
1794 A915 1fr olive green .30 .25
1795 A915 1.40fr green .65 .25
1796 A915 1.60fr green .75 .25
1797 A915 1.60fr red .75 .25
1798 A915 1.80fr red .85 .25
1799 A915 2fr brt yel grn .85 .25
1800 A915 2.30fr blue 1.50 1.25
1801 A915 2.60fr blue 1.25 1.00
1802 A915 3fr chocolate 1.40 .30
1803 A915 4fr brt carmine 1.75 .30
1804 A915 5fr gray blue 2.25 .25
Nos. 1783-1804 (22) 15.55 7.45

Coil Stamps

Perf. 13 Horiz.

1805 A915 1.40fr green 1.25 .90
1806 A915 1.60fr red 1.25 .90
1807 A915 1.60fr green .85 .50
1807A A915 1.80fr red .90 .50
Nos. 1805-1807A (4) 4.25 2.80

Issued: 5c-50c, 1fr-1.40fr, 2fr, 2.30fr, 5fr, No. 1797, 1/2; 1.80fr, 2.60fr, No. 1796, 6/1; 60c-90c, 3fr, 4fr, 11/3.

See Nos. 1878-1897A, 2077-2080, 3528, 4410h, 4521. For surcharge see No. 2115.

Tourist Issue

St. Pierre and Miquelon A916

Corsica A917

Renaissance Fountain, Aix-en Provence — A918

Collonges-la-Rouge — A919

Castle of Henry IV, Pau A920

Lille — A921

Chateau Ripaille, Haute-Savoie — A921a

1982 **Engr.** ***Perf. 12½***
1808 A916 1.60fr dk blue & blk 1.25 .30
1809 A917 1.90fr blue & red .90 .25

Perf. 13

1810 A918 2fr multicolored .90 .40
1811 A919 3fr multicolored 1.25 .40
1812 A920 3fr ultra & dk bl 1.25 .40

Issued: 1.60fr, 1.90fr, Jan. 9; 2fr, June 21, No. 1811, July 5, No. 1812, May 15.

Perf. 13x12½

1813 A921 1.80fr dull red & ol .85 .25
1813A A921a 2.90fr multicolored 1.40 .80
Nos. 1808-1813A (7) 7.80 2.80

Issue dates: 1.80fr, Oct. 16; 2.90fr, Sept. 4.

Tower Type of 1979

97c, Tanlay Castle, Yonne. 1.25fr, Salses Fort, Pyrenees-Orientales. 2.03fr, Montlhery Tower, Essonne. 3.36fr, Chateau d'If Bouches-du-Rhone.

1982, Jan. 11 **Engr.** ***Perf. 13***
1814 A841 97c olive grn & blk .45 .25
1815 A841 1.25fr red & blk .55 .25
1816 A841 2.03fr sepia & blk .95 .50
1817 A841 3.36fr ultra & blk 1.50 .80
Nos. 1814-1817 (4) 3.45 1.80

Nos. 1814-1817 are known only precanceled. See second note after No. 132.

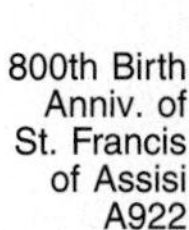

800th Birth Anniv. of St. Francis of Assisi A922

1982, Feb. 6 **Photo. & Engr.**
1818 A922 2fr black & blue .90 .40

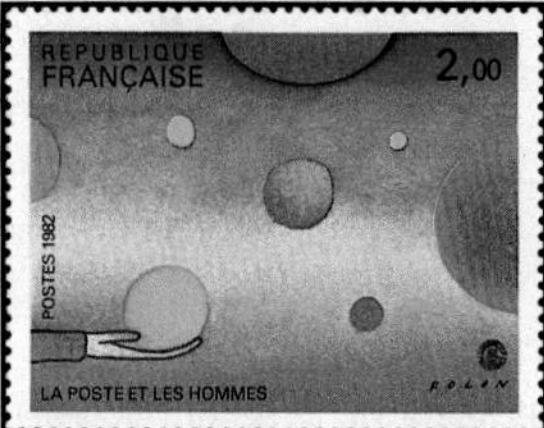

Posts and Mankind — A923

Posts and Technology — A924

1982, Feb. 13 **Photo.**
1819 A923 2fr multicolored 1.50 1.25
1820 A924 2fr multicolored 1.50 1.25
a. Pair, #1819-1820 + label 3.50 3.00

PHILEXFRANCE '82 Stamp Exhibition, Paris, June 11-21.

Souvenir Sheet

Marianne, by Jean Cocteau — A925

1982, June 11
1821 A925 Sheet of 2 10.00 9.00
a. 4fr red & blue *4.00 3.50*
b. 6fr blue & red *5.00 4.50*

Sold only with 20fr show admission ticket.

Scouting Year A926

1982, Feb. 20 **Engr.**
1822 A926 2.30fr yel grn & blk 1.00 .30

31st Natl. Census — A927

1982, Feb. 27 **Photo.**
1823 A927 1.60fr multicolored .75 .25

Bale-Mulhouse Airport Opening — A928

1982, Mar. 15 **Engr.** ***Perf. 13***
1824 A928 1.90fr multicolored .90 .50

Fight Against Racism A929

1982, Mar. 20
1825 A929 2.30fr brn & red org 1.00 .50

Blacksmith — A930

1982, Apr. 17
1826 A930 1.40fr multicolored .65 .40

Europa 1982 A931

1982, Apr. 24
1827 A931 1.60fr Treaty of Rome, 1957 .90 .30
1828 A931 2.30fr Treaty of Verdun, 843 1.20 .40

1982 World Cup A932

1982, Apr. 28
1829 A932 1.80fr multicolored .90 .30

Young Greek Soldier, Hellenic Sculpture, Agde A933

1982, May 15 ***Perf. 12½x13***
1830 A933 4fr multicolored 1.90 1.00

Embarkation for Ostia, by Claude Gellee — A934

The Lacemaker, by Vermeer A935

Turkish Chamber, by Balthus — A936

1982 **Photo.** ***Perf. 13x12½, 12½x13***
1831 A934 4fr multicolored 1.90 1.00
1832 A935 4fr multicolored 1.90 1.00
1833 A936 4fr multicolored 1.90 1.00
Nos. 1831-1833 (3) 5.70 3.00

Issued: No. 1831, 6/19; No. 1832, 9/4; No. 1833, 11/6.

35th Intl. Film Festival, Cannes — A937

1982, May 15 **Photo.** ***Perf. 13***
1834 A937 2.30fr multicolored 1.00 .75

Natl. Space Studies Center, 20th Anniv. — A938

1982, May 15 **Engr.**
1835 A938 2.60fr multicolored 1.20 .50

A939

1982, June 4 **Photo.**
1836 A939 2.60fr multicolored 1.20 .50

Industrialized Countries' Summit Meeting, Versailles, June 4-6.

A940

1982, June 4 **Engr.** ***Perf. 13***
1837 A940 1.60fr ol grn & dk grn .75 .25

Jules Valles (1832-1885), writer.

Frederic and Irene Curie, Radiation Diagrams A941

1982, June 26
1838 A941 1.80fr multicolored .85 .30

Electric Street Lighting Centenary A942

1982, July 10
1839 A942 1.80fr dk blue & vio .90 .30

The Family, by Marc Boyan A943

Photogravure and Engraved

1982, Sept. 18 ***Perf. 12½x13***
1840 A943 4fr multicolored 1.75 1.00

Natl. Fed. of Firemen, Cent. — A944

1982, Sept. 18 **Engr.** ***Perf. 13***
1841 A944 3.30fr red & sepia 1.60 .40

Marionettes — A945

1982, Sept. 25
1842 A945 1.80fr multicolored .90 .30

Rugby A946

1982, Oct. 9
1843 A946 1.60fr multicolored 1.50 .30

Higher Education A947

1982, Oct. 16
1844 A947 1.80fr red & black .90 .30

TB Bacillus Centenary A948

1982, Nov. 13
1845 A948 2.60fr red & black 1.10 .40

St. Teresa of Avila (1515-82) — A949

1982, Nov. 20
1846 A949 2.10fr multicolored 1.00 .45

Leon Blum (1872-1950), Politician — A950

1982, Dec. 18 **Engr.** ***Perf. 13***
1847 A950 1.80fr dk brn & brn .85 .25

Cavelier de la Salle (1643-1687), Explorer — A951

1982, Dec. 18 ***Perf. 13x12½***
1848 A951 3.25fr multicolored 1.25 .50

Spring — A952

1983, Jan. 17 **Engr.** ***Perf. 13***
1849 A952 1.05fr shown .45 .25
1850 A952 1.35fr Summer .50 .30
1851 A952 2.19fr Autumn 1.00 .75
1852 A952 3.63fr Winter 1.40 1.10
Nos. 1849-1852 (4) 3.35 2.40

Nos. 1849-1852 known only precanceled. See second note after No. 132.

Provence-Alpes-Cote d'Azur — A953

Brantome (Perigord) A954

Concarneau — A955

Noirlac Abbey A956

1983 **Photo.** ***Perf. 13***
1853 A953 1fr multicolored .45 .25
Engr.
Perf. 13x12½
1854 A954 1.80fr multicolored .85 .25
Perf. 13
1855 A955 3fr multicolored 1.25 .60
Perf. 13x12½
1856 A956 3.60fr multicolored 1.60 .30

Issued: 1fr, 1/8; 1.80fr, 2/5; 3fr, 6/11; 3.60fr, 7/2.

Jarnac A957

Charleville-Mezieres — A958

1983 ***Perf. 13x12½***
1857 A957 2fr multicolored .90 .35
1858 A958 3.10fr multicolored 1.40 .85
Nos. 1853-1858 (6) 6.45 2.60

Issued: 2fr, Oct. 8; 3.10fr, Sept. 17.

Martin Luther (1483-1546) — A959

1983, Feb. 12 **Engr.** ***Perf. 13***
1859 A959 3.30fr dk brn & tan 1.40 .55

Alliance Francaise Centenary A960

1983, Feb. 19
1860 A960 1.80fr multicolored .85 .30

Danielle Casanova (d. 1942), Resistance Leader A961

1983, Mar. 8
1861 A961 3fr blk & red brn 1.25 .30

World Communications Year — A962

1983, Mar. 12 **Photo.**
1862 A962 2.60fr multicolored 1.10 .65

Manned Flight Bicentenary — A963

1983, Mar. 19 **Photo.** ***Perf. 13***
1863 2fr Hot air balloon .80 .55
1864 3fr Hydrogen balloon 1.25 .70
a. A963 Pair, #1863-1864 + label 2.25 2.25

Female Nude, by Raphael A964

Aurora-Set, by Dewasne — A965

1983 **Engr.** ***Perf. 13***
1865 A964 4fr multicolored 1.75 1.00
Photo.
1866 A965 4fr multicolored 1.75 1.00

Issued: No. 1866, 3/19; No. 1865, 4/9.

Illustration from Perrault's Folk Tales, by Gustave Dore A966

1983, June 18 **Engr.** ***Perf. 13***
1867 A966 4fr red & black 1.75 1.00

Homage to Jean Effel A967

1983, Oct. 15
1868 A967 4fr multicolored 1.75 1.00

Le Lapin Agile, by Utrillo — A968

1983, Dec. 3 ***Perf. 13x12½***
1869 A968 4fr multicolored 1.75 1.00

Thistle — A969

1983, Apr. 23 **Engr.** ***Perf. 12½x12***
1870 A969 1fr shown .35 .30
1871 A969 2fr Martagon lily .80 .30
1872 A969 3fr Aster 1.25 .60
1873 A969 4fr Aconite 1.75 .60
Nos. 1870-1873 (4) 4.15 1.80

Europa 1983 — A970

1.80fr, Symbolic shutter. 2.60fr, Lens-to-screen diagram.

1983, Apr. 29 *Perf. 13*

1874 A970 1.80fr multi 1.00 .40
1875 A970 2.60fr multi 1.25 .75

Centenary of Paris Convention for the Protection of Industrial Property — A971

1983, May 14 **Photo.** *Perf. 13*

1876 A971 2fr multicolored .85 .30

French Philatelic Societies Congress, Marseille A972

1983, May 21 **Engr.** *Perf. 13*

1877 A972 1.80fr multicolored .85 .35

Liberty Type of 1982

1983-87 **Engr.** *Perf. 13*

1878 A915 1.70fr green .75 .25
1879 A915 1.80fr green .80 .25
1880 A915 1.90fr green 1.25 .25
1881 A915 2fr red .90 .25
1882 A915 2fr green .90 .25
1883 A915 2.10fr red .95 .25
1884 A915 2.20fr red 2.00 .25
a. Booklet pane of 10 20.00
b. Bklt. pane, #1788, 4 #1884 8.50
c. With label ('87) 1.00 .25
1885 A915 2.80fr blue 1.25 .90
1886 A915 3fr blue 1.25 .50
1887 A915 3.20fr blue 1.50 .90
1888 A915 3.40fr blue 1.60 .75
1889 A915 3.60fr blue 1.60 .65
1890 A915 10fr purple 4.50 .25
1891 A915 (1.90fr) green .90 .25
1892 A915 (2fr) green .90 .25
Nos. 1878-1892 (15) 21.05 6.20

Coil Stamps

Engr. *Perf. 13 Horiz.*

1893 A915 1.70fr green .90 .80
1894 A915 1.80fr green 1.00 .50
1895 A915 1.90fr green 1.25 .30
1896 A915 2fr red 1.00 .30
1897 A915 2.10fr red 1.10 .60
1897A A915 2.20fr red 1.00 .50
Nos. 1893-1897A (6) 6.25 3.00

No. 1891 is inscribed "A," No. 1892 "B."

No. 1884c was issued in sheets of 50 plus 50 alternating labels picturing the PHILEX-FRANCE '89 emblem to publicize the international philatelic exhibition.

Issued: 2.80fr, 10fr, No. 1881, 6/1; 1.70fr, 2.10fr, 3fr, 7/1/84; 1.80fr, 2.20fr, 3.20fr, 8/1/85; 3.40fr, No. 1891, 8/1/86; 1.90fr, 9/13/86; No. 1882, 10/15/87; 3.60fr, No. 1892, 8/1/87.

For surcharge see No. 2115.

50th Anniv. of Air France A973

1983, June 18

1898 A973 3.45fr multicolored 1.50 .85

Treaties of Versailles and Paris Bicentenary — A974

1983, Sept. 2 *Perf. 13x12½*

1899 A974 2.80fr multicolored 1.40 .60

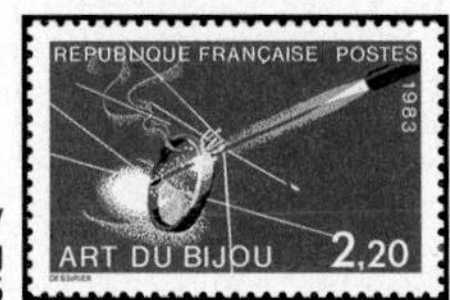

Jewelry Making A975

1983, Sept. 10 **Photo.** *Perf. 13*

1900 A975 2.20fr multicolored .90 .35

30th Anniv. of Customs Cooperation Council — A976

1983, Sept. 22 **Engr.** *Perf. 13x12½*

1901 A976 2.30fr multicolored 1.00 .40

Michaux's Bicycle A977

1983, Oct. 1 **Engr.** *Perf. 13*

1902 A977 1.60fr multicolored 1.10 .30

Natl. Weather Forecasting — A978

1983, Oct. 22 **Engr.** *Perf. 12½x13*

1903 A978 1.50fr multicolored .70 .25

Berthie Albrecht (1893-1943) — A979

1983, Nov. 5

1904 A979 1.60fr dk brown & olive .75 .30
1905 A979 1.60fr Rene Levy (1906-1943) .75 .30

Resistance heroines.

A980

1983, Dec. 16

1906 A980 2fr dk gray & red .80 .25

Pierre Mendes France (1907-1982), Premier.

Union Leader Waldeck-Rousseau A981

1984, Mar. 22 *Perf. 13*

1907 A981 3.60fr multi 1.60 .30

Trade Union centenary.

Homage to the Cinema, by Cesar A982

1984, Feb. 4 **Engr.** *Perf. 12½x13*

1908 A982 4fr multicolored 1.75 1.00

Four Corners of the Sky, by Jean Messagier — A983

1984, Mar. 31 **Photo.** *Perf. 13x12½*

1909 A983 4fr multicolored 1.75 1.00

Dining Room Corner, at Cannet, by Pierre Bonnard — A984

Photogravure and Engraved

1984, Apr. 14 *Perf. 12½x12*

1910 A984 4fr multicolored 1.75 1.00

Pythia, by Andre Masson A985

Painter at the Feet of His Model, by Helion A986

1984 **Photo.** *Perf. 12x13*

1911 A985 5fr multicolored 2.25 1.00
1912 A986 5fr multicolored 2.25 1.00

Issue dates: No. 1911, 10/13; No. 1912, 12/1.

Guadeloupe — A987

Design: Map, West Indian dancers.

1984, Feb. 25 *Perf. 13*

1913 A987 2.30fr multicolored 1.00 .30

Vauban Citadel, Belle Ile-en-Mer A988

Cordouan Lighthouse — A989

1984 **Engr.** *Perf. 13*

1914 A988 2.50fr multicolored 1.10 .35
1915 A989 3.50fr multicolored 1.60 .40

Issued: No. 1914, 5/26; No. 1915, 6/23.

La Grande Chartreuse Monastery, 900th Anniv. A990

Palais Ideal, Hauterives-Drome — A991

Montsegur Chateau A992

1984
1916 A990 1.70fr multicolored .80 .40
1917 A991 2.10fr multicolored .95 .30
1917A A992 3.70fr multicolored 1.60 .40
Nos. 1914-1917A (5) 6.05 1.85

Issued: 1.70fr, 7/7; 2.10fr, 6/30; 3.70fr, 9/15.

Flora Tristan (1803-44), Feminist A992a

1984, Mar. 8
1918 A992a 2.80fr multicolored 1.25 .50

Playing Card Suits — A993

1984, Apr. 11 **Engr.**
1919 A993 1.14fr Hearts .50 .45
1920 A993 1.47fr Spades .65 .55
1921 A993 2.38fr Diamonds 1.00 .75
1922 A993 3.95fr Clubs 1.60 1.25
Nos. 1919-1922 (4) 3.75 3.00

Nos. 1919-1922 known only precanceled. See second note after No. 132.

450th Anniv. of Cartier's Landing in Quebec A994

1984, Apr. 20 **Photo. & Engr.**
1923 A994 2fr multicolored .90 .25

See Canada No. 1011.

Philex '84, Dunkirk A995

1984, Apr. 21 ***Perf. 13x12½***
1924 A995 1.60fr multicolored .75 .35

Europa (1959-84) A996

1984, Apr. 28 **Engr.** ***Perf. 13***
1925 A996 2fr red brown .80 .30
1926 A996 2.80fr blue 1.25 .50

2nd European Parliament Election A997

1984, Mar. 24 **Photo.** ***Perf. 13***
1927 A997 2fr multicolored .90 .25

Foreign Legion A998

1984, Apr. 30 **Engr.** ***Perf. 13x12½***
1928 A998 3.10fr multicolored 1.40 .50

40th Anniv. of Liberation A999

Photogravure and Engraved

1984, May 8 ***Perf. 12½x13***
1929 A999 2fr Resistance .85 .50
1930 A999 3fr Landing 1.25 .60
a. Pair, #1929-1930 + label 2.50 2.00

Olympic Events — A1000

1984, June 1 ***Perf. 13***
1931 A1000 4fr multicolored 1.75 1.00

Intl. Olympic Committee, 90th anniv. and 1984 Summer Olympics.

Engraving — A1001

1984, June 8 **Engr.**
1932 A1001 2fr multicolored .90 .25

Bordeaux A1002

1984, June 9 ***Perf. 13x12½***
1933 A1002 2fr red .85 .25

French Philatelic Societies Congress, Bordeaux.

Natl. Telecommunications College, 40th Anniv. — A1003

Design: Satellite, phone, keyboard.

1984, June 16 **Photo.** ***Perf. 13***
1934 A1003 3fr multicolored 1.25 .30

25th Intl. Geography Congress, Paris — A1004

1984, Aug. 25 **Engr.** ***Perf. 13x12½***
1935 A1004 3fr Alps 1.25 .45

Telecom I Satellite A1005

1984, Sept. 1 **Photo.** ***Perf. 13***
1936 A1005 3.20fr multicolored 1.50 .50

High-speed Train Mail Transport A1006

Design: Electric train, Paris-Lyon.

1984, Sept. 8
1937 A1006 2.10fr multicolroed 1.00 .25

Local Birds — A1007

Design: 1fr, Gypaetus barbatus. 2fr, Circaetus gallicus. 3fr, Accipiter nisus. 5fr, Peregrine falcon.

Photogravure and Engraved

1984, Sept. 22 ***Perf. 12½x12***
1938 A1007 1fr multi .45 .25
1939 A1007 2fr multi .90 .25
1940 A1007 3fr multi 1.40 .75
1941 A1007 5fr multi 2.25 .55
Nos. 1938-1941 (4) 5.00 1.80

Marx Dormoy (1888-1941) A1008

1984, Sept. 22 **Engr.** ***Perf. 13***
1942 A1008 2.40fr multicolored 1.00 .30

A1009

1984, Oct. 6 **Engr.** ***Perf. 12½x13***
1943 A1009 3fr Automobile plans 1.40 .30

100th anniv. of the automobile.

A1010

1984, Nov. 3
1944 A1010 2.10fr multicolored .95 .30

Pres. Vincent Auriol (1884-1966).

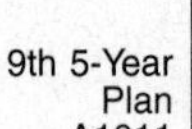
9th 5-Year Plan A1011

1984, Dec. 8 **Photo.** ***Perf. 13***
1945 A1011 2.10fr dk blue & scar .95 .25

French Language Promotion — A1012

1985, Jan. 15 **Engr.** ***Perf. 12½x13***
1946 A1012 3fr multicolored 1.25 .30

Tourism Issue

View of Vienne A1013

Cathedral at Montpelier A1014

St. Michel de Cuxa (Codalet) Abbey — A1015

Talmont Church, Saintonge Romane A1016

Solutre A1017

1985 ***Perf. 13x12½***
1947 A1013 1.70fr ol blk & dk grn .75 .25
1948 A1014 2.10fr sepia & org .90 .25
1949 A1015 2.20fr multicolored .90 .35
1950 A1016 3fr multicolored 1.25 .55
1951 A1017 3.90fr multicolored 1.50 .40
Nos. 1947-1951 (5) 5.30 1.80

Issue dates: 1.70fr, Jan. 19; 2.10fr, Mar. 30; 2.20fr, July 6; 3fr, June 15; 3.90fr, Sept. 28.

French TV, 50th Anniv. A1018

1985, Jan. 26 **Photo.** ***Perf. 13***
1952 A1018 2.50fr multicolored 1.10 .50

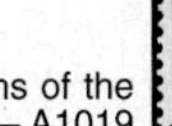
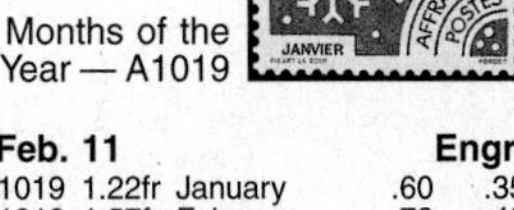

Months of the Year — A1019

1985, Feb. 11 **Engr.**
1953 A1019 1.22fr January .60 .35
1954 A1019 1.57fr February .70 .40
1955 A1019 2.55fr March 1.25 .90
1956 A1019 4.23fr April 2.00 1.25

1986, Feb. 10 **Engr.** ***Perf. 13***
1957 A1019 1.28fr May .65 .35
1958 A1019 1.65fr June .75 .40
1959 A1019 2.67fr July 1.25 1.00
1960 A1019 4.44fr August 2.25 1.60

1987, Feb. 16 **Engr.**
1961 A1019 1.31fr September .70 .35
1962 A1019 1.69fr October .75 .40
1963 A1019 2.74fr November 1.25 1.00
1964 A1019 4.56fr December 2.25 1.75
Nos. 1953-1964 (12) 14.40 9.75

Nos. 1953-1964 are known only precanceled. See second note after No. 132.

St. Valentine, by Raymond Peynet A1020

1985, Feb. 14 **Photo.** ***Perf. 13x12½***
1965 A1020 2.10fr multicolored .95 .25

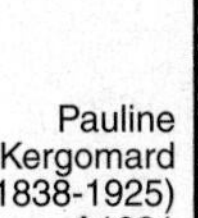

Pauline Kergomard (1838-1925) A1021

1985, Mar. 8 **Engr.** ***Perf. 13x12½***
1966 A1021 1.70fr int bl & cop red .75 .25

Stained Glass Window, Strasbourg Cathedral A1022

Still-life with Candle, Nicolas de Stael — A1023

1985 **Engraved** ***Perf. 12x13***
1967 A1022 5fr multicolored 2.25 1.25

Photo.
Perf. 13x12
1968 A1023 5fr multicolored 2.25 1.00

Issue dates: No. 1967, 4/13; No. 1968, 6/1.

Untitled Abstract by Jean Dubuffet — A1024

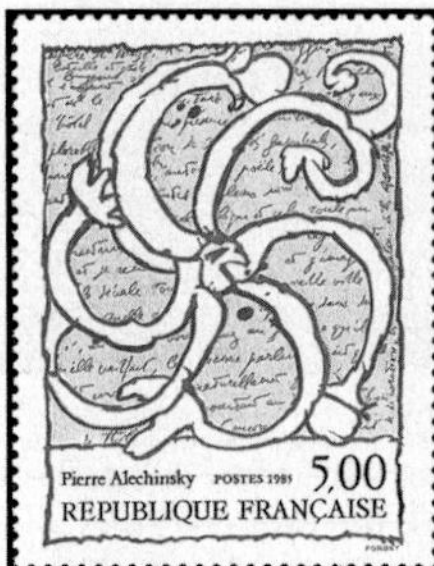

Octopus Overlaid on Manuscript, by Pierre Alechinsky — A1025

Photogravure; Engraved (#1970)
1985 ***Perf. 13x12½***
1969 A1024 5fr multicolored 2.25 1.00
1970 A1025 5fr multicolored 2.25 1.00

Issued: No. 1969, 10/14; No. 1970, 10/12.

The Dog, Abstract by Alberto Giacometti (1901-1966) — A1026

1985, Dec. 7 **Engr.** ***Perf. 13x12½***
1971 A1026 5fr grnsh blk & lt lem 2.25 1.00

Housing in Givors A1027

Contemporary architecture by Jean Renaude.

1985, Apr. 20 **Engr.** ***Perf. 13***
1972 A1027 2.40fr blk, yel org & ol grn 1.00 .50

Landevennec Abbey, 1500th Anniv. — A1028

1985, Apr. 20 ***Perf. 13x12½***
1973 A1028 1.70fr green & brn vio .75 .25

A1029

Europa: 2.10fr, Adam de la Halle (1240-1285), composer. 3fr, Darius Milhaud (1892-1974), composer.

1985, Apr. 27 ***Perf. 12½x13***
1974 A1029 2.10fr dr bl, blk, & brt bl .95 .30
1975 A1029 3fr dk bl, brt bl & blk 1.40 .50

A1030

1985, May 8 ***Perf. 13x12½***
1976 A1030 2fr Return of peace .75 .50
1977 A1030 3fr Return of liberty 1.25 .50
a. Pair, #1976-1977 + label 2.25 2.00

Liberation of France from German occupation forces, 40th anniv.

Natl. Philatelic Congress, Tours — A1031

Design: Tours Cathedral.

1985, May 25 ***Perf. 12½x13***
1978 A1031 2.10fr multicolored .95 .30

Rabies Vaccine Cent. A1032

Design: Pasteur inoculating patient.

1985, June 1 ***Perf. 13x12½***
1979 A1032 1.50fr multicolored .70 .30

Mystere Falcon-900 A1033

1985, June 1 ***Perf. 13***
1980 A1033 10fr blue 4.50 2.00

Lake Geneva Life-Saving Society Cent. A1034

1985, June 15
1981 A1034 2.50fr blk, red & brt ultra 1.00 .40

UN, 40th Anniv. — A1035

1985, June 26 ***Perf. 13x12½***
1982 A1035 3fr multicolored 1.10 .30

Huguenot Cross — A1036

1985, Aug. 31 **Engr.** ***Perf. 12½x13***
1983 A1036 2.50fr dp vio, dk red brn & dk red 1.00 .30

King Louis XIV revoked the Edict of Nantes on Oct. 18, 1685, dispossessing French Protestants of religious and civil liberty.

A1037

Trees, leaves and fruit of the beech, elm, oak and spruce varieties: 2fr, Ulmus montana. 3fr, Quercus pedunculata. 5fr, Picea abies.

1985, Sept. 21 **Engr.** ***Perf. 12½***
1984 A1037 1fr shown .45 .25
1985 A1037 2fr multicolored .90 .25
1986 A1037 3fr multicolored 1.25 .60
1987 A1037 5fr multicolored 2.25 .30
Nos. 1984-1987 (4) 4.85 1.40

A1038

La France Mourning the Dead, Eternal Flame.

1985, Nov. 2 **Engr.** ***Perf. 12½x13***
1988 A1038 1.80fr brn, org & lake .85 .25

Memorial Day.

A1039

1985, Nov. 9 **Engr.**
1989 A1039 3.20fr black & blue 1.25 .40

Charles Dullin, 1885-1949, impresario, theater.

A1040

1985, Nov. 16 **Engr.** ***Perf. 13x12½***
1990 A1040 2.20fr red & black .90 .25

National information system.

Thai Ambassadors at the Court of King Louis XIV, Painting
A1041

1986, Jan. 25 Engr. *Perf. 13*

1991 A1041 3.20fr rose lake & blk 1.25 .65

Normalization of diplomatic relations with Thailand, 300th anniv.

Leisure, by Fernand Leger
A1042

1986, Feb. 1 Photo. *Perf. 13*

1992 A1042 2.20fr multicolored .90 .25

1936 Popular Front, 50th anniv.

Venice Carnival, Paris — A1043

1986, Feb. 12 *Perf. 12½x13*

1993 A1043 2.20fr multicolored .90 .25

La Marianne, Typograph by Raymond Gid
A1044

Photogravure & Engraved

1986, Mar. 3 *Perf. 12½x13½*

1994 A1044 5fr black & dk red 2.25 1.00

Tourism Issue

Filitosa, South Corsica
A1045

Loches Chateau
A1046

Norman Manor, St. Germain de Livet
A1047

Notre-Dame-en-Vaux Monastery, Marne — A1048

Market Square, Bastide de Monpazier, Dordogne — A1049

1986 Engr. *Perf. 13*

1995 A1045 1.80fr multicolored .85 .25
1996 A1046 2fr int blue & blk .90 .50
1997 A1047 2.20fr grnsh bl, brn & grn 1.00 .35
1998 A1048 2.50fr henna brn & sepia 1.10 .40

Perf. 13x12½

1999 A1049 3.90fr blk & yel org 1.75 .90
Nos. 1995-1999 (5) 5.60 2.40

Issued: 2.20fr, 3/3; 2fr, 6/14; 2.50fr, 6/9; 1.80fr, 3.90fr, 7/5.

Louise Michel (1830-1905), Anarchist — A1050

1986, Mar. 10 Engr.

2000 A1050 1.80fr dk red & gray blk .80 .25

City of Science and Industry, La Villette — A1051

1986, Mar. 17

2001 A1051 3.90fr multicolored 1.60 .50

Center for Modern Asia-Africa Studies
A1052

1986, Apr. 12 Photo. *Perf. 13*

2002 A1052 3.20fr Map 1.25 .25

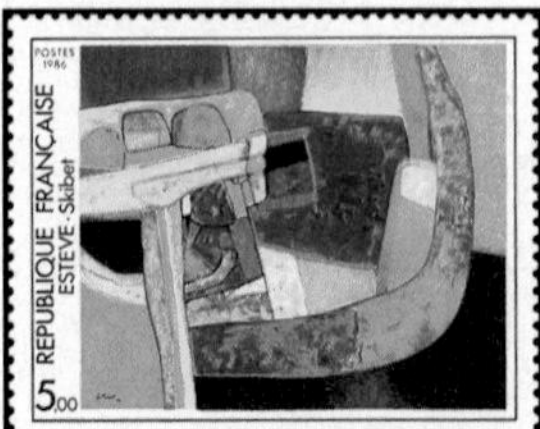

Skibet, Abstract by Maurice Esteve — A1053

Virginia, Abstract by Alberto Magnelli — A1054

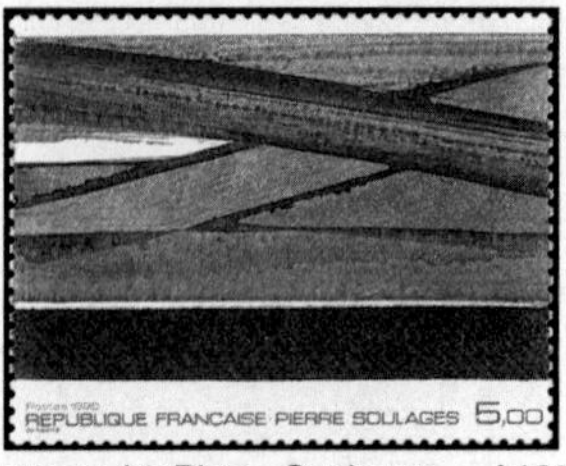

Abstract, by Pierre Soulages — A1055

The Dancer, by Jean Arp
A1056

Isabelle d'Este, by Leonardo da Vinci
A1057

Perf. 12½x13, 13x12½ (#2005, 2006)

1986 Photo., Engr. (#2005, 2007)

2003 A1053 5fr multicolored 2.25 1.00
2004 A1054 5fr multicolored 2.25 1.00
2005 A1055 5fr brt vio, blk & brn gray 2.25 1.00
2006 A1056 5fr multicolored 2.25 1.00
2007 A1057 5fr blk, red brn & grnsh yel 2.25 1.00
Nos. 2003-2007 (5) 11.25 5.00

Issued: No. 2003, 4/14; No. 2004, 6/25; No. 2005, 6/22; Nos. 2006, 2007, 11/10.

Victor Basch (1863-1944), IPY Emblem — A1058

1986, Apr. 28 Engr. *Perf. 13*

2008 A1058 2.50fr black & yel grn 1.10 .25

International Peace Year.

Europa 1986
A1059

1986, Apr. 28 *Perf. 13x12½*

2009 A1059 2.20fr Civet cat 1.00 .30
2010 A1059 3.20fr Bat 1.40 .60

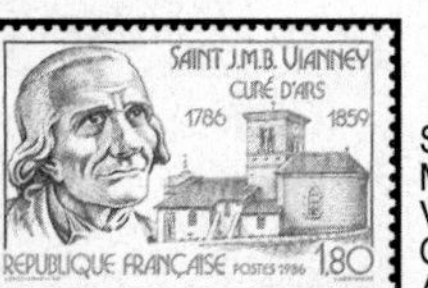

St. Jean-Marie Vianney, Curé of Ars
A1060

1986, May 3 Engr. *Perf. 13x12½*

2011 A1060 1.80fr sepia, brn org & brn .80 .25

Philatelic Societies Federation Congress, Nancy — A1061

1986, May 17 *Perf. 13*

2012 A1061 2.20fr Exposition Center .90 .25

Mens World Volleyball Championship
A1062

1986, May 24 Engr. *Perf. 13*

2013 A1062 2.20fr dk vio, brn vio & scar .90 .30

Statue of Liberty, Cent. — A1063

1986, July 4 *Perf. 13*

2014 A1063 2.20fr scar & dk blue 1.00 .30

See US No. 2224.

1st Ascent of Mt. Blanc, 1786
A1064

1986, Aug. 8 Engr. *Perf. 13x12½*

2015 A1064 2fr J. Balmat, M.G. Paccard .90 .50

Pierre-Louis Moreau de Maupertuis (1698-1759), La Condamine and Sextant — A1065

1986, Sept. 5

2016 A1065 3fr multicolored 1.25 .55

Lapland Expedition, 250th anniv., proved Earth's poles are flattened.

See Finland No. 741.

Marcassite A1066

1986, Sept. 13 *Perf. 12½*

2017	A1066	2fr shown	.90	.25
2018	A1066	3fr Quartz	1.40	.25
2019	A1066	4fr Calcite	1.75	.70
2020	A1066	5fr Fluorite	2.25	.70
		Nos. 2017-2020 (4)	6.30	1.90

Souvenir Sheet

Natl. Film Industry, 50th Anniv. — A1067

Personalities and film scenes: a, Louis Feuillade, The Vampires. b, Max Linder. c, Sacha Guitry, Romance of the Trickster. d, Jean Renoir, The Grand Illusion. e, Marcel Pagnol, The Baker's Woman. f, Jean Epstein, The Three-Sided Mirror. g, Rene Clair, Women of the Night. h, Jean Gremillon, Talk of Love. i, Jacques Becker, Helmet of Gold. j, Francois Truffaut, The Young Savage.

1986, Sept. 20 Photo. *Perf. 13x12½*

2021	A1067	Sheet of 10	10.00	10.00
a.-j.		2.20fr any single	1.00	1.00

Scene from Le Grand Meaulnes, by Henry Alain-Fournier (b. 1886), Novelist — A1068

1986, Oct. 4 Engr. *Perf. 12½x13*

2022 A1068 2.20fr black & dk red .90 .25

Professional Education, Cent. — A1069

1986, Oct. 4

2023 A1069 1.90fr brt vio & dp lil rose .85 .25

World Energy Conf., Cannes — A1070

1986, Oct. 5 Photo. *Perf. 13*

2024 A1070 3.40fr multicolored 1.50 .50

Mulhouse Technical Museum — A1071

1986, Dec. 1 Engr.

2025 A1071 2.20fr int blue, dk red & blk 1.00 .50

Museum at Orsay, Opening — A1072

1986, Dec. 10 Photo.

2026 A1072 3.70fr bluish blk & pck bl 1.60 .60

Fulgence Bienvenue (1852-1934), and the Metro — A1073

1987, Jan. 17 Engr. *Perf. 13*

2027 A1073 2.50fr vio brn, brn & dk grn 1.10 .30

A1074

1987, Jan. 24

2028 A1074 1.90fr grn & grnsh blk .85 .25

Raoul Follereau (1903-1977), care for lepers.

A1075

1987, Mar. 7 Engr. *Perf. 12½x13*

2029 A1075 1.90fr black & red .85 .25

Cutlery industry, Thiers.

Tourist Issue

Redon, Ille et Vilaine A1076

Azay-le-Rideau Chateau — A1077

Meuse District — A1078

Etretat A1079

Les Baux-de-Provence — A1080

1987 Engr. *Perf. 13*

2030	A1076	2.20fr dp rose lil, blk & brn ol	1.00	.25
2031	A1077	2.50fr Prus blue & olive grn	1.25	.55

Perf. 12½

2032 A1078 3.70fr multicolored 1.75 1.40

Photo. *Perf. 13*

2033 A1079 2.20fr multicolored 1.00 .25

Engr.

2034	A1080	3fr dk ol bis & dp vio	1.25	.40
		Nos. 2030-2034 (5)	6.25	2.85

Issued: No. 2030, 3/7; No. 2033, 6/12; 2.50fr, 5/9; 3fr, 6/27; 3.70fr, 5/30.

Charles Edouard Jenneret (Le Corbusier) (1887-1965), Architect — A1081

1987, Apr. 11 Photo. *Perf. 13x12½*

2035 A1081 3.70fr Abstract 1.60 .50

Europa 1987 A1082

Modern architecture: 2.20fr, Metal factory at Boulogne-Billancourt, by architect Claude Vasconi. 3.40fr, Rue Mallet-Stevens housing, by Robert Mallet-Stevens.

1987, Apr. 25 Engr. *Perf. 13x12½*

2036	A1082	2.20fr dk blue & grn	1.00	.50
2037	A1082	3.40fr brn & dk grn	1.50	.65

Abstract Painting, by Bram van Velde — A1083

Woman under Parasol, by Eugene Boudin (1824-1898) — A1084

Precambrien, by Camille Bryen — A1085

World, Bronze Sculpture by Antoine Pevsner — A1086

Perf. 12½x13, 13x12½ (Nos. 2039, 2041)

Photo., Engr. (Nos. 2039, 2041)

1987

2038	A1083	5fr multicolored	2.25	1.00
2039	A1084	5fr multicolored	2.25	1.00
2040	A1085	5fr multicolored	2.25	1.00
2041	A1086	5fr bister & blk	2.25	1.00
		Nos. 2038-2041 (4)	9.00	4.00

Issue dates: No. 2038, 4/25; No. 2039, 5/23; No. 2040, 9/12; No. 2041, 11/14.

Gaspard de Montagnes, from a Manuscript Illustration — A1087

1987, May 9 Engr. *Perf. 13*

2042 A1087 1.90fr dp grn & sepia .85 .25

Henri Pourrat (1887-1959), novelist.

Natl. Philatelic Societies Congress, Lens A1088

1987, June 6 ***Perf. 13x13½***
2043 A1088 2.20fr choc & red .90 .30

Involvement of U.S. Forces in WW I, 70th Anniv. A1089

Design: Stars and Stripes, troops, Gen. John J. Pershing (1860-1948), American army commander.

1987, June 13 ***Perf. 13***
2044 A1089 3.40fr olive grn, saph & ver 1.50 .70

A1090

1987, June 17 **Photo.**
2045 A1090 2fr multicolored .90 .50

6th Intl. Cable Car Transport Congress, Grenoble.

A1091

1987, June 20 **Litho.**
2046 A1091 1.90fr pale chalky blue & blk .90 .50

Accession of Hugh Capet (c.938-996), 1st king of France, millenary.

A1092

1987, June 20 **Engr.** ***Perf. 12½x13***
2047 A1092 2.20fr multicolored .90 .30

La Fleche Natl. Military School.

A1093

1987, June 27 **Photo.** ***Perf. 13***
2048 A1093 1.90fr multicolored .90 .55

World Assembly of Expatriate Algerians, Nice.

World Wrestling Championships — A1094

1987, Aug. 21 **Engr.**
2049 A1094 3fr brt pur, vio gray & brt olive grn 1.25 .60

Mushrooms A1095

2fr, Gyroporus cyanescens. 3fr, Gomphus clavatus. 4fr, Morchella conica. 5fr, Russula virescens.

1987, Sept. 5 ***Perf. 12½***
2050 A1095 2fr multicolored .90 .25
2051 A1095 3fr multicolored 1.25 .30
2052 A1095 4fr multicolored 1.75 .60
2053 A1095 5fr multicolored 2.25 .60
Nos. 2050-2053 (4) 6.15 1.75

William the Conqueror (c. 1027-1087) A1096

1987, Sept. 5 ***Perf. 13***
2054 A1096 2fr Bayeux Tapestry detail .90 .30

Montbenoit Le Saugeais A1097

Design: Abbey of Medieval Knights, cloisters, winter scene.

1987, Sept. 19
2055 A1097 2.50fr saph, blk & scar 1.10 .55

Pasteur Institute, Cent. — A1098

1987, Oct. 3
2056 A1098 2.20fr dp blue & dk red .85 .25

Blaise Cendrars (1887-1961), Poet and Novelist — A1099

Pen and ink portrait by Modigliani.

1987, Nov. 6 ***Perf. 12½***
2057 A1099 2fr brt grn, buff & blk .90 .35

Treaty of Andelot, 1400th Anniv. — A1100

1987, Nov. 28 ***Perf. 12½x13***
2058 A1100 3.70fr multicolored 1.60 .55

Gen. Leclerc (1902-1947), Marshal of France — A1101

1987, Nov. 28 ***Perf. 13x12½***
2059 A1101 2.20fr multicolored .90 .25

Liberty Type of 1982

1987-90 ***Perf. 13***
2077 A915 3.70fr brt lilac rose 1.75 .30
2078 A915 (2.10fr) green ('90) .95 .25
2079 A915 (2.30fr) red ('90) 1.00 .25
Nos. 2077-2079 (3) 3.70 .80

Coil Stamp
Engr.
Perf. 13 Horiz.
2080 A915 2fr emerald green .90 .30

Issued: 2fr, 8/1; 3.70fr, 11/16; Nos. 2078-2079, 1/2.
Nos. 2078-2079 are inscribed "C."

Franco-German Cooperation Treaty, 25th Anniv. — A1102

1988, Jan. 15 ***Perf. 13***
2086 A1102 2.20fr Adenauer, De Gaulle 1.00 .30

See Fed. Rep. of Germany No. 1546.

Marcel Dassault (1892-1986), Aircraft Designer — A1103

1988, Jan. 23 **Photo.**
2087 A1103 3.60fr brt ultra, gray blk & dk red 1.60 .70

Communications A1104

Angouleme Festival prize-winning cartoons.

1988, Jan. 29 **Photo.** ***Perf. 13½x13***
Booklet Stamps
2088 A1104 2.20fr Pellos 1.00 .40
2089 A1104 2.20fr Reiser 1.00 .40
2090 A1104 2.20fr Marijac 1.00 .40
2091 A1104 2.20fr Fred 1.00 .40
2092 A1104 2.20fr Moebius 1.00 .40
2093 A1104 2.20fr Gillon 1.00 .40
2094 A1104 2.20fr Bretecher 1.00 .40
2095 A1104 2.20fr Forest 1.00 .40
2096 A1104 2.20fr Mezieres 1.00 .40
2097 A1104 2.20fr Tardi 1.00 .40
2098 A1104 2.20fr Lob 1.00 .40
2099 A1104 2.20fr Bilal 1.00 .40
a. Bklt. pane of 12, #2088-2099 12.00 8.50

Great Synagogue, Rue Victoire, Paris — A1105

1988, Feb. 7 **Litho.** ***Perf. 13***
2100 A1105 2fr black & gold .90 .25

The Four Elements — A1106

1988, Feb. 1 **Engr.** ***Perf. 13***
2101 A1106 1.36fr Air .65 .40
2102 A1106 1.75fr Water .80 .40
2103 A1106 2.83fr Fire 1.25 1.00
2104 A1106 4.75fr Earth 2.25 1.75
Nos. 2101-2104 (4) 4.95 3.55

Nos. 2101-2104 known only precanceled. See second note after No. 132.

PHILEXFRANCE '89 — A1107

1988, Mar. 4
2105 A1107 2.20fr #1885, emblem 1.00 .25

Postal Training College, Cent. A1108

1988, Mar. 29
2106 A1108 3.60fr multicolored 1.60 .40

Philex-Jeunes '88, Youth Stamp Show — A1109

1988, Apr. 8 ***Perf. 13x12½***
2107 A1109 2fr multicolored .90 .25

Blood Donation — A1110

1988, Apr. 9 Photo. ***Perf. 13½x13***
2108 A1110 2.50fr multicolored 1.10 .40

Europa 1988 A1111

Communication and transportation.

1988, Apr. 30 Engr. ***Perf. 13***
2109 A1111 2.20fr Cables, satellites 1.00 .30
2110 A1111 3.60fr Rail cars 1.75 .40

Jean Monnet (1888-1979), Economist — A1112

1988, May 10 ***Perf. 12½x13***
2111 A1112 2.20fr black & brn ol 1.00 .25

Philatelic Congress, Valence A1113

1988, May 21 ***Perf. 13x12½***
2112 A1113 2.20fr multicolored 1.00 .35

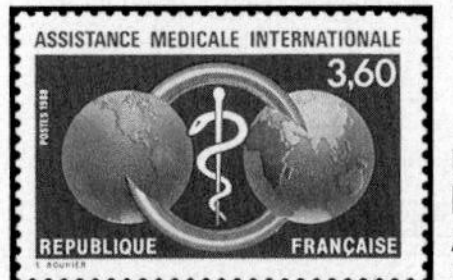

Intl. Medical Assistance A1114

1988, May 28 Photo. ***Perf. 13***
2113 A1114 3.60fr multicolored 1.60 .50

Aid to the Handicapped — A1115

1988, May 28
2114 A1115 3.70fr multicolored 1.60 .50

No. 1884 Surcharged in European Currency Units

1988, Apr. 16 **Engr.**
2115 A915 2.20fr red 1.00 .25

Tourist Issue

Hermes Dicephalus (Roman Empire), Frejus — A1116

1988, June 12 Engr. ***Perf. 13x12½***
2116 A1116 3.70fr multicolored 1.75 .80

Ship Museum, Douarnenez — A1117

Chateau Sedieres, Correze — A1118

Cirque de Gavarnie A1119

1988 ***Perf. 13, 12½x13 (#2118)***
2117 A1117 2fr multicolored .90 .25
2118 A1118 2.20fr multicolored 1.00 .35
2119 A1119 3fr multicolored 1.25 .40

Issued: 2.20fr, 7/2; 2fr, 7/4; 3fr, 7/23.

View of Perouges, Ain A1120

1988, Sept. 10 ***Perf. 13x12½***
2120 A1120 2.20fr multicolored 1.00 .25
Nos. 2116-2120 (5) 5.90 2.05

French Revolution, Bicent. — A1121

Designs: 3fr, Assembly of the Three Estates, Vizille. 4fr, Day of the Tiles (Barricades), Grenoble.

1988, June 18 **Engr.**
2121 A1121 3fr multicolored 1.25 1.00
2122 A1121 4fr multicolored 1.75 1.00
a. Pair, #2121-2122 + label 3.50 3.00

PHILEXFRANCE '89.

Buffon's Natural History — A1122

1988, June 18 ***Perf. 12½***
2123 A1122 2fr Otters .90 .25
2124 A1122 3fr Stag 1.25 .30
2125 A1122 4fr Fox 1.75 .70
2126 A1122 5fr Badger 2.25 .60
Nos. 2123-2126 (4) 6.15 1.85

Alpine Troops, Cent. — A1123

1988, June 25 ***Perf. 13***
2127 A1123 2.50fr multicolored 1.10 .60

Roland Garros (1888-1918), 1st Pilot to Fly Across the Mediterranean, Sept. 23, 1913 — A1124

1988, July 2 Engr. ***Perf. 13x12½***
2128 A1124 2fr brt grn bl & olive .90 .25

A1125

1988, Sept. 10 Engr. ***Perf. 13***
2129 A1125 2.20fr brt blue, gray & blk 1.00 .25

Nov. 11, 1918 Armistice Ending World War I, 70th anniv.

Homage to Leon Degand, Sculpture by Robert Jacobsen A1126

1988, Sept. 22 ***Perf. 12½x13***
2130 A1126 5fr blk & dp claret 2.25 1.00

French-Danish cultural exchange program, 10th anniv. See Denmark No. 860.

Strasbourg, 2000th Anniv. — A1127

1988, Sept. 24 ***Perf. 13***
2131 A1127 2.20fr Municipal arms 1.00 .25

St. Mihiel Sepulcher, by Ligier Richier (c. 1500-1567), Sculptor — A1128

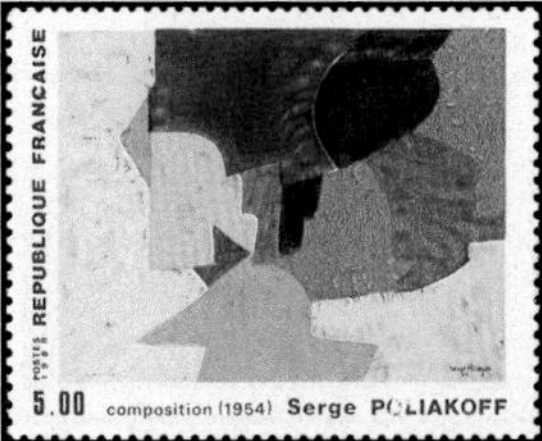

Composition, 1954, by Serge Poliakoff (1906-1969) — A1129

La Pieta de Villeneuve-les-Avignon, by Enguerrand Quarton (1444-1466) — A1130

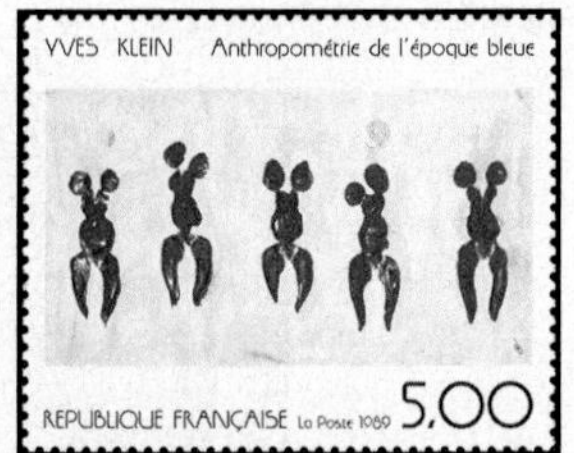

Anthropometry of the Blue Period, by Yves Klein — A1131

1988-89 Engr. *Perf. 13x12½*
2132 A1128 5fr black brown 2.25 1.00

Photo.

2133 A1129 5fr multicolored 2.25 1.00
2134 A1130 5fr multicolored 2.25 1.00
2135 A1131 5fr multi ('89) 2.25 1.00
Nos. 2132-2135 (4) 9.00 4.00

Issue dates: No. 2132, 10/15; No. 2133, 10/22; No. 2134, 12/10; No. 2135, 1/21.

Thermal Springs A1132

1988, Nov. 21 Engr. *Perf. 13x12½*
2136 A1132 2.20fr multicolored 1.00 .25

Metamecanique, by Jean Tinguely — A1133

1988, Nov. 25 Photo.
2137 A1133 5fr multicolored 2.25 1.00

See Switzerland No. 828.

UN Declaration of Human Rights, 40th Anniv. A1134

1988, Dec. 12 Litho. *Perf. 13*
2138 A1134 2.20fr dk bl & grnsh bl 1.00 .25

French Revolution, Bicent. — A1135

1989, Jan. 1 Photo. *Perf. 13x12½*
2139 A1135 2.20fr red & vio blue 1.00 .25

Valentin Hauy (1745-1822), Founder of the School for the Blind, Paris, 1791 — A1136

Photo. & Embossed

1989, Jan. 28
2140 A1136 2.20fr multicolored 1.00 .40

Estienne School, Cent. — A1137

1989, Feb. 4 Engr. *Perf. 12½*
2141 A1137 2.20fr gray, black & red 1.00 .25

European Parliament Elections A1138

1989, Mar. 4 Litho. *Perf. 13*
2142 A1138 2.20fr multicolored 1.00 .25

A1139

1989 Engr. *Perf. 12½x13*
2143 A1139 2.20fr Liberty 1.00 .25
2144 A1139 2.20fr Equality 1.00 .25
2145 A1139 2.20fr Fraternity 1.00 .25
a. Strip of 3, #2143-2145 + label 3.00 2.50

Bicent. of the French revolution and the Declaration of Rights of Man and the Citizen. No. 2145a contains inscribed label picturing PHILEXFRANCE '89 emblem.

Issue dates: No. 2143, 3/18; No. 2144, 4/22; No. 2145, 5/27; No. 2145a, 7/14.

French-Soviet Joint Space Flight — A1140

1989, Mar. 4 Litho. *Perf. 13*
2146 A1140 3.60fr multicolored 1.60 .50

Historic Sights, Paris — A1141

Designs: No. 2147, Arche de la Defense. No. 2148, Eiffel Tower. No. 2149, Grand Louvre. No. 2150, Notre Dame Cathedral. No. 2151, Bastille Monument and Opera de la Bastille. No. 2151a has a continuous design.

1989, Apr. 21 Engr. *Perf. 13x12½*
2147 A1141 2.20fr multicolored 1.00 .75
2148 A1141 2.20fr multicolored 1.00 .75
2149 A1141 2.20fr multicolored 1.00 .75
2150 A1141 2.20fr multicolored 1.00 .75
2151 A1141 2.20fr multicolored 1.00 .75
a. Strip of 5, #2147-2151 5.00 5.00

Europa 1989 A1142

Children's games.

1989, Apr. 29 *Perf. 13*
2152 A1142 2.20fr Hopscotch 1.00 .30
2153 A1142 3.60fr Catch (ball) 1.60 .60

ITU Plenipotentiaries Conference, Nice — A1143

1989, May 23 Litho.
2154 A1143 3.70fr dk bl, dl org & red 1.60 .40

Tourist Issue

Fontainebleau Forest — A1144

Vaux le Vicomte — A1145

La Brenne — A1146

1989, May 20 Engr. *Perf. 13*
2155 A1144 2.20fr multicolored .90 .30

Perf. 13x12½

2156 A1145 3.70fr ol bis & blk 1.60 .75
2157 A1146 4fr violet blue 1.60 .75
Nos. 2155-2157 (3) 4.10 1.80

Issued: 2.20fr, 5/20; 3.70fr, 7/14; 4fr, 8/25.

World Cycling Championships, Chambery — A1147

1989, June 3 Litho. *Perf. 13*
2158 A1147 2.20fr multi 1.00 .25

Jehan de Malestroit, Dept. of Morbihan — A1148

1989, June 10 Engr. *Perf. 12½x13*
2159 A1148 3.70fr multicolored 1.60 .55

Preliminary Sketch (Detail) for *Oath of the Tennis Court,* by David — A1149

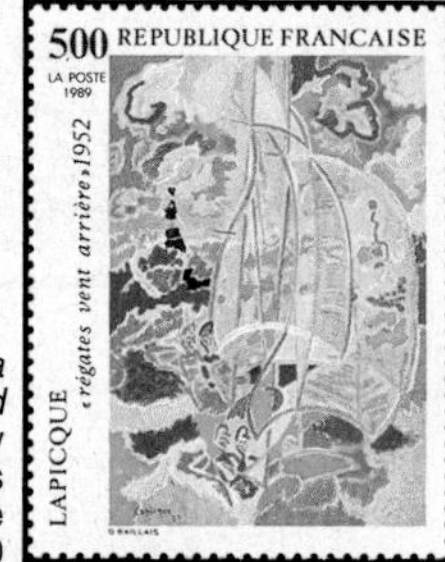

Regatta with Wind Astern, by Charles Lapicque A1150

1989, June 19 Photo. *Perf. 13x12½*
2160 A1149 5fr multicolored 2.25 1.00

Perf. 12½

2161 A1150 5fr multicolored 2.25 1.00

No. 2160 for French revolution bicent. Issued: No. 2160, 6/19; No. 2161, 9/23.

Souvenir Sheet

Revolution Bicentennial — A1151

Revolutionaries: a, Madame Roland (1754-1793). b, Camille Desmoulins (1760-1794). c, Condorcet (1743-1794). d, Kellermann (1735-1820).

1989, June 26 Engr. *Perf. 13*
2162 A1151 Sheet of 4 4.00 3.50
a.-d. 2.20fr any single 1.00 .60

A1152

2.20fr, 15th Summit of the Arch Meeting of Leaders from Industrial Nations, July 14-16.

1989, July 14 Photo.
2163 A1152 2.20fr multicolored 1.00 .35

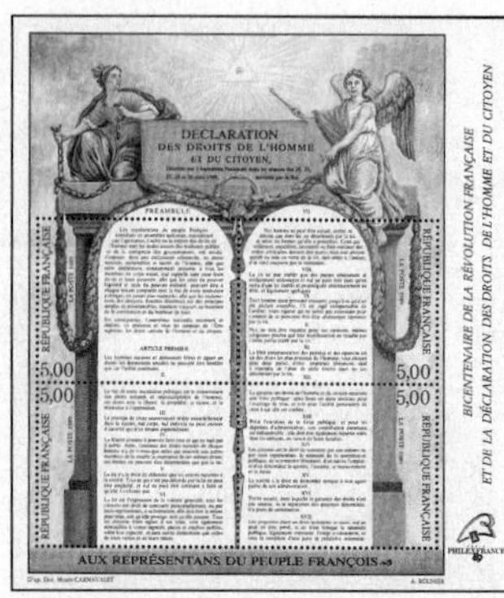

Declaration of the Rights of Man and the Citizen, Versailles, Aug. 26, 1789 — A1153

Details of an anonymous 18th-19th cent. painting in Carnavalet Museum: No. 2168a, Preamble, Article I. No. 2168b, Articles VII-XI. No. 2168c, Articles II-VI. No. 2168d, Articles XII-XVII.

Litho. & Engr.

1989, Aug. 26 *Perf. 13x11½*

2164 A1153 2.50fr Preamble, Article I 1.00 .80
2165 A1153 2.50fr Art. II-VI 1.00 .80
2166 A1153 2.50fr Art. VII-XI 1.00 .80
2167 A1153 2.50fr Art. XII-XVII 1.00 .80
a. Strip, #2164-2167 + label 4.50 3.25

Souvenir Sheet

Perf. 13x12½

2168 A1153 Sheet of 4 10.00 10.00
a.-d. 5fr any single 2.25 2.00

No. 2168 contains 4 52x41mm stamps. Sold for 50fr, including admission fee to PHILEX-FRANCE '89.

Value of No. 2168 is for examples on plain paper. Examples on fluorescent paper seem to have been distributed in North America, and may not have been distributed widely or made available in Europe. Value $400.

Musical Instruments — A1154

1989 **Litho.** *Perf. 12x12½*

2169 A1154 1.39fr Harp .65 .50
2170 A1154 1.79fr Piano .80 .50
2171 A1154 2.90fr Trumpet 1.25 1.00
2172 A1154 4.84fr Violin 2.25 1.75
Nos. 2169-2172 (4) 4.95 3.75

Nos. 2169-2172 are known only precanceled. See second note after No. 132.

See Nos. 2233-2239, 2273-2283, 2303-2306, 2368-2371.

TGV Atlantic A1155

1989, Sept. 23 **Photo.** *Perf. 13*

2173 A1155 2.50fr dk bl, sil & red 1.10 .50

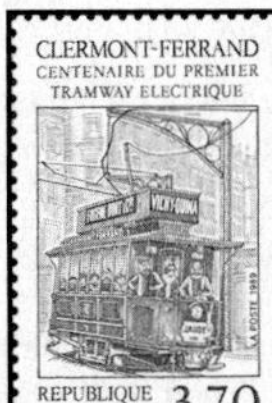

Clermont-Ferrand Tramway, Cent. — A1156

1989, Oct. 28 **Engr.**

2174 A1156 3.70fr blk & dk ol bis 1.75 .40

Villers-Cotterets Ordinance, 450th Anniv. — A1157

1989, Oct. 28 **Engr.**

2175 A1157 2.20fr blk, dp cl & red 1.00 .25

Baron Augustin-Louis Cauchy (1789-1857), Mathematician — A1158

1989, Nov. 10 *Perf. 13x12½*

2176 A1158 3.60fr red, blk & bl grn 1.60 .50

Marshal Jean de Lattre de Tassigny (1889-1952) — A1159

1989, Nov. 18 *Perf. 13*

2177 A1159 2.20fr bl, blk & red 1.00 .25

Harki Soldiers of France A1160

1989, Dec. 9 **Photo.**

2178 A1160 2.20fr multicolored 1.00 .30

Marianne — A1161

1990-92 **Engr.** *Perf. 13*

2179 A1161 10c brn blk .25 .25
a. Bklt. pane, #2180, 4 #2179 1.00
2180 A1161 20c lt green .25 .25
2181 A1161 50c brt violet .25 .25
2182 A1161 1fr orange .45 .25
2183 A1161 2fr apple grn .90 .25
2184 A1161 2.10fr dark grn .95 .25
2185 A1161 2.20fr dark grn 1.00 .25
2186 A1161 2.20fr emerald 1.00 .25
2187 A1161 2.30fr red 1.00 .25
a. Bklt. pane, #2180, 4 #2187 5.00
2188 A1161 2.50fr red 1.10 .25
2189 A1161 3.20fr blue 1.50 .75
2190 A1161 3.40fr blue 1.60 .40
2191 A1161 3.80fr lilac rose 1.75 .30
2192 A1161 4fr lilac rose 1.90 .25
2193 A1161 4.20fr lilac rose 1.90 .25
2194 A1161 5fr greenish blue 2.25 .25
2195 A1161 10fr violet 4.50 .25
2196 A1161 (2.20fr) dk grn 1.00 .25
2197 A1161 (2.50fr) red 1.10 .25
Nos. 2179-2197 (19) 24.65 5.45

Coil Stamps

Perf. 13 Horiz.

2198 A1161 2.10fr dk grn 1.00 .25
2199 A1161 2.20fr dk grn 1.00 .60
2200 A1161 2.30fr red 1.00 .25
2201 A1161 2.50fr red 1.10 .25
Nos. 2198-2201 (4) 4.10 1.35

Die Cut

Self-Adhesive

2202 A1161 2.30fr red 1.00 .25
a. Booklet pane of 10 10.00
2203 A1161 2.50fr red 1.10 .25
a. Booklet pane of 10 11.00
b. Booklet pane of 5 5.50
2204 A1161 (2.50fr) red 1.10 .25
a. Booklet pane of 10 11.00
Nos. 2202-2204 (3) 3.20 .75

Issued: No. 2187, 1/2; No. 2198, 1/1; 10c, 20c, 50c, 3.20fr, 3.80fr, 3/26; No. 2202, 1/29; Nos. 2182-2183, 2194-2195, 5/21; Nos. 2196-2197, 8/19/91; 2.20fr, 2.50fr, 3.40fr, 4fr, 9/30/91; Nos. 2179a, 2187a, 2199, 2201, 1991; 4.20fr, 9/24/92; Nos. 2203-2204, 1992; 2.10fr, 1993.

Peelable paper backing serves as booklet cover for Nos. 2202, 2203. No. 2203b has separate backing with no printing.

Nos. 2196-2197, 2204 inscribed "D."

See Nos. 2333-2348, 3529, 4410i, 4522.

Lace Work A1162

1990, Feb. 3 **Engr.** *Perf. 13x12½*

2205 A1162 2.50fr red 1.00 .40

1992 Winter Olympics, Albertville — A1163

1990, Feb. 9 **Photo.** *Perf. 13*

2206 A1163 2.50fr multicolored 1.00 .25

Charles de Gaulle (1890-1970) A1164

1990, Feb. 24 **Engr.** *Perf. 12½x13*

2207 A1164 2.30fr brt vio, vio bl & blk 1.00 .25

Max Hymans (1900-1961), Planes and ACC Emblem — A1165

1990, Mar. 3 *Perf. 13*

2208 A1165 2.30fr brt vio, brt bl & dk ol grn 1.00 .25

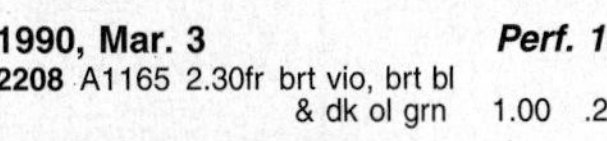

Profile of a Woman, by Odilon Redon A1166

Head of Christ, Wissembourg — A1167

Cambodian Dancer by Auguste Rodin — A1168

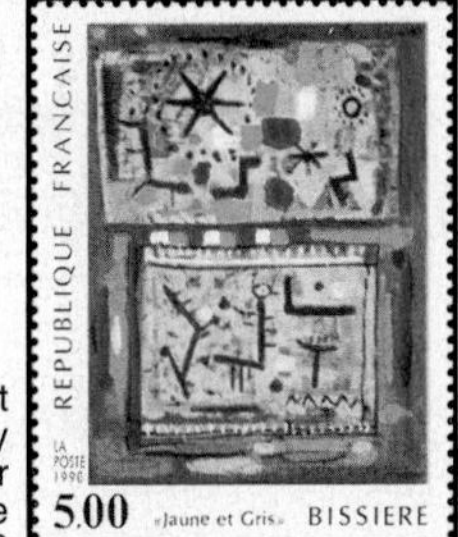

Jaune et Gris by Roger Bissiere A1169

1990 **Litho.** *Perf. 13½x14*

2209 A1166 5fr multicolored 2.25 1.00

Perf. 12½x13

Engr.

2210 A1167 5fr multicolored 2.25 1.00
2211 A1168 5fr multicolored 2.25 1.00

Photo.

2212 A1169 5fr multicolored 2.25 1.00
Nos. 2209-2212 (4) 9.00 4.00

Issue dates: No. 2209, Mar. 3; No. 2210, June 16; No. 2211, June 9; No. 2212, Dec. 8.

Jean Guehenno (1890-1978) A1170

Litho. & Engr.

1990, Mar. 24 *Perf. 13*

2213 A1170 3.20fr buff & red brn 1.50 .40

Tourism Series

Flaran Abbey, Gers A1171

1990, Apr. 21 **Engr.** *Perf. 13*

2214 A1171 3.80fr sepia & blk 1.75 .50

Cluny A1172

Pont Canal de Briare A1173

Cap Canaille, Cassis A1174

1990

2215 A1172 2.30fr multicolored 1.00 .25
2216 A1173 2.30fr multicolored 1.00 .25
2217 A1174 3.80fr multicolored 1.75 .50
Nos. 2215-2217 (3) 3.75 1.00

Issued: No. 2215, 6/23; No. 2216, 7/7; 3.80fr, 7/14.

Europa 1990 A1175

Post offices.

1990, Apr. 28 Engr. *Perf. 13*

2218 A1175 2.30fr Macon 1.00 .30
2219 A1175 3.20fr Cerizay 1.50 .60

Arab World Institute — A1176

1990, May 5 *Perf. 12½x13*

2220 A1176 3.80fr brt bl, dk red & dp bl 1.75 .40

Labor Day, Cent. A1177

1990, May 1 Photo. *Perf. 13*

2221 A1177 2.30fr multicolored 1.00 .25

Villefranche-sur-Saone — A1178

1990, June 2 Engr. *Perf. 13x12½*

2222 A1178 2.30fr multicolored 1.00 .25

National philatelic congress.

A1179

1990, June 6 *Perf. 13x12½*

2223 A1179 2.30fr La Poste 1.00 .25

Whitbread trans-global yacht race.

A1181

1990, June 17 *Perf. 12½x13*

2225 A1181 2.30fr multicolored 1.00 .25

De Gaulle's Call for French Resistance, 50th anniv.

Franco-Brazilian House, Rio de Janeiro — A1182

1990, July 14 *Perf. 13*

2226 A1182 3.20fr multicolored 1.50 .70

See Brazil No. 2255.

A1183

1990, Oct. 6 Engr. *Perf. 12½*

2227 A1183 2fr Rutilus rutilus .90 .25
2228 A1183 3fr Perca fluviatilis 1.25 .25
2229 A1183 4fr Salmo salar 1.75 .40
2230 A1183 5fr Esox lucius 2.25 .40
Nos. 2227-2230 (4) 6.15 1.30

A1184

1990, Sept. 29 Photo. *Perf. 12½x13*

2231 A1184 2.30fr multicolored 1.00 .30

Natl. Institute of Geography, 50th anniv.

Souvenir Sheet

French Revolution, Bicentennial — A1185

Designs: a, Gaspard Monge. b, Abbe Gregoire. c, Creation of the Tricolor. d, Creation of the French departments.

1990, Oct. 15 Engr. *Perf. 13*

2232 A1185 Sheet of 4 4.50 4.00
a.-d. 2.50fr any single 1.10 .90

Musical Instrument Type of 1989

Designs: 1.46fr, Accordion. 1.89fr, Breton bagpipe. 3.06fr, Tambourin. 5.10fr, Hurdy-gurdy.

1990, Sept. 1 Litho. *Perf. 13*

2233 A1154 1.46fr multi .65 .40
2234 A1154 1.89fr multi .75 .60
2235 A1154 3.06fr multi 1.50 1.50
2236 A1154 5.10fr multi 2.50 2.40
Nos. 2233-2236 (4) 5.40 4.90

1990, Nov. Litho. *Perf. 13*

2237 A1154 1.93fr like #2169 1.00 .60
2238 A1154 2.39fr like #2170 1.10 .80
2239 A1154 2.74fr like #2172 1.25 1.25
Nos. 2237-2239 (3) 3.35 2.65

Nos. 2233-2239 are known only precanceled. See second note after No. 132.

Maurice Genevoix (1890-1980), Novelist — A1186

1990, Nov. 12 Engr. *Perf. 13*

2240 A1186 2.30fr lt green & blk 1.00 .25

A1187

1990, Dec. 15 Litho.

2241 A1187 3.20fr dk & lt blue 1.50 .70

Organization for Economic Cooperation and Development, 30th Anniv.

"The Swing" by Auguste Renoir (1841-1919) — A1188

1991, Feb. 23 Engr. *Perf. 12½x13*

2242 A1188 5fr multicolored 2.25 1.00

Youth Philatelic Exhibition, Cholet A1189

1991, Mar. 30 Litho. *Perf. 13*

2243 A1189 2.50fr multicolored 1.10 .40

Art Series

Le Noeud Noir by Georges Seurat (1859-1891) — A1190

Apres Nous La Maternite, by Max Ernst (1891-1976) — A1191

Volte Faccia by Francois Rouan A1192

O Tableau Noir by Roberto Matta (b. 1911) — A1193

1991 Engr. *Perf. 12½x13*

2244 A1190 5fr pale yellow & blk 2.25 1.00

Photo. *Perf. 13*

2245 A1191 2.50fr multicolored 1.00 .70

Engr. *Perf. 12½x13*

2246 A1192 5fr black 2.25 1.00

Photo. *Perf. 13x12½*

2247 A1193 5fr multicolored 2.25 1.00
Nos. 2244-2247 (4) 7.75 3.70

Issued: No. 2244, 4/13: No. 2245, 10/10; No. 2246, 11/9; No. 2247, 11/30.

Wolfgang Amadeus Mozart (1756-1791), Composer — A1194

1991, Apr. 9 Photo. *Perf. 13*

2248 A1194 2.50fr bl, blk & red 1.10 .60

National Printing Office, 350th Anniv. — A1195

1991, Apr. 13

2249 A1195 4fr multicolored 1.75 .75

Tourism Series

Chevire Bridge, Nantes — A1196

Carennac Castle A1197

Pipe Organ, Wasquehal A1198

Valley of Munster A1199

1991 **Engr.** ***Perf. 13***
2250 A1196 2.50fr multicolored 1.10 .25

Perf. 12x13
2251 A1197 2.50fr multicolored 1.10 .30

Perf. 12
2252 A1198 4fr black & buff 1.75 .55

Perf. 13x12½
2253 A1199 4fr violet 1.75 .55
Nos. 2250-2253 (4) 5.70 1.65

Issue dates: No. 2250, Apr. 27; Nos. 2251, 2253, July 6; No. 2252, June 22.

Europa — A1200

2.50fr, Ariane launch site, French Guiana. 3.50fr, Television satellite.

1991, Apr. 27 ***Perf. 12½x13***
2254 A1200 2.50fr multi 1.10 .25
2255 A1200 3.50fr multi 1.60 .55

Compare with No. 2483.

Concours Lepine, 90th Anniv. — A1201

1991, Apr. 27 ***Perf. 13***
2256 A1201 4fr multicolored 1.75 .75

French Assoc. of Small Manufacturers and Inventors.

Philatelic Society Congress, Perpignan A1202

1991, May 18
2257 A1202 2.50fr multicolored 1.10 .25

French Open Tennis Championships, Cent. — A1203

1991, May 24 **Engr.** ***Perf. 13***
2258 A1203 3.50fr multicolored 1.60 .50

Souvenir Sheet

French Revolution, Bicent. — A1204

Designs: a, Theophile Malo Corret, La Tour d'Auvergne (1743-1800). b, Liberty Tree. c, National police, bicent. d, Louis Antoine-Leon de St. Just (1767-1794).

1991, June 1 **Engr.** ***Perf. 13***
2259 A1204 Sheet of 4 4.50 3.50
a.-d. 2.50fr any single 1.10 .80

A1205

1991, June 13 **Photo.** ***Perf. 13***
2260 A1205 2.50fr multicolored 1.10 .40

Gaston III de Foix (Febus) (1331-1391), general.

Wildlife — A1206

Designs: 2fr, Ursus arctos. 3fr, Testudo hermanni. 4fr, Castor fiber. 5fr, Alcedo atthis.

1991, Sept. 14 **Engr.** ***Perf. 12½***
2261 A1206 2fr multi .90 .30
2262 A1206 3fr multi 1.25 .30
2263 A1206 4fr multi 1.75 .70
2264 A1206 5fr multi 2.25 .70
Nos. 2261-2264 (4) 6.15 2.00

10th World Forestry Congress A1207

1991, Sept. 22 **Engr.** ***Perf. 13x12½***
2265 A1207 2.50fr multicolored 1.10 .25

School of Public Works, Cent. A1208

1991, Oct. 5 **Litho. & Engr.** ***Perf. 13***
2266 A1208 2.50fr multicolored 1.10 .30

Marcel Cerdan (1916-1949), Middleweight Boxing Champion — A1209

1991, Oct. 19 **Photo.** ***Perf. 13***
2267 A1209 2.50fr black & red 1.00 .30

Amnesty International, 30th Anniv. — A1210

1991, Oct. 19
2268 A1210 3.40fr multicolored 1.50 .60

1992 Winter Olympics, Albertville — A1211

1991, Nov. 14 **Engr.** ***Perf. 13***
2269 A1211 2.50fr Olympic flame 1.10 .25

Fifth Handicapped Olympics — A1212

1991, Dec. 7 ***Perf. 13***
2270 A1212 2.50fr dk & lt blue 1.10 .25

Voluntary Attachment of Mayotte to France, Sesquicentennial — A1213

1991, Dec. 21 **Engr.**
2271 A1213 2.50fr multicolored 1.10 .25

French Pavilion, Expo '92, Seville A1214

Litho. & Engr.
1992, Jan. 18 ***Perf. 13***
2272 A1214 2.50fr multicolored 1.10 .25

Musical Instruments Type of 1989

1992, Jan. 31 **Litho.** ***Perf. 13***
2273 A1154 1.60fr Guitar 60.00 25.00
2274 A1154 1.98fr like #2233 3.00 2.25
2275 A1154 2.08fr Saxophone 1.25 1.00
2276 A1154 2.46fr like #2234 1.25 1.00
2277 A1154 2.98fr Banjo 1.50 1.50
2278 A1154 3.08fr like #2235 6.00 4.00
2279 A1154 3.14fr like #2236 2.00 1.50
2280 A1154 3.19fr like #2169 7.00 4.00
2281 A1154 5.28fr Xylophone 3.00 1.50
2282 A1154 5.30fr like #2170 3.00 1.50
2283 A1154 5.32fr like #2172 3.00 1.50
Nos. 2273-2283 (11) 91.00 44.75

Perf. 12

2273a	A1154	1.60fr	Guitar	*7.50*	*4.50*
2274a	A1154	1.98fr	like #2233	*150.00*	*140.00*
2275a	A1154	2.08fr	Saxophone	*40.00*	*30.00*
2276a	A1154	2.46fr	like #2234	*12.00*	*7.50*
2278a	A1154	3.08fr	like #2235	*12.00*	*7.50*
2279a	A1154	3.14fr	like #2236	60.00	*50.00*
2280a	A1154	3.19fr	like #2169	*8.00*	*5.00*
2281a	A1154	5.28fr	Xylophone	*30.00*	*20.00*
2282a	A1154	5.30fr	like #2170	*75.00*	*60.00*
2283a	A1154	5.32fr	like #2172	*25.00*	*20.00*
	Nos. 2273a-2283a (10)			*419.50*	*344.50*

Nos. 2273-2283 are known only precanceled. See 2nd note after No. 132. See Nos. 2303-2306.

1992 Summer Olympics, Barcelona A1215

1992, Apr. 3 **Photo.** ***Perf. 13***
2284 A1215 2.50fr multicolored 1.10 .25

See Greece No. 1730.

Marguerite d'Angouleme (1492-1549) A1216

1992, Apr. 11 **Litho.** ***Perf. 13***
2285 A1216 3.40fr multicolored 1.60 .75

Founding of Ajaccio, 500th Anniv. A1217

Virgin and Child Beneath a Garland by Botticelli.

1992, Apr. 30 **Photo.** ***Perf. 13***
2286 A1217 4fr multicolored 1.75 .60

Europa — A1218

Discovery of America, 500th Anniv.: 2.50fr, Map, navigation instruments. 3.40fr, Sailing ship, map.

1992, May 9 Engr. *Perf. 13x12½*

2287 A1218 2.50fr multicolored 1.25 .30
2288 A1218 3.40fr multicolored 1.75 .60

Intl. Bread and Cereal Congress — A1219

1992, May 30 Litho. *Perf. 13*

2289 A1219 3.40fr multicolored 1.60 .70

Tourism Series

Ourcq Canal A1220

1992, May 30 Engr. *Perf. 13*

2290 A1220 4fr black, blue & grn 1.75 .40

Mt. Aiguille — A1221

1992, June 27 Engr. *Perf. 13*

2291 A1221 3.40fr multicolored 1.60 .70

First ascension of Mt. Aiguille, 500th anniv.

Lorient A1222

1992, July 4 Engr. *Perf. 13*

2292 A1222 4fr multicolored 1.25 .25

Biron Castle — A1223

1992, July 4 *Perf. 12½x13*

2293 A1223 2.50fr multicolored 1.75 .40

Natl. Philatelic Societies Congress, Niort A1224

1992, June 6 Photo. *Perf. 13*

2294 A1224 2.50fr multicolored 1.10 .25

Natl. Art Festival.

1992 Olympic Games, Albertville and Barcelona A1225

1992, June 19 *Perf. 12½x13½*

2295 A1225 2.50fr multicolored 1.10 .30

Tautavel Man A1226

1992, June 20 Photo. *Perf. 13*

2296 A1226 3.40fr multicolored 1.60 .60

Portrait of Jacques Callot (1592-1635), by Claude Deruet — A1227

1992, June 27 Engr. *Perf. 12x13*

2297 A1227 5fr buff & brown 2.25 1.00

Flowers — A1228

2fr, Pancratium maritimum. 3fr, Drosera rotundifolia. 4fr, Orchis palustris. 5fr, Nuphar luteum.

1992, Sept. 12 Engr. *Perf. 12½*

2298 A1228 2fr multicolored .90 .30
2299 A1228 3fr multicolored 1.25 .30
2300 A1228 4fr multicolored 1.75 .60
2301 A1228 5fr multicolored 2.25 .60
Nos. 2298-2301 (4) 6.15 1.80

First French Republic, Bicent. A1229

1992, Sept. 26 *Perf. 13*

2302 A1229 2.50fr multicolored 1.10 .25

Musical Instruments Type of 1989

1992, Oct. Litho. *Perf. 13*

2303 A1154 1.73fr like #2273 .80 .25
2304 A1154 2.25fr like #2275 1.00 .50
2305 A1154 3.51fr like #2277 2.00 1.00
2306 A1154 5.40fr like #2281 2.75 1.75
Nos. 2303-2306 (4) 6.55 3.50

Nos. 2303-2306 are known only precanceled. See second note after No. 132.

Proclamation of First French Republic, Bicent. — A1230

Paintings or drawings by contemporary artists: No. 2307, Tree of Freedom, by Pierre Alechinsky. No. 2308, Portrait of a Young Man, by Martial Raysse. No. 2309, Marianne with Body and Head of Rooster, by Gerard Garouste. No. 2310, "Republique Francaise," by Jean-Charles Blais.

1992, Sept. 26 Engr. *Perf. 13*

2307 A1230 2.50fr red 1.10 .25
2308 A1230 2.50fr red 1.10 .25
2309 A1230 2.50fr red 1.10 .25
2310 A1230 2.50fr red 1.10 .25
Nos. 2307-2310 (4) 4.40 1.00

Single European Market A1231

1992, Nov. 6 Photo. *Perf. 12½x13½*

2311 A1231 2.50fr multicolored 1.10 .30

First Mail Flight from Nancy to Luneville, 80th Anniv. A1232

1992, Nov. 12 *Perf. 13*

2312 A1232 2.50fr multicolored 1.10 .40

Marcel Paul (1900-1982), Minister of Industrial Production — A1233

1992, Nov. 13 Engr.

2313 A1233 4.20fr claret & blue 1.90 .50

Contemporary Art — A1234

No. 2314, Le Rendezvous d'Ephese, by Paul Delvaux, Belgium. No. 2315, Abstract painting, by Alberto Burri, Italy. No. 2316, Abstract painting, by Antoni Tapies, Spain. No. 2317, Portrait of John Edwards, by Francis Bacon, Great Britain.

1992 Photo. *Perf. 13x12½*

2314 A1234 5fr multicolored 2.25 1.00
2315 A1234 5fr multicolored 2.25 1.00
2316 A1234 5fr multicolored 2.25 1.00
2317 A1234 5fr multicolored 2.25 1.00
Nos. 2314-2317 (4) 9.00 4.00

Issued: No. 2314, 11/20; Nos. 2315-2317, 11/21.

See Nos. 2379-2390.

Gypsy Culture — A1235

1992, Dec. 5 Photo. *Perf. 13*

2318 A1235 2.50fr multicolored 1.10 .25

Yacht "La Poste," Entrant in Whitbread Trans-Global Race — A1236

1993, Feb. 6 Engr. *Perf. 12*

2319 A1236 2.50fr multicolored 1.10 .30

See No. 2375.

Water Birds — A1237

1993, Feb. 6 *Perf. 12½x12*

2320 A1237 2fr Harle piette .90 .30
2321 A1237 3fr Fuligule nyroca 1.25 .30
2322 A1237 4fr Tadorne de belon 1.75 .60
2323 A1237 5fr Harle huppe 2.25 .70
Nos. 2320-2323 (4) 6.15 1.90

Memorial to Indochina War, Frejus A1238

Litho. & Engr.

1993, Feb. 16 *Perf. 13x13½*

2324 A1238 4fr multicolored 1.75 .60

Stamp Day — A1239

1993, Mar. 6 Photo. *Perf. 13*

2325 A1239 2.50fr red & multi 1.50 .80
2326 A1239 2.50fr +60c red & multi 1.25 1.00
a. Bklt. pane of 4 #2325, 3 #2326 + label 10.00

Mediterranean Youth Games, Agde — A1240

1993, Mar. 13 Photo. *Perf. 13*
2327 A1240 2.50fr multicolored 1.10 .25

Human Rights, Intl. Mixed Masonic Order, Cent. — A1241

1993, Apr. 3 Engr. *Perf. 13*
2328 A1241 3.40fr blue & black 1.60 .50

Contemporary Art — A1242

Europa: 2.50fr, Painting, Rouge Rythme Bleu, by Olivier Debre. 3.40fr, Sculpture, Le Griffu, by Germaine Richier, vert.

Perf. 13x12½, 12½x13
1993, Apr. 17 Litho.
2329 A1242 2.50fr multicolored 1.10 .30
2330 A1242 3.40fr multicolored 1.60 .80

Marianne Type of 1990

1993-96 Engr. *Perf. 13*
2333 A1161 2fr blue 1.00 .25
2334 A1161 2.40fr emerald 1.25 .25
2335 A1161 2.70fr emerald 1.40 .25
2336 A1161 3.50fr apple green 1.60 .30
2337 A1161 3.80fr blue 1.75 .50
2338 A1161 4.40fr blue 2.00 .40
2339 A1161 4.50fr mag 2.00 .40
2340 A1161 (2.50fr) red 1.75 .25
Complete booklet, 10 #2340 17.50
Nos. 2333-2340 (8) 12.75 2.60

Perf. 13 Horiz.
Coil Stamps
2341 A1161 2.40fr emerald 1.10 .60
2342 A1161 2.70fr emerald 1.60 .25
2343 A1161 (2.80fr) red 1.75 .25

Self-Adhesive
Die Cut
2344 A1161 70c brown 13.00 9.00

Serpentine Die Cut Vert.
2345 A1161 70c brown 13.00 9.00
2346 A1161 1fr orange 4.25 2.50
a. Booklet pane, 3 #2348, 1 #2346 9.00
Complete bklt., 2 #2346a 20.00

Die Cut
2347 A1161 (2.50fr) red 1.75 .25
a. Booklet pane of 10 (see footnote) 17.50
b. Bklt. pane of 4 + label 7.00
c. Booklet pane, #2344, 3 #2347 + label 30.00
d. Booklet pane of 10 (see footnote) 15.00

Serpentine Die Cut 6¾ Vert.
2348 A1161 (2.80fr) red 1.75 .25
a. Bklt. pane of 4 + label 7.00
b. Booklet pane of 10 (see footnote) 17.50
c. Booklet pane, #2345, 3 #2348 + label 19.00
d. Booklet pane of 10 (see footnote) 17.50
e. Booklet pane of 10 (see footnote) 17.50
f. Booklet pane of 10 (see footnote) —

Nos. 2340, 2347 pay postage for the first class letter rate and sold for 2.50fr when first released. They have no denomination or letter inscription. Nos. 2343 and 2348 had a face value of 2.80fr when released.

No. 2347a has all stamps adjoining and has selvage covering backing paper (booklet cover), No. 2347d is comprised of two strips of 5 stamps each with yellow backing paper showing.

No. 2348b has the same format as No. 2347a. No. 2348d has a format similar to No. 2347d except there is a narrow selvage strip between the left six stamps and the right four stamps. No. 2348e is like No. 2348f but lacks the selvage strip. No. 2348f has a format similar to No. 2347a except it has a wide selvage strip between the left four stamps and the right six stamps.

Backing paper of Nos. 2347b and 2347c may have cuts along fold and were sold in a booklet for 20fr.

Issued: #2340, 2347, 4/19/93; 70c, July; 2fr, 7/31/94; Nos. 2341-2343, 4/1/94; Nos. 2345, 2348, 2/14/94; 1fr, 2.70fr, 3.80fr, 4.50fr, 3/18/96.

Tourism Series

Chinon — A1243

1993, Apr. 24 Engr. *Perf. 13x12½*
2355 A1243 4.20fr dk grn, ol grn & brn 2.00 .80

Village of Minerve — A1244

1993, July 17 *Perf. 13*
2356 A1244 4.20fr red brown & yel grn 2.00 .50

Chaise-Dieu Abbey — A1245

Montbeliard — A1246

1993
2357 A1245 2.80fr multicolored 1.25 .30
2358 A1246 4.40fr multicolored 2.00 .60
Nos. 2355-2358 (4) 7.25 2.20

Issued: No. 2357, 9/4; No. 2358, 9/11.

Ninth European Conference on Protection of Human Rights — A1247

1993, May 8 Engr. *Perf. 12½x13*
2359 A1247 2.50fr multicolored 1.10 .30

Django Reinhardt (1910-1953), Musician — A1248

1993, May 14 Litho. *Perf. 13*
2360 A1248 4.20fr multicolored 1.90 .50

Louise Weiss (1893-1983), Suffragist — A1249

1993, May 15 Engr. *Perf. 13x12½*
2361 A1249 2.50fr blk, buff & red 1.10 .30

Philatelic Society Congress, Lille A1250

1993, May 29 Engr. *Perf. 13x12½*
2362 A1250 2.50fr bl, dk bl & lil 1.10 .40

Natural History Museum, Bicent. A1251

Litho. & Engr.
1993, June 5 *Perf. 13*
2363 A1251 2.50fr multicolored 1.10 .30

Martyrs and Heroes of the Resistance — A1252

1993, June 18 Photo. *Perf. 13*
2364 2.50fr red, black & gray 1.10 .60
2365 4.20fr red, black & gray 1.90 1.00
a. A1252 Pair, #2364-2365 3.00 2.50

A1254

1993, July 10 Engr. *Perf. 13x12½*
2366 A1254 2.50fr multicolored 1.10 .30

Claude Chappe's Semaphore Telegraph, bicent.

A1255

1993, July 10 Engr. *Perf. 12½x13*
2367 A1255 3.40fr bl, grn & red 1.50 .70

Train to Lake Artouste, Laruns, highest train ride in Europe.

Musical Instruments Type of 1989

1993, July 1 Litho. *Perf. 13*
2368 A1154 1.82fr like #2171 .80 .25
2369 A1154 2.34fr like #2235 1.10 .60
2370 A1154 3.86fr like #2236 1.75 .90
2371 A1154 5.93fr like #2281 2.75 1.75
Nos. 2368-2371 (4) 6.40 3.50

Nos. 2368-2371 are known only precanceled. See note after No. 132.

Liberation of Corsica, 50th Anniv. — A1256

1993, Sept. 9 Engr. *Perf. 13*
2372 A1256 2.80fr lake, bl & blk 1.25 .30

Saint Thomas, by Georges de la Tour (1593-1652) — A1257

1993, Sept. 9 Photo. *Perf. 12½x13*
2373 A1257 5fr multicolored 2.25 1.00

Service as Military Hospital of Val de Grace Monastery, Bicent. — A1258

1993, Sept. 25 Engr. *Perf. 13*
2374 A1258 3.70fr multicolored 1.60 .30

Whitbread Trans-Global Race Type

1993, Sept. 27 Engr. *Perf. 12*
2375 A1236 2.80fr multicolored 1.25 .40

The Muses, by Maurice Denis (1870-1943) — A1259

1993, Oct. 2 Photo. *Perf. 12½x13*
2376 A1259 5fr multicolored 2.25 1.00

The Clowns, by Albert Gleizes (1881-1953) A1260

1993, Oct. 2 Photo. *Perf. 13½x12½*
2377 A1260 2.80fr multicolored 1.25 .30

Natl. Circus Center, Chalons-sur-Marne.

Clock Tower Bellringer Statues of Lambesc — A1261

1993, Oct. 9 Engr. *Perf. 13x12½*
2378 A1261 4.40fr multicolored 2.00 .60

European Contemporary Art Type

Designs: No. 2379, Abstract, by Takis. No. 2380, Abstract, by Maria Helena Vieira da Silva. No. 2381, Abstract Squares, by Sean Scully. No. 2382, Abstract, by Georg Baselitz, Germany.

1993-94 Photo. *Perf. 13x12½*
2379 A1234 5fr blk & ver 2.25 1.00
2380 A1234 5fr multicolored 2.25 1.00
2381 A1234 6.70fr multicolored 3.00 1.00

Perf. 13

2382 A1234 6.70fr multicolored 3.00 1.00
Nos. 2379-2382 (4) 10.50 4.00

Issued: No. 2379, 10/9/93; No. 2380, 12/11/93; No. 2381, 1/29/94; No. 2382, 11/19/94.

Greetings A1266

Greeting, artist: No. 2383, Happy Birthday, Claire Wendling. No. 2384, Happy Birthday, Bernard Olivie. No. 2385, Happy Anniversary, Stephane Colman. No. 2386, Happy Anniversary, Guillaune Sorel. No. 2387, With Love, Jean-Michel Thiriet. No. 2388, Please Write, Etienne Davodeau. No. 2389, Congratulations, Johan de Moor. No. 2390, Good luck, "Mezzo." No. 2391, Best Wishes, Nicolas de Crecy. No. 2392, Best Wishes, Florence Magnin. No. 2393, Merry Christmas, Thierry Robin. No. 2394, Merry Christmas, Patrick Prugne.

1993, Oct. 21 Photo. *Perf. 13½x13*
Booklet Stamps

2383 A1266 2.80fr multicolored 1.25 .30
2384 A1266 2.80fr multicolored 1.25 .30
2385 A1266 2.80fr multicolored 1.25 .30
2386 A1266 2.80fr multicolored 1.25 .30
2387 A1266 2.80fr multicolored 1.25 .30
2388 A1266 2.80fr multicolored 1.25 .30
2389 A1266 2.80fr multicolored 1.25 .30
2390 A1266 2.80fr multicolored 1.25 .30
2391 A1266 2.80fr multicolored 1.25 .30
2392 A1266 2.80fr multicolored 1.25 .30
2393 A1266 2.80fr multicolored 1.25 .30
2394 A1266 2.80fr multicolored 1.25 .30
a. Bklt. pane, #2383-2394 15.00

Perf. 12½

2383a A1266 2.80fr 1.25 .30
2384a A1266 2.80fr 1.25 .30
2385a A1266 2.80fr 1.25 .30
2386a A1266 2.80fr 1.25 .30
2387a A1266 2.80fr 1.25 .30
2388a A1266 2.80fr 1.25 .30
2389a A1266 2.80fr 1.25 .30
2390a A1266 2.80fr 1.25 .30
2391a A1266 2.80fr 1.25 .30
2392a A1266 2.80fr 1.25 .30
2393a A1266 2.80fr 1.25 .30
2394b A1266 2.80fr 1.25 .30
c. Booklet pane of 12, #2383a-2393a, 2394b 16.50

Souvenir Sheet

European Stamp Exhibition, Salon du Timbre — A1267

a, Rhododendrons. b, Flowers in park, Paris.

1993, Nov. 10 *Perf. 13*
2395 A1267 2.40fr #a.-b.+ 2 labels 12.00 10.00

Sold for 15fr.

Louvre Museum, Bicent. A1268

1993, Nov. 20
2396 A1268 2.80fr Louvre, 1793 1.25 1.00
2397 A1268 4.40fr Louvre, 1993 2.00 1.25
a. Pair, #2396-2397 3.50 2.50

Glassware, 1901 — A1269

Cast Iron, c. 1900 — A1270

Furniture, c. 1902 — A1271

Stoneware, c. 1898 — A1272

Decorative arts by: No. 2398, Emile Galle (1846-1904). No. 2399, Hector Guimard (1867-1942). No. 2400, Louis Majorelle (1859-1926). No. 2401, Pierre-Adrien Dalpayrat (1844-1910).

Perf. 13½x12½
1994. Jan. 22 Photo.
2398 A1269 2.80fr multicolored 1.25 .35
2399 A1270 2.80fr multicolored 1.25 .35
2400 A1271 4.40fr multicolored 2.00 .65
2401 A1272 4.40fr multicolored 2.00 .65
Nos. 2398-2401 (4) 6.50 2.00

Stained Glass Window, St. Julian's Cathedral, Le Mans A1273

1994, Feb. 12 Engr. *Perf. 12½x13*
2402 A1273 6.70fr multicolored 3.00 1.00

City of Bastia — A1274

1994, Feb. 19 *Perf. 13x12½*
2403 A1274 4.40fr blue & brown 2.00 .60

Tourism Series

Argentat A1275

1994, June 18 Engr. *Perf. 12x12½*
2404 A1275 4.40fr red brn & rose car 2.00 .60

European Parliamentary Elections — A1276

1994, Feb. 26 Litho. *Perf. 13*
2405 A1276 2.80fr multicolored 1.25 .25

Laurent Mourguet (1769-1844), Creator of Puppet, Guignol — A1277

1994, Mar. 4 Photo. *Perf. 13*
2406 A1277 2.80fr multicolored 1.25 .30

French Polytechnic Institute, Bicent. A1277a

1994, Mar. 11
2407 A1277a 2.80fr multicolored 1.25 .30

Stamp Day A1278

1994, Mar. 12 Engr. *Perf. 13*
2408 A1278 2.80fr blue & red *2.00 1.60*
2409 A1278 2.80fr +60c blue & red *1.40 1.25*
a. Booklet pane of 4 #2408, 3 #2409 + 1 label *25.00*

No. 2408 issued only in booklets.

Swedish Ballet Costume — A1279

Banquet for Gustavus III at the Trianon, 1784, by Lafrensen — A1280

French-Swedish cultural relations: No. 2411, Tuxedo costume for Swedish ballet. No. 2412, Viking ships. No. 2413, Viking ship. No. 2415, Swedish, French flags.

1994, Mar. 18 Engr. *Perf. 13*
2410 A1279 2.80fr multicolored 1.25 1.00
2411 A1279 2.80fr multicolored 1.25 1.00
2412 A1279 2.80fr multicolored 1.25 1.00
2413 A1279 2.80fr multicolored 1.25 1.00

2414 A1280 3.70fr multicolored 3.00 2.00
2415 A1280 3.70fr multicolored 3.00 2.00
a. Booklet pane of #2410-2415 16.00

See Sweden Nos. 2065-2070.

Pres. Georges Pompidou (1911-1974) A1281

1994, Apr. 9 Engr. *Perf. 13*
2416 A1281 2.80fr olive brown 1.25 .30

Resistance of the Maquis, 50th Anniv. A1282

1994, Apr. 9
2417 A1282 2.80fr multicolored 1.25 .30

Philexjeunes '94, Grenoble — A1283

1994, Apr. 22 Photo.
2418 A1283 2.80fr multicolored 1.25 .30

Europa A1284

Discoveries: 2.80fr, AIDS virus, by scientists of Pasteur Institute. 3.70fr, Formula for wave properties of matter, developed by Louis de Brogile.

1994, Apr. 30 Photo. & Engr.
2419 A1284 2.80fr multicolored 1.25 .30
a. With label 1.25 .75
2420 A1284 3.70fr multicolored 1.75 .85

No. 2419a issued Dec. 1, 1994.

Opening of Channel Tunnel — A1285

Designs: Nos. 2421, 2423, British lion, French rooster, meeting over Channel. Nos. 2422, 2424, Joined hands above speeding train.

1994, May 3 Photo. *Perf. 13*
2421 A1285 2.80fr dk blue & multi 1.25 .30
2422 A1285 2.80fr dk blue & multi 1.25 .30
a. Pair, #2421-2422 2.75 1.50
2423 A1285 4.30fr lt blue & multi 2.00 .90
2424 A1285 4.30fr multicolored 2.00 .90
a. Pair, #2423-2424 4.50 2.25
Nos. 2421-2424 (4) 6.50 2.40

See Great Britain Nos. 1558-1561.

Asian Development Bank, Board of Governors Meeting, Nice — A1286

1994, May 3 Photo. *Perf. 13*
2425 A1286 2.80fr multicolored 1.25 .30

Federation of French Philatelic Societies, 67th Congress, Martigues A1287

1994, May 20 Engr. *Perf. 12x12½*
2426 A1287 2.80fr multicolored 1.25 .30

Court of Cassation A1288

Litho. & Engr.
1994, June 3 *Perf. 13*
2427 A1288 2.80fr multicolored 1.25 .30

D-Day, 50th Anniv. A1289

No. 2429, Tank, crowd waving Allied flags.

1994, June 4 Engr.
2428 A1289 4.30fr multicolored 2.00 .50
2429 A1289 4.30fr multicolored 2.00 .50

Liberation of Paris, 50th anniv. (No. 2429).

Mount St. Victoire, by Paul Cezanne (1839-1906) — A1290

1994, June 18 Photo. *Perf. 13*
2430 A1290 2.80fr multicolored 1.25 .30

Intl. Olympic Committee, Cent. A1291

1994, June 23 Litho. *Perf. 13*
2431 A1291 2.80fr multicolored 1.25 .25

Saulx River Bridge, Rupt aux Nonains A1292

1994, July 2 Engr.
2432 A1292 2.80fr blackish blue 1.25 .25

Organ, Poitiers Cathedral — A1293

1994, July 2 *Perf. 13x12½*
2433 A1293 4.40fr multicolored 2.00 .55

Allied Landings in Provence, 50th Anniv. A1294

1994, Aug. 13 Engr. *Perf. 13*
2434 A1294 2.80fr multicolored 1.25 .30

Moses and the Daughters of Jethro, by Nicolas Poussin (1594-1665) — A1295

1994, Sept. 10
2435 A1295 4.40fr yel brn & blk 1.90 .90

Natl. Conservatory of Arts and Crafts, Bicent. — A1296

1994, Sept. 24 *Perf. 13x12½*
2436 A1296 2.80fr Foucault's pendulum 1.25 .25

The Great Cascade, St. Cloud Park — A1297

1994, Sept. 24 *Perf. 12½x13*
2437 A1297 3.70fr multicolored 1.75 .60

Leaves — A1298

1994 Litho. *Perf. 13*
2438 A1298 1.91fr Oak .85 .40
2439 A1298 2.46fr Sycamore 1.10 .70
2440 A1298 4.24fr Chestnut 2.00 1.00
2441 A1298 6.51fr Holly 3.00 1.75
Nos. 2438-2441 (4) 6.95 3.85

Nos. 2438-2441 are known only precanceled. See second note after No. 132.
See Nos. 2517-2520.

Ecole Normale Superieure (Teachers' School), Bicent. — A1299

1994, Oct. 8 Engr. *Perf. 13*
2442 A1299 2.80fr red & dk bl 1.25 .25

Georges Simenon (1903-89), Writer A1300

Litho. & Engr.
1994, Oct. 15 *Perf. 13*
2443 A1300 2.80fr multicolored 1.25 .25

See Belgium No. 1567, Switzerland No. 948.

Souvenir Sheet

European Stamp Exhibition — A1301

a, Flowers in park, Paris. b, Dahlias, vert.

1994, Oct. 15 Photo. *Perf. 13*
2444 A1301 2.80fr Sheet of 2, #a.-b. 10.00 9.00

No. 2444 sold for 16fr.

Natl. Drug Addiction Prevention Day — A1302

1994, Oct. 15
2445 A1302 2.80fr multicolored 1.25 .25

Grand Lodge of France, Cent. A1303

1994, Nov. 5 Engr.
2446 A1303 2.80fr multicolored 1.25 .25

Alain Colas (1943-78), Sailor A1304

1994, Nov. 19
2447 A1304 3.70fr green & black 1.60 .60

French Natl. Press Federation, 50th Anniv. A1305

1994, Dec. 9 Photo. *Perf. 13*
2448 A1305 2.80fr multicolored 1.25 .30

Champs Elysees — A1306

1994, Dec. 31
2449 A1306 4.40fr multicolored 2.00 .75

No. 2449 printed with se-tenant label.

Souvenir Sheet

Motion Pictures, Cent. — A1307

Faces on screen and: a, Projector at right. b, Projector facing away from screen. c, Projector facing screen. d, Reels of film.

1995, Jan. 14 Photo. *Perf. 13*
2450 A1307 Sheet of 4 5.00 5.00
a.-d. 2.80fr any single 1.00 1.00

Normandy Bridge — A1308

1995, Jan. 20 Engr. *Perf. 13*
2451 A1308 4.40fr multicolored 2.00 .75

European Notaries Public — A1309

1995, Jan. 21 *Perf. 13x12*
2452 A1309 2.80fr multicolored 1.25 .30

Louis Pasteur (1822-95) — A1310

1995, Feb. 18 Photo. *Perf. 13*
2453 A1310 3.70fr multicolored 1.60 1.00

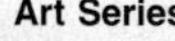

Art Series

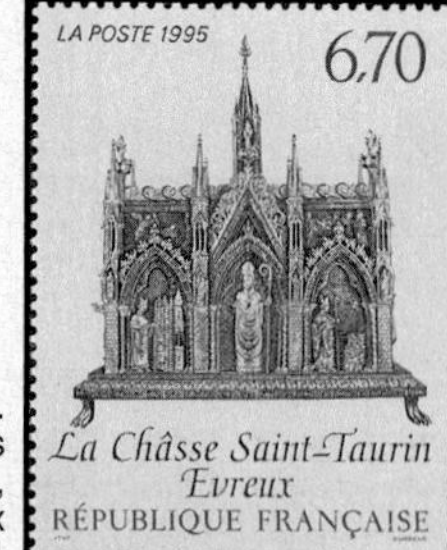

St. Taurin's Reliquary, Evreaux A1311

Study for the Dream of Happiness, by Pierre Prud'hon (1758-1823) — A1312

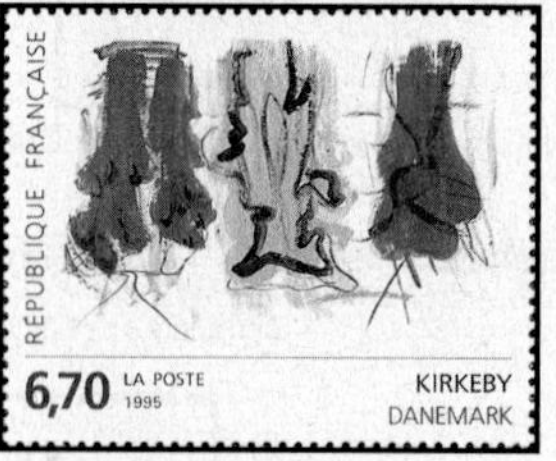

Abstract, by Zao Wou-ki — A1313

Abstract, by Per Kirkeby, Denmark — A1314

1995 Photo. & Engr. *Perf. 12x13*
2454 A1311 6.70fr multicolored 3.00 1.10

Engr.
Perf. 13x12
2455 A1312 6.70fr slate & blue 3.00 1.10

Litho.
Perf. 14
2456 A1313 6.70fr multicolored 3.00 1.10

Photo.
Perf. 13
2457 A1314 6.70fr multicolored 3.00 1.10
Nos. 2454-2457 (4) 12.00 4.40

Issued: No. 2454, 2/25; No. 2455, 5/12; No. 2456, 6/10; No. 2457, 9/23.

Tourism Series

Stenay Malt Works A1315

Remiremont, Vosges — A1316

Nyons Bridge, Drome A1317

Barbizon, Home of Landscape Artists A1318

1995 Engr. *Perf. 13x12½*
2458 A1315 2.80fr ol & dk grn 1.25 .30
2459 A1316 2.80fr brn, grn & bl 1.25 .30

Perf. 12½x13
2460 A1317 4.40fr multicolored 2.00 .75

Photo.
Perf. 13½
2461 A1318 4.40fr multicolored 2.00 .75
Nos. 2458-2461 (4) 6.50 2.10

Issued: No. 2458, 2/25; No. 2459, 5/13; No. 2460, 5/20; No. 2461, 9/30.

A1319

John J. Audubon (1785-1851) A1320

Designs: No. 2462, Snowy egret. No. 2463, Band-tailed pigeon. 4.30fr, Common tern. 4.40fr, Brown-colored rough-legged buzzard.

1995, Feb. 25 Photo. *Perf. 12½x12*
2462 A1319 2.80fr multicolored 1.25 .40
2463 A1320 2.80fr multicolored 1.25 .40
2464 A1319 4.30fr multicolored 2.00 .75
2465 A1320 4.40fr multicolored 2.00 .75
a. Souvenir sheet of 4, #2462-2465, perf. 13 7.00 7.00
Nos. 2462-2465 (4) 6.50 2.30

Stamp Day A1321

1995, Mar. 4 Engr. *Perf. 13*
2466 A1321 2.80fr multicolored 2.00 1.00
2467 A1321 2.80fr +60c multi 1.50 1.25
a. Booklet pane, 4 #2466, 3 #2467+label 15.00
Complete booklet, #2467 16.00

No. 2466 issued only in booklets.

Work Councils, 50th Anniv. — A1322

1995, Mar. 7 Engr. *Perf. 13*
2468 A1322 2.80fr dk bl, brn & sky bl 1.25 .30

Advanced Institute of Electricity, Cent. A1323

1995, Mar. 11 Photo.
2469 A1323 3.70fr multicolored 1.75 .60

Institute of Oriental Languages, Bicent. A1324

1995, Mar. 25 Photo. *Perf. 13*
2470 A1324 2.80fr multicolored 1.25 .30

Jean Giono (1895-1970), Writer — A1325

1995, Mar. 25 Engr.
2471 A1325 3.70fr multicolored 1.75 .60

Iron and Steel Industry in Lorraine — A1326

1995, Apr. 1 *Perf. 13x12*
2472 A1326 2.80fr multicolored 1.25 .30

End of World War II, 50th Anniv. A1327

Europa: 2.80fr, Barbed wire, laurel wreath. 3.70fr, Broken sword, emblem of Europe Union.

1995, Apr. 29 Photo. *Perf*
2473 A1327 2.80fr multicolored 1.25
2474 A1327 3.70fr multicolored 1.75 1

Forestry Profession, Ardennes — A1328

1995, May 2 Engr. *Perf. 12½x13*
2475 A1328 4.40fr multicolored 2.00 .60

End of World War II, 50th Anniv. A1329

1995, May 8 Photo. *Perf. 13*
2476 A1329 2.80fr multicolored 1.25 .30

Natl. Assembly — A1330

1995, May 13 Photo. *Perf. 13x12½*
2477 A1330 2.80fr multicolored 1.25 .60

French's People's Relief Assoc., 50th Anniv. A1331

1995, May 20 Engr. *Perf. 12½x13*
2478 A1331 2.80fr multicolored 1.25 .30

Scenes of France — A1332

No. 2479, Forest, Vosges. No. 2480, Massif, Brittany. No. 2481, Wetlands, cattle, Camargue. No. 2482, Volcanoes, Auvergne.

1995, May 27 *Perf. 13*
2479 A1332 2.40fr green 1.10 .25
2480 A1332 2.40fr green 1.10 .25
2481 A1332 2.80fr red 1.25 .30
2482 A1332 2.80fr red 1.25 .30
Nos. 2479-2482 (4) 4.70 1.10

Ariane Rocket on Launch Pad, French Guiana — A1333

1995, March 28 Engr. *Perf. 12½x13*
2483 A1333 2.80fr bl, grn & red 1.25 .30

Compare with No. 2254.

A1334

1995, June 2 Engr. *Perf. 13*
2484 A1334 2.80fr multicolored 1.25 .30

68th Congress of French Federation of Philatelic Organizations, Orleans.

Town of Correze — A1335

1995, June 3
2485 A1335 4.40fr multi 2.00 .60

A1336

Fables of Jean de la Fontaine (1621-95): No. 2486, The Grasshopper and The Ant. No. 2487, The Frog Who Could Make Himself Larger than an Ox. No. 2488, The Wolf and the Lamb. No. 2489, The Crow and the Fox. No. 2490, The Cat, the Weasel, and the Small Rabbit. No. 2491, The Tortoise and the Hare.

1995, June 24 Photo. *Perf. 13*
2486 A1336 2.80fr multicolored 1.40 .50
2487 A1336 2.80fr multicolored 1.40 .50
2488 A1336 2.80fr multicolored 1.40 .50
2489 A1336 2.80fr multicolored 1.40 .50
2490 A1336 2.80fr multicolored 1.40 .50
2491 A1336 2.80fr multicolored 1.40 .50
a. Strip, #2486-2491 + 2 labels 9.00 8.00

Velodrome d'Hiver Raid — A1337

1995, July 9 Photo. *Perf. 13*
2492 A1337 2.80fr multicolored 1.25 .30

André Maginot (1877-1932), Creator of Maginot Line — A1338

1995, Sept. 9 Engr. *Perf. 13*
2493 A1338 2.80fr multicolored 1.25 .30

Women's Grand Masonic Lodge of France, 50th Anniv. — A1339

1995, Sept. 16 *Perf. 13x12½*
2494 A1339 2.80fr multicolored 1.25 .30

Hospital Pharmacies, 500th Anniv. — A1340

1995, Sept. 23 *Perf. 12½x13*
2495 A1340 2.80fr multicolored 1.25 .30

Natl. School of Administration, 50th Anniv. — A1341

1995, Oct. 5 Photo. *Perf. 13*
2496 A1341 2.80fr multicolored 1.25 .30

The Cradle, by Berthe Morisot (1841-95) A1342

1995, Oct. 7 Litho. *Perf. 13½x14*
2497 A1342 6.70fr multicolored 3.00 1.00

The French Institute, Bicent. — A1343

1995, Oct. 14 Engr. *Perf. 12½x13*
2498 A1343 2.80fr blk, grn & red 1.25 .30

Automobile Club of France, Cent. A1344

1995, Nov. 4 Engr. *Perf. 13x12½*
2499 A1344 4.40fr blk, bl & red 2.00 .60

UN, 50th Anniv. A1345

1995, Nov. 16 Photo. *Perf. 13*
2500 A1345 4.30fr multicolored 2.00 .60

Francis Jammes (1868-1938), Poet — A1346

1995, Dec. 2 Engr. *Perf. 13*
2501 A1346 3.70fr black & blue 1.60 .60

A1347

1995, Dec. 9 Litho. & Engr.
2502 A1347 2.80fr Evry Cathedral 1.25 .30

A1348

1995, Dec. 12 Photo. *Perf. 13*
2503 A1348 2.80fr multicolored 1.25 .30

1998 World Cup Soccer Championships, France.

Art Series

Abstract, by Lucien Wercollier — A1349

Design: No. 2505, The Netherlands (Horizon), abstract photograph, by Jan Dibbets.

1996 *Perf. 13x12½*
2504 A1349 6.70fr multicolored 3.00 1.00
2505 A1349 6.70fr multicolored 3.00 1.00

Issued: No. 2504, 1/20; No. 2505, 2/10.

Arawak Civilization, Saint Martin — A1350

Design: 2.80fr, Dog figurine, 550 B.C.

1996, Feb. 10 Engr. *Perf. 13*
2506 A1350 2.80fr multicolored 1.25 .30

The Augustus Bridge over the Nera River, by Camille Corot (1796-1875) — A1351

1996, Mar. 2 Litho. *Perf. 13*

2507 A1351 6.70fr multicolored 3.00 1.00

St. Patrick A1352

1996, Mar. 16 Photo. *Perf. 13*

2508 A1352 2.80fr multicolored 1.25 .30

The Sower, 1903 — A1353

1996, Mar. 16 Litho. & Engr.

2509 A1353 2.80fr multicolored 2.00 1.50

2510 A1353 2.80fr +60c multi 1.50 1.25

a. Booklet pane, 4 #2509, 3 #2510 + label 13.00

Complete booklet, #2510a 15.00

Stamp Day.

Jacques Rueff (1896-1978), Economist — A1354

1996, Mar. 23 Engr. *Perf. 13x12½*

2511 A1354 2.80fr multicolored 1.25 .30

René Descartes (1596-1650) A1355

1996, Mar. 30 Engr. *Perf. 12½x13*

2512 A1355 4.40fr red 2.00 .75

Gas & Electric Industries, 50th Anniv. A1356

1996, Apr. 6 Photo. *Perf. 13*

2513 A1356 3fr multicolored 1.25 .30

Natl. Parks A1357

1996, Apr. 20

2514 A1357 3fr Cévennes 1.25 .40

2515 A1357 4.40fr Vanoise 2.00 .75

2516 A1357 4.40fr Mercantour 2.00 .75

Nos. 2514-2516 (3) 5.25 1.90

See Nos. 2569-2572.

Leaf Type of 1994

1996, Mar. Litho. *Perf. 13*

2517 A1298 1.87fr Ash .85 .25

2518 A1298 2.18fr Beech 1.00 .50

2519 A1298 4.66fr Walnut 2.10 1.00

2520 A1298 7.11fr Elm 3.00 1.75

Nos. 2517-2520 (4) 6.95 3.50

Nos. 2517-2520 are known only precanceled. Values for precanceled stamps in first column are for those which have not been through the post and have original gum. Values in second column are for postally used, gumless stamps.

Madame Marie de Sévigné (1626-96), Writer — A1358

1996, Apr. 27 Photo. *Perf. 13*

2521 A1358 3fr multicolored 1.25 .40

Europa.

Natl. Institute of Agronomy Research, 50th Anniv. A1359

1996, May 4 Photo. *Perf. 13*

2522 A1359 3.80fr multicolored 1.75 .60

Joan of Arc's House, Domremy-La-Pucelle — A1360

1996, May 11

2523 A1360 4.50fr multicolored 2.10 .75

RAMOGE Agreement Between France, Italy, Monaco, 20th Anniv. A1361

1996, May 14 Photo. & Engr.

2524 A1361 3fr multicolored 1.25 .30

See Monaco No. 1998, Italy No. 2077.

69th Congress of Federation of Philatelic Assoc., Clermont-Ferrand — A1362

1996, May 24 Engr. *Perf. 13*

2525 A1362 3fr brn, red & grn 1.25 .30

Tourism Series

Bitche, Moselle A1363

Iles Sanguinaires, Ajaccio, Southern Corsica — A1364

Thoronet Abbey, Var A1365

Chambéry Cathedral, Savoie A1366

1996 Engr. *Perf. 12½x13*

2526 A1363 3fr multicolored 1.25 .30

2527 A1364 3fr multicolored 1.25 .30

Perf. 13x12½

2528 A1365 3.80fr brn & claret 1.75 .60

Photo.

Perf. 13

2529 A1366 4.50fr multicolored 2.00 .75

Issued: No. 2526, 5/25; No. 2527, 6/1; 3.80fr, 7/6; 4.50fr, 6/8.

1998 World Cup Soccer Championships, France — A1367

Various stylized soccer plays, name of host city in France.

1996, June 1 Photo. *Perf. 13*

2530 A1367 3fr Lens 1.25 .30

2531 A1367 3fr Toulouse 1.25 .30

2532 A1367 3fr Saint-Etienne 1.25 .30

2533 A1367 3fr Montpellier 1.25 .30

Nos. 2530-2533 (4) 5.00 1.20

See Nos. 2584-2587, 2623-2624, sheet of 10, No. 2624a.

Art Series

Gallo-Roman Bronze Statue of Horse, Neuvy-en-Sullias, Loiret — A1368

Imprints of Cello Fragments, by Arman — A1369

1996 Engr. *Perf. 13*

2534 A1368 6.70fr multicolored 3.00 1.00

Photo.

2535 A1369 6.70fr multicolored 3.00 1.00

Issued: No. 2534, 6/8; No. 2535, 9/21.

Modern Olympic Games, Cent. — A1371

1996, June 15 Photo. *Perf. 13*

2537 A1371 3fr multicolored 1.25 .30

A1372

1996, June 15 Engr. *Perf. 12½x13*

2538 A1372 4.40fr deep purple 2.00 .70

Jacques Marette (1922-84), Member of Parliament.

A1373

1996, June 29 Photo. *Perf. 13*

2539 A1373 3fr multicolored 1.25 .30

Train between Ajaccio and Vizzavona, cent.

A1374

1996, Sept. 6 Engr. *Perf. 13x12½*
2540 A1374 3fr dark blue & yel 1.25 .30

Notre Dame de Fourvière Basilica, Lyon, cent.

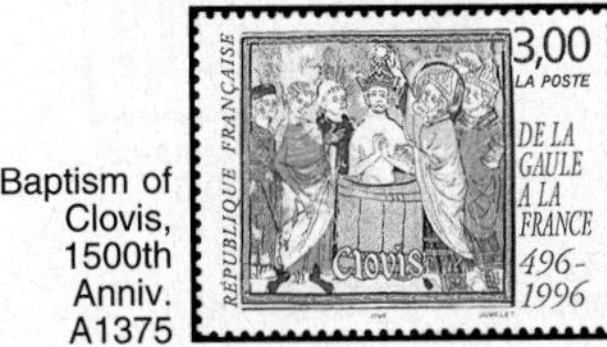
Baptism of Clovis, 1500th Anniv. A1375

1996, Sept. 14 *Perf. 13*
2541 A1375 3fr multicolored 1.25 .30

Henri IV High School, Bicent. — A1376

1996, Oct. 12 Engr. *Perf. 12½x13*
2542 A1376 4.50fr brown & blue 2.00 .80

UNICEF, 50th Anniv. A1377

1996, Oct. 19 Photo. *Perf. 13*
2543 A1377 4.50fr multicolored 2.00 .80

Economic and Social Council, 50th Anniv. — A1378

1996, Oct. 26 Engr. *Perf. 13*
2544 A1378 3fr red, black & blue 1.25 .30

UNESCO, 50th Anniv. A1379

1996, Nov. 2 Litho. *Perf. 13*
2545 A1379 3.80fr multicolored 1.75 .60

Autumn Stamp Show, 50th Anniv. — A1380

1996, Nov. 7 Photo. *Perf. 13*
2546 A1380 3fr multicolored 1.25 .30

A1381

1996, Nov. 16
2547 A1381 3fr multicolored 1.25 .30

Creation of French Overseas Departments, 50th anniv.

André Malraux (1901-76), Writer A1382

1996, Nov. 23 Engr. *Perf. 13*
2548 A1382 3fr deep green black 1.25 .30

French School in Athens, 150th Anniv. A1383

1996, Nov. 23 Photo.
2549 A1383 3fr multicolored 1.25 .30

Cannes Film Festival, 50th Anniv. A1384

1996, Nov. 30
2550 A1384 3fr multicolored 1.25 .30

New National Library of France A1385

1996, Dec. 14
2551 A1385 3fr multicolored 1.25 .30

Francois Mitterrand (1916-96) — A1386

1997, Jan. 4
2552 A1386 3fr multicolored 1.25 .30

Participatory Innovation A1387

1997, Jan. 24 Photo. *Perf. 13*
2553 A1387 3fr multicolored 1.25 .30

A1388

1997, Jan. 31 Engr. *Perf. 12½x13*
2554 A1388 3fr multicolored 1.25 .30

Georges Pompidou Natl. Center of Art and Culture, 20th Anniv.

Happy Holiday A1389

1997, Feb. 8 Photo. *Perf. 13*
2555 A1389 3fr shown 1.25 .30
2556 A1389 3fr Happy birthday 1.25 .30

A1390

Photo. & Engr.

1997, Feb. 14 *Perf. 12½x13*
2557 A1390 3fr multicolored 1.25 .30

Natl. School of Bridges and Highways, 250th Anniv.

Saint-Laurent-du-Maroni, French Guiana — A1391

Photo. & Engr.

1997, Feb. 22 *Perf. 12½x13*
2558 A1391 3fr multicolored 1.25 .30

Art Series

Church Fresco, Tavant A1392

Painting by Bernard Moninot — A1393

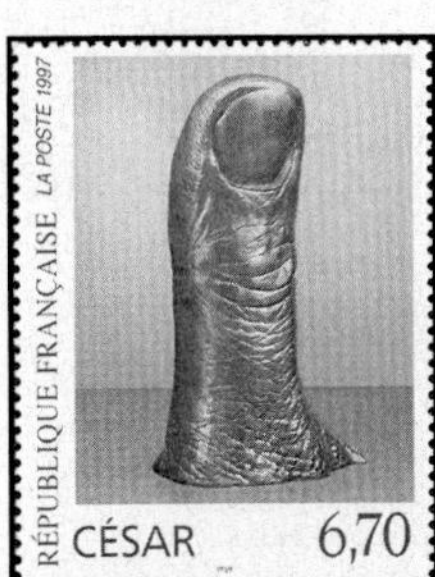
The Thumb, Polished Bronze, by César A1394

Grapes and Pomegranates, by Jean Baptiste Chardin — A1395

1997 Engr. *Perf. 13*
2559 A1392 6.70fr multicolored 3.00 1.00

Photo.

2560 A1393 6.70fr multicolored 3.00 1.00
2561 A1394 6.70fr multicolored 3.00 1.00
2562 A1395 6.70fr multicolored 3.00 1.00
Nos. 2559-2562 (4) 12.00 4.00

Issued: No. 2559, 3/1; No. 2560, 3/29; No. 2561, 9/13; No. 2562, 9/27.

Tourism Series

Millau — A1396

Guimiliau Church Close — A1398

Fresco, Saint Eutrope des Salles-Lavauguyon — A1397

Sablé-Sur-Sarthe — A1399

1997 Engr. *Perf. 12½x13*
2563 A1396 3fr grn & dk bl grn 1.25 .30

Perf. 13

2564 A1397 4.50fr multicolored 2.10 .75
2565 A1398 3fr multicolored 1.25 .30

Perf. 12½x13

2566 A1399 3fr multicolored 1.25 .30
Nos. 2563-2566 (4) 5.85 1.65

Issued: No. 2563, 3/15; No. 2564, 6/14; No. 2565, 7/12; No. 2566, 9/20.

Vignette of Type A17 — A1400

Litho. & Engr.

1997, Mar. 15 ***Perf. 13½x13***

2567 A1400 3fr multicolored 2.50 1.50
2568 A1400 3fr +60c multi 1.50 1.25
a. Booklet pane, 4 #2567, 3 #2568 + label 15.00
Complete booklet, #2568a 16.00

Stamp Day.
No. 2567 issued only in booklets.

National Parks Type of 1996

No. 2569, Parc des Ecrins. No. 2570, Guadeloupe Park. No. 2571, Parc des Pyrénées. No. 2572, Port-Cros Park.

1997, Apr. 12 **Photo.** ***Perf. 13***

2569 A1357 3fr multi 1.25 .40
2570 A1357 3fr multi 1.25 .40
2571 A1357 4.50fr multi 2.00 .70
2572 A1357 4.50fr multi 2.00 .70
Nos. 2569-2572 (4) 6.50 2.20

Puss-in-Boots A1401

1997, Apr. 26 **Engr.** ***Perf. 13***

2573 A1401 3fr blue 1.25 .30

Europa.

Philexjeunes '97, Nantes — A1402

1997, May 2 **Litho.** ***Perf. 13***

2574 A1402 3fr multicolored 1.25 .30

Cartoon Journey of a Letter A1403

"Envelope": No. 2575, Writing letter. No. 2576, Climbing ladder to go into letter box. No. 2577, On wheels. No. 2578, Following postman carrying another "Envelope." No. 2579, Held by girl. No. 2580, At feet of girl reading long letter.

1997, May 8 **Photo.** ***Perf. 13***

2575 A1403 3fr multicolored 1.25 1.00
2576 A1403 3fr multicolored 1.25 1.00
2577 A1403 3fr multicolored 1.25 1.00
2578 A1403 3fr multicolored 1.25 1.00
2579 A1403 3fr multicolored 1.25 1.00
2580 A1403 3fr multicolored 1.25 1.00
a. Strip of 6, #2575-2580 + label 8.00 8.00

Self-Adhesive

Serpentine Die Cut 11

2580B A1403 3fr like #2575 1.25 1.00
2580C A1403 3fr like #2576 1.25 1.00
2580D A1403 3fr like #2577 1.25 1.00
2580E A1403 3fr like #2578 1.25 1.00
2580F A1403 3fr like #2579 1.25 1.00
2580G A1403 3fr like #2580 1.25 1.00
h. Booklet pane, 2 each #2580B-2580G 15.00 15.00

By its nature No. 2580h is a complete booklet. The peelable paper backing serves as a booklet cover.

See Nos. 2648-2659.

Honoring French Soldiers in North Africa (1952-62) A1404

1997, May 10 **Litho.** ***Perf. 13***

2581 A1404 3fr multicolored 1.25 .30

French Federation of Philatelic Associations, 70th Congress, Versailles — A1405

1997, May 17 **Photo.** ***Perf. 13***

2582 A1405 3fr multicolored 1.25 .40

Printed with se-tenant label.

Château de Plessis-Bourré, Maine and Loire Rivers — A1406

1997, May 24 **Litho. & Engr.**

2583 A1406 4.40fr multicolored 2.00 1.25

1998 World Cup Soccer Championships Type

Stylized action scenes, name of host city in France.

1997, May 31 **Photo.** ***Perf. 13½***

2584 A1367 3fr Lyon 1.25 .30
2585 A1367 3fr Marseilles 1.25 .30
2586 A1367 3fr Nantes 1.25 .30
2587 A1367 3fr Paris 1.25 .30
Nos. 2584-2587 (4) 5.00 1.20

Saint Martin of Tours (316-97) Apostle of the Gauls A1408

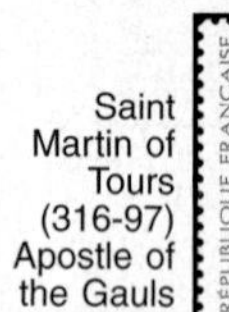

1997, July 5 **Engr.** ***Perf. 13***

2588 A1408 4.50fr multicolored 2.00 .75

Marianne — A1409

1997, July 14 **Engr.** ***Perf. 13***

2589 A1409 10c brown .25 .25
2590 A1409 20c brt blue grn .25 .25
2591 A1409 50c purple .25 .25
2592 A1409 1fr bright org .45 .25
2593 A1409 2fr bright blue 1.00 .30
2594 A1409 2.70fr bright grn 1.25 .25
2595 A1409 (3fr) red 1.90 .25
2596 A1409 3.50fr apple grn 1.60 .25
2597 A1409 3.80fr blue 1.75 .25
2598 A1409 4.20fr dark org 1.90 .30
2599 A1409 4.40fr blue 2.00 .30
2600 A1409 4.50fr bright pink 2.10 .30
2601 A1409 5fr brt grn blue 5.25 .30
2602 A1409 6.70fr dark grn 3.00 .30
a. Souvenir sheet, #2594-2600, 2602 14.00 14.00
2603 A1409 10fr violet 4.50 .35
a. Souvenir sheet, #2589-2593, 2601, 2603 12.00 12.00
Nos. 2589-2603 (15) 27.45 4.15

Self-Adhesive

Booklet Stamps

Die Cut x Serpentine Die Cut 7

2603B A1409 1fr brt org 2.25 .50
c. Booklet pane, #2603B, 3 #2604 7.75
Booklet, 2 #2603Bc 16.00
2604 A1409 (3fr) red 1.40 .25
a. Booklet pane of 10 14.00

Coil Stamps

Perf. 13 Horiz.

2604B A1409 2.70fr bright grn 1.25 .50
2605 A1409 (3fr) red 1.75 .25

Nos. 2595, 2604-2605 were valued at 3fr on day of issue.

Issued: Nos. 2602a, 2603a, 11/12/01. No. 2603B, 9/1/97.

See Nos. 2835-2835C, 2921-2922, 3530, 4410j, 4523.

1997 World Rowing Championships, Savoie — A1410

1997, Aug. 30 **Engr.** ***Perf. 13x12½***

2606 A1410 3fr blue & magenta 1.25 .30

Basque Corsairs A1411

1997, Sept. 13 ***Perf. 13***

2607 A1411 3fr multicolored 1.25 .30

Saint-Maurice Basilica, Epinal — A1412

1997, Sept. 20 ***Perf. 13x12½***

2608 A1412 3fr multicolored 1.25 .30

Fresh Fish Merchants, Port of Boulogne A1413

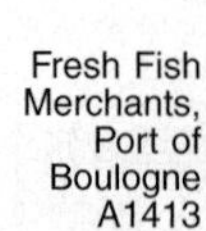

1997, Sept. 26 ***Perf. 13***

2609 A1413 3fr multicolored 1.25 .30

Japan Year — A1414

1997, Oct. 4 **Engr.** ***Perf. 13***

2610 A1414 4.90fr multicolored 1.00 1.25

1997 World Judo Championships — A1415

1997, Oct. 9 **Photo.** ***Perf. 13***

2611 A1415 3fr multicolored 1.25 .30

Sceaux Estate, Hauts-de-Seine — A1416

1997, Oct. 11

2612 A1416 3fr multicolored 1.25 .30

Saar-Lorraine-Luxembourg Summit — A1417

1997, Oct. 16 **Photo.** ***Perf. 13***

2613 A1417 3fr multicolored 1.25 .30

See Germany No. 1982, Luxembourg No. 972.

College of France A1418

1997, Oct. 18 **Engr.**

2614 A1418 4.40fr multicolored 2.00 .70

Quality — A1419

1997, Oct. 18 **Photo.**

2615 A1419 4.50fr multicolored 2.00 .80

A1420

Season's Greetings A1421

1997 **Photo.** ***Perf. 13***

2616 A1420 3fr Cat & mouse 1.50 .30

Photo. & Embossed

2617 A1421 3fr Mailman 1.25 .30

Issued: No. 2616, 11/8; No. 2617, 11/22.

Protection of Abused Children — A1422

1997, Nov. 20 **Photo.**
2618 A1422 3fr multicolored 1.25 .30

A1423

Design: Marshal Jacques Leclerc (Philippe de Haute Cloque) (1902-47).

1997, Nov. 28 **Photo.** ***Perf. 13***
2619 A1423 3fr multicolored 1.25 .30

Philexfrance '99, World Stamp Exposition — A1424

1997, Dec. 6 **Engr.**
2620 A1424 3fr red & blue 1.25 .30

Abbey of Moutier D'Ahun, Creuse A1425

1997, Dec. 13
2621 A1425 4.40fr multicolored 2.00 .70

Michel Debré (1912-96), Politician A1426

1998, Jan. 15 **Photo.**
2622 A1426 3fr multicolored 1.25 .30

1998 World Cup Soccer Championships Type

Stylized action scenes, name of host city in France.

1998, Jan. 24 ***Perf. 13½***
2623 A1367 3fr Saint-Denis 1.25 .30
2624 A1367 3fr Bordeaux 1.25 .30
a. Sheet of 10, #2530-2533, #2584-2587, #2623-2624 + label 14.00 14.00

National Assembly, Bicent. — A1427

1998, Jan. 24 ***Perf. 13***
2625 A1427 3fr multicolored 1.25 .30

Valentine's Day A1428

1998, Jan. 31
2626 A1428 3fr multicolored 1.25 .30

Office of Mediator of the Republic, 25th Anniv. A1429

1998, Feb. 5
2627 A1429 3fr multicolored 1.25 .30

A1430

1998, Feb. 28 **Photo.** ***Perf. 12½***
2628 A1430 3fr multicolored 1.25 .30

Self-Adhesive

Serpentine Die Cut

2629 A1430 3fr like #2628 1.25 .30
a. Booklet pane of 10 14.00 14.00
b. Sheet of 1 + 7 labels 17.00 16.00

1998 World Cup Soccer Championships, France.

The peelable paper backing of No. 2629a serves as a booklet cover.

See No. 2665.

A1431

1998, Feb. 21 **Engr.** ***Perf. 13½x13***
2630 A1431 3fr Detail of design A16 3.00 1.60
2631 A1431 3fr +60c like #2630 1.50 1.40
a. Booklet pane, 4 #2630, 3 #2631 + label 14.00
Complete booklet, #2631a 15.00

Stamp Day. No. 2630 issued only in booklets.

A1432

1998, Feb. 28 **Engr.** ***Perf. 13***
2632 A1432 4.50fr blue 2.00 .75

Father Franz Stock (1904-48), prison chaplain.

Happy Birthday A1433

1998, Mar. 13 **Photo.** ***Perf. 13x13½***
2633 A1433 3fr multicolored 1.25 .30

Union of Mulhouse with France, Bicent. A1434

1998, Mar. 14
2634 A1434 3fr multicolored 1.25 .30

Citeaux Abbey, 900th Anniv. A1435

1998, Mar. 14 **Engr.** ***Perf. 13***
2635 A1435 3fr multicolored 1.25 .30

Sous-Préfecture Hotel, Saint-Pierre, Réunion — A1436

1998, Apr. 4 **Engr.** ***Perf. 13***
2636 A1436 3fr multicolored 1.25 .30

Réunion's architectural heritage.

"The Return," by René Magritte — A1437

1998, Apr. 18 **Photo.**
2637 A1437 3fr multicolored 1.40 .50

See Belgium No. 1691.

Edict of Nantes, 400th Anniv. A1438

1998, Apr. 18 **Litho.**
2638 A1438 4.50fr Henry IV 2.00 .75

Art Series

Detail from "Entry of the Crusaders into Constantinople," by Delacroix (1798-1863) — A1439

Le Printemps, by Pablo Picasso (1881-1973) — A1440

Neuf Moules Malic, by Marcel Duchamp (1887-1968) — A1441

Vision After the Sermon, by Paul Gauguin (1848-1903) — A1442

1998 **Engr.** ***Perf. 12x13***
2639 A1439 6.70fr multicolored 3.00 1.00

Litho.

Perf. 13

2640 A1440 6.70fr multicolored 3.00 1.00

Photo.

2641 A1441 6.70fr multicolored 3.00 1.00
2642 A1442 6.70fr multicolored 3.00 1.00

Issued: No. 2639, 4/25; No. 2640, 5/15; No. 2641, 10/17; No. 2642, 12/5.

Abolition of Slavery, 150th Anniv. A1443

1998, Apr. 25 **Litho.** ***Perf. 13***
2643 A1443 3fr multicolored 1.25 .30

Tourism Series

Le Gois Causeway, Island of Noirmoutier, Vendée — A1444

Bay of Somme, Picardy — A1445

Château de Crussol, Ardèche A1446

Collegiate Church of Mantes — A1447

1998, May 2 **Photo.**

2644 A1444 3fr multicolored 1.25 .30
2645 A1445 3fr multicolored 1.25 .30

Engr.

2646 A1446 3fr multicolored 1.25 .30
2647 A1447 4.40fr multicolored 2.00 .70
Nos. 2644-2647 (4) 5.75 1.60

Issued: No. 2644, 5/2; No. 2645, 6/27; No. 2646, 7/4; No. 2647, 9/19.

Journey of a Letter Type

Historic "letters:" No. 2648, Dove carrying letter, Noah's Ark. No. 2649, Egyptian writing letter on papyrus. No. 2650, Soldier running to Athens with letter to victory at Marathon. No. 2651, Knight carrying letter on horseback. No. 2652, Writing letters with quill and ink. No. 2653, Astronaut carrrying letter in space from earth to the moon.

1998, May 9 **Photo.** ***Perf. 13x13½***

2648 A1403 3fr multicolored 1.25 1.00
2649 A1403 3fr multicolored 1.25 1.00
2650 A1403 3fr multicolored 1.25 1.00
2651 A1403 3fr multicolored 1.25 1.00
2652 A1403 3fr multicolored 1.25 1.00
2653 A1403 3fr multicolored 1.25 1.00
a. Strip, #2648-2653 + label 8.00 6.50

Booklet Stamps
Self-Adhesive
Serpentine Die Cut 11

2654 A1403 3fr like #2648 1.25 1.00
2655 A1403 3fr like #2649 1.25 1.00
2656 A1403 3fr like #2650 1.25 1.00
2657 A1403 3fr like #2651 1.25 1.00
2658 A1403 3fr like #2652 1.25 1.00
2659 A1403 3fr like #2653 1.25 1.00
a. Bklt. pane, 2 ea #2654-2659 16.00 14.00

By its nature No. 2659a is a complete booklet. The peelable paper backing serves as a booklet cover.

League of Human Rights, Cent. — A1448

1998, May 9 ***Perf. 13***

2660 A1448 4.40fr multicolored 2.00 .70

Henri Collet (1885-1951), Composer — A1449

1998, May 15 **Engr.** ***Perf. 12x13***

2661 A1449 4.50fr black, gray & buff 2.00 .80

French Federation of Philatelic Assoc., 71st Congress, Dunkirk — A1450

Photo. & Engr.

1998, May 29 ***Perf. 13***

2662 A1450 3fr multicolored 1.25 .30

Mont-Saint-Michel — A1451

1998, June 6 **Photo.** ***Perf. 13***

2663 A1451 3fr multicolored 1.40 .30

Natl. Music Festival — A1452

1998, June 13

2664 A1452 3fr multicolored 1.25 .50

Europa.

1998 World Cup Soccer Championships Type with Added Inscription, "Champion du Monde"

1998, July 12 **Photo.** ***Perf. 12½***

2665 A1430 3fr multicolored 1.25 .30

Stéphane Mallarmé (1842-98), Poet A1453

Photo. & Engr.

1998, Sept. 5 ***Perf. 13***

2666 A1453 4.40fr multicolored 2.00 .70

Flowers — A1453a

1.87fr, Liseron. 2.18fr, Coquelicot. 4.66fr, Violette. 7.11fr, Bouton d'or.

1998, Sept. 9 **Litho.** ***Perf. 13***

2666A A1453a 1.87fr multi .85 .25
2666B A1453a 2.18fr multi 1.00 .50
2666C A1453a 4.66fr multi 2.10 1.00
2666D A1453a 7.11fr multi 3.00 1.75
Nos. 2666A-2666D (4) 6.95 3.50

Nos. 2666A-2666D are known only precanceled. See second note after No. 132.

Aéro Club of France, Cent. — A1454

1998, Sept. 12 **Photo.**

2667 A1454 3fr multicolored 1.25 .30

A1455

"The Little Prince," by Antoine de Saint-Exupéry (1900-44): a, Standing in uniform with sword, horiz. b, Seated on wall. c, "The Little Prince on Asteroid B-612." d, Pouring water from sprinkling can. e, Walking along cliff, fox, horiz.

1998, Oct. 23 **Photo.** ***Perf. 13***

2668 Strip of 5 + 2 labels 6.50 4.00
a.-e. A1455 3fr any single 1.25 .70
f. Souv. sheet, #2668a-2668e 8.00 8.00

Philexfrance '99. No. 2668f was released 9/12 and sold for 25fr.

Hall of Heavenly Peace, Imperial Palace, Beijing, China A1456

1998, Sept. 12 **Photo.** ***Perf. 13x13½***

2669 A1456 3fr shown 1.25 .40
2670 A1456 4.90fr The Louvre, France 2.40 1.25

See People's Republic of China Nos. 2895-2896.

Garnier Palace, Home of the Paris Opera — A1457

1998, Sept. 19 **Photo.** ***Perf. 13***

2671 A1457 4.50fr multicolored 2.00 .70

Horses A1458

1998, Sept. 27

2672 A1458 2.70fr Camargue 1.10 .30
2673 A1458 3fr Pottok 1.25 .40
2674 A1458 3fr French trotter 1.25 .40
2675 A1458 4.50fr Ardennais 2.10 .80
Nos. 2672-2675 (4) 5.70 1.90

Paris Auto Show, Cent. A1459

1998, Oct. 1 ***Perf. 12***

2676 A1459 3fr multicolored 1.25 .30

5th Republic, 40th Anniv. A1460

1998, Oct. 3 **Photo.** ***Perf. 13***

2677 A1460 3fr blue, gray & red 1.25 .30

Saint-Dié, Capital of Vosges Mountain Region — A1461

1998, Oct. 3 **Engr.** ***Perf. 13***

2678 A1461 3fr Tower of Liberty 1.25 .30

End of World War I, 80th Anniv. A1462

1998, Oct. 17 **Photo.** ***Perf. 13x13½***

2679 A1462 3fr multicolored 1.25 .30

Intl. Union for the Conservation of Nature and Natural Resources, 50th Anniv. — A1463

1998, Nov. 3 **Litho.**

2680 A1463 3fr multicolored 1.25 .40

New Year A1464

Christmas A1465

1998, Nov. 7 **Photo.** ***Perf. 13***

Background Colors

2681 A1464 3fr deep blue 1.60 .70
2682 A1465 3fr green 1.60 .70
2683 A1464 3fr yellow 1.60 .70
2684 A1465 3fr red 1.60 .70
2685 A1464 3fr green 1.60 .70
a. Strip of 5, #2681-2685 6.50 3.50

Issued in sheets of 10 stamps. Location of "Bonne Annee" and "Meilleurs Voeux" varies.

Doctors Without Borders A1466

1998, Nov. 21 *Perf. 13x13½*
2686 A1466 3fr multicolored 1.25 .30

European Parliament, Strasbourg A1467

1998, Dec. 5 **Photo.** *Perf. 13*
2687 A1467 3fr multicolored 1.25 .30

Universal Declaration of Human Rights, 50th Anniv. A1468

No. 2688, Faces of people of various races, globe. No. 2689, René Cassin (1887-1976), principal author of Declaration, Eleanor Roosevelt (1884-1962), Chaillot Palace, Paris.

1998, Dec. 10 **Litho.** *Perf. 13*
2688 A1468 3fr multicolored 1.25 .40
2689 A1468 3fr multicolored 1.25 .40

Discovery of Radium, Cent., ZOE Reactor, 50th Anniv. A1469

1998, Dec. 15 **Photo.** *Perf. 13*
2690 A1469 3fr multicolored 1.25 .30

Introduction of the Euro — A1470

1999 **Engr.** *Perf. 13*
2691 A1470 3fr red & blue 1.25 .25

Booklet Stamps
Self-Adhesive
Die Cut x Serpentine Die Cut 7

2691A A1470 3fr red & blue 1.25 .25
b. Booklet pane of 10 12.50

Issued: No. 2691, 1/1/99. No. 2691A, 2/15/99. Values are shown in both Francs and Euros on Nos. 2691-2691A. No. 2691Ab is a complete booklet.
Euro currency did not circulate until 2002.

French Postage Stamps, 150th Anniv. A1471

1999, Jan. 1 **Photo.** *Perf. 13*
Booklet Stamps

2692 A1471 3fr black & red 7.00 6.00
2693 A1471 3fr red & black 1.25 1.00
a. Booklet pane, #2692, 4 #2693 + label 13.00
Complete booklet, #2693a 14.00

No. 2692 has black denomination; No. 2693 has red denomination.
Stamp Day.

Public Assistance Hospital, Paris, 150th Anniv. A1472

1999, Jan. 9
2694 A1472 3fr multicolored 1.25 .30

Diplomatic Relations with Israel, 50th Anniv. — A1473

1999, Jan. 24
2695 A1473 4.40fr multicolored 2.00 .75

Festival Stamps A1474

1999, Feb. 6 **Photo.** *Perf. 13*
2696 A1474 3fr Stars, "Je t'aime" 1.25 .30
2697 A1474 3fr Rose 1.25 .30

Booklet Stamps
Self-Adhesive
Die Cut Perf. 10

2698 A1474 3fr like #2696 1.25 .30
2699 A1474 3fr like #2697 1.25 .30
a. Bklt. pane, 5 ea #2698-2699 14.00

No. 2699a is a complete booklet.

Art Series

St. Luke the Evangelist, Sculpture by Jean Goujon (1510-66) A1475

Painting, "Waterlillies in Moonlight," by Claude Monet (1840-1926) — A1476

Stained Glass, Cathedral of Auch, by Arnauld de Moles, 16th Cent. A1477

Charles I, King of England, by Sir Anthony Van Dyck A1478

1999 **Engr.** *Perf. 13*
2700 A1475 6.70fr multicolored 3.00 1.00

Litho.
2701 A1476 6.70fr multicolored 3.00 1.00

Engr.
2702 A1477 6.70fr multicolored 3.00 1.00

Photo.
Perf. 13¼x13
2703 A1478 6.70fr multicolored 3.00 1.00
Nos. 2700-2703 (4) 12.00 4.00

Issued: No. 2700, 2/13; No. 2701, 5/29; No. 2702, 6/19; No. 2703, 11/11.

National Census — A1479

1999, Feb. 20 **Photo.** *Perf. 13½*
2704 A1479 3fr multicolored 1.25 .30

Cultural Heritage of Lebanon A1480

Mosaic illustrating transformation of Zeus into bull, Natl. Museum of Beirut.

1999, Feb. 27 *Perf. 12½*
2705 A1480 4.40fr multicolored 2.00 .70

Asterix, by Albert Uderzo and Rene Goscinny A1481

1999, Mar. 6 **Photo.** *Perf. 13¼*
2706 A1481 3fr multicolored 1.25 .30
a. Perf. 13¼x12¾ 1.40 1.20

Booklet Stamp
Perf. 13¼x12¾

2707 A1481 3fr +60c like #2706 3.00 1.50
b. Booklet pane, 4 #2706a, 3 #2707 + label 14.00
Complete booklet, #2707b 15.00

Souvenir Sheet

2707A A1481 3fr +60c like #2706 2.50 2.00

Stamp Day. Stamp design in No. 2707A continues into the margins.

Council of Europe, 50th Anniv. A1482

1999, Mar. 19
2708 A1482 3fr multicolored 1.25 .30

A1483

Announcements — A1483a

No. 2709, Marriage (Oui). No. 2710, It's a boy (C'est un garcon). No. 2711, It's a girl (C'est une fille). No. 2712, Thank you.

1999, Mar. 20 *Perf. 13*
2709 A1483 3fr multi 1.25 .30
2710 A1483 3fr multi 1.25 .30
2711 A1483 3fr multi 1.25 .30
2712 A1483a 3fr multi 1.25 .30
Nos. 2709-2712 (4) 5.00 1.20

See Nos. 2721-2722.

Souvenir Sheet

PhilexFrance '99 — A1484

Works of art: a, Venus de Milo. b, Mona Lisa, by Da Vinci. c, Liberty Guiding the People, by Delacroix.

Litho. & Engr.

1999, Mar. 26 *Perf. 13¼*
2713 A1484 Sheet of 3 80.00 60.00
a.-b. 5fr each 17.50 12.50
c. 10fr multicolored 37.50 30.00

No. 2713 sold for 50fr, with 30fr serving as a donation to the Assoc. for the Development of Philately.

Elections to the European Parliament A1485

1999, Mar. 27 **Photo.** *Perf. 13*
2714 A1485 3fr multicolored 1.25 .30

Richard I, the Lion-Hearted (1157-1199), King of England — A1486

1999, Apr. 10 Engr. *Perf. 13x12½*
2715 A1486 3fr multicolored 1.25 .35

Tourism Series

Dieppe A1487

Haut-Koenigsbourg Castle, Bas-Rhin — A1488

Birthpalce of Champollion, Figeac — A1489

Chateau, Arnac-Pompadour — A1490

1999 Engr. *Perf. 13½*
2716 A1487 3fr multicolored 1.25 .30

Litho. & Engr.
Perf. 13

2717 A1488 3fr multicolored 1.40 .50
2718 A1489 3fr multicolored 1.25 .30

Engr.

2719 A1490 3fr multicolored 1.25 .30
Nos. 2716-2719 (4) 5.15 1.40

Issued: No. 2716, 4/17; No. 2717, 5/15; No. 2718, 6/26; No. 2719, 7/10.

The Camargue Nature Preserve A1491

1999, Apr. 24 Photo. *Perf. 13x13½*
2720 A1491 3fr multicolored 1.25 .30

Europa.

Announcements Type of 1999 and

A1492

No. 2721, Nice Holiday (bonnes vacances). No. 2722, Happy Birthday (joyeux anniversaire). No. 2723, Long Live Vacations (Vive les vacances).

1999, May 13 Photo. *Perf. 13*
2721 A1483 3fr multi 1.25 .30
2722 A1483 3fr multi 1.25 .30
2723 A1492 3fr multi 1.25 .30
Nos. 2721-2723 (3) 3.75 .90

Saint Pierre, Martinique A1493

1999, May 15
2724 A1493 3fr multicolored 1.25 .30

Detail of "Noctuelles" Dish, by Émile Gallé, School of Nancy Museum A1494

1999, May 22
2725 A1494 3fr multicolored 1.25 .30

Souvenir Sheet

World Old Roses Competition, Lyon — A1495

a, 4.50fr, Mme. Caroline Testout. b, 3fr, Mme. Alfred Carrière. c, 4.50fr, La France.

1999, May 28 *Perf. 13½x13*
2726 A1495 Sheet of 3, #a.-c. 5.50 4.50

Court of Saint-Emilion, 800th Anniv. — A1496

1999, May 29 Engr. *Perf. 13¼x13*
2727 A1496 3.80fr multicolored 1.75 .60

Hotel de la Monnaie, French Mint Headquarters — A1497

1999, June 5 Engr. *Perf. 13*
2728 A1497 4.50fr brn org & bl 2.00 .75

A1498

1999, June 12 Photo. *Perf. 13¼*
2729 A1498 3fr multicolored 1.25 .30

Countess of Segur (1799-1874), children's storyteller.

Loving Welcome — A1499

1999, June 19 *Perf. 13*
2730 A1499 3fr multicolored 1.25 .30

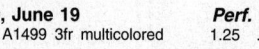

René Caillié (1799-1838), Explorer of Africa — A1500

1999, June 26 Engr. *Perf. 13¼*
2731 A1500 4.50fr multicolored 2.00 .75

1st French Postage Stamps, 150th Anniv. A1501

1999, July 2 Photo. *Perf. 11¾x13*
2732 A1501 6.70fr multicolored 3.00 1.00

PhilexFrance '99, World Philatelic Exhibition.

No. 2732 was printed with a se-tenant label and contains a holographic image. Soaking in water may affect the hologram.

Celebrating the Year 2000 A1502

1999, July 5 Photo. *Perf. 13*
2733 A1502 3fr multicolored 1.25 .30

Year 2000 Stamp Design Contest Winner — A1503

1999, July 6
2734 A1503 3fr multicolored 1.25 .30

Total Solar Eclipse, Aug. 11, 1999 A1504

1999, July 8 *Perf. 12x12¼*
2735 A1504 3fr multicolored 1.25 .30

Gathering of Tall Ships, Rouen, July 9-18 A1505

Sailing ships: a, Simón Bolivar. b, Iskra. c, Statsraad Lehmkuhl. d, Asgard II. e, Belle Poule. f, Belem. g, Amerigo Vespucci. h, Sagres. i, Europa. j, Cuauhtemoc.

1999, July 10 Photo. *Perf. 13*
2736 1fr Sheet of 10 6.50 6.50
a.-j. A1505 any single .60 .50

1999 Rugby World Cup, Cardiff, Wales A1506

1999, Sept. 11 Photo. *Perf. 13¼*
2737 A1506 3fr multicolored 1.25 .40
a. Miniature sheet of 10 12.50

Value is for stamp with surrounding selvage.

One stamp in No. 2737a has a missing "F" in the printer's mark.

Frédéric Ozanam (1813-53), Historian — A1507

1999, Sept. 11 Engr. *Perf. 13*
2738 A1507 4.50fr multicolored 2.00 .75

Emmaus Movement, 50th Anniv. A1508

1999, Sept. 26 Photo. *Perf. 13*
2739 A1508 3fr multicolored 1.25 .30

Cats and Dogs — A1509

Designs: No. 2740, Chartreux cat. No. 2741, European cat. No. 2742, Pyrenean Mountain dog. No. 2743, Brittany spaniel.

1999, Oct. 2 Photo. *Perf. 13¼*

2740 A1509 2.70fr multi 1.25 .30
2741 A1509 3fr multi 1.25 .30
2742 A1509 3fr multi 1.25 .30
2743 A1509 4.50fr multi 2.00 .75
Nos. 2740-2743 (4) 5.75 1.65

Frédéric Chopin (1810-49), Composer A1510

1999, Oct. 17 Engr. *Perf. 13¼*

2744 A1510 3.80fr multicolored 1.75 .75

See Poland No. 3484.

A1511

Best Wishes for Year 2000 A1512

1999, Nov. 20 Photo. *Perf. 13x13¼*

2745 A1511 3fr multi 1.25 .30
2746 A1512 3fr multi 1.25 .30

No. 2746 was printed with se-tenant label.

Paris Metro, Cent. A1513

1999, Dec. 4 Photo. *Perf. 13*

2747 A1513 3fr multi 1.25 .30

Council of State, Bicent. — A1514

1999, Dec. 11

2748 A1514 3fr multi 1.25 .30

Reconstruction of Lighthouses — A1515

2000, Jan. 1 Photo. *Perf. 13x12¾*

2749 A1515 3fr multi 1.25 .30

Reconstruction of San Juan de Salvamento Lighthouse, Argentina and replication of its design at La Rochelle, France.

Hearts A1516

2000, Jan. 8 Photo. *Perf. 13*

2750 A1516 3fr Snakes 1.25 .30
2751 A1516 3fr Face 1.25 .30
a. Souvenir sheet, 3 #2750, 2 #2751 8.00 6.50

Self-Adhesive Booklet Stamps

Serpentine Die-Cut

2752 A1516 3fr Like #2750 1.25 .30
2753 A1516 3fr Like #2751 1.25 .30
a. Bklt. pane, 5 ea #2752-2753 12.50

Values for Nos. 2750-2751 are for stamps with surrounding selvage. No. 2753a is a complete booklet.

Bank of France, Bicent. — A1517

2000, Jan. 15 Litho. *Perf. 13*

2754 A1517 3fr multi 1.25 .30

Prefectorial Corps, Bicent. — A1518

2000, Feb. 17 Photo. *Perf. 13x12¼*

2755 A1518 3fr multi 1.25 .30

Art Series

Venus and the Graces Offering Gifts to a Young Girl, by Sandro Botticelli (1445-1510) — A1519

The Waltz, by Camille Claudel A1520

Visage Rouge, by Gaston Chaissac A1521

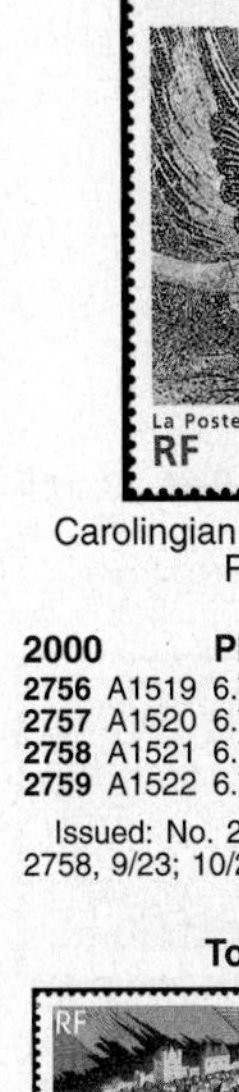

Carolingian Mosaic, Germigny-des-Prés — A1522

2000 Photo. *Perf. 13¼x13*

2756 A1519 6.70fr multi 3.00 1.00
2757 A1520 6.70fr multi 3.00 1.00
2758 A1521 6.70fr multi 3.00 1.00
2759 A1522 6.70fr multi 3.00 1.00

Issued: No. 2756, 2/25; No. 2757, 4/8; No. 2758, 9/23; 10/21.

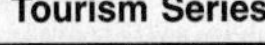

Tourism Series

Carcassonne — A1523

Saint-Guilhem-Le-Désert — A1524

Gérardmer A1525

Abbey Church of Ottmarsheim — A1526

2000 Photo. *Perf. 13*

2760 A1523 3fr multi 1.25 .30

Engr.

Perf. 13¼

2761 A1524 3fr multi 1.25 .30
2762 A1525 3fr multi 1.25 .30

Perf. 12¼x13

2763 A1526 3fr multi 1.25 .30
Nos. 2760-2763 (4) 5.00 1.20

Issued: No. 2760, 3/3; No. 2761, 4/8; No. 2762, 4/17; No. 2763, 6/17.

Tintin — A1527

2000, Mar. 11 Photo. *Perf. 13¼*

2764 A1527 3fr multi 1.25 .30
a. Perf. 13½x13 1.40 1.20

Perf. 13½x13

2765 A1527 3fr + 60c multi 2.50 2.00
a. Booklet pane, 4 #2764a, 3 #2765 + label 14.00
Complete booklet, #2765a 15.00
b. Souvenir sheet of 1 2.50 2.00

Stamp Day.

Bretagne Parliament Building Restoration — A1528

2000, Mar. 25 Photo. *Perf. 13¼*

2766 A1528 3fr multi 1.25 .30

Madagascar Periwinkles — A1529

2000, Mar. 25 Litho. *Perf. 13x13¼*

2767 A1529 4.50fr multi 2.00 .80

Felicitations A1530

2000, Apr. 7 Photo. *Perf. 13x13¼*

2768 A1530 3fr multi 1.25 .30

The 20th Century — A1531

No. 2769: a, France as World Cup soccer champions, 1998, vert. b, Marcel Cerdan wins middleweight boxing title, 1948. c, Charles Lindbergh flies solo across Atlantic, 1927. d, Jean-Claude Killy wins three Winter Olympics gold medals, 1968, vert. e, Carl Lewis wins four Olympic gold medals, 1984, vert.

Perf. 13¼x13 (vert. stamps), 13x13¼

2000, Apr. 15

2769 A1531 Sheet, 2 ea #a-e 14.00 14.00
a.-e. 3fr any single 1.40 .75

Top part of No. 2769 contains Nos. 2769a-2769e and is separated from bottom part of sheet by a row of rouletting.

See No. 2787, 2804, 2837, 2881, 2915.

Automobiles — A1532

No. 2770: a, Bugatti 35. b, Citroen Traction. c, Renault 4CV. d, Simca Chambord. e, Hispano-Suiza K6. f, Volkswagen Beetle. g, 1962 Cadillac. h, Peugeot 203. i, Citroen DS19. j, Ferrari 250 GTO.

2000, May 5 ***Perf. 13¼x13***

2770 A1532 Sheet of 10, #a.-j. 7.50 7.50
a.-e. 1fr any single .45 .35
f.-j. 2fr any single .90 .60

Europa, 2000

Common Design Type

2000, May 9 **Photo.** ***Perf. 13¼***

2771 CD17 3fr multi 1.25 .40

Henry-Louis Duhamel du Monceau (1700-82), Agronomist — A1533

2000, May 13 **Engr.** ***Perf. 13***

2772 A1533 4.50fr multi 2.00 .80

French Federation of Philatelic Associations, 73rd Congress, Nevers — A1534

2000, May 19 **Engr.** ***Perf. 13¼***

2773 A1534 3fr multi 1.25 .30

Happy Vacation — A1535

2000, June 1 **Photo.** ***Perf. 13¼x13***

2774 A1535 3fr multi 1.25 .30

A1536

2000, June 3 **Engr.** ***Perf. 13x12¼***

2775 A1536 3fr multi 1.25 .30

First Ascent of Annapurna, 50th anniv.

Nature A1537

2.70fr, Agrias sardanapalus butterfly. No. 2777, Giraffe. No. 2778, Allosaurus. 4.50fr, Tulipa lutea.

2000, June 17 **Photo.** ***Perf. 13¼***

2776 A1537 2.70fr multi 1.25 .30
2777 A1537 3fr multi, vert. 1.25 .30
2778 A1537 3fr multi 1.25 .30
2779 A1537 4.50fr multi, vert 2.00 .75
a. Souvenir sheet, #2776-2779 6.00 6.00
Nos. 2776-2779 (4) 5.75 1.65

Antoine de Saint-Exupéry (1900-44), Aviator, Writer — A1538

2000, June 24 **Photo.** ***Perf. 13¼x13***

2780 A1538 3fr multi 1.25 .30

Yellow Train of Cerdagne, Cent. A1539

2000, July 14 ***Perf. 13x13¼***

2781 A1539 3fr multi 1.25 .30

Folklore A1540

2000, Aug. 12 **Photo.** ***Perf. 13***

2782 A1540 4.50fr multi 2.00 .80

2000 Summer Olympics, Sydney A1541

Designs: No. 2783, Cycling, fencing, relay racer. No. 2784, Relay racer, judo, diving.

2000, Sept. 9

2783 A1541 3fr multi 1.40 .30
2784 A1541 3fr multi 1.40 .30
a. Pair, #2783-2784 3.00 2.00
b. Sheet, 5 #2784a + label 15.00 15.00

Olymphilex 2000, Sydney (No. 2784b).

Brother Alfred Stanke (1904-75) A1542

2000, Sept. 23 **Engr.**

2785 A1542 4.40fr multi 2.00 .70

S.O.S. Amitié, 40th Anniv. A1543

2000, Sept. 30 **Litho.** ***Perf. 13***

2786 A1543 3fr multi 1.40 .30

20th Century Type

No. 2787: a, Man on the Moon, 1969, vert. b, Paid vacations, 1936. c, Invention of washing machine, 1901, vert. d, Woman suffrage, 1944, vert. e, Universal Declaration of Human Rights, 1948.

Perf. 13¼x13 (vert. stamps), 13x13¼

2000, Sept. 30 **Photo.**

2787 A1531 Sheet, 2 each #a-e 14.00 14.00
a.-e. 3fr Any single 1.40 .50

The top and bottom parts of No. 2787 contains Nos. 2787a-2787e and are separated by a row of rouletting.

2001, Start of New Millennium A1544

2000, Oct. 14 **Litho.** ***Perf. 13***

2788 A1544 3fr multi 1.40 .30

The Lovers' Kiosk, by Peynet A1545

2000, Nov. 4 **Engr.** ***Perf. 13¼x13***

2789 A1545 3fr multi 1.40 .50

Endangered Birds — A1546

2000, Nov. 4 **Photo.** ***Perf. 13¼***

2790 A1546 3fr Kiwi 1.40 .40
2791 A1546 5.20fr Falcon 2.50 1.50

See New Zealand Nos. 1688, 1694.

Start of the 3rd Millennium — A1547

2000, Nov. 9 **Photo.** ***Perf. 13x13¼***

2792 A1547 3fr multi + label 1.40 .30

Issued in sheets of 10 stamps + 10 labels, which could be personalized for an extra fee.

Holiday Greetings A1548

2000, Nov. 11 ***Perf. 12¼x13***

2793 A1548 3fr Meilleurs voeux 1.40 .30

Perf. 13¼

2794 A1548 3fr Bonne année 1.40 .30

Union of Metallurgical & Mining Industries, Cent. — A1549

Engr. with Foil Application

2000, Dec. 9 ***Perf. 13x13¼***

2795 A1549 4.50fr multi 2.10 .90

World Handball Championships — A1550

2001, Jan. 20 **Photo.** ***Perf. 13¼***

2796 A1550 3fr multi 1.40 .30

Heart A1551

2001, Jan. 27

2797 A1551 3fr multi 1.40 .30
a. Souvenir sheet of 5 10.00 10.00

Value of No. 2797 is for stamp with surrounding selvage.

Art Series

The Peasant Dance, by Pieter Breughel, the Elder — A1552

Hotel des Chevaliers de Saint-Jean-de-Jérusalem — A1553

Yvette Guilbert Singing "Linger, Longer, Loo," by Henri de Toulouse-Lautrec (1864-1901) — A1554

Honfleur at Low Tide, by Johan Barthold Jongkind — A1555

Engr., Photo (#2800), Litho (#2801)

2001 *Perf. 13x13¼, 13¼x13 (#2800)*

2798 A1552 6.70fr multi 3.00 1.00
2799 A1553 6.70fr multi 3.00 1.00
2800 A1554 6.70fr multi 3.00 1.00
2801 A1555 6.70fr multi 3.00 1.00
Nos. 2798-2801 (4) 12.00 4.00

Issued: No. 2798, 2/3; No. 2799, 4/21; No. 2800, 9/8; No. 2801, 10/27.

Gaston Lagaffe, by André Franquin A1556

2001, Feb. 24 Photo. *Perf. 13¼*

2802 A1556 3fr multi 1.40 .30
a. Perf. 13¼x13 1.40 1.20

Perf. 13¼x13

2803 A1556 3fr +60c multi 3.00 1.50
a. Souvenir sheet of 1 6.00 3.50
b. Booklet pane, 5 #2802a, 3 #2803 18.00
Booklet, #2803b 19.00

Stamp Day.

20th Century Type of 2000

No. 2804 — Communications: a, Television. b, Compact disc. c, Advertisements, vert. d, Radio, vert. e, Portable telephone, vert.

Perf. 13¼x13 (vert. stamps), 13x13¼

2001, Mar. 17 Photo.

2804 A1531 Sheet, 2 each #a-e 14.00 14.00
a.-e. 3fr Any single 1.40 .75

Top part of No. 2804 contains Nos. 2804a-2804e and is separated from bottom part by a row of rouletting.

Announcements — A1557

Designs: No. 2805, It's a girl. No. 2806, It's a boy. No. 2807, Thank you. 4.50fr, Yes (marriage).

2001 Frame Color *Perf. 13*

2805 A1557 3fr brt pink 1.40 .30
a. Litho., stamp + label 6.50 6.50
2806 A1557 3fr brt blue 1.40 .30
a. Litho., stamp + label 6.50 6.50
2807 A1557 3fr brt yel grn 1.40 .30
a. Litho., stamp + label 6.50 6.50
2808 A1557 4.50fr orange 2.10 .75
Nos. 2805-2808 (4) 6.30 1.65

Issued: Nos. 2805-2808, 3/23; Nos. 2805a-2807a, 11/8.

Nos. 2805a-2807a were issued in sheets of 10 stamps and 10 labels that sold for 60fr on day of issue. The labels could be personalized. Frames on Nos. 2805 and 2806 look splotchy, while those on Nos. 2805a and 2806a have a distinct dot structure. The frame on No. 2807 has tightly spaced small dots, while on No. 2807a, the dots are more widely spaced.

Wildlife — A1558

2001, Apr. 21 Photo. *Perf. 13¼*

2809 A1558 2.70fr Squirrel 1.25 .40
2810 A1558 3fr Roe deer 1.40 .40
2811 A1558 3fr Hedgehog, horiz. 1.40 .40
2812 A1558 4.50fr Ermine 2.10 .75
a. Souvenir sheet, #2809-2812 7.00 6.50

Tourism Issue

Nogent-le-Rotrou A1559

Besançon A1560

Calais A1561

Château de Grignan A1562

Engr., Litho & Engr. (#2813)

2001 *Perf. 13¼x13 (#2813), 13*

2813 A1559 3fr multi 1.40 .40
2814 A1560 3fr multi 1.40 .30
2815 A1561 3fr multi 1.40 .30
2816 A1562 3fr multi 1.40 .30
Nos. 2813-2816 (4) 5.60 1.30

Issued: No. 2813, 4/28; No. 2814, 5/5; No. 2815, 6/16; No. 2816, 7/7.

Europa — A1563

2001, May 8 Photo. *Perf. 13*

2817 A1563 3fr multi 1.40 .35

Gardens of Versailles — A1564

2001, May 12

2818 A1564 4.40fr multi 2.00 .80

Singers — A1565

Designs: No. 2819, Claude François (1939-78). No. 2820, Léo Ferré (1916-93). No. 2821, Serge Gainsbourg (1928-91). No. 2822, Dalida (1933-87). No. 2823, Michel Berger (1947-92). No. 2824, Barbara (1930-97).

2001, May 19 Photo. *Perf. 13*

2819 A1565 3fr multi 1.40 .75
2820 A1565 3fr multi 1.40 .75
2821 A1565 3fr multi 1.40 .75
2822 A1565 3fr multi 1.40 .75
2823 A1565 3fr multi 1.40 .75
2824 A1565 3fr multi 1.40 .75
a. Souvenir sheet, #2819-2824 12.00 12.00
Nos. 2819-2824 (6) 8.40 4.50

No. 2824a sold for 28fr with the Red Cross receiving 10fr of that.

Old Lyon — A1566

2001, May 19 Engr. *Perf. 13¼*

2825 A1566 3fr multi 1.40 .30

French Federation of Philatelic Associations 74th Congress, Tours — A1567

2001, June 1

2826 A1567 3fr multi 1.40 .30

Jean Vilar (1912-71), Actor A1568

Litho. & Engr.

2001, June 7 *Perf. 13*

2827 A1568 3fr multi 1.40 .40

Vacation A1569

2001, June 10 Litho. *Perf. 13*

2828 A1569 3fr multi 1.40 .30

Booklet Stamp

Self-Adhesive

2829 A1569 3fr multi 1.40 .30
a. Booklet of 10 14.00

1 Euro Coin A1570

2001, June 23 Photo. *Perf. 12½*

2830 A1570 3fr multi 1.40 .30

Value is for copy with surrounding selvage.

Albert Caquot (1881-1976), Engineer — A1571

2001, June 30 Engr. *Perf. 13¼*

2831 A1571 4.50fr multi 2.00 .75

Law Guaranteeing Freedom of Association, Cent. — A1572

2001, July 1 Photo. *Perf. 13*

2832 A1572 3fr multi 1.40 .30

Trains — A1573

No. 2833: a, Eurostar. b, American 220. c, Crocodile. d, Crampton. e, Garratt 59. f, Pacific Chapelon. g, Mallard. h, Capitole. i, Autorail Panoramique. j, 230 Class P8.

2001, July 6 Photo. *Perf. 13¼*

2833	A1573 Sheet of 10		10.00	8.00
a.-j.	1.50fr Any single		.90	.65

Geneva Convention on Refugees, UN High Commisioner for Refugees, 50th Anniv. — A1574

2001, July 28 *Perf. 13*

2834	A1574 4.50fr multi	2.00	.75

Marianne Type of 1997 Inscribed "RF" at Lower Left Instead of "La Poste"

2001 Engr. *Perf. 13*

2835	A1409 (3fr) red	1.40	.25
d.	Sheet of 15 + 15 labels	60.00	—

Serpentine Die Cut 6¾ Vert.

Self-Adhesive

2835A	A1409 (3fr) red	1.40	.25
b.	Booklet of 10	15.00	
e.	No. 2835 with attached label	6.00	

No. 2835Ae is from a sheet having either small or large-sized labels that could be personalized.

2001, Aug. 1 Engr. *Perf. 13 Horiz.*

Coil Stamp

Water-Activated Gum

2835C	A1409 (3fr) red	1.40	.25

Issued: Nos. 2835, 2835C, 8/1; No. 2835A, 9/24. No. 2835Ae, 2004.

No. 2835d sold for €10.03. Labels could be personalized for an additional price.

Pierre de Fermat (1601-65), Mathematician — A1575

2001, Aug. 19 Engr. *Perf. 13¼x13*

2836	A1575 4.50fr multi	2.00	.75

20th Century Type of 2000

No. 2837 — Science: a, First man in space. b, DNA. c, Chip cards. d, Laser. e, Penicillin.

Perf. 13¼x13 (vert. stamps), 13

2001, Sept. 22 Photo.

2837	A1531 Sheet, 2 each #a-e	14.00	14.00
a.-e.	3fr Any single	1.40	.70

Top part of No. 2837 contains Nos. 2837a-2837e and is separated from bottom part of sheet by a row of rouletting.

Astrolabe Sculpture, Val-de-Reuil A1576

2001, Sept. 29 *Perf. 13*

2838	A1576 3fr multi	1.40	.30

Halloween A1577

2001, Oct. 20

2839	A1577 3fr multi	1.40	.30
a.	Souvenir sheet of 5 + 4 labels	8.00	8.00

Jean Pierre-Bloch (1905-99), Human Rights Advocate — A1578

2001, Nov. 8 Engr. *Perf. 13*

2840	A1578 4.50fr multi	2.00	.75

Albert Decaris (1901-88), Artist A1579

2001, Nov. 9 Engr. *Perf. 13¼x13*

2841	A1579 3fr multi	1.40	.40

Jacques Chaban-Delmas (1915-2000), Politician — A1580

2001, Nov. 10 Engr. *Perf. 13x13¼*

2842	A1580 3fr multi	1.40	.40

Holiday Greetings A1581

Designs: Nos. 2843, 2845 Bonne Année (Happy New Year). Nos. 2844, 2846 Meilleurs Voeux (Best wishes).

2001, Nov. 9 Litho. *Perf. 13*

2843	A1581 3fr multi	1.40	.30
2844	A1581 3fr multi	1.40	.30

Serpentine Die Cut 11

Self-Adhesive

Booklet Stamps

2845	A1581 3fr multi	1.40	.30
2846	A1581 3fr multi	1.40	.30
a.	Booklet, 5 each # 2845-2846	14.00	

Fountains A1582

Designs: 3fr, Nejjarine Fountain, Fez, Morocco. 3.80fr, Wallace Fountain, Paris.

2001, Dec. 14 Photo. *Perf. 13¼*

2847	A1582 3fr multi	1.40	.40
2848	A1582 3.80fr multi	1.75	1.00

See Morocco Nos. 914-915.

100 Cents = 1 Euro (€)

Marianne (With Euro Denominations) A1583

2002, Jan. 1 Engr. *Perf. 13*

2849	A1583	1c yellow	.25	.25
2850	A1583	2c brown	.25	.25
2851	A1583	5c brt bl grn	.25	.25
2852	A1583	10c purple	.25	.25
2853	A1583	20c brt org	.60	.30
2854	A1583	41c brt green	1.20	.25
2855	A1583	50c dk blue	1.50	.25
2856	A1583	53c apple grn	1.60	.40
2857	A1583	58c blue	1.75	.50
2858	A1583	64c dark org	1.90	.50
2859	A1583	67c brt blue	2.00	.50
a.	67c deep blue		2.00	.50
2860	A1583	69c brt pink	2.10	.60
2861	A1583	€1 Prus blue	3.00	.80
2862	A1583	€1.02 dk green	3.00	.90
a.	Souvenir sheet, #2835, 2854, 2856-2858, 2859a, 2860, 2862		15.00	15.00
2863	A1583	€2 violet	6.00	1.50
a.	Souvenir sheet, #2849-2853, 2855, 2861, 2863		12.00	12.00
	Nos. 2849-2863 (15)		25.65	7.50

Coil Stamp

Perf. 13 Horiz.

2864	A1583	41c brt green	1.50	.30

See Nos. 2952-2957, 3043, 3043P-3043Q.

Orchids — A1584

Designs: 29c, Orchis insularis. 33c, Ophrys fuciflora.

2002, Jan. 2 Litho. *Perf. 13*

2865	A1584 29c multi	1.00	.30
2866	A1584 33c multi	1.50	.40

Nos. 2865-2866 are known only precanceled. See second note after No. 132.

See Nos. 2958-2959, 3046, 3168.

Heart of Voh, Photograph by Yann Arthurs-Bertrand — A1585

2002, Jan. 18 Photo. *Perf. 13¼*

2867	A1585 46c multi	1.40	.40
a.	Souvenir sheet of 5	7.00	7.00

Value of No. 2867 is for stamp with surrounding selvage.

2002 Winter Olympics, Salt Lake City — A1586

2002, Jan. 26 *Perf. 13*

2868	A1586 46c multi	1.40	.30

Art Series

Sphere Concorde, by Jesús Rafael Soto A1587

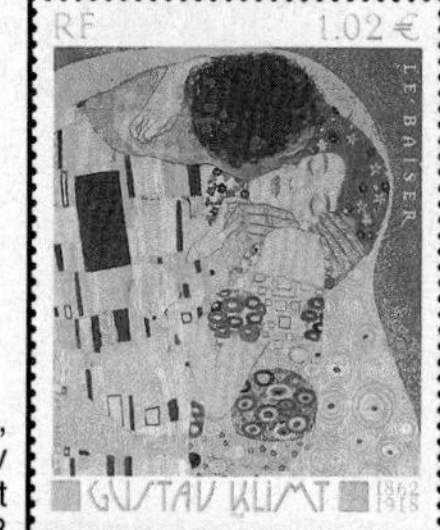

The Kiss, by Gustav Klimt A1588

The Dancers, by Fernando Botero A1589

Self-Portrait, by Elisabeth Vigée-Lebrun — A1590

2002 Photo. *Perf. 13¼x13*

2869	A1587	75c multi	2.25	1.00
2870	A1588	€1.02 multi	3.00	1.00
2871	A1589	€1.02 multi	3.00	1.00

Engr.

2872	A1590	€1.02 multi	3.00	1.00
	Nos. 2869-2872 (4)		11.25	4.00

Issued: No. 2869, 11/11. No. 2870, 2/8; No. 2871, 4/27. No. 2872, 10/12.

Alain Bosquet (1919-98), Poet — A1591

2002, Feb. 16 Engr. *Perf. 13*

2873 A1591 58c multi 1.75 .80

It's A Girl A1592

It's A Boy A1593

Yes A1594

2002, Feb. 23 Photo.

2874 A1592 46c multi 1.40 .30
2875 A1593 46c multi 1.40 .30
2876 A1594 69c multi 2.00 .80
Nos. 2874-2876 (3) 4.80 1.40

Europa — A1595

2002, Mar. 2 *Perf. 13¼*

2877 A1595 46c multi 1.40 .30

Boule and Bill, by Jean Roba — A1596

Designs: 46c, Boule, Bill, bird. 46c+9c, Boule, Bill, ball.

2002, Mar. 16 *Perf. 13¼*

2878 A1596 46c multi 1.40 .50
a. Perf. 13¼x13 1.40 1.20

Perf. 13¼x13

2879 A1596 46c +9c multi 3.00 1.50
a. Souvenir sheet of 1 3.00 2.50
b. Booklet pane, 5 #2878a, 3 #2879 18.00 —
Booklet, #2879b 19.00

Stamp Day. No. 2879 surtax for Red Cross. Stamp on No. 2879a has continuous design.

Nimes Amphitheater — A1597

Litho. & Engr.

2002, Mar. 22 *Perf. 13*

2880 A1597 46c multi 1.40 .30

20th Century Type of 2000

No. 2881 — Transportation: a, Concorde supersonic airplane. b, TGV train. c, Ocean liner France, vert. d, Mobylette motor scooter, vert. e, Citroen 2 CV automobile, vert.

Perf. 13, 13¼x13 (vert. stamps)

2002, Mar. 23 Photo.

2881 A1531 Sheet, 2 each #a-e 14.00 14.00
a.-e. 46c Any single 1.40 .75

Top part of No. 2881 contains Nos. 2881a-2881e and is separated from bottom part of sheet by a row of rouletting.

Encounter of Matthew Flinders and Nicolas Boudin, Bicent. A1598

Map of Australia, portrait and ship of: 46c, Flinders. 79c, Boudin.

2002, Apr. 4 *Perf. 13¼*

2882 A1598 46c multi 1.40 .40
2883 A1598 79c multi 2.25 1.50

See Australia Nos. 2053-2054.

Tourism Series

La Charité-sur-Loire — A1599

Collioure A1600

Locronan A1601

Neufchateau — A1602

Engraved (#2884, 2886), Photo. (#2885)

2002 *Perf. 13¼*

2884 A1599 46c multi 1.40 .30
2885 A1600 46c multi 1.40 .30
2886 A1601 46c multi 1.40 .30
2887 A1602 46c multi 1.40 .30
Nos. 2884-2887 (4) 5.60 1.20

Issue dates: No. 2884, 4/6; No. 2885, 6/22; No. 2886, 7/13; No. 2887, 10/12/02.

Numbers have been reserved for additional stamps in this set.

Birthday Greetings A1603

Invitation A1604

2002, Apr. 6 Photo. *Perf. 13*

2888 A1603 46c multi 1.40 .30
a. Litho., stamp + label 6.00 6.00
2889 A1604 46c multi 1.40 .30
a. Litho., stamp + label 6.00 6.00

Issued: Nos. 2888a, 2889a, 11/7. Nos. 2888a and 2889a were issued in sheets of 10 stamps and 10 labels that sold for €6.19 on day of issue. The labels could be personalized.

No. 2888a has a duller blue in "Anniversaire" than No. 2888, but is otherwise quite similar in appearance. The gold ink on No. 2889a has a more coppery look than that on No. 2889.

100th Paris-Roubaix Bicycle Race — A1605

2002, Mar. 13

2890 A1605 46c multi 1.40 .30

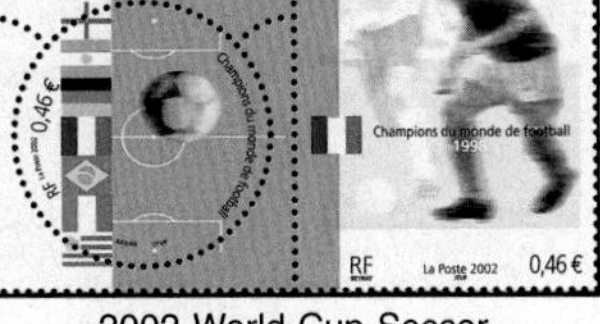

2002 World Cup Soccer Championships, Japan and Korea — A1606

No. 2891: a, Flags, soccer ball and field (32mm diameter). b, Soccer player, year of French championship.

2002, Apr. 27 *Perf. 12¾*

2891 A1606 Horiz. pair 2.75 2.50
a.-b. 46c Any single 1.40 .30
c. Sheet, 5 #2891 15.00 15.00

Issued: No. 2891c, 5/18.

See Argentina No. 2184, Brazil No. 2840, Germany No. 2163, Italy No. 2526 and Uruguay No. 1946.

Marine Life A1607

Designs: 41c, Sea turtle (tortue luth), vert. No. 2893, Killer whale (orque). No. 2894, Dolphin (grand dauphin). 69c, Seal (phoque veau marin).

2002, May 4 *Perf. 13¼*

2892 A1607 41c multi 1.25 .30
2893 A1607 46c multi 1.25 .30
2894 A1607 46c multi 1.25 .30
2895 A1607 69c multi 2.00 .75
a. Souvenir sheet, #2892-2895 6.50 6.50
Nos. 2892-2895 (4) 5.75 1.65

Worldwide Fund for Nature (No. 2895a).

French Federation of Philatelic Associations 75th Congress, Marseilles — A1608

2002, May 17 Engr. *Perf. 13*

2896 A1608 46c multi 1.40 .40

Legion of Honor, Bicent. — A1609

2002, May 18 Photo.

2897 A1609 46c multi 1.40 .30

Rocamadour A1610

2002, May 25 *Perf. 13¼*

2898 A1610 46c multi 1.40 .30

Louis Delgrés (1766-1802), Soldier — A1611

2002, May 25

2899 A1611 46c multi 1.40 .30

Vacation A1612

2002, June 8 Litho. *Perf. 13*

2900 A1612 46c multi 1.40 .30

Self-Adhesive

Serpentine Die Cut 11

2901 A1612 46c multi 1.40 .30
a. Booklet pane of 10 14.00

World Disabled Athletics Championships — A1613

2002, June 15 Photo. *Perf. 13¼*

2902 A1613 46c multi 1.40 .30

Saint-Ser Chapel — A1614

2002, June 22 Engr. *Perf. 13x13¼*

2903 A1614 46c multi 1.40 .30

Metz Cathedral Stained Glass A1615

2002, July 6 Engr. *Perf. 13¼x13*
2904 A1615 46c multi 1.40 .40

Jazz Musicians — A1616

Designs: No. 2905, Louis Armstrong (1901-71). No. 2906, Ella Fitzgerald (1918-96). No. 2907, Duke Ellington (1899-1974). No. 2908, Stéphane Grappelli (1908-97). No. 2909, Michel Petrucciani (1962-99), horiz. No. 2910, Sidney Bechet (1897-1959), horiz.

2002, July 13 Photo. *Perf. 13*
2905 A1616 46c multi 1.40 .75
2906 A1616 46c multi 1.40 .75
2907 A1616 46c multi 1.40 .75
2908 A1616 46c multi 1.40 .75
2909 A1616 46c multi 1.40 .75
2910 A1616 46c multi 1.40 .75
a. Souvenir sheet, #2905-2910 12.00 12.00
Nos. 2905-2910 (6) 8.40 4.50

No. 2910a sold for €4.36, with the Red Cross receiving €1.60 of that.

Pilgrimages to Notre Dame de la Salette, 150th Anniv. A1617

2002, Aug. 15 Engr. *Perf. 13¼x13*
2911 A1617 46c multi 1.40 .30

Choreography — A1618

2002, Sept. 13 Photo. *Perf. 13x13¼*
2912 A1618 53c multi 1.60 .70

Motorcycles — A1619

No. 2913: a, Honda 750 four. b, Terrot 500 RGST. c, Majestic. d, Norton Commando 750. e, Voxan 1000 Café Racer. f, BMW R90S. g, Harley Davidson Hydra Glide. h, Triumph Bonneville 650. i, Ducati 916. j, Yamaha 500 XT.

2002, Sept. 14 *Perf. 13¼x13*
2913 A1619 Sheet of 10 12.00 12.00
a.-e. 16c any single .75 .60
f.-j. 30c any single .90 .75

Georges Perec (1936-82), Writer — A1620

2002, Sept. 21 Engr. *Perf. 13¼*
2914 A1620 46c multi 1.40 .30

20th Century Type of 2000

No. 2915 — Photographs of everyday life: a, Family on motor scooter, 1955, vert. b, Man, horse and wagon, 1947. c, Woman ironing, 1950. d, Boy at fountain, 1950, vert. e, Girl in classroom, 1965, vert.

Perf. 13¼x13 (vert. stamps), 13
2002, Sept. 28 Photo.
2915 A1531 Sheet, 2 each #a-e 14.00 14.00
a.-e. 46c Any single 1.40 .75

Top part of No. 2915 contains Nos. 2915a-2915e and is separated from bottom part of sheet by a row of rouletting.

Emile Zola (1840-1902), Novelist — A1621

2002, Oct. 5 *Perf. 13*
2916 A1621 46c multi 1.40 .30

Souvenir Sheet

European Capitals — A1622

Attractions in Rome: a, Trevi Fountain. b, Coliseum, horiz. c, Trinità de Monti Church and Spanish Steps. d, St. Peter's Basilica, horiz.

2002, Nov. 7 *Perf. 13¼x13, 13x13¼*
2917 A1622 Sheet of 4 6.00 6.00
a.-d. 46c Any single 1.40 .90

See Nos. 2985, 3052, 3138, 3223, 3340, 3535, 3728, 3908, 3986, 4183, 4365.

Globe and Microcircuits A1623

2002, Nov. 8 Photo. *Perf. 13*
2918 A1623 46c multi 1.40 .30
a. Litho., stamp + label 6.00 6.00

Issued: No. 2918a, 11/7. No. 2918a was issued in sheets of 10 stamps and 10 labels that sold for €6.19 on day of issue. The labels could be personalized.

No. 2918a has a hairline at top, above "RF" that No. 2918 does not have, but is otherwise quite similar in appearance.

Holiday Greetings A1624

2002, Nov. 8 Photo. *Perf. 13*
2919 A1624 46c multi 1.40 .30
a. Litho., stamp + label 6.00 6.00

Booklet Stamp
Self-Adhesive
Serpentine Die Cut 11

2920 A1624 46c multi 1.40 .30
a. Booklet pane of 10 14.00

Issued: No. 2919a, 11/7. No. 2919a was issued in sheets of 10 stamps and 10 labels that sold for €6.19 on day of issue. The labels could be personalized.

No. 2919a has a finer dot structure, which is most noticeable in the chimney smoke, than No. 2919.

Marianne Type of 1997 Inscribed "RF" at Lower Left

2002, Nov. 9 Engr. *Perf. 13*
2921 A1409 (41c) bright green 1.20 .25

Coil Stamp
Perf. 13 Horiz.

2922 A1409 (41c) bright green 1.20 .25

Alexandre Dumas (Father) (1802-70), Writer A1625

2002, Nov. 30 Photo. *Perf. 13*
2924 A1625 46c multi 1.40 .30

Léopold Sédar Senghor (1906-2001), President of Senegal, Poet — A1626

2002, Dec. 20
2925 A1626 46c multi 1.40 .30

Hearts A1627

2003, Jan. 11 *Perf. 13¼*
2926 A1627 46c Four hearts 1.40 .30
a. Souvenir sheet of 5 7.00 7.00
2927 A1627 69c Roses 2.00 .75

Values for Nos. 2926-2927 are for examples with surrounding selvage.

Thank You A1628

Birth A1629

2003, Jan. 11 *Perf. 13*
2928 A1628 46c multi 1.40 .30
2929 A1629 46c brt org & brt bl 1.40 .30

Franco-German Cooperation Treaty, 40th Anniv. — A1630

2003, Jan. 16 *Perf. 13¼*
2930 A1630 46c multi 1.40 .40

A1631

2003, Feb. 8 Photo. *Perf. 13*
2931 A1631 46c multi 1.40 .30

Delegation for Land-use Planning and Regional Action, 40th Anniv.

Geneviève de Gaulle Anthonioz (1920-2002), World War II Resistance Fighter — A1632

2003, Feb. 11
2932 A1632 46c blk & ol brn 1.40 .30

Paris Chamber of Commerce and Industry, Bicent. — A1633

2003, Feb. 22 ***Perf. 13¼***

2933 A1633 46c multi 1.40 .30

Lucky Luke, by Morris (Maurice De Bevere) — A1634

Lucky Luke and Jolly Jumper: 46c, Skipping rope on ball on high wire. 46c+9c, Following dog, Rantanplan.

2003, Mar. 15 **Photo.** ***Perf. 13¼***

2934 A1634 46c multi 1.40 .65
a. Perf. 13¼x13 1.40 .65

Perf. 13¼x13

2935 A1634 46c +9c multi 3.50 2.00
a. Souvenir sheet of 1 3.00 2.50
b. Booklet pane, 5 #2934a, 3 #2935 17.50 —
Complete booklet, #2935b 18.00

Stamp Day.

Birds A1635

Designs: 41c, Colibri à tete bleue (Cyanophaia bicolor). No. 2937, Toucan ariel (Ramphastos vitellinus). No. 2938, Colibri grenat (Eulampis jugularis), vert. 69c, Terpsiphone de Bourbon (Terpsiphone bourbonnensis).

2003, Mar. 22 **Photo.** ***Perf. 13¼***

2936 A1635 41c multi 1.20 .30
2937 A1635 46c multi 1.40 .30
2938 A1635 46c multi 1.40 .30
2939 A1635 69c multi 2.00 .75
a. Souvenir sheet, #2936-2939 7.00 7.00
Nos. 2936-2939 (4) 6.00 1.65

Nantes A1636

2003, Apr. 4 **Engr.**

2940 A1636 46c multi 1.40 .30

Pierre Bérégovoy (1925-93), Prime Minister — A1637

2003, Apr. 30 **Engr.** ***Perf. 13x13¼***

2941 A1637 46c multi 1.40 .30

Milan Stefanik (1880-1919), Czechoslovakian General — A1638

2003, May 3 ***Perf. 13¼***

2942 A1638 50c multi 1.50 .40

See Slovakia No. 428.

Europa — A1639

2003, May 8 **Photo.**

2943 A1639 50c multi 1.50 .40

Charter of Fundamental Rights of the European Union — A1640

2003, May 8

2944 A1640 50c multi 1.50 .30

Aircraft Carrier "Charles de Gaulle" A1641

2003, May 8 **Engr.**

2945 A1641 50c multi 1.50 .30

Aspects of Life in the French Regions A1642

No. 2946: a, Beach cabins. b, Fishing net. c, Vineyards of Champagne. d, Camembert cheese, vert. e, Foie gras, vert. f, Petanque. g, Puppet show (Guignol), vert. h, Crepe, vert. i, Cassoulet. j, Limoges porcelain.

2003, May 24 **Photo.** ***Perf. 13***

2946 Sheet of 10 16.00 16.00
a.-j. A1642 50c Any single 1.50 1.30

No. 2946 has three vertical rows of rouletting, separating sheet into quarters.

Nos. 2946a-2946j were also issued in large booklets containing panes of 1 of each stamp. The booklet sold for €19.

See Nos. 2978, 3007, 3047, 3106, 3139, 3192, 3234, 3299, 3300-3301, 3357, 3427, 3505.

Art Series

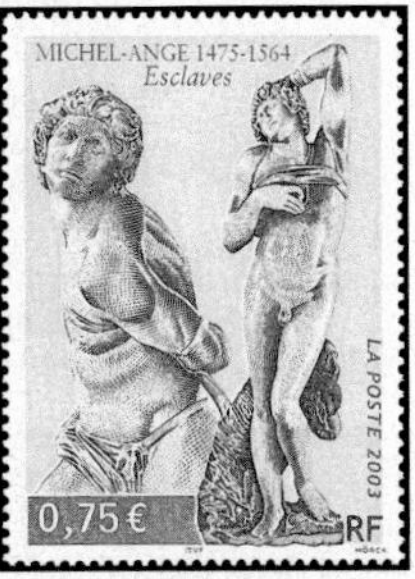

"The Dying Slave" and "The Rebel Slave," by Michelangelo — A1643

The Red Buoy, by Paul Signac A1644

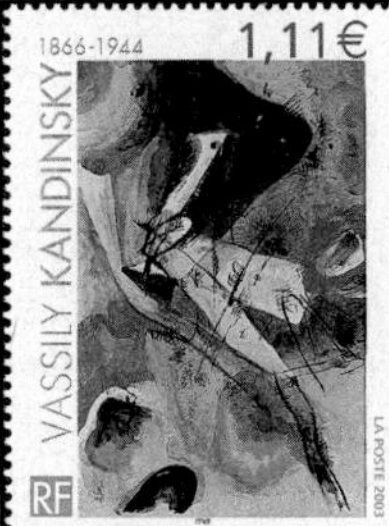

Untitled Abstract by Vassily Kandinsky A1645

Marilyn, by Andy Warhol A1646

2003 **Engr.** ***Perf. 13¼x13***

2947 A1643 75c multi 2.50 1.25

Photo.

2948 A1644 75c multi 2.50 1.25

Litho.

2949 A1645 €1.11 multi 3.50 1.25
2950 A1646 €1.11 multi 3.50 1.40
Nos. 2947-2950 (4) 12.00 5.15

Issued: No. 2947, 5/24. Nos. 2948, 2949, 7/5. No. 2950, 11/8.

A sheet containing 3 No. 2949 and 12 imperforate color progressive proofs was bound in a book that sold for €60.

Happy Birthday A1647

2003, May 31 **Photo.** ***Perf. 13¼***

2951 A1647 50c multi 1.50 .35
a. Souvenir sheet of 5 7.50 7.50
b. Litho., stamp + label 1.75 1.75

Issued: No. 2951b, 2004. No. 2951b was issued in sheets of 10 stamps + 10 labels that sold for €6.67 on day of issue. The labels could be personalized. The background on No. 2951 looks splotchy while that of No. 2951b has a dot structure.

Marianne With Euro Denominations Type of 2002

2003, June 1 **Engr.** ***Perf. 13***

2952 A1583 58c apple grn 1.75 .40
2953 A1583 70c yellow grn 2.00 .50
2954 A1583 75c bright blue 2.25 .25
2955 A1583 90c dark blue 2.60 1.00
2956 A1583 €1.11 red lilac 3.25 .25
2957 A1583 €1.90 vio brn 5.75 .40
a. Souvenir sheet, #2835, 2921, 2952-2957 22.00 22.00
Nos. 2952-2957 (6) 17.60 2.80

No. 2957a issued 2/28/04.

Orchids Type of 2002

Designs: 30c, Platanthera chlorantha. 35c, Dactylorhiza savogiensis.

2003, June 1 **Litho.** ***Perf. 13***

2958 A1584 30c multi 1.00 .30
2959 A1584 35c multi 1.50 .40

Nos. 2958-2959 are known only precanceled, See second note after No. 132.

French Federation of Philatelic Associations 76th Congress, Mulhouse A1648

2003, June 6 **Engr.** ***Perf. 13¼***

2960 A1648 50c multi 1.50 .30

Vacation — A1649

Perf. 12¾x13¼

2003, June 14 **Litho.**

2961 A1649 50c multi 1.50 .30

Self-Adhesive

Booklet Stamp

Serpentine Die Cut 11

2962 A1649 50c multi 1.50 .30
a. Booklet pane of 10 15.00

Tourism Issue

Notre Dame de l'Epine Basilica — A1650

Tulle A1651

Arras — A1652

Pontarlier A1653

Perf. 13x13¼, 13 (#2965)

2003, June 21 **Engr.**

2963 A1650 50c multi		1.50	.30
2964 A1651 50c multi		1.50	.30
2965 A1652 50c multi		1.50	.30
2966 A1653 50c multi		1.50	.30
	Nos. 2963-2966 (4)	6.00	1.20

Issued: Nos. 2963, 2964, 6/21. No. 2965, 9/20. No. 2966, 10/11.

French Freemasonry, 275th Anniv. — A1654

2003, June 28 Engr. ***Perf. 13¼x13***

2967 A1654 50c multi	1.50	.30

Tour de France Bicycle Race, Cent. A1655

No. 2968: a, Maurice Garin, winner of 1903 race. b, Cyclist with arms raised.

2003, June 28 Photo. ***Perf. 13***

2968 A1655 Vert. pair	3.00	2.00
a.-b. 50c Either single	1.50	.30

Values are for stamps with surrounding selvage.

Saint-Père Church, Yonne — A1656

2003, July 12 Engr. ***Perf. 13¼***

2969 A1656 50c multi	1.50	.30

World Track and Field Championships, Paris — A1657

2003, July 19 Photo. ***Perf. 13***

2970 A1657 50c multi	1.50	.30

Characters From French Literature — A1658

Designs: No. 2971, Eugène-François Vidocq (1775-1857), convict and police official. No. 2972, Esmerelda, from *Notre-Dame de Paris,* by Victor Hugo. No. 2973, Claudine, from *Claudine* novels, by Colette. No. 2974, Nana, from *Rougon-Macquart,* by Emile Zola. No. 2975, La Comte de Monte-Cristo, from *La Comte de Monte-Cristo,* by Alexandre Dumas (pere). No. 2976, Gavroche, from *Les Miserables,* by Hugo.

2003, Aug. 30 Photo. ***Perf. 13***

2971 A1658 50c multi	1.50	.75
2972 A1658 50c multi	1.50	.75
2973 A1658 50c multi	1.50	.75
2974 A1658 50c multi	1.50	.75
2975 A1658 50c multi	1.50	.75
2976 A1658 50c multi	1.50	.75
a. Souvenir sheet, #2971-2976	14.00	14.00
Nos. 2971-2976 (6)	9.00	4.50

No. 2976a sold for €4.60, with the Red Cross receiving €1.60 of that.

Ahmad Shah Massoud (1953-2001), Afghan Northern Alliance Leader — A1659

2003, Sept. 9

2977 A1659 50c multi	1.50	.30

Aspects of Life in French Regions Type of 2003

No. 2978: a, Chateau de Chenonceau. b, House, Alsace. c, Roof, Bourgogne. d, Genoese Tower, Corsica, vert. e, Arc de Triomphe, vert. f, Farm house, Provence. g, Pointe du Raz, vert. h, Mont Blanc, vert. i, Basque house. j, Pont du Gard.

2003, Sept. 20 Photo. ***Perf. 13***

2978 Sheet of 10	15.00	15.00
a.-j. A1642 50c Any single	1.50	1.25

No. 2978 has three vertical rows of rouletting, separating sheet into quarters.

Nos. 2978a-2978j were also issued in large booklets containing panes of 1 of each stamp. The booklet sold for €19.

Gardens and Parks — A1660

No. 2979: a, Buttes-Chaumont Park. b, Jardin du Luxembourg.

2003, Sept. 27 ***Perf. 13¼x13***

2979 Sheet of 2	12.00	12.00
a.-b. A1660 €1.90 Either single	6.00	6.00

Salon du Timbre 2004. No. 2979 has four vertical rows of rouletting, separating sheet into fifths, with the two stamps in the central fifth.

See Nos. 3029, 3118, 3201, 3316, 3429.

Motor Vehicles — A1661

No. 2980: a, 1954 Isobloc 648 DP 102 bus (Autocar). b, 1950 SFV 302 Tractor. c, 1938 Delahaye fire truck with mechanical aerial ladder. d, Renault Kangaroo Express postal van. e, 1932 Renault TN6 Paris city bus. f, 1910 Berliet 22hp Type M delivery truck. g, 1957 Berliet T100 heavy-duty truck. h, Citroen police van. i, Citroen DS ambulance. j, 1964 Hotchkiss fire truck.

2003, Oct. 24 Photo. ***Perf. 13¼***

2980 A1661 Sheet of 10	9.00	9.00
a.-e. 20c Any single	.55	.45
f.-j. 30c Any single	1.00	.75

Philexjeunes 2003 Philatelic Exhibition, Dunkerque.

A1662

Holiday Greetings A1663

2003, Nov. 6 Photo. ***Perf. 13***

2981 A1662 50c multi	1.50	.35
a. Litho., stamp + label	6.00	6.00

Litho.

2982 A1663 50c multi	1.50	.35
a. Sheet of 10 + 10 labels	60.00	60.00

Booklet Stamp
Self-Adhesive

Serpentine Die Cut 11¼

2983 A1663 50c multi	1.50	.35
a. Booklet pane of 10	16.00	

Nos. 2981a, 2982a, 2004. Nos. 2981a and 2982 were issued in sheets of 10 stamps + 10 labels that sold for €6.67 each on day of issue. The labels could be personalized. The background on No. 2981 looks splotchy while that of No. 2981a has a dot structure.

A souvenir sheet containing No. 2982 was sold for €6 by mail order only. It was not available through standing order subscriptions and was not offered in the philatelic bureau's sales catalog. 50,000 copies of this sheet were printed. Value $100.

Sower Type of 1903, Cent. — A1664

Serpentine Die Cut 6¾ Vert.

2003, Nov. 6 **Engr.**

Booklet Stamp

2984 A1664 50c red	3.50	2.00
a. Booklet pane, 5 each # 2984, 2835A	25.00	

See No. 4727b.

European Capitals Type of 2002

No. 2985 — Attractions in Luxembourg: a, Citadelle Saint-Esprit. b, Notre Dame Cathedral, horiz. c, Adolphe Bridge, horiz. d, Grand Duke's Palace.

Perf. 13¼x13, 13x13¼

2003, Nov. 7 **Photo.**

2985 A1622 Sheet of 4	7.50	7.50
a.-d. 50c Any single	1.50	1.00

Indian and French Artisan's Work A1665

Designs: 50c, Illumination depicting rooster, France, 15th cent. 90c, Jewelry design, India, 19th cent.

2003, Nov. 29 Engr. ***Perf. 13¼x13***

2986 A1665 50c multi	1.50	.45
2987 A1665 90c multi	2.60	1.50

See India No. 2040.

Launch of the Queen Mary 2 — A1666

2003, Dec. 12 Photo. ***Perf. 13¼***

2988 A1666 50c multi	1.50	.30

Greetings A1667

Holes punched through dots in "i's."

2004, Jan. 9 Photo. ***Perf. 13***

2989 A1667 50c shown	1.50	.30
2990 A1667 50c Un grand merci	1.50	.30

No Holes Punched Through Dots of "i's"

Stamp + Label

2991 A1667 50c Like No. 2989	6.00	6.00
2992 A1667 50c Like No. 2990	6.00	6.00

Nos. 2991-2992 were issued in sheets of 10 stamps + 10 labels that sold for €6.67 on day of issue. The labels could be personalized.

Compare with Type A2203. See Nos. 3096-3097D, 3569A-3569B.

It's a Boy A1668

It's a Girl A1669

2004 Litho. *Perf. 13*
Stamp + Label

2993 A1668 50c multi 6.00 6.00
2994 A1669 50c multi 6.00 6.00

Booklet Stamps
Self-Adhesive
Serpentine Die Cut 11

2995 A1668 50c multi 1.50 .35
a. Booklet pane of 10 15.00
2996 A1669 50c multi 1.50 .35
a. Booklet pane of 10 15.00

Nos. 2993-2994 were issued in sheets of 10 stamps + 10 labels that sold for €6.67 on day of issue. The labels could be personalized.

Nos. 2995-2996 issued 1/9/04.

Hearts A1670

Designs: 50c, Chanel No. 5 perfume bottle. 75c, Woman, Eiffel Tower.

2004, Jan. 9 Photo. *Perf. 13*

2997 A1670 50c multi 1.50 .35
a. Souvenir sheet of 5 7.50 7.50
b. Litho., stamp + label, perf. 13¼ 6.00 6.00
2998 A1670 75c multi 2.25 .75
a. Litho., stamp + label, perf. 13¼ 6.00 6.00

Nos. 2997b and 2998a were each printed in sheets of 10 stamps + 10 labels that could be personalized and sold for €6.69 and €10 respectively. On No. 2997b, there are large brown dots arranged in circles in the shading on the green rectangles, while on No. 2997 the brown dots are small and arranged in rows. On No. 2998a, the dots in the sky are larger and father apart than the tiny dots found on No. 2998.

Values are for stamps with surrounding selvage.

See Nos. 3133, 3135.

Tourism Issue

Lille, 2004 European Cultural Capital A1671

2004, Jan. 10 Photo. *Perf. 13*

2999 A1671 50c multi 1.50 .35

Art Series

Statue of Liberty, Sculpted by Frederic Auguste Bartholdi (1834-1904) — A1672

2004, Feb. 21 Engr. *Perf. 13¼x13*

3000 A1672 90c multi 2.60 1.50

Queen Eleanor of Aquitaine (c. 1122-1204) A1673

2004, Feb. 28 *Perf. 13x13¼*

3001 A1673 50c multi 1.50 .35

Stamp Day — A1674

Characters of Walt Disney: 45c, Donald Duck. 50c, Mickey Mouse. 75c, Minnie Mouse.

2004, Mar. 6 Photo. *Perf. 13¼*

3002 A1674 50c multi 1.50 .35
a. Perf. 13¼x13 (from booklet pane) 1.50 .35

Booklet Stamps
Perf. 13¼x13

3003 A1674 45c multi 2.25 1.00
3004 A1674 75c multi 2.25 .75
a. Booklet pane, 2 #3003, 4 each #3002a, 3004 23.00 —
Complete booklet, #3004a 24.00

Civil Code, Bicent. A1675

2004, Mar. 12 Engr. *Perf. 13¼x13*

3005 A1675 50c multi 1.50 .35

George Sand (1804-76), Writer A1676

2004, Mar. 20 Engr. *Perf. 13¼x13*

3006 A1676 50c multi 1.50 .35

Aspects of Life in French Regions
Type of 2003

No. 3007: a, Cutlery. b, Produce of Provence, vert. c, Beaujolais grapes, vert. d, Bread. e, Woman wearing coif, vert. f, Oysters, vert. g, Quiche Lorraine. h, Bullfighting. i, Clafoutis. j, Bagpipers.

2004, Mar. 26 Photo. *Perf. 13*

3007 Sheet of 10 15.00 15.00
a.-j. A1642 50c Any single 1.50 1.25

No. 3007 has three vertical rows of rouletting, separating sheet into quarters.

Clermont-Ferrand — A1677

2004, Mar. 26 Engr. *Perf. 13¼*

3008 A1677 50c multi 1.50 .30

Entente Cordiale, Cent. — A1678

Designs: 50c, Coccinelle, by Sonia Delaunay. 75c, Lace 1 (trial proof) 1968, by Sir Terry Frost.

2004, Apr. 6 Photo. *Perf. 13¼*

3009 A1678 50c multi 1.50 .35
3010 A1678 75c multi 2.25 .85

See Great Britain Nos. 2200-2201.

Road Safety — A1679

2004, Apr. 7

3011 A1679 50c multi 1.50 .30

See United Nations Offices in Geneva No. 424.

Art Series

La Méridienne d'Après Millet, by Vincent van Gogh — A1680

2004, July 2 Photo. *Perf. 13x13¼*

3012 A1680 75c multi 2.50 .95

Art Series

Un Combat de Coqs, by Jean-Léon Gérôme — A1681

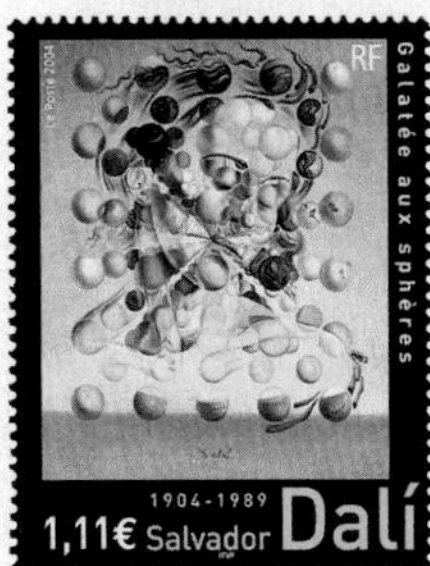

Galatée aux Sphères, by Salvador Dali A1682

2004 Photo. *Perf. 13x13¼*

3013 A1681 €1.11 multi 3.50 1.25
3014 A1682 €1.11 multi 3.50 1.25

Issued: No. 3013, 4/17; No. 3014, 6/19.

Tourism Issue

Bordeaux — A1683

Vaux-sur-Mer — A1684

Notre Dame de l'Assomption Cathedral, Luçon — A1685

2004 Litho. & Engr. *Perf. 13*

3015 A1683 50c multi 1.50 .30

Engr.
Perf. 13¼

3016 A1684 50c multi 1.50 .30
3017 A1685 50c multi 1.50 .30

Issued: No. 3015, 4/26; No. 3016, 7/17; No. 3017, 10/2.

Farm Animals A1686

2004, Apr. 26 Photo. *Perf. 13¼*

3018 A1686 45c Rabbit 1.25 .30
3019 A1686 50c Cow, vert. 1.50 .30
3020 A1686 50c Chicken 1.50 .30
3021 A1686 75c Burro, vert. 2.25 .90
a. Souvenir sheet, #3018-3021 7.00 7.00

Expansion of the European Union A1687

2004, May 1 Photo. *Perf. 13¼*

3022 A1687 50c multi 1.50 .30

Battle of Dien Bien Phu, 50th Anniv. — A1688

2004, May 7 *Perf. 13¼x13*

3023 A1688 50c multi 1.50 .30

Europa A1689

2004 Photo. *Perf. 13x13¼*

3024 A1689 50c multi 1.50 .30

Litho.

Booklet Stamp

Self-Adhesive

Serpentine Die Cut 11

3025 A1689 50c multi 1.50 .30
a. Booklet pane of 10 15.00

Issued: No. 3024, 5/9; No. 3025, 6/4.

Blake and Mortimer, Comic Book Characters by Edgar P. Jacobs A1690

Blake and Mortimer and: 50c, Brick wall, vert. €1, Blue background.

2004, May 15 Photo. *Perf. 13¼*

3026 A1690 50c multi 1.50 .30
3027 A1690 €1 multi 3.00 1.25

See Belgium No. 2020.

FIFA (Fédération Internationale de Football Association), Cent. — A1691

2004, May 20 *Perf. 13¼x13*

3028 A1691 50c multi 1.50 .30

Gardens and Parks Type of 2003

No. 3029: a, Jardin des Tuileries. b, Parc Floral de Paris.

2004, June 4 *Perf. 13¼x13*

3029 Sheet of 2 12.00 12.00
a.-b. A1660 €1.90 Either single 5.75 5.00
c. Souvenir sheet, #2979a-2979b, 3029a-3029b 35.00 35.00

Salon du Timbre 2004. No. 3029 has four vertical rows of rouletting, separating sheet into fifths, with the two stamps in the central fifth.

D-Day Invasion of France, 60th Anniv. — A1692

2004, June 5 *Perf. 13*

3030 A1692 50c multi 1.50 .30

Organ Donation A1693

2004, June 22 *Perf. 13¼*

3031 A1693 50c multi 1.50 .30

Pierre Dugua de Mons, Leader of First French Settlement in Acadia, and Ship A1694

Litho. & Engr.

2004, June 26 *Perf. 13*

3032 A1694 90c multi 2.75 1.00

See Canada No. 2044.

Napoleon I and the Imperial Guard — A1695

Designs: No. 3033, Light cavalry (Chasseur à cheval). No. 3034, Artilleryman and cannon (Artilleur à pied), horiz. No. 3035, Dragoon. No. 3036, Mameluke. No. 3037, Napoleon I. No. 3038, Grenadier (Grenadier à pied).

2004, June 26 Photo.

3033 A1695 50c multi 1.50 .75
3034 A1695 50c multi 1.50 .75
3035 A1695 50c multi 1.50 .75
3036 A1695 50c multi 1.50 .75
3037 A1695 50c multi 1.50 .75
3038 A1695 50c multi 1.50 .75
a. Souvenir sheet, #3033-3038 12.50 12.50
Nos. 3033-3038 (6) 9.00 4.50

No. 3038a sold for €4.60, with the Red Cross receiving €1.60 of that.

French Federation of Philatelic Associations 77th Congress, Paris — A1696

Litho. & Engr.

2004, June 27 *Perf. 13¼x13*

3039 A1696 50c multi 1.50 .30

2004 Summer Olympics, Athens — A1697

2004, June 28 Photo. *Perf. 13¼*

3040 50c Modern athletes 1.50 .75
3041 50c Ancient athletes 1.50 .75
a. A1697 Pair, #3040-3041 3.25 2.25

Printed in sheets containing five of each stamp.

A souvenir sheet containing No. 3041 was issued Aug. 2 and sold for €2.51. Value $20.

Happy Birthday A1698

2004, June 30 Photo. *Perf. 13¼*

3042 A1698 50c multi 1.50 .30
a. Souvenir sheet of 5 7.50 7.50
b. Litho. stamp + label 6.00 6.00

No. 3042b printed in sheets of 10 stamps + 10 labels that could be personalized that sold for €8. No. 3042b has a dark green inscription at left with a distinct dot pattern. No. 3042 has a lighter green inscription.

Marianne Type of 1997 Inscribed "RF" at Lower Left and Type of 2002 With Euro Denominations

2004 Litho. *Perf. 13*

3043 Sheet of 15 + 15 labels 60.00 60.00
a. A1583 1c orange yellow .25 .25
b. A1583 2c brown .25 .25
c. A1583 5c brt bl green .25 .25
d. A1583 10c purple .30 .30
e. A1583 20c orange .60 .60
f. A1583 58c apple green 1.75 1.75
g. A1583 70c olive 2.10 2.10
h. A1583 75c sky blue 2.25 2.25
i. A1583 90c dark blue 2.75 2.75
j. A1583 €1 Prussian blue 3.00 3.00
k. A1583 €1.11 red lilac 3.25 3.25
l. A1583 €1.90 violet brown 5.75 5.75
m. A1583 €2 violet 6.00 6.00
n. A1409 (45c) green 1.40 1.40
o. A1409 (50c) red 1.50 1.50

Engr.

Serpentine Die Cut 6¾ Vert

Self-Adhesive

3043P A1583 75c brt blue + label 8.75 8.75
3043Q A1583 €1.11 purple + label 10.50 10.50
3043R A1583 €1.11 chocolate + label — —

No. 3043 sold for €10.03. Stamps have a glossy varnish.

Labels on Nos. 3043P-3043R could be personalized.

Marianne and Emblem of World Fund to Combat AIDS, Tuberculosis and Smoking — A1699

2004, July 1 Engr. *Perf. 13*

3044 A1699 (50c) red 1.50 .35

Extreme Sports — A1700

No. 3045: a, Skateboarding. b, Parachuting. c, Sailboarding. d, Surfing. e, Luge. f, BMX bicycling. g, Paragliding. h, Jetskiing. i, Snowboarding. j, Rollerblading.

2004, July 3 Photo. *Perf. 13¼x13*

3045 A1700 Sheet of 10 7.50 7.50
a.-e. 20c Any single .60 .50
f.-j. 30c Any single .90 .75

Orchid Type of 2002

Design: 39c, Orchis insularis.

2004, Sept. 1 Litho. *Perf. 13*

3046 A1584 39c multi 1.50 .75

No. 3046 known only precanceled. See second note after No. 132.

Aspects of Life in the French Regions Type of 2003

No. 3047: a, House, Normandy. b, Chambord Chateau. c, Gorges, Tarn, vert. d, Notre Dame Cathedral, Paris, vert. e, Windmill, vert. f, Cave dwellings. g, Creek, Cassis, vert. h, Cap-Ferret Lighthouse, vert. i, Castle ruins. j, Alpine chalet.

2004, Sept. 18 Photo. *Perf. 13*

3047 Sheet of 10 15.00 15.00
a.-j. A1642 50c Any single 1.50 1.25

No. 3047 has three vertical rows of rouletting separating sheet into quarters.

Each stamp exists in booklet pane of 1 from booklet that sold for €19.

Halloween A1701

2004, Oct. 9 Litho. *Perf. 13*

3048 A1701 50c multi 1.50 .30

Félix Eboué (1884-1944), Colonial Governor — A1702

2004, Oct. 16 Photo.

3049 A1702 50c multi 1.50 .30

Ouistreham Lighthouse A1703

2004, Oct. 30 *Perf. 13¼*

3050 A1703 50c multi 1.50 .30

Marianne — A1704

Serpentine Die Cut 6¾ Vert.

2004, Nov. 10 Engr.

Booklet Stamp

Self-Adhesive

3051 A1704 50c multi 3.00 2.00
a. Booklet pane, 5 each #2835A, 3051 22.50

European Capitals Type of 2002

No. 3052 — Attractions in Athens: a, Greek Academy. b, Parthenon. c, Odeon of Herodes Atticus. d, Church of the Holy Apostles, vert.

Perf. 13x13¼, 13¼x13

2004, Nov. 11 **Photo.**

3052 A1622 Sheet of 4 7.50 7.50
a.-d. 50c Any single 1.50 .90

A1705

A1706

A1707

A1708

A1709

Holiday Greetings A1710

2004, Nov. 12 **Photo.** ***Perf. 13***

3053 A1705 50c multi 1.50 .30

Litho.

3054 A1706 50c multi + label 6.00 6.00
3055 A1707 50c multi + label 6.00 6.00
3056 A1708 50c multi + label 6.00 6.00
3057 A1709 50c multi + label 6.00 6.00
3058 A1710 50c multi + label 6.00 6.00
a. Vert. strip of 5, #3054-3059 + 5 labels 30.00 30.00
Miniature sheet, 2 #3058a + 10 labels 70.00 70.00

Booklet Stamps

Self-Adhesive

Serpentine Die Cut 11¼x11

3059 A1706 50c multi 1.50 .30
3060 A1707 50c multi 1.50 .30
3061 A1708 50c multi 1.50 .30
3062 A1709 50c multi 1.50 .30
3063 A1710 50c multi 1.50 .30
a. Booklet pane, 2 each #3059-3063 15.00
Nos. 3053-3063 (11) 39.00 31.80

Miniature sheet containing Nos. 3054-3058 sold for €6.69. Labels could be personalized.

No. 3055 exists in a souvenir sheet of 1 stamp without label that sold for €3. Value $35.

Henri Wallon (1812-1904), Historian and Politician — A1711

2004, Nov. 13 **Photo.** ***Perf. 13***

3064 A1711 50c multi 1.50 .30

Opening of Millau Viaduct — A1712

2004, Dec. 14 **Photo.** ***Perf. 13***

3065 A1712 50c multi 2.50 1.00

Marianne — A1713

Inscribed "ITVF" at Bottom

2005-07 **Engr.** ***Perf. 13***

3066 A1713 1c yellow .25 .25
a. Inscribed "Phil@poste" at bottom .25 .25
3067 A1713 5c brn blk .25 .25
a. Inscribed "Phil@poste" at bottom .25 .25
3068 A1713 10c violet .25 .25
3069 A1713 (45c) green 1.60 .25
a. Inscribed "Phil@poste" at bottom 1.60 .25
3070 A1713 (50c) red 3.00 .25
a. Sheet of 15 + 15 labels 70.00 70.00
b. Inscribed "Phil@poste" at bottom 2.00 .25
3071 A1713 55c dark blue 1.60 .50
3072 A1713 58c olive green 1.75 .40
3073 A1713 64c dark green 1.90 .40
3074 A1713 70c dark green 2.10 .50
3075 A1713 75c light blue 2.25 .25
3076 A1713 82c fawn 4.00 .50
3077 A1713 90c dark blue 2.75 .80
3078 A1713 €1 orange 3.00 .25
a. Inscribed "Phil@poste" at bottom 3.25 .75
3079 A1713 €1.11 red violet 3.25 .25
3080 A1713 €1.22 red violet 3.00 .30
3081 A1713 €1.90 chocolate 5.75 .30
3082 A1713 €1.98 chocolate 6.00 1.25
Nos. 3066-3082 (17) 42.70 6.95

Self-Adhesive (#3083-3085)

Serpentine Die Cut 6¾ Vert.

3083 A1713 (50c) red 1.50 .25
a. Booklet pane of 10 (see footnote) 15.00
b. Booklet pane of 10 (see footnote) 15.00
c. Booklet pane of 20 30.00
d. As #3083, with "Phil@poste" inscription 1.50 .25
e. Booklet pane, 10 #3083d 15.00
f. Booklet pane of 12 #3083d 17.00
g. No. 3083 with attached label 7.50
3084 A1713 82c fawn + label 12.00 12.00
3085 A1713 €1.22 red violet 15.00 15.00

Coil Stamps

Perf. 13 Horiz.

3086 A1713 (45c) green 2.00 .30
a. Inscribed "Phil@poste" at bottom 1.40 .25
3087 A1713 (50c) red 2.00 .25
c. Inscribed "Phil@poste" at bottom — —
3087A A1713 55c dark blue 2.50 1.25
b. Inscribed "Phil@poste" at bottom 1.60 .25
Nos. 3083-3087A (6) 35.00 29.05

Issued: Nos. 1c, 10c, (45c), (50c), 58c, 70c, 75c, 90c, €1, €1.11, €1.90, 1/8. 5c, No. 3071, 64c, 82c, €1.22, €1.98, 3/1. No. 3087A, 7/15. Nos. 3083d, 3083e, 10/1/06. Nos. 3066a, 3067a, 3069a, 3070b, 2006. No. 3083f, Jan. 2007. Nos. 3083g, 3084-3085, Apr. 2007. No. 3086a was issued in 2008 and sold for 50c. No. 3087b was issued in 2008 and sold for 55c.

Face values shown for Nos. 3069, 3070, 3083, 3086 and 3087 are those the stamps sold for on the day of issue. On day of issue, No. 3069a sold for 49c; No. 3070b for 54c.

No. 3070a sold for €10.03 and the labels could be personalized for an additional fee.

No. 3083a has a narrow strip of selvage separating the four stamps at left, from the six stamps, at right, and is on a white backing paper. No. 3083b is comprised of two horizontal strips of five stamps on a yellow backing paper. No. 3083d sold for 54c on day of issue.

No. 3083g was printed in sheets containing 15 stamps + 15 small or large-sized labels that could be personalized. Nos. 3084 and 3085 were each printed in sheets of 30 stamps + 30 large-sized labels that could be personalized.

A sheet of 10 litho. stamps similar to No. 3068 + 10 labels exists, but was not sold.

See Nos. 3211, 3211N, 3212, 3247-3255E, 3302, 3302N, 3383-3388A, 3389, 3531, 4410k, 4524.

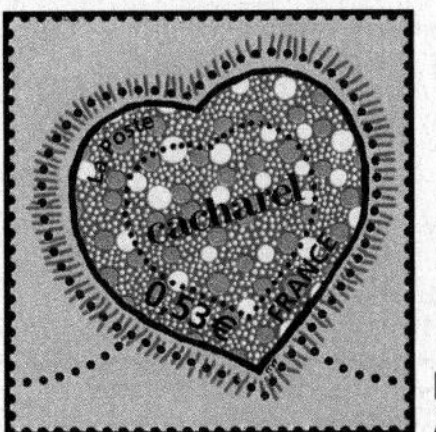

Rabbi Shlomo Yitshaqi (Rashi) (1040-1105) — A1714

2005, Jan. 16 **Engr.** ***Perf. 13¼***

3088 A1714 50c multi 1.75 .30

Hearts A1715

Designs: 53c, Polka dots. 82c, Bird and flowers.

2005, Jan. 29 **Photo.** ***Perf. 13¼***

3089 A1715 53c multi 1.50 .30
a. Souvenir sheet of 5 7.50 7.50
b. Litho, stamp + label 6.00 6.00
3090 A1715 82c multi 2.50 1.00
a. Litho, stamp + label 6.00 6.00

Values are for stamps with surrounding selvage.

Sheets of 10 of No. 3089b sold for €6.86, and sheets of 10 of No. 3090a sold for €8.78. Labels could be personalized for an additional fee.

See Nos. 3134, 3136.

New Year 2005 (Year of the Rooster) A1716

Photo. & Embossed

2005, Jan. 29 ***Perf. 13½x13***

3091 A1716 (50c) multi 1.75 .30

Printed in sheets of 10. See No. 4969a.

Rotary International, Cent. — A1717

2005, Feb. 19 **Photo.** ***Perf. 13¼***

3092 A1717 53c multi 1.50 .30

See No. 3227A.

Titeuf — A1718

Nadia — A1719

Manu — A1720

2005, Feb. 28 **Photo.** ***Perf. 13¼***

3093 A1718 (50c) red & multi 1.50 .30
a. Perf. 13¼x13 (booklet stamp) 1.50 .30

Booklet Stamps

3094 A1719 (45c) green & multi 3.00 .60
3095 A1720 (90c) blue & multi 2.50 1.00
a. Booklet pane, 2 #3094, 4 each #3093a, 3095 22.00 —
Complete booklet, #3095a 23.00

Characters from Titeuf, comic strip by Zep. Stamp Day.

Greetings Type of 2004 Inscribed "Lettre 20g"

Designs: Nos. 3096, 3097A, "Ceci est une invitation." Nos. 3097, 3097B, "Un grand merci."

No. 3097C, "Ceci est une invitation." No. 3097D, "Un grand merci."

2005-06 **Photo.** ***Perf. 13***

Holes Punched Through Dots of "i's"

3096 A1667 (53c) brt lil rose & yel 2.00 .30
3097 A1667 (53c) brt yel grn & red lil 2.00 .30

Litho.

No Holes Punched Through Dots of "i's"

Stamp + Label

3097A A1667 (53c) brt lil rose & yel 5.00
3097B A1667 (53c) brt yel grn & red lil 5.00

Self-Adhesive

No Holes Punched Through Dots of "i's"

Serpentine Die Cut 11¼x11

Stamp + Label

3097C A1667 (53c) brt lil rose & yel 5.00 5.00
3097D A1667 (53c) brt yel grn & rrd lil 5.00 5.00

Nos. 3097A-3097B were issued in sheets of 10 stamps + 10 labels that sold for €8 on day of issue. The labels could be personalized.

Nos. 3097C-3097D were each issued in sheets of 10 stamps + 10 labels that sold for €8.61. Labels could be personalized.

Issued: Nos. 2096-3097B, 3/1/05. Nos. 3097C-3097D, 2006.

Art Series

The Guitarist, by Jean-Baptiste Greuze (1725-1805) — A1721

White Bear, Sculpture by François Pompon — A1722

Sicile, by Nicolas de Stael — A1723

2005 Photo. *Perf. 13x13¼*

3098 A1721 82c multi 2.50 .50
3099 A1722 90c multi 3.00 1.25
3100 A1723 €1.22 multi 3.75 1.25

Issued: €1.22, 3/5. 90c, 7/2. 82c, 9/24.

Orchids — A1725

Designs: No. 3102, Cypripedium calceolus. No. 3103, Paphiopedilum Mabel Sanders. 55c, Oncidium papilio. 82c, Paphinia cristata, horiz.

2005, Mar. 11 Photo. *Perf. 13¼*

3102 A1725 53c multi 1.60 .30
3103 A1725 53c multi 1.60 .30
3104 A1725 55c multi 1.60 .30
3105 A1725 82c multi 2.50 .60
a. Souvenir sheet, #3102-3105 7.50 7.50
Nos. 3102-3105 (4) 7.30 1.50

Aspects of Life in French Regions Type of 2003

No. 3106: a, Nautical jousting. b, Clocks of Franche-Comte, vert. c, Cantal cheese and bread, vert. d, Dancers and accordion player. e, Bouillabaisse. f, P'tit Quinquin statue, vert. g, Rillettes (chopped pork). h, Sauerkraut and sausage, beer stein. i, Pelota, vert. j, Sugar cane, vert.

2005, Mar. 19 Photo. *Perf. 13*

3106 Sheet of 10 16.00 16.00
a.-j. A1642 53c Any single 1.50 1.25

No. 3106 has three vertical rows of rouletting, separating sheet into quarters.

Each stamp exists in a booklet pane of 1 from a booklet that sold for €19. Value $50.

Tourism Issue

Aix-en-Provence — A1726

Gulf of Morbihan — A1727

Villefranche-sur-Mer — A1728

La Roque-Gageac — A1729

2005 Engr. *Perf. 13¼, 13 (#3108)*

3107 A1726 53c multi 1.60 .30

Photo.

3108 A1727 53c multi 1.60 .30
3109 A1728 53c multi 1.60 .30

Engr.

3110 A1729 53c multi 1.60 .30

Issued: No. 3107, 4/1; No. 3108, 5/5; No. 3109, 6/4; No. 3110, 7/23.

Happy Birthday A1730

2005, Apr. 2 Photo. *Perf. 13*

3111 A1730 (53c) multi 2.00 .30
a. Souvenir sheet of 5 10.00 9.00
b. Litho., stamp + label 8.00 8.00

Litho.

Serpentine Die Cut 11

Self-Adhesive

3111C A1730 (53c) multi + label — —

Sheets of 10 and 10 labels of No. 3111b and 3111C each sold for €6.86. Labels could be personalized for an additional fee.

Albert Einstein (1879-1955), Physicist — A1731

2005, Apr. 16 *Perf. 13¼*

3112 A1731 53c multi 1.60 .30

Alexis de Tocqueville (1805-59), Writer — A1732

2005, Apr. 23 Engr. *Perf. 13x13¼*

3113 A1732 90c multi 2.75 1.00

Liberation of Concentration Camp Internees, 60th Anniv. — A1733

2005, Apr. 24 Photo. *Perf. 13¼*

3114 A1733 53c multi 1.60 .30

Battle of Austerlitz, Bicent. A1734

Litho. & Engr.

2005, May 4 *Perf. 13¼*

3115 A1734 55c multi 1.60 .45

See Czech Republic No. 3273.

French Federation of Philatelic Associations, 78th Congress, Nancy — A1735

2005, May 5 Engr. *Perf. 13*

3116 A1735 53c multi + label 1.60 .30

A souvenir sheet of one stamp without label exists. Value $12.

Europa — A1736

2005, May 8 Photo. *Perf. 13¼*

3117 A1736 53c multi 1.60 .30

Gardens and Parks Type of 2003

Souvenir Sheet

No. 3118 — Sculptures in Jardin de la Fontaine, Nimes: a, Denomination in green. b, Denomination in white.

2005, May 15 *Perf. 13¼x13*

3118 Sheet of 2 12.00 12.00
a.-b. A1660 €1.98 Either single 6.00 6.00

Salon du Timbre 2005. No. 3118 has four vertical rows of rouletting, separating sheet into fifths, with the two stamps in the central fifth.

Vacation A1737

Serpentine Die Cut 11

2005, May 23 Litho.

Booklet Stamp

Self-Adhesive

3119 A1737 (53c) multi 2.00 .25
a. Booklet pane of 10 20.00

Stories by Jules Verne (1828-1905) A1738

Designs: No. 3120, Five Weeks in a Balloon (Cinq Semaines en Ballon). No. 3121, From the Earth to the Moon (De la Terre à la Lune). No. 3122, Journey to the Center of the Earth (Voyage au Centre de la Terre), horiz. No. 3123, Michael Strogoff, horiz. No. 3124, Around the World in Eighty Days (Le Tour du Monde en Quatre-vingts Jours). No. 3125, 20,000 Leagues Under the Sea (Vingt Mille Lieues Sous les Mers).

2005, May 28 Photo. *Perf. 13*

3120 A1738 53c multi 1.60 .75
3121 A1738 53c multi 1.60 .75
3122 A1738 53c multi 1.60 .75
3123 A1738 53c multi 1.60 .75
3124 A1738 53c multi 1.60 .75
3125 A1738 53c multi 1.60 .75
a. Souvenir sheet, #3120-3125 12.00 12.00
Nos. 3120-3125 (6) 9.60 4.50

No. 3125a sold for €4.80 with the Red Cross receiving €1.62 of that.

Miniature Sheet

Gordon Bennett Cup, Cent. — A1739

No. 3126 — Inscriptions: a, La Coupe Gordon Bennett (Car No. 1 facing right). b, La Coupe Gordon Bennett (Car No. 1 facing left). c, La Formule 1, vert. d, Le Rallye-Raid, vert. e, Les Rallyes. f, La Course d'endurance.

2005, June 2 Photo. *Perf.*

3126 A1739 Sheet of 10, #a-b, 2 each #c-f 19.00 19.00
a.-f. 53c Any single 1.75 .85

A souvenir sheet containing No. 3126a sold for €3. Value $100.

Environmental Charter — A1740

2005, June 5 Litho. *Perf. 13*

3127 A1740 53c multi, *lt green* 1.60 .30

Enactment of Handicapped Persons Rights Law — A1741

2005, June 18 Photo. *Perf. 13¼*
3128 A1741 53c multi 1.60 .30

It's a Boy A1742

It's a Girl A1743

2005 Litho. *Perf. 13x13¼*
3129 A1742 (53c) multi + label 5.00 5.00
3130 A1743 (53c) multi + label 5.00 5.00

Booklet Stamps
Self-Adhesive
Serpentine Die Cut 11¼x11

3131 A1742 (53c) multi 2.00 .30
a. Booklet pane of 10 20.00
b. Sheet of 10 + 10 labels 50.00
3132 A1743 (53c) multi 2.00 .30
a. Booklet pane of 10 20.00
b. Sheet of 10 + 10 labels 50.00

Sheets of 10 stamps and 10 labels of Nos. 3129 and 3130 each sold for €6.86. Nos. 3131b and 3132b each sold for €8.61. Labels could be personalized for an additional fee.

Hearts Types of 2004-05
Serpentine Die Cut
2005, July 15 Photo.
Self-Adhesive

3133 A1670 50c Like #2997 4.00 2.50
3134 A1715 53c Like #3089 4.00 3.00
3135 A1670 75c Like #2998 6.00 3.50
3136 A1715 82c Like #3090 6.00 4.00
Nos. 3133-3136 (4) 20.00 13.00

Haras du Pin Natl. Stud Farm A1744

2005, July 16 *Perf. 13*
3137 A1744 53c multi 1.60 .30

European Capitals Type of 2002

No. 3138 — Attractions in Berlin: a, Brandenburg Gate. b, Kaiser Wilhelm Memorial Church, vert. c, Philharmonic Hall. d, Reichstag.

Perf. 13x13¼, 13¼x13
2005, Aug. 27 Photo.
3138 A1622 Sheet of 4 7.00 7.00
a.-d. 53c Any single 1.75 1.00

Aspects of Life in the French Regions Type of 2003

No. 3139: a, Lake Annecy. b, Etretat Cliffs, vert. c, Pigeon house, vert. d, Wash house (lavoir). e, Banks of the Seine. f, Carnac megaliths. g, House, Sologne. h, Pilat Sand Dune. i, Stiff Lighthouse, vert. j, Stone hut (borie), vert.

2005, Sept. 17 *Perf. 13*
3139 Sheet of 10 17.00 17.00
a.-j. A1642 53c Any single 1.60 1.25

No. 3139 has three vertical rows of rouletting, separating sheet into quarters.

Nos. 3139a-3139j were also issued in large booklets containing panes of 1 of each stamp. The booklet sold for €19. Value $60.

Art Series

Les Halles Centrales, Designed by Victor Baltard (1805-74) — A1745

2005, Sept. 17 Engr. *Perf. 13x13¼*
3140 A1745 €1.22 multi 3.75 1.10

Breast Cancer Awareness A1746

2005, Oct. 1 Photo. *Perf. 13¼*
3141 A1746 53c multi 1.60 .30

A1747

A1748

A1749

A1750

A1751

A1752

A1753

A1754

A1755

Cat, Comics by Philippe Geluck A1756

Serpentine Die Cut 11¼x11
2005, Oct. 1 Litho.
Booklet Stamps
Self-Adhesive

3142 A1747 (53c) multi 2.00 .30
3143 A1748 (53c) multi 2.00 .30
3144 A1749 (53c) multi 2.00 .30
3145 A1750 (53c) multi 2.00 .30
3146 A1751 (53c) multi 2.00 .30
3147 A1752 (53c) multi 2.00 .30
3148 A1753 (53c) multi 2.00 .30
3149 A1754 (53c) multi 2.00 .30
3150 A1755 (53c) multi 2.00 .30
3151 A1756 (53c) multi 2.00 .30
a. Booklet pane of 10, #3142-3151 20.00

Raymond Aron (1905-83), Philosopher A1757

2005, Oct. 7 Engr. *Perf. 13¼x13*
3152 A1757 53c multi 1.60 .30

Souvenir Sheet

The Annunciation, by Raphael — A1758

No. 3153: a, Drawing of Angel, painting of Virgin Mary. b, Painting of Angel, drawing of Virgin Mary.

Litho. & Engr.
2005, Nov. 10 *Perf. 13x13¼*
3153 A1758 Sheet of 2 4.00 4.00
a. 53c multi 1.60 1.60
b. 55c multi 1.75 1.75

See Vatican City Nos. 1312-1314.

Marianne — A1759

Serpentine Die Cut 6¾ Vert.
2005, Nov. 11 Engr.
Booklet Stamp
Self-Adhesive

3154 A1759 53c red 3.50 3.00
a. Booklet pane, 5 each #3083, 3154 25.00

See No. 4911.

Video Game Characters — A1760

No. 3155: a, Link. b, Pac-Man. c, Prince of Persia. d, Spyro. e, Donkey Kong. f, Mario. g, Adibou. h, Rayman. i, Lara Croft. j, The Sims.

2005, Nov. 11 Photo. *Perf. 13¼x13*
3155 A1760 Sheet of 10 9.00 9.00
a.-e. 20c Any single .60 .50
f.-j. 33c Any single 1.00 .75

Avicenna (980-1037), Scientist — A1761

2005, Nov. 12 Engr. *Perf. 13x13¼*
3156 A1761 53c multi 1.60 .30

Holiday Greetings A1762

Designs: Nos. 3157, 3162, Bear, three penguins and sled. Nos. 3158, 3163, Two penguins, reindeer and sled. Nos. 3159, 3164, Two penguins, bear and sled. Nos. 3160, 3165, Three penguins. Nos. 3161, 3166, Two penguins, reindeer and snowman.

2005, Nov. 12 Litho. *Perf. 13*
3157 A1762 (53c) multi + label 6.00 4.00
3158 A1762 (53c) multi + label 6.00 4.00
3159 A1762 (53c) multi + label 6.00 4.00
3160 A1762 (53c) multi + label 6.00 4.00
3161 A1762 (53c) multi + label 6.00 4.00
a. Vert. strip of 5, #3157-3161, + 5 labels *30.00 30.00*
Miniature sheet, 2 #3161a *60.00 60.00*

Booklet Stamps
Self-Adhesive
Serpentine Die Cut 11¼x11

3162 A1762 (53c) multi 2.00 .30
3163 A1762 (53c) multi 2.00 .30
3164 A1762 (53c) multi 2.00 .30
3165 A1762 (53c) multi 2.00 .30
3166 A1762 (53c) multi 2.00 .30
a. Booklet pane, 2 each #3162-3166 16.00
Nos. 3157-3166 (10) 40.00 21.50

Miniature sheet containing Nos. 3157-3161 sold for €6.86. Labels could be personalized.

No. 3161 exists in a souvenir sheet of one stamp without label, that sold for €3. Value $30.

Jacob Kaplan (1895-1994), Grand Rabbi of France — A1763

2005, Nov. 14 Engr. *Perf. 13*
3167 A1763 53c multi 1.60 .30

Orchid Type of 2002

Design: Orchis insularis.

2005 Litho. *Perf. 13*
3168 A1584 42c multi 2.50 .75

No. 3168 is known only precanceled. See second note after No. 132.

Law Separating Church and State, Cent. — A1764

2005, Dec. 3 Photo. *Perf. 13¼x13*
3169 A1764 53c multi 1.60 .30

Hearts A1765

Designs: (53c), Hearts, octagons and diamonds. (82c), Heart and stripes.

2006, Jan. 7 Photo. *Perf. 13¼*
3170 A1765 (53c) multi 1.60 .30
a. Souvenir sheet of 5 10.00 8.00
b. Litho., stamp + label 5.00 5.00
3171 A1765 (82c) multi 3.00 1.00
a. Litho., stamp + label 12.00 12.00

Self-Adhesive
Serpentine Die Cut

3172 A1765 (53c) Like #3170 4.00 3.00
a. Sheet of 10 + 10 labels 40.00
3173 A1765 (82c) Like #3171 6.00 4.50
a. Sheet of 10 + 10 labels 60.00

Values are for stamps with surrounding selvage. Sheets of 10 of No. 3170b sold for €6.86, and sheets of No. 3172a. No. 3172a sold for €8.61; No. 3173a for €11.54. Labels could be personalized for an additional fee.

New Year 2006 (Year of the Dog) — A1766

2006, Jan. 21 Photo. *Perf. 13¼x13*
3174 A1766 (53c) multi 1.60 .30

A souvenir sheet containing No. 3174 sold for €3. Value $8.
See No. 4969b.

Impressionist Paintings — A1767

Designs: Nos. 3175a, 3176, Portraits from the Country, by Gustave Caillebotte. Nos. 3175b, 3183, Dancers, by Edgar Degas. Nos. 3175c, 3181, Marguerite Gachet in the Garden, by Vincent van Gogh. Nos. 3175d, 3179, Two Young Girls at the Piano, by Auguste Renoir. Nos. 3175e, 3177, The Butterfly Hunt, by Berthe Morisot. Nos. 3175f, 3184, Luncheon on the Grass, by Edouard Manet. Nos. 3175g, 3182, Evening Air, by Henri-Edmond Cross. Nos. 3175h, 3180, The Shepherdess (Young Peasant Girl with a Stick), by Camille Pissarro. Nos. 3175i, 3178, Mother and Child, by Mary Cassatt. Nos. 3175j, 3185, Women of Tahiti on the Beach, by Paul Gauguin.

2006 Litho. *Perf. 13¼*
3175 Sheet of 10 +10 labels 60.00 60.00
a.-j. A1767 (53c) Any single + label 5.00 5.00

Booklet Stamps
Self-Adhesive
Serpentine Die Cut 11¼x11

3176 A1767 (53c) multi 2.00 .30
3177 A1767 (53c) multi 2.00 .30
3178 A1767 (53c) multi 2.00 .30
3179 A1767 (53c) multi 2.00 .30
3180 A1767 (53c) multi 2.00 .30
3181 A1767 (53c) multi 2.00 .30
3182 A1767 (53c) multi 2.00 .30
3183 A1767 (53c) multi 2.00 .30
3184 A1767 (53c) multi 2.00 .30
3185 A1767 (53c) multi 2.00 .30
a. Booklet pane of 10, #3176-3185 20.00
b. Sheet of 10, #3176-3185, + 10 labels *110.00*

Issued: No. 3175, 6/1; Nos. 3176-3185, 1/21. No. 3175 sold for €6.86. No. 3185b sold for €8.61. Labels could be personalized.

2006 Winter Olympics, Turin — A1768

2006, Feb. 4 Photo. *Perf. 13*
3186 A1768 53c multi 1.60 .30

Spirou — A1769

Fantasio, Spip and Spirou — A1770

Fantasio A1771

2006, Feb. 25 *Perf. 13¼*
3187 A1769 (53c) multi 2.00 .30
a. Perf. 13¼x13 (booklet stamp) 1.25 .30

Booklet Stamps
Perf. 13¼x13

3188 A1770 (48c) multi 2.50 1.00
3189 A1771 (90c) multi 3.00 .75
a. Booklet pane, 4 each #3187a, 3188, 2 #3189 23.00 —
Complete booklet, #3189a 24.00

Characters from Spirou, by Robert Velter. Stamp Day.

Courrières Coal Mine Disaster, Cent. — A1772

2006, Feb. 25 *Perf. 13¼*
3190 A1772 53c multi 1.60 .30

Douaumont Ossuary — A1773

2006, Mar. 4 Engr.
3191 A1773 53c multi 1.60 .30

Aspects of Life in the French Regions Type of 2003

No. 3192: a, Yellow plums (mirabelle). b, Salt marsh (marais salants). c, Butter (beurre). d, Roquefort cheese, vert. e, Olive oil, vert. f, Carnival, vert. g, Grape harvests (vendanges), vert. h, Waiter at café, vert. i, Transhumance of livestock. j, Marshland gardens (hortillonages).

2006, Mar. 25 Photo. *Perf. 13*
3192 Sheet of 10 16.00 16.00
a.-j. A1642 53c Any single 1.60 1.25

No. 3192 has three vertical rows of rouletting, separating sheet into quarters.
Nos. 3192a-3192j were also issued in large booklets containing panes of 1 of each stamp. The booklet sold for €19. Value $35.

Tourism Issue

Yvoire A1774

Dijon A1775

Antibes Juan-les-Pins — A1776

Thionville A1777

2006 Photo. *Perf. 13*
3193 A1774 53c multi 1.60 .30

Engr.
Perf. 13¼
3194 A1775 53c multi 1.60 .30

Litho. & Engr.
Perf. 13x13¼
3195 A1776 53c multi 1.60 .30

Engraved
3196 A1777 54c multi 1.60 .40
Nos. 3193-3196 (4) 6.40 1.30

Issued: No. 3193, 3/25; No. 3194, 4/7. No. 3195, 7/15. No. 3196, 9/16.

Art Series

Prehistoric Drawings in Rouffignac Cave — A1778

Bathers, by Paul Cézanne — A1779

Untitled Painting by Claude Viallat A1780

Beggars Receiving Alms at the Door of a House, by Rembrandt A1781

Engr., Photo (#3198, 3199)

2006 *Perf. 13x13¼*

3197 A1778 55c multi 2.25 .75
3198 A1779 82c multi 2.50 1.00

Perf. 13¼x13

3199 A1780 €1.22 brt pink & bl grn 3.75 1.25
3200 A1781 €1.30 multi 4.75 1.25
Nos. 3197-3200 (4) 13.25 4.25

Issued: 82c, 4/8; 55c, 5/27; No. 3199, 6/3. No. 3200, 11/10.

Gardens and Parks Type of 2003

Souvenir Sheet

No. 3201: a, Vallée-aux-Loups Park. b, Albert Kahn Gardens.

2006, Apr. 22 Photo. *Perf. 13¼x13*

3201 Sheet of 2 13.00 13.00
a.-b. A1660 €1.98 Either single 6.00 5.00
c. Souvenir sheet, #3118a, 3118b, 3201a, 3201b 50.00 50.00

Salon du Timbre 2006. No. 3201 has four vertical rows of rouletting, separating sheet into fifths, with the two stamps in the central fifth.

No. 3201c issued 6/16.

Young Animals A1782

Designs: No. 3202, Puppy. No. 3203, Kitten. 55c, Foal, horiz. 82c, Lamb, horiz..

2006, Apr. 22 *Perf. 13¼*

3202 A1782 53c multi 1.60 .30
3203 A1782 53c multi 1.60 .30
3204 A1782 55c multi 1.60 .30
3205 A1782 82c multi 2.40 .75
a. Souvenir sheet, #3202-3205 7.50 7.50
Nos. 3202-3205 (4) 7.20 1.65

Europa A1783

2006, Apr. 30

3206 A1783 53c multi 1.60 .30

Pierre Bayle (1647-1706), Philiosopher A1784

2006, May 2 Engr. *Perf. 13x13¼*

3207 A1784 53c blk & brn 1.60 .30

Remembrance of Slavery Day, 5th Anniv. — A1785

2006, May 10 Photo. *Perf. 13¼*

3208 A1785 53c multi 1.60 .30

Vacation A1786

Serpentine Die Cut 11¼x11

2006, May 27 Litho.

Booklet Stamp

Self-Adhesive

3209 A1786 (53c) multi 2.00 .25
a. Booklet pane of 10 20.00

Miniature Sheet

2006 World Cup Soccer Championships, Germany — A1787

No. 3210: a, Replacement players (39x25mm). b, Fans (39x25mm). c, Player with ball near chest (32mm diameter). d, Player kicking ball (32mm diameter). e, Goalie throwing ball (32mm diameter). f, Player making scissor kick (32mm diameter). g, Two players (32mm diameter). h, Referee (25x39mm). i, Coach (39x25mm). j, Cameramen (39x25mm).

2006, May 27 Photo. *Perf. 12¾*

3210 A1787 Sheet of 10 16.00 16.00
a.-j. 53c Any single 1.60 1.25

Marianne Type of 2005

2006 Litho. *Perf. 13*

3211 Sheet of 15, #a-k, 2 each #l-m, + 15 labels 70.00 70.00
a. A1713 1c yellow orange .35 .35
b. A1713 5c dark brown .35 .35
c. A1713 10c violet .55 .55
d. A1713 55c blue 2.75 2.75
e. A1713 64c olive green 3.25 3.25
f. A1713 75c light blue 3.50 3.50
g. A1713 82c fawn 4.25 4.25
h. A1713 90c dark blue 4.50 4.50
i. A1713 €1 dull orange 5.00 5.00
j. A1713 €1.22 red violet 6.00 6.00
k. A1713 €1.98 brown 9.50 9.50
l. A1713 (48c) green 2.50 2.50
m. A1713 (53c) red 2.60 2.60

Serpentine Die Cut 11¼

Self-Adhesive

3211N Sheet of 15, #3211No-3211Ny, 2 each #3211Nz, 3211Naa, + 15 labels *250.00*
o. A1713 1c yellow orange .75 .75
p. A1713 5c dark brown .75 .75
q. A1713 10c violet 1.25 1.25
r. A1713 55c blue 6.75 6.75
s. A1713 64c olive green 7.50 7.50
t. A1713 75c light blue 8.75 8.75
u. A1713 82c fawn 9.50 9.50
v. A1713 90c dark blue 11.00 11.00
w. A1713 €1 dull orange 12.00 12.00
x. A1713 €1.22 red violet 15.00 15.00
y. A1713 €1.98 brown 20.00 20.00
z. A1713 (48c) green 5.50 5.50
aa. A1713 (53c) red 6.25 6.25

Etched on Foil

Die Cut Perf. 13

3212 A1713 €5 *silver* 17.50 12.50

Nos. 3211a-3211m, 3211No-3211Naa and 3212 have "Phil@poste" inscription at bottom. Nos. 3211 and 3211N have stamps with a glossy varnish. No. 3211 sold for €12.04 and labels could be personalized. No. 3211N sold for €15.05 and labels could be personalized. No. 3212 was sold in a protective package.

Costumes From Operas by Wolfgang Amadeus Mozart — A1788

Designs: No. 3213, The Magic Flute. No. 3214, Don Giovanni. No. 3215, The Marriage of Figaro. No. 3216, The Clemency of Titus. No. 3217, The Abduction from the Seraglio (L'enlèvement au Sérail). No. 3218, Cosi Fan Tutte.

2006, June 17 Photo. *Perf. 13*

3213 A1788 53c multi 1.60 .75
3214 A1788 53c multi 1.60 .75
3215 A1788 53c multi 1.60 .75
3216 A1788 53c multi 1.60 .75
3217 A1788 53c multi 1.60 .75
3218 A1788 53c multi 1.60 .75
a. Souvenir sheet, #3213-3218 12.00 12.00
Nos. 3213-3218 (6) 9.60 4.50

Nos. 3213-3218 were each printed in souvenir sheets containing one stamp that sold as a set for €15, and in booklet panes containing one stamp in a large book that sold for €19. Value: set of 6 sheets $40; set of 6 panes in book $50. No. 3218a sold for €4.80, with the Red Cross receiving €1.62 of that.

UNESCO World Heritage Sites A1789

Designs: 53c, Provins. 90c, Mont Saint-Michel.

2006, June 17 Photo. *Perf. 13¼*

3219 A1789 53c multi 1.60 .30
3220 A1789 90c multi 2.75 1.20

See United Nations Offices in Geneva Nos. 459-461.

Garnier Opera House, Paris — A1790

2006, June 18 Engr. *Perf. 13x13¼*

3221 A1790 53c multi + label 1.60 .40

French Federation of Philatelic Associations 79th Congress, Paris. No. 3221 exists in a souvenir sheet of 1 (without label), issued in 2007 that sold for €3. Value, $12.

Happy Birthday A1791

2006, June 19 Photo. *Perf. 13*

3222 A1791 (53c) multi 2.00 .30
a. Souvenir sheet of 5 10.00 10.00
b. Litho. stamp + label 6.00 6.00

Serpentine Die Cut 11

Self-Adhesive

3222C A1791 (53c) multi + label 15.00 15.00

Sheets of 10 of No. 3222b sold for €6.86. No. 3222C was printed in sheets of 10 stamps + 10 labels that sold for €8.61. Labels could be personalized for an additional fee.

European Capitals Type of 2002

Souvenir Sheet

No. 3223 — Attractions in Nicosia, Cyprus: a, Chrysaliniotissa Church. b, Archaeological Museum. c, Famagusta Gate. d, Archbishop's residence (Archevеché).

2006, June 20 Photo. *Perf. 13x13¼*

3223 A1622 Sheet of 4 7.00 7.00
a.-d. 53c Any single 1.60 1.00

Tango Dancing A1792

2006, June 21 Photo. *Perf. 12¼*

3224 A1792 53c Dancers 1.60 .30
3225 A1792 90c Musician 2.75 1.20

See Argentina Nos. 2395-2396.

La Poste's Business Foundation, 10th Anniv. — A1793

2006, June 22 Litho. *Perf. 13*

3226 A1793 (53c) multi, *tan* 2.00 .30

French Open Golf Championship, Cent. — A1794

Photo. & Embossed

2006, June 24 *Perf. 13*

3227 A1794 53c multi 1.60 .30

A souvenir sheet containing No. 3227 sold for €3. Value $8.

Rotary International Type of 2005

Serpentine Die Cut 11

2006, July 1 Photo.

Self-Adhesive

3227A A1717 53c multi 5.00 4.00

French Soccer Team's Second-Place Showing in 2006 World Cup — A1795

2006, July 5 Photo. *Perf. 13¼*

Size: 35x26mm

3228 A1795 53c multi 1.60 .40

Litho.

Size: 35x22mm

Perf. 13

3229 A1795 53c multi + label 5.00 4.00

Serpentine Die Cut 11¼x11

Self-Adhesive

3229A A1795 53c multi + label 13.00 13.00

No. 3229 was printed in sheets of 10 stamps and 10 labels that sold for €6.94. Value $55. No. 3229A was printed in sheets of 10 stamps + 10 labels that sold for €8.61. Value $150. Labels could be personalized.

Quai Branly Museum — A1796

2006, July 8 Photo. *Perf. 13x13¼*

3230 A1796 53c multi 1.60 .40

Reinstatement of Capt. Alfred Dreyfus, Cent. — A1797

2006, July 12 Engr.

3231 A1797 53c multi 1.60 .30

Claude-Joseph Rouget de Lisle (1760-1836), Composer of "La Marseillaise" — A1798

2006, July 13 Photo. *Perf. 13¼*

3232 A1798 53c multi 1.60 .30

Pablo Casals (1876-1973), Cellist — A1799

2006, July 29

3233 A1799 53c multi 1.60 .30

Aspects of Life in French Regions Type of 2003

No. 3234: a, Catalan Towers. b, La Croisette, Cannes. c, Brocéliande Forest. d, Volcanic craters, Auvergne, vert. e, Les Invalides, Paris, vert. f, Chateau de Chaumont, Chaumont-sur-Loire. g, Ardèche Gorges, vert. h, Flour mill, Valmy, vert. i, Grotto of Messabielle, Lourdes. j, Calanches de Piana, Corsica.

2006, Sept. 2 Photo. *Perf. 13*

3234 Sheet of 10 16.00 16.00
a.-j. A1642 54c Any single 1.60 1.25

No. 3234 has three vertical rows of rouletting, separating sheet into quarters.

Nos. 3234a-3234j were also issued in large booklets containing panes of 1 of each stamp. The booklet sold for €19. Value $35.

A1800

A1801

A1802

A1803

A1804

A1805

A1806

A1807

A1808

Cubitus, Comics by Michel Rodrigue and Pierre Aucaigne A1809

Serpentine Die Cut 11¼x11

2006, Sept. 20 Litho.

Self-Adhesive

Booklet Stamps

3235	A1800	(54c) multi	2.00	.30
3236	A1801	(54c) multi	2.00	.30
3237	A1802	(54c) multi	2.00	.30
3238	A1803	(54c) multi	2.00	.30
3239	A1804	(54c) multi	2.00	.30
3240	A1805	(54c) multi	2.00	.30
3241	A1806	(54c) multi	2.00	.30
3242	A1807	(54c) multi	2.00	.30
3243	A1808	(54c) multi	2.00	.30
3244	A1809	(54c) multi	2.00	.30
a.		Booklet pane of 10, #3235-3244	20.00	

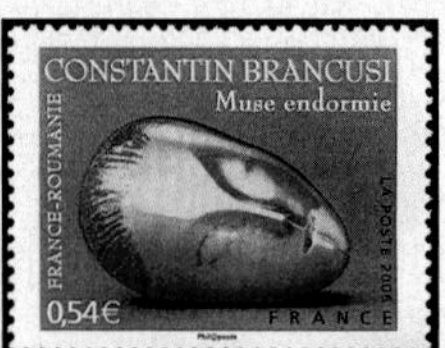

Sculptures by Constantin Brancusi (1876-1957) — A1810

Designs: 54c, Sleeping Muse. 85c, Sleep.

2006, Sept. 25 Photo. *Perf. 13¼*

3245 A1810 54c multi 1.60 .30
3246 A1810 85c multi 2.75 .90

See Romania Nos. 4878-4879.

Marianne Type of 2005

2006 Engr. *Perf. 13*

Inscribed "Phil@poste" at Bottom

3247	A1713	10c gray	.30	.25
3248	A1713	60c dark blue	1.75	.40
3249	A1713	70c yel green	2.10	.40
3250	A1713	85c purple	2.75	.50
3251	A1713	86c fawn	2.75	.50
3252	A1713	€1.15 blue	3.50	.75
3253	A1713	€1.30 red violet	4.00	1.00
3254	A1713	€2.11 chocolate	6.25	.50
		Nos. 3247-3254 (8)	23.40	4.30

Coil Stamp

Perf. 13 Horiz.

3255 A1713 60c dark blue 2.00 .75

Serpentine Die Cut 11¼

Self-Adhesive

3255A A1713 (54c) red + label 12.00 12.00
f. Inscribed "ITVF" at bottom + label — —

Inscribed "Phila@poste" at Bottom

3255B	A1713	55c dk blue + label	—	—
3255C	A1713	60c dark blue + label	13.00	13.00
3255D	A1713	82c fawn + label	15.00	15.00
3255E	A1713	86c fawn + label	13.00	13.00
		Nos. 3255A-3255E (4)	53.00	53.00

Issued: Nos. 3247-3255, 10/1, others, 2006. Nos. 3255A, 3255Af, 3255C and 3255E were printed in sheets of 15 stamps + 15 labels that could be personalized. Nos. 3255B and 3255D were printed in sheets containing 10 stamps + 10 large labels or 15 stamps and 15 small labels. Labels could be personalized. Sheets of Nos. 3255A and 3255Af each sold for €13.29; No. 3255C, €14.04; No. 3255E, €17.31. For Nos. 3255A, 3255C, 3255D and 3255E, adjacent labels came in large and small sizes.

Aviation Without Borders — A1811

2006, Oct. 7 Photo. *Perf. 13*

3256 A1811 54c multi 1.60 .30

Henri Moissan (1852-1907), 1906 Nobel Chemistry Laureate — A1812

2006, Oct. 14 Engr. *Perf. 13¼x13*

3257 A1812 54c multi 1.60 .30

"Shared Memories," Intl. Conference on Veterans, Paris — A1813

2006, Oct. 26 Photo. *Perf. 13¼*

3258 A1813 54c multi 1.60 .30

Marianne — A1814

Serpentine Die Cut 6¾ Vert.

2006, Nov. 8 Engr.

Self-Adhesive

Booklet Stamp

3259 A1814 54c red 4.00 3.00
a. Booklet pane, 5 each #3083d, 3259 30.00

See No. 4910.

Miniature Sheet

Flying Machines — A1815

No. 3260: a, Gustave Ponton d'Amécourt's helicopter. b, Alberto Santos-Dumont's monoplane, "Demoiselle," horiz. c, Jean Marie Le Bris's bird-shaped glider, horiz. d, Clément Ader's "Avion III," horiz. e, Henri Fabré's seaplane, horiz. f, Jean-Pierre Blanchard's balloon.

Litho. & Engr.

2006, Nov. 9 *Perf. 13*

3260 A1815 Sheet of 6 10.00 10.00
a.-f. 54c Any single 1.60 1.40

Inauguration of Aulnay-sous-Bois to Bondy Tram-Train Line — A1816

2006, Nov. 18 Photo. *Perf. 13x13¼*

3261 A1816 54c multi 1.60 .30

Holiday Greetings A1817

Designs: No. 3262, Reindeer, sleigh, four penguins. No. 3263, Reindeer with fishing pole, three penguins. No. 3264, Reindeer, Christmas tree, two penguins. No. 3265, Reindeer skating, three penguins. No. 3266, Reindeer with gift boxes, three penguins.

2006, Nov. 25 Litho. *Perf. 13¼*

3261A	A1817	(54c) multi + label	2.00	.30
3261B	A1817	(54c) multi + label	2.00	.30
3261C	A1817	(54c) multi + label	2.00	.30
3261D	A1817	(54c) multi + label	2.00	.30
3261E	A1817	(54c) multi + label	2.00	.30
f.		Vert. strip of 5, #3261A-3261E, + 5 labels	12.00	12.00
		Miniature sheet, 2 #3261Ef	30.00	30.00

Self-Adhesive

Booklet Stamps

Serpentine Die Cut 11¼x11

3262	A1817	(54c) multi	2.00	.30
3263	A1817	(54c) multi	2.00	.30
3264	A1817	(54c) multi	2.00	.30
3265	A1817	(54c) multi	2.00	.30
3266	A1817	(54c) multi	2.00	.30
a.		Booklet pane, 2 each #3262-3266	20.00	
		Nos. 3262-3266 (5)	10.00	1.50

Miniature sheet containing Nos. 3261A-3261E sold for €6.94. Value $60. Labels could be personalized. Value $60.

A souvenir sheet containing a perf. 13 example of No. 3266 sold for €3. Value $17.50. A sheet containing 5 No. 3261A + 5 labels exists, but was not sold.

Grand Masonic Lodge of France A1818

2006, Dec. 1 Photo. *Perf. 13x13¼*
3267 A1818 54c multi 1.60 .30

Alain Poher (1909-96), Politician, and Senate Building A1819

2006, Dec. 2 Engr. *Perf. 13¼*
3268 A1819 54c multi 1.60 .30

Opening of New Paris Tramway A1820

2006, Dec. 16 Photo. *Perf. 13¼*
3269 A1820 54c multi 1.75 .30

Orchids Type of 2002

Designs: 31c, Platanthera chlorantha. 36c, Dactylorhiza savogiensis. 43c, Orchis insularis.

2007, Jan. 2 Litho. *Perf. 13*
3270 A1584 31c multi 1.50 .50
3271 A1584 36c multi 1.50 .60
3272 A1584 43c multi 2.50 .75
Nos. 3270-3272 (3) 5.50 1.85

Nos. 3270-3272 are known only precanceled. See second note after No. 132.

Hearts A1821

"Givenchy" in: (54c), Black and white. (86c), Red.

2007, Jan. 6 Photo. *Perf. 13¼*
Inscribed "Lettre 20 g"
3273 A1821 (54c) red & black 2.00 .30
a. Souvenir sheet of 5 10.00 10.00

Inscribed "Lettre 50 g"
3274 A1821 (86c) black & red 3.00 1.00

Values are for stamps with surrounding selvage.

Serpentine Die Cut
Self-Adhesive
3275 A1821 (54c) Like #3273 16.00 13.00

Inscribed "Lettre 50 g"
3276 A1821 (86c) Like #3274 16.00 13.00

New Year 2007 (Year of the Pig) — A1822

2007, Jan. 27 Photo. *Perf. 13¼x13*
3277 A1822 (54c) multi 2.00 .30
a. Litho., stamp + label 8.00 8.00

Serpentine Die Cut 11
Self-Adhesive
3277B A1822 (54c) multi + label 15.00 15.00

No. 3277 has a somewhat blurrier image than No. 3277a. Sheets of 5 #3277a + 5 labels sold for €3.51. Value $15. Labels could be personalized. No. 3277 exists in a souvenir sheet of 1 that sold for €3. Value $12.

No. 3277B was printed in sheets of 10 + 10 labels that sold for €8.86. Value $150. Labels could be personalized.

See No. 4969c.

Egyptian Hippopotamus Figurine — A1823

Head of Aphrodite A1824

Winged Victory of Samothrace A1825

Fresco, Pompeii A1826

King Amenemhet III of Egypt A1827

Statue of Juno A1828

Egyptian Harpist A1829

Etruscan Sarcophagus of Husband and Wife — A1830

Egyptian Statue of Seated Scribe A1831

Head of Pericles A1832

Serpentine Die Cut 11¼x11
2007, Jan. 27 Litho.
Booklet Stamps
Self-Adhesive
3279 A1823 (54c) multi 2.00 .30
3280 A1824 (54c) multi 2.00 .30
3281 A1825 (54c) multi 2.00 .30
3282 A1826 (54c) multi 2.00 .30
3283 A1827 (54c) multi 2.00 .30
3284 A1828 (54c) multi 2.00 .30
3285 A1829 (54c) multi 2.00 .30
3286 A1830 (54c) multi 2.00 .30
3287 A1831 (54c) multi 2.00 .30
3288 A1832 (54c) multi 2.00 .30
a. Booklet pane of 10, #3279-3288 20.00

Tourism Issue

Valenciennes A1833

2007 Engr. *Perf. 13¼*
3289 A1833 54c red & blue 1.50 .30

Issued: No. 3289, 2/3.

Tourism Issue

Limoges A1834

2007 Engr. *Perf. 13¼*
3290 A1834 54c multi 2.25 .30

Issued: No. 3290, 3/23.

Tourism Issue

Arcachon A1835

2007, May 19 Photo. *Perf. 13¼*
3291 A1835 54c multi 2.25 .30

Tourism Issue

Castres A1836

2007, July 20 Engr. *Perf. 13¼*
3292 A1836 54c multi 1.60 .30

Tourism Issue

Firminy — A1837

2007, Sept. 15 Engr. *Perf. 13¼*
3293 A1837 54c multi 1.75 .30

Rights of France A1838

2007, Feb. 5 Photo. *Perf. 13¼*
3294 A1838 54c multi 2.00 .30

Art Issue

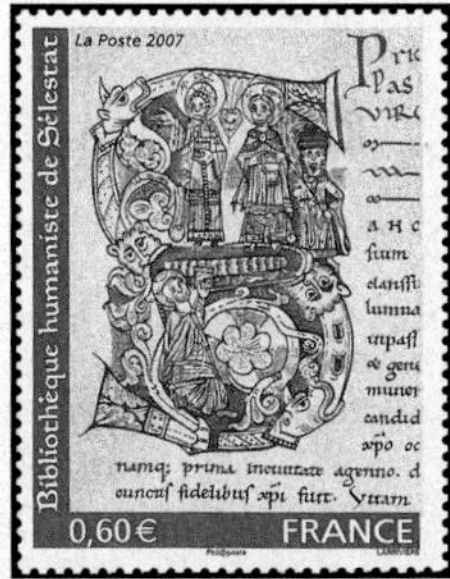

Book Illumination from Sélestat Library — A1839

Galerie des Glaces, Versailles Palace — A1840

La Barrière Fleurie, by Paul Sérusier A1841

Gallic Boar Ensign — A1842

Perf. 12¼x13, 13¼x13 (#3297), 13x13¼ (#3296, 3298)
Engraved, Photo. (#3296, 3297, 3298A)

2007-08
3295 A1839 60c multi 1.75 .60
3296 A1840 85c multi 3.50 1.00
3297 A1841 86c multi 3.00 1.00
3298 A1842 €1.30 multi 4.50 1.25
Nos. 3295-3298 (4) 12.75 3.85

Self-Adhesive
Serpentine Die Cut 11
3298A A1840 85c multi 20.00 12.00

Issued: No. 3295, 2/10. No. 3297, 10/13. No. 3298, 6/2. No. 3296, 11/10. No. 3298A, 2008.

Aspects of Life in the French Regions Type of 2003

No. 3299: a, Baux-de-Provence. b, Banks of the Loire. c, Grande-Chartreuse Massif. d, Saint-Tropez. e, Doubs Waterfall, vert. f, Fontainebleau Forest, vert. g, Chantilly Castle. h, Saint-Malo. i, Ballon d'Alsace, vert. j, Midi Canal, vert.

2007, Feb. 24 Photo. *Perf. 13*
3299 Sheet of 10 16.00 16.00
a.-j. A1642 54c Any single 1.50 1.25

No. 3299 has three vertical rows of rouletting, separating sheet into quarters.

Nos. 3299a-3299j were also issued in large booklets containing panes of 1 of each stamp. The booklet sold for €19.

Aspects of Life in French Regions Type of 2003 Inscribed "Lettre Prioritaire 20g"

Designs: Nos. 3300-3301, Arc de Triomphe, vert.

2007, Feb. Photo. *Perf. 13*
3300 A1642 (54c) multi + label 8.00 8.00

Serpentine Die Cut 11x11¼
3301 A1642 (54c) multi + label 45.00 45.00

Nos. 3300-3301 each were printed in sheets of 10 stamps + 10 different labels that sold for €6.85. Value of sheets: No. 3300, $80; No. 3301, $450.

Marianne Type of 2005

2007 Litho. *Perf. 13*
Stamps Inscribed "Phil@poste"
Without Varnish

3302 Sheet of 15, #a-k, 2 each #l-m, + 15 labels 250.00 250.00
a. A1713 1c yellow orange 1.25 1.25
b. A1713 5c brown 1.65 1.65
c. A1713 10c gray 3.00 3.00
d. A1713 60c blue 11.50 11.50
e. A1713 70c lt yellow green 13.50 13.50
f. A1713 85c purple 16.00 16.00
g. A1713 86c pink 17.00 17.00
h. A1713 €1 orange 21.00 21.00
i. A1713 €1.15 light blue 23.00 23.00
j. A1713 €1.30 red violet 25.00 25.00
k. A1713 €2.11 maroon 37.50 37.50
l. A1713 (49c) blue green 10.00 10.00
m. A1713 (54c) red 11.50 11.50

Litho.
Serpentine Die Cut 11¼
Self-Adhesive
Stamps Inscribed "Phil@poste"
Without Varnish

3302N Sheet of 15, #3302No-3302Ny, 2 each #3302Nz, 3302Naa, + 15 labels —
o. A1713 1c yellow orange — —
p. A1713 5c brown — —
q. A1713 10c gray — —
r. A1713 60c blue — —
s. A1713 70c lt yellow green — —
t. A1713 85c purple — —
u. A1713 86c pink — —
v. A1713 €1 orange — —
w. A1713 €1.15 light blue — —
x. A1713 €1.30 red violet — —
y. A1713 €2.11 maroon — —
z. A1713 (49c) blue green — —
aa. A1713 (54c) red — —

Nos. 3302 and 3302N each sold for €14.40 and have personalizable labels.

Albert Londres (1884-1932), Journalist — A1844

2007, Mar. 16 Engr. *Perf. 13x13¼*
3306 A1844 54c multi 1.60 .30

Six different souvenir sheets containing one No. 3306 exist. The set sold for €15. Value, set $45.

Audit Office, Bicent. A1845

2007 *Perf. 13¼x13*
3307 A1845 54c multi 2.00 .30

Serpentine Die Cut 11
Self-Adhesive
3307A A1845 54c multi 5.00 4.00

Issued: No. 3307, 3/17; No. 3307A, 7/20.

Treaty of Rome, 50th Anniv. A1846

2007, Mar. 23 Photo. *Perf. 13¼*
3308 A1846 54c multi 1.50 .30

Sébastaen Le Prestre de Vauban (1633-1707), Military Engineer — A1847

2007, Mar. 30 Engr.
3309 A1847 54c multi 1.50 .30

2007 Rugby World Cup A1848

2007, Apr. 14 Photo. *Perf. 13¼*
3310 A1848 54c multi 1.50 .30
a. Perf. 13x13¼ + label 5.00 5.00

Serpentine Die Cut 11¼
Self-Adhesive
3311 A1848 54c multi + label 12.50 12.50

No. 3310a was printed in sheets of 5 stamps and 5 labels that could be personalized that sold for €4.20. Value $60.

No. 3311 was printed in sheets of 10 + 10 labels that could be personalized. Sheets sold for €10.60. Value, sheet $125.

Endangered Animals in Overseas Departments A1849

Designs: No. 3312, Antillean iguana. No. 3313, Raccoon, horiz. 60c, Jaguar, horiz. 86c, Barau's petrel, horiz..

2007, Apr. 28 Photo. *Perf. 13¼*
3312 A1849 54c multi 1.50 .30
3313 A1849 54c multi 1.50 .30
3314 A1849 60c multi 1.75 .60
3315 A1849 86c multi 2.40 .60
a. Souvenir sheet, #3312-3315 7.25 7.25
Nos. 3312-3315 (4) 7.15 1.80

Gardens and Parks Type of 2003
Souvenir Sheet

No. 3316 — Parc de la Tete d'Or, Lyon: a, Red flowers. b, White flowers.

2007, Apr. 28 *Perf. 13¼x13*
3316 Sheet of 2 12.00 12.00
a.-b. A1660 €2.11 Either single 6.00 5.00

Salon du Timbre. No. 3316 has four vertical rows of rouletting, separating sheet into fifths, with the two stamps in the central fifth.

Vacations A1850

Designs: No. 3317, Wooden fence and red hollyhocks. No. 3318, Angelfish. No. 3319, Blue flowers. No. 3320, Blueberries. No. 3321, Canoes. No. 3322, Dyed wool hanging on rods. No. 3323, Glacier. No. 3324, Palm tree. No. 3325, Beach umbrellas and woman. No. 3326, Boxes of color pigments.

Serpentine Die Cut 11¼x11
2007, Apr. 28 Litho.
Booklet Stamps
Self-Adhesive

3317 A1850 (54c) multi 1.75 .30
3318 A1850 (54c) multi 1.75 .30
3319 A1850 (54c) multi 1.75 .30
3320 A1850 (54c) multi 1.75 .30
3321 A1850 (54c) multi 1.75 .30
3322 A1850 (54c) multi 1.75 .30
3323 A1850 (54c) multi 1.75 .30
3324 A1850 (54c) multi 1.75 .30
3325 A1850 (54c) multi 1.75 .30
3326 A1850 (54c) multi 1.75 .30
a. Booklet pane of 10, #3317-3326 17.50

Europa A1851

2007, May 1 Photo. *Perf. 13¼*
3327 A1851 60c multi 1.50 .40

Scouting, cent.

Intl. Sailing Federation, Cent. — A1852

2007, May 4 *Perf. 13*
3328 A1852 85c multi 2.25 .80

A souvenir sheet containing No. 3328 sold for €3. Value, $12.

Tintin and Snowy — A1853

Characters from Tintin comic strips and books, by Hergé: No. 3330, Professor Calculus (Tournesol). No. 3331, Captain Haddock. No. 3332, Thomson and Thompson (Dupondt). No. 3333, Bianca Castafiore. No. 3334, Chang (Tchang).

2007, May 12
3329 A1853 54c multi 1.50 .50
3330 A1853 54c multi 1.50 .50
3331 A1853 54c multi 1.50 .50
3332 A1853 54c multi 1.50 .50
3333 A1853 54c multi 1.50 .50
3334 A1853 54c multi 1.50 .50
a. Souvenir sheet, #3329-3334 13.50 13.50

No. 3334a sold for €5, with the Red Cross receiving €1.76 of that.

Religious Art — A1854

Designs: 54c, Nativity, 15th cent. miniature, from Armenia. 85c, The Smile of Reims.

2007, May 22 *Perf. 13¼*
3335 A1854 54c multi 1.60 .30
3336 A1854 85c multi 2.50 1.00

See Armenia Nos. 749-750.

Inauguration of Eastern France TGV Train Service — A1855

2007, June 9 *Perf. 13*
3337 A1855 54c multi 1.50 .30

French Federation of Philatelic Associations 80th Congress, Poitiers — A1856

2007, June 15 Engr. *Perf. 13x13¼*
3338 A1856 54c multi + label 1.75 .30

Miniature Sheet

2007 Rugby World Cup, France — A1857

No. 3339 — Inscriptions: a, Touche (Throw-in, 30x39mm elliptical). b, Melée (scrum). c, Attaque (player running with ball). d, Essai (try). e, Transformation (kick, 30x39mm elliptical). f, Passe (pass). g, Raffut (stiff-arm). h, Haka (dance). i, Plaquage (tackle). j, Supporteurs (fans).

2007, June 23 *Perf. 13x13¼*
3339 A1857 Sheet of 10 17.00 17.00
a.-j. 54c Any single 1.50 1.25

European Capitals Type of 2002
Souvenir Sheet

No. 3340 — Attractions in Brussels: a, Maison du Roi (Royal Palace). b, Hotel du Ville (City Hall), vert. c, Mannekin Pis, vert. d, Atomium.

Perf. 13x13¼, 13¼x13 (vert. stamps)
2007, June 30
3340 A1622 Sheet of 4 7.50 7.50
a.-d. 54c Any single 1.60 .90

Association of French Mayors, Cent. — A1858

2007, July 5 Photo. *Perf. 13¼*
3341 A1858 54c multi 1.50 .30

Pierre Pfimlin (1907-2000), Mayor of Strasbourg A1859

2007, July 7 Photo. *Perf. 13¼*
3342 A1859 60c multi 1.75 .60

2007 Rugby World Cup, France A1860

Litho. With Three-Dimensional Plastic Affixed
2007, Sept. 5 *Serpentine Die Cut 11*
Self-Adhesive
3343 A1860 €3 multi 10.00 6.00

Happy Birthday A1861

2007, Sept. 8 Photo. *Perf. 13x13¼*
3344 A1861 (54c) multi 5.00 .30
a. Litho., with attached label 2.40 2.40

No. 3344 was printed in a sheet of 5; No. 3344a was printed in a sheet of 5 + 5 labels that sold for €4.20.

Gift Boxes — A1862

Boxes and: Nos. 3345a, 3346, Butterflies. Nos. 3345b, 3348, Flowers. Nos. 3345c, 3347, Hearts. Nos. 3345d, 3350, Musical notes. Nos. 3345e, 3349, Bubbles.

2007, Sept. 8 Litho. *Perf. 13¼*
3345 Sheet of 5 + 5 labels 12.00 12.00
a.-e. A1862 (54c) Any single + label 2.40 2.40

Self-Adhesive
Booklet Stamps
Serpentine Die Cut 11

3346 A1862 (54c) multi 1.60 .55
3347 A1862 (54c) multi 1.60 .55
3348 A1862 (54c) multi 1.60 .55
3349 A1862 (54c) multi 1.60 .55
3350 A1862 (54c) multi 1.60 .55
a. Booklet pane of 5 #3346-3350 8.00

No. 3345 sold for €4.20.

Sully Prudhomme (1839-1907), Poet — A1863

2007, Sept. 15 Engr. *Perf. 13¼*
3351 A1863 €1.30 multi 3.75 1.25

A1864

A1865

A1866

A1867

Cows A1868

Serpentine Die Cut 11
2007, Sept. 20 Litho.
Self-Adhesive
Booklet Stamps

3352 A1864 (54c) multi 1.60 .55
3353 A1865 (54c) multi 1.60 .55
3354 A1866 (54c) multi 1.60 .55
3355 A1867 (54c) multi 1.60 .55
3356 A1868 (54c) multi 1.60 .55
a. Booklet pane, 2 each #3352-3356 16.00
Nos. 3352-3356 (5) 8.00 2.75

Aspects of Life in French Regions Type of 2003

No. 3357: a, Sèvres porcelain. b, Grasse perfume. c, Christmas market. d, Marseille soap. e, Giants, vert. f, Basque beret, vert. g, Aubusson tapestries. h, Lyonnaise tavern. i, Slipper, vert. j, Canteloupe, vert.

2007, Sept. 29 Photo. *Perf. 13*
3357 Sheet of 10 16.00 16.00
a.-j. A1642 54c Any single 1.60 .55

No. 3357 has three vertical rows of rouletting separating sheet into quarters.

Nos. 3357a-3357j were also issued in large booklets containing panes of 1 of each stamp. The booklet sold for €19. Value $55.

Space Age, 50th Anniv. — A1869

2007, Oct. 4 *Perf. 13x12½*
3358 A1869 85c multi 2.40 1.00

Medical Research Foundation, 60th Anniv. — A1870

2007, Oct. 20 *Perf. 13¼*
3359 A1870 54c multi 1.60 .30

Guy Moquet (1924-41), World War II Resistance Fighter — A1871

2007, Oct. 22 Engr.
3360 A1871 54c multi 1.60 .30

Dole A1872

2007, Nov. 2
3361 A1872 54c multi 1.60 .30

Personalized Stamp With Country Name on Short Side — A1873

Personalized Stamp With Country Name on Long Side A1874

Serpentine Die Cut 11¼ Syncopated
2007, Nov. Litho.
Self-Adhesive

Inscribed: "Lettre Prioritaire 20 g"

3362 A1873 (54c) multi 6.00 6.00
3363 A1874 (54c) multi 6.00 6.00

Inscribed: "Monde 20 g"

3364 A1873 (85c) multi 6.00 6.00
3365 A1874 (85c) multi 6.00 6.00

Inscribed: "Lettre Prioritaire 50 g"

3366 A1873 (86c) multi 6.00 6.00
3367 A1874 (86c) multi 6.00 6.00
Nos. 3362-3367 (6) 36.00 36.00

Nos. 3362-3367 were each printed in sheets of ten, having vignettes that could be personalized or chosen from a library of stock designs, two of which are shown on the illustrated stamps. Sheets of Nos. 3362 and 3363 each sold for €10.03, and sheets of Nos. 3364-3367 each sold for €13.38. Sheets were made available with different frame colors. Starting in 2008, numerous sheets containing a varying number of stamps with these frames and having various pre-selected vignettes were produced and sold by La Poste for various prices per sheet, each well above the franking value of the stamps at the time of issue. Any stamp with a vignette and/or frame color differing from the items shown is an equivalent item to those shown. Also starting in 2008, stamps were created having dozens of different rate inscriptions other than "Lettre Prioritaire 20g," "Monde 20g," and "Lettre Prioritaire 50g" inscriptions listed here.

Jean-Baptiste Charcot (1867-1936), Polar Explorer A1875

Ship Pourquoi-Pas? — A1876

2007, Nov. 8 Engr. *Perf. 13x12¾*
3368 A1875 54c multi 1.60 .55
3369 A1876 60c multi 1.75 .60
a. Horiz. pair, #3368-3369 3.50 1.25

See Greenland No. 505. A sheet containing Nos. 3368-3369 sold for €4 in 2008.

Marianne — A1877

Serpentine Die Cut 6¾ Vert.
2007, Nov. 8 Engr.
Self-Adhesive
Booklet Stamp

3370 A1877 54c red 3.00 2.00
a. Booklet pane, 6 each #3083d, 3370 27.50

Miniature Sheet

Lighthouses — A1878

No. 3371: a, Cap Fréhel Lighthouse. b, Espiguette Lighthouse. c, D'ar-Men Lighthouse. d, Grand-Léjon Lighthouse. e, Porquerolles Lighthouse, horiz. f, Chassiron Lighthouse, horiz.

Litho. & Engr.
2007, Nov. 9 *Perf. 13*
3371 A1878 Sheet of 6 9.75 9.75
a.-f. 54c Any single 1.60 .55

2007 Women's World Handball Championships, France — A1879

2007, Nov. 10 Photo. *Perf. 13¼*
3372 A1879 54c multi 1.60 .30

Holiday Greetings
A1880

No. 3377: a, Squirrel with stocking cap. b, Bird with party hat. c, Hedgehog with party cap. d, Dog with stocking cap. e, Deer with stocking cap.

No. 3378, Squirrel with stocking cap. No. 3379, Bird with party hat. No. 3380, Deer with stocking cap. No. 3381, Hedgehog with party hat. No. 3382, Dog with stocking cap.

2007, Nov. 24 Litho. *Perf. 13¼*

3377	Sheet of 5 + 5 labels	20.00	20.00
a.-e.	A1880 (54c) Any single + label	2.50	2.50

Booklet Stamps

Self-Adhesive

Serpentine Die Cut 11

3378	A1880 (54c)	multi	2.00	.30
3379	A1880 (54c)	multi	2.00	.30
3380	A1880 (54c)	multi	2.00	.30
3381	A1880 (54c)	multi	2.00	.30
3382	A1880 (54c)	multi	2.00	.30
a.	Booklet pane, 2 each #3378-3382		20.00	

No. 3377 sold for €4.20 and had labels that could not be personalized.

A souvenir sheet of 1 of No. 3381 sold for €3. Value, $12.

Marianne Type of 2005

2008 Engr. *Perf. 13*

3383	A1713	(65c) dk blue	2.50	.40
3384	A1713	72c yel green	2.25	.40
3385	A1713	88c fawn	2.75	.50
3386	A1713	€1.25 blue	4.00	.80
3387	A1713	€1.33 red vio	4.25	.85
3388	A1713	€2.18 choc	6.50	1.40
	Nos. 3383-3388 (6)		22.25	4.35

Coil Stamp

Perf. 13 Horiz.

3388A	A1713	(65c) dk blue	3.00	.40

Issued: Nos. 3383-3388A, 3/1.

Marianne Type of 2005

Serpentine Die Cut 6¾ Vert.

2008 Self-Adhesive Engr.

Booklet Stamp

3389	A1713 (60c) blue	2.50	.50
a.	Booklet pane of 12	30.00	

Issued: No. 3389, 1/2.

Hearts
A1881

Designs: (54c), Face. (86c), (88c), Plant with heart-shaped leaves.

2008, Jan. 5 Photo. *Perf. 13¼*

3390	A1881	(54c) multi	1.60	.30
a.	Souvenir sheet of 5		8.00	8.00
b.	Sheet of 10 + 10 labels		20.00	—
3391	A1881	(86c) multi	2.60	1.00

Self-Adhesive

Serpentine Die Cut

3392	A1881	(54c) multi	16.00	12.00
3392A	A1881	(88c) multi	16.00	12.00

Values are for stamps with surrounding selvage.

Nos. 3390, 3390a, 3390b, 3391-3392 issued 1/5/08. No. 3390b was sold for €6.86. Labels could not be personalized.

New Year 2008 (Year of the Rat) — A1882

2008, Jan. 26 Photo. *Perf. 13¼x13*

3393	A1882 (54c) multi	1.60	.30

Printed in sheets of 5. A souvenir sheet of one No. 3393 sold for €3.

See No. 4969d.

Paintings
A1883

Designs: No. 3394, Legend of St. Francis: Sermon to the Birds, by Giotto di Bondone. No. 3395, Seaport at Sunset, by Claude Lorrain. No. 3396, The Birth of Venus, by Sandro Botticelli. No. 3397, Napoleon Bonaparte Crossing the Alps, by Jacques-Louis David. No. 3398, La Belle Jardinière (Madonna and Child with St. John the Baptist), by Raphael, vert. No. 3399, Head of a Girl in a Turban, by Jan Vermeer, vert. No. 3400, Summer, by Giuseppe Arcimboldo, vert. No. 3401, Mona Lisa, by Leonardo da Vinci, vert. No. 3402, Infant Maria Marguerita, by Diego Velásquez, vert. No. 3403, Money Changer with Wife, by Quentin Massys (Metsys), vert.

Serpentine Die Cut 11

2008, Jan. 26 Litho.

Booklet Stamps

Self-Adhesive

3394	A1883 (54c) multi	1.60	.55
3395	A1883 (54c) multi	1.60	.55
3396	A1883 (54c) multi	1.60	.55
3397	A1883 (54c) multi	1.60	.55
3398	A1883 (54c) multi	1.60	.55
3399	A1883 (54c) multi	1.60	.55
3400	A1883 (54c) multi	1.60	.55
3401	A1883 (54c) multi	1.60	.55
3402	A1883 (54c) multi	1.60	.55
3403	A1883 (54c) multi	1.60	.55
a.	Booklet pane of 10, #3394-3403	16.00	

France Stadium, 10th Anniv.
A1884

2008, Jan. 28 Photo. *Perf. 13¼*

3404	A1884 54c multi	1.60	.30

Tourism Issue

Vendôme
A1885

La Rochelle — A1886

Toulon
A1887

Richelieu
A1888

Le Havre — A1889

2008 Engr. *Perf. 13¼*

3405	A1885 54c multi	1.60	.30

Perf. 13

3406	A1886 55c multi	1.50	.30
3407	A1887 55c multi	1.50	.30
3408	A1888 55c multi	1.50	.30
3409	A1889 55c multi	1.50	.30
	Nos. 3405-3409 (5)	7.60	1.50

Issued: No. 3405, 2/2; No. 3406, 4/5; Nos. 3407-3408, 7/5; No. 3409, 9/13. A souvenir sheet of one of No. 3406 sold for €3.

Art Issue

Globes of Vincenzo Coronelli
A1890

Young Girl Warming Her Hands at a Large Stove, by Jean-Jacues Henner — A1891

Untitled Work by Gérard Garouste
A1892

A Theater Box Office, by Honoré Daumier
A1893

Litho. & Engr., Photo (A1891-A1892), Engr. (A1893)

2008 *Perf. 13¼x13*

3410	A1890	85c multi	3.00	1.25
3411	A1891	88c multi	3.00	.60
3412	A1892	€1.33 multi	4.00	1.25
3413	A1893	€1.33 choc & bl gray	4.50	1.00
	Nos. 3410-3413 (4)		14.50	4.10

Self-Adhesive

Serpentine Die Cut 11

3413A	A1891	88c multi	6.00	4.00
3413B	A1892	€1.33 multi	12.00	50.00
3413C	A1893	€1.33 choc & bl gray	200.00	75.00
	Nos. 3413A-3413C (3)		218.00	129.00

Issued: No. 3410, 2/11; No. 3412, 6/19; No. 3411, 10/18; No. 3413, 11/7.

A souvenir sheet containing No. 3410 sold for €3.

Emir Abdelkader (1808-83), Algerian Leader — A1894

2008, Feb. 20 Engr. *Perf. 13¼*

3414	A1894 54c multi	1.75	.30

Droopy Dog
A1895

Red-haired Woman
A1896

The Wolf
A1897

Design: €2.18, Droopy Dog, diff.

2008, Mar. 1 Photo. *Perf. 13¼*

3415	A1895	(55c) multi	1.75	.30
3416	A1896	(55c) multi	1.75	.30
3417	A1897	(55c) multi	1.75	.30
a.	Strip of 3, #3415-3417		5.25	1.90

Souvenir Sheet

Perf. 13x13¼

3418	A1895 €2.18 multi	6.75	6.75

Booklet Stamps

Self-Adhesive

Serpentine Die Cut 11

3419	A1895	(55c) multi	1.75	.30
3420	A1896	(55c) multi	1.75	.30
3421	A1897	(55c) multi	1.75	.30
a.	Booklet pane of 10, 4 #3419, 3 each #3420-3421		17.50	

Cartoon characters created by Tex Avery; Stamp Day. No. 3418 contains one 35x27mm stamp that has thermographic ink (on cartoon balloon) that when warmed, changes color allowing a message below the ink to appear.

Nos. 3419-3421 exist in three sheets, each containing 5 of each stamp + 5 non-personalizable labels. Each sheet sold for €6.50. Value, each $40.

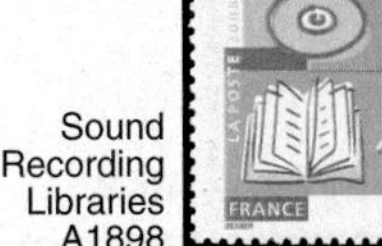

Sound Recording Libraries A1898

2008, Mar. 15 Photo. *Perf. 13¼*
3422 A1898 55c multi 1.75 .30

Flowers — A1899

Designs: 37c, Aquilegia. 38c, Tulipa sp. 44c, Bellis perennis. 45c, Primula veris.

2008, Mar. 1 Litho. *Perf. 13*
3423 A1899 37c multi 1.25 .60
3424 A1899 38c multi 1.25 .60
3425 A1899 44c multi 1.75 .70
3426 A1899 45c multi 1.75 .70
Nos. 3423-3426 (4) 6.00 2.60

Nos. 3423-3426 are known only precanceled. See second note after No. 132.

Compare with types A2174-A2177.

Aspects of Life in French Regions Type of 2003

No. 3427: a, Chateau d'Ussé, Rigny-Ussé. b, Vézelay. c, Place des Vosges, Le Marais district, Paris. d, Le Marais Poitevin (Poitevin Marsh). e, Cugarel Windmill, Castelnaudary, vert. f, Red granite coastal rocks, vert. g, Honfleur. h, La Petite France district, Strasbourg. i, La Boétie House, Sarlat-la-Canéda, vert. j, Marfate Cirque, Reunion, vert.

2008, Mar. 29 Photo. *Perf. 13*
3427 Sheet of 10 17.50 17.50
a.-j. A1642 55c Any single 1.75 1.25

No. 3427 has three vertical rows of rouletting, separating sheet into quarters. Nos. 3427a-3427j were also issued in a large booklet containing panes of 1 of each stamp. The booklet sold for €19.

Lyon — A1900

Litho. & Engr.

2008, Apr. 4 *Perf. 13*
3428 A1900 55c multi 1.75 .30

Gardens and Parks Type of 2003

No. 3429: a, Parc Longchamp, Marseille. b, Parc Borely, Marseille.

2008 Photo. *Perf. 13¼x13*
3429 Sheet of 2 13.50 13.50
a.-b. A1660 €2.18 Either single 6.75 3.50
c. Miniature sheet of 4, #3316a, 3316b, 3429a, 3429b 50.00 50.00

Salon du Timbre. No. 3429 has four vertical rows of rouletting, separating sheet into fifths, with the two stamps in the central fifth.

Issued: No. 3429, 4/12; No. 3429c, 6/14.

Prehistoric Animals A1901

Designs: No. 3430, Phorusrhacos. No. 3431, Smilodon. 65c, Megaloceros, horiz. 88c, Mammoth, horiz.

2008, Apr. 19 *Perf. 13¼*
3430 A1901 55c multi 1.75 .30
3431 A1901 55c multi 1.75 .30
3432 A1901 65c multi 2.00 .50
3433 A1901 88c multi 2.75 1.00
a. Miniature sheet, #3430-3433 8.25 8.25
Nos. 3430-3433 (4) 8.25 2.10

First Heart Transplant in Europe, 40th Anniv. — A1902

2008, Apr. 24 *Perf. 13¼x13*
3434 A1902 55c red & black 1.60 .30

Valentré Bridge, Cahors A1903

2008, Apr. 26 Engr. *Perf. 13x13¼*
3435 A1903 55c multi 1.60 .30

Europa A1904

2008, May 4 Photo. *Perf. 13x13¼*
3436 A1904 55c multi 1.75 .30

Self-Adhesive

Serpentine Die Cut 11

3436A A1904 55c multi 3.00 3.00

Quebec City, Canada, 400th Anniv. A1905

2008, May 16 Engr. *Perf. 13*
3437 A1905 85c multi 2.75 1.00

See Canada No. 2269.

A souvenir sheet containing No. 3437 and Canada No. 2269 sold for $4.99 in Canada and was sold in France for €15 as part of a set additionally containing six different souvenir sheets containing only No. 3437.

Happy Birthday A1906

2008, May 28 Photo.
3438 A1906 (55c) multi 1.75 .30

Printed in sheets of 5.

It's a Boy A1907

It's a Girl A1908

2008, May 28 *Serpentine Die Cut 11*

Booklet Stamps

Self-Adhesive

3439 A1907 (55c) multi, unscratched panel 2.00 2.00
a. Scratched panel .60
b. Booklet pane of 10 #3439 20.00
3440 A1908 (55c) multi, unscratched panel 2.00 2.00
a. Scratched panel .60
b. Booklet pane of 10 #3440 20.00

Scratch-off panels on Nos. 3439-3440 cover pictures and text for baby boy and girl, respectively.

Vacations A1909

Designs: No. 3441, Ferns. No. 3442, Butterfly on leaf. No. 3443, Hands holding plant's leaves. No. 3444, Coconut palm tree. No. 3445, Path beside forest lake. No. 3446, Golf ball, putter and hole. No. 3447, Water lily and lily pads. No. 3448, Watering cans and foliage. No. 3449, Sliced kiwi fruit. No. 3450, Shelled and unshelled peas.

Serpentine Die Cut 11

2008, May 28 Litho.

Booklet Stamps

Self-Adhesive

3441 A1909 (55c) multi 1.75 .60
3442 A1909 (55c) multi 1.75 .60
3443 A1909 (55c) multi 1.75 .60
3444 A1909 (55c) multi 1.75 .60
3445 A1909 (55c) multi 1.75 .60
3446 A1909 (55c) multi 1.75 .60
3447 A1909 (55c) multi 1.75 .60
3448 A1909 (55c) multi 1.75 .60
3449 A1909 (55c) multi 1.75 .60
3450 A1909 (55c) multi 1.75 .60
a. Booklet pane of 10, #3441-3450 17.50

Evreux Belfry — A1910

2008, May 31 Engr. *Perf. 13*
3451 A1910 55c multi 1.60 .60

French Federation of Philatelic Associations 81st Congress, Paris — A1911

2008, June 14 *Perf. 13x13¼*
3452 A1911 55c multi + label 1.60 .60

Marianne and Stars A1912

Hand Depositing Ballot A1913

Tree in Hand A1914

Dove A1915

2008 Engr. *Perf. 13*
3453 A1912 1c yellow .25 .25
3454 A1912 5c gray brown .25 .25
3455 A1912 10c gray .30 .25
3456 A1912 (50c) green 1.60 .25
3457 A1912 (55c) red 1.75 .40
3458 A1912 (65c) dark blue 2.10 .50
3459 A1912 72c olive green 2.25 .60
3460 A1912 85c purple 2.75 .70
3461 A1912 88c fawn 2.75 .70
3462 A1912 €1 orange 3.25 .80
3463 A1912 €1.25 blue 4.00 1.00
3464 A1912 €1.33 red violet 4.25 1.10
3465 A1912 €2.18 chocolate 7.00 2.40

Self-Adhesive (#3466)

Etched on Foil

Die Cut Perf. 13

3466 A1912 *€5 silver* 16.00 16.00
Nos. 3453-3466 (14) 48.50 25.20

Litho.

Perf. 13

3467 Sheet of 15, #3467a-3467k, 2 each #3467l-3467m, + 15 labels 40.00 40.00
a. A1912 1c yellow .25 .25
b. A1912 5c brown .25 .25
c. A1912 10c gray .35 .35
d. A1912 (65c) dark blue 2.40 2.40
e. A1912 72c olive green 2.60 2.60
f. A1912 85c purple 3.00 3.00
g. A1912 88c fawn 3.25 3.25
h. A1912 €1 orange 3.50 3.50
i. A1912 €1.25 blue 4.50 4.50
j. A1912 €1.33 red violet 4.75 4.75
k. A1912 €2.18 brn violet 7.75 7.75
l. A1912 (50c) green 1.75 1.75
m. A1912 (55c) red 2.00 2.00

Coil Stamps

Perf. 13 Horiz.

Engr.

3468 A1912 (50c) green 3.50 2.00
3469 A1912 (55c) red 4.00 2.00
3470 A1912 (65c) dark blue 4.50 2.00

Booklet Stamps (Types A1913-A1915)

Self-Adhesive

Serpentine Die Cut 6¾ Vert.

3471 A1912 (55c) red 2.50 1.00
a. Booklet pane of 20 50.00
b. Booklet pane of 10 25.00
c. Booklet pane of 12 30.00
3472 A1913 55c red 2.50 1.00
3473 A1914 55c red 2.50 1.00
3474 A1915 55c red 2.50 1.00
a. Booklet pane of 12, 6 #3471, 2 each #3472-3474 30.00
3475 A1912 (65c) dark blue 2.50 1.00
a. Booklet pane of 12 30.00
3476 A1913 65c dark blue 2.50 1.00
3477 A1914 65c dark blue 2.50 1.00

3478 A1915 65c dark blue 2.50 1.00
a. Booklet pane of 12, 6 #3475, 2 each #3476-3478 30.00
Nos. 3471-3478 (8) 20.00 8.00

Issued: No. 3457, 6/17; No. 3741c, 9/8; No. 3466, 7/1; No. 3475a, 2009; others, 6/14. On day of issue, No. 3467 sold for €12.54. Labels on No. 3467 could not be personalized.

No. 3471b is comprised of two horizontal strips of five stamps on a yellow backing paper. Nos. 3471 and 3475 were also printed in sheets of 100 later in 2008.

See Nos. 3532, 3551-3566, 3612-3616E, 3730, 3871-3882, 4410l, 4525.

Typographed, engraved and silk-screened perf. 13 stamps of types A486 and A1912 with denomination of €1 in red were produced in pairs with 2 labels and photogravure perf. 13 stamps of these types with denominations of €1 in blue, green and multicolored were printed in blocks of 8 + 8 labels. These items were created in very limited quantities in 2010.

Ecology A1916

Designs: No. 3479, Tree. No. 3480, Bicycle. No. 3481, World map. No. 3482, Computer. No. 3483, Water droplets. No. 3484, Sun. No. 3485, Two plastic bottles. No. 3486, Three plastic bottles. No. 3487, Apple core. No. 3488, Strawberry.

Serpentine Die Cut 11

2008, June 14 **Photo.**

Booklet Stamps

Self-Adhesive

3479 A1916 (55c) multi 1.75 .50
3480 A1916 (55c) multi 1.75 .50
3481 A1916 (55c) multi 1.75 .50
3482 A1916 (55c) multi 1.75 .50
3483 A1916 (55c) multi 1.75 .50
3484 A1916 (55c) multi 1.75 .50
3485 A1916 (55c) multi 1.75 .50
3486 A1916 (55c) multi 1.75 .50
3487 A1916 (55c) multi 1.75 .50
3488 A1916 (55c) multi 1.75 .50
a. Booklet pane of 10, #3479-3488 17.50

Trapeze Artist — A1917

Bareback Rider — A1918

Clown — A1919

Lion Tamer — A1920

Clown — A1921

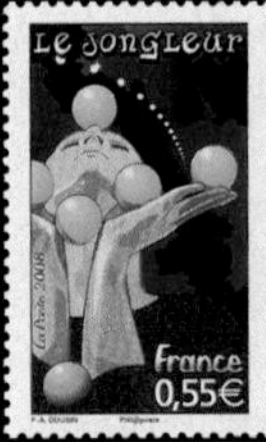

Juggler — A1922

2008, June 15 **Photo.** ***Perf. 13***

3489 A1917 55c multi 1.75 .60
3490 A1918 55c multi 1.75 .60
3491 A1919 55c multi 1.75 .60
3492 A1920 55c multi 1.75 .60
3493 A1921 55c multi 1.75 .60
3494 A1922 55c multi 1.75 .60
a. Souvenir sheet, #3489-3494 16.50 16.50
Nos. 3489-3494 (6) 10.50 3.60

No. 3494a sold for €5.10, with the Red Cross receiving €1.80 of that.

2008 Summer Olympics, Beijing — A1923

Designs: No. 3495, Equestrian, cycling. No. 3496, Swimming, rowing, horiz. No. 3497, Judo, fencing, horiz. No. 3498, Tennis, running.

Perf. 13¼x13, 13x13¼

2008, June 16

3495 A1923 55c multi 1.75 .60
3496 A1923 55c multi 1.75 .60
3497 A1923 55c multi 1.75 .60
a. Pair, #3496-3497 3.50 1.75
3498 A1923 55c multi 1.75 .60
a. Vert. pair, #3495, 3498 3.50 1.75
Nos. 3495-3498 (4) 7.00 2.40

Nos. 3495-3498 were printed in a sheet of 10 containing 2 each #3495 and #3498 and 3 each #3496-3497.

Charles de Gaulle Memorial, Paris A1924

2008, June 18 **Engr.** ***Perf. 13¼***

3499 A1924 55c multi 1.75 .60

Miniature Sheet

European Projects — A1925

No. 3500: a, Map of Europe, 1-euro coin. b, Flags of France and European Union, horiz (French Presidency of European Union). c, Earth and Galileo satellite, horiz. d, Students and flags (Erasmus higher education program).

2008, June 19 **Photo.** ***Perf. 13***

3500 A1925 Sheet of 4 7.00 7.00
a.-d. 55c Any single 1.75 .60

Miniature Sheet

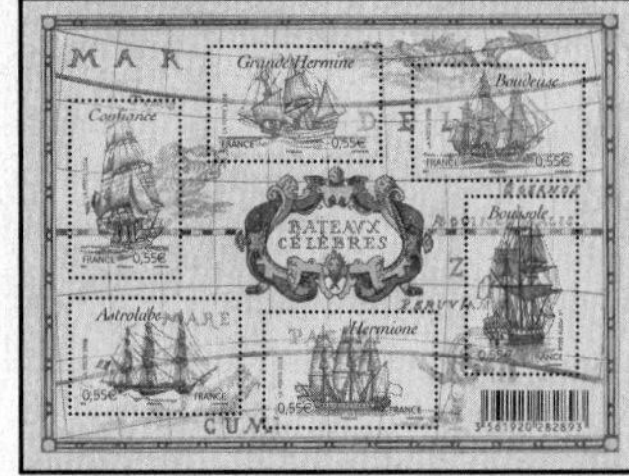

Famous Ships — A1926

No. 3501: a, Confiance. b, Grande Hermine, horiz. c, Boudeuse, horiz. d, Astrolabe, horiz. e, Hermione, horiz. f, Boussole.

2008, June 20

3501 A1926 Sheet of 6 10.50 10.50
a.-f. 55c Any single 1.75 .60

French and Brazilian Landscapes — A1927

Designs: 55c, Amazonian forest, Brazil. 85c, Glacier, France.

2008, July 13

3502 A1927 55c multi 1.75 .60
3503 A1927 85c multi 2.75 .90
a. Horiz. pair, #3502-3503 4.50 2.25

See Brazil No. 3052.

Mediterranean Summit, Paris — A1928

2008, July 13 ***Perf. 13¼***

3504 A1928 55c multi 1.75 .60

Aspects of Life in French Regions Type of 2003

No. 3505: a, Espadrilles. b, Stew (pot au feu). c, Chestnuts (chataigne). d, Fireworks (feu d'artifice). e, Epinal prints (l'image d'Epinal), vert. f, Lentils (lentille), vert. g, Reblochon cheese. h, Calissons (candy). i, Stilt walker (les échasses), vert. j, Mustard (moutarde), vert.

2008, Sept. 6 **Photo.** ***Perf. 13***

3505 Sheet of 10 15.00 15.00
a.-j. A1642 55c Any single 1.50 .50

No. 3505 has three vertical rows of rouletting, separating sheet into quarters.

Nos. 3505a-3505j also were issued in large booklets containing panes of 1 of each stamp. The booklet sold for €19.

Josselin A1929

2008, Sept. 20 **Engr.** ***Perf. 13¼***

3506 A1929 55c multi 1.75 .50

A1930

A1931

A1932

A1933

A1934

A1935

A1936

A1937

A1938

Garfield, Comic Strip by Jim Davis A1939

Serpentine Die Cut 11¼x11

2008, Sept. 18 **Photo.**

Booklet Stamps

Self-Adhesive

3507 A1930 (55c) multi 1.75 .50
3508 A1931 (55c) multi 1.75 .50
3509 A1932 (55c) multi 1.75 .50
3510 A1933 (55c) multi 1.75 .50
3511 A1934 (55c) multi 1.75 .50
3512 A1935 (55c) multi 1.75 .50
3513 A1936 (55c) multi 1.75 .50
3514 A1937 (55c) multi 1.75 .50
3515 A1938 (55c) multi 1.75 .50
3516 A1939 (55c) multi 1.75 .50
a. Booklet pane of 10, #3507-3516 17.50
Nos. 3507-3516 (10) 17.50 5.00

"I Am Sport"
A1940

2008, Oct. 2 Photo. *Perf. 12½*
3517 A1940 55c multi 1.50 .50

Values are for stamps with surrounding selvage.

Fifth Republic, 50th Anniv.
A1941

2008. Oct. 4 *Perf. 13¼*
3518 A1941 55c multi 1.50 .50

Seascapes of Viet Nam and France — A1942

Designs: 55c, Along Bay, Viet Nam. 85, Strait of Bonifacio, France.

2008, Oct. 15 Photo. *Perf. 13x12¾*
3519 A1942 55c multi 1.40 .45
3520 A1942 85c multi 2.25 .75

See Viet Nam Nos. 3340-3341.

Types of 1959-2008
Serpentine Die Cut 6¾ Vert.
2008, Nov. 6 Photo.
Booklet Stamps
Self-Adhesive

3521 A328 55c multi 1.40 .45
3522 A349 55c multi 1.40 .45
3523 A360 55c multi 1.40 .45
3524 A379 55c multi 1.40 .45
3525 A486 55c dark red 1.40 .45
3526 A555 55c rose carmine 1.40 .45
3527 A771 55c bright red 1.40 .45
3528 A915 55c red 1.40 .45
3529 A1161 55c red 1.40 .45
3530 A1409 55c red 1.40 .45
3531 A1713 55c red 1.40 .45
3532 A1912 55c red 1.40 .45
a. Booklet pane of 12, #3521-3532 17.00
Nos. 3521-3532 (12) 16.80 5.40

Landmarks of France and Israel — A1943

Airplane, stamped first flight cover and: 55c, Haifa waterfront, Israel. 85c, Eiffel Tower, Paris.

2008, Nov. 6 Photo. *Perf. 13*
3533 A1943 55c multi 1.40 .45
3534 A1943 85c multi 2.25 .75

First flight between France and Israel, 60th anniv. See Israel Nos. 1750-1751.

European Capitals Type of 2002

No. 3535 — Attractions in Prague: a, Tour du Petit Coté (Charles Bridge and Tower), vert. b, Hotel de ville horloge astronomique et calandrier (City Hall astronomical clock), vert. c, Eglise Notre-Dame-de-Tyn (Tyn Cathedral), vert. d, Le Chateau (Hradcany Castle).

Perf. 13¼x13, 13x13¼ (#3535d)
2008, Nov. 7 Photo.
3535 A1622 Sheet of 4 5.75 5.75
a.-d. 55c Any single 1.40 .45

A1944 A1945

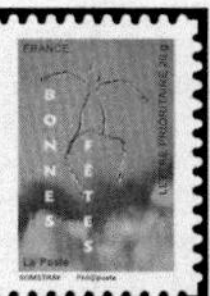

A1946 A1947

A1948 A1949

A1950

A1951

A1952

A1953

A1954

A1955

A1956

Happy Holidays
A1957

Serpentine Die Cut 11¼x11
2008, Nov. 8 Photo.
Booklet Stamps
Self-Adhesive

3536 A1944 (55c) multi 1.40 .45
3537 A1945 (55c) multi 1.40 .45
3538 A1946 (55c) multi 1.40 .45
3539 A1947 (55c) multi 1.40 .45
3540 A1948 (55c) multi 1.40 .45
3541 A1949 (55c) multi 1.40 .45

Serpentine Die Cut 11x11¼

3542 A1950 (55c) multi 1.40 .45
3543 A1951 (55c) multi 1.40 .45
3544 A1952 (55c) multi 1.40 .45
3545 A1953 (55c) multi 1.40 .45
3546 A1954 (55c) multi 1.40 .45
3547 A1955 (55c) multi 1.40 .45
3548 A1956 (55c) multi 1.40 .45
3549 A1957 (55c) multi 1.40 .45
a. Booklet pane of 14, #3536-3549 20.00
Nos. 3536-3549 (14) 19.60 6.30

A souvenir sheet containing one perf. 13x13¼ stamp like No. 3543 with water-activated gum sold for €3.

End of World War I, 90th Anniv.
A1958

2008, Nov. 11 Engr. *Perf. 13¼*
3550 A1958 55c multi 1.40 .45

Marianne and Stars Type of 2008
Serpentine Die Cut 6¾ Vert.
2008 Engr. Self-Adhesive

3551 A1912 1c yellow .25 .25
3552 A1912 5c gray brown .25 .25
3553 A1912 10c gray .30 .30
3554 A1912 (50c) green 1.40 1.40
3555 A1912 72c olive green 2.00 2.00
3556 A1912 85c purple 2.40 2.40
3557 A1912 88c fawn 2.50 2.50
3558 A1912 €1 orange 2.75 2.75
3559 A1912 €1.25 blue 3.50 3.50
3560 A1912 €1.33 red violet 3.75 3.75
3561 A1912 €2.18 chocolate 6.00 6.00
Nos. 3551-3561 (11) 25.10 25.10

Serpentine Die Cut 6¾ Horiz.
Coil Stamps

3564 A1912 (50c) green 1.40 1.40
3565 A1912 (55c) red 1.50 1.50
3566 A1912 (65c) dark blue 1.90 1.90
Nos. 3564-3566 (3) 4.80 4.80

Nos. 3551-3561 each were printed in sheets of 100.

Flowers — A1959

Designs: 31c, Helianthus annuus. 33c, Magnolia.

2008, Nov. 12 Litho. *Perf. 13*
3567 A1959 31c multi .80 .25
3568 A1959 33c multi .85 .25

Nos. 3567-3568 are known only precanceled. See note under No. 132.

Trees and Map of Mediterranean Area — A1960

2008, Nov. 20 Photo. *Perf. 13x12¾*
3569 A1960 85c multi 2.50 .75

See Lebanon No. 645.

Greetings Type of 2004 Inscribed "Lettre Prioritaire 20g"

Designs: No. 3569A, "Ceci est une invitation." No. 3569B, "Un grand merci."

2008 Photo. *Serpentine Die Cut 11*
Self-Adhesive
3569A A1667 (55c) brt lil rose & yel 1.60 1.60
3569B A1667 (55c) brt yel grn & red lil 1.60 1.60

Louis Braille (1809-52), Educator of the Blind — A1961

Engr. & Embossed
2009, Jan. 4 *Perf. 13x12¾*
3570 A1961 55c blk & violet 1.50 .50

New Year 2009 (Year of the Ox) — A1962

2009, Jan. 10 Photo. *Perf. 13¼x13*
3571 A1962 (55c) multi 1.50 .50

No. 3571 was printed in sheets of 5. A souvenir sheet of 1 sold for €3. Value, $8.
See No. 4970a.

Decorated Glasses, Nancy Museum
A1963

Decorated Clock, Louvre Museum
A1964

Marquetry, Valençay Chateau
A1965

Quimper Faience, Sèvres Museum
A1966

Enamelwork, Apt Cathedral — A1967

Tapestry, Malmaison Chateau
A1968

Stained Glass, St. Joan of Arc Church, Rouen
A1969

Cabinetwork, Louvre Museum — A1970

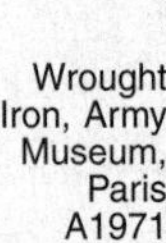

Wrought Iron, Army Museum, Paris A1971

Mosaic, Palace of Versailles A1972

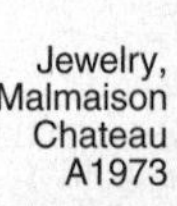
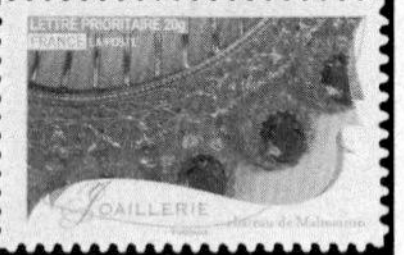

Jewelry, Malmaison Chateau A1973

Crystal, Clichy Glassworks A1974

Booklet Stamps

Serpentine Die Cut 11

2009, Jan. 10 Self-Adhesive

3572	A1963 (55c) multi		1.50	.50
3573	A1964 (55c) multi		1.50	.50
3574	A1965 (55c) multi		1.50	.50
3575	A1966 (55c) multi		1.50	.50
3576	A1967 (55c) multi		1.50	.50
3577	A1968 (55c) multi		1.50	.50
3578	A1969 (55c) multi		1.50	.50
3579	A1970 (55c) multi		1.50	.50
3580	A1971 (55c) multi		1.50	.50
3581	A1972 (55c) multi		1.50	.50
3582	A1973 (55c) multi		1.50	.50
3583	A1974 (55c) multi		1.50	.50
a.	Booklet pane of 12, #3572-3583		18.00	
	Nos. 3572-3583 (12)		18.00	6.00

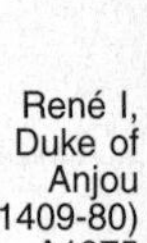

René I, Duke of Anjou (1409-80) A1975

2009, Jan. 16 Engr. *Perf. 13¼*

3584	A1975 55c multi	1.50	.50

Hearts A1976

Flowers and: (55c), One parrot. (88c), Two parrots.

2009, Jan. 17 Photo. *Perf. 13¼*

3585	A1976 (55c) multi	1.50	.50
a.	Souvenir sheet of 5	7.50	7.50
3586	A1976 (88c) multi	2.40	1.25

Self-Adhesive

Serpentine Die Cut

3587	A1976 (55c) multi	1.50	.50
3588	A1976 (88c) multi	2.40	1.25
a.	Booklet pane of 12	29.00	
	Nos. 3585-3588 (4)	7.80	3.50

Tourism Issue

Les Sables D'Olonne A1977

Menton — A1978

Chaumont A1979

Château de la Bâtie d'Urfé A1980

Bordeaux — A1981

Abbey of Royaumont A1982

Photo., Engr. (#3590, 3592-3594)

2009 *Perf. 13¼, 13 (#3593)*

3589	A1977 55c multi	1.40	.45
3590	A1978 56c multi	1.40	.45
3591	A1979 56c multi	1.60	.55
3592	A1980 56c multi	1.60	.55

Perf. 13

3593	A1981 56c multi	1.60	.55
3594	A1982 56c multi	1.75	.60
	Nos. 3589-3594 (6)	9.35	3.15

Self-Adhesive

Serpentine Die Cut 11

3594A	A1981 56c multi	1.60	1.60

Issued: No. 3589, 1/31; No. 3590, 2/21; No. 3591, 5/16. No. 3592, 6/6; Nos. 3593, 3594A, 6/20. No. 3594, 9/26.

Miniature Sheet

World Alpine Skiing Championships, Val d'Isère — A1983

No. 3595: a, Super combined skier. b, Slalom skier. c, Downhill (Descente) skier. d, Giant slalom skier. e, Skiers at Val d'Isère.

2009, Jan. 31 Photo. *Perf. 13x13¼*

3595	A1983 Sheet of 5	7.00	7.00
a.-e.	55c Any single	1.40	.45

France Foundation, 40th Anniv. — A1984

2009, Feb. 5 Photo. *Perf. 13¼*

3596	A1984 55c multi	1.40	.45

Art Series

Angel, St. Cecilia Cathedral, Albi A1985

La Promenade, by Hansi (Jean-Jacques Waltz) — A1986

Wrapping of Pont-Neuf, by Christo and Jeanne-Claude — A1987

Paintings by Pierre-Auguste Renoir — A1988

No. 3600: a, Monsieur et Madame Bernheim de Villers. b, Gabrielle à la Rose.

Perf. 13, 13x13¼ (#3598), 13¼x13 (#3599)

2009 Litho. (#3597), Photo.

3597	A1985 85c multi	2.25	1.10
3598	A1986 90c multi	2.75	1.40
3599	A1987 €1.35 multi	3.75	1.90
	Nos. 3597-3599 (3)	8.75	4.40

Souvenir Sheet

Perf. 13¼

3600	A1988 Sheet of 2	6.50	6.50
a.	85c multi	2.50	1.25
b.	€1.35 multi	4.00	2.00

Self-Adhesive

Serpentine Die Cut 11

3601	A1985 85c multi	2.50	2.50
3602	A1986 90c multi	2.75	2.75
3603	A1987 €1.35 multi	3.75	3.75

Issued: No. 3597, 2/7; No. 3598, 10/24; Nos. 3599, 3603, 6/13 No. 3600, 11/5. A souvenir sheet of 1 of No. 3597 sold for €3.

Road Runner and Wile E. Coyote A1989

Sylvester and Tweety Bird A1990

Daffy Duck and Bugs Bunny A1991

Design: €1, Yosemite Sam, Wile E. Coyote, Sylvester, Tasmanian Devil, Bugs Bunny, Daffy Duck, Road Runner, Marvin the Martian and Tweety Bird.

2009, Feb. 28 Photo. *Perf. 13x13¼*

3605	A1989 56c multi	1.40	.45
3606	A1990 56c multi	1.40	.45
3607	A1991 56c multi	1.40	.45
a.	Strip of 3, #3605-3607	4.25	1.40
	Nos. 3605-3607 (3)	4.20	1.35

Souvenir Sheet

3608	A1989 €1 multi	2.60	1.25

Booklet Stamps

Self-Adhesive

Litho.

Serpentine Die Cut 11

3609	A1989 (56c) multi	1.40	.45
3610	A1991 (56c) multi	1.40	.45
3611	A1990 (56c) multi	1.40	.45
a.	Booklet pane of 12, 4 each #3609-3611	17.00	
	Nos. 3609-3611 (3)	4.20	1.35

Stamp Day. No. 3608 contains one 80x26mm stamp. Sheets of five serpentine die cut 11 self-adhesive stamps like Nos. 3605-3607 and 5 labels each sold for €6.50.

Marianne and Stars Type of 2008

2009, Feb. 28 Engr. *Perf. 13*

3612	A1912 73c ol grn	1.90	.50
3613	A1912 90c fawn	2.25	.55
3614	A1912 €1.30 blue	3.25	.85
3615	A1912 €1.35 red vio	3.50	.90
3616	A1912 €2.22 choc	5.75	1.40
	Nos. 3612-3616 (5)	16.65	4.20

Serpentine Die Cut 6¾ Vert.

Self-Adhesive

3616A	A1912 73c ol grn	1.90	1.90
3616B	A1912 90c fawn	2.25	2.25
3616C	A1912 €1.30 blue	3.25	3.25
3616D	A1912 €1.35 red vio	3.50	3.50
3616E	A1912 €2.22 choc	5.75	5.75
	Nos. 3616A-3616E (5)	16.65	16.65

Constitutional Council — A1992

2009, Mar. 5 Photo. *Perf. 13¼*

3617	A1992 56c multi	1.40	.45

Self-Adhesive

Serpentine Die Cut 11

3617A	A1992 56c multi	1.60	1.60

Papal Palace, Avignon — A1993

2009, Mar. 7 Engr. ***Perf. 13x12¾***
3618 A1993 70c multi 1.90 .65

Portraits of Women by Titouan Lamazou A1994

Designs: No. 3619, Helena, United States. No. 3620, Dayu, Indonesia. No. 3621, Deborah, France. No. 3622, Kabari, Bangladesh. No. 3623, Mei Mei, China. No. 3624, Malika, Morocco. No. 3625, Dayan, Colombia. No. 3626, Francine, Rwanda. No. 3627, Blessing, Nigeria. No. 3628, Nandita, India. No. 3629, Elmas, Turkey. No. 3630, Nadia, Brazil.

Serpentine Die Cut 11
2009, Mar. 9 Litho.
Booklet Stamps
Self-Adhesive

3619 A1994 (56c) multi 1.50 .50
3620 A1994 (56c) multi 1.50 .50
3621 A1994 (56c) multi 1.50 .50
3622 A1994 (56c) multi 1.50 .50
3623 A1994 (56c) multi 1.50 .50
3624 A1994 (56c) multi 1.50 .50
3625 A1994 (56c) multi 1.50 .50
3626 A1994 (56c) multi 1.50 .50
3627 A1994 (56c) multi 1.50 .50
3628 A1994 (56c) multi 1.50 .50
3629 A1994 (56c) multi 1.50 .50
3630 A1994 (56c) multi 1.50 .50
a. Booklet pane of 12, #3619-3630 18.00
Nos. 3619-3630 (12) 18.00 6.00

Mâcon — A1995

2009, Mar. 27 Engr. ***Perf. 13x12¾***
3631 A1995 56c multi 1.50 .50

Souvenir Sheet

Protection of Polar Regions — A1996

No. 3632: a, Iceberg and bird. b, Emperor penguins, vert.

Perf. 13x13¼, 13¼x13 (85c)
2009, Mar. 28 Litho. & Engr.
3632 A1996 Sheet of 2 4.00 4.00
a. 56c multi 1.50 .50
b. 85c multi 2.50 .85

Aimé Césaire (1913-2008), Martinique Politician A1997

2009, Apr. 17 Photo. ***Perf. 13¼x13***
3633 A1997 56c multi 1.50 .50

Flora of the French Regions A1998

Designs: No. 3634, Plum (quetsche), Alsace. No. 3635, Plum (mirabelle), Lorraine. No. 3636, Birch tree, Centre. No. 3637, Bee orchid, Champagne-Ardenne. No. 3638, Lily, Paris. No. 3639, Bluebells, Ile de France. No. 3640, Gorse, Bretagne. No. 3641, Lily-of-the-valley, Pays de la Loire. No. 3642, Apples, Basse-Normandie. No. 3643, Beech leaves, Haute-Normandie. No. 3644, Rose, Picardie. No. 3645, Potatoes, Nord-Pas de Calais. No. 3646, Olives, Provence-Alpes-Côte d'Azur. No. 3647, Chestnut, Corse. No. 3648, Wild thyme, Languedoc-Roussillon. No. 3649, Yellow gentian, Auvergne. No. 3650, Boletus mushroom, Limousin. No. 3651, Saltwort, Poitou-Charentes. No. 3652, Maritime pine, Aquitaine. No. 3653, Norway spruce, Franche-Comté. No. 3654, Awara palm, French Guiana. No. 3655, Toulouse violet, Midi-Pyrénées. No. 3656, Blueberries, Rhône-Alpes. No. 3657, Black currants, Bourgogne.

Serpentine Die Cut 11
2009, Apr. 25 Photo.
Booklet Stamps
Self-Adhesive

3634 A1998 (56c) multi 1.50 .50
3635 A1998 (56c) multi 1.50 .50
a. Booklet pane of 2, #3634-3635 3.00
3636 A1998 (56c) multi 1.50 .50
3637 A1998 (56c) multi 1.50 .50
a. Booklet pane of 2, #3636-3637 3.00
3638 A1998 (56c) multi 1.50 .50
3639 A1998 (56c) multi 1.50 .50
a. Booklet pane of 2, #3638-3639 3.00
3640 A1998 (56c) multi 1.50 .50
3641 A1998 (56c) multi 1.50 .50
a. Booklet pane of 2, #3640-3641 3.00
3642 A1998 (56c) multi 1.50 .50
3643 A1998 (56c) multi 1.50 .50
a. Booklet pane of 2, #3642-3643 3.00
3644 A1998 (56c) multi 1.50 .50
3645 A1998 (56c) multi 1.50 .50
a. Booklet pane of 2, #3644-3645 3.00
Complete booklet, #3635a, 3637a, 3639a, 3641a, 3643a, 3645a 18.00
3646 A1998 (56c) multi 1.50 .50
3647 A1998 (56c) multi 1.50 .50
a. Booklet pane of 2, #3646-3647 3.00
3648 A1998 (56c) multi 1.50 .50
3649 A1998 (56c) multi 1.50 .50
a. Booklet pane of 2, #3648-3649 3.00
3650 A1998 (56c) multi 1.50 .50
3651 A1998 (56c) multi 1.50 .50
a. Booklet pane of 2, #3650-3651 3.00
3652 A1998 (56c) multi 1.50 .50
3653 A1998 (56c) multi 1.50 .50
a. Booklet pane of 2, #3652-3653 3.00
3654 A1998 (56c) multi 1.50 .50
3655 A1998 (56c) multi 1.50 .50
a. Booklet pane of 2, #3654-3655 3.00
3656 A1998 (56c) multi 1.50 .50
3657 A1998 (56c) multi 1.50 .50
a. Booklet pane of 2, #3656-3657 3.00
Complete booklet, #3647a, 3649a, 3651a, 3653a, 3655a, 3657a 18.00
Nos. 3634-3657 (24) 36.00 12.00

Souvenir Sheet

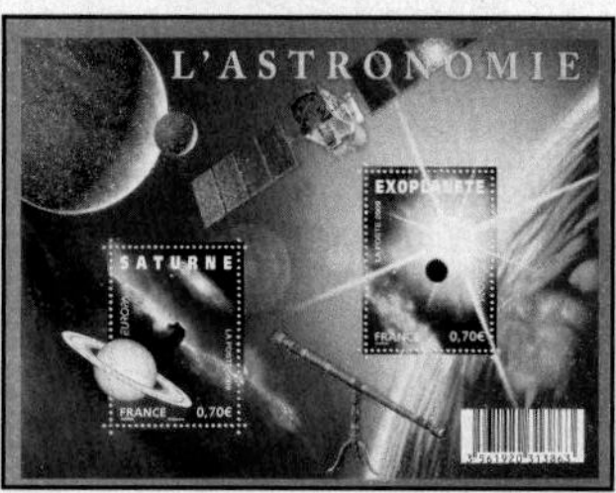

Europa — A1999

No. 3658: a, Saturn. b, Exoplanet.

2009, May 3 Litho. ***Perf. 13¼x13***
3658 A1999 Sheet of 2 4.00 4.00
a.-b. 70c Either single 2.00 .65

Intl. Year of Astronomy.

A2000

Vacations A2001

Designs: No. 3659, Tennis ball on red clay court. No. 3660, Red-striped director's chair. No. 3661, Red turban. No. 3662, Ladybug. No. 3663, Red air mattress. No. 3664, Cherry tomatoes. No. 3665, Rooster. No. 3666, Poppy. No. 3667, License plate of Bonaire, Netherlands Antilles. No. 3668, Monarch butterfly. No. 3669, Raspberries. No. 3670, Door-knocker on red door. No. 3671, Flowers near house number. No. 3672, Red boat, rope and cleat.

Serpentine Die Cut 11
2009, May 13 Litho.
Booklet Stamps
Self-Adhesive

3659 A2000 (56c) multi 1.60 .55
3660 A2000 (56c) multi 1.60 .55
3661 A2000 (56c) multi 1.60 .55
3662 A2000 (56c) multi 1.60 .55
3663 A2000 (56c) multi 1.60 .55
3664 A2000 (56c) multi 1.60 .55
3665 A2001 (56c) multi 1.60 .55
3666 A2001 (56c) multi 1.60 .55
3667 A2001 (56c) multi 1.60 .55
3668 A2001 (56c) multi 1.60 .55
3669 A2001 (56c) multi 1.60 .55
3670 A2001 (56c) multi 1.60 .55
3671 A2001 (56c) multi 1.60 .55
3672 A2001 (56c) multi 1.60 .55
a. Booklet pane of 14, #3659-3672 22.50
Nos. 3659-3672 (14) 22.40 7.70

Timber-frame Houses, Alsace — A2002

Azay-le-Rideau Chateau — A2003

Notre Dame Cathedral, Paris A2004

Vineyards, Bordeaux A2005

Nice A2006

Mont-Saint-Michel — A2007

Eiffel Tower A2008

Provence A2009

Serpentine Die Cut 11
2009, May 13 Litho.
Booklet Stamps
Self-Adhesive

3673 A2002 (85c) multi 2.40 .80
3674 A2003 (85c) multi 2.40 .80
3675 A2004 (85c) multi 2.40 .80
3676 A2005 (85c) multi 2.40 .80
3677 A2006 (85c) multi 2.40 .80
3678 A2007 (85c) multi 2.40 .80
3679 A2008 (85c) multi 2.40 .80
3680 A2009 (85c) multi 2.40 .80
a. Booklet pane of 8, #3673-3680 19.50
Nos. 3673-3680 (8) 19.20 6.40

Nos. 3678 and 3679 each were printed in sheets of 50 in 2010.

John Calvin (1509-64), Theologian and Religious Reformer A2010

2009, May 22 Engr. ***Perf. 13¼***
3681 A2010 56c multi 1.60 .55

Miniature Sheet

Chocolate — A2011

No. 3682: a, Cacao leaves, pods and beans. b, Aztec Indian. c, Spanish soldier. d, Castle. e, Map of French Atlantic coast. f, European man and woman of 16th cent. g, Production of chocolate. h, Chocolate bar. i, Cocoa service. j, Person eating chocolate bar.

2009, May 23 Photo. ***Perf. 13***
3682 A2011 Sheet of 10 16.00 16.00
a.-j. 56c Any single 1.60 .55

No. 3682 is impregnated with a chocolate scent.

French Federation Of Philatelic Associations 82nd Congress, Tarbes — A2012

2009, June 12 Engr. ***Perf. 13x13¼***
3683 A2012 56c multi + label 1.60 .55

Jean Moulin Memorial, Rhône A2013

2009, June 20 Engr. *Perf. 13¼*

3684	A2013 56c multi		1.60	.55

Serpentine Die Cut 11

Self-Adhesive

3685	A2013 56c multi	1.60	1.60

Endangered Animals A2014

Designs: No. 3686, Giant panda. No. 3687, Rhinoceros. 70c, Aurochs, horiz. 90c, California condor, horiz.

2009, June 20 Photo. *Perf. 13¼*

3686	A2014 56c multi	1.60	.55
3687	A2014 56c multi	1.60	.55
3688	A2014 70c multi	2.00	.65
3689	A2014 90c multi	2.50	.85
a.	Souvenir sheet of 4, #3686-3689	7.75	7.75
	Nos. 3686-3689 (4)	7.70	2.60

Gordon Bennett Aviation Cup, Cent. A2015

2009, June 27 Engr. *Perf. 13¼*

3690	A2015 56c blk & brn	1.60	.55

Etienne Dolet (1509-46), Printer and Translator — A2016

2009, July 4 Engr. *Perf. 13x13¼*

3691	A2016 56c multi	1.60	.55

Miniature Sheet

Fair Attractions — A2017

Designs: a, Parachute jump. b, Ferris wheel. c, Roller coaster. d, Carousel. e, Candy apple. f, Fishing arcade game.

2009, Sept. 5 Photo. *Perf. 13*

3692	A2017 Sheet of 6	10.50	10.50
a.-f.	56c Any single	1.75	.60

A2018

Invitation — A2019

Designs: No. 3693, Yellow background, man with red violet pants and shoes. No. 3694, Red background, woman wearing dress. No. 3695, Red violet background, woman scattering papers. No. 3696, Light blue background, cow with flowers. No. 3697, Blue background, man with red violet pants and blue shoes. No. 3698, Brown black background, birthday cake with slice on cake server. No. 3699. Yellow green background, woman with brown pants and green shoes. No. 3700, Green background, man with blue pants and shoes. No. 3701, Brown background, cut birthday cake. No. 3702, Red violet background, woman with red violet pants and shoes. No. 3703, Pink background, woman with balloons. No. 3704, Red background, bird. No. 3705, Yellow green background, woman with green skirt and shoes. No. 3706, Orange background, woman scattering papers.

Serpentine Die Cut 11

2009, Sept. 5 Litho.

Booklet Stamps

Self-Adhesive

3693	A2018 (56c) multi	1.75	.60
3694	A2018 (56c) multi	1.75	.60
3695	A2018 (56c) multi	1.75	.60
3696	A2018 (56c) multi	1.75	.60
3697	A2018 (56c) multi	1.75	.60
3698	A2018 (56c) multi	1.75	.60
3699	A2018 (56c) multi	1.75	.60
3700	A2018 (56c) multi	1.75	.60
3701	A2019 (56c) multi	1.75	.60
3702	A2019 (56c) multi	1.75	.60
3703	A2019 (56c) multi	1.75	.60
3704	A2019 (56c) multi	1.75	.60
3705	A2019 (56c) multi	1.75	.60
3706	A2019 (56c) multi	1.75	.60
a.	Booklet pane of 14, #3693-3706	24.50	
	Nos. 3693-3706 (14)	24.50	8.40

Eugène Vaillé (1875-1959), First Conservator of the Postal Museum — A2020

2009, Sept. 19 Engr. *Perf. 13¼*

3707	A2020 56c multi	1.75	.60

Self-Adhesive

Serpentine Die Cut 11

3708	A2020 56c multi	1.75	1.75

Souvenir Sheet

Jardin des Plantes, Paris — A2021

No. 3709: a, Gazebo. b, Mexican Hothouse.

2009, Sept. 19 Photo. *Perf. 13¼x13*

3709	A2021 Sheet of 2	13.00	13.00
a.-b.	€2.22 Either single	6.50	3.25

Salon du Timbre.

A2022

Le Petit Nicolas, by René Goscinny A2023

Designs: No. 3710, Nicolas, wearing striped shirt, holding envelope and book bag. No. 3711, Geoffroy. No. 3712, Eudes. No. 3713, Nicolas, wearing scarf, holding envelope and book bag. No. 3714, Nicolas writing. No. 3715, Joachim. No. 3716, "Chouette, des nouvelles!" No. 3717, Character at typewriter. No. 3718, "Vous me ferez cent lignes!" No. 3719, "Chère Maman. . ." No. 3720, "C'est toi la plus jolie!", vert. No. 3721, "J'ai fait le bonheur de tout le monde.", vert. No. 3722, "Moi, je veux pas grand chose réellement. . .", vert. No. 3723, "C'est pout toi, Maman!", vert.

Serpentine Die Cut 11

2009, Sept. 19 Litho.

Booklet Stamps

Self-Adhesive

3710	A2022 (56c) multi	1.75	.60
3711	A2022 (56c) multi	1.75	.60
3712	A2022 (56c) multi	1.75	.60
3713	A2022 (56c) multi	1.75	.60
3714	A2022 (56c) multi	1.75	.60
3715	A2022 (56c) multi	1.75	.60
3716	A2023 (56c) multi	1.75	.60
3717	A2023 (56c) multi	1.75	.60
3718	A2023 (56c) multi	1.75	.60
3719	A2023 (56c) multi	1.75	.60
3720	A2023 (56c) multi	1.75	.60
3721	A2023 (56c) multi	1.75	.60
3722	A2023 (56c) multi	1.75	.60
3723	A2023 (56c) multi	1.75	.60
a.	Booklet pane of 14, #3710-3723	24.50	
	Nos. 3710-3723 (14)	24.50	8.40

René de Saint-Marceaux (1845-1915), Sculptor of UPU Monument — A2024

Litho. & Engr.

2009, Oct. 9 *Perf. 13x13¼*

3724	A2024 70c multi	2.10	.70

See Switzerland No. 9O22.

Miniature Sheet

Dolls — A2025

No. 3725: a, Porcelain doll. b, GéGé doll, horiz. c, Rag doll, horiz. d, Bella doll, horiz. e, Baigneur Petitcollin, horiz. f, Unglazed porcelain doll (poupée en biscuit).

2009, Oct. 17 *Perf. 13*

3725	A2025 Sheet of 6	10.50	10.50
a.-f.	56c Any single	1.75	.60

Juliette Dodu (1848-1909), Spy — A2026

2009, Oct. 28 Engr. *Perf. 13¼*

3726	A2026 56c multi	1.75	.60

Self-Adhesive

Serpentine Die Cut 11

3727	A2026 56c multi	1.75	1.75

European Capitals Type of 2002

Miniature Sheet

No. 3728 — Attractions in Lisbon: a, Hieronymites Monastery. b, Bairro Alto Quarter, vert. c, Belém Tower. d, Monument to the Discoveries.

Perf. 13x13¼, 13¼x13 (#3728b)

2009, Nov. 5 Photo.

3728	A1622 Sheet of 4	7.00	7.00
a.-d.	56c Any single	1.75	.60

Francisco de Miranda (1750-1816), Revolutionist in France and Venezuela — A2027

2009, Nov. 6 Photo. *Perf. 13¼*

3729	A2027 85c multi	2.60	.90

See Venezuela No. 1693.

Marianne and Stars Type of 2008

Miniature Sheet

Photo., Engr. (#3456-3458)

2009, Nov. 6 *Perf. 13*

3730	Sheet of 13, #3456-3458, 3730a-3730j + label	31.00	31.00
a.	A1912 1c yellow	.25	.25
b.	A1912 5c gray brown	.25	.25
c.	A1912 10c gray	.30	.30
d.	A1912 73c olive green	2.25	2.25
e	A1912 85c purple	2.60	2.60
f.	A1912 90c fawn	2.75	2.75
g.	A1912 €1 orange	3.00	3.00
h.	A1912 €1.30 blue	4.00	4.00
i.	A1912 €1.35 red violet	4.00	4.00
j.	A1912 €2.22 chocolate	6.50	6.50

Euromed Postal Conference — A2028

2009, Nov. 7 Engr. *Perf. 13¼*

3731	A2028 56c multi	1.75	.60

A2029

A2030

A2031

A2032

A2033

A2034

A2035 A2036

A2037

A2038

A2039

A2040

A2041 A2042

Serpentine Die Cut 11

2009, Nov. 7 Photo.

Booklet Stamps

Self-Adhesive

3732	A2029 (56c) multi		1.75	.60
3733	A2030 (56c) multi		1.75	.60
3734	A2031 (56c) multi		1.75	.60
3735	A2032 (56c) multi		1.75	.60
3736	A2033 (56c) multi		1.75	.60
3737	A2034 (56c) multi		1.75	.60
3738	A2035 (56c) multi		1.75	.60
3739	A2036 (56c) multi		1.75	.60
3740	A2037 (56c) multi		1.75	.60
3741	A2038 (56c) multi		1.75	.60
3742	A2039 (56c) multi		1.75	.60
3743	A2040 (56c) multi		1.75	.60
3744	A2041 (56c) multi		1.75	.60
3745	A2042 (56c) multi		1.75	.60
a.	Booklet pane of 14, #3732-3745		24.50	
	Nos. 3732-3745 (14)		24.50	8.40

A souvenir sheet containing one No. 3743 sold for €3.

Helicopter Carrier Jeanne d'Arc — A2043

Sailors of the Jeanne d'Arc — A2044

2009, Nov. 21 Engr. *Perf. 13x12¾*

3746	A2043 56c multi	1.75	.60
3747	A2044 56c multi	1.75	.60
a.	Horiz. pair, #3746-3747	3.50	1.20

A souvenir sheet containing Nos. 3746-3747 sold for €3.

Asterix, Comic Strip by René Goscinny and Albert Uderzo — A2045

No. 3749: a, Assurancetorix on rope (40x30mm). b, Eight characters, horiz. (80x26mm). c, Falbala with basket (30x40mm). d, Idefix and bone, horiz. (22x19mm). e, Obelix carrying rock (50x100mm).

2009, Dec. 2 Photo. *Perf. 13*

3748	A2045 56c multi	1.75	.60
3749	Sheet of 6, #3748, 3749a-3749e	15.50	15.50
a.	A2045 56c multi, perf. 13x13¼	2.50	2.50
b.	A2045 56c multi, perf. 13	2.50	2.50
c.	A2045 56c multi, perf. 13¼x13	2.50	2.50
d.	A2045 56c multi, perf. 13¼x12½	2.50	2.50
e.	A2045 56c multi, perf. 13x12¼	2.50	2.50

No. 3749 sold for €5.20, with the Red Cross receiving €1.84 of that. No. 3749e has a gritty substance affixed to the rock.

A2046

Hearts A2047

Type I — Bow ties extend to perforations.
Type II — Bow ties do not touch perforations (red frame all around).

2010, Jan. 8 Photo. *Perf. 13¼*

3750	A2046 56c multi, type I	1.60	.55

Perf.

3751	A2046 56c multi, type II	1.60	.55

Perf. 13¼

3752	A2047 90c multi	2.50	1.25
	Nos. 3750-3752 (3)	5.70	2.35

Self-Adhesive

Serpentine Die Cut

3753	A2046 56c multi, type I	1.60	1.60
3754	A2047 90c multi	2.50	2.50

Values for Nos. 3750, 3752 are for stamps with surrounding selvage. No. 3751 was printed in sheets of 5.

New Year 2010 (Year of the Tiger) — A2048

2010, Jan. 15 Photo. *Perf. 13¼x13*

3755	A2048 56c multi	1.60	.55

No. 3755 was printed in sheets of 5. A souvenir sheet of 1 sold for €3.

See No. 4970b.

Abbé Pierre (1912-2007), Founder of Emmaus Movement A2049

2010, Jan. 22 Engr. *Perf. 13¼*

3756	A2049 56c multi	1.60	.55

Self-Adhesive

Serpentine Die Cut 11

3757	A2049 56c multi	1.60	1.60

A souvenir sheet containing No. 3756 was printed in 2011 and sold for €3.

Musical Instruments in Art — A2050

Designs: No. 3758, Lyre, by Gustave Moreau. No. 3759, Harp (Harpe), by François André Vincent. No. 3760, Violincello (Violincelle), by Karl Gustav Klingstedt. No. 3761, Guitar (Guitare), by Camille Roqueplan. No. 3762, Horn (Cor), by Daniel Rabel. No. 3763, Saxophone, by Marthe and Juliette Vesque. No. 3764, Organ (Orgue), by François Garas. No. 3765, Bugle (Clairon), by Auguste Mayer. No. 3766, Clavecin, by Louis Carrogis Carmontelle. No. 3767, Piano, by Pierre-Désiré Lamy. No. 3768, Tambourine (Tambourin), by Théodore Chassériau. No. 3769, Drums (Tambour), by Jacques-Antoine Delaistre.

Serpentine Die Cut 11

2010, Jan. 30 Photo.

Booklet Stamps

Self-Adhesive

3758	A2050 (56c) multi	1.60	.55
3759	A2050 (56c) multi	1.60	.55
3760	A2050 (56c) multi	1.60	.55
3761	A2050 (56c) multi	1.60	.55
3762	A2050 (56c) multi	1.60	.55
3763	A2050 (56c) multi	1.60	.55
3764	A2050 (56c) multi	1.60	.55
3765	A2050 (56c) multi	1.60	.55
3766	A2050 (56c) multi	1.60	.55
3767	A2050 (56c) multi	1.60	.55
3768	A2050 (56c) multi	1.60	.55
3769	A2050 (56c) multi	1.60	.55
a.	Booklet pane of 12, #3758-3769	19.50	
	Nos. 3758-3769 (12)	19.20	6.60

See Nos. 3882A-3882B.

2010 Winter Olympics, Vancouver A2051

2010, Feb. 6 *Perf. 13x13¼*

3770	A2051 85c Figure skaters	2.40	1.25
3771	A2051 85c Skier	2.40	1.25
a.	Horiz. pair, #3770-3771	4.80	2.50
b.	Tete-beche block of 4, 2 #3771a	9.60	5.00

Art Issue

Museum of Art and Industry (La Piscine), Roubaix — A2052

The Beach at Calais at Ebb Tide, by Joseph Mallord William Turner — A2053

Maman, by Louise Bourgeois — A2054

Allegory of Spring, by Sandro Botticelli — A2055

No. 3775: a, Flora, Zephyrus and Chloris. b, The Three Graces.

2010 Photo. *Perf. 13x13¼*

3772	A2052	85c multi	2.10	1.10
3773	A2053	€1.35 multi	3.75	1.90
3774	A2054	€1.35 multi	3.50	1.75
		Nos. 3772-3774 (3)	9.35	4.75

Perf. 13¼x13

3775	A2055	Sheet of 2	6.25	6.25
a.		87c multi	2.40	1.25
b.		€1.40 multi	3.75	1.90

Self-Adhesive

Serpentine Die Cut 11

Photo.

3776	A2052	85c multi	2.10	2.10
3776A	A2055	87c Like #3775b	2.40	2.40
3777	A2053	€1.35 multi	3.75	3.75
3778	A2054	€1.35 multi	3.50	3.50
3779	A2055	€1.40 Like #3775a	3.75	3.75
		Nos. 3776-3779 (5)	15.50	15.50

Issued: Nos. 3772, 3776, 5/15; Nos. 3773, 3777, 2/19; Nos. 3774, 3778, 6/17; No. 3775, 11/8/10; Nos. 3776A, 3779, 11/18/10.

A2056

Stamp Day — A2057

2010, Feb. 27 Engr. *Perf. 13*
3780 A2056 56c blue & red 1.60 .55

Souvenir Sheet
Litho. & Embossed
Perf. 13¼x13
3781 A2057 €2 multi 5.50 2.75

Protection of Water A2058

Inscriptions: No. 3782, Grands mammifères marins (large marine mammals). No. 3783, Marée noire (black tide). No. 3784, Irrigation. No. 3785, Plaisir de l'eau (pleasure of water). No. 3786, Inondation (flood). No. 3787, Source. No. 3788, Aigues vertes (green water). No. 3789, Secheresse (drought). No. 3790, Hydro-électricité (hydroelectricity). No. 3791, Géothermie (geothermal energy). No. 3792, Pluies acides (acid rain). No. 3793, Fonte des glaciers (melting of glaciers).

Serpentine Die Cut 11
2010, Feb. 27 Photo.
Booklet Stamps
Self-Adhesive

3782 A2058 (56c) multi 1.60 .55
3783 A2058 (56c) multi 1.60 .55
3784 A2058 (56c) multi 1.60 .55
3785 A2058 (56c) multi 1.60 .55
3786 A2058 (56c) multi 1.60 .55
3787 A2058 (56c) multi 1.60 .55
3788 A2058 (56c) multi 1.60 .55
3789 A2058 (56c) multi 1.60 .55
3790 A2058 (56c) multi 1.60 .55
3791 A2058 (56c) multi 1.60 .55
3792 A2058 (56c) multi 1.60 .55
3793 A2058 (56c) multi 1.60 .55
a. Booklet pane of 12, #3782-3793 19.50
Nos. 3782-3793 (12) 19.20 6.60

Savoy as Part of France, 150th Anniv. A2059

2010, Mar. 27 Engr. *Perf. 13¼x13*
3794 A2059 56c multi 1.60 .55

Self-Adhesive
Serpentine Die Cut 11
3795 A2059 56c multi 1.60 1.60

Tourism Issue

Villeneuve lez Avignon A2060

Orcival Basilica — A2061

Pornic — A2062

Arcueil-Cachan Aqueduct Bridge — A2063

2010 Engr. *Perf. 13¼*
3796 A2060 56c multi 1.50 .50
3797 A2061 56c multi 1.40 .45

Perf. 13
3798 A2062 56c multi 1.40 .45

Perf. 13¼
3799 A2063 58c multi 1.60 .55
Nos. 3796-3799 (4) 5.90 1.95

Self-Adhesive
Engr.
Serpentine Die Cut 11
3800 A2060 56c multi 1.50 1.50

Issued: Nos. 3796, 3800, 4/17; No. 3797, 5/13; No. 3798, 5/25; No. 3799, 9/24.

A2064

A2065

A2066

A2067

A2068

A2069

A2070

A2071

A2072

A2073

A2074

Campaign Against Violence Toward Women — A2075

Serpentine Die Cut 11
2010, Apr. 20 Litho.
Booklet Stamps
Self-Adhesive

3801 A2064 (56c) multi 1.50 .50
3802 A2065 (56c) multi 1.50 .50
3803 A2066 (56c) multi 1.50 .50
3804 A2067 (56c) multi 1.50 .50
3805 A2068 (56c) multi 1.50 .50
3806 A2069 (56c) multi 1.50 .50
3807 A2070 (56c) multi 1.50 .50
3808 A2071 (56c) multi 1.50 .50
3809 A2072 (56c) multi 1.50 .50
3810 A2073 (56c) multi 1.50 .50
3811 A2074 (56c) multi 1.50 .50
3812 A2075 (56c) multi 1.50 .50
a. Booklet pane of 12, #3801-3812 18.00
Nos. 3801-3812 (12) 18.00 6.00

Colmar A2076

2010, Apr. 23 Engr. *Perf. 13¼*
3813 A2076 56c multi 1.50 .50

Self-Adhesive
Serpentine Die Cut 11
3814 A2076 56c multi 1.50 1.50

National Sheepcote, Rambouillet — A2077

2010, May 1 *Perf. 13¼*
3815 A2077 90c multi 2.40 1.25

Europa A2078

2010, May 9 Photo.
3816 A2078 70c multi 1.75 .60

Miniature Sheet

Stamp Bourse in Paris, 150th Anniv. — A2079

No. 3817 — Famous philatelists: a, Pres. Franklin Delano Roosevelt (1882-1945). b, Lucien Berthelot (1903-85), President of International Philatelic Federation. c, Louis Yvert (1866-1950), stamp catalogue publisher, horiz. d, Arthur Maury (1844-1907), stamp catalogue publisher, horiz. e, Alberto Bolaffi (1874-1944), stamp catalogue publisher.

2010, May 13 Engr. *Perf. 13*
3817 A2079 Sheet of 5 7.00 7.00
a.-e. 56c Any single 1.40 .45

Deauville, 150th Anniv. A2080

2010, May 14 Photo. *Perf. 13¼*
3818 A2080 85c multi 2.10 1.10

Mother Teresa (1910-97), Humanitarian A2081

2010, May 27 Engr. *Perf. 13¼x13*
3819 A2081 85c multi 2.10 1.10

Self-Adhesive
Serpentine Die Cut 11
3820 A2081 85c multi 2.10 2.10

Institute of Human Paleontology, Paris, Cent. — A2082

2010, June 1 *Perf. 13x12¾*

3821 A2082 56c multi 1.40 .45

See Monaco No. 2597.

Nice as Part of France, 150th Anniv. A2083

2010, June 11 **Photo.** *Perf. 13¼*

3822 A2083 56c multi 1.40 .45

Self-Adhesive

Serpentine Die Cut 11

3823 A2083 56c multi 1.40 1.40

Front Side of No. 3824

Rear Side of No. 3824 — A2084

A2085

2010 World Cup Soccer Championships, South Africa — A2086

No. 3825: a, Soccer player and ball. b, Soccer players, vert. c, South African building, vert. d, Aerial view of Cape Town.

2010 **Photo.** *Perf. 13x12¾*

3824 A2084 56c multi 2.75 .50

Perf. 13x13¼, 13¼x13

3825 A2085 Sheet of 4 8.50 8.50
a.-d. 85c Any single 2.10 1.10

Embossed and Etched on Silver

Die Cut Perf. 12¾

Self-Adhesive

3826 A2086 €5 *silver* 12.50 12.50

Issued: Nos. 3824, 3825, 6/13; No. 3826, 6/1.1. No. 3824 is gummed on both sides and sold for €1.12. Both sides of the stamp could be used. Values for used examples of No. 3824 are for stamps canceled on either or both sides.

Launch of Soyuz Space Flights From French Guiana A2087

2010, June 12 **Photo.** *Perf. 13¼*

3827 A2087 85c multi 2.25 1.10

Self-Adhesive

Serpentine Die Cut 11

3828 A2087 85c multi 2.25 2.25

Souvenir Sheet

Jardins de Giverny, by Claude Monet — A2088

No. 3829: a, Bridge. b, Pond.

2010, June 12 *Perf. 13¼x13*

3829 A2088 Sheet of 2 11.50 11.50
a.-b. €2.22 Either single 5.75 3.00
c. Souvenir sheet, #3709a, 3709b, 3829a, 3829b 22.50 22.50

2010 Salon du Timbre (No. 3829c).

Regional Cuisine A2089

Designs: No. 3830, Eclade (grilled mussels), Poitou-Charentes. No. 3831, Baeckaoffe (stew), Alsace. No. 3832, Tomme des Pyrénées cheese, Midi-Pyrénées. No. 3833, Tarte aux mirabelles (plum tart), Lorraine. No. 3834, Potage aux cresson (watercress soup), Ile-de-France. No. 3835, Flamiche (leek pie), Picardy. No. 3836, Pont l'Evêque cheese, Basse-Normandie. No. 3837, Blanc-manger (blancmange), Antilles. No. 3838, Caviar, Aquitaine. No. 3839, Chapon (capon), Franche-Comté. No. 3840, Fourme d'Ambert cheese, Auvergne. No. 3841, Tarte tatin (upside-down apple tart), Centre.

No. 3842, Quenelles (dumplings), Rhône-Alpes. No. 3843, Escalope normande (veal cutlet), Haute-Normandie. No. 3844, Maroilles cheese, Nord-Pas-de-Calais. No. 3845, Clafoutis (baked fruit and batter), Limousin. No. 3846, Gougères (cheese pastry), Bourgogne. No. 3847, Tian (baked vegetables), Provence-Alpes-Côte d'Azur. No. 3848, Brocciu cheese, Corsica. No. 3849, Abricots rouges au miel (apricots in honey), Languedoc-Roussillon. No. 3850, Homard breton (lobster), Bretagne. No. 3851, Brochet au beurre blanc (pike with white butter), Pays de la Loire. No. 3852, Chaource cheese, Champagne-Ardennes. No. 3853, Paris-Brest (butter cream-filled pastry), Paris.

Serpentine Die Cut 11

2010, June 12 **Photo.**

Booklet Stamps

Self-Adhesive

3830 A2089 (56c) multi 1.40 .45
3831 A2089 (56c) multi 1.40 .45
3832 A2089 (56c) multi 1.40 .45
3833 A2089 (56c) multi 1.40 .45
a. Booklet pane of 4, #3830-3833 5.60
3834 A2089 (56c) multi 1.40 .45
3835 A2089 (56c) multi 1.40 .45
3836 A2089 (56c) multi 1.40 .45
3837 A2089 (56c) multi 1.40 .45
a. Booklet pane of 4, #3834-3837 5.60
3838 A2089 (56c) multi 1.40 .45
3839 A2089 (56c) multi 1.40 .45
3840 A2089 (56c) multi 1.40 .45
3841 A2089 (56c) multi 1.40 .45
a. Booklet pane of 4, #3838-3841 5.60
Complete booklet, #3833a, 3837a, 3841a 17.00
3842 A2089 (56c) multi 1.40 .45
3843 A2089 (56c) multi 1.40 .45
3844 A2089 (56c) multi 1.40 .45
3845 A2089 (56c) multi 1.40 .45
a. Booklet pane of 4, #3842-3845 5.60
3846 A2089 (56c) multi 1.40 .45
3847 A2089 (56c) multi 1.40 .45
3848 A2089 (56c) multi 1.40 .45
3849 A2089 (56c) multi 1.40 .45
a. Booklet pane of 4, #3846-3849 5.60
3850 A2089 (56c) multi 1.40 .45
3851 A2089 (56c) multi 1.40 .45
3852 A2089 (56c) multi 1.40 .45
3853 A2089 (56c) multi 1.40 .45
a. Booklet pane of 4, #3850-3853 5.60
Complete booklet, #3845a, 3849a, 3853a 17.00
Nos. 3830-3853 (24) 33.60 10.80

Romanesque Art — A2090

Designs: No. 3854, Bas-relief, Tournus. No. 3855, Interior of Cistercian Abbey, Léoncel. No. 3856, Painting, St. Sever. No. 3857, Serrabone Priory, Boule d'Amont. No. 3858, Sculpture, L'Ile-Bouchard. No. 3859, Painting, Citeaux Abbey. No. 3860, Fresco from St. Martin's Church, Nohant-Vic. No. 3861, Bas-relief, Clermont-Ferrand. No. 3862, Fresco, St. Jacques-des-Guérets. No. 3863, Bas-relief, Angouleme. No. 3864, Painting of the Consecration of the third Abbey Church, Cluny. No. 3865, Bas-reliefs, tympanum of Saint-Foy Abbey Church, Conques.

Serpentine Die Cut 11

2010, June 14 **Photo.**

Booklet Stamps

Self-Adhesive

3854 A2090 (56c) multi 1.40 .45
3855 A2090 (56c) multi 1.40 .45
3856 A2090 (56c) multi 1.40 .45
3857 A2090 (56c) multi 1.40 .45
3858 A2090 (56c) multi 1.40 .45
3859 A2090 (56c) multi 1.40 .45
3860 A2090 (56c) multi 1.40 .45
3861 A2090 (56c) multi 1.40 .45
3862 A2090 (56c) multi 1.40 .45
3863 A2090 (56c) multi 1.40 .45
3864 A2090 (56c) multi 1.40 .45
3865 A2090 (56c) multi 1.40 .45
a. Booklet pane of 12, #3854-3865 17.00
Nos. 3854-3865 (12) 16.80 5.40

See Nos. 3870A-3870B.

Miniature Sheet

Mills — A2091

No. 3866: a, Windmill, Montbrun-Lauragais. b, Windmill, Cassel. c, Aigremonts Windmill, Bléré, horiz. d, Daudet Windmill, Fontvieille, horiz. e, Flour mill, Villeneuve-d'Ascq. f, Birlot Watermill, Ile-de-Bréhat, horiz.

Litho. & Engr.

2010, June 15 *Perf. 13*

3866 A2091 Sheet of 6 8.50 8.50
a.-f. 56c Any single 1.40 .45

2010 Youth Olympics, Singapore A2092

2010, June 16 **Photo.** *Perf. 13¼*

3867 A2092 85c multi 2.25 1.10

Souvenir Sheet

Charles de Gaulle's Appeal of June 18 Speech, 70th Anniv. — A2093

2010, June 18 **Engr.** *Perf. 13x13¼*

3868 A2093 56c multi 1.40 .45

Conciergerie, Paris — A2094

2010, June 19

3869 A2094 56c multi + label 1.40 .45

French Federation of Philatelic Associations, 83rd Congress, Paris.

French Pavilion, Expo 2010, Shanghai A2095

2010, June 20 **Photo.** *Perf. 13¼*

3870 A2095 85c multi 2.25 1.10

Romanesque Art Type of 2010

Designs: No. 3870A, Like #3855. No. 3870B, Like #3858.

Serpentine Die Cut 11

2010, June 21 **Litho.**

Self-Adhesive

3870A A2090 (56c) multi 1.40 1.40
3870B A2090 (56c) multi 1.40 1.40

Nos. 3870A-3870B each were printed in sheets of 50. The red panels of Nos. 3855 and 3858 are splotchy, typical of photogravure printings. Under magnification black dots can be seen in the red panels on Nos. 3870A-3870B.

Marianne and Stars Type of 2008

2010, July 1 **Engr.** *Perf. 13*

3871 A1912 75c olive green 1.90 .50
3872 A1912 87c purple 2.25 .55
3873 A1912 95c fawn 2.40 .60
3874 A1912 €1.35 blue 3.50 .90
3875 A1912 €1.40 red violet 3.50 .90
3876 A1912 €2.30 chocolate 5.75 1.50
Nos. 3871-3876 (6) 19.30 4.95

Self-Adhesive

Serpentine Die Cut 6¾ Vert.

3877 A1912 75c olive green 1.90 1.90
3878 A1912 87c purple 2.25 2.25
3879 A1912 95c fawn 2.40 2.40
3880 A1912 €1.35 blue 3.50 3.50
3881 A1912 €1.40 red violet 3.50 3.50
3882 A1912 €2.30 chocolate 5.75 5.75
Nos. 3877-3882 (6) 19.30 19.30

Musical Instruments Type of 2010

Designs: No. 3882A, Like #3761. No. 3882B, Like #3767.

Serpentine Die Cut 11

2010, July 1 **Litho.**

Self-Adhesive

3882A A2050 (58c) multi 1.50 1.50
3882B A2050 (58c) multi 1.50 1.50

Nos. 3882A-3882B were each printed in sheets of 50. The gray blue portions of Nos. 3761 and 3767 are splotchy, typical of photogravure printings, and not splotchy on Nos. 3882A and 3882B.

Independence of French Colonies in Africa, 50th Anniv. — A2096

2010, July 15 **Photo.** ***Perf. 13¼***

3883 A2096 87c multi 2.25 1.10

Self-Adhesive

Serpentine Die Cut 11

3884 A2096 87c multi 2.25 2.25

Butterflies A2097

Designs: Nos. 3885, 3886b, Morpho menelaus. No. 3886a, Cerura vinula caterpillar. 75c, Thersamolycaena dispar, vert. 95c, Callophrys rubi.

Litho. (#3885, 3886a), Litho. & Embossed

2010, Sept. 3 ***Perf. 13¼***

3885 A2097 58c multi 1.50 .50
3886 Sheet of 4 7.50 7.50
a. A2097 58c multi 1.50 .50
b. A2097 58c multi 1.50 .50
c. A2097 75c multi 2.00 .65
d. A2097 95c multi 2.50 .85

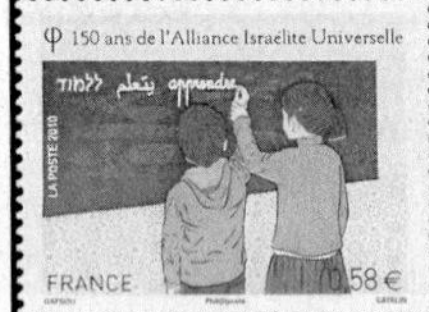

Universal Israelite Alliance, 150th Anniv. A2098

Litho. & Engr.

2010, Sept. 7 ***Perf. 13¼***

3887 A2098 58c multi 1.50 .50

A2099

A2100

A2101

A2102

A2103

A2104

A2105

A2106

A2107

A2108

A2109

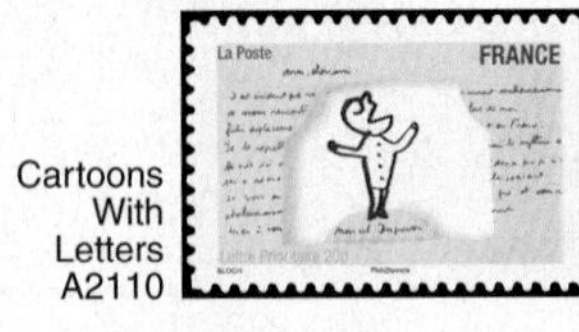

Cartoons With Letters A2110

Serpentine Die Cut 11

2010, Oct. 11 **Photo.**

Booklet Stamps

Self-Adhesive

3888 A2099 (58c) multi 1.75 .60
3889 A2100 (58c) multi 1.75 .60
3890 A2101 (58c) multi 1.75 .60
3891 A2102 (58c) multi 1.75 .60
3892 A2103 (58c) multi 1.75 .60
3893 A2104 (58c) multi 1.75 .60
3894 A2105 (58c) multi 1.75 .60
3895 A2106 (58c) multi 1.75 .60
3896 A2107 (58c) multi 1.75 .60
3897 A2108 (58c) multi 1.75 .60
3898 A2109 (58c) multi 1.75 .60
3899 A2110 (58c) multi 1.75 .60
a. Booklet pane of 12, #3888-3899 21.00
Nos. 3888-3899 (12) 21.00 7.20

Aviation Pioneers — A2111

Designs: Nos. 3900, 3902, Elise Deroche (1882-1919).

No. 3901: a, Hubert Latham (1883-1912). b, Orville (1871-1948) and Wilbur Wright (1867-1912). c, Henry Farman (1874-1958). d, Jules Védrines (1881-1919). e, Léon Delagrange (1872-1910).

2010, Oct. 15 **Photo.** ***Perf. 13***

3900 A2111 58c multi 1.75 .60
3901 Sheet of 6, #3900, 3901a-3901e 15.00 15.00
a.-e. A2111 58c Any single 2.50 2.50

Self-Adhesive

Serpentine Die Cut 11

3902 A2111 58c multi 1.75 1.75

No. 3901 sold for € 5.40, with the Red Cross receiving €1.92 of that.

World Fencing Championships, Paris — A2112

Designs: 58c, Wheelchair fencing. 87c, Fencing.

2010, Oct. 22 **Engr.** ***Perf. 13x13¼***

3903 A2112 58c multi 1.75 .60
3904 A2112 87c multi 2.50 .85
a. Horiz. pair, #3903-3904 + central label 4.25 1.50

Paris Bar Association, Bicent. — A2113

2010, Oct. 28 **Photo.** ***Perf. 13¼***

3905 A2113 58c black & lt blue 1.75 .60

Self-Adhesive

Serpentine Die Cut 11

3906 A2113 58c black & lt blue 1.75 1.75

Villeneuve-sur-Lot — A2114

2010, Oct. 30 **Engr.** ***Perf. 13¼***

3907 A2114 58c multi 1.75 .60

European Capitals Type of 2002

Miniature Sheet

No. 3908 — Attractions in Paris: a, Arc de Triomphe de l'Etoile. b, Notre Dame Cathedral. c, Garnier Opera House. d, Eiffel Tower, vert.

Perf. 13x13¼, 13¼x13 (#3908d)

2010, Nov. 4 **Photo.**

3908 A1622 Sheet of 4 7.00 7.00
a.-d. 58c Any single 1.75 .60

A2115

A2116

A2117

A2118

A2119

A2120

A2121

A2122

A2123

A2124

A2125

A2126

A2127

"Best Wishes" — A2128

Serpentine Die Cut 11

2010, Nov. 5 **Photo.**

Booklet Stamps

Self-Adhesive

3909 A2115 (58c) multi 1.75 .60
3910 A2116 (58c) multi 1.75 .60
3911 A2117 (58c) multi 1.75 .60
3912 A2118 (58c) multi 1.75 .60
3913 A2119 (58c) multi 1.75 .60
3914 A2120 (58c) multi 1.75 .60
3915 A2121 (58c) multi 1.75 .60
3916 A2122 (58c) multi 1.75 .60
3917 A2123 (58c) multi 1.75 .60
3918 A2124 (58c) multi 1.75 .60
3919 A2125 (58c) multi 1.75 .60
3920 A2126 (58c) multi 1.75 .60
3921 A2127 (58c) multi 1.75 .60
3922 A2128 (58c) multi 1.75 .60
a. Booklet pane of 14, #3909-3922, + 14 stickers 24.50
Nos. 3909-3922 (14) 24.50 8.40

A souvenir sheet containing one perf. 13x13¼ example of No. 3915 with water-activated gum sold for €3.

First French Revenue Stamp, 150th Anniv. — A2129

Serpentine Die Cut 6¾ Vert.

2010, Nov. 6 Engr.

Booklet Stamp
Self-Adhesive

3923 A2129 (58c) brown 1.60 .40
a. Booklet pane of 12, 6 each #3471, 3923 19.50

Souvenir Sheet

Primitive Flemish Paintings — A2130

No. 3924: a, Madonna and Child, by Roger de la Pasture. b, Portrait of Laurent Froimont, by Rogier van der Weyden.

2010, Nov. 6 Photo. *Perf. 13*

3924 A2130 Sheet of 2 10.00 10.00
a.-b. €1.80 Either single 5.00 2.50

See Belgium No. 2478.

Independence Movements of Latin America and the Caribbean, Bicent. — A2131

2010, Nov. 27 *Perf. 13¼*

3925 A2131 87c multi 2.40 .80

Hearts A2132

Designs: 58c, Multicolored outlines of hearts. 95c, Red heart.

Photo., Photo. With Foil Application (95c)

2011, Jan. 7 *Perf. 13*

3926 A2132 58c multi 1.60 .55
a. Sheet of 5 8.00 8.00
3927 A2132 95c black & red 2.60 .85

Self-Adhesive

Serpentine Die Cut

3928 A2132 58c multi 1.60 1.60
3929 A2132 95c black & red 2.60 2.60

New Year 2011 (Year of the Rabbit) — A2133

2011, Jan. 14 Photo. *Perf. 13¼x13*

3930 A2133 58c multi 1.60 .55

No. 3930 was printed in sheets of 5. A souvenir sheet of 1 sold for €3.

See No. 4970c.

Mulhouse Tram-Train A2134

2011, Jan. 14 Engr. *Perf. 13¼*

3931 A2134 58c multi 1.60 .55

Fabric Designs A2135

Fabric designs from: Nos. 3932, 3936, French Polynesia. Nos. 3933, 3942, Japan. No. 3934, France, from 1780. No. 3935, Ivory Coast. No. 3937, Italy. No. 3938, Iran. No. 3939, Egypt. No. 3940, India. No. 3941, China. No. 3943, Peru. No. 3944, Morocco. No. 3945, France, from First Empire period.

Serpentine Die Cut 11

2011, Jan. 21 Photo.

Self-Adhesive
With Faint Blue Dots Behind Type in Area Below Vignette

3932 A2135 (58c) multi 1.60 1.60
3933 A2135 (58c) multi 1.60 1.60

Booklet Stamps
Without Dots Behind Type In Area Below Vignette

3934 A2135 (58c) multi 1.60 .55
3935 A2135 (58c) multi 1.60 .55
3936 A2135 (58c) multi 1.60 .55
3937 A2135 (58c) multi 1.60 .55
3938 A2135 (58c) multi 1.60 .55
3939 A2135 (58c) multi 1.60 .55
3940 A2135 (58c) multi 1.60 .55
3941 A2135 (58c) multi 1.60 .55
3942 A2135 (58c) multi 1.60 .55
3943 A2135 (58c) multi 1.60 .55
3944 A2135 (58c) multi 1.60 .55
3945 A2135 (58c) multi 1.60 .55
a. Booklet pane of 12, #3934-3945 19.50
Nos. 3934-3945 (12) 19.20 6.60

Marie Curie (1867-1934), Chemist A2136

2011, Jan. 27 Engr. *Perf. 13¼*

3946 A2136 87c red & dk blue 2.40 .80

Self-Adhesive

Serpentine Die Cut 11

3947 A2136 87c red & dk blue 2.40 2.40

Intl. Year of Chemistry.

Art Issue

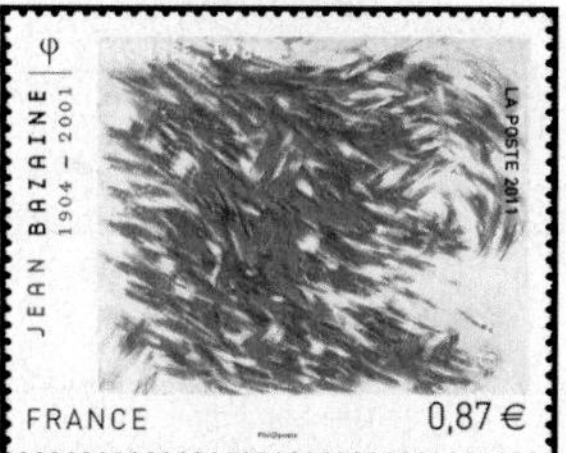

Plongée, by Jean Bazaine — A2137

Le Kiosque des Noctambules, Sculpture by Jean-Michel Othoniel — A2138

Buddha, by Odilon Redon A2139

Dying Centaur, Sculpture, by Antoine Bourdelle (1861-1929) — A2140

The Three Nymphs, Sculpture by Aristide Maillol (1861-1944) — A2140a

2011 Photo. *Perf. 13x13¼*

3948 A2137 87c multi 2.50 1.25

Perf. 13¼x13

3949 A2138 €1.40 multi 3.75 1.90
3950 A2139 €1.40 multi 3.75 1.90
Nos. 3948-3950 (3) 10.00 5.05

Souvenir Sheet

Engr.

3951 Sheet of 2 6.50 6.50
a. A2140 89c multi 2.50 1.25
b. A2140a €1.45 multi 4.00 2.00

Self-Adhesive

Serpentine Die Cut 11

3952 A2137 87c multi 2.50 2.50
3953 A2138 €1.40 multi 3.75 3.75
3954 A2139 €1.40 multi 3.75 3.75
3955 A2140 89c multi 2.50 2.50
3955A A2140a €1.45 multi 4.00 4.00
Nos. 3952-3955A (5) 16.50 16.50

Issued: Nos. 3948, 3952, 3/18; Nos. 3949, 3953, 2/11; Nos. 3950, 3954, 4/1; Nos. 3951, 3955, 3955A, 11/4.

Marianne and Hand Planting Seedling A2141

Strawberry and Strawberry Plant — A2142

2011, Feb. 26 Engr. *Perf. 13*

3956 A2141 58c multi 1.75 .60

Souvenir Sheet

Photo. & Engr.

Perf. 13¼x13

3957 A2142 €2 multi 5.75 3.00

Stamp Day. No. 3957 has printing and a strawberry-scented scratch-and-sniff panel on the reverse.

Hand Planting Seedling A2143

Leaf on Edge of Cliff A2144

Flora and Earth A2145

Hedgehog and Plants A2146

Field A2147

Tree With Various Fruits A2148

Man Carrying Earth in Wheelbarrow — A2149

Heart-shaped Plants in Flower Pots — A2150

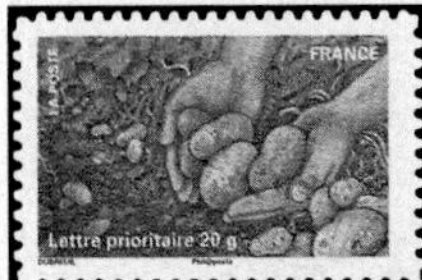

Hands Holding Potatoes A2151

Man Watering Tree on Earth A2152

Earth on Plant A2153

Farmer's Field and House A2154

Serpentine Die Cut 11

2011, Feb. 26 Photo.

Self-Adhesive

Smooth, Glossy Paper

3958 A2143 (58c) multi 1.75 1.75
3959 A2144 (58c) multi 1.75 1.75
3960 A2145 (58c) multi 1.75 1.75
Nos. 3958-3960 (3) 5.25 5.25

Booklet Stamps

Rough, Textured Paper

3961 A2143 (58c) multi 1.75 .60
3962 A2144 (58c) multi 1.75 .60
3963 A2146 (58c) multi 1.75 .60
3964 A2147 (58c) multi 1.75 .60
3965 A2148 (58c) multi 1.75 .60
3966 A2149 (58c) multi 1.75 .60
3967 A2150 (58c) multi 1.75 .60
3968 A2151 (58c) multi 1.75 .60
3969 A2152 (58c) multi 1.75 .60
3970 A2153 (58c) multi 1.75 .60
3971 A2154 (58c) multi 1.75 .60
3972 A2145 (58c) multi 1.75 .60
a. Booklet pane of 12, #3961-3972 21.00
Nos. 3961-3972 (12) 21.00 7.20

Stamp Day.

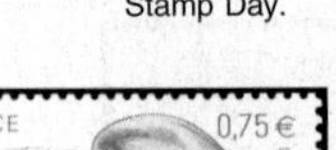

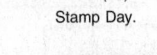

Tristan Corbière (1845-75), Poet A2155

2011, Mar. 4 Engr. *Perf. 13*
3973 A2155 75c multi 2.10 .70

Art of Miss.Tic (Radhia de Ruiter) A2156

Woman and text: No. 3974, Femme de lêtre. No. 3975, Je suis la votelle du mot voyou. No. 3976, Femme de tête mais l'esprit de corps. No. 3977, Tout achever sauf le désir. No. 3978, Soyons heureuses en attendant le bonneur. No. 3979, Je crois en l'éternel féminin. No. 3980, L'homme est le passé de la femme. No. 3981, Le masculin l'emporte mais où? No. 3982, Je ne me suis pas laissé défaire. No. 3983, Mieux que rien c'est pas assez. No. 3984, Il fait un temps de chienne. No. 3985, Cueillir l'éros de la vie.

Serpentine Die Cut 11

2011, Mar. 8 Photo.

Booklet Stamps

Self-Adhesive

3974 A2156 (58c) black & red 1.75 .60
3975 A2156 (58c) black & red 1.75 .60
3976 A2156 (58c) black & red 1.75 .60
3977 A2156 (58c) black & red 1.75 .60
3978 A2156 (58c) black & red 1.75 .60
3979 A2156 (58c) black & red 1.75 .60
3980 A2156 (58c) black & red 1.75 .60
3981 A2156 (58c) black & red 1.75 .60
3982 A2156 (58c) black & red 1.75 .60
3983 A2156 (58c) black & red 1.75 .60
3984 A2156 (58c) black & red 1.75 .60
3985 A2156 (58c) black & red 1.75 .60
a. Booklet pane of 12, #3974-3985 21.00
Nos. 3974-3985 (12) 21.00 7.20

Intl. Women's Day.

European Capitals Type of 2002

Miniature Sheet

No. 3986 — Attractions in Budapest: a, Parliament. b, Pont des Chaînes (Chain Bridge). c, Royal Palace. d, Bains Széchenyi (Szechenyi Baths), vert.

Perf. 13x13¼, 13¼x13 (#3986d)

2011, Mar. 25 Photo.
3986 A1622 Sheet of 4 7.00 7.00
a.-d. (58c) Any single 1.75 .60

Tourism Issue

Angers A2157

Wooden Bridge, Crest A2158

Autun — A2159

Varengeville-sur-Mer — A2160

Notre Dame Church, Royan — A2161

2011 Engr. *Perf. 13¼*
3987 A2157 58c multi 1.75 .60
3988 A2158 58c multi 1.75 .60

Perf. 13
3989 A2159 58c multi 1.75 .60

Perf. 13¼
3990 A2160 58c multi 1.75 .60
3991 A2161 60c multi 1.75 .60
Nos. 3987-3991 (5) 8.75 3.00

Issued: No. 3990, 6/24. No. 3991, 10/23.

Gothic Houses of Worship A2162

Designs: Nos. 3992, 4001, Notre Dame Cathedral, Strasbourg. Nos. 3993, 4002, Notre Dame Cathedral, Amiens. Nos. 3994, 4005, Sainte-Chapelle, Paris. No. 3995, St. Etienne Cathedral, Sens. No. 3996, Notre Dame Cathedral, Chartres. No. 3997, Notre Dame Cathedral, Laon. No. 3998, St. Etienne Cathedral, Metz. No. 3999, St. Pierre Cathedral, Beauvais. No. 4000, St. Etienne Cathedral, Bourges. No. 4003, Notre Dame Cathedral, Bayeux. No. 4004, Notre Dame Cathedral, Rouen. No. 4006, St. Denis Basilica, Saint-Denis.

Serpentine Die Cut 11

2011, Apr. 15 Litho.
3992 A2162 (58c) multi 1.75 1.75
3993 A2162 (58c) multi 1.75 1.75
3994 A2162 (58c) multi 1.75 1.75
Nos. 3992-3994 (3) 5.25 5.25

Photo.

Booklet Stamps

3995 A2162 (58c) multi 1.75 .60
3996 A2162 (58c) multi 1.75 .60
3997 A2162 (58c) multi 1.75 .60
3998 A2162 (58c) multi 1.75 .60
3999 A2162 (58c) multi 1.75 .60
4000 A2162 (58c) multi 1.75 .60
4001 A2162 (58c) multi 1.75 .60
4002 A2162 (58c) multi 1.75 .60
4003 A2162 (58c) multi 1.75 .60
4004 A2162 (58c) multi 1.75 .60
4005 A2162 (58c) multi 1.75 .60
4006 A2162 (58c) multi 1.75 .60
a. Booklet pane of 12, #3995-4006 21.00
Nos. 3995-4006 (12) 21.00 7.20

On lithographed stamps, "Phil@poste" is sharp and crisp, while on photogravure stamps it is muddy and unclear.

Dogs A2163

Designs: No. 4007, Labrador retriever. No. 4008a, Berger allemand (German shepherd), vert. 75c, Caniche (poodle). 95c, Yorkshire terrier, vert.

Perf. 13¼, 13¼x13¼x12¾x13¼ (#4008b)

2011, Apr. 28 Photo.
4007 A2163 58c multi 1.75 .60
4008 Sheet of 4, #4008a-4008c, 4007 8.50 8.50
a. A2163 58c multi 1.75 .60
b. A2163 75c multi 2.25 .75
c. A2163 95c multi 2.75 .90

Souvenir Sheet

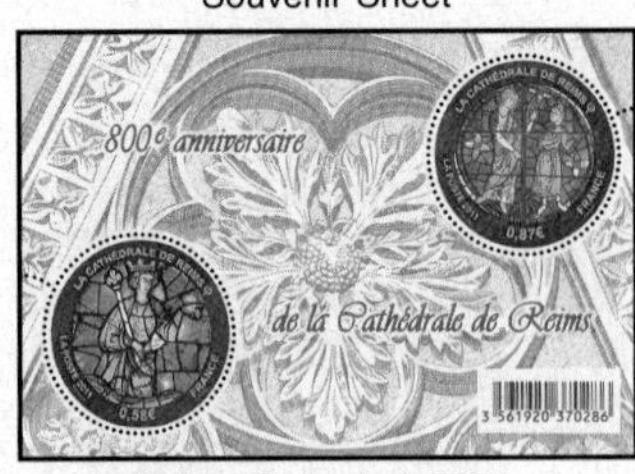

Reims Cathedral, 800th Anniv. — A2164

No. 4009 — Stained-glass window depicting: a, King. b, Saint and man.

2011, May 6 Engr. *Perf.*
4009 A2164 Sheet of 2 4.25 4.25
a. 58c multi 1.75 .60
b. 87c multi 2.50 .85

A souvenir sheet containing Nos. 4009a-4009b with a different sheet margin sold for €3.

Europa A2165

2011, May 8 Photo. *Perf. 13¼*
4010 A2165 75c multi 2.10 .70

Self-Adhesive

Serpentine Die Cut 11
4011 A2165 75c multi 2.10 2.10

Intl. Year of Forests.

Claude Bourgelat (1712-79), Founder of World's First Veterinary School A2166

2011, May 14 Engr. *Perf. 13¼*
4012 A2166 58c dark blue 1.75 .60

Self-Adhesive

Serpentine Die Cut 11
4013 A2166 58c dark blue 1.75 1.75

Regional Festivals and Traditions A2167

Inscriptions and location: Nos. 4014, 4018, La Braderie, Lille. Nos. 4015, 4033, La Saint-Vincent Tournante, Bourgogne. No. 4016, Le Théâtre des Cabotans, Amiens. No. 4017, Le Feu d'Artifices du 14 Juillet, Paris. No. 4019, Les Médiévales, Provins. No. 4020, La Bénédiction de la Mer, Port-en-Bessin-Huppain. No. 4021, La Fête du Hareng, Haute-Normandie. No. 4022, La Fête des Brodeuses, Pont-l'Abbé. No. 4023, La Fête des Chalands Fleuris, Saint-André-des-Eaux. No. 4024, La Force Basque, Biarritz, Hendaye and Esplette. No. 4025, Les Nuits Romanes, Poitou-Charentes. No. 4026, La Sardane, Céret. No. 4027, La Fête de la Transhumance, Midi-Pyrénées. No. 4028, La Saint Nicolas, Lorraine. No. 4029, Le Mariage de l'Ami Fritz, Marlenheim. No. 4030, Les Fêtes Johanniques, Reims. No. 4031, Les Soufflaculs, Saint-Claude. No. 4032, La Fête de l'Estive, allanche. No. 4034, La Foire aux Potirons, Tranzault. No. 4035, La Frairie des Petits Ventres, Limoges. No. 4036, La Fête du Citron, Menton. No. 4037, La Fête des Lumières, Lyon. No. 4038, L'Abolition de l'Esclavage, Réunion. No. 4039, Les Chants Corses, Corsica.

2011 Litho. *Serpentine Die Cut 11*

Self-Adhesive

4014 A2167 (58c) multi 1.75 1.75
4015 A2167 (58c) multi 1.75 1.75

Photo.

Booklet Stamps

4016 A2167 (58c) multi 1.75 .60
4017 A2167 (58c) multi 1.75 .60
4018 A2167 (58c) multi 1.75 .60
4019 A2167 (58c) multi 1.75 .60
a. Booklet pane of 4, #4016-4019 7.00
4020 A2167 (58c) multi 1.75 .60
4021 A2167 (58c) multi 1.75 .60
4022 A2167 (58c) multi 1.75 .60
4023 A2167 (58c) multi 1.75 .60
a. Booklet pane of 4, #4020-4023 7.00
4024 A2167 (58c) multi 1.75 .60
4025 A2167 (58c) multi 1.75 .60
4026 A2167 (58c) multi 1.75 .60
4027 A2167 (58c) multi 1.75 .60
a. Booklet pane of 4, #4024-4027 7.00
Complete booklet, #4019a, 4023a, 4027a 21.00
4028 A2167 (58c) multi 1.75 .60
4029 A2167 (58c) multi 1.75 .60
4030 A2167 (58c) multi 1.75 .60
4031 A2167 (58c) multi 1.75 .60
a. Booklet pane of 4, #4028-4031 7.00
4032 A2167 (58c) multi 1.75 .60
4033 A2167 (58c) multi 1.75 .60
4034 A2167 (58c) multi 1.75 .60

4035 A2167 (58c) multi 1.75 .60
a. Booklet pane of 4, #4032-4035 7.00
4036 A2167 (58c) multi 1.75 .60
4037 A2167 (58c) multi 1.75 .60
4038 A2167 (58c) multi 1.75 .60
4039 A2167 (58c) multi 1.75 .60
a. Booklet pane of 4, #4036-4039 7.00
Complete booklet, #4031a, 4035a, 4039a 21.00
Nos. 4016-4039 (24) 42.00 14.40

The black text on No. 4014 is sharper than that on No. 4018. The black text on No. 4015 is sharper than that on No. 4033.

Issued: No. 4014, 6/30, Nos. 4016-4039, 5/28.

French Federation of Philatelic Associations 84th Congress, Metz — A2168

2011, June 10 Engr. ***Perf. 13x13¼***
4040 A2168 58c multi + label 1.75 .60

A souvenir sheet containing No. 4040 was issued in 2012 and sold fro €3.

Miniature Sheet

Bicycles — A2169

No. 4041 — Inscriptions: a, Bicyclette à Pneumatiques. b, Draisenne, horiz. c, Vélocipède à Pédales, horiz. d, Vélo de Ville, horiz. e, Bicyclette à Chaine, horiz. f, Grand Bi.

Litho. & Engr.

2011, June 17 ***Perf. 13***
4041 A2169 Sheet of 6 10.50 10.50
a.-f. 58c Any single 1.75 .60

Pres. Georges Pompidou (1911-74), and Pompidou Center, Paris A2170

2011, June 22 Engr. ***Perf. 13¼***
4042 A2170 58c gray grn & brt bl 1.75 .60

Train des Pignes, Provence, Cent. A2171

2011, June 24
4043 A2171 58c multi 1.75 .60

Organization for Economic Cooperation and Development, 50th Anniv. — A2172

2011, June 24 **Photo.**
4044 A2172 87c multi 2.50 .85

World Judo Championships, Paris — A2173

2011, July 1 ***Perf. 13x12¾***
4045 A2173 89c multi 2.50 .85

Aquilegia A2174

Tulipa Sp. A2175

Bellis Perennis A2176

Primula Veris A2177

2011, July 1 Litho. ***Perf. 13***
4046 A2174 (38c) multi 1.10 .25
4047 A2175 (39c) multi 1.10 .25
4048 A2176 (46c) multi 1.40 .30
4049 A2177 (47c) multi 1.40 .30
Nos. 4046-4049 (4) 5.00 1.10

Nos. 4046-4049 are known only precanceled. See note after No. 132.

Compare with Nos. 3423-3426.

"Ecopli 20g" — A2178

"Lettre Prioritaire 20g" — A2179

"Europe 20g" — A2180

"Monde 20g" — A2181

"Lettre Prioritaire 50g" A2182

"Lettre Prioritaire 100g" A2183

"Lettre Prioritaire 250g" — A2184

Engr., Litho. (#4057a-4057d)

2011 ***Perf. 13***
4050 A2178 (55c) gray 1.60 .25
4051 A2179 (60c) red 1.75 .40
4052 A2180 (77c) dark blue 2.25 .60
4053 A2181 (89c) purple 2.50 .65
4054 A2182 (€1) fawn 3.00 .75
4055 A2183 (€1.45) red violet 4.25 1.10
4056 A2184 (€2.40) chocolate 6.75 2.40
Nos. 4050-4056 (7) 22.10 6.15

Souvenir Sheet

4057 Sheet of 7, #4050-4052, 4057a-4057d, + label 21.50 21.50
a. A2181 (89c) purple, litho. 2.50 2.50
b. A2182 (€1) fawn, litho. 2.75 2.75
c. A2183 (€1.45) red violet, litho. 4.00 4.00
d. A2184 (€2.40) chocolate, litho. 6.75 6.75

Coil Stamps

Perf. 13 Horiz.

4058 A2179 (60c) red 1.75 .40
4059 A2180 (77c) blue 2.25 .60

Self-Adhesive

Serpentine Die Cut 6¾ Vert.

4060 A2178 (55c) gray 1.60 1.60
4061 A2179 (60c) red 1.75 1.75
a. Booklet pane of 12 21.00
b. Booklet pane of 20 35.00
c. Booklet pane of 10 17.50
4062 A2180 (77c) blue 2.25 2.25
a. Booklet pane of 12 27.00
4063 A2181 (89c) purple 2.50 2.50
4064 A2182 (€1) fawn 3.00 3.00
4065 A2183 (€1.45) red violet 4.25 4.25
4066 A2184 (€2.40) chocolate 6.75 6.75
Nos. 4060-4066 (7) 22.10 22.10

Issued: Nos. 4050-4056, Nos. 4060-4066, 7/1; No. 4057, 11/3; Nos. 4058-4059, 7/6; No. 4061a, 7/1; Nos. 4061b-4061c, 4/16/12; No. 4062a, 8/16. See Nos. 4089-4090.

G20 and G8 Summits, Cannes and Deauville A2185

2011, July 8 Photo. ***Perf. 12¼***
4067 A2185 89c multi 2.50 .85

Self-Adhesive

Serpentine Die Cut 11

4068 A2185 89c multi 2.50 2.50

A2186

2011 Rugby World Cup, New Zealand A2187

No. 4069: a, Player with ball behind scrum. b, Player carrying ball, vert. c, Auckland skyline, vert. d, Lake and mountains, New Zealand.

€5, Two players.

Perf. 13¼x13, 13x13¼

2011, July 8 **Photo.**
4069 A2186 Sheet of 4 10.00 10.00
a.-d. 89c Any single 2.50 .85

Embossed and Etched on Silver

Self-Adhesive

Die Cut Perf. 12¾

4070 A2187 €5 silver 14.00 14.00

Protection of Water Type of 2010

Serpentine Die Cut 11

2011, Sept. 9 **Litho.**

Self-Adhesive

4071 A2058 (60c) Like #3782 1.75 1.75
4072 A2058 (60c) Like #3787 1.75 1.75

Nos. 4071-4072 have a dot structure not found on Nos. 3782 and 3787, which are printed by photogravure.

Souvenir Sheet

Gardens — A2188

No. 4073: a, Cheverny Gardens. b, Villandry Gardens.

2011, Sept. 16 Photo. ***Perf. 13¼x13***
4073 A2188 Sheet of 2 13.00 13.00
a.-b. €2.40 Either single 6.50 3.25

Salon du Timbre 2012.

Firefighters of Paris, Bicent. — A2189

No. 4074: a, Horse-drawn fire wagon (38x38mm). b, Fireman holding hose (26x40mm). c, Firemen attending to victim on gurney, ambulance (26x40mm). d, Fireman with rescue dog (30x40mm). e, Firefighter's badge (26x40mm). f, Firemen in truck holding flag, Arc de Triomphe (26x40mm). g, Fireman wearing helmet without visor (30x40mm). h, Firemen in antique fire truck (40x26mm). i, Fireman and modern ladder truck (40x26mm). j, j, Fireman wearing helmet with visor (30x40mm).

Perf. 13, 13¼ (#4074a), 13¼x13 (#4074d, 4074g, 4074j)

2011, Sept. 16
4074 A2189 Sheet of 10 17.50 17.50
a.-j. 60c Any single 1.75 .60

Self-Adhesive

Serpentine Die Cut 11

4075 A2189 60c Like #4074b 1.75 1.75
4076 A2189 60c Like #4074i 1.75 1.75

A set of six souvenir sheets, each containing one example of Nos. 4074a, 4074b, 4074f, 4074h, 4074i, and 4074j, sold for €15.

TGV Train Service, 30th Anniv. A2190

2011, Sept. 27 ***Perf. 13¼***
4077 A2190 60c multi 1.75 .60

Self-Adhesive

Serpentine Die Cut 11

4078 A2190 60c multi 1.75 1.75

A2191 A2192

Marianne, Stars and Leaf
A2193 A2194

2011, Sept. 30 **Engr.** ***Perf. 13***
4079 A2191 (57c) green 1.60 .25
4080 A2192 (95c) yellow green 2.60 .55
4081 A2193 (€1.40) blue green 4.00 .80
4082 A2194 (€2.30) dk bl green 6.25 1.25
Nos. 4079-4082 (4) 14.45 2.85

Coil Stamp

Perf. 13 Horiz.

4083 A2191 (57c) green 1.60 .25

Self-Adhesive

Serpentine Die Cut 6¾ Vert.

4084 A2191 (57c) green 1.60 1.60
a. Booklet pane of 10 16.00
b. Booklet pane of 12 19.50
c. Booklet pane of 20 32.00
4085 A2192 (95c) yellow green 2.60 2.60
4086 A2193 (€1.40) blue green 4.00 4.00
4087 A2194 (€2.30) dk bl green 6.25 6.25

Serpentine Die Cut 6¾ Horiz.

4088 A2191 (57c) green 1.60 .40
Nos. 4084-4088 (5) 16.05 14.85

Marianne and Stars Types of 2011

Serpentine Die Cut 6¾ Horiz.

2011, Oct. 1 **Engr.**

Coil Stamps
Self-Adhesive

4089 A2179 (60c) red 1.75 .40
4090 A2180 (77c) dark blue 2.10 .60

Souvenir Sheet

World Weight Lifting Championships, Paris — A2195

No. 4091: a, Male weight lifter (43mm diameter). b, Female weight lifter (49mm diameter).

2011, Oct. 7 **Photo.** ***Perf.***
4091 A2195 Sheet of 2 4.25 4.25
a. 60c multi 1.75 .60
b. 89c multi 2.50 .85

Souvenir Sheets

Chantilly Lace — A2196

Lace of Puy-en-Velay Region — A2197

Alençon Lace — A2198

Calais Lace — A2199

Litho. with Lace Affixed

2011, Oct. 8
4092 A2196 €2.50 multi 7.00 7.00
4093 A2197 €2.50 multi 7.00 7.00
4094 A2198 €2.50 multi 7.00 7.00
4095 A2199 €2.50 multi 7.00 7.00
Nos. 4092-4095 (4) 28.00 28.00

National Center for Space Studies, 50th Anniv. A2200

2011, Oct. 12 **Engr.** ***Perf. 13¼***
4096 A2200 60c multi 1.75 .60

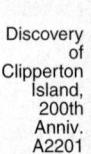

Discovery of Clipperton Island, 200th Anniv. A2201

2011, Oct. 21
4097 A2201 €1 multi 2.75 .90

Second-Place Finish of French Team in 2011 Rugby World Cup Championships — A2202

2011, Oct. 23 **Photo.**
4098 A2202 60c multi 1.75 .60

Values are for stamp with surrounding selvage.

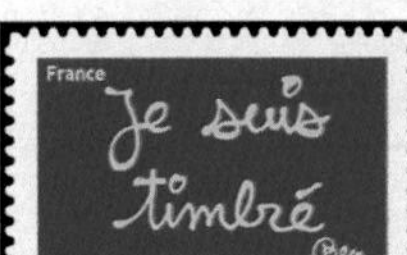

Words of Ben A2203

"Ben" (artist Benjamin Vautier) and inscription: No. 4099, Je suis timbré. No. 4100, J'aime écrire. No. 4101, Les mots c'est la vie. No. 4102, Entre nous. . . No. 4103, Cette idée. . . voyage. No. 4104, Pour l'instant tout va bien. No. 4105, Enfin de l'art. No. 4106, J'ai quelque chose à dire. No. 4107, Mots d'amour. No. 4108, Ceci est un lettre. No. 4109, Garderem lo moral. No. 4110, Vous êtes formidables!

Serpentine Die Cut 11

2011, Oct. 24 **Photo.**

Booklet Stamps
Self-Adhesive

4099 A2203 (60c) multi 1.75 .60
4100 A2203 (60c) multi 1.75 .60
4101 A2203 (60c) multi 1.75 .60
4102 A2203 (60c) multi 1.75 .60
4103 A2203 (60c) multi 1.75 .60
4104 A2203 (60c) multi 1.75 .60
4105 A2203 (60c) multi 1.75 .60
4106 A2203 (60c) multi 1.75 .60
4107 A2203 (60c) multi 1.75 .60
4108 A2203 (60c) multi 1.75 .60
4109 A2203 (60c) multi 1.75 .60
4110 A2203 (60c) multi 1.75 .60
a. Booklet pane of 12, #4099-4110 21.00
Nos. 4099-4110 (12) 21.00 7.20

Compare with type A1667.

Gaston Monnerville (1897-1991), Senate President A2204

2011, Nov. 7 **Engr.** ***Perf. 13¼***
4111 A2204 60c multi 1.75 .60

Henri Mouhot (1826-61), Explorer of Southeast Asia A2205

2011, Nov. 7
4112 A2205 89c multi 2.50 .85

Christmas A2206

Paintings: No. 4113, Adoration of the Shepherds, by Robert Campin, Master of Flémalle. No. 4114, Adoration of the Shepherds, by Mathias Stormer. No. 4115, The Newborn, by Georges de La Tour. No. 4116, Adoration of the Magi, by Italian School artist. No. 4117, Adoration of the Magi, by Francisco de Zurbaran. No. 4118, Nativity, by Jean Fouquet. No. 4119, Nativity, by the Master of the Nativity in the Louvre. No. 4120, Triptych of the Adoration of the Magi, by the Master of 1518. No. 4121, Adoration of the Magi, by Peter Paul Rubens. No. 4122, Adoration of the Infant Jesus, by the Master of Moulins. No. 4123, Adoration of the Child, by the Master of the St. Bartholomew Altarpiece. No. 4124, Scenes from the Life of Christ — Nativity, by Mariotto di Nardo.

Serpentine Die Cut 11

2011, Nov. 7 **Photo.**

Booklet Stamps
Self-Adhesive

4113 A2206 (60c) multi 1.75 .60
4114 A2206 (60c) multi 1.75 .60
4115 A2206 (60c) multi 1.75 .60
4116 A2206 (60c) multi 1.75 .60
4117 A2206 (60c) multi 1.75 .60
4118 A2206 (60c) multi 1.75 .60
4119 A2206 (60c) multi 1.75 .60
4120 A2206 (60c) multi 1.75 .60
4121 A2206 (60c) multi 1.75 .60
4122 A2206 (60c) multi 1.75 .60
4123 A2206 (60c) multi 1.75 .60
4124 A2206 (60c) multi 1.75 .60
a. Booklet pane of 12, #4113-4124 21.00
Nos. 4113-4124 (12) 21.00 7.20

A souvenir sheet containing one perf. 13x13¼ example of No. 4115 with water-activated gum sold for €3.

Discovery of Insulin, 90th Anniv. A2207

2011, Nov. 17 **Photo.** ***Perf. 13¼***
4125 A2207 60c multi 1.75 .60

Serpentine Die Cut 11

Self-Adhesive

4126 A2207 60c multi 1.75 .60

Year of Overseas Territories A2208

Drawings of: No. 4127, Carved rocks, Guadeloupe. No. 4128, Harbor, Cayenne, French Guiana. No. 4129, Beach scence, New Caledonia. No. 4130, Tattoo designs of tiki and compass rose, French Polynesia. No. 4131, Tree blossoms, St. Martin. No. 4132, Buildings, St. Pierre and Miquelon. No. 4133, House, Martinique. No. 4134, Man on path near Morne Langevin, Reunion. No. 4135, Pirogue, near Mt. Choungi, Mayotte. No. 4136, Building, Saint-Barthélemy. No. 4137, Kava bowl and building, Wallis and Futuna Islands. No. 4138, Penguins, French Southern and Antarctic Territories (T.A.A.F).

Serpentine Die Cut 11

2011, Nov. 25 **Photo.**

Booklet Stamps
Self-Adhesive

4127 A2208 (60c) multi 1.75 .60
4128 A2208 (60c) multi 1.75 .60
4129 A2208 (60c) multi 1.75 .60
4130 A2208 (60c) multi 1.75 .60
4131 A2208 (60c) multi 1.75 .60
4132 A2208 (60c) multi 1.75 .60
4133 A2208 (60c) multi 1.75 .60
4134 A2208 (60c) multi 1.75 .60
4135 A2208 (60c) multi 1.75 .60
4136 A2208 (60c) multi 1.75 .60
4137 A2208 (60c) multi 1.75 .60
4138 A2208 (60c) multi 1.75 .60
a. Booklet pane of 12, #4127-4138 21.00
Nos. 4127-4138 (12) 21.00 7.20

New Year 2012 (Year of the Dragon)
A2209

2012, Jan. 6 ***Perf. 13¼x13***
4139 A2209 60c multi 1.60 .55

No. 4139 was printed in sheets of 5. A souvenir sheet of one sold for €3.
See No. 4970d.

A2210

Hearts
A2211

2012, Jan. 13 **Photo.** ***Perf. 13***
4140 A2210 €1 red & black 2.75 .95

Self-Adhesive
Serpentine Die Cut
4141 A2210 €1 red & black 2.75 2.75

On Plastic
4142 A2211 60c red & black 1.60 1.60
a. Souvenir sheet of 5 8.00

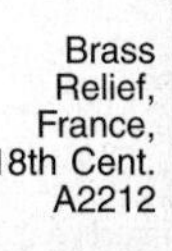

Brass Relief, France, 18th Cent.
A2212

Bronze Relief, China, 2nd Cent.
A2213

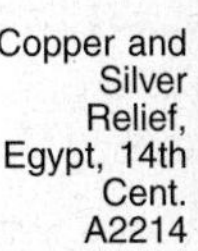

Copper and Silver Relief, Egypt, 14th Cent.
A2214

Marble Relief, Andalusia, 11th Cent.
A2215

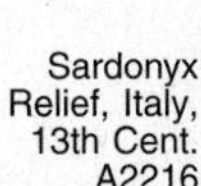

Sardonyx Relief, Italy, 13th Cent.
A2216

Stone Relief, Egypt, 1440 B.C.
A2217

Litho., Engr. (olive gray stamps)
Serpentine Die Cut 11
2012, Jan. 20 **Self-Adhesive**
Booklet Stamps
4143 A2212 (60c) multi 1.60 .55
4144 A2212 (60c) olive gray 1.60 .55
4145 A2213 (60c) multi 1.60 .55
4146 A2213 (60c) olive gray 1.60 .55
4147 A2214 (60c) multi 1.60 .55
4148 A2214 (60c) olive gray 1.60 .55
4149 A2215 (60c) multi 1.60 .55
4150 A2215 (60c) olive gray 1.60 .55
4151 A2216 (60c) multi 1.60 .55
4152 A2216 (60c) olive gray 1.60 .55
4153 A2217 (60c) multi 1.60 .55
4154 A2217 (60c) olive gray 1.60 .55
a. Booklet pane of 12, #4143-4154 19.50
Nos. 4143-4154 (12) 19.20 6.60

Art Issue

Morning Sun, by Edward Hopper — A2218

2012, Feb. 3 **Photo.** ***Perf. 13x13¼***
4155 A2218 €1.45 multi 4.00 2.00

Self-Adhesive
Serpentine Die Cut 11
4156 A2218 €1.45 multi 4.00 4.00

Flowers — A2219

Designs: No. 4157, Arums. No. 4158, Tulips. No. 4159, Roses. No. 4160, Violets. No. 4161, Pansies (Pensée). No. 4162, Lily of the valley (Muguet). No. 4163, Irises. No. 4164, Dahlias. No. 4165, Poppies (Coquelicot). No. 4166, Peonies (Pivoine). No. 4167, Daisies (Marguerite). No. 4168, Pinks (Oeillet).

Serpentine Die Cut 11
2012, Feb. 10 **Self-Adhesive**
Booklet Stamps
4157 A2219 (60c) multi 1.60 .55
4158 A2219 (60c) multi 1.60 .55
4159 A2219 (60c) multi 1.60 .55
4160 A2219 (60c) multi 1.60 .55
4161 A2219 (60c) multi 1.60 .55
4162 A2219 (60c) multi 1.60 .55
4163 A2219 (60c) multi 1.60 .55
4164 A2219 (60c) multi 1.60 .55
4165 A2219 (60c) multi 1.60 .55
4166 A2219 (60c) multi 1.60 .55
4167 A2219 (60c) multi 1.60 .55
4168 A2219 (60c) multi 1.60 .55
a. Booklet pane of 12, #4157-4168 19.50
Nos. 4157-4168 (12) 19.20 6.60

Grand Mosque of Paris, 90th Anniv. — A2220

2012, Feb. 11 **Engr.** ***Perf. 13¼***
4169 A2220 60c multi 1.60 .55

Henri Queuille (1884-1970), Prime Minister — A2221

2012, Feb. 17
4170 A2221 €1 black & brown 2.75 .95

Portraits of Women — A2222

Details of paintings: No. 4171, Young Woman in a Ball Gown, by Berthe Morisot. No. 4172, Portrait of Lydia Cassat, by Mary Cassatt. No. 4173, Biskra Woman, by Marie Caire. No. 4174, Woman with Turban, by Marie Laurencin. No. 4175, Madame Molé-Raymond, by Elisabeth Vigée-Lebrun. No. 4176, Portrait of a Young Woman, by Edgar Degas. No. 4177, Mandy, by Edouard Barnard Lintott. No. 4178, Orphan Girl at the Cemetery, by Eugène Delacroix. No. 4179, Woman with a Mirror, by Titian. No. 4180, Madeleine Bernard, by Paul Gauguin. No. 4181, Young Woman, by Hippolyte Flandrin. No. 4182, Portrait of Berthe Morisot with a Bouquet of Violets, by Edouard Manet.

Serpentine Die Cut 11
2012, Mar. 8 **Photo.**
Booklet Stamps
Self-Adhesive
4171 A2222 (60c) multi 1.60 .55
4172 A2222 (60c) multi 1.60 .55
4173 A2222 (60c) multi 1.60 .55
4174 A2222 (60c) multi 1.60 .55
4175 A2222 (60c) multi 1.60 .55
4176 A2222 (60c) multi 1.60 .55
4177 A2222 (60c) multi 1.60 .55
4178 A2222 (60c) multi 1.60 .55
4179 A2222 (60c) multi 1.60 .55
4180 A2222 (60c) multi 1.60 .55
4181 A2222 (60c) multi 1.60 .55
4182 A2222 (60c) multi 1.60 .55
a. Booklet pane of 12, #4171-4182 19.50
Nos. 4171-4182 (12) 19.20 6.60

European Capitals Type of 2002
Miniature Sheet

No. 4183 — Attractions in Copenhagen, Denmark: a, The Little Mermaid statue. b, Amalienborg Palace, horiz. c, Rosenborg Castle. d, Nyhavn, horiz.

Perf. 13¼x13, 13x13¼ (horiz. stamps)
2012, Mar. 23 **Photo.**
4183 A1622 Sheet of 4 6.50 6.50
a.-d. 60c Any single 1.60 .55

Tourism Issue

Moulins — A2223

2012, Mar. 23 **Engr.** ***Perf. 13x12¾***
4184 A2223 60c multi 1.60 .55

Miniature Sheet

Way of St. James — A2224

No. 4185: a, Via Turonensis in Paris. b, Via Lemovicensis in Vézelay, horiz. c, Via Podiensis in Puy-en Velay, horiz. d, Via Tolosana in Arles.

Litho. & Engr.
2012, Mar. 30 ***Perf. 13***
4185 A2224 Sheet of 4 8.50 8.50
a.-d. 77c Any single 2.10 .70

Fruits
A2225

Designs: No. 4186, Pineapple (Ananas). No. 4187, Melon. No. 4188, White grapes (Raisins blancs). No. 4189, Hazel nuts (Noisettes). No. 4190, Kiwis. No. 4191, Gooseberries (Groseilles à maquereaux). No. 4192, Green papayas (Papayes vertes). No. 4193, Dates (Dattes). No. 4194, Bananas (Bananes vertes). No. 4195, Mangos (Mangues). No. 4196, Pippin apples (Pommes "Reinette grise"). No. 4197, Pear (Poire William).

Serpentine Die Cut 11
2012, Mar. 30 **Photo.**
Booklet Stamps
Self-Adhesive
4186 A2225 (57c) multi 1.50 .50
4187 A2225 (57c) multi 1.50 .50
4188 A2225 (57c) multi 1.50 .50
4189 A2225 (57c) multi 1.50 .50
4190 A2225 (57c) multi 1.50 .50
4191 A2225 (57c) multi 1.50 .50
4192 A2225 (57c) multi 1.50 .50
4193 A2225 (57c) multi 1.50 .50
4194 A2225 (57c) multi 1.50 .50
4195 A2225 (57c) multi 1.50 .50
4196 A2225 (57c) multi 1.50 .50
4197 A2225 (57c) multi 1.50 .50
a. Booklet pane of 12, #4186-4197 18.00
Nos. 4186-4197 (12) 18.00 6.00

Tourism Issue

Epernay
A2226

2012, Apr. 13 **Engr.** ***Perf. 13¼***
4198 A2226 60c multi 1.60 .55

Tropical Fish — A2227

Designs: No. 4199, Amphiprion ocellaris. No. 4200a, Phycodurus eques, hoirz. No. 4200b, Heniochus acuminatus, horiz. No. 4200c, Pomacanthus imperator.

2012, Apr. 20 Photo. *Perf. 13¼*

4199 A2227 60c multi 1.60 .55
4200 Sheet of 4, #4199, 4200a-4200c 8.00 8.00
a. A2227 60c multi 1.60 .55
b. A2227 77c multi 2.10 .70
c. A2227 €1 multi 2.60 .90

Art A2228

Designs: No. 4201, Douglas Castle, painting by unknown Chinese artist. No. 4202, Crab, sculpture by Cheung Yee. Nos. 4203, 4205, The Racecourse — Amateur Jockeys Close to a Carriage, painting by Edgar Degas. No. 4204, The Horse, sculpture by Raymnond Duchamp-Villon.

2012, May 3 Photo. *Perf. 13¼*

4201 A2228 60c multi 1.60 .55
4202 A2228 60c multi 1.60 .55
4203 A2228 89c multi 2.40 .80
4204 A2228 89c multi 2.40 .80
Nos. 4201-4204 (4) 8.00 2.70

Self-Adhesive

Serpentine Die Cut 11

4205 A2228 89c multi 2.40 2.40

See Hong Kong Nos. 1490-1493.

Cubist Art A2229

Designs: No. 4206, La Table Louis-Philippe, by Roger de La Fresnaye. No. 4207, Three Figures Under a Tree, by Pablo Picasso. No. 4208, The Three Poets, by Louis Marcoussis, vert. No. 4209, Still Life with a Red Ball, by Auguste Herbin, vert. No. 4210, The Blue Bird, by Jean Metzinger, vert. No. 4211, The 14th of July, by Fernand Léger, vert. No. 4212, Music, by Frantisek Kupka. No. 4213, Rugby, by André Lhote. No. 4214, The War Song, Portrait of Florent Schmitt, by Albert Gleizes, vert. No. 4215, The Book, by Juan Gris, vert. No. 4216, Compotier et Cartes, by Georges Braque, vert. No. 4217, Marine, by Lyonel Feininger, vert.

2012, May 10 *Serpentine Die Cut 11*

Booklet Stamps

Self-Adhesive

4206 A2229 (60c) multi 1.50 .50
4207 A2229 (60c) multi 1.50 .50
4208 A2229 (60c) multi 1.50 .50
4209 A2229 (60c) multi 1.50 .50
4210 A2229 (60c) multi 1.50 .50
4211 A2229 (60c) multi 1.50 .50
4212 A2229 (60c) multi 1.50 .50
4213 A2229 (60c) multi 1.50 .50
4214 A2229 (60c) multi 1.50 .50
4215 A2229 (60c) multi 1.50 .50
4216 A2229 (60c) multi 1.50 .50
4217 A2229 (60c) multi 1.50 .50
a. Booklet pane of 12, #4206-4217 18.00
Nos. 4206-4217 (12) 18.00 6.00

Pacific 231 K8 Locomotive, Cent. — A2230

2012, May 11 Engr. *Perf. 13¼*

4218 A2230 60c multi 1.50 .50

Self-Adhesive

Serpentine Die Cut 11

4219 A2230 60c multi 1.50 1.50

A souvenir sheet of one of No. 4218 sold for €3.

St. Joan of Arc (c. 1412-31) — A2231

Photo. & Engr.

2012, May 11 *Perf. 13*

4220 A2231 77c multi 2.00 .65

See Vatican City No. 1499.

Souvenir Sheet

Battle of Denain, 300th Anniv. — A2232

2012, May 12 Photo. *Perf. 13¼*

4221 A2232 77c multi 2.00 .65

Birds — A2233

Designs: No. 4222a, Little bustard (Outarde canepetière). No. 4222b, Bluethroat (Gorgebleue à miroir), horiz. No. 4222c, Osprey (Balbuzard pêcheur). Nos. 4222d, 4223, Atlantic puffin (Macareux moine).

Perf. 13¼x13, 13x13¼ (#4222b)

2012, May 12

4222 Sheet of 4 6.00 6.00
a.-d. A2233 57c Any single 1.50 .50

Self-Adhesive

Serpentine Die Cut 11

4223 A2233 57c multi 1.50 1.50

Bird Protection League, cent.

Europa — A2234

2012, May 20 Engr. *Perf. 13*

4224 A2234 77c multi 2.00 .65

Self-Adhesive

Serpentine Die Cut 11

4225 A2234 77c multi 2.00 2.00

Tourism Issue

Chateau de Suscinio A2235

2012, May 26 *Perf. 13¼*

4226 A2235 60c multi 1.50 .50

Souvenir Sheet

Saint-Cloud Park, Paris — A2236

No. 4227: a, Cascade. b, Reflecting ponds,

2012, June 9 Photo. *Perf. 13x13¼*

4227 A2236 Sheet of 2 12.00 12.00
a.-b. €2.40 Either single 6.00 3.00
c. Souvenir sheet of 4, #4073a, 4073b, 4227a, 4227b 24.00 24.00

2012 Salon du Timbre, Paris.

Historic Residences — A2237

Designs: Nos. 4228, 4245, Palais du Luxembourg, Paris. No. 4229, Château Guillaume-le-Conquérant, Falaise. No. 4230, Château des Comtes de Foix. No. 4231, Château de Boulogne sur Mer. No. 4232, Château de Saumur. No. 4233, Château d' Anjony, Tournemire. No. 4234, Château de Pompadour. No. 4235, Citadelle de Corte. No. 4236, Forteresse de Salses. No. 4237, Château d'If. No. 4238, Hôtel de Mauroy, Troyes. No. 4239, Maison Pfister, Colmar. No. 4240, Château du Taureau, Baie de Morlaix. No. 4241, Palais Ducal de Nevers. No. 4242, Château d'Azay-le-Rideau. No. 4243, Château de Puyguilhem. No. 4244, Château de Crazannes. No. 4246, Château de Vaux-le-Vicomte. No. 4247, Château de Brémontier-Merval. No. 4248, Château de Lesdiguières, Vixille. No. 4249, Château de Pierrefonds. No. 4250, Villa Palladienne de Syam. No. 4251, Maison Souques-Pagès, Pointe-à-Pitre. No. 4252, Villa Majorelle, Nancy.

Serpentine Die Cut 11

2012, June 9 Litho.

Self-Adhesive

4228 A2237 (60c) multi 1.50 1.50

Photo.

Booklet Stamps

4229 A2237 (60c) multi 1.50 .50
4230 A2237 (60c) multi 1.50 .50
4231 A2237 (60c) multi 1.50 .50
4232 A2237 (60c) multi 1.50 .50
a. Booklet pane of 4, #4229-4232 6.00
4233 A2237 (60c) multi 1.50 .50
4234 A2237 (60c) multi 1.50 .50
4235 A2237 (60c) multi 1.50 .50
4236 A2237 (60c) multi 1.50 .50
a. Booklet pane of 4, #4233-4236 6.00
4237 A2237 (60c) multi 1.50 .50
4238 A2237 (60c) multi 1.50 .50
4239 A2237 (60c) multi 1.50 .50
4240 A2237 (60c) multi 1.50 .50
a. Booklet pane of 4, #4237-4240 6.00
Complete booklet, #4232a, 4236a, 4240a 18.00
4241 A2237 (60c) multi 1.50 .50
4242 A2237 (60c) multi 1.50 .50
4243 A2237 (60c) multi 1.50 .50
4244 A2237 (60c) multi 1.50 .50
a. Booklet pane of 4, #4241-4244 6.00
4245 A2237 (60c) multi 1.50 .50
4246 A2237 (60c) multi 1.50 .50
4247 A2237 (60c) multi 1.50 .50
4248 A2237 (60c) multi 1.50 .50
a. Booklet pane of 4, #4245-4248 6.00
4249 A2237 (60c) multi 1.50 .50
4250 A2237 (60c) multi 1.50 .50
4251 A2237 (60c) multi 1.50 .50
4252 A2237 (60c) multi 1.50 .50
a. Booklet pane of 4, #4249-4252 6.00
Complete booklet, #4244a, 4248a, 4252a 18.00
Nos. 4229-4252 (24) 36.00 12.00

Lettering, most evident in the "Phil@poste" inscription at bottom, is sharp on No. 4228 and fuzzy on No. 4245.

Miniature Sheet

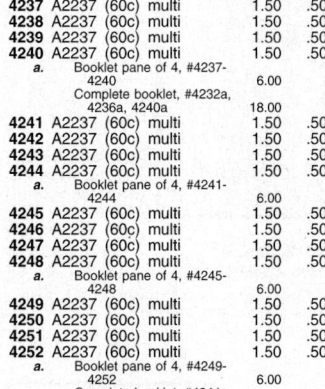

Soldiers — A2238

No. 4253: a, Croisé (crusader), 12th cent. b, Vercingetorix (c. 82-46 B.C.), Gallic chieftain, horiz. c, Fantassin (foot soldier), 16th cent. d, Tambour (drummer), 18th cent. e, Grognard (member of Napoleon's Old Guard). f, Fantassin (foot soldier), 1914.

Litho. & Engr.

2012, June 10 *Perf. 13*

4253 A2238 Sheet of 6 9.00 9.00
a.-f. 60c Any single 1.50 .50

A set of six souvenir sheets, each containing one example of Nos. 4253a-4253f, sold for €15.

Handball A2239

Embossed and Etched on Silver

2012, June 11 *Die Cut Perf. 12¾*

Self-Adhesive

4254 A2239 €5 silver 12.50 12.50

2012 Summer Olympics, London — A2240

2012, June 12 Photo. *Perf. 13*

4255 A2240 89c multi 2.25 .75

Miles Davis (1926-91), Jazz Trumpet Player — A2241

Edith Piaf (1915-63), Singer — A2242

2012, June 12 ***Perf. 13***

4256	A2241 60c multi		1.50	.50
4257	A2242 89c multi		2.25	.75
a.	Horiz. pair, #4256-4257		3.75	1.25

See United States Nos. 4692-4693.

Vegetables A2243

Designs: No. 4258, Peas (petits pois). No. 4259, Salad greens (salades). Nos. 4260, Pimentos (piments). No. 4261, Green beans (haricots verts). No. 4262, Broccoli (chou brocoli). No. 4263, Zucchini (courgettes). No. 4264, Snap beans (haricots mange-tout). No. 4265, Leeks (poireaux). No. 4266, Green peppers (poivron "Lamuyo"). No. 4267, Artichoke (artichaut "Gros Camus"). No. 4268, Squashes (potirons vers). No. 4269, Cabbage (chou cabus).

Serpentine Die Cut 11

2012, June 13 **Self-Adhesive**

Booklet Stamps

4258	A2243 (57c) multi	1.40	.45
4259	A2243 (57c) multi	1.40	.45
4260	A2243 (57c) multi	1.40	.45
4261	A2243 (57c) multi	1.40	.45
4262	A2243 (57c) multi	1.40	.45
4263	A2243 (57c) multi	1.40	.45
4264	A2243 (57c) multi	1.40	.45
4265	A2243 (57c) multi	1.40	.45
4266	A2243 (57c) multi	1.40	.45
4267	A2243 (57c) multi	1.40	.45
4268	A2243 (57c) multi	1.40	.45
4269	A2243 (57c) multi	1.40	.45
a.	Booklet pane of 12, #4258-4269	17.00	
	Nos. 4258-4269 (12)	16.80	5.40

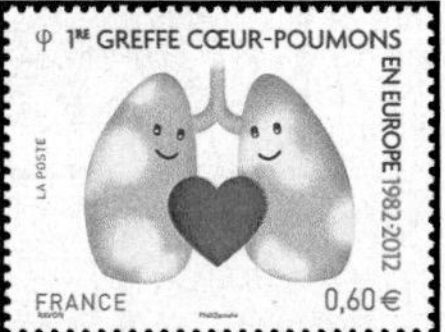

First Heart-Lung Transplant in Europe, 30th Anniv. — A2244

2012, June 14 ***Perf. 13¼***

4270	A2244 60c multi	1.50	.50

Issenheim Altarpiece, 500th Anniv. — A2245

Sheet with Altarpiece Doors Closed (Covering Stamps)

No. 4271: a, St. Augustine, "Le Retable d'Issenheim" at right (19x56mm). b, St. Hieronymus, "Le Retable d'Issenheim" at left (19x56mm). c, St. Anthony (34x65mm).

Perf. 13¼x13, 13 (#4271c)

2012, June 15 **Litho.**

4271	A2245	Sheet of 3	12.50	12.50
a.-b.		€1.50 Either single	3.75	1.25
c.		€2 multi	5.00	1.75

Card stock doors printed on both sides that depict artwork on the two alterpiece doors, are pasted on top of each other at the left and right of the stamps. Values for the sheet are for examples with all four doors affixed.

Musée d'Orsay, Paris — A2246

2012, June 16 **Engr.** ***Perf. 13x13¼***

4272	A2246 60c multi + label	1.50	.50

French Federation of Philatelic Associations, 85th Congress, Paris.

Tourism Issue

Pointe Saint-Mathieu — A2247

2012, June 22 ***Perf. 13¼***

4273	A2247 57c multi	1.40	.45

Souvenir Sheet

2012 World Karate Championships, Paris — A2248

No. 4274: a, Karateka kicking. b, Eiffel Tower. c, Karateka kicking, horiz.

Perf. 13¼x13, 13x13¼ (#4274c)

2012, Sept. 7 **Photo.**

4274	A2248	Sheet of 3	7.25	7.25
a.-c.		89c Any single	2.40	.80

2012 World Pétanque Championships, Marseille — A2249

Photo. & Embossed

2012, Sept. 14 ***Perf. 13x13¼***

4275	A2249 89c multi	2.40	.80

Art Issue

Figures Representing Seven Continents, by Jaume Plensa, Place Masséna, Nice — A2250

2012, Sept. 14 **Photo.**

4276	A2250 €1.45 multi	3.75	1.90

Camp des Milles, World War II Internment Camp — A2251

2012, Sept. 21 **Engr.**

4277	A2251 60c multi	1.60	.55

Tourism Issue

Verneuil-sur-Avre — A2252

2012, Sept. 21 ***Perf. 13¼***

4278	A2252 60c multi	1.60	.55

Marianne and Stars A2253

2012, Oct. 1 ***Perf. 13***

4279	Souvenir sheet of 3, #4051, 4079, 4279a	5.00	5.00
a.	A2253 60c orange	1.60	.55

Torch, Marianne and Stars A2254

The Temptation of St. Anthony, by Hieronymus Bosch — A2255

Items on Fire A2256

Designs: No. 4282, Lava (La lave). No. 4283, Welder (la soudure). No. 4284, Glassblowing (Le travail du verre). No. 4285, Flame of the Unknown Soldier, Paris (La flamme du soldat inconnu). No. 4286, Halloween jack o'lantern. No. 4287, People around Midsummer's Eve bonfire (Feu de la Saint-Jean). No. 4288, Fire fighters and fire (Les pompiers). No. 4289, Charcoal fire (Les braises). No. 4290, Candles (bougies). No. 4291, Light show (Spectacle). No. 4292, Sunset (Coucher de soleil). No. 4293, Birthday candles on cake (Bougies d'anniversaire).

2012, Oct. 13 **Engr.** ***Perf. 13***

4280	A2254 60c orange & red	1.60	.55

Souvenir Sheet

Litho. & Engr.

Perf. 13x13¼

4281	A2255	€2 multi	5.25	2.60

Photo.

Booklet Stamps

Self-Adhesive

4282	A2256 (60c) multi	1.60	.55
4283	A2256 (60c) multi	1.60	.55
4284	A2256 (60c) multi	1.60	.55
4285	A2256 (60c) multi	1.60	.55
4286	A2256 (60c) multi	1.60	.55
4287	A2256 (60c) multi	1.60	.55
4288	A2256 (60c) multi	1.60	.55
4289	A2256 (60c) multi	1.60	.55
4290	A2256 (60c) multi	1.60	.55
4291	A2256 (60c) multi	1.60	.55
4292	A2256 (60c) multi	1.60	.55
4293	A2256 (60c) multi	1.60	.55
a.	Booklet pane of 12, #4282-4293	19.50	
	Nos. 4282-4293 (12)	19.20	6.60

Stamp Day. An illustration and a bar code is found on the reverse of the sheet margin of No. 4281.

Historic Residences Type of 2012

Design: (60c), Chaâteau d'If.

Serpentine Die Cut 11

2012, Oct. 29 **Litho.**

Self-Adhesive

4294	A2237 (60c) multi	1.60	1.60

Lettering, most evident in the "Phil@poste" inscription at bottom, is sharp on No. 4294 and fuzzy on No. 4237.

Court House, Lyon — A2257

2012, Oct. 26 **Engr.** ***Perf. 13***

4295	A2257 60c multi	1.60	.55

Lion of Belfort Statue, by Frédéric Auguste Bartholdi — A2258

2012, Nov. 2 ***Perf. 13x13¼***

4296 A2258 60c multi + label 1.60 .55

Timbres Passion 2012 Stamp Exhibition, Belfort. A souvenir sheet containing No. 4296 was issued in 2013 and sold for €3.

King Henri IV of France (1553-1610), Co-Prince of Andorra — A2259

2012, Nov. 8

4297 A2259 60c multi 1.60 .55
a. Sheet of 10, 5 each #4297, French Andorra #710 16.00 16.00

See French Andorra No. 710.

Souvenir Sheet

The Masked Ball, Opera by Daniel Auber — A2260

No. 4298: a, Auber (1782-1871). b, King Gustav III of Sweden (1746-92), main character in opera.

Litho. & Engr.

2012, Nov. 9 ***Perf. 13¼***

4298 A2260 Sheet of 2 3.75 3.75
a. 60c multi 1.60 .55
b. 77c multi 2.00 .65

See Sweden No. 2697.

Souvenir Sheet

Organ from Church of St. Jacques, Lunéville — A2261

No. 4299 — Various details of organ's ornamentation: a, 89c. b, €1.45, vert.

Perf. 13x13¼, 13¼x13

2012, Nov. 10 **Engr.**

4299 A2261 Sheet of 2 6.25 6.25
a. 89c multi 2.40 .80
b. €1.45 multi 3.75 1.25

Laurent Bonnevay (1870-1957), Politician, and Apartment Building — A2262

2012, Nov. 12 **Engr.** ***Perf. 13¼***

4300 A2262 57c multi 1.50 .50

Bonnevay Law on rent-controlled housing, cent.

Souvenir Sheet

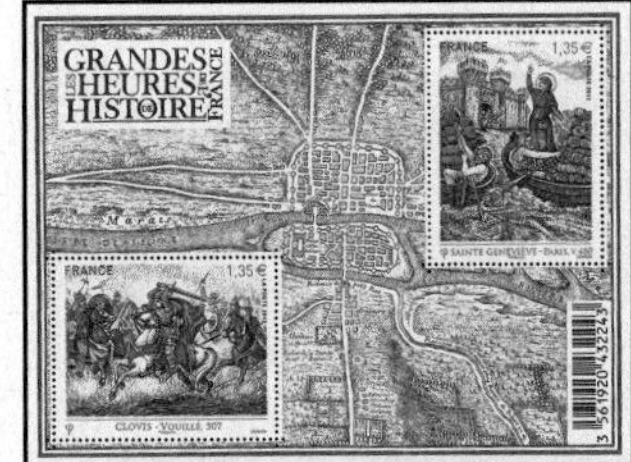

French History — A2263

No. 4301: a, Intercession by St. Geneviève on behalf of Paris, c. 480. b, Clovis at Battle of Vouillé, 507, horiz.

Perf. 13¼x13, 13x13¼

2012, Nov. 12

4301 A2263 Sheet of 2 7.00 7.00
a.-b. €1.35 Either single 3.50 1.10

A2264

A2265

A2266

A2267

A2268

A2269

A2270

A2271

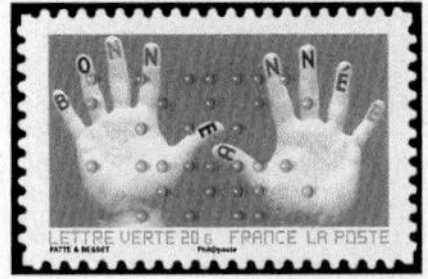
A2272

A2273

A2274

Greetings Stamps A2275

Booklet Stamps

Serpentine Die Cut 11

2012, Nov. 12 **Photo.**

Self-Adhesive

4302	A2264	(57c)	multi	1.50	.50
4303	A2265	(57c)	multi	1.50	.50
4304	A2266	(57c)	multi	1.50	.50
4305	A2267	(57c)	multi	1.50	.50
4306	A2268	(57c)	multi	1.50	.50
4307	A2269	(57c)	multi	1.50	.50
4308	A2270	(57c)	multi	1.50	.50
4309	A2271	(57c)	multi	1.50	.50
4310	A2272	(57c)	multi	1.50	.50
4311	A2273	(57c)	multi	1.50	.50
4312	A2274	(57c)	multi	1.50	.50
4313	A2275	(57c)	multi	1.50	.50
a.	Booklet pane of 12, #4302-4313			18.00	
	Nos. 4302-4313 (12)			18.00	6.00

A souvenir sheet containing one perf. 13x13¼ example of No. 4309 with water-activated gum sold for €3.

See No. 4329.

Elysée Treaty, 50th Anniv. A2276

2013, Jan. 2 **Litho.** ***Perf. 13***

4314 A2276 80c multi 2.25 .75

See Germany No. 2703.

New Year 2013 (Year of the Snake) — A2277

2013, Jan. 4 **Photo.** ***Perf. 13¼x13***

4315 A2277 63c multi 1.75 .60

No. 4315 was printed in sheets of 5. A souvenir sheet of one sold for €3.

See No. 4971a.

Bronze Sculpture of Goat A2278

Terra Cotta Figurine of Rabbit, From Studio of Bernard Palissy A2279

Bronze Sculpture of Buffalo A2280

Brass Sculpture of Rooster A2281

Bronze Sculpture of Tiger, by Antoine Louis Barye A2282

Porcelain Figurine of Rats and Egg A2283

Glazed Clay Figurine of Pig A2284

Bronze Sculpture of Monkey, by Jacques Lehmann A2285

Enameled Stone Sculpture of Dog A2286

Earthenware Figurine of Dragon A2287

Gold Sculpture of Snake A2288

Bronze Sculpture of Horse, by Edgar Degas A2289

2013, Jan. 4 ***Serpentine Die Cut 11***
Booklet Stamps
Self-Adhesive

4316 A2278 (58c) multi 1.60 .55
4317 A2279 (58c) multi 1.60 .55
4318 A2280 (58c) multi 1.60 .55
4319 A2281 (58c) multi 1.60 .55
4320 A2282 (58c) multi 1.60 .55
4321 A2283 (58c) multi 1.60 .55
4322 A2284 (58c) multi 1.60 .55
4323 A2285 (58c) multi 1.60 .55
4324 A2286 (58c) multi 1.60 .55
4325 A2287 (58c) multi 1.60 .55
4326 A2288 (58c) multi 1.60 .55
4327 A2289 (58c) multi 1.60 .55
a. Booklet pane of 12, #4316-4327 19.50
Nos. 4316-4327 (12) 19.20 6.60

Marseille, 2013 European Capital of Culture
A2290

2013, Jan. 12 **Photo.** ***Perf. 13¼***
4328 A2290 80c multi 2.25 .75

Greetings Type of 2012
Serpentine Die Cut 11
2013, Jan. 14 **Litho.**
Self-Adhesive

4329 A2265 (58c) multi 1.60 1.60

Lettering, most evident in the "Phil@poste" inscription at bottom, is sharp on No. 4329 and fuzzy on No. 4303.

Souvenir Sheet

Notre Dame Cathedral, Paris, 850th Anniv. — A2291

No. 4330 — Stained-glass window depicting: a, Peasant with scythe (44x44mm). b, Madonna and Child (42mm diameter).

Litho., Sheet Margin Litho. & Engr.
2013, Jan. 19 ***Perf.***

4330 A2291 Sheet of 2 7.25 7.25
a. €1.05 multi 3.00 1.00
b. €1.55 multi 4.25 1.40
c. Sheet of 2, #4330a, 4330b, lithographed sheet margin 13.50 13.50

No. 4330c has a different margin design and sold for €5.

Art Issue

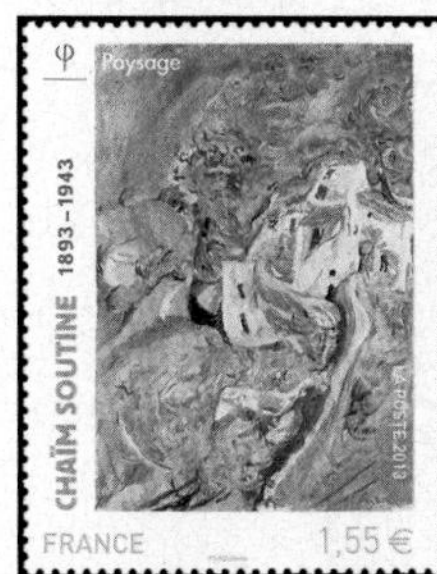

Landscape, by Chaim Soutine (1893-1943) — A2292

2013, Jan. 25 **Photo.** ***Perf. 13¼x13***
4331 A2292 €1.55 multi 4.25 2.10

A2293

A2294

Hearts — A2295

No. 4334: a, Two white hearts embellished with flowers. b, Bird with long tail. c, Swan facing left. d, Swan facing right.

2013, Jan. 25 ***Perf. 13¼***
4332 A2293 58c multi 1.60 .55
4333 A2294 97c multi 2.75 .90

Souvenir Sheet
Perf.

4334 A2295 Sheet of 5, #4332, 4334a-4334d 8.00 8.00
a.-d 58c Any single 1.60 .55

Self-Adhesive
Serpentine Die Cut

4335 A2293 58c multi 1.60 1.60
4336 A2294 97c multi 2.75 2.75

Values for Nos. 4332-4333 are for stamps with surrounding selvage.

Art Issue

85.8 Degree Arc x 16, Sculpture, by Bernar Venet — A2296

2013, Feb. 1 ***Perf. 13x13¼***
4337 A2296 €1.55 multi 4.25 2.10

Animal Proverbs and Idioms
A2297

Designs: No. 4338, Qui vole un oeuf vole un boeuf ("Who steals an egg steals an ox"). No. 4339, Etre serrés come des sardines ("Be packed like sardines"). No. 4340, Etre heureux comme un poisson dans l'eau ("Be happy as a fish in water"). No. 4341, Pleurer des larmes de crocodile ("Cry crocodile tears"). No. 4342, Quand les poules auront des dents ("When chickens have teeth" or "When pigs fly"). No. 4343, Avaler des couleuvres ("To swallow snakes" or "To endure affronts"). No. 4344, Le chat parti, les souris dansent ("The cat's away, the mice will play"). No. 4345, Sauter du coq à l'âne ("Jump from the rooster to the donkey" or "Jump from one thing to another"). No. 4346, Se regarder en chiens de faience ("To stare like clay dogs" or "To stare menacingly at each other"). No. 4347, Ménager la chèvre et le chou ("To take care of the goat and the cabbage" or "To run with the hares and hunt with the hounds"). No. 4348, Ca ne se trouve pas sous les sabots d'un cheval ("That is not under the hooves of a horse"). No. 4349, Pratique la politique de l'autruche ("Practice the policy of an ostrich" or "Bury one's head in the sand like an ostrich").

2013, Feb. 4 ***Serpentine Die Cut 11***
Booklet Stamps
Self-Adhesive

4338 A2297 (58c) multi 1.60 .55
4339 A2297 (58c) multi 1.60 .55
4340 A2297 (58c) multi 1.60 .55
4341 A2297 (58c) multi 1.60 .55
4342 A2297 (58c) multi 1.60 .55
4343 A2297 (58c) multi 1.60 .55
4344 A2297 (58c) multi 1.60 .55
4345 A2297 (58c) multi 1.60 .55
4346 A2297 (58c) multi 1.60 .55
4347 A2297 (58c) multi 1.60 .55
4348 A2297 (58c) multi 1.60 .55
4349 A2297 (58c) multi 1.60 .55
a. Booklet pane of 12, #4338-4349 19.50
Nos. 4338-4349 (12) 19.20 6.60

Compare types A2297 and A2498.

Raphael Elizé (1891-1945), First Black Mayor in France — A2298

2013, Feb. 15 **Engr.** ***Perf. 13¼***
4350 A2298 63c multi 1.75 .60

Miniature Sheet

Way of St. James — A2299

No. 4351: a, Via Lemovicensis in Neuvy-Saint-Sépulchre. b, Via Turonensis in Aulnay. c, Via Tolosana in Saint-Gilles, horiz. d, Via Podiensis in Conques, horiz.

Litho. & Engr.
2013, Feb. 22 ***Perf. 13***
4351 A2299 Sheet of 4 8.50 8.50
a.-d. 80c Any single 2.10 .70

50th International Agricultural Show, Paris — A2300

2013, Feb. 25 **Photo.** ***Perf. 13¼***
4352 A2300 95c multi 2.50 .85

Intl. Women's Day
A2301

Qualities of women in Aicha des Gazelles Rally, Morocco: No. 4353, Courage. No. 4354, Partage (sharing). No. 4355, Dépassement de soi (surpassing oneself). No. 4356, Entraide (mutual aid). No. 4357, Enthusiasme (enthusiasm). No. 4358, Solidarité (solidarity). No. 4359, Esprit d'équipe (team spirit). No. 4360, Engagement. No. 4361, Emotion. No. 4362, Performance. No. 4363, Confiance (confidence). No. 4364, Respect.

2013, Mar. 8 ***Serpentine Die Cut 11***
Booklet Stamps
Self-Adhesive

4353 A2301 (58c) multi 1.50 .50
4354 A2301 (58c) multi 1.50 .50
4355 A2301 (58c) multi 1.50 .50
4356 A2301 (58c) multi 1.50 .50
4357 A2301 (58c) multi 1.50 .50
4358 A2301 (58c) multi 1.50 .50
4359 A2301 (58c) multi 1.50 .50
4360 A2301 (58c) multi 1.50 .50
4361 A2301 (58c) multi 1.50 .50
4362 A2301 (58c) multi 1.50 .50
4363 A2301 (58c) multi 1.50 .50
4364 A2301 (58c) multi 1.50 .50
a. Booklet pane of 12, #4353-4364 18.00
Nos. 4353-4364 (12) 18.00 6.00

See No. 4406.

European Capitals Type of 2002
Miniature Sheet

No. 4365 — Attractions in Madrid, Spain: a, Plaza Mayor. b, Almudena Cathedral, horiz. c, Palace of Communication (Cibeles Palace), horiz. d, Royal Palace, horiz.

Perf. 13¼x13 (#4365a), 13x13¼
2013, Mar. 15
4365 A1622 Sheet of 4 6.50 6.50
a.-d. 63c Any single 1.60 .55

Opening of Jacques Chaban-Delmas Vertical Lift Bridge, Bordeaux — A2302

2013, Mar. 16 ***Perf. 13¼***
4366 A2302 58c multi 1.50 .50

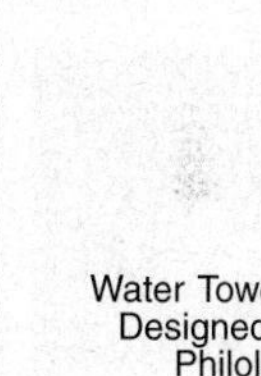

Water Towers, Designed by Philolaos Tloupas, Valence — A2303

2013, Mar. 22 **Engr.**
4367 A2303 58c multi 1.50 .50

Spring Philatelic Show, Mâcon — A2304

2013, Apr. 5 ***Perf. 13¼***
4368 A2304 63c multi 1.75 .60

Horses
A2305

Horse breeds and horses at work: No. 4369, Breton horse. No. 4370, Norman Cob horse. No. 4371, Boulonnais horse. No. 4372, Trait du Nord horse. No. 4373, Ardennais horse. No. 4374, Comtois horse. No. 4375, Poitevin Mulsassier horse. No. 4376, Horse pulling wagon (Attelage en roulotte). No. 4377, Percheron horse. No. 4378, Horse working in vineyard (Travail de la vigne). No. 4379, Auxois horse. No. 4380, Horse pulling logs in forest (Débardage en forêt).

Serpentine Die Cut 11

2013, Apr. 5 Photo.

Booklet Stamps
Self-Adhesive

4369	A2305 (58c) multi	1.50	.50
4370	A2305 (58c) multi	1.50	.50
4371	A2305 (58c) multi	1.50	.50
4372	A2305 (58c) multi	1.50	.50
4373	A2305 (58c) multi	1.50	.50
4374	A2305 (58c) multi	1.50	.50
4375	A2305 (58c) multi	1.50	.50
4376	A2305 (58c) multi	1.50	.50
4377	A2305 (58c) multi	1.50	.50
4378	A2305 (58c) multi	1.50	.50
4379	A2305 (58c) multi	1.50	.50
4380	A2305 (58c) multi	1.50	.50
a.	Booklet pane of 12, #4369-4380	18.00	
	Nos. 4369-4380 (12)	18.00	6.00

Champs-Elysées Theater, Paris, Cent. — A2306

2013, Apr. 8 Engr. *Perf. 13¼*

4381	A2306 €1.05 multi	2.75	.90

Chateau des Vaux, Home of Apprentices of Auteuil — A2307

2013, Apr. 12

4382	A2307 58c multi	1.50	.50

Bats A2308

Designs: No. 4383, Rhinolophus ferrumequinum.

No. 4384: a, Pteropus seychellensis comorensis, vert. b, Plecotus macrobullaris, vert. c, Myotis nattereri.

2013, Apr. 19 Photo.

4383	A2308 58c multi	1.50	.50

Miniature Sheet

4384	Sheet of 4, #4383, 4384a-4384c	8.00	8.00
a.	A2308 58c multi	1.50	.50
b.	A2308 80c multi	2.10	.70
c.	A2308 €1.05 multi	2.75	.90

Notre Dame de Melun Collegiate Church, 1000th Anniv. A2309

2013, Apr. 20 Engr.

4385	A2309 63c multi	1.75	.60

Impressionist Paintings Depicting Water — A2310

Designs: No. 4386, L'Ile de la Grande Jatte, Neuilly-sur-Seine, by Alfred Sisley. No. 4387, L'Estaque - Vue du Golfe de Marseille (Gulf of Marseille as Seen from L'Estaque), by Paul Cézanne. No. 4388, Sur la Plage (On the Beach), by Edouard Manet. No. 4389, L'Anse des Pilotes au Havre, Haute Mer Après Midi, Soleil, by Camille Pissarro. No. 4390, Régates à Argenteuil (Regatta at Argenteuil), by Claude Monet. No. 4391, Alphonsine Fournaise, by Pierre-Auguste Renoir. No. 4392, La Rivière Blanche (Breton Boy by the Aven River), by Paul Gauguin. No. 4393, L'Homme à la Barre (Man at the Helm), by Théo van Rysselberghe. No. 4394, Les Pecheurs à la Ligne, Étude pour la Grande Jatte (Fishermen), by Georges Seurat. No. 4395, Dans le Port de Rouen (In the Port of Rouen), by Albert Lebourg. No. 4396, La Nuit Etoilée, Arles (Starry Night Over the Rhone), by Vincent van Gogh. No. 4397, La Jetée de Deauville (The Jetty at Deauville), by Louis-Eugène Boudin.

Serpentine Die Cut 11

2013, Apr. 29 Photo.

Booklet Stamps
Self-Adhesive

4386	A2310 (58c) multi	1.50	.50
4387	A2310 (58c) multi	1.50	.50
4388	A2310 (58c) multi	1.50	.50
4389	A2310 (58c) multi	1.50	.50
4390	A2310 (58c) multi	1.50	.50
4391	A2310 (58c) multi	1.50	.50
4392	A2310 (58c) multi	1.50	.50
4393	A2310 (58c) multi	1.50	.50
4394	A2310 (58c) multi	1.50	.50
4395	A2310 (58c) multi	1.50	.50
4396	A2310 (58c) multi	1.50	.50
4397	A2310 (58c) multi	1.50	.50
a.	Booklet pane of 12, #4386-4397	18.00	
	Nos. 4386-4397 (12)	18.00	6.00

See Nos. 4449-4452.

Rixheim — A2311

2013, May 3 Litho. & Engr. *Perf. 13*

4398	A2311 63c multi	1.75	.60

A souvenir sheet of one No. 4398 sold for €3.

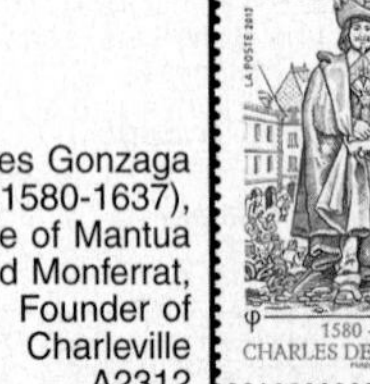

Charles Gonzaga (1580-1637), Duke of Mantua and Monferrat, Founder of Charleville A2312

2013, May 6 Engr. *Perf. 13¼*

4399	A2312 80c red & black	2.25	.75

World Table Tennis Championships, Paris — A2313

Designs: 63c, Female player (blue shirt). 95c, Male player (red shirt).

2013, May 13 *Perf. 13x13¼*

4400	A2313 63c multi	1.75	.60
4401	A2313 95c multi	2.50	.80
a.	Horiz. pair, #4400-4401, + central label	4.25	1.40

Cathedral and Jules Verne Circus, Amiens — A2314

2013, May 17

4402	A2314 63c multi + label	1.75	.60

French Federation of Philatelic Associations, 86th Congress, Amiens. A souvenir sheet containing No. 4402 was issued in 2014 and sold for €3.20.

Europa — A2315

Designs: No. 4403, Mail coach, 1840. No. 4404, Renault Kangoo ZE mail van.

2013, May 19 Photo.

4403	80c multi	2.25	.75
4404	80c multi	2.25	.75
a.	A2315 Horiz. pair, #4403-4404	4.50	1.50

Souvenir Sheet

Works of André Le Nôtre (1613-1700), Landscape Architect for King Louis XVI — A2316

No. 4405 — Fountains and gardens at: a, Versailles. b, Chantilly.

2013, May 31 *Perf. 13x13¼*

4405	A2316 Sheet of 2	14.00	14.00
a.-b.	€2.55 Either single	7.00	2.50
c.	Sheet of 2, #4405a-4405b, different sheet margin	24.00	24.00

No. 4405c sold for €9.

Intl. Women's Day Type of 2013

Serpentine Die Cut 11

2013, June 1 Litho.

Self-Adhesive

4406	A2301 (58c) Like #4359	1.60	1.60

No. 4406 has a dot structure not found on No. 4359, which is printed by photogravure.

Abbaye-aux-Dames, Saintes — A2317

2013, June 14 Engr. *Perf. 13¼*

4407	A2317 63c multi	1.75	.60

Jacques Baumel (1918-2006), Politician — A2318

2013, June 15

4408	A2318 €1.05 multi	3.00	1.00

Miniature Sheet

100th Tour de France Bicycle Race — A2319

No. 4409: a, Rider wearing yellow jersey, Annecy in background (40x30mm). b, Rider wearing polka-dot jersey near Bagnères-de-Bigorre (26x40mm). c, Rider wearing light blue and dark blue jersey near Mont Ventoux (26x40mm). d, Peloton going along Alpe d'Huez mountain road (40x40mm). e, Rider wearing green jersey in foreground, Calvi in background (40x26mm). f, Rider wearing white jersey, Versailles Palace in background (40x30mm). g, Rider wearing yellow jersey winning race, Arc de Triomphe, Paris (30x40mm). h, Rider in red and black jersey, Mont-Saint-Michel (40x26mm).

Perf. 13x13¼ (#4409a, 4409f), 13¼x13 (#4409g), 13

2013, June 29 Photo.

4409	A2319 Sheet of 8	15.50	15.50
a.-d.	58c Any single	1.50	.50
e.-f.	80c Either single	2.10	.70
g.-h.	95c Either single	2.50	.85

A souvenir sheet containing Nos. 4409e and 4409g sold for €4.

Types of 1959-2008

Miniature Sheet

2013 Engr. *Perf. 13*

4410	Sheet of 12	21.00	21.00
a.	A328 63c black	1.75	.60
b.	A349 63c black	1.75	.60
c.	A360 63c black	1.75	.60
d.	A379 63c black	1.75	.60
e.	A486 63c black	1.75	.60
f.	A555 63c black	1.75	.60
g.	A771 63c black	1.75	.60
h.	A915 63c black	1.75	.60
i.	A1161 63c black	1.75	.60
j.	A1409 63c black	1.75	.60
k.	A1713 63c black	1.75	.60
l.	A1912 63c black	1.75	.60
m.	Booklet pane of 12, #4410a-4410l	21.00	—

No. 4410 was only sold together with No. 4437a.

Issued: No. 4410, 7/15; No. 4410m, 11/6

Marianne and Children A2320

Marianne and Children "Ecopli" A2321

Marianne and Children "Lettre Prioritaire" A2322

Marianne and Children "Europe" A2323

Marianne and Children "Monde" — A2324

Type A2322 gram limits (at LL): Nos. 4415, 4422, 4428, 4435, 20g. Nos. 4419, 4432, 50g. Nos. 4420, 4433, 100g. Nos. 4421, 4434, 250g.

2013, July 15 Engr. *Perf. 13*

4411 A2320 1c yellow .25 .25
4412 A2320 5c dk brown .25 .25
4413 A2320 10c brown .25 .25
4414 A2321 (56c) dk gray 1.50 .30
4415 A2322 (63c) red 1.75 .35
- *a.* As No. 4415, engraved, glossy paper (#4437g) 1.75 1.75
- *b.* As No. 4415, photogravure, glossy paper (#4437g) 1.75 1.75
- *c.* As No. 4415, litho., glossy paper (#4437g) 1.75 1.75
- *d.* As No. 4415, typo., glossy paper (#4437g) 1.75 1.75
- *e.* As No. 4415, silk-screened, glossy paper (#4437g) 1.75 1.75
- *f.* No. 4415a with overprint "Marianne 1944-2014" (#4437o) 1.75 1.75
- *g.* No. 4415b with overprint "Marianne 1944-2014" (#4437o) 1.75 1.75
- *h.* No. 4415c with overprint "Marianne 1944-2014" (#4437o) 1.75 1.75
- *i.* No. 4415d with overprint "Marianne 1944-2014" (#4437o) 1.75 1.75
- *j.* No. 4415e with overprint "Marianne 1944-2014" (#4437o) 1.75 1.75

4416 A2323 (80c) blue 2.10 .45
4417 A2324 (95c) purple 2.50 .65
4418 A2320 €1 orange 2.60 .65
4419 A2322 (€1.05) fawn 2.75 .70
4420 A2322 (€1.55) red violet 4.00 1.00
4421 A2322 (€2.55) chocolate 6.75 2.40
Nos. 4411-4421 (11) 24.70 7.25

Coil Stamps

Perf. 13 Horiz.

4422 A2322 (63c) red 1.75 .35
4423 A2323 (80c) blue 2.10 .45

Self-Adhesive

Serpentine Die Cut 6¾ Vert.

4424 A2320 1c yellow .25 .25
4425 A2320 5c dk brown .25 .25
4426 A2320 10c brown .25 .25
4427 A2321 (56c) dk gray 1.50 1.50
4428 A2322 (63c) red 1.75 .35
- *a.* Booklet pane of 10 17.50
- *b.* Booklet pane of 12 21.00
- *c.* Booklet pane of 20 35.00

4429 A2323 (80c) blue 2.10 .45
- *a.* Booklet pane of 12 25.50

4430 A2324 (95c) purple 2.50 2.50
4431 A2320 €1 orange 2.60 2.60
4432 A2322 (€1.05) fawn 2.75 2.75
4433 A2322 (€1.55) red violet 4.00 4.00
4434 A2322 (€2.55) chocolate 6.75 6.75
Nos. 4424-4434 (11) 24.70 21.65

Coil Stamps

Serpentine Die Cut 6¾ Horiz.

4435 A2322 (63c) red 1.75 .35
4436 A2323 (80c) blue 2.10 .45

Issued: Nos. 4415a-4415e, 11/6; Nos. 4415f-4415j, 11/6/14. No. 4415e uses an ink that is shinier than that used on No. 4415a that causes the small lettering at the base of the stamp to be indistinct. Nos. 4415f-4415j had a franking value of 66c on day of issue. Compare with types A2534, A2536. See No. 4519. For overprint, see No. 5447.

Marianne and Tree "Lettre Verte" — A2325

Type A2325 gram limits (at LL): Nos. 4437, 4441, 4442, 4446, 20g. Nos. 4438, 4443, 50g. Nos. 4439, 4444, 100g. Nos. 4440, 4445, 250g.

2013, July 15 Engr. *Perf. 13*

4437 A2325 (58c) green 1.50 .25
- *a.* Souvenir sheet of 2, #4415, 4437 3.25 3.25
- *b.* As No. 4437, engraved, glossy paper (#4437g) 1.60 1.60
- *c.* As No. 4437, photogravure, glossy paper (#4437g) 1.60 1.60
- *d.* As No. 4437, litho., glossy paper (#4437g) 1.60 1.60
- *e.* As No. 4437, typo., glossy paper (#4437g) 1.60 1.60
- *f.* As No. 4437, silk-screened, glossy paper (#4437g) 1.60 1.60
- *g.* Sheet of 40, 8 each #4415a, 4437b, 4 each #4415b, 4415e, 4437d, 4437e, 2 each #4415c, 4415d, 4437c, 4437f, + label 67.00 67.00
- *h.* Booklet pane of 2, #4415, 4437 3.50 —
- Complete booklet, #4410m, 4437h 24.50
- *i.* Booklet pane of 2, #4079, 4437 3.00 —
- *j.* No. 4437b with overprint "Marianne 1944-2014" (#4437o) 1.60 1.60
- *k.* No. 4437c with overprint "Marianne 1944-2014" (#4437o) 1.60 1.60
- *l.* No. 4437d with overprint "Marianne 1944-2014" (#4437o) 1.60 1.60
- *m.* No. 4437e with overprint "Marianne 1944-2014" (#4437o) 1.60 1.60
- *n.* No. 4437f with overprint "Marianne 1944-2014" (#4437o) 1.60 1.60
- *o.* Sheet of 40, 8 each #4415f, 4437j, 4 each #4415g, 4415j, 4437l, 4437m, 2 each #4415h, 4415i, 4437k, 4437n, + label 67.00 67.00

4438 A2325 (97c) yel grn 2.60 .55
4439 A2325 (€1.45) dk bl grn 3.75 .80
4440 A2325 (€2.35) dk bl grn 6.25 1.25
Nos. 4437-4440 (4) 14.10 2.85

Coil Stamp

Perf. 13 Horiz.

4441 A2325 (58c) green 1.50 .25

Self-Adhesive

Serpentine Die Cut 6¾ Vert.

4442 A2325 (58c) green 1.50 .25
- *a.* Booklet pane of 10 15.00
- *b.* Booklet pane of 12 18.00

4443 A2325 (97c) yel grn 2.60 2.60
4444 A2325 (€1.45) dk bl grn 3.75 3.75
4445 A2325 (€2.35) dk bl grn 6.25 6.25
Nos. 4442-4445 (4) 14.10 12.85

Coil Stamp

Serpentine Die Cut 6¾ Horiz.

4446 A2325 (58c) green 1.50 .25

Issued: Nos. 4437b-4437h, 11/6, No. 4437i-4437o, 11/6/14. No. 4437a was only sold together with No. 4410. No. 4437a is 144x106mm. A 209x103mm sheet similar to No. 4473a was sold with a folder for €4.

No. 4437f uses an ink that is shinier than that used on No. 4437b that causes the small lettering at the base of the stamp to be indistinct. Nos. 4437j-4437n each had a franking value of 61c on day of issue.

The 80x52mm label on No. 4437g depicting an enlarged example of Type A2325 is not valid for postage. The 80x52mm label on No. 4437o was also overprinted "Marianne 1944-2014" but is not valid for postage.

Compare with type A2535.

See No. 4512. For overprint, see No. 5448.

Gaston Doumergue (1863-1937), Politician A2326

2013, Aug. 1 Engr. *Perf. 13¼*

4447 A2326 58c dark blue 1.60 .55

Pierre-Georges Latécoère (1883-1943), Aircraft Manufacturer — A2327

2013, Aug. 15 Photo.

4448 A2327 €1.05 multi 3.00 1.00

Impressionist Paintings Type of 2013

Designs: No. 4449, Like #4387. No. 4450, Like #4389. No. 4451, Like #4390. No. 4452, Like #4396.

Serpentine Die Cut 11

2013, Aug. 26 Litho.

Self-Adhesive

4449 A2310 (58c) multi 1.60 1.60
4450 A2310 (58c) multi 1.60 1.60
4451 A2310 (58c) multi 1.60 1.60
4452 A2310 (58c) multi 1.60 1.60
Nos. 4449-4452 (4) 6.40 6.40

Nos. 4449-4452 each have a dot structure in the colored panels at right that is not found on the photogravure stamps. The appearance of "France" on Nos. 4449-4452 appears lighter and grayer than that found on the photogravure stamps.

Patronage Law, 10th Anniv. — A2328

2013, Sept. 5 Photo. *Perf. 13¼*

4453 A2328 63c multi 1.75 .60

Sculpture of Virgin Mary and Infant Jesus A2329

Keystone, Sainte-Chapelle de Vincennes — A2330

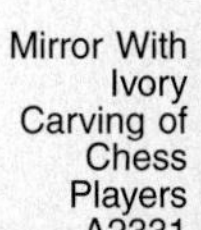

Mirror With Ivory Carving of Chess Players A2331

Annunciation of the Virgin, Reims Cathedral A2332

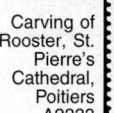

Carving of Rooster, St. Pierre's Cathedral, Poitiers A2333

Decorated Mirror of Louis d'Anjou A2334

Marriage of the Virgin, Notre Dame Cathedral, Paris A2335

Angel From Canopy of King Charles VII — A2336

Illumination From Les Très Riches Heures du Duc de Berry A2337

Reliquary Medallion A2338

Illumination from Heures de François de Guise A2339

Bas-relief of Man Presenting Flower to Woman A2340

Serpentine Die Cut 11

2013, Sept. 6 Photo.

Booklet Stamps

Self-Adhesive

4454 A2329 (63c) multi 1.75 .60
4455 A2330 (63c) multi 1.75 .60
4456 A2331 (63c) multi 1.75 .60
4457 A2332 (63c) multi 1.75 .60
4458 A2333 (63c) multi 1.75 .60
4459 A2334 (63c) multi 1.75 .60
4460 A2335 (63c) multi 1.75 .60
4461 A2336 (63c) multi 1.75 .60
4462 A2337 (63c) multi 1.75 .60
4463 A2338 (63c) multi 1.75 .60
4464 A2339 (63c) multi 1.75 .60
4465 A2340 (63c) multi 1.75 .60
- *a.* Booklet pane of 12, #4454-4465 21.00

Nos. 4454-4465 (12) 21.00 7.20

Gothic art.

French Heritage A2341

Designs: No. 4466, House of the Lumière Brothers, Lyon. No. 4467, Buffon Museum, Montbard. No. 4468, House of George Sand, Nohant. No. 4469, House of Georges Clemenceau, Saint-Vincent-sur-Jard. No. 4470, Château de La Motte-Tilly, La Motte-Tilly. No. 4471, Castle and ramparts, Carcassonne. No. 4472, Château de Carrouges, Carrouges. No. 4473, Château de Champs-sur-Marne, Champs-sur-Marne. No. 4474, Aligned stones of Carnac. No. 4475, Roman structures (Mausoleum of the Julii, Triumphal arch of Glanum), Saint-Rémy-de-Provence. No. 4476, Mosaics at Montcaret archaeological site. No. 4477, Gallo-Roman Villa, Montmaurin.

Serpentine Die Cut 11

2013, Sept. 6 Photo.

Booklet Stamps
Self-Adhesive

4466	A2341 (58c) multi		1.60	.55
4467	A2341 (58c) multi		1.60	.55
4468	A2341 (58c) multi		1.60	.55
4469	A2341 (58c) multi		1.60	.55
a.	Booklet pane of 4, #4466-4469		6.50	
4470	A2341 (58c) multi		1.60	.55
4471	A2341 (58c) multi		1.60	.55
4472	A2341 (58c) multi		1.60	.55
4473	A2341 (58c) multi		1.60	.55
a.	Booklet pane of 4, #4470-4473		6.50	
4474	A2341 (58c) multi		1.60	.55
4475	A2341 (58c) multi		1.60	.55
4476	A2341 (58c) multi		1.60	.55
4477	A2341 (58c) multi		1.60	.55
a.	Booklet pane of 4, #4474-4477		6.50	
	Complete booklet, #4469a, 4473a, 4477a		19.50	
	Nos. 4466-4477 (12)		19.20	6.60

Judicial Police of Paris, Cent. — A2342

2013, Sept. 13 Photo. *Perf. 13¼*

4478	A2342 63c multi	1.75	.60

Art Issue

Faience Vase, by Théodore Deck (1823-91) A2343

2013, Sept. 20 Photo. *Perf. 13¼x13*

4479	A2343 €1.55 multi	4.25	2.10

Alexandre Yersin (1863-1943), Bacteriologist — A2344

Yersin as: 63c, Older man. 95c, Young man.

2013, Sept. 20 Engr. *Perf. 13x13¼*

4480	A2344 63c multi	1.75	.60
4481	A2344 95c multi	2.60	.85

See Viet Nam Nos. 3488-3489.

Art Issue
Souvenir Sheet

Paintings by Georges Braque (1882-1963) — A2345

No. 4482: a, Le Guéridon. b, Le Salon.

2013, Sept. 27 Photo. *Perf. 13x13¼*

4482	A2345 Sheet of 2	8.50	8.50
a.-b.	€1.55 Either single	4.25	2.10

St. Bernard of Clairvaux (1090-1153), Abbot, and His Birthplace, Fontaine-lès-Dijon — A2346

2013, Oct. 4 Engr. *Perf. 13¼*

4483	A2346 58c multi	1.60	.55

Miniature Sheet

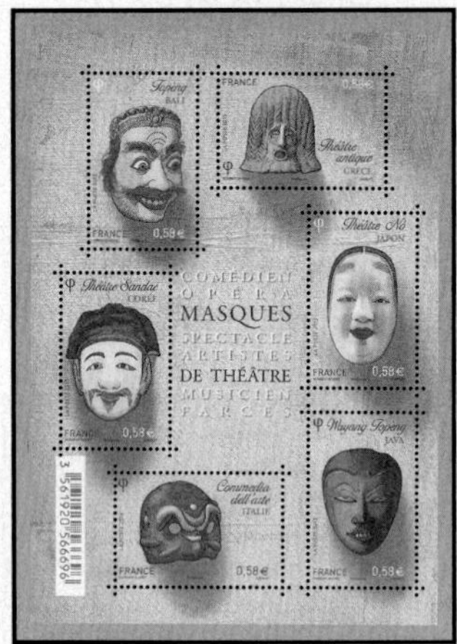

Theatrical Masks — A2347

No. 4484: a, Balinese Topeng. b, Greek theater mask, horiz. c, Korean Sandae mask. d, Japanese Noh theater mask. e, Italian Commedia dell'arte mask, horiz. f, Javanese shadow theater mask.

2013, Oct. 4 Litho. & Engr. *Perf. 13*

4484	A2347 Sheet of 6	9.75	9.75
a.-f.	58c Any single	1.60	.55

A set of six souvenir sheets, each containing one each of Nos. 4484a-4484f, sold for €15.

Marianne and Balloon A2348

Balloons and Paraglider — A2349

Man Blowing on Fire A2350

Bottle of Air in Water A2351

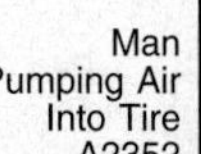

Man Pumping Air Into Tire A2352

Paramedics Tending to Man Wearing Oxygen Mask A2353

Hang Glider A2354

Sailboat A2355

Birds A2356

Hummingbird and Flowers — A2357

Horn Player A2358

Runner A2359

Polynesian Canoe A2360

Wind Turbine A2361

2013, Oct. 12 Engr. *Perf. 13*

4485	A2348 58c multi	1.60	.55

Photo. & Embossed
Souvenir Sheet
Perf. 13¼x13

4486	A2349 €2.35 multi	6.50	3.25

Photo.
Booklet Stamps
Self-Adhesive
Serpentine Die Cut 11

4487	A2350 (63c) multi	1.75	.60
4488	A2351 (63c) multi	1.75	.60
4489	A2352 (63c) multi	1.75	.60
4490	A2353 (63c) multi	1.75	.60
4491	A2354 (63c) multi	1.75	.60
4492	A2355 (63c) multi	1.75	.60
4493	A2356 (63c) multi	1.75	.60
4494	A2357 (63c) multi	1.75	.60
4495	A2358 (63c) multi	1.75	.60
4496	A2359 (63c) multi	1.75	.60
4497	A2360 (63c) multi	1.75	.60
4498	A2361 (63c) multi	1.75	.60
a.	Booklet pane of 12, #4487-4498	21.00	
	Nos. 4487-4498 (12)	21.00	7.20

Stamp Day. See Nos. 4535-4536.

Miniature Sheet

Television Personalities — A2362

No. 4499: a, Pierre Sabbagh (1918-94), news reporter and producer. b, Léon Zitrone (1914-95), news and sports reporter. c, Catherine Langeais (1923-98), show host. d, Denise Glaser (1920-83), show host and producer. e, Jacqueline Joubert (1921-2005), show host and producer, horiz. f, Pierre Desgraupes (1918-93), news reporter, horiz.

2013, Oct. 18 Photo. *Perf. 13*

4499	A2362 Sheet of 6	9.75	9.75
a.-f.	58c Any single	1.60	.55

Little Pleasures A2363

Designs: No. 4500, People and tea set (Thé partagé). No. 4501, Tree of life (Arbre de vie). No. 4502, Peacock holding letter (Paon messager). No. 4503, Carousel (Carrousel). No. 4504, Tree and falling coins (Pluie d'écus). No. 4505, Robin (Le rouge-gorge). No. 4506, Child and dove (Enfant de paix). No. 4507, Flying horse and rider (Cheval porte-bonheur). No. 4508, Cookies, pastries and snacks (Gourmandises). No. 4509, Citrus fruit and blossoms (Magie d'agrumes). No. 4510, Mother, child and flowers (Bienveillance). No. 4511, Shoe filled with gifts (L'escarpin).

Serpentine Die Cut 11

2013, Oct. 25 Photo.

Booklet Stamps
Self-Adhesive

4500	A2363 (58c) multi	1.60	.55
4501	A2363 (58c) multi	1.60	.55
4502	A2363 (58c) multi	1.60	.55
4503	A2363 (58c) multi	1.60	.55
4504	A2363 (58c) multi	1.60	.55
4505	A2363 (58c) multi	1.60	.55
4506	A2363 (58c) multi	1.60	.55
4507	A2363 (58c) multi	1.60	.55
4508	A2363 (58c) multi	1.60	.55
4509	A2363 (58c) multi	1.60	.55
4510	A2363 (58c) multi	1.60	.55
4511	A2363 (58c) multi	1.60	.55
a.	Booklet pane of 12, #4500-4511	19.50	
	Nos. 4500-4511 (12)	19.20	6.60

A souvenir sheet containing a perf. 12¾ example of No. 4510 with water-activated gum sold for €3.

Types of 1959-2013
Serpentine Die Cut 11

2013, Nov. 6 Engr.

Booklet Stamps
Self-Adhesive

4512	A2325 (58c) green	1.60	.35
4513	A328 63c black	1.75	.60
4514	A349 63c black	1.75	.60
4515	A360 63c black	1.75	.60
4516	A379 63c black	1.75	.60
4517	A486 63c black	1.75	.60
4518	A555 63c black	1.75	.60
4519	A2322 (63c) red	1.75	.60
4520	A771 63c black	1.75	.60
4521	A915 63c black	1.75	.60
4522	A1161 63c black	1.75	.60
4523	A1409 63c black	1.75	.60

4524 A1713 63c black 1.75 .60
4525 A1912 63c black 1.75 .60
a. Booklet pane of 14, #4512-4525 24.50
Nos. 4512-4525 (14) 24.35 8.15

Trade Treaty Between France and Denmark, 350th Anniv. A2364

Map and compass rose with ship at: 63c, Right. 80c, Left.

2013, Nov. 7 Engr. *Perf. 13*
4526 A2364 63c multi 1.75 .60
4527 A2364 80c multi 2.25 .75

See Denmark Nos. 1663-1664.

Fashion A2365

Designs: No. 4528, Finished dresses on three dress forms. No. 4529, Flower, three women wearing white dresses. No. 4530, Three dress forms. No. 4531, Three women wearing white dresses.

2013, Nov. 8 Photo. *Perf. 13¼*
4528 A2365 63c multi 1.75 .60
4529 A2365 63c multi 1.75 .60
4530 A2365 95c multi 2.60 .85
4531 A2365 95c multi 2.60 .85
Nos. 4528-4531 (4) 8.70 2.90

See Singapore Nos. 1640-1643.

Souvenir Sheet

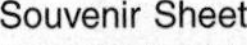

French History — A2366

No. 4532: a, Battle of Muret, 1213. b, Capture of Tournoel, 1212.

2013, Nov. 8 Engr. *Perf. 13x13¼*
4532 A2366 Sheet of 2 8.00 8.00
a.-b. €1.45 Either single 4.00 1.40

National Order of Merit, 50th Anniv. — A2367

2013, Nov. 9 Engr. *Perf. 13¼*
4533 A2367 63c blue 1.75 .60

2013 French Kickboxing World Championships, Clermont-Ferrand — A2368

2013, Nov. 16 Photo. *Perf. 13*
4534 A2368 95c multi 2.60 .85

Sailboat and Horn Player Types of 2013

Serpentine Die Cut 11

2013, Nov. 18 Litho.

Self-Adhesive

4535 A2355 (63c) multi 1.75 1.75
4536 A2358 (63c) multi 1.75 1.75

"Phil@poste" is sharper on Nos. 4535-4536 than on Nos. 4492 and 4495.

Items with Spirals A2369

Spirals in: No. 4537, Solarium shell (Coquillage solarium). No. 4538, Pottery design from Iznik, Turkey (Céramique Iznik). No. 4539, Spirograph. No. 4540, Red rose (Rose rouge). No. 4541, Ammonite fossil (Fossile d'ammonite). No. 4542, Chinese highway interchange (Echangeur Shanghai Nanpu). No. 4543, Kite (Cerf-volant). No. 4544, Cyclone Ingrid. No. 4545, Tree rings (Sapincoupe transversale). No. 4546, Basket (Vannerie). No. 4547, Lighthouse staircase (Phare de la Coubre). No. 4548, School of barracudas (Banc des barracudas).

Serpentine Die Cut 11

2014, Jan. 4 Photo.

Booklet Stamps

Self-Adhesive

4537 A2369 (66c) multi 1.75 .60
4538 A2369 (66c) multi 1.75 .60
4539 A2369 (66c) multi 1.75 .60
4540 A2369 (66c) multi 1.75 .60
4541 A2369 (66c) multi 1.75 .60
4542 A2369 (66c) multi 1.75 .60
4543 A2369 (66c) multi 1.75 .60
4544 A2369 (66c) multi 1.75 .60
4545 A2369 (66c) multi 1.75 .60
4546 A2369 (66c) multi 1.75 .60
4547 A2369 (66c) multi 1.75 .60
4548 A2369 (66c) multi 1.75 .60
a. Booklet pane of 12, #4537-4548 21.00
Nos. 4537-4548 (12) 21.00 7.20

See Nos. 4566-4567, 4698.

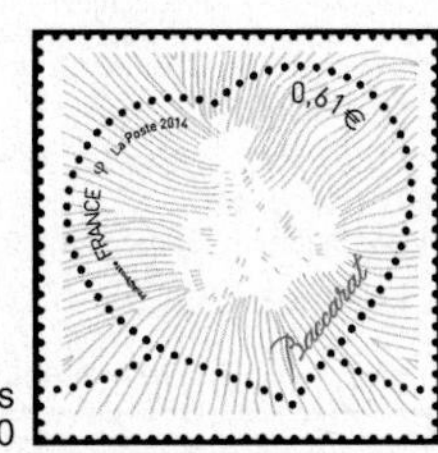

Hearts A2370

"Baccarat" and: 61c, Chandelier. €1.02, Goblet.

Silk-Screened, Engraved & Embossed

2014, Jan. 7 *Perf. 13*
4549 A2370 61c multi 1.75 .60
a. Souvenir sheet of 5 8.75 8.75
4550 A2370 €1.02 multi 2.75 .90

Silk-Screened & Engraved

Serpentine Die Cut

Self-Adhesive

4551 A2370 61c multi 1.75 1.75
4552 A2370 €1.02 multi 2.75 2.75

See No. 4651.

Anne, Duchess of Brittany (1477-1514) A2371

Litho. & Engr.

2014, Jan. 11 *Perf. 13*
4553 A2371 66c multi 1.75 .60

A souvenir sheet of one sold for €3.20.

Signs of the Zodiac A2372

Designs: No. 4554, Aries (Bélier). No. 4555, Taurus (Taureau). No. 4556, Gemini (Gémeaux). No. 4557, Cancer. No. 4558, Leo (Lion). No. 4559, Virgo (Vierge). No. 4560, Libra (Balance). No. 4561, Scorpio (Scorpion). No. 4562, Sagittarius (Sagittaire). No. 4563, Capricorn (Capricorne). No. 4564, Aquarius (Verseau). No. 4565, Pisces (Poissons).

Serpentine Die Cut 11

2014, Jan. 20 Photo.

Booklet Stamps

Self-Adhesive

4554 A2372 (61c) multi 1.75 .60
4555 A2372 (61c) multi 1.75 .60
4556 A2372 (61c) multi 1.75 .60
4557 A2372 (61c) multi 1.75 .60
4558 A2372 (61c) multi 1.75 .60
4559 A2372 (61c) multi 1.75 .60
4560 A2372 (61c) multi 1.75 .60
4561 A2372 (61c) multi 1.75 .60
4562 A2372 (61c) multi 1.75 .60
4563 A2372 (61c) multi 1.75 .60
4564 A2372 (61c) multi 1.75 .60
4565 A2372 (61c) multi 1.75 .60
a. Booklet pane of 12, #4554-4565 21.00
Nos. 4554-4565 (12) 21.00 7.20

Items With Spirals Type of 2014

Designs: No. 4566, Like #4542. No. 4567, Like #4543.

Serpentine Die Cut 11

2014, Jan. 27 Litho.

Self-Adhesive

4566 A2369 (66c) multi 1.75 1.75
4567 A2369 (66c) multi 1.75 1.75

"Phil@poste" is sharper on Nos. 4566-4567 than on Nos. 4542-4543.

New Year 2014 (Year of the Horse) — A2373

2014, Jan. 31 Photo. *Perf. 13¼x13*
4568 A2373 66c multi 1.75 .60

No. 4568 was printed in sheets of 5. A souvenir sheet of one sold for €3.20.

See No. 4971b.

Art Issue

Bust of Julius Caesar A2374

2014, Feb. 14 Engr. *Perf. 13¼x13*
4569 A2374 €1.65 multi 4.50 2.25

Cattle Breeds A2375

Inscriptions: No. 4570, La Bretonne Pie Noir. No. 4571, L'Armoricaine. No. 4572, La Béarnaise. No. 4573, La Maraîchine. No. 4574, La Mirandaise. No. 4575, La Villard de Lans. No. 4576, La Saosnoise. No. 4577, La Nantaise. No. 4578, La Bordelaise. No. 4579, La Lourdaise. No. 4580, La Casta. No. 4581, La Ferrandaise.

Serpentine Die Cut 11

2014, Feb. 22 Photo.

Booklet Stamps

Self-Adhesive

4570 A2375 (61c) multi 1.75 .60
4571 A2375 (61c) multi 1.75 .60
4572 A2375 (61c) multi 1.75 .60
4573 A2375 (61c) multi 1.75 .60
4574 A2375 (61c) multi 1.75 .60
4575 A2375 (61c) multi 1.75 .60
4576 A2375 (61c) multi 1.75 .60
4577 A2375 (61c) multi 1.75 .60
4578 A2375 (61c) multi 1.75 .60
4579 A2375 (61c) multi 1.75 .60
4580 A2375 (61c) multi 1.75 .60
4581 A2375 (61c) multi 1.75 .60
a. Booklet pane of 12, #4570-4581 21.00
Nos. 4570-4581 (12) 21.00 7.20

Art Issue

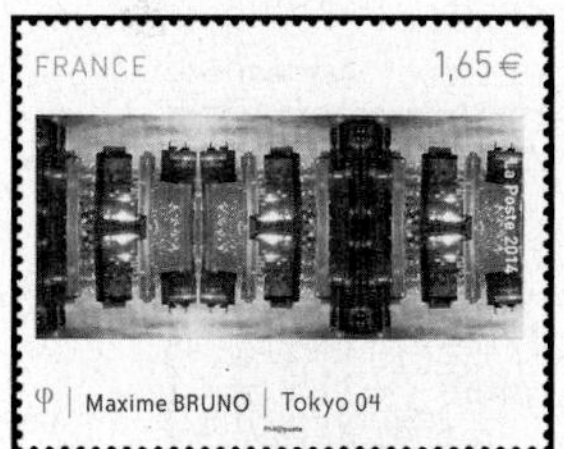

Tokyo 04, Photograph by Maxime Bruno — A2376

2014, Feb. 28 Litho. *Perf. 13x13¼*
4582 A2376 €1.65 multi 4.50 2.25

Miniature Sheet

Way of St. James — A2377

No. 4583: a, Via Lemovicensis in Bazas. b, Via Podiensis in Moissac. c, Via Tolosana in Auch. d, Via Turonensis in Pons.

Litho. & Engr.

2014, Mar. 14 *Perf. 13*
4583 A2377 Sheet of 4 9.00 9.00
a.-d. 83c Any single 2.25 .75

Alexandre Glais-Bizoin (1800-77), Politician — A2378

2014, Mar. 15 Engr. *Perf. 13x13¼*

4584 A2378 66c multi 1.90 .65

Bears A2379

Designs: No. 4585, Giant panda (Panda géant).
No. 4586: a, Spectacled bear (Ours andin). b, Kermode bear (Ours Kermode). c, Polar bear (Ours polaire).

2014, Mar. 21 Photo. *Perf. 13¼*

4585 A2379 61c multi 1.75 .60

Miniature Sheet

4586 Sheet of 4, #4585, 4586a-4586c 7.00 7.00
a.-c. A2379 61c Any single 1.75 .60

Diplomatic Relations Between France and People's Republic of China, 50th Anniv. — A2380

Designs: 66c, Qinhuai River, Nanjing. 98c, Seine River, Paris.

2014, Mar. 27 Engr. *Perf. 13x13¼*

4587 A2380 66c multi 1.90 .65
4588 A2380 98c multi 2.75 .90

See People's Republic of China Nos. 4172-4173.

Art Issue

Painting by Joan Mitchell (1925-92) A2381

2014, Mar. 28 Litho. *Perf. 13¼x13*

4589 A2381 €1.65 multi 4.50 2.25

Sell and Buy Used Items A2382

Turn Off Appliances A2383

Fruits and Vegetables A2384

Fix Leaks Quickly A2385

Sort and Recycle Paper A2386

Control Indoor Temperatures — A2387

Conserve Water A2388

People in Carpool A2389

Use Public Transportation — A2390

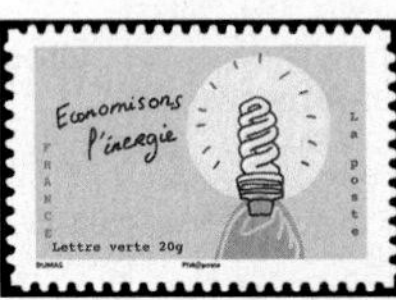

Save Energy A2391

Drive Ecologically Friendly Automobiles A2392

Recycle Waste Products A2393

Serpentine Die Cut 11

2014, Apr. 3 Photo.

Booklet Stamps Self-Adhesive

4590 A2382 (61c) multi 1.75 .60
4591 A2383 (61c) multi 1.75 .60
4592 A2384 (61c) multi 1.75 .60
4593 A2385 (61c) multi 1.75 .60
4594 A2386 (61c) multi 1.75 .60
4595 A2387 (61c) multi 1.75 .60
4596 A2388 (61c) multi 1.75 .60
4597 A2389 (61c) multi 1.75 .60
4598 A2390 (61c) multi 1.75 .60
4599 A2391 (61c) multi 1.75 .60
4600 A2392 (61c) multi 1.75 .60
4601 A2393 (61c) multi 1.75 .60
a. Booklet pane of 12, #4590-4601 21.00
Nos. 4590-4601 (12) 21.00 7.20

Opera Theater, Clermont-Ferrand — A2394

2014, Apr. 4 Engr. *Perf. 13¼*

4602 A2394 61c multi 1.75 .60

Spring Philatelic Show, Clermont-Ferrand.

Marguerite Duras (1914-96), Writer and Film Director — A2395

2014, Apr. 4 Engr. *Perf. 13¼*

4603 A2395 €1.10 multi 3.00 1.00

Arrest and Deportation of Jews at Izieu Orphanage, 70th Anniv. A2396

Litho. & Engr.

2014, Apr. 6 *Perf. 13x13¼*

4604 A2396 61c multi 1.75 .60

Miniature Sheet

European Capitals — A2397

No. 4605 — Attractions in Vienna: a, Secession Building. b, Belvedere Palace, horiz. c, Karlskirche (St. Charles' Church). d, Hofburg Palace, horiz.

Perf. 13¼x13, 13x13¼

2014, Apr. 18 Photo.

4605 A2397 Sheet of 4 + 3 labels 7.75 7.75
a.-d. 66c Any single 1.90 .65

Souvenir Sheet

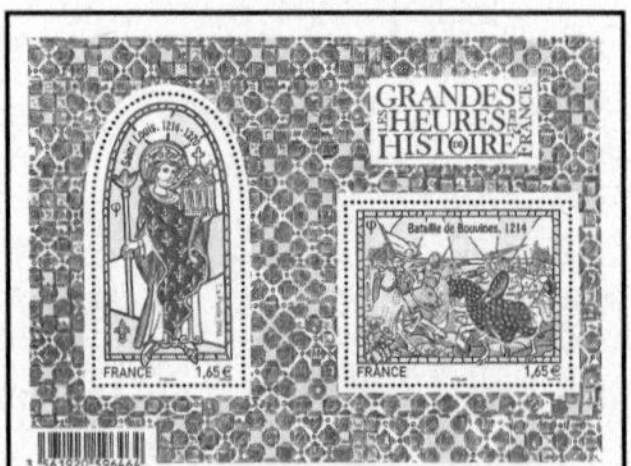

French History — A2398

No. 4606: a, St. Louis (1214-70) (35x66mm). b, Battle of Bouvines, 1214 (52x41mm)

2014, Apr. 25 Engr. *Perf. 13x13¼*

4606 A2398 Sheet of 2 9.50 9.50
a.-b. €1.65 Either single 4.75 2.25
c. Souvenir sheet of 4, #4532a, 4532b, 4606a, 4606b 17.00 17.00

Salon du Timbre 2014 (No. 4606c). Issued: No. 4606c, 6/23/14.

Palace of Poitiers — A2399

2014, May 1 Engr. *Perf. 13x13¼*

4607 A2399 61c multi + label 1.75 .60

Vacation A2400

Designs: No. 4608, Dog with sunglasses eating ice cream bar. No. 4609, Snail with trailer for shell. No. 4610, Crab building sand castle. No. 4611, Cats dancing. No. 4612, Turtle playing lute, turtle dancing. No. 4613, Lobster holding beach gear. No. 4614, Chicken and egg wearing headphones. No. 4615, Fish surfing. No. 4616, Ram with backpack and mountain climbing gear. No. 4617, Rabbits on tandem bicycle. No. 4618. Frogs with umbrellas in swan boat. No. 4619, Geese, tent, snails on picnic plate.

Serpentine Die Cut 11

2014, May 3 Photo.

Booklet Stamps Self-Adhesive

4608 A2400 (61c) multi 1.75 .60
4609 A2400 (61c) multi 1.75 .60
4610 A2400 (61c) multi 1.75 .60
4611 A2400 (61c) multi 1.75 .60
4612 A2400 (61c) multi 1.75 .60
4613 A2400 (61c) multi 1.75 .60
4614 A2400 (61c) multi 1.75 .60
4615 A2400 (61c) multi 1.75 .60
4616 A2400 (61c) multi 1.75 .60
4617 A2400 (61c) multi 1.75 .60
4618 A2400 (61c) multi 1.75 .60
4619 A2400 (61c) multi 1.75 .60
a. Booklet pane of 12, #4608-4619 21.00
Nos. 4608-4619 (12) 21.00 7.20

Harp Created by Jean Henri Naderman, 1787 A2401

2014, May 4 Photo. *Perf. 13¼x13*

4620 A2401 83c multi 2.25 .75

Europa.

Opening of English Channel Tunnel, 20th Anniv. A2402

2014, May 6 Engr. *Perf. 13¼*

4621 A2402 66c multi 1.90 .65

Tourism Series

Boulogne-sur-Mer — A2403

2014, May 9 Engr. ***Perf. 13x12¾***
4622 A2403 61c multi 1.75 .60

D-Day, 70th Anniv. — A2404

2014, June 5 Photo. ***Perf. 13x12¾***
4623 A2404 66c multi 1.90 .65

Two souvenir sheets of one, issued in 2014 and in 2015, each sold for €3.20.

Tourism Issue

Pontigny Abbey, Yonne — A2405

2014, June 7 Engr. ***Perf. 13¼***
4624 A2405 61c multi 1.75 .60

Massacre of Tulle, 70th Anniv. A2406

2014, June 9 Photo. ***Perf. 13¼***
4625 A2406 66c multi 1.90 .65

Souvenir Sheet

Benjamin Rabier (1864-1939), Comic Book Illustrator — A2407

No. 4626: a, Duckling hatching, ring with rabbits, chick and chicken (41x41mm). b, Rabier, chicken, rabbit and duck (30x41mm).

2014, June 14 Engr. ***Perf. 13¼***
4626 A2407 Sheet of 2 5.00 5.00
a. 66c multi 1.90 .65
b. €1.10 multi 3.00 1.00

A 200x95mm sheet containing Nos. 4626a and 4626b, but having a different margin design sold for €6.
See Nos. 4676, 4680.

Trains A2408

Designs: No. 4627, Buddicom No. 33, Haute-Normandie. No. 4628, Z 209, Vallée de Chamonix. No. 4629, Pacific Chapelon Nord 3.1192, Paris, Gare du Nord. No. 4630, Micheline XM 5005, Haute-Marne. No. 4631, Mikado 141 R 1187, Côte Vermeille. No. 4632, BB 12125, Moselle. No. 4633, Z 6181, Ile-de-France. No. 4634, BB 66001, Les Cévennes. No. 4635, BB 9004, Les Landes. No. 4636, RTG T 2057, Gare de Boulogne-Aroglisseurs. No. 4637, CC 6572, Limoges, Gare des Bénédictins. No. 4638, TGV Duplex, Gare de Belfort-Montbéliard TGV.

Serpentine Die Cut 11

2014, June 14 Photo.

Booklet Stamps
Self-Adhesive

4627 A2408 (66c) multi 1.90 .65
4628 A2408 (66c) multi 1.90 .65
4629 A2408 (66c) multi 1.90 .65
4630 A2408 (66c) multi 1.90 .65
a. Booklet pane of 4, #4627-4630 7.60
4631 A2408 (66c) multi 1.90 .65
4632 A2408 (66c) multi 1.90 .65
4633 A2408 (66c) multi 1.90 .65
4634 A2408 (66c) multi 1.90 .65
a. Booklet pane of 4, #4631-4634 7.60
4635 A2408 (66c) multi 1.90 .65
4636 A2408 (66c) multi 1.90 .65
4637 A2408 (66c) multi 1.90 .65
4638 A2408 (66c) multi 1.90 .65
a. Booklet pane of 4, #4635-4638 7.60
Complete booklet, #4630a, 4634a, 4638a 23.00
Nos. 4627-4638 (12) 22.80 7.80

Paris Zoo, 80th Anniv. — A2409

2014, June 15 Photo. ***Perf. 13***
4639 A2409 98c multi 2.75 .95

A souvenir sheet containing No. 4639 sold for €3.20.

Jean Jaurès (1859-1914), Assassinated Socialist Party Leader — A2410

Jaurès: 61c, Without hat. €1.02, With hat.

2014, June 17 Engr. ***Perf. 13¼***
4640 A2410 61c blue 1.75 .60
4641 A2410 €1.02 red 2.75 .95
a. Horiz. pair, #4640-4641 4.50 2.25

See Nos. 4675, 4679.

Miniature Sheet

The 1950s — A2411

No. 4642: a, Automobile. b, Electricity advertisement, vert. c, People packing for vacation, vert. d, Vendor in movie theater. e, Musicians. f, Two women modeling fashions, veret.

2014, June 18 Photo. ***Perf. 13***
4642 A2411 Sheet of 6 11.50 11.50
a.-f. 66c Any single 1.90 .65

See Nos. 4677, 4678.

A set of 10 miniature sheets containing reproductions of old French stamps (Nos. 641, 722, 764, 850, B34, B92, B97, B172, B248 and C22) with denominations was produced in limited quantities and offered only as a complete set. Each sheet contained five reproductions of one of the ten stamps in different colors, one with a €2.20 denomination and four with €2.45 denominations. **Similar sets were produced in limited quantities in subsequent years with reproductions of different stamps having different new denomninations of more than €1.40.**

Ceres — A2412

2014, June 18 Engr. ***Imperf.***
With Printer's Inscription at Base of Stamp

4643 A2412 €1 rose carmine 2.75 1.40
4644 A2412 €1 red 2.75 1.40

Typo.

4645 A2412 €1 vermilion 2.75 1.40
a. With printer information at top of stamp 2.75 1.40
4646 A2412 €1 rose 2.75 1.40
a. With printer information at top of stamp 2.75 1.40
Nos. 4643-4646 (4) 11.00 5.60

Printed in sheets of 20 containing Nos. 4645a, 4646a, 5 each Nos. 4643-4644, 4 each Nos. 4645-4646. See No. 4727a.

Tourism Issue

Coareze A2413

Locmariaquer — A2414

2014 Engr. ***Perf. 13¼***
4647 A2413 61c multi 1.75 .60
4648 A2414 61c multi 1.75 .60

Issued: No. 4647, 6/19; No. 4648, 6/20. See Nos. 4673, 4674.

French Institute, Paris — A2415

2014, June 21 Engr. ***Perf. 13x13¼***
4649 A2415 61c multi + label 1.75 .60

French Federation of Philatelic Associations, 87th Congress, Paris. See No. 4672.

Art Issue

The Seine at Pont du Carrousel, by Jean Dufy (1888-1964) — A2416

2014, June 22 Litho. ***Perf. 13x13¼***
4650 A2416 €1.65 multi 4.50 2.25

See No. 4681.

Baccarat Hearts Type of 2014
Silk-Screened & Engraved

2014, June 23 ***Perf.***
4651 A2370 €3 multi 8.25 4.25

No. 4651 was printed in sheets of 5.

National Institute of Health and Medical Research, 50th Anniv. A2417

2014, July 3 Photo. ***Perf. 13¼***
4652 A2417 66c multi 1.75 .60

Jeanne Antoine Poisson, Marquise de Pompadour (1721-64), Patron of the Arts — A2418

2014, July 4 Engr. ***Perf. 13¼***
4653 A2418 66c multi 1.75 .60

Art Issue

Les Boîtes de Conserve, by Jean Fautrier (1898-1964) — A2419

2014, July 11 Engr. ***Perf. 13x13¼***
4654 A2419 €1.65 multi 4.50 2.25

General Mobilization of World War I Troops, Cent. — A2420

2014, Aug. 2 Engr. ***Perf. 13x13¼***
4655 A2420 66c blue & red 1.75 .60

Miniature Sheet

2014 World Equestrian Games, Normandy — A2421

No. 4656: a, Dressage (40x30mm). b, Endurance (40x30mm). c, Concours complet d'équitation (40x40mm). d, Para-dressage (30x40mm). e, Voltige (30x40mm). f, Attelage (40x40mm). g, Saut d'obstacles (40x30mm). h, Reining (40x30mm).

2014, Aug. 23 Photo. *Perf. 13x13¼*

4656	A2421	Sheet of 8	17.50	8.75
a.-d.		61c Any single	1.60	.55
e.-h.		€1.02 Any single	2.75	.90

A souvenir sheet containing examples of Nos. 4656e and 4656f with different perforations, sold for €6.

Charles Péguy (1873-1914), Writer — A2422

2014, Sept. 5 Engr. *Perf. 13¼*

4657	A2422	€1.55 multi	4.00	1.40

Renaissance Objets d'Art — A2423

Designs: No. 4658, Gardens of Château de Villandry. No. 4659, Clock, Rouen. No. 4660, Stairway sculpture, by Jean Goujon. No. 4661, Sculpture of salamander, Château de Fontainbleau. No. 4662, Buckle of King Charles IX. No. 4663, Detail of tapestry depicting Jupiter and Latona. No. 4664, Portrait of King Francis I, by Jean Clouet. No. 4665, Stainedd-glass window depicting angel playing flute, Sainte-Etienne Cathedral, Sens. No. 4666, Enamel painting of Ulysses, by Léonard Limousin. No. 4667, Book cover by Étienne Roffet. No. 4668, Armor of King Henri II. No. 4669, Stained-glass emblem of Queen Anne of Brittany depicting ermine and crown.

Serpentine Die Cut 11

2014, Sept. 6 Photo.

Booklet Stamps
Self-Adhesive

4658	A2423	(61c) multi	1.60	.55
4659	A2423	(61c) multi	1.60	.55
4660	A2423	(61c) multi	1.60	.55
4661	A2423	(61c) multi	1.60	.55
4662	A2423	(61c) multi	1.60	.55
4663	A2423	(61c) multi	1.60	.55
4664	A2423	(61c) multi	1.60	.55
4665	A2423	(61c) multi	1.60	.55
4666	A2423	(61c) multi	1.60	.55
4667	A2423	(61c) multi	1.60	.55
4668	A2423	(61c) multi	1.60	.55
4669	A2423	(61c) multi	1.60	.55
a.		Booklet pane of 12, #4658-4669	19.50	
		Nos. 4658-4669 (12)	19.20	6.60

Souvenir Sheet

First Battle of the Marne, Cent. — A2424

No. 4670: a, Troops and automobile. b, Troops on horseback.

Photo. & Litho.

2014, Sept. 12 *Perf. 13¼*

4670	A2424	Sheet of 2	4.25	2.10
a.		66c multi	1.75	.60
b.		98c multi	2.50	.85

A souvenir sheet containing Nos. 4670a and 4670b but with as different margin sold for €5.

Art Issue

Mural on Necker Hospital Staircase, by Keith Haring (1958-90) A2425

2014, Sept. 19 Photo. *Perf. 12¼x13*

4671	A2425	€2.65 multi	6.75	3.50

Types of 2014

Serpentine Die Cut 11

2014, Sept. 25 Photo.

Booklet Stamps
Self-Adhesive

4672	A2415	61c	Like #4649 + label (22x16mm)	1.60	.55
4673	A2413	61c	Like #4647 (22x16mm)	1.60	.55
4674	A2414	61c	Like #4648 (21x16mm)	1.60	.55
4675	A2410	61c	Like #4640 (15x22mm)	1.60	.55
4676	A2407	66c	Like #4626a (21x22mm)	1.75	.60
4677	A2411	66c	Like #4642e (30x22mm)	1.75	.60
4678	A2411	66c	Like #4642a (30x22mm)	1.75	.60
4679	A2410	€1.02	Like #4641 (15x22mm)	2.60	.85
4680	A2407	€1.10	Like #4626b (15x22mm)	2.75	.90
4681	A2416	€1.65	Like #4650 (46x38mm)	4.25	1.40
a.			Booklet pane of 10, #4672-4681 + label	21.50	
			Nos. 4672-4681 (10)	21.25	7.15

Sense of Smell A2426

Designs: No. 4682, Man and woman in love. No. 4683, Dog with magnifying glass. No. 4684, Coffee pot and cup. No. 4685, Skunks. No. 4686, Perfume atomizer. No. 4687, Athletic shoe and flowers. No. 4688, Fish with clothespin on nose. No. 4689, Cheese and foxes. No. 4690, Roast chicken. No. 4691, Woman smelling rose. No. 4692, Mother and baby. No. 4693, Face, herbs and spices.

Serpentine Die Cut 11

2014, Oct. 1 Photo.

Booklet Stamps
Self-Adhesive

4682	A2426	(61c) multi	1.60	.55
4683	A2426	(61c) multi	1.60	.55
4684	A2426	(61c) multi	1.60	.55
4685	A2426	(61c) multi	1.60	.55
4686	A2426	(61c) multi	1.60	.55
4687	A2426	(61c) multi	1.60	.55
4688	A2426	(61c) multi	1.60	.55
4689	A2426	(61c) multi	1.60	.55
4690	A2426	(61c) multi	1.60	.55
4691	A2426	(61c) multi	1.60	.55
4692	A2426	(61c) multi	1.60	.55
4693	A2426	(61c) multi	1.60	.55
a.		Booklet pane of 12, #4682-4693	19.50	
		Nos. 4682-4693 (12)	19.20	6.60

Douai Court House 300th Anniv. A2427

2014, Oct. 3 Engr. *Perf. 13¼*

4694	A2427	83c multi	2.10	.70

Green Turtle A2428

2014, Oct. 9 Litho. *Perf. 13x13¼*

4695	A2428	98c multi	2.50	.85

See Comoro Islands No. , French Southern & Antarctic Territories No. 511, Malagasy Republic No. 1637, Mauritius No. 1144, Seychelles No. 904.

Salsa Dancers — A2429

Break Dancers — A2430

2014, Oct. 11 Engr. *Perf. 13¼*

4696	A2429	61c multi	1.50	.50

Souvenir Sheet

Litho.

Perf. 13¼x13

4697	A2430	€2.45 multi	6.25	2.10

Stamp Day.

Items With Spirals Type of 2014

Serpentine Die Cut 11

2014, Oct. 15 Litho.

Self-Adhesive

4698	A2369	(66c) Like #4540	1.75	1.75

"Phil@poste" is sharper on No. 4698 than on No. 4540.

Maximilien Vox (1894-1974), Creator of Typographical Classification System — A2431

2014, Oct. 17 Engr. *Perf. 13¼*

4699	A2431	€1.10 multi	2.75	.90

Miniature Sheet

Cameras — A2432

No. 4700: a, 1865 Derogy four-lens camera. b, 1902 Girard Le Reve folding camera. c, 1930 Kodak Beau Brownie camera. d, 1898 Bazin & Leroy Stereocycle camera. e, 1910 folding camera, horiz. f, 1935 Gaumont Spido Reportage camera.

Litho. & Engr.

2014, Oct. 24 *Perf. 13*

4700	A2432	Sheet of 6	10.50	5.25
a.-f.		66c Any single	1.75	.60

A set of six souvenir sheets containing one example of Nos. 4700a-4700f sold as a set for €16.

A2433

A2434

A2435

A2436

A2437

A2438

A2439

A2440

A2441

A2442

A2443

A2444

Serpentine Die Cut 11

2014, Oct. 24 Photo.

Booklet Stamps
Self-Adhesive

No.	Design	Value	Color	Unused	Used
4701	A2433	(61c)	multi	1.50	.50
4702	A2434	(61c)	multi	1.50	.50
4703	A2435	(61c)	multi	1.50	.50
4704	A2436	(61c)	multi	1.50	.50
4705	A2437	(61c)	multi	1.50	.50
4706	A2438	(61c)	multi	1.50	.50
4707	A2439	(61c)	multi	1.50	.50
4708	A2440	(61c)	multi	1.50	.50
4709	A2441	(61c)	multi	1.50	.50
4710	A2442	(61c)	multi	1.50	.50
4711	A2443	(61c)	multi	1.50	.50
4712	A2444	(61c)	multi	1.50	.50
a.	Booklet pane of 12, #4701-4712			18.00	
	Nos. 4701-4712 (12)			18.00	6.00

A souvenir sheet containing one perf. 13¼ example of a stamp like No. 4706 sold for €3.20.

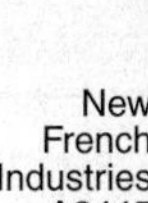

New French Industries A2445

Serpentine Die Cut 11

2014, Oct. 27 Photo.

Self-Adhesive

No.	Design	Value	Color	Unused	Used
4713	A2445	(98c)	multi	—	—

New French Industries A2446

Inscriptions: No. 4714, Usine du futur. No. 4715, Transition numérique. No. 4716, Développement durable. No. 4717, Patrimoine. No. 4718, Gastronomie. No. 4719, Transition énergétique. No. 4720, Elégance. No. 4721, Economi sociale et solidaire. No. 4722, Electromobilité. No. 4723, Exportations. No. 4724, Métiers d'art. No. 4725, Innovation 2030.

Serpentine Die Cut 11

2014, Oct. 27 Photo.

Booklet Stamps
Self-Adhesive

No.	Design	Value	Color	Unused	Used
4714	A2446	(61c)	multi	1.50	.50
4715	A2446	(61c)	multi	1.50	.50
4716	A2446	(61c)	multi	1.50	.50
4717	A2446	(61c)	multi	1.50	.50
4718	A2446	(61c)	multi	1.50	.50
4719	A2446	(61c)	multi	1.50	.50
4720	A2446	(61c)	multi	1.50	.50
4721	A2446	(61c)	multi	1.50	.50
4722	A2446	(61c)	multi	1.50	.50
4723	A2446	(61c)	multi	1.50	.50
4724	A2446	(61c)	multi	1.50	.50
4725	A2446	(61c)	multi	1.50	.50
a.	Booklet pane of 12, #4714-4725			18.00	
	Nos. 4714-4725 (12)			18.00	6.00

Public Sale of Blue Cornflowers Made by World War I Veterans, 80th Anniv. — A2447

2014, Nov. 6 Photo. *Perf. 13¼*

No.	Design	Value	Color	Unused	Used
4726	A2447	€1.10	multi	2.75	.90

Types of 2003-14

2014, Nov. 6 Engr. *Perf. 13*

No.	Description	Unused	Used
4727	Sheet of 4, #4079, 4437, 4727a, 4727b	6.00	3.00
a.	A2412 61c green (20x26mm)	1.50	.50
b.	A1664 61c green	1.50	.50
c.	Booklet pane of 12, 6 each #4727a-4727b	18.00	—
	Complete booklet, #4437b, 4727c	21.00	

Evariste de Parny (1753-1814), Poet — A2448

2014, Nov. 7 Engr. *Perf. 13¼*

No.	Design	Value	Color	Unused	Used
4728	A2448	83c	multi	2.10	.70

Republican Security Companies (Riot Control Forces), 70th Anniv. — A2449

2014, Dec. 8 Photo. *Perf. 13x12¾*

No.	Design	Value	Color	Unused	Used
4729	A2449	€1.10	multi	2.75	.90

Handicrafts A2450

Inscriptions: Nos. 4730, 4742, Pierres précieuses (jewelery making). No. 4731, Bois (sanding wood). No. 4732, Verre (glass making). No. 4733, Métal (blacksmithing). No. 4734, Tissu (embroidery). No. 4735, Terre (pottery making). No. 4736, Papier (paper making). No. 4737, Tissu (weaving). No. 4738, Cuir (leather work). No. 4739, Bois (barrel making). No. 4740, Pierre (sculpting). No. 4741, Végétal (flower arranging).

2015 Litho. *Serpentine Die Cut 11*

Self-Adhesive

No.	Design	Value	Color	Unused	Used
4730	A2450	(76c)	multi	1.75	1.75

Photo.

Booklet Stamps

No.	Design	Value	Color	Unused	Used
4731	A2450	(76c)	multi	1.75	.60
4732	A2450	(76c)	multi	1.75	.60
4733	A2450	(76c)	multi	1.75	.60
4734	A2450	(76c)	multi	1.75	.60
4735	A2450	(76c)	multi	1.75	.60
4736	A2450	(76c)	multi	1.75	.60
4737	A2450	(76c)	multi	1.75	.60
4738	A2450	(76c)	multi	1.75	.60
4739	A2450	(76c)	multi	1.75	.60
4740	A2450	(76c)	multi	1.75	.60
4741	A2450	(76c)	multi	1.75	.60
4742	A2450	(76c)	multi	1.75	.60
a.	Booklet pane of 12, #4731-4742			21.00	
	Nos. 4731-4742 (12)			21.00	7.20

No. 4730 has a visible dot pattern in the upper right part of the vignette and a sharper "Phil@poste" than No. 4742. Issued: Nos. 4730, 1/5; others 1/3.

Marianne and Children "Lettre Suivie" — A2450a

2015-16 Litho. *Die Cut*

Self-Adhesive

No.	Design	Description	Unused	Used
4742B	A2450a	(€1.08) red lilac + label, background dots close together	—	—
c.		red lilac, background dots farther apart	—	—
d.		€1.10 As "c," magenta		—
e.		lt magenta, finer background dots	—	—
f.		As "e," dots and circles in background, coarse portrait with jagged curved lines	—	—

Issued: No. 4742B, 1/1. No. 4742Bd, 1/1/16. Sheet margins differ. No. 4742B has a green panel at left and destination and date lines over green background. No. 4742Bc is like No. 4742B, but with destination and date lines over a white background. No. 4742Bd has a magenta panel at left with "Indemnisation**" and "€" at lower left. Nos. 4742Be and 4742Bf are like No. 4742Bd, but with "Epaisseur 3cm max" at lower left.

Art Issue

The Great Wave, by Katsushika Hokusai (1760-1849) — A2451

2015, Jan. 16 Photo. *Perf. 13x13¼*

No.	Design	Value	Color	Unused	Used
4743	A2451	€1.90	multi	4.50	2.25

Hearts — A2452

"JC de Castelbajac," people kissing and: 68c, Hearts. €1.15, Flowers.

2015, Jan. 23 Photo. *Perf.*

With White Frame Around Stamp

No.	Design	Value	Color	Unused	Used
4744	A2452	68c	multi	1.60	.55

Without White Frame Around Stamp

Perf. 13

No.	Design	Value	Color	Unused	Used
4745	A2452	68c	multi	1.60	.55
4746	A2452	€1.15	multi	2.60	.85

Self-Adhesive

Serpentine Die Cut

No.	Design	Value	Color	Unused	Used
4747	A2452	68c	multi	1.60	1.60
4748	A2452	€1.15	multi	2.60	2.60

No. 4744 was printed in sheets of 5. Values for Nos. 4745-4748 are for examples with surrounding selvage. Designs on Nos. 4745-4748 continue onto the surrounding selvage.

New Year 2015 (Year of the Goat) — A2453

2015, Jan. 30 Photo. *Perf. 13¼x13*

No.	Design	Value	Color	Unused	Used
4749	A2453	76c	multi	1.75	.60

No. 4749 was printed in sheets of 5. A souvenir sheet of one sold for €3.20. See No. 4971c.

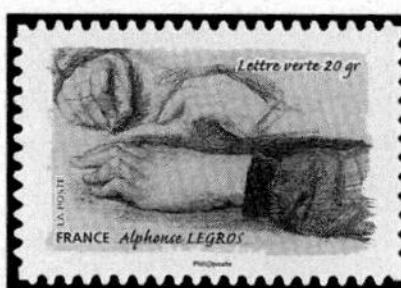

Drawings of Hands A2454

Drawing by: No. 4750, Alphonse Legros. No. 4751, Unknown 18th century Italian School artist. No. 4752, Paul Delaroche. No. 4753, Gustave Moreau. No. 4754, Eugène Carrière. No. 4755, Pablo Picasso. No. 4756, Annibale Carrache. No. 4757, Unknown 17th century Italian School artist (four hands holding handles). No. 4758, Louis Tocque (one hand). No. 4759, Pierre Mignard. No. 4760, Tocque (two hands holding hoop with flowers). No. 4761, Unknown 17th Italian School artist (hand, water drop and goblet).

Serpentine Die Cut 11

2015, Jan. 30 Litho.

Booklet Stamps
Self-Adhesive

No.	Design	Value	Color	Unused	Used
4750	A2454	(68c)	multi	1.60	.55
4751	A2454	(68c)	multi	1.60	.55
4752	A2454	(68c)	multi	1.60	.55
4753	A2454	(68c)	multi	1.60	.55
4754	A2454	(68c)	multi	1.60	.55
4755	A2454	(68c)	multi	1.60	.55
4756	A2454	(68c)	multi	1.60	.55
4757	A2454	(68c)	multi	1.60	.55
4758	A2454	(68c)	multi	1.60	.55
4759	A2454	(68c)	multi	1.60	.55
4760	A2454	(68c)	multi	1.60	.55
4761	A2454	(68c)	multi	1.60	.55
a.	Booklet pane of 12, #4750-4761			19.50	
	Nos. 4750-4761 (12)			19.20	6.60

Landmine Removal Service, 70th Anniv. A2455

2015, Feb. 20 Photo. *Perf. 13¼*

No.	Design	Value	Color	Unused	Used
4762	A2455	€1.20	multi	2.75	.90

Goat Breeds A2456

Inscriptions: No. 4763, La Créole. No. 4764, La Poitevine. No. 4765, L'Alpine. No. 4766, La Chèvre du Massif Central. No. 4767, La Lorraine. No. 4768, La Rove. No. 4769, La Chèvre des Fossés. No. 4770, La Saanen. No. 4771, La Pyrénéenne. No. 4772, L'Angora. No. 4773, La Provençale. No. 4774, La Corse.

Serpentine Die Cut 11

2015, Feb. 21 Photo.

Booklet Stamps
Self-Adhesive

No.	Design	Value	Color	Unused	Used
4763	A2456	(68c)	multi	1.50	.50
4764	A2456	(68c)	multi	1.50	.50
4765	A2456	(68c)	multi	1.50	.50
4766	A2456	(68c)	multi	1.50	.50
4767	A2456	(68c)	multi	1.50	.50
4768	A2456	(68c)	multi	1.50	.50
4769	A2456	(68c)	multi	1.50	.50
4770	A2456	(68c)	multi	1.50	.50
4771	A2456	(68c)	multi	1.50	.50
4772	A2456	(68c)	multi	1.50	.50
4773	A2456	(68c)	multi	1.50	.50

4774 A2456 (68c) multi 1.50 .50
a. Booklet pane of 12, #4763-4774 18.00
Nos. 4763-4774 (12) 18.00 6.00

Souvenir Sheet

Enamel Art of Léonard Limosin (c. 1505-77) — A2457

No. 4775: a, The Judgment of Paris. b, Eritrean Sibyl (Sybila Richea), vert.

Perf. 13x13¼, 13¼x13

2015, Feb. 27 **Photo.**

4775 A2457 Sheet of 2 8.50 8.50
a.-b. €1.90 Either single 4.25 1.40
c. Souvenir sheet of 2, #4775a-4775b, #4775a at right 14.00 14.00

No. 4775c sold for €6.20.

Souvenir Sheet

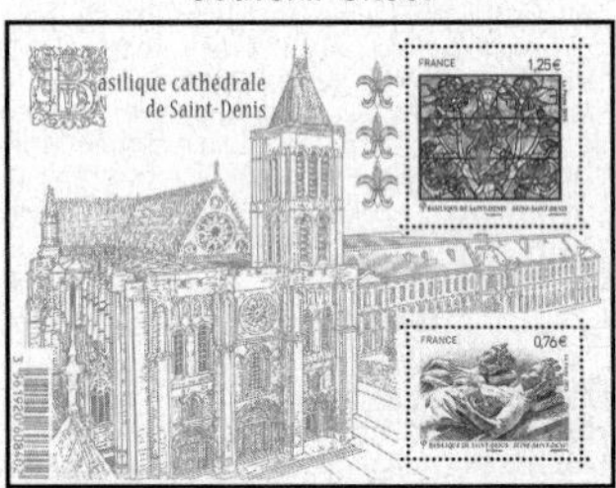

Basilica of Saint-Denis — A2458

No. 4776: a, Tombs (41x30mm). b, Stained-glass window (41x41mm).

2015, Mar. 14 **Engr.** ***Perf. 13¼***

4776 A2458 Sheet of 2 4.50 4.50
a. 76c multi 1.75 .60
b. €1.25 multi 2.75 .90

A souvenir sheet of 2, containing Nos. 4776a-4776b, with No. 4776a at left sold for €6.20.

Spring Philatelic Show, Paris — A2459

2015, Mar. 19 **Engr.** ***Perf. 13x12¾***

4777 A2459 68c multi 1.50 .50

Belgian Government in Exile in Sainte-Adresse, Cent. — A2460

Mailboxes, Belgian government officials in exile and: 76c, French and Belgian flags, building. 95c, Ministerial residence.

2015, Mar. 19 **Photo.** ***Perf. 13¼***

4778 A2460 76c multi 1.75 .60
4779 A2460 95c multi 2.10 .70
a. Souvenir sheet of 2, #4778-4779 7.00 7.00

No. 4779a sold for €3.20. See Belgium No. 2748.

Art Issue

L'O, Light Sculpture by Yann Kersalé A2461

2015, Mar. 20 **Photo.** ***Perf. 13¼***

4780 A2461 €1.90 multi 4.25 2.10

Nicole Mangin (1878-1919), World War I Physician — A2462

2015, Mar. 21 **Engr.** ***Perf. 13x13¼***

4781 A2462 68c multi 1.50 .50

Renaissance Architecture A2463

Designs: No. 4782, Château d'Amboise. No. 4783, Château de Valençay. No. 4784, Palais Ducal de Nevers. No. 4785, Château de Villandry. No. 4786, Château d'Ancy-le-Franc. No. 4787, Palais du Louvre. No. 4788, Château de Chambord. No. 4789, Château d'Ecouen. No. 4790, Château d'Azay-le-Rideau. No. 4791, Château de Chenonceau. No. 4792, Château d'Anet. No. 4793, Château de Blois.

Serpentine Die Cut 11

2015, Mar. 27 **Litho.**

Booklet Stamps Self-Adhesive

4782 A2463 (68c) multi 1.50 .50
4783 A2463 (68c) multi 1.50 .50
4784 A2463 (68c) multi 1.50 .50
4785 A2463 (68c) multi 1.50 .50
4786 A2463 (68c) multi 1.50 .50
4787 A2463 (68c) multi 1.50 .50
4788 A2463 (68c) multi 1.50 .50
4789 A2463 (68c) multi 1.50 .50
4790 A2463 (68c) multi 1.50 .50
4791 A2463 (68c) multi 1.50 .50
4792 A2463 (68c) multi 1.50 .50
4793 A2463 (68c) multi 1.50 .50
a. Booklet pane of 12, #4782-4793 18.00
Nos. 4782-4793 (12) 18.00 6.00

Saintes-Maries-de-la-Mer Religious Procession, 700th Anniv. — A2464

2015, Mar. 29 **Engr.** ***Perf. 13¼***

4794 A2464 68c multi 1.50 .50

Miniature Sheet

European Capitals — A2465

No. 4795 — Attractions in Riga, Latvia: a, Nativity Cathedral. b, St. Peter's Church, horiz. c, House of the Blackheads, horiz. d, National Opera.

Perf. 13¼x13, 13x13¼

2015, Apr. 3 **Photo.**

4795 A2465 Sheet of 4 7.00 7.00
a.-d. 76c Any single 1.75 .60

Croix de Guerre, Cent. — A2466

2015, Apr. 8 **Engr.** ***Perf. 13¼***

4796 A2466 76c multi 1.75 .60

Souvenir Sheet

French History — A2467

No. 4797: a, Coronation of Charlemagne, 768. b, Educational reforms of Charlemagne, 789, horiz.

Perf. 13¼x13, 13x13¼

2015, Apr. 10 **Engr.**

4797 A2467 Sheet of 2 8.50 8.50
a.-b. €1.90 Either single 4.25 1.40

French and Indian Cooperation in Space, 50th Anniv. — A2468

Designs: 76c, Saral satellite. €1.20, Megha-Tropiques satellite.

2014, Apr. 10 **Photo.** ***Perf. 13¼***

4798 A2468 76c multi 1.75 .60
4799 A2468 €1.20 multi 2.75 .90

See India Nos. 2725-2726.

Chalon-sur-Saône A2469

2015, Apr. 17 **Engr.** ***Perf. 13¼***

4800 A2469 68c multi 1.60 .55

Liberation of Concentration Camps, 70th Anniv. — A2470

2015, Apr. 24 **Photo.** ***Perf. 13¼***

4801 A2470 76c multi 1.75 .60

Miniature Sheet

Way of St. James — A2471

No. 4802 — Sites in: a, Oloron-Sainte-Marie. b, Aire-sur l'Adour, vert. c, Saint-Jean-Pied-de Port. d, Blaye.

Litho. & Engr.

2015, Apr. 24 ***Perf. 13***

4802 A2471 Sheet of 4 9.00 9.00
a.-d. 95c Any single 2.25 .75

Europa — A2472

2015, May 2 **Photo.** ***Perf. 13¼***

4803 A2472 95c multi 2.25 .75

Paintings of Flowers — A2473

Designs: No. 4804, Irises and Red Geraniums, by Paul Cézanne. No. 4805, Peonies, by Paul Gauguin. No. 4806, Carnations, by Jeanne Magnin. No. 4807, Wisteria, by Pierre Bracquemond. No. 4808, Daisies and Hydrangea, by Emile Boutin. No. 4809, Roses and Anémones, by Vincent van Gogh. No. 4810, Gladioluses, by Auguste Renoir. No. 4811, Wildflowers by Odilon Redon. No. 4812, Peonies, by Edouard Manet. No. 4813, Roses, by Gustave Caillebotte. No. 4814, Queens Daisies, by Marie Duhem. No. 4815, Roses, by Henri Fantin-Latour.

Serpentine Die Cut 11

2015, May 2 Litho.

Booklet Stamps
Self-Adhesive

4804	A2473 (68c) multi		1.60	.55
4805	A2473 (68c) multi		1.60	.55
4806	A2473 (68c) multi		1.60	.55
4807	A2473 (68c) multi		1.60	.55
4808	A2473 (68c) multi		1.60	.55
4809	A2473 (68c) multi		1.60	.55
4810	A2473 (68c) multi		1.60	.55
4811	A2473 (68c) multi		1.60	.55
4812	A2473 (68c) multi		1.60	.55
4813	A2473 (68c) multi		1.60	.55
4814	A2473 (68c) multi		1.60	.55
4815	A2473 (68c) multi		1.60	.55
a.	Booklet pane of 12, #4804-4815		19.50	
	Nos. 4804-4815 (12)		19.20	6.60

Victory in World War II, 70th Anniv. — A2474

2015, May 7 Photo. *Perf. 13¼*

4816 A2474 68c multi 1.50 .50

Marshal Jacques II de Chabannes, Lord of La Palice (1470-1525) — A2475

2015, May 15 Engr. *Perf. 13¼*

4817 A2475 76c multi 1.75 .60

Mâcon — A2476

2015, May 22 Engr. *Perf. 13x13¼*

4818 A2476 68c multi + label 1.50 .50

French Federation of Philatelic Associations, 88th Congress, Mâcon.

17th World Convention of Rose Societies, Lyon A2477

Designs: 76c, Red and pink roses. €1.20, Pink and yellow roses.

2015, May 29 Photo. *Perf. 13¼*

4819	A2477 76c multi	1.75	.60
4820	A2477 €1.20 multi	2.75	.90
a.	Horiz. pair, #4819-4820	4.50	2.25

A souvenir sheet containing Nos. 4819-4820 sold for €6.20.

Service Central d'Etat Civil, 50th Anniv. — A2478

2015, June 6 Engr. *Perf. 13¼*

4821 A2478 €1.25 multi 2.75 .90

The 1960's — A2479

No. 4822: a, Radio France Headquarters. b, Men and women dancing, vert. c, Movie poster for *Les Demoiselles de Rochefort*, vert. d, 1961 Peugeot 404 convertible. e, Ocean liner SS France. f, Women wearing short dresses, vert.

2015, June 12 Photo. *Perf. 13*

4822	A2479 Sheet of 6	10.50	10.50
a.-f.	76c Any single	1.75	.60

Hartmannswillerkopf National Monument — A2480

2015, June 19 Engr. *Perf. 13¼*

4823 A2480 95c multi 2.10 .70

Saint-Martial Church, Lestards — A2481

2015, June 24 Engr. *Perf. 13¼*

4824 A2481 68c multi 1.50 .50

A2482

A2483

A2484

A2485

A2486

A2487

A2488

A2489

A2490

A2491

A2492

Vacations A2493

Serpentine Die Cut 11

2015, June 29 Photo.

Booklet Stamps
Self-Adhesive

4825	A2482 (68c) multi	1.50	.50
4826	A2483 (68c) multi	1.50	.50
4827	A2484 (68c) multi	1.50	.50
4828	A2485 (68c) multi	1.50	.50
4829	A2486 (68c) multi	1.50	.50
4830	A2487 (68c) multi	1.50	.50
4831	A2488 (68c) multi	1.50	.50
4832	A2489 (68c) multi	1.50	.50
4833	A2490 (68c) multi	1.50	.50
4834	A2491 (68c) multi	1.50	.50
4835	A2492 (68c) multi	1.50	.50
4836	A2493 (68c) multi	1.50	.50
a.	Booklet pane of 12, #4825-4836	18.00	
	Nos. 4825-4836 (12)	18.00	6.00

Haguenau, 900th Anniv. A2494

2015, July 3 Engr. *Perf. 13¼*

4837 A2494 68c multi 1.50 .50

Martin Nadaud (1815-98), Mason and Politician A2495

2015, July 3 Engr. *Perf. 13¼*

4838 A2495 68c multi 1.50 .50

Gilberto Bosques (1892-1995), Mexican Diplomat Who Saved Jews In World War II — A2496

Bosques and: 76c, Notre Dame de la Garde Basilica, Marseilles, and signed travel visa. €1.20, Embassy, Mexican consular handstamp.

2015, July 16 Litho. *Perf. 13*

4839	A2496 76c multi	1.75	.60
4840	A2496 €1.20 multi	2.75	.90
a.	Horiz. pair, #4839-4840	4.50	2.25

See Mexico Nos. 2940-2941.

Animal Eyes A2497

Eye of: No. 4841, Requin à aileron blanc du lagon (whitetip reef shark). No. 4842, Petit-duc du Grant (southern white-faced owl). No. 4843, Rainette à yeux rouges (red-eyed tree frog). No. 4844, Toucan. No. 4845, Coq de race Brahma (Brahma chicken). No. 4846, Agame (agama lizard). No. 4847, Ara hyacinthe (hyacinth macaw). No. 4848, Iguane des Fidji (Fiji banded iguana). No. 4849, Tarente géante (giant wall gecko). No. 4850, Serpentaire (serpent eagle). No. 4851, Poisson-lime gribouillé (scrawled filefish). No. 4852, Gypaète barbu (bearded vulture).

Serpentine Die Cut 11

2015, July 31 Photo.

Booklet Stamps
Self-Adhesive

4841	A2497 (76c) multi	1.75	.60
4842	A2497 (76c) multi	1.75	.60
4843	A2497 (76c) multi	1.75	.60
4844	A2497 (76c) multi	1.75	.60
4845	A2497 (76c) multi	1.75	.60
4846	A2497 (76c) multi	1.75	.60
4847	A2497 (76c) multi	1.75	.60
4848	A2497 (76c) multi	1.75	.60
4849	A2497 (76c) multi	1.75	.60
4850	A2497 (76c) multi	1.75	.60
4851	A2497 (76c) multi	1.75	.60
4852	A2497 (76c) multi	1.75	.60
a.	Booklet pane of 12, #4841-4852	21.00	
	Nos. 4841-4852 (12)	21.00	7.20

Animal Proverbs and Idioms A2498

Designs: No. 4853, Un froid de canard ("Freezing cold"). No. 4854, Rire comme une baleine ("Laughing like a whale"). No. 4855, Comme un chien dans un jeu de quilles ("Like a bull in a China shop"). No. 4856, Prendre le taureau par les cornes ("Take the bull by the horns"). No. 4857, Fier comme un paon ("Proud as a peacock"). No. 4858, Donner de la confiture aux cochons ("Cast pearls before swine"). No. 4859, Avoir un appétit d'oiseau ("Have the appetite of a bird"). No. 4860, Donner sa langue au chat ("Cat got your tongue?"). No. 4861, Etre le bouc émissaire ("Be the scapegoat"). No. 4862, Faire le pied de grue ("To cool one's heels"). No. 4863, Araignée du soir espoir ("A spider in the evening, hope"). No. 4864, Poser un lapin ("To stand someone up").

Serpentine Die Cut 11

2015, Aug. 28 Photo.

Booklet Stamps
Self-Adhesive

4853 A2498 (68c) multi 1.60 .55
4854 A2498 (68c) multi 1.60 .55
4855 A2498 (68c) multi 1.60 .55
4856 A2498 (68c) multi 1.60 .55
4857 A2498 (68c) multi 1.60 .55
4858 A2498 (68c) multi 1.60 .55
4859 A2498 (68c) multi 1.60 .55
4860 A2498 (68c) multi 1.60 .55
4861 A2498 (68c) multi 1.60 .55
4862 A2498 (68c) multi 1.60 .55
4863 A2498 (68c) multi 1.60 .55
4864 A2498 (68c) multi 1.60 .55
a. Booklet pane of 12, #4853-4864 19.50
Nos. 4853-4864 (12) 19.20 6.60

Compare types A2498 and A2297.

Souvenir Sheet

Battle of Huningue, 200th Anniv. — A2499

2015, Aug. 29 Photo. *Perf. 13¼*
4865 A2499 €1.25 multi 3.00 1.00

2015 World Rowing Championships, Aiguebelette A2500

Boat with: 76c, Two female rowers. €1.20, Male rowers (35x26mm).

2015, Aug. 30 Photo. *Perf. 13x13¼*
4866 A2500 76c multi 1.75 .60
4867 A2500 €1.20 multi 2.75 .90
a. Horiz. pair, #4866-4867 4.50 2.25

Marianne and Children "Europe" With Data Matrix Code A2501

Marianne and Children "Monde" With Data Matrix Code A2502

2015, Sept. 4 Engr. *Perf. 13*
4868 A2501 (95c) blue 2.25 .75
4869 A2502 (€1.20) purple 2.75 .90

Self-Adhesive

Serpentine Die Cut 6¾ Vert.
4870 A2501 (95c) blue 2.25 .75
a. Booklet pane of 6 13.50
4871 A2502 (€1.20) purple 2.75 .90

The Data Matrix codes on types A2501 and A2502 differ, but all examples of stamps of either type have identical codes. Compare with Types A2538-A2539.

Art Issue

Woman with White Stockings, by Suzanne Valadon (1865-1938) — A2503

2015, Sept. 18 Photo. *Perf. 13¼x13*
4872 A2503 €1.90 multi 4.25 2.10

Freedom, Equality, Fraternity, Painting by Jonone in National Assembly A2504

2015, Sept. 19 Photo. *Perf. 13¼*
4873 A2504 76c multi 1.75 .60

Landing of French on Mauritius, 300th Anniv. — A2505

2015, Sept. 25 Photo. *Perf. 13¼*
4874 A2505 76c multi 1.75 .60

See Mauritius No. 1147.

Sense of Sight A2506

Designs: No. 4875, Room with a window (Chambre avec vue). No. 4876, Eye chart (A ma vue). No. 4877, Land in sight (Terre en vue). No. 4878, Eye (A vue d'oeil). No. 4879, Sun on horizon (Déjà vue). No. 4880, Women viewed through binoculars (Jumelles en vue). No. 4881, Planets (Vue imprenable). No. 4882, Nose and butterfly (A vue de nez). No. 4883, Diver and pool (Vue plongeante). No. 4884, Clouds (A perte de vue). No. 4885, Woman wearing mask (Ni vue, ni connue). No. 4886, Ghost and pink flying elephant (Vue de l'esprit).

Serpentine Die Cut 11

2015, Sept. 25 Photo.

Booklet Stamps
Self-Adhesive

4875 A2506 (68c) multi 1.60 .55
4876 A2506 (68c) multi 1.60 .55
4877 A2506 (68c) multi 1.60 .55
4878 A2506 (68c) multi 1.60 .55
4879 A2506 (68c) multi 1.60 .55
4880 A2506 (68c) multi 1.60 .55
4881 A2506 (68c) multi 1.60 .55
4882 A2506 (68c) multi 1.60 .55
4883 A2506 (68c) multi 1.60 .55
4884 A2506 (68c) multi 1.60 .55
4885 A2506 (68c) multi 1.60 .55
4886 A2506 (68c) multi 1.60 .55
a. Booklet pane of 12, #4875-4886 19.50
Nos. 4875-4886 (12) 19.20 6.60

Jean-Henri Fabre (1823-1915), Entomologist — A2507

2015, Oct. 2 Litho. *Perf. 13¼*
4887 A2507 €2.60 multi 6.00 2.00

A souvenir sheet of one of No. 4887 sold for €6.20.

A2508

Design: Pierre Laroque (1907-97), Director of Social Security, and Ambroise Croizat (1901-51), Politician.

2015, Oct. 6 Photo. *Perf. 13x13¼*
4888 A2508 68c multi 1.50 .50

French Social Security System, 70th anniv.

Tango Dancers — A2509

Ballet Preljocaj — A2510

Litho. & Engr.

2015, Oct. 10 *Perf. 13¼*
4889 A2509 68c multi 1.50 .50

Photo.

Souvenir Sheet

4890 A2510 €1.15 multi 2.60 .85

Stamp Day. A souvenir sheet of one No. 4889 was produced in 2016 and sold for €3.20.

Saint-Gobain Corporation, 350th Anniv. — A2511

Litho. & Engr.

2015, Oct. 14 *Perf. 13¼*
4891 A2511 68c multi 1.50 .50

Laure Diebold-Mutschler (1915-65), Resistance Leader in World War II — A2512

2015, Oct. 16 Engr. *Perf. 13¼*
4892 A2512 68c multi 1.50 .50

A2513

A2514

A2515

A2516

A2517

A2518

A2519

A2520

A2521

A2522

A2523

Happy New Year — A2524

Serpentine Die Cut 11

2015, Oct. 30 Photo.

Booklet Stamps
Self-Adhesive

4893 A2513 (68c) multi 1.50 .50
4894 A2514 (68c) multi 1.50 .50
4895 A2515 (68c) multi 1.50 .50
4896 A2516 (68c) multi 1.50 .50
4897 A2517 (68c) multi 1.50 .50
4898 A2518 (68c) multi 1.50 .50
4899 A2519 (68c) multi 1.50 .50
4900 A2520 (68c) multi 1.50 .50
4901 A2521 (68c) multi 1.50 .50
4902 A2522 (68c) multi 1.50 .50
4903 A2523 (68c) multi 1.50 .50
4904 A2524 (68c) multi 1.50 .50
a. Booklet pane of 12, #4893-4904 18.00
Nos. 4893-4904 (12) 18.00 6.00

A souvenir sheet containing one perf. 12¾ example of a stamp like No. 4902 sold for €3.20.

Types of 1944-45 with Denominations in Euro Currency and Types of 2005-06

2015, Nov. 5 Engr. *Perf. 13x12¾*
4905 A144 €1 dark blue 2.10 .70

Perf. 12¾x13
4906 A147 €1 dark blue 2.10 .70

Perf. 13
4907 A151 €4 dark blue 8.50 2.60
Nos. 4905-4907 (3) 12.70 4.00

Booklet Stamps

4908 A147 76c red, 15x19mm design 1.60 .55
4909 A144 76c red, 15x19mm design 1.60 .55
a. Booklet pane of 2, #4908-4909 3.25 —
4910 A1814 76c red 1.60 .55
4911 A1759 76c red 1.60 .55
a. Booklet pane of 12, 6 each #4910-4911 19.50 —
Complete booklet, #4909a, 4911a 23.00
Nos. 4908-4911 (4) 6.40 2.20

Nos. 4905-4907 were printed in sheets of 14 containing 6 each Nos. 4905-4906 and 2 No. 4907.

Tapestry Depicting the Sacrifice of Abraham — A2525

Unicorn Hide, Tapetry by Nicolas Buffe — A2526

2015, Nov. 6 Litho. *Perf. 13*
Flocked Paper

4912 A2525 76c multi 1.60 .55
4913 A2526 €1.20 multi 2.60 .85
a. Horiz. pair, #4912-4913, + central label 4.25 1.40

Aubusson, International City of Tapestries.

Miniature Sheet

Music Boxes — A2527

No. 4914 — Inscriptions: a, La pendule à orgues. b, La leçon de chant. c, L'automate magicien. d, Boîte à musique danseuse. e, L'oiseau chanteur, horiz. f, La joueuse de typanon.

Litho. & Engr.

2015, Nov. 6 *Perf. 13*
4914 A2527 Sheet of 6 9.00 9.00
a.-f. 68c Any single 1.50 .50

Nos. 4914a-4914f were each printed in souvenir sheets containing one stamp that sold as a set for €16.

Souvenir Sheet

Roland Barthes (1915-80), Semiotician — A2528

2015, Nov. 12 Engr. *Perf. 13¼*
4915 A2528 €1.15 multi 2.50 .85

Roosters
A2529

Designs: No. 4916, Coq gaulois.
No. 4917: a, Coq de Houdan. b, Coq meusien. c, Coq de Marans.

2015, Nov. 13 Photo. *Perf. 13¼*
4916 A2529 68c multi 1.50 .50
4917 Sheet of 4, #4916, 4917a-4917c 6.00 6.00
a.-c. A2529 68c Any single 1.50 .50

Two souvenir sheets, one containing Nos. 4916 and 4917b, and the other containing Nos. 4917a and 4917c, sold as a set for €6.20.

National Forestry Office, 50th Anniv.
A2530

2015, Nov. 20 Photo. *Perf. 13¼*
4918 A2530 68c multi 1.50 .50

COP21 Climate Conference, Paris
A2531

2015, Nov. 24 Photo. *Perf. 13¼*
4919 A2531 (€1.20) multi 2.60 .85

Values are for stamps with surrounding selvage.

Launch of Astérix Satellite, 50th Anniv. — A2532

2015, Nov. 26 Photo. *Perf. 13¼*
4920 A2532 68c multi 1.50 .50
a. Tete-beche pair 3.00 1.00

City Halls
A2533

City Hall in: No. 4921, La Pernelle. No. 4922, Brunstatt. No. 4923, Chambourcy. No. 4924, Châteaugiron. No. 4925, Sennecey-le-Grand. No. 4926, Saint-Nicolas-de-la-Grave. No. 4927, Caudebec-en-Caux. No. 4928, Cercy-la-Tour. No. 4929, Clamart. No. 4930, Créteil. No. 4931, Toul. No. 4932, Le Pêchereau.

Serpentine Die Cut 11

2015, Dec. 10 Photo.

Booklet Stamps
Self-Adhesive

4921 A2533 (70c) multi 1.60 .55
4922 A2533 (70c) multi 1.60 .55
4923 A2533 (70c) multi 1.60 .55
4924 A2533 (70c) multi 1.60 .55
4925 A2533 (70c) multi 1.60 .55
4926 A2533 (70c) multi 1.60 .55
4927 A2533 (70c) multi 1.60 .55
4928 A2533 (70c) multi 1.60 .55
4929 A2533 (70c) multi 1.60 .55
4930 A2533 (70c) multi 1.60 .55
4931 A2533 (70c) multi 1.60 .55
4932 A2533 (70c) multi 1.60 .55
a. Booklet pane of 12, #4921-4932 19.50
Nos. 4921-4932 (12) 19.20 6.60

Marianne and Children, "Ecopli" Without Gram Limit Inscription
A2534

Marianne and Tree, "Lettre Verte" Without Gram Limit Inscription
A2535

Marianne and Children, "Lettre Prioritaire" Without Gram Limit Inscription — A2536

2016, Jan. 1 Engr. *Perf. 13*
4933 A2534 (68c) gray black 1.50 .30
4934 A2535 (70c) emerald 1.60 .35
4935 A2536 (80c) red 1.75 .45
Nos. 4933-4935 (3) 4.85 1.10

Coil Stamps
Perf. 13 Horiz.

4936 A2535 (70c) green 1.60 .35
4937 A2536 (80c) red 1.75 .45

Self-Adhesive
Serpentine Die Cut 6¾ Vert.

4938 A2534 (68c) gray black 1.50 .30
4939 A2535 (70c) emerald 1.60 .35
a. Booklet pane of 10 16.00
b. Booklet pane of 12 19.50
4940 A2536 (80c) scarlet 1.75 .45
a. Booklet pane of 10 17.50
b. Booklet pane of 12 21.00
c. Booklet pane of 20 35.00
Nos. 4938-4940 (3) 4.85 1.10

Compare with types A2321, A2322 and A2325. See No. B775.

Marianne and Children "Europe" With Data Matrix Code Without Gram Limit Inscription
A2538

Marianne and Children "Monde" With Data Matrix Code Without Gram Limit Inscription
A2539

2016, Jan. 1 Engr. *Perf. 13*
4942 A2538 (€1) blue 2.25 .75
4943 A2539 (€1.25) purple 2.75 .90

Self-Adhesive
Serpentine Die Cut 6¾ Vert.

4944 A2538 (€1) blue 2.25 .75
a. Booklet pane of 6 —
4945 A2539 (€1.25) dp reddish vio 2.75 .90

Compare with types A2501-A2502. Data Matrix codes differ on types A2501 and A2538, and on types A2502 and A2539.

Minerals — A2540

Designs: No. 4946, Gold (or), No. 4947, Labradorite. No. 4948, Topaz (topaze). No. 4949, Amethyst (amethyste). No. 4950, Olivine. No. 4951, Quartz. No. 4952, Turquoise. No. 4953, Fluorite. No. 4954, Sulfur (soufre). No. 4955, Ruby (rubis). No. 4956, Silver (argent). No. 4957, Copper (cuivre).

Serpentine Die Cut 11

2016, Jan. 7 **Photo.**

Booklet Stamps
Self-Adhesive

4946 A2540 (80c) multi 1.75 .60
4947 A2540 (80c) multi 1.75 .60
4948 A2540 (80c) multi 1.75 .60
4949 A2540 (80c) multi 1.75 .60
4950 A2540 (80c) multi 1.75 .60
4951 A2540 (80c) multi 1.75 .60
4952 A2540 (80c) multi 1.75 .60
4953 A2540 (80c) multi 1.75 .60
4954 A2540 (80c) multi 1.75 .60
4955 A2540 (80c) multi 1.75 .60
4956 A2540 (80c) multi 1.75 .60
4957 A2540 (80c) multi 1.75 .60
a. Booklet pane of 12, #4946-4957 21.00
Nos. 4946-4957 (12) 21.00 7.20

A2541

A2542

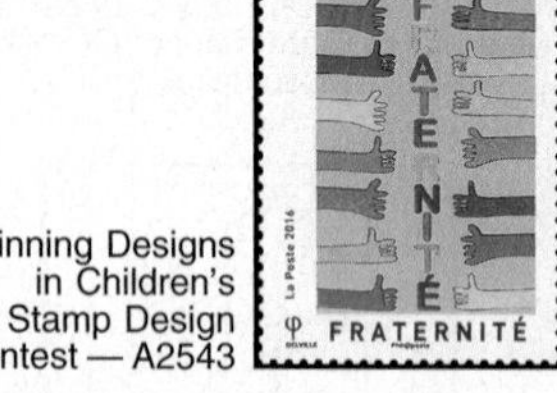

Winning Designs in Children's Stamp Design Contest — A2543

2016, Jan. 11 **Photo.** ***Perf. 13¼***

4958 A2541 70c multi 1.60 .55
4959 A2542 70c multi 1.60 .55
4960 A2543 70c multi 1.60 .55
a. Horiz. strip of 3, #4958-4960 5.00 1.75
Nos. 4958-4960 (3) 4.80 1.65

Hearts A2544

"Courrèges" and: Nos. 4961, 4965, Light blue heart, bright pink denomination. No. 4962, No. 4966, White heart, slate denomination.

No. 4963 — "Courrèges," light blue heart and denomination in: a, Pale yellow. b, Light blue. c, Dark blue. d, Bright orange.

No. 4964 — "Courrèges," and heart in: a, Bright pink. b, Bright green. c, Bright yellow. d, Dark blue. e, Bright orange.

Photo., Litho. (#4964)

2016 ***Perf. 13***

4961 A2544 70c multi 1.60 .55
4962 A2544 €1.40 multi 3.25 1.10

Perf.

4963 Sheet of 5, #4961, 4963a-4963d 8.00 8.00
a.-d. A2544 70c Any single 1.60 .55
4964 Sheet of 5 34.00 34.00
a.-e. A2544 €3 Any single 6.75 3.50

Self-Adhesive

Serpentine Die Cut

4965 A2544 70c multi 1.60 .55
4966 A2544 €1.40 multi 3.25 1.10

Issued: No. 4964, 5/19; others, 1/15. Values for Nos. 4961-4962 are for stamps with surrounding selvage.

Art Issue

Black, Red Over Black on Red, by Mark Rothko (1903-70) A2545

2016, Jan. 22 **Photo.** ***Perf. 13¼x13***

4967 A2545 €1.60 multi 3.50 1.75

New Year Types of 2005-15 and

New Year 2016 (Year of the Monkey) A2546

2016, Jan. 29 **Photo.** ***Perf. 13¼x13***

4968 A2546 80c multi 1.75 .60
4969 Sheet of 4 8.75 8.75
a. A1716 80c multi 2.10 2.10
b. A1766 80c multi 2.10 2.10
c. A1822 80c multi 2.10 2.10
d. A1882 80c multi 2.10 2.10
4970 Sheet of 4 8.75 8.75
a. A1962 80c multi 2.10 2.10
b. A2048 80c multi 2.10 2.10
c. A2133 80c multi 2.10 2.10
d. A2209 80c multi 2.10 2.10
4971 Sheet of 4, #4968, 4971a-4971c 8.75 8.75
a. A2277 80c multi 2.10 2.10
b. A2373 80c multi 2.10 2.10
c. A2453 80c multi 2.10 2.10
Nos. 4969-4971 (3) 26.25 26.25

No. 4968 was printed in sheets of 5. A souvenir sheet of 1 #4968 sold for €3.20. Nos. 4969-4971 sold as a set for €12.

Sense of Hearing A2549

Ear, playback buttons and: No. 4972, Cricket. No. 4973, Various insects. No. 4974, Man's head and singing angels. No. 4975, Marbles rolling down stairs. No. 4976, Pinball game. No. 4977, Water drip. No. 4978, Bird. No. 4979, Lion. No. 4980, Musicians. No. 4981, Sea shell. No. 4982, Harp, lyre, hands, butterflies and flowers. No. 4983, Children.

Serpentine Die Cut 11

2016, Jan. 30 **Litho.**

Booklet Stamps
Self-Adhesive

4972 A2549 (70c) multi 1.60 .55
4973 A2549 (70c) multi 1.60 .55
4974 A2549 (70c) multi 1.60 .55
4975 A2549 (70c) multi 1.60 .55
4976 A2549 (70c) multi 1.60 .55
4977 A2549 (70c) multi 1.60 .55
4978 A2549 (70c) multi 1.60 .55
4979 A2549 (70c) multi 1.60 .55
4980 A2549 (70c) multi 1.60 .55
4981 A2549 (70c) multi 1.60 .55
4982 A2549 (70c) multi 1.60 .55
4983 A2549 (70c) multi 1.60 .55
a. Booklet pane of 12, #4972-4983 19.50
Nos. 4972-4983 (12) 19.20 6.60

Marguerite Long (1874-1966), Pianist — A2550

2016, Feb. 12 **Engr.** ***Perf. 13¼***

4984 A2550 70c multi 1.50 .50

Art Issue

Annie Hall, by Jan Toorop (1858-1928) — A2551

2016, Feb. 19 **Litho.** ***Perf. 13***

4985 A2551 €2.80 multi 6.25 3.25

Georges Charpak (1924-2010), 1992 Nobel Laureate in Physics — A2552

2016, Feb. 26 **Engr.** ***Perf. 13¼***

4986 A2552 70c gold & multi 1.50 .50

Roosters — A2557

Inscriptions: No. 4987, Coq Barbezieux. No. 4988, Coq Bourbonnais. No. 4989, Coq Gaulois, No. 4990, Coq Gournay. No. 4991, Coc Coucou de Rennes. No. 4992, Coq Faverolles. No. 4993, Coq d'Alsace. No. 4994, Coq Bresse. No. 4995, Coq Meusien. No. 4996, Coq Marans. No. 4997, Coq Gâtinais. No. 4998, Coq La Flèche.

Serpentine Die Cut 11

2016, Feb. 27 **Photo.**

Booklet Stamps
Self-Adhesive

4987 A2557 (70c) multi 1.50 .50
4988 A2557 (70c) multi 1.50 .50
4989 A2557 (70c) multi 1.50 .50
4990 A2557 (70c) multi 1.50 .50
4991 A2557 (70c) multi 1.50 .50
4992 A2557 (70c) multi 1.50 .50
4993 A2557 (70c) multi 1.50 .50
4994 A2557 (70c) multi 1.50 .50
4995 A2557 (70c) multi 1.50 .50
4996 A2557 (70c) multi 1.50 .50
4997 A2557 (70c) multi 1.50 .50
4998 A2557 (70c) multi 1.50 .50
a. Booklet pane of 12, #4987-4998 18.00
Nos. 4987-4998 (12) 18.00 6.00

Pierre Messmer (1916-2007), Prime Minister — A2558

2016, Mar. 11 **Engr.** ***Perf. 13¼***

4999 A2558 80c multi 1.90 .65

Sophie Germain (1776-1831), Mathematician — A2559

2016, Mar. 18 **Engr.** ***Perf. 13¼***

5000 A2559 70c multi 1.60 .55

Notre-Dame-des-Missions Church, Epinay-sur-Seine — A2560

2016, Mar. 18 **Engr.** ***Perf. 13¼***

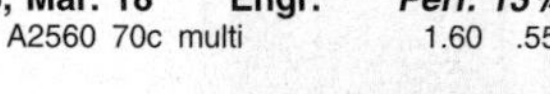

5001 A2560 70c multi 1.60 .55

Auteuil Apprentices, 150th Anniv. — A2561

2016, Mar. 18 **Photo.** ***Perf. 13¼***

5002 A2561 70c multi 1.60 .55

2016 European Soccer Championships, France — A2562

2016 **Photo.** ***Perf. 13***

5003 A2562 €1 multi 2.25 .75
a. Souvenir sheet of 5 11.50 11.50
5004 A2562 €2 multi 4.50 2.25

Issued: No. 5003, 3/26; No. 5004, 5/19. Values are for stamps with surrounding selvage. No. 5004 was printed in sheets of 5 and has varnish covering the trophy in the design.

Sculptor A2563

2016, Mar. 31 Engr. *Perf. 12¼*

5005 A2563 70c multi 1.60 .55

Spring Philatelic Show, Belfort — A2564

2016, Apr. 1 Engr. *Perf. 13x12¾*

5006 A2564 70c multi 1.60 .55

Portraits — A2565

Designs: No. 5007, Portrait of a Young Boy, by Paul Gauguin. No. 5008, Portrait of the Artist's Son, by Paul Cézanne. No. 5009, Young Woman Wearing a Black Hat, by Pierre-Auguste Renoir. No. 5010, Young Woman with a Low-cut Dress and Flower in Hair, by Berthe Morisot. No. 5011, Margot Lux with a Wide Hat, by Mary Cassatt. No. 5012, Portrait of Irma Brunner, La Viennoise, by Edouard Manet. No. 5013, Portrait of Léon Bonnat, by Edgar Degas. No. 5014, Self-portrait, by Gustave Caillebotte. No. 5015, Portrait of a Young Girl, by Armand Guillaumin. No. 5016, Self-portrait, by Vincent van Gogh. No. 5017, Portrait of Blanche Hoschedé, by Claude Monet. No. 5018, Woman with a Green Scarf, by Camille Pissarro.

Serpentine Die Cut 11

2016, Apr. 2 Litho.

Booklet Stamps
Self-Adhesive

5007 A2565 (70c) multi 1.60 .55
5008 A2565 (70c) multi 1.60 .55
5009 A2565 (70c) multi 1.60 .55
5010 A2565 (70c) multi 1.60 .55
5011 A2565 (70c) multi 1.60 .55
5012 A2565 (70c) multi 1.60 .55
5013 A2565 (70c) multi 1.60 .55
5014 A2565 (70c) multi 1.60 .55
5015 A2565 (70c) multi 1.60 .55
5016 A2565 (70c) multi 1.60 .55
5017 A2565 (70c) multi 1.60 .55
5018 A2565 (70c) multi 1.60 .55
a. Booklet pane of 12, #5007-5018 19.50
Nos. 5007-5018 (12) 19.20 6.60

National Center of Costume and Scenography, Moulins — A2566

Litho. & Engr.

2016, Apr. 8 *Perf. 13x13¼*

5019 A2566 80c multi 1.90 .65

A souvenir sheet containing No. 5019 sold for €3.20.

Edmond Locard (1877-1966), Forensic Scientist A2567

2016, Apr. 15 Engr. *Perf. 13¼*

5020 A2567 70c multi 1.60 .55

Marquis de Jouffroy d'Abbans (1751-1832) and Steamboat — A2568

2016, Apr. 22 Engr. *Perf. 13¼*

5021 A2568 €1.25 red & blue 3.00 1.00

Steamboat navigation on the Seine, 200th anniv.

Deposits and Consignments Fund, 200th Anniv. — A2569

Engr. & Embossed

2016, Apr. 28 *Perf. 13¼*

5022 A2569 80c black & red 1.90 .60

A self-adhesive version of this stamp on a cream-colored paper was printed in sheets of 4 that were produced in limited quantities.

Europa A2570

2016, May 8 Photo. *Perf. 13¼*

5023 A2570 €1 multi 2.25 .75

Think Green Issue.

Saint-Brevin-les-Pins — A2571

2016, May 13 Photo. *Perf. 13¼*

5024 A2571 70c multi 1.60 .55

Soccer Plays — A2572

Inscriptions: No. 5025, Frappe (kick). No. 5026, Coup du sombrero (heading ball). No. 5027, Amorti poitrine (chest stop). No. 5028, Coup franc laucarne (corner kick). No. 5029, Reprise de volée (volley). No. 5030, Aile de pigeon (pigeon wing). No. 5031, Arrêt gardien (goalie's save). No. 5032, Coup du foulard (behind-the-planted-leg kick). No. 5033, Coup de pied retourné (bicycle kick). No. 5034, Joueuse qui gagne (winning player).

Serpentine Die Cut 11

2016, May 19 Litho.

Booklet Stamps
Self-Adhesive

5025 A2572 (70c) multi 1.60 .55
5026 A2572 (70c) multi 1.60 .55
5027 A2572 (70c) multi 1.60 .55
5028 A2572 (70c) multi 1.60 .55
5029 A2572 (70c) multi 1.60 .55
5030 A2572 (70c) multi 1.60 .55
5031 A2572 (70c) multi 1.60 .55
5032 A2572 (70c) multi 1.60 .55
5033 A2572 (70c) multi 1.60 .55
5034 A2572 (70c) multi 1.60 .55
a. Booklet pane of 10, #5025-5034 16.00
Nos. 5025-5034 (10) 16.00 5.50

Types of 1947-78

Souvenir Sheet

Engr., Sheet Margin Photo. & Embossed With Foil Application

2016, May 19 *Perf. 13*

5035 Sheet of 3 13.50 13.50
a. A169 €2 blue 4.50 2.25
b. A791 €2 gray & dull brown 4.50 2.25
c. SP171 €2 gray black 4.50 2.25

2016 Paris-Philex Stamp Show.

Bees A2573

Inscriptions: No. 5036, Collète.
No. 5037: a, Osmie, vert. b, Anthophore. c, Mégachile, vert.

2016, May 20 Photo. *Perf. 13¼*

5036 A2573 70c multi 1.60 .55
5037 Sheet of 4, #5036, 5037a-5073c 6.50 6.50
a.-c. A2573 70c Any single 1.60 .55

Two souvenir sheets, one containing Nos. 5036 and 5037a, and the other containing Nos. 5037b and 5037c, sold as a set for €6.20.

Place des Vosges, Paris — A2574

2016, May 21 Engr. *Perf. 13x13¼*

5038 A2574 70c multi + label 1.60 .55

French Federation of Philatelic Associations, 89th Congress, Paris.

Miniature Sheet

The 1970's — A2575

No. 5039: a, Renault 5 automobile. b, Women's fashions, vert. c, Skiers, chair lift and resort, vert. d, L'île aux Enfants children's televison show. e, Parc des Princes Stadium, Paris. f, People dancing at discotheque, vert.

2016, May 21 Photo. *Perf. 13*

5039 A2575 Sheet of 6 11.50 11.50
a.-f. 80c Any single 1.90 .60

Louise Labé (c. 1524-1566), Poet — A2576

2016, May 22 Engr. *Perf. 13x13¼*

5040 A2576 €1.40 multi 3.25 1.10

Battle of Verdun, Cent. — A2577

Litho. & Engr.

2016, May 29 *Perf. 13x12¾*

5041 A2577 70c multi 1.60 .55

A souvenir sheet containing No. 5041 sold for €3.20. A souvenir sheet issued in 2017 containing No. 5041, a denominated proof of No. 5041 with black, brown and yellow inks, and a non-denominated proof of No. 5041 with red, yellow and blue inks sold for €6.20.

Saint-Etienne School of Mines, 200th Anniv. — A2578

2016, June 3 Engr. *Perf. 13¼*

5042 A2578 70c multi 1.60 .55

Diplomatic Relations Between France and South Korea, 130th Anniv. — A2579

Designs: 80c, Korean Celadon incense burner, 12th. cent. €1.25, French reliquary.

2016, June 3 Photo. *Perf. 13¼*

5043 A2579 80c multi 1.90 .60
5044 A2579 €1.25 multi 2.75 .90

See South Korea No. 2469.

French History — A2580

No. 5045: a, Catherine de Medici (1519-89), Queen of France. b, 1520 meeting of King Henry VIII of England and King François I of France at Field of the Cloth of Gold, horiz.

Perf. 13¼x13, 13x13¼

2016, June 3 Engr.

5045	A2580	Sheet of 2	6.50	6.50
a.-b.		€1.40 Either single	3.25	1.60

A 200x95mm sheet containing Nos. 5045a and 5045b, but with a different margin design sold for €6.20.

First Women in French Government, 80th Anniv. — A2581

2016, June 4 Photo. *Perf. 13*

5046	A2581	70c red & black	1.60	.55

Cécile Brunschvicg (1877-1946), Undersecretary of State for National Education; Irène Joliot-Curie (1897-1956), Undersecretary of State for Scientific Research; Suzanne Lacore (1875-1975), Undersecretary of State for Public Health.

Art Issue

Lost Illusions, by Charles Gleyre (1806-74) — A2582

2016, June 5 Engr. *Perf. 13x13¼*

5047	A2582	€1.60 multi	3.75	1.90

Holy Cross Abbey, Quimperlé A2583

2016, June 17 Engr. *Perf. 13¼*

5048	A2583	70c multi	1.60	.55

League of Education, 150th Anniv. A2584

2016, June 23 Photo. *Perf. 13¼*

5049	A2584	€1 multi	2.25	.75

Pierre Mauroy (1928-2013), Prime Minister — A2585

2016, June 24 Engr. *Perf. 13¼*

5050	A2585	80c multi	1.90	.60

Academy of Sciences, 350th Anniv. A2586

2016, June 28 Photo. *Perf. 13¼*

5051	A2586	€2.50 multi	5.75	1.90

Souvenir Sheet

Battle of the Somme, Cent. — A2587

No. 5052: a, Soldiers shaking hands, castle and British tank. b, Damaged Albert Cathedral, Theipval Memorial, Visitor's Center.

2016, July 1 Photo. *Perf. 13¼*

5052	A2587	Sheet of 2	4.25	4.25
a.		80c multi	1.90	.60
b.		€1 multi	2.25	.75

A 200x95mm sheet containing Nos. 5052a and 5052b, but with a different margin design sold for €6.20.

A2588

A2589

A2590

A2591

A2592

A2593

A2594

A2595

A2596

A2597

A2598

Summer Vacation A2599

Serpentine Die Cut 11

2016, July 2 Photo.

Booklet Stamps Self-Adhesive

5053	A2588	(70c) multi	1.60	.55
5054	A2589	(70c) multi	1.60	.55
5055	A2590	(70c) multi	1.60	.55
5056	A2591	(70c) multi	1.60	.55
5057	A2592	(70c) multi	1.60	.55
5058	A2593	(70c) multi	1.60	.55
5059	A2594	(70c) multi	1.60	.55
5060	A2595	(70c) multi	1.60	.55
5061	A2596	(70c) multi	1.60	.55
5062	A2597	(70c) multi	1.60	.55
5063	A2598	(70c) multi	1.60	.55
5064	A2599	(70c) multi	1.60	.55
a.		Booklet pane of 12, #5053-5064	19.50	
		Nos. 5053-5064 (12)	19.20	6.60

Mediterranean Sea Fish — A2600

2016, July 9 Photo. *Perf. 13x12½*

5065	A2600	€1 multi	2.25	.75

Flowers — A2601

Inscriptions: No. 5066, Oiseau de paradis (bird-of-paradise flower). No. 5067, Coquelicot (poppy). No. 5068, Muguet (lily-of-the-valley). No. 5069, Balisier (heliconia). No. 5070, Lys rouge (red lily). No. 5071, Iris. No. 5072, Rose. No. 5073, Tournesol (sunflower). No. 5074, Jonquille (jonquil). No. 5075, Marguerite (daisy). No. 5076, Belle-de-nuit (four o'clock flower). No. 5077, Passiflore (passionflower).

Serpentine Die Cut 11

2016, July 30 Photo.

Booklet Stamp Self-Adhesive

5066	A2601	(80c) multi	1.75	.60
5067	A2601	(80c) multi	1.75	.60
5068	A2601	(80c) multi	1.75	.60
5069	A2601	(80c) multi	1.75	.60
5070	A2601	(80c) multi	1.75	.60
5071	A2601	(80c) multi	1.75	.60
5072	A2601	(80c) multi	1.75	.60
5073	A2601	(80c) multi	1.75	.60
5074	A2601	(80c) multi	1.75	.60
5075	A2601	(80c) multi	1.75	.60
5076	A2601	(80c) multi	1.75	.60
5077	A2601	(80c) multi	1.75	.60
a.		Booklet pane of 12, #5066-5077	21.00	
		Nos. 5066-5077 (12)	21.00	7.20

Eagle Dam, Soursac, and World War II Resistance Fighters — A2602

2016, Sept. 2 Engr. *Perf. 13x12¾*

5078	A2602	€3.20 multi	7.25	2.40

Animal Proverbs and Idioms A2603

Designs: No. 5079, Courir plusieurs lièvres à la fois ("to try to do more than one thing at once"). No. 5080, Quand on parle du loup on en voit la queue ("speak of the devil and he appears"). No. 5081, Avoir des oursins dans le porte-monnaie ("to be stingy"). No. 5082, Avoir une mémoire d'éléphant ("have the memory of an elephant"). No. 5083, Muet comme une carpe ("silent like a carp"). No. 5084, La part du lion ("the lion's share"). No. 5085, Dormir comme un loir ("to sleep like a log"). No. 5086, Etre le dindon de la farce ("being the butt of the joke"). No. 5087, Peigner la girafe ("to do nothing effective"). No. 5088, C'est le serpent qui se mord la queue ("to be in a vicious cycle"). No. 5089, Monter sur ses grands chevaux ("to get carried away"). No. 5090, Bayer aux corneilles ("to stand and gape").

Serpentine Die Cut 11

2016, Sept. 3 Photo.

Booklet Stamps Self-Adhesive

5079	A2603	(70c) multi	1.60	.55
5080	A2603	(70c) multi	1.60	.55
5081	A2603	(70c) multi	1.60	.55
5082	A2603	(70c) multi	1.60	.55
5083	A2603	(70c) multi	1.60	.55
5084	A2603	(70c) multi	1.60	.55
5085	A2603	(70c) multi	1.60	.55
5086	A2603	(70c) multi	1.60	.55
5087	A2603	(70c) multi	1.60	.55
5088	A2603	(70c) multi	1.60	.55
5089	A2603	(70c) multi	1.60	.55
5090	A2603	(70c) multi	1.60	.55
a.		Booklet pane of 12, #5079-5090	19.50	
		Nos. 5079-5090 (12)	19.20	6.60

Léo Ferré (1916-93), Musician A2604

2016, Sept. 8 Photo. *Perf. 12¼*

5091	A2604	€1.40 multi	3.25	1.10

Françoise Giroud (1916-2003), Minister of Culture — A2605

2016, Sept. 9 Engr. *Perf. 13x13¼*
5092 A2605 80c lt blue & maroon 1.75 .60

Characters From *Les Legendaires,* Cartoons by Patrick Sobral A2606

Designs: No. 5093, Danael. No. 5094, Jadina and Shimy.

2016, Sept. 16 Photo. *Perf. 13¼*
5093 A2606 70c multi 1.60 .55
5094 A2606 70c multi 1.60 .55
a. Horiz. pair, #5093-5094, + 2 alternating labels 3.20 1.10

A2607

A2608

A2609

A2610

A2611

A2612

A2613

A2614

A2615

A2616

A2617

Stars and Heavenly Bodies A2618

Serpentine Die Cut 11
2016, Oct. 1 Photo.
Booklet Stamps
Self-Adhesive

5095 A2607 (70c) multi 1.60 .55
5096 A2608 (70c) multi 1.60 .55
5097 A2609 (70c) multi 1.60 .55
5098 A2610 (70c) multi 1.60 .55
5099 A2611 (70c) multi 1.60 .55
5100 A2612 (70c) multi 1.60 .55
5101 A2613 (70c) multi 1.60 .55
5102 A2614 (70c) multi 1.60 .55
5103 A2615 (70c) multi 1.60 .55
5104 A2616 (70c) multi 1.60 .55
5105 A2617 (70c) multi 1.60 .55
5106 A2618 (70c) multi 1.60 .55
a. Booklet pane of 12, #5095-5106 19.50
Nos. 5095-5106 (12) 19.20 6.60

Charleston Dancers A2619

Ballet Dancer in *Swan Lake* — A2620

2016, Oct. 8 Engr. *Perf. 13¼*
5107 A2619 70c multi 1.60 .55

Souvenir Sheet
Photo. & Embossed
Perf. 13¼x13

5108 A2620 €1.40 multi 3.25 1.10
Stamp Day.

Eclair Airplane Propellers, Cent. A2621

2016, Oct. 13 Photo. *Perf. 13¼*
5109 A2621 70c multi 1.60 .55

St. Étienne Cathedral, Toul — A2622

2016, Oct. 21 Engr. *Perf. 13x13¼*
5110 A2622 70c multi + label 1.60 .55

Architecture of Paris and Lisbon — A2623

Designs: 80c, Rua Augusta Arch, Lisbon. €1, Buildings along Rue Royale, Paris.

2016, Oct. 21 Engr. *Perf. 13x12½*
5111 A2623 80c multi 1.75 .60
5112 A2623 €1 multi 2.25 .75

See Portugal Nos. 3847-3848.

Pres. François Mitterrand (1916-96) A2624

2016, Oct. 26 Engr. *Perf. 13¼*
5113 A2624 80c multi 1.75 .60

Miniature Sheet

European Capitals — A2625

No. 5114 — Attractions in Amsterdam, Netherlands: a, Begijnhof (Le Béguinage). b, Rijksmuseum. c, Westerkerk, vert. d, Canals and buildings.

Perf. 13¼x13½, 13½x13¼
2016, Nov. 3 Photo.
5114 A2625 Sheet of 4 7.00 7.00
a.-d. 80c Any single 1.75 .60

Peace and Commerce ("Type Sage" With Denominations in Euro Currency) — A2626a A2626

Type I: The "N" of "INV" is under the "B" of "REPUBLIQUE."
Type II: The "N" of "INV" is under the "U" of "REPUBLIQUE."

2016, Nov. 3 Engr. *Perf. 12¾x13¼*
Type I
5115 A2626 €1 dark green 2.25 .75
Type II
5116 A2626 €1 dark green 2.25 .75
a. Pair, #5115-5116 4.50 1.50

Booklet Stamps
Type I
Design Size: 15x19mm
Perf. 12¾x13

5117 A2626 80c red 1.75 .45
5118 A2626a 80c black 1.75 .45
a. Booklet pane of 2, #5117-5118 3.50 —
b. Booklet pane of 12, 6 each #5117-5118 21.00 —
Complete booklet, #5118a, 5118b 24.50

Nos. 5115-5116 were printed in sheets containing 10 of each stamp.

Brive-la-Gaillarde — A2627

2016, Nov. 4 Engr. *Perf. 13x12¾*
5119 A2627 70c multi 1.50 .50

Miniature Sheet

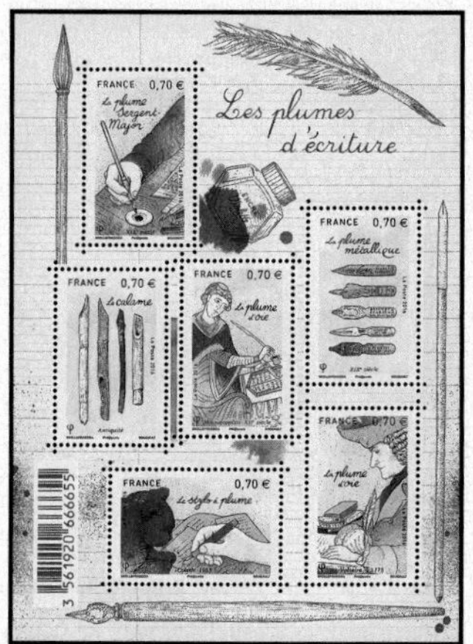

Pens — A2628

No. 5120: a, Person dipping Sergent-Major pen into ink, 19th cent. b, Calames (ancient reed pen). c, Monk with quill pen, 12th cent. d, Metallic pen nibs, 19th cent. e, Cat, writer with fountain pen, horiz. f, Voltaire writing with quill pen, 1775.

Litho. & Engr.

2016, Nov. 4 *Perf. 13*

5120	A2628	Sheet of 6	9.00	9.00
a.-f.		70c Any single	1.50	.50
g.		Souvenir sheet of 3, #5120a, 5120d, 5120e	6.75	6.75
h.		Souvenir sheet of 3, #5120b, 5120c, 5120f	6.75	6.75

Nos. 5120g and 5120h were sold as a set for €6.20.

Restoration and Reopening of Bièvre River — A2629

2016, Nov. 5 **Photo.** *Perf. 13¼*

5121 A2629 70c multi 1.50 .50

Art Issue

Souvenir Sheet

Paintings by Marie Laurencin (1883-1956) — A2630

No. 5122: a, Portrait of Baroness Gourgaud in Black Mantilla, 1923. b, Young Girl with Guitar, 1940.

2016, Nov. 6 **Photo.** *Perf. 13¼x13*

5122	A2630	Sheet of 2	7.00	7.00
a.-b.		€1.60 Either single	3.50	1.75

National Office of Veterans and War Victims, Cent. — A2631

2016, Nov. 9 **Photo.** *Perf. 13¼*

5123 A2631 70c multi 1.50 .50

Jewelery Making A2632

2016, Nov. 10 **Engr.** *Perf. 12¼*

5124 A2632 €1 multi 2.25 .75

A2633

A2634

A2635

A2636

A2637

A2638

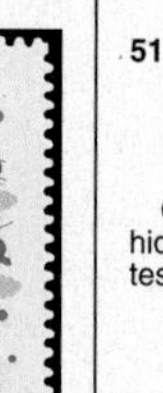

A2639

A2640

A2641

A2642

A2643

Contest Stamps With Scratch-off Panel — A2644

Serpentine Die Cut 11

2016, Nov. 14 **Photo.**

Booklet Stamps

Self-Adhesive

Unscrached Panels

5125	A2633 (70c) multi		1.50	.50
a.	Scratched panel			.35
5126	A2634 (70c) multi		1.50	.50
a.	Scratched panel			.35
5127	A2635 (70c) multi		1.50	.50
a.	Scratched panel			.35
5128	A2636 (70c) multi		1.50	.50
a.	Scratched panel			.35
5129	A2637 (70c) multi		1.50	.50
a.	Scratched panel			.35
5130	A2638 (70c) multi		1.50	.50
a.	Scratched panel			.35
5131	A2639 (70c) multi		1.50	.50
a.	Scratched panel			.35
5132	A2640 (70c) multi		1.50	.50
a.	Scratched panel			.35
5133	A2641 (70c) multi		1.50	.50
a.	Scratched panel			.35
5134	A2642 (70c) multi		1.50	.50
a.	Scratched panel			.35
5135	A2643 (70c) multi		1.50	.50
a.	Scratched panel			.35
5136	A2644 (70c) multi		1.50	.50
a.	Scratched panel			.35
b.	Booklet pane of 12, #5125-5136		18.00	
	Nos. 5125-5136 (12)		18.00	6.00

Gold scratch-off panels on Nos. 5125-5136 hide codes that could be entered at the contest website for a chance to win various prizes.

Stained-Glass Windows — A2645

Window from: No. 5137, Notre Dame Cathedral, Coutances. No. 5138, Saint-Denis Chapel, Paris. No. 5139, Notre Dame Cathedral, Chartres. No. 5140, Saint-Nazaire Basilica, Carcassonne. No. 5141, Notre Dame Cathedral, Strasbourg. No. 5142, Saint-Savin-de-Gartempe Abbey, Saint-Savin. No. 5143, Saint-Etienne Cathedral, Bourges. No. 5144, Saint-Julien Cathedral, Le Mans. No. 5145, Saint-Denis Basilica, Saint-Denis. No. 5146, Notre Dame Cathedral, Bayeux. No. 5147, Saint-Pierre Cathedral, Beauvais. No. 5148, Notre Dame Cathedral, Paris.

Serpentine Die Cut 11

2016, Nov. 26 **Photo.**

Booklet Stamps

Self-Adhesive

5137	A2645 (70c) multi		1.50	.50
5138	A2645 (70c) multi		1.50	.50
5139	A2645 (70c) multi		1.50	.50
5140	A2645 (70c) multi		1.50	.50
5141	A2645 (70c) multi		1.50	.50
5142	A2645 (70c) multi		1.50	.50
5143	A2645 (70c) multi		1.50	.50
5144	A2645 (70c) multi		1.50	.50
5145	A2645 (70c) multi		1.50	.50
5146	A2645 (70c) multi		1.50	.50
5147	A2645 (70c) multi		1.50	.50
5148	A2645 (70c) multi		1.50	.50
a.	Booklet pane of 12, #5137-5148		18.00	
	Nos. 5137-5148 (12)		18.00	6.00

French Academy in Rome, 350th Anniv. A2646

2016, Nov. 30 **Photo.** *Perf. 13¼*

5149 A2646 €1 chestnut & red 2.25 .75

A souvenir sheet of one sold for €3.50. See Italy No. 3433

Landscape Reflections A2647

Designs: No. 5150, Nusa Dua, Bali, Indonesia. No. 5151, Siwa Oasis, Egypt. No. 5152, Mont Blanc, France. No. 5153, Laguna Colorada, Bolivia. No. 5154, Mount Shompole, Tanzania. No. 5155, Moremi Game Reserve, Botswana. No. 5156, Mount Fuji, Japan. No. 5157, Dolomites, Italy. No. 5158, Avenue of Baobabs, Madagascar. No. 5159, Mountains, Sermersooq Municipality, Greenland. No. 5160, Everglades, United States. No. 5161, Mountains, Ultima Esperanza Province, Chile.

Serpentine Die Cut 11

2017, Jan. 7 **Photo.**

Booklet Stamps

Self-Adhesive

5150	A2647 (85c) multi	1.90	.65
5151	A2647 (85c) multi	1.90	.65
5152	A2647 (85c) multi	1.90	.65
5153	A2647 (85c) multi	1.90	.65
5154	A2647 (85c) multi	1.90	.65
5155	A2647 (85c) multi	1.90	.65
5156	A2647 (85c) multi	1.90	.65
5157	A2647 (85c) multi	1.90	.65
5158	A2647 (85c) multi	1.90	.65
5159	A2647 (85c) multi	1.90	.65
5160	A2647 (85c) multi	1.90	.65

5161	A2647 (85c) multi		1.90	.65
a.	Booklet pane of 12, #5150-5161		23.00	
	Nos. 5150-5161 (12)		22.80	7.80

Art Issue

Souvenir Sheet

Art by Marc Chagall (1887-1985) — A2648

No. 5162: a, Peace (stained-glass window), 1976. b, Paradise (painting), 1961.

2017, Jan. 13 Photo. *Perf. 13¼*

5162	A2648	Sheet of 2	7.50	4.00
a.-b.	€1.70 Either single		3.75	1.90

A2649

Hearts A2650

2017, Jan. 20 Photo. *Perf. 13¼*

5163	A2649	73c multi	1.60	.55
a.	Souvenir sheet of 5		8.00	8.00
5164	A2650	€1.46 multi	3.25	1.10

Self-Adhesive

Serpentine Die Cut

5165	A2649	73c multi	1.60	.55
5166	A2650	€1.46 multi	3.25	1.10

Values for Nos. 5163-5164 are for stamps with surrounding selvage.

Tourism Issue

Chateau de Pailly A2651

2017, Jan. 28 Engr. *Perf. 13¼*

5167	A2651	73c multi	1.60	.55

Rat — A2652

Ox — A2653

Tiger — A2654

Rabbit A2655

Dragon A2656

Snake — A2657

Horse — A2658

Goat — A2659

Monkey A2660

Rooster A2661

Dog — A2662

Pig — A2663

Serpentine Die Cut 11

2017, Jan. 28 Photo.

Booklet Stamps Self-Adhesive

5168	A2652 (73c) multi		1.60	.55
5169	A2653 (73c) multi		1.60	.55
5170	A2654 (73c) multi		1.60	.55
5171	A2655 (73c) multi		1.60	.55
5172	A2656 (73c) multi		1.60	.55
5173	A2657 (73c) multi		1.60	.55
5174	A2658 (73c) multi		1.60	.55
5175	A2659 (73c) multi		1.60	.55
5176	A2660 (73c) multi		1.60	.55
5177	A2661 (73c) multi		1.60	.55
5178	A2662 (73c) multi		1.60	.55
5179	A2663 (73c) multi		1.60	.55
a.	Booklet pane of 12, #5168-5179		19.50	
	Nos. 5168-5179 (12)		19.20	6.60

New Year 2017 (Year of the Rooster).

Women and Lucien Neuwirth (1924-2013), Politician — A2664

2017, Feb. 9 Photo. *Perf. 13¼*

5180	A2664	85c multi	1.90	.65

Passage of Neuwirth Law legalizing birth control, 50th anniv.

Art Issue

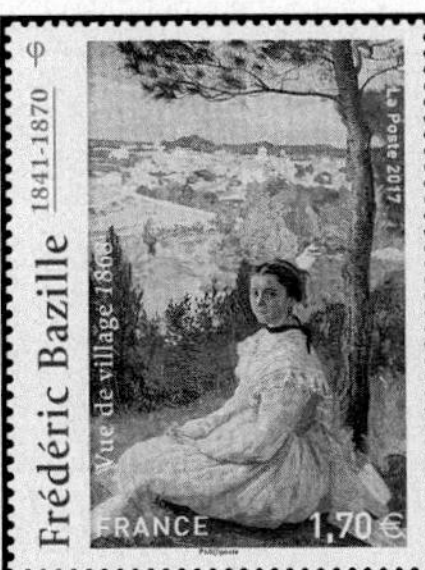

La Vue de Village, by Frédéric Bazille (1841-70) A2665

2017, Feb. 17 Photo. *Perf. 13¼x13*

5181	A2665	€1.70 multi	3.75	1.90

Farm Animals A2666

Designs: No. 5182, Bélier (ram). No. 5183, Laperau (rabbit). No. 5184, Anesse (female donkey). No. 5185, Dindon (turkey). No. 5186, Oie (goose). No. 5187, Veau (calf). No. 5188, Porcelet (piglet). No. 5189, Anon (male donkey). No. 5190, Canard (duck). No. 5191, Brebis (ewe). No. 5192, Vache (cow). No. 5193, Poule (hen).

Serpentine Die Cut 11

2017, Feb. 24 Photo.

Booklet Stamps Self-Adhesive

5182	A2666 (73c) multi		1.60	.55
5183	A2666 (73c) multi		1.60	.55
5184	A2666 (73c) multi		1.60	.55
5185	A2666 (73c) multi		1.60	.55
5186	A2666 (73c) multi		1.60	.55
5187	A2666 (73c) multi		1.60	.55
5188	A2666 (73c) multi		1.60	.55
5189	A2666 (73c) multi		1.60	.55
5190	A2666 (73c) multi		1.60	.55
5191	A2666 (73c) multi		1.60	.55
5192	A2666 (73c) multi		1.60	.55
5193	A2666 (73c) multi		1.60	.55
a.	Booklet pane of 12, #5182-5193		19.50	
	Nos. 5182-5193 (12)		19.20	6.60

Anne Morgan (1873-1952), Philanthropist and Provider of War Relief — A2667

2017, Feb. 24 Engr. *Perf. 13¼*

5194	A2667	85c multi	1.90	.65

Montmartre — A2668

2017, Mar. 9 Engr. *Perf. 13x12¾*

5195	A2668	73c multi	1.60	.55

Spring Philatelic Show, Paris.

Miniature Sheet

European Capitals — A2669

No. 5196 — Attractions in Valletta, Malta: a, Palais des Grand Maîtres (Grandmaster's Palace). b, Gallarija (building balconies). c, St. John's Co-cathedral, vert. d, Fort Saint Elmo (canals and buildings).

Perf. 13x13¼, 13¼x13

2017, Mar. 10 Photo.

5196	A2669	Sheet of 4	7.75	7.75
a.-d.	85c Any single		1.90	.65

Germaine Ribière (1917-99), Resistance Fighter Who Saved Jews in World War II — A2670

2017, Mar. 10 Engr. *Perf. 13¼*

5197	A2670	€1.10 multi	2.40	.80

Waltzers A2671

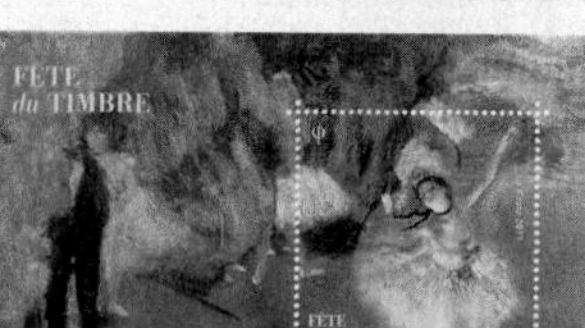

The Star, by Edgar Degas (1834-1917) — A2672

2017, Mar. 11 Engr. *Perf. 13¼*

5198 A2671 73c multi 1.60 .55

Souvenir Sheet

Photo.

Perf. 13¼x13

5199 A2672 €1.46 multi 3.25 1.10

Stamp Day. A souvenir sheet containing No. 5198 was issued in 2018 and sold for €4.

Law on Commercial And Industrial Credit, Cent. — A2673

2017, Mar. 13 Photo. *Perf. 13¼*

5200 A2673 85c multi 1.90 .65

French-Algerian War Ceasefire, 55th Anniv. — A2674

2017, Mar. 15 Photo. *Perf. 13¼*

5201 A2674 €1.30 multi 2.75 .90

Maurice Faure (1922-2014), Politician A2675

2017, Mar. 25 Engr. *Perf. 13¼*

5202 A2675 85c multi 1.90 .65

Photographs of Items Looking Like Masks, by Michelangelo Durazzo — A2676

Mask number: No. 5203, 7. No. 5204, 13. No. 5205, 12. No. 5206, 9. No. 5207, 32. No. 5208, 29. No. 5209, 26. No. 5210, 35. No. 5211, 3. No. 5212, 17. No. 5213, 21. No. 5214, 44.

Serpentine Die Cut 11

2017, Mar. 31 Photo.

Booklet Stamps Self-Adhesive

5203	A2676 (73c) multi		1.60	.55
5204	A2676 (73c) multi		1.60	.55
5205	A2676 (73c) multi		1.60	.55
5206	A2676 (73c) multi		1.60	.55
5207	A2676 (73c) multi		1.60	.55
5208	A2676 (73c) multi		1.60	.55
5209	A2676 (73c) multi		1.60	.55
5210	A2676 (73c) multi		1.60	.55
5211	A2676 (73c) multi		1.60	.55
5212	A2676 (73c) multi		1.60	.55
5213	A2676 (73c) multi		1.60	.55
5214	A2676 (73c) multi		1.60	.55
a.	Booklet pane of 12, #5203-5214		19.50	
	Nos. 5203-5214 (12)		19.20	6.60

Ironwork A2677

2017, Mar. 31 Engr. *Perf. 12¼*

5215 A2677 73c multi 1.60 .55

Souvenir Sheet

Battle of Vimy Ridge, Cent. — A2678

No. 5216: a, Pillars and statue. b, Statue of weeping woman.

2017, Apr. 7 Engr. *Perf. 13¼*

5216 A2678 Sheet of 2	5.00	5.00
a. 85c multi	1.90	.65
b. €1.30 multi	3.00	1.00

See Canada Nos. 2981-2982.

Souvenir Sheet

Second Battle of Chemin des Dames, Cent. — A2679

No. 5217: a, Seven Senegalese soldiers. b, Eight soldiers in Dragon Cavern.

2017, Apr. 14 Photo. *Perf. 13¼*

5217 A2679 Sheet of 2	5.00	5.00
a.-b. €1.10 Either single	2.40	.80

A 200x95mm sheet containing Nos. 5217a and 5217b, but with a different margin design sold for €6.20.

Jean-Baptiste Charcot (1867-1936), Polar Explorer, and Ship Pourquoi-Pas? — A2680

2017, Apr. 22 Engr. *Perf. 13x12¾*

5218 A2680 €1.30 multi 3.00 1.00

A souvenir sheet containing No. 5218 sold for €3.20.

Concours Lépine Inventor's Show — A2681

2017, Apr. 27 Photo. *Perf. 13¼*

5219 A2681 €1.30 multi 3.00 1.00

Flowers in Objets d' Art — A2682

Inscription: No. 5220, Cristal pierres & or (crystal stones and gold). No. 5221, Bois peint & doré (painted and gilded wood). No. 5222, Argent travaillé (worked silver). No. 5223, Faience & glaçure, peinte (glazed and painted faience). No. 5224, Bronze doré (gilded bronze). No. 5225, Mosaique, pierres dures (stone mosaic). No. 5226, Porcelaine tendre (soft porcelain). No. 5227, Bois sculpté (sculpted wood). No. 5228, Laine & soie (wool and silk). No. 5229, Bois gravé (engraved wood). No. 5230, Perles, diamants, or & argent (pearls, diamonds, gold and silver). No. 5231, Coton & fil de soie, broderie (cotton and silk thread embroidery).

Serpentine Die Cut 11

2017, Apr. 28 Photo.

Booklet Stamps Self-Adhesive

5220	A2682 (73c) multi	1.60	.55
5221	A2682 (73c) multi	1.60	.55
5222	A2682 (73c) multi	1.60	.55
5223	A2682 (73c) multi	1.60	.55
5224	A2682 (73c) multi	1.60	.55
5225	A2682 (73c) multi	1.60	.55
5226	A2682 (73c) multi	1.60	.55
5227	A2682 (73c) multi	1.60	.55
5228	A2682 (73c) multi	1.60	.55
5229	A2682 (73c) multi	1.60	.55
5230	A2682 (73c) multi	1.60	.55
5231	A2682 (73c) multi	1.60	.55
a.	Booklet pane of 12, #5220-5231	19.50	
	Nos. 5220-5231 (12)	19.20	6.60

Cholet — A2683

2017, Apr. 28 Engr. *Perf. 13x13¼*

5232 A2683 73c multi + label 1.60 .55

French Federation of Philatelic Associations, 90th Congress, Cholet.

Bid of Paris to Host 2024 Summer Olympics and Paralympics — A2684

2017, May 13 Photo. *Perf. 13x13¼*

5233 A2684 73c multi + label 1.75 .60

For overprint, see No. 5303.

Chambord, Azay-le-Rideau and Chenonceau Chateaus — A2685

2017, May 14 Photo. *Perf. 13x12¾*

5234 A2685 €1.10 multi 2.50 .85

Europa.

Coupe de France Soccer Tournament, Cent. — A2686

2017, May 19 Photo. *Perf. 13¼*

5235 A2686 73c multi 1.75 .60

Saint-Benoît-sur-Loire Abbey — A2687

2017, May 19 Engr. *Perf. 13¼*

5236 A2687 73c multi 1.75 .60

Insects A2688

Designs: No. 5237, Coccinelle (ladybug). No. 5238: a, Demoiselle (banded damselfly). b, Hanneton (cockchafer), vert. c, Carabe (beetle), vert.

2017, May 19 Photo. *Perf. 13¼*

5237 A2688 73c multi	1.75	.60
5238 Sheet of 4, #5237, 5238a-5238c	7.00	7.00
a.-c. A2688 73c Any single	1.75	.60

Two souvenir sheets, one containing Nos. 5237 and 5238c, and the other containing Nos. 5238a and 5238b, sold as a set for €6.20.

National Sea Rescue Society, 50th Anniv. A2689

2017, May 23 Photo. *Perf. 13¼*

5239 A2689 85c multi 1.90 .65

Lions Clubs International, Cent. — A2690

2017, May 27 Photo. *Perf. 13¼*

5240 A2690 85c multi	1.90	.65

Haunted House Ride A2691

Bumper Cars A2692

Cotton Candy A2693

Carousel A2694

Candy Apples A2695

Duck Hooking Game A2696

Stuffed Animal Prizes A2697

Ferris Wheel A2698

Roller Coaster A2699

Bowling A2700

Swing Ride A2701

Slide A2702

Serpentine Die Cut 11

2017, June 2 Photo.

Booklet Stamps Self-Adhesive

5241 A2691 (73c) multi	1.75	.60
5242 A2692 (73c) multi	1.75	.60
5243 A2693 (73c) multi	1.75	.60
5244 A2694 (73c) multi	1.75	.60
5245 A2695 (73c) multi	1.75	.60
5246 A2696 (73c) multi	1.75	.60
5247 A2697 (73c) multi	1.75	.60
5248 A2698 (73c) multi	1.75	.60
5249 A2699 (73c) multi	1.75	.60
5250 A2700 (73c) multi	1.75	.60
5251 A2701 (73c) multi	1.75	.60
5252 A2702 (73c) multi	1.75	.60
a. Booklet pane of 12, #5241-5252	21.00	
Nos. 5241-5252 (12)	21.00	7.20

Louis Vicat (1786-1861), Buildings and Bridge — A2703

2017, June 2 Photo. *Perf. 13¼*

5253 A2703 €1.30 multi	3.00	1.00

Invention of artificial cement by Vicat, 200th anniv.

Art Issue

Woman, Sculpture by Jeanne Bardey (1872-1954) — A2704

2017, June 2 Engr. *Perf. 13¼x13*

5254 A2704 €1.70 multi	4.00	2.00

Rochefort-en-Terre — A2705

2017, June 14 Engr. *Perf. 13¼*

5255 A2705 73c multi	1.75	.60

Arrival of American Troops in World War I, Cent. A2706

2017, June 23 Engr. *Perf. 13¼*

5256 A2706 €1.30 multi	3.00	1.00

Joachim Murat (1767-1815), French Marshal and Admiral and King of Naples — A2707

2017, June 23 Engr. *Perf. 13¼*

5257 A2707 85c multi	2.00	.70

Harness Race at Rambouillet Hippodrome — A2708

2017, June 24 Photo. *Perf. 13¼*

5258 A2708 73c multi	1.75	.60

Diplomatic Relations Between France and the Philippines, 70th Anniv. A2709

Unnamed painting by: 85c, Philippine painter Macario Vitalis (1898-1989). €1.30, French painter Jacques Villon (1875-1963).

2017, June 26 Photo. *Perf. 13¼*

5259 A2709 85c multi	2.00	.70
5260 A2709 €1.30 multi	3.00	1.00
a. Souvenir sheet of 2, #5259-5260	7.50	7.50

No. 5260a sold for €3.20. See Philippines No. 3732.

Souvenir Sheet

French History — A2710

No. 5261: a, Anne of France (1461-1522), Duchess of Beaujeu (41x53mm oval stamp). b, Treaty of Picquigny, 1475 (53x42mm).

Perf., Perf. 13x13¼ (#5261b)

2017, June 30 Engr.

5261 A2710 Sheet of 2	7.00	7.00
a.-b. €1.46 Either single	3.50	1.25

A 200x95mm sheet containing Nos. 5261a and 5261b, but with a different margin design sold for €6.50.

Grains A2711

Designs: No. 5262, Avoine (oats). No. 5263, Blé dur (durum wheat). No. 5264, Mais (corn). No. 5265, Millet. No. 5266, Riz (rice). No. 5267, Seigle (rye). No. 5268, Blé tendre (soft wheat). No. 5269, Epeautre (spelt). No. 5270, Orge (barley). No. 5271, Petit épautre (einkorn wheat). No. 5272, Sorgho (sorghum). No. 5273, Triticale.

Serpentine Die Cut 11

2017, June 30 Photo.

Booklet Stamps Self-Adhesive

5262 A2711 (85c) multi	2.00	.70
5263 A2711 (85c) multi	2.00	.70
5264 A2711 (85c) multi	2.00	.70
5265 A2711 (85c) multi	2.00	.70
5266 A2711 (85c) multi	2.00	.70
5267 A2711 (85c) multi	2.00	.70
5268 A2711 (85c) multi	2.00	.70
5269 A2711 (85c) multi	2.00	.70
5270 A2711 (85c) multi	2.00	.70
5271 A2711 (85c) multi	2.00	.70
5272 A2711 (85c) multi	2.00	.70
5273 A2711 (85c) multi	2.00	.70
a. Booklet pane of 12, #5262-5273	24.00	
Nos. 5262-5273 (12)	24.00	8.40

Cherbourg-en-Cotentin — A2712

2017, July 7 Engr. *Perf. 13¼*

5274 A2712 73c multi	1.75	.60

Trees of the Mediterranean Area — A2713

2017, July 10 Photo. *Perf. 13¼*

5275 A2713 €1.10 multi	2.60	.90

2017 World Wrestling Championships, Paris — A2714

2017, July 22 Photo. *Perf. 13x12¾*

5276 A2714 €1.30 multi	3.25	1.10

Espelette Pepper A2715

Woman Holding Strawberry A2716

Loaf of Bread, Croissant and Roll A2717

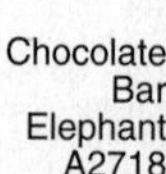

Chocolate Bar Elephant A2718

Beans A2719

Lobster A2720

Woman Drinking Citrus Juice A2721

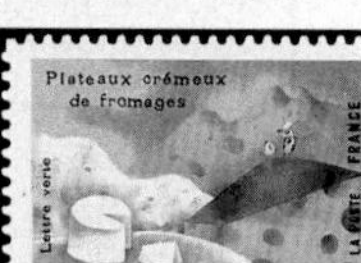

Cows and Cheese A2722

Tomato and Olive Salad A2723

Toucan With Cup of Coffee A2724

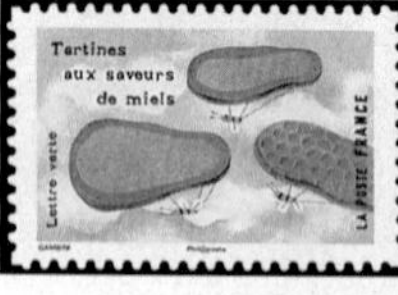

Toast With Flavored Honey A2725

People Drinking Mint Tea A2726

Serpentine Die Cut 11

2017, Aug. 5 **Photo.**

Booklet Stamps
Self-Adhesive

5277	A2715	(73c) multi		1.75	.60
5278	A2716	(73c) multi		1.75	.60
5279	A2717	(73c) multi		1.75	.60
5280	A2718	(73c) multi		1.75	.60
5281	A2719	(73c) multi		1.75	.60
5282	A2720	(73c) multi		1.75	.60
5283	A2721	(73c) multi		1.75	.60
5284	A2722	(73c) multi		1.75	.60
5285	A2723	(73c) multi		1.75	.60
5286	A2724	(73c) multi		1.75	.60
5287	A2725	(73c) multi		1.75	.60
5288	A2726	(73c) multi		1.75	.60
a.	Booklet pane of 12, #5277-5288			21.00	
	Nos. 5277-5288 (12)			21.00	7.20

Sense of taste.

Le Havre, 500th Anniv. A2727

2017, Aug. 31 **Engr.** ***Perf. 13¼***

5289	A2727	85c multi	2.10	.70

Bridges A2728

Designs: No. 5290, Pont du Gard, Vers-Pont-du-Gard, France. No. 5291, Pont du Diable, Saint-Jean-de-Fos, France. No. 5292, Morlaix Viaduct, Morlaix, France. No. 5293, Digoin Canal Bridge, Digoin, France. No. 5294, Garabit Viaduct, Ruynes-en-Margeride, France. No. 5295, Tower Bridge, London. No. 5296, Pont Valentré, Cahors, France. No. 5297, Ponte Vecchio, Florence. No. 5298, U Bein Bridge, Amarapura, Myanmar. No. 5299, Manhattan and Brooklyn Bridges, New York City. No. 5300, Pont Alexandre III and Pont de la Concorde, Paris. No. 5301, Rochefort-Martrou Transporter Bridge, Rochefort, France.

Serpentine Die Cut 11

2017, Sept. 1 **Photo.**

Booklet Stamps
Self-Adhesive

5290	A2728	(73c) multi		1.75	.60
5291	A2728	(73c) multi		1.75	.60
5292	A2728	(73c) multi		1.75	.60
5293	A2728	(73c) multi		1.75	.60
5294	A2728	(73c) multi		1.75	.60
5295	A2728	(73c) multi		1.75	.60
5296	A2728	(73c) multi		1.75	.60
5297	A2728	(73c) multi		1.75	.60
5298	A2728	(73c) multi		1.75	.60
5299	A2728	(73c) multi		1.75	.60
5300	A2728	(73c) multi		1.75	.60
5301	A2728	(73c) multi		1.75	.60
a.	Booklet pane of 12, #5290-5301			21.00	
	Nos. 5290-5301 (12)			21.00	7.20

Normandie-Niemen Air Regiment, 75th Anniv. — A2729

2017, Sept. 1 **Engr.** ***Perf. 13x12¾***

5302	A2729	€1.30 multi	3.25	1.10

A souvenir sheet containing No. 5302, a denominated example of No. 5302 with black and red inks only, and a non-denominated example of No. 5302 without the black and red inks sold for €6.20. See Russia No. 7843.

No. 5233 Overprinted in Dark Blue

Method and Perf. As Before

2017, Sept. 13

5303	A2684	73c multi + label	1.75	.60

Selection of Paris as host city of 2024 Summer Olympics.

Art Issue

The Kiss, Sculpture by Auguste Rodin (1840-1917) — A2730

2017, Sept. 15 **Engr.** ***Perf. 13¼x13***

5304	A2730	€1.30 multi	3.25	1.60

A souvenir sheet containing No. 5304 sold for €3.20.

Nadia Boulanger (1887-1979), Conductor and Teacher — A2731

2017, Sept. 16 **Engr.** ***Perf. 13¼x13***

5305	A2731	85c multi	2.00	.70

Jeanne Lanvin (1867-1946), Fashion Designer — A2732

2017, Sept. 23 **Photo.** ***Perf. 13¼x13***

5306	A2732	€1.46 multi	3.50	1.25

A souvenir sheet containing No. 5306 sold for €3.20.

Characters Maestro, Nabot and Globus From *Hello Maestro!* Animated Television Series A2733

2017, Sept. 23 **Photo.** ***Perf. 13¼***

5307	A2733	73c multi	1.75	.60
a.	Miniature sheet of 10		—	—

Woman in Hoop — A2734

Elephant Act — A2735

Rabbit in Magician's Hat — A2736

Mime — A2737

Lion Tamer A2738

Acrobat A2739

Human Tower — A2740

Clown Playing Guitar — A2741

Ringmaster A2742

Unicyclist A2743

Trick Rider on Horse A2744

Aerial Contortionist A2745

Serpentine Die Cut 11

2017, Sept. 29 **Photo.**

Booklet Stamps
Self-Adhesive

5308	A2734	(73c) multi		1.75	.60
5309	A2735	(73c) multi		1.75	.60
5310	A2736	(73c) multi		1.75	.60
5311	A2737	(73c) multi		1.75	.60
5312	A2738	(73c) multi		1.75	.60
5313	A2739	(73c) multi		1.75	.60
5314	A2740	(73c) multi		1.75	.60
5315	A2741	(73c) multi		1.75	.60
5316	A2742	(73c) multi		1.75	.60
5317	A2743	(73c) multi		1.75	.60
5318	A2744	(73c) multi		1.75	.60
5319	A2745	(73c) multi		1.75	.60
a.	Booklet pane of 12, #5308-5319			21.00	
	Nos. 5308-5319 (12)			21.00	7.20

Circus acts.

Electronic Military Transmissions, 150th Anniv. — A2746

2017, Sept. 29 **Photo.** ***Perf. 13¼***

5320	A2746	€1.46 multi	3.50	1.25

Father Victor Dillard (1897-1945), Minister to Deported French Slaves of Germany in World War II — A2747

2017, Oct. 6 **Engr.** ***Perf. 13¼***

5321	A2747	73c multi	1.75	.60

Miniature Sheet

Actors and Actresses — A2748

No. 5322: a, Magali Noel (1931-2015). b, Bruno Crémer (1929-2010). c, Odile Versois (1930-80). d, Jean-Claude Brialy (1933-2007).

2017, Oct. 13 **Photo.** ***Perf. 13¼***

5322	A2748	Sheet of 4	8.00	8.00
a.-d.		85c Any single	2.00	.70

Joseph Peyré (1892-1968), Writer — A2749

2017, Oct. 20 **Engr.** ***Perf. 13¼***

5323	A2749	€1.10 multi	2.60	.90

A2750

A2751

A2752

A2753

A2754

A2755

A2756

A2757

A2758

A2759

A2760

Contest Stamps With Scratch-off Panel A2761

Serpentine Die Cut 11

2017, Nov. 6 **Photo.**

Booklet Stamps
Self-Adhesive

5324	A2750	(73c) gold & multi	1.75	.60
a.		Scratched panel		.40
5325	A2751	(73c) gold & multi	1.75	.60
a.		Scratched panel		.40
5326	A2752	(73c) gold & multi	1.75	.60
a.		Scratched panel		.40
5327	A2753	(73c) gold & multi	1.75	.60
a.		Scratched panel		.40
5328	A2754	(73c) gold & multi	1.75	.60
a.		Scratched panel		.40
5329	A2755	(73c) gold & multi	1.75	.60
a.		Scratched panel		.40
5330	A2756	(73c) gold & multi	1.75	.60
a.		Scratched panel		.40
5331	A2757	(73c) gold & multi	1.75	.60
a.		Scratched panel		.40
5332	A2758	(73c) gold & multi	1.75	.60
a.		Scratched panel		.40
5333	A2759	(73c) gold & multi	1.75	.60
a.		Scratched panel		.40
5334	A2760	(73c) gold & multi	1.75	.60
a.		Scratched panel		.40
5335	A2761	(73c) gold & multi	1.75	.60
a.		Scratched panel		.40
b.		Booklet pane of 12, #5324-5335	21.00	
		Nos. 5324-5335 (12)	21.00	7.20

Sabine Type of 1977-78

2017, Nov. 9 **Engr.** ***Perf. 13***

5336	A771	€1 red	2.40	.80
5337	A771	€1 green	2.40	.80
a.		Pair, #5336-5337	4.80	1.60

Size: 30x47mm

5338	A771	€5 red	12.00	4.00
5339	A771	€5 green	12.00	4.00
a.		Horiz. pair, #5338-5339	24.00	8.00
		Nos. 5336-5339 (4)	28.80	9.60

Booklet Stamps

5340	A771	73c green	1.75	.60
5341	A771	85c red	2.00	.65
a.		Booklet pane of 12, 6 each #5340-5341	22.50	—

Size: 30x47mm

5342	A771	€1.46 green	3.50	1.25
5343	A771	€1.70 red	4.00	1.40
a.		Booklet pane of 2, #5342-5343	7.50	—
		Complete booklet, #5341a, 5343a	30.00	
		Nos. 5340-5343 (4)	11.25	3.90

Nos. 5336-5339 were printed in sheets of 12 containing 5 each Nos. 5336-5337 and 1 each Nos. 5338-5339.

Souvenir Sheet

Tulle Lace — A2762

No. 5344: a, Butterfly. b, Rose.

Photo. & Engr.

2017, Nov. 9 ***Perf. 13¼***

5344	A2762	Sheet of 2	4.00	4.00
a.-b.		85c Either single	2.00	.65

Augustin-Alphonse Marty (1862-1940), Reformer of Military Postal System — A2763

2017, Nov. 10 **Engr.** ***Perf. 13¼x13***

5345	A2763	73c multi	1.75	.60

Art Issue

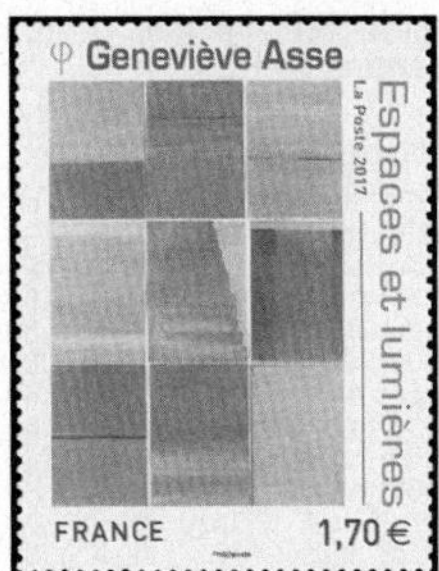

Spaces and Lights, by Geneviève Asse A2764

2017, Nov. 10 **Photo.** ***Perf. 13¼x13***

5346	A2764	€1.70 multi	4.00	2.00

Miniature Sheet

Postal Balances and Scales — A2765

No. 5347 — Inscription: a, Balance Romaine. b, Pèse-lettres Type "Roberval," horiz. c, Balance de Guichet. d, Balance à Fléau. e, Balance à Trébuchet, horiz. f, Pèse-lettres de Poche.

Litho. & Engr.

2017, Nov. 11 ***Perf. 13***

5347	A2765	Sheet of 6	10.50	10.50
a.-f.		73c Any single	1.75	.60
g.		Souvenir sheet of 3, #5347a, 5347c, 5347e	7.50	7.50
h.		Souvenir sheet of 3, #5347b, 5347d, 5347f	7.50	7.50

Nos. 5347g and 5347h were sold together for €6.20.

Cabinetmaking — A2766

2017, Nov. 12 **Engr.** ***Perf. 12¼***

5348	A2766	€1.10 multi	2.60	.85

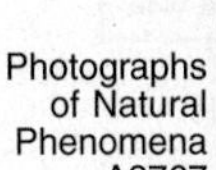

Photographs of Natural Phenomena A2767

Inscriptions: No. 5357, Détail de marbre (detail of marble, buff panel). No. 5358, Détail de marbre (detail of marble, red panel). No. 5359, Tronc d'arbre (tree trunk). No. 5360, Eau gelée (ice crystals). No. 5361, Sable-traces de crabes (sand balls made by crabs). No. 5362, Bulles d'air dans la glace (air bubbles in ice). No. 5363, Lichen crustacé sur un rocher (lichen covering rock). No. 5364, Roche chargeé de fer (iron in rock). No. 5365, Flyschs à helminthoides (worm trails). No. 5366, Concrétions (rock concretions). No. 5367, Début de rouille (beginnings of rust).

No. 5368, Minerai de fer sur la roche (iron ore in rock).

Serpentine Die Cut 11

2018, Jan. 5 **Photo.**

Booklet Stamps
Self-Adhesive

5357 A2767 (95c) multi 2.40 .80
5358 A2767 (95c) multi 2.40 .80
5359 A2767 (95c) multi 2.40 .80
5360 A2767 (95c) multi 2.40 .80
5361 A2767 (95c) multi 2.40 .80
5362 A2767 (95c) multi 2.40 .80
5363 A2767 (95c) multi 2.40 .80
5364 A2767 (95c) multi 2.40 .80
5365 A2767 (95c) multi 2.40 .80
5366 A2767 (95c) multi 2.40 .80
5367 A2767 (95c) multi 2.40 .80
5368 A2767 (95c) multi 2.40 .80
a. Booklet pane of 12, #5357-5368 29.00
Nos. 5357-5368 (12) 28.80 9.60

Heart and Faces
A2768

Heart and Lips
A2769

2018, Jan. 12 **Photo.** ***Perf. 13¼***
5369 A2768 80c blk & red 2.00 .65
a. Souvenir sheet of 5 10.00 10.00
5370 A2769 €1.60 blk & red 4.00 1.40

Self-Adhesive
Serpentine Die Cut

5371 A2768 80c blk & red 2.00 .65
5372 A2769 €1.60 blk & red 4.00 1.40

Values for Nos. 5369-5370 are for stamps with surrounding selvage.

Art Issue

Le Quai aux Fleurs, Notre-Dame, by Léonard Foujita (1886-1968) — A2770

2018, Jan. 26 **Photo.** ***Perf. 13x13¼***
5373 A2770 €1.90 multi 4.75 2.40

Clermont-Ferrand Short Film Festival, 40th Anniv. — A2771

2018, Feb. 2 **Photo.** ***Perf. 13¼***
5374 A2771 €1.30 multi 3.25 1.10

Sculptures of Dogs
A2772

Designs: No. 5375, African wooden sculpture of dog. No. 5376, Sculpture of spaniel by Antoine-Louis Barye (1795-1875). No. 5377, Sculpture of Boston terrier by François Pompon (1855-1933). No. 5378, Japanese sculpture of dog on table. No. 5379, Oriental sculptures of two dogs facing left. No. 5380, Egyptian sculpture of dog. No. 5381, Oriental sculpture of dog and bowl. No. 5382, Sculpture of basset hound by Barye. No. 5383, Chinese sculpture of dog. No. 5384, Two European sculptures of spaniels. No. 5385, Sculpture of dog by Louis de Monard (1873-1939). No. 5386, Asian sculpture of dog with ball.

Serpentine Die Cut 11

2018, Feb. 2 **Photo.**

Booklet Stamp
Self-Adhesive

5375 A2772 (80c) multi 2.00 .65
5376 A2772 (80c) multi 2.00 .65
5377 A2772 (80c) multi 2.00 .65
5378 A2772 (80c) multi 2.00 .65
5379 A2772 (80c) multi 2.00 .65
5380 A2772 (80c) multi 2.00 .65
5381 A2772 (80c) multi 2.00 .65
5382 A2772 (80c) multi 2.00 .65
5383 A2772 (80c) multi 2.00 .65
5384 A2772 (80c) multi 2.00 .65
5385 A2772 (80c) multi 2.00 .65
5386 A2772 (80c) multi 2.00 .65
a. Booklet pane of 12, #5375-5386 24.00
Nos. 5375-5386 (12) 24.00 7.80

Art Issue

Desir, Sculpture by Annette Messager — A2773

2018, Feb. 16 **Photo.** ***Perf. 13x13¼***
5387 A2773 €1.90 multi 4.75 2.40

Suzanne Noel (1878-1954), Plastic Surgeon — A2774

2018, Mar. 2 **Photo.** ***Perf. 13¼***
5388 A2774 95c multi 2.40 .80

17th Century Tableware
A2775

Designs: No. 5389, Cup made in Nevers. No. 5390, Plate made in Lille. No. 5391, Terrine made in Vincennes. No. 5392, Plate made in Moustiers-Sainte-Marie. No. 5393, Decorative cruet made in Strasbourg. No. 5394, Plate made in Limoges. No. 5395, Plate made in Moulins. No. 5396, Dessert service made in Gien. No. 5397, Tureen made in Sceaux. No. 5398, Plates made in Lyon. No. 5399, Plate and ewer made in Sèvres. No. 5400, Pot with lid made in Chantilly.

Serpentine Die Cut 11

2018, Mar. 2 **Photo.**

Booklet Stamp
Self-Adhesive

5389 A2775 (80c) multi 2.00 .65
5390 A2775 (80c) multi 2.00 .65
5391 A2775 (80c) multi 2.00 .65
5392 A2775 (80c) multi 2.00 .65
5393 A2775 (80c) multi 2.00 .65
5394 A2775 (80c) multi 2.00 .65
5395 A2775 (80c) multi 2.00 .65
5396 A2775 (80c) multi 2.00 .65
5397 A2775 (80c) multi 2.00 .65
5398 A2775 (80c) multi 2.00 .65
5399 A2775 (80c) multi 2.00 .65
5400 A2775 (80c) multi 2.00 .65
a. Booklet pane of 12, #5389-5400 24.00
Nos. 5389-5400 (12) 24.00 7.80

Stamp Day
A2776

Automobiles: 80c, Alpine Renault A110. €1.60, Renault Maxi 5 Turbo.

2018, Mar. 10 **Engr.** ***Perf. 13¼***
5401 A2776 80c multi 2.00 .65

Souvenir Sheet
Photo.
Perf. 13

5402 A2776 €1.60 multi 4.00 1.40

No. 5402 contains one 52x41mm stamp.

Art Issue

Plans Par Couleurs, by Frantisek Kupka (1871-1957) — A2777

2018, Mar. 18 **Photo.** ***Perf. 12¼x13***
5403 A2777 €1.90 multi 4.75 2.40

A souvenir sheet containing a perf. 13¼ example of No. 5403 and three labels sold for €4.

Savings Banks, 200th Anniv. — A2778

2018, Mar. 22 **Photo.** ***Perf. 13¼***
5404 A2778 95c multi 2.40 .80

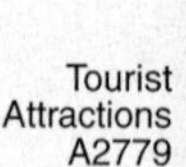

Tourist Attractions
A2779

Designs: No. 5405, Umbrellas on beach, Deauville. No. 5406, Chaîne des Puys. No. 5407, Dune of Pilat. No. 5408, Eiffel Tower and Tour Montparnasse, Paris. No. 5409, Vineyard, Bourgogne. No. 5410, Mont Blanc massif. No. 5411, Field, Alpes-de-Haute-Provence. No. 5412, Rocks on beach, Belle-Ile-en-Mer.

Serpentine Die Cut 11

2018, Mar. 23 **Photo.**

Booklet Stamps
Self-Adhesive

5405 A2779 (€1.30) multi 3.25 1.10
5406 A2779 (€1.30) multi 3.25 1.10
5407 A2779 (€1.30) multi 3.25 1.10
5408 A2779 (€1.30) multi 3.25 1.10
5409 A2779 (€1.30) multi 3.25 1.10
5410 A2779 (€1.30) multi 3.25 1.10
5411 A2779 (€1.30) multi 3.25 1.10
5412 A2779 (€1.30) multi 3.25 1.10
a. Booklet pane of 8, #5405-5412 26.00
Nos. 5405-5412 (8) 26.00 8.80

A2780

2018, Mar. 24 **Photo.** ***Perf. 13x13¼***
5413 A2780 80c multi + label 2.00 .65

Posts, Telegraphs and Telecommunications Sporting Association, 120th Anniv.

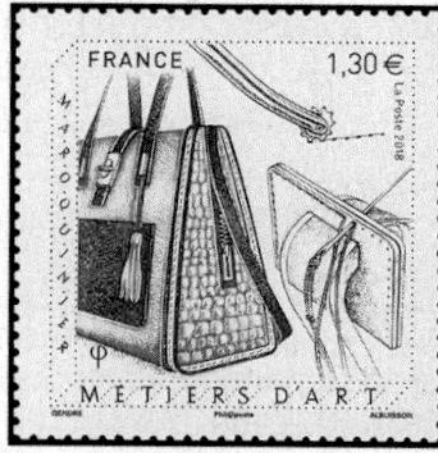

Leatherwork — A2781

2018, Mar. 30 **Engr.** ***Perf. 12¼***
5414 A2781 €1.30 multi 3.25 1.10

Sorgues — A2782

2018, Apr. 6 **Engr.** ***Perf. 13***
5415 A2782 95c multi 2.25 .75

Spring Philatelic Show, Sorgues.

Sosthène Mortenol (1859-1930), Naval Hero — A2783

Litho. & Engr.

2018, Apr. 13 ***Perf. 13x13¼***
5416 A2783 €1.20 multi 3.00 1.00

Miniature Sheet

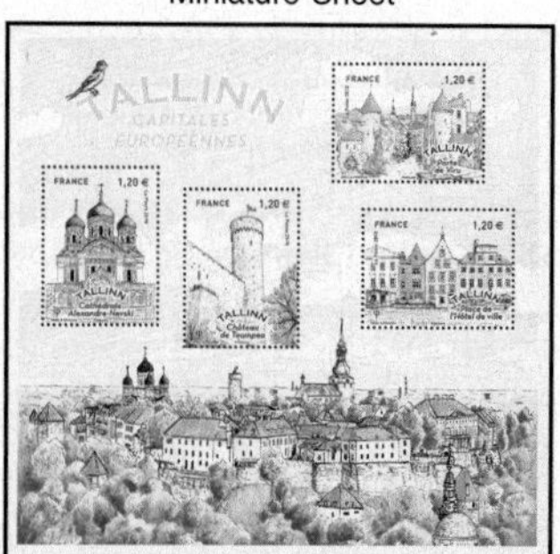

European Capitals — A2784

No. 5417 — Attractions in Tallinn, Estonia: a, Viru Gate. b, Alexander Nexsky Cathedral, vert. c, Toompea Castle, vert. d, Town Hall Square.

Perf. 13x13¼, 13¼x13

2018, Apr. 20 **Photo.**
5417 A2784 Sheet of 4 12.00 12.00
a.-d. €1.20 Any single 3.00 1.00

Souvenir Sheet

Vrai Guignolet Puppet Theater, Paris, 200th Anniv. — A2785

No. 5418: a, Two puppets with red and green headdresses. b, Two puppets, hot air balloon in background.

2018, May 10 Engr. *Perf. 13*

5418	A2785	Sheet of 2	12.00	12.00
a.-b.		€2.60 Either single	6.00	2.00

Deux Rives Pedestrian Bridge, Strasbourg A2786

2018, May 18 Photo. *Perf. 13¼*

5419	A2786	€1.20 multi	3.00	1.00

Europa.

A2787

A2788

A2789

A2790

A2791

A2792

A2793

A2794

A2795

A2796

A2797

Emojis A2798

Serpentine Die Cut 11

2018, May 18 Photo.

Booklet Stamps Self-Adhesive

5420	A2787	(80c) multi	1.90	.65
5421	A2788	(80c) multi	1.90	.65
5422	A2789	(80c) multi	1.90	.65
5423	A2790	(80c) multi	1.90	.65
5424	A2791	(80c) multi	1.90	.65
5425	A2792	(80c) multi	1.90	.65
5426	A2793	(80c) multi	1.90	.65
5427	A2794	(80c) multi	1.90	.65
5428	A2795	(80c) multi	1.90	.65
5429	A2796	(80c) multi	1.90	.65
5430	A2797	(80c) multi	1.90	.65
5431	A2798	(80c) multi	1.90	.65
a.		Booklet pane of 12, #5420-5431	23.00	
		Nos. 5420-5431 (12)	22.80	7.80

Lucie (1912-2007) and Raymond Aubrac (1914-2012), World War II Resistance Leaders — A2799

2018, May 26 Engr. *Perf. 13x13¼*

5432	A2799	€1.30 multi	3.00	1.00

United Nations Peacekeepers, 70th Anniv. — A2800

2018, May 29 Photo. *Perf. 13*

5433	A2800	€1.30 multi	3.00	1.00

A2801

Photographs of Earth Features Taken By Thomas Pesquet on the International Space Station: No. 5434, Snow and three lines of trees, Russia, taken Feb. 16, 2017. No. 5435, Paris, France, taken Apr. 14, 2017. No. 5436, Betsiboka River, Madagascar, taken May 6, 2017. No. 5437, Bijagos Archipelago, Guinea-Bissau, taken Feb. 4, 2017. No. 5438, Green River, Utah, taken Apr. 14, 2017. No. 5439, Persian Gulf islands, taken Dec. 31, 2016. No. 5440, Irrigated fields in desert, Saudi Arabia, taken Jan. 1, 2017. No. 5441, Fields, Spain, taken Apr. 12, 2017. No. 5442, Road in wilderness, Canada, taken Dec. 26, 2016. No. 5443, Melting ice in Himalayas, People's Republic of China, taken Apr. 27, 2017. No. 5444, Ile de Noirmoutier, France, taken Feb. 16, 2017. No. 5445, Coral reef and volcanic islands, French Polynesia, taken Mar. 16, 2017.

Serpentine Die Cut 11

2018, June 2 Photo.

Self-Adhesive Booklet Stamps

5434	A2801	(80c) multi	1.90	.65
5435	A2801	(80c) multi	1.90	.65
5436	A2801	(80c) multi	1.90	.65
5437	A2801	(80c) multi	1.90	.65
5438	A2801	(80c) multi	1.90	.65
5439	A2801	(80c) multi	1.90	.65
5440	A2801	(80c) multi	1.90	.65
5441	A2801	(80c) multi	1.90	.65
5442	A2801	(80c) multi	1.90	.65
5443	A2801	(80c) multi	1.90	.65
5444	A2801	(80c) multi	1.90	.65
5445	A2801	(80c) multi	1.90	.65
a.		Booklet pane of 12, #5434-5445	23.00	
		Nos. 5434-5445 (12)	22.80	7.80

Elysée Palace, Paris — A2802

2018, June 7 Engr. *Perf. 13*

5446	A2802	95c multi + label	2.25	.75

French Federation of Philatelic Associations, 91st Congress, Paris.

Nos. 4413 and 4437 Overprinted in Blue or Red

2018, June 8 Engr. *Perf. 13*

5447	A2320	10c brown (Bl)	—	—
5448	A2325	(80c) green (R)	—	—

Nos. 5447-5448 were sold only at the Paris Philex show on the day of issue. The entire 250,000-stamp print run of No. 5448 sold out on the day of issue.

Miniature Sheets

A2803

Paris Philex 2018 Stamp Show — A2804

No. 5449 — French stamps depicting Paris landmarks of 1939-56 redrawn: a, Grand Trianon, Versailles (like #794). b, Church of the Invalides, vert. (like #B203). c, Eiffel Tower, vert. (like #B85). d, Alexander III Bridge, Petit Palais (like #C24).

No. 5450 — French Orphan Relief stamps of 1917-19 redrawn: a, Widow at gate, vert. (like #B3). b, War orphans, vert. (like #B4). c, Woman plowing (like #B5). d, Woman plowing (like #B6). e, "Trench of Bayonets" (like #B7). f, Lion of Belfort (like #B8). g, "La Marseillaise" (like #B9). h, "La Marseillaise" (like #B10).

Engr., Sheet Margin Litho. With Foil Application

2018, June 7 *Perf. 13*

5449	A2803	Sheet of 4	23.50	23.50
a.		€2 brown lake	4.75	4.75
b.		€2 brown lake	4.75	4.75
c.		€2 brown lake	4.75	4.75
d.		€4 brown lake	9.25	9.25

Typo.

5450	A2804	Sheet of 8	71.00	71.00
a.		€1 violet brown	2.40	2.40
b.		€1 sage green	2.40	2.40
c.		€2 sage green	4.75	4.75
d.		€2 light blue	4.75	4.75
e.		€3 gray grn & lilac	7.00	7.00
f.		€3 brn pur & lt brn	7.00	7.00
g.		€3 brn rose & maroon	7.00	7.00
h.		€15 lt blue & gray grn	35.00	35.00

Art Issue

Self-portrait, by Edouard Vuillard (1868-1940) A2805

2018, June 8 Photo. *Perf. 13x12¾*

5451	A2805	€1.30 multi	3.00	1.50

No. 5451 was printed in sheets of 9 + 8 triangular labels.

Souvenir Sheet

French History — A2806

No. 5452: a, Treaty of the Pyrenees, 1659. b, Queen Maria Theresa (1638-83).

2018, June 9 Engr. *Perf. 13*

5452	A2806	Sheet of 2	12.00	12.00
a.-b.		€2.60 Either single	6.00	6.00
c.		Souvenir sheet of 2, #5452a-5452b, with different sheet margin	18.50	18.50

No. 5452c sold for €8.

Birds A2807

Designs: No. 5453, Mésange bleue (European blue tit).

No. 5454: a, Rouge-gorge (European robin). b, Moineau (sparrow). c, Pie (magpie).

2018, June 10 Photo. *Perf. 13¼*

5453	A2807	80c multi	1.90	.65

Souvenir Sheet

5454		Sheet of 4, #5453, 5454a-5454c	7.75	7.75
a.-c.	A2807	80c Any single	1.90	.95
d.		Souvenir sheet of 2, #5454a-5454b	7.00	7.00
e.		Souvenir sheet of 2, #5453, 5454c	7.00	7.00

Nos. 5454d-5454e sold together as a set for €6.

Trois-Fontaines Abbey, 900th Anniv. — A2808

2018, June 15 Photo. *Perf. 13¼x13*

5455 A2808 95c multi 2.25 .75

Tourism Issue

Kayserberg — A2809

2018, June 20 Photo. *Perf. 13x12¾*

5456 A2809 80c multi 1.90 .65

Ploumanc'h Lighthouse, Perros-Guirec A2810

2018, June 22 Photo. *Perf. 13¼*

5457 A2810 80c multi 1.90 .65

Mickey Mouse and Eiffel Tower A2811

Mickey Mouse and Mont-Saint-Michel Abbey — A2812

Mickey Mouse and Azay-le-Rideau Chateau — A2813

Mickey Mouse and Pont Saint-Bénézet, Avignon — A2814

Mickey Mouse and Bonifacio, Corsica A2815

Mickey Mouse and Beach A2816

Mickey Mouse and Etretat Cliffs A2817

Mickey Mouse and Auvergne Region Volcano A2818

Mickey Mouse and Cable Car A2819

Mickey Mouse and Lumière Monument, Lyon A2820

Mickey Mouse and Saint-Tropez A2821

Mickey Mouse and Strasbourg Cathedral A2822

Serpentine Die Cut 11

2018, June 29 Photo.

Booklet Stamps
Self-Adhesive

5458	A2811	(80c)	multi	1.90	.65
5459	A2812	(80c)	multi	1.90	.65
5460	A2813	(80c)	multi	1.90	.65
5461	A2814	(80c)	multi	1.90	.65
5462	A2815	(80c)	multi	1.90	.65
5463	A2816	(80c)	multi	1.90	.65
5464	A2817	(80c)	multi	1.90	.65
5465	A2818	(80c)	multi	1.90	.65
5466	A2819	(80c)	multi	1.90	.65
5467	A2820	(80c)	multi	1.90	.65
5468	A2821	(80c)	multi	1.90	.65
5469	A2822	(80c)	multi	1.90	.65
a.	Booklet pane of 12, #5458-5869			23.00	
	Nos. 5458-5469 (12)			22.80	7.80

Ryder Cup, Flags of United States and European Union — A2823

2018 Photo. *Perf. 13x13¼*

5470	A2823	€1.30	multi + label	3.00	1.00
a.	Sheet of 4 + 4 labels, sheet margin with white background			12.00	12.00
5470B	A2823	€2.60	multi + label	6.00	2.00

42nd Ryder Cup Matches, Guyancourt. Issued: No. 5470, 6/30; No. 5470B, 9/15. No. 5470B was printed in sheets of 4.

Camargue Region House A2824

2018, July 6 Photo. *Perf. 13¼*

5471 A2824 €1.30 multi 3.00 1.00

Viaur Viaduct — A2825

2018, July 6 Photo. *Perf. 13x12¾*

5472 A2825 95c multi 2.25 .75

Marianne and Denomination A2826

Marianne "Ecopli" A2827

Marianne "Lettre Verte" A2828

Marianne "Lettre Prioritaire" A2829

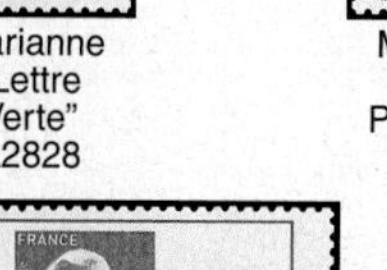

Marianne "Europe" With Data Matrix Code A2830

Marianne "Monde" With Data Matrix Code A2831

2018, July 20 Engr. *Perf. 13*

5473	A2826	1c	yellow	.25	.25
5474	A2826	5c	dk brown	.25	.25
5475	A2826	10c	brown	.25	.25
a.	Souvenir sheet of 3, #5473-5475			.60	.60
5476	A2827	(78c)	dk gray	1.90	.50
5477	A2828	(80c)	emerald	1.90	.50
5478	A2829	(95c)	red	2.25	.55
a.	Souvenir sheet of 2, #5477-5478			6.75	6.75
b.	Booklet pane of 12, 6 each #5477-5478			25.00	—
5479	A2826	€1	orange	2.40	.60
a.	Souvenir sheet of 2, #5476, 5479			6.75	6.75
5480	A2830	(€1.20)	dull blue	2.75	.70
5481	A2831	(€1.30)	purple	3.00	.75
a.	Souvenir sheet of 5, #5476-5478, 5480-5481			12.00	12.00
b.	Souvenir sheet of 5, #5480-5481			9.50	9.50
	Nos. 5473-5481 (9)			14.95	4.35

Coil Stamps

Perf. 13 Horiz.

5482	A2828	(80c)	emerald	1.90	.50
5483	A2829	(95c)	red	2.25	.55

Self-Adhesive

Serpentine Die Cut 6¾ Vert.

5484	A2826	1c	yellow	.25	.25
5485	A2826	5c	dk brown	.25	.25
5486	A2826	10c	brown	.25	.25
5487	A2827	(78c)	dk gray	1.90	.50
5488	A2828	(80c)	emerald	1.90	.50
5489	A2829	(95c)	red	2.25	.55
a.	Booklet pane of 10			22.50	
b.	Booklet pane of 12			27.00	
c.	Booklet pane of 20			45.00	
5490	A2826	€1	orange	2.40	.60
5491	A2830	(€1.20)	dull blue	2.75	.70
5492	A2831	(€1.30)	purple	3.00	.75
	Nos. 5484-5492 (9)			14.95	4.35

Coil Stamps

Serpentine Die Cut 6¾ Horiz.

5493	A2828	(80c)	emerald	1.90	.50
5494	A2829	(95c)	red	2.25	.55

Issued: No. 5478b, 11/12/18. Nos. 5475a, 5478a, 5479a and 5481b sold as a set for €10.

See Nos. 5558-5561. For overprints, see Nos. 5539-5540.

Trees — A2832

Designs: No. 5495, Betula papyrifera. No. 5496, Adansonia digitata. No. 5497, Cedrus libani. No. 5498, Carpinus betulus. No. 5499, Quercus robur. No. 5500, Fraxinus excelsior. No. 5501, Acer saccharum. No. 5502, Pinus sylvestris. No. 5503, Sequoiadendron giganteum. No. 5504, Ginkgo biloba. No. 5505, Olea europaea. No. 5506, Fagus sylvatica.

Serpentine Die Cut 11

2018, Aug. 3 Photo.

Booklet Stamps
Self-Adhesive

5495	A2832	(95c)	multi	2.25	.75
5496	A2832	(95c)	multi	2.25	.75
5497	A2832	(95c)	multi	2.25	.75
5498	A2832	(95c)	multi	2.25	.75
5499	A2832	(95c)	multi	2.25	.75
5500	A2832	(95c)	multi	2.25	.75
5501	A2832	(95c)	multi	2.25	.75
5502	A2832	(95c)	multi	2.25	.75
5503	A2832	(95c)	multi	2.25	.75
5504	A2832	(95c)	multi	2.25	.75
5505	A2832	(95c)	multi	2.25	.75
5506	A2832	(95c)	multi	2.25	.75
a.	Booklet pane of 12, #5495-5506			27.00	
	Nos. 5495-5506 (12)			27.00	9.00

Teapot From Jiangsu, China A2833

Teapot From China A2834

Teapot From England A2835

Teapot From Sèvres, France A2836

Teapot From Delft, Netherlands A2837

Teapot From Jingdezhen, China A2838

Teapot From Sèvres, France A2839

Teapot From Kyoto, Japan A2840

Teapot From Paris, France A2841

Teapot From Moscow, Russia A2842

Teapot From Venice, Italy A2843

Teapot From Lille, France A2844

Serpentine Die Cut 11

2018, Aug. 31 **Photo.**

Booklet Stamps Self-Adhesive

5507	A2833 (80c) multi		1.90	.65
5508	A2834 (80c) multi		1.90	.65
5509	A2835 (80c) multi		1.90	.65
5510	A2836 (80c) multi		1.90	.65
5511	A2837 (80c) multi		1.90	.65
5512	A2838 (80c) multi		1.90	.65
5513	A2839 (80c) multi		1.90	.65
5514	A2840 (80c) multi		1.90	.65
5515	A2841 (80c) multi		1.90	.65
5516	A2842 (80c) multi		1.90	.65
5517	A2843 (80c) multi		1.90	.65
5518	A2844 (80c) multi		1.90	.65
a.	Booklet pane of 12, #5507-5518		23.00	
	Nos. 5507-5518 (12)		22.80	7.80

Mickey Mouse, 90th Anniv. A2845

2018, Sept. 5 **Photo.** ***Perf. 13¼x13***

5519 A2845 €1.30 multi 3.00 1.00

Miniature Sheet

Stage Actors and Actresses — A2846

No. 5520: a, François-Joseph Talma (1763-1826). b, Rachel Félix (1821-58). c, Sarah Bernhardt (1844-1923). d, Benoît-Constant Coquelin (Coquelin Aîné) (1841-1909).

2018, Sept. 7 **Photo.** ***Perf. 13¼***

5520	A2846 Sheet of 4 + 5 labels	11.00	11.00
a.-d.	€1.20 Any single	2.75	.90

Ceramics A2847

2018, Sept. 15 **Engr.** ***Perf. 13***

5521 A2847 €1.30 multi 3.00 1.00

A souvenir sheet of 1 sold for €4.

Pierre Schoendoerffer (1928-2012), Film Director and War Reporter — A2848

2018, Sept. 21 **Engr.** ***Perf. 13¼***

5522 A2848 €1.30 multi 3.00 1.00

Louise de Bettignies (1880-1918), World War I Secret Agent — A2849

2018, Sept. 28 **Photo.** ***Perf. 13¼***

5523 A2849 80c multi 1.90 .65

Rose Valland (1898-1980), Art Historian and World War II Resistance Leader — A2850

2018, Sept. 28 **Photo.** ***Perf. 13¼***

5524 A2850 €1.20 multi 2.75 .90

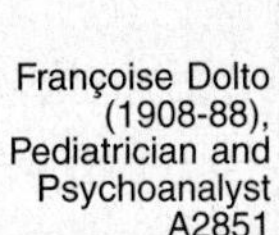

Françoise Dolto (1908-88), Pediatrician and Psychoanalyst A2851

2018, Oct. 5 **Photo.** ***Perf. 13¼***

5525 A2851 95c multi 2.25 .75

A2852 A2853

A2854 A2855

A2856 A2857

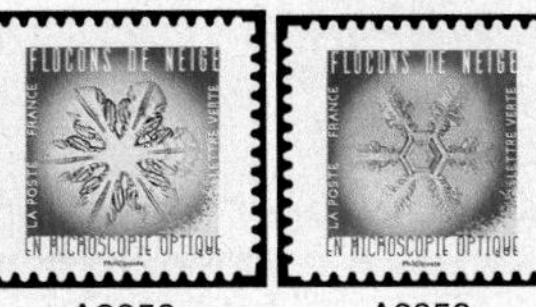

A2858 A2859

A2860 A2861

Photographs of Snowflakes

A2862 A2863

Serpentine Die Cut 11

2018, Oct. 5 **Photo.**

Booklet Stamps Self-Adhesive

5526	A2852 (80c) multi		1.90	.65
5527	A2853 (80c) multi		1.90	.65
5528	A2854 (80c) multi		1.90	.65
5529	A2855 (80c) multi		1.90	.65
5530	A2856 (80c) multi		1.90	.65
5531	A2857 (80c) multi		1.90	.65
5532	A2858 (80c) multi		1.90	.65
5533	A2859 (80c) multi		1.90	.65
5534	A2860 (80c) multi		1.90	.65
5535	A2861 (80c) multi		1.90	.65
5536	A2862 (80c) multi		1.90	.65
5537	A2863 (80c) multi		1.90	.65
a.	Booklet pane of 12, #5526-5537		23.00	
	Nos. 5526-5537 (12)		22.80	7.80

Elise (1898-1983) and Célestin (1896-1966) Freinet, Educational Reformers — A2864

2018, Oct. 12 **Photo.** ***Perf. 13¼***

5538 A2864 95c multi 2.25 .75

Nos. 5480-5481 Overprinted in Red or Blue

Methods and Perfs. As Before

2018, Oct. 15

5539	A2830 (€1.20) dull blue (R)	2.75	1.40
5540	A28310 (€1.30) purple (Bl)	3.00	1.50

Art Issue

Photograph of Woman Reading Letter by Sophie Calle — A2865

2018, Oct. 19 **Photo.** ***Perf. 13x13¼***

5541 A2865 €1.90 multi 4.50 2.25

Périgueux — A2866

2018, Oct. 26 **Engr.** ***Perf. 13x13¼***

5542 A2866 80c multi + label 1.90 .65

Postal Checks, Cent. A2867

2018, Oct. 31 **Photo.** ***Perf. 12¼***

5543 A2867 80c multi 1.90 .65

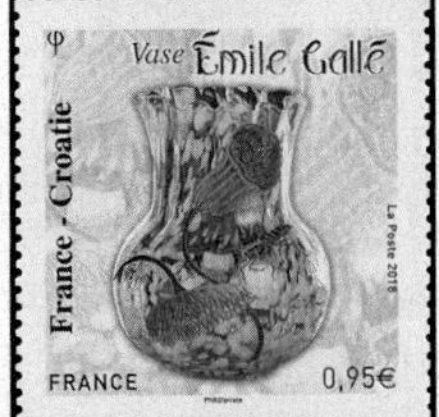

Vases A2868

Vase by: 95c, Emile Gallé (1846-1904), France. €1.20, Antonija Krasnik (1874-1956), Croatia.

2018, Nov. 8 Photo. *Perf. 12¼*

5544	A2868	95c multi	2.25	.75
5545	A2868	€1.20 multi	2.75	.90

Joint Issue between France and Croatia. See Croatia Nos. 1092-1093.

"Bonne Année" — A2869

House and Trees — A2870

Heart and Flowers A2871

Reindeer and Flowers — A2872

"Bonne Année" — A2873

Candle, Flowers and Hearts — A2874

Christmas Ornament A2875

Reindeer A2876

Gift — A2877

"Joyeuses Fêtes" — A2878

"Joie" — A2879

Head of Reindeer A2880

Serpentine Die Cut 11

2018, Nov. 8 Photo.

Booklet Stamps
Self-Adhesive

5546	A2869 (80c) gold & multi		1.90	.65
	Scratched panel			.40
5547	A2870 (80c) gold & multi		1.90	.65
	Scratched panel			.40
5548	A2871 (80c) gold & multi		1.90	.65
	Scratched panel			.40
5549	A2872 (80c) gold & multi		1.90	.65
	Scratched panel			.40
5550	A2873 (80c) gold & multi		1.90	.65
	Scratched panel			.40
5551	A2874 (80c) gold & multi		1.90	.65
	Scratched panel			.40
5552	A2875 (80c) gold & multi		1.90	.65
	Scratched panel			.40
5553	A2876 (80c) gold & multi		1.90	.65
	Scratched panel			.40
5554	A2877 (80c) gold & multi		1.90	.65
	Scratched panel			.40
5555	A2878 (80c) gold & multi		1.90	.65
	Scratched panel			.40
5556	A2879 (80c) gold & multi		1.90	.65
	Scratched panel			.40
5557	A2880 (80c) gold & multi		1.90	.65
	Scratched panel			.40
a.	Booklet pane of 12, #5546-5557		23.00	
	Nos. 5546-5557 (12)		22.80	7.80

Christmas and New Year's greetings.

Marianne Types of 2018 and

Marianne A2881

2018, Nov. 12 Engr. *Perf. 13*

Booklet Stamps
Size: 30x46mm

5558	A2826	€1.60 green	3.75	1.25
5559	A2826	€1.90 red	4.50	1.50
a.		Booklet pane of 2, #5558-5559	8.25	—
		Complete booklet, #5478b, 5559a	33.50	

Self-Adhesive
Design Size: 15x23mm (Nos. 5560-5561)
Photo.
Serpentine Die Cut 11

5560	A2828	(80c) green	1.90	.50
5561	A2829	(95c) red	2.25	.60
5562	A2881	(€3.20) black & gray	7.25	2.40
a.		Bklt. pane of 13, #5562, 6 each #5560-5561	32.50	
		Nos. 5560-5562 (3)	11.40	3.50

Marianne "Lettre Suivie" — A2881a

2018 ? Litho. *Die Cut*
Self-Adhesive

5563	A2881a	(€1.28) cerise + label	—	—

Ivan Turgenev (1818-83), Writer A2882

2018, Nov. 9 Photo. *Perf. 13¼*

5565	A2882	€1.30 multi	3.00	1.00

Miniature Sheet

Hats — A2883

No. 5566: a, Capeline. b, Haut de forme (top hat). c, Cloche. d, Mambo (pork pie hat), horiz. e, Toque. f, Chapeau melon (bowler hat), horiz.

Litho. & Engr.

2018, Nov. 9 *Perf. 13*

5566	A2883	Sheet of 6	13.50	13.50
a.-f.		95c Any single	2.25	.75
g.		Souvenir sheet of 3, #5566a, 5566d, 5566f	9.25	9.25
h.		Souvenir sheet of 3, #5566b, 5566c, 5566e	9.25	9.25

Nos. 5566g and 5566h were sold together for €8.

Souvenir Sheet

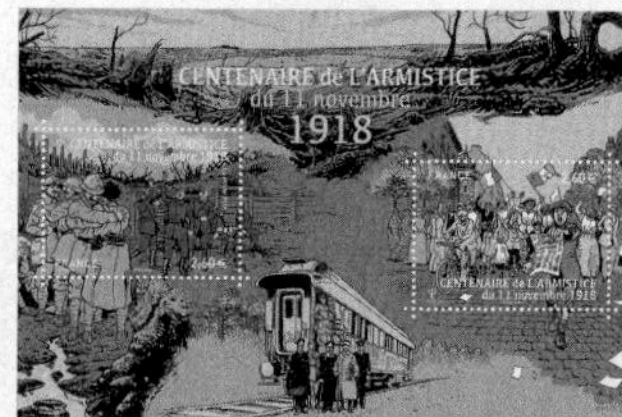

World War I Armistice, Cent. — A2884

No. 5567: a, Soldiers celebrating. b, Civilians celebrating.

2018, Nov. 11 Photo. *Perf. 13¼*

5567	A2884	Sheet of 2	12.00	12.00
a.-b.		€2.60 Either stamp	6.00	2.00
c.		Souvenir sheet of 2, #5567a-5567b, different sheet margin	18.50	18.50

No. 5567c sold for €8.

A2885

General Henri M. Berthelot (1861-1931) — A2886

2018, Nov. 27 Photo. *Perf. 13¼*

5568	A2885	€1.30 multi	3.00	1.00
5569	A2886	€1.30 multi	3.00	1.00
a.		Souvenir sheet of 2, #5568-5569	9.25	9.25

No. 5569a sold for €4. See Romania Nos. 6201-6202.

Universal Declaration of Human Rights, 70th Anniv. — A2887

2018, Dec. 10 Photo. *Perf. 13¼*

5570	A2887	88c multi	2.00	.65

Marianne "International" and Data Matrix Code — A2888

2019, Jan. 1 Engr. *Perf. 13*

5571	A2888	(€1.30) purple	3.00	.75

Self-Adhesive
Serpentine Die Cut 6¾ Vert.

5572	A2888	(€1.30) purple	3.00	.75

A2889

A2890

A2891

A2892

A2893

A2894

A2895

A2896

A2897

A2898

A2899

African Fabric Patterns A2900

Serpentine Die Cut 11

2019, Jan. 4 **Photo.**

Booklet Stamps
Self-Adhesive

5573 A2889 (88c) multi 2.10 .70
5574 A2890 (88c) multi 2.10 .70
5575 A2891 (88c) multi 2.10 .70
5576 A2892 (88c) multi 2.10 .70
a. Larger dots in flowers and background 2.10 .70
5577 A2893 (88c) multi 2.10 .70
5578 A2894 (88c) multi 2.10 .70
5579 A2895 (88c) multi 2.10 .70
5580 A2896 (88c) multi 2.10 .70
5581 A2897 (88c) multi 2.10 .70
5582 A2898 (88c) multi 2.10 .70
5583 A2899 (88c) multi 2.10 .70
5584 A2900 (88c) multi 2.10 .70
a. Booklet pane of 12, #5573-5584 25.50
Nos. 5573-5584 (12) 25.20 8.40

No. 5576a was printed only in sheets of 50.

Emilie du Châtelet (1706-49), Philosopher, Mathematician and Physicist A2901

2019, Jan. 18 **Photo.** ***Perf. 13¼***
5585 A2901 88c multi 2.10 .70

Heart and Vine A2902

Heart and Vendôme Column, Paris A2903

2019, Jan. 18 **Photo.** ***Perf. 13¼***
5586 A2902 88c multi 2.10 .70
a. Souvenir sheet of 5 10.50 10.50
5587 A2903 €1.76 multi 4.00 1.40

Self-Adhesive
Serpentine Die Cut
5588 A2902 88c multi 2.10 .70
5589 A2903 €1.76 multi 4.00 1.40

Values for Nos. 5586-5589 are for stamps with surrounding selvage.

New Year 2019 (Year of the Pig) — A2904

Designs: 88c, Pig holding Chinese lantern. €1.30, Three pigs on Chinese lantern.

2019, Jan. 25 **Photo.** ***Perf. 13***
5590 Sheet of 5, #5590a, 4 #5590b 10.50 10.50
a. A2904 88c 33x40mm stamp 2.10 .70
b. A2904 88c 29x35mm stamp 2.10 .70
5591 Sheet of 5, #5591a, 4 #5591b 15.00 15.00
a. A2904 €1.30 33x40mm stamp 3.00 1.00
b. A2904 €1.30 29x35mm stamp 3.00 1.00

Architectural Details of French Buildings A2905

Designs: No. 5592, Chapelle Sainte-Marie, Nevers. No. 5593, Château de Vitré. No. 5594, Grand Palais, Paris. No. 5595, Château de Chambord. No. 5596, Notre Dame Cathedral, Strasbourg. No. 5597, Pavilion de l'Horloge, Louvre Museum, Paris. No. 5598, Saline Royale (Royal Saltworks), Arc-et-Senans. No. 5599, Museum of Grenoble. No. 5600, Church, Saint-Nectaire. No. 5601, Notre-Dame-des-Champs Church, Avranches. No. 5602, Maison Carrée, Nîmes. No. 5603, Saint-Front Cathedral, Périgueux.

Serpentine Die Cut 11

2019, Feb. 1 **Photo.**

Booklet Stamps
Self-Adhesive

5592 A2905 (€1.05) multi 2.40 .80
5593 A2905 (€1.05) multi 2.40 .80
5594 A2905 (€1.05) multi 2.40 .80
5595 A2905 (€1.05) multi 2.40 .80
a. Larger and coarser dot structure 2.40 .80
5596 A2905 (€1.05) multi 2.40 .80
a. Larger and coarser dot structure 2.40 .80
5597 A2905 (€1.05) multi 2.40 .80
5598 A2905 (€1.05) multi 2.40 .80
5599 A2905 (€1.05) multi 2.40 .80
5600 A2905 (€1.05) multi 2.40 .80
5601 A2905 (€1.05) multi 2.40 .80
5602 A2905 (€1.05) multi 2.40 .80
5603 A2905 (€1.05) multi 2.40 .80
a. Booklet pane of 12, #5592-5603 29.00
Nos. 5592-5603 (12) 28.80 9.60

Nos. 5595a and 5596a were both printed in sheets of 50. The larger and coarser dot structure can best be seen in the upper left triangle.

Louise de Vilmorin (1902-69), Writer — A2906

2019, Feb. 8 **Photo.** ***Perf. 13¼***
5604 A2906 €1.05 multi 2.40 .80

Sister Cities of Dinan, France and Dinant, Belgium — A2907

2019, Feb. 15 **Photo.** ***Perf. 13x12¾***
5605 A2907 €1.30 multi 3.00 1.00

Saltwater Fish A2908

Designs: No. 5606, Thunnus thynnus. No. 5607, Scorpaena scrofa. No. 5608, Dicentrarchus labrax. No. 5609, Zeus faber. No. 5610, Sparus aurata. No. 5611, Scophthalmus maximus. No. 5612, Solea solea. No. 5613, Scomber scombrus. No. 5614, Epinephelus marginatus. No. 5615, Ssrdina pilchardus. No. 5616, Raja clavata. No. 5617, Gadus morhua.

Serpentine Die Cut 11

2019, Feb. 22 **Photo.**

Booklet Stamps
Self-Adhesive

5606 A2908 (88c) multi 2.00 .65
5607 A2908 (88c) multi 2.00 .65
5608 A2908 (88c) multi 2.00 .65
5609 A2908 (88c) multi 2.00 .65
5610 A2908 (88c) multi 2.00 .65
5611 A2908 (88c) multi 2.00 .65
5612 A2908 (88c) multi 2.00 .65
5613 A2908 (88c) multi 2.00 .65
5614 A2908 (88c) multi 2.00 .65
5615 A2908 (88c) multi 2.00 .65
5616 A2908 (88c) multi 2.00 .65
5617 A2908 (88c) multi 2.00 .65
a. Booklet pane of 12, #5606-5617 24.00
Nos. 5606-5617 (12) 24.00 7.80

Art Series

Calendula (Marigold), Photograph by Valérie Belin A2909

2019, Feb. 22 **Litho.** ***Perf. 13***
5618 A2909 €2.10 multi 4.75 2.40

Citroen Automobiles — A2910

Designs: 88c, Citroen Type A 10 HP. €1.76, Citroen Traction.

2019, Mar. 9 **Photo.** ***Perf. 13¼***
5619 A2910 88c multi 2.00 .65

Souvenir Sheet
Perf. 13x13¼
5620 A2910 €1.76 sil & multi 4.00 1.40

Stamp Day. No. 5620 contains one 52x41mm stamp.

Fontaine Saint-Michel, Paris — A2911

2019, Mar. 14 **Engr.** ***Perf. 13***
5621 A2911 88c multi 2.00 .65

Spring Philatelic Show, Paris.

Ceres — A2912

Photo. & Typo.

2019, Mar. 14 ***Imperf.***
5622 A2912 20c black .85 .85
a. Tête bêche pair — —
5623 A2912 88c black 2.00 .65
a. As #5623, with inverted vignette — —
b. Pair, #5623-5623a — —

No. 5622 was printed in sheets of 150 (with one stamp inverted) that sold for €55. No. 5623 was printed in sheets of 20 (with one stamp with inverted vignette).

Crystal Production A2913

2019, Mar. 15 **Engr.** ***Perf. 13¼***
5624 A2913 €1.30 indigo & slate vio 3.00 1.00

A souvenir sheet containing No. 5624 sold for €4.

Miniature Sheet

European Capitals — A2914

No. 5625 — Attractions in Helsinki, Finland: a, Lutheran Cathedral. b, Kruununhaka. c, Suomenlinna. d, Sibelius Monument.

2019, Mar. 16 Photo. ***Perf. 13x13¼***

5625	A2914	Sheet of 4	12.00	12.00
a.-d.		€1.30 Any single	3.00	1.00

Sculptures of Nude Women — A2915

Designs: No. 5626, Sculpture by Charles Despiau. No. 5627, Sculpture by Antoine Bourdelle. No. 5628, Ancient Egyptian sculpture. No. 5629, Ancient Greek sculpture (Venus de Milo). No. 5630, Sculpture by Edgar Degas. No. 5631, Ancient Oriental sculpture. No. 5632, Sculpture by Jacquio Ponce. No. 5633, Sculpture by Aristide Maillol. No. 5634, Nepalese sculpture. No. 5635, Statue by unknown artist in style of Etienne Maurice Falconet. No. 5636, Statue from Upper Paleolithic era. No. 5637, Sculpture from Ivory Coast (Côte d'Ivoire).

Serpentine Die Cut 11

2019, Mar. 29 Photo.

Booklet Stamps
Self-Adhesive

5626	A2915 (88c) multi		2.00	.65
5627	A2915 (88c) multi		2.00	.65
5628	A2915 (88c) multi		2.00	.65
5629	A2915 (88c) multi		2.00	.65
5630	A2915 (88c) multi		2.00	.65
5631	A2915 (88c) multi		2.00	.65
5632	A2915 (88c) multi		2.00	.65
5633	A2915 (88c) multi		2.00	.65
5634	A2915 (88c) multi		2.00	.65
5635	A2915 (88c) multi		2.00	.65
5636	A2915 (88c) multi		2.00	.65
5637	A2915 (88c) multi		2.00	.65
a.	Booklet pane of 12, #5626-5637		24.00	
	Nos. 5626-5637 (12)		24.00	7.80

Souvenir Sheet

Diplomatic Relations Between France and Poland, Cent. — A2916

No. 5638: a, Charles de Gaulle (1890-1970), as army captain (later president of France). b, Józef Haller (1873-1960), Polish lieutenant general.

2019, Apr. 2 Photo. ***Perf. 13¼***

5638	A2916	Sheet of 2	5.00	5.00
a.		88c multi	2.00	.65
b.		€1.30 multi	3.00	1.00

A souvenir sheet containing Nos. 5638a-5638b with a different sheet margin sold for €6. See Poland No. 4409.

Souvenir Sheet

Mogador Theater, Paris, Cent. — A2917

No. 5639: a, Seats in theater. b, Architectural detail depicting ram's head.

2019, Apr. 2 Photo. ***Perf. 13¼***

5639	A2917	Sheet of 2	6.00	6.00
a.-b.		€1.30 Either single	3.00	1.00

A souvenir sheet containing Nos. 5639a-5639b with a different sheet margin sold for €6.

Woman's Suffrage in France, 75th Anniv. A2918

2019, Apr. 19 Photo. ***Perf. 13¼***

5640	A2918	88c multi	2.00	.65

Souvenir Sheet

Paintings — A2919

No. 5641: a, The Gulf of Marseille Seen From L'Estaque, by Paul Cézanne (1839-1906). b, Mohammed V Square, Casablanca, by Jacques Majorelle (1886-1962).

2019, Apr. 26 Photo. ***Perf. 13¼***

5641	A2919	Sheet of 2	5.00	5.00
a.		88c multi	2.00	.65
b.		€1.30 multi	3.00	1.00

See Morocco No. 1269.

Art Issue

Lascaux Cave Drawings — A2920

2019, Apr. 26 Engr. ***Perf. 13x12***

5642	A2920	88c multi	2.00	1.00

A souvenir sheet containing a perf. 13x13¼ example of No. 5642 sold for €4.

A2921

A2922

A2923

A2924

A2925

A2926

A2927

A2928

A2929

A2930

A2931

Photographs of Flowers by Jacques du Sordet A2932

Serpentine Die Cut 11

2019, May 3 Photo.

Booklet Stamps
Self-Adhesive

5643	A2921 (88c) multi		2.00	.65
5644	A2922 (88c) multi		2.00	.65
5645	A2923 (88c) multi		2.00	.65
5646	A2924 (88c) multi		2.00	.65
5647	A2925 (88c) multi		2.00	.65
5648	A2926 (88c) multi		2.00	.65
5649	A2927 (88c) multi		2.00	.65
5650	A2928 (88c) multi		2.00	.65
5651	A2929 (88c) multi		2.00	.65
5652	A2930 (88c) multi		2.00	.65
5653	A2931 (88c) multi		2.00	.65
5654	A2932 (88c) multi		2.00	.65
a.	Booklet pane of 12, #5643-5654		24.00	
	Nos. 5643-5654 (12)		24.00	7.80

Lighthouse, Fresnel Lens and Augustin Fresnel (1788-1827), Physicist — A2933

2019, May 3 Engr. ***Perf. 13¼***

5655	A2933	€1.05 multi	2.40	.80

Stylized Birds — A2934

2019, May 10 Photo. ***Perf. 13***

5656	A2934	€1.30 multi	3.00	1.00

Europa.

Endangered Flora — A2935

Designs: No. 5657, Violette de Rouen.

No. 5658: a, Saxifrage oeil-de-bouc. b, Faujasie écailleuse. c, Dracocépahale d'Autriche.

2019, May 17 Photo. ***Perf. 13¼***

5657	A2935	88c multi	2.00	.65

Miniature Sheet

5658	Sheet of 4, #5657, 5658a-5658c	8.00	8.00
a.-c.	A2935 88c Any single	2.00	.65
d.	Souvenir sheet of 2, #5657, 5658b	6.75	6.75
e.	Souvenir sheet of 2, #5658a, 5658c	6.75	6.75

Nos. 5658d and 5658e were sold together for €6.

Miniature Sheet

Sports — A2936

No. 5659: a, Volleyball. b, Table tennis, horiz. c, Soccer, horiz. d, Field hockey. e, Kayaking, horiz. f, Wheelchair basketball.

2019, May 18 Litho. *Perf. 13*

5659	A2936	Sheet of 6	18.00	18.00
a.-f.		€1.30 Any single	3.00	1.00

Château de Chambord, 500th Anniv. — A2937

2019, May 31 Engr. *Perf. 13x12¾*

5660	A2937	88c multi	2.00	.65

A souvenir sheet containing No. 5660 sold for €4.

Characters from Astérix Comic Strips — A2938

Designs: No. 5661, Falbala. No. 5662, Obélix. No. 5663, Panoramix. No. 5664, Ordralfabétix. No. 5665, Abraracourcix. No. 5666, Bonemine. No. 5667, Cétautomatix. No. 5668, Assurancetourix. No. 5669, Agecanonix. No. 5670, Mrs. Agecanonix. No. 5671, Idéfix. No. 5672, Astérix.

Serpentine Die Cut 11

2019, June 6 Photo.

Booklet Stamps
Self-Adhesive

5661	A2938	(88c) multi	2.00	.65
5662	A2938	(88c) multi	2.00	.65
5663	A2938	(88c) multi	2.00	.65
5664	A2938	(88c) multi	2.00	.65
5665	A2938	(88c) multi	2.00	.65
5666	A2938	(88c) multi	2.00	.65
5667	A2938	(88c) multi	2.00	.65
5668	A2938	(88c) multi	2.00	.65
5669	A2938	(88c) multi	2.00	.65
5670	A2938	(88c) multi	2.00	.65
5671	A2938	(88c) multi	2.00	.65
5672	A2938	(88c) multi	2.00	.65
a.		Booklet pane of 12, #5661-5672	24.00	
		Nos. 5661-5672 (12)	24.00	7.80

Art Issue

Self-Portrait with a Black Dog, by Gustave Courbet (1819-77) — A2939

2019, June 7 Photo. *Perf. 13x13¼*

5673	A2939	€2.10 multi	4.75	2.40

Opéra Comédie, Montpellier — A2940

2019, June 7 Engr. *Perf. 13x13¼*

5674	A2940	€1.05 multi + label	2.40	.80

French Federation of Philatelic Associations, 92nd Congress, Montpellier.

Saint-Philbert-de-Grand-Lieu Abbey — A2941

2019, June 14 Photo. *Perf. 13¼*

5675	A2941	88c multi	2.00	.65

Fountain of the Quatre-Vallées, Tarbes — A2942

2019, June 21 Photo. *Perf. 13¼*

5676	A2942	88c multi	2.00	.65

Reuze-Papa and Reuze-Maman Statues, Cassel — A2943

2019, June 27 Photo. *Perf. 13x12¾*

5677	A2943	88c multi	2.00	.65

A2944

A2945

A2946

A2947

A2948

A2949

A2950

A2951

A2952

A2953

A2954

Vacation A2955

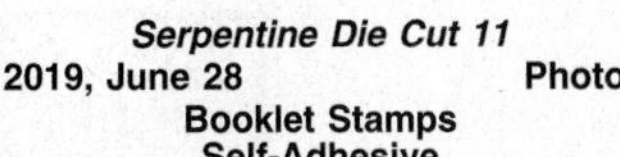

Serpentine Die Cut 11

2019, June 28 Photo.

Booklet Stamps
Self-Adhesive

5678	A2944	(88c) multi	2.00	.65
5679	A2945	(88c) multi	2.00	.65
5680	A2946	(88c) multi	2.00	.65
5681	A2947	(88c) multi	2.00	.65
5682	A2948	(88c) multi	2.00	.65
5683	A2949	(88c) multi	2.00	.65
5684	A2950	(88c) multi	2.00	.65
5685	A2951	(88c) multi	2.00	.65
5686	A2952	(88c) multi	2.00	.65
5687	A2953	(88c) multi	2.00	.65
5688	A2954	(88c) multi	2.00	.65
5689	A2955	(88c) multi	2.00	.65
a.		Booklet pane of 12, #5678-5689	24.00	
		Nos. 5678-5689 (12)	24.00	7.80

Françoise d'Aubigne, Marquise de Maintenon (1635-1719), Second Wife of King Louis XIV — A2956

2019, June 28 Photo. *Perf. 13*

5690	A2956	€1.05 multi	2.40	.80

Values are for stamps with surrounding selvage.

Awarding of Legion of Honor and Croix de Guerre to City of Reims, Cent. A2957

2019, July 5 Engr. *Perf. 13*

5691	A2957	€1.05 multi	2.40	.80

Mediterranean Women's Costumes and Euromed Postal Emblem — A2958

2019, July 5 Photo. *Perf. 13¼*

5692	A2958	€1.30 multi	3.00	1.00

First Man on the Moon, 50th Anniv. A2959

2019, July 19 Photo. *Perf. 13x13¼*

5693	A2959	€1.30 multi	3.00	1.00

Lighthouses
A2960

Designs: No. 5694, Dunkerque Lighthouse. No. 5695, Goury Lighthouse. No. 5696, Ile Vierge Lighthouse. No. 5697, Kéréon Lighthouse. No. 5698, Ar-Men Lighthouse. No. 5699, Pilier Lighthouse. No. 5700, Chassiron Lighthouse. No. 5701, Cordouon Lighthouse. No. 5702, Biarritz Lighthouse. No. 5703, Cap Béar Lighthouse. No. 5704, Cap Camarat Lighthouse. No. 5705, Lavezzi Lighthouse.

Serpentine Die Cut 11

2019, Aug. 2 **Photo.**

Booklet Stamps
Self-Adhesive

5694	A2960	(€1.05) multi	2.40	.80
5695	A2960	(€1.05) multi	2.40	.80
5696	A2960	(€1.05) multi	2.40	.80
5697	A2960	(€1.05) multi	2.40	.80
5698	A2960	(€1.05) multi	2.40	.80
5699	A2960	(€1.05) multi	2.40	.80
5700	A2960	(€1.05) multi	2.40	.80
5701	A2960	(€1.05) multi	2.40	.80
5702	A2960	(€1.05) multi	2.40	.80
5703	A2960	(€1.05) multi	2.40	.80
5704	A2960	(€1.05) multi	2.40	.80
5705	A2960	(€1.05) multi	2.40	.80
a.		Booklet pane of 12, #5694-5705	29.00	
		Nos. 5694-5705 (12)	28.80	9.60

Liberation of Paris, 75th
Anniv. — A2961

2019, Aug. 25 **Photo.** *Perf. 13x12¾*

5706	A2961	€1.30 multi	3.00	1.00

A souvenir sheet containing No. 5706 sold for €4.

Monte
Cinto,
Corsica
A2962

2019, Sept. 6 **Photo.** *Perf. 13¼*

5707	A2962	88c multi	1.90	.65

Astérix
Comic
Strips,
60th Anniv.
A2963

2019, Sept. 6 **Photo.** *Perf. 13x13¼*

5708	A2963	88c multi	1.90	.65

No. 5708 was printed in sheets of 5.

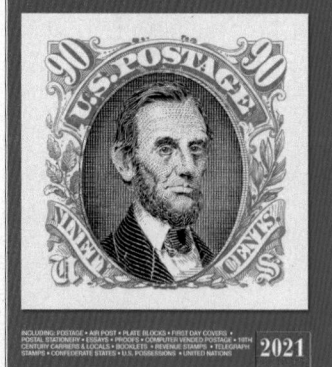

Subject Index of French Commemorative Issues

FRANCE

SEMI-POSTAL STAMPS

No. 162 Surcharged in Red

and

SP2

1914 Unwmk. Typo. *Perf. 14x13½*

B1 A22 10c + 5c red 5.00 4.25
Never hinged 7.00
B2 SP2 10c + 5c red 32.50 3.25
Never hinged 90.00
a. Booklet pane of 10 600.00
Never hinged 800.00

Issue dates: No. B1, Aug. 11; No. B2, Sept. 10.

See Nos. B746a, B746b.

For overprint see Offices in Morocco No. B8.

Widow at Grave SP3

War Orphans SP4

Woman Plowing — SP5

"Trench of Bayonets" SP6

Lion of Belfort SP7

"La Marseillaise" — SP8

1917-19

B3 SP3 2c + 3c vio brn 4.50 5.00
Never hinged 10.00
B4 SP4 5c + 5c grn ('19) 21.00 9.50
Never hinged 60.00
B5 SP5 15c + 10c gray green 30.00 27.50
Never hinged 85.00
B6 SP5 25c + 15c dp bl 80.00 57.50
Never hinged 175.00
B7 SP6 35c + 25c slate & vio 135.00 125.00
Never hinged 350.00
B8 SP7 50c + 50c pale brn & dk brn 225.00 180.00
Never hinged 650.00
B9 SP8 1fr + 1fr cl & mar 425.00 400.00
Never hinged 1,100.
B10 SP8 5fr + 5fr dp bl & blk 1,600. 1,550.
Never hinged 4,000.
Nos. B3-B10 (8) 2,521. 2,355.

See No. B20-B23. For surcharges see No. B12-B19. For similar stamps with euro denominations, see No. 5450.

Hospital Ship and Field Hospital SP9

1918, Aug.

B11 SP9 15c + 5c sl & red 125.00 60.00
Never hinged 250.00

See No. B746d.

Semi-Postal Stamps of 1917-19 Surcharged

1922, Sept. 1

B12 SP3 2c + 1c violet brn .50 *.80*
Never hinged 1.00
B13 SP4 5c + 2½c green .80 *1.25*
Never hinged 1.50
B14 SP5 15c + 5c gray grn 1.25 *1.60*
Never hinged 2.60
B15 SP5 25c + 5c deep bl 2.30 *2.50*
Never hinged 4.75
B16 SP6 35c + 5c slate & vio 13.00 *15.00*
Never hinged 30.00
B17 SP7 50c + 10c pale brn & dk brn 19.00 *24.00*
Never hinged 39.00
a. Pair, one without surcharge
B18 SP8 1fr + 25c cl & mar 32.50 *37.50*
Never hinged 60.00
B19 SP8 5fr + 1fr bl & blk 150.00 *155.00*
Never hinged 275.00
Nos. B12-B19 (8) 219.35 237.65
Set, never hinged 415.00

Style and arrangement of surcharge differs for each denomination.

Types of 1917-19

1926-27

B20 SP3 2c + 1c violet brn 1.50 1.40
Never hinged 4.00
B21 SP7 50c + 10c ol brn & dk brn 20.00 12.50
Never hinged 72.50
B22 SP8 1fr + 25c dp rose & red brn 55.00 42.50
Never hinged 150.00
B23 SP8 5fr + 1fr sl bl & blk 105.00 100.00
Never hinged 240.00
Nos. B20-B23 (4) 181.50 156.40

Sinking Fund Issues

Types of Regular Issues of 1903-07 Surcharged in Red or Blue

1927, Sept. 26

B24 A22 40c + 10c lt blue (R) 5.75 5.75
Never hinged 10.50
B25 A20 50c + 25c green (Bl) 8.25 *9.00*
Never hinged 14.00

Surcharge on No. B25 differs from illustration.

Type of Regular Issue of 1923 Surcharged in Black

B26 A23 1.50fr + 50c orange 14.50 14.00
Never hinged 37.50
a. Pair, one without surcharge *2,000.*
Nos. B24-B26 (3) 28.50 28.75

See Nos. B28-B33, B35-B37, B39-B41.

Industry and Agriculture SP10

1928, May Engr. *Perf. 13½*

B27 SP10 1.50fr + 8.50fr dull blue 140.00 *150.00*
Never hinged 225.00
a. Blue green 500.00 *550.00*
Never hinged 725.00

Types of 1903-23 Issues Surcharged like Nos. B24-B26

1928, Oct. 1 *Perf. 14x13½*

B28 A22 40c + 10c gray lil (R) 13.00 *14.00*
Never hinged 32.50
B29 A20 50c + 25c org brn (Bl) 32.50 29.00
Never hinged 60.00
B30 A23 1.50fr + 50c rose lilac (Bk) 52.50 42.50
Never hinged 100.00
Nos. B28-B30 (3) 98.00 85.50

Types of 1903-23 Issues Surcharged like Nos. B24-B26

1929, Oct. 1

B31 A22 40c + 10c green 18.00 *19.00*
Never hinged 37.50
B32 A20 50c + 25c lilac rose 30.00 30.00
Never hinged 60.00
B33 A23 1.50fr + 50c chestnut 60.00 *65.00*
Never hinged 130.00
Nos. B31-B33 (3) 108.00 114.00

"The Smile of Reims" SP11

1930, Mar. 15 Engr. *Perf. 13*

B34 SP11 1.50fr + 3.50fr red vio 80.00 *82.50*
Never hinged 130.00
a. Booklet pane of 4 300.00
Never hinged 525.00
b. Booklet pane of 8 600.00
Never hinged 1,050.
Complete booklet, #B34b 1,100.

Booklets containing No. B34 have two panes of 4 (No. B34a) connected by a gutter, the complete piece constituting #B34b, which is stapled into the booklet through the gutter. See footnote after No. 4642.

Types of 1903-07 Issues Surcharged like Nos. B24-B25

1930 Oct. 1 *Perf. 14x13½*

B35 A22 40c + 10c cerise 20.00 *21.00*
Never hinged 70.00
B36 A20 50c + 25c gray brown 37.50 *42.50*
Never hinged 120.00
B37 A22 1.50fr + 50c violet 65.00 *70.00*
Never hinged 190.00
Nos. B35-B37 (3) 122.50 133.50

Allegory, French Provinces SP12

1931, Mar. 1 *Perf. 13*

B38 SP12 1.50fr + 3.50fr green 125.00 *140.00*
Never hinged 300.00

Types of 1903-07 Issues Surcharged like Nos. B24-B25

1931, Oct. 1 *Perf. 14x13½*

B39 A22 40c + 10c ol grn 40.00 *45.00*
Never hinged 100.00
B40 A20 50c + 25c gray vio 100.00 *110.00*
Never hinged 235.00
B41 A22 1.50fr + 50c deep red 100.00 *110.00*
Never hinged 200.00
Nos. B39-B41 (3) 240.00 265.00

Catalogue values for unused stamps in this section, from this point to the end of the section, are for Never Hinged items.

"France" Giving Aid to an Intellectual SP13

Symbolic of Music SP14

1935, Dec. 9 Engr. *Perf. 13*

B42 SP13 50c + 10c ultra 4.00 2.50
Hinged 2.50
B43 SP14 50c + 2fr dull red 125.00 45.00
Hinged 55.00

The surtax was for the aid of distressed and exiled intellectuals.

For surcharge see No. B47.

Statue of Liberty — SP15

1936-37

B44 SP15 50c + 25c dk blue ('37) 7.50 5.00
Hinged 4.00
B45 SP15 75c + 50c violet 20.00 10.00
Hinged 9.50

Surtax for the aid of political refugees.

For surcharge see No. B47.

Children of the Unemployed SP16

1936, May

B46 SP16 50c + 10c copper red 7.50 5.00
Hinged 4.50

The surtax was for the aid of children of the unemployed.

No. B43 Surcharged in Black

1936, Nov.

B47 SP14 20c on 50c + 2fr dull red 4.75 3.50
Hinged 3.25

Jacques Callot SP17

Anatole France (Jacques Anatole Thibault) — SP18

Hector Berlioz SP19

Victor Hugo SP20

Auguste Rodin SP21

Louis Pasteur SP22

1936-37 **Engr.**

B48 SP17 20c + 10c brn car 4.50 2.50
Hinged 2.25
B49 SP18 30c + 10c emer ('37) 5.00 2.75
Hinged 2.25
B50 SP19 40c + 10c emer 4.50 2.75
Hinged 2.25
B51 SP20 50c + 10c copper red 8.75 3.75
Hinged 3.75
B52 SP21 90c + 10c rose red ('37) 13.00 6.50
Hinged 6.00
B53 SP22 1.50fr + 50c deep ultra 40.00 20.00
Hinged 20.00
Nos. B48-B53 (6) 75.75 38.25

The surtax was used for relief of unemployed intellectuals.

1938

B54 SP18 30c + 10c brn car 3.00 1.75
Hinged 1.75
B55 SP17 35c + 10c dull green 3.50 2.40
Hinged 2.40
B56 SP19 55c + 10c dull vio 10.00 4.00
Hinged 6.00
B57 SP20 65c + 10c ultra 11.50 4.00
Hinged 6.00
B58 SP21 1fr + 10c car lake 8.50 4.50
Hinged 4.75
B59 SP22 1.75fr + 25c dp blue 35.00 17.00
Hinged 17.00
Nos. B54-B59 (6) 71.50 33.65

Tug of War SP23

Foot Race SP24

Hiking — SP25

1937, June 16

B60 SP23 20c + 10c brown 3.00 2.25
Hinged 1.60
B61 SP24 40c + 10c red brn 3.00 2.25
Hinged 1.60
B62 SP25 50c + 10c black brn 3.00 2.25
Hinged 1.60
Nos. B60-B62 (3) 9.00 6.75

The surtax was for the Recreation Fund of the employees of the Post, Telephone and Telegraph.

Pierre Loti (Louis Marie Julien Viaud) SP26

1937, Aug.

B63 SP26 50c + 20c rose car 7.50 5.00
Hinged 3.75

The surtax was for the Pierre Loti Monument Fund.

"France" and Infant SP27

1937-39

B64 SP27 65c + 25c brown vio 5.25 2.75
Hinged 3.25
B65 SP27 90c + 30c pck bl ('39) 3.50 2.75
Hinged 2.10

The surtax was used for public health work.

Winged Victory of Samothrace — SP28

1937, Aug.

B66 SP28 30c blue green 175.00 40.00
Hinged 65.00
B67 SP28 55c red 175.00 40.00
Hinged 65.00

On sale at the Louvre for 2.50fr. The surtax of 1.65fr was for the benefit of the Louvre Museum.

Jean Baptiste Charcot — SP29

1938-39

B68 SP29 65c + 35c dk bl grn 3.00 3.00
Hinged 1.60
B69 SP29 90c + 35c brt red vio ('39) 30.00 13.50
Hinged 11.00

Surtax for the benefit of French seamen.

Palace of Versailles SP30

1938, May 9

B70 SP30 1.75fr + 75c dp bl 37.50 19.00
Hinged 19.00

Natl. Exposition of Painting and Sculpture at Versailles.

The surtax was for the benefit of the Versailles Concert Society.

French Soldier — SP31

1938, May 16

B71 SP31 55c + 70c brown vio 8.50 5.25
Hinged 4.75
B72 SP31 65c + 1.10fr pck bl 8.50 5.25
Hinged 4.75

The surtax was for a fund to erect a monument to the glory of the French Infantrymen.

Monument — SP32

1938, May 25

B73 SP32 55c + 45c vermilion 22.50 12.50
Hinged 10.00

The surtax was for a fund to erect a monument in honor of the Army Medical Corps.

Reims Cathedral — SP33

1938, July 10

B74 SP33 65c + 35c ultra 17.50 10.50
Hinged 8.50

Completion of the reconstruction of Reims Cathedral, July 10, 1938.

"France" Welcoming Her Sons — SP34

1938, Aug. 8

B75 SP34 65c + 60c rose car 8.50 5.75
Hinged 4.00

The surtax was for the benefit of French volunteers repatriated from Spain.

Curie Issue

Common Design Type

1938, Sept. 1

B76 CD80 1.75fr + 50c dp ultra 21.00 12.50
Hinged 8.75

Victory Parade Passing Arc de Triomphe SP36

1938, Oct. 8

B77 SP36 65c + 35c brown car 5.75 4.50
Hinged 3.25

20th anniversary of the Armistice.

Student and Nurse — SP37

1938, Dec. 1

B78 SP37 65c + 60c pck blue 15.00 8.25
Hinged 8.00

The surtax was for Student Relief.

Blind Man and Radio SP38

1938, Dec.

B79 SP38 90c + 25c brown vio 15.00 9.00
Hinged 8.00

The surtax was used to help provide radios for the blind.

Civilian Facing Firing Squad — SP39

1939, Feb. 1

B80 SP39 90c + 35c black brn 17.00 10.50
Hinged 8.75

The surtax was used to erect a monument to civilian victims of World War I.

Red Cross Nurse — SP40

1939, Mar. 24

B81 SP40 90c + 35c dk sl grn, turq bl & red 13.00 8.25
Hinged 6.75

75th anniv. of the Intl. Red Cross Society. See No. B746c.

Army Engineer SP41

1939, Apr. 3

B82 SP41 70c + 50c vermilion 12.50 8.25
Hinged 6.00

Army Engineering Corps. The surtax was used to erect a monument to those members who died in World War I.

Ministry of Post, Telegraph and Telephone SP42

1939, Apr. 8

B83 SP42 90c + 35c turq blue 37.50 20.00
Hinged 19.00

The surtax was used to aid orphans of employees of the postal system. Opening of the new building for the Ministry of Post, Telegraph and Telephones.

Mother and Child — SP43

1939, Apr. 24

B84 SP43 90c + 35c red 3.75 2.50
Hinged 2.40

The surtax was used to aid children of the unemployed.

50th Anniv. of the Eiffel Tower — SP44

1939, May 5

B85 SP44 90c + 50c red violet 15.00 9.00
Hinged 8.75

The surtax was used for celebration festivities. For stamp with euro denominations see No. 5449c.

Puvis de Chavannes — SP45

Claude Debussy SP46

Honoré de Balzac SP47

Claude Bernard SP48

1939-40

B86 SP45 40c + 10c ver 1.75 1.00
Hinged .80
B87 SP46 70c + 10c brn vio 8.25 2.50
Hinged 3.50
B87A SP46 80c + 10c brn vio ('40) 9.00 7.50
Hinged 4.25
B88 SP47 90c + 10c brt red vio 7.25 2.50
Hinged 3.25
B88A SP47 1fr + 10c brt red vio ('40) 9.00 7.50
Hinged 4.25
B89 SP48 2.25fr + 25c brt ultra 28.00 11.50
Hinged 14.50
B89A SP48 2.50fr + 25c brt ultra ('40) 9.00 7.50
Hinged 4.25
Nos. B86-B89A (7) 72.25 40.00

The surtax was used to aid unemployed intellectuals.

Mothers and Children
SP49 SP50

1939, June 15

B90 SP49 70c + 80c bl, grn & vio 5.25 4.50
Hinged 3.25
B91 SP50 90c + 60c dk brn, dl vio & brn 8.50 5.25
Hinged 4.75

The surtax was used to aid France's repopulation campaign.

"The Letter" by Jean Honoré Fragonard — SP51

1939, July 6

B92 SP51 40c + 60c multi 4.25 2.75
Hinged 2.40

The surtax was used for the Postal Museum. See footnote after No. 4642.

Statue of Widow and Children — SP52

1939, July 20

B93 SP52 70c + 30c brown vio 25.00 12.00
Hinged 12.00

Surtax for the benefit of French seamen.

French Soldier SP53

Colonial Trooper SP54

1940, Feb. 15

B94 SP53 40c + 60c sepia 3.25 2.75
Hinged 1.50
B95 SP54 1fr + 50c turq blue 3.25 2.75
Hinged 1.50

The surtax was used to assist the families of mobilized men.

World Map Showing French Possessions — SP55

1940, Apr. 15

B96 SP55 1fr + 25c scarlet 2.50 1.50
Hinged 1.50

Marshal Joseph J. C. Joffre SP56

Marshal Ferdinand Foch — SP57

Gen. Joseph S. Gallieni SP58

Woman Plowing SP59

1940, May 1

B97 SP56 80c + 45c choc 6.00 3.75
Hinged 3.00
B98 SP57 1fr + 50c dk vio 4.50 3.00
Hinged 2.50
B99 SP58 1.50fr + 50c brown red 4.50 3.00
Hinged 2.50
B100 SP59 2.50fr + 50c indigo & dl bl 12.00 7.50
Hinged 6.00
Nos. B97-B100 (4) 27.00 17.25

The surtax was used for war charities. See footnote after No. 4642.

Doctor, Nurse, Soldier and Family SP60

Nurse and Wounded Soldier SP61

1940, May 12

B101 SP60 80c + 1fr dk grn & red 7.25 3.50
Hinged 3.50
B102 SP61 1fr + 2fr sep & red 9.00 3.50
Hinged 3.50

The surtax was used for the Red Cross. See Nos. B747a, B747e.

Nurse with Injured Children — SP62

1940, Nov. 12

B103 SP62 1fr + 2fr sepia 1.25 .80
Hinged .80

The surtax was used for victims of the war.

Wheat Harvest SP63

Sowing SP64

Picking Grapes SP65

Grazing Cattle SP66

1940, Dec. 2

B104 SP63 80c + 2fr brn blk 3.00 1.50
Hinged 1.40
B105 SP64 1fr + 2fr chestnut 3.00 1.50
Hinged 1.40
B106 SP65 1.50fr + 2fr brt vio 3.00 1.50
Hinged 1.40
B107 SP66 2.50fr + 2fr dp grn 3.25 1.75
Hinged 1.75
Nos. B104-B107 (4) 12.25 6.25

The surtax was for national relief.

Prisoners of War
SP67 SP68

1941, Jan. 1

B108 SP67 80c + 5fr dark grn 1.50 1.50
B109 SP68 1fr + 5fr rose brn 1.50 1.50

The surtax was for prisoners of war.

Science Fighting Cancer SP69

1941, Feb. 20

B110 SP69 2.50fr + 50c slate blk & brn 1.50 1.25

Surtax used for the control of cancer.

No. 417 Surcharged in Blue

1941, Mar. 4

B111 A109 1fr + 10c crimson .25 .25

Men Hauling Coal SP70

"France" Aiding Needy Man SP71

1941

B112	SP70	1fr + 2fr sepia	2.25	1.00
B113	SP71	2.50fr + 7.50fr dk bl	7.50	2.00

The surtax was for Marshal Pétain's National Relief Fund.

Liner Pasteur SP72

1941, July 17 **Red Surcharge**

B114 SP72 1fr + 1fr on 70c dk bl grn .30 .30

World Map, Mercator Projection SP73

1941

B115 SP73 1fr + 1fr multi .65 .45

Fisherman — SP74

1941, Oct. 23

B116 SP74 1fr + 9fr dk blue grn .80 .70

Surtax for benefit of French seamen.

Arms of Various Cities

Nancy SP75

Lille SP76

Rouen SP77

Bordeaux SP78

Toulouse SP79

Clermont-Ferrand SP80

Marseille SP81

Lyon SP82

Rennes SP83

Reims SP84

Montpellier SP85

Paris SP86

1941 ***Perf. 14x13***

B117	SP75	20c + 30c brn blk	2.75	2.00
B118	SP76	40c + 60c org brn	2.75	2.00
B119	SP77	50c + 70c grnsh blue	2.75	2.00
B120	SP78	70c + 80c rose vio	2.75	2.00
B121	SP79	80c + 1fr dp rose	2.75	2.00
B122	SP80	1fr + 1fr black	2.75	2.00
B123	SP81	1.50fr + 2fr dk bl	2.75	2.00
B124	SP82	2fr + 2fr dk vio	2.75	2.00
B125	SP83	2.50fr + 3fr brt grn	2.75	2.00
B126	SP84	3fr + 5fr org brn	2.75	2.00
B127	SP85	5fr + 6fr brt ultra	2.75	2.00
B128	SP86	10fr + 10fr dk red	2.75	2.00
		Nos. B117-B128 (12)	33.00	24.00

Count de La Pérouse SP87

1942, Mar. 23 ***Perf. 13***

B129 SP87 2.50fr + 7.50fr ultra 1.25 1.40

Jean Francois de Galaup de La Pérouse, (1741-88), French navigator and explorer. The surtax was for National Relief.

Planes over Fields SP88

1942, Apr. 4

B130 SP88 1.50fr + 3.50fr lt vio 2.40 2.40

The surtax was for the benefit of French airmen and their familes.

Alexis Chabrier SP89

1942, May 18

B131 SP89 2fr + 3fr sepia 1.25 1.25

Emmanuel Chabrier (1841-1894), composer, birth centenary. The surtax was for works of charity among musicians.

Symbolical of French Colonial Empire SP90

1942, May 18

B132 SP90 1.50fr + 8.50fr black 1.10 1.10

The surtax was for National Relief.

Jean de Vienne SP91

1942, June 16

B133 SP91 1.50fr + 8.50fr sepia 1.10 1.10

600th anniv. of the birth of Jean de Vienne, 1st admiral of France. The surtax was for the benefit of French seamen.

Type of Regular Issue, 1941 Surcharged in Carmine

1942, Sept. 10 ***Perf. 14x13½***

B134 A116 1.50fr + 50c brt ultra .25 .25

The surtax was for national relief ("Secours National").

Arms of Various Cities

Chambéry SP92

La Rochelle SP93

Poitiers SP94

Orléans SP95

Grenoble SP96

Angers SP97

Dijon SP98

Limoges SP99

Le Havre SP100

Nantes SP101

Nice SP102

St. Etienne SP103

Perf. 14x13

1942, Oct. **Unwmk.** **Engr.**

B135	SP92	50c + 60c blk	3.50	3.25
B136	SP93	60c + 70c grnsh blue	3.50	3.25
B137	SP94	80c + 1fr rose	3.50	3.25
B138	SP95	1fr + 1.30fr dk green	3.50	3.25
B139	SP96	1.20fr + 1.50fr rose vio	3.50	3.25
B140	SP97	1.50fr + 1.80fr slate bl	3.50	3.25
B141	SP98	2fr + 2.30fr deep rose	3.50	3.25
B142	SP99	2.40fr + 2.80fr slate grn	3.50	3.25
B143	SP100	3fr + 3.50fr dp violet	3.50	3.25
B144	SP101	4fr + 5fr lt ultra	3.50	3.25
B145	SP102	4.50fr + 6fr red	3.50	3.25
B146	SP103	5fr + 7fr brt red vio	3.50	3.25
		Nos. B135-B146 (12)	42.00	39.00

The surtax was for national relief.

Tricolor Legion SP104

1942, Oct. 12 ***Perf. 13***

B147	SP104	1.20 + 8.80fr dk blue	10.00	10.00
a.		Vert. pair, #B147, B148 + albino impression	22.50	25.00
B148	SP104	1.20 + 8.80fr crim	10.00	10.00

These stamps were printed in sheets of 20 stamps and 5 albino impressions arranged: 2 horizontal rows of 5 dark blue stamps, 1 row of 5 albino impressions, and 2 rows of 5 crimson stamps.

Marshal Henri Philippe Pétain SP105 SP106

1943, Feb. 8

No.	Design	Description	Unused	Used
B149	SP105	1fr + 10fr rose red	2.75	2.75
B150	SP105	1fr + 10fr blue	2.75	2.75
B151	SP106	2fr + 12fr rose red	2.75	2.75
B152	SP106	2fr + 12fr blue	2.75	2.75
a.		Strip, #B149-B152 + label	12.50	12.50

The surtax was for national relief. Printed in sheets of 20, the 10 blue stamps at left, the 10 rose red at right, separated by a vert. row of 5 white labels bearing a tri-colored battle-ax.

Marshal Pétain — SP107

"Work" — SP108

"Family" SP109

"State" SP110

Marshal Pétain — SP111

1943, June 7

No.	Design	Description	Unused	Used
B153	SP107	1.20fr + 1.40fr dull vio	12.00	11.00
B154	SP108	1.50fr + 2.50fr red	12.00	11.00
B155	SP109	2.40fr + 7fr brn	12.00	11.00
B156	SP110	4fr + 10fr dk violet	12.00	11.00
B157	SP111	5fr + 15fr red brn	12.00	11.00
a.		Strip of 5, #B153-B157	100.00	100.00

Pétain's 87th birthday.

The surtax was for national relief.

Civilians Under Air Attack — SP112

1943, Aug. 23

No.	Design	Description	Unused	Used
B158	SP112	1.50fr + 3.50fr black	.40	.40

Surtax was for bomb victims at Billancourt, Dunkirk, Lorient, Saint-Nazaire.

Civilians Doing Farm Work — SP113

Prisoner's Family Doing Farm Work SP114

1943, Sept. 27

No.	Design	Description	Unused	Used
B159	SP113	1.50fr + 8.50fr sepia	.75	.75
B160	SP114	2.40fr + 7.60fr dk grn	.80	.80

The surtax was for families of war prisoners.

Michel de Montaigne — SP115

1.20fr+1.50fr, Francois Clouet. 1.50fr+3fr, Ambrose Paré. 2.40fr+4fr, Chevalier Pierre de Bayard. 4fr+6fr, Duke of Sully. 5fr+10fr, Henri IV.

1943, Oct. 2

No.	Design	Description	Unused	Used
B161	SP115	60c + 80c Prus green	1.75	1.75
B162	SP115	1.20fr + 1.50fr black	1.50	1.50
B163	SP115	1.50fr + 3fr deep ultra	1.50	1.50
B164	SP115	2.40fr + 4fr red	1.50	1.50
B165	SP115	4fr + 6fr dull brn red	1.75	1.75
B166	SP115	5fr + 10fr dull green	1.75	1.75
		Nos. B161-B166 (6)	9.75	9.75

The surtax was for national relief. Issued to honor famous 16th century Frenchmen.

Picardy Costume — SP121

Designs: 18th Century Costumes: 1.20fr+2fr, Brittany. 1.50fr+4fr, Ile de France. 2.40+5fr, Burgundy. 4fr+6fr, Auvergne. 5fr+7fr, Provence.

1943, Dec. 27

No.	Design	Description	Unused	Used
B167	SP121	60c + 1.30fr sepia	1.60	1.60
B168	SP121	1.20fr + 2fr lt vio	1.60	1.60
B169	SP121	1.50fr + 4fr turq blue	1.60	1.60
B170	SP121	2.40fr + 5fr rose car	1.60	1.60
B171	SP121	4fr + 6fr chlky blue	2.50	2.50
B172	SP121	5fr + 7fr red	2.50	2.50
		Nos. B167-B172 (6)	11.40	11.40

The surtax was for national relief. See footnote after No. 4642.

Admiral Tourville — SP127

1944, Feb. 21

No.	Design	Description	Unused	Used
B173	SP127	4fr + 6fr dull red brn	.60	.60

300th anniv. of the birth of Admiral Anne-Hilarion de Cotentin Tourville (1642-1701).

Charles Gounod — SP128

1944, Mar. 27 ***Perf. 14x13***

No.	Design	Description	Unused	Used
B174	SP128	1.50fr + 3.50fr sepia	.75	.60

50th anniv. of the death of Charles Gounod, composer (1818-1893).

Marshal Pétain SP129

Farming SP130

Industry SP131

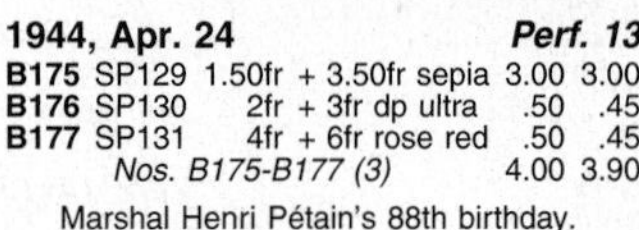

1944, Apr. 24 ***Perf. 13***

No.	Design	Description	Unused	Used
B175	SP129	1.50fr + 3.50fr sepia	3.00	3.00
B176	SP130	2fr + 3fr dp ultra	.50	.45
B177	SP131	4fr + 6fr rose red	.50	.45
		Nos. B175-B177 (3)	4.00	3.90

Marshal Henri Pétain's 88th birthday.

Modern Streamliner, 19th Cent. Train — SP132

1944, Aug. 14

No.	Design	Description	Unused	Used
B178	SP132	4fr + 6fr black	1.50	1.50

Centenary of the Paris-Rouen, Paris-Orléans railroad.

Molière (Jean-Baptiste Poquelin) — SP133

Designs: 80c+2.20fr, Jules Hardouin Mansart. 1.20fr+2.80fr, Blaise Pascal. 1.50fr+3.50fr, Louis II of Bourbon. 2fr+4fr, Jean-Baptiste Colbert. 4fr+6fr, Louis XIV.

1944, July 31

No.	Design	Description	Unused	Used
B179	SP133	50c + 1.50fr rose car	1.50	1.00
B180	SP133	80c + 2.20fr dk green	1.50	1.00
B181	SP133	1.20fr + 2.80fr black	1.50	1.00
B182	SP133	1.50fr + 3.50fr brt ultra	1.50	1.00
B183	SP133	2fr + 4fr dull brn red	1.50	1.00
B184	SP133	4fr + 6fr red	1.50	1.00
		Nos. B179-B184 (6)	9.00	6.00

Noted 17th century Frenchmen.

Angoulême SP139

Chartres SP140

Amiens SP141

Beauvais SP142

Albi — SP143

1944, Nov. 20

No.	Design	Description	Unused	Used
B185	SP139	50c + 1.50fr black	.60	.40
B186	SP140	80c + 2.20fr rose vio	.60	.40
B187	SP141	1.20fr + 2.80fr brn car	.60	.40
B188	SP142	1.50fr + 3.50fr dp blue	.60	.40
B189	SP143	4fr + 6fr orange red	.60	.40
		Nos. B185-B189 (5)	3.00	2.00

French Cathedrals.

Coat of Arms of Renouard de Villayer — SP144

1944, Dec. 9 **Engr.**

No.	Design	Description	Unused	Used
B190	SP144	1.50fr + 3.50fr dp brn	.25	.25

Stamp Day.

Sarah Bernhardt — SP145

1945, May 16 **Unwmk.** ***Perf. 13***

No.	Design	Description	Unused	Used
B191	SP145	4fr + 1fr dk violet brn	.30	.25

100th anniv. of the birth of Sarah Bernhardt, actress.

War Victims SP146

1945, May 16
B192 SP146 4fr + 6fr dk violet brn .25 .25

The surtax was for war victims of the P.T.T.

Tuberculosis Patient — SP147

1945, May 16 Typo. *Perf. 14x13½*
B193 SP147 2fr + 1fr red orange .25 .25

Surtax for the aid of tuberculosis victims.
For surcharge see No. 561.

Boy and Girl — SP148

1945, July 9 Engr. *Perf. 13*
B194 SP148 4fr + 2fr Prus green .25 .25

The surtax was used for child welfare.

Burning of Oradour Church — SP149

1945, Oct. 13
B195 SP149 4fr + 2fr sepia .25 .25

Destruction of Oradour, June, 1944.

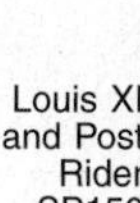

Louis XI and Post Rider SP150

1945, Oct. 13
B196 SP150 2fr + 3fr deep ultra .35 .25

Stamp Day.
For overprint see French West Africa No. B2.

Ruins of Dunkirk SP151

Ruins of Rouen SP152

Ruins of Caen SP153

Ruins of Saint-Malo SP154

1945, Nov. 5
B197 SP151 1.50fr + 1.50fr red brown .40 .30
B198 SP152 2fr + 2fr violet .40 .30
B199 SP153 2.40fr + 2.60fr blue .40 .30
B200 SP154 4fr + 4fr black .40 .30
Nos. B197-B200 (4) 1.60 1.20

The surtax was to aid the suffering residents of Dunkirk, Rouen, Caen and Saint Malo.

Alfred Fournier SP155

Henri Becquerel SP156

1946, Feb. 4 Engr. *Perf. 13*
B201 SP155 2fr + 3fr red brown .30 .25
B202 SP156 2fr + 3fr violet .30 .25

Issued to raise funds for the fight against venereal disease (No. B201) and for the struggle against cancer (No. B202).
No. B202 for the 50th anniv. of the discovery of radioactivity by Henri Becquerel.
See No. B221.

Church of the Invalides, Paris — SP157

1946, Mar. 11
B203 SP157 4fr + 6fr red brown .30 .25

The surtax was to aid disabled war veterans. For stamp with euro denominations, see No. 5449b.

French Warships SP158

1946, Apr. 8
B204 SP158 2fr + 3fr gray black .75 .40

The surtax was for naval charities.

"The Letter" by Jean Siméon Chardin — SP159

1946, May 25
B205 SP159 2fr + 3fr brown red .40 .30

The surtax was used for the Postal Museum.

Fouquet de la Varane — SP160

1946, June 29
B206 SP160 3fr + 2fr sepia .50 .25

Stamp Day.

François Villon — SP161

Designs: 3fr+1fr, Jean Fouquet. 4fr+3fr, Philippe de Commynes. 5fr+4fr, Joan of Arc. 6fr+5fr, Jean de Gerson. 10fr+6fr, Charles VII.

1946, Oct. 28
B207 SP161 2fr + 1fr dk Prus grn 1.25 .90
B208 SP161 3fr + 1fr dk blue vio 1.25 .90
B209 SP161 4fr + 3fr henna brn 1.25 .90
B210 SP161 5fr + 4fr ultra 1.25 .90
B211 SP161 6fr + 5fr sepia 1.25 .90
B212 SP161 10fr + 6fr red 1.25 .90
Nos. B207-B212 (6) 7.50 5.40

Church of St. Sernin, Toulouse SP167

Notre Dame du Port, Clermont-Ferrand SP168

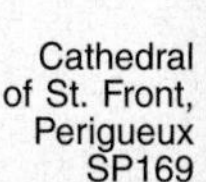
Cathedral of St. Front, Perigueux SP169

Cathedral of St. Julien, Le Mans SP170

Cathedral of Notre Dame, Paris — SP171

1947 Engr.
B213 SP167 1fr + 1fr car rose .85 .60
B214 SP168 3fr + 2fr dk bl vio 2.25 1.40
B215 SP169 4fr + 3fr henna brn 1.10 .90
B216 SP170 6fr + 4fr dp bl 1.10 .90
B217 SP171 10fr + 6fr dk gray grn 2.25 1.60
Nos. B213-B217 (5) 7.55 5.40

See No. 5035c.

François Michel le Tellier de Louvois — SP172

1947, Mar. 15
B218 SP172 4.50fr + 5.50fr car rose 1.10 .55

Stamp Day, Mar. 15, 1947.

Submarine Pens, Shipyard and Monument SP173

1947, Aug. 2
B219 SP173 6fr + 4fr bluish black .50 .30

British commando raid on the Nazi U-boat base at St. Nazaire, 1942.

Liberty Highway Marker — SP174

1947, Sept. 5
B220 SP174 6fr + 4fr dk green .75 .55

The surtax was to help defray maintenance costs of the Liberty Highway.

Fournier Type of 1946

1947, Oct. 20
B221 SP155 2fr + 3fr indigo .30 .25

Louis Braille — SP175

1948, Jan. 19
B222 SP175 6fr + 4fr purple .30 .25

Etienne Arago — SP176

1948, Mar. 6

B223 SP176 6fr + 4fr black brn .45 .25

Stamp Day, March 6-7, 1948.

Alphonse de Lamartine — SP177

Designs: 3fr+2fr, Alexandre A. Ledru-Rollin. 4fr+3fr, Louis Blanc. 5fr+4fr, Albert (Alexandre Martin). 6fr+5fr, Pierre J. Proudhon. 10fr+6fr, Louis Auguste Blanqui. 15fr+7fr, Armand Barbés. 20fr+8fr, Dennis A. Affre.

1948, Apr. 5 Engr. *Perf. 13*

B224	SP177	1fr + 1fr dk grn	1.10	.75
B225	SP177	3fr + 2fr henna brn	1.10	.75
B226	SP177	4fr + 3fr vio brn	1.10	.75
B227	SP177	5fr + 4fr lt bl grn	2.50	1.50
B228	SP177	6fr + 5fr indigo	2.25	1.10
B229	SP177	10fr + 6fr car rose	2.25	1.10
B230	SP177	15fr + 7fr sl blk	2.50	1.50
B231	SP177	20fr + 8fr purple	2.50	1.50
		Nos. B224-B231 (8)	15.30	8.95

Centenary of the Revolution of 1848.

Dr. Léon Charles Albert Calmette SP178

1948, June 18

B232 SP178 6fr + 4fr dk grnsh bl .75 .35

1st Intl. Congress on the Calmette-Guerin bacillus vaccine.

Farmer — SP179

Designs: 5fr+3fr, Fisherman. 8fr+4fr, Miner. 10fr+6fr, Metal worker.

1949, Feb. 14

B233	SP179	3fr + 1fr claret	.65	.45
B234	SP179	5fr + 3fr dk blue	.75	.45
B235	SP179	8fr + 4fr indigo	.75	.45
B236	SP179	10fr + 6fr dk red	.80	.45
		Nos. B233-B236 (4)	2.95	1.80

Étienne François de Choiseul and Post Cart — SP180

1949, Mar. 26

B237 SP180 15fr + 5fr dk green .80 .45

Stamp Day, Mar. 26-27, 1949.

Baron de la Brède et de Montesquieu SP181

Designs: 8fr+2fr, Voltaire. 10fr+3fr, Antoine Watteau. 12fr+4fr, Georges de Buffon. 15fr+5fr, Joseph F. Dupleix. 25fr+10fr, A. R. J. Turgot.

1949, Nov. 14

B238	SP181	5fr + 1fr dk grn	2.50	1.50
B239	SP181	8fr + 2fr indigo	2.50	1.50
B240	SP181	10fr + 3fr brn red	3.00	1.90
B241	SP181	12fr + 4fr purple	3.50	1.90
B242	SP181	15fr + 5fr rose car	3.75	2.25
B243	SP181	25fr + 10fr ultra	4.50	3.00
		Nos. B238-B243 (6)	19.75	12.05

"Spring" SP182

Designs: 8fr+2fr, Summer. 12fr+3fr, Autumn. 15fr+4fr, Winter.

1949, Dec. 19

B244	SP182	5fr + 1fr green	1.50	.90
B245	SP182	8fr + 2fr yel org	1.90	1.10
B246	SP182	12fr + 3fr purple	1.90	1.50
B247	SP182	15fr + 4fr dp blue	3.50	1.75
		Nos. B244-B247 (4)	8.80	5.25

Postman — SP183

1950, Mar. 11

B248 SP183 12fr + 3fr dp bl 3.00 1.75

Stamp Day, Mar. 11-12, 1950. See footnote after No. 4642.

André de Chénier — SP184

8fr+3fr, J. L. David. 10fr+4fr, Lazare Carnot. 12fr+5fr, G. J. Danton. 15fr+6fr, Maximilian Robespierre. 20fr+10fr, Louis Hoche.

1950, July 10 Engr. *Perf. 13*

Frames in Indigo

B249	SP184	5fr + 2fr brn vio	10.00	5.25
B250	SP184	8fr + 3fr blk brn	10.00	5.50
B251	SP184	10fr + 4fr lake	11.00	5.75
B252	SP184	12fr + 5fr red brn	13.00	6.00
B253	SP184	15fr + 6fr dk grn	14.00	6.00
B254	SP184	20fr + 10fr dk vio bl	14.00	6.00
		Nos. B249-B254 (6)	72.00	34.50

Alexandre Brongniart, Bust by Houdon — SP185

15fr+3fr, "L'Amour" by Etienne M. Falconet.

1950, Dec. 22

B255	SP185	8fr + 2fr ind & car	2.00	1.25
B256	SP185	15fr + 3fr red brn & car	2.25	1.25

The surtax was for the Red Cross.

Mail Car Interior — SP186

1951, Mar. 10 Unwmk. *Perf. 13*

B257 SP186 12fr + 3fr lilac gray 3.00 2.25

Stamp Day, Mar. 10-11, 1951.

Alfred de Musset — SP187

8fr+2fr, Eugène Delacroix. 10fr+3fr, J.-L. Gay-Lussac. 12fr+4fr, Robert Surcouf. 15fr+5fr, C. M. Talleyrand. 30fr+10fr, Napoleon I.

Frames in Dark Brown

1951, June 2

B258	SP187	5fr + 1fr dk grn	5.25	3.00
B259	SP187	8fr + 2fr vio brn	7.50	3.00
B260	SP187	10fr + 3fr grnsh black	6.75	3.00
B261	SP187	12fr + 4fr dk vio brn	6.75	3.75
B262	SP187	15fr + 5fr brn car	6.75	3.75
B263	SP187	30fr + 10fr indigo	12.00	6.00
		Nos. B258-B263 (6)	45.00	22.50

Child at Prayer by Le Maître de Moulins SP188

18th Century Child by Quentin de la Tour SP189

1951, Dec. 15 Cross in Red

B264	SP188	12fr + 3fr dk brown	3.00	1.75
B265	SP189	15fr + 5fr dp ultra	3.50	2.00

The surtax was for the Red Cross.

Stagecoach of 1844 SP190

1952, Mar. 8 *Perf. 13*

B266 SP190 12fr + 3fr dp green 3.50 2.25

Stamp Day, Mar. 8, 1952.

Gustave Flaubert — SP191

Portraits: 12fr+3fr, Edouard Manet. 15fr+4fr, Camille Saint-Saens. 18fr+5fr, Henri Poincaré. 20fr+6fr, Georges-Eugene Haussmann. 30fr+7fr, Adolphe Thiers.

1952, Oct. 18

Frames in Dark Brown

B267	SP191	8fr + 2fr dk blue	6.75	3.00
B268	SP191	12fr + 3fr vio blue	6.75	3.00
B269	SP191	15fr + 4fr dk grn	6.75	3.00
B270	SP191	18fr + 5fr dk brn	7.50	3.75
B271	SP191	20fr + 6fr car	8.25	4.50
B272	SP191	30fr + 7fr purple	9.00	4.50
		Nos. B267-B272 (6)	45.00	21.75

Cupid from Diana Fountain Versailles SP192

15fr+5fr, Similar detail, cupid facing left.

1952, Dec. 13 Cross in Red

B273	SP192	12fr + 3fr dk grn	4.25	2.50
B274	SP192	15fr + 5fr indigo	4.25	2.50
a.		Booklet pane of 10	225.00	
		Complete booklet	375.00	

The surtax was for the Red Cross.

Count d'Argenson SP193

1953, Mar. 14

B275 SP193 12fr + 3fr dp blue 2.50 1.50

Day of the Stamp. Surtax for the Red Cross.

St. Bernard — SP194

12fr+3fr, Olivier de Serres. 15fr+4fr, Jean Philippe Rameau. 18fr+5fr, Gaspard Monge. 20fr+6fr, Jules Michelet. 30fr+7fr, Marshal Hubert Lyautey.

1953, July 9

B276	SP194	8fr + 2fr ultra	6.00	3.00
B277	SP194	12fr + 3fr dk grn	6.00	3.00
B278	SP194	15fr + 4fr brn car	9.00	4.50
B279	SP194	18fr + 5fr dk blue	10.00	5.25
B280	SP194	20fr + 6fr dk pur	10.00	5.25
B281	SP194	30fr + 7fr brown	10.00	5.25
		Nos. B276-B281 (6)	51.00	26.25

The surtax was for the Red Cross.

Madame Vigée-Lebrun and her Daughter — SP195

Design: 15fr+5fr, "The Return from Baptism," by Louis Le Nain.

1953, Dec. 12 **Cross in Red**

B282 SP195 12fr + 3fr red brn 7.50 3.75
a. Bklt. pane, 4 each, gutter btwn. 85.00
B283 SP195 15fr + 5fr indigo 10.00 5.25

The surtax was for the Red Cross.

Count Antoine de La Vallette — SP196

1954, Mar. 20 **Engr.** ***Perf. 13***

B284 SP196 12fr + 3fr dp grn & choc 3.75 2.25

Stamp Day, Mar. 20, 1954.

Louis IX — SP197

Portraits: 15fr+5fr, Jacques Benigne Bossuet. 18fr+6fr, Sadi Carnot. 20fr+7fr, Antoine Bourdelle. 25fr+8fr, Dr. Emile Roux. 30fr+10fr, Paul Valéry.

1954, July 10

B285 SP197 12fr + 4fr dp bl 17.50 10.00
B286 SP197 15fr + 5fr pur 21.00 10.00
B287 SP197 18fr + 6fr dk brn 21.00 10.00
B288 SP197 20fr + 7fr crim 26.00 13.00
B289 SP197 25fr + 8fr ind 26.00 13.00
B290 SP197 30fr + 10fr dp claret 26.00 13.00
Nos. B285-B290 (6) 137.50 69.00

See Nos. B303-B308, B312-B317.

"The Sick Child," by Eugene Carrière — SP198

Design: 15fr+5fr, "Young Girl with Doves," by Jean Baptiste Greuze.

1954, Dec. 18 **Cross in Red**

B291 SP198 12fr + 3fr vio gray & indigo 10.00 4.50
a. Bklt. pane, 4 each, gutter btwn. 110.00
B292 SP198 15fr + 5fr dk brn & org brn 10.50 6.00

No. B291a for 90th anniv. of the Red Cross.
The surtax was for the Red Cross.

Balloon Post, 1870 SP199

1955, Mar. 19 **Unwmk.** ***Perf. 13***

B293 SP199 12fr + 3fr multi 3.75 2.25

Stamp Day, Mar. 19-20, 1955.

King Philip II — SP200

Portraits: 15fr+6fr, Francois de Malherbé. 18fr+7fr, Sebastien de Vauban. 25fr+8fr, Charles G. de Vergennes. 30fr+9fr, Pierre S. de Laplace. 50fr+15fr, Pierre Auguste Renoir.

1955, June 11

B294 SP200 12fr + 5fr brt pur 13.50 7.50
B295 SP200 15fr + 6fr dp bl 13.50 7.50
B296 SP200 18fr + 7fr dp green 13.50 7.50
B297 SP200 25fr + 8fr gray 19.00 9.00
B298 SP200 30fr + 9fr rose brn 26.00 10.00
B299 SP200 50fr + 15fr blue grn 26.00 11.00
Nos. B294-B299 (6) 111.50 52.50

See Nos. B321-B326.

Child with Cage by Pigalle — SP201

Design: 15fr+5fr, Child with Goose, by Boethus of Chalcedon.

1955, Dec. 17 **Cross in Red**

B300 SP201 12fr + 3fr claret 6.50 3.75
B301 SP201 15fr + 5fr dk bl 5.25 3.00
a. Booklet pane of 10 150.00
Complete booklet 300.00

The surtax was for the Red Cross.

Francois of Taxis SP202

1956, Mar. 17 **Engr.** ***Perf. 13***

B302 SP202 12fr + 3fr ultra, grn & dk brn 2.25 1.10

Stamp Day, Mar. 17-18, 1956.

Portrait Type of 1954

Portraits: No. 303, Guillaume Budé. No. B304, Jean Goujon. No. B305, Samuel de Champlain. No. B306, Jean Simeon Chardin. No. B307, Maurice Barrès. No. B308, Maurice Ravel.

1956, June 9 ***Perf. 13***

B303 SP197 12fr + 3fr saph 4.00 3.00
B304 SP197 12fr + 3fr lil gray 4.00 3.00
B305 SP197 12fr + 3fr brt red 5.25 3.00
B306 SP197 15fr + 5fr green 6.75 4.50
B307 SP197 15fr + 5fr vio brn 6.75 4.50
B308 SP197 15fr + 5fr dp vio 9.00 4.50
Nos. B303-B308 (6) 35.75 22.50

Peasant Boy by Le Nain — SP203

Design: 15fr+5fr, Gilles by Watteau.

1956, Dec. 8 **Unwmk.**
Cross in Red

B309 SP203 12fr + 3fr ol gray 2.25 1.10
a. Bklt. pane, 4 ea, gutter btwn. 40.00
B310 SP203 15fr + 5fr rose lake 2.50 1.25

The surtax was for the Red Cross.

Genoese Felucca, 1750 SP204

1957, Mar. 16 ***Perf. 13***

B311 SP204 12fr +3fr bluish gray & brn blk 1.60 1.00

Day of the Stamp, Mar. 16, 1957, and honoring the Maritime Postal Service.

Portrait Type of 1954

1957, June 15

Portraits: No. B312, Jean de Joinville. No. B313, Bernard Palissy. No. B314, Quentin de la Tour. No. B315, Hugues Félicité Robert de Lamennais. No. B316, George Sand. No. B317, Jules Guesde.

B312 SP197 12fr + 3fr ol gray & ol grn 1.90 1.10
B313 SP197 12fr + 3fr grnsh blk & grnsh bl 1.90 1.10
B314 SP197 15fr + 5fr cl & brt red 3.00 1.40
B315 SP197 15fr + 5fr ultra & ind 2.75 1.40
B316 SP197 18fr + 7fr grnsh blk & dk grn 3.25 1.60
B317 SP197 18fr + 7fr dk vio brn & red brn 3.25 1.60
Nos. B312-B317 (6) 16.05 8.20

Blind Man and Beggar, Engraving by Jacques Callot — SP205

Design: 20fr+8fr, Women beggars.

1957, Dec. 7 **Engr.** ***Perf. 13***

B318 SP205 15fr + 7fr ultra & red 3.50 1.75
a. Bklt. pane, 4 ea, gutter btwn. 45.00 45.00
B319 SP205 20fr + 8fr dk vio brn & red 4.50 2.40

The surtax was for the Red Cross.

Motorized Mail Distribution SP206

1958, Mar. 15

B320 SP206 15fr + 5fr multi 1.20 .75

Stamp Day, Mar. 15.

Portrait Type of 1955

Portraits: No. B321, Joachim du Bellay. No. B322, Jean Bart. No. B323, Denis Diderot. No. B324, Gustave Courbet. 20fr+8fr, J. B. Carpeaux. 35fr+15fr, Toulouse-Lautrec.

1958, June 7 **Engr.** ***Perf. 13***

B321 SP200 12fr + 4fr yel grn 1.40 .90
B322 SP200 12fr + 4fr dk blue 1.40 .90
B323 SP200 15fr + 5fr dull cl 1.50 1.00
B324 SP200 15fr + 5fr ultra 1.60 1.10
B325 SP200 20fr + 8fr brt red 1.60 1.00
B326 SP200 35fr + 15fr green 2.10 1.10
Nos. B321-B326 (6) 9.60 6.00

St. Vincent de Paul — SP207

Portrait: 20fr+8fr, J. H. Dunant.

1958, Dec. 6 **Unwmk.**
Cross in Carmine

B327 SP207 15fr + 7fr grayish grn 1.00 .45
a. Bklt. pane, 4 each, gutter btwn. 20.00
B328 SP207 20fr + 8fr violet 1.00 .45

The surtax was for the Red Cross. See No. B747d.

Plane Landing at Night SP208

1959, Mar. 21

B329 SP208 20fr + 5fr sl grn, blk & rose .45 .30

Issued for Stamp Day, Mar. 21, and to publicize night air mail service.
The surtax was for the Red Cross.
See No. 1089.

Geoffroi de Villehardouin and Ships — SP209

Designs: No. B331, André Le Nôtre and formal garden. No. B332, Jean Le Rond d'Alembert, books and wheel. No. B333, David d'Angers, statue and building. No. B334, M. F. X. Bichat and torch. No. B335, Frédéric Auguste Bartholdi, Statue of Liberty and Lion of Belfort.

1959, June 13 **Engr.** ***Perf. 13***

B330 SP209 15fr + 5fr vio blue 1.00 .60
B331 SP209 15fr + 5fr dk sl grn 1.00 .60
B332 SP209 20fr + 10fr olive bis .90 .60
B333 SP209 20fr + 10fr dk gray 1.10 .65
B334 SP209 30fr + 10fr dk car rose 1.00 .65
B335 SP209 30fr + 10fr org brn 1.20 .65
Nos. B330-B335 (6) 6.20 3.75

The surtax was for the Red Cross.

No. 927 Surcharged

1959, Dec. **Typo.** ***Perf. 14x13½***

B336 A328 25fr + 5fr black & red .25 .25

Surtax for the flood victims at Frejus.

Charles Michel de l'Épée — SP210

Design: 25fr+10fr, Valentin Hauy.

1959, Dec. 5 Engr. *Perf. 13*

Cross in Carmine

B337 SP210 20fr + 10fr blk & cl 1.60 1.00
a. Bklt. pane, 4 each, gutter btwn. 30.00
B338 SP210 25fr + 10fr dk blue & blk 2.00 1.10

The surtax was for the Red Cross.

Ship Laying Underwater Cable SP211

1960, Mar. 12

B339 SP211 20c + 5c grnsh bl & dk bl 1.10 .90

Issued for the Day of the Stamp. The surtax went to the Red Cross.

Refugee Girl Amid Ruins — SP212

1960, Apr. 7

B340 SP212 25c + 10c grn, brn & ind .30 .25

World Refugee Year, July 1, 1959-June 30, 1960. The surtax was for aid to refugees.

Michel de L'Hospital SP213

No. B342, Henri de la Tour D'Auvergne, Viscount of Turenne. No. B343, Nicolas Boileau (Despreaux). No. B344, Jean-Martin Charcot, M.D. No. B345, Georges Bizet. 50c+15c, Edgar Degás.

1960, June 11 Engr. *Perf. 13*

B341 SP213 10c + 5c pur & rose car 1.10 .90
B342 SP213 20c + 10c ol & vio brn 1.90 1.60
B343 SP213 20c + 10c Prus grn & dp yel grn 1.50 1.25
B344 SP213 30c + 10c rose car & rose red 2.60 2.25
B345 SP213 30c + 10c dk bl & vio bl 3.00 2.50
B346 SP213 50c + 15c sl bl & gray 3.50 2.75
Nos. B341-B346 (6) 13.60 11.25

The surtax was for the Red Cross.
See Nos. B350-B355.

Staff of the Brotherhood of St. Martin — SP214

25c+10c, St. Martin, 16th cent. wood sculpture.

1960, Dec. 3 Unwmk. *Perf. 13*

B347 SP214 20c + 10c rose cl & red 2.60 2.25
a. Bklt. pane, 4 each, gutter btwn. 32.50
B348 SP214 25c + 10c lt ultra & red 2.60 2.25

The surtax was for the Red Cross.

Letter Carrier, Paris 1760 — SP215

1961, Mar. 18 *Perf. 13*

B349 SP215 20c + 5c sl grn, brn & red .60 .45

Stamp Day. Surtax for Red Cross.

Famous Men Type of 1960

Designs: 15c+5c, Bertrand Du Guesclin. No. B351, Pierre Puget. No. B352, Charles Coulomb. 30c+10c, Antoine Drouot. 45c+10c, Honoré Daumier. 50c+15c, Guillaume Apollinaire.

1961, May 20 Engr.

B350 SP213 15c + 5c red brn & blk 1.60 1.50
B351 SP213 20c + 10c dk grn & lt bl 1.50 1.50
B352 SP213 20c + 10c ver & rose car 1.75 1.50
B353 SP213 30c + 10c blk & brn org 1.75 1.50
B354 SP213 45c + 10c choc & dk grn 2.60 2.25
B355 SP213 50c + 15c dk car rose & vio 2.60 2.25
Nos. B350-B355 (6) 11.80 10.50

"Love" by Rouault — SP216

Designs from "Miserere" by Georges Rouault: 25c+10c, "The Blind Consoles the Seeing."

1961, Dec. 2 *Perf. 13*

B356 SP216 20c + 10c brn, blk & red 1.90 1.50
a. Bklt. pane, 4 each, gutter btwn. 30.00
B357 SP216 25c + 10c brn, blk & red 2.25 1.90

The surtax was for the Red Cross.

Medieval Royal Messenger SP217

1962, Mar. 17

B358 SP217 20c + 5c rose red, bl & sepia .60 .55

Stamp Day. Surtax for Red Cross.

Denis Papin, Scientist — SP218

Portraits: No. B360, Edme Bouchardon, sculptor. No. B361, Joseph Lakanal, educator. 30c+10c, Gustave Charpentier, composer. 45c+15c, Edouard Estaunié, writer. 50c+20c, Hyacinthe Vincent, physician and bacteriologist.

1962, June 2 Engr.

B359 SP218 15c + 5c bluish grn & dk gray 1.50 1.25
B360 SP218 20c + 10c cl brn 1.50 1.25
B361 SP218 20c + 10c gray & sl 1.50 1.25
B362 SP218 30c + 10c brt bl & ind 1.90 1.60
B363 SP218 45c + 15c org brn & choc 2.10 1.75
B364 SP218 50c + 20c grnsh bl & blk 2.00 1.75
Nos. B359-B364 (6) 10.50 8.85

The surtax was for the Red Cross.

Rosalie Fragonard by Fragonard — SP219

Design: 25c+10c, Child dressed as Pierrot.

1962, Dec. 8 Cross in Red

B365 SP219 20c + 10c redsh brown .90 .75
a. Bklt. pane, 4 ea, gutter btwn. 32.00
B366 SP219 25c + 10c dull grn 1.50 1.40

The surtax was for the Red Cross.
For surcharges see Reunion Nos. B16-B17.

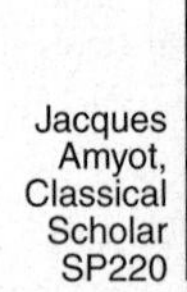

Jacques Amyot, Classical Scholar SP220

30c+10c, Pierre de Marivaux, playwright. 50c+20c, Jacques Daviel, surgeon.

1963, Feb. 23 Unwmk. *Perf. 13*

B367 SP220 20c + 10c mar, gray & pur .75 .65
B368 SP220 30c + 10c Prus grn & mar .75 .65
B369 SP220 50c + 20c ultra, ocher & ol .90 .75
Nos. B367-B369 (3) 2.40 2.05

The surtax was for the Red Cross.

Roman Chariot SP221

1963, Mar. 16 Engr.

B370 SP221 20c + 5c brn org & vio brn .25 .25

Stamp Day. Surtax for Red Cross.

Étienne Méhul, Composer SP222

Designs: 30c+10c, Nicolas-Louis Vauquelin, chemist. 50c+20c, Alfred de Vigny, poet.

1963, May 25 Unwmk. *Perf. 13*

B371 SP222 20c + 10c dp bl, dk brn & dp org .90 .75
B372 SP222 30c + 10c mag, gray ol & blk .75 .65
B373 SP222 50c + 20c sl, blk & brn 1.20 1.00
Nos. B371-B373 (3) 2.85 2.40

The surtax was for the Red Cross.

"Child with Grapes" by David d'Angers and Centenary Emblem — SP223

25c+10c, "The Fifer," by Edouard Manet.

1963, Dec. 9 Unwmk. *Perf. 13*

B374 SP223 20c + 10c black & red .65 .55
a. Bklt. pane, 4 each, gutter btwn. 9.00 9.00
B375 SP223 25c + 10c sl grn & red .65 .55

Cent. of the Intl. and French Red Cross. Surtax for the Red Cross.
For surcharges see Reunion Nos. B18-B19.

Post Rider, 18th Century SP224

1964, Mar. 14 Engr.

B376 SP224 20c + 5c Prus green .25 .25

Issued for Stamp Day.

Resistance Memorial by Watkin, Luxembourg Gardens — SP225

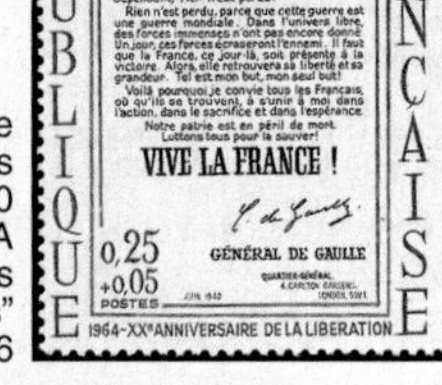

De Gaulle's 1940 Poster "A Tous les Francais" SP226

Street Fighting in Paris and Strasbourg. SP227

Designs: 20c+5c, "Deportation," concentration camp with watchtower and barbed wire.

No. B379, Allied troops landing in Normandy and Provence.

1964 Engr. *Perf. 13*
B377 SP225 20c + 5c slate blk .45 .40

Perf. 12x13
B378 SP226 25c + 5c dk red, bl, red & blk .75 .60

Perf. 13
B379 SP227 30c + 5c blk, bl & org brn .60 .55
B380 SP227 30c + 5c org brn, cl & blk .60 .55
B381 SP225 50c + 5c dk grn .60 .55
Nos. B377-B381 (5) 3.00 2.65

20th anniv. of liberation from the Nazis.
Issue dates: Noz. B377, B381, 3/21; No. B378, 6/18; No. B379, 6/6; No. B380, 8/22.

President René Coty — SP229

Portraits: No. B383, John Calvin. No. B384, Pope Sylvester II (Gerbert).

1964 Unwmk. *Perf. 13*
B382 SP229 30c + 10c dp cl & blk .30 .25
B383 SP229 30c + 10c dk grn, blk & brn .30 .25
B384 SP229 30c + 10c slate & cl .30 .25
Nos. B382-B384 (3) .90 .75

The surtax was for the Red Cross.
Issued: No. B382, 4/25; No. B383, 5/25; No. B384, 6/1.

Jean Nicolas Corvisart — SP230

Portrait: 25c+10c, Dominique Larrey.

Cross in Carmine

1964, Dec. 12 Engr.
B385 SP230 20c + 10c black .30 .25
a. Bklt. pane, 4 ea, gutter btwn. 3.50
B386 SP230 25c + 10c black .30 .25

Jean Nicolas Corvisart (1755-1821), physician of Napoleon I, and Dominique Larrey (1766-1842), Chief Surgeon of the Imperial Armies. The surtax was for the Red Cross.
For surcharges see Reunion Nos. B20-B21.

Paul Dukas, Composer — SP231

No. B387, Duke François de La Rochefoucauld, writer. No. B388, Nicolas Poussin, painter. No. B389, Duke Charles of Orléans, poet.

1965, Feb. Engr. *Perf. 13*
B387 SP231 30c + 10c org brn & dk bl .30 .25
B388 SP231 30c + 10c car & dk red brn .30 .25
B389 SP231 40c + 10c dk red brn, dk red & Prus bl .45 .40
B390 SP231 40c + 10c dk brn & sl bl .45 .40
Nos. B387-B390 (4) 1.50 1.30

The surtax was for the Red Cross.
Issued: Nos. B387, B390 2/13; Nos. B388-B389 2/20.

Packet "La Guienne" SP232

1965, Mar. 29 Unwmk. *Perf. 13*
B391 SP232 25c + 10c multi .40 .40

Issued for Stamp Day, 1965. "La Guienne" was used for transatlantic mail service. Surtax was for the Red Cross.

Infant with Spoon by Auguste Renoir — SP233

Design: 30c+10c, Coco Writing (Renoir's son Claude).

1965, Dec. 11 Engr. *Perf. 13*
Cross in Carmine
B392 SP233 25c + 10c slate .25 .25
a. Bklt. pane, 4 ea, gutter btwn. 2.75
B393 SP233 30c + 10c dull red brn .25 .25

The surtax was for the Red Cross.
For surcharges see Reunion Nos. B22-B23.

Francois Mansart and Carnavalet Palace, Paris SP234

No. B395, St. Pierre Fourier and Basilica of St. Pierre Fourier, Mirecourt. No. B396, Marcel Proust and St. Hilaire Bridge, Illiers. No. B397, Gabriel Fauré, monument and score of "Penelope." No. B398, Elie Metchnikoff, microscope and Pasteur Institute. No. B399, Hippolyte Taine and birthplace.

1966 Engr. *Perf. 13*
B394 SP234 30c + 10c dk red brn & grn .25 .25
B395 SP234 30c + 10c blk & gray grn .25 .25
B396 SP234 30c + 10c ind, sep & grn .25 .25
B397 SP234 30c + 10c bis brn & ind .25 .25
B398 SP234 30c + 10c blk & dl brn .25 .25
B399 SP234 30c + 10c grn & ol brn .25 .25
Nos. B394-B399 (6) 1.50 1.50

The surtax was for the Red Cross.
Issued: Nos. B394-B396, 2/12; others, 6/25.

Engraver Cutting Die and Tools SP235

1966, Mar. 19 Engr. *Perf. 13*
B400 SP235 25c + 10c slate, dk brn & dp org .25 .25

Stamp Day. Surtax for Red Cross.

Angel of Victory, Verdun Fortress, Marching Troops — SP236

1966, May 28 *Perf. 13*
B401 SP236 30c + 5c Prus bl, ultra & dk bl .25 .25

Victory of Verdun, 50th anniversary.

First Aid on Battlefield, 1859 — SP237

No. B403, Nurse giving first aid to child, 1966.

Cross in Carmine

1966, Dec. 10 Engr. *Perf. 13*
B402 SP237 25c + 10c green .25 .25
a. Bklt. pane, 4 ea, gutter btwn. 3.50
B403 SP237 30c + 10c slate .30 .25

The surtax was for the Red Cross.
See No. B746e. For surcharges see Reunion Nos. B24-B25.

Emile Zola — SP238

No. B405, Beaumarchais (pen name of Pierre Augustin Caron). No. B406, St. Francois de Sales (1567-1622). No. B407, Albert Camus (1913-1960).

1967 Engr. *Perf. 13*
B404 SP238 30c + 10c sl bl & bl .30 .25
B405 SP238 30c + 10c rose brn & lil .30 .25
B406 SP238 30c + 10c dl vio & pur .30 .25
B407 SP238 30c + 10c brn & dl cl .30 .25
Nos. B404-B407 (4) 1.20 1.00

The surtax was for the Red Cross.
Issued: Nos. B404-B405, 2/4; others, 6/24.

Letter Carrier, 1865 — SP239

1967, Apr. 8
B408 SP239 25c + 10c indigo, grn & red .30 .25

Issued for Stamp Day.

Ivory Flute Player — SP240

30c+10c, Violin player, ivory carving.

Cross in Carmine

1967, Dec. 16 Engr. *Perf. 13*
B409 SP240 25c + 10c dl vio & lt brn .30 .25
a. Bklt. pane, 4 ea, gutter btwn. 3.50
B410 SP240 30c + 10c grn & lt brn .35 .25

The surtax was for the Red Cross.
For surcharges see Reunion Nos. B26-B27.

Ski Jump and Long Distance Skiing — SP241

Designs: 40c+10c, Ice hockey. 60c+20c, Olympic flame and snowflakes. 75c+25c, Woman figure skater. 95c+35c, Slalom.

1968, Jan. 27
B411 SP241 30c + 10c ver, gray & brn .30 .30
B412 SP241 40c + 10c lil, lem & brt mag .30 .30
B413 SP241 60c + 20c dk grn, org & brt vio .40 .40
B414 SP241 75c + 25c brt pink, yel grn & blk .50 .50
B415 SP241 95c + 35c bl, brt pink & red brn .60 .50
Nos. B411-B415 (5) 2.10 2.00

Issued for the 10th Winter Olympic Games, Grenoble, Feb. 6-18.

Rural Mailman, 1830 — SP242

1968, Mar. 16 Engr. *Perf. 13*
B416 SP242 25c + 10c multi .25 .25

Issued for Stamp Day.

François Couperin, Composer, and Instruments SP243

Portraits: No. B418, Gen. Louis Desaix de Veygoux (1768-1800) and scene showing his death at the Battle of Marengo, Italy. No. B419, Saint-Pol-Roux (pen name of Paul-Pierre Roux, 1861-1940), Christ on the Cross and ruins of Camaret-sur-Mer. No. B420, Paul Claudel (poet and diplomat, 1868-1955) and Joan of Arc at the stake.

1968 Engr. *Perf. 13*
B417 SP243 30c + 10c pur & rose lil .25 .25
B418 SP243 30c + 10c dk grn & brn .25 .25
B419 SP243 30c + 10c cop red & ol bis .25 .25
B420 SP243 30c + 10c dk brn & lil .25 .25
Nos. B417-B420 (4) 1.00 1.00

Issue dates: Nos. B417-B418, Mar. 23; Nos. B419-B420, July 6.

Spring, by Nicolas Mignard — SP244

Paintings by Nicolas Mignard; 30c+10c, Fall. No. B423, Summer. No. B424, Winter.

1968-69 Engr. *Perf. 13*
Cross in Carmine
B421 SP244 25c + 10c pur & dk bl .30 .25
a. Bklt. pane, 4 ea #B421-B422 with gutter btwn.) 3.00
B422 SP244 30c + 10c brn & car red .30 .30

B423 SP244 40c + 15c dk brn & brn ('69) .45 .30
a. Bklt. pane, 4 ea #B423, B424 with gutter btwn.) 3.50
B424 SP244 40c + 15c pur & Prus bl ('69) .45 .30
Nos. B421-B424 (4) 1.50 1.15

The surtax was for the Red Cross.
For surcharges see Reunion Nos. B28-B31.

Mailmen's Omnibus, 1881 SP245

1969, Mar. 15 **Engr.** ***Perf. 13***
B425 SP245 30c + 10c brn, grn & blk .25 .25

Issued for Stamp Day.
For surcharge see Reunion No. B32.

Gen. Francois Marceau — SP246

Portraits: No. B427, Charles Augustin Sainte-Beuve (1804-1869), writer. No. B428, Albert Roussel (1869-1937), musician. No. B429, Marshal Jean Lannes (1769-1809). No. B430, Georges Cuvier (1769-1832), naturalist. No. B431, André Gide, (1869-1951), writer.

1969
B426 SP246 50c + 10c brn red .40 .35
B427 SP246 50c + 10c slate bl .40 .35
B428 SP246 50c + 10c dp vio bl .40 .35
B429 SP246 50c + 10c choc .40 .35
B430 SP246 50c + 10c dp plum .40 .35
B431 SP246 50c + 10c blue grn .40 .35
Nos. B426-B431 (6) 2.40 2.10

The surtax was for the Red Cross.
Issued: Nos. B426-B428, Mar. 24; No. B429, May 10; Nos. B430-B431, May 17.

Gen. Jacques Leclerc, La Madeleine and Battle — SP247

1969, Aug. 23 **Engr.** ***Perf. 13***
B432 SP247 45c + 10c slate & ol .75 .60

Liberation of Paris, 8/25/44, 25th anniv.

Inscribed Liberation de Strasbourg

1969, Nov. 22 **Engr.** ***Perf. 13***
B433 SP247 70c + 10c brn, choc & olive 2.75 2.00

25th anniv. of the liberation of Strasbourg.

Philibert Delorme, Architect, and Chateau d'Anet SP248

Designs: No. B435, Louis Le Vau (1612-1670), architect, and Vaux-le-Vicomte Chateau, Paris. No. B436, Prosper Merimée (1803-1870), writer, and Carmen. No. B437, Alexandre Dumas (1802-1870), writer, and Three Musketeers. No. B438, Edouard Branly (1844-1940), physicist, electric circuit and convent of the Carmes, Paris. No. B439, Maurice de Broglie (1875-1960), physicist, and X-ray spectrograph.

1970 **Engr.** ***Perf. 13***
B434 SP248 40c + 10c slate grn .40 .35
B435 SP248 40c + 10c dk car .40 .35
B436 SP248 40c + 10c Prus blue .40 .35
B437 SP248 40c + 10c violet bl .40 .35
B438 SP248 40c + 10c dp brown .40 .35
B439 SP248 40c + 10c dk gray .40 .35
Nos. B434-B439 (6) 2.40 2.10

The surtax was for the Red Cross.
Issued: No. B434-B436, 2/14; others, 4/11.

City Mailman, 1830 — SP249

1970, Mar. 14
B440 SP249 40c + 10c blk, ultra & dk car rose .30 .25

Issued for Stamp Day.
For surcharge see Reunion No. B33.

"Life and Death" — SP250

1970, Apr. 4
B441 SP250 40c + 10c brt bl, ol & car rose .25 .25

Issued to publicize the fight against cancer in connection with Health Day, Apr. 7.

Marshal de Lattre de Tassigny — SP251

1970, May 8 **Engr.** ***Perf. 13***
B442 SP251 40c + 10c slate & vio bl .50 .30

25th anniv. of the entry into Berlin of French troops under Marshal Jean de Lattre de Tassigny, May 8, 1945.

Lord and Lady, Dissay Chapel Fresco — SP252

No. B444, Angel holding whips, from fresco in Dissay Castle Chapel, Vienne, c. 1500.

1970, Dec. 12 **Engr.** ***Perf. 13***
Cross in Carmine
B443 SP252 40c + 15c green .30 .25
a. Bklt. pane, 4 ea, gutter btwn. 12.50
B444 SP252 40c + 15c cop red .30 .25

The surtax was for the Red Cross.
For surcharges see Reunion Nos. B34-B35.

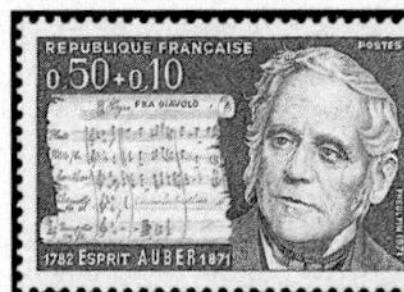

Daniel-Francois Auber and "Fra Diavolo" Music — SP253

No. B446, Gen. Charles Diego Brosset (1898-1944), Basilica of Fourvière. No. B447, Victor Grignard (1871-1935), chemist, Nobel Prize medal. No. B448, Henri Farman (1874-1958), plane. No. B449, Gen. Charles Georges Delestraint (1879-1945), scroll. No. B450, Jean Eugène Robert-Houdin (1805-71), magician's act.

1971 **Engr.** ***Perf. 13***
B445 SP253 50c + 10c brn vio & brn .50 .30
B446 SP253 50c + 10c dk sl grn & ol gray .50 .30
B447 SP253 50c + 10c brn red & olive .50 .30
B448 SP253 50c + 10c vio bl & vio .50 .30
B449 SP253 50c + 10c pur & cl .60 .45
B450 SP253 50c + 10c sl grn & bl grn .60 .45
Nos. B445-B450 (6) 3.20 2.10

The surtax was for the Red Cross.
Issued: Nos. B445-B446, 3/6; No. B447, 5/8; No. B448, 5/29; Nos. B449-B450, 10/16.

Army Post Office, 1914-1918 SP254

1971, Mar. 27 **Engr.** ***Perf. 13***
B451 SP254 50c + 10c ol, brn & bl .40 .30

Stamp Day, 1971.
For surcharge see Reunion No. B36.

Girl with Dog, by Greuze — SP255

Design: 50c+10c, "The Dead Bird," by Jean-Baptiste Greuze (1725-1805).

1971, Dec. 11 **Cross in Carmine**
B452 SP255 30c + 10c violet bl .55 .45
a. Bklt. pane, 4 each, gutter btwn. 6.00
B453 SP255 50c + 10c dp car .55 .45

The surtax was for the Red Cross.
For surcharges see Reunion Nos. B37-B38.

Aristide Bergès (1833-1904) SP256

No. B455, Paul de Chomedey (1612-76), founder of Montreal, and arms of Neuville-sur-Vanne. No. B456, Edouard Belin (1876-1963), inventor. No. B457, Louis Blériot (1872-1936), aviation pioneer. No. B458, Adm. François Joseph, Count de Grasse (1722-88), hero of the American Revolution. No. B459, Théophile Gautier (1811-72), writer.

1972 **Engr.** ***Perf. 13***
B454 SP256 50c + 10c blk & grn .50 .40
B455 SP256 50c + 10c blk & bl .50 .40
B456 SP256 50c + 10c blk & lil rose .50 .40
B457 SP256 50c + 10c red & blk .50 .40
B458 SP256 50c + 10c org & blk .50 .40
B459 SP256 50c + 10c blk & brn .50 .40
Nos. B454-B459 (6) 3.00 2.40

The surtax was for the Red Cross.
Issued: Nos. B454-B455, 2/19; No. B456, 6/24; No. B457, 7/1; Nos. B458-B459, 9/9.

Rural Mailman, 1894 — SP257

1972, Mar. 18 **Engr.** ***Perf. 13***
B460 SP257 50c + 10c bl, yel & ol gray .50 .40

Stamp Day 1972.
For surcharge see Reunion No. B39.

Nicolas Desgenettes SP258

Designs: 30c+10c, René Nicolas Dufriche, Baron Desgenettes, M.D. (1762-1837). 50c+10c, François Joseph Broussais, M.D. (1772-1838).

1972, Dec. 16 **Engr.** ***Perf. 13***
B461 SP258 30c + 10c sl grn & red .40 .30
a. Bklt. pane, 4 ea, gutter btwn. 7.00
B462 SP258 50c + 10c red .45 .40

The surtax was for the Red Cross.
See No. B747b. For surcharges see Reunion Nos. B40-B41.

Tony Garnier (1869-1948), architect — SP259

No. B463, Gaspard de Coligny (1519-1572), admiral and Huguenot leader. No. B464, Ernest Renan (1823-1892), philologist and historian. No. B465, Alberto Santos Dumont (1873-1932), Brazilian aviator. No. B466, Gabrielle-Sidonie Colette (1873-1954), writer. No. B467, René Duguay-Trouin (1673-1736), naval commander. No. B468, Louis Pasteur (1822-1895), chemist, bacteriologist. No. B469, Tony Garnier (1869-1948), architect.

1973 **Engr.** ***Perf. 13***
B463 SP259 50c + 10c multi .50 .40
B464 SP259 50c + 10c multi .50 .40
B465 SP259 50c + 10c multi .50 .40
B466 SP259 50c + 10c multi .50 .40
B467 SP259 50c + 10c multi .50 .40
B468 SP259 50c + 10c multi .50 .40
B469 SP259 50c + 10c multi .50 .40
Nos. B463-B469 (7) 3.50 2.80

Issued: No. B463, 2/17; No. B464, 4/28; No. B465, 5/26; No. B466, 6/2; No. B467, 6/9; No. B468, 10/6; No. B469, 11/17.

Mail Coach, 1835 SP260

1973, Mar. 24 **Engr.** ***Perf. 13***
B470 SP260 50c + 10c grnsh blue .40 .25

Stamp Day, 1973.
For surcharge see Reunion No. B42.

Mary Magdalene SP261

50c+10c, Mourning woman. Designs are from 15th cent. Tomb of Tonnerre.

1973, Dec. 1

B471 SP261 30c + 10c sl grn & red .40 .30
a. Bklt. pane, 4 each, gutter btwn. 6.00
B472 SP261 50c + 10c dk gray & red .45 .40

Surtax was for the Red Cross.
For surcharges see Reunion Nos. B43-B44.

St. Louis-Marie de Montfort — SP262

Portraits: No. B474, Francis Poulenc (1899-1963), composer. No. B475, Jules Barbey d'Aurevilly (1808-1889), writer. No. B476, Jean Giraudoux (1882-1944), writer.

1974, Feb. 23 Engr. *Perf. 13*

B473 SP262 50c + 10c multi .50 .40
B474 SP262 50c + 10c multi .50 .40
B475 SP262 80c + 15c multi .60 .50
B476 SP262 80c + 15c multi .60 .50
Nos. B473-B476 (4) 2.20 1.80

Issue dates: No. B473, Mar. 9; No. B474, July 20; Nos. B475-B476, Nov. 16.

Automatically Sorted Letters — SP263

1974, Mar. 9 Engr. *Perf. 13*

B477 SP263 50c + 10c multi .30 .25

Stamp Day 1974. Automatic letter sorting center, Orleans-la-Source, opened 1/30/73.
For surcharge see Reunion No. B45.

Order of Liberation and 5 Honored Cities — SP264

1974, June 15 Engr. *Perf. 13*

B478 SP264 1fr + 10c multi .55 .30

30th anniv. of liberation from the Nazis.

"Summer" — SP265

Designs: B481, "Spring" (girl on swing). B482, "Fall" (umbrella and rabbits).

1974, Nov. 30 Engr. *Perf. 13*

B479 SP265 60c + 15c multi .45 .40
a. Bklt. pane, 4 ea, gutter btwn. 6.00
B480 SP266 80c + 15c multi .45 .40

For surcharges see Reunion Nos. B46-B47.

"Winter" — SP266

1975, Nov. 29

B481 SP265 60c + 15c multi .40 .30
a. Bklt. pane, 4 ea, gutter btwn. 4.75
B482 SP266 80c + 20c multi .50 .40

Surtax was for the Red Cross.

Dr. Albert Schweitzer SP267

Edmond Michelet SP268

André Siegfried and Map SP269

No. B483, Albert Schweitzer (1875-1965), medical missionary. No. B484, Edmond Michelet (1899-1970), Resistance hero, statesman. No. B485, Robert Schuman (1886-1963), promoter of United Europe. No. B486, Eugene Thomas (1903-69), minister of PTT. No. B487, André Siegfried (1875-1959), political science professor, writer.

1975 Engr. *Perf. 13*

B483 SP267 80c + 20c multi .50 .40
B484 SP268 80c + 20c bl & ind .50 .40
B485 SP268 80c + 20c blk & ind .50 .40
B486 SP268 80c + 20c blk & sl .50 .40
B487 SP269 80c + 20c blk & bl .50 .40
Nos. B483-B487 (5) 2.50 2.00

Issued: No. B483, 1/11; No. B484, 2/22; No. B485, 5/10; No. B486, 6/28; No. B487, 11/15.

Second Republic Mailman's Badge — SP270

1975, Mar. 8 Photo.

B488 SP270 80c + 20c multi .45 .35

Stamp Day.

"Sage" Type of 1876 — SP271

1976, Mar. 13 Engr. *Perf. 13*

B489 SP271 80c + 20c blk & lil .40 .35

Stamp Day 1976.

Marshal A. J. de Moncey — SP272

No. B491, Max Jacob (1876-1944), Dadaist writer, by Picasso. No. B492, Jean Mounet-Sully (1841-1916), actor. No. B493, Gen. Pierre Daumesnil (1776-1832). No. B494, Eugène Fromentin (1820-1876), painter.

1976 Engr. *Perf. 13*

B490 SP272 80c + 20c multi .40 .30
B491 SP272 80c + 20c red brn & ol .40 .30
B492 SP272 80c + 20c multi .40 .30
B493 SP272 1fr + 20c multi .50 .30
B494 SP272 1fr + 20c multi .50 .30
Nos. B490-B494 (5) 2.20 1.50

Issued: No. B490, 5/22; No. B491, 7/22; No. B492, 8/28; No. B493, 9/4; No. B494, 9/25.

Anna de Noailles — SP273

1976, Nov. 6 Engr. *Perf. 13*

B495 SP273 1fr + 20c multi .50 .30

Anna de Noailles (1876-1933), writer & poet.

St. Barbara — SP274

Design: 1fr+25c, Cimmerian Sibyl. Sculptures from Brou Cathedral.

1976, Nov. 20 Cross in Carmine

B496 SP274 80c + 20c violet .45 .40
a. Bklt. pane, 4 ea, gutter btwn. 6.00
B497 SP274 1fr + 25c dk brown .65 .45

Surtax was for the Red Cross.

Marckolsheim Relay Station Sign — SP275

1977, Mar. 26 Engr. *Perf. 13*

B498 SP275 1fr + 20c multi .40 .25

Stamp Day.

Edouard Herriot, Statesman and Writer — SP276

Designs: No. B500, Abbé Breuil (1877-1961), archaeologist. No. B501, Guillaume de Machault (1305-1377), poet and composer. No. B502, Charles Cross (1842-1888).

1977 Engr. *Perf. 13*

B499 SP276 1fr + 20c blk .40 .30
B500 SP276 1fr + 20c multi .40 .30
B501 SP276 1fr + 20c multi .40 .30
B502 SP276 1fr + 20c multi .40 .30
Nos. B499-B502 (4) 1.60 1.20

Issued: No. B499, 10/8; No. B500, 10/15; No. B501, 11/12; No. B502, 12/3.

Christmas Figurine, Provence — SP277

1fr+25c, Christmas figurine (woman), Provence.

1977, Nov. 26

B503 SP277 80c + 20c red & ind .40 .30
a. Bklt. pane, 4 ea, gutter btwn. 4.50
B504 SP277 1fr + 25c red & sl grn .45 .30

Surtax was for the Red Cross.

Marie Noel, Writer — SP278

No. B506, Georges Bernanos (1888-1948), writer. No. B507, Leo Tolstoy (1828-1910), Russian writer. No. B508, Charles Marie Leconte de Lisle (1818-1894), poet. No. B509, Voltaire (1694-1778) and Jean Jacques Rousseau (1712-1778). No. B510, Claude Bernard (1813-1878), physiologist.

1978 Engr. *Perf. 13*

B505 SP278 1fr + 20c multi .40 .30
B506 SP278 1fr + 20c multi .40 .30
B507 SP278 1fr + 20c multi .40 .30
B508 SP278 1fr + 20c multi .40 .30
B509 SP278 1fr + 20c multi .40 .30
B510 SP278 1fr + 20c multi .40 .30
Nos. B505-B510 (6) 2.40 1.80

Issued: No. B505, 2/11; No. B506, 2/18; No. B507, 4/15; No. B508, 3/26; No. B509, 7/1; No. B510, 9/16.

Mail Collection, 1900 — SP279

1978, Apr. 8 Engr. *Perf. 13*

B511 SP279 1fr + 20c multi .40 .30

Stamp Day 1978.

SP280

1fr+25c, The Hare & the Tortoise. 1.20fr+30c, The City Mouse & the Country Mouse.

1978, Dec. 2 **Engr.** ***Perf. 13***

B512 SP280 1fr + 25c multi .60 .50
a. Bklt. pane, 4 ea, gutter btwn. 6.00
B513 SP280 1.20fr + 30c multi .65 .55

Surtax was for the Red Cross.

SP281

No. B514, Ladislas Marshal de Berchény (1689-1778). No. B515, Leon Jouhaux (1879-1954), labor leader. No. B516, Peter Abelard (1079-1142), theologian and writer. No. B517, Georges Courteline (1860-1929), humorist. No. B518, Simone Weil (1909-1943), social philosopher. No. B519, André Malraux (1901-1976), novelist.

1979 **Engr.** ***Perf. 13***

B514 SP281 1.20fr + 30c multi .50 .40
B515 SP281 1.20fr + 30c multi .50 .40
B516 SP281 1.20fr + 30c multi .50 .40
B517 SP281 1.20fr + 30c multi .50 .40
B518 SP281 1.30fr + 30c multi .60 .40
B519 SP281 1.30fr + 30c multi .60 .40
Nos. B514-B519 (6) 3.20 2.40

Issued: No. B514, 1/13; No. B515, 5/12; No. B516, 6/9; No. B517, 6/25; No. B518, 11/12; No. B519, 11/26.

General Post Office, from 1908 Post Card SP282

1979, Mar. 10 **Engr.** ***Perf. 13***

B520 SP282 1.20fr + 30c multi .50 .30

Stamp Day 1979.

Woman, Stained-Glass Window — SP283

Stained-glass windows, Church of St. Joan of Arc, Rouen: 1.30fr+30c, Simon the Magician.

1979, Dec. 1 ***Perf. 13***

B521 SP283 1.10fr + 30c multi .50 .40
B522 SP283 1.30fr + 30c multi .60 .45
a. Bklt. pane, 4 each #521-522, with gutter btwn., perf. 12½x13 6.00

Surtax was for the Red Cross.

Eugene Viollet le Duc (1814-1879), Architect — SP284

Jean-Marie de Le Mennais (1780-1860), Priest and Educator — SP285

No. B524, Jean Monnet (1888-1979), economist and diplomat. No. B525, Viollet le Duc (1814-1879), architect and writer. No. B526, Frederic Mistral (1830-1914), poet. No. B527, Saint-John Perse (Alexis Leger, 1887-1975), poet and diplomat. No. B528, Pierre Paul de Riquet (1604-1680), canal builder.

1980 **Engr.** ***Perf. 13***

B523 SP284 1.30fr + 30c multi .60 .55
B524 SP285 1.30fr + 30c multi .60 .55
B525 SP285 1.40fr + 30c blue .60 .55
B526 SP285 1.40fr + 30c black .60 .55
B527 SP285 1.40fr + 30c multi .60 .55
B528 SP284 1.40fr + 30c multi .60 .55
Nos. B523-B528 (6) 3.60 3.30

Issued: No. B523, Feb. 16; Nos. B524-B526, Sept. 6; Nos. B527-B528, Oct. 11.

The Letter to Melie, by Avati, Stamp Day, 1980 — SP286

1980, Mar. 8 **Photo.**

B529 SP286 1.30fr + 30c multi .50 .40

Filling the Granaries, Choir Stall Detail, Amiens Cathedral — SP287

No. B531, Grapes from the Promised Land.

1980, Dec. 6 **Engr.** ***Perf. 13***

B530 SP287 1.20fr + 30c red & dk red brn .50 .40
B531 SP287 1.40fr + 30c red & dk red brn .60 .40
a. Bklt. pane, 4 #B530-B531, with gutter btwn., perf. 12½x13 6.50

Sister Anne-Marie Javouhey (1779-1851), Founded Congregation of St. Joseph of Cluny — SP288

No. B532, Louis Armand (1905-71), railway engineer. No. B533, Louis Jouvet (1887-1951), theater director. No. B534, Marc Boegner (1881-1970), peace worker. No. B536, Jacques Offenbach (1819-80), composer. No. B537, Pierre Teilhard de Chardin (1881-1955), philosopher.
Nos. B532-B533, B537 vert.

1981 **Engr.** ***Perf. 13***

B532 SP288 1.20 + 30c multi .55 .45
B533 SP288 1.20 + 30c multi .55 .45
B534 SP288 1.40 + 30c multi .55 .45
B535 SP288 1.40 + 30c multi .55 .45
B536 SP288 1.40 + 30c multi .55 .45
B537 SP288 1.40 + 30c multi .55 .45
Nos. B532-B537 (6) 3.30 2.70

Issued: No. B532, 5/23; No. B533, 6/13; No. B534, 11/14; No. B535, 2/7; No. B536, 2/14; No. B537, 5/23.

The Love Letter, by Goya — SP289

1981, Mar. 7 ***Perf. 13x12½***

B538 SP289 1.40 + 30c multi .65 .60

Stamp Day 1981.

Scourges of the Passion SP290

Stained-glass Windows, Church of the Sacred Heart, Audincourt: 1.60fr+30c, "Peace."

1981, Dec. 5 **Photo.** ***Perf. 13***

B539 SP290 1.40 + 30c multi .60 .55
B540 SP290 1.60 + 30c multi .75 .65
a. Bklt. pane, 4 ea, gutter btwn. 6.00

Guillaume Postel (1510-1581), Theologian — SP291

No. B542, Henri Mondor (1885-1962), physician. No. B543, Andre Chantemesse (1851-1919), Scientist. No. B544, Louis Pergaud (1882-1915), writer. No. B545, Robert Debre (1882-1978), writer. No. B546, Gustave Eiffel (1832-1923), engineer.

1982 **Engr.** ***Perf. 13***

B541 SP291 1.40 + 30c multi .60 .50
B542 SP291 1.40 + 30c dk brn & dk bl .60 .50
B543 SP291 1.60 + 30c multi .60 .50
B544 SP291 1.60 + 40c multi .60 .50
B545 SP291 1.60 + 40c dk blue .65 .60
B546 SP291 1.80 + 40c sepia .65 .60
Nos. B541-B546 (6) 3.70 3.20

Woman Reading, by Picasso — SP292

1982, Mar. 27 ***Perf. 13x12½***

B547 SP292 1.60 + 40c multi .75 .60

Stamp Day.

SP293

Jules Verne books: 1.60fr+30c, Five Weeks in a Balloon. 1.80fr+40c, 20,000 Leagues under the Sea.

1982, Nov. 20 ***Perf. 13***

B548 SP293 1.60 + 30c multi .65 .50
B549 SP293 1.80 + 40c multi .75 .60
a. Bklt. pane, 4 each #B548-B549, with gutter btwn., perf. 12½x13 8.00

Surtax was for Red Cross.

SP294

No. B550, Andre Messager (1853-1929). No. B551, J.A. Gabriel (1698-1782), architect. No. B552, Hector Berlioz (1803-69), composer. No. B553, Max Fouchet (1913-80). No. B554, Rene Cassin (1887-1976). No. B555, Stendhal (Marie Henri Beyle, 1783-1842).

1983 **Engr.** ***Perf. 12½x13***

B550 SP294 1.60 + 30c multi .65 .60
B551 SP294 1.60 + 30c multi .65 .60
B552 SP294 1.80 + 40c dp lil & blk .65 .60
B553 SP294 1.80 + 40c multi .75 .60
B554 SP294 2fr + 40c multi .80 .65
B555 SP294 2fr + 40c multi .80 .65
Nos. B550-B555 (6) 4.30 3.70

Issued: No. B550, 1/15; No. B551, 4/16; No. B552, 1/22; No. B553, 4/30; No. B554, 6/25; No. B555, 11/12.

Man Dictating a Letter, by Rembrandt — SP295

Photo. & Engr.

1983, Feb. 26 ***Perf. 13X12½***

B556 SP295 1.80 + 40c multi .90 .60

Stamp Day.

Virgin with Child, Baillon, 14th Cent. — SP296

Design: No. B558, Virgin with Child, Genainville, 16th Cent.

1983, Nov. 26 **Engr.** ***Perf. 13***

B557 SP296 1.60 + 40c shown .65 .45
B558 SP296 2fr + 40c multi .75 .45
a. Bklt. pane, 4 #B557-B558, with gutter btwn., perf. 12½x13 6.50

Emile Littre (1801-1881), Physician — SP297

No. B560, Jean Zay (1904-44). No. B561, Pierre Corneille (1606-1684. No. B562, Gaston Bachelard (1884-1962). No. B563, Jean Paulhan (1884-1968). No. B564, Evariste Galois (1811-1832).

1984 Engr. *Perf. 13*

B559 SP297 1.60fr + 40c plum & blk .65 .60
B560 SP297 1.60fr + 40c dk grn & blk .65 .60
B561 SP297 1.70fr + 40c dp vio & blk .75 .60
B562 SP297 2fr + 40c gray & blk .75 .60
B563 SP297 2.10fr + 40c dk brn & blk .90 .65
B564 SP297 2.10fr + 40c ultra & blk .90 .65
Nos. B559-B564 (6) 4.60 3.70

SP298

Diderot Holding a Letter, by L.M. Van Loo.

1984, Mar. 17 Engr. *Perf. 12½x13*

B565 SP298 2fr + 40c multi .90 .60

SP299

The Rose Basket, by Caly.

1984, Nov. 24 Photo. *Perf. 12½x13*

B566 SP299 2.10fr + 50c pnksh (basket) & multi .80 .60
a. Salmon (basket) & multi, perf. 13½x13 .90 .60
b. As "a," bklt. pane of 10 + 2 labels 9.00

Surtax was for the Red Cross.

Jules Romains (1885-1972) — SP300

Authors: No. B568, Jean-Paul Sartre (1905-1980). No. B569, Romain Rolland (1866-1944). No. B570, Roland Dorgeles (1885-1973). No. B571, Victor Hugo (1802-1885). No. B572, Francois Mauriac (1885-1970).

1985, Feb. 23 Engr. *Perf. 13*

B567 SP300 1.70fr + 40c 1.10 .90
B568 SP300 1.70fr + 40c 1.10 .90
B569 SP300 1.70fr + 40c 1.10 .90
B570 SP300 2.10fr + 50c 1.25 1.00
B571 SP300 2.10fr + 50c 1.25 1.00
B572 SP300 2.10fr + 50c 1.25 1.00
a. Bklt. pane, 1 each + 2 labels, perf. 15x14½ 15.00
Nos. B567-B572 (6) 7.05 5.70

SP301

Stamp Day: Canceling apparatus invented by Eugene Daguin (1849-1888).

1985, Mar. 16 Engr. *Perf. 12½x13*

B573 SP301 2.10fr + 50c brn blk & bluish gray .90 .60

SP302

Issenheim Altarpiece retable.

1985, Nov. 23 Photo.

B574 SP302 2.20fr + 50c multi .80 .60
a. As "b," bklt. pane of 10 8.00
b. Perf. 13½x13 .90 .60

Surtax for the Red Cross.

SP303

Famous men: No. B575, Francois Arago (1786-1853), physician, politician. No. B576, Henri Moissan (1852-1907), chemist. No. B577, Henri Fabre (1882-1984), engineer. No. B578, Marc Seguin (1786-1875), engineer. No. B579, Paul Heroult (1863-1914), chemist.

1986, Feb. 22 Engr. *Perf. 13*

B575 SP303 1.80fr + 40c multi .75 .65
B576 SP303 1.80fr + 40c multi .75 .65
B577 SP303 1.80fr + 40c multi .75 .65
B578 SP303 2.20fr + 50c multi .80 .65
B579 SP303 2.20fr + 50c multi .80 .65
a. Bklt. pane of 5, #B575-B579, + 3 labels 6.00
Nos. B575-B579 (5) 3.85 3.25

SP304

1986, Mar. 1 Engr. *Perf. 13x12½*

B580 SP304 2.20fr + 50c brn blk *4.50 4.50*

Pierre Cot (1895-1977).

Mail Britzska SP305

1986, Apr. 5 *Perf. 13*

B581 SP305 2.20fr + 60c pale tan & dk vio brn .85 .60

Booklet Stamp

B582 SP305 2.20fr + 60c buff & blk .85 .60
a. Bklt. pane of 6 + 2 labels 6.00

Stamp Day. See Nos. B590-B591, B599-B600, B608-B609.

Stained Glass Window (detail), by Vieira da Silva, St. Jacques of Reims Church, Marne — SP306

1986, Nov. 24 Photo. *Perf. 12½x13*

B583 SP306 2.20fr + 60c multi .85 .60
a. As "b," bklt. pane of 10 9.00
b. Perf. 13½x13 .90 .60

Surtaxed to benefit the natl. Red Cross.

Physicians and Biologists SP307

No. B584, Charles Richet (1850-1935). No. B585, Eugene Jamot (1879-1937). No. B586, Bernard Halpern (1904-1978). No. B587, Alexandre Yersin (1863-1943). No. B588, Jean Rostand (1894-1977). No. B589, Jacques Monod (1910-1976).

1987, Feb. 21 Engr. *Perf. 13*

B584 SP307 1.90fr + 50c deep ultra .75 .60
B585 SP307 1.90fr + 50c dull lil .75 .60
B586 SP307 1.90fr + 50c grnsh gray .75 .60
B587 SP307 2.20fr + 50c grnsh gray .85 .65
B588 SP307 2.20fr + 50c deep ultra .85 .65
B589 SP307 2.20fr + 50c dull lil .85 .65
a. Bklt. pane of 6, #B584-B589 *5.00*
Nos. B584-B589 (6) 4.80 3.75

Stamp Day Type of 1986

Stamp Day 1987: Berline carriage.

1987, Mar. 14 Engr.

B590 SP305 2.20fr + 60c buff & sepia .85 .60

Booklet Stamp

B591 SP305 2.20fr + 60c pale & dk bl .85 .60
a. Bklt. pane of 6 + 2 labels 6.00

Flight Into Egypt, Retable by Melchior Broederlam SP308

1987, Nov. 21 Photo. *Perf. 12½x13*

B592 SP308 2.20fr +60c multi .85 .60
a. As "b," bklt. pane of 10 + 2 labels 8.00
b. Perf. 13½x13 .90 .60

Surtaxed to benefit the Red Cross.

Explorers SP309

Profiles & maps: No. B593, Marquis Abraham Duquesne (1610-1688), naval commander. No. B594, Pierre Andre de Suffren (1729-1788). No. B595, Jean-Francois de La Perouse (1741-1788). No. B596, Mahe de La Bourdonnais (1699-1753). No. B597, Louis-Antoine de Bougainville (1729-1811). No. B598, Jules Dumont d'Urville (1790-1842).

1988, Feb. 20 Engr. *Perf. 13*

B593 SP309 2fr + 50c multi .75 .50
B594 SP309 2fr + 50c multi .75 .50
B595 SP309 2fr + 50c multi .75 .50
B596 SP309 2.20fr + 50c multi .85 .60
B597 SP309 2.20fr + 50c multi .85 .60
B598 SP309 2.20fr + 50c multi .85 .60
a. Bklt. pane of 6, #B593-B598 4.50

Stamp Day Type of 1986

Stamp Day 1988: Postal coach.

1988, Mar. 29 Engr.

B599 SP305 2.20fr +60c dk lilac .85 .60

Booklet Stamp

B600 SP305 2.20fr +60c sepia .85 .60
a. Bklt. pane of 6 + 2 labels 5.00

Intl. Red Cross, 125th Anniv. — SP310

1988, Nov. 19 Engr. *Perf. 12½x13*

B601 SP310 2.20fr +60c multi .85 .60
a. As "b," bklt. pane of 10+2 labels 8.00
b. Perf. 13½x13 .85 .75

See No. B747c.

Revolution Leaders and Heroes SP311

No. B602, Emmanuel Joseph Sieyes (1748-1836). No. B603, Honore Gabriel Riqueti, Comte de Mirabeau (1749-91). No. B604, Louis Marie de Noailles (1756-1804). No. B605, Lafayette. No. B606, Antoine Pierre Joseph Marie Barnave (1761-93). No. B607, Jean Baptiste Drouet (1763-1824).

1989, Feb. 25 Engr. *Perf. 13*

B602 SP311 2.20fr +50c multi .85 .60
B603 SP311 2.20fr +50c multi .85 .60
B604 SP311 2.20fr +50c multi .85 .60
B605 SP311 2.20fr +50c multi .85 .60
B606 SP311 2.20fr +50c multi .85 .60
B607 SP311 2.20fr +50c multi .85 .60
a. Bklt. pane, 1 each + 2 labels 5.00

French Revolution, bicent.

Stamp Day Type of 1986

Design: Paris-Lyon stagecoach.

1989, Apr. 15 Engr. *Perf. 13*

B608 SP305 2.20fr +60c pale bl & dk bl .85 .60

Booklet Stamp

B609 SP305 2.20fr +60c pale lil & pur .85 .60
a. Bklt. pane of 6 + 2 labels 6.00

Stamp Day 1989.

Bird From a Silk Tapestry, Lyon, 18th Cent. — SP312

1989, Nov. 18 Photo. *Perf. 12½x13*

B610 SP312 2.20fr +60c multi .85 .60
a. As "b," bklt. pane of 10 9.00
b. Perf. 13½x13 .90 .60

Surtax for the natl. Red Cross.

1992 Winter Olympics, Albertville SP313

1990, Feb. 9 Engr. *Perf. 13*

B611 SP313 2.30fr +20c red, bl & blk .90 .70

See Nos. B621-B627, B636-B637, B639.

Stamp Day SP314

1990, Mar. 17 Photo.

B612 SP314 2.30fr +60c ultra, bl & brt yel .90 .70

Booklet Stamp

B613 SP314 2.30fr +60c ultra, grn, yel & brt grn .90 .70
a. Bklt. pane of 6 + 2 labels 6.00

SP315

Quimper or Brittany Ware Faience plate.

1990, May 5 Photo. *Perf. 12½x13*

B614 SP315 2.30fr +60c multi .90 .70
a. As "b," bklt. pane of 10+2 labels 9.00
b. Perf. 13½x13 .95 .70

Surcharge benefited the Red Cross.

SP316

No. B615, Aristide Bruant. No. B616, Maurice Chevalier. No. B617, Tino Rossi. No. B618, Edith Piaf. No. B619, Jacques Brel. No. B620, Georges Brassens.

1990, June 16 Photo. *Perf. 13*

B615 SP316 2.30fr +50c multi .90 .70
B616 SP316 2.30fr +50c multi .90 .70
B617 SP316 2.30fr +50c multi .90 .70
B618 SP316 2.30fr +50c multi .90 .70
B619 SP316 2.30fr +50c multi .90 .70
B620 SP316 2.30fr +50c multi .90 .70
a. Bklt. pane, 1 each +2 labels 5.00

Albertville Olympic Type

Designs: No. B621, Ski jumping. No. B622, Speed skiing. No. B623, Slalom skiing. No. B624, Cross-country skiing. No. B625, Ice hockey. No. B626, Luge. No. B627, Curling.

1990-91 Engr. *Perf. 13*

B621 SP313 2.30fr +20c multi .90 .70
B622 SP313 2.30fr +20c multi .90 .70
B623 SP313 2.30fr +20c multi .90 .70
B624 SP313 2.30fr +20c multi .90 .70
B625 SP313 2.30fr +20c multi .90 .70
B626 SP313 2.50fr +20c multi .90 .70
B627 SP313 2.50fr +20c multi .90 .70
Nos. B621-B627 (7) 6.30 4.90

Issued: No. B621, 12/22/90; No. B622, 12/29/90; No. B623, 1/19/91; No. B624, 2/2/91; No. B625, 2/9/91; No. B626, 3/2/91; No. B627, 4/20/91.

No. B624 inscribed "La Poste 1992."

Paul Eluard (1895-1952) — SP317

Poets: No. B629, Andre Breton (1896-1966). No. B630, Louis Aragon (1897-1982). No. B631, Francis Ponge (1899-1988). No. B632, Jacques Prevert (1900-1977). No. B633, Rene Char (1907-1988).

1991, Feb. 23 Engr. *Perf. 12½x13*

B628 SP317 2.50fr +50c multi 1.00 .75
B629 SP317 2.50fr +50c multi 1.00 .75
B630 SP317 2.50fr +50c multi 1.00 .75
B631 SP317 2.50fr +50c multi 1.00 .75
B632 SP317 2.50fr +50c multi 1.00 .75
B633 SP317 2.50fr +50c multi 1.00 .75
a. Bklt. pane, 1 each +2 labels, perf. 13 6.00

Stamp Day SP318

Designs: No. B634, Postal sorting with blue machine. No. B635, Postal sorting with purple machine.

1991, Mar. 16 Photo. *Perf. 13*

B634 SP318 2.50fr +60c multi 1.00 .75
B635 SP318 2.50fr +60c multi 1.00 .75
a. Bklt. pane of 6 + 2 labels 6.00

Winter Olympics Type of 1990

No. B636, Acrobatic skiing. No. B637, Alpine skiing.

1991 Engr. *Perf. 13*

B636 SP313 2.50fr +20c multi 1.00 .75
B637 SP313 2.50fr +20c multi 1.00 .75

Issued: No. B636, Aug. 3; No. B637, Aug. 17.

Nos. B636-B637 inscribed "La Poste 1992."

The Harbor of Toulon by Francois Nardi SP319

1991, Dec. 2 Photo. *Perf. 13x12½*

B638 SP319 2.50fr +60c multi 1.00 .75
a. Perf. 13x13½ 1.10 .75
b. As "a," bklt. pane of 10 + 2 labels 9.00

Surtax for the Red Cross.

Winter Olympics Type of 1990
Miniature Sheet

No. B639: a, like #B611. b, like #B621. c, like #B622. d, like #B623. e, like #B624. f, like #B625.

1992, Feb. 8 Engr. *Perf. 13*

B639 Sheet of 10 + label 15.00 15.00
a.-f. SP313 2.50fr +20c multi 1.00 .75

No. B639 contains one each B626-B627, B636-B637, B639a-B639f. Central label is litho.

Stamp Day SP320

Designs: Careers in Post, Welcome — No. B640, gray people. No. B641, red people.

1992, Mar. 7 Litho. *Perf. 13*

B640 SP320 2.50fr +60c gray people 1.00 .75

Booklet Stamp
Photo.

B641 SP320 2.50fr +60c red people 1.00 .75
a. Bklt. pane of 6 + 2 labels 6.00

SP321

Composers: No. B642, Cesar Franck (1822-1890). No. B643, Erik Satie (1866-1925). No. B644, Florent Schmitt (1870-1958). No. B645, Arthur Honegger (1892-1955). No. B646, Georges Auric (1899-1983). No. B647, Germaine Tailleferre (1892-1983).

1992, Apr. 11 Photo. *Perf. 13*

B642 SP321 2.50fr +50c multi 1.00 .75
B643 SP321 2.50fr +50c multi 1.00 .75
B644 SP321 2.50fr +50c multi 1.00 .75
B645 SP321 2.50fr +50c multi 1.00 .75
B646 SP321 2.50fr +50c multi 1.00 .75
B647 SP321 2.50fr +50c multi 1.00 .75
a. Bklt. pane of 6, #B642-B647 6.00

SP322

1992, Nov. 28 Photo. *Perf. 13½x13*

B648 SP322 2.50fr +60c multi 1.00 .70
a. Bklt. pane of 10 + 2 labels 9.00

Mutual Aid, Strasbourg. Surtax for the Red Cross.

Writers SP323

No. B649, Guy de Maupassant (1850-93). No. B650, Alain (Emile Chartier) (1868-1951). No. B651, Jean Cocteau (1889-1963). No. B652, Marcel Pagnol (1895-1974). No. B653, Andre Chamson (1900-83). No. B654, Marguerite Yourcenar (1903-87).

1993, Apr. 24 Engr. *Perf. 13*

B649 SP323 2.50fr +50c multi 1.00 .75
B650 SP323 2.50fr +50c multi 1.00 .75
B651 SP323 2.50fr +50c multi 1.00 .75
B652 SP323 2.50fr +50c multi 1.00 .75
B653 SP323 2.50fr +50c multi 1.00 .75
B654 SP323 2.50fr +50c multi 1.00 .75
a. Bklt. pane of 6, #B649-B654 + 2 labels 6.00

When Nos. B650-B654 are normally centered, inscriptions at base of the lower panel are not parallel to the perforations at bottom. On all six stamps the lower panel is not centered between the side perforations.

SP324

St. Nicolas, Image of Metz.

1993, Nov. 27 Engr. *Perf. 12½x13*

B655 SP324 2.80fr +60c multi 1.10 .75
a. Perf. 13½x13 1.20 .75
b. As "a," Bklt. pane of 10 +2 labels 12.00

Surtax for Red Cross.

SP325

Stage and Screen Personalities: No. B656, Yvonne Printemps (1894-1977). No. B657, Fernandel (1903-71). No. B658, Josephine Baker (1906-75). No. B659, Bourvil (1917-70). No. B660, Yves Montand (1921-91). No. B661, Coluche (1944-86).

1994, Sept. 17 Photo. *Perf. 13*

B656 SP325 2.80fr +60c multi 1.10 .75
B657 SP325 2.80fr +60c multi 1.10 .75
B658 SP325 2.80fr +60c multi 1.10 .75
B659 SP325 2.80fr +60c multi 1.10 .75
B660 SP325 2.80fr +60c multi 1.10 .75
B661 SP325 2.80fr +60c multi 1.10 .75
a. Bklt. pane, #B656-B661 + 2 labels 6.00

SP326

Designs: No. B662, St. Vaast, Arras Tapestry. No. B663, Brussels tapestry from Reydams workshop, Horse Museum, Saumur.

1994-95 Photo. *Perf. 12½x13*

B662 SP326 2.80fr +60c multi 1.10 .75
a. Perf. 13½x13 1.20 .75
b. Bklt. pane, 10 #B662a + 2 labels 12.00
Complete booklet, #B662b 13.00
B663 SP326 2.80fr +60c multi 1.10 .75
a. Perf. 13½x13 1.20 .75
b. Bklt. pane, 10 #B663a + 2 labels 12.00
Complete booklet, #B663b 13.00

Surtax for Red Cross.

Issued: No. B662, 11/26/94; No. B663, 5/13/95.

SP327

Provencal Nativity Figures: No. B664, The Shepherd. No. B665, The Miller. No. B666, The Simpleton and the Tambour Player. No. B667, The Fishmonger. No. B668, The Scissor Grinder. No. B669, The Elders.

1995, Nov. 25 Engr. *Perf. 13*

B664 SP327 2.80fr +60c multi 1.10 .85
B665 SP327 2.80fr +60c multi 1.10 .85
B666 SP327 2.80fr +60c multi 1.10 .85
B667 SP327 2.80fr +60c multi 1.10 .85
B668 SP327 2.80fr +60c multi 1.10 .85
B669 SP327 2.80fr +60c multi 1.10 .85
a. Booklet pane, Nos. B664-B669 + 2 labels 7.50
Complete booklet, No. B669a 11.00

SP328

Famous Fictional Detectives and Criminals: No. B670, Rocambole. No. B671, Arsène Lupin. No. B672, Joseph Rouletabille. No. B673, Fantômas. No. B674, Commissioner Maigret. No. B675, Nestor Burma.

1996, Oct. 5 Photo. *Perf. 13*

B670 SP328 3fr +60c multi 1.10 .85
B671 SP328 3fr +60c multi 1.10 .85
B672 SP328 3fr +60c multi 1.10 .85
B673 SP328 3fr +60c multi 1.10 .85
B674 SP328 3fr +60c multi 1.10 .85
B675 SP328 3fr +60c multi 1.10 .85
a. Booklet pane, #B670-B675 + 2 labels 7.50
Complete booklet, #B675a 11.00

Christmas SP329

1996, Nov. 16 Photo. *Perf. 12¾x13*

B676 SP329 3fr +60c multi 1.10 .85
a. Perf. 13¼x13 1.20 .85
b. Booklet pane, 10 #B676a + 2 labels 12.00 —
Complete booklet, #B676b 13.00

Surtax for Red Cross.

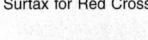

Adventure Heroes SP330

No. B677, Sir Lancelot. No. B678, Pardaillan. No. B679, D'Artagnan. No. B680, Cyrano de Bergerac. No. B681, Captain Fracasse. No. B682, Le Bossu.

1997, Oct. 25 Photo. *Perf. 13*

B677 SP330 3fr +60c multi 1.10 .85
B678 SP330 3fr +60c multi 1.10 .85
B679 SP330 3fr +60c multi 1.10 .85
B680 SP330 3fr +60c multi 1.10 .85
B681 SP330 3fr +60c multi 1.10 .85
B682 SP330 3fr +60c multi 1.10 .85
a. Booklet pane, #B677-B682 + 2 labels 7.50
Complete booklet, #B682a 7.50

Christmas, New Year — SP331

1997, Nov. 6 Photo. *Perf. 12¾x13*

B683 SP331 3fr +60c multi 1.10 .90
a. Perf. 13¼x13 1.20 .95
b. Booklet pane, 10 #B683a + 2 labels 12.00 —
Complete booklet, #B683b 13.00

Surtax for the Red Cross.

SP332

Actors of the French Cinema: No. B684, Romy Schneider (1938-82). No. B685, Simone Signoret (1921-85). No. B686, Jean Gabin (1904-76). No. B687, Louis de Funés (1914-83). No. B688, Bernard Blier (1916-89). No. B689, Lino Ventura (1919-87).

1998, Oct. 3 Photo. *Perf. 13*

B684 SP332 3fr +60c multi 1.10 .85
B685 SP332 3fr +60c multi 1.10 .85
B686 SP332 3fr +60c multi 1.10 .85
B687 SP332 3fr +60c multi 1.10 .85
B688 SP332 3fr +60c multi 1.10 .85
B689 SP332 3fr +60c multi 1.10 .85
a. Booklet pane, #B684-B689 + label 7.50
Complete booklet, #B689a 8.00

Christmas SP333

1998, Nov. 5 Photo. *Perf. 12½x13*

B690 SP333 3fr +60c multi 1.10 .85
a. Perf. 13½x13 1.20 .85
b. Booklet pane, 10 #B690a + 2 labels 12.00
Complete booklet, #B690b 13.00

Surtax for Red Cross.

Famous Photographers — SP334

Photographs by: No. B691, Robert Doisneau (1912-94). No. B692, Brassai (Gyula Halasz) (1899-1984). No. B693, Jacques Lartigue (1894-1986). No. B694, Henri Cartier-Bresson (1908-2004). No. B695, Eugene Atget (1857-1927). No. B696, Felix Nadar (1820-1910).

1999, July 10 Photo. *Perf. 13*

B691 SP334 3fr +60c multi 1.10 .85
B692 SP334 3fr +60c multi 1.10 .85
B693 SP334 3fr +60c multi 1.10 .85
B694 SP334 3fr +60c multi 1.10 .85
B695 SP334 3fr +60c multi 1.10 .85
B696 SP334 3fr +60c multi 1.10 .85
a. Booklet pane, #B691-B696 7.50
Complete booklet, #B696a 8.00

New Year 2000 — SP335

1999, Nov. 10 Photo. *Perf. 12¾x13*

B697 SP335 3fr +60c multi 1.20 .85
a. Perf. 13½x13 1.25 .85
b. Booklet pane, 10 #B697a + 2 labels 9.00
Complete booklet, #B697b 10.00

Surtax for Red Cross.

Adventurers SP336

No. B698, Eric Tabarly (1931-98), sailor. No. B699, Alexandra David-Néel (1868-1969), opera singer, Asian traveler. No. B700, Haroun Tazieff (1914-98), vulcanologist. No. B701, Paul-Emile Victor (1907-55), ethnologist, polar explorer. No. B702, Jacques-Yves Cousteau (1910-97), oceanographer. No. B703, Norbert Casteret (1897-1987), speleologist.

2000, Sept. 16 Photo. *Perf. 13¼x13*

B698 SP336 3fr +60c multi 1.20 .85
B699 SP336 3fr +60c multi 1.20 .85
B700 SP336 3fr +60c multi 1.20 .85
B701 SP336 3fr +60c multi 1.20 .85
B702 SP336 3fr +60c multi 1.20 .85
B703 SP336 3fr +60c multi 1.20 .85
a. Booklet pane, #B698-B703 7.00
Booklet, #B703a 7.50

Toy Airplane — SP337

2000, Nov. 9 Photo. *Perf. 13¼x13*

B704 SP337 3fr +60c multi 1.10 .85
a. Booklet pane of 10 + 2 labels 12.00
Booklet, #B704a 13.00

Surtax for Red Cross.

Santa Claus and Tree Ornaments SP338

2001, Nov. 8 Photo. *Perf. 12¾x13*

B705 SP338 3fr +60c multi 1.10 .85
a. Perf 13½x13 1.20 .85
b. Booklet pane of 10 11.00 —
Booklet, #B705a 11.00

Surtax for Red Cross.

Infant Jesus Asleep, by Giovanni Battista Salvi — SP339

2002, Nov. 7 Photo. *Perf. 12¾x13*

B706 SP339 46c +9c multi 1.10 .85
a. Perf. 13½x13 1.20 .85
b. As "a," booklet pane of 10 11.00 —
Booklet, #B706b 11.00

Surtax for Red Cross.

Virgin with Grapes, by Pierre Mignard — SP340

2003, Nov. 6 Photo. *Perf. 13¼x13*
Booklet Stamp

B707 SP340 50c +(16c) multi 1.50 1.00
a. Booklet pane of 10 15.00 —
Complete booklet, #B707a 15.00

Surtax for Red Cross.

Virgin With Child, Attributed to Cretan School — SP341

2004, Nov. 10 Photo. *Perf. 13¼x13*
Booklet Stamp

B708 SP341 50c +(16c) multi 1.50 1.00
a. Booklet pane of 10 + 2 labels 15.00 —
Complete booklet, #B708a 15.00

Surtax for Red Cross.

Dec. 26, 2004 Tsunami Victim Relief SP342

2005, Jan. 13 Engr. *Perf. 13*

B709 SP342 (50c) +20c red 1.75 .50

Virgin and Child, by Hans Memling SP343

2005, Nov. 10 Photo. *Perf. 13½x13*
Booklet Stamp

B710 SP343 53c +(17c) multi 1.50 1.00
a. Booklet pane of 10 + 2 labels 15.00 —
Complete booklet, #B710a 15.00

Surtax for Red Cross.

SP344

Children's Art — SP345

2006, Nov. 25 Photo. *Perf. 13½x13*
Booklet Stamps

B711 SP344 (54c) +(17c) multi 1.90 .85
B712 SP345 (54c) +(17c) multi 1.90 .85
a. Booklet pane, 5 each #B711-B712, + 2 labels 19.00 —
Complete booklet, #B712a 19.00

Surtax for Red Cross.

Red Cross
SP346 SP347

Serpentine Die Cut 11
2007, Nov. 24 Photo.
Self-Adhesive
Booklet Stamps

B713 SP346 (54c) +(17c) multi 1.90 .85
B714 SP347 (54c) +(17c) multi 1.90 .85
a. Booklet pane, 5 each #B713-B714 19.00

Surtax for Red Cross.

Red Cross
SP348 SP349

Serpentine Die Cut 11x11¼
2008, Nov. 8 Photo.
Booklet Stamps
Self-Adhesive

B715 SP348 (55c) +(18c) multi 1.90 .85
B716 SP349 (55c) +(18c) multi 1.90 .85
a. Booklet pane of 10, 2 each #B715-B716 19.00

Surtax for Red Cross.

Miniature Sheet

Red Cross — SP350

No. B717: a, Henri Dunant. b, Battle of Solferino. c, Pélias et Nélée, by Georges Braque, horiz. d, Geneva Conventions. e, Globe and symbols of the International Red Cross and Red Crescent Societies.

2009, Sept. 19 Photo. *Perf. 13*

B717 SP350 Sheet of 5 12.00 12.00
a.-e. 56c +(40c) Any single 2.50 2.50

Surtax for Red Cross.

Haiti Earthquake Relief — SP351

2010, Jan. 19 Engr. *Perf. 13*

B718 SP351 (56c) +44c red 2.25 1.50

Self-Adhesive

Serpentine Die Cut 11

B719 SP351 (56c) +44c red 4.50 4.00

Surtax was for French Red Cross relief efforts in Haiti.

Miniature Sheet

Red Cross — SP352

No. B720: a, Woman on telephone. b, Man assisting unconscious woman. c, Red Cross emblem, horiz. d, Woman performing Heimlich maneuver on choking man. e, Cardio-pulmonary resuscitation.

Photo., Photo. & Embossed (#B720c)

2010, Nov. 5 *Perf. 13*

B720 SP352 Sheet of 5 12.00 8.00
a.-e. 58c +(40c) Any single 2.00 1.25

Surtax for Red Cross.

Miniature Sheet

Singers — SP353

No. B721: a, Colette Renard (1924-2010). b, Henri Salvador (1917-2008). c, Serge Reggiani (1922-2004). d, Claude Nougaro (1929-2004). e, Daniel Balavoine (1952-86). f, Gilbert Bécaud (1927-2001).

2011, Oct. 14 Photo. *Perf. 13*

B721 SP353 Sheet of 6 12.00 9.00
a.-f. 60c + (33⅓c) Any single 2.00 1.50

Surtax for Red Cross.

Miniature Sheet

Red Cross — SP354

No. B722: a, People carrying person on litter. b, Three hands. c, Red Cross, horiz. d, Red Cross volunteer teaching illiterates. e, Red Cross volunteer giving bottle to infant.

2011, Nov. 4

B722 SP354 Sheet of 5 10.00 7.50
a.-e. 60c + (40c) Any single 2.00 1.50

Surtax for Red Cross.

Miniature Sheet

Movie Stars — SP355

No. B723: a, Françoise Dorléac (1942-67). b, Jean Marais (1913-98). c, Jacqueline Maillan (1923-92). d, Michel Serrault (1928-2007). e, Philippe Noiret (1930-2006). f, Annie Girardot (1931-2011).

2012, Oct. 19

B723 SP355 Sheet of 6 12.00 9.00
a.-f. 60c + (33⅓c) Any single 2.00 1.50

Surtax for Red Cross.

Miniature Sheet

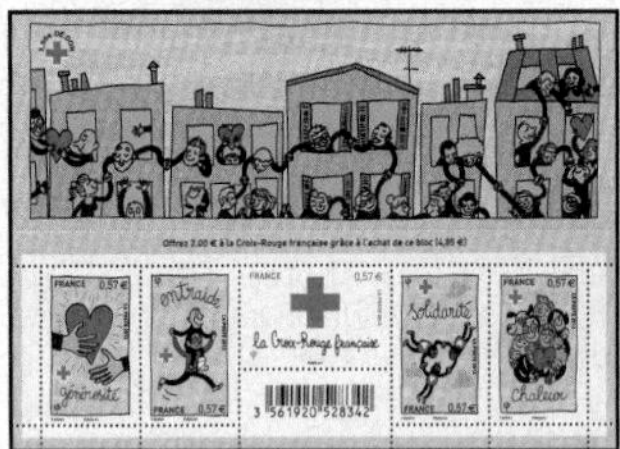

Red Cross — SP356

No. B724: a, Heart and hands. b, Man carrying man with injured foot. c, Red Cross, horiz. d, Three parachutists. e, People and dog hugging heart.

2012, Nov. 8

B724 SP356 Sheet of 5 12.50 12.50
a.-e. 57c + (40c) Any single 2.50 2.50

Surtax for Red Cross.

Loire River SP357

The Loire River at: No. B725, Mont Gerbier de Jonc. No. B726, Lac de Grangent. No. B727, Bec d'Allier. No. B728, Gien. No. B729, Pointe de Coupain. No. B730, Blois. No. B731, Candes-Saint-Martin. No. B732, Ingrandes-sur-Loire. No. B733, Champtoceaux. No. B734, Marais de Brière.

2013, June 1 *Serpentine Die Cut 11*

Booklet Stamps
Self-Adhesive

B725 SP357 (58c+20c) multi 1.60 .50
B726 SP357 (58c+20c) multi 1.60 .50
B727 SP357 (58c+20c) multi 1.60 .50
B728 SP357 (58c+20c) multi 1.60 .50
B729 SP357 (58c+20c) multi 1.60 .50
B730 SP357 (58c+20c) multi 1.60 .50
B731 SP357 (58c+20c) multi 1.60 .50
B732 SP357 (58c+20c) multi 1.60 .50
B733 SP357 (58c+20c) multi 1.60 .50
B734 SP357 (58c+20c) multi 1.60 .50
a. Booklet pane of 10, #B725-B734 18.00
Nos. B725-B734 (10) 16.00 5.00

Surtax for the Red Cross.

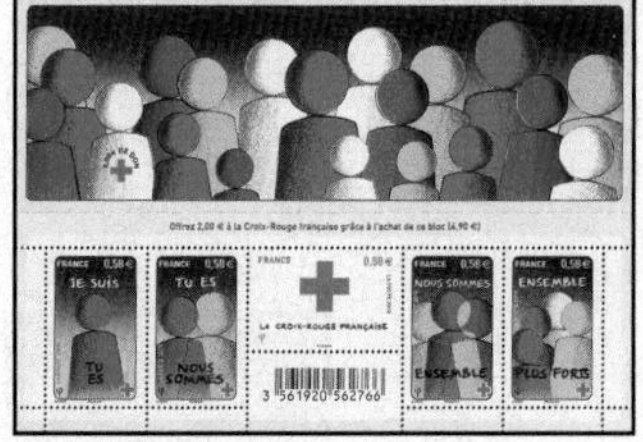

Red Cross — SP358

No. B735: a, One stylized person. b, Two stylized people. c, Red Cross, horiz. d, Three stylized people. e, Four stylized people.

2013, Nov. 7 Photo. *Perf. 13*

B735 SP358 Sheet of 5 10.00 7.50
a.-e. 58c + (40c) Any single 1.75 1.25

Surtax for Red Cross.

Flowers SP359

Designs: No. B736, Roses. No. B737, Daisies (Marguerite). No. B738, Tulips (Tulipe). No. B739, Sunflowers (Tournesol). No. B740, Irises. No. B741, Orchids (Orchidée). No. B742, Jonquils (Jonquille). No. B743, Lilies (Lys). No. B744, Carnations (Oeillet). No. B745, Gardenias (Gardénia).

Serpentine Die Cut 11

2014, May 24 Photo.

Booklet Stamps
Self-Adhesive

B736 SP359 (61c) + (20c) multi 1.75 1.00
B737 SP359 (61c) + (20c) multi 1.75 1.00
B738 SP359 (61c) + (20c) multi 1.75 1.00
B739 SP359 (61c) + (20c) multi 1.75 1.00
B740 SP359 (61c) + (20c) multi 1.75 1.00
B741 SP359 (61c) + (20c) multi 1.75 1.00
B742 SP359 (61c) + (20c) multi 1.75 1.00
B743 SP359 (61c) + (20c) multi 1.75 1.00
B744 SP359 (61c) + (20c) multi 1.75 1.00
B745 SP359 (61c) + (20c) multi 1.75 1.00
a. Booklet pane of 10, #B736-B745 20.00
Nos. B736-B745 (10) 17.50 10.00

Red Cross, 150th anniv. Surtax for Red Cross.

Semi-Postal Stamps of 1914-88 Redrawn

2014, June 14 Litho.

B746 Sheet of 5 14.00 14.00
a. SP2 61c +30c like #B2, perf. 13¼ 2.50 2.50
b. A22 61c +30c like #B1, perf. 13¼ 2.50 2.50
c. SP40 61c +30c like #B81, perf. 13 2.50 2.50
d. SP9 61c +30c like #B11, perf. 13x13¼ 2.50 2.50
e. SP237 61c +30c like #B403, perf. 13 2.50 2.50

B747 Sheet of 5 14.00 14.00
a. SP60 61c +30c like #B101, perf. 13x13¼ 2.50 2.50
b. SP258 61c +30c like #B462, perf. 13 2.50 2.50
c. SP310 61c +30c like #B601, perf. 13¼x13 2.50 2.50
d. SP207 61c +30c like #B328, perf. 13 2.50 2.50
e. SP61 61c +30c like #B102, perf. 13x13¼ 2.50 2.50

Nos. B746-B747 sold together as a set for €12.

Miniature Sheet

French Red Cross, 150th Anniv. — SP360

No. B748: a, Jean-Henri Dunant, 1864. b, White angel with Red Cross arm band treating soldier, 1914. c, Red cross and 150th anniv. emblem, horiz. d, Red Cross worker giving aid to refugee, 1945. e, Red Cross workers in Haiti, 2010.

2014, Nov. 7 Photo. *Perf. 13*

B748 SP360 Sheet of 5 10.00 8.00
a.-e. 61c+(30c) Any single 2.00 1.25

Surtax for the Red Cross.

SP361

SP362

SP363

SP364

SP366

SP367

Red Cross Workers in Action SP368

Serpentine Die Cut 11

2015, May 16 **Litho.**

Booklet Stamps
Self-Adhesive

B749	SP361 (68c+25c) multi		2.10	2.10
B750	SP362 (68c+25c) multi		2.10	2.10
B751	SP363 (68c+25c) multi		2.10	2.10
B752	SP364 (68c+25c) multi		2.10	2.10
B753	SP365 (68c+25c) multi		2.10	2.10
B754	SP366 (68c+25c) multi		2.10	2.10
B755	SP367 (68c+25c) multi		2.10	2.10
B756	SP368 (68c+25c) multi		2.10	2.10
a.	Booklet pane of 8, #B749-B756		17.00	
	Nos. B749-B756 (8)		16.80	16.80

Surtax for the Red Cross.

Miniature Sheet

Red Cross — SP369

No. B757: a, Red cross, heart and arrows. b, Sun, red crosses, ambulance. c, Red cross and text, horiz. d, Red cross and heart. e, Red Cross and text, diff.

2015, Nov. 7 **Photo.** ***Perf. 13***

B757	SP369 Sheet of 5	11.50	11.50
a.-e.	68c+(40c) Any single	2.25	2.25

Surtax for the Red Cross.

SP370

SP371

SP372

SP373

SP374

SP375

SP376

Red Cross Workers SP377

Serpentine Die Cut 11

2016, Apr. 30 **Litho.**

Booklet Stamps
Self-Adhesive

B758	SP370 (70c+25c) multi	2.25	2.25
B759	SP371 (70c+25c) multi	2.25	2.25
B760	SP372 (70c+25c) multi	2.25	2.25
B761	SP373 (70c+25c) multi	2.25	2.25
B762	SP374 (70c+25c) multi	2.25	2.25
B763	SP375 (70c+25c) multi	2.25	2.25
B764	SP376 (70c+25c) multi	2.25	2.25
B765	SP377 (70c+25c) multi	2.25	2.25
a.	Booklet pane of 8, #B758-B765	18.00	
	Nos. B758-B765 (8)	18.00	18.00

Surtax for the Red Cross.

Miniature Sheet

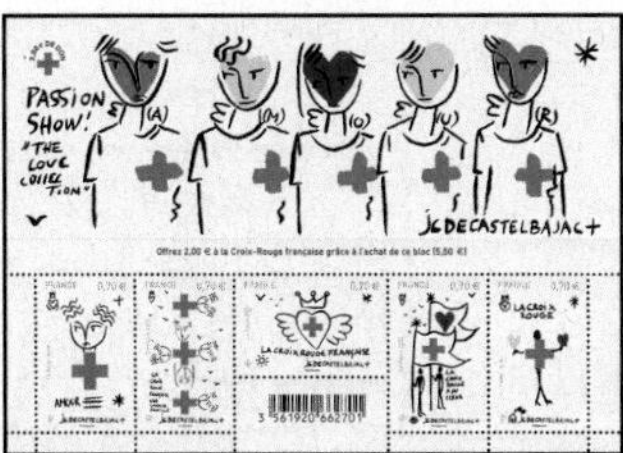

Red Cross — SP378

No. B766: a, Head on top of cross. b, Heads and three crosses. c, Cross in winged and crowned heart, horiz. d, Flags with cross and heart. e, Stylized person with cross as torso and arms.

2016, Nov. 5 **Photo.** ***Perf. 13***

B766	SP378 Sheet of 5	12.00	12.00
a.-e.	70c+(40c) Any single	2.40	2.40

Surtax for the Red Cross.

SP379

SP380

SP381

SP382

SP383

SP384

SP385

Work of the Red Cross SP386

Serpentine Die Cut 11

2017, May 5 **Photo.**

Booklet Stamps
Self-Adhesive

B767	SP379 (73c+25c) multi	2.25	2.25
B768	SP380 (73c+25c) multi	2.25	2.25
B769	SP381 (73c+25c) multi	2.25	2.25
B770	SP382 (73c+25c) multi	2.25	2.25
B771	SP383 (73c+25c) multi	2.25	2.25
B772	SP384 (73c+25c) multi	2.25	2.25
B773	SP385 (73c+25c) multi	2.25	2.25
B774	SP386 (73c+25c) multi	2.25	2.25
a.	Booklet pane of 8, #B767-B774	18.00	
	Nos. B767-B774 (8)	18.00	18.00

Surtax for Red Cross.

Marianne and Children "Lettre Prioritaire" Without Gram Limit Inscription Type of 2016

2017, Oct. 20 **Photo.** ***Perf. 13***

B775	A2536 (85c+66c) red	3.50	3.50

No. B775 was printed in sheets of 3 that sold for €4.55, €2 of which was for the Red Cross.

Flowers SP387

Designs: No. B776, Anemones and shell. No. B777, Asters and daisies (asters et marguerites), keys. No. B778, Dahlias, eglantine roses and peaches. No. B779, Snapdragons and cornflowers (moufliers et bleuets), elephant figurine. No. B780, Peonies (pivoines), cat figurine. No. B781, Ranunculus (renoncules), letter and shell. No. B782, Roses, hourglass. No. B783, Calendulas (soucis) and oranges. No. B784, Sunflowers and blue thistles (tournesols et chardons bleus), teapot and owl figurine. No. B785, Zinnias, snail and butterflies.

Serpentine Die Cut 11

2018, May 4 **Photo.**

Booklet Stamps
Self-Adhesive

B776	SP387 (80c+20c) multi	2.40	2.40
B777	SP387 (80c+20c) multi	2.40	2.40
B778	SP387 (80c+20c) multi	2.40	2.40
B779	SP387 (80c+20c) multi	2.40	2.40
B780	SP387 (80c+20c) multi	2.40	2.40
B781	SP387 (80c+20c) multi	2.40	2.40
B782	SP387 (80c+20c) multi	2.40	2.40
B783	SP387 (80c+20c) multi	2.40	2.40
B784	SP387 (80c+20c) multi	2.40	2.40
B785	SP387 (80c+20c) multi	2.40	2.40
a.	Booklet pane of 10, #B776-B785	24.00	
	Nos. B776-B785 (10)	24.00	24.00

Surtax was for Red Cross.

Marianne and Red Cross SP388

2018, Oct. 26 **Photo.** ***Perf. 13***

B786	SP388 (95c+66c) multi	3.75	3.75

No. B786 was printed in sheets of 3 that sold for €4.85, €2 of which was for the Red Cross.

SP389

SP390

SP391

SP392

SP393

SP394

SP395

SP396

SP397

Photographs of People by Christian Guémy — SP398

Serpentine Die Cut 11

2019, May 10 **Photo.**

Booklet Stamps
Self-Adhesive

B787	SP389 (88c+20c) multi	2.50	2.50
B788	SP390 (88c+20c) multi	2.50	2.50
B789	SP391 (88c+20c) multi	2.50	2.50
B790	SP392 (88c+20c) multi	2.50	2.50
B791	SP393 (88c+20c) multi	2.50	2.50
B792	SP394 (88c+20c) multi	2.50	2.50
B793	SP395 (88c+20c) multi	2.50	2.50
B794	SP396 (88c+20c) multi	2.50	2.50
B795	SP397 (88c+20c) multi	2.50	2.50
B796	SP398 (88c+20c) multi	2.50	2.50
a.	Booklet pane of 10, #B787-B796	25.00	
	Nos. B787-B796 (10)	25.00	25.00

Surtax for Red Cross.

AIR POST STAMPS

Nos. 127, 130 Overprinted in Dark Blue or Black

Perf. 14x13½

1927, June 25 **Unwmk.**

C1	A18 2fr org & bl (DB)	200.00	225.00
	Never hinged	400.00	
C2	A18 5fr dk bl & buff	200.00	225.00
	Never hinged	400.00	

On sale only at the Intl. Aviation Exhib. at Marseilles, June, 1927. One set could be purchased by each holder of an admission ticket. Excellent counterfeits exist.

Nos. 242, 196 Surcharged

1928, Aug. 23

C3	A33 10fr on 90c	2,400.	1,800.
	Never hinged	3,500.	
a.	Inverted surcharge	16,500.	16,500.
	Never hinged	25,000.	
b.	Space between "10" and bars 6½mm	3,100.	3,100.
	Never hinged	5,100.	
C4	A23 10fr on 1.50fr	10,000.	8,250.
	Never hinged	14,000.	
a.	Space between "10" and bars 6½mm	13,000.	13,000.
	Never hinged	20,000.	

Nos. C3-C4 received their surcharge in New York by order of the French consul general. They were for use in paying the 10fr fee for letters leaving the liner Ile de France on a catapulted hydroplane when the ship was one day off the coast of France on its eastward voyage.

The normal space between "10" and bars is 4½mm, but on 10 stamps in each pane of 50 the space is 6½mm. Counterfeits exist.

View of Marseille, Church of Notre Dame at Left — AP1

1930-31 **Engr.** ***Perf. 13***

C5	AP1 1.50fr dp car	21.00	4.00
	Never hinged	40.00	
a.	With perf. initials "E.I.P.A.30"	2,750.	3,750.
	Never hinged	3,600.	
C6	AP1 1.50fr dk bl ('31)	19.00	2.25
	Never hinged	35.00	
a.	1.50fr ultramarine	50.00	21.00
	Never hinged	90.00	
b.	As "a," with perf. initials "E.I.P.A.30"	450.00	350.00
	Never hinged	700.00	

Nos. C5a, C6a were sold at the Intl. Air Post Exhib., Paris, Nov. 6-20, 1930, at face value plus 5fr, the price of admission.

Forgeries abound of Nos. C5a and C6b. Certificates from recognized authorities are recommended.

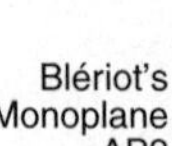

Blériot's Monoplane AP2

1934, Sept. 1 ***Perf. 13***

C7	AP2 2.25fr violet	24.00	6.00
	Never hinged	32.50	

1st flight across the English Channel, by Louis Blériot.

Plane over Paris AP3

1936

C8	AP3 85c deep green	2.25	2.25
	Never hinged	6.50	
C9	AP3 1.50fr blue	10.50	5.50
	Never hinged	18.00	
C10	AP3 2.25fr violet	18.00	7.00
	Never hinged	35.00	
C11	AP3 2.50fr rose	32.50	8.25
	Never hinged	45.00	
C12	AP3 3fr ultra	26.00	2.50
	Never hinged	37.50	
C13	AP3 3.50fr orange brn	62.50	24.00
	Never hinged	105.00	
C14	AP3 50fr emerald	825.00	325.00
	Never hinged	1,450.	
b.	50fr green	850.00	350.00
	Never hinged	1,500.	
	Nos. C8-C14 (7)	976.75	374.50

Monoplane over Paris — AP4

Paper with Red Network Overprint

1936, July 10 ***Perf. 12½***

C15	AP4 50fr ultra	625.00	310.00
	Never hinged	1,700.	

Airplane and Galleon — AP5

Airplane and Globe AP6

1936, Aug. 17 ***Perf. 13***

C16	AP5 1.50fr dk ultra	17.50	5.25
	Never hinged	35.00	
C17	AP6 10fr Prus green	290.00	130.00
	Never hinged	700.00	

100th air mail flight across the South Atlantic.

Catalogue values for unused stamps in this section, from this point to the end of the section, are for Never Hinged items.

Centaur and Plane — AP7

Iris — AP8

Zeus Carrying Hebe AP9

Chariot of the Sun AP10

1946-47 **Engr.** **Unwmk.**

C18	AP7 40fr dk green	.55	.25
C19	AP8 50fr rose pink	.60	.25
C20	AP9 100fr dk blue ('47)	6.25	3.25
C21	AP10 200fr red	5.25	1.50
	Nos. C18-C21 (4)	12.65	5.25

Issued: 50fr, 200fr, 5/27; 40fr, 7/1; 100fr, Jan.

For surcharges see Reunion Nos. C35-C38.

Ile de la Cité, Paris, and Gull — AP11

1947, May 7

C22	AP11 500fr dk Prus grn	45.00	27.50

UPU 12th Cong., Paris, May 7-July 7. See footnote after No. 4642.

View of Lille AP12

Air View of Paris — AP13

200fr, Bordeaux. 300fr, Lyon. 500fr, Marseille.

1949-50 **Unwmk.** ***Perf. 13***

C23	AP12 100fr sepia	1.20	.40
C24	AP12 200fr dk bl grn	11.50	.75
C25	AP12 300fr purple	15.00	9.00
C26	AP12 500fr brt red	55.00	4.75
C27	AP13 1000fr blk, dull gray vio ('50)	130.00	24.00
	Nos. C23-C27 (5)	212.70	38.90

For surcharges see Reunion Nos. C39-C41.

Alexander III Bridge and Petit Palais, Paris — AP14

1949, June 13

C28	AP14 100fr brown car	5.25	5.25

International Telegraph and Telephone Conference, Paris, May-July 1949.

Jet Plane, Mystère IV — AP15

Planes: 200fr, Noratlas. 500fr, Miles Magister. 1000fr, Provence.

1954, Jan. 16

C29	AP15 100fr red brn & bl	2.25	.25
C30	AP15 200fr blk brn & vio bl	9.00	.25
C31	AP15 500fr car & org	175.00	10.50
C32	AP15 1000fr vio brn, bl grn & ind	95.00	14.00
	Nos. C29-C32 (4)	281.25	25.00

See No. C37. For surcharges see Reunion Nos. C42-C45, C48.

Maryse Bastié and Plane AP16

1955, June 4 **Unwmk.** ***Perf. 13***

C33	AP16 50fr dp plum & rose pink	5.25	3.75

Issued to honor Maryse Bastié, 1898-1952.

Morane Saulnier 760 Paris AP17

Designs: 500fr, Caravelle. 1000fr, Alouette helicopter.

1957-59 **Engr.** ***Perf. 13***

C34	AP17 300fr sl grn, grnsh bl & sep ('59)	5.00	2.25
C35	AP17 500fr dp ultra & blk	21.00	3.00
C36	AP17 1000fr lil, ol blk & blk ('58)	45.00	19.00
	Nos. C34-C36 (3)	71.00	24.25

See Nos. C38-C41. For surcharges see Reunion Nos. C46-C47, C49-C51.

Types of 1954-59

Planes: 2fr, Noratlas. 3fr, MS760, Paris. 5fr, Caravelle. 10fr, Alouette helicopter.

1960, Jan. 11

C37	AP15 2fr vio bl & ultra	1.10	.25
a.	2fr ultramarine	3.00	.75
C38	AP17 3fr sl grn, grnsh bl & sep	1.20	.25
C39	AP17 5fr dp ultra & blk	2.25	.65
C40	AP17 10fr lil, ol blk & blk	10.00	2.00
	Nos. C37-C40 (4)	14.55	3.15

Type of 1957-59

Design: 2fr, Jet plane, Mystère 20.

1965, June 12 **Engr.** ***Perf. 13***

C41	AP17 2fr slate bl & indigo	.75	.25

Concorde Issue

Common Design Type

1969, Mar. 2 **Engr.** ***Perf. 13***

C42	CD129 1fr indigo & brt bl	.75	.35

The 0.95fr stamp in this design was prepared but not issued. Value $30,000.

Jean Mermoz, Antoine de Saint-Exupéry and Concorde — AP19

1970, Sept. 19 **Engr.** ***Perf. 13***

C43	AP19 20fr blue & indigo	8.00	.55

Jean Mermoz (1901-36) and writer Antoine de Saint-Exupéry (1900-44), aviators and air mail pioneers.

Balloon, Gare d'Austerlitz, Paris — AP20

1971, Jan. 16 Engr. *Perf. 13*

C44 AP20 95c bl, vio bl, org & sl grn .75 .55

Centenary of the balloon post from besieged Paris, 1870-71.

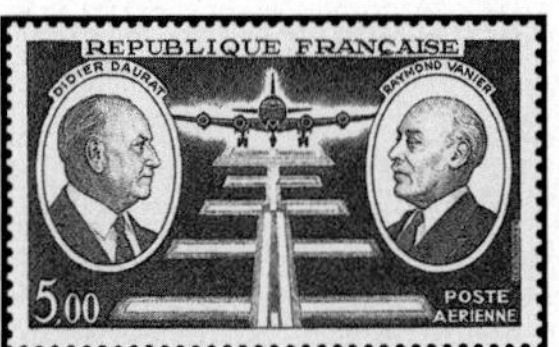

Didier Daurat, Raymond Vanier and Plane Landing at Night — AP21

1971, Apr. 17 Engr. *Perf. 13*

C45 AP21 5fr Prus bl, blk & lt grn 1.75 .25

Didier Daurat (1891-1969) and Raymond Vanier (1895-1965), aviation pioneers.

For surcharge see Reunion No. C52.

Hélène Boucher, Maryse Hilsz and Caudron-Renault and Moth-Morane Planes — AP22

Design: 15fr, Henri Guillaumet, Paul Codos, Latécoère 521, Guillaumet's crashed plane in Andes, skyscrapers.

1972-73 Engr. *Perf. 13*

C46 AP22 10fr plum, red & sl 3.50 .40
C47 AP22 15fr dp car, gray & brn ('73) 5.25 .75

Hélène Boucher (1908-34), Maryse Hilsz (1901-46), Henri Guillaumet (1902-40) and Paul Codos (1896-1960), aviation pioneers. Issue dates: 10fr, June 10; 15fr, Feb. 24.

Concorde AP23

1976, Jan. 10 Engr. *Perf. 13*

C48 AP23 1.70fr brt bl, red & blk .75 .40

First flight of supersonic jet Concorde from Paris to Rio de Janeiro, Jan. 21.

Planes over the Atlantic, New York-Paris — AP24

1977, June 4 Engr. *Perf. 13*

C49 AP24 1.90fr multicolored .75 .40

1st transatlantic flight by Lindbergh from NY to Paris, 50th anniv., and 1st attempted west-bound flight by French aviators Charles Nungesser and Francois Coli.

Plane over Flight Route AP25

1978, Oct. 14 Engr. *Perf. 13*

C50 AP25 1.50fr multicolored .60 .35

65th anniversary of first airmail route from Villacoublay to Pauillac, Gironde.

Rocket, Concorde, Exhibition Hall — AP26

1979, June 9 Engr. *Perf. 13*

C51 AP26 1.70fr ultra, org & brn .75 .60

33rd International Aerospace and Space Show, Le Bourget, June 11-15.

First Nonstop Transatlantic Flight, Paris-New York — AP27

1980, Aug. 30 Engr. *Perf. 13*

C52 AP27 2.50fr vio brn & ultra .90 .30

34th Intl. Space and Aeronautics Exhibition, June 5-14 AP28

1981, June 6 Engr. *Perf. 13*

C53 AP28 2fr multicolored 1.20 .40

Dieudonné Costes and Joseph Le Brix and their Breguet Bi-plane — AP29

1981, Sept. 12 Engr.

C54 AP29 10fr dk brown & red 3.50 .40

1st So. Atlantic crossing, Oct. 14-15, 1927.

Seaplane Late-300 — AP30

1982, Dec. 4 Engr.

C55 AP30 1.60fr multicolored .75 .40

Farman F-60 Goliath — AP31

Planes: 20fr, CAMS-53 seaplane. 30fr, Wibault 283 Monoplane. 50fr, Dewoitine 338.

1984-87 Engr.

C56 AP31	15fr dark blue		5.00	.75
C57 AP31	20fr dp org ('85)		6.50	.75
C58 AP31	30fr brt vio ('86)		10.00	1.50
C59 AP31	50fr green ('87)		15.00	4.50
	Nos. C55-C59 (5)		37.25	7.90

Issued: 15fr, 3/3; 20fr, 3/2; 30fr, 10/11; 50fr, 4/11.

Breguet XIV — AP32

1997, Nov. 15 Photo. *Perf. 13x13¼*

C60 AP32 20fr shown 9.00 3.00
a. Perf. 13x12½ 6.00 1.50
C61 AP32 30fr Potez 25 12.50 3.50
a. Perf. 13x12½ 10.00 2.25

Issued: No. C60 11/15/97; No. C60a, 7/13/98; 30fr, 7/13/98.

Airbus A300-B4 — AP33

1999, Apr. 10 Photo. *Perf. 13x13¼*

C62 AP33 15fr multicolored 15.00 3.00
a. Perf. 13x12½ 5.25 1.25

Couzinet 70 — AP34

2000, Feb. 12 *Perf. 13¼x13¼*

C63 AP34 50fr multi 17.50 6.00
a. Perf. 13x12½ 22.50 7.50

First Flight of Airbus A300, 30th Anniv. — AP35

2002, Oct. 26 Photo. *Perf. 13x13¼*

C64 AP35 €3 multi 7.00 1.50

No. C64 was issued both in panes of 40 and 10, same perforation.

Jacqueline Auriol (1917-2000), Pilot, and Jet — AP36

Litho. & Engr.

2003, June 21 *Perf. 13*

C65 AP36 €4 multi 9.00 2.25
a. Miniature sheet of 10 90.00 —

Marie Marvingt (1875-1963), Pilot — AP37

Litho. & Engr.

2004, June 29 *Perf. 13¼x13*

C66 AP37 €5 multi 11.00 3.00
a. Sheet of 10 110.00 —

Adrienne Bolland (1895-1975), Pilot — AP38

Litho. & Engr.

2005, Oct. 22 *Perf. 13*

C67 AP38 €2 multi 4.50 1.50
a. Miniature sheet of 10 45.00 —

Airbus A380 — AP39

2006, June 23 Photo. *Perf. 13x13¼*

C68 AP39 €3 multi 6.50 1.50
a. Miniature sheet of 10 65.00 —

Helicopters, Cent. — AP40

2007, Feb. 19 Photo. *Perf. 13x12½*

C69 AP40 €3 multi 6.50 1.50
a. Perf. 13x13¼ 9.00 2.25

No. C69 was issued in panes of 40; No. C69a in panes of 10.

French Acrobatic Patrol — AP41

Litho. & Engr.

2008, Sept. 13 *Perf. 13*
C70 AP41 €3 multi 6.50 1.50

Louis Blériot (1872-1936) and Blériot XI Airplane — AP42

Litho. & Engr.

2009, July 25 *Perf. 13x12¾*
C71 AP42 €2 multi 4.50 1.25

First flight across English Channel, cent.

Henri Fabre (1882-1984) and Le Canard Seaplane — AP43

Litho. & Engr.

2010, Mar. 27 *Perf. 13*
C72 AP43 €3 multi 6.50 1.50

First seaplane flight, cent.

Henri Pequet (1888-1974), Pilot for First Official Air Mail Flight in India — AP44

2011, Feb. 18
C73 AP44 €2 multi 4.50 1.25

First French Airmail Flight Between Nancy and Luneville, Cent. — AP45

2012, July 30
C74 AP45 €3 multi 6.50 1.50

First Parachute Jump by Adolphe Pégoud (1889-1915), Cent. — AP46

2013, June 13
C75 AP46 €2.55 multi 5.50 1.50
a. Miniature sheet of 10 65.00 65.00

First Trans-Mediterranean Flight by Roland Garros, Cent. — AP47

2013, Sept. 21 Photo. *Perf. 13x12¾*
C76 AP47 €3.40 multi 8.00 1.50

Caroline Aigle (1974-2007), First Female Fighter Pilot in French Air Force — AP48

Litho. & Engr.

2014, Apr. 5 *Perf. 13*
C77 AP48 €3.55 multi 8.50 1.50

Gaston Caudron (1882-1915), Pilot and Aircraft Manufacturer — AP49

Litho & Engr.

2015, June 15 *Perf. 13*
C78 AP49 €4.10 multi 9.00 2.00

Edouard Nieuport (1875-1911), Aviator and Airplane Manufacturer, and Nieuport 11 — AP50

Litho. & Engr.

2016, June 10 *Perf. 13*
C79 AP50 €4.80 multi 11.00 5.50

Georges Guynemer (1894-1917), Ace Fighter Pilot in World War I, and Spad XIII — AP51

Litho. & Engr.

2017, Sept. 8 *Perf. 13*
C80 AP51 €5.10 multi 12.00 6.00
a. Miniature sheet of 10 — —

Michel Coiffard (1892-1918), and Maurice Boyau (1888-1918), World War I Flying Aces — AP52

Litho. & Engr.

2018, Nov. 10 *Perf. 13*
C81 AP52 €3.80 multi 8.75 4.50

First Flight of the Concorde, 50th Anniv. — AP53

2019, Mar. 1 Photo. *Perf. 13*
C82 AP53 €4.20 multi 9.50 4.75

AIR POST SEMI-POSTAL STAMPS

Catalogue values for unused stamps in this section are for Never Hinged items.

Antoine de Saint-Exupéry — SPAP1

Col. Jean Dagnaux SPAP2

1948 Unwmk. Engr. *Perf. 13*
CB1 SPAP1 50fr + 30fr vio brn 2.75 1.60
CB2 SPAP2 100fr + 70fr dk blue 3.75 2.25

Modern Plane and Ader's "Eole" SPAP3

1948, Feb.
CB3 SPAP3 40fr + 10fr dk blue 1.60 1.50

50th anniv. of the flight of Clément Ader's plane, the Eole, in 1897.

POSTAGE DUE STAMPS

D1

1859-70 Unwmk. Litho. *Imperf.*
J1 D1 10c black 30,500. 240.00
J2 D1 15c black ('70) 140.00 *250.00*

In the lithographed stamps the central bar of the "E" of "CENTIMES" is very short, and the accent on "a" slants at an angle of 30 degree, for the 10c and 17 degree for the 15c, while on the typographed the central bar of the "E" is almost as wide as the top and bottom bars and the accent on the "a" slants at an angle of 47 degree.

No. J2 is known rouletted unofficially.

1859-78 **Typo.**
J3 D1 10c black 30.00 17.50
J4 D1 15c black ('63) 35.00 15.00
J5 D1 20c black ('77) 4,100.
J6 D1 25c black ('71) 150.00 50.00
a. Double impression 6,000.
J7 D1 30c black ('78) 225.00 125.00
J8 D1 40c blue ('71) 325.00 *425.00*
a. 40c ultramarine 6,500. 5,700.
b. 40c Prussian blue 2,600.
J9 D1 60c bister ('71) 475.00 *1,050.*
J10 D1 60c blue ('78) 60.00 *110.00*
a. 60c dark blue 600.00 *725.00*
J10B D1 60c black 2,700.

The 20c & 60c black were not put into use.

Nos. J3, J4, J6, J8 and J9 are known rouletted unofficially and Nos. J4, J6, J7 and J10 pin-perf. unofficially.

D2

1882-92 *Perf. 14x13½*
J11 D2 1c black 2.50 2.50
J12 D2 2c black 30.00 26.00
J13 D2 3c black 30.00 25.00
J14 D2 4c black 60.00 40.00
J15 D2 5c black 130.00 32.50
J16 D2 10c black 110.00 2.50
J17 D2 15c black 77.50 10.50
J18 D2 20c black 350.00 140.00
J19 D2 30c black 210.00 2.50
J20 D2 40c black 140.00 60.00
J21 D2 50c blk ('92) 600.00 175.00
J22 D2 60c blk ('84) 600.00 57.50
J23 D2 1fr black 750.00 350.00
J24 D2 2fr blk ('84) 1,400. 825.00
J25 D2 5fr blk ('84) 3,000. 1,600.

Excellent counterfeits exist of Nos. J23-J25.

See Nos. J26-J45A. For overprints and surcharges see Offices in China Nos. J1-J6, J33-J40, Offices in Egypt, Alexandria J1-J5, Port Said J1-J8, Offices in Zanzibar 60-62, J1-J5, Offices in Morocco 9-10, 24-25, J1-J5, J10-J12, J17-J22, J35-J41.

1884
J26 D2 1fr brown 400.00 90.00
J27 D2 2fr brown 190.00 130.00
J28 D2 5fr brown 450.00 325.00

1893-1941
J29 D2 5c blue ('94) .25 .30
J30 D2 10c brown .25 .30
J31 D2 15c lt grn ('94) 28.00 1.40
J32 D2 20c ol grn ('06) 6.50 .65
J33 D2 25c rose ('23) 6.50 3.75
J34 D2 30c red ('94) .25 .25
J35 D2 30c org red ('94) 475.00 85.00
J36 D2 40c rose ('25) 11.50 4.50
J37 D2 45c grn ('24) 9.00 5.25
J38 D2 50c brn vio ('95) .50 .30
a. 50c lilac .50 .30
J39 D2 60c bl grn ('25) 1.00 .55
J40 D2 1fr rose, *straw* ('96) 475.00 375.00
J41 D2 1fr red brn, *straw* ('20) 9.50 .30
J42 D2 1fr red brn ('35) 1.25 .40
J43 D2 2fr red org ('10) 225.00 65.00
J44 D2 2fr brt vio ('26) .65 *.75*
J45 D2 3fr magenta ('26) .65 *.75*
J45A D2 5fr red org ('41) 1.40 *2.25*

D3

1908-25
J46 D3 1c olive grn 1.00 *1.25*
J47 D3 10c violet 1.10 .30
a. Imperf., pair 175.00
J48 D3 20c bister ('19) 40.00 1.25
J49 D3 30c bister ('09) 14.00 .40
J50 D3 50c red ('09) 275.00 60.00
J51 D3 60c red ('25) 2.75 *3.75*
Nos. J46-J51 (6) 333.85 66.95

"Recouvrements" stamps were used to recover charges due on undelivered or refused mail which was returned to the sender.

For surcharges see Offices in Morocco Nos. J6-J9, J13-J16, J23-J26, J42-J45.

Nos. J49-J50 Surcharged

1917
J52 D3 20c on 30c bister 20.00 4.00
J53 D3 40c on 50c red 10.50 4.00
a. Double surcharge 475.00

In Jan. 1917 several values of the current issue of postage stamps were handstamped "T" in a triangle and used as postage due stamps.

Recouvrements Stamps of 1908-25 Surcharged

1926

No.	Type	Description	Unused	Used
J54	D3	50c on 10c lilac	3.50	3.25
J55	D3	60c on 1c ol grn	7.00	5.00
J56	D3	1fr on 60c red	18.00	10.00
J57	D3	2fr on 60c red	18.00	10.50
		Nos. J54-J57 (4)	46.50	28.75

D4

1927-31

No.	Type	Description	Unused	Used
J58	D4	1c olive grn ('28)	1.00	1.00
J59	D4	10c rose ('31)	1.90	1.40
J60	D4	30c bister	4.50	.50
J61	D4	60c red	4.50	.50
J62	D4	1fr violet	14.00	3.25
J63	D4	1fr Prus grn ('31)	17.00	.55
J64	D4	2fr blue	80.00	42.50
J65	D4	2fr olive brn ('31)	150.00	26.00
		Nos. J58-J65 (8)	272.90	75.70

Nos. J62 to J65 have the numerals of value double-lined.

Nos. J64, J62 Surcharged in Red or Black

1929

No.	Type	Description	Unused	Used
J66	D4	1.20fr on 2fr blue	42.50	11.00
J67	D4	5fr on 1fr vio (Bk)	65.00	15.00

No. J61 Surcharged

1931

No.	Type	Description	Unused	Used
J68	D4	1fr on 60c red	30.00	2.75

Catalogue values for unused stamps in this section, from this point to the end of the section, are for Never Hinged items.

Sheaves of Wheat — D5

Perf. 14x13½

1943-46 Unwmk. Typo.

No.	Type	Description	Unused	Used
J69	D5	10c sepia	.25	.25
J70	D5	30c brt red vio	.25	.25
J71	D5	50c blue grn	.25	.25
J72	D5	1fr brt ultra	.25	.25
J73	D5	1.50fr rose red	.25	.25
J74	D5	2fr turq blue	.25	.25
J75	D5	3fr brn org	.30	.25
J76	D5	4fr dp vio ('45)	4.50	2.25
J77	D5	5fr brt pink	.40	.25
J78	D5	10fr red org ('45)	2.50	.60
J79	D5	20fr ol bis ('46)	8.00	2.25
		Nos. J69-J79 (11)	17.20	7.10

Type of 1943 Inscribed "Timbre Taxe"

1946-53

No.	Type	Description	Unused	Used
J80	D5	10c sepia ('47)	.75	.40
J81	D5	30c brt red vio ('47)	.75	.40
J82	D5	50c blue grn ('47)	19.00	6.50
J83	D5	1fr brt ultra ('47)	.25	.25
J85	D5	2fr turq blue	.25	.25
J86	D5	3fr brown org	.25	.25
J87	D5	4fr deep violet	.25	.25
J88	D5	5fr brt pink ('47)	.25	.25
J89	D5	10fr red org ('47)	.25	.25
J90	D5	20fr olive bis ('47)	1.25	.30
J91	D5	50fr dk green ('50)	19.00	.75
J92	D5	100fr dp green ('53)	65.00	6.00
		Nos. J80-J92 (12)	107.25	15.85

For surcharges see Reunion Nos. J36-J44.

Sheaves of Wheat — D6

1960 Typo. *Perf. 14x13½*

No.	Type	Description	Unused	Used
J93	D6	5c bright pink	2.75	.40
J94	D6	10c red orange	3.75	.25
J95	D6	20c olive bister	3.50	.75
J96	D6	50c dark green	9.75	.75
J97	D6	1fr deep green	40.00	1.50
		Nos. J93-J97 (5)	59.75	3.65

For surcharges see Reunion Nos. J46-J48. For overprints see Algeria Nos. J49-J53.

D7

Flowers: 5c, Centaury. 10c, Gentian. 15c, Corn poppy. 20c, Violets. 30c, Forget-me-not. 40c, Columbine. 50c, Clover. 1fr, Soldanel.

1964-71 Typo. *Perf. 14x13½*

No.	Type	Description	Unused	Used
J98	D7	5c car rose, red & grn ('65)	.25	.25
J99	D7	10c car rose, brt bl & grn ('65)	.25	.25
J100	D7	15c brn, grn & red	.25	.25
J101	D7	20c dk grn, grn & vio ('71)	.25	.25
J102	D7	30c brn, ultra & grn	.25	.25
J103	D7	40c dk grn, scar & yel ('71)	.25	.25
J104	D7	50c vio bl, car & grn ('65)	.25	.25
J105	D7	1fr vio bl, lil & grn ('65)	.40	.25
		Nos. J98-J105 (8)	2.15	2.00

For surcharges see Reunion Nos. J49-J55.

D8

Designs: 10c, Ampedus Cinnabarinus. 20c, Dorcadion fuliginator. 30c, Leptura cordigera. 40c, Paederus littoralis. 50c, Pyrochroa coccinea. 1fr, Scarites laevigatus. 2fr, Trichius gallicus. 3fr, Adalia alpina. 4fr, Apoderus coryli. 5fr, Trichodes alvearius.

1982-83 Engr. *Perf. 13*

No.	Type	Description	Unused	Used
J106	D8	10c multicolored	.25	.25
J107	D8	20c multicolored	.25	.25
J108	D8	30c multicolored	.25	.25
J109	D8	40c multicolored	.25	.25
J110	D8	50c multicolored	.25	.25
J111	D8	1fr multicolored	.40	.25
J112	D8	2fr multicolored	.65	.25
J113	D8	3fr multicolored	1.00	.25
J114	D8	4fr multicolored	1.40	.25
J115	D8	5fr multicolored	1.75	.25
		Nos. J106-J115 (10)	6.45	2.50

Issued: 30c, 40c, 3fr, 5fr, 1/3/83; others, 1/4/82.

MILITARY STAMPS

Regular Issue Overprinted in Black or Red

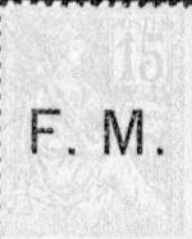

1901-39 Unwmk. *Perf. 14x13½*

No.	Type	Description	Unused	Used
M1	A17	15c orange ('01)	65.00	6.00
a.		Inverted overprint	300.00	150.00
b.		Imperf., pair	425.00	
M2	A19	15c pale red ('03)	65.00	6.00
M3	A20	15c slate grn ('04)	52.50	6.00
a.		No period after "M"	110.00	57.50
b.		Imperf., pair	290.00	
M4	A20	10c rose ('06)	30.00	8.25
a.		No period after "M"	82.50	45.00
b.		Imperf., pair	350.00	
M5	A22	10c red ('07)	1.75	1.00
a.		Inverted overprint	105.00	65.00
b.		Imperf., pair	190.00	
M6	A20	50c vermilion ('29)	4.75	1.00
a.		No period after "M"	32.50	18.00
b.		Period in front of F	32.50	18.00
M7	A45	50c rose red ('34)	2.75	.55
a.		No period after "M"	29.00	16.00
b.		Inverted overprint	150.00	110.00
M8	A45	65c brt ultra (R) ('38)	.30	.30
a.		No period after "M"	29.00	16.00
M9	A45	90c ultra (R) ('39)	.40	.35
		Nos. M1-M9 (9)	222.45	29.45

"F. M." are initials of Franchise Militaire (Military Frank). See No. S1.

Catalogue values for unused stamps in this section, from this point to the end of the section, are for Never Hinged items.

M1

1946-47 Typo.

No.	Type	Description	Unused	Used
M10	M1	dark green	1.75	.65
M11	M1	rose red ('47)	.30	.25

Nos. M10-M11 were valid also in the French colonies.

Flag — M2

1964, July 20 *Perf. 13x14*

No.	Type	Description	Unused	Used
M12	M2	multicolored	.30	.35

OFFICIAL STAMPS

FOR THE COUNCIL OF EUROPE

For use only on mail posted in the post office in the Council of Europe Building, Strasbourg.

Catalogue values for unused stamps in this section are for Never Hinged items.

For French stamp inscribed "Conseil de l'Europe" see No. 679.

France No. 854 Overprinted: "CONSEIL DE L'EUROPE"

Unwmk.

1958, Jan. 14 Engr. *Perf. 13*

No.	Type	Description	Unused	Used
1O1	A303	35fr car rose & lake	.75	*2.00*

Council of Europe Flag — O1

1958-59 Flag in Ultramarine

No.	Type	Description	Unused	Used
1O2	O1	8fr red org & brn vio	.25	.25
1O3	O1	20fr yel & lt brn	.25	.25
1O4	O1	25fr lil rose & sl grn ('59)	.60	.30
1O5	O1	35fr red	.40	.25
1O6	O1	50fr lilac rose ('59)	.75	.75
		Nos. 1O2-1O6 (5)	2.25	1.80

1963, Jan. 3 Flag in Ultramarine

No.	Type	Description	Unused	Used
1O7	O1	20c yel & lt brn	.90	.65
1O8	O1	25c lil rose & sl grn	1.40	1.10
1O9	O1	50c lilac rose	1.90	1.60
		Nos. 1O7-1O9 (3)	4.20	3.35

Centime value stamps shown the denomination as "0,20," etc.

1965-71

Flag in Ultramarine & Yellow

No.	Type	Description	Unused	Used
1O10	O1	25c ver, yel & sl grn	.75	.55
1O11	O1	30c ver & yel	.35	.35
1O12	O1	40c ver, yel & gray	.75	.55
1O13	O1	50c red, yel & grn	1.50	1.10
1O14	O1	60c ver, yel & vio	1.10	1.00
1O15	O1	70c ver, yel & dk brn	2.25	2.10
		Nos. 1O10-1O15 (6)	6.70	5.65

Issue dates: 25c, 30c, 60c, 1/16/65; 50c, 2/20/71; others, 3/24/69.

Type of 1958 Inscribed "FRANCE" Flag in Ultramarine & Yellow

1975-76 Engr. *Perf. 13*

No.	Type	Description	Unused	Used
1O16	O1	60c org, yel & emer	.60	.55
1O17	O1	80c yel & mag	.75	.60
1O18	O1	1fr car, yel & gray ol ('76)	1.50	1.25
1O19	O1	1.20fr org, yel & bl	4.00	2.25
		Nos. 1O16-1O19 (4)	6.85	4.65

Issue dates: 1fr, 10/16; others, 11/22.

New Council Headquarters, Strasbourg — O2

1977, Jan. 22 Engr. *Perf. 13*

No.	Type	Description	Unused	Used
1O20	O2	80c car & multi	.80	.50
1O21	O2	1fr brown & multi	.75	.30
1O22	O2	1.40fr gray & multi	1.50	.75
		Nos. 1O20-1O22 (3)	3.05	1.55

Human Rights Emblem in Upper Left Corner

1978, Oct. 14

No.	Type	Description	Unused	Used
1O23	O2	1.20fr red lilac & multi	.45	.40
1O24	O2	1.70fr blue & multi	.60	.55

30th anniversary of the Universal Declaration of Human Rights.

Council Headquarters Type of 1977

1980, Nov. 24 Engr. *Perf. 13*

No.	Type	Description	Unused	Used
1O25	O2	1.40fr olive	.50	.50
1O26	O2	2fr blue gray	.75	.75

New Council Headquarters, Strasbourg — O3

1981-84 Engr.

No.	Type	Description	Unused	Used
1O27	O3	1.40fr multicolored	.50	.50
1O28	O3	1.60fr multicolored	.50	.40
1O29	O3	1.70fr emerald	.60	.40
1O30	O3	1.80fr multicolored	.70	.60
1O31	O3	2fr multicolored	.75	.40
1O32	O3	2.10fr red	.75	.60
1O33	O3	2.30fr multicolored	.85	.60
1O34	O3	2.60fr multicolored	.90	.75
1O35	O3	2.80fr multicolored	1.00	.75
1O36	O3	3fr brt blue	1.10	.90
		Nos. 1O27-1O36 (10)	7.65	5.90

Issued: 1.40, 1.60, 2.30fr, 11/21; 1.80, 2.60fr, 11/13/82; 2, 2.80fr, 11/21/83; 1.70, 2.10, 3fr, 11/5/84.

Youth's Leg, Sneaker, Shattered Eggshell O4

1985, Aug. 31 **Engr.** ***Perf. 13***

1037	O4	1.80fr brt green	.70	.60
1038	O4	2.20fr vermilion	.75	.60
1039	O4	3.20fr brt blue	1.10	1.00
		Nos. 1037-1039 (3)	2.55	2.20

New Council Headquarters, Strasbourg — O5

1986-87 **Engr.** ***Perf. 13***

1040	O5	1.90fr green	.70	.60
1041	O5	2fr brt yel grn	.90	.60
1042	O5	2.20fr red	.75	.60
1043	O5	3.40fr blue	1.20	1.00
1044	O5	3.60fr brt blue	1.40	1.10
		Nos. 1040-1044 (5)	4.95	3.90

Issued: 1.90, 2.20, 3.40fr, 12/13; 2, 3.60fr, 10/10/87.

Council of Europe, 40th Anniv. O6

1989, Feb. 4 **Litho. & Engr.**

1045	O6	2.20fr multicolored	.90	.70
1046	O6	3.60fr multicolored	1.40	1.10

Denominations also inscribed in European Currency Units (ECUs).

Map of Europe O7

1990-91 **Litho.** ***Perf. 13***

1047	O7	2.30fr multicolored	.90	.75
1048	O7	2.50fr multicolored	.90	.75
1049	O7	3.20fr multicolored	1.10	1.00
1050	O7	3.40fr multicolored	1.10	1.00
		Nos. 1047-1050 (4)	4.00	3.50

Issued: 2.30fr, 3.20fr, 5/26/90; 2.50fr, 3.40fr, 11/23/91.

36 Heads, by Hundertwasser O8

1994, Jan. 15 **Litho.** ***Perf. 13***

1051	O8	2.80fr multicolored	1.40	.75
1052	O8	3.70fr multicolored	2.25	1.00

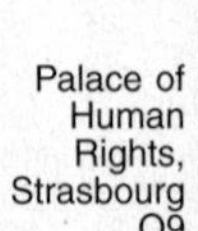

Palace of Human Rights, Strasbourg O9

1996, June 1 **Litho.** ***Perf. 13***

1053	O9	3fr multicolored	1.50	.75
1054	O9	3.80fr multicolored	1.75	1.00

Charioteer of Delphi — O10

1999, Sept. 18 **Photo.** ***Perf. 13***

1055	O10	3fr shown	1.40	.75
1056	O10	3.80fr Nike	1.75	1.00

Girl, Penguin and Boy — O11

2001, Dec. 1 **Litho.** ***Perf. 13***

1057	O11	3fr red & multi	2.00	.70
1058	O11	3.80fr grn & multi	2.40	1.00

Hiker on Stars — O12

2003, Oct. 18 **Litho.** ***Perf. 13***

1059	O12	50c Hiker facing left	2.00	.70
1060	O12	75c Hiker facing right	2.50	1.20

O13

O14

2005, Sept. 18 **Litho.** ***Perf. 13***

1061	O13	55c multi	2.00	.75
1062	O14	75c multi	2.50	1.20

Map of Europe O15

Sculpture by Mariano González Beltrán O16

2007, June 23 **Litho.** ***Perf. 13***

1063	O15	60c multi	2.00	.75
1064	O16	85c multi	2.50	1.25

Council of Europe, 60th Anniv. O17

European Court of Human Rights, 50th Anniv. O18

2009, May 16 **Litho.** ***Perf. 13***

1065	O17	56c multi	2.00	.75
1066	O18	70c multi	2.50	1.25

Tree — O19

Chain — O20

2010, Sept. 17 **Litho.** ***Perf. 13***

1067	O19	75c multi	2.10	.75
1068	O20	87c multi	2.40	1.25

European Human Rights Convention, 60th anniv. (No. 1068).

Map of Europe and Flags — O21

2011, Sept. 9 **Litho.** ***Perf. 13***

1069	O21	89c multi	2.50	1.25

European Social Charter, 50th anniv.

European Youth Center, Strasbourg, 40th Anniv. — O22

2012, Sept. 28

1070	O22	89c multi	2.40	1.25

Balance of Rights and Responsibilties of Citizens in a Democracy — O23

2013, Sept. 27 **Litho.** ***Perf. 13***

1071	O23	95c multi	2.60	1.25

European Directorate for the Quality of Medicines and Health Care, 50th Anniv. — O24

European Cultural Cooperation, 60th Anniv. — O25

2014, Oct. 3 **Photo.** ***Perf. 13***

1072	O24	83c multi	2.10	1.00
1073	O25	98c multi	2.50	1.25

European Union Flag, 60th Anniv. O26

2015, Oct. 2 **Litho.** ***Perf. 13***

1074	O26	95c multi	2.25	1.10

European Social Charter O27

2016, Oct. 14 **Litho.** ***Perf. 13***

1075	O27	€1 multi	2.25	2.25

Council of Europe Cultural Routes 30th Anniv. — O28

2017, Oct. 13 **Litho.** ***Perf. 13***

1076	O28	€1.10 multi	2.60	2.60

Framework Convention for the Protection of National Minorities, 20th Anniv. O29

2018, Oct. 12 **Litho.** ***Perf. 13***

1077	O29	€1.20 multi	2.75	2.75

Council of Europe, 70th Anniv. — O30

European Court of Human Rights, 60th Anniv. — O31

2019, May 5 **Litho.** ***Perf. 13¼***

1078	O30	€1.30 multi	3.00	3.00
1079	O31	€1.30 multi	3.00	3.00

FOR THE UNITED NATIONS EDUCATIONAL, SCIENTIFIC AND CULTURAL ORGANIZATION

For use only on mail posted in the post office in the UNESCO Building, Paris.

Catalogue values for unused stamps in this section are for Never Hinged items.

For French stamps inscribed "UNESCO" see Nos. 572, 893-894, 2545.

Khmer Buddha and Hermes by Praxiteles O1

1961-65 Unwmk. Engr. *Perf. 13*

2O1 O1 20c dk gray, ol bis & bl .25 *.55*
2O2 O1 25c blk, lake & grn .40 *.90*
2O3 O1 30c choc & bis brn ('65) .90 *.60*
2O4 O1 50c blk, red & vio bl .90 *1.75*
2O5 O1 60c grnsh bl, red brn & rose lil ('65) 1.00 1.40
Nos. 2O1-2O5 (5) 3.45 5.20

Book and Globe — O2

1966, Dec. 17

2O6 O2 25c gray .30 .25
2O7 O2 30c dark red .45 .35
2O8 O2 60c green .75 .65
Nos. 2O6-2O8 (3) 1.50 1.25

20th anniversary of UNESCO.

Human Rights Flame — O3

1969-71 Engr. *Perf. 13*

2O9 O3 30c sl grn, red & dp brn .30 .30
2O10 O3 40c dk car rose, red & dp brn .45 .40
2O11 O3 50c ultra, car & brn ('71) .75 .60
2O12 O3 70c pur, red & sl 1.50 1.40
Nos. 2O9-2O12 (4) 3.00 2.70

Universal Declaration of Human Rights.

Type of 1969 Inscribed "FRANCE" — O3a

1975, Nov. 15 Engr. *Perf. 13*

2O13 O3a 60c bl grn, red & choc .60 .55
2O14 O3a 80c ocher, red & red brn .90 .60
2O15 O3a 1.20fr ind, red & brn 3.00 2.25
Nos. 2O13-2O15 (3) 4.50 3.40

O4

1976-78 Engr. *Perf. 13*

2O16 O4 80c multi .65 .55
2O17 O4 1fr multi .35 .30
2O18 O4 1.20fr multi .50 .40
2O19 O4 1.40fr multi 1.25 .90
2O20 O4 1.70fr multi .75 .60
Nos. 2O16-2O20 (5) 3.50 2.75

Issued: 1.20, 1.70fr, 10/14/78; others, 10/23/76.

Slave Quarters, Senegal O5

Designs: 1.40fr, Mohenjo-Daro excavations, Pakistan. 2fr, Sans-Souci Palace, Haiti.

1980, Nov. 17 Engr. *Perf. 13*

2O21 O5 1.20fr multi .50 .50
2O22 O5 1.40fr multi .55 .50
2O23 O5 2fr multi .80 .65
Nos. 2O21-2O23 (3) 1.85 1.65

Hue, Vietnam — O7

Designs: 1.40fr, Building, Fez, Morocco. 1.60fr, Seated deity, Sukhotai, Thailand. 2.30fr, Fort St. Elmo, Malta, horiz. 2.60fr, St. Michael Church ruins, Brazil.

1981-82

2O24 O7 1.40fr multi .50 .35
2O25 O7 1.60fr multi .50 .35
2O26 O7 1.80fr shown .70 .55
2O27 O7 2.30fr multi .60 .50
2O28 O7 2.60fr multi .75 .55
Nos. 2O24-2O28 (5) 3.05 2.30

Issued: 1.80fr, 2.60fr, 10/23/82; others, 12/12/81.

Mosque, Chinguetti, Mauritania O8

Roman Theater and Female Standing Sculpture, Carthage, Tunisia — O8a

Architecture: 1.70fr, Church, Lalibela, Ethiopia. 2.10fr, San'a, Yemen. 2.20fr, Old Town Square and wrought iron latticework, Havana. 2.80fr, Enclosure wall interior, Istanbul. 3fr, Church, Kotor, Yugoslavia. 3.20fr, Temple of Anuradhapura and bas-relief of two women, Sri Lanka.

1983-85 Engr.

2O29 O8 1.70fr multi .55 .35
2O30 O8a 1.80fr multi .65 .55
2O31 O8 2fr multi .75 .40
2O32 O8 2.10fr multi .75 .60
2O33 O8a 2.20fr multi .75 .60
2O34 O8 2.80fr multi 1.00 .60
2O35 O8 3fr multi 1.10 .90
2O36 O8a 3.20fr multi 1.10 1.00
Nos. 2O29-2O36 (8) 6.65 5.00

Issued: 2fr, 2.80fr, 10/10; 1.70fr, 2.10fr, 3fr, 10/22/84; 1.80fr, 2.20fr, 3.20fr, 10/26/85.

Tikal Temple, Guatemala — O9

3.40fr, Bagerhat Mosque, Bangladesh.

1986, Dec. 6 Engr. *Perf. 13*

2O37 O9 1.90fr shown .75 .65
2O38 O9 3.40fr multicolored 1.25 1.20

The Parthenon, Athens O10

3.60fr, Temple of Philae, Egypt.

1987, Dec. 5 Engr. *Perf. 13x12½*

2O39 O10 2fr shown .90 .60
2O40 O10 3.60fr multicolored 1.40 1.20

Shibam, Yemen People's Democratic Republic O11

2.30fr, San Francisco de Lima, Peru, vert.

Perf. 13x12½, 12½x13

1990, Apr. 7 Engr.

2O41 O11 2.30fr multicolored .90 .75
2O42 O11 3.20fr shown 1.20 1.00

Bagdaon Temple, Nepal — O12

3.40fr, Citadel of Harat, Afghanistan, horiz.

1991, Nov. 23

2O43 O12 2.50fr choc & dk red .90 .75
2O44 O12 3.40fr grn, brn & ol 1.20 1.00

Tassili N'Ajjer Natl. Park, Algeria O13

Design: 2.80fr, Angkor Wat Archaeological Park, Cambodia, vert.

1993, Oct. 23 Litho. *Perf. 13*

2O45 O13 2.80fr multicolored 1.25 .75
2O46 O13 3.70fr multicolored 1.50 1.00

UNESCO, 50th Anniv. O14

Designs: 3fr, Uluru Natl. Park, Australia. 3.80fr, Los Glaciares Natl. Park, Argentina.

1996, June 1 Litho. *Perf. 13*

2O47 O14 3fr multicolored 1.50 .75
2O48 O14 3.80fr multicolored 2.00 1.00

Detail of Dionysus Fresco, Pompeii — O15

Moai Statues, Easter Island O16

1998, Oct. 24 Litho. *Perf. 13*

2O49 O15 3fr multicolored 1.50 .75
2O50 O16 3.80fr multicolored 1.90 1.25

Sphinx and Pyramids, Egypt O17

Komodo Dragon, Komodo Natl. Park, Indonesia O18

2001, Dec. 1 Litho. *Perf. 13*

2O51 O17 3fr multi 2.00 .75
2O52 O18 3.80fr multi 2.50 1.00

Reindeer, Lapland O19

Church of the Resurrection, St. Petersburg, Russia — O20

2003, Dec. 6 Litho. *Perf. 13*

2O53 O19 50c multi 2.00 .75
2O54 O20 75c multi 2.50 1.40

Bison in Bialowieza Forest, Poland — O21

Petra, Jordan O22

2005, Nov. 26 Litho. *Perf. 13*

2O55 O21 55c multi 2.00 .75
2O56 O22 90c multi 2.50 1.40

Siberian Tiger — O23

Luang Prabang, Laos O24

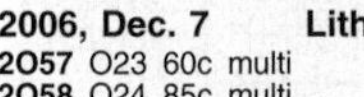

2006, Dec. 7 Litho. *Perf. 13*

2O57 O23 60c multi	2.00	.75
2O58 O24 85c multi	2.50	1.25

Ksar d'Ait-Ben-Haddou, Morocco — O25

Koala, Australia — O26

2007, Dec. 13 Litho. *Perf. 13*

2O59 O25 60c multi	2.00	.75
2O60 O26 85c multi	2.50	1.40

Gorilla — O27

Machu Picchu, Peru O28

2008, Dec. 3 Litho. *Perf. 13*

2O61 O27 65c multi	2.00	1.00
2O62 O28 85c multi	2.50	1.25

Polar Bear O29

Suzhou, China O30

2009, Dec. 9 Litho. *Perf. 13*

2O63 O29 70c multi	2.10	1.00
2O64 O30 85c multi	2.50	1.25

Alhambra, Spain O31

Alpaca O32

2010, Dec. 1 Litho. *Perf. 13*

2O65 O31 75c multi	2.00	1.00
2O66 O32 87c multi	2.40	1.20

Bactrian Camel O33

Milford Sound, New Zealand O34

2011, Oct. 19

2O67 O33 77c multi	2.10	1.00
2O68 O34 89c multi	2.50	1.25

Stonehenge, Great Britain — O35

African Elephants O36

2012, Nov. 22

2O69 O35 77c multi	2.00	1.00
2O70 O36 89c multi	2.40	1.20

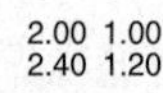

Japanese Cranes — O37

Sigiriya UNESCO World Heritage Site, Sri Lanka O38

2013, Nov. 7 Litho. *Perf. 13*

2O71 O37 58c multi	1.60	.80
2O72 O38 95c multi	2.60	1.25

Trulli of Alberobello UNESCO World Heritage Site, Italy — O39

Hyacinth Macaw — O40

2014, Nov. 8 Litho. *Perf. 13x13¼*

2O73 O39 83c multi	2.10	1.00

Perf. 13¼x13

2O74 O40 98c multi	2.50	1.25

African Gnu — O41

Sagrada Familia Basilica, Barcelona — O42

2015, Nov. 6 Litho. *Perf. 13*

2O75 O41 95c multi	2.00	2.00
2O76 O42 €1.20 multi	2.60	2.60

UNESCO, 70th anniv.

Florida Panther — O43

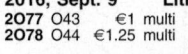

Ruins, Ephesus, Turkey — O44

2016, Sept. 9 Litho. *Perf. 13*

2O77 O43 €1 multi	2.25	2.25
2O78 O44 €1.25 multi	2.75	2.75

Samarkand, Uzbekistan — O45

Orangutan — O46

2017, June 30 Litho. *Perf. 13*

2O79 O45 €1.10 multi	2.50	2.50
2O80 O46 €1.30 multi	3.00	3.00

UNESCO Man and Biosphere Program O47

2018, Sept. 7 Photo. *Perf. 12¼*

2O81 O47 €1.30 multi	3.00	3.00

International Year of Indigenous Languages — O48

2019, Sept. 13 Litho. *Perf. 13¼*

2O82 O48 €1.30 multi	3.00	3.00

NEWSPAPER STAMPS

Coat of Arms — N1

1868 Unwmk. Typo. *Imperf.*

P1 N1 2c lilac	300.00	65.00
P2 N1 2c (+ 2c) blue	600.00	275.00

Perf. 12½

P3 N1 2c lilac	52.50	25.00
P4 N1 2c (+ 4c) rose	250.00	100.00
P5 N1 2c (+ 2c) blue	75.00	35.00
P6 N1 5c lilac	1,250.	550.00

Nos. P2, P4, and P5 were sold for face plus an added fiscal charge indicated in parenthesis. Nos. P1, P3 and P6 were used simply as fiscals.

The 2c rose and 5c lilac imperforate and the 5c rose and 5c blue, both imperforate and perforated, were never put into use.

Nos. P1-P6 were reprinted for the 1913 Ghent Exhibition and the 1937 Paris Exhibition (PEXIP).

No. 109 Surcharged in Red

1919 *Perf. 14x13½*

P7 A16 ½c on 1c gray	.30	.30
a. Inverted surcharge	1,200.	1,150.

No. 156 Surcharged

1933

P8 A22 ½c on 1c olive bister	.30	.30

PARCEL POST STAMPS

Inscribed "I APPORT A LA GARE" — PP1

Perfs As Noted

1892 Unwmk. Typo.

Q1 PP1 25c brown, *yel*, perf 13½ 825.00 290.00
Never hinged 1,500.

Q2 PP1 25c brown, *yel*, perf 11 30.00 24.00
Never hinged 45.00
a. Printed on both sides 400.00
Never hinged 650.00

Inscribed "II VALEUR DECLAREE" — PP2

Q3 PP2 10c red, perf 13½ 1,000. 275.00
Never hinged 1,750.

Q4 PP2 10c red, perf 10x13½ 875.00 325.00
Never hinged 1,600.

Q5 PP2 10c org red, perf 11 30.00 14.00
Never hinged 42.50

Q6 PP2 10c red, imperf 22.50 16.50
Never hinged 32.50

Inscribed "III LIVRAISON PAR EXPRESS" — PP3

Q7 PP3 25c green, perf 13½ 57.50 32.50
Never hinged 115.00

Q8 PP3 25c green, perf 11 45.00 24.00
Never hinged 70.00

See Nos. Q22-Q26.

Locomotive — PP4

A set of six stamps, in the design above, was prepared in 1901 as postal tax stamps for expedited parcels but were not issued. All are perf 14x13½. Values: 5c gray, $3, never hinged $4; 10c yellow green, $3, never hinged $5; 20c rose, $20, never hinged $29; 50c blue, $7, never hinged $11.50; 1fr brown, $8, never hinged $12; 2fr brown red, $37.50, never hinged $57.50.

PP5

Large Trefoil

Type I: Large Trefoil Under "N" of "MAJORATION"

1918 ***Perf. 11***

Q9 PP5 5c black 1.25 .85
Never hinged 2.00

Q10 PP5 15c brn lilac 1.25 .85
Never hinged 2.00

Imperforate

Q11 PP5 5c black 3.25 2.50
Never hinged 6.25

Q12 PP5 15c brn lilac 9.00 4.25
Never hinged 14.00
Nos. Q9-Q12 (4) 14.75 8.45

40c values, perforated 11 and imperf, in orange, were prepared but not issued. Value, perf or imperf, $375.

PP5a

Small Trefoil

Type II: Small Trefoil Under "O" of "MAJORATION"

Q13 PP5a 5c black 140.00 45.00
Never hinged 275.00

Q14 PP5a 35c red 3.75 2.50
Never hinged 5.00

Q15 PP5a 50c vio blue 4.50 1.60
Never hinged 7.00

Q16 PP5a 1fr yellow 4.25 1.60
Never hinged 7.00

Imperforate

Q17 PP5a 5c black 130.00 45.00
Never hinged 260.00

Q18 PP5a 15c brn lilac 30.00 16.50
Never hinged 50.00

Q19 PP5a 35c red 3.25 2.50
Never hinged 6.75

Q20 PP5a 50c vio blue 24.00 14.00
Never hinged 40.00

Q21 PP5a 1fr yellow 18.50 12.50
Never hinged 30.00
Nos. Q13-Q21 (9) 358.25 141.20

See Nos. Q41-Q44, Q143-Q145.
For surcharges, see Nos. Q28-Q40.

Type of 1892

1918-23 ***Perf. 10½x11***

Q22 PP1 30c brn, *yel* 37.50 16.50
Never hinged 55.00
a. Imperf 200.00
Never hinged 290.00

Q23 PP1 60c brn, *straw* ('23) 47.50 30.00
Never hinged 70.00
a. Imperf 190.00
Never hinged 275.00

Q24 PP2 15c vermilion ('22) 16.00 11.00
Never hinged 23.00

Q25 PP3 30c green 40.00 21.00
Never hinged 57.50
a. Imperf 240.00
Never hinged 325.00

Q26 PP3 60c green ('23) 75.00 50.00
Never hinged 110.00
Nos. Q22-Q26 (5) 216.00 128.50

PP6

1924, Oct. ***Perf. 14***

Q27 PP6 15c rose & blue 4.00 3.75
Never hinged 5.00
a. Imperf 550.00
Never hinged 750.00

No. Q27 is a postal tax stamp, issued to show the collection of a new 15c excise fee on rail parcels. On July 3, 1925, its use was extended to all fiscal categories.

Surcharged in Black or Red (R) on Nos. Q9//Q16 and Types of 1918

0F.20

1926 ***Perf. 13***

Q28 PP5 20c on 2fr rose 1.90 1.10
Never hinged 2.75

Q29 PP5 30c on 2fr yellow 1.90 1.10
Never hinged 2.75
a. "0f30" omitted 190.00
Never hinged 250.00

Q30 PP5 40c on 3fr gray 1.90 1.40
Never hinged 2.75

Q31 PP5 45c on 3fr orange 1.90 1.40
Never hinged 2.75
a. Period after "f" omitted 19.00 19.00
Never hinged 30.00

Q32 PP5 95c on 1fr yel 8.00 2.75
Never hinged 12.50
a. Imperf 90.00
Never hinged 150.00

Q33 PP5 1.35fr on 3fr vio 10.50 4.50
Never hinged 14.00
On postal document 70.00
a. Imperf 150.00
Never hinged 225.00

Q34 PP5 1.45fr on 5fr blk (R) 1.90 1.00
Never hinged 2.75

Q35 PP5 1.75fr on 2fr blue 10.50 4.50
Never hinged 14.00

Q36 PP5 1.85fr on 10c org 1.90 1.20
Never hinged 2.75

Q37 PP5 1.95fr on 15c brn lilac 2.50 1.75
Never hinged 3.50
a. Imperf 110.00
Never hinged 175.00

Q38 PP5 2.35fr on 25c grn 1.90 1.00
Never hinged 2.75
a. Imperf 110.00
Never hinged 175.00

Q39 PP5 2.90fr on 35c red 2.50 1.00
Never hinged 3.50
a. Dots before and after "f" 140.00
Never hinged 200.00
b. Imperf 125.00
Never hinged 190.00

Q40 PP5 3.30fr on 50c blue violet (R) 2.50 1.25
Never hinged 3.50
a. Double surcharge 250.00
Never hinged 375.00
b. Imperf 90.00
Never hinged 140.00
Nos. Q28-Q40 (13) 49.80 23.95

Type of 1918

1926 ***Perf. 11***

Q41 PP5 10c orange 2.00 1.25
Never hinged 3.75
a. Imperf 4.00
Never hinged 6.50

Q42 PP5 25c pale green 2.00 1.25
Never hinged 3.75
a. Imperf 4.00
Never hinged 6.50

Q43 PP5 2fr pale blue 25.00 14.50
Never hinged 42.50
a. Imperf 50.00
Never hinged 80.00

Q44 PP5 3fr violet 110.00 67.50
Never hinged 190.00
a. Imperf 225.00
Never hinged 360.00
Nos. Q41-Q44 (4) 139.00 84.50

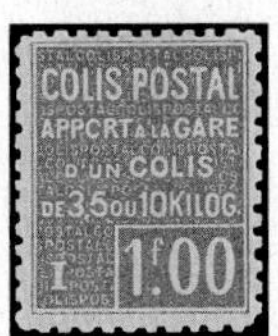

Inscribed "APPORT A LA GARE" — PP7

No. 51

1926

Q45 PP7 1fr on 60c brn, *yel* 13.50 10.50
Never hinged 24.00
a. Imperf 190.00
Never hinged 300.00

Q46 PP7 1fr brn, *yel* 17.50 13.00
Never hinged 30.00

Q47 PP7 1.30fr on 1fr brn, *yel* 17.50 12.50
Never hinged 30.00

Q48 PP7 1.50fr brn, *yel* 20.00 11.50
Never hinged 32.50

Q49 PP7 1.65fr brn, *yel* 15.00 12.50
Never hinged 24.00

Q50 PP7 1.90fr on 1fr brn, *yel* 17.50 12.50
Never hinged 30.00

Q51 PP7 2.10fr on 1.65fr brn, *yel* 17.50 12.50
Never hinged 30.00
Nos. Q45-Q51 (7) 118.50 85.00

See Nos. Q91-Q95, footnote following No. Q102, Q143-Q145.

For overprints and surcharges, see Nos. Q76-Q78, Q83-Q86, Q91-Q92, boxed note following Q95, Q96-Q99, Q107-QQ109, boxed note following Q159.

PP8

Type I

Type II

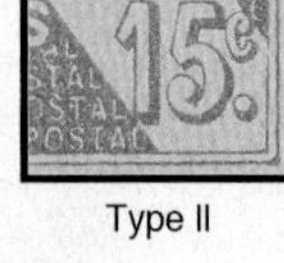

Type III

1926-38

Q52 PP8 15c brown, *yel*, type I 7.50 3.00
Never hinged 11.00
a. Imperf 180.00
Never hinged 275.00

Q53 PP8 15c brown, *yel*, type II ('32) 8.00 4.25
Never hinged 11.50
a. Type III ('38) 210.00
Never hinged 275.00
b. As "a," imperf 240.00
Never hinged 300.00

Nos. Q52-Q53a were issued for use in Paris only. No. Q53a was prepared but not issued.

Inscribed "VALEUR DECLAREE" — PP9

The additional numerals overprinted on Nos. Q56-Q63 and on Nos. Q72-Q75 indicate the weight category of the parcels being sent.

1926

Q54 PP9 50c on 15c red 3.00 1.60
Never hinged 5.00
a. Imperf 180.00
Never hinged 275.00

Q55 PP9 50c red 750.00 750.00
Never hinged 1,200.
a. Imperf 1,200.
Never hinged 1,650.

Q56 PP9 50c red, ovptd. "1" 4.50 2.00
Never hinged 7.00
a. Imperf 200.00
Never hinged 300.00
b. Double overprint "1" 300.00
Never hinged 400.00

Q57 PP9 55c on 15c red, ovptd. "1" 6.75 5.00
Never hinged 11.50
a. Imperf 190.00
Never hinged —

Q58 PP9 55c on 50c red, ovptd. "1" 6.75 5.00
Never hinged 11.50

Q59 PP9 65c on 50c red 2.50 2.50
Never hinged 4.25

Q60 PP9 65c on 50c red, ovptd. "1" 15.00 8.25
Never hinged 27.50

Q61 PP9 1.50fr on 50c red, ovptd. "3" 7.00 5.00
Never hinged 12.00
a. Imperf 275.00
Never hinged 375.00

Q62 PP9 2.00fr on 50c red, ovptd. "4" 8.25 3.75
Never hinged 14.00

Q63 PP9 2.50fr on 50c red, ovptd. "5" 15.00 8.25
Never hinged 26.50
Nos. Q54-Q63 (10) 818.75 791.35

See Nos. Q79, Q93, Q150-Q152.

For overprints and surcharges, see No. Q87, boxed note following No. Q95, Q100, Q110, Q123-Q124, Q138.

Inscribed "LIVRAISON PAR EXPRESS" — PP10

Q64 PP10 1.00fr on 60c grn 13.50 10.50
Never hinged 24.00
a. Imperf 225.00
Never hinged 325.00
Q65 PP10 1.00fr green 125.00 75.00
Never hinged 250.00
Q66 PP10 1.30fr on 1fr grn 16.50 12.50
Never hinged 29.00
Q67 PP10 1.50fr green 16.50 15.00
Never hinged 32.50
Q68 PP10 1.65fr green 16.50 15.00
Never hinged 32.50
Q69 PP10 1.90fr on 1.50fr grn 16.50 12.50
Never hinged 30.00
Q70 PP10 2.10fr on 1.65fr grn 30.00 14.00
Never hinged 50.00
Nos. Q64-Q70 (7) 234.50 154.50

For overprints and surcharges, see Nos. Q80-Q82, Q88-Q90, Q94, boxed note following Q95, Q101-Q105, Q111-Q113, Q125-Q132, Q139-Q141, Q146-Q149.

Inscribed "INTERETS A LA LIVRAISON" — PP11

No. Q72

No. Q73

Q71 PP11 50c lilac 3.00 1.60
Never hinged 5.00
a. Imperf 225.00 190.00
Never hinged 325.00
Q72 PP11 50c lil, ovptd. "1" 6.75 4.25
Never hinged 10.00
a. Imperf 200.00
Never hinged 300.00
Q73 PP11 1.50fr on 50c lil, ovptd. "3" 7.50 5.00
Never hinged 11.50
a. Imperf 200.00
Never hinged 300.00
Q74 PP11 2.00fr on 50c lil ovptd. "4" 10.00 7.00
Never hinged 16.00
Q75 PP11 2.50fr on 50c lil ovptd. "5" 10.00 7.00
Never hinged 16.50
a. Imperf 210.00
Never hinged 310.00
Nos. Q71-Q75 (5) 37.25 24.85

1926 Issues Overprinted

1928

Inscribed "APPORT A LA GARE"

Q76 PP7 1.00fr brn, *yel* 16.50 14.00
Never hinged 25.00
a. Imperf 190.00 190.00
Never hinged 300.00
Q77 PP7 1.50fr brn, *yel* 16.50 13.00
Never hinged 25.00
Q78 PP7 1.65fr brn, *yel* 16.50 13.00
Never hinged 25.00

Inscribed "VALEUR DECLAREE"

Q79 PP9 50c red 5.75 4.25
Never hinged 8.25
a. Imperf 190.00 190.00
Never hinged 300.00
b. Inverted overprint 210.00
Never hinged 310.00

Inscribed "LIVRAISON PAR EXPRESS"

Q80 PP10 1.00fr green 17.00 13.50
Never hinged 26.00
Q81 PP10 1.50fr green 17.00 13.50
Never hinged 26.00
Q82 PP10 1.65fr green 17.00 13.50
Never hinged 27.50
Nos. Q76-Q82 (7) 106.25 84.75

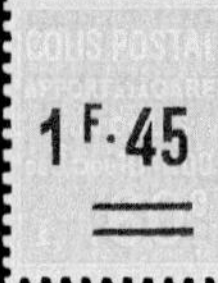

1926 Issues Surcharged

1928

Inscribed "APPORT A LA GARE"

Q83 PP7 1.45fr on 60c brn, *yel* 7.00 6.75
Never hinged 10.00
Q84 PP7 1.45fr on 1fr brn, *yel* 40.00 32.50
Never hinged 70.00
Q85 PP7 2.15fr on 1.50fr brn, *yel* 62.50 42.50
Never hinged 105.00
Q86 PP7 2.35fr on 1.65fr brn, *yel* 62.50 42.50
Never hinged 105.00

Inscribed "VALEUR DECLAREE"

Q87 PP9 75c on 50c red 2.10 1.60
Never hinged 3.25
a. Imperf 210.00
Never hinged 400.00

Inscribed "LIVRAISON PAR EXPRESS"

Q88 PP10 1.45fr on 1fr green 62.50 42.50
Never hinged 105.00
Q89 PP10 2.15fr on 1.50fr green 62.50 42.50
Never hinged 105.00
Q90 PP10 2.35fr on 1.65fr green 62.50 42.50
Never hinged 105.00
Nos. Q83-Q90 (8) 361.60 253.35

Types of 1926

1933

Inscribed "APPORT A LA GARE"

Q91 PP7 1.45fr brn, *yel* 55.00 25.00
Never hinged 82.50
Q92 PP7 2.35fr brn, *yel* 1,400.
Never hinged 1,900.

A 2.15fr value, brown on yellow paper, was prepared but not issued without overprint or surcharge.

For overprints and surcharges, see Nos. Q96, Q98, Q99, Q107-Q109, Q115, Q116, Q118, Q120-Q122, Q135-Q137.

Inscribed "VALEUR DECLAREE"

Q93 PP9 75c red 18.00 3.25
Never hinged 22.50
a. Imperf 180.00

For overprints and surcharges on No. Q93, see Nos. Q110, Q123, Q124, Q138.

A 1.15fr black in this design, imperf, was prepared but not issued. Value, $400.

Inscribed "LIVRAISON PAR EXPRESS"

Q94 PP10 1.45fr yel grn 450.00 300.00
Never hinged 675.00

Two other values, 2.15fr and 2.35fr were prepared but not issued without overprint or surcharge.

For overprints and surcharges, see Nos. Q101, Q103, Q105, Q111-Q113, Q125, Q126, Q128, Q130-Q132, Q139-Q141.

PP12

Inscribed "COLIS ENCOMBRANT"

1934

Q95 PP12 2fr blue 45.00 21.00
Never hinged 70.00

For overprints and surcharges, see Nos. Q106, Q114, Q133, Q134, Q142.

Nos. Q46, Q48, Q49, Q55, Q65, Q67 and Q68 overprinted "B" were not issued. Values: 1fr (No. Q46), $95; never hinged $130; 1.50fr (No. Q48), $95, never hinged $130; 1.65fr (No. Q49), $95, never hinged $130; 50c (No. Q55), $95, never hinged $130; 1fr (No. Q65), $92.50, never hinged $140; 1.50fr (No. Q67), $92.50, never hinged $140; 1.65fr (No. Q68), $92.50, never hinged $140.

Stamps and Types of 1926-34 Overprinted

1937

Inscribed "APPORT A LA GARE"

Q96 PP7 1.45fr brn, *yel* 6.75 6.75
Never hinged 10.00
Q97 PP7 2.15fr on 1.50fr brn, *yel* 37.50 31.00
Never hinged 57.50
Q98 PP7 2.15fr brn, *yel* 25.00 19.00
Never hinged 37.50
Q99 PP7 2.35fr brn, *yel* 25.00 19.00
Never hinged 37.50

Inscribed "VALEUR DECLAREE"

Q100 PP9 75c red 17.50 16.50
Never hinged 25.00
a. Imperf 225.00
Never hinged 325.00

Inscribed "LIVRAISON PAR EXPRESS"

Q101 PP10 1.45fr green 17.50 16.50
Never hinged 25.00
Q102 PP10 2.15fr on 1.50fr grn 17.50 16.50
Never hinged 25.00
Q103 PP10 2.15fr green 42.50 30.00
Never hinged 67.50
a. Imperf 210.00
Never hinged 315.00
Q104 PP10 2.35fr on 1.65fr grn 250.00 110.00
Never hinged 350.00
Q105 PP10 2.35fr green 17.50 12.50
Never hinged 26.00

Inscribed "COLIS ENCOMBRANT"

Q106 PP12 2fr blue 37.50 35.00
Never hinged 57.50
Nos. Q96-Q106 (11) 494.25 312.75

For overprints and surcharges, see Nos. Q146-Q149.

Types of 1933-34 Surcharged

1937

Inscribed "APPORT A LA GARE"

Q107 PP7 1.85fr on 1.45fr brn, *yel* 15.00 12.50
Never hinged 26.00
Q108 PP7 2.75fr on 2.15fr brn, *yel* 26.00 17.50
Never hinged 45.00
Q109 PP7 3.05fr on 2.55fr brn, *yel* 50.00 26.00
Never hinged 90.00

Inscribed "VALEUR DECLAREE"

Q110 PP9 .95fr on 75c red 42.50 25.00
Never hinged 67.50

Inscribed "LIVRAISON PAR EXPRESS"

Q111 PP10 1.85fr on 1.45fr grn 70.00 45.00
Never hinged 120.00
Q112 PP10 2.75fr on 2.15fr grn 70.00 45.00
Never hinged 120.00
Q113 PP10 3.05fr on 2.35fr grn 70.00 45.00
Never hinged 120.00

Inscribed "COLIS ENCOMBRANT"

Q114 PP12 2.60fr on 2fr bl 17.50 17.50
Never hinged 26.00
Nos. Q107-Q114 (8) 361.00 233.50

Stamps and Types of 1926-34 Overprinted

1937

Inscribed "APPORT A LA GARE"

Q115 PP7 1.45fr brn, *yel* 3.00 2.50
Never hinged 4.50
Q116 PP7 1.85fr on 1.45fr brn, *yel* 3.00 2.50
Never hinged 4.50
Q117 PP7 2.15fr on 1.50fr brn, *yel* 2.50 2.50
Never hinged 4.25
Q118 PP7 2.15fr brn, *yel* 42.50 35.00
Never hinged 62.50
Q119 PP7 2.35fr on 1.65fr brn, *yel* 575.00 475.00
Never hinged 800.00
Q120 PP7 2.35fr brn, *yel* 3.00 2.50
Never hinged 4.50
Q121 PP7 2.75fr on 2.15fr brn, *yel* 3.25 2.50
Never hinged 5.75
Q122 PP7 3.05fr on 2.35fr brn, *yel* 6.50 6.25
Never hinged 10.00

Inscribed "VALEUR DECLAREE"

Q123 PP9 75c red 3.75 3.50
Never hinged 5.50
a. Pair, one without overprint 225.00
Never hinged 350.00
Q124 PP9 95c on 75c red 3.00 3.00
Never hinged 3.75

Inscribed "LIVRAISON PAR EXPRESS"

Q125 PP10 1.45fr green 4.25 3.25
Never hinged 6.25
Q126 PP10 1.85fr on 1.45fr green 5.75 4.25
Never hinged 8.25
Q127 PP10 2.15fr on 1.50fr grn 375.00 325.00
Never hinged 500.00
Q128 PP10 2.15fr green 18.50 16.50
Never hinged 27.50
Q129 PP10 2.35fr on 1.65fr grn 675.00 725.00
Never hinged 775.00
Q130 PP10 2.35fr green 11.00 10.50
Never hinged 15.00
Q131 PP10 2.75fr on 2.15fr grn 35.00 45.00
Never hinged 55.00
Q132 PP10 3.05fr on 2.35fr grn 35.00 45.00
Never hinged 55.00

Inscribed "COLIS ENCOMBRANT"

Q133 PP12 2fr blue 3.00 2.10
Never hinged 4.50
a. Pair, imperf between 130.00
Never hinged 210.00
Q134 PP12 2.60fr on 2fr bl 3.25 2.50
Never hinged 5.50
Nos. Q115-Q134 (20) 1,811. 1,714.

For additional surcharges, see Nos. Q146-Q149.

Stamps and Types of 1933-34 Surcharged

1938

Inscribed "APPORT A LA GARE"

Q135 PP7 2.30fr on 1.45fr brn, *yel* 3.75 3.00
Never hinged 5.50
Q136 PP7 3.45fr on 2.15fr brn, *yel* 3.75 3.00
Never hinged 5.50
Q137 PP7 3.85fr on 1.45fr brn, *yel* 3.75 3.00
Never hinged 5.50

Inscribed "VALEUR DECLAREE"

Q138 PP9 1.15fr on 75c red 1.60 1.60
Never hinged 2.50

Inscribed "LIVRAISON PAR EXPRESS"

Q139 PP10 2.30fr on 1.45fr grn 3.75 3.00
Never hinged 5.50

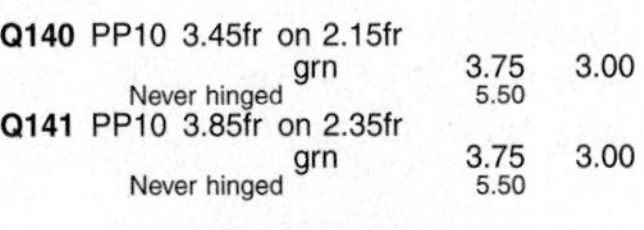

Q140	PP10 3.45fr on 2.15fr grn	3.75	3.00
	Never hinged	5.50	
Q141	PP10 3.85fr on 2.35fr grn	3.75	3.00
	Never hinged	5.50	

Inscribed "COLIS ENCOMBRANT"

Q142	PP12 3.25fr on 2fr bl	1.60	1.60
	Never hinged	2.50	
	Nos. Q135-Q142 (8)	25.70	21.20

For Nos. Q135-Q138, Q140-Q142 overprinted "E," see editor's note following No. Q159.

Type of 1918

1938		*11, Imperf (#Q161)*	
Q143	PP5 10c gray black	17.50	16.00
	Never hinged	26.00	
a.	Imperf	26.00	
	Never hinged	42.50	
Q144	PP5 20c brown lilac	17.50	16.00
	Never hinged	26.00	
a.	Imperf	42.50	
	Never hinged	62.50	
Q145	PP5 25c green, imperf	*50.00*	*20.00*
	Never hinged	*80.00*	
	Nos. Q143-Q145 (3)	85.00	52.00

Two additional values, a 10c rose lilac and a 15c ultramarine, were prepared with this set but not issued. Values, each stamp: $90, never hinged $150. Both stamps also exist imperf. Values, each: $82.50; never hinged $150.

Nos. Q103, Q105, Q112, Q113 Overprinted

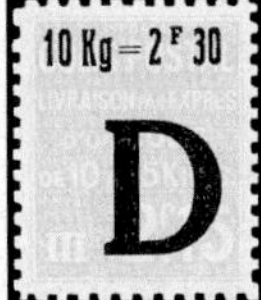

1938		*Perf. 11*	
Q146	PP10 2.30fr on 2.15fr green	62.50	62.50
	Never hinged	80.00	
Q147	PP10 2.30fr on 2.35fr green	62.50	62.50
	Never hinged	80.00	
Q148	PP10 2.30fr on 2.75fr on 2.15fr green	125.00	100.00
	Never hinged	175.00	
Q149	PP10 2.30fr on 3.05fr on 2.35fr green	125.00	100.00
	Never hinged	175.00	
	Nos. Q146-Q149 (4)	375.00	325.00

Types of 1926 and

PP13

PP13a

PP14

PP15

PP16

1938-39			
Q150	PP9 1fr red ('39)	2.50	2.50
	Never hinged	4.00	
Q151	PP9 1.15fr red	1.25	1.25
	Never hinged	2.10	
	Imperf	140.00	
	Never hinged	225.00	
Q152	PP9 5fr red ('39)	2.50	*2.75*
	Never hinged	4.00	
Q153	PP13 2.40fr brown, *yel*	2.50	*2.75*
	Never hinged	4.00	
Q154	PP13a 3.50fr brown, *yel*	2.50	*2.75*
	Never hinged	4.00	
Q155	PP13 3.80fr brown, *yel*	2.50	*2.75*
	Never hinged	4.00	
	Imperf	125.00	
	Never hinged	190.00	
Q156	PP14 2.50fr grn yel ('39)	2.50	2.25
	Never hinged	4.00	
Q157	PP14 7.50fr grn yel ('39)	2.75	2.50
	Never hinged	4.25	
Q158	PP15 1fr lilac ('39)	9.50	6.75
	Never hinged	14.00	
Q159	PP16 3.20fr blue	11.00	7.50
	Never hinged	16.00	
	Nos. Q150-Q159 (10)	39.50	33.75

Two additional values, 3.45fr and 3.85fr, type PP7, brown on yellow paper, imperforate, were prepared but not issued. Values, each: $140; never hinged, $225.

Nos. Q135-Q138, Q140-Q142 were overprinted "E" in 1939, in anticipation of new rates to take effect April 1, but were not issued. Values: 2.30fr on 1.45fr, $675, never hinged $1,000; 3.45fr on 2.15fr, $875, never hinged $1,300; 3.85fr on 2.35fr, $875, never hinged $1,300; 1.15fr on 75c, $300, never hinged $450; 3.45fr on 2.15fr, $2,800, never hinged $4,000; 3.85fr on 2.35fr, $2,800, never hinged $4,000; 3.25fr on 2fr, $675, never hinged $1,000.

In 1941, two sets were prepared in anticipation of new rate increases on April 1. They were not issued.

Six stamps in a new design, consisting of a 10c greenish gray, 30c blue, 50c brown, 1fr blue violet, 2fr orange and 5fr red. Values: 10c $185, never hinged $275; 30c $240, never hinged $350; 50c $240, never hinged $350; 1fr $185, never hinged $275; 2fr $185, never hinged $275; 5fr $185, never hinged $275.

Nos. Q93, Q153-Q155 and Q159 overprinted "E." Values: 75c; other values $575, never hinged.

PP17

PP18

Without Denominations

1941		*Perf. 12½*	
Q160	PP17 (2.70fr) brown	5.00	4.00
	Never hinged	8.25	
Q161	PP17 (3.90fr) blue	5.00	4.00
	Never hinged	8.25	
Q162	PP17 (4.20fr) green	5.00	4.00
	Never hinged	8.25	
Q163	PP18 (3.50fr) blue	9.50	8.50
	Never hinged	12.50	
	Nos. Q160-Q163 (4)	24.50	20.50

Five stamps in the designs of PP20-PP22 below, but with blank value tablets, were prepared with Nos. Q160-Q163 but were not issued. Values: (1fr) brown, (5fr) red and (2.50fr) blue, each $60, never hinged $80; (7.50fr) green, $260, never hinged $360; (1fr) violet, $110, never hinged $160.

See Nos. Q178-Q181, Q200-Q206.

"Domicile" PP19

"Valeur Declaree" PP20

"Remboursement" PP21

"Interet A La Livraison" PP22

"Encombrant" — PP23

1941		*Perf. 12½, 13 (#Q167-171)*	
Q164	PP19 2.70fr brown	6.00	5.00
	Never hinged	10.00	
Q165	PP19 3.90fr blue	6.00	5.00
	Never hinged	10.00	
Q166	PP19 4.20fr green	6.00	5.00
	Never hinged	10.00	
Q167	PP20 1fr brown	2.40	1.10
	Never hinged	3.75	
Q168	PP20 5fr red	1.20	*1.50*
	Never hinged	1.90	
Q169	PP21 2.50fr blue	1.20	*1.50*
	Never hinged	1.90	
Q170	PP21 7.50fr green	3.50	3.00
	Never hinged	5.25	
Q171	PP22 1fr violet	.85	.75
	Never hinged	1.50	
Q172	PP23 3.50fr blue	32.50	16.00
	Never hinged	47.50	
	Nos. Q164-Q172 (9)	59.65	38.85

See Nos. Q173-Q177, Q186-Q194, Q200-Q206.

For surcharges, see footnote following No. Q177, Nos. Q182-Q185, Q207-Q210.

Types of 1941 with Bold Numerals

1942, Feb.		*Perf. 13*	
Q173	PP20 1fr brown	1.25	1.10
	Never hinged	1.90	
Q174	PP20 5fr red	4.00	5.00
	Never hinged	6.00	
Q175	PP21 2.50fr blue	1.25	1.10
	Never hinged	1.90	
Q176	PP21 7.50fr green	6.00	*6.50*
	Never hinged	9.75	
Q177	PP22 1fr violet	60.00	
	Never hinged	95.00	
	Nos. Q173-Q177 (5)	72.50	13.70

See Nos. Q173-Q177, Q186-Q194, Q200-Q206. See No. Q194.

Nine stamps from the 1941-42 issues were surcharged "+3F / C.N.S. / Cheminots" to raise funds for a philatelic exhibition organized by railroad employees, which took place in Paris on Dec. 26 and 27, 1942. They were not valid for postage. Value, set: $110; never hinged $150.

Type of 1941 Inscribed in Value Tablets

1943		*Perf. 12½*	
Q178	PP17 (3fr) brown	2.60	2.60
	Never hinged	4.00	
Q179	PP17 (4.30fr) blue	2.60	2.60
	Never hinged	4.00	
Q180	PP17 (4.70fr) green	2.60	2.60
	Never hinged	4.00	
Q181	PP18 (3.50fr) blue	6.00	6.00
	Never hinged	12.00	
	Nos. Q178-Q181 (4)	13.80	13.80

Stamps of 1941 Surcharged in Deep Blue or Red

1943			
Q182	PP19 3fr on 2.70fr brn	12.50	12.50
	Never hinged	19.00	
Q183	PP19 4.3fr on 3.90fr blue (R)	2.25	*2.60*
	Never hinged	4.00	
Q184	PP19 4.7fr on 4.20fr green (R)	3.00	2.60
	Never hinged	4.50	
Q185	PP23 3.9fr on 3.50fr blue (R)	3.00	3.00
	Never hinged	4.50	
	Nos. Q182-Q185 (4)	20.75	20.70

Denominations in Black or Red

1943		**Unwmk.**	
Q186	PP19 3fr brn	3.50	*3.75*
	Never hinged	5.00	
Q187	PP19 4.3fr blue (R)	9.00	5.25
	Never hinged	11.50	
Q188	PP19 4.7fr green (R)	10.00	2.25
	Never hinged	13.50	
Q189	PP23 3.9fr blue (R)	65.00	52.50
	Never hinged	97.50	
	Nos. Q186-Q189 (4)	87.50	63.75

1943		**Wmk. 407**	
Q190	PP19 3fr brn	11.00	9.75
	Never hinged	19.00	

Q191 PP19 4.3fr blue 19.00 12.00
Never hinged 30.00
Q192 PP19 4.7fr green 19.00 12.00
Never hinged 30.00
Q193 PP23 3.9fr blue 12.00 12.00
Never hinged 19.00
Nos. Q190-Q193 (4) 61.00 45.75

1944
Q194 PP21 20fr orange 4.50 *6.00*
Never hinged 6.00

Hydroelectric Dam — PP24

Electric Train — PP25

Power Line — PP26

1944 ***Perf. 12½***
Q195 PP24 1fr dk mauve 6.00 6.00
Never hinged 8.25
Q196 PP24 5fr red brn 6.00 6.00
Never hinged 8.25
Q197 PP25 2.5fr blue 6.00 6.00
Never hinged 8.25
Q198 PP25 7.5fr green 6.00 6.00
Never hinged 8.25
Q199 PP26 1fr violet 6.00 6.00
Never hinged 8.25
Nos. Q195-Q199 (5) 30.00 30.00

A 20fr orange, design PP25, was prepared but not issued. Values: $1,050; never hinged, $1,600.

Nos. Q195-Q199 exist unwatermarked, but were not issued in this form Values, each: $275; never hinged $375.

Types of 1941 Inscribed "G" in Value Tablets

1945 **Unwmk.**
Q200 PP17 (5fr) brown 5.00 *5.25*
Never hinged 6.50
Q201 PP17 (7.20fr) blue 5.00 *5.25*
Never hinged 6.50
Q202 PP17 (7.60fr) green 5.00 *5.25*
Never hinged 6.50
Q203 PP18 (6.60fr) blue 5.50 *6.00*
Never hinged 8.00
Nos. Q200-Q203 (4) 20.50 *21.75*

Wmk. 407
Q204 PP17 (5fr) brown 15.00 15.00
Never hinged 21.00
Q205 PP17 (7.20fr) blue 11.00 *11.00*
Never hinged 16.50
Q206 PP17 (7.60fr) green 11.00 *11.00*
Never hinged 16.50
Nos. Q204-Q206 (3) 37.00 37.00

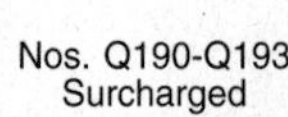

Nos. Q190-Q193 Surcharged

1945 **Wmk. 407**
Q207 PP19 5fr on 3fr brown 5.50 5.50
Never hinged 8.00
Q208 PP19 7.2fr on 4fr blue 5.50 5.50
Never hinged 8.00
Q209 PP19 7.8fr on 4.70fr green 5.50 5.50
Never hinged 8.00
Q210 PP23 6.6fr on 3.90fr blue 6.75 6.75
Never hinged 10.00
Nos. Q207-Q210 (4) 23.25 23.25

Nos. Q186-Q189 were also surcharged but were not issued. Values, each: $40; never hinged $67.50.

Electric Train — PP27

Transformer PP28

1945 **Denominations in Black**
Q211 PP27 5fr mauve 14.00 14.00
Never hinged 20.00
Q212 PP27 7.2fr blue 13.50 13.50
Never hinged 20.00
Q213 PP27 7.8fr green 13.50 13.50
Never hinged 20.00

Denomination in Purple
Q214 PP28 6.6fr blue 6.00 6.00
Never hinged 8.25
Nos. Q211-Q214 (4) 47.00 47.00

Nos. Q211-Q213 without watermark were not issued. Value, set: $45; never hinged, $72.50.

A set of ten stamps in the design of the first three images were prepared in 1945 but were not issued. Value, each: $300; never hinged $475.

Four stamps of types PP27-PP28, inscribed "H" in the value tablet, were prepared but not issued. Value, set: $2,400; never hinged $4,000.

Locomotive — PP29

Nos. Q215-216, Q222-Q223: 16x22mm; Nos. Q217-Q221, Q224-Q228: 18.5x22mm

1944 **Wmk. 407** ***Perf. 13***
Q215 PP29 1fr deep green 3.75 1.10
Never hinged 7.50
Q216 PP29 2fr violet 5.25 1.50
Never hinged 11.00
Q217 PP29 5fr ultramarine 24.00 1.50
Never hinged 32.50
Q218 PP29 10fr red 12.00 1.50
Never hinged 20.00
Q219 PP29 20fr olive green 10.00 1.50
Never hinged 16.00
Q220 PP29 50fr red orange 19.00 1.50
Never hinged 26.00
Q221 PP29 100fr gray black 35.00 1.50
Never hinged 52.50
Nos. Q215-Q221 (7) 109.00 10.10

Unwmk.
Q222 PP29 1fr deep green 9.75 4.75
Never hinged 15.00
Q223 PP29 2fr violet 12.50 4.75
Never hinged 19.00
Q224 PP29 5fr ultramarine 40.00 4.75
Never hinged 65.00
Q225 PP29 10fr red 26.00 4.75
Never hinged 37.50
Q226 PP29 20fr olive green 19.00 4.75
Never hinged 30.00
Q227 PP29 50fr red orange 37.50 4.75
Never hinged 55.00
Q228 PP29 100fr gray black 67.50 5.25
Never hinged 97.50
Nos. Q222-Q228 (7) 212.25 33.75

Nos. Q215-Q234 were issued for use on small packets. Effective January 1, 1946, the parcel and small packet services were unified, and all issued thereafter were valid for both services.

See Nos. Q229-Q254.

Nos. Q229-Q230: 16x22mm; Nos. Q231-Q254: 18.5x22mm

1944-45 **Wmk. 407**
Q229 PP29 3fr gray 6.00 1.50
Never hinged 11.00
Q230 PP29 4fr black 9.75 2.25
Never hinged 15.00
Q231 PP29 7fr violet 62.50 2.60
Never hinged 100.00
Q232 PP29 8fr yel grn 18.00 2.25
Never hinged 30.00
Q233 PP29 9fr dk blue 30.00 4.00
Never hinged 50.00
Q234 PP29 30fr red brn 82.50 1.50
Never hinged 125.00
Nos. Q229-Q234 (6) 208.75 14.10

1946
Q235 PP29 6fr claret 16.00 1.50
Never hinged 23.00
Q236 PP29 40fr yel brn 24.00 1.50
Never hinged 35.00
Q237 PP29 60fr lake red 26.00 1.50
Never hinged 37.50
Q238 PP29 70fr violet 175.00 26.00
Never hinged 260.00
Q239 PP29 80fr yel grn 24.00 2.25
Never hinged 35.00
Q240 PP29 90fr dk blue 140.00 25.00
Never hinged 225.00
Q241 PP29 200fr emer grn 30.00 2.25
Never hinged 47.50
Nos. Q235-Q241 (7) 435.00 60.00

1947
Q242 PP29 5fr pale blue 19.00 1.90
Never hinged 30.00
Q243 PP29 7fr pale vio 250.00 16.00
Never hinged 400.00
Q244 PP29 9fr pale bl 190.00 15.00
Never hinged 290.00
Q245 PP29 30fr pale gray brn 67.50 1.90
Never hinged 100.00
Q246 PP29 70fr pale viol 175.00 6.75
Never hinged 260.00
Q247 PP29 90fr pale ultra 130.00 2.25
Never hinged 200.00
Q248 PP29 100fr yellow 350.00 2.25
Never hinged 490.00
Nos. Q242-Q248 (7) 1,182. 46.05

1948
Q249 PP29 500fr yel org 80.00 2.25
Never hinged 120.00
Q250 PP29 1000fr yel 290.00 16.00
Never hinged 425.00

1951-52
Q251 PP29 10fr grn 52.50 7.50
Never hinged 82.50
Q252 PP29 20fr vio 52.50 13.50
Never hinged 82.50
Q253 PP29 50fr blue 65.00 9.00
Never hinged 100.00
Q254 PP29 100fr rose ver 19.00 1.50
Never hinged 26.00
Nos. Q251-Q254 (4) 189.00 31.50

Electric Train — PP30

1960
Q255 PP30 5c orange 11.50 2.10
Never hinged 17.50
Q256 PP30 10c red 10.50 8.25
Never hinged 16.00
Q257 PP30 20c dp red 8.75 3.75
Never hinged 13.50
Q258 PP30 30c dp red 8.75 3.75
Never hinged 13.50
Q259 PP30 40c dp red 8.75 7.50
Never hinged 13.50
Q260 PP30 50c dp red 8.75 4.25
Never hinged 13.50
Q261 PP30 60c dp red 7.50 4.25
Never hinged 11.00
Q262 PP30 70c dp red 7.50 4.25
Never hinged 11.00
Q263 PP30 80c dp red 11.50 4.25
Never hinged 17.50
Q264 PP30 90c dp red 11.50 4.25
Never hinged 17.50
Q265 PP30 1fr blue 13.00 2.25
Never hinged 20.00
Q266 PP30 2fr blue 13.00 2.25
Never hinged 20.00
Q267 PP30 3fr blue 13.00 2.25
Never hinged 20.00
Q268 PP30 4fr blue 13.00 2.25
Never hinged 20.00
Q269 PP30 5fr blue 13.00 2.25
Never hinged 20.00
Q270 PP30 10fr yellow 15.00 2.50
Never hinged 22.50
Q271 PP30 20fr dp grn 20.00 16.00
Never hinged 30.00
Nos. Q255-Q271 (17) 195.00 76.35

1960 **Unwmk.**
Q272 PP30 5c orange 14.00 6.25
Never hinged 32.50
Q273 PP30 20c dp red 210.00 55.00
Never hinged 325.00
Q274 PP30 30c dp red 150.00 55.00
Never hinged 325.00
Q275 PP30 40c dp red 110.00 30.00
Never hinged 160.00
Q276 PP30 70c dp red 22.50 7.50
Never hinged 32.50
Q277 PP30 80c dp red 22.50 6.50
Never hinged 32.50
Q278 PP30 90c dp red 22.50 6.50
Never hinged 32.50
Q279 PP30 1fr blue 20.00 3.75
Never hinged 30.00
Q280 PP30 2fr blue 20.00 3.75
Never hinged 30.00
Q281 PP30 3fr blue 20.00 3.75
Never hinged 30.00
Q282 PP30 4fr blue 20.00 3.75
Never hinged 30.00
Q283 PP30 5fr blue 20.00 3.75
Never hinged 30.00
Q284 PP30 10fr yellow 25.00 6.25
Never hinged 37.50
Q285 PP30 20fr dp grn 30.00 21.00
Never hinged 45.00
Nos. Q272-Q285 (14) 706.50 212.75

FRANCHISE STAMPS

No. 276 Overprinted

1939 **Unwmk.** ***Perf. 14x13½***
S1 A45 90c ultramarine 1.90 *2.50*
Never hinged 2.75
a. Period following "F" 30.00 30.00
Never hinged 50.00

No. S1 was for the use of Spanish refugees in France. "F" stands for "Franchise."

OCCUPATION STAMPS

FRANCO-PRUSSIAN WAR
Issued under German Occupation (Alsace and Lorraine)

OS1

Network Points Up

1870 Typo. Unwmk. *Perf. 13½x14*
Network with Points Up

N1 OS1 1c bronze green 75.00 *100.00*
a. 1c olive grn 75.00 *100.00*
N2 OS1 2c dark brown 125.00 *175.00*
a. 2c red brown 115.00 *175.00*
N3 OS1 4c gray 135.00 100.00
N4 OS1 5c yel grn 125.00 14.00
N5 OS1 10c bistre brn 110.00 5.75
a. 10c yellow brown 110.00 6.50
b. Network lemon yellow 135.00 10.00
N6 OS1 20c ultra 115.00 16.50
N7 OS1 25c brown 150.00 100.00
a. 25c black brown 145.00 100.00

There are three varieties of the 4c and two of the 10c, differing in the position of the figures of value, and several other setting varieties.

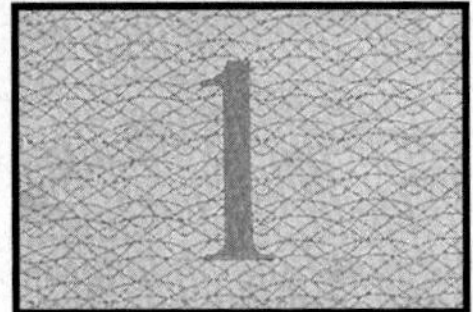

Network Points Down

Network with Points Down

N8 OS1 1c olive grn 350.00 *625.00*
N9 OS1 2c red brn 150.00 *550.00*
N10 OS1 4c gray 150.00 200.00
N11 OS1 5c yel grn 6,500. 650.00
N12 OS1 10c bister 150.00 21.50
a. Network lemon yellow 225.00 50.00
N13 OS1 20c ultra 225.00 90.00
N14 OS1 25c brown 450.00 300.00

Official imitations have the network with points downward. The "P" of "Postes" is 2½mm from the border in the imitations and 3mm in the originals.

The word "Postes" measures 12¾ to 13mm on the imitations, and from 11 to 12½mm on the originals.

The imitations are perf. 13½x14½; originals, perf. 13½x14¼.

The stamps for Alsace and Lorraine were replaced by stamps of the German Empire on Jan. 1, 1872.

WORLD WAR I
German Stamps of 1905-16 Surcharged

1916 Wmk. 125 *Perf. 14, 14½*

N15 A16 3c on 3pf brown 1.25 1.25
N16 A16 5c on 5pf green 1.25 1.25
N17 A22 8c on 7½pf org 2.00 2.00
N18 A16 10c on 10pf car 2.00 2.00
N19 A22 15c on 15pf yel brn 1.25 1.25
N20 A16 25c on 20pf blue 1.25 1.25
a. 25c on 20pf ultramarine 2.00 2.00
N21 A16 40c on 30pf org & blk, *buff* 2.90 2.75
N22 A16 50c on 40pf lake & blk 2.90 2.75
N23 A16 75c on 60pf mag 12.50 12.50
N24 A16 1fr on 80pf lake & blk, *rose* 12.50 12.50

N25 A17 1fr25c on 1m car 47.50 47.50
a. Double surcharge —
N26 A21 2fr50c on 2m gray bl 47.50 47.50
a. Double surcharge —
Nos. N15-N26 (12) 134.80 134.50

These stamps were also used in parts of Belgium occupied by the German forces.

Catalogue values for unused stamps in this section, from this point to the end of the section, are for Never Hinged items.

WORLD WAR II
Alsace
Issued under German Occupation

Stamps of Germany 1933-36 Overprinted in Black

1940 Wmk. 237 *Perf. 14*

N27 A64 3pf olive bister .80 *.55*
N28 A64 4pf dull blue .80 *.55*
N29 A64 5pf brt green .80 *.55*
N30 A64 6pf dark green .80 *.55*
a. Inverted overprint 1,500.
N31 A64 8pf vermilion .80 *.55*
a. Inverted overprint 4,000.
N32 A64 10pf chocolate .80 *.55*
N33 A64 12pf dp carmine 1.00 *.55*
N34 A64 15pf maroon 1.00 *.55*
N35 A64 20pf brt blue 1.65 *.75*
N36 A64 25pf ultra 1.65 *.75*
N37 A64 30pf olive grn 1.65 *.75*
N38 A64 40pf red violet 2.90 *1.00*
N39 A64 50pf dk grn & blk 7.00 *3.25*
N40 A64 60pf claret & blk 7.00 *3.25*
N41 A64 80pf dk blue & blk 17.50 *7.00*
N42 A64 100pf orange & blk 17.50 7.00
Nos. N27-N42 (16) 63.65 28.15

Lorraine
Issued under German Occupation

Stamps of Germany 1933-36 Overprinted in Black

1940 Wmk. 237 *Perf. 14*

N43 A64 3pf olive bister 1.00 .75
N44 A64 4pf dull blue 1.00 .75
N45 A64 5pf brt green 1.00 *4.00*
N46 A64 6pf dark green 1.00 .75
N47 A64 8pf vermilion 1.00 .75
N48 A64 10pf chocolate 1.50 .85
N49 A64 12pf deep carmine 1.50 .85
N50 A64 15pf maroon 1.50 .75
a. Inverted surcharge —
N51 A64 20pf brt blue 1.65 1.00
N52 A64 25pf ultra 1.40 1.00
N53 A64 30pf olive grn 2.10 1.00
N54 A64 40pf red violet 2.50 1.25
N55 A64 50pf dk grn & blk 6.00 3.00
N56 A64 60pf claret & blk 6.00 3.00
N57 A64 80pf dk blue & blk 18.00 7.50
N58 A64 100pf orange & blk 18.00 7.50
Nos. N43-N58 (16) 65.15 *34.70*

Besetztes Gebiet Nordfrankreich

These three words, in a rectangular frame covering two stamps, were handstamped in black on Nos. 267, 367 and 369 and used in the Dunkerque region in July-August, 1940. The German political officer of Dunkerque authorized the overprint. The prevalence of forgeries and later favor overprints make expertization mandatory.

ALLIED MILITARY GOVERNMENT

Stamps formerly listed in this section as Nos. 2N1-2N20 are now listed with regular stamps of France as Nos. 475-476H and 523A-523J.

FRANCE OFFICES ABROAD

OFFICES IN CHINA

Prior to 1923 several of the world powers maintained their own post offices in China for the purpose of sending and receiving overseas mail. French offices were maintained in Canton, Hoi Hao (Hoihow), Kwangchowan (Kouang-tchéou-wan), Mongtseu (Mong-tseu), Packhoi (Paknoi), Tong King (Tchongking), Yunnan Fou (Yunnanfu).

100 Centimes = 1 Franc
100 Cents = 1 Piaster
100 Cents = 1 Dollar

Peace and Commerce Stamps of France Ovptd. in Red, Carmine or Black

1894-1900 Unwmk. *Perf. 14x13½*

1 A15 5c grn, *grnsh* (R) 3.25 3.00
2 A15 5c yel grn, I (R) ('00) 4.25 3.00
a. Type II 47.50 32.50
3 A15 10c blk, *lav*, I (R) 9.25 3.00
a. Type II 27.50 *17.50*
4 A15 15c bl (R) 12.50 4.25
5 A15 20c red, *grn* 7.50 5.00
6 A15 25c blk, *rose* (C) 9.25 2.50
a. Double overprint 225.00
b. Pair, one without overprint 550.00
d. Imperf 120.00 45.00
7 A15 30c brn, *bis* 9.25 6.25
8 A15 40c red, *straw* 9.25 7.50
9 A15 50c car, *rose*, I 26.00 17.50
a. Carmine overprint 62.50
b. Type II (Bk) 25.00 16.00
10 A15 75c dp vio, *org* (R) 80.00 60.00
11 A15 1fr brnz grn, *straw* 17.00 8.50
a. Double overprint 425.00 *450.00*
12 A15 2fr brn, *az* ('00) 30.00 29.00
12A A15 5fr red lil, *lav* 75.00 60.00
b. Red overprint 525.00
Nos. 1-12A (13) 292.50 209.50

For surcharges and overprints see Nos. 13-17, J7-J10, J20-J23.

No. 11 Surcharged in Black

13 A15 25c on 1fr brnz grn, *straw* 125.00 75.00

No. 6 Surcharged in Red

1901

14 A15 2c on 25c blk, *rose* 1,100. 340.00
15 A15 4c on 25c blk, *rose* 1,350. 450.00
16 A15 6c on 25c blk, *rose* 1,100. 375.00
17 A15 16c on 25c blk, *rose* 325.00 200.00
a. Black surcharge *7,250.*
Nos. 14-17 (4) 3,875. 1,365.

Stamps of Indo-China Surcharged in Black

Two types of Nos. 18-33: type I, 13mmx3mm, "C" and "H" wide, "E" with fine serifs; type II, 12½mmx2¾mm, "C" and "H" narrower, "E" with heavy serifs.

1902-04

18a A3 1c blk, *lil bl* 2.50 2.50
19 A3 2c brn, *buff* 4.25 4.25
20a A3 4c claret, *lav* 4.25 3.40
21a A3 5c yellow grn 5.00 3.40
22 A3 10c red 6.75 6.00
23 A3 15c gray 7.50 6.75
24a A3 20c red, *grn* 9.25 8.50
25a A3 25c blk, *rose* 12.50 12.50
26 A3 25c blue 10.00 8.50
27a A3 30c brn, *bis* 9.25 8.50
28a A3 40c red, *straw* 25.00 21.00
29 A3 50c car, *rose* 67.50 67.50
30 A3 50c brn, *azure* 10.00 9.25
31a A3 75c vio, *org* 40.00 37.50
32a A3 1fr brnz grn, *straw* 45.00 42.50
33a A3 5fr red lil, *lav* 97.50 90.00
Nos. 18a-33a (16) 356.25 332.05

The Chinese characters surcharged on Nos. 18-33 are the Chinese equivalents of the French values and therefore differ on each denomination. Two printings exist, differing slightly in the size of "CHINE." Values above are for the less expensive variety. See the *Scott Classic Specialized Cataloue of Stamps and Covers* for detailed listings. Many varieties of surcharge exist.

Liberty, Equality and Fraternity
A3

"Rights of Man"
A4

A5

1902-03 Typo.

34 A3 5c green 6.00 3.75
35 A4 10c rose red ('03) 3.00 2.10
36 A4 15c pale red 3.00 2.10
37 A4 20c brn vio ('03) 8.50 7.25
38 A4 25c blue ('03) 6.75 3.40
39 A4 30c lilac ('03) 9.25 7.50
40 A5 40c red & pale bl 19.00 16.00
41 A5 50c bis brn & lav 23.00 19.00
42 A5 1fr claret & ol grn 30.00 19.00
43 A5 2fr gray vio & yel 62.50 45.00
44 A5 5fr dk bl & buff 92.50 72.50
Nos. 34-44 (11) 263.50 197.60

For surcharges and overprints see Nos. 45, 57-85, J14-J16, J27-J30.

Surcharged in Black

1903

45 A4 5c on 15c pale red 17.50 12.00
a. Inverted surcharge 135.00 75.00

Stamps of Indo-China, 1904-06, Surcharged as Nos. 18-33 in Black

1904-05

46 A4 1c olive grn 2.10 2.10
47 A4 2c vio brn, *buff* 2.10 2.10
47A A4 4c cl, *bluish* 975.00 800.00
48 A4 5c deep grn 2.10 2.10
49 A4 10c carmine 3.00 3.00
50 A4 15c org brn, *bl* (I) 3.00 3.00
51 A4 20c red, *grn* 11.50 11.00
52 A4 25c deep blue 10.00 6.00
53 A4 40c blk, *bluish* 8.50 6.00
54 A4 1fr pale grn 360.00 300.00

55 A4 2fr brn, *org* 42.50 37.50
56 A4 10fr org brn, *grn* 165.00 155.00
Nos. 46-56 (12) 1,585. 1,328.

Many varieties of the surcharge exist.

Stamps of 1902-03 Surcharged in Black

1907
57 A3 2c on 5c green 2.50 1.60
58 A4 4c on 10c rose red 2.50 1.75
a. Pair, one without surcharge —
59 A4 6c on 15c pale red 3.40 2.50
60 A4 8c on 20c brn vio 6.00 6.00
a. "8" inverted 75.00 75.00
61 A4 10c on 25c blue 2.10 1.25
62 A5 20c on 50c bis brn & lav 6.25 3.75
a. Double surcharge
b. Triple surcharge 440.00 440.00
63 A5 40c on 1fr claret & ol grn 22.00 13.50
64 A5 2pi on 5fr dk bl & buff 23.00 13.50
a. Double surcharge *2,300.* *1,900.*
Nos. 57-64 (8) 67.75 43.85

Stamps of 1902-03 Surcharged in Black

1911-22
65 A3 2c on 5c green 2.10 1.50
66 A4 4c on 10c rose red 2.50 1.75
67 A4 6c on 15c org 5.00 2.10
68 A4 8c on 20c brn vio 2.10 1.80
69 A4 10c on 25c bl ('21) 4.25 2.10
70 A4 20c on 50c bl ('22) 55.00 55.00
71 A5 40c on 1fr cl & ol grn 7.50 6.00

No. 44 Surcharged

73 A5 $2 on 5fr bl & buff ('22) 175.00 *200.00*
Nos. 65-73 (8) 253.45 270.25

Types of 1902-03 Surcharged like Nos. 65-71

1922
75 A3 1c on 5c org 6.00 *6.75*
76 A4 2c on 10c grn 6.75 *7.50*
77 A4 3c on 15c org 9.25 *11.00*
78 A4 4c on 20c red brn 11.00 *13.50*
79 A4 5c on 25c dk vio 6.00 6.00
80 A4 6c on 30c red 12.00 11.00
82 A4 10c on 50c blue 14.50 12.00
83 A5 20c on 1fr claret & ol grn 35.00 *40.00*
84 A5 40c on 2fr org & pale bl 45.00 *55.00*
85 A5 $1 on 5fr dk bl & buff 150.00 *160.00*
Nos. 75-85 (10) 295.50 322.75

POSTAGE DUE STAMPS

Postage Due Stamps of France Handstamped in Red or Black

1901-07 Unwmk. *Perf. 14x13½*
J1 D2 5c lt bl (R) 7.50 4.25
a. Double overprint 160.00
J2 D2 10c choc (R) 11.00 6.00
a. Double overprint 160.00
J3 D2 15c lt grn (R) 11.00 7.50
a. Pair, one stamp without ovpt. 275.00
b. Imperf, single 160.00
J4 D2 20c ol grn (R) ('07) 12.50 11.00
J5 D2 30c carmine 17.00 12.00
a. Double overprint 160.00
J6 D2 50c lilac 17.00 12.50
a. Triple overprint 160.00
b. Pair, one stamp without overprint 275.00
Nos. J1-J6 (6) 76.00 53.25

Stamps of 1894-1900 Handstamped in Carmine

1903
J7 A15 5c yel grn — 2,250.
a. Purple handstamp —
b. 5c green, *greenish* —
J8 A15 10c blk, *lavender* — —
a. Purple handstamp — —
J9 A15 15c blue *2,750.* 1,250.
a. Purple handstamp — —
J10 A15 30c brn, *bister* *1,500.* 350.00
a. Purple handstamp — —

Same Handstamp on Stamps of 1902-03 in Carmine

1903
J14 A3 5c green — 2,000.
a. Purple handstamp — —
J15 A4 10c rose red 750. 425.00
a. Purple handstamp — —
J16 A4 15c pale red 750. 325.00
a. Purple handstamp — —

Stamps of 1894-1900 Handstamped in Carmine

1903
J20 A1 5c yellow green — 1,100.
a. Purple handstamp — —
b. 5c green, *greenish* — —
J21 A1 10c blk, *lavender* — —
a. Purple handstamp — —
J22 A1 15c blue 1,250. 350.
a. Purple handstamp — —
J23 A1 30c brn, *bister* 600. 325.
a. Purple handstamp — —

Same Handstamp on Stamps of 1902-03 in Carmine or Purple

1903
J27 A3 5c green (C) — 1,750.
a. Purple handstamp — —
J28 A4 10c rose red (C) 340. 225.
a. Purple handstamp — —
J29 A4 15c pale red (C) 675. 225.
a. Purple handstamp — —
J30 A4 30c lilac (P) — —

The handstamps on Nos. J7-J30 are found inverted, double, etc.

The cancellations on these stamps should have dates between Sept. 1, and Nov. 30, 1903, to be genuine.

Postage Due Stamps of France, 1893-1910 Surcharged like Nos. 65-71

1911
J33 D2 2c on 5c blue 3.00 2.50
a. Double surcharge 140.00 —
J34 D2 4c on 10c choc 3.00 2.50
a. Double surcharge 140.00 —
J35 D2 8c on 20c ol grn 3.40 3.00
a. Double surcharge 140.00 —
J36 D2 20c on 50c lilac 3.40 3.00
Nos. J33-J36 (4) 12.80 11.00

1922
J37 D2 1c on 5c blue 82.50 *95.00*
J38 D2 2c on 10c brn 145.00 *165.00*
J39 D2 4c on 20c ol grn 145.00 *165.00*
J40 D2 10c on 50c brn vio 125.00 *185.00*
Nos. J37-J40 (4) 497.50 610.00

CANTON

Stamps of Indo-China, 1892-1900, Overprinted in Red

1901 Unwmk. *Perf. 14x13½*
1 A3 1c blk, *lil bl* 2.10 2.10
1A A3 2c brn, *buff* 2.50 2.50
2 A3 4c claret, *lav* 4.25 4.25
2A A3 5c grn, *grnsh* 600.00 600.00
3 A3 5c yel grn 3.40 3.40
4 A3 10c blk, *lavender* 7.25 7.25
5 A3 15c blue, quadrille paper 6.75 6.75
6 A3 15c gray 7.50 7.50
a. Double overprint 19.00
7 A3 20c red, *grn* 22.50 22.50
8 A3 25c blk, *rose* 13.50 13.50
9 A3 30c brn, *bister* 32.50 32.50
10 A3 40c red, *straw* 32.50 32.50
11 A3 50c car, *rose* 35.00 35.00
12 A3 75c dp vio, *org* 35.00 35.00
13 A3 1fr brnz grn, *straw* 45.00 45.00
14 A3 5fr red lil, *lav* 250.00 250.00
Nos. 1-14 (16) 1,100. 1,100.

The Chinese characters in the overprint on Nos. 1-14 read "Canton." On Nos. 15-64, they restate the denomination of the basic stamp.

Surcharged in Black

1903-04
15 A3 1c blk, *lil bl* 4.25 4.25
16 A3 2c brn, *buff* 4.50 4.25
17 A3 4c claret, *lav* 4.50 4.25
18 A3 5c yellow green 4.25 4.25
19 A3 10c rose red 4.50 4.25
20 A3 15c gray 4.50 4.25
21 A3 20c red, *grn* 21.00 17.50
22 A3 25c blue 7.50 7.50
23 A3 25c blk, *rose* ('04) 10.00 8.50
24 A3 30c brn, *bister* 27.50 21.00
25 A3 40c red, *straw* 67.50 55.00
26 A3 50c car, *rose* 340.00 310.00
27 A3 50c brn, *az* ('04) 85.00 72.50
28 A3 75c dp vio, *org* 67.50 67.50
a. "INDO-CHINE" inverted *55,000.*
29 A3 1fr brnz grn, *straw* 67.50 67.50
30 A3 5fr red lil, *lav* 67.50 67.50
Nos. 15-30 (16) 787.50 720.00

Many varieties of the surcharge exist on Nos. 15-30.

Stamps of Indo-China, 1892-1906, Surcharged in Red or Black

A second printing of the 1906 surcharges of Canton, Hoi Hao, Kwangchowan, Mongtseu, Packhoi, Tong King and Yunnan Fou was made in 1908. The inks are grayish instead of full black and vermilion instead of carmine. Values are for the cheaper variety which usually is the second printing.

The 4c and 50c of the 1892 issue of Indo-China are known with this surcharge and similarly surcharged for other cities in China. The surcharges on these two stamps are always inverted. It is stated that they were irregularly produced and never issued.

1906
31 A4 1c ol grn (R) 2.50 2.50
32 A4 2c vio brn, *buff* 2.50 2.50
33 A4 4c cl, *bluish* (R) 2.50 2.50
34 A4 5c dp grn (R) 2.10 2.10
35 A4 10c carmine 3.00 3.00
36 A4 15c org brn, *bl* 22.50 22.50
37 A4 20c red, *grn* 12.50 12.50
38 A4 25c deep blue 5.00 5.00
39 A4 30c pale brn 17.00 17.00
40 A4 35c blk, *yel* (R) 12.50 12.50
41 A4 40c blk, *bluish* (R) 21.00 21.00
42 A4 50c bister brn 14.50 14.50
43 A4 75c dp vio, *org* (R) 67.50 67.50
44 A4 1fr pale grn 30.00 30.00
45 A4 2fr brn, *org* (R) 42.50 42.50
46 A4 5fr red lil, *lav* 92.50 92.50
47 A4 10fr org brn, *grn* 85.00 85.00
Nos. 31-47 (17) 435.10 435.10

Surcharge exists inverted on 1c, 25c & 1fr.

Stamps of Indo-China, 1907, Srchd. in Red or Blue

Chinese Characters

1908
48 A5 1c ol brn & blk 1.25 1.25
49 A5 2c brn & blk 1.25 1.25
50 A5 4c bl & blk 2.50 1.25
51 A5 5c grn & blk 2.50 2.10
52 A5 10c red & blk (Bl) 3.40 2.50
53 A5 15c vio & blk 4.25 3.40
54 A6 20c vio & blk 5.00 5.00
55 A6 25c bl & blk 5.00 4.25
56 A6 30c brn & blk 8.50 8.50
57 A6 35c ol grn & blk 8.50 8.50
58 A6 40c brn & blk 11.00 8.50
59 A6 50c car & blk (Bl) 11.00 8.50
60 A7 75c ver & blk (Bl) 11.00 10.00
61 A8 1fr car & blk (Bl) 18.00 15.00
62 A9 2fr grn & blk 45.00 37.50
63 A10 5fr bl & blk 62.50 55.00
64 A11 10fr pur & blk 92.50 92.50
Nos. 48-64 (17) 293.15 265.00

Nos. 48-64 Surcharged with New Values in Cents or Piasters in Black, Red or Blue

1919
65 A5 ⅖c on 1c 1.25 1.25
66 A5 ⅘c on 2c 1.25 1.25
67 A5 1⅗c on 4c (R) 1.25 1.25
68 A5 2c on 5c 1.60 1.60
69 A5 4c on 10c (Bl) 2.10 1.60
a. Chinese "2" instead of "4" 42.50 42.50
70 A5 6c on 15c 2.50 2.10
71 A6 8c on 20c 4.25 2.10
72 A6 10c on 25c 5.00 1.60
73 A6 12c on 30c 2.10 2.10
a. Double surcharge 140.00 140.00
74 A6 14c on 35c 2.10 1.60
a. Closed "4" 10.00 10.00
75 A6 16c on 40c 2.50 1.60
76 A6 20c on 50c (Bl) 2.50 2.10
77 A7 30c on 75c (Bl) 2.50 2.10
78 A8 40c on 1fr (Bl) 12.50 7.50
79 A9 80c on 2fr (R) 19.00 12.00
80 A10 2pi on 5fr (R) 32.50 32.50
81 A11 4pi on 10fr (R) 32.50 32.50
Nos. 65-81 (17) 127.40 106.75

HOI HAO

Stamps of Indo-China Overprinted in Red

1901 Unwmk. *Perf. 14x13½*
1 A3 1c blk, *lil bl* 3.40 3.40
2 A3 2c brn, *buff* 4.25 4.25
3 A3 4c claret, *lav* 4.25 4.25
4 A3 5c yel grn 5.00 5.00
5 A3 10c blk, *lavender* 13.50 12.00
6 A3 15c blue 1,850. 800.00
7 A3 15c gray 7.50 5.00
8 A3 20c red, *grn* 32.50 25.00
9 A3 25c blk, *rose* 17.00 12.50
10 A3 30c brn, *bister* 67.50 67.50
11 A3 40c red, *straw* 67.50 67.50
12 A3 50c car, *rose* 67.50 67.50
13 A3 75c dp vio, *org* 250.00 225.00
14 A3 1fr brnz grn, *straw* 800.00 740.00
15 A3 5fr red lil, *lav* 800.00 675.00
Nos. 1-15 (15) 3,990. 2,714.

The Chinese characters in the overprint on Nos. 1-15 read "Hoi Hao." On Nos. 16-66, they restate the denomination of the basic stamp.

Surcharged in Black

1903-04
16 A3 1c blk, *lil bl* 2.50 2.50
17 A3 2c brn, *buff* 2.50 2.50
18 A3 4c claret, *lav* 4.25 4.25
19 A3 5c yel grn 4.25 4.25
20 A3 10c red 4.25 4.25
21 A3 15c gray 5.00 5.00
22 A3 20c red, *grn* 7.50 7.50
23 A3 25c blue 5.00 5.00
24 A3 25c blk, *rose* ('04) 8.50 8.50
25 A3 30c brn, *bister* 6.75 6.75
26 A3 40c red, *straw* 32.50 32.50
27 A3 50c car, *rose* 30.00 30.00
28 A3 50c brn, *az* ('04) 170.00 170.00
29 A3 75c dp vio, *org* 50.00 50.00
a. "INDO-CHINE" inverted *45,000.*
30 A3 1fr brnz grn, *straw* 67.50 67.50
31 A3 5fr red lil, *lav* 225.00 225.00
Nos. 16-31 (16) 625.50 625.50

Many varieties of the surcharge exist on Nos. 1-31.

Stamps of Indo-China, 1892-1906, Surcharged in Red or Black

1906

No.	Type	Description	Unused	Used
32	A4	1c ol grn (R)	8.50	8.50
33	A4	2c vio brn, *buff*	8.50	8.50
34	A4	4c cl, *bluish* (R)	8.50	8.50
35	A4	5c dp grn (R)	8.50	8.50
36	A4	10c carmine	8.50	8.50
37	A4	15c org brn, *bl*	32.50	32.50
38	A4	20c red, *grn*	13.50	13.50
39	A4	25c deep blue	11.00	11.00
40	A4	30c pale brn	13.50	13.50
41	A4	35c blk, *yel* (R)	21.00	21.00
42	A4	40c blk, *bluish* (R)	21.00	21.00
43	A4	50c gray brn	21.00	21.00
44	A3	75c dp vio, *org* (R)	62.50	62.50
45	A4	1fr pale grn	62.50	62.50
46	A4	2fr brn, *org* (R)	62.50	62.50
47	A3	5fr red lil, *lav*	135.00	135.00
48	A4	10fr org brn, *grn*	150.00	150.00
		Nos. 32-48 (17)	648.50	648.50

Stamps of Indo-China, 1907, Srchd. in Red or Blue

Chinese Characters

1908

No.	Type	Description	Unused	Used
49	A5	1c ol brn & blk	1.70	1.70
50	A5	2c brn & blk	1.70	1.70
51	A5	4c bl & blk	1.70	1.70
52	A5	5c grn & blk	3.00	3.00
53	A5	10c red & blk (Bl)	3.00	3.00
54	A5	15c vio & blk	6.75	6.75
55	A6	20c vio & blk	7.50	7.50
56	A6	25c bl & blk	7.50	7.50
57	A6	30c brn & blk	7.50	7.50
58	A6	35c ol grn & blk	7.50	7.50
59	A6	40c brn & blk	8.50	8.50
61	A6	50c car & blk (Bl)	10.00	10.00
62	A7	75c ver & blk (Bl)	10.00	10.00
63	A8	1fr car & blk (Bl)	29.00	29.00
64	A9	2fr grn & blk	42.50	42.50
65	A10	5fr bl & blk	75.00	75.00
66	A11	10fr pur & blk	110.00	110.00
		Nos. 49-66 (17)	332.85	332.85

Nos. 49-66 Surcharged with New Values in Cents or Piasters in Black, Red or Blue

1919

No.	Type	Description	Unused	Used
67	A5	⅖c on 1c	1.25	1.25
68	A5	⅘c on 2c	1.25	1.25
69	A5	1⅗c on 4c (R)	2.10	2.10
70	A5	2c on 5c	2.50	2.50
71	A5	4c on 10c (Bl)	3.00	3.00
a.		Chinese "2" instead of "4"	14.50	14.50
72	A5	6c on 15c	2.50	2.50
73	A6	8c on 20c	4.25	4.25
a.		"S" of "CENTS" omitted	170.00	170.00
74	A6	10c on 25c	6.75	6.75
75	A6	12c on 30c	4.25	4.25
76	A6	14c on 35c	3.40	3.40
a.		Closed "4"	42.50	42.50
77	A6	16c on 40c	4.25	4.25
79	A6	20c on 50c (Bl)	3.40	3.40
80	A7	30c on 75c (Bl)	11.00	11.00
81	A8	40c on 1fr (Bl)	22.00	22.00
82	A9	80c on 2fr (R)	62.50	62.50
83	A10	2pi on 5fr (R)	92.50	92.50
a.		Triple surch. of new value	750.00	*750.00*
84	A11	4pi on 10fr (R)	225.00	225.00
		Nos. 67-84 (17)	451.90	451.90

KWANGCHOWAN

A Chinese Territory leased to France, 1898 to 1945.

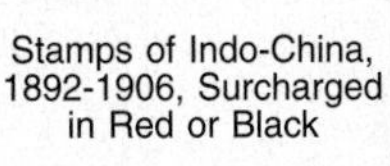

Stamps of Indo-China, 1892-1906, Surcharged in Red or Black

1906 **Unwmk.** ***Perf. 14x13½***

No.	Type	Description	Unused	Used
1	A4	1c ol grn (R)	8.50	8.50
2	A4	2c vio brn, *buff*	8.50	8.50
3	A4	4c cl, *bluish* (R)	8.50	8.50
4	A4	5c dp grn (R)	8.50	8.50
5	A4	10c carmine	8.50	8.50
6	A4	15c org brn, *bl*	32.50	32.50
7	A4	20c red, *grn*	13.50	13.50
8	A4	25c deep blue	11.00	11.00
9	A4	30c pale brn	13.50	13.50
10	A4	35c blk, *yel* (R)	21.00	21.00
11	A4	40c blk, *bluish* (R)	21.00	21.00
12	A4	50c bister brn	25.00	25.00
13	A3	75c dp vio, *org* (R)	67.50	67.50
14	A4	1fr pale grn	42.50	42.50
15	A4	2fr brn, *org* (R)	55.00	55.00
16	A3	5fr red lil, *lav*	225.00	225.00
17	A4	10fr org brn, *grn*	275.00	275.00
		Nos. 1-17 (17)	845.00	845.00

Various varieties of the surcharge exist on Nos. 2-10.

Stamps of Indo-China, 1907, Srchd. in Red or Blue

Value in Chinese

1908

No.	Type	Description	Unused	Used
18	A5	1c ol brn & blk	1.70	1.70
19	A5	2c brn & blk	1.70	1.70
20	A5	4c bl & blk	1.70	1.70
21	A5	5c grn & blk	1.70	1.70
22	A5	10c red & blk (Bl)	1.70	1.70
23	A5	15c vio & blk	4.25	4.25
24	A6	20c vio & blk	6.75	6.75
25	A6	25c bl & blk	6.75	6.75
26	A6	30c brn & blk	10.00	10.00
27	A6	35c ol grn & blk	14.50	14.50
28	A6	40c brn & blk	14.50	14.50
30	A6	50c car & blk (Bl)	17.00	17.00
31	A7	75c ver & blk (Bl)	17.00	17.00
32	A8	1fr car & blk (Bl)	24.00	24.00
33	A9	2fr grn & blk	32.50	32.50
34	A10	5fr bl & blk	75.00	75.00
35	A11	10fr pur & blk	105.00	105.00
a.		Double surcharge	1,050.	
b.		Triple surcharge	1,050.	
		Nos. 18-35 (17)	335.75	335.75

The Chinese characters overprinted on Nos. 1 to 35 repeat the denomination of the basic stamp.

Nos. 18-35 Srchd. in Cents or Piasters in Black, Red or Blue

1919

No.	Type	Description	Unused	Used
36	A5	⅖c on 1c	1.25	.85
37	A5	⅘c on 2c	1.25	1.25
38	A5	1⅗c on 4c (R)	1.25	.85
39	A5	2c on 5c	2.10	1.25
a.		"2 CENTS" inverted	97.50	
40	A5	4c on 10c (Bl)	3.75	3.40
41	A5	6c on 15c	2.10	2.10
42	A6	8c on 20c	4.25	4.25
43	A6	10c on 25c	14.50	13.50
44	A6	12c on 30c	3.40	3.40
45	A6	14c on 35c	3.40	3.40
a.		Closed "4"	45.00	37.50
46	A6	16c on 40c	2.10	2.10
48	A6	20c on 50c (Bl)	2.10	2.10
49	A7	30c on 75c (Bl)	11.00	11.00
50	A8	40c on 1fr (Bl)	12.00	12.00
a.		"40 CENTS" inverted		
51	A9	80c on 2fr (R)	20.00	20.00
52	A10	2pi on 5fr (R)	175.00	175.00
53	A11	4pi on 10fr (R)	32.50	32.50
		Nos. 36-53 (17)	291.95	288.55

Stamps of Indo-China, 1922-23, Overprinted in Black, Red or Blue

1923

No.	Type	Description	Unused	Used
54	A12	⅒c blk & sal (Bl)	.35	.35
55	A12	⅕c dp bl & blk (R)	.35	.35
a.		Black overprint	135.00	
56	A12	⅖c ol brn & blk (R)	.40	.40
57	A12	⅘c brt rose & blk	.60	.60
58	A12	1c yel brn & blk (Bl)	.60	.60
59	A12	2c gray grn & blk (R)	.95	.95
60	A12	3c vio & blk (R)	1.00	1.00
61	A12	4c org & blk	1.25	1.25
62	A12	5c car & blk	1.25	1.25
63	A13	6c dl red & blk	1.25	1.25
64	A13	7c ol grn & blk	1.70	1.70
65	A13	8c black (R)	2.50	2.50
66	A13	9c yel & blk	2.50	2.50
67	A13	10c bl & blk	2.10	2.10
68	A13	11c vio & blk	2.10	2.10
69	A13	12c brn & blk	2.10	2.10
70	A13	15c org & blk	3.00	3.00
71	A13	20c bl & blk, *straw* (R)	3.00	3.00
72	A13	40c ver & blk, *bluish* (Bl)	3.40	3.40
73	A13	1pi bl grn & blk, *grnsh*	7.50	7.50
74	A13	2pi vio brn & blk, *pnksh* (Bl)	17.00	17.00
		Nos. 54-74 (21)	54.90	54.90

Accent omitted varieties exist for Nos. 54-74. For detailed listings, see "Scott Classic Specialized Catalogue of Stamps and Covers 1840-1940".

Indo-China Stamps of 1927 Overprinted in Black or Red

1927

No.	Type	Description	Unused	Used
75	A14	⅒c lt ol grn (R)	.35	.35
76	A14	⅕c yellow	.35	.35
77	A14	⅖c lt blue (R)	.50	.50
78	A14	⅘c dp brown	.50	.50
79	A14	1c orange	.85	.85
80	A14	2c blue grn (R)	1.25	1.25
81	A14	3c indigo (R)	1.25	1.25
82	A14	4c lilac rose	1.25	1.25
83	A14	5c deep violet	1.25	1.25
84	A15	6c deep red	1.25	1.25
85	A15	7c lt brown	1.25	1.25
86	A15	8c gray grn (R)	1.25	1.25
87	A15	9c red violet	1.70	1.70
88	A15	10c lt bl (R)	1.70	1.70
89	A15	11c orange	1.70	1.70
90	A15	12c myr grn (R)	1.70	1.70
91	A16	15c dl rose & ol brn	3.00	3.00
92	A16	20c vio & sl (R)	2.50	2.50
93	A17	25c org brn & lil rose	2.50	2.50
94	A17	30c dp bl & ol gray (R)	1.70	1.70
95	A18	40c ver & lt bl	1.70	1.70
96	A18	50c lt grn & sl (R)	2.50	2.50
97	A19	1pi dk bl, blk & yel (R)	4.25	4.25
98	A19	2pi red, dp bl & org (R)	6.00	6.00
a.		Double overprint	160.00	
		Nos. 75-98 (24)	42.25	42.25

Accent omitted varieties exist for Nos. 75-90. For detailed listings, see "Scott Classic Specialized Catalogue of Stamps and Covers 1840-1940".

Stamps of Indo-China, 1931-41, Overprinted in Black or Red

1937-41 ***Perf. 13, 13½***

No.	Type	Description	Unused	Used
99	A20	⅒c Prus blue	.25	.25
100	A20	⅕c lake	.25	.25
101	A20	⅖c orange red	.40	.40
102	A20	½c red brown	.35	.35
103	A20	⅘c dk violet	.35	.35
104	A20	1c black brown	.35	.35
105	A20	2c dk green	.35	.35
a.		Inverted overprint	140.00	
106	A21	3c dk green	.75	.75
107	A21	3c yel brn ('41)	.35	.35
108	A21	4c dk blue (R)	1.00	1.00
109	A21	4c dk green ('41)	.35	.35
110	A21	4c yel org ('41)	2.75	2.75
111	A21	5c dp violet	.95	.95
112	A21	5c dp green ('41)	.50	.50
113	A21	6c orange red	.65	.65
114	A21	7c black (R) ('41)	.65	.65
115	A21	8c rose lake ('41)	.75	.75
116	A21	9c blk, *yel* (R) ('41)	1.00	1.00
d.		Black overprint	9.25	9.25
117	A22	10c dk blue (R)	1.10	1.10
118	A22	10c ultra, *pink* (R) ('41)	.85	.85
119	A22	15c dk bl (R)	.75	.75
120	A22	18c bl (R) ('41)	.65	.65
121	A22	20c rose	.75	.75
122	A22	21c olive grn	.75	.75
123	A22	22c green ('41)	.60	.60
124	A22	25c dp violet	3.00	3.00
125	A22	25c dk bl (R) ('41)	.85	.85
126	A22	30c orange brn	.85	.85
127	A23	50c dk brown	1.10	1.10
128	A23	60c dl violet	1.10	1.10
129	A23	70c lt bl (R) ('41)	.85	.85
130	A23	1pi yel green	2.10	2.10
131	A23	2pi red	2.25	2.25
		Nos. 99-131 (33)	29.55	29.55

Accent omitted varieties exist for Nos. 99-124 and No. 126. For detailed listings, see "Scott Classic Specialized Catalogue of Stamps and Covers 1840-1940".

Common Design Types pictured following the introduction.

Colonial Arts Exhibition Issue

Common Design Type

Souvenir Sheet

1937 **Engr.** ***Imperf.***

No.	Type	Description	Unused	Used
132	CD79	30c grn & sepia	9.25	*11.00*

New York World's Fair Issue

Common Design Type

1939 **Unwmk.** ***Perf. 12½x12***

No.	Type	Description	Unused	Used
133	CD82	13c car lake	1.25	1.25
134	CD82	23c ultra	1.25	1.25

Petain Issue

Indo-China Nos. 209-209A Overprinted "KOUANG TCHEOU" in Blue or Red

1941 **Engr.** ***Perf. 12½x12***

No.	Type	Description	Unused	Used
135	A27a	10c car lake (B)	.85	
136	A27a	25c blue (R)	.85	

Nos. 135-136 were issued by the Vichy government in France, but were not placed on sale in Kwangchowan.

For surcharges, see Nos. B9-B10.

Indo-China Types of 1937-41 without "RF" Overprinted "KOUANG TCHEOU" in Blue or Red

1942-44

No.	Type	Description	Unused	Used
137	A20	⅖c orange red	.25	
138	A20	½c red brown	.25	
139	A20	1c black brown	.35	
140	A20	2c dark green	.65	
141	A21	3c yellow brown	.65	
142	A21	4c yellow orange	.35	
143	A21	5c deep green	.50	
144	A21	9c black, *yellow*	.35	
145	A22	10c ultra, *pink* (R)	.60	
146	A22	18c blue (R)	190.00	
147	A22	22c green	.60	
148	A22	30c orange brown	.65	
149	A23	50c dark brown	.60	
150	A23	60c dull violet	.65	
151	A23	70c light blue (R)	.85	
152	A23	1pi yellow green	1.30	
153	A23	2pi red	1.40	
		Nos. 137-153 (17)	200.00	

Nos. 137-153 were issued by the Vichy government in France, but were not placed on sale in Kwangchowan.

SEMI-POSTAL STAMPS

French Revolution Issue

Common Design Type

1939 **Unwmk.** **Photo.** ***Perf. 13***

Name and Value typo. in Black

No.	Type	Description	Unused	Used
B1	CD83	6c + 2c green	9.25	9.25
B2	CD83	7c + 3c brown	9.25	9.25
B3	CD83	9c + 4c red org	9.25	9.25
B4	CD83	13c + 10c rose pink	9.25	9.25
B5	CD83	23c + 20c blue	9.25	9.25
		Nos. B1-B5 (5)	46.25	46.25

Indo-China Nos. B19A and B19C Overprinted "KOUANG-TCHEOU" in Blue or Red, and Common Design Type

1941 **Photo.** ***Perf. 13½***

No.	Type	Description	Unused	Used
B6	SP1	10c + 10c red (B)	.85	
B7	CD86	15c + 30c mar & car	.85	
B8	SP2	25c + 10c blue (R)	.85	
		Nos. B6-B8 (3)	2.55	

Nos. B6-B8 were issued by the Vichy government in France, but were not placed on sale in Kwangchowan.

Indo-China Nos. B21A-B21B Overprinted in Blue or Red

1944 **Engr.** ***Perf. 12½x12***

No.	Type	Description	Unused	Used
B9	A27a	5c + 15c on 25c deep blue (R)	1.00	
B10	A27a	+25c on 10c car lake	1.10	

Colonial Development Fund.

Nos. B9-B10 were issued by the Vichy government in France, but were not placed on sale in Kwangchowan.

AIR POST SEMI-POSTAL STAMPS

Indo-China Nos. CB2-CB4 Overprinted "KOUANG-TCHEOU" in Blue or Red

Methods and Perfs as Before

1942, June 22

CB1	SPAP1	15c + 35c green (R)	.95
CB2	SPAP2	20c + 60c brown	.95
CB3	SPAP3	30c +90c car red	.95
		Nos. CB1-CB3 (3)	2.85

Native children's welfare fund.

Nos. CB1-CB3 were issued by the Vichy government in France, but were not placed on sale in Kwangchowan.

Colonial Education Fund

Indo-China No. CB5 Overprinted "KOUANG-TCHEOU" in Blue or Red

Perf. 12½x13½

1942, June 22 **Engr.**

CB4 CD86a 12c + 18c blue & red 1.00

No. CB4 was issued by the Vichy government in France, but was not placed on sale in Kwangchowan.

MONGTSEU (MENGTSZ)

Stamps of Indo-China Surcharged in Black

1903-04 **Unwmk.** ***Perf. 14x13½***

1	A3	1c blk, *lil bl*	7.50	7.50
2	A3	2c brn, *buff*	6.75	6.75
3	A3	4c claret, *lav*	8.50	8.50
4	A3	5c yel grn	6.00	6.00
5	A3	10c red	9.25	9.25
6	A3	15c gray	10.00	10.00
7	A3	20c red, *grn*	12.50	12.50
7C	A3	25c blk, *rose*	725.00	725.00
8	A3	25c blue	12.50	12.50
9	A3	30c brn, *bister*	11.00	11.00
10	A3	40c red, *straw*	75.00	75.00
11	A3	50c car, *rose*	440.00	440.00
12	A3	50c brn, *az* ('04)	150.00	150.00
13	A3	75c dp vio, *org*	120.00	120.00
a.		"INDO-CHINE" inverted	*67,500.*	
14	A3	1fr brnz grn, *straw*	110.00	110.00
15	A3	5fr red lil, *lav*	110.00	110.00
		Nos. 1-15 (16)	1,814.	1,814.

Many surcharge varieties exist on Nos. 1-15.

Stamps of Indo-China, 1892-1906, Surcharged in Red or Black

1906

16	A4	1c ol grn (R)	5.00	5.00
17	A4	2c vio brn, *buff*	5.00	5.00
18	A4	4c cl, *bluish* (R)	5.00	5.00
19	A4	5c dp grn (R)	6.00	6.00
20	A4	10c carmine	5.00	5.00
21	A4	15c org brn, *bl*	35.00	35.00
22	A4	20c red, *grn*	13.50	13.50
23	A4	25c deep blue	10.00	10.00
24	A4	30c pale brn	13.50	13.50
25	A4	35c blk, *yel* (R)	12.50	12.50
26	A4	40c blk, *bluish* (R)	20.00	20.00
27	A4	50c bister brn	21.00	21.00
28	A3	75c dp vio, *org* (R)	67.50	67.50
a.		"INDO-CHINE" inverted	*67,500.*	
29	A4	1fr pale grn	42.50	42.50
30	A4	2fr brn, *org* (R)	55.00	55.00
31	A4	5fr red lil, *lav*	140.00	140.00
32	A4	10fr org brn, *grn*	150.00	150.00
a.		Chinese characters inverted	1,750.	*2,100.*
		Nos. 16-32 (17)	606.50	606.50

Inverted varieties of the surcharge exist on Nos. 19, 22 and 32.

Stamps of Indo-China, 1907, Srchd. in Red or Blue

Value in Chinese

1908

33	A5	1c ol brn & blk	1.25	1.25
34	A5	2c brn & blk	1.25	1.25
35	A5	4c bl & blk	1.25	1.25
36	A5	5c grn & blk	1.25	1.25
37	A5	10c red & blk (Bl)	3.00	3.00
38	A5	15c vio & blk	3.00	3.00
39	A6	20c vio & blk	6.00	6.00
40	A6	25c bl & blk	15.00	15.00
41	A6	30c brn & blk	6.75	6.75
42	A6	35c ol grn & blk	7.50	7.50
43	A6	40c brn & blk	5.00	5.00
45	A6	50c car & blk (Bl)	6.75	6.75
46	A7	75c ver & blk (Bl)	14.50	14.50
47	A8	1fr car & blk (Bl)	13.50	13.50
48	A9	2fr grn & blk	19.00	19.00
49	A10	5fr bl & blk	105.00	105.00
50	A11	10fr pur & blk	125.00	125.00
		Nos. 33-50 (17)	335.00	335.00

The Chinese characters overprinted on Nos. 1 to 50 repeat the denomination of the basic stamp.

Nos. 33-50 Srchd. in Cents or Piasters in Black, Red or Blue

1919

51	A5	2/5c on 1c	1.70	1.70
52	A5	4/5c on 2c	1.70	1.70
53	A5	1 3/5c on 4c	1.70	1.70
54	A5	2c on 5c	1.70	1.70
55	A5	4c on 10c (Bl)	3.00	3.00
56	A5	6c on 15c	3.00	3.00
57	A6	8c on 20c	6.75	6.75
58	A6	10c on 25c	5.00	5.00
59	A6	12c on 30c	5.00	5.00
60	A6	14c on 35c	3.40	3.40
a.		Closed "4"	21.00	21.00
61	A6	16c on 40c	4.25	4.25
63	A6	20c on 50c (Bl)	5.00	5.00
64	A7	30c on 75c (Bl)	9.25	9.25
65	A8	40c on 1fr (Bl)	10.00	10.00
66	A9	80c on 2fr (R)	10.00	10.00
a.		Triple surch., one inverted	550.00	550.00
67	A10	2pi on 5fr (R)	200.00	200.00
a.		Triple surch., one inverted	625.00	625.00
b.		Double surcharge	925.00	925.00
68	A11	4pi on 10fr (R)	30.00	30.00
		Nos. 51-68 (17)	301.45	301.45

PAKHOI

Stamps of Indo-China Surcharged in Black

1903-04 **Unwmk.** ***Perf. 14x13½***

1	A3	1c blk, *lil bl*	6.75	6.75
2	A3	2c brn, *buff*	6.75	6.75
3	A3	4c claret, *lav*	6.75	6.75
4	A3	5c yel grn	5.00	5.00
5	A3	10c red	5.00	5.00
6	A3	15c gray	5.00	5.00
7	A3	20c red, *grn*	11.00	11.00
8	A3	25c blue	9.25	9.25
9	A3	25c blk, *rose*('04)	6.75	6.75
10	A3	30c brn, *bister*	8.50	8.50
11	A3	40c red, *straw*	57.50	57.50
12	A3	50c car, *rose*	340.00	340.00
13	A3	50c brn, *az* ('04)	47.50	47.50
14	A3	75c dp vio, *org*	67.50	67.50
a.		"INDO-CHINE" inverted	*47,500.*	
15	A3	1fr brnz grn, *straw*	67.50	67.50
16	A3	5fr red lil, *lav*	135.00	135.00
		Nos. 1-16 (16)	785.75	785.75

Many varieties of the surcharge exist.

Stamps of Indo-China 1892-1906, Surcharged in Red or Black

1906

17	A4	1c ol grn (R)	8.50	8.50
18	A4	2c vio brn, *buff*	8.50	8.50
19	A4	4c cl, *bluish* (R)	8.50	8.50
20	A4	5c dp grn (R)	8.50	8.50
21	A4	10c carmine	8.50	8.50
22	A4	15c org brn,*bl*	32.50	32.50
23	A4	20c red, *grn*	13.50	13.50
24	A4	25c deep blue	11.00	11.00
25	A4	30c pale brn	13.50	13.50
26	A4	35c blk, *yel* (R)	21.00	21.00
27	A4	40c blk, *bluish*(R)	21.00	21.00
28	A4	50c bister brn	21.00	21.00
29	A3	75c dp vio, *org* (R)	67.50	67.50
30	A4	1fr pale grn	42.50	42.50
31	A4	2fr brn, *org*(R)	55.00	55.00
32	A3	5fr red lil, *lav*	140.00	140.00
33	A4	10fr org brn, *grn*	150.00	150.00
		Nos. 17-33 (17)	631.00	631.00

Various surcharge varieties exist on Nos. 17-24.

Stamps of Indo-China, 1907, Surcharged "PAKHOI" and Value in Chinese in Red or Blue

1908

34	A5	1c ol brn & blk	1.25	1.25
35	A5	2c brn & blk	1.25	1.25
36	A5	4c bl & blk	1.25	1.25
37	A5	5c grn & blk	1.70	1.70
38	A5	10c red & blk (Bl)	1.70	1.70
39	A5	15c vio & blk	2.10	2.10
40	A6	20c vio & blk	2.50	2.50
41	A6	25c bl & blk	3.00	3.00
42	A6	30c brn & blk	3.40	3.40
43	A6	35c ol grn & blk	3.40	3.40
44	A6	40c brn & blk	3.40	3.40
46	A6	50c car & blk (Bl)	3.40	3.40
47	A7	75c ver & blk (Bl)	7.25	7.25
48	A8	1fr car & blk (Bl)	7.50	7.50
49	A9	2fr grn & blk	16.00	16.00
50	A10	5fr bl & blk	85.00	85.00
51	A11	10fr pur & blk	150.00	150.00
		Nos. 34-51 (17)	294.10	294.10

The Chinese characters overprinted on Nos. 1 to 51 repeat the denomination of the basic stamps.

Nos. 34-51 Surcharged with New Values in Cents or Piasters in Black, Red or Blue

1919

52	A5	2/5c on 1c	1.25	1.25
a.		"PAK-HOI" and Chinese double	170.00	
53	A5	4/5c on 2c	1.25	1.25
54	A5	1 3/5c on 4c (R)	1.25	1.25
55	A5	2c on 5c	2.50	2.50
56	A5	4c on 10c (Bl)	3.40	3.40
57	A5	6c on 15c	1.70	1.70
58	A6	8c on 20c	3.40	3.40
59	A6	10c on 25c	5.00	5.00
60	A6	12c on 30c	1.70	1.70
a.		"12 CENTS" double	675.00	
61	A6	14c on 35c	1.25	1.25
a.		Closed "4"	14.50	14.50
62	A6	16c on 40c	3.00	3.00
64	A6	20c on 50c (Bl)	2.10	2.10
65	A7	30c on 75c (Bl)	9.25	9.25
66	A8	40c on 1fr (Bl)	12.50	12.50
67	A9	80c on 2fr (R)	10.00	10.00
68	A10	2pi on 5fr (R)	16.00	16.00
69	A11	4pi on 10fr (R)	35.00	35.00
		Nos. 52-69 (17)	110.55	110.55

TCHONGKING (CHUNGKING)

Stamps of Indo-China Surcharged in Black

1903-04 **Unwmk.** ***Perf. 14x13½***

1	A3	1c blk, *lil bl*	5.00	5.00
2	A3	2c brn, *buff*	5.00	5.00
3	A3	4c claret, *lav*	6.00	6.00
4	A3	5c yel grn	6.00	6.00
5	A3	10c red	6.00	6.00
6	A3	15c gray	6.00	6.00
7	A3	20c red, *grn*	8.50	8.50
8	A3	25c blue	55.00	55.00
9	A3	25c blk, *rose* ('04)	10.00	10.00
10	A3	30c brn, *bister*	15.00	15.00
11	A3	40c red, *straw*	62.50	62.50
12	A3	50c car, *rose*	225.00	225.00
13	A3	50c brn, *az* ('04)	140.00	140.00
14	A3	75c vio, *org*	45.00	45.00
15	A3	1fr brnz grn, *straw*	60.00	60.00
16	A3	5fr red lil, *lav*	105.00	105.00
		Nos. 1-16 (16)	760.00	760.00

Many surcharge varieties exist on Nos. 1-14.

Stamps of Indo-China and French China, issued in 1902 with similar overprint, but without Chinese characters, were not officially authorized.

Stamps of Indo-China, 1892-1906, Surcharged in Red or Black

1906

17	A4	1c ol grn (R)	8.50	8.50
18	A4	2c vio brn, *buff*	8.50	8.50
19	A4	4c cl, *bluish* (R)	8.50	8.50
20	A4	5c dp grn (R)	8.50	8.50
21	A4	10c carmine	8.50	8.50
22	A4	15c org brn, *bl*	32.50	32.50
23	A4	20c red, *grn*	13.50	13.50
24	A4	25c deep blue	11.00	11.00
25	A4	30c pale brn	13.50	13.50
26	A4	35c blk, *yellow* (R)	21.00	21.00
27	A4	40c blk, *bluish* (R)	21.00	21.00
28	A4	50c bis brn	25.00	25.00
29	A3	75c dp vio, *org* (R)	67.50	67.50
30	A4	1fr pale grn	42.50	42.50
31	A4	2fr brn, *org* (R)	55.00	55.00
32	A3	5fr red lil, *lav*	140.00	140.00
33	A4	10fr org brn, *grn*	150.00	150.00
		Nos. 17-33 (17)	635.00	635.00

Variety "T" omitted in surcharge occurs once in each sheet of Nos. 17-33. For detailed listings, see "Scott Classic Specialized Catalogue of Stamps and Values". Other surcharge varieties exist. Inverted surcharge on 1c and 2c are of private origin.

Stamps of Indo-China, 1907, Surcharged "TCHONGKING" and Value in Chinese in Red or Blue

1908

34	A5	1c ol brn & blk	.85	.85
35	A5	2c brn & blk	.85	.85
36	A5	4c bl & blk	1.25	1.25
37	A5	5c grn & blk	2.10	2.10
38	A5	10c red & blk (Bl)	2.10	2.10
39	A5	15c vio & blk	3.00	3.00
40	A6	20c vio & blk	3.00	3.00
41	A6	25c bl & blk	5.50	5.50
42	A6	30c brn & blk	3.40	3.40
43	A6	35c ol grn & blk	7.50	7.50
44	A6	40c brn & blk	15.00	15.00
45	A6	50c car & blk (Bl)	12.00	12.00
46	A7	75c ver & blk (Bl)	10.00	10.00
47	A8	1fr car & blk (Bl)	13.50	13.50
48	A9	2fr grn & blk	85.00	85.00
49	A10	5fr bl & blk	37.50	37.50
50	A11	10fr pur & blk	225.00	225.00
		Nos. 34-50 (17)	427.55	427.55

The Chinese characters overprinted on Nos. 1 to 50 repeat the denomination of the basic stamp.

Nos. 34-50 Surcharged with New Values in Cents or Piasters in Black, Red or Blue

1919

51	A5	2/5c on 1c	1.25	1.25
52	A5	4/5c on 2c	1.25	1.25
53	A5	1 3/5c on 4c (R)	1.25	1.25
54	A5	2c on 5c	1.70	1.70
55	A5	4c on 10c (Bl)	1.25	1.25
56	A5	6c on 15c	1.70	1.70
57	A6	8c on 20c	3.00	1.25
58	A6	10c on 25c	8.50	8.50
59	A6	12c on 30c	3.00	1.25
60	A6	14c on 35c	2.10	1.70
a.		Closed "4"	35.00	35.00
61	A6	16c on 40c	2.10	1.70
a.		"16 CENTS" double	125.00	125.00
62	A6	20c on 50c (Bl)	11.00	10.00
63	A7	30c on 75c (Bl)	9.25	6.75
64	A8	40c on 1fr (Bl)	9.25	6.75
65	A9	80c on 2fr (R)	9.25	6.75
66	A10	2pi on 5fr (R)	9.25	9.25
67	A11	4pi on 10fr (R)	17.50	17.50
		Nos. 51-67 (17)	92.60	79.80

YUNNAN FOU

(Formerly Yunnan Sen, later known as Kunming)

Stamps of Indo-China Surcharged in Black

1903-04 **Unwmk.** ***Perf. 14x13½***

1	A3	1c blk, *lil bl*	6.75	6.75
2	A3	2c brn, *buff*	6.75	6.75
3	A3	4c claret, *lav*	7.50	7.50
4	A3	5c yel green	6.75	6.75
5	A3	10c red	7.50	7.50
6	A3	15c gray	7.50	7.50
7	A3	20c red, *grn*	12.50	12.50
8	A3	25c blue	7.50	7.50
9	A3	30c brn, *bister*	12.50	12.50
10	A3	40c red, *straw*	75.00	60.00
11	A3	50c car, *rose*	350.00	350.00
12	A3	50c brn, *az* ('04)	180.00	180.00
13	A3	75c dp vio, *org*	67.50	62.50
a.		"INDO-CHINE" inverted	*47,500.*	

14 A3 1fr brnz grn, *straw* 67.50 62.50
15 A3 5fr red lil, *lav* 125.00 125.00
Nos. 1-15 (15) 940.25 915.25

The Chinese characters overprinted on Nos. 1 to 15 repeat the denomination of the basic stamp.

Many varieties of the surcharge exist.

Stamps of Indo-China, 1892-1906, Surcharged in Red or Black

1906 Unwmk. *Perf. 14x13½*

17 A4 1c ol grn (R) 5.00 5.00
18 A4 2c vio brn, *buff* 5.00 5.00
19 A4 4c cl, *bluish* (R) 5.00 5.00
20 A4 5c dp grn (R) 5.00 5.00
21 A4 10c carmine 5.00 5.00
22 A4 15c org brn, *bl* 35.00 35.00
23 A4 20c red, *grn* 13.50 13.50
24 A4 25c deep blue 11.00 11.00
25 A4 30c pale brn 13.50 13.50
26 A4 35c blk, *yel* (R) 17.00 17.00
27 A4 40c blk, *bluish* (R) 17.00 17.00
28 A4 50c bister brn 21.00 21.00
29 A3 75c dp vio, *org* (R) 67.50 67.50
30 A4 1fr pale grn 42.50 42.50
31 A4 2fr brn, *org* (R) 55.00 55.00
32 A3 5fr red lil, *lav* 140.00 140.00
33 A4 10fr org brn, *grn* 150.00 150.00
Nos. 17-33 (17) 608.00 608.00

Various varieties of the surcharge exist on Nos. 18, 20, 21 and 27.

Stamps of Indo-China, 1907, Surcharged "YUNNANFOU," and Value in Chinese in Red or Blue

1908

34 A5 1c ol brn & blk 1.25 1.25
35 A5 2c brn & blk 1.25 1.25
36 A5 4c bl & blk 2.10 2.10
37 A5 5c grn & blk 3.00 3.00
38 A5 10c red & blk (Bl) 3.00 3.00
39 A5 15c vio & blk 6.75 6.75
40 A6 20c vio & blk 6.25 6.25
41 A6 25c bl & blk 9.25 9.25
42 A6 30c brn & blk 7.50 7.50
43 A6 35c ol grn & blk 7.50 7.50
44 A6 40c brn & blk 8.50 8.50
45 A6 50c car & blk (Bl) 9.25 9.25
46 A7 75c ver & blk (Bl) 11.00 11.00
47 A8 1fr car & blk (Bl) 17.00 17.00
48 A9 2fr grn & blk 29.00 29.00
a. "YUNANNFOU" 2,500. 2,500.
49 A10 5fr bl & blk 60.00 60.00
a. "YUNANNFOU" 2,500. 2,500.
50 A11 10fr pur & blk 120.00 120.00
a. "YUNANNFOU" 2,500. 2,500.
Nos. 34-50 (17) 302.60 302.60

The Chinese characters overprinted on Nos. 17-50 repeat the denomination of the basic stamp.

Nos. 34-50 Surcharged with New Values in Cents or Piasters in Black, Red or Blue

1919

51 A5 ⅖c on 1c 1.25 1.25
a. New value double 140.00
52 A5 ⅘c on 2c 1.25 1.25
53 A5 1⅗c on 4c (R) 1.25 1.25
54 A5 2c on 5c 2.10 2.10
a. Triple surcharge 210.00
55 A5 4c on 10c (Bl) 1.70 1.70
56 A5 6c on 15c 3.00 3.00
57 A6 8c on 20c 2.10 2.10
58 A6 10c on 25c 3.75 3.75
59 A6 12c on 30c 9.25 9.25
60 A6 14c on 35c 14.50 14.50
a. Closed "4" 140.00 140.00
61 A6 16c on 40c 9.25 9.25
62 A6 20c on 50c (Bl) 3.00 3.00
63 A7 30c on 75c (Bl) 9.25 9.25
64 A8 40c on 1fr (Bl) 35.00 35.00
65 A9 80c on 2fr (R) 14.50 14.50
a. Triple surch., one inverted 250.00
66 A10 2pi on 5fr (R) 67.50 67.50
67 A11 4pi on 10fr (R) 35.00 35.00
Nos. 51-67 (17) 213.65 213.65

OFFICES IN CRETE

Austria, France, Italy and Great Britain maintained their own post offices in Crete during the period when that country was an autonomous state.

100 Centimes = 1 Franc

Liberty, Equality and Fraternity
A1

"Rights of Man"
A2

Liberty and Peace (Symbolized by Olive Branch) — A3

Perf. 14x13½

1902-03 Unwmk. Typo.

1 A1 1c dark gray 2.35 2.75
a. A1 1c light gray 2.35 2.75
2 A1 2c violet brown 2.35 2.75
3 A1 3c red orange 2.35 2.75
4 A1 4c yellow brown 2.35 2.75
5 A1 5c green 2.35 2.75
6 A2 10c rose red 2.75 2.75
7 A2 15c pale red ('03) 4.25 3.00
8 A2 20c brown vio ('03) 5.25 4.00
9 A2 25c blue ('03) 6.75 4.50
10 A2 30c lilac ('03) 6.75 4.50
11 A3 40c red & pale bl 13.00 13.00
12 A3 50c bis brn & lav 18.00 15.00
13 A3 1fr claret & ol grn 24.50 22.50
14 A3 2fr gray vio & yel 25.00 37.50
a. Imperf, pair 675.00
15 A3 5fr dk blue & buff 62.50 60.00
Nos. 1-15 (15) 180.50 180.50
Set, never hinged 375.00

A4

A5

1903 Black Surcharge

16 A4 1pi on 25c blue 55.00 47.50
17 A5 2pi on 50c bis brn & lav 75.00 57.50
18 A5 4pi on 1fr claret & ol grn 110.00 100.00
19 A5 8pi on 2fr gray vio & yel 140.00 *145.00*
20 A5 20pi on 5fr dk bl & buff 235.00 225.00
Nos. 16-20 (5) 615.00 575.00

OFFICES IN EGYPT

French post offices formerly maintained in Alexandria and Port Said.

100 Centimes = 1 Franc

ALEXANDRIA

Stamps of France Ovptd. in Red, Blue or Black

1899-1900 Unwmk. *Perf. 14x13½*

1 A15 1c blk, *lil bl* (R) 2.10 2.10
a. Double overprint 150.00
b. Triple overprint 180.00
2 A15 2c brn, *buff* (Bl) 3.25 2.50
3 A15 3c gray, *grysh* (Bl) 3.25 2.50
4 A15 4c cl, *lav* (Bl) 4.25 3.25
5 A15 5c yel grn, (I) (R) 6.00 3.25
a. Type II (R) 160.00 97.50
6 A15 10c blk, *lav*, (I) (R) 9.25 7.50
a. Type II (R) 62.50 37.50
7 A15 15c blue (R) 9.25 4.25
8 A15 20c red, *grn* 14.50 7.50
9 A15 25c blk, *rose* (R) 7.50 4.25
a. Inverted overprint 97.50
b. Double ovpt., one invtd. 160.00
10 A15 30c brn, *bis* 15.00 12.00
11 A15 40c red, *straw* 13.50 13.50
12 A15 50c car, *rose* (II) 35.00 17.50
a. Type I 150.00 27.50
13 A15 1fr brnz grn, *straw* 32.50 22.50
14 A15 2fr brn, *az* ('00) 82.50 80.00
15 A15 5fr red lil, *lav* 120.00 110.00
Nos. 1-15 (15) 357.85 292.60

A2

A3

A4

1902-13

16 A2 1c pale gray .80 .65
17 A2 2c violet brn .75 .75
18 A2 3c red orange .75 .75
19 A2 4c yellow brn 1.00 .85
20 A2 5c green 5.00 4.25
21 A3 10c rose red 1.50 .75
22 A3 15c orange ('13) 1.75 1.25
a. 15c pale red ('03) 4.75 1.60
23 A3 20c brn vio ('03) 3.00 1.50
24 A3 25c blue ('03) 1.75 .75
25 A3 30c violet ('03) 7.50 4.25
26 A4 40c red & pale bl 5.00 2.50
27 A4 50c bis brn & lav 11.00 3.00
28 A4 1fr cl & ol grn 10.00 4.25
29 A4 2fr gray vio & yel 24.00 12.00
30 A4 5fr dk bl & buff 29.00 17.00
Nos. 16-30 (15) 102.80 54.50

The 2c, 5c, 10c, 20c and 25c exist imperf. Value, each $55.

See #77-86. For surcharges see #31-73, B1-B4.

Stamps of 1902-03 Surcharged Locally in Black

1921

31 A2 2m on 5c green 7.50 5.00
32 A2 3m on 3c red org 14.50 12.00
a. Larger numeral 140.00 125.00
33 A3 4m on 10c rose 6.75 6.00
34 A2 5m on 1c gray 14.50 12.00
35 A2 5m on 4c yel brn 19.00 13.50
36 A3 6m on 15c orange 6.75 6.00
a. Larger numeral 110.00 110.00
37 A3 8m on 20c brn vio 7.50 6.00
a. Larger numeral 80.00 60.00
38 A3 10m on 25c blue 4.25 4.25
a. Inverted surcharge 45.00 45.00
b. Double surcharge 45.00 45.00
39 A3 12m on 30c vio 17.50 17.50
40 A2 15m on 2c vio brn 14.50 14.50

Nos. 26-30 Surcharged

41 A4 15m on 40c 25.00 19.00
42 A4 15m on 50c (#27a) 12.00 12.00
43 A4 30m on 1fr 175.00 175.00
44 A4 60m on 2fr 250.00 250.00
a. Larger numeral 1,050. 1,050.
45 A4 150m on 5fr 350.00 350.00

Port Said Nos. 20 and 19 Surcharged like Nos. 32 and 40

45A A2 3m on 3c red org 150.00 150.00
46 A2 15m on 2c vio brn 150.00 150.00
Nos. 31-46 (17) 1,225. 1,203.

Alexandria No. 28 Srchd.

1921

46A A4 30m on 15m on 1fr 1,200. *1,350.*

The surcharge "15 Mill." was made in error and is canceled by a bar.

The surcharges were lithographed on Nos. 31, 33, 38, 39 and 42 and typographed on the other stamps of the 1921 issue. Nos. 34, 36 and 37 were surcharged by both methods.

Alexandria Stamps of 1902-03 Surcharged in Paris

1921-23

47 A2 1m on 1c slate 3.25 2.50
48 A2 2m on 5c green 2.25 1.90
49 A3 4m on 10c rose 2.75 2.50
50 A3 4m on 10c green ('23) 2.50 2.50
51 A2 5m on 3c red org ('23) 6.75 5.00
52 A3 6m on 15c orange 2.25 1.90
53 A3 8m on 20c brn vio 2.25 1.25
54 A3 10m on 25c blue 1.40 1.25
55 A3 10m on 30c vio 4.25 3.25
56 A3 15m on 50c bl ('23) 3.25 3.00

Nos. 27-30 and Type of 1902 Surcharged

57 A4 15m on 50c 5.00 3.25
58 A4 30m on 1fr 4.25 3.00
59 A4 60m on 2fr 2,250. *2,400.*
60 A4 60m on 2fr org & pale bl ('23) 13.50 13.00
61 A4 150m on 5fr 13.50 8.50
Nos. 47-58,60-61 (14) 67.15 52.80

Stamps and Types of 1902-03 Surcharged with New Values and Bars in Black

1925

62 A2 1m on 1c slate 1.25 1.25
63 A2 2m on 5c orange 1.25 1.25
64 A2 2m on 5c green 1.75 1.75
65 A3 4m on 10c green 1.10 .85
66 A2 5m on 3c red org 1.50 1.25
67 A3 6m on 15c orange 1.40 1.25
68 A3 8m on 20c brn vio 1.75 1.40
69 A3 10m on 25c blue 1.10 1.00
70 A3 15m on 50c blue 2.40 1.40
71 A4 30m on 1fr cl & ol grn 3.50 2.90
72 A4 60m on 2fr org & pale bl 4.25 3.50
73 A4 150m on 5fr dk bl & buff 6.00 5.00
Nos. 62-73 (12) 27.25 22.80

Types of 1902-03 Issue

1927-28

77 A2 3m orange ('28) 2.50 2.10
81 A3 15m slate blue 2.50 2.10
82 A3 20m rose lil ('28) 6.75 5.00
84 A4 50m org & blue 11.00 9.35
85 A4 100m sl bl & buff 15.00 12.00
86 A4 250m gray grn & red 25.00 16.00
Nos. 77-86 (6) 62.75 46.55

SEMI-POSTAL STAMPS

Regular Issue of 1902-03 Surcharged in Carmine

1915 Unwmk. *Perf. 14x13½*

B1 A3 10c + 5c rose 1.25 1.25

Sinking Fund Issue

Type of 1902-03 Issue Surcharged in Blue or Black

1927-30

B2 A3 15m + 5m deep org 6.00 6.00
B3 A3 15m + 5m red vio ('28) 9.25 9.25
a. 15m + 5m violet ('30) 15.00 15.00

Type of 1902-03 Issue Surcharged as in 1927-28

1929

B4 A3 15m + 5m fawn 12.00 12.00

POSTAGE DUE STAMPS

Postage Due Stamps of France, 1893-1920, Surcharged in Paris in Black

1922 Unwmk. *Perf. 14x13½*

J1 D2 2m on 5c blue 2.50 2.50
J2 D2 4m on 10c brown 2.50 2.50
J3 D2 10m on 30c rose red 3.00 3.00
J4 D2 15m on 50c brn vio 3.25 3.25
J5 D2 30m on 1fr red brn, *straw* 4.50 4.50
Nos. J1-J5 (5) 15.75 15.75

D3

1928 Typo.

J6 D3 1m slate 1.60 1.60
J7 D3 2m light blue 1.25 1.25
J8 D3 4m lilac rose 1.75 1.75
J9 D3 5m gray green 2.00 2.00
J10 D3 10m light red 2.50 2.50
J11 D3 20m violet brn 2.25 2.25
J12 D3 30m green 5.00 5.00
J13 D3 40m lt violet 6.25 6.25
Nos. J6-J13 (8) 22.60 22.60

Nos. J6-J13 were also available for use in Port Said.

PORT SAID

Stamps of France Overprinted in Red, Blue or Black

1899-1900 Unwmk. *Perf. 14x13½*

1 A15 1c blk, *lil bl* (R) 2.10 1.70
2 A15 2c brn, *buff* (bl) 2.10 1.70
3 A15 3c gray, *grysh* (Bl) 2.10 2.10
4 A15 4c claret, *lav* (Bl) 1.75 *2.10*
5 A15 5c yel grn (I) (R) 11.00 5.00
  a. Type II (R) 55.00 25.00
6 A15 10c blk, *lav* (I) (R) 14.00 12.50
  a. Type II (R) 72.50 55.00
7 A15 15c blue (R) 14.00 8.50
8 A15 20c red, *grn* 17.00 11.00
9 A15 25c blk, *rose* (R) 14.00 5.00
  a. Double overprint 300.00
  b. Inverted overprint 300.00
10 A15 30c brn, *bister* 17.00 14.00
  a. Inverted overprint 325.00
11 A15 40c red, *straw* 14.00 14.00
12 A15 50c car, *rose* (II) 20.00 14.00
  a. Type I 300.00 100.00
  b. Double overprint (II) 425.00
13 A15 1fr brnz grn, *straw* 30.00 17.50
14 A15 2fr brn, *az* ('00) 75.00 65.00
15 A15 5fr red lil, *lav* 120.00 92.50
Nos. 1-15 (15) 354.05 266.60

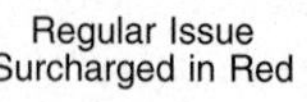

Regular Issue Surcharged in Red

1899

16 A15 25c on 10c blk, *lav* 130.00 32.50
  a. Inverted surcharge 250.00

With Additional Surcharge "25c" in Red

17 A15 25c on 10c blk, *lav* 475.00 160.00
  a. "25" inverted 1,500. 1,400.
  b. "25" in black 2,600.
  c. As "b," "VINGT CINQ" inverted 3,400.
  d. As "b," "25" vertical 3,400.
  e. As "c" and "d" 3,400.

A2

A3

A4

1902-03 Typo.

18 A2 1c pale gray ('16) .65 .65
19 A2 2c violet brn .75 .75
20 A2 3c red orange .85 .75
21 A2 4c yellow brown 1.10 .90
22 A2 5c blue green ('04) 1.20 .85
  a. 5c yellow green 5.00 3.00
23 A3 10c rose red 1.60 1.10
24 A3 15c pale red ('03) 3.25 2.25
  a. 15c orange 5.00 3.00
25 A3 20c brn vio ('03) 3.25 2.25
26 A3 25c blue ('03) 2.50 1.60
27 A3 30c gray violet ('03) 6.75 5.00
28 A4 40c red & pale bl 6.00 4.25
29 A4 50c bis brn & lav 9.25 6.75
30 A4 1fr claret & ol grn 12.00 9.25
31 A4 2fr gray vio & yel 15.00 15.00
32 A4 5fr dk bl & buff 35.00 32.50
Nos. 18-32 (15) 99.15 83.85

See Nos. 83-92. For surcharges see Nos. 33-80, B1-B4.

Stamps of 1902-03 Surcharged Locally

1921

33 A2 2m on 5c green 10.00 10.00
  a. Inverted surcharge 50.00 50.00
34 A3 4m on 10c rose 9.25 9.25
  a. Inverted surcharge 50.00 50.00
35 A2 5m on 1c slate 14.00 14.00
  b. 5m on 1c light gray 26.00 26.00
  c. Surcharged "2 Milliemes" on #35 67.50 67.50
36 A2 5m on 2c 24.00 24.00
  a. Surcharged "2 Milliemes" 75.00 75.00
  b. As "a," inverted 160.00 160.00
37 A2 5m on 3c 15.00 15.00
  a. Inverted surcharge 62.50 62.50
  b. On Alexandria #18 400.00 400.00
38 A2 5m on 4c 11.00 11.00
  a. Inverted surcharge 80.00 80.00
39 A2 10m on 2c 25.00 25.00
40 A2 10m on 4c 35.00 35.00
  a. Inverted surcharge 85.00 85.00
  b. Double surcharge 100.00 105.00
41 A3 10m on 25c 9.25 9.25
  a. Inverted surcharge 85.00 85.00
42 A3 12m on 30c 42.50 42.50
43 A2 15m on 4c 10.00 10.00
  a. Inverted surcharge 85.00 85.00
  b. Double surcharge 92.50 97.50
44 A3 15m on 15c pale red 67.50 67.50
  a. Inverted surcharge 160.00 160.00
45 A3 15m on 20c 67.50 67.50
  a. Inverted surcharge 160.00 160.00
46 A4 30m on 50c 300.00 300.00
47 A4 60m on 50c 350.00 350.00
48 A4 150m on 50c 400.00 400.00

Nos. 46, 47 and 48 have a bar between the numerals and "Millièmes," which is in capital letters.

Same Surcharge on Stamps of French Offices in Turkey, 1902-03

49 A2 2m on 2c vio brn 160.00 160.00
50 A2 5m on 1c gray 150.00 150.00
  a. "5" inverted 7,250.
Nos. 33-50 (18) 1,700. 1,700.

Nos. 28-32 Surcharged

51 A4 15m on 40c 60.00 60.00
52 A4 15m on 50c 85.00 85.00
  b. Bar below 15 50.00 50.00
53 A4 30m on 1fr 300.00 300.00
54 A4 60m on 2fr 85.00 *92.50*
55 A4 150m on 5fr 250.00 *275.00*
Nos. 51-55 (5) 780.00 812.50

Overprinted "MILLtEMES"

51a A4 15m on 40c 425.00 425.00
52a A4 15m on 50c 500.00 500.00
53a A4 30m on 1fr 1,400. 1,400.
54a A4 60m on 2fr 400.00 400.00
55a A4 150m on 5fr 1,050. 1,050.
Nos. 51a-55a (5) 3,775. 3,775.

Stamps of 1902-03 Surcharged in Paris

1921-23

56 A2 1m on 1c slate 1.60 1.60
57 A2 2m on 5c green 1.60 1.60
58 A3 4m on 10c rose 2.50 2.50
59 A2 5m on 3c red org 9.25 9.25
60 A3 6m on 15c orange 3.25 3.25
  a. 6m on 15c pale red 14.00 14.00
61 A3 8m on 20c brn vio 5.00 5.00
62 A3 10m on 25c blue 2.50 2.50
63 A3 10m on 30c violet 7.50 7.50
64 A3 15m on 50c blue 6.75 6.75

Nos. 29-32 and Type of 1902 Surcharged

65 A4 15m on 50c 6.00 6.00
66 A4 30m on 1fr 9.25 9.25
67 A4 60m on 2fr 130.00 130.00
68 A4 60m on 2fr org & pale blue 12.50 12.50
69 A4 150m on 5fr 20.00 20.00
Nos. 56-69 (14) 217.70 217.70

Stamps and Types of 1902-03 Surcharged

1925

70 A2 1m on 1c light gray .75 .75
71 A2 2m on 5c green 1.10 1.10
72 A3 4m on 10c rose red .90 .90
73 A2 5m on 3c red org 1.10 1.10
74 A3 6m on 15c orange 1.10 1.10
75 A3 8m on 20c brn vio 1.00 1.00
76 A3 10m on 25c blue 1.40 1.40
77 A3 15m on 50c blue 1.60 1.60
78 A4 30m on 1fr cl & ol grn 2.75 2.75
79 A4 60m on 2fr org & pale blue 2.50 2.50
80 A4 150m on 5fr dk bl & buff 4.25 4.25
Nos. 70-80 (11) 18.45 18.45

Type of 1902-03 Issue and

A5

1927-28

83 A5 3m orange ('28) 2.10 2.10
87 A3 15m slate bl 2.50 2.50
88 A3 20m rose lil ('28) 2.50 2.50
90 A4 50m org & blue 4.50 4.50
91 A4 100m slate bl & buff 6.00 6.00
92 A4 250m gray grn & red 9.25 9.25
Nos. 83-92 (6) 26.85 26.85

SEMI-POSTAL STAMPS

Regular Issue of 1902-03 Surcharged in Carmine

1915 Unwmk. *Perf. 14x13½*

B1 A3 10c + 5c rose 1.60 1.60

Sinking Fund Issue

Type of 1902-03 Issue Surcharged like Alexandria Nos. B2-B3 in Blue or Black

1927-30

B2 A3 15m + 5m dp org (Bl) 5.00 5.00
B3 A3 15m + 5m red vio ('28) 8.50 8.50
  b. 15m + 5m violet ('30) 14.00 14.00
B4 A3 15m + 5m fawn ('29) 10.00 10.00
Nos. B2-B4 (3) 23.50 23.50

POSTAGE DUE STAMPS

Postage Due Stamps of France, 1893-1906, Srchd. Locally in Black

1921 Unwmk. *Perf. 14x13½*

J1 D2 12m on 10c brown 62.50 *67.50*
J2 D2 15m on 5c blue 92.50 *105.00*
J3 D2 30m on 20c ol grn 92.50 *105.00*
  a. Inverted surcharge 1,100. 1,100.
J4 D2 30m on 50c red vio 3,000. 3,400.

Same Surcharged in Red or Blue

1921

J5 D2 2m on 5c bl (R) 55.00 *60.00*
  a. Blue surcharge 300.00 300.00
  b. Accent omitted from "è" of "Millièmes" 190.00 200.00
  c. Second "m" of "Millièmes" inverted 190.00 200.00
  d. "S" of "Millièmes" omitted 190.00 225.00
J6 D2 4m on 10c brn (Bl) 55.00 *62.50*
  a. Surcharged "15 Millièmes" 725.00 725.00
  b. Accent omitted from "è" of "MILLIèMES" 190.00 200.00
  c. Second "m" of "Millièmes" inverted 190.00 200.00
  d. "S" of "Millièmes" omitted 190.00 225.00
J7 D2 10m on 30c red (Bl) 55.00 *60.00*
  a. Inverted surcharge 160.00 160.00
  b. Accent omitted from "è" of "Millièmes" 190.00 190.00
  c. Second "M" of "Millièmes" inverted 190.00 190.00
  d. "S" of "Millièmes" omitted 190.00 225.00
  e. "Q" for "0" in surcharge (1Qm) 1,450. 1,500.
J8 D2 15m on 50c brn vio (Bl) 67.50 *72.50*
  a. Inverted surcharge 160.00 160.00
  b. Accent omitted from "è" of "Millièmes" 190.00 190.00
  c. Second "m" of "Millièmes" inverted 190.00 190.00
  d. "S" of "Millièmes" omitted 210.00 240.00
  e. As "a," accent omitted from è of "Millièmes" 425.00
Nos. J5-J8 (4) 232.50 255.00

Alexandria Nos. J6-J13 were also available for use in Port Said.

OFFICES IN TURKEY (LEVANT)

Various powers maintained post offices in the Turkish Empire before World War I by authority of treaties which ended with the signing of the Treaty of Lausanne in 1923. The foreign post offices were closed Oct. 27, 1923.

100 Centimes = 1 Franc
25 Centimes = 40 Paras = 1 Piaster

Stamps of France Surcharged in Black or Red

1885-1901 Unwmk. *Perf. 14x13½*

1 A15 1pi on 25c yel, *straw* 550.00 16.00
  a. Inverted surcharge 2,500. 2,400.

2 A15 1pi on 25c blk, *rose* (R) ('86) 4.25 1.25
Never hinged 8.00
a. Inverted surcharge 400.00 325.00
3 A15 2pi on 50c car, *rose* (II) ('90) 18.00 3.00
Never hinged 35.00
a. Type I ('01) 375.00 50.00
Never hinged 725.00
4 A15 3pi on 75c car, *rose* 30.00 15.00
Never hinged 60.00
5 A15 4pi on 1fr brnz grn, *straw* 30.00 15.00
Never hinged 60.00
6 A15 8pi on 2fr brn, *az* ('00) 37.50 25.00
Never hinged 67.50
7 A15 20pi on 5fr red lil, *lav* ('90) 110.00 60.00
Never hinged 225.00
Nos. 1-7 (7) 779.75 135.25

A2

A3

A4

Nos. 29, 32, 36 and Types of A4 Surcharged

No. 34

No. 35

1902-07 Typo. *Perf. 14x13½*

21 A2 1c gray .65 .65
Never hinged 1.25
22 A2 2c vio brn .65 .65
23 A2 3c red org .65 .65
24 A2 4c yel brn 3.00 1.10
a. Imperf., pair 90.00
25 A2 5c lt yel green ('03) 2.00 .80
26 A3 10c rose red 1.00 .65
27 A3 15c pale red ('03) 3.00 1.25
28 A3 20c brn vio ('03) 3.25 2.00
29 A3 25c blue ('07) 45.00 *60.00*
a. Imperf., pair 425.00
30 A3 30c lilac ('03) 6.00 3.00
31 A4 40c red & pale bl 6.00 3.25
32 A4 50c bis brn & lav ('07) 190.00 *225.00*
a. Imperf., pair 925.00
33 A4 1fr claret & ol grn ('07) 425.00 450.00
a. Imperf., pair 1,100.

Black Surcharge

34 A3 1pi on 25c bl ('03) 1.20 .65
a. Second "I" omitted 32.50 25.00
b. Double surcharge 72.50 60.00
35 A4 2pi on 50c bis brn & lavender 4.25 1.60
36 A4 4pi on 1fr cl & ol grn 5.00 2.10
a. Imperf., pair 750.00
37 A4 8pi on 2fr gray vio & yel 20.00 15.00
38 A4 20pi on 5fr dk bl & buff 10.00 6.00
Nos. 21-38 (18) 726.65 774.35

Nos. 29, 32-33 were used during the early part of 1907 in the French Offices at Harar and Diredawa, Ethiopia. Djibouti and Port Said stamps were also used.

No. 27 Surcharged in Green

1905

39 A3 1pi on 15c pale red 2,100. 325.
a. "Piastte" 6,500. 1,700.

Stamps of France 1900-21 Surcharged

On A22

On A20

On A18

1921-22

40 A22 30pa on 5c grn 1.00 1.00
41 A22 30pa on 5c org 1.00 .85
42 A22 1pi20pa on 10c red 1.10 1.10
43 A22 1pi20pa on 10c grn 1.10 .85
44 A22 3pi30pa on 25c bl 1.60 1.00
45 A22 4pi20pa on 30c org 1.60 1.10
a. "4" omitted 1,050.
46 A20 7pi20pa on 50c bl 1.60 1.25
47 A18 15pi on 1fr car & ol grn 3.00 2.10
48 A18 30pi on 2fr org & pale bl 12.50 10.00
49 A18 75pi on 5fr dk bl & buff 11.00 7.50
Nos. 40-49 (10) 35.50 26.75

Stamps of France, 1903-07, Handstamped

1923

52 A22 1pi20pa on 10c red 62.50 60.00
54 A20 3pi30pa on 15c gray grn (GC) 25.00 25.00
55 A22 7pi20pa on 35c vio 30.00 30.00
b. 1pi20pa on 35c violet 1,400. 1,400.
Nos. 52-55 (3) 117.50 115.00

CAVALLE (CAVALLA)

Stamps of France Ovptd. or Srchd. in Carmine, Red, Blue or Black

1893-1900 Unwmk. *Perf. 14x13½*

1 A15 5c grn, *grnsh* (R) 25.00 21.00
a. Type II (C) 25.00 21.00
2 A15 5c yel grn (I) ('00) (R) 21.00 21.00
3 A15 10c blk, *lav* (II) 26.00 26.00
a. 10c black, *lavender* (I) 180.00 150.00
4 A15 15c blue (R) 47.50 30.00
a. 15c blue (C) 47.50 30.00
5 A15 1pi on 25c blk, *rose* 28.00 20.00
6 A15 2pi on 50c car, *rose* 92.50 65.00
7 A15 4pi on 1fr brnz grn, *straw* (R) 97.50 87.50
b. 4pi on 1fr brnz grn, *straw* (C) 95.00 87.50
8 A15 8pi on 2fr brn, *az* ('00) (Bk) 120.00 120.00
Nos. 1-8 (8) 457.50 390.50
Set, never hinged 1,000.

A3

A4

A5

A6

1902-03

9 A3 5c green 2.25 1.75
a. 5c yel grn 2.50 2.00
10 A4 10c rose red ('03) 2.25 1.75
11 A4 15c orange 2.25 1.75
a. 15c pale red ('03) 12.50 12.50

Surcharged in Black

12 A5 1pi on 25c bl 4.75 3.00
13 A6 2pi on 50c bis brn & lav 13.00 7.00
14 A6 4pi on 1fr cl & ol grn 16.00 13.00
15 A6 8pi on 2fr gray vio & yel 21.00 19.00
Nos. 9-15 (7) 61.50 47.25

DEDEAGH (DEDEAGATCH)

Stamps of France Ovptd. or Srchd. in Carmine, Red, Blue or Black

1893-1900 Unwmk. *Perf. 14x13½*

1 A15 5c grn, *grnsh* (II) (R) 18.00 15.00
a. Type II (C) 18.00 15.00
2 A15 5c yel grn (I) ('00) (R) 14.50 14.00
3 A15 10c blk, *lav* (II) 27.50 20.00
a. Type I 47.50 32.50
b. As "a," double overprint 300.00
4 A15 15c blue (II) (R) 37.50 30.00
a. Type II (C) 37.50 30.00
5 A15 1pi on 25c blk, *rose* 42.50 37.50
6 A15 2pi on 50c car, *rose* 70.00 50.00
7 A15 4pi on 1fr brnz grn, *straw* (R) 82.50 70.00
8 A15 8pi on 2fr brn, *az* ('00) (Bk) 120.00 95.00
Nos. 1-8 (8) 412.50 331.50
Set, never hinged 1,000.

A3

A4

A5

A6

1902-03

9 A3 5c green ('03) 3.00 2.50
a. 5c yellow green 3.50 3.00
10 A4 10c rose red ('03) 3.50 2.75
11 A4 15c orange 5.00 3.75
a. 15c rose red ('03) 7.00 6.00
15 A5 1pi on 25c bl ('03) 3.50 2.75
16 A6 2pi on 50c bis brn & lav 11.50 10.00
a. Double surcharge 300.00
17 A6 4pi on 1fr cl & ol grn 22.50 18.50
18 A6 8pi on 2fr gray vio & yel 32.50 27.50
Nos. 9-18 (7) 81.50 67.75
Set, never hinged 175.00

PORT LAGOS

Stamps of France Ovptd. or Srchd. in Carmine, Red or Blue

1893 Unwmk. *Perf. 14x13½*

1 A15 5c grn, *grnsh* (R) 30.00 *32.50*
a. 5c grn, *grnsh* (C) 30.00 32.50
2 A15 10c blk, *lav* 62.50 47.50
3 A15 15c blue (R) 92.50 72.50
a. 15c blue (C) 97.50 77.50
4 A15 1pi on 25c blk, *rose* 77.50 62.50
5 A15 2pi on 50c car, *rose* 185.00 97.50
6 A15 4pi on 1fr brnz grn, *straw* (R) 112.50 97.50
Nos. 1-6 (6) 560.00 410.00
Set, never hinged 1,300.

VATHY (SAMOS)

Stamps of France Ovptd. or Srchd. in Carmine, Red, Blue or Black

1894-1900 Unwmk. *Perf. 14x13½*

1 A15 5c grn, *grnsh* (R) 8.75 8.00
a. 5c grn, *grnsh* (II) (C) 10.00 8.75
2 A15 5c yel grn (I) ('00) (R) 8.75 7.50
a. Type II 87.50 87.50
3 A15 10c blk, *lav* (I) 17.50 15.00
a. Type II 50.00 47.50
4 A15 15c blue (R) 17.50 15.00
5 A15 1pi on 25c blk, *rose* 17.50 11.50
6 A15 2pi on 50c car, *rose* 30.00 27.50
7 A15 4pi on 1fr brnz grn, *straw* (R) 42.50 35.00
8 A15 8pi on 2fr brn, *az* ('00) (Bk) 75.00 75.00
9 A15 20pi on 5fr lil, *lav* ('00) (Bk) 110.00 110.00
Nos. 1-9 (9) 327.50 304.50
Set, never hinged 600.00

OFFICES IN ZANZIBAR

Until 1906 France maintained post offices in the Sultanate of Zanzibar, but in that year Great Britain assumed direct control over this protectorate and the French withdrew their postal system.

16 Annas = 1 Rupee

Stamps of France Surcharged in Red, Carmine, Blue or Black

1894-96 Unwmk. *Perf. 14x13½*

1 A15 ½a on 5c grn, *grnsh* 10.00 7.50
2 A15 1a on 10c blk, *lav* (Bl) 15.00 12.50
3 A15 1½a on 15c bl ('96) 22.50 21.00
a. "ANNAS" 100.00 92.50
4 A15 2a on 20c red, *grn* ('96) (Bk) 19.00 15.00
a. "ANNA" 2,300. 2,300.
5 A15 2½a on 25c blk, *rose* (Bl) 12.50 9.25
a. Double surcharge 250.00 250.00
6 A15 3a on 30c brn, *bis* ('96) (Bk) 21.00 18.00
7 A15 4a on 40c red, *straw* ('96) (Bk) 29.00 25.00
8 A15 5a on 50c car, *rose* (Bl) 37.50 32.50
9 A15 7½a on 75c vio, *org* ('96) 500.00 400.00

10 A15 10a on 1fr brnz grn, *straw* 67.50 55.00
11 A15 50a on 5fr red lil, *lav* ('96) (Bk) 325.00 260.00
Nos. 1-11 (11) 1,059. 855.75

1894

12 A15 ½a & 5c on 1c blk, *lil bl* (R) 200.00 *220.00*
13 A15 1a & 10c on 3c gray, *grysh* (R) 180.00 *200.00*
14 A15 2½a & 25c on 4c cl, *lav* (Bk) 230.00 *275.00*
15 A15 5a & 50c on 20c red, *grn* (Bk) 250.00 *275.00*
16 A15 10a & 1fr on 40c red, *straw* (Bk) 475.00 *525.00*
Nos. 12-16 (5) 1,335. 1,495.

There are two distinct types of the figures 5c, four of the 25c and three of each of the others of this series.

Stamps of France Srchd. in Red, Carmine, Blue or Black

1896-1900

17 A15 ½a on 5c grn, *grnsh* (R) 11.00 8.50
18 A15 ½a on 5c yel grn (I) (R) 7.50 6.75
a. Type II 9.25 7.50
19 A15 1a on 10c blk, *lav* (II) (Bl) 9.25 7.50
a. Type I 22.50 19.00
20 A15 1½a on 15c bl (R) 11.00 9.25
21 A15 2a on 20c red, *grn* 9.25 9.25
a. "ZANZIBAR" double 210.00 210.00
b. "ZANZIBAR" triple 210.00 210.00
22 A15 2½a on 25c blk, *rose* (Bl) 11.00 9.25
a. Inverted surcharge 275.00 210.00
23 A15 3a on 30c brn, *bis* 11.00 9.25
24 A15 4a on 40c red, *straw* 13.50 10.00
25 A15 5a on 50c rose, *rose* (II) (Bl) 45.00 32.50
a. Type I 125.00 100.00
26 A15 10a on 1fr brnz grn, *straw* (R) 29.00 25.00
27 A15 20a on 2fr brn, *az* 35.00 29.00
a. "ZANZIBAS" 675.00 *750.00*
b. "ZANZIBAR" triple 1,600.
28 A15 50a on 5fr lil, *lav* 67.50 62.50
a. "ZANZIBAS" *9,250.*
Nos. 17-28 (12) 260.00 218.75

For surcharges see Nos. 50-54.

A4 A5

1897

29 A4 2½a & 25c on ½a on 5c grn, *grnsh* 1,300. 240.
30 A4 2½a & 25c on 1a on 10c *lav* *4,500.* 1,100.
31 A4 2½a & 25c on 1½a on 15c blue *4,400.* 950.
32 A5 5a & 50c on 3a on 30c brn, *bis* *4,400.* 950.
33 A5 5a & 50c on 4a on 40c red, *straw* *4,500.* 1,300.

Printed on the Margins of Sheets of French Stamps

A6

A7

Perf. 14x13½ on one or more sides

1897

34 A6 2½a & 25c grn, *grnsh* 1,300.
35 A6 2½a & 25c blk, *lav* *4,000.*
36 A6 2½a & 25c blue *3,000.*
37 A7 5a & 50c brn, *bis* *2,900.*
38 A7 5a & 50c red, *straw* *4,000.*

There are 5 varieties of figures in the above surcharges.

Surcharged in Red or Black

A8

A9

A10

1902-03 ***Perf. 14x13½***

39 A8 ½a on 5c grn (R) 6.75 6.00
40 A9 1a on 10c rose red ('03) 7.50 7.50
41 A9 1½a on 15c pale red ('03) 15.00 14.00
42 A9 2a on 20c brn vio ('03) 18.00 15.00
43 A9 2½a on 25c bl ('03) 18.00 15.00
44 A9 3a on 30c lil ('03) 13.00 13.00
a. 5a on 30c (error) 325.00 *375.00*
45 A10 4a on 40c red & pale bl 30.00 25.00
46 A10 5a on 50c bis brn & lav 25.00 21.00
47 A10 10a on 1fr cl & ol grn 32.50 29.00
48 A10 20a on 2fr gray vio & yel 85.00 75.00
49 A10 50a on 5fr dk bl & buff 100.00 92.50
Nos. 39-49 (11) 350.75 313.00

For see Reunion Nos. 55-59.

Nos. 23-24 Surcharged in Black

a

b

c

1904

50 A15 (a) 25c & 2½a on 4a on 40c 1,000.
51 A15 (b) 50c & 5a on 3a on 30c 1,200.
52 A15 (b) 50c & 5a on 4a on 40c 6,500. 1,200.
53 A15 (c) 1fr & 10a on 3a on 30c 2,000.
54 A15 (c) 1fr & 10a on 4a on 40c 2,000.

Nos. 39-40, 44 Surcharged in Red or Black

d

e

f

g

55 A8 (d) 25c & 2a on ½a on 5c (R) 3,100. 140.00
56 A9 (e) 25c & 2½a on 1a on 10c 6,500. 150.00
a. Inverted surcharge 1,500.
57 A9 (e) 25c & 2½a on 3a on 30c 2,400.
a. Inverted surcharge 4,100.
b. Double surch., both invtd. 2,600.
58 A9 (f) 50c & 5a on 3a on 30c 1,250.
59 A9 (g) 1fr & 10a on 3a on 30c 2,000.

No. J1-J3 With Various Surcharges Overprinted: "Timbre" in Red

60 D1 ½a on 5c blue 450.00

Overprinted "Affrancht" in Black

61 D1 1a on 10c brn 450.00

With Red Bars Across "CHIFFRE" and "TAXE"

62 D1 1½a on 15c grn 1,000.

The illustrations are not exact reproductions of the new surcharges but are merely intended to show their relative positions and general styles.

POSTAGE DUE STAMPS

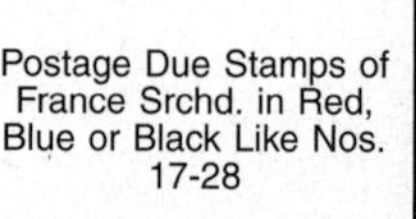

Postage Due Stamps of France Srchd. in Red, Blue or Black Like Nos. 17-28

1897 **Unwmk.** ***Perf. 14x13½***

J1 D2 ½a on 5c blue (R) 21.00 12.50
J2 D2 1a on 10c brn (Bl) 21.00 12.50
a. Inverted surcharge 160.00 *190.00*
J3 D2 1½aon 15c grn (R) 32.50 12.50
J4 D2 3a on 30c car (Bk) 29.00 21.00
J5 D2 5a on 50c lil (Bl) 32.50 25.00
a. 2½a on 50c lilac (Bl) 1,400. 1,300.
Nos. J1-J5 (5) 136.00 83.50

For overprints see Nos. 60-62.

REUNION

LOCATION — An island in the Indian Ocean about 400 miles east of Madagascar
GOVT. — Department of France
AREA — 970 sq. mi.
POP. — 490,000 (est. 1974)
CAPITAL — St. Denis

The colony of Réunion became an integral part of the Republic, acquiring the same status as the departments in metropolitan France, under a law effective Jan. 1, 1947.

On Jan. 1, 1975, stamps of France replaced those inscribed or overprinted "CFA."

100 Centimes = 1 Franc

Catalogue values for unused stamps in this country are for Never Hinged items, beginning with Scott 224 in the regular postage section, Scott B15 in the semi-postal section, Scott C18 in the airpost section, and Scott J26 in the postage due section.

For French stamps inscribed "Reunion" see Nos. 949, 1507.

A1

A2

1852 **Unwmk.** **Typo.** ***Imperf.***

1 A1 15c black, *blue* *39,000.* *25,000.*
2 A2 30c black, *blue* *39,000.* *25,000.*

Four varieties of each value.

The reprints are printed on a more bluish paper than the originals. They have a frame of a thick and a thin line, instead of one thick and two thin lines. Value, $62.50 each.

Stamps of French Colonies Surcharged or Overprinted in Black

a

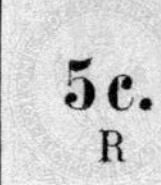

Overprint Type "a"

1885

3 A1(a) 5c on 40c org, *yelsh* 450.00 375.00
a. Inverted surcharge 2,250. 2,100.
b. Double surcharge 2,250. 2,100.
4 A1(a) 25c on 40c org, *yelsh* 70.00 55.00
a. Inverted surcharge 1,000. 900.00
b. Double surcharge 1,000. 900.00
5 A5(a) 5c on 30c brn, *yelsh* 70.00 57.50
a. "5" inverted 3,500. 3,000.
b. Double surcharge 1,100. 900.00
c. Inverted surcharge 1,000. 900.00
6 A4(a) 5c on 40c org, *yelsh* (I) 62.50 45.00
a. 5c on 40c org, *yelsh* (II) 2,500. 2,500.
b. Inverted surcharge (I) 1,100. 900.00
c. Double surcharge (I) 1,100. 900.00
7 A8(a) 5c on 30c brn, *yelsh* 22.50 18.00
8 A8(a) 5c on 40c ver, *straw* 135.00 115.00
a. Inverted surcharge 950.00 850.00
b. Double surcharge 925.00 850.00
9 A8(a) 10c on 40c ver, *straw* 27.50 22.50
a. Inverted surcharge 950.00 850.00
b. Double surcharge 950.00 850.00
10 A8(a) 20c on 30c brn, *yelsh* 90.00 75.00

b

Overprint Type "b" With or Without Accent on "E"

1891

11 A4 40c org, *yelsh* (I) 575.00 550.00
a. 40c orange, *yelsh* (II) *6,750.* *6,750.*
b. Double overprint 750.00 750.00
12 A7 80c car, *pnksh* 80.00 62.50
13 A8 30c brn, *yelsh* 52.50 52.50
14 A8 40c ver, *straw* 42.50 42.50
15 A8 75c car, *rose* 475.00 475.00
16 A8 1fr brnz grn, *straw* 62.50 52.50

Perf. 14x13½

17 A9 1c blk, *lil bl* 4.75 4.00
a. Inverted overprint 60.00 60.00
b. Double overprint 52.50 52.50
18 A9 2c brn, *buff* 6.50 5.00
a. Inverted overprint 40.00 40.00
19 A9 4c claret, *lav* 10.00 8.00
a. Inverted overprint 72.50 72.50
20 A9 5c grn, *grnsh* 11.50 9.00
a. Inverted overprint 60.00 60.00
b. Double overprint 60.00 57.50
21 A9 10c blk, *lav* 40.00 8.00
a. Inverted overprint 90.00 80.00
b. Double overprint 100.00 80.00
22 A9 15c blue 57.50 9.00
a. Inverted overprint 120.00 110.00
23 A9 20c red, *grn* 45.00 30.00
a. Inverted overprint 175.00 150.00
b. Double overprint 175.00 150.00
24 A9 25c blk, *rose* 50.00 7.25
a. Inverted overprint 125.00 120.00
25 A9 35c dp vio, *yel* 45.00 35.00
a. Inverted overprint 180.00 175.00
26 A9 40c red, *straw* 72.50 62.50
a. Inverted overprint 240.00 225.00
27 A9 75c car, *rose* 675.00 575.00
a. Inverted overprint 1,600. 1,400.
28 A9 1fr brnz grn, *straw* 575.00 500.00
a. Inverted overprint 1,600. 1,500.
b. Double overprint 1,500. 1,400.

The varieties "RUNION," "RUENION," "REUNIONR," "ERUNION," "EUNION,"

"REUNIN," "REUNIOU" and "REUNOIN" are found on most stamps of this group. See *Scott Classic Specialized Catalogue of Stamps and Covers* for detailed listings. There are also many broken letters.

For surcharges see Nos. 29-33, 53-55.

No. 23 with Additional Surcharge in Black

c

d

e

f

1891

29 A9(c) 02c on 20c red, *grn* 14.50 14.50
- *a.* Inverted surcharge 90.00 90.00
- *b.* No "c" after "02" 57.50 57.50

30 A9(c) 15c on 20c red, *grn* 18.00 18.00
- *a.* Inverted surcharge 70.00 70.00

31 A9(d) 2c on 20c red, *grn* 5.00 5.00
32 A9(e) 2c on 20c red, *grn* 6.00 5.75
33 A9(f) 2c on 20c red, *grn* 10.00 10.00
Nos. 29-33 (5) 53.50 53.25

The varieties "RUNION" and "RUENION" appear on several stamps from this set. See *Scott Classic Specialized Catalogue of Stamps and Covers* for listings.

Navigation and Commerce — A14

1892-1905 Typo. *Perf. 14x13½*
Name of Colony in Blue or Carmine

34 A14 1c blk, *lil bl* 2.00 1.25
35 A14 2c brn, *buff* 2.00 1.25
36 A14 4c claret, *lav* 3.25 2.25
37 A14 5c grn, *grnsh* 7.25 2.25
38 A14 5c yel grn ('00) 1.75 1.75
39 A14 10c blk, *lav* 9.50 3.50
40 A14 10c red ('00) 4.50 4.50
41 A14 15c bl, quadrille paper 30.00 3.50
42 A14 15c gray ('00) 10.00 3.50
43 A14 20c red, *grn* 20.00 9.00
44 A14 25c blk, *rose* 22.50 3.50
- *a.* "Reunion" double 425.00 *450.00*

45 A14 25c blue ('00) 29.00 27.50
46 A14 30c brn, *bis* 23.00 12.00
47 A14 40c red, *straw* 32.50 19.00
48 A14 50c car, *rose* 80.00 42.50
- *a.* "Reunion" in red and blue 500.00 500.00

49 A14 50c brn, *az* ("Reunion" in car) ('00) 57.50 50.00
50 A14 50c brn, *az* ("Reunion" in bl) ('05) 57.50 50.00
51 A14 75c dp vio, *org* 62.50 45.00
- *a.* "Reunion" double 375.00 375.00

52 A14 1fr brnz grn, *straw* 50.00 35.00
- *a.* "Reunion" double 360.00 *375.00*

Nos. 34-52 (19) 504.75 317.25

Perf. 13½x14 stamps are counterfeits.

For surcharges and overprint see Nos. 56-59, 99-106, Q1.

French Colonies No. 52 Surcharged in Black

g

h

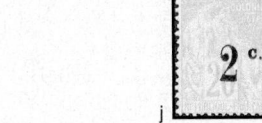
j

1893

53 A9(g) 2c on 20c red, *grn* 3.25 3.25
54 A9(h) 2c on 20c red, *grn* 6.00 6.00
55 A9(j) 2c on 20c red, *grn* 22.50 22.50
Nos. 53-55 (3) 31.75 31.75

Reunion Nos. 47-48, 51-52 Surcharged in Black

1901

56 A14 5c on 40c red, *straw* 7.00 7.00
- *a.* Inverted surcharge 47.50 47.50
- *b.* No bar 240.00 240.00
- *c.* Thin "5" —
- *d.* "5" inverted 1,400. 1,200.

57 A14 5c on 50c car, *rose* 7.75 7.25
- *a.* Inverted surcharge 47.50 47.50
- *b.* No bar 240.00 240.00
- *c.* Thin "5" —

58 A14 15c on 75c vio, *org* 22.50 22.50
- *a.* Inverted surcharge 57.50 57.50
- *b.* No bar 240.00 240.00
- *c.* Thin "5" and small "1" 47.50 47.50
- *d.* As "c," inverted 800.00 800.00

59 A14 15c on 1fr brnz grn, *straw* 19.00 19.00
- *a.* Inverted surcharge 57.50 57.50
- *b.* No bar 240.00 240.00
- *c.* Thin "5" and small "1" 47.50 47.50
- *d.* As "c," inverted —

Nos. 56-59 (4) 56.25 55.75

Map of Réunion A19

Coat of Arms and View of St. Denis A20

View of St. Pierre A21

1907-30 Typo.

60 A19 1c vio & lt rose .30 .30
61 A19 2c brn & ultra .30 .30
62 A19 4c ol grn & red .40 .40
- *a.* Center double 225.00

63 A19 5c grn & red 1.35 .40
64 A19 5c org & vio ('22) .30 .30
65 A19 10c car & grn 2.75 .40
66 A19 10c grn ('22) .30 .30
67 A19 10c brn red & org red, *bluish* ('26) .70 .70
68 A19 15c blk & ultra ('17) .55 .40
- *a.* Center double 250.00 250.00

69 A19 15c gray grn & bl grn ('26) .40 .40
70 A19 15c bl & lt red ('28) .55 .45
71 A20 20c gray grn & bl grn .45 .45
- *a.* Center omitted 1,100. 1,100.

72 A20 25c dp bl & vio brn 7.00 4.00
73 A20 25c lt brn & bl ('22) .55 .55
74 A20 30c yel brn & grn 1.50 1.00
75 A20 30c rose & pale rose ('22) 1.50 1.50
76 A20 30c gray & car rose ('26) .55 .55
77 A20 30c dp grn & yel grn ('28) 1.20 1.20
78 A20 35c ol grn & bl 1.75 1.10
79 A20 40c gray grn & brn ('25) .70 .70
80 A20 45c vio & car rose 1.90 1.10
81 A20 45c red brn & ver ('25) .90 .90
82 A20 45c vio & red org ('28) 3.00 2.75
83 A20 50c red brn & ultra 5.00 1.75
84 A20 50c bl & ultra ('22) 1.40 1.40
85 A20 50c yel & vio ('26) 1.10 1.10
86 A20 60c dk bl & yel brn ('25) 1.10 1.10
87 A20 65c vio & lt bl ('28) 1.60 1.40
88 A20 75c red & car rose .80 .70
89 A20 75c ol brn & red vio ('28) 2.50 2.25
90 A20 90c brn red & brt red ('30) 9.00 8.25
91 A21 1fr ol grn & bl 1.50 1.40
92 A21 1fr blue ('25) .95 .95
93 A21 1fr yel brn & lav ('28) 1.50 .70
94 A21 1.10fr org brn & rose lil ('28) 1.50 1.40
95 A21 1.50fr dk bl & ultra ('30) 16.00 16.00
96 A21 2fr red & grn 6.75 4.25
97 A21 3fr red vio ('30) 14.50 9.50
98 A21 5fr car & vio brn 11.50 6.75
Nos. 60-98 (39) 105.60 79.05

For surcharges see Nos. 107-121, 178-180, B1-B3.

Stamps of 1892-1900 Surcharged in Black or Carmine

1912

Spacing between figures of surcharge 1.5mm (5c), 2mm (10c)

99 A14 5c on 2c brn, *buff* 1.60 1.60
100 A14 5c on 15c gray (C) 1.40 1.40
- *a.* Inverted surcharge 210.00 210.00

101 A14 5c on 20c red, *grn* 2.40 2.40
102 A14 5c on 25c blk, *rose* (C) 1.60 1.60
103 A14 5c on 30c brn, *bis* (C) 1.40 1.40
104 A14 10c on 40c red, *straw* 1.40 1.40
105 A14 10c on 50c brn, *az* (C) 5.75 5.75
106 A14 10c on 75c dp vio, *org* 9.50 9.50
Nos. 99-106 (8) 25.05 25.05

Two spacings between the surcharged numerals are found on Nos. 99 to 106. For detailed listings, see the *Scott Classic Specialized Catalogue of Stamps and Covers.*

No. 62 Surcharged

1917

107 A19 1c on 4c ol grn & red 2.00 2.00
- *a.* Inverted surcharge 80.00 80.00
- *b.* Double surcharge 70.00 70.00
- *c.* In pair with unsurcharged #62 625.00 625.00

Stamps and Types of 1907-30 Surcharged in Black or Red

1922-33

108 A20 40c on 20c grn & yel .80 .80
- *a.* Double surcharge, one inverted 175.00 175.00
- *b.* Center double 175.00 175.00
- *c.* Surcharge omitted 1,200. 1,200.

109 A20 50c on 45c red brn & ver ('33) 1.20 1.20
109A A20 50c on 45c vio & red org ('33) 325.00 275.00
- *b.* Double surcharge 1,750.

110 A20 50c on 65c vio & lt bl ('33) 1.20 1.20
111 A20 60c on 75c red & rose .85 .85
- *a.* Double surcharge 225.00 225.00

112 A19 65c on 15c blk & ultra (R) ('25) 2.00 2.00
113 A19 85c on 15c blk & ultra (R) ('25) 2.00 2.00
114 A20 85c on 75c red & cer ('25) 2.25 2.25
115 A20 90c on 75 brn red & rose red ('27) 2.25 2.25
Nos. 108-109,110-115 (8) 12.55 12.55

Stamps and Type of 1907-30 Srchd. in Black or Red

1924-27

116 A21 25c on 5fr car & brn 1.10 1.10
- *a.* Double surcharge 110.00

117 A21 1.25fr on 1fr bl (R) ('26) 1.10 1.10
- *a.* Double surcharge 125.00

118 A21 1.50fr on 1fr ind & ultra, *bluish* ('27) 1.50 1.50
- *a.* Double surcharge 140.00
- *b.* Surcharge omitted 200.00

119 A21 3fr on 5fr dl red & lt bl ('27) 4.25 3.00
120 A21 10fr on 5fr bl grn & brn red ('27) 19.50 17.00
121 A21 20fr on 5fr blk brn & rose ('27) 24.00 19.00
Nos. 116-121 (6) 51.45 42.70

Common Design Types pictured following the introduction.

Colonial Exposition Issue
Common Design Types

1931 Engr. *Perf. 12½*
Name of Country Typo. in Black

122 CD70 40c dp green 5.50 5.50
123 CD71 50c violet 5.50 5.50
124 CD72 90c red orange 5.50 5.50
125 CD73 1.50fr dull blue 5.50 5.50
Nos. 122-125 (4) 22.00 22.00

Cascade of Salazie — A22

Waterfowl Lake and Anchain Peak — A23

Léon Dierx Museum, St. Denis — A24

Perf. 12, 12½ and Compound

1933-40 **Engr.**

126	A22	1c violet	.25	.25
127	A22	2c dark brown	.25	.25
128	A22	3c rose vio ('40)	.25	.25
129	A22	4c olive green	.25	.25
130	A22	5c red orange	.25	.25
131	A22	10c ultramarine	.25	.25
132	A22	15c black	.25	.25
133	A22	20c indigo	.30	.25
134	A22	25c red brown	.40	.30
135	A22	30c dark green	.40	.40
136	A23	35c green ('38)	.55	.55
137	A23	40c ultramarine	.55	.55
138	A23	40c brn blk ('40)	.40	.40
139	A23	45c red violet	1.00	1.00
140	A23	45c green ('40)	.45	.45
141	A23	50c red	.30	.25
142	A23	55c brn org ('38)	1.50	1.00
143	A23	60c dull bl ('40)	.45	.45
144	A23	65c olive green	1.10	.80
145	A23	70c ol grn ('40)	.65	.65
146	A23	75c dark brown	5.00	4.25
147	A23	80c black ('38)	1.00	.80
148	A23	90c carmine	2.50	2.10
149	A23	90c dl rose vio ('39)	1.00	1.00
150	A23	1fr green	2.00	.70
151	A23	1fr dk car ('38)	2.50	.70
152	A23	1fr black ('40)	.70	.70
153	A24	1.25fr orange brown	.70	.55
154	A24	1.25fr brt car rose ('39)	1.00	1.00
155	A22	1.40fr pck bl ('40)	1.00	1.00
156	A24	1.50fr ultramarine	.40	.40
157	A22	1.60fr dk car rose ('40)	1.40	1.40
158	A24	1.75fr olive green	1.00	.65
159	A22	1.75fr dk bl ('38)	1.40	.85
160	A24	2fr vermilion	.55	.55
161	A22	2.25fr brt ultra ('39)	2.00	2.00
162	A22	2.50fr chnt ('40)	1.40	1.40
163	A24	3fr purple	.55	.55
164	A24	5fr magenta	.55	.55
165	A24	10fr dark blue	1.10	1.10
166	A24	20fr red brown	1.50	1.50
		Nos. 126-166 (41)	39.05	32.55

For overprints and surcharges see Nos. 177A, 181-220, 223, C1.
60c, 1fr without "RF," see Nos. 237A-238B.

Paris International Exposition Issue
Common Design Types

1937 ***Perf. 13***

167	CD74	20c dp vio	2.25	2.25
168	CD75	30c dk grn	2.25	2.25
169	CD76	40c car rose	2.25	2.25
170	CD77	50c dk brn & blk	2.10	2.10
171	CD78	90c red	2.10	2.10
172	CD79	1.50fr ultra	2.25	2.25
		Nos. 167-172 (6)	13.20	13.20
		Set, never hinged	20.00	

Colonial Arts Exhibition Issue
Souvenir Sheet
Common Design Type

1937 ***Imperf.***

173 CD74 3fr ultra 8.50 *10.00*
Never hinged 16.00

New York World's Fair Issue
Common Design Type

1939 **Engr.** ***Perf. 12½x12***

174	CD82	1.25fr car lake	1.40	1.40
175	CD82	2.25fr ultra	1.40	1.40
		Set, never hinged	4.50	

For overprints, see Nos. 221-222.

St. Denis Roadstead and Marshal Pétain A25

1941 **Unwmk.** ***Perf. 11½x12***

176	A25	1fr brown	.80
177	A25	2.50fr blue	.80
		Set, never hinged	2.00

Nos. 176-177 were issued by the Vichy government in France, but were not placed on sale in Réunion.
For surcharges, see Nos. B13-B14.

No. 144 Surcharged in Carmine

1943

177A 1fr on 65c olive grn 1.10 .65
Never hinged 1.60

De Pronis Landing on Reunion — A25a

1943 ***Perf. 12½x12***

177B	A25a	60c blk brn & red	.55
177C	A25a	80c green & blue	.40
177D	A25a	1.50fr dk brn red	.35
177E	A25a	4fr ultra & red	.35
177F	A25a	5fr red brn & black	.55
177G	A25a	10fr violet & green	.65
		Nos. 177B-177G,C13A-C13F (12)	5.70
		Set, never hinged	8.00

300th Ann. of French settlement on Réunion.
Nos. 177B-177G were issued by the Vichy government in France, but were not placed on sale in Réunion.

Stamps of 1907 Overprinted in Blue Violet

q

1943 **Unwmk.** ***Perf. 14x13½***

178	A19(q)	4c ol gray & pale red	6.00	6.00
179	A20(q)	75c red & lil rose	1.75	1.75
180	A21(q)	5fr car & vio brn	60.00	60.00

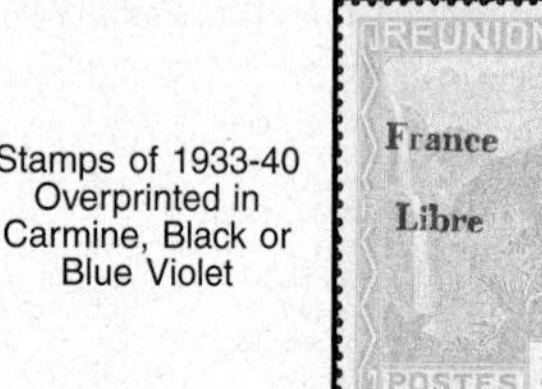

Stamps of 1933-40 Overprinted in Carmine, Black or Blue Violet

181	A22(r)	1c rose vio (C)	1.00	1.00
182	A22(r)	2c blk brn (C)	1.00	1.00
183	A22(r)	3c rose vio (C)	1.00	1.00
184	A22(r)	4c ol yel (C)	1.00	1.00
185	A22(r)	5c red org	1.00	1.00
186	A22(r)	10c ultra (C)	1.00	1.00
187	A22(r)	15c blk (C)	1.00	1.00
188	A22(r)	20c ind (C)	1.00	1.00
189	A22(r)	25c red brn (BlV)	1.25	1.25
190	A22(r)	30c dk grn (C)	1.40	1.40
191	A23(q)	35c green	1.00	1.00
192	A23(q)	40c dl ultra (C)	1.00	1.00
193	A23(q)	40c brn blk (C)	1.00	1.00
194	A23(q)	45c red vio	1.00	1.00
195	A23(q)	45c green	1.00	1.00
196	A23(q)	50c org red	1.00	1.00
197	A23(q)	55c brn org	1.00	1.00
198	A23(q)	60c dl bl (C)	3.00	3.00
199	A23(q)	65c ol grn	1.00	1.00
200	A23(q)	70c ol grn (C)	2.25	2.25
201	A23(q)	75c dk brn (C)	5.25	5.25
202	A23(q)	80c blk (C)	1.00	1.00
203	A23(q)	90c dl rose vio	1.00	1.00
204	A23(q)	1fr green	1.00	1.00
205	A23(q)	1fr dk car	1.00	1.00
206	A23(q)	1fr blk (C)	3.00	3.00
207	A24(q)	1.25fr org brn (BlV)	1.00	1.00
208	A24(q)	1.25fr brt car rose	3.00	3.00
209	A22(r)	1.40fr pck bl (C)	2.00	2.00
210	A24(q)	1.50fr ultra (C)	1.00	1.00
211	A22(r)	1.60fr dk car rose	2.10	2.10
212	A24(q)	1.75fr ol grn (C)	2.75	2.75
213	A22(r)	1.75fr dk bl (C)	4.50	4.50
214	A24(q)	2fr vermilion	1.00	1.00
215	A22(r)	2.25fr brt ultra (C)	4.50	4.50
216	A22(r)	2.50fr chnt (BlV)	7.50	7.50
217	A24(q)	3fr pur (C)	1.00	1.00
218	A24(q)	5fr brn lake (BlV)	2.10	2.10
219	A24(q)	10fr dk bl (C)	8.50	8.50
220	A24(q)	20fr red brn (BlV)	13.00	13.00

New York World's Fair Issue Overprinted in Black or Carmine

221	CD82(q)	1.25fr car lake	4.00	4.00
222	CD82(q)	2.25fr ultra (C)	4.00	4.00
		Nos. 178-222 (45)	165.85	165.85
		Set, never hinged	235.00	

No. 177A Overprinted

1943 **Unwmk.** ***Perf. 12½***

223 A23 1fr on 65c ol grn .85 .85

Catalogue values for unused stamps in this section, from this point to the end of the section, are for Never Hinged items.

Produce of Réunion A26

1943 **Photo.** ***Perf. 14½x14***

224	A26	5c dull brown	.25	.25
225	A26	10c blue & lt blue	.25	.25
226	A26	25c emerald	.25	.25
227	A26	30c dp orange	.25	.25
228	A26	40c dk slate grn	.25	.25
229	A26	80c rose violet	.65	.50
230	A26	1fr red brown	.25	.25
231	A26	1.50fr crimson	.65	.50
232	A26	2fr black	.65	.50
233	A26	2.50fr ultra	1.00	.70
234	A26	4fr dk violet	1.25	.90
235	A26	5fr bister	1.25	.90
236	A26	10fr dark brown	1.75	1.40
237	A26	20fr dark green	2.75	1.75
		Nos. 224-237 (14)	11.45	8.65

For surcharges see Nos. 240-247.

Type of 1933-40 without "RF"

1944 **Engr.** ***Perf. 12½***

237A	A23	60c dull blue	1.40	1.00
237B	A23	1fr black & blue	1.40	1.00

Nos. 237A-237B were issued by the Vichy government in France, but were not placed on sale in Réunion.

Eboue Issue
Common Design Type

1945 **Engr.** ***Perf. 13***

238	CD91	2fr black	1.00	1.00
239	CD91	25fr Prussian green	1.40	1.00

Nos. 224, 226 and 233 Surcharged in Carmine or Black

1945 ***Perf. 14½x14***

240	A26	50c on 5c dl brn (C)	.30	.25
241	A26	60c on 5c dl brn (C)	.30	.25
242	A26	70c on 5c dl brn (C)	.30	.25
243	A26	1.20fr on 5c dl brn (C)	.70	.50
244	A26	2.40fr on 25c emer	.70	.50
245	A26	3fr on 25c emer	1.25	.90
246	A26	4.50fr on 25c emer	1.25	.90
247	A26	15fr on 2.50fr ultra (C)	1.75	1.10
		Nos. 240-247 (8)	6.55	4.65

Various double and inverted overprints exist for Nos. 240-247.

Cliff — A27

Cutting Sugar Cane — A28

Cascade A29

Banana Tree A30

Mountain Scene A31

Ship Approaching Réunion — A32

1947 **Unwmk.** **Photo.** ***Perf. 13½***

249	A27	10c org & grnsh blk	.25	.25
250	A27	30c org & brt bl	.25	.25
251	A27	40c org & brn	.25	.25
252	A28	50c bl grn & brn	.25	.25
253	A28	60c dk bl & brn	.25	.25
254	A28	80c brn & ol brn	.55	.45
255	A29	1fr dl bl & vio brn	.55	.45
256	A29	1.20fr bl grn & gray	.80	.65
257	A29	1.50fr org & vio brn	.80	.65
258	A30	2fr gray bl & bl grn	.80	.65
259	A30	3fr vio brn & bl grn	.80	.65
260	A30	3.60fr dl red & rose red	.90	.70
261	A30	4fr gray bl & buff	.80	.70
262	A31	5fr rose lil & brn	1.25	.70
263	A31	6fr bl & brn	1.50	.75
264	A31	10fr org & ultra	3.25	1.50
265	A32	15fr gray bl & vio brn	4.75	2.75
266	A32	20fr bl & org	6.50	4.00
267	A32	25fr rose lil & brn	8.00	4.25
		Nos. 249-267 (19)	32.50	20.10

Nos. 249-267 exist imperf. Value, set $100.

Stamps of France, 1945-49, Surcharged type "a" or "b" in Black or Carmine

On A147

Others

1949 **Unwmk.** ***Perf. 14x13½, 13***

No.	Type	Description	Unused	Used
268	A153	10c on 30c	.30	.25
269	A153	30c on 50c	.60	.25
270	A146	50c on 1fr	1.40	.90
271	A146	60c on 2fr	8.00	1.40
272	A147	1fr on 3fr	2.00	.70
273	A147	2fr on 4fr	8.00	1.60
274	A147	2.50fr on 5fr	20.00	11.00
275	A147	3fr on 6fr	2.25	1.40
276	A147	4fr on 10fr	2.00	1.60
277	A162	5fr on 20fr (C)	10.00	1.40
278	A147	6fr on 12fr	29.00	2.25
279	A160	7fr on 12fr	9.00	3.00
280	A165	8fr on 25fr (C)	37.50	3.25
281	A165	10fr on 25fr (C)	2.75	1.40
282	A174	11fr on 18fr (C)	16.00	2.25
		Nos. 268-282 (15)	148.80	32.65

The letters "C. F. A." are the initials of "Colonies Francaises d'Afrique," referring to the currency which is expressed in French Africa francs.

The surcharge on Nos. 277, 279, 282 includes two bars.

1950 ***Perf. 14x13½***

No.	Type	Description	Unused	Used
283	A182	10c on 50c bl, red & yel	.55	.55
284	A182	1fr on 2fr grn, yel & red (#619)	10.00	3.50
285	A147	2fr on 5fr lt grn	18.00	4.25
		Nos. 283-285 (3)	28.55	8.30

France Nos. 630 & 623 Surcharged

1950-51 ***Perf. 13***

No.	Type	Description	Unused	Used
286	A188	5fr on 20fr dk red	10.00	1.75
287	A185	8fr on 25fr dp ultra ('51)	10.00	1.75

Stamps of France, 1951-52, Surcharged in Black or Red

No. 288

No. 292

1951-52 ***Perf. 14x13½, 13***

No.	Type	Description	Unused	Used
288	A182	50c on 1fr bl, red & yel	.70	.70
289	A182	1fr on 2fr vio bl, red & yel (#662)	.70	.70
290	A147	2fr on 5fr dl vio	4.25	2.00
291	A147	3fr on 6fr grn	8.00	1.60
292	A220	5fr on 20fr dk pur (R; '52)	3.00	1.75
293	A147	6fr on 12fr red org ('52)	9.00	2.00
294	A215	8fr on 40fr vio (R) ('52)	6.50	.70
295	A147	9fr on 18fr cerise	21.00	4.25
296	A208	15fr on 30fr ind (R)	11.00	2.25
		Nos. 288-296 (9)	64.15	15.95

The surcharge on Nos. 292, 294 and 296 include two bars.

France No. 697 Surcharged in Black

1953 ***Perf. 14x13½***

No.	Type	Description	Unused	Used
297	A182	50c on 1fr blk, red & yel	.35	.25

France No. 688 Surcharged Type "c" in Black

Perf. 13

No.	Type	Description	Unused	Used
298	A230	3fr on 6fr dp plum & car	1.20	.80

France Nos. 703 and 705 Surcharged in Red or Blue

No. 299

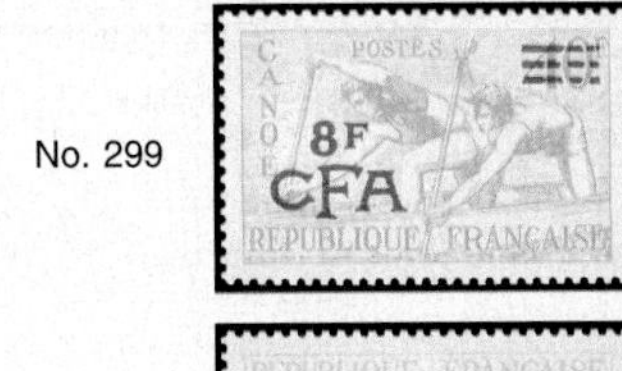

No. 300

1954

No.	Type	Description	Unused	Used
299	A235	8fr on 40fr (R)	38.50	7.50
300	A235	20fr on 75fr	80.00	32.50

France Nos. 698, 721, 713, and 715 Surcharged in Black

No. 301

No. 304

No.	Type	Description	Unused	Used
301	A182	1fr on 2fr	4.75	2.10
302	A241	4fr on 10fr	4.50	1.25
303	A238	8fr on 40fr	11.00	1.60
304	A238	20fr on 75fr	14.50	1.60

The surcharge on Nos. 303 and 304 includes two bars.

France Nos. 737, 719 and 722-724 Surcharged in Black or Red

a

b

No.	Type	Description	Unused	Used
305	A182(b)	1fr on 2fr	.50	.50
306	A241(a)	2fr on 6fr (R)	.80	.50
307	A242(a)	6fr on 12fr	11.00	1.75
308	A241(b)	9fr on 18fr	12.00	5.00
309	A241(a)	10fr on 20fr	8.00	1.40
		Nos. 299-309 (11)	185.55	55.70

The surcharge on Nos. 306-308 includes two bars; on No. 309 three bars.

France No. 720 Surcharged in Red

1955 ***Perf. 13***

No.	Type	Description	Unused	Used
310	A241	3fr on 8fr brt bl & dk grn	1.40	1.10

France Nos. 785, 774-779 Surcharged in Black or Red

No. 311

No. 317

Perf. 14x13½, 13

1955-56 **Typo., Engr.**

No.	Type	Description	Unused	Used
311	A182	50c on 1fr	.45	.30
312	A265	2fr on 6fr ('56)	1.20	.70
313	A265	3fr on 8fr	1.00	.50
314	A265	4fr on 10fr	1.25	.50
315	A265	5fr on 12fr (R)	1.30	.50
316	A265	6fr on 18fr (R)	1.00	.50
317	A265	10fr on 25fr	1.75	.50
		Nos. 311-317 (7)	7.95	3.50

The surcharge on Nos. 312-317 includes two bars.

France Nos. 801-804 Surcharged in Black or Red

No. 318

No. 319

No. 320

No. 321

1956 **Engr.** ***Perf. 13***

No.	Type	Description	Unused	Used
318	A280(a)	8fr on 30fr (R)	5.25	1.10
319	A280(b)	9fr on 40fr	7.75	3.00
320	A280(a)	15fr on 50fr	9.25	1.60
321	A280(a)	20fr on 75fr (R)	8.50	2.25
		Nos. 318-321 (4)	30.75	7.95

The surcharge on Nos. 318, 319 and 321 includes two bars.

France Nos. 837 and 839 Surcharged in Red

1957 ***Perf. 13***

No.	Type	Description	Unused	Used
322	A294	7fr on 15fr	1.20	.55
323	A265	17fr on 70fr	6.75	2.10

The surcharge on Nos. 322-323 includes two bars.

No. 322 has three types of "7" in the sheet of 50. There are 34 of the "normal" 7; 10 of a slightly thinner 7, and 6 of a slightly thicker 7.

France Nos. 755-756, 833-834, 851-855, 908, 949 Surcharged in Black or Red Type "a", "b" or

d

Typographed, Engraved

1957-60 ***Perf. 14x13½, 13***

No.	Type	Description	Unused	Used
324	A236(b)	2fr on 6fr	.30	.30
325	A302(b)	3fr on 10fr ('58)	.50	.50
326	A236(b)	4fr on 12fr	3.50	.75
327	A236(b)	5fr on 10fr	2.25	1.10
328	A303(b)	6fr on 18fr	1.25	.50
329	A302(a)	9fr on 25fr (R) ('58)	1.25	.65
330	A252(a)	10fr on 20fr (R)	1.75	.30
331	A252(a)	12fr on 25fr	6.75	.50
332	A303(a)	17fr on 35fr	3.75	1.75
333	A302(a)	20fr on 50fr	1.75	.80
334	A302(a)	25fr on 85fr	4.00	1.60
335	A339(d)	50fr on 1fr ('60)	3.00	.75
		Nos. 324-335 (12)	30.05	9.50

The surcharge includes two bars on Nos. 324, 326-327, 329-331, 333 and 335.

France Nos. 973, 939 and 968 Surcharged

e

f

1961-63 **Typo.** ***Perf. 14x13½***

No.	Type	Description	Unused	Used
336	A318(e)	2fr on 5c multi	.30	.25
a.		Double surcharge	300.00	—
b.		Inverted surcharge	1,000.	—
337	A336(e)	5fr on 10c brt grn	1.30	.50
338	A336(b)	5fr on 10c brt grn ('63)	1.60	.75
339	A349(f)	12fr on 25c lake & gray	.30	.30
		Nos. 336-339 (4)	3.50	1.80

The surcharge on No. 337 includes three bars. No. 338 has "b" surcharge and two bars.

France Nos. 943, 941 and 946 Surcharged in Black or Red

Engraved, Typographed

1961 Unwmk. ***Perf. 13, 14x13½***

340 A338 7fr on 15c 1.00 .80
341 A337 10fr on 20c .30 .30
342 A339 20fr on 50c (R) 17.00 4.50
Nos. 340-342 (3) 18.30 5.60

Surcharge on No. 342 includes 3 bars.

France Nos. 1047-1048 Surcharged

No. 343

No. 344

1963, Jan. 2 Engr. ***Perf. 13***

343 A394 12fr on 25c 1.00 .95
344 A395 25fr on 50c 1.00 .95

1st television connection of the US and Europe through the Telstar satellite, July 11-12, 1962.

France Nos. 1040-1041, 1007 and 1009 Surcharged

No. 345

No. 346

No. 347

No. 348

Typographed, Engraved

1963 ***Perf. 14x13½, 13***

345 A318 2fr on 5c .30 .30
346 A318 5fr on 10c .25 .25
347 A372 7fr on 15c .60 .50
348 A372 20fr on 45c 1.25 .75
Nos. 345-348 (4) 2.40 1.80

Two-line surcharge on No. 345; No. 347 has currency expressed in capital "F" and two heavy bars through old value; two thin bars on No. 348.

France No. 1078 Surcharged

1964, Feb. 8 Engr. ***Perf. 13***

349 CD118 12fr on 25c 1.25 1.25

"PHILATEC," Intl. Philatelic and Postal Techniques Exhib., Paris, June 5-21, 1964.

France Nos. 1092, 1094 and 1102 Surcharged

Typographed, Engraved

1964 ***Perf. 14x13½, 13***

350 A318 1fr on 2c .25 .25
351 A318 6fr on 18c .30 .30
352 A420 35fr on 70c 1.50 .95
Nos. 350-352 (3) 2.05 1.50

Surcharge on No. 352 includes two bars.

France Nos. 1095, 1126, 1070 Surcharged

No. 353

No. 354

No. 355

1965

353 A318 15fr on 30c .50 .30
354 A440 25fr on 50c 1.00 .95
355 A408 30fr on 60c 1.50 1.00
Nos. 353-355 (3) 3.00 2.25

Two bars obliterate old denomination on Nos. 354-355.

Etienne Regnault, "Le Taureau" and Coast of Reunion — A33

1965, Oct. 3 Engr. ***Perf. 13***

356 A33 15fr bluish blk & dk car 1.00 .65

Tercentenary of settlement of Reunion.

France No. 985 Surcharged

1966, Feb. 13 Engr. ***Perf. 13***

357 A360 10fr on 20c bl & car 1.60 .70

French Satellite A-1 Issue
France Nos. 1137-1138 Surcharged in Red

1966, Mar. 27 Engr. ***Perf. 13***

358 CD121 15fr on 30c 1.10 1.00
359 CD121 30fr on 60c 1.30 1.10
a. Strip of 2 + label 3.50 3.00

France Nos. 1142, 1143, 1101 and 1127 Surcharged

No. 360

No. 361

1967-69 Typo. ***Perf. 14x13***

360 A446 2fr on 5c bl & red .30 .30

Photo. ***Perf. 13***

360A A446 10fr on 20c multi ('69) .30 .30

Engr.

361 A421 20fr on 40c multi 1.10 .95
362 A439 30fr on 60c bl & red brn 1.30 .75

EXPO '67 Issue
France No. 1177 Surcharged

1967, June 12 Engr. ***Perf. 13***

363 A473 30fr on 60c dl bl & bl grn 2.40 1.75

EXPO '67, Montreal, Apr. 28-Oct. 27.

Lions Issue
France No. 1196 Surcharged in Violet Blue

1967, Oct. 29 Engr. ***Perf. 13***

364 A485 20fr on 40c 3.00 1.20

50th anniversary of Lions International.

France No. 1130 Surcharged in Violet Blue

1968, Feb. 26 Engr. ***Perf. 13***

365 A440 50fr on 1fr 2.75 1.60

France No. 1224 Surcharged

1968, Oct. 21 Engr. ***Perf. 13***

366 A508 20fr on 40c multi 1.50 1.00

20 years of French Polar expeditions.

France Nos. 1230-1231 Surcharged

1969, Apr. 13 Engr. ***Perf. 13***

367 A486 15fr on 30c green .65 .50
368 A486 20fr on 40c dp car .70 .30

France No. 1255 Surcharged

1969, Aug. 18 Engr. ***Perf. 13***

370 A526 35fr on 70c multi 1.60 1.35

Napoleon Bonaparte (1769-1821).

France No. 1293 Surcharged

1971, Jan. 16 Engr. ***Perf. 13***

371 A555 25fr on 50c rose car .90 .30

France No. 1301 Surcharged

1971, Apr. 13 Engr. ***Perf. 13***

372 A562 40fr on 80c multi 2.00 1.40

France No. 1309 Surcharged

1971, June 5 Engr. ***Perf. 13***

373 A569 15fr on 40c multi 1.00 .70

Aid for rural families.

France No. 1312 Surcharged

1971, Aug. 30 Engr. *Perf. 13*
374 A571 45fr on 90c multi 1.15 .95

France No. 1320 Surcharged

1971, Oct. 18 Engr. *Perf. 13*
375 A573 45fr on 90c multi 1.40 1.00

40th anniversary of the first assembly of presidents of artisans' guilds.

Réunion Chameleon A34

1971, Nov. 8 Photo. *Perf. 13*
376 A34 25fr multi 1.40 1.10

Nature protection.

Common Design Type and

De Gaulle in Brazzaville, 1944 — A35

Designs: No. 377, Gen. de Gaulle, 1940. No. 379, de Gaulle entering Paris, 1944. No. 380, Pres. de Gaulle, 1970.

1971, Nov. 9 Engr.

377	CD134	25fr black	1.60	1.60
378	A35	25fr ultra	1.60	1.60
379	A35	25fr rose red	1.60	1.60
380	CD134	25fr black	1.60	1.60
a.		Strip of 4 + label	9.25	8.00

Charles de Gaulle (1890-1970), president of France.

Nos. 377-380 printed se-tenant in sheets of 20 containing 5 strips of 4 plus labels with Cross of Lorraine and inscription. Exists imperf. Value, strip $200.

France No. 1313 Surcharged

1972, Jan. 17 Engr. *Perf. 13*
381 A570 50fr on 1.10fr multi 1.40 1.15

Map of South Indian Ocean, Penguin and Ships — A36

1972, Jan. 31 Engr. *Perf. 13*
382 A36 45fr blk, bl & ocher 2.25 2.25

Bicentenary of the discovery of the Crozet and Kerguelen Islands.

France No. 1342 Surcharged in Red

1972, May. 8 Engr. *Perf. 13*
383 A590 15fr on 40c red 1.00 .95

20th anniv. of Blood Donors' Assoc. of Post and Telecommunications Employees.

France Nos. 1345-1346 Surcharged

1972, June 5 Typo. *Perf. 14x13*
384 A593 15fr on 30c multi .45 .45
385 A593 25fr on 50c multi .75 .65

Introduction of postal code system.

France No. 1377 Surcharged in Ultramarine

1973, June 12 Engr. *Perf. 13*
386 A620 45fr on 90c multi 2.00 1.35

France No. 1374 Surcharged in Ultramarine

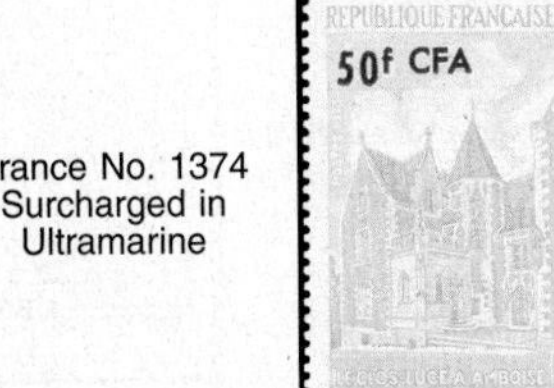

France No. 1336 Srchd. in Red

1973 Engr. *Perf. 13*
387 A617 50fr on 1fr multi (U) 1.15 .95
388 A586 100fr on 2fr multi (R) 2.00 1.10

On No. 388, two bars cover "2.00".
Issue dates: 50fr, June 24; 100fr, Oct. 13.

France No. 1231C Surcharged in Black

1973, Nov. Typo. *Perf. 14x13*
389 A486 15fr on 30c bl grn 5.00 .80

France No. 1390 Surcharged in Red

1974, Jan. 20 Engr. *Perf. 13*
390 A633 25fr on 50c multi .70 .70

ARPHILA 75 Phil. Exhib., Paris, June 1975.

France Nos. 1394-1397 Surcharged in Black, Ultramarine or Brown

No. 391

No. 394

Engr. (#391, 393), Photo. (#392, 394)
1974 *Perf. 12x13, 13x12*

391	A637	100fr on 2fr (Blk)	2.50	2.40
392	A638	100fr on 2fr (U)	3.25	2.40
393	A639	100fr on 2fr (Br)	3.25	2.40
394	A640	100fr on 2fr (U)	3.25	2.40
		Nos. 391-394 (4)	12.25	9.60

Nos. 391-394 printed in sheets of 25 with alternating labels publicizing "ARPHILA 75," Paris June 6-16, 1975.

Two bars obliterate original denomination on Nos. 391-393.

France No. 1401 Surcharged in Red

1974, Apr. 29 Engr. *Perf. 13*
395 A644 45fr on 90c multi 1.90 1.40

Reorganized sea rescue organization.

France No. 1415 Surcharged in Ultramarine

1974, Oct. 6 Engr. *Perf. 13*
396 A657 60fr on 1.20fr multi 1.60 1.35

Centenary of Universal Postal Union.

France Nos. 1292A and 1294B Surcharged in Ultramarine

1974, Oct. 19 Typo. *Perf. 14x13*
397 A555 30fr on 60c grn 1.75 1.60

Engr.
Perf. 13
398 A555 40fr on 80c car rose 2.10 1.75

SEMI-POSTAL STAMPS

No. 65 Surcharged in Black or Red

1915 Unwmk. *Perf. 14x13½*

B1	A19	10c + 5c (Bk)	160.00	120.00
a.		Inverted surcharge	450.00	350.00
B2	A19	10c + 5c (R)	1.75	1.75
a.		Inverted surcharge	77.50	77.50
b.		Double surcharge, both inverted	675.00	675.00

No. 65 Surcharged in Red

1916
B3 A19 10c + 5c 1.90 1.90

Curie Issue
Common Design Type

1938 *Perf. 13*
B4 CD80 1.75fr + 50c brt ultra 14.00 14.00
Never hinged 24.00

French Revolution Issue
Common Design Type

1939 Photo. Unwmk.
Name and Value Typo. in Black

B5	CD83	45c + 25c grn	12.50	12.50
B6	CD83	70c + 30c brn	12.50	12.50
B7	CD83	90c + 35c red org	12.50	12.50
B8	CD83	1.25fr + 1fr rose pink	12.50	12.50
B9	CD83	2.25fr + 2fr blue	12.50	12.50
		Nos. B5-B9 (5)	62.50	62.50
		Set, never hinged	110.00	

See CB1.

Common Design Type and

Artillery Colonel — SP1

Colonial Infantry SP2

1941 **Unwmk.** ***Perf. 13½***

B10 SP1 1fr + 1fr red 1.60
B11 CD86 1.50fr + 3fr claret 1.60
B12 SP2 2.50fr + 1fr blue 1.60
Nos. B10-B12 (3) 4.80
Set, never hinged 6.50

Nos. B10-B12 were issued by the Vichy government in France, but were not placed on sale in Reunion. Nos. B10-B12 exist imperf. Value, set $200.

Nos. 176-177 Surcharged in Black or Red

1944 **Engr.** ***Perf. 12½x12***

B13 50c + 1.50fr on 2.50fr deep blue (R) .80
B14 + 2.50fr on 1fr yel brn .80
Set, never hinged 2.00

Colonial Development Fund.

Nos. B13-B14 were issued by the Vichy government in France, but were not placed on sale in Réunion.

Catalogue values for unused stamps in this section, from this point to the end of the section, are for Never Hinged items.

Red Cross Issue

Common Design Type

1944 ***Perf. 14½x14***

B15 CD90 5fr + 20fr black 1.60 1.10

The surtax was for the French Red Cross and national relief.

France Nos. B365-B366 Surcharged in Black

1962, Dec. 10 **Engr.** ***Perf. 13***

B16 SP219 10 + 5fr on 20 + 10c 2.50 2.50
B17 SP219 12 + 5fr on 25 + 10c 2.75 2.75

The surtax was for the Red Cross.

France Nos. B374-B375 Surcharged in Red

1963, Dec. 9

B18 SP223 10 + 5fr on 20 + 10c 3.00 3.00
B19 SP223 12 + 5fr on 25 + 10c 3.00 3.00

Centenary of the Intl. Red Cross. The surtax was for the Red Cross.

France Nos. B385-B386 Surcharged in Dark Blue

1964, Dec. 13 **Unwmk.** ***Perf. 13***

B20 SP230 10 + 5fr on 20 + 10c 1.75 1.75
B21 SP230 12 + 5fr on 25 + 10c 1.90 1.90

Jean Nicolas Corvisart (1755-1821) and Dominique Larrey (1766-1842), physicians. The surtax was for the Red Cross.

France Nos. B392-B393 Surcharged in Black

1965, Dec. 12 **Engr.** ***Perf. 13***

B22 SP233 12 + 5fr on 25 + 10c 1.60 1.60
B23 SP233 15 + 5fr on 30 + 10c 1.60 1.60

The surtax was for the Red Cross.

France Nos. B402-B403 Surcharged in Black

1966, Dec. 11 **Engr.** ***Perf. 13***

B24 SP237 12 + 5fr on 25 + 10c 1.50 1.50
B25 SP237 15 + 5fr on 30 + 10c 1.50 1.50

The surtax was for the Red Cross.

France Nos. B409-B410 Surcharged in Black

1967, Dec. 17 **Engr.** ***Perf. 13***

B26 SP240 12 + 5fr on 25 + 10c 3.00 3.00
B27 SP240 15 + 5fr on 30 + 10c 3.75 3.75

Surtax for the Red Cross.

France Nos. B421-B424 Surcharged in Black

1968-69 **Engr.** ***Perf. 13***

B28 SP244 12 + 5fr on 25 + 10c 1.70 1.50
B29 SP244 15 + 5fr on 30 + 10c 1.90 1.50
B30 SP244 20 + 7fr on 40 + 15c ('69) 1.60 1.50
B31 SP244 20 + 7fr on 40 + 15c ('69) 1.60 1.50
Nos. B28-B31 (4) 6.80 6.00

The surtax was for the Red Cross.

France No. B425 Surcharged in Black

1969, Mar. 17 **Engr.** ***Perf. 13***

B32 SP245 15fr + 5fr on 30c + 10c 1.40 1.40

Stamp Day.

France No. B440 Surcharged in Black

1970, Mar. 16 **Engr.** ***Perf. 13***

B33 SP249 20fr + 5fr on 40c + 10c 1.10 .95

Stamp day.

France Nos. B443-B444 Surcharged in Black

1970, Dec. 14 **Engr.** ***Perf. 13***

B34 SP252 20 + 7fr on 40 + 15c 2.40 2.00
B35 SP252 20 + 7fr on 40 + 15c 2.40 2.40

The surtax was for the Red Cross.

France No. B451 Surcharged in Black

1971, Mar. 29 **Engr.** ***Perf. 13***

B36 SP254 25fr + 5fr on 50c + 10c 1.10 .90

Stamp Day.

France Nos. B452-B453 Surcharged in Black

1971, Dec. 13

B37 SP255 15fr + 5fr on 30c + 10c 1.40 1.40
B38 SP255 25fr + 5fr on 50c + 10c 1.40 1.40

The surtax was for the Red Cross.

France No. B460 Surcharged in Black

1972, Mar. 20 **Engr.** ***Perf. 13***

B39 SP257 25fr + 5fr on 50c + 10c 1.20 1.20

Stamp Day.

France Nos. B461-B462 Surcharged in Red or Green

1972, Dec. 16 **Engr.** ***Perf. 13***

B40 SP258 15 + 5fr on 30 + 10c 1.20 1.20
B41 SP258 25 + 5fr on 50 + 10c (G) 1.40 1.40

Surtax was for the Red Cross.

France No. B470 Surcharged in Red

1973, Mar. 26 **Engr.** ***Perf. 13***

B42 SP260 25fr +5fr on 50c +10c 1.40 1.40

Stamp Day.

France Nos. B471-B472 Surcharged in Red

1973, Dec. 3 **Engr.** ***Perf. 13***

B43 SP261 15 +5fr on 30c +10c 1.40 1.40
B44 SP261 25 +5fr on 50c +10c 1.40 1.40

Surtax was for the Red Cross.

France No. B477 Surcharged

1974, Mar. 11 **Engr.** ***Perf. 13***

B45 SP263 25fr + 5fr on 50c + 10c 1.10 1.10

Stamp Day.

France Nos. B479-B480 Surcharged in Green or Red

1974, Nov. 30 **Engr.** ***Perf. 13***

B46 SP265 30 + 7fr on 60 + 15c (G) 1.40 1.40
B47 SP266 40 + 7fr on 80 + 15c (R) 1.40 1.40

Surtax was for the Red Cross.

AIR POST STAMPS

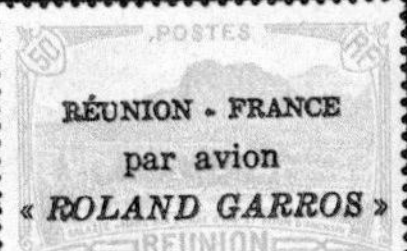

No. 141 Ovptd. in Blue

1937, Jan. 23 **Unwmk.** ***Perf. 12½***

C1 A23 50c red 290.00 250.00
a. Vert. pair, one without overprint 1,800. 1,800.
b. Inverted overprint 6,000.
c. As "b," in pair with unoverprinted stamp 26,000.

Flight of the "Roland Garros" from Reunion to France by aviators Laurent, Lenier and Touge in Jan.-Feb., 1937.

Airplane and Landscape — AP2

1938, Mar. 1 **Engr.** ***Perf. 12½***

C2 AP2 3.65fr slate blue & car 1.00 .90
C3 AP2 6.65fr brown & org red 1.00 .90
C4 AP2 9.65fr car & ultra 1.00 .90
C5 AP2 12.65fr brown & green 2.00 1.50
Nos. C2-C5 (4) 5.00 4.20
Set, never hinged 7.00

For overprints see Nos. C14-C17.

Plane and Bridge over East River AP3

Plane and Landscape AP4

1942, Oct. 19 ***Perf. 12x12½***

C6 AP3 50c olive & pur .35
C7 AP3 1fr dk bl & scar .35
C8 AP3 2fr brn & blk .60
C9 AP3 3fr rose lil & grn 1.10
C10 AP3 5fr red org & red brn 1.10

Frame Engr., Center Photo.

C11 AP4 10fr dk grn, red org & vio 1.10
C12 AP4 20fr dk bl, brn vio & red 1.10
C13 AP4 50fr brn car, Prus grn & bl 1.60
Nos. C6-C13 (8) 7.30
Set, never hinged 9.50

Nos. C6-C13 were issued by the Vichy government in France, but were not placed on sale in Réunion.

De Poivre AP4a

1943 ***Perf. 12½x12***

C13A AP4a 1fr sepia & red .25
C13B AP4a 2fr green & blue .35
C13C AP4a 3fr dk brown red .40
C13D AP4a 5fr ultra & red .55
C13E AP4a 10fr red brn & blk .55
C13F AP4a 20fr violet & green .75
Nos. C13A-C13F (6) 2.85
Set, never hinged 4.00

300th Ann. of French settlement on Réunion.

Nos. C13A-C13F were issued by the Vichy government in France, but were not placed on sale in Réunion.

Nos. C2-C5 Overprinted in Black or Carmine

1943 **Unwmk.** ***Perf. 12½***

C14 AP2 3.65fr sl bl & car 5.50 5.50
C15 AP2 6.65fr brn & org red 5.50 5.50
C16 AP2 9.65fr car & ultra (C) 5.50 5.50
C17 AP2 12.65fr brn & grn 5.50 5.50
Nos. C14-C17 (4) 22.00 22.00
Set, never hinged 32.50

Catalogue values for unused stamps in this section, from this point to the end of the section, are for Never Hinged items.

Common Design Type

1944 **Photo.** ***Perf. 14½x14***

C18 CD87 1fr dk org .50 .30
C19 CD87 1.50fr brt red .50 .30
C20 CD87 5fr brn red .70 .45
C21 CD87 10fr black 1.10 .80
C22 CD87 25fr ultra 1.25 .95
C23 CD87 50fr dk grn 1.25 .95
C24 CD87 100fr plum 1.75 1.25
Nos. C18-C24 (7) 7.05 5.00

Victory Issue
Common Design Type

1946, May 8 **Engr.** ***Perf. 12½***

C25 CD92 8fr olive gray 1.10 .90

European victory of the Allied Nations in WWII.

Chad to Rhine Issue
Common Design Types

1946, June 6

C26 CD93 5fr orange 1.40 .85
C27 CD94 10fr sepia 1.40 .85
C28 CD95 15fr grnsh blk 1.40 .85
C29 CD96 20fr lilac rose 1.90 1.25
C30 CD97 25fr greenish blue 1.90 1.25
C31 CD98 50fr green 2.25 1.50
Nos. C26-C31 (6) 10.25 6.55

Shadow of Plane — AP5

Plane over Réunion — AP6

Air View of Réunion and Shadow of Plane — AP7

Perf. 13x12½

1947, Mar. 24 **Photo.** **Unwmk.**

C32 AP5 50fr ol grn & bl gray 11.00 8.00
C33 AP6 100fr dk brn & org 17.00 12.50
C34 AP7 200fr dk bl & org 21.00 14.00
Nos. C32-C34 (3) 49.00 34.50

France, Nos. C18-C21 Surcharged in Carmine or Black

1949 **Unwmk.** ***Perf. 13***

C35 AP7 20fr on 40fr (C) 3.75 1.25
C36 AP8 25fr on 50fr 4.75 1.40
C37 AP9 50fr on 100fr (C) 11.00 4.25
C38 AP10 100fr on 200fr 55.00 21.00
Nos. C35-C38 (4) 74.50 27.90

France Nos. C24, C26 and C27 Surcharged in Black

No. C39

No. C40

No. C41

1949-51

C39 AP12 100fr on 200fr ('51) 145.00 26.50
C40 AP12 200fr on 500fr 55.00 21.00
C41 AP13 500fr on 1000fr ('51) 325.00 210.00
Nos. C39-C41 (3) 525.00 257.50

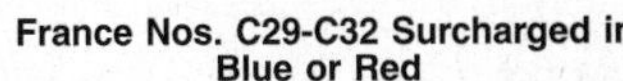

France Nos. C29-C32 Surcharged in Blue or Red

No. C42

No. C43

No. C44

No. C45

1954, Feb. 10

C42 AP15 50fr on 100fr 3.50 1.25
C43 AP15 100fr on 200fr (R) 5.50 1.40
C44 AP15 200fr on 500fr 45.00 12.50
C45 AP15 500fr on 1000fr 37.50 12.50
Nos. C42-C45 (4) 91.50 27.65

France Nos. C35-C36 Surcharged in Red or Black

No. C46

No. C47

1957-58 **Engr.** ***Perf. 13***

C46 AP17 200fr on 500fr (R) 25.00 6.75
C47 AP17 500fr on 1000fr ('58) 25.00 13.00

France Nos. C37, C39-C40 Surcharged in Red or Black

No. C48

No. C49

No. C50

1961-64

C48	AP15 100fr on 2fr	6.75	1.40
C49	AP17 200fr on 5fr	7.00	3.25
C50	AP17 500fr on 10fr (B;'64)	16.00	6.25
	Nos. C48-C50 (3)	29.75	10.90

France No. C41 Surcharged in Red

1967, Jan. 27 Engr. *Perf. 13*

C51	AP17 100fr on 2fr sl bl & ind	2.25	.80

France No. C45 Surcharged in Red

1972, May 14 Engr. *Perf. 13*

C52	AP21 200fr on 5fr multi	5.00	1.75

AIR POST SEMI-POSTAL STAMP

French Revolution Issue
Common Design Type

1939 Unwmk. *Perf. 13*
Name and Value Typo. in Orange

CB1	CD83 3.65fr + 4fr brn blk	25.00	25.00
	Never hinged	37.50	

Felix Guyon Hospital, St. Denis — SPAP1

Perf. 13½x12½

1942, June 22 Engr.

CB2	SPAP1 1.50fr + 3.50fr lt grn	1.00	
CB3	SPAP1 2fr + 6fr yel brn	1.00	
	Set, never hinged	2.50	

Native children's welfare fund.

Nos. CB2-CB3 were issued by the Vichy government in France, but were not placed on sale in Réunion.

Colonial Education Fund
Common Design Type

1942, June 22

CB4	CD86a 1.20fr + 1.80fr blue & red	.90	
	Never hinged	1.25	

No. CB4 was issued by the Vichy government in France, but was not placed on sale in Réunion.

POSTAGE DUE STAMPS

D1

1889-92 Unwmk. Type-set *Imperf.*
Without Gum

J1	D1	5c black	29.00	16.00
J2	D1	10c black	35.00	16.00
J3	D1	15c black ('92)	67.50	42.50
J4	D1	20c black	50.00	27.50
J5	D1	30c black	45.00	27.50
		Nos. J1-J5 (5)	226.50	129.50

Ten varieties of each value.

Nos. J1-J2, J4-J5 issued on yellowish paper in 1889; Nos. J1-J3, J5 on bluish white paper in 1892.

Nos. J1-J5 exist with double impression. Values, each $125-$190.

D2

1907 Typo. *Perf. 14x13½*

J6	D2	5c carmine, *yel*	.90	.90
J7	D2	10c blue, *bl*	.90	.90
J8	D2	15c black, *bluish*	1.50	1.50
J9	D2	20c carmine	1.50	1.50
J10	D2	30c green, *grnsh*	2.25	2.25
J11	D2	50c red, *green*	2.60	2.60
J12	D2	60c carmine, *bl*	2.60	2.60
J13	D2	1fr violet	3.00	3.00
		Nos. J6-J13 (8)	15.25	15.25
		Set, never hinged	27.50	

Type of 1907 Issue Surcharged

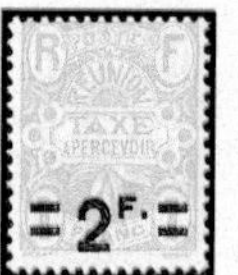

1927

J14	D2	2fr on 1fr org red	12.50	12.50
J15	D2	3fr on 1fr org brn	12.50	12.50
		Set, never hinged	40.00	

Arms of Réunion — D3

1933 Engr. *Perf. 13x13½*

J16	D3	5c deep violet	.25	.25
J17	D3	10c dark green	.25	.25
J18	D3	15c orange brown	.25	.25
J19	D3	20c light red	.35	.35
J20	D3	30c olive green	.35	.35
J21	D3	50c ultramarine	.80	.80
J22	D3	60c black brown	.80	.80
J23	D3	1fr light violet	.80	.80
J24	D3	2fr deep blue	.80	.80
J25	D3	3fr carmine	1.00	1.00
		Nos. J16-J25 (10)	5.65	5.65
		Set, never hinged	8.75	

Catalogue values for unused stamps in this section, from this point to the end of the section, are for Never Hinged items.

Numeral — D4

1947 Unwmk. Photo. *Perf. 13*

J26	D4	10c dark violet	.25	.25
J27	D4	30c brown	.25	.25
J28	D4	50c blue green	.25	.25
J29	D4	1fr orange	.60	.45
J30	D4	2fr red violet	.60	.45
J31	D4	3fr red brown	.85	.65
J32	D4	4fr blue	1.50	1.10
J33	D4	5fr henna brown	2.00	1.40
J34	D4	10fr slate green	2.00	1.40
J35	D4	20fr violet blue	2.00	.90
		Nos. J26-J35 (10)	10.30	7.10

France, Nos. J83-J92 Surcharged in Black

1949-53

J36	D5	10c on 1fr brt ultra	.25	.25
J37	D5	50c on 2fr turq bl	.45	.40
J38	D5	1fr on 3fr brn org	.60	.40
J39	D5	2fr on 4fr dp vio	.60	.40
J40	D5	3fr on 5fr brt pink	6.50	2.75
J41	D5	5fr on 10fr red org	1.10	.70
J42	D5	10fr on 20fr ol bis	2.00	2.00
J43	D5	20fr on 50fr dk grn ('50)	12.50	5.50
J44	D5	50fr on 100fr dp grn ('53)	30.00	13.00
		Nos. J36-J44 (9)	54.00	25.40

France Nos. J93, J95-J96 Surcharged

1962-63 Typo. *Perf. 14x13½*

J46	D6	1fr on 5c brt pink ('63)	3.00	1.10
J47	D6	10fr on 20c ol bis ('63)	5.50	2.75
J48	D6	20fr on 50c dk grn	22.00	12.50
		Nos. J46-J48 (3)	30.50	16.35

France Nos. J98-J102, J104-J105 Surcharged

1964-71 Unwmk. *Perf. 14x13½*

J49	D7	1fr on 5c	.25	.25
J50	D7	5fr on 10c	.30	.25
J51	D7	7fr on 15c	.50	.45
J52	D7	10fr on 20c ('71)	1.40	.55
J53	D7	15fr on 30c	.65	.45
J54	D7	20fr on 50c	.80	.55
J55	D7	50fr on 1fr	1.40	1.25
		Nos. J49-J55 (7)	5.30	3.75

PARCEL POST STAMP

Frame Typographed; Center Handstamped — PP1

1890-1903 Unwmk. Typo. *Imperf.*

Q1	PP1	10c black, *yellow*, black frame	400.00	200.00
Q2	PP1	10c black, *yellow*, ultra frame	110.00	100.00
Q3	PP1	10c black, *yellow*, bl grn frame	30.00	27.50

No. 40 Overprinted

1906 Unwmk. *Perf. 14x13½*

Q4	A14	10c red	22.50	22.50

Fiscal Stamps Surcharged — PP2

1907-23 Unwmk. Typo. *Perf. 14*

Q5	PP2	10c blk on grayish brn ('07)	17.50	15.00
Q6	PP2	10c red on gray ('23)	17.50	15.00

FRENCH COLONIES

ˈfrench ˈkä-lə-nēz

From 1859 to 1906 and from 1943 to 1945 special stamps were issued for use in all French Colonies which did not have stamps of their own.

100 Centimes = 1 Franc

Catalogue values for unused stamps in this country are for Never Hinged items, beginning with Scott B1 in the semi-postal section and Scott J23 in the postage due section.

Perforations: Nos. 1-45 are known variously perforated privately.

Gum: Many of Nos. 1-45 were issued without gum. Some were gummed locally.

Reprints: Nos. 1-7, 9-12, 24, 26-42, 44 and 45 were reprinted officially in 1887. These reprints are ungummed and the colors of both design and paper are deeper or brighter than the originals. Value for Nos. 1-6, $20 each.

Eagle and Crown — A1

1859-65 Unwmk. Typo. *Imperf.*

1	A1	1c ol grn, *pale bl* ('62)	24.00	*27.50*
2	A1	5c yel grn, *grnsh* ('62)	24.00	16.00
3	A1	10c bister, *yel*	32.50	8.00
a.		Pair, one sideways	1,000.	525.00
4	A1	20c bl, *bluish* ('65)	35.00	13.50
5	A1	40c org, *yelsh*	27.50	13.50
6	A1	80c car rose, *pnksh* ('65)	110.00	60.00
		Nos. 1-6 (6)	253.00	138.50

For surcharges, see Reunion Nos. 1-4.

Napoleon III
A2 A3

Ceres
A4

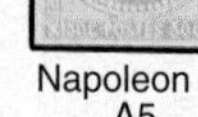

Napoleon III
A5

1871-72 *Imperf.*

7	A2	1c ol grn, *pale bl* ('72)	80.00	80.00
8	A3	5c yel grn, *grnsh* ('72)	1,000.	400.00
9	A4	10c bis, *yelsh*	375.00	130.00
a.		Tête bêche pair	*55,000.*	*22,500.*
10	A4	15c bis, *yelsh* ('72)	325.00	13.00
11	A4	20c blue, *bluish*	750.00	125.00
a.		Tête bêche pair	—	18,000.
12	A4	25c bl, *bluish* ('72)	175.00	13.00
13	A5	30c brn, *yelsh*	175.00	60.00
14	A4	40c org, *yelsh* (I)	250.00	13.00
a.		Type II	*3,500.*	*650.00*
b.		Pair, types I & II	*7,250.*	*1,750.*
15	A5	80c rose, *pnksh*	1,100.	115.00
		Nos. 7-15 (9)	4,230.	949.00

For 40c types I-II see illustrations over France #1.

For surcharges, see Reunion Nos. 5-6.

See note after France No. 9 for additional information on Nos. 8-9, 11-12, 14.

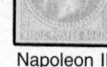

Ceres
A6 A7

1872-77 ***Imperf.***

16 A6	1c ol grn, *pale bl* ('73)	13.00	*14.50*
17 A6	2c red brn, *yelsh* ('76)	475.00	750.00
18 A6	4c gray ('76)	*11,000.*	475.00
19 A6	5c grn, *pale bl*	17.50	9.50
20 A7	10c bis, *rose* ('76)	240.00	13.00
21 A7	15c bister ('77)	525.00	100.00
22 A7	30c brn, *yelsh*	130.00	21.00
23 A7	80c rose, *pnksh* ('73)	625.00	140.00

No. 17 was used only in Cochin China, 1876-77. Excellent forgeries of Nos. 17 and 18 exist.

With reference to the stamps of France and French Colonies in the same designs and colors see the note after France No. 9.

Peace and Commerce — A8

1877-78 **Type I** ***Imperf.***

24	A8	1c grn, *grnsh*	35.00	*45.00*
25	A8	4c grn, *grnsh*	24.00	14.50
26	A8	30c brn, *yelsh* ('78)	52.50	52.50
27	A8	40c ver, *straw*	35.00	21.00
28	A8	75c rose, *rose* ('78)	75.00	*100.00*
29	A8	1fr brnz grn, *straw*	60.00	67.50
		Nos. 24-29 (6)	281.50	300.50

Type II

30	A8	2c grn, *grnsh*	17.50	11.00
31	A8	5c grn, *grnsh*	24.00	5.50
32	A8	10c grn, *grnsh*	125.00	24.00
33	A8	15c gray, *grnsh*	250.00	72.50
34	A8	20c red brn, *straw*	52.50	9.50
35	A8	25c ultra *bluish*	52.50	8.75
a.		25c blue, *bluish* ('78)	*4,250.*	175.00
36	A8	35c vio blk, *org* ('78)	67.50	32.50
		Nos. 30-36 (7)	589.00	163.75
		Nos. 24-36 (13)	870.50	464.25

Type II

1878-80

38	A8	1c blk, *lil bl*	21.00	21.00
39	A8	2c brn, *buff*	21.00	*24.00*
40	A8	4c claret, *lav*	32.50	*45.00*
41	A8	10c blk, *lav* ('79)	120.00	27.50
42	A8	15c blue ('79)	35.00	17.50
43	A8	20c red, *grn* ('79)	87.50	17.50
44	A8	25c blk, *red* ('79)	600.00	275.00
45	A8	25c yel, *straw* ('80)	725.00	32.50
		Nos. 38-45 (8)	1,642.	460.00

No. 44 was used only in Mayotte, Nossi-Be and New Caledonia. Forgeries exist.

The 3c yellow, 3c gray, 15c yellow, 20c blue, 25c rose and 5fr lilac were printed together with the reprints, and were never issued.

For stamps of type A8 surcharged and with "SPM" see St. Pierre & Miquelon Nos. 1-8.

Commerce — A9

1881-86 ***Perf. 14x13½***

46	A9	1c blk, *lil bl*	5.50	4.75
47	A9	2c brn, *buff*	5.50	4.75
48	A9	4c claret, *lav*	5.50	5.50
49	A9	5c grn, *grnsh*	6.50	3.25
50	A9	10c blk, *lavender*	11.00	4.75
51	A9	15c blue	16.00	3.25
52	A9	20c red, *yel grn*	52.50	18.00
53	A9	25c yel, *straw*	17.50	5.50
54	A9	25c blk, *rose* ('86)	24.00	3.25
55	A9	30c brn, *bis*	45.00	21.00
56	A9	35c vio blk, *yel org*	40.00	30.00
a.		35c violet black, *yellow*	100.00	52.50
57	A9	40c ver, *straw*	45.00	27.50
58	A9	75c car, *rose*	120.00	60.00
59	A9	1fr brnz grn, *straw*	80.00	45.00
		Nos. 46-59 (14)	474.00	236.50

Nos. 46-59 exist imperforate. They are proofs and were not used for postage, except the 10c.

For stamps of type A9 surcharged with numerals see: Cochin China, Diego Suarez, Gabon, Malagasy (Madagascar), Nossi-Be, New Caledonia, Reunion, Senegal, Tahiti.

For stamps of type A9 surcharged and with "MQE" see Martinique Nos. 3-4. For stamps of type A9 surcharged and with "SPM" see St. Pierre & Miquelon Nos. 9-11, 15-18.

SEMI-POSTAL STAMPS

Catalogue values for unused stamps in this section are for Never Hinged items.

Resistance Fighters — SP1

1943 Unwmk. Litho. ***Rouletted***

B1	SP1	1.50fr + 98.50fr ind & gray	47.50	*65.00*
		Without label	21.00	*35.00*

The surtax was for the benefit of patriots and the French Committee of Liberation.

No. B1 was printed in sheets of 10 (5x2) with adjoining labels showing the Lorraine cross.

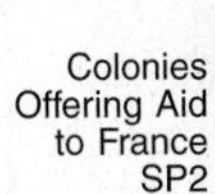

Colonies Offering Aid to France SP2

1943 ***Perf. 12***

B2	SP2	9fr + 41fr red violet	3.50	10.50

Surtax for the benefit of French patriots.

Patriots and Map of France SP3

1943

B3	SP3	50c + 4.50fr yel grn	1.25	*10.50*
B4	SP3	1.50fr + 8.50fr cerise	1.25	*10.50*
B5	SP3	3fr + 12fr grnsh bl	1.25	*10.50*
B6	SP3	5fr + 15fr olive gray	1.25	*1.50*
		Nos. B3-B6 (4)	5.00	33.00

Surtax for the aid of combatants and patriots.

Refugee Family SP4

1943

B7	SP4	10fr + 40fr dull blue	5.25	*12.50*

The surtax was for refugee relief work.

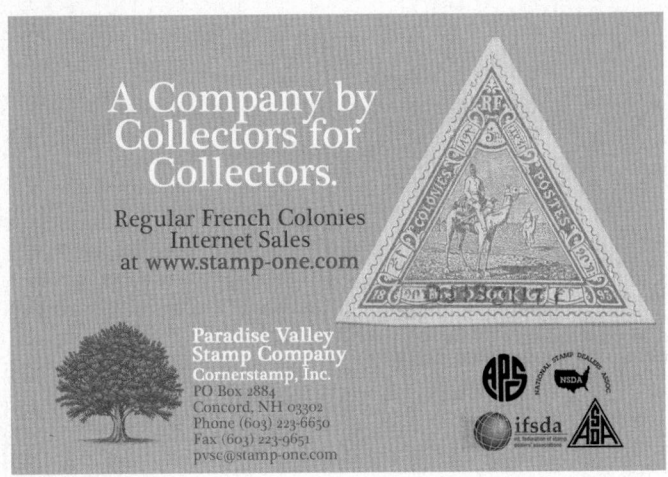

Woman and Child with Wing — SP5

1944

B8	SP5	10fr + 40fr grnsh blk	6.75	*21.00*

Surtax for the benefit of aviation.

Nos. B1-B8 were prepared for use in the French Colonies, but after the landing of Free French troops in Corsica they were used there and later also in Southern France. They became valid throughout France in Nov. 1944.

POSTAGE DUE STAMPS

D1

1884-85 Unwmk. Typo. ***Imperf.***

J1	D1	1c black	4.00	4.00
J2	D1	2c black	4.00	4.00
J3	D1	3c black	4.00	4.00
J4	D1	4c black	4.75	4.00
J5	D1	5c black	6.50	3.25
J6	D1	10c black	8.75	6.50
J7	D1	15c black	13.00	10.50
J8	D1	20c black	16.00	10.50
J9	D1	30c black	17.50	8.75
J10	D1	40c black	21.00	8.75
J11	D1	60c black	27.50	16.00
J12	D1	1fr brown	35.00	27.50
a.		1fr black	300.00	
J13	D1	2fr brown	35.00	27.50
a.		2fr black	300.00	*325.00*
J14	D1	5fr brown	110.00	67.50
a.		5fr black	425.00	*450.00*

Nos. J12a, J13a and J14a were not regularly issued.

1894-1906

J15	D1	5c blue	1.60	1.60
J16	D1	10c brown	1.60	1.60
J17	D1	15c pale green	1.60	1.60
J18	D1	20c olive grn ('06)	1.60	1.60
J19	D1	30c carmine	2.75	1.60
J20	D1	50c lilac	2.75	1.60
J21	D1	60c brown, *buff*	4.50	2.75
a.		60c dark violet, *buff*	4.75	2.75
J22	D1	1fr red, *buff*	7.50	4.50
a.		1fr rose, *buff*	27.50	19.00
		Nos. J15-J22 (8)	23.90	16.85

For overprints see New Caledonia Nos. J1-J8.

Catalogue values for unused stamps in this section, from this point to the end of the section, are for Never Hinged items.

D2

1945 Litho. ***Perf. 12***

J23	D2	10c slate blue	.45	*16.00*
J24	D2	15c yel green	.45	*16.00*
J25	D2	25c deep orange	.45	*16.00*
J26	D2	50c greenish blk	1.00	*16.00*
J27	D2	60c copper brn	1.00	*16.00*
J28	D2	1fr deep red lil	1.00	*16.00*
J29	D2	2fr red	1.00	*16.00*
J30	D2	4fr slate gray	4.50	*20.00*
J31	D2	5fr brt ultra	4.50	*20.00*
J32	D2	10fr purple	22.50	*52.50*
J33	D2	20fr dull brown	4.00	*20.00*
J34	D2	50fr deep green	7.25	*27.50*
		Nos. J23-J34 (12)	48.10	252.00

FRENCH CONGO

'french 'käŋ-ˌgō

LOCATION — Central Africa
GOVT. — French possession

French Congo was originally a separate colony, but was joined in 1888 to Gabon and placed under one commissioner-general with a lieutenant-governor presiding in Gabon and another in French Congo. In 1894 the military holdings in Ubangi were attached to French Congo, and in 1900 the Chad military protectorate was added. Postal service was not established in Ubangi or Chad, however, at that time. In 1906 Gabon and Middle Congo were separated and French Congo ceased to exist as such. Chad and Ubangi remained attached to Middle Congo as the joint dependency of "Ubangi-Chari-Chad," and Middle Congo stamps were used there.

Issues of the Republic of the Congo are listed under Congo People's Republic (ex-French).

100 Centimes = 1 Franc

Watermarks

Wmk. 122 Thistle Branch

Wmk. 123 — Rose Branch

Wmk. 124 Olive Branch

Stamps of French Colonies Surcharged Horizontally in Red or Black

1891 Unwmk. *Perf. 14x13½*

No.	Description	Unused	Used
1	A9 5c on 1c blk, *lil bl* (R)	*6,500.*	*4,750.*
a.	Double surcharge	20,000.	
2	A9 5c on 1c blk, *lil bl*	200.00	110.00
a.	Double surcharge	650.00	425.00
3	A9 5c on 15c blue	350.00	180.00
a.	Double surcharge	725.00	375.00
5	A9 5c on 25c blk, *rose*	130.00	52.50
a.	Inverted surcharge		
b.	Surcharge vertical	275.00	115.00
c.	Double surcharge	600.00	600.00

First "O" of "Congo" is a Capital, "Francais" with Capital "F"

1891-92

No.	Description	Unused	Used
6	A9 5c on 20c red, *grn*	1,300.	425.00
7	A9 5c on 25c blk, *rose*	200.00	100.00
a.	Surcharge vertical	250.00	110.00
8	A9 10c on 25c blk, *rose*	240.00	67.50
a.	Inverted surcharge	400.00	160.00
b.	Surcharge vertical	300.00	100.00
d.	Double surcharge	400.00	225.00
9	A9 10c on 40c red, *straw*	2,750.	400.00
10	A9 15c on 25c blk, *rose*	225.00	52.50
a.	Surcharge vertical	260.00	92.50
c.	Double surcharge	400.00	200.00

First "O" of Congo small Surcharge Vert., Down or Up No Period

No.	Description	Unused	Used
11	A9 5c on 25c blk, *rose*	300.00	135.00
12	A9 10c on 25c blk, *rose*		—
13	A9 15c on 25c blk, *rose*	425.00	190.00

The listings Nos. 5a and 12 are being re-evaluated. The Catalogue Editors would appreciate any information on these stamps.

Postage Due Stamps of French Colonies Surcharged in Red or Black Reading Down or Up

1892 *Imperf.*

No.	Description	Unused	Used
14	D1 5c on 5c blk (R)	200.00	140.00
a.	Double surcharge	1,450.	
15	D1 5c on 20c blk (R)	200.00	140.00
16	D1 5c on 30c blk (R)	260.00	180.00
17	D1 10c on 1fr brown	200.00	140.00
a.	Double surcharge	4,100.	
b.	Surcharge horiz.		*2,400.*
c.	"Congo" omitted		*475.00*
	Nos. 14-17 (4)	860.00	600.00

Excellent counterfeits of Nos. 1-17 exist.

Navigation and Commerce — A3

1892-1900 Typo. *Perf. 14x13½*

Colony Name in Blue or Carmine

No.	Description	Unused	Used
18	A3 1c blk, *lil bl*	1.60	1.60
a.	Name double	225.00	175.00
19	A3 2c brn, *buff*	4.00	3.25
a.	Name double	225.00	175.00
20	A3 4c claret, *lav*	4.00	3.25
a.	Name in blk and in blue	225.00	175.00
21	A3 5c grn, *grnsh*	8.00	8.00
22	A3 10c blk, *lavender*	24.00	20.00
a.	Name double	850.00	600.00
23	A3 10c red ('00)	4.00	4.00
24	A3 15c blue, quadrille paper	55.00	20.00
25	A3 15c gray ('00)	12.00	8.00
26	A3 20c red, *grn*	24.00	20.00
27	A3 25c blk, *rose*	24.00	16.00
28	A3 25c blue ('00)	12.00	*12.00*
29	A3 30c brn, *bis*	40.00	24.00
30	A3 40c red, *straw*	55.00	32.50
31	A3 50c car, *rose*	55.00	40.00
32	A3 50c brn, *az* ('00)	16.00	16.00
a.	Name double	775.00	775.00
33	A3 75c dp vio, *org*	47.50	40.00
34	A3 1fr brnz grn, *straw*	55.00	40.00
	Nos. 18-34 (17)	441.10	308.60

Perf. 13½x14 stamps are counterfeits.

For surcharges see Nos. 50-51.

No. 21 exists in yellow green on pale green. The stamp was prepared but not issued. Value, $4,000.

Leopard — A4

Type I

Type II

Bakalois Woman — A5

Coconut Grove — A6

Design A4 exists in two types. Type 1: end of left tusk extends behind and above right tusk. Type 2: end of left tusk does not appear behind right tusk. Type 2 of design A4 appears in position 91 of each pane of 100. For detailed listings, see the *Scott Catalogue Classic Specialized of Stamps & Covers.*

1900-04 Wmk. 122 *Perf. 11*

No.	Description	Unused	Used
35	A4 1c brn vio & gray lilac	.80	.80
a.	Background inverted	75.00	75.00
36	A4 2c brn & yel	.80	.80
a.	Imperf., pair	80.00	*80.00*
b.	Pair, imperf between	100.00	*110.00*
37	A4 4c scar & gray bl	1.60	1.20
a.	Background inverted	95.00	87.50
b.	Type 2	55.00	55.00
38	A4 5c grn & gray grn	2.75	1.60
a.	Imperf., pair	140.00	140.00
39	A4 10c red & rose pink	8.00	3.25
a.	Imperf., pair	140.00	140.00
40	A4 15c dl vio & ol grn	2.40	1.20
a.	Imperf. pair	110.00	

Wmk. 123

No.	Description	Unused	Used
41	A5 20c yel grn & org (1)	2.40	2.00
42	A5 25c bl & pale bl	3.50	2.40
43	A5 30c car rose & org	5.50	2.40
44	A5 40c org brn & brt grn	8.00	2.75
a.	Imperf., pair	110.00	110.00
b.	Center and value inverted	200.00	170.00
45	A5 50c gray vio & lil	8.00	6.50
46	A5 75c red vio & org	20.00	11.00
a.	Imperf., pair	110.00	110.00

Wmk. 124

No.	Description	Unused	Used
47	A6 1fr gray lil & ol	24.00	20.00
a.	Center and value inverted	300.00	300.00
b.	Imperf., pair	140.00	140.00
48	A6 2fr car & brn	47.50	32.50
a.	Imperf., pair	300.00	300.00
49	A6 5fr brn org & gray	87.50	72.50
a.	5fr ocher & gray	750.00	*950.00*
b.	Center and value inverted	450.00	450.00
c.	Wmk. 123	500.00	500.00
d.	Imperf., pair	800.00	800.00
	Nos. 35-49 (15)	222.75	160.90

For surcharges see Nos. 52-53.

Nos. 26 and 29 Surcharged in Black

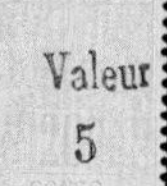

1900 Unwmk. *Perf. 14x13½*

No.	Description	Unused	Used
50	A3 5c on 20c red, *grn*	*26,000.*	*6,000.*
a.	Double surcharge		*18,000.*
51	A3 15c on 30c brn, *bis*	*20,000.*	*2,600.*
a.	Double surcharge		*6,000.*

Nos. 43 and 48 Surcharged in Black

a

b

1903 Wmk. 123 *Perf. 11*

No.	Description	Unused	Used
52	A5 5c on 30c	325.00	160.00
a.	Inverted surcharge	*2,750.*	

Wmk. 124

No.	Description	Unused	Used
53	A6 10c on 2fr	375.00	160.00
a.	Inverted surcharge	*2,750.*	
b.	Double surcharge	*3,250.*	

Counterfeits of the preceding surcharges are known.

FRENCH EQUATORIAL AFRICA

ˈfrench ˌē-kwə-ˈtōr-ē-əl ˈa-fri-kə

LOCATION — North of Belgian Congo and south of Libya
GOVT. — French Colony
AREA — 959,256 square miles
POP. — 4,491,785
CAPITAL — Brazzaville

In 1910 Gabon and Middle Congo, with its military dependencies, were politically united as French Equatorial Africa. The component colonies were granted administrative autonomy. In 1915 Ubangi-Chari-Chad was made an autonomous civilian colony and in 1920 Chad was made a civil colony. In 1934 the four colonies were administratively united as one colony, but this federation was not completed until 1936. Each colony had its own postal administration until 1936. The postal issues of the former colonial subdivisions are listed under the names of those colonies.

In 1958, French Equatorial Africa was divided into four republics: Chad, Congo, Gabon and Central African Republic (formerly Ubangi-Chari).

Stamps other than Nos. 189-192 are inscribed with "Afrique Equatoriale Francaise" or "AEF" and the name of one of the component colonies are listed under those colonies.

100 Centimes = 1 Franc

Catalogue values for unused stamps in this country are for Never Hinged items, beginning with Scott 142 in the regular postage section, Scott B8A in the semi-postal section, Scott C17 in the airpost section, and Scott J12 in the postage due section.

Stamps of Gabon, 1932, Overprinted "Afrique Equatoriale Francaise" and Bars Similar to "a" and "b" in Black

Perf. 13x13½, 13½x13

1936 **Unwmk.**

No.	Type	Value	Description	Unused	Used
1	A16	1c	brown violet	.40	*.80*
2	A16	2c	black, *rose*	.80	*.80*
3	A16	4c	green	1.20	1.60
4	A16	5c	grnsh blue	1.20	1.60
5	A16	10c	red, *yel*	1.20	1.60
6	A17	40c	brown violet	4.00	3.25
7	A17	50c	red brown	3.25	2.40
8	A17	1fr	yel grn, *bl*	32.50	16.00
9	A18	1.50fr	dull blue	8.00	4.00
10	A18	2fr	brown red	20.00	16.00
			Nos. 1-10 (10)	72.55	48.05

Stamps of Middle Congo, 1933 Overprinted in Black

a

b

c

1936

No.	Type	Value	Description	Unused	Used
11	A4 (b)	1c	lt brown	.40	*.50*
12	A4 (b)	2c	dull blue	.40	*.50*
13	A4 (b)	4c	olive green	1.60	1.60
14	A4 (b)	5c	red violet	.80	1.00
15	A4 (b)	10c	slate	1.60	1.25
16	A4 (b)	15c	dk violet	2.00	1.60
17	A4 (b)	20c	red, *pink*	2.00	1.60
18	A4 (b)	25c	orange	4.00	2.40
19	A5 (a)	40c	orange brn	5.50	2.75
20	A5 (c)	50c	black violet	5.50	2.40
21	A5 (c)	75c	black, *pink*	5.50	4.75
22	A5 (a)	90c	carmine	5.50	4.00
23	A5 (c)	1.50fr	dark blue	4.75	2.00
24	A6 (a)	5fr	slate blue	55.00	35.00
25	A6 (a)	10fr	black	35.00	30.00
26	A6 (a)	20fr	dark brown	35.00	32.50
			Nos. 11-26 (16)	164.55	123.85

Other overprints inscribed "Afrique Equitoriale Française" in a different type font on earlier Middle Congo stamps are listed under Middle Congo.

Common Design Types pictured following the introduction.

Paris International Exposition Issue

Common Design Types

1937, Apr. 15 **Engr.** ***Perf. 13***

No.	Type	Value	Description	Unused	Used
27	CD74	20c	dark violet	2.40	2.40
28	CD75	30c	dark green	2.40	2.40
29	CD76	40c	carmine rose	2.40	2.40
30	CD77	50c	dk brn & bl	2.40	2.40
31	CD78	90c	red	3.25	3.25
32	CD79	1.50fr	ultra	3.25	3.25
			Nos. 27-32 (6)	16.10	16.10

Logging on Loéme River — A1

People of Chad — A2

Pierre Savorgnan de Brazza A3

Emile Gentil — A4

Paul Crampel A5

Governor Victor Liotard A6

Two types of 25c:
Type I — Wide numerals (4mm).
Type II — Narrow numerals (3½mm).

1937-40 **Photo.** ***Perf. 13½x13***

No.	Type	Value	Description	Unused	Used
33	A1	1c	brown & yel	.25	.25
34	A1	2c	violet & grn	.25	.25
35	A1	3c	blue & yel ('40)	.25	.30
36	A1	4c	magenta & bl	.25	.30
37	A1	5c	dk & lt green	.25	.30
38	A2	10c	magenta & blue	.25	.30
39	A2	15c	blue & buff	.25	.30
40	A2	20c	brown & yellow	.25	*.30*
41	A2	25c	cop red & bl (I)	.80	.30
a.			Type II	2.75	2.00
42	A3	30c	gray grn & grn	.80	.55
43	A3	30c	chlky bl, ind & buff ('40)	.40	.50
44	A2	35c	dp grn & yel ('38)	.80	.80
45	A3	40c	cop red & bl	.40	.30
46	A3	45c	dk bl & lt grn	4.75	3.50
47	A3	45c	dp grn & yel grn ('40)	.40	.80
48	A3	50c	brown & yellow	.50	.25
49	A3	55c	pur & bl ('38)	.80	.80
50	A3	60c	mar & gray bl ('40)	.80	.85
51	A4	65c	dk bl & lt grn	.80	.40
52	A4	70c	dp vio & buff ('40)	.80	.95
53	A4	75c	ol blk & dl yel	5.50	4.50
54	A4	80c	brn & yel ('38)	.40	.80
55	A4	90c	copper red & buff	.55	.40
56	A4	1fr	dk vio & lt grn	2.40	1.20
57	A3	1fr	cer & dl org ('38)	4.00	1.60
58	A4	1fr	bl grn & sl grn ('40)	.40	.55
59	A5	1.25fr	cop red & buff	2.40	1.20
60	A5	1.40fr	dk brn & pale grn ('40)	1.20	1.25
61	A5	1.50fr	dk & lt blue	1.60	.80
62	A5	1.60fr	dp vio & buff ('40)	1.60	1.25
63	A5	1.75fr	brn & yel	2.00	1.20
64	A4	1.75fr	bl & lt bl ('38)	.80	.80
65	A5	2fr	dk & lt green	1.60	.80
66	A6	2.15fr	brn, vio & yel ('38)	1.20	.80
67	A6	2.25fr	bl & lt bl ('39)	1.60	1.60
68	A6	2.50fr	rose lake & buff ('40)	2.00	1.40
69	A6	3fr	dk blue & buff	.80	.50
70	A6	5fr	dk & lt green	1.60	1.20
71	A6	10fr	dk violet & bl	3.25	3.25
72	A6	20fr	ol blk & dl yel	4.00	3.50
			Nos. 33-72 (40)	52.95	40.90

For overprints and surcharges see Nos. 80-127, 129-141, B2-B3, B10-B13, B22-B23.

Colonial Arts Exhibition Issue

Souvenir Sheet

Common Design Type

1937 ***Imperf.***

No.	Type	Value	Description	Unused	Used
73	CD79	3fr	red brown	12.00	*16.00*
			Never hinged	16.00	

Count Louis Edouard Bouet-Willaumez and His Ship "La Malouine" — A7

1938, Dec. 5 ***Perf. 13½***

No.	Type	Value	Description	Unused	Used
74	A7	65c	gray brown	1.25	1.25
75	A7	1fr	deep rose	1.25	1.25
76	A7	1.75fr	blue	1.60	1.60
77	A7	2fr	dull violet	2.40	2.40
			Nos. 74-77 (4)	6.50	6.50
			Set, never hinged	8.85	

Centenary of Gabon.

New York World's Fair Issue

Common Design Type

1939, May 10 **Engr.** ***Perf. 12½x12***

No.	Type	Value	Description	Unused	Used
78	CD82	1.25fr	car lake	.80	1.60
79	CD82	2.25fr	ultra	.80	1.60
			Set, never hinged	2.40	

Libreville View and Marshal Petain A7a

1941 **Engr.** ***Perf. 12½x12***

No.	Type	Value	Description	Unused	Used
79A	A7a	1fr	bluish green	.40	
79B	A7a	2.50fr	blue	.40	
			Set, never hinged	1.60	

Nos. 79A-79B were issued by the Vichy government in France, but were not placed on sale in French Equatorial Africa.

For surcharges, see Nos. B36-B37.

Stamps of 1936-40, Overprinted in Carmine or Black

Nos. 80-82, 84-88, 93

Nos. 83, 89-92, 94-125

1940-41 ***Perf. 13½x13***

No.	Type	Value	Description	Unused	Used
80	A1	1c	brn & yel (C)	4.00	4.00
81	A1	2c	vio & grn (C)	4.00	4.00
82	A1	3c	blue & yel (C)	4.00	4.00
83	A4	4c	ol grn (No. 13)	24.00	16.00
b.			Inverted overprint	120.00	*150.00*
84	A1	5c	dk grn & lt grn (C)	4.00	4.00
85	A2	10c	magenta & bl	4.00	4.00
86	A2	15c	blue & buff (C)	4.00	4.00
87	A2	20c	brn & yel (C)	4.00	4.00
88	A2	25c	cop red & bl	4.00	4.00
89	A3	30c	gray grn & grn (C)	16.00	16.00
90	A3	30c	gray grn & grn ('41)	16.00	16.00
91	A3	30c	chlky bl, ind & buff (C) ('41)	16.00	16.00
92	A3	30c	chlky bl, ind & buff ('41)	16.00	16.00
93	A2	35c	dp grn & yel (C)	4.00	4.00
94	A3	40c	cop red & bl	4.00	4.00
b.			Inverted overprint		*100.00*
95	A3	45c	dp grn & yel grn (C)	4.00	4.00
96	A3	45c	dp grn & yel grn ('41)	16.00	16.00
97	A3	50c	brn & yel (C)	4.00	4.00
98	A3	50c	brn & yel ('41)	8.00	8.00
99	A3	55c	pur & bl (C)	4.00	4.00
100	A3	55c	pur & bl ('41)	16.00	16.00
101	A3	60c	mar & gray bl	4.00	4.00
102	A4	65c	dk bl & lt grn	4.00	4.00
103	A4	70c	dp vio & buff	4.00	4.00
104	A4	75c	ol blk & dl yel	80.00	80.00
105	A4	80c	brown & yellow	4.00	4.00
106	A4	90c	cop red & buff	4.00	4.00
107	A4	1fr	bl grn & sl grn	8.00	8.00
108	A4	1fr	bl grn & sl grn (C) ('41)	20.00	20.00
109	A3	1fr	cer & dl org	4.00	4.00
110	A5	1.40fr	dk brn & pale grn	4.00	4.00
111	A5	1.50fr	dk bl & lt bl	4.00	4.00
112	A5	1.60fr	dp vio & buff	4.00	4.00
113	A5	1.75fr	brown & yel	4.00	4.00
114	A6	2.15fr	brn, vio & yel	4.00	4.00
115	A6	2.25fr	bl & lt bl (C)	4.00	4.00
116	A6	2.25fr	bl & lt bl ('41)	16.00	16.00
117	A6	2.50fr	rose lake & buff	4.00	4.00
118	A6	3fr	dk bl & buff (C)	4.00	4.00
119	A6	3fr	dk bl & buff ('41)	16.00	16.00
120	A6	5fr	dk grn & lt grn (C)	4.00	4.00
121	A6	5fr	dk grn & lt grn ('41)	140.00	140.00
122	A6	10fr	dk vio & bl (C)	3.25	3.25
123	A6	10fr	dk vio & bl ('41)	130.00	130.00
124	A6	20fr	ol blk & dl yel (C)	4.00	4.00
125	A6	20fr	ol blk & dl yel ('41)	16.00	16.00
			Nos. 80-125 (46)	673.25	665.25

For overprints and surcharges see Nos. 129-132, B12-B13, B22-B23.

For types of Nos. 38//61 without "RF," see Nos. 155A-155B.

Double Overprint

No.	Type	Value		Unused	Used
80a	A1	1c		325.00	225.00
81a	A1	2c		32.50	
82a	A1	3c		32.50	
83a	A4	4c		75.00	
84a	A1	5c		32.50	
85a	A2	10c		32.50	40.00
86a	A2	15c		32.50	
87a	A2	20c		32.50	
88a	A2	25c		55.00	
89a	A3	30c		110.00	120.00
90a	A3	30c		47.50	55.00
91a	A3	30c		47.50	47.50
93a	A2	35c		250.00	
94a	A3	40c		47.50	
96a	A3	45c		75.00	
98a	A3	50c		110.00	75.00
100a	A3	55c		75.00	
102a	A4	65c		45.00	
103a	A4	70c		47.50	
104a	A4	75c		175.00	
105a	A4	80c		47.50	
106a	A4	90c		45.00	
b.		one inverted		120.00	
109a	A4	1fr	One inverted	120.00	
110a	A5	1.40fr		47.50	
111a	A5	1.50fr		47.50	
114a	A6	2.15fr		40.00	
115a	A6	2.25fr		60.00	
116a	A6	2.25fr		47.50	
117a	A6	2.50fr		47.50	
119a	A6	3fr		60.00	
123a	A6	10fr		60.00	*67.50*
124a	A6	20fr		60.00	
			Nos. 96a-124a (17)	1,035.	

Nos. 48, 51 Surcharged in Black or Carmine

1940

No.	Type	Value	Description	Unused	Used
126	A3	75c	on 50c	.80	.80
a.			Double surcharge	40.00	

127 A4 1fr on 65c (C) .80 .80
a. Double surcharge 32.50
Set, never hinged 3.20

Middle Congo No. 67 Overprinted in Carmine like No. 80
Perf. 13½

128 A4 4c olive green 65.00 65.00

Stamps of 1940 With Additional Overprint in Black

1940 ***Perf. 13½x13***

129 A4 80c brown & yel 24.00 16.00
a. Overprint without "2" 150.00
130 A4 1fr bl grn & sl grn 24.00 20.00
131 A3 1fr cer & dull org 24.00 16.00
132 A5 1.50fr dk bl & lt bl 24.00 16.00
Nos. 129-132 (4) 96.00 68.00

Arrival of General de Gaulle in Brazzaville, capital of Free France, Oct. 24, 1940.

These stamps were sold affixed to post cards and at a slight increase over face value to cover the cost of the cards. Values for unused stamps are for examples without gum.

For surcharges see Nos. B12-B13, B22-B23.

Stamps of 1937-40 Overprinted in Black

1 mm between lines

2 mm between lines

1941

133 A1 1c brown & yel 4.00 4.00
134 A1 2c violet & grn 4.00 4.00
135 A1 3c blue & yel 4.00 4.00
136 A1 5c dk & lt green 4.00 4.00
137 A2 10c magenta & bl 4.00 4.00
138 A2 15c blue & buff 4.00 4.00
139 A2 20c brown & yel 4.00 4.00
140 A2 25c copper red & bl 4.00 4.00
141 A2 35c dp grn & yel 4.00 4.00
a. Double overprint 120.00
Nos. 133-141 (9) 36.00 36.00
Set, never hinged 55.00

There are 2 settings of the overprint on Nos. 133-141 & C10. The 1st has 1mm between lines of the overprint (Nos. 133-141), the 2nd has 2mm. Value, set with 2mm spacing $95.

Catalogue values for unused stamps in this section, from this point to the end of the section, are for Never Hinged items.

Phoenix — A8

1941 Photo. ***Perf. 14x14½***

142 A8 5c brown .30 .25
143 A8 10c dark blue .30 .25
a. Denomination doubled 125.00 —
144 A8 25c emerald .30 .25
145 A8 30c deep orange .30 .25
146 A8 40c dk slate grn .55 .30
147 A8 80c red brown .55 .30
148 A8 1fr deep red lilac .55 .30
149 A8 1.50fr brt red .75 .40
150 A8 2fr gray .75 .40
151 A8 2.50fr brt ultra .95 .70
152 A8 4fr dull violet .95 .70
153 A8 5fr yellow bister .95 .70
154 A8 10fr deep brown 1.40 1.00
155 A8 20fr deep green 1.75 1.25
Nos. 142-155 (14) 10.35 7.05

For surcharges see #158-165, B14-B21, B24-B35.

Types of 1937-40 without "RF"

1944 ***Perf. 13½***

155A A2 10c magenta & blue 1.20
155B A2 15c blue & buff 1.60
155C A3 60c mar & gray blue 1.60
155D A5 1.50fr dk & lt blue 2.00
Nos. 155A-155D (4) 6.40

Nos. 155A-155D were issued by the Vichy government in France, but were not sold in French Equatorial Africa.

Eboue Issue
Common Design Type

1945 Unwmk. Engr. ***Perf. 13***

156 CD91 2fr black .65 .50
157 CD91 25fr Prussian green 1.90 1.50

Nos. 156-157 exist imperforate. Value, set $65.

Nos. 142, 144 and 151 Surcharged with New Values and Bars in Red, Carmine or Black

1946 ***Perf. 14x14½***

158 A8 50c on 5c (R) .80 .65
159 A8 60c on 5c (R) .80 .65
160 A8 70c on 5c (R) .80 .65
161 A8 1.20fr on 5c (C) .80 .65
162 A8 2.40fr on 25c 1.40 1.00
163 A8 3fr on 25c 1.40 1.00
164 A8 4.50fr on 25c 1.75 1.20
165 A8 15fr on 2.50fr (C) 1.90 1.40
Nos. 158-165 (8) 9.65 7.20

Black Rhinoceros and Rock Python A9

Jungle Scene — A10

Mountainous Shore Line — A11

Gabon Forest — A12

Niger Boatman — A13

Young Bacongo Woman — A14

1946 Unwmk. Engr. ***Perf. 12½***

166 A9 10c deep blue .40 .25
167 A9 30c violet blk .40 .25
168 A9 40c dp orange .40 .25
169 A10 50c violet bl .80 .50
170 A10 60c dk carmine .80 .50
171 A10 80c dk ol grn .80 .50
172 A11 1fr dp orange .80 .30
173 A11 1.20fr dp claret .80 .65
174 A11 1.50fr dk green 1.20 .95
175 A12 2fr dk vio brn .40 .25
176 A12 3fr rose carmine .80 .50
177 A12 3.60fr red brown 3.25 2.50
178 A12 4fr deep blue .80 .30
179 A13 5fr dk brown .80 .25
180 A13 6fr deep blue 1.25 .30
181 A13 10fr black 2.40 .75
182 A14 15fr brown 2.40 .80
183 A14 20fr dp claret 2.40 .80
184 A14 25fr black 3.25 .80
Nos. 166-184 (19) 24.15 11.40

Imperforates

Most French Equatorial Africa stamps from 1951 onward exist imperforate in issued and trial colors, and also in small presentation sheets in issued colors.

Pierre Savorgnan de Brazza — A15

1951, Nov. 5 ***Perf. 13***

185 A15 10fr indigo & dk grn 1.60 .40

Cent. of the birth of Pierre Savorgnan de Brazza, explorer.

Military Medal Issue
Common Design Type
Engraved and Typographed

1952, Dec. 1 ***Perf. 13***

186 CD101 15fr multicolored 8.00 5.50

Lt. Gov. Adolphe L. Cureau A16

1954, Sept. 20 Engr.

187 A16 15fr ol grn & red brn 2.00 .80

Savannah Monitor A17

1955, May 2 Unwmk.

188 A17 8fr dk grn & claret 2.40 1.25

International Exhibition for Wildlife Protection, Paris, May 1955.

FIDES Issue
Common Design Type

Designs: 5fr, Boali Waterfall and Power Plant, Ubangi-Chari. 10fr, Cotton, Chad. 15fr, Brazzaville Hospital, Middle Congo. 20fr, Libreville Harbor, Gabon.

1956, Apr. 25 ***Perf. 13x12½***

189 CD103 5fr dk brn & claret .65 .30
190 CD103 10fr blk & bluish grn .65 .30
191 CD103 15fr ind & gray vio .80 .40
192 CD103 20fr dk red & red org 1.10 .65
Nos. 189-192 (4) 3.20 1.65

Coffee Issue

Coffee A19

1956, Oct. Engr. ***Perf. 13***

193 A19 10fr brn vio & vio bl 1.60 .40

Leprosarium at Mayumba and Maltese Cross — A20

1957, Mar. 11

194 A20 15fr grn, bl grn & red 2.00 .80

Issued in honor of the Knights of Malta.

Giant Eland A21

1957, Nov. 4

195 A21 1fr shown .80 .40
196 A21 2fr Lions .80 .40
197 A21 3fr Elephant, vert. .80 .40
198 A21 4fr Greater kudu, vert. .90 .40
Nos. 195-198 (4) 3.30 1.60

WHO Building, Brazzaville A22

1958, May 19 Engr. ***Perf. 13***

199 A22 20fr dk green & org brn 1.60 .80

10th anniv. of WHO.

Flower Issue
Common Design Type

1958, July 7 Photo. ***Perf. 12x12½***

200 CD104 10fr Euadania 1.60 .65
201 CD104 25fr Spathodea 2.00 .95

Human Rights Issue
Common Design Type

1958, Dec. 10 Engr. ***Perf. 13***

202 CD105 20fr Prus grn & dk bl 2.40 1.25

SEMI-POSTAL STAMPS

Common Design Type

1938, Oct. 24 Engr.

B1 CD80 1.75fr + 50c brt ultra 24.00 24.00
Never hinged 32.50

Nos. 51, 64 Surcharged in Black or Red

1938, Nov. 7 ***Perf. 13x13½***

B2 A4 65c + 35c dk bl & lt grn (R) 2.40 2.40
B3 A4 1.75fr + 50c bl & lt bl 4.00 4.00
Set, never hinged 12.00

The surtax was for welfare.

French Revolution Issue
Common Design Type
Name and Value Typo. in Black

1939, July 5 Photo.

B4 CD83 45c + 25c green 16.00 16.00
B5 CD83 70c + 30c brown 16.00 16.00
B6 CD83 90c + 35c red org 16.00 16.00

No.	Type	Description	Unused	Used
B7	CD83	1.25fr + 1fr rose pink	16.00	16.00
B8	CD83	2.25fr + 2fr blue	16.00	16.00
		Nos. B4-B8 (5)	80.00	80.00
		Set, never hinged	120.00	

Surtax used for the defense of the colonies.

Catalogue values for unused stamps in this section, from this point to the end of the section, are for Never Hinged items.

Common Design Type and

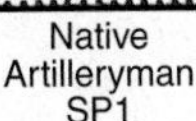

Native Artilleryman SP1

Gabon Infantryman SP2

1941 Photo. *Perf. 13½*

No.	Type	Description	Unused	Used
B8A	SP1	1fr + 1fr red	3.50	
B8B	CD86	1.50fr + 3fr maroon	3.50	
B8C	SP2	2.50fr + 1fr blue	3.50	
		Nos. B8A-B8C (3)	10.50	

Nos. B8A-B8C were issued by the Vichy government in France, but were not placed on sale in French Equatorial Africa.

Brazza and Stanley Pool SP3

1941 Photo. *Perf. 14½x14*

B9 SP3 1fr + 2fr dk brn & red 2.00 1.60

The surtax was for a monument to Pierre Savorgnan de Brazza.

Nos. 67, 71 Srchd. in Red

1943, June 28 *Perf. 13½x13*

No.	Type	Description	Unused	Used
B10	A6	2.25fr + 50fr	47.50	32.50
B11	A6	10fr + 100fr	120.00	80.00

Nos. 129 and 132 with Add'l. Srch. in Carmine

1944

No.	Type	Description	Unused	Used
B12	A4	80c + 10fr	65.00	40.00
B13	A5	1.50fr + 15fr	65.00	40.00

Surcharged Vertically on Nos. 142-146, 148, 150-151

Perf. 14x14½

No.	Type	Description	Unused	Used
B14	A8	5c + 10fr brown	40.00	27.50
B15	A8	10c + 10fr dk bl	40.00	27.50
B16	A8	25c + 10fr emer	40.00	27.50
B17	A8	30c + 10fr dp org	40.00	27.50
B18	A8	40c + 10fr dk sl grn	40.00	27.50
B19	A8	1fr + 10fr dp red lil	40.00	27.50
B20	A8	2fr + 20fr gray	40.00	27.50
B21	A8	2.50fr + 25fr brt ultra	40.00	27.50
		Nos. B12-B21 (10)	450.00	300.00

Nos. 129 and 132 with Add'l. Srch. in Carmine

1944 *Perf. 13½x13*

No.	Type	Description	Unused	Used
B22	A4	80c + 10fr	65.00	40.00
B23	A5	1.50fr + 15fr	65.00	40.00

Surcharged Vertically on Nos. 142-146, 148, 150-155

Perf. 14x14½

No.	Type	Description	Unused	Used
B24	A8	5c + 10fr brn	40.00	27.50
B25	A8	10c + 10fr dk bl	40.00	27.50
B26	A8	25c + 10fr emer	40.00	27.50
B27	A8	30c + 10fr dp org	40.00	27.50
B28	A8	40c + 10fr dk sl grn	40.00	27.50
B29	A8	1fr + 10fr dp red lil	40.00	27.50
B30	A8	2fr + 20fr gray	40.00	27.50
B31	A8	2.50fr + 25fr brt ultra	40.00	27.50
B32	A8	4fr + 40fr dl vio	40.00	27.50
B33	A8	5fr + 50fr yel bis	40.00	27.50
B34	A8	10fr + 100fr dp brn	40.00	27.50
B35	A8	20fr + 200fr dp grn	40.00	27.50
		Nos. B22-B35 (14)	610.00	410.00

Nos. B12 to B35 were issued to raise funds for the Committee to Aid the Fighting Men and Patriots of France.

Nos. 79A-79B Srchd. in Black or Red

1944 Engr. *Perf. 12½x12*

No.	Description	Unused
B36	50c + 1.50fr on 2.50fr deep blue (R)	.80
B37	+ 2.50fr on 1fr green	.80

Colonial Development Fund.

Nos. B36-B37 were issued by the Vichy government in France, but were not placed on sale in French Equatorial Africa.

Red Cross Issue

Common Design Type

1944 Photo. *Perf. 14½x14*

B38 CD90 5fr + 20fr royal blue 1.60 1.20

The surtax was for the French Red Cross and national relief.

Tropical Medicine Issue

Common Design Type

1950, May 15 Engr. *Perf. 13*

B39 CD100 10fr + 2fr dk bl grn & vio brn 7.25 5.50

The surtax was for charitable work.

AIR POST STAMPS

Hydroplane over Pointe-Noire — AP1

Trimotor over Stanley Pool — AP2

1937 Unwmk. Photo. *Perf. 13½*

No.	Type	Description	Unused	Used
C1	AP1	1.50fr ol blk & yel	.40	.40
C2	AP1	2fr mag & blue	.55	.55
C3	AP1	2.50fr grn & buff	.55	.55
C4	AP1	3.75fr brn & lt grn	.80	.80
C5	AP2	4.50fr cop red & bl	.90	.90
C6	AP2	6.50fr bl & lt grn	1.60	1.60
C7	AP2	8.50fr red brn & yel	1.60	1.60
C8	AP2	10.75fr vio & lt grn	1.60	1.60
		Nos. C1-C8 (8)	8.00	8.00

For overprints and surcharges see Nos. C9-C16, CB6.

Nos. C1, C3-C7 Overprinted in Black like Nos. 133-141

No. C10

1940-41

No.	Type	Description	Unused	Used
C9	AP1	1.50fr ('41)	240.00	240.00
C10	AP1	2.50fr	4.00	4.00
a.		Double overprint	275.00	275.00
b.		Inverted overprint	275.00	275.00
C11	AP1	3.75fr ('41)	240.00	240.00
C12	AP2	4.50fr	4.50	4.50
a.		Double overprint	275.00	275.00
C13	AP2	6.50fr	4.00	4.00
a.		Double overprint	130.00	130.00
C14	AP2	8.50fr	4.00	4.00

No. C8 Surcharged in Carmine

C15 AP2 50fr on 10.75fr 12.00 12.00

No. C3 Surcharged in Black

No.	Type	Description	Unused	Used
C16	AP1	10fr on 2.50fr ('41)	95.00	95.00
		Nos. C9-C16 (8)	603.50	603.50

Counterfeits of Nos. C9 and C11 exist. See note following No. 141.

Catalogue values for unused stamps in this section, from this point to the end of the section, are for Never Hinged items.

Common Design Type

1941 Photo. *Perf. 14½x14*

No.	Type	Description	Unused	Used
C17	CD87	1fr dark orange	.65	.30
C18	CD87	1.50fr brt red	.95	.50
C19	CD87	5fr brown red	1.60	.90
C20	CD87	10fr black	1.75	1.00
C21	CD87	25fr ultra	1.60	1.20
C22	CD87	50fr dark green	1.60	1.20
C23	CD87	100fr plum	2.25	1.25
		Nos. C17-C23 (7)	10.40	6.35

Types of 1937 without "RF" and

Sikorsky 5.43 Seaplane and Canoe — AP2a

Perf. 13½, 13 (#C23M)

1943, Oct. 18-1944 Unwmk.

No.	Type	Description	Unused	Used
C23A	AP1	1.50fr ol blk & yel	.40	
C23B	AP1	2fr mag & blue	.40	
C23C	AP1	2.50fr grn & buff	.40	
C23D	AP1	3.75fr brn & lt grn	.80	
C23E	AP2	4.50fr cop red & bl	.80	
C23F	AP2	5fr green	1.20	
C23G	AP2	6.50fr bl & lt grn	1.20	
C23H	AP2	8.50fr red brn & yel	1.20	
C23I	AP2	10fr gray & brn ('44)	1.20	
C23J	AP2	10.75fr vio & lt grn	1.20	
C23K	AP2	20fr yel & brn red ('44)	1.60	
C23L	AP2	50fr gray grn & blk ('44)	2.40	
C23M	AP2a	100fr red brn ('44)	1.60	
		Nos. C23A-C23M (13)	14.40	

Issue dates: Nos. C23I, C23K-L, 4/3/44; C23M, 6/26/44.

Nos. C23A-C23M were issued by the Vichy government in France, but were not sold in French Equatorial Africa.

Victory Issue

Common Design Type

Perf. 12½

1946, May 8 Unwmk. Engr.

C24 CD92 8fr lilac rose 1.60 1.25

Chad to Rhine Issue

Common Design Types

1946, June 6

No.	Type	Description	Unused	Used
C25	CD93	5fr dk violet	1.60	1.20
C26	CD94	10fr slate green	1.60	1.20
C27	CD95	15fr deep blue	2.75	2.00
C28	CD96	20fr red orange	2.75	2.00
C29	CD97	25fr sepia	2.75	2.00
C30	CD98	50fr brown carmine	3.25	2.40
		Nos. C25-C30 (6)	14.70	10.80

Palms and Village — AP3

Village and Waterfront — AP4

Bearers in Jungle — AP5

1946 Engr. *Perf. 13*

No.	Type	Description	Unused	Used
C31	AP3	50fr red brn	3.50	.80
C32	AP4	100fr grnsh blk	5.25	1.25
C33	AP5	200fr deep blue	12.00	2.00
		Nos. C31-C33 (3)	20.75	4.05

UPU Issue

Common Design Type

1949, July 4

C34 CD99 25fr green 16.00 12.00

Brazza Holding Map — AP6

1951, Nov. 5

C35 AP6 15fr brn, indigo & red 2.40 1.60

Cent. of the birth of Pierre Savorgnan de Brazza, explorer.

Archbishop Augouard and St. Anne Cathedral, Brazzaville — AP7

1952, Dec. 1

C36 AP7 15fr ol grn, dk brn & vio brn 6.50 2.40

Cent. of the birth of Archbishop Philippe-Prosper Augouard.

Anhingas — AP8

1953, Feb. 16

C37 AP8 500fr grnsh blk, blk & slate 47.50 8.00

Liberation Issue

Common Design Type

1954, June 6

C38 CD102 15fr vio & vio brn 12.00 8.00

Log Rafts — AP9

Designs: 100fr, Fishing boats and nets, Lake Chad. 200fr, Age of mechanization.

1955, Jan. 24 **Engr.**

C39 AP9 50fr ind, brn & dk grn 2.40 .80
C40 AP9 100fr aqua, dk grn & blk brn 8.00 1.60
C41 AP9 200fr red & deep plum 12.00 2.40
Nos. C39-C41 (3) 22.40 4.80

Gov. Gen. Félix Eboué, View of Brazzaville and the Pantheon — AP10

1955, Apr. 30 **Unwmk.** ***Perf. 13***

C42 AP10 15fr sep, brn & slate bl 6.50 2.40

Gen. Louis Faidherbé and African Sharpshooter AP11

1957, July 20

C43 AP11 15fr sepia & org ver 3.50 2.00

Centenary of French African Troops.

AIR POST SEMI-POSTAL STAMPS

French Revolution Issue

Common Design Type

1939 **Unwmk.** **Photo.** ***Perf. 13***

Name and Value Typo. in Orange

CB1 CD83 4.50fr + 4fr brn blk 40.00 40.00

SPAP1

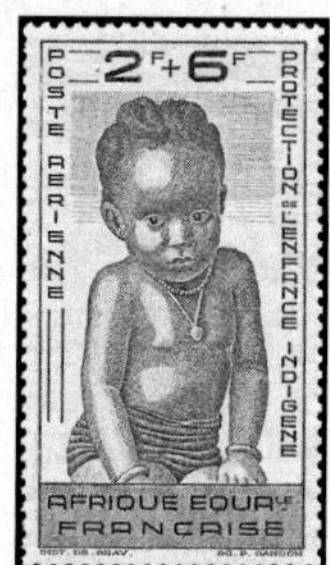

SPAP2

SPAP3

Unwmk.

1942, June 22 **Engr.** ***Perf. 13***

CB2 SPAP1 1.50fr + 3.50fr green .80
CB3 SPAP2 2fr + 6fr brown .80
CB4 SPAP3 3fr + 9fr carmine .80
Nos. CB2-CB4 (3) 2.40

Native children's welfare fund.

Nos. CB2-CB4 were issued by the Vichy government in France, but were not placed on sale in French Equatorial Africa.

Colonial Education Fund

Common Design Type

1942, June 22

CB5 CD86a 1.20fr + 1.80fr bl & red .80

No. CB5 was issued by the Vichy government in France, but was not placed on sale in French Equatorial Africa.

No. C8 Surcharged in Red like Nos. B10-B11

1943, June 28 ***Perf. 13½***

CB6 AP2 10.75fr + 200fr 400.00 240.00

Counterfeits exist.

POSTAGE DUE STAMPS

Numeral of Value on Equatorial Butterfly — D1

1937 **Unwmk.** **Photo.** ***Perf. 13***

J1 D1 5c redsh pur & lt bl .25 .40
J2 D1 10c cop red & buff .25 .40
J3 D1 20c dk grn & grn .30 .50
J4 D1 25c red brn & buff .30 .50
J5 D1 30c cop red & lt bl .50 .55
J6 D1 45c mag & yel grn .75 .80
J7 D1 50c dk ol grn & buff .80 .95
J8 D1 60c redsh pur & yel .95 1.10
J9 D1 1fr brown & yel 1.00 1.20
J10 D1 2fr dk bl & buff 1.40 1.50
J11 D1 3fr red brn & lt grn 1.50 1.75
Nos. J1-J11 (11) 8.00 9.65
Set, never hinged 12.00

Catalogue values for unused stamps in this section, from this point to the end of the section, are for Never Hinged items.

D2

1947 **Engr.**

J12 D2 10c red .40 .25
J13 D2 30c dp org .40 .25
J14 D2 50c greenish bl .50 .30
J15 D2 1fr carmine .55 .40
J16 D2 2fr emerald .65 .50
J17 D2 3fr dp red lil .65 .50
J18 D2 4fr dp ultra 1.60 1.20
J19 D2 5fr red brown 1.60 1.20
J20 D2 10fr peacock blue 2.00 1.60
J21 D2 20fr sepia 2.10 1.90
Nos. J12-J21 (10) 10.45 8.10

FRENCH GUIANA

'french gē-'a-nə

LOCATION — On the northeast coast of South America bordering on the Atlantic Ocean.
GOVT. — French colony
AREA — 34,740 sq. mi.
POP. — 28,537 (1946)
CAPITAL — Cayenne

French Guiana became an overseas department of France in 1946.

100 Centimes = 1 Franc

Catalogue values for unused stamps in this country are for Never Hinged items, beginning with Scott 171 in the regular postage section, Scott B12 in the semi-postal section, Scott C9 in the air-post section, and Scott J22 in the postage due section.

See France No. 1446 for French stamp inscribed "Guyane."

Stamps of French Colonies Surcharged in Black

1886, Dec. **Unwmk.** ***Imperf.***

1 A8 5c on 2c grn, *grnsh*, srch 12mm high 750.00 675.00
a. Double surcharge 1,900. 1,900.
b. Surcharge 10½mm high 900.00 825.00
c. No "f" after "O" 950.00 850.00

Perf. 14x13½

2 A9 5c on 2c brn, *buff*, srch 12mm high 650.00 600.00
a. No "f" after "O" 525.00 450.00
b. As "a," double surcharge 1,700. 1,700.

Nos. 1-2 unused are valued without gum.

Stamps of French Colonies Overprinted in Black

"Av" of Date Line Inverted-Reversed

1887, Apr. ***Imperf.***

4 A8 20c on 35c blk, *org* 70.00 57.50
a. Double surcharge 225.00 225.00
b. No "f" after "O" 150.00 150.00

Date Line Reads "Avril 1887"

5 A8 5c on 2c grn, *grnsh* 175.00 125.00
a. Double surcharge 900.00 900.00
b. No "f" after "O" 375.00 375.00
c. Pair, one stamp without surcharge 1,500.
6 A8 20c on 35c blk, *org* 375.00 375.00
a. Double surcharge 1,250. 1,250.
b. No "f" after "O" 850.00 850.00
c. Vertical pair, #6 + #4 2,200.
7 A7 25c on 30c brn, *yelsh* 55.00 47.50
a. Double surcharge 900.00 900.00
b. No "f" after "O" 275.00 275.00

Nos. 4-7 unused are valued without gum.

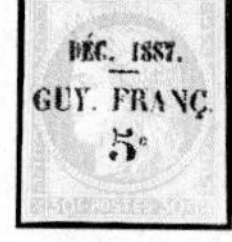

French Colonies Nos. 22 and 26 Surcharged

8 A7 5c on 30c brn, *yelsh* 155.00 140.00
a. Double surcharge 800.00 800.00
b. Inverted surcharge 1,200. 1,200.
c. Pair, one without surcharge 1,600.
9 A8 5c on 30c brn, *yelsh* 1,500. 1,500.

Nos. 8-9 unused are valued without gum.

French Colonies Nos. 22 and 28 Surcharged

1888

10 A7 5c on 30c brn, *yelsh* 155.00 140.00
b. Double surcharge 500.00 500.00
c. Inverted surcharge 600.00 600.00
11 A8 10c on 75c car, *rose* 400.00 290.00
No gum 290.00
a. Double surcharge 1,100. 1,100.
b. Pair, one stamp without surcharge 2,500.

No. 10 unused is valued without gum.

Stamps of French Colonies Overprinted in Black

1892, Feb. 20 ***Imperf.***

12 A8 2c grn, *grnsh* 850.00 *975.00*
a. Inverted overprint 3,500.
13 A7 30c brn, *yelsh* 155.00 155.00
a. Inverted overprint 575.00 575.00
14 A8 35c blk, *orange* *2,850.* *3,000.*
15 A8 40c red, *straw* 175.00 140.00
16 A8 75c car, *rose* 180.00 140.00
a. Inverted overprint 625.00 550.00
17 A8 1fr brnz grn, *straw* 210.00 160.00
a. Inverted overprint 800.00 800.00
b. Double overprint 800.00 800.00
c. Triple overprint 1,800. 1,800.

Nos. 12-14 unused are valued without gum.

1892 ***Perf. 14x13½***

18 A9 1c blk, *lil bl* 47.50 35.00
19 A9 2c brn, *buff* 45.00 37.50
20 A9 4c claret, *lav* 42.50 37.50
21 A9 5c grn, *grnsh* 47.50 35.00
a. Inverted overprint 150.00 150.00
b. Double overprint 150.00 150.00
22 A9 10c blk, *lavender* 67.50 40.00
a. Inverted overprint 200.00 200.00
b. Double overprint 275.00 275.00
23 A9 15c blue 67.50 45.00
a. Double overprint 275.00 200.00
24 A9 20c red, *grn* 55.00 42.50
a. Inverted overprint 225.00 225.00
25 A9 25c blk, *rose* 75.00 35.00
a. Double overprint 275.00 275.00
b. Triple overprint 300.00 300.00
26 A9 30c brn, *bis* 47.50 40.00
27 A9 35c blk, *orange* 225.00 225.00
a. Inverted overprint 575.00 575.00
28 A9 40c red, *straw* 135.00 135.00
a. Inverted overprint 300.00 300.00
29 A9 75c car, *rose* 145.00 125.00
30 A9 1fr brnz grn, *straw* 250.00 220.00
a. Double overprint 375.00
Nos. 18-30 (13) 1,250. 1,053.

French Colonies No. 51 Surcharged

1892, Dec.

31 A9 5c on 15c blue 70.00 47.50
a. Double surcharge 300.00 275.00
b. No "f" after "O" 160.00 135.00
c. Pair, one stamp without surcharge 1,700. 1,700.

Navigation and Commerce — A12

1892-1904 Typo. *Perf. 14x13½*

Name of Colony in Blue or Carmine

32 A12 1c blk, *lil bl* 2.00 1.75
33 A12 2c brn, *buff* 1.45 1.45
34 A12 4c claret, *lav* 2.00 1.90
a. "GUYANE" double 275.00
35 A12 5c grn, *grnsh* 12.50 11.00
36 A12 5c yel grn ('04) 2.40 1.60
37 A12 10c blk, *lavender* 13.50 8.25
38 A12 10c red ('00) 4.75 1.60
39 A12 15c blue, quadrille paper 42.50 4.00
40 A12 15c gray, *lt gray* ('00) 122.50 110.00
41 A12 20c red, *grn* 25.00 18.00
42 A12 25c blk, *rose* 20.00 5.50
43 A12 25c blue ('00) 22.50 *22.50*
44 A12 30c brn, *bis* 24.00 18.00
45 A12 40c red, *straw* 24.00 16.00
46 A12 50c car, *rose* 35.00 18.00
47 A12 50c brn, *az* ('00) 26.00 26.00
48 A12 75c dp vio, *org* 37.50 27.50
49 A12 1fr brn grn, *straw* 18.00 14.00
50 A12 2fr vio, *rose* ('02) 180.00 16.00
Nos. 32-50 (19) 615.60 323.05

Perf. 13½x14 stamps are counterfeits.
For surcharges see Nos. 87-93.

Great Anteater — A13

Washing Gold — A14

Palm Grove at Cayenne A15

1905-28

51 A13 1c black .40 .40
52 A13 2c blue .40 .40
a. Imperf 57.50
53 A13 4c red brn .40 .40
54 A13 5c green 1.25 1.10
55 A13 5c org ('22) .40 *.45*
56 A13 10c rose 1.50 1.10
57 A13 10c grn ('22) .65 .40
58 A13 10c red, *bluish* ('25) .45 .45
59 A13 15c violet 1.75 1.25
60 A14 20c red brn .65 .65
61 A14 25c blue 3.00 1.60
62 A14 25c vio ('22) .60 .50
63 A14 30c black 2.50 1.00
64 A14 30c rose ('22) .50 *.60*
65 A14 30c red org ('25) .45 .45
66 A14 30c dk grn, *grnsh* ('28) 1.35 1.35
67 A14 35c blk, *yel* ('06) .65 .65
68 A14 40c rose 1.50 .85
69 A14 40c black ('22) .40 *.45*
70 A14 45c olive ('07) 1.00 .95
71 A14 50c violet 4.25 3.50
72 A14 50c blue ('22) .55 *.65*
73 A14 50c gray ('25) .80 .80
74 A14 60c lil, *rose* ('25) .65 .65
75 A14 65c myr grn ('26) .85 .80
76 A14 75c green 1.60 1.40
77 A14 85c magenta ('26) .85 .80
78 A15 1fr rose .90 .85
a. Imperf 82.50
79 A15 1fr bl, *bluish* ('25) .85 .80
80 A15 1fr bl, *yel grn* ('28) 2.75 2.75
81 A15 1.10fr lt red ('28) 1.50 1.50
82 A15 2fr blue 1.35 1.35
83 A15 2fr org red, *yel* ('26) 2.75 2.40
84 A15 5fr black 8.50 6.50
a. Imperf 82.50
85 A15 10fr grn, *yel* ('24) 14.00 *14.50*
a. Printed on both sides 140.00
86 A15 20fr brn lake ('24) 17.50 17.50
Nos. 51-86 (36) 79.45 71.75

For surcharges see Nos. 94-108, B1-B2.

Issue of 1892 Surcharged in Black or Carmine

1912

Spacing between figures of surcharge 1.5mm (5c), 2mm (10c)

87 A12 5c on 2c brn, *buff* 1.60 *2.00*
88 A12 5c on 4c cl, *lav* (C) 1.20 *1.60*
89 A12 5c on 20c red, *grn* 1.75 *1.90*
90 A12 5c on 25c blk, *rose* (C) 4.00 4.75
91 A12 5c on 30c brn, *bis* (C) 1.75 *1.90*
92 A12 10c on 40c red, *straw* 1.40 *1.90*
a. Pair, one stamp without surcharge 1,250.
93 A12 10c on 50c car, *rose* 4.25 *5.25*
a. Double surcharge 550.00
Nos. 87-93 (7) 15.95 *19.30*

Two spacings between the surcharged numerals are found on Nos. 87 to 93. For detailed listings, see the *Scott Classic Specialized Catalogue of Stamps and Covers.*

No. 59 Surcharged in Various Colors

1922

94 A13 1c on 15c vio (Bk) .65 *.75*
a. Double surcharge 90.00
95 A13 2c on 15c vio (Bl) .65 *.75*
a. Inverted surcharge 97.50
b. In pair with unovptd. stamp 250.00
c. No. 95a, in pair with unovptd. stamp 850.00
96 A13 4c on 15c vio (G) .65 *.75*
a. Double surcharge 90.00
b. In pair with unovptd. stamp 275.00
97 A13 5c on 15c vio (R) .65 *.75*
a. In pair with unovptd. stamp 275.00
Nos. 94-97 (4) 2.60 3.00

Type of 1905-28 Srchd. in Blue

1923

98 A15 10fr on 1fr grn, *yel* 22.50 *24.00*
99 A15 20fr on 5fr lilac, *rose* 22.50 *24.00*

Stamps and Types of 1905-28 Srchd. in Black or Red

1924-27

100 A13 25c on 15c vio ('25) .85 *.85*
a. Triple surcharge 130.00 130.00
b. In pair with unovptd. stamp 260.00
101 A15 25c on 2fr bl ('24) .90 *.95*
a. Double surcharge 140.00
b. Triple surcharge 150.00
102 A14 65c on 45c ol (R) ('25) 1.75 *1.90*
103 A14 85c on 45c ol (R) ('25) 1.75 *1.90*
104 A14 90c on 75c red ('27) 1.50 1.50
105 A15 1.05fr on 2fr lt yel brn ('27) 1.50 1.50
106 A15 1.25fr on 1fr ultra (R) ('26) 1.60 *1.75*
107 A15 1.50fr on 1fr lt bl ('27) 1.60 *1.75*
108 A15 3fr on 5fr vio ('27) 1.75 *2.00*
a. No period after "F" 12.00 12.00
Nos. 100-108 (9) 13.20 14.10

Carib Archer — A16

Shooting Rapids, Maroni River A17

Government Building, Cayenne — A18

1929-40 *Perf. 13½x14*

109 A16 1c gray lil & grnsh bl .25 .25
a. Imperf 35.00
110 A16 2c dk red & bl grn .25 .25
a. Imperf 35.00
111 A16 3c gray lil & grnsh bl ('40) .30 .30
112 A16 4c ol brn & red vio .30 .30
113 A16 5c Prus bl & red org .30 .30
114 A16 10c mag & brn .30 .30
115 A16 15c yel brn & red org .30 .30
a. Imperf 35.00
116 A16 20c dk bl & ol grn .30 .30
117 A16 25c dk red & dk brn .50 .50

Perf. 14x13½

118 A17 30c dl & lt grn .70 .70
119 A17 30c grn & brn ('40) .50 .50
120 A17 35c Prus grn & ol grn ('38) 1.10 1.10
121 A17 40c org brn & ol gray .30 .30
122 A17 45c grn & dk brn 1.20 1.20
123 A17 45c ol grn & lt grn ('40) .70 .70
124 A17 50c dk bl & ol gray .40 .40
a. Imperf 35.00
125 A17 55c vio bl & car ('38) 1.50 1.50
126 A17 60c sal & grn ('40) .75 .75
a. Imperf 47.50
127 A17 65c sal & grn 1.10 1.10
128 A17 70c ind & sl bl ('40) 1.30 1.30
129 A17 75c ind & sl bl 1.15 1.15
130 A17 80c blk & vio bl ('38) .80 .80
131 A17 90c dk red & ver 1.10 1.10
132 A17 90c red vio & brn ('39) 1.30 1.30
133 A17 1fr lt vio & brn .70 .70
134 A17 1fr car & lt red ('38) 2.10 2.10
135 A17 1fr blk & vio bl ('40) .80 .80
136 A18 1.05fr ver & olive 6.25 6.25
137 A18 1.10fr ol brn & red vio 7.25 5.75
138 A18 1.25fr blk brn & bl grn ('33) .80 .80
139 A18 1.25fr rose & lt red ('39) 1.10 1.10
140 A18 1.40fr ol brn & red vio ('40) 1.30 1.30
141 A18 1.50fr dk bl & lt bl .40 .40
142 A18 1.60fr ol brn & bl grn ('40) 1.30 1.30
143 A18 1.75fr brn red & blk brn ('33) 2.25 2.25
144 A18 1.75fr vio bl ('38) 1.75 1.75
145 A18 2fr dk grn & rose red .65 .65
146 A18 2.25fr vio bl ('39) 1.30 1.30
147 A18 2.50fr cop red & brn ('40) 1.30 1.30
148 A18 3fr brn red & red vio .75 .75
149 A18 5fr dl vio & yel grn 1.25 1.25
150 A18 10fr ol gray & dp ultra 1.50 1.50
151 A18 20fr indigo & ver 2.50 2.50
Nos. 109-151 (43) 51.95 50.45

For types A16-A18 without "RF," see Nos. 170C-170E.

Common Design Types pictured following the introduction.

Colonial Exposition Issue

Common Design Types

1931 Engr. *Perf. 12½*

Name of Country in Black

152 CD70 40c dp green 5.50 5.50
153 CD71 50c violet 5.50 5.50
154 CD72 90c red orange 5.50 5.50
155 CD73 1.50fr dull blue 5.50 5.50
Nos. 152-155 (4) 22.00 22.00

Recapture of Cayenne by d'Estrées, 1676 — A19

Products of French Guiana A20

1935, Oct. 21 *Perf. 13*

156 A19 40c gray brn 5.75 5.75
157 A19 50c dull red 10.00 8.00
158 A19 1.50fr ultra 5.75 5.75
159 A20 1.75fr lilac rose 12.50 11.50
160 A20 5fr brown 10.00 9.00
161 A20 10fr blue green 10.50 10.00
Nos. 156-161 (6) 54.50 50.00

Tercentenary of the founding of French possessions in the West Indies.

Paris International Exposition Issue

Common Design Types

1937, Apr. 15

162 CD74 20c deep violet 1.75 1.75
163 CD75 30c dark green 1.75 1.75
164 CD76 40c car rose 1.75 1.75
165 CD77 50c dark brown 1.75 1.75
166 CD78 90c red 1.75 1.75
167 CD79 1.50fr ultra 2.25 2.25
Nos. 162-167 (6) 11.00 11.00

Colonial Arts Exhibition Issue

Souvenir Sheet

Common Design Type

1937 *Imperf.*

168 CD75 3fr violet 11.50 *13.50*

New York World's Fair Issue

Common Design Type

1939, May 10 Engr. *Perf. 12½x12*

169 CD82 1.25fr car lake 1.30 1.30
170 CD82 2.25fr ultra 1.30 1.30

View of Cayenne and Marshal Petain A21a

1941 Engr. *Perf. 12½x12*

170A A21a 1fr deep lilac .80 .80
170B A21a 2.50fr blue .80 .80

For surcharges, see Nos. B11A-B11B.

Types of 1929-40 without "RF"

1944 *Methods and Perfs as Before*

170C A16 15c yel brn & red org 1.10
170D A17 1fr black & vio blue 1.10
170E A18 1.50fr dk blue & lt blue 1.40
Nos. 170C-170E (3) 3.60

Nos. 170C-170E were issued by the Vichy government in France, but were not issued in French Guiana.

Catalogue values for unused stamps in this section, from this point to the end of the section, are for Never Hinged items.

Eboue Issue

Common Design Type

1945 Engr. *Perf. 13*

171 CD91 2fr black .95 .80
172 CD91 25fr Prussian green 1.50 1.20

This issue exists imperforate.

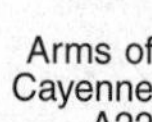

Arms of Cayenne
A22

1945 Litho. *Perf. 12*

No.	Type	Value	Color	Unused	Used
173	A22	10c	dp gray violet	.30	.25
174	A22	30c	brown org	.35	.25
175	A22	40c	lt blue	.35	.25
176	A22	50c	violet brn	.75	.60
177	A22	60c	orange yel	.75	.60
178	A22	70c	pale brown	.75	.60
179	A22	80c	lt green	.75	.60
180	A22	1fr	blue	.35	.25
181	A22	1.20fr	brt violet	.75	.60
182	A22	1.50fr	dp orange	1.00	.75
183	A22	2fr	black	1.10	.85
184	A22	2.40fr	red	1.10	.85
185	A22	3fr	pink	1.10	.85
186	A22	4fr	dp ultra	1.30	1.00
187	A22	4.50fr	dp yel grn	1.30	1.00
188	A22	5fr	orange brn	1.30	1.00
189	A22	10fr	dk violet	1.30	1.00
190	A22	15fr	rose carmine	1.30	1..00
191	A22	20fr	olive green	1.50	1.25
			Nos. 173-191 (19)	17.40	12.55

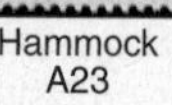

Hammock
A23

Guiana Girl
A26

Maroni River Bank
A24

Inini Scene
A25

Toucans
A27

Parrots
A28

Perf. 13.

1947, June 2 Unwmk. Engr.

No.	Type	Value	Color	Unused	Used
192	A23	10c	dk blue grn	.30	.25
193	A23	30c	brt red	.30	.25
194	A23	50c	dk vio brn	.30	.25
195	A24	60c	grnsh blk	.60	.45
196	A24	1fr	red brn	.85	.60
197	A24	1.50fr	black brn	.85	.60
198	A25	2fr	dp yel grn	1.10	.75
199	A25	2.50fr	dp ultra	1.10	.75
200	A25	3fr	red brn	1.00	.70
201	A26	4fr	black brn	2.50	1.25
202	A26	5fr	deep blue	1.75	1.10
203	A26	6fr	red brown	1.75	1.10
204	A27	10fr	deep ultra	7.25	4.75
205	A27	15fr	black brn	9.25	5.00
206	A27	20fr	red brn	9.25	5.00
207	A28	25fr	brt bl grn	13.00	8.50
208	A28	40fr	black brn	11.00	8.00
			Nos. 192-208 (17)	60.15	39.30

SEMI-POSTAL STAMPS

Regular Issue of 1905-28 Surcharged in Red

1915 Unwmk. *Perf. 13½x14*

No.		Unused	Used
B1 A13 10c + 5c rose		17.50	*18.00*
a.	Inverted surcharge	250.00	250.00
b.	Double surcharge	250.00	250.00

Regular Issue of 1905-28 Surcharged in Rose

B2 A13 10c + 5c rose 1.60 1.60

Curie Issue
Common Design Type

1938 *Perf. 13*

B3 CD80 1.75fr + 50c brt ultra 13.50 13.50

French Revolution Issue
Common Design Type

1939 Photo.

Name and Value in Black

No.	Type	Value	Unused	Used
B4	CD83	45c + 25c green	11.50	11.50
B5	CD83	70c + 30c brown	11.50	11.50
B6	CD83	90c + 35c red org	11.50	11.50
B7	CD83	1.25fr + 1fr rose pink	11.50	11.50
B8	CD83	2.25fr + 2fr blue	11.50	11.50
		Nos. B4-B8 (5)	57.50	57.50

Common Design Type and

Colonial Infantryman — SP1

Colonial Policeman
SP2

1941 Photo. *Perf. 13½*

No.	Type	Value	Unused
B9	SP1	1fr + 1fr red	1.30
B10	CD86	1.50fr + 3fr maroon	1.50
B11	SP2	2.50fr + 1fr blue	1.30
		Nos. B9-B11 (3)	4.10

Nos. B9-B11 were issued by the Vichy government in France, but were not placed on sale in French Guiana.

Nos. 170A-170B Srchd. in Black or Red

1944 Engr. *Perf. 12½x12*

No.	Value	Unused
B11A	50c + 1.50fr on 2.50fr deep blue (R)	.80
B11B	+ 2.50fr on 1fr dp lilac	.80

Colonial Development Fund.

Nos. B11A-B11B were issued by the Vichy government in France, but were not placed on sale in French Guiana.

Catalogue values for unused stamps in this section, from this point to the end of the section, are for Never Hinged items.

Red Cross Issue
Common Design Type

1944 *Perf. 14½x14*

B12 CD90 5fr + 20fr dk copper brn 1.75 1.25

The surtax was for the French Red Cross and national relief.

AIR POST STAMPS

Cayenne
AP1

Perf. 13½

1933, Nov. 20 Unwmk. Photo.

No.	Type	Value	Color	Unused	Used
C1	AP1	50c	orange brn	.30	.30
C2	AP1	1fr	yellow grn	.50	.50
C3	AP1	1.50fr	dk blue	.70	.70
C4	AP1	2fr	orange	.70	.70
C5	AP1	3fr	black	.85	.85
C6	AP1	5fr	violet	.85	.85
C7	AP1	10fr	olive grn	.85	.85
C8	AP1	20fr	scarlet	1.25	1.25
			Nos. C1-C8 (8)	6.00	6.00

For No. C1 without "RF," see No. C8A.

A 20fr violet exists, but was not regularly issued. Value, $175.

Catalogue values for unused stamps in this section, from this point to the end of the section, are for Never Hinged items.

Type of 1933 without "RF" and

AP1a

AP1b

Perf. 13½, 13 (#C8C)

1941-44 Photo, Engr. (#C8C)

No.	Type	Value	Color	Unused
C8A	AP1	50c	orange brn	1.00
C8B	AP1a	50f	bl grn & red brown ('42)	1.40
C8C	AP1b	100f	dk blue ('44)	1.60
			Nos. C8A-C8C (3)	4.00

Nos. C8A-C8C were issued by the Vichy government in France, but were not placed on sale in French Guiana.

Common Design Type

1945 Photo. *Perf. 14½x14*

No.	Type	Value	Color	Unused	Used
C9	CD87	50fr	dark green	1.30	1.10
C10	CD87	100fr	plum	2.50	2.00

Victory Issue
Common Design Type

1946, May 8 Engr. *Perf. 12½*

C11 CD92 8fr black 1.75 1.25

Chad to Rhine Issue
Common Design Types

1946, June 6

No.	Type	Value	Color	Unused	Used
C12	CD93	5fr	dk slate bl	1.75	1.50
C13	CD94	10fr	lilac rose	1.75	1.50
C14	CD95	15fr	dk vio brn	1.75	1.50
C15	CD96	20fr	dk slate grn	2.00	1.60
C16	CD97	25fr	vio brown	2.40	2.00
C17	CD98	50fr	bright lilac	3.00	2.25
			Nos. C12-C17 (6)	12.65	10.35

Eagles — AP2

Tapir — AP3

Toucans — AP4

1947, June 2 Engr. *Perf. 13*

No.	Type	Value	Color	Unused	Used
C18	AP2	50fr	deep green	22.50	17.50
C19	AP3	100fr	red brown	15.00	13.00
C20	AP4	200fr	dk gray bl	30.00	24.00
			Nos. C18-C20 (3)	67.50	54.50

AIR POST SEMI-POSTAL STAMP

French Revolution Issue
Common Design Type

Unwmk.

1939, July 5 Photo. *Perf. 13*

Name & Value Typo. in Orange

CB1 CD83 5fr + 4fr brn blk 22.00 22.00

Nurse with Mother & Child — SPAP1

Unwmk.

1942, June 22 Engr. *Perf. 13*

No.	Type	Value	Unused
CB2	SPAP1	1.50fr + 50c green	1.00
CB3	SPAP1	2fr + 6fr brn & red	1.00

Native children's welfare fund.

Nos. CB2-CB3 were issued by the Vichy government in France, but were not placed on sale in French Guiana.

Colonial Education Fund
Common Design Type

1942, June 22

CB4 CD86a 1.20fr + 1.80fr blue & red 1.10

No. CB4 was issued by the Vichy government in France, but was not placed on sale in French Guiana.

POSTAGE DUE STAMPS

Postage Due Stamps of France, 1893-1926, Overprinted

1925-27 Unwmk. *Perf. 14x13½*

No.	Type	Description	Unused	Used
J1	D2	5c light blue	.70	*.75*
a.		In pair with unovptd. stamp	375.00	
J2	D2	10c brown	1.00	*1.10*
J3	D2	20c olive green	1.10	*1.25*
J4	D2	50c violet brown	1.50	*1.60*
J5	D2	3fr magenta ('27)	11.00	*12.50*

Surcharged in Black

No.	Type	Description	Unused	Used
J6	D2	15c on 20c ol grn	1.00	*1.10*
a.		Blue surcharge	67.50	
J7	D2	25c on 5c lt bl	1.30	*1.40*
a.		In pair with unovptd. stamp	375.00	
J8	D2	30c on 20c ol grn	1.50	*1.60*
J9	D2	45c on 10c brn	1.50	*1.60*
J10	D2	60c on 5c lt bl	1.50	*1.60*
J11	D2	1fr on 20c ol grn	2.25	*2.40*
J12	D2	2fr on 50c vio brn	2.25	*2.40*
		Nos. J1-J12 (12)	26.60	*29.30*

Royal Palms — D3

Guiana Girl — D4

1929, Oct. 14 Typo. *Perf. 13½x14*

No.	Type	Description	Unused	Used
J13	D3	5c indigo & Prus bl	.45	*.50*
J14	D3	10c bis brn & Prus grn	.45	*.50*
J15	D3	20c grn & rose red	.45	*.50*
J16	D3	30c ol brn & rose red	.45	*.50*
J17	D3	50c vio & ol brn	.95	*1.00*
J18	D3	60c brn red & ol brn	1.30	*1.40*
J19	D4	1fr dp bl & org brn	1.75	*1.90*
J20	D4	2fr brn red & bluish grn	2.00	*2.10*
J21	D4	3fr violet & blk	4.25	*4.50*
		Nos. J13-J21 (9)	12.05	*12.90*

Catalogue values for unused stamps in this section, from this point to the end of the section, are for Never Hinged items.

D5

1947, June 2 Engr. *Perf. 14x13*

No.	Type	Description	Unused	Used
J22	D5	10c dk car rose	.35	.35
J23	D5	30c dull green	.45	.45
J24	D5	50c black	.45	.45
J25	D5	1fr brt ultra	.55	.55
J26	D5	2fr dk brown red	.55	.55
J27	D5	3fr deep violet	1.00	.80
J28	D5	4fr red	1.30	1.10
J29	D5	5fr brown violet	1.50	1.25
J30	D5	10fr blue green	2.25	1.90
J31	D5	20fr lilac rose	3.00	2.25
		Nos. J22-J31 (10)	11.40	9.65

FRENCH GUINEA

'french 'gi-nē

LOCATION — On the coast of West Africa, between Portuguese Guinea and Sierra Leone.
GOVT. — French colony
AREA — 89,436 sq. mi.
POP. — 2,058,442 (est. 1941)
CAPITAL — Conakry

French Guinea stamps were replaced by those of French West Africa around 1944-45. French Guinea became the Republic of Guinea Oct. 2, 1958. See "Guinea" for issues of the republic.

100 Centimes = 1 Franc

See French West Africa No. 66 for additional stamp inscribed "Guinee" and "Afrique Occidentale Francaise."

Navigation and Commerce — A1

Perf. 14x13½

1892-1900 Typo. Unwmk.

Name of Colony in Blue or Carmine

No.	Type	Description	Unused	Used
1	A1	1c black, *lilac bl*	2.40	1.60
2	A1	2c brown, *buff*	2.40	2.00
3	A1	4c claret, *lav*	3.25	2.00
4	A1	5c green, *grnsh*	8.00	8.00
5	A1	10c blk, *lavender*	8.00	4.75
6	A1	10c red ('00)	45.00	40.00
7	A1	15c blue, quadrille paper	16.00	8.00
8	A1	15c gray, *lt gray* ('00)	100.00	87.50
9	A1	20c red, *grn*	20.00	16.00
10	A1	25c black, *rose*	16.00	8.00
11	A1	25c blue ('00)	24.00	24.00
12	A1	30c brown, *bis*	40.00	32.50
13	A1	40c red, *straw*	40.00	32.50
a.		"GUINEE FRANCAISE" double	475.00	475.00
14	A1	50c car, *rose*	47.50	35.00
15	A1	50c brown, *az* ('00)	40.00	40.00
16	A1	75c dp vio, *org*	65.00	47.50
17	A1	1fr brnz grn, *straw*	50.00	40.00
		Nos. 1-17 (17)	527.55	429.35

Perf. 13½x14 stamps are counterfeits.
For surcharges see Nos. 48-54.

Fulah Shepherd — A2

1904

No.	Type	Description	Unused	Used
18	A2	1c black, *yel grn*	1.20	1.20
19	A2	2c vio brn, *buff*	1.20	1.20
20	A2	4c carmine, *bl*	1.60	1.60
21	A2	5c green, *grnsh*	1.60	1.60
22	A2	10c carmine	4.00	2.40
23	A2	15c violet, *rose*	12.00	5.50
24	A2	20c carmine, *grn*	16.00	16.00
25	A2	25c blue	16.00	10.00
26	A2	30c brown	24.00	24.00
27	A2	40c red, *straw*	35.00	24.00
28	A2	50c brown, *az*	32.50	24.00
29	A2	75c green, *org*	32.50	32.50
30	A2	1fr brnz grn, *straw*	47.50	47.50
31	A2	2fr red, *org*	87.50	87.50
32	A2	5fr green, *yel grn*	120.00	120.00
		Nos. 18-32 (15)	432.60	399.00

For surcharges see Nos. 55-62.

Gen. Louis Faidherbé A3

Oil Palm — A4

Dr. Noel Eugène Ballay A5

1906-07

Name of Colony in Red or Blue

No.	Type	Description	Unused	Used
33	A3	1c gray	.80	.80
34	A3	2c brown	1.20	1.20
35	A3	4c brown, *bl*	1.60	1.60
36	A3	5c green	4.00	2.00
37	A3	10c carmine (B)	24.00	1.60
38	A4	20c black, *blue*	8.00	4.00
39	A4	25c blue, *pnksh*	8.00	6.50
40	A4	30c brown, *pnksh*	8.00	4.00
41	A4	35c black, *yellow*	6.50	2.40
42	A4	45c choc, *grnsh gray*	8.00	4.00
43	A4	50c dp violet	16.00	12.00
44	A4	75c blue, *org*	12.00	4.00
45	A5	1fr black, *az*	20.00	*24.00*
46	A5	2fr blue, *pink*	40.00	*45.00*
47	A5	5fr car, *straw* (B)	60.00	*65.00*
		Nos. 33-47 (15)	218.10	*178.10*

Regular Issues Surcharged in Black or Carmine

1912

On Issue of 1892-1900

No.	Type	Description	Unused	Used
48	A1	5c on 2c brown, *buff*	1.60	*2.00*
49	A1	5c on 4c cl, *lav* (C)	1.25	*1.60*
50	A1	5c on 15c blue (C)	1.25	*1.60*
51	A1	5c on 20c red, *grn*	4.00	*5.25*
52	A1	5c on 30c brn, *bis* (C)	5.50	*6.50*
53	A1	10c on 40c red, *straw*	2.40	*3.25*
54	A1	10c on 75c dp vio, *org*	8.00	*9.50*
a.		Double surcharge, inverted	325.00	

On Issue of 1904

No.	Type	Description	Unused	Used
55	A2	5c on 2c vio brn, *buff*	1.20	*1.20*
a.		Pair, one without surcharge	650.00	
b.		Inverted surcharge	210.00	
56	A2	5c on 4c car, *blue*	1.20	*1.20*
57	A2	5c on 15c violet, *rose*	1.20	*1.20*
58	A2	5c on 20c car, *grn*	1.60	1.60
59	A2	5c on 25c blue (C)	1.60	*2.00*
60	A2	5c on 30c brown (C)	2.00	*3.25*
61	A2	10c on 40c red, *straw*	2.00	*3.25*
62	A2	10c on 50c brn, *az* (C)	5.50	*6.50*
		Nos. 48-62 (15)	40.30	49.90

Two spacings between the surcharged numerals are found on Nos. 48 to 62. For detailed listings, see the *Scott Classic Specialized Catalogue of Stamps and Covers.*

Ford at Kitim — A6

1913-33 *Perf. 13½x14*

No.	Type	Description	Unused	Used
63	A6	1c violet & bl	.25	.25
a.		Imperf.	72.50	
64	A6	2c brn & vio brn	.25	.25
a.		Double impression of vio brn	160.00	
65	A6	4c gray & black	.25	.25
66	A6	5c yel grn & bl grn	1.20	.40
a.		Booklet pane of 4	—	
		Complete booklet, 10 #66a	275.00	
67	A6	5c brn vio & grn ('22)	.40	.25
68	A6	10c red org & rose	1.20	.40
a.		Booklet pane of 4	—	
		Complete booklet, 10 #68a	550.00	
69	A6	10c yel grn & bl grn ('22)	.55	.25
70	A6	10c vio & ver ('25)	.80	.40
a.		Imperf.	45.00	
71	A6	15c vio brn & rose, chalky paper ('16)	.80	.40
a.		Booklet pane of 4	—	
		Complete booklet, 10 #71a	1,200.	
72	A6	15c gray grn & yel grn ('25)	.40	.40
73	A6	15c red brn & rose lil ('27)	.40	.30
74	A6	20c brn & vio	.40	.40
75	A6	20c grn & bl grn ('26)	.80	.80
76	A6	20c brn red & brn ('27)	.80	.50
77	A6	25c ultra & blue	2.75	1.60
78	A6	25c black & vio ('22)	.80	.80
79	A6	30c vio brn & grn	1.60	1.20
80	A6	30c red org & rose ('22)	1.20	1.10
81	A6	30c rose red & grn ('25)	.30	.30
82	A6	30c dl grn & bl grn ('28)	1.60	1.60
83	A6	35c blue & rose	.55	.55
84	A6	40c green & gray	1.20	1.20
85	A6	45c brown & red	1.20	1.20
86	A6	50c ultra & black	6.50	4.75
87	A6	50c ultra & bl ('22)	1.60	.80
88	A6	50c yel brn & ol ('25)	.80	.80
89	A6	60c vio, *pnksh* ('25)	.80	.80
90	A6	65c yel brn & sl bl ('26)	2.00	1.20
91	A6	75c red & ultra	1.60	1.60
92	A6	75c indigo & dl bl ('25)	.80	1.20
93	A6	75c mag & yel grn ('27)	1.60	1.20
94	A6	85c ol grn & red brn ('26)	1.20	1.20
95	A6	90c brn red & rose ('30)	5.50	4.75
96	A6	1fr violet & black	1.60	2.40
97	A6	1.10fr vio & ol brn ('28)	8.00	8.00
98	A6	1.25fr vio & yel brn ('33)	2.40	1.60
99	A6	1.50fr dk bl & lt bl ('30)	6.50	2.40
100	A6	1.75fr ol brn & vio ('33)	1.75	1.60
101	A6	2fr org & vio brn	4.00	4.00
102	A6	3fr red vio ('30)	8.00	5.50
103	A6	5fr black & vio	16.00	16.00
104	A6	5fr dl bl & blk ('22)	4.00	2.40
		Nos. 63-104 (42)	94.35	77.00

For surcharges see Nos. 105-115, B1.

Nos. 66, 68 and 77 pasted on colored cardboard and overprinted "VALEUR D'ECHANGE" were used as emergency currency in 1920.

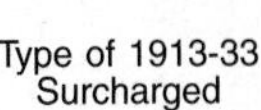

Type of 1913-33 Surcharged

1922

No.	Type	Description	Unused	Used
105	A6	60c on 75c violet, *pnksh*	.40	.40

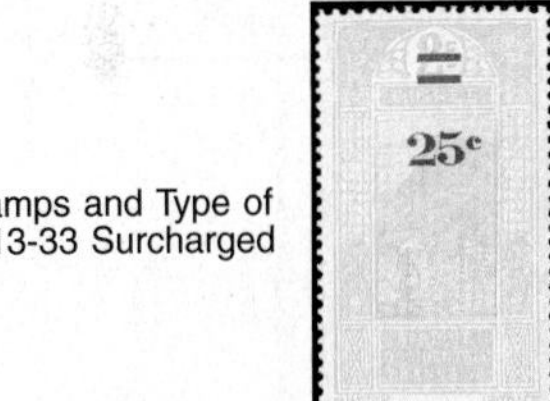

Stamps and Type of 1913-33 Surcharged

1924-27

No.	Type	Description	Unused	Used
106	A6	25c on 2fr org & brn (R)	.40	.40
107	A6	25c on 5fr dull bl & blk	.40	.40
108	A6	65c on 75c rose & ultra ('25)	1.60	1.60
109	A6	85c on 75c rose & ultra ('25)	2.40	2.00
110	A6	90c on 75c brn red & cer ('27)	3.25	3.25
111	A6	1.25fr on 1fr dk bl & ultra ('26)	1.20	1.60
112	A6	1.50fr on 1fr dp bl & lt bl ('27)	2.40	2.40
113	A6	3fr on 5fr mag & sl ('27)	4.00	4.00
114	A6	10fr on 5fr bl & bl grn, *bluish* ('27)	8.00	8.00
115	A6	20fr on 5fr rose lil & brn ol, *pnksh* ('27)	20.00	20.00
		Nos. 106-115 (10)	43.65	43.65

Common Design Types pictured following the introduction.

Colonial Exposition Issue
Common Design Types

1931 Engr. *Perf. 12½*
Name of Country in Black

116 CD70 40c deep green 4.75 4.75
a. "GUINÉE FRANCAISE" omitted 55.00 *67.50*
117 CD71 50c violet 4.75 4.75
118 CD72 90c red orange 4.75 4.75
a. "GUINÉE FRANCAISE" omitted 55.00 *70.00*
119 CD73 1.50fr dull blue 5.50 5.50
a. "GUINÉE FRANCAISE" omitted 55.00 *67.50*
Nos. 116-119 (4) 19.75 19.75
Set, never hinged 32.00

Paris International Exposition Issue
Common Design Types

1937 *Perf. 13*

120 CD74 20c deep violet 2.00 2.00
121 CD75 30c dark green 2.00 2.00
122 CD76 40c car rose 2.40 2.40
123 CD77 50c dark brown 1.60 1.60
124 CD78 90c red 1.60 1.60
125 CD79 1.50fr ultra 2.40 2.40
Nos. 120-125 (6) 12.00 12.00
Set, never hinged 20.25

Colonial Arts Exhibition Issue
Souvenir Sheet
Common Design Type

1937 *Imperf.*

126 CD76 3fr Prussian green 12.00 *16.00*
Never hinged 16.00

Guinea Village A7

Hausa Basket Workers A8

Forest Waterfall A9

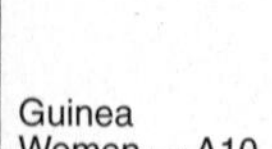
Guinea Women — A10

1938-40 *Perf. 13*

128 A7 2c vermilion .25 .25
129 A7 3c ultra .25 .25
130 A7 4c green .25 .25
131 A7 5c rose car .25 .25
132 A7 10c peacock blue .25 .25
133 A7 15c violet brown .25 .25
134 A8 20c dk carmine .30 .25
135 A8 25c pck blue .40 .25
136 A8 30c ultra .40 .25
137 A8 35c green .55 .50
138 A8 40c blk brn ('40) .40 .25
139 A8 45c dk green ('40) .40 .40
140 A8 50c red brown .55 .50
141 A9 55c dk ultra 1.20 .80
142 A9 60c dk ultra ('40) 1.20 1.20
143 A9 65c green 1.20 .80
144 A9 70c green ('40) 1.20 1.20
145 A9 80c rose violet .80 .55
146 A9 90c rose vio ('39) 1.25 1.25
147 A9 1fr orange red 2.40 2.00
148 A9 1fr brn blk ('40) .40 .40
149 A9 1.25fr org red ('39) 1.40 1.40
150 A9 1.40fr brown ('40) 1.20 1.20
151 A9 1.50fr violet 2.40 2.00
152 A10 1.60fr org red ('40) 1.60 1.60
153 A10 1.75fr ultra .80 .80
154 A10 2fr magenta 1.20 .80
155 A10 2.25fr brt ultra ('39) 1.75 1.75
156 A10 2.50fr brn blk ('40) 1.60 1.60
157 A10 3fr peacock blue .95 .40
158 A10 5fr rose violet .95 .80
159 A10 10fr slate green 1.60 1.60
160 A10 20fr chocolate 2.40 2.40
Nos. 128-160 (33) 32.00 28.60
Set, never hinged 45.00

For surcharges see Nos. B8-B11.

Caillié Issue
Common Design Type

1939 Engr. *Perf. 12½x12*

161 CD81 90c org brn & org .40 .80
162 CD81 2fr brt violet .40 1.20
163 CD81 2.25fr ultra & dk bl .40 1.20
Nos. 161-163 (3) 1.20 3.20
Set, never hinged 2.40

René Caillié, French explorer, death cent.

New York World's Fair Issue
Common Design Type

1939

164 CD82 1.25fr carmine lake .80 1.60
165 CD82 2.25fr ultra .80 1.60
Set, never hinged 2.40

Ford at Kitim and Marshal Petain — A11

1941 *Perf. 12x12½*

166 A11 1fr green .40 —
167 A11 2.50fr deep blue .40 —
Set, never hinged 1.60

For surcharges, see Nos. B15-B16.

Types of 1933-40 without "RF"

1943-44 *Perf. 13*

168 A7 10c peacock blue .40
169 A8 20c dk carmine .40
170 A8 30c ultramarine .40
171 A8 40c black brown 1.20
172 A9 60c dk ultramarine 1.20
173 A9 1.50fr violet 1.20
174 A10 2fr magenta 1.60
Nos. 168-174 (7) 6.40
Set, never hinged 9.50

Nos. 168-174 were issued by the Vichy government in France, but were not placed on sale in French Guinea.

SEMI-POSTAL STAMPS

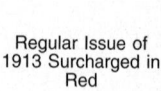

Regular Issue of 1913 Surcharged in Red

1915 Unwmk. *Perf. 13½x14*

B1 A6 10c + 5c org & rose 1.60 1.60

Curie Issue
Common Design Type

1938 Engr. *Perf. 13*

B2 CD80 1.75fr + 50c brt ultra 8.75 8.75
Never hinged 14.00

French Revolution Issue
Common Design Type

1939 Photo.
Name and Value Typo. in Black

B3 CD83 45c + 25c green 9.50 9.50
B4 CD83 70c + 30c brown 9.50 9.50
B5 CD83 90c + 35c red org 9.50 9.50
B6 CD83 1.25fr + 1fr rose pink 9.50 9.50
B7 CD83 2.25fr + 2fr blue 9.50 9.50
Nos. B3-B7 (5) 47.50 47.50
Set, never hinged 80.00

Stamps of 1938, Surcharged in Black

1941 Unwmk. *Perf. 13*

B8 A8 50c + 1fr red brn 4.00 4.00
B9 A9 80c + 2fr rose vio 8.00 8.00
B10 A9 1.50fr + 2fr brn 8.00 8.00
B11 A10 2fr + 3fr magenta 8.00 8.00
Nos. B8-B11 (4) 28.00 28.00
Set, never hinged 55.00

Common Design Type and

Senegalese Soldier SP1

Colonial Infantryman SP2

1941 Unwmk. *Perf. 13*

B12 SP1 1fr + 1fr red 1.25
B13 CD86 1.50fr + 3fr maroon 1.40
B14 SP2 2.50fr + 1fr blue 1.40
Nos. B12-B14 (3) 4.05
Set, never hinged 6.50

Nos. B12-B14 were issued by the Vichy government in France, but were not placed on sale in the French Guinea.

Nos. 166-167 Surcharged in Black or Red

1944 Engr. *Perf. 12½x12*

B15 50c + 1.50fr on 2.50fr deep blue (R) .40
B16 + 2.50fr on 1fr green .40
Set, never hinged 1.60

Colonial Development Fund.

Nos. B15-B16 were issued by the Vichy government in France, but were not placed on sale in French Guinea.

AIR POST STAMPS

Common Design Type

1940 Unwmk. Engr. *Perf. 12½x12*

C1 CD85 1.90fr ultra .40 .40
C2 CD85 2.90fr dark red .40 .40
C3 CD85 4.50fr dk gray grn .80 .80
C4 CD85 4.90fr yellow bis .80 .80
C5 CD85 6.90fr dp orange 1.60 1.60
Nos. C1-C5 (5) 4.00 4.00
Set, never hinged 6.00

Common Design Types

1942 Engr.

C6 CD88 50c car & blue .25
C7 CD88 1fr brown & blk .30
C8 CD88 2fr dk grn & red brn .30
C9 CD88 3fr dk bl & scar .50
C10 CD88 5fr vio & brn red .80

Frame Engraved, Center Typographed

C11 CD89 10fr multicolored .80
C12 CD89 20fr multicolored 1.20
C13 CD89 50fr multicolored 1.60 —
Nos. C6-C13 (8) 5.75
Set, never hinged 12.00

There is doubt whether Nos. C6-C12 were officially placed in use.

AIR POST SEMI-POSTAL STAMPS

Dahomey types SPAP1-SPAP3 inscribed "Guinée Frcaise" or "Guinée"

Perf. 13½x12½, 13 (#CB3)
Photo, Engr. (#CB3)

1942, June 22

CB1 SPAP1 1.50fr + 3.50fr grn .40 *5.50*
CB2 SPAP2 2fr + 6fr brown .40 *5.50*
CB3 SPAP3 3fr + 9fr car red .40 *5.50*
Nos. CB1-CB3 (3) 1.20 16.50
Set, never hinged 2.40

Native children's welfare fund.

Colonial Education Fund
Common Design Type
Perf. 12½x13½

1942, June 22 Engr.

CB4 CD86a 1.20fr + 1.80fr blue & red .40 *5.50*
Never hinged .80

POSTAGE DUE STAMPS

Fulah Woman — D1

1905 Unwmk. Typo. *Perf. 14x13½*

J1 D1 5c blue 1.60 *3.25*
J2 D1 10c brown 2.40 *3.25*
J3 D1 15c green 8.00 6.50
J4 D1 30c rose 8.00 6.50
J5 D1 50c black 12.00 *13.00*
J6 D1 60c dull orange 12.00 *16.00*
J7 D1 1fr violet 40.00 *47.50*
Nos. J1-J7 (7) 84.00 96.00

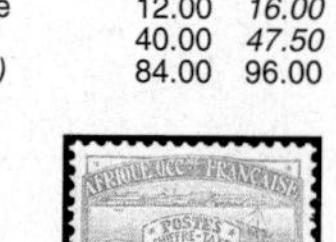

Heads and Coast — D2

1906-08

J8 D2 5c grn, *grnsh* ('08) 20.00 13.00
J9 D2 10c violet brn ('08) 8.00 5.50
J10 D2 15c dk blue ('08) 8.00 5.50
J11 D2 20c blk, *yellow* 8.00 5.50
J12 D2 30c red, *straw* ('08) 27.50 26.00
J13 D2 50c violet ('08) 24.00 *26.00*
J14 D2 60c blk, *buff* ('08) 24.00 21.00
J15 D2 1fr blk, *pnksh* ('08) 16.00 13.50
Nos. J8-J15 (8) 135.50 116.00

D3

1914

J16 D3 5c green .40 *.55*
J17 D3 10c rose .40 *.65*
J18 D3 15c gray .40 *.80*
J19 D3 20c brown .80 .80
J20 D3 30c blue .80 .80
J21 D3 50c black 1.00 *1.25*
J22 D3 60c orange 2.00 *2.40*
J23 D3 1fr violet 2.00 *2.40*
Nos. J16-J23 (8) 7.80 9.65

Type of 1914 Issue Surcharged

1927

J24 D3 2fr on 1fr lil rose 8.00 *8.00*
a. No period after "F" 27.50 *32.50*
J25 D3 3fr on 1fr org brn 8.00 *8.00*

D4

1938 **Engr.**

J26 D4	5c	dk violet	.25	.30
J27 D4	10c	carmine	.25	.30
J28 D4	15c	green	.25	.30
J29 D4	20c	red brown	.25	.40
J30 D4	30c	rose violet	.25	.40
J31 D4	50c	chocolate	.80	.70
J32 D4	60c	peacock blue	.80	1.10
J33 D4	1fr	vermilion	.80	1.10
J34 D4	2fr	ultra	.80	1.10
J35 D4	3fr	black	1.60	1.60
		Nos. J26-J35 (10)	6.05	7.30

For No. J27 without "RF," see No. J36.

Type of 1938 without "RF"

1944

J36 D4	10c	carmine	.80	
		Never hinged	1.20	

No. J36 was issued by the Vichy government in France, but was not placed on sale in French Guinea.

FRENCH INDIA

'french 'in-dē-ə

LOCATION — East coast of India bordering on Bay of Bengal.
GOVT. — French Territory
AREA — 196 sq. mi.
POP. — 323,295 (1941)
CAPITAL — Pondichéry

French India was an administrative unit comprising the five settlements of Chandernagor, Karikal, Mahé, Pondichéry and Yanaon. These united with India in 1949 and 1954.

100 Centimes = 1 Franc
24 Caches = 1 Fanon (1923)
8 Fanons = 1 Rupie

Catalogue values for unused stamps in this country are for Never Hinged items, beginning with Scott 210 in the regular postage section, Scott B14 in the semi-postal section, and Scott C7 in the airpost section.

Navigation and Commerce — A1

Perf. 14x13½

1892-1907 **Typo.** **Unwmk.**

Colony Name in Blue or Carmine

1 A1	1c	blk, *lil bl*	1.40	1.00
2 A1	2c	brn, *buff*	2.40	1.50
3 A1	4c	claret, *lav*	3.00	2.50
4 A1	5c	grn, *grnsh*	6.00	3.75
5 A1	10c	blk, *lavender*	13.50	2.75
6 A1	10c	red ('00)	5.00	2.40
7 A1	15c	blue, quadrille paper	16.00	5.50
8 A1	15c	gray, *lt gray* ('00)	30.00	30.00
9 A1	20c	red, *grn*	8.00	5.50
10 A1	25c	blk, *rose*	5.25	2.75
11 A1	25c	blue ('00)	19.00	16.00
12 A1	30c	brn, *bis*	57.50	50.00
13 A1	35c	blk, *yel* ('06)	19.00	9.00
14 A1	40c	red, *straw*	7.50	7.25
15 A1	45c	blk, *gray grn* ('07)	5.25	*6.00*
16 A1	50c	car, *rose*	7.25	7.25
17 A1	50c	brn, *az* ('00)	16.00	*17.50*
18 A1	75c	dp vio, *org*	9.75	*9.50*
19 A1	1fr	brnz grn, *straw*	14.00	*14.50*
		Nos. 1-19 (19)	245.80	*194.65*

Perf. 13½x14 stamps are counterfeits.

Nos. 10 and 16 Surcharged in Carmine or Black

1903

20 A1	5c on 25c	blk, *rose*	400.00	240.00
21 A1	10c on 25c	blk, *rose*	375.00	225.00
22 A1	15c on 25c	blk, *rose*	125.00	115.00
23 A1	40c on 50c	car, *rose* (Bk)	525.00	425.00
		Nos. 20-23 (4)	1,425.	1,005.

Counterfeits of Nos. 20-23 abound.

A2

Revenue Stamp Surcharged in Black

1903

24 A2	5c gray blue	30.00	30.00

The bottom of the revenue stamps were cut off.

Brahma — A5

Kali Temple near Pondichéry
A6

1914-22 ***Perf. 13½x14, 14x13½***

25 A5	1c	gray & blk	.30	.30
a.		1c light gray & black	.55	.55
26 A5	2c	brn vio & blk	.30	.30
27 A5	2c	grn & brn vio ('22)	.45	.45
28 A5	3c	brown & blk	.40	.40
29 A5	4c	orange & blk	.40	.40
30 A5	5c	bl grn & blk	.70	.70
31 A5	5c	vio brn & blk ('22)	.60	.60
32 A5	10c	dp rose & blk	1.25	1.25
33 A5	10c	grn & blk ('22)	.90	.90
34 A5	15c	vio & blk	1.10	1.10
35 A5	20c	org red & blk	2.00	2.00
36 A5	25c	blue & blk	2.00	2.00
37 A5	25c	ultra & fawn ('22)	1.60	1.60
38 A5	30c	ultra & blk	4.00	4.00
39 A5	30c	rose & blk ('22)	1.75	1.75
40 A6	35c	choc & blk	2.25	2.25
41 A6	40c	org red & blk	2.25	2.25
42 A6	45c	bl grn & blk	2.25	2.25
43 A6	50c	dp rose & blk	2.25	2.25
44 A6	50c	ultra & bl ('22)	3.00	3.00
45 A6	75c	blue & blk	4.50	4.50
46 A6	1fr	yellow & blk	4.50	4.50
47 A6	2fr	violet & blk	6.75	6.75
48 A6	5fr	ultra & blk	3.50	3.50
49 A6	5fr	rose & blk ('22)	5.50	5.50
		Nos. 25-49 (25)	54.50	54.50

For surcharges see Nos. 50-79, 113-116, 156A, B1-B5.

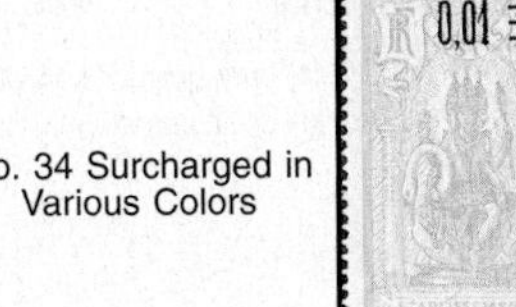
No. 34 Surcharged in Various Colors

1922

50 A5	1c on 15c (Bk)	.80	.80
51 A5	2c on 15c (Bl)	.80	.80
53 A5	5c on 15c (R)	.80	.80
	Nos. 50-53 (3)	2.40	2.40

Stamps and Types of 1914-22 Surcharged with New Values in Caches, Fanons and Rupies in Black, Red or Blue

No. 55

No. 69

No. 78

1923-28

54 A5	1ca	on 1c gray & blk (R)	.30	.30
a.		Imperf.	50.00	50.00
55 A5	2ca	on 5c vio brn & blk	.50	.50
a.		Horizontal pair, imperf. between	—	
b.		Imperf.	45.00	45.00
56 A5	3ca	on 3c brn & blk	.55	.55
57 A5	4ca	on 4c org & blk	.80	.80
58 A5	6ca	on 10c grn & blk	.95	.95
a.		Double surcharge	175.00	
59 A6	6ca	on 45c bl grn & blk (R)	.95	.95
60 A5	10ca	on 20c dp red & bl grn ('28)	2.50	2.50
61 A5	12ca	on 15c vio & blk	.95	.95
62 A5	15ca	on 20c org & blk	1.50	1.50
63 A6	16ca	on 35c lt bl & yel brn ('28)	2.60	2.60
64 A5	18ca	on 30c rose & blk	2.40	2.40
65 A6	20ca	on 45c grn & dl red ('28)	2.00	1.50
66 A5	1fa	on 25c dp grn & rose red ('28)	3.50	3.50
67 A6	1fa3ca	on 35c choc & blk (Bl)	1.10	1.10
68 A6	1fa6ca	on 40c org & blk (R)	1.50	1.25
69 A6	1fa12ca	on 50c ultra & bl (Bl)	1.75	1.50
70 A6	1fa12ca	on 75c bl & blk (Bl)	1.25	1.25
a.		Double surcharge	145.00	
71 A6	1fa16ca	on 75c brn red & grn ('28)	3.50	3.00
72 A5	2fa9ca	on 25c ultra & fawn (Bl)	1.50	1.20
73 A6	2fa12ca	on 1fr vio & dk brn ('28)	3.00	3.00
74 A6	3fa3ca	on 1fr yel & blk (R)	1.75	1.45
a.		Double surcharge	145.00	
75 A6	6fa6ca	on 2fr vio & blk (Bl)	5.25	4.50
76 A6	1r	on 1fr grn & dp bl (R) ('26)	9.50	7.75
77 A6	2r	on 5fr rose & blk (R)	7.50	7.00
a.		Double surcharge	145.00	
78 A6	3r	on 2fr gray & bl vio (R) ('26)	21.00	19.00
79 A6	5r	on 5fr rose & blk, *grnsh* ('26)	27.50	24.00
		Nos. 54-79 (26)	105.60	95.00

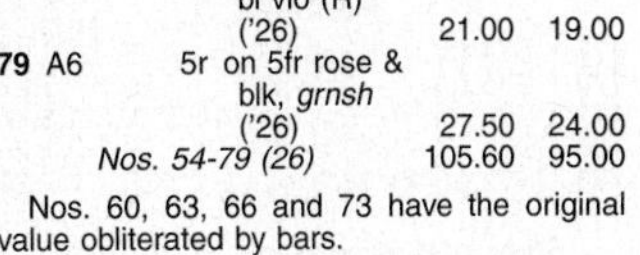

Nos. 60, 63, 66 and 73 have the original value obliterated by bars.

A7

A8

1929

80 A7	1ca	dk gray & blk	.25	.25
81 A7	2ca	vio brn & blk	.25	.25
82 A7	3ca	brn & blk	.25	.25
83 A7	4ca	org & blk	.30	.30
84 A7	6ca	gray grn & grn	.30	.30
85 A7	10ca	brn, red & grn	.30	.30
86 A8	12ca	grn & lt grn	.75	.70
87 A7	16ca	brt bl & blk	.95	.95
88 A7	18ca	brn red & ver	.95	.95
89 A7	20ca	dk bl & grn, *bluish*	.75	.75
90 A8	1fa	gray grn & rose red	.75	.70
91 A8	1fa6ca	red org & blk	.75	.70
92 A8	1fa12ca	dp bl & ultra	.75	.70
93 A8	1fa16ca	rose red & grn	.95	.95
94 A8	2fa12ca	brt vio & brn	1.20	1.00
95 A8	6fa6ca	dl vio & blk	1.20	1.00
a.		Imperf.	50.00	
96 A8	1r	gray grn & dp bl	1.10	1.00
97 A8	2r	rose & blk	1.60	1.20
a.		Imperf.	50.00	
98 A8	3r	lt gray & gray lil	3.00	2.25
99 A8	5r	rose & blk, *grnsh*	3.00	2.40
		Nos. 80-99 (20)	19.35	16.90

For overprints and surcharges see Nos. 117-134, 157-176, 184-209G.

Common Design Types pictured following the introduction.

Colonial Exposition Issue
Common Design Types

1931 **Engr.** ***Perf. 12½***

100 CD70	10ca	deep green	4.50	*4.50*
101 CD71	12ca	violet	4.50	*4.50*
102 CD72	18ca	red orange	4.50	*4.50*
103 CD73	1fa12ca	dull blue	4.50	*4.50*
		Nos. 100-103 (4)	18.00	*18.00*

Paris International Exposition Issue
Common Design Types

1937 ***Perf. 13***

104 CD74	8ca	dp violet	2.00	*4.00*
105 CD75	12ca	dk green	2.25	*4.00*
106 CD76	16ca	car rose	2.25	*4.00*
107 CD77	20ca	dk brown	1.40	*4.00*
108 CD78	1fa12ca	red	1.75	*4.00*
109 CD79	2fa12ca	ultra	2.25	*4.00*
		Nos. 104-109 (6)	11.90	*24.00*

For overprints see Nos. 135-139, 177-181.

Colonial Arts Exhibition Issue
Souvenir Sheet
Common Design Type

1937 ***Imperf.***

110 CD79	5fa	red violet	9.25	*12.50*

For overprint see No. 140.

New York World's Fair Issue
Common Design Type

1939 **Engr.** ***Perf. 12½x12***

111 CD82	1fa12ca	car lake	1.25	*4.00*
112 CD82	2fa12ca	ultra	1.75	*4.00*

For overprints see Nos. 141-142, 182-183.

Temple near Pondichéry and Marshal Petain
A9

1941 Engr. *Perf. 12½x12*

112A	A9 1fa16ca car & red	.80	
c.	Denomination omitted	55.00	
112B	A9 4fa4ca blue	.80	
d.	Denomination omitted	200.00	

Nos. 112A-112B were issued by the Vichy government in France, but were not placed on sale in French India.

For surcharges, see Nos. B13B-B13C.

Nos. 62, 64, 67, 72 Overprinted in Carmine or Blue (#116)

a

b

1941 Unwmk. *Perf. 13½x14*

113	A5 (a)	15ca on 20c	85.00	85.00
114	A5 (a)	18ca on 30c	16.00	16.00
115	A6 (a)	1fa3ca on 35c	130.00	130.00
a.		Horiz. overprint	125.00	125.00
116	A5 (b)	2fa9ca on 25c	1,600.	1,150.
a.		Overprint "a" (Bl)	1,400.	1,150.
b.		Overprint "b" (C)	*2,100.*	*2,100.*

Nos. 81-99 Overprinted Type "a" in Carmine or Blue

1941

117	A7	2ca (C)	12.50	12.50
118	A7	3ca (C)	4.75	4.75
119	A7	4ca (C)	13.50	13.50
120	A7	6ca (C)	4.75	4.75
121	A7	10ca (Bl)	6.50	6.50
122	A8	12ca (C)	4.75	4.75
123	A7	16ca (C)	4.75	4.75
123A	A7	18ca (Bl)	675.00	675.00
124	A7	20ca (C)	4.75	4.75
125	A8	1fa (Bl)	4.75	4.75
126	A8	1fa6ca (C)	4.75	4.75
127	A8	1fa12ca (C)	6.50	6.50
128	A8	1fa16ca (C)	4.75	4.75
129	A8	2fa12ca (C)	4.75	4.75
130	A8	6fa6ca (C)	4.75	4.75
131	A8	1r (C)	4.75	4.75
132	A8	2r (C)	4.75	4.75
133	A8	3r (C)	6.50	6.50
134	A8	5r (C)	10.50	10.50
		Nos. 117-123,124-134 (18)	113.00	113.00

Same Overprints on Paris Exposition Issue of 1937

1941 *Perf. 13*

135	CD74 (b)	8ca (C)	10.00	10.00
135A	CD74 (b)	8ca (Bl)	275.00	275.00
d.		Blk. overprint	1,000.	1,000.
135B	CD74 (a)	8ca (C)	180.00	180.00
135C	CD74 (a)	8ca (Bl)	250.00	250.00
136	CD75 (a)	12ca (C)	6.00	6.00
137	CD76 (a)	16ca (Bl)	6.00	6.00
a.		Blk. overprint	175.00	175.00
138	CD78 (a)	1fa12ca (Bl)	6.00	6.00
139	CD79 (a)	2fa12ca (C)	6.00	6.00
		Nos. 135-139 (8)	739.00	739.00

Inverted overprints exist.

Souvenir Sheet
No. 110 Overprinted "FRANCE LIBRE" Diagonally in Blue Violet

Two types of overprint:
I — Overprint 37mm. With serifs.
II — Overprint 24mm, as type "a" shown above No. 113. No serifs.

1941 Unwmk. *Imperf.*

140	CD79 5fa red vio (I)	800.00	725.00
a.	Type II	1,000.	1,000.
b.	As No. 140, inverted surcharge	5,000.	2,000.

Overprinted on New York World's Fair Issue, 1939

Perf. 12½x12

141	CD82 (a) 1fa12ca (Bl)	4.75	4.75
142	CD82 (a) 2fa12ca (C)	5.50	5.50

Lotus Flowers — A10

1942 Unwmk. Photo. *Perf. 14x14½*

143	A10	2ca brown	.30	.30
144	A10	3ca dk blue	.30	.30
145	A10	4ca emerald	.30	.30
146	A10	6ca dk orange	.30	.30
147	A10	12ca grnsh blk	.30	.30
148	A10	16ca rose violet	.30	.30
149	A10	20ca dk red brn	.65	.65
150	A10	1fa brt red	.70	.65
151	A10	1fa18ca slate blk	.90	.80
152	A10	6fa6ca brt ultra	1.60	1.50
153	A10	1r dull violet	1.40	1.40
154	A10	2r bister	1.75	1.60
155	A10	3r chocolate	1.75	1.60
156	A10	5r dk green	2.25	2.00
		Nos. 143-156 (14)	12.80	12.00

Stamps of 1923-39 Overprinted in Blue or Carmine

c

d

1942-43 *Perf. 13½x14, 14x13½*

Overprinted on No. 64

156A	A5 (c) 18ca on 30c (B)	300.00	230.00

Overprinted on #81-82, 84, 86-99

157	A7 (c)	2ca (C)	3.75	3.75
a.		"FRANCE LIBRE" in black	250.00	175.00
b.		As No. 157, blk. overprint	375.00	375.00
c.		As No. 157, bl. overprint	500.00	500.00
158	A7 (c)	3ca (C)	2.40	2.40
159	A7 (c)	6ca (Bl)	3.25	3.25
a.		Car. overprint	325.00	
b.		Blk. overprint	725.00	
c.		Bl.-Blk. overprint	50.00	35.00
160	A8 (d)	12ca (Bl)	3.75	3.75
161	A7 (c)	16ca (C)	3.25	3.25
162	A7 (c)	18ca (Bl)	2.40	2.40
163	A7 (c)	20ca (Bl) ('43)	7.25	5.50
164	A7 (c)	20ca (C)	2.40	2.40
a.		Double overprint, one bl. one car.	1,350.	475.00
165	A8 (d)	1fa (Bl)	2.40	2.40
166	A8 (d)	1fa6ca (C)	3.25	3.25
a.		Bl. overprint	300.00	225.00
167	A8 (d)	1fa12ca (C)	3.25	3.25
168	A8 (d)	1fa16ca (Bl)	3.25	3.25
169	A8 (d)	2fa12ca (Bl)	100.00	80.00
170	A8 (d)	2fa12ca (C)	3.25	3.25
171	A8 (d)	6fa6ca (C)	4.00	4.00
172	A8 (d)	1r (C)	7.25	7.25
173	A8 (d)	2r (C)	7.25	7.25
174	A8 (d)	3r (C)	7.25	7.25
175	A8 (d)	3r (Bl) ('43)	200.00	175.00
176	A8 (d)	5r (C)	7.25	7.25
		Nos. 156A-176 (21)	676.85	560.10

Same Overprints on Paris International Exposition Issue of 1937

Perf. 13

177	CD74 (c)	8ca (Bl)	7.25	7.25
178	CD75 (d)	12ca (Bl)	7.25	7.25
179	CD76 (d)	16ca (Bl)	1,300.	1,300.
180	CD78 (d)	1fa12ca (Bl)	7.25	7.25
181	CD79 (d)	2fa12ca (C)	7.25	7.25

Same Overprint on New York World's Fair Issue, 1939

Perf. 12½x12

182	CD82 (d) 1fa12ca (Bl)	7.25	7.25
183	CD82 (d) 2fa12ca (C)	7.25	7.25

No. 87 Surcharged in Carmine

1942-43 *Perf. 13½x14*

184	A7	1ca on 16ca	75.00	45.00
185	A7	4ca on 16ca ('43)	75.00	45.00
186	A7	10ca on 16ca	55.00	35.00
187	A7	15ca on 16ca	55.00	35.00
188	A7	1fa3ca on 16ca ('43)	72.50	45.00
189	A7	2fa9ca on 16ca ('43)	72.50	45.00
190	A7	3fa3ca on 16ca ('43)	55.00	35.00
		Nos. 184-190 (7)	460.00	285.00

Nos. 95-99 Srchd. in Carmine

1943 *Perf. 14x13½*

191	A8	1ca on 6fa6ca	11.00	11.00
192	A8	4ca on 6fa6ca	12.50	12.50
193	A8	10ca on 6fa6ca	11.00	11.00
194	A8	15ca on 6fa6ca	11.00	11.00
195	A8	1fa3ca on 6fa6ca	11.00	11.00
196	A8	2fa9ca on 6fa6ca	12.50	12.50
197	A8	3fa3ca on 6fa6ca	12.50	12.50
198	A8	1ca on 1r	4.75	4.75
199	A8	2ca on 1r	1.60	1.60
200	A8	4ca on 1r	1.60	1.60
201	A8	6ca on 2r	1.60	1.60
202	A8	10ca on 2r	1.75	1.75
203	A8	12ca on 2r	1.60	1.60
204	A8	15ca on 3r	1.60	1.60
205	A8	16ca on 3r	1.60	1.60
206	A8	1fa3ca on 3r	1.60	1.60
207	A8	1fa6ca on 5r	2.00	2.00
208	A8	1fa12ca on 5r	2.40	2.40
209	A8	1fa16ca on 5r	2.40	2.40
		Nos. 191-209 (19)	106.00	106.00

In 1943, 200 each of 27 stamps were overprinted in red or dark blue, "FRANCE TOUJOURS" and a Lorraine Cross within a circle measuring 17½mm in diameter. Overprinted were Nos. 81-99, 104-109, 111-112. Values, set: $25,000 unused; $6,000 used.

No. 95 Surcharged in Carmine

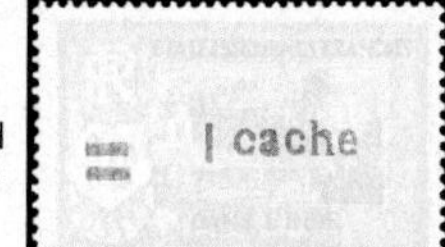

1943 Unwmk. *Perf. 14x13½*

209A	A8	1ca on 6fa6ca	35.00	27.50
209B	A8	4ca on 6fa6ca	35.00	27.50
209C	A8	10ca on 6fa6ca	24.00	16.00
209D	A8	15ca on 6fa6ca	24.00	16.00
209E	A8	1fa3ca on 6fa6ca	32.50	27.50
209F	A8	2fa9ca on 6fa6ca	32.50	27.50
209G	A8	3fa3ca on 6fa6ca	35.00	27.50
		Nos. 209A-209G (7)	218.00	169.50

Catalogue values for unused stamps in this section, from this point to the end of the section, are for Never Hinged items.

Eboue Issue
Common Design Type

1945 Engr. *Perf. 13*

210	CD91 3fa8ca black	.80	.70
211	CD91 5r1fa16ca Prus grn	1.40	1.25

Nos. 210 and 211 exist imperforate.

Apsaras — A11

Designs: 6ca, 8ca, 10ca, Dvarabalagar. 12ca, 15ca, 1fa, Vishnu. 1fa6ca, 2fa, 2fa2ca, Dvarabalagar (foot raised). 2fa12ca, 3fa, 5fa, Temple Guardian. 7fa12ca, 1r2fa, 1r4fa12ca, Tigoupalagar.

1948 Photo. *Perf. 13x13½*

212	A11	1ca dk ol grn	.50	.25
213	A11	2ca orange brn	.50	.25
214	A11	4ca vio, *cr*	.55	.30
215	A11	6ca yellow org	1.50	.65
216	A11	8ca gray blk	1.50	1.10
217	A11	10ca dl yel grn, *pale grn*	1.50	1.10
218	A11	12ca violet brn	1.00	.65
219	A11	15ca Prus grn	1.00	.65
220	A11	1fa vio, *pale rose*	1.50	.80
221	A11	1fa6ca brown red	1.50	.85
222	A11	2fa dk green	1.50	.85
223	A11	2fa2ca blue, *cr*	1.50	1.15
224	A11	2fa12ca brown	1.90	1.15
225	A11	3fa dp orange	3.25	1.25
226	A11	5fa red vio, *rose*	3.00	1.25
227	A11	7fa12ca dk brown	3.25	1.25
228	A11	1r2fa brown blk	6.00	4.50
229	A11	1r4fa12ca olive grn	6.50	5.00
		Nos. 212-229 (18)	37.95	23.00

Brahman Ascetic — A12

1952

230	A12	18ca rose red	2.75	2.00
231	A12	1fa15ca vio blue	3.75	2.50
232	A12	4fa olive grn	4.25	3.50
		Nos. 230-232 (3)	10.75	8.00

Military Medal Issue
Common Design Type

1952 Engr. and Typo. *Perf. 13*

233	CD101 1fa multi	5.50	*7.00*

SEMI-POSTAL STAMPS

Regular Issue of 1914 Surcharged in Red

Two printings: 1st, surcharge at bottom of stamp; 2nd, surcharge centered toward top.

1915 Unwmk. *Perf. 14x13½*

B1	A5 10c + 5c rose & blk (1st)	2.10	2.10
b.	Inverted surcharge	210.00	210.00

There were two printings of this surcharge. In the first, it was placed at the bottom of the stamp; in the second, it was centered toward the top.

Regular Issue of 1914 Surcharged in Red

1916

B2 A5 10c + 5c rose & blk 21.00 21.00
a. Inverted surcharge 210.00 210.00
b. Double surcharge 210.00 210.00

No. 32 Surcharged

B3 A5 10c + 5c rose & blk 3.50 3.50

No. 32 Surcharged

B4 A5 10c + 5c rose & blk 1.60 1.60

No. 32 Surcharged

B5 A5 10c + 5c rose & blk 2.25 2.25

Curie Issue
Common Design Type

1938 Engr. *Perf. 13*
B6 CD80 2fa12ca + 20ca brt ultra 10.00 10.00

French Revolution Issue
Common Design Type

1939 Photo.
Name and Value Typo. in Black
B7 CD83 18ca + 10ca grn 5.75 *6.50*
B8 CD83 1fa6ca + 12ca brn 5.75 *6.50*
B9 CD83 1fa12ca + 16ca red org 5.75 *6.50*
B10 CD83 1fa16ca + 1fa16ca rose pink 5.75 *6.50*
B11 CD83 2fa12ca + 3fa blue 5.75 *6.50*
Nos. B7-B11 (5) 28.75 *32.50*

Common Design Type and

Non-Commissioned Officer, Native Guard — SP1

Sepoy SP2

1941 Photo. *Perf. 13½*
B12 SP1 1fa16ca + 1fa16ca red 1.25
B13 CD86 2fa12ca + 5fa mar 1.25
B13A SP2 4fa4ca + 1fa16ca bl 1.25
Nos. B12-B13A (3) 3.75

Nos. B12-B13A were issued by the Vichy government in France, but were not placed on sale in French India.

Nos. 112A-112B Srchd. in Black or Red

1944 Engr. *Perf. 12½x12*
B13B 20ca + 2fa12ca on 4fa4ca deep blue (R) 1.00
B13C + 4fa4ca on 1fa16ca car & red 1.00

Colonial Development Fund.
Nos. B13B-B13C were issued by the Vichy government in France, but were not placed on sale in French India.

Catalogue values for unused stamps in this section, from this point to the end of the section, are for Never Hinged items.

Red Cross Issue
Common Design Type

1944 Photo. *Perf. 14½x14*
B14 CD90 3fa + 1r4fa dk ol brn 1.50 1.25

The surtax was for the French Red Cross and national relief.

Tropical Medicine Issue
Common Design Type

1950 Engr. *Perf. 13*
B15 CD100 1fa + 10ca ind & dp bl 6.00 4.00

The surtax was for charitable work.

AIR POST STAMPS

Common Design Type

1942 Unwmk. Photo. *Perf. 14½x14*
C1 CD87 4fa dark orange .90 *2.00*
C2 CD87 1r bright red .90 *2.00*
C3 CD87 2r brown red 1.50 *2.00*
C4 CD87 5r black 1.50 *3.00*
C5 CD87 8r ultra 2.25 *3.00*
C6 CD87 10r dark green 2.25 *3.00*
Nos. C1-C6 (6) 9.30 *15.00*

Catalogue values for unused stamps in this section, from this point to the end of the section, are for Never Hinged items.

Victory Issue
Common Design Type

1946 Engr. *Perf. 12½*
C7 CD92 4fa dk blue green 1.00 *4.00*

Chad to Rhine Issue
Common Design Types

1946, June 6
C8 CD93 2fa12ca olive bis 1.40 *2.00*
C9 CD94 5fa dark blue 1.40 *2.00*
C10 CD95 7fa12ca dk purple 2.25 *2.00*
C11 CD96 1r2fa green 2.25 *3.00*
C12 CD97 1r4fa12ca dk car 2.75 *3.00*
C13 CD98 3r1fa violet brn 2.75 *3.00*
Nos. C8-C13 (6) 12.80 *15.00*

A 3r ultramarine and red, picturing the Temple of Chindambaram, was sold at Paris June 7 to July 8, 1948, but not placed on sale in the colony. Values: $10 never hinged, $7 hinged.

Bas-relief Figure of Goddess — AP1

Wing and Temple — AP2

Bird over Palms — AP3

Perf. 12x13, 13x12
1949 Photo. Unwmk.
C14 AP1 1r yellow & plum 6.00 *10.00*
C15 AP2 2r green & dk grn 6.00 *10.00*
C16 AP3 5r lt bl & vio brn 27.50 *30.00*
Nos. C14-C16 (3) 39.50 *50.00*

UPU Issue
Common Design Type

1949 Engr. *Perf. 13*
C17 CD99 6fa lilac rose 11.50 8.75

Universal Postal Union, 75th anniv.

Liberation Issue
Common Design Type

1954, June 6
C18 CD102 1fa sepia & vio brn 11.00 8.00

AIR POST SEMI-POSTAL STAMPS

Girl's School SPAP1

Perf. 12½x13½
1942, June 22 Unwmk. Photo.
CB1 SPAP1 2fa12ca + 5fa20ca green .95
CB2 SPAP1 3fa8ca + 1r2fa yel brn .95

Native children's welfare fund.
Nos. CB1-CB2 were issued by the Vichy government in France, but were not placed on sale in French India.

Colonial Education Fund
Common Design Type

1942, June 22
CB3 CD86a 2fa + 3fa blue & red .90

No. CB3 was issued by the Vichy government in France, but was not placed on sale in French India.

POSTAGE DUE STAMPS

Postage Due Stamps of France Surcharged like Nos. 54-75 in Black, Blue or Red

1923 Unwmk. *Perf. 14x13½*
J1 D2 6ca on 10c brn 1.25 1.25
J2 D2 12ca on 25c rose (Bk) 1.25 1.25
J3 D2 15ca on 20c ol grn (R) 1.60 1.60
J4 D2 1fa6ca on 30c red 1.60 1.60
J5 D2 1fa12a on 50c brn vio 2.75 2.75
J6 D2 1fa15ca on 5c bl (Bk) 3.00 3.00
J7 D2 3fa3ca on 1fr red brn, *straw* 3.25 3.25
Nos. J1-J7 (7) 14.70 14.70

Types of Postage Due Stamps of French Colonies, 1884-85, Surcharged with New Values as in 1923 in Red or Black Bars over Original Values

1928
J8 D1 4ca on 20c gray lil 1.60 1.60
J9 D1 1fa on 30c orange 3.25 3.25
J10 D1 1fa16ca on 5c bl blk (R) 3.25 3.25
J11 D1 3fa on 1fr lt grn 3.75 3.75
Nos. J8-J11 (4) 11.85 11.85

D3

1929 Typo.
J12 D3 4ca deep red .50 .50
J13 D3 6ca blue .65 .65
J14 D3 12ca green .65 .65
J15 D3 1fa brown 1.25 1.25
J16 D3 1fa12ca lilac gray 1.25 1.25
J17 D3 1fa16ca buff 1.75 1.75
J18 D3 3fa lilac 2.10 2.10
Nos. J12-J18 (7) 8.15 8.15

D4

1948 Unwmk. Photo. *Perf. 13x13½*
J19 D4 1ca dk violet .30 .30
J20 D4 2ca dk brown .50 .50
J21 D4 6ca blue green .50 .50
J22 D4 12ca dp orange .70 .70
J23 D4 1fa dk car rose .80 .80
J24 D4 1fa12ca brown .80 .80
J25 D4 2fa dk slate bl 1.25 1.25
J26 D4 2fa12ca henna brn 1.60 1.60
J27 D4 5fa dk olive grn 2.25 2.25
J28 D4 1r dk blue vio 3.00 3.00
Nos. J19-J28 (10) 11.70 11.70

FRENCH MOROCCO

'french mə-'rä-ˌkō

LOCATION — Northwest coast of Africa
GOVT. — French Protectorate
AREA — 153,870 sq. mi.
POP. — 8,340,000 (estimated 1954)
CAPITAL — Rabat

French Morocco was a French Protectorate from 1912 until 1956 when it, along with the Spanish and Tangier zones of Morocco, became the independent country, Morocco.

Stamps inscribed "Tanger" were for use in the international zone of Tangier in northern Morocco.

100 Centimos = 1 Peseta
100 Centimes = 1 franc (1917)

Catalogue values for unused stamps in this country are for Never Hinged items, beginning with Scott 177 in the regular postage section, Scott B26 in the semi-postal section, Scott C27 in the airpost section, Scott CB23A in the airpost semi-postal section, and Scott J46 in the postage due section.

French Offices in Morocco

Stamps of France Surcharged in Red or Black

Type I. The "N" of "INV" is under the "B" of "REPUBLIQUE."
Type II. The "N" of "INV" is under the "U" of "REPUBLIQUE."

1891-1900 Unwmk. *Perf. 14x13½*

No.	Type	Description	Unused	Used
1	A15	5c on 5c grn, *grnsh* (R)	16.00	4.00
a.		Imperf., pair	175.00	
2	A15	5c on 5c yel grn (II) (R) ('99)	32.50	27.50
a.		Type I	32.50	27.50
3	A15	10c on 10c blk, *lav* (II) (R)	32.50	4.00
a.		Type I	45.00	20.00
b.		10c on 25c black, *rose*	1,100.	1,200.
4	A15	20c on 20c red, *grn*	40.00	32.50
5	A15	25c on 25c blk, *rose* (R)	32.50	4.00
a.		Double surcharge	225.00	
b.		Imperf., pair	175.00	
6	A15	50c on 50c car, *rose* (II)	105.00	47.50
a.		Type I	375.00	260.00
7	A15	1p on 1fr brnz grn, *straw*	120.00	80.00
8	A15	2p on 2fr brn, *az* (Bk) ('00)	240.00	240.00
		Nos. 1-8 (8)	618.50	439.50

No. 3b was never sent to Morocco.

France Nos. J15-J16 Overprinted in Carmine

1893

No.	Type	Description	Unused	Used
9	D2	5c black	3,250.	1,200.
10	D2	10c black	2,900.	800.

Counterfeits exist.

Surcharged in Red or Black

A3

A4

A5

1902-10

No.	Type	Description	Unused	Used
11	A3	1c on 1c gray (R) ('08)	2.40	1.20
12	A3	2c on 2c vio brn ('08)	2.40	1.20
13	A3	3c on 3c red org ('08)	3.25	1.60
14	A3	4c on 4c yel brn ('08)	13.00	8.00
15	A3	5c on 5c grn (R)	12.00	4.00
a.		Double surcharge		340.00
b.		Triple surcharge	340.00	
16	A4	10c on 10c rose red ('03)	8.00	4.00
a.		Surcharge omitted	225.00	
17	A4	20c on 20c brn vio ('03)	40.00	24.00
18	A4	25c on 25c bl ('03)	40.00	4.00
19	A4	35c on 35c vio ('10)	40.00	24.00
20	A5	50c on 50c bis brn & lav ('03)	67.50	16.00
21	A5	1p on 1fr cl & ol grn ('03)	120.00	80.00
22	A5	2p on 2fr gray vio & yel ('03)	160.00	120.00
		Nos. 11-22 (12)	508.55	288.00

Nos. 11-14 exist spelled CFNTIMOS or GENTIMOS.

The 25c on 25c with surcharge omitted is listed as No. 81a.

For overprints and surcharges see Nos. 26-37, 72-79, B1, B3.

Postage Due Stamps Nos. J1-J2 Handstamped

1903

No.	Type	Description	Unused	Used
24	D2	5c on 5c light blue	1,500.	1,400.
25	D2	10c on 10c chocolate	2,800.	2,600.

Nos. 24 and 25 were used only on Oct. 10, 1903. Used stamps were not canceled, the overprint serving as a cancellation.

Numerous counterfeits exist.

Types of 1902-10 Issue Surcharged in Red or Blue

1911-17

No.	Type	Description	Unused	Used
26	A3	1c on 1c gray (R)	1.20	.90
27	A3	2c on 2c vio brn	1.20	1.20
28	A3	3c on 3c orange	1.20	1.20
29	A3	5c on 5c green (R)	1.20	.80
30	A4	10c on 10c rose	1.20	.80
a.		Imperf., pair	275.00	
31	A4	15c on 15c org ('17)	3.50	2.40
32	A4	20c on 20c brn vio	5.50	4.00
33	A4	25c on 25c blue (R)	2.40	1.60
34	A4	35c on 35c violet (R)	12.00	5.50
35	A5	40c on 40c red & pale bl ('17)	8.00	5.50
36	A5	50c on 50c bis brn & lav (R)	27.50	16.00
37	A5	1p on 1fr cl & ol grn	24.00	12.00
		Nos. 26-37 (12)	88.90	51.90

For surcharges see Nos. B1, B3.

Stamps of this design were issued by the Cherifien posts in 1912-13. The Administration Cherifinne des Postes, Telegraphes et Telephones was formed in 1911 under French guidance. See Morocco in Vol. 4 for listings.

French Protectorate Issue of 1911-17 Overprinted "Protectorat Francais"

A6

A7

A8

1914-21

No.	Type	Description	Unused	Used
38	A6	1c on 1c lt gray	.40	.50
a.		1c dk gray ('22)	.55	.80
39	A6	2c on 2c vio brn	.80	.50
40	A6	3c on 3c orange	1.20	.65
41	A6	5c on 5c green	1.20	.50
a.		New value omitted	275.00	275.00
42	A7	10c on 10c rose	.80	.30
a.		New value omitted	550.00	550.00
43	A7	15c on 15c org ('17)	.80	.80
a.		New value omitted	120.00	120.00
44	A7	20c on 20c brn vio	4.75	3.50
a.		"Protectorat Francais" double	300.00	300.00
45	A7	25c on 25c blue	3.25	.80
a.		New value omitted	350.00	350.00
46	A7	25c on 25c violet ('21)	1.25	.40
a.		"Protectorat Francais" omitted	80.00	80.00
b.		"Protectorat Francais" double	175.00	175.00
c.		"Protectorat Francais" dbl. (R + Bk)	175.00	175.00
47	A7	30c on 30c vio ('21)	20.00	9.00
48	A7	35c on 35c violet	4.75	1.60
49	A8	40c on 40c red & pale bl	20.00	8.75
a.		New value omitted	375.00	375.00
50	A8	45c on 45c grn & bl ('21)	55.00	40.00
51	A8	50c on 50c bis brn & lav	2.40	.80
a.		"Protectorat Francais" invtd.	200.00	200.00
b.		"Protectorat Francais" double	450.00	450.00
52	A8	1p on 1fr cl & ol grn	5.50	.80
a.		"Protectorat Francais" invtd.	350.00	350.00
b.		New value double	200.00	200.00
c.		New value dbl., one invtd.	210.00	210.00
53	A8	2p on 2fr gray vio & yel	8.00	4.00
a.		New value omitted	175.00	175.00
b.		"Protectorat Francais" omitted	110.00	110.00
c.		New value double		225.00
d.		New value dbl., one invtd.		
54	A8	5p on 5fr dk bl & buff	15.00	8.00
		Nos. 38-54 (17)	145.10	80.90

For surcharges see Nos. B2, B4-B5.

Tower of Hassan, Rabat — A9

Mosque of the Andalusians, Fez — A10

City Gate Chella A11

Koutoubiah, Marrakesh A12

Bab Mansour, Meknes A13

Roman Ruins, Volubilis A14

1917 Engr. *Perf. 13½x14, 14x13½*

No.	Type	Description	Unused	Used
55	A9	1c grnsh gray	.40	.40
56	A9	2c brown lilac	.40	.40
57	A9	3c orange brn	.40	.80
a.		Imperf., pair	87.50	
58	A10	5c yellow grn	.40	.40
59	A10	10c rose red	.80	.40
60	A10	15c dark gray	.80	.40
a.		Imperf., pair	65.00	
61	A11	20c red brown	4.00	2.40
62	A11	25c dull blue	4.00	1.25
63	A11	30c gray violet	4.75	3.25
64	A12	35c orange	4.75	4.00
65	A12	40c ultra	1.60	1.60
66	A12	45c gray green	32.50	16.00
67	A13	50c dk brown	5.50	4.00
a.		Imperf., pair	65.00	
68	A13	1fr slate	16.00	4.00
a.		Imperf., pair	65.00	
69	A14	2fr black brown	160.00	95.00
70	A14	5fr dk gray grn	47.50	40.00
71	A14	10fr black	47.50	40.00
		Nos. 55-71 (17)	331.30	214.30

See note following No. 115. See Nos. 93-105. For surcharges see Nos. 120-121.

Types of the 1902-10 Issue Overprinted

1918-24 *Perf. 14x13½*

No.	Type	Description	Unused	Used
72	A3	1c dk gray	.40	.80
73	A3	2c violet brn	.40	.80
74	A3	3c red orange	1.20	1.20
75	A3	5c green	1.20	1.20
76	A3	5c orange ('23)	2.40	2.00
77	A4	10c rose	2.40	1.60
78	A4	10c green ('24)	2.40	1.60
79	A4	15c orange	1.60	1.20
80	A4	20c violet brn	2.40	2.40
81	A4	25c blue	2.40	2.40
a.		"TANGER" omitted	450.00	450.00
82	A4	30c red org ('24)	4.00	2.75
83	A4	35c violet	4.00	2.40
84	A5	40c red & pale bl	4.00	2.40
85	A5	50c bis brn & lav	27.50	16.00
86	A4	50c blue ('24)	24.00	13.50
87	A5	1fr claret & ol grn	16.00	8.00
88	A5	2fr org & pale bl ('24)	80.00	72.50
89	A5	5fr dk bl & buff ('24)	67.50	65.00
		Nos. 72-89 (18)	243.80	197.75

Types of 1917 and

Tower of Hassan, Rabat — A15

Bab Mansour, Meknes A16

Roman Ruins, Volubilis A17

1923-27 Photo. *Perf. 13½*

No.	Type	Denomination	Color	Unused	Used
90	A15	1c	olive green	.25	.25
91	A15	2c	brown vio	.25	.25
92	A15	3c	yellow brn	.25	.25
93	A10	5c	orange	.25	.25
94	A10	10c	yellow grn	.25	.25
95	A10	15c	dk gray	.25	.25
96	A11	20c	red brown	.25	.25
97	A11	20c	red vio ('27)	.40	.40
98	A11	25c	ultra	.40	.40
99	A11	30c	deep red	.40	.40
100	A11	30c	turq bl ('27)	1.20	.80
101	A12	35c	violet	1.20	.80
102	A12	40c	orange red	.25	.25
103	A12	45c	deep green	.40	.40
104	A16	50c	dull turq	.40	.40
105	A12	50c	ol grn ('27)	.80	.40
106	A16	60c	lilac	1.20	.80
107	A16	75c	red vio ('27)	.80	.40
108	A16	1fr	deep brown	.80	.80
109	A16	1.05fr	red brn ('27)	1.60	.80
110	A16	1.40fr	dull rose ('27)	.80	.80
111	A16	1.50fr	turq bl ('27)	1.20	.40
112	A17	2fr	olive brn	1.60	1.20
113	A17	3fr	dp red ('27)	1.60	1.20
114	A17	5fr	dk gray grn	4.00	2.75
115	A17	10fr	black	12.00	4.75
			Nos. 90-115 (26)	32.80	19.90

Nos. 90-110, 112-115 exist imperf. The stamps of 1917 were line engraved. Those of 1923-27 were printed by photogravure and have in the margin at lower right the imprint "Helio Vaugirard."

See No. B36. For surcharges see Nos. 122-123.

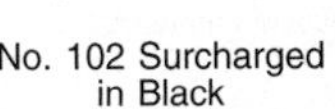

No. 102 Surcharged in Black

1930

No.	Type	Description	Unused	Used
120	A12	15c on 40c org red	1.60	1.60
a.		Surcharge bars omitted	72.50	72.50
b.		Pair, one with surcharge omitted	350.00	

Nos. 100, 106 and 110 Surcharged in Blue Similarly to No. 176

1931

No.	Type	Description	Unused	Used
121	A11	25c on 30c turq blue	2.50	2.10
a.		Inverted surcharge	140.00	140.00
122	A16	50c on 60c lilac	1.20	.40
a.		Inverted surcharge	150.00	150.00
b.		Double surcharge	150.00	150.00
c.		Surcharge bars omitted	90.00	
123	A16	1fr on 1.40fr rose	3.25	1.60
a.		Inverted surcharge	150.00	150.00
b.		Surcharge bars omitted	90.00	
		Nos. 121-123 (3)	6.95	4.10

Old Treasure House and Tribunal, Tangier A18

Roadstead at Agadir A19

Post Office at Casablanca A20

Moulay Idriss of the Zehroun A21

Kasbah of the Oudayas, Rabat A22

Court of the Medersa el Attarine at Fez — A23

Kasbah of Si Madani el Glaoui at Ouarzazat A24

Saadiens' Tombs at Marrakesh — A25

1933-34 Engr. *Perf. 13*

No.	Type	Denomination	Color	Unused	Used
124	A18	1c	olive blk	.25	.25
125	A18	2c	red violet	.25	.25
126	A19	3c	dark brown	.25	.25
127	A19	5c	brown red	.25	.25
128	A20	10c	blue green	.30	.30
129	A20	15c	black	.40	.30
130	A20	20c	red brown	.40	.30
131	A21	25c	dark blue	.40	.30
132	A21	30c	emerald	.40	.30
133	A21	40c	black brn	.40	.30
134	A22	45c	brown vio	.80	.65
135	A22	50c	dk blue grn	.80	.30
a.			Booklet pane of 10	—	
b.			Booklet pane of 20	—	
			Complete booklet, #135b	2,000.	
136	A22	65c	brown red	.40	.30
a.			Booklet pane of 10	—	
b.			Booklet pane of 20	—	
			Complete booklet, #136b	65.00	
137	A23	75c	red violet	.80	.30
138	A23	90c	orange red	.40	.30
139	A23	1fr	deep brown	1.20	.50
140	A23	1.25fr	black ('34)	1.60	1.50
141	A24	1.50fr	ultra	.40	.30
142	A24	1.75fr	myr grn ('34)	.80	.40
143	A24	2fr	yellow brn	4.75	.80
144	A24	3fr	car rose	55.00	6.50
145	A25	5fr	red brown	12.00	2.50
146	A25	10fr	black	10.00	6.50
147	A25	20fr	bluish gray	9.50	7.25
			Nos. 124-147 (24)	101.75	30.90

Booklets containing Nos. 135 and 136 each have two panes of 10 (Nos. 135a, 136a) connected by a gutter, the complete piece constituting No. 135b or 136b, which is stapled into the booklet through the gutter.

For surcharges see Nos. 148, 176, B13-B20.

No. 135 Srchd. in Red

1939

No.	Type	Description	Unused	Used
148	A22	40c on 50c dk bl grn	.95	.50

Mosque of Salé — A26

Sefrou — A27

Cedars — A28

Goatherd A29

Ramparts of Salé — A30

Scimitar-horned Oryxes — A31

Valley of Draa A32

Fez — A33

1939-42

No.	Type	Denomination	Color	Unused	Used
149	A26	1c	rose violet	.25	.25
150	A27	2c	emerald	.25	.25
151	A27	3c	ultra	.25	.25
152	A26	5c	dk bl grn	.25	.25
153	A27	10c	brt red vio	.25	.25
154	A28	15c	dk green	.25	.25
155	A28	20c	black grn	.25	.25
156	A29	30c	deep blue	.25	.25
157	A29	40c	chocolate	.25	.25
158	A29	45c	Prus green	.50	.50
159	A30	50c	rose red	1.40	.90
159A	A30	50c	Prus grn ('40)	.30	.25
160	A30	60c	turq blue	1.25	.75
160A	A30	60c	choc ('40)	.30	.25
161	A31	70c	dk violet	.25	.25
162	A32	75c	grnsh blk	.50	.50
163	A32	80c	pck bl ('40)	.30	.25
163A	A32	80c	dk grn ('42)	.40	.25
164	A30	90c	ultra	.30	.25
165	A28	1fr	chocolate	.30	.25
165A	A32	1.20fr	rose vio ('42)	.80	.40
166	A32	1.25fr	henna brn	1.10	.65
167	A32	1.40fr	rose violet	.65	.30
168	A30	1.50fr	cop red ('40)	.30	.25
168A	A30	1.50fr	rose ('42)	.25	.25
169	A33	2fr	Prus green	.25	.25
170	A33	2.25fr	dark blue	.65	.50
170A	A26	2.40fr	red ('42)	.30	.30
171	A26	2.50fr	scarlet	.90	.70
171A	A26	2.50fr	dp blue ('40)	1.10	.65
172	A33	3fr	black brown	.50	.30
172A	A26	4fr	dp ultra ('42)	.40	.40
172B	A32	4.50fr	grnsh blk ('42)	.80	.80
173	A31	5fr	dark blue	.65	.50
174	A31	10fr	red	1.25	.90
174A	A31	15fr	Prus grn ('42)	4.75	4.00
175	A31	20fr	dk vio brn	2.00	1.75
			Nos. 149-175 (37)	24.70	19.55
			Set, never hinged	32.50	

See Nos. 197-219. For surcharges see Nos. 244, 261-262, B21-B24, B26, B28, B32.

No. 136 Srchd. in Black

1940

No.	Type	Description	Unused	Used
176	A22	35c on 65c brown red	1.75	.95
a.		Pair, one without surcharge	3.25	2.40

The surcharge was applied on alternate rows in the sheet, making No. 176a. This was done to make a pair equal 1fr, the new rate.

Catalogue values for unused stamps in this section, from this point to the end of the section, are for Never Hinged items.

One Aim Alone-Victory — A34

1943 Litho. *Perf. 12*

No.	Type	Description	Unused	Used
177	A34	1.50fr deep blue	.40	.25

Tower of Hassan, Rabat — A35

1943

No.	Type	Denomination	Color	Unused	Used
178	A35	10c	rose lilac	.30	.25
179	A35	30c	blue	.30	.25
180	A35	40c	lake	.30	.25
181	A35	50c	blue green	.30	.25
182	A35	60c	dk vio brn	.30	.25
183	A35	70c	rose violet	.30	.25
184	A35	80c	gray green	.30	.30
185	A35	1fr	car lake	.30	.25
186	A35	1.20fr	violet	.30	.25
187	A35	1.50fr	red	.30	.25
188	A35	2fr	lt bl grn	.30	.25
189	A35	2.40fr	car rose	.30	.35
190	A35	3fr	olive brn	.30	.30
191	A35	4fr	dk ultra	.30	.30
192	A35	4.50fr	slate blk	.40	.25
193	A35	5fr	dull blue	.55	.25
194	A35	10fr	orange brn	.55	.40
195	A35	15fr	slate grn	1.60	.55
196	A35	20fr	deep plum	2.40	.80
			Nos. 178-196 (19)	9.70	6.00

Types of 1939-42

Perf. 13½x14, 14x13½

1945-47 Typo. Unwmk.

No.	Type	Denomination	Color	Unused	Used
197	A27	10c	red violet	.40	.25
199	A29	40c	chocolate	.40	.25
200	A30	50c	Prus grn	.40	.25
203	A28	1fr	choc ('46)	.40	.35
204	A32	1.20fr	vio brn ('46)	.40	.30
205	A27	1.30fr	blue ('47)	.80	.40
206	A30	1.50fr	deep red	.40	.25
207	A33	2fr	Prus grn	.40	.25
209	A33	3fr	black brn	.40	.25
210	A29	3.50fr	dk red ('47)	1.20	.80
212	A31	4.50fr	magenta ('47)	.80	.40
214	A31	5fr	indigo	1.20	.55
215	A32	6fr	chlky bl ('46)	.80	.35
216	A31	10fr	red	2.00	.80
217	A31	15fr	Prus grn	2.40	.80
218	A31	20fr	dk vio brn	3.25	1.40
219	A31	25fr	black brn	3.25	2.10
			Nos. 197-219 (17)	18.90	9.75

For surcharges see Nos. 261-263, B26, B28, B32.

The Terraces — A37

Mountain District — A39

Fortress A38

Marrakesh A40

Gardens of Fez — A41

Ouarzazat District — A42

1947 Engr. Unwmk. *Perf. 13*

221	A37	10c black brn	.40	.25
222	A37	30c brt red	.40	.25
223	A37	50c brt grnsh bl	.40	.25
224	A37	60c brt red vio	.40	.25
225	A38	1fr black	.40	.25
226	A38	1.50fr blue	.40	.25
227	A39	2fr brt green	.80	.40
228	A39	3fr brown red	.40	.25
229	A40	4fr dk bl vio	.40	.25
230	A41	5fr dk green	1.20	.55
231	A40	6fr crimson	.40	.25
232	A41	10fr dp blue	1.20	.40
233	A42	15fr dk grn	1.60	1.20
234	A42	20fr henna brn	1.60	.80
235	A42	25fr purple	2.40	1.20
		Nos. 221-235 (15)	12.40	6.80

1948-49

236	A37	30c purple	.40	.25
237	A38	2fr vio brn ('49)	.80	.40
238	A40	4fr green	.80	.35
239	A41	8fr org ('49)	1.60	.80
240	A41	10fr blue	1.20	.40
241	A42	10fr car rose	.80	.80
242	A38	12fr red	1.20	.80
243	A42	18fr deep blue	2.40	1.20
		Nos. 236-243 (8)	9.20	5.00

For surcharges see Nos. 263, 293-294.

No. 175 Surcharged with New Value and Wavy Lines in Carmine

1948

244	A31	8fr on 20fr dk vio brn	1.20	.80

Fortified Oasis A43

Walled City — A44

1949

245	A43	5fr blue green	1.20	.40
246	A44	15fr red	1.60	.80
247	A44	25fr ultra	1.60	.80
		Nos. 245-247 (3)	4.40	2.00

See No. 300.

Detail, Gate of Oudayas, Rabat — A45

Nejjarine Fountain, Fez — A46

Garden, Meknes — A47

1949 *Perf. 14x13*

248	A45	10c black	.40	.25
249	A45	50c rose brn	.40	.25
250	A45	1fr blue vio	.40	.25
251	A46	2fr dk car rose	.40	.25
252	A46	3fr dark blue	.80	.25
253	A46	5fr brt green	1.20	.25
254	A47	8fr dk bl grn	1.60	.80
255	A47	10fr brt red	1.60	.80
		Nos. 248-255 (8)	6.80	3.10

Postal Administration Building, Meknes — A48

1949, Oct. *Perf. 13*

256	A48	5fr dark green	2.40	2.00
257	A48	15fr deep carmine	2.40	2.00
258	A48	25fr deep blue	2.75	2.40
		Nos. 256-258 (3)	7.55	6.40

75th anniv. of the UPU.

Todra Valley A49

1950

259	A49	35fr red brown	1.60	.40
260	A49	50fr indigo	1.60	.40

See No. 270.

Nos. 204 and 205 Srchd. in Black or Blue

1950 *Perf. 14x13½, 13½x14*

261	A32	1fr on 1.20fr vio brn (Bk)	.40	.35
262	A27	1fr on 1.30fr blue (Bl)	.40	.25

The surcharge is transposed and spaced to fit the design on No. 262.

No. 231 Surcharged with New Value and Wavy Lines in Black

1951 *Perf. 13*

263	A40	5fr on 6fr crimson	.80	.25

Statue of Gen. Jacques Leclerc — A50

1951, Apr. 28 Engr.

264	A50	10fr blue green	2.40	2.00
265	A50	15fr deep carmine	2.75	2.00
266	A50	25fr indigo	2.75	2.00
		Nos. 264-266 (3)	7.90	6.00

Unveiling of a monument to Gen. Leclerc at Casablanca, Apr. 28, 1951. See No. C39.

Loustau Hospital, Oujda A51

Designs: 15fr, New Hospital, Meknes. 25fr, New Hospital, Rabat.

1951

267	A51	10fr indigo & pur	2.00	1.60
268	A51	15fr Prus grn & red brn	2.00	1.60
269	A51	25fr dk brn & ind	2.40	2.00
		Nos. 267-269 (3)	6.40	5.20

See No. C41.

Todra Valley Type of 1950

1951

270	A49	30fr ultramarine	1.60	.40

Pigeons at Fountain A52

Karaouine Mosque, Fez A53

Patio, Oudayas A54

Oudayas Point, Rabat A55

Patio of Old House — A56

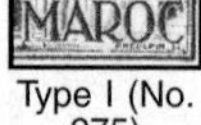

Type I (No. 275)

Type II (No. 276)

Perf. 14x13, 13

1951-53 Engr. Unwmk.

271	A52	5fr magenta ('52)	.40	.25
272	A53	6fr bl grn ('52)	.40	.40
273	A52	8fr brown ('52)	.40	.40
273A	A53	10fr rose red ('53)	.40	.35
274	A53	12fr dp ultra ('52)	.80	.40
275	A54	15fr red brn (I)	2.75	.25
276	A54	15fr red brn (II)	1.20	.25
277	A55	15fr pur ('52)	1.20	.40
278	A55	18fr red ('52)	2.00	1.20
279	A56	20fr dp grnsh bl ('52)	2.40	.80
		Nos. 271-279 (10)	11.95	4.70

See Nos. 297-299.

8th-10th Cent. Capital — A57

Capitals: 20fr, 12th Cent. 25fr, 13th-14th Cent. 50fr, 17th Cent.

1952, Apr. 5 *Perf. 13*

280	A57	15fr deep blue	3.25	2.40
281	A57	20fr red	3.25	2.40
282	A57	25fr purple	3.25	2.40
283	A57	50fr deep green	3.25	2.40
		Nos. 280-283 (4)	13.00	9.60

Casablanca Monument — A58

1952 Sept. 22 Engr. & Typo.

284	A58	15fr multicolored	3.50	2.40

Creation of the French Military Medal, cent.

Daggers of South Morocco — A59

Designs: 20fr and 25fr, Antique brooches.

1953, Mar. 27 Engr.

285	A59	15fr dk car rose	4.00	3.25
286	A59	20fr violet brn	4.00	3.25
287	A59	25fr dark blue	4.00	3.25
		Nos. 285-287 (3)	12.00	9.75

See No. C46.

Post Rider and Public Letter-writer — A60

1953, May 16

288	A60	15fr violet brown	2.00	1.60

Stamp Day, May 16, 1953.

Bine el Ouidane Dam — A61

1953, Nov. 3 *Perf. 13*

290	A61	15fr indigo	2.00	1.60

See No. 295.

Mogador Fortress — A62

Design: 30fr, Moorish knights.

1953, Dec. 4

291 A62 15fr green 2.40 1.60
292 A62 30fr red brown 2.40 1.60

Issued to aid Army Welfare Work.

Nos. 226 and 243 Surcharged with New Value and Wavy Lines in Black

1954

293 A38 1fr on 1.50fr blue .40 .25
294 A42 15fr on 18fr dp bl 1.20 .65

Dam Type of 1953

1954, Mar. 8

295 A61 15fr red brn & indigo 1.60 1.20

Station of Rural Automobile Post — A63

1954, Apr. 10

296 A63 15fr dk blue grn 1.40 .80

Stamp Day, April 10, 1954.

Types of 1951-53

1954 Engr. *Perf. 14x13*

297 A52 15fr dk blue green 1.20 .40

Typo.

298 A52 5fr magenta 1.20 .40
299 A55 15fr rose violet 1.60 .40
Nos. 297-299 (3) 4.00 1.20

Walled City Type of 1949

1954 Engr. *Perf. 13*

300 A44 25fr purple 2.40 .80

Marshal Lyautey at Rabat A64

Lyautey, Builder of Cities — A65

Designs: 15fr, Marshal Lyautey at Khenifra. 50fr, Hubert Lyautey, Marshal of France.

1954, Nov. 17

301 A64 5fr indigo 2.40 2.00
302 A64 15fr dark green 3.25 2.75
303 A65 30fr rose brown 4.00 3.25
304 A65 50fr dk red brn 4.00 3.25
Nos. 301-304 (4) 13.65 11.25

Marshal Hubert Lyautey, birth cent.

Franco-Moslem Education — A66

Moslem Student at Blackboard — A67

Designs: 30fr, Moslem school at Camp Boulhaut. 50fr, Moulay Idriss College at Fez.

1955, Apr. 16 Unwmk. *Perf. 13*

305 A66 5fr indigo 2.00 1.60
306 A67 15fr rose lake 2.40 2.00
307 A66 30fr chocolate 2.40 2.00
308 A67 50fr dk blue grn 2.75 2.40
Nos. 305-308 (4) 9.55 8.00

Franco-Moslem solidarity.

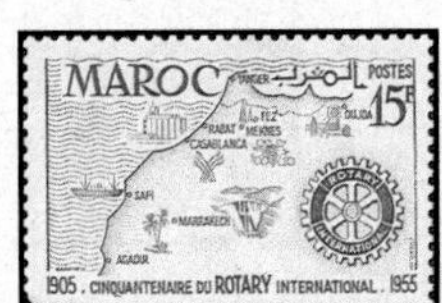

Map and Rotary Emblem A68

1955, June 11

309 A68 15fr bl & org brn 2.00 1.20

Rotary Intl., 50th anniv.

Post Office, Mazagan A69

1955, May 24

310 A69 15fr red 1.20 .80

Stamp Day.

Bab el Chorfa, Fez A70

Mahakma (Courthouse), Casablanca A71

Fortress, Safi — A72

Designs: 50c, 1fr, 2fr, 3fr, Mrissa Gate, Salé. 10fr, 12fr, 15fr, Minaret at Rabat. 30fr, Menara Garden Marrakesh. 40fr, Tafraout Village. 50fr, Portuguese cistern, Mazagan. 75fr, Garden of Oudaya, Rabat.

1955 *Perf. 13½x13, 13x13½, 13*

311 A70 50c brn vio .40 .25
312 A70 1fr blue .40 .25
313 A70 2fr red lilac .40 .25
314 A70 3fr bluish blk .40 .25
315 A70 5fr vermilion 1.60 .40
316 A70 6fr green .75 .35
317 A70 8fr orange brn 1.20 .40
318 A70 10fr violet brn 1.60 .40
319 A70 12fr greenish bl .80 .40
320 A70 15fr magenta 1.10 .25
321 A71 18fr dk green 2.00 .80
322 A71 20fr brown lake 1.20 .40
323 A72 25fr brt ultra 2.75 .40
324 A72 30fr green 2.40 .80
325 A72 40fr orange red 2.40 .40
326 A72 50fr black brn 8.00 .80
327 A71 75fr greenish bl 2.40 1.20
Nos. 311-327 (17) 29.80 8.00

Succeeding issues, released under the Kingdom, are listed under Morocco in Vol. 4.

SEMI-POSTAL STAMPS

French Protectorate

No. 30 Surcharged in Red

1914 Unwmk. *Perf. 14x13½*

B1 A4 10c + 5c on 10c *24,000. 28,000.*

Known only with inverted red surcharge.

No. 42 Surcharged in Red

B2 A7 10c + 5c on 10c rose 6.50 6.50
a. Double surcharge 175.00 175.00
b. Inverted surcharge 225.00 225.00
c. "c" omitted 110.00 110.00

On Nos. B1 and B2 the cross is set up from pieces of metal (quads), the horizontal bar being made from two long pieces, the vertical bar from two short pieces. Each cross in the setting of twenty-five differs from the others.

No. 30 Handstamp Surcharged in Red

B3 A4 10c + 5c on 10c rose *1,650. 1,300.*

No. B3 was issued at Oujda. The surcharge ink is water-soluble.

No. 42 Surcharged in Vermilion or Carmine

B4 A7 10c + 5c on 10c (V) 25.00 25.00
a. Double surcharge 240.00 240.00
b. Inverted surcharge 240.00 240.00
c. Double surch., one invtd. 200.00 200.00
B5 A7 10c +5c on 10c (C) 475.00 525.00
a. Inverted surcharge 1,600. 1,600.

On Nos. B4-B5 the horizontal bar of the cross is single and not as thick as on Nos. B1-B2.

No. B5 was sold largely at Casablanca.

Carmine Surcharge SP1

Black Overprint SP2

1915

B6 SP1 5c + 5c green 3.25 2.40
a. Inverted surcharge 300.00 300.00
B7 SP2 10c + 5c rose 4.75 4.75

No. B6 was not issued without the Red Cross surcharge. No. B7 was used in Tangier.

France No. B2 Overprinted in Black

B8 SP2 10c + 5c red 7.50 7.50

No. 30 Surcharged in Carmine — SP4

1917

B9 SP4 10c + 5c on 10c rose 3.25 3.25

On No. B9 the horizontal bar of the cross is made from a single, thick piece of metal.

Marshal Hubert Lyautey — SP5

1935, May 15 Photo. *Perf. 13x13½*

B10 SP5 50c + 50c red 9.50 9.50
B11 SP5 1fr + 1fr dk grn 11.00 11.00
B12 SP5 5fr + 5fr blk brn 45.00 45.00
Nos. B10-B12 (3) 65.50 65.50
Set, never hinged 98.00

Stamps of 1933-34 Surcharged in Blue or Red

1938 *Perf. 13*

B13 A18 2c + 2c red vio 5.50 5.50
B14 A19 3c + 3c dk brn 5.50 5.50
B15 A20 20c + 20c red brn 5.50 5.50
B16 A21 40c + 40c blk brn (R) 5.50 5.50
B17 A22 65c + 65c brn red 5.50 5.50
B18 A23 1.25fr + 1.25fr blk (R) 5.50 5.50
B19 A24 2fr + 2fr yel brn 5.50 5.50
B20 A25 5fr + 5fr red brn 5.50 5.50
Nos. B13-B20 (8) 44.00 44.00
Set, never hinged 64.00

Stamps of 1939 Srchd. in Black

1942

B21 A29 45c + 2fr Prus grn 6.75 4.75
B22 A30 90c + 4fr ultra 6.75 4.75
B23 A32 1.25fr + 6fr henna brn 8.00 6.50
B24 A26 2.50fr + 8fr scarlet 8.00 6.50
Nos. B21-B24 (4) 29.50 22.50
Set, never hinged 40.00

The arrangement of the surcharge differs slightly on each denomination.

Catalogue values for unused stamps in this section, from this point to the end of the section, are for Never Hinged items.

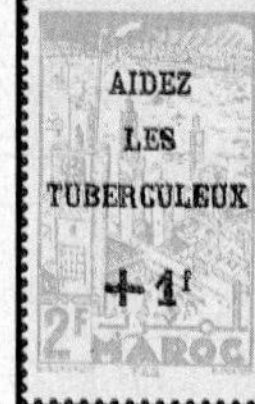

No. 207 Surcharged in Black

1945 Unwmk. *Perf. 13½x14*
B26 A33 2fr + 1fr Prus green .80 .50

For surcharge see No. B28.

Mausoleum of Marshal Lyautey — SP7

1945 Litho. *Perf. 11½*
B27 SP7 2fr + 3fr dark blue .80 .40

The surtax was for French works of solidarity.

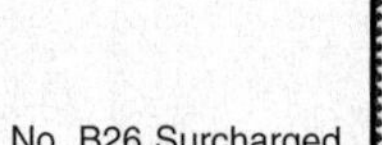

No. B26 Surcharged in Red

1946 *Perf. 13½x14*
B28 A33 3fr (+ 1fr) on 2fr + 1fr .40 .25

Statue of Marshal Lyautey — SP8

Perf. 13½x14, 13
1946, Dec. 16 Engr.
B29 SP8 2fr + 10fr black 2.40 1.60
B30 SP8 3fr + 15fr cop red 2.40 1.60
B31 SP8 10fr + 20fr brt bl 3.25 2.40
Nos. B29-B31 (3) 8.05 5.60

The surtax was for works of solidarity.

No. 212 Surcharged in Rose Violet

1947, Mar. 15 *Perf. 13½x14*
B32 A31 4.50fr + 5.50fr magenta 2.00 1.60

Stamp Day, 1947.

Map and Symbols of Prosperity from Phosphates SP9

1947 *Perf. 13*
B33 SP9 4.50fr + 5.50fr green 1.60 1.20

25th anniv. of the exploitations of the Cherifien Office of Phosphates.

Power — SP10

Health — SP11

1948, Feb. 9
B34 SP10 6fr + 9fr red brn 3.25 2.40
B35 SP11 10fr + 20fr dp ultra 3.25 2.40

The surtax was for combined works of Franco-Moroccan solidarity.

Type of Regular Issue of 1923, Inscribed: "Journee du Timbre 1948"

1948, Mar. 6
B36 A16 6fr + 4fr red brown 1.20 .80

Stamp Day, Mar. 6, 1948.

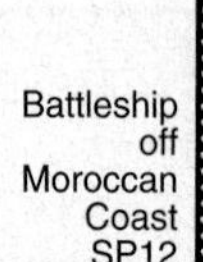

Battleship off Moroccan Coast SP12

1948, Aug.
B37 SP12 6fr + 9fr purple 2.00 1.60

The surtax was for naval charities.

Wheat Field near Meknes SP13

Designs: 2fr+5fr, Olive grove, Taroudant. 3fr+7fr, Net and coastal view. 5fr+10fr, Aguedal Gardens, Marrakesh.

1949, Apr. 12 Engr. Unwmk.
Inscribed: "SOLIDARITÉ 1948"
B38 SP13 1fr + 2fr orange 2.00 1.60
B39 SP13 2fr + 5fr car 2.00 1.60
B40 SP13 3fr + 7fr pck bl 2.00 1.60
B41 SP13 5fr + 10fr dk brn vio 2.00 1.60
a. Sheet of 4, #B38-B41 27.50 24.00
Nos. B38-B41,CB31-CB34 (8) 17.60 14.40

Gazelle Hunter, from 1899 Local Stamp SP14

1949, May 1
B42 SP14 10fr + 5fr choc & car rose 2.00 1.60

Stamp Day and 50th anniversary of Mazagan-Marrakesh local postage stamp.

Moroccan Soldiers, Flag — SP15

1949
B43 SP15 10fr + 10fr bright red 1.60 1.40

The surtax was for Army Welfare Work.

Rug Weaving — SP16

Designs: 2fr+5fr, Pottery making, 3fr+7fr, Bookbinding. 5fr+10fr, Copper work.

Inscribed: "SOLIDARITE 1949"

1950, Apr. 11
B44 SP16 1fr + 2fr dp car 2.75 2.40
B45 SP16 2fr + 5fr dk brnsh bl 2.75 2.40
B46 SP16 3fr + 7fr dk pur 2.75 2.40
B47 SP16 5fr + 10fr red brn 2.75 2.40
a. Sheet of 4, #B44-B47 32.50 24.00
Nos. B44-B47,CB36-CB39 (8) 20.60 17.60

Ruins of Sala Colonia at Chella SP17

1950, Sept. 25 Engr. *Perf. 13*
B48 SP17 10fr + 10fr dp mag 2.00 *1.60*
B49 SP17 15fr + 15fr indigo 2.00 1.60

The surtax was for Army Welfare Work.

AIR POST STAMPS

French Protectorate

Biplane over Casablanca AP1

1922-27 Photo. Unwmk. *Perf. 13½*
C1 AP1 5c dp org ('27) .50 .50
C2 AP1 25c dp ultra 1.20 1.20
C3 AP1 50c grnsh blue .40 .40
C4 AP1 75c dp blue 80.00 16.00
C5 AP1 75c dp green .80 .40
C6 AP1 80c vio brn ('27) 2.40 .80
C7 AP1 1fr vermilion 1.20 .80
C8 AP1 1.40fr brn lake ('27) 2.40 1.25
C9 AP1 1.90fr dp blue ('27) 2.75 1.60
C10 AP1 2fr black vio 2.40 1.20
a. 2fr deep violet 2.25 1.40
C11 AP1 3fr gray blk 2.75 2.00
Nos. C1-C11 (11) 96.80 26.15

The 25c, 50c, 75c deep green and 1fr each were printed in two of three types, differing in frameline thickness, or hyphen in "Helio-Vaugirard" imprint.Values are for the more common types.

Imperf., Pairs

C1a AP1 5c 65.00 65.00
C2a AP1 25c 72.50 72.50
C3a AP1 50c 72.50 72.50
C4a AP1 75c 550.00 550.00
C5a AP1 75c 72.50 72.50
C6a AP1 80c 72.50 72.50
C7a AP1 1fr 90.00 90.00
C10b AP1 2fr 225.00 225.00

Nos. C8-C9 Srchd. in Blue or Black

1931, Apr. 10
C12 AP1 1fr on 1.40fr (B) 2.40 2.40
a. Inverted surcharge 310.00 310.00
C13 AP1 1.50fr on 1.90fr (Bk) 2.40 2.40

Rabat and Tower of Hassan AP2

Casablanca AP3

1933, Jan. Engr.
C14 AP2 50c dark blue .80 .80
C15 AP2 80c orange brn .80 .65
C16 AP2 1.50fr brown red .80 .80
C17 AP3 2.50fr carmine rose 6.50 1.20
C18 AP3 5fr violet 3.25 1.75
C19 AP3 10fr blue green 1.20 1.20
Nos. C14-C19 (6) 13.35 6.40

For surcharges see Nos. CB22-CB23.

Storks and Minaret, Chella — AP4

Plane and Map of Morocco AP5

1939-40 *Perf. 13*
C20 AP4 80c Prus green .25 .25
C21 AP4 1fr dk red .25 .25
C22 AP5 1.90fr ultra .40 .30
C23 AP5 2fr red vio ('40) .40 .30
C24 AP5 3fr chocolate .50 .25
C25 AP4 5fr violet 1.40 .80
C26 AP5 10fr turq blue 1.25 .55
Nos. C20-C26 (7) 4.45 2.70

Catalogue values for unused stamps in this section, from this point to the end of the section, are for Never Hinged items.

Plane over Oasis — AP6

1944 Litho. *Perf. 11½*
C27 AP6 50c Prus grn .50 .35
C28 AP6 2fr ultra .50 .35
C29 AP6 5fr scarlet .50 .35
C30 AP6 10fr violet 1.40 1.10
C31 AP6 50fr black 2.00 1.60
C32 AP6 100fr dp bl & red 4.00 3.25
Nos. C27-C32 (6) 8.90 7.00

For surcharge see No. CB24.

Plane AP7

1945 Engr. *Perf. 13*

C33 AP7 50fr sepia	1.20	.95

Moulay Idriss — AP8

La Medina AP9

1947-48

C34 AP8 9fr dk rose car	.40	.30
C35 AP8 40fr dark blue	1.20	.80
C36 AP8 50fr dp claret ('47)	1.60	.40
C37 AP9 100fr dp grnsh bl	3.25	1.20
C38 AP9 200fr henna brn	8.00	1.60
Nos. C34-C38 (5)	14.45	4.30

Leclerc Type of Regular Issue

1951, Apr. 28

C39 A50 50fr purple	3.25	2.75

Unveiling of a monument to Gen. Leclerc at Casablanca, Apr. 28, 1951.

Kasbah of the Oudayas, Rabat AP11

1951, May 22

C40 AP11 300fr purple	24.00	12.00

Ben Smine Sanatorium AP12

1951, June 4

C41 AP12 50fr pur & Prus grn	3.50	2.75

Fortifications, Chella — AP13

Plane Near Marrakesh AP14

Fort, Anti-Atlas Mountains AP15

View of Fez AP16

1952, Apr. 19 Unwmk. *Perf. 13*

C42 AP13 10fr blue green	1.60	.80
C43 AP14 40fr red	2.40	.80
C44 AP15 100fr brown	5.50	1.60
C45 AP16 200fr purple	10.50	4.00
Nos. C42-C45 (4)	20.00	7.20

Antique Brooches — AP17

1953, Mar. 27

C46 AP17 50fr dark green	4.00	3.25

"City" of the Agdal, Meknes AP18

20fr, Yakoub el Mansour, Rabat. 40fr, Ainchock, Casablanca. 50fr, El Aliya, Fedala.

1954, Mar. 8

C47 AP18 10fr olive brown	4.00	2.75
C48 AP18 20fr purple	4.00	2.75
C49 AP18 40fr red brown	4.00	2.75
C50 AP18 50fr deep green	4.00	2.75
Nos. C47-C50 (4)	16.00	11.00

Franco-Moroccan solidarity.

Naval Vessel and Sailboat — AP19

1954, Oct. 18

C51 AP19 15fr dk blue green	2.00	1.60
C52 AP19 30fr violet blue	2.40	2.00

Village in the Anti-Atlas — AP20

"Ksar es Souk," Rabat and Plane AP21

200fr, Estuary of Bou Regreg, Rabat and Plane.

1955, July 25 Engr. *Perf. 13*

C53 AP20 100fr brt violet	2.75	.80
C54 AP20 200fr brt carmine	6.50	1.20
C55 AP21 500fr grnsh blue	16.00	4.00
Nos. C53-C55 (3)	25.25	6.00

AIR POST SEMI-POSTAL STAMPS

French Protectorate

Moorish Tribesmen SPAP1

Designs: 25c, Moor plowing with camel and burro. 50c, Caravan nearing Saffi. 75c, Walls, Marrakesh. 80c, Sheep grazing at Azrou. 1fr, Gate at Fez. 1.50fr, Aerial view of Tangier. 2fr, Aerial view of Casablanca. 3fr, Storks on old wall, Rabat. 5fr, Moorish fete.

Perf. 13½

1928, July 26 Photo. Unwmk.

CB1	SPAP1	5c dp blue	5.25	5.25
CB2	SPAP1	25c brn org	5.25	5.25
CB3	SPAP1	50c red	5.25	5.25
CB4	SPAP1	75c org brn	5.25	5.25
CB5	SPAP1	80c olive grn	5.25	5.25
CB6	SPAP1	1fr orange	5.25	5.25
CB7	SPAP1	1.50fr Prus bl	5.25	5.25
CB8	SPAP1	2fr dp brown	5.25	5.25
CB9	SPAP1	3fr dp violet	5.25	5.25
CB10	SPAP1	5fr brown blk	5.25	5.25
	Nos. CB1-CB10 (10)		52.50	52.50

These stamps were sold in sets only and at double their face value. The money received for the surtax was divided among charitable and social organizations. The stamps were not sold at post offices but solely by subscription to the Moroccan Postal Administration.

Overprinted in Red or Blue (25c, 50c, 75c, 1fr)

1929, Feb. 1

CB11	SPAP1	5c dp blue	5.25	5.25
CB12	SPAP1	25c brown org	5.25	5.25
CB13	SPAP1	50c red	5.25	5.25
CB14	SPAP1	75c org brn	5.25	5.25
CB15	SPAP1	80c olive grn	5.25	5.25
CB16	SPAP1	1fr orange	5.25	5.25
CB17	SPAP1	1.50fr Prus bl	5.25	5.25
CB18	SPAP1	2fr dp brown	5.25	5.25
CB19	SPAP1	3fr dp violet	5.25	5.25
CB20	SPAP1	5fr brown blk	5.25	5.25
	Nos. CB11-CB20 (10)		52.50	52.50

These stamps were sold at double their face values and only in Tangier. The surtax benefited various charities.

Marshal Hubert Lyautey SPAP10

1935, May 15 *Perf. 13½*

CB21 SPAP10 1.50fr + 1.50fr blue	20.00	20.00

Nos. C14, C19 Surcharged in Red

1938 *Perf. 13*

CB22 AP2 50c + 50c dk bl	8.00	8.00
CB23 AP3 10fr + 10fr bl grn	5.50	5.50

Catalogue values for unused stamps in this section, from this point to the end of the section, are for Never Hinged items.

Plane over Oasis — SPAP11

1944 Litho. *Perf. 11½*

CB23A SPAP11 1.50fr + 98.50fr	2.40	1.60

The surtax was for charity among the liberated French.

No. C29 Surcharged in Black

1946, June 18 *Perf. 11*

CB24 AP6 5fr + 5fr scarlet	1.60	1.20

6th anniv. of the appeal made by Gen. Charles de Gaulle, June 18, 1940. The surtax was for the Free French Association of Morocco.

Statue of Marshal Lyautey — SPAP12

1946, Dec. Engr. *Perf. 13*

CB25 SPAP12 10fr +30fr dk grn	6.50	2.75

The surtax was for works of solidarity.

Replenishing Stocks of Food — SPAP13

Agriculture SPAP14

1948, Feb. 9 Unwmk.

CB26 SPAP13 9fr +26fr dp grn	2.00	1.60
CB27 SPAP14 20fr +35fr brown	2.00	1.60

The surtax was for combined works of Franco-Moroccan solidarity.

Tomb of Marshal Hubert Lyautey — SPAP15

1948, May 18 *Perf. 13*

CB28 SPAP15 10fr +25fr dk grn	1.60	1.25

Lyautey Exposition, Paris, June, 1948.

P.T.T. Clubhouse SPAP16

1948, June 7 **Engr.**

CB29	SPAP16	6fr + 34fr dk grn	2.40	2.00
CB30	SPAP16	9fr + 51fr red brn	2.40	2.00

The surtax was used for the Moroccan P.T.T. employees vacation colony at Ifrane.

View of Agadir — SPAP17

Designs: 6fr+9fr, Fez. 9fr+16fr, Atlas Mountains. 15fr+25fr, Valley of Draa.

1949, Apr. 12 ***Perf. 13***

Inscribed: "SOLIDARITÉ 1948"

CB31	SPAP17	5fr +5fr dk grn	2.40	2.00
CB32	SPAP17	6fr +9fr org red	2.40	2.00
CB33	SPAP17	9fr +16fr blk brn	2.40	2.00
CB34	SPAP17	15fr +25fr ind	2.40	2.00
a.		Sheet of 4, #CB31-CB34	32.50	24.00
		Nos. CB31-CB34 (4)	9.60	8.00

Plane over Globe — SPAP18

1950, Mar. 11 **Engr. & Typo.**

CB35	SPAP18	15fr + 10fr bl grn & car	1.60	1.25

Day of the Stamp, Mar. 11-12, 1950, and 25th anniv. of the 1st post link between Casablanca and Dakar.

Scenes and Map: Northwest Corner SPAP19

Designs (quarters of map): 6fr+9fr, NE, 9fr+16fr, SW. 15fr+25fr, SE.

1950, Apr. 11 **Engr.**

Inscribed: "SOLIDARITE 1949"

CB36	SPAP19	5fr +5fr dp ultra	2.40	2.00
CB37	SPAP19	6fr +9fr Prus grn	2.40	2.00
CB38	SPAP19	9fr +16fr dk brn	2.40	2.00
CB39	SPAP19	15fr +25fr brn red	2.40	2.00
a.		Sheet of 4, #CB36-CB39	32.50	24.00
		Nos. CB36-CB39 (4)	9.60	8.00

Arch of Triumph of Caracalla at Volubilis SPAP20

1950, Sept. 25 **Unwmk.**

CB40	SPAP20	10fr + 10fr sepia	2.00	1.60
CB41	SPAP20	15fr + 15fr bl grn	2.00	1.60

The surtax was for Army Welfare Work.

Casablanca Post Office and First Air Post Stamp SPAP21

1952, Mar. 8 ***Perf. 13***

CB42	SPAP21	15fr + 5fr red brn & dp grn	4.75	4.00

Day of the Stamp, Mar. 8, 1952, and 30th anniv. of French Morocco's 1st air post stamp.

POSTAGE DUE STAMPS

French Offices in Morocco

France Postage Due Stamps and Types Surcharged in Red or Black

1896 **Unwmk.** ***Perf. 14x13½***

On Stamps of 1891-93

J1	D2	5c on 5c lt bl (R)	12.00	5.50
J2	D2	10c on 10c choc (R)	16.00	6.50
J3	D2	30c on 30c car	32.50	24.00
a.		Pair, one without surcharge		
J4	D2	50c on 50c lilac	32.50	27.50
a.		"S" of "CENTIMOS" omitted	340.00	250.00
J5	D2	1p on 1fr lil brn	350.00	325.00

1909-10 **On Stamps of 1908-10**

J6	D3	1c on 1c ol grn (R)	4.00	4.00
J7	D3	10c on 10c violet	40.00	32.50
J8	D3	30c on 30c bister	55.00	40.00
J9	D3	50c on 50c red	80.00	72.50
		Nos. J6-J9 (4)	179.00	149.00

Postage Due Stamps of France Surcharged in Red or Blue

1911 **On Stamps of 1893-96**

J10	D2	5c on 5c blue (R)	4.75	4.75
J11	D2	10c on 10c choc (R)	16.00	16.00
a.		Double surcharge	225.00	*260.00*
J12	D2	50c on 50c lil (Bl)	20.00	20.00

On Stamps of 1908-10

J13	D3	1c on 1c ol grn (R)	4.00	3.25
J14	D3	10c on 10c vio (R)	8.00	8.00
J15	D3	30c on 30c bis (R)	12.00	12.00
J16	D3	50c on 50c red (Bl)	16.00	16.00
		Nos. J10-J16 (7)	80.75	80.00

For surcharges see Nos. J23-J26.

French Protectorate

France Postage Due Stamps of 1911 Issue Overprinted

1915-17

J17	D4	1c on 1c black	.80	.80
a.		New value double	175.00	
J18	D4	5c on 5c blue	3.25	2.00
J19	D4	10c on 10c choc	4.00	2.00
J20	D4	20c on 20c ol grn	4.00	2.00
J21	D4	30c on 30c rose red, *grayish*	8.00	5.50
J22	D4	50c on 50c vio brn	12.00	8.00
		Nos. J17-J22 (6)	32.05	20.30

Nos. J13 to J16 With Additional Overprint "Protectorat Francais"

1915

J23	D3	1c on 1c ol grn	1.60	1.60
J24	D3	10c on 10c violet	4.00	3.25
J25	D3	30c on 30c bister	4.00	4.00
J26	D3	50c on 50c red	4.00	4.00
		Nos. J23-J26 (4)	13.60	12.85

D5

1917-26 **Typo.**

J27	D5	1c black	.25	.25
J28	D5	5c deep blue	.40	.25
J29	D5	10c brown	.40	.40
J30	D5	20c olive green	2.50	1.60
J31	D5	30c rose	.40	.40
J32	D5	50c lilac brown	.80	.40
J33	D5	1fr red brn, *straw* ('26)	.85	.80
J34	D5	2fr violet ('26)	2.40	1.60
		Nos. J27-J34 (8)	8.00	5.70

See #J49-J56, Morocco #J1-J4. For surcharges see #J46-J48.

Postage Due Stamps of France, 1882-1906 Overprinted

1918

J35	D2	1c black	1.20	1.20
J36	D2	5c blue	2.40	2.40
J37	D2	10c chocolate	2.00	2.00
J38	D2	15c green, *grayish*	4.75	4.75
J39	D2	20c olive green	6.50	6.50
J40	D2	30c rose red, *grayish*	16.00	16.00
J41	D2	50c violet brown	24.00	24.00
		Nos. J35-J41 (7)	56.85	56.85

Postage Due Stamps of France, 1908-19 Overprinted

1918

J42	D3	1c olive green	1.20	1.20
J43	D3	10c violet	2.75	2.75
J44	D3	20c bister, *grayish*	8.00	8.00
J45	D3	40c red	20.00	20.00
		Nos. J42-J45 (4)	31.95	31.95

Catalogue values for unused stamps in this section, from this point to the end of the section, are for Never Hinged items.

Nos. J31 and J29 Surcharged

1944 **Unwmk.** ***Perf. 14x13½***

J46	D5	50c on 30c rose	3.25	2.40
J47	D5	1fr on 10c brown	5.50	4.00
J48	D5	3fr on 10c brown	13.00	9.50
		Nos. J46-J48 (3)	21.75	15.90

Type of 1917-1926

1945-52 **Typo.**

J49	D5	1fr brn lake ('47)	1.20	.80
J50	D5	2fr rose lake ('47)	1.60	.80
J51	D5	3fr ultra	.80	.35
J52	D5	4fr red orange	.80	.30
J53	D5	5fr green	1.60	.50
J54	D5	10fr yellow brn	2.00	.50
J55	D5	20fr carmine ('50)	2.00	.90
J56	D5	30fr dull brn ('52)	2.75	1.60
		Nos. J49-J56 (8)	12.75	5.75

PARCEL POST STAMPS

French Protectorate

PP1

1917 **Unwmk.** ***Perf. 13½x14***

Q1	PP1	5c green	1.20	.80
Q2	PP1	10c carmine	1.20	.80
Q3	PP1	20c lilac brown	1.20	1.00
Q4	PP1	25c blue	1.60	.80
Q5	PP1	40c dark brown	2.40	1.60
Q6	PP1	50c red orange	4.00	.80
Q7	PP1	75c pale slate	4.00	2.40
Q8	PP1	1fr ultra	5.50	.80
Q9	PP1	2fr gray	12.00	1.60
Q10	PP1	5fr violet	12.00	1.60
Q11	PP1	10fr black	20.00	1.60
		Nos. Q1-Q11 (11)	65.10	13.80

FRENCH POLYNESIA

ˈfrench ˌpä-lə-ˈnē-zhə

(French Oceania)

LOCATION — South Pacific Ocean
GOVT. — French Overseas Territory
AREA — 1,522 sq. mi.
POP. — 242,073 (1999 est.)
CAPITAL — Papeete

In 1903 various French Establishments in the South Pacific were united to form a single colony. Most important of the island groups are the Society Islands, Marquesas Islands, the Tuamotu group and the Gambier, Austral, and Rapa Islands. Tahiti, largest of the Society group, ranks first in importance.

100 Centimes = 1 Franc

Catalogue values for unused stamps in this country are for Never Hinged items, beginning with Scott 136 in the regular postage section, Scott B11 in the semi-postal section, Scott C2 in the airpost section, Scott J18 in the postage due section, and Scott O1 in the officials section.

Navigation and Commerce — A1

Perf. 14x13½

1892-1907 Typo. Unwmk.
Name of Colony in Blue or Carmine

1 A1 1c black, *lil bl* 1.60 1.60
2 A1 2c brown, *buff* 2.75 2.75
3 A1 4c claret, *lav* 4.50 4.00
4 A1 5c green, *grnsh* 13.50 9.50
5 A1 5c yellow grn ('06) 5.00 2.40
6 A1 10c blk, *lavender* 30.00 12.50
7 A1 10c red ('00) 5.00 2.40
8 A1 15c blue, quadrille paper 35.00 12.00
9 A1 15c gray, *lt gray* ('00) 10.00 7.25
10 A1 20c red, *grn* 17.50 16.00
11 A1 25c black, *rose* 60.00 30.00
12 A1 25c blue ('00) 32.50 16.00
13 A1 30c brown, *bis* 16.00 14.50
14 A1 35c black, *yel* ('06) 11.00 9.50
15 A1 40c red, *straw* 132.50 80.00
16 A1 45c blk, *gray grn* ('07) 6.75 *6.75*
17 A1 50c car, *pale rose* 10.00 10.00
a. 50c rose, *pale rose* 10.00 9.00
18 A1 50c brown, *az* ('00) 275.00 250.00
19 A1 75c dp vio, *org* 12.00 12.00
20 A1 1fr brnz grn, *straw* 13.50 13.50
Nos. 1-20 (20) 694.10 512.65

Perf. 13½x14 stamps are counterfeits.

For overprint and surcharge see Nos. 55, B1.

Tahitian Girl — A2

Kanakas — A3

Fautaua Valley — A4

1913-30

21 A2 1c violet & brn .25 .25
22 A2 2c brown & blk .25 .25
23 A2 4c orange & bl .35 .35

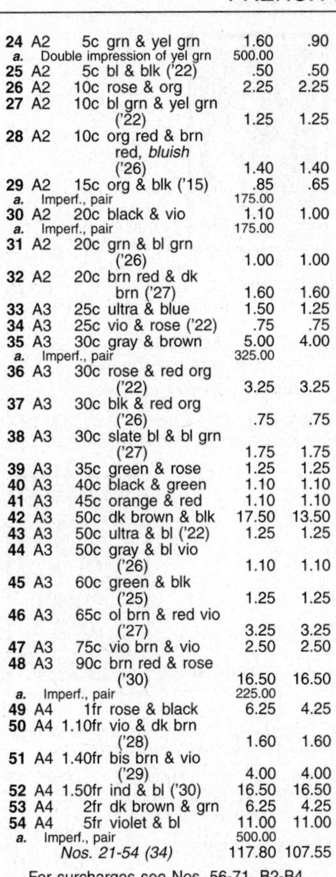

24 A2 5c grn & yel grn 1.60 .90
a. Double impression of yel grn 500.00
25 A2 5c bl & blk ('22) .50 .50
26 A2 10c rose & org 2.25 2.25
27 A2 10c bl grn & yel grn ('22) 1.25 1.25
28 A2 10c org red & brn red, *bluish* ('26) 1.40 1.40
29 A2 15c org & blk ('15) .85 .65
a. Imperf., pair 175.00
30 A2 20c black & vio 1.10 1.00
a. Imperf., pair 175.00
31 A2 20c grn & bl grn ('26) 1.00 1.00
32 A2 20c brn red & dk brn ('27) 1.60 1.60
33 A3 25c ultra & blue 1.50 1.25
34 A3 25c vio & rose ('22) .75 .75
35 A3 30c gray & brown 5.00 4.00
a. Imperf., pair 325.00
36 A3 30c rose & red org ('22) 3.25 3.25
37 A3 30c blk & red org ('26) .75 .75
38 A3 30c slate bl & bl grn ('27) 1.75 1.75
39 A3 35c green & rose 1.25 1.25
40 A3 40c black & green 1.10 1.10
41 A3 45c orange & red 1.10 1.10
42 A3 50c dk brown & blk 17.50 13.50
43 A3 50c ultra & bl ('22) 1.25 1.25
44 A3 50c gray & bl vio ('26) 1.10 1.10
45 A3 60c green & blk ('25) 1.25 1.25
46 A3 65c ol brn & red vio ('27) 3.25 3.25
47 A3 75c vio brn & vio 2.50 2.50
48 A3 90c brn red & rose ('30) 16.50 16.50
a. Imperf., pair 225.00
49 A4 1fr rose & black 6.25 4.25
50 A4 1.10fr vio & dk brn ('28) 1.60 1.60
51 A4 1.40fr bis brn & vio ('29) 4.00 4.00
52 A4 1.50fr ind & bl ('30) 16.50 16.50
53 A4 2fr dk brown & grn 6.25 4.25
54 A4 5fr violet & bl 11.00 11.00
a. Imperf., pair 500.00
Nos. 21-54 (34) 117.80 107.55

For surcharges see Nos. 56-71, B2-B4.

No. 7 Overprinted

1915

55 A1 10c red 6.75 6.75
a. Inverted overprint 225.00 225.00

For surcharge see No. B1.

No. 29 Surcharged

1916

56 A2 10c on 15c org & blk 3.50 3.50

No. 22 Surcharged

No. 41 Surcharged

No. 29 Surcharged

1921

57 A2 5c on 2c brn & blk 36.00 36.00
58 A3 10c on 45c org & red 36.00 36.00
59 A2 25c on 15c org & blk 9.00 9.00
Nos. 57-59 (3) 81.00 81.00

On No. 58 the new value and date are set wide apart and without bar.

Types of 1913-30 Issue Surcharged in Black or Red

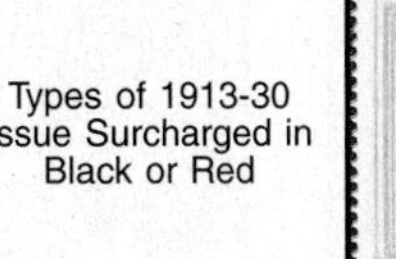

1923-27

60 A3 60c on 75c bl & brn .75 .75
61 A4 65c on 1fr dk bl & ol (R) ('25) 2.25 2.25
62 A4 85c on 1fr dk bl & ol (R) ('25) 2.25 2.25
63 A3 90c on 75c brn red & cer ('27) 3.00 3.00
Nos. 60-63 (4) 8.25 8.25

No. 26 Surcharged

1924

64 A2 45c on 10c rose & org 3.00 3.00
a. Inverted surcharge *2,400.* *2,400.*

Stamps and Type of 1913-30 Surcharged with New Value and Bars in Black or Red

1924-27

65 A4 25c on 2fr dk brn & grn 1.10 1.10
66 A4 25c on 5fr vio & bl 1.10 1.10
67 A4 1.25fr on 1fr dk bl & ultra (R) ('26) 1.20 1.20
68 A4 1.50fr on 1fr dk bl & lt bl ('27) 4.00 4.00
69 A4 20fr on 5fr org & brt vio ('27) 32.50 26.00
Nos. 65-69 (5) 39.90 33.40

Surcharged in Black or Red

1926

70 A4 3fr on 5fr gray & blue 3.25 2.50
71 A4 10fr on 5fr grn & blk (R) 7.25 7.25

Papetoai Bay, Moorea A5

1929, Mar. 25

72 A5 3fr green & dk brn 8.00 8.00
73 A5 5fr lt blue & dk brn 15.00 15.00
74 A5 10fr lt red & dk brn 45.00 45.00
75 A5 20fr lilac & dk brn 57.50 57.50
Nos. 72-75 (4) 125.50 125.50

For overprints see Nos. 128, 130, 132, 134.

Common Design Types pictured following the introduction.

Colonial Exposition Issue
Common Design Types

1931, Apr. 13 Engr. *Perf. 12½*
Name of Country Printed in Black

76 CD70 40c deep green 7.50 7.50
77 CD71 50c violet 7.50 7.50
78 CD72 90c red orange 7.50 7.50
79 CD73 1.50fr dull blue 7.50 7.50
Nos. 76-79 (4) 30.00 30.00

Spear Fishing A12

Tahitian Girl — A13

Idols A14

1934-40 Photo. *Perf. 13½, 13½x13*

80 A12 1c gray black .25 .25
81 A12 2c claret .35 .35
82 A12 3c lt blue ('40) .35 .35
83 A12 4c orange .60 .60
84 A12 5c violet .90 .90
85 A12 10c dark brown .40 .40
86 A12 15c green .60 .60
87 A12 20c red .60 .60
88 A13 25c gray blue .90 .90
89 A13 30c yellow green 1.20 1.20
90 A13 30c org brn ('40) .80 .80
91 A14 35c dp green ('38) 4.00 4.00
92 A13 40c red violet .60 .60
93 A13 45c brown orange 9.00 9.00
94 A13 45c dk green ('39) 1.60 1.60
95 A13 50c violet .60 .60
96 A13 55c blue ('38) 6.75 6.75
97 A13 60c black ('39) .75 .75
98 A13 65c brown 3.25 3.25
99 A13 70c brt pink ('39) 1.40 1.40
100 A13 75c olive green 9.00 9.00
101 A13 80c violet brn ('38) 2.00 2.00
102 A13 90c rose red .90 .90
103 A14 1fr red brown .90 .90
104 A14 1.25fr brown violet 8.25 8.25
105 A14 1.25fr rose red ('39) 1.25 1.25
106 A14 1.40fr org yel ('39) 1.25 1.25
107 A14 1.50fr blue .90 .90
108 A14 1.60fr dull vio ('39) 1.40 1.40
109 A14 1.75fr olive 6.75 6.75
110 A14 2fr red 1.10 1.10
111 A14 2.25fr dp blue ('39) 1.25 1.25
112 A14 2.50fr black ('39) 1.25 1.25
113 A14 3fr brn org ('39) 1.50 1.50
114 A14 5fr red violet ('39) 1.00 1.00
115 A14 10fr dk grn ('39) 3.00 3.00
116 A14 20fr dk brn ('39) 3.50 3.50
Nos. 80-116 (37) 80.10 80.10

For overprints see Nos. 126-127, 129, 131, 133, 135.

Paris International Exposition Issue
Common Design Types

1937 Engr. *Perf. 13*

117 CD74 20c deep violet 3.50 3.50
118 CD75 30c dark green 3.50 3.50
119 CD76 40c carmine rose 3.50 3.50
120 CD77 50c dk brn & blue 4.25 4.25
121 CD78 90c red 4.25 4.25
122 CD79 1.50fr ultra 5.00 5.00
Nos. 117-122 (6) 24.00 24.00

Colonial Arts Exhibition Issue
Souvenir Sheet
Common Design Type

1937 *Imperf.*

123 CD78 3fr emerald 36.00 *52.50*
Never hinged 55.00

New York World's Fair Issue
Common Design Type

1939, May 10 Engr. *Perf. 12½x12*

124 CD82 1.25fr carmine lake 2.40 2.40
125 CD82 2.25fr ultra 2.40 2.40
Set, never hinged 8.00

Fautaua Valley and Marshal Petain A15

1941 Engr. *Perf. 12½x12*

125A A15 1fr bluish green 1.10
c. Denomination ("1F") omitted 80.00
125B A15 2.50fr deep blue 1.25
Set, never hinged 3.25

Nos. 125A-125B were issued by the Vichy government in France, but were not placed on sale in the French Polynesia.

For surcharges, see Nos. B12B-B12C.

Stamps of 1929-39 Ovptd. in Black or Red

1941 *Perf. 14x13½, 13½x13*

126 A14 1fr red brn (BK) 7.00 *9.50*
a. Inverted overprint 1,200.
127 A14 2.50fr black 8.00 *11.00*
a. Inverted overprint 1,200.
128 A5 3fr grn & dk brn 9.00 9.00
129 A14 3fr brn org (Bk) 10.00 *12.00*
130 A5 5fr lt bl & dk brn 9.00 9.00
131 A14 5fr red vio (Bk) 10.00 10.00
132 A5 10fr lt red & dk brn 25.00 *30.00*
133 A14 10fr dark green 90.00 *110.00*
134 A5 20fr lil & dk brn 135.00 135.00
135 A14 20fr dark brown 75.00 *95.00*
Nos. 126-135 (10) 378.00 *430.50*
Set, never hinged 480.00

Types of 1934-39 without "RF"

1942-44 Photo. *Perf. 13½*

135A A12 10c dark brown .65
135B A13 30c orange brown .85
135C A14 1.50fr blue 1.00
135D A14 10fr dark green 1.75
135E A14 20fr dark brown 2.50
Nos. 135A-135E (5) 6.75

Nos. 135A-135E were issued by the Vichy government in France, but were not placed on sale in French Polynesia.

Catalogue values for unused stamps in this section, from this point to the end of the section, are for Never Hinged items.

Ancient Double Canoe A16

1942 Photo. *Perf. 14½x14*

136 A16 5c dark brown .40 .25
137 A16 10c dk gray bl .40 .25
138 A16 25c emerald .40 .25
139 A16 30c red orange .40 .25
140 A16 40c dk slate grn .40 .25
141 A16 80c red brown .40 .25
142 A16 1fr rose violet .50 .35
143 A16 1.50fr brt red .65 .50
144 A16 2fr gray black 1.00 .75
145 A16 2.50fr brt ultra 2.50 1.75
146 A16 4fr dull violet 1.75 1.25
147 A16 5fr bister 1.75 1.25
148 A16 10fr deep brown 2.50 1.90
149 A16 20fr deep green 3.00 2.10
Nos. 136-149 (14) 16.05 11.35

For surcharges see Nos. 152-159.

Eboue Issue
Common Design Type

1945 Engr. *Perf. 13*

150 CD91 2fr black 1.00 .75
151 CD91 25fr Prus green 2.60 2.10

Nos. 150 and 151 exist imperforate.

Nos. 136, 138 and 145 Surcharged with New Values and Bars in Carmine or Black

1946 *Perf. 14½x14*

152 A16 50c on 5c (C) .65 .50
153 A16 60c on 5c (C) .65 .50
154 A16 70c on 5c (C) .65 .50
155 A16 1.20fr on 5c (C) .80 .65
156 A16 2.40fr on 25c (Bk) 1.60 1.25
157 A16 3fr on 25c (Bk) 1.00 .75
158 A16 4.50fr on 25c (Bk) 2.00 1.50
159 A16 15fr on 2.50fr (C) 2.40 1.75
Nos. 152-159 (8) 9.75 7.40

Coast of Mooréa A17

Fisherman and Catch — A18

Tahitian Girl — A20

House at Faa — A19

Island of Borabora A21

Island Women A22

1948 Unwmk. Engr. *Perf. 13*

160 A17 10c brown .50 .35
161 A17 30c blue green .50 .35
162 A17 40c deep blue .50 .35
163 A18 50c red brown .50 .35
164 A18 60c dk brown ol .65 .50
165 A18 80c brt blue .65 .50
166 A19 1fr red brown .65 .35
167 A19 1.20fr slate .65 .50
168 A19 1.50fr deep ultra .65 .50
169 A20 2fr sepia 1.10 .75
170 A20 2.40fr red brown 1.25 1.00
171 A20 3fr purple 11.50 2.50
172 A20 4fr blue black 2.40 1.40
173 A21 5fr sepia 3.75 1.60
174 A21 6fr steel blue 3.75 2.10
175 A21 10fr dk brown ol 4.75 1.75
176 A22 15fr vermilion 7.25 2.75
177 A22 20fr slate 7.25 3.25
178 A22 25fr sepia 9.00 5.00
Nos. 160-178 (19) 57.25 25.85

Imperforates

Most French Polynesia stamps from 1948 onward exist imperforate in issued and trial colors, and also in small presentation sheets in issued colors.

Military Medal Issue
Common Design Type

1952, Dec. 1 Engr. & Typo.

179 CD101 3fr multicolored 13.50 10.00

Girl of Bora Bora — A23

1955, Sept. 26 Engr.

180 A23 9fr dk brn, blk & red 11.00 7.25

FIDES Issue
Common Design Type

Design: 3fr, Dry dock at Papeete.

1956, Oct. 22 Engr. *Perf. 13x12½*

181 CD103 3fr grnsh blue 4.00 2.00

Girl Playing Guitar — A24

Designs: 4fr, 7fr, 9fr, Man with headdress. 10fr, 20fr, Girl with shells on beach.

1958, Nov. 3 Unwmk. *Perf. 13*

182 A24 10c grn & redsh brn .65 .55
183 A24 25c slate grn, cl & car .80 .60
184 A24 1fr brt bl, brn & red org 1.00 .65
185 A24 2fr brn, vio brn & vio 1.10 .65
186 A24 4fr sl grn & org yel 1.50 1.00
187 A24 7fr red brn, grn & org 3.00 1.60
188 A24 9fr vio brn, grn & org 5.50 2.25
189 A24 10fr dk bl, brn & car 5.00 2.25
190 A24 20fr pur, rose red & brn 9.00 5.00
Nos. 182-190 (9) 27.55 14.55

See Nos. 304-306.

Human Rights Issue
Common Design Type

1958, Dec. 10

191 CD105 7fr dk gray & dk bl 13.00 8.75

Flower Issue
Common Design Type

1959, Jan. 3 Photo. *Perf. 12½x12*

192 CD104 4fr Breadfruit 6.50 4.00

Spear Fishing — A25

Tahitian Dancers A26

1960, May 16 Engr. *Perf. 13*

193 A25 5fr green, brn & lil 1.25 1.00
194 A26 17fr ultra, brt grn & red brn 6.00 2.50

Post Office, Papeete A27

1960, Nov. 19 Unwmk. *Perf. 13*

195 A27 16fr green, bl & claret 5.50 3.25

Saraca Indica — A28

1962, July 12 Photo. *Perf. 13*

196 A28 15fr shown 15.00 14.00
197 A28 25fr Hibiscus 24.00 16.00

Map of Australia and South Pacific — A29

1962, July 18 *Perf. 13x12*

198 A29 20fr multicolored 17.50 7.75

5th South Pacific Conf., Pago Pago, July 1962.

Spined Squirrelfish A30

Fish: 10fr, One-spot butterflyfish. 30fr, Radiate lionfish. 40fr, Horned boxfish.

1962, Dec. 15 Engr. *Perf. 13*

199 A30 5fr black, mag & bis 4.25 1.90
200 A30 10fr multicolored 6.25 2.75
201 A30 30fr multicolored 12.50 7.75
202 A30 40fr multicolored 15.50 11.50
Nos. 199-202 (4) 38.50 23.90

Soccer A30a

Design: 50fr, Throwing the javelin.

1963, Aug. 29 Photo. *Perf. 12½*

203 A30a 20fr brt ultra & brn 9.00 6.25
204 A30a 50fr brt car rose & ultra 16.00 9.25

South Pacific Games, Suva, 8/29-9/7.

Red Cross Centenary Issue
Common Design Type

1963, Sept. 2 Engr. *Perf. 13*

205 CD113 15fr vio brn, gray & car 15.00 12.00

Human Rights Issue
Common Design Type

1963, Dec. 10 Unwmk. *Perf. 13*

206 CD117 7fr green & vio bl 15.00 10.00

Philatec Issue
Common Design Type

1964, Apr. 9 Unwmk. *Perf. 13*
207 CD118 25fr grn, dk sl grn & red 18.00 12.50

Tahitian Dancer A31

1964, May 14 Engr. *Perf. 13*
208 A31 1fr multicolored .40 .40
209 A31 3fr dp claret, blk & org .90 .90

Soldiers, Truck and Battle Flag — A32

1964, July 10 Photo. *Perf. 12½*
210 A32 5fr multicolored 11.00 4.25

Issued to honor the Tahitian Volunteers of the Pacific Battalion. See No. C31.

Tuamotu Scene A33

Views: 4fr, Borabora. 7fr, Papeete Harbor. 8fr, Paul Gauguin's tomb, Marquesas. 20fr, Mangareva, Gambier Islands.

1964, Dec. 1 Litho. *Perf. 12½x13*
211 A33 2fr multicolored .90 .50
212 A33 4fr multicolored 1.50 .50
213 A33 7fr multicolored 3.00 1.25
214 A33 8fr multicolored 4.00 1.75
215 A33 20fr multicolored 9.50 2.50
Nos. 211-215,C32 (6) 28.40 10.50

Painting from a School Dining Room — A34

1965, Nov. 29 Engr. *Perf. 13*
216 A34 20fr dk brn, sl grn & dk car 20.00 12.00

Publicizing the School Canteen Program. See No. C38.

Outrigger Canoe on Lagoon A35

Ships: 11fr, Large cruising yacht, vert. 12fr, Motorboat for sport fishing. 14fr, Outrigger canoes with sails. 19fr, Schooner, vert. 22fr, Modern coaster "Oiseau des Iles II."

1966, Aug. 30 Engr. *Perf. 13*
217 A35 10fr brt ultra, emer & mar 2.75 .90
218 A35 11fr mar, dk bl & sl grn 2.75 1.60
219 A35 12fr emer, dk bl & red lil 3.75 1.75
220 A35 14fr brn, bl & slate grn 5.50 2.00
221 A35 19fr scar, sl grn & dp bl 6.50 2.10
222 A35 22fr multicolored 9.50 4.00
Nos. 217-222 (6) 30.75 12.35

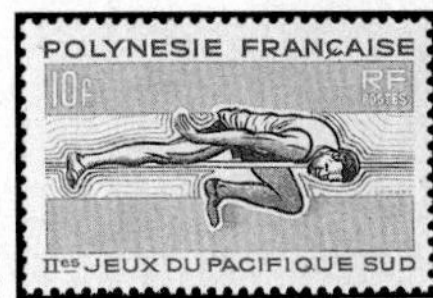

High Jump A36

Designs: 20fr, Pole vault, vert. 40fr, Women's basketball, vert. 60fr, Hurdling.

1966, Dec. 15 Engr. *Perf. 13*
223 A36 10fr dk red, lem & blk 2.25 1.50
224 A36 20fr blue, emer & blk 5.25 2.00
225 A36 40fr emer, brt pink & blk 10.00 5.00
226 A36 60fr dull yel, bl & blk 17.00 8.50
Nos. 223-226 (4) 34.50 17.00

2nd South Pacific Games, Nouméa, New Caledonia, Dec. 8-18.

Poi Pounder — A37

1967, June 15 Engr. *Perf. 13*
227 A37 50fr orange & blk 17.00 10.00

Society for Oceanic Studies, 50th anniv.

Javelin Throwing — A38

5fr, Spring dance. 15fr, Horse race. 16fr, Fruit carriers' race. 21fr, Canoe race.

1967, July 11
228 A38 5fr multi, horiz. 1.10 .90
229 A38 13fr multi 4.50 1.50
230 A38 15fr multi, horiz. 4.50 1.60
231 A38 16fr multi 4.50 2.75
232 A38 21fr multi, horiz. 9.50 5.00
Nos. 228-232 (5) 24.10 11.75

Issued to publicize the July Festival.

Earring — A39

Art of the Marquesas Islands: 10fr, Carved mother-of-pearl. 15fr, Decorated canoe paddle. 23fr, Oil vessel. 25fr, Carved stilt stirrups. 30fr, Fan handles. 35fr, Tattooed man. 50fr, Tikis.

1967-68 Engr. *Perf. 13*
233 A39 10fr dp cl, dl red & ultra 2.25 .65
234 A39 15fr black & emerald 3.00 1.25
235 A39 20fr ol gray, dk car & lt bl 5.25 2.00
236 A39 23fr dk brn, ocher & bl 6.50 4.00
237 A39 25fr dk brn, dk bl & lil 6.50 3.75
238 A39 30fr brown & red lilac 8.25 4.00
239 A39 35fr ultra & dk brn 14.00 6.25
240 A39 50fr brn, sl grn & lt bl 15.00 7.25
Nos. 233-240 (8) 60.75 29.15

Issued: 20fr, 25fr, 30fr, 50fr, 12/19/67; others 2/28/68.

WHO Anniversary Issue
Common Design Type

1968, May 4 Engr. *Perf. 13*
241 CD126 15fr bl grn, mar & dp vio 11.00 4.75
242 CD126 16fr org, lil & bl grn 11.00 8.00

Human Rights Year Issue
Common Design Type

1968, Aug. 10 Engr. *Perf. 13*
243 CD127 15fr blue, red & brn 12.00 6.00
244 CD127 16fr brn, brt pink & ultra 12.00 8.00

Tiare Apetahi A40

Flower: 17fr, Tiare Tahiti.

1969, Mar. 27 Photo. *Perf. 12½x13*
245 A40 9fr multicolored 2.10 1.10
246 A40 17fr multicolored 4.25 2.10

3rd South Pacific Games, Port Moresby, Papua and New Guinea, Aug. 13-23 — A41

1969, Aug. 13 Engr. *Perf. 13*
247 A41 9fr Boxer, horiz 3.25 1.25
248 A41 17fr High jump 7.25 2.00
249 A41 18fr Runner 9.00 3.50
250 A41 22fr Long jump 12.00 7.25
Nos. 247-250 (4) 31.50 14.00

ILO Issue
Common Design Type

1969, Nov. 24 Engr. *Perf. 13*
251 CD131 17fr org, emer & ol 12.00 5.75
252 CD131 18fr org, dk brn & vio bl 12.00 6.75

Territorial Assembly A42

Buildings: 14fr, Governor's Residence. 17fr, House of Tourism. 18fr, Maeva Hotel. 24fr, Taharaa Hotel.

1969, Dec. 22 Photo. *Perf. 12½x12*
253 A42 13fr black & multi 2.75 1.25
254 A42 14fr black & multi 4.25 1.50
255 A42 17fr black & multi 7.00 3.50
256 A42 18fr black & multi 7.75 4.00
257 A42 24fr black & multi 13.50 7.00
Nos. 253-257 (5) 35.25 17.25

Stone Figure with Globe — A43

Designs: 40fr, Globe, plane, map of Polynesia and men holding "PATA" sign, horiz. 60fr, Polynesian carrying globe.

1970, Apr. 7 Engr. *Perf. 13*
258 A43 20fr deep plum, gray & bl 6.75 3.25
259 A43 40fr emer, rose lil & ultra 11.00 5.25
260 A43 60fr red brn, bl & dk brn 19.00 10.00
Nos. 258-260 (3) 36.75 18.50

Issued to publicize the 1970 Pacific Area Travel Association Congress (PATA).

UPU Headquarters Issue
Common Design Type

1970, May 20 Engr. *Perf. 13*
261 CD133 18fr mar, pur & brn 10.00 4.75
262 CD133 20fr lil rose, ol & ind 10.00 5.25

Night Fishing — A44

1971, May 11 Photo. *Perf. 13*
263 A44 10fr multicolored 12.50 5.25
Nos. 263,C71-C73 (4) 37.50 19.75

Flowers — A45

Designs: Various flowers. 12fr is horiz.

Perf. 12½x13, 13x12½
1971, Aug. 27
264 A45 8fr multicolored 2.25 1.00
265 A45 12fr multicolored 3.50 1.75
266 A45 22fr multicolored 5.75 3.00
Nos. 264-266 (3) 11.50 5.75

Day of a Thousand Flowers.

Water-skiing Slalom — A46

Designs: 20fr, Water-skiing, jump, vert. 40fr, Figure water-skiing.

1971, Oct. 11 Engr. *Perf. 13*
267 A46 10fr grnsh bl, dk red & brn 6.25 2.00
268 A46 20fr car, emer & brn 9.00 4.00
269 A46 40fr brn, grn & lil 20.00 12.00
Nos. 267-269 (3) 35.25 18.00

World water-skiing championships, Oct. 1971.

De Gaulle Issue
Common Design Type

30fr, As general, 1940. 50fr, As president, 1970.

1971, Nov. 9 Engr. *Perf. 13*
270 CD134 30fr red lilac & blk 22.50 11.00
271 CD134 50fr red lilac & blk 29.00 18.50

Map of Tahiti and Jerusalem Cross A47

1971, Dec. 18 Photo. *Perf. 13x12½*
272 A47 28fr lt blue & multi 14.00 8.50

2nd rally of French Boy Scouts and Guides, Taravao, French Polynesia.

"Alcoholism" — A48

1972, Mar. 24 Photo. *Perf. 13*

273	A48 20fr brown & multi	11.50	5.75

Fight against alcoholism.

Mother and Child — A49

1973, Sept. 26 Photo. *Perf. 12½x13*

274	A49 28fr pale yellow & multi	9.50	5.00

Day nursery.

Polynesian Golfer — A50

Design: 24fr, Atimaono Golf Course.

1974, Feb. 27 Photo. *Perf. 13*

275	A50 16fr multicolored	8.50	3.25
276	A50 24fr multicolored	10.50	5.25

Atimaono Golf Course.

Hand Throwing Life Preserver to Puppy — A51

1974, May 9 Photo. *Perf. 13*

277	A51 21fr brt blue & multi	12.00	5.00

Society for the Protection of Animals.

Around a Fire, on the Beach A52

Polynesian Views: 2fr, Lagoons and mountains. 6fr, Pebble divers. 10fr, Lonely Mountain and flowers, vert. 15fr, Sailing ship at sunset. 20fr, Lagoon and mountain.

1974, May 22

278	A52 2fr multicolored	.90	.60
279	A52 5fr multicolored	1.10	.90
280	A52 6fr multicolored	1.90	1.10
281	A52 10fr multicolored	2.10	1.25
282	A52 15fr multicolored	4.25	1.75
283	A52 20fr multicolored	7.00	2.10
	Nos. 278-283 (6)	17.25	7.70

Polynesian Woman and UPU Emblem — A53

1974, Oct. 9 Engr. *Perf. 13*

284	A53 65fr multicolored	12.00	7.75

Centenary of Universal Postal Union.

Lion, Sun and Emblem — A54

1975, June 17 Photo.

285	A54 26fr multicolored	12.00	5.00

15th anniv. of Lions Intl. in Tahiti.

Fish and Leaf A55

1975, July 9 Litho. *Perf. 12*

286	A55 19fr dp ultra & green	10.00	4.25

Polynesian Association for the Protection of Nature.

Georges Pompidou, Pres. of France — A55a

1976, Feb. 16 Engr. *Perf. 13*

287	A55a 49fr dk violet & black	11.00	7.00

See France No. 1430.

Alain Gerbault and Sailboat A56

1976, May 25 Photo. *Perf. 13*

288	A56 90fr multicolored	13.50	9.00

Alain Gerbault's arrival in Bora Bora, 50th anniv.

Turtle — A57

Design: 42fr, Hand protecting bird.

1976, June 24 Litho. *Perf. 12½*

289	A57 18fr multicolored	14.00	4.25
290	A57 42fr multicolored	20.00	11.00

World Ecology Day.

A. G. Bell, Telephone, Radar and Satellite — A58

1976, Sept. 15 Engr. *Perf. 13*

291	A58 37fr multicolored	10.00	5.00

Centenary of first telephone call by Alexander Graham Bell, Mar. 10, 1876.

Dugout Canoes — A59

1976, Dec. 16 Litho. *Perf. 13x12½*

292	A59 25fr Marquesas	3.75	2.75
293	A59 30fr Raiatea	4.75	4.75
294	A59 75fr Tahiti	9.50	5.75
295	A59 100fr Tuamotu	12.00	7.00
	Nos. 292-295 (4)	30.00	20.25

Sailing Ship — A60

Designs: Various sailing vessels.

1977, Dec. 22 Litho. *Perf. 13*

296	A60 20fr multicolored	6.25	2.00
297	A60 50fr multicolored	7.25	2.25
298	A60 85fr multicolored	9.00	3.75
299	A60 120fr multicolored	15.00	5.75
	Nos. 296-299 (4)	37.50	13.75

Hibiscus — A61

Designs: 10fr, Vanda orchids. 16fr, Pua (fagraea berteriana). 22fr, Gardenia.

1978-79 Photo. *Perf. 12½x13*

300	A61 10fr multicolored	1.10	.50
301	A61 13fr multicolored	2.50	1.00
302	A61 16fr multicolored	2.75	1.75
303	A61 22fr multicolored	1.75	1.00
	Nos. 300-303 (4)	8.10	4.25

Issued: 13fr, 16fr, 8/23; 10fr, 22fr, 1/25/79.

Girl with Shells on Beach — A62

Design A24 with "1958 1978" added: 28fr, Man with headdress. 36fr, Girl playing guitar.

1978, Nov. 3 Engr. *Perf. 13*

304	A62 20fr multicolored	3.00	.75
305	A62 28fr multicolored	3.75	1.50
306	A62 36fr multicolored	5.75	2.25
a.	Souvenir sheet of 3	27.50	27.50
	Nos. 304-306 (3)	12.50	4.50

20th anniv. of stamps inscribed: Polynesie Francaise. No. 306a contains Nos. 304-306 in changed colors.

Ships — A63

1978, Dec. 29 Litho. *Perf. 13x12½*

307	A63 15fr Tahiti	1.50	.80
308	A63 30fr Monowai	2.75	1.25
309	A63 75fr Tahitien	4.50	3.25
310	A63 100fr Mariposa	8.50	3.25
	Nos. 307-310 (4)	17.25	8.55

Porites Coral A64

Design: 37fr, Montipora coral.

1979, Feb. 15 *Perf. 13x12½*

311	A64 32fr multicolored	2.50	1.25
312	A64 37fr multicolored	3.75	2.00

Raiatea A65

Landscapes: 1fr, Moon over Bora Bora. 2fr, Mountain peaks, Ua Pou. 3fr, Sunset over Motu Tapu. 5fr, Motu. 6fr, Palm and hut, Tuamotu.

1979, Mar. 8 Photo. *Perf. 13x13½*

313	A65 1fr multicolored	.25	.25
314	A65 2fr multicolored	.25	.25
315	A65 3fr multicolored	.30	.25
316	A65 4fr multicolored	.45	.25
317	A65 5fr multicolored	.80	.35
318	A65 6fr multicolored	1.00	.60
	Nos. 313-318 (6)	3.05	1.95

See Nos. 438-443 for redrawn designs.

Dance Costumes A66

1979, July 14 Litho. *Perf. 12½*

319	A66	45fr Fetia	1.75	1.00
320	A66	51fr Teanuanua	2.75	1.25
321	A66	74fr Temaeva	3.75	2.25
		Nos. 319-321 (3)	8.25	4.50

Hill, Great Britain No. 53, Tahiti No. 28 A67

1979, Aug. 1 Engr. *Perf. 13*

322	A67	100fr multicolored	5.00	3.00

Sir Rowland Hill (1795-1879), originator of penny postage.

Hastula Strigilata — A68

Shells: 28fr, Scabricola variegata. 35fr, Fusinus undatus.

1979, Aug. 22 Litho. *Perf. 12½*

323	A68	20fr multicolored	1.50	.50
324	A68	28fr multicolored	2.00	1.00
325	A68	35fr multicolored	2.75	2.00
		Nos. 323-325 (3)	6.25	3.50

Statue Holding Rotary Emblem — A69

1979, Nov. 30 Litho. *Perf. 13*

326	A69	47fr multicolored	2.75	2.00

Rotary International, 75th anniversary; Papeete Rotary Club, 20th anniversary.

For overprint see No. 330.

Myripristis Murdjan A70

Fish: 8fr, Napoleon. 12fr, Emperor.

1980, Jan. 21 Litho. *Perf. 12½*

327	A70	7fr multicolored	1.00	.50
328	A70	8fr multicolored	1.00	.65
329	A70	12fr multicolored	1.65	.95
		Nos. 327-329 (3)	3.65	2.10

No. 326 Overprinted and Surcharged in Gold

1980, Feb. 23 Litho. *Perf. 13*

330	A69	77fr on 47fr multi	5.75	3.25

Rotary International, 75th anniversary.

CNEXO Fish Hatchery A71

1980, Mar. 17 Photo. *Perf. 13x13½*

331	A71	15fr shown	1.75	.90
332	A71	22fr Crayfish	1.75	.90

Papeete Post Office Building Opening A72

1980, Apr. 30 Photo. *Perf. 13x12½*

333	A72	50fr multicolored	2.50	1.50

Tiki and Festival Emblem — A73

1980, June 30 Photo. *Perf. 13½*

334	A73	34fr shown	1.25	.90
335	A73	39fr Drum (pahu)	2.00	1.30
336	A73	49fr Ax (to'i)	2.75	1.75
a.		Souv. sheet of 3, #334-336	13.50	13.00
		Nos. 334-336 (3)	6.00	3.95

South Pacific Arts Festival, Port Moresby, Papua New Guinea.

Titmouse Henparrot — A74

25fr, White sea-swallow, horiz. 45fr, Minor frigate bird, horiz.

Perf. 13x12½, 12½x13

1980, Oct. 20 Photo.

337	A74	25fr multi	1.50	.70
338	A74	35fr shown	1.75	.90
339	A74	45fr multi	2.75	1.10
		Nos. 337-339 (3)	6.00	2.70

Charles de Gaulle — A75

1980, Nov. 9 Engr. *Perf. 12½x13*

340	A75	100fr multicolored	5.00	3.25

Naso Vlamingi (Karaua) A76

16fr, Lutjanus vaigensis (toau). 24fr, Plectropomus leopardus (tonu).

1981, Feb. 5 Litho. *Perf. 12½*

341	A76	13fr shown	1.00	.50
342	A76	16fr multi	1.10	.60
343	A76	24fr multi	2.25	.75
		Nos. 341-343 (3)	4.35	1.85

Indoor Fish Breeding Tanks, Cnexo Hatchery A77

1981, May 14 Photo. *Perf. 13x13½*

344	A77	23fr shown	1.10	.80
345	A77	41fr Mussels	2.00	1.10

Folk Dancers A78

Perf. 13x13½, 13½x13

1981, July 10 Litho.

346	A78	26fr shown	1.25	.65
347	A78	28fr Dancer	1.25	1.10
348	A78	44fr Dancers, vert.	2.10	1.50
		Nos. 346-348 (3)	4.60	3.25

Sterna Bergii — A79

53fr, Ptilinopus purpuratus, vert. 65fr, Estrilda astrild, vert.

1981, Sept. 24 Litho. *Perf. 13*

349	A79	47fr shown	1.75	1.00
350	A79	53fr multi	1.75	1.20
351	A79	65fr multi	2.25	1.50
		Nos. 349-351 (3)	5.75	3.70

See Nos. 370-372.

Huahine Island A80

1981, Oct. 22 Litho. *Perf. 12½*

352	A80	34fr shown	1.40	.75
353	A80	134fr Maupiti	3.25	2.00
354	A80	136fr Bora-Bora	3.25	2.00
		Nos. 352-354 (3)	7.90	4.75

A81

1982, Feb. 4 Photo. *Perf. 13x13½*

355	A81	30fr Parrotfish	1.00	.75
356	A81	31fr Regal angel	1.40	.75
357	A81	45fr Spotted bass	1.50	1.25
		Nos. 355-357 (3)	3.90	2.75

Pearl Industry A82

1982, Apr. 22 Photo. *Perf. 13x13½*

358	A82	7fr Pearl beds	.85	.45
359	A82	8fr Extracting pearls	.85	.45
360	A82	10fr Pearls	1.20	1.10
		Nos. 358-360 (3)	2.90	2.00

Tahiti "No. 1A," Emblem — A83

1982, May 12 Engr. *Perf. 13*

361	A83	150fr multicolored	4.75	3.50
a.		Souvenir sheet	16.00	16.00

PHILEXFRANCE Stamp Exhibition, Paris, June 11-21. No. 361a contains No. 361 in changed colors.

King Holding Carved Scepter — A84

Designs: Coronation ceremony.

1982, July 12 Photo. *Perf. 13½x13*

362	A84	12fr shown	.50	.25
363	A84	13fr King, priest	.50	.25
364	A84	17fr Procession	1.00	.50
		Nos. 362-364 (3)	2.00	1.00

Championship Emblem — A85

1982, Aug. 13 *Perf. 13*

365	A85	90fr multicolored	2.75	2.00

4th Hobie-Cat 16 World Catamaran Sailing Championship, Tahiti, Aug. 15-21.

First Colloquium on New Energy Sources — A86

1982, Sept. 29 **Litho.**

366 A86 46fr multicolored 1.75 1.00

Motu, Tuamotu Islet — A87

1982, Oct. 12 **Litho.** ***Perf. 13***

367 A87 20fr shown .70 .35
368 A87 33fr Tupai Atoll .90 .45
369 A87 35fr Gambier Islds. 1.25 .55
Nos. 367-369 (3) 2.85 1.35

Bird Type of 1981

37fr, Sacred egret. 39fr, Pluvialis dominica, vert. 42fr, Lonchura castaneothorax.

1982, Nov. 17 **Litho.** ***Perf. 13***

370 A79 37fr multi 1.40 .55
371 A79 39fr multi 1.40 .65
372 A79 42fr multi 1.75 .90
Nos. 370-372 (3) 4.55 2.10

Fish — A88

8fr, Acanthurus lineatus. 10fr, Caranx melampygus. 12fr, Carcharhinus melanopterus.

1983, Feb. 9 **Litho.** ***Perf. 13x13½***

373 A88 8fr multi .70 .35
374 A88 10fr multi .90 .35
375 A88 12fr multi 1.40 .50
Nos. 373-375 (3) 3.00 1.20

The Way of the Cross, Sculpture by Damien Haturau — A89

1983, Mar. 9 **Litho.** ***Perf. 13***

376 A89 7fr shown .25 .25
377 A89 21fr Virgin and Child .70 .60
378 A89 23fr Christ .90 .60
Nos. 376-378 (3) 1.85 1.45

Traditional Hats — A90

1983, May 24 **Litho.** ***Perf. 13x12½***

379 A90 11fr Acacia .45 .30
380 A90 13fr Niau .60 .30
381 A90 25fr Ofe .80 .50
382 A90 35fr Ofe, diff. 1.10 .60
Nos. 379-382 (4) 2.95 1.70

See Nos. 393-396.

Chieftain in Traditional Costume, Sainte-Christine Isld. — A91

Traditional Costumes, Marquesas Islds.

1983, July 12 **Photo.** ***Perf. 13***

383 A91 15fr shown .70 .30
384 A91 17fr Man .90 .40
385 A91 28fr Woman 1.10 .50
Nos. 383-385 (3) 2.70 1.20

See Nos. 397-399, 419-421.

Polynesian Crowns — A92

Various flower garlands.

1983, Oct. 19 **Litho.** ***Perf. 13***

386 A92 41fr multicolored 1.25 .90
387 A92 44fr multicolored 1.40 .95
388 A92 45fr multicolored 1.50 1.00
Nos. 386-388 (3) 4.15 2.85

See Nos. 400-402.

Martin Luther (1483-1546) A93

1983, Nov. 10 **Engr.** ***Perf. 13***

389 A93 90fr black, brn & lil gray 2.25 1.10

Tiki Carvings — A94

Various carvings.

1984, Feb. 8 **Litho.** ***Perf. 12½x13***

390 A94 14fr multicolored .50 .25
391 A94 16fr multicolored .60 .45
392 A94 19fr multicolored .75 .45
Nos. 390-392 (3) 1.85 1.15

Hat Type of 1983

1984, June 20 **Litho.** ***Perf. 13x12½***

393 A90 20fr Aeho ope .50 .35
394 A90 24fr Paeore .60 .35
395 A90 26fr Ofe fei .75 .50
396 A90 33fr Hua .80 .50
Nos. 393-396 (4) 2.65 1.70

Costume Type of 1983

34fr, Tahitian playing nose flute. 35fr, Priest, Oei-eitia. 39fr, Tahitian adult and child.

1984, July 11 **Litho.** ***Perf. 13***

397 A91 34fr multi .75 .50
398 A91 35fr multi .90 .50
399 A91 39fr multi .90 .50
Nos. 397-399 (3) 2.55 1.50

Garland Type of 1983

1984, Oct. 24 **Litho.** ***Perf. 13x12½***

400 A92 46fr Moto'i Lei .90 .50
401 A92 47fr Pitate Lei 1.00 .60
402 A92 53fr Bougainvillea Lei 1.25 .80
Nos. 400-402 (3) 3.15 1.90

4th Pacific Arts Festival, Noumea, New Caledonia, Dec. 8-22 — A95

1984, Nov. 20 **Litho.** ***Perf. 13***

403 A95 150fr Statue, head-dress 3.50 2.25

See No. C213.

Paysage D'Anaa, by Jean Masson — A96

Paintings: 50fr, Sortie Du Culte, by Jacques Boulaire. 75fr, La Fete, by Robert Tatin. 85fr, Tahitiennes Sur La Plage, by Pierre Heyman.

Perf. 12½x13, 13x12½

1984, Dec. 12 **Litho.**

404 A96 50fr multi, vert. 1.25 .70
405 A96 65fr multicolored 1.40 .90
406 A96 75fr multicolored 1.90 1.00
407 A96 85fr multicolored 2.25 1.75
Nos. 404-407 (4) 6.80 4.35

Tiki Carvings — A97

1985, Jan. 23 **Litho.** ***Perf. 13½***

408 A97 30fr multicolored .60 .35
409 A97 36fr multicolored .80 .45
410 A97 40fr multicolored .90 .75
Nos. 408-410 (3) 2.30 1.55

Polynesian Faces — A98

1985, Feb. 20 **Photo.** ***Perf. 12½x13***

411 A98 22fr multicolored .40 .30
412 A98 39fr multicolored .75 .40
413 A98 44fr multicolored .95 .70
Nos. 411-413 (3) 2.10 1.40

Early Tahiti — A99

Designs: 42fr, Entrance to Papeete. 45fr, Girls, vert. 48fr, Papeete market.

Perf. 13x12½, 12½x13

1985, Apr. 24 **Litho.**

414 A99 42fr multicolored .90 .55
415 A99 45fr multicolored 1.25 .75
416 A99 48fr multicolored 1.40 .85
Nos. 414-416 (3) 3.55 2.15

5th Intl. Congress on Coral Reefs, Tahiti A100

Design: Local reef formation.

1985, May 28 **Litho.** ***Perf. 13½***

417 A100 140fr multicolored 3.00 2.00

Printed se-tenant with label picturing congress emblem.

National Flag A101

1985, June 28

418 A101 9fr Flag, natl. arms .65 .30

Costume Type of 1983

18th-19th Cent. Prints, Beslu Collection: 38fr, Tahitian dancer. 55fr, Man and woman from Otahiti, 1806. 70fr, Traditional chief.

1985, July 17 ***Perf. 13***

419 A91 38fr multicolored .95 .65
420 A91 55fr multicolored 1.25 .90
421 A91 70fr multicolored 1.75 1.25
Nos. 419-421 (3) 3.95 2.80

Local Foods — A103

Designs: 25fr, Roasted pig. 35fr, Pit fire. 80fr, Fish in coconut milk. 110fr, Fafaru.

1985-86 **Litho.** ***Perf. 13***

422 A103 25fr multi .85 .60
423 A103 35fr multi 1.10 .65
423A A103 80fr multi 1.90 1.50
423B A103 110fr multi 2.40 1.90
Nos. 422-423B (4) 6.25 4.65

Issued: 25fr, 35fr, 11/14; 80fr, 110fr, 5/20/86.
See Nos. 458-459, 474-475.

Catholic Churches — A104

90fr, St. Anne's, Otepipi. 100fr, St. Michael's Cathedral, Rikitea. 120fr, Cathedral, exterior.

1985, Dec. 11 Litho. *Perf. 13*

424	A104	90fr multi	1.75	1.00
425	A104	100fr multi	1.90	1.00
426	A104	120fr multi	2.25	1.50
		Nos. 424-426 (3)	5.90	3.50

Nos. 424-426 printed se-tenant with labels picturing local religious art.

Crabs A105

1986, Jan. 22 *Perf. 13½*

427	A105	18fr Fiddler	.90	.50
428	A105	29fr Hermit	1.40	.65
429	A105	31fr Coconut	2.40	.65
		Nos. 427-429 (3)	4.70	1.80

Faces of Polynesia A106

1986, Feb. 19 *Perf. 12½x13, 13x12½*

430	A106	43fr Boy, fish	1.00	.50
431	A106	49fr Boy, coral	1.25	.50
432	A106	51fr Boy, turtle, vert.	1.40	.60
		Nos. 430-432 (3)	3.65	1.60

Old Tahiti — A107

Designs: 52fr, Papeete. 56fr, Harpoon fishing. 57fr, Royal Palace, Papeete.

1986, Mar. 18 *Perf. 13x12½*

433	A107	52fr multi	1.00	.55
434	A107	56fr multi	1.10	.55
435	A107	57fr multi	1.25	.70
		Nos. 433-435 (3)	3.35	1.80

Tiki Rock Carvings — A108

Designs: 58fr, Atuona, Hiva Oa. 59fr, Ua Huka Hill, Hane Valley.

1986, Apr. 16

436	A108	58fr multi	1.40	.70
437	A108	59fr multi	1.40	.70

Landscapes Type Redrawn

1986-88 Litho. *Perf. 13½*

438	A65	1fr multi, type 2 ('88)	2.50	.35
a.		Type 1 ('86)	4.50	1.25
b.		Type 3 ('91)	18.50	4.50
439	A65	2fr multicolored	.40	.25
440	A65	3fr multicolored	.45	.25
441	A65	4fr multicolored ('87)	1.75	.40
442	A65	5fr multicolored	.75	.30
443	A65	6fr multicolored	.65	.30
		Nos. 438-443 (6)	6.50	1.85

Nos. 438-443 printed in sharper detail, and box containing island name is taller. Nos. 439-443 margin is inscribed "CARTOR" instead of "DELRIEU."

No. 438 has three types of inscription below design: type 1, photographer's name at left, no inscription at right; type 2, photographer's name at left 9.5mm long, printer's name (Cartor) at right; type 3, photographer's name at left 12.5mm long, Cartor at right.

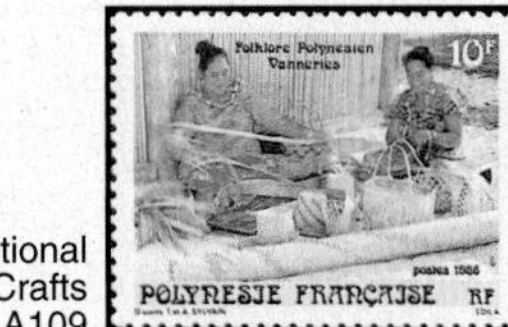

Traditional Crafts A109

Perf. 13x12½, 12½x13

1986, July 17 Litho.

444	A109	8fr Quilting, vert.	.25	.25
445	A109	10fr Baskets, hats	.25	.25
446	A109	12fr Grass skirts	.80	.30
		Nos. 444-446 (3)	1.30	.80

Building a Pirogue (Canoe) A110

1986, Oct. 21 Litho. *Perf. 13½*

447	A110	46fr Boat-builders	1.00	.65
448	A110	50fr Close-up	1.10	.85

Medicinal Plants — A111

Designs: 40fr, Phymatosorus. 41fr, Barringtonia asiatica. 60fr, Ocimum bacilicum.

1986, Nov. 19 *Perf. 13*

449	A111	40fr multi	.90	.50
450	A111	41fr multi	1.00	.50
451	A111	60fr multi	1.60	.90
		Nos. 449-451 (3)	3.50	1.90

See Nos. 495-497.

Polynesians A112

1987, Jan. 21 Litho. *Perf. 13½*

452	A112	28fr Old man	.60	.35
453	A112	30fr Mother and child	.75	.50
454	A112	37fr Old woman	1.00	.60
		Nos. 452-454 (3)	2.35	1.45

Crustaceans — A113

34fr, Carpilius maculatus. 35fr, Parribacus antarticus. 39fr, Justitia longimana.

1987, Feb. 18 *Perf. 12½x13*

455	A113	34fr multicolored	2.00	.65
456	A113	35fr multicolored	2.00	.65
457	A113	39fr multicolored	2.50	.65
		Nos. 455-457 (3)	6.50	1.95

Local Foods Type of 1985

1987, Mar. 19 Litho. *Perf. 13*

458	A103	33fr Papaya poe	1.10	.70
459	A103	65fr Chicken fafa	2.00	1.00

Polynesian Petroglyphs A114

1987, May 13 *Perf. 12½*

460	A114	13fr Tipaerui, Tahiti	.35	.25
461	A114	21fr Turtle, Raiatea Is.	.60	.35

Calling Devices and Musical Instruments, Museum of Tahiti and the Isles — A115

1987, July 1 *Perf. 13½*

462	A115	20fr Wood horn	.65	.30
463	A115	26fr Triton's conch	.80	.65
464	A115	33fr Nose flutes	1.00	.70
		Nos. 462-464 (3)	2.45	1.65

Medicinal Plants — A116

46fr, Thespesia populnea. 53fr, Ophioglossum reticulatum. 54fr, Dicrocephala latifolia.

1987, Sept. 16 *Perf. 12½x13*

465	A116	46fr olive green	1.00	.55
466	A116	53fr reddish lilac	1.40	.55
467	A116	54fr dp bluish grn	1.50	.55
		Nos. 465-467 (3)	3.90	1.65

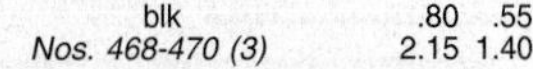

Ancient Weapons and Tools — A117

Designs: 25fr, Adze, war club, chisel, flute. 27fr, War clubs, tatooing comb, mallet. 32fr, Headdress, necklaces, nose flute.

1987, Oct. 14 Engr. *Perf. 13*

468	A117	25fr lt olive grn & blk	.60	.40
469	A117	27fr Prus grn & int blue	.75	.45
470	A117	32fr brt olive bis & brn blk	.80	.55
		Nos. 468-470 (3)	2.15	1.40

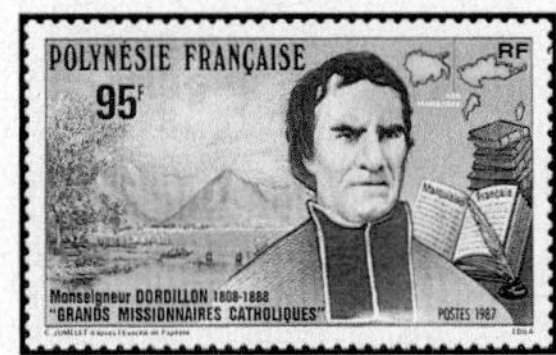

Catholic Missionaries — A118

Monsignors: 95fr, Rene Ildefonse Dordillon (1808-1888), bishop of the Marquesas Isls. 105fr, Tepano Jaussen (1815-1891), first bishop of Polynesia. 115fr, Paul Laurent Maze (1885-1976), archbishop of Papeete.

1987, Dec. 9 Litho.

471	A118	95fr multicolored	1.90	1.40
472	A118	105fr multicolored	2.10	1.50
473	A118	115fr multicolored	2.40	1.60
		Nos. 471-473 (3)	6.40	4.50

Local Foods Type of 1985

Designs: 40fr, Crayfish (varo). 75fr, Bananas in coconut milk.

1988, Jan. 12 Litho. *Perf. 13*

474	A103	40fr multi	1.90	.55
475	A103	75fr multi	2.75	1.10

Nos. 474-475 are vert.

Authors — A119

62fr, James Norman Hall (1887-1951). 85fr, Charles Bernard Nordhoff (1887-1947).

1988, Feb. 10

476	A119	62fr multicolored	1.40	.75
477	A119	85fr multicolored	1.90	.85

Traditional Housing — A120

11fr, Taranpoo Opoa Is., Raiatea. 15fr, Tahaa Village. 17fr, Community meeting house, Tahiti.

1988, Mar. 16 Litho. *Perf. 13x12½*

478	A120	11fr multicolored	.50	.30
479	A120	15fr multicolored	.60	.30
480	A120	17fr multicolored	.60	.30
		Nos. 478-480 (3)	1.70	.90

Point Venus Lighthouse, 120th Anniv. — A121

1988, Apr. 21 Litho. *Perf. 13*

481	A121	400fr multicolored	8.50	5.50

Tapa-cloth Paintings by Paul Engdahl A122

1988, May 20

482	A122	52fr multicolored	1.25	.75
483	A122	54fr multicolored	1.40	.85
484	A122	64fr multicolored	1.50	1.10
		Nos. 482-484 (3)	4.15	2.70

POLYSAT (Domestic Communications Network) — A123

1988, June 15 Litho. *Perf. 12½x12*

485 A123 300fr multicolored 6.00 4.75

Tahitian Dolls — A124

Designs: 42fr, Wearing grass skirt and headdress. 45fr, Wearing print dress and straw hat, holding guitar. 48fr, Wearing print dress and straw hat, holding straw bag.

1988, June 27 *Perf. 13x12½*

486 A124 42fr multicolored 1.00 .60
487 A124 45fr multicolored 1.25 .60
488 A124 48fr multicolored 1.50 .75
Nos. 486-488 (3) 3.75 1.95

Visiting a Marae at Nuku Hiva, Engraving by J. & E. Verreaux A125

1988, Aug. 1 Engr. *Perf. 13*

489 A125 68fr black brown 2.00 1.25

Size: 143x101mm

490 A125 145fr violet brn & grn 5.25 4.00

SYDPEX '88, July 30-Aug. 7, Australia. No. 490 pictures a Russian navy officer (probably Krusenstern) visiting the Marquesas Islanders; denomination LR.

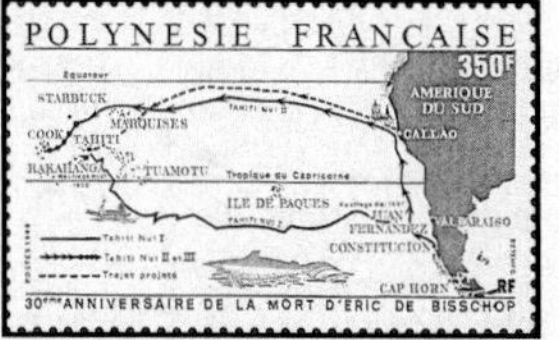

Map Linking South America and South Pacific Islands — A126

1988, Aug. 30 Engr.

491 A126 350fr multicolored 7.50 4.50

Eric de Bisschop (1890-1958), explorer who tried to prove that there was an exchange of peoples between the South Pacific islands and So. America, rather than that the island populations originated from So. America.

Seashells A127

1988, Sept. 21 Litho. *Perf. 13½*

492 A127 24fr Kermia barnardi .60 .35
493 A127 35fr Vexillum suavis 1.00 .50
494 A127 44fr Berthelinia 1.40 .75
Nos. 492-494 (3) 3.00 1.60

Medicinal Plants Type of 1986

23fr, Davallia solida. 36fr, Rorippa sarmentosa. 49fr, Lindernia crustacea.

1988, Oct. 18 Engr. *Perf. 13*

495 A111 23fr carmine lake .75 .30
496 A111 36fr purple brown 1.10 .45
497 A111 49fr deep blue 1.25 .70
Nos. 495-497 (3) 3.10 1.45

Protestant Missionaries — A128

80fr, Henry Nott (1774-1844). 90fr, Papeiha (1800-40). 100fr, Samuel Raapoto (1921-76).

1988, Dec. 7 Litho.

498 A128 80fr multi 1.50 .90
499 A128 90fr multi 2.00 1.25
500 A128 100fr multi 2.25 1.40
Nos. 498-500 (3) 5.75 3.55

Tahiti Post Office A129

1989, Jan. 12 Engr.

501 A129 30fr P.O., 1875 .75 .40
502 A129 40fr P.O., 1915 1.00 .55

Center for Arts and Crafts A130

29fr, Marquesas Is. lidded bowl. 31fr, Mother-of-pearl pendant.

1989, Feb. 15 Litho. *Perf. 12½*

503 A130 29fr multi .80 .40
504 A130 31fr multi .90 .45

Copra Industry

Extracting Coconut Meat From Shell — A131a

Drying Coconut Meat in Sun — A131

1989, Mar. 16 Litho. *Perf. 13*

505 A131a 55fr multicolored *55.00 40.00*
506 A131 70fr multicolored *2.50 2.00*

Tapa Art — A132

43fr, Wood statue (pole), Marquesas Islands, vert. 51fr, Hand-painted bark tapestry, Society Is. 56fr, Concentric circles, Tubuai, Austral Islands.

1989, Apr. 18 Litho. *Perf. 13½*

507 A132 43fr multicolored .90 .60
508 A132 51fr shown 1.25 .75
509 A132 56fr multicolored 1.50 .90
Nos. 507-509 (3) 3.65 2.25

Polynesian Environment A133

Design: 140fr, Diving for seashells.

1989, May 17 Litho. *Perf. 13x12½*

510 A133 120fr shown 2.25 1.50
511 A133 140fr multicolored 2.75 1.75

Polynesian Folklore A134

Designs: 47fr, Stone-lifting contest, vert. 61fr, Dancer, vert. 67fr, Folk singers.

Perf. 13x12½, 12½x13

1989, June 28 Litho.

512 A134 47fr multicolored 1.10 .55
513 A134 61fr multicolored 1.40 .70
514 A134 67fr multicolored 1.75 .75
Nos. 512-514 (3) 4.25 2.00

Bounty Castaways, from an Etching by Robert Dodd — A135

1989, July 7 Engr. *Perf. 13*

515 A135 100fr dp blue & bl grn 2.40 1.50

Souvenir Sheet

Imperf

516 A135 200fr dk ol grn & dk brn 12.00 12.00

PHILEXFRANCE '89 and 200th annivs. of the mutiny on the *Bounty* and the French revolution.

No. 515 printed se-tenant with label picturing exhibition emblem.

Reverend-Father Patrick O'Reilly (1900-1988) A136

1989, Aug. 7 Engr. *Perf. 13x13½*

517 A136 52fr yel brn & myrtle grn 1.40 .75

Miniature Sheet

Messages A137

a, Get well soon. b, Good luck. c, Happy birthday. d, Keep in touch. e, Congratulations.

1989, Sept. 27 Litho. *Perf. 12½*

518 A137 42fr Sheet of 5, #a.-e. 12.00 12.00

Sea Shells A138

1989, Oct. 12 Litho. *Perf. 13½*

523 A138 60fr Triphoridae 1.60 .80
524 A138 69fr Muricidae favartia 1.75 .90
525 A138 73fr Muricidae morula 2.00 1.00
Nos. 523-525 (3) 5.35 2.70

Te Faaturama, c. 1892, by Gauguin A139

1989, Nov. 19 Litho. *Perf. 12½x13*

526 A139 1000fr multicolored 22.00 12.50

Legends — A140

Designs: 66fr, Maui, birth of the islands, vert. 82fr, Mt. Rotui, the pierced mountain. 88fr, Princess Hina and the eel King of Lake Vaihiria.

1989, Dec. 6 Litho. *Perf. 13*

527 A140 66fr olive brn & blk 1.40 .90
528 A140 82fr buff & blk 1.90 1.10
529 A140 88fr cream & blk 2.00 1.15
Nos. 527-529 (3) 5.30 3.15

Vanilla Orchid — A141

1990, Jan. 11 **Litho.**

530 A141 34fr Flower 1.35 .60
531 A141 35fr Bean pods 1.60 .60

Marine Life A142

1990, Feb. 9 **Litho.** ***Perf. 13½***

532 A142 40fr Kuhlia marginata 1.30 .55
533 A142 50fr Macrobrachium 1.50 .70

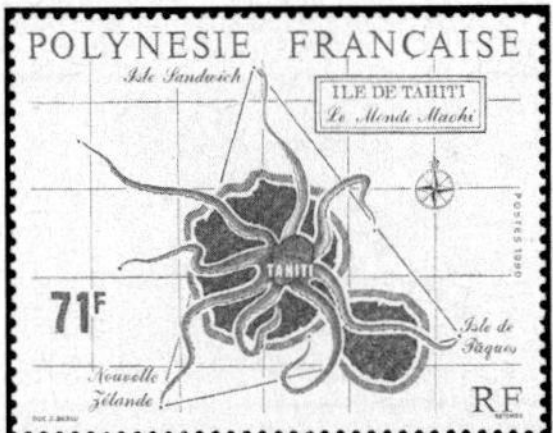
Tahiti, Center of Polynesian Triangle — A143

Maohi settlers and maps of island settlements: 58fr, Hawaiian Islands. 59fr, Easter Island. 63fr, New Zealand.

1990, Mar. 14 **Engr.** ***Perf. 13***

534 A143 58fr black 1.75 .85
535 A143 59fr bluish gray *45.00* 25.00
536 A143 63fr olive green 2.25 .95
537 A143 71fr Prussian blue 2.50 1.10
Nos. 534-537 (4) *51.50* 27.90

See Nos. 544-545.

Papeete Village, Cent. — A144

1990, May 16 **Litho.**

538 A144 150fr New City Hall 3.25 1.75
539 A144 250fr Old Town Hall 4.75 3.00

A145

Designs: Endangered birds.

1990, June 5 ***Perf. 13½***

540 A145 13fr Porzana tabuensis .75 .25
541 A145 20fr Vini ultramarina 1.75 .35

A146

1990, July 10 ***Perf. 13***

542 A146 39fr multicolored 1.10 .65

Lions Club in Papeete, 30th anniv.

Gen. Charles de Gaulle, Birth Cent. — A147

1990, Sept. 2 **Litho.**

543 A147 200fr multi 4.50 3.25

No. 536 with Different Colors and Inscriptions

1990, Aug. 24 **Engr.** ***Perf. 13***

544 A143 125fr Man, map 3.00 2.00

Souvenir Sheet

Imperf

545 A143 230fr like No. 544 6.00 6.00

New Zealand 1990.

Intl. Tourism Day — A148

1990, Sept. 27 **Litho.** ***Perf. 12½***

546 A148 8fr red & yellow pareo 1.10 .35
547 A148 10fr yellow pareo 1.10 .35
548 A148 12fr blue pareo 1.10 .75
Nos. 546-548 (3) 3.30 1.45

Polynesian Legends — A149

170fr, Legend of the Uru. 290fr, Pipiri-ma, vert. 375fr, Hiro, God of Thieves, vert.

1990, Nov. 7 **Litho.** ***Perf. 13***

549 A149 170fr multicolored 4.00 2.50
550 A149 290fr multicolored 7.50 4.00
551 A149 375fr multicolored 11.00 5.00
Nos. 549-551 (3) 22.50 11.50

Tiare Flower — A150

Designs: 28fr, Flower crown, lei. 30fr, Flowers in bloom. 37fr, Lei.

1990, Dec. 5 ***Perf. 12½***

552 A150 28fr multicolored .70 .45
553 A150 30fr multicolored .95 .45
554 A150 37fr multicolored 1.20 .55
Nos. 552-554 (3) 2.85 1.45

Pineapple A151

1991, Jan. 9 ***Die Cut***

Self-adhesive

555 A151 42fr shown 1.25 .90
556 A151 44fr Pineapple field 1.75 1.10

Nos. 555-556 are on paper backing perf. 12½.

Marine Life A152

1991, Feb. 7 ***Perf. 12½***

557 A152 7fr Nudibranch .45 .25
558 A152 9fr Galaxaura tenera .70 .25
559 A152 11fr Adusta cumingii .70 .25
Nos. 557-559 (3) 1.85 .75

Maohi Islands A153

18th Century scenes of: 68fr, Woman of Easter Island, vert. 84fr, Twin-hulled canoe, Hawaii. 94fr, Maori village, New Zealand.

1991, Mar. 13 **Engr.** ***Perf. 13***

560 A153 68fr olive 47.50 32.50
561 A153 84fr black 2.50 1.75
562 A153 94fr brown 3.00 1.75
Nos. 560-562 (3) 53.00 36.00

Basketball, Cent. — A154

1991, May 15 **Litho.** ***Perf. 13***

563 A154 80fr multicolored 1.75 1.25

Birds — A155

1991, June 5 ***Perf. 13½***

564 A155 17fr Halcyon gambieri .60 .25
565 A155 21fr Vini kuhlii .90 .35

Still Life with Oranges in Tahiti by Paul Gauguin — A156

1991, June 9 **Litho.** ***Perf. 13***

566 A156 700fr multicolored 17.50 9.50

Sculptures of the Marquesas Islands — A157

56fr, White Tiki with Club, vert. 102fr, Warriors Carrying Tired Man, vert. 110fr, Native Canoe.

1991, July 17 **Litho.** ***Perf. 13***

567 A157 56fr multicolored 1.25 .85
568 A157 102fr multicolored 2.25 1.50
569 A157 110fr multicolored 2.50 1.75
Nos. 567-569 (3) 6.00 4.10

Wolfgang Amadeus Mozart, Death Bicent. — A158

1991, Aug. 28 **Engr.** ***Perf. 13x12½***

570 A158 100fr multicolored 3.00 1.75

Stone Fishing — A159

25fr, Fishing boats, vert. 57fr, Man hurling stone, vert. 62fr, Trapped fish.

1991, Oct. 9 **Litho.** ***Perf. 13***

571 A159 25fr multi .60 .40
572 A159 57fr multi 1.25 .90
573 A159 62fr multi 1.50 1.25
Nos. 571-573 (3) 3.35 2.55

Phila Nippon '91
A160

Designs: 50fr, Drawings of marine life by Jules-Louis Lejeune, vert. 70fr, Sailing ship, La Coquille. 250fr, Contains designs from Nos. 574-575.

Perf. 12½x13, 13x12½

1991, Nov. 16 **Engr.**

574 A160 50fr multicolored 1.30 .55
575 A160 70fr multicolored 1.75 1.25

Size: 100x75mm

Imperf

576 A160 250fr multicolored 6.00 6.00
Nos. 574-576 (3) 9.05 7.80

Central Bank for Economic Co-operation, 50th Anniv. — A161

1991, Dec. 2 **Litho.** ***Perf. 13x12½***

577 A161 307fr multicolored 7.00 4.50

Christmas
A162

Perf. 12½x13, 13x12½

1991, Dec. 11 **Litho.**

578 A162 55fr Scuba divers 1.25 .75
579 A162 83fr Underwater scene 1.75 1.35
580 A162 86fr Nativity, vert. 1.75 1.35
Nos. 578-580 (3) 4.75 3.45

Tourism — A163

Designs: 2fr, Horses, beach. 3fr, Girl holding fish. 4fr, Waterfalls, vert. 5fr, Sailing. 6fr, Waterfalls, helicopter, vert.

1992, Feb. 12 ***Perf. 13***

581 A163 1fr shown .25 .25
582 A163 2fr multicolored .35 .25
583 A163 3fr multicolored .50 .30
584 A163 4fr multicolored .60 .35
585 A163 5fr multicolored .75 .40
586 A163 6fr multicolored 1.00 .45
Nos. 581-586 (6) 3.45 2.00

Views from Space — A164

Designs: 46fr, Tahiti. 72fr, Mataiva. 76fr, Bora Bora. 230fr, Satellite imaging system.

1992, Mar. 18 **Litho.** ***Perf. 13x12½***

587 A164 46fr multi 1.75 .90
588 A164 72fr multi 2.00 1.25
589 A164 76fr multi 2.25 1.40

Size: 130x100mm

Imperf

590 A164 230fr multi 6.00 5.75
Nos. 587-590 (4) 12.00 9.30

International Space Year.

World Health Day
A165

1992, Apr. 7 ***Perf. 13½***

591 A165 136fr multicolored 3.00 2.25

Discovery of America, 500th Anniv. — A166

1992, May 22 ***Perf. 13***

592 A166 130fr multicolored 3.00 2.25

Size: 140x100mm

Imperf

593 A166 250fr multicolored 6.00 6.00

World Columbian Stamp Expo '92, Chicago.

Traditional Dances — A167

Dance from: 95fr, Tahiti. 105fr, Hawaii. 115fr, Tonga.

1992, June 17 **Engr.** ***Perf. 13***

594 A167 95fr brown black 1.90 1.60
595 A167 105fr olive brown 2.10 1.75
596 A167 115fr red brn & olive grn 2.50 1.75
Nos. 594-596 (3) 6.50 5.10

Tattoos
A168

1992, July 8 **Litho.** ***Perf. 12½***

597 A168 61fr Hand 1.90 1.25
598 A168 64fr Man, vert. 2.00 1.25

Children's Games
A169

Designs: 22fr, Outrigger canoe models. 31fr, String game. 45fr, Stilt game, vert.

1992, Aug. 5 ***Perf. 13½***

599 A169 22fr multi .50 .35
600 A169 31fr multi .75 .45
601 A169 45fr multi 1.25 .70
Nos. 599-601 (3) 2.50 1.50

Herman Melville, 150th Anniv. of Arrival in French Polynesia — A170

1992, Sept. 16 ***Perf. 12½***

602 A170 78fr multicolored 4.50 1.25

6th Festival of Pacific Arts, Rarotonga — A171

40fr, Men on raft. 65fr, Pirogues, Tahiti.

1992, Oct. 16 **Engr.** ***Perf. 13***

603 A171 40fr lake 1.50 .60
604 A171 65fr blue 2.00 1.00

First French Polynesian Postage Stamps, Cent. — A172

1992, Nov. 18 **Photo.** ***Perf. 13***

605 A172 200fr multicolored 4.75 3.25

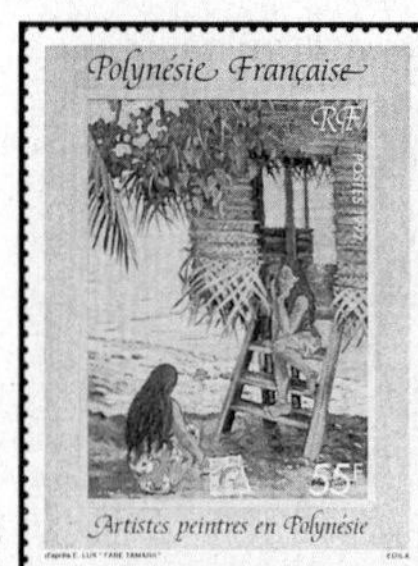

Paintings
A173

55fr, Two Women Talking, by Erhard Lux. 60fr, Bouquet of Flowers, by Uschi. 75fr, Spearfisherman, by Pierre Kienlen. 85fr, Mother Nursing Child, by Octave Morillot.

1992, Dec. 9 ***Perf. 12½x13***

606 A173 55fr multicolored 1.50 .75
607 A173 60fr multicolored 1.75 1.40
608 A173 75fr multicolored 1.90 1.50
609 A173 85fr multicolored 2.50 1.60
Nos. 606-609 (4) 7.65 5.25

Net Thrower — A174

1993, Feb. 10 **Litho.** ***Die Cut***

Self-Adhesive

Size: 26x36mm

610 A174 46fr blue & multi 1.50 1.00

Size: 17x23mm

611 A174 46fr green & multi 1.50 1.00
a. Booklet pane of 10 15.00

Bonito Fishing — A175

1993, Mar. 10 ***Perf. 13½***

612 A175 68fr Line & hook 1.60 1.25
613 A175 84fr Boat, horiz. 1.90 1.50
614 A175 86fr Drying catch 2.10 1.50
Nos. 612-614 (3) 5.60 4.25

Allied Airfield on Bora Bora, 50th Anniv. — A176

1993, Apr. 5 ***Perf. 13***

615 A176 120fr multicolored 3.00 2.25

Jacques Boullaire, Artist, Birth Cent. — A177

Various scenes depicting life on: 32fr, Moorea. 36fr, Tuamotu. 39fr, Rurutu. 51fr, Nuku Hiva.

1993, May 6 **Engr.**

616 A177 32fr brown black .90 .50
617 A177 36fr brick red .90 .65
618 A177 39fr violet 1.25 .90
619 A177 51fr light brown 1.50 1.00
Nos. 616-619 (4) 4.55 3.05

Sports Festival — A178

1993, May 15 **Litho.** ***Perf. 12½***

620 A178 30fr multicolored .85 .50

Australian Mathematics Competition, 15th Anniv. — A179

1993, July 1 Litho. *Perf. 13½*
621 A179 70fr multicolored 1.75 1.10

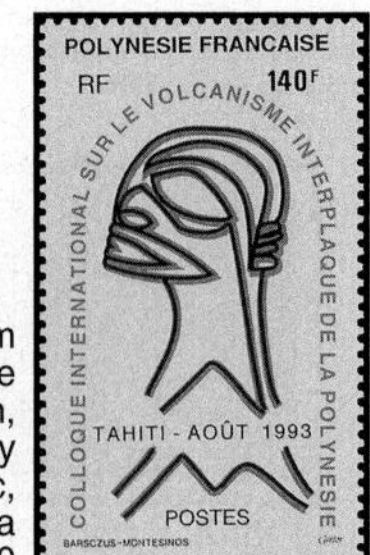

Intl. Symposium on Inter-Plate Volcanism, French University of the Pacific, Punaauia A180

1993, Aug. 2 Litho. *Perf. 13*
622 A180 140fr tan, blk & brn 3.50 2.50

Taipei '93 — A181

1993, Aug. 14 Litho. *Perf. 13½*
623 A181 46fr multicolored 1.75 .85

Exists without the Cartor imprint. Value, unused $17.50.

Tourism — A182

14fr, Boat tour. 20fr, Groom preparing for traditional wedding. 29fr, Beachside brunch.

1993, Sept. 27
624 A182 14fr multi, horiz. .60 .35
625 A182 20fr multi .65 .35
626 A182 29fr multi, horiz. .75 .45
Nos. 624-626 (3) 2.00 1.15

Exist without the Cartor imprint. Value, set unused $30.

Arrival of First French Gendarme in Tahiti, 150th Anniv. — A183

1993, Oct. 14 *Perf. 13*
627 A183 100fr multicolored 2.50 1.60

Exists without the Cartor imprint. Value, unused $17.50.

Alain Gerbault (1893-1941), Sailor — A184

1993, Nov. 17 Engr. *Perf. 13*
628 A184 150fr red, green & blue 4.00 2.75

Paintings — A185

Artists: 40fr, Vaea Sylvain. 70fr, A. Marere, vert. 80fr, J. Shelsher. 90fr, P.E. Victor, vert.

1993, Dec. 3 Photo. *Perf. 13*
629 A185 40fr multicolored 1.75 .70
630 A185 70fr multicolored 2.50 1.25
631 A185 80fr multicolored 3.00 1.25
632 A185 90fr multicolored 3.50 1.50
Nos. 629-632 (4) 10.75 4.70

French School of the Pacific, 30th Anniv. A186

1993, Dec. 7 Litho. *Perf. 12½*
633 A186 200fr multicolored 5.00 3.50

Whales and Dolphins A187

Designs: 25fr, Whale breeching. 68fr, Dolphins. 72fr, Humpback whales, vert.

1994, Jan. 12 Litho. *Perf. 13½*
634 A187 25fr multi .75 .45
635 A187 68fr multi 1.75 1.10
636 A187 72fr multi 2.00 1.25
Nos. 634-636 (3) 4.50 2.80

A188

1994, Feb. 18 Litho. *Perf. 13½*
637 A188 51fr multicolored 2.25 .95

Hong Kong '94. New Year 1994 (Year of the Dog).

Sister Germaine Bruel — A189

1994, Mar. 16
638 A189 180fr multicolored 4.00 3.00

Arrival of Nuns from St. Joseph of Cluny, 150th anniv.

A190

1994, Apr. 30 Litho. *Perf. 13½*
639 A190 154fr Tahiti temple 3.50 2.75

Church of Jesus Christ of Latter-day Saints in French Polynesia, 150th Anniv.

Conservatory of Arts and Crafts, Bicent. — A191

1994, May 25 Photo. *Perf. 13*
640 A191 316fr multicolored 7.50 5.50

Regional Associated Center of Papeete, 15th anniv.

Internal Self-Government, 10th Anniv. — A192

1994, June 29 Litho. *Perf. 13*
641 A192 500fr multicolored 12.00 7.50

Tahitian Academy, 20th Anniv. — A193

1994, July 2 Engr. *Perf. 13*
642 A193 136fr multicolored 3.00 2.00

Scenes of Old Tahiti — A194

1994, Aug. 10 Litho. *Perf. 13*
643 A194 22fr Papara .90 .50
644 A194 26fr Mataiea 1.10 .65
645 A194 51fr Taravao, vert. 1.90 .95
Nos. 643-645 (3) 3.90 2.10

See Nos. 673-675.

Faaturuma, by Paul Gauguin (1848-1903) A195

1994, Sept. 14 Litho. *Perf. 13*
646 A195 1000fr multicolored 24.00 16.00

Epiphyllum Oxypetalum A196

1994, Oct. 15 Litho. *Perf. 13½*
647 A196 51fr multicolored 1.75 .95

Hawaiki Nui Va'a '94 (Canoe Race) A197

Designs: a, 52fr, Yellow canoe, bow paddler. b, 76fr, Paddlers. c, 80fr, Paddlers, blue canoe. d, 94fr, Stern paddler, yellow canoe.

1994, Nov. 10 Litho. *Perf. 13½x13*
648 A197 Strip of 4, #a.-d. 8.00 4.75

No. 648 is a continuous design.

Paintings of French Polynesia — A198

62fr, Young girl, by Michelle Villemin. 78fr, Ocean tide, fish, by Michele Dallet. 102fr, Native carrying bundles of fruit, by Johel Blanchard. 110fr, View of coastline, by Pierre Lacouture.

1994, Dec. 19 Litho. *Perf. 13*
649 A198 62fr multi, vert. 1.75 .95
650 A198 78fr multi, vert. 2.00 1.25
651 A198 102fr multi, vert. 2.25 1.60
652 A198 110fr multi 2.75 1.75
Nos. 649-652 (4) 8.75 5.55

Don Domingo de Boenechea's Tautira Expedition, 220th Anniv. — A199

1995, Jan. 1
653 A199 92fr multicolored 2.25 1.25

South Pacific Tourism Year — A200

1995, Jan. 11 Litho. *Perf. 13½*
654 A200 92fr multicolored 2.25 1.40

New Year 1995 (Year of the Boar) A201

1995, Feb. 1 Litho.
655 A201 51fr multicolored 1.75 .80

Portions of the design on No. 655 were applied by a thermographic process producing a shiny, raised effect.

Exists without the Cartor imprint. Value, unused $9.

University Teacher's Training Institute of the Pacific — A202

1995, Mar. 8 Litho. *Perf. 13½*
656 A202 59fr multicolored 1.50 .95

See New Caledonia No. 710 and Wallis & Futuna No. C182.

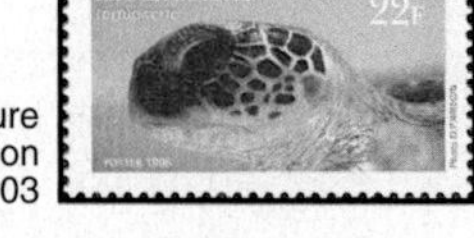

Nature Protection A203

1995, May 4 Litho. *Perf. 13*
657 Strip of 3 + 2 labels 4.25 4.25
a. A203 22fr Head of turtle .75 .35
b. A203 29fr Turtle swimming 1.00 .50
c. A203 91fr Black coral 2.50 1.50

Louis Pasteur (1822-95) — A204

1995, May 8
658 A204 290fr dk blue & blue 6.75 4.00

Loti's Marriage, Novel by Julien Viaud (1850-1923) — A205

1995, May 19 Photo. *Perf. 13*
659 A205 66fr multicolored 2.00 1.10

A206

1995, May 24 Litho. *Perf. 13½*
660 A206 150fr multicolored 3.50 2.25

Tahitian Monoi beauty aid.

Birds — A207

1995, June 7
661 A207 22fr Ptilinopus huttoni .65 .50
662 A207 44fr Ducula galeata 1.40 .75

Tahitian Pearls A208

1995, June 14
663 A208 66fr shown 1.60 1.10
664 A208 84fr Eight pearls 2.10 1.40

On Nos. 663-664 portions of the design were applied by a thermographic process producing a shiny, raised effect.

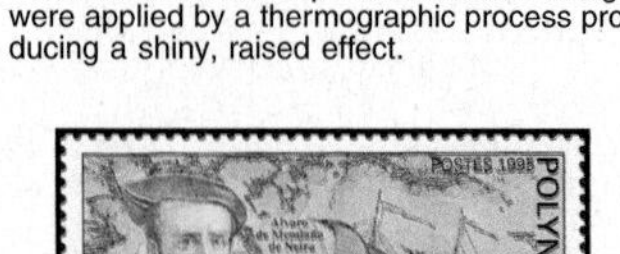

Discovery of Marquesas Islands, 400th Anniv. — A209

a, Alvaro de Mendana de Neira, sailing ships. b, Pedro Fernandez de Quiros, map of islands.

1995, July 21 Litho. *Perf. 13*
665 Pair + label 8.00 6.00
a. A209 161fr multicolored 3.50 2.75
b. A209 195fr multicolored 4.50 3.25

A210

1995, Aug. 12 Litho. *Perf. 13*
666 A210 83fr multicolored 2.00 1.40

10th South Pacific Games, Tahiti.

Pandanus Plant — A211

No. 667a, Entire plant. b, Flower. c, Fruit. d, Using dry leaves for weaving.

1995, Sept. 1 *Perf. 13½x13*
667 Strip of 4 8.50 6.00
a.-d. A211 91fr any single 2.00 1.50

Singapore '95.

UN, 50th Anniv. — A212

1995, Oct. 24 Litho. *Perf. 13*
668 A212 420fr multicolored 9.50 6.00

Paintings — A213

Designs: 57fr, The Paddler with the Yellow Dog, by Philippe Dubois, vert. 76fr, An Afternoon in Vaitape, by Maui Seaman, vert. 79fr, The Mama with the White Hat, by Simone Testeguide. 100fr, In Front of the Kellum House in Moorea, by Christian Deloffre.

1995, Dec. 6 Photo. *Perf. 13*
669 A213 57fr multicolored 1.50 .90
670 A213 76fr multicolored 1.75 1.25
671 A213 79fr multicolored 1.90 1.25
672 A213 100fr multicolored 2.50 1.60
Nos. 669-672 (4) 7.65 5.00

Scenes of Old Tahiti Type

Designs: 18fr, Fautaua. 30fr, District of Punaauia. 35fr, Tautira.

1996, Jan. 17 Litho. *Perf. 13*
673 A194 18fr multi .65 .45
674 A194 30fr multi .80 .50
675 A194 35fr multi .90 .60
Nos. 673-675 (3) 2.35 1.55

New Year 1996 (Year of the Rat) — A214

1996, Feb. 19 Photo. *Perf. 13*
676 A214 51fr multicolored 1.75 .80

Portions of the design on No. 676 were applied by a thermographic process producing a shiny, raised effect.

Paul-Emile Victor (1907-95), Explorer, Writer — A215

1996, Mar. 7 Litho.
677 A215 500fr multicolored 12.00 8.00

Queen Pomare IV — A216

1996, Mar. 1 Litho. *Perf. 13*
678 A216 (51fr) multicolored 1.50 .80

Serpentine Die Cut 7 Vert.
Self-Adhesive
Size: 17x24mm

678A A216 (51fr) multicolored 2.00 1.15
b. Booklet pane of 5 10.00
Complete booklet, 2 #678b 20.00

Sea Shells A217

10fr, Conus pertusus. 15fr, Cypraea alisonae. 25fr, Vexillum roseotinctum.

1996, Apr. 10 Photo. *Perf. 13½x13*
679 A217 10fr multicolored .45 .25
680 A217 15fr multicolored .50 .25
681 A217 25fr multicolored .95 .40
Nos. 679-681 (3) 1.90 .90

Portions of the designs on Nos. 679-681 were applied by a thermographic process producing a shiny, raised effect.

Return of the Pacific Battalion, 50th Anniv. — A218

1996, May 5 Litho. *Perf. 13*
682 A218 100fr multicolored 3.00 1.60

CHINA '96, 9th Asian Intl. Philatelic Exhibition A219

Design: 200fr, Chinese School, Tahiti, 1940.

1996, May 18 ***Perf. 13x13½***

683 A219 50fr multicolored 1.25 .80

Souvenir Sheet

Imperf

684 A219 200fr multicolored 4.50 3.40

Birds A220

1996, June 12 Litho. ***Perf. 13x13½***

685 A220 66fr Sula sula 1.50 1.10
686 A220 79fr Fregata minor 2.00 1.25
687 A220 84fr Anous stolidus 2.00 1.40
Nos. 685-687 (3) 5.50 3.75

Musical Instruments A221

Designs: 5fr, Pahu, ukulele, toere. 9fr, Toere. 14fr, Pu, vivo.

1996, July 10 ***Perf. 13x13½***

688 A221 5fr multicolored .30 .25
689 A221 9fr multicolored .40 .25
690 A221 14fr multicolored .50 .25
Nos. 688-690 (3) 1.20 .75

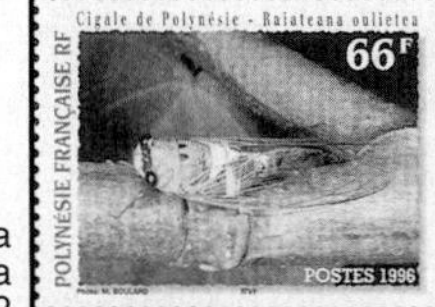

Raiateana Oulietea A222

1996, Aug. 7 Litho. ***Perf. 13x13½***

691 A222 66fr multicolored 1.75 1.10

Ruahatu, God of the Ocean — A223

1996, Sept. 9 Litho. ***Perf. 13***

692 A223 70fr multicolored 1.75 1.10

7th Pacific Arts Festival.

A224

Stamp Day: Young Tahitian girl (Type A2), Noho Mercier, taken from photo by Henry Lemasson (1870-1956), postal administrator.

1996, Oct. 16 Engr. ***Perf. 13***

693 A224 92fr black, red & blue 2.50 1.50

First Representative Assembly, 50th Anniv. — A225

1996, Nov. 7 Litho. ***Perf. 13***

694 A225 85fr multicolored 2.00 1.10

Paintings of Tahitian Women — A226

Designs: 70fr, Woman lounging on Bora Bora Beach, by Titi Bécaud. 85fr, "Woman with Crown of Auti leaves," by Maryse Noguier, vert. 92fr, "Dreamy Woman," by Christine de Dinechin, vert. 96fr, Two working women, by Andrée Lang, vert.

1996, Dec. 4 Litho. ***Perf. 13***

695 A226 70fr multicolored 2.00 .75
696 A226 85fr multicolored 2.25 .90
697 A226 92fr multicolored 2.50 1.00
698 A226 96fr multicolored 3.00 1.00
Nos. 695-698 (4) 9.75 3.65

A227

1997, Jan. 2 Litho. ***Perf. 13***

699 A227 55fr brown 1.25 .55

Society of South Sea Studies, 80th anniv.

A228

1997, Feb. 7 Photo. ***Perf. 13½x13***

700 A228 13fr multicolored 1.00 .30

New Year 1997 (Year of the Ox). Portions of the design were applied by a thermographic process producing a shiny, raised effect.

Arrival of Evangelists in Tahiti, Bicent. — A229

Designs: a, Sailing ship, "Duff." b, Painting, "Transfer of the Matavai District to the L.M.S. Missionaries," by Robert Smirke.

1997, Mar. 5 Litho. ***Perf. 13***

701 A229 43fr Pair, #a.-b. + label 2.00 1.25

Tifaifai (Tahitian Bedspread) A230

Various leaf and floral patterns.

1997, Apr. 16

702 A230 1fr multicolored .25 .25
703 A230 5fr multicolored .25 .25
704 A230 70fr multicolored 1.60 .70
Nos. 702-704 (3) 2.10 1.20

PACIFIC 97 — A231

Sailing ships carrying mail, passengers between Tahiti and San Francisco: No. 705, Tropic Bird, 1897. No. 706, Papeete/Zélee, 1892.

1997, May 29 Litho. ***Perf. 13***

705 A231 92fr multicolored 3.25 1.60
706 A231 92fr multicolored 3.25 1.60
a. Pair, #705-706 6.50 6.50
b. Souvenir sheet, #705-706 65.00 65.00

No. 706b sold for 400fr.

Island Scenes A232

No. 707, Flower. No. 708, Rowing canoe, sun behind mountain. No. 709, Throwing spears. No. 710. Aerial view of island. No. 711, Fish. No. 712, Women walking on beach. No. 713, Holding oyster shell with pearls. No. 714, Boat with sail down, sunset across water. No. 715, Snorkeling, sting ray. No. 716, Bananas, pineapples. No. 717, Palm tree, beach. No. 718, Women dancers in costume.

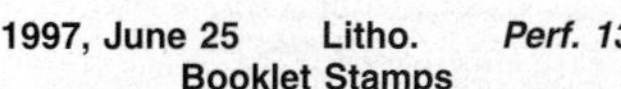

1997, June 25 Litho. ***Perf. 13***

Booklet Stamps

707 A232 85fr multicolored 14.00 14.00
708 A232 85fr multicolored 14.00 14.00
709 A232 85fr multicolored 14.00 14.00
710 A232 85fr multicolored 14.00 14.00
711 A232 85fr multicolored 14.00 14.00
712 A232 85fr multicolored 14.00 14.00
a. Bklt. pane of 6, #707-712 90.00
713 A232 85fr multicolored 14.00 14.00
714 A232 85fr multicolored 14.00 14.00
715 A232 85fr multicolored 14.00 14.00
716 A232 85fr multicolored 14.00 14.00
717 A232 85fr multicolored 14.00 14.00
718 A232 85fr multicolored 14.00 14.00
a. Bklt. pane of 6, #713-718 90.00
Complete booklet, 2 each #712a, #718a 350.00

Traditional Dance Costumes A233

Designs: 4fr, Warrior's costume. 9fr, Women's costume. 11fr, Couple.

1997, July 10 Litho. ***Perf. 13½x13***

719 A233 4fr multicolored 1.00 .30
720 A233 9fr multicolored 1.25 .30
721 A233 11fr multicolored 2.00 .30
Nos. 719-721 (3) 4.25 .90

Kon-Tiki Expedition, 50th Anniv. — A234

1997, Aug. 7 Litho. ***Perf. 13***

722 A234 88fr multicolored 2.25 .80

Artists in Tahiti — A235

Designs: 85fr, Painting, "The Fruit Carrier," by Monique "Mono" Garnier-Bissol. 96fr, "Revival of Our Resources," mother of pearl painting, by Camélia Maraea. 110fr, "Tahitian Spirit," pottery, by Peter Owen, vert. 126fr, "Monoi," surrealist painting, by Elisabeth Stefanovitch.

1997, Oct. 15 Litho. ***Perf. 13***

723 A235 85fr multicolored 1.90 .80
724 A235 96fr multicolored 2.00 .90
725 A235 110fr multicolored 2.50 1.00
726 A235 126fr multicolored 3.00 1.10
Nos. 723-726 (4) 9.40 3.80

Te Arii Vahine, by Paul Gauguin (1848-1903) — A236

1997, Nov. 6 Litho. ***Perf. 13***

727 A236 600fr multicolored 13.00 8.00

Christmas A237

1997, Dec. 3 Litho. *Perf. 13*
728 A237 118fr multicolored 3.00 1.10

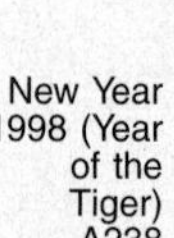

New Year 1998 (Year of the Tiger) A238

1998, Jan. 28 Photo. *Perf. 13*
729 A238 96fr multicolored 2.50 .90

Portions of the design on No. 729 were applied by a thermographic process producing a shiny, raised effect.

Domestic Airline Network — A239

Designs: a, 70fr, Grumman Widgeon, 1950. b, 85fr, DHC 6 Twin-Otter, 1968. c, 70fr, Fairchild FH 227, 1980. d, 85fr, ATR 42-500, 1998.

1998, Apr. 16 Photo. *Perf. 13*
730 A239 Strip of 4, #a.-d. + label 6.50 2.90

Orchids A240

5fr, Dendrobium "Royal King." 20fr, Oncidium "Ramsey." 50fr, Ascodenca "Laksi." 100fr, Cattleya "hybride."

1998, May 14 Photo. *Perf. 13*
731 A240 5fr multi .25 .25
732 A240 20fr multi, vert. .50 .25
733 A240 50fr multi, vert. 1.25 .45
734 A240 100fr multi 2.25 .95
Nos. 731-734 (4) 4.25 1.90

On Nos. 731-734 portions of the design were applied by a thermographic process producing a shiny, raised effect.

The Lovers, by Paul Gauguin (1848-1903) — A241

1998, June 7 Photo. *Perf. 13x12½*
735 A241 1000fr multicolored 22.50 9.00

Printed se-tenant with label.

1998 World Cup Soccer Championships, France — A242

1998, June 10
736 A242 85fr multicolored 2.00 .75

For overprint see No. 742.

Tahiti Festival of Flower and Shell Garlands — A243

Women wearing various garlands of flowers or shells.

1998, July 16 Photo. *Perf. 13½*
737 A243 55fr multicolored 1.50 .50
738 A243 65fr multicolored 1.75 .60
739 A243 70fr multicolored 2.00 .65
740 A243 80fr multicolored 2.25 .75
Nos. 737-740 (4) 7.50 2.50

Painting, "Underwater World of Polynesia," by Stanley Haumani A244

1998, Sept. 10 Photo. *Perf. 12½x13*
741 A244 200fr multicolored 4.00 2.00

No. 736 Overprinted in Blue & Black

1998, Oct. 28 Photo. *Perf. 13½*
742 A242 85fr multicolored 3.00 1.00

No. 742 has blue, white and red margins and No. 736 has white margins.

Autumn Philatelic Fair, Paris — A246

Watercolor paintings of Papeete Bay, by René Gillotin (1814-61), 250fr each: a, Beach at left, people. b, Beach at right, people.

1998, Nov. 5 *Perf. 13*
743 A246 Pair, #a.-b. + label 12.00 5.00
c. Souvenir sheet, #a.-b., imperf. 12.00 5.00

Life in Tahiti and the Islands A247

Paintings by André Deymonaz: 70fr, Return to the Market, vert. 100fr, Bonito Fish Stalls, vert. 102fr, Going Fishing. 110fr, Discussion after Church Services.

1998, Dec. 10 Photo. *Perf. 13*
744 A247 70fr multicolored 1.50 .80
745 A247 100fr multicolored 2.00 1.00
746 A247 102fr multicolored 2.25 1.00
747 A247 110fr multicolored 2.50 1.10
Nos. 744-747 (4) 8.25 3.90

St. Valentine's Day — A248

1999, Feb. 11 Litho. *Perf. 13*
748 A248 96fr multicolored 2.50 .90

New Year 1999 (Year of the Rabbit) A249

1999, Feb. 16
749 A249 118fr Rabbits, flowers 2.50 1.10

Portions of the design of No. 749 were applied by a thermographic process producing a shiny, raised effect.

Marine Life A250

Designs: 70fr, Ptérois volitans. 85fr, Hippocampus histrix. 90fr, Antennarius pictus. 120fr, Taenianotus triacanthus.

1999, Mar. 18 Photo. *Perf. 13*
750 A250 70fr multicolored 1.50 .65
751 A250 85fr multicolored 1.90 .80
752 A250 90fr multicolored 2.00 .80
753 A250 120fr multicolored 2.75 1.10
Nos. 750-753 (4) 8.15 3.35

Portions of the designs on Nos. 750-753 were applied by a thermographic process producing a shiny, raised effect.

IBRA '99, World Philatelic Exhibition, Nuremberg A251

Tatooed men of Marquesas Islands, 1804: 90fr, Holding staff, fan. 120fr, Wearing blue cape.

Photo. & Engr.

1999, Apr. 27 *Perf. 13¼*
754 A251 90fr multicolored 2.00 .90
755 A251 120fr multicolored 2.75 1.25

Mother's Day A252

1999, May 27 Litho. *Perf. 13¼*
756 A252 85fr Children, vert. 1.90 .75
757 A252 120fr shown 2.75 1.00

A253

Island Fruits A254

No. 758, Breadfruit, vert. 120fr, Coconut.
No. 760: a, Papaya. b, Guava (goyave). c, Mombin. d, Rambutan. e, Star apple (pomme-etoile). f, Otaheite gooseberry (seurette). g, Rose apple. h, Star fruit (carambole). i, Spanish lime (quenette). j, Sweetsop (pomme-cannelle). k, Cashew (pomme de cajou). l, Passion fruit.

1999 Litho. *Perf. 13½x13, 13x13½*
758 A253 85fr multicolored 1.90 .75
759 A253 120fr multicolored 2.75 1.10

Souvenir Booklet

760 Complete bklt. 32.50
a.-l. A254 85fr Any single 2.00 1.40

Issued: No. 758, 120fr, 7/21; No. 760, 7/21.
No. 760 sold for 1200fr, and contains two booklet panes, containing Nos. 760a-760f, and Nos. 760g-760l. A second variety of No. 760 exists with selling price on cover as 1020fr. Value, complete booklet, $100.

No. 720, 1856 Letter, 1864 Postmark — A255

1999, July 2 Litho. *Perf. 13*
761 A255 180fr multicolored 4.00 2.25
a. Souvenir sheet of 1 12.00 12.00

150th anniv. of French postage stamps, PhilexFrance 99.
No. 761 issued se-tenant with label. No. 761a sold for 500fr.

Frédéric Chopin (1810-49), Composer — A256

1999, July 2 Litho. *Perf. 13*
762 A256 250fr multicolored 5.50 2.50

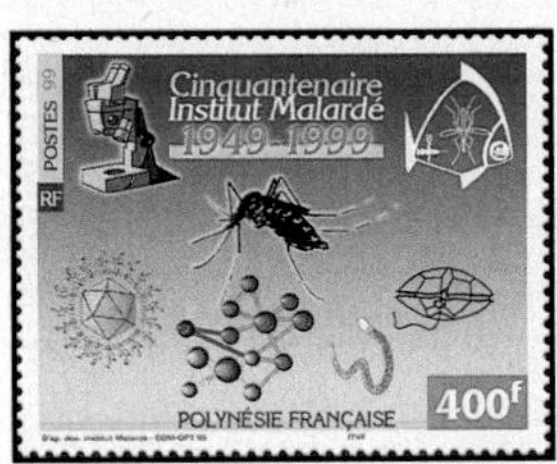

Malardé Medical Research Institute, 50th Anniv. — A257

1999, Sept. 27
763 A257 400fr multicolored 8.75 3.75

Nudes A258

Paintings by: 85fr, J. Sorgniard. 120fr, J. Dubrusk. 180fr, C. Deloffre. 250fr, J. Gandouin.

1999, Oct. 14 Litho. *Perf. 13*
764 A258 85fr multi 2.10 .75
765 A258 120fr multi 3.25 1.10
766 A258 180fr multi 4.50 1.60
767 A258 250fr multi 6.00 2.25
Nos. 764-767 (4) 15.85 5.70

Tahiti on the Eve of the Year 2000 A259

1999, Nov. 10 Litho. *Perf. 13*
768 A259 85fr multi 2.50 .75

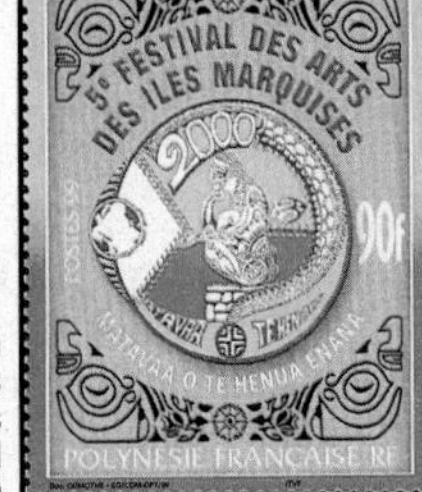

5th Marquesas Islands Arts Festival A260

1999, Dec. 10
769 A260 90fr multi 2.00 .80

Year 2000 — A261

85fr, Hands of adult and infant. 120fr, Eye.

2000, Jan. 3 *Perf. 13¼x13, 13x13¼*
770 A261 85fr multi, vert. 2.50 .75
771 A261 120fr multi 3.25 1.10

New Year 2000 (Year of the Dragon) A262

2000, Feb. 5 Litho. *Perf. 13x13¼*
772 A262 180fr multi 5.50 1.50

Portions of the design were applied by a thermographic process producing a shiny, raised effect.

Postal Service Emblem and Stamps A263

2000, Mar. 15 Litho. *Perf. 13x13¼*
773 A263 90fr multi 2.00 .75

First Intl. Tattoo Festival, Raiatea — A264

Various tattoos.

2000, Apr. 28 *Perf. 13*
774 A264 85fr multi 1.90 .70
775 A264 120fr multi 2.75 .95
776 A264 130fr multi 2.90 1.00
777 A264 160fr multi 3.50 1.25
Nos. 774-777 (4) 11.05 3.90

Beautiful Women of French Polynesia — A265

2000, May 30
778 A265 300fr multi 7.50 3.00
a. Souvenir sheet of 1 12.00 12.00

No. 778a sold for 500fr.

Traditional Dresses — A266

Denominations: 85fr, 120fr, 160fr, 250fr.

2000, June 21 Litho. *Perf. 13¼x13*
779-782 A266 Set of 4 13.50 6.00

Mountains A267

Designs: 90fr, Mts. Aorai and Orohena. 180fr, Mts. Orohena and Aorai.

2000, July 10 *Perf. 13x13¼*
783-784 A267 Set of 2 6.00 2.60

Traditional Sports A268

120fr, Fruit carrying. 250fr, Stone lifting, vert.

Perf. 13x13¼, 13¼x13
2000, Sept. 15
785-786 A268 Set of 2 8.25 3.50

Native Woven Crafts A269

No. 787, Fans. No. 788, Hat.

2000, Oct. 3 Litho. *Perf. 13x13¼*
787-788 A269 85fr Set of 2 3.75 1.75

Year of Ancient Tahitian Language Reo Ma'ohi A270

2000, Nov. 9 Litho. *Perf. 13x13¼*
789 A270 120fr multi 2.75 1.20

Portions of the design were applied by a thermographic process producing a shiny, raised effect.

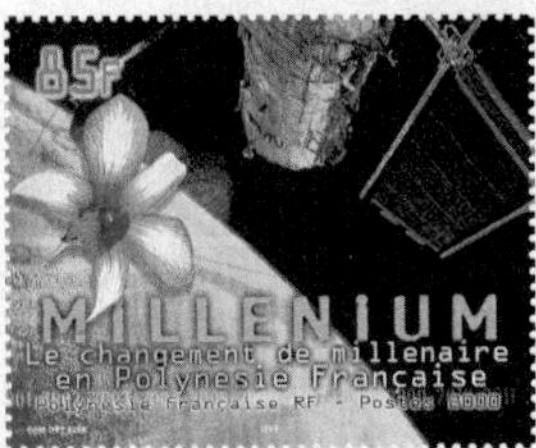

Advent of New Millennium — A271

2000, Dec. 28
790 A271 85fr multi 2.50 .90

Central School, Cent. — A272

Designs: No. 791, 85fr, Central School. No. 792, 85fr, Paul Gauguin High School.

2001, Jan. 16
791-792 A272 Set of 2 3.75 1.75

New Year 2001 (Year of the Snake) — A273

2001, Jan. 24 *Perf. 13¼x13*
793 A273 120fr multi 2.75 1.20

Portions of the design were applied by a thermographic process producing a shiny, raised effect.

Landscapes A274

Designs: 35fr, Vaiharuru Waterfall. 50fr, Vahiria Lake, horiz. 90fr, Hakaui Valley.

Perf. 13¼x13, 13x13¼
2001, Feb. 26 Litho.
794-796 A274 Set of 3 6.00 1.75

Year of the Polynesian Child — A275

2001, Mar. 28 Litho. *Perf. 13x13¼*
797 A275 55fr multi 1.25 .55

Polynesian Singers — A276

Designs: 85fr, Eddie Lund. 120fr, Charley Mauu. 130fr, Bimbo. 180fr, Marie Mariteragi and Emma Terangi, horiz.

2001, Apr. 12 *Perf. 13¼x13, 13x13¼*
798-801 A276 Set of 4 11.50 5.00

Volunteers of the Pacific Batallion, 60th Anniv. A277

2001, Apr. 21 *Perf. 13x13¼*
802 A277 85fr multi 2.25 .90

Surfing Waves of Teahupoo A278

2001, May 4
803 A278 120fr multi 2.75 1.20

Internal Autonomy, 17th Anniv. A279

2001, June 29 Litho. *Perf. 13*
804 A279 250fr multi 5.50 2.50
a. Souvenir sheet of 1 12.00 12.00

No. 804a sold for 500fr.

Pirogue Racing — A280

Designs: 85fr, Male racers. 120fr, Female racers.

2001, July 12 *Perf. 13¼x13*
805-806 A280 Set of 2 4.50 2.00
a. Souvenir sheet, #805-806, imperf. 5.50 5.50

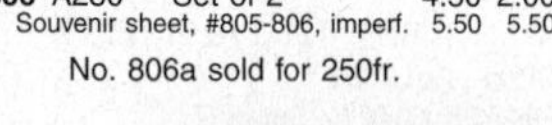

No. 806a sold for 250fr.

Hardwood Trees A281

Designs: 90fr, Tou. 130fr, Ati. 180fr, Miro.

2001, Oct. 23 Litho. *Perf. 13x13½*
807-809 A281 Set of 3 11.00 8.00

AIDS Prevention A282

2001, Sept. 20 Litho. *Perf. 13x13¼*
810 A282 55fr multi 2.75 1.10

Year of Dialogue Among Civilizations A283

2001, Oct. 9 *Perf. 13*
811 A283 500fr multi 11.50 10.00

Perfume Flowers — A284

Designs: 35fr, Gardenia tahitensis. 50fr, Fagraea berteriana. 85fr, Gardenia jasminoides.

2001, Nov. 8 *Perf. 13¼x13*
812-814 A284 Set of 3 6.00 3.50

Portions of the designs were applied by a thermographic process producing a shiny, raised effect.

Christmas A285

2001, Dec. 6 *Perf. 13x13¼*
815 A285 120fr multi 2.75 2.40

New Year 2002 (Year of the Horse) A286

2002, Feb. 12 Litho. *Perf. 13x13¼*
816 A286 130fr multi 3.25 2.60

Portions of the design were applied by a thermographic process producing a shiny, raised effect.

Happy Holidays A287

Greetings A288

2002, Feb. 28 Background Colors
817 A287 55fr red 1.25 1.10
818 A288 55fr blue 1.25 1.10
819 A287 85fr blue 1.90 1.75
820 A288 85fr green 1.90 1.75
Nos. 817-820 (4) 6.30 5.70

10th World Outrigger Canoe Championships — A289

Canoe rowers and emblems: 120fr, 180fr.

2002, Mar. 9 Photo. *Perf. 13¼*
821-822 A289 Set of 2 6.75 6.25

Sea Urchins A290

Designs: 35fr, Echinometra sp. 50fr, Heterocentrotus trigonarius. 90fr, Echinothrix calamaris. 120fr, Toxopneustes sp.

2002, Apr. 18 Litho. *Perf. 13x13¼*
823-826 A290 Set of 4 6.50 6.25

Blood Donation — A291

2002, May 3 Litho. *Perf. 13¼x13*
827 A291 130fr multi 4.00 3.25

2002 World Cup Soccer Championships, Japan and Korea — A292

2002, May 30
828 A292 85fr multi 2.10 1.75

Traditional Sports — A293

Designs: 85fr, Coconut husking. 120fr, Fruit carrying. 250fr, Javelin throwing.

2002, June 27
829-831 A293 Set of 3 10.00 9.00

House of James Norman Hall — A294

2002, July 4 *Perf. 13x13¼*
832 A294 90fr multi 2.00 1.90

Papeete Market — A295

2002, Aug. 30 Litho. *Perf. 13*
833 A295 400fr multi 8.75 8.00
a. Souvenir sheet of 1 11.00 11.00

Amphilex 2002 Stamp Exhibition, Amsterdam (No. 833a). No. 833a sold for 500fr.

Pacific Oceanology Center, Vairoa A296

Designs: 55fr, Research pond, fish, shrimp, oyster, and flasks. 90fr, Aeriel view of center, fish, shrimp and oyster.

2002, Sept. 26 Photo. *Perf. 13¼*
834-835 A296 Set of 2 3.50 2.40

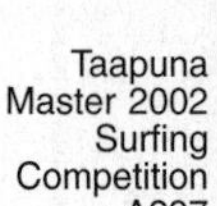

Taapuna Master 2002 Surfing Competition A297

2002, Oct. 21 Litho. *Perf. 13x13¼*
836 A297 120fr multi 2.75 2.00

Halophilic Flowers A298

Designs: 85fr, Hibiscus tiliaceus. 130fr, Scaveola sericea. 180fr, Guettarda speciosa.

2002, Nov. 7
837-839 A298 Set of 3 8.75 6.75

Polynesians at Festivals A299

Designs: 55fr, Dancers and bus. 120fr, Musicians, vert.

2002, Dec. 5 *Perf. 13x13¼, 13¼x13*
840-841 A299 Set of 2 3.75 3.00

New Year 2003 (Year of the Ram) — A300

2003, Feb. 1 Litho. *Perf. 13¼x13*
842 A300 120fr multi 3.00 2.25

Portions of the design was applied by a thermographic process producing a shiny, raised effect.

Polynesian Women — A301

2003, Mar. 8 Litho. *Perf. 13¼x13*
843 A301 55fr multi 1.25 1.00

Waterfalls — A302

2003, Apr. 10 *Perf. 13*
844 A302 330fr multi 7.25 6.00

Old Papeete A303

Designs: 55fr, Automobiles and buildings, vert. 85fr, Ship in harbor. 90fr, People with bicycles in front of buildings (50x28mm). 120fr, Tree-lined street (50x28mm).

Perf. 13¼x13, 13x13¼, 13

2003, May 15

845-848 A303 Set of 4 7.75 7.00
848a Souvenir sheet, #845-848 12.00 12.00

No. 848a sold for 550fr.

Fish — A304

2003, June 12 Litho. *Perf. 13*

849 A304 460fr multi 9.50 9.50

Portions of the design were applied by a thermographic process producing a shiny, raised effect.

Outrigger Canoes A305

Designs: No. 850, 85fr, shown. No. 851, 85fr, Three sailors on canoe at sea. No. 852, 85fr, Three sailors on canoe, vert. No. 853, 85fr, Sailor sitting on outrigger, vert.

Perf. 13x13¼, 13¼x13

2003, July 11 Litho.

850-853 A305 Set of 4 7.50 6.50

Firewalkers A306

Orange-banded Cowrie — A307

2003, Aug. 14 Photo. *Perf. 13¼*

854 A306 130fr multi 2.50 2.50

Perf. 13x13¼

855 A307 420fr multi 8.50 8.50

Are You Jealous? by Paul Gauguin (1848-1903) — A308

2003, Sept. 11 *Perf. 13x12¼*

856 A308 250fr multi 6.50 3.50

Office of Posts and Telecommunications Emblem — A308a

Type I: "Postes 2003" at right.
Type II: "Postes" only at right.

Serpentine Die Cut 6½ Vert.

2003, Oct. 1 Engr.

Booklet Stamp

Self-Adhesive

856A A308a (60fr) blue (type II), *2006* *10.00 1.00*
b. Booklet pane of 10 *100.00*
c. Type I *40.00 24.00*
d. As "c," booklet pane of 10 *400.00*
e. As #856A, inscribed "Phil@poste" *8.00 1.00*
f. Booklet pane of 10 #856Ae *80.00*

Issued: No. 856Ac, 10/1/03. No. 856A, 2006. No. 856Ae, 2007.

See Nos. 869, 1070-1070B.

French Polynesian Flag A309

2003, Oct. 1 Litho. *Perf. 13x13¼*

857 A309 (60fr) multi 1.50 1.25

Tiki — A310

2003, Oct. 1 *Perf. 13¼x13*

858 A310 100fr multi 3.00 2.00

Reissued in 2006 on shiny paper with much deeper colors. Values the same.

Flowers A311

Designs: 90fr, Orchid. 130fr, Rose de porcelain (torch ginger).

2003, Oct. 4 Litho. *Perf. 13x13¼*

859-860 A311 Set of 2 6.50 4.50

Portions of the designs were applied by a thermographic process producing a shiny, raised effect.

Bora Bora A312

Designs: No. 861, 60fr, Painting of Bora Bora by A. Van Der Heyde. No. 862, 60fr, Aerial photograph of Bora Bora.

2003, Nov. 6 Litho. *Perf. 13x13¼*

861-862 A312 Set of 2 5.00 2.75

Tiki — A313

2003, Dec. 6 *Perf. 13*

863 A313 190fr multi 4.00 4.00

Buildings and Palm Trees A314

2003, Dec. 19 *Perf. 13x13¼*

864 A314 90fr multi 3.00 1.90

New Year 2004 (Year of the Monkey) — A315

2004, Jan. 22 Litho. *Perf. 13¼x13*

865 A315 130fr multi 3.50 3.50

A portion of the design was applied by a thermographic process producing a shiny, raised effect.

Scenes From Everyday Life A316

Designs: 60fr, Women working with cloth. 90fr, Street scene, vert.

Perf. 13x13¼, 13¼x13

2004, Feb. 13 Litho.

866-867 A316 Set of 2 3.25 3.25

Polynesian Woman — A317

2004, Mar. 8 *Perf. 13¼x13*

868 A317 90fr multi 4.00 1.90

Post Emblem Type of 2003

Serpentine Die Cut 6¾ Vert.

2004, Apr. 22 Engr.

Booklet Stamp

Self-Adhesive

869 A308a (90fr) red *6.00 2.00*
a. Booklet pane of 10 *60.00*
b. As #869, inscribed "Phil@poste" — —
c. Booklet pane of 10 #869b —

No. 869 lacks year date.

Polynesian Economic Development — A318

2004, Apr. 23 Litho. *Perf. 13x12¾*

870 A318 500fr multi 11.00 10.00

Arahurahu Marae, Paea — A319

2004, Apr. 23

871 A319 500fr multi 11.00 10.00

Vanilla — A320

2004, May 14 *Perf. 13¼x13*

872 A320 90fr multi 2.10 1.90

No. 872 is impregnated with a vanilla scent.

Mobile Snack Bars — A321

2004, May 28 *Perf. 13x12¾*

873 A321 300fr multi 6.50 6.25

Handicrafts A322

Designs: No. 874, 60fr, Artisan braiding fibers. No. 875, 60fr, Mother-of-pearl carving. No. 876, 90fr, Artisan carving statue. No. 877, 90fr, Hat.

2004, June 26 *Perf. 13x13¼*

874-877 A322 Set of 4 10.00 6.25

Portion of the designs were applied by a thermographic process producing a shiny, raised effect.

Involvement in South Pacific Area of Office of Posts and Telecommunications — A323

Designs: 100fr, Earth, Sun on horizon. 130fr, Satellite dish, building.

2004, July 23 Photo. ***Perf. 13¼***
878-879 A323 Set of 2 5.50 4.75

Information Technology and Communications A324

Designs: No. 880, 190fr, Computer keyboard, "@." No. 881, 190fr, Satellite, satellite dish.

2004, Sept. 23 Litho. ***Perf. 13¼x13***
880-881 A324 Set of 2 8.00 8.00

Omai, Polynesian Capt. James Cook Brought to England — A325

2004, Oct. 14 ***Perf. 13***
882 A325 250fr multi 5.25 5.25

Shell Collectors A326

2004, Nov. 10 Photo. ***Perf. 13¼***
883 A326 60fr multi 1.60 1.40

A souvenir sheet of one sold for 250fr. Value $7.

Adenium Obesum A327

Alpinia Purpurata A328

Ixora Chinensis A329

Gardenia Taitensis A330

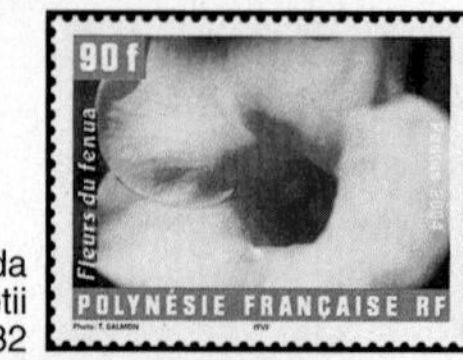

Heliconia Psittacorum — A331

Allamanda Blanchetii A332

Otacanthus Caeruleus — A333

Hibiscus Rosa-sinensis — A334

Euphorba Milii A335

Asocenda Hybrid of Vanda x Ascocentrum — A336

Mussaenda Erythrophylia — A337

Bougainvillea Glabra — A338

2004, Nov. 10 Litho. ***Perf. 13x13¼***

884	Booklet pane of 6	17.50	—
a.	A327 90fr multi	2.50	2.50
b.	A328 90fr multi	2.50	2.50
c.	A329 90fr multi	2.50	2.50
d.	A330 90fr multi	2.50	2.50
e.	A331 90fr multi	2.50	2.50
f.	A332 90fr multi	2.50	2.50
885	Booklet pane of 6	17.50	—
a.	A333 90fr multi	2.50	2.50
b.	A334 90fr multi	2.50	2.50
c.	A335 90fr multi	2.50	2.50
d.	A336 90fr multi	2.50	2.50
e.	A337 90fr multi	2.50	2.50
f.	A338 90fr multi	2.50	2.50
	Complete booklet, #884-885	30.00	

Complete booklet sold for 1200fr.

Christmas A339

2004, Dec. 17
886 A339 60fr multi 1.60 1.40

A portion of the design was applied by a thermographic process producing a shiny, raised effect.

Bamboo — A340

2005, Feb. 9 ***Perf. 13¼x13***
887 A340 130fr multi 3.00 3.00

New Year 2005. A portion of the design was applied by a thermographic process producing a shiny, raised effect.

People and Hut A341

2005, Feb. 25 ***Perf. 13x13¼***
888 A341 90fr multi 2.00 2.00

Polynesian Women — A342

Designs: 60fr, Woman wearing lei. 90fr, Woman wearing flower garland on head and robe.

2005, Mar. 8 ***Perf. 13¼x13***
889-890 A342 Set of 2 4.00 3.50

Woman Making Tapa Cloth — A343

2005, Apr. 22 ***Perf. 13***
891 A343 250fr multi 5.50 5.50

Tifaifai A344

2005, Mar. 23 Litho. ***Perf. 13x13¼***
892 A344 5fr multi .25 .25

Angelfish A345

Designs: No. 893, 90fr, Centropyge bispinosa. No. 894, 90fr, Centropyge loricula. No. 895, 130fr, Centropyge heraldi. No. 896, 130fr, Centropyge flavissima.

2005, May 27 Litho. ***Perf. 13x13¼***
893-896 A345 Set of 4 9.50 9.50
896a Souvenir sheet, #893-896 9.50 9.50

Portions of the designs were applied by a thermographic process producing a shiny, raised effect.

Historic Airplanes A346

Designs: No. 897, 60fr, TAI DC-8, first jet in Tahiti, 1961. No. 898, 60fr, Pan American Boeing 707, first foreign flight, 1963. No. 899, 100fr, Air France Boeing 707, first Air France flight to Tahiti, 1973. No. 900, 100fr, Air Tahiti Nui Airbus A340-300, first Tahitian airline, 2000.

2005, June 24
897-900 A346 Set of 4 6.50 6.50

Musical Instruments A347

Designs: No. 901, 130fr, Drum. No. 902, 130fr, Nose flutes, horiz.

2005, July 22 ***Perf. 13¼x13, 13x13¼***
901-902 A347 Set of 2 5.50 5.50

Polynesian Landscapes — A348

2005, Aug. 26 ***Perf. 13***
903 A348 300fr multi 6.25 6.25

Pineapples A349

Designs: 90fr, Close-up of spines. 130fr, Entire fruit.

2005, Sept. 23 Litho. *Perf. 13¼x13*
904-905 A349 Set of 2 4.75 4.50

Nos. 904-905 are impregnated with pineapple scent.

Marae — A350

Marquesan Tohua — A351

2005, Oct. 21 *Perf. 13*
906 A350 500fr multi 10.00 10.00
907 A351 500fr multi 10.00 10.00

Autonomy, 20th Anniv. (in 2004) — A352

2005, Nov. 10 *Perf. 13¼x13*
908 A352 60fr multi 4.00 1.75

No. 908 was printed in France and distributed there in June 2004 but was not sold in French Polynesia until 2005, where it was available from the philatelic bureau upon request, and not through standing orders.

O'Parrey Harbor, Tahiti A353

2005, Nov. 10 Engr. *Perf. 13x12½*
909 A353 100fr multi 2.00 2.00

Christmas A354

2005, Dec. 16 Litho. *Perf. 13x13¼*
910 A354 90fr multi 2.00 2.00

Lotus Flower A355

Litho. & Silk-screened

2006, Jan. 30 *Perf. 13x13¼*
911 A355 130fr multi 2.60 2.60

A356

Hearts A357

2006, Feb. 14 Photo. *Perf. 13*
912 A356 60fr multi 1.25 1.25
913 A357 90fr multi 1.90 1.90

Values are for stamps with surrounding selvage.

Polynesian Women — A358

Woman: 60fr, At water's edge. 90fr, With oil lamp.

2006, Mar. 8 Litho. *Perf. 13¼x13*
914-915 A358 Set of 2 3.75 3.25

Maupiti — A359

2006, Apr. 26 Engr. *Perf. 13x13¼*
916 A359 500fr multi 11.00 11.00

History of the Marquesas (Washington) Islands — A360

Designs: 60fr, Native man and woman. 130fr, Ships.

2006, May 27 Litho. *Perf. 13¼x13*
917-918 A360 Set of 2 4.00 4.00
918a Souvenir sheet, #917-918 4.00 4.00

Diners and Musicians — A361

2006, June 6 *Perf. 13*
919 A361 300fr multi 6.50 6.50

Polynesian Ground Dove A362

Tuamotu Sandpiper A363

2006, June 21 *Perf. 13x13¼*
920 A362 250fr multi 5.25 5.25
921 A363 250fr multi 5.25 5.25

Heiva — A364

Designs: 90fr, Canoe race. 130fr, Stone lifting. 190fr, Dancer.

2006, July 19 *Perf. 13¼x13*
922-924 A364 Set of 3 8.75 8.75

Frangipani Flowers A365

2006, Aug. 23 Litho. *Perf. 13x13½*
925 A365 90fr multi 2.25 1.90

No. 925 is impregnated with frangipani scent.

A366

World Tourism Day A367

Designs: 40fr, Ruins. No. 927, 90fr, Waterfall, woman and child. 130fr, Clothing at open-air market.

No. 929: a, Dancers with yellow skirts. b, Surfer. c, House and palm tree. d, Pearls. e, Fish and coral. f, Islanders in outrigger canoes.

No. 930: a, Woman in hammock. b, Stilt houses. c, Tower and boats. d, Horses and riders. e, Aerial view of island. f, Diver and sting ray.

2006, Sept. 22 *Perf. 13¼x13*
926-928 A366 Set of 3 6.00 6.00

Booklet Stamps

Perf. 13x13¼

929 Booklet pane of 6 15.00 —
a.-f. A367 90fr Any single 2.00 2.00
930 Booklet pane of 6 15.00 —
a.-f. A367 90fr Any single 2.00 2.00
Complete booklet, #929-930 30.00

Complete booklet sold for 1200fr.

Paintings A368

Designs: 60fr, Javelin Throwing, by Monique Garnier Bissol. 90fr, Market Life, by Albert Luzuy, horiz. 100fr, Island Quay, by Gilbert Chaussoy, horiz. 190fr, Vahine, by Olivier Louzé.

2006, Oct. 25 *Perf. 13*
931-934 A368 Set of 4 9.50 9.50

Engravings by Paul Gauguin (1848-1903) — A369

Engravings depicting: 60fr, Women. 130fr, Cow and man carrying items on stick.

2006, Nov. 8 Engr. *Perf. 13¼*
935-936 A369 Set of 2 4.25 4.25

Children's Art A370

2006, Dec. 13 Litho. *Perf. 13x13¼*
937 A370 90fr multi 2.00 2.00

Beach Gear — A371

Designs: 60fr, Flip-flops. 90fr, Surfboards.

Serpentine Die Cut 11x11¼

2007 Photo. Self-Adhesive
938 A371 60fr multicolored 1.25 1.25
a. Blue tips of die cutting along left side 1.25 1.25
939 A371 90fr multicolored 2.00 2.00
a. Light blue tips of die cutting along bottom 2.00 2.00

Issued: Nos. 938a, 939a, 1/24; Nos. 938-939, Feb. Nos. 938a and 939a are from the original printing, and are from sheets having adjacent stamps and die cutting that does not extend through the backing paper. Nos. 938-939, which were distributed to the philatelic trade, are from sheets with selvage around each stamp, and with rouletting that extends through the backing paper that allows the stamps to be removed from the sheet more easily.

New Year 2007 (Year of the Pig) A372

2007, Feb. 19 Litho. *Perf. 13x13¼*

940 A372 130fr multi 3.50 3.50

Portions of the design were applied by a thermographic process producing a shiny, raised effect.

Painting of Polynesian Woman by Mathius — A373

Photograph of Polynesian Woman by John Stember — A374

2007, Mar. 8 Litho. *Perf. 13¼x13*

941 A373 60fr multi 1.50 1.40

Perf. 13x13¼

942 A374 90fr multi 2.25 2.00

Audit Office, Bicent. A375

2007, Mar. 17 Engr. *Perf. 13¼x13*

943 A375 90fr multi 2.75 2.00

Shells — A376

Designs: 10fr, Lambis crocata pilsbryi. 60fr, Cypraea thomasi. 90fr, Cyrtulus serotinus. 130fr, Chicoreus laqueatus.

2007, Apr. 25 Litho.

944-947 A376 Set of 4 6.75 6.75

947a Souvenir sheet, #944-947 6.75 6.75

Coconut A377

2007, May 23 *Perf. 13x13¼*

948 A377 90fr multi 2.25 2.00

No. 948 is impregnated with a coconut scent.

Ships — A378

Designs: No. 949, 250fr, Gunboat Zélée. No. 950, 250fr, Passenger and cargo liner Sagittaire.

2007, June 22 *Perf. 13*

949-950 A378 Set of 2 12.00 11.50

Heiva Festival — A379

Various women dancers: 65fr, 100fr, 140fr.

2007, July 4 *Perf. 13¼x13*

951-953 A379 Set of 3 7.50 7.50

Arrival of Kon-Tiki Expedition in Polynesia, 60th Anniv. — A380

Litho. & Silk-screened

2007, Aug. 7 *Perf. 13*

954 A380 300fr multi 7.00 7.00

Arrival of Ship at Papeete Dock — A381

2007, Aug. 29 Litho. *Perf. 13*

955 A381 190fr multi 4.50 4.50

Old and Modern Photos of Papeete — A382

Designs: 65fr, Rue Gauguin, 2007. 100fr, Rue de la Petite-Pologne (now Rue Gauguin), 1907.

2007, Sept. 26

956-957 A382 Set of 2 4.75 4.00

Old Franc and Centime Notes — A383

Designs: 65fr, 1919 2-franc Chamber of Commerce note. 140fr, 1942 2-franc note. 500fr, 1943 50-centime note.

2007, Oct. 26 Engr. *Perf. 13*

958-960 A383 Set of 3 20.00 17.00

Flowers A384

Designs: 100fr, Hibiscus. 140fr, Bird-of-paradise (Oiseaux de paradis).

Litho. & Silk-screened

2007, Nov. 8 *Perf. 13x13¼*

961-962 A384 Set of 2 7.50 7.50

Christmas A385

2007, Dec. 6 Litho. *Perf. 13x13¼*

963 A385 100fr multi 2.50 2.50

Marine Life A386

Designs: 10fr, Himantura fai. 20fr, Tursiops truncatus. 40fr, Megaptera novaeangliae. 65fr, Negaprion acutidens.

2008, Jan. 10

964-967 A386 Set of 4 4.00 4.00

New Year 2008 (Year of the Rat) — A387

2008, Feb. 7 Photo. *Perf. 13¼x13*

968 A387 140fr multi 3.75 3.75

Paintings of Women by Bénilde Menghini — A388

Designs: 65fr, Woman picking mangos. 100fr, Women scaling fish.

2008, Mar. 7 Litho.

969-970 A388 Set of 2 4.25 4.25

Paintings by Polynesian Artists A389

Unnamed paintings depicting: No. 971, 100fr, Boat and reef, by Torea Chan. No. 972, 100fr, Polynesian man, by Raymond Vigor. No. 973, 100fr, Fruit bowl, by Teurarea Prokop, horiz.

2008, Apr. 10 *Perf. 13x13¼, 13¼x13*

971-973 A389 Set of 3 8.00 8.00

Pouvanaa a Oopa (1895-1977), Politician — A390

2008, May 20 Litho. *Perf. 13*

974 A390 500fr multi 13.00 13.00

Island Touring Vehicles — A391

Designs: 65fr, Motor scooter. 100fr, Bus, horiz.

Serpentine Die Cut 11

2008, June 12 Photo.

Self-Adhesive

975-976 A391 Set of 2 4.50 4.50

Heiva Festival A392

Designs: 65fr, Woman with floral headdress. 140fr, Tattooed man. 190fr, Girl dancing.

2008, July 16 Litho. *Perf. 13*
977-979 A392 Set of 3 11.00 11.00

Sports — A393

Designs: No. 980, 140fr, Table tennis. No. 981, 140fr, Weight lifting.

2008, Aug. 8 Litho. *Perf. 13¼x13*
980-981 A393 Set of 2 7.00 7.00

End of Tahiti Nui Expedition, 50th Anniv. — A394

2008, Aug. 29 Litho. *Perf. 13*
982 A394 190fr multi 4.50 4.50

Eric de Bisschop (1890-1958), expedition leader.

Polynesian Scenes A395

No. 983: a, Woman crouching. b, Woman under shelter. c, Boat in bay near cliffs. d, Orange flowers. e, Red hibiscus flower. f, Island. g, Woman with headdress. h, White flower. i, Woman with headdress and flower garland. j, Pink flower. k, Islands. l, Bay near mountains.

Serpentine Die Cut 11¼x11
2008, Sept. 8 Self-Adhesive
983 Booklet pane of 12 32.50
a.-d. A395 65fr Any single 1.50 1.50
e.-h. A395 100fr Any single 2.40 2.40
i.-l. A395 140fr Any single 3.25 3.25

Gardenia Taitensis in Bottle of Monoi Oil — A396

2008, Sept. 17 *Perf. 13¼x13*
984 A396 100fr multi 2.40 2.40

No. 984 is impregnated with a gardenia scent.

Aviation Anniversaries — A397

Designs: No. 985, 250fr, Air service between France and French Polynesia, 50th anniv. No. 986, 250fr, Air Tahiti Nui, 10th anniv.

2008, Oct. 15 Litho. *Perf. 13*
985-986 A397 Set of 2 11.00 11.00

French Polynesia Postage Stamps, 50th Anniv. — A398

Designs: 65fr, French Polynesia #185. 100fr, Vignette of French Polynesia #C24. 140fr, French Polynesia #J29.

2008, Nov. 6 Engr. *Perf. 13*
987-989 A398 Set of 3 6.75 6.75
989a Sheet of 3, #987-989 6.75 6.75

Boater and Dancer A399

2008, Dec. 5 Litho. *Perf. 13x13¼*
990 A399 100fr multi 2.25 2.25

Winning design in children's stamp design contest.

Hypolimnas Bolina A400

Litho. & Silk-screened
2009, Jan. 16 *Perf. 13*
991 A400 70fr multi 1.50 1.50

Fire Fighters — A401

Designs: 70fr, Fireman on aerial ladder. 140fr, Fireboat.

2009, Feb. 13 Litho. *Perf. 13*
992-993 A401 Set of 2 4.50 4.50

Paintings of Polynesian Women — A402

Designs: 70fr, Woman, by Myriam Stroken. 100fr, Woman with Guitar, by Stanley Haumani.

2009, Mar. 30 Litho. *Perf. 13¼x13*
994-995 A402 Set of 2 4.00 4.00

Jacques Brel (1929-78), Singer — A403

Colors: 70fr, Blue. 100fr, Brown.

2009, Apr. 8 Engr.
996-997 A403 Set of 2 4.25 4.25

Pareo Fabric A404

Pareo in: (70fr), Blue. (100fr), Red. (140fr), Green.

Serpentine Die Cut 11
2009, May 29 Litho.
Self-Adhesive
998-1000 A404 Set of 3 7.25 7.25

Heiva Celebrations of the Past — A405

Various Heiva dancers: 70fr, 100fr, 140fr. 100fr and 140fr are horiz.

Perf. 13¼x13, 13x13¼
2009, June 19
1001-1003 A405 Set of 3 7.50 7.50

First Man on the Moon, 40th Anniv. A406

2009, July 20 *Perf. 13¼*
1004 A406 140fr multi 3.50 3.50

Water Activities A407

Designs: 70fr, Surfing. 100fr, Canoeing (pirogue).

Serpentine Die Cut 11x11¼
2009, Aug. 7 Litho. Self-Adhesive
1005-1006 A407 Set of 2 4.00 4.00

Passion Fruit A408

2009, Aug. 14 *Perf. 13x13¼*
1007 A408 100fr multi 2.40 2.40

No. 1007 has a scratch-and-sniff coating on the fruit having a passion fruit scent.

Underwater Scenes — A409

Designs: 70fr, Scuba divers. 100fr, Turtles, horiz. 140fr, Whale, horiz.

Litho. & Silk-screened
Perf. 13¼x13, 13x13¼
2009, Sept. 11
1008-1010 A409 Set of 3 7.75 7.75
1010a Sheet of 3, #1008-1010 7.75 7.75

Fish — A410

No. 1011: a, Chaetodon lunula. b, Chaetodon trichrous. c, Chaetodon ornatissimus. d, Chaetodon pelewensis. e, Pterois antennata. f, Myripristis berndti. g, Priacanthus hamrur. h, Epinephelus polyphekadion. i, Thalassoma lutescens. j, Thalassoma hardwicke. k, Pygoplites diacanthus. l, Coris gaimard.

Serpentine Die Cut 11¼x11
2009, Sept. 11 Self-Adhesive
1011 Booklet pane of 12 31.00
a.-d. A410 70fr Any single 1.75 1.75
e.-h. A410 100fr Any single 2.50 2.50
i.-l. A410 140fr Any single 3.50 3.50

Paintings by Paul Gauguin (1848-1903) — A411

Designs: No. 1012, 250fr, Still Life with a Maori Statuette. No. 1013, 250fr, Still Life with Apples, horiz.

2009, Oct. 16 Litho. *Perf. 13*
1012-1013 A411 Set of 2 12.50 12.50

French Polynesia No. 180 — A412

2009, Nov. 5 **Engr.**
1014 A412 500fr multi 12.50 12.50

Legend of the Coconut Tree — A413

2009, Dec. 11 **Litho.** ***Perf. 13¼x13***
1015 A413 190fr multi 4.75 4.75

Papeete Post Office, 150th Anniv. — A414

2010, Jan. 20
1016 A414 70fr multi 1.60 1.60

New Year 2010 (Year of the Tiger) A415

Litho. & Silk-screened
2010, Feb. 15 ***Perf. 13x13¼***
1017 A415 140fr multi 3.25 3.25

Woman and Child — A416

Woman and child: 70fr, Facing forward. 100fr, Facing right.

2010, Mar. 8 **Litho.** ***Perf. 13¼x13***
1018-1019 A416 Set of 2 4.00 4.00

Tattoos A417

Tattooed: No. 1020, 250fr, Woman (green background). No. 1021, 250fr, Man (dark red background).

2010, Apr. 6
1020-1021 A417 Set of 2 11.50 11.50

Tiare Apetahi Flower A418

Litho. & Silk-screened
2010, Apr. 20 ***Perf. 13x13¼***
1022 A418 70fr multi 1.50 1.50

Captain Frederick William Beechey (1796-1856), Explorer — A419

2010, May 5 **Litho.**
1023 A419 140fr multi 3.00 3.00

Corals A420

Various corals: 70fr, 100fr, 140fr. 140fr is vert.

Litho. & Silk-screened
2010, June 4 ***Perf. 13x13¼, 13¼x13***
1024-1026 A420 Set of 3 6.50 6.50
1026a Sheet of 3, #1024-1026 6.50 6.50

Heiva Festival — A421

Various festival participants: 100fr, 140fr, 190fr.

2010, July 20 **Litho.** ***Perf. 13¼x13***
1027-1029 A421 Set of 3 9.50 9.50

Mango A422

2010, Aug. 8 ***Perf. 13x13¼***
1030 A422 100fr multi 2.25 2.25

No. 1030 has a scratch-and-sniff coating on the fruit having a mango scent.

Phosphate Mining at Makatea, Cent. A423

Designs: 70fr, Office. 100fr, Train. 140fr, Mining operations.

2010, Aug. 17 **Litho.** ***Perf. 13x13¼***
1031-1033 A423 Set of 3 6.75 6.75

Honotua Fiber Optic Submarine Cable Project — A424

Serpentine Die Cut 11
2010, Sept. 15 **Photo.**
Self-Adhesive
1034 A424 70fr multi 1.75 1.75

Birds A425

No. 1035: a, Lori de Kuhl (Kuhl's lorikeet). b, Bécasseau Sanderling (Sanderling). c, Carpophade de la Société (Imperial pigeon). d, Tangara à dos rouge (Crimson-backed tanager). e, Ptilope de Hutton (Rapa fruit dove). f, Sterne huppée (Great crested tern). g, Gygis blanche (White tern). h, Lori Nonnette (Blue lorikeet). i, Chevalier errant (Wandering tattler). j, Martin chasseur des Gambier (Tuamotu kingfisher). k, Fou brun (Brown booby). l, Pluvier fauve (Pacific golden plover).

Litho. & Silk-screened
2010, Sept. 15 **Self-Adhesive**
1035 Booklet pane of 12 28.00
a.-l. A425 100fr Any single 2.25 2.25

Tahiti Faa'a International Airport, 50th Anniv. — A426

2010, Oct. 14 **Litho.** ***Perf. 13***
1036 A426 500fr multi 11.50 11.50

Sphinx Moth A427

2010, Oct. 14 ***Perf. 13x13½***
1037 A427 5fr multi .25 .25

1948 Air Post Stamps of French Oceania — A428

Designs: 70fr, #C17. 100fr, #C18. 140fr, #C19.

2010, Nov. 4 **Engr.** ***Perf. 13***
1038-1040 A428 Set of 3 7.25 7.25

Legend of Moua Puta A429

2010, Dec. 9 **Litho.** ***Perf. 13x13¼***
1041 A429 70fr multi 1.60 1.60

Crabs A430

Designs: 20fr, Atergatopsis cf. germanini. 40fr, Zosimus aeneus. 70fr, Carpilius convexus. 100fr, Carpilius maculatus.

2011, Jan. 18
1042-1045 A430 Set of 4 5.25 5.25
1045a Souvenir sheet of 4, #1042-1045 5.25 5.25

New Year 2011 (Year of the Rabbit) — A431

Litho. & Silk-screened
2011, Feb. 3 ***Perf. 13¼x13***
1046 A431 140fr multi 3.25 3.25

Images of Polynesia — A432

No. 1047: a, Canoe race. b, Outrigger canoe. c, Aerial view of islands. d, Fish on reef. e, Pearls. f, Flowers.

Serpentine Die Cut 11¼
2011, Mar. 8 **Litho.**
Self-Adhesive
1047 Booklet pane of 6 14.50
a.-f. A432 100fr Any single 2.40 2.40

Intl. Women's Year — A433

Designs: 70fr, Two women weaving. 100fr, Woman standing.

2011, Mar. 8 ***Perf. 13¼x13***
1048-1049 A433 Set of 2 4.00 4.00

Pearl of Tahiti, 50th Anniv. — A434

2011, Apr. 7 **Litho.**
1050 A434 140fr multi 3.50 3.50

Portions of the design were applied by a thermographic process producing a shiny, raised effect.

Transportation of the Past — A435

Designs: 70fr, Truck, 1939. 100fr, Horse-drawn carriages, 1900.

2011, May 17 **Litho.** ***Perf. 13***
1051-1052 A435 Set of 2 4.25 4.25

Fishing — A436

Cartoons: 100fr, Fisherman in boat catching swordfish. 140fr, Spear fisherman and speared fish.

Serpentine Die Cut 11
2011, June 22 **Litho.**
Self-Adhesive
1053-1054 A436 Set of 2 5.75 5.75

Carved Items — A437

Designs: 70fr, Coral pestle. 140fr, Basalt tiki. 190fr, Oceania rosewood container with lid, hoirz.

2011, July 19 ***Perf. 13¼x13, 13x13¼***
1055-1057 A437 Set of 3 9.75 9.75

Orchid — A438

2011, Aug. 17 **Litho.** ***Perf. 13¼x13***
1058 A438 140fr multi 3.25 3.25

No. 1058 is impregnated with an orchid scent.

Islands A439

Photographs of: 10fr, Rangiroa. 100fr, Ua Pou. 140fr, Bora Bora.

2011, Sept. 27 ***Perf. 13x13¼***
1059-1061 A439 Set of 3 5.75 5.75

Marine Birds and Sea Life A440

No. 1062: a, Birds. b, Bird and whale. c, Dolphin and fish. d, Red striped fish, black and white striped angelfish. e, Blue and yellow striped fish. f, Lionfish, yellow fish. g, Ray. h, Shark. i, Sea turtle, fish, coral. j, Anemonefish, sea anemones. k, Crab. l, Moray eel, coral.

Serpentine Die Cut 11¼x11
2011, Sept. 27 **Self-Adhesive**
1062 Booklet pane of 12 29.00
a.-l. A440 100fr Any single 2.40 2.40

Filming of *Mutiny on the Bounty* in Tahiti, 50th Anniv. — A441

2011, Oct. 19 ***Perf. 13***
1063 A441 500fr multi 11.50 11.50

Fort Collet, Marquesas Islands — A442

No. 1064 — Engraving of Fort from 1854: a, Buildings without flags. b, Buildings with flags.

2011, Nov. 3 **Engr.** ***Perf. 13***
1064 A442 250fr Horiz. pair, #a-b 11.50 11.50

Ta'aroa, Polynesian God of Creation — A443

2011, Dec. 15 **Litho.** ***Perf. 13¼x13***
1065 A443 70fr multi 1.60 1.60

New Yeart 2012 (Year of the Dragon) A444

Litho & Silk-screened
2012, Jan. 23 ***Perf. 13***
1066 A444 140fr multi 3.25 3.25

Papeete Maritime Station — A445

Ships in Papeete Harbor — A446

2012, Jan. 27 **Litho.**
1067 A445 70fr multi 1.60 1.60
1068 A446 100fr multi 2.25 2.25

Port of Papeete Authority, 50th anniv.

Food Truck Vendors A447

Serpentine Die Cut 11
2012, Feb. 22 **Self-Adhesive**
1069 A447 100fr multi 2.25 2.25

Office of Posts and Telecommunications Emblem Type of 2003
Booklet Stamps
Serpentine Die Cut 6¾ Vert.
2012, Feb. 8 **Self-Adhesive**
1070 A308a 5fr red violet .25 .25
c. Booklet pane of 10 #1070 1.25
1070A A308a (75fr) blue, type II 1.75 1.75
d. Booklet pane of 10 #1070A 17.50
1070B A308a (100fr) rose 2.25 2.25
e. Booklet pane of 10 #1070B 22.50
Nos. 1070-1070B (3) 4.25 4.25

Intl. Women's Day — A448

Designs: 70fr, Woman. 100fr, Woman and child.

2012, Mar. 8 ***Perf. 13¼x13***
1071-1072 A448 Set of 2 3.75 3.75

Flowers — A449

No. 1073: a, Gingembre à abeilles. b, Reine de Malaisie. c, Opuhi alpinia rose. d, Zedoaire. e, Safran indien. f, Opuhi alpinia orchidée.

2012, Mar. 8 ***Serpentine Die Cut 11***
Self-Adhesive
1073 Booklet pane of 6 13.50
a.-f. A449 100fr Any single 2.25 2.25

Nudibranchs — A450

Designs: 75fr, Glossodoris rufomarginata. 100fr, Elysia ornata. 190fr, Cyerce nigricans.

Litho. & Silk-screened
2012, Apr. 26 ***Perf. 13x13¼***
1074-1076 A450 Set of 3 8.00 8.00
1076b Souvenir sheet of 3, #1074-1076 8.00 8.00

Tiurai (1842-1918), Healer — A451

2012, June 18 **Litho.** ***Perf. 13¼x13***
1077 A451 75fr multi 1.60 1.60

Tamanu Orange Picking Contest — A452

2012, June 27
1078 A452 75fr multi 1.60 1.60

Heiva Dancer A453

2012, July 18 ***Perf. 13x13¼***
1079 A453 100fr multi 2.10 2.10

Grapefruits A454

2012, Aug. 22
1080 A454 140fr multi 3.00 3.00

No. 1080 is impregnated with a grapefruit scent.

Airports A455

Airport at: 5fr, Bora Bora. 75fr, Tikehau. 100fr, Ua Pou.

2012, Sept. 27
1081-1083 A455 Set of 3 4.00 4.00

Landscapes — A456

No. 1084: a, Moorea. b, Mangareva. c, Rurutu. d, Kauehi. e, Hiva Oa. f, Rapa.

Serpentine Die Cut 11
2012, Sept. 27 Self-Adhesive
1084 Booklet pane of 6 13.50
a.-f. A456 100fr Any single 2.25 2.25

Turtles in Botanical Gardens, Papeari A457

Horses and Riders, Marquesas Islands A458

2012, Oct. 17 ***Perf. 13x13¼***
1085 A457 75fr multi 1.60 1.60
1086 A458 100fr multi 2.25 2.25

First Stamps of French Oceania, 120th Anniv. — A459

No. 1087: a, "Commerce," horse-drawn carriage, people near shore. b, People on rowboat, "Navigation."

2012, Nov. 8 Engr. ***Perf. 13xx13¼***
1087 Horiz. pair, #a-b, + central label 11.00 11.00
a.-b. A459 250fr Either single 5.50 5.50

Season of Matari'i i Ni'a — A460

2012, Nov. 20 Litho. ***Perf. 13***
1088 A460 75fr multi 1.75 1.75

Matavai Bay A461

2012, Dec. 13 Engr.
1089 A461 500fr blk & gray blue 11.00 11.00

Scenes of Everyday Life A462

Designs: 75fr, Street scene outside of Quinn's Bar, Papeete. 100fr, Street musicians.

2013, Jan. 2 Litho. ***Perf. 13x13¼***
1090-1091 A462 Set of 2 4.00 4.00

New Year 2013 (Year of the Snake) A463

Litho. & Silk-screened
2013, Feb. 11 ***Perf. 13***
1092 A463 140fr multi 3.00 3.00

Queen Pomare IV (1813-77) A464

Serpentine Die Cut 11
2013, Feb. 28 Photo.
Self-Adhesive
1093 A464 75fr multi 1.75 1.75

Legend of Tahiri Vahine — A465

Designs: 75fr, Tahiri Vahine (woman with fan). 100fr, Tahiri Vahine with other women.

2013, Mar. 8 Litho. ***Perf. 13¼x13***
1094-1095 A465 Set of 2 4.00 4.00

Intl. Women's Day.

Flora and Fauna — A466

Designs: 20fr, Lemon (citron). 40fr, Lizard (lézard), horiz. 190fr, Chestnut-breasted mannikin (capuchin).

Litho. & Silk-screened
2013, Apr. 26 ***Perf. 13¼x13, 13x13¼***
1096-1098 A466 Set of 3 5.50 5.50
1098a Souvenir sheet of 3, #1096-1098 5.50 5.50

Jacques Brel (1929-78), Singer — A467

2013, May 10 Engr. ***Perf. 13***
1099 A467 500fr multi 11.50 11.50

Fruits A468

No. 110: a, Pineapples. b, Mangos. c, Bananas. d, Coconuts. e, Papayas. f, Watermelon.

Litho. & Silk-screened
2013, May 10 ***Serpentine Die Cut 11***
Self-Adhesive
1100 Booklet pane of 6 13.50
a.-f. A468 100fr Any single 2.25 2.25

Marine Life — A469

Designs: 5fr, Starfish. 10fr, Giant clam. 75fr, Sea anemone and clown fish. 100fr, Sea turtle.

Litho. & Silk-screened
2013, June 7 ***Perf. 13x13¼***
1101-1104 A469 Set of 4 4.25 4.25
1104a Souvenir sheet of 4, #1101-1104 4.25 4.25

Carousel at Heiva Fairground — A470

2013, July 16 Litho. ***Perf. 13***
1105 A470 100fr multi 2.25 2.25

Jasmine Flowers A471

2013, Aug. 22 Litho. ***Perf. 13x13¼***
1106 A471 100fr multi 2.25 2.25

No. 1106 is impregnated with a jasmine scent.

FIFA Beach Soccer World Cup Tournament, Tahiti — A472

2013, Sept. 18 Litho. ***Perf. 13¼x13***
1107 A472 140fr multi 3.25 3.25

A473

A474

A475 A476

Women

A477 A478

Serpentine Die Cut 11
2013, Sept. 18 Litho.
Self-Adhesive

1108	Booklet pane of 6, #1108a-1108f	13.50	
a.	A473 100fr multi	2.25	2.25
b.	A474 100fr multi	2.25	2.25
c.	A475 100fr multi	2.25	2.25
d.	A476 100fr multi	2.25	2.25
e.	A477 100fr multi	2.25	2.25
f.	A478 100fr multi	2.25	2.25
g.	A473 100fr Dated "2015"	1.75	1.75
h.	A474 100fr Dated "2015"	1.75	1.75
i.	A475 100fr Dated "2015"	1.75	1.75
j.	A476 100fr Dated "2015"	1.75	1.75
k.	A477 100fr Dated "2015"	1.75	1.75
l.	A478 100fr Dated "2015"	1.75	1.75
m.	Booklet pane of 6, #1180g-1108l	10.50	

Issued: Nos. 1108g-1108m, 11/5/15.

Canoes — A479

Various canoes: 75fr, 100fr.

2013, Oct. 17 Litho. ***Perf. 13***
1109-1110 A479 Set of 2 4.00 4.00

Stock Certificates — A480

Stock certificate of: 250fr, Comptoirs Français d'Océanie. 300fr, Compagnie Française de Tahiti.

2013, Nov. 6 Engr. ***Perf. 13***
1111-1112 A480 Set of 2 12.50 12.50

Old Automobiles — A481

Designs: 75fr, 1915 Ford Model T. 100fr, 1950 Citroen Traction Avant.

2013, Dec. 12 Litho. *Perf. 13*
1113-1114 A481 Set of 2 4.00 4.00

New Banknotes — A482

Designs: 10fr, 500-franc banknote. 20fr, 1000-franc banknote. 75fr, 5000-franc banknote. 100fr, 10,000-franc banknote.

Litho. & Silk-Screened

2014, Jan. 20 *Perf. 13*
1115-1118 A482 Set of 4 4.75 4.75
1118a Souvenir sheet of 4, #1115-1118 4.75 4.75

Postal Check Center, 50th Anniv. A483

2014, Jan. 27 Litho. *Perf. 13x13¼*
1119 A483 75fr multi 1.75 1.75

New Year 2014 (Year of the Horse) A484

Litho. & Silk-Screened

2014, Jan. 31 *Perf. 13*
1120 A484 140fr multi 3.25 3.25

Intl. Year of Family Farming — A485

Designs: 75fr, Woman watering flower garden. 100fr, Farmers, fruits and vegetables.

2014, Feb. 21 Litho. *Perf. 13*
1121-1122 A485 Set of 2 4.00 4.00

Intl. Women's Day A486

Design: 75fr, Head of woman with floral headdress. 100fr, Woman, vert.

Perf. 13x13¼, 13¼x13

2014, Mar. 7 Litho.
1123-1124 A486 Set of 2 4.00 4.00

Wild Boars A487

Serpentine Die Cut 11

2014, Apr. 30 Photo.

Self-Adhesive

1125 A487 100fr multi 2.40 2.40

A488 A489

A490 A491

A492 A493

Serpentine Die Cut 11

2014, May 16 Litho.

Self-Adhesive

1126	Booklet pane of 6	13.50	
a.	A488 100fr multi	2.25	2.25
b.	A489 100fr multi	2.25	2.25
c.	A490 100fr multi	2.25	2.25
d.	A491 100fr multi	2.25	2.25
e.	A492 100fr multi	2.25	2.25
f.	A493 100fr multi	2.25	2.25

Graffiti art by Enos.

Sharks — A494

Designs: 10fr, Carcharhinus melanopterus. 40fr, Sphyrna mokarran. 75fr, Carcharhinus albimarginatus. 190fr, Galeocerdo cuvier.

Litho. & Silk-Screened

2014, June 10 *Perf. 13*
1127-1130 A494 Set of 4 7.25 7.25
1130a Souvenir sheet of 4, #1127-1130 7.25 7.25

Autonomy, 30th Anniv. — A495

2014, June 27 Litho. *Perf. 13¼x13*
1131 A495 75fr multi 1.75 1.75

Woman in Heiva Costume — A496

2014, July 3 Litho. *Perf. 13¼x13*
1132 A496 75fr multi 1.75 1.75

Jar of Honey, Honeybee and Honeycomb A497

2014, Aug. 28 Litho. *Perf. 13x13¼*
1133 A497 100fr multi 2.25 2.25

No. 1133 is impregnated with a honey scent.

Bombardment of Papeete, Cent. — A498

Litho. & Engr.

2014, Sept. 30 *Perf. 13*
1134 A498 300fr multi 6.50 6.50

World War I, cent.

Tiaré Flower A499

2014, Nov. 6 Litho. *Perf. 13x13¼*
1135 A499 2fr multi .25 .25

Sunset — A500

2014, Nov. 6 Litho. *Perf. 13¼x13*
1136 A500 77fr multi 1.60 1.60

Issuance of French Polynesia No. C30, 50th Anniv. A501

2014, Nov. 6 Litho. *Perf. 13*
1137 A501 500fr multi 10.50 10.50

Office of Posts and Telecommunications Emblem — A502

Serpentine Die Cut 6¾ Vert.

2014, Nov. 6 Litho.

Booklet Stamps

Self-Adhesive

1138	A502 (75fr) deep blue	1.60	1.60
a.	Booklet pane of 10	16.00	
1139	A502 (100fr) red	2.10	2.10
a.	Booklet pane of 10	21.00	

Legend of Pipiri Ma — A503

2014, Dec. 12 Litho. *Perf. 13*
1140 A503 75fr multi 1.50 1.50

Occupations A504

Designs: 10fr, Underwater spear fisherman. 20fr, Sculptor. 75fr, Masseuse, horiz. 100fr, Seamstress, horiz.

2015, Jan. 29 Litho. *Perf. 13¼x13*
1141 A504 10fr multi .25 .25
1142 A504 20fr multi .40 .40

Perf. 13x13¼

1143 A504 75fr multi 1.50 1.50
1144 A504 100fr multi 1.90 1.90
Nos. 1141-1144 (4) 4.05 4.05

New Year 2015 (Year of the Goat) A505

Litho. & Silk-Screened

2015, Feb. 19 *Perf. 13*
1145 A505 140fr multi 2.60 2.60

Mama Dolphin at Sea Post Office
A506

2015, Mar. 26 Litho. *Perf. 13x13¼*
1146 A506 75fr multi 1.40 1.40

Translation of Bible Into Tahitian by Henry Nott, 180th Anniv. — A507

Discovery of King George Islands by John Byron, 250th Anniv. — A508

Litho. & Engr.

2015, May 13 *Perf. 13*
1147 A507 140fr multi 2.60 2.60

Litho.

1148 A508 190fr multi 3.50 3.50
a. Souvenir sheet of 2, #1147-1148 6.25 6.25

Coffee
A509

2015, July 1 Litho. *Perf. 13x13¼*
1149 A509 100fr multi 1.90 1.90

No. 1149 is impregnated with a coffee scent.

Children's Art — A510

2015, Aug. 1 Litho. *Perf. 13¼*
1150 A510 1fr multi .25 .25

Orator
A511

2015, Aug. 5 Litho. *Perf. 13x13¼*
1151 A511 80fr multi 1.50 1.50

Tropical Architecture
A512

Designs: 80fr, Chez Vat Restaurant and Chez Alin Store. 100fr, Houses.

2015, Aug. 14 Litho. *Perf. 13x13¼*
1152-1153 A512 Set of 2 3.50 3.50

First Flight Between Tahiti and Santiago, Chile, 50th Anniv.
A513

2015, Aug. 31 Litho. *Perf. 13x13¼*
1154 A513 80fr multi 1.50 1.50

1915 Postcard Depicting Papeete — A514

2015, Sept. 29 Litho. *Perf. 13¼x13*
1155 A514 300fr multi 5.75 5.75

Issuance of Tahiti No. B2, Cent.
A515

Litho. & Engr.

2015, Nov. 5 *Perf. 13¼x13*
1156 A515 500fr multi 9.00 9.00
a. Souvenir sheet of 1 9.00 9.00

Sponges — A516

No. 1157: a, Clathrina n. sp. b, Dysidea n. sp. c, Haliclona n. sp. d, Ernstia n. sp. e, Stylissa flabelliformis. f, Darwinella n. sp.

Serpentine Die Cut 11

2015, Nov. 5 Litho.

Self-Adhesive

1157 Booklet pane of 6 10.50
a.-f. A516 100fr Any single 1.75 1.75

Papeete Market — A517

Designs: 80fr, Tower and awning. 100fr, Vendors and shoppers, horiz. 140fr, Fish vendors and shoppers, horiz.

2015, Dec. 16 Litho. *Perf. 13*
1158-1160 A517 Set of 3 6.00 6.00

Ancient Adornments — A518

Designs: 10fr, Pa'e kea and pavahina. 20fr, Hei ku'a. 80fr, Peue kavi'i.

2016, Jan. 29 Litho. *Perf. 13x13¼*
1161-1163 A518 Set of 3 2.00 2.00

New Year 2016 (Year of the Monkey)
A519

Litho. & Silk-screened

2016, Feb. 8 *Perf. 13*
1164 A519 140fr multi 2.60 2.60

Hikers — A520

Serpentine Die Cut 11

2016, Mar. 18 Litho.

Self-Adhesive

1165 A520 100fr multi 1.90 1.90

Ships — A521

Designs: 40fr, Queen Elizabeth 2. 80fr, France. 100fr, City of New York.

Litho. & Silk-screened

2016, Apr. 22 *Perf. 13*
1166-1168 A521 Set of 3 4.25 4.25

Street Art in Papeete by Seth and HTJ — A522

2016, May 27 Litho. *Perf. 13*
1169 A522 140fr multi 2.60 2.60

World Stamp Show 2016, New York.

Sandalwood — A523

2016, June 17 Litho. *Perf. 13x13¼*
1170 A523 100fr multi 1.90 1.90

No. 1170 is impregnated with a sandalwood scent.

Miss Tahiti Pageant Winners — A524

No. 1171: a, Marie Moua, 1965. b, Moea Amiot, 1975. c, Ruth Manea, 1985. d, Timeri Baudry, 1995. e, Mihimana Sachet, 2005. f, Vaimiti Teiefitu, 2015.

Serpentine Die Cut 11

2016, June 24 Litho.

Self-Adhesive

1171 Booklet pane of 6 11.50
a.-f. A524 100fr Any single 1.90 1.90

See Nos. 1191, 1211, 1230.

Famous People Wearing Heiva Costumes
A525

Designs: 80fr, Gilles Hollande. 100fr, Madeleine Moua (1899-1989).

2016, July 11 Litho. *Perf. 13¼x13*
1172-1173 A525 Set of 2 3.50 3.50

Premna Serratifolia
A526

2016, Aug. 12 Engr. *Perf. 13*
1174 A526 80fr multi 1.50 1.50

Woman and Plum Blossoms
A527

2016, Oct. 21 Litho. *Perf. 13x13¼*
1175 A527 300fr multi 5.75 5.75
a. Souvenir sheet of 1 5.75 5.75

PhilaTaipei 2016 International Philatelic Exhibition, Taipei.

Francis Ariioehau Sanford (1912-96), Politician
A528

2016, Nov. 3 Engr. *Perf. 13*

1176 A528 500fr multi 9.00 9.00

A529 A530

A531 A532

A533 Men — A534

Serpentine Die Cut 11

2016, Nov. 3 Litho.

Self-Adhesive

1177	Booklet pane of 6	10.50	
a.	A529 100fr multi	1.75	1.75
b.	A530 100fr multi	1.75	1.75
c.	A531 100fr multi	1.75	1.75
d.	A532 100fr multi	1.75	1.75
e.	A533 100fr multi	1.75	1.75
f.	A534 100fr multi	1.75	1.75

Birds — A535

Designs: 80fr, Striated heron (héron strié). 100fr, Southern Marquesan reed warbler (rousserolle des Marquises).

2016, Dec. 9 Litho. *Perf. 13*

1178-1179	A535 Set of 2	3.25	3.25
1179a	Souvenir sheet of 2, #1178-1179	3.25	3.25

Society for Oceania Studies, Cent. — A536

2017, Jan. 2 Litho. *Perf. 13¼x13*

1180 A536 100fr multi 1.75 1.75

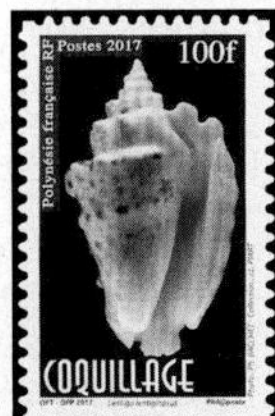

Shells — A537

No. 1181: a, Lentigo lentiginosus. b, Mitra papalis. c, Monoplex aquatilis. d, Conus nussatella. e, Oxymeris maculata. f, Drupa clathrata.

Serpentine Die Cut 11

2017, Jan. 3 Litho.

Self-Adhesive

1181	Booklet pane of 6	10.50	
a.-f.	A537 100fr Any single	1.75	1.75

New Year 2017 (Year of the Rooster) A538

Litho. & Silk-Screened

2017, Jan. 27 *Perf. 13*

1182 A538 140fr multi 2.60 2.60

Henri Cadousteau (1890-1946), Fighter Pilot, and Salmson 2A2 — A539

Litho. & Silk-Screened

2017, Feb. 17 *Perf. 13*

1183 A539 80fr multi 1.40 1.40

International Women's Day — A540

Women wearing headdresses: 80fr, 100fr.

2017, Mar. 8 Litho. *Perf. 13¼x13*

1184-1185 A540 Set of 2 3.25 3.25

Polynesian Women of the Bounty — A541

2017, Mar. 30 Litho. *Perf. 13*

1186 A541 140fr multi 2.50 2.50

See Pitcairn Islands No. 827.

Underwater Scenes A542

Designs: 10fr, Woman laying on sea floor and ray. 20fr, Diver and school of fish. 80fr, Diver on sea floor and school of fish. 100fr, Woman sitting on sea floor and ray, diff.

2017, May 5 Litho. *Perf. 13x13¼*

1187-1190	A542 Set of 4	4.00	4.00
1190a	Souvenir sheet of 4, #1187-1190	4.00	4.00

Miss Tahiti Pageant Winners Type of 2016

No. 1191: a, Sonia Agnieray, 1966. b, Patricia Servonnat, 1976. c, Loana Bohl, 1986. d, Hinerava Hiro, 1996. e, Tehere Pere, 2006. f, Vaea Ferrand, 2016.

Serpentine Die Cut 11

2017, June 23 Litho.

Self-Adhesive

1191	Booklet pane of 6	11.50	
a.-f.	A524 100fr Any single	1.90	1.90

Oranges A543

2017, June 23 Litho. *Perf. 13x13¼*

1192 A543 100fr multi 1.90 1.90

No. 1192 is impregnated with an orange scent.

Heiva Celebration Dancers — A544

2017, July 13 Litho. *Perf. 13¼x13*

1193 A544 80fr multi 1.60 1.60

Lions Clubs International, Cent. — A545

2017, Aug. 25 Litho. *Perf. 13¼x13*

1194 A545 190fr multi 3.75 3.75

Cats and Dogs — A546

No. 1195: a, Cat named Kitty. b, Cat named Gribouille. c, Cat named Caramel. d, Dog named Peanuts. e, Dog named Lolly. f, Dog named Sydney.

Serpentine Die Cut 11

2017, Aug. 25 Litho.

Self-Adhesive

1195	Booklet pane of 6	12.00	
a.-f.	A546 100fr Any single	2.00	2.00

Navigators and Boats — A547

Boat and: 40fr, Rodolphe Tuko Harry Wiliams (1920-86). 100fr, Francis Puara Cowan (1926-2009).

2017, Sept. 27 Engr. *Perf. 13*

1196-1197 A547 Set of 2 2.75 2.75

Hina Natua, 2017 Miss Heiva A548

2017, Oct. 24 Litho. *Perf. 13*

1198 A548 300fr multi 6.00 6.00

Brasilia 2017 International Philatelic Exhibition, Brasilia, Brazil.

Halloween A549

Serpentine Die Cut 11

2017, Oct. 27 Litho.

Self-Adhesive

1199 A549 80fr multi 1.60 1.60

Fautaua Waterfall A550

2017, Nov. 9 Engr. *Perf. 13*

1200 A550 500fr turq blue & slate grn 10.00 10.00

Souvenir Sheet
Litho.
Imperf

1200A A550 500fr multi 10.00 10.00

Pierre Loti (1850-1923), writer.

French Polynesia No. 527 — A551

2017, Dec. 15 Litho. *Perf. 13*
1201 A551 80fr multi 1.60 1.60

Air Tahiti, 60th Anniv. A552

Designs: 10fr, Sunderland Bermuda. 20fr, Douglas DC-4. 40fr, ATR 72-500. 80fr, ATR 72-600.

2018, Jan. 11 Litho. *Perf. 13x13¼*
1202-1205 A552 Set of 4 3.25 3.25

New Year 2018 (Year fo the Dog) A553

Litho. & Silk-Screened
2018, Feb. 16 *Perf. 13*
1206 A553 140fr multi 3.00 3.00

No. 1206 was printed in sheets of 10 + central label.

International Women's Day — A554

2018, Mar. 8 Litho. *Perf. 13¼x13*
1207 A554 80fr multi 1.75 1.75

Arrival of Louis-Antoine de Bougainville (1729-1811) in Tahiti, 250th Anniv. — A555

2018, Apr. 6 Engr. *Perf. 12¾x13*
1208 A555 250fr mar & dp bluish grn 5.00 5.00

Pointe Vénus Lighthouse, 150th Anniv. A556

2018, Apr. 23 Litho. *Perf. 13*
1209 A556 80fr multi 1.60 1.60

Bird and Kite — A557

Serpentine Die Cut 11
2018, May 25 Litho.
Self-Adhesive
1210 A557 100fr multi 2.00 2.00

Miss Tahiti Pageant Winners Type of 2016

No. 1211: a, Pageant emblem. b, Timia Teriiero, 1977. c, Meari Manoi, 1987. d, Hinano Teanotoga, 1997. e, Taoahere Richmond, 2007. f, Turouru Temorere, 2017.

Serpentine Die Cut 11
2018, June 1 Litho.
Self-Adhesive
1211 Booklet pane of 6 12.00
a.-f. A524 100fr Any single 2.00 2.00

Basil — A558

2018, June 22 Litho. *Perf. 13¼x13*
1212 A558 80fr multi 1.60 1.60

No. 1212 is impregnated with a basil scent.

Polynesian Canoes A559

2018, July 16 Litho. *Perf. 13x13¼*
1213 A559 80fr multi 1.60 1.60

Milan Rastislav Stefánik (1880-1919), Slovak General and His Tahitian Astronomical Observatory — A560

2018, Aug, 17 Litho. *Perf. 13*
1214 A560 140fr multi 2.75 2.75

Praga 2018 International Philatelic Exhibition, Prague.

Self-portrait with Yellow Christ, by Paul Gauguin (1848-1903) — A561

2018, Sept. 21 Litho. *Perf. 13*
1215 A561 300fr multi 6.00 6.00
a. Souvenir sheet of 1 6.00 6.00

Disappearance of Alain Colas (1943-78), Sailboat Racer, 40th Anniv. — A562

2018, Oct. 26 Litho. *Perf. 13x13¼*
1216 A562 100fr multi 1.90 1.90

Babies A563

No. 1217 — Names at lower right: a, Tahi. b, Hinarani. c, Nainoa. d, Imianau. e, Tevaihereiti. f, Kihani.

Serpentine Die Cut 11
2018, Oct. 26 Litho.
Booklet Stamps
Self-Adhesive
1217 Booklet pane of 6 11.50
a.-f. A563 100fr Any single 1.90 1.90

French Polynesia No. 184 — A564

2018, Nov. 8 Engr. *Perf. 13*
1218 A564 190fr multi 3.75 3.75

First stamps inscribed "Polynésie Française," 60th anniv.

End of World War I, Cent. — A565

2018, Nov. 8 Engr. *Perf. 13*
1219 A565 500fr multi 9.50 9.50
a. Souvenir sheet of 1 9.50 9.50

Taputapuatea UNESCO World Heritage Site — A566

2018, Dec. 14 Litho. *Perf. 13x13¼*
1220 A566 100fr multi 1.90 1.90

Endangered Birds A567

Designs: 10fr, Pseudobulweria rostrata. 80fr, Pomarea nigra, vert.

Perf. 13x13¼, 13¼x13
2019, Jan. 25 Litho.
1221-1222 A567 Set of 2 1.75 1.75

New Year 2019 (Year of the Pig) A568

Litho. & Silk-Screened
2019, Feb. 5 *Perf. 13*
1223 A568 140fr multi 2.75 2.75

International Women's Day — A569

Designs: 80fr, Woman and palm trees. 100fr, Woman with flower in hair.

2019, Mar. 8 Litho. *Perf. 13¼x13*
1224-1225 A569 Set of 2 3.50 3.50

Tupaia (c. 1725-70), Navigator, Capt. James Cook (1728-79), and Ship, Endeavour — A570

2019, Apr. 12 Engr. *Perf. 13*
1226 A570 250fr multi 4.75 4.75

Cook's arrival in Tahiti, 250th anniv.

Marine Life in Protected Reserve — A571

2019, May 24 Litho. *Perf. 13*

1227 A571 100fr multi 1.90 1.90

Campaign Against Obesity — A572

No. 1228: a, Lychee fruit on lollipop stick. b, Mango in ice cream cup. c, Pineapple surrounding soda can. d, Watermelon slice on ice cream stick. e, Peeled banana in candy wrapper. f, Coconut surrounding bottle and straw.

Serpentine Die Cut 11

2019, May 24 Litho.

Booklet Stamps

Self-Adhesive

1228 Booklet pane of 6 11.50
a.-f. A572 100fr Any single 1.90 1.90

Office of Posts and Telecommunications Emblem — A573

Serpentine Die Cut 6¾ Vert.

2019 Self-Adhesive Litho.

Booklet Stamp

1229 A573 (80fr) deep ultra — —
a. Booklet pane of 10 —

Miss Tahiti Pageant Winners Type of 2016

No. 1230: a, Viola Teriitahi, 1968. b, Moeata Schmouker, 1978. c, Teumrre Pater, 1988. d, Mareva Galanter, 1998. e, Hinatea Boosie, 2008. f, Vaimalama Chaves, 2018.

Serpentine Die Cut 11

2019, June 7 Litho.

Self-Adhesive

1230 Booklet pane of 6 11.50
a.-f. A524 100fr Any single 1.90 1.90

Cantaloupe A574

2019, June 7 Litho. *Perf. 13x13¼*

1231 A574 140fr multi 2.75 2.75

No. 1231 is impregnated with a cantaloupe scent.

Artistic Conservatory of French Polynesia, 40th Anniv. — A575

Serpentine Die Cut 11

2019, July 19 Litho.

Self-Adhesive

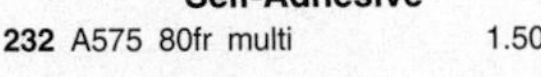

1232 A575 80fr multi 1.50 1.50

André Japy (1904-74), Aviator — A576

2019, Aug. 23 Litho. *Perf. 13*

1233 A576 100fr multi 1.90 1.90

General Milan Stefánik (1880-1919), Builder of Astronomical Observatory in French Polynesia — A577

2019, Sept. 6 Litho. *Perf. 13*

1234 A577 140fr multi 2.60 2.60

Fish A578

Designs: 40fr, Ruvettus pretiosus. 80fr, Pontinus macrocephalus. 100fr, Etelis carbunculus.

Litho. & Silk-Screened

2019, Oct. 18 *Perf. 13x13¼*

1235-1237 A578 Set of 3 4.25 4.25
1237a Souvenir sheet of 3, #1235-1237 4.25 4.25

Polynesia, the Sky, by Henri Matisse (1869-1954) — A579

Polynesia, the Sea, by Matisse — A580

2019, Nov. 7 Litho. *Perf. 13*

1238 A579 100fr multi 1.90 1.90
1239 A580 100fr multi 1.90 1.90

Cargo Vessel Hawaiki Nui — A581

Litho. & Engr.

2019, Nov. 7 *Perf. 13½x13*

1240 A581 500fr multi 9.25 9.25
a. Souvenir sheet of 1 9.25 9.25

See St. Pierre & Miquelon No.

SEMI-POSTAL STAMPS

Nos. 55 and 26 Surcharged in Red

1915 Unwmk. *Perf. 14x13½*

B1	A1 10c + 5c red	32.50	32.50
a.	"e" instead of "c"	87.50	87.50
b.	Inverted surcharge	225.00	225.00
c.	Double surcharge	525.00	525.00
B2	A2 10c + 5c rose & org	12.50	12.50
a.	"e" instead of "c"	65.00	65.00
b.	"c" inverted	65.00	65.00
c.	Inverted surcharge	300.00	300.00
d.	As "a," inverted surcharge	400.00	
e.	As "b," inverted surcharge	400.00	

Surcharged in Carmine

B3	A2 10c + 5c rose & org	5.50	5.50
a.	"e" instead of "c"	45.00	45.00
b.	Inverted surcharge	200.00	200.00
c.	Double surcharge	200.00	200.00
d.	As "a," inverted surcharge	325.00	

Surcharged in Carmine

1916

B4 A2 10c + 5c rose & org 5.50 5.50

Curie Issue

Common Design Type

1938 Engr. *Perf. 13*

B5 CD80 1.75fr + 50c brt ultra 20.00 20.00

French Revolution Issue

Common Design Type

1939 Photo.

Name and Value Typo. in Black

B6	CD83 45c + 25c grn	17.50	17.50
B7	CD83 70c + 30c brn	17.50	17.50
B8	CD83 90c + 35c red org	17.50	17.50
B9	CD83 1.25fr + 1fr rose pink	17.50	17.50
B10	CD83 2.25fr + 2fr blue	17.50	17.50
	Nos. B6-B10 (5)	87.50	87.50
	Set, never hinged	145.00	

Catalogue values for unused stamps in this section, from this point to the end of the section, are for Never Hinged items.

Common Design Type and

Marine Officer — SP1

"L'Astrolabe" — SP2

1941 Photo. *Perf. 13½*

B11	SP1 1fr + 1fr red	3.50
B12	CD86 1.50fr + 3fr maroon	3.50
B12A	SP2 2.50fr + 1fr blue	3.50
	Nos. B11-B12A (3)	10.50

Nos. B11-B12A were issued by the Vichy government in France, and were not placed on sale in French Polynesia.

Nos. 125A-125B Srchd. in Black or Red

1944 Engr. *Perf. 12½x12*

B12B	50c + 1.50fr on 2.50fr dp blue (R)	1.75
B12C	+ 2.50fr on 1fr green	1.75

Colonial Development Fund.

Nos. B12B-B12C were issued by the Vichy government in France, but were not placed on sale in French Polynesia.

Red Cross Issue

Common Design Type

1944 Photo. *Perf. 14½x14*

B13 CD90 5fr + 20fr pck blue 2.00 1.60

The surtax was for the French Red Cross and national relief.

Tropical Medicine Issue

Common Design Type

1950, July 17 Engr. *Perf. 13*

B14 CD100 10fr + 2fr dk bl grn & dk grn 10.50 8.00

The surtax was for charitable work.

AIR POST STAMPS

Seaplane in Flight AP1

Perf. 13½

1934, Nov. 5 Unwmk. Photo.

C1 AP1 5fr green 1.25 1.25

For overprint see No. C2.

For Type AP1 without "RF," see Nos. C1A-C1D.

Type of 1934 without "RF" and

Beach Scene — AP1a

Perf. 13½, 13 (#C1E)

1944 Photo, Engr. (#C1E)

C1A	AP1 5fr green	.70
C1B	AP1 10fr black	1.00
C1C	AP1 20fr orange	1.10
C1D	AP1 50fr gray blue	1.50
C1E	AP1a 100fr turquoise blue	2.00
	Nos. C1A-C1E (5)	6.30

Nos. C1A-C1E were issued by the Vichy government in France, but were not placed on sale in French Polynesia.

Catalogue values for unused stamps in this section, from this point to the end of the section, are for Never Hinged items.

No. C1 Overprinted in Red

1941
C2 AP1 5fr green 7.25 4.75

Common Design Type

1942 ***Perf. 14½x14***

C3 CD87 1fr dark orange .90 .65
C4 CD87 1.50fr bright red .95 .70
C5 CD87 5fr brown red 1.25 .95
C6 CD87 10fr black 1.90 1.40
C7 CD87 25fr ultra 2.75 2.10
C8 CD87 50fr dark green 3.00 2.10
C9 CD87 100fr plum 3.00 2.10
Nos. C3-C9 (7) 13.75 10.00

Victory Issue

Common Design Type

1946, May 8 Engr. ***Perf. 12½***
C10 CD92 8fr dark green 2.75 2.00

Chad to Rhine Issue

Common Design Types

1946, June 6
C11 CD93 5fr red orange 2.10 1.60
C12 CD94 10fr dk olive bis 2.10 1.60
C13 CD95 15fr dk yellow grn 2.10 1.60
C14 CD96 20fr carmine 2.75 2.10
C15 CD97 25fr dk rose violet 4.00 3.00
C16 CD98 50fr black 4.50 3.50
Nos. C11-C16 (6) 17.55 13.40

Shearwater and Moorea Landscape — AP2

Fishermen — AP3

Shearwater over Maupiti Shoreline — AP4

1948, Mar. 1 Unwmk. ***Perf. 13***
C17 AP2 50fr red brown 30.00 11.00
C18 AP3 100fr purple 24.00 8.00
C19 AP4 200fr blue green 52.50 17.50
Nos. C17-C19 (3) 106.50 36.50

UPU Issue

Common Design Type

1949
C20 CD99 10fr deep blue 20.00 15.00

Gauguin's "Nafea faaipoipo" — AP5

1953, Sept. 24
C21 AP5 14fr dk brn, dk gray grn & red 80.00 65.00

50th anniv. of the death of Paul Gauguin.

Liberation Issue

Common Design Type

1954, June 6
C22 CD102 3fr dk grnsh bl & bl grn 10.00 8.00

Bahia Peak, Borabora — AP6

1955, Sept. 26 Unwmk. ***Perf. 13***
C23 AP6 13fr indigo & blue 10.00 5.50

Mother-of-Pearl Artist — AP7

Designs: 50fr, "Women of Tahiti," Gauguin, horiz. 100fr, "The White Horse," Gauguin. 200fr, Night fishing at Moorea, horiz.

1958, Nov. 3 Engr. ***Perf. 13***
C24 AP7 13fr multicolored 13.00 4.50
C25 AP7 50fr multicolored 12.00 4.50
C26 AP7 100fr multicolored 20.00 7.25
C27 AP7 200fr lilac & slate 40.00 21.00
Nos. C24-C27 (4) 85.00 37.25

Airport, Papeete — AP8

1960, Nov. 19
C28 AP8 13fr rose lil, vio, & yel grn 3.50 2.40

Telstar Issue

Common Design Type

1962, Dec. 5 ***Perf. 13***
C29 CD111 50fr red lil, mar & vio bl 11.50 8.00

Tahitian Dancer — AP10

1964, May 14 Photo. ***Perf. 13***
C30 AP10 15fr multicolored 4.75 2.00

Map of Tahiti and Free French Emblems — AP11

1964, July 10 Unwmk.
C31 AP11 16fr multicolored 15.00 9.00

Issued to commemorate the rallying of French Polynesia to the Free French cause.

Moorea Scene — AP12

1964, Dec. 1 Litho. ***Perf. 13***
C32 AP12 23fr multicolored 9.50 4.00

ITU Issue

Common Design Type

1965, May 17 Engr. ***Perf. 13***
C33 CD120 50fr vio, red brn & bl 80.00 52.50

Paul Gauguin — AP13

Design: 25fr, Gauguin Museum (stylized). 40fr, Primitive statues at Gauguin Museum.

1965 Engr. ***Perf. 13***
C34 AP13 25fr olive green 7.50 4.50
C35 AP13 40fr blue green 15.00 8.00
C36 AP13 75fr brt red brown 20.00 15.00
Nos. C34-C36 (3) 42.50 27.50

Opening of Gauguin Museum, Papeete. Issued: 25fr, 75fr, 6/13. 40fr, 11/7.

Skin Diver with Spear Gun — AP14

1965, Sept. 1 Engr. ***Perf. 13***
C37 AP14 50fr red brn, dl bl & dk grn 90.00 55.00

World Championships in Underwater Fishing, Tuamotu Archipelago, Sept. 1965.

Painting from a School Dining Room — AP15

1965, Nov. 29
C38 AP15 80fr brn, bl, dl bl & red 22.50 17.50

School Canteen Program.

Radio Tower, Globe and Palm — AP16

1965, Dec. 29 Engr. ***Perf. 13***
C39 AP16 60fr org, grn & dk brn 19.00 15.00

50th anniversary of the first radio link between Tahiti and France.

French Satellite A-1 Issue

Common Design Type

Designs: 7fr, Diamant Rocket and launching installations. 10fr, A-1 satellite.

1966, Feb. 7
C40 CD121 7fr choc, dp grn & lil 6.75 6.00
C41 CD121 10fr lil, dp grn & dk brn 6.75 6.00
a. Pair, #C40-C41 + label 14.00 14.00

French Satellite D-1 Issue

Common Design Type

1966, May 10 Engr. ***Perf. 13***
C42 CD122 20fr multicolored 7.00 4.75

Papeete Harbor — AP17

1966, June 30 Photo. ***Perf. 13***
C43 AP17 50fr multicolored 15.00 11.00

"Vive Tahiti" by A. Benichou — AP18

1966, Nov. 28 Photo. ***Perf. 13***
C44 AP18 13fr multicolored 11.00 6.50

Explorer's Ship and Canoe — AP19

Designs: 60fr, Polynesian costume and ship. 80fr, Louis Antoine de Bougainville, vert.

1968, Apr. 6 Engr. ***Perf. 13***
C45 AP19 40fr multicolored 8.75 3.25
C46 AP19 60fr multicolored 11.50 6.50
C47 AP19 80fr multicolored 14.50 8.75
a. Souv. sheet, #C45-C47 160.00 160.00
Nos. C45-C47 (3) 34.75 18.50

200th anniv. of the discovery of Tahiti by Louis Antoine de Bougainville.
Issued: 40fr, 4/6/68.

The Meal, by Paul Gauguin — AP20

1968, July 30 Photo. *Perf. 12x12½*
C48 AP20 200fr multicolored 40.00 32.50

See Nos. C63-C67, C78-C82, C89-C93, C98.

Shot Put — AP21

1968, Oct. 12 Engr. *Perf. 13*
C49 AP21 35fr dk car rose & brt grn 16.00 9.00

19th Olympic Games, Mexico City, 10/12-27.

Concorde Issue
Common Design Type

1969, Apr. 17
C50 CD129 40fr red brn & car rose 55.00 35.00

PATA 1970 Poster — AP22

1969, July 9 Photo. *Perf. 12½x13*
C51 AP22 25fr blue & multi 17.50 7.25

Issued to publicize PATA 1970 (Pacific Area Travel Association Congress), Tahiti.

Underwater Fishing — AP23

52fr, Hand holding fish made up of flags, vert.

1969, Aug. 5 Photo. *Perf. 13*
C52 AP23 48fr blk, grnsh bl & red lil 35.00 13.50
C53 AP23 52fr bl, blk & red 40.00 22.50

Issued to publicize the World Underwater Fishing Championships.

Gen. Bonaparte as Commander of the Army in Italy, by Jean Sebastien Rouillard — AP24

1969, Oct. 15 Photo. *Perf. 12½x12*
C54 AP24 100fr car & multi 80.00 67.50

Bicentenary of the birth of Napoleon Bonaparte (1769-1821).

Eiffel Tower, Torii and EXPO Emblem — AP25

Design: 30fr, Mount Fuji, Tower of the Sun and EXPO emblem, horiz.

1970, Sept. 15 Photo. *Perf. 13*
C55 AP25 30fr multicolored 20.00 8.00
C56 AP25 50fr multicolored 27.50 12.00

EXPO '70 International Exposition, Osaka, Japan, Mar. 15-Sept. 13.

Pearl Diver Descending, and Basket — AP26

Designs: 5fr, Diver collecting oysters. 18fr, Implantation into oyster, horiz. 27fr, Open oyster with pearl. 50fr, Woman with mother of pearl jewelry.

1970, Sept. 30 Engr. *Perf. 13*
C57 AP26 2fr slate, grnsh bl & red brn 1.50 .90
C58 AP26 5fr grnsh blue, ultra & org 2.75 1.50
C59 AP26 18fr sl, mag & org 3.75 2.75
C60 AP26 27fr brt pink, brn & dl lil 9.25 4.75
C61 AP26 50fr gray, red brn & org 16.00 7.50
Nos. C57-C61 (5) 33.25 17.40

Pearl industry of French Polynesia.

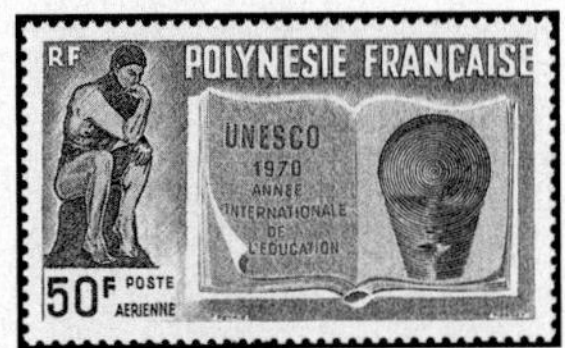

The Thinker, by Auguste Rodin and Education Year Emblem — AP27

1970, Oct. 15 Engr. *Perf. 13*
C62 AP27 50fr bl, ind & fawn 17.00 10.50

International Education Year.

Painting Type of 1968

Paintings by Artists Living in Polynesia: 20fr, Woman on the Beach, by Yves de Saint-Front. 40fr, Abstract, by Frank Fay. 60fr, Woman and Shells, by Jean Guillois. 80fr, Hut under Palms, by Jean Masson. 100fr, Polynesian Girl, by Jean-Charles Bouloc, vert.

Perf. 12x12½, 12½x12

1970, Dec. 14 Photo.
C63 AP20 20fr brn & multi 8.00 4.00
C64 AP20 40fr brn & multi 12.00 7.50
C65 AP20 60fr brn & multi 16.00 11.00
C66 AP20 80fr brn & multi 20.00 16.00
C67 AP20 100fr brn & multi 26.00 22.50
Nos. C63-C67 (5) 82.00 61.00

South Pacific Games Emblem — AP28

1971, Jan. 26 *Perf. 12½*
C68 AP28 20fr ultra & multi 8.00 5.00

Publicity for 4th South Pacific Games, held in Papeete, Sept. 8-19, 1971.

Memorial Flame — AP29

1971, Mar. 19 Photo. *Perf. 12½*
C69 AP29 5fr multicolored 8.00 5.00

In memory of Charles de Gaulle.

Soldier and Badge — AP30

1971, Apr. 21
C70 AP30 25fr multicolored 11.00 6.75

30th anniversary of departure of Tahitian volunteers to serve in World War II.

Water Sports Type

Designs: 15fr, Surfing, vert. 16fr, Skin diving, vert. 20fr, Water-skiing with kite.

1971, May 11 Photo. *Perf. 13*
C71 A44 15fr multicolored 6.50 3.50
C72 A44 16fr multicolored 7.50 3.25
C73 A44 20fr multicolored 11.00 7.75
Nos. C71-C73 (3) 25.00 14.50

Sailing AP31

1971, Sept. 8 *Perf. 12½*
C74 AP31 15fr shown 6.50 3.50
C75 AP31 18fr Golf 8.00 4.75
C76 AP31 27fr Archery 12.00 7.25
C77 AP31 53fr Tennis 20.00 13.50
a. Souv. sheet, #C74-C77 190.00 190.00
Nos. C74-C77 (4) 46.50 29.00

4th So. Pacific Games, Papeete, Sept. 8-19.

Painting Type of 1968

Paintings by Artists Living in Polynesia: 20fr, Hut and Palms, by Isabelle Wolf. 40fr, Palms on Shore, by André Dobrowolski. 60fr, Polynesian Woman, by Françoise Séli, vert. 80fr, Holy Family, by Pierre Heymann, vert. 100fr, Crowd, by Nicolai Michoutouchkine.

1971, Dec. 15 Photo. *Perf. 13*
C78 AP20 20fr multicolored 7.50 4.50
C79 AP20 40fr multicolored 11.00 7.50
C80 AP20 60fr multicolored 13.00 10.00
C81 AP20 80fr multicolored 18.00 12.50
C82 AP20 100fr multicolored 30.00 22.50
Nos. C78-C82 (5) 79.50 57.00

Papeete Harbor — AP32

1972, Jan. 13
C83 AP32 28fr violet & multi 11.00 8.00

Free port of Papeete, 10th anniversary.

Figure Skating and Dragon AP33

1972, Jan. 25 Engr. *Perf. 13*
C84 AP33 20fr ultra, lake & brt grn 9.00 7.00

11th Winter Olympic Games, Sapporo, Japan, Feb. 3-13.

South Pacific Commission Headquarters, Noumea — AP34

1972, Feb. 5 Photo. *Perf. 13*
C85 AP34 21fr blue & multi 11.00 5.25

South Pacific Commission, 25th anniv.

Festival Emblem — AP35

1972, May 9 Engr. *Perf. 13*
C86 AP35 36fr orange, bl & grn 8.00 5.25

So. Pacific Festival of Arts, Fiji, May 6-20.

Kon Tiki and Route, Callao to Tahiti — AP36

1972, Aug. 18 Photo. *Perf. 13*

C87 AP36 16fr dk & lt bl, blk & org 10.00 6.50

25th anniversary of the arrival of the raft Kon Tiki in Tahiti.

Charles de Gaulle and Memorial — AP37

1972, Dec. 9 Engr. *Perf. 13*

C88 AP37 100fr slate 62.50 42.50

Painting Type of 1968

Paintings by Artists Living in Polynesia: 20fr, Horses, by Georges Bovy. 40fr, Sailboats, by Ruy Juventin, vert. 60fr, Harbor, by André Brooke. 80fr, Farmers, by Daniel Adam, vert. 100fr, Dancers, by Aloysius Pilioko, vert.

1972, Dec. 14 Photo.

C89	AP20	20fr gold & multi	9.75	4.25
C90	AP20	40fr gold & multi	12.00	6.75
C91	AP20	60fr gold & multi	21.00	9.50
C92	AP20	80fr dk grn, buff & dk brn	27.50	13.00
C93	AP20	100fr gold & multi	32.50	25.00
		Nos. C89-C93 (5)	102.75	58.50

St. Teresa and Lisieux Basilica AP38

1973, Jan. 23 Engr. *Perf. 13*

C94 AP38 85fr multicolored 25.00 17.50

Centenary of the birth of St. Teresa of Lisieux (1873-1897), Carmelite nun.

Nicolaus Copernicus — AP39

1973, Mar. 7 Engr. *Perf. 13*

C95 AP39 100fr brn, vio bl & red lil 30.00 17.50

Copernicus (1473-1543), Polish astronomer.

Plane over Tahiti — AP40

1973, Apr. 3 Photo. *Perf. 13*

C96 AP40 80fr ultra, gold & lt grn 22.50 16.00

Air France's World Tour via Tahiti.

DC-10 at Papeete Airport — AP41

1973, May 18 Engr. *Perf. 13*

C97 AP41 20fr bl, ultra & sl grn 16.00 9.00

Start of DC-10 service.

Painting Type of 1968

Design: 200fr, "Ta Matete" (seated women), by Paul Gauguin.

1973, June 7 Photo. *Perf. 13*

C98 AP20 200fr multicolored 27.50 20.00

Paul Gauguin (1848-1903), painter.

Pierre Loti and Characters from his Books — AP42

1973, July 4 Engr. *Perf. 13*

C99 AP42 60fr multicolored 40.00 20.00

Pierre Loti (1850-1923), French naval officer and writer.

Woman with Flowers, by Eliane de Gennes AP43

Paintings by Artists Living in Polynesia: 20fr, Sun, by Jean Francois Favre. 60fr, Seascape, by Alain Sidet. 80fr, Crowded Bus, by Francois Ravello. 100fr, Stylized Boats, by Jackie Bourdin, horiz.

1973, Dec. 13 Photo. *Perf. 13*

C100	AP43	20fr gold & multi	8.00	2.75
C101	AP43	40fr gold & multi	11.50	6.00
C102	AP43	60fr gold & multi	17.00	10.50
C103	AP43	80fr gold & multi	22.50	17.00
C104	AP43	100fr gold & multi	27.50	20.00
		Nos. C100-C104 (5)	86.50	56.25

Bird, Fish, Flower and Water — AP44

1974, June 12 Photo. *Perf. 13*

C105 AP44 12fr blue & multi 7.50 5.25

Nature protection.

Catamaran under Sail — AP45

1974, July 22 Engr. *Perf. 13*

C106 AP45 100fr multicolored 27.50 16.00

2nd Catamaran World Championships.

Still-life, by Rosine Temarui-Masson — AP46

Paintings by Artists Living in Polynesia: 40fr, Palms and House on Beach, by Marcel Chardon. 60fr, Man, by Marie-Françoise Avril. 80fr, Polynesian Woman, by Henriette Robin. 100fr, Lagoon by Moon-light, by David Farsi, horiz.

1974, Dec. 12 Photo. *Perf. 13*

C107	AP46	20fr gold & multi	18.00	8.50
C108	AP46	40fr gold & multi	27.50	9.50
C109	AP46	60fr gold & multi	32.50	12.00
C110	AP46	80fr gold & multi	45.00	16.50
C111	AP46	100fr gold & multi	65.00	27.50
		Nos. C107-C111 (5)	188.00	74.00

See Nos. C122-C126.

Polynesian Gods of Travel — AP47

Designs: 75fr, Tourville hydroplane, 1929. 100fr, Passengers leaving plane.

1975, Feb. 7 Engr. *Perf. 13*

C112	AP47	50fr sep, pur & brn	11.00	6.00
C113	AP47	75fr grn, bl & red	16.00	8.00
C114	AP47	100fr grn, sep & car	25.00	15.00
		Nos. C112-C114 (3)	52.00	29.00

Fifty years of Tahitian aviation.

French Ceres Stamp and Woman — AP48

1975, May 29 Engr. *Perf. 13*

C115 AP48 32fr ver, brn & blk 8.00 5.00

ARPHILA 75 International Philatelic Exhibition, Paris, June 6-16.

Shot Put and Games' Emblem AP50

Designs: 30fr, Volleyball. 40fr, Women's swimming.

1975, Aug. 1 Photo. *Perf. 13*

C117	AP50	25fr shown	4.75	3.00
C118	AP50	30fr multicolored	7.00	3.75
C119	AP50	40fr multicolored	9.25	5.25
		Nos. C117-C119 (3)	21.00	12.00

5th South Pacific Games, Guam, Aug. 1-10.

Flowers, Athlete, View of Montreal — AP51

1975, Oct. 15 Engr. *Perf. 13*

C120 AP51 44fr brt bl, ver & blk 11.00 6.50

Pre-Olympic Year 1975.

UPU Emblem, Jet and Letters — AP52

1975, Nov. 5 Engr. *Perf. 13*

C121 AP52 100fr brn, bl & ol 22.50 13.00

World Universal Postal Union Day.

Paintings Type of 1974

Paintings by Artists Living in Polynesia: 20fr, Beach Scene, by R. Marcel Marius, horiz. 40fr, Roofs with TV antennas, by M. Anglade, horiz. 60fr, Street scene with bus, by J. Day, horiz. 80fr, Tropical waters (fish), by J. Steimetz. 100fr, Women, by A. van der Heyde.

1975, Dec. 17 Litho. *Perf. 13*

C122	AP46	20fr gold & multi	3.00	1.75
C123	AP46	40fr gold & multi	6.00	3.00
C124	AP46	60fr gold & multi	9.00	4.50
C125	AP46	80fr gold & multi	12.00	7.50
C126	AP46	100fr gold & multi	14.50	12.00
		Nos. C122-C126 (5)	44.50	28.75

Concorde — AP53

1976, Jan. 21 Engr. *Perf. 13*

C127 AP53 100fr car, bl & ind 19.00 13.00

First commercial flight of supersonic jet Concorde from Paris to Rio, Jan. 21.

Adm. Rodney, Count de la Perouse, "Barfleur" and "Triomphant" in Battle — AP54

31fr, Count de Grasse and Lord Graves, "Ville de Paris" & "Le Terible" in Chesapeake Bay Battle.

1976, Apr. 15 Engr. *Perf. 13*

C128	AP54	24fr grnsh bl, lt brn & blk	5.00	2.50
C129	AP54	31fr mag, red & lt brn	5.75	3.50

American Bicentennial.

King Pomaré I — AP55

Portraits: 21fr, King Pomaré II. 26fr, Queen Pomaré IV. 30fr, King Pomaré V.

1976, Apr. 28 Litho. *Perf. 12½*

C130	AP55	18fr olive & multi	1.75	.75
C131	AP55	21fr multicolored	2.00	1.10
C132	AP55	26fr gray & multi	2.75	1.25
C133	AP55	30fr plum & multi	3.00	1.90
		Nos. C130-C133 (4)	9.50	5.00

Pomaré Dynasty. See Nos. C141-C144.

Running and Maple Leaf — AP56

Designs: 34fr, Long jump, vert. 50fr, Olympic flame and flowers.

1976, July 19 Engr. *Perf. 13*

C134	AP56	26fr ultra & multi	4.25	2.10
C135	AP56	34fr ultra & multi	6.00	2.75
C136	AP56	50fr ultra & multi	11.50	5.00
a.		Min. sheet, #C134-C136	90.00	90.00
		Nos. C134-C136 (3)	21.75	9.85

21st Olympic Games, Montreal, Canada, July 17-Aug. 1.

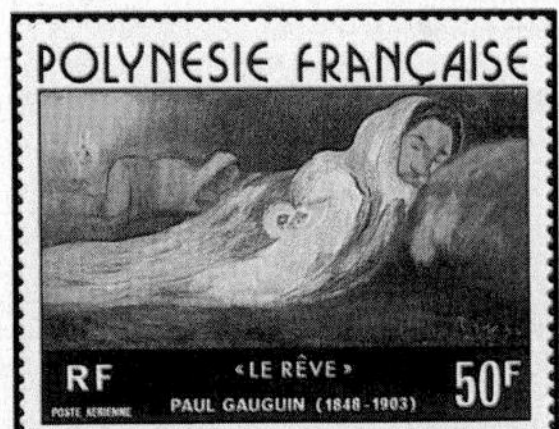

The Dream, by Paul Gauguin — AP57

1976, Oct. 17 Photo. *Perf. 13*

C137	AP57	50fr multicolored	11.00	7.25

Murex Steeriae — AP58

Sea Shells: 27fr, Conus Gauguini. 35fr, Conus marchionatus.

1977, Mar. 14 Photo. *Perf. 12½x13*

C138	AP58	25fr vio bl & multi	4.25	1.25
C139	AP58	27fr ultra & multi	4.25	1.50
C140	AP58	35fr blue & multi	5.00	2.00
		Nos. C138-C140 (3)	13.50	4.75

See Nos. C156-C158.

Royalty Type of 1976

19fr, King Maputeoa, Mangareva. 33fr, King Camatoa V, Raiatea. 39fr, Queen Vaekehu, Marquesas. 43fr, King Teurarii III, Rurutu.

1977, Apr. 19 Litho. *Perf. 12½*

C141	AP55	19fr dull red & multi	1.25	.95
C142	AP55	33fr dk blue & multi	1.90	1.25
C143	AP55	39fr ultra & multi	1.90	1.25
C144	AP55	43fr green & multi	2.75	1.90
		Nos. C141-C144 (4)	7.80	5.35

Polynesian rulers.

Pocillopora AP59

Design: 25fr, Acropora, horiz.

Perf. 13x12½, 12½x13

1977, May 23 Photo.

C145	AP59	25fr multicolored	1.90	1.10
C146	AP59	33fr multicolored	2.75	1.90

3rd Symposium on Coral Reefs, Miami, Fla. See Nos. C162-C163.

De Gaulle Memorial — AP60

Photogravure and Embossed

1977, June 18 *Perf. 13*

C147	AP60	40fr gold & multi	7.00	5.00

5th anniversary of dedication of De Gaulle memorial at Colombey-les-Deux-Eglises.

Tahitian Dancer — AP61

1977, July 14 Litho. *Perf. 12½*

C148	AP61	27fr multicolored	4.00	2.50

Charles A. Lindbergh and Spirit of St. Louis — AP62

1977, Aug. 18 Litho. *Perf. 12½*

C149	AP62	28fr multicolored	7.00	3.50

Lindbergh's solo transatlantic flight from New York to Paris, 50th anniv.

Mahoe — AP63

1977, Sept. 15 Photo. *Perf. 12½x13*

C150	AP63	8fr shown	1.40	.80
C151	AP63	12fr Frangipani	1.75	1.25

Palms on Shore — AP64

1977, Nov. 8 Photo. *Perf. 12½x13*

C152	AP64	32fr multicolored	10.00	4.50

Ecology, protection of trees.

Rubens' Son Albert AP65

1977, Nov. 28 Engr. *Perf. 13*

C153	AP65	100fr grnsh blk & rose cl	11.00	8.00

Peter Paul Rubens (1577-1640), painter, 400th birth anniversary.

Capt. Cook and "Discovery" — AP66

Design: 39fr, Capt. Cook and "Resolution."

1978, Jan. 20 Engr. *Perf. 13*

C154	AP66	33fr multicolored	2.50	3.00
C155	AP66	39fr multicolored	3.00	3.50

Bicentenary of Capt. James Cook's arrival in Hawaii.
For overprints see Nos. C166-C167.

Shell Type of 1977

Sea Shells: 22fr, Erosaria obvelata. 24fr, Cypraea ventriculus. 31fr, Lambis robusta.

1978, Apr. 13 Photo. *Perf. 13½x13*

C156	AP58	22fr brt blue & multi	2.25	1.25
C157	AP58	24fr brt blue & multi	2.25	1.50
C158	AP58	31fr brt blue & multi	3.50	2.50
		Nos. C156-C158 (3)	8.00	5.25

Tahitian Woman and Boy, by Gauguin AP67

1978, May 7 *Perf. 13*

C159	AP67	50fr multicolored	8.75	5.25

Paul Gauguin (1848-1903).

Antenna and ITU Emblem AP68

1978, May 17 Litho. *Perf. 13*

C160	AP68	80fr gray & multi	6.00	3.25

10th World Telecommunications Day.

Soccer and Argentina '78 Emblem — AP69

1978, June 1

C161	AP69	28fr multicolored	3.25	2.10

11th World Cup Soccer Championship, Argentina, June 1-25.

Coral Type of 1977

Designs: 26fr, Fungia, horiz. 34fr, Millepora.

Perf. 13x12½, 12½x13

1978, July 13 Photo.

C162	AP59	26fr multicolored	1.75	1.25
C163	AP59	34fr multicolored	2.25	1.60

Radar Antenna, Polynesian Woman — AP70

1978, Sept. 5 Engr. *Perf. 13*

C164	AP70	50fr blue & black	3.00	1.75

Papenoo earth station.

Bird and Rainbow over Island — AP71

1978, Oct. 5 **Photo.**
C165 AP71 23fr multicolored 6.00 1.75

Nature protection.

Nos. C154-C155 Overprinted

No. C166

No. C167

1979, Feb. 14 **Engr.** ***Perf. 13***
C166 AP66 33fr multi 4.00 2.50
C167 AP66 39fr multi (VBl) 5.00 3.50

Bicentenary of Capt. Cook's death. On No. C167 date is last line of overprint.

Children, Toys and IYC Emblem — AP72

1979, May 3 **Engr.** ***Perf. 13***
C168 AP72 150fr multicolored 12.00 7.00

International Year of the Child.

"Do you expect a letter?" by Paul Gauguin — AP73

1979, May 20 **Photo.** ***Perf. 13***
C169 AP73 200fr multicolored 16.00 8.00

Shell and Carved Head — AP74

1979, June 30 **Engr.** ***Perf. 13***
C170 AP74 44fr multicolored 3.50 2.00

Museum of Tahiti and the Islands.

Conference Emblem over Island AP75

1979, Oct. 6 **Photo.** ***Perf. 13***
C171 AP75 23fr multicolored 2.25 1.10

19th South Pacific Conf., Tahiti, Oct. 6-12.

Flying Boat "Bermuda" — AP76

Planes Used in Polynesia: 40fr, DC-4 over Papeete. 60fr, Britten-Norman "Islander." 80fr, Fairchild F-27A. 120fr, DC-8 over Tahiti.

1979, Dec. 19 **Litho.** ***Perf. 13***
C172 AP76 24fr multicolored 1.00 .50
C173 AP76 40fr multicolored 1.75 1.00
C174 AP76 60fr multicolored 2.75 1.50
C175 AP76 80fr multicolored 3.50 2.25
C176 AP76 120fr multicolored 6.00 3.00
Nos. C172-C176 (5) 15.00 8.25

See Nos. C180-C183.

Window on Tahiti, by Henri Matisse AP77

1980, Feb. 18 **Photo.**
C177 AP77 150fr multicolored 8.00 5.00

Marshi Metua No Tehamana, by Gauguin AP78

1980, Aug. 24 **Photo.** ***Perf. 13***
C178 AP78 500fr multicolored 18.00 13.00

Sydpex '80, Philatelic Exhibition, Sydney Town Hall — AP79

1980, Sept. 29 **Photo.** ***Perf. 13***
C179 AP79 70fr multicolored 8.00 5.25

Aviation Type of 1979

1980, Dec. 15 **Litho.** ***Perf. 13***
C180 AP76 15fr Catalina .75 .55
C181 AP76 26fr Twin Otter 1.00 .70
C182 AP76 30fr CAMS 55 1.25 .90
C183 AP76 50fr DC-6 2.00 1.40
Nos. C180-C183 (4) 5.00 3.55

And The Gold of their Bodies, by Gauguin — AP80

1981, Mar. 15 **Photo.** ***Perf. 13***
C184 AP80 100fr multicolored 4.50 2.50

20th Anniv. of Manned Space Flight AP81

1981, June 15 **Litho.** ***Perf. 12½***
C185 AP81 300fr multicolored 9.00 7.00

First Intl. Pirogue (6-man Canoe) Championship — AP82

1981, July 25 **Litho.** ***Perf. 13x12½***
C186 AP82 200fr multicolored 5.50 4.50

Matavai Bay, by William Hodges — AP83

Paintings: 60fr, Poedea, by John Weber, vert. 80fr, Omai, by Joshua Reynolds, vert. 120fr, Point Venus, by George Tobin.

1981, Dec. 10 **Photo.** ***Perf. 13***
C187 AP83 40fr multicolored 1.10 .90
C188 AP83 60fr multicolored 1.75 1.25
C189 AP83 80fr multicolored 2.75 1.75
C190 AP83 120fr multicolored 3.50 2.40
Nos. C187-C190 (4) 9.10 6.30

See Nos. C194-C197, C202-C205.

TB Bacillus Centenary — AP84

1982, Mar. 24 **Engr.** ***Perf. 13***
C191 AP84 200fr multicolored 5.00 3.00

1982 World Cup — AP85

1982, May 18 **Litho.** ***Perf. 13***
C192 AP85 250fr multicolored 6.50 4.50

French Overseas Possessions' Week, Sept. 18-25 — AP86

1982, Sept. 17 **Engr.**
C193 AP86 110fr multicolored 2.75 1.65

Painting Type of 1981

Designs: 50fr, The Tahitian, by M. Radiguet, vert. 70fr, Souvenir of Tahiti, by C. Giraud. 100fr, Beating Cloth Lengths, by Atlas JL the Younger. 160fr, Papeete Harbor, by C.F. Gordon Cumming.

1982, Dec. 15 **Photo.** ***Perf. 13***
C194 AP83 50fr multicolored 1.90 1.00
C195 AP83 70fr multicolored 2.25 1.50
C196 AP83 100fr multicolored 2.75 2.00
C197 AP83 160fr multicolored 4.50 2.75
Nos. C194-C197 (4) 11.40 7.25

Wood Cutter, by Gauguin AP87

Photo. & Engr.

1983, May 8 ***Perf. 12½x13***
C198 AP87 600fr multicolored 16.00 8.00

Voyage of Capt. Bligh — AP88

1983, June 9 **Litho.** ***Perf. 13***
C199 AP88 200fr Map, fruit 6.00 3.00

BRASILIANA '83 Intl. Stamp Exhibition, Rio de Janeiro, July 29-Aug. 7 — AP89

1983, July 29 **Litho.** ***Perf. 13x12½***
C200 AP89 100fr multicolored 2.50 1.75
a. Souvenir sheet 3.50 3.50

1983, Aug. 4 **Litho.** ***Perf. 13x12½***
C201 AP89 110fr Bangkok '83 3.00 2.00
a. Souvenir sheet 4.00 4.00

Painting Type of 1981

20th Cent. Paintings: 40fr, View of Moorea, by William Alister MacDonald (1861-1956). 60fr, The Fruit Carrier, by Adrian Herman Gouwe (1875-1965). 80fr, Arrival of the Destroyer Escort, by Nicolas Mordvinoff (1911-1977). 100fr, Women on a Veranda, by Charles Alfred Le Moine (1872-1918).

1983, Dec. 22 **Photo.** ***Perf. 13***
C202 AP83 40fr multi 1.00 .75
C203 AP83 60fr multi, vert. 1.50 1.00
C204 AP83 80fr multi, vert. 1.60 1.25
C205 AP83 100fr multi 2.00 1.60
Nos. C202-C205 (4) 6.10 4.60

ESPANA '84 — AP90

Design: Maori canoers.

1984, Apr. 27 **Engr.** ***Perf. 13***
C206 AP90 80fr brn red & dk bl 2.25 1.50

Souvenir Sheet

C207 AP90 200fr dk bl & dk red 7.25 7.25

Woman with Mango, by Gauguin AP91

Photo. & Engr.

1984, May 27 ***Perf. 12½x13***
C208 AP91 400fr multicolored 11.00 6.00

Ausipex '84 — AP92

Details from Human Sacrifice of the Maori in Tahiti, 18th cent. engraving.

1984, Sept. 5 **Litho.** ***Perf. 13x12½***
C209 AP92 120fr Worshippers 3.00 2.25
C210 AP92 120fr Preparation 3.00 2.25
a. Pair, #C209-C210 + label 7.50 7.50

Souvenir Sheet

C211 AP92 200fr Entire 9.50 9.50

Painting by Gaugin (1848-1903) — AP93

Design: Where have we come from? What are we? Where are we going?

1985, Mar. 17 **Litho.** ***Perf. 13½x13***
C212 AP93 550fr multi 14.00 7.50

4th Pacific Arts Festival Type

Design: Islander, tiki, artifacts.

1985, July 3 **Litho.** ***Perf. 13***
C213 A95 200fr multicolored 4.50 3.00

Intl. Youth Year — AP95

Design: Island youths, frigate bird.

1985, Sept. 18 **Litho.**
C214 AP95 250fr multi 5.50 3.25

ITALIA '85 — AP96

Designs: Ship sailing into Papeete Harbor, 19th century print.

1985, Oct. 22 **Engr.**
C215 AP96 130fr multicolored 2.75 2.50

Souvenir Sheet

C216 AP96 240fr multicolored 7.50 7.50

1st Intl. Marlin Fishing Contest, Feb. 27-Mar. 5 — AP97

1986, Feb. 27 **Litho.** ***Perf. 12½***
C217 AP97 300fr multicolored 6.50 4.00

Arrival of a Boat, c.1880 — AP98

1986, June 24 **Engr.** ***Perf. 13***
C218 AP98 400fr intense blue 8.75 5.25

STOCKHOLMIA '86 — AP99

Design: Dr. Karl Solander and Anders Sparrmann, Swedish scientists who accompanied Capt. Cook, and map of Tahiti.

1986, Aug. 28 **Engr.** ***Perf. 13***
C219 AP99 150fr multicolored 3.25 2.25

Souvenir Sheet

C220 AP99 210fr multicolored 4.75 4.75

Protestant Churches — AP100

1986, Dec. 17 **Litho.** ***Perf. 13***
C221 AP100 80fr Tiva, 1955 1.75 .90
C222 AP100 200fr Avera, 1880 4.50 2.10
C223 AP100 300fr Papetoai, 1822 6.50 3.25
Nos. C221-C223 (3) 12.75 6.25

Broche Barracks, 120th Anniv. — AP101

1987, Apr. 21 **Litho.** ***Perf. 12½x12***
C224 AP101 350fr multicolored 7.75 5.00

CAPEX '87 — AP102

Design: George Vancouver (1757-1798), English navigator and cartographer, chart and excerpt from ship's log.

1987, June 15 **Engr.** ***Perf. 13***
C225 AP102 130fr multi 2.90 2.25

Imperf

Size: 143x100mm

C226 AP102 260fr multicolored 5.75 5.75

Soyez Mysterieuses, from a 5-Panel Sculpture by Paul Gauguin, Gauguin Museum — AP103

1987, Nov. 15 ***Perf. 13***
C227 AP103 600fr multicolored 14.00 9.50

AIR POST SEMI-POSTAL STAMPS

Catalogue values for unused stamps in this section are for Never Hinged items.

French Revolution Issue

Common Design Type

Unwmk.

1939, July 5 **Photo.** ***Perf. 13***

Name and Value Typo. in Orange

CB1 CD83 5fr + 4fr brn blk 35.00 35.00

Mother & Children on Beach — SPAP1

Perf. 12½x13½

1942, June 22 **Engr.**
CB2 SPAP1 1.50fr + 3.50fr green 2.00
CB3 SPAP1 2fr + 6fr yel brn 2.00

Native children's welfare fund.

Nos. CB2-CB3 were issued by the Vichy government in France, but were not placed on sale in French Polynesia.

Colonial Education Fund

Common Design Type

1942, June 22
CB4 CD86a 1.20fr + 1.80fr blue & red 2.00

No. CB4 was issued by the Vichy government in France, but was not placed on sale in French Polynesia.

POSTAGE DUE STAMPS

Postage Due Stamps of French Colonies, 1894-1906, Overprinted

1926-27 Unwmk. *Perf. 14x13½*

J1 D1	5c light blue	.95	.95
J2 D1	10c brown	.95	.95
J3 D1	20c olive green	1.40	1.40
J4 D1	30c dull red	1.60	1.60
J5 D1	40c rose	3.50	3.50
J6 D1	60c blue green	3.50	3.50
J7 D1	1fr red brown, *straw*	3.75	3.75
J8 D1	3fr magenta ('27)	15.00	15.00

With Additional Surcharge of New Value

J9 D1	2fr on 1fr orange red	4.00	4.75
	Nos. J1-J9 (9)	34.65	35.40

Fautaua Falls, Tahiti — D2

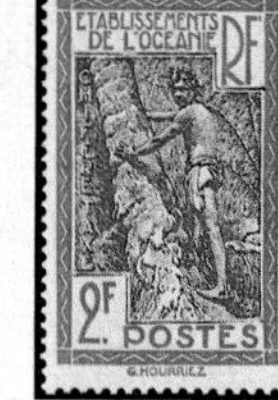

Tahitian Youth — D3

1929 Typo. *Perf. 13½x14*

J10 D2	5c lt blue & dk brn	.75	.75
J11 D2	10c vermilion & grn	.75	.75
J12 D2	30c dk brn & dk red	1.75	1.75
J13 D2	50c yel grn & dk brn	1.40	1.40
J14 D2	60c dl vio & yel grn	4.00	4.00
J15 D3	1fr Prus bl & red vio	3.50	3.50
J16 D3	2fr brn red & dk brn	2.00	2.10
J17 D3	3fr bl vio & bl grn	2.10	2.40
	Nos. J10-J17 (8)	16.25	16.65

Catalogue values for unused stamps in this section, from this point to the end of the section, are for Never Hinged items.

D4

1948 Engr. *Perf. 14x13*

J18 D4	10c brt blue grn	.40	.25
J19 D4	30c black brown	.40	.25
J20 D4	50c dk car rose	.50	.30
J21 D4	1fr ultra	.65	.50
J22 D4	2fr dk blue green	.95	.70
J23 D4	3fr red	1.90	1.40
J24 D4	4fr violet	2.00	1.60
J25 D4	5fr lilac rose	3.00	2.10
J26 D4	10fr slate	4.00	3.00
J27 D4	20fr red brown	5.50	4.25
	Nos. J18-J27 (10)	19.30	14.35

Polynesian Club — D5

1958 Unwmk. *Perf. 14x13*

J28 D5	1fr dk brn & grn	.65	.65
J29 D5	3fr bluish blk & hn brn	.90	.90
J30 D5	5fr brown & ultra	1.10	1.10
	Nos. J28-J30 (3)	2.65	2.65

Tahitian Bowl — D6

Designs: 1fr, Mother-of-pearl fish hook, vert. 5fr, Marquesan fan. 10fr, Lamp stand, vert. 20fr, Wood headrest ('87). 50fr, Wood scoop ('87).

1984-87 Litho. *Perf. 13*

J31 D6	1fr multicolored	.25	.25
J32 D6	3fr shown	.25	.25
J33 D6	5fr multicolored	.30	.30
J34 D6	10fr multicolored	.55	.55
J35 D6	20fr multicolored	.60	.60
J36 D6	50fr multicolored	1.50	1.50
	Nos. J31-J36 (6)	3.45	3.45

Issued: #J31-34, 3/15; #J35-J36, 8/18.

OFFICIAL STAMPS

Catalogue values for unused stamps in this section are for Never Hinged items.

Breadfruit O1

Polynesian Fruits: 2fr, 3fr, 5fr, like 1fr. 7fr, 8fr, 10fr, 15fr, "Vi Tahiti." 19fr, 20fr, 25fr, 35fr, Avocados. 50fr, 100fr, 200fr, Mangos.

1977, June 9 Litho. *Perf. 12½*

O1 O1	1fr ultra & multi	.40	*.65*
O2 O1	2fr ultra & multi	.40	*.65*
O3 O1	3fr ultra & multi	.40	*.65*
O4 O1	5fr ultra & multi	.40	*.65*
O5 O1	7fr red & multi	.65	*.95*
O6 O1	8fr red & multi	.65	*.95*
O7 O1	10fr red & multi	.95	*1.25*
O8 O1	15fr red & multi	1.40	*1.60*
O9 O1	19fr black & multi	1.60	*2.00*
O10 O1	20fr black & multi	1.75	*2.40*
O11 O1	25fr black & multi	2.50	*2.75*
O12 O1	35fr black & multi	3.25	*3.50*
O13 O1	50fr black & multi	3.25	*3.50*
O14 O1	100fr red & multi	7.25	*8.00*
O15 O1	200fr ultra & multi	14.00	*16.00*
	Nos. O1-O15 (15)	38.85	*45.50*

1982-86 *Perf. 13*

O1a O1	1fr ultra & multi	.70	*1.25*
O2a O1	2fr ultra & multi	.70	*1.25*
O3a O1	3fr ultra & multi	.95	*1.25*
O4a O1	5fr ultra & multi	2.25	*2.40*
O5a O1	7fr red & multi	2.25	*2.50*
O6a O1	8fr red & multi	3.25	*3.50*
O7a O1	10fr red & multi	3.50	*3.50*
O8a O1	15fr red & multi ('84)	3.50	*3.50*
O10a O1	20fr black & multi	3.50	*3.50*
O11a O1	25fr black & multi ('84)	3.50	*3.50*
O12a O1	35fr black & multi ('84)	8.00	*10.50*
O13a O1	50fr black & multi ('84)	20.00	*22.50*
O14a O1	100fr red & multi ('86)	52.50	*60.00*
O15a O1	200fr ultra & multi ('86)	67.50	*80.00*
	Nos. O1a-O15a (14)	172.10	*199.15*

Nos. O1-O15 have dull finish (matte) gum. Nos. O1a-O15a have shiny gum.

Stamps and Postmarks — O2

1fr, French Colonies #5. 2fr, French Colonies #27, #12. 3fr, French Colonies #29, 1884 Papeete postmark. 5fr, Newspaper franked with surcharge of Tahiti #2, 1884 Papeete postmark. 9fr, #176. 10fr, #4, 1894 octagonal postmark. 20fr, #6, #8. 46fr, #48. 51fr, #147-148, Vaitepaua-Makatea Island postmark. 70fr, Visit Tahiti postmark on postal card piece. 85fr, #59 with 1921 manuscript cancel, vert. 100fr, #181. 200fr, #C21, 1st day cancel.

Perf. 13¼, 13¼x13 (#O20), 13x13¼ (#O26)

1993-99 Litho.

O16 O2	1fr multicolored	.25	*.40*
a.	Perf. 13¼x13 ('98)	8.00	*9.50*
O17 O2	2fr multicolored	.25	*.40*
a.	Perf. 13¼x13 ('97)	1.00	*1.25*
O18 O2	3fr multicolored	.25	*.40*
a.	Perf. 13¼x13 ('98)	8.00	*9.50*
O19 O2	5fr multicolored	.30	*.55*
a.	Perf. 13¼x13 ('97)	1.00	*1.25*
O20 O2	9fr multicolored	.80	*1.25*
O21 O2	10fr multicolored	.30	*.55*
a.	Perf. 13¼x13 ('99)	1.00	.85
O22 O2	20fr multicolored	.65	*.95*
a.	Perf. 13¼x13 ('99)	8.00	*9.50*
O23 O2	46fr multicolored	1.40	*1.60*
O24 O2	51fr multicolored	2.50	*3.25*
O25 O2	70fr multicolored	2.40	*2.75*
a.	Perf. 13¼x13 ('97)	4.00	*6.50*
O26 O2	85fr multicolored	2.50	*3.25*
O27 O2	100fr multicolored	2.75	*3.50*
a.	Perf. 13¼x13 ('99)	2.40	1.90
O28 O2	200fr multicolored	5.25	*6.50*
a.	Perf. 13¼x13 ('97)	5.00	4.50
	Nos. O16-O28 (13)	19.60	*25.35*

Issued: 51fr, 4/6/94; 9fr, 85fr, 4/21/97; others, 1/13/93.

FRENCH SOUTHERN & ANTARCTIC TERRITORY

'french 'sə-thərn and ,ant-ärk-tik 'ter-ə-'tōr-ēs

POP. — 130 staff

Formerly dependencies of Madagascar, these areas, comprising the Kerguelen Archipelago; St. Paul, Amsterdam and Crozet Islands and Adelle Land in Antarctica achieved territorial status on August 6, 1955.

100 Centimes = 1 Franc
100 Cents = 1 Euro (2002)

Catalogue values for all unused stamps in this country are for Never Hinged items.

Madagascar No. 289 Ovptd. in Red

Unwmk.

1955, Oct. 28 Engr. *Perf. 13*

1 A25	15f dk grn & dp ultra	10.00	*27.50*

Rockhopper Penguins, Crozet Archipelago — A1

New Amsterdam A2

Design: 10fr, 15fr, Elephant seal.

1956, Apr. 25 Engr. *Perf. 13*

2 A1	50c dk blue, sepia & yel	.40	*1.00*
3 A1	1fr ultra, org & gray	.40	*1.00*
4 A2	5fr blue & dp ultra	2.40	*2.50*
5 A2	8fr gray vio & dk brn	14.00	*17.50*
6 A2	10fr indigo	5.00	5.00
7 A2	15fr indigo & brn vio	6.50	6.50
	Nos. 2-7 (6)	28.70	33.50

Polar Observation A3

1957, Oct. 11

8 A3	5fr black & violet	2.50	*4.25*
9 A3	10fr rose red	3.50	*5.00*
10 A3	15fr dark blue	4.00	*6.50*
	Nos. 8-10 (3)	10.00	15.75

International Geophysical Year, 1957-58.

Imperforates

Most stamps of this French possession exist imperforate in issued and trial colors, and also in small presentation sheets in issued colors.

Flower Issue

Common Design Type

Design: Pringlea, horiz.

1959 Photo. *Perf. 12½x12*

11 CD104	10fr sal, grn & yel	8.75	7.50

Common Design Types pictured following the introduction.

Light-mantled Sooty Albatross — A4

Designs: 40c, Skua, horiz. 12fr, King shag.

1959, Sept. 14 Engr. *Perf. 13*

12 A4	30c blue, grn & red brn	.55	*.85*
13 A4	40c blk, dl red brn & bl	.55	*.85*
14 A4	12fr lt blue & blk	10.00	8.00
	Nos. 12-14 (3)	11.10	9.70

Coat of Arms — A5

1959, Sept. 14 Typo. *Perf. 13x14*

15 A5	20fr ultra, lt bl & yel	13.50	11.00

Sheathbills — A6

4fr, Sea leopard, horiz. 25fr, Weddell seal at Kerguélen, horiz. 85fr, King penguin.

1960, Dec. 15 Engr. *Perf. 13*

16 A6	2fr grnsh bl, gray & choc	2.00	*2.50*
17 A6	4fr bl, dk brn & dk grn	8.00	7.75
18 A6	25fr sl grn, bis brn & blk	77.50	45.00
19 A6	85fr grnsh bl, org & blk	17.50	17.50
	Nos. 16-19 (4)	105.00	72.75

Yves-Joseph de Kerguélen-Trémarec — A7

1960, Nov. 22

20 A7	25fr red org, dk bl & brn	22.50	21.00

Yves-Joseph de Kerguélen-Trémarec, discoverer of the Kerguélen Archipelago.

Charcot, Compass Rose and "Pourquoi-pas?" — A8

1961, Dec. 26 Unwmk. *Perf. 13*
21 A8 25fr brn, grn & red 24.00 21.00

25th anniv. of the death of Commander Jean Charcot (1867-1936), Antarctic explorer.

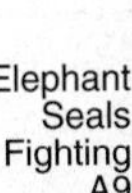

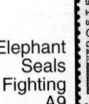

Elephant Seals Fighting A9

1963, Feb. 11 Engr. *Perf. 13*
22 A9 8fr dk blue, blk & claret 10.00 8.00

See No. C4.

Penguins and Camp on Crozet Island A10

20fr, Research station & IQSY emblem.

1963, Dec. 16 Unwmk. *Perf. 13*
23 A10 5fr blk, red brn & Prus bl 55.00 45.00
24 A10 20fr vio, sl & red brn 57.50 52.50

Intl. Quiet Sun Year, 1964-65. See No. C6.

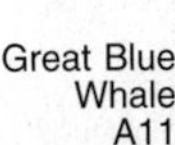

Great Blue Whale A11

Black-browed Albatross — A12

10fr, Cape pigeons. 12fr, Phylica trees, Amsterdam Island. 15fr, Killer whale (orca).

1966-69 Engr. *Perf. 13*

No.	Type	Description	Unused	Used
25	A11	5fr brt bl & indigo	18.50	12.50
26	A12	10fr sl, ind & ol brn	27.50	24.00
27	A11	12fr brt bl, sl grn & lemon	17.50	16.00
27A	A11	15fr ol, dk bl & ind	14.00	9.50
28	A12	20fr slate, ol & org	280.00	225.00
		Nos. 25-28 (5)	357.50	287.00

Issued: 5fr, 12/12; 20fr, 1/3/68; 10fr, 12fr, 1/6/69; 15fr, 12/21/69.

Aurora Australis, Map of Antarctica and Rocket — A13

1967, Mar. 4 Engr. *Perf. 13*
29 A13 20fr mag, blue & blk 22.00 20.00

Launching of the 1st space rocket from Adelie Land, Jan., 1967.

Dumont d'Urville A14

1968, Jan. 20
30 A14 30fr lt ultra, dk bl & dk brn 110.00 75.00

Jules Sébastien César Dumont D'Urville (1790-1842), French naval commander and South Seas explorer.

WHO Anniversary Issue
Common Design Type

1968, May 4 Engr. *Perf. 13*
31 CD126 30fr red, yel & bl 62.50 47.50

Human Rights Year Issue
Common Design Type

1968, Aug. 10 Engr. *Perf. 13*
32 CD127 30fr grnsh bl, red & brn 55.00 47.50

Polar Camp with Helicopter, Plane and Snocat Tractor — A15

1969, Mar. 17 Engr. *Perf. 13*
33 A15 25fr Prus bl, lt grnsh bl & brn red 19.00 11.00

20 years of French Polar expeditions.

ILO Issue
Common Design Type

1970, Jan. 1 Engr. *Perf. 13*
35 CD131 20fr org, dk bl & brn 15.00 10.00

UPU Headquarters Issue
Common Design Type

1970, May 20 Engr. *Perf. 13*
36 CD133 50fr blue, plum & ol bis 40.00 27.50

Ice Fish A16

Fish: Nos. 38-43, Antarctic cods, various species. 135fr, Zanchlorhynchus spinifer.

1971 Engr. *Perf. 13*

No.	Type	Description	Unused	Used
37	A16	5fr brt grn, ind & org	2.50	1.25
38	A16	10fr redsh brn & dp vio	3.50	1.50
39	A16	20fr dp cl, brt grn & org	4.75	2.50
40	A16	22fr pur, brn ol & mag	5.00	3.50
41	A16	25fr grn, ind & org	5.75	3.75
42	A16	30fr sep, gray & bl vio	6.00	4.50
43	A16	35fr sl grn, dk brn & ocher	6.25	3.75
44	A16	135fr Prus bl, dp org & ol grn	10.00	5.75
		Nos. 37-44 (8)	43.75	26.50

Issued: Nos. 37-39, 41-42, 1/1; Nos. 40, 43-44, 12/22.

Map of Antarctica — A17

1971, Dec. 22
45 A17 75fr red 19.00 19.00

Antarctic Treaty pledging peaceful uses of and scientific cooperation in Antarctica, 10th anniv.

Microzetia Mirabilis — A18

Insects: 15fr, Christiansenia dreuxi. 22f, Phtirocoris antarcticus. 30fr, Antarctophytosus atriceps. 40fr, Paractora drenxi. 140fr, Pringleophaga Kerguelenensis.

1972

No.	Type	Description	Unused	Used
46	A18	15fr cl, org & brn	8.50	5.50
47	A18	22fr vio bl, sl grn & yel	12.00	8.50
48	A18	25fr grn, rose lil & pur	5.25	3.50
49	A18	30fr blue & multi	15.00	9.00
50	A18	40fr dk brn, ocher & blk	7.50	4.25
51	A18	140fr bl, emer & brn	11.00	8.00
		Nos. 46-51 (6)	59.25	38.75

Issued: Nos. 48, 50-51, 1/3; Nos. 46-47, 49, 12/16.

De Gaulle Issue
Common Design Type

Designs: 50fr, Gen. de Gaulle, 1940. 100fr, Pres. de Gaulle, 1970.

1972, Feb. 1 Engr. *Perf. 13*
52 CD134 50fr brt grn & blk 17.50 13.00
53 CD134 100fr brt grn & blk 22.50 16.50

Kerguelen Cabbage — A19

Designs: 61fr, Azorella selago, horiz. 87fr, Acaena ascendens, horiz.

1972-73

No.	Type	Description	Unused	Used
54	A19	45fr multicolored	8.00	4.75
55	A19	61fr multicolored	3.00	2.50
56	A19	87fr multicolored	5.00	3.50
		Nos. 54-56 (3)	16.00	10.75

Issued: 45fr, 12/18; others, 12/13/73.

Mailship Sapmer and Map of Amsterdam Island — A20

1974, Dec. 31 Engr. *Perf. 13*
57 A20 75fr bl, blk & dk brn 6.00 5.00

25th anniversary of postal service.

Antarctic Tern — A21

Designs: 50c, Antarctic petrel. 90c, Sea lioness. 1fr, Weddell seal. 1.20fr, Kerguelen cormorant, vert. 1.40fr, Gentoo penguin, vert.

1976, Jan. Engr. *Perf. 13*

No.	Type	Description	Unused	Used
58	A21	40c multicolored	4.00	3.00
59	A21	50c multicolored	4.25	3.00
60	A21	90c multicolored	6.25	4.00
61	A21	1fr multicolored	10.00	9.25
62	A21	1.20fr multicolored	12.00	11.00
63	A21	1.40fr multicolored	13.00	11.50
		Nos. 58-63 (6)	49.50	41.75

Climbing Mount Ross — A22

James Clark Ross — A22a

1976, Dec. 16 Engr. *Perf. 13*

64 A22 30c multicolored 3.75 2.75
65 A22a 3fr multicolored 4.00 2.75

First climbing of Mount Ross, Kerguelen Island, Jan. 5, 1975.

James Cook — A23

1976, Dec. 16

66 A23 70c multicolored 10.00 9.00

Bicentenary of Capt. Cook's voyage past Kerguelen Island. See No. C46.

Commerson's Dolphins — A24

1977, Feb. 1 Engr. *Perf. 13*

67 A24 1.10fr Blue whale 5.25 3.75
68 A24 1.50fr shown 5.75 4.00

Macrocystis Algae — A25

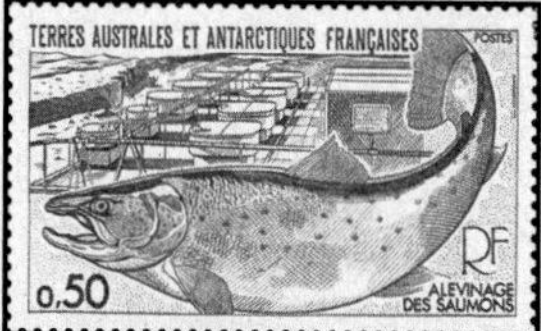

Salmon Hatchery — A26

Magga Dan — A27

Designs: 70c, Durvillea algae. 90c, Albatross. 1fr, Underwater sampling and scientists, vert. 1.40fr, Thala Dan and penguins.

1977, Dec. 20 Engr. *Perf. 13*

69 A25 40c ol brn & bis 1.20 .75
70 A26 50c dk bl & pur 1.25 1.10
71 A25 70c blk, grn & brn 1.40 1.00
72 A26 90c grn, brt bl & brn 1.50 1.10
73 A27 1fr slate 1.25 1.10
74 A27 1.20fr multi 2.50 1.75
75 A27 1.40fr multi 1.75 1.75
Nos. 69-75 (7) 10.85 8.55

See Nos. 77-79.

A28

Explorer with French and Expedition Flags.

1977, Dec. 24

76 A28 1.90fr multicolored 6.25 5.25

French Polar expeditions, 1947-48.

Types of 1977

40c, Forbin, destroyer. 50c Jeanne d'Arc, helicopter carrier. 1.40fr, Kerguelen cormorant.

1979, Jan. 1 Engr. *Perf. 13*

77 A27 40c black & blue 1.00 1.00
78 A27 50c black & blue 1.25 1.15
79 A26 1.40fr multicolored 1.25 1.25
Nos. 77-79 (3) 3.50 3.40

Raymond Rallier du Baty — A29

1979, Jan. 1

80 A29 1.20fr citron & indigo 1.10 1.00

See Nos. 97, 100, 111, 117, 129, 135, 188.

French Navigators Monument, Hobart — A30

1979, Jan. 1

81 A30 1fr multicolored .80 .75

French navigators and explorers.

Petrel — A31

Design: 70c, Rockhopper penguins, vert.

1979 Engr. *Perf. 13*

82 A31 70c multi .90 .90
83 A31 1fr shown 1.10 1.10

Commandant Bourdais — A32

Design: 1.10fr, Doudart de Lagree, vert.

1979

84 A32 1.10fr multicolored .95 .90
85 A32 1.50fr shown 1.10 1.10

Adm. Antoine d'Entrecasteaux A33

1979

86 A33 1.20fr multicolored 1.00 1.00

Sebastian de el Cano — A34

Discovery of Amsterdam Island, 1522: 4fr, Victoria, horiz.

1979

87 A34 1.40fr multicolored .85 .75
88 A34 4fr multicolored 1.75 1.40

Adelie Penguins — A35

Adelie Penguin — A36

Sea Leopard A37

1980, Dec. 15 Engr. *Perf. 13*

89 A35 50c rose violet 1.10 1.00
90 A36 60c multicolored 1.10 1.00
91 A35 1.20fr multicolored 1.75 1.25
92 A37 1.30fr multicolored 1.10 1.00
93 A37 1.80fr multicolored 1.10 1.00
Nos. 89-93 (5) 6.15 5.25

20th Anniv. of Antarctic Treaty — A38

1981, June 23 Engr. *Perf. 13*

94 A38 1.80fr multicolored 3.75 3.75

Alouette II — A39

1981-82 Engr. *Perf. 13*

95 A39 55c brown & multi .50 .45
96 A39 65c blue & multi .55 .45

Explorer Type of 1979

1981

97 A29 1.40fr Jean Loranchet .70 .50

Landing Ship Le Gros Ventre, Kerguelen — A41

1983, Jan. 3 Engr. *Perf. 13*

98 A41 55c multicolored .80 .60

Our Lady of the Winds Statue and Church, Kerguelen — A42

1983, Jan. 3

99 A42 1.40fr multicolored .80 .75

Explorer Type of 1979

Design: Martin de Vivies, Navigator.

1983, Jan. 3

100 A29 1.60fr multicolored .80 .70

Eaton's Ducks A44

1983, Jan. 3

101 A44 1.50fr multicolored .75 .55
102 A44 1.80fr multicolored .80 .75

2,30 Terres Australes et Antarctiques Françaises

Trawler Austral — A45

1983, Jan. 3

103 A45 2.30fr multicolored 1.25 1.00

Freighter Lady Franklin — A46

1983, Aug. 4 Engr. *Perf. 13*
104 A46 5fr multicolored 3.50 2.75

Glaciology — A47

Design: Scientists examining glacier, base.

1984, Jan. 1 Engr. *Perf. 13*
105 A47 15c multicolored .30 .25
106 A47 1.70fr multicolored .70 .60

Crab-eating Seal — A48

Penguins — A49

1984, Jan. 1
107 A48 60c multicolored .50 .50
108 A49 70c multicolored .40 .40
109 A49 2fr multicolored 1.10 .90
110 A48 5.90fr multicolored 1.75 1.50
Nos. 107-110 (4) 3.75 3.30

Explorer Type of 1979

1984, Jan. 1
111 A29 1.80fr Alfred Faure .80 .65

Biomass — A51

1985, Jan. 1 Engr. *Perf. 13*
112 A51 1.80fr multicolored .65 .50
113 A51 5.20fr multicolored 1.50 1.25

Emperor Penguins — A52

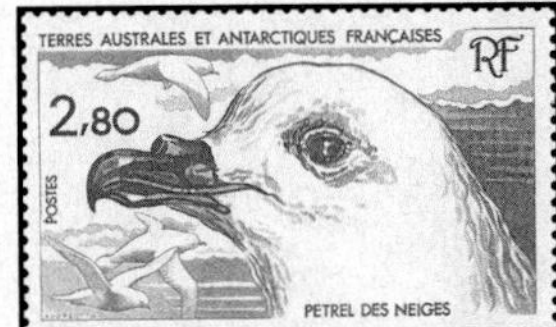

Snowy Petrel — A53

1985, Jan. 1 Engr. *Perf. 13*
114 A52 1.70fr multicolored .90 .75
115 A53 2.80fr multicolored 1.10 1.00

Port Martin — A54

1985, Jan. 1 Engr. *Perf. 13*
116 A54 2.20fr multicolored 1.10 .75

Explorer Type of 1979

1985, Jan. 1 Engr. *Perf. 13*
117 A29 2fr Andre-Frank Liotard .80 .65

Antarctic Fulmar — A56

1986, Jan. 1 Engr. *Perf. 13*
118 A56 1fr shown .50 .40
119 A56 1.70fr Giant petrels .75 .70
Nos. 118-119,C91 (3) 3.25 2.85

Echinoderms — A57

1986, Jan. 1
120 A57 1.90fr shown .85 .70

Cotula Plumosa — A58

Design: 6.20fr, Lycopodium. saururus.

1986, Jan. 1
121 A58 2.30fr shown .75 .70
122 A58 6.20fr multicolored 2.00 1.75

Shipping — A59

Designs: 2.10fr, Var research ship. 3fr, Polarbjorn support ship.

1986, Jan. 1
123 A59 2.10fr multicolored .85 .75
124 A59 3fr multicolored 1.10 1.00

Marine Life — A60

1987, Jan. 1 Engr. *Perf. 13½x13*
125 A60 50c dk blue & org .55 .45

Flora — A61

Designs: 1.80fr, Poa cookii. 6.50fr, Lichen, Neuropogon taylori.

1987, Jan. 1
126 A61 1.80fr multicolored .65 .45
127 A61 6.50fr multicolored 1.90 1.40

Marret Base, Adelie Land — A62

1987, Jan. 1
128 A62 2fr yel brn, dk ultra & lake .80 .65

Explorer Type of 1979

1987, Jan. 1
129 A29 2.20fr Adm. Mouchez .85 .65

Reindeer — A64

1987, Jan. 1
130 A64 2.50fr black 1.25 1.00

Transport Ship Eure — A65

1987, Jan. 1
131 A65 3.20fr dk ultra, Prus grn & dk grn 1.25 1.00

Macaroni Penguins — A66

1987, Jan. 1 *Perf. 13x12½*
132 A66 4.80fr multicolored 2.50 1.75

Elephant Grass — A67

1988, Jan. 1 Engr. *Perf. 13*
133 A67 1.70fr Prus grn, emer & olive .75 .60

Rev.-Father Lejay, Explorer — A68

1988, Jan. 1
134 A68 2.20fr vio, ultra & blk .85 .70

Explorer Type of 1979

Design: Robert Gessain (1907-86).

1988, Jan. 1
135 A29 3.40fr gray, dk red & blk 1.25 1.00

Le Gros Ventre, 18th Cent. — A70

1988, Jan. 1
136 A70 3.50fr dp ultra, bl grn & brn 1.25 1.10

Mermaid and B.A.P. Jules Verne, Research Vessel — A71

1988, Jan. 1
137 A71 4.90fr gray & dk blue 2.25 1.60

La Fortune, Early 19th Cent. — A72

1988, Jan. 1

138 A72 5fr blk & dull bl grn 2.00 1.60

Wilson's Petrel — A73

1988, Jan. 1

139 A73 6.80fr blk, sepia & dl bl grn 2.75 2.00

See Nos. 143-144.

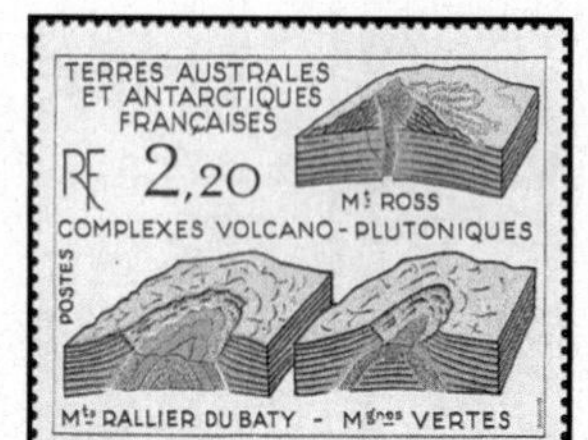

Mt. Ross Campaign (in 1987) — A74

Designs: 2.20fr, Volcanic rock cross-sections. 15.10fr, Kerguelen Is.

1988, Jan. 1 ***Perf. 13x12½***

140 A74 2.20fr multi .75 .60
141 A74 15.10fr multi 4.25 3.50
a. Pair, #140-141 + label 6.50 6.50

Darrieus System Wind Vane Electric Generator — A75

1988, Jan. 1 **Engr.** ***Perf. 13***

142 A75 1fr dark blue & blue .50 .30

Fauna Type of 1988

1989, Jan. 1 **Engr.**

143 A73 1.10fr Lithodes .35 .35
144 A73 3.60fr Blue petrel 1.40 1.10

Fern A76

Designs: Blechnum penna Marina.

1989, Jan. 1

145 A76 2.80fr multicolored 1.00 .85

Minerals A77

1989, Jan. 1

146 A77 5.10fr Mesotype 1.90 1.75
147 A77 7.30fr Analcime 2.75 2.75

Henri and Rene Bossiere, Pioneers of the Kerguelen Isls. — A78

1989, Jan. 1

148 A78 2.20fr multicolored 1.10 .65

Kerguelen Is. Sheep — A79

1989, Jan. 1 ***Perf. 13½x13***

149 A79 2fr multicolored .80 .60

Scuba Diver, Adelie Coast — A80

1989, Jan. 1

150 A80 1.70fr dk olive bis, blue & dk grn .75 .65

Map of Kerguelen Island, Protozoa and Copepod — A81

1990, Jan. 1 **Engr.** ***Perf. 13***

151 A81 1.10fr blk, brt blue & red brn .90 .50

Study of protista, Kerguelan Is.

Cattle on Farm, Sea Birds — A82

1990, Jan. 1

152 A82 1.70fr Prus blue, grn & brn blk .80 .65

Rehabilitation of the environment, Amsterdam Is.

Quoy and *Copendium decollata* — A83

1990, Jan. 1 ***Perf. 13½x13***

153 A83 2.20fr brt blue, blk & red brn .90 .70

Jean Rene C. Quoy (1790-1869), naturalist, navigator.

Dumont d'Urville (1790-1842), Explorer — A84

1990, Jan. 1

154 A84 3.60fr ultra & blk 1.50 1.00

Yellow-billed Albatross — A85

1990, Jan. 1 ***Perf. 13x12½***

155 A85 2.80fr multicolored 1.75 1.00

Aragonite A86

1990, Jan. 1

156 A86 5.10fr deep ultra & dark yel grn 2.75 2.00

Ranunculus pseudo trullifolius — A87

1990, Jan. 1 ***Perf. 13***

157 A87 8.40fr dp bl, org & emer grn 3.00 2.50

Penguin Type of Airpost 1974

1991, Jan. 1

158 AP18 50c blue grn, bl & blk .75 .45

Postal Service at Crozet Island, 30th anniv.

Moss — A88

1991, Jan. 1 ***Perf. 13x12½***

159 A88 1.70fr gray, brn & blk .80 .60

Adm. Max Douguet (1903-1989) A89

1991, Jan. 1

160 A89 2.30fr org brn, blk & bl 1.25 .90

Lighter L'Aventure — A90

1991, Jan. 1 **Engr.** ***Perf. 13***

161 A90 3.20fr brn, grn & bl 1.50 1.10

Sea Lions — A91

1991, Jan. 1 ***Perf. 13***

162 A91 3.60fr blue & ol brn 2.25 1.50

Mordenite — A92

1991, Jan. 1

163 A92 5.20fr blk, grn bl & grn 2.60 1.75

Champsocephalus Gunnari — A93

1991, Jan. 1

164 A93 7.80fr blue & green 3.00 2.50

Antarctic Treaty, 30th Anniv. — A94

1991, Jan. 1
165 A94 9.30fr ol grn & rose red 3.75 3.25

A95

Design: Colobanthus Kerguelensis.

1992, Jan. 1 Engr. *Perf. 13*
166 A95 1fr bl grn, grn & brn .85 .40

Globe Challenge Yacht Race — A96

1992, Jan. 1 Litho.
167 A96 2.20fr multicolored 1.75 1.10

Dissostichus Eleginoides — A97

1992, Jan. 1 Engr.
168 A97 2.30fr blue, ol grn & red brn 1.60 1.10

Paul Tchernia A98

1992, Jan. 1 Engr. *Perf. 13*
169 A98 2.50fr brown & green .95 .90

Capt. Marion Dufresne (1724-1772) — A99

1992, Jan. 1 Engr. *Perf. 13*
170 A99 3.70fr red, blk & bl 1.60 1.30

Supply Ship Tottan, 1951 — A100

1992, Jan. 1 Engr. *Perf. 13*
171 A100 14fr blue grn, brn & bl 5.50 4.50

WOCE Program — A101

1992, Jan. 1
172 A101 25.40fr multi 11.00 9.50

Coat of Arms — A102

1992-95 Engr. *Perf. 13*

173	A102	10c black	.25	.25
174	A102	20c greenish blue	.40	.25
175	A102	30c red	.50	.25
176	A102	40c green	.60	.25
177	A102	50c orange	.60	.25
		Nos. 173-177 (5)	2.35	1.25

Issued: 10c, 1/1/92; 20c, 30c, 1/1/93; 40c, 1/1/94; 50c, 1/2/95.
See Nos. 295-299.

Garnet A103

1993, Jan. 1 Engr. *Perf. 13*
183 A103 1fr multicolored 1.40 .35

See Nos. 194, 203, 212, 222, 235, 244, 259, 279, 300, 330.

Research Ship Marion Dufresne, 20th Anniv. — A104

1993, Jan. 1
184 A104 2.20fr multicolored 1.25 .70

Lyallia Kerguelensis A105

1993, Jan. 1
185 A105 2.30fr blue & green 1.25 .70

A106

A107

1993, Jan. 1
186 A106 2.50fr Killer whale 1.25 .80
187 A107 2.50fr Skua 6.50 1.50

A108

Design: 2.50fr, Andre Prudhomme (1930-1959), Meteorologist. 22fr, Weather station, Adelie Land.

1993, Jan. 1 *Perf. 12½x13*

188	2.50fr blue, blk & org	1.00	.75
189	22fr org, blk & bl	7.50	5.25
a.	A108 Pair, #188-189 + label	11.00	11.00

43rd Anniv. of Mèteo France in French Southern & Antarctic Territory.

Centriscops Obliquus — A109

1993, Jan. 1 *Perf. 13*
190 A109 3.40fr multicolored 1.50 1.00

Freighter Italo Marsano — A110

1993, Jan. 1
191 A110 3.70fr multicolored 1.75 .90

ECOPHY Program A111

1993, Jan. 1
192 A111 14fr black, blue & brn 6.25 3.50

L'Astrolabe on Northeast Route, 1991 A112

1993, Jan. 1
193 A112 22fr multicolored 9.00 6.25

Mineral Type of 1993

1994, Jan. 1 Engr. *Perf. 13*
194 A103 1fr Cordierite 1.25 .70

Felis Catus — A113

1994, Jan. 1
195 A113 2fr green & black 3.50 1.25

A114

1994, Jan. 1 Engr. *Perf. 13*
196 A114 2.40fr dk brn, blk & bl 1.50 .65

A115

1994, Jan. 1
197 A115 2.80fr slate blue 1.50 .80

Robert Pommier (1919-61) A116

1994, Jan. 1
198 A116 2.80fr multicolored 1.50 .85

A117

Designs: 2.80fr, C.A. Vincendon Dumoulin (1811-58), hydrographer. 23fr, Measuring Earth's magnetic field.

1994, Jan. 1 ***Perf. 12½x13***
199 2.80fr black & blue 1.50 1.00
200 23fr blue & black 7.25 5.00
a. A117 Pair, #199-200 + label 10.00 10.00

Rascasse — A119

1994, Jan. 1 ***Perf. 13***
201 A119 3.70fr bl grn & red brn 1.40 1.00

Kerguelen of Tremarec — A120

1994, Jan. 1
202 A120 4.30fr multicolored 1.75 1.25

Mineral Type of 1993

1995, Jan. 2 **Engr.** ***Perf. 13***
203 A103 1fr Olivine 1.50 .40

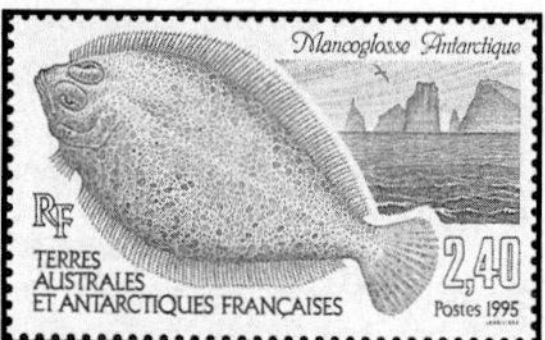

Mancoglosse Antarctique — A121

1995, Jan. 2
204 A121 2.40fr ol brn, vio & bl grn 1.25 1.00

Andree (1903-90) and Edgar de la Rue (1901-91) A122

1995, Jan. 2
205 A122 2.80fr bl, red brn & mag 1.40 .90

SODAR Station — A123

1995, Jan. 2
206 A123 2.80fr vio, mag & red brn 1.40 1.00

Mont D'Alsace — A124

1995, Jan. 2
207 A124 3.70fr dk bl, vio, red brn 1.75 1.10

Balaenoptera Acutorostrata — A125

1995, Jan. 2
208 A125 23fr blue, claret & ind 9.75 6.50

Sailing Ship Tamaris A126

1995, Jan. 2
209 A126 25.80fr multicolored 10.00 6.75

L'Heroine, Crozet Islands Mission, 1837 — A127

1995, Jan. 2
210 A127 27.30fr blue 11.00 7.25

Creation of the Territories, 40th Anniv. — A128

1995, Aug. 7 **Litho.** ***Imperf.***
Size: 143x84mm
211 A128 30fr multicolored 15.00 15.00

Mineral Type of 1993

1996, Jan. 1 **Engr.** ***Perf. 13***
212 A103 1fr Amazonite .90 .30

White-chinned Petrel — A129

1996, Jan. 1
213 A129 2.40fr blue black 1.40 .70

Expedition Ship Yves de Kerguelen — A130

1996, Jan. 1
214 A130 2.80fr multicolored 1.50 .75

Benedict Point Scientific Research Station, Amsterdam Island — A131

1996, Jan. 1
215 A131 2.80fr multicolored 1.50 .75

Paul-Emile Victor (1907-1995), Polar Explorer — A132

Designs: 2.80fr, Victor crossing Greenland with sled dogs, 1936. 23fr, Victor, penguins, Dumont d'Urville Base, Adélie Land.

1996, Jan. 1
216 A132 2.80fr multicolored 1.40 .85
217 A132 23fr multicolored 11.50 7.50
a. Pair, #216-217 + label 14.00 14.00

Admiral Jacquinot (1796-1879), Antarctic Explorer — A133

1996, Jan. 1
218 A133 3.70fr dark blue & blue 1.50 1.00

Trawler Austral — A134

1996, Jan. 1 **Photo. & Engr.**
219 A134 4.30fr multicolored 2.25 1.25

Lycopodium Magellanicum — A135

1996, Jan. 1 **Engr.**
220 A135 7.70fr multicolored 3.00 2.25

Search for Micrometeorites, Cape Prudhomme — A136

1996, Jan. 1
221 A136 15fr vio, blk & grn bl 8.00 5.00

Mineral Type of 1993

1997, Jan. 1 **Engr.** ***Perf. 13x12½***
222 A103 1fr Amethyst 1.25 .40

Storm Petrel — A137

1997, Jan. 1 ***Perf. 13***
223 A137 2.70fr blue & indigo 1.50 .80

Rene Garcia (1915-95), Windmill A138

1997, Jan. 1
224 A138 3fr multicolored 1.60 .90

Research Ship Marion Dufresne — A139

Photo. & Engr.

1997, Jan. 1 ***Perf. 13x12½***
225 A139 3fr multicolored 1.60 .90

Jean Turquet (1867-1945) — A140

1997, Jan. 1 Engr. *Perf. 13*
226 A140 4fr black & brown 1.60 1.10

A141

1997, Jan. 1
227 A141 5.20fr multicolored 2.40 1.50

Church of Our Lady of Birds, Crozet Island.

Army Health Service — A142

1997, Jan. 1
228 A142 8fr multicolored 3.75 2.50

Poa Kerguelensis A143

1997, Jan. 1
229 A143 29.20fr multi 12.50 8.50

French Polar Expeditions, 50th Anniv. — A144

Designs: No. 230, Greenland Expedition. No. 231, Port Martin, 1950-51, Marret Base, 1952, Adélie Land. No. 232, Dumont D'Urville, 1956, Charcot Station, Magnetic Pole, 1957.

Photo. & Engr.

1997, Feb. 28 *Perf. 13x12½*
230 1fr multicolored 1.10 .70
231 1fr multicolored 1.10 .70
232 1fr multicolored 1.10 .70
a. A144 Strip of 3, #230-232 8.00 6.00

Yves-Joseph de Kerguelen Trémarec (1734-97) — A145

3fr, Portrait. 24fr, Cook's landing at Kerguelen Island, Dec. 1776.

1997, Mar. 3 Engr. *Perf. 13*
233 3fr multicolored 1.25 .90
234 24fr multicolored 9.00 7.00
a. A145 Pair, #233-234 + label 14.00 11.00

No. 234 is 37x37mm.

Mineral Type of 1993

1998, Jan. 2 Engr. *Perf. 13*
235 A103 1fr Rock crystal 1.25 .40

Fisheries Management — A146

Designs: No. 236, Fishing boats. No. 237, Examining fish, performing research.

1998, Jan. 2
236 A146 2.60fr multicolored 1.40 .70
237 A146 2.60fr multicolored 1.40 .70
a. Pair, #236-237 + label 3.50 3.50

Gray-headed Albatross — A147

1998, Jan. 2
238 A147 2.70fr multicolored 1.75 .75

Ecology of St. Paul Island — A148

1998, Jan. 2
239 A148 3fr bl, brn & grn 2.25 1.00

Etienne Peau, Antarctic Explorer — A149

1998, Jan. 2 *Perf. 13x13½*
240 A149 3fr lilac, blue & black 1.75 .85

Georges Laclavere (1906-94), Geographer — A150

1998, Jan. 2
241 A150 4fr lt org, blk & red brn 1.75 1.00

Mole Shark — A151

1998, Jan. 2 *Perf. 13*
242 A151 27fr multicolored 11.00 6.75

"Le Cancalais" — A152

1998, Jan. 2
243 A152 29.20fr multicolored 11.50 7.00

Mineral Type of 1993

1999, Jan. 1 Engr. *Perf. 13*
244 A103 1fr Epidote, vert. 1.25 .40

Chinstrap Penguin — A153

1999, Jan. 1
245 A153 2.70fr brn, blk & bl 1.60 .85

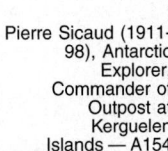

Pierre Sicaud (1911-98), Antarctic Explorer, Commander of Outpost at Kerguelen Islands — A154

1999, Jan. 1
246 A154 3fr black & green 1.25 .80

Penguins of Crozet Islands — A155

1999, Jan. 1
247 A155 3fr multicolored 3.00 .85

Jacques-André Martin (1911-49) — A156

1999, Jan. 1
248 A156 4fr multicolored 1.75 1.00

Ray — A157

1999, Jan. 1 *Perf. 12½*
249 A157 5.20fr mag, bl & brn 2.25 2.25

Value is for stamp with surrounding rectangular selvage.

F.S. Floreal — A158

1999, Jan. 1 Photo. *Perf. 13*
250 A158 5.20fr multicolored 2.25 1.75

No. 250 was printed se-tenant with label. Value is for stamp with label attached.

"Pop Cat" Program, Kerguelen Islands — A159

1999, Jan. 1 Engr.
251 A159 8fr multicolored 4.75 3.00

Study of Albatrosses on Artificial Nests A160

1999, Jan. 1
252 A160 16fr olive, grn & blk 6.50 4.25

Amsterdam Base, Kerguelen Base, 50th Anniv. — A161

Designs: 3fr, Amsterdam Base. 24fr, Kerguelen Base.

1999, Jan. 1
253 A161 3fr multi 4.50 1.00
254 A161 24fr multi 8.50 5.00
a. Pair, #253-254 + label 15.00 12.00

Festuca Contracta A162

1999, Jan. 1
255 A162 24fr dk grn, ol & bl grn 9.00 6.00

Geoleta Program — A163

1999, Jan. 1 ***Perf. 13x12½***
256 A163 29.20fr blk, bl & red brn 11.00 7.00

Voyage of Marion Dufresne II — A164

a, Docked, Reunion. b, Passengers in dining salon. c, Penguins, Crozet Island. d, Postal manager of Alfred Faure, Crozet Island, vert. e, Port of France, Kerguelen Island. f, Port Couvreux, Kerguelen Island. g, Offloading stores, Port of France, Kerguelen Island. h, Port Jeanne d'arc, Kerguelen Island. i, St. Paul Island. j, Ruins of lobster cannery, St. Paul Island. k, Martin de Vivies Base, Amsterdam Island. l, Offloading cargo, Amsterdam Island.

1999, May 1 **Litho.** ***Perf. 13***
257 A164 Souv. bklt., #a.-l. 90.00

Nos. 257a-257l are all non-denominated. Stamps are valid for 20 gram international letter rate. Each stamp appears on a separate booklet pane showing an enlarged design of the stamp. Booklet sold for 100fr.

See Nos. 294, 329, 359, 390, 420, 482, 573C.

Souvenir Sheet

PhilexFrance '99, World Philatelic Exhibition — A165

Antarctic postmarks on stamps: a, Malagasy Republic #280. b, Malagasy Republic #282. c, Malagasy Republic #C42. d, #21.

1999, July 2 **Litho. & Engr.** ***Perf. 13***
258 A165 5.20fr Sheet of 4, #a.-d. 10.00 7.50

Nos. 258b-258c are each 40x52mm.

Mineral Type of 1993

2000, Jan. **Engr.** ***Perf. 12¾x13***
259 A103 1fr Mica, *vert.* 1.25 .40

Puffin — A166

2000, Jan. ***Perf. 13x12¾***
260 A166 2.70fr multi 2.00 .80

André Beaugé (1913-97) A167

2000, Jan. ***Perf. 12¾x13***
261 A167 3fr multi 1.40 .60

Abby Jane Morrell — A168

2000, Jan. ***Perf. 13¼x13***
262 A168 4fr multi 1.75 .95

Oceanographic Survey — A169

2000, Jan. ***Perf. 13x12½***
263 A169 4.40fr multi 2.10 1.25

Sled Dog Hobbs — A170

2000, Jan. ***Perf. 12¾x13***
264 A170 5.20fr multi 2.25 1.25

Sleep Study — A171

2000, Jan. **Photo.** ***Perf. 13x12½***
265 A171 8fr multi + label 3.50 2.25

Ship "La Perouse" — A172

2000, Jan. **Engr.** ***Perf. 13x12½***
266 A172 16fr multi 7.00 4.25

Lantern Fish — A173

2000, Jan.
267 A173 24fr multi 10.50 6.00

Larose Bay — A174

2000, Jan.
268 A174 27fr multi 11.00 7.00

Explorers A175

No. 269, Yves Joseph de Kerguelen-Trémarec (1734-97). No. 270, Jules Sébastien César Dumont D'Urville (1790-1842). No. 271, Raymond Rallier du Baty (1881-1978). No. 272, Edgar Aubert de La Rüe (1901-91). #273, Paul-Emile Victor (1907-95).

2000, Jan. ***Perf. 13***

Booklet Stamps

269 A175 3fr multi 1.60 .75
270 A175 3fr multi 1.60 .75
271 A175 3fr multi 1.60 .75
272 A175 3fr multi 1.60 .75
273 A175 3fr multi 1.60 .75
a. Bklt. pane, #269-273 + 2 labels 9.00 —
Complete booklet, #273a 10.00

Souvenir Sheet

The Third Millennium — A176

No. 274: a, Penguins, Crozet Islands. b, Seals, Kerguelen Islands. c, Crustacean, Saint-Paul and Amsterdam Islands. d, Hovering vehicle, Adelie Land.

2000, Jan. **Photo.** ***Perf. 13***
274 A176 3fr Sheet of 4, #a.-d. 8.50 5.50

Bird Demographic Studies — A177

Designs: 5.20fr, Bird banding. 8fr, Albatross, graph. 16fr, Emperor penguins, graph.

2000, Jan. ***Perf. 13x13¼***
275 A177 5.20fr multi 2.00 1.00

Size: 50x28mm

276 A177 8fr multi 3.00 1.50
277 A177 16fr multi 6.50 4.00
a. Horiz. strip, #275-277 15.00 *15.00*

Relocation of Headquarters to Reunion — A178

2000, Aug. 6 **Litho.** ***Perf. 13***
278 A178 27fr multi 12.00 9.00

Mineral Type of 1993

2001, Jan. 1 **Engr.** ***Perf. 13x12¾***
279 A103 1fr Magnetite 1.25 .40

Diving Petrel — A179

2001, Jan. 1 ***Perf. 13x13¼***
280 A179 2.70fr multi 1.50 .60

High Mountain Military Group A180

2001, Jan. 1 ***Perf. 13¼x13***
281 A180 3fr multi 1.40 .65

Kerguelen Arch — A181

2001, Jan. 1 ***Perf. 13***
282 A181 3fr blue gray 2.00 .70

Xavier-Charles Richert (1913-92) — A182

2001, Jan. 1
283 A182 3fr multi 1.40 .65

Jean Coulomb — A183

2001, Jan. 1
284 A183 4fr multi 1.75 .85

Memorial to 1874 Astronomical Observation, St. Paul Island — A184

2001, Jan. 1
285 A184 8fr brn & blk 3.50 1.75

Frigate La Fayette — A185

2001, Jan. 1 *Perf. 13x13¼*
286 A185 16fr multi 7.00 3.50

Squid — A186

2001, Jan. 1
287 A186 24fr multi 10.50 5.00

Amateur Radio Link Between Space Station Mir and Crozet Island — A187

2001, Jan. 1 **Litho.** *Perf. 13*
288 A187 27fr multi 12.00 5.50

Bryum Laevigatum — A188

2001, Jan. 1 **Engr.** *Perf. 13x12½*
289 A188 29.20fr multi 13.00 6.00

Souvenir Sheet

Ships — A189

No. 290: a, Carmen. b, Austral. c, Ramuntcho. d, Samper 1.

2001, Jan. 1 *Perf. 13x13½*
290 A189 5.20fr Sheet of 4, #a-d 9.00 4.50

Souvenir Sheet

Wildlife — A190

No. 291: a, Albatrosses. b, Emperor penguins, horiz. c, Sea lions, horiz. d, Whales.

2001, Jan. 1 **Litho.** *Perf. 13*
291 A190 3fr Sheet of 4, #a-d 10.50 5.00

Antarctic Treaty, 40th Anniv. — A191

2001, June 23 **Engr.** *Perf. 13x12¾*
292 A191 5.20fr dark & sky blue 3.25 1.00

Commission for the Conservation of Antarctic Marine Living Resources, 20th Anniv. — A192

2001, Oct. 22 **Litho.** *Perf. 13*
293 A192 5.20fr multi 5.00 2.00

Voyage Booklet Type of 1999

Adélie Land: a, Boat in pack ice. b, Dumont d'Urville Base. c, Adélie penguin rookery. d, L'Astrolabe Glacier. e, Pointe Géologie Archipelago. f, Release of meteorological balloon. g, Equipment convoy. h, Helicopter transport of fresh supplies. i, Arrival of emperor penguins. j, Telecommunications center. k, Looking towards the Antarctic. l, Cape Prud'homme. m, Ship L'Astrolabe anchored. n, Dispatch of mail.

2001, Oct. 29 *Perf. 13*
294 A164 Souvenir booklet, 2 each #a-n 95.00

Nos. 294a-294n are all non-denominated. Stamps are valid for 20 gram international letter rate. Each stamp appears on a separate booklet pane showing an enlarged design of the stamp and on one pane with all of the stamps and four labels found at the center of the booklet. the booklet sold for 196.78fr.

100 Cents = 1 Euro (€)

Arms Type of 1992-95 with Euro Denominations

2002, Jan. 2 **Engr.** *Perf. 13*
295 A102 1c black .25 .25
296 A102 2c greenish blue .25 .25
297 A102 5c red .30 .25
298 A102 10c green .40 .25
299 A102 20c orange .70 .25
Nos. 295-299 (5) 1.90 1.25

Mineral Type of 1993 with Euro Denomination

2002, Jan. 2 **Engr.** *Perf. 12¾x13*
300 A103 15c Nepheline, vert. 1.00 .40

Albatross A193

2002, Jan. 2 *Perf. 13¼x13*
301 A193 41c multi 3.00 .80

Ship "Marion Dufresne" — A194

2002, Jan. 2 *Perf. 13x13¼*
302 A194 46c multi 1.40 .60

1963-83 Telegraph Station, Crozet Island A195

2002, Jan. 2 **Litho.** *Perf. 13*
303 A195 46c multi 1.50 .60

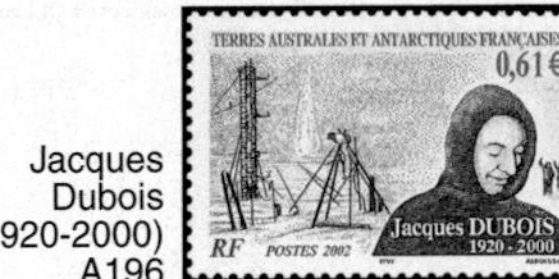

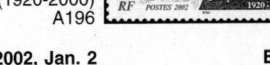

Jacques Dubois (1920-2000) A196

2002, Jan. 2 **Engr.**
304 A196 61c multi 2.25 .90

Engraved Rock, Saint Paul Island — A197

2002, Jan. 2 *Perf. 13x13¼*
305 A197 79c multi 2.40 1.25

Kerguelen Cabbage A198

2002, Jan. 2 *Perf. 12¼*
306 A198 €1.22 multi 3.50 1.75

Passage of the Ship "Gauss," Cent. — A199

2002, Jan. 2 *Perf. 13x12¼*
307 A199 €2.44 multi 7.25 3.50

Crab — A200

2002, Jan. 2 *Perf. 13x13¼*
308 A200 €3.66 multi 11.00 5.25

Pack Ice Diatoms — A201

2002, Jan. 2 **Litho.** *Perf. 13*
309 A201 €4.12 multi 12.50 6.00

French Geographic Society Building, Paris — A202

2002, Jan. 2 Engr. *Perf. 13¼x13*
310 A202 €4.45 multi + label 13.50 8.00

Cartoker Program — A203

No. 311: a, 46c, Diagram of plate tectonics. b, €3.66, Geological map of Kerguelen Island.

2002, Jan. 2 *Perf. 13x12¼*
311 A203 Horiz. pair, #a-b, + central label 12.50 12.50

Souvenir Sheet

Olympic Games for Antarctic Animals — A204

No. 312: a, Albatrosses flying marathon. b, Langoustines diving, vert. c, Penguins riding bobsled course, vert. d, Killer whales performing synchronized swimming, vert.

2002, Jan. 2 Litho. *Perf. 13*
312 A204 46c Sheet of 4, #a-d 6.50 5.50

Souvenir Sheet

Animals and Their Young — A205

No. 313: a, Penguins. b, Sea lions. c, Albatrosses. d, Elephant seals.

2002, Jan. 2
313 A205 79c Sheet of 4, #a-d 10.50 9.50

Introduction of the Euro A206

2002, Feb. 17
314 A206 46c blue & black 3.50 .60

Mineral Type of 1993

2003, Jan. Engr. *Perf. 13¼*
315 A103 15c Apatite, vert. 1.25 .40

Lobster Processing Plant, Saint-Paul — A207

2003, Jan. *Perf. 13x13¼*
316 A207 41c multi 1.25 .65

Luc Marie Bayle (1914-2000), Painter — A208

2003, Jan. Litho. *Perf. 13*
317 A208 46c multi 1.50 .70

Emperor Penguins — A209

2003, Jan.
318 A209 46c multi 2.75 .80

Otice Hydroacoustic Station — A210

2003, Jan. Engr. *Perf. 13x13¼*
319 A210 61c multi 1.90 1.00

Restoration of Port Jeanne d'Arc — A211

2003, Jan. *Perf. 13x12¼*
320 A211 79c multi 2.40 1.25

Phylica — A212

2003, Jan. *Perf. 13x13¼*
321 A212 €1.22 multi 4.50 2.25

Ship "Bougainville" A213

2003, Jan. *Perf. 13¼x13*
322 A213 €2.44 multi 7.25 4.25

Chub — A214

2003, Jan. Engr. *Perf. 13x13¼*
323 A214 €3.66 multi 11.00 6.50

Ile aux Pingouins — A215

2003, Jan. *Perf. 13x12¼*
324 A215 €3.66 black 11.00 6.50

Super Darn Antenna Array — A216

2003, Jan. *Perf. 13*
325 A216 €4.12 multi 12.50 7.00

Souvenir Sheet

Paintings Revised to Reflect a Less Southerly Antarctica — A217

No. 326: a, Triumph of Venus with fish and lobsters. b, King Louis XV and wife with penguins, vert. c, Jules Dumont d'Urville and wife in a grassy Adélie Land. d, Chevalier Yves de Kerguelin under umbrella, seal in pool, vert.

2003, Jan. Litho.
326 A217 46c Sheet of 4, #a-d 6.50 6.50

Protective Clothing — A218

Cold-weather outerwear from: a, 1898. b, 1912. c, 2002. d, 1980, e, 1996.

2003, Jan. Photo. *Perf. 13¼x13*
327 Booklet pane of 5 12.00 —
a.-e. A218 79c Any single 2.40 1.25
Booklet, #327 12.00

Voyage of the Ship "Français," Cent. — A219

2003, Aug. 31 Engr. *Perf. 13x13¼*
328 Horiz. strip of 3 15.00 13.50
a. A219 79c Capt. J.-B. Charcot 2.50 1.25
b. A219 €1.22 Ship in ice, horiz. 4.00 2.00
c. A219 €2.44 Ship in harbor, horiz. 7.50 4.25

Stamp size: Nos. 328b-328c, 49x29mm.

Voyage Booklet Type of 1999

Recipes: a, Truite aus deux citrons (trout and waterfall). b, Veau d'Amsterdam à la savoyarde (cattle). c, Lapin "Volage" à la cannelle (rabbits, penguins). d, Rôti de légine de l'ile de l'est (fish). e, Civet de renne "Volcan du diable," (reindeer). f, Iles antarctiques flottantes. g, Langouste à la mode de Saint-Paul (lobster). h, Gigot de mouflon aux 5 épices et aux pommes (sheep). i, Cabot tropical (fish, ship). j, Tagine d'agneau aux épices de la Réunion (sheep). k, Moules au pastis (mussels). l, Glace à la menthe sauvage d'Amsterdam (mint plant).

2003, Nov. 6 Litho. *Perf. 13*
329 A164 Souvenir booklet, #a-l 60.00

Nos. 329a-329l are all non-denominated. Stamps are valid for 20 gram international letter rate. Each stamp appears on a separate booklet pane showing an enlarged design of the stamp. The booklet sold for €17.

Mineral Type of 1993

2004, Jan. 1 Engr. *Perf. 13¼*
330 A103 15c Chalcedony, vert. 1.25 .40

A220

2004, Jan. 1 Engr. *Perf. 13x13¼*
331 A220 45c multi 1.40 .85

Mario Marret, director of film "Terre Adélie."

Col. Robert Genty (1910-2001) A221

2004, Jan. 1
332 A221 50c multi 1.75 .95

Albert Faure Base, Crozet Island, 40th Anniv. — A222

2004, Jan. 1 Litho. & Engr.
333 A222 50c multi 1.50 .95

Péron's Dolphins — A223

2004, Jan. 1 Litho. *Perf. 13*
334 A223 75c multi 3.00 1.50

Twin Otter Flights A224

2004, Jan. 1 Photo. *Perf. 12¾*
335 A224 90c multi 2.75 1.75

Values are for stamps with surrounding selvage.

Iceberg — A225

2004, Jan. 1 Engr. *Perf. 13x13¼*
336 A225 €1.30 multi 4.00 2.40

Grave of Sailors from the Volage — A226

2004, Jan. 1 *Perf. 13¼x13*
337 A226 €2.50 multi 7.50 5.00

Krill — A227

2004, Jan. 1 *Perf. 13x13¼*
338 A227 €4 multi 12.00 8.00

Ship "Dives" — A228

2004, Jan. 1
339 A228 €4.50 multi 13.50 9.25

Souvenir Sheet

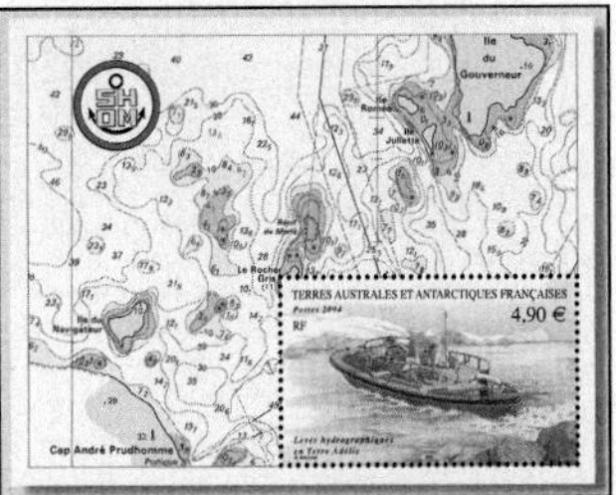
Hydrological Surveys, Adélie Land — A229

2004, Jan. 1 Litho. *Perf. 13*
340 A229 €4.90 multi 15.00 10.50

Souvenir Sheet

Imaginary "TAAFland" Theme Park — A230

No. 341: a, Whale statue, pyramidal entrance structure. b, Showgirls, seals, vert. c, Boy and girl with ice cream cones, vert. d, Woman in swimsuit, penguins.

2004, Jan. 1
341 A230 50c Sheet of 4, #a-d 8.00 8.00

Souvenir Sheet

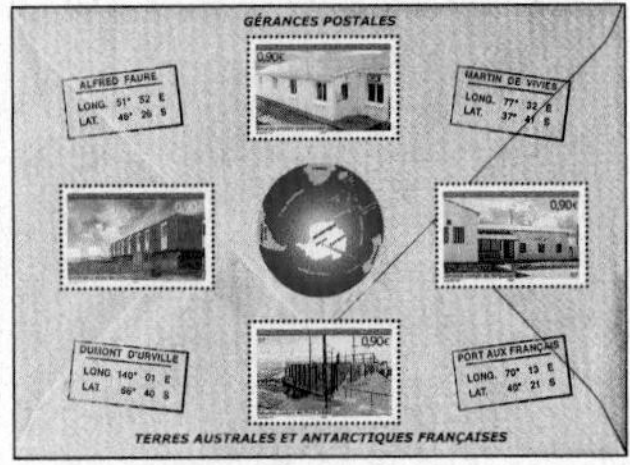
Post Offices — A231

No. 342: a, Amsterdam Island. b, Crozet Island. c, Kerguelen Island. d, Adélie Land.

2004, Jan. 1
342 A231 90c Sheet of 4, #a-d 12.00 12.00

Penguin and Liberty Cap — A232

2004, June 26 Engr. *Perf. 13¼x13*
343 A232 €4.50 multi 15.00 7.00

Mineral Type of 1993

2005, Jan. 1 Engr. *Perf. 13¼*
344 A103 15c Agate .80 .50

Albert Bauer (1916-2003), Glaciologist — A233

2005, Jan. 1 *Perf. 13x13¼*
345 A233 45c multi 2.00 1.75

Roger Barberot (1915-2002), Administrator A234

2005, Jan. 1
346 A234 50c multi 2.00 2.00

Ship "Cap Horn" — A235

2005, Jan. 1
347 A235 50c multi 2.00 2.00

Seal Pot A236

2005, Jan. 1 Litho. *Perf. 13*
348 A236 50c multi 2.25 2.25

Macgillivray's Prion — A237

2005, Jan. 1 Engr. *Perf. 13x13¼*
349 A237 75c multi 2.75 2.75

Studer Valley — A238

2005, Jan. 1 *Perf. 13x12½*
350 A238 90c multi 3.00 3.00

Peigne des Néréides A239

2005, Jan. 1 ***Perf. 12¼***
351 A239 €2.50 multi 8.00 7.50

Harpovoluta Charcoti — A240

2005, Jan. 1 ***Perf. 13x12½***
352 A240 €4 multi 14.00 14.00

Murray's Ray — A241

2005, Jan. 1 **Litho.** ***Perf. 13***
353 A241 €4.50 multi 14.00 14.00

Elephant Seal and Oceanographic Chart — A242

2005, Jan. 1 **Engr.**
354 A242 €4.90 multi 16.00 16.00

Concordia Station — A243

2005, Jan. 3 **Litho.** ***Perf. 13***
355 A243 50c multi 1.75 1.75

Return of the Ship "Français," Cent. — A244

2005, Mar. 4 **Engr.** ***Perf. 13x13¼***
356 A244 €4.50 multi + label 15.00 15.00

Disappearance of Paul-Emile Victor, 10th Anniv. — A245

2005, Mar. 7 **Litho.** ***Perf. 13***
357 A245 50c multi 2.50 2.50

50th Anniversary Coat of Arms — A246

2005, Aug. 6
358 A246 (90c) multi 3.00 3.00
a. Booklet pane of 1 4.00 —

No. 358a is found in No. 359.

Voyage Booklet Type of 1999

History: a, Discovery of Amsterdam Island, 1522. b, Discovery of Crozet Island, 1772. c, Discovery of Kerguelen Island, 1772, vert. d, Discovery of Adélie Land, 1840. e, Astronomers viewing 1874 transit of Venus on St. Paul Island. f, Wreck of the Strathmore, 1875. g, Port Jeanne d'Arc, 1908. h, Port-Couvreux, 1925. i, Building of Port-Martin, 1950. j, Antarctic Treaty, 1959. k, Building of fourth base, 1963-64.

2005, Aug. 6 **Litho.** ***Perf. 13***
359 A164 Souvenir booklet, #a-k, 358a 70.00

Nos. 359a-359k are all non-denominated. Stamps are valid for 90c, the 20 gram international letter rate. Each stamp appears on a separate booklet pane showing an enlarged design of the stamp. The booklet sold for €18.

Penguins and No. 1 — A247

2005, Nov. 2
360 A247 90c multi 3.25 3.25

French Southern & Antarctic Territories, 50th anniv.

Souvenir Sheet

Maps — A248

Maps of: a, Crozet Archipelago. b, Amsterdam and St. Paul Islands. c, Kerguelen Island. d, Adélie Land.

Litho. & Engr.

2005, Nov. 10 ***Perf. 13x13¼***
361 A248 50c Sheet of 4, #a-d 6.50 6.50

French Southern & Antarctic Territories, 50th anniv.

Rutile A249

2006, Jan. 1 **Engr.** ***Perf. 13x12½***
362 A249 15c multi .80 .80

Charles Vélain (1845-1925), Geologist — A250

2006, Jan. 1 ***Perf. 13x13¼***
363 A250 48c pur & red 1.60 1.60

Albert Seyrolle (1887-1919), Mariner — A251

2006, Jan. 1
364 A251 53c multi 1.60 1.60

Amsterdam Island Garden — A252

2006, Jan. 1 **Litho.** ***Perf. 13***
365 A252 53c multi 1.60 1.60

Ship "Osiris" — A253

2006, Jan. 1 **Photo.** ***Perf. 13x13¼***
366 A253 90c multi 3.00 3.00

Dumont d'Urville Base, 50th Anniv. — A254

2006, Jan. 1 **Engr.** ***Perf. 13x12½***
367 A254 90c multi 2.75 2.75

Virgin of the Seal Hunters — A255

2006, Jan. 1 ***Perf. 12½x13***
368 A255 €2.50 multi 7.50 7.50

Lagenorhynchus Cruciger — A256

2006, Jan. 1 ***Perf. 13x13¼***
369 A256 €4 multi 12.00 12.00

Keguelen Hake — A257

2006, Jan. 1
370 A257 €4.53 multi 13.50 13.50

Amsterdam Island Carbon Dioxide Measurements, 25th Anniv. — A258

2006, Jan. 1
371 A258 €4.90 multi 15.00 15.00

Miniature Sheet

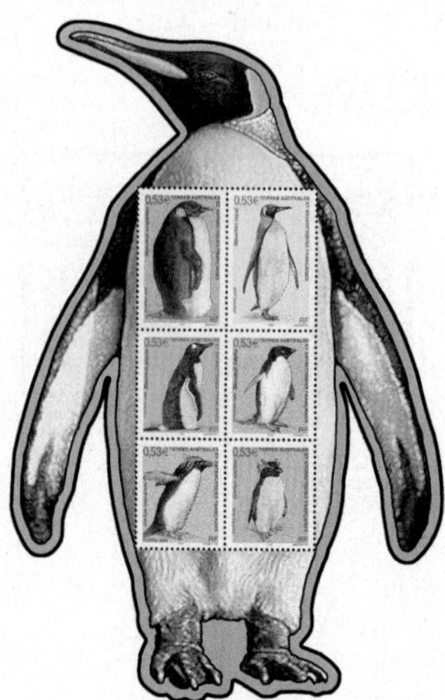

Penguins — A259

No. 372 — Penguin (background color): a, Emperor penguin (lilac, 22x36mm). b, King penguin (pale yellow green, 22x36mm). c, Gentoo penguin (green, 22x27mm). d, Adélie penguin (pink, 22x27mm). e, Macaroni penguin (orange, 22x27mm). f, Rockhopper penguin (blue, 22x27mm).

Litho. & Engr.

2006, Jan. 1 *Perf. 13*

372 A259 53c Sheet of 6, #a-f 12.00 12.00

Souvenir Sheet

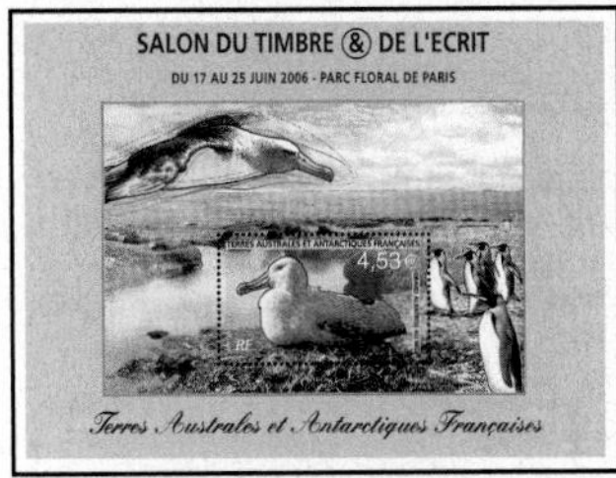

Albatross — A260

Litho. & Engr.

2006, June 1 *Perf. 13*

373 A260 €4.53 multi 14.50 14.50

Souvenir Sheet

Albatross — A261

Litho. & Engr.

2006, Nov. 8 *Perf. 13*

374 A261 90c multi 3.50 3.50

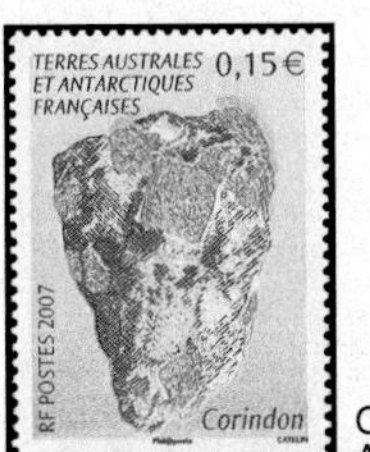

Corundum A262

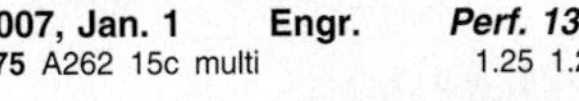

2007, Jan. 1 **Engr.** *Perf. 13¼*

375 A262 15c multi 1.25 1.25

A263

2007, Jan. 1 *Perf. 13x13¼*

376 A263 49c multi 1.50 1.50

Louis-Francois Aleno de Saint Aloüarn (1738-72), explorer who claimed Australia for France.

A264

2007, Jan. 1

377 A264 54c multi 1.60 1.60

Marthe Emmanuel (1901-97), assistant to explorer Jean Charcot.

Cattle, Amsterdam Island — A265

2007, Jan. 1 *Perf. 13x12½*

378 A265 54c multi 1.50 1.50

Ship Tonkinois — A266

2007, Jan. 1 *Perf. 13x13¼*

379 A266 90c multi 2.50 2.50

Ile de la Baleine — A267

2007, Jan. 1 *Perf. 13x12½*

380 A267 90c multi 2.50 2.50

Archaeology on Saint Paul Island — A268

2007, Jan. 1 *Perf. 12½x13*

381 A268 €2.50 multi 7.00 7.00

Lampris Immaculatus — A269

2007, Jan. 1 *Perf. 13x12½*

382 A269 €4 multi 11.00 11.00

Astonomy at Concordia — A270

Litho. & Engr.

2007, Jan. 1 *Perf. 13*

383 A270 €4.90 multi 14.00 14.00

French Polar Expeditions, 60th Anniv. — A271

No. 384: a, Expedition headquarters, Paris, men shaking hands over globe. b, Expedition headquarters.

2007, Jan. 1 **Engr.** *Perf. 13x13¼*

384 Horiz. pair + central label 13.50 13.50

a. A271 54c multi 1.75 1.75

b. A271 €4 multi 11.00 11.00

Miniature Sheet

Albatrosses — A272

No. 385: a, Amsterdam albatross. b, Great albatross (Grand albatros). c, Black-browed albatross (Albatros à sourcils noir). d, Yellow-beaked albatross (Albatros à bec jaune). e, Sooty albatross (Albatros fuligineux).

Litho. & Engr.

2007, Jan. 1 *Perf. 13*

385 A272 54c Sheet of 5, #a-e 8.00 8.00

Intl. Polar Year — A273

No. 386: a, Penguins. b, Map of Antarctica, French Southern & Antarctic Territories #9.

2007, Mar. 1 **Litho.** *Perf. 13*

386 Horiz. pair + central label 15.00 15.00

a. A273 90c multi 2.75 2.75

b. A273 €4 multi 12.00 12.00

Audit Office, Bicent. A274

2007 Mar. 19 **Engr.** *Perf. 13¼*

387 A274 90c multi 4.50 4.50

Miniature Sheet

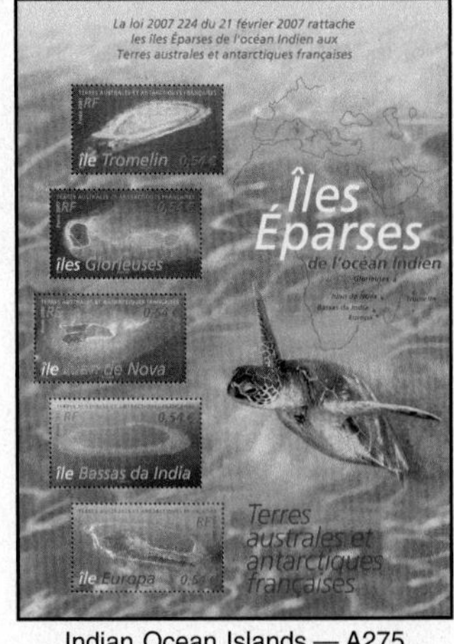

Indian Ocean Islands — A275

No. 388: a, Ile Tromelin. b, Iles Glorieuses. c, Ile Juan de Nova. d, Ile Bassas da India. e, Ile Europa.

2007, May 10 **Photo.** *Perf. 13x13¼*

388 A275 54c Sheet of 5, #a-e 9.00 9.00

Path of Sun on June 21 Over Dumont d'Urville Base — A276

2007, June 21

389 A276 90c multi 3.00 3.00

Voyage Booklet Type of 1999

No. 390 — Photographs of land features: a, Apostle Island, Crozet Archipelago. b, Chamonix Lake, Kerguelen Island. c, Phylicia forest, Amsterdam Island. d, Gulf of Morbihan, Kerguelen Islands. e, Mount Cook, Chamonix Lake and glacier, Kerguelen Islands. f, Tourbiéres Plateau, Amsterdam Island. g, Nuageuses Islands, Kerguelen Islands. h, Caldera, Amsterdam Island. i, Mount Cook, Kerguelen Island. j, Central Plateau, Kerguelen Island. k, Isle of Penguins, Crozet Archipelago. l, Antonelli Crater, Amsterdam Island. m, Lake on Possession Island, Crozet Archipelago. n, Rocks off Apostle Island, Crozet Archipelago. o, Geographic Society Peninsula, Kerguelen Island. p, Ronarch Peninsula, Kerguelen Island.

2007, Nov. 8 **Litho.** *Perf. 13*

390 A164 (90c) Souvenir booklet, #a-p 70.00

No. 390 sold for €20, and contains four panes, consisting of a block of four stamps of Nos. 390a-390d, 390e-390h, 390i-390l, and 390m-390p.

French Southern and Antarctic Territories Flag — A277

2008, Jan. 1 **Litho.** *Perf. 13*

Background Color

391	A277	1c black	.25	.25
392	A277	2c blue	.35	.35
393	A277	5c red	.40	.40
394	A277	10c green	.40	.40
395	A277	20c brn orange	.80	.80
		Nos. 391-395 (5)	2.20	2.20

Spinel — A278

2008, Jan. 1 **Engr.** *Perf. 13¼*

396 A278 15c multi .80 .45

Samivel (1907-92), Writer — A279

2008, Jan. 1 ***Perf. 13x13¼***
397 A279 54c grn & brown 1.60 1.60

St. Paul Island — A280

2008, Jan. 1
398 A280 54c blue & dk blue 1.60 1.60

Construction of Port Jeanne d'Arc, Cent. — A281

2008, Jan. 1 ***Perf. 13x12¾***
399 A281 90c multi 2.75 2.75

Rockhopper Penguins — A282

2008, Jan. 1 ***Perf. 13x12½***
400 A282 90c multi 2.75 2.75

Shipwreck of L'Esperance — A283

2008, Jan. 1 Litho. ***Perf. 13x12¾***
401 A283 90c multi 2.75 2.75

Macrourus Carinatus — A284

2008, Jan. 1 Engr. ***Perf. 13x12½***
402 A284 €4 multi 12.00 12.00

Galium Antarcticum A285

2008, Jan. 1 ***Perf. 12½x13***
403 A285 €4.54 multi 13.50 13.50

Adélie Land Coastal Ichthyology Program A286

2008, Jan. 1 Litho. ***Perf. 13***
404 A286 €4.90 multi 14.50 14.50

Souvenir Sheet

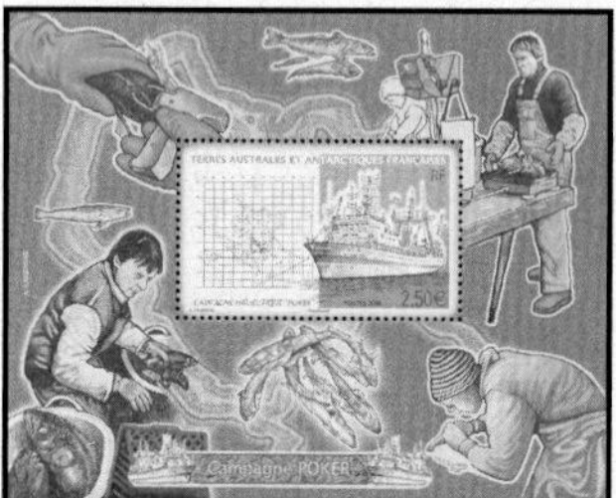

Kerguelen Fish Biomass Evaluation Project (POKER) — A287

2008, Jan. 1 Litho. & Engr.
405 A287 €2.50 multi 7.50 7.50

Souvenir Sheet

Elephant Seals — A288

No. 406: a, Head of adult female. b, Seals initiating combat. c, Juvenile seal. d, Head of adult male.

2008, Jan. 1
406 A288 54c Sheet of 4, #a-d 6.50 6.50

Gérard Mégie (1946-2004), Ozone Researcher — A289

2008, Feb. 15 Engr. ***Perf. 13x13¼***
407 A289 54c multi 1.75 1.75

Miniature Sheet

Birds — A290

No. 408: a, Sooty tern (Sterne fulgineuse). b, Red-footed booby (Fou a pieds rouges), vert. c, Masked booby (Fou masque), vert. d, Great frigatebird (Fregate du Pacifique), vert. e, Tropicbird (Paille en queue).

Perf. 13¼x13 (#408a, 408e), 13x13¼
2008, June 1 Litho. & Engr.
408 A290 54c Sheet of 5, #a-e 8.50 8.50

Earth and Birds — A291

2008, June 14 Photo. ***Perf. 13***
409 A291 €4.54 multi 14.50 14.50

Ship Marion Dufresne — A292

2008, Nov. 6 Litho. ***Perf. 13***
410 A292 (55c) multi 1.75 1.75

Compare with type A194.

Pyrite A293

2009, Jan. 1 Engr. ***Perf. 13¼***
411 A293 15c multi .60 .60

A294

2009, Jan. 1 ***Perf. 13x13¼***
412 A294 55c multi 1.60 1.60

Henri Paschal de Rochegude (1741-1834), naval officer.

A295

2009, Jan. 1 ***Perf. 13***
413 A295 55c multi 1.60 1.60

Charles Gaston Rouillon (1915-2007), director of French polar scientific expeditions.

Residence de France Seal of Kerguelen Islands, Cent. — A296

2009, Jan. 1 **Litho.**
414 A296 90c multi 2.50 2.50

Shark With Dorsal Spines — A297

2009, Jan. 1 Engr. ***Perf. 13x12½***
415 A297 €2.50 multi 7.00 7.00

Ship Jeanne d'Arc — A298

2009, Jan. 1
416 A298 €4 multi 11.00 11.00

MACARBI Program Scallop Research A299

2009, Jan. 1 ***Perf. 12½x13***
417 A299 €4.55 multi 13.00 13.00

Seaweed — A300

No. 418: a, Himantothallus grandifolius and iceberg. b, Laminaria pallida and seals.

2009, Jan. 1 *Perf. 13x13¼*
418 Horiz. pair + central label 13.50 13.50
a. A300 90c multi 2.50 2.50
b. A300 €4 multi 11.00 11.00

Miniature Sheet

Petrels — A301

No. 419: a, Soft-plumaged petrel (Petrel soyeux). b, Wilson's petrel (Petrel de Wilson). c, Gray petrel (Petrel gris). d, Diving petrel (Petrel plongeur). e, Snow petrel (Petrel des neiges).

Litho. & Engr.

2009, Jan. 1 *Perf. 13¼x13*
419 A301 55c Sheet of 5, #a-e 7.75 7.75

Voyage Booklet Type of 1999

No. 420 — Photographs: a, Frigatebirds, Europa Island. b, Beach on north coast of Europa Island. c, Mangroves, Europa Island. d, Flagpole, palm trees, Europa Island. e, Turtle on beach, Juan de Nova Island. f, Sandbanks off Juan de Nova Island. g, Tree, Juan de Nova Island. h, Grounded ship, Juan de Nova Island. i, Brown noddies, Glorioso Islands. j, Flower, Glorioso Islands. k, Pool of water, Glorioso Islands. l, Tree on islet, Glorioso Islands. m, Birds, Tromelin Island. n, Meteorological station, Tromelin Island. o, Coral fossil, Tromelin Island. p, Anchor, Tromelin Island.

2009, Nov. 5 **Litho.** *Perf. 13*
420 A164 (90c) Souvenir booklet, #a-p 65.00

No. 420 sold for €21.50, and contains four panes, consisting of a block of four stamps of Nos. 420a-420d, 420e-420h, 420i-4290l, and 420m-420p.

Antarctic Treaty, 50th Anniv. — A302

2009, Dec. 1 **Engr.** *Perf. 13x13¼*
421 A302 56c multi 1.75 1.75

Tourmaline A303

2010, Jan. 2 **Engr.** *Perf. 13¼*
422 A303 28c multi .80 .80

Dr. Jean Rivolier (1923-2007), Medical Researcher — A304

2010, Jan. 2 **Litho.** *Perf. 13*
423 A304 56c multi 1.60 1.60

Birds on Ile du Lys — A305

2010, Jan. 2 **Engr.** *Perf. 13x13¼*
424 A305 56c multi 1.60 1.60

Patureau House, Juan de Nova Island — A306

2010, Jan. 2
425 A306 56c multi 1.60 1.60

Program Crac-ice — A307

2010, Jan. 2
426 A307 90c multi 2.50 2.50

Supply Ship Ile St. Paul — A308

2010, Jan. 2
427 A308 €1.35 multi 3.75 3.75

Crozet Orca — A309

2010, Jan. 2
428 A309 €2.80 multi 7.75 7.75

Kerguelen Terns — A310

2010, Jan. 2
429 A310 €4.30 multi 12.00 12.00

Miniature Sheet

Sea Lions of Amsterdam Island — A311

No. 430: a, Sea lion and ship. b, Two sea lions on rocks, denomination at UR in black, horiz. c, Sea lion, denomination at UL in black, horiz. d, Two sea lions near water, denomination in white at UR, horiz. e, Two sea lions, denomination at LL in black, horiz.

Litho. & Engr.

2010, Jan. 2 *Perf. 13*
430 A311 56c Sheet of 5, #a-e 7.75 7.75

Miniature Sheet

Polar Transportation — A312

No. 431: a, Team of dogs pulling sled. b, Weasel M29C. c, Sno-cat 743. d, HB40-Castor. e, Challenger 65. f, PB 330.

2010, Jan. 2
431 A312 90c Sheet of 6, #a-f 15.00 15.00

Gabriel Pavilion, Paris — A313

2010, May 28 **Litho.** *Perf. 13*
432 A313 56c multi 1.40 1.40

Second Elysée Philatelic Club Show, Paris.

Miniature Sheet

Albatross Protection — A314

No. 433: a, Albatross and chick on nest. b, Albatross facing left. c, Albatross facing right. d, Two juvenile albatrosses.

Litho. & Engr.

2010, June 12 *Perf. 13*
433 A314 56c Sheet of 4, #a-d 5.75 5.75

French Southern & Antarctic Territories Booth at Espace Champerret Stamp Show — A315

2010, Nov. 5 **Litho.** *Perf. 13*
434 A315 56c multi 3.00 3.00

Self-Adhesive

Serpentine Die Cut 11

435 A315 56c multi 3.00 3.00

Astronomical Observatory, Concordia Base, Antarctica and Southern Cross — A316

Litho. & Engr.

2011, Jan. 2 *Perf. 13*
436 A316 56c multi 1.50 1.50

Martin de Viviès Base, Amsterdam Island — A317

2011, Jan. 2 **Engr.** *Perf. 13x13¼*
437 A317 90c multi 2.40 2.40

Josef Enzensperger (1873-1903), Meteorologist A318

2011, Jan. 2 *Perf. 13¼x13*
438 A318 90c multi 2.40 2.40

André Chastain (1906-62), Botanist A319

2011, Jan. 2
439 A319 €1.35 multi 3.75 3.75

Sheathbills — A320

2011, Jan. 2 *Perf. 13x13¼*
440 A320 €1.35 black & purple 3.75 3.75

Artedidraco Orianae — A321

2011, Jan. 2
441 A321 €1.35 multi 3.75 3.75

Cruiser Lapérouse — A322

2011, Jan. 2
442 A322 €4.30 multi 11.50 11.50

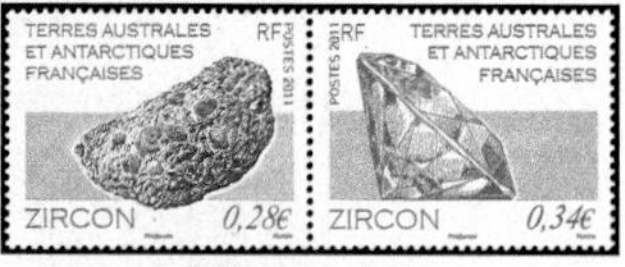

Zircons — A323

No. 443: a, Zircons embedded in rock. b, Cut and polished zircon.

Litho. & Engr.

2011, Jan. 2 ***Perf. 13¼***
443 A323 Horiz. pair 1.75 1.75
a. 28c multi .75 .75
b. 34c multi .90 .90

December 8, 1929 Mail Plane Crash — A324

No. 444: a, Farman F190 airplane. b, Map of flight. c, Crew and crash covers.

2011, Jan. 2 ***Perf. 13***
444 Horiz. strip of 3 7.75 7.75
a. A324 56c multi 1.50 1.50
b. A324 90c multi 2.40 2.40
c. A324 €1.35 multi 3.75 3.75

Miniature Sheet

Whales — A325

No. 445: a, Baleine à bosse (humpback whale). b, Baleine franche australe (southern right whale). c, Cachalot (sperm whale). d, Rorqual de Rudolphi (sei whale).

2011, Jan. 2
445 A325 56c Sheet of 4, #a-d 6.00 6.00

Patrol Boat Osiris — A326

2011, Apr. 1 **Litho.**
446 A326 (60c) multi 1.75 1.75

Gentoo Penguins — A327

2011, June 15 **Litho.** ***Perf. 13***
447 A327 €1 multi + label 3.00 3.00

Orré House (Prefect's Residence), St. Pierre, Reunion — A328

2011, Sept. 19
448 A328 60c multi 1.75 1.75

Souvenir Sheet

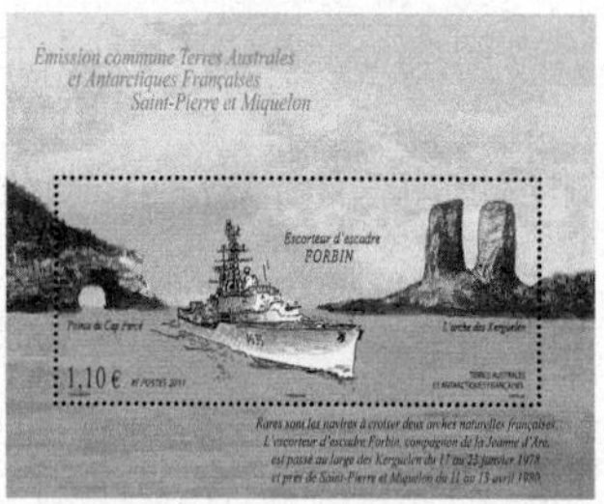

Squadron Escort Forbin — A329

2011, Nov. 3 **Litho. & Engr.**
449 A329 €1.10 multi 3.00 3.00

See St. Pierre & Miquelon No. 938.

Adélie Penguins — A330

2011, Dec. 2 **Litho.** ***Perf. 13***
450 A330 60c multi 1.60 1.60

Penguin Breeding Grounds, Baie du Marin, Crozet Island — A331

Views of Baie du Marin in: No. 451, 60c, 1961. No. 452, 60c, 2011.

2011, Dec. 23 ***Perf. 13x13¼***
451-452 A331 Set of 2 3.25 3.25

Ship Marion Dufresne in Mamoudzou Lagoon — A332

Serpentine Die Cut 11

2011, Dec. 31 **Self-Adhesive**
453 A332 60c multi 1.60 1.60

See Mayotte No. 288.

Notodiscus Hookeri — A333

2012, Jan. 2 **Engr.** ***Perf. 13x13¼***
454 A333 60c multi 1.60 1.60

Ship Marius Moutet — A334

2012, Jan. 2
455 A334 60c multi 1.60 1.60

Weddell Seals — A335

2012, Jan. 2 ***Perf. 13¼x13***
456 A335 €1 multi 2.60 2.60

Roald Amundsen (1872-1928), Polar Explorer A336

2012, Jan. 2
457 A336 €1 multi 2.60 2.60

René-Emile Bossière (1857-1941), Kerguelen Island Business Entrepreneur A337

2012, Jan. 2
458 A337 €1.45 multi 3.75 3.75

Lepidonotothen Larseni — A338

Litho. & Silk-screened

2012, Jan. 2 ***Perf. 13***
459 A338 €2.40 multi 6.25 6.25

Diopside — A339

No. 460: a, Crystals. b, Crystal and cut stone.

2012, Jan. 2 **Engr.** ***Perf. 13¼***
460 A339 Horiz. pair 1.75 1.75
a. 29c red & green .80 .80
b. 36c red & green .95 .95

Point Molloy, Kerguelen Island — A340

No. 461: a, Buildings at Point Molloy. b, Molloy seismological station, 1953-63.

Litho. & Engr.

2012, Jan. 2 ***Perf. 13x13¼***
461 Horiz. pair 3.25 3.25
a.-b. A340 60c Either single 1.60 1.60

Military Presence in French Southern & Antarctic Territories — A341

No. 462: a, Second Regiment of Marine Infantry Parachutists on Europa Island. b, Detachment of the Mayotte Foreign Legion on the Glorioso Islands.

Litho. & Silk-screened

2012, Jan. 2 ***Perf. 13***
462 Horiz. pair 3.25 3.25
a.-b. A341 60c Either single 1.60 1.60

Miniature Sheet

Derelict Whaling Station, Port-Jeanne d'Arc, Kerguelen Island — A342

No. 463: a, Eight storage tanks. b, Three boilers, vert. c, Two storage silos. d, House, vert.

2012, Jan. 2 **Photo.**
463 A342 60c Sheet of 4, #a-d 6.25 6.25

Miniature Sheet

Nature Reserve Flora and Fauna — A343

No. 464: a, Gentoo penguin (manchot papou). b, White-chinned petrel (petrel a menton blanc). c, Lyallia kerguelensis. d, Anatalanta aptera.

2012, Jan. 2 Litho. & Engr.

464	A343	Sheet of 4	8.50	8.50
a.		20c multi	.55	.55
b.		60c multi	1.60	1.60
c.		€1 multi	2.60	2.60
d.		€1.45 multi	3.75	3.75

Miniature Sheet

Aircraft Used in Polar Regions — A344

No. 465: a, B-24 Liberator. b, DC-4 Skymaster. c, Nord 2501 Noratlas. d, C-130 Hercules. e, DC-3 Basler BT-67. f, DHC-6 Twin Otter.

2012, Jan. 2
465 A344 €1 Sheet of 6, #a-f 16.00 16.00

Ile Longue, Kerguelen Islands A345

No. 466: a, 60c, Painting. b, €1, Painting, diff.

2012, Apr. 13 Litho. *Perf. 13x13¼*
466 A345 Pair, #a-b 4.25 4.25

No. 466 was printed in sheets containing two pairs.

Souvenir Sheet

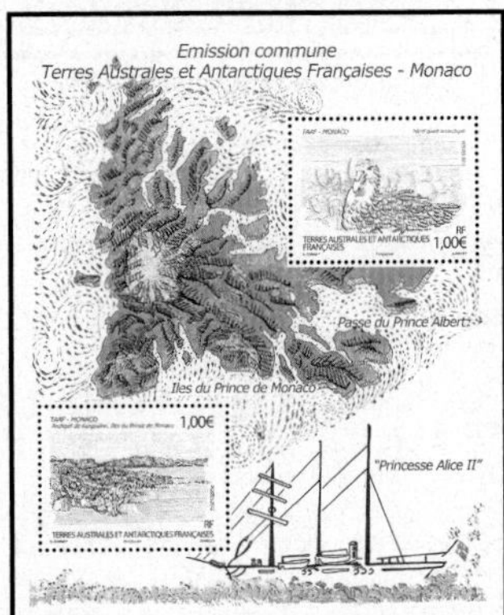

Prince of Monaco Islands — A346

No. 467: a, Giant Antarctic petrel. b, Coastline of Prince of Monaco Islands.

Litho. & Engr.

2012, June 9 *Perf. 13¼*
467 A346 €1 Sheet of 2, #a-b 5.00 5.00

See Monaco No. 2680.

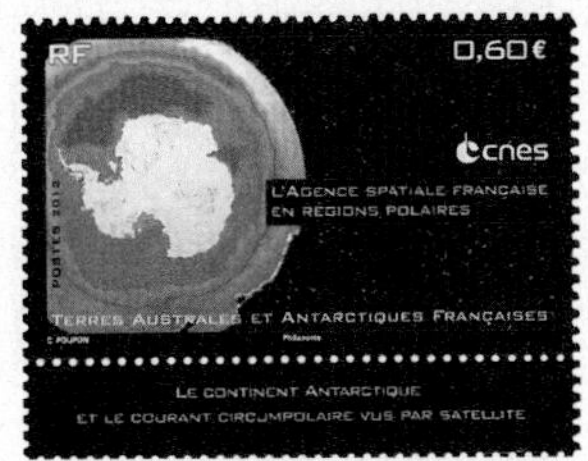

National Space Studies Center (CNES) Projects — A347

No. 468: a, Map of Antarctica. b, Penguin with tracking devices. c, Galileo satellite. d, Scientists deploying weather balloon. e, Pleaides satellite.

2012, June 9 Photo. *Perf. 13*

468		Vert. strip of 5 + 5 labels	12.00	12.00
a.-b.	A347	60c Either single + label	1.50	1.50
c.-d.	A347	€1 Either single + label	2.50	2.50
e.	A347	€1.45 multi + label	3.75	3.75

French Polar Institute, 20th Anniv. — A348

2012, July 12 Litho. *Perf. 13¼x13*
469 A348 60c multi 1.50 1.50

Souvenir Sheet

Bridge for Tracking Adélie Penguins — A349

Litho. & Engr.

2012, Nov. 2 *Perf. 13¼x13*
470 A349 €2 multi 5.25 5.25

Flight of Maryse Hilsz to Juan de Nova Island, 80th Anniv. — A350

No. 471: a, Airplane, map of route. b, Hilsz (1901-46) in airplane.

2012, Nov. 8 Litho. *Perf. 13*

471	A350	Horiz. pair	4.25	4.25
a.		60c multi	1.60	1.60
b.		€1 multi	2.60	2.60

Prasiola Crispa and Penguins — A351

2013, Jan. 1 Engr. *Perf. 13x13¼*
472 A351 65c multi 1.75 1.75

Charles Petitjean (1914-88), Pilot — A352

2013, Jan. 1 *Perf. 12½x13*
473 A352 65c multi 1.75 1.75

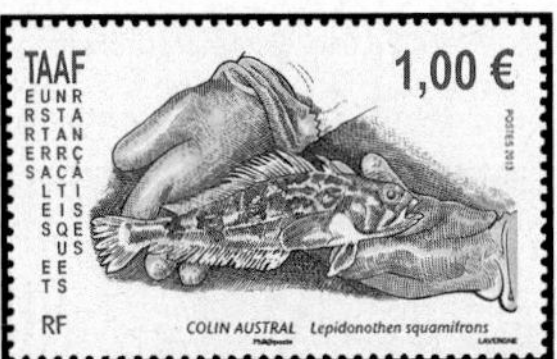

Lepidonothen Squamifrons — A353

2013, Jan. 1 *Perf. 13x13¼*
474 A353 €1 multi 2.75 2.75

Sailboat "Le Mischief" A354

2013, Jan. 1 *Perf. 12¼*
475 A354 €1 multi 2.75 2.75

Douglas Mawson (1882-1958), Antarctic Explorer, Huts and Penguins — A355

Litho. & Engr.

2013, Jan. 1 *Perf. 13*
476 A355 €1.45 multi 4.00 4.00

Bernard-Marie Boudin, Chevalier de Tromelin (1735-1816), Explorer and Colonial Administrator — A356

2013, Jan. 13 Litho.
477 A356 €2.40 multi 6.50 6.50

Hematite — A357

2013, Jan. 1 Engr. *Perf. 13¼*

478	A357	Horiz. pair	2.75	2.75
a.		40c Crystals	1.10	1.10
b.		60c Crystal	1.60	1.60

Miniature Sheet

Eaton's Pintail — A358

No. 479: a, Duck in water. b, Heads of two ducks, vert. c, Duck and egss. d, Head of duck, ducks in flight.

Litho. & Engr.

2013, Jan. 1 *Perf. 13*

479	A358	Sheet of 4	9.00	9.00
a.		20c multi	.55	.55
b.		60c multi	1.60	1.60
c.		€1 multi	2.75	2.75
d.		€1.45 multi	4.00	4.00

Miniature Sheet

Helicopters — A359

No. 480: a, Sud-Ouest Djinn 1221. b, Bell 47 G2. c, Hiller 360. d, Sud-Est Alouette II 3130. e, Écureuil AS 350. f, Panther AS 565

2013, Jan. 1
480 A359 €1 Sheet of 6, #a-f 16.00 16.00

Souvenir Sheet

Engravings of Amsterdam and St. Paul Islands — A360

2013, Jan. 1 Litho.
481 A360 €3.40 multi 9.00 9.00

Voyage Booklet Type of 1999

No. 482: a, Ship Astrolabe near Dumont d'Urville Station. b, The Astrolabe, helicopter and Adélie penguins. c, Astrolabe docked near Lion landing strip. d, Four Adélie penguins at Dumont d'Urville station. e, View of Dumont d'Urville Station taken from the Astrolabe. f, Aerial view of Dumont d'Urville Station. g, Aurora Australis. h, Colony of Emperor penguins. i, Five men and plow at Cap Prudhomme Base. j, Aerial view of Cap Prudhomme Base, island at right. k, View of Cap Prudhomme Base, island at center. l, Two penguins. m, Italian, French and European Union flags at Concordia Base. n, Snow vehicle moving containers. o, Astronomical equipment near Concordia Base. p, Steps leading to containers.

2013, Apr. 5 Litho. *Perf. 13*
482 A164 (€1) Souvenir booklet, #a-p 65.00

No. 482 sold for €25 and contains four panes, consisting of a block of four stamps of Nos. 482a-482d, 482e-482h, 482i-482l, and 482m-482p.

F.S. Floreal — A361

2013, Apr. 5 Litho. *Perf. 13*

483 A361 (63c) multi 1.75 1.75

A362

Silhouettes of Emblems — A363

Designs: 1c, Green turtle. 2c, Helicopter. 3c, Penguin. 4c, Ship "Marion Dufresne." 63c, Green turtle, helicopter, penguin, ship, "TAAF."

2013, Apr. 29 Engr. *Perf. 13*

484 A362 1c dk bl & bl .25 .25
485 A362 2c purple .25 .25
486 A362 3c dk grn & yel grn .25 .25
487 A362 4c brn org & org .25 .25

Litho. & Silk-screened

Perf. 13¼

488 A363 63c multi 1.75 1.75
Nos. 484-488 (5) 2.75 2.75

See Nos. 504-507, 568a.

Souvenir Sheet

Engraver, Map, Penguin — A364

Engr. (Litho. Margin)

2013, May 17 *Perf. 13*

489 A364 €5 multi 13.50 13.50

Souvenir Sheets

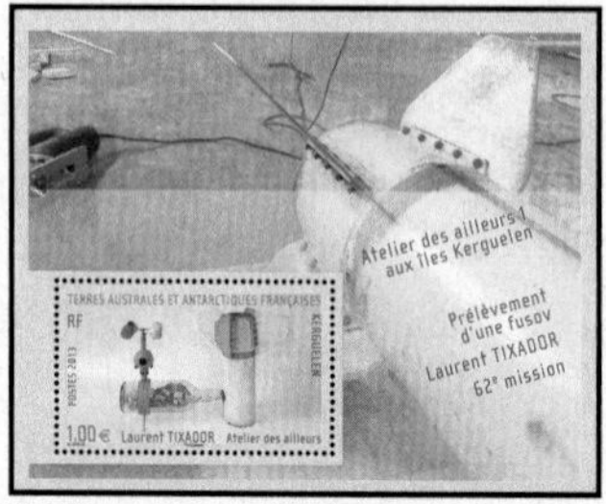

Prélèvement d'une Fusov, by Laurent Tixador — A365

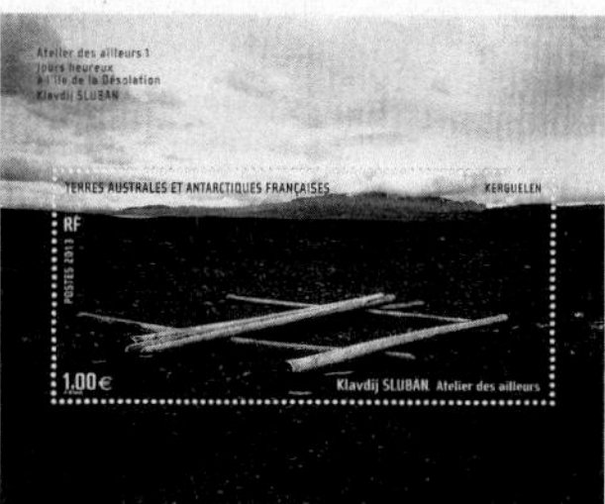

Jours Heureux à l'Ile de la Désolation, by Klavdij Sluban — A366

2013, June 17 Litho. *Perf. 13*

490 A365 €1 multi 2.75 2.75
491 A366 €1 black 2.75 2.75

Ateliers des Ailleurs art project.

Souvenir Sheet

Whale and Stock Certificate for Kerguelen Fisheries Society — A367

2013, Nov. 6 Litho. *Perf. 13¼x13*

492 A367 €1 multi 2.75 2.75

Louis Jacquinot (1898-1993), Minister of Overseas France — A368

2014, Jan. 2 Engr. *Perf. 13¼x13*

493 A368 66c multi 1.90 1.90

Bertrand Imbert (1924-2011), Leader of French Research for International Geophysical Year — A369

2014, Jan. 2 Engr. *Perf. 12¾x13*

494 A369 66c multi 1.90 1.90

Tromelin Meteorological Station, 60th Anniv. — A370

2014, Jan. 2 Engr. *Perf. 13x13¼*

495 A370 €1.55 multi 4.25 4.25

Rock Carvings of Amsterdam Island — A371

2014, Jan. 2 Engr. *Perf. 13x13¼*

496 A371 €1.55 multi 4.25 4.25

Supply Ship "Le Malin" — A372

2014, Jan. 2 Litho. *Perf. 13*

497 A372 €1.55 multi 4.25 4.25

Bren Carrier on Kerguelen Island — A373

2014, Jan. 2 Engr. *Perf. 13x13¼*

498 A373 €2 multi 5.50 5.50

White Tower (Basalt Columns), Crozet Islands — A374

2014, Jan. 2 Litho. *Perf. 13*

499 A374 €2 multi 5.50 5.50

Lepidonotothen Mizops — A375

2014, Jan. 2 Engr. *Perf. 13x13¼*

500 A375 €2.40 multi 6.50 6.50

Fluorite — A376

No. 501: a, Polished stones. b, Crystal.

2014, Jan. 2 Litho. *Perf. 13*

501 A376 Horiz. pair 2.75 2.75
a. 37c multi 1.00 1.00
b. 63c multi 1.75 1.75

Miniature Sheet

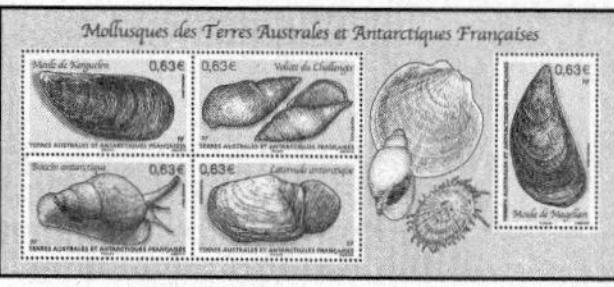

Mollusks — A377

No. 502: a, Moule de Kerguelen (Kerguelen mussel). b, Volute de Challenger (Challenger volute). c, Moule de Magellan (Magellan mussel), vert. d, Buccin antarctique (Antarctic whelk). e, Laternule antarctique (Antarctic clam).

Litho. & Engr.

2014, Jan. 2 *Perf. 13*

502 A377 63c Sheet of 5, #a-e 8.75 8.75

Miniature Sheet

Birds — A378

No. 503: a, Damier du Cap (Cape petrels). b, Manchot royal de Crozet (Crozet Island king penguins). c, Fulmar antarctique (Antarctic fulmars). d, Grand albatros de Crozet (Wandering albatrosses).

2014, Jan. 2 Engr. *Perf. 13x12¾*

503 A378 Sheet of 4 11.00 11.00
a.-b. 66c Either single 1.90 1.90
c. €1.05 multi 2.75 2.75
d. €1.55 multi 4.25 4.25

Silhouette of Emblems Type of 2013 and

Silhouettes of Emblems — A379

A362 designs as before.
€7, Map of District of Crozet, dolphin, penguin, ship, "TAAF."

2014, Mar. 7 Litho. *Perf. 13*

Dated "2014"

504 A362 1c dk bl & bl .25 .25
a. Litho. & silk-screened (varnish on silhouette), dated "2015" .25 .25
b. As "a," dated "2016" .25 .25
505 A362 2c purple .25 .25
a. Litho. & silk-screened (varnish on silhouette), dated "2015" .25 .25
b. As "a," dated "2016" .25 .25
506 A362 3c dk grn & yel grn .25 .25
a. Litho. & silk-screened (varnish on silhouette), dated "2015" .25 .25
b. As "a," dated "2016" .25 .25
c. Pair, #505b-506b .25 .25
507 A362 4c brn org & org .25 .25
a. Litho. & silk-screened (varnish on silhouette), dated "2015" .25 .25
b. As "a," dated "2016" .25 .25
c. Pair, #504b, 507b .25 .25

Litho. & Silk-Screened

Perf. 13¼

508 A379 €7 multi 19.00 19.00
Nos. 504-508 (5) 20.00 20.00

Issued: Nos. 504a, 505a, 506a, 507a, 3/19; Nos. 504b, 505b, 506b, 507b, 3/30/16. See No. 568b.

Miniature Sheet

Commerson's Dolphins — A380

No. 509: a, 63c, Dolphin sticking head out of water. b, 66c, Three dolphins underwater. c, 66c, Dolphin breaching surface. d, €1.05, Dolphin above water.

Litho. & Engr.

2014, June 26 ***Perf. 13¼x13***
509 A380 Sheet of 4, #a-d 8.25 8.25

Map of Madagascar to Tromelin Flight — A381

AAC-1 Toucan — A382

AAC-1 Toucan and Stamped Cover from Tromelin — A383

2014, Sept. 21 **Litho.** ***Perf. 13***
510 Horiz. strip of 3 8.50 8.50
a. A381 66c multi 1.75 1.75
b. A382 €1.05 multi 2.75 2.75
c. A383 €1.55 multi 4.00 4.00

First flight between Madagascar and Tromelin, 50th anniv.

Green Turtle A384

2014, Oct. 9 **Litho.** ***Perf. 13x13¼***
511 A384 €1.05 multi 2.60 2.60

See Comoro Islands No. , France No. 4695, Malagasy Republic No. 1637, Mauritius No. 1144, Seychelles No. 904.

Gendarmes — A385

No. 512 — Gendarme on: a, Iles Eparses. b, Iles Kerguelen.

Litho. & Silk-Screened

2014, Oct. 16 ***Perf. 13***
512 Horiz. pair + central label 3.50 3.50
a.-b A385 66c Either single 1.75 1.75

Souvenir Sheet

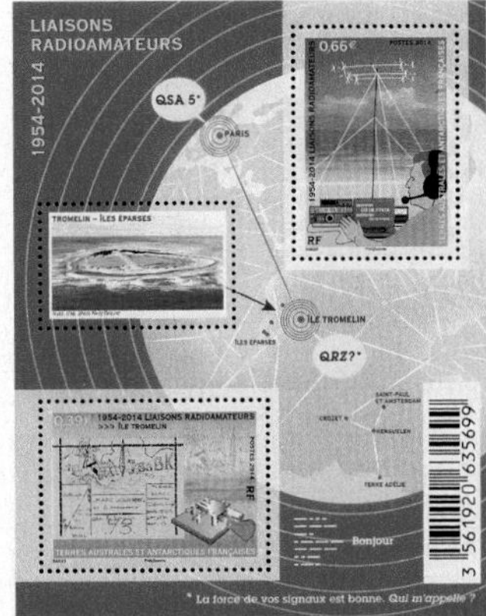

Amateur Radio — A386

No. 513: a, QSL card, radio key, amateur radio antenna on Tromelin Island. b, Radio operator, radio and antenna, vert.

Perf. 13x13¼, 13¼x13

2014, Nov. 6 **Litho.**
513 A386 Sheet of 2 2.75 2.75
a. 39c multi 1.00 1.00
b. 66c multi 1.75 1.75

Decauville Hopper Cars on Juan de Nova Island — A387

2015, Jan. 1 **Engr.** ***Perf. 13x13¼***
514 A387 66c multi 1.60 1.60

Euphausia Superba — A388

Litho. & Engr.

2015, Jan. 1 ***Perf. 13¼***
515 A388 66c multi 1.60 1.60

Emperor Penguin A389

2015, Jan. 1 **Litho.** ***Perf. 13***
516 A389 €1 multi 2.40 2.40

Leopard Seal in Adélie Land — A390

2015, Jan. 1 **Engr.** ***Perf. 13¼x13***
517 A390 €1.05 multi 2.60 2.60

Ship Radioleine — A391

2015, Jan. 1 **Engr.** ***Perf. 13x13¼***
518 A391 €2.40 multi 5.75 5.75

Antarctic Terns — A392

Litho. & Engr.

2015, Jan. 1 ***Perf. 13***
519 A392 €4.30 multi 10.50 10.50

Insects — A393

Designs: 66c, Amalopteryx maritima. €2, Ectemnorhinus vanhoeffenianus, horiz.

2015, Jan.1 **Litho.** ***Perf. 13¼***
520-521 A393 Set of 2 6.50 6.50

Beryl — A394

No. 522: a, Polihsed gemstones. b, Crystals in matrix.

Litho. & Engr.

2015, Jan. 1 ***Perf. 13***
522 A394 Horiz. pair 2.40 2.40
a. 34c multi .80 .80
b. 66c multi 1.60 1.60

Snowmobile Transport — A395

No. 523: a, Snowmobile pulling cargo. b, Snowmobile without cargo.

2015, Jan. 1 **Litho.** ***Perf. 13¼***
523 Horiz. pair 4.25 4.25
a. A395 66c multi 1.60 1.60
b. A395 €1.05 multi 2.60 2.60

Robert Guillard (1919-2013), Polar Explorations Chief of Operations — A396

No. 524 — Guillard and: a, Ship and penguins, Adélie Land. b, Expedition vehicles, Greenland.

2015, Jan. 1 **Engr.** ***Perf. 13x13¼***
524 Horiz. pair + central label 4.25 4.25
a. A396 66c multi 1.60 1.60
b. A396 €1.05 multi 2.60 2.60

Miniature Sheet

Fish — A397

No. 525: a, Chaenodraco wilsoni. b, Chaenodraco myersi. c, Pagetopsis macropterus. d, Pagetopsis maculatus.

2015, Jan. 1 **Engr.** ***Perf. 13***
525 A397 Sheet of 4 9.75 9.75
a.-b. 66c Either single 1.60 1.60
c. €1.05 multi 2.60 2.60
d. €1.55 multi 3.75 3.75

Paul-Emile Victor (1907-95), Polar Explorer — A398

2015, Mar. 7 **Engr.** ***Perf. 13x12½***
526 A398 €1 multi 2.25 2.25

Silhouettes of Saint-Paul & Amsterdam District Emblems — A399

Litho. & Silk-Screened

2015, Mar. 19 ***Perf. 13¼***
527 A399 50c multi 1.10 1.10

See No. 568d.

François Tabuteau (1921-2000), Polar Explorer — A400

2015, Apr. 17 **Litho.** ***Perf. 13***
528 A400 80c multi 1.90 1.90

French Southern and Antarctic Territories, 60th Anniv. — A401

No. 529 — Ship and: a, Airplane, seal, bird, turtle. b, Helicopter, birds, fish, killer whales. c, Penguins and birds in flight.

2015, July 14 Litho. *Perf. 13*
529 Horiz. strip of 3 5.25 5.25
a.-c. A401 80c Any single 1.75 1.75

People Stranded Without Supplies on Saint Paul Island, 1930 — A402

2015, Sept. 18 Engr. *Perf. 13*
530 A402 €1 multi 2.25 2.25

Ship *Marion Dufresne,* 20th Anniv. — A403

2015 Litho. & Engr. *Perf. 13*
Denomination Color
531 A403 80c red 1.90 1.90
532 A403 €1.35 blue 3.00 3.00

Issued: 80c, 10/4; €1.35, 11/5.

Souvenir Sheet

Penguin on Floating Ice — A404

Litho. & Embossed
2015, Nov. 5 *Perf. 13½x13*
533 A404 €1.24 multi 2.75 2.75

Ships A405

No. 534: a, Croix du Sud I. b, Albius. c, Le Saint-Andre. d, Mascareignes III. e, Ile de la Reunion. f, Cap Horn I. g, Ile Bourbon.

Litho. & Engr.
2015, Dec. 3 *Perf. 13*
534 Booklet pane of 7 19.50 —
a.-g. A405 €1.24 Any single 2.75 2.75
Complete booklet, #534 19.50

Lozère Waterfall A406

2016, Jan. 2 Engr. *Perf. 13¼x13*
535 A406 50c multi 1.10 1.10

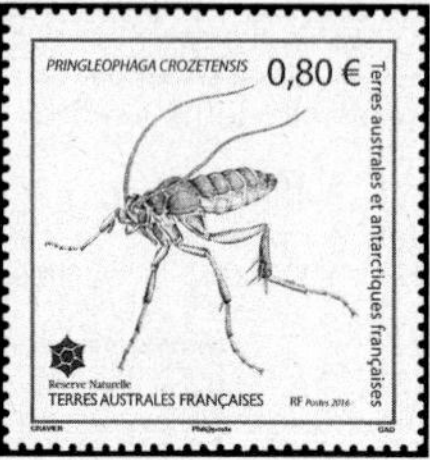

Pringleophaga Crozetensis — A407

2016, Jan. 2 Engr. *Perf. 12¼*
536 A407 80c black 1.75 1.75

Serge Frolow, Director of Meteorological Service — A408

2016, Jan. 2 Litho. *Perf. 13*
537 A408 80c multi 1.75 1.75

Point d'Entrecasteaux — A409

2016, Jan. 2 Engr. *Perf. 13x13¼*
538 A409 €1.05 multi 2.40 2.40

Valdivia, Ship From 1898-99 German Deep Sea Expedition — A410

2016, Jan. 2 Engr. *Perf. 13x12½*
539 A410 €1.24 multi 2.75 2.75

Jean Volot (1921-2012), Polar Expedition Engineer and Priest — A411

2016, Jan. 2 Engr. *Perf. 12½x13*
540 A411 €1.35 multi 3.00 3.00

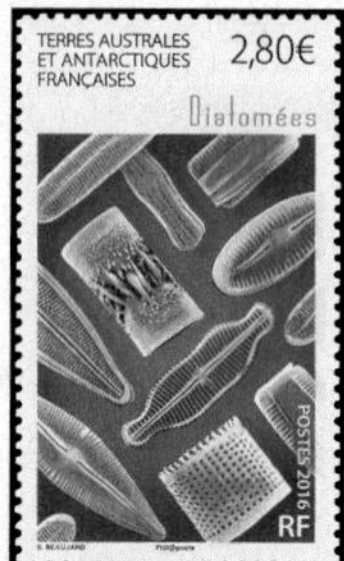

Diatoms — A412

Litho. & Silk-Screened
2016, Jan. 2 *Perf. 13*
541 A412 €2.80 multi 6.25 6.25

Schooner Rêve and Grave of Raoul Fleurié — A413

2016, Jan. 2 Engr. *Perf. 13x13¼*
542 A413 €2.80 multi 6.25 6.25

Sphene — A414

No. 543: a, Polished and cut gemstones. b, Crystal.

Litho. & Silk-Screened
2016, Jan. 2 *Perf. 13*
543 A414 Horiz. pair 2.25 2.25
a. 20c multi .50 .50
b. 80c multi 1.75 1.75

Kerguelen Island — A415

No. 544: a, Whaling. b, Ships from *The Ice Sphinx,* by Jules Verne. c, Cormoran-Vert Hostel, Christmas Harbor.

2016, Jan. 2 Litho. *Perf. 13*
544 Horiz. strip of 3 7.50 7.50
a. A415 80c cream & black 1.75 1.75
b. A415 €1.24 cream & black 2.75 2.75
c. A415 €1.35 cream & black 3.00 3.00

Souvenir Sheet

Flyovers of the Kerguelen Islands — A416

No. 545: a, RRS Discovery. b, De Havilland Gipsy Moth seaplane.

2016, Jan. 2 Litho. *Perf. 13*
545 A416 Sheet of 2 2.75 2.75
a. 44c multi 1.00 1.00
b. 80c multi 1.75 1.75

Miniature Sheet

Fish — A417

No. 546: a, Histiodraco velifer (52x41mm). b, Dolloidraco longedorsalis (60x27mm). c, Pogonophryne phyllopogon (60x27mm). d, Pogonophryne cf. barsukovi (52x31mm).

2016, Jan. 2 Engr. *Perf. 13*
546 A417 Sheet of 4 9.00 9.00
a.-b. 80c Either single 1.75 1.75
c. €1.05 multi 2.40 2.40
d. €1.35 multi 3.00 3.00

Miniature Sheet

Birds — A418

No. 547: a, Fulmar antarctique (Antarctic fulmar). b, Petrel geant (giant petrel), horiz. c, Damier du cap (cape petrel), horiz. d, Skua, horiz.

Litho. & Engr.
2016, Jan. 2 *Perf. 13*
547 A418 Sheet of 4 9.00 9.00
a. 70c multi 1.50 1.50
b. 80c multi 1.75 1.75
c. €1.05 multi 2.40 2.40
d. €1.45 multi 3.25 3.25

Silhouettes of Kerguelen District Emblems — A419

Litho. & Silk-Screened
2016, Mar. 31 *Perf. 13¼*
548 A419 80c multi 1.90 1.90

See No. 568c.

No. 2 and Rockhopper Penguin — A420

2016, May 19 Litho. *Perf. 13*
549 A420 €2 multi + label 4.50 4.50

Paris Philex 2016.

Souvenir Sheet

Albatrosses — A421

2016, May 21 Litho. *Perf. 13¼x13*
550 A421 €1 multi 2.25 2.25

Bernard Duboys de Lavigerie (1934-2008), Ionosphere Researcher A422

2016, Oct. 1 Engr. *Perf. 13¼x13*
551 A422 80c multi 1.90 1.90

Souvenir Sheet

Fillod Prefabricated Buildings In French Southern & Antarctic Territories, 60th Anniv. — A423

No. 552 — Prefabricated building and: a, Penguins. b, Ferdinand Fillod (1891-1956), building manufacturer.

Litho. & Embossed

2016, Nov. 3 *Perf. 13*
552 A423 Sheet of 2 9.25 9.25
a. €1.60 blue 3.50 3.50
b. €2.70 blue 5.75 5.75

Cirque du Château, Kerguelen Island — A424

2016, Nov. 25 Litho. *Perf. 13*
553 A424 50c multi 1.10 1.10

Cabins Near the Mortadella, Kerguelen Island — A425

2017, Jan. 2 Litho. *Perf. 13*
554 A425 80c multi 1.75 1.75

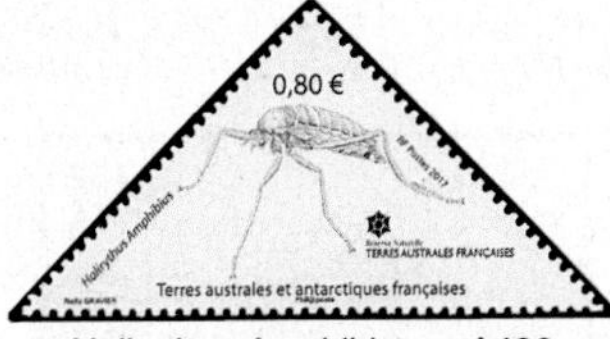

Halirythus Amphibius — A426

2017, Jan. 2 Litho. *Perf. 13x13¼*
555 A426 80c multi 1.75 1.75

1696 Landing of Willem de Vlamingh on Saint Paul and Amsterdam Islands — A427

2017, Jan. 2 Litho. *Perf. 13*
556 A427 €1 multi 2.10 2.10

Turborotalita Quinqueloba — A428

Photo. & Embossed

2017, Jan. 2 *Perf. 13¼*
557 A428 €1.24 multi 2.60 2.60

Values are for stamps with surrounding selvage.

Challenger 8 Tractor — A429

2017, Jan. 2 Engr. *Perf. 13x13¼*
558 A429 €1.24 multi 2.60 2.60

RV Ob, Flagship of 1956 Soviet Antarctic Expedition at Kerguelen Island — A430

2017, Jan. 2 Engr. *Perf. 13x13¼*
559 A430 €1.24 multi 2.60 2.60

Amalopteryx Maritima — A431

2017, Jan. 2 Engr. *Perf. 13x13¼*
560 A431 €1.55 multi 3.25 3.25

Slaves Abandoned on Tromelin Island After 1761 Shipwreck — A432

Litho. & Engr.

2017, Jan. 2 *Perf. 13x13¼*
561 A432 €1.55 multi 3.25 3.25

Pyroxene — A433

No. 562: a, Crystal. b, Polished and cut stones.

Litho. & Silk-Screened

2017, Jan. 2 *Perf. 13*
562 A433 Horiz. pair 2.25 2.25
a. 20c multi .45 .45
b. 80c multi 1.75 1.75

Founders of French Polar Expeditions — A434

Polar Expedition Port-Martin Station, Adélie Land — A435

2017, Jan. 2 Engr. *Perf. 13x13¼*
563 Horiz. pair + central label 4.50 4.50
a. A434 80c multi 1.75 1.75
b. A435 €1.24 multi 2.60 2.60

Souvenir Sheet

CASA CN-235 Over Island — A436

2017, Jan. 2 Litho. *Perf. 13*
564 A436 €3.90 multi 8.25 8.25

Souvenir Sheet

Tuna Fishing — A437

No. 565: a, Albacore tuna. b, Fishing trawler.

Litho. & Engr.

2017, Jan. 2 *Perf. 13*
565 A437 Sheet of 2 2.60 2.60
a. 44c multi .85 .85
b. 80c multi 1.75 1.75

Miniature Sheet

Gygis Alba — A438

No. 566: a, Two terns, blue background, vert. b, Chick, green background. c, Head of tern facing forward, blue background. d, Head of tern facing left, red background.

Litho. & Engr.

2017, Jan. 2 *Perf. 13*
566 A438 Sheet of 4 7.00 7.00
a.-d. 85c Any single 1.75 1.75

Miniature Sheet

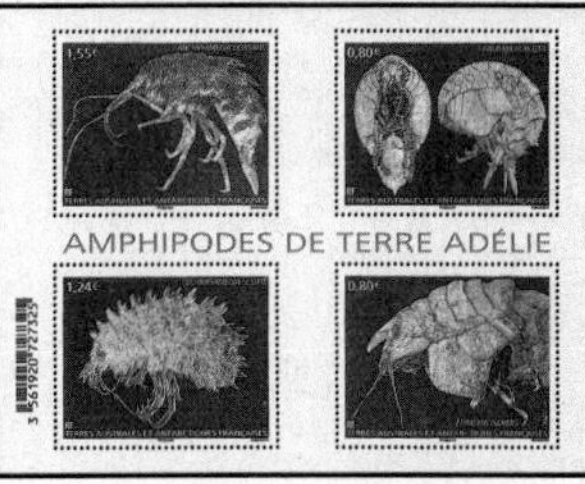

Amphipods — A439

No. 567: a, Epimeria robusta. b, Epimeria inermis. c, Echiniphimedia scotti. d, Anchiphimedia dorsalis.

2017, Jan. 2 Engr. *Perf. 13*
567 A439 Sheet of 4 9.50 9.50
a.-b. 80c Either single 1.75 1.75
c. €1.24 multi 2.60 2.60
d. €1.55 multi 3.25 3.25

Silhouettes of Emblems Types of 2013-16

Miniature Sheet

2017, Mar. 9 Litho. *Perf. 13*
568 Sheet of 4 16.00 16.00
a. A363 (€1.24) multi 4.00 4.00
b. A379 (€1.24) multi 4.00 4.00
c. A419 (€1.24) multi 4.00 4.00
d. A399 (€1.24) multi 4.00 4.00

No. 568 sold for €7.50. Nos. 568a-568d are each inscribed "Lettre 20g tarif international."

Ship Marion Dufresne — A440

Litho. & Engr.

2017, May 12 *Perf. 13*
569 A440 (€1.24) multi 2.75 2.75

Ship L'Astrolabe — A441

2017, Oct. 9 Engr. *Perf. 13x13¼*
570 A441 €1.30 multi 3.00 3.00

Birds of the Arctic and Antarctic — A442

Designs: €1.41, Stercorarius maccormicki. €3.63, Aptenodytes forsteri.

No. 573: a, Like No. 571. b, Like No. 572.

Litho. & Engr.

2017, Oct. 27 *Perf. 13x12¾*

Stamps With Gray Frames

571-572 A442 Set of 2 12.00 12.00

Souvenir Sheet

Stamps Without Gray Frames

573 Sheet of 2 + label 6.00 6.00
a. A442 €1 multi 2.40 2.40
b. A442 €1.50 multi 3.50 3.50

See Greenland Nos. 763-765.

Voyage Booklet Type of 1999

No. 573C: d, Morne Rouge, Crozet Island. e, Baie Larose, Kerguelen Island. f, Plateau des Tourbières, Amsterdam Island. g, Ile Saint-Paul. h, Diver observing seaweed off Kerguelen Island. i, Scientist measuring lobster. j, Photo-identification chart of orca dorsal fins. k, Photographer on ship near Kerguelen Island. l, Man uprooting invasive non-native plants, Crozet Island. m, Scientist on bird survey, Kerguelen Island. n, Flower and measuring gauge, Kerguelen Island. o, Man inspecting plants, Amsterdam Island. p, Stacks of wooden pathway segments, Crozet Island. q, Freight decontamination at port, Reunion. r, Aerial view of building site, Crozet Island. s, Fence, Kerguelen Island.

2017, Nov. 9 Litho. *Perf. 13*
573C A164 (€1.24) Souvenir booklet, #d-s 65.00

No. 573C sold for €27 and contains four panes consisting of a block of four of Nos. 573Cd-573Cg, 573Ch-573Ck, 573Cl-573Co and 573Cp-573Cs.

Miniature Sheet

Birds and Reptiles — A443

No. 574: a, Phaéton à bec jaune (yellow-billed tropicbird) (44x43mm). b, Scinque aux labiales tachetés (skink) (54x54mm diamond). c, Frégate du Pacifique (great frigatebird) (38x38mm). d, Tortue verte (green turtle) (43mm diameter).

Perf. 13, Perf. (#574a, 574d)

2017, Nov. 30 Litho. & Engr.
574 A443 Sheet of 4 10.00 10.00
a.-c. 85c Any single 2.10 2.10
d. €1.45 multi 3.50 3.50

Adélie Penguins — A444

Litho. & Silk-screened

2017, Dec. 8 *Perf. 13*
575 A444 €1 multi — —

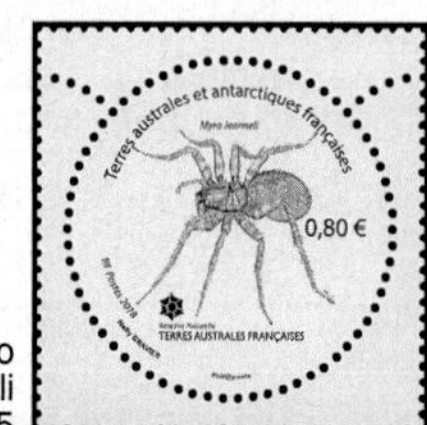

Myro Jeanneli A445

2018, Jan. 2 Photo. *Perf. 13¼*
576 A445 80c brnsh black 2.00 2.00

Cabin in Canyon des Sourcils Noirs, Kerguelen Island A446

2018, Jan. 2 Litho. *Perf. 13*
577 A446 85c multi 2.10 2.10

Kubota Snow Vehicle — A447

2018, Jan. 2 Litho. *Perf. 13*
578 A447 85c multi 2.10 2.10

Dr. Jean Sapin-Jaloustre (1917-99), Polar Expedition Physician — A448

2018, Jan. 2 Litho. *Perf. 13*
579 A448 85c multi 2.10 2.10

Pierre Etienne de Boynes (1718-83), French Secretary of the Navy — A449

2018, Jan. 2 Engr. *Perf. 13x12¾*
580 A449 85c multi 2.10 2.10

La Quille Island Near Saint Paul Island — A450

2018, Jan. 2 Engr. *Perf. 13x13¼*
581 A450 €1.05 multi 2.60 2.60

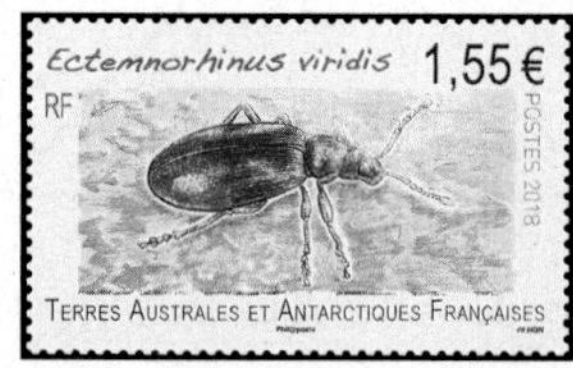

Ectemnorhinus Viridis — A451

2018, Jan. 2 Engr. *Perf. 13x13¼*
582 A451 €1.55 multi 3.75 3.75

Transport Ship La Grandière — A452

2018, Jan. 2 Engr. *Perf. 13x13¼*
583 A452 €1.70 multi 4.25 4.25

Ilmenite — A453

No. 584: a, Ilmenite in rock. b, Cut and polished ilmenite.

Litho. & Silk-Screened

2018, Jan. 2 *Perf. 13*
584 A453 50c Horiz. pair, #a-b 2.40 2.40

Renker Program, 2011-15 Study of Reindeer on Kerguelen Island — A454

No. 585: a, Head of reindeer. b, Herd of reindeer. c, Adult and juvenile reindeer.

2018, Jan. 2 Litho. *Perf. 13*
585 Horiz. strip of 3 6.50 6.50
a.-c. A454 85c Any single 2.10 2.10

Souvenir Sheet

Map of Antarctica — A455

2018, Jan. 2 Photo. *Perf. 13¼*
586 A455 85c multi 2.10 2.10

Madrid Protocol on Envrionmental Protection to the Antarctic Treaty, 20th anniv.

Souvenir Sheet

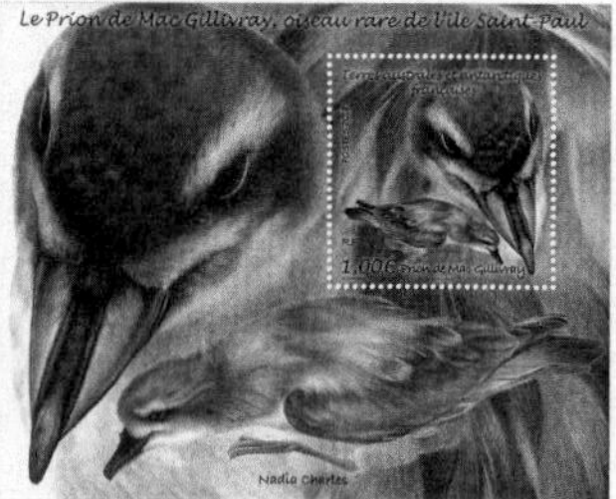

MacGillivray's Prions — A456

2018, Jan. 2 Litho. *Perf. 13*
587 A456 €1 multi 2.40 2.40

Souvenir Sheet

PBY Catalina, Ship La Pérouse, Map of Forgotten Airfield on Kerguelen Island — A457

2018, Jan. 2 Litho. *Perf. 13¼x13*
588 A457 €3.90 multi 9.50 9.50

Souvenir Sheet

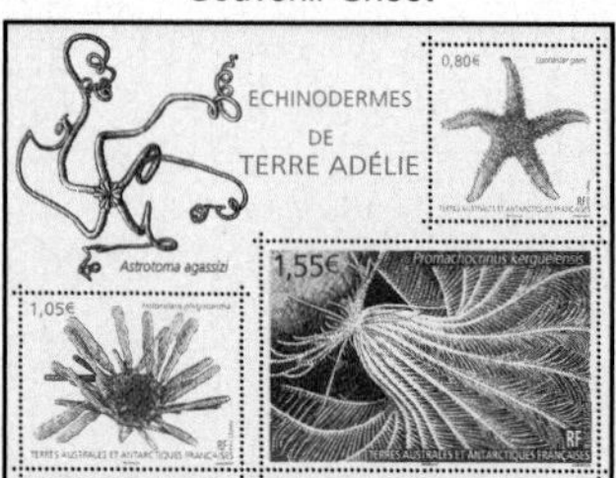

Echinoderms of Adélie Land — A458

No. 589: a, Lophaster gaini (40x40mm). b, Notocidaris platyacantha (52x40mm). c, Promachocrinus kerguelensis (80x53mm).

2018, Jan. 2 Engr. *Perf. 13*
589 A458 Sheet of 3 8.50 8.50
a. 80c multi 2.00 2.00
b. €1.05 multi 2.60 2.60
c. €1.55 multi 3.75 3.75

Miniature Sheet

Protected Animals — A459

No. 590: a, Amsterdam albatross. b, Emperor penguin, vert. c, Crozet elephant seal. d, Kerguelen fur seal.

2018, Jan. 2 Engr. *Perf. 13*
590 A459 Sheet of 4 13.00 13.00
a.-b. 85c Either single 2.10 2.10
c.-d. €1.70 Either single 4.25 4.25

Ship L'Astrolabe — A460

2018, Apr. 8 Litho. *Perf. 13*
591 A460 (85c) multi 2.10 2.10

Silhouettes of Adélie Land District Emblems — A461

Litho. & Silk-screened
2018, Apr. 8 *Perf. 13¼*
592 A461 €1 multi 2.40 2.40

A stamp similar to No. 592, with an inscription of "lettre - 20g tarif international" was issued on Nov. 7, 2019 in a sheet along with a similarly inscribed stamp similar to No. 617. The franking value of each of these stamps was €1.10, but the sheet sold for €5, along with a folder.

Souvenir Sheet

Symphonie Australe, Musical Composition by Julien Gauthier — A462

2018, Apr. 20 Litho. *Perf. 13¼*
593 A462 €2 multi 5.00 5.00

A463

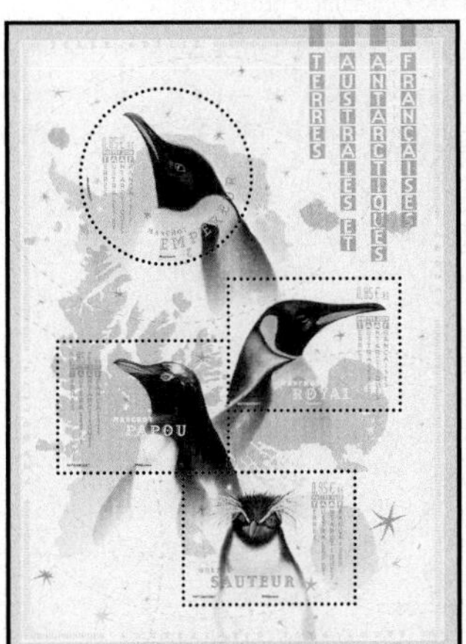

Penguins — A464

Designs: 10c, Rockhopper penguin (gorfou sauteur). 20c, King penguin (manchot royal). 30c, Gentoo penguin (manchot papou).

No. 597: a, Emperor penguin (manchot empereur, 40mm diameter). b, King penguin (40x30mm). c, Gentoo penguin (40x30mm). d, Rockhopper penguin (40x30mm).

2018, June 7 Litho. *Perf. 13*
594-596 A463 Set of 3 1.40 1.40
594a Dated "2019" .25 .25
595a Dated "2019" .45 .45
596a Dated "2019" .70 .70

Miniature Sheet
Perf. (#597a), Perf. 13¼ (#597b-597d)
597 A464 Sheet of 4 8.00 8.00
a.-d. 85c Any single 2.00 2.00

Issued: Nos. 594a, 595a, 596a, 3/14/19.

Souvenir Sheet

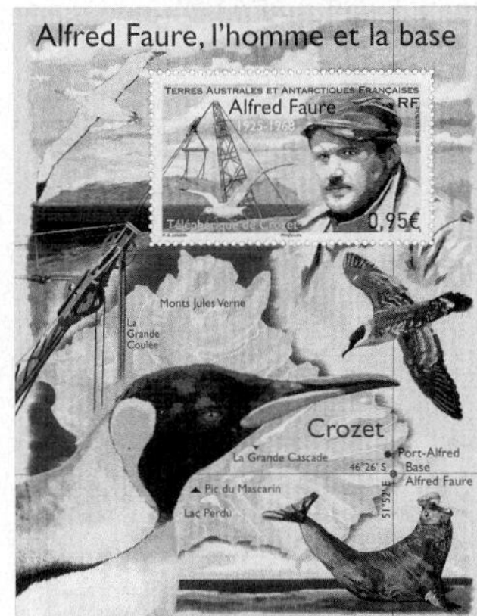

Alfred Faure (1925-68), Leader of Crozet Island Base — A465

2018, Oct. 17 Litho. *Perf. 13*
598 A465 95c multi 2.25 2.25

Eudyptes Chrysocome Moseleyi — A466

No. 599: a, Head of penguin and Ile Saint-Paul. b, Penguin and volcano cone.

2018, Oct. 26 Engr. *Perf. 13*
599 A466 Horiz. pair + central label 5.50 5.50
a. 95c dp bluish grn & blk lil 2.25 2.25
b. €1.35 dp bluish grn & blk lil 3.25 3.25

Souvenir Sheet

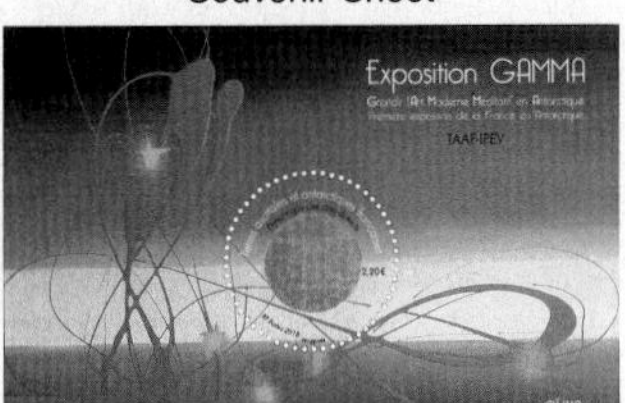

Modern Art Exhibition at Dumont d'Urville Station, Antarctica — A467

Photo. & Silk-Screened
2018, Nov. 8 *Perf.*
600 A467 €2.20 multi 5.00 5.00

Elephant Seal Observation Cabins Near American Bay, Crozet Island — A468

2019, Jan. 2 Litho. *Perf. 13*
601 A468 95c multi 2.25 2.25

Gygis Alba and Tromelin Island — A469

2019, Jan. 2 Engr. *Perf. 13*
602 A469 95c multi 2.25 2.25

Yves Vallette (1920-2014), Civil Engineer and Member of 1949-51 French Polar Expeditions A470

2019, Jan. 2 Engr. *Perf. 12½x13*
603 A470 95c multi 2.25 2.25

Mario Zucchelli (1944-2003), Director of Italian Antarctic Program — A471

2019, Jan. 2 Engr. *Perf. 13*
604 A471 €1.35 multi 3.25 3.25

Neomaso Antarcticus — A472

2019, Jan. 2 Engr. *Perf. 13*
605 A472 €1.55 multi 3.50 3.50

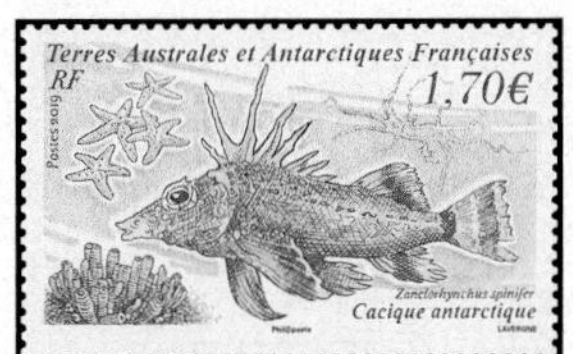

Zanclorhynchus Spinifer — A473

2019, Jan. 2 Engr. *Perf. 13*
606 A473 €1.70 multi 4.00 4.00

B2M Champlain — A474

2019, Jan. 2 Litho. *Perf. 13*
607 A474 €1.90 multi 4.50 4.50

Missile Cruiser Colbert — A475

2019, Jan. 2 Litho. *Perf. 13*
608 A475 €2.80 multi 6.50 6.50

Sapphirines — A476

No. 609: a, Raw sapphirine. b, Three cut and polished sapphirines.

Litho. & Silk-Screened
2019, Jan. 2 *Perf. 13*
609 A476 50c Horiz. pair, #a-b 2.25 2.25

Laboureur, Kerguelen Island A477

No. 610: a, Mairie Annexe Cabin (40x26mm). b, Laboureur (81x26mm).

2019, Jan. 2 Engr. *Perf. 13*
610 Horiz. pair + central label 5.50 5.50
a. A477 95c multi 2.25 2.25
b. A477 €1.35 multi 3.25 3.25

Study of Lake Sediment Cores — A478

No. 611: a, Workers on barge coring lake sediment. b, Barge on Lac d'Armor. c, Equipment for studying cores.

2019, Jan. 2 Litho. *Perf. 13*
611 Horiz. strip of 3 12.00 12.00
a. A478 95c multi 2.25 2.25
b. A478 €1.35 multi 3.25 3.25
c. A478 €2.70 multi 6.25 6.25

Souvenir Sheet

Restoration of Phylica Arborea on Amsterdam Island — A479

2019, Jan. 2 Litho. *Perf. 13*
612 A479 95c multi 2.25 2.25

Souvenir Sheet

Flesh-footed Shearwater — A480

2019, Jan. 2 Litho. *Perf. 13*
613 A480 €2 multi 4.50 4.50

Souvenir Sheet

Photovoltaic Solar Power Plant on Tromelin Island — A481

No. 614 — Power plant and: a, Bird at UL, sea turtle at LR (40x40mm). b, Bird at UR, sea turtle at LL (40x30mm).

Perf. 13 (#614a), 13x13¼ (#614b)
2019, Jan. 2 Litho.
614 A481 Sheet of 2 4.50 4.50
a.-b. 95c Either single 2.25 2.25

Souvenir Sheet

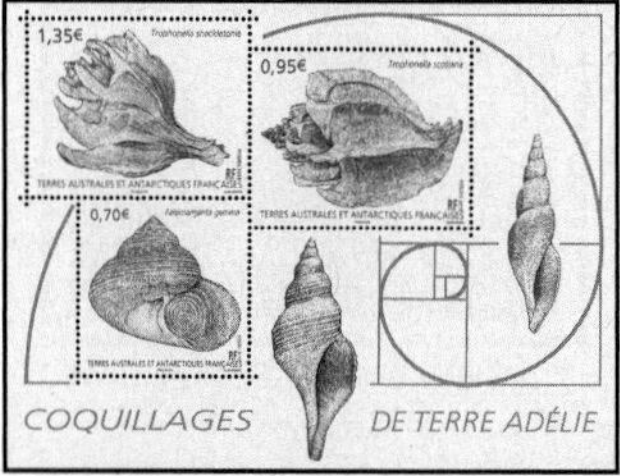

Shells of Adélie Land — A482

No. 615: a, Falsimargarita gemma (40x40mm). b, Trophonella scotiana (52x40mm). c, Trophonella shackletoni (52x40mm).

2019, Jan. 2 Engr. *Perf. 13*
615 A482 Sheet of 3 7.25 7.25
a. 70c multi 1.60 1.60
b. 95c multi 2.25 2.25
c. €1.35 multi 3.25 3.25

Gentoo Penguins — A483

2019, Mar. 16 Litho. *Perf. 13*
616 A483 €1 multi 2.25 2.25

Silhouettes of Scattered Islands of the Indian Ocean District Emblems — A484

Litho. & Silk-screened
2019, Mar. 16 *Perf. 13¼*
617 A484 €1.50 multi 3.50 3.50

A stamp similar to No. 617, with an inscription of "lettre - 20g tarif international" was issued on Nov. 7, 2019 in a sheet along with a similarly inscribed stamp similar to No. 592. The franking value of each of these stamps was €1.10, but the sheet sold for €5, along with a folder.

Oceanographic Ship La Curieuse — A485

2019, June 7 Litho. *Perf. 13*
618 A485 €1.35 multi 3.25 3.25

A sheet of two, containing stamps similar to Nos. 592 and 617, but with an inscription of "lettre - 20g tarif international" was issued on Nov. 7, 2019. The franking value of each of these stamps was €1.10, but the sheet sold for €5, along with a folder.

Souvenir Sheet

Aptenodytes Patagonicus — A486

No. 619: a, Three King penguins (40x40mm). b, One King penguin (40x30mm).

Perf. 13 (#619a), 13x13¼ (#619b)
2019, Nov. 28 Litho.
619 A486 Sheet of 2 7.00 7.00
a.-b. €1.50 Either single 3.50 3.50

AIR POST STAMPS

Emperor Penguins and Map of Antarctica — AP1

Unwmk.
1956, Apr. 25 Engr. *Perf. 13*
C1 AP1 50fr lt ol grn & dk grn 42.50 29.00
C2 AP1 100fr dl bl & indigo 35.00 25.00

Wandering Albatross — AP2

1959, Sept. 14
C3 AP2 200fr brn red, bl & blk 40.00 27.50

Adélie Penguins — AP3

1963, Feb. 11 Unwmk. *Perf. 13*
C4 AP3 50fr blk, dk bl & dp cl 42.50 32.50

Telstar Issue
Common Design Type
1962, Dec. 24
C5 CD111 50fr dp bl, ol & grn 29.00 21.00

Radio Towers, Adelie Penguins and IQSY Emblem — AP4

1963, Dec. 16 Engr.
C6 AP4 100fr bl, ver & blk 110.00 87.50

International Quiet Sun Year, 1964-65.

Discovery of Adelie Land — AP5

1965, Jan. 20 Engr. *Perf. 13*
C7 AP5 50fr blue & indigo 125.00 87.50

125th anniversary of the discovery of Adelie Land by Dumont d'Urville.

ITU Issue
Common Design Type
1965, May 17 Unwmk. *Perf. 13*
C8 CD120 30fr multi 200.00 160.00

French Satellite A-1 Issue
Common Design Type

Designs: 25fr, Diamant rocket and launching installations. 30fr, A-1 satellite.

1966, Mar. 2 Engr. *Perf. 13*
C9 CD121 25fr dk grn, choc & sl 13.50 10.00
C10 CD121 30fr choc, sl & dk grn 13.50 10.00
a. Pair, #C9-C10 + label 29.00 24.00

French Satellite D-1 Issue
Common Design Type
1966, Mar. 27
C11 CD122 50fr dk pur, lil & org 57.50 40.00

Ionospheric Research Pylon, Adelie Land — AP6

1966, Dec. 12
C12 AP6 25fr plum, bl & dk brn 32.50 17.50

Port aux Français, Emperor Penguin and Explorer — AP7

40fr, Aerial view of Saint Paul Island.

1968-69 Engr. *Perf. 13*
C13 AP7 40fr brt bl & dk gray 42.50 27.50
C14 AP7 50fr lt ultra, dk grn & blk 175.00 110.00

Issue dates: 50fr, Jan. 21; 40fr, Jan. 5, 1969.

Kerguelen Island and Rocket — AP8

Design: 30fr, Adelie Land.

1968, Apr. 22 Engr. *Perf. 13*
C15 AP8 25fr sl grn, dk brn & Prus bl 19.00 14.00
C16 AP8 30fr dk brn, sl grn & Prus bl 19.00 14.00
a. Pair, #C15-C16 + label 40.00 30.00

Space explorations with Dragon rockets, 1967-68.

Eiffel Tower, Antarctic Research Station, Ship from Paris Arms and Albatross AP9

1969, Jan. 13
C17 AP9 50fr bright blue 45.00 35.00

5th Consultative Meeting of the Antarctic Treaty Powers, Paris, Nov. 18, 1968.

Concorde Issue
Common Design Type

1969, Apr. 17
C18 CD129 85fr indigo & blue 55.00 37.50

Prepared but not issued with 87fr denomination. Value $3,000.

Map of Amsterdam Island AP10

Map of Kerguelen Island — AP11

Coat of Arms AP12

Designs: 50fr, Possession Island. 200fr, Point Geology Archipelago.

1969-71 Engr. *Perf. 13*
C19 AP10 30fr brown 19.00 12.50
C20 AP11 50fr sl grn, bl & dk red 21.00 14.00
C21 AP11 100fr blue & blk 85.00 40.00
C22 AP10 200fr sl grn, brn & Prus bl 70.00 42.50
C23 AP12 500fr pck blue 20.00 15.00
Nos. C19-C23 (5) 215.00 124.00

30fr for the 20th anniv. of the Amsterdam Island Meteorological Station.
Issued: 100fr, 500fr, 12/21; 30fr, 3/27/70; 50fr, 12/22/70; 200fr, 1/1/71.

Port-aux-Français, 1970 — AP13

Design: 40fr, Port-aux-Français, 1950.

1971, Mar. 9 Engr. *Perf. 13*
C24 AP13 40fr bl, ocher & sl grn 19.00 12.00
C25 AP13 50fr bl, grn ol & sl grn 19.00 12.00
a. Pair, #C24-C25 + label 40.00 27.50

20th anniversary of Port-aux-Français on Kerguelen Island.

Marquis de Castries Taking Possession of Crozet Island, 1772 — AP14

250fr, Fleur-de-lis flag raising on Kerguelen Is.

1972 Engr. *Perf. 13*
C26 AP14 100fr black 45.00 29.00
C27 AP14 250fr blk & dk brn 100.00 45.00

Bicentenary of the discovery of the Crozet and Kerguelen Islands.
Issue dates: 100fr, Jan. 24; 250fr, Feb. 23.

M. S. Galliéni — AP15

1973, Jan. 25 Engr. *Perf. 13*
C28 AP15 100fr black & blue 25.00 17.50

Exploration voyages of the Galliéni.

"Le Mascarin," 1772 — AP16

Sailing Ships: 145fr, "L'Astrolabe," 1840. 150fr, "Le Rolland," 1774. 185fr, "La Victoire," 1522.

1973, Dec. 13 Engr. *Perf. 13*
C29 AP16 120fr brown olive 6.75 4.75
C30 AP16 145fr brt ultra 6.75 4.75
C31 AP16 150fr slate 8.00 8.00
C32 AP16 185fr ocher 10.50 8.00
Nos. C29-C32 (4) 32.00 25.50

Ships used in exploring Antarctica.
See Nos. C37-C38.

Alfred Faure Base — AP17

Design: Nos. C33-C35 show panoramic view of Alfred Faure Base.

1974, Jan. 7 Engr. *Perf. 13*
C33 AP17 75fr Prus bl, ultra & brn 8.00 5.25
C34 AP17 110fr Prus bl, ultra & brn 11.00 8.00
C35 AP17 150fr Prus bl, ultra & brn 14.00 8.00
a. Triptych, Nos. C33-C35 37.50 30.00

Alfred Faure Antarctic Base, 10th anniv.

Penguin, Map of Antarctica, Letters — AP18

1974, Oct. 9 Engr. *Perf. 13*
C36 AP18 150fr multicolored 7.00 5.50

Centenary of Universal Postal Union.

Ship Type of 1973

100fr, "Le Français." 200fr, "Pourquoi-pas?"

1974, Dec. 16 Engr. *Perf. 13*
C37 AP16 100fr brt blue 5.50 3.00
C38 AP16 200fr dk car rose 9.00 4.50

Ships used in exploring Antarctica.

Rockets over Kerguelen Islands — AP19

Design: 90fr, Northern lights over map of northern coast of Russia.

1975, Jan. 26 Engr. *Perf. 13*
C39 AP19 45fr purple & multi 7.00 4.00
C40 AP19 90fr purple & multi 9.00 5.25
a. Pair, #C39-C40 + label 19.00 13.00

Franco-Soviet magnetosphere research.

"La Curieuse" — AP20

Ships: 2.70fr, Commandant Charcot. 4fr, Marion-Dufresne.

1976, Jan. Engr. *Perf. 13*
C41 AP20 1.90fr multicolored 3.25 2.00
C42 AP20 2.70fr multicolored 5.00 3.25
C43 AP20 4fr red & multi 9.00 4.25
Nos. C41-C43 (3) 17.25 9.50

Dumont d'Urville Base, 1956 — AP21

4fr, Dumont d'Urville Base, 1976, Adelie Land.

1976, Jan.
C44 AP21 1.20fr multicolored 9.00 4.00
C45 AP21 4fr multicolored 11.00 7.25
a. Pair, #C44-C45 + label 24.00 16.00

Dumont d'Urville Antarctic Base, 20th anniv.

Capt. Cook's Ships Passing Kerguelen Island — AP22

1976, Dec. 31 Engr. *Perf. 13*
C46 AP22 3.50fr slate & blue 13.00 8.00

Bicentenary of Capt. Cook's voyage past Kerguelen Island.

Sea Lion and Cub AP23

1977-79 Engr. *Perf. 13*
C47 AP23 4fr dk blue, grn ('79) 3.00 2.50
C48 AP23 10fr multicolored 10.00 9.00

Satellite Survey, Kerguelen — AP24

Designs: 50c, 2.70fr, Satellites, Kerguelen. 70c, Geophysical laboratory. 1.90fr, Satellite and Kerguelen tracking station. 3fr, Satellites, Adelie Land.

1977-79 Engr. *Perf. 13*
C49 AP24 50c multi ('79) .90 .70
C50 AP24 70c multi ('79) .90 .70
C51 AP24 1.90fr multi ('79) 1.60 1.40
C52 AP24 2.70fr multi ('78) 2.75 2.00
C53 AP24 3fr multicolored 4.25 3.25
Nos. C49-C53 (5) 10.40 8.05

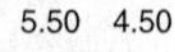
Elephant Seals — AP25

1979, Jan. 1
C54 AP25 10fr multicolored 5.50 4.50

Challenger — AP26

1979, Jan. 1
C55 AP26 2.70fr black & blue 2.25 1.75

Antarctic expeditions to Crozet and Kerguelen Islands, 1872-1876.

La Recherche and L'Esperance — AP27

1979
C56 AP27 1.90fr deep blue 1.50 1.10

Arrival of d'Entrecasteaux and Kermadec at Amsterdam Island, Mar. 28, 1792.

Lion Rock — AP28

1979
C57 AP28 90c multicolored 1.10 .70

Natural Arch, Kerguelen Island, 1840 — AP29

1979
C58 AP29 2.70fr multicolored 1.25 1.10

Phylica Nitida, Amsterdam Island — AP30

1979
C59 AP30 10fr multicolored 4.00 3.25

Charles de Gaulle, 10th Anniversary of Death AP31

1980, Nov. 9 Engr. *Perf. 13*
C60 AP31 5.40fr multicolored 11.00 8.00

HB-40 Castor Truck and Trailer — AP32

1980, Dec. 15
C61 AP32 2.40fr multicolored 1.25 1.00

Supply Ship Saint Marcouf — AP33

Design: 7.30fr, Icebreaker Norsel.

1980, Dec. 15
C62 AP33 3.50fr shown 1.60 1.10
C63 AP33 7.30fr multicolored 2.50 2.00

Glacial Landscape, Dumont d'Urville Sea — AP34

Chionis — AP35

Adele Dumont d'Urville (1798-1842) — AP36

Arcad III — AP37

25th Anniv. of Charcot Station — AP38

Antares — AP39

1981 Engr. *Perf. 13, 12½x13 (2fr)*

C64	AP34 1.30fr multicolored	.70	.45
C65	AP35 1.50fr black	.70	.50
C66	AP36 2fr black & lt brn	.90	.85
C67	AP37 3.85fr multicolored	1.60	1.25
C68	AP38 5fr multicolored	1.75	1.50
C69	AP39 8.40fr multicolored	2.75	2.25
	Nos. C64-C69 (6)	8.40	6.80

PHILEXFRANCE '82 Stamp Exhibition, Paris, June 11-21 — AP40

1982, June 11 Engr. *Perf. 13*
C70 AP40 8fr multicolored 5.50 5.25

French Overseas Possessions Week, Sept. 18-25 — AP41

1982, Sept. 17 Engr. *Perf. 13*
C71 AP41 5fr Commandant Charcot 1.75 1.75

Apostle Islands — AP42

1983, Jan. 3 Engr. *Perf. 13*
C72 AP42 65c multicolored .55 .35

Sputnik I, 25th Anniv. of Intl. Geophysical Year — AP43

Orange Bay Base, Cape Horn, 1883, Cent. — AP44

5.20fr, Scoresby Sound Base, Greenland, 50th anniv.

1983, Jan. 3

C73	AP43 1.50fr multicolored	.60	.60
C74	AP44 3.30fr multicolored	1.75	1.75
C75	AP44 5.20fr multicolored	2.00	2.00
a.	Strip of 3, #C73-C75	4.50	4.50

AP45

1983, Jan. 3
C76 AP45 4.55fr dark blue 4.00 3.00

Abstract, by G. Mathieu — AP46

1983, Jan. 3 Photo. *Perf. 13x13½*
C77 AP46 25fr multicolored 10.00 8.00

Erebus off Antarctic Ice Cap, 1842 — AP47

Port of Joan of Arc, 1930 — AP48

1984, Jan. 1 **Engr.** ***Perf. 13***
C78 AP47 2.60fr ultra & dk blue 1.10 1.00
C79 AP48 4.70fr multicolored 1.75 1.75

Aurora Polaris — AP49

1984, Jan. 1 **Photo.**
C80 AP49 3.50fr multicolored 2.00 1.25

Manned Flight Bicentenary (1983) — AP50

Various balloons and airships.

1984, Jan. 1 **Engr.**
C81 AP50 3.50fr multicolored 1.75 1.75
C82 AP50 7.80fr multicolored 2.75 2.75
a. Pair, #C81-C82 + label 5.00 5.00

Patrol Boat Albatros — AP51

1984, July 2 **Engr.** ***Perf. 13***
C83 AP51 11.30fr multi 4.25 4.25

NORDPOSTA Exhibition — AP52

Design: Scientific Vessel Gauss.

1984, Nov. 3 **Engr.** ***Perf. 13***
C84 AP52 9fr multicolored 4.50 3.50

Issued se-tenant with label.

Corsican Sheep — AP53

Amsterdam Albatross AP54

Designs: 70c, Mouflons. 3.90fr, Diomedia amsterdamensis.

1985, Jan. 1 **Engr.** ***Perf. 13***
C85 AP53 70c multicolored .70 .40
C86 AP54 3.90fr multicolored 1.60 1.25

La Novara, Frigate AP55

Design: La Novara at St. Paul.

1985, Jan. 1 **Engr.** ***Perf. 13***
C87 AP55 12.80fr multi 5.00 4.50

Explorer and Seal, by Tremois — AP56

Design: Explorer, seal, names of territories.

1985, Jan. 1 **Photo.** ***Perf. 13x12½***
C88 AP56 30fr + label 11.00 8.50

Sailing Ships, Ropes, Flora & Fauna — AP57

1985, Aug. 6 **Engr.** ***Perf. 13***
C89 AP57 2fr blk, brt bl & ol grn .70 .55
C90 AP57 12.80fr blk, ol grn & brt bl 3.75 3.75
a. Pair, #C89-C90 + label 5.50 5.50

French Southern & Antarctic Territories, 30th anniv. No. C90a has continuous design with center label.

Bird Type of 1986

1986, Jan. 1 **Engr.** ***Perf. 13½x13***
C91 A56 4.60fr Sea Gulls 2.00 1.75

Antarctic Atmospheric Research, 10th Anniv. — AP58

1986, Jan. 1
C92 AP58 14fr blk, dk red & brt org 5.00 4.00

Jean Charcot (1867-1936), Explorer — AP59

Designs: 2.10fr, Ship Pourquoi Pas. 14fr, Ship in storm.

1986, Jan. 1
C93 AP59 2.10fr multicolored .90 .60
C94 AP59 14fr multicolored 4.50 4.25
a. Pair, #C93-C94 + label 6.25 6.25

SPOT Satellite over the Antarctic — AP60

1986, May 26 **Engr.** ***Perf. 13***
C95 AP60 8fr dp ultra, sep & dk ol grn 3.25 2.50

J.B. Charcot — AP61

1987, Jan. 1 **Engr.** ***Perf. 13x13½***
C96 AP61 14.60fr multi 5.00 4.50

Ocean Drilling Program — AP62

1987, Jan. 1 ***Perf. 13½x13***
C97 AP62 16.80fr lem, dk ultra & bluish blk 5.50 4.50

INMARSAT — AP63

1987, Mar. 2 **Engr.** ***Perf. 13***
C98 AP63 16.80fr multi 8.00 7.50

French Polar Expeditions, 40th Anniv. — AP64

1988, Jan. 1
C99 AP64 20fr lake, ol grn & plum 8.00 6.75

Views of Penguin Is. — AP65

1988, Jan. 1
C100 AP65 3.90fr dk bl & sep 1.75 1.50
C101 AP65 15.10fr dp grn, choc brn & dk bl 5.50 5.00

See Nos. C103, C109.

Founding of Permanent Settlements in the Territories, 40th Anniv. — AP66

1989, Jan. 1 **Engr.** ***Perf. 13½x13***
C102 AP66 15.50fr black 5.00 4.75

Island View Type

1989, Jan. 1
C103 AP65 8.40fr Apostle Islands 2.75 2.50

La Curieuse — AP68

1989, Jan. 1 ***Perf. 13x12½***
C104 AP68 2.20fr multicolored .80 .70
C105 AP68 15.50fr multi, diff. 5.00 5.00
a. Pair, #C104-C105 + label 6.00 6.00

No. C105a label continues the design.

French Revolution, Bicent. — AP69

1989, July 14 Engr. *Perf. 13x12½*

C106 AP69 5fr pink, dark olive grn & dark blue 5.50 3.50

Souvenir Sheet

Perf. 13

C107 Sheet of 4 10.00 10.00
a. AP69 5fr Prus green, brt ultra & dark red 2.50 2.50

No. C107 for PHILEXFRANCE '89.

15th Antarctic Treaty Summit Conference — AP70

1989, Oct. 9 Engr. *Perf. 13*

C108 AP70 17.70fr multicolored 6.00 5.75

Island View Type

1990, Jan. 1 Engr. *Perf. 13*

C109 AP65 7.30fr Isle of Pigs, Crozet Isls. 3.00 2.40

L'Astrolabe, Expedition Team — AP72

1990, Jan. 1

C110 AP72 15.50fr dk red vio & blk 5.00 5.00

Discovery of Adelie Land by Dumont D'Urville, 150th anniv.

L'Astrolabe, Commanded by Dumont D'Urville, 1840 — AP73

1990, Jan. 1

C111 AP73 2.20fr *L'Astrolabe,* 1988 .80 .75
C112 AP73 15.50fr shown 5.00 5.00
a. Pair, #C111-C112 + label 6.50 6.50

Bird, by Folon — AP74

1990, Jan. 1 Litho. *Perf. 12½x13*

C113 AP74 30fr multicolored 10.00 9.50

Albatross, Argos Satellite AP75

1991, Jan. 1

C114 AP75 2.10fr red brn, bl & brn 1.50 .95

Climatological Research — AP76

3.60fr, Weather balloons, instruments. 20fr, Research ship.

1991, Jan. 1 Engr. *Perf. 13*

C115 AP76 3.60fr multi 1.40 1.40
C116 AP76 20fr multi 7.75 7.75
a. Pair, #C115-C116 + label 10.00 10.00

Charles de Gaulle (1890-1970) — AP77

1991, Jan. 1

C117 AP77 18.80fr blk, red & bl 7.75 7.75

Cape Petrel — AP78

1992, Jan. 1 Engr. *Perf. 13*

C118 AP78 3.40fr multicolored 2.25 1.40

French Institute of Polar Research and Technology — AP79

No. C120, Polar bear with man offering flowers.

1991, Dec. 16 Engr. *Perf. 13x12*

C119 AP79 15fr multicolored 5.75 5.75
C120 AP79 15fr multicolored 5.75 5.75
a. Strip, #C119-C120 + label 12.00 12.00

Christopher Columbus and Discovery of America — AP80

1992, Jan. 1 *Perf. 13*

C121 AP80 22fr multicolored 9.75 9.75

Mapping Satellite Poseidon — AP81

1992, Jan. 1 Engr. *Perf. 13*

C122 AP81 24.50fr multi 11.00 10.50

Dumont d'Urville Base, Adelie Land — AP82

1992, Jan. 1 Litho. *Perf. 13x12½*

C123 AP82 25.70fr multi 12.00 10.50

Amateur Radio — AP83

1993, Jan. 1 Engr. *Perf. 13*

C124 AP83 2fr multicolored 2.00 .75

New Animal Biology Laboratory, Adelie Land — AP84

1993, Jan. 1

C125 AP84 25.40fr multicolored 11.00 6.75

Support Base D10 — AP85

1993, Jan. 1

C126 AP85 25.70fr ol, red & bl 11.00 7.00

Opening of Adelie Land Airfield — AP86

1993, Jan. 1

C127 AP86 30fr multicolored 13.00 8.75

Krill — AP87

1994, Jan. 1 Engr. *Perf. 13*

C128 AP87 15fr black 6.50 4.00

Fishery Management — AP88

1994, Jan. 1

C129 AP88 23fr multicolored 10.00 6.00

Satellite, Ground Station — AP89

Design: 27.30fr, Lidar Station.

1994, Jan. 1

C130 AP89 26.70fr multicolored 12.00 7.00
C131 AP89 27.30fr multicolored 12.00 7.25

Arrival of Emperor Penguins — AP90

1994, Jan. 1 *Perf. 13x12½*

C132 AP90 28fr blue & black 13.00 8.00

Erebus Mission — AP91

1995, Jan. 2 Engr. *Perf. 13*

C133 AP91 4.30fr bl, vio & slate 2.25 1.50

Moving of Winter Station, Charcot — AP92

1995, Jan. 2 **Litho.**
C134 AP92 15fr multicolored 6.50 4.25

G. Lesquin (1803-30) — AP93

1995, Jan. 2
C135 AP93 28fr multicolored 12.00 8.00

Map of East Island — AP94

1996, Jan. 1 **Engr.** ***Perf. 13***
C136 AP94 20fr multicolored 8.50 6.00

Expedition to Dome/C — AP95

1996, Jan. 1
C137 AP95 23fr dark blue 10.00 7.00

Blue Whale, Southern Whale Sanctuary — AP96

1996, Jan. 1
C138 AP96 26.70fr multicolored 12.00 8.00

Port-Couvreux — AP97

1996, Jan. 1
C139 AP97 27.30fr multicolored 12.00 8.50

Jasus Paulensis AP98

1997, Jan. 1 **Engr.** ***Perf. 12½x13***
C140 AP98 5.20fr multicolored 3.00 1.75

Racing Yacht Charentes 2 — AP99

1997, Jan. 1 **Litho.** ***Perf. 13***
C141 AP99 16fr multicolored 8.00 5.50

John Nunn, Shipwrecked 1825-29, Hope Cottage — AP100

1997, Jan. 1 **Engr.**
C142 AP100 20fr multicolored 8.75 6.25

ICOTA Program — AP101

1997, Jan. 1
C143 AP101 24fr multicolored 10.50 7.50

Harpagifer Spinosus — AP102

1997, Jan. 1
C144 AP102 27fr multicolored 12.00 8.50

EPICA Program — AP103

1998, Jan. 2 **Engr.** ***Perf. 13***
C145 AP103 5.20fr dk brn & lil 2.50 1.40

First Radio Meteorological Station, Port Aux Francais — AP104

1998, Jan. 2
C146 AP104 8fr black, blue & red 4.25 2.25

King Penguin, Argos Satellite AP105

1998, Jan. 2 ***Perf. 12½x13***
C147 AP105 16fr multicolored 7.00 4.75

Ranunculas Moseleyi AP106

1998, Jan. 2
C148 AP106 24fr multicolored 10.50 6.50

Intl. Geophysical Year, 40th Anniv. — AP107

1998, Oct. **Engr.** ***Perf. 13x12½***
C149 AP107 5.20fr dk bl, blk & brick red 3.00 1.50

FRENCH SUDAN

'french sü-'dan

LOCATION — In northwest Africa, north of French Guinea and Ivory Coast
GOVT. — French Colony
AREA — 590,966 sq. mi.
POP. — 3,794,270 (1941)
CAPITAL — Bamako

In 1899 French Sudan was abolished as a separate colony and was divided among Dahomey, French Guinea, Ivory Coast, Senegal and Senegambia and Niger. Issues for French Sudan were resumed in 1921.

From 1906 to 1921 a part of this territory was known as Upper Senegal and Niger. A part of Upper Volta was added in 1933. See Mali.

100 Centimes = 1 Franc

See French West Africa No. 70 for stamp inscribed "Soudan Francais" and "Afrique Occidentale Francaise."

French Colonies Nos. 58-59 Srchd. in Black

Perf. 14x13½

1894, Apr. 12 **Unwmk.**
1 A9 15c on 75c car, *rose* *4,600. 2,300.*
2 A9 25c on 1fr brnz grn, *straw* *5,000. 1,700.*

The imperforate stamp like No. 1 was made privately in Paris from a fragment of the lithographic stone which had been used in the Colony for surcharging No. 1.

Counterfeit surcharges exist.

Navigation and Commerce — A2

1894-1900 **Typo.** ***Perf. 14x13½***
Name of colony in Blue or Carmine

No.	Type	Value	Description	Unused	Used
3	A2	1c	blk, *lil bl*	1.60	2.00
4	A2	2c	brn, *buff*	2.40	2.75
5	A2	4c	claret, *lav*	8.00	6.50
6	A2	5c	grn, *grnsh*	12.00	12.00
7	A2	10c	blk, *lav*	24.00	24.00
8	A2	10c	red ('00)	8.00	8.00
9	A2	15c	blue, quadrille paper	8.00	8.00
10	A2	15c	gray, *lt gray* ('00)	8.00	8.00
11	A2	20c	red, *grn*	40.00	35.00
12	A2	25c	blk, *rose*	32.50	27.50
13	A2	25c	blue ('00)	8.00	8.75
14	A2	30c	brn, *bister*	40.00	40.00
15	A2	40c	red, *straw*	40.00	35.00
16	A2	50c	car, *rose*	55.00	65.00
17	A2	50c	brn, *az* ('00)	16.00	16.00
18	A2	75c	dp vio, *org*	55.00	55.00
19	A2	1fr	brnz grn, *straw*	12.00	12.00
			Nos. 3-19 (17)	370.50	365.50

Perf. 13½x14 stamps are counterfeits.

Nos. 8, 10, 13, 17 were issued in error. They were accepted for use in the other colonies.

Stamps and Types of Upper Senegal and Niger, 1914-17, Overprinted

1921-30 ***Perf. 13½x14***

No.	Type	Value	Description	Unused	Used
21	A4	1c	brn vio & vio	.25	.40
22	A4	2c	dk gray & dl vio	.30	.50
23	A4	4c	blk & blue	.30	.50
24	A4	5c	ol brn & dk brn	.30	.40
25	A4	10c	yel grn & bl grn	.90	.55
26	A4	10c	red vio & bl ('25)	.40	.50
27	A4	15c	red brn & org	.50	.55
28	A4	15c	yel grn & dp grn ('25)	.40	.40
29	A4	15c	org brn & vio ('27)	1.60	1.60
30	A4	20c	brn vio & blk	.50	.55
31	A4	25c	blk & bl grn	1.25	.80
a.			Booklet pane of 4	—	
			Complete booklet, 5 #31a	650.00	
			Complete booklet, overprint omitted on one pane	16,000.	
32	A4	30c	red org & rose	1.60	1.60
33	A4	30c	bl grn & blk ('26)	.80	.70
34	A4	30c	dl grn & bl grn ('28)	2.00	2.00
35	A4	35c	rose & vio	.40	.55
36	A4	40c	gray & rose	1.25	1.25
37	A4	45c	bl & ol brn	1.25	1.25
38	A4	50c	ultra & bl	1.60	1.25
39	A4	50c	red org & bl ('26)	1.25	1.25
40	A4	60c	vio, *pnksh* ('26)	1.25	1.25
41	A4	65c	bis & pale bl ('28)	1.60	1.60
42	A4	75c	org & ol brn	1.60	2.00
43	A4	90c	brn red & pink ('30)	5.50	5.50
44	A4	1fr	dk brn & dl vio	1.60	2.00
45	A4	1.10fr	gray lil & red vio ('28)	3.25	4.00

46 A4 1.50fr dp bl & bl ('30) 5.50 5.50
47 A4 2fr grn & bl 2.40 2.75
48 A4 3fr red vio ('30) 12.00 12.00
a. Double overprint 190.00
49 A4 5fr vio & blk 8.00 7.25
Nos. 21-49 (29) 59.55 60.45

Type of 1921 Surcharged

1922, Sept. 28
50 A4 60c on 75c vio, *pnksh* .80 .80

Stamps and Type of 1921-30 Surcharged

1925-27
51 A4 25c on 45c .80 .80
52 A4 65c on 75c 2.00 2.40
53 A4 85c on 2fr 2.00 2.40
54 A4 85c on 5fr 2.00 2.40
55 A4 90c on 75c brn red & sal pink ('27) 2.40 2.75
56 A4 1.25fr on 1fr dp bl & lt bl (R) ('26) 1.25 1.60
57 A4 1.50fr on 1fr dp bl & ultra ('27) 1.60 2.00
58 A4 3fr on 5fr dl red & brn org ('27) 6.50 5.50
59 A4 10fr on 5fr brn red & bl grn ('27) 24.00 21.00
60 A4 20fr on 5fr vio & ver ('27) 29.00 29.00
Nos. 51-60 (10) 71.55 69.85

Sudanese Woman — A4

Entrance to the Residency at Djenné — A5

Sudanese Boatman — A6

1931-40 Typo. *Perf. 13x14*
61 A4 1c dk red & blk .25 .25
62 A4 2c dp blue & org .25 .25
63 A4 3c dk red & blk ('40) .25 .25
64 A4 4c gray lil & rose .25 .25
65 A4 5c indigo & grn .25 .25
66 A4 10c ol grn & rose .25 .25
67 A4 15c blk & brt vio .40 .30
68 A4 20c hn brn & lt bl .40 .30
69 A4 25c red vio & lt red .40 .30
70 A5 30c grn & lt grn .80 .50
71 A5 30c dk bl & red org ('40) .30 .30
72 A5 35c ol grn & grn ('38) .40 .40
73 A5 40c ol grn & pink .40 .30
74 A5 45c dk bl & red org 1.20 .65
75 A5 45c ol grn & grn ('40) .50 .50
76 A5 50c red & black .40 .30
77 A5 55c ultra & car ('38) .40 .40
78 A5 60c brt bl & brn ('40) 1.20 1.20
79 A5 65c brt vio & blk .80 .55
80 A5 70c vio bl & car rose ('40) .80 .80
81 A5 75c brt bl & ol brn 2.40 2.00
82 A5 80c car & brn ('38) .80 .80
83 A5 90c dp red & red org 1.60 .80
84 A5 90c brt vio & sl blk ('39) .90 1.00
85 A5 1fr indigo & grn 8.00 2.40
86 A5 1fr rose red ('38) 5.50 1.60
87 A5 1fr car & brn ('40) .80 .80
88 A6 1.25fr vio & dl vio ('33) .80 .80
89 A6 1.25fr red ('39) .90 1.00
90 A6 1.40fr brt vio & blk ('40) .90 .90
91 A6 1.50fr dk bl & ultra .80 .55
92 A6 1.60fr brn & dp bl ('40) .90 .90
93 A6 1.75fr dk brn & dp bl ('33) .80 .80
94 A6 1.75fr vio bl ('38) .80 .80
95 A6 2fr org brn & grn .80 .55
96 A6 2.25fr vio bl & ultra ('39) 1.00 1.10
97 A6 2.50fr lt brown ('40) 1.60 1.60
98 A6 3fr Prus grn & brn .80 .40
99 A6 5fr red & blk 2.00 1.20
100 A6 10fr dull bl & grn 2.40 2.00
101 A6 20fr red vio & brn 3.25 2.40
Nos. 61-101 (41) 47.65 32.70

For surcharges see Nos. B7-B10.
For 10c and 30c, without "RF," see Nos. 120-121

Common Design Types pictured following the introduction.

Colonial Exposition Issue
Common Design Types

1931, Apr. 13 Engr. *Perf. 12½*
Name of Country Printed in Black
102 CD70 40c deep green 4.75 4.75
103 CD71 50c violet 4.75 4.75
104 CD72 90c red orange 4.75 4.75
105 CD73 1.50fr dull blue 4.75 4.75
Set, never hinged 29.00

Paris International Exposition Issue
Common Design Types

1937, Apr. 15 *Perf. 13*
106 CD74 20c deep violet 2.00 2.00
107 CD75 30c dark green 2.00 2.00
108 CD76 40c car rose 2.40 2.40
109 CD77 50c dark brown 1.60 1.60
110 CD78 90c red 1.60 1.60
111 CD79 1.50fr ultra 2.40 2.40
Nos. 106-111 (6) 12.00 12.00
Set, never hinged 20.25

Colonial Arts Exhibition Issue
Souvenir Sheet
Common Design Type

1937 Engr. *Imperf.*
112 CD77 3fr magenta & blk 12.00 *16.00*
Never hinged 16.00

Caillie Issue
Common Design Type

1939, Apr. 5 *Perf. 12½x12*
113 CD81 90c org brn & org .40 .80
114 CD81 2fr brt violet .40 1.20
115 CD81 2.25fr ultra & dk bl .40 1.20
Nos. 113-115 (3) 1.20 3.20
Set, never hinged 2.40

New York World's Fair Issue
Common Design Type

1939, May 10
116 CD82 1.25fr car lake .80 1.60
117 CD82 2.25fr ultra .80 1.60
Set, never hinged 2.40

Entrance to the Residency at Djenné and Marshal Pétain — A7

1941 Engr. *Perf. 12x12½*
118 A7 1fr green .40 —
119 A7 2.50fr blue .40 —
Set, never hinged 1.60

For surcharges, see Nos. B14-B15.

Types of 1931-40 without "RF"

1943-44 Typo. *Perf. 13½x14*
120 A4 10c ol green & rose .65
121 A5 30c dk bl & red org .95
Set, never hinged 2.00

Nos. 120-121 were issued by the Vichy government in France, but were not placed on sale in French Sudan.

Stamps of French Sudan were superseded by those of French West Africa.

SEMI-POSTAL STAMPS

Curie Issue
Common Design Type
Unwmk.

1938, Oct. 24 Engr. *Perf. 13*
B1 CD80 1.75fr + 50c brt ultra 12.50 12.50
Never hinged 21.00

French Revolution Issue
Common Design Type

1939, July 5 Photo.
Name and Value Typo. in Black
B2 CD83 45c + 25c green 10.00 10.00
B3 CD83 70c + 30c brown 10.00 10.00
B4 CD83 90c + 35c red org 10.00 10.00
B5 CD83 1.25fr + 1fr rose pink 10.00 10.00
B6 CD83 2.25fr + 2fr blue 10.00 10.00
Nos. B2-B6 (5) 50.00 50.00
Set, never hinged 87.50

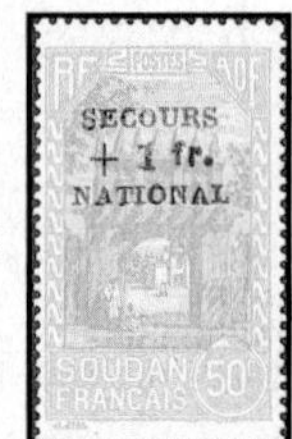

Stamps of 1931-40, Surcharged in Black or Red

1941 *Perf. 13x14*
B7 A5 50c + 1fr red & blk (R) 4.00 4.00
B8 A5 80c + 2fr car & brn 8.00 8.00
B9 A6 1.50fr + 2fr dk bl & ultra 8.00 8.00
B10 A6 2fr + 3fr org brn & grn 8.00 8.00
Nos. B7-B10 (4) 28.00 28.00
Set, never hinged 55.00

Common Design Type and

Native Officer — SP1

Aviation Officer — SP2

1941 Photo. *Perf. 13½*
B11 SP1 1fr + 1fr red 1.25
B12 CD86 1.50fr + 3fr claret 1.40
B13 SP2 2.50fr + 1fr blue 1.40
Nos. B11-B13 (3) 4.05
Set, never hinged 5.50

Surtax for the defense of the colonies. Issued by the Vichy government in France, but not placed on sale in French Sudan.

Petain type of 1941 Surcharged in Black or Red

1944 Engr. *Perf. 12x12½*
B14 50c + 1.50fr on 2.50fr deep blue (R) .40
B15 + 2.50fr on 1fr green .40
Set, never hinged 1.60

Colonial Development Fund.
Nos. B14-B15 were issued by the Vichy government in France, but were not placed on sale in French Sudan.

AIR POST STAMPS

Common Design Type
Perf. 12½x12

1940, Feb. 8 Unwmk. Engr.
C1 CD85 1.90fr ultra .40 .40
C2 CD85 2.90fr dark red .40 .40
C3 CD85 4.50fr dk gray green .80 .80
C4 CD85 4.90fr yellow bister .80 .80
C5 CD85 6.90fr deep orange 1.60 1.60
Nos. C1-C5 (5) 4.00 4.00
Set, never hinged 5.20

Common Design Types

1942, Oct. 19
C6 CD88 50c carmine & bl .40 —
C7 CD88 1fr brown & blk .40
C8 CD88 2fr dk grn & red brn .80
C9 CD88 3fr dk blue & scar .80
C10 CD88 5fr vio & brn red .80

Frame Engr., Center Typo.
C11 CD89 10fr ultra, ind & gray blk 1.20
C12 CD89 20fr rose car, mag & lt vio 1.60
C13 CD89 50fr yel grn, dl grn & dl bl 2.00 —
Nos. C6-C13 (8) 8.00
Set, never hinged 12.00

There is doubt whether Nos. C7-C12 were officially placed in use.

AIR POST SEMI-POSTAL STAMPS

Types of Dahomey Air Post Semi-Postal Issue
Perf. 13½x12½, 13 (#CB3)
Photo, Engr. (#CB3)

1942, June 22
CB1 SPAP1 1.50fr + 3.50fr grn .40 *5.50*
CB2 SPAP2 2fr + 6fr brown .40 *5.50*
CB3 SPAP2 3fr + 9fr car red .40 *5.50*
Nos. CB1-CB3 (3) 1.20 *16.50*
Set, never hinged 2.40

Native children's welfare fund.

Colonial Education Fund
Common Design Type
Perf. 12½x13½

1942, June 22 Engr.
CB4 CD86a 1.20fr + 1.80fr blue & red .40 *5.50*
Never hinged .80

POSTAGE DUE STAMPS

Upper Senegal and Niger Postage Due Stamps Overprinted

Perf. 14x13½
1921, Dec. Unwmk. Typo.
J1 D1 5c green .40 .40
J2 D1 10c rose .40 .40
J3 D1 15c gray .40 .80
J4 D1 20c brown 1.20 1.20
J5 D1 30c blue 1.20 1.20

J6 D1 50c black 2.00 2.40
J7 D1 60c orange 2.40 2.40
J8 D1 1fr violet 2.40 3.25
Nos. J1-J8 (8) 10.40 12.05

Type of 1921 Issue Surcharged

1927, Oct. 10

J9 D1 2fr on 1fr lilac rose 8.00 8.00
J10 D1 3fr on 1fr org brown 8.00 8.00

D2

1931, Mar. 9

J11 D2 5c green .25 .30
J12 D2 10c rose .25 .30
J13 D2 15c gray .25 .50
J14 D2 20c dark brown .25 .50
J15 D2 30c dark blue .40 .55
J16 D2 50c black .40 .55
J17 D2 60c deep orange .80 .80
J18 D2 1fr violet 1.20 1.20
J19 D2 2fr lilac rose 1.60 1.60
J20 D2 3fr red brown 1.60 1.60
Nos. J11-J20 (10) 7.00 7.90

FRENCH WEST AFRICA

ˈfrench ˈwest ˈa-fri-kə

LOCATION — Northwestern Africa
GOVT. — French colonial administrative unit
AREA — 1,821,768 sq. mi.
POP. — 18,777,163 (est.)
CAPITAL — Dakar

French West Africa comprised the former colonies of Senegal, French Guinea, Ivory Coast, Dahomey, French Sudan, Mauritania, Niger and Upper Volta.

In 1958, these former colonies became republics, eventually issuing their own stamps. Until the republic issues appeared, stamps of French West Africa continued in use. The Senegal and Sudanese Republics issued stamps jointly as the Federation of Mali, starting in 1959.

Catalogue values for all unused stamps in this country are for Never Hinged items.

Many stamps other than Nos. 65-72 and 77 are inscribed "Afrique Occidentale Francaise" and the name of one of the former colonies. See listings in these colonies for such stamps.

Senegal No. 156 Surcharged in Red

1943 Unwmk. *Perf. 12½x12*

1 A30 1.50fr on 65c dk vio 1.20 .90
2 A30 5.50fr on 65c dk vio 1.60 .80
3 A30 50fr on 65c dk vio 4.00 2.00

Mauritania No. 91 Surcharged in Red

1943 *Perf. 13*

4 A7 3.50fr on 65c dp grn .80 .40
5 A7 4fr on 65c dp grn .80 .40
6 A7 5fr on 65c dp grn 1.60 .80
7 A7 10fr on 65c dp grn 1.60 .80
Nos. 1-7 (7) 11.60 6.10

Senegal No. 143, 148 and 188 Surcharged with New Values in Black and Orange

1944 *Perf. 12½x12*

8 A29 1.50fr on 15c blk (O) .80 .65
9 A29 4.50fr on 15c blk (O) 1.20 .90
10 A29 5.50fr on 2c brn 2.40 1.60
11 A29 10fr on 15c blk (O) 4.00 1.75
12 CD81 20fr on 90c org brn & org 2.40 1.75
13 CD81 50fr on 90c org brn & org 6.50 3.25

Mauritania No. 109 Surcharged in Black

14 CD81 15fr on 90c org brn & org 2.40 1.60
Nos. 8-14 (7) 19.70 11.50

Common Design Types pictured following the introduction.

Eboue Issue
Common Design Type

1945 Engr. *Perf. 13*

15 CD91 2fr black .80 .80
16 CD91 25fr Prussian green 1.60 1.60

Nos. 15 and 16 exist imperforate.

Colonial Soldier — A1

1945 Litho. *Perf. 12½x12, 12*

17 A1 10c indigo & buff .40 .25
18 A1 30c olive & yel .40 .25
19 A1 40c blue & buff .40 .25
20 A1 50c red org & gray .40 .25
21 A1 60c ol brn & bl .80 .40
22 A1 70c mag & cit .80 .40
23 A1 80c bl grn & pale lem .80 .40
24 A1 1fr brn vio & cit .80 .40
25 A1 1.20fr gray brn & cit 4.00 2.40
26 A1 1.50fr choc & pink .80 .40
27 A1 2fr ocher and gray .80 .40
28 A1 2.40fr red & gray 1.25 .80
29 A1 3fr brn red & yelsh .80 .40
30 A1 4fr ultra & pink .80 .40
31 A1 4.50fr org brn & yelsh .80 .40
32 A1 5fr dk pur & yelsh .80 .40
33 A1 10fr ol grn & pink 1.60 .80
34 A1 15fr orange & yel 2.40 1.20
35 A1 20fr sl grn & grnsh 2.75 2.00
Nos. 17-35 (19) 21.60 12.20

Rifle Dance, Mauritania — A2

Bamako Dike, French Sudan — A3

Trading Canoe, Niger River — A4

Oasis of Bilma, Niger — A5

Shelling Coconuts, Togo — A6

Kouandé Weaving, Dahomey A7

Donkey Caravan, Senegal A8

Crocodile and Hippopotamus, Ivory Coast — A9

Gathering Coconuts, French Guinea — A10

Bamako Fountain, French Sudan A11

Peul Woman of Dienné — A12

Bamako Market — A13

Dahomey Laborer A14

Woman of Mauritania A15

Fula Woman, French Guinea — A16

Djenné Mosque, French Sudan A17

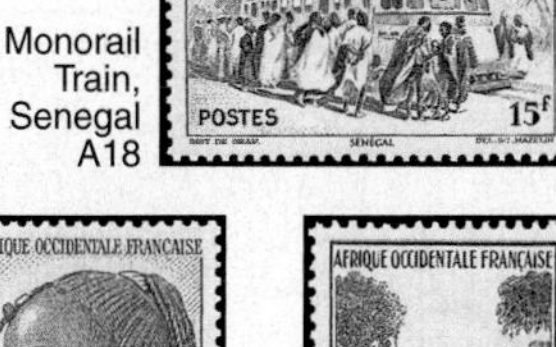

Monorail Train, Senegal A18

Agni Woman, Ivory Coast — A19

Azwa Women at Niger River — A20

1947 Engr. Unwmk. *Perf. 12½*

36 A2 10c blue .40 .25
37 A3 30c red brn .40 .25
38 A4 40c gray grn .40 .25
39 A5 50c red brn .40 .25
40 A6 60c gray blk .80 .50
41 A7 80c brown vio .80 .50
42 A8 1fr maroon .80 .30
43 A9 1.20fr dk blue grn 2.00 1.40
44 A10 1.50fr ultra 2.00 1.10
45 A11 2fr red orange .80 .25
46 A12 3fr chocolate .80 .30
47 A13 3.60fr brown red 1.60 1.40
48 A14 4fr deep blue .80 .30
49 A15 5fr gray green .40 .25
50 A16 6fr dark blue .80 .30
51 A17 10fr brn red .80 .25
52 A18 15fr sepia 2.40 .30
53 A19 20fr chocolate 1.60 .30
54 A20 25fr grnsh blk 2.40 .50
Nos. 36-54 (19) 20.40 8.95

Types of 1947

1948 Re-engraved

55 A6 60c brown olive 1.20 .80
56 A12 3fr chocolate 1.20 .55

Nos. 40 and 46 are inscribed "TOGO" in lower margin. Inscription omitted on Nos. 55 and 56.

Imperforates

Most stamps of French West Africa from 1949 onward exist imperforate in issued and trial colors, and also in small presentation sheets in issued colors.

Military Medal Issue
Common Design Type
Engraved and Typographed

1952, Dec. 1 *Perf. 13*

57 CD101 15fr multicolored 8.75 6.50

Treich Laplène and Map — A21

1952, Dec. 1 Engr.

58 A21 40fr brown lake 2.40 .40

Marcel Treich Laplène, a leading contributor to the development of Ivory Coast.

Medical Laboratory A22

1953, Nov. 18
59 A22 15fr brn, dk bl grn & blk brn 1.60 .40

Couple Feeding Antelopes A23

1954, Sept. 20
60 A23 25fr multicolored 2.00 .40

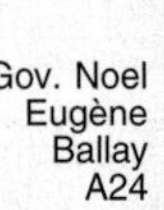

Gov. Noel Eugène Ballay A24

1954, Nov. 29
61 A24 8fr indigo & brown 2.00 .80

Chimpanzee — A25

Giant Pangolin A26

1955, May 2 Unwmk. *Perf. 13*
62 A25 5fr dp vio & dk brn 2.00 .80
63 A26 8fr brn & bl grn 2.00 .80

International Exhibition for Wildlife Protection, Paris, May 1955.

Map, Symbols of Industry, Rotary Emblem A27

1955, July 4
64 A27 15fr dark blue 2.40 .80

50th anniv. of the founding of Rotary Intl.

FIDES Issue
Common Design Type

Designs: 1fr, Date grove, Mauritania. 2fr, Milo Bridge, French Guinea. 3fr, Mossi Railroad, Upper Volta. 4fr, Cattle raising, Niger. 15fr, Farm machinery and landscape, Senegal. 17fr, Woman and Niger River, French Sudan. 20fr, Palm oil production, Dahomey. 30fr, Road construction, Ivory Coast.

1956 Engr. *Perf. 13x12½*
65 CD103 1fr dk grn & dk bl grn 1.60 .65
66 CD103 2fr dk bl grn & bl 1.60 .65
67 CD103 3fr dk brn & red brn 1.60 1.00
68 CD103 4fr dk car rose 2.40 1.10
69 CD103 15fr ind & ultra 1.60 .55
70 CD103 17fr dk bl & ind 2.40 .75
71 CD103 20fr rose lake 2.40 .65
72 CD103 30fr dk pur & claret 2.40 1.00
Nos. 65-72 (8) 16.00 6.35

Coffee A28a

1956, Oct. 22 *Perf. 13*
73 A28a 15fr dk blue green 1.60 .80

Mobile Leprosy Clinic and Maltese Cross A29

1957, Mar. 11
74 A29 15fr dk red brn, pur & red 2.40 .80

Issued in honor of the Knights of Malta.

Map of Africa — A30

1958, Feb. Unwmk. *Perf. 13*
75 A30 20fr multicolored 1.60 .80

6h Intl.Cong. for African Tourism at Dakar.

"Africa" and Communications Symbols — A31

1958, Mar. 15 Engr.
76 A31 15fr org, ultra & choc 2.00 .80

Stamp Day. See No. 86.

Abidjan Bridge A32

1958, Mar. 15
77 A32 20fr dk sl grn & grnsh bl 2.00 .80

Bananas A33

1958, May 19 *Perf. 13*
78 A33 20fr rose lil, dk grn & ol 1.60 .40

Flower Issue
Common Design Type

10fr, Gloriosa. 25fr, Adenopus. 30fr, Cyrtosperma. 40fr, Cistanche. 65fr, Crinum Moorei.

1958-59 Photo. *Perf. 12x12½*
79 CD104 10fr multicolored 1.20 .40
80 CD104 25fr red, yel & grn 1.60 .80
81 CD104 30fr multicolored 2.00 1.20
82 CD104 40fr blk brn, grn & yel 2.40 1.60
83 CD104 65fr multicolored 3.25 1.60
Nos. 79-83 (5) 10.45 5.60

Issued: 25fr, 40fr, 1/5/59; others, 7/7/58.

Moro Naba Sagha and Map — A34

1958, Nov. 1 Engr. *Perf. 13*
84 A34 20fr ol brn, car & vio 1.60 .80

10th anniv. of the reestablishment of the Upper Volta territory.

Human Rights Issue
Common Design Type

1958, Dec. 10
85 CD105 20fr maroon & dk bl 2.40 2.00

Type of 1958 Redrawn

1959, Mar. 21 Engr. *Perf. 13*
86 A31 20fr red, grnsh bl & sl grn 2.75 2.40

Name of country omitted on No. 86; "RF" replaced by "CF," inscribed "Dakar-Abidjan." Stamp Day.

SEMI-POSTAL STAMPS

Red Cross Issue
Common Design Type
Perf. 14½x14

1944, Dec. Photo. Unwmk.
B1 CD90 5fr + 20fr plum 6.50 4.75

The surtax was for the French Red Cross and national relief.

Type of France, 1945, Overprinted in Black

1945, Oct. 13 Engr. *Perf. 13*
B2 SP150 2fr + 3fr orange red 1.20 .80

Tropical Medicine Issue
Common Design Type

1950, May 15 *Perf. 13*
B3 CD100 10fr +2fr red brn & sep 9.50 7.25

The surtax was for charitable work.

AIR POST STAMPS

Common Design Type

1945 Photo. Unwmk. *Perf. 14½x14*
C1 CD87 5.50fr ultra 2.00 1.00
C2 CD87 50fr dark green 3.50 1.40
C3 CD87 100fr plum 4.00 1.50
Nos. C1-C3 (3) 9.50 3.90

Victory Issue
Common Design Type

1946, May 8 Engr. *Perf. 12½*
C4 CD92 8fr violet 1.60 1.20

Chad to Rhine Issue
Common Design Types

1946, June 6
C5 CD93 5fr brown car 2.00 1.60
C6 CD94 10fr deep blue 2.00 1.60
C7 CD95 15fr brt violet 2.40 1.60
C8 CD96 20fr dk slate grn 2.40 2.00
C9 CD97 25fr olive brn 3.25 2.40
C10 CD98 50fr brown 4.00 2.75
Nos. C5-C10 (6) 16.05 11.95

Antoine de Saint-Exupéry, Map and Natives — AP1

Plane over Dakar — AP2

Great White Egrets in Flight — AP3

Natives and Phantom Plane — AP4

1947, Mar. 24 Engr.
C11 AP1 8fr red brown 1.60 .80
C12 AP2 50fr rose violet 4.00 1.20
C13 AP3 100fr ultra 16.00 4.75
C14 AP4 200fr slate gray 14.00 5.25
Nos. C11-C14 (4) 35.60 12.00

UPU Issue
Common Design Type

1949, July 4 *Perf. 13*
C15 CD99 25fr multicolored 12.00 8.75

Vridi Canal, Abidjan — AP5

1951, Nov. 5 Unwmk. *Perf. 13*
C16 AP5 500fr red org, bl grn & dp ultra 32.50 4.75

Liberation Issue
Common Design Type

1954, June 6
C17 CD102 15fr indigo & ultra 12.00 5.50

Logging — AP6

Designs: 100fr, Radiotelephone exchange. 200fr, Baobab trees.

1954, Sept. 20
C18 AP6 50fr ol grn & org brn 4.00 .80
C19 AP6 100fr ind, dk brn & dk grn 6.50 1.20

C20	AP6	200fr bl grn, grnsh blk & brn lake	17.50	2.75
		Nos. C18-C20 (3)	28.00	4.75

Gen. Louis Faidherbé and African Sharpshooter AP7

1957, July 20 Unwmk. *Perf. 13*

C21	AP7	15fr indigo & blue	2.00	1.60

Centenary of French African troops.

Gorée Island and Woman — AP8

Designs: 20fr, Map with planes and ships. 25fr, Village and modern city. 40fr, Seat of Council of French West Africa. 50fr, Worker, ship and peanut plant. 100fr, Bay of N'Gor.

1958, Mar. 15 Engr.

C22	AP8	15fr blk brn, grn & vio	1.60	.80
C23	AP8	20fr blk brn, dk bl & red brn	1.60	.80
C24	AP8	25fr blk vio, bis & grn	1.60	1.20
C25	AP8	40fr dk bl, brn & grn	1.60	1.20
C26	AP8	50fr violet, brn & grn	3.25	1.60
C27	AP8	100fr brown, bl & grn	6.50	2.40
a.		Souvenir sheet of 6, #C22-C27	20.00	16.00
		Nos. C22-C27 (6)	16.15	8.00

Centenary of Dakar.

Woman Playing Native Harp — AP9

1958, Dec. 1 Unwmk. *Perf. 13*

C28	AP9	20fr red brn, blk & gray	1.60	.80

Inauguration of Nouakchott as capital of Mauritania.

POSTAGE DUE STAMPS

D1

1947 Engr. Unwmk. *Perf. 13*

J1	D1	10c red	.40	.25
J2	D1	30c deep orange	.40	.25
J3	D1	50c greenish blk	.40	.25
J4	D1	1fr carmine	.40	.25
J5	D1	2fr emerald	.50	.30
J6	D1	3fr red lilac	.90	.65
J7	D1	4fr deep ultra	1.10	.80
J8	D1	5fr red brown	2.25	1.60
J9	D1	10fr peacock blue	2.90	2.25
J10	D1	20fr sepia	5.25	3.75
		Nos. J1-J10 (10)	14.50	10.35

OFFICIAL STAMPS

Mask — O1

Designs: Various masks.

Perf. 14x13

1958, June 2 Typo. Unwmk.

O1	O1	1fr dk brn red	1.10	1.00
O2	O1	3fr brt green	.65	.55
O3	O1	5fr crim rose	.65	.50
O4	O1	10fr light ultra	.80	.65
O5	O1	20fr bright red	1.60	.80
O6	O1	25fr purple	1.60	.80
O7	O1	30fr green	2.75	1.60
O8	O1	45fr gray black	3.25	1.60
O9	O1	50fr dark red	3.25	1.60
O10	O1	65fr brt ultra	4.50	1.60
O11	O1	100fr olive bister	10.50	2.75
O12	O1	200fr deep green	21.00	5.50
		Nos. O1-O12 (12)	51.65	18.95

FUJEIRA

fü-'jī-rə

LOCATION — Oman Peninsula, Arabia, on Persian Gulf

GOVT. — Sheikdom under British protection

Fujeira is one of six Persian Gulf sheikdoms to join the United Arab Emirates which proclaimed independence Dec. 2, 1971. See United Arab Emirates.

100 Naye Paise = 1 Rupee

Catalogue values for all unused stamps in this country are for Never Hinged items.

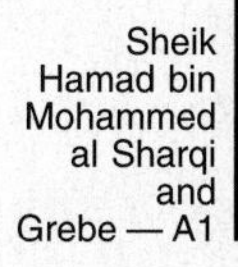

Sheik Hamad bin Mohammed al Sharqi and Grebe — A1

Sheik and: 2np, 50np, Arabian oryx. 3np, 70np, Hoopoe. 4np, 1r, Wild ass. 5np, 1.50r, Herons in flight. 10np, 2r, Arabian horses. 15np, 3r, Leopard. 20np, 5r, Camels. 30np, 10r, Hawks.

Photo. & Litho.

1964 Unwmk. *Perf. 14*

Size: 36x24mm

1	A1	1np gold & multi	.25	.25
2	A1	2np gold & multi	.25	.25
3	A1	3np gold & multi	.25	.25
4	A1	4np gold & multi	.25	.25
5	A1	5np gold & multi	.25	.25
6	A1	10np gold & multi	.25	.25
7	A1	15np gold & multi	.25	.25
8	A1	20np gold & multi	.25	.25
9	A1	30np gold & multi	.25	.25

Size: 43x28mm

10	A1	40np gold & multi	.35	.25
11	A1	50np gold & multi	.40	.25
12	A1	70np gold & multi	.45	.25
13	A1	1r gold & multi	.65	.25
14	A1	1.50r gold & multi	.95	.25
15	A1	2r gold & multi	1.50	.25

Size: 53½x35mm

16	A1	3r gold & multi	2.40	.25
17	A1	5r gold & multi	2.25	.35
18	A1	10r gold & multi	7.50	.50
		Nos. 1-18 (18)	18.70	4.85

Issued: 20np, 30np, 70np, 1.50r, 3r, 10r, Nov. 14; others, Sept. 22.

Exist imperf. Value, set $30.

Sheik Hamad and Shot Put A2

1964, Dec. 6 *Perf. 14*

Size: 43x28mm

19	A2	25np shown	.25	.25
20	A2	50np Discus	.25	.25
21	A2	75np Fencing	.25	.25
22	A2	1r Boxing	.35	.30
23	A2	1.50r Relay race	.50	.35
24	A2	2r Soccer	.60	.40

Size: 53½x35mm

25	A2	3r Pole vaulting	1.15	.50
26	A2	5r Hurdling	3.00	.75
27	A2	7.50r Equestrian	4.25	.90
		Nos. 19-27 (9)	10.60	3.95

18th Olympic Games, Tokyo, 10/10-25/64.
Exist imperf. Value, set $12.

John F. Kennedy — A3

Kennedy: 10np, As sailor in the Pacific. 15np, As naval lieutenant. 20np, On speaker's rostrum. 25np, Sailing with family. 50np, With crowd of people. 1r, With Mrs. Kennedy, Lyndon B. Johnson. 2r, With Eisenhower on White House porch. 3r, With Mrs. Kennedy & Caroline. 5r, Portrait.

1965, Feb. 23 Photo. *Perf. 13½*

Size: 29x44mm

Black Design with Gold Inscriptions

28	A3	5np pale gray	.25	.25
29	A3	10np pale yellow	.25	.25
30	A3	15np pink	.25	.25
31	A3	20np pale greenish gray	.25	.25
32	A3	25np pale blue	.25	.25
33	A3	50np pale rose	.30	.25

Size: 33x51mm

34	A3	1r pale gray	.75	.30
35	A3	2r pale green	1.25	.40
36	A3	3r pale gray	2.50	.50
37	A3	5r pale yellow	3.25	.80
		Nos. 28-37 (10)	9.30	3.50

Pres. John F. Kennedy (1917-1963). A souvenir sheet contains 2 29x44mm stamps similar to Nos. 36-37 with pale blue (3r) and pale rose (5r) backgrounds. Value (unused): perf $7; imperf $9.

Nos. 28-37 exist imperf. Value $14.

AIR POST STAMPS

Wild Ass AP1

Photo. & Litho.

1965, Aug. 16 Unwmk. *Perf. 13½*

Size: 43x28mm

C1	AP1	15np Grebe	.25	.25
C2	AP1	25np Arabian oryx	.25	.25
C3	AP1	35np Hoopoe	.35	.25
C4	AP1	50np Wild ass	.40	.25
C5	AP1	75np Herons in flight	.45	.25
C6	AP1	1r Arabian horses	.60	.25

Size: 53½x35mm

C7	AP1	2r Leopard	1.25	.25
C8	AP1	3r Camels	2.50	.25
C9	AP1	5r Hawks	4.50	.50
		Nos. C1-C9 (9)	10.55	2.50

Exist imperf. Value, set $11.

AIR POST OFFICIAL STAMPS

Type of Air Post Issue, 1965

Photo. & Litho.

1965, Nov. 10 Unwmk. *Perf. 13½*

Size: 43x28mm

CO1	AP1	75np Arabian horses	.60	.25

Perf. 13

Size: 53½x35mm

CO2	AP1	2r Leopard	1.50	.40
CO3	AP1	3r Camels	2.50	.60
CO4	AP1	5r Hawks	4.50	1.00
		Nos. CO1-CO4 (4)	9.10	2.25

Exist imperf. Values same as perf.

OFFICIAL STAMPS

Type of Air Post Issue, 1965

Photo. & Litho.

1965, Oct. 14 Unwmk. *Perf. 13½*

Size: 43x28mm

O1	AP1	25np Grebe	.25	.25
O2	AP1	40np Arabian oryx	.25	.25
O3	AP1	50np Hoopoe	.35	.25
O4	AP1	75np Wild ass	.55	.25
O5	AP1	1r Herons in flight	1.25	.25
		Nos. O1-O5 (5)	2.65	1.25

Exist imperf. Values same as perf.

FUNCHAL

fün-'shäl

LOCATION — A city and administrative district in the Madeira island group in the Atlantic Ocean northwest of Africa

GOVT. — A part of the Republic of Portugal

POP. — 150,574 (1900)

Postage stamps of Funchal were superseded by those of Portugal.

1000 Reis = 1 Milreis

King Carlos — A1

1892-93 Typo. Unwmk.

Perf. 11 ½, 12 ½, 13 ½

1	A1	5r yellow	4.25	2.00
2	A1	10r red violet	4.25	2.00
3	A1	15r chocolate	5.50	3.75
4	A1	20r lavender	5.50	3.00
5a	A1	25r dark green	8.00	1.75
6	A1	50r ultramarine	10.25	5.00
7	A1	75r carmine	10.25	6.75
8	A1	80r yellow green	20.00	12.00
9	A1	100r brn, *yel* ('93)	13.50	5.50
10	A1	150r car, *rose* ('93)	70.00	31.00
11	A1	200r dk bl, *bl* ('93)	80.00	45.00
12	A1	300r dk bl, *sal* ('93)	80.00	55.00
		Nos. 1-12 (12)	311.50	172.75

Nos. 1-12 were printed on both enamel-surfaced and chalky papers. Values are for the most common varieties. For detailed listings, see the *Scott Classic Specialized Catalogue.*

The reprints of this issue have shiny white gum and clean-cut perforation 13½. The shades differ from those of the originals and the uncolored paper is thin.

King Carlos — A2

Name and Value in Black except Nos. 25 and 34

1897-1905 ***Perf. 11¾***

13	A2	2½r gray	.60	.60
a.		Name and denomination inverted	275.00	
14	A2	5r orange	.60	.60
15	A2	10r light green	.60	.60
16	A2	15r brown	8.00	5.00
17	A2	15r gray grn ('99)	5.50	3.75
18	A2	20r gray vio	2.40	1.20
19	A2	25r sea green	3.75	1.20
20	A2	25r car rose ('99)	2.40	.60
a.		Booklet pane of 6	—	
21	A2	50r dark blue	9.25	5.00
a.		Perf. 12½	25.00	12.00
22	A2	50r ultra ('05)	2.40	1.20
23	A2	65r slate blue ('98)	1.25	1.20
24	A2	75r rose	2.40	1.20
25	A2	75r brn & red, *yel* ('05)	3.00	1.40
26	A2	80r violet	2.40	1.75
27	A2	100r dark blue, *blue*	2.40	1.75
28	A2	115r org brn, *pink* ('98)	3.50	1.75
29	A2	130r gray brown, *buff* ('98)	3.50	1.75
30	A2	150r lt brn, *buff*	4.25	1.75
31	A2	180r sl, *pnksh* ('98)	3.50	1.75
32	A2	200r red vio, *pale lil*	4.25	2.40
33	A2	300r blue, *rose*	4.25	2.40
34	A2	500r blk & red, *bl*	4.25	2.40
a.		Perf. 12½	17.50	9.00
		Nos. 13-34 (22)	74.45	41.25

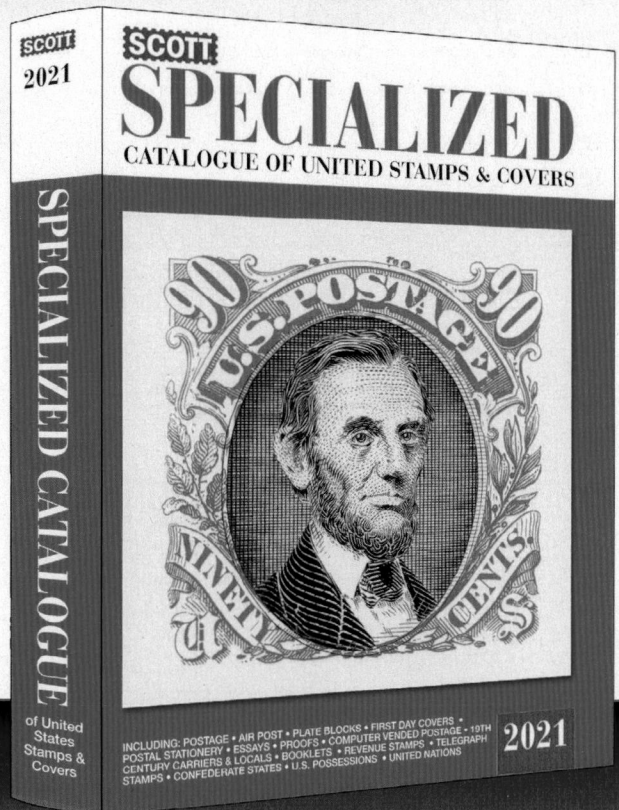

Pronunciation Symbols

ə .... banana, collide, abut

ˈə, ˌə .... humdrum, abut

ə .... immediately preceding \l\, \n\, \m\, \ŋ\, as in battle, mitten, eaten, and sometimes open \ˈō-pᵊm\, lock **and** key \-ᵊŋ-\; immediately following \l\, \m\, \r\, as often in French table, prisme, titre

ər .... further, merger, bird

ˈər- } .... as in two different pronunciations
ˈə-r } of hurry \ˈhər-ē, ˈhə-rē\

a .... mat, map, mad, gag, snap, patch

ā .... day, fade, date, aorta, drape, cape

ä .... bother, cot, and, with most American speakers, father, cart

ȧ .... father as pronounced by speakers who do not rhyme it with *bother*; French patte

au̇ .... now, loud, out

b .... baby, rib

ch .... chin, nature \ˈnā-chər\

d .... did, adder

e .... bet, bed, peck

ˈē, ˌē .... beat, nosebleed, evenly, easy

ē .... easy, mealy

f .... fifty, cuff

g .... go, big, gift

h .... hat, ahead

hw .... whale as pronounced by those who do not have the same pronunciation for both *whale* and *wail*

i .... tip, banish, active

ī .... site, side, buy, tripe

j .... job, gem, edge, join, judge

k .... kin, cook, ache

k̲ .... German ich, Buch; one pronunciation of loch

l .... lily, pool

m .... murmur, dim, nymph

n .... no, own

ⁿ .... indicates that a preceding vowel or diphthong is pronounced with the nasal passages open, as in French *un bon vin blanc* \œⁿ -bōⁿ -vaⁿ -bläⁿ\

ŋ .... sing \ˈsiŋ\, singer \ˈsiŋ-ər\, finger \ˈfiŋ-gər\, ink \ˈiŋk \

ō .... bone, know, beau

ȯ .... saw, all, gnaw, caught

œ .... French boeuf, German Hölle

œ̄ .... French feu, German Höhle

ȯi .... coin, destroy

p .... pepper, lip

r .... red, car, rarity

s .... source, less

sh .... as in shy, mission, machine, special (actually, this is a single sound, not two); with a hyphen between, two sounds as in *grasshopper* \ˈgras-ˌhä-pər\

t .... tie, attack, late, later, latter

th .... as in thin, ether (actually, this is a single sound, not two); with a hyphen between, two sounds as in *knighthood* \ˈnīt-ˌhu̇d\

t̲h̲ .... then, either, this (actually, this is a single sound, not two)

ü .... rule, youth, union \ˈyün-yən\, few \ˈfyü\

u̇ .... pull, wood, book, curable \ˈkyu̇r-ə-bəl\, fury \ˈfyu̇r-ē\

ue .... German füllen, hübsch

ue̅ .... French rue, German fühlen

v .... vivid, give

w .... we, away

y .... yard, young, cue \ˈkyü\, mute \ˈmyüt\, union \ˈyün-yən\

ʸ .... indicates that during the articulation of the sound represented by the preceding character the front of the tongue has substantially the position it has for the articulation of the first sound of *yard*, as in French *digne* \dēnʸ\

z .... zone, raise

zh .... as in vision, azure \ˈa-zhər\ (actually, this is a single sound, not two); with a hyphen between, two sounds as in *hogshead* \ˈhȯgz-ˌhed, ˈhägz-\

\ .... slant line used in pairs to mark the beginning and end of a transcription: \ˈpen\

ˈ .... mark preceding a syllable with primary (strongest) stress: \ˈpen-mən-ˌship\

ˌ .... mark preceding a syllable with secondary (medium) stress: \ˈpen-mən-ˌship\

- .... mark of syllable division

( ) .... indicate that what is symbolized between is present in some utterances but not in others: *factory* \ˈfak-t(ə-)rē\

÷ .... indicates that many regard as unacceptable the pronunciation variant immediately following: *cupola* \ˈkyü-pə-lə, ÷-ˌlō\

Illustrated Identifier

This section pictures stamps or parts of stamp designs that will help identify postage stamps that do not have English words on them.

Many of the symbols that identify stamps of countries are shown here as well as typical examples of their stamps.

See the Index and Identifier for stamps with inscriptions such as "sen," "posta," "Baja Porto," "Helvetia," "K.S.A.", etc.

1. HEADS, PICTURES AND NUMERALS

GREAT BRITAIN

Great Britain stamps never show the country name, but, except for postage dues, show a picture of the reigning monarch.

Victoria

Edward VII George V Edward VIII

George VI

Elizabeth II

Some George VI and Elizabeth II stamps are surcharged in annas, new paisa or rupees. These are listed under Oman.

Silhouette (sometimes facing right, generally at the top of stamp)

The silhouette indicates this is a British stamp. It is not a U.S. stamp.

VICTORIA

Queen Victoria

INDIA

Other stamps of India show this portrait of Queen Victoria and the words "Service" (or "Postage") and "Annas."

AUSTRIA

YUGOSLAVIA

(Also BOSNIA & HERZEGOVINA if imperf.)

BOSNIA & HERZEGOVINA

Denominations also appear in top corners instead of bottom corners.

HUNGARY

Another stamp has posthorn facing left

BRAZIL

AUSTRALIA

Kangaroo and Emu

GERMANY

Mecklenburg-Vorpommern

SWITZERLAND

PALAU

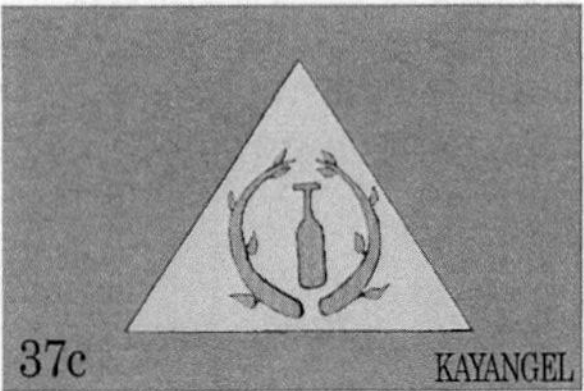

2. ORIENTAL INSCRIPTIONS

CHINA

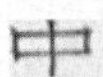

Any stamp with this one character is from China (Imperial, Republic or People's Republic). This character appears in a four-character overprint on stamps of Manchukuo. These stamps are local provisionals, which are unlisted. Other overprinted Manchukuo stamps show this character, but have more than four characters in the overprints. These are listed in People's Republic of China.

Some Chinese stamps show the Sun.

Most stamps of Republic of China show this series of characters.

Stamps with the China character and this character are from People's Republic of China. 人

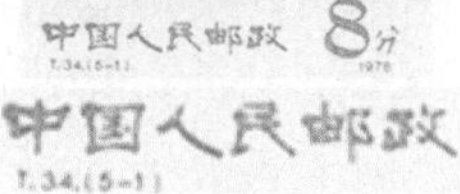

Calligraphic form of People's Republic of China

(一)	(二)	(三)	(四)	(五)	(六)
1	2	3	4	5	6
(七)	(八)	(九)	(十)	(一十)	(二十)
7	8	9	10	11	12

Chinese stamps without China character

REPUBLIC OF CHINA

PEOPLE'S REPUBLIC OF CHINA

Mao Tse-tung

MANCHUKUO

Temple Emperor Pu-Yi

The first 3 characters are common to many Manchukuo stamps.

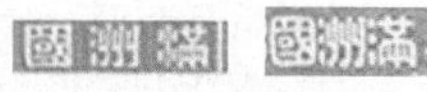

The last 3 characters are common to other Manchukuo stamps.

Orchid Crest

Manchukuo stamp without these elements

JAPAN

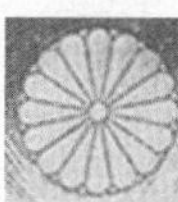
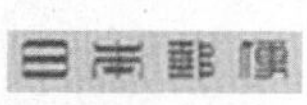

Chrysanthemum Crest Country Name

Japanese stamps without these elements

The number of characters in the center and the design of dragons on the sides will vary.

RYUKYU ISLANDS

Country Name

PHILIPPINES (Japanese Occupation)

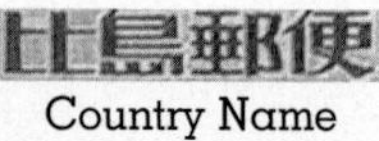

Country Name

NETHERLANDS INDIES (Japanese Occupation)

Indicates Japanese Occupation

Java Sumatra

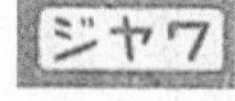

Country Name Country Name

Moluccas, Celebes and South Borneo

Country Name

NORTH BORNEO (Japanese Occupation)

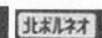

Indicates Japanese Occupation Country Name

MALAYA (Japanese Occupation)

Indicates Japanese Occupation Country Name

BURMA

Union of Myanmar

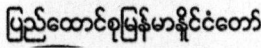

ပြည်ထောင်စုမြန်မာနိုင်ငံတော်

Union of Myanmar

(Japanese Occupation)

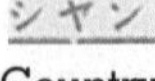

Indicates Japanese Occupation

Country Name

Other Burma Japanese Occupation stamps without these elements

Burmese Script

KOREA

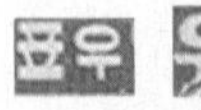

These two characters, in any order, are common to stamps from the Republic of Korea (South Korea) or of the People's Democratic Republic of Korea (North Korea).

This series of four characters can be found on the stamps of both Koreas. Most stamps of the Democratic People's Republic of Korea (North Korea) have just this inscription.

대한민국 우표

Indicates Republic of Korea (South Korea)

South Korean postage stamps issed after 1952 do not show currency expressed in Latin letters. Stamps wiith " HW," "HWAN," "WON," "WN," "W" or "W" with two lines through it, if not illustrated in listings of stamps before this date, are revenues. North Korean postage stamps do not have currency expressed in Latin letters.

Yin Yang appears on some stamps.

South Korean stamps show Yin Yang and starting in 1966, 'KOREA" in Latin letters

Example of South Korean stamps lacking Latin text, Yin Yang and standard Korean text of country name. North Korean stamps never show Yin Yang and starting in 1976 are inscribed "DPRK" or "DPR KOREA" in Latin letters.

THAILAND

Country Name

King Chulalongkorn

King Prajadhipok and Chao P'ya Chakri

3. CENTRAL AND EASTERN ASIAN INSCRIPTIONS

INDIA - FEUDATORY STATES

Alwar

Bhor

Bundi

Similar stamps come with different designs in corners and differently drawn daggers (at center of circle).

Dhar

Duttia

Faridkot

Hyderabad

Similar stamps exist with different central design which is inscribed "Postage" or "Post & Receipt."

Indore

Jammu & Kashmir

Text varies.

Jasdan

Jhalawar

Kotah

Size and text varies

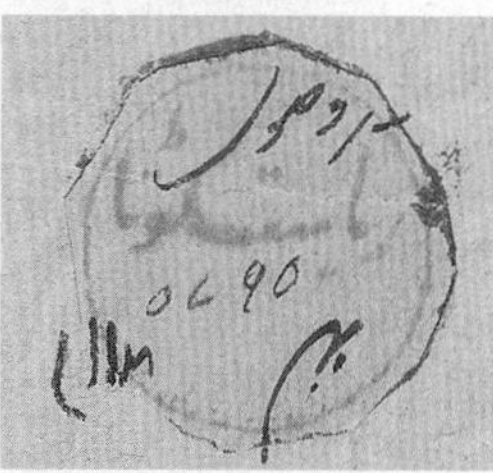

Nandgaon

Nowanuggur

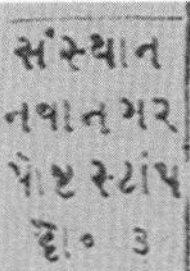

Poonch

Similar stamps exist in various sizes with different text

Rajasthan

Rajpeepla

Soruth

Tonk

BANGLADESH

Country Name

NEPAL

Similar stamps are smaller, have squares in upper corners and have five or nine characters in central bottom panel.

TANNU TUVA

ISRAEL

GEORGIA

This inscription is found on other pictorial stamps.

Country Name

ARMENIA

The four characters are found somewhere on pictorial stamps. On some stamps only the middle two are found.

4. AFRICAN INSCRIPTIONS

ETHIOPIA

5. ARABIC INSCRIPTIONS

١	٢	٣	٤	٥
1	2	3	4	5
٦	٧	٨	٩	٠
6	7	8	9	0

AFGHANISTAN

Many early Afghanistan stamps show Tiger's head, many of these have ornaments protruding from outer ring, others show inscriptions in black.

Arabic Script

Crest of King Amanullah

Mosque Gate & Crossed Cannons

The four characters are found somewhere on pictorial stamps. On some stamps only the middle two are found.

BAHRAIN

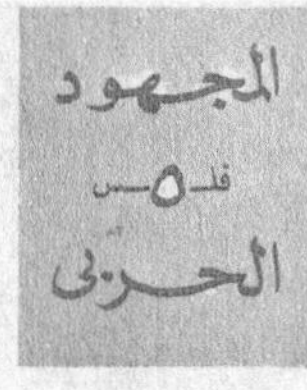

EGYPT

Postage

IRAN

Country Name

Royal Crown

Lion with Sword

Symbol

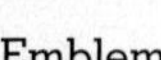

Emblem

IRAQ

JORDAN

LEBANON

Similar types have denominations at top and slightly different design.

LIBYA

Country Name in various styles

Other Libya stamps show Eagle and Shield (head facing either direction) or Red, White and Black Shield (with or without eagle in center).

Without Country Name

SAUDI ARABIA

Tughra (Central design)

Palm Tree and Swords

SYRIA

Arab Government Issues

THRACE

YEMEN

PAKISTAN

PAKISTAN - BAHAWALPUR

Country Name in top panel, star and crescent

TURKEY

Star & Crescent is a device found on many Turkish stamps, but is also found on stamps from other Arabic areas (see Pakistan-Bahawalpur)

Tughra (similar tughras can be found on stamps of Turkey in Asia, Afghanistan and Saudi Arabia)

Mohammed V

Mustafa Kemal

Plane, Star and Crescent

TURKEY IN ASIA

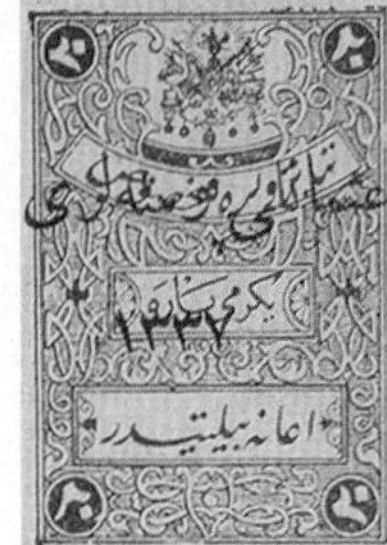

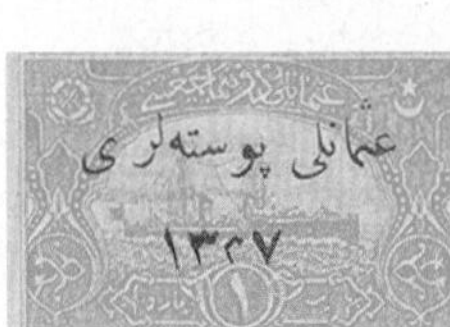

Other Turkey in Asia pictorials show star & crescent.
Other stamps show tughra shown under Turkey.

6. GREEK INSCRIPTIONS

GREECE

Country Name in various styles
(Some Crete stamps overprinted with the Greece country name are listed in Crete.)

Lepta

ΔΡΑΧΜΗ ΔΡΑΧΜΑΙ

Drachma Drachmas Lepton

Abbreviated Country Name ΕΛΛ

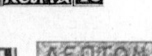

Other forms of Country Name

No country name

CRETE

Country Name

Crete stamps with a surcharge that have the year "1922" are listed under Greece.

EPIRUS

Similar stamps have text above the eagle.

IONIAN IS.

7. CYRILLIC INSCRIPTIONS

RUSSIA

Postage Stamp Imperial Eagle

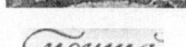

Postage in various styles

КОП РУБ РОССIЯ

Abbreviation for Kopeck Abbreviation for Ruble Russia

Abbreviation for Russian Soviet Federated Socialist Republic RSFSR stamps were overprinted (see below)

Abbreviation for Union of Soviet Socialist Republics

This item is footnoted in Latvia

RUSSIA - Army of the North

"OKCA"

RUSSIA - Wenden

RUSSIAN OFFICES IN THE TURKISH EMPIRE

РОПиТ

These letters appear on other stamps of the Russian offices.

The unoverprinted version of this stamp and a similar stamp were overprinted by various countries (see below).

ARMENIA

BELARUS

FAR EASTERN REPUBLIC

Country Name

FINLAND

Circles and Dots on stamps similar to Imperial Russia issues

SOUTH RUSSIA

Country Name

BATUM

БАТУМСКАЯ

Forms of Country Name

TRANSCAUCASIAN FEDERATED REPUBLICS

Abbreviation for Country Name

KAZAKHSTAN

ҚАЗАҚСТАН

KYRGYZSTAN

КЫРГЫЗСТАН Country Name

ROMANIA

TAJIKISTAN

Тадж.

Country Name & Abbreviation

UKRAINE

Пошта України Україhи

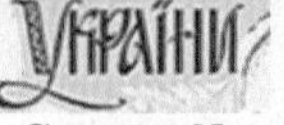

Україhu

Country Name in various forms

The trident appears on many stamps, usually as an overprint.

УС РР

Abbreviation for Ukrainian Soviet Socialist Republic

WESTERN UKRAINE

Abbreviation for Country Name

AZERBAIJAN

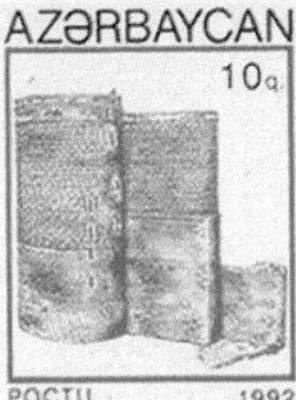

AZƏRBAYCAN

Country Name

A.C.C.P.

Abbreviation for Azerbaijan Soviet Socialist Republic

MONTENEGRO

ЦРНЕГОРЕ

ЦРНА ГОРА

Country Name in various forms

ЦР. ГОРЕ

Abbreviation for country name

No country name (A similar Montenegro stamp without country name has same vignette.)

SERBIA

СРПСКА СРБИЈА

Country Name in various forms

СРП. К.С.

Abbreviation for country name

No country name

MACEDONIA

МАКЕДОНИЈА

МАКЕДОНИЈА

Country Name

МАКЕДОНСКИ

Different form of Country Name

SERBIA & MONTENEGRO

YUGOSLAVIA

ЈУГОСЛАВИЈА

Showing country name

No Country Name

BOSNIA & HERZEGOVINA (Serb Administration)

РЕПУБЛИКА СРПСКА

Country Name

РЕПУБЛИКЕ СРПСКЕ

Different form of Country Name

No Country Name

BULGARIA

Country Name Postage

Stotinka

Stotinki (plural) Abbreviation for Stotinki

Country Name in various forms and styles

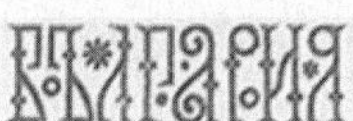

No country name

Abbreviation for Lev, leva

MONGOLIA

Country name in one word Tugrik in Cyrillic

Country name in two words Mung in Cyrillic

Mung in Mongolian

Tugrik in Mongolian

Arms

No Country Name

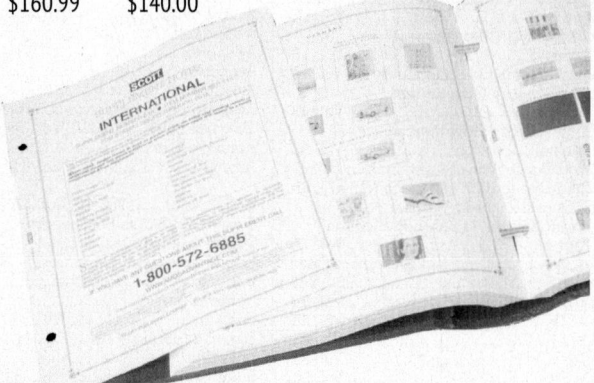

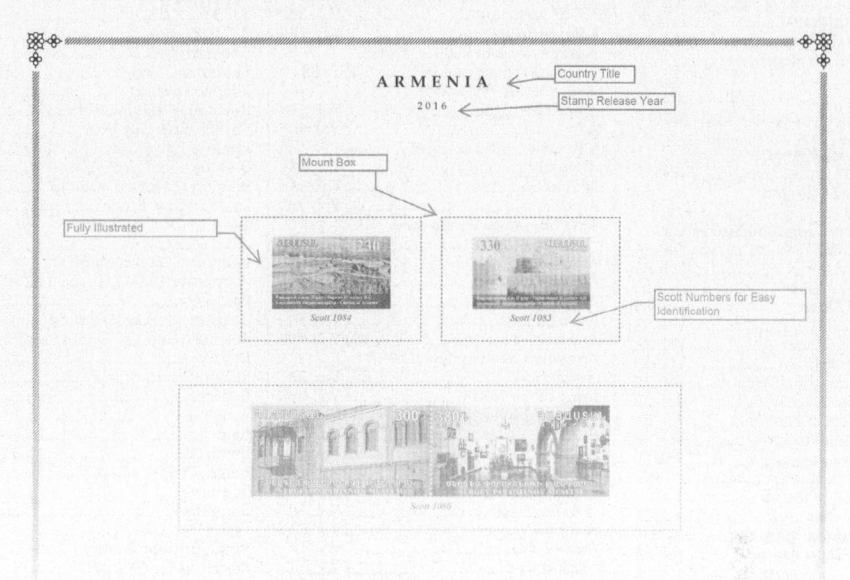

INDEX AND IDENTIFIER

All page numbers shown are those in this Volume 2B.

INDEX TO ADVERTISERS 2021 VOLUME 2B

Vols. 2A-2B Number Additions, Deletions & Changes

Number in 2020 Catalogue	Number in 2021 Catalogue
China	
new	75a
China, Republic of	
new	1606b
new	1607b
new	1608b
new	1609b
new	1791a
new	1792a
new	1793a
new	1794a
new	1796b
new	1797b
new	1798b
new	2154Ac
3165a	3165A
new	3165Ab
new	3165Ac
Crete	
96b	deleted
96c	deleted
Dahomey	
C191a	C191A
Fiji	
new	1254h
new	1370a
new	1407Bc

SCOTT® Specialty Series

Embark on a new collecting journey. There are Specialty pages available for more than 140 countries with some of them back in print after many years thanks to on-demand printing technology. Start a new collecting adventure with countries featured in Volume 2 of the new Scott Standard Postage Stamp Catalogue!

Specialty Series pages are sold as page units only. Binders, labels and slipcases are sold separately.

ALBUM SETS

These money-saving album sets include pages, binders and self-adhesive binder labels. Some set contents may vary, please call or visit or web site for specific information.

CANADA

Item		# of Pgs.	Retail	AA
240CAN1	1851-1952	64	$44.99	$38.24
240CAN2	1953-1978	57	$44.99	$38.24
240CAN3	1979-1990	54	$44.99	$38.24
240CAN4	1991-1995	40	$32.99	$28.04
240CAN5	1996-2000	60	$44.99	$38.24
240CAN6	2001-2006	80	$57.99	$49.29
240S007	2007 #59	14	$19.99	$16.99
240S008	2008 #60	9	$13.99	$11.89
240S009	2009 #61	16	$19.99	$16.99
240S010	2010 #62	17	$19.99	$16.99
240S011	2011 #63	19	$19.99	$16.99
240S012	2012 #64	18	$19.99	$16.99
240S013	2013 #65	23	$21.99	$18.69
240S014	2014 #66	25	$21.99	$18.69
240S015	2015 #67	20	$21.99	$18.69
240S016	2016 #68		$25.99	$21.99
240S017	2017 #69		$25.99	$21.99
240S018	2018 #70		$25.99	$21.99
240S019	2019 #71		$25.99	$21.99
240BLANK	Blank Pages	20	$19.99	$16.99
LB012	Label: Canada		$3.99	$2.99
240SET	Album Set 1851-2015		$569.99	$469.99

Supplemented in May

CAYMAN ISLANDS

Item		# of Pgs.	Retail	AA
261CYI0	1900-1995	78	$52.99	$45.04
261CYI2	1996-2006	42	$32.99	$28.04
261CI07	2007 #11	4	$9.99	$8.49
261CI08	2008 #12	7	$9.99	$8.49
261CI09	2009 #13	4	$9.99	$8.49
261CI11	2011 #14	5	$9.99	$8.49
261CI12	2012 #15	4	$9.99	$8.49
261CI13	2013 #16	4	$9.99	$8.49
261CI14	2014 #17	3	$6.99	$5.94
261CI16	2016 #18		$11.99	$9.99
261CI17	2017 #19		$11.99	$9.99
261CI18	2018 #20		$11.99	$9.99
CAYBLANK	Blank Pages	20	$19.99	$16.99
LB150	Label: Cayman Islands		$3.99	$2.99
261CISET	Album Set 1900-2015		$199.99	$149.99

Supplemented in June

CHILE

Item		# of Pgs.	Retail	AA
645CHL1	1853-1977	73	$49.99	$42.49
645CHL2	1978-1993	74	$49.99	$42.49
645CHL3	1994-1997	25	$21.99	$18.69
645CHL4	1998-2006	49	$49.99	$42.49
645S007	2007 #13	5	$9.99	$8.49
645S008	2008 #14	10	$13.99	$11.89
645S009	2009 #15	10	$13.99	$11.89
645S010	2010 #16	8	$13.99	$11.89
645S011	2011 #17	5	$9.99	$8.49
645S012	2012 #18	3	$6.99	$5.94
645S013	2013 #19	4	$9.99	$8.49
645S014	2014 #20	5	$9.99	$8.49
645S015	2015 #21	5	$9.99	$8.49
645S016	2016 #22		$11.99	$9.99
645S017	2017 #23		$11.99	$9.99
645SET	Album Set 1853-2015		$369.99	$279.99

Supplemented in September

CHINA

Item		# of Pgs.	Retail	AA
480CHN1	1878-1949	91	$57.99	$49.29
480CHN2	1865-1950	101	$69.99	$59.49
480SET	Album Set 1878-1950		$229.99	$169.99
CHINASET	China Complete 1878-2015		$1,249.99	$989.99

COLOMBIA

Item		# of Pgs.	Retail	AA
646COL1	1856-1976	151	$89.99	$76.49
646COL2	1977-1994	58	$44.99	$38.24
646COL3	1995-1997	15	$19.99	$16.99
646COL4	1998-2006	58	$44.99	$38.24
646S007	2007 #13	7	$9.99	$8.49
646S009	2008-2009 #14	11	$16.99	$14.44
646S010	2010 #15	14	$19.99	$16.99
646S011	2011 #16	8	$13.99	$11.89
646S012	2012 #17	9	$13.99	$11.89
646S013	2013 #18	4	$9.99	$8.49
646S015	2015 #19	4	$9.99	$8.49
646S016	2016 #20		$11.99	$9.99
646S018	2018 #21		$19.99	$16.99
LB194	Label: Colombia		$3.99	$2.99
646SET	Album Set 1856-2015		$399.99	$299.99

Supplemented in September

CYPRUS

Item		# of Pgs.	Retail	AA
203CYP0	1880-1997	85	$57.99	$49.29
203CYP2	1998-2006	33	$29.99	$25.49
203CY07	2007 #9	3	$6.99	$5.94
203CY08	2008 #10	5	$9.99	$8.49
203CY09	2009 #11	4	$9.99	$8.49
203CY10	2010 #12	4	$9.99	$8.49
203CY11	2011 #13	6	$9.99	$8.49
203CY12	2012 #14	4	$9.99	$8.49
203CY13	2013 #15	6	$9.99	$8.49
203CY14	2014 #16	3	$6.99	$5.94
203CY15	2015 #17	8	$13.99	$11.89
203CY16	2016 #18		$11.99	$9.99
203CY17	2017 #19		$11.99	$9.99
203CY18	2018 #20		$11.99	$9.99
CYPBLANK	Blank Pages	20	$19.99	$16.99
LB188	Label: Cyprus		$3.99	$2.99
203CYPSET	Album Set 1880-2015		$219.99	$159.99

Supplemented in May

CZECHOSLOVAKIA

Item		# of Pgs.	Retail	AA
307CZH1	1918-1959	121	$69.99	$59.49
307CZH2	1960-1972	89	$57.99	$49.29
307CZH3	1973-1986	82	$57.99	$49.29
307CZH4	1987-1994	46	$34.99	$29.74
307CZH5	1995-1999	37	$32.99	$28.04
307CZH6	2000-2006	58	$44.99	$38.24
307S007	2007 #58	10	$13.99	$11.89
307S008	2008 #59	10	$13.99	$11.89
307S009	2009 #60	13	$16.99	$14.44
307S010	2010 #61	10	$13.99	$11.89
307S011	2011 #62	18	$19.99	$16.99
307S012	2012 #63	15	$19.99	$16.99
307S013	2013 #64	11	$16.99	$14.44
307S014	2014 #65	11	$16.99	$14.44
307S015	2015 #66	13	$16.99	$14.44
307S016	2016 #67		$22.99	$19.99
307S017	2017 #68		$22.99	$19.99
307S018	2018 #69		$22.99	$19.99
307S019	2019 #70		$22.99	$19.99
CZEBLANK	Blank Pages	20	$19.99	$16.99
LB014	Label: Czechoslovakia		$3.99	$2.99
LB211	Label: Czech Republic		$3.99	$2.99
LB212	Label: Slovakia		$3.99	$2.99
307SET	Album Set 1913-2015		$599.99	$499.99

Supplemented in August

DENMARK

Item		# of Pgs.	Retail	AA
345DEN1	1851-1995	81	$57.99	$49.29
345DEN2	1996-2009	96	$64.99	$55.24
345DM10	2010 #15	19	$19.99	$16.99
345DM11	2011 #16	17	$19.99	$16.99
345DM12	2012 #17	15	$19.99	$16.99
345DM13	2013 #18	9	$13.99	$11.89
345DM14	2014 #19	7	$9.99	$8.49
345DM15	2015 #20	7	$9.99	$8.49
345DM16	2016 #21		$16.99	$13.99
345DM17	2017 #22		$16.99	$13.99
345DM18	2018 #23		$16.99	$13.99
345DM19	2019 #24		$16.99	$13.99
DENBLANK	Blank Pages	20	$19.99	$16.99
LB157	Label: Denmark		$3.99	$2.99

DENMARK

Item		# of Pgs.	Retail	AA
345DENSET	Album Set 1851-2015		$249.99	$189.99

Supplemented in June

FAROE ISLANDS

Item		# of Pgs.	Retail	AA
345FIS0	1919-1995	30	$29.99	$25.49
345FIS2	1996-2009	46	$34.99	$29.74
345FI10	2010 #14	5	$9.99	$8.49
345FI11	2011 #15	4	$9.99	$8.49
345FI12	2012 #16	5	$9.99	$8.49
345FI13	2013 #17	4	$9.99	$8.49
345FI14	2014 #18	5	$9.99	$8.49
345FI15	2015 #19	5	$9.99	$8.49
345FI16	2016 #20		$11.99	$9.99
345FI17	2017 #21		$11.99	$9.99
345FI18	2018 #22		$11.99	$9.99
345FI19	2019 #23		$11.99	$9.99
FAROBLANK	Blank Pages		$19.99	$16.99
LB158	Label: Faroe Islands		$3.99	$2.99
345FAISET	Album Set 1919-2015		$189.99	$139.99

Supplemented in June

FIJI

Item		# of Pgs.	Retail	AA
624FJI1	1870-1993	64	$44.99	$38.24
624FJI2	1994-1997	16	$19.99	$16.99
624FJI3	1998-2006	49	$39.99	$33.99
624S007	2007 #14	7	$9.99	$8.49
624S008	2008 #15	5	$9.99	$8.49
624S009	2009 #16	3	$6.99	$5.94
624S010	2010 #17	5	$9.99	$8.49
624S011	2011 #18	4	$9.99	$8.49
624S012	2012 #19	3	$6.99	$5.94
624S013	2013 #20	5	$9.99	$8.49
624S014	2014 #21	3	$6.99	$5.94
624S016	2016 #22		$11.99	$9.99
624S018	2018 #23		$11.99	$9.99
LB130	Label: Fiji		$3.99	$2.99
FIJISET	Album Set 1870-2014		$219.99	$159.99

Supplemented in August

FINLAND

Item		# of Pgs.	Retail	AA
345FIN1	1856-1995	108	$69.99	$59.49
345FIN2	1996-2003	45	$34.99	$29.74
345FN04	2004 #9	10	$13.99	$11.89
345FN05	2005 #10	9	$13.99	$11.89
345FN06	2006 #11	8	$13.99	$11.89
345FN07	2007 #12	9	$13.99	$11.89
345FN08	2008 #13	14	$19.99	$16.99
345FN09	2009 #14	7	$9.99	$8.49
345FN10	2010 #15	11	$16.99	$14.44
345FN11	2011 #16	15	$19.99	$16.99
345FN12	2012 #17	13	$16.99	$14.44
345FN13	2013 #18	11	$16.99	$14.44
345FN14	2014 #19	13	$16.99	$14.44
345FN15	2015 #20	13	$16.99	$14.44
345FN16	2016 #21		$22.99	$19.99
345FN17	2017 #22		$22.99	$19.99
345FN18	2018 #23		$22.99	$19.99
345FN19	2019 #24		$22.99	$19.99
FINBLANK	Blank Pages	20	$19.99	$16.99
LB017	Label: Finland		$3.99	$2.99
345FINSET	Album Set 1856-2015		$349.99	$269.99

Supplemented in June

FRANCE

Item		# of Pgs.	Retail	AA
310FRN1	1849-1958	70	$49.99	$42.49
310FRN2	1959-1976	66	$44.99	$38.24
310FRN3	1977-1987	59	$44.99	$38.24
310FRN4	1988-1994	54	$44.99	$38.24
310FRN5	1995-2000	55	$44.99	$38.24
310FRN6	2001-2005	98	$64.99	$55.24
310FRN7	2006-2009	107	$69.99	$59.49
310S010	2010 #45	20	$19.99	$16.99
310S011	2011 #46	24	$21.99	$18.69
310S012	2012 #47	39	$32.99	$28.04
310S013	2013 #48	29	$24.99	$21.24

FRANCE

Item		# of Pgs.	Retail	AA
310S014	2014 #49	28	$24.99	$21.24
310S015	2015 #50	34	$29.99	$25.49
310S016	2016 #51		$34.99	$29.99
310S017	2017 #52		$34.99	$29.99
310S018	2018 #54		$34.99	$29.99
310S019	2019 #55		$34.99	$29.99
310BLANK	Blank Pages	20	$19.99	$16.99
LB018	Label: France		$3.99	$2.99
310SET	Album Set 1849-2015		$669.99	$529.99

Supplemented in May

FRENCH AFRICA

Item		# of Pgs.	Retail	AA
310FRA1	1886-1977	252	$129.99	$110.49
310FRAS1	2010 Supplement (Addendum)	8	$13.99	$11.89
310FRA2	1888-1974	235	$129.99	$110.49
310FRAS2	2010 Supplement (Addendum)	22	$19.99	$16.99
LB073	Label: French Africa		$3.99	$2.99

FRENCH COLONIES

Item		# of Pgs.	Retail	AA
310FCP0	1859-1956	126	$72.99	$62.04
LB020	Label: French Colonies		$3.99	$2.99

FRENCH OFFICES ABROAD

Item		# of Pgs.	Retail	AA
310FOA0	1885-1941	40	$32.99	$28.04

FRENCH POLYNESIA

Item		# of Pgs.	Retail	AA
625FRP1	1892-1994	108	$69.99	$59.49
625FRP2	1995-2006	40	$32.99	$28.04
625S007	2007 #13	5	$9.99	$8.49
625S008	2008 #14	6	$9.99	$8.49
625S010	2010 #15	10	$13.99	$11.89
625S011	2011 #16	5	$9.99	$8.49
625S012	2012 #17	6	$9.99	$8.49
625S013	2013 #18	6	$9.99	$8.49
625S014	2014 #19	6	$9.99	$8.49
625S015	2015 #20	4	$9.99	$8.49
626S016	2016 #21		$11.99	$9.99
625S017	2017 #22		$11.99	$9.99
625S018	2018 #23		$11.99	$9.99
625S019	2019 #24		$11.99	$9.99
LB136	Label: French Polynesia		$3.99	$2.99
FRPOSET	Album Set 1892-2015		$229.99	$169.99

Supplemented in August

FRENCH SOUTHERN & ANTARCTIC TERRITORIES

Item		# of Pgs.	Retail	AA
626FSA1	1955-1994	38	$32.99	$28.04
626FSA2	1995-2006	37	$32.99	$28.04
626S007	2007 #10	6	$9.99	$8.49
626S008	2008 #11	6	$9.99	$8.49
626S010	2010 #12	6	$9.99	$8.49
626S011	2011 #13	4	$9.99	$8.49
626S012	2012 #14	7	$9.99	$8.49
626S013	2013 #15	7	$9.99	$8.49
626S014	2014 #16	9	$13.99	$11.89
626S015	2015 #17	3	$6.99	$5.94
626S016	2016 #18		$16.99	$13.99
626S017	2017 #19		$16.99	$13.99
626S018	2018 #20		$16.99	$13.99
626S019	2019 #21		$16.99	$13.99
LB141	Label: French & Antarctic Territories		$3.99	$2.99
FSASET	Album Set 1955-2015		$189.99	$139.99

Supplemented in August

ORDERING INFORMATION: *AA prices apply to paid subscribers of Amos Media titles, or for orders plwaced online. Prices, terms and product availability subject to change. Taxes will apply in CA, OH, & IL.

SHIPPING & HANDLING: United States – Order total $0-$10.00 charged $3.99 shipping; Order total $10.01-$79.99 charged $7.99 shipping; Order total $80.00 or more charged 10% of order total for shipping. Maximum Freight Charge $45.00. **Canada** – 20% of order total. Minimum charge $19.99 Maximum charge $200.00. **Foreign** – Orders are shipped via FedEx Int'l. or USPS and billed actual freight.

Visit www.AmosAdvantage.com

Call 800-572-6885

Outside U.S. & Canada call: (937) 498-0800 • P.O. Box 4129, Sidney, OH 45365

2021
VOLUME 2B
DEALER DIRECTORY
YELLOW PAGE LISTINGS

This section of your Scott Catalogue contains advertisements to help you conveniently find what you need, when you need it...!

Aerophilately

HENRY GITNER PHILATELISTS, INC.
PO Box 3077-S
Middletown, NY 10940
PH: 845-343-5151
PH: 800-947-8267
FAX: 845-343-0068
hgitner@hgitner.com
www.hgitner.com

Appraisals

DR. ROBERT FRIEDMAN & SONS STAMP & COIN BUYING CENTER
2029 W. 75th St.
Woodridge, IL 60517
PH: 800-588-8100
FAX: 630-985-1588
stampcollections@drbobstamps.com
www.drbobfriedmanstamps.com

Asia

KELLEHER & ROGERS LTD.
22 Shelter Rock Lane, Unit #53
Danbury, CT 06810
PH: 203-830-2500
Toll Free: 800-212-2830
info@kelleherauctions.com
www.kelleherauctions.com

THE STAMP ACT
PO Box 1136
Belmont, CA 94002
PH: 650-703-2342
thestampact@sbcglobal.net

Auctions

DUTCH COUNTRY AUCTIONS
The Stamp Center
4115 Concord Pike
Wilmington, DE 19803
PH: 302-478-8740
FAX: 302-478-8779
auctions@dutchcountryauctions.com
www.dutchcountryauctions.com

KELLEHER & ROGERS LTD.
22 Shelter Rock Lane, Unit #53
Danbury, CT 06810
PH: 203-830-2500
Toll Free: 800-212-2830
info@kelleherauctions.com
www.kelleherauctions.com

British Commonwealth

COLLECTORS EXCHANGE ORLANDO STAMP SHOP
1814A Edgewater Drive
Orlando, FL 32804
PH: 407-620-0908
PH: 407-947-8603
FAX: 407-730-2131
jlatter@cfl.rr.com
www.OrlandoStampShop.com

ARON R. HALBERSTAM PHILATELISTS, LTD.
PO Box 150168
Van Brunt Station
Brooklyn, NY 11215-0168
PH: 718-788-3978
arh@arhstamps.com
www.arhstamps.com

British Commonwealth

British Commonwealth

ROY'S STAMPS
PO Box 28001
600 Ontario Street
St. Catharines, ON
CANADA L2N 7P8
Phone: 905-934-8377
Email: roystamp@cogeco.ca

THE STAMP ACT
PO Box 1136
Belmont, CA 94002
PH: 650-703-2342
thestampact@sbcglobal.net

WORLDSTAMPS/ FRANK GEIGER PHILATELISTS
PO Box 4743
Pinehurst, NC 28374
PH: 910-295-2048
info@WorldStamps.com
www.WorldStamps.com

Buying

DR. ROBERT FRIEDMAN & SONS STAMP & COIN BUYING CENTER
2029 W. 75th St.
Woodridge, IL 60517
PH: 800-588-8100
FAX: 630-985-1588
stampcollections@drbobstamps.com
www.drbobfriedmanstamps.com

Canada

CANADA STAMP FINDER
PO Box 92591
Brampton, ON L6W 4R1
PH: 514-238-5751
Toll Free in North America:
877-412-3106
FAX: 323-315-2635
canadastampfinder@gmail.com
www.canadastampfinder.com

ROY'S STAMPS
PO Box 28001
600 Ontario Street
St. Catharines, ON
CANADA L2N 7P8
Phone: 905-934-8377
Email: roystamp@cogeco.ca

WORLDSTAMPS/ FRANK GEIGER PHILATELISTS
PO Box 4743
Pinehurst, NC 28374
PH: 910-295-2048
info@WorldStamps.com
www.WorldStamps.com

China

KELLEHER & ROGERS LTD.
22 Shelter Rock Lane, Unit #53
Danbury, CT 06810
PH: 203-830-2500
Toll Free: 800-212-2830
info@kelleherauctions.com
www.kelleherauctions.com

THE STAMP ACT
PO Box 1136
Belmont, CA 94002
PH: 650-703-2342
thestampact@sbcglobal.net

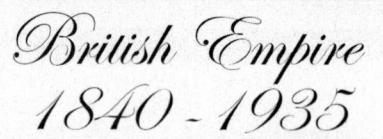

Collections

DR. ROBERT FRIEDMAN & SONS STAMP & COIN BUYING CENTER
2029 W. 75th St.
Woodridge, IL 60517
PH: 800-588-8100
FAX: 630-985-1588
stampcollections@drbobstamps.com
www.drbobfriedmanstamps.com

Czechoslovakia

WORLDSTAMPS/ FRANK GEIGER PHILATELISTS
PO Box 4743
Pinehurst, NC 28374
PH: 910-295-2048
info@WorldStamps.com
www.WorldStamps.com

Ducks

MICHAEL JAFFE
PO Box 61484
Vancouver, WA 98666
PH: 360-695-6161
PH: 800-782-6770
FAX: 360-695-1616
mjaffe@brookmanstamps.com
www.brookmanstamps.com

Europe-Western

WORLDSTAMPS/ FRANK GEIGER PHILATELISTS
PO Box 4743
Pinehurst, NC 28374
PH: 910-295-2048
info@WorldStamps.com
www.WorldStamps.com

Falkland Islands

WORLDSTAMPS/ FRANK GEIGER PHILATELISTS
PO Box 4743
Pinehurst, NC 28374
PH: 910-295-2048
info@WorldStamps.com
www.WorldStamps.com

France & Colonies

E. JOSEPH McCONNELL, INC.
PO Box 683
Monroe, NY 10949
PH: 845-783-9791
FAX: 845-782-0347
ejstamps@gmail.com
www.EJMcConnell.com

WORLDSTAMPS/ FRANK GEIGER PHILATELISTS
PO Box 4743
Pinehurst, NC 28374
PH: 910-295-2048
info@WorldStamps.com
www.WorldStamps.com

French S. Antarctic

E. JOSEPH McCONNELL, INC.
PO Box 683
Monroe, NY 10949
PH: 845-783-9791
FAX: 845-782-0347
ejstamps@gmail.com
www.EJMcConnell.com

WORLDSTAMPS/ FRANK GEIGER PHILATELISTS
PO Box 4743
Pinehurst, NC 28374
PH: 910-295-2048
info@WorldStamps.com
www.WorldStamps.com

Japan

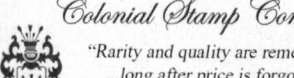

KELLEHER & ROGERS LTD.
22 Shelter Rock Lane, Unit #53
Danbury, CT 06810
PH: 203-830-2500
Toll Free: 800-212-2830
info@kelleherauctions.com
www.kelleherauctions.com

Korea

KELLEHER & ROGERS LTD.
22 Shelter Rock Lane, Unit #53
Danbury, CT 06810
PH: 203-830-2500
Toll Free: 800-212-2830
info@kelleherauctions.com
www.kelleherauctions.com

Manchukuo

KELLEHER & ROGERS LTD.
22 Shelter Rock Lane, Unit #53
Danbury, CT 06810
PH: 203-830-2500
Toll Free: 800-212-2830
info@kelleherauctions.com
www.kelleherauctions.com

Middle East - Arab

KELLEHER & ROGERS LTD.
22 Shelter Rock Lane, Unit #53
Danbury, CT 06810
PH: 203-830-2500
Toll Free: 800-212-2830
info@kelleherauctions.com
www.kelleherauctions.com

New Issues

DAVIDSON'S STAMP SERVICE
Personalized Service since 1970
PO Box 36355
Indianapolis, IN 46236-0355
PH: 317-826-2620
ed-davidson@earthlink.net
www.newstampissues.com

Proofs & Essays

HENRY GITNER PHILATELISTS, INC.
PO Box 3077-S
Middletown, NY 10940
PH: 845-343-5151
PH: 800-947-8267
FAX: 845-343-0068
hgitner@hgitner.com
www.hgitner.com

Stamp Stores

Delaware

DUTCH COUNTRY AUCTIONS
The Stamp Center
4115 Concord Pike
Wilmington, DE 19803
PH: 302-478-8740
FAX: 302-478-8779
auctions@dutchcountryauctions.com
www.dutchcountryauctions.com

Florida

DR. ROBERT FRIEDMAN & SONS STAMP & COIN BUYING CENTER
PH: 800-588-8100
FAX: 630-985-1588
stampcollections@drbobstamps.com
www.drbobfriedmanstamps.com

Illinois

DR. ROBERT FRIEDMAN & SONS STAMP & COIN BUYING CENTER
2029 W. 75th St.
Woodridge, IL 60517
PH: 800-588-8100
FAX: 630-985-1588
stampcollections@drbobstamps.com
www.drbobfriedmanstamps.com

Stamp Stores

New Jersey

BERGEN STAMPS & COLLECTIBLES
306 Queen Anne Rd.
Teaneck, NJ 07666
PH: 201-836-8987
bergenstamps@gmail.com

TRENTON STAMP & COIN
Thomas DeLuca
Store: Forest Glen Plaza
1800 Highway #33, Suite 103
Hamilton Square, NJ 08690
Mail: PO Box 8574
Trenton, NJ 08650
PH: 609-584-8100
FAX: 609-587-8664
TOMD4TSC@aol.com
www.trentonstampandcoin.com

New York

CK STAMPS
42-14 Union St. # 2A
Flushing, NY 11355
PH: 917-667-6641
ckstampsllc@yahoo.com

Ohio

HILLTOP STAMP SERVICE
Richard A. Peterson
PO Box 626
Wooster, OH 44691
PH: 330-262-8907 (0)
PH: 330-201-1377 (H)
hilltopstamps@sssnet.com
www.hilltopstamps.com

Supplies

BROOKLYN GALLERY COIN & STAMP, INC.
8725 4th Ave.
Brooklyn, NY 11209
PH: 718-745-5701
FAX: 718-745-2775
info@brooklyngallery.com
www.brooklyngallery.com

Topicals

E. JOSEPH McCONNELL, INC.
PO Box 683
Monroe, NY 10949
PH: 845-783-9791
FAX: 845-782-0347
ejstamps@gmail.com
www.EJMcConnell.com

WORLDSTAMPS/ FRANK GEIGER PHILATELISTS
PO Box 4743
Pinehurst, NC 28374
PH: 910-295-2048
info@WorldStamps.com
www.WorldStamps.com

Topicals - Columbus

MR. COLUMBUS
PO Box 1492
Fennville, MI 49408
PH: 269-543-4755
David@MrColumbus1492.com
www.MrColumbus1492.com

Topicals - Miscellaneous

HENRY GITNER PHILATELISTS, INC.
PO Box 3077-S
Middletown, NY 10940
PH: 845-343-5151
PH: 800-947-8267
FAX: 845-343-0068
hgitner@hgitner.com
www.hgitner.com

United Nations

BRUCE M. MOYER
Box 12031
Charlotte, NC 28220
PH: 908-237-6967
moyer@unstamps.com
www.unstamps.com

United States

ACS STAMP COMPANY
2914 W 135th Ave
Broomfield, Colorado 80020
303-841-8666
www.ACSStamp.com

BROOKMAN STAMP CO.
PO Box 90
Vancouver, WA 98666
PH: 360-695-1391
PH: 800-545-4871
FAX: 360-695-1616
info@brookmanstamps.com
www.brookmanstamps.com

U.S. Classics/Moderns

BARDO STAMPS
PO Box 7437
Buffalo Grove, IL 60089
PH: 847-634-2676
jfb7437@aol.com
www.bardostamps.com

U.S.-Collections Wanted

DUTCH COUNTRY AUCTIONS
The Stamp Center
4115 Concord Pike
Wilmington, DE 19803
PH: 302-478-8740
FAX: 302-478-8779
auctions@dutchcountryauctions.com
www.dutchcountryauctions.com

DR. ROBERT FRIEDMAN & SONS STAMP & COIN BUYING CENTER
2029 W. 75th St.
Woodridge, IL 60517
PH: 800-588-8100
FAX: 630-985-1588
stampcollections@drbobstamps.com
www.drbobfriedmanstamps.com

Wanted - Worldwide Collections

DUTCH COUNTRY AUCTIONS
The Stamp Center
4115 Concord Pike
Wilmington, DE 19803
PH: 302-478-8740
FAX: 302-478-8779
auctions@dutchcountryauctions.com
www.dutchcountryauctions.com

Websites

ACS STAMP COMPANY
2914 W 135th Ave
Broomfield, Colorado 80020
303-841-8666
www.ACSStamp.com

Wholesale

HENRY GITNER PHILATELISTS, INC.
PO Box 3077-S
Middletown, NY 10940
PH: 845-343-5151
PH: 800-947-8267
FAX: 845-343-0068
hgitner@hgitner.com
www.hgitner.com

Worldwide

KELLEHER & ROGERS LTD.
22 Shelter Rock Lane, Unit #53
Danbury, CT 06810
PH: 203-830-2500
Toll Free: 800-212-2830
info@kelleherauctions.com
www.kelleherauctions.com

GUILLERMO JALIL
Maipu 466, local 4
1006 Buenos Aires
Argentina
guillermo@jalilstamps.com
philatino@philatino.com
www.philatino.com (worldwide stamp auctions)
www.jalilstamps.com (direct sale, worldwide stamps)

Worldwide-Collections

DR. ROBERT FRIEDMAN & SONS STAMP & COIN BUYING CENTER
2029 W. 75th St.
Woodridge, IL 60517
PH: 800-588-8100
FAX: 630-985-1588
stampcollections@drbobstamps.com
www.drbobfriedmanstamps.com

Worldwide

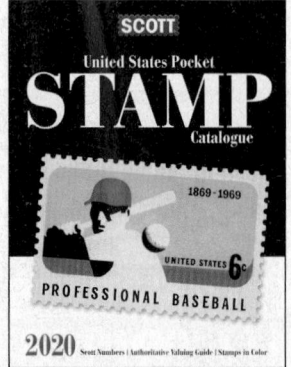